THE TIMES

English Dictionary & Thesaurus

THE TIMES

English Dictionary & Thesaurus

HarperCollins*Publishers* & TIMES BOOKS

second edition 2000

latest reprint 2002

HarperCollins Publishers
Westerhill Road, Bishopbriggs, Glasgow G64 2QT
Great Britain

www.collinsdictionaries.com

Standard Edition ISBN 0-00-472502-6
Thumb-indexed Edition ISBN 0-00-472503-4
Times Books Edition ISBN 0-00-710857-5

This edition prepared in conjunction with Market House Books Ltd, Aylesbury, England

---

Acknowledgements
We would like to thank those authors and publishers who kindly gave permission for copyright material to be used in the Bank of English. We would also like to thank Times Newspapers Ltd for providing valuable data.

Note
Entered words that we have reason to believe constitute trademarks have been designated as such. However, neither the presence nor absence of such designation should be regarded as affecting the legal status of any trademark.

A catalogue record for this book is available from the British Library

Typeset by Market House Books Ltd, Aylesbury, England

Printed and bound in Spain by Mateu Cromo

General Consultant

J M Sinclair
Formerly Professor, Department of English Language and Literature
University of Birmingham

Special Consultants

AUSTRALIAN ENGLISH
G A Wilkes
Challis Professor of English Literature,
University of Sydney

W A Krebs
Associate Professor in Literature and Communications,
Bond University, Queensland

W S Ramson
Reader in English,
Australian National University

BRITISH REGIONAL ENGLISH, URBAN DIALECTS
Harold Orton
Professor Emeritus, Department of English,
University of Leeds

CANADIAN ENGLISH
R J Gregg
Formerly Professor, Department of Linguistics,
University of British Columbia

Patrick Drysdale
Editor, *A Dictionary of Canadianisms on Historical Principles*

James Arthurs
Professor, Department of Linguistics,
University of Victoria

CARIBBEAN ENGLISH
S R R Allsopp
Coordinator, Caribbean Lexicography Project,
University of the West Indies,
Barbados

EAST AFRICAN ENGLISH
J Kalema
Department of Linguistic Science,
University of Reading

INDIAN ENGLISH
R K Bansal
Professor, Department of Phonetics and Spoken English,
Central Institute of English and Foreign Languages, Hyderabad

IRISH ENGLISH
R J Gregg
Formerly Professor, Department of Linguistics,
University of British Columbia

T de Bhaldraithe
Professor, Department of Irish Dialectology,
University College, Dublin

NEW ZEALAND ENGLISH
Ian A Gordon
Professor Emeritus,
University of Wellington

SCOTTISH ENGLISH
A J Aitken
Department of English Language
University of Edinburgh,
Formerly Editor, *Dictionary of the Older Scottish Tongue*

SOUTH AFRICAN ENGLISH
L W Lanham
Professor, Department of Phonetics and General Linguistics,
University of the Witwatersrand

M V Aldridge
Professor, Department of Phonetics and General Linguistics,
University of the Witwatersrand

Geoffrey Hughes
Professor, Department of English,
University of the Witwatersrand

WEST AFRICAN ENGLISH
J Spencer
Director, Institute of Modern English Language Studies,
University of Leeds

PRONUNCIATION
A C Gimson
Formerly Professor, Department of Phonetics and Linguistics,
University College,
University of London

Specialist Contributors

AERONAUTICS
T C Wooldridge, Angus Boyd
Senior Lecturer in Aerodynamics,
The College of Aeronautics,
Cranfield

ARCHITECTURE; CIVIL ENGINEERING
Bruce Martin

AUSTRALIAN ENGLISH
Steve Higgs
Melbourne Grammar School

BIOGRAPHIES, PLACES
Market House Books
Aylesbury

BROADCASTING, FILM, ETC.
Patrick Leggatt
Chief Engineer,
External Relations,
British Broadcasting Corporation

BUSINESS
Alan Isaacs

CHEMISTRY
John Daintith

COMPUTERS
Richard Fryer
Department of Computer Science,
University of Strathclyde

CONSTRUCTION
M J Walker
Construction Industry Research and Information Association

EARTH SCIENCES
Peter J Smith
Reader in Earth Sciences,
The Open University

ECONOMICS
P Donaldson
Ruskin College, Oxford

EDUCATION
Catherine Playford
Head Teacher of English,
Priestnall School

ENGINEERING
J P Quayle
Editor, *Kempe's Engineering Year-Book*

INDUSTRIAL RELATIONS
Professor Angela M Bowey
Strathclyde Business School,
University of Strathclyde
Alexander Purdie
Scottish College of Textiles,
Galashiels

INFORMATION TECHNOLOGY
Professor Thomas Carbery
Andrew Doswell
Catherine M Young
Department of Information Science,
University of Strathclyde

JUDAISM
Ephraim Borowski
Department of Philosophy,
University of Glasgow

LANGUAGES & PEOPLES
David Kilby
Formerly, Department of Language and Linguistics,
University of Essex

LAW
Richard Latham
Barrister-at-Law
Brian Russell Davis
Barrister-at-Law
Sandra Clarke

LIFE SCIENCES
Miranda Robertson
Life Sciences Editor,
Nature
Dr W Gratzer
MRC Cell Biophysics Unit

LINGUISTICS
Professor Yorick Wilks
New Mexico State University

LINGUISTICS AND GRAMMAR
Lloyd Humberstone

LOGIC
Ephraim Borowski
Department of Philosophy,
University of Glasgow

MALAYSIAN ENGLISH
U Yong-ee

MARKETING
Professor M Christopher
Department of Marketing and Logistics Systems,
Cranfield School of Management

METALLURGY
Stanley White

MILITARY
Major S R Elliot
Colonel Andrew Duncan
The International Institute for Strategic Studies

MILITARY AND NAUTICAL TERMS
Cmdr I Johnston RN

PHILOSOPHY
Christopher Sion
Ephraim Borowski
Department of Philosophy,
University of Glasgow

PHYSICAL SCIENCES
R Cutler

PHYSICS
J W Warren
Department of Physics,
Brunel University

PIDGINS AND CREOLES
Loreto Todd
The School of English,
University of Leeds

PLANTS
Sandra Holmes

POP MUSIC
Ingrid von Essen

PRINTING
C H Parsons
Laurence Chizlett

PSYCHOLOGY
Dr Eric Taylor
Professor Stuart Sutherland
Director, Centre for Research on Perception and Cognition, University of Sussex

RAILWAYS
James Barnes

RELIGION
The Rev D Lancashire
University of Essex

RELIGIOUS TERMS
David Bourke
Rev Canon D W Gundry
Chancellor of Leicester Cathedral

SOCIAL WELFARE
Bob Marsden
Harrow Social Services Department

SPORT
Stuart Bathgate
Freelance Journalist

STATISTICS
Ephraim Borowski
Department of Philosophy, University of Glasgow

TOOLS
N J Small
Associate of the Institute of Marine Engineers

Other Contributors

Jane Bartholomew ANIMALS
Jenny Baster COOKERY; CLOTHING AND FASHION; TEXTILES
Denise Bown PLACE NAMES
Ron Brown JAZZ
Daphne Butler CHEMISTRY
Christopher L Clarke HOROLOGY
Brian Dalgleish METALLURGY
Carolyn Eardley ANTIQUES; FURNITURE; TEXTILES
R J Edwards PSYCHOLOGY
Dennis Exton FILMS, TV, AND RADIO
Rosalind Fergusson BIOGRAPHIES
Ian Fuller PSYCHOLOGY
C Gallon PLANTS
Robert Hine BIOGRAPHIES
Amanda Isaacs BIOGRAPHIES
Cherry McDonald-Taylor EDUCATION; LIBRARY SCIENCE
Mary Marshall CARDS; DANCING AND BALLET
David Martin PSYCHOLOGY
Peter Miller SPORTS
Stewart Murray METALLURGY
Serena Penman ART
H G Procter PSYCHOLOGY
Mark Salad PLACE NAMES
David H Shaw ENGINEERING
Brian Street ANTHROPOLOGY
Andrew Treacher PSYCHOLOGY
Ralph Tyler FILMS, TV, AND RADIO; LITERATURE; MYTHOLOGY; THEATRE; BIOGRAPHIES
Jennifer Wearden ARCHAEOLOGY
Irene Wise BIOCHEMISTRY

This dictionary has been compiled by referring to the Bank of English, a unique database of the English language with examples of over 350 million words enabling lexicographers to analyse how English is actually used today and how it is changing. This is the evidence on which the changes in the dictionary are based.

The Bank of English was set up to be a resource for language research and lexicography. It contains a very wide range of material from books, newspapers, radio, TV, magazines, letters, and talks reflecting the whole spectrum of English today. Its size and range make it an unequalled resource and it has purpose-built software for its analysis.

This ensures that the text accurately reflects English as it is used today in a way that is most helpful to the dictionary user as well as including the full range of rarer and historical words and meanings.

Foreword

The **English Dictionary & Thesaurus** is a uniquely useful language reference book, combining as it does dictionary entries and thesaurus entries on the same page. This means that at one look-up you can find not only all the standard dictionary information – pronunciations, meaning, examples, etymologies, but also synonyms for the different meanings, and where applicable, antonyms as well.

The dictionary text includes over 105,000 references, and is a substantial work that provides extensive coverage of all aspects of today's English. It is up to date containing thousands of the most recent new words and terms to have entered the language, reflecting changes and developments in our society. Particular attention is given to the vocabulary of science, technology, and many other special interest subjects with entries based on the latest research and development.

Help is given with difficult or controversial points in the use of English. The dictionary definitions give clear guidance on many aspects of syntax and grammar, and contain thousands of examples of words in use. Particularly problematic words have notes after the main entry in the dictionary text showing the current view on their usage, especially in cases where this usage is changing.

The thesaurus section at the foot of the page provides lists of alternative words for some 16,000 entry words in the dictionary text, the most basic words of the language and therefore those for which an alternative expression is most likely to be needed. Antonyms are included where appropriate. The synonym lists are divided into numbered categories, each relating to the particular meaning of the word in the dictionary text, so that it is easy to identify the synonym that most closely relates to the context required. Italic labels in both the dictionary and the thesaurus text identify words which have a particular area of use; for example, words which are slang or literary, or which are restricted to a particular region of the world.

The book is easy to use, with clear typography, numbered meanings, and every dictionary item which needs a definition given as a main entry in its own right.

The **English Dictionary & Thesaurus** is thus the complete language reference book, providing the fullest, most up-to-date, and helpful range of information available.

Guide to the Text

THESAURUS

Headword	**build up** *vb* 2 = **increase**, add to, amplify, augment, develop, enhance, expand, extend, fortify, heighten, improve, intensify, reinforce, strengthen 4 = **hype**, advertise, boost, plug (*inf.*), promote, publicize, spotlight ◆ *n* **build-up** 5 = **increase**, accumulation, development, enlargement, escalation, expansion, gain, growth 7 = **hype**, ballyhoo (*inf.*), plug (*inf.*), promotion, publicity, puff	Synonyms; Key synonym
Usage label	**built-in** *adj* 2 = **integral**, essential, immanent, implicit, in-built, included, incorporated, inherent, inseparable, part and parcel of	
Dictionary sense number	**bulbous** *adj* 1, 4 = **bulging**, bloated, convex, rounded, swelling, swollen **bulge** *n* 1 = **swelling**, bump, hump, lump, projection, protrusion, protuberance 2 = **increase**, boost, intensification, rise, surge ◆ *vb* 3 = **swell out**, bag, dilate, distend, enlarge, expand, project, protrude, puff out, sag, stand out, stick out, swell	Part of speech
"Opposite to"	**Antonyms** *n* ≠ **swelling**: bowl, cave, cavity, concavity, crater, dent, depression, hole, hollow, indentation, pit, trough	
	bulk *n* 1 = **size**, amplitude, bigness, dimensions, immensity, largeness, magnitude, massiveness, substance, volume, weight 2 = **main part**, better part, body, generality, lion's share, majority, major part, mass, most, nearly all, plurality, preponderance ◆ *vb* 7 **bulk large** = **be important**, carry weight, dominate, loom, loom large, preponderate, stand out, threaten	Idiom or phrase
Antonyms	**bulky** *adj* = **large**, big, colossal, cumbersome, elephantine, enormous, heavy, huge, hulking, immense, mammoth, massive, massy, ponderous, substantial, unmanageable, unwieldy, voluminous, weighty **Antonyms** *adj* convenient, handy, manageable, neat, slim, small, wieldy	

Guide to the Text

DICTIONARY

Headword | Grammatical information | Subject-field label | Pronunciation | Regional label | Part of speech | Cross-reference | Etymology | Sense number | Inflected forms | Derived words | Thesaurus symbol | Example | Usage note | Definition | Related adjective | Usage label | Idiom or phrase

build up ❶ *vb* (*adv*) **1** (*tr*) to construct gradually, systematically, and in stages. **2** to increase, accumulate, or strengthen, esp. by degrees: *the murmur built up to a roar.* **3** (*tr*) to improve the health or physique of (a person). **4** (*intr*) to prepare for or gradually approach a climax. ◆ *n* **build-up. 5** progressive increase in number, size, etc.: *the build-up of industry.* **6** a gradual approach to a climax. **7** extravagant publicity or praise, esp. in the form of a campaign. **8** *Mil.* the process of attaining the required strength of forces and equipment.

built (bɪlt) *vb* the past tense and past participle of **build.**

built-in ❶ *adj* **1** made or incorporated as an integral part: *a built-in cupboard.* **2** essential; inherent. ◆ *n* **3** *Austral.* a built-in cupboard.

built-in obsolescence *n* See **planned obsolescence.**

built-up *adj* **1** having many buildings (esp. in **built-up area**). **2** increased by the addition of parts: *built-up heels.*

bulb ❶ (bʌlb) *n* **1** a rounded organ of vegetative reproduction in plants such as the tulip and onion: a flattened stem bearing a central shoot surrounded by fleshy nutritive inner leaves and thin brown outer leaves. **2** a plant, such as a hyacinth or daffodil, that grows from a bulb. **3** See **light bulb. 4** any bulb-shaped thing. [C16: from L *bulbus,* from Gk *bolbos* onion]

▸ **'bulbous** *adj*

bulbil ('bʌlbɪl) *n* **1** a small bulb produced from a parent bulb. **2** a bulb-like reproductive organ in a leaf axil of certain plants. **3** any small bulblike structure in an animal. [C19: from NL *bulbillus* BULB]

bulbul ('bʊlbʊl) *n* a songbird of tropical Africa and Asia having brown plumage and, in many species, a distinct crest. [C18: via Persian from Ar.]

Bulgarian (bʌl'gɛərɪən, bʊl-) *adj* **1** of or denoting Bulgaria, a country of SE Europe, on the Balkan Peninsula, its people, or their language. ◆ *n* **2** the official language of Bulgaria. **3** a native or inhabitant of Bulgaria.

bulge ❶ (bʌldʒ) *n* **1** a swelling or an outward curve. **2** a sudden increase in number, esp. of population. ◆ *vb* **bulges, bulging, bulged. 3** to swell outwards. [C13: from OF *bouge,* from L *bulga* bag, prob. of Gaulish origin]

▸ **'bulging** *adj* ▸ **'bulgy** *adj*

bulgur ('bʌlgə) *n* cracked wheat that has been hulled, steamed, and roasted so that it requires little or no cooking. [C20: from Ar. *burghul*]

bulimia (bju:'lɪmɪə) *n* **1** pathologically insatiable hunger. **2** Also called: **bulimia nervosa.** a disorder characterized by compulsive overeating followed by vomiting. [C17: from NL, from Gk *bous* ox + *limos* hunger]

bulk ❶ (bʌlk) *n* **1** volume, size, or magnitude, esp. when great. **2** the main part: *the bulk of the work is repetitious.* **3** a large body, esp. of a person. **4** the part of food which passes unabsorbed through the digestive system. **5 in bulk. 5a** in large quantities. **5b** (of a cargo, etc.) unpackaged. ◆ *vb* **6** to cohere or cause to cohere in a mass. **7 bulk large.** to be or seem important or prominent. [C15: from ON *bulki* cargo]

> **USAGE NOTE** The use of a plural noun after *bulk* was formerly considered incorrect, but is now acceptable.

bulk buying *n* the purchase of goods in large amounts, often at reduced prices.

bulkhead ('bʌlk,hɛd) *n* any upright wall-like partition in a ship, aircraft, etc. [C15: prob. from *bulk* projecting framework from ON *bálkr* +HEAD]

bulk modulus *n* a coefficient of elasticity of a substance equal to the ratio of the applied stress to the resulting fractional change in volume.

bulky ❶ ('bʌlkɪ) *adj* **bulkier, bulkiest.** very large and massive, esp. so as to be unwieldy.

▸ **'bulkily** *adv* ▸ **'bulkiness** *n*

bull[1] (bʊl) *n* **1** any male bovine animal, esp. one that is sexually mature. Related adj: **taurine. 2** the male of various other animals including the elephant and whale. **3** a very large, strong, or aggressive person. **4** *Stock Exchange.* **4a** a speculator who buys in anticipation of rising prices in order to make a profit on resale. **4b** (*as modifier*): *a bull market.* Cf. **bear**[2] (sense 5). **5** *Chiefly Brit.* short for **bull's-eye** (senses 1, 2). **6** *Sl.* short for **bullshit. 7 a bull in a china shop.** a clumsy person. **8 take the bull by the horns.** to face and tackle a difficulty without shirking. ◆ *adj* **9** male; masculine: *a bull elephant.* **10** large; strong. [OE *bula*]

Editorial Staff

EDITORIAL DIRECTOR
Diana Treffry

EDITORIAL CONSULTANT
Alan Isaacs

MANAGING EDITOR
Sheila Ferguson

LEXICOGRAPHERS
Elspeth Summers (Senior Lexicographer)
Ian Brookes **Lorna Gilmour**
Andrew Holmes **Mary O'Neill**

COMPUTER STAFF
Raymond Carrick

USAGE NOTES
John Todd

MARKET HOUSE EDITORS
John Daintith **Elizabeth Martin** **Fran Alexander**
Jonathan Law **Peter Blair**

COMPUTERS
Anne Stibbs

KEYBOARDERS
Jessica Scholes **Sandra McQueen** **Gwynneth Shaw** **Brenda Tomkins**

Guide to the Use of the Dictionary

The Guide that follows sets out the main principles on which the Dictionary is arranged and enables you to make full use of the Dictionary by showing the range of information that it contains.

HEADWORD

All main entries, including place names, biographies, abbreviations, prefixes, and suffixes, are printed in large boldface type and are listed in strict alphabetical order. This applies even if the headword consists of more than one word.

Order of entries

Words that have the same spelling but are derived from different sources (homographs) are entered separately with superscript numbers after the headwords.

> **saw**[1] (sɔː) *n* **1** any of various hand tools ...
> **saw**[2] (sɔː) *vb* the past tense of **see**[1].
> **saw**[3] (sɔː) *n* a wise saying, maxim, or proverb. ...

Abbreviations, acronyms, and symbols

Abbreviations, acronyms, and symbols are entered as headwords in the main alphabetical list. In linewith modern practice, full stops are generally not used but it can be assumed that nearly all abbreviations are equally acceptable with or without stops.

Prefixes, suffixes, and combining forms

Prefixes (e.g. **in-**, **pre-**, **sub-**), suffixes (e.g. **-able**, **-ation**, **-ity**), and combining forms (e.g. **psycho-**, **-iatry**) have been entered as headwords if they are still used freely to produce new words in English.

Variant spellings

Common acceptable variant spellings of English words are given as alternative forms of the headword.

> **capitalize** *or* **capitalise** (ˈkæpɪtəˌlaɪz) *vb* ...

US spellings

Where it is different, the US spelling of a word is also recorded in the headword.

> **centre** *or US* **center** (ˈsɛntə) *n*

PRONUNCIATION

Pronunciations of words in this Dictionary represent those that are common in educated British English speech. They are transcribed in the International Phonetic Alphabet (IPA). A *Pronunciation Key* is printed at the end of this Guide. The pronunciation is normally given in brackets immediately after the headword.

> **abase** (əˈbeɪs) *vb* **abases, abasing, abased.** (*tr*) **1** to humble ...

The stress pattern is marked by the symbols ˈ for primary stress and ˌ for secondary stress. The stress mark precedes the syllable to which it applies.

Variant pronunciations

When a headword has an acceptable variant pronunciation or stress pattern, the variant is given by repeating only the syllable or syllables that change.

> **economic** (ˌiːkəˈnɒmɪk, ˌɛkə-) *adj* **1** of or relating to ...

Pronunciations with different parts of speech

When two or more parts of speech of a word have different pronunciations, the pronunciations are shown in brackets before the relevant group of senses.

> **record** *n* (ˈrɛkɔːd). **1** an account in permanent form, ... ◆ *vb* (rɪˈkɔːd). (*mainly tr*) **18** to set down in some permanent form ...

Pronunciation of individual senses

If one sense of a headword has a different pronunciation from that of the rest, the pronunciation is given in brackets after the sense number.

> **conjure** (ˈkʌndʒə) *vb* **conjures, conjuring, conjured. 1** (*intr*) to practise conjuring. **2** (*intr*) to call upon supposed supernatural forces by spells and incantations. **3** (kənˈdʒʊə). (*tr*) to appeal earnestly to: *I conjure you to help me.* ...

INFLECTED FORMS

Inflected forms are shown for the following:

Nouns and verbs whose inflections involve a change in internal spelling.

> **goose**[1] (guːs) *n, pl* **geese.** ...
> **drive** (draɪv) *vb* **drives, driving, drove, driven.** ...

Nouns, verbs, and adjectives that end in a consonant plus *-y*, where *y* is changed to *i* before inflectional endings.

> **augury** (ˈɔːgjʊrɪ) *n, pl* **auguries.** ...

Nouns having identical singular and plural forms.

> **sheep** (ʃiːp) *n, pl* **sheep.** ...

Nouns that closely resemble others but form their plurals differently.

> **mongoose** (ˈmɒŋˌguːs) *n, pl* **mongooses.** ...

Nouns that end in *-ful*, *-o*, and *-us*.

handful ('hændful) *n, pl* **handfuls**. ...
tomato (tə'mɑːtəʊ) *n, pl* **tomatoes**. ...
prospectus (prə'spɛktəs) *n, pl* **prospectuses**. ...

Nouns whose plurals are not regular English inflections.

basis ('beɪsɪs) *n, pl* **bases** (-siːz) ...

Plural nouns whose singulars are not regular English forms.

bacteria (bæk'tɪərɪə) *pl n, sing* **bacterium**. ...

Nouns whose plurals have regular spellings but involve a change in pronunciation.

house *n* (haʊs), *pl* **houses** ('haʊzɪz). ...

Multiword nouns when it is not obvious which word takes a plural inflection.

attorney-at-law *n, pl* **attorneys-at-law**. ...

Adjectives that change their roots to form comparatives and superlatives.

good (gʊd) *adj* **better, best**. ...

Adjectives and verbs that double their final consonant before adding endings.

fat (fæt) ... ◆ *adj* **fatter, fattest**. ...
control (kən'trəʊl) *vb* **controls, controlling, controlled**. ...

Verbs that are regular and do not (as might be expected) double their final consonant before adding endings.

rivet ('rɪvɪt) ... ◆ *vb* **rivets, riveting, riveted**. ...

Verbs and adjectives that end in a vowel plus *-e*.

canoe (kə'nuː) ... ◆ *vb* **canoes, canoeing, canoed**. ...
free (friː) *adj* **freer, freest**. ... ◆ *vb* **frees, freeing, freed**. ...

Verbs that end in *-e*.

pace[1] (peɪs) ... ◆ *vb* **paces, pacing, paced**. ...

PARTS OF SPEECH

A part-of-speech label in italics precedes the sense or senses relating to that part of speech.

Standard parts of speech

The standard parts of speech, with the abbreviations used, are as follows: adjective (*adj*), adverb (*adv*), conjunction (*conj*), interjection (*interj*), noun (*n*), preposition (*prep*), pronoun (*pron*), verb (*vb*).

Less traditional parts of speech

Certain other less traditional parts of speech have been used in this Dictionary.

determiner. This denotes such words as *the*, *a*, *some*, *any*, *that*, *this*, as well as the numerals, and possessives such as *my* and *your*. Many determiners can have a pronoun function without change of meaning:

some (sʌm; *unstressed* səm) *determiner* ... **2a** an unknown or unspecified quantity or amount of: *there's some rice on the table; he owns some horses*. **2b** (*as pron; functioning as sing or pl*): *we'll buy some*. ...

sentence connector. This description replaces the traditional classification of certain words, such as *therefore* and *however*, as adverbs or conjunctions. These words link sentences together rather in the manner of conjunctions; however, they are not confined to the first position in a clause as conjunctions are.

sentence substitute. Sentence substitutes are words such as *yes*, *no*, *perhaps*, *definitely*, and *maybe*. They can stand as meaningful utterances by themselves.

Words used as more than one part of speech

If a word can be used as more than one part of speech, the senses of one part of speech are separated from the others by a lozenge (◆).

lure (lʊə) *vb* **lures, luring, lured**. (*tr*) ... **2** *Falconry*. to entice (a hawk or falcon) from the air to the falconer by a lure. ◆ *n* **3** a person or thing that lures. ...

Guide to the Use of the Dictionary

GRAMMATICAL INFORMATION

Grammatical information is provided in brackets and typically in italics to distinguish it from other types of information.

Adjectives and determiners

Some adjectives and determiners are restricted by usage to a particular position relative to the nouns they qualify. This is indicated by the following labels:

postpositive (used predicatively or after the noun, but not before the noun):

ablaze (ə'bleɪz) *adj (postpositive), adv* **1** on fire; burning. ...

immediately postpositive (always used immediately following the noun qualified and never used predicatively):

galore (gə'lɔː) *determiner (immediately postpositive)* in great numbers or quantity: *there were daffodils galore in the park. ...*

prenominal (used before the noun, and never used predicatively):

chief (tʃiːf) ... ◆ *adj* **4** *(prenominal)* **4a** most important; principal. ...

Intensifiers

Adjectives and adverbs that perform an exclusively intensifying function, with no addition of meaning, are described as (intensifier) without further explanation.

blooming ('bluːmɪŋ) *adv, adj Brit. inf.* (intensifier): *a blooming genius; blooming painful.*

Conjunctions

Conjunctions are divided into two classes, marked by the following labels:

coordinating. Coordinating conjunctions connect words, phrases, or clauses that perform an identical function and are not dependent on each other. They include *and*, *but*, and *or*.

subordinating. Subordinating conjunctions introduce clauses that are dependent on a main clause in a complex sentence. They include *where*, *until*, and *if*.

Some conjunctions, such as *while* and *whereas*, can function as either coordinating or subordinating conjunctions.

Singular and plural labelling of nouns

Headwords and senses that are apparently plural in form but that take a singular verb, etc., are marked *'functioning as sing'*.

physics ('fɪzɪks) *n (functioning as sing)* **1** the branch of science ...

Headwords and senses that appear to be singular, such as collective nouns, but that take a plural verb, etc., are marked *'functioning as pl'*.

cattle ('kætᵊl) *n (functioning as pl)* **1** bovid mammals of the tribe *Bovini* ...

Headwords and senses that may take either a singular or a plural verb, etc., are marked *'functioning as sing or pl'*.

bellows ('beləuz) *n (functioning as sing or pl)* **1** Also: **pair of bellows.** an instrument consisting of an air chamber ...

Modifiers

A noun that is commonly used as if it were an adjective is labelled *modifier.* If the sense of the modifier can be understood from the sense of the noun, the modifier is shown without further explanation, with an example to illustrate its use. Otherwise its meaning and/or usage is explained separately.

key[1] (kiː) *n* ... **8** *(modifier)* of great importance: *a key issue.*

Verbs

The principal parts given are: 3rd person singular of the present tense; present participle; past tense; past participle if different from the past tense.

Intransitive and transitive verbs

When a sense of a verb (*vb*) is restricted to transitive use, it is labelled (*tr*); if it is intransitive only, it is labelled (*intr*). If all the senses of a verb are transitive or all are intransitive, the appropriate label appears before the first numbered sense and is not repeated.

Absence of a label is significant: it indicates that the sense may be used both transitively and intransitively.

Guide to the Use of the Dictionary

If nearly all the senses of a verb are transitive, the label (*mainly tr*) appears immediately before the first numbered sense. This indicates that, unless otherwise labelled, any given sense of the verb is transitive. Similarly, all the senses of a verb may be labelled (*mainly intr*).

Copulas

A verb that takes a complement is labelled copula.

> **seem** (siːm) *vb* (*may take an infinitive*) **1** (*copula*) to appear to the mind or eye; look: *the car seems to be running well. ...*

Phrasal verbs

Verbal constructions consisting of a verb and a prepositional or an adverbial particle are given headword status if the meaning of the phrasal verb cannot be deduced from the separate meanings of the verb and the particle.

Phrasal verbs are labelled to show four possible distinctions: a transitive verb with an adverbial particle (*tr, adv*); a transitive verb with a prepositional particle (*tr, prep*); an intransitive verb with an adverbial particle (*intr, adv*); an intransitive verb with a prepositional particle (*intr, prep*):

> **turn on** ... **4** (*tr, adv*) *Inf.* to produce (charm, tears, etc.) suddenly or automatically.

> **take for** *vb* (*tr, prep*) *Inf.* to consider or suppose to be, esp. mistakenly: *the fake coins were taken for genuine; who do you take me for?*

> **break off** ... **3** (*intr, adv*) to stop abruptly: *he broke off in the middle of his speech.*

> **turn on** ... **2** (*intr, prep*) to depend or hinge on: *the success of the party turns on you.*

The absence of a label is significant. If there is no label (*tr*) or (*intr*), the verb may be used either transitively or intransitively. If there is no label (*adv*) or (*prep*), the particle may be either adverbial or prepositional.

Any noun, adjective, or modifier formed from a phrasal verb is entered under the phrasal-verb headword. In some cases, where the noun or adjective is more common than the verb, the phrasal verb is entered after the noun or adjective form:

> **breakaway** (ˈbreɪkəˌweɪ) *n* **1a** loss or withdrawal of a group of members from an association, club, etc. **1b** (*as modifier*): *a breakaway faction. ...* ◆ *vb* **break away.** (*intr, adv*) **3** (often foll. by *from*) to leave hastily or escape. **4** to withdraw or secede.

RESTRICTIVE LABELS

If a particular sense is restricted as to appropriateness, connotation, subject field, etc., an italic label is placed immediately before the relevant definition.

> **hang on** *vb* (*intr*) ... **5** (*adv*) *Inf.* to wait: *hang on for a few minutes.*

If a label applies to all senses of one part of speech, it is placed immediately after the part-of-speech label.

> **assured** (əˈʃʊəd) *adj* ... ◆ *n* **4** *Chiefly Brit.* **4a** the beneficiary under a life assurance policy. **4b** the person whose life is insured. ...

If a label applies to all senses of a headword, it is placed immediately after the pronunciation (or inflections).

> **con**[1] (kɒn) *Inf.* ◆ *n* **1a** short for **confidence trick. 1b** (*as modifier*): *con man.* ◆ *vb* **cons, conning, conned. 2** (*tr*) to swindle ...

Usage labels

Sl. (*Slang*). Refers to words or senses that are informal and restricted in context, for example, to members of a particular social or cultural group. Slang words are inappropriate in formal speech or writing.

Inf. (*Informal*). Applies to words or senses that may be widely used, especially in conversation, letter-writing, etc., but that are not common in formal writing. Such words are subject to fewer contextual restrictions than slang words.

Taboo. Indicates words that are not acceptable in polite use.

Offens. (*Offensive*). Indicates that a word might be regarded as offensive by the person described or referred to, even if the speaker uses the word without any malicious intention.

Derog. (*Derogatory*). Implies that the connotations of a word are unpleasant with intent on the part of the speaker or writer.

Not standard. Indicates words or senses that are frequently encountered but widely regarded as incorrect.

Arch. (*Archaic*). Denotes a word or sense that is no longer in common use but that may be found in literary works or used to impart a historical colour to contemporary writing.

Obs. (*Obsolete*). Denotes a word or sense that is no longer in use. In specialist or technical fields the label often implies that the term has been superseded.

The word 'formerly' is placed in brackets before a sense when the practice, concept, etc., being described, rather than the word itself, is obsolete or out-of-date.

A number of other usage labels, such as *Ironic*, *Facetious*, and *Euphemistic*, are used where appropriate.

More extended help on usage is provided in usage notes after certain entries.

Subject-field labels

A number of italic labels are used to indicate that a word or sense is used in a particular specialist or technical field.

MEANING

The meaning of each headword in this Dictionary is explained in one or more definitions, together with information about context and typical use.

Order of senses

As a general rule, where a headword has more than one sense, the first sense given is the one most common in current usage.

> **complexion** (kəm'plɛkʃən) *n* **1** the colour and general appearance of a person's skin, esp. of the face. **2** aspect or nature: *the general complexion of a nation's finances.* **3** *Obs.* temperament. ...

Where the lexicographers consider that a current sense is the 'core meaning' in that it illuminates the meaning of other senses, the core meaning may be placed first.

> **competition** (ˌkɒmpɪ'tɪʃən) *n* **1** the act of competing. **2** a contest in which a winner is selected from among two or more entrants. **3** a series of games, sports events, etc. **4** the opposition offered by competitors....

Subsequent senses are arranged so as to give a coherent account of the meaning of a headword. If a word is used as more than one part of speech, all the senses of each part of speech are grouped together in a single block. Within a part-of-speech block, closely related senses are grouped together; technical senses generally follow general senses; archaic and obsolete sense follow technical senses; idioms and fixed phrases are generally placed last.

Scientific and technical definitions

Units, physical quantities, formulas, etc. In accordance with the recommendations of the International Standards Organization, all scientific measurements are expressed in SI units (*Système International d'Unités*). Measurements and quantities in more traditional units are often given as well as SI units. The entries for chemical compounds give the systematic names as well as the more familiar popular names.

CROSS-REFERENCES

Cross-references introduced by the words 'See also' or 'Compare' refer the reader to additional information elsewhere in the Dictionary. If the cross-reference is preceded by a lozenge (◆), it applies to all senses of the headword that have gone before it, unless otherwise stated. If there is no lozenge, the cross-reference applies only to the sense immediately preceding it.

Variant spellings

Variant spellings (e.g. **foetus**...a variant spelling of **fetus**) are generally entered as cross-references if their place in the alphabetical list is more than ten entries distant from the main entry.

Alternative names

Alternative names or terms are printed in boldface type and introduced by the words 'Also' or 'Also called'. If the alternative name or term is preceded by a lozenge, it applies to the entire entry.

RELATED ADJECTIVES

Certain nouns, especially of Germanic origin, have related adjectives that are derived from Latin or French. For example, *mural* (from Latin) is an adjective related in meaning to *wall*. Such adjectives are shown in a number of cases after the sense (or part-of-speech block) to which they are related.

> **wall** (wɔːl) *n* **1a** a vertical construction made of stone, brick, wood, etc. ... Related adj: **mural**. ...

Guide to the Use of the Dictionary

IDIOMS

Fixed noun phrases, such as **dark horse**, and certain other idioms are given full headword status. Other idioms are placed under the key word of the idiom, as a separate sense, generally at the end of the appropriate part-of-speech block.

> **ground**[1] (graund) *n* ... **17 break new ground.** to do something that has not been done before. ...

ETYMOLOGIES

Etymologies are placed in bold square brackets after the definition. They are given for all headwords except those that are derivative forms (consisting of a base word and a suffix or prefix), compound words, inflected forms, and proper names.

Many headwords, such as **enlighten** and **prepossess**, consist of a prefix and a base word and are not accompanied by etymologies since the essential etymological information is shown for the component parts, all of which are entered in the Dictionary as headwords in their own right.

The purpose of the etymologies is to trace briefly the history of the word back from the present day, through its first recorded appearance in English, to its origin, often in some source language other than English. The etymologies show the history of the word both in English (wherever there has been significant change in form or sense) and in its pre-English source languages.

Words printed in SMALL CAPITALS refer to other headwords where relevant or additional information, either in the definition or in the etymology, may be found.

Dating

The etymology records the first known occurrence (a written citation) of a word in English. Words first appearing in the language during the Middle English period or later are dated by century, abbreviated **C**.

> **mantis** ('mæntɪs) ... [C17: NL, from Gk: prophet, alluding to its praying posture]

This indicates that there is a written citation for **mantis** in the seventeenth century. The absence of a New Latin or Greek form in the etymology means that the form of the word was the same in those languages as in English.

Old English

Native words from Old English are not dated, written records of Old English being scarce, but are simply identified as being of Old English origin.

DERIVED WORDS

Words derived from a base word by the addition of suffixes such as *-ly*, *-ness*, etc., are entered in boldface type immediately after the etymology or after the last definition if there is no etymology. They are preceded by an arrow head (▸). The meanings of such words may be deduced from the meanings of the suffix and the headword.

USAGE NOTES

A brief note introduced by the label **USAGE NOTE** has been added at the end of a number of entries in order to comment on matters of usage.

Guide to the Use of the Thesaurus

Entries

Main entry words are alphabetically arranged, with their synonyms also listed alphabetically. When a word has distinctly separate meanings, separate numbered lists are given for the different senses. The sense numbers in the thesaurus correspond to those of the dictionary. Where the listed synonyms can be used as alternatives for more than one dictionary sense, this is indicated, as in the entry for *academic*.

Key synonyms

Key synonyms are shown in bold type and placed first in each list. This feature helps to identify immediately which sense of the word is referred to and also offers the closest alternative to the word being looked up.

Parts of speech

Where it is desirable to distinguish between different parts of speech, labels have been added as follows:

n (noun), *vb* (verb), *adj* (adjective), *adv* (adverb), *pron* (pronoun), *conj* (conjunction), *prep* (preposition), *interj* (interjection). See entries for *living, loaf, loan, local.*

All the synonyms for a particular part of speech are grouped together. Thus, in the entry *catch*, synonyms for all verb senses are given first, followed by synonyms for all the noun senses.

Change of part of speech

When a headword has more than one meaning and can function as more than one part of speech, a new part-of-speech function is shown by a lozenge (◆), as in the entry for *glance* or *grasp*.

Phrases

Commonly used phrases appear as main entries; for instance, *give away* comes after *give*. Expressions such as *a priori* or *en route* are also given as main entries within the alphabetical listing. Short idiomatic phrases are entered under their key word at the end of the appropriate part-of-speech section. Thus, the phrase *take a dim view*, in which *dim* is an adjective, appears immediately after the other adjectival senses of *dim*.

Plurals

Plural forms with a distinct meaning, such as *damages*, are entered at their own alphabetical position, while those with a less distinct difference, such as *features*, are given as a separate sense under the singular form, e.g. *feature...1 plural...*

Antonyms

The antonym lists which follow many entries are also arranged alphabetically. Where there is more than one synonym sense, the corresponding antonym list is introduced with a = sign to indicate the sense to which the antonym list refers.

Labels

A label in brackets applies only to the synonym preceding it, while one which is not bracketed relates to the whole of that particular sense. Labels have been abbreviated when a readily understandable shortened form exists, such as *sl.* (slang), *inf.* (informal), and *arch.* (archaic).

List of Abbreviations Used in the Dictionary

abbrev. abbreviation
Abor. Aboriginal
adj adjective
adv adverb(ial)
Afrik. Afrikaans
Amerind American Indian
Anat. Anatomy
approx. approximate(ly)
Ar. Arabic
Arch. Archaic
Archaeol. Archaeology
Archit. Architecture
Astrol. Astrology
Astron. Astronomy
Austral. Australian

Biol. Biology
Bot. Botany
Brit. Britain; British

C century (e.g. **C14** = 14th century)
°C degrees Celsius
Canad. Canadian
cap. capital
cf. compare
Chem. Chemistry
comp. comparative
conj conjunction

Derog. Derogatory
dim. diminutive
Du. Dutch

E east(ern); (in etymologies) English
Econ. Economics
e.g. for example
esp. especially
est. estimate

F French
fem feminine
foll. followed
ft foot *or* feet

G German
Geog. Geography

Geol. Geology
Geom. Geometry
Gk Greek
Gmc Germanic

Heb. Hebrew

i.e. that is
imit. of imitative origin
in. inch(es)
Inf. Informal
infl. influence(d)
interj interjection
intr intransitive
It. Italian

km kilometre(s)

L Late; Latin
lit. literally
LL Late Latin

m metre(s)
M Middle
masc masculine
Maths Mathematics
Med. Medicine; (in etymologies) Medieval
MHG Middle High German
Mil. Military
Mod. Modern
Myth. Mythology

n noun
N north(ern)
Naut. Nautical
NE northeast(ern)
NL New Latin
no. number
NW northwest(ern)
NZ New Zealand

O Old
Obs. Obsolete
Offens. Offensive
OHG Old High German
ON Old Norse

orig. originally

Photog. Photography
pl plural
pop. population
Port. Portuguese
p.p. past participle
prep preposition(al)
prob. probably
pron pronoun
Psychol. Psychology
pt. point
p.t. past tense

rel. related

S south(ern)
S. African South African
Sansk. Sanskrit
Scand. Scandinavian
Scot. Scottish; Scots
SE southeast(ern)
sing singular
Sl. slang
Sp. Spanish
sq. square
sup. superlative
SW southwest(ern)

Theol. Theology
tr transitive

ult. ultimately
US United States

var. variant
vb verb
vol. volume

W west(ern)
wt. weight

Zool. Zoology

? in etymologies indicates "query"

Pronunciation Key

The symbols used in the pronunciation transcriptions are those of the International Phonetic Alphabet. The following consonant symbols have their usual English values: *b, d, f, h, k, l, m, n, p, r, s, t, v, w, z*. The remaining symbols and their interpretations are listed below.

English Sounds

ɑː as in *father* ('fɑːðə), *alms* (ɑːmz), *clerk* (klɑːk), *heart* (hɑːt), *sergeant* ('sɑːdʒənt)

æ as in *act* (ækt), *Caedmon* ('kædmən), *plait* (plæt)

aɪ as in *dive* (daɪv), *aisle* (aɪl), *guy* (gaɪ), *might* (maɪt), *rye* (raɪ)

aɪə as in *fire* ('faɪə), *buyer* ('baɪə), *liar* ('laɪə), *tyre* ('taɪə)

aʊ as in *out* (aʊt), *bough* (baʊ), *crowd* (kraʊd), *slouch* (slaʊtʃ)

aʊə as in *flour* ('flaʊə), *cower* ('kaʊə), *flower* ('flaʊə), *sour* ('saʊə)

ɛ as in *bet* (bɛt), *ate* (ɛt), *bury* ('bɛrɪ), *heifer* ('hɛfə), *said* (sɛd), *says* (sɛz)

eɪ as in *paid* (peɪd), *day* (deɪ), *deign* (deɪn), *gauge* (geɪdʒ), *grey* (greɪ), *neigh* (neɪ)

ɛə as in *bear* (bɛə), *dare* (dɛə), *prayer* (prɛə), *stairs* (stɛəz), *where* (wɛə)

g as in *get* (gɛt), *give* (gɪv), *ghoul* (guːl), *guard* (gɑːd), *examine* (ɪg'zæmɪn)

ɪ as in *pretty* ('prɪtɪ), *build* (bɪld), *busy* ('bɪzɪ), *nymph* (nɪmf), *pocket* ('pɒkɪt), *sieve* (sɪv), *women* ('wɪmɪn)

iː as in *see* (siː), *aesthete* ('iːsθiːt), *evil* ('iːvᵊl), *magazine* (ˌmægə'ziːn), *receive* (rɪ'siːv), *siege* (siːdʒ)

ɪə as in *fear* (fɪə), *beer* (bɪə), *mere* (mɪə), *tier* (tɪə)

j as in *yes* (jɛs), *onion* ('ʌnjən), *vignette* (vɪ'njɛt)

ɒ as in *pot* (pɒt), *botch* (bɒtʃ), *sorry* ('sɒrɪ)

əʊ as in *note* (nəʊt), *beau* (bəʊ), *dough* (dəʊ), *hoe* (həʊ), *slow* (sləʊ), *yeoman* ('jəʊmən)

ɔː as in *thaw* (θɔː), *broad* (brɔːd), *drawer* ('drɔːə), *fault* (fɔːlt), *halt* (hɔːlt), *organ* ('ɔːgən)

ɔɪ as in *void* (vɔɪd), *boy* (bɔɪ), *destroy* (dɪ'strɔɪ)

ʊ as in *pull* (pʊl), *good* (gʊd), *should* (ʃʊd), *woman* ('wʊmən)

uː as in *zoo* (zuː), *do* (duː), *queue* (kjuː), *shoe* (ʃuː), *spew* (spjuː), *true* (truː), *you* (juː)

ʊə as in *poor* (pʊə), *skewer* (skjʊə), *sure* (ʃʊə)

ə as in *potter* ('pɒtə), *alone* (ə'ləʊn), *furious* ('fjʊərɪəs), *nation* ('neɪʃən), *the* (ðə)

ɜː as in *fern* (fɜːn), *burn* (bɜːn), *fir* (fɜː), *learn* (lɜːn), *term* (tɜːm), *worm* (wɜːm)

ʌ as in *cut* (kʌt), *flood* (flʌd), *rough* (rʌf), *son* (sʌn)

ʃ as in *ship* (ʃɪp), *election* (ɪ'lɛkʃən), *machine* (mə'ʃiːn), *mission* ('mɪʃən), *pressure* ('prɛʃə), *schedule* ('ʃɛdjuːl), *sugar* ('ʃʊgə)

ʒ as in *treasure* ('trɛʒə), *azure* ('æʒə), *closure* ('kləʊʒə), *evasion* (ɪ'veɪʒən)

tʃ as in *chew* (tʃuː), *nature* ('neɪtʃə)

dʒ as in *jaw* (dʒɔː), *adjective* ('ædʒɪktɪv), *lodge* (lɒdʒ), *soldier* ('səʊldʒə), *usage* ('juːsɪdʒ)

θ as in *thin* (θɪn), *strength* (strɛŋθ), *three* (θriː)

ð as in *these* (ðiːz), *bathe* (beɪð), *lather* ('lɑːðə)

ŋ as in *sing* (sɪŋ), *finger* ('fɪŋgə), *sling* (slɪŋ)

ᵊ indicates that the following consonant (*l or n*) is syllabic, as in *bundle* ('bʌndᵊl), *button* ('bʌtᵊn)

Foreign Sounds

The symbols above are also used to represent foreign sounds where these are similar to English sounds. However, certain common foreign sounds require symbols with markedly different values, as follows:

a *a* in French *ami*, German *Mann*, Italian *pasta*: a sound between English (æ) and (ɑː), similar to the vowel in Northern English *cat* or London *cut*.

ɑ *a* in French *bas*: a sound made with the tongue position similar to that of English (ɑː), but shorter.

e *é* in French *été*, *eh* in German *sehr*, *e* in Italian *che*: a sound similar to the first part of the English diphthong (eɪ) in *day* or to the Scottish vowel in *day*.

i *i* in French *il*, German *Idee*, Spanish *filo*, Italian *signor*: a sound made with a tongue position similar to that of English (iː), but shorter.

ɔ *o* in Italian *no*, French *bonne*, German *Sonne*: a vowel resembling English (ɒ), but with a higher tongue position and more rounding of the lips.

o *o* in French *rose*, German *so*, Italian *voce*: a sound between English (ɔː) and (uː) with closely rounded lips, similar to the Scottish vowel in *so*.

u *ou* in French *genou*, *u* in German *kulant*, Spanish *puna*: a sound made with a tongue position similar to that of English (uː), but shorter.

y *u* in French *tu*, *ü* in German *über* or *fünf*: a sound made with a tongue position similar to that of English (iː), but with closely rounded lips.

ø *eu* in French *deux*, *ö* in German *schön*: a sound made with the tongue position of (e), but with closely rounded lips.

œ *œu* in French *œuf*, *ö* in German *zwölf*: a sound made with a tongue position similar to that of English (ɛ), but with open rounded lips.

~ above a vowel indicates nasalization, as in French *un* (œ̃), *bon* (bɔ̃), *vin* (vɛ̃), *blanc* (blɑ̃).

χ *ch* in Scottish *loch*, German *Buch*, *j* in Spanish *Juan*.

ç *ch* in German *ich*: a (j) sound as in *yes*, said without voice; similar to the first sound in *huge*.

β *b* in Spanish *Habana*: a voiced fricative sound similar to (v), but made by the two lips.

ʎ *ll* in Spanish *llamar*, *gl* in Italian *consiglio*: similar to the (lj) sequence in *million*, but with the tongue tip lowered and the sounds said simultaneously.

ɥ *u* in French *lui*: a short (y).

ɲ *gn* in French *vigne*, Italian *gnocchi*, *ñ* in Spanish *España*: similar to the (nj) sequence in *onion*, but with the tongue tip lowered and the two sounds said simultaneously.

ɣ *g* in Spanish *luego*: a weak (g) made with voiced friction.

Pronunciation Key

Length

The symbol : denotes length and is shown together with certain vowel symbols when the vowels are typically long.

Stress

Three grades of stress are shown in the transcriptions by the presence or absence of marks placed immediately *before* the affected syllable. Primary or strong stress is shown by ˈ, while secondary or weak stress is shown by ˌ. Unstressed syllables are not marked. In *photographic* (ˌfəʊtəˈgræfɪk), for example, the first syllable carries secondary stress and the third primary stress, while the second and fourth are unstressed.

Notes

(i) Though words like *castle, path,* and *fast* are shown as pronounced with an /ɑː/ sound, many speakers use an /æ/. Such variations are acceptable and are to be assumed by the reader.

(ii) The letter "r" in some positions is not sounded in the speech of Southern England and elsewhere. However, many speakers in other areas do sound the "r" in such positions with varying degrees of distinctness. Again such variations are to be assumed, and in such words as *fern, fear,* and *arm* the reader will sound or not sound the "r" according to his or her speech habits.

(iii) Though the widely received pronunciation of words like *which* and *why* is with a simple /w/ sound and is so shown in the dictionary, many speakers in Scotland and elsewhere preserve an aspirated sound: /hw/. Once again this variation is to be assumed.

English Dictionary & Thesaurus

Aa

a *or* **A** (eɪ) *n, pl* **a's, A's,** *or* **As. 1** the first letter and first vowel of the English alphabet. **2** any of several speech sounds represented by this letter, as in *take, bag,* or *calm.* **3** Also called: **alpha.** the first in a series, esp. the highest mark. **4 from A to Z.** from start to finish.

a[1] (ə; *emphatic* eɪ) *determiner* (*indefinite article;* used before an initial consonant. Cf. **an**[1]) **1** used preceding a singular countable noun, not previously specified: *a dog; a great pity.* **2** used preceding a noun or determiner of quantity: *a dozen eggs; a great many; to read a lot.* **3** (preceded by *once, twice, several times,* etc.) each or every; per: *once a day.* **4** a certain; one: *a Mr Jones called.* **5** (preceded by *not*) any at all: *not a hope.* ◆ Cf. **the**[1].

a[2] *symbol for:* **1** acceleration. **2** are(s) (metric measure of area). **3** atto-.

A *symbol for:* **1** *Music.* **1a** the sixth note of the scale of C major. **1b** the major or minor key having this note as its tonic. **2** a human blood type of the ABO group, containing the A antigen. **3** (in Britain) a major arterial road. **4** ampere(s). **5** absolute (temperature). **6** area. **7** (*in combination*) atomic: *an A-bomb; an A-plant.* **8a** a person whose job is in top management, or who holds a senior administrative or professional position. **8b** (*as modifier*): *an A worker.* ◆ See also **occupation groupings.**

Å *symbol for* angstrom unit.

a. *abbrev. for:* **1** acre(s). **2** Also: **A.** alto.

A. *abbrev. for:* **1** acre(s). **2** America(n). **3** answer.

a-[1] *or before a vowel* **an-** *prefix* not; without; opposite to: *atonal; asocial.* [from Gk *a-, an-* not, without]

a-[2] *prefix* **1** on; in; towards: *aground; aback.* **2** in the state of: *afloat; asleep.*

A1, A-1, *or* **A-one** (ˈeɪˈwʌn) *adj* **1** physically fit. **2** *Inf.* first class; excellent. **3** (of a vessel) in first-class condition.

A4 *n* a standard paper size, 297 × 210 mm.

AA *abbrev. for:* **1** Alcoholics Anonymous. **2** anti-aircraft. **3** (in Britain) Automobile Association.

AAA *abbrev. for:* **1** (formerly) *Brit.* Amateur Athletic Association. **2** *US.* Automobile Association of America.

A and E *abbrev. for* Accident and Emergency (in hospitals).

A and R *abbrev. for* artists and repertoire.

AAP *abbrev. for:* **1** Australian Associated Press. **2** (in the US) affirmative action programme.

aardvark (ˈɑːdˌvɑːk) *n* a nocturnal burrowing African mammal that has long ears and snout and feeds on termites. Also called: **ant bear.** [C19: from obs. Afrik., from *aarde* earth + *varken* pig]

aardwolf (ˈɑːdˌwʊlf) *n, pl* **aardwolves.** a nocturnal mammal of the hyena family that inhabits the plains of southern Africa and feeds on termites and insect larvae. [C19: from Afrik., from *aarde* earth + *wolf* wolf]

Aaron's beard (ˈɛərən) *n* another name for **rose of Sharon.**

Aaron's rod *n* a widespread Eurasian plant having tall erect spikes of yellow flowers.

A'asia *abbrev. for* Australasia.

AB *abbrev. for:* **1** Also: **a.b.** able-bodied seaman. **2** Alberta. **3** (in the US) Bachelor of Arts. ◆ **4** *symbol for* a human blood type of the ABO group, containing both the A antigen and the B antigen.

ab-[1] *prefix* away from; opposite to: *abnormal.* [from L *ab* away from]

ab-[2] *prefix* a cgs unit of measurement in the electromagnetic system: *abampere, abwatt, abvolt.* [from ABSOLUTE]

aba (ˈæbə) *n* **1** a type of cloth from Syria, made of goat or camel hair. **2** a sleeveless outer garment of such cloth. [from Ar.]

abaca (ˈæbəkə) *n* **1** a Philippine plant, the source of Manila hemp. **2** another name for **Manila hemp.** [via Sp. from Tagalog *abaká*]

aback ❶ (əˈbæk) *adv* **taken aback. 1** startled or disconcerted. **2** *Naut.* (of a vessel or sail) having the wind against the forward side so as to prevent forward motion. [OE *on bæc* to the back]

abacus (ˈæbəkəs) *n, pl* **abaci** (-ˌsaɪ) *or* **abacuses. 1** a counting device that consists of a frame holding rods on which a number of beads are free to move. **2** *Archit.* the flat upper part of the capital of a column. [C16: from L, from Gk *abax* board covered with sand, from Heb. *ābhāq* dust]

abaft (əˈbɑːft) *Naut.* ◆ *adv, adj* (*postpositive*) **1** closer to the stern than to another place on a vessel. ◆ *prep* **2** behind; aft of. [C13: *on baft; baft* from OE *beæftan,* from *be* by + *æftan* behind]

abalone (ˌæbəˈləʊnɪ) *n* an edible marine mollusc having an ear-shaped shell perforated with a row of respiratory holes and lined with mother-of-pearl. Also called: **ear shell.** [C19: from American Sp. *abulón*]

abandon ❶ (əˈbændən) *vb* (*tr*) **1** to forsake completely; desert; leave behind. **2** to give up completely: *to abandon hope.* **3** to give up (something begun) before completion: *the game was abandoned.* **4** to surrender (oneself) to emotion without restraint. **5** to give (insured property that has suffered partial loss or damage) to the insurers in order that a claim for a total loss may be made. ◆ *n* **6** freedom from inhibitions, restraint, or worry: *she danced with abandon.* [C14: *abandounen* (vb), from OF, from *a bandon* under one's control, from *a* at, to + *bandon* control]
▸**aˈbandonment** *n*

abandoned ❶ (əˈbændənd) *adj* **1** deserted: *an abandoned hut.* **2** forsaken: *an abandoned child.* **3** uninhibited.

abase ❶ (əˈbeɪs) *vb* **abases, abasing, abased.** (*tr*) **1** to humble or belittle (oneself, etc.). **2** to lower or reduce, as in rank. [C15 *abessen,* from OF *abaissier* to make low. See BASE[2]]
▸**aˈbasement** *n*

abash ❶ (əˈbæʃ) *vb* (*tr; usually passive*) to cause to feel ill at ease, embarrassed, or confused. [C14: from OF *esbair* to be astonished, from *es-* out + *bair* to gape]
▸**aˈbashed** *adj*

abate ❶ (əˈbeɪt) *vb* **abates, abating, abated. 1** to make or become less in amount, intensity, degree, etc. **2** (*tr*) *Law.* **2a** to suppress or terminate (a nuisance). **2b** to suspend or extinguish (a claim or action). **2c** to annul (a writ). **3** (*intr*) *Law.* (of a writ, etc.) to become null and void. [C14: from OF *abatre* to beat down]
▸**aˈbatement** *n*

abatis *or* **abattis** (ˈæbətɪs) *n* **1** a rampart of felled trees with their branches outwards. **2** a barbed-wire entanglement before a position. [C18: from F, from *abattre* to fell]

abattoir ❶ (ˈæbəˌtwɑː) *n* another name for **slaughterhouse.** [C19: F, from *abattre* to fell]

abbacy (ˈæbəsɪ) *n, pl* **abbacies.** the office, term of office, or jurisdiction of an abbot or abbess. [C15: from Church L *abbātia,* from *abbāt-* ABBOT]

abbatial (əˈbeɪʃəl) *adj* of an abbot, abbess, or abbey. [C17: from Church L *abbātiālis,* from *abbāt-* ABBOT]

abbé (ˈæbeɪ) *n* **1** a French abbot. **2** a title used in addressing any other French cleric, such as a priest.

abbess (ˈæbɪs) *n* the female superior of a convent. [C13: from OF, from Church L *abbātissa*]

Abbevillian (æbˈvɪlɪən) *Archaeol.* ◆ *n* **1** the period represented by

THESAURUS

aback *adv* **1 taken aback = surprised,** astonished, astounded, bewildered, disconcerted, flabbergasted (*inf.*), floored (*inf.*), nonplussed, staggered, startled, stunned

abandon *vb* **1, 2 = leave,** desert, forsake, jilt, leave behind, leave in the lurch, let (someone) stew in their own juice, strand **1 = evacuate,** quit, vacate, withdraw from **2 = give up,** abdicate, cede, relinquish, renounce, resign, surrender, waive, yield **3 = stop,** desist, discontinue, drop, forgo, kick (*inf.*) ◆ *n* **6 = wildness,** careless freedom, dash, recklessness, unrestraint, wantonness, wild impulse
Antonyms *vb* ≠ **evacuate:** defend, maintain, uphold ≠ **give up:** claim, hold, keep, take ≠ **stop:** continue ◆ *n* ≠ **wildness:** control, moderation, restraint

abandoned *adj* **1, 2 = left,** cast aside, cast away, cast out, derelict, deserted, discarded, ditched, dropped, forlorn, forsaken, jilted, neglected, outcast, out of the window, rejected, relinquished, stranded **1 = unoccupied,** vacant **3 = uninhibited,** uncontrolled, unrestrained, wild
Antonyms *adj* ≠ **unoccupied:** claimed, kept, maintained, occupied ≠ **uninhibited:** conscious, inhibited, restrained

abandonment *n* **1, 2 = leaving,** dereliction, desertion, forsaking, jilting **1 = evacuation,** quitting, withdrawal from **2 = giving up,** abdication, cession, relinquishment, renunciation, resignation, surrender, waiver **3 = stopping,** desistance, discontinuation, dropping

abase *vb* **1, 2 = humble,** belittle, bring low, cast down, debase, degrade, demean, demote, denigrate, depress, disgrace, dishonour, downgrade, humiliate, lower, mortify, put in one's place, reduce
Antonyms *vb* advance, aggrandize, dignify, elevate, exalt, glorify, honour, prefer, promote, raise, upgrade

abasement *n* **1, 2 = humbling,** belittlement, debasement, degradation, demotion, depression, disgrace, dishonour, downgrading, humiliation, lowering, mortification, reduction, shame

abashed *adj* **= embarrassed,** affronted, ashamed, astounded, bewildered, chagrined, confounded, confused, discomfited, discomposed, disconcerted, discountenanced, dismayed, humbled, humiliated, mortified, perturbed, shamefaced, taken aback
Antonyms *adj* at ease, blatant, bold, brazen, composed, confident, unabashed, unashamed, undaunted, undismayed, unperturbed

abate *vb* **1 = decrease,** alleviate, appease, attenuate, decline, diminish, dull, dwindle, ease, ebb, fade, lessen, let up, mitigate, moderate, quell, reduce, relax, relieve, sink, slacken, slake, slow, subside, taper off, wane, weaken
Antonyms *vb* add to, amplify, augment, boost, enhance, escalate, increase, intensify, magnify, multiply, strengthen

abatement *n* **1 = decrease,** alleviation, allowance, attenuation, cessation, decline, diminution, dulling, dwindling, easing, extenuation, fading, lessening, let-up (*inf.*), mitigation, moderation, quelling, reduction, relief, remission, slackening, slaking, slowing, tapering off, waning, weakening

abattoir *n* **= slaughterhouse,** butchery, shambles

Lower Palaeolithic European sites containing the earliest hand axes. ◆ *adj* **2** of this period.

abbey ➊ ('æbɪ) *n* **1** a building inhabited by a community of monks or nuns. **2** a church built in conjunction with such a building. **3** a community of monks or nuns. [C13: via OF *abeie* from Church L *abbātia* ABBACY]

abbot ('æbət) *n* the superior of an abbey of monks. [OE *abbod,* from Church L *abbāt-* (stem of *abbas*), ult. from Aramaic *abbā* father]
▸ **'abbotship** *or* **'abbotcy** *n*

abbreviate ➊ (ə'briːvɪ,eɪt) *vb* **abbreviates, abbreviating, abbreviated.** (*tr*) **1** to shorten (a word or phrase) by contraction or omission of some letters or words. **2** to cut short; curtail. [C15: from p.p. of LL *abbreviāre,* from L *brevis* brief]

abbreviation ➊ (ə,briːvɪ'eɪʃən) *n* **1** a shortened or contracted form of a word or phrase. **2** the process or result of abbreviating.

ABC[1] *n* **1** (*pl in US*) the rudiments of a subject. **2** an alphabetical guide. **3** (*often pl in US*) the alphabet.

ABC[2] *abbrev. for:* **1** American Broadcasting Company. **2** Australian Broadcasting Corporation.

abdicate ➊ ('æbdɪ,keɪt) *vb* **abdicates, abdicating, abdicated.** to renounce (a throne, rights, etc.), esp. formally. [C16: from L *abdicāre* to disclaim]
▸ **,abdi'cation** *n* ▸ **'abdi,cator** *n*

abdomen ➊ ('æbdəmən) *n* **1** the region of the body of a vertebrate that contains the viscera other than the heart and lungs. **2** the front or surface of this region; belly. **3** (in arthropods) the posterior part of the body behind the thorax. [C16: from L; from ?]
▸ **abdominal** (æb'dɒmɪnᵊl) *adj*

abduct ➊ (æb'dʌkt) *vb* (*tr*) **1** to remove (a person) by force or cunning; kidnap. **2** (of certain muscles) to pull (a leg, arm, etc.) away from the median axis of the body. [C19: from L *abdūcere* to lead away]
▸ **ab'duction** *n* ▸ **ab'ductor** *n*

abeam (ə'biːm) *adv, adj* (*postpositive*) at right angles to the length of a vessel or aircraft. [C19: A-[2] + BEAM]

abed (ə'bed) *adv Arch.* in bed.

Aberdeen Angus (,æbə'diːn 'æŋgəs) *n* a black hornless breed of beef cattle originating in Scotland.

aberrant ➊ (æ'berənt) *adj* **1** deviating from the normal or usual type. **2** behaving in an abnormal or untypical way. **3** deviating from morality. [rare before C19: from L *aberrāre* to wander away]
▸ **ab'errance** *or* **ab'errancy** *n*

aberration ➊ (,æbə'reɪʃən) *n* **1** deviation from what is normal, expected, or usual. **2** departure from truth, morality, etc. **3** a lapse in control of one's mental faculties. **4** *Optics.* a defect in a lens or mirror that causes either a distorted image or one with coloured fringes. **5** *Astron.* the apparent displacement of a celestial body due to the motion of the observer with the earth.

abet ➊ (ə'bet) *vb* **abets, abetting, abetted.** (*tr*) to assist or encourage, esp. in wrongdoing. [C14: from OF *abeter* to lure on, from *beter* to bait]
▸ **a'betment** *n* ▸ **a'better** *or* (*esp. Law*) **a'bettor** *n*

abeyance ➊ (ə'beɪəns) *n* **1** (usually preceded by *in* or *into*) a state of being suspended or put aside temporarily. **2** (usually preceded by *in*) *Law.* an indeterminate state of ownership. [C16–17: from Anglo-F, from OF *abeance* expectation, lit. a gaping after]

ABH *abbrev. for* actual bodily harm.

abhor ➊ (əb'hɔː) *vb* **abhors, abhorring, abhorred.** (*tr*) to detest vehemently; find repugnant. [C15: from L *abhorrēre,* from *ab-* away from + *horrēre* to shudder]
▸ **ab'horrer** *n*

abhorrence ➊ (əb'hɒrəns) *n* **1** a feeling of extreme loathing or aversion. **2** a person or thing that is loathsome.

abhorrent ➊ (əb'hɒrənt) *adj* **1** repugnant; loathsome. **2** (when *postpositive,* foll. by *of*) feeling extreme aversion (for): *abhorrent of vulgarity.* **3** (usually *postpositive* and foll. by *to*) conflicting (with): *abhorrent to common sense.*

abide ➊ (ə'baɪd) *vb* **abides, abiding, abode** *or* **abided. 1** (*tr*) to tolerate; put up with. **2** (*tr*) to accept or submit to. **3** (*intr;* foll. by *by*) **3a** to comply (with): *to abide by the decision.* **3b** to remain faithful (to): *to abide by your promise.* **4** (*intr*) to remain or continue. **5** (*intr*) *Arch.* to dwell. **6** (*tr*) *Arch.* to await in expectation. [OE *ābīdan,* from *a-* (intensive) + *bīdan* to wait]
▸ **a'bider** *n*

abiding ➊ (ə'baɪdɪŋ) *adj* permanent; enduring: *an abiding belief.*

ability ➊ (ə'bɪlɪtɪ) *n, pl* **abilities. 1** possession of necessary skill, competence, or power. **2** considerable proficiency; natural capability: *a man of ability.* **3** (*pl*) special talents. [C14: from OF from L *habilitās* aptitude, from *habilis* ABLE]

ab initio ➊ *Latin.* (æb ɪ'nɪʃɪ,əʊ) from the start.

abiogenesis (,eɪbaɪəʊ'dʒenɪsɪs) *n* the hypothetical process by which living organisms arise from inanimate matter. Also called: **spontaneous generation.** [C19: NL, from A-[1] + BIO- + GENESIS]

abject ➊ ('æbdʒekt) *adj* **1** utterly wretched or hopeless. **2** forlorn; dejected. **3** submissive: *an abject apology.* **4** contemptible; despicable: *an abject liar.* [C14 (in the sense: rejected, cast out): from L *abjectus* thrown away, from *abjicere,* from *ab-* away + *jacere* to throw]
▸ **ab'jection** *n* ▸ **'abjectly** *adv* ▸ **'abjectness** *n*

abjure (əb'dʒʊə) *vb* **abjures, abjuring, abjured.** (*tr*) **1** to renounce or retract, esp. formally or under oath. **2** to abstain from. [C15: from OF *abjurer* or L *abjurāre* to deny on oath]
▸ **,abju'ration** *n* ▸ **ab'jurer** *n*

ablation (æb'leɪʃən) *n* **1** the surgical removal of an organ, structure, or part. **2** the melting or wearing away of a part, such as the heat shield of a space re-entry vehicle on passing through the earth's atmo-

THESAURUS

abbey *n* **1, 2** = **monastery**, cloister, convent, friary, nunnery, priory

abbreviate *vb* **1, 2** = **shorten**, abridge, abstract, clip, compress, condense, contract, curtail, cut, digest, epitomize, précis, reduce, summarize, trim, truncate
Antonyms *vb* amplify, draw out, elongate, expand, extend, increase, lengthen, prolong, protract, spin out, stretch out

abbreviated *adj* **1, 2** = **shortened**, abridged, brief, compressed, concise, condensed, cut, potted, pruned, reduced, shorter, summarized, trimmed
Antonyms *adj* amplified, diffuse, drawn out, expanded, increased, prolonged, protracted, unabbreviated, unabridged

abbreviation *n* **1, 2** = **shortening**, abridgment, abstract, clipping, compendium, compression, condensation, conspectus, contraction, curtailment, digest, epitome, précis, reduction, résumé, summary, synopsis, trimming, truncation

abdicate *vb* = **give up**, abandon, abjure, abnegate, cede, forgo, quit, relinquish, renounce, resign, retire, step down (*inf.*), surrender, vacate, waive, yield

abdication *n* = **giving up**, abandonment, abjuration, abnegation, cession, quitting, relinquishment, renunciation, resignation, retiral (*especially Scot.*), retirement, surrender, waiver, yielding

abdomen *n* **2** = **stomach**, belly, breadbasket (*sl.*), corporation (*inf.*), guts (*sl.*), midriff, midsection, paunch, pot, tummy (*inf.*)

abdominal *adj* **1** = **gastric**, intestinal, stomachic, stomachical, visceral

abduct *vb* **1** = **kidnap**, carry off, make off with, run away with, run off with, seize, snatch (*sl.*)

abduction *n* **1** = **kidnapping**, carrying off, seizure

aberrance *n* **1, 2** = **abnormality**, anomaly, deviance, deviation, divergence, eccentricity, irregularity, oddness, peculiarity, variance
Antonyms *n* conformity, consistency, normality, regularity, uniformity

aberrant *adj* **1, 2** = **abnormal**, anomalous, defective, deviant, divergent, eccentric, irregular, odd, outré, peculiar, queer, rambling, straying, untypical, wandering **3** = **wrong**, corrupt, corrupted, degenerate, depraved, deviant, erroneous, perverse, perverted

aberration *n* **1** = **oddity**, aberrancy, abnormality, anomaly, defect, deviation, divergence, eccentricity, irregularity, lapse, peculiarity, quirk, rambling, straying, wandering

abet *vb* = **help**, aid, assist, back, condone, connive at, promote, sanction, second, succour, support, sustain, uphold = **encourage**, egg on, incite, prompt, spur, urge

abetting *n* = **help**, abetment, abettal, aid, assistance, encouragement, facilitation, furtherance, support

abettor *n* = **accomplice**, accessory = **accomplice**, assistant, associate, backer, confederate, conniver, cooperator, helper, henchman, second = **instigator**, encourager, fomenter, inciter = **instigator**, prompter

abeyance *n* **1 in abeyance** = **shelved**, hanging fire, in cold storage (*inf.*), on ice, pending, suspended

abhor *vb* = **hate**, abominate, detest, execrate, loathe, recoil from, regard with repugnance *or* horror, shrink from, shudder at
Antonyms *vb* admire, adore, cherish, covet, delight in, desire, enjoy, like, love, relish

abhorrence *n* **1** = **hatred**, abomination, animosity, aversion, detestation, disgust, distaste, enmity, execration, hate, horror, loathing, odium, repugnance, revulsion

abhorrent *adj* **1** = **hateful**, abominable, detestable, disgusting, distasteful, execrable, hated, heinous, horrible, horrid, loathsome, obnoxious, obscene, odious, offensive, repellent, repugnant, repulsive, revolting, yucky *or* yukky (*sl.*)

abide *vb* **1** = **tolerate**, accept, bear, brook, endure, hack (*sl.*), put up with, stand, stomach, submit to, suffer **3a** = **obey**, acknowledge, agree to, comply with, conform to, follow, observe, submit to, toe the line **3b** = **carry out**, adhere to, discharge, fulfil, hold to, keep to, persist in, stand by **4** = **last**, continue, endure, persist, remain, survive **5** = **stay**, dwell, linger, live, lodge, reside, rest, sojourn, stop, tarry, wait

abiding *adj* = **everlasting**, constant, continuing, durable, enduring, eternal, fast, firm, immortal, immutable, indissoluble, lasting, permanent, persistent, persisting, steadfast, surviving, tenacious, unchanging, unending
Antonyms *adj* brief, ephemeral, evanescent, fleeting, momentary, passing, short, short-lived, temporary, transient, transitory

ability *n* **1-3** = **skill**, adeptness, aptitude, capability, capacity, competence, competency, craft, dexterity, endowment, energy, expertise, expertness, facility, faculty, flair, force, gift, knack, know-how (*inf.*), potentiality, power, proficiency, qualification, talent
Antonyms *n* inability, incapability, incapacity, incompetence, powerlessness, weakness

ab initio *adv* = **from the beginning**, *ab ovo,* from first principles, from scratch (*inf.*), from the first, from the start, initially, originally, to begin *or* start with

abject *adj* **1, 2** = **miserable**, deplorable, forlorn, hopeless, outcast, pitiable, wretched **3, 4** = **servile**, base, contemptible, cringing, debased, degraded, despicable, dishonourable, fawning, grovelling, humiliating, ignoble, ignominious, low, mean, slavish, sordid, submissive, vile, worthless
Antonyms *adj* ≠ **servile**: august, dignified, distinguished, elevated, eminent, exalted, grand, great, high, lofty, noble, patrician, worthy

abjectness *n* **1, 2** = **misery**, destitution, forlornness, hopelessness, pitiableness, pitifulness, squalor, wretchedness **3, 4** = **degradation**, abjection, baseness, contemptibleness, debase-

sphere. **3** the wearing away of a rock or glacier. [C15: from LL *ablatiōn-*, from L *auferre* to carry away]
▸**ablate** (æb'leɪt) *vb*

ablative ('æblətɪv) *Grammar.* ◆ *adj* **1** (in certain inflected languages such as Latin) denoting a case of nouns, pronouns, and adjectives indicating the agent, or the instrument, manner, or place of the action. ◆ *n* **2** the ablative case or a speech element in it.

ablaut ('æblaut) *n Linguistics.* vowel gradation, esp. in Indo-European languages. See **gradation** (sense 5). [G, coined 1819 by Jakob Grimm from *ab* off + *Laut* sound]

ablaze ⓘ (ə'bleɪz) *adj (postpositive), adv* **1** on fire; burning. **2** brightly illuminated. **3** emotionally aroused.

able ⓘ ('eɪbᵊl) *adj* **1** (*postpositive*) having the necessary power, resources, skill, opportunity, etc., to do something. **2** capable; talented. **3** *Law.* competent or authorized. [C14: ult. from L *habilis* easy to hold, manageable, from *habēre* to have + *-ilis* -ILE]

-able *suffix forming adjectives.* **1** capable of or deserving of (being acted upon as indicated): *enjoyable; washable.* **2** inclined to; able to; causing: *comfortable; variable.* [via OF from L *-ābilis, -ībilis*, forms of *-bilis*, adjectival suffix]
▸**-ably** *suffix forming adverbs.* ▸**-ability** *suffix forming nouns.*

able-bodied ⓘ *adj* physically strong and healthy; robust.

able-bodied seaman *n* a seaman, esp. one in the merchant navy, who has been trained in certain skills. Also: **able seaman.** Abbrev.: **AB, a.b.**

abled ('eɪbᵊld) *adj* having a range of physical powers as specified (esp. in **less abled, differently abled**).

ableism ('eɪbᵊl,ɪzəm) *n* discrimination against disabled or handicapped people.

able rating *n* (esp. in the Royal Navy) a rating who is qualified to perform certain duties of seamanship.

abloom (ə'blu:m) *adj (postpositive)* in flower; blooming.

ablution ⓘ (ə'blu:ʃən) *n* **1** the ritual washing of a priest's hands or of sacred vessels. **2** (*often pl*) the act of washing: *perform one's ablutions.* **3** (*pl*) *Mil. inf.* a washing place. [C14: ult. from L *ablūere* to wash away]
▸**ab'lutionary** *adj*

ably ('eɪblɪ) *adv* in a competent or skilful manner.

ABM *abbrev. for* antiballistic missile.

abnegate ('æbnɪ,geɪt) *vb* **abnegates, abnegating, abnegated.** (*tr*) to deny to oneself; renounce. [C17: from L *abnegāre* to deny]
▸**,abne'gation** *n* ▸**'abne,gator** *n*

abnormal ⓘ (æb'nɔ:məl) *adj* **1** not normal; deviating from the usual or typical. **2** concerned with abnormal behaviour: *abnormal psychology.* **3** *Inf.* odd; strange. [C19: AB-¹ + NORMAL, replacing earlier *anormal* from Med. L *anormalus*, a blend of LL *anōmalus* ANOMALOUS + L *abnormis* departing from a rule]
▸**ab'normally** *adv*

abnormality ⓘ (,æbnɔ:'mælɪtɪ) *n, pl* **abnormalities. 1** an abnormal feature, event, etc. **2** a physical malformation. **3** deviation from the usual.

Abo ('æbəu) *n, pl* **Abos.** (*sometimes not cap.*) *Austral. inf., often derog.* short for **Aborigine** (sense 1).

aboard (ə'bɔ:d) *adv, adj (postpositive), prep* **1** on, in, onto, or into (a ship, train, etc.). **2** *Naut.* alongside. **3 all aboard!** a warning to passengers to board a vehicle, ship, etc.

abode¹ ⓘ (ə'bəud) *n* a place in which one lives; one's home. [C17: n formed from ABIDE]

abode² (ə'bəud) *vb* a past tense and past participle of **abide.**

abolish ⓘ (ə'bɒlɪʃ) *vb* (*tr*) to do away with (laws, regulations, customs, etc.). [C15: from OF, ult. from L *abolēre* to destroy]
▸**a'bolishable** *adj* ▸**a'bolisher** *n* ▸**a'bolishment** *n*

abolition ⓘ (,æbə'lɪʃən) *n* **1** the act of abolishing or the state of being abolished; annulment. **2** (*often cap.*) (in British territories) the ending of the slave trade (1807) or of slavery (1833). **3** (*often cap.*) (in the US) the emancipation of slaves, by the Emancipation Proclamation (1863, ratified 1865). [C16: from L *abolitio*, from *abolēre* to destroy]
▸**,abo'litionary** *adj* ▸**,abo'litionism** *n* ▸**,abo'litionist** *n, adj*

abomasum (,æbə'meɪsəm) *n* the fourth and last compartment of the stomach of ruminants. [C18: NL, from AB-¹ + *omāsum* bullock's tripe]

A-bomb *n* short for **atomic bomb.**

abominable ⓘ (ə'bɒmɪnəbᵊl) *adj* **1** offensive; loathsome; detestable. **2** *Inf.* very bad or inferior: *abominable workmanship.* [C14: from L, from *abōminārī* to ABOMINATE]
▸**a'bominably** *adv*

abominable snowman *n* a large manlike or apelike creature alleged to inhabit the Himalayas. Also called: **yeti.** [translation of Tibetan *metohkangmi*, from *metoh* foul + *kangmi* snowman]

abominate ⓘ (ə'bɒmɪ,neɪt) *vb* **abominates, abominating, abominated.** (*tr*) to dislike intensely; detest. [C17: from L *abōminārī* to regard as an ill omen, from *ab-* away from + *ōmin-*, from OMEN]
▸**a'bomi,nator** *n*

abomination ⓘ (ə,bɒmɪ'neɪʃən) *n* **1** a person or thing that is disgusting or loathsome. **2** an action that is vicious, vile, etc. **3** intense loathing or disgust.

aboriginal ⓘ (,æbə'rɪdʒɪnᵊl) *adj* existing in a place from the earliest known period; indigenous.
▸**,abo'riginally** *adv*

Aboriginal (,æbə'rɪdʒɪnᵊl) *adj* **1** of, relating to, or characteristic of the native peoples of Australia. ◆ *n* **2** another word for **Aborigine** (sense 1).
▸**,Abo,rigi'nality** *n*

aborigine ⓘ (,æbə'rɪdʒɪnɪ) *n* an original inhabitant of a country or region. [C16: back formation from *aborigines*, from L: inhabitants of Latium in pre-Roman times, associated in folk etymology with *ab origine* from the beginning]

Aborigine (,æbə'rɪdʒɪnɪ) *n* **1** Also called: **native Australian, Aboriginal.** a member of a dark-skinned hunting and gathering people who were living in Australia when European settlers arrived. **2** any of the languages of this people.

abort ⓘ (ə'bɔ:t) *vb* **1** to undergo or cause (a woman) to undergo the ter-

THESAURUS

ment, dishonour, humbleness, humiliation, ignominy, lowness, meanness, servility, slavishness, sordidness, submissiveness, vileness, worthlessness

ablaze *adj* **1** = **on fire**, afire, aflame, alight, blazing, burning, fiery, flaming, ignited, lighted **2** = **glowing**, aglow, brilliant, flashing, gleaming, illuminated, incandescent, luminous, radiant, sparkling **3** = **furious**, angry, fit to be tied (*sl.*), foaming at the mouth, fuming, incandescent, incensed, on the warpath, raging **3** = **aroused**, enthusiastic, excited, fervent, frenzied, impassioned, passionate, stimulated

able *adj* **1, 2** = **capable**, accomplished, adept, adequate, adroit, clever, competent, effective, efficient, experienced, expert, fit, fitted, gifted, highly endowed, masterful, masterly, powerful, practised, proficient, qualified, skilful, skilled, strong, talented
Antonyms *adj* amateurish, inadequate, incapable, incompetent, ineffective, inefficient, inept, mediocre, no great shakes (*inf.*), unfit, unskilful, weak

able-bodied *adj* = **strong**, firm, fit, hale, hardy, healthy, hearty, lusty, powerful, robust, sound, staunch, stout, strapping, sturdy, vigorous
Antonyms *adj* ailing, debilitated, feeble, fragile, frail, sickly, tender, weak

ablution *n* **2** *often plural* = **washing**, bath, bathing, cleansing, lavation, purification, shower, wash

abnormal *adj* **1, 3** = **unusual**, aberrant, anomalous, atypical, curious, deviant, eccentric, erratic, exceptional, extraordinary, irregular, monstrous, odd, outré, peculiar, queer, singular, strange, uncommon, unexpected, unnatural, untypical, weird
Antonyms *adj* common, conventional, customary, familiar, natural, normal, ordinary, regular, unexceptional, usual

abnormality *n* **1-3** = **oddity**, aberration, anomaly, atypicalness, bizarreness, deformity, deviation, eccentricity, exception, extraordinariness, flaw, irregularity, monstrosity, peculiarity, queerness, singularity, strangeness, uncommonness, unexpectedness, unnaturalness, untypicalness, unusualness, weirdness

abnormally *adv* **1, 3** = **unusually**, atypically, bizarrely, disproportionately, exceptionally, excessively, extraordinarily, extremely, fantastically, freakishly, inordinately, in the extreme, oddly, overly, particularly, peculiarly, prodigiously, singularly, strangely, subnormally, supernormally, uncannily, uncommonly, unnaturally

abode¹ *n* = **home**, domicile, dwelling, dwelling-place, habitat, habitation, house, lodging, pad (*sl.*), quarters, residence

abolish *vb* = **do away with**, abrogate, annihilate, annul, axe (*inf.*), cancel, destroy, eliminate, end, eradicate, expunge, exterminate, extinguish, extirpate, invalidate, nullify, obliterate, overthrow, overturn, put an end to, quash, repeal, repudiate, rescind, revoke, stamp out, subvert, suppress, terminate, vitiate, void, wipe out
Antonyms *vb* authorize, continue, create, establish, found, institute, introduce, legalize, promote, reinstate, reintroduce, restore, revive, sustain

abolition *n* **1** = **ending**, abrogation, annihilation, annulment, cancellation, destruction, elimination, end, eradication, expunction, extermination, extinction, extirpation, invalidation, nullification, obliteration, overthrow, overturning, quashing, repeal, repudiation, rescission, revocation, stamping out, subversion, suppression, termination, vitiation, voiding, wiping out, withdrawal

abominable *adj* **1** = **terrible**, abhorrent, accursed, atrocious, base, contemptible, despicable, detestable, disgusting, execrable, foul, hateful, heinous, hellish, horrible, horrid, loathsome, nauseous, obnoxious, obscene, odious, repellent, reprehensible, repugnant, repulsive, revolting, vile, villainous, wretched
Antonyms *adj* admirable, agreeable, charming, commendable, delightful, desirable, good, laudable, likable *or* likeable, lovable, pleasant, pleasing, wonderful

abominably *adv* **1** = **terribly**, abhorrently, contemptibly, deplorably, despicably, detestably, disgustingly, dreadfully, execrably, foully, heinously, hideously, horribly, horridly, nauseatingly, obnoxiously, odiously, offensively, reprehensibly, repugnantly, repulsively, revoltingly, shamefully, unpalatably, vilely
Antonyms *adv* admirably, commendably, delightfully, excellently, impeccably, perfectly, wonderfully

abominate *vb* = **hate**, abhor, detest, execrate, loathe, recoil from, regard with repugnance, shudder at
Antonyms *vb* admire, adore, cherish, dote on, esteem, idolize, love, revere, treasure, worship

abomination *n* **1** = **evil**, anathema, bête noire, bugbear, curse, disgrace, horror, plague, shame, torment **3** = **hatred**, abhorrence, antipathy, aversion, detestation, disgust, distaste, execration, hate, horror, loathing, odium, repugnance, revulsion

aboriginal *adj* = **native**, ancient, autochthonous, earliest, first, indigenous, original, primary, primeval, primitive, primordial, pristine

aborigine *n* = **native**, aboriginal, autochthon, indigene, original inhabitant

abort *vb* **1, 2, 5** = **terminate** (*a pregnancy*), mis-

DICTIONARY

mination of pregnancy before the fetus is viable. **2** (*tr*) to cause (a fetus) to be expelled from the womb before it is viable. **3** (*intr*) to fail to come to completion. **4** (*tr*) to stop the development of; cause to be abandoned. **5** (*intr*) to give birth to a dead or nonviable fetus. **6** (of a space flight or other undertaking) to fail or terminate prematurely. **7** (*intr*) (of an organism or part of an organism) to fail to develop into the mature form. ◆ *n* **8** the premature termination or failure of (a space flight, etc.). [C16: from L *abortāre,* from *aborīrī* to miscarry, from *ab-* wrongly + *orīrī* to be born]

abortifacient (əˌbɔːtɪˈfeɪʃənt) *adj* **1** causing abortion. ◆ *n* **2** a drug or agent that causes abortion.

abortion Ⓣ (əˈbɔːʃən) *n* **1** an operation or other procedure to terminate pregnancy before the fetus is viable. **2** the premature termination of pregnancy by spontaneous or induced expulsion of a nonviable fetus from the uterus. **3** an aborted fetus. **4** a failure to develop to completion or maturity. **5** a person or thing that is deformed.

abortionist (əˈbɔːʃənɪst) *n* a person who performs abortions, esp. illegally.

abortion pill *n* a drug, such as mifepristone (RU 486), used to terminate a pregnancy in its earliest stage.

abortive Ⓣ (əˈbɔːtɪv) *adj* **1** failing to achieve a purpose; fruitless. **2** (of organisms) imperfectly developed. **3** causing abortion.

ABO system *n* a system for classifying human blood on the basis of the presence or absence of two antigens in the red cells: there are four such blood types (A, B, AB, and O).

aboulia (əˈbuːlɪə, -ˈbjuː-) *n* a variant spelling of **abulia.**

abound Ⓣ (əˈbaʊnd) *vb* (*intr*) **1** to exist or occur in abundance. **2** (foll. by *with* or *in*) to be plentifully supplied (with): *the fields abound in corn.* [C14: via OF from L *abundāre* to overflow, from *undāre* to flow, from *unda* wave]

about Ⓣ (əˈbaʊt) *prep* **1** relating to; concerning. **2** near or close to. **3** carried on: *I haven't any money about me.* **4** on every side of. **5** active in or engaged in. ◆ *adv* **6** near in number, time, degree, etc.: *about 50 years old.* **7** nearby. **8** here and there: *walk about to keep warm.* **9** all around; on every side. **10** in or to the opposite direction. **11** in rotation or revolution: *turn and turn about.* **12** used in informal phrases to indicate understatement: *it's about time you stopped.* **13** *Arch.* around. **14 about to. 14a** on the point of; intending to: *she was about to jump.* **14b** (*with a negative*) determined not to: *nobody is about to miss it.* ◆ *adj* **15** (*predicative*) active; astir after sleep: *up and about.* **16** (*predicative*) in existence, current, or in circulation: *there aren't many about nowadays.* [OE *abūtan, onbūtan,* from ON + *būtan* outside]

about turn Ⓣ *or US* **about face** *sentence substitute.* **1** a military command to a formation of men to reverse the direction in which they are facing. ◆ *n* **about-turn** *or US* **about-face. 2** a complete change of opinion, direction, etc. ◆ *vb* **about-turn** *or US* **about-face. 3** (*intr*) to perform an about-turn.

above Ⓣ (əˈbʌv) *prep* **1** on top of or higher than; over. **2** greater than in quantity or degree: *above average.* **3** superior to or prior to: *to place honour above wealth.* **4** too high-minded for: *above petty gossiping.* **5** too respected for; beyond: *above suspicion.* **6** too difficult to be understood by: *the talk was above me.* **7** louder or higher than (other noise). **8** in preference to. **9** north of. **10** upstream from. **11 above all.** most of all; especially. **12 above and beyond.** in addition to. ◆ *adv* **13** in or to a higher place: *the sky above.* **14a** in a previous place (in something written). **14b** (*in combination*): *the above-mentioned clause.* **15** higher in rank or position. **16** in or concerned with heaven. ◆ *n* **17 the above.** something previously mentioned. ◆ *adj* **18** appearing in a previous place (in something written). [OE *abufan,* from *a-* on + *bufan* above]

above board Ⓣ *adj* (**aboveboard** *when prenominal*), *adv* in the open; without dishonesty, concealment, or fraud.

abracadabra Ⓣ (ˌæbrəkəˈdæbrə) *interj* **1** a spoken formula, used esp. by conjurors. ◆ *n* **2** a word used in incantations, etc., considered to possess magic powers. **3** gibberish. [C17: magical word used in certain Gnostic writings, ? rel. to Gk *Abraxas,* a Gnostic deity]

abrade Ⓣ (əˈbreɪd) *vb* **abrades, abrading, abraded.** (*tr*) to scrape away or wear down by friction. [C17: from L *abrādere,* from AB-[1] + *rādere* to scrape]
▸**aˈbrader** *n*

abranchiate (əˈbræŋkɪɪt, -ˌeɪt) *or* **abranchial** *adj Zool.* having no gills. [C19: A-[1] + BRANCHIATE]

abrasion Ⓣ (əˈbreɪʒən) *n* **1** the process of scraping or wearing down by friction. **2** a scraped area or spot; graze. **3** *Geog.* the effect of mechanical erosion of rock, esp. a river bed, by rock fragments scratching and scraping it. [C17: from Med. L *abrāsiōn-,* from L *abrādere* to ABRADE]

abrasive Ⓣ (əˈbreɪsɪv) *n* **1** a substance or material such as sandpaper, pumice, or emery, used for cleaning, smoothing, or polishing. ◆ *adj* **2** causing abrasion; rough. **3** irritating in manner or personality.

abreaction (ˌæbrɪˈækʃən) *n Psychoanal.* the release and expression of emotional tension associated with repressed ideas by bringing those ideas into consciousness.

abreast Ⓣ (əˈbrɛst) *adj* (*postpositive*) **1** alongside each other and facing in the same direction. **2** (foll. by *of* or *with*) up to date (with).

abridge Ⓣ (əˈbrɪdʒ) *vb* **abridges, abridging, abridged.** (*tr*) **1** to reduce the length of (a written work) by condensing. **2** to curtail. [C14: via OF *abregier* from LL *abbreviāre* to shorten]
▸**aˈbridgable** *or* **aˈbridgeable** *adj* ▸**aˈbridger** *n*

abridgment Ⓣ *or* **abridgement** (əˈbrɪdʒmənt) *n* **1** a shortened version of a written work. **2** the act of abridging or state of being abridged.

abroad Ⓣ (əˈbrɔːd) *adv, adj* (*postpositive*). **1** to or in a foreign country or countries. **2** (of rumours, etc.) in general circulation. **3** out in the open. **4** over a wide area. [C13: from A-[2] + BROAD]

abrogate (ˈæbrəʊˌgeɪt) *vb* **abrogates, abrogating, abrogated.** (*tr*) to cancel or revoke formally or officially. [C16: from L *abrogātus* repealed, from AB-[1] + *rogāre* to propose (a law)]
▸ˌ**abroˈgation** *n* ▸ˈ**abroˌgator** *n*

abrupt Ⓣ (əˈbrʌpt) *adj* **1** sudden; unexpected. **2** brusque or brief in speech, manner, etc. **3** (of a style of writing or speaking) disconnected. **4** precipitous; steep. **5** *Bot.* truncate. **6** *Geol.* (of strata) cropping out suddenly. [C16: from L *abruptus* broken off, from AB-[1] + *rumpere* to break]
▸**abˈruptly** *adv* ▸**abˈruptness** *n*

THESAURUS

carry **3, 4 = stop,** arrest, axe, call off, check, end, fail, halt, terminate

abortion *n* **1, 2 = termination,** aborticide, deliberate miscarriage, feticide, miscarriage **4, 5 = failure,** disappointment, fiasco, misadventure, monstrosity, vain effort

abortive *adj* **1 = failed,** bootless, failing, fruitless, futile, idle, ineffectual, miscarried, unavailing, unsuccessful, useless, vain **2 = imperfectly developed,** incomplete, rudimentary, stunted

abound *vb* **1, 2 = be plentiful,** be jammed with, be packed with, crowd, flourish, increase, infest, luxuriate, overflow, proliferate, superabound, swarm, swell, teem, thrive

about *prep* **1 = regarding,** anent (*Scot.*), as regards, concerned with, concerning, connected with, dealing with, on, re, referring to, relating to, relative to, respecting, touching, with respect to **2 = near,** adjacent to, beside, circa (*used with dates*), close to, nearby **4 = around,** encircling, on all sides, round, surrounding ◆ *adv* **6 = nearly,** almost, approaching, approximately, around, close to, more or less, nearing, roughly **8 = here and there,** from place to place, hither and thither, to and fro **14a about to = on the point of,** intending to, on the verge *or* brink of, ready to ◆ *adj* **15 = around,** active, astir, in motion, present, stirring

about-turn *n* **2 = change of direction,** reversal, reverse, right about (turn), turnabout, turnaround, U-turn, volte-face ◆ *vb* **3 = change direction,** do *or* perform a U-turn *or* volte-face, face the opposite direction, reverse, turn about *or* around, turn through 180 degrees, volte-face

above *prep* **1 = over,** atop, beyond, exceeding, higher than, on top of, upon **3 = superior to,** before, beyond, exceeding, prior to, surpassing ◆ *adv* **13 = overhead,** aloft, atop, in heaven, on high ◆ *adj* **14 = preceding,** aforementioned, aforesaid, earlier, foregoing, previous, prior
Antonyms *prep* ≠ **over:** below, beneath, under, underneath ≠ **superior to:** inferior, lesser, less than, lower than, subordinate

above board *adj* **1 = honest,** candid, fair and square, forthright, frank, guileless, honourable, kosher (*inf.*), legitimate, on the up and up, open, overt, square, straight, straightforward, true, trustworthy, truthful, upfront (*inf.*), upright, veracious ◆ *adv* **1 = honestly,** candidly, forthrightly, frankly, honourably, openly, overtly, straightforwardly, truly, truthfully, uprightly, veraciously, without guile
Antonyms *adj* ≠ **honest:** clandestine, crooked, deceitful, deceptive, devious, dishonest, fraudulent, furtive, secret, secretive, shady, sly, sneaky, underhand

abracadabra *n* **1, 2 = spell,** chant, charm, conjuration, hocus-pocus, incantation, invocation, magic, mumbo jumbo, sorcery, voodoo, witchcraft

abrade *vb* **= scrape,** erase, erode, file, grind, rub off, scour, scrape away, scrape out, wear away, wear down, wear off

abrasion *n* **1 = scraping,** abrading, chafing, erosion, friction, grating, rubbing, scouring, scratching, scuffing, wearing away, wearing down

abrasive *n* **1 = scourer,** abradant, burnisher, grinder, scarifier ◆ *adj* **2 = rough,** chafing, erosive, frictional, grating, scraping, scratching, scratchy, scuffing **3 = unpleasant,** annoying, biting, caustic, cutting, galling, grating, hurtful, irritating, nasty, rough, sharp, vitriolic

abreast *adj* **1 = alongside,** beside, level, neck and neck, shoulder to shoulder, side by side **2 abreast of = informed about,** acquainted with, *au courant* with, *au fait* with, conversant with, familiar with, in the picture about, in touch with, keeping one's finger on the pulse of, knowledgeable about, up to date with, up to speed with

abridge *vb* **1, 2 = shorten,** abbreviate, abstract, clip, compress, concentrate, condense, contract, curtail, cut, cut down, decrease, digest, diminish, downsize, epitomize, lessen, précis, reduce, summarize, synopsize (*US*), trim
Antonyms *vb* amplify, augment, enlarge, expand, extend, go into detail, lengthen, prolong, protract, spin out, stretch out

abridged *adj* **1, 2 = shortened,** abbreviated, brief, compressed, concise, condensed, curtailed, cut, diminished, potted (*inf.*), pruned, reduced, shorter, summarized, trimmed
Antonyms *adj* amplified, diffuse, drawn out, expanded, increased, prolonged, protracted, unabbreviated, unabridged

abridgment *n* **1, 2 = shortening,** abbreviation, abstract, compendium, condensation, conspectus, contraction, curtailment, cutting, decrease, digest, diminishing, diminution, epitome, lessening, limitation, outline, précis, reduction, restraint, restriction, résumé, summary, synopsis

abroad *adv* **1 = overseas,** beyond the sea, in foreign lands, out of the country **2-4 = about,** at large, away, circulating, current, elsewhere, extensively, far, far and wide, forth, in circulation, out, out-of-doors, outside, publicly, widely, without

abrupt *adj* **1 = sudden,** hasty, headlong, hurried, precipitate, quick, surprising, swift, unanticipated, unexpected, unforeseen **2 = curt,**

ABS brake *n* another name for **antilock brake.** [from G *Antiblockiersystem*]
abscess ❶ ('æbsɛs) *n* **1** a localized collection of pus formed as the product of inflammation. ◆ *vb* **2** (*intr*) to form such a collection of pus. [C16: from L *abscessus,* from *abscēdere* to go away]
▸'**abscessed** *adj*
abscissa (æb'sɪsə) *n, pl* **abscissas** *or* **abscissae** (-'sɪsiː). the horizontal or *x*-coordinate of a point in a two-dimensional system of Cartesian coordinates. It is the distance from the *y*-axis measured parallel to the *x*-axis. Cf. **ordinate.** [C17: NL, orig. *linea abscissa* a cut-off line]
abscission (æb'sɪʒən) *n* **1** the separation of leaves, branches, flowers, and bark from plants. **2** the act of cutting off. [C17: from L, from AB-[1] + *scissiō* a cleaving]
abscond ❶ (əb'skɒnd) *vb* (*intr*) to run away secretly, esp. to avoid prosecution or punishment. [C16: from L *abscondere,* from *abs-* AB-[1] + *condere* to stow]
▸**ab'sconder** *n*
abseil ('æbsaɪl) *Mountaineering.* ◆ *vb* (*intr*) **1** to descend a steep slope or vertical drop by a rope secured from above and coiled around one's body. ◆ *n* **2** an instance or the technique of abseiling. [C20: from G *abseilen,* from *ab-* down + *Seil* rope]
absence ❶ ('æbsəns) *n* **1** the state of being away. **2** the time during which a person or thing is away. **3** the fact of being without something; lack. [C14: via OF from L *absentia,* from *absēns* a being away]
absent ❶ *adj* ('æbsənt). **1** away or not present. **2** lacking. **3** inattentive. ◆ *vb* (æb'sɛnt). **4** (*tr*) to remove (oneself) or keep away. [C14: from L *absent-,* from *abesse* to be away]
▸**ab'senter** *n*
absentee ❶ (ˌæbsən'tiː) *n* **a** a person who is absent. **b** (*as modifier*): *an absentee landlord.*
absenteeism (ˌæbsən'tiːɪzəm) *n* persistent absence from work, school, etc.
absent-minded ❶ *adj* preoccupied; forgetful.
▸ˌ**absent-'mindedly** *adv* ▸ˌ**absent-'mindedness** *n*
absinthe *or* **absinth** ('æbsɪnθ) *n* **1** a potent green alcoholic drink, originally having high wormwood content. **2** another name for **wormwood** (the plant). [C15: via F and L from Gk *apsinthion* wormwood]
absolute ❶ ('æbsəˌluːt) *adj* **1** complete; perfect. **2** free from limitations, restrictions, or exceptions. **3** despotic: *an absolute ruler.* **4** undoubted; certain: *the absolute truth.* **5** not dependent on, conditioned by, or relative to anything else; independent: *absolute humidity; absolute units.* **6** pure; unmixed: *absolute alcohol.* **7** (of a grammatical construction) syntactically independent of the main clause, as for example the construction *Joking apart* in the sentence *Joking apart, we'd better leave now.* **8** *Grammar.* (of a transitive verb) used without a direct object, as the verb *intimidate* in the sentence *His intentions are good, but his rough manner tends to intimidate.* **9** *Grammar.* (of an adjective) used as a noun, as for instance *young* and *aged* in the sentence *The young care little for the aged.* ◆ *n* **10** something that is absolute. [C14: from L *absolūtus* unconditional, from *absolvere.* See ABSOLVE]
Absolute ('æbsəˌluːt) *n* (*sometimes not cap.*) *Philosophy.* **1** the ultimate basis of reality. **2** that which is totally unconditioned, unrestricted, pure, perfect, or complete.
absolutely ❶ (ˌæbsə'luːtlɪ) *adv* **1** in an absolute manner, esp. completely or perfectly. ◆ *sentence substitute.* **2** yes; certainly.
absolute magnitude *n* the magnitude a given star would have if it were 10 parsecs (32.6 light years) from earth.
absolute majority *n* a number of votes totalling over 50 per cent, such as the total number of votes or seats obtained by a party that beats the combined opposition.
absolute pitch *n* **1** Also called: **perfect pitch.** the ability to identify the pitch of a note, or to sing a given note, without reference to one previously sounded. **2** the exact pitch of a note determined by vibration per second.
absolute temperature *n* another name for **thermodynamic temperature.**
absolute value *n* **1** the positive real number equal to a given real but disregarding its sign: written $|x|$. Where x is positive, $|x| = x = |-x|$. **2** Also called: **modulus.** a measure of the magnitude of a complex number.
absolute zero *n* the lowest temperature theoretically attainable, at which the particles constituting matter would be at rest: equivalent to −273.15°C or −459.67°F.
absolution ❶ (ˌæbsə'luːʃən) *n* **1** the act of absolving or the state of being absolved; release from guilt, obligation, or punishment. **2** *Christianity.* **2a** a formal remission of sin pronounced by a priest in the sacrament of penance. **2b** the form of words granting such a remission. [C12: from L *absolūtiōn-* acquittal, from *absolvere* to ABSOLVE]
absolutism ❶ ('æbsəluːˌtɪzəm) *n* the principle or practice of a political system in which unrestricted power is vested in a monarch, dictator, etc.; despotism.
▸**abso'lutist** *n, adj*
absolve ❶ (əb'zɒlv) *vb* **absolves, absolving, absolved.** (*tr*) **1** (usually foll. by *from*) to release from blame, sin, obligation, or responsibility. **2** to pronounce not guilty. [C15: from L *absolvere,* from AB-[1] + *solvere* to make loose]
▸**ab'solver** *n*
absorb ❶ (əb'sɔːb) *vb* (*tr*) **1** to soak or suck up (liquids). **2** to engage or occupy (the interest or time) of (someone). **3** to receive or take in (the energy of an impact). **4** *Physics.* to take in (all or part of incident radiated energy) and retain it. **5** to take in or assimilate; incorporate. **6** to pay for as part of a commercial transaction: *the distributor absorbed the cost of transport.* **7** *Chem.* to cause to undergo a process in which one substance permeates into or is dissolved by a liquid or solid: *porous solids absorb water.* [C15: via OF from L *absorbēre,* from AB-[1] + *sorbēre* to suck]
▸**abˌsorba'bility** *n* ▸**ab'sorbable** *adj*

THESAURUS

blunt, brisk, brusque, clipped, direct, discourteous, gruff, impatient, impolite, monosyllabic, rough, rude, short, snappish, snappy, terse, unceremonious, uncivil, ungracious **3** = **uneven,** broken, disconnected, discontinuous, irregular, jerky **4** = **steep,** precipitous, sharp, sheer, sudden
Antonyms *adj* ≠ **sudden:** easy, leisurely, slow, thoughtful, unhurried ≠ **curt:** civil, courteous, gracious, polite ≠ **steep:** gradual

abruptly *adv* **1** = **suddenly,** all at once, all of a sudden, hastily, hurriedly, precipitately, quickly, sharply, short, unexpectedly **2** = **curtly,** bluntly, briskly, brusquely, gruffly, rudely, sharply, shortly, snappily, tersely
Antonyms *adv* ≠ **suddenly:** bit by bit, gently, gradually, little by little, progressively, slowly, steadily ≠ **curtly:** courteously, politely

abruptness *n* **1** = **suddenness,** precipitateness, unexpectedness **2** = **curtness,** bluntness, briskness, brusqueness, brusquerie, gruffness, sharpness, shortness, terseness
Antonyms *n* ≠ **suddenness:** gradualness, steadiness ≠ **curtness:** courteousness, politeness

abscess *n* **1** = **boil,** bubo, carbuncle, felon, furuncle (*Pathology*), gathering, gumboil, infection, inflammation, parulis (*Pathology*), pustule, whitlow

abscond *vb* = **flee,** bolt, clear out, decamp, disappear, escape, flit (*inf.*), fly, make off, run off, skedaddle (*inf.*), slip away, sneak away, steal away

absence *n* **1** = **nonattendance,** absenteeism, nonappearance, truancy **3** = **lack,** default, defect, deficiency, need, nonexistence, omission, privation, unavailability, want

absent *adj* **1** = **missing,** away, elsewhere, gone, lacking, nonattendant, nonexistent, not present, out, truant, unavailable, wanting **3** = **absent-minded,** absorbed, abstracted, bemused, blank, daydreaming, distracted, dreamy, empty, faraway, heedless, inattentive, musing, oblivious, preoccupied, unaware, unconscious, unheeding, unthinking, vacant, vague ◆ *vb* **4** = **stay away,** abscond, bunk off (*sl.*), depart, keep away, play truant, remove, slope off (*inf.*), truant, withdraw
Antonyms *adj* ≠ **missing:** attendant, in attendance, present ≠ **absent-minded:** alert, attentive, aware, conscious, thoughtful ◆ *vb* ≠ **stay away:** attend, show up (*inf.*)

absentee *n* = **nonattender,** no-show, stay-at-home, stayaway, truant

absent-minded *adj* = **vague,** absent, absorbed, abstracted, bemused, distracted, ditzy *or* ditsy (*sl.*), dreaming, dreamy, engrossed, faraway, forgetful, heedless, inattentive, musing, oblivious, preoccupied, unaware, unconscious, unheeding, unthinking
Antonyms *adj* alert, awake, observant, on one's toes, on the ball, perceptive, quick, vigilant, wary, wide-awake

absent-mindedness *n* = **vagueness,** absence of mind, abstraction, daydreaming, distractedness, forgetfulness, inattention, musing, obliviousness, preoccupation, woolgathering

absolute *adj* **1** = **total,** arrant, complete, consummate, deep-dyed (*usually derogatory*), downright, entire, full-on (*inf.*), out-and-out, outright, perfect, pure, sheer, thorough, unadulterated, unalloyed, unmitigated, unmixed, unqualified, utter **3** = **supreme,** absolutist, arbitrary, autarchical, autocratic, autonomous, despotic, dictatorial, full, peremptory, sovereign, tyrannical, unbounded, unconditional, unlimited, unqualified, unquestionable, unrestrained, unrestricted **4** = **definite,** actual, categorical, certain, conclusive, decided, decisive, exact, genuine, infallible, positive, precise, sure, unambiguous, unequivocal, unquestionable

absolutely *adv* **1** = **totally,** completely, consummately, entirely, every inch, fully, lock, stock and barrel, one hundred per cent, perfectly, purely, thoroughly, to the hilt, unmitigatedly, utterly, wholly **3** = **supremely,** arbitrarily, autocratically, autonomously, despotically, dictatorially, fully, peremptorily, sovereignly, tyrannically, unconditionally, unquestionably, unrestrainedly, without qualification **4** = **definitely,** actually, categorically, certainly, conclusively, decidedly, decisively, exactly, genuinely, infallibly, positively, precisely, surely, truly, unambiguously, unequivocally, unquestionably
Antonyms *adv* ≠ **totally:** fairly, probably, reasonably, somewhat

absolution *n* **1, 2** = **forgiveness,** acquittal, amnesty, deliverance, discharge, dispensation, exculpation, exemption, exoneration, freeing, indulgence, liberation, mercy, pardon, release, remission, setting free, shriving, vindication

absolutism *n* = **dictatorship,** absoluteness, arbitrariness, autarchy, authoritarianism, autocracy, despotism, totalitarianism, tyranny

absolutist *n* = **dictator,** arbiter, authoritarian, autocrat, despot, totalitarian, tyrant

absolve *vb* **1, 2** = **forgive,** acquit, clear, deliver, discharge, exculpate, excuse, exempt, exonerate, free, let off, liberate, loose, pardon, release, remit, set free, shrive, vindicate
Antonyms *vb* blame, censure, charge, condemn, convict, damn, denounce, excoriate, pass sentence on, reprehend, reproach, reprove, sentence, upbraid

absorb *vb* **1, 5** = **soak up,** assimilate, consume, devour, digest, drink in, exhaust, imbibe, incorporate, ingest, osmose, receive, suck up, take in **2** = **preoccupy,** captivate, engage, engross, en-

absorbed ➊ (əb'sɔːbd) *adj* engrossed; deeply interested.

absorbed dose *n* the amount of energy transferred by radiation to a unit mass of absorbing material.

absorbent ➊ (əb'sɔːbənt) *adj* **1** able to absorb. ◆ *n* **2** a substance that absorbs.
▸**ab'sorbency** *n*

absorbing ➊ (əb'sɔːbɪŋ) *adj* occupying one's interest or attention.
▸**ab'sorbingly** *adv*

absorptance (əb'sɔːptəns) *or* **absorption factor** *n Physics.* the ability of an object to absorb radiation, measured as the ratio of absorbed flux to incident flux. [C20: from ABSORPTION + -ANCE]

absorption ➊ (əb'sɔːpʃən) *n* **1** the process of absorbing or the state of being absorbed. **2** *Physiol.* **2a** normal assimilation by the tissues of the products of digestion. **2b** the process of taking up various fluids, drugs, etc., through the mucous membranes or skin. [C16: from L *absorptiōn-*, from *absorbēre* to ABSORB]
▸**ab'sorptive** *adj*

absorption spectrum *n* the characteristic pattern of dark lines or bands that occurs when electromagnetic radiation is passed through an absorbing medium into a spectroscope. See also **emission spectrum.**

abstain ➊ (əb'steɪn) *vb* (*intr;* usually foll. by *from*) **1** to choose to refrain. **2** to refrain from voting, esp. in a committee, legislature, etc. [C14: via OF from L *abstinēre*, from *abs-* AB-[1] + *tenēre* to hold]
▸**ab'stainer** *n*

abstemious ➊ (əb'stiːmɪəs) *adj* sparing, esp. in the consumption of alcohol or food. [C17: from L *abstēmius*, from *abs-* AB-[1] + *tēm-*, from *tēmētum* intoxicating drink]
▸**ab'stemiously** *adv* ▸**ab'stemiousness** *n*

abstention ➊ (əb'stenʃən) *n* **1** the act of refraining or abstaining. **2** the act of withholding one's vote. [C16: from LL *abstentiōn;* see ABSTAIN]

abstinence ➊ ('æbstɪnəns) *n* the act or practice of refraining from some action or from the use of something, esp. alcohol. [C13: via OF from L *abstinentia*, from *abstinēre* to ABSTAIN]
▸**'abstinent** *adj*

abstract ➊ *adj* ('æbstrækt). **1** having no reference to material objects or specific examples. **2** not applied or practical; theoretical. **3** hard to understand. **4** denoting art characterized by geometric, formalized, or otherwise nonrepresentational qualities. ◆ *n* ('æbstrækt). **5** a condensed version of a piece of writing, speech, etc.; summary. **6** an abstract term or idea. **7** an abstract painting, sculpture, etc. **8 in the abstract.** without reference to specific circumstances. ◆ *vb* (æb'strækt). (*tr*) **9** to regard theoretically. **10** to form a general idea of (something) by abstraction. **11** ('æbstrækt). (*also intr*) to summarize. **12** to remove or extract. [C14 (in the sense: extracted): from L *abstractus* drawn off, from *abs-* AB-[1] + *trahere* to draw]

abstracted ➊ (æb'stræktɪd) *adj* **1** lost in thought; preoccupied. **2** taken out or separated.
▸**ab'stractedly** *adv*

abstract expressionism *n* a school of painting in the 1940s that combined the spontaneity of expressionism with abstract forms in apparently random compositions.

abstraction ➊ (æb'strækʃən) *n* **1** preoccupation. **2** the process of formulating generalized concepts by extracting common qualities from specific examples. **3** a concept formulated in this way: *good and evil are abstractions.* **4** an abstract painting, sculpture, etc.
▸**ab'stractive** *adj*

abstract noun *n* a noun that refers to an abstract concept, as for example *peace, joy,* etc.

abstract term *n* in traditional logic, the name of an attribute of many individuals: *humanity is an abstract term.*

abstruse ➊ (əb'struːs) *adj* not easy to understand. [C16: from L *abstrūsus*, from *abs-* AB-[1] + *trūdere* to thrust]
▸**ab'strusely** *adv* ▸**ab'struseness** *n*

absurd ➊ (əb'sɜːd) *adj* **1** at variance with reason; manifestly false. **2** ludicrous; ridiculous. [C16: via F from L *absurdus*, from AB-[1] (intensive) + *surdus* dull-sounding]
▸**ab'surdity** *or* **ab'surdness** *n* ▸**ab'surdly** *adv*

ABTA ('æbtə) *n acronym for* Association of British Travel Agents.

abulia *or* **aboulia** (ə'buːlɪə, -'bjuː-) *n Psychiatry.* a pathological inability to take decisions. [C19: NL, from Gk *aboulia* lack of resolution, from A-[1] + *boulē* will]

abundance ➊ (ə'bʌndəns) *n* **1** a copious supply; great amount. **2** fullness or benevolence: *from the abundance of my heart.* **3** degree of plentifulness: *the abundance of uranium-235 in natural uranium.* **4** Also: **abondance.** a call in solo whist undertaking to make nine tricks. **5** affluence. [C14: via OF from L, from *abundāre* to ABOUND]

abundant ➊ (ə'bʌndənt) *adj* **1** existing in plentiful supply. **2** (*postpositive;* foll. by *in*) having a plentiful supply (of). [C14: from L *abundant-*, p.p. of *abundāre* to ABOUND]
▸**a'bundantly** *adv*

THESAURUS

wrap, fascinate, fill, fill up, fix, hold, immerse, monopolize, occupy, rivet

absorbed *adj* = **preoccupied**, captivated, concentrating, engaged, engrossed, fascinated, fixed, held, immersed, involved, lost, occupied, rapt, riveted, up to one's ears, wrapped up

absorbency *n* **1** = **permeability**, ability to soak up *or* take in, permeableness, perviousness, porousness, receptiveness, retentiveness, sponginess
Antonyms *n* impermeability, impermeableness, imperviousness

absorbent *adj* **1** = **permeable**, absorptive, assimilative, blotting, imbibing, penetrable, pervious, porous, receptive, spongy

absorbing *adj* = **fascinating**, arresting, captivating, engrossing, gripping, interesting, intriguing, riveting, spellbinding
Antonyms *adj* boring, dreary, dull, humdrum, mind-numbing, monotonous, tedious, tiresome, unexciting

absorption *n* **1** = **soaking up**, assimilation, consumption, digestion, exhaustion, incorporation, osmosis, sucking up **1** = **concentration**, captivation, engagement, fascination, holding, immersion, intentness, involvement, occupation, preoccupation, raptness

abstain *vb* **1** = **refrain**, avoid, cease, decline, deny (oneself), desist, fast, forbear, forgo, give up, keep from, kick (*inf.*), refuse, renounce, shun, stop, withhold
Antonyms *vb* abandon oneself, give in, indulge, partake, yield

abstemious *adj* = **self-denying**, abstinent, ascetic, austere, continent, frugal, moderate, sober, sparing, temperate
Antonyms *adj* edacious (*chiefly humorous*), gluttonous, greedy, immoderate, incontinent, intemperate, self-indulgent

abstemiousness *n* = **self-denial**, abstinence, asceticism, austerity, continence, forbearance, frugality, moderation, restraint, self-restraint, sobriety, temperance
Antonyms *n* dissipation, drunkenness, excess, gluttony, incontinence, self-indulgence

abstention *n* **1** = **refusal**, abstaining, abstinence, avoidance, desistance, eschewal, forbearance, nonindulgence, refraining, self-control, self-denial, self-restraint

abstinence *n* = **self-denial**, abstemiousness, asceticism, avoidance, continence, forbearance, moderation, refraining, self-restraint, soberness, sobriety, teetotalism, temperance
Antonyms *n* abandon, acquisitiveness, covetousness, excess, gluttony, greediness, indulgence, self-indulgence, wantonness

abstinent *adj* = **self-denying**, abstaining, abstemious, continent, forbearing, moderate, self-controlled, self-restraining, sober, temperate

abstract *adj* **1, 2** = **theoretical**, abstruse, arcane, complex, conceptual, deep, general, generalized, hypothetical, indefinite, intellectual, nonconcrete, notional, occult, philosophical, profound, recondite, separate, subtle, theoretic, unpractical, unrealistic ◆ *n* **5** = **summary**, abridgment, compendium, condensation, digest, epitome, essence, outline, précis, recapitulation, résumé, synopsis ◆ *vb* **11** = **summarize**, abbreviate, abridge, condense, digest, epitomize, outline, précis, shorten, synopsize (*US*) **12** = **remove**, detach, dissociate, extract, isolate, separate, steal, take away, take out, withdraw
Antonyms *adj* actual ≠ **theoretical:** concrete, definite, factual, material, real, specific ◆ *n* ≠ **summary:** enlargement, expansion ◆ *vb* ≠ **remove:** add, combine, inject

abstracted *adj* **1** = **preoccupied**, absent, absent-minded, bemused, daydreaming, dreamy, faraway, inattentive, remote, withdrawn, woolgathering

abstraction *n* **1** = **absent-mindedness**, absence, bemusedness, dreaminess, inattention, pensiveness, preoccupation, remoteness, woolgathering **3** = **idea**, concept, formula, generality, generalization, hypothesis, notion, theorem, theory, thought

abstruse *adj* = **obscure**, abstract, arcane, complex, dark, deep, Delphic, enigmatic, esoteric, hidden, incomprehensible, mysterious, mystical, occult, perplexing, profound, puzzling, recondite, subtle, unfathomable, vague
Antonyms *adj* apparent, bold, clear, conspicuous, evident, manifest, open, overt, patent, perceptible, plain, self-evident, transparent, unsubtle

abstruseness *n* = **obscurity**, arcaneness, complexity, deepness, depth, esotericism, incomprehensibility, mysteriousness, occultness, perplexity, profundity, reconditeness, subtlety, vagueness

absurd *adj* **2** = **ridiculous**, crazy (*inf.*), daft (*inf.*), farcical, foolish, idiotic, illogical, inane, incongruous, irrational, laughable, ludicrous, meaningless, nonsensical, preposterous, senseless, silly, stupid, unreasonable
Antonyms *adj* intelligent, logical, prudent, rational, reasonable, sagacious, sensible, smart, wise

absurdity *n* **2** = **ridiculousness**, craziness (*inf.*), daftness (*inf.*), farce, farcicality, farcicalness, folly, foolishness, idiocy, illogicality, illogicalness, incongruity, irrationality, joke, ludicrousness, meaninglessness, nonsense, preposterousness, senselessness, silliness, stupidity, unreasonableness

absurdly *adv* **2** = **ridiculously**, farcically, foolishly, idiotically, illogically, implausibly, inanely, inconceivably, incongruously, incredibly, irrationally, laughably, ludicrously, preposterously, senselessly, unbelievably, unreasonably

abundance *n* **1** = **plenty**, affluence, ampleness, bounty, copiousness, exuberance, fullness, heap (*inf.*), plenitude, plenteousness, profusion
Antonyms *n* ≠ **plenty:** dearth, deficiency, lack, need, paucity, scantiness, scarcity, sparseness

abundant *adj* **1, 2** = **plentiful**, ample, bounteous, bountiful, copious, exuberant, filled, full, lavish, luxuriant, overflowing, plenteous, profuse, rank, rich, teeming, two a penny, well-provided, well-supplied
Antonyms *adj* deficient, few, few and far between, inadequate, in short supply, insufficient, lacking, rare, scant, scanty, scarce, short, sparse

abundantly *adv* **1, 2** = **plentifully**, amply, bounteously, bountifully, copiously, extensively, exuberantly, freely, fully, in abundance, in great *or* large numbers, in plentiful supply, in profusion, lavishly, luxuriantly, plenteously, profusely, richly

abuse Ⓣ *vb* (ə'bju:z), **abuses, abusing, abused.** (*tr*) **1** to use incorrectly or improperly; misuse. **2** to maltreat, esp. physically or sexually. **3** to speak insultingly or cruelly to. ◆ *n* (ə'bju:s). **4** improper, incorrect, or excessive use. **5** maltreatment of a person; injury. **6** insulting or coarse speech. **7** an evil, unjust, or corrupt practice. **8** See **child abuse. 9** *Arch.* a deception. [C14 (vb): via OF from L *abūsus*, p.p. of *abūtī* to misuse, from AB-[1] + *ūtī* to USE]
▸**a'buser** *n*

abusive Ⓣ (ə'bju:sɪv) *adj* **1** characterized by insulting or coarse language. **2** characterized by maltreatment. **3** incorrectly used.
▸**a'busively** *adv* ▸**a'busiveness** *n*

abut Ⓣ (ə'bʌt) *vb* **abuts, abutting, abutted.** (usually foll. by *on*, *upon*, or *against*) to adjoin, touch, or border on (something) at one end. [C15: from OF *abouter* to join at the ends; infl. by *abuter* to touch at an end]

abutment Ⓣ (ə'bʌtmənt) *or* **abuttal** *n* **1** the state or process of abutting. **2a** something that abuts. **2b** the thing on which something abuts. **2c** the point of junction between them. **3** a construction that supports the end of a bridge.

abutter (ə'bʌtə) *n Property law.* the owner of adjoining property.

abuzz (ə'bʌz) *adj* (*postpositive*) humming, as with conversation, activity, etc.; buzzing.

abysm (ə'bɪzəm) *n* an archaic word for **abyss.** [C13: via OF from Med. L *abysmus* ABYSS]

abysmal Ⓣ (ə'bɪzməl) *adj* **1** immeasurable; very great. **2** *Inf.* extremely bad.
▸**a'bysmally** *adv*

abyss Ⓣ (ə'bɪs) *n* **1** a very deep gorge or chasm. **2** anything that appears to be endless or immeasurably deep, such as time, despair, or shame. **3** hell. [C16: via LL from Gk *abussos* bottomless, from A-[1] + *bussos* depth]

abyssal (ə'bɪsəl) *adj* **1** of or relating to an abyss. **2** of or belonging to the ocean depths, esp. below 2000 metres (6500 ft): *abyssal zone.*

Ac *the chemical symbol for* actinium.

AC *abbrev. for:* **1** Air Corps. **2** alternating current. Cf. **DC. 3** ante Christum. [L: before Christ] **4** athletic club. **5** Companion of the Order of Australia.

a/c *Book-keeping. abbrev. for:* **1** account. **2** account current.

acacia (ə'keɪʃə) *n* **1** a tropical or subtropical shrub or tree, having small yellow or white flowers. In Australia, the term is applied esp. to the wattle. **2 false acacia.** another name for **locust** (senses 2, 3). **3 gum acacia.** another name for **gum arabic.** [C16: from L, from Gk *akakia*, ? rel. to *akē* point]

academe ('ækəˌdi:m) *n Literary.* any place of learning, such as a college or university. [C16: first used by Shakespeare in *Love's Labour's Lost* (1594); see ACADEMY]

academic Ⓣ (ˌækə'dɛmɪk) *adj* **1** belonging or relating to a place of learning, esp. a college, university, or academy. **2** of purely theoretical or speculative interest. **3** (esp. of pupils) having an aptitude for study. **4** excessively concerned with intellectual matters. **5** conforming to set rules and traditions: *an academic painter.* **6** relating to studies such as languages and pure science rather than technical, applied, or professional studies. ◆ *n* **7** a member of a college or university.
▸**ˌaca'demically** *adv*

academician (əˌkædə'mɪʃən) *n* a member of an academy (senses 1, 2).

academy Ⓣ (ə'kædəmɪ) *n, pl* **academies. 1** an institution or society for the advancement of literature, art, or science. **2** a school for training in a particular skill or profession: *a military academy.* **3** a secondary school, esp. in Scotland: now only used as part of a name. [C16: via L from Gk *akadēmeia* the grove where Plato taught, named after the legendary hero *Akadēmos*]
▸**ˌaca'demical** *adj*

Academy Award *n* the official name for an **Oscar.**

acanthus (ə'kænθəs) *n, pl* **acanthuses** *or* **acanthi** (-θaɪ). **1** a shrub or herbaceous plant, native to the Mediterranean region but widely cultivated as an ornamental plant, having large spiny leaves and spikes of white or purplish flowers. **2** a carved ornament based on the leaves of the acanthus plant, esp. as used on the capital of a Corinthian column. [C17: NL, from Gk *akanthos*, from *akantha* thorn, spine]

a cappella (ɑ: kə'pɛlə) *adj, adv Music.* without instrumental accompaniment. [It.: lit., according to (the style of the) chapel]

acariasis (ˌækə'raɪəsɪs) *n* infestation with mites or ticks. [C19: NL: see ACARID, -IASIS]

acarid ('ækərɪd) *or* **acaridan** (ə'kærɪdən) *n* any of an order of small arachnids that includes the ticks and mites. [C19: from Gk *akari* a small thing, mite]

acarpous (eɪ'kɑ:pəs) *adj* (of plants) producing no fruit. [from Gk *akarpos*, from A-[1] + *karpos* fruit]

ACAS *or* **Acas** ('eɪkæs) *n* (in Britain) *acronym for* Advisory Conciliation and Arbitration Service.

acc. *abbrev. for:* **1** accompanied. **2** according. **3** *Book-keeping.* account. **4** *Grammar.* accusative.

accede Ⓣ (æk'si:d) *vb* **accedes, acceding, acceded.** (*intr;* usually foll. by *to*) **1** to assent or give one's consent. **2** to enter upon or attain (to an office, right, etc.): *the prince acceded to the throne.* **3** *International law.* to become a party (to an agreement between nations, etc.). [C15: from L *accēdere*, from *ad-* to + *cēdere* to yield]
▸**ac'cedence** *n*

accelerando (ækˌsɛlə'rændəʊ) *adj, adv Music.* (to be performed) with increasing speed. [It.]

accelerate Ⓣ (æk'sɛləˌreɪt) *vb* **accelerates, accelerating, accelerated. 1** to go, occur, or cause to go or occur more quickly; speed up. **2** (*tr*) to cause to happen sooner than expected. **3** (*tr*) to increase the velocity of (a body, reaction, etc.). [C16: from L *accelerātus*, from *accelerāre*, from *ad-* (intensive) + *celerāre* to hasten, from *celer* swift]
▸**ac'celerative** *adj*

acceleration Ⓣ (ækˌsɛlə'reɪʃən) *n* **1** the act of accelerating or the state of being accelerated. **2** the rate of increase of speed or the rate of change of velocity. **3** the power to accelerate.

acceleration of free fall *n* the acceleration of a body falling freely in a vacuum in the earth's gravitational field. Symbol: *g* Also called: **acceleration due to gravity.**

accelerator (æk'sɛləˌreɪtə) *n* **1** a device for increasing speed, esp. a pedal for controlling the fuel intake in a motor vehicle; throttle. **2** *Physics.* a machine for increasing the kinetic energy of subatomic particles or atomic nuclei. **3** Also: **accelerant.** *Chem.* a substance that increases the speed of a chemical reaction; catalyst.

accelerometer (ækˌsɛlə'rɒmɪtə) *n* an instrument for measuring acceleration, esp. of an aircraft or rocket.

accent Ⓣ *n* ('æksənt). **1** the characteristic mode of pronunciation of a person or group, esp. one that betrays social or geographical origin. **2** the relative prominence of a spoken or sung syllable, esp. with regard to stress or pitch. **3** a mark (such as ', ˌ, ´, or `) used in writing to indicate the stress or prominence of a syllable. **4** any of various marks or symbols conventionally used in writing certain languages to indicate the quality of a vowel. See **acute** (sense 8), **grave**[2] (sense 5), **circumflex. 5** rhythmic stress in verse or prose. **6** *Music.* **6a** stress placed on certain notes in a piece of music, indicated by a symbol printed over the note concerned. **6b** the rhythmic pulse of a piece or passage, usually represented as the stress on the first beat of each bar. **7** a distinctive characteristic of anything, such as taste, pattern, style, etc. **8** particular attention or emphasis: *an accent on learning.* **9** a strongly contrasting detail. ◆ *vb* (æk'sɛnt). (*tr*) **10** to mark with an accent in writing, speech, music, etc. **11** to lay particular emphasis or stress on. [C14: via OF from L *accentus*, from *ad-* to + *cantus* chant]

accentor (æk'sɛntə) *n* a small sparrow-like songbird, which inhabits

THESAURUS

Antonyms *adv* inadequately, in short supply, insufficiently, rarely, scantily, scarcely, sparsely

abuse *vb* **1, 2** = **ill-treat**, damage, exploit, harm, hurt, impose upon, injure, maltreat, manhandle, mar, misapply, misuse, oppress, spoil, take advantage of, wrong **3** = **insult**, calumniate, castigate, curse, defame, disparage, inveigh against, libel, malign, revile, scold, slander, slate (*inf., chiefly Brit.*), smear, swear at, traduce, upbraid, vilify, vituperate ◆ *n* **4, 5** = **ill-treatment**, damage, exploitation, harm, hurt, imposition, injury, maltreatment, manhandling, oppression, spoiling, wrong **4** = **misuse**, misapplication **6** = **insults**, blame, calumniation, castigation, censure, character assassination, contumely, curses, cursing, defamation, derision, disparagement, invective, libel, opprobrium, reproach, revilement, scolding, slander, swearing, tirade, traducement, upbraiding, vilification, vituperation
Antonyms *vb* ≠ **ill-treat**: care for, protect ≠ **insult**: acclaim, commend, compliment, extol, flatter, praise, respect

abusive *adj* **1** = **insulting**, calumniating, castigating, censorious, contumelious, defamatory, derisive, disparaging, invective, libellous, maligning, offensive, opprobrious, reproachful, reviling, rude, scathing, scolding, slanderous, traducing, upbraiding, vilifying, vituperative **2** = **harmful**, brutal, cruel, destructive, hurtful, injurious, rough
Antonyms *adj* ≠ **insulting**: approving, complimentary, eulogistic, flattering, laudatory, panegyrical, praising

abusiveness *n* **1** = **insults**, calumniation, coarse language, contumely, derisiveness, foul language, invective, offensiveness, philippics, rudeness, traducement, vilification, vitriol, vituperation **2** = **ill-treatment**, abuse, brutality, cruelty, exploitation, maltreatment

abut *vb* = **adjoin**, border, impinge, join, meet, touch, verge

abutment *n* **2, 3** = **support**, brace, bulwark, buttress, pier, prop, strut

abutting *adj* = **adjoining**, adjacent, bordering, contiguous, joining, meeting, next to, touching, verging

abysmal *adj* **2** = **terrible**, appalling, awful, bad, dire, dreadful

abyss *n* **1** = **pit**, abysm, bottomless depth, chasm, crevasse, fissure, gorge, gulf, void

academic *adj* **1, 3** = **scholarly**, bookish, campus, college, collegiate, erudite, highbrow, learned, lettered, literary, scholastic, school, studious, university **2** = **hypothetical**, abstract, conjectural, impractical, notional, speculative, theoretical ◆ *n* **7** = **scholar**, academician, don, fellow, lecturer, master, professor, pupil, scholastic, schoolman, student, tutor

academy *n* **2, 3** = **college**, centre of learning, institute, institution, school

accede *vb* **1** = **agree**, accept, acquiesce, admit, assent, comply, concede, concur, consent, endorse, grant, own, yield **2** = **inherit**, assume, attain, come to, enter upon, succeed, succeed to (*as heir*)

accelerate *vb* **1, 2** = **speed up**, advance, expedite, forward, further, hasten, hurry, pick up speed, precipitate, quicken, speed, spur, step up (*inf.*), stimulate
Antonyms *vb* decelerate, delay, hinder, impede, obstruct, slow down

acceleration *n* **1** = **speeding up**, expedition, hastening, hurrying, quickening, spurring, stepping up (*inf.*), stimulation

accent *n* **1** = **pronunciation**, articulation, brogue, enunciation, inflection, intonation, modulation, tone **2, 5, 6** = **emphasis**, beat, ca-

mainly mountainous regions of Europe and Asia. See also **hedge sparrow.**

accentual (æk'sɛntʃʊəl) *adj* **1** of, relating to, or having accents; rhythmic. **2** *Prosody.* of or relating to verse based on the number of stresses in a line.
▸**ac'centually** *adv*

accentuate Ⓣ (æk'sɛntʃʊˌeɪt) *vb* **accentuates, accentuating, accentuated.** (*tr*) to stress or emphasize.
▸**acˌcentu'ation** *n*

accept Ⓣ (ək'sɛpt) *vb* (*mainly tr*) **1** to take or receive (something offered). **2** to give an affirmative reply to. **3** to take on the responsibilities, duties, etc., of: *he accepted office.* **4** to tolerate. **5** to consider as true or believe in (a philosophy, theory, etc.). **6** (*may take a clause as object*) to be willing to believe: *you must accept that he lied.* **7** to receive with approval or admit, as into a community, group, etc. **8** *Commerce.* to agree to pay (a bill, draft, etc.). **9** to receive as adequate or valid. [C14: from L *acceptāre,* from *ad-* to + *capere* to take]
▸**ac'cepter** *n*

acceptable Ⓣ (ək'sɛptəbᵊl) *adj* **1** satisfactory; adequate. **2** pleasing; welcome. **3** tolerable.
▸**acˌcepta'bility** *or* **ac'ceptableness** *n* ▸**ac'ceptably** *adv*

acceptance Ⓣ (ək'sɛptəns) *n* **1** the act of accepting or the state of being accepted or acceptable. **2** favourable reception. **3** (often foll. by *of*) belief (in) or assent (to). **4** *Commerce.* a formal agreement by a debtor to pay a draft, bill, etc. **5** (*pl*) *Austral. & NZ.* a list of horses accepted as starters in a race.

acceptation (ˌæksɛp'teɪʃən) *n* the accepted meaning, as of a word, phrase, etc.

accepted Ⓣ (ək'sɛptɪd) *adj* commonly approved or recognized; customary; established.

acceptor (ək'sɛptə) *n* **1** *Commerce.* the person or organization on which a draft or bill of exchange is drawn. **2** *Electronics.* an impurity, such as gallium, added to a semiconductor material to increase its p-type semiconductivity.

access Ⓣ ('æksɛs) *n* **1** the act of approaching or entering. **2** the condition of allowing entry, esp. (of a building, etc.) entry by prams, wheelchairs, etc. **3** the right or privilege to approach, enter, or make use of something. **4** a way or means of approach or entry. **5** the opportunity or right to see or approach someone: *my ex-wife sabotages my access to the children.* **6** (*modifier*) designating programmes made by the general public: *access television.* **7** a sudden outburst or attack, as of rage or disease. ◆ *vb* (*tr*) **8** *Computing.* **8a** to obtain or retrieve (information) from a storage device. **8b** to place (information) in a storage device. **9** to gain access to; make accessible or available. [C14: from OF or from L *accessus,* from *accēdere* to ACCEDE]

accessible Ⓣ (ək'sɛsəbᵊl) *adj* **1** easy to approach, enter, or use. **2 accessible to.** likely to be affected by. **3** obtainable; available.
▸**acˌcessi'bility** *n*

accession Ⓣ (ək'sɛʃən) *n* **1** the act of attaining to an office, right, condition, etc. **2** an increase due to an addition. **3** an addition, as to a collection. **4** *Property law.* an addition to land or property by natural increase or improvement. **5** *International law.* the formal acceptance of a convention or treaty. **6** agreement. ◆ *vb* **7** (*tr*) to make a record of (additions to a collection).
▸**ac'cessional** *adj*

accessory Ⓣ (ək'sɛsərɪ) *n, pl* **accessories. 1** a supplementary part or object, as of a car, appliance, etc. **2** (*often pl*) a small accompanying item of dress, esp. of women's dress. **3** (formerly) a person involved in a crime although absent during its commission. ◆ *adj* **4** supplementary; additional. **5** assisting in or having knowledge of an act, esp. a crime. [C17: from LL *accessōrius:* see ACCESS]
▸**accessorial** (ˌæksɛ'sɔːrɪəl) *adj* ▸**ac'cessorily** *adv*

access road *n* a road giving entry to a region or, esp., a motorway.

access time *n Computing.* the time required to retrieve a piece of stored information.

acciaccatura (əˌtʃækə'tʊərə) *n, pl* **acciaccaturas** *or* **acciaccature** (-reɪ). a small grace note melodically adjacent to a principal note and played simultaneously with or immediately before it. [C18: It.: lit., a crushing sound]

accidence ('æksɪdəns) *n* the part of grammar concerned with changes in the form of words for the expression of tense, person, case, number, etc. [C15: from L *accidentia* accidental matters, from *accidere* to happen. See ACCIDENT]

accident Ⓣ ('æksɪdənt) *n* **1** an unforeseen event or one without an apparent cause. **2** anything that occurs unintentionally or by chance: *I met him by accident.* **3** a misfortune or mishap, esp. one causing injury or death. **4** *Geol.* a surface irregularity in a natural formation. [C14: via OF from L *accident-,* from the p.p. of *accidere* to happen, from *ad-* to + *cadere* to fall]

accidental Ⓣ (ˌæksɪ'dɛntᵊl) *adj* **1** occurring by chance, unexpectedly, or unintentionally. **2** nonessential; incidental. **3** *Music.* denoting sharps, flats, or naturals that are not in the key signature of a piece. ◆ *n* **4** an incidental or supplementary circumstance, factor, or attribute. **5** *Music.* a symbol denoting a sharp, flat, or natural that is not a part of the key signature.
▸ˌ**acci'dentally** *adv*

accident-prone *adj* liable to become involved in accidents.

accidie ('æksɪdɪ) *or* **acedia** *n* spiritual sloth; apathy; indifference. [in use C13 to C16 and revived C19: via LL from Gk *akēdia,* from A-[1] + *kēdos* care]

accipiter (æk'sɪpɪtə) *n* any of a genus of hawks having short rounded wings and a long tail. [C19: NL, from L: hawk]
▸**ac'cipitrine** *adj*

acclaim Ⓣ (ə'kleɪm) *vb* **1** (*tr*) to acknowledge publicly the excellence of (a person, act, etc.). **2** to applaud. **3** (*tr*) to acknowledge publicly: *they acclaimed him king.* ◆ *n* **4** an enthusiastic expression of approval, etc. [C17: from L *acclāmāre,* from *ad-* to + *clamāre* to shout]
▸**ac'claimer** *n*

THESAURUS

dence, force, ictus, pitch, rhythm, stress, timbre, tonality ◆ *vb* **11** = **emphasize**, accentuate, stress, underline, underscore

accentuate *vb* = **emphasize**, accent, draw attention to, foreground, highlight, stress, underline, underscore
Antonyms *vb* gloss over, make light *or* little of, minimize, play down, soft-pedal (*inf.*), underplay

accept *vb* **1** = **receive**, acquire, gain, get, have, obtain, secure, take **3** = **take on**, acknowledge, admit, assume, avow, bear, undertake **4** = **stand**, bear, bow to, brook, defer to, like it or lump it (*inf.*), put up with, submit to, suffer, take, tolerate, yield to **5, 6** = **agree to**, accede, acknowledge, acquiesce, admit, adopt, affirm, approve, believe, concur with, consent to, cooperate with, recognize, swallow (*inf.*), take on board
Antonyms *vb* ≠ **agree to:** decline, deny, disown, rebut, refuse, reject, repudiate, spurn

acceptability *n* **1, 3** = **adequacy**, acceptableness, admissibility, appropriateness, fitness, permissibility, propriety, satisfactoriness, suitability
Antonyms *n* impropriety, inadequacy, inadmissibility, inappropriateness, unacceptability, unsatisfactoriness, unsuitability

acceptable *adj* **1, 3** = **satisfactory**, adequate, admissible, all right, fair, moderate, passable, so-so (*inf.*), standard, suitable, tolerable, up to scratch (*inf.*) **2** = **pleasant**, agreeable, delightful, grateful, gratifying, pleasing, welcome
Antonyms *adj* ≠ **satisfactory:** unacceptable, unsatisfactory, unsuitable

acceptably *adv* **1, 3** = **adequately**, passably, satisfactorily, tolerably **2** = **pleasantly**, agreeably, delightfully, gratifyingly, pleasingly
Antonyms *adv* ≠ **adequately:** unacceptably, unsatisfactorily, unsuitably

acceptance *n* **1** = **accepting**, acquiring, gaining, getting, having, obtaining, receipt, securing, taking **3** = **agreement**, accedence, accession, acknowledgment, acquiescence, admission, adoption, affirmation, approbation, approval, assent, belief, compliance, concession, concurrence, consensus, consent, cooperation, credence, O.K. *or* okay (*inf.*), permission, recognition

accepted *adj* = **agreed**, acceptable, acknowledged, admitted, agreed upon, approved, authorized, common, confirmed, conventional, customary, established, normal, received, recognized, regular, sanctioned, standard, time-honoured, traditional, universal, usual
Antonyms *adj* abnormal, irregular, strange, unconventional, uncustomary, unorthodox, unusual, unwonted

access *n* **1, 4** = **entrance**, admission, admittance, approach, avenue, course, door, entering, entrée, entry, gateway, key, passage, passageway, path, road, way in **7** = **attack**, fit, onset, outburst, paroxysm

accessibility *n* **1** = **approachability**, affability, conversableness, cordiality, friendliness, informality **2** = **openness**, exposedness, susceptibility **3** = **handiness**, approachability, attainability, availability, nearness, obtainability, possibility, readiness

accessible *adj* **1** = **approachable**, affable, available, conversable, cordial, friendly, informal **2** = **open**, exposed, liable, subject, susceptible, vulnerable, wide-open **3** = **handy**, achievable, at hand, at one's fingertips, attainable, available, near, nearby, obtainable, on hand, possible, reachable, ready
Antonyms *adj* ≠ **handy:** far-off, hidden, inaccessible, secreted, unavailable, unobtainable, unreachable

accession *n* **1** = **taking up**, assumption, attaining to, attainment of, entering upon, succession (*to a throne, dignity, or office*), taking on, taking over **2, 3** = **increase**, addition, augmentation, enlargement, extension **6** = **agreement**, accedence, acceptance, acquiescence, assent, concurrence, consent

accessory *n* **1** = **addition**, accent, accompaniment, add-on, adjunct, adornment, aid, appendage, attachment, component, convenience, decoration, extension, extra, frill, help, supplement, trim, trimming **3** = **accomplice**, abettor, assistant, associate (*in crime*), colleague, confederate, helper, partner ◆ *adj* **4, 5** = **additional**, abetting, aiding, ancillary, assisting in, auxiliary, contributory, extra, secondary, subordinate, supplemental, supplementary

accident *n* **1, 2** = **chance**, fate, fluke, fortuity, fortune, hazard, luck **3** = **misfortune**, blow, calamity, casualty, chance, collision, crash, disaster, misadventure, mischance, mishap, pile-up (*inf.*)

accidental *adj* **1, 2** = **unintentional**, adventitious, casual, chance, contingent, fortuitous, haphazard, inadvertent, incidental, inessential, nonessential, random, uncalculated, uncertain, unessential, unexpected, unforeseen, unintended, unlooked-for, unplanned, unpremeditated, unwitting
Antonyms *adj* calculated, designed, expected, foreseen, intended, intentional, planned, prepared

accidentally *adv* **1, 2** = **unintentionally**, adventitiously, by accident, by chance, by mistake, casually, fortuitously, haphazardly, inadvertently, incidentally, randomly, unconsciously, undesignedly, unexpectedly, unwittingly
Antonyms *adv* by design, consciously, deliberately, designedly, on purpose, wilfully

acclaim *vb* **1, 2** = **praise**, applaud, approve, celebrate, cheer, clap, commend, crack up (*inf.*), eulogize, exalt, extol, hail, honour, laud, salute, welcome ◆ *n* **4** = **praise**, acclamation,

acclamation Ⓣ (ˌækləˈmeɪʃən) *n* **1** an enthusiastic reception or exhibition of welcome, approval, etc. **2** an expression of approval with shouts or applause. **3** *Canad.* an instance of electing or being elected without opposition.
▸**acclamatory** (əˈklæmətərɪ) *adj*

acclimatize Ⓣ *or* **acclimatise** (əˈklaɪməˌtaɪz) *vb* **acclimatizes, acclimatizing, acclimatized** *or* **acclimatises, acclimatising, acclimatised.** to adapt or become accustomed to a new climate or environment.
▸**acˈclimaˌtizable** *or* **acˈclimaˌtisable** *adj* ▸**acˌclimatiˈzation** *or* **acˌclimatiˈsation** *n*

acclivity (əˈklɪvɪtɪ) *n, pl* **acclivities.** an upward slope, esp. of the ground. Cf. **declivity.** [C17: from L, from *acclīvis* sloping up]
▸**acˈclivitous** *adj*

accolade Ⓣ (ˈækəˌleɪd) *n* **1** strong praise or approval. **2** an award or honour. **3** the ceremonial gesture used to confer knighthood, a touch on the shoulder with a sword. **4** a rare word for **brace** (sense 7). [C17: via F & It. from Vulgar L *accollāre* (unattested) to hug; rel. to L *collum* neck]

accommodate Ⓣ (əˈkɒməˌdeɪt) *vb* **accommodates, accommodating, accommodated. 1** (*tr*) to supply or provide, esp. with lodging. **2** (*tr*) to oblige or do a favour for. **3** to adapt. **4** (*tr*) to bring into harmony. **5** (*tr*) to allow room for. **6** (*tr*) to lend money to. [C16: from L *accommodāre*, from *ad-* to + *commodus* having the proper measure]

accommodating Ⓣ (əˈkɒməˌdeɪtɪŋ) *adj* willing to help; kind; obliging.

accommodation Ⓣ (əˌkɒməˈdeɪʃən) *n* **1** lodging or board and lodging. **2** adjustment, as of differences or to new circumstances; settlement or reconciliation. **3** something fulfilling a need, want, etc. **4** *Physiol.* the automatic or voluntary adjustment of the thickness of the lens of the eye for far or near vision. **5** willingness to help or oblige. **6** *Commerce.* a loan.

accommodation address *n* an address on letters, etc., to a person or business that does not wish or is not able to receive post at a permanent or actual address.

accommodation ladder *n Naut.* a flight of stairs or a ladder for lowering over the side of a ship for access to and from a small boat, pier, etc.

accompaniment Ⓣ (əˈkʌmpənɪmənt) *n* **1** something that accompanies or is served or used with something else. **2** *Music.* a subordinate or supporting part for an instrument, voices, or an orchestra.

accompanist (əˈkʌmpənɪst) *n* a person who plays a musical accompaniment for another performer.

accompany Ⓣ (əˈkʌmpənɪ) *vb* **accompanies, accompanying, accompanied. 1** (*tr*) to go along with, so as to be in company with. **2** (*tr; foll. by* with) to supplement. **3** (*tr*) to occur or be associated with. **4** to provide a musical accompaniment for (a soloist, etc.). [C15: from OF *accompaignier*, from *compaing* COMPANION[1]]

accomplice Ⓣ (əˈkɒmplɪs, əˈkʌm-) *n* a person who has helped another in committing a crime. [C15: from *a complice*, interpreted as one word, from OF, from LL *complex* partner, from L *complicāre* to COMPLICATE]

accomplish Ⓣ (əˈkɒmplɪʃ, əˈkʌm-) *vb* (*tr*) **1** to manage to do; achieve. **2** to complete. [C14: from OF *acomplir*, ult. from L *complēre* to fill up. See COMPLETE]

accomplished Ⓣ (əˈkɒmplɪʃt, əˈkʌm-) *adj* **1** successfully completed; achieved. **2** expert; proficient.

accomplishment Ⓣ (əˈkɒmplɪʃmənt, əˈkʌm-) *n* **1** the act of achieving. **2** something successfully completed. **3** (*often pl*) skill or talent. **4** (*often pl*) social grace and poise.

accord Ⓣ (əˈkɔːd) *n* **1** agreement; accordance (esp. in **in accord with**). **2** concurrence of opinion. **3 with one accord.** unanimously. **4** pleasing relationship between sounds, colours, etc. **5 of one's own accord.** voluntarily. ◆ *vb* **6** to be or cause to be in harmony or agreement. **7** (*tr*) to grant; bestow. [C12: via OF from L *ad-* to + *cord-*, stem of *cor* heart]

accordance Ⓣ (əˈkɔːdəns) *n* conformity; agreement; accord (esp. in **in accordance with**).

according Ⓣ (əˈkɔːdɪŋ) *adj* **1** (foll. by *to*) in proportion. **2** (foll. by *to*) as stated (by). **3** (foll. by *to*) in conformity (with). **4** (foll. by *as*) depending (on whether).

accordingly Ⓣ (əˈkɔːdɪŋlɪ) *adv* **1** in an appropriate manner; suitably. ◆ *sentence connector.* **2** consequently.

accordion (əˈkɔːdɪən) *n* **1** a portable box-shaped instrument consisting of metallic reeds that are made to vibrate by air from a set of bellows controlled by the player's hands. Notes are produced by means of studlike keys. **2** short for **piano accordion.** [C19: from G, from *Akkord* harmony]
▸**acˈcordionist** *n*

accordion pleats *pl n* tiny knife pleats.

accost Ⓣ (əˈkɒst) *vb* (*tr*) to approach, stop, and speak to (a person), as to ask a question, solicit sexually, etc. [C16: from LL *accostāre*, from L *costa* side, rib]
▸**acˈcostable** *adj*

accouchement *French.* (akuʃmɑ̃) *n* childbirth or the period of confinement. [C19: from *accoucher* to put to bed. See COUCH]

account Ⓣ (əˈkaʊnt) *n* **1** a verbal or written report, description, or narration of some occurrence, event, etc. **2** an explanation of conduct, esp. one made to someone in authority. **3** basis; consideration: *on this account.* **4** importance, consequence, or value: *of little account.* **5** assessment; judgment. **6** profit or advantage: *to good account.* **7** part or be-

THESAURUS

applause, approbation, approval, celebration, cheering, clapping, commendation, eulogizing, exaltation, honour, kudos, laudation, plaudits, welcome
Antonyms *n* ≠ **praise:** bad press, brickbats, censure, criticism, denigration, disparagement, fault-finding, flak (*inf.*), panning (*inf.*), stick (*sl.*), vituperation

acclaimed *adj* **1, 2** = **praised**, acknowledged, admired, celebrated, distinguished, famed, famous, highly esteemed, highly rated, highly thought of, much touted, much vaunted, noted, renowned, well received, well thought of
Antonyms *adj* badly *or* poorly received, criticized, unacclaimed, unacknowledged, undistinguished

acclamation *n* **1, 2** = **praise**, acclaim, adulation, approbation, approval, cheer, cheering, cheers, enthusiasm, kudos, laudation, loud homage, ovation, plaudit, salutation, shouting, tribute

acclimatization *n* = **adaptation**, acclimation, accommodation, acculturation, adjustment, habituation, inurement, naturalization

acclimatize *vb* = **adapt**, accommodate, accustom, adjust, become seasoned to, get used to, habituate, inure, naturalize

acclimatized *adj* = **adapted**, acclimated, accustomed, adjusted, familiarized, inured, orientated, oriented, seasoned, used

accolade *n* **1, 2** = **praise**, acclaim, acclamation, applause, approval, commendation, compliment, congratulation, eulogy, homage, honour, laud (*literary*), laudation (*formal*), ovation, plaudit, recognition, tribute

accommodate *vb* **1** = **house**, billet, board, cater for, entertain, harbour, lodge, put up, quarter, shelter **2** = **help**, afford, aid, assist, furnish, oblige, provide, purvey, serve, supply **3** = **adapt**, accustom, adjust, comply, compose, conform, fit, harmonize, modify, reconcile, settle

accommodating *adj* = **helpful**, complaisant, considerate, cooperative, friendly, hospitable, kind, obliging, polite, unselfish, willing
Antonyms *adj* disobliging, inconsiderate, rude, uncooperative, unhelpful

accommodation *n* **1** = **housing**, board, digs (*Brit. inf.*), harbouring, house, lodging(s), quartering, quarters, shelter, sheltering **2** = **adaptation**, adjustment, compliance, composition, compromise, conformity, fitting, harmony, modification, reconciliation, settlement **5** = **help**, aid, assistance, provision, service, supply

accompaniment *n* **1** = **supplement**, accessory, companion, complement **2** = **backing music**, backing

accompany *vb* **1** = **go with**, attend, chaperon, conduct, convoy, escort, hold (someone's) hand, squire, usher **2, 3** = **occur with**, belong to, coexist with, coincide with, come with, follow, go cheek by jowl, go together with, join with, supplement

accompanying *adj* **1-3** = **additional**, accessory, added, appended, associate, associated, attached, attendant, complementary, concomitant, concurrent, connected, fellow, joint, related, supplemental, supplementary

accomplice *n* = **helper**, abettor, accessory, ally, assistant, associate, coadjutor, collaborator, colleague, confederate, henchman, partner

accomplish *vb* **1, 2** = **do**, achieve, attain, bring about, bring off (*inf.*), carry out, complete, conclude, consummate, effect, effectuate, execute, finish, fulfil, manage, perform, produce, put the tin lid on, realize
Antonyms *vb* fail, fall short, forsake, give up

accomplished *adj* **1** = **done**, achieved, attained, brought about, carried out, completed, concluded, consummated, effected, executed, finished, fulfilled, in the can (*inf.*), managed, performed, produced, realized **2** = **skilled**, adept, consummate, cultivated, expert, gifted, masterly, polished, practised, proficient, skilful, talented
Antonyms *adj* ≠ **skilled:** amateurish, incapable, incompetent, inexpert, unestablished, unproven, unrealized, unskilled, untalented

accomplishment *n* **1** = **completion**, achievement, attainment, bringing about, carrying out, conclusion, consummation, doing, effecting, execution, finishing, fulfilment, management, performance, production, realization **2** = **achievement**, act, attainment, coup, deed, exploit, feat, stroke, triumph **3** *often plural* = **skill**, ability, achievement, art, attainment, capability, craft, gift, proficiency = **skill**, talent

accord *n* **1, 2** = **agreement**, accordance, assent, concert, concurrence, conformity, congruence, correspondence, harmony, rapport, sympathy, unanimity, unison ◆ *vb* **6** = **agree**, assent, be in tune (*inf.*), concur, conform, correspond, fit, harmonize, match, suit, tally **7** = **grant**, allow, bestow, concede, confer, endow, give, present, render, tender, vouchsafe
Antonyms *n* ≠ **agreement:** conflict, contention, disagreement, discord ≠ **agree:** conflict, contrast, differ, disagree, discord ◆ *vb* ≠ **grant:** hold back, refuse, withhold

accordance *n As in* **in accordance with** = **agreement**, accord, assent, concert, concurrence, conformity, congruence, correspondence, harmony, rapport, sympathy, unanimity

according *adj* **1** *foll. by* **to** = **in relation**, commensurate with, in proportion **2** *foll. by* **to** = **as stated by**, as believed by, as maintained by, in the light of, on the authority of, on the report of **3** *foll. by* **to** = **in keeping with**, after, after the manner of, consistent with, in accordance with, in compliance with, in conformity with, in harmony with, in line with, in obedience to, in step with, in the manner of, obedient to

accordingly *adv* **1** = **appropriately**, correspondingly, fitly, properly, suitably ◆ *sentence connector* **2** = **consequently**, as a result, ergo, hence, in consequence, so, therefore, thus

accost *vb* = **approach**, address, buttonhole, confront, greet, hail, halt, salute, solicit (*as a prostitute*), stop

account *n* **1, 2** = **description**, chronicle, detail, explanation, history, narration, narrative, recital, record, relation, report, statement, story, tale, version **3** = **reason**, basis, cause, consider-

half (only in **on one's** *or* **someone's account**). 8 *Finance.* **8a** a business relationship between a bank, department store, etc., and a depositor, customer, or client permitting the latter certain banking or credit services. **8b** the sum of money deposited at a bank. **8c** the amount of credit available to the holder of an account. **8d** a record of these. **9** a statement of monetary transactions with the resulting balance. **10** (formerly, on the London Stock Exchange) the period, ordinarily of a fortnight's duration, at the end of which settlements were made. **11a** a regular client or customer. **11b** an area of business assigned to another: *they transferred their publicity account to a new agent.* **12 call** (*or* **bring**) **to account. 12a** to insist on explanation. **12b** to reprimand. **12c** to hold responsible. **13 give a good** (**bad**, etc.) **account of oneself.** to perform well (badly, etc.). **14 on account. 14a** on credit. **14b** Also: **to account.** as partial payment. **15 on account of.** (*prep*) because of. **16 take account of** *or* **take into account.** to take into consideration; allow for. **17 settle** *or* **square accounts with. 17a** to pay or receive a balance due. **17b** to get revenge on (someone). **18** See **bank account.** ♦ *vb* **19** (*tr*) to consider or reckon: *he accounts himself poor.* [C13: from OF *acont,* from *conter* to COUNT[1]]

accountable ⓘ (əˈkauntəbᵊl) *adj* **1** responsible to someone or for some action. **2** able to be explained.
▸**ac,countaˈbility** *n* ▸**acˈcountably** *adv*

accountancy (əˈkauntənsɪ) *n* the profession or business of an accountant.

accountant ⓘ (əˈkauntənt) *n* a person concerned with the maintenance and audit of business accounts.

account executive *n* an executive in an advertising agency or public relations firm who manages a client's account.

account for ⓘ *vb* (*intr, prep*) **1** to give reasons for (an event, act, etc.). **2** to make or provide a reckoning of (expenditure, etc.). **3** to be responsible for destroying or putting (people, aircraft, etc.) out of action.

accounting ⓘ (əˈkauntɪŋ) *n* **a** the skill or practice of maintaining and auditing accounts and preparing reports on the assets, liabilities, etc., of a business. **b** (*as modifier*): *an accounting period.*

accoutre *or US* **accouter** (əˈkuːtə) *vb* **accoutres, accoutring, accoutred** *or US* **accouters, accoutering, accoutered.** (*tr; usually passive*) to provide with equipment or dress, esp. military. [C16: from OF *accoustrer,* ult. rel. to L *consuere* to sew together]

accoutrement ⓘ (əˈkuːtrəmənt, əˈkuːtə-) *or US* **accouterment** (əˈkuːtərmənt) *n* **1** equipment worn by soldiers in addition to their clothing and weapons. **2** (*usually pl*) clothing, equipment, etc.; trappings: *the correct accoutrements for any sport.*

accredit ⓘ (əˈkrɛdɪt) *vb* (*tr*) **1** to ascribe or attribute. **2** to give official recognition to. **3** to certify as meeting required standards. **4** (often foll. by *at* or *to*) **4a** to send (an envoy, etc.) with official credentials. **4b** to appoint (someone) as an envoy, etc. **5** to believe. **6** *NZ.* to pass (a candidate) for university entrance on school recommendation, without external examination. [C17: from F *accréditer,* from *mettre à crédit* to put to CREDIT]
▸**ac,crediˈtation** *n*

accredited ⓘ (əˈkrɛdɪtɪd) *adj* **1** officially authorized; recognized. **2** (of milk, cattle, etc.) certified as free from disease; meeting certain standards. **3** *NZ.* accepted for university entrance on school recommendation, without external examination.

accrete (əˈkriːt) *vb* **accretes, accreting, accreted. 1** to grow or cause to grow together. **2** to make or become bigger, as by addition. [C18: back formation from ACCRETION]

accretion (əˈkriːʃən) *n* **1** any gradual increase in size, as through growth or external addition. **2** something added, esp. extraneously, to cause growth or an increase in size. **3** the growing together of normally separate plant or animal parts. [C17: from L *accretiō* increase, from *accrēscere.* See ACCRUE]
▸**acˈcretive** *adj*

accrual (əˈkruːəl) *n* **1** the act of accruing. **2** something that has accrued. **3** *Accounting* a charge incurred in one accounting period that has not been paid by the end of it.

accrue ⓘ (əˈkruː) *vb* **accrues, accruing, accrued.** (*intr*) **1** to increase by growth or addition, esp. (of capital) to increase by periodic addition of interest. **2** (often foll. by *to*) to fall naturally (to). [C15: from OF *accreue,* ult. from L *accrēscere,* from *ad-* to, in addition + *crēscere* to grow]

acct *Book-keeping. abbrev. for* account.

acculturate (əˈkʌltʃə,reɪt) *vb* **acculturates, acculturating, acculturated.** (of a cultural or social group) to assimilate the cultural traits of another group. [C20: from AD- + CULTURE + -ATE[1]]
▸**ac,culturˈation** *n*

accumulate ⓘ (əˈkjuːmjʊ,leɪt) *vb* **accumulates, accumulating, accumulated.** to gather or become gathered together in an increasing quantity; collect. [C16: from L *accumulāre* to heap up, from *cumulus* a heap]
▸**acˈcumulable** *adj* ▸**acˈcumulative** *adj*

accumulation ⓘ (ə,kjuːmjʊˈleɪʃən) *n* **1** the act or process of collecting together or becoming collected. **2** something that has been collected, gathered, heaped, etc. **3** *Finance.* the continuous growth of capital by retention of interest or earnings.

accumulator (əˈkjuːmjʊ,leɪtə) *n* **1** Also called: **battery, storage battery.** a rechargeable device for storing electrical energy in the form of chemical energy. **2** *Horse racing, Brit.* a collective bet on successive races, with both stake and winnings being carried forward to accumulate progressively. **3** a register in a calculator or computer used for holding the results of a computation or data transfer.

accuracy ⓘ (ˈækjʊrəsɪ) *n, pl* **accuracies.** faithful measurement or representation of the truth; correctness; precision.

accurate ⓘ (ˈækjərɪt) *adj* **1** faithfully representing or describing the truth. **2** showing a negligible or permissible deviation from a standard: *an accurate ruler.* **3** without error; precise. **4** *Maths.* (of a number) correctly represented to a specified number of decimal places or significant figures. [C16: from L *accūrāre* to perform with care, from *cūra* care]
▸ˈ**accurately** *adv*

accursed ⓘ (əˈkɜːsɪd, əˈkɜːst) *or* **accurst** (əˈkɜːst) *adj* **1** under or subject to a curse. **2** (*prenominal*) hateful; detestable. [OE *ācursod,* p.p. of *ācursian* to put under a CURSE]
▸**accursedly** (əˈkɜːsɪdlɪ) *adv* ▸**acˈcursedness** *n*

accusation ⓘ (,ækjuˈzeɪʃən) *n* **1** an allegation that a person is guilty of some fault or crime. **2** a formal charge brought against a person.

accusative (əˈkjuːzətɪv) *adj* **1** *Grammar.* denoting a case of nouns, pronouns, and adjectives in inflected languages that is used to identify the direct object of a finite verb, of certain prepositions, and for certain other purposes. **2** another word for **accusatorial.** ♦ *n* **3** *Grammar.* the accusative case or a speech element in it. [C15: from L; in grammar, from *cāsus accūsātīvus* accusative case, a mistaken translation of Gk *ptōsis aitiatikē* the case indicating causation. See ACCUSE]
▸**accusatival** (ə,kjuːzəˈtaɪvᵊl) *adj* ▸**acˈcusatively** *adv*

accusatorial ⓘ (ə,kjuːzəˈtɔːrɪəl) *or* **accusatory** (əˈkjuːzətərɪ) *adj* **1** containing or implying blame or strong criticism. **2** *Law.* denoting a legal system in which the defendant is prosecuted before a judge in public. Cf. **inquisitorial.**

THESAURUS

ation, ground, grounds, interest, motive, regard, sake, score **4** = **importance,** advantage, benefit, consequence, distinction, esteem, honour, import, merit, note, profit, rank, repute, significance, standing, use, value, worth **8, 9** = **statement,** balance, bill, book, books, charge, computation, inventory, invoice, ledger, reckoning, register, score, tally ♦ *vb* **19** = **consider,** appraise, assess, believe, calculate, compute, count, deem, esteem, estimate, explain, gauge, hold, judge, rate, reckon, regard, think, value, weigh

accountability *n* **1** = **responsibility,** answerability, chargeability, culpability, liability

accountable *adj* **1** = **responsible,** amenable, answerable, charged with, liable, obligated, obliged

accountant *n* = **auditor,** bean counter (*inf.*), book-keeper

account for *vb* **1** = **explain,** answer for, clarify, clear up, elucidate, illuminate, justify, rationalize **3** = **put out of action,** destroy, incapacitate, kill, put paid to

accounting *n* = **accountancy,** auditing, book-keeping

accoutrements *pl n* **1, 2** = **equipment,** adornments, appurtenances, array, bells and whistles, clothing, decorations, dress, equipage, fittings, fixtures, furnishings, garb, gear, kit, ornamentation, outfit, paraphernalia, tackle, trappings, trimmings

accredit *vb* **1** = **attribute,** ascribe, assign, credit **2-4** = **authorize,** appoint, certify, commission, depute, empower, endorse, entrust, guarantee, license, recognize, sanction, vouch for

accredited *adj* **1** = **authorized,** appointed, certified, commissioned, deputed, deputized, empowered, endorsed, guaranteed, licensed, official, recognized, sanctioned, vouched for

accrue *vb* **1** = **increase,** accumulate, amass, arise, be added, build up, collect, enlarge, ensue, flow, follow, grow, issue, spring up

accumulate *vb* = **collect,** accrue, amass, build up, cumulate, gather, grow, hoard, increase, pile up, stockpile, store
Antonyms *vb* diffuse, disperse, disseminate, dissipate, distribute, propagate, scatter

accumulation *n* **1, 2** = **collection,** aggregation, augmentation, build-up, conglomeration, gathering, growth, heap, hoard, increase, mass, pile, rick, stack, stock, stockpile, store

accuracy *n* = **exactness,** accurateness, authenticity, carefulness, closeness, correctness, exactitude, faithfulness, faultlessness, fidelity, meticulousness, niceness, nicety, precision, strictness, truth, truthfulness, veracity, verity
Antonyms *n* carelessness, erroneousness, imprecision, inaccuracy, incorrectness, inexactitude, laxity, laxness

accurate *adj* **1, 3** = **exact,** authentic, careful, close, correct, faithful, faultless, just, meticulous, nice, precise, proper, regular, right, scrupulous, spot-on (*Brit. inf.*), strict, true, truthful, unerring, veracious
Antonyms *adj* careless, defective, faulty, imperfect, imprecise, inaccurate, incorrect, inexact, slovenly, wrong

accurately *adv* **1, 3** = **exactly,** authentically, carefully, closely, correctly, faithfully, faultlessly, justly, meticulously, nicely, precisely, properly, regularly, rightly, scrupulously, strictly, to the letter, truly, truthfully, unerringly, veraciously

accursed *adj* **1** = **cursed,** bedevilled, bewitched, condemned, damned, doomed, hopeless, ill-fated, ill-omened, jinxed, luckless, ruined, undone, unfortunate, unlucky, wretched **2** = **hateful,** abominable, despicable, detestable, execrable, hellish, horrible
Antonyms *adj* ≠ **cursed:** blessed, charmed, favoured, fortunate, lucky

accusation *n* **1, 2** = **charge,** allegation, arraignment, attribution, citation, complaint, denunciation, impeachment, imputation, incrimination, indictment, recrimination

accusatorial *adj* **1** = **accusing,** accusative, censorious, condemnatory, critical, denunciatory, imputative, incriminatory, recriminatory, reproachful

accuse ⓣ (əˈkju:z) *vb* **accuses, accusing, accused.** to charge (a person or persons) with some fault, offence, crime, etc. [C13: via OF from L *accūsāre* to call to account, from *ad-* to + *causa* lawsuit]
▸**acˈcuser** *n* ▸**acˈcusing** *adj* ▸**acˈcusingly** *adv*

accused (əˈkju:zd) *n* (preceded by *the*) *Law.* the defendant or defendants on a criminal charge.

accustom ⓣ (əˈkʌstəm) *vb* (*tr;* usually foll. by *to*) to make (oneself) familiar (with) or used (to), as by habit or experience. [C15: from OF *acostumer,* from *costume* CUSTOM]

accustomed ⓣ (əˈkʌstəmd) *adj* **1** usual; customary. **2** (*postpositive;* foll. by *to*) used (to). **3** (*postpositive;* foll. by *to*) in the habit (of).

AC/DC *adj Inf.* (of a person) bisexual. [C20: humorous reference to electrical apparatus that is adaptable for ALTERNATING CURRENT and DIRECT CURRENT]

ace ⓣ (eɪs) *n* **1** any die, domino, or any of four playing cards with one spot. **2** a single spot or pip on a playing card, die, etc. **3** *Tennis.* a winning serve that the opponent fails to reach. **4** a fighter pilot accredited with destroying several enemy aircraft. **5** *Inf.* an expert: *an ace at driving.* **6 an ace up one's sleeve.** a hidden and powerful advantage. ◆ *adj* **7** *Inf.* superb; excellent. [C13: via OF from L *as* a unit]

-acea *suffix forming plural proper nouns.* denoting animals belonging to a class or order: *Crustacea* (class); *Cetacea* (order). [NL, from L, neuter pl of *-āceus* -ACEOUS]

-aceae *suffix forming plural proper nouns.* denoting plants belonging to a family: *Liliaceae.* [NL, from L, fem pl of *-āceus* -ACEOUS]

acedia (əˈsi:dɪə) *n* another word for **accidie.**

ACE inhibitor (eɪs) *n* any one of a class of drugs, including captopril and enalapril, that cause the arteries to widen by preventing the synthesis of angiotensin: used to treat high blood pressure and heart failure. [C20: from *a(ngiotensin-)c(onverting) e(nzyme) inhibitor*]

-aceous *suffix forming adjectives.* relating to, having the nature of, or resembling: *herbaceous.* [NL, from L *-āceus* of a certain kind; rel. to *-āc, -āx,* adjectival suffix]

acephalous (əˈsɛfələs) *adj* having no head or one that is reduced and indistinct, as certain insect larvae. [C18: via Med. L from Gk *akephalos.* See A-[1], -CEPHALIC]

acer (ˈeɪsə) *n* any tree or shrub of the genus *Acer,* often cultivated for their brightly coloured foliage. See also **maple.**

acerbate (ˈæsəˌbeɪt) *vb* **acerbates, acerbating, acerbated.** (*tr*) **1** to embitter or exasperate. **2** to make sour or bitter. [C18: from L *acerbāre* to make sour]

acerbic ⓣ (əˈsɜ:bɪk) *adj* harsh, bitter, or astringent; sour. [C17: from L *acerbus* sour, bitter]

acerbity (əˈsɜ:bɪtɪ) *n, pl* **acerbities. 1** vitriolic or embittered speech, temper, etc. **2** sourness or bitterness of taste.

acetabulum (ˌæsɪˈtæbjʊləm) *n, pl* **acetabula** (-lə). the deep cuplike cavity on the side of the hipbone that receives the head of the thighbone. [L: vinegar cup, hence a cuplike cavity, from *acētum* vinegar + *-abulum,* suffix denoting a container]

acetal (ˈæsɪˌtæl) *n* **1** a type of organic compound formed by addition of an alcohol to an aldehyde or ketone. **2** a colourless pleasant-smelling volatile liquid used in perfumes.

acetaldehyde (ˌæsɪˈtældɪˌhaɪd) *n* a colourless volatile pungent liquid, used in the manufacture of organic compounds and as a solvent. Formula: CH_3CHO. Systematic name: **ethanal.**

acetanilide (ˌæsɪˈtænɪˌlaɪd) *n* a white crystalline powder used in the manufacture of dyes and as an analgesic in medicine.

acetate (ˈæsɪˌteɪt) *n* **1** any salt or ester of acetic acid. Systematic name: **ethanoate. 2** short for **acetate rayon** *or* **cellulose acetate. 3** an audio disc with an acetate lacquer coating: used for demonstration purposes, etc. [C19: from ACETIC + -ATE[1]]

acetate rayon *n* a synthetic textile fibre made from cellulose acetate.

acetic (əˈsi:tɪk) *adj* of, containing, producing, or derived from acetic acid or vinegar. [C19: from L *acētum* vinegar]

acetic acid *n* a colourless pungent liquid widely used in the manufacture of plastics, pharmaceuticals, dyes, etc. Formula: CH_3COOH. Systematic name: **ethanoic acid.** See also **vinegar.**

acetify (əˈsɛtɪˌfaɪ) *vb* **acetifies, acetifying, acetified.** to become or cause to become acetic acid or vinegar.
▸**aˌcetifiˈcation** *n*

aceto- *or before a vowel* **acet-** *combining form.* containing an acetyl group or derived from acetic acid: *acetone.* [from L *acētum* vinegar]

acetone (ˈæsɪˌtəʊn) *n* a colourless volatile pungent liquid used in the manufacture of chemicals and as a solvent for paints, varnishes, and lacquers. Formula: CH_3COCH_3. Systematic name: **propanone.** [C19: from G *Azeton,* from ACETO- + -ONE]

acetous (ˈæsɪtəs) *or* **acetose** (ˈæsɪˌtəʊs) *adj* **1** producing or resembling acetic acid or vinegar. **2** tasting like vinegar. [C18: from LL *acētōsus* vinegary, from *acētum* vinegar]

acetyl (ˈæsɪˌtaɪl, əˈsi:taɪl) *n* (*modifier*) of or containing the monovalent group CH_3CO-. [C19: from ACET(IC) + -YL]

acetylcholine (ˌæsɪtaɪlˈkəʊli:n, -lɪn) *n* a chemical substance secreted at the ends of many nerve fibres, responsible for the transmission of nervous impulses.

acetylene (əˈsɛtɪˌli:n) *n* **1** a colourless soluble flammable gas used in the manufacture of organic chemicals and in cutting and welding metals. Formula: C_2H_2. Systematic name: **ethyne. 2** another name for **alkyne.**

acetylene series *n* another name for **alkyne series.**

acetylsalicylic acid (ˌæsɪtaɪlˌsælɪˈsɪlɪk) *n* the chemical name for **aspirin.**

Achaean (əˈki:ən) *or* **Achaian** (əˈkaɪən) *n* **1** a member of a principal Greek tribe in the Mycenaean era. ◆ *adj* **2** of or relating to the Achaeans.

Achates (əˈkeɪti:z) *n* a loyal friend. [from Aeneas' faithful companion in Virgil's *Aeneid*]

ache ⓣ (eɪk) *vb* **aches, aching, ached.** (*intr*) **1** to feel, suffer, or be the source of a continuous dull pain. **2** to suffer mental anguish. ◆ *n* **3** a continuous dull pain. [OE *ācan* (vb), *æce* (n), ME *aken* (vb), *ache* (n)]
▸ˈ**aching** *adj*

achene (əˈki:n) *n* a dry one-seeded indehiscent fruit with the seed distinct from the fruit wall. [C19: from NL *achaenium* that which does not open, from A-[1] + Gk *khainein* to yawn]

Acheulian *or* **Acheulean** (əˈʃu:lɪən) *Archaeol.* ◆ *n* **1** (in Europe) the period in the Lower Palaeolithic following the Abbevillian, represented by the use of soft hammerstones in hand-axe production. **2** (in Africa) the period represented by every stage of hand-axe development. ◆ *adj* **3** of or relating to this period. [C20: after *St Acheul,* town in N France]

achieve ⓣ (əˈtʃi:v) *vb* **achieves, achieving, achieved.** (*tr*) **1** to bring to a successful conclusion. **2** to gain as by hard work or effort: *to achieve success.* [C14: from OF *achever* to bring to an end, from *a chef* to a head]
▸**aˈchievable** *adj* ▸**aˈchiever** *n*

achievement ⓣ (əˈtʃi:vmənt) *n* **1** something that has been accomplished, esp. by hard work, ability, or heroism. **2** successful completion; accomplishment.

achillea (ˌækɪˈli:ə) *n* any of several cultivated varieties of yarrow.

Achilles heel (əˈkɪli:z) *n* a small but fatal weakness.

Achilles tendon *n* the fibrous cord that connects the muscles of the calf to the heelbone.

achromat (ˈækrəˌmæt) *or* **achromatic lens** *n* a lens designed to reduce chromatic aberration.

achromatic (ˌækrəˈmætɪk) *adj* **1** without colour. **2** capable of reflecting or refracting light without chromatic aberration. **3** *Music.* involving no sharps or flats.
▸ˌ**achroˈmatically** *adv* ▸**achromatism** (əˈkrəʊməˌtɪzəm) *or* **achromaticity** (əˌkrəʊməˈtɪsɪtɪ) *n*

acid ⓣ (ˈæsɪd) *n* **1** any substance that dissociates in water to yield a sour corrosive solution containing hydrogen ions, and turning litmus red. **2** a sour-tasting substance. **3** a slang name for **LSD.** ◆ *adj* **4** *Chem.* **4a** of, derived from, or containing acid. **4b** being or having the properties of an acid. **5** sharp or sour in taste. **6** cutting, sharp, or hurtful in speech, manner, etc. [C17: from F *acide* or L *acidus,* from *acēre* to be sour]
▸ˈ**acidly** *adv* ▸ˈ**acidness** *n*

THESAURUS

accuse *vb* = **charge,** allege, arraign, attribute, blame, censure, cite, denounce, impeach, impute, incriminate, indict, point a *or* the finger at, recriminate, tax
Antonyms *vb* absolve, answer, defend, deny, exonerate, plead, reply, vindicate

accustom *vb* = **adapt,** acclimatize, acquaint, discipline, exercise, familiarize, habituate, inure, season, train

accustomed *adj* **1** = **usual,** common, conventional, customary, established, everyday, expected, fixed, general, habitual, normal, ordinary, regular, routine, set, traditional, wonted **2, 3** = **used,** acclimatized, acquainted, adapted, disciplined, exercised, familiar, familiarized, given to, habituated, in the habit of, inured, seasoned, trained
Antonyms *adj* ≠ **usual:** abnormal, infrequent, occasional, odd, peculiar, rare, strange, unaccustomed, uncommon, unfamiliar, unusual ≠ **used:** unaccustomed, unfamiliar, unused

ace *n* **1, 2** = **one,** single point **5** *Informal* = **expert,** adept, buff (*inf.*), champion, dab hand (*Brit. inf.*), genius, hotshot (*inf.*), master, maven (*US*), star, virtuoso, whizz (*inf.*), winner, wizard (*inf.*) ◆ *adj* **7** *Informal* = **excellent,** awesome (*sl.*), brilliant, champion, expert, fine, great, masterly, outstanding, superb, virtuoso

acerbic *adj* = **bitter,** acid, acrid, acrimonious, brusque, churlish, harsh, nasty, rancorous, rude, severe, sharp, stern, unfriendly, unkind = **bitter,** acetic, acid, acidulous, acrid, astringent, bitter, harsh, sharp, sour, tart, vinegary

ache *vb* **1** = **hurt,** pain, pound, smart, suffer, throb, twinge **2** = **suffer,** agonize, eat one's heart out, grieve, mourn, sorrow ◆ *n* **3** = **pain,** hurt, pang, pounding, smart, smarting, soreness, suffering, throb, throbbing

achievable *adj* **1, 2** = **attainable,** accessible, accomplishable, acquirable, feasible, obtainable, possible, practicable, reachable, realizable, winnable, within one's grasp

achieve *vb* **1, 2** = **attain,** accomplish, acquire, bring about, carry out, complete, consummate, do, earn, effect, execute, finish, fulfil, gain, get, obtain, perform, procure, put the tin lid on, reach, realize, win

achievement *n* **1** = **accomplishment,** act, deed, effort, exploit, feat, feather in one's cap, stroke **2** = **accomplishment,** accomplishment = **fulfilment,** acquirement, attainment, completion, execution, performance, production, realization

aching *adj* **1** = **painful,** hurting, pounding, smarting, sore, suffering, throbbing, tired

acid *adj* **5** = **sour,** acerb, acerbic, acetic, acidulous, acrid, biting, pungent, sharp, tart, vinegarish, vinegary **6** = **sharp,** acerbic, biting, bitter, caustic, cutting, harsh, hurtful, mordacious, mordant, pungent, stinging, trenchant, vitriolic
Antonyms *adj* ≠ **sour:** alkaline, bland, mild, pleas-

acid-fast *adj* (of bacteria and tissues) resistant to decolorization by mineral acids after staining.

Acid House *or* **Acid** *n* a dance music dominated by beat and bass line, created with synthesizers and digital sampling; popular in the late 1980s. [C20: from ACID (LSD) + HOUSE (MUSIC)]

acidic (əˈsɪdɪk) *adj* another word for **acid.**

acidify (əˈsɪdɪˌfaɪ) *vb* **acidifies, acidifying, acidified.** to convert into or become acid.
▸**aˈcidiˌfiable** *adj* ▸**aˌcidifiˈcation** *n*

acidity Ⓣ (əˈsɪdɪtɪ) *n, pl* **acidities. 1** the quality or state of being acid. **2** the amount of acid present in a solution.

acidosis (ˌæsɪˈdəʊsɪs) *n* a condition characterized by an abnormal increase in the acidity of the blood.
▸**acidotic** (ˌæsɪˈdɒtɪk) *adj*

acid rain *n* rain containing pollutants, chiefly sulphur dioxide and nitrogen oxide, released into the atmosphere by burning coal or oil.

acid rock *n* rock music characterized by bizarre amplified instrumental effects. [C20: from ACID (LSD)]

acid test *n* a rigorous and conclusive test to establish worth or value. [C19: from the testing of gold with nitric acid]

acidulate (əˈsɪdjʊˌleɪt) *vb* **acidulates, acidulating, acidulated.** (*tr*) to make slightly acid or sour. [C18: ACIDULOUS + -ATE[1]]
▸**aˌciduˈlation** *n*

acidulous Ⓣ (əˈsɪdjʊləs) *or* **acidulent** *adj* **1** rather sour. **2** sharp or sour in speech, manner, etc.; acid. [C18: from L *acidulus* sourish, dim. of *acidus* sour]

acinus (ˈæsɪnəs) *n, pl* **acini** (-ˌnaɪ). **1** *Anat.* any of the terminal saclike portions of a compound gland. **2** *Bot.* any of the small drupes that make up the fruit of the raspberry, etc. **3** *Bot., obs.* a collection of berries, such as a bunch of grapes. [C18: NL, from L: grape, berry]

ack-ack (ˈækˌæk) *n Mil.* **a** anti-aircraft fire. **b** (*as modifier*): *ack-ack guns.* [C20: British Army World War I phonetic alphabet for AA, abbrev. of *anti-aircraft*]

acknowledge Ⓣ (əkˈnɒlɪdʒ) *vb* **acknowledges, acknowledging, acknowledged.** (*tr*) **1** (*may take a clause as object*) to recognize or admit the existence, truth, or reality of. **2** to indicate recognition or awareness of, as by a greeting, glance, etc. **3** to express appreciation or thanks for. **4** to make the receipt of known: *to acknowledge a letter.* **5** to recognize, esp. in legal form, the authority, rights, or claims of. [C15: prob. from earlier *knowledge*, on the model of OE *oncnāwan*, ME *aknowen* to confess, recognize]
▸**acˈknowledgeable** *adj*

acknowledgment Ⓣ *or* **acknowledgement** (əkˈnɒlɪdʒmənt) *n* **1** the act of acknowledging or state of being acknowledged. **2** something done or given as an expression of thanks. **3** (*pl*) an author's statement acknowledging his use of the works of other authors.

aclinic line (əˈklɪnɪk) *n* another name for **magnetic equator.** [C19 *aclinic*, from Gk *aklinēs* not bending, from A-[1] + *klinein* to bend]

acme Ⓣ (ˈækmɪ) *n* the culminating point, as of achievement or excellence. [C16: from Gk *akmē*]

acne (ˈæknɪ) *n* a chronic skin disease common in adolescence, characterized by pustules on the face. [C19: NL, from a misreading of Gk *akmē* eruption on the face. See ACME]

acolyte Ⓣ (ˈækəˌlaɪt) *n* **1** a follower or attendant. **2** *Christianity.* an officer who assists a priest. [C16: via OF & Med. L from Gk *akolouthos* a follower]

aconite (ˈækəˌnaɪt) *n* **1** any of a genus of N temperate plants, such as monkshood and wolfsbane, many of which are poisonous. Cf. **winter aconite. 2** the dried poisonous root of many of these plants, sometimes used as a narcotic. [C16: via OF or L from Gk *akoniton* aconite]
▸**aconitic** (ˌækəˈnɪtɪk) *adj*

acorn (ˈeɪkɔːn) *n* the fruit of the oak tree, consisting of a smooth thick-walled nut in a woody scaly cuplike base. [C16: var. (infl. by *corn*) of OE *æcern* the fruit of a tree, acorn]

acoustic (əˈkuːstɪk) *or* **acoustical** *adj* **1** of or related to sound, hearing, or acoustics. **2** designed to respond to or absorb sound: *an acoustic tile.* **3** (of a musical instrument or recording) without electronic amplification: *an acoustic guitar.* [C17: from Gk *akoustikos*, from *akouein* to hear]
▸**aˈcoustically** *adv*

acoustics (əˈkuːstɪks) *n* **1** (*functioning as sing*) the scientific study of sound and sound waves. **2** (*functioning as pl*) the characteristics of a room, auditorium, etc., that determine the fidelity with which sound can be heard within it.

acquaint Ⓣ (əˈkweɪnt) *vb* (*tr*) (foll. by *with* or *of*) to make (a person) familiar (with). [C13: via OF & Med. L from L *accognitus*, from *accognōscere* to know perfectly, from *ad-* (intensive) + *cognōscere* to know]

acquaintance Ⓣ (əˈkweɪntəns) *n* **1** a person whom one knows but who is not a close friend. **2** knowledge of a person or thing, esp. when slight. **3 make the acquaintance of.** to come into social contact with. **4** those persons collectively whom one knows.
▸**acˈquaintanceship** *n*

acquainted Ⓣ (əˈkweɪntɪd) *adj* (*postpositive*) **1** (sometimes foll. by *with*) on terms of familiarity but not intimacy. **2** (foll. by *with*) familiar (with).

acquiesce Ⓣ (ˌækwɪˈɛs) *vb* **acquiesces, acquiescing, acquiesced.** (*intr*; often foll. by *in* or *to*) to comply (with); assent (to) without protest. [C17: from L *acquiēscere*, from *ad-* at + *quiēscere* to rest, from *quiēs* QUIET]
▸**ˌacquiˈescence** *n* ▸**ˌacquiˈescent** *adj*

> **USAGE NOTE** The use of *to* after *acquiesce* was formerly regarded as incorrect, but is now acceptable.

acquire Ⓣ (əˈkwaɪə) *vb* **acquires, acquiring, acquired.** (*tr*) to get or gain (something, such as an object, trait, or ability). [C15: via OF from L *acquīrere*, from *ad-* in addition + *quaerere* to get, seek]
▸**acˈquirable** *adj* ▸**acˈquirement** *n*

acquired behaviour *n Psychol.* the behaviour of an organism resulting from the effects of the environment.

acquired characteristic *n* a characteristic of an organism resulting from the effects of the environment.

acquired immune deficiency syndrome *or* **acquired immunodeficiency syndrome** *n* the full name for **AIDS.**

acquired immunity *n* the immunity produced by exposure of an organism to antigens, which stimulates the production of antibodies.

acquired taste *n* **1** a liking for something at first considered unpleasant. **2** the thing liked.

acquisition Ⓣ (ˌækwɪˈzɪʃən) *n* **1** the act of acquiring or gaining possession. **2** something acquired. **3** a person or thing of special merit added to a group. [C14: from L *acquīsītiōn-*, from *acquīrere* to ACQUIRE]

acquisitive Ⓣ (əˈkwɪzɪtɪv) *adj* inclined or eager to acquire things, esp. material possessions.
▸**acˈquisitively** *adv* ▸**acˈquisitiveness** *n*

THESAURUS

ant, sweet ≠ **sharp:** benign, bland, gentle, kindly, mild, pleasant, sweet

acidity *n* **1** = **sourness**, acerbity, acidulousness, acridity, acridness, bitterness, pungency, sharpness, tartness, vinegariness, vinegarishness **1** = **sharpness**, acerbity, acridity, acridness, bitterness, causticity, causticness, harshness, hurtfulness, mordancy, pungency, trenchancy

acidly *adv* **6** = **sharply**, acerbically, acridly, bitingly, bitterly, caustically, cuttingly, harshly, hurtfully, mordantly, pungently, stingingly, tartly, trenchantly
Antonyms *adv* benignly, blandly, gently, kindly, mildly, pleasantly, sweetly

acidulous *adj* **1** = **sour**, acerb, acerbic, acetic, acid, bitter, harsh, sharp, tart, vinegarish, vinegary **2** = **sharp**, acid, biting, bitter, caustic, cutting, harsh, pungent, sour, vitriolic

acknowledge *vb* **1** = **accept**, accede, acquiesce, admit, allow, concede, confess, declare, grant, own, profess, recognize, yield **2** = **greet**, address, hail, notice, recognize, salute **4** = **reply to**, answer, notice, react to, recognize, respond to, return
Antonyms *vb* ≠ **accept:** contradict, deny, disclaim, discount, reject, renounce, repudiate ≠ **greet:** disdain, disregard, ignore, reject, snub, spurn ≠ **reply to:** deny, disavow, disregard, ignore, rebut

acknowledged *adj* **1** = **accepted**, accredited, admitted, answered, approved, conceded, confessed, declared, professed, recognized, returned

acknowledgment *n* **1** = **acceptance**, accession, acquiescence, admission, allowing, confession, declaration, profession, realization, yielding **1** = **greeting**, addressing, hail, hailing, notice, recognition, salutation, salute **2** = **appreciation**, answer, credit, gratitude, reaction, recognition, reply, response, return, thanks

acme *n* = **high point**, apex, climax, crest, crown, culmination, height, optimum, peak, pinnacle, summit, top, vertex, zenith
Antonyms *n* bottom, depths, low point, minimum, nadir, rock bottom, zero

acolyte *n* **1, 2** = **attendant**, adherent, admirer, altar boy, assistant, follower, helper

acquaint *vb* = **tell**, advise, announce, apprise, disclose, divulge, enlighten, familiarize, inform, let (someone) know, notify, reveal

acquaintance *n* **1** = **associate**, colleague, contact **2** = **knowledge**, association, awareness, cognizance, companionship, conversance, conversancy, experience, familiarity, fellowship, intimacy, relationship, social contact, understanding
Antonyms *n* ≠ **associate:** buddy, good friend, intimate ≠ **knowledge:** ignorance, unfamiliarity

acquaintanceship *n* **2** = **relationship**, acquaintance, association, companionship, fellowship, knowledge, social contact

acquainted *adj* **2** *foll. by* **with** = **familiar with**, alive to, apprised of, *au fait* with, aware of, cognizant of, conscious of, conversant with, experienced in, informed of, in on, knowledgeable about, privy to, up to speed with, versed in

acquiesce *vb* = **agree**, accede, accept, allow, approve, assent, bow to, comply, concur, conform, consent, give in, go along with, play ball (*inf.*), submit, yield
Antonyms *vb* balk at, contest, demur, disagree, dissent, fight, object, protest, refuse, resist, veto

acquiescence *n* = **agreement**, acceptance, accession, approval, assent, compliance, concurrence, conformity, consent, giving in, obedience, submission, yielding

acquiescent *adj* = **agreeing**, acceding, accepting, agreeable, approving, assenting, compliant, concurrent, conforming, consenting, obedient, submissive, yielding

acquire *vb* = **get**, achieve, amass, attain, buy, collect, earn, gain, gather, land, obtain, pick up, procure, realize, receive, score (*sl.*), secure, win
Antonyms *vb* be deprived of, forfeit, forgo, give up, lose, relinquish, renounce, surrender, waive

acquirement *n* = **acquisition**, accomplishment, achievement, attainment, gathering, grip

acquisition *n* **1** = **acquiring**, achievement, acquirement, attainment, gaining, obtainment, procurement, pursuit **2** = **possession**, buy, gain, prize, property, purchase

acquisitive *adj* = **greedy**, avaricious, avid, cov-

acquit ❶ (əˈkwɪt) *vb* **acquits, acquitting, acquitted.** (*tr*) **1** (foll. by *of*) **1a** to free or release (from a charge of crime). **1b** to pronounce not guilty. **2** (foll. by *of*) to free or relieve (from an obligation, duty, etc.). **3** to repay or settle (a debt or obligation). **4** to conduct (oneself). [C13: from OF *aquiter*, from *quiter* to release, QUIT]
▸**acˈquittal** *n* ▸**acˈquitter** *n*

acquittance (əˈkwɪtəns) *n* **1** a release from or settlement of a debt, etc. **2** a record of this, such as a receipt.

acre (ˈeɪkə) *n* **1** a unit of area used in certain English-speaking countries, equal to 4840 square yards or 4046.86 square metres. **2** (*pl*) **2a** land, esp. a large area. **2b** *Inf.* a large amount. **3 farm the long acre.** *NZ.* to graze stock on the grass along a highway. [OE *æcer* field, acre]

acreage (ˈeɪkərɪdʒ) *n* **1** land area in acres. ◆ *adj* **2** *Austral.* of or relating to a large residential block of land, esp. in a rural area.

acrid ❶ (ˈækrɪd) *adj* **1** unpleasantly pungent or sharp to the smell or taste. **2** sharp or caustic, esp. in speech or nature. [C18: from L *ācer* sharp, sour; prob. infl. by ACID]
▸**acridity** (əˈkrɪdɪtɪ) *n* ▸**ˈacridly** *adv*

acridine (ˈækrɪˌdiːn) *n* a colourless crystalline solid used in the manufacture of dyes.

acriflavine (ˌækrɪˈfleɪvɪn) *n* a brownish or orange-red powder used in medicine as an antiseptic. [C20: from ACRIDINE + FLAVIN]

acriflavine hydrochloride *n* a red crystalline substance obtained from acriflavine and used as an antiseptic.

Acrilan (ˈækrɪˌlæn) *n Trademark.* an acrylic fibre or fabric, characterized by strength and resistance to creasing and used for clothing, carpets, etc.

acrimony ❶ (ˈækrɪmənɪ) *n, pl* **acrimonies.** bitterness or sharpness of manner, speech, temper, etc. [C16: from L *ācrimōnia*, from *ācer* sharp, sour]
▸**acrimonious** (ˌækrɪˈməʊnɪəs) *adj*

acro- *combining form.* **1** denoting something at a height, top, beginning, or end: *acropolis*. **2** denoting an extremity of the human body: *acromegaly*. [from Gk *akros* extreme, topmost]

acrobat ❶ (ˈækrəˌbæt) *n* **1** an entertainer who performs acts that require skill, agility, and coordination, such as swinging from a trapeze or walking a tightrope. **2** a person noted for his frequent and rapid changes of position or allegiance. [C19: via F from Gk *akrobatēs*, one who walks on tiptoe, from ACRO- + *bat-*, from *bainein* to walk]
▸ˌ**acroˈbatic** *adj* ▸ˌ**acroˈbatically** *adv*

acrobatics (ˌækrəˈbætɪks) *pl n* **1** the skills or feats of an acrobat. **2** any activity requiring agility and skill: *mental acrobatics*.

acrogen (ˈækrədʒən) *n* any flowerless plant, such as a fern or moss, in which growth occurs from the tip of the main stem.
▸**acrogenous** (əˈkrɒdʒɪnəs) *adj*

acromegaly (ˌækrəʊˈmɛgəlɪ) *n* a chronic disease characterized by enlargement of the bones of the head, hands, and feet, and swelling and enlargement of soft tissue. It is caused by excessive secretion of growth hormone by the pituitary gland. [C19: from F *acromégalie*, from ACRO- + Gk *megal-*, stem of *megas* big]
▸**acromegalic** (ˌækrəʊmɪˈgælɪk) *adj, n*

acronym (ˈækrənɪm) *n* a pronounceable name made from a series of initial letters or parts of a group of words; for example, *UNESCO* for the *United Nations Educational, Scientific, and Cultural Organization.* [C20: from ACRO- + -ONYM]

acrophobia (ˌækrəˈfəʊbɪə) *n* abnormal fear or dread of being at a great height. [C19: from ACRO- + -PHOBIA]
▸ˌ**acroˈphobic** *adj, n*

acropolis (əˈkrɒpəlɪs) *n* the citadel of an ancient Greek city. [C17: from Gk, from ACRO- + *polis* city]

across ❶ (əˈkrɒs) *prep* **1** from one side to the other side of. **2** on or at the other side of. **3** so as to transcend the boundaries or barriers of: *across religious divisions*. ◆ *adv* **4** from one side to the other. **5** on or to the other side. [C13 *on croice, acros*, from OF *a croix* crosswise]

across-the-board ❶ *adj* (**across the board** *when postpositive*) (of salary increases, taxation cuts, etc.) affecting all levels or classes equally.

acrostic (əˈkrɒstɪk) *n* a number of lines of writing, such as a poem, certain letters of which form a word, proverb, etc. A **single acrostic** is formed by the initial letters of the lines, a **double acrostic** by the initial and final letters, and a **triple acrostic** by the initial, middle, and final letters. [C16: via F from Gk, from ACRO- + *stikhos* line of verse]

acrylic (əˈkrɪlɪk) *adj* **1** of, derived from, or concerned with acrylic acid. ◆ *n* **2** short for **acrylic fibre, acrylic resin.** [C20: from L *ācer* sharp + *olēre* to smell + -IC]

acrylic acid *n* a colourless corrosive pungent liquid, used in the manufacture of acrylic resins. Formula: CH_2: CHCOOH. Systematic name: **propenoic acid.**

acrylic fibre *n* a man-made fibre used in blankets, knitwear, etc.

acrylic resin *n* any of a group of polymers of acrylic acid, its esters, or amides, used as synthetic rubbers, paints, and as plastics such as Perspex.

act ❶ (ækt) *n* **1** something done or performed. **2** the performance of some physical or mental process; action. **3** (*cap. when part of a name*) the formally codified result of deliberation by a legislative body. **4** (*often pl*) a formal written record of transactions, proceedings, etc., as of a society, committee, or legislative body. **5** a major division of a dramatic work. **6a** a short performance of skill, a comic sketch, dance, etc. **6b** those giving such a performance. **7** an assumed attitude or pose, esp. one intended to impress. **8 get in on the act.** *Inf.* to become involved in a profitable situation in order to share in the benefit. **9 get one's act together.** *Inf.* to organize oneself. ◆ *vb* **10** (*intr*) to do something. **11** (*intr*) to operate; react: *his mind acted quickly.* **12** to perform (a part or role) in a play, etc. **13** (*tr*) to present (a play, etc.) on stage. **14** (*intr;* usually foll. by *for* or *as*) to be a substitute (for). **15** (*intr;* foll. by *as*) to serve the function or purpose (of). **16** (*intr*) to conduct oneself or behave (as if one were): *she usually acts like a lady.* **17** (*intr*) to behave in an unnatural or affected way. **18** (*copula*) to play the part of: *to act the fool.* **19** (*copula*) to behave in a manner appropriate to: *to act one's age.* ◆ See also **act on, act up.** [C14: from L *actus* a doing, & *actum* a thing done, from the p.p. of *agere* to do]
▸ˈ**actable** *adj* ▸ˌ**actaˈbility** *n*

ACT *abbrev. for:* **1** Australian Capital Territory. **2** advance corporation tax.

ACTH *n* adrenocorticotrophic hormone; a hormone, secreted by the anterior lobe of the pituitary gland, that stimulates growth of the adrenal gland. It is used in treating rheumatoid arthritis, allergic and skin diseases, etc.

acting ❶ (ˈæktɪŋ) *adj* (*prenominal*) **1** taking on duties temporarily, esp. as a substitute for another. **2** performing the duties of though not yet holding the rank of: *acting lieutenant.* **3** operating or functioning. **4** intended for stage performance; provided with directions for actors: *an acting version of "Hedda Gabler".* ◆ *n* **5** the art or profession of an actor.

actinia (ækˈtɪnɪə) *n, pl* **actiniae** (-ˈtɪnɪˌiː) *or* **actinias.** a sea anemone common in rock pools. [C18: NL, lit.: things having a radial structure]

actinic (ækˈtɪnɪk) *adj* (of radiation) producing a photochemical effect. [C19: from ACTINO- + -IC]
▸**acˈtinically** *adv* ▸ˈ**actinˌism** *n*

actinide series (ˈæktɪˌnaɪd) *n* a series of 15 radioactive elements with increasing atomic numbers from actinium to lawrencium.

actinium (ækˈtɪnɪəm) *n* a radioactive element of the actinide series, occurring as a decay product of uranium. It is used in neutron production. Symbol: Ac; atomic no.: 89; half-life of most stable isotope, ^{227}Ac: 22 years. [C19: NL, from ACTINO- + -IUM]

actino- *or before a vowel* **actin-** *combining form.* **1** indicating a radial

THESAURUS

etous, grabbing, grasping, predatory, rapacious
Antonyms *adj* bounteous, bountiful, generous, lavish, liberal, munificent, open-handed, unselfish, unstinting

acquisitiveness *n* = **greed**, avarice, avidity, avidness, covetousness, graspingness, predatoriness, rapaciousness, rapacity

acquit *vb* **1, 2** = **clear**, absolve, deliver, discharge, exculpate, exonerate, free, fulfil, liberate, release, relieve, vindicate **3** = **pay off**, discharge, pay, repay, satisfy, settle **4** = **behave**, bear, comport, conduct, perform
Antonyms *vb* ≠ **clear:** blame, charge, condemn, convict, damn, find guilty, sentence

acquittal *n* **1, 2** = **clearance**, absolution, deliverance, discharge, exculpation, exoneration, freeing, liberation, release, relief, vindication

acrid *adj* **1** = **pungent**, acerb, acid, astringent, biting, bitter, burning, caustic, harsh, irritating, sharp, stinging, vitriolic **2** = **sharp**, acrimonious, biting, bitter, caustic, cutting, harsh, mordacious, mordant, nasty, sarcastic, trenchant, vitriolic

acrimonious *adj* = **bitter**, acerbic, astringent, biting, caustic, censorious, churlish, crabbed, cutting, irascible, mordacious, mordant, peevish, petulant, pungent, rancorous, sarcastic, severe, sharp, spiteful, splenetic, tart, testy, trenchant, vitriolic
Antonyms *adj* affable, benign, forgiving, good-tempered

acrimony *n* = **bitterness**, acerbity, asperity, astringency, churlishness, harshness, ill will, irascibility, mordancy, peevishness, pungency, rancour, sarcasm, spleen, tartness, trenchancy, virulence
Antonyms *n* amity, friendliness, friendship, good feelings, goodwill, liking, warmth

acrobat *n* **1** = **gymnast**, tumbler

across *prep* **1** = **throughout**, all through, covering, over, over the length and breadth of, straddling **2** = **opposite**, facing **2** = **over**, beyond, on the other *or* far side of, past ◆ *adv* **4** = **from side to side**, athwart, crossways *or* crosswise, transversely **5** = **over**, beyond, past, to the other *or* far side

across-the-board *adj* = **general**, all-embracing, all-encompassing, all-inclusive, blanket, complete, comprehensive, full, indiscriminate, overarching, sweeping, thorough, thoroughgoing, total, universal, wall-to-wall, wholesale, widespread, without exception *or* omission
Antonyms *adj* discriminate, limited, partial, restricted, selective, specific

act *n* **1, 2** = **deed**, accomplishment, achievement, action, blow, doing, execution, exertion, exploit, feat, move, operation, performance, step, stroke, undertaking **3** = **law**, bill, decree, edict, enactment, measure, ordinance, resolution, statute **6a** = **performance**, routine, show, sketch, turn **7** = **pretence**, affectation, attitude, counterfeit, dissimulation, fake, feigning, front, performance, pose, posture, sham, show, stance ◆ *vb* **11, 16** = **do**, acquit, bear, behave, carry, carry out, comport, conduct, enact, execute, exert, function, go about, make, move, operate, perform, react, serve, strike, take effect, undertake, work **12** = **perform**, act out, characterize, enact, impersonate, mime, mimic, personate, personify, play, play *or* take the part of, portray, represent **14** = **stand in for**, cover for, deputize for, fill in for, function in place of, replace, represent, serve, substitute for, take the place of **17** = **pretend**, affect, assume, counterfeit, dissimulate, feign, imitate, perform, pose, posture, put on, seem, sham

acting *adj* **1, 2** = **temporary**, interim, pro tem, structure: *actinomorphic.* **2** indicating radioactivity or radiation: *actinometer.* [from Gk, from *aktis* ray]

actinobiology (ˌæktɪnəʊbaɪˈɒlədʒɪ) *n* the branch of biology concerned with the effects of radiation on living organisms.

actinoid (ˈæktɪˌnɔɪd) *adj* having a radiate form, as a sea anemone or starfish.

actinometer (ˌæktɪˈnɒmɪtə) *n* an instrument for measuring the intensity of radiation, esp. of the sun's rays.

actinomycin (ˌæktɪnəʊˈmaɪsɪn) *n* any of several toxic antibiotics obtained from soil bacteria, used in treating some cancers.

actinozoan (ˌæktɪnəʊˈzəʊən) *n, adj* another word for **anthozoan.**

action ➊ (ˈækʃən) *n* **1** the state or process of doing something or being active. **2** something done, such as an act or deed. **3** movement or posture during some physical activity. **4** activity, force, or energy: *a man of action.* **5** (*usually pl*) conduct or behaviour. **6** *Law.* a legal proceeding brought by one party against another; lawsuit. **7** the operating mechanism, esp. in a piano, gun, watch, etc. **8** the force applied to a body. **9** the way in which something operates or works. **10** **out of action.** not functioning. **11** the events that form the plot of a story, play, or other composition. **12** *Mil.* **12a** a minor engagement. **12b** fighting at sea or on land: *he saw action in the war.* **13** *Inf.* the profits of an enterprise or transaction (esp. in **a piece of the action**). **14** *Sl.* the main activity, esp. social activity. **15** short for **industrial action.** ◆ *vb* (*tr*) **16** to put into effect; take action concerning. ◆ *sentence substitute.* **17** a command given by a film director to indicate that filming is to begin. [C14 *accioun*, ult. from L *āctiōn-*, from *agere* to do]

actionable (ˈækʃənəbᵊl) *adj Law.* affording grounds for legal action.
▸ˈ**actionably** *adv*

action committee *or* **group** *n* a committee or group formed to pursue an end, usually political, using petitions, marches, etc.

action painting *n* a development of abstract expressionism characterized by accidental effects of thrown, smeared, dripped, or spattered paint. Also called: **tachisme.**

action replay *n* the rerunning of a small section of a television film or tape of a match or other sporting contest, often in slow motion.

action stations *pl n* **1** *Mil.* the positions taken up by individuals in preparation for or during a battle. ◆ *sentence substitute.* **2** a command to take up such positions. **3** *Inf.* a warning to get ready for something.

activate ➊ (ˈæktɪˌveɪt) *vb* **activates, activating, activated.** (*tr*) **1** to make active or capable of action. **2** *Physics.* to make radioactive. **3** *Chem.* to increase the rate of (a reaction). **4** to purify (sewage) by aeration. **5** *US mil.* to mobilize or organize (a unit).
▸ˌ**actiˈvation** *n* ▸ˈ**actiˌvator** *n*

activated carbon *n* a highly adsorptive form of carbon used to remove colour or impurities from liquids and gases.

activated sludge *n* a mass of aerated precipitated sewage added to untreated sewage to bring about purification by hastening bacterial decomposition.

active ➊ (ˈæktɪv) *adj* **1** moving, working, or doing something. **2** busy or involved: *an active life.* **3** physically energetic. **4** effective: *an active ingredient.* **5** *Grammar.* denoting a voice of verbs used to indicate that the subject of a sentence is performing the action or causing the event or process described by the verb, as *kicked* in *The boy kicked the football.* **6** being fully engaged in military service. **7** (of a volcano) erupting periodically; not extinct. **8** *Astron.* (of the sun) exhibiting a large number of sunspots, solar flares, etc., and a marked variation in intensity and frequency of radio emission. ◆ *n* **9** *Grammar.* **9a** the active voice. **9b** an active verb. [C14: from L *āctīvus*. See ACT, -IVE]
▸ˈ**actively** *adv* ▸ˈ**activeness** *n*

active list *n Mil.* a list of officers available for full duty.

activism (ˈæktɪˌvɪzəm) *n* a policy of taking direct and often militant action to achieve an end, esp. a political or social one.
▸ˈ**activist** *n*

activity ➊ (ækˈtɪvɪtɪ) *n, pl* **activities. 1** the state or quality of being active. **2** lively action or movement. **3** any specific action, pursuit, etc.: *recreational activities.* **4** the number of disintegrations of a radioactive substance in a given unit of time. **5** *Chem.* a measure of the ability of a substance to take part in a chemical reaction.

act of God *n Law.* a sudden and inevitable occurrence caused by natural forces, such as a flood or earthquake.

act on ➊ *or* **upon** *vb* (*intr, prep*) **1** to regulate one's behaviour in accordance with (advice, information, etc.). **2** to have an effect on (illness, a part of the body, etc.).

actor ➊ (ˈæktə) *or* (*fem*) **actress** (ˈæktrɪs) *n* a person who acts in a play, film, broadcast, etc.

actual ➊ (ˈæktʃʊəl) *adj* **1** existing in reality or as a matter of fact. **2** real or genuine. **3** existing at the present time; current. ◆ See also **actuals.** [C14 *actuel* existing, from LL, from L *āctus* ACT]

> **USAGE NOTE** The excessive use of *actual* and *actually* should be avoided. They are unnecessary in sentences such as *in actual fact, he is forty-two,* and *he did actually go to the play but did not enjoy it.*

actual bodily harm *n Criminal law.* injury caused by one person to another that is less serious than grievous bodily harm. Abbrev.: **ABH.**

actuality ➊ (ˌæktʃʊˈælɪtɪ) *n, pl* **actualities. 1** true existence; reality. **2** (*sometimes pl*) a fact or condition that is real.

actualize ➊ *or* **actualise** (ˈæktʃʊəˌlaɪz) *vb* **actualizes, actualizing, actualized** *or* **actualises, actualising, actualised.** (*tr*) **1** to make actual or real. **2** to represent realistically.
▸ˌ**actualiˈzation** *or* ˌ**actualiˈsation** *n*

actually ➊ (ˈæktʃʊəlɪ) *adv* **1a** as an actual fact; really. **1b** (*as sentence modifier*): *actually, I haven't seen him.* **2** at present.

actuals (ˈæktʃʊəlz) *pl n Commerce.* commodities that can be purchased and used, as opposed to those bought and sold in a futures market. Also called: **physicals.**

actuarius (ˈæktʃʊˌeərɪəs) *n S. African history.* an official of the synod of a Dutch Reformed Church. [from L; see ACTUARY]

actuary (ˈæktʃʊərɪ) *n, pl* **actuaries.** a person qualified to calculate commercial risks and probabilities involving uncertain future events, esp. in such contexts as life assurance. [C16 (meaning: registrar): from L *āctuārius* one who keeps accounts, from *actum* public business, & *acta* documents]
▸**actuarial** (ˌæktʃʊˈeərɪəl) *adj*

actuate ➊ (ˈæktʃʊˌeɪt) *vb* **actuates, actuating, actuated.** (*tr*) **1** to put into action or mechanical motion. **2** to motivate: *actuated by unworthy desires.* [C16: from Med. L *actuātus*, from *actuāre* to incite to action, from L *āctus* ACT]
▸ˌ**actuˈation** *n* ▸ˈ**actuˌator** *n*

act up ➊ *vb* (*intr, adv*) *Inf.* to behave in a troublesome way: *the engine began to act up.*

acuity (əˈkjuːɪtɪ) *n* keenness or acuteness, esp. in vision or thought. [C15: from OF, from L *acūtus* ACUTE]

aculeus (əˈkjuːlɪəs) *n* **1** a prickle, such as the thorn of a rose. **2** a sting. [C19: from L, dim. of *acus* needle]
▸**aˈculeate** *adj*

THESAURUS

provisional, substitute, surrogate ◆ *n* **5** = **performance**, characterization, dramatics, enacting, impersonation, performing, playing, portrayal, portraying, stagecraft, theatre

action *n* **1, 2** = **deed**, accomplishment, achievement, act, blow, exercise, exertion, exploit, feat, move, operation, performance, step, stroke, undertaking **4** = **energy**, activity, force, liveliness, spirit, vigour, vim, vitality **4** = **movement**, activity, effect, effort, exertion, force, functioning, influence, motion, operation, power, process, work, working **5** *usually plural* = **behaviour**, bearing, comportment, conduct, demeanour, deportment, manners, ways **6** = **lawsuit**, case, cause, litigation, proceeding, prosecution, suit **12** = **battle**, affray, clash, combat, conflict, contest, encounter, engagement, fight, fighting, fray, skirmish, sortie, warfare

activate *vb* = **start**, actuate, animate, arouse, energize, galvanize, get going, impel, initiate, kick-start (*inf.*), mobilize, motivate, move, prod, prompt, propel, rouse, set going, set in motion, set off, stimulate, stir, switch on, trigger (off), turn on
Antonyms *vb* arrest, check, deactivate, halt, impede, stall, stop, terminate, turn off

activation *n* = **start**, actuation, animation, arousal, initiation, mobilization, setting in motion, switching on, triggering, turning on

active *adj* **1** = **in operation**, acting, astir, at work, doing, effectual, functioning, in action, in business, in force, live, moving, operative, running, stirring, working **2** = **busy**, bustling, engaged, full, hard-working, involved, occupied, on the go (*inf.*), on the move, strenuous **3** = **energetic**, alert, alive and kicking, animated, diligent, industrious, lively, nimble, on the go (*inf.*), quick, spirited, sprightly, spry, vibrant, vigorous, vital, vivacious
Antonyms *adj* dormant, dull, idle, inactive, inoperative, lazy, sedentary, slow, sluggish, torpid, unimaginative, unoccupied

activist *n* = **militant**, organizer, partisan

activity *n* **1, 2** = **action**, activeness, animation, bustle, enterprise, exercise, exertion, hurly-burly, hustle, labour, life, liveliness, motion, movement, stir, work **3** = **pursuit**, act, avocation, deed, endeavour, enterprise, hobby, interest, job, labour, occupation, pastime, project, scheme, task, undertaking, venture, work
Antonyms *n* ≠ **action:** dullness, idleness, immobility, inaction, inactivity, indolence, inertia, lethargy, passivity, sluggishness, torpor

act on *vb* **1** = **obey**, act in accordance with, carry out, comply with, conform to, follow, heed, yield to **2** = **affect**, alter, change, impact, influence, modify, sway, transform

actor *n* = **performer**, dramatic artist, leading man *or* lady, play-actor, player, Thespian, tragedian *or* tragedienne, trouper

actual *adj* **1** = **definite**, absolute, categorical, certain, concrete, corporeal, factual, indisputable, indubitable, physical, positive, real, substantial, tangible, undeniable, unquestionable **2** = **real**, authentic, confirmed, genuine, realistic, true, truthful, verified
Antonyms *adj* fictitious, hypothetical, made-up, probable, supposed, theoretical, unreal, untrue

actuality *n* **1** = **reality**, corporeality, factuality, materiality, realness, substance, substantiality, truth, verity **2** = **fact**, reality, truth, verity

actualize *vb* **1** = **make real**, bring about, bring into being, bring to life, effect, effectuate, give life *or* substance to, incarnate, make concrete, make happen, objectify, put into effect, realize, reify

actually *adv* **1** = **really**, absolutely, as a matter of fact, de facto, essentially, indeed, in fact, in point of fact, in reality, in truth, literally, truly, veritably

actuate *vb* **1, 2** = **motivate**, animate, arouse, cause, dispose, drive, excite, get going, impel, incite, induce, influence, inspire, instigate, move, prompt, quicken, rouse, spur, stimulate, stir, urge

act up *vb* = **misbehave**, be naughty, carry on, cause trouble, give bother, give trouble, horse

acumen ➊ ('ækjʊˌmɛn, ə'kju:mən) *n* the ability to judge well; insight. [C16: from L: sharpness, from *acuere* to sharpen]
▸**a'cuminous** *adj*

acuminate *adj* (ə'kju:mɪnɪt). **1** narrowing to a sharp point, as some types of leaf. ◆ *vb* (ə'kju:mɪˌneɪt), **acuminates, acuminating, acuminated. 2** (*tr*) to make pointed or sharp. [C17: from L *acūmināre* to sharpen]
▸**aˌcumi'nation** *n*

acupoint ('ækjʊˌpɔɪnt) *n* any of the specific points on the body into which a needle is inserted in acupuncture or onto which pressure is applied in shiatsu. [C19: from ACU(PUNCTURE) + POINT]

acupressure ('ækjʊˌprɛʃə) *n* another name for **shiatsu.** [C19: from ACU(PUNCTURE) + PRESSURE]

acupuncture ('ækjʊˌpʌŋktʃə) *n* the insertion of the tips of needles into the skin at specific points for the purpose of treating various disorders by stimulating nerve impulses. [C17: from L *acus* needle + PUNCTURE]
▸**'acuˌpuncturist** *n*

acute ➊ (ə'kju:t) *adj* **1** penetrating in perception or insight. **2** sensitive to details; keen. **3** of extreme importance; crucial. **4** sharp or severe; intense. **5** having a sharp end or point. **6** *Maths.* (of an angle) less than 90°. **7** (of a disease) **7a** arising suddenly and manifesting intense severity. **7b** of relatively short duration. **8** *Phonetics.* of or relating to an accent (´) placed over vowels, denoting that the vowel is pronounced with higher musical pitch (as in ancient Greek) or with certain special quality (as in French). **9** (of a hospital, hospital bed, or ward) intended to accommodate short-term patients. ◆ *n* **10** an acute accent. [C14: from L *acūtus*, p.p. of *acuere* to sharpen, from *acus* needle]
▸**a'cutely** *adv* ▸**a'cuteness** *n*

acute accent *n* the diacritical mark (´), used in some languages to indicate that the vowel over which it is placed has a special quality (as in French *été*) or that it receives the strongest stress in the word (as in Spanish *hablé*).

acute dose *n* a fatal dose of radiation.

ad (æd) *n Inf.* short for **advertisement.**

A.D. *or* **AD** (indicating years numbered from the supposed year of the birth of Christ) *abbrev. for* anno Domini: *70* A.D. [L: in the year of the Lord]

> **USAGE NOTE** In strict usage, A.D. is only employed with specific years: *he died in 1621* A.D., but *he died in the 17th century* (and not *the 17th century* A.D.). Formerly the practice was to write A.D. preceding the date (A.D. *1621*), and it is also strictly correct to omit *in* when A.D. is used, since this is already contained in the meaning of the Latin *anno Domini* (in the year of Our Lord), but this is no longer general practice. B.C. is used with both specific dates and indications of the period: *Heraclitus was born about 540* B.C.; *the battle took place in the 4th century* B.C.

ad- *prefix* **1** to; towards: *adsorb.* **2** near; next to: *adrenal.* [from L: towards. As a prefix in words of L origin, *ad-* became *ac-, af-, ag-, al-, an-, acq-, ar-, as-*, and *at-* before *c, f, g, l, n, q, r, s*, and *t*, and became *a-* before *gn, sc, sp, st*]

adage ➊ ('ædɪdʒ) *n* a traditional saying that is accepted by many as true; proverb. [C16: via OF from L *adagium*; rel. to *āio* I say]

adagio (ə'dɑ:dʒɪˌəʊ) *Music.* ◆ *adj, adv* **1** (to be performed) slowly. ◆ *n, pl* **adagios. 2** a movement or piece to be performed slowly. [C18: It., from *ad* at + *agio* ease]

Adam[1] ('ædəm) *n* **1** *Bible.* the first man, created by God (Genesis 2–3). **2 not know (someone) from Adam.** to have no knowledge of or acquaintance with someone. **3 Adam's ale** *or* **wine.** water.

Adam[2] ('ædəm) *adj* in the neoclassical style made popular by Robert *Adam* (1728–92), Scottish architect and furniture designer.

adamant ➊ ('ædəmənt) *adj* **1** unshakable in determination, purpose, etc.; inflexible. **2** unbreakable; impenetrable. ◆ *n* **3** any extremely hard substance. **4** a legendary stone said to be impenetrable. [OE: from L *adamas*, from Gk, lit.: unconquerable, from A-[1] + *daman* to conquer]
▸ˌ**ada'mantine** *adj*

Adam's apple *n* the visible projection of the thyroid cartilage of the larynx at the front of the neck.

adapt ➊ (ə'dæpt) *vb* **1** (often foll. by *to*) to adjust (someone or something) to different conditions. **2** (*tr*) to fit, change, or modify to suit a new or different purpose. [C17: from L *adaptāre*, from *ad-* to + *aptāre* to fit]
▸**a'daptable** *adj* ▸**aˌdapta'bility** *n* ▸**a'daptive** *adj*

adaptation ➊ (ˌædæp'teɪʃən) *n* **1** the act or process of adapting or the state of being adapted. **2** something that is produced by adapting something else. **3** something that is changed or modified to suit new conditions. **4** *Biol.* a modification in organisms that makes them better suited to survive and reproduce in a particular environment.

adaptor *or* **adapter** (ə'dæptə) *n* **1** a person or thing that adapts. **2** any device for connecting two parts, esp. ones that are of different sizes. **3a** a plug used to connect an electrical device to a mains supply when they have different types of terminals. **3b** a device used to connect several electrical appliances to a single socket.

ADC *abbrev. for:* **1** aide-de-camp. **2** analogue-digital converter.

add ➊ (æd) *vb* **1** to combine (two or more numbers or quantities) by addition. **2** (*tr*; foll. by *to*) to increase (a number or quantity) by another number or quantity using addition. **3** (*tr*; often foll. by *to*) to join (something) to something else in order to increase the size, effect, or scope: *to add insult to injury.* **4** (*intr*; foll. by *to*) to have an extra and increased effect (on). **5** (*tr*) to say or write further. **6** (*tr*; foll. by *in*) to include. ◆ See also **add up.** [C14: from L *addere*, from *ad-* to + *-dere*, *dare* to put]

ADD *abbrev. for* attention deficit disorder.

addax ('ædæks) *n* a large light-coloured antelope having ribbed loosely spiralled horns and inhabiting desert regions in N Africa. [C17: L, from an unidentified ancient N African language]

addend ('ædɛnd) *n* any of a set of numbers that is to be added. [C20: short for ADDENDUM]

addendum ➊ (ə'dɛndəm) *n, pl* **addenda** (-də). **1** something added; an addition. **2** a supplement or appendix to a book, magazine, etc. [C18: from L, gerundive of *addere* to ADD]

adder ('ædə) *n* **1** Also called: **viper.** a common viper that is widely distributed in Europe, including Britain, and Asia and is dark grey with a black zigzag pattern along the back. **2** any of various similar venomous or nonvenomous snakes. ◆ See also **death adder, puff adder.** [OE *nǣdre* snake; in ME *a naddre* was mistaken for *an addre*]

adder's-tongue *n* any of several ferns that grow in the N hemisphere and have a narrow spore-bearing body that sticks out like a spike from the leaf.

addict ➊ *vb* (ə'dɪkt). **1** (*tr; usually passive;* often foll. by *to*) to cause (someone or oneself) to become dependent (on something, esp. a narcotic drug). ◆ *n* ('ædɪkt). **2** a person who is addicted, esp. to narcotic drugs. **3** *Inf.* a person devoted to something: *a jazz addict.* [C16 (as adj and as vb; n use C20): from L *addictus* given over, from *addīcere*, from *ad-* to + *dīcere* to say]
▸**ad'diction** *n* ▸**ad'dictive** *adj*

Addison's disease ('ædɪsᵊnz) *n* a disease characterized by bronzing of the skin, anaemia, and extreme weakness, caused by underactivity of

THESAURUS

around (*inf.*), malfunction, mess about, play up (*Brit. inf.*), raise Cain

acumen *n* = **judgment**, acuteness, astuteness, cleverness, discernment, ingenuity, insight, intelligence, keenness, penetration, perception, perspicacity, perspicuity, sagacity, sharpness, shrewdness, smartness, wisdom, wit

acute *adj* **1, 2** = **perceptive**, astute, canny, clever, discerning, discriminating, incisive, ingenious, insightful, intuitive, keen, observant, on the ball (*inf.*), penetrating, perspicacious, piercing, sensitive, sharp, smart, subtle **3** = **serious**, critical, crucial, dangerous, decisive, essential, grave, important, severe, sudden, urgent, vital **4** = **sharp**, cutting, distressing, excruciating, exquisite, fierce, harrowing, intense, overpowering, overwhelming, piercing, poignant, powerful, racking, severe, shooting, shrill, stabbing, sudden, violent
Antonyms *adj* ≠ **perceptive:** dense, dim, dim-witted, dull, obtuse, slow, stupid, unintelligent

acuteness *n* **1, 2** = **perceptiveness**, acuity, astuteness, canniness, cleverness, discernment, discrimination, ingenuity, insight, intuition, intuitiveness, keenness, perception, perspicacity, sensitivity, sharpness, smartness, subtleness, subtlety, wit **3** = **seriousness**, criticality, criticalness, cruciality, danger, dangerousness, decisiveness, essentiality, gravity, importance, severity, suddenness, urgency, vitalness **4** = **sharpness**, distressingness, exquisiteness, fierceness, intenseness, intensity, poignancy, powerfulness, severity, shrillness, suddenness, violence

adage *n* = **saying**, aphorism, apophthegm, axiom, by-word, dictum, maxim, motto, precept, proverb, saw

adamant *adj* **1** = **determined**, firm, fixed, immovable, inexorable, inflexible, insistent, intransigent, obdurate, relentless, resolute, rigid, set, stiff, stubborn, unbending, uncompromising, unrelenting, unshakable, unyielding
Antonyms *adj* compliant, compromising, easy-going, flexible, lax, pliant, receptive, responsive, susceptible, tensile, tractable, yielding

adapt *vb* **1, 2** = **adjust**, acclimatize, accommodate, alter, apply, change, comply, conform, convert, customize, familiarize, fashion, fit, habituate, harmonize, make, match, modify, prepare, qualify, remodel, shape, suit, tailor, tweak (*inf.*)

adaptability *n* **1, 2** = **flexibility**, adaptableness, adjustability, alterability, changeability, compliancy, convertibility, malleability, modifiability, plasticity, pliability, pliancy, resilience, variability, versatility

adaptable *adj* **1, 2** = **flexible**, adjustable, alterable, changeable, compliant, conformable, convertible, easy-going, easy-oasy (*sl.*), malleable, modifiable, plastic, pliant, resilient, variable, versatile

adaptation *n* **1** = **conversion**, adjustment, alteration, change, modification, refitting, remodelling, reworking, shift, transformation, variation, version

add *vb* **1** = **count up**, add up, compute, reckon, sum up, total, tot up **3, 6** = **include**, adjoin, affix, amplify, annex, append, attach, augment, enlarge by, increase by, supplement
Antonyms *vb* deduct, diminish, lessen, reduce, remove, subtract, take away, take from

addendum *n* **1, 2** = **addition**, adjunct, affix, appendage, appendix, attachment, augmentation, codicil, extension, extra, postscript, supplement

addict *n* **2** = **junkie** (*inf.*), dope-fiend, fiend (*inf.*), freak (*inf.*), head (*sl.*), pill-popper (*inf.*), user (*inf.*) **3** = **fan**, adherent, buff (*inf.*), devotee, enthusiast, follower, freak (*inf.*), nut (*sl.*)

addicted *adj* **1** = **hooked** (*sl.*), absorbed, accustomed, dedicated, dependent, devoted, disposed, fond, habituated, inclined, obsessed, prone

addiction *n* **1** = **dependence**, craving, enslavement, habit, obsession

addictive *adj* **1** = **habit-forming**, causing addicthe adrenal glands. [C19: after Thomas *Addison* (1793–1860), E physician who identified it]

addition ❶ (əˈdɪʃən) *n* **1** the act, process, or result of adding. **2** a person or thing that is added or acquired. **3** a mathematical operation in which the sum of two numbers or quantities is calculated. Usually indicated by the symbol + **4** *Obs.* a title. **5 in addition.** (*adv*) also; as well. **6 in addition to.** (*prep*) besides; as well as. [C15: from L *additiōn-*, from *addere* to ADD]
▸**adˈditional** *adj*

additionality (əˌdɪʃəˈnælɪtɪ) *n* (in the European Union) the principle that the EU contributes to the funding of a project in a member country provided that the member country also contributes.

Additional Member System *n* a system of voting in which people vote separately for the candidate and the party of their choice. Parties are allocated extra seats if the number of constituencies they win does not reflect their overall share of the vote. See also **proportional representation.**

additive ❶ (ˈædɪtɪv) *adj* **1** characterized or produced by addition. ◆ *n* **2** any substance added to something to improve it, prevent deterioration, etc. **3** short for **food additive.** [C17: from LL *additīvus*, from *addere* to ADD]

addle ❶ (ˈædᵊl) *vb* **addles, addling, addled. 1.** to make or become confused or muddled. **2** to make or become rotten. ◆ *adj* **3** (*in combination*) indicating a confused or muddled state: *addle-brained.* [C18 (vb), back formation from *addled*, from C13 *addle* rotten, from OE *adela* filth]

add-on *n* a feature that can be added to a standard model or package to give increased benefits.

address ❶ (əˈdrɛs) *n* **1** the conventional form by which the location of a building is described. **2** the written form of this, as on a letter or parcel. **3** the place at which someone lives. **4** a speech or written communication, esp. one of a formal nature. **5** skilfulness or tact. **6** *Arch.* manner of speaking. **7** *Computing.* a number giving the location of a piece of stored information. **8** (*usually pl*) expressions of affection made by a man in courting a woman. ◆ *vb* (*tr*) **9** to mark (a letter, parcel, etc.) with an address. **10** to speak to, refer to in speaking, or deliver a speech to. **11** (used reflexively; foll. by *to*) **11a** to speak or write to. **11b** to apply oneself to: *he addressed himself to the task.* **12** to direct (a message, warning, etc.) to the attention of. **13** to adopt a position facing (the ball in golf, etc.). [C14 (in the sense: to make right, adorn) and C15 (in the modern sense: to direct words): via OF from Vulgar L *addrictiāre* (unattested), from L *ad-* to + *dīrectus* DIRECT]
▸**adˈdresser** *or* **adˈdressor** *n*

addressee (ˌædrɛˈsiː) *n* a person or organization to whom a letter, etc., is addressed.

adduce (əˈdjuːs) *vb* **adduces, adducing, adduced.** (*tr*) to cite (reasons, examples, etc.) as evidence or proof. [C15: from L *addūcere* to lead to]
▸**adˈducent** *adj* ▸**adˈducible** *adj* ▸**adduction** (əˈdʌkʃən) *n*

adduct (əˈdʌkt) *vb* (*tr*) **1** (of a muscle) to draw or pull (a leg, arm, etc.) towards the median axis of the body. ◆ *n* **2** *Chem.* a compound formed by direct combination of two or more different compounds or elements. [C19: from L *addūcere*; see ADDUCE]
▸**adˈduction** *n* ▸**adˈductor** *n*

add up ❶ *vb* (*adv*) **1** to find the sum (of). **2** (*intr*) to result in a correct total. **3** (*intr*) *Inf.* to make sense. **4** (*intr*; foll. by *to*) to amount to.

-ade *suffix forming nouns.* a sweetened drink made of various fruits: *lemonade.* [from F, from L *-āta* made of, fem p.p. of verbs ending in *-āre*]

adenine (ˈædənɪn) *n* a purine base present in animal and plant tissues as a constituent of the nucleic acids DNA and RNA.

adeno- *or before a vowel* **aden-** *combining form.* gland or glandular: *adenoid; adenology.* [NL, from Gk *adēn* gland]

adenoidal (ˌædɪˈnɔɪdᵊl) *adj* **1** having the nasal tones or impaired breathing of one with enlarged adenoids. **2** of adenoids.

adenoids (ˈædɪˌnɔɪdz) *pl n* a mass of lymphoid tissue at the back of the throat behind the uvula: when enlarged it often restricts nasal breathing, esp. in young children. [C19 : from Gk *adenoeidēs.* See ADENO-, -OID]

adenoma (ˌædɪˈnəʊmə) *n, pl* **adenomas** *or* **adenomata** (-mətə). **1** a tumour occurring in glandular tissue. **2** a tumour having a glandlike structure.

adenopathy (ˌædɪˈnɒpəθɪ) *n Pathol.* **1** enlargement of the lymph nodes. **2** enlargement of a gland.

adenosine (æˈdɛnəˌsiːn) *n Biochem.* a compound formed by the condensation of adenine and ribose. It is present in all living cells in a combined form. See also **ADP, AMP, ATP.** [C20: a blend of ADENINE + RIBOSE]

adept ❶ *adj* (əˈdɛpt). **1** proficient in something requiring skill or manual dexterity. **2** expert. ◆ *n* (ˈædɛpt). **3** a person who is skilled or proficient in something. [C17: from Med. L *adeptus*, from L *adipiscī*, from *ad-* to + *apiscī* to attain]
▸**aˈdeptness** *n*

adequate ❶ (ˈædɪkwɪt) *adj* able to fulfil a need without being abundant, outstanding, etc. [C17: from L *adaequāre*, from *ad-* to + *aequus* EQUAL]
▸**adequacy** (ˈædɪkwəsɪ) *n* ▸ˈ**adequately** *adv*

à deux *French.* (a dø) *adj, adv* of or for two persons.

ADFA *abbrev. for* Australian Defence Force Academy.

ADH *abbrev. for* antidiuretic hormone. See **vasopressin.**

adhere ❶ (ədˈhɪə) *vb* **adheres, adhering, adhered.** (*intr*) **1** (usually foll. by *to*) to stick or hold fast. **2** (foll. by *to*) to be devoted (to a political party, religion, etc.). **3** (foll. by *to*) to follow exactly. [C16: via Med. L, from L *adhaerēre* to stick to]

adherent ❶ (ədˈhɪərənt) *n* **1** (usually foll. by *of*) a supporter or follower. ◆ *adj* **2** sticking, holding fast, or attached.
▸**adˈherence** *n*

> **USAGE NOTE** See at **adhesion.**

adhesion ❶ (ədˈhiːʒən) *n* **1** the quality or condition of sticking together or holding fast. **2** ability to make firm contact without slipping. **3** attachment, as to a political party, cause, etc. **4** an attraction or repulsion between the molecules of unlike substances in contact. **5** *Pathol.* abnormal union of structures or parts. [C17: from L *adhaesiōn-* a sticking. See ADHERE]

> **USAGE NOTE** *Adhesion* is the preferred term when talking about sticking or holding fast in a physical sense. *Adherence* is preferred when talking about attachment to a political party, cause, etc.

adhesive ❶ (ədˈhiːsɪv) *adj* **1** able or designed to adhere: *adhesive tape.* **2** tenacious or clinging. ◆ *n* **3** a substance used for sticking, such as glue or paste.
▸**adˈhesively** *adv* ▸**adˈhesiveness** *n*

THESAURUS

tion *or* dependency, compelling, moreish *or* morish (*inf.*)

addition *n* **1 = counting up**, adding up, computation, reckoning, summation, summing up, totalling, totting up **1 = inclusion**, accession, adding, adjoining, affixing, amplification, annexation, attachment, augmentation, enlargement, extension, increasing **2 = extra**, addendum, additive, adjunct, affix, appendage, appendix, extension, gain, increase, increment, supplement **5, 6 in addition (to) = as well (as)**, additionally, also, besides, into the bargain, moreover, over and above, to boot, too, withal
Antonyms *n* ≠ **inclusion, counting up:** deduction, detachment, diminution, lessening, reduction, removal, subtraction

additional *adj* **2 = extra**, added, add-on, affixed, appended, fresh, further, increased, more, new, other, over-and-above, spare, supplementary

additive *n* **2, 3 = added ingredient**, artificial *or* synthetic ingredient, E number, extra, supplement

addle *vb* **1 = confuse**, befuddle, bewilder, fluster, fuddle, mix up, muddle, perplex, stupefy **2 = go off** (*Brit. inf.*), go bad, rot, spoil, turn, turn bad

addled *adj* **1 = confused**, at sea, befuddled, bewildered, flustered, foolish, mixed-up, muddled, perplexed, silly **2 = off**, bad, gone bad, rancid, rotten, turned

address *n* **2 = direction**, inscription, superscription **3 = location**, abode, domicile, dwelling, home, house, lodging, pad (*sl.*), place, residence, situation, whereabouts **4 = speech**, discourse, disquisition, dissertation, harangue, lecture, oration, sermon, talk ◆ *vb* **10 = speak to**, accost, apostrophize, approach, greet, hail, invoke, salute, talk to **10 = give a speech**, discourse, give a talk, harangue, lecture, orate, sermonize, speak, spout, talk **11 address (oneself) to = concentrate on**, apply (oneself) to, attend to, devote (oneself) to, engage in, focus on, knuckle down to, look to, take care of, take up, turn to, undertake

add up *vb* **1 = count up**, add, compute, count, reckon, sum up, total, tot up **3 = make sense**, be plausible, be reasonable, hold water, ring true, stand to reason **4 = mean**, amount, come to, imply, indicate, reveal, signify

adept *adj* **1, 2 = skilful**, able, accomplished, adroit, dexterous, expert, masterful, masterly, practised, proficient, skilled, versed ◆ *n* **3 = expert**, buff (*inf.*), dab hand (*Brit. inf.*), genius, hotshot (*inf.*), master, maven (*US*), whizz (*inf.*)
Antonyms *adj* ≠ **skilful:** amateurish, awkward, clumsy, inept, unskilled

adeptness *n* **1, 2 = skill**, ability, adroitness, aptitude, deftness, dexterity, expertise, facility, knack, mastery, proficiency, skilfulness
Antonyms *n* amateurishness, awkwardness, clumsiness, ineptitude, inexpertness

adequacy *n* **= sufficiency**, capability, commensurateness, competence, fairness, requisiteness, satisfactoriness, suitability, tolerability

adequate *adj* **= enough**, capable, commensurate, competent, fair, passable, requisite, satisfactory, sufficient, suitable, tolerable, up to scratch (*inf.*)
Antonyms *adj* deficient, inadequate, insufficient, lacking, meagre, scant, short, unsatisfactory, unsuitable

adhere *vb* **1 = stick**, attach, cement, cleave, cling, cohere, fasten, fix, glue, glue on, hold fast, paste, stick fast, unite **2, 3 = support**, abide by, be attached, be constant, be devoted, be faithful, be loyal, be true, cleave to, cling, follow, fulfil, heed, keep, keep to, maintain, mind, obey, observe, respect, stand by

adherent *n* **1 = supporter**, admirer, advocate, devotee, disciple, fan, follower, hanger-on, henchman, partisan, protagonist, sectary, upholder, votary ◆ *adj* **2 = sticky**, adhering, adhesive, clinging, gluey, glutinous, gummy, holding, mucilaginous, sticking, tacky, tenacious
Antonyms *n* ≠ **supporter:** adversary, antagonist, disputant, dissentient, enemy, foe, opponent, opposer, opposition, rival

adhesion *n* **1, 2 = sticking**, adherence, adhesiveness, attachment, coherence, cohesion, grip, holding fast, union **3 = support**, allegiance, attachment, constancy, devotion, faithfulness, fidelity, fulfilment, heed, loyalty, obedience, observation, respect, troth (*arch.*)

adhesive *adj* **1, 2 = sticky**, adhering, attaching, clinging, cohesive, gluey, glutinous, gummy, holding, mucilaginous, sticking,

ad hoc Ⓣ (æd 'hɒk) *adj, adv* for a particular purpose only: *an ad hoc committee.* [L, lit.: to this]
ad hominem *Latin.* (æd 'hɒmɪˌnem) *adj, adv* directed against a person rather than his arguments. [lit.: to the man]
adiabatic (ˌædɪə'bætɪk) *adj* **1** (of a thermodynamic process) taking place without loss or gain of heat. ◆ *n* **2** a curve on a graph representing the changes in a system undergoing an adiabatic process. [C19: from Gk, from A-[1] + *diabatos* passable]
adieu Ⓣ (ə'djuː) *sentence substitute, n, pl* **adieus** *or* **adieux** (ə'djuːz). goodbye. [C14: from OF, from *a* to + *dieu* God]
ad infinitum Ⓣ (æd ˌɪnfɪ'naɪtəm) *adv* without end; endlessly; to infinity. Abbrev.: **ad inf.** [L]
ad interim (æd 'ɪntərɪm) *adj, adv* for the meantime: *ad interim measures.* Abbrev.: **ad int.** [L]
adipocere (ˌædɪpəʊ'sɪə) *n* a waxlike fatty substance sometimes formed during the decomposition of corpses. [C19: from NL *adiposus* fat + F *cire* wax]
adipose ('ædɪˌpəʊs) *adj* **1** of, resembling, or containing fat; fatty. ◆ *n* **2** animal fat. [C18: from NL *adiposus,* from L *adeps* fat]
adit ('ædɪt) *n* an almost horizontal shaft into a mine, for access or drainage. [C17: from L *aditus,* from *adīre,* from *ad-* towards + *īre* to go]
adj. *abbrev. for:* **1** adjective. **2** adjunct. **3** Also: **adjt.** adjutant.
adjacent Ⓣ (ə'dʒeɪsᵊnt) *adj* being near or close, esp. having a common boundary; contiguous. [C15: from L *adjacēre,* from *ad-* near + *jacēre* to lie]
▸**ad'jacency** *n* ▸**ad'jacently** *adv*
adjacent angles *pl n* two angles having the same vertex and a side in common.
adjective ('ædʒɪktɪv) *n* **1a** a word imputing a characteristic to a noun or pronoun. **1b** *(as modifier): an adjective phrase.* Abbrev.: **adj.** ◆ *adj* **2** additional or dependent. [C14: from LL, from L from *adjicere,* from *ad-* to + *jacere* to throw]
▸**adjectival** (ˌædʒɪk'taɪvᵊl) *adj*
adjoin Ⓣ (ə'dʒɔɪn) *vb* **1** to be next to (an area of land, etc.). **2** *(tr;* foll. by *to)* to join; attach. [C14: via OF from L, from *ad-* to + *jungere* to join]
▸**ad'joining** *adj*
adjourn Ⓣ (ə'dʒɜːn) *vb* **1** *(intr)* (of a court, etc.) to close at the end of a session. **2** to postpone or be postponed, esp. temporarily. **3** *(tr)* to put off (a problem, discussion, etc.) for later consideration. **4** *(intr) Inf.* to move elsewhere: *let's adjourn to the kitchen.* [C14: from OF *ajourner* to defer to an arranged day, from *a-* to + *jour* day, from LL *diurnum,* from L *diēs* day]
▸**ad'journment** *n*
adjudge Ⓣ (ə'dʒʌdʒ) *vb* **adjudges, adjudging, adjudged.** *(tr; usually passive)* **1** to pronounce formally; declare. **2a** to judge. **2b** to decree: *he was adjudged bankrupt.* **2c** to award (costs, damages, etc.). **3** *Arch.* to condemn. [C14: via OF from L *adjūdicāre.* See ADJUDICATE]
adjudicate Ⓣ (ə'dʒuːdɪˌkeɪt) *vb* **adjudicates, adjudicating, adjudicated. 1** (when *intr,* usually foll. by *upon)* to give a decision (on), esp. a formal or binding one. **2** *(intr)* to serve as a judge or arbiter, as in a competition. [C18: from L *adjūdicāre,* from *ad-* to + *jūdicāre* to judge, from *jūdex* judge]
▸**ad,judi'cation** *n* ▸**ad'judi,cator** *n*
adjunct Ⓣ ('ædʒʌŋkt) *n* **1** something incidental or not essential that is added to something else. **2** a person who is subordinate to another. **3** *Grammar.* **3a** part of a sentence other than the subject or the predicate. **3b** a modifier. ◆ *adj* **4** added or connected in a secondary position. [C16: from L *adjunctus,* p.p. of *adjungere* to ADJOIN]
▸**adjunctive** (ə'dʒʌŋktɪv) *adj* ▸**'adjunctly** *adv*
adjure Ⓣ (ə'dʒʊə) *vb* **adjures, adjuring, adjured.** *(tr)* **1** to command, often by exacting an oath. **2** to appeal earnestly to. [C14: from L *adjūrāre,* from *ad-* to + *jūrāre* to swear, from *jūs* oath]
▸**adjuration** (ˌædʒʊə'reɪʃən) *n* ▸**ad'juratory** *adj* ▸**ad'jurer** *or* **ad'juror** *n*
adjust Ⓣ (ə'dʒʌst) *vb* **1** *(tr)* to alter slightly, esp. to achieve accuracy. **2** to adapt, as to a new environment, etc. **3** *(tr)* to put into order. **4** *(tr) Insurance.* to determine the amount payable in settlement of (a claim). [C17: from OF *adjuster,* from *ad-* to + *juste* right, JUST]
▸**ad'justable** *adj* ▸**ad'juster** *n*
adjustment Ⓣ (ə'dʒʌstmənt) *n* **1** the act of adjusting or state of being adjusted. **2** a control for regulating.
adjutant ('ædʒətənt) *n* an officer who acts as administrative assistant to a superior officer. [C17: from L *adjūtāre* to AID]
▸**'adjutancy** *n*
adjutant bird *or* **stork** *n* either of two large carrion-eating storks which are similar to the marabou and occur in S and SE Asia. [so called for its supposedly military gait]
adjutant general *n, pl* **adjutants general. 1** *Brit. Army.* a member of the Army Board responsible for personnel and administrative functions. **2** *US Army.* the adjutant of a military unit with general staff.
adjuvant ('ædʒəvənt) *adj* **1** aiding or assisting. ◆ *n* **2** something that aids or assists; auxiliary. [C17: from L *adjuvāre,* from *juvāre* to help]
Adlerian (æd'lɪərɪən) *adj* of or relating to the work of Alfred Adler (1870–1937), Austrian psychiatrist.
ad-lib Ⓣ (æd'lɪb) *vb* **ad-libs, ad-libbing, ad-libbed. 1** to improvise and deliver spontaneously (a speech, etc.). ◆ *adj* (**ad lib** *when predicative)* **2** improvised. ◆ *adv* **ad lib. 3** spontaneously; freely. ◆ *n* **4** an improvised performance, often humorous. [C18: short for L *ad libitum,* lit.: according to pleasure]
ad libitum (ˌæd 'lɪbɪtəm) *adv, adj Music.* at the performer's discretion. [L.: see AD-LIB]
Adm. *abbrev. for:* **1** Admiral. **2** Admiralty.
adman ('ædˌmæn) *n, pl* **admen.** *Inf.* a man who works in advertising.
admass ('ædmæs) *n* the section of the public that is susceptible to advertising, etc., and the processes involved in influencing them. [C20: from AD + MASS]
admeasure (æd'meʒə) *vb* **admeasures, admeasuring, admeasured.** to measure out (land, etc.) as a share; apportion. [C14 *amesuren,* from OF, from *mesurer* to MEASURE; the modern form derives from AD- + MEASURE]
admin ('ædmɪn) *n Inf.* short for **administration.**
administer Ⓣ (əd'mɪnɪstə) *vb (mainly tr)* **1** *(also intr)* to direct or control (the affairs of a business, etc.). **2** to dispense: *administer justice.* **3** (when *intr,* foll. by *to)* to give or apply (medicine, etc.). **4** to supervise the taking of (an oath, etc.). **5** to manage (an estate, property, etc.). [C14 *amynistre* via OF from L, from *ad-* to + *ministrāre* to MINISTER]
administrate Ⓣ (əd'mɪnɪˌstreɪt) *vb* **administrates, administrating, administrated.** to manage or direct (the affairs of a business, institution, etc.).
administration Ⓣ (ədˌmɪnɪ'streɪʃən) *n* **1** management of the affairs of an organization, such as a business or institution. **2** the duties of an administrator. **3** the body of people who administer an organization. **4** the conduct of the affairs of government. **5** term of office: used of governments, etc. **6** the government as a whole. **7** *(often cap.) Chiefly US.* the political executive, esp. of the US. **8** *Property law.* **8a** the con-

THESAURUS

tacky, tenacious ◆ *n* **3** = **glue**, cement, gum, mucilage, paste
ad hoc *adj* = **makeshift**, expedient, impromptu, improvised, jury-rigged (*chiefly Nautical*), stopgap ◆ *adv* = **for present purposes**, as the need arises
Antonyms *adj* ≠ **makeshift**: fixed, lasting, permanent, regular, standing (*of a committee*)
adieu *n* = **goodbye**, congé, farewell, leave-taking, parting, valediction
ad infinitum *adv* = **endlessly**, always, boundlessly, eternally, evermore, for all time, for ever (and ever), infinitely, in perpetuity, *in perpetuum*, interminably, limitlessly, perpetually, to infinity, unceasingly, unendingly, without end *or* limit
adjacent *adj* = **next**, abutting, adjoining, alongside, beside, bordering, cheek by jowl, close, contiguous, near, neighbouring, next door, proximate, touching, within sniffing distance (*inf.*)
Antonyms *adj* distant, far away, remote, separated
adjoin *vb* **1, 2** = **connect**, abut, add, affix, annex, append, approximate, attach, border, combine, communicate with, couple, impinge, interconnect, join, link, neighbour, touch, unite, verge
adjoining *adj* **1, 2** = **connecting**, abutting, adjacent, bordering, contiguous, interconnecting, joined, joining, near, neighbouring, next door, touching, verging
adjourn *vb* **1, 2** = **postpone**, defer, delay, discontinue, interrupt, prorogue, put off, put on the back burner (*inf.*), recess, stay, suspend, take a rain check on (*US & Canad. inf.*)
Antonyms *vb* assemble, continue, convene, gather, open, remain, reopen, stay
adjournment *n* **1, 2** = **postponement**, deferment, deferral, delay, discontinuation, interruption, prorogation, putting off, recess, stay, suspension
adjudge *vb* **1, 2** = **judge**, adjudicate, allot, apportion, assign, award, decide, declare, decree, determine, distribute, order, pronounce
adjudicate *vb* **1, 2** = **judge**, adjudge, arbitrate, decide, determine, mediate, referee, settle, umpire
adjudication *n* **1** = **judgment**, adjudgment, arbitration, conclusion, decision, determination, finding, pronouncement, ruling, settlement, verdict
adjudicator *n* **1, 2** = **judge**, arbiter, arbitrator, moderator, referee, umpire
adjunct *n* **1** = **addition**, accessory, addendum, add-on, appendage, appurtenance, auxiliary, complement, supplement
adjure *vb* **1** = **order**, charge, command, direct, enjoin **2** = **beg**, appeal to, beseech, entreat, implore, invoke, pray, supplicate
adjust *vb* **1-3** = **alter**, acclimatize, accommodate, accustom, adapt, arrange, compose, convert, customize, dispose, fit, fix, harmonize, make conform, measure, modify, order, reconcile, rectify, redress, regulate, remodel, set, settle, suit, tune (up), tweak (*inf.*)
adjustable *adj* **1-3** = **alterable**, adaptable, flexible, malleable, modifiable, mouldable, movable, tractable
adjustment *n* **1** = **alteration**, adaptation, arrangement, arranging, fitting, fixing, modification, ordering, rectification, redress, regulation, remodelling, setting, tuning **1** = **acclimatization**, harmonization, orientation, reconciliation, settlement, settling in
ad-lib *vb* **1** = **improvise**, busk, extemporize, make up, speak extemporaneously, speak impromptu, speak off the cuff, vamp, wing it (*inf.*) ◆ *adj* **2** = **improvised**, extemporaneous, extempore, extemporized, impromptu, made up, off-the-cuff (*inf.*), off the top of one's head, unprepared, unrehearsed ◆ *adv* **3 ad lib** = **off the cuff**, extemporaneously, extempore, impromptu, off the top of one's head (*inf.*), spontaneously, without preparation, without rehearsal
administer *vb* **1, 5** = **manage**, conduct, control, direct, govern, handle, oversee, run, superintend, supervise **2, 3** = **give**, apply, contribute, dispense, distribute, execute, impose, mete out, perform, provide
administrate *vb* = **manage**, administer, conduct, control, direct, govern, handle, oversee, run, superintend, supervise
administration *n* **1** = **management**, administering, application, conduct, control, direction, dispensation, distribution, execution, governing, government, overseeing, performance, provision, running, superintendence, supervi-

duct or disposal of the estate of a deceased person. **8b** the management by a trustee of an estate. **9a** the administering of something, such as a sacrament or medical treatment. **9b** the thing that is administered.
▸**ad'ministrative** *adj* ▸**ad'ministratively** *adv*

administration order *n Law.* **1** an order by a court appointing a person to manage a company that is in financial difficulty. **2** an order by a court for the administration of the estate of a debtor who has been ordered by the court to pay money that he owes.

administrator Ⓣ (əd'mɪnɪˌstreɪtə) *n* **1** a person who administers the affairs of an organization, official body, etc. **2** *Property law.* a person authorized to manage an estate.

admirable Ⓣ ('ædmərəbᵊl) *adj* deserving or inspiring admiration; excellent.
▸**'admirably** *adv*

admiral ('ædmərəl) *n* **1** the supreme commander of a fleet or navy. **2** Also called: **admiral of the fleet, fleet admiral.** a naval officer of the highest rank. **3** a senior naval officer entitled to fly his own flag. See also **rear admiral, vice admiral. 4** *Chiefly Brit.* the master of a fishing fleet. **5** any of various brightly coloured butterflies, esp. the red admiral or white admiral. [C13 *amyral,* from OF *amiral* emir, & from Med. L *admīrālis* (spelling prob. infl. by *admīrābilis* admirable); both from Ar. *amīr* emir, commander, esp. in *amīr-al* commander of]
▸**'admiralship** *n*

admiralty ('ædmərəltɪ) *n, pl* **admiralties. 1** the office or jurisdiction of an admiral. **2** jurisdiction over naval affairs.

Admiralty Board *n* **the.** a department of the British Ministry of Defence, responsible for the administration of the Royal Navy.

Admiralty House *n* the official residence of the Governor General of Australia, in Sydney.

admiration Ⓣ (ˌædmə'reɪʃən) *n* **1** pleasurable contemplation or surprise. **2** a person or thing that is admired.

admire Ⓣ (əd'maɪə) *vb* **admires, admiring, admired.** *(tr)* **1** to regard with esteem, approval, or pleased surprise. **2** *Arch.* to wonder at. [C16: from L *admīrārī,* from *ad-* to, at + *mīrārī* to wonder]
▸**ad'mirer** *n* ▸**ad'miring** *adj* ▸**ad'miringly** *adv*

admissible Ⓣ (əd'mɪsəbᵊl) *adj* **1** able or deserving to be considered or allowed. **2** deserving to be allowed to enter. **3** *Law.* (esp. of evidence) capable of being admitted in a court of law.
▸**adˌmissi'bility** *n*

admission Ⓣ (əd'mɪʃən) *n* **1** permission to enter or the right to enter. **2** the price charged for entrance. **3** acceptance for a position, etc. **4** a confession, as of a crime, etc. **5** an acknowledgment of the truth of something. [C15: from L *admissiōn-,* from *admittere* to ADMIT]
▸**ad'missive** *adj*

admit Ⓣ (əd'mɪt) *vb* **admits, admitting, admitted.** *(mainly tr)* **1** *(may take a clause as object)* to confess or acknowledge (a crime, mistake, etc.). **2** *(may take a clause as object)* to concede (the truth of something). **3** to allow to enter. **4** (foll. by *to*) to allow participation (in) or the right to be part (of). **5** (when *intr,* foll. by *of*) to allow (of). [C14: from L *admittere,* from *ad-* to + *mittere* to send]

admittance Ⓣ (əd'mɪtᵊns) *n* **1** the right or authority to enter. **2** the act of giving entrance. **3** *Electricity.* the reciprocal of impedance.

admittedly Ⓣ (əd'mɪtɪdlɪ) *adv (sentence modifier)* willingly conceded: *admittedly I am afraid.*

admix (əd'mɪks) *vb (tr) Rare.* to mix or blend. [C16: back formation from obs. *admixt,* from L *admīscēre* to mix with]

admixture Ⓣ (əd'mɪkstʃə) *n* **1** a less common word for **mixture. 2** an ingredient.

admonish Ⓣ (əd'mɒnɪʃ) *vb (tr)* **1** to reprove firmly but not harshly. **2** to warn; caution. [C14: via OF from Vulgar L *admonestāre* (unattested), from L *admonēre,* from *monēre* to advise]
▸**admonition** (ˌædmə'nɪʃən) *n* ▸**ad'monitory** *adj*

ad nauseam Ⓣ (æd 'nɔːzɪˌæm) *adv* to a disgusting extent. [L: to (the point of) nausea]

ado Ⓣ (ə'duː) *n* bustling activity; fuss; bother; delay (esp. in **without more ado, with much ado**). [C14: from *at do* a to-do, from ON *at* to (marking the infinitive) + DO[1]]

adobe (ə'dəʊbɪ) *n* **1** a sun-dried brick used for building. **2** a building constructed of such bricks. **3** the clayey material from which such bricks are made. [C19: from Sp.]

adolescence Ⓣ (ˌædə'lɛsəns) *n* the period in human development that occurs between the beginning of puberty and adulthood. [C15: via OF from L, from *adolēscere* to grow up]

adolescent Ⓣ (ˌædə'lɛsᵊnt) *adj* **1** of or relating to adolescence. **2** *Inf.* behaving in an immature way. ◆ *n* **3** an adolescent person.

Adonis (ə'dəʊnɪs) *n* **1** *Greek myth.* a handsome youth loved by Aphrodite. **2** a handsome young man. [C16: from L via Gk from Phoenician *adōni* my lord; rel. to Heb. *Adonai* Lord]

adopt Ⓣ (ə'dɒpt) *vb (tr)* **1** *Law.* to take (another's child) as one's own child. **2** to choose and follow (a plan, method, etc.). **3** to take over (an idea, etc.) as if it were one's own. **4** to assume: *to adopt a title.* **5** to accept (a report, etc.). [C16: from L *adoptāre,* from *optāre* to choose]
▸**ˌadop'tee** *n* ▸**a'doption** *n*

adopted (ə'dɒptɪd) *adj* having been adopted.

adoptive (ə'dɒptɪv) *adj* **1** acquired or related by adoption: *an adoptive father.* Cf. **adopted. 2** of or relating to adoption.

adorable Ⓣ (ə'dɔːrəbᵊl) *adj* **1** very attractive; lovable. **2** *Becoming rare.* deserving adoration.
▸**a'dorably** *adv*

adoration Ⓣ (ˌædə'reɪʃən) *n* **1** deep love or esteem. **2** the act of worshipping.

adore Ⓣ (ə'dɔː) *vb* **adores, adoring, adored. 1** *(tr)* to love intensely or deeply. **2** to worship (a god) with religious rites. **3** *(tr) Inf.* to like very much. [C15: via F from L *adōrāre,* from *ad-* to + *ōrāre* to pray]
▸**a'dorer** *n* ▸**a'doring** *adj* ▸**a'doringly** *adv*

THESAURUS

sion **3, 5, 6** = **government**, executive, governing body, management, ministry, term of office

administrative *adj* **1, 3, 5, 6** = **managerial**, directorial, executive, governmental, gubernatorial (*chiefly US*), management, organizational, regulatory, supervisory

administrator *n* **1** = **manager**, agent, bureaucrat, executive, functionary, mandarin, minister, officer, official, organizer, supervisor

admirable *adj* = **excellent**, choice, commendable, estimable, exquisite, fine, laudable, meritorious, praiseworthy, rare, sterling, superior, valuable, wonderful, worthy
Antonyms *adj* bad, commonplace, deplorable, disappointing, displeasing, mediocre, no great shakes (*inf.*), worthless

admiration *n* **1** = **regard**, adoration, affection, amazement, appreciation, approbation, approval, astonishment, delight, esteem, pleasure, praise, respect, surprise, veneration, wonder, wonderment

admire *vb* **1** = **respect**, adore, appreciate, approve, esteem, idolize, look up to, praise, prize, take one's hat off to, think highly of, value, venerate, worship **2** = **marvel at**, appreciate, delight in, take pleasure in, wonder at
Antonyms *vb* contemn, deride, despise, look down on, look down one's nose at (*inf.*), misprize, scorn, sneer at, spurn, undervalue

admirer *n* **1** = **suitor**, beau, boyfriend, lover, sweetheart, wooer **1** = **fan**, adherent, buff (*inf.*), devotee, disciple, enthusiast, follower, partisan, protagonist, supporter, votary, worshipper

admissible *adj* **1** = **permissible**, acceptable, allowable, allowed, passable, permitted, tolerable, tolerated
Antonyms *adj* disallowed, inadmissible, intolerable, unacceptable

admission *n* **1** = **entrance**, acceptance, access, admittance, entrée, entry, ingress, initiation, introduction **4, 5** = **confession**, acknowledgment, admitting, affirmation, allowance, avowal, concession, declaration, disclosure, divulgence, profession, revelation

admit *vb* **1, 2** = **confess**, acknowledge, affirm, avow, concede, cough (*sl.*), declare, disclose, divulge, own, profess, reveal **3** = **let in**, accept, allow, allow to enter, give access, initiate, introduce, receive, take in **4, 5** = **allow**, agree, grant, let, permit, recognize
Antonyms *vb* ≠ **let in:** exclude, keep out ≠ **allow:** deny, dismiss, forbid, negate, prohibit, reject

admittance *n* **1, 2** = **letting in**, acceptance, access, admitting, allowing, entrance, entry, passage, reception

admittedly *adv* = **it must be admitted**, allowedly, avowedly, certainly, confessedly, it cannot be denied, it must be allowed, it must be confessed, it must be said, to be fair *or* honest, undeniably

admixture *n* **1** = **mixture**, alloy, amalgamation, blend, combination, compound, fusion, intermixture, medley, meld **2** = **ingredient**, component, constituent, element

admonish *vb* **1, 2** = **reprimand**, advise, bawl out (*inf.*), berate, carpet (*inf.*), caution, censure, check, chide, counsel, enjoin, exhort, forewarn, rap over the knuckles, read the riot act, rebuke, reprove, scold, slap on the wrist, tear into (*inf.*), tell off (*inf.*), upbraid, warn
Antonyms *vb* applaud, commend, compliment, congratulate, praise

admonition *n* **1, 2** = **reprimand**, advice, berating, caution, chiding, counsel, rebuke, remonstrance, reproach, reproof, scolding, telling off (*inf.*), upbraiding, warning

admonitory *adj* **1, 2** = **reprimanding**, admonishing, advisory, cautionary, rebuking, reproachful, reproving, scolding, warning

ad nauseam *adv* = **again and again**, ad infinitum, on and on, over and over (again), time after time, time and (time) again, times without number

ado *n* = **fuss**, agitation, bother, bustle, commotion, confusion, delay, disturbance, excitement, flurry, pother, stir, to-do, trouble

adolescence *n* = **youth**, boyhood, girlhood, juvenescence, minority, teens = **youthfulness**, boyishness, childishness, girlishness, immaturity, juvenility, puerility

adolescent *adj* **1, 2** = **young**, boyish, girlish, growing, immature, juvenile, puerile, teenage, youthful ◆ *n* **3** = **youth**, juvenile, minor, teenager, youngster

adopt *vb* **1** = **foster**, take in **2-5** = **choose**, accept, appropriate, approve, assume, embrace, endorse, espouse, follow, maintain, ratify, select, support, take on, take over, take up
Antonyms *vb* ≠ **choose:** abandon, abnegate, cast aside, cast off, disavow, disclaim, disown, forswear, give up, reject, renounce, repudiate, spurn, wash one's hands of

adoption *n* **1** = **fostering**, adopting, fosterage, taking in **2-5** = **choice**, acceptance, approbation, appropriation, approval, assumption, embracing, endorsement, espousal, following, maintenance, ratification, selection, support, taking on, taking over, taking up

adorable *adj* **1** = **lovable**, appealing, attractive, captivating, charming, cute, darling, dear, delightful, fetching, pleasing, precious, sweet
Antonyms *adj* despicable, displeasing, hateful, unlikable *or* unlikeable, unlovable

adoration *n* **1, 2** = **love**, admiration, esteem, estimation, exaltation, glorification, honour, idolatry, idolization, reverence, veneration, worship, worshipping

adore *vb* **1, 2** = **love**, admire, bow to, cherish, dote on, esteem, exalt, glorify, honour, idolize, revere, reverence, venerate, worship
Antonyms *vb* abhor, abominate, despise, detest, execrate, hate, loathe

adorn Ⓣ (əˈdɔːn) *vb* (*tr*) **1** to decorate. **2** to increase the beauty, distinction, etc., of. [C14: via OF from L *adōrnāre*, from *ōrnāre* to furnish]
▸**aˈdornment** *n*

ADP *n Biochem.* adenosine diphosphate; a substance derived from ATP with the liberation of energy that is then used in the performance of muscular work.

ad rem *Latin.* (æd ˈrɛm) *adj, adv* to the point; without digression.

adrenal (əˈdriːnᵊl) *adj* **1** on or near the kidneys. **2** of or relating to the adrenal glands or their secretions. ◆ *n* **3** an adrenal gland. [C19: from AD- (near) + RENAL]

adrenal gland *n* an endocrine gland at the anterior end of each kidney. It secretes adrenaline. Also called: **suprarenal gland.**

adrenaline *or* **adrenalin** (əˈdrenəlɪn) *n* a hormone that is secreted by the adrenal medulla in response to stress and increases heart rate, pulse rate, and blood pressure. It is extracted from animals or synthesized for medical use. US name: **epinephrine.**

adrift Ⓣ (əˈdrɪft) *adj* (*postpositive*), *adv* **1** floating without steering or mooring; drifting. **2** without purpose; aimless. **3** *Inf.* off course.

adroit Ⓣ (əˈdrɔɪt) *adj* **1** skilful or dexterous. **2** quick in thought or reaction. [C17: from F *à droit* rightly]
▸**aˈdroitly** *adv* ▸**aˈdroitness** *n*

adsorb (ədˈsɔːb) *vb* to undergo or cause to undergo a process in which a substance, usually a gas, accumulates on the surface of a solid forming a thin film. [C19: AD- + *-sorb* as in ABSORB]
▸**adˈsorbable** *adj* ▸**adˈsorbent** *adj* ▸**adˈsorption** *n*

adsorbate (ədˈsɔːbeɪt) *n* a substance that has been or is to be adsorbed.

ADT (in the US and Canada) *abbrev. for* Atlantic Daylight Time.

adulate Ⓣ (ˈædjʊˌleɪt) *vb* **adulates, adulating, adulated.** (*tr*) to flatter or praise obsequiously. [C17: back formation from C15 *adulation*, from L *adūlārī* to flatter]
▸ˌ**aduˈlation** *n* ▸ˈ**aduˌlator** *n* ▸**adulatory** (ˌædjʊˈleɪtərɪ) *adj*

adult Ⓣ (ˈædʌlt, əˈdʌlt) *adj* **1** having reached maturity; fully developed. **2** of or intended for mature people: *adult education.* **3** suitable only for adults because of being pornographic. ◆ *n* **4** a person who has attained maturity. **5** a mature fully grown animal or plant. **6** *Law.* a person who has attained the age of legal majority. [C16: from L *adultus*, from *adolēscere* to grow up]
▸**aˈdulthood** *n*

adulterant (əˈdʌltərənt) *n* **1** a substance that adulterates. ◆ *adj* **2** adulterating.

adulterate Ⓣ *vb* (əˈdʌltəˌreɪt), **adulterates, adulterating, adulterated.** **1** (*tr*) to debase by adding inferior material: *to adulterate milk with water.* ◆ *adj* (əˈdʌltərɪt). **2** debased or impure. [C16: from L *adulterāre* to corrupt, commit adultery, prob. from *alter* another]
▸**aˌdulterˈation** *n* ▸**aˈdulterˌator** *n*

adulterer Ⓣ (əˈdʌltərə) *or* (*fem*) **adulteress** *n* a person who has committed adultery. [C16: orig. also *adulter*, from L *adulter*, back formation from *adulterāre* to ADULTERATE]

adulterous Ⓣ (əˈdʌltərəs) *adj* of, characterized by, or inclined to adultery.
▸**aˈdulterously** *adv*

adultery Ⓣ (əˈdʌltərɪ) *n, pl* **adulteries.** voluntary sexual intercourse between a married man or woman and a partner other than the legal spouse. [C15 *adulterie*, altered from C14 *avoutrie*, via OF from L *adulterium*, from *adulter*, back formation from *adulterāre*. See ADULTERATE]

adumbrate (ˈædʌmˌbreɪt) *vb* **adumbrates, adumbrating, adumbrated.** (*tr*) **1** to outline; give a faint indication of. **2** to foreshadow. **3** to obscure. [C16: from L *adumbrāre* to cast a shadow on, from *umbra* shadow]
▸ˌ**adumˈbration** *n* ▸**adumbrative** (ædˈʌmbrətɪv) *adj*

adv. *abbrev. for:* **1** adverb. **2** adverbial. **3** adversus. [L: against] **4** advertisement. **5** advocate.

ad valorem (æd vəˈlɔːrəm) *adj, adv* (of taxes) in proportion to the estimated value of the goods taxed. Abbrev.: **ad val., a.v., A/V.** [from L]

advance Ⓣ (ədˈvɑːns) *vb* **advances, advancing, advanced.** **1** to go or bring forward in position. **2** (foll. by *on*) to move (towards) in a threatening manner. **3** (*tr*) to present for consideration. **4** to improve; further. **5** (*tr*) to cause (an event) to occur earlier. **6** (*tr*) to supply (money, goods, etc.) beforehand, either for a loan or as an initial payment. **7** to increase (a price, etc.) or (of a price, etc.) to be increased. **8** (*intr*) to be promoted. ◆ *n* **9** forward movement; progress in time or space. **10** improvement; progress in development. **11** *Commerce.* **11a** the supplying of commodities or funds before receipt of an agreed consideration. **11b** the commodities or funds supplied in this manner. **12** Also called: **advance payment.** a money payment made before it is legally due: *this is an advance on your salary.* **13** a loan of money. **14** an increase in price, etc. **15 in advance. 15a** beforehand: *payment in advance.* **15b** (foll. by *of*) ahead in time or development: *ideas in advance of the time.* **16** (*modifier*) forward in position or time: *advance booking.* ◆ See also **advances.** [C15 *advauncen*, altered from C13 *avauncen*, via OF from L *abante*, from *ab-* away + *ante* before]
▸**adˈvancer** *n*

advance corporation tax *n* a British tax in which a company paying a dividend must deduct the basic rate of income tax from the grossed-up value of the dividend and pay it to the Inland Revenue. Abbrev.: **ACT.**

advanced Ⓣ (ədˈvɑːnst) *adj* **1** being ahead in development, knowledge, progress, etc. **2** having reached a comparatively late stage: *a man of advanced age.* **3** ahead of the times.

advanced gas-cooled reactor *n* a nuclear reactor using carbon dioxide as the coolant, and ceramic uranium dioxide cased in stainless steel as the fuel. Abbrev.: **AGR.**

advance directive *n* another name for **living will.**

Advanced level *n* a formal name for **A level.**

advancement Ⓣ (ədˈvɑːnsmənt) *n* **1** promotion in rank, status, etc. **2** a less common word for **advance** (senses 9, 10).

advances Ⓣ (ədˈvɑːnsɪz) *pl n* (*sometimes sing;* often foll. by *to* or *towards*) overtures made in an attempt to become friendly, etc.

advantage Ⓣ (ədˈvɑːntɪdʒ) *n* **1** (often foll. by *over* or *of*) a more favourable position; superiority. **2** benefit or profit (esp. in **to one's advantage**). **3** *Tennis.* the point scored after deuce. **4 take advantage of. 4a** to make good use of. **4b** to impose upon the weakness, good nature, etc., of. **4c** to seduce. **5 to advantage.** to good effect. ◆ *vb* **advantages, advantaging, advantaged.** **6** (*tr*) to put in a better position; favour. [C14 *avantage* (later altered to *advantage*), from OF *avant* before, from L *abante* from before. See ADVANCE]

THESAURUS

adoring *adj* **1 = loving**, admiring, adulatory, affectionate, ardent, devoted, doting, enamoured, fond, idolizing, reverent, reverential, venerating, worshipping
Antonyms *adj* abhorring, abominating, despising, detesting, hating, loathing

adorn *vb* **1, 2 = decorate**, array, beautify, bedeck, deck, embellish, emblazon, engarland, enhance, enrich, festoon, garnish, gild the lily, grace, ornament, trim

adornment *n* **1 = decoration**, accessory, embellishment, festoon, frill, frippery, ornament, supplement, trimming **2 = ornamentation**, beautification, decorating, decoration, embellishment, trimming

adrift *adj* **1 = drifting**, afloat, unanchored, unmoored **2 = aimless**, directionless, goalless, purposeless ◆ *adv* **3 = wrong**, amiss, astray, off course

adroit *adj* **1, 2 = skilful**, able, adept, apt, artful, bright (*inf.*), clever, cunning, deft, dexterous, expert, ingenious, masterful, neat, nimble, proficient, quick-witted, skilled
Antonyms *adj* awkward, blundering, bungling, cack-handed (*inf.*), clumsy, ham-fisted *or* ham-handed (*inf.*), inept, inexpert, maladroit, uncoordinated, unhandy, unskilful

adroitness *n* **1, 2 = skill**, ability, ableness, address, adeptness, aptness, artfulness, cleverness, craft, cunning, deftness, dexterity, expertise, ingeniousness, ingenuity, knack, masterfulness, mastery, nimbleness, proficiency, quick-wittedness, skilfulness

adulation *n* **= worship**, blandishment, bootlicking (*inf.*), extravagant flattery, fawning, fulsome praise, servile flattery, sycophancy
Antonyms *n* abuse, calumniation, censure, condemnation, disparagement, revilement, ridicule, vilification, vituperation

adulatory *adj* **= worshipping**, blandishing, bootlicking (*inf.*), fawning, flattering, obsequious, praising, servile, slavish, sycophantic

adult *adj* **1 = fully grown**, full grown, fully developed, grown-up, mature, of age, ripe ◆ *n* **4, 6 = grown-up**, grown *or* grown-up person (man *or* woman), person of mature age

adulterate *vb* **1 = debase**, attenuate, bastardize, contaminate, corrupt, depreciate, deteriorate, devalue, make impure, mix with, thin, vitiate, water down, weaken ◆ *adj* **2 = debased**, adulterated, attenuated, bastardized, contaminated, corrupt, depreciated, deteriorated, devalued, mixed, thinned, vitiated, watered down, weakened

adulterer *n* **= cheat** (*inf.*), fornicator

adulterous *adj* **= unfaithful**, cheating, extramarital, fornicating, unchaste

adultery *n* **= unfaithfulness**, cheating (*inf.*), extracurricular sex (*inf.*), extramarital congress, extramarital relations, extramarital sex, fornication, having an affair *or* a fling, illicit sex, infidelity, playing away from home (*sl.*), playing the field (*sl.*), unchastity
Antonyms *n* chastity, faithfulness, fidelity

advance *vb* **1 = progress**, accelerate, come forward, go ahead, go forward, go on, make inroads, move onward, move up, press on, proceed **3 = suggest**, adduce, allege, cite, offer, present, proffer, put forward, submit **4 = benefit**, further, grow, improve, multiply, prosper, thrive **5 = promote**, accelerate, bring forward, bring up, elevate, hasten, send forward, send up, speed, upgrade **6 = lend**, pay beforehand, supply on credit ◆ *n* **9 = progress**, advancement, development, forward movement, headway, inroads, onward movement **10 = improvement**, advancement, amelioration, betterment, breakthrough, furtherance, gain, growth, progress, promotion, step **12-14 = loan**, credit, deposit, down payment, increase (*in price*), prepayment, retainer, rise (*in price*) ◆ *modifier* **16 = prior**, beforehand, early, foremost, forward, in front, leading **16 in advance = beforehand**, ahead, earlier, in the forefront, in the lead, in the van, previously
Antonyms *vb* ≠ **progress:** decrease, diminish, lessen, move back, regress, retreat, weaken ≠ **suggest:** hide, hold back, suppress, withhold ≠ **promote:** demote, hold back, impede, retard, set back ≠ **lend:** defer payment, withhold payment

advanced *adj* **1, 3 = foremost**, ahead, avant-garde, extreme, forward, higher, leading, precocious, progressive
Antonyms *adj* backward, behind, late, retarded, underdeveloped, undeveloped

advancement *n* **1 = promotion**, advance, amelioration, betterment, gain, growth, improvement, preferment, progress, rise **2 = progress**, advance, forward movement, headway, onward movement

advances *pl n* **advances = overtures**, approach, approaches, moves, proposals, proposition

advantage *n* **1, 2 = benefit**, ace in the hole, ace up one's sleeve, aid, ascendancy, asset, assistance, avail, blessing, boon, convenience, dominance, edge, gain, good, help, inside track, interest, lead, mileage (*inf.*), precedence, pre-eminence, profit, service, start, superiority, sway, upper hand, use, utility, welfare

advantageous Ⓣ (ˌædvənˈteɪdʒəs) *adj* producing advantage. ▸ˌ**advanˈtageously** *adv*

advection (ədˈvɛkʃən) *n* the transference of heat energy in a horizontal stream of gas, esp. of air. [C20: from L *advectiō*, from *advehere*, from *ad-* to + *vehere* to carry]

advent Ⓣ (ˈædvɛnt, -vənt) *n* an arrival or coming, esp. one which is awaited. [C12: from L *adventus*, from *advenīre*, from *ad-* to + *venīre* to come]

Advent (ˈædvɛnt) *n* the season including the four Sundays preceding Christmas.

Advent calendar *n* a large card with small numbered doors for children to open on each of the days of Advent, revealing pictures beneath them.

Adventist (ˈædvɛntɪst) *n* a member of a Christian group that holds that the Second Coming of Christ is imminent.

adventitious (ˌædvɛnˈtɪʃəs) *adj* **1** added or appearing accidentally. **2** (of a plant or animal part) developing in an abnormal position. [C17: from L *adventīcius* coming from outside, from *adventus* a coming] ▸ˌ**advenˈtitiously** *adv*

adventure Ⓣ (ədˈvɛntʃə) *n* **1** a risky undertaking of unknown outcome. **2** an exciting or unexpected event or course of events. **3** a hazardous financial operation. ◆ *vb* **adventures, adventuring, adventured. 4** to take a risk or put at risk. **5** (*intr;* foll. by *into, on,* or *upon*) to dare to enter (into a place, dangerous activity, etc.). **6** to dare to say (something): *he adventured his opinion.* [C13 *aventure* (later altered to *adventure*), via OF ult. from L *advenīre* to happen to (someone), arrive]

adventure playground *n Brit.* a playground for children that contains building materials, etc., used to build with, climb on, etc.

adventurer Ⓣ (ədˈvɛntʃərə) *or* (*fem*) **adventuress** *n* **1** a person who seeks adventure, esp. one who seeks success or money through daring exploits. **2** a person who seeks money or power by unscrupulous means. **3** a speculator.

adventurism (ədˈvɛntʃəˌrɪzəm) *n* recklessness, esp. in politics and finance. ▸**adˈventurist** *n*

adventurous Ⓣ (ədˈvɛntʃərəs) *adj* **1** Also: **adventuresome.** daring or enterprising. **2** dangerous; involving risk.

adverb (ˈædˌvɜːb) *n* **a** a word or group of words that serves to modify a whole sentence, a verb, another adverb, or an adjective; for example, *easily, very,* and *happily* respectively in the sentence *They could easily envy the very happily married couple.* **b** (*as modifier*): *an adverb marker.* Abbrev.: **adv.** [C15–C16: from L *adverbium* adverb, lit.: added word] ▸**adˈverbial** *adj*

adversarial (ˌædvɜːˈsɛərɪəl) *adj* (of political parties) hostile to and opposing each other on party lines; antagonistic.

adversary Ⓣ (ˈædvəsərɪ) *n, pl* **adversaries. 1** a person or group that is hostile to someone. **2** an opposing contestant in a sport. [C14: from L *adversārius*, from *adversus* against]

adversative (ədˈvɜːsətɪv) *Grammar.* ◆ *adj* **1** (of a word, phrase, or clause) implying opposition. *But* and *although* are adversative conjunctions. ◆ *n* **2** an adversative word or speech element.

adverse Ⓣ (ˈædvɜːs) *adj* **1** antagonistic; hostile: *adverse criticism.* **2** unfavourable to one's interests: *adverse circumstances.* **3** contrary or opposite: *adverse winds.* [C14: from L *adversus*, from *advertere*, from *ad-* towards + *vertere* to turn] ▸**adˈversely** *adv* ▸**adˈverseness** *n*

adversity Ⓣ (ədˈvɜːsɪtɪ) *n, pl* **adversities. 1** distress; affliction; hardship. **2** an unfortunate event.

advert[1] Ⓣ (ədˈvɜːt) *vb* (*intr;* foll. by *to*) to draw attention (to). [C15: from L *advertere* to turn one's attention to]

advert[2] Ⓣ (ˈædvɜːt) *n Brit. inf.* short for **advertisement.**

advertise Ⓣ *or US* (*sometimes*) **advertize** (ˈædvəˌtaɪz) *vb* **advertises, advertising, advertised** *or US* (*sometimes*) **advertizes, advertizing, advertized. 1** to present or praise (goods, a service, etc.) to the public, esp. in order to encourage sales. **2** to make (a vacancy, article for sale, etc.) publicly known: *to advertise a job.* **3** (*intr;* foll. by *for*) to make a public request (for): *she advertised for a cook.* [C15: from OF *avertir*, ult. from L *advertere* to turn one's attention to. See ADVERSE] ▸ˈ**adverˌtiser** *or US* (*sometimes*) ˈ**adverˌtizer** *n*

advertisement Ⓣ *or US* (*sometimes*) **advertizement** (ədˈvɜːtɪsmənt) *n* any public notice, as a printed display in a newspaper, short film on television, etc., designed to sell goods, publicize an event, etc.

advertising *or US* (*sometimes*) **advertizing** (ˈædvəˌtaɪzɪŋ) *n* **1** the promotion of goods or services for sale through impersonal media such as television. **2** the business that specializes in creating such publicity. **3** advertisements collectively.

Advertising Standards Authority *n* (in Britain) an independent body set up by the advertising industry to ensure that all advertisements comply with the British Code of Advertising Practice. Abbrev.: **ASA.**

advertorial (ˌædvɜːˈtɔːrɪəl) *n* **1** advertising presented under the guise of editorial material. ◆ *adj* **2** presented in such a manner. [C20: from blend of ADVERT[2] + EDITORIAL]

advice Ⓣ (ədˈvaɪs) *n* **1** recommendation as to appropriate choice of action. **2** (*sometimes pl*) formal notification of facts. [C13 *avis* (later *advise*), via OF from Vulgar L, from L *ad* to + *vīsum* view]

advisable Ⓣ (ədˈvaɪzəbᵊl) *adj* worthy of recommendation; prudent. ▸**adˈvisably** *adv* ▸**adˌvisaˈbility** *or* **adˈvisableness** *n*

advise Ⓣ (ədˈvaɪz) *vb* **advises, advising, advised.** (*when tr, may take a clause as object or an infinitive*) **1** to offer advice (to a person or persons): *he advised caution.* **2** (*tr;* sometimes foll. by *of*) to inform or notify. **3** (*intr;* foll. by *with*) *Chiefly US, obs. in Britain.* to consult. [C14: via OF from Vulgar L *advīsāre* (unattested), from L *ad-* to + *vidēre* to see]

advised Ⓣ (ədˈvaɪzd) *adj* resulting from deliberation. See also **ill-advised, well-advised.** ▸**advisedly** (ədˈvaɪzɪdlɪ) *adv*

adviser Ⓣ *or* **advisor** (ədˈvaɪzə) *n* **1** a person who advises. **2** *Education.* a person responsible for advising students on career guidance, etc. **3** *Brit. education.* a subject specialist who advises on current teaching methods and facilities.

advisory Ⓣ (ədˈvaɪzərɪ) *adj* **1** empowered to make recommendations: *an advisory body.* ◆ *n, pl* **advisories. 2** a statement issued to give advice, recommendations, or a warning: *a travel advisory.* **3** a person or organization with an advisory function: *the Prime Minister's media advisory.*

advocaat (ˈædvəʊˌkɑː) *n* a liqueur having a raw egg base. [C20: Du.]

advocacy Ⓣ (ˈædvəkəsɪ) *n, pl* **advocacies.** active support, esp. of a cause.

advocate Ⓣ *vb* (ˈædvəˌkeɪt), **advocates, advocating, advocated. 1** (*tr; may*

THESAURUS

Antonyms *n* curse, difficulty, disadvantage, downside, drawback, handicap, hindrance, inconvenience, snag

advantageous *adj* = **beneficial**, convenient, expedient, helpful, of service, profitable, useful, valuable, worthwhile
Antonyms *adj* detrimental, unfavourable, unfortunate, unhelpful, useless

advent *n* = **coming**, appearance, approach, arrival, entrance, occurrence, onset, visitation

adventure *n* **1-3** = **escapade**, chance, contingency, enterprise, experience, exploit, hazard, incident, occurrence, risk, speculation, undertaking, venture ◆ *vb* **4, 5** = **dare**, endanger, hazard, imperil, jeopardize, risk, venture

adventurer *n* **1** = **hero**, daredevil, heroine, knight-errant, soldier of fortune, swashbuckler, traveller, venturer, voyager, wanderer **2, 3** = **mercenary**, charlatan, fortune-hunter, gambler, opportunist, rogue, speculator

adventurous *adj* **1, 2** = **daring**, adventuresome, audacious, bold, dangerous, daredevil, enterprising, foolhardy, have-a-go (*inf.*), hazardous, headstrong, intrepid, rash, reckless, risky, temerarious (*rare*), venturesome
Antonyms *adj* careful, cautious, chary, circumspect, hesitant, prudent, safe, tentative, timid, timorous, unadventurous, wary

adversary *n* **1, 2** = **opponent**, antagonist, competitor, contestant, enemy, foe, opposer, rival
Antonyms *n* accomplice, ally, associate, collaborator, colleague, confederate, co-worker, friend, helper, partner, supporter

adverse *adj* **1-3** = **unfavourable**, antagonistic, conflicting, contrary, detrimental, disadvantageous, hostile, inexpedient, inimical, injurious, inopportune, negative, opposing, opposite, reluctant, repugnant, unfortunate, unfriendly, unlucky, unpropitious, unwilling
Antonyms *adj* advantageous, auspicious, beneficial, favourable, fortunate, helpful, lucky, opportune, promising, propitious, suitable

adversity *n* **1, 2** = **hardship**, affliction, bad luck, calamity, catastrophe, deep water, disaster, distress, hard times, ill-fortune, ill-luck, misery, misfortune, mishap, reverse, sorrow, suffering, trial, trouble, woe, wretchedness

advert[1] *vb* = **refer**, allude, draw attention (to), mention, notice, observe, regard, remark

advert[2] *n Informal* = **advertisement**, ad (*inf.*), announcement, bill, blurb, circular, commercial, display, notice, placard, plug (*inf.*), poster, promotion, publicity, puff

advertise *vb* **1-3** = **publicize**, advise, announce, apprise, blazon, crack up (*inf.*), declare, display, flaunt, inform, make known, notify, plug (*inf.*), praise, proclaim, promote, promulgate, publish, puff, push (*inf.*), tout

advertisement *n* = **advert** (*Brit. inf.*), ad (*inf.*), announcement, bill, blurb, circular, commercial, display, notice, placard, plug (*inf.*), poster, promotion, publicity, puff

advice *n* **1** = **guidance**, admonition, caution, counsel, help, injunction, opinion, recommendation, suggestion, view **2** = **notification**, information, instruction, intelligence, notice, warning, word

advisability *n* = **wisdom**, appropriateness, aptness, desirability, expediency, fitness, judiciousness, profitability, propriety, prudence, seemliness, soundness, suitability

advisable *adj* = **wise**, appropriate, apt, desirable, expedient, fit, fitting, judicious, politic, profitable, proper, prudent, recommended, seemly, sensible, sound, suggested, suitable
Antonyms *adj* ill-advised, impolitic, improper, imprudent, inappropriate, inexpedient, injudicious, silly, stupid, undesirable, unfitting, unprofitable, unseemly, unsound, unsuitable, unwise

advise *vb* **1** = **recommend**, admonish, caution, commend, counsel, enjoin, prescribe, suggest, urge **2** = **notify**, acquaint, apprise, inform, let (someone) know, make known, report, tell, warn

advisedly *adv* = **deliberately**, after careful consideration, by design, calculatedly, designedly, intentionally, judiciously, on purpose, premeditatedly, prudently, with intent

adviser *n* **1, 2** = **guide**, aide, authority, coach, confidant, consultant, counsel, counsellor, guru, helper, lawyer, mentor, right-hand man, solicitor, teacher, tutor

advisory *adj* **1** = **advising**, consultative, counselling, helping, recommending

advocacy *n* = **recommendation**, advancement, argument for, backing, campaigning for, championing, defence, encouragement, espousal, justification, pleading for, promotion, promulgation, propagation, proposal, spokesmanship, support, upholding, urging

advocate *vb* **1** = **recommend**, advise, argue for, campaign for, champion, commend, countenance, defend, encourage, espouse, favour, justify, plead for, prescribe, press for, promote, propose, speak for, support, uphold, *take a clause as object*) to support or recommend publicly. ◆ *n* ('ædvəkɪt). **2** a person who upholds or defends a cause. **3** a person who intercedes on behalf of another. **4** a person who pleads his client's cause in a court of law. **5** *Scots Law.* the usual word for **barrister.** [C14: via OF from L *advocātus* legal witness, from *advocāre,* from *vocāre* to call]

advowson (əd'vauzᵊn) *n English ecclesiastical law.* the right of presentation to a vacant benefice. [C13: via OF from L *advocātiōn-,* from *advocāre* to summon]

advt *abbrev. for* advertisement.

adze *or US* **adz** (ædz) *n* a hand tool with a steel blade attached at right angles to a wooden handle, used for dressing timber. [OE *adesa*]

AEA (in Britain) *abbrev. for* Atomic Energy Authority.

AEC (in the US) *abbrev. for* Atomic Energy Commission.

aedes (eɪ'i:di:z) *n* a mosquito of tropical and subtropical regions which transmits yellow fever. [C20: NL, from Gk *aēdēs* unpleasant, from A-[1] + *ēdos* pleasant]

aedile *or US (sometimes)* **edile** ('i:daɪl) *n* a magistrate of ancient Rome in charge of public works, games, buildings, and roads. [C16: from L *aedīlis,* from *aedēs* a building]

AEEU (in Britain) *abbrev. for* Amalgamated Engineering and Electrical Union.

Aegean (i:'dʒi:ən) *adj* of or relating to the Aegean Sea or Islands.

aegis ❶ *or US (sometimes)* **egis** ('i:dʒɪs) *n* **1** sponsorship or protection (esp. in **under the aegis of**). **2** *Greek myth.* the shield of Zeus. [C18: from L, from Gk *aigis* shield of Zeus]

aegrotat ('aɪgrəuˌtæt, 'i:-) *n* **1** (in British and certain other universities, and, sometimes, schools) a certificate allowing a candidate to pass an examination although he has missed all or part of it through illness. **2** a degree or other qualification obtained in such circumstances. [C19: L, lit.: he is ill]

-aemia, -haemia, *or US* **-emia, -hemia** *n combining form.* denoting blood, esp. a specified condition of the blood in diseases: *leukaemia.* [NL, from Gk, from *haima* blood]

Aeneid (ɪ'ni:ɪd) *n* an epic poem in Latin by Virgil relating the experiences of Aeneas after the fall of Troy.

aeolian harp (i:'əulɪən) *n* a stringed instrument that produces a musical sound when wind passes over the strings. Also called: **wind harp.**

aeolotropic (ˌi:ələu'trɒpɪk) *adj* a less common word for **anisotropic.** [C19: from Gk *aiolos* fickle + -TROPIC]
▸**aeolotropy** (ˌi:ə'lɒtrəpɪ) *n*

aeon *or esp. US* **eon** ('i:ən, 'i:ɒn) *n* **1** an immeasurably long period of time. **2** *Astron.* a period of one thousand million years. [C17: from Gk *aiōn* an infinitely long time]

aerate ('ɛəreɪt) *vb* **aerates, aerating, aerated.** (*tr*) **1** to charge (a liquid) with a gas, as in the manufacture of effervescent drink. **2** to expose to the action or circulation of the air.
▸**aer'ation** *n* ▸**'aerator** *n*

aeri- *combining form.* a variant of **aero-.**

aerial ('ɛərɪəl) *adj* **1** of or resembling air. **2** existing, moving, or operating in the air: *aerial cable car.* **3** ethereal; light and delicate. **4** imaginary. **5** extending high into the air. **6** of or relating to aircraft: *aerial combat.* ◆ *n* **7** Also called: **antenna**. the part of a radio or television system by means of which radio waves are transmitted or received. [C17: via L from Gk *aērios,* from *aēr* air]

aerialist ('ɛərɪəlɪst) *n* a trapeze artist or tightrope walker.

aerie ('ɛərɪ) *n* a variant spelling (esp. US) of **eyrie.**

aeriform ('ɛərɪˌfɔ:m) *adj* **1** having the form of air; gaseous. **2** unsubstantial.

aero ('ɛərəu) *n* (*modifier*) of or relating to aircraft or aeronautics: *an aero engine.*

aero-, aeri-, *or before a vowel* **aer-** *combining form.* **1** denoting air, atmosphere, or gas: *aerodynamics.* **2** denoting aircraft: *aeronautics.* [ult. from Gk *aēr* air]

aerobatics (ˌɛərəu'bætɪks) *n* (*functioning as sing or pl*) spectacular or dangerous manoeuvres, such as loops or rolls, performed in an aircraft or glider. [C20: from AERO- + (ACRO)BATICS]

aerobe ('ɛərəub) *or* **aerobium** (ɛə'rəubɪəm) *n, pl* **aerobes** *or* **aerobia** (-'əubɪə). an organism that requires free oxygen or air for respiration. [C19: from AERO- + Gk *bios* life]

aerobic (ɛə'rəubɪk) *adj* **1** (of an organism or process) depending on free oxygen or air. **2** of or relating to aerobes. **3** designed for or relating to aerobics: *aerobic shoes; aerobic dances.*

aerobics (ɛə'rəubɪks) *n* (*functioning as sing*) any system of exercises designed to increase the amount of oxygen in the blood.

aerodrome ('ɛərəˌdrəum) *n* a landing area that is smaller than an airport.

aerodynamic braking *n* **1** the use of aerodynamic drag to slow spacecraft re-entering the atmosphere. **2** the use of airbrakes to retard flying vehicles or objects. **3** the use of a parachute or reversed thrust to decelerate an aircraft before landing.

aerodynamics (ˌɛərəudaɪ'næmɪks) *n* (*functioning as sing*) the study of the dynamics of gases, esp. of the forces acting on a body passing through air.
▸ˌ**aerody'namic** *adj* ▸ˌ**aerody'namically** *adv* ▸ˌ**aerody'namicist** *n*

aeroembolism (ˌɛərəu'ɛmbəˌlɪzəm) *n* the presence in the blood of nitrogen bubbles, caused by an abrupt reduction in atmospheric pressure. See **decompression sickness.**

aero engine *n* an engine for powering an aircraft.

aerofoil ('ɛərəuˌfɔɪl) *n* a cross section of a wing, rotor blade, etc.

aerogram *or* **aerogramme** ('ɛərəˌgræm) *n* an air-mail letter written on a single sheet of lightweight paper that folds and is sealed to form an envelope. Also called: **air letter.**

aerolite ('ɛərəˌlaɪt) *n* a stony meteorite consisting of silicate minerals.

aerology (ɛə'rɒlədʒɪ) *n* the study of the atmosphere, including its upper layers.
▸**aerological** (ˌɛərə'lɒdʒɪkᵊl) *adj* ▸**aer'ologist** *n*

aeromechanics (ˌɛərəumɪ'kænɪks) *n* (*functioning as sing*) the mechanics of gases, esp. air.
▸ˌ**aerome'chanical** *adj*

aeronautics (ˌɛərə'nɔ:tɪks) *n* (*functioning as sing*) the study or practice of all aspects of flight through the air.
▸ˌ**aero'nautical** *adj*

aeropause ('ɛərəˌpɔ:z) *n* the region of the upper atmosphere above which aircraft cannot fly.

aeroplane ('ɛərəˌpleɪn) *or US* **airplane** ('ɛəˌpleɪn) *n* a heavier-than-air powered flying vehicle with fixed wings. [C19: from F *aéroplane,* from AERO- + Gk *-planos* wandering]

aerosol ('ɛərəˌsɒl) *n* **1** a colloidal dispersion of solid or liquid particles in a gas. **2** a substance, such as a paint or insecticide, dispensed from a small metal container by a propellant under pressure. **3** Also called: **air spray.** such a substance together with its container. [C20: from AERO- + SOL(UTION)]

aerospace ('ɛərəˌspeɪs) *n* **1** the atmosphere and space beyond. **2** (*modifier*) of rockets, missiles, space vehicles, etc.: *the aerospace industry.*

aerostat ('ɛərəˌstæt) *n* a lighter-than-air craft, such as a balloon. [C18: from F *aérostat,* from AERO- + Gk *-statos* standing]
▸ˌ**aero'static** *adj*

aerostatics (ˌɛərə'stætɪks) *n* (*functioning as sing*) **1** the study of gases in equilibrium and bodies held in equilibrium in gases. Cf. **aerodynamics. 2** the study of lighter-than-air craft, such as balloons.

aerugo (ɪ'ru:gəu) *n* (esp. of old bronze) another name for **verdigris.** [C18: from L, from *aes* copper, bronze]
▸**aeruginous** (ɪ'ru:dʒɪnəs) *adj*

aery ('ɛərɪ) *n, pl* **aeries.** a variant of **eyrie.**

Aeschylean (ˌi:skə'li:ən) *adj* of or relating to the works of Aeschylus, 5th-century B.C. Greek dramatist.

Aesculapian (ˌi:skju'leɪpɪən) *adj* of or relating to Aesculapius, the Roman god of medicine, or to the art of medicine.

aesthesia *or US* **esthesia** (i:s'θi:zɪə) *n* the normal ability to experience sensation. [C20: back formation from ANAESTHESIA]

aesthete *or US* **esthete** ('i:sθi:t) *n* a person who has or who affects a highly developed appreciation of beauty. [C19: back formation from AESTHETICS]

aesthetic ❶ (i:s'θɛtɪk, ɪs-) *or US (sometimes)* **esthetic** *adj also* **aesthetical** *or US (sometimes)* **esthetical. 1** connected with aesthetics. **2a** relating to pure beauty rather than to other considerations. **2b** artistic: *an aesthetic consideration.* ◆ *n* **3** a principle of taste or style adopted by a particular person, group, or culture: *the Bauhaus aesthetic of functional modernity.* [C19: from Gk *aisthētikos,* from *aisthanesthai* to perceive, feel]
▸**aes'thetically** *or US (sometimes)* **es'thetically** *adv* ▸**aes'thetiˌcism** *or US (sometimes)* **es'thetiˌcism** *n*

aesthetics *or US (sometimes)* **esthetics** (i:s'θɛtɪks) *n* (*functioning as sing*) **1** the branch of philosophy concerned with the study of such concepts as beauty, taste, etc. **2** the study of the rules and principles of art.

aestival *or US* **estival** (i:'staɪvᵊl) *adj Rare.* of or occurring in summer. [C14: from F, from LL *aestīvālis,* from L *aestās* summer]

aestivate *or US* **estivate** ('i:stɪˌveɪt) *vb* **aestivates, aestivating, aestivated** *or US* **estivates, estivating, estivated.** (*intr*) **1** to pass the summer. **2** (of animals) to pass the summer or dry season in a dormant condition. [C17: from L, from *aestīvāre,* from *aestās* summer]
▸ˌ**aesti'vation** *or US* ˌ**esti'vation** *n*

aet. *or* **aetat.** *abbrev. for* aetatis. [L: at the age of]

aether ('i:θə) *n* a variant spelling of **ether** (senses 3, 4).

aetiology *or* **etiology** (ˌi:tɪ'ɒlədʒɪ) *n, pl* **aetiologies** *or* **etiologies. 1** the philosophy or study of causation. **2** the study of the causes of diseases. **3** the cause of a disease. [C16: from LL *aetologia,* from Gk *aitiologia,* from *aitia* cause]
▸ˌ**aetio'logical** *or* ˌ**etio'logical** *adj* ▸ˌ**aetio'logically** *or* ˌ**etio'logically** *adv* ▸ˌ**aeti'ologist** *or* ˌ**eti'ologist** *n*

AEU (in Britain) *abbrev. for* Amalgamated Engineering Union.

a.f. *abbrev. for* audio frequency.

afar (ə'fɑ:) *adv* **1** at, from, or to a great distance. ◆ *n* **2** a great distance (esp. in **from afar**). [C14 *a fer,* altered from earlier *on fer* & *of fer;* see A-[2], FAR]

THESAURUS

urge ◆ *n* **2, 3** = **supporter**, apologist, apostle, backer, campaigner, champion, counsellor, defender, pleader, promoter, proponent, proposer, speaker, spokesman, upholder **4, 5** = **lawyer**, attorney, barrister, counsel, solicitor

Antonyms *vb* ≠ **recommend:** contradict, oppose, resist, speak against, take a stand against, take issue with

aegis *n* **1** *As in* **under the aegis of** = **protection**, advocacy, auspices, backing, favour, guardianship, patronage, shelter, sponsorship, support, wing

aesthetic *adj* **2** = **tasteful**, artistic, in good taste, pleasing

AFC *abbrev. for:* **1** Air Force Cross. **2** Association Football Club. **3** automatic frequency control.

afeard *or* **afeared** (əˈfɪəd) *adj* (*postpositive*) an archaic or dialect word for **afraid**. [OE *āfǣred,* from *afǣran* to frighten]

affable ➊ (ˈæfəbᵊl) *adj* **1** showing warmth and friendliness. **2** easy to converse with; approachable. [C16: from L *affābilis,* from *affārī,* from *ad-* to + *fārī* to speak]
▸ˌ**affaˈbility** *n* ▸ˈ**affably** *adv*

affair ➊ (əˈfɛə) *n* **1** a thing to be done or attended to; matter. **2** an event or happening: *a strange affair.* **3** (*qualified by an adjective or descriptive phrase*) something previously specified: *our house is a tumbledown affair.* **4** a sexual relationship between two people who are not married to each other. [C13: from OF, from *à faire* to do]

affairs (əˈfɛəz) *pl n* **1** personal or business interests. **2** matters of public interest: *current affairs.*

affect[1] ➊ *vb* (əˈfɛkt). (*tr*) **1** to act upon or influence, esp. in an adverse way. **2** to move or disturb emotionally or mentally. **3** (of pain, disease, etc.) to attack. ◆ *n* (ˈæfɛkt). **4** *Psychol.* the emotion associated with an idea or set of ideas. [C17: from L *affectus,* p.p. of *afficere,* from *ad-* to + *facere* to do]

affect[2] ➊ (əˈfɛkt) *vb* (*mainly tr*) **1** to put on an appearance or show of: *to affect ignorance.* **2** to imitate or assume, esp. pretentiously. **3** to have or use by preference. **4** to adopt the character, manner, etc., of. **5** to incline habitually towards. [C15: from L *affectāre* to strive after; rel. to *afficere* to AFFECT[1]]

affectation ➊ (ˌæfɛkˈteɪʃən) *n* **1** an assumed manner of speech, dress, or behaviour, esp. one that is intended to impress others. **2** (often foll. by *of*) deliberate pretence. [C16: from L *affectātiōn-,* from *affectāre;* see AFFECT[2]]

affected[1] ➊ (əˈfɛktɪd) *adj* (*usually postpositive*) **1** deeply moved, esp. by sorrow or grief. **2** changed, esp. detrimentally. [C17: from AFFECT[1]]

affected[2] ➊ (əˈfɛktɪd) *adj* **1** behaving, speaking, etc., in an assumed way, esp. in order to impress others. **2** feigned: *affected indifference.* [C16: from AFFECT[2]]
▸**afˈfectedly** *adv*

affecting ➊ (əˈfɛktɪŋ) *adj* evoking feelings of pity; moving.
▸**afˈfectingly** *adv*

affection ➊ (əˈfɛkʃən) *n* **1** a feeling of fondness or tenderness for a person or thing. **2** (*often pl*) emotion, feeling, or sentiment: *to play on a person's affections.* **3** *Pathol.* any disease or pathological condition. **4** the act of affecting or the state of being affected. [C13: from L *affectiōn-,* from *afficere* to AFFECT[1]]
▸**afˈfectional** *adj*

affectionate ➊ (əˈfɛkʃənɪt) *adj* having or displaying tender feelings, affection, or warmth.
▸**afˈfectionately** *adv*

affective (əˈfɛktɪv) *adj* concerned with the emotions or affection.
▸**affectivity** (ˌæfɛkˈtɪvɪtɪ) *n*

affective disorder *n* any mental disorder, such as depression or mania, that is characterized by abnormal disturbances of mood.

affectless (ˈæfɛktˌlɪs, əˈfɛktlɪs) *adj* **a** showing no emotion or concern for others. **b** not giving rise to any emotion or feeling: *an affectless novel.* [C20: from AFFECT[1] (sense 4) + -LESS]

afferent (ˈæfərənt) *adj* bringing or directing inwards to a part or an organ of the body, esp. towards the brain or spinal cord. [C19: from L *afferre,* from *ad-* to + *ferre* to carry]

affiance ➊ (əˈfaɪəns) *vb* **affiances, affiancing, affianced.** (*tr*) to bind (a person or oneself) in a promise of marriage; betroth. [C14: via OF from Med. L *affīdāre* to trust (oneself) to, from *fīdāre* to trust]

affidavit (ˌæfɪˈdeɪvɪt) *n Law.* a declaration in writing made upon oath before a person authorized to administer oaths. [C17: from Med. L, lit.: he declares on oath, from *affīdare;* see AFFIANCE]

affiliate ➊ *vb* (əˈfɪlɪˌeɪt), **affiliates, affiliating, affiliated. 1** (*tr;* foll. by *to* or *with*) to receive into close connection or association (with a larger body, group, organization, etc.). **2** (foll. by *with*) to associate (oneself) or be associated, esp. as a subordinate or subsidiary. ◆ *n* (əˈfɪlɪɪt). **3a** a person or organization that is affiliated with another. **3b** (*as modifier*): *an affiliate member.* [C18: from Med. L *affiliātus* adopted as a son, from *affīliāre,* from L *filius* son]
▸**afˌfiliˈation** *n*

affiliation order *n Law.* an order that a man adjudged to be the father of an illegitimate child shall contribute towards the child's maintenance.

affine (ˈæfaɪn) *adj Maths.* denoting transformations which preserve collinearity, esp. those of translation, rotation, and reflection. [C16: from F: see AFFINITY]

affinity ➊ (əˈfɪnɪtɪ) *n, pl* **affinities. 1** a natural liking, taste, or inclination for a person or thing. **2** the person or thing so liked. **3** a close similarity in appearance or quality. **4** relationship by marriage. **5** similarity in structure, form, etc., between different animals, plants, or languages. **6** *Chem.* chemical attraction. **7** *Immunol.* a measure of the degree of interaction between an antigen and an antibody. [C14: via OF from L *affīnitāt-,* from *affīnis* bordering on, related]
▸**afˈfinitive** *adj*

affinity card *n* a credit card issued by a bank or credit-card company, which donates a small percentage of the money spent using the card to a specified charity.

affirm ➊ (əˈfɜːm) *vb* (*mainly tr*) **1** (*may take a clause as object*) to declare to be true. **2** to uphold, confirm, or ratify. **3** (*intr*) *Law.* to make an affirmation. [C14: via OF from L *affirmāre,* from *ad-* to + *firmāre* to make FIRM[1]]
▸**afˈfirmer** *or* **afˈfirmant** *n*

affirmation ➊ (ˌæfəˈmeɪʃən) *n* **1** the act of affirming or the state of being affirmed. **2** a statement of the truth of something; assertion. **3** *Law.* a solemn declaration permitted on grounds of conscientious objection to taking an oath.

affirmative ➊ (əˈfɜːmətɪv) *adj* **1** confirming or asserting something as true or valid. **2** indicating agreement or assent. **3** *Logic.* (of a categorical proposition) affirming the satisfaction by the subject of the predicate, as in the proposition *some men are married.* ◆ *n* **4** a positive assertion. **5** a word or phrase stating agreement or assent, such as *yes: to answer in the affirmative.* ◆ *sentence substitute.* **6** *Mil., etc.* a signal codeword used to express assent or confirmation.
▸**afˈfirmatively** *adv*

affix ➊ *vb* (əˈfɪks). (*tr;* usually foll. by *to* or *on*) **1** to attach, fasten, join, or stick. **2** to add or append: *to affix a signature to a document.* **3** to attach or attribute (guilt, blame, etc.). ◆ *n* (ˈæfɪks). **4** a linguistic element

THESAURUS

affability *n* **1, 2** = **friendliness**, amiability, amicability, approachability, benevolence, benignity, civility, congeniality, cordiality, courtesy, geniality, good humour, good nature, graciousness, kindliness, mildness, obligingness, pleasantness, sociability, urbanity, warmth

affable *adj* **1, 2** = **friendly**, amiable, amicable, approachable, benevolent, benign, civil, congenial, cordial, courteous, genial, good-humoured, good-natured, gracious, kindly, mild, obliging, pleasant, sociable, urbane, warm
Antonyms *adj* brusque, cold, discourteous, distant, haughty, rude, stand-offish, surly, unapproachable, uncivil, unfriendly, ungracious, unpleasant, unsociable

affair *n* **1, 2** = **event**, activity, business, circumstance, concern, episode, happening, incident, interest, matter, occurrence, proceeding, project, question, subject, transaction, undertaking **4** = **relationship**, amour, intrigue, liaison, romance

affect[1] *vb* **1** = **influence**, act on, alter, bear upon, change, concern, impact, impinge upon, interest, involve, modify, prevail over, regard, relate to, sway, transform **2** = **move**, disturb, impress, overcome, perturb, stir, touch, upset

affect[2] *vb* **1, 2, 4** = **put on**, adopt, aspire to, assume, contrive, counterfeit, feign, imitate, pretend, sham, simulate

affectation *n* **1, 2** = **pretence**, act, affectedness, appearance, artificiality, assumed manners, façade, fakery, false display, insincerity, mannerism, pose, pretension, pretentiousness, sham, show, simulation, unnatural imitation

affected[1] *adj* **1, 2** = **influenced**, afflicted, altered, changed, concerned, damaged, deeply moved, distressed, hurt, impaired, impressed, injured, melted, stimulated, stirred, touched, troubled, upset
Antonyms *adj* cured, unaffected, unconcerned, unharmed, uninjured, unmoved, untouched

affected[2] *adj* **1, 2** = **pretended**, artificial, arty-farty (*inf.*), assumed, camp (*inf.*), conceited, contrived, counterfeit, feigned, insincere, la-di-da (*inf.*), mannered, mincing, phoney *or* phony (*inf.*), pompous, precious, pretentious, put-on, sham, simulated, spurious, stiff, studied, unnatural
Antonyms *adj* genuine, natural, real, unaffected

affecting *adj* = **moving**, pathetic, piteous, pitiable, pitiful, poignant, sad, saddening, touching

affection *n* **1, 2** = **fondness**, amity, attachment, care, desire, feeling, friendliness, goodwill, inclination, kindness, liking, love, passion, propensity, tenderness, warmth

affectionate *adj* = **fond**, attached, caring, devoted, doting, friendly, kind, loving, tender, warm, warm-hearted
Antonyms *adj* cold, cool, glacial, indifferent, stony, uncaring, undemonstrative, unfeeling, unresponsive

affianced *adj* = **engaged**, betrothed, bound, pledged, promised

affiliate *vb* **1, 2** = **join**, ally, amalgamate, annex, associate, band together, combine, confederate, connect, incorporate, link, unite

affiliated *adj* **1, 2** = **connected**, allied, amalgamated, associated, confederated, conjoined, federated, incorporated, joined, linked, united

affiliation *n* **1, 2** = **connection**, alliance, amalgamation, association, banding together, coalition, combination, confederation, incorporation, joining, league, merging, relationship, union

affinity *n* **1** = **attraction**, fondness, inclination, leaning, liking, partiality, rapport, sympathy **3** = **similarity**, alliance, analogy, closeness, compatibility, connection, correspondence, kinship, likeness, relation, relationship, resemblance
Antonyms *n* ≠ **attraction:** abhorrence, animosity, antipathy, aversion, dislike, hatred, hostility, loathing, repugnance, revulsion ≠ **similarity:** difference, disparity, dissimilarity

affirm *vb* **1, 2** = **declare**, assert, asseverate, attest, aver, avouch, avow, certify, confirm, maintain, pronounce, ratify, state, swear, testify
Antonyms *vb* deny, disallow, rebut, refute, reject, renounce, repudiate, rescind, retract

affirmation *n* **1, 2** = **declaration**, assertion, asseveration, attestation, averment, avouchment, avowal, certification, confirmation, oath, pronouncement, ratification, statement, testimony

affirmative *adj* **1, 2** = **agreeing**, approving, assenting, concurring, confirming, consenting, corroborative, favourable, positive
Antonyms *adj* denying, disagreeing, disapproving, dissenting, negating, negative

affix *vb* **1, 2** = **attach**, add, annex, append, bind, fasten, glue, join, paste, put on, stick, subjoin, tack, tag
Antonyms *vb* detach, disconnect, remove, take off, unfasten, unglue

added to a word or root to produce a derived or inflected form, as *-ment* in *establishment.* See also **prefix, suffix, infix.** **5** something fastened or attached. [C15: from Med. L *affixāre,* from *ad-* to + *fixāre* to FIX]
▸**affixture** (ə'fɪkstʃə) *n*

afflatus (ə'fleɪtəs) *n* an impulse of creative power or inspiration considered to be of divine origin. [C17: L, from *afflātus,* from *afflāre,* from *flāre* to blow]

afflict ❶ (ə'flɪkt) *vb* (*tr*) to cause suffering or unhappiness to; distress greatly. [C14: from L *afflictus,* p.p. of *afflīgere* to knock against, from *flīgere* to strike]
▸**af'flictive** *adj*

affliction ❶ (ə'flɪkʃən) *n* **1** a condition of great distress or suffering. **2** something responsible for physical or mental suffering.

affluence ❶ ('æfluəns) *n* **1** an abundant supply of money, goods, or property; wealth. **2** *Rare.* abundance or profusion.

affluent ❶ ('æfluənt) *adj* **1** rich; wealthy. **2** abundant; copious. **3** flowing freely. ◆ *n* **4** a tributary stream. [C15: from L *affluent-,* present participle of *affluere,* from *fluere* to flow]

affluent society *n* a society in which the material benefits of prosperity are widely available.

afflux ('æflʌks) *n* a flowing towards a point: *an afflux of blood to the head.* [C17: from L *affluxus,* from *fluxus* FLUX]

afford ❶ (ə'fɔːd) *vb* **1** (preceded by *can, could,* etc.) to be able to do or spare something, esp. without incurring financial difficulties or without risk of undesirable consequences. **2** to give, yield, or supply. [OE *geforthian* to further, promote, from *forth* FORTH]
▸**af'fordable** *adj* ▸**af,forda'bility** *n*

afforest (ə'fɒrɪst) *vb* (*tr*) to plant trees on. [C15: from Med. L *afforestāre,* from *forestis* FOREST]
▸**af,forest'ation** *n*

affranchise (ə'fræntʃaɪz) *vb* **affranchises, affranchising, affranchised.** (*tr*) to release from servitude or an obligation. [C15: from OF *afranchir*]
▸**af'franchisement** *n*

affray ❶ (ə'freɪ) *n* a fight, noisy quarrel, or disturbance between two or more persons in a public place. [C14: via OF from Vulgar L *exfridāre* (unattested) to break the peace]

affricate ('æfrɪkɪt) *n* a composite speech sound consisting of a stop and a fricative articulated at the same point, such as the sound written *ch,* as in *chair.* [C19: from L *affricāre,* from *fricāre* to rub]

affright (ə'fraɪt) *Arch. or poetic.* ◆ *vb* **1** (*tr*) to frighten. ◆ *n* **2** a sudden terror. [OE *āfyrhtan,* from *a-* + *fyrhtan* to FRIGHT]

affront ❶ (ə'frʌnt) *n* **1** a deliberate insult. ◆ *vb* (*tr*) **2** to insult, esp. openly. **3** to offend the pride or dignity of. [C14: from OF *afronter* to strike in the face, from L *ad frontem* to the face]

afghan ('æfgæn, -gən) *n* **1** a knitted or crocheted wool blanket or shawl, esp. one with a geometric pattern. **2** a sheepskin coat, often embroidered.

Afghan ('æfgæn) *or* **Afghani** (æf'gænɪ) *n* **1** a native, citizen, or inhabitant of Afghanistan. **2** another name for **Pashto** (the language). ◆ *adj* **3** denoting Afghanistan, its people, or their language.

Afghan hound *n* a tall graceful breed of hound with a long silky coat.

aficionado ❶ (ə,fɪʃjə'nɑːdəʊ) *n, pl* **aficionados. 1** an ardent supporter or devotee: *a jazz aficionado.* **2** a devotee of bullfighting. [Sp., from *aficionar,* from *aficion* AFFECTION]

afield (ə'fiːld) *adv, adj* (*postpositive*) **1** away from one's usual surroundings or home (esp. in **far afield**). **2** off the subject (esp. in **far afield**). **3** in or to the field.

afire ❶ (ə'faɪə) *adv, adj* (*postpositive*) **1** on fire. **2** intensely interested or passionate: *he was afire with enthusiasm for the new plan.*

aflame ❶ (ə'fleɪm) *adv, adj* (*postpositive*) **1** in flames. **2** deeply aroused, as with passion: *he was aflame with desire.*

aflatoxin (,æflə'tɒksɪn) *n* a toxin produced by a fungus growing on peanuts, maize, etc., causing liver disease (esp. cancer) in man. [C20: from L name of fungus *A*(*spergillus*) *fla*(*vus*) + TOXIN]

afloat ❶ (ə'fləʊt) *adj* (*postpositive*), *adv* **1** floating. **2** aboard ship; at sea. **3** covered with water. **4** aimlessly drifting. **5** in circulation: *nasty rumours were afloat.* **6** free of debt.

aflutter (ə'flʌtə) *adj* (*postpositive*), *adv* in or into a nervous or excited state.

AFM *abbrev. for* Air Force Medal.

afoot ❶ (ə'fʊt) *adj* (*postpositive*), *adv* **1** in operation; astir: *mischief was afoot.* **2** on or by foot.

afore (ə'fɔː) *adv, prep, conj* an archaic or dialect word for **before.**

aforementioned (ə'fɔː,mɛnʃənd) *adj* (*usually prenominal*) (chiefly in legal documents) stated or mentioned before.

aforesaid (ə'fɔː,sɛd) *adj* (*usually prenominal*) (chiefly in legal documents) spoken of or referred to previously.

aforethought (ə'fɔː,θɔːt) *adj* (*immediately postpositive*) premeditated (esp. in **malice aforethought**).

a fortiori ('eɪ ,fɔːtɪ'ɔːraɪ) *adv* for similar but more convincing reasons. [L]

afp *abbrev. for* alpha-fetoprotein.

Afr. *abbrev. for* Africa(n).

afraid ❶ (ə'freɪd) *adj* (*postpositive*) **1** (often foll. by *of*) feeling fear or apprehension. **2** reluctant (to do something), as through fear or timidity. **3** (often foll. by *that;* used to lessen the effect of an unpleasant statement) regretful: *I'm afraid that I shall have to tell you to go.* [C14 *affraied,* p.p. of AFFRAY (*obs.*) to frighten]

afreet *or* **afrit** ('æfriːt, ə'friːt) *n Arabian myth.* a powerful evil demon. [C19: from Ar. *'ifrīt*]

afresh ❶ (ə'frɛʃ) *adv* once more; again; anew.

African ('æfrɪkən) *adj* **1** denoting or relating to Africa or any of its peoples, languages, nations, etc. ◆ *n* **2** a native or inhabitant of any of the countries of Africa. **3** a member or descendant of any of the peoples of Africa, esp. a Black person.

Africana (,æfrɪ'kɑːnə) *n* objects of cultural or historical interest of southern African origin.

African-American *or* **Afro-American** *n* **1** an American of African descent. ◆ *adj* **2** of or relating to Americans of African descent.

Africander (,æfrɪ'kændə) *n* a breed of hump-backed beef cattle originally raised in southern Africa. [C19: from South African Du., formed on the model of *Hollander*]

African National Congress *n* (in South Africa) a political party, founded in 1912 in South Africa as an African nationalist movement and banned from 1960 until 1990 because of its opposition to apartheid. In 1994 the ANC won South Africa's first multiracial elections. Abbrev.: **ANC.**

African violet *n* a tropical African plant cultivated as a house plant, with violet, white, or pink flowers and hairy leaves.

Afrikaans (,æfrɪ'kɑːns, -'kɑːnz) *n* one of the official languages of the Republic of South Africa, closely related to Dutch. Sometimes called: **South African Dutch.** [C20: from Du.: African]

Afrikaner (,æfrɪ'kɑːnə) *n* a White native of the Republic of South Africa whose mother tongue is Afrikaans. See also **Boer.**

afrit ('æfriːt, ə'friːt) *n* a variant spelling of **afreet.**

THESAURUS

afflict *vb* = **torment**, ail, beset, burden, distress, grieve, harass, hurt, oppress, pain, plague, rack, smite, trouble, try, wound

affliction *n* **1, 2** = **suffering**, adversity, calamity, cross, curse, depression, disease, distress, grief, hardship, misery, misfortune, ordeal, pain, plague, scourge, sickness, sorrow, torment, trial, tribulation, trouble, woe, wretchedness

affluence *n* **1** = **wealth**, abundance, big bucks (*inf., chiefly US*), big money, exuberance, fortune, megabucks (*US & Canad. sl.*), opulence, plenty, pretty penny (*inf.*), profusion, prosperity, riches, tidy sum (*inf.*)

affluent *adj* **1** = **wealthy**, loaded (*sl.*), moneyed, opulent, prosperous, rich, rolling in money (*sl.*), well-heeled (*inf.*), well-off, well-to-do **2** = **plentiful**, abundant, copious, exuberant, plenteous
Antonyms *adj* ≠ **wealthy:** broke (*inf.*), destitute, down at heel, hard-up (*inf.*), impecunious, impoverished, indigent, on the breadline, penniless, penurious, poor, poverty-stricken, skint (*Brit. sl.*), stony-broke (*Brit. sl.*)

afford *vb* **1** *As in* **can afford** = **spare**, bear, manage, stand, sustain **2** = **give**, bestow, furnish, grant, impart, offer, produce, provide, render, supply, yield

affordable *adj* **1** = **inexpensive**, cheap, economical, fair, low-cost, low-price, moderate, modest, reasonable
Antonyms *adj* ≠ **inexpensive:** beyond one's means, costly, dear, exorbitant, expensive, prohibitively expensive, unaffordable, uneconomical

affray *n* = **fight**, brawl, contest, disturbance, dogfight, encounter, feud, fracas, free-for-all (*inf.*), mêlée, outbreak, quarrel, scrap, scrimmage, scuffle, set-to (*inf.*), skirmish, tumult

affront *n* **1** = **insult**, abuse, indignity, injury, offence, outrage, provocation, slap in the face (*inf.*), slight, slur, vexation, wrong ◆ *vb* **2, 3** = **offend**, abuse, anger, annoy, displease, insult, outrage, pique, provoke, put *or* get one's back up, slight, vex

affronted *adj* **2, 3** = **offended**, angry, annoyed, cross, displeased, incensed, indignant, insulted, irate, miffed (*inf.*), outraged, peeved (*inf.*), piqued, slighted, stung, upset

aficionado *n* **1** = **fan**, addict, adherent, admirer, buff (*inf.*), connoisseur, devotee, disciple, enthusiast, fanatic, follower, freak (*inf.*), lover, nut (*sl.*), supporter, votary

afire *adj* **1** = **burning**, ablaze, aflame, alight, blazing, fiery, flaming, ignited, lighted, lit, on fire **2** = **passionate**, aglow, aroused, excited, fervent, impassioned, stimulated

aflame *adj* **1** = **burning**, ablaze, afire, alight, blazing, fiery, flaming, ignited, lighted, lit, on fire **2** = **passionate**, afire, aroused, excited, fervent, impassioned, stimulated

afloat *adj* **1** = **floating**, buoyant, keeping one's head above water, on the surface, unsubmerged ◆ *adv* **2** = **at sea**, aboard, on board (ship), on shipboard, sailing, under sail ◆ *adj* **3** = **flooded**, awash, inundated, submerged, swamped, under water **4** = **drifting**, adrift, aweigh, cast off, unanchored, unmoored **5** = **going about** *or* **around**, afoot, current, in circulation, in the air **6** = **solvent**, above water, in business
Antonyms *adj* ≠ **floating:** capsized, immersed, submerged, sunken, under water ≠ **drifting:** anchored, held fast, moored ≠ **solvent:** bankrupt, bust (*inf.*), in receivership, insolvent, out of business

afoot *adj* **1** = **going on**, about, abroad, afloat, astir, brewing, circulating, current, happening, hatching, in preparation, in progress, in the wind, on the go (*inf.*), operating, up (*inf.*)

afraid *adj* **1, 2** = **scared**, alarmed, anxious, apprehensive, cowardly, faint-hearted, fearful, frightened, intimidated, nervous, reluctant, suspicious, timid, timorous **3** = **sorry**, regretful, unhappy
Antonyms *adj* ≠ **scared:** audacious, bold, fearless, inapprehensive, indifferent, unafraid ≠ **sorry:** happy, pleased

afresh *adv* = **again**, anew, newly, once again, once more, over again

Afro ('æfrəʊ) *n, pl* **Afros.** a hairstyle in which the hair is shaped into a wide frizzy bush. [C20: independent use of AFRO-]
Afro- *combining form.* indicating Africa or African: *Afro-Asiatic.*
Afro-American *n, adj* another word for **African-American.**
Afro-Caribbean *adj* **1** denoting or relating to Caribbean people of African descent or their culture. ◆ *n* **2** a Caribbean of African descent.
afrormosia (ˌæfrɔːˈməʊzɪə) *n* a hard teaklike wood obtained from a genus of tropical African trees. [C20: from AFRO- + *Ormosia* (genus name)]
aft (ɑːft) *adv, adj Chiefly naut.* towards or at the stern or rear: *the aft deck.* [C17: ? shortened from earlier ABAFT]
after Ⓣ ('ɑːftə) *prep* **1** following in time; in succession to: *after dinner.* **2** following; behind. **3** in pursuit or search of: *he's only after money.* **4** concerning: *to inquire after his health.* **5** considering: *after what you have done, you shouldn't complain.* **6** next in excellence or importance to. **7** in imitation of; in the manner of. **8** in accordance with or in conformity to: *a man after her own heart.* **9** with a name derived from. **10** *US.* past (the hour of): *twenty after three.* **11 after all. 11a** in spite of everything: *it's only a game after all.* **11b** in spite of expectations, efforts, etc. **12 after you.** please go, enter, etc., before me. ◆ *adv* **13** at a later time; afterwards. **14** coming afterwards. **15** *Naut.* further aft. ◆ *conj* **16** (*subordinating*) at a time later than that at which. ◆ *adj* **17** *Naut.* further aft: *the after cabin.* [OE *æfter*]
afterbirth ('ɑːftəˌbɜːθ) *n* the placenta and fetal membranes expelled from the uterus after the birth of offspring.
afterburner ('ɑːftəˌbɜːnə) *n* **1** a device in the exhaust system of an internal-combustion engine for removing dangerous exhaust gases. **2** a device in an aircraft jet engine to produce extra thrust by igniting additional fuel.
aftercare ('ɑːftəˌkɛə) *n* **1** support services by a welfare agency for a person discharged from a hospital, prison, etc. **2** *Med.* the care of a patient after a serious illness or operation. **3** any system of maintenance or upkeep of an appliance or product: *contact-lens aftercare.*
afterdamp ('ɑːftəˌdæmp) *n* a poisonous gas, consisting mainly of carbon monoxide, formed after the explosion of firedamp in coal mines.
aftereffect Ⓣ ('ɑːftərɪˌfɛkt) *n* any result occurring some time after its cause.
afterglow ('ɑːftəˌgləʊ) *n* **1** the glow left after a light has disappeared, such as that sometimes seen after sunset. **2** the glow of an incandescent metal after the source of heat has been removed.
afterimage ('ɑːftərˌɪmɪdʒ) *n* a sustained or renewed sensation, esp. visual, after the original stimulus has ceased.
afterlife ('ɑːftəˌlaɪf) *n* life after death or at a later time in a person's lifetime.
aftermath Ⓣ ('ɑːftəˌmæθ) *n* **1** signs or results of an event or occurrence considered collectively: *the aftermath of war.* **2** *Agriculture.* a second crop of grass from land that has already yielded one crop earlier in the same year. [C16: AFTER + *math* a mowing, from OE *mæth*]
aftermost ('ɑːftəˌməʊst) *adj* closer or closest to the rear or (in a vessel) the stern; last.
afternoon (ˌɑːftəˈnuːn) *n* **1a** the period between noon and evening. **1b** (*as modifier*): *afternoon tea.* **2** a later part: *the afternoon of life.*
afternoons (ˌɑːftəˈnuːnz) *adv Inf.* during the afternoon, esp. regularly.
afterpains ('ɑːftəˌpeɪnz) *pl n* cramplike pains caused by contraction of the uterus after childbirth.
afters ('ɑːftəz) *n* (*functioning as sing or pl*) *Brit. inf.* dessert; sweet.
aftershave lotion ('ɑːftəˌʃeɪv) *n* a lotion, usually perfumed, for application to the face after shaving. Often shortened to **aftershave.**
aftertaste ('ɑːftəˌteɪst) *n* **1** a taste that lingers on after eating or drinking. **2** a lingering impression or sensation.
afterthought ('ɑːftəˌθɔːt) *n* **1** a comment, reply, etc., that occurs to one after the opportunity to deliver it has passed. **2** an addition to something already completed.
afterwards Ⓣ ('ɑːftəwədz) *or* **afterward** *adv* after an earlier event or time. [OE *æfterweard, æfteweard,* from AFT + WARD]
Ag *the chemical symbol for* silver. [from L *argentum*]
AG *abbrev. for:* **1** Adjutant General. **2** Attorney General.
aga *or* **agha** ('ɑːgə) *n* (in the Ottoman Empire) a title of respect, often used with the title of a senior position. [C17: Turkish, lit.: lord]
again Ⓣ (əˈgɛn, əˈgeɪn) *adv* **1** another or a second time: *he had to start again.* **2** once more in a previously experienced state or condition: *he is ill again.* **3** in addition to the original amount, quantity, etc. (esp. in **as much again; half as much again**). **4** (*sentence modifier*) on the other hand. **5** besides; also. **6** *Arch.* in reply; back: *he answered again.* **7 again and again.** continuously; repeatedly. ◆ *sentence connector.* **8** moreover; furthermore. [OE *ongegn* opposite to, from A-[2] + *gegn* straight]
against Ⓣ (əˈgɛnst, əˈgeɪnst) *prep* **1** opposed to; in conflict or disagreement with. **2** standing or leaning beside: *a ladder against the wall.* **3** coming in contact with. **4** in contrast to: *silhouettes are outlines against a light background.* **5** having an unfavourable effect on: *the system works against small companies.* **6** as a protection from: *a safeguard against contaminated water.* **7** in exchange for or in return for. **8** *Now rare.* in preparation for: *he gave them warm clothing against their journey.* **9 as against.** as opposed to or as compared with. [C12 *ageines,* from *again, ageyn,* etc. AGAIN + *-es,* genitive ending]
Aga Khan ('ɑːgə 'kɑːn) *n* the hereditary title of the head of the Ismaili Islamic sect.
agamic (əˈgæmɪk) *adj* asexual; occurring or reproducing without fertilization. [C19: from Gk *agamos* unmarried, from A-[1] + *gamos* marriage]
agamogenesis (ˌægəməʊˈdʒɛnɪsɪs) *n* asexual reproduction, such as fission or parthenogenesis. [C19: AGAMIC + GENESIS]
agapanthus (ˌægəˈpænθəs) *n* a South African plant with blue funnel-shaped flowers, widely cultivated for ornament. [C19: NL, from Gk *agapē* love + *anthos* flower]
agape Ⓣ (əˈgeɪp) *adj* (*postpositive*) **1** (esp. of the mouth) wide open. **2** very surprised, expectant, or eager. [C17: A-[2] + GAPE]
Agape ('ægəpɪ) *n* **1** Christian love, esp. as contrasted with erotic love; charity. **2** a communal meal in the early Church in commemoration of the Last Supper. [C17: Gk *agapē* love]
agar ('eɪgə) *n* a gelatinous carbohydrate obtained from seaweeds, used as a culture medium for bacteria, as a laxative, a thickening agent (**E406**) in food, etc. Also called: **agar-agar.** [C19: Malay]
agaric ('ægərɪk) *n* a fungus having gills on the underside of the cap. The group includes the edible mushrooms and poisonous forms such as the fly agaric. [C16: via L from Gk *agarikon*]
agate ('ægɪt) *n* **1** an impure form of quartz consisting of a variegated, usually banded chalcedony, used as a gemstone and in making pestles and mortars. **2** a playing marble of this quartz or resembling it. [C16: via F from L, from Gk *akhatēs*]
agave (əˈgeɪvɪ) *n* a plant native to tropical America with tall flower stalks rising from thick fleshy leaves. Some species are the source of fibres such as sisal. [C18: NL, from Gk *agauē,* fem. of *agauos* illustrious]
age Ⓣ (eɪdʒ) *n* **1** the period of time that a person, animal, or plant has lived or is expected to live. **2** the period of existence of an object, material, group, etc.: *the age of this table is 200 years.* **3a** a period or state of human life: *he should know better at his age.* **3b** (*as modifier*): *age group.* **4** the latter part of life. **5a** a period of history marked by some feature or characteristic. **5b** (*cap. when part of a name*): *the Middle Ages.* **6** generation: *the Edwardian age.* **7** *Geol., palaeontol.* **7a** a period of the earth's history distinguished by special characteristics: *the age of reptiles.* **7b** a subdivision of an epoch. **8** (*often pl*) *Inf.* a relatively long time: *I've been waiting ages.* **9** *Psychol.* the level in years that a person has reached in any area of development, compared with the normal level for his chronological age. **10 of age.** adult and legally responsible for one's actions (usually at 18 years). ◆ *vb* **ages, ageing** *or* **aging, aged. 11** to become or cause to become old or aged. **12** (*intr*) to begin to seem older: *to have aged a lot in the past year.* **13** *Brewing.* to mature or cause to mature. [C13: via OF from Vulgar L, from L *aetās*]
-age *suffix forming nouns.* **1** indicating a collection, set, or group: *baggage.* **2** indicating a process or action or the result of an action: *breakage.* **3** indicating a state or relationship: *bondage.* **4** indicating a house or place: *orphanage.* **5** indicating a charge or fee: *postage.* **6** indicating a rate: *dosage.* [from OF, from LL *-āticum* belonging to]
aged Ⓣ ('eɪdʒɪd) *adj* **1a** advanced in years; old. **1b** (*as collective n;* preceded by *the*): *the aged.* **2** of, connected with, or characteristic of old age. **3** (eɪdʒd). (*postpositive*) having the age of: *a woman aged twenty.*
ageing Ⓣ *or* **aging** ('eɪdʒɪŋ) *n* **1** the process of growing old or developing the appearance of old age. ◆ *adj* **2** becoming or appearing older: *an ageing car.* **3** giving the appearance of elderliness: *that dress is really ageing.*

THESAURUS

after *adv* **13, 14** = **following,** afterwards, behind, below, later, subsequently, succeeding, thereafter
Antonyms *adv* before, earlier, in advance, in front, previously, prior to, sooner
aftereffect *n* = **consequence,** delayed response, hangover (*inf.*), repercussion, spin-off
aftermath *n* **1** = **effects,** aftereffects, consequences, end, end result, outcome, results, sequel, upshot, wake
afterwards *adv* = **later,** after, after that, at a later date *or* time, following that, subsequently, then, thereafter
again *adv* **1** = **once more,** afresh, anew, another time **4** = **on the other hand,** on the contrary **5** = **also,** besides, furthermore, in addition, moreover
against *prep* **1** = **opposed to,** anti, averse to, contra (*inf.*), counter, hostile to, in defiance of, in opposition to, in the face of, opposing, resisting, versus **2, 3** = **beside,** abutting, close up to, facing, fronting, in contact with, on, opposite to, touching, upon **8** = **in preparation for,** in anticipation of, in expectation of, in provision for
agape *adj* **1** = **wide open,** gaping, wide, yawning **2** = **amazed,** agog, astonished, astounded, awe-stricken, dumbfounded, eager, expectant, flabbergasted, gobsmacked (*Brit. sl.*), spellbound, surprised, thunderstruck
age *n* **1, 2** = **time,** date, day(s), duration, epoch, era, generation, lifetime, period, span **4** = **old age,** advancing years, decline (*of life*), majority, maturity, senescence, senility, seniority **8** *often plural Informal* = **a long time** *or* **while,** aeons, a month of Sundays (*inf.*), an age *or* eternity, centuries, coon's age (*US sl.*), donkey's years (*inf.*), for ever (*inf.*), years, yonks (*inf.*) ◆ *vb* **11** = **grow old,** decline, deteriorate, mature, mellow, ripen
Antonyms *n* a flash, a jiffy (*inf.*), a little while, a moment, an instant, a second, a short time, a split second, no time at all, the twinkling *or* wink of an eye, two shakes of a lamb's tail (*inf.*)
aged *adj* **1, 2** = **old,** age-old, ancient, antiquated, antique, cobwebby, elderly, getting on, grey, hoary, past it (*inf.*), senescent, superannuated
Antonyms *adj* adolescent, boyish *or* girlish, childish, immature, juvenile, young, youthful
ageing *n* **1** = **growing old,** decay, decline, degeneration, deterioration, maturation, senescence, senility ◆ *adj* **2** = **growing old** *or* **older,** declining, deteriorating, getting on *or* past it (*inf.*), in decline, long in the tooth, maturing, mellowing, senescent, senile

ageism *or* **agism** ('eɪdʒɪzəm) *n* discrimination against people on the grounds of age.
▸'**ageist** *or* '**agist** *adj*

ageless ❶ ('eɪdʒlɪs) *adj* **1** apparently never growing old. **2** timeless; eternal: *an ageless quality.*

agency ❶ ('eɪdʒənsɪ) *n, pl* **agencies. 1** a business or other organization providing a specific service: *an employment agency.* **2** the place where an agent conducts business. **3** the business, duties, or functions of an agent. **4** action, power, or operation: *the agency of fate.* [C17: from Med. L *agentia,* from L *agere* to do]

agenda ❶ (ə'dʒendə) *n* **1** (*functioning as sing*) Also: **agendum.** a schedule or list of items to be attended to. **2** (*functioning as pl*) Also: **agendas, agendums.** matters to be attended to, as at a meeting. [C17: L, lit.: things to be done, from *agere* to do]

agent ❶ ('eɪdʒənt) *n* **1** a person who acts on behalf of another person, business, government, etc. **2** a person or thing that acts or has the power to act. **3** a substance or organism that exerts some force or effect: *a chemical agent.* **4** the means by which something occurs or is achieved. **5** a person representing a business concern, esp. a travelling salesman. [C15: from L *agent-,* noun use of the present participle of *agere* to do]
▸**agential** (eɪ'dʒenʃəl) *adj*

agent-general *n, pl* **agents-general.** a representative in London of a Canadian province or an Australian state.

Agent Orange *n* a highly poisonous herbicide used as a spray for defoliation and crop destruction, esp. by US forces during the Vietnam War. [C20: named after the identifying colour stripe on its container]

agent provocateur *French.* (aʒɑ̃ prɔvɔkatœr) *n, pl* **agents provocateurs** (aʒɑ̃ prɔvɔkatœr). a secret agent employed to provoke suspected persons to commit illegal acts and so be discredited or liable to punishment.

age of consent *n* **1** the age at which a person, esp. a female, is considered legally competent to consent to marriage or sexual intercourse. **2** the age at which a person can enter into a legally binding contract.

Age of Reason *n* (usually preceded by *the*) the 18th century in W Europe. See also **Enlightenment.**

age-old *or* **age-long** *adj* very old or of long duration; ancient.

ageratum (ˌædʒə'reɪtəm) *n* a tropical American plant with thick clusters of purplish-blue flowers. [C16: NL, via L from Gk *agēraton* that does not age, from A-[1] + *gērat-,* stem of *gēras* old age]

agglomerate *vb* (ə'glɒməˌreɪt), **agglomerates, agglomerating, agglomerated. 1** to form or be formed into a mass or cluster. ◆ *n* (ə'glɒmərɪt, -ˌreɪt). **2** a confused mass. **3** a volcanic rock consisting of angular fragments within a groundmass of lava. ◆ *adj* (ə'glɒmərɪt, -ˌreɪt). **4** formed into a mass. [C17: from L *agglomerāre,* from *glomerāre* to wind into a ball]
▸**agˌglomer'ation** *n* ▸**ag'glomerative** *adj*

agglutinate (ə'gluːtɪˌneɪt) *vb* **agglutinates, agglutinating, agglutinated. 1** to adhere or cause to adhere, as with glue. **2** *Linguistics.* to combine or be combined by agglutination. **3** (*tr*) to cause (bacteria, red blood cells, etc.) to clump together. [C16: from L *agglūtināre* to glue to, from *gluten* glue]
▸**ag'glutinable** *adj* ▸**ag'glutinant** *adj*

agglutination (əˌgluːtɪ'neɪʃən) *n* **1** the act or process of agglutinating. **2** a united mass of parts. **3** *Chem.* the formation of clumps of particles in a suspension. **4** *Immunol.* the formation of a mass of particles, such as red blood cells, by the action of antibodies. **5** *Linguistics.* the building up of words from component morphemes in such a way that these undergo little or no change of form or meaning.

aggrandize ❶ *or* **aggrandise** (ə'grændaɪz) *vb* **aggrandizes, aggrandizing, aggrandized** *or* **aggrandises, aggrandising, aggrandised.** (*tr*) **1** to increase the power, wealth, prestige, scope, etc., of. **2** to cause (something) to seem greater. [C17: from OF *aggrandiss-,* stem of *aggrandir,* from L *grandis* GRAND]
▸**aggrandizement** *or* **aggrandisement** (ə'grændɪzmənt) *n* ▸'**aggranˌdizer** *or* '**aggranˌdiser** *n*

aggravate ❶ ('ægrəˌveɪt) *vb* **aggravates, aggravating, aggravated.** (*tr*) **1** to make (a disease, situation, problem, etc.) worse. **2** *Inf.* to annoy. [C16: from L *aggravāre* to make heavier, from *gravis* heavy]
▸'**aggraˌvating** *adj* ▸ˌ**aggra'vation** *n*

aggregate ❶ *adj* ('ægrɪgɪt). **1** formed of separate units collected into a whole. **2** (of fruits and flowers) composed of a dense cluster of florets. ◆ *n* ('ægrɪgɪt, -ˌgeɪt). **3** a sum or assemblage of many separate units. **4** *Geol.* a rock, such as granite, consisting of a mixture of minerals. **5** the sand and stone mixed with cement and water to make concrete. **6 in the aggregate.** taken as a whole. ◆ *vb* ('ægrɪˌgeɪt). **7** to combine or be combined into a body, etc. **8** (*tr*) to amount to (a number). [C16: from L *aggregāre* to add to a flock or herd, from *grex* flock]
▸ˌ**aggre'gation** *n* ▸**aggregative** ('ægrɪˌgeɪtɪv) *adj*

aggress ❶ (ə'gres) *vb* (*intr*) to attack first or begin a quarrel. [C16: from Med. L *aggressāre,* from L *aggredī* to attack]
▸**aggressor** (ə'gresə) *n*

aggression ❶ (ə'greʃən) *n* **1** an attack or harmful action, esp. an unprovoked attack by one country against another. **2** any offensive activity, practice, etc. **3** *Psychol.* a hostile or destructive mental attitude. [C17: from L *aggression-,* from *aggredī* to attack]

aggressive ❶ (ə'gresɪv) *adj* **1** quarrelsome or belligerent. **2** assertive; vigorous.
▸**ag'gressively** *adv* ▸**ag'gressiveness** *n*

aggrieve (ə'griːv) *vb* **aggrieves, aggrieving, aggrieved.** (*tr*) **1** (*often impersonal or passive*) to grieve; distress; afflict. **2** to injure unjustly, esp. by infringing a person's legal rights. [C14 *agreven,* via OF from L *aggravāre* to AGGRAVATE]
▸**ag'grieved** *adj* ▸**aggrievedly** (ə'griːvɪdlɪ) *adv*

aggro ('ægrəʊ) *n Brit. sl.* aggressive behaviour. [C20: from AGGRAVATION]

aghast ❶ (ə'gɑːst) *adj* (*postpositive*) overcome with amazement or horror. [C13 *agast,* from OE *gæstan* to frighten]

agile ❶ ('ædʒaɪl) *adj* **1** quick in movement; nimble. **2** mentally quick or acute. [C15: from L *agilis,* from *agere* to do, act]
▸'**agilely** *adv* ▸**agility** (ə'dʒɪlɪtɪ) *n*

agin (ə'gɪn) *prep Inf. or dialect.* against. [C19: from obs. *again* AGAINST]

Agincourt ('ædʒɪnˌkɔːt; *French* aʒɛ̃kur) *n* a battle fought in 1415 near the village of Azincourt, N France: a decisive victory for English longbowmen under Henry V over French forces vastly superior in number.

agio ('ædʒɪəʊ) *n, pl* **agios. a** the difference between the nominal and actual values of a currency. **b** the charge payable for conversion of the less valuable currency. [C17: from It., lit.: ease]

agitate ❶ ('ædʒɪˌteɪt) *vb* **agitates, agitating, agitated. 1** (*tr*) to excite, disturb, or trouble (a person, the mind or feelings). **2** (*tr*) to shake, stir, or disturb. **3** (*intr; often foll. by for or against*) to attempt to stir up public

THESAURUS

ageless *adj* **1, 2 = eternal,** abiding, deathless, enduring, immortal, perennial, timeless, unchanging, unfading
Antonyms *adj* ephemeral, fleeting, momentary, passing, temporary, transitory

agency *n* **1 = business,** bureau, department, office, organization **4 = medium,** action, activity, auspices, efficiency, force, influence, instrumentality, intercession, intervention, means, mechanism, mediation, operation, power, work

agenda *n* **1 = list,** calendar, diary, plan, programme, schedule, timetable

agent *n* **1, 2, 5 = representative,** advocate, deputy, emissary, envoy, factor, go-between, negotiator, rep (*inf.*), substitute, surrogate **1, 2 = worker,** actor, author, doer, executor, mover, officer, operative, operator, performer **4 = force,** agency, cause, instrument, means, power, vehicle

aggrandize *vb* **1, 2 = enlarge,** advance, amplify, augment, dignify, elevate, ennoble, enrich, exaggerate, exalt, inflate, intensify, magnify, promote, widen

aggravate *vb* **1 = make worse,** add insult to injury, exacerbate, exaggerate, fan the flames of, heighten, increase, inflame, intensify, magnify, worsen **2** *Informal* **= annoy,** be on one's back (*sl.*), bother, exasperate, gall, get on one's nerves (*inf.*), get up one's nose (*inf.*), hassle (*inf.*), irk, irritate, nark (*Brit., Austral., & NZ sl.*), needle (*inf.*), nettle, pester, provoke, rub (someone) up the wrong way (*inf.*), tease, vex
Antonyms *vb* ≠ **make worse:** alleviate, assuage, calm, diminish, ease, improve, lessen, mitigate, smooth ≠ **annoy:** assuage, calm, pacify, please

aggravating *adj* **1 = worsening,** exacerbating, exaggerating, heightening, increasing, inflaming, intensifying, magnifying **2** *Informal* **= annoying,** exasperating, galling, irksome, irritating, provoking, teasing, vexing

aggravation *n* **1 = worsening,** exacerbation, exaggeration, heightening, increase, inflaming, intensification, magnification **2** *Informal* **= annoyance,** exasperation, gall, grief (*inf.*), hassle (*inf.*), irksomeness, irritation, provocation, teasing, vexation

aggregate *adj* **1 = total,** accumulated, added, assembled, collected, collective, combined, composite, corporate, cumulative, mixed ◆ *n* **2 = total,** accumulation, agglomeration, amount, assemblage, body, bulk, collection, combination, heap, lump, mass, mixture, pile, sum, whole ◆ *vb* **7 = combine,** accumulate, amass, assemble, collect, heap, mix, pile

aggregation *n* **7 = collection,** accumulation, agglomeration, assemblage, body, bulk, combination, heap, lump, mass, mixture, pile

aggression *n* **1 = attack,** assault, encroachment, injury, invasion, offence, offensive, onslaught, raid **2 = hostility,** aggressiveness, antagonism, belligerence, destructiveness, pugnacity

aggressive *adj* **1 = hostile,** belligerent, destructive, offensive, pugnacious, quarrelsome **2 = forceful,** assertive, bold, dynamic, energetic, enterprising, in-your-face (*sl.*), militant, pushing, pushy (*inf.*), vigorous, zealous
Antonyms *adj* ≠ **hostile:** friendly, peaceful ≠ **forceful:** mild, quiet, retiring, submissive

aggressor *n* **= attacker,** assailant, assaulter, invader

aggrieved *adj* **1, 2 = hurt,** afflicted, distressed, disturbed, harmed, ill-used, injured, peeved (*inf.*), saddened, unhappy, woeful, wronged

aghast *adj* **= horrified,** afraid, amazed, appalled, astonished, astounded, awestruck, confounded, frightened, horror-struck, shocked, startled, stunned, thunder-struck

agile *adj* **1 = nimble,** active, brisk, limber, lissom(e), lithe, lively, quick, sprightly, spry, supple, swift **2 = acute,** alert, bright (*inf.*), clever, lively, nimble, prompt, quick, quick-witted, sharp
Antonyms *adj* ≠ **nimble:** awkward, clumsy, heavy, lumbering, ponderous, slow, slow-moving, stiff, ungainly, unsupple

agility *n* **1 = nimbleness,** activity, briskness, litheness, liveliness, quickness, sprightliness, spryness, suppleness, swiftness **2 = acuteness,** alertness, cleverness, liveliness, promptitude, promptness, quickness, quick-wittedness, sharpness

agitate *vb* **1, 3 = upset,** alarm, arouse, confuse, disconcert, disquiet, distract, disturb, excite, faze, ferment, fluster, incite, inflame, perturb, rouse, ruffle, stimulate, trouble, unnerve, work up, worry **2 = stir,** beat, churn, convulse, disturb, rock, rouse, shake, toss

opinion for or against something. [C16: from L *agitātus*, from *agitāre* to set into motion, from *agere* to act]
▸**'agi,tated** *adj* ▸**'agi,tatedly** *adv* ▸**,agi'tation** *n*
agitato (,ædʒɪ'tɑːtəʊ) *adj, adv Music.* (to be performed) in an agitated manner.
agitator ❶ ('ædʒɪ,teɪtə) *n* **1** a person who agitates for or against a cause, etc. **2** a device for mixing or shaking.
agitprop ('ædʒɪt,prɒp) *n* **a** any promotion, as in the arts, of political propaganda, esp. of a Communist nature. **b** (*as modifier*): *agitprop theatre.* [C20: short for Russian *Agitpropbyuro*]
agleam (ə'gliːm) *adj* (*postpositive*) glowing; gleaming.
aglet ('æglɪt) *or* **aiglet** *n* **1** a metal sheath or tag at the end of a shoelace, ribbon, etc. **2** a variant spelling of **aiguillette.** [C15: from OF *aiguillette* a small needle]
agley (ə'gleɪ, ə'gliː, ə'glaɪ) *or* **aglee** (ə'gliː) *adv, adj Scot.* awry; askew. [from *gley* squint]
aglitter (ə'glɪtə) *adj* (*postpositive*) sparkling; glittering.
aglow (ə'gləʊ) *adj* (*postpositive*) glowing.
aglu *or* **agloo** ('ægluː) *n Canad.* a breathing hole made in ice by a seal. [C19: from Eskimo]
AGM *abbrev. for* annual general meeting.
agnail ('æg,neɪl) *n* another name for **hangnail.**
agnate ('ægneɪt) *adj* **1** related by descent from a common male ancestor. **2** related in any way. ◆ *n* **3** a male or female descendant by male links from a common male ancestor. [C16: from L *agnātus* born in addition, from *agnāsci*, from *ad-* in addition + *gnāsci* to be born]
agnostic (æg'nɒstɪk) *n* **1** a person who holds that knowledge of a Supreme Being, ultimate cause, etc., is impossible. Cf. **atheist, theist. 2** a person who claims, with respect to any particular question, that the answer cannot be known with certainty. ◆ *adj* **3** of or relating to agnostics. [C19: coined 1869 by T. H. Huxley from A-[1] + GNOSTIC]
▸**ag'nosti,cism** *n*
Agnus Dei ('ægnʊs 'deɪɪ) *n* **1** the figure of a lamb bearing a cross or banner, emblematic of Christ. **2** a chant beginning with these words or a translation of them, forming part of the Roman Catholic Mass. [L: Lamb of God]
ago (ə'gəʊ) *adv* in the past: *five years ago; long ago.* [C14 *ago*, from OE *āgān* to pass away]

> **USAGE NOTE** The use of *ago* with *since* (*it's ten years ago since he wrote the novel*) is redundant and should be avoided: *it is ten years since he wrote the novel.*

agog ❶ (ə'gɒg) *adj* (*postpositive*) eager or curious. [C15: ?from OF *en gogues* in merriments]
-agogue *or esp. US* **-agog** *n combining form.* indicating a person or thing that leads or incites to action: *demagogue.* [via LL from Gk *agōgos*, from *agein* to lead]
▸**-agogic** *adj combining form.* ▸**-agogy** *n combining form.*
agonic (ə'gɒnɪk) *adj* forming no angle. [C19: from Gk *agōnos*, from A-[1] + *gōnia* angle]
agonic line *n* an imaginary line on the surface of the earth connecting points of zero magnetic declination.
agonize ❶ *or* **agonise** ('ægə,naɪz) *vb* **agonizes, agonizing, agonized** *or* **agonises, agonising, agonised. 1** to suffer or cause to suffer agony. **2** (*intr*) to struggle; strive. [C16: via Med. L from Gk *agōnizesthai* to contend for a prize, from *agōn* contest]
▸**'ago,nizingly** *or* **'ago,nisingly** *adv*
agony ❶ ('ægənɪ) *n, pl* **agonies. 1** acute physical or mental pain; anguish. **2** the suffering or struggle preceding death. [C14: via LL from Gk *agōnia* struggle, from *agōn* contest]
agony aunt *n* (*sometimes cap.*) a person who replies to readers' letters in an agony column.
agony column *n* **1** a newspaper or magazine feature offering sympathetic advice to readers on their personal problems. **2** *Inf.* a newspaper or magazine column devoted to advertisements relating esp. to personal problems.
agora ('ægərə) *n, pl* **agorae** (-riː, -raɪ) *or* **agoras.** (*often cap.*) **a** the marketplace in Athens, used for popular meetings in ancient Greece. **b** the meeting itself. [from Gk, from *agorein* to gather]
agoraphobia (,ægərə'fəʊbɪə) *n* a pathological fear of being in public spaces.
▸**,agora'phobic** *adj, n*
agouti (ə'guːtɪ) *n, pl* **agoutis** *or* **agouties.** a rodent of Central and South America and the Caribbean. Agoutis are agile and long-legged, with hooflike claws, and are valued for their meat. [C18: via F & Sp. from Guarani]
AGR *abbrev. for* advanced gas-cooled reactor.
agrarian ❶ (ə'grɛərɪən) *adj* **1** of or relating to land or its cultivation. **2** of or relating to rural or agricultural matters. ◆ *n* **3** a person who favours the redistribution of landed property. [C16: from L *agrārius*, from *ager* field, land]
▸**a'grarian,ism** *n*
agree ❶ (ə'griː) *vb* **agrees, agreeing, agreed.** (*mainly intr*) **1** (often foll. by *with*) to be of the same opinion. **2** (*also tr;* when *intr*, often foll. by *to;* when *tr, takes a clause as object or an infinitive*) to give assent; consent. **3** (*also tr;* when *intr*, foll. by *on* or *about;* when *tr, may take a clause as object*) to come to terms (about). **4** (foll. by *with*) to be similar or consistent; harmonize. **5** (foll. by *with*) to be agreeable or suitable (to one's health, etc.). **6** (*tr; takes a clause as object*) to concede: *they agreed that the price was too high.* **7** *Grammar.* to undergo agreement. [C14: from OF *agreer*, from *a gre* at will or pleasure]
agreeable ❶ (ə'grɪəbᵊl) *adj* **1** pleasing; pleasant. **2** prepared to consent. **3** (foll. by *to* or *with*) in keeping. **4** (foll. by *to*) to one's liking.
▸**a'greeableness** *n* ▸**a'greeably** *adv*
agreed ❶ (ə'griːd) *adj* **1** determined by common consent: *the agreed price.* ◆ *sentence substitute.* **2** an expression of consent or agreement.
agreement ❶ (ə'griːmənt) *n* **1** the act of agreeing. **2** a settlement, esp. one that is legally enforceable. **3** a contract or document containing such a settlement. **4** the state of being of the same opinion. **5** the state of being similar or consistent. **6** *Grammar.* the determination of the inflectional form of one word by some grammatical feature, such as number or gender, of another word. [C14: from OF]
agribusiness ('ægrɪ,bɪznɪs) *n* the various businesses that process and distribute farm products. [C20: from AGRI(CULTURE) + BUSINESS]
agriculture ❶ ('ægrɪ,kʌltʃə) *n* the science or occupation of cultivating land and rearing crops and livestock; farming. [C17: from L *agricultūra*, from *ager* field, land + *cultūra* CULTURE]
▸**,agri'cultural** *adj* ▸**,agri'culturist** *or* **,agri'culturalist** *n*
agrimony ('ægrɪmənɪ) *n* **1** any of various plants of the rose family, which have compound leaves, long spikes of small yellow flowers, and bristly burlike fruits. **2** any of several other plants, such as hemp agrimony. [C15: via OF from L, from Gk *argemōnē* poppy]
agro- *combining form.* denoting fields, soil, or agriculture: *agrobiology.* [from Gk *agros* field]

THESAURUS

Antonyms *vb* ≠ **upset:** appease, assuage, calm, calm down, mollify, pacify, placate, quiet, quieten, soothe, still, tranquillize
agitated *adj* **1** = **upset,** alarmed, anxious, discomposed, disconcerted, disquieted, distracted, distressed, disturbed, edgy, excited, fazed, flustered, ill at ease, nervous, on edge, perturbed, rattled (*inf.*), ruffled, shaken, troubled, uneasy, unnerved, unsettled, worked up, worried
Antonyms *adj* at ease, calm, collected, composed, cool, relaxed, sedate, unexcited, unfazed (*inf.*), unperturbed, unruffled, untroubled
agitation *n* **1, 3** = **turmoil,** alarm, arousal, clamour, commotion, confusion, discomposure, disquiet, distraction, disturbance, excitement, ferment, flurry, fluster, incitement, lather (*inf.*), outcry, stimulation, tizzy, tizz *or* tiz-woz (*inf.*), trouble, tumult, upheaval, upset, worry **2** = **turbulence,** churning, convulsion, disturbance, rocking, shake, shaking, stir, stirring, tossing, upheaval
agitator *n* **1** = **troublemaker,** agent provocateur, demagogue, firebrand, inciter, instigator, rabble-rouser, revolutionary, stirrer (*inf.*)
agog *adj* = **eager,** avid, curious, enthralled, enthusiastic, excited, expectant, impatient, in suspense, keen
Antonyms *adj* apathetic, incurious, indifferent, unconcerned, uninterested
agonize *vb* **1, 2** = **suffer,** be distressed, be in agony, be in anguish, go through the mill, labour, strain, strive, struggle, worry, writhe
agonized *adj* **1** = **suffering,** anguished, broken-hearted, distressed, grief-stricken, racked, tormented, tortured, wounded, wretched
agonizing *adj* **1** = **painful,** bitter, distressing, excruciating, grievous, gut-wrenching, harrowing, heartbreaking, heart-rending, hellish, torturous
agony *n* **1, 2** = **suffering,** affliction, anguish, distress, misery, pain, pangs, throes, torment, torture, woe
agrarian *adj* **1, 2** = **agricultural,** agrestic, country, farming, land, rural, rustic
Antonyms *adj* industrial, urban
agree *vb* **1, 2** = **concur,** accede, acquiesce, admit, allow, assent, be of the same mind, be of the same opinion, comply, concede, consent, engage, grant, permit, see eye to eye, settle, shake hands **4** = **get on (together),** accord, answer, chime, coincide, conform, correspond, fit, harmonize, match, square, suit, tally
Antonyms *vb* ≠ **concur:** contradict, deny, differ, disagree, dispute, dissent, rebut, refute, retract
agreeable *adj* **1** = **pleasant,** acceptable, congenial, delightful, enjoyable, gratifying, likable *or* likeable, pleasing, pleasurable, satisfying, to one's liking, to one's taste **2** = **consenting,** acquiescent, agreeing, amenable, approving, complying, concurring, in accord, onside (*inf.*), responsive, sympathetic, well-disposed, willing
Antonyms *adj* ≠ **pleasant:** disagreeable, displeasing, horrid, offensive, unlikable *or* unlikeable, unpleasant
agreed *adj* **1** = **settled,** arranged, definite, established, firm, fixed, given, guaranteed, predetermined, stipulated ◆ *sentence substitute* **2** = **all right,** done, it's a bargain *or* deal, O.K. *or* okay (*inf.*), settled, you're on (*inf.*)
Antonyms *adj* ≠ **settled:** indefinite, negotiable, to be arranged *or* decided, up in the air, variable
agreement *n* **1, 4** = **concurrence,** agreeing, assent, compliance, concord, consent, harmony, union, unison **2** = **contract,** arrangement, bargain, compact, covenant, deal (*inf.*), pact, settlement, treaty, understanding **5** = **correspondence,** accord, accordance, affinity, agreeing, analogy, compatibility, conformity, congruity, consistency, similarity, suitableness
Antonyms *n* ≠ **concurrence:** altercation, argument, clash, conflict, discord, dispute, dissent, division, falling-out, quarrel, row, squabble, strife, tiff, wrangle ≠ **correspondence:** difference, discrepancy, disparity, dissimilarity, diversity, incompatibility, incongruity
agricultural *adj* = **farming,** agrarian, agrestic, agronomic, agronomical, country, rural, rustic
agriculture *n* = **farming,** agronomics, agronomy, cultivation, culture, husbandry, tillage

agrobiology (ˌæɡrəʊbaɪˈɒlədʒɪ) *n* the science of plant growth and nutrition in relation to agriculture.

agroforestry (ˌæɡrəʊˈfɒrɪstrɪ) *n* a method of farming integrating herbaceous and tree crops.

agronomics (ˌæɡrəˈnɒmɪks) *n* (*functioning as sing*) the branch of economics dealing with the distribution, management, and productivity of land.
▸ˌ**agroˈnomic** *adj*

agronomy (əˈɡrɒnəmɪ) *n* the science of cultivation of land, soil management, and crop production.
▸**aˈgronomist** *n*

agrostemma (ˌæɡrəʊˈstɛmə) *n* any cultivated variety of corncockle. [NL, from Gk *agros* field + *stemma* wreath]

aground Ⓣ (əˈɡraʊnd) *adv, adj* (*postpositive*) on or onto the ground or bottom, as in shallow water.

agterskot (ˈaxtəˌskɒt) *n* (in South Africa) the final payment to a farmer for crops. Cf. **voorskot.** [C20: Afrikaans *agter* after + *skot* shot, payment]

ague (ˈeɪɡjuː) *n* **1** malarial fever with successive stages of fever and chills. **2** a fit of shivering. [C14: from OF (*fievre*) *ague* acute fever; see ACUTE]
▸ˈ**aguish** *adj*

ah (ɑː) *interj* an exclamation expressing pleasure, pain, sympathy, etc., according to the intonation of the speaker.

AH (indicating years in the Muslim system of dating, numbered from the Hegira (622 A.D.)) *abbrev. for* anno Hegirae. [L]

aha (ɑːˈhɑː) *interj* an exclamation expressing triumph, surprise, etc., according to the intonation of the speaker.

ahead Ⓣ (əˈhɛd) *adj* **1** (*postpositive*) in front; in advance. ◆ *adv* **2** at or in the front; before. **3** forwards: *go straight ahead.* **4 ahead of. 4a** in front of; at a further advanced position than. **4b** *Stock Exchange.* in anticipation of: *the share price rose ahead of the annual figures.* **5 be ahead.** *Inf.* to have an advantage; be winning. **6 get ahead.** to attain success.

ahem (əˈhɛm) *interj* a clearing of the throat, used to attract attention, express doubt, etc.

ahimsa (ɑːˈhɪmsɑː) *n* (in Hindu, Buddhist, and Jainist philosophy) the law of reverence for, and nonviolence to, every form of life. [Sansk., from *a* without + *himsā* injury]

ahoy (əˈhɔɪ) *interj Naut.* a hail used to call a ship or to attract attention.

Ahriman (ˈɑːrɪmən) *n Zoroastrianism.* the supreme evil spirit and diabolical opponent of Ormazd.

Ahura Mazda (əˈhʊərə ˈmæzdə) *n Zoroastrianism.* another name for **Ormazd.**

ai (ˈɑːɪ) *n, pl* **ais.** another name for **three-toed sloth** (see **sloth** (sense 1)). [C17: from Port., from Tupi]

AI *abbrev. for:* **1** Amnesty International. **2** artificial insemination. **3** artificial intelligence.

aid Ⓣ (eɪd) *vb* **1** to give support to (someone to do something); help or assist. **2** (*tr*) to assist financially. ◆ *n* **3** assistance; help; support. **4** a person, device, etc., that helps or assists. **5** *Mountaineering.* a device such as a piton when used as a direct help in the ascent. **6** (in medieval Europe) a feudal payment made to the king or any lord by his vassals on certain occasions such as the knighting of an eldest son. [C15: via OF *aidier* from L *adjūtāre,* from *juvāre* to help]
▸ˈ**aider** *n*

Aid *or* **-aid** *n combining form.* denoting a charitable organization or function that raises money for a cause: *Band Aid; Ferryaid.*

AID *abbrev. for:* **1** *US.* Agency for International Development. **2** artificial insemination (by) donor: former name for donor insemination (DI).

aide Ⓣ (eɪd) *n* **1** an assistant. **2** short for **aide-de-camp.**

aide-de-camp *or* **aid-de-camp** (ˈeɪd də ˈkɒŋ) *n, pl* **aides-de-camp** *or* **aids-de-camp.** a military officer serving as personal assistant to a senior. Abbrev.: **ADC.** [C17: from F: camp assistant]

aide-mémoire (ˈeɪdmɛmˈwɑː) *n, pl* **aides-mémoire** (ˈeɪdzmɛmˈwɑː). **1** a note serving as a reminder. **2** a summarized diplomatic communication. [F, from *aider* to help + *mémoire* memory]

AIDS *or* **Aids** (eɪdz) *n acronym for* acquired immune (*or* immuno-) deficiency syndrome: a condition, caused by a virus, in which the body loses its ability to resist infection. AIDS is transmitted by sexual intercourse, through infected blood and blood products, and through the placenta.

AIDS-related complex *n* See **ARC.**

AIF (formerly) *abbrev. for* Australian Imperial Force.

aiglet (ˈeɪɡlɪt) *n* a variant of **aglet.**

aigrette *or* **aigret** (ˈeɪɡrɛt) *n* **1** a long plume worn on hats or as a headdress, esp. one of long egret feathers. **2** an ornament in imitation of a plume of feathers. [C17: from F; see EGRET]

aiguille (eɪˈɡwiːl) *n* **1** a rock mass or peak shaped like a needle. **2** an instrument for boring holes in rocks or masonry. [C19: F, lit.: needle]

aiguillette (ˌeɪɡwɪˈlɛt) *n* **1** an ornamentation worn by certain military officers, consisting of cords with metal tips. **2** a variant of **aglet.** [C19: F; see AGLET]

AIH *abbrev. for* artificial insemination (by) husband.

aikido (aɪˈkiːdəʊ) *n* a Japanese system of self-defence employing similar principles to judo, but including blows from the hands and feet. [from Japanese, from *ai* to join, receive + *ki* spirit, force + *do* way]

ail Ⓣ (eɪl) *vb* **1** (*tr*) to trouble; afflict. **2** (*intr*) to feel unwell. [OE *eglan,* from *egle* painful]

ailanthus (eɪˈlænθəs) *n, pl* **ailanthuses.** an E Asian deciduous tree having pinnate leaves, small greenish flowers, and winged fruits. Also called: **tree of heaven.** [C19: NL, from native name in the Moluccas in the Indian and Pacific Oceans]

aileron (ˈeɪlərɒn) *n* a flap hinged to the trailing edge of an aircraft wing to provide lateral control. [C20: from F, dim. of *aile* wing]

ailing Ⓣ (ˈeɪlɪŋ) *adj* unwell or unsuccessful, esp. over a long period.

ailment Ⓣ (ˈeɪlmənt) *n* a slight but often persistent illness.

aim Ⓣ (eɪm) *vb* **1** to point (a weapon, missile, etc.) or direct (a blow) at a particular person or object. **2** (*tr*) to direct (satire, criticism, etc.) at a person, object, etc. **3** (*intr;* foll. by *at* or an infinitive) to propose or intend. **4** (*intr;* often foll. by *at* or *for*) to direct one's efforts or strive (towards). ◆ *n* **5** the action of directing something at an object. **6** the direction in which something is pointed: *to take aim.* **7** the object at which something is aimed. **8** intention; purpose. [C14: via OF *aesmer* from L *aestimāre* to ESTIMATE]

AIM *abbrev. for* Alternative Investment Market.

aimless Ⓣ (ˈeɪmlɪs) *adj* having no purpose or direction.
▸ˈ**aimlessly** *adv* ▸ˈ**aimlessness** *n*

ain't (eɪnt) *Not standard. contraction of* am not, is not, are not, have not, *or* has not: *I ain't seen it.*

Ainu (ˈaɪnuː) *n* **1** (*pl* **Ainus** *or* **Ainu**) a member of the aboriginal people of Japan. **2** the language of this people, sometimes tentatively associated with Altaic, still spoken in parts of Hokkaido. [Ainu: man]

air Ⓣ (ɛə) *n* **1** the mixture of gases that forms the earth's atmosphere. It consists chiefly of nitrogen, oxygen, argon, and carbon dioxide. **2** the space above and around the earth; sky. Related adj: **aerial. 3** breeze; slight wind. **4** public expression; utterance. **5** a distinctive quality: *an air of mystery.* **6** a person's distinctive appearance, manner, or bearing. **7** *Music.* a simple tune for either vocal or instrumental performance. **8** transportation in aircraft (esp. in **by air**). **9** an archaic word for **breath** (senses 1–3). **10 in the air. 10a** in circulation; current. **10b** unsettled. **11 into thin air.** leaving no trace behind. **12 on** (*or* **off**) **the air.** (not) in the act of broadcasting or (not) being broadcast on radio or television. **13 take the air.** to go out of doors, as for a short walk. **14 up in the air. 14a** uncertain. **14b** *Inf.* agitated or excited. **15** (*modifier*) *Astrol.* of or relating to a group of three signs of the zodiac, Gemini, Libra, and Aquarius. ◆ *vb* **16** to expose or be exposed to the air so as to cool or freshen. **17** to expose or be exposed to warm or heated air so as to dry: *to air linen.* **18** (*tr*) to make known publicly: *to air one's opinions.* **19** (*intr*) (of a television or radio programme) to be broadcast. ◆ See also **airs.** [C13: via OF & L from Gk *aēr* the lower atmosphere]

air bag *n* a safety device in a car, consisting of a bag that inflates automatically in an accident and prevents the passengers from being thrown forwards.

air base *n* a centre from which military aircraft operate.

air bladder *n* **1** an air-filled sac, lying above the alimentary canal in bony fishes, that regulates buoyancy at different depths by a variation in the pressure of the air. **2** any air-filled sac, such as one in seaweeds.

THESAURUS

aground *adv* = **beached,** ashore, foundered, grounded, high and dry, on the rocks, stranded, stuck

ahead *adv* **2, 3** = **in front,** along, at an advantage, at the head, before, forwards, in advance, in the foreground, in the lead, in the vanguard, leading, on, onwards, to the fore, winning

aid *vb* **1, 2** = **help,** abet, assist, befriend, encourage, favour, give a leg up (*inf.*), promote, relieve, second, serve, subsidize, succour, support, sustain ◆ *n* **3** = **help,** assistance, benefit, encouragement, favour, promotion, relief, service, succour, support **4** = **helper,** abettor, adjutant, aide, aide-de-camp, assistant, second, supporter
Antonyms *vb* ≠ **help:** detract from, harm, hinder, hurt, impede, obstruct, oppose, thwart ◆ *n* ≠ **help:** hindrance

aide *n* **1** = **assistant,** adjutant, attendant, coadjutor (*rare*), deputy, helper, helpmate, henchman, right-hand man, second, supporter

ail *vb* **1** = **trouble,** afflict, annoy, be the matter with, bother, distress, irritate, pain, sicken, upset, worry **2** = **be ill,** be indisposed, be *or* feel off colour, be sick, be unwell, feel unwell

ailing *adj* = **ill,** debilitated, diseased, feeble, indisposed, infirm, invalid, off colour, poorly, sick, sickly, suffering, under the weather (*inf.*), unsound, unwell, weak

ailment *n* = **illness,** affliction, complaint, disease, disorder, infirmity, lurgy (*inf.*), malady, sickness

aim *vb* **1, 3, 4** = **intend,** aspire, attempt, design, direct, draw a bead (on), endeavour, level, mean, plan, point, propose, purpose, resolve, seek, set one's sights on, sight, strive, take aim (at), train, try, want, wish ◆ *n* **7, 8** = **intention,** ambition, aspiration, course, design, desire, direction, end, goal, Holy Grail (*inf.*), intent, mark, object, objective, plan, purpose, scheme, target, wish

aimless *adj* = **purposeless,** chance, directionless, erratic, frivolous, goalless, haphazard, pointless, random, stray, undirected, unguided, unpredictable, vagrant, wayward
Antonyms *adj* decided, deliberate, determined, firm, fixed, positive, purposeful, resolute, resolved, settled, single-minded

air *n* **2** = **atmosphere,** heavens, sky **3** = **wind,** blast, breath, breeze, draught, puff, waft, whiff, zephyr **4** = **circulation,** display, dissemination, exposure, expression, publicity, utterance, vent, ventilation **5** = **manner,** ambience, appearance, atmosphere, aura, bearing, character, demeanour, effect, feeling, flavour, impression, look, mood, quality, style, tone, vibes (*sl.*) **7** = **tune,** aria, lay, melody, song ◆ *vb* **16** = **ventilate,** aerate, expose, freshen **18** = **publicize,** circulate, communicate, declare, disclose, display, disseminate, divulge, exhibit, expose, express,

airborne ⓣ (ˈɛəˌbɔːn) *adj* **1** conveyed by or through the air. **2** (of aircraft) flying; in the air.
air brake *n* **1** a brake operated by compressed air, esp. in heavy vehicles and trains. **2** an articulated flap or small parachute for reducing the speed of an aircraft.
airbrick (ˈɛəˌbrɪk) *n Chiefly Brit.* a brick with holes in it, put into the wall of a building for ventilation.
airbrush (ˈɛəˌbrʌʃ) *n* **1** an atomizer for spraying paint or varnish by means of compressed air. ◆ *vb (tr)* **2** to paint or varnish (something) by using an airbrush. **3** to improve the image of (a person or thing) by concealing defects beneath a bland exterior: *an airbrushed version of the government's record.*
air chief marshal *n* a senior officer of the Royal Air Force and certain other air forces, of equivalent rank to admiral in the Royal Navy.
air cleaner *n* a filter that prevents dust and other particles from entering the air intake of an internal-combustion engine. Also called: **air filter.**
air commodore *n* a senior officer of the Royal Air Force and certain other air forces, of equivalent rank to brigadier in the Army.
air conditioning *n* a system or process for controlling the temperature and sometimes the humidity of the air in a house, etc.
▸**ˈair-conˌdition** *vb (tr)* ▸**air conditioner** *n*
air-cool *vb (tr)* to cool (an engine) by a flow of air. Cf. **water-cool.**
aircraft ⓣ (ˈɛəˌkrɑːft) *n, pl* **aircraft.** any machine capable of flying by means of buoyancy or aerodynamic forces, such as a glider, helicopter, or aeroplane.
aircraft carrier *n* a warship with an extensive flat deck for the launch of aircraft.
aircraftman (ˈɛəˌkrɑːftmən) *n, pl* **aircraftmen.** a serviceman of the most junior rank in the Royal Air Force.
▸**ˈaircraftˌwoman** *fem n*
air curtain *n* an air stream across a doorway to exclude draughts, etc.
air cushion *n* **1** an inflatable cushion. **2** the pocket of air that supports a hovercraft.
airdrop (ˈɛəˌdrɒp) *n* **1** a delivery of supplies, troops, etc., from an aircraft by parachute. ◆ *vb* **airdrops, airdropping, airdropped. 2** *(tr)* to deliver (supplies, etc.) by an airdrop.
Airedale (ˈɛəˌdeɪl) *n* a large rough-haired tan-coloured breed of terrier with a black saddle-shaped patch covering most of the back. Also called: **Airedale terrier.** [C19: from district in Yorkshire]
air engine *n* **1** an engine that uses the expansion of heated air to drive a piston. **2** a small engine that uses compressed air to drive a piston.
airfield ⓣ (ˈɛəˌfiːld) *n* a landing and taking-off area for aircraft.
air filter *n* another name for **air cleaner.**
airfoil (ˈɛəˌfɔɪl) *n* the US and Canad. name for **aerofoil.**
air force *n* **a** the branch of a nation's armed services primarily responsible for air warfare. **b** *(as modifier): an air-force base.*
airframe (ˈɛəˌfreɪm) *n* the body of an aircraft, excluding its engines.
air guitar *n* an imaginary guitar played while miming to rock music.
air gun *n* a gun discharged by means of compressed air.
airhead (ˈɛəˌhɛd) *n Sl.* a stupid or simple-minded person; idiot. [C20: from AIR + HEAD]
air hole *n* **1** a hole that allows the passage of air, esp. for ventilation. **2** a section of open water in a frozen surface.
air hostess *n* a stewardess on an airliner.
airily ⓣ (ˈɛərɪlɪ) *adv* **1** in a jaunty or high-spirited manner. **2** in a light or delicate manner.
airiness ⓣ (ˈɛərɪnɪs) *n* **1** the quality or condition of being fresh, light, or breezy. **2** gaiety.
airing ⓣ (ˈɛərɪŋ) *n* **1a** exposure to air or warmth, as for drying or ventilation. **1b** *(as modifier): airing cupboard.* **2** an excursion in the open air. **3** exposure to public debate.
airless ⓣ (ˈɛəlɪs) *adj* **1** lacking fresh air; stuffy or sultry. **2** devoid of air.
▸**ˈairlessness** *n*
air letter *n* another name for **aerogram.**
airlift (ˈɛəˌlɪft) *n* **1** the transportation by air of passengers, troops, cargo, etc., esp. when other routes are blocked. ◆ *vb* **2** *(tr)* to transport by an airlift.
airline (ˈɛəˌlaɪn) *n* **1a** a system or organization that provides scheduled flights for passengers or cargo. **1b** *(as modifier): an airline pilot.* **2** a hose or tube carrying air under pressure.
airliner (ˈɛəˌlaɪnə) *n* a large passenger aircraft.
airlock (ˈɛəˌlɒk) *n* **1** a bubble in a pipe causing an obstruction. **2** an airtight chamber with regulated air pressure used to gain access to a space that has air under pressure.
airmail (ˈɛəˌmeɪl) *n* **1** the system of conveying mail by aircraft. **2** mail conveyed by aircraft. ◆ *adj* **3** of or for airmail.
airman (ˈɛəmən) *n, pl* **airmen.** a man who serves in his country's air force.
air marshal *n* **1** a senior Royal Air Force officer of equivalent rank to a vice admiral in the Royal Navy. **2** a Royal Australian Air Force officer of the highest rank. **3** a Royal New Zealand Air Force officer of the highest rank when chief of defence forces.
air mass *n* a large body of air having characteristics of temperature, moisture, and pressure that are approximately uniform horizontally.
Air Miles *pl n* points awarded by certain companies to purchasers of flight tickets and some other products that may be used to pay for other flights.
air miss *n* a situation in which two aircraft pass very close to one another in the air; near miss.
airplane (ˈɛəˌpleɪn) *n* the US and Canad. name for **aeroplane.**
airplay (ˈɛəˌpleɪ) *n* (of recorded music) radio exposure.
air pocket *n* a localized region of low air density or a descending air current, causing an aircraft to suffer an abrupt decrease in height.
airport ⓣ (ˈɛəˌpɔːt) *n* a landing and taking-off area for civil aircraft, usually with runways and aircraft maintenance and passenger facilities.
air power *n* the strength of a nation's air force.
air pump *n* a device for pumping air into or out of something.
air raid *n* **a** an attack by hostile aircraft or missiles. **b** *(as modifier): an air-raid shelter.*
air-raid warden *n* a member of a civil defence organization responsible for enforcing regulations, etc., during an air attack.
air rifle *n* a rifle discharged by compressed air.
airs ⓣ (ɛəz) *pl n* affected manners intended to impress others: *to give oneself airs; put on airs.*
air sac *n* any of the membranous air-filled extensions of the lungs of birds, which increase the efficiency of respiration.
airscrew (ˈɛəˌskruː) *n Brit.* an aircraft propeller.
air-sea rescue *n* an air rescue at sea.
air shaft *n* a shaft for ventilation, esp. in a mine or tunnel.
airship (ˈɛəˌʃɪp) *n* a lighter-than-air self-propelled craft. Also called: **dirigible.**
airshow (ˈɛəˌʃəʊ) *n* an occasion when an air base is open to the public and a flying display and, usually, static exhibitions are held.
airsick (ˈɛəˌsɪk) *adj* nauseated from travelling in an aircraft.
airside (ˈɛəˌsaɪd) *n* the part of an airport nearest the aircraft, the boundary of which is the security check, customs, passport control, etc. Cf. **landside** (sense 1).
airspace (ˈɛəˌspeɪs) *n* the atmosphere above the earth or part of the earth, esp. the atmosphere above a particular country.
airspeed (ˈɛəˌspiːd) *n* the speed of an aircraft relative to the air in which it moves.
airstrip (ˈɛəˌstrɪp) *n* a cleared area for the landing and taking-off of aircraft; runway. Also called: **landing strip.**
air terminal *n Brit.* a building in a city from which air passengers are taken to an airport.
airtight (ˈɛəˌtaɪt) *adj* **1** not permitting the passage of air. **2** having no weak points; rigid or unassailable.
air-to-air *adj* operating between aircraft in flight.
air-traffic control *n* an organization that determines the altitude, speed, and direction at which planes fly in a given area, giving instructions to pilots by radio.
▸**air-traffic controller** *n*
air vice-marshal *n* **1** a senior Royal Air Force officer of equivalent rank to a rear admiral in the Royal Navy. **2** a Royal Australian Air Force officer of the second highest rank. **3** a Royal New Zealand Air Force officer of the highest rank.
airwaves (ˈɛəˌweɪvz) *pl n Inf.* radio waves used in radio and television broadcasting.
airway (ˈɛəˌweɪ) *n* **1** an air route, esp. one that is fully equipped with navigational aids, etc. **2** a passage for ventilation, esp. in a mine. **3** the passage of air from the nose or mouth to the lungs. **4** *Med.* a tubelike device inserted via the throat to keep open the airway of an unconscious patient.
air waybill *n* a document made out by the consigner of goods by air freight giving details of the goods and the name of the consignee.
airworthy (ˈɛəˌwɜːðɪ) *adj* (of an aircraft) safe to fly.
airy ⓣ (ˈɛərɪ) *adj* **airier, airiest. 1** abounding in fresh air. **2** spacious or uncluttered. **3** nonchalant. **4** visionary; fanciful: *airy promises.* **5** of or relating to air. **6** weightless and insubstantial. **7** light and graceful in movement. **8** high up in the air.

THESAURUS

give vent to, make known, make public, proclaim, reveal, tell, utter, ventilate, voice
airborne *adj* **1, 2 = flying**, floating, gliding, hovering, in flight, in the air, on the wing, soaring, volitant, wind-borne
aircraft *n* = **plane**, aeroplane, airplane, flying machine, kite *(Brit. sl.)*
airfield *n* = **airport**, aerodrome, airdrome *(US)*, air station, airstrip, landing strip
airily *adv* **1 = light-heartedly**, animatedly, blithely, breezily, buoyantly, gaily, happily, high-spiritedly, jauntily
airiness *n* **1 = freshness**, breeziness, draughtiness, gustiness, lightness, openness, windiness **2 = light-heartedness**, animation, blitheness, breeziness, buoyancy, gaiety, happiness, high spirits, jauntiness, lightness of heart
airing *n* **1 = ventilation**, aeration, drying, freshening **3 = exposure**, circulation, display, dissemination, expression, publicity, utterance, vent, ventilation
airless *adj* **1, 2 = stuffy**, breathless, close, heavy, muggy, oppressive, stale, stifling, suffocating, sultry, unventilated
Antonyms *adj* airy, blowy, breezy, draughty, fresh, gusty, light, open, spacious, well- ventilated
airport *n* = **airfield**, aerodrome, airdrome *(US)*
airs *pl n* = **affectation**, affectedness, arrogance, haughtiness, hauteur, pomposity, pretensions, superciliousness, swank *(inf.)*
airy *adj* **1 = well-ventilated**, blowy, breezy, draughty, fresh, gusty, light, lofty, open, spacious, uncluttered, windy **3 = light-hearted**, animated, blithe, buoyant, cheerful, cheery, chirpy *(inf.)*, debonair, frolicsome, gay, genial, happy, high-spirited, jaunty, light, lively, merry, nonchalant, sprightly, upbeat *(inf.)* **4, 6 = insubstantial**, aerial, delicate, ethereal, fanciful, flimsy, illusory, imaginary, immaterial, in-

aisle Ⓣ (aɪl) *n* **1** a passageway separating seating areas in a theatre, church, etc. **2** a lateral division in a church flanking the nave or chancel. [C14 *ele* (later *aile, aisle,* through confusion with *isle*), via OF from L *āla* wing]
▸**aisled** *adj*

ait (eɪt) *or* **eyot** *n Dialect.* an islet, esp. in a river. [OE *ȳgett* small island, from *ieg* ISLAND]

aitch (eɪtʃ) *n* the letter *h* or the sound represented by it. [C16: a phonetic spelling]

aitchbone ('eɪtʃˌbəʊn) *n* **1** the rump bone in cattle. **2** a cut of beef from or including the rump bone. [C15 *hach-boon,* altered from earlier *nache-bone* (*a nache* mistaken for *an ache, an aitch*); *nache* buttock, via OF from LL *natica,* from L *natis* buttock]

ajar Ⓣ (ə'dʒɑː) *adj* (*postpositive*), *adv* (esp. of a door) slightly open. [C18: altered form of obs. *on char,* lit.: on the turn; from OE *cierran* to turn]

AK-47 *n Trademark.* a type of Kalashnikov.

a.k.a. *or* **AKA** *abbrev. for* also known as.

akene (ə'kiːn) *n* a variant spelling of **achene.**

akimbo (ə'kɪmbəʊ) *adj, adv* (**with**) **arms akimbo.** with hands on hips and elbows out. [C15 *in kenebowe,* lit.: in keen bow, that is, in a sharp curve]

akin Ⓣ (ə'kɪn) *adj* (*postpositive*) **1** related by blood. **2** (often foll. by *to*) having similar characteristics, properties, etc.

Akkadian *or* **Accadian** (ə'kædɪən) *n* **1** a member of an ancient Semitic people who lived in Mesopotamia in the third millennium B.C. **2** the extinct language of this people.

Al *the chemical symbol for* aluminium.

-al[1] *suffix forming adjectives.* of; related to: *functional; sectional; tonal.* [from L *-ālis*]

-al[2] *suffix forming nouns.* the act or process of doing what is indicated by the verb stem: *renewal.* [via OF *-aille, -ail,* from L *-ālia,* neuter pl used as substantive, from *-ālis* -AL[1]]

-al[3] *suffix forming nouns.* **1** (*not used systematically*) indicating any aldehyde: *ethanal.* **2** indicating a pharmaceutical product: *phenobarbital.* [shortened from ALDEHYDE]

ala ('eɪlə) *n, pl* **alae** ('eɪliː). **1** *Zool.* a wing or flat winglike process or structure. **2** *Bot.* a winglike part, such as one of the wings of a sycamore seed. [C18: from L *āla* a wing]

à la (ɑː lɑː) *prep* **1** in the manner or style of. **2** as prepared in (a particular place) or by or for (a particular person). [C17: from F, short for *à la mode de* in the style of]

alabaster ('ælәˌbɑːstə) *n* **1** a fine-grained usually white, opaque, or translucent variety of gypsum. **2** a variety of hard semitranslucent calcite. ◆ *adj* **3** of or resembling alabaster. [C14: from OF *alabastre,* from L *alabaster,* from Gk *alabastros*]
▸ˌ**ala'bastrine** *adj*

à la carte (ɑː lɑː 'kɑːt) *adj, adv* (of a menu) having dishes listed separately and individually priced. Cf. **table d'hôte.** [C19: from F, lit.: according to the card]

alack (ə'læk) *or* **alackaday** (ə'lækəˌdeɪ) *interj* an archaic or poetic word for **alas.** [C15: from *a* ah! + *lack* loss, LACK]

alacrity Ⓣ (ə'lækrɪtɪ) *n* liveliness or briskness. [C15: from L, from *alacer* lively]

à la mode Ⓣ (ɑː lɑː 'məʊd) *adj* **1** fashionable in style, design, etc. **2** (of meats) braised with vegetables in wine. [C17: from F: according to the fashion]

Al-Anon ('ælәˌnɒn) *n* an association for the families and friends of alcoholics to give mutual support.

alar ('eɪlə) *adj* relating to, resembling, or having wings or alae. [C19: from L *āla* a wing]

Alar ('eɪlɑː) *n* a chemical sprayed on cultivated apple trees in certain countries to increase fruit set; daminozide.

alarm Ⓣ (ə'lɑːm) *vb* (*tr*) **1** to fill with apprehension, anxiety, or fear. **2** to warn about danger; alert. **3** to fit or activate a burglar alarm on (a house, car, etc.). ◆ *n* **4** fear or terror aroused by awareness of danger. **5** apprehension or uneasiness. **6** a noise, signal, etc., warning of danger. **7** any device that transmits such a warning: *a burglar alarm.* **8a** the device in an alarm clock that triggers off the bell or buzzer. **8b** short for **alarm clock. 9** *Arch.* a call to arms. [C14: from OF *alarme,* from OIt. *all'arme* to arms; see ARM[2]]
▸**a'larming** *adj*

alarm clock *n* a clock with a mechanism that sounds at a set time: used esp. for waking a person up.

alarmist (ə'lɑːmɪst) *n* **1** a person who alarms or attempts to alarm others needlessly. **2** a person who is easily alarmed. ◆ *adj* **3** characteristic of an alarmist.

alarum (ə'lærəm, -'lɑːr-) *n* **1** *Arch.* an alarm, esp. a call to arms. **2** (used as a stage direction, esp. in Elizabethan drama) a loud disturbance or conflict (esp. in **alarums and excursions**). [C15: var. of ALARM]

alas (ə'læs) *sentence connector.* **1** unfortunately; regrettably: *there were, alas, none left.* ◆ *interj* **2** *Arch.* an exclamation of grief or alarm. [C13: from OF *ha las!* oh wretched!; *las* from L *lassus* weary]

alate ('eɪleɪt) *adj* having wings or winglike extensions. [C17: from L, from *āla* wing]

alb (ælb) *n Christianity.* a long white linen vestment with sleeves worn by priests and others. [OE *albe,* from Med. L *alba* (*vestis*) white (clothing)]

albacore ('ælbəˌkɔː) *n* a tunny occurring mainly in warm regions of the Atlantic and Pacific. It has very long pectoral fins and is a valued food fish. [C16: from Port., from Ar.]

Albanian (æl'beɪnɪən) *n* **1** the official language of Albania. **2** a native, citizen, or inhabitant of Albania. ◆ *adj* **3** of or relating to Albania, its people, or their language.

albatross ('ælbəˌtrɒs) *n* **1** a large bird of cool southern oceans, with long narrow wings and a powerful gliding flight. See also **wandering albatross. 2** a constant and inescapable burden or handicap. **3** *Golf.* a score of three strokes under par for a hole. [C17: from Port. *alcatraz* pelican, from Ar., from *al* the + *ghattās* white-tailed sea eagle; infl. by L *albus* white: C20 in sense 2, from Coleridge's poem *The Rime of the Ancient Mariner* (1798)]

albedo (æl'biːdəʊ) *n* the ratio of the intensity of light reflected from an object, such as a planet, to that of the light it receives from the sun. [C19: from Church L: whiteness, from L *albus* white]

albeit Ⓣ (ɔːl'biːɪt) *conj* even though. [C14 *al be it,* that is, although it be (that)]

albert ('ælbət) *n* a kind of watch chain usually attached to a waistcoat.

Albertan (æl'bɜːtən) *adj* **1** of or denoting Alberta, a province of W Canada. ◆ *n* **2** a native or inhabitant of Alberta.

albescent (æl'bes(ə)nt) *adj* shading into or becoming white. [C19: from L *albēscere,* from *albus* white]
▸**al'bescence** *n*

Albigenses (ˌælbɪ'dʒensiːz) *pl n* members of a Manichean sect that flourished in S France from the 11th to the 13th century.

albino (æl'biːnəʊ) *n, pl* **albinos. 1** a person with congenital absence of pigmentation in the skin, eyes, and hair. **2** any animal or plant that is deficient in pigment. [C18: via Port. & Sp. from L *albus* white]
▸**albinism** ('ælbɪˌnɪzəm) *n* ▸**albinotic** (ˌælbɪ'nɒtɪk) *adj*

Albion ('ælbɪən) *n Arch. or poetic.* Britain or England. [C13: from L, of Celtic origin]

albite ('ælbaɪt) *n* a white, bluish-green, or reddish-grey feldspar mineral used in the manufacture of glass and as a gemstone. [C19: from L *albus* white]

album Ⓣ ('ælbəm) *n* **1** a book or binder consisting of blank pages, for keeping photographs, stamps, autographs, etc. **2** one or more long-playing CDs, cassettes, or records released as a single item. **3** a booklike holder containing sleeves for gramophone records. **4** *Chiefly Brit.* an anthology. [C17: from L: blank tablet, from *albus* white]

albumen ('ælbjʊmɪn) *n* **1** the white of an egg; the nutritive substance that surrounds the yolk. **2** a variant spelling of **albumin.** [C16: from L: white of an egg, from *albus* white]

albumin *or* **albumen** ('ælbjʊmɪn) *n* any of a group of simple water-soluble proteins that are found in blood plasma, egg white, etc. [C19: from ALBUMEN + -IN]
▸**al'buminous** *adj*

albuminoid (æl'bjuːmɪˌnɔɪd) *adj* **1** resembling albumin. ◆ *n* **2** another name for **scleroprotein.**

albuminuria (ælˌbjuːmɪ'njʊərɪə) *n* the presence of albumin in the urine. Also called: **proteinuria.**

alburnum (æl'bɜːnəm) *n* a former name for **sapwood.** [C17: from L: sapwood, from *albus* white]

Alcaic (æl'keɪɪk) *adj* **1** of a metre used by the Greek poet Alcaeus (7th

THESAURUS

corporeal, light, vaporous, visionary, weightless, wispy
Antonyms *adj* ≠ **well-ventilated:** airless, close, heavy, muggy, oppressive, stale, stifling, stuffy, suffocating, unventilated ≠ **light-hearted:** cheerless, dismal, gloomy, glum, melancholy, miserable, morose, sad ≠ **insubstantial:** concrete, corporeal, material, real, realistic, substantial, tangible

aisle *n* **1** = **passageway,** alley, corridor, gangway, lane, passage, path

ajar *adj* = **open,** agape, gaping, partly open, unclosed

akin *adj* **1, 2 akin to** = **similar to,** affiliated with, allied with, analogous to, cognate with, comparable to, congenial with, connected with *or* to, consanguineous with, corresponding to, kin to, like, of a piece with, parallel to, related to

alacrity *n* = **eagerness,** alertness, avidity, briskness, cheerfulness, dispatch, enthusiasm, gaiety, hilarity, joyousness, liveliness, promptness, quickness, readiness, speed, sprightliness, willingness, zeal
Antonyms *n* apathy, dullness, inertia, lethargy, reluctance, slowness, sluggishness, unconcern, unwillingness

à la mode *adj* **1** = **fashionable,** all the go (*inf.*), all the rage (*inf.*), chic, in (*inf.*), in fashion, in vogue, latest, modish, popular, stylish, the latest rage (*inf.*), with it (*inf.*)

alarm *vb* **1** = **frighten,** daunt, dismay, distress, give (someone) a turn (*inf.*), make (someone's) hair stand on end, panic, put the wind up (someone) (*inf.*), scare, startle, terrify, unnerve ◆ *n* **4, 5** = **fear,** anxiety, apprehension, consternation, dismay, distress, fright, nervousness, panic, scare, terror, trepidation, unease, uneasiness **6** = **danger signal,** alarm bell, alert, bell, distress signal, hooter, siren, tocsin, warning
Antonyms *vb* ≠ **frighten:** assure, calm, comfort, reassure, relieve, soothe ◆ *n* ≠ **fear:** calm, calmness, composure, sang-froid, serenity

alarmed *adj* **1** = **frightened,** anxious, apprehensive, daunted, dismayed, distressed, disturbed, fearful, in a panic, nervous, scared, shocked, startled, terrified, troubled, uneasy, unnerved
Antonyms *adj* assured, calm, composed, fearless, serene, undaunted, untroubled

alarming *adj* **1** = **frightening,** daunting, dismaying, distressing, disturbing, dreadful, scaring, shocking, startling, terrifying, unnerving

albeit *conj* = **even though,** although, even if, notwithstanding that, tho' (*US. or poetic*), though

album *n* **1** = **book,** collection, scrapbook **2** = **record,** cassette, CD, LP century B.C.), consisting of a strophe of four lines each with four feet. ◆ *n* 2 (*usually pl*) verse written in the Alcaic form.

alcalde (æl'kældɪ) *or* **alcade** (æl'keɪd) *n* (in Spain and Spanish America) the mayor or chief magistrate in a town. [C17: from Sp., from Ar. *al-qāḍī* the judge]

alcazar (ˌælkə'zɑː; *Spanish* al'kaθar) *n* any of various palaces or fortresses built in Spain by the Moors. [C17: from Sp., from Ar. *al-qasr* the castle]

alchemist ('ælkəmɪst) *n* a person who practises alchemy.

alchemize *or* **alchemise** ('ælkəˌmaɪz) *vb* **alchemizes, alchemizing, alchemized** *or* **alchemises, alchemising, alchemised.** (*tr*) to alter (an element, metal, etc.) by alchemy.

alchemy Ⓣ ('ælkəmɪ) *n, pl* **alchemies. 1** the pseudoscientific predecessor of chemistry that sought a method of transmuting base metals into gold, and an elixir to prolong life indefinitely. **2** a power like that of alchemy: *her beauty had a potent alchemy.* [C14 *alkamye*, via OF from Med. L, from Ar., from *al* the + *kīmiyā'* transmutation, from LGk *khēmeia* the art of transmutation]
▸**alchemic** (æl'kɛmɪk) *or* **al'chemical** *adj*

alcheringa (ˌæltʃə'rɪŋgə) *n* another name for **Dreamtime.** [from Abor., lit.: dream time]

ALCM *abbrev. for* air-launched cruise missile: a type of cruise missile that can be launched from an aircraft.

alcohol Ⓣ ('ælkəˌhɒl) *n* **1** a colourless flammable liquid, the active principle of intoxicating drinks, produced by the fermentation of sugars. Formula: C_2H_5OH. Also called: **ethanol, ethyl alcohol. 2** a drink or drinks containing this substance. **3** *Chem.* any one of a class of organic compounds that contain one or more hydroxyl groups bound to carbon atoms that are not part of an aromatic ring. Cf. **phenol** (sense 2). [C16: via NL from Med. L, from Ar. *al-kuhl* powdered antimony]

alcohol-free *adj* **1** (of beer or wine) containing only a trace of alcohol. Cf. **low-alcohol. 2** (of a period of time) during which no alcoholic drink is consumed: *there should be one or two alcohol-free days per week.*

alcoholic Ⓣ (ˌælkə'hɒlɪk) *n* **1** a person affected by alcoholism. ◆ *adj* **2** of, relating to, containing, or resulting from alcohol.

Alcoholics Anonymous *n* an association of alcoholics who try, esp. by mutual assistance, to overcome alcoholism.

alcoholism ('ælkəhɒˌlɪzəm) *n* a condition in which dependence on alcohol harms a person's health, family life, etc.

alcoholize *or* **alcoholise** ('ælkəhɒˌlaɪz) *vb* **alcoholizes, alcoholizing, alcoholized** *or* **alcoholises, alcoholising, alcoholised.** (*tr*) to turn into alcoholic drink, as by fermenting or mixing with alcohol.
▸ˌ**alcoˌholi'zation** *or* ˌ**alcoˌholi'sation** *n*

alcopop ('ælkəʊˌpɒp) *n Inf.* an alcoholic drink that tastes like a soft drink. [C20: from ALCO(HOL) + POP[1] (sense 11)]

Alcoran *or* **Alkoran** (ˌælkɒ'rɑːn) *n* another name for the **Koran.**
▸ˌ**Alco'ranic** *or* ˌ**Alko'ranic** *adj*

alcove Ⓣ ('ælkəʊv) *n* **1** a recess or niche in the wall of a room, as for a bed, books, etc. **2** any recessed usually vaulted area, as in a garden wall. **3** any covered or secluded spot. [C17: from F, from Sp. *alcoba*, from Ar. *al-qubbah* the vault]

aldehyde ('ældɪˌhaɪd) *n* **1** any organic compound containing the group -CHO. Aldehydes are oxidized to carboxylic acids. **2** (*modifier*) consisting of, containing, or concerned with the group -CHO. [C19: from NL *al*(*cohol*) *dehyd*(*rogenātum*) dehydrogenated alcohol]
▸**aldehydic** (ˌældə'hɪdɪk) *adj*

al dente (ˌæl 'dɛntɪ) *adj* (of pasta) still firm after cooking. [It., lit: to the tooth]

alder ('ɔːldə) *n* **1** a shrub or tree of the birch family, having toothed leaves and conelike fruits. The wood is used for bridges, etc., because it resists underwater rot. **2** any of several similar trees or shrubs. [OE *alor*]

alderman ('ɔːldəmən) *n, pl* **aldermen. 1** (in England and Wales until 1974) one of the senior members of a local council, elected by other councillors. **2** (in the US, Canada, Australia, etc.) a member of the governing body of a municipality. **3** *History.* a variant spelling of **ealdorman.** [OE *aldormann*, from *ealdor* chief (comp. of *eald* OLD) + *mann* MAN]
▸**aldermanic** (ˌɔːldə'mænɪk) *adj*

Alderney ('ɔːldənɪ) *n* any of a breed of dairy cattle originating from Alderney, one of the Channel Islands.

Aldis lamp ('ɔːldɪs) *n* a portable signalling lamp. [C20: after its inventor A.C.W. *Aldis*]

aldrin ('ɔːldrɪn) *n* a poisonous crystalline solid, mostly $C_{12}H_8Cl_6$, used as an insecticide. [C20: after K. *Alder* (1902–58), G chemist]

ale (eɪl) *n* **1** a beer fermented in an open vessel using yeasts that rise to the top of the brew. Compare **beer, lager. 2** (formerly) an alcoholic drink made by fermenting a cereal, esp. barley, but differing from beer by being unflavoured by hops. **3** *Chiefly Brit.* another word for **beer.** [OE *alu, ealu*]

aleatory ('eɪlɪətərɪ) *or* **aleatoric** (ˌeɪlɪə'tɒrɪk) *adj* **1** dependent on chance. **2** (esp. of a musical composition) involving elements chosen at random by the performer. [C17: from L, from *āleātor* gambler, from *ālea* game of chance]

alee (ə'liː) *adv, adj* (*postpositive*) *Naut.* on or towards the lee: *with the helm alee.*

alehouse ('eɪlˌhaʊs) *n* **1** *Arch.* a place where ale was sold; tavern. **2** *Inf.* a pub.

alembic (ə'lɛmbɪk) *n* **1** an obsolete type of retort used for distillation. **2** anything that distils or purifies. [C14: from Med. L, from Ar. *al-anbīq* the still, from Gk *ambix* cup]

aleph ('ɑːlɪf; *Hebrew* 'alɛf) *n* the first letter in the Hebrew alphabet. [Heb.: ox]

aleph-null *or* **aleph-zero** *n* the smallest infinite cardinal number; the cardinal number of the set of positive integers.

alert Ⓣ (ə'lɜːt) *adj* (*usually postpositive*) **1** vigilantly attentive: *alert to the problems.* **2** brisk, nimble, or lively. ◆ *n* **3** an alarm or warning. **4** the period during which such a warning remains in effect. **5 on the alert. 5a** on guard against danger, attack, etc. **5b** watchful; ready. ◆ *vb* (*tr*) **6** to warn or signal (troops, police, etc.) to prepare for action. **7** to warn of danger, an attack, etc. [C17: from It. *all'erta* on the watch, from *erta* lookout post]
▸**a'lertly** *adv* ▸**a'lertness** *n*

aleurone (ə'lʊərən) *or* **aleuron** (ə'lʊərɒn) *n* a protein that occurs in the form of storage granules in plant cells, esp. in seeds such as maize. [C19: from Gk *aleuron* flour]

Aleut (æ'luːt) *n* **1** a member of a people inhabiting the Aleutian Islands and SW Alaska, related to the Eskimos. **2** the language of this people, related to Eskimo. [from Russian *aleút*, prob. of native origin]
▸**Aleutian** (ə'luːʃən) *n, adj*

A level *n Brit.* **1a** the advanced level of a subject taken for the General Certificate of Education. **1b** (*as modifier*): *A-level maths.* **2** a pass in a subject at A level: *he has two A levels.*

alewife ('eɪlˌwaɪf) *n, pl* **alewives.** A North American fish similar to the herring. [C19: ?from F *alose* shad]

Alexander technique *n* a technique for developing awareness of one's posture and movement in order to improve it. [C20: named after Frederick Matthias *Alexander* (d. 1955), Australian actor who originated it]

Alexandrine (ˌælɪg'zændraɪn) *n* **1** a line of verse having six iambic feet, usually with a caesura after the third foot. ◆ *adj* **2** of or written in Alexandrines. [C16: from F, from *Alexandre*, 15th-cent. poem in this metre]

alexandrite (ˌælɪg'zændraɪt) *n* a green variety of chrysoberyl used as a gemstone.

alexia (ə'lɛksɪə) *n* a disorder of the central nervous system characterized by impaired ability to read. [C19: from NL, from A-[1] + Gk *lexis* speech]

alfalfa (æl'fælfə) *n* a leguminous plant of Europe and Asia, widely cultivated for forage. Also called: **lucerne.** [C19: from Sp., from Ar. *al-fasfasah*]

alfresco (æl'frɛskəʊ) *adj, adv* in the open air. [C18: from It.: in the cool]

alg. *abbrev. for* algebra or algebraic.

algae ('ældʒiː) *pl n, sing* **alga** ('ælgə). unicellular or multicellular organisms formerly classified as plants, occurring in water or moist ground, that have chlorophyll but lack true stems, roots, and leaves. [C16: from L, pl of *alga* seaweed, from ?]
▸**algal** ('ælgəl) *or* **algoid** ('ælgɔɪd) *adj*

algebra ('ældʒɪbrə) *n* **1** a branch of mathematics in which arithmetical operations and relationships are generalized by using symbols to represent numbers. **2** any abstract calculus, a formal language in which functions and operations can be defined and their properties studied. [C14: from Med. L, from Ar. *al-jabr* the bone-setting, mathematical reduction]
▸**algebraic** (ˌældʒɪ'breɪɪk) *or* ˌ**alge'braical** *adj* ▸**algebraist** (ˌældʒɪ'breɪɪst) *n*

Algerian (æl'dʒɪərɪən) *adj* **1** of or denoting Algeria, a republic in NW Africa, or its inhabitants, their customs, etc. ◆ *n* **2** a native or inhabitant of Algeria.

-algia *n combining form.* denoting pain in the part specified: *neuralgia; odontalgia.* [from Gk *algos* pain]
▸**-algic** *adj combining form.*

THESAURUS

alchemy *n* **1 = magic,** sorcery, witchcraft, wizardry

alcohol *n* **1 = ethanol,** ethyl alcohol **2 = drink,** booze, Dutch courage (*inf.*), firewater, grog (*inf., chiefly Austral. & NZ*), hooch *or* hootch (*inf., chiefly US & Canad.*), intoxicant, John Barleycorn, juice (*inf.*), liquor, spirits, strong drink, the bottle (*inf.*), the hard stuff (*inf.*)

alcoholic *n* **1 = drunkard,** bibber, boozer (*inf.*), dipsomaniac, drinker, drunk, hard drinker, inebriate, soak (*sl.*), sot, sponge (*inf.*), tippler, toper, tosspot (*inf.*), wino (*inf.*) ◆ *adj* **2 = intoxicating,** brewed, distilled, fermented, hard, inebriant, inebriating, spirituous, strong, vinous

alcove *n* **1 = recess,** bay, bower, compartment, corner, cubbyhole, cubicle, niche, nook

alert *adj* **1 = watchful,** active, agile, attentive, awake, bright-eyed and bushy-tailed (*inf.*), careful, circumspect, heedful, keeping a weather eye on, lively, observant, on guard, on one's toes, on the ball (*inf.*), on the lookout, on the watch, perceptive, quick, ready, spirited, vigilant, wary, wide-awake ◆ *n* **3 = warning,** alarm, signal, siren ◆ *vb* **7 = warn,** alarm, forewarn, inform, notify, signal
Antonyms *adj* ≠ **watchful:** careless, heedless, inactive, languid, lethargic, listless, oblivious, slow, unaware, unconcerned, unwary ◆ *n* ≠ **warning:** all clear ◆ *vb* ≠ **warn:** lull

alertness *n* **1, 2 = watchfulness,** activeness, agility, attentiveness, briskness, carefulness, circumspection, heedfulness, liveliness, nimbleness, perceptiveness, promptitude, quickness, readiness, spiritedness, sprightliness, vigilance, wariness

algid ('ældʒɪd) *adj Med.* chilly or cold. [C17: from L *algidus*, from *algēre* to be cold]
▸**al'gidity** *n*

alginate ('ældʒɪˌneɪt) *n* a salt or ester of alginic acid.

alginic acid (æl'dʒɪnɪk) *n* a white or yellowish powdery substance having hydrophilic properties. Extracted from kelp, it is used mainly in the food and textile industries.

Algol ('ælgɒl) *n* a computer-programming language designed for mathematical and scientific purposes. [C20: *alg(orithmic) o(riented) l(anguage)*]

algolagnia (ˌælgə'lægnɪə) *n* sexual pleasure got from suffering or inflicting pain. [ML, from Gk *algos* pain + *lagneiā* lust]

Algonquian (æl'gɒŋkɪən, -kwɪ-) *or* **Algonkian** *n* **1** a widespread family of North American Indian languages. **2** (*pl* **Algonquians** *or* **Algonquian**) a member of any of the North American Indian peoples that speak any of these languages. ◆ *adj* **3** denoting or relating to this linguistic family or its speakers.

Algonquin (æl'gɒŋkɪn, -kwɪn) *or* **Algonkin** (æl'gɒŋkɪn) *n* **1** (*pl* **Algonquins, Algonquin** *or* **Algonkins, Algonkin**) a member of a North American Indian people formerly living along the St Lawrence and Ottawa Rivers in Canada. **2** the language of this people, a dialect of Ojibwa. ◆ *n, adj* **3** a variant of **Algonquian.** [C17: from Canad. F., earlier written as *Algoumequin;* perhaps rel. to Micmac *algoomaking* at the fish-spearing place]

algorism ('ælgəˌrɪzəm) *n* **1** the Arabic or decimal system of counting. **2** the skill of computation. **3** an algorithm. [C13: from OF, from Med. L, from Ar., from the name of abu-Ja'far Mohammed ibn-Mūsa *al-Khuwārizmi*, 9th-cent. Persian mathematician]

algorithm ('ælgəˌrɪðəm) *n* **1** a logical arithmetical or computational procedure that if correctly applied ensures the solution of a problem. **2** *Logic, maths.* a recursive procedure whereby an infinite sequence of terms can be generated. ◆ Also called: **algorism.** [C17: changed from ALGORISM, infl. by Gk *arithmos* number]
▸ˌ**algo'rithmic** *adj*

Al Hijrah *or* **Al Hijra** (æl 'hɪdʒrə) *n* an annual Muslim festival marking the beginning of the Muslim year. It commemorates Mohammed's move from Mecca to Medina. See also **Hegira.** [from Ar. *hijrah* emigration or flight]

alias Ⓣ ('eɪlɪəs) *adv* **1** at another time or place known as or named: *Dylan, alias Zimmerman.* ◆ *n, pl* **aliases. 2** an assumed name. [C16: from L *aliās* (adv) otherwise, from *alius* other]

aliasing ('eɪlɪəsɪŋ) *n Radio & TV.* the error in a vision or sound signal arising from limitations in the system that generates or processes the signal.

alibi Ⓣ ('ælɪˌbaɪ) *n, pl* **alibis. 1** *Law.* **1a** a defence by an accused person that he was elsewhere at the time the crime was committed. **1b** the evidence given to prove this. **2** *Inf.* an excuse. ◆ *vb* **alibis, alibiing, alibied. 3** (*tr*) to provide with an alibi. [C18: from L *alibī* elsewhere, from *alius* other + *-bī* as in *ubī* where]

Alice band ('ælɪs) *n* an ornamental band worn across the front of the hair to hold it back from the face.

Alice-in-Wonderland *adj* fantastic; irrational. [C20: alluding to the absurdities of Wonderland in Lewis Carroll's book]

alicyclic (ˌælɪ'saɪklɪk, -'sɪk-) *adj* (of an organic compound) having essentially aliphatic properties, in spite of the presence of a ring of carbon atoms. [C19: from ALI(PHATIC) + CYCLIC]

alidade ('ælɪˌdeɪd) *or* **alidad** ('ælɪˌdæd) *n* **1** a surveying instrument used for drawing lines of sight on a distant object and taking angular measurements. **2** the upper rotatable part of a theodolite. [C15: from F, from Med. L, from Ar. *al-'idāda* the revolving radius of a circle]

alien Ⓣ ('eɪlɪən) *n* **1** a person owing allegiance to a country other than that in which he lives. **2** any being or thing foreign to its environment. **3** (in science fiction) a being from another world. ◆ *adj* **4** unnaturalized; foreign. **5** having foreign allegiance: *alien territory.* **6** unfamiliar: *an alien quality.* **7** (*postpositive;* foll. by *to*) repugnant or opposed (to): *war is alien to his philosophy.* **8** (in science fiction) of or from another world. [C14: from L *aliēnus* foreign, from *alius* other]

alienable ('eɪlɪənəbᵊl) *adj Law.* (of property) transferable to another owner.
▸ˌ**aliena'bility** *n*

alienate Ⓣ ('eɪlɪəˌneɪt) *vb* **alienates, alienating, alienated.** (*tr*) **1** to cause (a friend, etc.) to become unfriendly or hostile. **2** to turn away: *to alienate the affections of a person.* **3** *Law.* to transfer the ownership of (property, etc.) to another person.
▸ˌ**alien'ation** *n* ▸'**alienˌator** *n*

alienee (ˌeɪlɪə'niː) *n Law.* a person to whom a transfer of property is made.

alienist ('eɪlɪənɪst) *n US.* a psychiatrist who specializes in the legal aspects of mental illness.

alienor ('eɪlɪənə) *n Law.* a person who transfers property to another.

aliform ('ælɪˌfɔːm) *adj* wing-shaped. [C19: from NL *āliformis*, from L *āla* a wing]

alight[1] Ⓣ (ə'laɪt) *vb* **alights, alighting, alighted** *or* **alit.** (*intr*) **1** (usually foll. by *from*) to step out (of): *to alight from a taxi.* **2** to come to rest; land: *a thrush alighted on the wall.* [OE *ālīhtan*, from A-[2] + *līhtan* to make less heavy]

alight[2] Ⓣ (ə'laɪt) *adj* (*postpositive*), *adv* **1** burning; on fire. **2** illuminated. [OE, from *ālīhtan* to light up]

align Ⓣ (ə'laɪn) *vb* **1** to place or become placed in a line. **2** to bring (components or parts) into proper coordination or relation. **3** (*tr;* usually foll. by *with*) to bring (a person, country, etc.) into agreement with the policy, etc., of another. [C17: from OF, from *à ligne* into line]

alignment Ⓣ (ə'laɪnmənt) *n* **1** arrangement in a straight line. **2** the line or lines formed in this manner. **3** alliance with a party, cause, etc. **4** proper coordination or relation of components. **5** a ground plan of a railway, road, etc.

alike Ⓣ (ə'laɪk) *adj* (*postpositive*) **1** possessing the same or similar characteristics: *they all look alike.* ◆ *adv* **2** in the same or a similar manner or degree: *they walk alike.* [OE *gelīc*]

aliment ('ælɪmənt) *n* something that nourishes or sustains the body or mind. [C15: from L *alimentum* food, from *alere* to nourish]
▸ˌ**ali'mental** *adj*

alimentary Ⓣ (ˌælɪ'mentərɪ) *adj* **1** of or relating to nutrition. **2** providing sustenance or nourishment.

alimentary canal *n* the tubular passage extending from the mouth to the anus, through which food is passed and digested.

alimentation (ˌælɪmen'teɪʃən) *n* **1** nourishment. **2** sustenance; support.

alimony ('ælɪmənɪ) *n Law.* (formerly) an allowance paid under a court order by one spouse to another when they are separated but not divorced. See also **maintenance.** [C17: from L, from *alere* to nourish]

A-line ('eɪˌlaɪn) *adj* (of garments) flaring out slightly from the waist or shoulders.

aliphatic (ˌælɪ'fætɪk) *adj* (of an organic compound) not aromatic, esp. having an open chain structure. [C19: from Gk *aleiphat-*, *aleiphar* oil]

aliquant ('ælɪkwənt) *adj Maths.* of or signifying a quantity or number that is not an exact divisor of a given quantity or number: *5 is an aliquant part of 12.* [C17: from NL, from L *aliquantus* somewhat, a certain quantity of]

aliquot ('ælɪˌkwɒt) *adj Maths.* of or signifying an exact divisor of a quantity or number: *3 is an aliquot part of 12.* [C16: from L: several, a few]

A list *n* **a** the most socially desirable category. **b** (*as modifier*): *an A-list event.* ◆ Cf. **B list.**

alit (ə'lɪt) *vb* a rare past tense and past participle of **alight**[1].

aliterate (eɪ'lɪtərɪt) *n* **1** a person who is able to read but disinclined to do so. ◆ *adj* **2** of or relating to aliterates.

alive Ⓣ (ə'laɪv) *adj* (*postpositive*) **1** living; having life. **2** in existence; active: *they kept hope alive.* **3** (*immediately postpositive*) now living: *the happiest woman alive.* **4** full of life; lively. **5** (usually foll. by *with*) animated: *a face alive with emotion.* **6** (foll. by *to*) aware (of); sensitive (to). **7** (foll. by *with*) teeming (with): *the mattress was alive with fleas.* **8** *Electronics.* another word for **live**[2] (sense 10). [OE *on līfe* in LIFE]

THESAURUS

alias *adv* **1 = also known as,** also called, otherwise, otherwise known as ◆ *n* **2 = pseudonym,** assumed name, nom de guerre, nom de plume, pen name, stage name

alibi *n* **1, 2 = excuse,** defence, explanation, justification, plea, pretext, reason

alien *n* **1 = foreigner,** newcomer, outsider, stranger ◆ *adj* **4, 6, 7 = strange,** adverse, beyond one's ken, conflicting, contrary, estranged, exotic, foreign, inappropriate, incompatible, incongruous, not native, not naturalized, opposed, outlandish, remote, repugnant, separated, unfamiliar
Antonyms *n* ≠ **foreigner:** citizen, countryman, dweller, inhabitant, national, resident ◆ *adj* ≠ **strange:** affiliated, akin, alike, allied, analogous, cognate, connected, corresponding, kindred, like, parallel, related, similar

alienate *vb* **1, 2 = set against,** break off, disaffect, divert, divorce, estrange, make unfriendly, separate, turn away, withdraw **3** *Law* **= transfer,** abalienate, convey

alienation *n* **1, 2 = setting against,** breaking off, disaffection, diversion, divorce, estrangement, indifference, remoteness, rupture, separation, turning away, withdrawal **3** *Law* **= transfer,** abalienation, conveyance

alight[1] *vb* **1 = get off,** descend, disembark, dismount, get down **2 = land,** come down, come to rest, descend, light, perch, settle, touch down
Antonyms *vb* ≠ **land:** ascend, climb, float up, fly up, go up, lift off, mount, move up, rise, scale, soar, take off

alight[2] *adj* **1 = on fire,** ablaze, aflame, blazing, burning, fiery, flaming, flaring, ignited, lighted, lit **2 = lit up,** bright, brilliant, illuminated, shining

align *vb* **1 = line up,** arrange in line, coordinate, even, even up, make parallel, order, range, regulate, sequence, straighten **3 = ally,** affiliate, agree, associate, cooperate, join, side, sympathize

alignment *n* **1 = lining up,** adjustment, arrangement, coordination, evening, evening up, line, order, ranging, regulating, sequence, straightening up **3 = alliance,** affiliation, agreement, association, cooperation, sympathy, union

alike *adj* **1 = similar,** akin, analogous, corresponding, cut from the same cloth, duplicate, equal, equivalent, even, identical, like two peas in a pod, of a piece, parallel, resembling, the same, uniform ◆ *adv* **2 = similarly,** analogously, correspondingly, equally, evenly, identically, uniformly
Antonyms *adj* ≠ **similar:** different, dissimilar, diverse, separate, unlike ◆ *adv* ≠ **similarly:** differently, distinctly, unequally

alimentary *adj* **1, 2 = nutritional,** beneficial, nourishing, nutritious, nutritive, sustaining, wholesome

alive *adj* **1 = living,** animate, breathing, having life, in the land of the living (*inf.*), subsisting **2 = in existence,** active, existent, existing, extant, functioning, in force, operative, unquenched **4,**

alizarin (əˈlɪzərɪn) *n* a brownish-yellow powder or orange-red crystalline solid used as a dye. [C19: prob. from F, from Ar. *al-ʿasārah* the juice, from *ʿasara* to squeeze]

alkali (ˈælkəˌlaɪ) *n, pl* **alkalis** *or* **alkalies. 1** *Chem.* a soluble base or a solution of a base. **2** a soluble mineral salt that occurs in arid soils. [C14: from Med. L, from Ar. *al-qili* the ashes (of saltwort)]

alkali metal *n* any of the monovalent metals lithium, sodium, potassium, rubidium, caesium, and francium.

alkaline (ˈælkəˌlaɪn) *adj* having the properties of or containing an alkali.
▸**alkalinity** (ˌælkəˈlɪnɪtɪ) *n*

alkaline earth *n* **1** Also called: **alkaline earth metal, alkaline earth element.** any of the divalent electropositive metals beryllium, magnesium, calcium, strontium, barium, and radium. **2** an oxide of one of the alkaline earth metals.

alkalize *or* **alkalise** (ˈælkəˌlaɪz) *vb* **alkalizes, alkalizing, alkalized** *or* **alkalises, alkalising, alkalised.** (*tr*) to make alkaline.
▸**ˈalkaˌlizable** *or* **ˈalkaˌlisable** *adj*

alkaloid (ˈælkəˌlɔɪd) *n* any of a group of nitrogenous compounds found in plants. Many are poisonous and some are used as drugs.

alkane (ˈælkeɪn) *n* any saturated aliphatic hydrocarbon with the general formula C_nH_{2n+2}. Former name: **paraffin.**

alkane series *n* a homologous series of saturated hydrocarbons starting with methane and having the general formula C_nH_{2n+2}. Also called: **methane series.**

alkanet (ˈælkəˌnɛt) *n* **1** a European plant, the roots of which yield a red dye. **2** the dye obtained. [C14: from Sp., from Med. L, from Ar. *al* the + *hinnāʾ* henna]

alkene (ˈælkiːn) *n* any unsaturated aliphatic hydrocarbon with the general formula C_nH_{2n}. Former name: **olefine.**

alkene series *n* a homologous series of unsaturated hydrocarbons starting with ethylene (ethene) and having the general formula C_nH_{2n}. Also called: **ethylene series, ethene series.**

Alkoran *or* **Alcoran** (ˌælkɒˈrɑːn) *n* a less common name for the **Koran.**

alkyd resin (ˈælkɪd) *n* any of several synthetic resins made from a dicarboxylic acid, used in paints and adhesives.

alkyl (ˈælkɪl) *n* (*modifier*) of or containing the monovalent group C_nH_{2n+1}: *alkyl radical.* [C19: from G, from *Alk(ohol)* ALCOHOL + -YL]

alkylating agent (ˈælkɪˌleɪtɪŋ) *n* any cytotoxic drug containing alkyl groups that acts by damaging DNA; widely used in chemotherapy.

alkyne (ˈælkaɪn) *n* any unsaturated aliphatic hydrocarbon with the general formula C_nH_{2n-2}.

alkyne series *n* a homologous series of unsaturated hydrocarbons starting with acetylene (ethyne) and having the general formula C_nH_{2n-2}. Also called: **acetylene series.**

all ❶ (ɔːl) *determiner* **1a** the whole quantity or amount of; everyone of a class: *all the rice; all men are mortal.* **1b** (*as pronoun; functioning as sing or pl*): *all of it is nice; all are welcome.* **1c** (*in combination with a noun used as a modifier*): *an all-night sitting; an all-ticket match.* **2** the greatest possible: *in all earnestness.* **3** any whatever: *beyond all doubt.* **4 all along.** all the time. **5 all but.** nearly: *all but dead.* **6 all of.** no less or smaller than: *she's all of thirteen years.* **7 all over. 7a** finished. **7b** everywhere (in, on, etc.): *all over England.* **7c** *Inf.* typically (in **that's me** (**him**, etc.) **all over**). **7d** unduly effusive towards. **8 all in all. 8a** everything considered: *all in all, it was a great success.* **8b** the object of one's attention: *you are my all in all.* **9 all the.** (foll. by a comp. adj or adv) so much (more or less) than otherwise: *we must work all the faster now.* **10 all too.** definitely but regrettably: *it's all too true.* **11 at all. 11a** (*used with a negative or in a question*) in any way or to any degree: *I didn't know that at all.* **11b** anyway: *I'm surprised you came at all.* **12 be all for.** *Inf.* to be strongly in favour of. **13 for all. 13a** in so far as: *for all anyone knows, he was a baron.* **13b** notwithstanding: *for all my pushing, I still couldn't move it.* **14 for all that.** in spite of that: *he was a nice man for all that.* **15 in all.** altogether: *there were five in all.* ◆ *adv* **16** (in scores of games) apiece; each: *the score was three all.* ◆ *n* **17** (preceded by *my, his,* etc.) (one's) complete effort or interest: *to give your all.* **18** totality or whole. [OE *eall*]

all- *combining form.* a variant of **allo-** before a vowel.

alla breve (ˈælə ˈbreɪvɪ) *Music.* ◆ *adj, adv* **1** with two beats to the bar instead of four, i.e. twice as fast as written. ◆ *n* **2** (formerly) a time of two or four minims to the bar. Symbol: ¢ [C19: It., lit.: according to the breve]

Allah (ˈælə) *n* the name of God in Islam. [C16: from Ar., from *al* the + *Ilāh* god]

all-American *adj US.* **1** representative of the whole of the United States. **2** composed exclusively of American members. **3** (of a person) typically American.

allantois (ˌælənˈtəʊɪs, əˈlæntɔɪs) *n* a membranous sac growing out of the ventral surface of the hind gut of embryonic reptiles, birds, and mammals. [C17: NL, from Gk *allantoeidēs* sausage-shaped]
▸**allantoic** (ˌælənˈtəʊɪk) *adj*

allay ❶ (əˈleɪ) *vb* **1** to relieve (pain, grief, etc.) or be relieved. **2** (*tr*) to reduce (fear, anger, etc.). [OE *ālecgan* to put down]

All Blacks *pl n* **the.** the international Rugby Union football team of New Zealand. [so named because of the players' black strip]

all clear *n* **1** a signal indicating that some danger, such as an air raid, is over. **2** permission to proceed.

all-dayer (ˌɔːlˈdeɪə) *n* an entertainment, such as a pop concert or film screening, that lasts all day.

allegation ❶ (ˌælɪˈgeɪʃən) *n* **1** the act of alleging. **2** an unproved assertion, esp. an accusation.

allege ❶ (əˈlɛdʒ) *vb* **alleges, alleging, alleged.** (*tr; may take a clause as object*) **1** to state without or before proof: *he alleged malpractice.* **2** to put forward (an argument or plea) for or against an accusation, claim, etc. [C14 *aleggen,* ult. from L *allēgāre* to dispatch on a mission, from *lēx* law]

alleged ❶ (əˈlɛdʒd) *adj* (*prenominal*) **1** stated to be such: *the alleged murderer.* **2** dubious: *an alleged miracle.*
▸**allegedly** (əˈlɛdʒɪdlɪ) *adv*

allegiance ❶ (əˈliːdʒəns) *n* **1** loyalty, as of a subject to his sovereign. **2** (in feudal society) the obligations of a vassal to his liege lord. [C14: from OF, from *lige* LIEGE]

allegorical ❶ (ˌælɪˈgɒrɪkᵊl) *or* **allegoric** *adj* used in, containing, or characteristic of allegory.

allegorize *or* **allegorise** (ˈælɪgəˌraɪz) *vb* **allegorizes, allegorizing, allegorized** *or* **allegorises, allegorising, allegorised. 1** to transform (a story, fable, etc.) into or compose in the form of allegory. **2** (*tr*) to interpret allegorically.
▸**ˌallegoriˈzation** *or* **ˌallegoriˈsation** *n*

allegory ❶ (ˈælɪgərɪ) *n, pl* **allegories. 1** a poem, play, picture, etc., in which the apparent meaning of the characters and events is used to symbolize a moral or spiritual meaning. **2** use of such symbolism. **3** anything used as a symbol. [C14: from OF, from L, from Gk *allēgorein* to speak figuratively, from *allos* other + *agoreuein* to make a speech in public]
▸**ˈallegorist** *n*

allegretto (ˌælɪˈgrɛtəʊ) *Music.* ◆ *adj, adv* **1** (to be performed) fairly quickly or briskly. ◆ *n, pl* **allegrettos. 2** a piece or passage to be performed in this manner. [C19: dim. of ALLEGRO]

allegro (əˈleɪgrəʊ, -ˈlɛg-) *Music.* ◆ *adj, adv* **1** (to be performed) in a brisk lively manner. ◆ *n, pl* **allegros. 2** a piece or passage to be performed in this manner. [C17: from It.: cheerful, from L *alacer* brisk, lively]

allele (əˈliːl) *n* any of two or more genes that are responsible for alternative characteristics, such as smooth or wrinkled seeds in peas. Also called: **allelomorph** (əˈliːləˌmɔːf). [C20: from G *Allel,* from *Allelomorph,* from Gk *allēl-* one another + *morphē* form]

alleluia (ˌælɪˈluːjə) *interj* praise the Lord! Used in liturgical contexts in place of *hallelujah.* [C14: via Med. L from Heb. *hallelūyāh*]

allemande (ˈælɪmænd) *n* **1** the first movement of the classical suite, composed in a moderate tempo. **2** any of several German dances. **3** a figure in country dancing or square dancing by which couples change position in the set. [C17: from F *danse allemande* German dance]

allergen (ˈæləˌdʒɛn) *n* any substance capable of inducing an allergy.
▸**ˌallerˈgenic** *adj*

allergic ❶ (əˈlɜːdʒɪk) *adj* **1** of, having, or caused by an allergy. **2** (*postpositive;* foll. by *to*) *Inf.* having an aversion (to): *allergic to work.*

allergist (ˈælədʒɪst) *n* a physician skilled in the treatment of allergies.

allergy ❶ (ˈælədʒɪ) *n, pl* **allergies. 1** a hypersensitivity to a substance

THESAURUS

5 = **lively**, active, alert, animated, awake, brisk, cheerful, chirpy (*inf.*), eager, energetic, full of beans (*inf.*), full of life, quick, spirited, sprightly, spry, vigorous, vital, vivacious, zestful **6** *foll. by* **to** = **aware of**, alert to, awake to, cognizant of, eager for, sensible of, sensitive to, susceptible to **7** *foll. by* **with** = **swarming with**, abounding in, bristling with, bustling with, buzzing with, crawling with, hopping with, infested with, jumping with, lousy with (*sl.*), overrun by, packed with, teeming with, thronged with
Antonyms *adj* ≠ **living:** dead, deceased, departed, expired, extinct, gone, inanimate, lifeless ≠ **in existence:** extinct, inactive, inoperative, lost ≠ **lively:** apathetic, dull, inactive, lifeless, spiritless

all *determiner* **1** = **the whole of**, every bit of, the complete, the entire, the sum of, the totality of, the total of **1** = **every**, each, each and every, every one of, every single

allay *vb* **1, 2** = **reduce**, alleviate, appease, assuage, blunt, calm, check, compose, diminish, dull, ease, lessen, mitigate, moderate, mollify, pacify, quell, quiet, relax, relieve, smooth, soften, soothe, subdue

allegation *n* **2** = **claim**, accusation, affirmation, assertion, asseveration, averment, avowal, charge, declaration, deposition, plea, profession, statement

allege *vb* **1, 2** = **claim**, advance, affirm, assert, asseverate, aver, avow, charge, declare, depose, maintain, plead, profess, put forward, state
Antonyms *vb* abjure, contradict, deny, disagree with, disavow, disclaim, gainsay (*arch. or literary*), oppose, refute, renounce, repudiate

alleged *adj* **1** = **stated**, affirmed, asserted, averred, declared, described, designated **2** = **supposed**, doubtful, dubious, ostensible, professed, purported, so-called, suspect, suspicious, unproved

allegedly *adv* **1** = **supposedly**, apparently, by all accounts, purportedly, reportedly, reputedly

allegiance *n* **1** = **loyalty**, adherence, constancy, devotion, duty, faithfulness, fealty, fidelity, homage, obedience, obligation, troth (*arch.*)
Antonyms *n* disloyalty, faithlessness, falseness, inconstancy, infidelity, perfidy, treachery, treason, unfaithfulness

allegorical *adj* = **symbolic**, emblematic, figurative, parabolic, symbolizing

allegory *n* **1** = **symbol**, apologue, emblem, fable, myth, parable, story, symbolism, tale

allergic *adj* **1** = **sensitive**, affected by, hypersensitive, sensitized, susceptible **2** *Informal* = **averse**, antipathetic, disinclined, hostile, loath, opposed

allergy *n* **1** = **sensitivity**, antipathy, hypersensitivity, susceptibility **2** *Informal* = **dislike**, antipa-

that causes the body to react to any contact with it. Hay fever is an allergic reaction to pollen. **2** *Inf.* an aversion. [C20: from G *Allergie* (indicating a changed reaction), from Gk *allos* other + *ergon* activity]

alleviate ❶ (əˈliːvɪˌeɪt) *vb* **alleviates, alleviating, alleviated.** (*tr*) to make (pain, sorrow, etc.) easier to bear; lessen. [C15: from LL, from L *levis* light]
▸**alˌleviˈation** *n* ▸**alˈleviˌator** *n*

USAGE NOTE See at **ameliorate.**

alley[1] ❶ (ˈælɪ) *n* **1** a narrow passage, esp. one between or behind buildings. **2** See **bowling alley. 3** *Tennis, chiefly US.* the space between the singles and doubles sidelines. **4** a walk in a garden, esp. one lined with trees. **5 up** (*or* **down**) **one's alley.** *Sl.* suited to one's abilities or interests. [C14: from OF, from *aler* to go, ult. from L *ambulāre* to walk]

alley[2] (ˈælɪ) *n* a large playing marble. [C18: shortened and changed from ALABASTER]

alleyway (ˈælɪˌweɪ) *n* a narrow passage; alley.

All Fools' Day *n* another name for **April Fools' Day** (see **April fool**).

all found *adj* (of charges for accommodation) inclusive of meals, heating, etc.

all hail *sentence substitute.* an archaic greeting or salutation. [C14, lit.: all health (to someone)]

Allhallows (ˌɔːlˈhæləuz) *n* a less common term for **All Saints' Day.**

alliaceous (ˌælɪˈeɪʃəs) *adj* **1** of or relating to a genus of plants that have a strong smell and often have bulbs. The genus occurs in the N hemisphere and includes onion and garlic. **2** tasting or smelling like garlic or onions. [C18: from L *allium* garlic]

alliance ❶ (əˈlaɪəns) *n* **1** the act of allying or state of being allied; union. **2** a formal agreement, esp. a military one, between two or more countries. **3** the countries involved. **4** a union between families through marriage. **5** affinity or correspondence in characteristics. **6** *Bot.* a taxonomic category consisting of a group of related families. [C13: from OF, from *alier* to ALLY]

allied ❶ (əˈlaɪd, ˈælaɪd) *adj* **1** joined, as by treaty or marriage; united. **2** of the same type or class.

Allied (ˈælaɪd) *adj* of or relating to the Allies.

Allies (ˈælaɪz) *pl n* **1** (in World War I) the powers of the Triple Entente (France, Russia, and Britain) together with the nations allied with them. **2** (in World War II) the countries that fought against the Axis and Japan, esp. Britain and the Commonwealth countries, the US, the Soviet Union, China, Poland, and France.

alligator (ˈælɪˌgeɪtə) *n* **1** a large crocodilian of the southern US, having powerful jaws but differing from the crocodiles in having a shorter and broader snout. **2** a similar but smaller species occurring in China. **3** any of various tools or machines having adjustable toothed jaws. [C17: from Sp. *el lagarto* the lizard, from L *lacerta*]

alligator pear *n* another name for **avocado.**

all-important ❶ *adj* crucial; vital.

all in *adj* **1** (*postpositive*) *Inf.* completely exhausted. ◆ *adv, adj* (**all-in** *when prenominal*). **2** with all expenses included: *one hundred pounds a week all in.* **3** (of wrestling) in freestyle.

alliterate (əˈlɪtəˌreɪt) *vb* **alliterates, alliterating, alliterated. 1** to contain or cause to contain alliteration. **2** (*intr*) to speak or write using alliteration.

alliteration (əˌlɪtəˈreɪʃən) *n* the use of the same consonant (**consonantal alliteration**) or of a vowel (**vocalic alliteration**), at the beginning of each word or stressed syllable in a line of verse, as in *around the rock the ragged rascal ran.* [C17: from L *litera* letter]
▸**alˈliterative** *adj*

allium (ˈælɪəm) *n* a genus of liliaceous plants that includes the onion, garlic, shallot, leek, and chive. [C19: from L: garlic]

all-nighter (ˌɔːlˈnaɪtə) *n* an entertainment, such as a pop concert or film screening, that lasts all night.

allo- *or before a vowel* **all-** *combining form.* indicating difference, variation, or opposition: *allopathy; allomorph.* [from Gk *allos* other, different]

allocate ❶ (ˈæləˌkeɪt) *vb* **allocates, allocating, allocated.** (*tr*) **1** to assign for a particular purpose. **2** a less common word for **locate** (sense 2). [C17: from Med. L, from L *locus* a place]
▸**ˈalloˌcatable** *adj* ▸**ˌalloˈcation** *n*

allocution (ˌæləˈkjuːʃən) *n Rhetoric.* a formal or authoritative speech or address. [C17: from LL *allocūtiō*, from L *alloquī* to address]

allomerism (əˈlɒməˌrɪzəm) *n* similarity of crystalline structure in substances of different chemical composition.
▸**allomeric** (ˌæləˈmɛrɪk) *or* **alˈlomerous** *adj*

allomorph (ˈæləˌmɔːf) *n* **1** *Linguistics.* any of the representations of a single morpheme. For example, the final (s) and (z) sounds of *bets* and *beds* are allomorphs. **2** any of the different crystalline forms of a chemical compound, such as a mineral.
▸**ˌalloˈmorphic** *adj*

allopath (ˈæləˌpæθ) *or* **allopathist** (əˈlɒpəθɪst) *n* a person who practises or is skilled in allopathy.

allopathy (əˈlɒpəθɪ) *n* the usual method of treating disease, by inducing a condition different from the cause of the disease. Cf. **homeopathy.**
▸**allopathic** (ˌæləˈpæθɪk) *adj*

allophone (ˈæləˌfəun) *n* **1** any of several speech sounds regarded as variants of the same phoneme. In English the aspirated initial (p) in *pot* and the unaspirated (p) in *spot* are allophones of the phoneme /p/. **2** *Canad.* a Canadian whose native language is neither French nor English.
▸**allophonic** (ˌæləˈfɒnɪk) *adj*

All-Ordinaries Index *n* an index of share prices on the Australian Stock Exchange giving a weighted arithmetic average of 245 ordinary shares.

allot ❶ (əˈlɒt) *vb* **allots, allotting, allotted.** (*tr*) **1** to assign or distribute (shares, etc.). **2** to designate for a particular purpose; apportion: *we allotted two hours to the case.* [C16: from OF, from *lot* portion]

allotment ❶ (əˈlɒtmənt) *n* **1** the act of allotting. **2** a portion or amount allotted. **3** *Brit.* a small piece of land rented by an individual for cultivation.

allotrope (ˈæləˌtrəup) *n* any of two or more physical forms in which an element can exist.

allotropy (əˈlɒtrəpɪ) *or* **allotropism** *n* the existence of an element in two or more physical forms.
▸**allotropic** (ˌæləˈtrɒpɪk) *adj*

all-out ❶ *Inf.* ◆ *adj* **1** using one's maximum powers: *an all-out effort.* ◆ *adv* **all out. 2** to one's maximum capacity: *he went all out.*

allow ❶ (əˈlau) *vb* **1** (*tr*) to permit (to do something). **2** (*tr*) to set aside: *five hours were allowed to do the job.* **3** (*tr*) to let enter or stay: *they don't allow dogs.* **4** (*tr*) to acknowledge (a point, claim, etc.). **5** (*tr*) to let have: *he was allowed few visitors.* **6** (*intr;* foll. by *for*) to take into account. **7** (*intr;* often foll. by *of*) to permit: *a question that allows of only one reply.* **8** (*tr; may take a clause as object*) *US dialect.* to assert; maintain. [C14: from OF, from LL *allaudāre* to extol, infl. by Med. L *allocāre* to assign]
▸**alˈlowable** *adj* ▸**alˈlowably** *adv*

allowance ❶ (əˈlauəns) *n* **1** an amount of something, esp. money or food, given at regular intervals. **2** a discount, as in consideration for something given in part exchange; rebate. **3** (in Britain) an amount of a person's income that is not subject to income tax. **4** a portion set aside to cover special expenses. **5** admission; concession. **6** the act of allowing; toleration. **7 make allowances** (*or* **allowance**). (usually foll. by *for*) **7a** to take mitigating circumstances into account. **7b** to allow (for). ◆ *vb* **allowances, allowancing, allowanced.** (*tr*) **8** to supply (something) in limited amounts.

THESAURUS

thy, aversion, disinclination, hostility, loathing, opposition

alleviate *vb* = **ease**, abate, allay, assuage, blunt, check, diminish, dull, lessen, lighten, mitigate, moderate, mollify, palliate, quell, quench, quiet, reduce, relieve, slacken, slake, smooth, soften, soothe, subdue

alleviation *n* = **easing**, diminution, dulling, lessening, lightening, mitigation, moderation, palliation, quelling, quenching, reduction, relief, slackening, slaking

alley[1] *n* **1** = **passage**, alleyway, backstreet, lane, passageway, pathway, walk

alliance *n* **1, 2, 4** = **union**, affiliation, affinity, agreement, association, coalition, combination, compact, concordat, confederacy, confederation, connection, federation, league, marriage, pact, partnership, treaty
Antonyms *n* alienation, breach, break, disaffection, dissociation, disunion, disunity, division, rupture, separation, severance, split, split-up

allied *adj* **1, 2** = **united**, affiliated, amalgamated, associated, bound, combined, confederate, connected, hand in glove (*inf.*), in cahoots (*US inf.*), in league, joined, joint, kindred, leagued, linked, married, related, unified, wed

all-important *adj* = **essential**, central, consequential, critical, crucial, key, momentous, necessary, pivotal, significant, urgent, vital

allocate *vb* **1** = **assign**, allot, allow, apportion, appropriate, budget, designate, earmark, mete, set aside, share out

allocation *n* **1** = **assignment**, allotment, allowance, apportionment, appropriation, grant, lot, measure, portion, quota, ration, share, stint, stipend

allot *vb* **1, 2** = **assign**, allocate, apportion, appropriate, budget, designate, earmark, mete, set aside, share out

allotment *n* **1, 2** = **assignment**, allocation, allowance, apportionment, appropriation, grant, lot, measure, portion, quota, ration, share, stint, stipend **3** = **plot**, kitchen garden, patch, tract

allotted *vb* **1, 2** = **assigned**, allocated, apportioned, designated, earmarked, given, set aside

all-out *adj* **1** = **total**, complete, determined, exhaustive, full, full-on (*inf.*), full-scale, maximum, optimum, outright, resolute, supreme, thorough, thoroughgoing, undivided, unlimited, unremitting, unrestrained, unstinted, utmost
Antonyms *adj* careless, cursory, half-hearted, negligent, off-hand, perfunctory, unenthusiastic

allow *vb* **1** = **permit**, approve, authorize, bear, brook, enable, endure, give leave, let, put up with (*inf.*), sanction, stand, suffer, tolerate **2** = **give**, allocate, allot, assign, deduct, grant, provide, remit, set aside, spare **4** = **acknowledge**, acquiesce, admit, concede, confess, grant, own **6** *foll. by* **for** = **take into account**, arrange for, consider, foresee, keep in mind, make allowances for, make concessions for, make provision for, plan for, provide for, set (something) aside for, take into consideration
Antonyms *vb* ≠ **permit:** ban, disallow, forbid, prohibit, proscribe, refuse ≠ **give:** deny, forbid, refuse ≠ **acknowledge:** contradict, deny, disagree with, gainsay (*arch. or literary*), oppose

allowable *adj* **1** = **permissible**, acceptable, admissible, all right, appropriate, approved, sanctionable, sufferable, suitable, tolerable

allowance *n* **1** = **portion**, allocation, allotment, amount, annuity, apportionment, grant, lot, measure, pension, quota, ration, remittance, share, stint, stipend, subsidy **2** = **concession**, deduction, discount, rebate, reduction

allowedly (ə'laʊɪdlɪ) *adv* (*sentence modifier*) by general admission or agreement; admittedly.

alloy Ⓣ *n* ('ælɔɪ, ə'lɔɪ). **1** a metallic material, such as steel, consisting of a mixture of two or more metals or of metallic with nonmetallic elements. **2** something that impairs the quality of the thing to which it is added. ◆ *vb* (ə'lɔɪ). (*tr*) **3** to add (one metal or element to another) to obtain a substance with a desired property. **4** to debase (a pure substance) by mixing with an inferior element. **5** to diminish or impair. [C16: from OF *aloi* a mixture, from *aloier* to combine, from L *alligāre*]

all-purpose *adj* useful for many things.

all right Ⓣ *adj* (*postpositive except in slang use*), *adv* **1** adequate; satisfactory. **2** unharmed; safe. **3 all-right.** *US sl.* acceptable; reliable. ◆ *sentence substitute.* **4** very well: used to express assent. ◆ *adv* **5** satisfactorily: *the car goes all right.* **6** without doubt. ◆ Also **alright.**

> **USAGE NOTE** See at **alright.**

all-round *adj* **1** efficient in all respects, esp. in sport: *an all-round player.* **2** comprehensive; many-sided: *an all-round education.*

all-rounder *n* a versatile person, esp. in a sport.

All Saints' Day *n* a Christian festival celebrated on Nov. 1 to honour all the saints.

all-singing all-dancing *adj* having every desirable feature possible: *an all-singing all-dancing computer.*

All Souls' Day *n RC Church.* a day of prayer (Nov. 2) for the dead in purgatory.

allspice ('ɔːlˌspaɪs) *n* **1** a tropical American tree, having small white flowers and aromatic berries. **2** the seeds of this berry used as a spice, having a flavour said to resemble a mixture of cinnamon, cloves, and nutmeg. ◆ Also called: **pimento.**

all-star *adj* (*prenominal*) consisting of star performers.

all-time *adj* (*prenominal*) *Inf.* unsurpassed.

all told *adv* (*sentence modifier*) in all: *we were seven all told.*

allude Ⓣ (ə'luːd) *vb* **alludes, alluding, alluded.** (*intr*; foll. by *to*) **1** to refer indirectly. **2** (loosely) to mention. [C16: from L *allūdere,* from *lūdere* to sport, from *lūdus* a game]

> **USAGE NOTE** Avoid confusion with **elude.**

allure Ⓣ (ə'lʊə) *vb* **allures, alluring, allured. 1** (*tr*) to entice or tempt (someone); attract. ◆ *n* **2** attractiveness; appeal. [C15: from OF *alurer,* from *lure* bait]
▸**al'lurement** *n* ▸**al'luring** *adj*

allusion Ⓣ (ə'luːʒən) *n* **1** the act of alluding. **2** a passing reference. [C16: from LL *allūsiō,* from L *allūdere* to sport with]

allusive (ə'luːsɪv) *adj* containing or full of allusions.
▸**al'lusiveness** *n*

alluvial (ə'luːvɪəl) *adj* **1** of or relating to alluvium. ◆ *n* **2** another name for **alluvium.**

alluvion (ə'luːvɪən) *n* **1a** the wash of the sea or a river. **1b** a flood. **1c** sediment; alluvium. **2** *Law.* the gradual formation of new land, as by the recession of the sea. [C16: from L *alluviō* an overflowing, from *luere* to wash]

alluvium (ə'luːvɪəm) *n, pl* **alluviums** *or* **alluvia** (-vɪə). a fine-grained fertile soil consisting of mud, silt, and sand deposited by flowing water. [C17: from L; see ALLUVION]

ally Ⓣ *vb* (ə'laɪ), **allies, allying, allied.** (usually foll. by *to* or *with*) **1** to unite or be united, esp. formally, as by treaty. **2** (*tr*; *usually passive*) to be related, as through being similar. ◆ *n* ('ælaɪ), *pl* **allies. 3** a country, person, or group allied with another. **4** a plant, animal, etc., closely related to another in characteristics or form. [C14: from OF *alier* to join, from L *ligāre* to bind]

allyl resin ('ælɪl) *n* any of several thermosetting synthetic resins, containing the CH_2:$CHCH_2$– group, used as adhesives. [C19: from L *allium* garlic + -YL]

alma mater ('ælmə 'mɑːtə, 'meɪtə) *n* (*often caps.*) one's school, college, or university. [C17: from L: bountiful mother]

almanac ('ɔːlməˌnæk) *n* a yearly calendar giving statistical information, such as the phases of the moon, tides, anniversaries, etc. Also (archaic): **almanack.** [C14: from Med. L *almanachus,* ?from LGk *almenikhiaka*]

almandine ('ælməndɪn) *n* a deep violet-red garnet. [C17: from F, from Med. L, from *Alabanda,* ancient city of Asia Minor where these stones were cut]

almighty Ⓣ (ɔːl'maɪtɪ) *adj* **1** omnipotent. **2** *Inf.* (intensifier): *an almighty row.* ◆ *adv* **3** *Inf.* (intensifier): *an almighty loud bang.*

almond ('ɑːmənd) *n* **1** a small widely cultivated rosaceous tree that is native to W Asia and has pink flowers and an edible nutlike seed. **2** the seed, which has a yellowish-brown shell. **3** (*modifier*) made of or containing almonds: *almond cake.* [C13: from OF *almande,* ult. from Gk *amugdalē*]

almond-eyed *adj* having narrow oval eyes.

almoner ('ɑːmənə) *n* **1** *Brit.* a former name for a trained hospital social worker. **2** (formerly) a person who distributes charity on behalf of a household or institution. [C13: from OF, from *almosne* alms, ult. from LL *eleēmosyna*]

almost Ⓣ ('ɔːlməʊst) *adv* very nearly.

alms Ⓣ (ɑːmz) *pl n* charitable donations of money or goods to the poor or needy. [OE *ælmysse,* from LL, from Gk *eleēmosunē* pity]

almshouse ('ɑːmzˌhaʊs) *n Brit. history.* a privately supported house offering accommodation to the aged or needy.

almucantar *or* **almacantar** (ˌælmə'kæntə) *n* **1** a circle on the celestial sphere parallel to the horizon. **2** an instrument for measuring altitudes. [C14: from F, from Ar. *almukantarāt* sundial]

aloe ('æləʊ) *n, pl* **aloes. 1** any plant of the genus *Aloe,* chiefly native to southern Africa, with fleshy spiny-toothed leaves. **2 American aloe.** Also called: **century plant.** a tropical American agave which blooms only once in 10 to 30 years. [C14: from L *aloē,* from Gk]

aloes ('æləʊz) *n* (*functioning as sing*) a bitter purgative drug made from the leaves of several species of aloe. Also called: **bitter aloes.**

aloe vera ('vɪərə) *n* **1** a plant of the species *Aloe vera,* the leaves of which yield a juice used as an emollient. **2** the juice of this plant, used in skin and hair preparations.

aloft Ⓣ (ə'lɒft) *adv, adj* (*postpositive*) **1** in or into a high or higher place. **2** *Naut.* in or into the rigging of a vessel. [C12: from ON *ā lopt* in the air]

alone Ⓣ (ə'ləʊn) *adj* (*postpositive*), *adv* **1** apart from another or others. **2** without anyone or anything else: *one man alone could lift it.* **3** without equal: *he stands alone in the field of microbiology.* **4** to the exclusion of others: *she alone believed him.* **5 leave** *or* **let alone.** to refrain from annoying or interfering with. **6 leave well alone.** to refrain from interfering with something that is satisfactory. **7 let alone.** not to mention; much less: *he can't afford beer, let alone whisky.* [OE *al one,* lit.: all (entirely) one]

along (ə'lɒŋ) *prep* **1** over or for the length of: *along the road.* ◆ *adv* **2** continuing over the length of some specified thing. **3** together with some specified person or people: *he'd like to come along.* **4** forward: *the horse trotted along.* **5** to a more advanced state: *he got the work moving along.* **6 along with.** together with: *consider the advantages along with the disadvantages.* [OE *andlang,* from *and-* against + *lang* LONG[1]]

> **USAGE NOTE** See at **plus.**

alongshore (əˌlɒŋ'ʃɔː) *adv, adj* (*postpositive*) close to, by, or along a shore.

alongside (ə'lɒŋˌsaɪd) *prep* **1** (often foll. by *of*) close beside: *alongside the quay.* ◆ *adv* **2** near the side of something: *come alongside.*

THESAURUS

alloy *n* **1** = **mixture**, admixture, amalgam, blend, combination, composite, compound, hybrid, meld ◆ *vb* **3** = **mix**, admix, amalgamate, blend, combine, compound, fuse, meld

all right *adj* **1** = **satisfactory**, acceptable, adequate, average, fair, O.K. *or* okay (*inf.*), passable, so-so (*inf.*), standard, unobjectionable, up to scratch (*inf.*) **2** = **well**, hale, healthy, O.K. *or* okay (*inf.*), out of the woods, safe, sound, unharmed, unimpaired, uninjured, whole ◆ *adv* **5** = **satisfactorily**, acceptably, adequately, O.K. *or* okay (*inf.*), passably, unobjectionably, well enough
Antonyms *adj* ≠ **satisfactory:** bad, inadequate, not good enough, not up to scratch (*inf.*), objectionable, poor, unacceptable, unsatisfactory ≠ **well:** ailing, bad, ill, injured, off colour, out of sorts, poorly, sick, sickly, unhealthy, unwell

allude *vb* **1, 2** = **refer**, advert, glance, hint, imply, insinuate, intimate, mention, remark, speak of, suggest, tip the wink, touch upon

allure *vb* **1** = **attract**, beguile, cajole, captivate, charm, coax, decoy, enchant, entice, inveigle, lead on, lure, persuade, seduce, tempt, win over ◆ *n* **2** = **attractiveness**, appeal, attraction, charm, enchantment, enticement, glamour, lure, persuasion, seductiveness, temptation

alluring *adj* **1** = **attractive**, beguiling, bewitching, captivating, come-hither, enchanting, fascinating, fetching, glamorous, intriguing, seductive, sexy, tempting
Antonyms *adj* abhorrent, off-putting (*Brit. inf.*), repellent, repugnant, repulsive, unattractive

allusion *n* **2** = **reference**, casual remark, glance, hint, implication, indirect reference, innuendo, insinuation, intimation, mention, suggestion

ally *vb* **1** = **unite**, affiliate, associate, band together, collaborate, combine, confederate, connect, join, join battle with, join forces, league, marry, unify ◆ *n* **3** = **partner**, abettor, accessory, accomplice, associate, coadjutor, collaborator, colleague, confederate, co-worker, friend, helper
Antonyms *vb* ≠ **unite:** alienate, disaffect, disunite, divide, drive apart, separate, set at odds ◆ *n* ≠ **partner:** adversary, antagonist, competitor, enemy, foe, opponent, rival

almighty *adj* **1** = **all-powerful**, absolute, invincible, omnipotent, supreme, unlimited **2** *Informal* = **great**, awful, desperate, enormous, excessive, intense, loud, severe, terrible
Antonyms *adj* ≠ **all-powerful:** helpless, impotent, powerless, weak ≠ **great:** feeble, insignificant, paltry, poor, slight, tame, weak

almost *adv* = **nearly**, about, all but, approximately, as good as, close to, just about, not far from, not quite, on the brink of, practically, so near (and) yet so far, virtually, well-nigh

alms *pl n* = **donation**, benefaction, bounty, charity, gift, relief

aloft *adv* **1** = **in the air**, above, heavenward, higher, high up, in the sky, on high, overhead, skyward, up, up above, upward

alone *adj* **1, 2** = **by oneself**, abandoned, apart, by itself, deserted, desolate, detached, forlorn, forsaken, isolated, lonely, lonesome, only, on one's tod (*sl.*), out on a limb, separate, single, single-handed, sole, solitary, unaccompanied, unaided, unassisted, unattended, uncombined, unconnected, under one's own steam, unescorted

aloof ❶ (əˈluːf) *adj* distant, unsympathetic, or supercilious in manner. [C16: from A-[1] + *loof*, var. of LUFF]
▸**aˈloofly** *adv* ▸**aˈloofness** *n*

alopecia (ˌæləˈpiːʃɪə) *n* baldness. [C14: from L, from Gk *alōpekia*, orig.: mange in foxes]

aloud ❶ (əˈlaʊd) *adv, adj (postpositive)* **1** in a normal voice. **2** in a spoken voice; not silently.

alp (ælp) *n* **1** (in Switzerland) a mountain pasture. **2** a high mountain. **3 the Alps.** a high mountain range in S central Europe. [C16: from L *Alpes*]

ALP *abbrev. for* Australian Labor Party.

alpaca (ælˈpækə) *n* **1** a domesticated South American mammal related to the llama, with dark shaggy hair. **2** the cloth made from the wool of this animal. **3** a glossy fabric simulating this. [C18: via Sp. from Aymara *allpaca*]

alpenhorn (ˈælpənˌhɔːn) *n* another name for **alphorn.**

alpenstock (ˈælpənˌstɒk) *n* a stout stick with an iron tip used by hikers, mountain climbers, etc. [C19: from G, from *Alpen* Alps + *Stock* STICK[1]]

alpha (ˈælfə) *n* **1** the first letter in the Greek alphabet (Α, α). **2** *Brit.* the highest grade or mark, as in an examination. **3** *(modifier)* **3a** involving helium nuclei. **3b** denoting an isomeric or allotropic form of a substance. [via L from Gk, of Phoenician origin]

alpha and omega *n* the first and last, a phrase used in Revelation 1:8 to signify God's eternity.

alphabet ❶ (ˈælfəˌbɛt) *n* **1** a set of letters or other signs used in a writing system, each letter or sign being used to represent one or sometimes more than one phoneme in the language being transcribed. **2** any set of characters, esp. one representing sounds of speech. **3** basic principles or rudiments. [C15: from LL, from the first two letters of the Gk alphabet; see ALPHA, BETA]

alphabetical (ˌælfəˈbɛtɪkᵊl) *or* **alphabetic** *adj* **1** in the conventional order of the letters of an alphabet. **2** of or expressed by an alphabet.
▸ˌ**alphaˈbetically** *adv*

alphabetize *or* **alphabetise** (ˈælfəbəˌtaɪz) *vb* **alphabetizes, alphabetizing, alphabetized** *or* **alphabetises, alphabetising, alphabetised.** *(tr)* **1** to arrange in conventional alphabetical order. **2** to express by an alphabet.
▸ˌ**alphabetiˈzation** *or* ˌ**alphabetiˈsation** *n*

alpha-blocker *n* any of a class of drugs that prevent the stimulation of alpha receptors, a type of receptor in the sympathetic nervous system, by adrenaline and that therefore cause widening of blood vessels: used in the treatment of high blood pressure.

alpha decay *n* the radioactive decay process resulting in emission of alpha particles.

alpha-fetoprotein (ˌælfəˌfiːtəʊˈprəʊtiːn) *n* a protein that forms in the liver of the human fetus; excessive quantities in the amniotic fluid may indicate spina bifida in the fetus; low levels may point to Down's syndrome. Abbrev.: **afp.**

alphanumeric (ˌælfənjuːˈmɛrɪk) *or* **alphameric** *adj* (of a character set or file of data) consisting of alphabetical and numerical symbols.

alpha particle *n* a helium nucleus, containing two neutrons and two protons, emitted during some radioactive transformations.

alpha ray *n* ionizing radiation consisting of a stream of alpha particles.

alpha rhythm *or* **wave** *n Physiol.* the normal bursts of electrical activity from the cerebral cortex of a person at rest. See also **brain wave.**

alpha stock *n* any of the most active securities on the London stock exchange of which there are between 100 and 200.

alphorn (ˈælpˌhɔːn) *or* **alpenhorn** *n* a wind instrument used in the Swiss Alps, made from a very long tube of wood. [C19: from G: Alps horn]

alpine (ˈælpaɪn) *adj* **1** of or relating to high mountains. **2** (of plants) growing on mountains above the limit for tree growth. **3** connected with mountaineering. **4** *Skiing.* of racing events on steep prepared slopes, such as the slalom and downhill. Cf. **nordic.** ◆ *n* **5** a plant grown in or native to high altitudes.

alpinist (ˈælpɪnɪst) *n* a mountain climber.

already ❶ (ɔːlˈrɛdɪ) *adv* **1** by or before a stated or implied time: *he is already here.* **2** at a time earlier than expected: *is it ten o'clock already?*

alright (ɔːlˈraɪt) *adv, sentence substitute, adj* a variant spelling of **all right.**

> **USAGE NOTE** The form *alright,* though very common, is still considered by many people to be wrong or less acceptable

Alsatian (ælˈseɪʃən) *n* **1** Also called: **German shepherd (dog).** a large wolflike breed of dog often used as a guard dog and by the police. **2** a native or inhabitant of Alsace, a region of NE France. ◆ *adj* **3** of or relating to Alsace or its inhabitants.

also ❶ (ˈɔːlsəʊ) *adv* **1** *(sentence modifier)* in addition; as well; too. ◆ *sentence connector.* **2** besides; moreover. [OE *alswā;* see ALL, SO[1]]

also-ran *n* **1** a contestant, horse, etc., failing to finish among the first three. **2** a loser.

alstroemeria (ˌælstrəʊˈmɪərɪə) *n* any of several plants with fleshy roots and brightly coloured flowers in summer, esp. the Peruvian lily. [C18: NL, after Claude *Alstroemer* (1736–96), Swedish naturalist]

alt. *abbrev. for:* **1** alternate. **2** altitude. **3** alto.

Alta. *abbrev. for* Alberta.

Altaic (ælˈteɪɪk) *n* **1** a postulated family of languages of Asia and SE Europe, including the Turkic, Tungusic, and Mongolic subfamilies. See also **Ural-Altaic.** ◆ *adj* **2** denoting or relating to this linguistic family or its speakers.

altar (ˈɔːltə) *n* **1** a raised place or structure where sacrifices are offered and religious rites performed. **2** (in Christian churches) the communion table. **3** a step in the wall of a dry dock. [OE, ult. from L *altus* high]

altar boy *n RC Church, Church of England.* a boy serving as an acolyte.

altarpiece (ˈɔːltəˌpiːs) *n* a work of art set above and behind an altar; a reredos.

altazimuth (ælˈtæzɪməθ) *n* an instrument for measuring the altitude and azimuth of a celestial body. [C19: from ALT(ITUDE) + AZIMUTH]

altazimuth mounting *n* a telescope mounting that allows motion of the telescope about a vertical axis (in altitude) and a horizontal axis (in azimuth).

alter ❶ (ˈɔːltə) *vb* **1** to make or become different in some respect; change. **2** *(tr) Inf., chiefly US.* a euphemistic word for **castrate** or **spay.** [C14: from OF, ult. from L *alter* other]
▸ˈ**alterable** *adj*

alteration ❶ (ˌɔːltəˈreɪʃən) *n* **1** a change or modification. **2** the act of altering.

alterative (ˈɔːltərətɪv) *adj* **1** likely or able to produce alteration. **2** (of a drug) able to restore health. ◆ *n* **3** such a drug.

altercate (ˈɔːltəˌkeɪt) *vb* **altercates, altercating, altercated.** *(intr)* to argue, esp. heatedly; dispute. [C16: from L *altercārī* to quarrel with another, from *alter* other]

altercation ❶ (ˌɔːltəˈkeɪʃən) *n* an angry or heated discussion or quarrel; argument.

alter ego (ˈæltər ˈiːgəʊ, ˈɛgəʊ) *n* **1** a second self. **2** a very close friend. [L: other self]

alternate ❶ *vb* (ˈɔːltəˌneɪt), **alternates, alternating, alternated. 1** (often foll. by *with*) to occur or cause to occur by turns: *day and night alternate.* **2** *(intr;* often foll. by *between)* to swing repeatedly from one condition, action, etc., to another. **3** *(tr)* to interchange regularly or in succession. **4** *(intr)* (of an electric current, voltage, etc.) to reverse direction or sign at regular intervals. ◆ *adj* (ɔːlˈtɜːnɪt). **5** occurring by turns: *alternate feelings of love and hate.* **6** every other or second one of a series: *he came on alternate days.* **7** being a second choice; alternative: *alternate director.* **8** *Bot.* (of leaves, flowers, etc.) arranged singly at different heights on either side of the stem. ◆ *n* (ˈɔːltənɪt, ɔːlˈtɜːnɪt). **9** *US & Canad.* a person who substitutes for another; stand-in. [C16: from L *alternāre* to do one thing and then another, ult. from *alter* other]
▸ˌ**alterˈnation** *n*

alternate angles *pl n* two angles at opposite ends and on opposite sides of a transversal cutting two lines.

alternately (ɔːlˈtɜːnɪtlɪ) *adv* in an alternating sequence or position.

alternating current *n* an electric current that periodically reverses direction. Abbrev.: **AC.**

alternation of generations *n* the occurrence in the life cycle of many plants and lower animals of alternating sexual and asexual reproductive forms.

alternative ❶ (ɔːlˈtɜːnətɪv) *n* **1** a possibility of choice, esp. between two things. **2** either of such choices: *we took the alternative of walking.* ◆ *adj*

THESAURUS

Antonyms *adj* accompanied, aided, among others, assisted, escorted, helped, joint, together

aloof *adj* = **distant**, chilly, cold, cool, detached, forbidding, formal, haughty, indifferent, remote, reserved, standoffish, supercilious, unapproachable, unfriendly, uninterested, unresponsive, unsociable, unsympathetic
Antonyms *adj* friendly, gregarious, neighbourly, open, sociable, sympathetic, warm

aloud *adv* **1, 2** = **out loud**, audibly, clearly, distinctly, intelligibly, plainly

alphabet *n* **1** = **letters**, script, syllabary, writing system

already *adv* **1** = **before now**, as of now, at present, before, by now, by that time, by then, by this time, even now, heretofore, just now, previously

also *adv* **1** = **too**, additionally, along with, and, as well, as well as, besides, further, furthermore, in addition, including, into the bargain, moreover, on top of that, plus, to boot

alter *vb* **1** = **change**, adapt, adjust, amend, convert, diversify, metamorphose, modify, recast, reform, remodel, reshape, revise, shift, transform, transmute, turn, tweak (*inf.*), vary

alteration *n* **1, 2** = **change**, adaptation, adjustment, amendment, conversion, difference, diversification, metamorphosis, modification, reformation, remodelling, reshaping, revision, shift, transformation, transmutation, variance, variation

altercation *n* = **argument**, bickering, clash, contention, controversy, disagreement, discord, dispute, dissension, quarrel, row, squabble, wrangle

alternate *vb* **1, 3** = **change**, act reciprocally, alter, fluctuate, follow in turn, follow one another, interchange, intersperse, oscillate, rotate, substitute, take turns ◆ *adj* **5, 6** = **every other**, alternating, every second, interchanging, rotating **7** = **second**, alternative, another, different, substitute

alternating *adj* **1, 3** = **changing**, fluctuating, interchanging, occurring by turns, oscillating, rotating, seesawing, shifting, swinging, vacillating

alternation *n* **1, 3** = **change**, fluctuation, oscillation, rotation, swing, vacillation, variation, vicissitude

alternative *n* **1, 2** = **choice**, option, other (*of two*), preference, recourse, selection, substitute ◆ *adj* **3** = **different**, alternate, another, other, second, substitute

alternatively *adv* **3** = **or**, as an alternative, by

3 presenting a choice, esp. between two possibilities only. 4 (of two things) mutually exclusive. 5 denoting a lifestyle, culture, art form, etc., that is regarded as preferable to that of contemporary society because it is less conventional, materialistic, or institutionalized.
▸**al'ternatively** *adv*

alternative curriculum *n Brit. education.* any course of study offered as an alternative to the National Curriculum.

alternative energy *n* a form of energy derived from a natural source, such as the sun, wind, tides, or waves. Also called: **renewable energy.**

Alternative Investment Market *n* a market on the London Stock Exchange for small companies that want to avoid the expenses of a main-market listing. Abbrev.: **AIM.**

alternative medicine *n* the treatment or alleviation of disease by techniques such as osteopathy and acupuncture, allied with attention to a person's general wellbeing. Also called: **complementary medicine.**

alternative society *n* a group of people who agree in rejecting the traditional values of the society around them.

Alternative Vote *n* (*modifier*) of or relating to a system of voting in which voters list the candidates in order of preference. If no candidate obtains more than 50% of first-preference votes, the votes for the bottom candidate are redistributed according to the voters' next preference. See **proportional representation.**

alternator ('ɔːltəˌneɪtə) *n* an electrical machine that generates an alternating current.

althaea *or US* **althea** (æl'θiːə) *n* any Eurasian plant of the genus *Althaea,* such as the hollyhock, having tall spikes of showy flowers. [C17: from L, from Gk *althaia* marsh mallow]

althorn ('ælt,hɔːn) *n* a valved brass musical instrument belonging to the saxhorn family.

although ➊ (ɔːl'ðəʊ) *conj* (*subordinating*) even though: *although she was ill, she worked hard.*

altimeter (æl'tɪmɪtə, 'æltɪˌmiːtə) *n* an instrument that indicates height above sea level, esp. one based on an aneroid barometer and fitted to an aircraft. [C19: from L *altus* high + -METER]

altitude ➊ ('æltɪˌtjuːd) *n* **1** the vertical height of an object, esp. above sea level. **2** *Geom.* the perpendicular distance from the vertex to the base of a geometrical figure or solid. **3** Also called: **elevation.** *Astron., navigation.* the angular distance of a celestial body from the horizon. **4** *Surveying.* the angle of elevation of a point above the horizontal plane of the observer. **5** (*often pl*) a high place or region. [C14: from L *altus* high, deep]

alto ('æltəʊ) *n, pl* **altos. 1** (in choral singing) short for **contralto. 2** the highest adult male voice; countertenor. **3** a singer with such a voice. **4** a flute, saxophone, etc., that is the third or fourth highest instrument in its group. ◆ *adj* **5** denoting such an instrument. [C18: from It.: high, from L *altus*]

alto clef *n* the clef that establishes middle C as being on the third line of the staff.

altocumulus (ˌæltəʊ'kjuːmjʊləs) *n, pl* **altocumuli** (-laɪ). a globular cloud at an intermediate height of about 2400 to 6000 m (8000 to 20 000 ft).

altogether ➊ (ˌɔːltə'geðə, 'ɔːltəˌgeðə) *adv* **1** with everything included: *altogether he owed me sixty pounds.* **2** completely; utterly: *altogether mad.* **3** on the whole: *altogether it was very good.* ◆ *n* **4 in the altogether.** *Inf.* naked.

altoist ('æltəʊɪst) *n* a person who plays the alto saxophone.

altostratus (ˌæltəʊ'streɪtəs, -'strɑː-) *n, pl* **altostrati** (-taɪ). a layer cloud at an intermediate height of about 2400 to 6000 m (8000 to 20 000 ft).

altricial (æl'trɪʃəl) *adj* **1** denoting birds whose young, after hatching, are naked, blind, and dependent on the parents for food. ◆ *n* **2** an altricial bird. ◆ Cf. **precocial.** [C19: from NL, from L *altrix* a nurse]

altruism ➊ ('æltruːˌɪzəm) *n* unselfish concern for the welfare of others. [C19: from F, from It. *altrui* others, from L]
▸**'altruist** *n* ▸**ˌaltru'istic** *adj* ▸**ˌaltru'istically** *adv*

ALU *Computing. abbrev. for* arithmetical and logical unit.

alum ('æləm) *n* **1** a colourless soluble hydrated double sulphate of aluminium and potassium used in manufacturing and in medicine. Formula: $K_2SO_4.Al_2(SO_4)_3.24H_2O$. **2** any of a group of similar hydrated double sulphates of a monovalent metal or group and a trivalent metal. [C14: from OF, from L *alūmen*]

alumina (ə'luːmɪnə) *n* another name for **aluminium oxide.** [C18: from NL, pl of L *alūmen* ALUM]

aluminium (ˌæljʊ'mɪnɪəm) *or US & Canad.* **aluminum** (ə'luːmɪnəm) *n* a light malleable silvery-white metallic element that resists corrosion; the third most abundant element in the earth's crust, occurring as a compound, principally in bauxite. Symbol: Al; atomic no.: 13; atomic wt.: 26.981.

aluminium oxide *n* a powder occurring naturally as corundum and used in the production of aluminium, abrasives, glass, and ceramics. Formula: Al_2O_3. Also called: **alumina.**

aluminize *or* **aluminise** (ə'luːmɪˌnaɪz) *vb* **aluminizes, aluminizing, aluminized** *or* **aluminises, aluminising, aluminised.** (*tr*) to cover with aluminium or aluminium paint.

aluminous (ə'luːmɪnəs) *adj* resembling aluminium.

alumnus (ə'lʌmnəs) *or* (*fem*) **alumna** (ə'lʌmnə) *n, pl* **alumni** (-naɪ) *or* **alumnae** (-niː). *Chiefly US & Canad.* a graduate of a school, college, etc. [C17: from L: nursling, pupil, from *alere* to nourish]

alveolar (æl'vɪələ, ˌælvɪ'əʊlə) *adj* **1** *Anat.* of an alveolus. **2** denoting the part of the jawbone containing the roots of the teeth. **3** (of a consonant) articulated with the tongue in contact with the part of the jawbone immediately behind the upper teeth. ◆ *n* **4** an alveolar consonant, such as *t, d,* and *s* in English.

alveolate (æl'vɪəlɪt, -ˌleɪt) *adj* having many small cavities. [C19: from LL *alveolātus* hollowed, from L: ALVEOLUS]
▸**ˌalveo'lation** *n*

alveolus (æl'vɪələs) *n, pl* **alveoli** (-ˌlaɪ). any small pit, cavity, or saclike dilation, such as a honeycomb cell, a tooth socket, or the tiny air sacs in the lungs. [C18: from L: a little hollow, dim. of *alveus*]

always ➊ ('ɔːlweɪz) *adv* **1** without exception; every time: *he always arrives on time.* **2** continually; repeatedly. **3** in any case: *you could always take a day off work.* ◆ Also (archaic): **alway.** [C13 *alles weiss,* from OE *ealne weg,* lit.: all the way]

alyssum ('ælɪsəm) *n* a widely cultivated herbaceous garden plant, having clusters of small yellow or white flowers. [C16: from NL, from Gk *alusson,* from *alussos* (adj) curing rabies]

Alzheimer's disease ('ælts,haɪməz) *n* a disorder of the brain resulting in progressive decline and eventual dementia. Often shortened to **Alzheimer's.** [C20: after A. *Alzheimer* (1864–1915), G physician who first identified it]

am (æm; *unstressed* əm) *vb* (used with *I*) a form of the present tense of **be.** [OE *eam*]

Am *the chemical symbol for* americium.

AM *abbrev. for:* **1** Also: **am.** amplitude modulation. **2** *US.* Master of Arts. **3** Member of the Order of Australia.

Am. *abbrev. for* America(n).

a.m., A.M., am, *or* **AM** (indicating the period from midnight to midday) *abbrev. for* ante meridiem. [L: before noon]

amabokoboko (ama'bɒkɒbɒkɒ) *pl n S. African.* an African name for the **Springbok** rugby team. [C20: from Nguni *ama,* a plural prefix + *bokoboko,* from *bok* a diminutive of SPRINGBOK]

Amadhlozi *or* **Amadlozi** (ˌæmæ'hlɒʒiː) *pl n S. African.* the ancestral spirits. [from Zulu, pl. *amadlozi*]

amadoda (ˌæmæ'dɒdə) *pl n S. African.* grown men. [from Nguni *ama,* a plural prefix + *doda* men]

amadou ('æməˌduː) *n* a spongy substance got from some fungi, used (formerly) as tinder, a styptic, and by fishermen to dry flies. [C18: from F, from Provençal: lover, from L *amāre* to love (because easily set alight)]

amah ('ɑːmə) *n* (in the East, esp. formerly) a nurse or maidservant. [C19: from Port. *ama* nurse]

amain (ə'meɪn) *adv Arch. or poetic.* with great strength or haste. [C16: from A-[2] + MAIN[1]]

amalgam ➊ (ə'mælgəm) *n* **1** an alloy of mercury with another metal, esp. silver: *dental amalgam.* **2** a blend or combination. [C15: from Med. L *amalgama,* from ?]

amalgamate ➊ (ə'mælgəˌmeɪt) *vb* **amalgamates, amalgamating, amalgamated. 1** to combine or cause to combine; unite. **2** to alloy (a metal) with mercury.

amalgamation ➊ (əˌmælgə'meɪʃən) *n* **1** the process of amalgamating.

THESAURUS

way of alternative, if not, instead, on the other hand, otherwise

although *conj* = **though,** albeit, despite the fact that, even if, even supposing, even though, notwithstanding, tho' (*US or poetic*), while

altitude *n* **1** = **height,** elevation, loftiness, peak, summit

altogether *adv* **1** = **in total,** all told, everything included, in all, in sum, *in toto,* taken together **2** = **completely,** absolutely, every inch, fully, lock, stock and barrel, perfectly, quite, thoroughly, totally, utterly, wholly **3** = **on the whole,** all in all, all things considered, as a whole, collectively, generally, in general, *in toto*
Antonyms *adv* ≠ **completely:** halfway, incompletely, in part, in some measure, not fully, partially, relatively, slightly, somewhat, to a certain degree *or* extent, up to a certain point

altruism *n* = **selflessness,** beneficence, benevolence, bigheartedness, charitableness, charity, consideration, generosity, goodwill, greatheartedness, humanitarianism, magnanimity, philanthropy, self-sacrifice, unselfishness
Antonyms *n* egoism, egotism, greed, meanness, mercenariness, narrowness, self-absorption, self-centredness, self-interest, selfishness, self-seeking

altruist *n* = **humanitarian,** philanthropist

altruistic *adj* = **selfless,** benevolent, charitable, considerate, generous, humanitarian, philanthropic, public-spirited, self-sacrificing, unselfish
Antonyms *adj* egoistic(al), egotistic(al), greedy, mean, self-centred, self-interested, selfish, self-seeking, ungenerous

always *adv* **1, 2** = **continually,** aye (*Scot.*), consistently, constantly, eternally, ever, everlastingly, evermore, every time, forever, *in perpetuum,* invariably, perpetually, repeatedly, unceasingly, without exception
Antonyms *adv* hardly, hardly ever, infrequently, once in a blue moon, once in a while, only now and then, on rare occasions, rarely, scarcely ever, seldom

amalgam *n* **2** = **combination,** admixture, alloy, amalgamation, blend, composite, compound, fusion, meld, mixture, union

amalgamate *vb* **1** = **combine,** alloy, ally, blend, coalesce, commingle, compound, fuse, incorporate, integrate, intermix, meld, merge, mingle, unite
Antonyms *vb* disunite, divide, part, separate, split, split up

amalgamation *n* **1, 2, 4** = **combination,** ad-

2 the state of being amalgamated. 3 a method of extracting precious metals by treatment with mercury. 4 a merger.

amanuensis (ə,mænju'ɛnsɪs) *n, pl* **amanuenses** (-siːz). a person employed to take dictation or to copy manuscripts. [C17: from L, from *servus ā manū* slave at hand (that is, handwriting)]

amaranth ('æmə,rænθ) *n* **1** *Poetic.* an imaginary flower that never fades. **2** any of numerous plants having tassel-like heads of small green, red, or purple flowers. **3** a synthetic red food colouring (**E123**), used in packet soups, cake mixes, etc. [C17: from L *amarantus,* from Gk, from A-[1] + *marainein* to fade]

amaretto (,æmə'retəu) *n* an Italian liqueur with a flavour of almonds. [C20: from It. *amaro* bitter]

amaryllis (,æmə'rɪlɪs) *n* **1** a plant native to southern Africa having large lily-like reddish or white flowers. **2** any of several related plants. [C18: from NL, from L: after *Amaryllis,* Gk conventional name for a shepherdess]

amass ❶ (ə'mæs) *vb* **1** (*tr*) to accumulate or collect (esp. riches, etc.). **2** to gather in a heap. [C15: from OF, from *masse* MASS]
▸**a'masser** *n*

amateur ❶ ('æmətə) *n* **1** a person who engages in an activity, esp. a sport, as a pastime rather than for gain. **2** a person unskilled in a subject or activity. **3** a person who is fond of or admires something. **4** (*modifier*) of or for amateurs: *an amateur event.* ◆ *adj* **5** not professional or expert: *an amateur approach.* [C18: from F, from L *amātor* lover, from *amāre* to love]
▸**'amateurism** *n*

amateurish ❶ ('æmətərɪʃ) *adj* lacking professional skill or expertise.
▸**'amateurishly** *adv*

amative ('æmətɪv) *adj* a rare word for **amorous.** [C17: from Med. L, from L *amāre* to love]

amatory ('æmətərɪ) *or* **amatorial** (,æmə'tɔːrɪəl) *adj* of, relating to, or inciting sexual love or desire. [C16: from L *amātōrius,* from *amāre* to love]

amaurosis (,æmɔː'rəusɪs) *n* blindness, esp. when occurring without observable damage to the eye. [C17: via NL from Gk: darkening, from *amauroun* to dim]
▸**amaurotic** (,æmɔː'rɒtɪk) *adj*

amaze ❶ (ə'meɪz) *vb* **amazes, amazing, amazed.** (*tr*) **1** to fill with incredulity or surprise; astonish. ◆ *n* **2** an archaic word for **amazement.** [OE *āmasian*]
▸**a'mazing** *adj*

amazement ❶ (ə'meɪzmənt) *n* incredulity or great astonishment; complete wonder.

Amazon ('æməzᵊn) *n* **1** *Greek myth.* one of a race of women warriors of Scythia. **2** (*often not cap.*) any tall, strong, or aggressive woman. [C14: via L from Gk *Amazōn,* from ?]
▸ **Amazonian** (,æmə'zəunɪən) *adj*

ambassador ❶ (æm'bæsədə) *n* **1** a diplomat of the highest rank, accredited as permanent representative to another country. **2 ambassador extraordinary.** a diplomat of the highest rank sent on a special mission. **3 ambassador plenipotentiary.** a diplomat of the first rank with treaty-signing powers. **4 ambassador-at-large.** *US.* an ambassador with special duties who may be sent to more than one government. **5** an authorized representative or messenger. [C14: from OF, from It., from OProvençal *ambaisador,* from *ambaisa* (unattested) mission, errand]
▸**am'bassadress** *fem n* ▸**ambassadorial** (æm,bæsə'dɔːrɪəl) *adj* ▸**am'bassador,ship** *n*

amber ('æmbə) *n* **1** a yellow translucent fossil resin derived from extinct coniferous trees and often containing trapped insects. **2a** a brownish-yellow colour. **2b** (*as adj*): *an amber dress.* **3** an amber traffic light used as a warning between red and green. [C14: from Med. L *ambar,* from Ar. *'anbar* ambergris]

amber gambler *n Brit. inf.* a driver who races through traffic lights when they are at amber.

ambergris ('æmbə,griːs, -grɪs) *n* a waxy substance secreted by the intestinal tract of the sperm whale and often found floating in the sea: used in the manufacture of some perfumes. [C15: from OF *ambre gris* grey amber]

amberjack ('æmbə,dʒæk) *n* any of several large fishes occurring in tropical and subtropical Atlantic waters. [C19: from AMBER + JACK]

ambi- *combining form.* indicating both: *ambidextrous; ambivalence.* [from L: round, on both sides, both, from *ambo* both]

ambidextrous (,æmbɪ'dɛkstrəs) *adj* **1** equally expert with each hand. **2** *Inf.* skilled or adept. **3** underhanded.
▸**ambidexterity** (,æmbɪdɛk'stɛrɪtɪ) *or* **,ambi'dextrousness** *n*

ambience ❶ *or* **ambiance** ('æmbɪəns) *n* the atmosphere of a place. [C19: from F, from *ambiant* surrounding]

ambient ('æmbɪənt) *adj* **1** surrounding. **2** creating a relaxing atmosphere: *ambient music.* [C16: from L *ambiēns* going round, from AMBI- + *īre* to go]

ambiguity ❶ (,æmbɪ'gjuːɪtɪ) *n, pl* **ambiguities. 1** the possibility of interpreting an expression in more than one way. **2** an instance or example of this, as in the sentence *they are cooking apples.* **3** vagueness or uncertainty of meaning.

ambiguous ❶ (æm'bɪgjuəs) *adj* **1** having more than one possible interpretation. **2** difficult to understand; obscure. [C16: from L *ambiguus* going here and there, uncertain, from *ambigere* to go around]
▸**am'biguously** *adv* ▸**am'biguousness** *n*

ambisexual (,æmbɪ'sɛksjuəl) *or* **ambosexual** *adj Biol.* relating to or affecting both the male and female sexes.

ambit ❶ ('æmbɪt) *n* **1** scope or extent. **2** limits or boundary. [C16: from L *ambitus* a going round, from *ambīre* to go round]

ambition ❶ (æm'bɪʃən) *n* **1** strong desire for success or distinction. **2** something so desired; goal. [C14: from OF, from L *ambitiō* a going round (of candidates), from *ambīre* to go round]

ambitious ❶ (æm'bɪʃəs) *adj* **1** having a strong desire for success or achievement. **2** necessitating extraordinary effort or ability: *an ambitious project.* **3** (often foll. by *of*) having a great desire (for something or to do something).
▸**am'bitiousness** *n*

ambivalence ❶ (æm'bɪvələns) *or* **ambivalency** *n* the coexistence of two opposed and conflicting emotions, etc.
▸**am'bivalent** *adj*

amble ❶ ('æmbᵊl) *vb* **ambles, ambling, ambled.** (*intr*) **1** to walk at a leisurely relaxed pace. **2** (of a horse) to move, lifting both legs on one side together. **3** to ride a horse at an amble. ◆ *n* **4** a leisurely motion in walking. **5** a leisurely walk. **6** the ambling gait of a horse. [C14: from OF, from L *ambulāre* to walk]

amblyopia (,æmblɪ'əupɪə) *n* impaired vision with no discernible damage to the eye or optic nerve. [C18: NL, from Gk *ambluōpia,* from *amblus* dull, dim + *ōps* eye]
▸**amblyopic** (,æmblɪ'ɒpɪk) *adj*

amboyna *or* **amboina** (æm'bɔɪnə) *n* the mottled curly-grained wood of an Indonesian tree, used in making furniture.

ambrosia (æm'brəuzɪə) *n* **1** *Classical myth.* the food of the gods, said to bestow immortality. Cf. **nectar** (sense 2). **2** anything particularly delightful to taste or smell. **3** another name for **beebread.** [C16: via L from Gk: immortality, from A-[1] + *brotos* mortal]
▸**am'brosial** *or* **am'brosian** *adj*

ambry ('æmbrɪ) *or* **aumbry** ('ɔːmbrɪ) *n, pl* **ambries** *or* **aumbries. 1** a recessed cupboard in the wall of a church near the altar, used to store sacred vessels, etc. **2** *Obs.* a small cupboard. [C14: from OF *almarie,* ult. from L *armārium* chest for storage, from *arma* arms]

ambulance ('æmbjuləns) *n* a motor vehicle designed to carry sick or

THESAURUS

mixture, alliance, alloy, amalgam, amalgamating, blend, coalition, commingling, composite, compound, fusion, incorporation, integration, joining, meld, merger, mingling, mixing, mixture, union

amass *vb* **1, 2** = **collect**, accumulate, aggregate, assemble, compile, garner, gather, heap up, hoard, pile up, rake up, scrape together

amateur *n* **1** = **nonprofessional**, dabbler, dilettante, layman

amateurish *adj* = **unprofessional**, amateur, bungling, clumsy, crude, inexpert, unaccomplished, unskilful
Antonyms *adj* experienced, expert, practised, professional, skilled

amaze *vb* **1** = **astonish**, alarm, astound, bewilder, boggle the mind, bowl over (*inf.*), confound, daze, dumbfound, electrify, flabbergast, shock, stagger, startle, stun, stupefy, surprise

amazement *n* = **astonishment**, admiration, bewilderment, confusion, marvel, perplexity, shock, stupefaction, surprise, wonder

amazing *adj* **1** = **astonishing**, astounding, breathtaking, eye-opening, jaw-dropping, mind-boggling, overwhelming, staggering, startling, stunning, surprising

ambassador *n* **1, 5** = **representative**, agent, consul, deputy, diplomat, emissary, envoy, legate, minister, plenipotentiary

ambience *n* = **atmosphere**, air, aura, character, complexion, feel, flavour, impression, milieu, mood, quality, setting, spirit, surroundings, temper, tenor, tone, vibes (*sl.*), vibrations (*sl.*)

ambiguity *n* **3** = **vagueness**, doubt, doubtfulness, dubiety, dubiousness, enigma, equivocacy, equivocality, equivocation, inconclusiveness, indefiniteness, indeterminateness, obscurity, puzzle, tergiversation, uncertainty

ambiguous *adj* **1, 2** = **unclear**, clear as mud (*inf.*), cryptic, Delphic, doubtful, dubious, enigmatic, enigmatical, equivocal, inconclusive, indefinite, indeterminate, obscure, oracular, puzzling, uncertain, vague
Antonyms *adj* clear, definite, explicit, obvious, plain, simple, specific, unequivocal, unmistakable, unquestionable

ambit *n* **1** = **range**, extent, radius, reach, scope, sweep **2** = **limit**, border, boundary, circumference, circumscription, compass, confine, edge, extremity, frontier, margin, parameter, perimeter, restraint, restriction, verge

ambition *n* **1** = **enterprise**, aspiration, avidity, desire, drive, eagerness, get-up-and-go (*inf.*), hankering, longing, striving, yearning, zeal **2** = **goal**, aim, aspiration, desire, dream, end, Holy Grail (*inf.*), hope, intent, objective, purpose, wish

ambitious *adj* **1** = **enterprising**, aspiring, avid, desirous, driving, eager, hopeful, intent, purposeful, striving, zealous **2** = **demanding**, arduous, bold, challenging, difficult, elaborate, energetic, exacting, formidable, grandiose, hard, impressive, industrious, pretentious, severe, strenuous
Antonyms *adj* ≠ **enterprising:** apathetic, good-for-nothing, lazy, unambitious, unaspiring ≠ **demanding:** easy, modest, simple, unambitious

ambivalence *n* = **indecision**, clash, conflict, contradiction, doubt, equivocation, fluctuation, hesitancy, irresolution, opposition, uncertainty, vacillation, wavering

ambivalent *adj* = **undecided**, clashing, conflicting, contradictory, debatable, doubtful, equivocal, fluctuating, hesitant, inconclusive, in two minds, irresolute, mixed, opposed, uncertain, unresolved, unsure, vacillating, warring, wavering
Antonyms *adj* certain, clear, conclusive, convinced, decided, definite, free from doubt, positive, sure, unwavering

amble *vb* **1** = **stroll**, dawdle, meander, mosey (*inf.*), ramble, saunter, walk, wander

injured people. [C19: from F, based on (*hôpital*) *ambulant* mobile or field (hospital), from L *ambulāre* to walk]
ambulance chaser *n US sl.* a lawyer who seeks to encourage and profit from the lawsuits of accident victims.
▸**ambulance chasing** *n*
ambulance stocks *pl n* high-performance stocks and shares recommended by a broker to a dissatisfied client to improve their relationship.
ambulant ('æmbjʊlənt) *adj* **1** moving about from place to place. **2** *Med.* another word for **ambulatory** (sense 3).
ambulate ('æmbjʊˌleɪt) *vb* **ambulates, ambulating, ambulated.** (*intr*) to wander about or move from place to place. [C17: from L *ambulāre* to walk]
▸ˌ**ambu'lation** *n*
ambulatory ('æmbjʊlətərɪ) *adj* **1** of or designed for walking. **2** changing position; not fixed. **3** Also: **ambulant.** able to walk. ◆ *n, pl* **ambulatories. 4** a place for walking, such as an aisle or a cloister.
ambuscade (ˌæmbə'skeɪd) *n* **1** an ambush. ◆ *vb* **ambuscades, ambuscading, ambuscaded. 2** to ambush or lie in ambush. [C16: from F, from OIt. *imboscata,* prob. of Gmc origin; cf. AMBUSH]
ambush ➊ ('æmbʊʃ) *n* **1** the act of waiting in a concealed position in order to launch a surprise attack. **2** a surprise attack from such a position. **3** the concealed position from which such an attack is launched. **4** the person or persons waiting to launch such an attack. ◆ *vb* **5** to lie in wait (for). **6** (*tr*) to attack suddenly from a concealed position. [C14: from OF *embuschier* to position in ambush, from *em-* IM- + *-buschier,* from *busche* piece of firewood, prob. of Gmc origin]
ameba (ə'mi:bə) *n, pl* **amebae** (-bi:) *or* **amebas.** the usual US spelling of **amoeba.**
▸**a'mebic** *adj*
ameer (ə'mɪə) *n* a variant spelling of **emir.**
ameliorate ➊ (ə'mi:ljəˌreɪt) *vb* **ameliorates, ameliorating, ameliorated.** to make or become better. [C18: from F *améliorer* to improve, from OF, from *meillor* better, from L *melior*]
▸**aˌmelio'ration** *n* ▸**a'meliorative** *adj* ▸**a'melioˌrator** *n*

> **USAGE NOTE** *Ameliorate* is often wrongly used where *alleviate* is meant. *Ameliorate* is properly used to mean 'improve', not 'make easier to bear', so one should talk about *alleviating* pain or hardship, not *ameliorating* it.

amen (ˌeɪ'mɛn, ˌɑ:'mɛn) *sentence substitute.* **1** so be it!: a term used at the end of a prayer. ◆ *n* **2** the use of the word *amen.* [C13: via LL via Gk from Heb. *āmēn* certainly]
amenable ➊ (ə'mi:nəbᵊl) *adj* **1** likely to listen, cooperate, etc. **2** accountable to some authority; answerable. **3** capable of being tested, judged, etc. [C16: from Anglo-F, from OF, from L *mināre* to drive (cattle), from *minārī* to threaten]
▸**aˌmena'bility** *or* **a'menableness** *n* ▸**a'menably** *adv*
amend ➊ (ə'mɛnd) *vb* (*tr*) **1** to improve; change for the better. **2** to correct. **3** to alter or revise (legislation, etc.) by formal procedure. [C13: from OF, from L *ēmendāre* to EMEND]
▸**a'mendable** *adj* ▸**a'mender** *n*
amendment ➊ (ə'mɛndmənt) *n* **1** correction. **2** an addition or alteration to a document, etc.
amends ➊ (ə'mɛndz) *n* (*functioning as sing*) recompense or compensation for some injury, insult, etc.: *to make amends.* [C13: from OF, from *amende* compensation, from *amender* to EMEND]
amenity ➊ (ə'mi:nɪtɪ) *n, pl* **amenities. 1** (*often pl*) a useful or pleasant facility: *a swimming pool was one of the amenities.* **2** the fact or condition of being agreeable. **3** (*usually pl*) a social courtesy. [C14: from L, from *amoenus* agreeable]
amenorrhoea *or esp. US* **amenorrhea** (æˌmɛnə'rɪə, eɪ-) *n* abnormal absence of menstruation. [C19: from A-[1] + MENO- + -RRHOEA]
ament ('æmənt) *n* another name for **catkin.** Also called: **amentum** (ə'mɛntəm). [C18: from L *āmentum* thong]
▸ˌ**amen'taceous** *adj*
amentia (ə'mɛnʃə) *n* severe mental deficiency, usually congenital. [C14: from L: insanity, from *āmēns* mad, from *mēns* mind]
amerce (ə'mɜ:s) *vb* **amerces, amercing, amerced.** (*tr*) *Obs.* **1** *Law.* to punish by a fine. **2** to punish with any arbitrary penalty. [C14: from Anglo-F, from OF *à merci* at the mercy; see MERCY]
▸**a'mercement** *n*
American ➊ (ə'mɛrɪkən) *adj* **1** of or relating to the United States of America, its inhabitants, or their form of English. **2** of or relating to the American continent. ◆ *n* **3** a native or citizen of the US. **4** a native or inhabitant of any country of North, Central, or South America. **5** the English language as spoken or written in the United States.
Americana (əˌmɛrɪ'kɑ:nə) *pl n* objects, such as documents, relics, etc., relating to America.
American aloe *n* See **aloe** (sense 2).
American Civil War *n* see **Civil War** (sense 2).
American Dream *n* **the.** the notion that the American social, economic, and political system makes success possible for every individual.
American football *n* **1** a team game similar to rugby, with 11 players on each side. **2** the oval-shaped inflated ball used in this game.
American Indian *n* **1** Also called: **Indian, Amerindian, Native American.** a member of any of the indigenous peoples of America, typically having straight black hair and a yellow-to-brown skin. ◆ *adj* **2** Also called: **Amerindian.** of or relating to any of these peoples, their languages, or their cultures.
Americanism (ə'mɛrɪkəˌnɪzəm) *n* **1** a custom, linguistic usage, or other feature peculiar to or characteristic of the United States. **2** loyalty to the United States.
Americanize *or* **Americanise** (ə'mɛrɪkəˌnaɪz) *vb* **Americanizes, Americanizing, Americanized** *or* **Americanises, Americanising, Americanised.** to make or become American in outlook, attitudes, etc.
▸**Aˌmericani'zation** *or* **Aˌmericani'sation** *n*
American Revolution *n* the usual US term for War of American Independence.
americium (ˌæmə'rɪsɪəm) *n* a white metallic transuranic element artificially produced from plutonium. It is used as an alpha-particle source. Symbol: Am; atomic no.: 95; half-life of most stable isotope, ^{243}Am: 7.4×10^3 years.
Amerindian (ˌæmə'rɪndɪən) *n also* **Amerind** ('æmərɪnd), *adj* another word for **American Indian.**
▸ˌ**Amer'indic** *adj*
amethyst ('æmɪθɪst) *n* **1** a purple or violet variety of quartz used as a gemstone. **2** a purple variety of sapphire. **3a** the purple colour of amethyst. **3b** (*as adj*): *amethyst shadow.* [C13: from OF, from L, from Gk *amethustos,* lit.: not drunken, from A-[1] + *methuein* to make drunk; from the belief that the stone could prevent intoxication]
▸**amethystine** (ˌæmɪ'θɪstaɪn) *adj*
Amex ('æmɛks) *n acronym for* **1** *Trademark.* American Express. **2** American Stock Exchange.
AMF *abbrev. for* Australian Military Forces.
Amharic (æm'hærɪk) *n* **1** the official language of Ethiopia. ◆ *adj* **2** denoting this language.
amiable ➊ ('eɪmɪəbᵊl) *adj* having or displaying a pleasant or agreeable nature; friendly. [C14: from OF, from LL *amīcābilis* AMICABLE]
▸ˌ**amia'bility** *or* **'amiableness** *n* ▸**'amiably** *adv*
amianthus (ˌæmɪ'ænθəs) *n* any of the fine silky varieties of asbestos. [C17: from L *amiantus,* from Gk *amiantos* unsullied, from A-[1] + *miainein* to pollute]
amicable ➊ ('æmɪkəbᵊl) *adj* characterized by friendliness: *an amicable agreement.* [C15: from LL *amīcābilis,* from L *amīcus* friend]
▸ˌ**amica'bility** *or* **'amicableness** *n* ▸**'amicably** *adv*

THESAURUS

ambush *n* **1-3** = **trap**, ambuscade, attack, concealment, cover, hiding, hiding place, lying in wait, retreat, shelter, waylaying ◆ *vb* **5, 6** = **trap**, ambuscade, attack, bushwhack (*US*), ensnare, surprise, waylay
ameliorate *vb* = **improve**, advance, allay, alleviate, amend, assuage, benefit, better, ease, elevate, make better, meliorate, mend, mitigate, promote, raise, reform, relieve
amelioration *n* = **improvement**, advance, amendment, betterment, change for the better, correction, enhancement, melioration, recovery, upswing
amenability *n* **1** = **receptiveness**, accessibility, acquiescence, agreeableness, compliance, cooperativeness *or* co-operativeness, impressionability, malleability, open-mindedness, openness, persuadability, perviousness, pliancy *or* pliantness, readiness, responsiveness, suggestibleness, susceptibility, tractability, willingness
Antonyms *n* doggedness, fixedness, headstrongness, imperviousness, obduracy *or* obdurateness, obstinacy, self-willedness, single-mindedness, steadfastness, stubbornness
amenable *adj* **1** = **receptive**, able to be influenced, acquiescent, agreeable, compliant, open, persuadable, responsive, susceptible, tractable
Antonyms *adj* inflexible, intractable, mulish, obdurate, obstinate, pig-headed, recalcitrant, stiff-necked, stubborn, unbending, unyielding
amend *vb* **1-3** = **change**, alter, ameliorate, better, correct, enhance, fix, improve, mend, modify, rectify, reform, remedy, repair, revise, tweak (*inf.*)
amendment *n* **1** = **change**, alteration, amelioration, betterment, correction, emendation, enhancement, improvement, mending, modification, rectification, reform, remedy, repair, revision **2** = **alteration**, addendum, addition, adjunct, attachment, clarification
amends *pl n* = **compensation**, apology, atonement, expiation, indemnity, recompense, redress, reparation, requital, restitution, restoration, satisfaction
amenity *n* **1** = **facility**, advantage, comfort, convenience, service **2** = **courtesy**, affability, agreeableness, amiability, complaisance, mildness, pleasantness, politeness, refinement, suavity
Antonyms *n* ≠ **courtesy:** bad manners, discourtesy, impoliteness, incivility, rudeness, ungraciousness
American *adj* **1** = **Yankee** *or* **Yank**, stateside, U.S. ◆ *n* **3** = **Yankee** *or* **Yank**, Yankee Doodle
amiability *n* = **pleasantness**, affability, agreeableness, amiableness, attractiveness, benignity, charm, cheerfulness, delightfulness, engagingness, friendliness, friendship, geniality, good humour, good nature, kindliness, kindness, lovableness, pleasingness, sociability, sweetness, winsomeness
amiable *adj* = **pleasant**, affable, agreeable, attractive, benign, charming, cheerful, congenial, delightful, engaging, friendly, genial, good-humoured, good-natured, kind, kindly, likable *or* likeable, lovable, obliging, pleasing, sociable, sweet-tempered, winning, winsome
Antonyms *adj* disagreeable, displeasing, hostile, ill-natured, loathsome, repellent, sour, unfriendly, unpleasant
amicability *n* = **friendliness**, amiability, amicableness, amity, brotherliness, civility, cordiality, courtesy, fraternity, friendship, goodwill,

amice ('æmɪs) *n Christianity.* a rectangular piece of white linen worn by priests around the neck and shoulders under the alb or, formerly, on the head. [C15: from OF, from L *amictus* cloak]

amicus curiae (æ'mi:kʊs 'kjʊərɪ,i:) *n, pl* **amici curiae** (æ'mi:kaɪ) *Law.* a person, not directly engaged in a case, who advises the court. [L, lit.: friend of the court]

amid ❶ (ə'mɪd) *or* **amidst** *prep* in the middle of; among. [OE *on middan* in the middle]

amide ('æmaɪd) *n* **1** any organic compound containing the group $-CONR_2$, where R denotes a hydrogen atom or a hydrocarbon group. **2** (*modifier*) containing the group $-CONR_2$: *amide group or radical.* **3** an inorganic compound containing the NH_2^- ion and having the general formula $M(NH_2)_x$, where M is a metal atom. [C19: from AM(MONIA) + -IDE]

amidships (ə'mɪdʃɪps) *adv, adj (postpositive) Naut.* at, near, or towards the centre of a vessel.

amigo (æ'mi:gəʊ, ə-) *n, pl* **amigos.** a friend; comrade. [Sp., from L *amicus*]

amine (ə'mi:n, 'æmɪn) *n* an organic base formed by replacing one or more of the hydrogen atoms of ammonia by hydrocarbon groups. [C19: from AM(MONIUM) + -INE[2]]

amino (ə'mi:nəʊ) *n (modifier)* of or containing the group of atoms $-NH_2$: *amino radical.*

amino acid *n* **1** any of a group of organic compounds containing one or more amino groups, $-NH_2$, and one or more carboxyl groups, -COOH. **2** any of a group of organic nitrogenous compounds that form the component molecules of proteins.

amino resin *n* a thermosetting synthetic resin used as an adhesive and coating for paper and textiles.

amir (ə'mɪə) *n* a variant spelling of **emir.** [C19: from Ar., var. of EMIR]
▸**a'mirate** *n*

Amish ('æmɪʃ, 'ɑ:-) *adj* of a US and Canadian Mennonite sect. [C19: from G *Amisch*, after Jakob *Amman*, 17th-cent. Swiss Mennonite bishop]

amiss ❶ (ə'mɪs) *adv* **1** in an incorrect or defective manner. **2 take (something) amiss.** to be annoyed or offended by (something). ◆ *adj* **3** (*postpositive*) wrong or faulty. [C13 *a mis*, from *mis* wrong]

amitosis (,æmɪ'təʊsɪs) *n* a form of cell division in which the nucleus and cytoplasm divide without the formation of chromosomes. [C20: from A-[1] + MITOSIS]
▸**amitotic** (,æmɪ'tɒtɪk) *adj*

amity ❶ ('æmɪtɪ) *n, pl* **amities.** friendship; cordiality. [C15: from OF *amité*, ult. from L *amīcus* friend]

ammeter ('æm,mi:tə) *n* an instrument for measuring an electric current in amperes. [C19: AM(PERE) + -METER]

ammo ('æməʊ) *n Inf.* short for **ammunition.**

ammonia (ə'məʊnɪə) *n* **1** a colourless pungent gas used in the manufacture of fertilizers and as a refrigerant and solvent. Formula: NH_3. **2** a solution of ammonia in water, containing ammonium hydroxide. [C18: from NL, from L (*sal*) *ammōniacus* (sal) AMMONIAC]

ammoniac (ə'məʊnɪ,æk) *n* a gum resin obtained from the stems of an Asian plant and formerly used as a stimulant, perfume, and in porcelain cement. Also called: **gum ammoniac.** [C14: from L, from Gk *ammōniakos* belonging to Ammon (apparently the gum resin was extracted from plants found in Libya near the temple of Ammon)]

ammoniacal (,æmə'naɪək^{ə}l) *adj* of, containing, or resembling ammonia.

ammoniate (ə'məʊnɪ,eɪt) *vb* **ammoniates, ammoniating, ammoniated.** to unite or treat with ammonia.
▸**am,moni'ation** *n*

ammonify (ə'mɒnɪ,faɪ) *vb* **ammonifies, ammonifying, ammonified.** to treat or impregnate with ammonia or a compound of ammonia.
▸**am,monifi'cation** *n*

ammonite ('æmə,naɪt) *n* **1** any extinct marine cephalopod mollusc of the order *Ammonoidea*, which were common in Mesozoic times and had a coiled partitioned shell. **2** the shell of any of these animals, commonly occurring as a fossil. [C18: from L *cornū Ammōnis*, lit.: horn of Ammon]

ammonium (ə'məʊnɪəm) *n (modifier)* of or containing the monovalent group NH_4– or the ion NH_4^+: *ammonium compounds.*

ammonium chloride *n* a white soluble crystalline solid used as an electrolyte in dry batteries. Formula: NH_4Cl. Also called: **sal ammoniac.**

ammonium hydroxide *n* a compound existing in solution when ammonia is dissolved in water. Formula: NH_4OH.

ammonium sulphate *n* a white soluble crystalline solid used mainly as a fertilizer and in water purification. Formula: $(NH_4)_2SO_4$.

ammunition ❶ (,æmjʊ'nɪʃən) *n* **1** any projectiles, such as bullets, rockets, etc., that can be discharged from a weapon. **2** bombs, missiles, chemicals, etc., capable of use as weapons. **3** any means of defence or attack, as in an argument. [C17: from obs. F *amunition*, by mistaken division from earlier *la munition*; see MUNITION]

amnesia (æm'ni:zjə, -ʒjə, -zɪə) *n* a defect in memory, esp. one resulting from a pathological cause. [C19: via NL from Gk: forgetfulness, prob. from *amnēstia* oblivion]
▸**amnesiac** (æm'ni:zɪ,æk) *or* **amnesic** (æm'ni:sɪk, -zɪk) *adj, n*

amnesty ❶ ('æmnɪstɪ) *n, pl* **amnesties. 1** a general pardon, esp. for offences against a government. **2** a period during which a law is suspended to allow offenders to admit their crime without fear of prosecution. ◆ *vb* **amnesties, amnestying, amnestied. 3** (*tr*) to overlook or forget (an offence). [C16: from L *amnēstia*, from Gk: oblivion, from A-[1] + *-mnēstos*, from *mnasthai* to remember]

Amnesty International *n* an international organization that works to secure the release of people imprisoned for their beliefs, to ban the use of torture, and to abolish the death penalty. Abbrev.: **AI.**

amniocentesis (,æmnɪəʊsen'ti:sɪs) *n, pl* **amniocenteses** (-si:z). removal of amniotic fluid for diagnostic purposes by the insertion into the womb of a hollow needle. [C20: from AMNION + *centesis* from Gk *kentēsis* from *kentein* to prick]

amnion ('æmnɪən) *n, pl* **amnions** *or* **amnia** (-nɪə). the innermost of two membranes enclosing an embryonic reptile, bird, or mammal. [C17: via NL from Gk: a little lamb, from *amnos* a lamb]
▸**amniotic** (,æmnɪ'ɒtɪk) *adj*

amniotic fluid *n* the fluid surrounding the fetus in the womb.

amoeba *or US* **ameba** (ə'mi:bə) *n, pl* **amoebae** (-bi:) *or* **amoebas** *or US* **amebae** *or* **amebas.** any of a phylum of protozoans able to change shape because of the movements of cell processes. They live in fresh water or soil or as parasites in man and animals. [C19: from NL, from Gk, from *ameibein* to change, exchange]
▸**a'moebic** *or US* **a'mebic** *adj*

amok ❶ (ə'mʌk, ə'mɒk) *or* **amuck** (ə'mʌk) *n* **1** a state of murderous frenzy. ◆ *adv* **2 run amok.** to run about as with a frenzied desire to kill. [C17: from Malay *amoq* furious assault]

among ❶ (ə'mʌŋ) *or* **amongst** *prep* **1** in the midst of: *he lived among the Indians.* **2** to each of: *divide the reward among yourselves.* **3** in the group, class, or number of: *among the greatest writers.* **4** taken out of (a group): *he is one among many.* **5** with one another within a group: *decide it among yourselves.* **6** in the general opinion or practice of: *accepted among experts.* [OE *amang*, contracted from *on gemang* in the group of, from ON + *gemang* crowd]

USAGE NOTE See at **between.**

amontillado (ə,mɒntɪ'lɑ:dəʊ) *n* a medium-dry sherry. [C19: from Sp. *vino amontillado* wine of *Montilla*, town in Spain]

amoral ❶ (,eɪ'mɒrəl) *adj* **1** having no moral quality; nonmoral. **2** without moral standards or principles.
▸**amorality** (,eɪmɒ'rælɪtɪ) *n*

USAGE NOTE *Amoral* is often wrongly used where *immoral* is meant. *Immoral* is properly used to talk about the breaking of moral rules, *amoral* about people who have no moral code or about places or situations where moral considerations do not apply.

amorist ('æmərɪst) *n* a lover or a writer about love.

amoroso (,æmə'rəʊsəʊ) *adj, adv* **1** *Music.* (to be played) tenderly. ◆ *n* **2** a rich sweet sherry. [from It. & Sp.: AMOROUS]

amorous ❶ ('æmərəs) *adj* **1** inclined towards or displaying love or de-

THESAURUS

harmony, kindliness, kindness, neighbourliness, peace, peaceableness, peacefulness, politeness, sociability

amicable *adj* = **friendly**, amiable, brotherly, civil, cordial, courteous, fraternal, good-humoured, harmonious, kind, kindly, neighbourly, peaceable, peaceful, polite, sociable
Antonyms *adj* antagonistic, bellicose, belligerent, disagreeable, hostile, ill-disposed, impolite, inimical, pugnacious, quarrelsome, uncivil, unfriendly, unkind, unsociable

amid *prep* = **in the middle of**, among, amongst, in the midst of, in the thick of, surrounded by

amiss *adv* **1** = **wrongly**, erroneously, faultily, improperly, inappropriately, incorrectly, mistakenly, unsuitably **2** *As in* **take (something) amiss** = **as an insult**, as offensive, out of turn, wrongly ◆ *adj* **3** = **wrong**, awry, confused, defective, erroneous, fallacious, false, faulty, improper, inaccurate, inappropriate, incorrect, mistaken, out of order, unsuitable, untoward
Antonyms *adv* ≠ **wrongly**: appropriately, correctly, properly, rightly, suitably, well ◆ *adj* ≠ **wrong**: accurate, appropriate, correct, in order, O.K. *or* okay (*inf.*), perfect, proper, right, suitable, true

amity *n* = **friendship**, accord, amicability, brotherhood, comity, comradeship, concord, cordiality, fellowship, fraternity, friendliness, goodwill, harmony, kindliness, peace, peacefulness, tranquillity, understanding

ammunition *n* **1** = **munitions**, armaments, cartridges, explosives, materiel, powder, rounds, shells, shot, shot and shell

amnesty *n* **1** = **general pardon**, absolution, condonation, dispensation, forgiveness, immunity, oblivion, remission (*of penalty*), reprieve

amok *adv* **2** *As in* **run amok** = **madly**, berserk, destructively, ferociously, frenziedly, in a frenzy, insanely, maniacally, murderously, savagely, uncontrollably, violently, wildly

among *prep* **1** = **in the midst of**, amid, amidst, in association with, in the middle of, in the thick of, midst, surrounded by, together with, with **2** = **to each of**, between **3** = **in the group of**, in the class of, in the company of, in the number of, out of

amoral *adj* **1, 2** = **unethical**, nonmoral, unvirtuous

amorous *adj* **1, 2** = **loving**, affectionate, amatory, ardent, attached, doting, enamoured, erotic, fond, impassioned, in love, lovesick, lustful, passionate, tender

sire. **2** in love. **3** of or relating to love. [C14: from OF, from Med. L, from L *amor* love]
▸**'amorously** *adv* ▸**'amorousness** *n*

amorphous ❶ (ə'mɔːfəs) *adj* **1** lacking a definite shape. **2** of no recognizable character or type. **3** (of rocks, etc.) not having a crystalline structure. [C18: from NL, from Gk, from A-[1] + *morphē* shape]
▸**a'morphism** *n* ▸**a'morphousness** *n*

amortize *or* **amortise** (ə'mɔːtaɪz) *vb* **amortizes, amortizing, amortized** *or* **amortises, amortising, amortised.** (*tr*) **1** *Finance.* to liquidate (a debt, mortgage, etc.) by payments or by periodic transfers to a sinking fund. **2** to write off (a wasting asset) by transfers to a sinking fund. **3** *Property law.* (formerly) to transfer (lands, etc.) in mortmain. [C14: from Med. L, from OF *amortir* to reduce to the point of death, ult. from L *ad* to + *mors* death]
▸**a,morti'zation** *or* **a,morti'sation** *n*

amount ❶ (ə'maʊnt) *n* **1** extent; quantity. **2** the total of two or more quantities. **3** the full value or significance of something. **4** a principal sum plus the interest on it, as in a loan. ◆ *vb* **5** (*intr*; usually foll. by *to*) to be equal or add up. [C13: from OF *amonter* to go up, from *amont* upwards, from *a* to + *mont* mountain (from L *mōns*)]

> **USAGE NOTE** The use of a plural noun after *amount of* (*an amount of bananas; the amount of refugees*) should be avoided: *a quantity of bananas; the number of refugees.*

amount of substance *n* a measure of the number of entities (atoms, molecules, ions, electrons, etc.) present in a substance, expressed in moles.

amour ❶ (ə'mʊə) *n* a love affair, esp. a secret or illicit one. [C13: from OF, from L *amor* love]

amour-propre *French.* (amurprɔprə) *n* self-respect.

amp (æmp) *n* **1** an ampere. **2** *Inf.* an amplifier.

AMP *n Biochem.* adenosine monophosphate; a substance produced by hydrolysis of ATP with the liberation of energy. The cyclic form (**cyclic AMP**) acts as a messenger in many hormone-induced biochemical reactions.

ampelopsis (,æmpɪ'lɒpsɪs) *n* any of a genus of woody climbing plants of tropical and subtropical Asia and America. [C19: from NL, from Gk *ampelos* grapevine]

amperage ('æmpərɪdʒ) *n* the strength of an electric current measured in amperes.

ampere ('æmpɛə) *n* **1** the basic SI unit of electric current; the constant current that, when maintained in two parallel conductors of infinite length and negligible cross section placed 1 metre apart in free space, produces a force of 2×10^{-7} newton per metre between them. **2** a former unit of electric current (**international ampere**); the current that, when passed through a solution of silver nitrate, deposits silver at the rate of 0.001118 gram per second. ◆ Abbrev.: **amp.** Symbol: A

ampere-turn *n* a unit of magnetomotive force; the magnetomotive force produced by a current of 1 ampere passing through one complete turn of a coil.

ampersand ('æmpə,sænd) *n* the character (&), meaning *and*: *John Brown & Co.* [C19: shortened from *and per se and*, that is, the symbol & by itself (represents) *and*]

amphetamine (æm'fɛtə,miːn) *n* a synthetic colourless liquid used medicinally as the white crystalline sulphate, mainly for its stimulant action on the central nervous system. [C20: from A(LPHA) + M(ETHYL) + PH(ENYL) + ET(HYL) + AMINE]

amphi- *prefix* **1** on both sides; at both ends; of both kinds: *amphipod; amphibious.* **2** around: *amphibole.* [from Gk]

amphibian (æm'fɪbɪən) *n* **1** any cold-blooded vertebrate of the class *Amphibia*, typically living on land but breeding in water. The class includes newts, frogs, and toads. **2** an aircraft able to land and take off from both water and land. **3** any vehicle able to travel on both water and land. ◆ *adj* **4** another word for **amphibious. 5** of or belonging to the class *Amphibia*.

amphibious (æm'fɪbɪəs) *adj* **1** able to live both on land and in the water, as frogs, etc. **2** designed for operation on or from both water and land. **3** relating to military forces and operations launched from the sea against an enemy shore. **4** having a dual or mixed nature. [C17: from Gk *amphibios*, lit.: having a double life, from AMPHI- + *bios* life]
▸**am'phibiousness** *n*

amphibole ('æmfɪ,bəʊl) *n* any of a large group of minerals consisting of the silicates of calcium, iron, magnesium, sodium, and aluminium, which are common constituents of igneous rocks. [C17: from F, from Gk *amphibolos* uncertain; so called from the large number of varieties in the group]

amphibology (,æmfɪ'bɒlədʒɪ) *or* **amphiboly** (æm'fɪbəlɪ) *n, pl* **amphibologies** *or* **amphibolies.** ambiguity of expression, esp. when due to a grammatical construction, as in *save rags and waste paper.* [C14: from LL, ult. from Gk *amphibolos* ambiguous]

amphimixis (,æmfɪ'mɪksɪs) *n, pl* **amphimixes** (-'mɪksiːz). true sexual reproduction, esp. the fusion of gametes from two organisms. [C19: from AMPHI- + Gk *mixis* a blending]
▸**amphimictic** (,æmfɪ'mɪktɪk) *adj*

amphioxus (,æmfɪ'ɒksəs) *n, pl* **amphioxi** (-'ɒksaɪ) *or* **amphioxuses.** another name for the **lancelet.** [C19: from NL, from AMPHI- + Gk *oxus* sharp]

amphipod ('æmfɪ,pɒd) *n* **1** any marine or freshwater crustacean of the order *Amphipoda*, such as the sand hoppers, in which the body is laterally compressed. ◆ *adj* **2** of or belonging to the *Amphipoda*.

amphiprostyle (æm'fɪprə,staɪl) *adj* **1** (esp. of a classical temple) having a set of columns at both ends but not at the sides. ◆ *n* **2** a temple of this kind.

amphisbaena (æmfɪs'biːnə) *n, pl* **amphisbaenae** (-niː) *or* **amphisbaenas. 1** a genus of wormlike lizards of tropical America. **2** *Classical myth.* a fabulous serpent with a head at each end. [C16: from L, from Gk *amphisbaina*, from *amphis* both ways + *bainein* to go]

amphitheatre *or US* **amphitheater** ('æmfɪ,θɪətə) *n* **1** a building, usually circular or oval, in which tiers of seats rise from a central open arena. **2** a place where contests are held. **3** any level circular area of ground surrounded by higher ground. **4** a gallery in a theatre. **5** a lecture room in which seats are tiered away from a central area.

amphora ('æmfərə) *n, pl* **amphorae** (-fə,riː) *or* **amphoras.** a Greek or Roman two-handled narrow-necked jar for oil, etc. [C17: from L, from Gk, from AMPHI- + *phoreus* bearer, from *pherein* to bear]

amphoteric (,æmfə'tɛrɪk) *adj Chem.* able to function as either a base or an acid. [C19: from Gk *amphoteros* each of two (from *amphō* both) + -IC]

ampicillin (,æmpɪ'sɪlɪn) *n* a form of penicillin used to treat various infections.

ample ❶ ('æmp[ə]l) *adj* **1** more than sufficient: *an ample helping.* **2** large: *of ample proportions.* [C15: from OF, from L *amplus* spacious]
▸**'ampleness** *n*

amplification ❶ (,æmplɪfɪ'keɪʃən) *n* **1** the act or result of amplifying. **2** material added to a statement, story, etc., to expand or clarify it. **3** a statement, story, etc., with such additional material. **4** *Electronics.* the increase in strength of an electrical signal by means of an amplifier.

amplifier ('æmplɪ,faɪə) *n* **1** an electronic device used to increase the strength of the current fed into it, esp. one for the amplification of sound signals in a radio, record player, etc. **2** *Photog.* an additional lens for altering focal length. **3** a person or thing that amplifies.

amplify ❶ ('æmplɪ,faɪ) *vb* **amplifies, amplifying, amplified. 1** (*tr*) to increase in size, extent, effect, etc., as by the addition of extra material. **2** *Electronics.* to produce amplification of (electrical signals). **3** (*intr*) to expand a speech, narrative, etc. [C15: from OF, ult. from L *amplificāre* to enlarge, from *amplus* spacious + *facere* to make]

amplitude ❶ ('æmplɪ,tjuːd) *n* **1** greatness of extent; magnitude. **2** abundance. **3** breadth or scope, as of the mind. **4** *Astron.* the angular distance along the horizon measured from true east or west to the point of intersection of the vertical circle passing through a celestial body. **5** *Physics.* the maximum displacement from the zero or mean position of a periodic motion. [C16: from L, from *amplus* spacious]

amplitude modulation *n* one of the principal methods of transmitting information using radio waves, the relevant signal being superimposed onto a radio-frequency carrier wave. The frequency of the carrier wave remains unchanged but its amplitude is varied in accordance with the amplitude of the input signal. Cf. **frequency modulation.**

THESAURUS

Antonyms *adj* aloof, cold, distant, frigid, frosty, indifferent, passionless, stand-offish, undemonstrative, unfeeling, unloving

amorousness *n* **1, 2** = **desire**, affection, ardour, concupiscence, fondness, lovingness, lust, passion, the hots (*sl.*)

amorphous *adj* **1, 2** = **shapeless**, characterless, formless, inchoate, indeterminate, irregular, nebulous, nondescript, unformed, unshaped, unshapen, unstructured, vague
Antonyms *adj* definite, distinct, regular, shaped, structured

amount *n* **1** = **quantity**, bulk, expanse, extent, lot, magnitude, mass, measure, number, supply, volume **2** = **total**, addition, aggregate, entirety, extent, lot, sum, sum total, whole **3** = **importance**, full effect, full value, import, result, significance ◆ *vb* **5** = **add up to**, aggregate, become, come to, develop into, equal, grow, mean, purport, total

amour *n* = **love affair**, affair, *affaire de coeur*, intrigue, liaison, relationship, romance

ample *adj* **1, 2** = **plenty**, abounding, abundant, big, bountiful, broad, capacious, commodious, copious, enough and to spare, expansive, extensive, full, generous, great, large, lavish, liberal, plenteous, plentiful, profuse, rich, roomy, spacious, substantial, two a penny, unrestricted, voluminous, wide
Antonyms *adj* inadequate, insufficient, little, meagre, restricted, scant, skimpy, small, sparse, unsatisfactory

amplification *n* **1** = **increase**, augmentation, boosting, deepening, dilation, enlargement, expansion, extension, heightening, intensification, lengthening, magnification, raising, strengthening, stretching, widening **2** = **explanation**, augmentation, development, elaboration, expansion, expatiation, fleshing out, rounding out, supplementing

amplify *vb* **1** = **expand**, augment, boost, deepen, dilate, enlarge, extend, heighten, increase, intensify, lengthen, magnify, raise, strengthen, stretch, widen **3** = **go into detail**, augment, develop, elaborate, enlarge, expand, expatiate, explain, flesh out, round out, supplement
Antonyms *vb* ≠ **expand:** boil down, condense, curtail, cut down, decrease, reduce ≠ **go into detail:** abbreviate, abridge, simplify

amplitude *n* **1, 3** = **extent**, bigness, breadth, bulk, capaciousness, compass, dimension, expanse, greatness, hugeness, largeness, magnitude, mass, range, reach, scope, size, spaciousness, sweep, vastness, width **2** = **fullness**, abundance, ampleness, completeness,

amply ➊ (ˈæmplɪ) *adv* fully; generously.

ampoule (ˈæmpuːl, -pjuːl) *or esp. US* **ampule** *n Med.* a small glass vessel in which liquids for injection are hermetically sealed. [C19: from F, from L: see AMPULLA]

ampulla (æmˈpʊlə) *n, pl* **ampullae** (-ˈpʊliː). **1** *Anat.* the dilated end part of certain ducts or canals. **2** *Christianity.* **2a** a vessel for the wine and water used at the Eucharist. **2b** a small flask for consecrated oil. **3** a Roman two-handled bottle for oil, wine, or perfume. [C16: from L, dim. of AMPHORA]

amputate ➊ (ˈæmpjʊˌteɪt) *vb* **amputates, amputating, amputated.** *Surgery.* to remove (all or part of a limb). [C17: from L, from *am-* around + *putāre* to trim, prune]
▸ˌ**ampuˈtation** *n*

amputee (ˌæmpjʊˈtiː) *n* a person who has had a limb amputated.

amu *abbrev. for* atomic mass unit.

amuck ➊ (əˈmʌk) *n, adv* a variant spelling of **amok.**

amulet ➊ (ˈæmjʊlɪt) *n* a trinket or piece of jewellery worn as a protection against evil; charm. [C17: from L *amulētum,* from ?]

amuse ➊ (əˈmjuːz) *vb* **amuses, amusing, amused.** (*tr*) **1** to entertain; divert. **2** to cause to laugh or smile. [C15: from OF *amuser* to cause to be idle, from *muser* to MUSE[1]]

amusement ➊ (əˈmjuːzmənt) *n* **1** something that amuses, such as a game or pastime. **2** a mechanical device used for entertainment, as at a fair. **3** the act of amusing or the state or quality of being amused.

amusement arcade *n Brit.* a covered area having coin-operated game machines.

amusing ➊ (əˈmjuːzɪŋ) *adj* entertaining; causing a smile or laugh.
▸**aˈmusingly** *adv*

amygdalin (əˈmɪgdəlɪn) *n* a white soluble bitter-tasting glycoside extracted from bitter almonds. [C17: from Gk: ALMOND + -IN]

amyl (ˈæmɪl) *n* (*modifier*) (no longer in technical usage) of or containing any of eight isomeric forms of the monovalent group C_5H_{11}–: *amyl group or radical.* [C19: from L: AMYLUM]

amylaceous (ˌæmɪˈleɪʃəs) *adj* of or resembling starch.

amyl alcohol *n* **1** any of eight isomeric alcohols with the general formula $C_5H_{11}OH$. **2** a mixture of these alcohols, used in preparing amyl nitrite.

amylase (ˈæmɪˌleɪz) *n* any of several enzymes that hydrolyse starch and glycogen to simple sugars, such as glucose.

amyl nitrite *n* an ester of amyl alcohol and nitrous acid used as a vasodilator, esp. to treat angina.

amyloid (ˈæmɪˌlɔɪd) *n* **1** any substance resembling starch. ◆ *adj* **2** starchlike.

amylopsin (ˌæmɪˈlɒpsɪn) *n* an enzyme of the pancreatic juice that converts starch into sugar; pancreatic amylase. [C19: from AMYL + (PE)PSIN]

amylum (ˈæmɪləm) *n* another name for **starch** (senses 1,2). [L, from Gk *amulon* fine meal, starch]

amyotrophic lateral sclerosis (ˌæmɪəʊˈtrəʊfɪk) *n* a form of motor neurone disease in which degeneration of motor tracts in the spinal cord causes progressive muscular paralysis starting in the limbs. Also called: **Lou Gehrig's disease.**

Amytal (ˈæmɪˌtæl) *n Trademark.* sodium amytal, used as a sedative and hypnotic.

an[1] (æn; *unstressed* ən) *determiner* (*indefinite article*) a form of **a**[1], used before an initial vowel sound: *an old car; an elf; an hour.* [OE *ān* ONE]

> **USAGE NOTE** *An* was formerly often used before words that begin with *h* and are unstressed on the first syllable: *an hotel; an historic meeting.* Sometimes the initial *h* was not pronounced. This usage is now becoming obsolete.

an[2] *or* **an'** (æn; *unstressed* ən) *conj* (*subordinating*) an obsolete or dialect word for **if.** See **and** (sense 8).

An *the chemical symbol for* actinon.

an. *abbrev. for* anno. [L: in the year]

an- *or before a consonant* **a-** *prefix* not; without: *anaphrodisiac.* [from Gk]

-an, -ean, *or* **-ian** *suffix.* **1** (*forming adjectives and nouns*) belonging to; coming from; typical of; adhering to: *European; Elizabethan; Christian.* **2** (*forming nouns*) a person who specializes or is expert in: *dietitian.* [from L *-ānus,* suffix of adjectives]

ana- *or before a vowel* **an-** *prefix* **1** up; upwards: *anadromous.* **2** again: *anagram.* **3** back; backwards: *anapaest.* [from Gk *ana*]

-ana *or* **-iana** *suffix forming nouns.* denoting a collection of objects or information relating to a particular individual, subject or place: *Victoriana, Americana.* [NL, from L *-āna,* lit.: matters relating to, neuter pl of *-ānus;* see -AN]

Anabaptist (ˌænəˈbæptɪst) *n* **1** a member of any of various Protestant movements, esp. of the 16th century, that rejected infant baptism, insisted that adults be rebaptized, and sought to establish Christian communism. ◆ *adj* **2** of these sects or their doctrines. [C16: from Ecclesiastical L, from *anabaptīzāre* to baptize again, from LGk *anabaptizein*]
▸ˌ**Anaˈbaptism** *n*

anabas (ˈænəˌbæs) *n* any of several freshwater fishes, esp. the climbing perch, that can travel on land. [C19: from NL, from Gk *anabainein* to go up]

anabasis (əˈnæbəsɪs) *n, pl* **anabases** (-ˌsiːz). **1** the march of Cyrus the Younger from Sardis to Cunaxa in Babylonia in 401 B.C., described by Xenophon in his *Anabasis.* **2** any military expedition, esp. one from the coast to the interior. [C18: from Gk: a going up, from *anabainein* to go up]

anabatic (ˌænəˈbætɪk) *adj Meteorol.* (of air currents) rising upwards. [C19: from Gk *anabatikos* relating to ascents, from *anabainein* to go up]

anabiosis (ˌænəbaɪˈəʊsɪs) *n* the ability to return to life after apparent death; suspended animation. [C19: via NL from Gk, from *anabioein* to come back to life]
▸**anabiotic** (ˌænəbaɪˈɒtɪk) *adj*

anabolic steroid *n* any of a group of synthetic steroid hormones (androgens) used to stimulate muscle and bone growth for athletic or therapeutic purposes.

anabolism (əˈnæbəˌlɪzəm) *n* a metabolic process in which complex molecules are synthesized from simpler ones with the storage of energy; constructive metabolism. [C19: from ANA- + (META)BOLISM]
▸**anabolic** (ˌænəˈbɒlɪk) *adj*

anachronism (əˈnækrəˌnɪzəm) *n* **1** the representation of an event, person, or thing in a historical context in which it could not have occurred or existed. **2** a person or thing that belongs or seems to belong to another time. [C17: from L, from Gk *anakhronismos* a mistake in chronology, from ANA- + *khronos* time]
▸**aˌnachroˈnistic** *adj* ▸**aˌnachroˈnistically** *adv*

anacoluthon (ˌænəkəˈluːθɒn) *n, pl* **anacolutha** (-θə). a construction that involves the change from one grammatical sequence to another within a single sentence. [C18: from LL, from Gk, from *anakolouthos* not consistent, from AN- + *akolouthos* following]

anaconda (ˌænəˈkɒndə) *n* a very large nonvenomous arboreal and semiaquatic snake of tropical South America, which kills its prey by constriction. [C18: prob. changed from Sinhalese *henakandayā* whip snake; orig. referring to a snake of Sri Lanka]

anacrusis (ˌænəˈkruːsɪs) *n, pl* **anacruses** (-siːz). **1** *Prosody.* one or more unstressed syllables at the beginning of a line of verse. **2** *Music.* an unstressed note or group of notes immediately preceding the strong first beat of the first bar. [C19: from Gk, from *anakrouein* to strike up, from ANA- + *krouein* to strike]

anadromous (əˈnædrəməs) *adj* (of fishes such as the salmon) migrating up rivers from the sea in order to breed. [C18: from Gk *anadromos* running upwards]

anaemia *or US* **anemia** (əˈniːmɪə) *n* a deficiency in the number of red blood cells or in their haemoglobin content, resulting in pallor and lack of energy. [C19: from NL, from Gk *anaimia* lack of blood, from AN- + *haima* blood]

anaemic ➊ *or US* **anemic** (əˈniːmɪk) *adj* **1** relating to or suffering from anaemia. **2** pale and sickly looking; lacking vitality.

anaerobe (æˈnɛərəʊb, ˈænərəʊb) *or* **anaerobium** (ˌænɛəˈrəʊbɪəm) *n, pl* **anaerobes** *or* **anaerobia** (-ˈəʊbɪə). an organism that does not require, or requires the absence of, free oxygen or air.
▸ˌ**anaerˈobic** *adj*

anaesthesia *or US* **anesthesia** (ˌænɪsˈθiːzɪə) *n* **1** loss of bodily sensation, esp. of touch, as the result of nerve damage or other abnormality. **2** loss of sensation, esp. of pain, induced by drugs: called **general anaesthesia** when consciousness is lost and **local anaesthesia** when only a specific area of the body is involved. [C19: from NL, from Gk *anaisthēsia* absence of sensation]

anaesthetic ➊ *or US* **anesthetic** (ˌænɪsˈθɛtɪk) *n* **1** a substance that causes anaesthesia. ◆ *adj* **2** causing or characterized by anaesthesia.

THESAURUS

copiousness, plenitude, plethora, profusion, richness

amply *adv* = **fully**, abundantly, bountifully, capaciously, completely, copiously, extensively, generously, greatly, lavishly, liberally, plenteously, plentifully, profusely, richly, substantially, thoroughly, unstintingly, well, without stinting
Antonyms *adv* inadequately, insufficiently, meagrely, poorly, scantily, skimpily, sparsely, thinly

amputate *vb* = **cut off**, curtail, lop, remove, separate, sever, truncate

amuck *see* **amok**

amulet *n* = **charm**, fetish, juju, periapt (*rare*), talisman

amuse *vb* **1, 2** = **entertain**, beguile, charm, cheer, delight, divert, enliven, gladden, gratify, interest, occupy, please, recreate, regale, tickle
Antonyms *vb* be tedious, bore, jade, pall on, send to sleep, tire, weary

amusement *n* **1** = **pastime**, distraction, diversion, entertainment, game, hobby, joke, lark, prank, recreation, sport **3** = **entertainment**, beguilement, cheer, delight, diversion, enjoyment, fun, gladdening, gratification, hilarity, interest, laughter, merriment, mirth, pleasing, pleasure, recreation, regalement, sport
Antonyms *n* ≠ **entertainment**: boredom, displeasure, monotony, sadness, tedium

amusing *adj* = **funny**, charming, cheerful, cheering, comical, delightful, diverting, droll, enjoyable, entertaining, facetious, gladdening, gratifying, humorous, interesting, jocular, laughable, lively, merry, pleasant, pleasing, rib-tickling, waggish, witty
Antonyms *adj* boring, dead, dull, flat, humdrum, monotonous, stale, tedious, tiresome, unamusing, unexciting, unfunny, uninteresting, wearisome

anaemic *adj* **2** = **pale**, ashen, bloodless, characterless, colourless, dull, enervated, feeble, frail, infirm, like death warmed up (*inf.*), pallid, sickly, wan, weak
Antonyms *adj* blooming, florid, full-blooded, glowing, hearty, radiant, rosy, rosy-cheeked, rubicund, ruddy, sanguine

anaesthetic *n* **1** = **painkiller**, analgesic, ano-

anaesthetics (ˌænɪsˈθɛtɪks) *n (functioning as sing)* the science of anaesthesia and its application. US name: **anesthesiology.**
anaesthetist (əˈniːsθətɪst) *n* **1** *Brit.* a doctor specializing in the administration of anaesthetics. US name: **anesthesiologist. 2** *US.* See **anesthetist.**
anaesthetize, anaesthetise, *or US* **anesthetize** (əˈniːsθəˌtaɪz) *vb* **anaesthetizes, anaesthetizing, anaesthetized** *or* **anaesthetises, anaesthetising, anaesthetised** *or* **anesthetizes, anesthetizing, anesthetized.** *(tr)* to render insensible to pain by administering an anaesthetic.
▸**aˌnaestheti'zation, aˌnaestheti'sation,** *or US* **aˌnestheti'zation** *n*
anaglyph (ˈænəˌglɪf) *n* **1** *Photog.* a stereoscopic picture consisting of two images of the same object, taken from slightly different angles, in two complementary colours. When viewed through coloured spectacles, the images merge to produce a stereoscopic sensation. **2** anything cut to stand in low relief, such as a cameo. [C17: from Gk *anagluphē* carved in low relief, from ANA- + *gluphē* carving, from *gluphein* to carve]
▸**ˌana'glyphic** *adj*
Anaglypta (ˌænəˈglɪptə) *n Trademark.* a type of thick embossed wallpaper designed to be painted. [C19: from Gk *anagluptos;* see ANAGLYPH]
anagram (ˈænəˌgræm) *n* a word or phrase the letters of which can be rearranged into another word or phrase. [C16: from NL, from Gk, from *anagrammatizein* to transpose letters, from ANA- + *gramma* a letter]
▸**anagrammatic** (ˌænəgrəˈmætɪk) *or* **ˌanagram'matical** *adj*
anagrammatize *or* **anagrammatise** (ˌænəˈgræməˌtaɪz) *vb* **anagrammatizes, anagrammatizing, anagrammatized** *or* **anagrammatises, anagrammatising, anagrammatised.** to arrange into an anagram.
anal (ˈeɪnᵊl) *adj* **1** of or near the anus. **2** *Psychoanal.* relating to a stage of psychosexual development during which the child's interest is concentrated on the anal region and excremental functions. [C18: from NL *ānālis;* see ANUS]
▸**'anally** *adv*
analects (ˈænəˌlɛkts) *or* **analecta** (ˌænəˈlɛktə) *pl n* selected literary passages from one or more works. [C17: via L from Gk, from *analegein* to collect up, from *legein* to gather]
analeptic (ˌænᵊˈlɛptɪk) *adj* **1** (of a drug, etc.) restorative or invigorating. ◆ *n* **2** a restorative remedy or drug. [C17: from NL, from Gk *analēptikos* stimulating, from *analambanein* to take up]
anal fin *n* an unpaired fin between the anus and tail fin in fishes that maintains equilibrium.
analgesia (ˌænᵊlˈdʒiːzɪə) *or* **analgia** (ænˈældʒɪə) *n* inability to feel pain. [C18: via NL from Gk: insensibility, from AN- + *algēsis* sense of pain]
analgesic (ˌænᵊlˈdʒiːzɪk) *adj* **1** of or causing analgesia. ◆ *n* **2** a substance that produces analgesia.
analog (ˈænəˌlɒg) *n* a variant spelling of **analogue.**

> **USAGE NOTE** The spelling *analog* is a US variant of *analogue* in all its senses, and is also the generally preferred spelling in the computer industry.

analog computer *n* a computer that performs arithmetical operations using a variable physical quantity, such as mechanical movement or voltage, to represent numbers.
analogize *or* **analogise** (əˈnæləˌdʒaɪz) *vb* **analogizes, analogizing, analogized** *or* **analogises, analogising, analogised. 1** *(intr)* to make use of analogy, as in argument. **2** *(tr)* to make analogous or reveal analogy in.
analogous ❶ (əˈnæləgəs) *adj* **1** similar or corresponding in some respect. **2** *Biol.* (of organs and parts) having the same function but different evolutionary origin. **3** *Linguistics.* formed by analogy: *an analogous plural.* [C17: from L, from Gk *analogos* proportionate, from ANA- + *logos* speech, ratio]

> **USAGE NOTE** The use of *with* after *analogous* should be avoided: *swimming has no event that is analogous to* (not *with*) *the 100 metres in athletics.*

analogue *or US (sometimes)* **analog** (ˈænᵊˌlɒg) *n* **1a** a physical object or quantity used to measure or represent another quantity. **1b** *(as modifier): analogue watch; analogue recording.* **2** something analogous to something else. **3** *Biol.* an analogous part or organ.

> **USAGE NOTE** See at **analog.**

analogy ❶ (əˈnælədʒɪ) *n, pl* **analogies. 1** agreement or similarity, esp. in a limited number of features. **2** a comparison made to show such a similarity: *an analogy between an atom and the solar system.* **3** *Biol.* the relationship between analogous organs or parts. **4** *Logic, maths, philosophy.* a form of reasoning in which a similarity between two or more things is inferred from a known similarity between them in other respects. **5** *Linguistics.* imitation of existing models or regular patterns in the formation of words, etc.: *a child may use "sheeps" as the plural of "sheep" by analogy with "cat," "cats," etc.* [C16: from Gk *analogia* correspondence, from *analogos* ANALOGOUS]
▸**analogical** (ˌænəˈlɒdʒɪkᵊl) *adj*
anal retentive *Psychoanal.* ◆ *n* **1** a person who exhibits anal personality traits, such as orderliness, meanness, stubbornness, etc. ◆ *adj* **anal-retentive. 2** exhibiting anal personality traits, such as orderliness, meanness, stubbornness, etc.
analysand (əˈnælɪˌsænd) *n* any person who is undergoing psychoanalysis. [C20: from ANALYSE + *-and,* on the model of *multiplicand*]
analyse ❶ *or US* **analyze** (ˈænᵊˌlaɪz) *vb* **analyses, analysing, analysed** *or US* **analyzes, analyzing, analyzed.** *(tr)* **1** to examine in detail in order to discover meaning, essential features, etc. **2** to break down into components or essential features. **3** to make a mathematical, chemical, etc., analysis of. **4** another word for **psychoanalyse.** [C17: back formation from ANALYSIS]
▸**'anaˌlyser** *or US* **'anaˌlyzer** *n*
analysis ❶ (əˈnælɪsɪs) *n, pl* **analyses** (-ˌsiːz). **1** the division of a physical or abstract whole into its constituent parts to examine or determine their relationship. **2** a statement of the results of this. **3** short for **psychoanalysis. 4** *Chem.* **4a** the decomposition of a substance in order to determine the kinds of constituents present (**qualitative analysis**) or the amount of each constituent (**quantitative analysis**). **4b** the result obtained by such a determination. **5** *Linguistics.* the use of word order together with word function to express syntactic relations in a language, as opposed to the use of inflections. **6** *Maths.* the branch of mathematics principally concerned with the properties of functions. **7 in the last, final,** *or* **ultimate analysis.** after everything has been given due consideration. [C16: from NL, from Gk *analusis,* lit.: a dissolving, from ANA- + *luein* to loosen]
analysis of variance *n Statistics.* a technique for analysing the total variation of a set of observations as measured by the variance of the observations multiplied by their number.
analyst (ˈænəlɪst) *n* **1** a person who analyses or is skilled in analysis. **2** short for **psychoanalyst.**
analytic ❶ (ˌænəˈlɪtɪk) *or* **analytical** *adj* **1** relating to analysis. **2** capable of or given to analysing: *an analytic mind.* **3** *Linguistics.* denoting languages characterized by analysis. **4** *Logic.* (of a proposition) true or false by virtue of the meanings of the words alone: *all spinsters are unmarried* is analytically true. [C16: via LL from Gk *analutikos,* from *analuein* to dissolve, break down]
▸**ˌana'lytically** *adv* ▸**analyticity** (ˌænəlɪˈtɪsɪtɪ) *n*
analytical geometry *n* the branch of geometry that uses algebraic notation to locate a point; coordinate geometry.
analytic philosophy *n* See **philosophical analysis.**
anandrous (ænˈændrəs) *adj* (of flowers) having no stamens. [C19: from Gk *anandros* lacking males, from AN- + *anēr* man]
anapaest *or* **anapest** (ˈænəpɛst, -piːst) *n Prosody.* a metrical foot of three syllables, the first two short, the last long (⏑⏑–). [C17: via L from Gk *anapaistos* reversed, from *ana-* back + *paiein* to strike]
▸**ˌana'paestic** *or* **ˌana'pestic** *adj*
anaphora (əˈnæfərə) *n* **1** *Grammar.* the use of a word such as a pronoun to avoid repetition, as for example *one* in *He offered me a drink but I didn't want one.* **2** *Rhetoric.* the repetition of a word or phrase at the beginning of successive clauses. [C16: via L from Gk: repetition, from ANA- + *pherein* to bear]
anaphrodisiac (ˌænæfrəˈdɪzɪˌæk) *adj* **1** tending to lessen sexual desire. ◆ *n* **2** an anaphrodisiac drug.
anaphylaxis (ˌænəfɪˈlæksɪs) *n* extreme sensitivity to an injected antigen following a previous injection. [C20: from ANA- + (PRO)PHYLAXIS]
anaplasmosis (ˌænəplæzˈməʊsɪs) *n* another name for **gallsickness.**
anaptyxis (ˌænæpˈtɪksɪs) *n, pl* **anaptyxes** (-ˈtɪksiːz). the insertion of a short vowel between consonants in order to make a word more easily pronounceable. [C19: via NL from Gk *anaptuxis,* from *anaptussein* to unfold, from ANA- + *ptussein* to fold]
anarchism (ˈænəˌkɪzəm) *n* **1** *Political theory.* a doctrine advocating the abolition of government. **2** the principles or practice of anarchists.
anarchist ❶ (ˈænəkɪst) *n* **1** a person who advocates a society based on

THESAURUS

dyne, narcotic, opiate, sedative, soporific, stupefacient, stupefactive ◆ *adj* **2** = **pain-killing,** analgesic, anodyne, deadening, dulling, narcotic, numbing, opiate, sedative, sleep-inducing, soporific, stupefacient, stupefactive
analogous *adj* **1** = **similar,** agreeing, akin, alike, comparable, corresponding, equivalent, homologous, like, of a piece, parallel, related, resembling
Antonyms *adj* contrasting, different, discrepant, disparate, dissimilar, diverse, unlike
analogy *n* **1, 2** = **similarity,** agreement, comparison, correlation, correspondence, equivalence, homology, likeness, parallel, relation, resemblance, similitude
analyse *vb* **1** = **examine,** assay, estimate, evaluate, interpret, investigate, judge, research, test, work over **2** = **break down,** anatomize, consider, dissect, dissolve, divide, resolve, separate, study, think through
analysis *n* **1** = **finding,** estimation, evaluation, interpretation, judgment, opinion, reasoning, study **1** = **examination,** anatomization, anatomy, assay, breakdown, dissection, dissolution, division, inquiry, investigation, perusal, resolution, scrutiny, separation, sifting, test
analytic *adj* **1, 2** = **rational,** detailed, diagnostic, discrete, dissecting, explanatory, expository, inquiring, inquisitive, interpretative, interpretive, investigative, logical, organized, problem-solving, questioning, searching, studious, systematic, testing
anarchic *adj* **1-4** = **lawless,** chaotic, confused, disordered, disorganized, misgoverned, misruled, off the rails, rebellious, revolutionary, rioting, riotous, ungoverned
Antonyms *adj* controlled, decorous, disciplined, law-abiding, ordered, peaceable, peaceful, quiet, restrained, well-behaved
anarchist *n* **1, 2** = **revolutionary,** insurgent, nihilist, rebel, terrorist

voluntary cooperation and the abolition of government. **2** a person who causes disorder or upheaval.

anarchy Ⓣ (ˈænəkɪ) *n* **1** general lawlessness and disorder, esp. when thought to result from an absence or failure of government. **2** the absence of government. **3** the absence of any guiding or uniting principle; chaos. **4** political anarchism. [C16: from Med. L, from Gk, from *anarkhos* without a ruler, from AN- + *arkh-* leader, from *arkhein* to rule]
▸**anarchic** (ænˈɑːkɪk) *or* **anˈarchical** *adj*

anastigmat (æˈnæstɪgmæt, ˌænəˈstɪgmæt) *n* a lens system designed to be free of astigmatism. [C19: from AN- + ASTIGMATIC]
▸**ˌanastigˈmatic** *adj*

anastomose (əˈnæstəˌməʊz) *vb* **anastomoses, anastomosing, anastomosed.** to join (two parts of a blood vessel, etc.) by anastomosis.

anastomosis (əˌnæstəˈməʊsɪs) *n, pl* **anastomoses** (-siːz). **1** a natural connection between two tubular structures, such as blood vessels. **2** the union of two hollow parts that are normally separate. [C16: via NL from Gk: opening, from *anastomoun* to equip with a mouth, from *stoma* mouth]

anastrophe (əˈnæstrəfɪ) *n Rhetoric.* another term for **inversion** (sense 3). [C16: from Gk, from *anastrephein* to invert]

anathema Ⓣ (əˈnæθəmə) *n, pl* **anathemas. 1** a detested person or thing: *he is anathema to me.* **2** a formal ecclesiastical excommunication, or denunciation of a doctrine. **3** the person or thing so cursed. **4** a strong curse. [C16: via Church L from Gk: something accursed, from *anatithenai* to dedicate, from ANA- + *tithenai* to set]

anathematize *or* **anathematise** (əˈnæθɪməˌtaɪz) *vb* **anathematizes, anathematizing, anathematized** *or* **anathematises, anathematising, anathematised.** to pronounce an anathema (upon a person, etc.); curse.

anatomical (ˌænəˈtɒmɪkᵊl) *adj* of anatomy.

anatomist (əˈnætəmɪst) *n* an expert in anatomy.

anatomize *or* **anatomise** (əˈnætəˌmaɪz) *vb* **anatomizes, anatomizing, anatomized** *or* **anatomises, anatomising, anatomised.** (*tr*) **1** to dissect (an animal or plant). **2** to examine in minute detail.

anatomy Ⓣ (əˈnætəmɪ) *n, pl* **anatomies. 1** the science concerned with the physical structure of animals and plants. **2** the physical structure of an animal or plant or any of its parts. **3** a book or treatise on this subject. **4** dissection of an animal or plant. **5** any detailed analysis: *the anatomy of a crime.* **6** *Inf.* the human body. [C14: from L, from Gk *anatomē*, from ANA- + *temnein* to cut]

anatto (əˈnætəʊ) *n, pl* **anattos.** a variant spelling of **annatto.**

ANC *abbrev. for* African National Congress.

-ance *or* **-ancy** *suffix forming nouns.* indicating an action, state or condition, or quality: *resemblance; tenancy.* [via OF from L *-antia*]

ancestor Ⓣ (ˈænsɛstə) *n* **1** a person from whom another is directly descended; forefather. **2** an early animal or plant from which a later type has evolved. **3** a person or thing regarded as a forerunner: *the ancestor of the modern camera.* [C13: from OF, from LL *antecēssor* one who goes before, from L *antecēdere*]
▸**ˈancestress** *fem n*

ancestral Ⓣ (ænˈsɛstrəl) *adj* of or inherited from ancestors.

ancestry Ⓣ (ˈænsɛstrɪ) *n, pl* **ancestries. 1** lineage or descent, esp. when noble or distinguished. **2** ancestors collectively.

anchor Ⓣ (ˈæŋkə) *n* **1** a device attached to a vessel by a cable and dropped overboard so as to grip the bottom and restrict movement. **2** an object used to hold something else firmly in place: *the rock provided an anchor for the rope.* **3** a source of stability or security. **4** short for **anchorman** *or* **anchorwoman. 5 cast, come to,** *or* **drop anchor.** to anchor a vessel. **6 ride at anchor.** to be anchored. ◆ *vb* **7** to use an anchor to hold (a vessel) in one place. **8** to fasten or be fastened securely; fix or become fixed firmly. ◆ See also **anchors.** [OE *ancor*, from L, from Gk *ankura*]

anchorage Ⓣ (ˈæŋkərɪdʒ) *n* **1** the act of anchoring. **2** any place where a vessel is anchored. **3** a place designated for vessels to anchor. **4** a fee imposed for anchoring. **5** anything used as an anchor. **6** a source of security or strength.

anchorite Ⓣ (ˈæŋkəˌraɪt) *n* a person who lives in seclusion, esp. a religious recluse; hermit. [C15: from Med. L, from LL, from Gk, from *anakhōrein* to retire, from *khōra* a space]
▸**ˈanchoress** *fem n*

anchorman (ˈæŋkəmæn) *n, pl* **anchormen. 1** *Sport.* the last person in a team to compete, esp. in a relay race. **2** (in broadcasting) a person in a central studio who links up and maintains contact with various outside camera units, reporters, etc.
▸**ˈanchorˌwoman** *fem n*

anchors (ˈæŋkəz) *pl n Sl.* the brakes of a motor vehicle: *he rammed on the anchors.*

anchovy (ˈæntʃəvɪ) *n, pl* **anchovies** *or* **anchovy.** any of various small marine food fishes which have a salty taste and are often tinned or made into a paste or essence. [C16: from Sp. *anchova*, ? ult. from Gk *aphuē* small fish]

anchusa (æŋˈkjuːsə) *n* any of several Eurasian plants having rough hairy stems and leaves and blue flowers. [C18: from L]

anchylose (ˈæŋkɪˌləʊz) *vb* a variant spelling of **ankylose.**

ancien régime *French.* (ɑ̃sjɛ̃ reʒim) *n, pl* ***anciens régimes*** (ɑ̃sjɛ̃ reʒim). the political and social system of France before the Revolution of 1789. [lit.: old regime]

ancient Ⓣ (ˈeɪnʃənt) *adj* **1** dating from very long ago: *ancient ruins.* **2** very old. **3** of the far past, esp. before the collapse of the Western Roman Empire (476 A.D.). ◆ *n* **4** (*often pl*) a member of a civilized nation in the ancient world, esp. a Greek or Roman. **5** (*often pl*) one of the classical authors of Greek or Roman antiquity. **6** *Arch.* an old man. [C14: from OF *ancien*, from Vulgar L *anteanus* (unattested), from L *ante* before]
▸**ˈancientness** *n*

ancient lights *n* (*usually functioning as sing*) the legal right to receive, by a particular window or windows, adequate and unobstructed daylight.

anciently (ˈeɪnʃəntlɪ) *adv* in ancient times.

ancillary Ⓣ (ænˈsɪlərɪ) *adj* **1** subsidiary. **2** auxiliary; supplementary: *ancillary services.* ◆ *n, pl* **ancillaries. 3** a subsidiary or auxiliary thing or person. [C17: from L *ancillāris* concerning maidservants, ult. from *ancŭla* female servant]

ancon (ˈæŋkɒn) *or* **ancone** (ˈæŋkəʊn) *n, pl* **ancones** (æŋˈkəʊniːz). *Architect.* a projecting bracket or console supporting a cornice. [C18: from Gk *ankōn* a bend]

-ancy *suffix forming nouns.* a variant of **-ance,** indicating condition or quality: *poignancy.*

ancylostomiasis (ˌænsɪˌlɒstəˈmaɪəsɪs) *or* **ankylostomiasis** (ˌæŋkɪˌlɒstəˈmaɪəsɪs) *n* infestation of the intestine with blood-sucking hookworms; hookworm disease. [from NL, ult. from Gk *ankulos* hooked + *stoma* mouth]

and Ⓣ (ænd; *unstressed* ənd, ən) *conj* (*coordinating*) **1** in addition to: *boys and girls.* **2** as a consequence: *he fell down and cut his knee.* **3** afterwards: *we pay and go through that door.* **4** plus: *two and two equals four.* **5** used to give emphasis or indicate repetition or continuity: *it rained and rained.* **6** used to express a contrast between instances of what is named: *there are jobs and jobs.* **7** *Inf.* used in place of *to* in infinitives after verbs such as *try, go,* and *come: try and see it my way.* **8** an obsolete word for **if:** *and it please you.* [OE *and*]

> **USAGE NOTE** See at **to.**

-and *or* **-end** *suffix forming nouns.* indicating a person or thing that is to be dealt with in a specified way: *dividend; multiplicand.* [from L gerundives ending in *-andus, -endus*]

andante (ænˈdæntɪ) *Music.* ◆ *adj, adv* **1** (to be performed) at a moderately slow tempo. ◆ *n* **2** a passage or piece to be performed in this manner. [C18: from It., from *andare* to walk, from L *ambulāre*]

andantino (ˌændænˈtiːnəʊ) *Music.* ◆ *adj, adv* **1** (to be performed) slightly faster or slower than andante. ◆ *n, pl* **andantinos. 2** a passage or piece to be performed in this manner. [C19: dim. of ANDANTE]

AND circuit *or* **gate** (ænd) *n Computing.* a logic circuit that has a high-voltage output signal if and only if all input signals are at a high voltage simultaneously. Cf. **NAND circuit, NOR circuit, OR circuit.** [C20: from similarity of operation of *and* in logical conjunctions]

andiron (ˈændˌaɪən) *n* either of a pair of metal stands for supporting logs in a hearth. [C14: from OF *andier*, from ?; infl. by IRON]

and/or *conj* (*coordinating*) used to join terms when either one or the other or both is indicated: *passports and/or other means of identification.*

> **USAGE NOTE** Many people think that *and/or* is only acceptable in legal and commercial contexts. In other contexts, it is better to use *or both: some alcoholics lose their jobs or their driving licences or both* (not *their jobs and/or their driving licences*).

andro- *or before a vowel* **andr-** *combining form.* **1** male; masculine:

THESAURUS

anarchy *n* **1-4** = **lawlessness**, chaos, confusion, disorder, disorganization, misgovernment, misrule, rebellion, revolution, riot
Antonyms *n* control, discipline, government, law, law and order, order, peace, rule

anathema *n* **1** = **abomination**, bane, bête noire, bugbear, enemy, pariah

anatomy *n* **2** = **structure**, build, composition, frame, framework, make-up **4, 5** = **examination**, analysis, dismemberment, dissection, division, inquiry, investigation, study

ancestor *n* **1, 2** = **forefather**, forebear, forerunner, precursor, predecessor, progenitor
Antonyms *n* descendant, inheritor, issue, offspring, progeny, successor

ancestral *adj* = **inherited**, ancestorial, antecedent, forefatherly, genealogical, hereditary, lineal, patriarchal

ancestry *n* **1, 2** = **origin**, ancestors, antecedents, blood, derivation, descent, extraction, family, forebears, forefathers, genealogy, house, line, lineage, parentage, pedigree, progenitors, race, stock

anchor *n* **1** = **mooring**, bower (*Nautical*), drogue, hook (*Nautical*), kedge, sheet anchor ◆ *vb* **5 cast anchor** = **moor**, come to anchor, dock, drop anchor, drop the hook, kedge, kedge off, lay anchor, let go the anchor, tie up **8** = **secure**, attach, bolt, chain, fasten, fix, tie

anchorage *n* **2, 3** = **berth**, dock, dockage, harbour, harbourage, haven, moorage, port, quay

anchorite *n* = **hermit**, eremite, recluse

ancient *adj* **1-3** = **old**, aged, age-old, antediluvian, antiquated, antique, archaic, bygone, cobwebby, early, hoary, obsolete, old as the hills, olden, old-fashioned, outmoded, out-of-date, primeval, primordial, superannuated, timeworn
Antonyms *adj* current, fresh, in vogue, late, modern, modish, new, newfangled, new-fashioned, novel, recent, state-of-the-art, up-to-date, with it (*inf.*), young

ancillary *adj* **1, 2** = **supplementary**, accessory, additional, auxiliary, contributory, extra, secondary, subordinate, subsidiary, supporting
Antonyms *adj* cardinal, chief, main, major, premier, primary, prime, principal

and *conj* **1** = **also**, along with, as well as, further-

androsterone. **2** (in botany) stamen or anther: *androecium.* [from Gk *anēr* (genitive *andros*) man]

androecium (æn'driːsɪəm) *n, pl* **androecia** (-sɪə). the stamens of a flowering plant collectively. [C19: from NL, from ANDRO- + Gk *oikion* a little house]

androgen ('ændrədʒən) *n* any of several steroids that promote development of male sexual characteristics.
▸**androgenic** (ˌændrə'dʒɛnɪk) *adj*

androgyne ('ændrəˌdʒaɪn) *n* another word for **hermaphrodite.** [C17: from OF, via L from Gk *androgunos,* from *anēr* man + *gunē* woman]

androgynous ⓣ (æn'drɒdʒɪnəs) *adj* **1** *Bot.* having male and female flowers in the same inflorescence. **2** having male and female characteristics; hermaphrodite.
▸**an'drogyny** *n*

android ⓣ ('ændrɔɪd) *n* **1** (in science fiction) a robot resembling a human being. ◆ *adj* **2** resembling a human being. [C18: from LGk *androeidēs* manlike; see ANDRO-, -OID]

andrology (æn'drɒlədʒɪ) *n* the branch of medicine concerned with diseases in men, esp. of the reproductive organs. [C20: from ANDRO- + -LOGY]
▸**an'drologist** *n*

androsterone (æn'drɒstəˌrəʊn) *n* an androgenic steroid hormone produced in the testes.

-androus *adj combining form.* (in botany) indicating number or type of stamens: *diandrous.* [from NL, from Gk *-andros,* from *anēr* man]

ane (eɪn) *determiner, pron, n* a Scottish word for **one.**

-ane *suffix forming nouns.* indicating a hydrocarbon of the alkane series: *hexane.* [coined to replace *-ene, -ine,* and *-one*]

anecdotage ('ænɪkˌdəʊtɪdʒ) *n Humorous.* garrulous old age. [from ANECDOTE + -AGE, with play on *dotage*]

anecdote ⓣ ('ænɪkˌdəʊt) *n* a short usually amusing account of an incident. [C17: from Med. L, from Gk *anekdotos* unpublished, from AN- + *ekdotos* published]
▸ˌ**anec'dotal** *or* ˌ**anec'dotic** *adj* ▸ˌ**anec'dotalist** *or* '**anecˌdotist** *n*

anechoic (ˌænɪ'kəʊɪk) *adj* having a low degree of reverberation: *an anechoic recording studio.*

anemia (ə'niːmɪə) *n* the usual US spelling of **anaemia.**
▸**anemic** (ə'niːmɪk) *adj*

anemo- *combining form.* indicating wind: *anemometer; anemophilous.* [from Gk *anemos* wind]

anemograph (ə'nɛməʊˌgrɑːf) *n* a self-recording anemometer.

anemometer (ˌænɪ'mɒmɪtə) *n* an instrument for recording the speed and often the direction of winds. Also called: **wind gauge.**
▸ˌ**ane'mometry** *n* ▸**anemometric** (ˌænɪməʊ'mɛtrɪk) *adj*

anemone (ə'nɛmənɪ) *n* any woodland plant of the genus *Anemone* of N temperate regions, such as the white-flowered **wood anemone** or **windflower.** Some cultivated anemones have coloured flowers. [C16: via L from Gk: windflower, from *anemos* wind]

anemophilous (ˌænɪ'mɒfɪləs) *adj* (of flowering plants such as grasses) pollinated by the wind.
▸ˌ**ane'mophily** *n*

anent (ə'nɛnt) *prep Arch. or Scot.* **1** lying against; alongside. **2** concerning; about. [OE *on efen,* lit.: on even (ground)]

aneroid barometer ('ænəˌrɔɪd) *n* a device for measuring atmospheric pressure without the use of fluids. It consists of a partially evacuated chamber, the lid of which is displaced by variations in air pressure. This displacement is magnified by levers and made to operate a pointer. [C19 *aneroid,* from F, from AN- + Gk *nēros* wet + -OID]

anesthesia (ˌænɪs'θiːzɪə) *n* the usual US spelling of **anaesthesia.**

anesthesiologist (ˌænɪsˌθiːzɪ'ɒlədʒɪst) *n* the US name for an **anaesthetist.**

anesthesiology (ˌænɪsˌθiːzɪ'ɒlədʒɪ) *n* the US name for **anaesthetics.**

anesthetic (ˌænɪs'θɛtɪk) *n, adj* the usual US spelling of **anaesthetic.**

anesthetist (ə'nesθətɪst) *n* (in the US) a person qualified to administer anaesthesia, often a nurse or someone other than a physician.

aneurysm *or* **aneurism** ('ænjəˌrɪzəm) *n* a sac formed by abnormal dilation of the weakened wall of a blood vessel. [C15: from Gk *aneurusma,* from *aneurunein* to dilate]

anew ⓣ (ə'njuː) *adv* **1** once more. **2** in a different way; afresh. [OE *of nīwe;* see OF, NEW]

angary ('æŋgərɪ) *n Law.* the right of a belligerent state to use the property of a neutral state or to destroy it subject to payment of compensation to the owners. [C19: from F, from LL *angaria* enforced service, from Gk *angaros* courier]

angel ⓣ ('eɪndʒəl) *n* **1** one of a class of spiritual beings attendant upon God. In medieval angelology they are divided by rank into nine orders. **2** a divine messenger from God. **3** a guardian spirit. **4** a conventional representation of any of these beings, depicted in human form with wings. **5** *Inf.* a person who is kind, pure, or beautiful. **6** *Inf.* an investor, esp. in a theatrical production. **7** Also called: **angel-noble.** a former English gold coin with a representation of the archangel Michael on it. **8** *Inf.* an unexplained signal on a radar screen. [OE, from LL *angelus,* from Gk *angelos* messenger]

angel cake *or esp. US* **angel food cake** *n* a very light sponge cake made without egg yolks.

angel dust *n* a slang name for **PCP.**

angelfish ('eɪndʒəlˌfɪʃ) *n, pl* **angelfish** *or* **angelfishes. 1** any of various small tropical marine fishes which have a deep flattened brightly coloured body. **2** a South American freshwater fish having a compressed body and large dorsal and anal fins: a popular aquarium fish. **3** a shark with flattened pectoral fins.

angelic ⓣ (æn'dʒɛlɪk) *adj* **1** of or relating to angels. **2** Also: **angelical.** resembling an angel in beauty, etc.
▸**an'gelically** *adv*

angelica (æn'dʒɛlɪkə) *n* **1** an umbelliferous plant, the aromatic seeds, leaves, and stems of which are used in medicine and cookery. **2** the candied stems of this plant, used for decorating and flavouring sweet dishes. [C16: from Med. L *(herba) angelica* angelic (herb)]

Angelus ('ændʒɪləs) *n RC Church.* **1** a series of prayers recited in the morning, at midday, and in the evening. **2** the bell (**Angelus bell**) signalling the times of these prayers. [C17: L, from *Angelus domini nuntiavit Mariae* the angel of the Lord brought tidings to Mary]

anger ⓣ ('æŋgə) *n* **1** a feeling of great annoyance or antagonism as the result of some real or supposed grievance; rage; wrath. ◆ *vb (tr)* **2** to make angry; enrage. [C12: from ON *angr* grief]

angina (æn'dʒaɪnə) *n* **1** any disease marked by painful attacks of spasmodic choking. **2** Also called: **angina pectoris** ('pɛktərɪs). a sudden intense pain in the chest, caused by momentary lack of adequate blood supply to the heart muscle. [C16: from L: quinsy, from Gk *ankhonē* a strangling]

angio- *or before a vowel* **angi-** *combining form.* indicating a blood or lymph vessel; seed vessel. [from Gk *angeion* vessel]

angioma (ˌændʒɪ'əʊmə) *n, pl* **angiomas** *or* **angiomata** (-mətə). a tumour consisting of a mass of blood vessels or a mass of lymphatic vessels.

angioplasty ('ændʒɪəˌplæstɪ) *n* a surgical technique for restoring normal blood flow through an artery narrowed or blocked by atherosclerosis, either by inserting a balloon into it or by using a laser beam.

angiosperm ('ændʒɪəˌspɜːm) *n* any seed-bearing plant in which the ovules are enclosed in an ovary which develops into the fruit after fertilization; any flowering plant. Cf. **gymnosperm.**
▸ˌ**angio'spermous** *adj*

angle[1] ⓣ ('æŋgᵊl) *n* **1** the space between two straight lines or two planes that extend from a common point. **2** the shape formed by two such lines or planes. **3** the extent to which one such line or plane diverges from the other, measured in degrees or radians. **4** a recess; corner. **5** point of view: *look at the question from another angle.* **6** See **angle iron.** ◆ *vb* **angles, angling, angled. 7** to move in or bend into angles or an angle. **8** *(tr)* to produce (an article, statement, etc.) with a particular point of view. **9** *(tr)* to present or place at an angle. **10** *(intr)* to turn in a different direction. [C14: from F, from OL *angulus* corner]

angle[2] ⓣ ('æŋgᵊl) *vb* **angles, angling, angled.** *(intr)* **1** to fish with a hook and line. **2** (often foll. by *for*) to attempt to get: *he angled for a compliment.* ◆ *n* **3** *Obs.* a fish-hook. [OE *angul* fish-hook]

Angle ('æŋgᵊl) *n* a member of a people from N Germany who invaded and settled large parts of E and N England in the 5th and 6th centuries A.D. [from L *Anglus,* of Gmc origin, an inhabitant of *Angul,* a district in Schleswig, a name identical with OE *angul* hook, ANGLE[2], referring to its shape]
▸'**Anglian** *adj, n*

angle iron *n* an iron or a steel structural bar that has an L-shaped cross section. Also called: **angle, angle bar.**

angle of incidence *n* **1** the angle that a line or beam of radiation makes with a line perpendicular to the surface at the point of incidence. **2** the angle between the chord line of an aircraft wing or tailplane and the aircraft's longitudinal axis.

angle of reflection *n* the angle that a beam of reflected radiation makes with the normal to a surface at the point of reflection.

angle of refraction *n* the angle that a refracted beam of radiation

THESAURUS

more, in addition to, including, moreover, plus, together with

androgynous *adj* **2** = **hermaphrodite,** androgyne, bisexual, epicene, hermaphroditic

android *n* **1** = **robot,** automaton, bionic man *or* woman, cyborg, humanoid, mechanical man

anecdote *n* = **story,** reminiscence, short story, sketch, tale, urban legend, urban myth, yarn

anew *adv* **1** = **again,** afresh, another time, from scratch, from the beginning, once again, once more, over again

angel *n* **1-4** = **divine messenger,** archangel, cherub, guardian spirit, seraph, spiritual being **5** *Informal* = **dear,** beauty, darling, dream, gem, ideal, jewel, paragon, saint, treasure

angelic *adj* **1** = **heavenly,** celestial, cherubic, ethereal, seraphic **2** = **pure,** adorable, beatific, beautiful, entrancing, innocent, lovely, saintly, virtuous
Antonyms *adj* ≠ **heavenly:** demonic, devilish, diabolic, diabolical, fiendish, hellish, infernal, satanic

anger *n* **1** = **rage,** annoyance, antagonism, choler, displeasure, exasperation, fury, ill humour, ill temper, indignation, ire, irritability, irritation, outrage, passion, pique, resentment, seeing red, spleen, temper, vexation, wrath ◆ *vb* **2** = **enrage,** affront, aggravate *(inf.),* annoy, antagonize, displease, exasperate, excite, fret, gall, hassle *(inf.),* incense, infuriate, irritate, madden, make one's blood boil, nettle, offend, outrage, pique, provoke, put one's back up, rile, vex
Antonyms *n* ≠ **rage:** acceptance, amiability, approval, calmness, forgiveness, goodwill, gratification, liking, patience, peace, pleasure ◆ *vb* ≠ **enrage:** appease, calm, pacify, placate, please, soothe

angle[1] *n* **1, 2** = **intersection,** bend, corner, crook, crotch, cusp, edge, elbow, knee, nook, point **5** = **point of view,** approach, aspect, outlook, perspective, position, side, slant, standpoint, take *(inf.),* viewpoint

angle[2] *vb* **1** = **fish,** cast **2** = **be after** *(inf.),* aim for, cast about *or* around for, contrive, fish for, makes with the normal to the surface between two media at the point of refraction.

angle of repose *n* the maximum angle to the horizontal at which rock, soil, etc., will remain without sliding.

angler Ⓣ ('æŋglə) *n* **1** a person who fishes with a hook and line. **2** Also called: **angler fish.** any of various spiny-finned fishes which live at the bottom of the sea and typically have a long movable dorsal fin with which they lure their prey.

Anglican ('æŋglɪkən) *adj* **1** denoting or relating to the Church of England or one of the churches in communion with it. ◆ *n* **2** a member of the Anglican Church. [C17: from Med. L, from *Anglicus* English, from L *Anglī* the Angles]
▸**'Anglican,ism** *n*

Anglicism ('æŋglɪ,sɪzəm) *n* **1** a word, or idiom peculiar to the English language, esp. as spoken in England. **2** an English mannerism, custom, etc. **3** the fact of being English.

anglicize *or* **anglicise** ('æŋglɪ,saɪz) *vb* **anglicizes, anglicizing, anglicized** *or* **anglicises, anglicising, anglicised.** (*sometimes cap.*) to make or become English in outlook, form, etc.

angling Ⓣ ('æŋglɪŋ) *n* the art or sport of catching fish with a baited hook or other lure, such as a fly; fishing.

Anglo ('æŋgləʊ) *n, pl* **Anglos. 1** *US.* a White inhabitant of the US who is not of Latin extraction. **2** *Canad.* an English-speaking Canadian, esp. one of Anglo-Celtic origin; an Anglo-Canadian.

Anglo- *combining form.* denoting English or England: *Anglo-Saxon.* [from Med. L *Anglii*]

Anglo-American *adj* **1** of relations between England and the United States. ◆ *n* **2** *Chiefly US.* an inhabitant of the United States who was or whose ancestors were born in England.

Anglo-Catholic *adj* **1** of or relating to a group within the Anglican Church that emphasizes the Catholic elements in its teaching and practice. ◆ *n* **2** a member of this group.
▸**,Anglo-Ca'tholi,cism** *n*

Anglo-French *adj* **1** of England and France. **2** of Anglo-French. ◆ *n* **3** the Norman-French language of medieval England.

Anglo-Indian *adj* **1** of England and India. **2** denoting or relating to Anglo-Indians. **3** (of a word) introduced into English from an Indian language. ◆ *n* **4** a person of mixed English and Indian descent. **5** an English person who lives or has lived for a long time in India.

Anglomania (,æŋgləʊ'meɪnɪə) *n* excessive respect for English customs, etc.
▸**,Anglo'mani,ac** *n*

Anglo-Norman *adj* **1** relating to the Norman conquerors of England, their society, or their language. ◆ *n* **2** a Norman inhabitant of England after 1066. **3** the Anglo-French language.

Anglophile ('æŋgləʊfɪl, -,faɪl) *or* **Anglophil** *n* a person having admiration for England or the English.

Anglophobe ('æŋgləʊ,fəʊb) *n* **1** a person who hates or fears England or its people. **2** *Canad.* a person who hates or fears Canadian Anglophones.

Anglophone ('æŋglə,fəʊn) (*often not cap.*) ◆ *n* **1** a person who speaks English. ◆ *adj* **2** speaking English.

Anglo-Saxon *n* **1** a member of any of the West Germanic tribes that settled in Britain from the 5th century A.D. **2** the language of these tribes. See **Old English. 3** any White person whose native language is English. **4** *Inf.* plain blunt English. ◆ *adj* **5** forming part of the Germanic element in Modern English: *"forget" is an Anglo-Saxon word.* **6** of the Anglo-Saxons or the Old English language. **7** of the White Protestant culture of Britain, Australia, and the US.

angora (æŋ'gɔːrə) *n* (*sometimes cap.*) **1** the long soft hair of the Angora goat or the fur of the Angora rabbit. **2** yarn, cloth, or clothing made from this hair or fur. **3** (*as modifier*): *an angora sweater.* ◆ See also **mohair.** [from *Angora*, former name of Ankara, in Turkey]

Angora goat (æŋ'gɔːrə) *n* a breed of domestic goat with long soft hair.

Angora rabbit *n* a breed of rabbit with long silky fur.

angostura bark (,æŋgə'stjʊərə) *n* the bitter aromatic bark of certain South American trees, formerly used to reduce fever.

angostura bitters *pl n* (*often cap.*) *Trademark.* a bitter aromatic tonic, used as a flavouring in alcoholic drinks.

angry Ⓣ ('æŋgrɪ) *adj* **angrier, angriest. 1** feeling or expressing annoyance, animosity, or resentment. **2** suggestive of anger: *angry clouds.* **3** severely inflamed: *an angry sore.*
▸**'angrily** *adv*

> **USAGE NOTE** It was formerly considered incorrect to talk about being *angry at* a person, but this use is now acceptable.

angst Ⓣ (æŋst) *n* an acute but nonspecific sense of anxiety or remorse. [G]

angstrom ('æŋstrəm) *n* a unit of length equal to 10^{-10} metre, used principally to express the wavelengths of electromagnetic radiations. Symbol: Å or A Also called: **angstrom unit.**

anguine ('æŋgwɪn) *adj* of or similar to a snake. [C17: from L *anguīnus*, from *anguis* snake]

anguish Ⓣ ('æŋgwɪʃ) *n* **1** extreme pain or misery; mental or physical torture; agony. ◆ *vb* **2** to afflict or be afflicted with anguish. [C13: from OF *angoisse* a strangling, from L, from *angustus* narrow]
▸**'anguished** *adj*

angular Ⓣ ('æŋgjʊlə) *adj* **1** lean or bony. **2** awkward or stiff. **3** having an angle or angles. **4** placed at an angle. **5** measured by an angle or by the rate at which an angle changes; *angular momentum; angular velocity.* [C15: from L *angulāris*, from *angulus* ANGLE[1]]

angularity (,æŋgjʊ'lærɪtɪ) *n, pl* **angularities. 1** the condition of being angular. **2** an angular shape.

anhedral (æn'hiːdrəl) *n* the downward inclination of an aircraft wing in relation to the lateral axis.

anhydride (æn'haɪdraɪd) *n* **1** a compound that has been formed from another compound by dehydration. **2** a compound that forms an acid or base when added to water. [C19: from ANHYDR(OUS) + -IDE]

anhydrous (æn'haɪdrəs) *adj* containing no water, esp. no water of crystallization. [C19: from Gk *anudros*; see AN-, HYDRO-]

anil ('ænɪl) *n* a leguminous West Indian shrub which is a source of indigo. Also called: **indigo.** [C16: from Port., from Ar. *an-nīl*, the indigo]

aniline ('ænɪlɪn, -,liːn) *n* a colourless oily poisonous liquid used in the manufacture of dyes, plastics, and explosives. Formula: $C_6H_5NH_2$.

aniline dye *n* any synthetic dye originally made from aniline, obtained from coal tar.

anima ('ænɪmə) *n* (in Jungian psychology) **a** the feminine principle as present in the male unconscious. **b** the inner personality. [L: air, breath, spirit, fem of ANIMUS]

animadversion (,ænɪmæd'vɜːʃən) *n* criticism or censure.

animadvert (,ænɪmæd'vɜːt) *vb* (*intr*) **1** (usually foll. by *on* or *upon*) to comment with strong criticism (upon); make censorious remarks (about). **2** to make an observation or comment. [C16: from L *animadvertere* to notice, from *animus* mind + *advertere* to turn to]

animal Ⓣ ('ænɪməl) *n* **1** *Zool.* any living organism characterized by voluntary movement, the possession of specialized sense organs enabling rapid response to stimuli, and the ingestion of complex organic substances. **2** any mammal, esp. except man. **3** a brutish person. **4** *Facetious.* a person or thing (esp. in **no such animal**). ◆ *adj* **5** of, relating to, or derived from animals. **6** of or relating to physical needs or desires; carnal; sensual. [C14: from L, from *animālis* (adj) living, breathing; see ANIMA]

animalcule (,ænɪ'mælkjuːl) *n* a microscopic animal such as an amoeba or rotifer. [C16: from NL *animalculum* a small animal]
▸**,ani'malcular** *adj*

animal husbandry *n* the science of breeding, rearing, and caring for farm animals.

animalism ('ænɪmə,lɪzəm) *n* **1** preoccupation with physical matters; sensuality. **2** the doctrine that man lacks a spiritual nature. **3** a mode of behaviour typical of animals.

animality (,ænɪ'mælɪtɪ) *n* **1** the animal side of man, as opposed to the intellectual or spiritual. **2** the characteristics of an animal.

animalize *or* **animalise** ('ænɪmə,laɪz) *vb* **animalizes, animalizing, animalized** *or* **animalises, animalising, animalised.** (*tr*) to rouse to brutality or sensuality or make brutal or sensual.
▸**,animali'zation** *or* **,animali'sation** *n*

animal magnetism *n* **1** the quality of being attractive, esp. to members of the opposite sex. **2** *Obs.* hypnotism.

animal rights *pl n* **a** the rights of animals to be protected from exploitation and abuse by humans. **b** (*as modifier*): *the animal-rights lobby.*

animal spirits *pl n* boisterous exuberance. [from a vital force once supposed to be dispatched by the brain to all points of the body]

animate Ⓣ *vb* ('ænɪ,meɪt), **animates, animating, animated.** (*tr*) **1** to give life to or cause to come alive. **2** to make energetic or lively. **3** to encourage or inspire. **4** to impart motion to. **5** to record on film or video tape so

THESAURUS

hunt, invite, look for, scheme, seek, set one's sights on, solicit, try for

angler *n* **1** = **fisherman**, fisher

angling *n* = **fishing**

angry *adj* **1** = **furious**, annoyed, antagonized, at daggers drawn, choked, choleric, cross, displeased, enraged, exasperated, heated, hot, ill-tempered, incandescent, incensed, indignant, infuriated, in high dudgeon, irascible, irate, ireful, irritable, irritated, mad (*inf.*), nettled, on the warpath, outraged, passionate, piqued, provoked, raging, resentful, riled, splenetic, tumultuous, up in arms, wrathful
Antonyms *adj* agreeable, amiable, calm, congenial, friendly, gratified, happy, loving, mild, peaceful, pleasant, pleased

angst *n* = **anxiety**, agitation, apprehension, care, disquietude, distress, fretfulness, inquietude, malaise, perturbation, torment, unease, vexation, worry
Antonyms *n* calmness, collectedness, composure, contentment, ease, fulfilment, nonchalance, peace of mind, satisfaction

anguish *n* **1** = **suffering**, agony, distress, grief, heartache, heartbreak, misery, pain, pang, sorrow, throe, torment, torture, woe

anguished *adj* **1** = **suffering**, afflicted, agonized, brokenhearted, distressed, grief-stricken, tormented, tortured, wounded, wretched

angular *adj* **1** = **skinny**, bony, gaunt, lank, lanky, lean, rangy, rawboned, scrawny, spare

animal *n* **1, 2** = **creature**, beast, brute **3** = **brute**, barbarian, beast, monster, savage, wild man ◆ *adj* **6** = **physical**, bestial, bodily, brutish, carnal, fleshly, gross, sensual

animate *vb* **1-3** = **enliven**, activate, breathe life into, embolden, encourage, energize, excite, fire, gee up, gladden, impel, incite, inspire, inspirit, instigate, invigorate, kindle, liven up, move, prod, quicken, revive, rouse, spark, spur, stimulate, stir, urge, vitalize, vivify ◆ *adj* **6** = **liv-**

as to give movement to. ◆ *adj* ('ænɪmɪt). **6** having life. **7** spirited, or lively. [C16: from L *animāre* to make alive, from *anima* breath, spirit]
▸**'ani,matedly** *adv*

animated cartoon *n* a film produced by photographing a series of gradually changing drawings, etc., which give the illusion of movement when the series is projected rapidly.

animation ❶ (,ænɪ'meɪʃən) *n* **1** vivacity. **2** the condition of being alive. **3** the techniques used in the production of animated cartoons.

animato (,ænɪ'mɑːtəʊ) *adj, adv Music.* lively; animated. [It.]

animatronics (,ænɪmə'trɒnɪks) *n* (*functioning as sing*) a branch of film and theatre technology that combines traditional puppetry techniques with electronics to create lifelike animated effects. [C20: from ANIMA(TION) + (ELEC)TRONICS]

animé ('ænɪ,meɪ, -mɪ) *n* any of various resins, esp. that obtained from a tropical American leguminous tree. [F: from ?]

animism ('ænɪ,mɪzəm) *n* **1** the belief that natural objects have desires and intentions. **2** (in the philosophies of Plato and Pythagoras) the hypothesis that there is an immaterial force that animates the universe. [C19: from L *anima* vital breath, spirit]
▸**animistic** (,ænɪ'mɪstɪk) *adj*

animosity ❶ (,ænɪ'mɒsɪtɪ) *n, pl* **animosities.** a powerful and active dislike or hostility. [C15: from LL *animōsitās*, from ANIMUS]

animus ❶ ('ænɪməs) *n* **1** intense dislike; hatred; animosity. **2** motive or purpose. **3** (in Jungian psychology) the masculine principle present in the female unconscious. [C19: from L: mind, spirit]

anion ('æn,aɪən) *n* a negatively charged ion; an ion that is attracted to the anode during electrolysis. Cf. **cation.** [C19: from ANA- + ION]
▸**anionic** (,ænaɪ'ɒnɪk) *adj*

anise ('ænɪs) *n* a Mediterranean umbelliferous plant having clusters of small yellowish-white flowers and liquorice-flavoured seeds. [C13: from OF *anis*, via L from Gk *anison*]

aniseed ('ænɪ,siːd) *n* the liquorice-flavoured aromatic seeds of the anise plant, used medicinally for expelling intestinal gas and in cookery.

anisette (,ænɪ'zɛt, -'sɛt) *n* a liquorice-flavoured liqueur made from aniseed. [C19: from F]

anisotropic (æn,aɪsəʊ'trɒpɪk) *adj* **1** having different physical properties in different directions: *anisotropic crystals.* **2** (of a plant) responding unequally to an external stimulus in different parts.
▸**an,iso'tropically** *adv* ▸**anisotropy** (,ænaɪ'sɒtrəpɪ) *n*

ankh (æŋk) *n* a tau cross with a loop on the top, symbolizing eternal life: often appearing in Egyptian personal names, such as Tutankhamen. [from Egyptian *'nh* life, soul]

ankle ('æŋkᵊl) *n* **1** the joint connecting the leg and the foot. **2** the part of the leg just above the foot. [C14: from ON]

ankle biter *n Austral. sl.* a child.

anklebone ('æŋkᵊl,bəʊn) *n* the nontechnical name for **talus**[1].

anklet ('æŋklɪt) *n* an ornamental chain worn around the ankle.

ankylose *or* **anchylose** ('æŋkɪ,ləʊz) *vb* **ankyloses, ankylosing, ankylosed** *or* **anchyloses, anchylosing, anchylosed.** (of bones in a joint, etc.) to fuse or stiffen by ankylosis.

ankylosis *or* **anchylosis** (,æŋkɪ'ləʊsɪs) *n* abnormal adhesion or immobility of the bones in a joint, as by a fibrous growth of tissues within the joint. [C18: from NL, from Gk *ankuloun* to crook]
▸**ankylotic** *or* **anchylotic** (,æŋkɪ'lɒtɪk) *adj*

anna ('ænə) *n* a former Indian coin, worth one sixteenth of a rupee. [C18: from Hindi *ānā*]

annals ❶ ('ænᵊlz) *pl n* **1** yearly records of events. **2** history in general. **3** regular reports of the work of a society, learned body, etc. [C16: from L (*librī*) *annālēs* yearly (books), from *annus* year]
▸**'annalist** *n* ▸**,annal'istic** *adj*

annates ('æneɪts, -əts) *pl n RC Church.* the first year's revenue of a see, etc., paid to the pope. [C16: from F, from Med. L *annāta*, from L *annus* year]

annatto *or* **anatto** (ə'nætəʊ) *n, pl* **annattos** *or* **anattos. 1** a small tropical American tree having pulpy seeds that yield a dye. **2** the yellowish-red dye obtained from the seeds of this tree, used for colouring fabrics, butter, varnish, etc. [from Carib]

anneal (ə'niːl) *vb* **1** to temper or toughen (something) by heat treatment to remove internal stress, crystal defects, and dislocations. **2** (*tr*) to toughen or strengthen (the will, determination, etc.). ◆ *n* **3** an act of annealing. [OE *onǣlan*, from ON + *ǣlan* to burn, from *āl* fire]
▸**an'nealer** *n*

annelid ('ænəlɪd) *n* **1** a worm in which the body is divided into segments both externally and internally, as the earthworms. ◆ *adj* **2** of such worms. [C19: from NL *Annelida*, from OF, ult. from L *ānulus* ring]
▸**annelidan** (ə'nɛlɪdən) *n, adj*

annex ❶ *vb* (æ'nɛks). (*tr*) **1** to join or add, esp. to something larger. **2** to add (territory) by conquest or occupation. **3** to add or append as a condition, etc. **4** to appropriate without permission. ◆ *n* ('ænɛks). **5** a variant spelling (esp. US) of **annexe.** [C14: from Med. L, from L *annectere* to attach to, from *nectere* to join]
▸**an'nexable** *adj* ▸**,annex'ation** *n*

annexe ❶ *or esp. US* **annex** ('ænɛks) *n* **1a** an extension to a main building. **1b** a building used as an addition to a main one nearby. **2** something added, esp. a supplement to a document.

annihilate ❶ (ə'naɪə,leɪt) *vb* **annihilates, annihilating, annihilated.** (*tr*) **1** to destroy completely; extinguish. **2** *Inf.* to defeat totally, as in argument. [C16: from LL, from L *nihil* nothing]
▸**an,nihi'lation** *n* ▸**an'nihi,lator** *n*

anniversary (,ænɪ'vɜːsərɪ) *n, pl* **anniversaries. 1** the date on which an event occurred in some previous year: *a wedding anniversary.* **2** the celebration of this. ◆ *adj* **3** of or relating to an anniversary. [C13: from L *anniversārius* returning every year, from *annus* year + *vertere* to turn]

anno Domini ('ænəʊ 'dɒmɪ,naɪ, -,niː) **1** the full form of **A.D.** ◆ *n* **2** *Inf.* advancing old age. [L: in the year of our Lord]

annotate ❶ ('ænəʊ,teɪt, 'ænə,teɪt) *vb* **annotates, annotating, annotated.** to supply (a written work) with critical or explanatory notes. [C18: from L *annotāre*, from *nota* mark]
▸**'anno,tative** *adj* ▸**'anno,tator** *n*

annotation ❶ (,ænəʊ'teɪʃən, ,ænə'teɪʃən) *n* **1** the act of annotating. **2** a note added in explanation, etc., esp. of some literary work.

announce ❶ (ə'naʊns) *vb* **announces, announcing, announced. 1** (*tr; may take a clause as object*) to make known publicly. **2** (*tr*) to declare the arrival of: *to announce a guest.* **3** (*tr; may take a clause as object*) to presage: *the dark clouds announced rain.* **4** (*intr*) to work as an announcer, as on radio or television. [C15: from OF, from L *annuntiāre*, from *nuntius* messenger]
▸**an'nouncement** *n*

announcer ❶ (ə'naʊnsə) *n* a person who announces, esp. one who reads the news, etc., on radio or television.

annoy ❶ (ə'nɔɪ) *vb* **1** to irritate or displease. **2** to harass with repeated attacks. [C13: from OF, from LL *inodiāre* to make hateful, from L *in odiō* (*esse*) (to be) hated, from *odium* hatred]
▸**an'noyer** *n* ▸**an'noying** *adj* ▸**an'noyingly** *adv*

THESAURUS

ing, alive, alive and kicking, breathing, live, moving
Antonyms *vb* ≠ **enliven:** check, curb, deaden, deter, devitalize, discourage, dull, inhibit, kill, make lifeless, put a damper on, restrain

animated *adj* **1-3** = **lively**, active, airy, alive and kicking, ardent, brisk, buoyant, dynamic, ebullient, elated, energetic, enthusiastic, excited, fervent, full of beans (*inf.*), gay, passionate, quick, sparky, spirited, sprightly, vibrant, vigorous, vital, vivacious, vivid, zealous, zestful
Antonyms *adj* apathetic, boring, dejected, depressed, dull, inactive, lethargic, lifeless, listless, monotonous, passive

animation *n* **1** = **liveliness**, action, activity, airiness, ardour, brio, briskness, buoyancy, dynamism, ebullience, elation, energy, enthusiasm, excitement, exhilaration, fervour, gaiety, high spirits, life, passion, pep, sparkle, spirit, sprightliness, verve, vibrancy, vigour, vitality, vivacity, zeal, zest, zing (*inf.*)

animosity *n* = **hostility**, acrimony, animus, antagonism, antipathy, bad blood, bitterness, enmity, hate, hatred, ill will, malevolence, malice, malignity, rancour, resentment, virulence
Antonyms *n* amity, benevolence, congeniality, friendliness, friendship, goodwill, harmony, kindness, love, rapport, sympathy

animus *n* **1** = **ill will**, acrimony, animosity, antagonism, antipathy, bad blood, bitterness, enmity, hate, hatred, hostility, malevolence, malice, malignity, rancour, resentment, virulence **2** = **animating force**, intention, motive, purpose, will

annals *pl n* **1-3** = **records**, accounts, archives, chronicles, history, journals, memorials, registers

annex *vb* **1** = **join**, add, adjoin, affix, append, attach, connect, fasten, subjoin, tack, unite **2, 4** = **seize**, acquire, appropriate, arrogate, conquer, expropriate, occupy, take over
Antonyms *vb* ≠ **join:** detach, disconnect, disengage, disjoin, disunite, remove, separate, unfasten

annexation *n* **2, 4** = **seizure**, annexing, appropriation, arrogation, conquest, expropriation, occupation, takeover

annexe *n* **1** = **extension**, ell, supplementary building, wing **2** = **addition**, addendum, adjunct, affix, appendix, attachment, supplement

annihilate *vb* **1** = **destroy**, abolish, eradicate, erase, exterminate, extinguish, extirpate, liquidate, nullify, obliterate, root out, wipe from the face of the earth, wipe out

annihilation *n* **1** = **destruction**, abolition, eradication, erasure, extermination, extinction, extinguishing, extirpation, liquidation, nullification, obliteration, rooting out, wiping out

annihilator *n* **1** = **destroyer**, eradicator, expunger, exterminator, extinguisher, extirpator, nullifier, obliterator

annotate *vb* = **make notes**, commentate, comment on, elucidate, explain, footnote, gloss, illustrate, interpret, make observations, note

annotation *n* **2** = **note**, comment, commentary, elucidation, exegesis, explanation, explication, footnote, gloss, illustration, interpretation, observation

announce *vb* **1** = **make known**, advertise, broadcast, declare, disclose, divulge, give out, intimate, proclaim, promulgate, propound, publish, report, reveal, tell **3** = **be a sign of**, augur, betoken, foretell, harbinger, herald, portend, presage, signal, signify
Antonyms *vb* ≠ **make known:** bury, conceal, cover up, hide, hold back, hush (up), keep back, keep quiet, keep secret, suppress, withhold

announcement *n* **1** = **statement**, advertisement, broadcast, bulletin, communiqué, declaration, disclosure, divulgence, intimation, proclamation, promulgation, publication, report, revelation

announcer *n* = **presenter**, anchor man, anchor woman, broadcaster, commentator, master of ceremonies, newscaster, newsreader, reporter

annoy *vb* **1** = **irritate**, aggravate (*inf.*), anger, badger, bedevil, bore, bother, bug, displease, disturb, exasperate, gall, get (*inf.*), get up one's nose (*inf.*), harass, harry, hassle (*inf.*), incom-

annoyance Ⓣ (ə'nɔɪəns) *n* **1** the feeling of being annoyed. **2** the act of annoying. **3** a person or thing that annoys.

annual Ⓣ ('ænjʊəl) *adj* **1** occurring, done, etc., once a year or every year; yearly: *an annual income.* **2** lasting for a year: *an annual subscription.* ◆ *n* **3** a plant that completes its life cycle in one year. **4** a book, magazine, etc., published once every year. [C14: from LL, from L *annuus* yearly, from *annus* year]
▸ **'annually** *adv*

annual general meeting *n* the statutory meeting of the directors and shareholders of a company or of the members of a society, held once every financial year. Abbrev.: **AGM.**

annualize *or* **annualise** ('ænjʊə,laɪz) *vb* **annualizes, annualizing, annualized** *or* **annualises, annualising, annualised.** (*tr*) to convert (a rate of interest) to an annual rate when it is quoted for a period less than a year: *an annualized percentage rate.*

annual percentage rate *n* the annual equivalent of a rate of interest when the rate is quoted more frequently than annually, usually monthly. Abbrev.: **APR.**

annual ring *n* a ring indicating one year's growth, seen in the transverse section of stems and roots of woody plants. Also called: **tree ring.**

annuitant (ə'njuːɪtənt) *n* a person in receipt of or entitled to an annuity.

annuity (ə'njuːɪtɪ) *n, pl* **annuities.** a fixed sum payable at specified intervals over a period, such as the recipient's life, or in perpetuity, in return for a premium paid either in instalments or in a single payment. [C15: from F, from Med. L *annuitās,* from L *annuus* ANNUAL]

annul Ⓣ (ə'nʌl) *vb* **annuls, annulling, annulled.** (*tr*) to make (something, esp. a law or marriage) void; abolish. [C14: from OF, from LL *adnullāre* to bring to nothing, from L *nullus* not any]
▸ **an'nullable** *adj*

annular ('ænjʊlə) *adj* ring-shaped. [C16: from L *annulāris,* from *annulus, ānulus* ring]

annular eclipse *n* an eclipse of the sun in which the moon does not cover the entire disc of the sun, so that a ring of sunlight surrounds the shadow of the moon.

annular ligament *n Anat.* any of various ligaments that encircle a part, such as the wrist.

annulate ('ænjʊlɪt, -,leɪt) *adj* having, composed of, or marked with rings. [C19: from L *ānulātus,* from *ānulus* a ring]
▸ **,annu'lation** *n*

annulet ('ænjʊlɪt) *n* **1** *Archit.* a moulding in the form of a ring. **2** *Heraldry.* a ring-shaped device on a shield. **3** a little ring. [C16: from L *ānulus* ring + -ET]

annulment Ⓣ (ə'nʌlmənt) *n* **1** a formal invalidation, as of a marriage, judicial proceeding, etc. **2** the act of annulling.

annulus ('ænjʊləs) *n, pl* **annuli** (-,laɪ) *or* **annuluses. 1** the area between two concentric circles. **2** a ring-shaped part. [C16: from L, var. of *ānulus* ring]

annunciate (ə'nʌnsɪ,eɪt, -ʃɪ-) *vb* **annunciates, annunciating, annunciated.** (*tr*) a less common word for **announce.** [C16: from Med L from L *annuntiāre;* see ANNOUNCE]

Annunciation (ə,nʌnsɪ'eɪʃən) *n* **1 the.** the announcement of the Incarnation by the angel Gabriel to the Virgin Mary (Luke 1:26–38). **2** Also called: **Annunciation Day.** the festival commemorating this, on March 25 (Lady Day).

annunciator (ə'nʌnsɪ,eɪtə) *n* **1** a device that gives a visual indication as to which of a number of electric circuits has operated, such as an indicator showing in which room a bell has been rung. **2** a device giving an audible signal indicating the position of a train. **3** an announcer.

annus horribilis ('ænʊs hɒ'riːbɪlɪs) *n* a terrible year. [C20: from L, modelled on ANNUS MIRABILIS, first used by Elizabeth II of the year 1992]

annus mirabilis ('ænʊs mɪ'ræbɪlɪs) *n, pl* **anni mirabiles** ('ænaɪ mɪ'ræbɪliːz). a year of wonders, catastrophes, or other notable events. [L: wonderful year]

anoa (ə'nəʊə) *n* the smallest of the cattle tribe, having small straight horns and inhabiting the island of Celebes in Indonesia. [from a native name in Celebes]

anode ('ænəʊd) *n* **1** the positive electrode in an electrolytic cell or in an electronic valve. **2** the negative terminal of a primary cell. Cf. **cathode.** [C19: from Gk *anodos* a way up, from *hodos* a way; alluding to the movement of the current]
▸ **anodal** (eɪ'nəʊdᵊl) *or* **anodic** (ə'nɒdɪk) *adj*

anodize *or* **anodise** ('ænə,daɪz) *vb* **anodizes, anodizing, anodized** *or* **anodises, anodising, anodised.** to coat (a metal, such as aluminium) with a protective oxide film by electrolysis.

anodyne Ⓣ ('ænə,daɪn) *n* **1** a drug that relieves pain. **2** anything that alleviates mental distress. ◆ *adj* **3** capable of relieving pain or distress. [C16: from L, from Gk *anōdunos* painless, from AN- + *odunē* pain]

anoint Ⓣ (ə'nɔɪnt) *vb* (*tr*) **1** to smear or rub over with oil. **2** to apply oil to as a sign of consecration or sanctification. [C14: from OF, from L *inunguere,* from IN-² + *unguere* to smear with oil]
▸ **a'nointer** *n* ▸ **a'nointment** *n*

anointing of the sick *n RC Church.* a sacrament in which a person who is seriously ill or dying is anointed by a priest with consecrated oil. Former name: **extreme unction.**

anomalistic (ə,nɒmə'lɪstɪk) *adj* **1** *Astron.* **1a** (of a month) measured between successive perigees of the moon. **1b** (of a year) between successive perihelia of the earth. **2** anomalous.

anomalous Ⓣ (ə'nɒmələs) *adj* deviating from the normal or usual order, type, etc. [C17: from LL, from Gk *anōmalos* uneven, inconsistent, from AN- + *homalos* even, from *homos* one and the same]
▸ **a'nomalousness** *n*

anomaly Ⓣ (ə'nɒməlɪ) *n, pl* **anomalies. 1** something anomalous. **2** deviation from the normal; irregularity. **3** *Astron.* the angle between a planet, the sun, and the previous perihelion of the planet.

anomie *or* **anomy** ('ænəʊmɪ) *n Sociol.* lack of social or moral standards in an individual or society. [from Gk *anomia* lawlessness, from A-¹ + *nomos* law]
▸ **anomic** (ə'nɒmɪk) *adj*

anon Ⓣ (ə'nɒn) *adv Arch. or literary.* **1** soon. **2 ever and anon.** now and then. [OE *on āne,* lit.: in one, that is, immediately]

anon. *abbrev. for* anonymous.

anonym ('ænənɪm) *n* **1** a less common word for **pseudonym. 2** an anonymous person or publication.

anonymize *or* **anonymise** (ə'nɒnɪ,maɪz) *vb* **anonymizes, anonymizing, anonymized** *or* **anonymises, anonymising, anonymised.** (*tr*) to carry out or organize in such a way as to preserve anonymity: *anonymized AIDS screening.*

anonymous Ⓣ (ə'nɒnɪməs) *adj* **1** from or by a person, author, etc., whose name is unknown or withheld. **2** having no known name. **3** lacking individual characteristics. **4** (*often cap.*) denoting an organization which provides help to applicants who remain anonymous: *Alcoholics Anonymous.* [C17: via LL from Gk *anōnumos,* from AN- + *onoma* name]
▸ **anonymity** (,ænə'nɪmɪtɪ) *n*

anopheles (ə'nɒfɪ,liːz) *n, pl* **anopheles.** any of various mosquitoes constituting the genus *Anopheles,* some species of which transmit the malaria parasite to man. [C19: via NL from Gk *anōphelēs* useless, from AN- + *ōphelein* to help]

anorak ('ænə,ræk) *n* **1** a warm waterproof hip-length jacket usually with a hood. **2** *Inf.* a boring or socially inept person. [from Eskimo *ánoráq*]

anorexia (,ænɒ'reksɪə) *n* **1** loss of appetite. **2** Also called: **anorexia nervosa** (nɜː'vəʊsə). a disorder characterized by fear of becoming fat and refusal of food, leading to debility and even death. [C17: via NL from Gk, from AN- + *orexis* appetite]
▸ **,ano'rectic** *or* **,ano'rexic** *adj, n*

THESAURUS

mode, irk, madden, make one's blood boil, molest, needle (*inf.*), nettle, peeve, pester, piss one off (*taboo sl.*), plague, provoke, put one's back up, rile, ruffle, tease, trouble, vex
Antonyms *vb* appease, calm, comfort, console, mollify, solace, soothe

annoyance *n* **1, 2** = **irritation,** aggravation, anger, bedevilment, bother, displeasure, disturbance, exasperation, grief (*inf.*), harassment, hassle (*inf.*), nuisance, provocation, trouble, vexation **3** = **nuisance,** bind (*inf.*), bore, bother, drag (*inf.*), gall, pain (*inf.*), pain in the neck (*inf.*), pest, plague, tease

annoyed *adj* **1** = **irritated,** aggravated (*inf.*), bothered, browned off (*inf.*), displeased, exasperated, harassed, harried, hassled (*inf.*), irked, maddened, miffed (*inf.*), nettled, peeved (*inf.*), piqued, pissed off (*taboo sl.*), riled, ruffled, vexed

annoying *adj* **1** = **irritating,** aggravating, bedevilling, boring, bothersome, displeasing, disturbing, exasperating, galling, harassing, irksome, maddening, peeving (*inf.*), provoking, teasing, troublesome, vexatious
Antonyms *adj* agreeable, amusing, charming, delightful, diverting, enjoyable, entertaining, gratifying, pleasant

annual *adj* **1, 2** = **yearly,** once a year, yearlong

annually *adv* **1** = **yearly,** by the year, each year, every year, once a year, per annum, per year, year after year

annul *vb* = **invalidate,** abolish, abrogate, cancel, countermand, declare *or* render null and void, negate, nullify, obviate, recall, repeal, rescind, retract, reverse, revoke, void
Antonyms *vb* bring back, re-enforce, re-establish, reimpose, reinstate, reintroduce, restore

annulment *n* **1, 2** = **invalidation,** abolition, abrogation, cancellation, countermanding, negation, nullification, recall, repeal, rescindment, rescission, retraction, reversal, revocation, voiding

anodyne *n* **1** = **painkiller,** analgesic, narcotic, pain reliever, palliative ◆ *adj* **3** = **pain-killing,** analgesic, deadening, dulling, narcotic, numbing, pain-relieving, palliative

anoint *vb* **1** = **smear,** daub, embrocate, grease, oil, rub, spread over **2** = **consecrate,** anele (*arch.*), bless, hallow, sanctify

anomalous *adj* = **unusual,** aberrant, abnormal, atypical, bizarre, deviating, eccentric, exceptional, incongruous, inconsistent, irregular, odd, outré, peculiar, rare
Antonyms *adj* common, customary, familiar, natural, normal, ordinary, regular, typical, usual

anomaly *n* **1, 2** = **irregularity,** aberration, abnormality, departure, deviation, eccentricity, exception, incongruity, inconsistency, oddity, peculiarity, rarity

anon *adv* **1** *Archaic or literary* = **soon,** before long, betimes (*arch.*), erelong (*arch. or poetic*), forthwith, in a couple of shakes (*inf.*), presently, promptly, shortly

anonymity *n* **1, 2** = **namelessness,** innominateness **3** = **unremarkability** *or* **unremarkableness,** characterlessness, unsingularity

anonymous *adj* **1, 2** = **unnamed,** incognito, innominate, nameless, unacknowledged, unattested, unauthenticated, uncredited, unidentified, unknown, unsigned **3** = **nondescript,** characterless, undistinguished, unexceptional
Antonyms *adj* ≠ **unnamed:** accredited, acknowledged, attested, authenticated, credited, identified, known, named, signed

anosmia (æn'ɒzmɪə, -'ɒs-) *n* loss of the sense of smell. [C19: from NL, from AN- + Gk *osmē* smell]
▸**anosmatic** (ˌænɒz'mætɪk) *or* **an'osmic** *adj*

another (ə'nʌðə) *determiner* **1a** one more: *another chance.* **1b** (*as pron*): *help yourself to another.* **2a** a different: *another era from ours.* **2b** (*as pron*): *to try one, then another.* **3a** a different example of the same sort. **3b** (*as pron*): *we got rid of one, but I think this is another.* [C14: orig. *an other*]

A.N. Other *n Brit.* an unnamed person: used in team lists, etc., to indicate a place that remains to be filled.

anoxia (æn'ɒksɪə) *n* lack or deficiency of oxygen. [C20: from AN- + OX(YGEN) + -IA]
▸**an'oxic** *adj*

Anschluss ('ænʃlʊs) *n* a political or economic union, esp. the annexation of Austria by Nazi Germany (1938). [G, from *anschliessen* to join]

anserine ('ænsəˌraɪn) *adj* of or resembling a goose. [C19: from L *anserīnus,* from *anser* goose]

answer 🅣 ('ɑːnsə) *n* **1** a reply, either spoken or written, as to a question, request, letter, or article. **2** a reaction or response: *drunkenness was his answer to disappointment.* **3** a solution, esp. of a mathematical problem. ◆ *vb* **4** (when *tr, may take a clause as object*) to reply or respond (to) by word or act: *to answer a question; to answer the door.* **5** (*tr*) to reply correctly to; solve: *I could answer only three questions.* **6** (*intr;* usually foll. by *to*) to respond or react: *the steering answers to the slightest touch.* **7a** (when *intr,* often foll. by *for*) to meet the requirements (of); be satisfactory (for): *this will answer his needs.* **7b** to be responsible (to a person or for a thing). **8** (when *intr,* foll. by *to*) to match or correspond (esp. in **answer** (*or* **answer to**) **the description**). **9** (*tr*) to give a defence or refutation of (a charge) or in (an argument). [OE *andswaru* an answer; see SWEAR]

answerable 🅣 ('ɑːnsərəbᵊl) *adj* **1** (*postpositive;* foll. by *for* or *to*) responsible or accountable: *answerable to one's boss.* **2** able to be answered.

answer back 🅣 *vb* (*adv*) to reply rudely to (a person, esp. someone in authority) when one is expected to remain silent.

answering machine *n* a device by which a telephone call is answered automatically and the caller leaves a recorded message. In full: **telephone answering machine.** Also called: **answerphone.**

ant (ænt) *n* **1** a small social insect of a widely distributed hymenopterous family, typically living in highly organized colonies of winged males, wingless sterile females (workers), and fertile females (queens). Related adj: **formic. 2 white ant.** another name for a **termite.** [OE *ǣmette*]

-ant *suffix forming adjectives and nouns.* causing or performing an action or existing in a certain condition: *pleasant; deodorant; servant.* [from L *-ant,* ending of present participles of the first conjugation]

antacid (ænt'æsɪd) *n* **1** a substance used to treat acidity, esp. in the stomach. ◆ *adj* **2** having the properties of this substance.

antagonism 🅣 (æn'tægəˌnɪzəm) *n* **1** openly expressed and usually mutual opposition. **2** the inhibiting or nullifying action of one substance or organism on another.

antagonist 🅣 (æn'tægənɪst) *n* **1** an opponent or adversary. **2** any muscle that opposes the action of another. **3** a drug that counteracts the effects of another drug.
▸**anˌtago'nistic** *adj* ▸**anˌtago'nistically** *adv*

antagonize 🅣 *or* **antagonise** (æn'tægəˌnaɪz) *vb* **antagonizes, antagonizing, antagonized** *or* **antagonises, antagonising, antagonised.** (*tr*) **1** to make hostile; annoy or irritate. **2** to act in opposition to or counteract. [C17: from Gk, from ANTI- + *agōnizesthai* to strive, from *agōn* contest]
▸**anˌtagoni'zation** *or* **anˌtagoni'sation** *n*

antalkali (ænt'ælkəˌlaɪ) *n, pl* **antalkalis** *or* **antalkalies.** a substance that neutralizes alkalis.

Antarctic (ænt'ɑːktɪk) *adj* of or relating to the south polar regions. [C14: via L from Gk *antarktikos;* see ANTI-, ARCTIC]

Antarctic Circle *n* the imaginary circle around the earth, parallel to the equator, at latitude 66° 32′ S.

ant bear *n* another name for **aardvark.**

ante ('æntɪ) *n* **1** the gaming stake put up before the deal in poker by the players. **2** *Inf.* a sum of money representing a person's share, as in a syndicate. **3 up the ante.** *Inf.* to increase the costs, risks, or considerations involved in taking an action or reaching a conclusion. ◆ *vb* **antes, anteing, anted** *or* **anteed. 4** to place (one's stake) in poker. **5** (usually foll. by *up*) *Inf.* to pay.

ante- *prefix* before in time or position: *antedate; antechamber.* [from L]

anteater ('æntˌiːtə) *n* any of several toothless mammals having a long tubular snout used for eating termites.

antebellum (ˌæntɪ'bɛləm) *adj* of or during the period before a war, esp. the American Civil War. [L *ante bellum,* lit.: before the war]

antecede (ˌæntɪ'siːd) *vb* **antecedes, anteceding, anteceded.** (*tr*) to go before; precede. [C17: from L *antecēdere,* from *cēdere* to go]

antecedent 🅣 (ˌæntɪ'siːdᵊnt) *n* **1** an event, etc., that happens before another. **2** *Grammar.* a word or phrase to which a pronoun refers. In "People who live in glass houses shouldn't throw stones," *people* is the antecedent of *who.* **3** *Logic.* the first hypothetical clause in a conditional statement. ◆ *adj* **4** preceding in time or order; prior.
▸ˌ**ante'cedence** *n*

antecedents 🅣 (ˌæntɪ'siːdᵊnts) *pl n* **1** ancestry. **2** a person's past history.

antechamber ('æntɪˌtʃeɪmbə) *n* an anteroom. [C17: from OF, from It. *anticamera;* see ANTE-, CHAMBER]

antedate 🅣 ('æntɪˌdeɪt) *vb* (*tr*) **1** to be or occur at an earlier date than. **2** to affix or assign a date to (a document, event, etc.) that is earlier than the actual date. **3** to cause to occur sooner. ◆ *n* **4** an earlier date.

antediluvian 🅣 (ˌæntɪdɪ'luːvɪən) *adj* **1** of the ages before the biblical Flood. **2** old-fashioned. ◆ *n* **3** an antediluvian person or thing. [C17: from ANTE- + L *dīluvium* flood]

antelope ('æntɪˌləʊp) *n, pl* **antelopes** *or* **antelope.** any of a group of mammals of Africa and Asia. They are typically graceful, having long legs and horns, and include the gazelles, springbok, impala, and dik-diks. [C15: from OF, from Med. L, from LGk *antholops* a legendary beast]

antemeridian (ˌæntɪmə'rɪdɪən) *adj* before noon; in the morning. [C17: from L]

ante meridiem ('æntɪ mə'rɪdɪəm) the full form of **a.m.** [L, from ANTE- + *merīdiēs* midday]

antenatal (ˌæntɪ'neɪtᵊl) *adj* occurring or present before birth; during pregnancy.

antenna (æn'tɛnə) *n* **1** (*pl* **antennae** (-niː)) one of a pair of mobile appendages on the heads of insects, crustaceans, etc., that often respond to touch and taste but may be specialized for swimming. **2** (*pl* **antennas**) an aerial. [C17: from L: sail yard, from ?]
▸**an'tennal** *or* **an'tennary** *adj*

antenuptial contract (ˌæntɪ'nʌpʃəl) *n* (in South Africa) a marriage contract effected prior to the wedding giving each partner control over his or her property.

antependium (ˌæntɪ'pɛndɪəm) *n, pl* **antependia** (-dɪə). a covering hung over the front of an altar. [C17: from Med. L, from L ANTE- + *pendēre* to hang]

antepenult (ˌæntɪpɪ'nʌlt) *n* the third last syllable in a word. [C16: shortened from L (*syllaba*) *antepaenultima;* see ANTE-, PENULT]

antepenultimate (ˌæntɪpɪ'nʌltɪmɪt) *adj* **1** third from last. ◆ *n* **2** anything that is third from last.

ante-post *adj Brit.* (of a bet) placed before the runners in a race are confirmed.

anterior 🅣 (æn'tɪərɪə) *adj* **1** at or towards the front. **2** earlier. **3** *Zool.* of or near the head end. **4** *Bot.* (of part of a flower or leaf) farthest away from the main stem. [C17: from L, comp. of *ante* before]

anteroom 🅣 ('æntɪˌruːm, -ˌrʊm) *n* a room giving entrance to a larger room, often used as a waiting room.

anthelion (æn'θiːlɪən) *n, pl* **anthelia** (-lɪə). **1** a faint halo sometimes seen in high altitude regions around a shadow cast onto fog. **2** a white spot occasionally appearing at the same height as and opposite to the sun.

THESAURUS

answer *n* **1, 2** = **reply,** acknowledgment, comeback, counterattack, defence, explanation, plea, reaction, refutation, rejoinder, report, resolution, response, retort, return, riposte, solution, vindication ◆ *vb* **4-6** = **reply,** acknowledge, explain, react, refute, rejoin, resolve, respond, retort, return, solve **7a** = **do,** conform, correlate, correspond, fill, fit, fulfil, measure up, meet, pass, qualify, satisfy, serve, suffice, suit, work **7b** = **be responsible for,** be accountable for, be answerable for, be chargeable for, be liable for, be to blame for, take the rap for (*sl.*) **8** = **fit,** agree, confirm, correspond, match, meet
Antonyms *n* ≠ **reply:** inquiry, interrogation, query, question ◆ *vb* ≠ **reply:** ask, inquire, interrogate, query, question

answerable *adj* **1** *usually foll. by* **for** *or* **to** = **responsible,** accountable, amenable, chargeable, liable, subject, to blame

answer back *vb* = **be impertinent,** argue, be cheeky, cheek (*inf.*), contradict, disagree, dispute, rebut, retort, talk back

antagonism *n* **1** = **hostility,** antipathy, competition, conflict, contention, discord, dissension, friction, opposition, rivalry
Antonyms *n* accord, agreement, amity, friendship, harmony, love, peacefulness, sympathy

antagonist *n* **1** = **opponent,** adversary, competitor, contender, enemy, foe, opposer, rival

antagonistic *adj* **1** = **hostile,** adverse, antipathetic, at odds, at variance, averse, conflicting, contentious, ill-disposed, incompatible, in dispute, inimical, opposed, unfriendly

antagonization *n* **1** = **annoyance,** aggravation (*inf.*), exacerbation, grief (*inf.*), hassle (*inf.*), infuriation, irritation, offence, provocation **2** = **hostility,** adverseness, antipathy, aversion, competition, conflict, contention, counteraction, enmity, friction, inimicalness *or* inimicality, opposition, oppugnancy (*rare*), rivalry, variance

antagonize *vb* **1** = **annoy,** aggravate (*inf.*), alienate, anger, disaffect, estrange, gall, hassle (*inf.*), insult, irritate, offend, piss one off (*taboo sl.*), repel, rub (someone) up the wrong way (*inf.*)
Antonyms *vb* appease, calm, conciliate, disarm, mollify, pacify, placate, propitiate, soothe, win over

antecedent *adj* **4** = **preceding,** anterior, earlier, foregoing, former, precursory, preliminary, previous, prior
Antonyms *adj* after, coming, consequent, ensuing, following, later, posterior, subsequent, succeeding, successive

antecedents *pl n* **1** = **ancestors,** ancestry, blood, descent, extraction, family, forebears, forefathers, genealogy, line, progenitors, stock **2** = **past,** background, history

antedate *vb* **1** = **come first** *or* **before,** anticipate, forego, go before, precede, predate

antediluvian *adj* **1** = **prehistoric,** primeval, primitive, primordial **2** = **old-fashioned,** ancient, antiquated, antique, archaic, obsolete, old as the hills, out-of-date, out of the ark (*inf.*), passé

anterior *adj* **1** = **front,** fore, forward, frontward **2** = **earlier,** antecedent, foregoing, former, introductory, preceding, previous, prior

anteroom *n* = **outer room,** antechamber, foyer, lobby, reception room, vestibule, waiting room

[C17: from LGk, from *anthēlios* opposite the sun, from ANTE- + *hēlios* sun]

anthelmintic (ˌænθɛlˈmɪntɪk) *or* **anthelminthic** (ˌænθɛlˈmɪnθɪk) *n Med.* another name for **vermifuge.**

anthem Ⓣ (ˈænθəm) *n* **1** a song of loyalty: *a national anthem.* **2** a musical composition for a choir, usually set to words from the Bible. **3** a religious chant sung antiphonally. [OE *antemne,* from LL *antiphōna* ANTIPHON]

anthemis (ænˈθiːmɪs) *n* any of several cultivated varieties of camomile. [NL, from L, from Gk *anthos* flower]

anther (ˈænθə) *n* the terminal part of a stamen consisting of two lobes each containing two sacs in which the pollen matures. [C18: from NL, from L, from Gk *anthēros* flowery, from *anthos* flower]

antheridium (ˌænθəˈrɪdɪəm) *n, pl* **antheridia** (-ɪə). the male sex organ of algae, fungi, mosses, etc. [C19: from NL, dim. of *anthēra* ANTHER]

ant hill *n* a mound of soil, leaves, etc., near the entrance of an ants' or termites' nest, deposited there by the ants or termites while constructing the nest.

anthologize *or* **anthologise** (ænˈθɒləˌdʒaɪz) *vb* **anthologizes, anthologizing, anthologized** *or* **anthologises, anthologising, anthologised.** to compile or put into an anthology.

anthology Ⓣ (ænˈθɒlədʒɪ) *n, pl* **anthologies. 1** a collection of literary passages, esp. poems, by various authors. **2** any printed collection of literary pieces, songs, etc. [C17: from Med. L, from Gk, lit.: a flower gathering, from *anthos* flower + *legein* to collect]
▸**anˈthologist** *n*

anthozoan (ˌænθəˈzəʊən) *n* **1** any of the sessile marine coelenterates of the class *Anthozoa,* including corals and sea anemones, in which the body is in the form of a polyp. ◆ *adj* also: **actinozoan. 2** of or relating to these.

anthracene (ˈænθrəˌsiːn) *n* a colourless crystalline solid, used in the manufacture of chemicals and as crystals in scintillation counters. [C19: from ANTHRAX + -ENE]

anthracite (ˈænθrəˌsaɪt) *n* a hard coal that burns slowly with a nonluminous flame giving out intense heat. Also called: **hard coal.** [C19: from L, from Gk *anthrakitēs* coal-like, from *anthrax* coal]
▸**anthracitic** (ˌænθrəˈsɪtɪk) *adj*

anthracosis (ˌænθrəˈkəʊsɪs) *n* a lung disease due to inhalation of coal dust.

anthrax (ˈænθræks) *n, pl* **anthraces** (-θrəˌsiːz). **1** a highly infectious bacterial disease of animals, esp. cattle and sheep, which can be transmitted to man. **2** a pustule caused by this disease. [C19: from LL, from Gk: carbuncle]

anthropic principle *n Astron.* the cosmological theory that the presence of life in the universe limits the ways in which the very early universe could have evolved.

anthropo- *combining form.* indicating man or human: *anthropology.* [from Gk *anthrōpos*]

anthropocentric (ˌænθrəpəʊˈsɛntrɪk) *adj* regarding humans as the central factor in the universe.

anthropogenesis (ˌænθrəpəʊˈdʒɛnɪsɪs) *or* **anthropogeny** (ˌænθrəˈpɒdʒɪnɪ) *n* the study of the origins of humans.

anthropoid (ˈænθrəˌpɔɪd) *adj* **1** resembling humans. **2** resembling an ape; apelike. ◆ *n* **3** any primate of the suborder *Anthropoidea,* including monkeys, apes, and humans.

anthropoid ape *n* any of a group of primates having no tail, elongated arms, and a highly developed brain, including gibbons, orang-utans, chimpanzees, and gorillas.

anthropology (ˌænθrəˈpɒlədʒɪ) *n* the study of human beings, their origins, institutions, religious beliefs, social relationships, etc.
▸ˌ**anthropoˈlogical** *adj* ▸ˌ**anthroˈpologist** *n*

anthropometry (ˌænθrəˈpɒmɪtrɪ) *n* the comparative study of sizes and proportions of the human body.
▸ˌ**anthropoˈmetric** *or* ˌ**anthropoˈmetrical** *adj*

anthropomorphic (ˌænθrəpəˈmɔːfɪk) *adj* **1** of or relating to anthropomorphism. **2** resembling the human form.
▸ˈ**anthropoˌmorph** *n* ▸ˌ**anthropoˈmorphically** *adv*

anthropomorphism (ˌænθrəpəˈmɔːfɪzəm) *n* the attribution of human form or behaviour to a deity, animal, etc.

anthropomorphous (ˌænθrəpəˈmɔːfəs) *adj* **1** shaped like a human being. **2** another word for **anthropomorphic.**

anthropophagi (ˌænθrəˈpɒfəˌgaɪ) *pl n, sing* **anthropophagus** (-gəs). cannibals. [C16: from L, from Gk *anthrōpophagos;* see ANTHROPO-, -PHAGE]

anthroposophy (ˌænθrəˈpɒsəfɪ) *n* the spiritual and mystical teachings of Rudolph Steiner, based on the belief that creative activities are psychologically valuable, esp. for educational and therapeutic purposes.
▸ˌ**anthropoˈsophic** *adj*

anti (ˈæntɪ) *Inf.* ◆ *adj* **1** opposed to a party, policy, attitude, etc. ◆ *n* **2** an opponent.

anti- *prefix* **1** against; opposing: *anticlerical.* **2** opposite to: *anticlimax.* **3** rival; false: *antipope.* **4** counteracting or neutralizing: *antifreeze; antihistamine.* **5** designating the antiparticle of the particle specified: *antineutron.* [from Gk *anti*]

anti-aircraft (ˌæntɪˈɛəkrɑːft) *n* (*modifier*) of or relating to defence against aircraft attack: *anti-aircraft batteries.*

anti-apartheid *adj* opposed to a policy of racial segregation.

antiar (ˈæntɪˌɑː) *n* another name for **upas** (senses 1, 2). [from Javanese]

antiballistic missile (ˌæntɪbəˈlɪstɪk) *n* a ballistic missile designed to destroy another ballistic missile in flight.

antibiosis (ˌæntɪbaɪˈəʊsɪs) *n* an association between two organisms, esp. microorganisms, that is harmful to one of them.

antibiotic (ˌæntɪbaɪˈɒtɪk) *n* **1** any of various chemical substances, such as penicillin, produced by microorganisms, esp. fungi, or made synthetically, and capable of destroying microorganisms, esp. bacteria. ◆ *adj* **2** of or relating to antibiotics.

antibody (ˈæntɪˌbɒdɪ) *n, pl* **antibodies.** any of various proteins produced in the blood in response to an antigen. By becoming attached to antigens on infectious organisms antibodies can render them harmless.

antic (ˈæntɪk) *Arch.* ◆ *n* **1** an actor in a ludicrous or grotesque part; clown. ◆ *adj* **2** fantastic; grotesque. ◆ See also **antics.** [C16: from It. *antico* something grotesque (from its application to fantastic carvings found in ruins of ancient Rome)]

anticathode (ˌæntɪˈkæθəʊd) *n* the target electrode for the stream of electrons in a vacuum tube, esp. an X-ray tube.

Antichrist (ˈæntɪˌkraɪst) *n* **1** *Bible.* the antagonist of Christ, expected by early Christians to appear and reign over the world until overthrown at Christ's Second Coming. **2** (*sometimes not cap.*) an enemy of Christ or Christianity.

anticipant (ænˈtɪsɪpənt) *adj* **1** operating in advance. ◆ *n* **2** a person who anticipates.

anticipate Ⓣ (ænˈtɪsɪˌpeɪt) *vb* **anticipates, anticipating, anticipated.** (*mainly tr*) **1** (*may take a clause as object*) to foresee and act in advance of; forestall: *I anticipated his punch.* **2** (*also intr*) to mention (something) before its proper time: *don't anticipate the climax of the story.* **3** (*may take a clause as object*) to regard as likely; expect. **4** to make use of in advance of possession: *he anticipated his salary in buying a leather jacket.* [C16: from L *anticipāre* to take before, from *anti-* ANTE- + *capere* to take]
▸**anˈticiˌpator** *n* ▸**anˈticiˌpatory** *or* **anˈticipative** *adj*

> **USAGE NOTE** The use of *anticipate* to mean *expect* should be avoided.

anticipation Ⓣ (ænˌtɪsɪˈpeɪʃən) *n* **1** the act of anticipating; expectation, premonition, or foresight. **2** *Music.* an unstressed, usually short note introduced before a downbeat.

anticlerical (ˌæntɪˈklɛrɪkᵊl) *adj* **1** opposed to the power and influence of the clergy, esp. in politics. ◆ *n* **2** a supporter of an anticlerical party.
▸ˌ**antiˈclericalism** *n*

anticlimax Ⓣ (ˌæntɪˈklaɪmæks) *n* **1** a disappointing or ineffective conclusion to a series of events, etc. **2** a sudden change from a serious subject to one that is disappointing or ludicrous.
▸**anticlimactic** (ˌæntɪklaɪˈmæktɪk) *adj*

anticline (ˈæntɪˌklaɪn) *n* a formation of stratified rock raised up, by folding, into a broad arch so that the strata slope down on both sides from a common crest.
▸ˌ**antiˈclinal** *adj*

anticlockwise (ˌæntɪˈklɒkˌwaɪz) *adv, adj* in the opposite direction to the rotation of the hands of a clock. US equivalent: **counterclockwise.**

anticoagulant (ˌæntɪkəʊˈægjʊlənt) *adj* **1** acting to prevent or retard coagulation, esp. of blood. ◆ *n* **2** an agent that prevents or retards coagulation.

anti-Communist *adj* opposed to Communism or its principles.

anticonvulsant (ˌæntɪkənˈvʌlsənt) *n* **1** any of a class of drugs used to relieve convulsions. ◆ *adj* **2** of or relating to such drugs.

antics Ⓣ (ˈæntɪks) *pl n* absurd acts or postures.

anticyclone (ˌæntɪˈsaɪkləʊn) *n Meteorol.* a body of moving air of higher pressure than the surrounding air, in which the pressure decreases away from the centre. Also called: **high.**
▸**anticyclonic** (ˌæntɪsaɪˈklɒnɪk) *adj*

antidazzle mirror (ˌæntɪˈdæzᵊl) *n* a rear-view mirror for road vehicles that only partially reflects headlights behind.

antidepressant (ˌæntɪdɪˈprɛsᵊnt) *n* **1** any of a class of drugs used to alleviate depression. ◆ *adj* **2** of this class of drugs.

antidiuretic hormone (ˌæntɪˌdaɪjʊˈrɛtɪk) *n* another name for **vasopressin.** Abbrev.: **ADH.**

antidote Ⓣ (ˈæntɪˌdəʊt) *n* **1** *Med.* a drug or agent that counteracts or neutralizes the effects of a poison. **2** anything that counteracts or re-

THESAURUS

anthem *n* **1 = song of praise,** paean **2, 3 = hymn,** canticle, carol, chant, chorale, psalm

anthology *n* **1 = collection,** analects, choice, compendium, compilation, digest, garland, miscellany, selection, treasury

anticipate *vb* **1 = forestall,** antedate, beat (someone) to it (*inf.*), intercept, prevent **1, 3 = expect,** apprehend, await, count upon, forecast, foresee, foretell, hope for, look for, look forward to, predict, prepare for

anticipation *n* **1 = expectation,** apprehension, awaiting, expectancy, foresight, foretaste, forethought, hope, preconception, premonition, prescience, presentiment

anticipatory *adj* **1, 3 = expectant,** apprehensive, forecasting, foreseeing, foretelling, forethoughtful, predicting, provident

anticlimax *n* **1, 2 = disappointment,** bathos, comedown, letdown
Antonyms *n* climax, culmination, height, highlight, high point, peak, summit, top, zenith

antics *pl n* **= clowning,** buffoonery, capers, escapades, foolishness, frolics, horseplay, larks, mischief, monkey tricks, playfulness, pranks, silliness, skylarking, stunts, tomfoolery, tricks

lieves a harmful condition. [C15: from L, from Gk *antidoton* something given as a countermeasure, from ANTI- + *didonai* to give]
▸ ˌ**anti'dotal** *adj*

antiemetic (ˌæntɪ'mɛtɪk) *adj* **1** preventing vomiting. ◆ *n* **2** any antiemetic drug, such as promethazine.

antifreeze ('æntɪˌfriːz) *n* a liquid, usually ethylene glycol (ethanediol), added to water to lower its freezing point, esp. for use in an internal-combustion engine.

antifungal (ˌæntɪ'fʌŋgᵊl) *adj* **1** inhibiting the growth of fungi. **2** (of a drug) possessing antifungal activity and therefore used to treat fungal infections. ◆ Also: **antimycotic.**

antigen ('æntɪdʒən, -ˌdʒɛn) *n* a substance, usually a toxin produced by a bacterium, that stimulates the production of antibodies. [C20: from ANTI(BODY) + -GEN]

antihero ('æntɪˌhɪərəʊ) *n, pl* **antiheroes.** a central character in a novel, play, etc., who lacks the traditional heroic virtues.

antihistamine (ˌæntɪ'hɪstəˌmiːn, -mɪn) *n* any drug that neutralizes the effects of histamine, used esp. in the treatment of allergies.

anti-inflammatory *adj* **1** reducing inflammation. ◆ *n, pl* **anti-inflammatories. 2** any anti-inflammatory drug, such as cortisone, aspirin, or ibuprofen.

anti-inflationary *adj* (of an economic policy) designed to reduce or counteract the effects of inflation.

antiknock (ˌæntɪ'nɒk) *n* a compound, such as lead tetraethyl, added to petrol to reduce knocking in the engine.

antilock brake ('æntɪˌlɒk) *n* a brake fitted to some road vehicles that prevents skidding and improves control by sensing and compensating for overbraking. Also called: **ABS brake.**

antilogarithm (ˌæntɪ'lɒgəˌrɪðəm) *n* a number whose logarithm to a given base is a given number: *100 is the antilogarithm of 2 to base 10.* Often shortened to **antilog.**
▸ ˌ**antiˌloga'rithmic** *adj*

antilogy (æn'tɪlədʒɪ) *n, pl* **antilogies.** a contradiction in terms. [C17: from Gk *antilogia*]

antimacassar (ˌæntɪmə'kæsə) *n* a cloth covering the back and arms of chairs, etc., to prevent soiling. [C19: from ANTI- + MACASSAR (OIL)]

antimagnetic (ˌæntɪmæg'nɛtɪk) *adj* of a material that does not acquire permanent magnetism when exposed to a magnetic field.

antimalarial (ˌæntɪmə'lɛərɪəl) *adj* **1** effective in the treatment of malaria. ◆ *n* **2** an antimalarial drug or agent.

antimasque ('æntɪˌmɑːsk) *n* a comic dance, presented between the acts of a masque.

antimatter ('æntɪˌmætə) *n* a form of matter composed of antiparticles, such as antihydrogen, consisting of antiprotons and positrons.

antimetabolite (ˌæntɪmɪ'tæbəˌlaɪt) *n* any drug that acts by disrupting the normal growth of a cell. Antimetabolites are used in cancer treatment.

antimissile (ˌæntɪ'mɪsaɪl) *adj* **1** relating to defensive measures against missile attack: *an antimissile system.* ◆ *n* **2** Also called: **antimissile missile.** a defensive missile used to intercept and destroy attacking missiles.

antimony ('æntɪmənɪ) *n* a toxic metallic element that exists in two allotropic forms and is added to alloys to increase their strength and hardness. Symbol: Sb; atomic no.: 51; atomic wt.: 121.75. [C15: from Med. L *antimōnium*, from ?]
▸ **antimonial** (ˌæntɪ'məʊnɪəl) *adj*

antimuon (ˌæntɪ'mjuːɒn) *n* the antiparticle of a muon.

antimycotic (ˌæntɪmaɪ'kɒtɪk) *adj* another word for **antifungal.**

anti-Nazi *adj* opposed to Nazism or its principles.

antinoise ('æntɪˌnɔɪz) *n* sound generated so that it is out of phase with a noise, such as that made by an engine, in order to reduce the noise level by interference.

antinomian (ˌæntɪ'nəʊmɪən) *adj* **1** relating to the doctrine that by faith a Christian is released from the obligation of adhering to any moral law. ◆ *n* **2** a member of a Christian sect holding such a doctrine.
▸ ˌ**anti'nomianism** *n*

antinomy (æn'tɪnəmɪ) *n, pl* **antinomies. 1** opposition of one law, principle, or rule to another. **2** *Philosophy.* contradiction existing between two apparently indubitable propositions. [C16: from L, from Gk: conflict between laws, from ANTI- + *nomos* law]
▸ **antinomic** (ˌæntɪ'nɒmɪk) *adj*

antinovel ('æntɪˌnɒvᵊl) *n* a type of prose fiction in which conventional or traditional novelistic elements are rejected.

antinuclear (ˌæntɪ'njuːklɪə) *adj* opposed to nuclear weapons or nuclear power.

antioxidant (ˌæntɪ'ɒksɪdənt) *n* **1** any substance that retards deterioration by oxidation, esp. of fats, oils, foods, or rubber. **2** *Biol.* a substance, such as vitamin C, vitamin E, or beta carotene, that counteracts the damaging effects of oxidation in a living organism.

antiparticle ('æntɪˌpɑːtɪkᵊl) *n* any of a group of elementary particles that have the same mass as their corresponding particle but have a charge of equal magnitude but opposite sign. When a particle collides with its antiparticle mutual annihilation occurs.

antipasto (ˌæntɪ'pɑːstəʊ, -'pæs-) *n, pl* **antipastos.** a course of hors d'oeuvres in an Italian meal. [It.: before food]

antipathetic (ænˌtɪpə'θɛtɪk, ˌæntɪpə-) *or* **antipathetical** *adj* (often foll. by *to*) having or arousing a strong aversion.

antipathy ❶ (æn'tɪpəθɪ) *n, pl* **antipathies. 1** a feeling of dislike or hostility. **2** the object of such a feeling. [C17: from L, from Gk, from ANTI- + *patheia* feeling]

antipersonnel (ˌæntɪpɜːsə'nɛl) *adj* (of weapons, etc.) designed to cause casualties to personnel rather than to destroy equipment.

antiperspirant (ˌæntɪ'pɜːspərənt) *n* **1** a substance applied to the skin to reduce or prevent perspiration. ◆ *adj* **2** reducing perspiration.

antiphlogistic (ˌæntɪflə'dʒɪstɪk) *adj* **1** of or relating to the prevention or alleviation of inflammation. ◆ *n* **2** an antiphlogistic drug.

antiphon ('æntɪfən) *n* **1** a short passage, usually from the Bible, recited or sung as a response after certain parts of a liturgical service. **2** a psalm, hymn, etc., chanted or sung in alternate parts. **3** any response. [C15: from LL *antiphōna* sung responses, from LGk, pl of *antiphōnon* (something) responsive, from ANTI- + *phōnē* sound]
▸ **antiphonal** (æn'tɪfənəl) *adj*

antiphonary (æn'tɪfənərɪ) *n, pl* **antiphonaries.** a bound collection of antiphons.

antiphony (æn'tɪfənɪ) *n, pl* **antiphonies. 1** antiphonal singing. **2** any musical or other sound effect that answers or echoes another.

antipode ('æntɪpəʊd) *n* the exact or direct opposite.
▸ **antipodal** (æn'tɪpədᵊl) *adj*

antipodes (æn'tɪpəˌdiːz) *pl n* **1** either or both of two places that are situated diametrically opposite one another on the earth's surface. **2** the people who live there. **3** (*often cap.*) **the.** Australia and New Zealand. [C16: via LL from Gk, pl of *antipous* having the feet opposite, from ANTI- + *pous* foot]
▸ **antipodean** (ænˌtɪpə'diːən) *adj*

antipope ('æntɪˌpəʊp) *n* a rival pope elected in opposition to one who has been canonically chosen.

anti-Protestant *adj* opposed to Protestantism.

antipsychotic (ˌæntɪsaɪ'kɒtɪk) *adj* **1** preventing or treating psychosis. ◆ *n* **2** any antipsychotic drug, such as chlorpromazine: used to treat such conditions as schizophrenia.

antipyretic (ˌæntɪpaɪ'rɛtɪk) *adj* **1** preventing or alleviating fever. ◆ *n* **2** an antipyretic remedy or drug.

antiquarian (ˌæntɪ'kwɛərɪən) *adj* **1** concerned with the study of antiquities or antiques. ◆ *n* **2** a less common name for **antiquary.**
▸ ˌ**anti'quarianism** *n*

antiquark ('æntɪˌkwɑːk) *n* the antiparticle of a quark.

antiquary ('æntɪkwərɪ) *n, pl* **antiquaries.** a person who collects, deals in, or studies antiques or ancient works of art. Also called: **antiquarian.**

antiquate ❶ ('æntɪˌkweɪt) *vb* **antiquates, antiquating, antiquated.** (*tr*) to make obsolete or old-fashioned. [C15: from L *antīquāre* to make old, from *antīquus* ancient]
▸ **'antiˌquated** *adj*

antique ❶ (æn'tiːk) *n* **1a** a decorative object, piece of furniture, or other work of art created in an earlier period, that is valued for its beauty, workmanship, and age. **1b** (*as modifier*): *an antique shop.* **2** any object made in an earlier period. **3 the.** the style of ancient art, esp. Greek or Roman. ◆ *adj* **4** made in or in the style of an earlier period. **5** of or belonging to the distant past, esp. of ancient Greece or Rome. **6** *Inf.* old-fashioned. **7** *Arch.* aged or venerable. ◆ *vb* **antiques, antiquing, antiqued. 8** (*tr*) to give an antique appearance to. [C16: from L *antīquus* ancient, from *ante* before]

antiquities (æn'tɪkwɪtɪz) *pl n* remains or relics, such as statues, buildings, or coins, that date from ancient times.

antiquity ❶ (æn'tɪkwɪtɪ) *n, pl* **antiquities. 1** the quality of being ancient: *a vase of great antiquity.* **2** the far distant past, esp. preceding the Middle Ages. **3** the people of ancient times collectively.

antiracism (ˌæntɪ'reɪsɪzəm) *n* the policy of challenging racism and promoting racial tolerance.
▸ ˌ**anti'racist** *n, adj*

anti-riot *adj* designed for or employed in controlling crowds: *anti-riot police.*

anti-roll bar *n* a crosswise rubber-mounted bar in the suspension of a motor vehicle, which counteracts the movement downwards on one side when cornering.

antirrhinum (ˌæntɪ'raɪnəm) *n* any plant of the genus *Antirrhinum*, esp. the snapdragon, which has two-lipped flowers of various colours. [C16: via L from Gk *antirrhinon*, from ANTI- (imitating) + *rhis* nose]

THESAURUS

antidote *n* **1, 2 = cure**, antitoxin, antivenin, corrective, counteragent, countermeasure, neutralizer, nostrum, preventive, remedy, specific

antipathy *n* **1 = hostility**, abhorrence, animosity, animus, antagonism, aversion, bad blood, contrariety, disgust, dislike, distaste, enmity, hatred, ill will, incompatibility, loathing, odium, opposition, rancour, repugnance, repulsion

Antonyms *n* affection, affinity, attraction, bond, empathy, fellow-feeling, goodwill, harmony, partiality, rapport, sympathy, tie

antiquated *adj* **= obsolete**, antediluvian, antique, archaic, dated, old-fashioned, old hat, outmoded, out-of-date, outworn, passé, past it (*inf.*), superannuated

Antonyms *adj* **≠ obsolete:** all-singing, all-dancing, current, fashionable, fresh, modern, modish, new, state-of-the-art, stylish, up-to-date, young

antique *n* **1, 2 = period piece**, bygone, heirloom, object of virtu, relic ◆ *adj* **4 = vintage**, antiquarian, classic, olden **6** *Inf.* **= old-fashioned**, archaic, obsolete, outdated

antiquity *n* **1 = old age**, age, ancientness, elderliness, oldness **2 = distant past**, ancient times, olden days, time immemorial

antiscorbutic (ˌæntɪskɔːˈbjuːtɪk) *adj* **1** preventing or curing scurvy. ◆ *n* **2** an antiscorbutic agent.

anti-Semite *n* a person who persecutes or discriminates against Jews. ▸ˌ**anti-Seˈmitic** *adj* ▸ˌ**anti-ˈSemitism** *n*

antisepsis (ˌæntɪˈsɛpsɪs) *n* **1** destruction of undesirable microorganisms, such as those that cause disease or putrefaction. **2** the state of being free from such microorganisms.

antiseptic ❶ (ˌæntɪˈsɛptɪk) *adj* **1** of or producing antisepsis. **2** entirely free from contamination. **3** *Inf.* lacking spirit or excitement. ◆ *n* **4** an antiseptic agent.
▸ˌ**antiˈseptically** *adv*

antiserum (ˌæntɪˈsɪərəm) *n, pl* **antiserums** *or* **antisera** (-rə). blood serum containing antibodies against a specific antigen, used to treat or provide immunity to a disease.

antisocial ❶ (ˌæntɪˈsəʊʃəl) *adj* **1** avoiding the company of other people; unsociable. **2** contrary or injurious to the interests of society in general.

antispasmodic (ˌæntɪspæzˈmɒdɪk) *adj* **1** preventing or arresting spasms. ◆ *n* **2** an antispasmodic drug.

antistatic (ˌæntɪˈstætɪk) *adj* (of a substance, textile, etc.) retaining sufficient moisture to provide a conducting path, thus avoiding the effects of static electricity.

antistrophe (ænˈtɪstrəfɪ) *n* (in ancient Greek drama) **a** the second of two movements made by a chorus during the performance of a choral ode. **b** the second part of a choral ode sung during this movement. ◆ See **strophe.** [C17: via LL from Gk *antistrophē* an answering turn, from ANTI- + *strophē* a turning]
▸**antistrophically** (ˌæntɪˈstrɒfɪkəlɪ) *adv*

antitank (ˌæntɪˈtæŋk) *adj* designed to immobilize or destroy armoured vehicles.

antithesis ❶ (ænˈtɪθɪsɪs) *n, pl* **antitheses** (-ˌsiːz). **1** the exact opposite. **2** contrast or opposition. **3** *Rhetoric.* the juxtaposition of contrasting ideas or words to produce an effect of balance, such as *my words fly up, my thoughts remain below.* [C15: via L from Gk: a setting against, from ANTI- + *tithenai* to place]
▸**antithetical** (ˌæntɪˈθɛtɪkᵊl) *adj*

antitoxin (ˌæntɪˈtɒksɪn) *n* **1** an antibody that neutralizes a toxin. **2** blood serum that contains a specific antibody.
▸ˌ**antiˈtoxic** *adj*

antitrades (ˈæntɪˌtreɪdz) *pl n* winds in the upper atmosphere blowing in the opposite direction from and above the trade winds.

antitrust (ˌæntɪˈtrʌst) *n* (*modifier*) *Chiefly US.* regulating or opposing trusts, monopolies, cartels, or similar organizations.

antitussive (ˌæntɪˈtʌsɪv) *n* **1** any of a class of drugs used to suppress or alleviate coughing. ◆ *adj* **2** of or relating to such drugs. [from ANTI- + L *tussis* a cough]

antitype (ˈæntɪˌtaɪp) *n* **1** a person or thing that is foreshadowed or represented by a type or symbol. **2** an opposite type.
▸**antitypical** (ˌæntɪˈtɪpɪkᵊl) *adj*

antivenin (ˌæntɪˈvɛnɪn) *or* **antivenene** (ˌæntɪvɪˈniːn) *n* an antitoxin that counteracts a specific venom, esp. snake venom. [C19: from ANTI- + VEN(OM) + -IN]

antiviral (ˌæntɪˈvaɪrəl) *adj* **1** inhibiting the growth of viruses. ◆ *n* **2** any antiviral drug.

antler (ˈæntlə) *n* one of a pair of bony outgrowths on the heads of male deer and some related species of either sex. [C14: from OF *antoillier*]
▸ˈ**antlered** *adj*

antlion (ˈæntˌlaɪən) *n* **1** any of various insects which resemble dragonflies and are most common in tropical regions. **2** the larva of this insect, which buries itself in the sand to await its prey.

antonomasia (ˌæntənəˈmeɪzɪə) *n* **1** the substitution of a title or epithet for a proper name, such as *his highness.* **2** the use of a proper name for an idea: *he is a Daniel come to judgment.* [C16: via L from Gk, from *antonomazein* to name differently, from *onoma* name]

antonym (ˈæntənɪm) *n* a word that means the opposite of another. [C19: from Gk, from ANTI- + *onoma* name]
▸**antonymous** (ænˈtɒnɪməs) *adj*

antrum (ˈæntrəm) *n, pl* **antra** (-trə). *Anat.* a natural cavity, hollow, or sinus, esp. in a bone. [C14: from L: cave, from Gk *antron*]
▸ˈ**antral** *adj*

ANU *abbrev. for* Australian National University.

anuresis (ˌænjʊˈriːsɪs) *n* inability to urinate. [C20: NL, from AN- + Gk *ouresis* urination]

anus (ˈeɪnəs) *n* the excretory opening at the end of the alimentary canal. [C16: from L]

anvil (ˈænvɪl) *n* **1** a heavy iron or steel block on which metals are hammered during forging. **2** any part having a similar shape or function, such as the lower part of a telegraph key. **3** *Anat.* the nontechnical name for **incus.** [OE *anfealt*]

anxiety ❶ (æŋˈzaɪɪtɪ) *n, pl* **anxieties. 1** a state of uneasiness or tension caused by apprehension of possible misfortune, danger, etc. **2** intense desire; eagerness. **3** *Psychol.* a state of intense apprehension, common in mental illness or after a very distressing experience. [C16: from L *anxietas*]

anxiety disorder *n* any of various mental disorders characterized by extreme anxiety.

anxious ❶ (ˈæŋkʃəs, ˈæŋʃəs) *adj* **1** worried and tense because of possible misfortune, danger, etc. **2** causing anxiety; worrying; distressing: *an anxious time.* **3** intensely desirous: *anxious for promotion.* [C17: from L *anxius;* rel. to L *angere* to torment]
▸ˈ**anxiously** *adv* ▸ˈ**anxiousness** *n*

any (ˈɛnɪ) *determiner* **1a** one, some, or several, as specified, no matter how much, what kind, etc.: *you may take any clothes you like.* **1b** (*as pron; functioning as sing or pl*): *take any you like.* **2** (*usually used with a negative*) **2a** even the smallest amount or even one: *I can't stand any noise.* **2b** (*as pron; functioning as sing or pl*): *don't give her any.* **3** whatever or whichever: *any dictionary will do.* **4** an indefinite or unlimited (amount or number): *any number of friends.* ◆ *adv* **5** (*usually used with a negative*) (foll. by a comp. adj) to even the smallest extent: *it isn't any worse.* [OE *ǣnig*]

anybody (ˈɛnɪˌbɒdɪ) *pron* **1** any person; anyone. **2** (*usually used with a negative or a question*) a person of any importance: *he isn't anybody.* ◆ *n, pl* **anybodies. 3** (often preceded by *just*) any person at random.

anyhow (ˈɛnɪˌhaʊ) *adv* **1** in any case. **2** by any means whatever. **3** carelessly.

any more *or esp. US* **anymore** (ˌɛnɪˈmɔː) *adv* any longer; still; nowadays.

anyone (ˈɛnɪˌwʌn) *pron* **1** any person; anybody. **2** (*used with a negative or a question*) a person of any importance: *is he anyone?* **3** (often preceded by *just*) any person at random.

anyplace (ˈɛnɪˌpleɪs) *adv US & Canad. inf.* anywhere.

anything (ˈɛnɪˌθɪŋ) *pron* **1** any object, event, action, etc., whatever: *anything might happen.* ◆ *n* **2** a thing of any kind: *have you anything to declare?* ◆ *adv* **3** in any way: *he wasn't anything like his father.* **4 anything but.** not in the least: *she was anything but happy.* **5 like anything.** (intensifier): *he ran like anything.*

anyway (ˈɛnɪˌweɪ) *adv* **1** in any case; at any rate; nevertheless. **2** in a careless manner. **3** Usually **any way.** in any manner.

anywhere (ˈɛnɪˌwɛə) *adv* **1** in, at, or to any place. **2 get anywhere.** to be successful.

anywise (ˈɛnɪˌwaɪz) *adv Chiefly US.* in any way.

ANZAAS (ˈænzəs, -zæs) *n acronym for* Australian and New Zealand Association for the Advancement of Science.

Anzac (ˈænzæk) *n* **1** (in World War I) a soldier serving with the Australian and New Zealand Army Corps. **2** (now) any Australian or New Zealand soldier. **3** the Anzac landing at Gallipoli in 1915.

Anzac Day *n* April 25, a public holiday in Australia and New Zealand commemorating the Anzac landing at Gallipoli in 1915.

ANZUS (ˈænzəs) *n acronym for* Australia, New Zealand, and the United States, with reference to the security alliance between them.

AO *abbrev. for* Officer of the Order of Australia.

A/O *or* **a/o** (accounting, etc.) *abbrev. for* account of.

AOB *or* **a.o.b.** *abbrev. for* any other business.

AOC *abbrev. for* appellation d'origine contrôlée: the highest French wine classification; indicates that the wine meets strict requirements concerning area of production, strength, etc. Cf. **VDQS, vin de pays.**

AONB (in England and Wales) *abbrev. for* area of outstanding natural beauty: an area officially designated as requiring protection to conserve and enhance its natural beauty.

aorist (ˈeɪərɪst, ˈɛərɪst) *n Grammar.* a tense of the verb, esp. in classical Greek, indicating past action without reference to whether the action involved was momentary or continuous. [C16: from Gk *aoristos* not limited, from A-[1] + *horistos,* from *horizein* to define]

aorta (eɪˈɔːtə) *n, pl* **aortas** *or* **aortae** (-tiː). the main vessel in the arterial network, which conveys oxygen-rich blood from the heart. [C16: from NL, from Gk *aortē,* lit.: something lifted, from *aeirein* to raise]
▸**aˈortic** *or* **aˈortal** *adj*

Aotearoa (ˈæɒˌtɪəˌrɔːə) *n NZ.* the Maori name for New Zealand. [Maori: the long white cloud]

aoudad (ˈɑːʊˌdæd) *n* a wild mountain sheep of N Africa. Also called: **Barbary sheep.** [from F, from Berber *audad*]

THESAURUS

antiseptic *adj* **2** = **hygienic**, aseptic, clean, germ-free, pure, sanitary, sterile, uncontaminated, unpolluted ◆ *n* **4** = **disinfectant**, bactericide, germicide, purifier
Antonyms *adj* ≠ **hygienic:** contaminated, dirty, impure, infected, insanitary, polluted, septic, unhygienic

antisocial *adj* **1** = **unsociable**, alienated, asocial, misanthropic, reserved, retiring, uncommunicative, unfriendly, withdrawn **2** = **disruptive**, antagonistic, belligerent, disorderly, hostile, menacing, rebellious, uncooperative
Antonyms *adj* ≠ **unsociable:** companionable, friendly, gregarious, philanthropic, sociable, social

antithesis *n* **1** = **opposite**, antipode, contrary, contrast, converse, inverse, reverse **2** = **contrast**, contradiction, contraposition, contrariety, inversion, opposition, reversal

anxiety *n* **1** = **uneasiness**, angst, apprehension, care, concern, disquiet, disquietude, distress, foreboding, fretfulness, misgiving, nervousness, restlessness, solicitude, suspense, tension, trepidation, unease, watchfulness, worry
Antonyms *n* assurance, calmness, confidence, contentment, relief, security, serenity

anxious *adj* **1** = **uneasy**, apprehensive, careful, concerned, disquieted, distressed, disturbed, fearful, fretful, in suspense, nervous, neurotic, on tenterhooks, overwrought, restless, solicitous, taut, tense, troubled, twitchy (*inf.*), unquiet (*chiefly literary*), watchful, worried **3** = **eager**, ardent, avid, desirous, expectant, impatient, intent, itching, keen, yearning
Antonyms *adj* ≠ **uneasy:** assured, calm, certain, collected, composed, confident, cool, nonchalant, unfazed (*inf.*), unperturbed ≠ **eager:** disinclined, hesitant, loath, nonchalant, reluctant

ap (æp) son of: occurring as part of some surnames of Welsh origin: *ap Thomas.* [from Welsh *mab* son]

apace ➊ (ə'peɪs) *adv* quickly; rapidly. [C14: prob. from OF *à pas,* at a (good) pace]

apache (ə'pæʃ) *n* a Parisian gangster or ruffian. [from F: APACHE]

Apache (ə'pætʃɪ) *n* **1** (*pl* **Apaches** *or* **Apache**) a member of a North American Indian people inhabiting the southwestern US and N Mexico. **2** the language of this people. [from Mexican Sp.]

apanage ('æpənɪdʒ) *n* a variant spelling of **appanage.**

apart ➊ (ə'pɑːt) *adj* (*postpositive*), *adv* **1** to or in pieces: *he had the television apart.* **2** placed or kept separately or for a particular purpose, etc.; aside (esp. in **set** *or* **put apart**). **3** separate in time, place, or position: *he stood apart from the group.* **4** not being taken into account: *these difficulties apart, the project ran smoothly.* **5** individual; distinct: *a race apart.* **6** separately or independently: *considered apart, his reasoning was faulty.* **7** **apart from.** (*prep*) besides. ◆ See also **take apart, tell apart.** [C14: from OF *a part* at (the) side]

apartheid (ə'pɑːthaɪt, -heɪt) *n* (formerly, in South Africa) the government policy of racial segregation; officially renounced in 1992. [C20: Afrik., from *apart* APART + *-heid* -HOOD]

apartment ➊ (ə'pɑːtmənt) *n* **1** (*often pl*) any room in a building, usually one of several forming a suite, used as living accommodation, offices, etc. **2a** another name (esp. US and Canad.) for **flat**[2] (sense 1). **2b** (*as modifier*): *apartment house.* [C17: from F *appartement,* from It., from *appartare* to separate]

apathetic ➊ (ˌæpə'θetɪk) *adj* having or showing little or no emotion or interest. [C18: from APATHY + PATHETIC]
▸ **ˌapa'thetically** *adv*

apathy ➊ ('æpəθɪ) *n* **1** absence of interest in or enthusiasm for things generally considered interesting or moving. **2** absence of emotion. [C17: from L, from Gk *apatheia,* from A-[1] + *pathos* feeling]

apatite ('æpəˌtaɪt) *n* a common naturally occurring mineral consisting basically of calcium fluorophosphate. It is a source of phosphorus and is used in fertilizers. [C19: from G *Apatit,* from Gk *apatē* deceit; from its misleading similarity to other minerals]

ape ➊ (eɪp) *n* **1** any of various primates in which the tail is very short or absent. **2** (not in technical use) any monkey. **3** an imitator; mimic. ◆ *vb* **apes, aping, aped. 4** (*tr*) to imitate. [OE *apa*]
▸ **'apeˌlike** *adj*

APEC *Canad. abbrev. for* Atlantic Provinces Economic Council.

apeman ('eɪpˌmæn) *n, pl* **apemen.** any of various extinct apelike primates thought to have been the forerunners of modern man.

aperçu *French.* (apersy) *n* **1** an outline. **2** an insight. [from *apercevoir* to PERCEIVE]

aperient (ə'pɪərɪənt) *Med.* ◆ *adj* **1** laxative. ◆ *n* **2** a mild laxative. [C17: from L *aperīre* to open]

aperiodic (ˌeɪpɪərɪ'ɒdɪk) *adj* **1** not periodic; not occurring at regular intervals. **2** *Physics.* **2a** (of a system or instrument) being damped sufficiently to reach equilibrium without oscillation. **2b** (of an oscillation or vibration) not having a regular period. **2c** (of an electrical circuit) not having a measurable resonant frequency.
▸ **aperiodicity** (ˌeɪpɪərɪə'dɪsɪtɪ) *n*

apéritif (əˌperɪ'tiːf) *n* an alcoholic drink before a meal to whet the appetite. [C19: from F, from Med. L, from L *aperīre* to open]

aperture ➊ ('æpətʃə) *n* **1** a hole; opening. **2** *Physics.* a usually circular and often variable opening in an optical instrument or device that controls the quantity of radiation entering or leaving it. [C15: from LL *apertūra* opening, from *aperīre* to open]

apetalous (eɪ'petələs) *adj* (of flowering plants such as the wood anemone) having no petals. [C18: from NL; see A-[1], PETAL]

apex ➊ ('eɪpeks) *n, pl* **apexes** *or* **apices. 1** the highest point; vertex. **2** the pointed end or tip of something. **3** a high point, as of a career. [C17: from L: point]

APEX ('eɪpeks) *n acronym for:* **1** Advance Purchase Excursion, a reduced airline or long-distance rail fare that must be paid a specified number of days in advance. **2** Association of Professional, Executive, Clerical, and Computer Staff.

Apex Club ('eɪpeks) *n* (in Australia) an association of business and professional men to promote community welfare.
▸ **Apexian** (eɪ'peksɪən) *adj, n*

apgar score *or* **rating** ('æpgɑː) *n* a system for determining the condition of an infant at birth by allotting a maximum of 2 points to each of the following: heart rate, breathing effort, muscle tone, response to stimulation, and colour. [C20: after V. *Apgar* (1909–74), US anaesthetist]

aphaeresis *or* **apheresis** (ə'fɪərɪsɪs) *n* the omission of a letter or syllable at the beginning of a word. [C17: via LL from Gk, from *aphairein* to remove]

aphasia (ə'feɪzɪə) *n* a disorder of the central nervous system characterized by loss of the ability to communicate, esp. in speech. [C19: via NL from Gk, from A-[1] + *-phasia,* from *phanai* to speak]

aphelion (æp'hiːlɪən, ə'fiː-) *n, pl* **aphelia** (-lɪə). the point in its orbit when a planet or comet is at its greatest distance from the sun. [C17: from NL *aphēlium,* from AP(O)- + Gk *hēlios* sun]

aphesis ('æfɪsɪs) *n* the gradual disappearance of an unstressed vowel at the beginning of a word, as in *squire* from *esquire.* [C19: from Gk, from *aphienai* to set free]
▸ **aphetic** (ə'fetɪk) *adj*

aphid ('eɪfɪd) *n* any of the small homopterous insects of the family Aphididae, which feed by sucking the juices from plants. [C19: from *aphides,* pl. of APHIS]

aphis ('eɪfɪs) *n, pl* **aphides** ('eɪfɪˌdiːz). any of a genus of aphids such as the blackfly. [C18: from NL (coined by Linnaeus for obscure reasons)]

aphonia (ə'fəʊnɪə) *or* **aphony** ('æfənɪ) *n* loss of voice caused by damage to the vocal tract. [C18: NL, from Gk, from A-[1] + *phōnē* sound]

aphorism ➊ ('æfəˌrɪzəm) *n* a short pithy saying expressing a general truth; maxim. [C16: from LL, from Gk *aphorismos,* from *aphorizein* to define]
▸ **'aphorist** *n* ▸ **ˌapho'ristic** *adj*

aphrodisiac ➊ (ˌæfrə'dɪzɪæk) *n* **1** a drug, food, etc., that excites sexual desire. ◆ *adj* **2** exciting sexual desire. [C18: from Gk, from *aphrodisios* belonging to *Aphrodite,* goddess of love]

aphyllous (ə'fɪləs) *adj* (of plants) having no leaves. [C19: from NL, from Gk A-[1] + *phullon* leaf]

apian ('eɪpɪən) *adj* of, relating to, or resembling bees. [C19: from L *apiānus,* from *apis* bee]

apiarist ('eɪpɪərɪst) *n* a person who studies or keeps bees.

apiary ('eɪpɪərɪ) *n, pl* **apiaries.** a place where bees are kept. [C17: from L *apiārium,* from *apis* bee]

apical ('æpɪkᵊl, 'eɪ-) *adj* of, at, or being the apex. [C19: from NL *apicālis*]
▸ **'apically** *adv*

apices ('æpɪˌsiːz, 'eɪ-) *n* a plural of **apex.**

apiculture ('eɪpɪˌkʌltʃə) *n* the breeding and care of bees. [C19: from L *apis* bee + CULTURE]
▸ **ˌapi'cultural** *adj* ▸ **ˌapi'culturist** *n*

apiece ➊ (ə'piːs) *adv* (*postpositive*) for, to, or from each one: *they were given two apples apiece.*

apish ('eɪpɪʃ) *adj* **1** stupid; foolish. **2** resembling an ape. **3** slavishly imitative.
▸ **'apishly** *adv* ▸ **'apishness** *n*

aplanatic (ˌæplə'nætɪk) *adj* (of a lens or mirror) free from spherical aberration. [C18: from Gk *aplanetos* free from error, from A-[1] + *planaein* to wander]

aplenty ➊ (ə'plentɪ) *adj* (*postpositive*), *adv* in plenty.

aplomb ➊ (ə'plɒm) *n* equanimity, self-confidence, or self-possession. [C18: from F: uprightness, from *à plomb* according to the plumb line]

apnoea *or US* **apnea** (æp'nɪə) *n* a temporary inability to breathe. [C18: from NL, from Gk *apnoia,* from A-[1] + *pnein* to breathe]

apo- *or* **ap-** *prefix* **1** away from; off: *apogee.* **2** separation of: *apocarpous.* [from Gk *apo* away, off]

Apoc. *abbrev. for:* **1** Apocalypse. **2** Apocrypha *or* Apocryphal.

THESAURUS

apace *adv* = **quickly,** at full speed, expeditiously, posthaste, rapidly, speedily, swiftly, with dispatch, without delay

apart *adv* **1** = **to pieces,** asunder, in bits, in pieces, into parts, to bits **2** = **separate,** afar, alone, aloof, aside, away, by itself, by oneself, cut off, distant, distinct, divorced, excluded, independent, independently, isolated, out on a limb, piecemeal, separated, separately, singly, to itself, to oneself, to one side **7** **apart from** = **except for,** aside from, besides, but, excluding, not counting, other than, save

apartment *n* **1, 2** = **room,** accommodation, chambers, compartment, flat, living quarters, penthouse, quarters, rooms, suite

apathetic *adj* = **uninterested,** cold, cool, emotionless, impassive, indifferent, insensible, listless, passive, phlegmatic, sluggish, stoic, stoical, torpid, unconcerned, unemotional, unfeeling, unmoved, unresponsive
Antonyms *adj* active, anxious, aroused, bothered, caring, committed, concerned, emotional, enthusiastic, excited, interested, moved, passionate, responsive, troubled, worried, zealous

apathy *n* **1, 2** = **lack of interest,** coldness, coolness, emotionlessness, impassibility, impassivity, indifference, inertia, insensibility, listless- ness, nonchalance, passiveness, passivity, phlegm, sluggishness, stoicism, torpor, unconcern, unfeelingness, uninterestedness, unresponsiveness
Antonyms *n* anxiety, attention, concern, emotion, enthusiasm, feeling, interest, zeal

ape *vb* **4** = **imitate,** affect, caricature, copy, counterfeit, echo, mimic, mirror, mock, parody, parrot

aperture *n* **1** = **opening,** breach, chink, cleft, crack, eye, eyelet, fissure, gap, hole, interstice, orifice, passage, perforation, rent, rift, slit, slot, space, vent

apex *n* **1-3** = **highest point,** acme, apogee, climax, crest, crown, culmination, height, peak, pinnacle, point, summit, tip, top, vertex, zenith
Antonyms *n* base, bottom, depths, lowest point, nadir, perigee, rock bottom

aphorism *n* = **saying,** adage, apothegm, axiom, dictum, gnome, maxim, precept, proverb, saw

aphrodisiac *n* **1** = **love potion,** philter ◆ *adj* **2** = **erotic** *or* **erotical,** arousing, exciting, stimulating, venereal

apiece *adv* = **each,** for each, from each, individually, respectively, separately, severally, to each
Antonyms *adv* all together, as a group, collectively, en masse, overall, together

aplenty *adj* = **in plenty,** à gogo, galore, in abundance, in profusion, in quantity, to spare ◆ *adv* = **plentifully,** abundantly, copiously, in abundance, in plenty, in quantity, plenteously

aplomb *n* = **self-possession,** balance, calmness, composure, confidence, coolness, equanimity, level-headedness, poise, sang-froid, self-assurance, self-confidence, stability
Antonyms *n* awkwardness, chagrin, confusion, discomfiture, discomposure, embarrassment, self-consciousness

apocalypse ⓣ (əˈpɒkəlɪps) *n* **1** a prophetic disclosure or revelation. **2** an event of great importance, violence, etc., like the events described in the Apocalypse. [C13: from LL *apocalypsis,* from Gk, from APO- + *kaluptein* to hide]
▸**aˌpocaˈlyptic** *adj*

Apocalypse (əˈpɒkəlɪps) *n Bible.* another name for the Book of Revelation.

apocarpous (ˌæpəˈkɑːpəs) *adj* (of the ovaries of flowering plants) consisting of separate carpels. [C19: from NL, from Gk APO- + *karpos* fruit]

apochromat (ˌæpəˈkrəʊmæt) *or* **apochromatic lens** (ˌæpəkrəˈmætɪk) *n* a lens system designed to bring trichromatic light to a single focus and reduce chromatic aberration.

apocope (əˈpɒkəpɪ) *n* omission of the final sound or sounds of a word. [C16: via LL from Gk, from *apokoptein* to cut off]

apocrine (ˈæpəkraɪn, -krɪn) *adj* losing cellular tissue in the process of secreting, as in mammary glands. Cf. **eccrine.** [C20: from APO- + *-crine,* from Gk *krinein* to separate]

Apocrypha (əˈpɒkrɪfə) *n* **the.** (*functioning as sing or pl*) the 14 books included as an appendix to the Old Testament in the Septuagint and the Vulgate but not in the Hebrew canon. [C14: via LL *apocrypha* (*scripta*) hidden (writings), from Gk, from *apokruptein* to hide away]

apocryphal ⓣ (əˈpɒkrɪfəl) *adj* **1** of questionable authenticity. **2** (*sometimes cap.*) of or like the Apocrypha. **3** untrue; counterfeit.

apodal (ˈæpədᵊl) *or* **apodous** (ˈæpədəs) *adj* without feet; having no pelvic fins. [C18: from Gk A-[1] + *pous* foot]

apodosis (əˈpɒdəsɪs) *n, pl* **apodoses** (-ˌsiːz). *Logic, grammar.* the consequent of a conditional statement, as *I won't go* in *if it rains I won't go.* [C17: via LL from Gk, from *apodidonai* to give back]

apogee ⓣ (ˈæpəˌdʒiː) *n* **1** the point in its orbit around the earth when the moon or an artificial satellite is at its greatest distance from the earth. **2** the highest point. [C17: from NL, from Gk, from *apogaios* away from the earth]
▸**ˌapoˈgean** *adj*

apolitical (ˌeɪpəˈlɪtɪkᵊl) *adj* politically neutral; without political attitudes, content, or bias.

Apollyon (əˈpɒljən) *n* the destroyer, a name given to the Devil (Revelation 9:11). [C14: via LL from Gk, from *apollunai* to destroy totally]

apologetic ⓣ (əˌpɒləˈdʒɛtɪk) *adj* **1** expressing or anxious to make apology; contrite. **2** defending in speech or writing.
▸**aˌpoloˈgetically** *adv*

apologetics (əˌpɒləˈdʒɛtɪks) *n* (*functioning as sing*) **1** the branch of theology concerned with the rational justification of Christianity. **2** a defensive method of argument.

apologia (ˌæpəˈləʊdʒɪə) *n* a formal written defence of a cause or one's beliefs or conduct.

apologist (əˈpɒlədʒɪst) *n* a person who offers a defence by argument.

apologize ⓣ *or* **apologise** (əˈpɒləˌdʒaɪz) *vb* **apologizes, apologizing, apologized** *or* **apologises, apologising, apologised.** (*intr*) **1** to express or make an apology; acknowledge faults. **2** to make a formal defence.

apologue (ˈæpəˌlɒg) *n* an allegory or moral fable. [C17: from L, from Gk *apologos*]

apology ⓣ (əˈpɒlədʒɪ) *n, pl* **apologies. 1** a verbal or written expression of regret or contrition for a fault or failing. **2** a poor substitute. **3** another word for **apologia.** [C16: from OF, from LL, from Gk: a verbal defence, from APO- + *logos* speech]

apophthegm *or* **apothegm** (ˈæpəˌθɛm) *n* a short remark containing some general or generally accepted truth; maxim. [C16: from Gk *apophthegma,* from *apophthengesthai* to speak frankly]

apoplectic ⓣ (ˌæpəˈplɛktɪk) *adj* **1** of apoplexy. **2** *Inf.* furious.
▸**ˌapoˈplectically** *adv*

apoplexy ⓣ (ˈæpəˌplɛksɪ) *n* sudden loss of consciousness, often followed by paralysis, caused by rupture or occlusion of a blood vessel in the brain. [C14: from OF *apoplexie,* from LL, from Gk, from *apoplēssein* to cripple by a stroke]

aport (əˈpɔːt) *adv, adj* (*postpositive*) *Naut.* on or towards the port side: *with the helm aport.*

apostasy ⓣ (əˈpɒstəsɪ) *n, pl* **apostasies.** abandonment of one's religious faith, party, a cause, etc. [C14: from Church L *apostasia,* from Gk *apostasis* desertion]

apostate ⓣ (əˈpɒsteɪt, -tɪt) *n* **1** a person who abandons his religion, party, etc. ◆ *adj* **2** guilty of apostasy.
▸**apostatical** (ˌæpəˈstætɪkᵊl) *adj*

apostatize *or* **apostatise** (əˈpɒstəˌtaɪz) *vb* **apostatizes, apostatizing, apostatized** *or* **apostatises, apostatising, apostatised.** (*intr*) to abandon one's belief, faith, or allegiance.

a posteriori (eɪ pɒsˌtɛrɪˈɔːraɪ, -rɪ; ɑː) *adj Logic.* **1** relating to inductive reasoning from particular facts to a general principle. **2** derived from or requiring evidence for its validation; empirical. [C18: from L, lit.: from the latter]

apostle ⓣ (əˈpɒsᵊl) *n* **1** (*often cap.*) one of the 12 disciples chosen by Christ to preach his gospel. **2** any prominent Christian missionary, esp. one who first converts a people. **3** an ardent early supporter of a cause, movement, etc. [OE *apostol,* from Church L, from Gk *apostolos* a messenger]

Apostles' Creed *n* a concise statement of Christian beliefs dating from about 500 A.D., traditionally ascribed to the Apostles.

apostolate (əˈpɒstəlɪt, -ˌleɪt) *n* the office, authority, or mission of an apostle.

apostolic (ˌæpəˈstɒlɪk) *adj* **1** of or relating to the Apostles or their teachings or practice. **2** of or relating to the pope as successor of the Apostles.
▸**ˌaposˈtolical** *adj*

Apostolic See (ˌæpəˈstɒlɪk) *n* the see of the pope.

Apostolic succession *n* the doctrine that the authority of Christian bishops derives from the Apostles through an unbroken line of consecration.

apostrophe[1] (əˈpɒstrəfɪ) *n* the punctuation mark ' used to indicate the omission of a letter or number, such as *he's* for *he has* or *he is,* also used in English to form the possessive, as in *John's father.* [C17: from LL, from Gk *apostrophos* mark of elision, from *apostrephein* to turn away]

apostrophe[2] (əˈpɒstrəfɪ) *n Rhetoric.* a digression from a discourse, esp. an address to an imaginary or absent person or a personification. [C16: from L *apostrophē,* from Gk: a turning away]

apostrophize *or* **apostrophise** (əˈpɒstrəˌfaɪz) *vb* **apostrophizes, apostrophizing, apostrophized** *or* **apostrophises, apostrophising, apostrophised.** (*tr*) to address an apostrophe to.

apothecaries' measure *n* a system of liquid volume measure used in pharmacy in which 20 fluid ounces equal 1 pint.

apothecaries' weight *n* a system of weights formerly used in pharmacy based on the Troy ounce.

apothecary (əˈpɒθɪkərɪ) *n, pl* **apothecaries. 1** an archaic word for **chemist. 2** *Law.* a chemist licensed by the Society of Apothecaries of London to prescribe, prepare, and sell drugs. [C14: from OF, from LL, from Gk *apothēkē* storehouse]

apothegm (ˈæpəˌθɛm) *n* a variant spelling of **apophthegm.**

apothem (ˈæpəˌθɛm) *n* the perpendicular from the centre of a regular polygon to any of its sides. [C20: from APO- + Gk *thema,* from *tithenai* to place]

apotheosis ⓣ (əˌpɒθɪˈəʊsɪs) *n, pl* **apotheoses** (-siːz). **1** elevation to the rank of a god; deification. **2** glorification of a person or thing. **3** a glorified ideal. [C17: via LL from Gk: deification]

apotheosize *or* **apotheosise** (əˈpɒθɪəˌsaɪz) *vb* **apotheosizes, apotheosizing, apotheosized** *or* **apotheosises, apotheosising, apotheosised.** (*tr*) **1** to deify. **2** to glorify or idealize.

app. *abbrev. for:* **1** apparatus. **2** appendix (of a book). **3** applied. **4** appointed. **5** apprentice. **6** approved. **7** approximate.

appal ⓣ *or US* **appall** (əˈpɔːl) *vb* **appals, appalling, appalled** *or US* **appalls, appalling, appalled.** (*tr*) to fill with horror; shock or dismay. [C14: from OF *appalir* to turn pale]

appalling ⓣ (əˈpɔːlɪŋ) *adj* **1** causing dismay, horror, or revulsion. **2** *Inf.* very bad.
▸**apˈpallingly** *adv*

Appaloosa (ˌæpəˈluːsə) *n* a breed of horse, originally from America, having a spotted rump. [C19: ?from *Palouse,* river in Idaho]

appanage *or* **apanage** (ˈæpənɪdʒ) *n* **1** land or other provision granted by a king for the support of esp. a younger son. **2** a customary accompaniment or perquisite, as to a job or position. [C17: from OF, from Med. L, from *appānāre* to provide for, from L *pānis* bread]

THESAURUS

apocalypse *n* **2** = **destruction**, carnage, conflagration, devastation, havoc, holocaust

apocryphal *adj* **1** = **dubious**, doubtful, equivocal, fictitious, legendary, mythical, questionable, spurious, unauthenticated, uncanonical, unsubstantiated, unverified
Antonyms *adj* attested, authentic, authenticated, authorized, canonical, credible, factual, substantiated, true, undisputed, unquestionable, verified

apogee *n* **1, 2** = **highest point**, acme, apex, climax, crest, crown, culmination, height, peak, pinnacle, summit, tip, top, vertex, zenith

apologetic *adj* **1** = **regretful**, contrite, penitent, remorseful, rueful, sorry

apologize *vb* **1** = **say sorry**, ask forgiveness, beg pardon, express regret, say one is sorry

apology *n* **1** = **defence**, acknowledgment, confession, excuse, explanation, extenuation, justification, plea, vindication **2** *As in* **an apology for** = **mockery**, caricature, excuse, imitation, travesty

apoplectic *adj* **2** *Informal* = **furious**, beside oneself, boiling, enraged, frantic, frenzied, fuming, incandescent, incensed, infuriated, livid (*inf.*), mad, raging

apoplexy *n* = **fit**, attack, convulsion, paroxysm, seizure

apostasy *n* = **desertion**, backsliding, defection, disloyalty, faithlessness, falseness, heresy, perfidy, recreance *or* recreancy (*arch.*), treachery, unfaithfulness

apostate *n* **1** = **deserter**, backslider, defector, heretic, recreant (*arch.*), renegade, traitor, turncoat ◆ *adj* **2** = **disloyal**, backsliding, faithless, false, heretical, perfidious, recreant, traitorous, treacherous, unfaithful, untrue

apostle *n* **2** = **evangelist**, herald, messenger, missionary, preacher, proselytizer **3** = **supporter**, advocate, champion, pioneer, propagandist, propagator, proponent

apotheosis *n* **1, 2** = **deification**, elevation, exaltation, glorification, idealization, idolization

appal *vb* = **horrify**, alarm, astound, daunt, dishearten, dismay, frighten, harrow, intimidate, make one's hair stand on end (*inf.*), outrage, petrify, scare, shock, terrify, unnerve

appalled *adj* = **horrified**, alarmed, astounded, daunted, disheartened, dismayed, disquieted, frightened, outraged, petrified, scared, shocked, stunned, terrified, unnerved

appalling *adj* **1** = **horrifying**, alarming, astounding, awful, daunting, dire, disheartening, dismaying, dreadful, fearful, frightening, frightful, from hell (*inf.*), ghastly, grim, harrowing, hideous, horrible, horrid, horrific, intimidating, petrifying, scaring, shocking, terrible, terrifying, unnerving

apparatchik (ˌæpəˈrɑːtʃɪk) *n* **1** a member of a Communist Party organization. **2** a bureaucrat in any organization. [C20: from Russian, from *apparat* apparatus, instrument + *-ckik*, suffix denoting agent]

apparatus ➊ (ˌæpəˈreɪtəs, -ˈrɑːtəs) *n, pl* **apparatus** *or* **apparatuses.** **1** a collection of equipment used for a particular purpose. **2** a machine having a specific function: *breathing apparatus.* **3** the means by which something operates; organization. **4** *Anat.* any group of organs having a specific function. [C17: from L, from *apparāre* to make ready]

apparel ➊ (əˈpærəl) *n* **1** *Arch.* clothing. **2** *Naut.* a vessel's gear and equipment. ◆ *vb* **apparels, apparelling, apparelled** *or US* **apparels, appareling, appareled.** **3** (*tr*) *Arch.* to clothe, adorn, etc. [C13: from OF *apareillier* to make ready, from Vulgar L *apparicu̇lāre* (unattested), from L *parāre* to prepare]

apparent ➊ (əˈpærənt) *adj* **1** readily seen or understood; obvious. **2** (*usually prenominal*) seeming, as opposed to real: *his apparent innocence.* **3** *Physics.* as observed but ignoring such factors as the motion of the observer, etc. [C14: from L *apparēns,* from *appārēre* to APPEAR]
▸**apˈparently** *adv*

apparent magnitude *n* See **magnitude** (sense 4).

apparition ➊ (ˌæpəˈrɪʃən) *n* **1** an appearance, esp. of a ghost or ghostlike figure. **2** the figure so appearing; spectre. **3** the act of appearing. [C15: from LL *appāritiō,* from L *appārēre* to APPEAR]

appassionato (əˌpæsjəˈnɑːtəʊ) *adj, adv Music.* (to be performed) with passion. [It.]

appeal ➊ (əˈpiːl) *n* **1** a request for relief, aid, etc. **2** the power to attract, please, stimulate, or interest. **3** an application or resort to another authority, esp. a higher one, as for a decision. **4** *Law.* **4a** the judicial review by a superior court of the decision of a lower tribunal. **4b** a request for such review. **5** *Cricket.* a request to the umpire to declare a batsman out. ◆ *vb* **6** (*intr*) to make an earnest request. **7** (*intr*) to attract, please, stimulate, or interest. **8** *Law.* to apply to a superior court to review (a case or issue decided by a lower tribunal). **9** (*intr*) to resort (to), as for a decision. **10** (*intr*) *Cricket.* to ask the umpire to declare a batsman out. **11** (*intr*) to challenge the umpire's or referee's decision. [C14: from OF *appeler,* from L *appellāre* to entreat, from *pellere* to drive]
▸**apˈpealable** *adj* ▸**apˈpealer** *n* ▸**apˈpealing** *adj* ▸**apˈpealingly** *adv*

appear ➊ (əˈpɪə) *vb* (*intr*) **1** to come into sight. **2** (*copula; may take an infinitive*) to seem: *the evidence appears to support you.* **3** to be plain or clear, as after further evidence, etc.: *it appears you were correct after all.* **4** to develop; occur: *faults appeared during testing.* **5** to be published: *his biography appeared last month.* **6** to perform: *he has appeared in many London productions.* **7** to be present in court before a magistrate or judge: *he appeared on two charges of theft.* [C13: from OF *aparoir,* from L *appārēre* to become visible, attend upon, from *pārēre* to appear]

appearance ➊ (əˈpɪərəns) *n* **1** the act or an instance of appearing. **2** the outward aspect of a person or thing. **3** an outward show; pretence: *he gave an appearance of not caring.* **4 keep up appearances.** to maintain the public impression of wellbeing or normality. **5 put in** *or* **make an appearance.** to attend briefly, as out of politeness. **6 to all appearances.** apparently.
▸**apˈpeaser** *n*

appearance money *n* money paid by a promoter of an event to a particular celebrity in order to ensure that the celebrity takes part in the event.

appease ➊ (əˈpiːz) *vb* **appeases, appeasing, appeased.** (*tr*) **1** to calm or pacify, esp. by acceding to the demands of. **2** to satisfy or quell (a thirst, etc.). [C16: from OF *apaisier,* from *pais* peace, from L *pax*]

appeasement ➊ (əˈpiːzmənt) *n* **1** the policy of acceding to the demands of a potentially hostile nation in the hope of maintaining peace. **2** the act of appeasing.

appellant (əˈpɛlənt) *n* **1** a person who appeals. **2** *Law.* the party who appeals to a higher court from the decision of a lower tribunal. ◆ *adj* **3** *Law.* another word for **appellate.** [C14: from OF; see APPEAL]

appellate (əˈpɛlɪt) *adj Law.* **1** of appeals. **2** (of a tribunal) having jurisdiction to review cases on appeal. [C18: from L *appellātus* summoned, from *appellāre* to APPEAL]

appellation ➊ (ˌæpɪˈleɪʃən) *n* **1** a name or title. **2** the act of naming.

appellative (əˈpɛlətɪv) *n* **1** a name or title. **2** *Grammar.* another word for **common noun.** ◆ *adj* **3** of or relating to a name. **4** (of a proper noun) used as a common noun.

append ➊ (əˈpɛnd) *vb* (*tr*) **1** to add as a supplement: *to append a footnote.* **2** to attach; hang on. [C15: from LL *appendere* to hang (something) from, from L *pendere* to hang]

appendage ➊ (əˈpɛndɪdʒ) *n* an ancillary or secondary part attached to a main part; adjunct, such as an organ that projects from the trunk of an animal.

appendant (əˈpɛndənt) *adj* **1** attached or added. **2** attendant or associated as an accompaniment or result. ◆ *n* **3** a person or thing attached or added.

appendicectomy (əˌpɛndɪˈsɛktəmɪ) *or esp. US & Canad.* **appendectomy** (ˌæpənˈdɛktəmɪ) *n, pl* **appendicectomies** *or* **appendectomies.** surgical removal of any appendage, esp. the vermiform appendix.

appendicitis (əˌpɛndɪˈsaɪtɪs) *n* inflammation of the vermiform appendix.

appendix ➊ (əˈpɛndɪks) *n, pl* **appendices** (-dɪˌsiːz) *or* **appendixes.** **1** a body of separate additional material at the end of a book, etc. **2** any part that is dependent or supplementary. **3** *Anat.* See **vermiform appendix.** [C16: from L: an appendage, from *appendere* to APPEND]

apperceive (ˌæpəˈsiːv) *vb* **apperceives, apperceiving, apperceived.** (*tr*) **1** to be aware of perceiving. **2** *Psychol.* to comprehend by assimilating (a perception) to ideas already in the mind. [C19: from OF, from L *percipere* to PERCEIVE]

apperception (ˌæpəˈsɛpʃən) *n* **1** *Psychol.* the attainment of full awareness of a sensation or idea. **2** the act of apperceiving.
▸ˌ**apperˈceptive** *adj*

appertain ➊ (ˌæpəˈteɪn) *vb* (*intr;* usually foll. by *to*) to belong (to) as a part, function, right, etc.; relate (to) or be connected (with). [C14: from OF *apertenir,* from LL, from L AD- + *pertinēre* to PERTAIN]

appetence (ˈæpɪtəns) *or* **appetency** *n, pl* **appetences** *or* **appetencies.** **1** a craving or desire. **2** an attraction or affinity. [C17: from L *appetentia,* from *appetere* to crave]

appetite ➊ (ˈæpɪˌtaɪt) *n* **1** a desire for food or drink. **2** a desire to satisfy a bodily craving, as for sexual pleasure. **3** (usually foll. by *for*) a liking

THESAURUS

Antonyms *adj* comforting, consolatory, consoling, encouraging, heartening, reassuring

apparatus *n* **1, 2 = equipment,** appliance, contraption (*inf.*), device, gear, implements, machine, machinery, materials, means, mechanism, outfit, tackle, tools, utensils **3 = organization,** bureaucracy, chain of command, hierarchy, network, setup (*inf.*), structure, system

apparel *n* **1** *Archaic* **= clothing,** accoutrements, array (*poetic*), attire, clothes, costume, dress, equipment, garb, garments, gear (*inf.*), habiliments, habit, outfit, raiment (*arch. or poetic*), robes, threads (*sl.*), trappings, vestments

apparent *adj* **1 = obvious,** blatant, bold, clear, conspicuous, discernible, distinct, evident, indubitable, manifest, marked, open, overt, patent, plain, salient, understandable, unmistakable, visible **2 = seeming,** ostensible, outward, specious, superficial
Antonyms *adj* ≠ **obvious:** ambiguous, doubtful, dubious, hazy, indefinite, indistinct, obscure, uncertain, unclear, vague ≠ **seeming:** actual, authentic, bona fide, genuine, honest, intrinsic, real, sincere, true

apparently *adv* **2 = it appears that,** it seems that, on the face of it, ostensibly, outwardly, seemingly, speciously, superficially

apparition *n* **2 = ghost,** chimera, eidolon, phantom, revenant, shade (*literary*), spectre, spirit, spook (*inf.*), visitant, wraith

appeal *n* **1, 3 = plea,** adjuration, application, entreaty, invocation, petition, prayer, request, solicitation, suit, supplication **2 = attraction,** allure, attractiveness, beauty, charm, engagingness, fascination, interestingness, pleasingness ◆ *vb* **6, 9 = plead,** adjure, apply, ask, beg, beseech, call, call upon, entreat, implore, petition, pray, refer, request, resort to, solicit, sue, supplicate **7 = attract,** allure, charm, engage, entice, fascinate, interest, invite, please, tempt
Antonyms *n* ≠ **plea:** denial, refusal, rejection, repudiation ≠ **attraction:** repulsiveness ◆ *vb* ≠ **plead:** deny, refuse, reject, repudiate, repulse ≠ **attract:** alienate, bore, repulse, revolt

appealing *adj* **2 = attractive,** alluring, charming, desirable, endearing, engaging, inviting, prepossessing, taking, winning, winsome
Antonyms *adj* disgusting, forbidding, loathsome, objectionable, obnoxious, odious, offensive, repellent, repugnant, repulsive, revolting, sickening, unalluring, unappealing, unattractive, undesirable, uninviting, unprepossessing

appear *vb* **1, 4 = come into view,** arise, arrive, attend, be present, come forth, come into sight, come out, come to light, crop up (*inf.*), develop, emerge, issue, loom, materialize, occur, show (*inf.*), show one's face, show up (*inf.*), surface, turn out, turn up **2 = look (like** *or* **as if),** occur, seem, strike one as **3 = be obvious,** be apparent, be clear, be evident, be manifest, be patent, be plain **5 = come into being,** become available, be created, be developed, be invented, be published, come into existence, come out **6 = perform,** act, be exhibited, come on, come onstage, enter, play, play a part, take part
Antonyms *vb* ≠ **come into view:** disappear, vanish ≠ **be obvious:** be doubtful, be unclear

appearance *n* **1 = arrival,** advent, appearing, coming, debut, emergence, introduction, presence, showing up (*inf.*), turning up **2 = look,** air, aspect, bearing, demeanour, expression, face, figure, form, image, looks, manner, mien (*literary*) **3 = impression,** front, guise, illusion, image, outward show, pretence, semblance

appease *vb* **1 = pacify,** calm, conciliate, mollify, placate, pour oil on troubled waters, quiet, satisfy, soothe **2 = ease,** allay, alleviate, assuage, blunt, calm, compose, diminish, lessen, lull, mitigate, quell, quench, quiet, relieve, satisfy, soothe, subdue, tranquillize
Antonyms *vb* ≠ **pacify:** aggravate (*inf.*), anger, annoy, antagonize, arouse, disturb, enrage, incense, inflame, infuriate, irritate, madden, provoke, rile, upset

appeasement *n* **1 = pacification,** acceding, accommodation, compromise, concession, conciliation, mollification, placation, propitiation **2 = easing,** abatement, alleviation, assuagement, blunting, lessening, lulling, mitigation, quelling, quenching, quieting, relieving, satisfaction, softening, solace, soothing, tranquillization

appellation *n* **1 = name,** address, description, designation, epithet, sobriquet, style, term, title

append *vb* **1, 2 = add,** adjoin, affix, annex, attach, fasten, hang, join, subjoin, tack on, tag on
Antonyms *vb* detach, disconnect, disengage, remove, separate, take off

appendage *n* **= attachment,** accessory, addendum, addition, adjunct, affix, ancillary, annexe, appendix, appurtenance, auxiliary, supplement **= limb,** extremity, member, projection, protuberance

appendix *n* **1 = supplement,** addendum, addition, add-on, adjunct, appendage, codicil, postscript

appertain *vb, foll. by* **to = relate to,** apply to, bear upon, be characteristic of, be connected to, belong to, be part of, be pertinent to, be proper to, be relevant to, have to do with, inhere in, pertain to, refer to, touch upon

appetite *n* **1-3 = desire,** appetence, appetency, craving, demand, hankering, hunger, inclination, liking, longing, passion, proclivity,

or willingness: *a great appetite for work.* [C14: from OF *apetit,* from L, from *appetere* to desire ardently]
▸**appetitive** (ə'pɛtɪtɪv) *adj*

appetizer ❶ *or* **appetiser** ('æpɪˌtaɪzə) *n* **1** a small amount of food or drink taken to stimulate the appetite. **2** any stimulating foretaste.

appetizing ❶ *or* **appetising** ('æpɪˌtaɪzɪŋ) *adj* pleasing or stimulating to the appetite; delicious; tasty.

applaud ❶ (ə'plɔːd) *vb* **1** to indicate approval of (a person, performance, etc.) by clapping the hands. **2** (*usually tr*) to express approval or praise of: *I applaud your decision.* [C15: from L *applaudere,* from *plaudere* to beat, applaud]

applause ❶ (ə'plɔːz) *n* appreciation or praise, esp. as shown by clapping the hands.

apple ('æpᵊl) *n* **1** a rosaceous tree, widely cultivated in temperate regions in many varieties. **2** the fruit of this tree, having red, yellow, or green skin and crisp whitish flesh. **3** the wood of this tree. **4** any of several unrelated trees that have fruit similar to the apple. **5 apple of one's eye.** a person or thing that is very much loved. [OE *æppel*]

apple green *n* **a** a bright light green. **b** (*as adj*): *an apple-green carpet.*

apple-pie bed *n Brit.* a bed made with the sheets folded so as to prevent the person from entering it.

apple-pie order *n Inf.* perfect order or condition.

applet ('æplɪt) *n Computing.* a computer program that runs within a page on the World Wide Web. [C20: from APP(LICATION) + -LET]

appliance ❶ (ə'plaɪəns) *n* **1** a machine or device, esp. an electrical one used domestically. **2** any piece of equipment having a specific function. **3** another name for a **fire engine.**

applicable ❶ ('æplɪkəbᵊl, ə'plɪkə-) *adj* being appropriate or relevant; able to be applied; fitting.
▸ˌ**applica'bility** *n* ▸'**applicably** *adv*

applicant ❶ ('æplɪkənt) *n* a person who applies, as for a job, grant, support, etc.; candidate. [C15: from L *applicāns,* from *applicāre* to APPLY]

application ❶ (ˌæplɪ'keɪʃən) *n* **1** the act of applying to a particular use. **2** relevance or value: *the practical applications of space technology.* **3** the act of asking for something. **4** a written request, as for a job, etc. **5** diligent effort: *a job requiring application.* **6** something, such as a lotion, that is applied, esp. to the skin.

applicator ('æplɪˌkeɪtə) *n* a device, such as a spatula or rod, for applying a medicine, glue, etc.

applicatory ('æplɪkətərɪ) *adj* suitable for application.

applied (ə'plaɪd) *adj* put to practical use: *applied mathematics.* Cf. **pure** (sense 5).

appliqué (æ'pliːkeɪ) *n* **1** a decoration of one material sewn or fixed onto another. **2** the practice of decorating in this way. ◆ *vb* **appliqués, appliquéing, appliquéd. 3** (*tr*) to sew or fix (a decoration) on as an appliqué. [C18: from F, lit.: applied]

apply ❶ (ə'plaɪ) *vb* **applies, applying, applied. 1** (*tr*) to put to practical use; employ. **2** (*intr*) to be relevant or appropriate. **3** (*tr*) to cause to come into contact with. **4** (*intr; often foll. by for*) to put in an application or request. **5** (*tr; often foll. by to*) to devote (oneself or one's efforts) with diligence. **6** (*tr*) to bring into use: *the police only applied the law to aliens.* [C14: from OF *aplier,* from L *applicāre* to attach to]
▸**ap'plier** *n*

appoggiatura (əˌpɒdʒə'tʊərə) *n, pl* **appoggiaturas** *or* **appoggiature** (-reɪ). *Music.* an ornament consisting of a nonharmonic note preceding a harmonic one either before or on the stress. [C18: from It., lit.: a propping]

appoint ❶ (ə'pɔɪnt) *vb* (*mainly tr*) **1** (*also intr*) to assign officially, as to a position, responsibility, etc. **2** to establish by agreement or decree. **3** to prescribe: *laws appointed by tribunal.* **4** *Property law.* to nominate (a person) to take an interest in property. **5** to equip with usual features; furnish: *a well-appointed hotel.* [C14: from OF *apointer* to put into a good state]
▸**appoin'tee** *n* ▸**ap'pointer** *n*

appointive (ə'pɔɪntɪv) *adj Chiefly US.* filled by appointment: *an appointive position.*

appointment ❶ (ə'pɔɪntmənt) *n* **1** an arrangement to meet a person or be at a place at a certain time. **2** the act of placing in a job or position. **3** the person who receives such a job. **4** the job or position to which such a person is appointed. **5** (*usually pl*) a fixture or fitting.

apportion ❶ (ə'pɔːʃən) *vb* (*tr*) to divide, distribute, or assign shares of; allot proportionally.
▸**ap'portionable** *adj* ▸**ap'portionment** *n*

appose (ə'pəʊz) *vb* **apposes, apposing, apposed.** (*tr*) **1** to place side by side. **2** (usually foll. by *to*) to place (something) near or against another thing. [C16: from OF *apposer,* from *poser* to put, from L *pōnere*]
▸**ap'posable** *adj*

apposite ❶ ('æpəzɪt) *adj* appropriate; apt. [C17: from L *appositus,* from *appōnere,* from *pōnere* to put]
▸'**appositely** *adv* ▸'**appositeness** *n*

apposition (ˌæpə'zɪʃən) *n* **1** a putting into juxtaposition. **2** a grammatical construction in which a word, esp. a noun, is placed after another to modify its meaning.
▸ˌ**appo'sitional** *adj*

appositive (ə'pɒzɪtɪv) *Grammar.* ◆ *adj* **1** in, of, or relating to apposition. ◆ *n* **2** an appositive word or phrase.
▸**ap'positively** *adv*

appraisal ❶ (ə'preɪzᵊl) *or* **appraisement** *n* **1** an assessment of the worth or quality of a person or thing. **2** a valuation.

appraise ❶ (ə'preɪz) *vb* **appraises, appraising, appraised.** (*tr*) **1** to assess the worth, value, or quality of. **2** to make a valuation of, as for taxation. [C15: from OF, from *prisier* to PRIZE²]
▸**ap'praisable** *adj* ▸**ap'praiser** *n*

> **USAGE NOTE** *Appraise* is sometimes wrongly used where *apprise* is meant: *they had been apprised* (not *appraised*) *of my arrival.*

appreciable ❶ (ə'priːʃəbᵊl) *adj* sufficient to be easily measured or noticed.
▸**ap'preciably** *adv*

THESAURUS

propensity, relish, stomach, taste, willingness, yearning, zeal, zest
Antonyms *n* abhorrence, aversion, disgust, disinclination, dislike, distaste, loathing, repugnance, repulsion, revulsion

appetizer *n* **1** = **hors d'oeuvre**, antipasto, canapé, titbit **1** = **apéritif**, cocktail

appetizing *adj* = **delicious**, appealing, inviting, mouthwatering, palatable, savoury, scrumptious (*inf.*), succulent, tasty, tempting
Antonyms *adj* distasteful, nauseating, unappetizing, unpalatable, unsavoury

applaud *vb* **1, 2** = **praise**, acclaim, approve, cheer, clap, commend, compliment, crack up (*inf.*), encourage, eulogize, extol, give (someone) a big hand, laud, magnify (*arch.*)
Antonyms *vb* blast, boo, censure, condemn, criticize, decry, deprecate, deride, disparage, excoriate, hiss, lambast(e), pan (*inf.*), put down, ridicule, run down, slag (off) (*sl.*), tear into (*inf.*), vilify

applause *n* = **ovation**, acclaim, acclamation, accolade, approbation, approval, big hand, cheering, cheers, clapping, commendation, eulogizing, hand, hand-clapping, laudation, plaudit, praise

appliance *n* **1, 2** = **device**, apparatus, gadget, implement, instrument, machine, mechanism, tool

applicable *adj* = **appropriate**, apposite, apropos, apt, befitting, fit, fitting, germane, pertinent, relevant, suitable, suited, to the point, to the purpose, useful
Antonyms *adj* inapplicable, inappropriate, irrelevant, unsuitable, wrong

applicant *n* = **candidate**, aspirant, claimant, inquirer, petitioner, postulant, suitor, suppliant

application *n* **2** = **relevance**, appositeness, appropriateness, exercise, function, germaneness, pertinence, practice, purpose, use, value **3, 4** = **request**, appeal, claim, inquiry, petition, requisition, solicitation, suit **5** = **effort**, assiduity, attention, attentiveness, commitment, dedication, diligence, hard work, industry, perseverance, study **6** = **lotion**, balm, cream, dressing, emollient, ointment, poultice, salve, unguent

apply *vb* **1, 6** = **use**, administer, assign, bring into play, bring to bear, carry out, employ, engage, execute, exercise, exert, implement, practise, put to use, utilize **2** = **be relevant**, appertain, be applicable, be appropriate, bear upon, be fitting, fit, pertain, refer, relate, suit **3** = **put on**, anoint, bring into contact with, cover with, lay on, paint, place, smear, spread on, touch to **4** = **request**, appeal, claim, inquire, make application, petition, put in, requisition, solicit, sue **5 apply oneself** = **try**, address oneself, be assiduous, be diligent, be industrious, buckle down (*inf.*), commit oneself, concentrate, dedicate oneself, devote oneself, make an effort, pay attention, persevere, study, work hard

appoint *vb* **1** = **assign**, choose, commission, delegate, elect, install, name, nominate, select **2** = **decide**, allot, arrange, assign, choose, designate, determine, establish, fix, set, settle **5** = **equip**, fit out, furnish, provide, supply
Antonyms *vb* ≠ **assign**: discharge, dismiss, fire, give the sack (*inf.*), sack (*inf.*) ≠ **decide**: cancel ≠ **equip**: dismantle, divest, strip

appointed *adj* **1** = **assigned**, chosen, commissioned, delegated, elected, installed, named, nominated, selected **2** = **decided**, allotted, arranged, assigned, chosen, designated, determined, established, fixed, set, settled **5** = **equipped**, fitted out, furnished, provided, supplied

appointment *n* **1** = **meeting**, arrangement, assignation, consultation, date, engagement, interview, rendezvous, session, tryst (*arch.*) **2** = **selection**, allotment, assignment, choice, choosing, commissioning, delegation, designation, election, installation, naming, nomination **3** = **appointee**, candidate, delegate, nominee, office-holder, representative **4** = **job**, assignment, berth (*inf.*), office, place, position, post, situation, station **5** *usually plural* = **fittings**, accoutrements, appurtenances, equipage, fixtures, furnishings, gear, outfit, paraphernalia, trappings

apportion *vb* = **divide**, allocate, allot, assign, deal, dispense, distribute, dole out, give out, measure out, mete out, parcel out, ration out, share

apportionment *n* = **division**, allocation, allotment, assignment, dealing out, dispensing, distribution, doling out, measuring out, meting out, parcelling out, rationing out, sharing

apposite *adj* = **appropriate**, appertaining, applicable, apropos, apt, befitting, fitting, germane, pertinent, proper, relevant, suitable, suited, to the point, to the purpose
Antonyms *adj* inapplicable, inappropriate, inapt, irrelevant, unsuitable, unsuited

appraisal *n* **1** = **assessment**, estimate, estimation, evaluation, judgment, opinion, recce (*sl.*), sizing up (*inf.*) **2** = **valuation**, assay, pricing, rating, reckoning, survey

appraise *vb* **1** = **assess**, assay, estimate, evaluate, eye up, gauge, inspect, judge, price, rate, recce (*sl.*), review, size up (*inf.*), survey, value

appreciable *adj* = **significant**, ascertainable, clear-cut, considerable, definite, detectable,

appreciate ❶ (ə'pri:ʃɪ,eɪt, -sɪ-) *vb* **appreciates, appreciating, appreciated.** (*mainly tr*) **1** to feel thankful or grateful for. **2** (*may take a clause as object*) to take sufficient account of: *to appreciate a problem.* **3** to value highly. **4** (*usually intr*) to increase in value. [C17: from Med. L *appretiāre* to value, from L *pretium* PRICE]
▸**ap'preci,ator** *n*

appreciation ❶ (ə,pri:ʃɪ'eɪʃən, -sɪ-) *n* **1** thanks or gratitude. **2** assessment of the true worth of persons or things. **3** perceptive recognition of qualities, as in art. **4** an increase in value. **5** a review of a book, etc., esp. when favourable.

appreciative ❶ (ə'pri:ʃɪətɪv) *or* **appreciatory** *adj* feeling or expressing appreciation.
▸**ap'preciatively** *adv* ▸**ap'preciativeness** *n*

apprehend ❶ (,æprɪ'hɛnd) *vb* **1** (*tr*) to arrest and escort into custody. **2** to grasp mentally; understand. **3** to await with fear or anxiety. [C14: from L *apprehendere* to lay hold of]

apprehensible (,æprɪ'hɛnsɪbᵊl) *adj* capable of being comprehended or grasped mentally.
▸**,appre,hensi'bility** *n*

apprehension ❶ (,æprɪ'hɛnʃən) *n* **1** anxiety over what may happen. **2** the act of arresting. **3** understanding. **4** a notion or conception.

apprehensive ❶ (,æprɪ'hɛnsɪv) *adj* **1** fearful or anxious. **2** (*usually postpositive* and foll. by *of*) *Arch.* intelligent, perceptive.
▸**,appre'hensively** *adv* ▸**,appre'hensiveness** *n*

apprentice ❶ (ə'prɛntɪs) *n* **1** someone who works for a skilled or qualified person in order to learn a trade, esp. for a recognized period. **2** any beginner or novice. ◆ *vb* **apprentices, apprenticing, apprenticed. 3** (*tr*) to take, place, or bind as an apprentice. [C14: from OF *aprentis*, from *aprendre* to learn, from L *apprehendere* to APPREHEND]
▸**ap'prenticeship** *n*

apprise ❶ *or* **apprize** (ə'praɪz) *vb* **apprises, apprising, apprised** *or* **apprizes, apprizing, apprized.** (*tr*; often foll. by *of*) to make aware; inform. [C17: from F *appris*, from *apprendre* to teach; learn]

> **USAGE NOTE** See at **appraise.**

appro ('æprəʊ) *n* an informal shortening of **approval**: *on appro.*

approach ❶ (ə'prəʊtʃ) *vb* **1** to come nearer in position, time, quality, character, etc., to (someone or something). **2** (*tr*) to make a proposal or suggestion to. **3** (*tr*) to begin to deal with. ◆ *n* **4** the act of drawing close or closer. **5** a close approximation. **6** the way or means of entering or leaving. **7** (*often pl*) an overture to a person. **8** a means adopted in tackling a problem, job of work, etc. **9** Also called: **approach path.** the course followed by an aircraft preparing for landing. **10** Also called: **approach shot.** *Golf.* a shot made to or towards the green after a tee shot. [C14: from OF *aprochier*, from LL *appropiāre* to draw near, from L *prope* near]
▸**ap'proachable** *adj* ▸**ap,proacha'bility** *n*

approbation ❶ (,æprə'beɪʃən) *n* **1** commendation; praise. **2** official recognition.
▸**'appro,bative** *or* **'appro,batory** *adj*

appropriate ❶ *adj* (ə'prəʊprɪɪt). **1** right or suitable; fitting. ◆ *vb* (ə'prəʊprɪ,eɪt), **appropriates, appropriating, appropriated.** (*tr*) **2** to take for one's own use, esp. illegally. **3** to put aside (funds, etc.) for a particular purpose or person. [C15: from LL *appropriāre* to make one's own, from L *proprius* one's own]
▸**ap'propriately** *adv* ▸**ap'propriateness** *n* ▸**ap'propri,ator** *n*

appropriation ❶ (ə,prəʊprɪ'eɪʃən) *n* **1** the act of setting apart or taking for one's own use. **2** a sum of money set apart for a specific purpose.

THESAURUS

discernible, distinguishable, evident, marked, material, measurable, noticeable, obvious, perceivable, perceptible, pronounced, recognizable, substantial, visible
Antonyms *adj* immaterial, imperceptible, inappreciable, indiscernible, indistinguishable, insignificant, invisible, minor, minute, negligible, small, trivial, undetectable, unnoticeable, unsubstantial

appreciably *adv* = **significantly**, ascertainably, considerably, definitely, detectably, discernibly, distinguishably, evidently, markedly, measurably, noticeably, obviously, palpably, perceivably, perceptively, recognizably, substantially, visibly

appreciate *vb* **1** = **be grateful for**, be appreciative, be indebted, be obliged, be thankful for, give thanks for **2** = **be aware of**, acknowledge, be alive to, be cognizant of, be conscious of, comprehend, estimate, know, perceive, realize, recognize, sympathize with, take account of, understand **3** = **value**, admire, cherish, enjoy, esteem, like, prize, rate highly, regard, relish, respect, savour, treasure **4** = **increase**, enhance, gain, grow, improve, inflate, raise the value of, rise
Antonyms *vb* ≠ **be grateful for:** be ungrateful for ≠ **be aware of:** be unaware of, misunderstand, underrate ≠ **value:** belittle, denigrate, disdain, disparage, scorn ≠ **increase:** deflate, depreciate, devaluate, fall

appreciation *n* **1** = **gratitude**, acknowledgment, gratefulness, indebtedness, obligation, thankfulness, thanks **2, 3** = **awareness**, admiration, appraisal, assessment, cognizance, comprehension, enjoyment, esteem, estimation, knowledge, liking, perception, realization, recognition, regard, relish, respect, responsiveness, sensitivity, sympathy, understanding, valuation **4** = **increase**, enhancement, gain, growth, improvement, inflation, rise **5** = **praise**, acclamation, criticism, critique, notice, recognition, review, tribute
Antonyms *n* ≠ **gratitude:** ingratitude ≠ **awareness:** ignorance, incomprehension ≠ **increase:** decline, depreciation, devaluation, fall

appreciative *adj* = **aware**, admiring, cognizant, conscious, enthusiastic, in the know (*inf.*), knowledgeable, mindful, perceptive, pleased, regardful, respectful, responsive, sensitive, supportive, sympathetic, understanding

apprehend *vb* **1** = **arrest**, bust (*inf.*), capture, catch, collar (*inf.*), feel one's collar (*sl.*), lift (*sl.*), nab (*inf.*), nail (*inf.*), nick (*sl., chiefly Brit.*), pinch (*inf.*), run in (*sl.*), seize, take, take prisoner **2** = **understand**, appreciate, believe, comprehend, conceive, get the message, get the picture, grasp, imagine, know, perceive, realize, recognize, think
Antonyms *vb* ≠ **arrest:** discharge, free, let go, liberate, release ≠ **understand:** be at cross-purposes, be unaware of, be unconscious of, get one's lines crossed, misapprehend, misconceive, miss, misunderstand

apprehension *n* **1** = **anxiety**, alarm, apprehensiveness, concern, disquiet, doubt, dread, fear, foreboding, misgiving, mistrust, pins and needles, premonition, suspicion, trepidation, unease, uneasiness, worry **2** = **arrest**, capture, catching, seizure, taking **3** = **awareness**, comprehension, grasp, intellect, intelligence, ken, knowledge, perception, understanding **4** = **idea**, belief, concept, conception, conjecture, impression, notion, opinion, sentiment, thought, view
Antonyms *n* ≠ **anxiety:** assurance, composure, confidence, nonchalance, serenity, unconcern ≠ **arrest:** discharge, liberation, release ≠ **awareness:** incomprehension

apprehensive *adj* **1** = **anxious**, afraid, alarmed, concerned, disquieted, doubtful, fearful, foreboding, mistrustful, nervous, neurotic, suspicious, twitchy (*inf.*), uneasy, worried
Antonyms *adj* assured, at ease, composed, confident, nonchalant, unafraid

apprehensiveness *n* **1** = **anxiety**, alarm, anxiousness, concern, disquietedness *or* disquietness, disquietude, doubtfulness, fear, fearfulness, foreboding, forebodingness, misgiving, mistrustfulness, nervousness, suspiciousness, trepidation, uneasiness, worry

apprentice *n* **1, 2** = **trainee**, beginner, learner, neophyte, novice, probationer, pupil, student, tyro
Antonyms *n* ace (*inf.*), adept, dab hand (*Brit. inf.*), expert, master, past master, pro

apprenticeship *n* **1, 2** = **traineeship**, novitiate *or* noviciate, probation, studentship

apprise *vb* = **make aware**, acquaint, advise, communicate, enlighten, give notice, inform, make cognizant, notify, tell, warn

approach *vb* **1** = **move towards**, advance, catch up, come close, come near, come to, draw near, gain on, meet, near, push forward, reach **1** = **be like**, approximate, be comparable to, come close to, come near to, compare with, resemble **2** = **make a proposal to**, appeal to, apply to, broach the matter with, make advances to, make overtures to, sound out **3** = **set about**, begin work on, commence, embark on, enter upon, make a start, undertake ◆ *n* **4** = **coming**, advance, advent, arrival, drawing near, nearing **5** = **likeness**, approximation, semblance **6** = **access**, avenue, entrance, passage, road, way **7** *often plural* = **proposal**, advance, appeal, application, invitation, offer, overture, proposition **8** = **way**, attitude, course, manner, means, method, mode, modus operandi, procedure, style, technique

approachability *n* **1** = **accessibility**, attainability, openness **2** = **friendliness**, affability, congeniality, conversableness, cordiality, expansiveness, sociability
Antonyms *n* ≠ **accessibility:** inaccessibility, remoteness ≠ **friendliness:** aloofness, chilliness, coolness, detachment, distance, frigidity, frostiness, remoteness, reservedness, standoffishness, unaffability, uncongeniality, unexpansiveness, unfriendliness, unsociability, withdrawnness

approachable *adj* **1** = **accessible**, attainable, come-at-able (*inf.*), get-at-able (*inf.*), reachable **2** = **friendly**, affable, congenial, cordial, open, sociable
Antonyms *adj* ≠ **accessible:** inaccessible, out of reach, out-of-the-way, remote, unreachable ≠ **friendly:** aloof, chilly, cold as ice, cool, distant, frigid, remote, reserved, standoffish, unfriendly, unsociable, withdrawn

approbation *n* **1, 2** = **approval**, acceptance, acclaim, applause, assent, commendation, congratulation, encouragement, endorsement, favour, laudation, praise, ratification, recognition, sanction, support
Antonyms *n* blame, censure, condemnation, disapprobation, disapproval, disfavour, dislike, displeasure, dissatisfaction, reproof, stricture

approbative *adj* **1** = **approving**, accepting, acclamatory, applauding, commendatory, congratulatory, encouraging, favourable, laudatory, supportive

appropriate *adj* **1** = **suitable**, adapted, applicable, apposite, appurtenant, apropos, apt, becoming, befitting, belonging, congruous, correct, felicitous, fit, fitting, germane, meet (*arch.*), opportune, pertinent, proper, relevant, right, seemly, to the point, to the purpose, well-suited, well-timed ◆ *vb* **2** = **seize**, annex, arrogate, assume, commandeer, confiscate, expropriate, impound, pre-empt, take, take over, take possession of, usurp **2** = **steal**, embezzle, filch, misappropriate, pilfer, pocket **3** = **allocate**, allot, apportion, assign, devote, earmark, set aside
Antonyms *adj* ≠ **suitable:** improper, inappropriate, incompatible, incorrect, inopportune, irrelevant, unfitting, unsuitable, untimely ◆ *vb* ≠ **seize:** cede, donate, give, relinquish ≠ **allocate:** withhold

appropriateness *n* **1** = **suitability**, applicability, appositeness, aptness, becomingness, congruousness, correctness, felicitousness, felicity, fitness, fittingness, germaneness, opportuneness, pertinence, properness, relevance, rightness, seemliness, timeliness, well-suitedness

appropriation *n* **1** = **setting aside**, allocation, allotment, apportionment, assignment, earmarking **1** = **seizure**, annexation, arrogation, assumption, commandeering, confiscation, expropriation, impoundment, pre-emption, takeover, taking, usurpation

approval ❶ (əˈpruːvᵊl) *n* **1** the act of approving. **2** formal agreement. **3** a favourable opinion. **4 on approval.** (of articles for sale) for examination with an option to buy or return.

approve ❶ (əˈpruːv) *vb* **approves, approving, approved. 1** (when *intr*, often foll. by *of*) to consider fair, good, or right. **2** (*tr*) to authorize or sanction. [C14: from OF *aprover*, from L *approbāre* to approve, from *probāre* to test, PROVE]

approved school *n* (in Britain) a former name for **community home.**

approx. *abbrev. for* approximate(ly).

approximate ❶ *adj* (əˈprɒksɪmɪt). **1** almost accurate or exact. **2** inexact; rough; loose. **3** much alike; almost the same. **4** near; close together. ◆ *vb* (əˈprɒksɪˌmeɪt), **approximates, approximating, approximated. 5** (usually foll. by *to*) to come or bring near or close; be almost the same (as). **6** *Maths.* to find an expression for (some quantity) accurate to a specified degree. [C15: from LL *approximāre*, from L *proximus* nearest]
▸**apˈproximately** *adv*

approximation ❶ (əˌprɒksɪˈmeɪʃən) *n* **1** the process or result of making a rough calculation, estimate, or guess. **2** an imprecise or unreliable record or version. **3** *Maths.* an inexact number, relationship, or theory that is sufficiently accurate for a specific purpose.

appurtenance ❶ (əˈpɜːtɪnəns) *n* **1** a less significant thing or part. **2** (*pl*) accessories. **3** *Property law.* a minor right, interest, or privilege. [C14: from Anglo-F *apurtenance*, from OF *apartenance*, from *apartenir* to APPERTAIN]

APR *abbrev. for* annual percentage rate.

Apr. *abbrev. for* April.

apraxia (əˈpræksɪə) *n* a disorder of the central nervous system characterized by impaired ability to carry out certain purposeful muscular movements. [C19: via NL from Gk: inactivity, from A-[1] + *praxis* action]

après-ski (ˌæpreɪˈskiː) *n* a social activity following a day's skiing. **b** (*as modifier*): *an après-ski outfit.* [F, lit.: after ski]

apricot (ˈeɪprɪˌkɒt) *n* **1** a tree native to Africa and W Asia, but widely cultivated for its edible fruit. **2** the yellow juicy fruit of this tree, which resembles a small peach. [C16: from Port., from Ar., from LGk, from L *praecox* early-ripening]

April (ˈeɪprəl) *n* the fourth month of the year, consisting of 30 days. [C14: from L *Aprīlis*]

April fool *n* a victim of a practical joke performed on the first of April (**April Fools' Day** *or* **All Fools' Day**).

a priori ❶ (eɪ praɪˈɔːraɪ, ɑː prɪˈɔːrɪ) *adj* **1** *Logic.* relating to or involving deductive reasoning from a general principle to the expected facts or effects. **2** known to be true independently of experience of the subject matter. [C18: from L, lit.: from the previous]
▸**apriority** (ˌeɪpraɪˈɒrɪtɪ) *n*

apron ❶ (ˈeɪprən) *n* **1** a protective or sometimes decorative garment worn over the front of the body and tied around the waist. **2** the part of a stage extending in front of the curtain. **3** a hard-surfaced area in front of an aircraft hangar, terminal building, etc. **4** a continuous conveyor belt composed of metal slats. **5** a protective plate screening the operator of a machine, artillery piece, etc. **6** *Geol.* a sheet of sand, gravel, etc., deposited at the front of a moraine. **7** another name for **skirt** (sense 3). **8 tied to someone's apron strings.** dominated by someone, esp. a mother or wife. ◆ *vb* **9** (*tr*) to protect or provide with an apron. [C16: mistaken division of *a napron*, from OF, from L *mappa* napkin]

apron stage *n* a stage that projects into the auditorium so that the audience sits on three sides of it.

apropos ❶ (ˌæprəˈpəʊ) *adj* **1** appropriate. ◆ *adv* **2** appropriately. **3** by the way; incidentally. **4 apropos of.** (*prep*) in respect of. [C17: from F *à propos* to the purpose]

apse (æps) *n* a domed or vaulted semicircular or polygonal recess, esp. at the east end of a church. Also called: **apsis.** [C19: from L *apsis*, from Gk: a fitting together, from *haptein* to fasten]
▸**ˈapsidal** *adj*

apsis (ˈæpsɪs) *n, pl* **apsides** (æpˈsaɪdiːz). either of two points lying at the extremities of an eccentric orbit of a planet, satellite, etc. Also called: **apse.** [C17: via L from Gk; see APSE]
▸**apsidal** (ˈæpsɪdᵊl) *adj*

apt ❶ (æpt) *adj* **1** suitable; appropriate. **2** (*postpositive;* foll. by an infinitive) having a tendency (to behave as specified). **3** having the ability to learn and understand easily. [C14: from L *aptus* fitting, from *apere* to fasten]
▸**ˈaptly** *adv* ▸**ˈaptness** *n*

APT *abbrev. for* Advanced Passenger Train.

apterous (ˈæptərəs) *adj* **1** (of insects) without wings, as silverfish. **2** without winglike expansions, as some seeds and fruits. [C18: from Gk, from A-[1] + *pteron* wing]
▸**ˈapterˌism** *n*

apteryx (ˈæptərɪks) *n* another name for **kiwi** (the bird). [C19: from NL; see APTEROUS]

aptitude ❶ (ˈæptɪˌtjuːd) *n* **1** inherent or acquired ability. **2** ease in learning or understanding. **3** the quality of being apt. [C15: via OF from LL, from L *aptus* APT]

aqua (ˈækwə) *n, pl* **aquae** (ˈækwiː) *or* **aquas. 1** water: used in compound names of certain liquid substances or solutions of substances in water. ◆ *n, adj* **2** short for **aquamarine** (the colour). [L: water]

aquaculture (ˈækwəˌkʌltʃə) *or* **aquiculture** *n* the cultivation of freshwater and marine organisms for human consumption or use.

aquaerobics *or* **aquarobics** (ˌækwəˈrəʊbɪks) *n* (*functioning as sing*) the practice of exercising to music in a swimming pool. [C20: from L *aqua* water + AEROBICS]

aqua fortis (ˈfɔːtɪs) *n* an obsolete name for **nitric acid.** [C17: from L, lit.: strong water]

aqualung (ˈækwəˌlʌŋ) *n* breathing apparatus used by divers, etc., consisting of a mouthpiece attached to air cylinders strapped to the back.

aquamarine (ˌækwəməˈriːn) *n* **1** a pale greenish-blue transparent variety of beryl used as a gemstone. **2a** a pale blue to greenish-blue colour. **2b** (*as adj*): *an aquamarine dress.* [C19: from NL, from L: sea water (referring to the gem's colour)]

aquanaut (ˈækwəˌnɔːt) *n* a person who works, swims, or dives underwater. [C20: from AQUA + *-naut*, as in ASTRONAUT]

aquaplane (ˈækwəˌpleɪn) *n* **1** a board on which a person stands and is towed by a motorboat. ◆ *vb* **aquaplanes, aquaplaning, aquaplaned.** (*intr*) **2** to ride on an aquaplane. **3** (of a motor vehicle travelling at high speeds on wet roads) to rise up onto a thin film of water so that contact with the road is lost.

aqua regia (ˈriːdʒɪə) *n* a mixture of nitric acid and hydrochloric acid. [C17: from NL: royal water; referring to its use in dissolving gold, the royal metal]

THESAURUS

approval *n* **1, 2** = **consent**, acquiescence, agreement, assent, authorization, blessing, compliance, concurrence, confirmation, countenance, endorsement, imprimatur, leave, licence, mandate, O.K. *or* okay (*inf.*), permission, ratification, recommendation, sanction, the go-ahead (*inf.*), the green light, validation **3** = **favour**, acclaim, admiration, applause, appreciation, approbation, Brownie points, commendation, esteem, good opinion, liking, praise, regard, respect
Antonyms *n* ≠ **favour:** denigration, disapproval, dislike, disparagement, displeasure, dissatisfaction

approve *vb* **1** = **favour**, acclaim, admire, applaud, appreciate, be pleased with, commend, esteem, have a good opinion of, like, praise, regard highly, respect, think highly of **2** = **agree to**, accede to, accept, advocate, allow, assent to, authorize, bless, buy into (*inf.*), concur in, confirm, consent to, countenance, endorse, go along with, mandate, O.K. *or* okay (*inf.*), pass, permit, ratify, recommend, sanction, second, subscribe to, uphold, validate
Antonyms *vb* ≠ **favour:** blame, censure, condemn, deplore, deprecate, disapprove, dislike, find unacceptable, frown on, look down one's nose at (*inf.*), object to, take exception to ≠ **agree to:** disallow, discountenance, veto

approving *adj* **1** = **favourable**, acclamatory, admiring, applauding, appreciative, commendatory, respectful

approximate *adj* **1** = **close**, almost accurate, almost exact, near **2** = **rough**, estimated, inexact, loose **3** = **like**, analogous, close, comparable, near, relative, similar, verging on ◆ *vb* **5** = **come close**, approach, border on, come near, reach, resemble, touch, verge on
Antonyms *adj* ≠ **close, rough:** accurate, correct, definite, exact, precise, specific

approximately *adv* **1, 2** = **almost**, about, around, circa (*used with dates*), close to, generally, in the neighbourhood of, in the region of, in the vicinity of, just about, loosely, more or less, nearly, not far off, relatively, roughly

approximation *n* **1** = **guess**, ballpark estimate (*inf.*), ballpark figure (*inf.*), conjecture, estimate, estimation, guesswork, rough calculation, rough idea

appurtenance *n* **2** *plural* = **accompaniments**, accessories, accoutrements, appendages, equipment, impedimenta, paraphernalia, trappings

a priori *adj* **1** = **deduced**, deductive, from cause to effect, inferential

apron *n* **1** = **pinny** (*inf.*), pinafore

apropos *adj* **1** = **appropriate**, applicable, apposite, apt, befitting, belonging, correct, fit, fitting, germane, meet (*arch.*), opportune, pertinent, proper, related, relevant, right, seemly, suitable, to the point, to the purpose ◆ *adv* **2** = **appropriately**, aptly, opportunely, pertinently, relevantly, suitably, timely, to the point, to the purpose **3** = **incidentally**, by the bye, by the way, in passing, parenthetically, while on the subject **4 apropos of** = **regarding**, in respect of, on the subject of, re, respecting, with reference to, with regard to, with respect to

apt *adj* **1** = **appropriate**, applicable, apposite, apropos, befitting, correct, fit, fitting, germane, meet (*arch.*), pertinent, proper, relevant, seemly, suitable, timely, to the point, to the purpose **2** = **inclined**, disposed, given, liable, likely, of a mind, prone, ready **3** = **gifted**, astute, bright, clever, expert, ingenious, intelligent, prompt, quick, sharp, skilful, smart, talented, teachable
Antonyms *adj* ≠ **appropriate:** ill-fitted, ill-suited, ill-timed, improper, inapplicable, inapposite, inappropriate, infelicitous, inopportune, irrelevant, unsuitable, untimely ≠ **gifted:** awkward, clumsy, dull, gauche, incompetent, inept, inexpert, maladroit, slow, stupid

aptitude *n* **1** = **tendency**, bent, disposition, inclination, leaning, predilection, proclivity, proneness, propensity **2** = **gift**, ability, aptness, capability, capacity, cleverness, faculty, flair, giftedness, intelligence, knack, proficiency, quickness, talent

aptness *n* **1** = **appropriateness**, applicability, appositeness, becomingness, congruousness, correctness, felicitousness, felicity, fitness, fittingness, germaneness, opportuneness, pertinence, properness, relevance, rightness, seemliness, suitability, timeliness, well-suitedness **2** = **tendency**, aptitude, bent, disposition, inclination, leaning, liability, likelihood, likeliness, predilection, proclivity, proneness, propensity, readiness **3** = **gift**, ability, capability, capacity, cleverness, faculty, fitness, flair, giftedness, intelligence, knack, proficiency, quickness, suitability, talent

aquarist ('ækwərɪst) *n* **1** the curator of an aquarium. **2** a person who studies aquatic life.

aquarium (ə'kwɛərɪəm) *n, pl* **aquariums** *or* **aquaria** (-rɪə). **1** a tank, bowl, or pool in which aquatic animals and plants are kept for pleasure, study, or exhibition. **2** a building housing a collection of aquatic life, as for exhibition. [C19: from L *aquārius* relating to water, on the model of VIVARIUM]

Aquarius (ə'kwɛərɪəs) *n, Latin genitive* **Aquarii** (ə'kwɛərɪ,aɪ). **1** *Astron.* a S constellation. **2** *Astrol.* also called: the **Water Carrier.** the eleventh sign of the zodiac. The sun is in this sign between about Jan. 20 and Feb. 18. [L]

aquatic (ə'kwætɪk) *adj* **1** growing, living, or found in water. **2** *Sport.* performed in or on water. ◆ *n* **3** a marine animal or plant. [C15: from L *aquāticus,* from *aqua* water]

aquatics (ə'kwætɪks) *pl n* sports or pastimes performed in or on the water.

aquatint ('ækwə,tɪnt) *n* **1** a technique of etching copper with acid to produce an effect resembling watercolour. **2** an etching made in this way. ◆ *vb* **3** (*tr*) to etch (a block, etc.) in aquatint. [C18: from It. *acqua tinta* dyed water]

aquavit ('ækwə,vɪt) *n* a grain- or potato-based spirit flavoured with aromatic seeds. Also called: **akvavit.** [of Scandinavian origin: see AQUA VITAE]

aqua vitae ('viːtaɪ, 'vaɪtiː) *n* an archaic name for **brandy.** [Med. L: water of life]

aqueduct ('ækwɪ,dʌkt) *n* **1** a conduit used to convey water over a long distance. **2** a structure, often a bridge, that carries such a conduit or a canal across a valley or river. **3** a channel or conduit in the body. [C16: from L *aquaeductus,* from *aqua* water + *dūcere* to convey]

aqueous ('eɪkwɪəs) *adj* **1** of, like, or containing water. **2** dissolved in water: *aqueous ammonia.* **3** (of rocks, etc.) formed from material laid down in water. [C17: from Med. L *aqueus,* from L *aqua* water]

aqueous humour *n Physiol.* the watery fluid within the eyeball between the cornea and the lens.

aquiculture ('eɪkwɪ,kʌltʃə, 'ækwɪ-) *n* **1** another name for **hydroponics.** **2** a variant of **aquaculture.**
▸ **'aqui,culturist** *n* ▸ **'aqui,cultural** *adj*

aquifer ('ækwɪfə) *n* a deposit or rock, such as a sandstone, containing water that can be used to supply wells.

aquilegia (,ækwɪ'liːdʒɪə) *n* another name for **columbine.** [C19: from Med. L, from ?]

aquiline ('ækwɪ,laɪn) *adj* **1** (of a nose) having the curved shape of an eagle's beak. **2** of or like an eagle. [C17: from L, from *aquila* eagle]

Ar *the chemical symbol for* argon.

ar. *abbrev. for:* **1** arrival. **2** arrive(s).

Ar. *abbrev. for:* **1** Arabia(n). **2** Also: **Ar** Arabic. **3** Aramaic.

a.r. *abbrev. for* anno regni. [L: in the year of the reign]

-ar *suffix forming adjectives.* of; belonging to; like: *linear; polar.* [via OF *-er* from L *-āris*]

ARA *abbrev. for:* **1** (in Britain) Associate of the Royal Academy. **2** (in New Zealand) Auckland Regional Authority.

Arab ('ærəb) *n* **1** a member of a Semitic people originally inhabiting Arabia. **2** a small breed of horse, used for riding. **3** (*modifier*) of or relating to the Arabs. [C14: from L, from Gk *Araps,* from Ar. *'Arab*]

arabesque (,ærə'bɛsk) *n* **1** *Ballet.* a classical position in which the dancer has one leg raised behind. **2** *Music.* a piece or movement with a highly ornamented melody. **3** *Arts.* a type of curvilinear decoration in painting, metalwork, etc., with intricate intertwining designs. [C18: from F, from It. *arabesco* in the Arabic style]

Arabian (ə'reɪbɪən) *adj* **1** of or relating to Arabia or the Arabs. ◆ *n* **2** another word for **Arab.**

Arabian camel *n* a domesticated camel with one hump on its back, used as a beast of burden in the deserts of N Africa and SW Asia.

Arabic ('ærəbɪk) *n* **1** the Semitic language of the Arabs, which has its own alphabet and is spoken in Algeria, Egypt, Iraq, Jordan, Saudi Arabia, Syria, Tunisia, etc. ◆ *adj* **2** denoting or relating to this language, any of the peoples that speak it, or the countries in which it is spoken.

arabica bean (ə'ræbɪkə) *n* a high-quality coffee bean, obtained from the tree *Coffea arabica.*

Arabic numeral *n* one of the numbers 0, 1, 2, 3, 4, 5, 6, 7, 8, 9. Cf. **Roman numerals.**

arabis ('ærəbɪs) *n* any of several trailing plants having pink or white flowers in spring. Also called: **rock cress.** [C16: from Med. L, from Gk *arabis,* ult. from *Arābios* Arabian, prob. from growing in sandy or stony soil]

Arabist ('ærəbɪst) *n* a student of Arabic culture, language, history, etc.

arable Ⓣ ('ærəb^{ə}l) *adj* **1** (of land) being or capable of being tilled for the production of crops. **2** of, relating to, or using such land. [C15: from L *arābilis,* from *arāre* to plough]

Araby ('ærəbɪ) *n* an archaic or poetic name for Arabia.

arachnid (ə'ræknɪd) *n* any of a class of arthropods characterized by simple eyes and four pairs of legs, including the spiders, scorpions, and ticks. [C19: from NL *Arachnida,* from Gk *arakhnē* spider]
▸ **a'rachnidan** *adj, n*

arachnoid (ə'ræknɔɪd) *n* **1** the middle one of three membranes that cover the brain and spinal cord. ◆ *adj* **2** of or relating to this membrane. **3** *Bot.* consisting of or covered with soft fine hairs or fibres.

arachnophobia (ə,ræknə'fəʊbɪə) *n* an abnormal fear of spiders. [C20: from Gk *arakhnē* spider + -PHOBIA]

arak ('ærək) *n* a variant spelling of **arrack.**

Araldite ('ærəldaɪt) *n Trademark.* an epoxy resin used as a glue for mending glass, plastic, and china.

Aram. *abbrev. for* Aramaic.

Aramaic (,ærə'meɪɪk) *n* **1** an ancient Semitic language of the Middle East, still spoken in parts of Syria and the Lebanon. ◆ *adj* **2** of, relating to, or using this language.

Aran ('ærən) *adj* **1** of or relating to the Aran Islands, off the W coast of Ireland. **2** made of thick natural wool: *an Aran sweater.*

araucaria (,ærɔː'kɛərɪə) *n* any of a group of coniferous trees of South America, Australia, and Polynesia, such as the monkey puzzle. [C19: from NL (*arbor*) *Araucaria* (tree) from *Arauco,* a province in Chile]

arbalest *or* **arbalist** ('ɑːbəlɪst) *n* a large medieval crossbow, usually cocked by mechanical means. [C11: from OF, from LL *arcuballista,* from L *arcus* bow + BALLISTA]

arbiter Ⓣ ('ɑːbɪtə) *n* **1** a person empowered to judge in a dispute; referee. **2** a person having control of something. [C15: from L, from ?]
▸ **'arbitress** *fem n*

arbitrament (ɑː'bɪtrəmənt) *n* **1** the decision or award made by an arbitrator upon a disputed matter. **2** another word for **arbitration.**

arbitrary Ⓣ ('ɑːbɪtrərɪ) *adj* **1** founded on or subject to personal whims, prejudices, etc. **2** not absolute. **3** (of a government, ruler, etc.) despotic or dictatorial. **4** *Law.* (esp. of a penalty) within the court's discretion. [C15: from L *arbitrārius* arranged through arbitration]
▸ **'arbitrarily** *adv* ▸ **'arbitrariness** *n*

arbitrate Ⓣ ('ɑːbɪ,treɪt) *vb* **arbitrates, arbitrating, arbitrated.** **1** to achieve a settlement between parties. **2** to submit to or settle by arbitration. [C16: from L *arbitrārī* to give judgment]
▸ **'arbi,trator** *n*

arbitration Ⓣ (,ɑːbɪ'treɪʃən) *n* the hearing and determination of a dispute, esp. an industrial one, by an impartial referee selected or agreed upon by the parties concerned.

arbor[1] ('ɑːbə) *n* the US spelling of **arbour.**

arbor[2] ('ɑːbə) *n* **1** a rotating shaft in a machine on which a milling cutter or grinding wheel is fitted. **2** a rotating shaft. [C17: from L: tree]

arboraceous (,ɑːbə'reɪʃəs) *adj Literary.* **1** resembling a tree. **2** wooded.

arboreal (ɑː'bɔːrɪəl) *adj* **1** of or resembling a tree. **2** living in or among trees.

arborescent (,ɑːbə'rɛs^{ə}nt) *adj* having the shape or characteristics of a tree.
▸ **,arbo'rescence** *n*

arboretum (,ɑːbə'riːtəm) *n, pl* **arboreta** (-tə) *or* **arboretums.** a place where trees or shrubs are cultivated. [C19: from L, from *arbor* tree]

arboriculture ('ɑːbərɪ,kʌltʃə) *n* the cultivation of trees or shrubs.
▸ **,arbori'culturist** *n*

arbor vitae ('ɑːbɔː 'viːtaɪ, 'vaɪtiː) *n* any of several Asian and North American evergreen coniferous trees having tiny scalelike leaves and egglike cones. [C17: from NL, lit.: tree of life]

arbour ('ɑːbə) *n* a leafy glade or bower shaded by trees, vines, shrubs, etc. [C14 *erber,* from OF, from L *herba* grass]

arbutus (ɑː'bjuːtəs) *n, pl* **arbutuses.** any of a genus of shrubs having clusters of white or pinkish flowers, broad evergreen leaves, and strawberry-like berries. [C16: from L; rel. to *arbor* tree]

arc Ⓣ (ɑːk) *n* **1** something curved in shape. **2** part of an unbroken curved line. **3** a luminous discharge that occurs when an electric current flows between two electrodes separated by a small gap. **4** *Maths.* a section of a curve, graph, or geometric figure. ◆ *vb* **arcs, arcing, arced** *or* **arcs, arcking, arcked.** **5** (*intr*) to form an arc. ◆ *adj* **6** *Maths.* specifying an inverse trigonometric function: *arcsin, arccos, arctan.* [C14: from OF, from L *arcus* bow, arch]

ARC *abbrev. for* AIDS-related complex: a condition in which a person infected with the AIDS virus suffers from relatively mild symptoms, such as loss of weight, fever, etc.

THESAURUS

arable *adj* **1** = **productive**, cultivable, farmable, fecund, fertile, fruitful, ploughable, tillable

arbiter *n* **1** = **judge**, adjudicator, arbitrator, referee, umpire **2** = **authority**, controller, dictator, expert, governor, lord, master, pundit, ruler

arbitrariness *n* **1** = **randomness**, capriciousness, fancifulness, inconsistency, subjectivity, unreasonableness, whimsicality, wilfulness **3** = **dictatorialness**, absoluteness, despotism, dogmatism, domineeringness, high-handedness, imperiousness, magisterialness, overbearingness, peremptoriness, summariness, tyrannicalness, tyrannousness, tyranny, uncontrolledness, unlimitedness, unrestrainedness

arbitrary *adj* **1** = **random**, capricious, chance, discretionary, erratic, fanciful, inconsistent, optional, personal, subjective, unreasonable, whimsical, wilful **3** = **dictatorial**, absolute, autocratic, despotic, dogmatic, domineering, high-handed, imperious, magisterial, overbearing, peremptory, summary, tyrannical, tyrannous, uncontrolled, unlimited, unrestrained
Antonyms *adj* ≠ **random:** consistent, judicious, logical, objective, rational, reasonable, reasoned, sensible, sound

arbitrate *vb* **1, 2** = **settle**, adjudge, adjudicate, decide, determine, judge, mediate, pass judgment, referee, sit in judgment, umpire

arbitration *n* = **settlement**, adjudication, arbitrament, decision, determination, judgment

arbitrator *n* **1, 2** = **judge**, adjudicator, arbiter, referee, umpire

arc *n* **1, 2** = **curve**, arch, bend, bow, crescent, half-moon

arcade ➊ (ɑːˈkeɪd) *n* **1** a set of arches and their supporting columns. **2** a covered and sometimes arched passageway, usually with shops on one or both sides. [C18: from F, from It. *arcata,* from L *arcus* bow, arch]

Arcadian (ɑːˈkeɪdɪən) *adj* **1** of Arcadia, the idealized setting of pastoral poetry. **2** rustic or bucolic. ◆ *n* **3** a person who leads a quiet simple rural life.

arcane ➊ (ɑːˈkeɪn) *adj* requiring secret knowledge to be understood; esoteric. [C16: from L *arcānus* secret, from *arcēre* to keep safe]

arcanum (ɑːˈkeɪnəm) *n, pl* **arcana** (-nə). (*sometimes pl*) a secret or mystery. [C16: from L; see ARCANE]

arch[1] ➊ (ɑːtʃ) *n* **1** a curved structure that spans an opening. **2** Also called: **archway.** a structure in the form of an arch that serves as a gateway. **3** something curved like an arch. **4** any of various parts or structures of the body having a curved or archlike outline, such as the raised vault formed by the tarsal and metatarsal bones (**arch of the foot**). ◆ *vb* **5** (*tr*) to span (an opening) with an arch. **6** to form or cause to form an arch or a curve resembling that of an arch. **7** (*tr*) to span or extend over. [C14: from OF *arche,* from L *arcus* bow, ARC]

arch[2] ➊ (ɑːtʃ) *adj* **1** (*prenominal*) chief; principal; leading. **2** (*prenominal*) expert: *an arch criminal.* **3** knowing or superior; coyly playful: *an arch look.* [C16: independent use of ARCH-]
▸**ˈarchly** *adv* ▸**ˈarchness** *n*

arch. *abbrev. for:* **1** archaic. **2** archaism. **3** archipelago. **4** architect. **5** architectural. **6** architecture.

arch- ➊ *or* **archi-** *combining form.* **1** chief; principal: *archbishop.* **2** eminent above all others of the same kind: *archenemy.* [ult. from Gk *arkhi-,* from *arkhein* to rule]

-arch *n combining form.* leader; ruler; chief: *patriarch; monarch.* [from Gk *-arkhēs,* from *arkhein* to rule]

Archaean *or esp. US* **Archean** (ɑːˈkiːən) *adj* of the metamorphosed rocks formed in the early Precambrian era.

archaeology *or* **archeology** (ˌɑːkɪˈɒlədʒɪ) *n* the study of man's past by scientific analysis of the material remains of his cultures. [C17: from LL, from Gk *arkhaiologia* study of what is ancient, from *arkhē* beginning]
▸**archaeological** *or* **archeological** (ˌɑːkɪəˈlɒdʒɪkᵊl) *adj* ▸**ˌarchaeˈologist** *or* **ˌarcheˈologist** *n*

archaeopteryx (ˌɑːkɪˈɒptərɪks) *n* any of several extinct primitive birds which occurred in Jurassic times and had teeth, a long tail, and well-developed wings. [C19: from Gk *arkhaios* ancient + *pterux* winged creature]

archaic ➊ (ɑːˈkeɪɪk) *adj* **1** belonging to or characteristic of a much earlier period. **2** out of date; antiquated. **3** (of vocabulary, etc.) characteristic of an earlier period of a language. [C19: from F, from Gk *arkhaïkos,* from *arkhaios* ancient, from *arkhē* beginning, from *arkhein* to begin]
▸**arˈchaically** *adv*

archaism (ˈɑːkeɪˌɪzəm) *n* **1** the adoption or imitation of archaic words or style. **2** an archaic word, style, etc. [C17: from NL, from Gk, from *arkhaizein* to model one's style upon that of ancient writers; see ARCHAIC]
▸**ˈarchaist** *n* ▸**ˌarchaˈistic** *adj*

archangel (ˈɑːkˌeɪndʒəl) *n* a principal angel.
▸**archangelic** (ˌɑːkænˈdʒelɪk) *adj*

archbishop (ˈɑːtʃˈbɪʃəp) *n* a bishop of the highest rank. Abbrev.: **abp, Abp, Arch., Archbp.**

archbishopric (ˈɑːtʃˈbɪʃəprɪk) *n* the rank, office, or jurisdiction of an archbishop.

archdeacon (ˈɑːtʃˈdiːkən) *n* **1** an Anglican clergyman ranking just below a bishop. **2** a clergyman of similar rank in other Churches.
▸**ˈarchˈdeaconry** *n*

archdiocese (ˌɑːtʃˈdaɪəˌsiːs) *n* the diocese of an archbishop.
▸**archdiocesan** (ˌɑːtʃdaɪˈɒsɪsᵊn) *adj*

archducal (ˈɑːtʃˈdjuːkᵊl) *adj* of or relating to an archduke, archduchess, or archduchy.

archduchess (ˈɑːtʃˈdʌtʃɪs) *n* **1** the wife or widow of an archduke. **2** (since 1453) a princess of the Austrian imperial family.

archduchy (ˈɑːtʃˈdʌtʃɪ) *n, pl* **archduchies.** the territory ruled by an archduke or archduchess.

archduke (ˈɑːtʃˈdjuːk) *n* a chief duke, esp. (since 1453) a prince of the Austrian imperial dynasty.

Archean (ɑːˈkiːən) *adj* a variant spelling (esp. US) of **Archaean.**

archegonium (ˌɑːkɪˈgəʊnɪəm) *n, pl* **archegonia** (-nɪə). a female sex organ, occurring in mosses, ferns, etc. [C19: from NL, from Gk, from *arkhe-* chief, first + *gonos* seed, race]

archenemy (ˈɑːtʃˈenɪmɪ) *n, pl* **archenemies. 1** a chief enemy. **2** (*often cap.;* preceded by *the*) the devil.

archeology (ˌɑːkɪˈɒlədʒɪ) *n* a variant of **archaeology.**

archer ➊ (ˈɑːtʃə) *n* a person skilled in the use of a bow and arrow. [C13: from OF, from LL, from L *arcus* bow]

Archer (ˈɑːtʃə) *n* **the.** the constellation Sagittarius, the ninth sign of the zodiac.

archerfish (ˈɑːtʃəˌfɪʃ) *n, pl* **archerfish** *or* **archerfishes.** a freshwater fish, related to the perch, of SE Asia and Australia, that catches insects by spitting water at them.

archery (ˈɑːtʃərɪ) *n* **1** the art or sport of shooting with bows and arrows. **2** archers or their weapons collectively.

archetype ➊ (ˈɑːkɪˌtaɪp) *n* **1** a perfect or typical specimen. **2** an original model; prototype. **3** *Psychoanal.* one of the inherited mental images postulated by Jung. **4** a recurring symbol or motif in literature, etc. [C17: from L *archetypum* an original, from Gk, from *arkhetupos* first-moulded; see ARCH-, -TYPE]
▸**ˌarcheˈtypal** *adj*

archfiend (ˌɑːtʃˈfiːnd) *n* (*often cap.*) **the.** the devil; Satan.

archidiaconal (ˌɑːkɪdaɪˈækənᵊl) *adj* of or relating to an archdeacon or his office.
▸**ˌarchidiˈaconate** *n*

archiepiscopal (ˌɑːkɪɪˈpɪskəpᵊl) *adj* of or associated with an archbishop.
▸**ˌarchieˈpiscopate** *n*

archil (ˈɑːtʃɪl) *n* a variant of **orchil.**

archimandrite (ˌɑːkɪˈmændraɪt) *n Greek Orthodox Church.* the head of a monastery. [C16: from LL, from LGk *arkhimandritēs,* from ARCHI- + *mandra* monastery]

Archimedes' principle (ˌɑːkɪˈmiːdiːz) *n* a law of physics stating that the apparent loss in weight of a body immersed in a fluid is equal to the weight of the displaced fluid. [after *Archimedes* (?287–212 BC), Gk mathematician and physicist]

Archimedes' screw *or* **Archimedean screw** (ˌɑːkɪˈmiːdɪən) *n* an ancient water-lifting device using a spiral passage in an inclined cylinder.

archipelago (ˌɑːkɪˈpeləˌgəʊ) *n, pl* **archipelagos** *or* **archipelagoes. 1** a group of islands. **2** a sea studded with islands. [C16 (meaning: the Aegean Sea): from It., from L *pelagus,* from Gk, from ARCH- + *pelagos* sea]
▸**archipelagic** (ˌɑːkɪpəˈlædʒɪk) *adj*

architect ➊ (ˈɑːkɪˌtekt) *n* **1** a person qualified to design buildings and to supervise their erection. **2** a person similarly qualified in another form of construction: *a naval architect.* **3** any planner or creator. [C16: from F, from L, from Gk *arkhitektōn* director of works, from ARCHI- + *tektōn* workman; rel. to *tekhnē* art, skill]

architectonic (ˌɑːkɪtekˈtɒnɪk) *adj* **1** denoting, relating to, or having architectural qualities. **2** *Metaphysics.* of the systematic classification of knowledge. [C16: from LL *architectonicus* concerning architecture; see ARCHITECT]

architectonics (ˌɑːkɪtekˈtɒnɪks) *n* (*functioning as sing*) **1** the science of architecture. **2** *Metaphysics.* the scientific classification of knowledge.

architecture ➊ (ˈɑːkɪˌtektʃə) *n* **1** the art and science of designing and superintending the erection of buildings, etc. **2** a style of building or structure. **3** buildings or structures collectively. **4** the structure or design of anything.
▸**ˌarchiˈtectural** *adj*

architrave (ˈɑːkɪˌtreɪv) *n Archit.* **1** the lowest part of an entablature that bears on the columns. **2** a moulding around a doorway, window opening, etc. [C16: via F from It., from ARCHI- + *trave* beam, from L *trabs*]

archive ➊ (ˈɑːkaɪv) *n* (*often pl*) **1** a collection of records of an institution, family, etc. **2** a place where such records are kept. **3** *Computing.* data transferred to a tape or disk for long-term storage rather than frequent use. ◆ *vb* **4** (*tr*) to store (documents, data, etc.) in an archive or other repository. [C17: from LL, from Gk *arkheion* repository of official records, from *arkhē* government]
▸**arˈchival** *adj*

archivist (ˈɑːkɪvɪst) *n* a person in charge of archives.

archon (ˈɑːkɒn) *n* (in ancient Athens) one of the nine chief magistrates. [C17: from Gk *arkhōn* ruler, from *arkhein* to rule]
▸**ˈarchonˌship** *n*

THESAURUS

arcade *n* **1, 2** = **gallery,** cloister, colonnade, covered walk, mall, peristyle, portico

arcane *adj* = **mysterious,** cabbalistic, esoteric, hidden, occult, recondite, secret

arch[1] *n* **1, 2** = **archway,** curve, dome, span, vault **3** = **curve,** arc, bend, bow, curvature, hump, semicircle ◆ *vb* **5, 6** = **curve,** arc, bend, bow, bridge, embow, span

arch[2] *adj* **3** = **playful,** frolicsome, mischievous, pert, roguish, saucy, sly, waggish

arch- *adj* **1, 2** = **chief,** accomplished, consummate, expert, finished, first, foremost, greatest, head, highest, lead, leading, main, major, master, pre-eminent, primary, principal, top

archaic *adj* **1** = **old,** ancient, antique, bygone, olden (*arch.*), primitive **2** = **old-fashioned,** antiquated, behind the times, obsolete, old hat, outmoded, out of date, passé, superannuated
Antonyms *adj* ≠ **old:** contemporary, current, modern, new, present, recent ≠ **old-fashioned:** fresh, latest, modern, modish, new, newfangled, novel, state-of-the-art, up-to-date, up-to-the-minute, with it (*inf.*)

arched *adj* **6** = **curved,** domed, embowed, vaulted

archer *n* = **bowman** (*arch.*), toxophilite (*formal*)

archetypal *adj* **1** = **typical,** classic, exemplary, ideal, model, normal, paradigmatic, standard **2** = **original,** prototypal, prototypic *or* prototypical

archetype *n* **1** = **standard,** classic, exemplar, form, ideal, model, norm, paradigm, pattern, prime example **2** = **original,** prototype

architect *n* **1, 2** = **designer,** master builder, planner **3** = **creator,** author, contriver, deviser, engineer, founder, instigator, inventor, maker, originator, planner, prime mover, shaper

architecture *n* **1** = **design,** architectonics, building, construction, planning **2, 4** = **structure,** construction, design, framework, make-up, style

archive *n often plural* **1** = **records,** annals, chronicles, documents, papers, registers, rolls **2** = **record office,** museum, registry, repository

archpriest ('ɑːtʃ'priːst) *n* **1** (formerly) a chief assistant to a bishop. **2** a senior priest.
archway ('ɑːtʃ,weɪ) *n* a passageway or entrance under an arch or arches.
-archy *n combining form.* government; rule: *anarchy; monarchy.* [from Gk *-arkhia;* see -ARCH]
arc light *n* a light source in which an arc between two electrodes produces intense white illumination. Also called: **arc lamp.**
arctic ❶ ('ɑːktɪk) *adj* **1** of or relating to the Arctic. **2** *Inf.* cold; freezing. ◆ *n* **3** (*modifier*) suitable for conditions of extreme cold: *arctic clothing.* [C14: from L *arcticus,* from Gk *arktikos* northern, lit.: pertaining to (the constellation of) the Bear, from *arktos* bear]
Arctic ❶ ('ɑːktɪk) *adj* of or relating to the regions north of the Arctic Circle.
Arctic Circle *n* the imaginary circle round the earth, parallel to the equator, at latitude 66° 32′ N.
arctic hare *n* a large hare of the Canadian Arctic whose fur is white in winter.
arctic willow *n* a low-growing shrub of the Canadian tundra.
Arcturus (ɑːk'tjʊərəs) *n* the brightest star in the constellation Boötes: a red giant. [C14: from L, from Gk *Arktouros,* from *arktos* bear + *ouros* guard, keeper]
arcuate ('ɑːkjʊɪt) *adj* shaped or bent like an arc or bow. [C17: from L *arcuāre,* from *arcus* ARC]
arc welding *n* a technique in which metal is welded by heat generated by an electric arc.
▸**arc welder** *n*
-ard *or* **-art** *suffix forming nouns.* indicating a person who does something, esp. to excess: *braggart; drunkard.* [via OF, of Gmc origin]
ardent ❶ ('ɑːdᵊnt) *adj* **1** expressive of or characterized by intense desire or emotion. **2** intensely enthusiastic; eager. **3** glowing or shining: *ardent eyes.* **4** **ardent spirits.** alcoholic drinks. [C14: from L *ārdēre* to burn]
▸ **'ardency** *n* ▸ **'ardently** *adv*
ardour ❶ *or US* **ardor** ('ɑːdə) *n* **1** feelings of great intensity and warmth. **2** eagerness; zeal. [C14: from OF, from L *ārdor,* from *ārdēre* to burn]
arduous ❶ ('ɑːdjuːəs) *adj* **1** difficult to accomplish; strenuous. **2** hard to endure; harsh. **3** steep or difficult: *an arduous track.* [C16: from L *arduus* steep, difficult]
▸ **'arduously** *adv* ▸ **'arduousness** *n*
are[1] (ɑː; *unstressed* ə) *vb* the plural form of the present tense of **be** and the singular form used with *you.* [OE *aron,* second person pl of *bēon* to BE]
are[2] (ɑː) *n* a unit of area equal to 100 square metres. [C19: from F, from L *ārea* piece of ground; see AREA]
area ❶ ('ɛərɪə) *n* **1** any flat, curved, or irregular expanse of a surface. **2a** the extent of a two-dimensional surface: *the area of a triangle.* **2b** the two-dimensional extent of a plane or surface: *the area of a sphere.* **3** a section or part. **4** region; district. **5a** a geographical division of administrative responsibility. **5b** (*as modifier*): *area manager.* **6** a part or section, as of a building, town, etc., having some specified function: *reception area; commercial area.* **7** the range or scope of anything. **8** a subject field or field of study. **9** Also called: **areaway.** a sunken area, usually enclosed, giving light, air, and sometimes access to a cellar basement. [C16: from L: level ground, threshing-floor; rel. to *ārēre* to be dry]
▸ **'areal** *adj*
arena ❶ (ə'riːnə) *n* **1** an enclosure or platform, usually surrounded by seats, in which sports events, entertainments, etc., take place: *a boxing arena.* **2** the central area of an ancient Roman amphitheatre, in which gladiatorial contests were held. **3** a sphere of intense activity: *the political arena.* [C17: from L *harēna* sand, place where sand was strewn for the combats]
arenaceous (,ærɪ'neɪʃəs) *adj* **1** (of sedimentary rocks) composed of sand. **2** (of plants) growing in a sandy soil. [C17: from L *harēnāceus* sandy, from *harēna* sand]
aren't (ɑːnt) **1** *contraction of* are not. **2** *Inf., chiefly Brit.* (used in interrogative sentences) *contraction of* am not.
areola (ə'rɪələ) *n, pl* **areolae** (-,liː) *or* **areolas.** *Anat.* any small circular area, such as the pigmented ring around the human nipple. [C17: from L: dim. of AREA]
▸**a'reolar** *or* **areolate** (ə'rɪəlɪt, -,leɪt) *adj*
areole ('ærɪəʊl) *n* **1** *Biol.* a space outlined on a surface, such as an area between veins on a leaf. **2** a sunken area on a cactus from which spines, hairs, etc., arise.
▸ **'areo,late** *adj*
arête (ə'reɪt, ə'rɛt) *n* a sharp ridge that separates glacial valleys. [C19: from F: fishbone, ridge, from L *arista* ear of corn, fishbone]
argal ('ɑːgəl) *n* another name for **argol.**
argali ('ɑːgəlɪ) *or* **argal** *n, pl* **argali** *or* **argals.** a wild sheep, with massive horns in the male, inhabiting semidesert regions in central Asia. [C18: from Mongolian]
argent ('ɑːdʒənt) *n* **a** an archaic or poetic word for **silver. b** (*as adj; often postpositive, esp. in heraldry*): *a bend argent.* [C15: from OF, from L]
argentiferous (,ɑːdʒən'tɪfərəs) *adj* containing or bearing silver.
argentine ('ɑːdʒən,taɪn) *adj* **1** of or resembling silver. ◆ *n* **2** a small marine fish characterized by a long silvery body.
Argentine ('ɑːdʒən,tiːn, -,taɪn) *or* **Argentinian** (,ɑːdʒən'tɪnɪən) *adj* **1** of or relating to Argentina, a republic in South America. ◆ *n* **2** a native or inhabitant of Argentina.
argillaceous (,ɑːdʒɪ'leɪʃəs) *adj* (of sedimentary rocks) composed of very fine-grained material, such as clay. [C18: from L *argilla* white clay, from Gk, from *argos* white]
Argive ('ɑːdʒaɪv, -gaɪv) *adj* **1** of or relating to Argos, a city of ancient Greece. **2** a literary word for **Greek.** ◆ *n* **3** an ancient Greek, esp. one from Argos.
argol ('ɑːgɒl) *or* **argal** ('ɑːgəl) *n* crude potassium hydrogentartrate. [C14: from Anglo-F *argoil,* from ?]
argon ('ɑːgɒn) *n* an unreactive colourless odourless element of the rare gas series that forms almost 1 per cent of the atmosphere. It is used in electric lights. Symbol: Ar; atomic no.: 18; atomic wt.: 39.95. [C19: from Gk, from *argos* inactive, from A-[1] + *ergon* work]
argosy ('ɑːgəsɪ) *n, pl* **argosies.** *Arch. or poetic.* a large abundantly laden merchant ship, or a fleet of such ships. [C16: from It. *Ragusea* (*nave*) (ship) of Ragusa]
argot ❶ ('ɑːgəʊ) *n* slang or jargon peculiar to a particular group, esp. (formerly) a group of thieves. [C19: from F, from ?]
arguable ❶ ('ɑːgjʊəbᵊl) *adj* **1** capable of being disputed. **2** plausible; reasonable.
▸ **'arguably** *adv*
argue ❶ ('ɑːgjuː) *vb* **argues, arguing, argued. 1** (*intr*) to quarrel; wrangle. **2** (*intr; often foll. by for or against*) to present supporting or opposing reasons or cases in a dispute. **3** (*tr; may take a clause as object*) to try to prove by presenting reasons. **4** (*tr; often passive*) to debate or discuss. **5** (*tr*) to persuade. **6** (*tr*) to suggest: *her looks argue despair.* [C14: from OF *arguer* to assert, from L *arguere* to make clear, accuse]
▸ **'arguer** *n*
argufy ('ɑːgjʊ,faɪ) *vb* **argufies, argufying, argufied.** *Facetious or dialect.* to argue or quarrel, esp. over something trivial.
argument ❶ ('ɑːgjʊmənt) *n* **1** a quarrel; altercation. **2** a discussion in which reasons are put forward; debate. **3** (*sometimes pl*) a point or series of reasons presented to support or oppose a proposition. **4** a summary of the plot or subject of a book, etc. **5** *Logic.* **5a** a process of reasoning in which the conclusion can be shown to be true or false. **5b** the middle term of a syllogism. **6** *Maths.* another name for **independent variable** of a function.
argumentation (,ɑːgjʊmɛn'teɪʃən) *n* **1** the process of reasoning methodically. **2** argument; debate.
argumentative ❶ (,ɑːgjʊ'mɛntətɪv) *adj* **1** given to arguing. **2** characterized by argument; controversial.
Argus ('ɑːgəs) *n* **1** *Greek myth.* a giant with a hundred eyes who was made guardian of the heifer Io. **2** a vigilant person.
Argus-eyed (,ɑːgəs'aɪd) *adj* observant; vigilant.

THESAURUS

arctic *adj* **2** *Informal* = **freezing,** chilly, cold, cold as ice, frigid, frost-bound, frosty, frozen, gelid, glacial, icy
Arctic *adj* = **polar,** far-northern, hyperborean
ardent *adj* **1** = **passionate,** ablaze, amorous, fervent, fervid, fierce, fiery, flaming, hot, hot-blooded, impassioned, intense, lusty, spirited, vehement, warm, warm-blooded **2** = **enthusiastic,** avid, eager, keen, keen as mustard, zealous
Antonyms *adj* ≠ **passionate:** cold, cool, frigid, impassive ≠ **enthusiastic:** apathetic, indifferent, lukewarm, unenthusiastic
ardour *n* **1** = **passion,** devotion, feeling, fervour, fierceness, fire, heat, intensity, spirit, vehemence, warmth **2** = **enthusiasm,** avidity, eagerness, earnestness, keenness, zeal
arduous *adj* **1-3** = **difficult,** backbreaking, burdensome, exhausting, fatiguing, formidable, gruelling, hard, harsh, heavy, laborious, onerous, painful, punishing, rigorous, severe, steep, strenuous, taxing, tiring, toilsome, tough, troublesome, trying
Antonyms *adj* child's play (*inf.*), easy, easy-peasy (*sl.*), effortless, facile, light, no bother, no trouble, painless, simple, undemanding
area *n* **3** = **part,** portion, section, sector **4** = **region,** district, domain, locality, neck of the woods (*inf.*), neighbourhood, patch, plot, realm, sector, sphere, stretch, territory, tract, turf (*US sl.*), zone **7** = **range,** ambit, breadth, compass, expanse, extent, scope, size, width **8** = **field,** arena, department, domain, province, realm, sphere, territory **9** = **sunken space,** yard
arena *n* **1, 2** = **ring,** amphitheatre, bowl, coliseum, enclosure, field, ground, park (*US & Canad.*), stadium, stage **3** = **sphere,** area, domain, field, province, realm, scene, scope, sector, territory, theatre
argot *n* = **jargon,** cant, dialect, idiom, lingo (*inf.*), parlance, patois, patter, slang, vernacular
arguably *adv* **1** = **debatably,** contestably, controversially, controvertibly, deniably, disputably, dubitably, questionably, refutably **2** = **possibly,** conceivably, feasibly, plausibly, potentially
argue *vb* **1** = **quarrel,** altercate, bandy words, bicker, cross swords, disagree, dispute, fall out (*inf.*), feud, fight, fight like cat and dog, have an argument, squabble, wrangle **3, 4** = **discuss,** assert, claim, contend, controvert, debate, dispute, expostulate, hold, maintain, plead, question, reason, remonstrate **5** = **persuade,** convince, prevail upon, talk into, talk round **6** = **suggest,** demonstrate, denote, display, evince, exhibit, imply, indicate, manifest, point to, show
argument *n* **1** = **quarrel,** altercation, barney (*inf.*), bickering, clash, controversy, difference of opinion, disagreement, dispute, falling out (*inf.*), feud, fight, row, squabble, wrangle **2** = **discussion,** assertion, claim, contention, debate, dispute, expostulation, plea, pleading, questioning, remonstrance, remonstration **3** = **reason,** argumentation, case, defence, dialectic, ground(s), line of reasoning, logic, polemic, reasoning
Antonyms *n* ≠ **quarrel:** accord, agreement, concurrence
argumentative *adj* **1** = **quarrelsome,** belligerent, combative, contentious, contrary, disputatious, litigious, opinionated

argy-bargy or **argie-bargie** (ˈɑːdʒɪˈbɑːdʒɪ) *n, pl* **argy-bargies.** *Brit. inf.* a wrangling argument or verbal dispute. [C19: from Scot., from dialect *argle,* prob. from ARGUE]

aria (ˈɑːrɪə) *n* an elaborate accompanied song for solo voice from a cantata, opera, or oratorio. [C18: from It.: tune, AIR]

Arian (ˈɛərɪən) *adj* **1** of or relating to Arius, 3rd-century A.D. Greek Christian theologian, or to Arianism. ◆ *n* **2** an adherent of Arianism.

-arian *suffix forming nouns.* indicating a person or thing that advocates, believes, or is associated with something: *vegetarian; librarian.* [from L *-ārius* -ARY + -AN]

Arianism (ˈɛərɪəˌnɪzəm) *n* the doctrine of Arius, declared heretical, which asserted that Christ was not of one substance with the Father.

arid ❶ (ˈærɪd) *adj* **1** having little or no rain; dry. **2** devoid of interest. [C17: from L *āridus,* from *ārēre* to be dry]
▸**aridity** (əˈrɪdɪtɪ) *or* ˈ**aridness** *n*

arid zone *n* either of the zones of latitude 15–30° N and S, with low rainfall and desert or semidesert terrain.

Aries (ˈɛəriːz) *n, Latin genitive* **Arietis** (əˈraɪɪtɪs). **1** *Astron.* a N constellation. **2** *Astrol.* Also called: the **Ram.** the first sign of the zodiac. The sun is in this sign between about March 21 and April 19. [C14: from L: ram]

aright ❶ (əˈraɪt) *adv* correctly; rightly; properly.

aril (ˈærɪl) *n* an additional covering formed on certain seeds, such as those of the yew and nutmeg, after fertilization. [C18: from NL, from Med. L *arilli* raisins, pips of grapes]
▸ˈ**arilˌlate** *adj*

arioso (ˌɑːrɪˈəʊzəʊ) *n, pl* **ariosos** *or* **ariosi** (-siː). *Music.* a recitative with the lyrical quality of an aria. [C18: from It., from ARIA]

arise ❶ (əˈraɪz) *vb* **arises, arising, arose, arisen** (əˈrɪzᵊn). (*intr*) **1** to come into being; originate. **2** (foll. by *from*) to proceed as a consequence. **3** to get or stand up, as from a sitting or lying position. **4** to come into notice. **5** to ascend. [OE *ārīsan*]

aristo (ˈærɪstəʊ, əˈrɪstəʊ) *n, pl* **aristos.** *Inf.* short for **aristocrat.**

aristocracy ❶ (ˌærɪˈstɒkrəsɪ) *n, pl* **aristocracies. 1** a privileged class of people usually of high birth; the nobility. **2** such a class as the ruling body of a state. **3** government by such a class. **4** a state governed by such a class. **5** a class of people considered to be outstanding in a sphere of activity. [C16: from LL, from Gk *aristokratia* rule by the best-born, from *aristos* best; see -CRACY]

aristocrat ❶ (ˈærɪstəˌkræt) *n* **1** a member of the aristocracy. **2** a person who has the manners or qualities of a member of a privileged class. **3** a supporter of aristocracy as a form of government.

aristocratic ❶ (ˌærɪstəˈkrætɪk) *adj* **1** relating to or characteristic of aristocracy or an aristocrat. **2** elegant or stylish in appearance and behaviour.
▸ˌ**aristoˈcratically** *adv*

Aristotelian (ˌærɪstəˈtiːlɪən) *adj* **1** of or relating to Aristotle, 4th-century B.C. Greek philosopher, or to his philosophy. ◆ *n* **2** a follower of Aristotle.

Aristotelian logic *n* **1** traditional logic, esp. relying on the theory of syllogism. **2** the logical method of Aristotle, esp. as developed in the Middle Ages.

arithmetic *n* (əˈrɪθmətɪk). **1** the branch of mathematics concerned with numerical calculations, such as addition, subtraction, multiplication, and division. **2** calculations involving numerical operations. **3** knowledge of or skill in using arithmetic. ◆ *adj* (ˌærɪθˈmɛtɪk) *also* **arithmetical. 4** of, relating to, or using arithmetic. [C13: from L, from Gk *arithmētikē,* from *arithmein* to count, from *arithmos* number]
▸ˌ**arithˈmetically** *adv* ▸**aˌrithmeˈtician** *n*

arithmetic mean *n* the average value of a set of terms or quantities, expressed as their sum divided by their number: *the arithmetic mean of 3, 4, and 8 is 5.* Also called: **average.**

arithmetic progression *n* a sequence, each term of which differs from the succeeding term by a constant amount, such as 3,6,9,12.

-arium *suffix forming nouns.* indicating a place for or associated with something: *aquarium; solarium.* [from L *-ārium,* neuter of *-ārius* -ARY]

ark (ɑːk) *n* **1** the vessel that Noah built which survived the Flood (Genesis 6–9). **2** a place or thing offering shelter or protection. **3** *Dialect.* a box. [OE *arc,* from L *arca* box, chest]

Ark (ɑːk) *n Judaism.* **1** Also called: **Holy Ark.** the cupboard in a synagogue in which the Torah scrolls are kept. **2** Also called: **Ark of the Covenant.** the most sacred symbol of God's presence among the Hebrew people, carried in their journey from Sinai to the Promised Land (Canaan).

arm[1] ❶ (ɑːm) *n* **1** (in man) either of the upper limbs from the shoulder to the wrist. Related adj: **brachial. 2** the part of either of the upper limbs from the elbow to the wrist; forearm. **3a** the corresponding limb of any other vertebrate. **3b** an armlike appendage of some invertebrates. **4** an object that covers or supports the human arm, esp. the sleeve of a garment or the side of a chair, etc. **5** anything considered to resemble an arm in appearance, function, etc.: *an arm of the sea; the arm of a record player.* **6** an administrative subdivision of an organization: *an arm of the government.* **7** power; authority: *the arm of the law.* **8 arm in arm.** with arms linked. **9 at arm's length.** at a distance. **10 in the arms of Morpheus.** sleeping. **11 with open arms.** with great warmth and hospitality. [OE]

arm[2] ❶ (ɑːm) *vb* **1** to equip with weapons as a preparation for war. **2** (*tr*) to provide (a person or thing) with something that strengthens, protects, or increases efficiency. **3a** (*tr*) to activate (a fuse) so that it will explode at the required time. **3b** to prepare (an explosive device) for use by introducing a detonator, etc. ◆ *n* **4** (*usually pl*) a weapon, esp. a firearm. [C14: from OF *armes,* from L *arma* arms, equipment]

armada ❶ (ɑːˈmɑːdə) *n* **1** a large number of ships or aircraft. **2** (*cap.*) **the.** Also called: **Spanish Armada.** the great fleet sent by Philip II of Spain against England in 1588. [C16: from Sp., from Med. L *armāta* fleet, armed forces, from L *armāre* to provide with arms]

armadillo (ˌɑːməˈdɪləʊ) *n, pl* **armadillos.** a burrowing mammal of Central and South America with a covering of strong horny plates over most of the body. [C16: from Sp., dim. of *armado* armed (man), from L *armātus* armed; cf. ARMADA]

Armageddon (ˌɑːməˈgɛdᵊn) *n* **1** *New Testament.* the final battle between good and evil at the end of the world. **2** a catastrophic and extremely destructive conflict. [C19: from LL, from Gk, from Heb. *har megiddōn,* mountain district of *Megiddo* (in N Palestine)]

Armalite (ˈɑːməlaɪt) *n Trademark.* a lightweight high-velocity rifle of various calibres, capable of automatic and semiautomatic operation. [C20: from *Armalite* Division, Fairchild Engine and Airplane Company, manufacturers]

armament ❶ (ˈɑːməmənt) *n* **1** (*often pl*) the weapon equipment of a military vehicle, ship, or aircraft. **2** a military force raised and armed ready for war. **3** preparation for war. [C17: from L *armāmenta* utensils, from *armāre* to equip]

armature (ˈɑːmətjʊə) *n* **1** a revolving structure in an electric motor or generator, wound with the coils that carry the current. **2** any part of an electric machine or device that moves under the influence of a magnetic field or within which an electromotive force is induced. **3** Also called: **keeper.** a soft iron or steel bar placed across the poles of a magnet to close the magnetic circuit. **4** *Sculpture.* a framework to support the clay or other material used in modelling. **5** the protective outer covering of an animal or plant. [C15: from L *armātūra* armour, equipment, from *armāre* to furnish with equipment]

armchair (ˈɑːmˌtʃɛə) *n* **1** a chair, esp. an upholstered one, that has side supports for the arms or elbows. **2** (*modifier*) taking or involving no active part: *an armchair strategist.*

armed[1] ❶ (ɑːmd) *adj* **1** equipped with or supported by arms, armour, etc. **2** prepared for conflict or any difficulty. **3** (of an explosive device) prepared for use. **4** (of plants) having the protection of thorns, spines, etc.

armed[2] (ɑːmd) *adj* **a** having an arm or arms. **b** (*in combination*): *long-armed; one-armed.*

THESAURUS

Antonyms *adj* accommodating, amenable, complaisant, compliant, conciliatory, easy-going, obliging

arid *adj* **1** = **dry**, barren, desert, dried up, moistureless, parched, sterile, torrid, waterless **2** = **boring**, as dry as dust, colourless, dreary, dry, dull, flat, jejune, lifeless, spiritless, tedious, tiresome, uninspired, uninteresting, vapid
Antonyms *adj* ≠ **dry:** fertile, fruitful, lush, rich, verdant ≠ **boring:** exciting, interesting, lively, sexy (*inf.*), spirited, stimulating, vivacious

aridity *n* **1** = **dryness**, barrenness, moisturelessness, parchedness, sterility, waterlessness **2** = **boredom**, colourlessness, dreariness, dryness, dullness, flatness, jejuneness, jejunity, lifelessness, spiritlessness, tediousness, tedium, uninspiredness, uninterestingness, vapidity, vapidness

aright *adv* = **correctly**, accurately, appropriately, aptly, duly, exactly, fitly, in due order, justly, properly, rightly, suitably, truly, without error

arise *vb* **1, 2** = **happen**, appear, begin, come into being, come to light, commence, crop up (*inf.*), emanate, emerge, ensue, follow, issue, occur, originate, proceed, result, set in, spring, start, stem **3** = **get up**, get to one's feet, go up, rise, stand up, wake up **5** = **ascend**, climb, lift, mount, move upward, rise, soar, tower

aristocracy *n* **1** = **upper class**, body of nobles, elite, gentry, *haut monde*, nobility, noblesse (*literary*), patricians, patriciate, peerage, ruling class, upper crust (*inf.*)
Antonyms *n* commoners, common people, hoi polloi, lower classes, masses, plebeians, plebs, proles (*derogatory sl., chiefly Brit.*), proletariat, working classes

aristocrat *n* **1** = **noble**, aristo (*inf.*), childe (*arch.*), grandee, lady, lord, nobleman, noblewoman, patrician, peer, peeress

aristocratic *adj* **1** = **upper-class**, blue-blooded, elite, gentle (*arch.*), gentlemanly, highborn, lordly, noble, patrician, titled, well-born **2** = **refined**, courtly, dignified, elegant, fine, haughty, polished, snobbish, stylish, well-bred
Antonyms *adj* ≠ **upper-class:** common, lower-class, plebeian, proletarian, working-class ≠ **refined:** boorish, coarse, common, crass, crude, ill-bred, uncouth, unrefined, vulgar

arm[1] *n* **1-3** = **upper limb**, appendage, limb **6** = **section**, bough, branch, department, detachment, division, extension, offshoot, projection, sector **7** = **power**, authority, command, force, might, potency, strength, sway

arm[2] *vb* **1** = **equip**, accoutre, array, deck out, furnish, issue with, outfit, provide, rig, supply **1** = **mobilize**, muster forces, prepare for war, take up arms **2** = **provide**, brace, equip, forearm, fortify, gird one's loins, guard, make ready, outfit, prepare, prime, protect, strengthen

armada *n* **1** = **fleet**, flotilla, navy, squadron

armaments *pl n* **1** = **weapons**, ammunition, arms, guns, materiel, munitions, ordnance, weaponry

armed[1] *adj* **1-3** = **carrying weapons**, accoutred, arrayed, equipped, fitted out, forearmed, fortified, furnished, girded, guarded, in arms, prepared, primed, protected, provided, ready, rigged out, strengthened, supplied, tooled up (*sl.*), under arms

DICTIONARY

armed forces *pl n* the military forces of a nation or nations, including the army, navy, air force, marines, etc.

Armenian (ɑː'miːnɪən) *n* **1** a native or inhabitant of Armenia, a republic in NW Asia, or of the ancient kingdom of Armenia in W Asia. **2** the Indo-European language of the Armenians. ◆ *adj* **3** of Armenia, its inhabitants, or their language.

armful ('ɑːmfʊl) *n, pl* **armfuls.** the amount that can be held by one or both arms.

armhole ('ɑːmˌhəʊl) *n* the opening in an article of clothing through which the arm passes.

armillary sphere (ɑː'mɪlərɪ) *n* a model of the celestial sphere formerly used in fixing the positions of heavenly bodies.

Arminian (ɑː'mɪnɪən) *adj* denoting, relating to, or believing in the Protestant doctrines of Jacobus Arminius, 16th-century Dutch theologian, which rejected absolute predestination and stressed free will in man.
▸**Ar'minianˌism** *n*

armistice Ⓣ ('ɑːmɪstɪs) *n* an agreement between opposing armies to suspend hostilities; truce. [C18: from NL, from L *arma* arms + *sistere* to stop]

Armistice Day ('ɑːmɪstɪs) *n* the anniversary of the signing of the armistice that ended World War I, on Nov. 11, 1918. See also **Remembrance Sunday.**

armlet ('ɑːmlɪt) *n* **1** a small arm, as of a lake. **2** a band or bracelet worn round the arm.

armoire (ɑːm'wɑː) *n* a large cabinet, originally used for storing weapons. [C16: from F, from OF *armaire,* from L *armārium* chest, closet; see AMBRY]

armorial (ɑː'mɔːrɪəl) *adj* of or relating to heraldry or heraldic arms.

armour Ⓣ *or US* **armor** ('ɑːmə) *n* **1** any defensive covering, esp. that of metal, chain mail, etc., worn by medieval warriors. **2** the protective metal plates on a tank, warship, etc. **3** *Mil.* armoured fighting vehicles in general. **4** any protective covering, such as the shell of certain animals. **5** heraldic insignia; arms. ◆ *vb* **6** (*tr*) to equip or cover with armour. [C13: from OF *armure,* from L *armātūra* armour, equipment]

armoured Ⓣ *or US* **armored** ('ɑːməd) *adj* **1** having a protective covering. **2** comprising units making use of armoured vehicles: *an armoured brigade.*

armourer *or US* **armorer** ('ɑːmərə) *n* **1** a person who makes or mends arms and armour. **2** a person employed in the maintenance of small arms and weapons in a military unit.

armour plate *n* a tough heavy steel often hardened on the surface, used for protecting warships, tanks, etc.

armoury Ⓣ *or US* **armory** ('ɑːmərɪ) *n, pl* **armouries** *or* **armories. 1** a secure place for the storage of weapons. **2** armour generally; military supplies. **3** resources, such as arguments, on which to draw: *a few choice terms from her armoury of invective.*

armpit ('ɑːmˌpɪt) *n* **1** the small depression beneath the arm where it joins the shoulder. Technical name: **axilla. 2** *Sl.* an extremely unpleasant place: *the armpit of the Middle West.*

armrest ('ɑːmˌrest) *n* the part of a chair, sofa, etc., that supports the arm. Sometimes shortened to **arm.**

arms Ⓣ (ɑːmz) *pl n* **1** weapons collectively. See also **small arms. 2** military exploits: *prowess in arms.* **3** the official heraldic symbols of a family, state, etc. **4 bear arms. 4a** to carry weapons. **4b** to serve in the armed forces. **4c** to have a coat of arms. **5 in** *or* **under arms.** armed and prepared for war. **6 lay down one's arms.** to stop fighting; surrender. **7 take (up) arms.** to prepare to fight. **8 up in arms.** indignant; prepared to protest strongly. [C13: from OF, from L *arma;* see ARM[2]]

arm wrestling *n* a contest of strength in which two people rest the elbow of one arm on a flat surface, grasp each other's hand, and try to force their opponent's forearm down flat.

army Ⓣ ('ɑːmɪ) *n, pl* **armies. 1** the military land forces of a nation. **2** a military unit usually consisting of two or more corps with supporting arms and services. **3** (*modifier*) of or characteristic of an army. **4** any large body of people united for some specific purpose. **5** a large number of people, animals, etc. [C14: from OF, from Med. L *armāta* armed forces]

army ant *n* any of various tropical American predatory ants which travel in vast hordes preying on other animals. Also called: **legionary ant.**

army worm *n* a type of caterpillar which travels in vast hordes and is a serious pest of cereal crops.

arnica ('ɑːnɪkə) *n* **1** any of a genus of N temperate or arctic plants having yellow flowers. **2** the tincture of the dried flower heads of any of these plants, used in treating bruises. [C18: from NL, from ?]

aroha ('ɑːrɒhə) *n NZ.* love, compassion, or affectionate regard. [Maori]

aroid ('ærɔɪd, 'ɛər-) *adj* of or relating to a plant family that includes the arum, calla, and anthurium. [C19: from ARUM + -OID]

aroint thee *or* **ye** (ə'rɔɪnt) *sentence substitute. Arch.* away! begone! [C17: from ?]

aroma Ⓣ (ə'rəʊmə) *n* **1** a distinctive usually pleasant smell, esp. of spices, wines, and plants. **2** a subtle pervasive quality or atmosphere. [C18: via L from Gk: spice]

aromatherapy (əˌrəʊmə'θerəpɪ) *n* the use of fragrant essential oils as a treatment in alternative medicine to relieve tension and cure certain minor ailments.
▸**aˌroma'therapist** *n*

aromatic Ⓣ (ˌærə'mætɪk) *adj* **1** having a distinctive, usually fragrant smell. **2** (of an organic compound) having an unsaturated ring, esp. containing a benzene ring. Cf. **aliphatic.** ◆ *n* **3** something, such as a plant or drug, giving off a fragrant smell.
▸**ˌaro'matically** *adv* ▸**aˌroma'ticity** *n*

aromatize *or* **aromatise** (ə'rəʊməˌtaɪz) *vb* **aromatizes, aromatizing, aromatized** *or* **aromatises, aromatising, aromatised.** (*tr*) to make aromatic.
▸**aˌromati'zation** *or* **aˌromati'sation** *n*

arose (ə'rəʊz) *vb* the past tense of **arise.**

around Ⓣ (ə'raʊnd) *prep* **1** situated at various points in: *a lot of shelves around the house.* **2** from place to place in: *driving around Ireland.* **3** somewhere in or near. **4** approximately in: *it happened around 1957.* ◆ *adv* **5** in all directions from a point of reference: *he owns the land for ten miles around.* **6** in the vicinity, esp. restlessly but idly: *to stand around.* **7** in no particular place or direction: *dotted around.* **8** *Inf.* (of people) active and prominent in a particular area or profession. **9** *Inf.* present in some place (the exact location being unknown or unspecified). **10** *Inf.* in circulation; available: *that type of phone has been around for some years now.* **11** *Inf.* to many places, so as to have gained considerable experience, often of a worldly or social nature: *I've been around.* [C17 (rare earlier): from A-[2] + ROUND]

> **USAGE NOTE** In American English, *around* is usually used instead of *round* in adverbial and prepositional senses, except in a few fixed phrases such as *all year round.* The use of *around* in adverbial senses is less common in British English.

arouse Ⓣ (ə'raʊz) *vb* **arouses, arousing, aroused. 1** (*tr*) to evoke or elicit (a reaction, emotion, or response). **2** to awaken from sleep.
▸**a'rousal** *n* ▸**a'rouser** *n*

arpeggio (ɑː'pedʒɪəʊ) *n, pl* **arpeggios.** a chord whose notes are played or sung in rapid succession rather than simultaneously. [C18: from It., from *arpeggiare* to perform on the harp, from *arpa* HARP]

arquebus ('ɑːkwɪbəs) *or* **harquebus** *n* a portable long-barrelled gun dating from the 15th century. [C16: via OF from MDu. *hakebusse,* lit.: hook gun, from the shape of the butt, from *hake* hook + *busse* box, gun, from LL *busis* box]

arr. *abbrev. for:* **1** arranged (by). **2** arrival. **3** arrive(d).

arrack *or* **arak** ('ærək) *n* a coarse spirit distilled in various Eastern countries from grain, rice, sugar cane, etc. [C17: from Ar. *'araq* sweat, sweet juice, liquor]

arraign Ⓣ (ə'reɪn) *vb* (*tr*) **1** to bring (a prisoner) before a court to answer an indictment. **2** to call to account; accuse. [C14: from OF, from Vulgar L *ratiōnāre* (unattested) to talk, argue, from L *ratiō* a reasoning]
▸**ar'raigner** *n* ▸**ar'raignment** *n*

arrange Ⓣ (ə'reɪndʒ) *vb* **arranges, arranging, arranged. 1** (*tr*) to put into a proper or systematic order. **2** (*tr; may take a clause as object or an infinitive*) to arrive at an agreement about. **3** (when *intr,* often foll. by *for;*

THESAURUS

armistice *n* = **truce,** ceasefire, peace, suspension of hostilities

armour *n* **1, 4** = **protection,** armour plate, covering, sheathing, shield

armoured *adj* **1** = **protected,** armour-plated, bombproof, bulletproof, ironclad, mailed, steel-plated

armoury *n* **1** = **arsenal,** ammunition dump, arms depot, magazine, ordnance depot

arms *pl n* **1** = **weapons,** armaments, firearms, guns, instruments of war, ordnance, weaponry **3** = **heraldry,** blazonry, crest, escutcheon, insignia

army *n* **1, 2** = **soldiers,** armed force, host (*arch.*), land forces, legions, military, military force, soldiery, troops **5** = **vast number,** array, horde, host, multitude, pack, swarm, throng

aroma *n* **1** = **scent,** bouquet, fragrance, odour, perfume, redolence, savour, smell

aromatic *adj* **1** = **fragrant,** balmy, odoriferous, perfumed, pungent, redolent, savoury, spicy, sweet-scented, sweet-smelling
Antonyms *adj* acrid, bad-smelling, fetid, foul, foul-smelling, malodorous, noisome, offensive, olid, rank, reeking, smelly, stinking

around *prep* **4** = **approximately,** about, circa (*used with dates*), roughly ◆ *adv* **5** = **everywhere,** about, all over, here and there, in all directions, on all sides, throughout, to and fro **6** = **near,** at hand, close, close at hand, close by, nearby, nigh (*arch. or dialect*)

arousal *n* **1** = **stimulation,** agitation, animation, enlivenment, excitement, exhilaration, incitement, inflammation, movement, provocation, reaction, response, stirring up **2** = **awakening,** rousedness

arouse *vb* **1** = **stimulate,** agitate, animate, call forth, enliven, excite, foment, foster, goad, incite, inflame, instigate, kindle, move, prod, provoke, quicken, sharpen, spark, spur, stir up, summon up, warm, whet, whip up **2** = **awaken,** rouse, waken, wake up
Antonyms *vb* ≠ **stimulate:** allay, alleviate, assuage, calm, dampen, dull, end, lull, pacify, quell, quench, still

arraign *vb* **1, 2** = **accuse,** call to account, charge, complain about, denounce, impeach, incriminate, indict, prosecute, take to task

arraignment *n* **1, 2** = **accusation,** charge, complaint, denunciation, impeachment, incrimination, indictment, prosecution

arrange *vb* **1** = **put in order,** align, array, class, classify, dispose, file, form, group, line up, marshal, order, organize, position, range, rank, sequence, set out, sort, sort out (*inf.*), systematize, tidy **2, 5** = **agree,** adjust, come to terms, compromise, determine, settle **3** = **plan,** construct, contrive, devise, fix up, organize, prepare, project, schedule **4** = **adapt,** instrument, orchestrate, score

when *tr, may take a clause as object or an infinitive*) to make plans or preparations in advance (for something): *we arranged for her to be met.* **4** (*tr*) to adapt (a musical composition) for performance in a different way, esp. on different instruments. **5** (*intr; often foll. by with*) to come to an agreement. [C14: from OF *arangier*, from A-[2] + *rangier* to put in a row, RANGE]
▸**ar'rangeable** *adj* ▸**ar'ranger** *n*

arrangement ⓘ (ə'reɪndʒmənt) *n* **1** the act of arranging or being arranged. **2** the form in which things are arranged. **3** a thing composed of various ordered parts: *a flower arrangement.* **4** (*often pl*) a preparation. **5** an understanding. **6** an adaptation of a piece of music for performance in a different way, esp. on different instruments.

arrant ⓘ ('ærənt) *adj* utter; out-and-out: *an arrant fool.* [C14: var. of ERRANT (wandering, vagabond)]
▸**'arrantly** *adv*

arras ('ærəs) *n* a wall hanging, esp. of tapestry.

array ⓘ (ə'reɪ) *n* **1** an impressive display or collection. **2** an orderly arrangement, esp. of troops in battle order. **3** *Poetic.* rich clothing. **4** *Maths.* a set of numbers or symbols arranged in rows and columns, as in a determinant or matrix. **5** *Law.* a panel of jurors. **6** *Computing.* a regular data structure in which elements may be located by reference to index numbers. ◆ *vb* (*tr*) **7** to dress in rich attire. **8** to arrange in order (esp. troops for battle). **9** *Law.* to draw up (a panel of jurors). [C13: from OF, from *arayer* to arrange, of Gmc origin]
▸**ar'rayal** *n*

arrears (ə'rɪəz) *n* (*sometimes sing*) **1** Also called: **arrearage.** something outstanding or owed. **2 in arrears** *or* **arrear.** late in paying a debt or meeting an obligation. [C18: from obs. *arrear* (adv) behindhand, from OF, from Med. L *adretrō*, from L *ad* to + *retrō* backwards]

arrest ⓘ (ə'rɛst) *vb* (*tr*) **1** to deprive (a person) of liberty by taking him into custody, esp. under lawful authority. **2** to seize (a ship) under lawful authority. **3** to slow or stop the development of (a disease, growth, etc.). **4** to catch and hold (one's attention, etc.). ◆ *n* **5** the act of taking a person into custody, esp. under lawful authority. **6** the act of seizing and holding a ship under lawful authority. **7** the state of being held: *under arrest.* **8** the slowing or stopping of something: *a cardiac arrest.* [C14: from OF, from Vulgar L *arrestāre* (unattested), from L *ad* at, to + *restāre* to stand firm, stop]

arresting ⓘ (ə'rɛstɪŋ) *adj* attracting attention; striking.
▸**ar'restingly** *adv*

arrhythmia (ə'rɪðmɪə) *n* any variation from the normal rhythm in the heartbeat. [C19: NL, from Gk *arrhuthmia*, from A-[1] + *rhuthmos* RHYTHM]

arrière-pensée *French.* (arjerpɑ̃se) *n* an unrevealed thought or intention. [C19: lit.: behind thought]

arris ('ærɪs) *n, pl* **arris** *or* **arrises.** a sharp edge at the meeting of two surfaces at an angle with one another. [C17: from OF *areste* beard of grain, sharp ridge; see ARÊTE]

arrival ⓘ (ə'raɪvᵊl) *n* **1** the act or time of arriving. **2** a person or thing that arrives or has arrived.

arrive ⓘ (ə'raɪv) *vb* **arrives, arriving, arrived.** (*intr*) **1** to come to a certain place during or after a journey. **2** to reach: *to arrive at a decision.* **3** to occur eventually: *the moment arrived when pretence was useless.* **4** *Inf.* (of a baby) to be born. **5** *Inf.* to attain success. [C13: from OF, from Vulgar L *arrīpāre* (unattested) to land, reach the bank, from L *ad* to + *rīpa* river bank]

arrivederci *Italian.* (arrive'dertʃi) *sentence substitute.* goodbye.

arriviste ⓘ (ˌæriː'viːst) *n* a person who is unscrupulously ambitious. [F: see ARRIVE, -IST]

arrogant ⓘ ('ærəgənt) *adj* having or showing an exaggerated opinion of one's own importance, merit, ability, etc.: *an arrogant assumption.* [C14: from L *arrogāre* to claim as one's own; see ARROGATE]
▸**'arrogance** *n* ▸**'arrogantly** *adv*

arrogate ('ærəˌgeɪt) *vb* **arrogates, arrogating, arrogated.** (*tr*) **1** to claim or appropriate for oneself without justification. **2** to attribute or assign to another without justification. [C16: from L *arrogāre*, from *rogāre* to ask]
▸ˌ**arro'gation** *n* ▸**arrogative** (ə'rɒgətɪv) *adj*

arrondissement (*French* arɔ̃dismɑ̃) *n* (in France) **1** the largest subdivision of a department. **2** a municipal district of large cities, esp. Paris. [C19: from *arrondir* to make round]

arrow ⓘ ('ærəʊ) *n* **1** a long slender pointed weapon, usually having feathers fastened at the end as a balance, that is shot from a bow. **2** any of various things that resemble an arrow in shape, function, or speed. [OE *arwe*]

arrowhead ('ærəʊˌhɛd) *n* **1** the pointed tip of an arrow, often removable from the shaft. **2** something that resembles the head of an arrow in shape. **3** an aquatic herbaceous plant having arrow-shaped leaves.

arrowroot ('ærəʊˌruːt) *n* **1** a white-flowered West Indian plant, whose rhizomes yield an easily digestible starch. **2** the starch obtained from this plant.

arroyo (ə'rɔɪəʊ) *n, pl* **arroyos.** *Chiefly southwestern US.* a steep-sided stream bed that is usually dry except after heavy rain. [C19: from Sp.]

arse (ɑːs) *or US & Canad.* **ass** *n Taboo.* **1** the buttocks. **2** the anus. **3** a stupid person; fool. ◆ Also called (for senses 2, 3): **arsehole,** (US & Canad.) **asshole.** [OE]

arsenal ⓘ ('ɑːsənᵊl) *n* **1** a store for arms, ammunition, and other military items. **2** a workshop that produces munitions. **3** a store of anything regarded as weapons. [C16: from It. *arsenale* dockyard, from Ar., from *dār* house + *sinā'ah* manufacture]

arsenate ('ɑːsəˌneɪt, -nɪt) *n* a salt or ester of arsenic acid.

arsenic *n* ('ɑːsnɪk). **1** a toxic metalloid element used in transistors, lead-based alloys, and high-temperature brasses. Symbol: As; atomic no.: 33; atomic wt.: 74.92. **2** a nontechnical name for **arsenic trioxide** (As_2O_3), used as rat poison and an insecticide. ◆ *adj* (ɑː'sɛnɪk). **3** of or containing arsenic, esp. in the pentavalent state; designating an arsenic(V) compound. [C14: from L, from Gk *arsenikon* yellow arsenic ore, from Syriac *zarnīg* (infl. by Gk *arsenikos* virile)]

arsenic acid *n* a white poisonous soluble crystalline solid used in the manufacture of insecticides.

arsenical (ɑː'sɛnɪkᵊl) *adj* **1** of or containing arsenic. ◆ *n* **2** a drug or insecticide containing arsenic.

arsenious (ɑː'siːnɪəs) *or* **arsenous** ('ɑːsɪnəs) *adj* of or containing arsenic in the trivalent state; designating an arsenic(III) compound.

arson ('ɑːsᵊn) *n Criminal law.* the act of intentionally or recklessly setting fire to property for some improper reason. [C17: from OF, from Med. L *ārsiō*, from L *ārdēre* to burn]
▸**'arsonist** *n*

art[1] ⓘ (ɑːt) *n* **1a** the creation of works of beauty or other special significance. **1b** (*as modifier*): *an art movement.* **2** the exercise of human skill (as distinguished from *nature*). **3** imaginative skill as applied to repre-

THESAURUS

Antonyms *vb* ≠ **put in order:** disarrange, disorganize, disturb, mess up, scatter

arrangement *n* **1, 2, 3** = **order,** alignment, array, classification, design, display, disposition, form, grouping, line-up, marshalling, ordering, organization, ranging, rank, setup (*inf.*), structure, system **4** *often plural* = **plan,** construction, devising, organization, planning, preparation, provision, schedule **5** = **agreement,** adjustment, compact, compromise, deal, settlement, terms, understanding **6** = **adaptation,** instrumentation, interpretation, orchestration, score, version

arrant *adj* = **total,** absolute, atrocious, blatant, complete, deep-dyed (*usually derogatory*), downright, egregious, extreme, flagrant, gross, infamous, monstrous, notorious, out-and-out, outright, rank, thorough, thoroughgoing, undisguised, unmitigated, utter, vile

array *n* **1, 2** = **arrangement,** collection, display, disposition, exhibition, formation, line-up, marshalling, muster, order, parade, show, supply **3** *Poetic* = **clothing,** apparel, attire, clothes, dress, finery, garb, garments, raiment (*arch. or poetic*), regalia ◆ *vb* **7** = **dress,** accoutre, adorn, apparel (*arch.*), attire, bedeck, caparison, clothe, deck, decorate, equip, festoon, fit out, garb, get ready, outfit, robe, supply, wrap **8** = **arrange,** align, display, dispose, draw up, exhibit, form up, group, line up, marshal, muster, order, parade, place in order, range, sequence, set in line (*Military*), show

arrest *vb* **1** = **capture,** apprehend, bust, catch, collar (*inf.*), detain, feel one's collar (*sl.*), lay hold of, lift (*sl.*), nab (*inf.*), nail (*inf.*), nick (*sl., chiefly Brit.*), pinch (*inf.*), run in (*sl.*), seize, take, take into custody, take prisoner **3** = **stop,** block, check, delay, end, halt, hinder, hold, inhibit, interrupt, obstruct, restrain, retard, slow, stall, stay, suppress **4** = **grip,** absorb, catch, engage, engross, fascinate, hold, intrigue, occupy ◆ *n* **5** = **capture,** apprehension, bust (*inf.*), cop (*sl.*), detention, seizure **8** = **stopping,** blockage, check, delay, end, halt, hindrance, inhibition, interruption, obstruction, restraint, stalling, stay, suppression
Antonyms *vb* ≠ **capture:** free, let go, release, set free ≠ **stop:** accelerate, encourage, precipitate, promote, quicken, speed up ◆ *n* ≠ **capture:** freeing, release ≠ **stopping:** acceleration, encouragement, precipitation, promotion, quickening

arresting *adj* = **striking,** conspicuous, dramatic, engaging, extraordinary, impressive, jaw-dropping, noticeable, outstanding, remarkable, salient, stunning, surprising
Antonyms *adj* inconspicuous, unimpressive, unnoticeable, unremarkable

arrival *n* **1** = **coming,** advent, appearance, arriving, entrance, happening, occurrence, taking place **2** = **newcomer,** arriver, caller, comer, entrant, incomer, visitant, visitor

arrive *vb* **1, 2** = **come,** appear, attain, befall, enter, get to, happen, occur, reach, show up (*inf.*), take place, turn up **5** *Informal* = **succeed,** achieve recognition, become famous, make good, make it, make one's mark (*inf.*), make the grade (*inf.*), reach the top
Antonyms *vb* ≠ **come:** depart, disappear, exit, go, go away, leave, pack one's bags (*inf.*), retire, take (one's) leave, vanish, withdraw

arriviste *n* = **upstart,** adventurer *or* adventuress, climber, parvenu *or* parvenue, social climber, status seeker, would-be

arrogance *n* = **conceit,** bluster, conceitedness, contemptuousness, disdainfulness, haughtiness, hauteur, high-handedness, hubris, imperiousness, insolence, loftiness, lordliness, overweeningness, pomposity, pompousness, presumption, pretension, pretentiousness, pride, scornfulness, superciliousness, swagger
Antonyms *n* bashfulness, diffidence, humility, meekness, modesty, politeness, shyness

arrogant *adj* = **conceited,** assuming, blustering, contemptuous, disdainful, haughty, high and mighty (*inf.*), high-handed, imperious, insolent, looking down one's nose at, lordly, overbearing, overweening, pompous, presumptuous, pretentious, proud, scornful, supercilious, swaggering
Antonyms *adj* bashful, deferential, diffident, humble, modest, polite, servile, shy, unassuming

arrow *n* **1** = **dart,** bolt, flight, quarrel, reed (*arch.*), shaft (*arch.*)

arsenal *n* **1** = **armoury,** ammunition dump, arms depot, magazine, ordnance depot, stock, stockpile, store, storehouse, supply

art[1] *n* **7** = **skill,** adroitness, aptitude, artifice (*arch.*), artistry, craft, craftsmanship, dexterity, expertise, facility, ingenuity, knack, knowledge, mastery, method, profession, trade, virtuosity **9** = **cunning,** artfulness, artifice, astuteness, craftiness, deceit, duplicity, guile, trickery, wiliness sentations of the natural world or figments of the imagination. **4a** works of art collectively, esp. of the visual arts. **4b** (*as modifier*): *an art gallery*. **5** any branch of the visual arts, esp. painting. **6a** any field using the techniques of art to display artistic qualities. **6b** (*as modifier*): *art film*. **7** method, facility, or knack: *the art of threading a needle*. **8** skill governing a particular human activity: *the art of government*. **9** cunning. **10 get something down to a fine art.** to become highly proficient at something through practice. ◆ See also **arts.** [C13: from OF, from L *ars* craftsmanship]

art^{2} (ɑːt) *vb Arch.* (used with the pronoun *thou*) a singular form of the present tense of **be.** [OE *eart*, part of *bēon* to BE]

art. *abbrev. for:* **1** article. **2** artificial. **3** Also: **arty.** artillery.

-art *suffix forming nouns.* a variant of **-ard.**

Art Deco (ˈdɛkəʊ) *n* a style of interior decoration, architecture, etc., at its height in the 1930s and characterized by geometrical shapes. [C20: from *art décoratif*, after the *Exposition des arts décoratifs* held in Paris in 1925]

art director *n* a person responsible for the sets and costumes in a film.

artefact *or* **artifact** (ˈɑːtɪˌfækt) *n* **1** something made or given shape by man, such as a tool or a work of art, esp. an object of archaeological interest. **2** anything man-made, such as a spurious experimental result. **3** *Cytology.* a structure seen in dead tissue that is not normally present in the living tissue. [C19: from L *arte factum*, from *ars* skill + *facere* to make]

artel (ɑːˈtɛl) *n* (in the former Soviet Union) a cooperative union or organization, esp. of producers, such as peasants. [from Russian *artel'*, from It. *artieri* artisans, from *arte* work, from L *ars* ART^{1}]

arterial (ɑːˈtɪərɪəl) *adj* **1** of or affecting an artery or arteries. **2** denoting or relating to the bright red reoxygenated blood that circulates in the arteries. **3** being a major route, esp. one with many minor branches.
▸**arˈterially** *adv*

arterialize *or* **arterialise** (ɑːˈtɪərɪəˌlaɪz) *vb* **arterializes, arterializing, arterialized** *or* **arterialises, arterialising, arterialised.** (*tr*) **1** to change (venous blood) into arterial blood by replenishing the depleted oxygen. **2** to provide with arteries.
▸**arˌterialiˈzation** *or* **arˌterialiˈsation** *n*

arteriole (ɑːˈtɪərɪˌəʊl) *n Anat.* any of the small subdivisions of an artery that form thin-walled vessels ending in capillaries. [C19: from NL, from L *artēria* ARTERY]

arteriosclerosis (ɑːˌtɪərɪəʊsklɪəˈrəʊsɪs) *n, pl* **arterioscleroses** (-siːz). a thickening and loss of elasticity of the walls of the arteries. Nontechnical name: **hardening of the arteries.**
▸**arteriosclerotic** (ɑːˌtɪərɪəʊsklɪəˈrɒtɪk) *adj*

artery (ˈɑːtərɪ) *n, pl* **arteries. 1** any of the tubular thick-walled muscular vessels that convey oxygenated blood from the heart to various parts of the body. Cf. **pulmonary artery, vein. 2** a major road or means of communication. [C14: from L *artēria*, rel. to Gk *aortē* the great artery, AORTA]

artesian well (ɑːˈtiːzɪən) *n* a well sunk through impermeable strata into strata receiving water from an area at a higher altitude than that of the well, so the water is forced to flow upwards. [C19: from F, from OF *Arteis* Artois, old province, where such wells were common]

Artex (ˈɑːtɛks) *n Trademark.* a textured coating for walls and ceilings.

art form *n* **1** an accepted mode of artistic composition, such as the sonnet, symphony, etc. **2** a recognized medium of artistic expression.

artful Ⓣ (ˈɑːtfʊl) *adj* **1** cunning or tricky. **2** skilful in achieving a desired end.
▸**ˈartfully** *adv* ▸**ˈartfulness** *n*

art house *n* **1** a cinema that specializes in showing films that are not part of the commercial mainstream. ◆ *adj* **2** of or relating to such films or a cinema that specializes in showing them.

arthralgia (ɑːˈθrældʒə) *n Pathol.* pain in a joint.
▸**arˈthralgic** *adj*

arthritis (ɑːˈθraɪtɪs) *n* inflammation of a joint or joints characterized by pain and stiffness of the affected parts. [C16: via L from Gk *arthron* joint + -ITIS]
▸**arthritic** (ɑːˈθrɪtɪk) *adj, n*

arthropod (ˈɑːθrəˌpɒd) *n* an invertebrate having jointed limbs, a segmented body, and an exoskeleton made of chitin, as the crustaceans, insects, arachnids, and centipedes. [C19: from NL, from Gk *arthron* joint + *-podus* footed, from *pous* foot]

artic (ɑːˈtɪk) *n Inf.* short for **articulated lorry.**

artichoke (ˈɑːtɪˌtʃəʊk) *n* **1** Also called: **globe artichoke.** a thistle-like Eurasian plant, cultivated for its large edible flower head. **2** the unopened flower head of this plant, which can be cooked and eaten. **3** See **Jerusalem artichoke.** [C16: from It., from OSp., from Ar. *al-kharshūf*]

article Ⓣ (ˈɑːtɪk^{ə}l) *n* **1** one of a class of objects; item. **2** an unspecified or previously named thing, esp. a small object. **3** a written composition on a subject, often being one of several found in a magazine, newspaper, etc. **4** *Grammar.* a kind of determiner, occurring in many languages including English, that lacks independent meaning. See also **definite article, indefinite article. 5** a clause or section in a written document. **6** (*often cap.*) *Christianity.* See **Thirty-nine Articles.** ◆ *vb* **articles, articling, articled.** (*tr*) **7** to bind by a written contract, esp. one that governs a period of training: *an articled clerk*. [C13: from OF, from L *articulus* small joint, from *artus* joint]

articular (ɑːˈtɪkjʊlə) *adj* of or relating to joints or to the structural components in a joint. [C15: from L *articulāris* concerning the joints, from *articulus* small joint]

articulate Ⓣ *adj* (ɑːˈtɪkjʊlɪt). **1** able to express oneself fluently and coherently. **2** having the power of speech. **3** distinct, clear, or definite: *an articulate document*. **4** *Zool.* (of arthropods and higher vertebrates) possessing joints or jointed segments. ◆ *vb* (ɑːˈtɪkjʊˌleɪt), **articulates, articulating, articulated. 5** to speak or enunciate (words, syllables, etc.) clearly and distinctly. **6** (*tr*) to express coherently in words. **7** (*intr*) *Zool.* to be jointed or form a joint. [C16: from L *articulāre* to divide into joints]
▸**arˈticulately** *adv* ▸**arˈticulateness** *n* ▸**arˈticuˌlator** *n*

articulated lorry *n* a large lorry made in two separate sections, a tractor and a trailer, connected by a pivoted bar.

articulation Ⓣ (ɑːˌtɪkjʊˈleɪʃən) *n* **1** the act or process of speaking or expressing in words. **2a** the process of articulating a speech sound. **2b** the sound so produced, esp. a consonant. **3** the act or the state of being jointed together. **4** *Zool.* **4a** a joint such as that between bones or arthropod segments. **4b** the way in which jointed parts are connected. **5** *Bot.* the part of a plant at which natural separation occurs.

artifact (ˈɑːtɪˌfækt) *n* a variant spelling of **artefact.**

artifice Ⓣ (ˈɑːtɪfɪs) *n* **1** a clever expedient. **2** crafty or subtle deception. **3** skill; cleverness. **4** a skilfully contrived device. [C16: from OF, from L *artificium* skill, from *artifex* one possessed of a specific skill, from *ars* skill + *-fex*, from *facere* to make]

artificer (ɑːˈtɪfɪsə) *n* **1** a skilled craftsman. **2** a clever or inventive designer. **3** a serviceman trained in mechanics.

artificial Ⓣ (ˌɑːtɪˈfɪʃəl) *adj* **1** produced by man; not occurring naturally. **2** made in imitation of a natural product: *artificial cream*. **3** pretended; insincere. **4** lacking in spontaneity; affected: *an artificial laugh*. [C14: from L *artificiālis* belonging to art, from *artificium* skill, ARTIFICE]
▸**artificiality** (ˌɑːtɪˌfɪʃɪˈælɪtɪ) *n* ▸**ˌartiˈficially** *adv*

artificial daylight *n Physics.* artificial light having approximately the same spectral characteristics as natural daylight.

artificial disintegration *n Physics.* radioactive transformation of a substance by bombardment with high-energy particles, such as alpha particles or neutrons.

artificial insemination *n* introduction of spermatozoa into the vagina or uterus by means other than sexual union.

artificial intelligence *n* the ability of a machine, such as a computer, to imitate intelligent human behaviour.

artificial respiration *n* **1** any of various methods of restarting breathing after it has stopped. **2** any method of maintaining respiration, as by use of an iron lung.

artillery Ⓣ (ɑːˈtɪlərɪ) *n* **1** guns, cannon, mortars, etc., of calibre greater than 20mm. **2** troops or military units specializing in using such guns. **3** the science dealing with the use of guns. [C14: from OF, from *artillier* to equip with weapons, from ?]

artiodactyl (ˌɑːtɪəʊˈdæktɪl) *n* an ungulate with an even number of toes, as pigs, camels, deer, cattle, etc. [C19: from Gk *artios* even-numbered + *daktulos* finger]
▸**ˌartioˈdactylous** *adj*

artisan Ⓣ (ˈɑːtɪˌzæn, ˌɑːtɪˈzæn) *n* a skilled workman; craftsman. [C16: from F, from OIt. *artigiano*, from *arte* ART^{1}]
▸**artisanal** (ɑːˈtɪzən^{ə}l, ˈɑːtɪzən^{ə}l) *adj*

THESAURUS

artful *adj* **1 = cunning,** clever, crafty, deceitful, designing, foxy, intriguing, politic, scheming, sharp, shrewd, sly, smart, subtle, tricky, wily **2 = skilful,** adept, adroit, clever, dexterous, ingenious, masterly, proficient, resourceful, smart, subtle
Antonyms *adj* **≠ cunning:** artless, frank, ingenuous, open, simple, straightforward **≠ skilful:** artless, clumsy, unadept, unskilled, untalented

article *n* **1 = thing,** commodity, item, object, piece, substance, unit **3 = piece,** composition, discourse, essay, feature, item, paper, story, treatise **5 = clause,** branch, detail, division, head, heading, item, paragraph, part, passage, piece, point, portion, section

articulate *adj* **1 = expressive,** clear, coherent, comprehensible, eloquent, fluent, intelligible, lucid, meaningful, understandable, vocal, well-spoken ◆ *vb* **5 = express,** enounce, enunciate, pronounce, say, speak, state, talk, utter, verbalize, vocalize, voice
Antonyms *adj* **≠ expressive:** dumb, faltering, halting, hesitant, incoherent, incomprehensible, indistinct, mumbled, mute, poorly-spoken, silent, speechless, stammering, stuttering, tongue-tied, unclear, unintelligible, voiceless

articulation *n* **1 = expression,** delivery, diction, enunciation, pronunciation, saying, speaking, statement, talking, utterance, verbalization, vocalization, voicing **3, 4 = joint,** connection, coupling, hinge, jointing, juncture

artifice *n* **1 = trick,** contrivance, device, dodge, expedient, hoax, machination, manoeuvre, ruse, stratagem, subterfuge, tactic, wile **2 = cunning,** artfulness, chicanery, craft, craftiness, deception, duplicity, guile, scheming, slyness, trickery **3 = cleverness,** adroitness, deftness, facility, finesse, ingenuity, invention, inventiveness, skill

artificial *adj* **1 = synthetic,** man-made, manufactured, non-natural, plastic **2 = fake,** bogus, counterfeit, ersatz, imitation, mock, phoney *or* phony (*inf.*), pseudo (*inf.*), sham, simulated, specious, spurious **3, 4 = insincere,** affected, assumed, contrived, false, feigned, forced, hollow, meretricious, phoney *or* phony (*inf.*), pretended, spurious, unnatural
Antonyms *adj* **≠ fake:** authentic **≠ insincere:** frank, genuine, honest, natural, sincere, true, unaffected

artillery *n* **1 = big guns,** battery, cannon, cannonry, gunnery, ordnance

artisan *n* **= craftsman,** artificer, handicraftsman, journeyman, mechanic, skilled workman, technician

artist ➊ ('ɑːtɪst) *n* **1** a person who practises or is skilled in an art, esp. painting, drawing, or sculpture. **2** a person who displays in his work qualities required in art, such as sensibility and imagination. **3** a person whose profession requires artistic expertise. **4** a person skilled in some task or occupation. **5** *Sl.* a person devoted to or proficient in something: *a con artist; a booze artist.*
▸**ar'tistic** *adj* ▸**ar'tistically** *adv*

artiste ➊ (ɑː'tiːst) *n* **1** an entertainer, such as a singer or dancer. **2** a person who is highly skilled in some occupation: *a hair artiste.* [F]

artistry ➊ ('ɑːtɪstrɪ) *n* **1** artistic workmanship, ability, or quality. **2** artistic pursuits. **3** great skill.

artless ➊ ('ɑːtlɪs) *adj* **1** free from deceit; ingenuous: *an artless remark.* **2** natural; unpretentious. **3** without art or skill.
▸**'artlessly** *adv*

Art Nouveau (ɑː nuː'vəʊ; *French* ar nuvo) *n* a style of art and architecture of the 1890s, characterized by sinuous outlines and stylized natural forms. [F, lit.: new art]

art paper *n* a high-quality type of paper having a smooth coating of china clay or similar substance on it.

arts (ɑːts) *pl n* **1a the.** imaginative, creative, and nonscientific branches of knowledge considered collectively, esp. as studied academically. **1b** (*as modifier*): *an arts degree.* **2** See **fine art. 3** cunning actions or schemes.

Arts and Crafts *pl n* decorative handicraft and design, esp. that of the **Arts and Crafts movement**, in late nineteenth-century Britain, which sought to revive medieval craftsmanship.

art union *n Austral. & NZ.* an officially approved lottery for prizes other than cash (formerly works of art).

arty ➊ ('ɑːtɪ) *adj* **artier, artiest.** *Inf.* having an affected interest in artists or art.
▸**'artiness** *n*

arugula (ə'ruːgjʊlə) *n* a Mediterranean plant of the mustard family with yellowish-white flowers and pungent leaves that are used as a salad; rocket. See also **rocket**[2] (sense 1). [C20: from N It. dialect]

arum ('ɛərəm) *n* **1** any of various aroid plants of Europe and the Mediterranean region, having arrow-shaped leaves and a typically white spathe, such as the cuckoopint. **2 arum lily.** another name for **calla** (sense 1). [C16: from L, var. of *aros* wake-robin, from Gk *aron*]

arvo ('ɑːvəʊ) *n Austral. inf.* afternoon.

-ary *suffix.* **1** (*forming adjectives*) of; related to; belonging to: *cautionary.* **2** (*forming nouns*) a person or thing connected with: *missionary; aviary.* [from L *-ārius, -āria, -ārium*]

Aryan ('ɛərɪən) *n* **1** (in Nazi ideology) a Caucasian of non-Jewish descent. **2** a member of any of the peoples supposedly descended from the Indo-Europeans. ◆ *adj* **3** of or characteristic of an Aryan or Aryans. ◆ *adj, n* **4** *Arch.* Indo-European. [C19: from Sansk. *ārya* of noble birth]

as[1] ➊ (æz; *unstressed* əz) *conj* (*subordinating*) **1** (often preceded by *just*) while; when: *he caught me as I was leaving.* **2** in the way that: *dancing as only she can.* **3** that which; what: *I did as I was told.* **4** (of) which fact, event, etc. (referring to the previous statement): *to become wise, as we all know, is not easy.* **5 as it were.** in a way; as if it were really so. **6** since; seeing that. **7** in the same way that: *he died of cancer, as his father had done.* **8** for instance: *capital cities, as London.* ◆ *adv, conj* **9a** used to indicate identity of extent, amount, etc.: *she is as heavy as her sister.* **9b** used with this sense after a noun phrase introduced by *the same: the same height as her sister.* ◆ *prep* **10** in the role of; being: *as his friend, I am probably biased.* **11 as for** *or* **to.** with reference to: *as for my past, I'm not telling you anything.* **12 as if** *or* **though.** as it would be if: *he talked as if he knew all about it.* **13 as (it) is.** in the existing state of affairs. **14 as was.** in a previous state. [OE *alswā* likewise]

USAGE NOTE See at **like.**

as[2] (æs) *n* **1** an ancient Roman unit of weight approximately equal to 1 pound troy (373 grams). **2** a copper coin of ancient Rome. [C17: from L *ās* unity]

As *symbol for:* **1** altostratus. **2** *Chem.* arsenic.

AS *abbrev. for:* **1** Also: **A.S.** Anglo-Saxon. **2** antisubmarine.

ASA *abbrev. for:* **1** (in Britain) Amateur Swimming Association. **2** (in Britain) Advertising Standards Authority. **3** (in the US) American Standards Association.

ASA/BS *abbrev.* an obsolete expression of the speed of a photographic film, replaced by the ISO rating. [C20: from *American Standards Association/British Standard*]

asafoetida *or* **asafetida** (ˌæsə'fetɪdə) *n* a bitter resin with an unpleasant onion-like smell, obtained from the roots of some umbelliferous plants: formerly used to treat flatulence, etc. [C14: from Med. L, from *asa* gum (cf. Persian *azā* mastic) + L *foetidus* evil-smelling]

a.s.a.p. *abbrev. for* as soon as possible.

asbestos (æs'bestɒs) *n* **a** any of the fibrous amphibole minerals that are incombustible and resistant to chemicals. It was formerly widely used in the form of fabric or board as a heat-resistant structural material. **b** (*as modifier*): *asbestos matting.* [C14: via L from Gk: from *asbestos* inextinguishable, from A-[1] + *sbennunai* to extinguish]

asbestosis (ˌæsbes'təʊsɪs) *n* inflammation of the lungs resulting from chronic inhalation of asbestos particles.

ascarid ('æskərɪd) *n* a parasitic nematode worm such as the common roundworm of man and pigs. [C14: from NL, from Gk *askarides,* pl. of *askaris*]

ascend ➊ (ə'send) *vb* **1** to go or move up (a ladder, hill, slope, etc.). **2** (*intr*) to slope or incline upwards. **3** (*intr*) to rise to a higher point, level, etc. **4** to trace (a genealogy, etc.) back in time. **5** to sing or play (a scale, etc.) from the lower to higher notes. **6 ascend the throne.** to become king or queen. [C14: from L *ascendere,* from *scandere*]

ascendancy ➊, **ascendency** (ə'sendənsɪ) *or* **ascendance, ascendence** *n* the condition of being dominant.

ascendant ➊ *or* **ascendent** (ə'sendənt) *adj* **1** proceeding upwards; rising. **2** dominant or influential. ◆ *n* **3** a position or condition of dominance. **4** *Astrol.* (*sometimes cap.*) **4a** a point on the ecliptic that rises on the eastern horizon at a particular moment. **4b** the sign of the zodiac containing this point. **5 in the ascendant.** increasing in influence, etc.

ascender (ə'sendə) *n* **1** *Printing.* the part of certain lower-case letters, such as *b* or *h,* that extends above the body of the letter. **2** a person or thing that ascends.

ascension ➊ (ə'senʃən) *n* the act of ascending.
▸**as'censional** *adj*

Ascension (ə'senʃən) *n Bible.* the passing of Jesus Christ from earth into heaven (Acts 1:9).

Ascension Day *n* the 40th day after Easter, when the Ascension of Christ into heaven is celebrated.

ascent ➊ (ə'sent) *n* **1** the act of ascending; upward movement. **2** an upward slope. **3** movement back through time (esp. in **line of ascent**).

ascertain ➊ (ˌæsə'teɪn) *vb* (*tr*) **1** to determine definitely. **2** *Arch.* to make certain. [C15: from OF *acertener* to make certain]
▸**ˌascer'tainable** *adj* ▸**ˌascer'tainment** *n*

ascetic ➊ (ə'setɪk) *n* **1** a person who practises great self-denial and abstains from worldly comforts and pleasures, esp. for religious reasons. ◆ *adj also* **ascetical. 2** rigidly abstinent or abstemious. **3** of or relating to ascetics or asceticism. [C17: from Gk *askētikos,* from *askētēs,* from *askein* to exercise]
▸**as'cetically** *adv* ▸**a'sceti,cism** *n*

ascidian (ə'sɪdɪən) *n* any of a class of minute marine invertebrate animals, such as the sea squirt, the adults of which are degenerate and sedentary.

ascidium (ə'sɪdɪəm) *n, pl* **ascidia** (-'sɪdɪə). part of a plant that is shaped

THESAURUS

artist *n* **1, 4 = creator**, artisan (*obs.*), craftsman, maker, master

artiste *n* **1 = performer**, entertainer

artistic *adj* **1 = creative**, aesthetic, beautiful, cultivated, cultured, decorative, elegant, exquisite, graceful, imaginative, ornamental, refined, sensitive, sophisticated, stylish, tasteful
Antonyms *adj* inartistic, inelegant, tasteless, unattractive, untalented

artistry *n* **1, 3 = skill**, accomplishment, art, artistic ability, brilliance, craft, craftsmanship, creativity, finesse, flair, genius, mastery, proficiency, sensibility, style, talent, taste, touch, virtuosity, workmanship

artless *adj* **1 = straightforward**, candid, direct, fair, frank, genuine, guileless, honest, open, plain, round, sincere, true, undesigning, upfront (*inf.*) **2 = natural**, humble, plain, pure, simple, unadorned, unaffected, uncontrived, unpretentious **3 = unskilled**, awkward, bungling, clumsy, crude, incompetent, inept, maladroit, primitive, rude, untalented
Antonyms *adj* ≠ **straightforward:** artful, crafty, cunning, designing, dishonest, false, insincere ≠ **natural:** affected, artificial, unnatural ≠ **unskilled:** aesthetic, artful, artistic, crafty, cunning, sophisticated

arty *adj Informal* = **artistic**, arty-crafty (*inf.*), arty-farty (*derogatory sl.*)

as[1] *conj* **1 = when**, at the time that, during the time that, just as, while **2 = in the way that**, in the manner that, like **3 = what**, that which **5 as it were = in a way**, in a manner of speaking, so to say, so to speak **6 = since**, because, considering that, seeing that **8 = for instance**, like, such as ◆ *prep* **10 = being**, in the character of, in the role of, under the name of **11 as for = with regard to**, as regards, in reference to, on the subject of, with reference to, with respect to

ascend *vb* **1-3 = move up**, climb, float up, fly up, go up, lift off, mount, rise, scale, slope upwards, soar, take off, tower
Antonyms *vb* alight, descend, dip, drop, fall, go down, incline, move down, plummet, plunge, sink, slant, slope, subside, tumble

ascendancy *n* = **influence**, authority, command, control, dominance, domination, dominion, hegemony, mastery, power, predominance, pre-eminence, prevalence, reign, rule, sovereignty, superiority, supremacy, sway, upper hand
Antonyms *n* inferiority, servility, subjection, subordination, weakness

ascendant *adj* **2 = influential**, authoritative, commanding, controlling, dominant, powerful, predominant, pre-eminent, prevailing, ruling, superior, supreme, uppermost ◆ *n* **5 in the ascendant = rising**, ascending, climbing, commanding, dominant, dominating, flourishing, growing, increasing, influential, mounting, on the rise, on the way up, powerful, prevailing, supreme, up-and-coming, uppermost, winning

ascension *n* = **rise**, ascending, ascent, climb, mounting, moving upwards, rising

ascent *n* **1 = rise**, ascending, ascension, clambering, climb, climbing, mounting, rising, scaling, upward movement **2 = upward slope**, acclivity, gradient, incline, ramp, rise, rising ground

ascertain *vb* **1 = find out**, confirm, determine, discover, establish, ferret out, fix, identify, learn, make certain, settle, suss (out) (*sl.*), verify

ascetic *n* **1 = monk**, abstainer, anchorite, hermit, nun, recluse, self-denier ◆ *adj* **2 = self-denying**, abstemious, abstinent, austere, celibate, frugal, harsh, plain, puritanical, rigorous, self-disciplined, severe, Spartan, stern
Antonyms *n* ≠ **monk:** hedonist, sensualist, voluptuary ◆ *adj* ≠ **self-denying:** abandoned, comfortable, luxurious, self-indulgent, sensuous, voluptuous

like a pitcher, such as the modified leaf of the pitcher plant. [C18: from NL, from Gk *askidion* a little bag, from *askos* bag]

ascomycete (ˌæskəmaɪˈsiːt) *n* any of a phylum of fungi in which the spores (ascospores) are formed inside a club-shaped cell (ascus). The group includes yeast, penicillium, and certain mildews.
▸**ˌascomyˈcetous** *adj*

ascorbic acid (əˈskɔːbɪk) *n* a white crystalline vitamin present in plants, esp. citrus fruits, tomatoes, and green vegetables. A deficiency in the diet of man leads to scurvy. Also called: **vitamin C.**

ascribe Ⓣ (əˈskraɪb) *vb* **ascribes, ascribing, ascribed.** (*tr*) **1** to credit or assign, as to a particular origin or period. **2** to consider as belonging to: *to ascribe beauty to youth.* [C15: from L *ascrībere* to enrol, from *ad* in addition + *scrībere* to write]
▸**asˈcribable** *adj*

> **USAGE NOTE** *Ascribe* is sometimes wrongly used where *subscribe* is meant: *I do not subscribe* (not *ascribe*) *to this view.*

ascription (əˈskrɪpʃən) *n* **1** the act of ascribing. **2** a statement ascribing something to someone. [C16: from L *ascriptiō,* from *ascrībere* to ASCRIBE]

asdic (ˈæzdɪk) *n* an early form of **sonar.** [C20: from *A(nti-)S(ubmarine) D(etection) I(nvestigation) C(ommittee)*]

-ase *suffix forming nouns.* indicating an enzyme: *oxidase.* [from DIASTASE]

ASEAN (ˈæsɪˌæn) *n acronym for* Association of South-East Asian Nations.

asepsis (əˈsɛpsɪs, eɪ-) *n* **1** the state of being free from living pathogenic organisms. **2** the methods of achieving a germ-free condition.
▸**aˈseptic** *adj*

asexual Ⓣ (eɪˈsɛksjʊəl) *adj* **1** having no apparent sex or sex organs. **2** (of reproduction) not involving the fusion of male and female gametes.
▸**ˌasexuˈality** *n* ▸**aˈsexually** *adv*

ash[1] (æʃ) *n* **1** the residue formed when matter is burnt. **2** fine particles of lava thrown out by an erupting volcano. **3** a light silvery-grey colour. ◆ See also **ashes.** [OE *æsce*]

ash[2] (æʃ) *n* **1** a tree having compound leaves, clusters of small greenish flowers, and winged seeds. **2** the wood of this tree, used for tool handles, etc. **3** any of several trees resembling the ash, such as the mountain ash. **4** *Austral.* any of various eucalypts. [OE *æsc*]

ash[3] (æʃ) *n* the digraph æ, as in Old English, representing a vowel approximately like that of the *a* in Modern English *hat.*

ASH (æʃ) *n* (in Britain) *acronym for* Action on Smoking and Health.

ashamed Ⓣ (əˈʃeɪmd) *adj* (*usually postpositive*) **1** overcome with shame or remorse. **2** (foll. by *of*) suffering from feelings of shame in relation to (a person or deed). **3** (foll. by *to*) unwilling through fear of humiliation, shame, etc. [OE *āscamod,* p.p. of *āscamian* to shame, from *scamu* SHAME]
▸**ashamedly** (əˈʃeɪmɪdlɪ) *adv*

A shares *pl n* ordinary shares in a company which carry restricted voting rights.

ash can *n* a US word for **dustbin.** Also called: **garbage can, ash bin, trash can.**

ashen[1] Ⓣ (ˈæʃən) *adj* **1** drained of colour. **2** consisting of or resembling ashes. **3** of a pale greyish colour.

ashen[2] (ˈæʃən) *adj* of, relating to, or made from the ash tree or its timber.

ashes (ˈæʃɪz) *pl n* **1** ruins or remains, as after burning. **2** the remains of a human body after cremation.

Ashes (ˈæʃɪz) *pl n* **the.** a cremated cricket stump constituting a trophy competed for by England and Australia in test cricket since 1882. [from a mock obituary of English cricket after a great Australian victory]

Ashkenazi (ˌæʃkəˈnɑːzɪ) *n, pl* **Ashkenazim** (-zɪm). **1** (*modifier*) of or relating to the Jews of Germany and E Europe. **2** a Jew of German or E European descent. Cf. **Sephardi.** [C19: LHeb., from Heb. *Ashkenaz,* the son of Gomer (Genesis 10:3; I Chronicles 1:6)]

ashlar *or* **ashler** (ˈæʃlə) *n* **1** a square block of hewn stone for use in building. **2** a thin dressed stone with straight edges, used to face a wall. **3** masonry made of ashlar. [C14: from OF *aisselier* crossbeam, from *ais* board, from L *axis* axletree]

ashore Ⓣ (əˈʃɔː) *adv* **1** towards or onto land from the water. ◆ *adj* (*postpositive*), *adv* **2** on land: *a day ashore before sailing.*

ashram (ˈæʃrəm) *n* a religious retreat or community where a Hindu holy man lives. [from Sansk. *āśrama,* from *ā-* near + *śrama* religious exertion]

ashtray (ˈæʃˌtreɪ) *n* a receptacle for tobacco ash, cigarette butts, etc.

Ash Wednesday *n* the first day of Lent, named from the Christian custom of sprinkling ashes on penitents' heads.

ashy (ˈæʃɪ) *adj* **ashier, ashiest. 1** of a pale greyish colour; ashen. **2** consisting of, covered with, or resembling ash.

Asian (ˈeɪʃən, ˈeɪʒən) *adj* **1** of or relating to Asia, the largest of the continents, or to any of its people or languages. **2** *Brit.* of or relating to natives of the Indian subcontinent or their descendants, esp. when living in Britain. ◆ *n* **3** a native or inhabitant of Asia or a descendant of one. **4** *Brit.* a native of the Indian subcontinent or a descendant of one.

> **USAGE NOTE** The use of *Asian* or *Asiatic* as a noun can be offensive and should be avoided.

Asian flu *n* a type of influenza caused by a virus which apparently originated in China in 1957.

Asian pear *n* a variety of pear, apple-shaped with crisp juicy flesh.

Asiatic (ˌeɪʃɪˈætɪk, -zɪ-) *n, adj* another word for **Asian.**

> **USAGE NOTE** See at **Asian.**

Asiatic cholera *n* another name for **cholera.**

aside Ⓣ (əˈsaɪd) *adv* **1** on or to one side. **2** out of hearing; in or into seclusion. **3** away from oneself: *he threw the book aside.* **4** out of mind or consideration: *he put aside all fears.* **5** in or into reserve: *to put aside money for old age.* ◆ *n* **6** something spoken by an actor, intended to be heard by the audience, but not by the others on stage. **7** any confidential statement spoken in undertones. **8** an incidental remark, note, etc.

A-side *n* the side of a gramophone record regarded as more important.

asinine Ⓣ (ˈæsɪˌnaɪn) *adj* **1** obstinate or stupid. **2** resembling an ass. [C16: from L *asinīnus,* from *asinus* ASS[1]]
▸**ˈasiˌninely** *adv* ▸**asininity** (ˌæsɪˈnɪnɪtɪ) *n*

ASIO *abbrev. for* Australian Security Intelligence Organization.

ask Ⓣ (ɑːsk) *vb* **1** (often foll. by *about*) to put a question (to); request an answer (from). **2** (*tr*) to inquire about: *she asked the way.* **3** (*tr*) to direct or put (a question). **4** (*may take a clause as object or an infinitive;* often foll. by *for*) to make a request or demand: *they asked for a deposit.* **5** (*tr*) to demand or expect (esp. in **ask a lot of, ask too much of**). **6** (*tr*) Also: **ask out, ask over.** to request (a person) politely to come or go to a place: *he asked her to the party.* [OE *āscian*]
▸**ˈasker** *n*

ask after *vb* (*prep*) to make inquiries about the health of (someone): *he asked after her mother.*

askance Ⓣ (əˈskæns) *or* **askant** (əˈskænt) *adv* **1** with an oblique glance. **2** with doubt or mistrust. [C16: from ?]

askew Ⓣ (əˈskjuː) *adv, adj* at an oblique angle; towards one side; awry.

ask for *vb* (*prep*) **1** to try to obtain by requesting. **2** (*intr*) *Inf.* to behave in a provocative manner that is regarded as inviting (trouble, etc.): *you're asking for it.*

asking price *n* the price suggested by a seller but usually considered to be subject to bargaining.

aslant Ⓣ (əˈslɑːnt) *adv* **1** at a slant. ◆ *prep* **2** at a slant across or athwart.

THESAURUS

asceticism *n* **2 = self-denial**, abstemiousness, abstinence, austerity, celibacy, frugality, harshness, mortification of the flesh, plainness, puritanism, rigorousness, rigour, self-abnegation, self-discipline, self-mortification

ascribe *vb* **1 = attribute**, assign, charge, credit, impute, put down, refer, set down

asexual *adj* **1 = sexless**, neuter, neutral

asexuality *n* **1 = sexlessness**, neutrality

ashamed *adj* **1, 2 = embarrassed**, abashed, bashful, blushing, chagrined, conscience-stricken, crestfallen, discomfited, distressed, guilty, humbled, humiliated, mortified, prudish, reluctant, remorseful, shamefaced, sheepish, shy, sorry
Antonyms *adj* gratified, honoured, pleased, proud, satisfied, unashamed, vain

ashen[1] *adj* **1, 3 = pale**, anaemic, ashy, colourless, grey, leaden, like death warmed up (*inf.*), livid, pallid, pasty, wan, white
Antonyms *adj* blooming, blushing, florid, flushed, glowing, radiant, red, reddish, rosy, rosy-cheeked, rubicund, ruddy

ashore *adv* **1 = on land**, aground, landwards, on dry land, on the beach, on the shore, shorewards, to the shore

aside *adv* **1 = to one side**, alone, alongside, apart, away, beside, in isolation, in reserve, on one side, out of mind, out of the way, privately, separately, to the side ◆ *n* **8 = interpolation**, interposition, parenthesis **8 = digression**, departure, excursion, excursus, tangent

asinine *adj* **1 = stupid**, braindead (*inf.*), brainless, daft (*inf.*), dunderheaded, fatuous, foolish, goofy (*inf.*), gormless (*Brit. inf.*), halfwitted, idiotic, imbecile, imbecilic, inane, moronic, senseless, silly, thickheaded, thick-witted
Antonyms *adj* brainy (*inf.*), bright, clever, intelligent, quick-witted, sage, sane, sensible, sharp, smart, wise

asininity *n* **1 = stupidity**, brainlessness, cloddishness, daftness, doltishness, fatuity, fatuousness, foolishness (*inf.*), goofiness, gormlessness (*Brit. inf.*), idiocy, imbecility, inanity, moronism, moronity, oafishness, senselessness, silliness, thickheadedness, thick-wittedness
Antonyms *adj* braininess (*inf.*), brightness, cleverness, intelligence, keenness, quickness, quick-wittedness, sagacity, sageness, saneness, sensibleness, sharpness, sharp-wittedness, smartness, wisdom

ask *vb* **1-3 = inquire**, interrogate, query, question, quiz **4 = request**, appeal, apply, beg, beseech, claim, crave, demand, entreat, implore, petition, plead, pray, seek, solicit, sue, supplicate **6 = invite**, bid, summon
Antonyms *vb* ≠ **inquire:** answer, reply, respond

askance *adv As in* **look askance at 1 = out of the corner of one's eye**, awry, indirectly, obliquely, sideways, with a side glance **2 = suspiciously**, disapprovingly, distrustfully, doubtfully, dubiously, mistrustfully, sceptically

askew *adv* **= crookedly**, aslant, awry, obliquely, off-centre, to one side ◆ *adj* **= crooked**, awry, cockeyed (*inf.*), lopsided, oblique, off-centre, skewwhiff (*Brit. inf.*)
Antonyms *adv* ≠ **crookedly:** aligned, evenly, in line, level, right, squarely, straight, true ◆ *adj* ≠ **crooked:** aligned, even, in line, level, right, square, straight, true

aslant *adv* **1 = at a slant**, aslope, atilt, slantingly, slopingly ◆ *prep* **2 = across**, athwart

asleep 🅣 (əˈsliːp) *adj (postpositive)* **1** in or into a state of sleep. **2** in or into a dormant or inactive state. **3** (of limbs) numb; lacking sensation. **4** *Euphemistic.* dead.

ASLEF (ˈæzlɛf) *n* (in Britain) *acronym for* Associated Society of Locomotive Engineers and Firemen.

AS level *n Brit.* **1a** an advanced level of a subject taken for the General Certificate of Education, with a smaller course content than an A level. **1b** (*as modifier*): *AS-level English.* **2** a pass in a subject at AS level: *I've got three AS levels.*

ASM *abbrev. for:* **1** air-to-surface missile. **2** *Theatre.* assistant stage manager.

asocial (eɪˈsəʊʃəl) *adj* **1** avoiding contact. **2** unconcerned about the welfare of others. **3** hostile to society.

asp (æsp) *n* **1** the venomous snake that caused the death of Cleopatra. **2** Also called: **asp viper.** a viper that occurs in S Europe and is very similar to but smaller than the adder. **3 horned asp.** another name for **horned viper.** [C15: from L *aspis,* from Gk]

asparagus (əˈspærəgəs) *n* **1** a plant of the lily family, having small scaly or needle-like leaves. **2** the succulent young shoots, which may be cooked and eaten. **3 asparagus fern.** a fernlike species of asparagus, native to southern Africa. [C15: from L, from Gk *asparagos,* from ?]

aspartame (əˈspɑːˌteɪm) *n* an artificial sweetener produced from a nonessential amino acid. [C20: from *aspart(ic acid)* + *(phenyl)a(lanine) m(ethyl) e(ster)*]

aspect 🅣 (ˈæspɛkt) *n* **1** appearance to the eye; visual effect. **2** a distinct feature or element in a problem, situation, etc.; facet. **3** the way in which a problem, idea, etc., may be considered. **4** a facial expression: *a severe aspect.* **5** a position facing a particular direction: *the southern aspect of a house.* **6** a view in a certain direction. **7** *Astrol.* any of several specific angular distances between two planets. **8** *Grammar.* a category of verbal inflections that expresses such features as the continuity, repetition, or completedness of the action described. [C14: from L *aspectus* a sight, from *ad-* to, at + *specere* to look]

aspect ratio *n* **1** the ratio of width to height of a picture on a television or cinema screen. **2** *Aeronautics.* the ratio of the span of a wing to its mean chord.

aspen (ˈæspən) *n* a kind of poplar tree in which the leaves are attached to the stem by long flattened stalks so that they quiver in the wind. [OE *æspe*]

Asperger's syndrome (ˈæspəgəz) *n* a form of autism in which the sufferer has limited but obsessive interests and has difficulty relating to other people. [C20: after Hans *Asperger* (20th cent.), Austrian physician who first described it]

asperity 🅣 (æˈspɛrɪtɪ) *n, pl* **asperities. 1** roughness or sharpness of temper. **2** roughness or harshness of a surface, sound, etc. **3** *Physics.* the elongated compressed region of contact between two surfaces caused by the normal force. [C16: from L *asperitās,* from *asper* rough]

asperse (əˈspɜːs) *vb* **asperses, aspersing, aspersed.** (*tr*) to spread false rumours about; defame. [C15: from L *aspersus,* from *aspergere* to sprinkle]
▸**asˈperser** *n* ▸**asˈpersive** *adj*

aspersion 🅣 (əˈspɜːʃən) *n* **1** a disparaging or malicious remark (esp. in **cast aspersions (on)**). **2** the act of defaming.

asphalt (ˈæsfælt) *n* **1** any of several black semisolid substances composed of bitumen and inert mineral matter. They occur naturally and as a residue from petroleum distillation. **2** a mixture of this substance with gravel, used in road-surfacing and roofing materials. **3** (*modifier*) containing or surfaced with asphalt. ◆ *vb* **4** (*tr*) to cover with asphalt. [C14: from LL *aspaltus,* from Gk *asphaltos,* prob. from A-[1] + *sphallein* to cause to fall; referring to its use as a binding agent]
▸**asˈphaltic** *adj*

asphodel (ˈæsfəˌdɛl) *n* **1** any of various S European plants of the lily family having clusters of white or yellow flowers. **2** an unidentified flower of Greek legend said to cover the Elysian fields. [C16: from L *asphodelus,* from Gk *asphodelos,* from ?]

asphyxia (æsˈfɪksɪə) *n* lack of oxygen in the blood due to restricted respiration; suffocation. [C18: from NL, from Gk *asphuxia* a stopping of the pulse, from A-[1] + *sphuxis* pulse, from *sphuzein* to throb]
▸**asˈphyxial** *adj* ▸**asˈphyxiant** *adj*

asphyxiate 🅣 (æsˈfɪksɪˌeɪt) *vb* **asphyxiates, asphyxiating, asphyxiated.** to cause asphyxia in or undergo asphyxia; smother; suffocate.
▸**asˌphyxiˈation** *n* ▸**asˈphyxiˌator** *n*

aspic (ˈæspɪk) *n* a savoury jelly based on meat or fish stock, used as a relish or as a mould for meat, vegetables, etc. [C18: from F: aspic (jelly), asp]

aspidistra (ˌæspɪˈdɪstrə) *n* a popular house plant of the lily family with long tough evergreen leaves. [C19: from NL, from Gk *aspis* shield, on the model of *Tupistra,* genus of liliaceous plants]

aspirant 🅣 (ˈæspɪrənt) *n* **1** a person who aspires, as to a high position. ◆ *adj* **2** aspiring.

aspirate *vb* (ˈæspɪˌreɪt), **aspirates, aspirating, aspirated.** (*tr*) **1** *Phonetics.* **1a** to articulate (a stop) with some force, so that breath escapes audibly. **1b** to pronounce (a word or syllable) with an initial *h.* **2** to remove by inhalation or suction, esp. to suck (air or fluid) from a body cavity. **3** to supply air to (an internal-combustion engine). ◆ *n* (ˈæspɪrɪt). **4** *Phonetics.* **4a** a stop pronounced with an audible release of breath. **4b** the glottal fricative represented in English and several other languages as *h.* ◆ *adj* (ˈæspɪrɪt). **5** *Phonetics.* (of a stop) pronounced with a forceful expulsion of breath.

aspiration 🅣 (ˌæspɪˈreɪʃən) *n* **1** strong desire to achieve something, such as success. **2** the aim of such desire. **3** the act of breathing. **4** *Phonetics.* **4a** the pronunciation of an aspirated consonant. **4b** an aspirated consonant. **5** *Med.* **5a** the sucking of fluid or foreign matter into the air passages of the body. **5b** the removal of air or fluid from the body by suction.
▸**ˌaspiˈrational** *adj* ▸**aspiratory** (əˈspaɪrətərɪ) *adj*

aspirator (ˈæspɪˌreɪtə) *n* a device employing suction, such as a jet pump or one for removing fluids from a body cavity.

aspire 🅣 (əˈspaɪə) *vb* **aspires, aspiring, aspired.** (*intr*) **1** (usually foll. by *to* or *after*) to yearn (for), desire, or hope (to do or be something): *to aspire to be a great leader.* **2** to rise to a great height. [C15: from L *aspīrāre* to breathe upon, from *spīrāre* to breathe]
▸**asˈpiring** *adj*

aspirin (ˈæsprɪn) *n, pl* **aspirin** *or* **aspirins. 1** a white crystalline compound widely used in the form of tablets to relieve pain, fever, and colds. Chemical name: **acetylsalicylic acid. 2** a tablet of aspirin. [C19: from G, from *A(cetyl)* + *Spir(säure)* spiraeic acid (modern salicylic acid) + -IN]

Aspirin (ˈæsprɪn) *n* (in Canada) a trademark for **aspirin.**

asquint (əˈskwɪnt) *adv, adj* (*postpositive*) with a glance from the corner of the eye, esp. a furtive one. [C13: ?from Du. *schuinte* slant, from ?]

ass[1] 🅣 (æs) *n* **1** a mammal related to the horse. It is hardy and sure-footed, having longer ears than the horse. **2** (not in technical use) the donkey. **3** a foolish or ridiculously pompous person. [OE *assa,* prob. from OIrish *asan,* from L *asinus;* rel. to Gk *onos* ass]

ass[2] (æs) *n* the usual US and Canad. word for **arse.** [OE *ærs*]

assagai (ˈæsəˌgaɪ) *n, pl* **assagais.** a variant spelling of **assegai.**

assai (æˈsaɪ) *adv Music.* (usually preceded by a musical direction) very: *allegro assai.* [It.: enough]

assail 🅣 (əˈseɪl) *vb* (*tr*) **1** to attack violently; assault. **2** to criticize or ridicule vehemently. **3** to beset or disturb: *his mind was assailed by doubts.* **4** to encounter with the intention of mastering. [C13: from OF *asalir,* from L *assilīre,* from *salīre* to leap]
▸**asˈsailable** *adj* ▸**asˈsailer** *n*

assailant 🅣 (əˈseɪlənt) *n* a person who attacks another, either physically or verbally.

assassin 🅣 (əˈsæsɪn) *n* a murderer, esp. one who kills a prominent political figure. [C16: from Med. L *assassīnus,* from Ar. *hashshāshīn,* pl. of *hashshāsh* one who eats HASHISH]

assassinate 🅣 (əˈsæsɪˌneɪt) *vb* **assassinates, assassinating, assassinated.** (*tr*) **1** to murder (a political figure). **2** to ruin or harm (a person's reputation, etc.) by slander.
▸**asˌsassiˈnation** *n*

assault 🅣 (əˈsɔːlt) *n* **1** a violent attack, either physical or verbal. **2** *Law.*

THESAURUS

asleep *adj* **1** = **sleeping,** crashed out, dead to the world (*inf.*), dormant, dozing, fast asleep, napping, out for the count, slumbering, snoozing (*inf.*), sound asleep

aspect *n* **1, 4** = **appearance,** air, attitude, bearing, condition, countenance, demeanour, expression, look, manner, mien (*literary*) **2** = **feature,** angle, facet, side **3, 6** = **position,** bearing, direction, exposure, outlook, point of view, prospect, scene, situation, view

asperity *n* **1** = **sharpness,** acerbity, acrimony, bitterness, churlishness, crabbedness, crossness, harshness, irascibility, irritability, moroseness, peevishness, ruggedness, severity, sourness, sullenness

aspersion *n* **1** *As in* **cast aspersions on** = **slander,** abuse, calumny, censure, character assassination, defamation, denigration, detraction, disparagement, obloquy, reproach, slur, smear, traducement, vilification, vituperation

asphyxiate *vb* = **suffocate,** choke, smother, stifle, strangle, strangulate, throttle

asphyxiation *n* = **suffocation,** strangulation

aspirant *n* **1** = **candidate,** applicant, aspirer, hopeful, postulant, seeker, suitor ◆ *adj* **2** = **hopeful,** ambitious, aspiring, eager, endeavouring, longing, striving, wishful

aspiration *n* **1, 2** = **aim,** ambition, craving, desire, dream, eagerness, endeavour, goal, hankering, Holy Grail (*inf.*), hope, longing, object, objective, wish, yearning

aspire *vb* **1** = **aim,** be ambitious, be eager, crave, desire, dream, hanker, hope, long, pursue, seek, set one's heart on, wish, yearn

aspiring *adj* **1** = **hopeful,** ambitious, aspirant, eager, endeavouring, longing, striving, wannabe (*inf.*), wishful, would-be

ass[1] *n* **2** = **donkey,** jennet, moke (*sl.*) **3** = **fool,** airhead, berk (*Brit. sl.*), blockhead, coot, daftie (*inf.*), dolt, dope (*inf.*), dunce, fathead (*inf.*), geek (*sl.*), halfwit, idiot, jackass, jerk (*sl., chiefly US & Canad.*), nerd *or* nurd (*sl.*), nincompoop, ninny, nitwit (*inf.*), numbskull *or* numskull, oaf, pillock (*Brit. sl.*), prat (*sl.*), simpleton, twerp *or* twirp (*inf.*), twit (*inf., chiefly Brit.*), wally (*sl.*)

assail *vb* **1** = **attack,** assault, belabour, beset, charge, encounter, fall upon, invade, lay into (*inf.*), maltreat, set about, set upon **2** = **criticize,** abuse, berate, blast, go for the jugular, impugn, lambast(e), malign, put down, revile, tear into (*inf.*), vilify

assailant *n* = **attacker,** aggressor, assailer, assaulter, invader

assassin *n* = **murderer,** eliminator (*sl.*), executioner, hatchet man, hit man (*sl.*), killer, liquidator, slayer

assassinate *vb* **1** = **murder,** blow away (*sl., chiefly US*), eliminate (*sl.*), hit (*sl.*), kill, liquidate, slay, take out (*sl.*)

assassination *n* **1** = **murder,** elimination (*sl.*), hit (*sl.*), killing, liquidation, purge, removal (*euphemistic*), slaying

assault *n* **1** = **attack,** aggression, campaign, charge, incursion, inroad, invasion, offensive, onset, onslaught, storm, storming, strike ◆ *vb* **5**

an act that threatens violence to another. **3a** the culmination of a military attack. **3b** (*as modifier*): *assault troops.* **4** rape or attempted rape. ◆ *vb* (*tr*) **5** to make an assault upon. **6** to rape or attempt to rape. [C13: from OF *asaut,* from Vulgar L, from *assalīre* (unattested) to leap upon; see ASSAIL]
▸**as'saultive** *adj*

assault and battery *n Criminal law.* a threat of attack to another person followed by actual attack.

assault course *n* an obstacle course designed to give soldiers practice in negotiating hazards.

assay ❶ *vb* (ə'seɪ). **1** to subject (a substance, such as silver or gold) to chemical analysis, as in the determination of the amount of impurity. **2** (*tr*) to attempt (something or to do something). ◆ *n* (ə'seɪ, 'æseɪ). **3a** an analysis, esp. a determination of the amount of metal in an ore or the amounts of impurities in a precious metal. **3b** (*as modifier*): *an assay office.* **4** a substance undergoing an analysis. **5** a written report on the results of an analysis. **6** a test. [C14: from OF *assai;* see ESSAY]
▸**as'sayer** *n*

assegai *or* **assagai** ('æsə,gaɪ) *n, pl* **assegais** *or* **assagais. 1** a southern African tree, the wood of which is used for making spears. **2** a sharp light spear. [C17: from Port. *azagaia,* from Ar. *az zaghāyah,* from *al* the + *zaghāyah* assegai, from Berber]

assemblage ❶ (ə'semblɪdʒ) *n* **1** a number of things or persons assembled together. **2** the act of assembling or the state of being assembled. **3** (,æsəm'blɑːʒ). a three-dimensional work of art that combines various objects.

assemble ❶ (ə'semb^{ə}l) *vb* **assembles, assembling, assembled. 1** to come or bring together; collect or congregate. **2** to fit or join together (the parts of something, such as a machine). [C13: from OF *assembler,* from Vulgar L *assimulāre* (unattested) to bring together, from L *simul* together]

assembler (ə'semblə) *n* **1** a person or thing that assembles. **2** a computer program that converts a program written in assembly language into machine code. Cf. **compiler. 3** another name for **assembly language.**

assembly ❶ (ə'semblɪ) *n, pl* **assemblies. 1** a number of people gathered together, esp. for a formal meeting held at regular intervals. **2** the act of assembling or the state of being assembled. **3** the process of putting together a number of parts to make a machine. **4** *Mil.* a signal for personnel to assemble.

Assembly (ə'semblɪ) *n, pl* **Assemblies. 1** the lower chamber in various state legislatures, esp. in Australia and America. See also **House of Assembly, legislative assembly. 2** *NZ.* short for **General Assembly.**

assembly language *n Computing.* a low-level programming language that allows a programmer complete control of the machine code to be generated.

assembly line *n* a sequence of machines, tools, operations, workers, etc., in a factory, arranged so that at each stage a further process is carried out.

assent ❶ (ə'sent) *n* **1** agreement, as to a statement, proposal, etc. **2** compliance. ◆ *vb* (*intr; usually foll. by to*) **3** to agree or express agreement. [C13: from OF *assenter,* from L *assentīrī,* from *sentīre* to think]

assert ❶ (ə'sɜːt) *vb* (*tr*) **1** to insist upon (rights, etc.). **2** (*may take a clause as object*) to state to be true; declare. **3** to put (oneself) forward in an insistent manner. [C17: from L *asserere* to join to oneself, from *serere* to join]
▸**as'serter** *or* **as'sertor** *n*

assertion ❶ (ə'sɜːʃən) *n* **1** a positive statement, usually made without evidence. **2** the act of asserting.

assertion sign *n* a sign 0 used in symbolic logic to introduce the conclusion of a valid argument: often read as "therefore."

assertive ❶ (ə'sɜːtɪv) *adj* **1** confident and direct in dealing with others. **2** given to making assertions; dogmatic or aggressive.
▸**as'sertively** *adv* ▸**as'sertiveness** *n*

assess ❶ (ə'ses) *vb* (*tr*) **1** to evaluate. **2** (foll. by *at*) to estimate the value of (income, property, etc.) for taxation purposes. **3** to determine the amount of (a fine, tax, etc.). **4** to impose a tax, fine, etc., on (a person or property). [C15: from OF *assesser,* from L *assidēre* to sit beside, from *sedēre* to sit]
▸**as'sessable** *adj*

assessment ❶ (ə'sesmənt) *n* **1** the act of assessing, esp. (in Britain) the evaluation of a student's achievement on a course. **2** an amount determined as payable. **3** a valuation set on taxable property, etc. **4** evaluation.

assessment tests *pl n Brit. education.* nationally standardized tests for pupil assessment based on attainment targets in the National Curriculum. Formal name: **standard assessment tasks, SATs.**

assessor (ə'sesə) *n* **1** a person who evaluates the merits of something. **2** a person who values property for taxation. **3** a person who estimates the value of damage to property for insurance purposes. **4** a person with technical expertise called in to advise a court.
▸**assessorial** (,æse'sɔːrɪəl) *adj*

asset ❶ ('æset) *n* anything valuable or useful. [C19: back formation from ASSETS]

assets ❶ ('æsets) *pl n* **1** *Accounting.* the property and claims against debtors that are shown balanced against liabilities. **2** *Law.* the property available to an executor for settling a deceased person's estate. **3** any property owned by a person or firm. [C16: from OF *asez* enough, from Vulgar L *ad satis* (unattested) from L *ad* up to + *satis* enough]

asset-stripping *n Commerce.* the practice of taking over a failing company at a low price and then selling the assets piecemeal.
▸**'asset-,stripper** *n*

asset value *n* the value of a share in a company calculated by dividing the difference between the total of its assets and its liabilities by the number of ordinary shares issued.

asseverate (ə'sevə,reɪt) *vb* **asseverates, asseverating, asseverated.** (*tr*) to declare solemnly. [C18: from L *asseverāre* to do (something) earnestly, from *sevērus* SEVERE]
▸**as,sever'ation** *n*

assibilate (ə'sɪbɪ,leɪt) *vb* **assibilates, assibilating, assibilated.** (*tr*) *Phonetics.* to pronounce (a speech sound) with or as a sibilant. [C19: from LL *assībilāre* to hiss at, from *sībilāre* to hiss]
▸**as,sibi'lation** *n*

assiduity (,æsɪ'djuːɪtɪ) *n, pl* **assiduities. 1** constant and close application. **2** (*often pl*) devoted attention.

assiduous ❶ (ə'sɪdjuəs) *adj* **1** hard-working; persevering. **2** undertaken

THESAURUS

= **attack**, assail, belabour, beset, charge, fall upon, invade, lay into (*inf.*), set about, set upon, storm, strike at
Antonyms *n* ≠ **attack:** defence, protection, resistance ◆ *vb* ≠ **attack:** defend, protect, resist

assay *vb* **1** = **analyse**, appraise, assess, evaluate, examine, inspect, investigate, prove, test, try, weigh ◆ *n* **3, 6** = **analysis**, examination, inspection, investigation, test, trial

assemblage *n* **1, 2** = **group**, accumulation, aggregation, assembly, body, collection, company, conclave, congregation, convocation, crowd, flock, gathering, mass, meeting, multitude, rally, throng

assemble *vb* **1** = **gather**, accumulate, amass, bring together, call together, collect, come together, congregate, convene, convoke, flock, foregather, marshal, meet, muster, rally, round up, summon **2** = **put together**, build up, connect, construct, erect, fabricate, fit together, join, make, manufacture, piece together, set up
Antonyms *vb* ≠ **gather:** adjourn, break up (*inf.*), disband, dismiss, disperse, distribute, scatter ≠ **put together:** disassemble, divide, take apart

assembly *n* **1** = **gathering**, accumulation, aggregation, assemblage, body, collection, company, conclave, conference, congregation, congress, convention, convocation, council, crowd, diet, flock, group, house, mass, meeting, multitude, rally, synod, throng **2, 3** = **putting together**, building up, connecting, construction, erection, fabrication, fitting together, joining, manufacture, piecing together, setting up

assent *n* **1, 2** = **agreement**, acceptance, accession, accord, acquiescence, approval, compliance, concurrence, consent, permission, sanction ◆ *vb* **3** = **agree**, accede, accept, acquiesce, allow, approve, comply, concur, consent, fall in with, go along with, grant, permit, sanction, subscribe
Antonyms *n* ≠ **agreement:** denial, disagreement, disapproval, dissension, dissent, objection, refusal ◆ *vb* ≠ **agree:** deny, differ, disagree, dissent, object, protest, rebut, reject, retract

assert *vb* **1** = **insist upon**, claim, defend, press, put forward, stand up for, stress, uphold, vindicate **2** = **state**, affirm, allege, asseverate, attest, aver, avouch (*arch.*), avow, contend, declare, maintain, predicate, profess, pronounce, swear **3** = **be forceful**, exert one's influence, make one's presence felt, put oneself forward, put one's foot down (*inf.*)
Antonyms *vb* ≠ **insist upon, state:** deny, disavow, disclaim, rebut, refute, retract

assertion *n* **1** = **statement**, affirmation, allegation, asseveration, attestation, avowal, claim, contention, declaration, predication, profession, pronouncement **2** = **insistence**, defence, maintenance, stressing, vindication

assertive *adj* **1, 2** = **confident**, aggressive, can-do, decided, decisive, demanding, dogmatic, domineering, emphatic, feisty (*inf., chiefly US & Canad.*), firm, forceful, forward, insistent, in-your-face (*Brit. sl.*), overbearing, positive, pushy (*inf.*), self-assured, strong-willed
Antonyms *adj* backward, bashful, diffident, hesitant, insecure, meek, modest, reserved, retiring, self-conscious, self-effacing, sheepish, shrinking, shy, timid, timorous, unassertive, unobtrusive

assertiveness *n* **1, 2** = **confidence**, aggressiveness, decidedness, decisiveness, dogmatism, domineeringness, firmness, forcefulness, forwardness, insistence, positiveness, pushiness (*inf.*), self-assuredness
Antonyms *n* backwardness, bashfulness, diffidence, hesitancy, insecurity, meekness, modesty, reservedness, self-consciousness, self-effacement, sheepishness, shyness, tentativeness, timidity, timidness, timorousness

assess *vb* **1** = **judge**, appraise, compute, determine, estimate, evaluate, eye up, fix, gauge, rate, size up (*inf.*), value, weigh **2-4** = **evaluate**, demand, fix, impose, levy, rate, tax, value

assessable *adj* **1-4** = **measurable**, appraisable, computable, determinable, estimable (*rare*), gaugeable *or* gageable, judgeable, ratable *or* rateable

assessment *n* **1** = **judgment**, appraisal, computation, determination, estimate, estimation, evaluation, rating, valuation **2-4** = **evaluation**, charge, demand, duty, fee, impost, levy, rate, rating, tariff, tax, taxation, toll, valuation

asset *n* = **benefit**, ace in the hole, ace up one's sleeve, advantage, aid, blessing, boon, feather in one's cap, help, resource, service
Antonyms *n* albatross, burden, disadvantage, drag, drawback, encumbrance, handicap, hindrance, impediment, liability, millstone, minus (*inf.*), nuisance

assets *pl n* **1, 3** = **property**, capital, estate, funds, goods, holdings, means, money, possessions, reserves, resources, valuables, wealth

assiduous *adj* **1** = **diligent**, attentive, constant, hard-working, indefatigable, industrious, labo-

with perseverance and care. [C16: from L, from *assidēre* to sit beside, from *sedēre* to sit]
▸**as'siduousness** *n*

assign ⓘ (əˈsaɪn) *vb* (*mainly tr*) **1** to select for and appoint to a post, etc. **2** to give out or allot (a task, problem, etc.). **3** to set apart (a place, person, time, etc.) for a particular function or event: *to assign a day for the meeting.* **4** to attribute to a specified cause, origin, or source. **5** to transfer (one's right, interest, or title to property) to someone else. ◆ *n* **6** *Law.* a person to whom property is assigned; assignee. [C14: from OF, from L *assignāre*, from *signāre* to mark out]
▸**as'signable** *adj* ▸**as'signer** *or* ˌ**assign'or** *n*

assignation ⓘ (ˌæsɪgˈneɪʃən) *n* **1** a secret or forbidden arrangement to meet, esp. one between lovers. **2** the act of assigning; assignment. [C14: from OF, from L *assignātiō* a marking out]

assignee (ˌæsaɪˈniː) *n Law.* a person to whom some right, interest, or property is transferred.

assignment ⓘ (əˈsaɪnmənt) *n* **1** something that has been assigned, such as a mission or task. **2** a position or post to which a person is assigned. **3** the act of assigning or state of being assigned. **4** *Law.* **4a** the transfer to another of a right, interest, or title to property. **4b** the document effecting such a transfer.

assimilate ⓘ (əˈsɪmɪˌleɪt) *vb* **assimilates, assimilating, assimilated. 1** (*tr*) to learn (information, etc.) and understand it thoroughly. **2** (*tr*) to absorb (food). **3** (*intr*) to become absorbed, incorporated, or learned and understood. **4** (usually foll. by *into* or *with*) to adjust or become adjusted: *the new immigrants assimilated easily.* **5** (usually foll. by *to* or *with*) to become or cause to become similar. **6** (usually foll. by *to*) *Phonetics.* to change (a consonant) or (of a consonant) to be changed into another under the influence of one adjacent to it. [C15: from L *assimilāre* to make one thing like another, from *similis* like, SIMILAR]
▸**as'similable** *adj* ▸**asˌsimi'lation** *n* ▸**as'similative** *or* **as'similatory** *adj* ▸**as'simiˌlator** *n*

assist ⓘ (əˈsɪst) *vb* **1** to give help or support to (a person, cause, etc.). **2** to work or act as an assistant or subordinate to (another). ◆ *n* **3** *US.* the act of helping. [C15: from F, from L *assistere* to stand by, from *sistere* to cause to stand, from *stāre* to stand]
▸**as'sister** *n*

assistance ⓘ (əˈsɪstəns) *n* **1** help; support. **2** the act of assisting. **3** *Brit. inf.* See **national assistance.**

assistant ⓘ (əˈsɪstənt) *n* **1a** a person who assists, esp. in a subordinate position. **1b** (*as modifier*): *assistant manager.* **2** See **shop assistant.**

assistant referee *n Soccer.* the official name for **linesman** (sense 1).

assize (əˈsaɪz) *n Scots Law.* **a** trial by a jury. **b** a jury. [C13: from OF *assise* session, from *asseoir* to seat, from L *assidēre* to sit beside]

assizes (əˈsaɪzɪz) *pl n* (formerly in England and Wales) the sessions of the principal court in each county, exercising civil and criminal jurisdiction: replaced in 1971 by crown courts.

assoc. *abbrev. for:* **1** associate(d). **2** association.

associate ⓘ *vb* (əˈsəʊʃɪˌeɪt, -sɪ-). (usually foll. by *with*) **associates, associating, associated. 1** (*tr*) to link or connect in the mind or imagination. **2** (*intr*) to mix socially: *to associate with writers.* **3** (*intr*) to form or join an association, group, etc. **4** (*tr; usually passive*) to consider in conjunction: *rainfall is associated with humidity.* **5** (*tr*) to bring (a person, esp. oneself) into friendship, partnership, etc. **6** (*tr; often passive*) to express agreement (with): *Bertrand Russell was associated with the CND movement.* ◆ *n* (əˈsəʊʃɪɪt, -sɪ-). **7** a person joined with another or others in an enterprise, business, etc. **8** a companion or friend. **9** something that usually accompanies another thing. **10** a person having a subordinate position in or admitted to only partial membership of an institution, association, etc. ◆ *adj* (əˈsəʊʃɪɪt, -sɪ-). (*prenominal*) **11** joined with another or others in an enterprise, business, etc.: *an associate director.* **12** having partial rights or subordinate status: *an associate member.* **13** accompanying; concomitant. [C14: from L *associāre* to ally with, from *sociāre* to join, from *socius* an ally]
▸**as'sociable** *adj* ▸**as'sociˌator** *n* ▸**as'sociateˌship** *n*

association ⓘ (əˌsəʊsɪˈeɪʃən, -ʃɪ-) *n* **1** a group of people having a common purpose or interest; a society or club. **2** the act of associating or the state of being associated. **3** friendship or companionship: *their association will not last.* **4** a mental connection of ideas, feelings, or sensations. **5** *Chem.* the formation of groups of molecules and ions held together by weak chemical bonds. **6** *Ecology.* a group of similar plants that grow in a uniform environment.

association football *n* a more formal name for **soccer.**

associative (əˈsəʊʃɪətɪv, -sɪ-) *adj* **1** of, relating to, or causing association or union. **2** *Maths, logic.* **2a** of an operation, such as multiplication or addition, in which the answer is the same regardless of the way in which the elements are grouped: $(2 \times 3) \times 4 = 2 \times (3 \times 4)$. **2b** referring to this property: *the associative laws of arithmetic.*

assonance (ˈæsənəns) *n* **1** the use of the same vowel sound with different consonants or the same consonant with different vowels, as in a line of verse. Examples are *time* and *light* or *mystery* and *mastery.* **2** partial correspondence. [C18: from F, from L *assonāre* to sound, from *sonāre* to sound]
▸**'assonant** *adj, n*

assort (əˈsɔːt) *vb* **1** (*tr*) to arrange or distribute into groups of the same type; classify. **2** (*intr;* usually foll. by *with*) to fit or fall into a class or group. **3** (*tr*) to supply with an assortment of merchandise. **4** (*tr*) to put in the same category as others. [C15: from OF *assorter*, from *sorte* SORT]
▸**as'sortative** *adj*

assorted ⓘ (əˈsɔːtɪd) *adj* **1** consisting of various kinds mixed together. **2** classified: *assorted categories.* **3** matched (esp. in **well-assorted, ill-assorted**).

assortment ⓘ (əˈsɔːtmənt) *n* **1** a collection or group of various things or sorts. **2** the act of assorting.

ASSR (formerly) *abbrev. for* Autonomous Soviet Socialist Republic.

asst *abbrev. for* assistant.

assuage ⓘ (əˈsweɪdʒ) *vb* **assuages, assuaging, assuaged.** (*tr*) **1** to soothe, moderate, or relieve (grief, pain, etc.). **2** to give relief to (thirst, etc.). **3** to pacify; calm. [C14: from OF, from Vulgar L *assuāviāre* (unattested) to sweeten, from L *suāvis* pleasant]
▸**as'suagement** *n* ▸**as'suager** *n*

assume ⓘ (əˈsjuːm) *vb* **assumes, assuming, assumed.** (*tr*) **1** (*may take a clause as object*) to take for granted; suppose. **2** to undertake or take on or over (a position, responsibility, etc.): *to assume office.* **3** to pretend to; feign: *he assumed indifference.* **4** to take or put on; adopt: *the problem*

THESAURUS

rious, persevering, persistent, sedulous, steady, studious, unflagging, untiring, unwearied
Antonyms *adj* careless, idle, inattentive, indolent, lax, lazy, negligent, slack

assign *vb* **1 = select**, appoint, choose, delegate, designate, name, nominate **2 = give**, allocate, allot, apportion, consign, distribute, give out, grant, make over **3 = fix**, appoint, appropriate, determine, set apart, stipulate **4 = attribute**, accredit, ascribe, put down

assignation *n* **1 = secret meeting**, clandestine meeting, illicit meeting, rendezvous, tryst (*arch.*)

assignment *n* **1, 2 = task**, appointment, charge, commission, duty, job, mission, position, post, responsibility **3 = selection**, appointment, choice, delegation, designation, nomination

assimilate *vb* **1, 3 = learn**, absorb, digest, imbibe (*literary*), incorporate, ingest, take in **4, 5 = adjust**, acclimatize, accommodate, acculturate, accustom, adapt, become like, become similar, blend in, conform, fit, homogenize, intermix, mingle

assist *vb* **1, 2 = help**, abet, aid, back, benefit, boost, collaborate, cooperate, encourage, expedite, facilitate, further, give a leg up (*inf.*), lend a helping hand, promote, reinforce, relieve, second, serve, succour, support, sustain, work for, work with
Antonyms *vb* frustrate, hamper, handicap, hinder, hold back, hold up, impede, obstruct, resist, thwart, work against

assistance *n* **1 = help**, abetment, aid, backing, benefit, boost, collaboration, cooperation, encouragement, furtherance, helping hand, promotion, reinforcement, relief, service, succour, support, sustenance
Antonyms *n* hindrance, obstruction, opposition, resistance

assistant *n* **1 = helper**, abettor, accessory, accomplice, aide, aider, ally, associate, auxiliary, backer, coadjutor, collaborator, colleague, confederate, cooperator, helpmate, henchman, partner, protagonist, right-hand man, second, supporter

associate *vb* **1, 3 = connect**, affiliate, ally, combine, confederate, conjoin, correlate, couple, identify, join, league, link, lump together, mention in the same breath, mix, pair, relate, think of together, unite, yoke **2 = mix**, accompany, befriend, be friends, consort, fraternize, hang, hang about, hang out (*inf.*), hobnob, mingle, run around (*inf.*), socialize ◆ *n* **7 = partner**, collaborator, colleague, confederate, co-worker **8 = friend**, ally, companion, compeer, comrade, confrère, mate (*inf.*)
Antonyms *vb* ≠ **connect:** detach, disconnect, dissociate, distance, distinguish, divorce, isolate, segregate, separate, set apart ≠ **mix:** avoid, be alienated, be estranged, break off, part company

associated *adj* **1, 3 = connected**, affiliated, allied, bound, combined, confederated, correlated, involved, joined, leagued, linked, related, syndicated, tied, united, yoked

association *n* **1 = group**, affiliation, alliance, band, clique, club, coalition, combine, company, confederacy, confederation, cooperative, corporation, federation, fraternity, league, order, organization, partnership, society, syndicate, union **2, 4 = connection**, blend, bond, combination, concomitance, correlation, identification, joining, juxtaposition, linkage, linking, lumping together, mixing, mixture, pairing, relation, tie, union, yoking **3 = friendship**, affinity, companionship, comradeship, familiarity, fellowship, fraternization, intimacy, liaison, partnership, relations, relationship

assorted *adj* **1 = various**, different, diverse, diversified, heterogeneous, manifold, miscellaneous, mixed, motley, sundry, varied, variegated **2 = grouped**, arranged, arrayed, categorized, classified, disposed, filed, graded, matched, ranged, ranked, sorted, typed
Antonyms *adj* ≠ **various:** alike, homogeneous, identical, like, same, similar, uniform, unvaried

assortment *n* **1 = variety**, array, choice, collection, diversity, farrago, hotchpotch, jumble, medley, *mélange*, miscellany, mishmash, mixed bag (*inf.*), mixture, pick 'n' mix, potpourri, salmagundi, selection **2 = sorting**, arrangement, categorizing, classification, disposition, distribution, filing, grading, grouping, ranging, ranking, typing

assuage *vb* **1, 2 = relieve**, allay, alleviate, calm, ease, lessen, lighten, mitigate, moderate, palliate, quench, soothe, temper **3 = calm**, appease, lull, mollify, pacify, pour oil on troubled waters, quiet, relax, satisfy, soften, soothe, still, tranquillize
Antonyms *vb* ≠ **relieve:** aggravate, exacerbate, heighten, increase, intensify, worsen ≠ **calm:** aggravate, embitter, enrage, infuriate, madden, provoke

assume *vb* **1 = take for granted**, accept, believe, expect, fancy, guess (*inf., chiefly US & Canad.*), imagine, infer, presume, presuppose, suppose, surmise, suspect, think **2 = take on**, accept, ac-

assumed gigantic proportions. **5** to appropriate or usurp (power, control, etc.). [C15: from L *assūmere* to take up, from *sūmere* to take up, from SUB- + *emere* to take]
▸**as'sumable** *adj* ▸**as'sumer** *n*

assumed ❶ (ə'sju:md) *adj* **1** false; fictitious: *an assumed name.* **2** taken for granted. **3** usurped.

assuming (ə'sju:mɪŋ) *adj* **1** expecting too much; presumptuous. ◆ *conj* **2** (often foll. by *that*) if it is assumed or taken for granted.

assumption ❶ (ə'sʌmpʃən) *n* **1** the act of taking something for granted or something that is taken for granted. **2** an assuming of power or possession. **3** presumption. **4** *Logic.* a statement that is used as the premise of a particular argument but may not be otherwise accepted. [C13: from L *assūmptiō* a taking up, from *assūmere* to ASSUME]
▸**as'sumptive** *adj*

Assumption (ə'sʌmpʃən) *n Christianity.* **1** the taking up of the Virgin Mary (body and soul) into heaven when her earthly life was ended. **2** the feast commemorating this.

assurance ❶ (ə'ʃʊərəns) *n* **1** a statement, assertion, etc., intended to inspire confidence. **2** a promise or pledge of support. **3** freedom from doubt; certainty. **4** forwardness; impudence. **5** *Chiefly Brit.* insurance providing for certainties such as death as contrasted with fire.

assure ❶ (ə'ʃʊə) *vb* **assures, assuring, assured.** (*tr; may take a clause as object*) **1** to convince: *to assure a person of one's love.* **2** to promise; guarantee. **3** to state positively. **4** to make (an event) certain. **5** *Chiefly Brit.* to insure against loss, esp. of life. [C14: from OF, from Med. L *assēcūrāre* to secure or make sure, from *sēcūrus* SECURE]
▸**as'surable** *adj* ▸**as'surer** *n*

assured ❶ (ə'ʃʊəd) *adj* **1** sure; guaranteed. **2** self-assured. **3** *Chiefly Brit.* insured. ◆ *n* **4** *Chiefly Brit.* **4a** the beneficiary under a life assurance policy. **4b** the person whose life is insured.
▸**assuredly** (ə'ʃʊərɪdlɪ) *adv*

asswipe ('æs,waɪp) *n US sl.* a despicable or stupid person. [C20: orig.: toilet paper, from ASS[2] + WIPE]

Assyrian (ə'sɪrɪən) *n* **1** an inhabitant of ancient Assyria, a kingdom of Mesopotamia. **2** the extinct Semitic language of the Assyrians. ◆ *adj* **3** of or characteristic of the ancient Assyrians, their language, or culture.

AST *abbrev. for* Atlantic Standard Time.

astatic (æ'stætɪk, eɪ-) *adj* **1** not static; unstable. **2** *Physics.* having no tendency to assume any particular position or orientation. [C19: from Gk *astatos* unsteady]
▸**a'statically** *adv*

astatine ('æstə,ti:n) *n* a radioactive element that occurs naturally in minute amounts and is artificially produced by bombarding bismuth with alpha particles. Symbol: At; atomic no.: 85; half-life of most stable isotope, ^{210}At: 8.1 hours. [C20: from Gk *astatos* unstable]

aster ('æstə) *n* **1** a plant having white, blue, purple, or pink daisy-like flowers. **2 China aster.** a related Chinese plant widely cultivated for its showy brightly coloured flowers. [C18: from NL, from L *aster* star, from Gk]

-aster *suffix forming nouns.* a person or thing that is inferior to what is specified: *poetaster.* [from L]

asterisk ('æstərɪsk) *n* **1** a star-shaped character (*) used in printing or writing to indicate a cross-reference to a footnote, an omission, etc. ◆ *vb* **2** (*tr*) to mark with an asterisk. [C17: from LL *asteriscus* a small star, from Gk, from *astēr* star]

asterism ('æstə,rɪzəm) *n* **1** three asterisks arranged in a triangle (⁂ or ⁂), to draw attention to the text that follows. **2** a cluster of stars or a constellation. [C16: from Gk *asterismos* arrangement of constellations, from *astēr* star]

astern (ə'stɜ:n) *adv, adj* (*postpositive*) *Naut.* **1** at or towards the stern. **2** with the stern first: *full speed astern!* **3** aft of the stern of a vessel.

asteroid ('æstə,rɔɪd) *n* **1** Also called: **minor planet, planetoid.** any of numerous small celestial bodies that move around the sun mainly between the orbits of Mars and Jupiter. **2** a starfish. ◆ *adj also* **,aste'roidal. 3** of a starfish. **4** shaped like a star. [C19: from Gk *asteroeidēs* starlike, from *astēr* a star]

asthenia (æs'θi:nɪə) *n Pathol.* an abnormal loss of strength; debility. [C19: via NL from Gk *astheneia* weakness, from A-[1] + *sthenos* strength]

asthenic (æs'θɛnɪk) *adj* **1** of or having asthenia; weak. **2** referring to a physique characterized by long limbs and a small trunk. ◆ *n* **3** a person with long limbs and a small trunk.

asthma ('æsmə) *n* a respiratory disorder, often of allergic origin, characterized by difficulty in breathing. [C14: from Gk: laborious breathing, from *azein* to breathe hard]

asthmatic (æs'mætɪk) *adj* **1** of or having asthma. ◆ *n* **2** a person who has asthma.
▸**asth'matically** *adv*

astigmatic (,æstɪg'mætɪk) *adj* relating to or affected with astigmatism. [C19: from A-[1] + Gk *stigmat-, stigma* spot, focus]
▸**,astig'matically** *adv*

astigmatism (ə'stɪgmə,tɪzəm) *or* **astigmia** (ə'stɪgmɪə) *n* **1** a defect of a lens resulting in the formation of distorted images, caused by light rays not meeting at a single focal point. **2** faulty vision resulting from defective curvature of the cornea or lens of the eye.

astilbe (ə'stɪlbɪ) *n* any perennial plant of the genus *Astilbe*, cultivated for its spikes of ornamental pink or white flowers. [C19: NL, from Gk A-[1] + *stilbē*, from *stilbein* to glitter; referring to its inconspicuous individual flowers]

astir ❶ (ə'stɜ:) *adj* (*postpositive*) **1** awake and out of bed. **2** in motion; on the move.

astonish ❶ (ə'stɒnɪʃ) *vb* (*tr*) to fill with amazement; surprise greatly. [C15: from earlier *astonyen*, from OF, from Vulgar L *extonāre* (unattested) to strike with thunder, from L *tonāre* to thunder]
▸**a'stonishing** *adj*

astonishment ❶ (ə'stɒnɪʃmənt) *n* **1** extreme surprise; amazement. **2** a cause of amazement.

astound ❶ (ə'staʊnd) *vb* (*tr*) to overwhelm with amazement; bewilder. [C17: from *astoned* amazed, from OF, from *estoner* to ASTONISH]
▸**a'stounding** *adj*

astraddle (ə'stræd^{ə}l) *adj* **1** (*postpositive*) with a leg on either side of something. ◆ *prep* **2** astride.

astragal ('æstrəg^{ə}l) *n* **1** *Archit.* Also called: **bead.** a small convex moulding, usually with a semicircular cross section. **2** *Anat.* the ankle or anklebone. [C17: from L, from Gk *astragalos* anklebone, hence, small round moulding]

astragalus (æ'strægələs) *n, pl* **astragali** (-,laɪ). *Anat.* another name for **talus**[1]. [C16: via NL from L: ASTRAGAL]

astrakhan (,æstrə'kæn) *n* **1** a fur, usually black or grey, made of the closely curled wool of lambs from Astrakhan, a city in S Russia. **2** a cloth with curled pile resembling this. **3** (*modifier*) made of such fur or cloth.

astral ('æstrəl) *adj* **1** relating to or resembling the stars. **2** *Theosophy.* re-

THESAURUS

quire, attend to, begin, don, embark upon, embrace, enter upon, put on, set about, shoulder, take over, take responsibility for, take up, undertake **3, 4 = put on,** adopt, affect, counterfeit, feign, imitate, impersonate, mimic, pretend to, sham, simulate **5 = take over,** acquire, appropriate, arrogate, commandeer, expropriate, pre-empt, seize, take, usurp
Antonyms *vb* ≠ **take for granted:** know, prove ≠ **take on, take over:** give up, hand over, leave, put aside, relinquish

assumed *adj* **1 = false,** affected, bogus, counterfeit, fake, feigned, fictitious, imitation, made-up, make-believe, phoney *or* phony (*inf.*), pretended, pseudonymous, sham, simulated, spurious **2 = taken for granted,** accepted, expected, hypothetical, presumed, presupposed, supposed, surmised
Antonyms *adj* ≠ **false:** actual, authentic, natural, real ≠ **taken for granted:** known, positive, stated, true

assumption *n* **1 = presumption,** acceptance, belief, conjecture, expectation, fancy, guess, hypothesis, inference, postulate, postulation, premise, premiss, presupposition, supposition, surmise, suspicion, theory **2 = taking on,** acceptance, acquisition, adoption, embracing, entering upon, putting on, shouldering, takeover, taking up, undertaking **2 = taking,** acquisition, appropriation, arrogation, expropriation, pre-empting, seizure, takeover, usurpation **3 = presumptuousness,** arrogance, conceit, imperiousness, pride, self-importance

assurance *n* **1, 2 = assertion,** affirmation, declaration, guarantee, oath, pledge, profession, promise, protestation, statement, vow, word, word of honour **3 = confidence,** assertiveness, assuredness, boldness, certainty, certitude, conviction, coolness, courage, faith, firmness, nerve, poise, positiveness, security, self-confidence, self-reliance, sureness
Antonyms *n* ≠**assertion:** falsehood, lie ≠**confidence:** apprehension, diffidence, distrust, doubt, self-doubt, self-effacement, shyness, timidity, uncertainty

assure *vb* **1 = convince,** comfort, embolden, encourage, hearten, persuade, reassure, soothe **2, 3 = promise,** affirm, attest, certify, confirm, declare confidently, give one's word to, guarantee, pledge, swear, vow **4 = make certain,** clinch, complete, confirm, ensure, guarantee, make sure, seal, secure

assured *adj* **1 = certain,** beyond doubt, clinched, confirmed, dependable, ensured, fixed, guaranteed, indubitable, in the bag (*sl.*), irrefutable, made certain, sealed, secure, settled, sure, unquestionable **2 = confident,** assertive, audacious, bold, brazen, certain, complacent, overconfident, poised, positive, pushy (*inf.*), self-assured, self-confident, self-possessed, sure of oneself
Antonyms *adj* ≠ **certain:** ambiguous, doubtful, indefinite, questionable, uncertain, unconfirmed, unsettled, unsure ≠ **confident:** bashful, diffident, hesitant, retiring, self-conscious, self-effacing, timid

astir *adj* **1 = out of bed,** awake, roused, up and about, up and around **2 = in motion,** active, afoot, on the go (*inf.*), on the move (*inf.*)

astonish *vb* **= amaze,** astound, bewilder, boggle the mind, confound, daze, dumbfound, flabbergast (*inf.*), stagger, stun, stupefy, surprise

astonished *adj* **= amazed,** astounded, bewildered, confounded, dazed, dumbfounded, flabbergasted (*inf.*), gobsmacked (*inf.*), perplexed, staggered, stunned, stupefied, surprised

astonishing *adj* **= amazing,** astounding, bewildering, breathtaking, brilliant, impressive, jaw-dropping, sensational (*inf.*), staggering, striking, stunning, stupefying, surprising, wondrous (*arch. or literary*)

astonishment *n* **1 = amazement,** awe, bewilderment, confusion, consternation, stupefaction, surprise, wonder, wonderment

astound *vb* **= amaze,** astonish, bewilder, boggle the mind, confound, daze, dumbfound, flabbergast (*inf.*), overwhelm, stagger, stun, stupefy, surprise, take one's breath away

astounding *adj* **= amazing,** astonishing, bewildering, breathtaking, brilliant, impressive, jaw-dropping, sensational (*inf.*), staggering, striking, stunning, stupefying, surprising, wondrous (*arch. or literary*) lating to a supposed supersensible substance taking the form of an aura discernible to certain gifted individuals. [C17: from LL *astrālis*, from L *astrum* star, from Gk *astron*]

astray ❶ (əˈstreɪ) *adj (postpositive), adv* **1** out of the correct path or direction. **2** out of the right or expected way. [C13: from OF, from *estraier* to STRAY]

astride (əˈstraɪd) *adj (postpositive)* **1** with a leg on either side. **2** with the legs far apart. ◆ *prep* **3** with a leg on either side of. **4** with a part on both sides of; spanning.

astringent ❶ (əˈstrɪndʒənt) *adj* **1** severe; harsh. **2** sharp or invigorating. **3** causing contraction of body tissues, checking blood flow; styptic. ◆ *n* **4** an astringent drug or lotion. [C16: from L *astringēns* drawing together]
▸**asˈtringency** *n* ▸**asˈtringently** *adv*

astro- *combining form.* indicating a star or star-shaped structure: *astrology*. [from Gk, from *astron* star]

astrobiology (ˌæstrəʊbaɪˈɒlədʒɪ) *n* the branch of biology that investigates the possibility of life on other planets.

astrochemistry (ˌæstrəʊˈkɛmɪstrɪ) *n* the study of the chemistry of celestial bodies and space.

astrodome (ˈæstrəˌdəʊm) *n* a transparent dome on the top of an aircraft, through which observations can be made.

astrol. *abbrev. for:* **1** astrologer. **2** astrological. **3** astrology.

astrolabe (ˈæstrəˌleɪb) *n* an instrument used by early astronomers to measure the altitude of stars and planets and also as a navigational aid. [C13: via OF & Med. L from Gk, from *astrolabos*, from *astron* star + *lambanein* to take]

astrology (əˈstrɒlədʒɪ) *n* **1** the study of the motions and relative positions of the planets, sun, and moon, interpreted in terms of human characteristics and activities. **2** primitive astronomy. [C14: from OF, from L *astrologia*, from Gk, from *astrologos* (orig.: astronomer); see ASTRO-, -LOGY]
▸**asˈtrologer** *or* **asˈtrologist** *n* ▸**astrological** (ˌæstrəˈlɒdʒɪkᵊl) *adj*

astron. *abbrev. for:* **1** astronomer. **2** astronomical. **3** astronomy.

astronaut ❶ (ˈæstrəˌnɔːt) *n* a person trained for travelling in space. See also **cosmonaut.** [C20: from ASTRO- + *-naut*, from Gk *nautēs* sailor, on the model of *aeronaut*]

astronautics (ˌæstrəˈnɔːtɪks) *n* (*functioning as sing*) the science and technology of space flight.
▸ˌ**astroˈnautical** *adj*

Astronomer Royal *n* an honorary title awarded to an eminent British astronomer: until 1972, the Astronomer Royal was also director of the Royal Greenwich Observatory.

astronomical ❶ (ˌæstrəˈnɒmɪkᵊl) *or* **astronomic** *adj* **1** enormously large. **2** of or relating to astronomy.
▸ˌ**astroˈnomically** *adv*

astronomical clock *n* **1** a complex clock showing astronomical phenomena, such as the phases of the moon. **2** any clock showing sidereal time used in observatories.

astronomical unit *n* a unit of distance used in astronomy equal to the mean distance between the earth and the sun. 1 astronomical unit is equivalent to 1.495×10^{11} metres.

astronomy (əˈstrɒnəmɪ) *n* the scientific study of the individual celestial bodies (excluding the earth) and of the universe as a whole. [C13: from OF, from L *astronomia*, from Gk; see ASTRO-, -NOMY]
▸**asˈtronomer** *n*

astrophysics (ˌæstrəʊˈfɪzɪks) *n* (*functioning as sing*) the branch of physics concerned with the physical and chemical properties of the celestial bodies.
▸ˌ**astroˈphysicist** *n*

Astroturf (ˈæstrəʊˌtɜːf) *n Trademark.* a type of grasslike artificial surface used for playing fields and lawns. [C20: from *Astro(dome)* the baseball stadium in Texas where it was first used + *turf*]

astute ❶ (əˈstjuːt) *adj* having insight or acumen; perceptive; shrewd. [C17: from L *astūtus* cunning, from *astus* (n) cleverness]
▸**asˈtutely** *adv* ▸**asˈtuteness** *n*

asunder ❶ (əˈsʌndə) *adv, adj (postpositive)* in or into parts or pieces; apart: *to tear asunder.* [OE *on sundran* apart]

asylum ❶ (əˈsaɪləm) *n* **1** shelter; refuge; sanctuary. **2** a safe or inviolable place of refuge, esp. as formerly offered by the Christian Church. **3** *International law.* refuge afforded to a person whose extradition is sought by a foreign government: *political asylum.* **4** an institution for the care or confinement of individuals, esp. (formerly) a mental hospital. [C15: via L from Gk *asulon* refuge, from A-[1] + *sulon* right of seizure]

asymmetric (ˌæsɪˈmɛtrɪk, ˌeɪ-) *or* **asymmetrical** *adj* **1** not symmetrical; lacking symmetry; misproportioned. **2** *Logic, maths.* (of a relation) never holding between a pair of values *x* and *y* when it holds between *y* and *x*, as in *John is the father of David.*
▸ˌ**asymˈmetrically** *adv*

asymmetric bars *pl n Gymnastics.* **a** (*functioning as pl*) a pair of wooden or fibreglass bars placed parallel to each other but set at different heights, for various exercises. **b** (*functioning as sing*) an event in a gymnastic competition in which competitors exercise on such bars.

asymmetry (æˈsɪmɪtrɪ, eɪ-) *n* lack or absence of symmetry.

asymptomatic (ˌeɪsɪmptəˈmætɪk) *adj* not showing any symptoms of disease.

asymptote (ˈæsɪmˌtəʊt) *n* a straight line that is closely approached by a curve so that the distance between them decreases to zero as the distance from the origin increases to infinity. [C17: from Gk *asumptōtos* not falling together, from A-[1] + SYN- + *ptōtos* inclined to fall, from *piptein* to fall]
▸**asymptotic** (ˌæsɪmˈtɒtɪk) *or* ˌ**asympˈtotical** *adj*

asystole (əˈsɪstəlɪ) *n Pathol.* the absence of heartbeat; cardiac arrest.
▸**asystolic** (ˌæsɪsˈtɒlɪk) *adj*

at (æt) *prep* **1** used to indicate location or position: *are they at the table?* **2** towards; in the direction of: *looking at television.* **3** used to indicate position in time: *come at three o'clock.* **4** engaged in; in a state of (being): *children at play.* **5** (in expressions concerned with habitual activity) during the passing of: *he used to work at night.* **6** for; in exchange for: *it's selling at four pounds.* **7** used to indicate the object of an emotion: *shocked at his behaviour.* **8 where it's at.** *Sl.* the real place of action. [OE *æt*]

At *the chemical symbol for* astatine.

AT *Brit. education. abbrev. for* attainment target.

at. *abbrev. for:* **1** atmosphere (unit of pressure). **2** atomic.

ataractic (ˌætəˈræktɪk) *or* **ataraxic** (ˌætəˈræksɪk) *adj* **1** able to calm or tranquillize. ◆ *n* **2** an ataractic drug.

ataraxia (ˌætəˈræksɪə) *or* **ataraxy** (ˈætəˌræksɪ) *n* calmness or peace of mind; emotional tranquillity. [C17: from Gk: serenity, from A-[1] + *tarassein* to trouble]

atavism (ˈætəˌvɪzəm) *n* **1** the recurrence in a plant or animal of certain primitive characteristics that were present in an ancestor but have not occurred in intermediate generations. **2** reversion to a former type. [C19: from F, from L *atavus* strictly: great-grandfather's grandfather, prob. from *atta* daddy + *avus* grandfather]
▸ˌ**ataˈvistic** *adj*

ataxia (əˈtæksɪə) *or* **ataxy** (əˈtæksɪ) *n Pathol.* lack of muscular coordination. [C17: via NL from Gk: lack of coordination, from A-[1] + *-taxia*, from *tassein* to put in order]
▸**aˈtaxic** *adj*

ATB *abbrev. for* Advanced Technology Bomber.

ATC *abbrev. for:* **1** air-traffic control. **2** (in Britain) Air Training Corps.

ate (ɛt, eɪt) *vb* the past tense of **eat.**

-ate[1] *suffix.* **1** (*forming adjectives*) having the appearance or characteristics of: *fortunate.* **2** (*forming nouns*) a chemical compound, esp. a salt or ester of an acid: *carbonate.* **3** (*forming nouns*) the product of a process: *condensate.* **4** forming verbs from nouns and adjectives: *hyphenate.* [from L *-ātus*, p.p. ending of verbs ending in *-āre*]

-ate[2] *suffix forming nouns.* denoting office, rank, or a group having a certain function: *episcopate.* [from L *-ātus*, suffix of collective nouns]

atelier (ˈætəlˌjeɪ) *n* an artist's studio or workshop. [C17: from OF, from *astele* chip of wood, from L *astula* splinter, from *assis* board]

a tempo (ɑː ˈtɛmpəʊ) *Music.* ◆ *adj, adv* **1** to the original tempo. ◆ *n* **2** a passage thus marked. ◆ Also: **tempo primo.** [It.: in (the original) time]

Athanasian Creed (ˌæθəˈneɪʃən) *n Christianity.* a profession of faith widely used in the Western Church formerly attributed to Athanasius, 4th-century A.D. patriarch of Alexandria.

Athapascan, Athapaskan (ˌæθəˈpæskən) *or* **Athabascan, Athabaskan** (ˌæθəˈbæskən) *n* a group of North American Indian languages including Apache and Navaho. [from Cree *athapaskaaw* scattered grass]

atheism ❶ (ˈeɪθɪˌɪzəm) *n* rejection of belief in God or gods. [C16: from F, from Gk *atheos* godless, from A-[1] + *theos* god]
▸ˈ**atheist** *n, adj* ▸**atheˈistic** *adj*

athematic (ˌæθɪˈmætɪk) *adj* **1** *Music.* not based on themes. **2** *Linguistics.* (of verbs) having a suffix attached with no intervening vowel.

athenaeum *or US* **atheneum** (ˌæθɪˈniːəm) *n* **1** an institution for the

THESAURUS

astray *adj, adv* **1** = **off the right track**, adrift, afield, amiss, lost, off, off course, off the mark, off the subject **2** = **into sin**, into error, to the bad, wrong

astringent *adj* **1** = **severe**, acerbic, austere, caustic, exacting, grim, hard, harsh, rigid, rigorous, stern, strict, stringent **3** = **contractive**, contractile, styptic

astronaut *n* = **space traveller**, cosmonaut, spaceman, space pilot, spacewoman

astronomical *adj* **1** = **huge**, boundless, colossal, enormous, galactic, Gargantuan, giant, gigantic, great, immeasurable, immense, infinite, massive, monumental, titanic, vast

astute *adj* = **intelligent**, adroit, artful, bright, calculating, canny, clever, crafty, cunning, discerning, foxy, insightful, keen, knowing, on the ball (*inf.*), penetrating, perceptive, politic, sagacious, sharp, shrewd, sly, subtle, wily
Antonyms *adj* dull, ingenuous, naive, slow, straightforward, stupid, unintelligent, unknowing

astuteness *n* = **intelligence**, acumen, adroitness, artfulness, brightness, canniness, cleverness, craftiness, cunning, discernment, foxiness, insight, keenness, knowledge, penetration, perceptiveness, sagacity, sharpness, shrewdness, slyness, subtlety, suss (*sl.*), wiliness

asunder *adv, adj* = **to pieces**, apart, in pieces, into pieces, rent, to bits, torn, to shreds

asylum *n* **1, 2** = **refuge**, harbour, haven, preserve, retreat, safety, sanctuary, shelter **4** = **mental hospital**, funny farm (*facetious*), hospital, institution, laughing academy (*US. sl.*), loony bin (*sl.*), madhouse (*inf.*), nuthouse (*sl.*), psychiatric hospital

atheism *n* = **nonbelief**, disbelief, freethinking, godlessness, heathenism, infidelity, irreligion, paganism, scepticism, unbelief

atheist *n* = **nonbeliever**, disbeliever, freethinker, heathen, infidel, irreligionist, pagan, sceptic, unbeliever promotion of learning. **2** a building containing a reading room or library. [C18: from LL, from Gk *Athēnaion* temple of Athene, frequented by poets and teachers]

Athenian (ə'θiːnɪən) *n* **1** a native or inhabitant of Athens, the capital of Greece. ◆ *adj* **2** of or relating to Athens.

atherosclerosis (ˌæθərəʊsklɪə'rəʊsɪs) *n, pl* **atheroscleroses** (-siːz). a degenerative disease of the arteries characterized by thickening of the arterial walls, caused by deposits of fatty material. [C20: from NL, from Gk *athērōma* tumour full of grainy matter + SCLEROSIS]
▸**atherosclerotic** (ˌæθərəʊsklɪə'rɒtɪk) *adj*

athirst (ə'θɜːst) *adj* (*postpositive*) **1** (often foll. by *for*) having an eager desire; longing. **2** *Arch.* thirsty.

athlete ⓘ ('æθliːt) *n* **1** a person trained to compete in sports or exercises. **2** a person who has a natural aptitude for physical activities. **3** *Chiefly Brit.* a competitor in track and field events. [C18: from L via Gk, from *athlein* to compete for a prize, from *athlos* a contest]

athlete's foot *n* a fungal infection of the skin of the foot, esp. between the toes and on the soles.

athletic ⓘ (æθ'letɪk) *adj* **1** physically fit or strong. **2** of, relating to, or suitable for an athlete or for athletics.
▸**ath'letically** *adv* ▸**ath'leticism** *n*

athletics ⓘ (æθ'letɪks) *n* (*functioning as sing or pl*) **1** *Chiefly Brit.* **1a** track and field events. **1b** (*as modifier*): *an athletics meeting.* **2** sports or exercises engaged in by athletes.

athletic support *n* a more formal term for **jockstrap**.

at-home *n* **1** a social gathering in a person's home. **2** another name for **open day**.

-athon *suffix forming nouns.* a variant of **-thon**.

athwart (ə'θwɔːt) *adv* **1** transversely; from one side to another. ◆ *prep* **2** across the path or line of (esp. a ship). **3** in opposition to; against. [C15: from A-[2] + THWART]

-atic *suffix forming adjectives.* of the nature of the thing specified: *problematic.* [from F, from Gk *-atikos*]

-ation *suffix forming nouns.* indicating an action, process, state, condition, or result: *arbitration; hibernation.* [from L *-ātiōn-*, suffix of abstract nouns]

-ative *suffix forming adjectives.* of, relating to, or tending to: *authoritative; informative.* [from L *-ātīvus*]

Atlantean (ˌætlæn'tiːən) *adj Literary.* of, relating to, or like Atlas; extremely strong.

Atlantic (ət'læntɪk) *n* **1 the.** short for the **Atlantic Ocean**, the world's second largest ocean. ◆ *adj* **2** of, relating to, or bordering the Atlantic Ocean. **3** of or relating to Atlas or the Atlas Mountains. [C15: from L, from Gk (*pelagos*) *Atlantikos* (the sea) of Atlas (so called because it lay beyond the Atlas Mountains)]

Atlanticism (ət'læntɪˌsɪzəm) *n* advocacy of close cooperation in military, political, and economic matters between Western Europe, esp. the UK, and the US.
▸**At'lanticist** *n*

Atlantis (ət'læntɪs) *n* (in ancient legend) a continent said to have sunk beneath the Atlantic west of Gibraltar.

atlas ('ætləs) *n* **1** a collection of maps, usually in book form. **2** a book of charts, graphs, etc.: *an anatomical atlas.* **3** *Anat.* the first cervical vertebra, supporting the skull in man. **4** (*pl* **atlantes**) *Archit.* another name for **telamon**.

Atlas ('ætləs) *n Greek myth.* **1** a Titan compelled to support the sky on his shoulders as punishment for rebelling against Zeus. **2** a US intercontinental ballistic missile, also used in launching spacecraft.

ATM *abbrev. for* automated teller machine.

atm. *abbrev. for:* **1** atmosphere (unit of pressure). **2** atmospheric.

atman ('ɑːtmən) *n Hinduism.* **1** the personal soul or self. **2** Brahman considered as the Universal Soul. [from Sansk. *ātman* breath]

atmolysis (æt'mɒlɪsɪs) *n, pl* **atmolyses** (-ˌsiːz). the separation of gases by differential diffusion through a porous substance.

atmosphere ⓘ ('ætməsˌfɪə) *n* **1** the gaseous envelope surrounding the earth or any other celestial body. **2** the air or climate in a particular place. **3** a general pervasive feeling or mood. **4** the prevailing tone or mood of a novel, symphony, painting, etc. **5** any local gaseous environment or medium: *an inert atmosphere.* **6** Abbrev: **at., atm.** a unit of pressure; the pressure that will support a column of mercury 760 mm high at 0°C at sea level.
▸**atmospheric** (ˌætməs'ferɪk) *adj* ▸ˌ**atmos'pherically** *adv*

atmospheric pressure *n* the pressure exerted by the atmosphere at the earth's surface. It has an average value of 1 atmosphere.

atmospherics (ˌætməs'ferɪks) *pl n* radio interference, heard as crackling or hissing in receivers, caused by electrical disturbance.

at. no. *abbrev. for* atomic number.

atoll ('ætɒl) *n* a circular coral reef or string of coral islands surrounding a lagoon. [C17: from *atollon*, native name in the Maldive Islands]

atom ⓘ ('ætəm) *n* **1a** the smallest quantity of an element that can take part in a chemical reaction. **1b** this entity as a source of nuclear energy: *the power of the atom.* **2** the hypothetical indivisible particle of matter postulated by certain ancient philosophers. **3** a very small amount or quantity: *to smash something to atoms.* [C16: via OF & L, from Gk, from *atomos* (adj) that cannot be divided, from A-[1] + *temnein* to cut]

atomic (ə'tɒmɪk) *adj* **1** of, using, or characterized by atomic bombs or atomic energy: *atomic warfare.* **2** of or comprising atoms: *atomic hydrogen.*
▸**a'tomically** *adv*

atomic bomb *or* **atom bomb** *n* a type of bomb in which the energy is provided by nuclear fission. Also called: **A-bomb, fission bomb.** Cf. **fusion bomb.**

atomic clock *n* an extremely accurate clock in which an electrical oscillator is controlled by the natural vibrations of an atomic or molecular system such as caesium or ammonia.

atomic energy *n* another name for **nuclear energy**.

atomicity (ˌætə'mɪsɪtɪ) *n* **1** the state of being made up of atoms. **2** the number of atoms in the molecules of an element. **3** a less common name for **valency**.

atomic mass unit *n* a unit of mass used to express atomic and molecular weights that is equal to one-twelfth of the mass of an atom of carbon-12. Abbrev.: **amu.**

atomic number *n* the number of protons in the nucleus of an atom of an element. Abbrev.: **at. no.**

atomic pile *n* the original name for a **nuclear reactor**.

atomic sentence *n Logic.* a sentence consisting of one predicate and a finite number of terms: *"it is raining" is an atomic sentence.*

atomic structure *n* the concept of an atom as a central positively charged nucleus consisting of protons and neutrons surrounded by a number of electrons. The number of electrons is equal to the number of protons: the whole entity is thus electrically neutral.

atomic theory *n* **1** any theory in which matter is regarded as consisting of atoms. **2** the current concept of the atom as an entity with a definite structure. See **atomic structure**.

atomic weight *n* the former name for **relative atomic mass.** Abbrev.: **at. wt.**

atomize *or* **atomise** ('ætəˌmaɪz) *vb* **atomizes, atomizing, atomized** *or* **atomises, atomising, atomised. 1** to separate or be separated into free atoms. **2** to reduce (a liquid or solid) to fine particles or spray or (of a liquid or solid) to be reduced in this way. **3** (*tr*) to destroy by weapons, esp. nuclear weapons.

atomizer *or* **atomiser** ('ætəˌmaɪzə) *n* a device for reducing a liquid to a fine spray, such as a bottle with a fine outlet used to spray perfumes.

atom smasher *n Physics.* the nontechnical name for **accelerator** (sense 2).

atomy ('ætəmɪ) *n, pl* **atomies.** *Arch.* a minute particle or creature. [C16: from L *atomi* atoms, used as sing]

atonal (eɪ'təʊnᵊl) *adj Music.* having no established key.

atonality (ˌeɪtəʊ'nælɪtɪ) *n* **1** absence of or disregard for an established musical key in a composition. **2** the principles of composition embodying this.

atone ⓘ (ə'təʊn) *vb* **atones, atoning, atoned.** (*intr;* foll. by *for*) to make amends or reparation (for a crime, sin, etc.). [C16: back formation from ATONEMENT]
▸**a'toner** *n*

atonement ⓘ (ə'təʊnmənt) *n* **1** satisfaction, reparation, or expiation given for an injury or wrong. **2** (*often cap.*) *Christian theology.* **2a** the reconciliation of man with God through the sacrificial death of Christ. **2b** the sufferings and death of Christ. [C16: from ME *at onement* in harmony]

atonic (eɪ'tɒnɪk, æ-) *adj* **1** (of a syllable, word, etc.) carrying no stress; unaccented. **2** lacking body or muscle tone. ◆ *n* **3** an unaccented or unstressed syllable, word, etc. [C18: from L, from Gk *atonos* lacking tone]

atop (ə'tɒp) *adv* **1** on top; at the top. ◆ *prep* **2** on top of; at the top of.

-ator *suffix forming nouns.* a person or thing that performs a certain action: *agitator; radiator.* [from L *-ātor*]

-atory *suffix forming adjectives.* of, relating to, characterized by, or serving to: *circulatory; explanatory.* [from L *-ātōrius*]

ATP *n* adenosine triphosphate; a substance found in all plant and animal cells. It is the major source of energy for cellular reactions.

atrabilious (ˌætrə'bɪlɪəs) *or* **atrabiliar** *adj Rare.* irritable or gloomy. [C17: from L *ātra bīlis* black bile, from *āter* black + *bīlis* BILE[1]]
▸ˌ**atra'biliousness** *n*

THESAURUS

atheistic *adj* = **nonbelieving**, disbelieving, faithless, freethinking, godless, heathen, infidel, irreligious, nullifidian, paganistic, sceptic, unbelieving

athlete *n* **1, 3** = **sportsperson**, competitor, contender, contestant, games player, gymnast, player, runner, sportsman, sportswoman

athletic *adj* **1** = **fit**, able-bodied, active, brawny, energetic, herculean, husky (*inf.*), lusty, muscular, powerful, robust, sinewy, strapping, strong, sturdy, vigorous, well-proportioned

Antonyms *adj* delicate, feeble, frail, puny, sickly, weedy (*inf.*)

athletics *pl n* **1, 2** = **sports**, contests, exercises, games of strength, gymnastics, races, track and field events

atmosphere *n* **1** = **air**, aerosphere, heavens, sky **2, 3** = **feeling**, air, ambience, aura, character, climate, environment, feel, flavour, mood, quality, spirit, surroundings, tone, vibes (*sl.*)

atom *n* **3** = **particle**, bit, crumb, dot, fragment, grain, iota, jot, mite, molecule, morsel, mote, scintilla (*rare*), scrap, shred, speck, spot, tittle, trace, whit

atone *vb, foll. by* **for** = **make amends**, answer for, compensate, do penance, make redress, make reparation, make up for, pay for, recompense, redress

atonement *n* **1** = **amends**, compensation, expiation, payment, penance, propitiation, recompense, redress, reparation, restitution, satisfaction

atrazine ('ætrəzi:n) *n* a white crystalline compound widely used as a weedkiller. Formula: $C_8H_{14}N_5Cl$. [C20: from A(MINO) *tr(i)azine*]

atrium ('eɪtrɪəm, 'ɑ:-) *n, pl* **atria** ('eɪtrɪə, 'ɑ:-). **1** the open main court of a Roman house. **2** a central often glass-roofed hall that extends through several storeys in a building, such as a shopping centre or hotel. **3** a court in front of an early Christian or medieval church. **4** *Anat.* a cavity or chamber in the body, esp. the upper chamber of each half of the heart. [C17: from L; rel. to *āter* black]
▸**'atrial** *adj*

atrocious ❶ (ə'trəʊʃəs) *adj* **1** extremely cruel or wicked: *atrocious deeds.* **2** horrifying or shocking. **3** *Inf.* very bad: *atrocious writing.* [C17: from L *ātrōx* dreadful, from *āter* black]
▸**a'trociousness** *n*

atrocity ❶ (ə'trɒsɪtɪ) *n, pl* **atrocities. 1** behaviour or an action that is wicked or ruthless. **2** the fact or quality of being atrocious. **3** (*usually pl*) acts of extreme cruelty.

atrophy ❶ ('ætrəfɪ) *n, pl* **atrophies. 1** a wasting away of an organ or part, or a failure to grow to normal size. **2** any degeneration or diminution. ◆ *vb* **atrophies, atrophying, atrophied. 3** to waste away or cause to waste away. [C17: from LL, from Gk, from *atrophos* ill-fed, from A-[1] + -*trophos*, from *trephein* to feed]
▸**atrophic** (ə'trɒfɪk) *adj*

atropine ('ætrəˌpi:n) *n* a poisonous alkaloid obtained from the deadly nightshade, used to treat peptic ulcers, biliary and renal colic, etc. [C19: from NL *atropa* deadly nightshade, from Gk *atropos* unchangeable, inflexible]

attach ❶ (ə'tætʃ) *vb* (*mainly tr*) **1** to join, fasten, or connect. **2** (*reflexive or passive*) to become associated with or join. **3** (*intr; foll. by to*) to be connected (with): *responsibility attaches to the job.* **4** to attribute or ascribe. **5** to include or append: *a proviso is attached to the contract.* **6** (*usually passive*) *Mil.* to place on temporary duty with another unit. **7** to appoint officially. **8** *Law.* to arrest or take (a person, property, etc.) with lawful authority. [C14: from OF *atachier* to fasten, changed from *estachier* to fasten with a stake]
▸**at'tachable** *adj* ▸**at'tacher** *n*

attaché (ə'tæʃeɪ) *n* a specialist attached to a diplomatic mission: *military attaché.* [C19: from F: someone attached (to a mission)]

attaché case *n* a small flat rectangular briefcase used for carrying documents, papers, etc.

attached ❶ (ə'tætʃt) *adj* **1** (foll. by *to*) fond (of). **2** married, engaged, or associated in an exclusive sexual relationship.

attachment ❶ (ə'tætʃmənt) *n* **1** a fastening. **2** (often foll. by *to*) affection or regard (for). **3** an object to be attached: *an attachment for an electric drill.* **4** the act of attaching or the state of being attached. **5a** the lawful seizure of property and placing of it under control of a court. **5b** a writ authorizing such seizure.

attack ❶ (ə'tæk) *vb* **1** to launch a physical assault (against) with or without weapons. **2** (*intr*) to take the initiative in a game, sport, etc. **3** (*tr*) to criticize or abuse vehemently. **4** (*tr*) to turn one's mind or energies to (a job, problem, etc.). **5** (*tr*) to begin to injure or affect adversely: *rust attacked the metal.* ◆ *n* **6** the act or an instance of attacking. **7** strong criticism or abuse. **8** an offensive move in a game, sport, etc. **9 the attack.** *Ball games.* the players in a team whose main role is to attack the opponents. **10** commencement of a task, etc. **11** any sudden and usually severe manifestation of a disease or disorder: *a heart attack.* **12** *Music.* **12a** decisiveness in beginning a passage, movement, or piece. **12b** (in electronic instruments) the time between the start of a note and its maximum volume. [C16: from F, from OIt. *attaccare* to attack, attach, from *estaccare* to attach]
▸**at'tacker** *n*

attain ❶ (ə'teɪn) *vb* **1** (*tr*) to achieve or accomplish (a task, aim, etc.). **2** (*tr*) to reach in space or time. **3** (*intr; often foll. by to*) to arrive (at) with effort or exertion. [C14: from OF, from L *attingere* to reach, from *tangere* to touch]
▸**at'tainable** *adj* ▸**at,taina'bility** *or* **at'tainableness** *n*

attainder (ə'teɪndə) *n* (formerly) the extinction of a person's civil rights resulting from a sentence of death or outlawry on conviction for treason or felony. [C15: from Anglo-F *attaindre* to convict, from OF *ateindre* to ATTAIN]

attainment ❶ (ə'teɪnmənt) *n* an achievement or the act of achieving; accomplishment.

attainment target *n Brit. education.* a general defined level of ability that a pupil is expected to achieve in every subject at each key stage in the National Curriculum. Abbrev.: **AT.**

attaint (ə'teɪnt) *vb* (*tr*) *Arch.* **1** to pass judgment of death or outlawry upon (a person). **2** (of sickness) to affect or strike (somebody). ◆ *n* **3** a less common word for **attainder.** [C14: from OF *ateint* convicted, from *ateindre* to ATTAIN]

attar ('ætə), **otto** ('ɒtəʊ), *or* **ottar** ('ɒtə) *n* an essential oil from flowers, esp. the damask rose: *attar of roses.* [C18: from Persian, from *'itr* perfume, from Ar.]

attempt ❶ (ə'tempt) *vb* (*tr*) **1** to make an effort (to do something) or to achieve (something); try. **2** to try to surmount (an obstacle). **3** to try to climb. ◆ *n* **4** an endeavour to achieve something; effort. **5** a result of an attempt or endeavour. **6** an attack, esp. with the intention to kill. [C14: from OF, from L *attemptāre* to strive after, from *tentāre* to try]
▸**at'temptable** *adj*

> **USAGE NOTE** *Attempt* should not be used in the passive when followed by an infinitive: *attempts were made to find a solution* (not *a solution was attempted to be found*).

attend ❶ (ə'tend) *vb* **1** to be present at (an event, etc.). **2** (when *intr,* foll. by *to*) to give care (to); minister (to). **3** (when *intr,* foll. by *to*) to pay attention. **4** (*tr; often passive*) to accompany or follow: *a high temperature attended by a severe cough.* **5** (*intr;* foll. by *on* or *upon*) to follow as a consequence (of). **6** (*intr;* foll. by *to*) to apply oneself: *to attend to the garden.* **7** (*tr*) to escort or accompany. **8** (*intr;* foll. by *on* or *upon*) to provide for the needs (of): *to attend on a guest.* [C13: from OF, from L *attendere* to stretch towards, from *tendere* to extend]

THESAURUS

atrocious *adj* **1 = cruel,** barbaric, brutal, diabolical, fiendish, flagrant, heinous, infamous, infernal, inhuman, monstrous, nefarious, ruthless, savage, vicious, villainous, wicked **2 = shocking,** appalling, detestable, execrable, grievous, horrible, horrifying, terrible
Antonyms *adj* ≠ **cruel:** civilized, generous, gentle, good, honourable, humane, kind, merciful ≠ **shocking:** admirable, fine, tasteful

atrocity *n* **1, 2 = cruelty,** atrociousness, barbarity, barbarousness, brutality, enormity, fiendishness, grievousness, heinousness, horror, infamy, inhumanity, monstrousness, nefariousness, ruthlessness, savagery, shockingness, viciousness, villainousness, wickedness **3 = act of cruelty,** abomination, barbarity, brutality, crime, cruelty, enormity, evil, horror, monstrosity, outrage, villainy

atrophy *n* **1, 2 = wasting away,** decay, decaying, decline, degeneration, deterioration, diminution, meltdown (*inf.*), shrivelling, wasting, withering ◆ *vb* **3 = waste away,** decay, decline, degenerate, deteriorate, diminish, dwindle, fade, shrink, shrivel, waste, wilt, wither

attach *vb* **1 = connect,** add, adhere, affix, annex, append, bind, couple, fasten, fix, join, link, make fast, secure, stick, subjoin, tie, unite **2 = join,** accompany, affiliate oneself with, associate with, become associated with, combine with, join forces with, latch on to, sign on with, sign up with, unite with **4 = put,** ascribe, assign, associate, attribute, connect, impute, invest with, lay, place
Antonyms *vb* ≠ **connect:** detach, disconnect, dissociate, loosen, remove, retire, separate, untie, withdraw

attached *adj* **1** *foll. by* **to = fond of,** affectionate towards, devoted to, full of regard for **2 = spoken for,** accompanied, engaged, married, partnered

attachment *n* **1 = connector,** adaptor *or* adapter, bond, clamp, connection, coupling, fastener, fastening, joint, junction, link, tie **2 = fondness,** affection, affinity, attraction, bond, devotion, fidelity, friendship, liking, love, loyalty, partiality, possessiveness, predilection, regard, tenderness **3 = accessory,** accoutrement, adaptor *or* adapter, addition, add-on, adjunct, appendage, appurtenance, auxiliary, extension, extra, fitting, fixture, supplement, supplementary part
Antonyms *n* ≠ **fondness:** animosity, antipathy, aversion, disinclination, distaste, hatred, hostility, loathing

attack *vb* **1 = assault,** assail, charge, fall upon, invade, lay into (*inf.*), raid, rush, set about, set upon, storm, strike (at) **3 = criticize,** abuse, berate, bite someone's head off, blame, blast, censure, excoriate, have a go (at) (*inf.*), impugn, lambast(e), malign, put down, revile, snap someone's head off, tear into (*inf.*), vilify ◆ *n* **6 = assault,** aggression, campaign, charge, foray, incursion, inroad, invasion, offensive, onset, onslaught, raid, rush, strike **7 = criticism,** abuse, blame, calumny, censure, character assassination, denigration, impugnment, stick (*sl.*), vilification **11 = bout,** access, convulsion, fit, paroxysm, seizure, spasm, spell, stroke
Antonyms *vb* ≠ **assault:** defend, guard, protect, retreat, support, sustain, withdraw ◆ *n* ≠ **assault:** defence, retreat, support, withdrawal

attacker *n* **1 = assailant,** aggressor, assaulter, intruder, invader, raider

attain *vb* **1 = achieve,** accomplish, acquire, arrive at, bring off, complete, earn, effect, fulfil, gain, get, grasp, land, obtain, procure, reach, realize, reap, score (*sl.*), secure, win

attainable *adj* **1 = achievable,** accessible, accomplishable, at hand, feasible, gettable, graspable, likely, obtainable, possible, potential, practicable, probable, procurable, reachable, realizable, within reach
Antonyms *adj* impossible, impracticable, improbable, inaccessible, out of reach, unattainable, unfeasible, unlikely, unobtainable, unprocurable, unreachable

attainment *n* **= achievement,** accomplishment, acquirement, acquisition, arrival at, completion, feat, fulfilment, gaining, getting, obtaining, procurement, reaching, realization, reaping, winning

attempt *vb* **1 = try,** endeavour, essay, experiment, have a crack (*inf.*), have a go (*inf.*), have a shot (*inf.*), have a stab (*inf.*), seek, strive, tackle, take on, try one's hand at, undertake, venture ◆ *n* **4 = try,** assault, attack, bid, crack (*inf.*), effort, endeavour, essay, experiment, go (*inf.*), shot (*inf.*), stab (*inf.*), trial, undertaking, venture

attempted *vb* **1 = tried,** assayed, endeavoured, undertaken, ventured

attend *vb* **1 = be present,** appear, be at, be here, be there, frequent, go to, haunt, make one (*arch.*), put in an appearance, show oneself, show up (*inf.*), turn up, visit **2 = look after,** care for, mind, minister to, nurse, take care of, tend **3 = pay attention,** follow, hear, hearken (*arch.*), heed, listen, look on, mark, mind, note, notice, observe, pay heed, regard, take to heart, watch **4, 5 = accompany,** arise from, be associated with, be connected with, be consequent on, follow, go hand in hand with, issue from, occur with, result from **6 = apply oneself to,** concentrate on, devote oneself to, get to work on, look after, occupy oneself with, see to, take care of **7 = escort,** accompany, chaperon, companion,

attendance ❶ (ə'tɛndəns) *n* **1** the act or state of attending. **2** the number of persons present.

attendant ❶ (ə'tɛndənt) *n* **1** a person who accompanies or waits upon another. **2** a person employed to assist, guide, or provide a service for others. **3** a person who is present. ◆ *adj* **4** being in attendance. **5** associated: *attendant problems.*

attendee (ə,tɛn'di:) *n* a person who is present at a specified event.

attention ❶ (ə'tɛnʃən) *n* **1** concentrated direction of the mind, esp. to a problem or task. **2** consideration, notice, or observation. **3** detailed care or special treatment: *to pay attention to one's appearance.* **4** (*usually pl*) an act of courtesy or gallantry indicating affection or love. **5** the motionless position of formal military alertness, an upright position with legs and heels together. ◆ *sentence substitute.* **6** the order to be alert or to adopt a position of formal military alertness. [C14: from L, from *attendere* to apply the mind to]

attention deficit disorder *n* a disorder, particularly of children, characterized by excessive activity and inability to concentrate on one task for any length of time. Abbrev.: **ADD.**

attentive ❶ (ə'tɛntɪv) *adj* **1** paying attention; listening carefully. **2** (*postpositive;* often foll. by *to*) careful to fulfil the needs or wants (of).
▸**at'tentively** *adv* ▸**at'tentiveness** *n*

attenuate ❶ *vb* (ə'tɛnjʊ,eɪt) **attenuates, attenuating, attenuated. 1** to weaken or become weak. **2** to make or become thin or fine; extend. ◆ *adj* (ə'tɛnjʊɪt, -,eɪt). **3** weakened or reduced. **4** *Bot.* tapering. [C16: from L *attenuāre* to weaken, from *tenuis* thin]
▸**at,tenu'ation** *n*

attest ❶ (ə'tɛst) *vb* **1** (*tr*) to affirm the correctness or truth of. **2** (when *intr,* usually foll. by *to*) to witness (an act, event, etc.) or bear witness (to an act, event, etc.). **3** (*tr*) to make evident; demonstrate. **4** (*tr*) to provide evidence for. [C16: from L, from *testārī* to bear witness, from *testis* a witness]
▸**at'testable** *adj* ▸**at'testant, at'tester** *or esp. in legal usage* **at'testor** *n* ▸**attestation** (,ætɛ'steɪʃən) *n*

attested (ə'tɛstɪd) *adj Brit.* (of cattle, etc.) certified to be free from a disease, esp. from tuberculosis.

attic ❶ ('ætɪk) *n* **1** a space or room within the roof of a house. **2** *Archit.* a storey or low wall above the cornice of a classical façade. [C18: special use of ATTIC, from use of Attic-style pilasters on façade of top storey]

Attic ❶ ('ætɪk) *adj* **1** of or relating to Attica, the area around Athens, its inhabitants, or the dialect of Greek spoken there. **2** (*often not cap.*) classically elegant, simple, or pure. ◆ *n* **3** the dialect of Ancient Greek spoken and written in Athens.

Atticism ('ætɪ,sɪzəm) *n* **1** the idiom or character of the Attic dialect of Ancient Greek. **2** an elegant, simple expression.

Attic salt *or* **wit** *n* refined incisive wit.

attire ❶ (ə'taɪə) *vb* **attires, attiring, attired. 1** (*tr*) to dress, esp. in fine elegant clothes; array. ◆ *n* **2** clothes or garments, esp. if fine or decorative. [C13: from OF *atirier* to put in order, from *tire* row]

attitude ❶ ('ætɪ,tju:d) *n* **1** the way a person views something or tends to behave towards it, often in an evaluative way. **2** a theatrical pose created for effect (esp. in **strike an attitude**). **3** a position of the body indicating mood or emotion. **4** *Inf.* a hostile manner: *don't give me attitude, my girl.* **5** the orientation of an aircraft's axes or a spacecraft in relation to some plane or the direction of motion. [C17: from F, from It. *attitudine* disposition, from LL *aptitūdō* fitness, from L *aptus* APT]
▸**,atti'tudinal** *adj*

attitudinize *or* **attitudinise** (,ætɪ'tju:dɪ,naɪz) *vb* **attitudinizes, attitudinizing, attitudinized** *or* **attitudinises, attitudinising, attitudinised.** (*intr*) to adopt a pose or opinion for effect; strike an attitude.

attn *abbrev. for* attention.

atto- *prefix* denoting 10^{-18}: *attotesla.* Symbol: a [from Norwegian & Danish *atten* eighteen]

attorney (ə'tɜ:nɪ) *n* **1** a person legally appointed or empowered to act for another. **2** *US.* a lawyer qualified to represent clients in legal proceedings. [C14: from OF, from *atourner* to direct to, from *tourner* to TURN]
▸**at'torney,ship** *n*

attorney-at-law *n, pl* **attorneys-at-law.** *Law, now chiefly US.* a lawyer.

attorney general *n, pl* **attorneys general** *or* **attorney generals.** a chief law officer and senior legal adviser of some national and state governments.

attract ❶ (ə'trækt) *vb* (*mainly tr*) **1** to draw (notice, a crowd of observers, etc.) to oneself (esp. in **attract attention**). **2** (*also intr*) to exert a force on (a body) that tends to oppose a separation: *the gravitational pull of the earth attracts objects to it.* **3** to possess some property that pulls or draws (something) towards itself. **4** (*also intr*) to exert a pleasing or fascinating influence (upon). [C15: from L *attrahere* to draw towards, from *trahere* to pull]
▸**at'tractable** *adj* ▸**at'tractor** *n*

attraction ❶ (ə'trækʃən) *n* **1** the act or quality of attracting. **2** a person or thing that attracts or is intended to attract. **3** a force by which one object attracts another: *magnetic attraction.*

attractive ❶ (ə'træktɪv) *adj* **1** appealing to the senses or mind through beauty, form, character, etc. **2** arousing interest: *an attractive opportunity.* **3** possessing the ability to draw or pull: *an attractive force.*
▸**at'tractively** *adv*

attrib. *abbrev. for:* **1** attribute. **2** attributive.

attribute ❶ *vb* (ə'trɪbju:t). **attributes, attributing, attributed. 1** (*tr;* usually foll. by *to*) to regard as belonging (to), produced (by), or resulting (from): *to attribute a painting to Picasso.* ◆ *n* ('ætrɪ,bju:t). **2** a property, quality, or feature belonging to or representative of a person or thing. **3** an object accepted as belonging to a particular office or position. **4** *Grammar.* **4a** an adjective or adjectival phrase. **4b** an attributive adjective. **5** *Logic.* the property or feature that is affirmed or denied concerning the subject of a proposition. [C15: from L *attribuere* to associate with, from *tribuere* to give]
▸**at'tributable** *adj* ▸**attribution** (,ætrɪ'bju:ʃən) *n*

attributive (ə'trɪbjʊtɪv) *adj* **1** relating to an attribute. **2** *Grammar.* (of an adjective or adjectival phrase) preceding the noun modified. Cf. **predicative. 3** *Philosophy.* relative to an understood domain, as *small* in *that elephant is small.*

THESAURUS

convoy, guard, squire, usher **8** = **serve**, be in the service of, wait upon, work for

Antonyms *vb* ≠ **be present:** be absent, miss, play truant ≠ **look after, apply oneself to:** neglect ≠ **pay attention:** discount, disregard, ignore, neglect ≠ **accompany:** dissociate

attendance *n* **1** = **presence**, appearance, attending, being there **2** = **turnout**, audience, crowd, gate, house, number present

attendant *n* **1, 2** = **assistant**, aide, auxiliary, chaperon, companion, custodian, escort, flunky, follower, guard, guide, helper, lackey, menial, page, servant, steward, underling, usher, waiter ◆ *adj* **5** = **accompanying**, accessory, associated, concomitant, consequent, related

attention *n* **1** = **concentration**, consideration, contemplation, deliberation, heed, heedfulness, intentness, mind, scrutiny, thinking, thought, thoughtfulness **2** = **notice**, awareness, consciousness, consideration, observation, recognition, regard **3** = **care**, concern, looking after, ministration, treatment **4** *usually plural* = **courtesy**, assiduities, care, civility, compliment, consideration, deference, gallantry, mindfulness, politeness, regard, respect, service

Antonyms *n* ≠ **concentration, notice:** carelessness, disregard, disrespect, distraction, inattention, laxity, laxness, thoughtlessness, unconcern ≠ **care:** negligence ≠ **courtesy:** discourtesy, impoliteness

attentive *adj* **1** = **intent**, alert, awake, careful, concentrating, heedful, listening, mindful, observant, on one's toes, regardful, studious, watchful **2** = **considerate**, accommodating, civil, conscientious, courteous, devoted, gallant, gracious, helpful, kind, obliging, polite, respectful, thoughtful

Antonyms *adj* ≠ **intent:** absent-minded, careless, distracted, dreamy, heedless, inattentive, preoccupied, unheeding, unmindful ≠ **considerate:** neglectful, negligent, remiss, thoughtless

attenuate *vb* **1** = **weaken**, adulterate, contract, decrease, devaluate, dilute, diminish, enervate, enfeeble, lessen, lower, reduce, sap, water down **2** = **stretch out**, draw out, elongate, extend, lengthen, make fine, make slender, rarefy, refine, slim, spin out, thin ◆ *adj* **3** = **weakened**, adulterated, contracted, decreased, devalued, dilute, diluted, diminished, enervated, enfeebled, lessened, lowered, reduced, sapped, watered down

attest *vb* **1-4** = **testify**, adjure, affirm, assert, authenticate, aver, bear out, bear witness, certify, confirm, corroborate, declare, demonstrate, display, evince, exhibit, give evidence, invoke, manifest, prove, ratify, seal, show, substantiate, swear, verify, vouch for, warrant, witness

Antonyms *vb* contradict, controvert, deny, disprove, gainsay (*arch. or literary*), give the lie to, make a nonsense of, prove false, rebut, refute

attic *n* **1** = **loft**, garret

Attic *adj* **2** = **classical**, chaste, correct, elegant, graceful, polished, pure, refined, simple, tasteful

attire *vb* **1** = **dress**, accoutre, apparel, array, clothe, costume, deck out, equip, fit out, garb, get ready, rig out, robe, turn out ◆ *n* **2** = **clothes**, accoutrements, apparel, array (*poetic*), clothing, costume, dress, garb, garments, gear (*inf.*), habiliments, habit, outfit, raiment (*arch. or poetic*), robes, uniform, vestment, wear

attitude *n* **1** = **disposition**, approach, frame of mind, mood, opinion, outlook, perspective, point of view, position, stance, view **2** = **position**, pose, posture, stance **3** = **manner**, air, aspect, bearing, carriage, condition, demeanour, mien (*literary*)

attract *vb* **4** = **appeal to**, allure, bewitch, captivate, catch (someone's) eye, charm, decoy, draw, enchant, endear, engage, entice, fascinate, incline, induce, interest, invite, lure, pull (*inf.*), tempt

Antonyms *vb* disgust, give one the creeps (*inf.*), put one off, repel, repulse, revolt, turn one off (*inf.*)

attraction *n* **1, 3** = **appeal**, allure, attractiveness, bait, captivation, charm, come-on (*inf.*), draw, enchantment, endearment, enticement, fascination, incentive, inducement, interest, invitation, lure, magnetism, pull (*inf.*), temptation, temptingness

attractive *adj* **1, 2** = **appealing**, agreeable, alluring, beautiful, bonny, captivating, charming, comely, cute, engaging, enticing, fair, fascinating, fetching, glamorous, good-looking, gorgeous, handsome, interesting, inviting, likable *or* likeable, lovely, magnetic, pleasant, pleasing, prepossessing, pretty, seductive, tempting, winning, winsome

Antonyms *adj* disagreeable, displeasing, distasteful, offensive, repulsive, ugly, unappealing, unbecoming, uninviting, unlikable *or* unlikeable, unpleasant, unsightly

attributable *adj* **1** = **ascribable**, accountable, applicable, assignable, blamable *or* blameable, explicable, imputable, placeable, referable *or* referrable, traceable

attribute *vb* **1** = **ascribe**, apply, assign, blame, charge, credit, impute, lay at the door of, put down to, refer, set down to, trace to ◆ *n* **2** = **quality**, aspect, character, characteristic, facet, feature, idiosyncrasy, indication, mark, note, peculiarity, point, property, quirk, sign, symbol, trait, virtue

attribution *n* **1** = **ascription**, assignation, as-

attrition ❶ (əˈtrɪʃən) *n* **1** the act of wearing away or the state of being worn away, as by friction. **2** constant wearing down to weaken or destroy (often in **war of attrition**). **3** *Geog.* the grinding down of rock particles by friction. **4** *Theol.* sorrow for sin arising from fear of damnation, esp. as contrasted with contrition. [C14: from LL *attrītiō* a rubbing against something, from L *atterere* to weaken, from *terere* to rub]
attune ❶ (əˈtjuːn) *vb* **attunes, attuning, attuned.** (*tr*) to adjust or accustom (a person or thing); acclimatize.
ATV *abbrev. for* all-terrain vehicle.
at. vol. *abbrev. for* atomic volume.
at. wt. *abbrev. for* atomic weight.
atypical ❶ (eɪˈtɪpɪkᵊl) *adj* not typical; deviating from or not conforming to type.
▸**aˈtypically** *adv*
Au *the chemical symbol for* gold. [from NL *aurum*]
aubade (əʊˈbɑːd) *n* a poem or short musical piece to greet the dawn. [C19: F, from OProvençal *auba* dawn, ult. from L *albus* white]
aubergine (ˈəʊbəˌʒiːn) *n* **1** *Chiefly Brit.* a tropical Old World plant widely cultivated for its egg-shaped typically dark purple fruit. US, Canad., and Austral. name: **eggplant. 2** the fruit of this plant, which is cooked and eaten as a vegetable. **3a** a dark purple colour. **3b** (*as adj*): *an aubergine dress.* [C18: from F, from Catalan *albergínia*, from Ar. *al-bādindjān*, ult. from Sansk. *vatin-ganah*, from ?]
aubrietia, aubrieta, *or* **aubretia** (ɔːˈbriːʃə) *n* a trailing purple-flowered plant native to European mountains but widely planted in rock gardens. [C19: from NL, after Claude *Aubriet*, 18th-cent. F painter of flowers and animals]
auburn ❶ (ˈɔːbᵊn) *n* **a** a moderate reddish-brown colour. **b** (*as adj*): *auburn hair.* [C15 (orig. meaning: blond): from OF *alborne* blond, from Med. L, from L *albus* white]
au courant *French.* (o kurɑ̃) *adj* up-to-date, esp. in knowledge of current affairs. [lit.: in the current]
auction (ˈɔːkʃən) *n* **1** a public sale of goods or property in which prospective purchasers bid until the highest price is reached. **2** the competitive calls made in bridge before play begins. ◆ *vb* **3** (*tr*; *often foll. by off*) to sell by auction. [C16: from L *auctiō* an increasing, from *augēre* to increase]
auction bridge *n* a variety of bridge in which all the tricks made score towards game.
auctioneer (ˌɔːkʃəˈnɪə) *n* **1** a person who conducts an auction. ◆ *vb* **2** (*tr*) to sell by auction.
auctorial (ɔːkˈtɔːrɪəl) *adj* of or relating to an author. [C19: from L *auctor* AUTHOR]
audacious ❶ (ɔːˈdeɪʃəs) *adj* **1** recklessly bold or daring. **2** impudent or presumptuous. [C16: from L *audāx* bold, from *audēre* to dare]
▸**auˈdaciousness** *or* **audacity** (ɔːˈdæsɪtɪ) *n*
audible ❶ (ˈɔːdɪbᵊl) *adj* perceptible to the hearing; loud enough to be heard. [C16: from LL, from L *audīre* to hear]
▸ˌ**audiˈbility** *or* ˈ**audibleness** *n* ▸ˈ**audibly** *adv*
audience ❶ (ˈɔːdɪəns) *n* **1** a group of spectators or listeners, esp. at a concert or play. **2** the people reached by a book, film, or radio or television programme. **3** the devotees or followers of a public entertainer, etc. **4** a formal interview with a monarch or head of state. [C14: from OF, from L *audientia* a hearing, from *audīre* to hear]
audio (ˈɔːdɪəʊ) *n* (*modifier*) **1** of or relating to sound or hearing: *audio frequency.* **2** relating to or employed in the transmission or reproduction of sound. [C20: from L *audīre* to hear]
audio book *n* a reading of a book recorded on tape.
audio frequency *n* a frequency in the range 20 hertz to 20 000 hertz. A sound wave of this frequency would be audible to the human ear.
audiology (ˌɔːdɪˈɒlədʒɪ) *n* the scientific study of hearing, often including the treatment of persons with hearing defects.
▸ˌ**audiˈologist** *n*
audiometer (ˌɔːdɪˈɒmɪtə) *n* an instrument for testing hearing.
▸ˌ**audiˈometrist** *n* ▸ˌ**audiˈometry** *n*
audiophile (ˈɔːdɪəʊˌfaɪl) *n* a person who has a great interest in high-fidelity sound reproduction.
audiotypist (ˈɔːdɪəʊˌtaɪpɪst) *n* a typist trained to type from a dictating machine.
▸ˈ**audioˌtyping** *n*
audiovisual (ˌɔːdɪəʊˈvɪʒʊəl) *adj* (esp. of teaching aids) involving or directed at both hearing and sight.
▸ˌ**audioˈvisually** *adv*
audit ❶ (ˈɔːdɪt) *n* **1a** an inspection, correction, and verification of business accounts, conducted by an independent qualified accountant. **1b** (*as modifier*): *audit report.* **2** *US.* an audited account. **3** any thorough-going examination or check. ◆ *vb* **audits, auditing, audited. 4** to inspect, correct, and certify (accounts, etc.). [C15: from L *audītus* a hearing, from *audīre* to hear]
audition (ɔːˈdɪʃən) *n* **1** a test at which a performer or musician is asked to demonstrate his ability for a particular role, etc. **2** the act or power of hearing. ◆ *vb* **3** to judge by means of or be tested in an audition. [C16: from L *audītiō* a hearing, from *audīre* to hear]
auditor (ˈɔːdɪtə) *n* **1** a person qualified to audit accounts. **2** a person who hears or listens. [C14: from OF, from L *audītor* a hearer]
▸ˌ**audiˈtorial** *adj*
Auditor General *n* (in Canada) an officer appointed by the Governor General to audit the accounts of the Federal Government and report to Parliament.
auditorium (ˌɔːdɪˈtɔːrɪəm) *n, pl* **auditoriums** *or* **auditoria** (-ˈtɔːrɪə). **1** the area of a concert hall, theatre, etc., in which the audience sits. **2** *US & Canad.* a building for public meetings. [C17: from L: a judicial examination]
auditory (ˈɔːdɪtərɪ) *adj* of or relating to hearing or the sense of hearing. [C14: from L *audītōrius* relating to hearing, from *audīre* to hear]
au fait ❶ *French.* (o fɛ) *adj* fully informed; in touch or expert. [C18: lit.: to the point]
au fond *French.* (o fɔ̃) *adv* fundamentally; essentially. [lit.: at the bottom]
auf Wiedersehen *German.* (auf ˈviːdərzeːən) *sentence substitute.* goodbye, until we see each other again.
Aug. *abbrev. for* August.
Augean (ɔːˈdʒiːən) *adj* extremely dirty or corrupt. [C16: from *Augeas*, in Gk myth., king whose filthy stables Hercules cleaned in one day]
augend (ˈɔːdʒɛnd, ɔːˈdʒɛnd) *n* a number to which another number, the addend, is added. [from L *augendum*, from *augēre* to increase]
auger (ˈɔːgə) *n* **1** a hand tool with a bit shaped like a corkscrew, for boring holes in wood. **2** a larger tool of the same kind for boring holes in the ground. [C15: *an augur*, mistaken division of *a nauger*, from OE *nafugār* nave (of a wheel) spear, from *nafu* NAVE² + *gār* spear]
aught *or* **ought** (ɔːt) (*used with a negative or in conditional or interrogative sentences or clauses*) *Arch. or literary.* ◆ *pron* **1** anything whatever (esp. in **for aught I know**). ◆ *adv* **2** *Dialect.* to any degree. [OE *āwiht*, from *ā* ever, + *wiht* thing]
augment ❶ (ɔːgˈmɛnt) *vb* to make or become greater in number, strength, etc. [C15: from LL, from *augmentum* growth, from L *augēre* to increase]
▸**augˈmentable** *adj* ▸**augˈmenter** *n*
augmentation ❶ (ˌɔːgmɛnˈteɪʃən) *n* **1** the act of augmenting or the state of being augmented. **2** the amount by which something is increased.
augmentative (ɔːgˈmɛntətɪv) *adj* **1** tending or able to augment. **2** *Grammar.* denoting an affix that may be added to a word to convey the meaning *large* or *great*: for example, the suffix *-ote* in Spanish, where *hombre* means man and *hombrote* big man.
augmented (ɔːgˈmɛntɪd) *adj* **1** *Music.* (of an interval) increased from

THESAURUS

signment, attachment, blame, charge, credit, imputation, placement, referral
attrition *n* **1, 2** = **wearing down**, attenuation, debilitation, harassment, harrying, thinning out, weakening
attune *vb* = **accustom**, acclimatize, accord, adapt, adjust, coordinate, familiarize, harmonize, modulate, regulate, set, tune
attuned *adj* = **accustomed**, acclimatized, adjusted, coordinated, familiarized, harmonized, in accord, in harmony, in tune
atypical *adj* = **unusual**, deviant, exceptional, nonconforming, out of keeping, out of the ordinary, singular, uncharacteristic, uncommon, unconforming, unconventional, uncustomary, unique, unorthodox, unrepresentative
Antonyms *adj* archetypal, average, characteristic, classic, conforming, conventional, customary, illustrative, in character, in keeping, model, normal, ordinary, orthodox, representative, standard, stock, true to type, unexceptional, unsingular, usual
auburn *adj* = **reddish-brown**, chestnut-coloured, copper-coloured, henna, nutbrown, russet, rust-coloured, tawny, Titian red
audacious *adj* **1** = **daring**, adventurous, bold, brave, courageous, daredevil, dauntless, death-defying, enterprising, fearless, intrepid, rash, reckless, risky, valiant, venturesome **2** = **cheeky**, assuming, brazen, defiant, disrespectful, forward, fresh (*inf.*), impertinent, impudent, insolent, in-your-face (*Brit. sl.*), pert, presumptuous, rude, sassy (*US inf.*), shameless
Antonyms *adj* ≠ **daring:** careful, cautious, cowardly, frightened, guarded, prudent, timid, unadventurous, unenterprising ≠ **cheeky:** deferential, gracious, tactful, unassuming
audacity *n* **1** = **daring**, adventurousness, audaciousness, boldness, bravery, courage, dauntlessness, enterprise, face (*inf.*), fearlessness, front, guts (*inf.*), intrepidity, nerve, rashness, recklessness, valour, venturesomeness **2** = **cheek**, audaciousness, brass neck (*Brit. inf.*), chutzpah (*US & Canad. inf.*), defiance, disrespectfulness, effrontery, forwardness, gall (*inf.*), impertinence, impudence, insolence, neck (*inf.*), nerve, pertness, presumption, rudeness, sassiness (*US inf.*), shamelessness
audible *adj* = **clear**, detectable, discernible, distinct, hearable, perceptible
Antonyms *adj* faint, imperceptible, inaudible, indistinct, low, out of earshot
audience *n* **1** = **spectators**, assemblage, assembly, congregation, crowd, gallery, gathering, house, listeners, onlookers, turnout, viewers **3** = **public**, devotees, fans, following, market **4** = **interview**, consultation, hearing, meeting, reception
audit *n* **1** = **inspection**, balancing, check, checking, examination, investigation, review, scrutiny, verification ◆ *vb* **4** = **inspect**, balance, check, examine, go over, go through, investigate, review, scrutinize, verify
au fait *adj* = **fully informed**, abreast of, *au courant*, clued-up (*inf.*), conversant, expert, familiar, in the know, in the loop, in touch, knowledgeable, on the ball (*inf.*), up to speed, well-acquainted, well up
augment *vb* = **increase**, add to, amplify, boost, build up, dilate, enhance, enlarge, expand, extend, grow, heighten, inflate, intensify, magnify, multiply, raise, reinforce, strengthen, swell
Antonyms *vb* contract, curtail, cut down, decrease, diminish, lessen, lower, reduce, shrink
augmentation *n* **1, 2** = **increase**, accession, addition, amplification, boost, build-up, dilation, enhancement, enlargement, expansion, extension, growth, heightening, inflation, in-

being perfect or major by the raising of the higher note or the dropping of the lower note by one semitone: *C to G sharp is an augmented fifth.* **2** having been increased, esp. in number: *an augmented orchestra.*

au gratin (*French* o gratẽ) *adj* covered and cooked with browned breadcrumbs and sometimes cheese. [F, lit.: with the grating]

augur ➊ ('ɔ:gə) *n* **1** (in ancient Rome) a religious official who observed and interpreted omens and signs. **2** any prophet or soothsayer. ◆ *vb* **3** to predict (some future event), as from signs or omens. **4** (*tr; may take a clause as object*) to be an omen (of). **5** (*intr*) to foreshadow future events: *this augurs well for us.* [C14: from L: a diviner, ?from *augēre* to increase]
▸**augural** ('ɔ:gjurəl) *adj*

augury ➊ ('ɔ:gjurɪ) *n, pl* **auguries. 1** the art of or a rite conducted by an augur. **2** a sign or portent; omen.

august ➊ (ɔ:'gʌst) *adj* **1** dignified or imposing. **2** of noble birth or high rank: *an august lineage.* [C17: from L *augustus;* rel. to *augēre* to increase]
▸**au'gustness** *n*

August ('ɔ:gəst) *n* the eighth month of the year, consisting of 31 days.

Augustan (ɔ:'gʌstən) *adj* **1** characteristic of or relating to the Roman emperor Augustus Caesar (63 B.C.–14 A.D.), his period, or the poets writing during his reign. **2** of or characteristic of any literary period noted for refinement and classicism, esp. the 18th century in England. ◆ *n* **3** an author in an Augustan Age.

Augustinian (ˌɔ:gə'stɪnɪən) *adj* **1** of Saint Augustine of Hippo (354–430 A.D.), his doctrines, or the Christian religious orders founded on his doctrines. ◆ *n* **2** a member of any of several religious orders that are governed by the rule of Saint Augustine. **3** a person who follows the doctrines of Saint Augustine.

auk (ɔ:k) *n* **1** a diving bird of northern oceans having a heavy body, short tail, narrow wings, and a black-and-white plumage. See also **great auk, razorbill. 2 little auk.** a small short-billed auk, abundant in Arctic regions. [C17: from ON *ālka*]

au lait (əʊ 'leɪ) *adj* prepared or served with milk. [F, lit.: with milk]

auld (ɔ:ld) *adj* a Scottish word for **old.** [OE *āld*]

auld lang syne ('ɔ:ld læŋ 'saɪn) *n* times past, esp. those remembered with nostalgia. [Scot., lit.: old long since]

aumbry ('ɔ:mbrɪ) *n, pl* **aumbries.** a variant of **ambry.**

au naturel *French.* (o natyrɛl) *adj, adv* **1** naked; nude. **2** uncooked or plainly cooked. [lit.: in (a) natural (condition)]

aunt (ɑ:nt) *n* (*often cap., esp. as a term of address*) **1** a sister of one's father or mother. **2** the wife of one's uncle. **3** a term of address used by children for a female friend of the parents. **4 my (sainted) aunt!** an exclamation of surprise. [C13: from OF, from L *amita* a father's sister]

auntie *or* **aunty** ('ɑ:ntɪ) *n, pl* **aunties.** a familiar or diminutive word for **aunt.**

Auntie ('ɑ:ntɪ) *n Brit. inf.* the BBC.

Aunt Sally ('sælɪ) *n, pl* **Aunt Sallies.** *Brit.* **1** a figure of an old woman used in fairgrounds and fêtes as a target. **2** any person who is a target for insults or criticism.

au pair (əʊ 'pɛə) *n* **a** a young foreigner, usually a girl, who undertakes housework in exchange for board and lodging, esp. in order to learn the language. **b** (*as modifier*): *an au pair girl.* [C20: from F: on an equal footing]

aura ➊ ('ɔ:rə) *n, pl* **auras** *or* **aurae** ('ɔ:ri:). **1** a distinctive air or quality considered to be characteristic of a person or thing. **2** any invisible emanation, esp. surrounding a person or object. **3** *Pathol.* strange sensations, such as noises in the ears or flashes of light, that immediately precede an attack, esp. of epilepsy. [C18: via L from Gk: breeze]

aural ('ɔ:rəl) *adj* of or relating to the sense or organs of hearing; auricular. [C19: from L *auris* ear]
▸**'aurally** *adv*

aureate ('ɔ:rɪɪt) *adj* **1** covered with gold; gilded. **2** (of a style of writing or speaking) excessively elaborate. [C15: from LL, from L *aureus* golden, from *aurum* gold]

aureole ('ɔ:rɪˌəʊl) *or* **aureola** (ɔ:'ri:ələ) *n* **1** a border of light or radiance enveloping the head of a figure represented as holy. **2** a less common word for **halo. 3** another name for **corona** (sense 2). [C13: from OF, from Med. L (*corōna*) *aureola* golden (crown), from L, from *aurum* gold]

au revoir *French.* (o rəvwar) *sentence substitute.* goodbye. [lit.: to the seeing again]

auric ('ɔ:rɪk) *adj* of or containing gold, esp. in the trivalent state; designating a gold(III) compound. [C19: from L *aurum* gold]

auricle ('ɔ:rɪk^{ə}l) *n* **1** the upper chamber of the heart; atrium. **2** Also called: **pinna.** *Anat.* the external part of the ear. **3** *Biol.* an ear-shaped part or appendage. [C17: from L *auricula* the external ear, from *auris* ear]
▸**'auricled** *adj*

auricula (ɔ:'rɪkjulə) *n, pl* **auriculae** (-ˌli:) *or* **auriculas. 1** Also called: **bear's-ear.** a widely cultivated alpine primrose with leaves shaped like a bear's ear. **2** another word for **auricle** (sense 3). [C17: from NL, from L; see AURICLE]

auricular (ɔ:'rɪkjulə) *adj* **1** of, relating to, or received by the sense or organs of hearing; aural. **2** shaped like an ear. **3** of or relating to an auricle of the heart.

auriferous (ɔ:'rɪfərəs) *adj* (of rock) containing gold; gold-bearing. [C18: from L, from *aurum* gold + *ferre* to bear]

Aurignacian (ˌɔ:rɪg'neɪʃən) *adj* of or produced during a flint culture of the Upper Palaeolithic type characterized by the use of bone and antler tools, and also by cave art. [C20: after *Aurignac,* France, near the cave where remains were discovered]

aurochs ('ɔ:rɒks) *n, pl* **aurochs.** a recently extinct member of the cattle tribe that inhabited forests in N Africa, Europe, and SW Asia. Also called: **urus.** [C18: from G, from OHG *ūrohso,* from *ūro* bison + *ohso* OX]

aurora (ɔ:'rɔ:rə) *n, pl* **auroras** *or* **aurorae** (-ri:). **1** an atmospheric phenomenon consisting of bands, curtains, or streamers of light, that move across the sky. **2** *Poetic.* the dawn. [C14: from L: dawn]
▸**au'roral** *adj*

aurora australis (ɒ'streɪlɪs) *n* (*sometimes cap.*) the aurora seen around the South Pole. Also called: **southern lights.** [NL: southern aurora]

aurora borealis (ˌbɔ:rɪ'eɪlɪs) *n* (*sometimes cap.*) the aurora seen around the North Pole. Also called: **northern lights.** [C17: NL: northern aurora]

aurous ('ɔ:rəs) *adj* of or containing gold, esp. in the monovalent state; designating a gold(I) compound. [C19: from F *aureux,* LL *aurōsus* gold-coloured, from L *aurum* gold]

auscultation (ˌɔ:skəl'teɪʃən) *n* **1** the diagnostic technique in medicine of listening to the various internal sounds made by the body, usually with the aid of a stethoscope. **2** the act of listening. [C19: from L, from *auscultāre* to listen attentively; rel. to L *auris* ear]
▸**'auscul,tate** *vb* ▸**auscultatory** (ɔ:'skʌltətərɪ) *adj*

auspice ➊ ('ɔ:spɪs) *n* **1** (*usually pl*) patronage (esp. in **under the auspices of**). **2** (*often pl*) an omen, esp. one that is favourable. [C16: from L *auspicium* augury from birds]

auspicious ➊ (ɔ:'spɪʃəs) *adj* **1** favourable or propitious. **2** *Arch.* fortunate.
▸**aus'piciously** *adv* ▸**aus'piciousness** *n*

> **USAGE NOTE** The use of *auspicious* to mean 'very special' (as in *this auspicious occasion*) should be avoided.

Aussie ('ɒzɪ) *n, adj Inf.* Australian.

Aust. *abbrev. for:* **1** Australia(n). **2** Austria(n).

austere ➊ (ɒ'stɪə) *adj* **1** stern or severe in attitude or manner. **2** grave, sober, or serious. **3** self-disciplined, abstemious, or ascetic: *an austere life.* **4** severely simple or plain: *an austere design.* [C14: from OF, from L *austērus* sour, from Gk *austēros* astringent; rel. to Gk *hauein* to dry]
▸**aus'terely** *adv*

austerity ➊ (ɒ'stɛrɪtɪ) *n, pl* **austerities. 1** the state or quality of being austere. **2** (*often pl*) an austere habit, practice, or act. **3a** reduced availability of luxuries and consumer goods. **3b** (*as modifier*): *an austerity budget.*

austral[1] ('ɔ:strəl) *adj* of or coming from the south: *austral winds.* [C14: from L *austrālis,* from *auster* the south wind]

austral[2] (aʊ'strɑ:l) *n, pl* **australes** (-'strɑ:les). a former monetary unit of Argentina. [from Sp.; see AUSTRAL[1]]

Austral. *abbrev. for:* **1** Australasia. **2** Australia(n).

Australasian (ˌɒstrə'leɪzɪən) *adj* **1** of or relating to Australia, New Zealand, and neighbouring islands. **2** (of organizations) having members in Australia and New Zealand.

THESAURUS

tensification, magnification, multiplication, reinforcement, rise, strengthening, swelling

augur *vb* **3-5** = **bode,** be an omen of, bespeak (*arch.*), betoken, foreshadow, harbinger, herald, portend, predict, prefigure, presage, promise, prophesy, signify

augury *n* **1** = **prediction,** divination, prophecy, soothsaying, sortilege **2** = **omen,** auspice, forerunner, forewarning, harbinger, herald, portent, precursor, presage, prognostication, promise, prophecy, sign, token, warning

august *adj* **1, 2** = **noble,** dignified, exalted, glorious, grand, high-ranking, imposing, impressive, kingly, lofty, magnificent, majestic, monumental, regal, solemn, stately, superb

aura *n* **1** = **air,** ambience, aroma, atmosphere, emanation, feel, feeling, mood, odour, quality, scent, suggestion, tone, vibes (*sl.*), vibrations (*sl.*)

auspice *n* **1** *usually plural As in* **under the auspices of** = **support,** advocacy, aegis, authority, backing, care, championship, charge, control, countenance, guidance, influence, patronage, protection, sponsorship, supervision

auspicious *adj* **1** = **favourable,** bright, encouraging, felicitous, fortunate, happy, hopeful, lucky, opportune, promising, propitious, prosperous, rosy, timely
Antonyms *adj* bad, black, discouraging, ill-omened, inauspicious, infelicitous, ominous, unfavourable, unfortunate, unlucky, unpromising, unpropitious

austere *adj* **1, 2** = **stern,** cold, exacting, forbidding, formal, grave, grim, hard, harsh, inflexible, rigorous, serious, severe, solemn, stiff, strict, stringent, unfeeling, unrelenting **3** = **ascetic,** abstemious, abstinent, chaste, continent, economical, exacting, puritanical, rigid, self-denying, self-disciplined, sober, solemn, Spartan, strait-laced, strict, unrelenting **4** = **plain,** bleak, economical, harsh, severe, simple, spare, Spartan, stark, subdued, unadorned, unornamented
Antonyms *adj* ≠ **stern:** affable, cheerful, convivial, flexible, free-and-easy, genial, indulgent, jovial, kindly, permissive, sweet ≠ **ascetic:** abandoned, free-and-easy, immoral, indulgent, loose, permissive ≠ **plain:** comfortable, indulgent, luxurious

austerity *n* **1** = **sternness,** coldness, exactingness, forbiddingness, formality, gravity, grimness, hardness, harshness, inflexibility, rigour, seriousness, severity, solemnity, stiffness, strictness **1** = **asceticism,** abstemiousness, abstinence, chasteness, chastity, continence, economy, exactingness, puritanism, rigidity, self-denial, self-discipline, sobriety, solemnity,

Australian (ɒ'streɪlɪən) *n* **1** a native or inhabitant of Australia, the smallest continent. **2** the form of English spoken in Australia. ◆ *adj* **3** of, relating to, or characteristic of Australia, the Australians, or their form of English.

Australiana (ɒˌstreɪlɪ'ɑːnə) *pl n* objects, books, documents, etc. relating to Australia and its history and culture.

Australian Rules *n* (*functioning as sing*) a game resembling rugby, played in Australia between teams of 18 men each on an oval pitch, with a ball resembling a large rugby ball. Players attempt to kick the ball between posts (without crossbars) at either end of the pitch.

Australoid ('ɒstrəˌlɔɪd) *adj* **1** denoting, relating to, or belonging to a racial group that includes the native Australians and certain other peoples of southern Asia and the Pacific islands. ◆ *n* **2** any member of this racial group.

australopithecine (ˌɒstrələʊ'pɪθɪˌsiːn) *n* any of various extinct apelike primates whose remains have been found in southern and E Africa. Some species are estimated to be over 4.5 million years old. [C20: from NL, from L *austrālis* southern + Gk *pithēkos* ape]

Australorp ('ɒstrəˌlɔːp) *n* a heavy black breed of domestic fowl laying brown eggs. [shortened from *Austral(ian Black) Orp(ington)*]

Austrian ('ɒstrɪən) *adj* **1** of or relating to Austria, a republic in Central Europe. ◆ *n* **2** a native or inhabitant of Austria.

Austrian blind *n* a window blind consisting of rows of vertically gathered fabric that may be drawn up to form a series of ruches.

Austro-[1] ('ɒstrəʊ) *combining form.* southern: *Austro-Asiatic.* [from L *auster* the south wind]

Austro-[2] ('ɒstrəʊ) *combining form.* Austrian: *Austro-Hungarian.*

AUT (in Britain) *abbrev. for* Association of University Teachers.

autarchy ('ɔːtɑːkɪ) *n, pl* **autarchies.** unlimited rule; autocracy. [C17: from Gk *autarkhia,* from *autarkhos* autocratic]
▸**au'tarchic** *or* **au'tarchical** *adj*

autarky ('ɔːtɑːkɪ) *n, pl* **autarkies.** (esp. of a political unit) a system or policy of economic self-sufficiency. [C17: from Gk *autarkeia,* from *autarkēs* self-sufficient, from AUTO- + *arkein* to suffice]
▸**au'tarkic** *adj* ▸**'autarkist** *n*

auteur (əʊ'tɜː) *n* a director whose creative influence on a film is so great as to be considered its author. [F: author]
▸**au'teurism** *n* ▸**au'teurist** *n*

authentic ➊ (ɔː'θentɪk) *adj* **1** of undisputed origin or authorship; genuine. **2** trustworthy; reliable: *an authentic account.* **3** (of a deed, etc.) duly executed. **4** *Music.* **4a** using period instruments and historically researched scores and playing techniques. **4b** (*in combination*): *an authentic-instrument performance.* **5** *Music.* commencing on the perfect and ending an octave higher. Cf. **plagal.** [C14: from LL *authenticus* coming from the author, from Gk, from *authentēs* one who acts independently, from AUTO- + *hentēs* a doer]
▸**au'thentically** *adv* ▸**authenticity** (ˌɔːθen'tɪsɪtɪ) *n*

authenticate ➊ (ɔː'θentɪˌkeɪt) *vb* **authenticates, authenticating, authenticated.** (*tr*) **1** to establish as genuine or valid. **2** to give authority or legal validity to.
▸**auˌthenti'cation** *n* ▸**au'thentiˌcator** *n*

author ➊ ('ɔːθə) *n* **1** a person who composes a book, article, or other written work. Related adj: **auctorial. 2** a person who writes books as a profession; writer. **3** an originator or creator: *the author of this plan.* ◆ *vb* (*tr*) **4** to write or originate. [C14: from OF, from L *auctor* author, from *augēre* to increase]
▸**authorial** (ɔː'θɔːrɪəl) *adj*

authoritarian ➊ (ɔːˌθɒrɪ'teərɪən) *adj* **1** favouring or characterized by strict obedience to authority. **2** favouring or relating to government by a small elite. **3** dictatorial; domineering. ◆ *n* **4** a person who favours or practises authoritarian policies.

authoritative ➊ (ɔː'θɒrɪtətɪv) *adj* **1** recognized or accepted as being true or reliable. **2** commanding: *an authoritative manner.* **3** possessing or supported by authority; official.
▸**au'thoritatively** *adv* ▸**au'thoritativeness** *n*

authority ➊ (ɔː'θɒrɪtɪ) *n, pl* **authorities. 1** the power or right to control, judge, or prohibit the actions of others. **2** (*often pl*) a person or group of people having this power, such as a government, police force, etc. **3** a position that commands such a power or right (often in **in authority**). **4** such a power or right delegated: *she has his authority.* **5** the ability to influence or control others. **6** an expert or an authoritative written work in a particular field. **7** evidence or testimony. **8** confidence resulting from great expertise. **9** (*cap. when part of a name*) a public board or corporation exercising governmental authority: *Advertising Standards Authority.* [C14: from OF, from L, from *auctor* author]

authorize ➊ *or* **authorise** ('ɔːθəˌraɪz) *vb* **authorizes, authorizing, authorized** *or* **authorises, authorising, authorised.** (*tr*) **1** to confer authority upon (someone to do something). **2** to permit (someone to do or be something) with official sanction.
▸**ˌauthori'zation** *or* **ˌauthori'sation** *n*

Authorized Version *n* **the.** an English translation of the Bible published in 1611 under James I. Also called: **King James Version.**

authorship ('ɔːθəˌʃɪp) *n* **1** the origin or originator of a written work, plan, etc. **2** the profession of writing books.

autism ('ɔːtɪzəm) *n Psychiatry.* abnormal self-absorption, usually affecting children, characterized by lack of response to people and limited ability to communicate. [C20: from Gk *autos* self + -ISM]
▸**au'tistic** *adj*

auto ('ɔːtəʊ) *n, pl* **autos.** *US & Canad. inf.* **a** short for **automobile. b** (*as modifier*): *auto parts.*

auto. *abbrev. for:* **1** automatic. **2** automobile. **3** automotive.

auto- *or sometimes before a vowel* **aut-** *combining form.* **1** self; same; of or by the same one: *autobiography.* **2** self-caused: *autohypnosis.* **3** self-propelling: *automobile.* [from Gk *autos* self]

autobahn ('ɔːtəˌbɑːn) *n* a motorway in German-speaking countries. [C20: from G from *Auto* car + *Bahn* road, track]

autobiography ➊ (ˌɔːtəʊbaɪ'ɒgrəfɪ) *n, pl* **autobiographies.** an account of a person's life written or otherwise recorded by that person.
▸**ˌautobi'ographer** *n* ▸**autobiographical** (ˌɔːtəˌbaɪə'græfɪk°l) *adj*

autocephalous (ˌɔːtəʊ'sefələs) *adj* (of an Eastern Christian Church) governed by its own national synods and appointing its own patriarchs or prelates.

autochthon (ɔː'tɒkθən) *n, pl* **autochthons** *or* **autochthones** (-θəˌniːz). **1** (*often pl*) one of the earliest known inhabitants of any country. **2** an animal or plant that is native to a particular region. [C17: from Gk *autokhthōn* from the earth itself, from AUTO- + *khthōn* the earth]
▸**au'tochthonous** *adj*

autoclave ('ɔːtəˌkleɪv) *n* **1** a strong sealed vessel used for chemical reactions at high pressure. **2** an apparatus for sterilizing objects (esp. surgical instruments) by means of steam under pressure. [C19: from F AUTO- + *-clave,* from L *clāvis* key]

autocracy ➊ (ɔː'tɒkrəsɪ) *n, pl* **autocracies. 1** government by an individual with unrestricted authority. **2** a country, society, etc., ruled by an autocrat.

autocrat ➊ ('ɔːtəˌkræt) *n* **1** a ruler who possesses absolute and unrestricted authority. **2** a domineering or dictatorial person.
▸**ˌauto'cratic** *adj* ▸**ˌauto'cratically** *adv*

autocross ('ɔːtəʊˌkrɒs) *n* a motor sport in which cars race over a half-mile circuit of rough grass.

THESAURUS

Spartanism, strictness **1 = plainness,** economy, severity, simplicity, spareness, Spartanism, starkness

authentic *adj* **1, 2 = genuine,** accurate, actual, authoritative, bona fide, certain, dependable, factual, faithful, legitimate, on the level (*inf.*), original, pure, real, reliable, simon-pure (*rare*), the real McCoy, true, true-to-life, trustworthy, valid, veritable
Antonyms *adj* counterfeit, fake, false, fictitious, fraudulent, hypothetical, imitation, misleading, mock, pseudo (*inf.*), spurious, supposed, synthetic, unfaithful, unreal, untrue

authenticate *vb* **1, 2 = verify,** attest, authorize, avouch, certify, confirm, endorse, guarantee, validate, vouch for, warrant
Antonyms *vb* annul, invalidate, render null and void

authenticity *n* **1, 2 = genuineness,** accuracy, actuality, authoritativeness, certainty, dependability, factualness, faithfulness, legitimacy, purity, realness, reliability, trustworthiness, truth, truthfulness, validity, veritableness, verity

author *n* **1, 2 = writer,** composer, creator **3 = creator,** architect, designer, doer, fabricator, father, founder, framer, initiator, inventor, maker, mover, originator, parent, planner, prime mover, producer

authoritarian *adj* **1, 3 = strict,** absolute, autocratic, despotic, dictatorial, disciplinarian, doctrinaire, dogmatic, domineering, harsh, imperious, rigid, severe, tyrannical, unyielding ◆ *n* **4 = disciplinarian,** absolutist, autocrat, despot, dictator, tyrant
Antonyms *adj* ≠ **strict:** broad-minded, democratic, flexible, indulgent, lenient, liberal, permissive, tolerant

authoritative *adj* **1 = reliable,** accurate, authentic, definitive, dependable, factual, faithful, learned, scholarly, sound, true, trustworthy, truthful, valid, veritable **2 = commanding,** assertive, autocratic, confident, decisive, dictatorial, dogmatic, dominating, imperative, imperious, imposing, lordly, masterly, peremptory, self-assured **3 = official,** approved, authorized, commanding, legitimate, sanctioned, sovereign
Antonyms *adj* ≠ **reliable:** deceptive, undependable, unreliable ≠ **commanding:** humble, subservient, timid, weak ≠ **official:** unauthorized, unofficial, unsanctioned

authority *n* **1 = power,** ascendancy, charge, command, control, direction, domination, dominion, force, government, influence, jurisdiction, might, prerogative, right, rule, say-so, strength, supremacy, sway, weight **2** *often plural* **= powers that be,** administration, government, management, officialdom, police, the Establishment **4 = permission,** authorization, justification, licence, permit, sanction, say-so, warrant **6 = expert,** arbiter, bible, connoisseur, guru, judge, master, professional, scholar, specialist, textbook

authorization *n* **1 = power,** ability, authority, right, say-so, strength **2 = permission,** approval, credentials, leave, licence, permit, sanction, say-so, warrant

authorize *vb* **1 = empower,** accredit, commission, enable, entitle, give authority **2 = permit,** accredit, allow, approve, confirm, countenance, give authority for, give leave, give the green light for, license, ratify, sanction, vouch for, warrant
Antonyms *vb* ban, debar, disallow, exclude, forbid, outlaw, preclude, prohibit, proscribe, rule out, veto

authorized *adj* **1 = official,** approved, commissioned, licensed, ratified, signed and sealed **2 = permitted,** allowed, approved, countenanced, licensed, sanctioned, warranted

autobiography *n* **= life story,** history, memoirs, record, résumé

autocracy *n* **1 = dictatorship,** absolutism, despotism, tyranny

autocrat *n* **1 = dictator,** absolutist, despot, tyrant

autocratic *adj* **1 = dictatorial,** absolute,

Autocue ('ɔːtəʊˌkjuː) *n Trademark.* an electronic television prompting device whereby a script, unseen by the audience, is displayed for the speaker.

auto-da-fé (ˌɔːtəʊdəˈfeɪ) *n, pl* **autos-da-fé. 1** *History.* a ceremony of the Spanish Inquisition including the pronouncement and execution of sentences passed on sinners or heretics. **2** the burning to death of people condemned as heretics by the Inquisition. [C18: from Port., lit.: act of the faith]

autoeroticism (ˌɔːtəʊɪˈrɒtɪˌsɪzəm) *or* **autoerotism** (ˌɔːtəʊˈɛrəˌtɪzəm) *n Psychol.* the arousal and use of one's own body as a sexual object.
▸ **ˌautoeˈrotic** *adj*

autoexposure (ˌɔːtəʊɪkˈspəʊʒə) *n* another name for **automatic exposure.**

autofocus ('ɔːtəʊˌfəʊkəs) *n* another name for **automatic focus.**

autogamy (ɔːˈtɒgəmɪ) *n* self-fertilization.
▸ **auˈtogamous** *adj*

autogenic training (ˌɔːtəʊˈdʒɛnɪk) *n* a technique for reducing stress through mental exercises. Also called: **autogenics.**

autogenous (ɔːˈtɒdʒɪnəs) *adj* **1** originating within the body. **2** self-produced. **3** denoting a weld in which the filler metal and the parent metal are of similar composition.
▸ **auˈtogenously** *adv*

autogiro *or* **autogyro** (ˌɔːtəʊˈdʒaɪrəʊ) *n, pl* **autogiros** *or* **autogyros.** a self-propelled aircraft supported in flight mainly by unpowered rotating horizontal blades. [C20: orig. a trademark]

autograph ('ɔːtəˌgrɑːf) *n* **1a** a handwritten signature, esp. that of a famous person. **1b** *(as modifier): an autograph album.* **2** a person's handwriting. **3a** a book, document, etc., handwritten by its author. **3b** *(as modifier): an autograph letter.* ◆ *vb (tr)* **4** to write one's signature on or in; sign. **5** to write with one's own hand.
▸ **autographic** (ˌɔːtəˈgræfɪk) *adj* ▸ **ˌautoˈgraphically** *adv*

autohypnosis (ˌɔːtəʊhɪpˈnəʊsɪs) *n Psychol.* the process or result of self-induced hypnosis.

autoimmune (ˌɔːtəʊɪˈmjuːn) *adj* (of a disease) caused by the action of antibodies produced against substances normally present in the body.
▸ **ˌautoimˈmunity** *n*

autointoxication (ˌɔːtəʊɪnˌtɒksɪˈkeɪʃən) *n* self-poisoning caused by toxic products originating within the body.

autologous (ɔːˈtɒləgəs) *adj* (of a tissue graft, blood transfusion, etc.) originating from the recipient rather than from a donor.

autolysis (ɔːˈtɒlɪsɪs) *n* the destruction of cells and tissues of an organism by enzymes produced by the cells themselves.
▸ **autolytic** (ˌɔːtəˈlɪtɪk) *adj*

automat ('ɔːtəˌmæt) *n* another name, esp. US, for **vending machine.**

automate ('ɔːtəˌmeɪt) *vb* **automates, automating, automated.** to make (a manufacturing process, factory, etc.) automatic, or (of a manufacturing process, etc.) to be made automatic.

automated teller machine *n* a computerized cash dispenser. Abbrev.: **ATM.**

automatic ❶ (ˌɔːtəˈmætɪk) *adj* **1** performed from force of habit or without conscious thought: *an automatic smile.* **2a** (of a device, mechanism, etc.) able to activate, move, or regulate itself. **2b** (of an act or process) performed by such automatic equipment. **3** (of the action of a muscle, etc.) involuntary or reflex. **4** occurring as a necessary consequence: *promotion is automatic after a year.* **5** (of a firearm) utilizing some of the force of each explosion to eject the empty shell, replace it with a new one, and fire continuously until release of the trigger. ◆ *n* **6** an automatic firearm. **7** a motor vehicle having automatic transmission. **8** a machine that operates automatically. [C18: from Gk *automatos* acting independently]
▸ **ˌautoˈmatically** *adv*

automatic data processing *n* data processing performed by automatic electromechanical devices. Abbrev.: **ADP, A.D.P., a.d.p.**

automatic door *n* a self-opening door.

automatic exposure *n* the automatic adjustment of the lens aperture and shutter speed of a camera by a control mechanism. Also called: **autoexposure.**

automatic focus *n* **a** a system in a camera that automatically adjusts the lens so that the object being photographed is in focus. **b** *(as modifier): automatic-focus lens.* Also called: **autofocus.**

automatic gain control *n* a control of a radio receiver which adjusts the magnitude of the input so that the output (or volume) remains approximately constant.

automatic pilot *n* **1** a device that automatically maintains an aircraft on a preset course. **2** *Inf.* a state of mind in which a person performs familiar tasks automatically: *I was on automatic pilot all day.* ◆ Also called: **autopilot.**

automatic transmission *n* a transmission system in a motor vehicle in which the gears change automatically.

automation (ˌɔːtəˈmeɪʃən) *n* **1** the use of methods for controlling industrial processes automatically, esp. by electronically controlled systems. **2** the extent to which a process is so controlled.

automatism (ɔːˈtɒməˌtɪzəm) *n* **1** the state or quality of being automatic; mechanical or involuntary action. **2** *Psychol.* the performance of actions, such as sleepwalking, without conscious knowledge or control.
▸ **auˈtomatist** *n*

automatize *or* **automatise** (ɔːˈtɒməˌtaɪz) *vb* **automatizes, automatizing, automatized** *or* **automatises, automatising, automatised.** to make (a process, etc.) automatic or (of a process, etc.) to be made automatic.
▸ **auˌtomatiˈzation** *or* **auˌtomatiˈsation** *n*

automaton (ɔːˈtɒmətᵊn) *n, pl* **automatons** *or* **automata. 1** a mechanical device operating under its own hidden power. **2** a person who acts mechanically. [C17: from L, from Gk, from *automatos* spontaneous]

automobile ('ɔːtəməˌbiːl) *n* another word (esp. US) for **car** (sense 1).
▸ **ˌautomoˈbilist** *n*

automobilia (ˌɔːtəməˈbiːlɪə) *pl n* items connected with cars and motoring that are of interest to the collector.

automotive (ˌɔːtəˈməʊtɪv) *adj* **1** relating to motor vehicles. **2** self-propelling.

autonomic (ˌɔːtəˈnɒmɪk) *adj* **1** occurring spontaneously. **2** of or relating to the autonomic nervous system. **3** Also: **autonomous.** (of plant movements) occurring as a result of internal stimuli.
▸ **ˌautoˈnomically** *adv*

autonomic nervous system *n* the section of the nervous system of vertebrates that controls the involuntary actions of the smooth muscles, heart, and glands.

autonomics (ˌɔːtəˈnɒmɪks) *n (functioning as sing) Electronics.* the study of self-regulating systems for process control.

autonomous ❶ (ɔːˈtɒnəməs) *adj* **1** (of a community, country, etc.) possessing a large degree of self-government. **2** of or relating to an autonomous community. **3** independent of others. **4** *Biol.* existing as an organism independent of other organisms or parts. [C19: from Gk *autonomos* living under one's own laws, from AUTO- + *nomos* law]
▸ **auˈtonomously** *adv*

autonomy ❶ (ɔːˈtɒnəmɪ) *n, pl* **autonomies. 1** the right or state of self-government, esp. when limited. **2** a state or individual possessing autonomy. **3** freedom to determine one's own actions, behaviour, etc. **4** *Philosophy.* the doctrine that the individual human will is, or ought to be, governed only by its own principles and laws. [C17: from Gk *autonomia* freedom to live by one's own laws]

autopilot (ˌɔːtəˈpaɪlət) *n* short for **automatic pilot.**

autopsy ❶ ('ɔːtəpsɪ, ɔːˈtɒp-) *n, pl* **autopsies. 1** Also called: **postmortem examination.** dissection and examination of a dead body to determine the cause of death. **2** an eyewitness observation. **3** any critical analysis. [C17: from NL, from Gk: seeing with one's own eyes, from AUTO- + *opsis* sight]

autoroute ('ɔːtəʊˌruːt) *n* a motorway in French-speaking countries. [C20: from F from *auto* car + *route* road]

autostrada ('ɔːtəʊˌstrɑːdə) *n* a motorway in Italian-speaking countries. [C20: from It. from *auto* car + *strada* road]

autosuggestion (ˌɔːtəʊsəˈdʒɛstʃən) *n* a process of suggestion in which the person unconsciously supplies the means of influencing his own behaviour or beliefs.

autotelic (ˌɔːtəʊˈtɛlɪk) *adj* being or having an end or justification in itself. [C20: from AUTO- + Gk *telos* end]

autotomy (ɔːˈtɒtəmɪ) *n, pl* **autotomies.** the casting off by an animal of a part of its body, to facilitate escape when attacked.
▸ **autotomic** (ˌɔːtəˈtɒmɪk) *adj*

autotrophic (ˌɔːtəˈtrɒfɪk) *adj* (of organisms such as green plants) capable of manufacturing complex organic nutritive compounds from simple inorganic sources.
▸ **ˈautoˌtroph** *n*

autumn ('ɔːtəm) *n* **1** *(sometimes cap.)* **1a** Also called (esp. US): **fall.** the season of the year between summer and winter, astronomically from the September equinox to the December solstice in the N hemisphere and from the March equinox to the June solstice in the S hemisphere. **1b** *(as modifier): autumn leaves.* **2** a period of late maturity, esp. one followed by a decline. [C14: from L *autumnus*]
▸ **autumnal** (ɔːˈtʌmnᵊl) *adj*

autumn crocus *n* a plant of the lily family having pink or purplish autumn flowers, found in Europe and N Africa.

aux. *abbrev. for* auxiliary.

auxanometer (ˌɔːksəˈnɒmɪtə) *n* an instrument that measures the linear growth of plant shoots. [C19: from Gk *auxanein* to increase + -METER]

auxiliaries (ɔːgˈzɪljərɪz, -ˈzɪlə-) *pl n* foreign troops serving another nation; mercenaries.

auxiliary ❶ (ɔːgˈzɪljərɪ, -ˈzɪlə-) *adj* **1** secondary or supplementary. **2** supporting. ◆ *n, pl* **auxiliaries. 3** a person or thing that supports or supplements. **4** *Naut.* **4a** a sailing vessel with an engine. **4b** the engine of

THESAURUS

all-powerful, despotic, domineering, imperious, tyrannical, tyrannous, unlimited

automatic *adj* **1, 3** = **involuntary**, instinctive, instinctual, mechanical, natural, reflex, spontaneous, unconscious, unwilled **2** = **mechanical**, automated, mechanized, push-button, robot, self-acting, self-activating, self-moving, self-propelling, self-regulating **4** = **inevitable**, assured, certain, inescapable, necessary, routine, unavoidable
Antonyms *adj* ≠ **involuntary**: conscious, deliberate, intentional, voluntary ≠ **mechanical**: done by hand, hand-operated, human, manual, physical

autonomous *adj* **1, 3** = **self-ruling**, free, independent, self-determining, self-governing, sovereign

autonomy *n* **1, 3** = **independence**, freedom, home rule, self-determination, self-government, self-rule, sovereignty
Antonyms *n* dependency, foreign rule, subjection

autopsy *n* **1** = **postmortem**, dissection, necropsy, postmortem examination

auxiliary *adj* **1** = **supplementary**, back-up, emergency, fall-back, reserve, secondary, sub-

such a vessel. [C17: from L, from *auxilium* help, from *augēre* to increase, strengthen]

auxiliary rotor *n* the tail rotor of a helicopter, used for directional and rotary control.

auxiliary verb *n* a verb used to indicate the tense, voice, or mood of another verb where this is not indicated by inflection, such as English *will* in *he will go.*

auxin ('ɔːksɪn) *n* a plant hormone that promotes growth. [C20: from Gk *auxein* to grow]

AV *abbrev. for* Authorized Version (of the Bible).

av. *abbrev. for:* **1** average. **2** avoirdupois.

Av. *or* **av.** *abbrev. for* avenue.

a.v. *or* **A/V** *abbrev. for* ad valorem.

avadavat (ˌævədə'væt) *or* **amadavat** (ˌæmədə'væt) *n* either of two Asian weaverbirds having a red plumage: often kept as cagebirds. [C18: from *Ahmadabad,* Indian city from which these birds were brought to Europe]

avail ⓣ (ə'veɪl) *vb* **1** to be of use, advantage, profit, or assistance (to). **2 avail oneself of.** to make use of to one's advantage. ◆ *n* **3** use or advantage (esp. in **of no avail, to little avail**). [C13 *availen,* from OF *valoir,* from L *valēre* to be strong]

available ⓣ (ə'veɪləbᵊl) *adj* **1** obtainable or accessible; capable of being made use of. **2** *Arch.* advantageous.
▸**aˌvaila'bility** *or* **a'vailableness** *n* ▸**a'vailably** *adv*

avalanche ⓣ ('ævəˌlɑːntʃ) *n* **1a** a fall of large masses of snow and ice down a mountain. **1b** a fall of rocks, sand, etc. **2** a sudden or overwhelming appearance of a large quantity of things. ◆ *vb* **avalanches, avalanching, avalanched. 3** to come down overwhelmingly (upon). [C18: from F, by mistaken division from *la valanche,* from *valanche,* from dialect *lavantse*]

avant- ('ævɒŋ) *prefix* of or belonging to the avant-garde of a specified field.

avant-garde ⓣ (ˌævɒŋ'gɑːd) *n* **1** those artists, writers, musicians, etc., whose techniques and ideas are in advance of those generally accepted. ◆ *adj* **2** of such artists, their ideas, or techniques. [from F: VANGUARD]

avarice ⓣ ('ævərɪs) *n* extreme greed for riches. [C13: from OF, from L, from *avārus* covetous, from *avēre* to crave]
▸**avaricious** (ˌævə'rɪʃəs) *adj*

avast (ə'vɑːst) *sentence substitute. Naut.* stop! cease! [C17: ?from Du. *hou'vast* hold fast]

avatar ('ævəˌtɑː) *n* **1** *Hinduism.* the manifestation of a deity in human or animal form. **2** a visible manifestation of an abstract concept. [C18: from Sansk. *avatāra* a going down, from *ava* down + *tarati* he passes over]

avaunt (ə'vɔːnt) *sentence substitute. Arch.* go away! depart! [C15: from OF *avant!* forward! from LL *ab ante* forward, from L *ab* from + *ante* before]

avdp. *abbrev. for* avoirdupois.

ave ('ɑːvɪ, 'ɑːveɪ) *sentence substitute.* welcome or farewell. [L]

Ave[1] ('ɑːvɪ) *n RC Church.* short for **Ave Maria:** see **Hail Mary.** [C13: from L: hail!]

Ave[2] *or* **ave** *abbrev. for* avenue.

avenge ⓣ (ə'vendʒ) *vb* **avenges, avenging, avenged.** (*usually tr*) to inflict a punishment in retaliation for (harm, injury, etc.) done to (a person or persons): *to avenge a crime; to avenge a murdered friend.* [C14: from OF, from *vengier,* from L *vindicāre;* see VENGEANCE, VINDICATE]
▸**a'venger** *n*

> **USAGE NOTE** The use of *avenge* with a reflexive pronoun was formerly considered incorrect, but is now acceptable: *she avenged herself on the man who killed her daughter.*

avens ('ævɪnz) *n, pl* **avens.** (*functioning as sing*) **1** any of a genus of plants, such as **water avens,** which has a purple calyx and orange-pink flowers. **2 mountain avens.** a trailing evergreen white-flowered shrub that grows on mountains in N temperate regions. [C15: from OF, from Med. L *avencia* variety of clover]

aventurine (ə'ventjʊrɪn) *or* **avanturine** (ə'væntjʊrɪn) *n* **1** a dark-coloured glass, usually green or brown, spangled with fine particles of gold, copper, or some other metal. **2** a variety of quartz containing red or greenish particles of iron oxide or mica. [C19: from F, from It., from *avventura* chance; so named because usually found by accident]

avenue ⓣ ('ævɪnjuː) *n* **1a** a broad street, often lined with trees. **1b** (*cap. as part of a street name*) a road, esp. in a built-up area. **2** a main approach road, as to a country house. **3** a way bordered by two rows of trees. **4** a line of approach: *explore every avenue.* [C17: from F, from *avenir* to come to, from L, from *venīre* to come]

aver (ə'vɜː) *vb* **avers, averring, averred.** (*tr*) **1** to state positively. **2** *Law.* to allege as a fact or prove to be true. [C14: from OF, from Med. L *adverāre,* from L *vērus* true]
▸**a'verment** *n*

average ⓣ ('ævərɪdʒ, 'ævrɪdʒ) *n* **1** the typical or normal amount, quality, degree, etc.: *above average in intelligence.* **2** Also called: **arithmetic mean.** the result obtained by adding the numbers or quantities in a set and dividing the total by the number of members in the set: *the average of 3, 4, and 8 is 5.* **3** a similar mean for continuously variable ratios, such as speed. **4** *Maritime law.* **4a** a loss incurred or damage suffered by a ship or its cargo at sea. **4b** the equitable apportionment of such loss among the interested parties. **5 on (the** *or* **an) average.** usually; typically. ◆ *adj* **6** usual or typical. **7** mediocre or inferior: *his performance was only average.* **8** constituting a numerical average: *an average speed.* **9** approximately typical of a range of values: *the average contents of a matchbox.* ◆ *vb* **averages, averaging, averaged. 10** (*tr*) to obtain or estimate a numerical average of. **11** (*tr*) to assess the general quality of. **12** (*tr*) to perform or receive a typical number of: *to average eight hours' work a day.* **13** (*tr*) to divide up proportionately. **14** to amount to or be on average: *the children averaged 15 years of age.* [C15 *averay* loss arising from damage to ships, from OIt. *avaria,* ult. from Ar. *awār* damage, blemish]
▸**'averagely** *adv*

averse ⓣ (ə'vɜːs) *adj* (*postpositive;* usually foll. by *to*) opposed, disinclined, or loath. [C16: from L, from *āvertere* to turn from, from *vertere* to turn]
▸ **a'versely** *adv* ▸ **a'verseness** *n*

aversion ⓣ (ə'vɜːʃən) *n* **1** (usually foll. by *to* or *for*) extreme dislike or disinclination. **2** a person or thing that arouses this: *he is my pet aversion.*

aversion therapy *n Psychiatry.* a way of suppressing an undesirable habit, such as smoking, by associating an unpleasant effect, such as an electric shock, with the habit.

avert ⓣ (ə'vɜːt) *vb* (*tr*) **1** to turn away or aside: *to avert one's gaze.* **2** to ward off: *to avert danger.* [C15: from OF, from L *āvertere;* see AVERSE]
▸**a'vertible** *or* **a'vertable** *adj*

THESAURUS

sidiary, substitute **2** = **supporting**, accessory, aiding, ancillary, assisting, helping ◆ *n* **3** = **helper**, accessory, accomplice, ally, assistant, associate, companion, confederate, henchman, partner, protagonist, subordinate, supporter **3** = **backup**, reserve
Antonyms *adj* ≠ **supplementary, supporting:** cardinal, chief, essential, first, leading, main, primary, prime, principal

avail *vb* **1** = **benefit**, aid, assist, be effective, be of advantage, be of use, be useful, help, profit, serve, work **2 avail oneself of** = **make use of**, employ, exploit, have recourse to, make the most of, profit from, take advantage of, turn to account, use, utilize ◆ *n* **3** = **benefit**, advantage, aid, assistance, boot (*obs.*), effectiveness, efficacy, good, help, mileage (*inf.*), profit, purpose, service, use, usefulness, utility

availability *n* **1** = **accessibility**, attainability, handiness, obtainability, readiness

available *adj* **1** = **accessible**, applicable, at hand, at one's disposal, at one's fingertips, attainable, convenient, free, handy, obtainable, on hand, on tap, ready, ready for use, to hand, vacant
Antonyms *adj* busy, engaged, inaccessible, in use, occupied, spoken for, taken, unattainable, unavailable, unobtainable

avalanche *n* **1** = **snow-slide**, landslide, landslip, snow-slip **2** = **flood**, barrage, deluge, inundation, torrent

avant-garde *adj* **2** = **progressive**, experimental, far-out (*sl.*), ground-breaking, innovative, innovatory, pioneering, unconventional, way-out (*inf.*)
Antonyms *adj* conservative, conventional, hidebound, reactionary, traditional

avarice *n* = **greed**, acquisitiveness, close-fistedness, covetousness, cupidity, grasping-ness, greediness, meanness, miserliness, niggardliness, parsimony, penny-pinching, penuriousness, rapacity, stinginess
Antonyms *n* benevolence, bountifulness, extravagance, generosity, largesse *or* largess, liberality, unselfishness

avaricious *adj* = **grasping**, acquisitive, close-fisted, covetous, greedy, mean, miserable, miserly, niggardly, parsimonious, penny-pinching, penurious, rapacious, stingy, tight as a duck's arse (*taboo sl.*)

avenge *vb* = **get revenge for**, even the score for, get even for (*inf.*), get one's own back, hit back, pay (someone) back for, pay (someone) back in his *or* her own coin, punish, repay, requite, retaliate, revenge, take revenge for, take satisfaction for, take vengeance

avenue *n* **1, 2** = **street**, access, alley, approach, boulevard, channel, course, drive, driveway, entrance, entry, pass, passage, path, pathway, road, route, thoroughfare, way

average *n* **1, 2** = **usual**, common run, mean, medium, midpoint, norm, normal, par, rule, run, run of the mill, standard **5 on average** = **usually**, as a rule, for the most part, generally, normally, typically ◆ *adj* **6** = **usual**, common, commonplace, fair, general, normal, ordinary, regular, standard, typical **7** = **mediocre**, banal, bog-standard (*Brit. & Irish sl.*), indifferent, middle-of-the-road, middling, moderate, no great shakes (*inf.*), not bad, passable, run-of- the-mill, so-so (*inf.*), tolerable, undistinguished, unexceptional **8** = **mean**, intermediate, median, medium, middle ◆ *vb* **14** = **make on average**, balance out to, be on average, do on average, even out to
Antonyms *adj* ≠ **usual:** abnormal, awful, bad, different, exceptional, great, memorable, notable, outstanding, remarkable, special, terrible, unusual ≠ **mean:** maximum, minimum

averse *adj* = **opposed**, antipathetic, backward, disinclined, hostile, ill-disposed, indisposed, inimical, loath, reluctant, unfavourable, unwilling
Antonyms *adj* agreeable, amenable, disposed, eager, favourable, inclined, keen, sympathetic, willing

aversion *n* **1** = **hatred**, abhorrence, animosity, antipathy, detestation, disgust, disinclination, dislike, distaste, hate, horror, hostility, indisposition, loathing, odium, opposition, reluctance, repugnance, repulsion, revulsion, unwillingness
Antonyms *n* desire, inclination, liking, love, willingness

avert *vb* **1** = **turn away**, turn, turn aside **2** = **ward**

Avesta (ə'vɛstə) *n* a collection of sacred writings of Zoroastrianism, including the Songs of Zoroaster.

Avestan (ə'vɛstən) *n* **1** the earliest recorded form of the Iranian language, formerly called **Zend.** ◆ *adj* **2** of the Avesta or its language.

avian ('eɪvɪən) *adj* of, relating to, or resembling a bird. [C19: from L *avis* bird]

aviary ('eɪvjərɪ) *n, pl* **aviaries.** a large enclosure in which birds are kept. [C16: from L, from *aviārius* concerning birds, from *avis* bird]

aviation ➊ (ˌeɪvɪ'eɪʃən) *n* **1** the art or science of flying aircraft. **2** the design, production, and maintenance of aircraft. [C19: from F, from L *avis* bird]

aviator ➊ ('eɪvɪˌeɪtə) *n Old-fashioned.* the pilot of an aeroplane or airship; flyer.
▸**'aviˌatrix** *or* **'aviˌatress** *fem n*

avid ➊ ('ævɪd) *adj* **1** very keen; enthusiastic: *an avid reader.* **2** (*postpositive;* often foll. by *for* or *of*) eager (for): *avid for revenge.* [C18: from L, from *avēre* to long for]
▸**avidity** (ə'vɪdɪtɪ) *n* ▸**'avidly** *adv*

avifauna (ˌeɪvɪ'fɔːnə) *n* all the birds in a particular region.
▸ˌ**avi'faunal** *adj*

avionics (ˌeɪvɪ'ɒnɪks) *n* **1** (*functioning as sing*) the science and technology of electronics applied to aeronautics. **2** (*functioning as pl*) the electronic circuits and devices of an aerospace vehicle. [C20: from *avi(ation electr)onics*]
▸ˌ**avi'onic** *adj*

avitaminosis (æˌvɪtəmɪn'əʊsɪs) *n, pl* **avitaminoses** (-siːz). any disease caused by a vitamin deficiency in the diet.

avocado (ˌævə'kɑːdəʊ) *n, pl* **avocados. 1** a pear-shaped fruit having a leathery green or blackish skin, a large stony seed, and a greenish-yellow edible pulp. **2** the tropical American tree that bears this fruit. **3a** a dull greenish colour. **3b** (*as adj*): *an avocado bathroom suite.* ◆ Also called (for senses 1 & 2): **avocado pear, alligator pear.** [C17: from Sp. *aguacate,* from Nahuatl *ahuacatl* testicle, alluding to the shape of the fruit]

avocation (ˌævə'keɪʃən) *n* **1** *Formal.* a minor occupation undertaken as a diversion. **2** *Not standard.* a person's regular job. [C17: from L, from *āvocāre* to distract, from *vocāre* to call]

avocet ('ævəˌsɛt) *n* a long-legged shore bird having black-and-white plumage and a long slender upward-curving bill. [C18: from F, from It. *avocetta,* from ?]

Avogadro constant *or* **number** (ˌævə'gɑːdrəʊ) *n* the number of atoms or molecules in a mole of a substance, equal to 6.02252×10^{23} per mole. [C19: after Amedeo *Avogadro* (1776–1856), It. physicist]

Avogadro's law *or* **hypothesis** *n* the principle that equal volumes of all gases contain the same number of molecules at the same temperature and pressure.

avoid ➊ (ə'vɔɪd) *vb* (*tr*) **1** to keep out of the way of. **2** to refrain from doing. **3** to prevent from happening: *to avoid damage to machinery.* **4** *Law.* to invalidate; quash. [C14: from Anglo-F, from OF *esvuidier,* from *vuidier* to empty]
▸**a'voidable** *adj* ▸**a'voidably** *adv* ▸**a'voidance** *n* ▸**a'voider** *n*

avoirdupois *or* **avoirdupois weight** (ˌævwɑːdjuː'pwɑː) *n* a system of weights used in many English-speaking countries. It is based on the pound, which contains 16 ounces or 7000 grains. [C14: from OF *aver de peis* goods of weight]

avouch ➊ (ə'vaʊtʃ) *vb* (*tr*) *Arch.* **1** to vouch for; guarantee. **2** to acknowledge. **3** to assert. [C16: from OF *avochier* to summon, call on, from L *advocāre;* see ADVOCATE]
▸**a'vouchment** *n*

avow ➊ (ə'vaʊ) *vb* (*tr*) **1** to state or affirm. **2** to admit openly. [C13: from OF *avouer* to confess, from L *advocāre* to appeal to, call upon]
▸**a'vowal** *n* ▸**a'vowed** *adj* ▸**avowedly** (ə'vaʊɪdlɪ) *adv* ▸**a'vower** *n*

avuncular (ə'vʌŋkjʊlə) *adj* **1** of or concerned with an uncle. **2** resembling an uncle; friendly. [C19: from L *avunculus* (maternal) uncle, dim. of *avus* grandfather]

AWACS *or* **Awacs** ('eɪwæks) *n acronym for* Airborne Warning and Control System.

await ➊ (ə'weɪt) *vb* **1** (*tr*) to wait for. **2** (*tr*) to be in store for. **3** (*intr*) to wait, esp. with expectation.

awake ➊ (ə'weɪk) *vb* **awakes, awaking, awoke** *or* **awaked, awoken** *or* **awaked. 1** to emerge or rouse from sleep. **2** to become or cause to become alert. **3** (usually foll. by *to*) to become or make aware (of). **4** Also: **awaken.** (*tr*) to arouse (feelings, etc.) or cause to remember (memories, etc.). ◆ *adj* (*postpositive*) **5** not sleeping. **6** (sometimes foll. by *to*) lively or alert. [OE *awacian, awacan*]

USAGE NOTE See at **wake**[1].

award ➊ (ə'wɔːd) *vb* (*tr*) **1** to give (something due), esp. as a reward for merit: *to award prizes.* **2** *Law.* to declare to be entitled, as by decision of a court or an arbitrator. ◆ *n* **3** something awarded, such as a prize or medal. **4** *Austral. & NZ.* the amount of an **award wage** (esp. in **above award**). **5** *Law.* **5a** the decision of an arbitrator. **5b** a grant made by a court of law. [C14: from Anglo-F *awarder,* from OF *eswarder* to decide after investigation, from *es-* EX-[1] + *warder* to observe]
▸**a'warder** *n*

award wage *n* (in Australia and New Zealand) statutory minimum pay for a particular group of workers. Sometimes shortened to **award.**

aware ➊ (ə'wɛə) *adj* **1** (*postpositive;* foll. by *of*) having knowledge: *aware of his error.* **2** informed of current developments: *politically aware.* [OE *gewær*]
▸**a'wareness** *n*

awash ➊ (ə'wɒʃ) *adv, adj* (*postpositive*) *Naut.* **1** level with the surface of the sea. **2** washed over by the waves.

away ➊ (ə'weɪ) *adv* **1** from a particular place: *to swim away.* **2** in or to another, a usual, or a proper place: *to put toys away.* **3** apart; at a distance: *to keep away from strangers.* **4** out of existence: *the music faded away.* **5** indicating motion, displacement, transfer, etc., from a normal or proper place: *to turn one's head away.* **6** indicating activity that is wasteful or designed to get rid of something: *to sleep away the hours.* **7** continuously: *laughing away.* **8 away with.** a command for a person to go or be removed: *away with him to prison!* ◆ *adj* (*usually postpositive*) **9** not present: *away from school.* **10** distant: *he is a good way away.* **11** having started; released: *he was away before sunrise.* **12** (*also prenominal*) *Sport.* played on an opponent's ground. ◆ *n* **13** *Sport.* a game played or

THESAURUS

off, avoid, fend off, forestall, frustrate, preclude, prevent, stave off

aviation *n* **1** = **flying**, aeronautics, flight, powered flight

aviator *n* = **pilot**, aeronaut, airman, flyer

avid *adj* **1** = **enthusiastic**, ardent, devoted, eager, fanatical, fervent, intense, keen, keen as mustard, passionate, zealous
Antonyms *adj* apathetic, impassive, indifferent, lukewarm, unenthusiastic

avidity *n* **1** = **enthusiasm**, ardour, devotion, eagerness, fervour, keenness, zeal

avoid *vb* **1** = **keep away from**, body-swerve (*Scot.*), bypass, circumvent, dodge, elude, escape, evade, give a wide berth to, keep aloof from, shun, sidestep, slip through the net, steer clear of **2** = **refrain from**, dodge, duck (out of) (*inf.*), eschew, fight shy of, shirk **3** = **prevent**, avert
Antonyms *vb* ≠ **keep away from:** approach, confront, contact, face, face up to, find, invite, pursue, seek out, solicit

avoidable *adj* **1** = **escapable**, evadable **3** = **preventable**, avertible *or* avertable, stoppable
Antonyms *adj* ≠ **escapable:** inescapable, inevitable, necessary, unavoidable ≠ **preventable:** unpreventable, unstoppable

avoidance *n* **1** = **evasion**, body swerve (*Scot.*), circumvention, dodging, eluding, escape, keeping away, shunning, steering clear **2** = **refraining**, dodging, eschewal, shirking **3** = **prevention**

avouch *vb* **1-3** = **vouch for**, acknowledge, affirm, allege, assert, asseverate, aver, avow, declare, guarantee, maintain, proclaim, profess, pronounce, state, swear

avow *vb* **1** = **state**, affirm, allege, assert, asseverate, aver, declare, maintain, proclaim, profess, recognize, swear **2** = **confess**, acknowledge, admit, own

avowal *n* **1** = **statement**, affirmation, allegation, assertion, asseveration, averment, declaration, maintenance, oath, proclamation, profession, recognition **2** = **confession**, acknowledgment, admission, owning

avowed *adj* **1** = **declared**, open, professed, self-proclaimed, sworn **2** = **confessed**, acknowledged, admitted

await *vb* **1, 3** = **wait for**, abide, anticipate, expect, look for, look forward to, stay for **2** = **be in store for**, attend, be in readiness for, be prepared for, be ready for, wait for

awake *vb* **1** = **wake up**, awaken, rouse, wake **2, 4** = **alert**, activate, animate, arouse, awaken, breathe life into, call forth, enliven, excite, fan, incite, kick-start (*inf.*), kindle, provoke, revive, stimulate, stir up, vivify ◆ *adj* **5** = **not sleeping**, aroused, awakened, aware, bright-eyed and bushy-tailed, conscious, wakeful, waking, wide-awake **6** = **alert**, alive, attentive, aware, heedful, observant, on guard, on one's toes, on the alert, on the lookout, vigilant, watchful
Antonyms *adj* ≠ **not sleeping:** asleep, crashed out (*sl.*), dead to the world (*inf.*), dormant, dozing, napping, sleeping, unconscious ≠ **alert:** inattentive, unaware

awaken *vb* = **awake**, arouse, revive, rouse, wake = **alert**, activate, animate, breathe life into, call forth, enliven, excite, fan, incite, kick-start (*inf.*), kindle, provoke, stimulate, stir up, vivify

award *vb* **1** = **give**, accord, adjudge, allot, apportion, assign, bestow, confer, decree, distribute, endow, gift, grant, hand out, present, render ◆ *n* **3** = **prize**, decoration, gift, grant, trophy, verdict **3** = **giving**, allotment, bestowal, conferment, conferral, endowment, hand-out, order, presentation, stipend **5** *Law* = **decision**, adjudication, decree

aware *adj* **1** *foll. by* **of** = **knowing about**, acquainted with, alive to, appreciative of, apprised of, attentive to, cognizant of, conscious of, conversant with, familiar with, hip to (*sl.*), mindful of, sensible of, wise to (*sl.*) **2** = **informed**, *au courant,* clued-up (*inf.*), enlightened, in the loop, in the picture, knowledgeable
Antonyms *adj* ignorant, insensible, oblivious, unaware, unfamiliar with, unknowledgeable

awareness *n* **1, 2** = **knowledge**, acquaintance, appreciation, attention, cognizance, consciousness, enlightenment, familiarity, mindfulness, perception, realization, recognition, sensibility, sentience, understanding

awash *adj* **2** = **flooded**, afloat, deluged, drowned, engulfed, immersed, inundated, overburdened, overwhelmed, submerged, submersed, swamped, swept

away *adv* **1** = **off**, abroad, elsewhere, from here, from home, hence **3** = **at a distance**, apart, far, remote **7** = **continuously**, incessantly, interminably, relentlessly, repeatedly, uninterruptedly, unremittingly ◆ *adj* **9** = **not present**, abroad, absent, elsewhere, gone, not at home, not here, not there, out ◆ *sentence substitute* **14** = **go**

won at an opponent's ground. ◆ *sentence substitute.* **14** an expression of dismissal. [OE *on weg* on way]

awayday (ə'weɪ,deɪ) *n* a day trip taken for pleasure, relaxation, etc.; day excursion. [C20: from *awayday ticket,* name applied to some special-rate railway day returns]

awe ❶ (ɔː) *n* **1** overwhelming wonder, respect, or dread. **2** *Arch.* power to inspire fear or reverence. ◆ *vb* **awes, awing, awed.** **3** (*tr*) to inspire with reverence or dread. [C13: from ON *agi*]

aweigh (ə'weɪ) *adj* (*postpositive*) *Naut.* (of an anchor) no longer hooked into the bottom; hanging by its rope or chain.

awe-inspiring ❶ *adj* causing or worthy of admiration or respect; amazing or magnificent.

awesome ❶ ('ɔːsəm) *adj* **1** inspiring or displaying awe. **2** *Sl.* excellent or outstanding.
▸ **'awesomely** *adv* ▸ **'awesomeness** *n*

awestruck ❶ *or* **awe-stricken** *adj* overcome or filled with awe.

awful ❶ ('ɔːfʊl) *adj* **1** very bad; unpleasant. **2** *Arch.* inspiring reverence or dread. **3** *Arch.* overcome with awe. ◆ *adv* **4** *Not standard.* (intensifier): *an awful cold day.* [C13: see AWE, -FUL]
▸ **'awfulness** *n*

awfully ❶ ('ɔːfəlɪ) *adv* **1** in an unpleasant, bad, or reprehensible manner. **2** *Inf.* (intensifier): *I'm awfully keen to come.* **3** *Arch.* so as to express or inspire awe.

awhile ❶ (ə'waɪl) *adv* for a brief period.

awkward ❶ ('ɔːkwəd) *adj* **1** lacking dexterity, proficiency, or skill; clumsy. **2** ungainly or inelegant in movements or posture. **3** unwieldy; difficult to use. **4** embarrassing: *an awkward moment.* **5** embarrassed: *he felt awkward about leaving.* **6** difficult to deal with; requiring tact: *an awkward customer.* **7** deliberately unhelpful. **8** dangerous or difficult. [C14: *awk,* from ON *öfugr* turned the wrong way round + -WARD]
▸ **'awkwardly** *adv* ▸ **'awkwardness** *n*

awl (ɔːl) *n* a pointed hand tool with a fluted blade used for piercing wood, leather, etc. [OE *ǣl*]

awn (ɔːn) *n* any of the bristles growing from the flowering parts of certain grasses and cereals. [OE *agen* ear of grain]
▸ **awned** *adj*

awning ('ɔːnɪŋ) *n* a roof of canvas or other material supported by a frame to provide protection from the weather, esp. one placed over a doorway or part of a deck of a ship. [C17: from ?]

awoke (ə'wəʊk) *vb* a past tense and (now rare or dialectal) past participle of **awake.**

AWOL ('eɪwɒl) *or* **A.W.O.L.** *adj Mil.* absent without leave but without intending to desert.

awry ❶ (ə'raɪ) *adv, adj* (*postpositive*) **1** with a slant or twist to one side; askew. **2** away from the appropriate or right course; amiss. [C14 *on wry;* see A-[2], WRY]

axe ❶ *or US* **ax** (æks) *n, pl* **axes.** **1** a hand tool with one side of its head forged and sharpened to a cutting edge, used for felling trees, splitting timber, etc. **2 an axe to grind.** **2a** an ulterior motive. **2b** a grievance. **2c** a pet subject. **3 the axe.** *Inf.* **3a** dismissal, esp. from employment (esp. in **get the axe**). **3b** *Brit.* severe cutting down of expenditure, esp. in a public service. ◆ *vb* **axes, axing, axed.** (*tr*) **4** to chop or trim with an axe. **5** *Inf.* to dismiss (employees), restrict (expenditure or services), or terminate (a project, etc.). [OE *æx*]

axel ('æksəl) *n Skating.* a jump of one and a half, two and a half, or three and a half turns, taking off from the forward outside edge of one skate and landing on the backward outside edge of the other. [C20: after *Axel* Paulsen (d. 1938), Norwegian skater]

axeman ('æksmən) *n, pl* **axemen.** **1** a man who wields an axe, esp. to cut down trees. **2** a person who makes cuts in expenditure or services, esp. on behalf of another: *the chancellor's axeman.*

axes[1] ('æksiːz) *n* the plural of **axis**[1].

axes[2] ('æksɪz) *n* the plural of **axe.**

axial ('æksɪəl) *adj* **1** forming or characteristic of an axis. **2** situated in, on, or along an axis.
▸ **,axi'ality** *n* ▸ **'axially** *adv*

axil ('æksɪl) *n* the upper angle between a branch or leafstalk and the stem from which it grows. [C18: from L *axilla* armpit]

axilla (æk'sɪlə) *n, pl* **axillae** (-liː). **1** the technical name for the **armpit.** **2** the area under a bird's wing corresponding to the armpit. [C17: from L: armpit]

axillary (æk'sɪlərɪ) *adj* **1** of, relating to, or near the armpit. **2** *Bot.* growing in or related to the axil. ◆ *n, pl* **axillaries.** **3** (*usually pl*) Also called: **axillar** (æk'sɪlə). one of the feathers growing from the axilla of a bird's wing.

axiom ❶ ('æksɪəm) *n* **1** a generally accepted proposition or principle, sanctioned by experience. **2** a universally established principle or law that is not a necessary truth. **3** a self-evident statement. **4** *Logic, maths.* a statement that is stipulated to be true for the purpose of a chain of reasoning. [C15: from L *axiōma* a principle, from Gk, from *axioun* to consider worthy, from *axios* worthy]

axiomatic ❶ (,æksɪə'mætɪk) *adj* **1** self-evident. **2** containing maxims; aphoristic.
▸ **,axio'matically** *adv*

axis[1] ❶ ('æksɪs) *n, pl* **axes.** **1** a real or imaginary line about which a body, such as an aircraft, can rotate or about which an object, form, composition, or geometrical construction is symmetrical. **2** one of

THESAURUS

away, beat it (*sl.*), begone, be off, bugger off (*taboo sl.*), get lost, get out, go, on your bike (*sl.*), on your way

awe *n* **1** = **wonder**, admiration, amazement, astonishment, dread, fear, horror, respect, reverence, terror, veneration ◆ *vb* **3** = **impress**, amaze, astonish, cow, daunt, frighten, horrify, intimidate, put the wind up (*inf.*), stun, terrify
Antonyms *n* ≠ **wonder:** arrogance, boldness, contempt, disrespect, fearlessness, irreverence, scorn

awed *adj* **1** = **impressed**, afraid, amazed, astonished, cowed, daunted, dumbfounded, fearful, frightened, horrified, intimidated, shocked, stunned, terrified, wonder-stricken, wonder-struck

awe-inspiring *adj* = **impressive**, amazing, astonishing, awesome, breathtaking, daunting, fearsome, intimidating, jaw-dropping, magnificent, striking, stunning (*inf.*), wonderful, wondrous (*arch. or literary*)
Antonyms *adj* bland, boring, dull, flat, humdrum, insipid, prosaic, tame, tedious, unimpressive, uninspiring, vapid

awesome *adj* **1** = **awe-inspiring**, alarming, amazing, astonishing, awful, breathtaking, daunting, dreadful, fearful, fearsome, formidable, frightening, horrible, horrifying, imposing, impressive, intimidating, jaw-dropping, magnificent, majestic, overwhelming, redoubtable, shocking, solemn, striking, stunning, stupefying, terrible, terrifying, wonderful, wondrous (*arch. or literary*)

awestruck *adj* = **impressed**, afraid, amazed, astonished, awed, awe-inspired, cowed, daunted, dumbfounded, fearful, frightened, horrified, intimidated, shocked, struck dumb, stunned, terrified, wonder-stricken, wonder-struck

awful *adj* **1** = **terrible**, abysmal, alarming, appalling, deplorable, dire, distressing, dreadful, fearful, frightful, from hell (*inf.*), ghastly, harrowing, hideous, horrendous, horrible, horrid, horrific, horrifying, nasty, shocking, tremendous, ugly, unpleasant, unsightly **2** *Archaic* = **awe-inspiring**, amazing, awesome, dread, fearsome, majestic, portentous, solemn
Antonyms *adj* ≠ **terrible:** amazing, brilliant, excellent, fabulous (*inf.*), fantastic, great (*inf.*), magnificent, marvellous, miraculous, sensational (*inf.*), smashing (*inf.*), super (*inf.*), superb, terrific, tremendous, wonderful

awfully *adv* **1** = **badly**, disgracefully, disreputably, dreadfully, inadequately, reprehensibly, shoddily, unforgivably, unpleasantly, wickedly, woefully, wretchedly **2** *Informal* = **very**, badly, dreadfully, exceedingly, exceptionally, excessively, extremely, greatly, immensely, quite, seriously (*inf.*), terribly, very much

awhile *adv* = **for a while**, briefly, for a little while, for a moment, for a short time

awkward *adj* **1, 2** = **clumsy**, all thumbs, artless, blundering, bungling, clownish, coarse, gauche, gawky, graceless, ham-fisted *or* ham-handed (*inf.*), ill-bred, inelegant, inept, inexpert, lumbering, maladroit, oafish, rude, skill-less, stiff, uncoordinated, uncouth, ungainly, ungraceful, unpolished, unrefined, unskilful, unskilled **3** = **inconvenient**, clunky (*inf.*), cumbersome, difficult, troublesome, unhandy, unmanageable, unwieldy **4, 5** = **embarrassing**, compromising, cringe-making (*Brit. inf.*), cringeworthy (*Brit. inf.*), delicate, difficult, embarrassed, ill at ease, inconvenient, inopportune, painful, perplexing, sticky (*inf.*), thorny, ticklish, toe-curling (*sl.*), troublesome, trying, uncomfortable, unpleasant, untimely **6, 7** = **uncooperative**, annoying, bloody-minded (*Brit. inf.*), difficult, disobliging, exasperating, hard to handle, intractable, irritable, perverse, prickly, stubborn, touchy, troublesome, trying, unhelpful, unpredictable, vexatious, vexing **8** = **risky**, chancy (*inf.*), dangerous, difficult, hazardous, perilous
Antonyms *adj* ≠ **clumsy:** adept, adroit, dexterous, graceful, skilful ≠ **inconvenient:** convenient, easy, handy ≠ **embarrassing:** comfortable, pleasant

awkwardness *n* **1, 2** = **clumsiness**, artlessness, clownishness, coarseness, gaucheness, gaucherie, gawkiness, gracelessness, ill-breeding, inelegance, ineptness, inexpertness, maladroitness, oafishness, rudeness, stiffness, uncoordination, uncouthness, ungainliness, unskilfulness, unskilledness **3** = **unwieldiness**, cumbersomeness, difficulty, inconvenience, troublesomeness, unhandiness, unmanageability **4, 5** = **embarrassment**, delicacy, difficulty, discomfort, inconvenience, inopportuneness, painfulness, perplexingness, stickiness (*inf.*), thorniness, ticklishness, unpleasantness, untimeliness **6, 7** = **uncooperativeness**, bloody-mindedness (*Brit. inf.*), difficulty, disobligingness, intractability, irritability, perversity, prickliness, stubbornness, touchiness, unhelpfulness, unpredictability **8** = **difficulty**, chanciness (*inf.*), danger, hazardousness, peril, perilousness, risk, riskiness

awry *adv* **1** = **askew**, cockeyed (*inf.*), crookedly, obliquely, off-centre, off course, out of line, out of true, skew-whiff (*inf.*), to one side, unevenly ◆ *adj* **1** = **askew**, asymmetrical, cockeyed (*inf.*), crooked, misaligned, off-centre, off course, out of line, out of true, skew-whiff (*inf.*), to one side, twisted, uneven ◆ *adv, adj* **2** = **wrong**, amiss

axe *n* **1** = **hatchet**, adze, chopper **2 an axe to grind** = **pet subject**, grievance, personal consideration, private ends, private purpose, ulterior motive **3 the axe** *Informal* = **the sack** (*inf.*), cancellation, cutback, discharge, dismissal, termination, the boot (*sl.*), the chop (*sl.*), the (old) heave-ho (*inf.*) ◆ *vb* **4** = **cut down**, chop, fell, hew **5** *Informal* = **cut back**, cancel, discharge, dismiss, dispense with, eliminate, fire (*inf.*), get rid of, give the push, oust, pull, pull the plug on, relegate, remove, sack (*inf.*), terminate, throw out, turn off (*inf.*)

axiom *n* **1** = **principle**, adage, aphorism, apophthegm, dictum, fundamental, gnome, maxim, postulate, precept, truism

axiomatic *adj* **1** = **self-evident**, absolute, accepted, apodictic *or* apodeictic, assumed, certain, fundamental, given, granted, indubitable, manifest, presupposed, understood, unquestioned **2** = **epigrammatic**, aphoristic, apophthegmatic, gnomic, pithy, terse

axis[1] *n* **1** = **pivot**, axle, centre line, shaft, spindle two or three reference lines used in coordinate geometry to locate a point in a plane or in space. **3** *Anat.* the second cervical vertebra. **4** *Bot.* the main central part of a plant, typically consisting of the stem and root. **5** an alliance between a number of states to coordinate their foreign policy. **6** Also called: **principal axis.** *Optics.* the line of symmetry of an optical system, such as the line passing through the centre of a lens. [C14: from L: axletree, earth's axis; rel. to Gk *axōn* axis]

axis[2] ('æksɪs) *n, pl* **axises.** a S Asian deer with a reddish-brown white-spotted coat and slender antlers. [C18: from L: Indian wild animal, from ?]

Axis ('æksɪs) *n* **a the.** the alliance (1936) of Nazi Germany and Fascist Italy, later joined by Japan and other countries, and lasting until their defeat in World War II. **b** *(as modifier): the Axis powers.*

axle **T** ('æksəl) *n* a bar or shaft on which a wheel, pair of wheels, or other rotating member revolves. [C17: from ON *öxull*]

axletree ('æksəl,triː) *n* a bar fixed across the underpart of a wagon or carriage that has rounded ends on which the wheels revolve.

Axminster carpet ('æks,mɪnstə) *n* a type of patterned carpet with a cut pile. Often shortened to **Axminster.** [after *Axminster* in Devon]

axolotl (ˌæksə'lɒtᵊl) *n* an aquatic salamander of N America, such as the **Mexican axolotl,** in which the larval form (including external gills) is retained throughout life under natural conditions. [C18: from Nahuatl, from *atl* water + *xolotl* servant, doll]

axon ('æksɒn) *n* the long threadlike extension of a nerve cell that conducts nerve impulses from the cell body. [C19: via NL from Gk: axis, axle, vertebra]

ay[1] *or* **aye** (eɪ) *adv Arch., poetic* always.

ay[2] (aɪ) *sentence substitute, n* a variant spelling of **aye.**

ayah ('aɪə) *n* (in parts of the former British Empire) a native maidservant or nursemaid. [C18: from Hindi *āyā,* from Port. *aia,* from L *avia* grandmother]

ayatollah (ˌaɪə'tɒlə) *n* one of a class of Shiite religious leaders in Iran. [via Persian from Ar., from *aya* creation + ALLAH]

aye *or* **ay** (aɪ) *sentence substitute.* **1** yes: archaic or dialectal except in voting by voice. ◆ *n* **2a** a person who votes in the affirmative. **2b** an affirmative vote. ◆ Cf. **nay.** [C16: prob. from pron *I,* expressing assent]

aye-aye ('aɪ,aɪ) *n* a rare nocturnal arboreal primate of Madagascar related to the lemurs. It has long bony fingers and rodent-like incisor teeth. [C18: from F, from Malagasy *aiay,* prob. imit.]

Aymara (ˌaɪmə'rɑː) *n* **1** *(pl* **-ras** *or* **-ra)** a member of a S American Indian people of Bolivia and Peru. **2** the language of this people. [from Sp. *aimará,* from Amerind]

Ayrshire ('ɛəʃə) *n* any one of a hardy breed of brown-and-white dairy cattle. [from *Ayrshire,* former Scot. county]

azalea (ə'zeɪljə) *n* an ericaceous plant cultivated for its showy pink or purple flowers. [C18: via NL from Gk, from *azaleos* dry; from its supposed preference for a dry situation]

azeotrope (ə'ziːəˌtrəʊp) *n* a mixture of liquids that boils at a constant temperature, at a given pressure, without change of composition. [C20: from A-[1] + *zeo-,* from Gk *zein* to boil + -TROPE] ▸**azeotropic** (ˌeɪzɪə'trɒpɪk) *adj*

azerty *or* **AZERTY keyboard** (ə'zɜːtɪ) *n* a common European version of typewriter keyboard layout with the characters a, z, e, r, t, and y positioned at the top left of the keyboard.

azide ('eɪzaɪd) *n* **a** an acyl derivative or salt of hydrazoic acid, used as a coating to enhance electron emission. **b** *(as modifier): an azide group or radical.*

Azilian (ə'zɪlɪən) *n* **1** a Palaeolithic culture of Spain and SW France that can be dated to the 10th millennium B.C., characterized by flat bone harpoons and schematically painted pebbles. ◆ *adj* **2** of or relating to this culture. [C19: after Mas d'*Azil,* France, where artefacts were found]

azimuth ('æzɪməθ) *n* **1** *Astron., navigation.* the angular distance usually measured clockwise from the south point of the horizon in astronomy or from the north point in navigation to the intersection with the horizon of the vertical circle passing through a celestial body. **2** *Surveying.* the horizontal angle of a bearing clockwise from north. [C14: from OF *azimut,* from Ar. *as-sumūt,* pl. of *as-samt* the path, from L *semita* path] ▸**azimuthal** (ˌæzɪ'mʌθəl) *adj*

azine ('eɪziːn) *n* an organic compound having a six-membered ring with at least one nitrogen atom, the other atoms in the ring being carbon atoms.

azo ('eɪzəʊ, 'æ-) *adj* of, consisting of, or containing the divalent group -N:N-: *an azo group or radical.* See also **diazo.** [from F *azote* nitrogen, from Gk *azōos* lifeless]

azoic (ə'zəʊɪk) *adj* without life; characteristic of the ages that have left no evidence of life in the form of organic remains. [C19: from Gk *azōos* lifeless]

AZT *abbrev. for* azidothymidine: another name for **zidovudine.**

Aztec ('æztɛk) *n* **1** a member of a Mexican Indian people who established a great empire, centred on the valley of Mexico, that was overthrown by Cortés in the early 16th century. **2** the language of the Aztecs. See also **Nahuatl.** ◆ *adj also* **Aztecan. 3** of, relating to, or characteristic of the Aztecs, their civilization, or their language. [C18: from Sp., from Nahuatl *Aztecatl,* from *Aztlan,* their traditional place of origin, lit.: near the cranes]

azure **T** ('æʒə, 'eɪ-) *n* **1** a deep blue similar to the colour of a clear blue sky. **2** *Poetic.* a clear blue sky. ◆ *adj* **3** of the colour azure. **4** *(usually postpositive) Heraldry.* of the colour blue. [C14: from OF, from OSp., from Ar. *lāzaward* lapis lazuli, from Persian *lāzhuward*]

azurite ('æʒuˌraɪt) *n* a deep blue mineral consisting of hydrated basic copper carbonate. It is used as an ore of copper and as a gemstone.

azygous ('æzɪgəs) *adj Biol.* developing or occurring singly. [C17: via NL from Gk *azugos,* from A-[1] + *zugon* YOKE]

THESAURUS

axle *n* = **shaft,** arbor, axis, mandrel, pin, pivot, rod, spindle

azure *adj* **3** = **sky-blue,** blue, cerulean, clear blue, sky-coloured, ultramarine

Bb

b *or* **B** (bi:) *n, pl* **b's, B's,** *or* **Bs. 1** the second letter of the English alphabet. **2** a speech sound represented by this letter **3** Also: **beta.** the second in a series, class, or rank.

B *symbol for:* **1** *Music.* **1a** the seventh note of the scale of C major. **1b** the major or minor key having this note as its tonic. **2** the less important of two things. **3** a human blood type of the ABO group, containing the B antigen. **4** (in Britain) a secondary road. **5** *Chem.* boron. **6** magnetic flux density. **7** *Chess.* bishop. **8** (on Brit. pencils, signifying degree of softness of lead) black. **9** Also: **b** *Physics.* bel. **10** *Physics.* baryon number. **11a** a person whose job is in middle management, or who holds an intermediate administrative or professional position. **11b** (*as modifer*): *a B worker.* ◆ See also **occupation groupings.**

b. *abbrev. for:* **1** born. **2** *Cricket.* **2a** bowled. **2b** bye.

b. *or* **B.** *abbrev. for:* **1** *Music.* bass *or* basso. **2** billion. **3** book. **4** breadth.

B. *abbrev. for:* **1** (on maps, etc.) bay. **2** Bible.

B- (of US military aircraft) *abbrev. for* bomber.

Ba the chemical symbol for barium.

BA *abbrev. for:* **1** Bachelor of Arts. **2** British Academy. **3** British Airways. **4** British Association (for the Advancement of Science). **5** British Association screw thread.

baa (bɑ:) *vb* **baas, baaing, baaed. 1** (*intr*) to make the cry of a sheep; bleat. ◆ *n* **2** the cry made by sheep.

BAA *abbrev. for* British Airports Authority.

Baader-Meinhof Gang (*German* 'ba:dər 'mainho:f) *n* **the.** a group of West German guerrillas dedicated to the violent overthrow of capitalist society. Also called: **Red Army Faction.** [C20: named after its leading members, Andreas *Baader* (1943–77) and Ulrike *Meinhof* (1934–76).

baas (bɑ:s) *n* a South African word for **boss**[1] (sense 1): used by Africans and Coloured people in addressing European managers or overseers. [C17: from Afrik., from MDu. *baes* master]

baaskap *or* **baasskap** ('bɑ:s,kap) *n* (*sometimes cap.*) (in South Africa) control by Whites of non-Whites. [from Afrik., from BAAS + *-skap* -SHIP]

baba ('bɑ:bɑ:) *n* a small cake, usually soaked in rum (**rum baba**). [C19: from F, from Polish, lit.: old woman]

babalas ('bæbə,læs) *n S. African.* a hangover. [from Zulu *ibhabhalasi*]

babbitt ('bæbɪt) *vb* (*tr*) to line (a bearing) or face (a surface) with Babbitt metal.

Babbitt ('bæbɪt) *n US derog.* a narrow-minded and complacent member of the middle class. [C20: after George *Babbitt,* central character in the novel *Babbitt* (1922) by Sinclair Lewis]
▸ **'Babbittry** *n*

Babbitt metal *n* any of a number of alloys originally based on tin, antimony, and copper but now often including lead: used esp. in bearings. [C19: after Isaac *Babbitt* (1799–1862), US inventor]

babble ⓣ ('bæb°l) *vb* **babbles, babbling, babbled. 1** to utter (words, sounds, etc.) in an incoherent jumble. **2** (*intr*) to talk foolishly, incessantly, or irrelevantly. **3** (*tr*) to disclose (secrets, etc.) carelessly. **4** (*intr*) (of streams, birds, etc.) to make a low murmuring sound. ◆ *n* **5** incoherent or foolish speech. **6** a murmuring sound. [C13: prob. imit.]

babbler ('bæblə) *n* **1** a person or thing that babbles. **2** any of various birds of the Old World tropics and subtropics having an incessant song.

babe ⓣ (beɪb) *n* **1** a baby. **2** *Inf.* a naive or gullible person. **3** *Sl.* a girl or young woman, esp. an attractive one.

Babel ⓣ ('beɪb°l) *n* **1** *Old Testament.* Also called: **Tower of Babel.** a tower presumptuously intended to reach from earth to heaven, the building of which was frustrated when Jehovah confused the language of the builders (Genesis 11:1–10). **2** (*often not cap.*) **2a** a confusion of noises or voices. **2b** a scene of noise and confusion. [from Heb. *Bābhél,* from Akkadian *Bāb-ilu,* lit.: gate of God]

babirusa (,bɑ:bɪ'ru:sə) *n* a wild pig of Indonesia. It has an almost hairless wrinkled skin and enormous curved canine teeth. [C17: from Malay, from *bābī* hog + *rūsa* deer]

Babism ('bɑ:bɪzəm) *n* a pantheistic Persian religious sect, founded in 1844, forbidding polygamy, concubinage, begging, trading in slaves, and indulgence in alcohol and drugs. [C19: from the *Bab,* title of Mirza Ali Mohammed (1819–50), Persian religious leader]

baboon (bə'bu:n) *n* any of several medium-sized Old World monkeys. They have an elongated muzzle, large teeth, and a fairly long tail. [C14 *babewyn* gargoyle, later, baboon, from OF]

babu ('bɑ:bu:) *n* (in India) **1** a form of address more or less equivalent to *Mr.* **2** (formerly) an Indian clerk who could write English. [Hindi, lit.: father]

babushka (bə'bu:ʃkə) *n* **1** a headscarf tied under the chin, worn by Russian peasant women. **2** (in Russia) an old woman. [Russian: grandmother, from *baba* old woman]

baby ⓣ ('beɪbɪ) *n, pl* **babies. 1a** a newborn child; infant. **1b** (*as modifier*): *baby food.* **2** an unborn child; fetus. **3** the youngest or smallest of a family or group. **4** a newborn or recently born animal. **5** *Usually derog.* an immature person. **6** *Sl.* a young woman or sweetheart. **7** a project of personal concern. **8 be left holding the baby.** to be left with the responsibility. ◆ *adj* **9** (*prenominal*) comparatively small of its type: *a baby car.* ◆ *vb* **babies, babying, babied. 10** (*tr*) to treat with love and attention. **11** to treat (someone) like a baby; pamper or overprotect. [C14: prob. childish reduplication]
▸ **'baby,hood** *n* ▸ **'babyish** *adj*

baby bonus *n Canad. inf.* Family Allowance.

baby boomer *n* a person born during a **baby boom,** a sharp increase in the birth rate, esp. (in Britain and the US) one born during the years 1945–55.

baby buggy *n* **1** *Brit. Trademark.* a child's pushchair. **2** *US & Canad. inf.* a small pram.

baby carriage *n* the US and Canad. name for **pram**[1].

Babylon ('bæbɪlən) *n* **1** *Derog.* (in Protestant polemic) the Roman Catholic Church, regarded as the seat of luxury and corruption. **2** *Derog.* any society or group in a society considered as corrupt or as a place of exile by another society or group, esp. White Britain as viewed by Rastafarians. [via L and Gk from Heb. *Bābhel;* see BABEL]
▸ **Babylonian** (bæbɪ'ləʊnɪən) *adj n*

baby-sit *vb* **baby-sits, baby-sitting, baby-sat.** (*intr*) to act or work as a baby-sitter.
▸ **'baby-,sitting** *n, adj*

baby-sitter *n* a person who takes care of a child or children while the parents are out.

baby snatcher *n Inf.* **1** a person who steals a baby from its pram. **2** someone who marries or has an affair with a much younger person.

baby wipe *n* a disposable moistened medicated paper towel used for cleaning babies.

baccalaureate (,bækə'lɔ:rɪɪt) *n* the university degree of Bachelor of Arts. [C17: from Med. L *baccalaureātus,* from *baccalaureus* advanced student from *baccalārius* BACHELOR]

baccarat ('bækə,rɑ:, ,bækə'rɑ:) *n* a card game in which two or more punters gamble against the banker. [C19: from F *baccara* from ?]

baccate ('bækeɪt) *adj Bot.* **1** like a berry. **2** bearing berries. [C19: from L *bāca* berry]

bacchanal ⓣ ('bækən°l) *n* **1** a follower of Bacchus, Greek god of wine. **2** a drunken and riotous celebration. **3** a participant in such a celebration. ◆ *adj* **4** of or relating to Bacchus. [C16: from L *Bacchānālis*]

bacchanalia (,bækə'neɪlɪə) *pl n* **1** (*often cap.*) orgiastic rites associated with Bacchus. **2** any drunken revelry.
▸ **,baccha'nalian** *adj, n*

bacchant ('bækənt) *or* (*fem*) **bacchante** (bə'kæntɪ) *n, pl* **bacchants** *or* **bacchantes** (bə'kæntɪz). **1** a priest, priestess, or votary of Bacchus. **2** a drunken reveller. [C17: from L *bacchāns,* from *bacchārī* to celebrate the BACCHANALIA]

Bacchic ('bækɪk) *adj* **1** of or relating to Bacchus, the Greek and Roman god of wine. **2** (*often not cap.*) riotously drunk.

baccy ('bækɪ) *n* a Brit. informal name for **tobacco.**

bach (bætʃ) *NZ.* ◆ *n* **1** a seaside, bush, or country cottage. ◆ *vb* **2** a variant spelling of **batch**[2].

bachelor ('bætʃələ, 'bætʃlə) *n* **1a** an unmarried man. **1b** (*as modifier*): *a bachelor flat.* **2** a person who holds the degree of Bachelor of Arts, Bachelor of Education, Bachelor of Science, etc. **3** (in the Middle Ages) a young knight serving a great noble. **4 bachelor seal.** a young male seal that has not yet mated. [C13: from OF *bacheler* youth, squire, from Vulgar L *baccalāris* (unattested) farm worker]
▸ **'bachelor,hood** *n*

bachelor girl *n* a young unmarried woman, esp. one who is self-supporting.

Bachelor of Arts *n* **1** a degree conferred on a person who has successfully completed undergraduate studies in the liberal arts or humanities. **2** a person who holds this degree.

Bachelor of Science *n* **1** a degree conferred on a person who has suc-

THESAURUS

babble *vb* **1 = gibber,** gurgle **2 = gabble,** burble, chatter, jabber, prate, prattle, rabbit (on) (*Brit. inf.*), waffle (*inf., chiefly Brit.*) **3 = blab,** run off at the mouth (*sl.*) ◆ *n* **5 = gabble,** burble, drivel, gibberish, waffle (*inf., chiefly Brit.*)

babe *n* **1 = baby,** ankle-biter (*Austral. sl.*), bairn (*Scot.*), child, infant, nursling, rug rat (*sl.*), sprog (*sl.*), suckling **2** *Informal* **= innocent,** babe in arms, ingénue *or* (*masc.*) ingénu

Babel *n, often not cap.* **2 = din,** bedlam, clamour, confusion, disorder, hubbub, hullabaloo, hurly-burly, pandemonium, tumult, turmoil, uproar

baby *n* **1 = infant,** ankle-biter (*Austral. sl.*), babe, babe in arms, bairn (*Scot.*), child, newborn child, rug rat (*sl.*), sprog (*sl.*) ◆ *adj* **9 = small,** diminutive, dwarf, little, midget, mini, miniature, minute, pygmy *or* pigmy, teensy-weensy, teeny-weeny, tiny, wee ◆ *vb* **11 = mollycoddle,** coddle, cosset, humour, indulge, overindulge, pamper, pet, spoil, spoon-feed

babyish *adj* **5 = childish,** foolish, immature, infantile, juvenile, puerile
Antonyms *adj* adult, grown-up, mature, of age

bacchanal *n* **2 = orgy,** debauch, debauchery, revel, revelry **3 = reveller,** carouser, debauchee, drunkard, roisterer, winebibber cessfully completed undergraduate studies in a science. **2** a person who holds this degree.

bachelor's-buttons *n* (*functioning as sing or pl*) any of various plants with button-like flower heads, esp. a double-flowered buttercup.

Bach flower remedy (bɑːx) *n Trademark.* an alternative medicine consisting of a distillation from various flowers, supposed to counteract negative states of mind and restore emotional balance. [C20: after Dr E. *Bach* (1886–1936), homeopath who developed this system]

bacillary (bəˈsɪlərɪ) *or* **bacillar** (bəˈsɪlə) *adj* **1** of, relating to, or caused by bacilli. **2** Also: **bacilliform** (bəˈsɪlɪˌfɔːm). shaped like a short rod.

bacillus (bəˈsɪləs) *n, pl* **bacilli** (-ˈsɪlaɪ). **1** any rod-shaped bacterium. **2** any of various rodlike spore-producing bacteria constituting the family Bacillaceae. [C19: from L, from *baculum* walking stick]

back ➊ (bæk) *n* **1** the posterior part of the human body, from the neck to the pelvis. **2** the corresponding or upper part of an animal. **3** the spinal column. **4** the part or side of an object opposite the front. **5** the part or side of anything less often seen or used. **6** the part or side of anything that is furthest from the front or from a spectator: *the back of the stage.* **7** something that supports, covers, or strengthens the rear of an object. **8** *Ball games.* **8a** a mainly defensive player behind a forward. **8b** the position of such a player. **9** the part of a book to which the pages are glued or that joins the covers. **10 at the back of one's mind.** not in one's conscious thoughts. **11 back of Bourke.** *Austral.* a remote or backward place. **12 behind one's back.** secretly or deceitfully. **13 break one's back.** to overwork or work very hard. **14 break the back of.** to complete the greatest or hardest part of (a task). **15 get off someone's back.** *Inf.* to stop criticizing or pestering someone. **16 put one's back into.** to devote all one's strength to (a task). **17 put** (*or* **get**) **someone's back up.** to annoy someone. **18 the back of beyond.** a very remote place. **19 turn one's back on. 19a** to turn away from in anger or contempt. **19b** to refuse to help; abandon. ◆ *vb* (*mainly tr*) **20** (*also intr*) to move or cause to move backwards. **21 back water.** to reverse the direction of a boat, esp. to push the oars of a rowing boat. **22** to provide support, money, or encouragement for (a person, enterprise, etc.). **23** to bet on the success of: *to back a horse.* **24** to provide with a back, backing, or lining. **25** to provide with a musical accompaniment. **26** to countersign or endorse. **27** (*intr; foll. by on or onto*) to have the back facing (towards): *the house backs onto a river.* **28** (*intr*) (of the wind) to change direction anticlockwise. Cf. **veer** (sense 3). ◆ *adj* (*prenominal*) **29** situated behind: *a back lane.* **30** of the past: *back issues of a magazine.* **31** owing from an earlier date: *back rent.* **32** remote: *a back road.* **33** *Phonetics.* of or denoting a vowel articulated with the tongue retracted towards the soft palate, as for the vowels in English *hard, fall, hot, full, fool.* ◆ *adv* **34** at, to, or towards the rear; behind. **35** in, to, or towards the original starting point, place, or condition: *to go back home; put the book back.* **36** in or into the past: *to look back on one's childhood.* **37** in reply, repayment, or retaliation: *to hit someone back.* **38** in check: *the dam holds back the water.* **39** in concealment; in reserve: *to keep something back.* **40 back and forth.** to and fro. **41 back to front. 41a** in reverse. **41b** in disorder. ◆ See also **back down, back off, back out, back up.** [OE *bæc*]

backbencher (ˈbækˈbɛntʃə) *n Brit., Austral., NZ., etc.* a Member of Parliament who does not hold office in the government or opposition.

backbite ➊ (ˈbækˌbaɪt) *vb* **backbites, backbiting, backbit; backbitten** *or* **backbit.** to talk spitefully about (an absent person).
▸ˈ**backˌbiter** *n*

backboard (ˈbækˌbɔːd) *n* **1** a board that is placed behind something to form or support its back. **2** a board worn to straighten or support the back, as after surgery. **3** (in basketball) a flat upright surface supported on a high frame, under which the basket is attached.

back boiler *n* a tank or series of pipes at the back of a fireplace for heating water.

backbone ➊ (ˈbækˌbəʊn) *n* **1** a nontechnical name for **spinal column. 2** something that resembles the spinal column in function, position, or appearance. **3** strength of character; courage.

backbreaking ➊ (ˈbækˌbreɪkɪŋ) *adj* exhausting.

backburn (ˈbækˌbɜːn) *Austral. & NZ.* ◆ *vb* **1** (*tr*) to clear (an area of scrub, bush, etc.) by creating a new fire that burns in the opposite direction to the line of advancing fire. ◆ *n* **2** the act or result of backburning.

back-calculate *vb* **back-calculates, back-calculating, back-calculated.** to estimate (the probable amount of alcohol in a person's blood) at an earlier time than that at which the blood test was taken, based on an average rate at which alcohol leaves the bloodstream: used to determine whether a driver had more than the legal limit of alcohol at the time of an accident.
▸ˈ**back-ˌcalcuˈlation** *n*

back catalogue *n* the recordings that a musician has made in the past, as distinct from his or her current recording: *favourites from his back catalogue.*

backchat ➊ (ˈbækˌtʃæt) *n Inf.* the act of answering back, esp. impudently.

backcloth (ˈbækˌklɒθ) *n* a painted curtain at the back of a stage set. Also called: **backdrop.**

backcomb (ˈbækˌkəʊm) *vb* to comb the under layers of (the hair) towards the roots to give more bulk to a hairstyle. Also: **tease.**

back country *n Austral. & NZ.* land remote from settled areas.

backdate (ˌbækˈdeɪt) *vb* **backdates, backdating, backdated.** (*tr*) to make effective from an earlier date.

back door *n* **1** a door at the rear or side of a building. **2** a means of entry to a job, etc., that is secret or obtained through influence.

back down ➊ *vb* **1** (*intr, adv*) to withdraw an earlier claim. ◆ *n* **back-down. 2** abandonment of an earlier claim.

backed (bækt) *adj* **a** having a back or backing. **b** (*in combination*): *high-backed; black-backed.*

backer ➊ (ˈbækə) *n* **1** a person who gives financial or other support. **2** a person who bets on a competitor or contestant.

backfield (ˈbækˌfiːld) *n American football.* **1** (usually preceded by *the*) the quarterback and running backs in a team. **2** the area behind the line of scrimmage from which the backfield begin each play.

backfill (ˈbækˌfɪl) *vb* (*tr*) to refill an excavated trench, esp. (in archaeology) at the end of an investigation.

backfire ➊ (ˌbækˈfaɪə) *vb* **backfires, backfiring, backfired.** (*intr*) **1** (of an internal-combustion engine) to emit a loud noise as a result of an explosion in the exhaust system. **2** to fail to have the desired effect, and, instead, recoil upon the originator. **3** to start a controlled fire in order to halt an advancing forest or prairie fire by creating a barren area. ◆ *n* **4** (in an internal-combustion engine) an explosion of unburnt gases in the exhaust system. **5** a controlled fire started to create a barren area that will halt an advancing forest or prairie fire.

back formation *n* **1** the invention of a new word on the assumption that a familiar word is derived from it. The verbs *edit* and *burgle* in English were so created from *editor* and *burglar.* **2** a word formed by this process.

backgammon (ˈbækˌgæmən) *n* **1** a game for two people played on a board with pieces moved according to throws of the dice. **2** the most complete form of win in this game. [C17: BACK + *gammon,* var. of GAME[1]]

background ➊ (ˈbækˌgraʊnd) *n* **1** the part of a scene furthest from the viewer. **2a** an inconspicuous or unobtrusive position (esp. in **in the background**). **2b** (*as modifier*): *a background influence.* **3** the plane or ground in a picture upon which all other planes or forms appear superimposed. **4** a person's social class, education, or experience. **5a** the circumstances that lead up to or help to explain something. **5b** (*as modifier*): *background information.* **6a** a low level of sound, lighting, etc., whose purpose is to be an unobtrusive accompaniment to something else. **6b** (*as modifier*): *background music.* **7** Also called: **background radiation.** *Physics.* low-intensity radiation from small amounts of radioisotopes in soil, air, etc. **8** *Electronics.* unwanted effects, such as noise, occurring in a measuring instrument, electronic device, etc.

backhand (ˈbækˌhænd) *n* **1** *Tennis, etc.* a stroke made across the body with the back of the hand facing the direction of the stroke. **2** the side on which backhand strokes are made. **3** handwriting slanting to the left. ◆ *adv* **4** with a backhand stroke.

backhanded ➊ (ˌbækˈhændɪd) *adj* **1** (of a blow, shot, etc.) performed with the arm moving across the body. **2** double-edged; equivocal: *a backhanded compliment.* **3** (of handwriting) slanting to the left. ◆ *adv* **4** in a backhanded manner.

THESAURUS

back *n* **1, 2** = **rear,** backside, end, hind part, hindquarters, posterior **4** = **end,** far end, reverse, stern, tail end **12 behind one's back** = **secretly,** covertly, deceitfully, sneakily, surreptitiously ◆ *vb* **22** = **support,** abet, advocate, assist, champion, countenance, encourage, endorse, espouse, favour, finance, promote, sanction, second, side with, sponsor, subsidize, sustain, underwrite ◆ *adj* **29** = **rear,** end, hind, hindmost, posterior, tail **30** = **previous,** earlier, former, past **31** = **overdue,** delayed, elapsed

Antonyms *n* ≠ **rear:** face, fore, front, head ◆ *vb* ≠ **support:** attack, combat, hinder, thwart, undermine, weaken ◆ *adj* ≠ **rear:** advance, fore, front ≠ **previous:** future

backbite *vb* = **slander,** abuse, bad-mouth (*sl., chiefly US & Canad.*), calumniate, defame, denigrate, detract, disparage, knock (*inf.*), libel, malign, revile, rubbish (*inf.*), slag (off) (*sl.*), traduce, vilify, vituperate

backbiting *n* = **slander,** abuse, aspersion, bitchiness (*sl.*), calumniation, calumny, cattiness (*inf.*), defamation, denigration, detraction, disparagement, gossip, malice, maligning, scandalmongering, spite, spitefulness, vilification, vituperation

backbone *n* **1** = **spinal column,** spine, vertebrae, vertebral column **2** = **foundation,** basis, mainstay, support **3** = **strength of character,** bottle (*Brit. sl.*), character, courage, determination, firmness, fortitude, grit, hardihood, mettle, moral fibre, nerve, pluck, resolution, resolve, stamina, steadfastness, tenacity, toughness, will, willpower

backbreaking *adj* = **exhausting,** arduous, crushing, gruelling, hard, killing, laborious, punishing, strenuous, toilsome, wearing, wearying

backchat *n Informal* = **cheek,** answering back, impertinence, impudence, insolence, lip (*sl.*), sass (*US & Canad. inf.*), talking back, verbals (*Brit. sl.*)

back down *vb* **1** = **give in,** accede, admit defeat, back-pedal, cave in (*inf.*), concede, surrender, withdraw, yield

backer *n* **1** = **supporter,** advocate, angel (*inf.*), benefactor, patron, promoter, second, sponsor, subscriber, underwriter, well-wisher

backfire *vb* **2** = **fail,** boomerang, disappoint, flop (*inf.*), miscarry, rebound, recoil

background *n* **4** = **credentials,** breeding, culture, education, environment, experience, grounding, milieu, preparation, qualifications, tradition, upbringing **5** = **history,** circumstances

backhanded *adj* **2** = **ambiguous,** double-edged, equivocal, indirect, ironic, oblique, sarcastic, sardonic, two-edged, with tongue in cheek

backhander ('bæk,hændə) *n* **1** a backhanded stroke or blow. **2** *Inf.* an indirect attack. **3** *Sl.* a bribe.

backing ⓘ ('bækɪŋ) *n* **1** support. **2** a body of supporters. **3** something that forms, protects, or strengthens the back of something. **4** musical accompaniment, esp. for a pop singer. **5** *Meteorol.* an anticlockwise change in wind direction.

backing dog *n NZ.* a dog that moves a flock of sheep by jumping on their backs.

backlash ⓘ ('bæk,læʃ) *n* **1** a sudden and adverse reaction. **2** a reaction or recoil between interacting worn or badly fitting parts in a mechanism. **3** the excessive play between such parts.

backlog ⓘ ('bæk,lɒg) *n* an accumulation of uncompleted work, unsold stock, etc., to be dealt with.

back marker *n* a competitor who is at the back of a field in a race.

back matter *n* the parts of a book, such as the index and appendices, that follow the text.

backmost ('bæk,məʊst) *adj* furthest back.

back number *n* **1** an issue of a newspaper, magazine, etc., that appeared on a previous date. **2** *Inf.* a person or thing considered to be old-fashioned.

back off ⓘ *vb* (*adv*) *Inf.* **1** (*intr*) to retreat. **2** (*tr*) to abandon (an intention, objective, etc.).

back out ⓘ *vb* (*intr, adv;* often foll. by *of*) to withdraw (from an agreement, etc.).

backpack ('bæk,pæk) *n* **1** a rucksack. **2** a pack carried on the back of an astronaut, containing oxygen cylinders, etc. ◆ *vb* (*intr*) **3** to travel about with a backpack.

back passage *n* the rectum.

back-pedal *vb* **back-pedals, back-pedalling, back-pedalled** *or US* **back-pedals, back-pedaling, back-pedaled.** (*intr*) **1** to turn the pedals of a bicycle backwards. **2** to retract or modify a previous opinion, principle, etc.

back projection *n* a method of projecting pictures onto a translucent screen so that they are viewed from the opposite side, used esp. in films to create the illusion that the actors in the foreground are moving.

back room *n* **a** a place where important and usually secret research or planning is done. **b** (*as modifier*): *back-room boys.*

back seat *n* **1** a seat at the back, esp. of a vehicle. **2** *Inf.* a subordinate or inconspicuous position (esp. in **take a back seat**).

back-seat driver *n Inf.* **1** a passenger in a car who offers unwanted advice to the driver. **2** a person who offers advice on or tries to direct matters that are not his or her concern.

backsheesh ('bækʃi:ʃ) *n* a variant spelling of **baksheesh.**

back shift *n Brit.* **1** a group of workers who work a shift from late afternoon to midnight in an industry or occupation where a day or a night shift is also worked. **2** the period worked. ◆ US and Canad. name: **swing shift.**

backside ⓘ (,bæk'saɪd) *n Inf.* the buttocks.

backslide ⓘ (,bæk'slaɪd) *vb* **backslides, backsliding, backslid.** (*intr*) to relapse into former bad habits.
▸ ,**back'slider** *n*

backspace ('bæk,speɪs) *vb* **backspaces, backspacing, backspaced.** to move (a typewriter carriage, etc.) backwards.

backspin ('bæk,spɪn) *n Sport.* a backward spin imparted to a ball to reduce its speed at impact.

backstage (,bæk'steɪdʒ) *adv* **1** behind the part of the theatre in view of the audience. **2** towards the rear of the stage. ◆ *adj* **3** situated backstage. **4** *Inf.* away from public view.

backstairs (,bæk'stɛəz) *pl n* **1** a secondary staircase in a house, esp. one originally for the use of servants. ◆ *adj also* **backstair. 2** underhand: *backstairs gossip.*

backstay ('bæk,steɪ) *n Naut.* a stay leading aft from the upper mast to the deck or stern.

backstreet ('bæk,stri:t) *n* **1** a street in a town remote from the main roads. **2** (*modifier*) denoting illicit activities regarded as likely to take place in such a street: *a backstreet abortion.*

backstroke ('bæk,strəʊk) *n Swimming.* a stroke performed on the back, using backward circular strokes of each arm and flipper movements of the feet. Also called: **back crawl.**

back-to-back *adj* (*usually postpositive*) **1** facing in opposite directions, often with the backs touching. **2** *Chiefly Brit.* (of urban houses) built so that their backs are joined or separated only by a narrow alley.

backtrack ⓘ ('bæk,træk) *vb* (*intr*) **1** to return by the same route by which one has come. **2** to retract or reverse one's opinion, policy, etc.

back up ⓘ *vb* (*adv*) **1** (*tr*) to support. **2** (*intr*) *Cricket.* (of a nonstriking batsman) to move down the wicket in readiness for a run as a ball is bowled. **3** (of water) to accumulate. **4** (of traffic) to become jammed behind an accident or other obstruction. **5** *Computing.* to make a copy of (a data file), esp. as a security copy. **6** (*intr;* usually foll. by *on*) *Austral.* to repeat an action immediately. ◆ *n* **backup. 7** a support or reinforcement. **8a** a substitute. **8b** (*as modifier*): *a backup copy.* **9** the overflow from a blocked drain or pipe.

backward ⓘ ('bækwəd) *adj* **1** (*usually prenominal*) directed towards the rear: *a backward glance.* **2** retarded in physical, material, or intellectual development. **3a** conservative or reactionary. **3b** (*in combination*): *backward-looking.* **4** reluctant or bashful: *a backward lover.* ◆ *adv* **5** a variant of **backwards.**
▸ **'backwardness** *n*

backwardation (,bækwə'deɪʃən) *n* **1** the difference between the spot price for a commodity, including rent and interest, and the forward price. **2** (formerly, on the Stock Exchange) postponement of delivery by a seller of securities until the next settlement period.

backwards ⓘ ('bækwədz) *or* **backward** *adv* **1** towards the rear. **2** with the back foremost. **3** in the reverse of usual order or direction. **4** to or towards the past. **5** into a worse state. **6** towards the point of origin. **7 bend, lean,** *or* **fall over backwards.** *Inf.* to make a special effort, esp. in order to please.

backwash ('bæk,wɒʃ) *n* **1** water washed backwards by the motion of oars or other propelling devices. **2** the backward flow of air set up by aircraft engines. **3** a repercussion.

backwater ('bæk,wɔ:tə) *n* **1** a body of stagnant water connected to a river. **2** an isolated or backward place or condition.

backwoods ⓘ ('bækwʊdz) *pl n* **1** partially cleared, sparsely populated forests. **2** any remote sparsely populated place. **3** (*modifier*) of or like the backwoods. **4** (*modifier*) uncouth; rustic.
▸ **'back,woodsman** *n*

backword ('bæk,wɜ:d) *n Dialect.* a failure to keep a promise.

back yard *n* **1** a yard at the back of a house, etc. **2 in one's own back yard. 2a** close at hand. **2b** involving or implicating one.

baclava ('bɑ:klə,vɑ:) *n* a variant spelling of **baklava.**

bacon ('beɪkən) *n* **1** meat from the back and sides of a pig, dried, salted, and usually smoked. **2 bring home the bacon.** *Inf.* **2a** to achieve success. **2b** to provide material support. **3 save (someone's) bacon.** *Brit. inf.* to help (someone) to escape from danger. [C12: from OF *bacon,* from OHG *bahho*]

Baconian (beɪ'kəʊnɪən) *adj* **1** of or relating to Francis Bacon (1561–1626), English philosopher, or his inductive method of reasoning. ◆ *n* **2** a follower of Bacon's philosophy. **3** one who believes that plays attributed to Shakespeare were written by Bacon.

BACS (bæks) *n acronym for* Bankers Automated Clearing System; a method of making payments direct to a creditor's bank without using a cheque.

bacteria ⓘ (bæk'tɪərɪə) *pl n, sing* **bacterium.** a large group of typically unicellular microorganisms, many of which cause disease. [C19: NL, from Gk *baktērion,* from *baktron* rod, staff]
▸ **bac'terial** *adj* ▸ **bac'terially** *adv*

bactericide (bæk'tɪərɪ,saɪd) *n* a substance able to destroy bacteria.
▸ **bac,teri'cidal** *adj*

bacterio-, bacteri-, *or sometimes before a vowel* **bacter-** *combining form.* indicating bacteria or an action or condition relating to bacteria: *bacteriology; bactericide.*

bacteriology (bæk,tɪərɪ'ɒlədʒɪ) *n* the study of bacteria.
▸ **bacteriological** (bæk,tɪərɪə'lɒdʒɪk'l) *adj* ▸ **bac,teri'ologist** *n*

THESAURUS

backing *n* **1 = support,** abetment, accompaniment, advocacy, aid, assistance, championing, encouragement, endorsement, espousal, funds, grant, moral support, patronage, promotion, sanction, seconding, sponsorship, subsidy

backlash *n* **1 = reaction,** backfire, boomerang, counteraction, repercussion, resentment, resistance, response, retaliation, retroaction **2 = recoil,** counterblast, kickback, reaction

backlog *n* **= build-up,** accumulation, excess, hoard, reserve, reserves, resources, stock, supply

back off *vb* **1 = move back,** backtrack, go back, regress, retire, retreat, reverse, turn tail, withdraw advance, approach, move forward, progress

back out *vb* **= withdraw,** abandon, cancel, chicken out, cop out (*sl.*), give up, go back on, recant, renege, resign, retreat

backside *n Informal* **= buttocks,** arse (*taboo sl.*), ass (*US & Canad. taboo sl.*), behind (*inf.*), bottom, bum (*Brit. sl.*), buns (*US sl.*), butt (*US & Canad. inf.*), coit (*Austral. sl.*), derrière (*euphemistic*), fanny (*sl., chiefly US & Canad.*), jacksy (*Brit. sl.*), keister *or* keester (*sl., chiefly US*), posterior, rear, rear end, rump, seat, tail (*US*)

backslide *vb* **= relapse,** fall from grace, go astray, go wrong, lapse, regress, renege, retrogress, revert, sin, slip, stray, weaken

backslider *n* **= relapser,** apostate, deserter, recidivist, recreant, renegade, reneger, turncoat

backtrack *vb* **1 = retrace one's steps,** back, back-pedal, go back, move back, retreat, reverse **2 = retract,** draw back, eat one's words, recant, retreat, withdraw

back up *vb* **1 = support,** aid, assist, bolster, confirm, corroborate, reinforce, second, stand by, substantiate ◆ *n* **backup 7 = support,** aid, assistance, backing, help, reinforcement, reserves **8 = substitute,** locum, relief, replacement, reserve, second string, stand-by, stand-in, understudy

backward *adj* **2 = slow,** behind, braindead (*inf.*), dead from the neck up (*inf.*), dense, dozy (*Brit. inf.*), dull, obtuse, retarded, stupid, subnormal, underdeveloped, undeveloped ◆ *adv* **5 = towards the rear,** behind, in reverse, rearward
Antonyms *adv* ≠ **towards the rear:** forward, frontward

backwardness *n* **2 = slowness,** arrested development, denseness, doziness (*inf.*), dullness, learning difficulties, retardation, underdevelopment
Antonyms *n* brightness, precociousness, precocity, quickness, smartness

backwards *adv* **1 = towards the rear,** behind, rearward **3 = in reverse**

backwoods *pl n* **2 = sticks** (*inf.*), back country, backlands (*US*), back of beyond, middle of nowhere, outback

bacteria *pl n* **= microorganisms,** bacilli, bugs (*sl.*), germs, microbes, pathogens, viruses

bad[1] *adj* **1 = inferior,** defective, deficient, duff (*Brit. inf.*), erroneous, fallacious, faulty, imper-

bacteriophage (bæk'tɪərɪəˌfeɪdʒ) *n* a virus that is parasitic in a bacterium and destroys its host. Often shortened to **phage.**
bacterium (bæk'tɪərɪəm) *n* the singular of **bacteria.**
Bactrian camel ('bæktrɪən) *n* a two-humped camel, used in the cold deserts of central Asia. [from *Bactria*, ancient country of SW Asia]
bad[1] ❶ (bæd) *adj* **worse, worst. 1** not good; of poor quality; inadequate. **2** (often foll. by *at*) lacking skill or talent; incompetent. **3** (often foll. by *for*) harmful. **4** immoral; evil. **5** naughty; mischievous. **6** rotten; decayed: *a bad egg.* **7** severe; intense: *a bad headache.* **8** incorrect; faulty: *bad pronunciation.* **9** ill or in pain (esp. in **feel bad**). **10** sorry or upset (esp. in **feel bad about**). **11** unfavourable; distressing: *bad news.* **12** offensive; unpleasant: *bad language; bad temper.* **13** not valid or sound: *a bad cheque.* **14** not recoverable: *a bad debt.* **15** (**badder, baddest**) *Sl.* good, excellent. **16 go bad.** to putrefy; spoil. **17 in a bad way.** *Inf.* **17a** seriously ill. **17b** in trouble. **18 make the best of a bad job.** to manage as well as possible in unfavourable circumstances. **19 not bad** *or* **not so bad.** *Inf.* passable; fairly good. **20 too bad.** *Inf.* (often used dismissively) regrettable. ◆ *n* **21** unfortunate or unpleasant events (often in **take the bad with the good**). **22** an immoral or degenerate state (often in **go to the bad**). **23** the debit side of an account: *£200 to the bad.* **24 go from bad to worse.** to deteriorate even more. ◆ *adv* **25** *Not standard.* badly: *to want something bad.* [C13: prob. from *bæd-*, as the first element of OE *bǣddel* hermaphrodite]
▸'**baddish** *adj* ▸'**badness** *n*

USAGE NOTE See at **good.**

bad[2] (bæd) *vb* a variant spelling of **bade.**
bad blood ❶ *n* a feeling of intense hatred or hostility; enmity.
baddie *or* **baddy** ❶ ('bædɪ) *n, pl* **baddies.** *Inf.* a bad character in a film, etc., esp. an opponent of the hero.
bade (bæd, beɪd) *or* **bad** *vb* past tense of **bid.**
badge ❶ (bædʒ) *n* **1** a distinguishing emblem or mark worn to signify membership, employment, achievement, etc. **2** any revealing feature or mark. [C14: from OF *bage*]
badger ❶ ('bædʒə) *n* **1** any of various stocky omnivorous mammals occurring in Europe, Asia, and N America. They are large burrowing animals, with strong claws and a thick coat striped black and white on the head. ◆ *vb* **2** (*tr*) to pester or harass. [C16: var. of *badgeard*, prob. from BADGE (from the white mark on its forehead) + -ARD]
bad hair day *n Inf.* **1** a day on which one's hair is untidy and unmanageable. **2** a day of mishaps and general irritation.
badinage ❶ ('bædɪˌnɑːʒ) *n* playful or frivolous repartee or banter. [C17: from F, from *badiner* to jest]
badlands ('bædˌlændz) *pl n* any deeply eroded barren area.
badly ❶ ('bædlɪ) *adv* **worse, worst. 1** poorly; defectively; inadequately. **2** unfavourably; unsuccessfully: *our scheme worked out badly.* **3** severely; gravely: *badly hurt.* **4** incorrectly or inaccurately: *to speak German badly.* **5** improperly; wickedly: *to behave badly.* **6** cruelly: *to treat badly.* **7** very much (esp. in **need badly, want badly**). **8** regretfully: *he felt badly about it.* **9 badly off.** poor.
badminton ('bædmɪntən) *n* **1** a game played with rackets and a shuttlecock which is hit back and forth across a high net. **2** Also called: **badminton cup.** a long drink of claret with soda water and sugar. [from *Badminton* House, Glos]
bad-mouth *vb* (*tr*) *Sl., chiefly US & Canad.* to speak unfavourably about.
bad-tempered ❶ *adj* angry; irritable.
BAe *abbrev. for* British Aerospace.
Baedeker ('beɪdɪkə) *n* any of a series of travel guidebooks issued by the German publisher Karl Baedeker (1801–59) or his firm.
BAF *abbrev. for* British Athletics Federation.
baffle ❶ ('bæf°l) *vb* **baffles, baffling, baffled.** (*tr*) **1** to perplex; bewilder; puzzle. **2** to frustrate (plans, efforts, etc.). **3** to check, restrain, or regulate (the flow of a fluid or the emission of sound or light). ◆ *n* **4** Also called: **baffle board, baffle plate.** a plate or mechanical device to restrain or regulate the flow of fluid, light, or sound, esp. in a loudspeaker or microphone. [C16: ?from Scot. dialect *bachlen* to condemn publicly]
▸'**bafflement** *n* ▸'**baffler** *n* ▸'**baffling** *adj* ▸'**bafflingly** *adv*
BAFTA ('bæftə) *n acronym for* British Academy of Film and Television Arts.
bag ❶ (bæg) *n* **1** a flexible container with an opening at one end. **2** Also: **bagful.** the contents of or amount contained in such a container. **3** a piece of portable luggage. **4** short for **handbag. 5** anything that sags, or is shaped like a bag, such as a loose fold of skin under the eyes. **6** any pouch or sac forming part of the body of an animal. **7** the quantity of quarry taken in a single hunting trip or by a single hunter. **8** *Derog. sl.* an ugly or bad-tempered woman or girl (often in **old bag**). **9 bag and baggage.** *Inf.* **9a** with all one's belongings. **9b** entirely. **10 bag of bones.** a lean creature. **11 in the bag.** *Sl.* almost assured of succeeding or being obtained. **12 rough as bags.** *Austral. sl.* **12a** uncouth. **12b** shoddy. ◆ *vb* **bags, bagging, bagged. 13** (*tr*) to put into a bag. **14** to bulge or cause to bulge. **15** (*tr*) to capture or kill, as in hunting. **16** (*tr*) to catch, seize, or steal. **17** (*intr*) to hang loosely; sag. **18** (*tr*) *Brit. & Austral. inf.* to secure the right to do or to have: *he bagged the best chair.* **19** (*tr*) to achieve or accomplish: *she bagged seven birdies.* ◆ See also **bags.** [C13: prob. from ON *baggi*]
bagasse (bə'gæs) *n* the dry pulp remaining after the extraction of juice from sugar cane or similar plants: used as fuel, for making fibreboard, etc. [C19: from F, from Sp. *bagazo* dregs]
bagatelle (ˌbægə'tel) *n* **1** something of little value. **2** a board game in which balls are struck into holes, with pins as obstacles. **3** a short light piece of music. [C17: from F, from It. *bagattella*, from (dialect) *bagatta* a little possession]
bagel *or* **beigel** ('beɪg°l) *n* a hard ring-shaped bread roll. [C20: from Yiddish *beygel*]
baggage ❶ ('bægɪdʒ) *n* **1** suitcases, bags, etc., packed for a journey; luggage. **2** an army's portable equipment. **3** *Inf., old-fashioned.* **3a** a pert young woman. **3b** an immoral woman. **4** *Irish inf.* a cantankerous old woman. **5** *Inf.* previous knowledge and experience that a person may use or be influenced by in new circumstances: *cultural baggage.* [C15: from OF *bagage*, from *bague* a bundle]
baggy ❶ ('bægɪ) *adj* **baggier, baggiest.** (of clothes) hanging loosely; puffed out.
▸'**baggily** *adv* ▸'**bagginess** *n*
bag lady *n* a homeless woman who wanders city streets with all her possessions in shopping bags.
bagman ('bægmən) *n, pl* **bagmen. 1** *Brit. inf.* a travelling salesman. **2** *Sl., chiefly US.* a person who collects or distributes money for racketeers. **3** *Austral.* a tramp or swagman, esp. one on horseback. **4** *Inf., chiefly Canad.* a person who solicits money for a political party.
bagnio ('bɑːnjəʊ) *n, pl* **bagnios. 1** a brothel. **2** *Obs.* an oriental prison for slaves. **3** *Obs.* an Italian or Turkish bathhouse. [C16: from It. *bagno*, from L *balneum* bath]
bagpipes ('bægˌpaɪps) *pl n* any of a family of musical wind instruments in which sounds are produced in reed pipes by air from a bag inflated either by the player's mouth or by arm-operated bellows.
bags (bægz) *pl n* **1** *Inf.* a lot. **2** *Brit. inf.* trousers. ◆ *interj* **3** Also: **bags I.**

THESAURUS

fect, inadequate, incorrect, low-rent (*inf., chiefly US*), of a sort *or* of sorts, pathetic, poor, poxy (*sl.*), substandard, unsatisfactory **3** = **harmful**, damaging, dangerous, deleterious, detrimental, hurtful, injurious, ruinous, unhealthy **4** = **wicked**, base, corrupt, criminal, delinquent, evil, immoral, mean, sinful, vile, villainous, wrong **5** = **naughty**, disobedient, mischievous, unruly **6** = **rotten**, decayed, mouldy, off, putrid, rancid, sour, spoiled **7** = **severe**, distressing, grave, painful, serious, terrible **9** = **ill**, ailing, diseased, sick, unwell **10** = **sorry**, apologetic, conscience-stricken, contrite, guilty, regretful, remorseful, sad, upset **11** = **unfavourable**, adverse, discouraging, distressing, gloomy, grim, melancholy, troubling, unfortunate, unpleasant **19 not bad** *Informal* = **O.K.** *or* **okay** (*inf.*), all right, average, fair, fair to middling (*inf.*), moderate, passable, respectable, so-so (*inf.*), tolerable
Antonyms *adj* ≠ **inferior:** adequate, fair, satisfactory ≠ **harmful:** agreeable, beneficial, good, healthful, safe, sound, wholesome ≠ **wicked:** ethical, fine, first-rate, good, moral, righteous, virtuous ≠ **naughty:** biddable, docile, good, obedient, well-behaved

bad blood *n* = **ill feeling**, acrimony, anger, animosity, antagonism, dislike, enmity, feud, hatred, ill will, malevolence, malice, rancour, resentment

baddie *n Informal* = **villain**, antihero, bad guy
Antonyms *n* good guy, goody, hero, heroine

badge *n* **1** = **mark**, brand, device, emblem, identification, insignia, sign, stamp, token

badger *vb* **2** = **pester**, bend someone's ear (*inf.*), bully, chivvy, goad, harass, harry, hound, importune, nag, plague, torment

badinage *n* = **wordplay**, banter, chaff, mockery, pleasantry, repartee, teasing

badly *adv* **1** = **poorly**, carelessly, defectively, erroneously, faultily, imperfectly, inadequately, incorrectly, ineptly, shoddily, wrong, wrongly **2** = **unfavourably**, unfortunately, unsuccessfully **3** = **severely**, acutely, deeply, desperately, gravely, greatly, intensely, painfully, seriously
Antonyms *adv* ≠ **poorly:** ably, competently, correctly, properly, rightly, satisfactorily, splendidly, well

badness *n* **4** = **wickedness**, baseness, corruption, delinquency, evil, foulness, immorality, impropriety, meanness, naughtiness, shamefulness, sin, sinfulness, vileness, villainy, wrong
Antonyms *n* excellence, good, goodness, morality, rectitude, righteousness, uprightness, virtue

bad-tempered *adj* = **irritable**, angry, cantankerous, crabbed, cross, crotchety (*inf.*), grouchy (*inf.*), grumbling, huffy, ill-tempered, irascible, peevish, petulant, querulous, ratty (*Brit. & NZ inf.*), sulky, sullen, surly, testy, tetchy
Antonyms *adj* affable, amiable, cheerful, genial, good-humoured, good-tempered, happy, pleasant, sanguine

baffle *vb* **1** = **puzzle**, amaze, astound, bewilder, boggle the mind, confound, confuse, daze, disconcert, dumbfound, flummox, mystify, nonplus, perplex, stump, stun **2** = **frustrate**, balk, check, defeat, foil, hinder, thwart, upset
Antonyms *vb* ≠ **puzzle:** clarify, clear up, elucidate, explain, explicate, interpret, make plain, shed *or* throw light upon, spell out

baffling *adj* **1** = **puzzling**, bewildering, confusing, difficult, enigmatic, inexplicable, mysterious, mystifying, perplexing, strange, unaccountable, unfathomable, weird
Antonyms *adj* clear, easy, intelligible, obvious, simple, understandable

bag *n* **1** = **container**, poke (*Scot.*), receptacle, sac, sack ◆ *vb* **14** = **bulge**, balloon, droop, sag, swell **15** = **catch**, acquire, capture, gain, get, kill, land, shoot, take, trap

baggage *n* **1** = **luggage**, bags, belongings, gear, suitcases, things **2** = **equipment**, accoutrements, impedimenta, paraphernalia

baggy *adj* = **loose**, billowing, bulging, droopy, floppy, ill-fitting, oversize, roomy, sagging, seated, slack
Antonyms *adj* close, close-fitting, constricted, cramped, narrow, snug, stretched, taut, tight, tight-fitting

Children's sl., Brit. & Austral. an indication of the desire to do, be, or have something.

baguette *or* **baguet** (bæ'get) *n* **1** a narrow French stick loaf. **2** a small gem cut as a long rectangle. **3** *Archit.* a small moulding having a semicircular cross section. [C18: from F, from It. *bacchetta* a little stick, from *bacchio* rod]

bah (bɑː, bæ) *interj* an expression of contempt or disgust.

Bahá'í (bə'hɑːɪ) *n* **1** an adherent of the Bahá'í Faith. ◆ *adj* **2** of or relating to the Bahá'í Faith. [from Persian *bahā'ī*, lit.: of glory]

Bahá'í Faith *or* **Bahí'í** *n* a religious system founded in 1863, based on Babism and emphasizing the value of all religions and the spiritual unity of mankind.

Bahá'ísm (bə'hɑːˌɪzəm) *n* another name, not in Bahá'í use, for the **Bahá'í Faith.**

bail[1] ⓣ (beɪl) *Law.* ◆ *n* **1** a sum of money by which a person is bound to take responsibility for the appearance in court of another person or himself, forfeited if the person fails to appear. **2** the person or persons so binding themselves; surety. **3** the system permitting release of a person from custody where such security has been taken: *he was released on bail.* **4 jump bail** *or* (*formal*) **forfeit bail.** to fail to appear in court to answer to a charge. **5 stand** *or* **go bail.** to act as surety (for someone). ◆ *vb* (*tr*) **6** (often foll. by *out*) to release or obtain the release of (a person) from custody, security having been made. [C14: from OF: custody, from *baillier* to hand over, from L *bāiulāre* to carry burdens]

bail[2] ⓣ *or* **bale** (beɪl) *vb* **bails, bailing, bailed** *or* **bales, baling, baled.** (often foll. by *out*) to remove (water) from (a boat). See also **bail out.** [C13: from OF *baille* bucket, from L *bāiulus* carrier]
▸ **'bailer** *or* **'baler** *n*

bail[3] (beɪl) *n* **1** *Cricket.* either of two small wooden bars across the tops of the stumps. **2** a partition between stalls in a stable or barn. **3** *Austral. & NZ.* a framework in a cowshed used to secure the head of a cow during milking. **4** a movable bar on a typewriter that holds the paper against the platen. ◆ *vb* **5** See **bail up.** [C18: from OF *baile* stake, fortification, prob. from L *baculum* stick]

bail[4] *or* **bale** (beɪl) *n* the semicircular handle of a kettle, bucket, etc. [C15: prob. of Scand. origin]

bailey ('beɪlɪ) *n* the outermost wall or court of a castle. [C13: from OF *baille* enclosed court, from *bailler* to enclose]

Bailey bridge ('beɪlɪ) *n* a temporary bridge made of prefabricated steel parts that can be rapidly assembled. [C20: after Sir Donald Coleman *Bailey* (1901–85), its Brit. designer]

bailie ('beɪlɪ) *n* (in Scotland) a municipal magistrate. [C13: from OF *bailli*, from earlier *baillif* BAILIFF]

bailiff ('beɪlɪf) *n* **1** *Brit.* the agent of a landlord or landowner. **2** a sheriff's officer who serves writs and summonses, makes arrests, and ensures that the sentences of the court are carried out. **3** *Chiefly Brit.* (formerly) a high official having judicial powers. **4** *Chiefly US.* an official having custody of prisoners appearing in court. [C13: from OF *baillif*, from *bail* custody; see BAIL[1]]

bailiwick ('beɪlɪwɪk) *n* **1** *Law.* the area over which a bailiff has jurisdiction. **2** a person's special field of interest. [C15: from BAILIE + WICK[2]]

bail out ⓣ *or* **bale out** *vb* (*adv*) **1** (*intr*) to make an emergency parachute jump from an aircraft. **2** (*tr*) *Inf.* to help (a person, organization, etc.) out of a predicament.

bail up *vb* (*adv*) **1** *Austral. & NZ.* to confine (a cow) or (of a cow) to be confined by the head in a bail. See **bail**[3] (sense 3). **2** (*tr*) *Austral.* (of a bushranger) to hold under guard in order to rob. **3** (*intr*) *Austral.* to submit to robbery without offering resistance. **4** (*tr*) *Austral. inf.* to accost or detain, esp. in conversation.

bain-marie *French.* (bɛ̃mari) *n, pl* **bains-marie** (bɛ̃mari). a vessel for holding hot water, in which sauces and other dishes are gently cooked or kept warm. [C19: from F, from Med. L *balneum Mariae*, lit.: bath of Mary, inaccurate translation of Med. Gk *kaminos Marios*, lit.: furnace of *Miriam*, alleged author of a treatise on alchemy]

Bairam (baɪ'ræm, 'baɪræm) *n* either of two Muslim festivals, one (**Lesser Bairam**) at the end of Ramadan, the other (**Greater Bairam**) at the end of the Islamic year. [from Turkish *bayrām*]

bairn (beən) *n Scot. & N English.* a child. [OE *bearn*]

bait[1] ⓣ (beɪt) *n* **1** something edible fixed to a hook or in a trap to attract fish or animals. **2** an enticement; temptation. **3** a variant spelling of **bate**[3]. **4** *Arch.* a short stop for refreshment during a journey. ◆ *vb* **5** (*tr*) to put a piece of food on or in (a hook or trap). **6** (*tr*) to persecute or tease. **7** (*tr*) to entice; tempt. **8** (*tr*) to set dogs upon (a bear, etc.). **9** (*intr*) *Arch.* to stop for rest and refreshment during a journey. [C13: from ON *beita* to hunt]

> **USAGE NOTE** The phrase *with bated breath* is sometimes wrongly spelled *with baited breath.*

bait[2] (beɪt) *vb* a variant spelling of **bate**[2].

baize (beɪz) *n* a woollen fabric resembling felt, usually green, used mainly for the tops of billiard tables. [C16: from OF *baies*, pl. of *baie* baize, from *bai* reddish brown, BAY[5]]

bake ⓣ (beɪk) *vb* **bakes, baking, baked. 1** (*tr*) to cook by dry heat as in an oven. **2** (*intr*) to cook bread, pastry, etc. **3** to make or become hardened by heat. **4** (*intr*) *Inf.* to be extremely hot. ◆ *n* **5** a batch of things baked at one time. **6** *Caribbean.* a small flat fried cake. [OE *bacan*]

baked Alaska (ə'læskə) *n* a dessert made of cake and ice cream covered with meringue and cooked very quickly.

baked beans *pl n* haricot beans, baked and tinned in tomato sauce.

Bakelite ('beɪkəˌlaɪt) *n Trademark.* any one of a class of thermosetting resins used as electric insulators and for making plastic ware, etc. [C20: after L. H. *Baekeland* (1863–1944), Belgian-born US inventor]

baker ('beɪkə) *n* a person whose business or employment is to make or sell bread, cakes, etc.

baker's dozen *n* thirteen. [C16: from the bakers' former practice of giving thirteen rolls where twelve were requested, to protect themselves against accusations of giving light weight]

bakery ('beɪkərɪ) *n, pl* **bakeries. 1** a room or building equipped for baking. **2** a shop in which bread, cakes, etc., are sold.

baking powder *n* a powdered mixture that contains sodium bicarbonate and one or more acidic compounds, such as cream of tartar: used in baking as a raising agent.

baklava *or* **baclava** ('bɑːkləˌvɑː) *n* a rich cake consisting of thin layers of pastry filled with nuts and honey. [from Turkish]

baksheesh *or* **backsheesh** ('bækʃiːʃ) *n* (in some Eastern countries, esp. formerly) money given as a tip, a present, or alms. [C17: from Persian *bakhshīsh*, from *bakhshīdan* to give]

bal. *Book-keeping. abbrev. for* balance.

Balaclava *or* **Balaclava helmet** (ˌbælə'klɑːvə) *n* (*often not caps.*) a close-fitting woollen hood that covers the ears and neck, as originally worn by soldiers in the Crimean War. [C19: from *Balaklava*, Ukrainian port]

balalaika (ˌbælə'laɪkə) *n* a Russian plucked musical instrument, usually having a triangular body and three strings. [C18: from Russian]

balance ⓣ ('bæləns) *n* **1** a weighing device, generally consisting of a horizontal beam pivoted at its centre, from the ends of which two pans are suspended. The substance to be weighed is placed in one pan and weights are placed in the other until the beam returns to the horizontal. **2** a state of equilibrium. **3** something that brings about such a state. **4** equilibrium of the body; steadiness: *to lose one's balance.* **5** emotional stability. **6** harmony in the parts of a whole. **7** the act of weighing factors, quantities, etc., against each other. **8** the power to influence or control: *the balance of power.* **9** something that remains: *the balance of what you owe.* **10** *Accounting.* **10a** equality of debit and credit totals in an account. **10b** a difference between such totals. **11 in the balance.** in an uncertain or undecided condition. **12 on balance.** after weighing up all the factors. **13 strike a balance.** to make a compromise. ◆ *vb* **balances, balancing, balanced. 14** (*tr*) to weigh in or as if in a balance. **15** (*intr*) to be or come into equilibrium. **16** (*tr*) to bring into or hold in equilibrium. **17** (*tr*) to compare the relative weight, importance, etc., of. **18** (*tr*) to be equal to. **19** (*tr*) to arrange so as to create a state of harmony. **20** (*tr*) *Accounting.* **20a** to compare the credit and debit totals of (an account). **20b** to equalize the credit and debit totals of (an account) by making certain entries. **20c** to settle or adjust (an account) by paying any money due. **21** (*intr*) (of a balance sheet, etc.) to have the debit and credit totals equal. [C13: from OF, from Vulgar L *bilancia* (unattested), from LL *bilanx* having two scales, from BI- + *lanx* scale]
▸ **'balanceable** *adj* ▸ **'balancer** *n*

Balance ('bæləns) *n* **the.** the constellation Libra, the seventh sign of the zodiac.

balance of payments *n* the difference over a given time between total payments to foreign nations and total receipts from foreign nations.

balance of power *n* the distribution of power among countries so that no one nation can seriously threaten another.

balance of trade *n* the difference in value between total exports and total imports of goods.

balance sheet ⓣ *n* a statement that shows the financial position of a business by listing the asset balances and the claims on such assets.

THESAURUS

bail[1] *n Law* **1, 3** = **security**, bond, guarantee, guaranty, pledge, surety, warranty

bail[2] *vb* = **scoop**, dip, drain off, ladle

bail out *vb* **1** = **escape**, quit, retreat **2** *Informal* = **help**, aid, relieve, rescue, save (someone's) bacon (*inf., chiefly Brit.*)

bait[1] *n* **1** = **lure**, decoy **2** = **enticement**, allurement, attraction, bribe, carrot and stick, incentive, inducement, snare, temptation ◆ *vb* **6** = **tease**, aggravate (*inf.*), annoy, be on one's back (*sl.*), bother, gall, get in one's hair (*inf.*), get one's back up, get on one's nerves (*inf.*), get *or* take a rise out of, harass, hassle (*inf.*), hound, irk, irritate, nark (*Brit., Austral., & NZ sl.*), needle (*inf.*), persecute, provoke, put one's back up, torment, wind up (*Brit. sl.*) **7** = **lure**, allure, beguile, entice, seduce, tempt

baked *adj* **3** = **dry**, arid, desiccated, parched, scorched, seared, sun-baked, torrid

balance *n* **2** = **equilibrium**, equipoise **4** = **stability**, poise, steadiness **5** = **composure**, equanimity, self-control, self-possession **6** = **harmony**, correspondence, equity, equivalence, evenness, parity, symmetry **9** = **remainder**, difference, residue, rest, surplus ◆ *vb* **15, 16** = **stabilize**, level, parallel, poise, steady **17** = **compare**, assess, consider, deliberate, estimate, evaluate, weigh **19** = **equalize**, adjust, compensate for, counteract, counterbalance, counterpoise, equate, make up for, neutralize, offset **20** *Accounting* = **calculate**, compute, settle, square, tally, total
Antonyms *n* ≠ **equilibrium:** disproportion, instability, unbalance ◆ *vb* ≠ **stabilize:** outweigh, overbalance, upset

balanced *adj* **17** = **unbiased**, disinterested, equitable, even-handed, fair, impartial, just, unprejudiced
Antonyms *adj* biased, distorted, jaundiced, lopsided, one-sided, partial, predisposed, prejudiced, slanted, unfair, warped, weighted

balance sheet *n* = **statement**, account, budget, credits and debits, ledger, report

DICTIONARY

balance wheel *n* a wheel oscillating against the hairspring of a timepiece, regulating its beat.

balata ('bælətə) *n* **1** a tropical American tree, yielding a latex-like sap. **2** a rubber-like gum obtained from this sap: a substitute for gutta-percha. [from American Sp., of Carib origin]

balcony Ⓣ ('bælkənɪ) *n, pl* **balconies. 1** a platform projecting from a building with a balustrade along its outer edge, often with access from a door or window. **2** a gallery in a theatre, above the dress circle. **3** *US & Canad.* any circle in a theatre. [C17: from It. *balcone*, prob. from OHG *balko* beam]
▸ **'balconied** *adj*

bald Ⓣ (bɔːld) *adj* **1** having no hair or fur, esp. (of a man) having no hair on the scalp. **2** lacking natural growth or covering. **3** plain or blunt: *a bald statement.* **4** bare or unadorned. **5** Also: **baldfaced.** (of birds and animals) having white markings on the head and face. **6** (of a tyre) having a worn tread. [C14 *ballede* (lit.: having a white spot)]
▸ **'baldish** *adj* ▸ **'baldly** *adv* ▸ **'baldness** *n*

baldachin *or* **baldaquin** ('bɔːldəkɪn) *n* **1** a richly ornamented brocade. **2** a canopy over an altar, shrine, or throne or carried in Christian religious processions over an object of veneration. [OE *baldekin*, from It. *baldacchino*, lit.: stuff from Baghdad]

bald eagle *n* a large eagle of North America, having a white head and tail. It is the US national bird.

balderdash Ⓣ ('bɔːldəˌdæʃ) *n* stupid or illogical talk; senseless rubbish. [C16: from ?]

balding Ⓣ ('bɔːldɪŋ) *adj* somewhat bald or becoming bald.

baldric ('bɔːldrɪk) *n* a sash or belt worn over the right shoulder to the left hip for carrying a sword, etc. [C13: from OF *baudrei*, of Frankish origin]

baldy ('bɔːldɪ) *Inf.* ◆ *adj* **1** bald. ◆ *n, pl* **baldies. 2** a bald person.

bale[1] (beɪl) *n* **1** a large bundle, package, or carton of goods bound by ropes, wires, etc., for storage or transportation. **2** *US.* 500 pounds of cotton. ◆ *vb* **bales, baling, baled. 3** to make (hay, etc.) or put (goods) into a bale or bales. [C14: prob. from OF *bale*, from OHG *balla* BALL[1]]

bale[2] (beɪl) *n Arch.* **1** evil; injury. **2** woe; suffering; pain. [OE *bealu*]

bale[3] Ⓣ (beɪl) *vb* a variant spelling of **bail**[2].

bale[4] (beɪl) *n* a variant spelling of **bail**[4].

baleen (bəˈliːn) *n* whalebone. [C14: from L *bālaena* whale]

baleen whale *n* another name for **whalebone whale.**

baleful Ⓣ ('beɪlfʊl) *adj* harmful, menacing, or vindictive.
▸ **'balefully** *adv* ▸ **'balefulness** *n*

baler ('beɪlə) *n* a machine for making bales of hay, etc. Also called: **baling machine.**

balk Ⓣ *or* **baulk** (bɔːk, bɔːlk) *vb* **1** (*intr;* usually foll. by *at*) to stop short; jib: *the horse balked at the jump.* **2** (*intr;* foll. by *at*) to recoil: *he balked at the idea of murder.* **3** (*tr*) to thwart, check, or foil: *he was balked in his plans.* ◆ *n* **4** a roughly squared heavy timber beam. **5** a timber tie beam of a roof. **6** an unploughed ridge between furrows. **7** an obstacle; hindrance; disappointment. **8** *Baseball.* an illegal motion by a pitcher. ◆ See also **baulk.** [OE *balca*]

Balkan ('bɔːlkən) *adj* of or denoting a large peninsula in SE Europe, between the Adriatic and Aegean Seas, or its inhabitants, countries, etc.

balky *or* **baulky** ('bɔːkɪ, 'bɔːlkɪ) *adj* **balkier, balkiest** *or* **baulkier, baulkiest.** inclined to stop abruptly and unexpectedly: *a balky horse.*

ball[1] Ⓣ (bɔːl) *n* **1** a spherical or nearly spherical body or mass. **2** a round or roundish body, of a size and composition suitable for any of various games. **3** a ball propelled in a particular way: *a high ball.* **4** any rudimentary game with a ball: *to play ball.* **5** a single delivery of the ball in cricket and other games. **6a** a solid nonexplosive projectile for a firearm, cannon, etc. **6b** such projectiles collectively. **7** any more or less rounded part: *the ball of the foot.* **8 ball of muscle.** *Austral.* a very strong, fit person. **9 have the ball at one's feet.** to have the chance of doing something. **10 keep the ball rolling.** to maintain the progress of a project, plan, etc. **11 on the ball.** *Inf.* alert; informed. **12 play ball.** *Inf.* to cooperate. **13 set** *or* **start the ball rolling.** to initiate an action, discussion, etc. ◆ *vb* **14** to make, form, wind, gather, etc., into a ball or balls. ◆ See also **balls, balls-up.** [C13: from ON *böllr*]

ball[2] (bɔːl) *n* **1** a social function for dancing, esp. one that is lavish or formal. **2** *Inf.* a very enjoyable time (esp. in **have a ball**). [C17: from F *bal* (n), from OF *baller* (vb), from LL *ballāre* to dance]

ballad ('bæləd) *n* **1** a narrative song with a recurrent refrain. **2** a narrative poem in short stanzas of popular origin. **3** a slow sentimental song, esp. a pop song. [C15: from OF *balade*, from OProvençal *balada* song accompanying a dance]

ballade (bæˈlɑːd) *n* **1** *Prosody.* a verse form consisting of three stanzas and an envoy, all ending with the same line. **2** *Music.* an instrumental composition based on or intended to evoke a narrative.

balladeer (ˌbæləˈdɪə) *n* a singer of ballads.

ball-and-socket joint *n Anat.* a joint in which a rounded head fits into a rounded cavity, allowing a wide range of movement.

ballast Ⓣ ('bæləst) *n* **1** any heavy material used to stabilize a vessel, esp. one that is not carrying cargo. **2** crushed rock, broken stone, etc., used for the foundation of a road or railway track or in making concrete. **3** anything that provides stability or weight. **4** *Electronics.* a device for maintaining the current in a circuit. ◆ *vb* (*tr*) **5** to give stability or weight to. [C16: prob. from Low G]

ball bearing *n* **1** a bearing consisting of steel balls rolling between a metal sleeve fitted over the rotating shaft and an outer sleeve held in the bearing housing, so reducing friction. **2** a metal ball, esp. one used in such a bearing.

ball boy *or* (*fem*) **ball girl** *n* (esp. in tennis) a person who retrieves balls that go out of play.

ballbreaker ('bɔːlˌbreɪkə) *n Sl.* someone, esp. a woman, whose behaviour may be regarded as threatening a man's sense of power. [C20: from BALLS (in the sense: testicles) + BREAKER]

ball cock *n* a device for regulating the flow of a liquid into a tank, cistern, etc., consisting of a floating ball mounted at one end of an arm and a valve on the other end that opens and closes as the ball falls and rises.

ballerina (ˌbæləˈriːnə) *n* a female ballet dancer. [C18: from It., fem of *ballerino* dancing master, from *ballare* to dance]

ballet ('bæleɪ, bæˈleɪ) *n* **1** a classical style of expressive dancing based on precise conventional steps. **2** a theatrical representation of a story or theme performed by ballet dancers. **3** a troupe of ballet dancers. **4** music written for a ballet. [C17: from F, from It. *balletto*, lit.: a little dance, from *ballare* to dance]
▸ **balletic** (bæˈletɪk) *adj*

balletomane ('bælɪtəʊˌmeɪn) *n* a ballet enthusiast.

balletomania (ˌbælɪtəʊˈmeɪnɪə) *n* passionate enthusiasm for ballet.

ball game *n* **1** any game played with a ball. **2** *US & Canad.* a game of baseball. **3** *Inf.* a situation; state of affairs (esp. in **a whole new ball game**).

ballista (bəˈlɪstə) *n, pl* **ballistae** (-tiː). an ancient catapult for hurling stones, etc. [C16: from L, ult. from Gk *ballein* to throw]

ballistic (bəˈlɪstɪk) *adj* **1** of or relating to ballistics. **2** denoting or relating to the flight of projectiles moving under their own momentum and the force of gravity. **3** (of a measurement or measuring instrument) depending on a brief impulse or current that causes a movement related to the quantity to be measured: *a ballistic pendulum.* **4 go ballistic.** *Inf.* to become enraged or frenziedly violent.
▸ **bal'listically** *adv*

ballistic missile *n* a missile that has no wings or fins and that follows a ballistic trajectory when its propulsive power is discontinued.

ballistics (bəˈlɪstɪks) *n* (*functioning as sing*) **1** the study of the flight dynamics of projectiles. **2** the study of the effects of firing on firearms and their projectiles.

ball lightning *n Meteorol.* a luminous ball occasionally seen during electrical storms.

ballocks ('bɒləks) *pl n, interj* a variant spelling of **bollocks.**

ball of fire *n Inf.* a very lively person.

balloon Ⓣ (bəˈluːn) *n* **1** an inflatable rubber bag used as a plaything or party decoration. **2** a large bag inflated with a lighter-than-air gas, designed to rise and float in the atmosphere. It may have a basket or gondola for carrying passengers, etc. **3** an outline containing the words or thoughts of a character in a cartoon. **4** a large rounded brandy glass. **5** *Commerce.* **5a** a large sum paid as an irregular instalment of a loan repayment. **5b** (*as modifier*): *a balloon loan.* **6** *Surgery.* **6a** an inflatable plastic tube used for dilating obstructed blood vessels or parts of the alimentary canal. **6b** (*as modifier*): *balloon angioplasty.* **7 go down like a lead balloon.** to prove unsuccessful or unpopular; fail: *the suggestion that the chairman should get a 77% pay rise went down like a lead balloon.* **8 when the balloon goes up.** *Inf.* when the action starts. ◆ *vb* **9** (*intr*) to go up or fly in a balloon. **10** to inflate or be inflated: *the wind ballooned the sails.* **11** (*intr*) to increase or expand significantly and rapidly: *losses ballooned to £278 million.* **12** (*tr*) *Brit.* to propel (a ball) high

THESAURUS

balcony *n* **1 = terrace,** veranda **2 = upper circle,** gallery, gods

bald *adj* **1 = hairless,** baldheaded, baldpated, depilated **2 = barren,** bleak, exposed, naked, stark, treeless, uncovered **3 = blunt,** direct, downright, forthright, outright, straight, straightforward, unvarnished, upfront (*inf.*) **4 = plain,** bare, severe, simple, unadorned

balderdash *n* **= nonsense,** bilge (*inf.*), bosh (*inf.*), bunk (*inf.*), bunkum *or* buncombe (*chiefly US*), claptrap (*inf.*), cobblers (*Brit. taboo sl.*), crap (*sl.*), drivel, garbage (*inf.*), hogwash, hot air (*inf.*), piffle (*inf.*), poppycock (*inf.*), rot, rubbish, tommyrot, tosh (*sl., chiefly Brit.*), trash, tripe (*inf.*), twaddle, waffle

balding *adj* **= losing one's hair,** becoming bald, receding, thin on top

baldness *n* **1 = losing one's hair,** alopecia (*Pathology*), baldheadedness, baldpatedness, hairlessness **2 = barrenness,** bleakness, nakedness, sparseness, starkness, treelessness **4 = plainness,** austerity, bluntness, severity, simplicity

bale[3] *see* **bail**[2]

baleful *adj* **= menacing,** calamitous, deadly, evil, harmful, hurtful, injurious, maleficent, malevolent, malignant, noxious, ominous, pernicious, ruinous, sinister, venomous, vindictive
Antonyms *adj* beneficial, benevolent, benign, friendly, good, healthy, salubrious

balk *vb* **1 = jib,** refuse **2 = recoil,** demur, dodge, evade, flinch, hesitate, resist, shirk, shrink from **3 = foil,** baffle, bar, check, counteract, defeat, disconcert, forestall, frustrate, hinder, obstruct, prevent, thwart
Antonyms *vb* ≠ **recoil:** accede, accept, acquiesce, comply, relent, submit, yield ≠ **foil:** abet, advance, aid, assist, further, help, promote, support, sustain

ball[1] *n* **1 = sphere,** drop, globe, globule, orb, pellet, spheroid **6 = shot,** ammunition, bullet, grapeshot, pellet, slug **12 play ball** *Informal* **= cooperate,** collaborate, go along, play along, reciprocate, respond, show willing

ballast *n* **3 = counterbalance,** balance, counterweight, stabilizer, weight

balloon *vb* **10 = inflate,** belly, billow, puff out,

into the air. [C16 (in the sense: ball, ball game): from It. dialect *ballone*]
▸**bal'loonist** *n* ▸**bal'loon-,like** *adj*

balloon loan *n* a loan in respect of which interest and capital are paid off in instalments at regular intervals.

ballot ➊ ('bælət) *n* **1** the practice of selecting a representative, course of action, etc., by submitting the options to a vote of all qualified persons. **2** an instance of voting, usually in secret. **3** a list of candidates standing for office. **4** the number of votes cast in an election. ◆ *vb* **ballots, balloting, balloted. 5** to vote or elicit a vote from: *we balloted the members on this issue.* **6** (*tr;* usually foll. by *for*) to vote for or decide on by lot or ballot. [C16: from It. *ballotta*, lit.: a little ball]

ballot box *n* a box into which ballot papers are dropped after voting.

ballotini (,bælə'ti:nɪ) *pl n* small glass beads used in reflective paints. [C20: from Italian *ballotini* small balls]

ballot paper *n* a paper used for voting.

ballpark ('bɔ:l,pɑ:k) *n* **1** *US & Canad.* a stadium used for baseball games. **2** *Inf.* **2a** approximate range: *in the right ballpark.* **2b** (*as modifier*): *a ballpark figure.* **3** *Inf.* a situation; state of affairs: *it's a whole new ballpark.*

ball-peen hammer *n* a hammer with one end of the head rounded for beating metal.

ballpoint *or* **ballpoint pen** ('bɔ:l,pɔɪnt) *n* a pen having a small ball bearing as a writing point.

ballroom ('bɔ:l,ru:m, -,rum) *n* a large hall for dancing.

ballroom dancing *n* social dancing, popular since the beginning of the 20th century, to dances in conventional rhythms (**ballroom dances**).

balls (bɔ:lz) *Taboo sl.* ◆ *pl n* **1** the testicles. **2** nonsense; rubbish. **3** courage; determination. ◆ *interj* **4** an exclamation of disagreement, contempt, etc.

balls-up *Taboo sl.* ◆ *n* **1** something botched or muddled. ◆ *vb* **balls up. 2** (*tr, adv*) to muddle or botch.

ballsy ('bɔ:lzɪ) *adj* **ballsier, ballsiest.** *Sl., chiefly US.* showing courage or determination; bold. [C20: from BALLS (sense 3) + -Y[1]]
▸**'ballsiness** *n*

bally ('bælɪ) *adj, adv* (intensifier) *Brit. sl.* a euphemistic word for **bloody** (sense 5).

ballyhoo ➊ (,bælɪ'hu:) *Inf.* ◆ *n* **1** a noisy, confused, or nonsensical situation. **2** sensational or blatant advertising or publicity. ◆ *vb* **ballyhoos, ballyhooing, ballyhooed. 3** (*tr*) *Chiefly US.* to advertise by sensational or blatant methods. [C19: from ?]

balm ➊ (bɑ:m) *n* **1** any of various oily aromatic substances obtained from certain tropical trees and used for healing and soothing. See also **balsam** (sense 1). **2** any plant yielding such a substance, esp. the balm of Gilead. **3** something comforting or soothing. **4** Also called: **lemon balm.** an aromatic Eurasian plant, having clusters of small fragrant white flowers. **5** a pleasant odour. [C13: from OF *basme*, from L *balsamum* BALSAM]

balm of Gilead ('gɪlɪ,æd) *n* **1** any of several trees of Africa and W Asia that yield a fragrant oily resin. **2** the resin exuded by these trees. **3** a North American poplar tree. **4** a fragrant resin obtained from the balsam fir.

Balmoral (bæl'mɒrəl) *n* (*sometimes not cap.*) **1** a laced walking shoe. **2** a Scottish brimless hat usually with a cockade and plume. [from *Balmoral* Castle, Scotland]

balmy ➊ ('bɑ:mɪ) *adj* **balmier, balmiest. 1** (of weather) mild and pleasant. **2** having the qualities of balm; fragrant or soothing. **3** a variant spelling of **barmy.**
▸**'balmily** *adv* ▸**'balminess** *n*

balneology (,bælnɪ'ɒlədʒɪ) *n* the branch of medical science concerned with the therapeutic value of baths, esp. with natural mineral waters. [C19: from L *balneum* bath]
▸**balneological** (,bælnɪə'lɒdʒɪk'l) *adj* ▸**,balne'ologist** *n*

baloney *or* **boloney** (bə'ləunɪ) *n Inf.* foolish talk; nonsense. [C20: from *Bologna* (sausage)]

BALPA ('bælpə) *n acronym for* British Airline Pilots' Association.

balsa ('bɔ:lsə) *n* **1** a tree of tropical America. **2** Also called: **balsawood.** the very light wood of this tree, used for making rafts, etc. **3** a light raft. [C18: from Sp.: raft]

balsam ('bɔ:lsəm) *n* **1** any of various fragrant oleoresins, such as balm, obtained from any of several trees and shrubs and used as a base for medicines and perfumes. **2** any of various similar substances used as ointments. **3** any of certain aromatic resinous turpentines. See **Canada balsam. 4** any plant yielding balsam. **5** Also called: **busy Lizzie.** any of several plants of the genus *Impatiens.* **6** anything healing or soothing. [C15: from L *balsamum*, from Gk *balsamon*, from Heb. *bāśām* spice]
▸**balsamic** (bɔ:l'sæmɪk) *adj*

balsam fir *n* a fir tree of NE North America, that yields Canada balsam.

balti ('bɔ:ltɪ, 'bæltɪ) *n* **a** a spicy Indian dish, stewed until most of the liquid has evaporated, and served in a woklike pot. **b** (*as modifier*): *a balti house.* [C20: from ?]

Baltic ('bɔ:ltɪk) *adj* **1** denoting or relating to the Baltic Sea in N Europe or the states bordering it. **2** of or characteristic of Baltic as a group of languages. ◆ *n* **3** a branch of the Indo-European family of languages consisting of Lithuanian, Latvian, and Old Prussian. **4** Also called: **Baltic Exchange.** a former commodity and freight-chartering market in the City of London.

baluster ('bæləstə) *n* any of a set of posts supporting a rail or coping. [C17: from F *balustre*, from It. *balaustro* pillar resembling a pomegranate flower, ult. from Gk *balaustion*]

balustrade ('bælə,streɪd) *n* an ornamental rail or coping with its supporting set of balusters. [C17: from F, from *balustre* BALUSTER]

bambino (bæm'bi:nəu) *n, pl* **bambinos** *or* **bambini** (-ni:). *Inf.* a young child, esp. Italian. [C18: from It.]

bamboo (bæm'bu:) *n* **1** a tall treelike tropical or semitropical grass having hollow stems with ringed joints. **2** the stem, used for building, poles, and furniture. [C16: prob. from Malay *bambu*]

bamboozle ➊ (bæm'bu:z[ə]l) *vb* **bamboozles, bamboozling, bamboozled.** (*tr*) *Inf.* **1** to cheat; mislead. **2** to confuse. [C18: from ?]
▸**bam'boozlement** *n* ▸**bam'boozler** *n*

ban ➊ (bæn) *vb* **bans, banning, banned. 1** (*tr*) to prohibit, esp. officially, from action, display, entrance, sale, etc.; forbid. ◆ *n* **2** an official prohibition or interdiction. **3** a public proclamation, esp. of outlawry. **4** *Arch.* a curse; imprecation. [OE *bannan* to proclaim]

banal ➊ (bə'nɑ:l) *adj* lacking force or originality; trite; commonplace. [C18: from OF: relating to compulsory feudal service, hence common to all, commonplace]
▸**banality** (bə'nælɪtɪ) *n* ▸**ba'nally** *adv*

banana (bə'nɑ:nə) *n* **1** any of several tropical and subtropical treelike plants, esp. a widely cultivated species having hanging clusters of edible fruit. **2** the crescent-shaped fruit of any of these plants. [C16: from Sp. or Port., of African origin]

banana republic *n Inf. & derog.* a small country, esp. in Central America, that is politically unstable and has an economy dominated by foreign interest, usually dependent on one export.

banana skin *n* **1** the soft outer covering of a banana. **2** *Inf.* something unforeseen that causes an obvious and embarrassing mistake. [sense 2 from the common slapstick joke of slipping on a banana skin]

band[1] ➊ (bænd) *n* **1** a company of people having a common purpose; group: *a band of outlaws.* **2** a group of musicians playing either brass and percussion instruments only (**brass band**) or brass, woodwind, and percussion instruments (**concert band** or **military band**). **3** a group of musicians who play popular music, jazz, etc., often for dancing. ◆ *vb* **4** (usually foll. by *together*) to unite; assemble. [C15: from F *bande*, prob. from OProvençal *banda*, of Gmc origin]

band[2] ➊ (bænd) *n* **1** a thin flat strip of some material, used esp. to encircle objects and hold them together: *a rubber band.* **2a** a strip of fabric or other material used as an ornament or to reinforce clothing. **2b** (*in combination*): *waistband; hatband.* **3** a stripe of contrasting colour or texture. **4** a driving belt in machinery. **5** a range of values that are close or related in number, degree, or quality. **6** *Physics.* a range of frequencies or wavelengths between two limits. **7** short for **energy band. 8** *Computing.* one or more tracks on a magnetic disk or drum. **9** *Anat.* any structure resembling a ribbon or cord that connects, encircles, or binds different parts. **10** *Archit.* a strip of flat panelling, such as a fascia, usually attached to a wall. **11** either of a pair of hanging extensions of the collar, forming part of academic, legal, or (formerly) clerical dress. ◆ *vb* (*tr*) **12** to fasten or mark with a band. [C15: from OF *bende*, of Gmc origin]

bandage ➊ ('bændɪdʒ) *n* **1** a piece of material used to dress a wound, bind a broken limb, etc. ◆ *vb* **bandages, bandaging, bandaged. 2** to cover or bind with a bandage. [C16: from F, from *bande* strip, BAND[2]]

THESAURUS

swell **11** = **expand**, bloat, blow up, dilate, distend, enlarge, grow rapidly

ballot *n* **1, 2, 4** = **vote**, election, poll, polling, voting

ballyhoo *n Informal* **1** = **fuss**, babble, commotion, hubbub, hue and cry, hullabaloo, noise, racket, to-do **2** = **publicity**, advertising, build-up, hype, PR, promotion, propaganda

balm *n* **1** = **ointment**, balsam, cream, embrocation, emollient, lotion, salve, unguent **3** = **comfort**, anodyne, consolation, curative, palliative, restorative, solace

balmy *adj* **1** = **mild**, clement, pleasant, summery, temperate
Antonyms *adj* harsh, inclement, rough, stormy

bamboozle *vb Informal* **1** = **cheat**, con (*inf.*), deceive, defraud, delude, dupe, fool, hoax, hoodwink, pull a fast one on (*inf.*), skin (*sl.*), swindle, trick **2** = **puzzle**, baffle, befuddle, confound, confuse, mystify, perplex, stump

ban *vb* **1** = **prohibit**, banish, bar, black, blackball, block, boycott, debar, disallow, disqualify, exclude, forbid, interdict, outlaw, proscribe, restrict, suppress ◆ *n* **2** = **prohibition**, block, boycott, censorship, disqualification, embargo, interdict, interdiction, proscription, restriction, stoppage, suppression, taboo
Antonyms *vb* ≠ **prohibit**: allow, approve, authorize, enable, let, permit, sanction ◆ *n* ≠ **prohibition**: allowance, approval, permission, sanction

banal *adj* = **unoriginal**, clichéd, cliché-ridden, commonplace, everyday, hackneyed, humdrum, mundane, old hat, ordinary, pedestrian, platitudinous, stale, stereotyped, stock, threadbare, tired, trite, unimaginative, vanilla (*sl.*), vapid
Antonyms *adj* challenging, distinctive, fresh, ground-breaking, imaginative, interesting, new, novel, original, stimulating, unique, unusual

banality *n* = **unoriginality**, bromide (*inf.*), cliché, commonplace, platitude, triteness, trite phrase, triviality, truism, vapidity

band[1] *n* **1** = **gang**, assembly, association, bevy, body, camp, clique, club, company, coterie, crew, group, horde, party, posse (*inf.*), society, troop **2, 3** = **ensemble**, combo, group, orchestra ◆ *vb* **4** = **unite**, affiliate, ally, consolidate, federate, gather, group, join, merge
Antonyms *vb* ≠ **unite**: cleave, disperse, disunite, divide, part, segregate, separate, split, sunder

band[2] *n* **1, 2** = **strip**, belt, binding, cord, fillet, ligature, ribbon, strap, tie

bandage *n* **1** = **dressing**, compress, gauze, plaster ◆ *vb* **2** = **dress**, bind, cover, swathe

bandanna *or* **bandana** (bæn'dænə) *n* a large silk or cotton handkerchief or neckerchief. [C18: from Hindi *bāndhnū* tie-dyeing]

B & B *abbrev. for* bed and breakfast.

bandbox ('bænd,bɒks) *n* a lightweight usually cylindrical box for small articles, esp. hats.

bandeau ('bændəʊ) *n, pl* **bandeaux** (-dəʊz). a narrow band of ribbon, velvet, etc., worn round the head. [C18: from F, from OF *bandel* a little BAND[2]]

banderole *or* **banderol** ('bændə,rəʊl) *n* **1** a long narrow flag, usually with forked ends, esp. one attached to the mast of a ship. **2** a ribbon-like scroll or sculptured band bearing an inscription. [C16: from OF, from It. *banderuola,* lit.: a little banner]

bandicoot ('bændɪ,ku:t) *n* **1** an agile terrestrial marsupial of Australia and New Guinea with a long pointed muzzle and a long tail. **2 bandicoot rat.** Also called: **mole rat.** any of three burrowing rats of S and SE Asia. [C18: from Telugu *pandikokku*]

banding ('bændɪŋ) *n Brit.* the practice of putting schoolchildren into ability groups to ensure a balanced intake to secondary school.

bandit ❶ ('bændɪt) *n, pl* **bandits** *or* **banditti** (bæn'dɪtɪ). a robber, esp. a member of an armed gang. [C16: from It. *bandito,* from *bandire* to proscribe, from *bando* edict]
▸ **'banditry** *n*

bandmaster ('bænd,mɑ:stə) *n* the conductor of a band.

Band of Hope *n* a society devoted to abstinence from alcohol.

bandolier *or* **bandoleer** (,bændə'lɪə) *n* a soldier's broad shoulder belt having small pockets or loops for cartridges. [C16: from OF *bandouliere*]

band-pass filter *n* **1** *Electronics.* a filter that transmits only currents having frequencies within specified limits. **2** an optical device for transmitting waves of predetermined wavelengths.

band saw *n* a power-operated saw consisting of an endless toothed metal band running over and driven by two wheels.

bandsman ('bændzmən) *n, pl* **bandsmen.** a player in a musical band, esp. a brass or military band.

bandstand ('bænd,stænd) *n* a platform for a band, usually out of doors and roofed.

band theory *n* the theory that electrons in solids have a range of energies falling into allowed bands, between which are forbidden bands.

bandwagon ('bænd,wægən) *n* **1** *US.* a wagon for the band in a parade. **2 jump, climb,** *or* **get on the bandwagon.** to join or support a party or movement that seems assured of success.

bandwidth ('bænd,wɪdθ) *n* the range of frequencies within a given waveband used for a particular radio transmission.

bandy ❶ ('bændɪ) *adj* **bandier, bandiest. 1** Also: **bandy-legged.** having legs curved outwards at the knees. **2** (of legs) curved thus. ◆ *vb* **bandies, bandying, bandied.** (*tr*) **3** to exchange (words) in a heated or hostile manner. **4** to give and receive (blows). **5** (often foll. by *about*) to circulate (a name, rumour, etc.). [C16: prob. from OF *bander* to hit the ball back and forth at tennis]

bane ❶ (beɪn) *n* **1** a person or thing that causes misery or distress (esp. in **bane of one's life**). **2** something that causes death or destruction. **3a** a fatal poison. **3b** (*in combination*): *ratsbane.* **4** *Arch.* ruin or distress. [OE *bana*]
▸ **'baneful** *adj*

baneberry ('beɪnbərɪ) *n, pl* **baneberries. 1** Also called: **herb Christopher** (Brit.). a plant which has small white flowers and red or white poisonous berries. **2** the berry.

bang[1] ❶ (bæŋ) *n* **1** a short loud explosive noise, as of the report of a gun. **2** a hard blow or knock, esp. a noisy one. **3** *Sl.* an injection of heroin or other narcotic. **4** *Taboo sl.* an act of sexual intercourse. **5 with a bang.** successfully: *the party went with a bang.* ◆ *vb* **6** to hit or knock, esp. with a loud noise. **7** to move noisily or clumsily: *to bang about the house.* **8** to close (a door, window, etc.) or (of a door, etc.) be closed noisily; slam. **9** (*tr*) to cause to move by hitting vigorously: *he banged the ball over the fence.* **10** to make or cause to make a loud noise, as of an explosion. **11** *Taboo sl.* to have sexual intercourse (with). **12** (*intr*) *Sl.* to inject heroin, etc. **13 bang one's head against a brick wall.** to try to achieve something impossible. ◆ *adv* **14** with a sudden impact or effect: *the car drove bang into a lamppost.* **15** precisely: *bang in the middle.* **16 go bang.** to burst, shut, etc., with a loud noise. [C16: from ON *bang, banga* hammer]

bang[2] (bæŋ) *n* **1** (*usually pl*) a section of hair cut straight across the forehead. ◆ *vb* (*tr*) **2** to cut (the hair) in such a style. **3** to dock (the tail of a horse, etc.). [C19: prob. short for *bangtail* short tail]

banger ('bæŋə) *n Brit.* **1** *Sl.* a sausage. **2** *Inf.* an old decrepit car. **3** a firework that explodes loudly.

Bangla ('bæŋglə) *n* another name for **Bengali** (sense 2).

bangle ('bæŋg[ə]l) *n* a bracelet, usually without a clasp, often worn round the arm or sometimes round the ankle. [C19: from Hindi *bangrī*]

bang on *adj, adv Brit. inf.* **1** with absolute accuracy. **2** excellent or excellently.

bangtail ('bæŋ,teɪl) *n* **1** a horse's tail cut straight across but not through the bone. **2** a horse with a tail cut in this way. [C19: from *bangtail* short tail]

banian ('bænjən) *n* a variant spelling of **banyan.**

banish ❶ ('bænɪʃ) *vb* (*tr*) **1** to expel from a place, esp. by an official decree as a punishment. **2** to drive away: *to banish gloom.* [C14: from OF *banir,* of Gmc origin]
▸ **'banishment** *n*

banisters ❶ *or* **bannisters** ('bænɪstəz) *pl n* the railing and supporting balusters on a staircase; balustrade. [C17: altered from BALUSTER]

banjo ('bændʒəʊ) *n, pl* **banjos** *or* **banjoes.** a stringed musical instrument with a long neck and a circular drumlike body overlaid with parchment, plucked with the fingers or a plectrum. [C18: var. (US Southern pronunciation) of earlier *bandore,* ult. from Gk *pandora*]
▸ **'banjoist** *n*

bank[1] ❶ (bæŋk) *n* **1** an institution offering certain financial services, such as the safekeeping of money and lending of money at interest. **2** the building used by such an institution. **3** a small container used at home for keeping money. **4** the funds held by a banker or dealer in some gambling games. **5** (in various games) **5a** the stock, as of money, etc., on which players may draw. **5b** the player holding this stock. **6** any supply, store, or reserve: *a data bank.* ◆ *vb* **7** (*tr*) to deposit (cash, cheques, etc.) in a bank. **8** (*intr*) to transact business with a bank. **9** (*intr*) to engage in banking. ◆ See also **bank on.** [C15: prob. from It. *banca* bench, moneychanger's table, of Gmc origin]

bank[2] ❶ (bæŋk) *n* **1** a long raised mass, esp. of earth; ridge. **2** a slope, as of a hill. **3** the sloping side of any hollow in the ground, esp. when bordering a river. **4** the ground beside a river or canal. **5a** an elevated section of the bed of a sea, lake, or river. **5b** (*in combination*): *sandbank.* **6** the face of a body of ore in a mine. **7** the lateral inclination of an aircraft about its longitudinal axis during a turn. **8** a bend on a road, athletics track, etc., having the outside built higher than the inside to reduce the effects of centrifugal force on vehicles, runners, etc., rounding it at speed. Also called: **camber, superelevation.** ◆ *vb* **9** (when *tr,* often foll. by *up*) to form into a bank or mound. **10** (*tr*) to border or enclose (a road, etc.) with a bank. **11** (*tr;* sometimes foll. by *up*) to cover (a fire) with ashes, fresh fuel, etc., so that it will burn slowly. **12** to cause (an aircraft) to tip laterally about its longitudinal axis or (of an aircraft) to tip in this way, esp. while turning. [C12: of Scand. origin]

bank[3] ❶ (bæŋk) *n* **1** an arrangement of similar objects in a row or in tiers: *a bank of dials.* **2** a tier of oars in a galley. ◆ *vb* **3** (*tr*) to arrange in a bank. [C17: from OF *banc* bench, of Gmc origin]

bankable ('bæŋkəb[ə]l) *adj* **1** appropriate for receipt by a bank. **2** dependable or reliable: *a bankable promise.* **3** (esp. of a star) likely to ensure the financial success of a film.
▸ **,banka'bility** *n*

bank account *n* **1** an account created by the deposit of money at a bank by a customer. **2** the amount credited to a depositor at a bank.

bank bill *n* **1** Also called: **bank draft.** a bill of exchange drawn by one bank on another. **2** *US.* a banknote.

bankbook ('bæŋk,bʊk) *n* a book held by depositors at certain banks, in which the bank enters a record of deposits, withdrawals, and earned interest. Also called: **passbook.**

bank card *or* **banker's card** *n* any plastic card issued by a bank, such as a cash card or cheque card.

bank draft *n* a cheque drawn by a bank on itself, which is bought by a person to pay a supplier unwilling to accept a normal cheque. Also called: **banker's cheque.**

banker[1] ('bæŋkə) *n* **1** a person who owns or is an executive in a bank. **2** an official or player in charge of the bank in various games. **3** a result

THESAURUS

bandit *n* = **robber**, brigand, crook, desperado, footpad, freebooter, gangster, gunman, highwayman, hijacker, marauder, outlaw, pirate, racketeer, thief

bandy *adj* **1, 2** = **bow-legged**, bandy-legged, bent, bowed, crooked, curved ◆ *vb* **3, 4** = **exchange**, barter, interchange, swap, throw, toss, trade

bane *n* **1** = **plague**, affliction, bête noire, blight, burden, curse, despair, misery, nuisance, pest, scourge, torment, trial, trouble, woe **2** = **destruction**, calamity, disaster, downfall, ruin
Antonyms *n* ≠ **plague**: blessing, comfort, consolation, joy, pleasure, relief, solace, support

bang[1] *n* **1** = **explosion**, boom, burst, clang, clap, clash, detonation, peal, pop, report, shot, slam, thud, thump **2** = **blow**, belt (*inf.*), box, bump, cuff, hit, knock, punch, smack, stroke, wallop (*inf.*), whack ◆ *vb* **6** = **hit**, bash (*inf.*), beat, belt (*inf.*), bump, clatter, crash, hammer, knock, pound, pummel, rap, slam, strike, thump **10** = **explode**, boom, burst, clang, detonate, drum, echo, peal, resound, thump, thunder ◆ *adv* **14** = **hard**, abruptly, headlong, noisily, suddenly **15** = **straight**, precisely, slap, smack

banish *vb* **1** = **expel**, deport, eject, evict, exclude, excommunicate, exile, expatriate, ostracize, outlaw, shut out, transport **2** = **get rid of**, ban, cast out, discard, dislodge, dismiss, dispel, drive away, eliminate, eradicate, oust, remove, shake off
Antonyms *vb* ≠ **expel**: accept, admit, embrace, hail, invite, offer hospitality to, receive, welcome

banishment *n* **1** = **expulsion**, deportation, exile, expatriation, proscription, transportation

banisters *pl n* = **railing**, balusters, balustrade, handrail, rail

bank[1] *n* **1, 2** = **storehouse**, depository, repository **6** = **store**, accumulation, fund, hoard, reserve, reservoir, savings, stock, stockpile ◆ *vb* **7** = **save**, deposit, keep **8** = **deal with**, transact business with

bank[2] *n* **1** = **mound**, heap, mass, pile, ridge **3** = **embankment**, banking **4** = **side**, brink, edge, margin, shore ◆ *vb* **9** = **pile**, amass, heap, mass, mound, stack **12** = **tilt**, camber, cant, heel, incline, pitch, slant, slope, tip

bank[3] *n* **1** = **row**, arrangement, array, file, group, line, rank, sequence, series, succession, tier, train that has been forecast identically in a series of entries on a football pool coupon. **4** a person whose performance can be relied on.

banker[2] ('bæŋkə) *n Austral. & NZ inf.* a stream almost overflowing its banks (esp. in **run a banker**).

banker's order *n* another name for **standing order** (sense 1).

bank holiday *n* (in Britain) any of several weekdays on which banks are closed by law and which are observed as national holidays.

banking ('bæŋkɪŋ) *n* the business engaged in by a bank.

bank manager *n* a person who directs the business of a local branch of a bank.

banknote ('bæŋk,nəʊt) *n* a promissory note, esp. one issued by a central bank, serving as money.

Bank of England ('ɪŋglənd) *n* the central bank of the United Kingdom, which acts as banker to the government and the commercial banks.

bank on ⓣ *vb (intr, prep)* to expect or rely with confidence on: *you can bank on him.*

bankroll ('bæŋk,rəʊl) *Chiefly US & Canad.* ◆ *n* **1** a roll of currency notes. **2** the financial resources of a person, organization, etc. ◆ *vb* **3** *(tr) Sl.* to provide the capital for; finance.

bankrupt ⓣ ('bæŋkrʌpt, -rəpt) *n* **1** a person adjudged insolvent by a court, his property being administered for the benefit of his creditors. **2** any person unable to discharge all his debts. **3** a person whose resources in a certain field are exhausted: *a spiritual bankrupt.* ◆ *adj* **4** adjudged insolvent. **5** financially ruined. **6** depleted in resources: *spiritually bankrupt.* **7** (foll. by *of*) *Brit.* lacking: *bankrupt of intelligence.* ◆ *vb* **8** *(tr)* to make bankrupt. [C16: from OF *banqueroute,* from OIt. *bancarotta,* from *banca* BANK[1] + *rotta* broken, from L *ruptus*]

▸**'bankruptcy** *n*

banksia ('bæŋksɪə) *n* any shrub or tree of the Australian genus *Banksia,* having dense cylindrical heads of flowers that are often yellowish. [C19: NL, after Sir Joseph *Banks* (1743–1820), E botanist]

bank statement *n* a statement of transactions in a bank account, esp. one of a series sent at regular intervals to the depositor.

banner ⓣ ('bænə) *n* **1** a long strip of material displaying a slogan, advertisement, etc. **2** a placard carried in a procession or demonstration. **3** something that represents a belief or principle. **4** the flag of a nation, army, etc. **5** Also called: **banner headline.** a large headline in a newspaper, etc., extending across the page. [C13: from OF *baniere,* of Gmc origin]

▸**'bannered** *adj*

bannisters ('bænɪstəz) *pl n* a variant spelling of **banisters.**

bannock ('bænək) *n* a round flat cake originating in Scotland, made from oatmeal or barley and baked on a griddle. [OE *bannuc*]

banns *or* **bans** (bænz) *pl n* **1** the public declaration of an intended marriage, usually on three successive Sundays in the parish churches of the betrothed. **2 forbid the banns.** to raise an objection to a marriage announced in this way. [C14: pl of *bann* proclamation]

banquet ⓣ ('bæŋkwɪt) *n* **1** a sumptuous meal; feast. **2** a ceremonial meal for many people. ◆ *vb* **banquets, banqueting, banqueted. 3** *(intr)* to hold or take part in a banquet. **4** *(tr)* to entertain (a person) with a banquet. [C15: from OF, from It. *banchetto,* from *banco* a table, of Gmc origin]

▸**'banqueter** *n*

banquette (bæŋ'ket) *n* **1** an upholstered bench. **2** (formerly) a raised part behind a parapet. [C17: from F, from Provençal *banqueta,* lit.: a little bench]

banshee ('bænʃiː, bæn'ʃiː) *n* (in Irish folklore) a female spirit whose wailing warns of impending death. [C18: from Irish Gaelic *bean sídhe,* lit.: woman of the fairy mound]

bantam ('bæntəm) *n* **1** any of various very small breeds of domestic fowl. **2** a small but aggressive person. **3** *Boxing.* short for **bantamweight.** [C18: after *Bantam,* village in Java, said to be the original home of this fowl]

bantamweight ('bæntəm,weɪt) *n* **1a** a professional boxer weighing 112–118 pounds (51–53.5 kg). **1b** an amateur boxer weighing 51–54 kg (112–119 pounds). **2** an amateur wrestler weighing usually 52–57 kg (115–126 pounds).

banter ⓣ ('bæntə) *vb* **1** to speak or tease lightly or jokingly. ◆ *n* **2** teasing or joking language or repartee. [C17: from ?]

▸**'banterer** *n*

Bantu ('bɑːntuː) *n* **1** a group of languages of Africa, including most of the principal languages spoken from the equator to the Cape of Good Hope. **2** (*pl* **Bantu** *or* **Bantus**) *Derog.* a Black speaker of a Bantu language. ◆ *adj* **3** of or relating to this group of peoples or their languages. [C19: from Bantu *Ba-ntu* people]

Bantustan ('bɑːntuː,stɑːn) *n Derog.* (formerly, in South Africa) an area reserved for occupation by a Black African people, with limited self-government; abolished in 1993. Official name: **homeland.** [from BANTU + Hindi *-stan* country of]

banyan *or* **banian** ('bænjən) *n* **1** an Indian tree with aerial roots that grow down into the soil forming additional trunks. **2** a member of the Hindu merchant caste of India. **3** a loose-fitting shirt, or robe, worn originally in India. [C16: from Hindi *baniyā,* from Sansk. *vānija* merchant]

banzai ('bɑːnzaɪ, bɑːn'zaɪ) *interj* a patriotic cheer, battle cry, or salutation. [Japanese: lit.: (may you live for) ten thousand years]

baobab ('beɪəʊ,bæb) *n* a tree native to Africa and N Australia that has a very thick trunk, angular branches, and a gourdlike fruit with an edible pulp. [C17: prob. from a native African word]

BAOR *abbrev. for* British Army of the Rhine.

bap (bæp) *n Brit.* a large soft bread roll. [from ?]

baptism ⓣ ('bæp,tɪzəm) *n* a Christian religious rite consisting of immersion in or sprinkling with water as a sign that the subject is cleansed from sin and constituted as a member of the Church.

▸**bap'tismal** *adj* ▸**bap'tismally** *adv*

baptism of fire *n* **1** a soldier's first experience of battle. **2** any initiating ordeal.

Baptist ('bæptɪst) *n* **1** a member of any of various Christian sects that affirm the necessity of baptism (usually of adults and by immersion). **2 the Baptist.** John the Baptist, the cousin and forerunner of Jesus, whom he baptized. ◆ *adj* **3** denoting or characteristic of any Christian sect of Baptists.

baptistry *or* **baptistery** ('bæptɪstrɪ) *n, pl* **baptistries** *or* **baptisteries. 1** a part of a Christian church in which baptisms are carried out. **2** a tank in a Baptist church in which baptisms are carried out.

baptize ⓣ *or* **baptise** (bæp'taɪz) *vb* **baptizes, baptizing, baptized** *or* **baptises, baptising, baptised. 1** *Christianity.* to immerse (a person) in water or sprinkle water on (a person) as part of the rite of baptism. **2** *(tr)* to give a name to; christen. [C13: from LL *baptīzāre,* from Gk, from *baptein* to bathe, dip]

bar[1] ⓣ (bɑː) *n* **1** a rigid usually straight length of metal, wood, etc., used esp. as a barrier or as a structural part: *a bar of a gate.* **2** a solid usually rectangular block of any material: *a bar of soap.* **3** anything that obstructs or prevents. **4** an offshore ridge of sand, mud, or shingle across the mouth of a river, bay, or harbour. **5** a counter or room where alcoholic drinks are served. **6** a counter, room, or establishment where a particular range of goods, food, services, etc., are sold: *a coffee bar; a heel bar.* **7** a narrow band or stripe, as of colour or light. **8** a heating element in an electric fire. **9** See **Bar. 10** the place in a court of law where the accused stands during his trial. **11** a particular court of law. **12** *Brit.* (in Parliament) the boundary where nonmembers wishing to address either House appear and where persons are arraigned. **13** a plea showing that a plaintiff has no cause of action. **14** anything referred to as an authority or tribunal: *the bar of decency.* **15** *Music.* a group of beats that is repeated with a consistent rhythm throughout a piece of music. The number of beats in the bar is indicated by the time signature. Also called: **measure. 16a** *Brit.* insignia added to a decoration indicating a second award. **16b** *US.* a strip of metal worn with uniform, esp. to signify rank or as an award for service. **17** *Football, etc.* See **crossbar. 18** *Gymnastics.* See **horizontal bar. 19** *Heraldry.* a narrow horizontal line across a shield. **20 behind bars.** in prison. **21 won't have a bar of.** *Austral. & NZ inf.* cannot tolerate; dislikes. ◆ *vb* **bars, barring, barred.** *(tr)* **22** to secure with a bar: *to bar the door.* **23** to shut in or out with or as if with barriers: *to bar the entrances.* **24** to obstruct: *the fallen tree barred the road.* **25** (usually foll. by *from*) to prohibit; forbid: *to bar a couple from meeting.* **26** (usually foll. by *from*) to keep out; exclude: *to bar a person from membership.* **27** to mark with a bar or bars. **28** *Law.* to prevent or halt (an action) by showing that the plaintiff has no cause. ◆ *prep* **29** except for. **30 bar none.** without exception. [C12: from OF *barre,* from Vulgar L *barra* (unattested) bar, rod, from ?]

bar[2] (bɑː) *n* a cgs unit of pressure equal to 10^6 dynes per square centimetre. [C20: from Gk *baros* weight]

Bar ⓣ (bɑː) *n* **the. 1** (in England and elsewhere) barristers collectively. **2** *US.* the legal profession collectively. **3 be called to the Bar.** *Brit.* to become a barrister. **4 be called within the Bar.** *Brit.* to be appointed as a Queen's Counsel.

bar. *abbrev. for:* **1** barometric. **2** barrel. **3** barrister.

THESAURUS

bank on *vb* = **rely on,** assume, believe in, count on, depend on, lean on, look to, trust

bankrupt *adj* **4, 5** = **insolvent,** beggared, broke (*inf.*), destitute, failed, impoverished, in queer street, in the red, on one's uppers, on the rocks, ruined, wiped out (*inf.*) **6** = **exhausted,** depleted, spent

Antonyms *adj* ≠ **insolvent:** in the money (*inf.*), on the up and up, prosperous, solvent, sound, wealthy

bankruptcy *n* **4, 5** = **insolvency,** crash, disaster, failure, indebtedness, liquidation, ruin **6** = **lack,** exhaustion

banner *n* **1** = **flag,** colours, ensign, pennant, pennon, standard, streamer **2** = **placard**

banquet *n* **1** = **feast,** dinner, meal, repast

banter *vb* **1** = **joke,** chaff, deride, jeer, jest, josh (*sl., chiefly US & Canad.*), kid (*inf.*), make fun of, rib (*inf.*), ridicule, take the mickey (*inf.*), taunt, tease, twit ◆ *n* **2** = **joking,** badinage, chaff, chaffing, derision, jeering, jesting, kidding (*inf.*), mockery, pleasantry, repartee, ribbing (*inf.*), ridicule, teasing

baptism *n* = **christening,** immersion, purification, sprinkling

baptize *vb* **1** *Christianity* = **purify,** besprinkle, cleanse, immerse **2** = **name,** call, christen, dub, title

bar[1] *n* **1** = **rod,** batten, crosspiece, paling, palisade, pole, rail, shaft, stake, stick **3** = **obstacle,** barricade, barrier, block, deterrent, hindrance, impediment, interdict, obstruction, rail, railing, stop **5** = **public house,** boozer (*Brit., Austral., & NZ inf.*), canteen, counter, hostelry (*arch. or facetious*), inn, lounge, pub (*inf., chiefly Brit.*), saloon, taproom, tavern, watering hole (*facetious sl.*) **10, 11** = **dock,** bench, court, courtroom, law court ◆ *vb* **22** = **fasten,** barricade, bolt, latch, lock, secure **24** = **obstruct,** hinder, prevent, restrain **26** = **exclude,** ban, black, blackball, forbid, keep out, prohibit

Antonyms *n* ≠ **obstacle:** aid, benefit, help ◆ *vb* ≠ **exclude:** accept, admit, allow, let, permit, receive

Bar *n* **the Bar 1, 2** = **barristers,** body of lawyers, counsel, court, judgment, tribunal

barathea (ˌbærəˈθɪə) *n* a fabric made of silk and wool or cotton and rayon. [C19: from ?]

barb[1] Ⓣ (bɑːb) *n* **1** a point facing in the opposite direction to the main point of a fish-hook, harpoon, etc., intended to make extraction difficult. **2** any of various pointed parts. **3** a cutting remark. **4** any of the hairlike filaments that form the vane of a feather. **5** a beardlike growth, hair, or projection. ◆ *vb* **6** (*tr*) to provide with a barb or barbs. [C14: from OF *barbe* beard, point, from L *barba* beard]
▸**barbed** *adj*

barb[2] (bɑːb) *n* a breed of horse of North African origin, similar to the Arab but less spirited. [C17: from F *barbe,* from It. *barbero* a Barbary (horse)]

Barbadian (bɑːˈbeɪdɪən) *adj* **1** of Barbados, an island in the Caribbean. ◆ *n* **2** a native or inhabitant of Barbados.

barbarian Ⓣ (bɑːˈbɛərɪən) *n* **1** a member of a primitive or uncivilized people. **2** a coarse or uncultured person. **3** a vicious person. ◆ *adj* **4** of an uncivilized culture. **5** uncultured or brutal. [C16: see BARBAROUS]

barbaric Ⓣ (bɑːˈbærɪk) *adj* **1** of or characteristic of barbarians. **2** primitive; unrestrained. **3** brutal. [C15: from L *barbaricus* outlandish; see BARBAROUS]
▸**barˈbarically** *adv*

barbarism Ⓣ (ˈbɑːbəˌrɪzəm) *n* **1** a brutal, coarse, or ignorant act. **2** the condition of being backward, coarse, or ignorant. **3** a substandard word or expression; solecism. **4** any act or object that offends against accepted taste. [C16: from L *barbarismus* error of speech, from Gk *barbarismos,* from *barbaros* BARBAROUS]

barbarity Ⓣ (bɑːˈbærɪtɪ) *n, pl* **barbarities. 1** the state of being barbaric or barbarous. **2** a vicious act.

barbarize *or* **barbarise** (ˈbɑːbəˌraɪz) *vb* **barbarizes, barbarizing, barbarized** *or* **barbarises, barbarising, barbarised. 1** to make or become barbarous. **2** to use barbarisms in (language).
▸ˌ**barbariˈzation** *or* ˌ**barbariˈsation** *n*

barbarous Ⓣ (ˈbɑːbərəs) *adj* **1** uncivilized; primitive. **2** brutal or cruel. **3** lacking refinement. [C15: via L from Gk *barbaros* barbarian, non-Greek, imit. of incomprehensible speech]
▸ˈ**barbarously** *adv* ▸ˈ**barbarousness** *n*

Barbary ape (ˈbɑːbərɪ) *n* a tailless macaque that inhabits NW Africa and Gibraltar. [from *Barbary,* old name for region in N Africa]

barbate (ˈbɑːbeɪt) *adj Biol.* having tufts of long hairs; bearded. [C19: from L *barba* a beard]

barbecue (ˈbɑːbɪˌkjuː) *n* **1** a meal cooked out of doors over an open fire. **2** a grill or fireplace used in barbecuing. **3** the food so cooked. **4** a party or picnic at which barbecued food is served. ◆ *vb* **barbecues, barbecuing, barbecued.** (*tr*) **5** to cook (meat, fish, etc.) on a grill, usually over charcoal and often with a highly seasoned sauce. [C17: from American Sp. *barbacoa:* frame made of sticks]

barbed wire *n* strong wire with sharply pointed barbs at close intervals.

barbel (ˈbɑːbᵊl) *n* **1** any of several slender tactile spines or bristles that hang from the jaws of certain fishes, such as the carp. **2** any of several European cyprinid fishes that resemble the carp. [C14: from OF, from LL from L *barba* beard]

barbell (ˈbɑːˌbɛl) *n* a long metal rod to which heavy discs are attached at each end for weightlifting.

barber (ˈbɑːbə) *n* **1** a person whose business is cutting men's hair and shaving beards. ◆ *vb* (*tr*) **2** to cut the hair of. [C13: from OF *barbeor,* from *barbe* beard, from L *barba*]

barberry (ˈbɑːbərɪ) *n, pl* **barberries.** any spiny Asian shrub of the genus *Berberis,* having clusters of yellow flowers and orange or red berries. [C15: from OF *berberis,* from Ar. *barbāris*]

barbershop (ˈbɑːbəˌʃɒp) *n* **1** *Now chiefly US.* the premises of a barber. **2** (*modifier*) denoting a type of close four-part harmony for male voices: *a barbershop quartet.*

barber's pole *n* a barber's sign consisting of a pole painted with red-and-white spiral stripes.

barbican (ˈbɑːbɪkən) *n* **1** a walled outwork to protect a gate or drawbridge of a fortification. **2** a watchtower projecting from a fortification. [C13: from OF *barbacane,* from Med. L, from ?]

barbicel (ˈbɑːbɪˌsɛl) *n Ornithol.* any of the minute hooks on the barbules of feathers that interlock with those of adjacent barbules. [C19: from NL *barbicella,* lit.: a small beard]

barbitone (ˈbɑːbɪˌtəʊn) *or US* **barbital** (ˈbɑːbɪˌtæl) *n* a long-acting barbiturate. [C20: from BARBIT(URIC ACID) + -ONE]

barbiturate (bɑːˈbɪtjʊrɪt, -ˌreɪt) *n* a derivative of barbituric acid, such as barbitone, used in medicine as a sedative or hypnotic.

barbituric acid (ˌbɑːbɪˈtjʊərɪk) *n* a white crystalline solid used in the preparation of barbiturate drugs. [C19: partial translation of G *Barbitursäure*]

Barbour jacket *or* **Barbour** (ˈbɑːbə) *n Trademark.* a hard-wearing waterproof waxed jacket.

barbule (ˈbɑːbjuːl) *n Ornithol.* any of the minute hairs that project from a barb and in some feathers interlock. [C19: from L *barbula* a little beard]

barcarole *or* **barcarolle** (ˈbɑːkəˌrəʊl, -ˌrɒl; ˌbɑːkəˈrəʊl) *n* **1** a Venetian boat song. **2** an instrumental composition resembling this. [C18: from F, from It. *barcarola,* from *barcaruolo* boatman, from *barca* boat]

bar chart *n* another term for **bar graph.**

bar code *n Commerce.* a machine-readable arrangement of numbers and parallel lines printed on a package, which can be electronically scanned at a checkout to register the price of the goods and to activate computer stock checking and reordering.

bard[1] Ⓣ (bɑːd) *n* **1a** (formerly) one of an ancient Celtic order of poets. **1b** a poet who wins a verse competition at a Welsh eisteddfod. **2** *Arch. or literary.* any poet. [C14: from Scot. Gaelic]
▸ˈ**bardic** *adj*

bard[2] (bɑːd) *n* **1** a piece of bacon or pork fat placed on meat during roasting to prevent drying out. ◆ *vb* (*tr*) **2** to place a bard on. [C15: from OF *barde,* from OIt. *barda,* from Ar. *barda'ah* packsaddle]

bardie (ˈbɑːdɪ) *n* **1** an edible white wood-boring grub of Australia. **2** **starve the bardies!** *Austral.* an exclamation of surprise or protest. [from Abor.]

bare[1] Ⓣ (bɛə) *adj* **1** unclothed: used esp. of a part of the body. **2** without the natural, conventional, or usual covering. **3** lacking appropriate furnishings, etc. **4** unembellished; simple: *the bare facts.* **5** (*prenominal*) just sufficient: *the bare minimum.* **6** **with one's bare hands.** without a weapon or tool. ◆ *vb* **bares, baring, bared. 7** (*tr*) to make bare; uncover. [OE *bær*]
▸ ˈ**bareness** *n*

bare[2] (bɛə) *vb Arch.* a past tense of **bear**[1].

bareback (ˈbɛəˌbæk) *or* **barebacked** *adj, adv* (of horse-riding) without a saddle.

barefaced Ⓣ (ˈbɛəˌfeɪst) *adj* unconcealed or shameless: *a barefaced lie.*
▸**barefacedly** (ˈbɛəˌfeɪsɪdlɪ) *adv* ▸ˈ**bareˌfacedness** *n*

barefoot (ˈbɛəˌfʊt) *or* **barefooted** *adj, adv* **1** with the feet uncovered. ◆ *adj* **2** denoting a worker with basic training sent to help people in remote rural areas, esp. of developing countries: *barefoot doctor.*

bareheaded (ˌbɛəˈhɛdɪd) *adj, adv* with the head uncovered.

bare-knuckle *adj* **1** without boxing gloves: *a bare-knuckle fighter.* **2** aggressive; without civilized restraint: *a bare-knuckle confrontation.*

barely Ⓣ (ˈbɛəlɪ) *adv* **1** only just: *barely enough.* **2** *Inf.* not quite: *barely old enough.* **3** scantily: *barely furnished.* **4** *Arch.* openly.

> **USAGE NOTE** See at **hardly.**

barf (bɑːf) *vb* (*intr*) *Sl.* to vomit. [C20: prob. imit.]

bargain Ⓣ (ˈbɑːgɪn) *n* **1** an agreement establishing what each party will give, receive, or perform in a transaction. **2** something acquired or received in such an agreement. **3a** something bought or offered at a low price. **3b** (*as modifier*): *a bargain price.* **4** **into the bargain.** in excess; besides. **5** **make** *or* **strike a bargain.** to agree on terms. ◆ *vb* **6** (*intr*) to negotiate the terms of an agreement, transaction, etc. **7** (*tr*) to exchange, as

THESAURUS

barb[1] *n* **2** = **point**, bristle, prickle, prong, quill, spike, spur, thorn **3** = **dig**, affront, cut, gibe, insult, rebuff, sarcasm, scoff, sneer

barbarian *n* **1** = **savage**, brute, yahoo **2** = **lout**, bigot, boor, hooligan, ignoramus, illiterate, lowbrow, philistine, ruffian, vandal ◆ *adj* **4** = **uncivilized**, primitive, wild **5** = **uncultured**, boorish, crude, lowbrow, philistine, rough, uncouth, uncultivated, unsophisticated, vulgar
Antonyms *adj* ≠ **uncultured:** civil, civilized, cultured, genteel, highbrow, refined, sophisticated, urbane, well-mannered

barbaric *adj* **1, 2** = **uncivilized**, primitive, rude, wild **3** = **brutal**, barbarous, cruel, fierce, inhuman, savage
Antonyms *adj* ≠ **uncivilized:** civilized, cultivated, cultured, gentlemanly, gracious, refined, sophisticated, urbane ≠ **brutal:** humane

barbarism *n* **1, 4** = **atrocity**, barbarity, enormity, outrage **2** = **savagery**, coarseness, crudity, uncivilizedness **3** = **misuse**, corruption, misusage, solecism, vulgarism

barbarity *n* **1** = **viciousness**, brutality, cruelty, inhumanity, ruthlessness, savagery

barbarous *adj* **1** = **uncivilized**, barbarian, brutish, primitive, rough, rude, savage, uncouth, wild **2** = **brutal**, barbaric, cruel, ferocious, heartless, inhuman, monstrous, ruthless, vicious **3** = **ignorant**, coarse, crude, uncultured, unlettered, unrefined, vulgar

barbed *adj* **2** = **spiked**, hooked, jagged, prickly, pronged, spiny, thorny, toothed **3** = **cutting**, acid, acrid, catty (*inf.*), critical, hostile, hurtful, nasty, pointed, scathing, unkind

bard[1] *n* **2** *Archaic or literary* = **poet**, minstrel, rhymer, singer, troubadour

bare *adj* **1** = **naked**, buck naked (*sl.*), denuded, exposed, in the bare scud (*sl.*), in the raw (*inf.*), naked as the day one was born (*inf.*), nude, peeled, shorn, stripped, unclad, unclothed, uncovered, undressed, without a stitch on (*inf.*) **2** = **empty**, barren, open, poor, scanty, scarce, unfurnished, vacant, void, wanting **3** = **unadorned**, austere, basic, severe, simple, spare, spartan, unembellished, unfussy, unvarnished **4** = **plain**, bald, basic, cold, essential, hard, literal, sheer, simple, stark, unembellished
Antonyms *adj* ≠ **naked:** attired, clad, clothed, concealed, covered, dressed, hidden ≠ **empty:** abundant, full, plentiful, profuse, well-stocked ≠ **unadorned:** adorned

barefaced *adj* = **shameless**, audacious, bald, blatant, bold, brash, brazen, flagrant, glaring, impudent, insolent, manifest, naked, open, palpable, patent, transparent, unconcealed
Antonyms *adj* concealed, covered, hidden, inconspicuous, masked, obscured, secret, tucked away, unseen

barely *adv* **1** = **only just**, almost, at a push, by the skin of one's teeth, hardly, just, scarcely
Antonyms *adv* amply, completely, fully, profusely

bargain *n* **1** = **agreement**, arrangement, business, compact, contract, convention, engagement, negotiation, pact, pledge, promise, stipulation, transaction, treaty, understanding **3** = **good buy**, (cheap) purchase, discount, giveaway, good deal, good value, reduction, snip (*inf.*), steal (*inf.*) ◆ *vb* **6** = **negotiate**, agree, con-

in a bargain. **8** to arrive at (an agreement or settlement). [C14: from OF *bargaigne*, from *bargaignier* to trade, of Gmc origin]
▸ **'bargainer** *n*

bargain away *vb (tr, adv)* to lose (rights, etc.) in return for something valueless.

bargain for ❶ *vb (intr, prep)* to expect; anticipate: *he got more than he bargained for.*

bargain on ❶ *vb (intr, prep)* to rely or depend on (something): *he bargained on her support.*

barge ❶ (bɑːdʒ) *n* **1** a vessel, usually flat-bottomed and with or without its own power, used for transporting freight, esp. on canals. **2** a vessel, often decorated, used in pageants, etc. **3** *Navy.* a boat allocated to a flag officer, used esp. for ceremonial occasions. ◆ *vb* **barges, barging, barged. 4** *(intr;* foll. by *into) Inf.* to bump (into). **5** *Inf.* to push (someone or one's way) violently. **6** *(intr;* foll. by *into* or *in) Inf.* to interrupt rudely or clumsily: *to barge into a conversation.* [C13: from OF, from Med. L *barga*, prob. from LL *barca* a small boat]

bargeboard ('bɑːdʒˌbɔːd) *n* a board, often decorated, along the gable end of a roof.

bargee (bɑːˈdʒiː) *n* a person employed on or in charge of a barge.

bargepole ('bɑːdʒˌpəʊl) *n* **1** a long pole used to propel a barge. **2 not touch with a bargepole.** *Inf.* to refuse to have anything to do with.

bar graph *n* a graph consisting of vertical or horizontal bars whose lengths are proportional to amounts or quantities.

bariatrics (ˌbærɪˈætrɪks) *n (functioning as sing)* the branch of medicine concerned with the treatment of obese people. [C20: from Gk *barōs* weight + -IATRICS]

barite ('beəraɪt) *n* the usual US and Canad. name for **barytes.** [C18: from BAR(IUM) + -ITE[1]]

baritone ('bærɪˌtəʊn) *n* **1** the second lowest adult male voice. **2** a singer with such a voice. **3** the second lowest instrument in the families of the saxophone, horn, oboe, etc. ◆ *adj* **4** relating to or denoting a baritone. [C17: from It., from Gk, from *barus* heavy, low + *tonos* TONE]

barium ('beərɪəm) *n* a soft silvery-white metallic element of the alkaline earth group. Symbol: Ba; atomic no.: 56; atomic wt.: 137.34. [C19: from BAR(YTA) + -IUM]

barium meal *n* a preparation of barium sulphate, which is opaque to X-rays, swallowed by a patient before X-ray examination of the upper part of his or her alimentary canal.

bark[1] ❶ (bɑːk) *n* **1** the loud abrupt usually harsh cry of a dog or certain other animals. **2** a similar sound, such as one made by a person, gun, etc. **3 his bark is worse than his bite.** he is bad-tempered but harmless. ◆ *vb* **4** *(intr)* (of a dog, etc.) to make its typical cry. **5** *(intr)* (of a person, gun, etc.) to make a similar loud harsh sound. **6** to say or shout in a brusque or angry tone: *he barked an order.* **7 bark up the wrong tree.** *Inf.* to misdirect one's attention, efforts, etc.; be mistaken. [OE *beorcan*]

bark[2] ❶ (bɑːk) *n* **1** a protective layer of dead corky cells on the outside of the stems of woody plants. **2** any of several varieties of this, used in tanning, dyeing, or in medicine. ◆ *vb (tr)* **3** to scrape or rub off skin, as in an injury. **4** to remove the bark or a circle of bark from (a tree). **5** to tan (leather), principally by the tannins in barks. [C13: from ON *börkr*]

bark[3] (bɑːk) *n* a variant spelling of **barque.**

barkentine ('bɑːkənˌtiːn) *n* the usual US and Canad. spelling of **barquentine.**

barker ('bɑːkə) *n* **1** an animal or person that barks. **2** a person at a fair booth, etc., who loudly addresses passers-by to attract customers.

barking ('bɑːkɪŋ) *Sl.* ◆ *adj* **1** mad; crazy. ◆ *adv* **2** (intensifier): *barking mad.*

barley ('bɑːlɪ) *n* **1** any of various annual temperate grasses that have dense bristly flower spikes and are widely cultivated for grain and forage. **2** the grain of any of these grasses, used in making beer and whisky and for soups, puddings, etc. [OE *bærlīc* (adj); rel. to *bere* barley]

barleycorn ('bɑːlɪˌkɔːn) *n* **1** a grain of barley, or barley itself. **2** an obsolete unit of length equal to one third of an inch.

barley sugar *n* a brittle clear amber-coloured sweet.

barley water *n* a drink made from an infusion of barley.

barm (bɑːm) *n* **1** the yeasty froth on fermenting malt liquors. **2** an archaic or dialect word for **yeast.** [OE *beorma*]

barmaid ('bɑːˌmeɪd) *n* a woman who serves in a pub.

barman ('bɑːmən) *n, pl* **barmen.** a man who serves in a pub.

Barmecide ('bɑːmɪˌsaɪd) *adj* lavish in imagination only; illusory; sham: *a Barmecide feast.* [C18: from a prince in the *Arabian Nights' Entertainment* who served empty plates to beggars, alleging that they held sumptuous food]

Bar Mitzvah (bɑː ˈmɪtsvə) *(sometimes not caps.) Judaism.* ◆ *adj* **1** (of a Jewish boy) having assumed full religious obligations, being at least thirteen years old. ◆ *n* **2** the occasion or celebration of this. **3** the boy himself. [Heb.: son of the law]

barmy ❶ ('bɑːmɪ) *adj* **barmier, barmiest.** *Sl.* insane. [C16: orig., full of BARM, hence frothing, excited]

barn[1] (bɑːn) *n* **1** a large farm outbuilding, chiefly for storing grain, etc., but also for livestock. **2** *US & Canad.* a large shed for railroad cars, trucks, etc. **3** any large building, esp. an unattractive one. **4** *(modifier)* relating to a system of poultry farming in which birds are allowed to move freely within a barn: *barn eggs.* [OE *beren*, from *bere* barley + *ærn* room]

barn[2] (bɑːn) *n* a unit of nuclear cross section equal to 10^{-28} square metres. Symbol: b [C20: from BARN[1]; so called because of the relatively large cross section]

barnacle ('bɑːnəkᵊl) *n* **1** any of various marine crustaceans that, as adults, live attached to rocks, ship bottoms, etc. **2** a person or thing that is difficult to get rid of. [C16: from earlier *bernak*, from OF *bernac*, from LL, from ?]
▸ **'barnacled** *adj*

barnacle goose *n* a N European goose that has a black-and-white head and body. [C13 *bernekke*: it was formerly believed that the goose developed from a shellfish]

barn dance *n* **1** *Brit.* a progressive round country dance. **2** *Brit.* a disco or party held in a barn. **3** *US & Canad.* a party with hoedown music and square-dancing.

barney ('bɑːnɪ) *Inf.* ◆ *n* **1** a noisy fight or argument. ◆ *vb* **2** *(intr) Chiefly Austral. & NZ.* to argue or quarrel. [C19: from ?]

barn owl *n* an owl with a pale brown and white plumage and a heart-shaped face.

barnstorm ('bɑːnˌstɔːm) *vb (intr)* **1** to tour rural districts putting on shows. **2** *Chiefly US & Canad.* to tour rural districts making speeches in a political campaign.
▸ **'barnˌstorming** *n, adj*

barnyard ('bɑːnˌjɑːd) *n* **1** a yard adjoining a barn. **2** *(modifier)* characteristic of a barnyard. **3** *(modifier)* crude or earthy.

baro- *combining form.* indicating weight or pressure: *barometer.* [from Gk *baros* weight]

baroceptor ('bærəʊˌseptə) *n* another name for **baroreceptor.**

barogram ('bærəˌgræm) *n Meteorol.* the record of atmospheric pressure traced by a barograph or similar instrument.

barograph ('bærəˌgrɑːf) *n Meteorol.* a self-recording aneroid barometer.
▸ **barographic** (ˌbærəˈgræfɪk) *adj*

barometer (bəˈrɒmɪtə) *n* **1** an instrument for measuring atmospheric pressure, usually to determine altitude or weather changes. **2** anything that shows change.
▸ **barometric** (ˌbærəˈmetrɪk) *or* ˌ**baroˈmetrical** *adj* ▸ **baˈrometry** *n*

baron ('bærən) *n* **1** a member of a specific rank of nobility, esp. the lowest rank in the British Isles. **2** (in Europe from the Middle Ages) originally any tenant-in-chief of a king or other overlord. **3** a powerful businessman or financier: *a press baron.* [C12: from OF, of Gmc origin]

baronage ('bærənɪdʒ) *n* **1** barons collectively. **2** the rank or dignity of a baron.

baroness ('bærənɪs) *n* **1** the wife or widow of a baron. **2** a woman holding the rank of baron.

baronet ('bærənɪt, -ˌnet) *n* (in Britain) a commoner who holds the lowest hereditary title of honour, ranking below a baron. Abbrev.: **Bart, Bt.**
▸ **'baronetage** *n* ▸ **'baronetcy** *n*

baronial (bəˈrəʊnɪəl) *adj* of, relating to, or befitting a baron or barons.

baron of beef *n* a cut of beef consisting of a double sirloin joined at the backbone.

barony ('bærənɪ) *n, pl* **baronies. 1a** the domain of a baron. **1b** (in Ireland) a division of a county. **1c** (in Scotland) a large estate or manor. **2** the rank or dignity of a baron.

baroque ❶ (bəˈrɒk, bəˈrəʊk) *n (often cap.)* **1** a style of architecture and decorative art in Europe from the late 16th to the early 18th century, characterized by extensive ornamentation. **2** a 17th-century style of music characterized by extensive use of ornamentation. **3** any ornate or heavily ornamented style. ◆ *adj* **4** denoting, in, or relating to the baroque. **5** (of pearls) irregularly shaped. [C18: from F, from Port. *barroco* a rough or imperfectly shaped pearl]

baroreceptor ('bærəʊrɪˌseptə) *or* **baroceptor** *n* a collection of sensory nerve endings, principally in the carotid sinuses and the aortic arch, that monitor blood-pressure changes in the body.

baroscope ('bærəˌskəʊp) *n* any instrument for measuring atmospheric pressure.
▸ **baroscopic** (ˌbærəˈskɒpɪk) *adj*

barouche (bəˈruːʃ) *n* a four-wheeled horse-drawn carriage, popular in the 19th century, having a retractable hood over the rear half. [C19: from G (dialect) *Barutsche*, from It. *baroccio*, from LL *birotus*, from BI- + *rota* wheel]

barperson ('bɑːˌpɜːsᵊn) *n, pl* **barpersons.** a person who serves in a pub: used esp. in advertisements.

THESAURUS

tract, covenant, cut a deal, promise, stipulate, transact **7** = **exchange**, barter, buy, deal, haggle, sell, trade, traffic

bargain for *vb* = **anticipate**, contemplate, expect, foresee, imagine, look for, plan for

bargain on *vb* = **depend on**, assume, bank on, count on, plan on, rely on

barge *n* **1** = **canal boat**, flatboat, lighter, narrow boat, scow ◆ *vb* **4** *foll. by* **into** *Informal* = **bump into**, cannon into, collide with, hit **5** *Informal* = **push**, shove **6** *foll. by* **into** *or* **in** *Informal* = **interrupt**, break in, burst in, butt in, infringe, intrude, muscle in *(inf.)*

bark[1] *n, vb* **1, 4** = **yap**, bay, growl, howl, snarl, woof, yelp **6** = **shout**, bawl, bawl at, berate, bluster, growl, snap, snarl, yell

bark[2] *n* **1** = **covering**, casing, cortex *(Anatomy, botany)*, crust, husk, rind, skin ◆ *vb* **3** = **scrape**, abrade, flay, rub, shave, skin, strip

barmy *adj Slang* = **insane**, crackpot *(inf.)*, crazy, daft, dippy, doolally *(sl.)*, loony *(sl.)*, loopy *(inf.)*, nuts *(sl.)*, nutty *(sl.)*, odd, off one's rocker *(sl.)*, off one's trolley *(sl.)*, out of one's mind, out to lunch *(inf.)*, round the twist *(Brit. sl.)*, up the pole *(inf.)*
Antonyms *adj* all there *(inf.)*, in one's right mind, of sound mind, rational, reasonable, sane, sensible

baroque *adj* **4** = **ornate**, elaborate, extravagant, flamboyant, florid, overdecorated, rococo

barque (bɑːk) *n* **1** a sailing ship of three or more masts having the foremasts rigged square and the aftermast rigged fore-and-aft. **2** *Poetic.* any boat. [C15: from OF, from OProvençal *barca*]
barquentine *or* **barquantine** (ˈbɑːkənˌtiːn) *n* a sailing ship of three or more masts rigged square on the foremast and fore-and-aft on the others. [C17: from BARQUE + (BRIG)ANTINE]
barrack[1] (ˈbærək) *vb* to house (soldiers, etc.) in barracks.
barrack[2] Ⓣ (ˈbærək) *vb Brit., Austral., & NZ inf.* **1** to criticize loudly or shout against (a team, speaker, etc.); jeer. **2** (*intr;* foll. by *for*) to shout support (for). [C19: from Irish: to boast]
barrack-room lawyer *n* a person who freely offers opinions, esp. in legal matters, that he is unqualified to give.
barracks Ⓣ (ˈbærəks) *pl n* (*sometimes sing; when pl, sometimes functions as sing*) **1** a building or group of buildings used to accommodate military personnel. **2** any large building used for housing people, esp. temporarily. **3** a large and bleak building. [C17: from F *baraque,* from OCatalan *barraca* hut, from ?]
barracouta (ˌbærəˈkuːtə) *n* a large predatory Pacific fish. [C17: var. of BARRACUDA]
barracuda (ˌbærəˈkjuːdə) *n, pl* **barracuda** *or* **barracudas.** a predatory marine mostly tropical fish, which attacks man. [C17: from American Sp., from ?]
barrage Ⓣ (ˈbærɑːʒ) *n* **1** *Mil.* the firing of artillery to saturate an area, either to protect against an attack or to support an advance. **2** an overwhelming and continuous delivery of something, as questions. **3** a construction across a watercourse, esp. one to increase the depth. [C19: from F, from *barrer* to obstruct; see BAR[1]]
barrage balloon *n* one of a number of tethered balloons with cables or net suspended from them, used to deter low-flying air attack.
barramundi (ˌbærəˈmʌndɪ) *n, pl* **barramundis, barramundies, barramundi.** a large edible Australian estuary fish of the perch family. [from Abor.]
barratry *or* **barretry** (ˈbærətrɪ) *n* **1** *Criminal law.* (formerly) the vexatious stirring up of quarrels or bringing of lawsuits. **2** *Maritime law.* a fraudulent practice committed by the master or crew of a ship to the prejudice of the owner. **3** the purchase or sale of public or Church offices. [C15: from OF *baraterie* deception, from *barater* to BARTER]
▸ **ˈbarratrous** *or* **ˈbarretrous** *adj* ▸ **ˈbarrator** *n*
barre *French.* (bar) *n* a rail at hip height used for ballet practice and leg exercises. [lit.: bar]
barrel (ˈbærəl) *n* **1** a cylindrical container usually bulging outwards in the middle and held together by metal hoops. **2** Also called: **barrelful.** the amount that a barrel can hold. **3** a unit of capacity of varying amount in different industries. **4** a thing shaped like a barrel, esp. a tubular part of a machine. **5** the tube through which the projectile of a firearm is discharged. **6** the trunk of a four-legged animal: *the barrel of a horse.* **7 over a barrel.** *Inf.* powerless. **8 scrape the barrel.** *Inf.* to be forced to use one's last and weakest resource. ◆ *vb* **barrels, barrelling, barrelled** *or US* **barrels, barreling, barreled. 9** (*tr*) to put into a barrel or barrels. [C14: from OF *baril,* ?from *barre* BAR[1]]
barrel-chested *adj* having a large rounded chest.
barrel organ *n* an instrument consisting of a cylinder turned by a handle and having pins on it that interrupt the air flow to certain pipes or pluck strings, thereby playing tunes.
barrel roll *n* a flight manoeuvre in which an aircraft rolls about its longitudinal axis while following a spiral course in line with the direction of flight.
barrel vault *n Archit.* a vault in the form of a half cylinder.
barren Ⓣ (ˈbærən) *adj* **1** incapable of producing offspring, seed, or fruit; sterile. **2** unable to support the growth of crops, etc.: *barren land.* **3** lacking in stimulation; dull. **4** not producing worthwhile results; unprofitable: *a barren period.* **5** (foll. by *of*) devoid (of): *barren of wit.* **6** (of rock strata) having no fossils. [C13: from OF *brahain,* from ?]
▸ **ˈbarrenness** *n*
barricade (ˌbærɪˈkeɪd, ˈbærɪˌkeɪd) *n* **1** a barrier for defence, esp. one erected hastily, as during street fighting. ◆ *vb* **barricades, barricading, barricaded.** (*tr*) **2** to erect a barricade across (an entrance, etc.) or at points of access to (a room, district, etc.). [C17: from OF, from *barriquer* to barricade, from *barrique* a barrel, from Sp. *barrica,* from *barril* BARREL]
barrier Ⓣ (ˈbærɪə) *n* **1** anything serving to obstruct passage or to maintain separation, such as a fence or gate. **2** anything that prevents progress. **3** anything that separates or hinders union: *a language barrier.* [C14: from OF *barriere,* from *barre* BAR[1]]
barrier cream *n* a cream used to protect the skin, esp. the hands.
barrier-nurse *vb* (*tr*) to tend (infectious patients) in isolation, to prevent the spread of infection.
▸ **barrier nursing** *n*
barrier reef *n* a long narrow coral reef near the shore, separated from it by deep water.
barring (ˈbɑːrɪŋ) *prep* unless (something) occurs; except for.
barrister (ˈbærɪstə) *n* **1** Also called: **barrister-at-law.** (in England) a lawyer who has been called to the bar and is qualified to plead in the higher courts. Cf. **solicitor. 2** (in Canada) a lawyer who pleads in court **3** *US.* a less common word for **lawyer.** [C16: from BAR[1]]
barrow[1] (ˈbærəʊ) *n* **1** See **wheelbarrow, handbarrow. 2** Also called: **barrowful.** the amount contained in or on a barrow. **3** *Chiefly Brit.* a handcart with a canvas roof, used esp. by street vendors. [OE *bearwe*]
barrow[2] (ˈbærəʊ) *n* a heap of earth placed over one or more prehistoric tombs, often surrounded by ditches. [OE *beorg*]
barrow boy *n Brit.* a man who sells his wares from a barrow; street vendor.
bar sinister *n* **1** (not in heraldic usage) another name for **bend sinister. 2** the condition or stigma of being of illegitimate birth.
Bart. *abbrev. for* Baronet.
bartender (ˈbɑːˌtendə) *n* another name (esp. US and Canad.) for **barman** or **barmaid.**
barter Ⓣ (ˈbɑːtə) *vb* **1** to trade (goods, services, etc.) in exchange for other goods, services, etc., rather than for money. **2** (*intr*) to haggle over such an exchange; bargain. ◆ *n* **3** trade by the exchange of goods. [C15: from OF *barater* to cheat]
bartizan (ˈbɑːtɪzən, ˌbɑːtɪˈzæn) *n* a small turret projecting from a wall, parapet, or tower. [C19: var. of *bertisene,* erroneously for *bretising,* from *bretasce* parapet; see BRATTICE]
▸ **bartizaned** (ˈbɑːtɪzənd, ˌbɑːtɪˈzænd) *adj*
baryon (ˈbærɪˌɒn) *n* any of a class of elementary particles that have a mass greater than or equal to that of the proton. Baryons are either nucleons or hyperons. The **baryon number** is the number of baryons in a system minus the number of antibaryons. [C20: from Gk *barus* heavy + -ON]
▸ **ˌbaryˈonic** *adj*
baryta (bəˈraɪtə) *n* another name for barium oxide or barium hydroxide. [C19: NL, from Gk *barutēs* weight, from *barus* heavy]
barytes (bəˈraɪtiːz) *n* a colourless or white mineral occurring in sedimentary rocks and with sulphide ores: a source of barium. [C18: from Gk *barus* heavy + *-ités* -ITE[1]]
basal (ˈbeɪsᵊl) *adj* **1** at, of, or constituting a base. **2** of or constituting a basis; fundamental.
basal metabolism *n* the amount of energy required by an individual in the resting state, for such functions as breathing and blood circulation.
basalt (ˈbæsɔːlt) *n* **1** a dark basic igneous rock: the most common volcanic rock. **2** a form of black unglazed pottery resembling basalt. [C18: from LL *basaltēs,* var. of *basanītēs,* from Gk *basanitēs* touchstone]
▸ **baˈsaltic** *adj*
bascule (ˈbæskjuːl) *n* **1** a bridge with a movable section hinged about a horizontal axis and counterbalanced by a weight. **2** a movable roadway forming part of such a bridge. [C17: from F: seesaw, from *bas* low + *cul* rump]
base[1] Ⓣ (beɪs) *n* **1** the bottom or supporting part of anything. **2** the fundamental principle or part. **3a** a centre of operations, organization, or supply. **3b** (*as modifier*): *base camp.* **4** starting point: *the new discovery became the base for further research.* **5** the main ingredient of a mixture: *to use rice as a base in cookery.* **6** a chemical compound that combines with an acid to form a salt and water. A solution of a base in water turns litmus paper blue and produces hydroxyl ions. **7** a medium such as oil or water in which the pigment is dispersed in paints, inks, etc. **8** *Biol.* the point of attachment of an organ or part. **9** the bottommost layer or part of anything. **10** *Archit.* the part of a column between the pedestal and the shaft. **11** the lower side or face of a geometric construction. **12** *Maths.* the number of units in a counting system that is equivalent to one in the next higher counting place: *10 is the base of the decimal system.* **13** *Maths.* the number that when raised to a certain power has a logarithm (based on that number) equal to that power: *the logarithm to the base 10 of 1000 is 3.* **14** *Linguistics.* a root or stem. **15** *Electronics.* the region in a transistor between the emitter and collector. **16** a starting or finishing point in any of various games. ◆ *vb* **bases, basing, based. 17** (*tr;* foll. by *on* or *upon*) to use as a basis (for); found (on). **18** (often foll. by *at* or *in*) to station, post, or place (a person or oneself). [C14: from OF, from L *basis* pedestal; see BASIS]

THESAURUS

barrack[2] *vb Brit., Austral., & N.Z. informal* **1** = **heckle**, abuse, boo, criticize, gibe *or* jibe, jeer, mock, taunt
barracks *pl n* **1** = **camp**, billet, cantonment, encampment, garrison, quarters
barrage *n* **1** *Military* = **bombardment**, battery, cannonade, curtain of fire, fusillade, gunfire, salvo, shelling, volley **2** = **torrent**, assault, attack, burst, deluge, hail, mass, onslaught, plethora, profusion, rain, storm, stream
barren *adj* **1** = **infertile**, childless, infecund, sterile, unprolific **2** = **unproductive**, arid, desert, desolate, dry, empty, unfruitful, waste **3** = **dull**, boring, flat, lacklustre, stale, uninformative, uninspiring, uninstructive, uninteresting, unrewarding, vapid **4** = **unprofitable**, fruitless, unsuccessful, useless
Antonyms *adj* ≠ **unproductive:** fecund, fertile, fruitful, lush, productive, profitable, rich, useful ≠ **dull:** instructive, interesting ≠ **unprofitable:** productive, profitable, useful
barricade *n* **1** = **barrier**, blockade, bulwark, fence, obstruction, palisade, rampart, stockade ◆ *vb* **2** = **bar**, block, blockade, defend, fortify, obstruct, protect, shut in
barrier *n* **1** = **barricade**, bar, block, blockade, boundary, ditch, fence, fortification, obstacle, obstruction, pale, railing, rampart, stop, wall **2** = **hindrance**, check, difficulty, drawback, handicap, hazard, hurdle, impediment, limitation, obstacle, restriction, stumbling block
barter *vb* **1** = **trade**, exchange, sell, swap, traffic **2** = **bargain**, drive a hard bargain, haggle
base[1] *n* **1** = **bottom**, bed, foot, foundation, groundwork, pedestal, rest, stand, support **2** = **basis**, core, essence, essential, fundamental, heart, key, origin, principle, root, source **3a** = **centre**, camp, headquarters, home, post, settlement, starting point, station ◆ *vb* **17** = **found**, build, construct, depend, derive, establish, ground, hinge **18** = **place**, locate, post, station

base[2] Ⓣ (beɪs) *adj* **1** devoid of honour or morality; contemptible. **2** of inferior quality or value. **3** debased; alloyed; counterfeit: *base currency.* **4** *English history.* (of land tenure) held by villein or other ignoble service. **5** *Arch.* born of humble parents. **6** *Arch.* illegitimate. [C14: from OF *bas,* from LL *bassus* of low height]
▸'**baseness** *n*

baseball ('beɪsˌbɔːl) *n* **1** a team game with nine players on each side, played on a field with four bases connected to form a diamond. The object is to score runs by batting the ball and running round the bases. **2** the hard rawhide-covered ball used in this game.

baseball cap *n* a close-fitting thin cap with a deep peak.

baseborn ('beɪsˌbɔːn) *adj Arch.* **1** born of humble parents. **2** illegitimate.

base hospital *n Austral.* a hospital serving a large rural area.

baseless Ⓣ ('beɪslɪs) *adj* not based on fact; unfounded.
▸'**baselessness** *n*

baseline ('beɪsˌlaɪn) *n* **1** *Surveying.* a measured line through a survey area from which triangulations are made. **2** a line at each end of a tennis court that marks the limit of play.

basement ('beɪsmənt) *n* **1a** a partly or wholly underground storey of a building, esp. one used for habitation rather than storage. **1b** (*as modifier*): *a basement flat.* **2** the foundation of a wall or building.

base metal *n* any of certain common metals, such as copper and lead, as distinct from precious metals.

basenji (bə'sendʒɪ) *n* a small African breed of dog that is unable to bark. [C20: from Bantu]

base rate *n* **1** *Brit.* the rate of interest used by individual commercial banks as a basis for their lending rates. **2** *Brit. inf.* the rate at which the Bank of England lends to the discount houses, which effectively controls the interest rates charged throughout the banking system. **3** *Statistics.* the average number of times an event occurs divided by the average number of times on which it might occur.

bases[1] ('beɪsiːz) *n* the plural of **basis.**

bases[2] ('beɪsɪz) *n* the plural of **base.**

base unit *n Physics.* any of the fundamental units in a system of measurement. The base SI units are the metre, kilogram, second, ampere, kelvin, candela, and mole.

bash Ⓣ (bæʃ) *Inf.* ◆ *vb* **1** (*tr*) to strike violently or crushingly. **2** (*tr;* often foll. by *in, down,* etc.) to smash, break, etc., with a crashing blow. **3** (*intr;* foll. by *into*) to crash (into); collide (with). **4** to dent or be dented. ◆ *n* **5** a heavy blow. **6** a party. **7 have a bash.** *Inf.* to make an attempt. [C17: from ?]

bashful Ⓣ ('bæʃful) *adj* **1** shy or modest; diffident. **2** indicating or characterized by shyness or modesty. [C16: from *bash,* short for ABASH + -FUL]
▸'**bashfully** *adv* ▸'**bashfulness** *n*

-bashing *n and adj combining form. Inf. or sl.* **a** indicating a malicious attack on members of a particular group: *union-bashing.* **b** indicating any of various other activities: *Bible-bashing.*
▸**-basher** *n combining form.*

basho ('bæʃəʊ) *n, pl* **basho.** a grand tournament in sumo wrestling. [C20: from Japanese, lit.: place]

basic Ⓣ ('beɪsɪk) *adj* **1** of, relating to, or forming a base or basis; fundamental. **2** elementary or simple: *a few basic facts.* **3** excluding additions or extras: *basic pay.* **4** *Chem.* of, denoting, or containing a base; alkaline. **5** *Metallurgy.* of or made by a process in which the furnace or converter is made of a basic material, such as magnesium oxide. **6** (of such igneous rocks as basalt) containing between 52 and 45 per cent silica. ◆ *n* **7** (*usually pl*) a fundamental principle, fact, etc.
▸'**basically** *adv*

BASIC *or* **Basic** ('beɪsɪk) *n* a computer programming language that uses common English terms. [C20: *b(eginner's) a(ll-purpose) s(ymbolic) i(nstruction) c(ode)*]

Basic Curriculum *n Brit. education.* the National Curriculum plus religious education.

basic English *n* a simplified form of English with a vocabulary of approximately 850 common words, intended as an international language.

basic industry *n* an industry which is highly important in a nation's economy.

basicity (beɪ'sɪsɪtɪ) *n Chem.* **a** the state of being a base. **b** the number of molecules of acid required to neutralize one molecule of a given base.

basic slag *n* a slag produced in steel-making, containing calcium phosphate.

basic wage *n* **1** a person's wage excluding overtime, bonuses, etc. **2** *Austral.* the statutory minimum wage for any worker.

basidiomycete (bæˌsɪdɪəʊmaɪ'siːt) *n* any of a class of fungi, including puffballs and rusts, which produce spores at the tips of slender projecting stalks. [C19: see BASIS, -MYCETE]
▸**baˌsidiomy'cetous** *adj*

basil ('bæz°l) *n* a Eurasian plant having spikes of small white flowers and aromatic leaves used as herbs for seasoning. Also called: **sweet basil.** [C15: from OF *basile,* from LL, from Gk *basilikos* royal]

basilar ('bæsɪlə) *adj Chiefly anat.* of or at a base. Also: **basilary** ('bæsɪlərɪ, -sɪlrɪ). [C16: from NL *basilaris*]

basilica (bə'zɪlɪkə) *n* **1** a Roman building, used for public administration, having a large rectangular central nave with an aisle on each side and an apse at the end. **2** a Christian church of similar design. **3** a Roman Catholic church having special ceremonial rights. [C16: from L, from Gk, from *basilikē oikia* the king's house]
▸**ba'silican** *or* **ba'silic** *adj*

basilisk ('bæzɪˌlɪsk) *n* **1** (in classical legend) a serpent that could kill by its breath or glance. **2** a small semiaquatic lizard of tropical America. The males have an inflatable head crest, used in display. [C14: from L *basiliscus,* from Gk *basiliskos* royal child]

basin ('beɪs°n) *n* **1** a round container open and wide at the top with sides sloping inwards towards the bottom. **2** Also called: **basinful.** the amount a basin will hold. **3** a washbasin or sink. **4** any partially enclosed or sheltered area where vessels may be moored. **5** the catchment area of a particular river and its tributaries. **6** a depression in the earth's surface. **7** *Geol.* a part of the earth's surface consisting of rock strata that slope down to a common centre. [C13: from OF *bacin,* from LL *bacchīnon*]

basis Ⓣ ('beɪsɪs) *n, pl* **bases** (-siːz). **1** something that underlies, supports, or is essential to something else, esp. an idea. **2** a principle on which something depends or from which something has issued. [C14: via L from Gk: step]

bask Ⓣ (bɑːsk) *vb* (*intr;* usually foll. by *in*) **1** to lie in or be exposed to pleasant warmth, esp. that of the sun. **2** to flourish or feel secure under some benevolent influence or favourable condition. [C14: from ON *bathask* to BATHE]

basket ('bɑːskɪt) *n* **1** a container made of interwoven strips of pliable materials, such as cane, and often carried by a handle. **2** Also called: **basketful.** the amount a basket will hold. **3** something resembling such a container, such as the structure suspended from a balloon. **4** *Basketball.* **4a** the hoop fixed to the backboard, through which a player must throw the ball to score points. **4b** a point or points scored in this way. **5** a group of similar or related things: *a basket of currencies.* **6** *Inf.* a euphemism for **bastard** (senses 1–3). [C13: prob. from OF *baskot* (unattested), from L *bascauda* wickerwork holder]

basketball ('bɑːskɪtˌbɔːl) *n* **1** a game played by two teams of five men (or six women), usually on an indoor court. Points are scored by throwing the ball through an elevated horizontal hoop. **2** the ball used in this game.

basket case *n Sl.* **1** *Chiefly US & Canad.* a person who has had both arms and both legs amputated. **2** a person who is suffering from extreme nervous strain; nervous wreck. **3a** someone or something that is incapable of functioning effectively. **3b** (*as modifier*): *a basket-case economy.*

basket chair *n* a chair made of wickerwork.

basketry ('bɑːskɪtrɪ) *n* **1** the art or practice of making baskets. **2** baskets collectively.

basket weave *n* a weave of yarns, resembling that of a basket.

THESAURUS

Antonyms *n* ≠ **bottom:** apex, crest, crown, peak, summit, top, vertex

base[2] *adj* **1** = **dishonourable,** abject, contemptible, corrupt, depraved, despicable, disreputable, evil, ignoble, immoral, infamous, scandalous, shameful, sordid, vile, villainous, vulgar, wicked **2** = **inferior,** downtrodden, grovelling, low, lowly, mean, menial, miserable, paltry, pitiful, poor, servile, slavish, sorry, subservient, worthless, wretched **3** = **counterfeit,** adulterated, alloyed, debased, fake, forged, fraudulent, impure, pinchbeck, spurious
Antonyms *adj* ≠ **dishonourable:** admirable, good, honest, honourable, just, moral, noble, pure, rare, righteous, upright, valuable, virtuous ≠ **inferior:** lofty, noble ≠ **counterfeit:** pure, unalloyed

baseless *adj* = **unfounded,** groundless, unconfirmed, uncorroborated, ungrounded, unjustifiable, unjustified, unsubstantiated, unsupported
Antonyms *adj* authenticated, confirmed, corroborated, proven, substantiated, supported, validated, verified, well-founded

baseness *n* **1** = **depravity,** contemptibility, degradation, depravation, despicability, disgrace, ignominy, infamy, notoriety, obloquy, turpitude **2** = **inferiority,** lowliness, meanness, misery, poverty, servility, slavishness, subservience, worthlessness, wretchedness

bash *Informal vb* **1-3** = **hit,** belt, biff (*sl.*), break, chin (*sl.*), crash, crush, deck (*sl.*), punch, slosh (*Brit. sl.*), smash, sock (*sl.*), strike, wallop (*inf.*) ◆ *n* **7** = **attempt,** crack (*inf.*), go (*inf.*), shot (*inf.*), stab (*inf.*), try

bashful *adj* **1, 2** = **shy,** abashed, blushing, confused, constrained, coy, diffident, easily embarrassed, nervous, overmodest, reserved, reticent, retiring, self-conscious, self-effacing, shamefaced, sheepish, shrinking, timid, timorous
Antonyms *adj* aggressive, arrogant, bold, brash, conceited, confident, egoistic, fearless, forward, immodest, impudent, intrepid, pushy (*inf.*), self-assured

bashfulness *n* **1, 2** = **shyness,** constraint, coyness, diffidence, embarrassment, hesitation, modesty, reserve, self-consciousness, sheepishness, timidity, timorousness

basic *adj* **1** = **essential,** bog-standard (*inf.*), central, fundamental, immanent, indispensable, inherent, intrinsic, key, necessary, primary, radical, underlying, vital ◆ *n* **7** *usually plural* = **essentials,** brass tacks (*inf.*), core, facts, funda-m entals, hard facts, necessaries, nitty-gritty (*inf.*), nuts and bolts (*inf.*), practicalities, principles, rudiments
Antonyms *adj* ≠ **essential:** complementary, minor, peripheral, secondary, supplementary, supporting, trivial, unessential

basically *adv* **1** = **essentially,** at bottom, at heart, *au fond,* firstly, fundamentally, inherently, in substance, intrinsically, mostly, primarily, radically

basis *n* **1** = **foundation,** base, bottom, footing, ground, groundwork, support **2** = **principle,** chief ingredient, core, essential, fundamental, heart, premise, principal element, theory

bask *vb* **1** = **lie in,** laze, loll, lounge, relax, sunbathe, swim in, toast oneself, warm oneself **2** = **enjoy,** delight in, indulge oneself, luxuriate, relish, revel, savour, take pleasure, wallow

basketwork ('bɑːskɪtˌwɜːk) *n* another word for **wickerwork.**
basking shark *n* a very large plankton-eating shark, often floating at the sea surface.
basmati rice (bəz'mætɪ) *n* a variety of long-grain rice with slender aromatic grains, used for savoury dishes. [from Hindi, lit.: aromatic]
basophil ('beɪsəfɪl) *or* **basophile** *adj also* **basophilic** (ˌbeɪsə'fɪlɪk). **1** (of cells or cell contents) easily stained by basic dyes. ◆ *n* **2** a basophil cell, esp. a leucocyte. [C19: from Gk; see BASIS, -PHILE]
basque (bæsk) *n* a type of tight-fitting bodice for women. [from F, from BASQUE]
Basque (bæsk, bɑːsk) *n* **1** a member of a people living around the W Pyrenees in France and Spain. **2** the language of this people, of no known relationship with any other language. ◆ *adj* **3** of or relating to this people or their language. [C19: from F, from L *Vascō* a Basque]
bas-relief (ˌbɑːrɪ'liːf, 'bæsrɪˌliːf) *n* sculpture in low relief, in which the forms project slightly from the background. [C17: from F, from It. *basso rilievo* low relief]
bass[1] ❶ (beɪs) *n* **1** the lowest adult male voice. **2** a singer with such a voice. **3 the bass.** the lowest part in a piece of harmony. **4** *Inf.* short for **bass guitar, double bass. 5a** the low-frequency component of an electrical audio signal, esp. in a record player or tape recorder. **5b** the knob controlling this. ◆ *adj* **6** relating to or denoting the bass. [C15 *bas* BASE[1]; modern spelling infl. by BASSO]
bass[2] (bæs) *n* **1** any of various sea perches. **2** a European spiny-finned freshwater fish. **3** any of various predatory North American freshwater fishes. [C15: from BASE[2], infl. by It. *basso* low]
bass clef (beɪs) *n* the clef that establishes F a fifth below middle C on the fourth line of the staff.
bass drum (beɪs) *n* a large drum of low pitch.
basset ('bæsɪt) *n* a smooth-haired breed of hound with short legs and long ears. Also: **basset hound.** [C17: from F, from *basset* short, from *bas* low]
basset horn *n* an obsolete woodwind instrument. [C19: prob. from G *Bassetthorn,* from It. *bassetto,* dim. of BASSO + HORN]
bass guitar (beɪs) *n* a guitar that has the same pitch and tuning as a double bass, usually electrically amplified.
bassinet (ˌbæsɪ'nɛt) *n* a wickerwork or wooden cradle or pram, usually hooded. [C19: from F: little basin; associated in folk etymology with F *barcelonnette* a little cradle]
bassist ('beɪsɪst) *n* a player of a double bass or bass guitar.
basso ('bæsəʊ) *n, pl* **bassos** *or* **bassi** (-sɪ). (esp. in operatic or solo singing) a singer with a bass voice. [C19: from It., from LL *bassus* low; see BASE[1]]
bassoon (bə'suːn) *n* **1** a woodwind instrument, the tenor of the oboe family. **2** an orchestral musician who plays a bassoon. [C18: from F *basson,* from It., from *basso* deep]
▸**bas'soonist** *n*
basso rilievo (*Italian* 'basso ri'ljɛːvo) *n, pl* **basso rilievos.** Italian name for **bas-relief.**
bass viol (beɪs) *n* **1** another name for **viola da gamba. 2** *US.* a less common name for **double bass** (sense 1).
bast (bæst) *n* **1** *Bot.* another name for **phloem. 2** fibrous material obtained from the phloem of jute, flax, etc., used for making rope, matting, etc. [OE *bæst*]
bastard ❶ ('bɑːstəd, 'bæs-) *n* **1** *Inf., offens.* an obnoxious or despicable person. **2** *Inf.* a person, esp. a man: *lucky bastard.* **3** *Inf.* something extremely difficult or unpleasant. **4** *Arch. or offens.* a person born of parents not married to each other. **5** something irregular, abnormal, or inferior. **6** a hybrid, esp. an accidental or inferior one. ◆ *adj* (*prenominal*) **7** *Arch. or offens.* illegitimate by birth. **8** irregular, abnormal, or inferior. **9** resembling a specified thing, but not actually being such: *a bastard cedar.* **10** counterfeit; spurious. **11** hybrid. [C13: from OF *bastart,* ?from *fils de bast* son of the packsaddle]
▸'**bastardy** *n*
bastardize ❶ *or* **bastardise** ('bɑːstəˌdaɪz, 'bæs-) *vb* **bastardizes, bastardizing, bastardized** *or* **bastardises, bastardising, bastardised.** (*tr*) **1** to debase. **2** *Arch.* to declare illegitimate.
baste[1] (beɪst) *vb* **bastes, basting, basted.** (*tr*) to sew with loose temporary stitches. [C14: from OF *bastir* to build, of Gmc origin]
▸'**basting** *n*
baste[2] (beɪst) *vb* **bastes, basting, basted.** (*tr*) to moisten (meat) during cooking with hot fat and the juices produced. [C15: from ?]
baste[3] (beɪst) *vb* **bastes, basting, basted.** (*tr*) to beat thoroughly; thrash. [C16: prob. from ON *beysta*]
Bastille (bæ'stiːl) *n* a fortress in Paris: a prison until its destruction in 1789, at the beginning of the French Revolution. [C14: from OF *bastile* fortress, from OProvençal *bastida,* from *bastir* to build]
bastinado (ˌbæstɪ'neɪdəʊ) *n, pl* **bastinadoes. 1** punishment or torture in which the soles of the feet are beaten with a stick. ◆ *vb* **bastinadoes, bastinadoing, bastinadoed. 2** (*tr*) to beat (a person) thus. [C16: from Sp. *bastonada,* from *baston* stick]
bastion ❶ ('bæstɪən) *n* **1** a projecting part of a fortification, designed to permit fire to the flanks along the the face of the wall. **2** any fortified place. **3** a thing or person regarded as defending a principle, etc. [C16: from F, from earlier *bastillon* bastion, from *bastille* BASTILLE]
bat[1] ❶ (bæt) *n* **1** any of various types of club with a handle, used to hit the ball in certain sports, such as cricket. **2** a flat round club with a short handle used by a man on the ground to guide the pilot of an aircraft when taxiing. **3** *Cricket.* short for **batsman. 4** *Inf.* a blow from a stick. **5** *Sl.* speed; pace: *they went at a fair bat.* **6 carry one's bat.** *Cricket.* (of an opening batsman) to reach the end of an innings without being dismissed. **7 off one's own bat. 7a** of one's own accord. **7b** by one's own unaided efforts. ◆ *vb* **bats, batting, batted. 8** (*tr*) to strike with or as if with a bat. **9** (*intr*) *Cricket, etc.* (of a player or a team) to take a turn at batting. [OE *batt* club, prob. of Celtic origin]
bat[2] (bæt) *n* **1** a nocturnal mouselike animal flying with a pair of membranous wings. **2** *Sl.* an irritating or eccentric woman. **3 blind as a bat.** having extremely poor eyesight. **4 have bats in the** (*or* **one's**) **belfry.** *Inf.* to be mad or eccentric. [C14 *bakke,* prob. of Scand. origin]
bat[3] (bæt) *vb* **bats, batting, batted.** (*tr*) **1** to wink or flutter (one's eyelids). **2 not bat an eye** (*or* **eyelid**). *Inf.* to show no surprise or concern. [C17: prob. var. of BATE[2]]
batch[1] ❶ (bætʃ) *n* **1** a group or set of usually similar objects or people, esp. if sent off, handled, or arriving at the same time. **2** the bread, cakes, etc., produced at one baking. **3** the amount of a material needed for an operation. ◆ *vb* **4** to group (items) for efficient processing. **5** to handle by batch processing. [C15 *bache;* rel. to OE *bacan* to BAKE]
batch[2] *or* **bach** (bætʃ) *vb* (*intr*) *Austral. & NZ inf.* (of a man) to do his own cooking and housekeeping.
batch processing *n* a system by which the computer programs of a number of individual users are submitted as a single batch.
bate[1] (beɪt) *vb* **bates, bating, bated. 1** another word for **abate. 2 with bated breath.** in suspense or fear.
bate[2] (beɪt) *vb* **bates, bating, bated.** (*intr*) (of a hawk) to jump violently from a perch or the falconer's fist, often hanging from the leash while struggling to escape. [C13: from OF *batre* to beat]
bate[3] (beɪt) *n Brit. Sl.* a bad temper or rage. [C19: from BAIT[1], alluding to the mood of a person who is being baited]
bateau (bæ'təʊ) *n, pl* **bateaux** (-'təʊz). a light flat-bottomed boat used on rivers in Canada and the northern US. [C18: from F: boat]
bateleur eagle ('bætəlɜː) *n* an African short-tailed bird of prey. [C19: from F *bateleur* juggler]
bath ❶ (bɑːθ) *n, pl* **baths** (bɑːðz). **1** a large container used for washing the body. **2** the act or an instance of washing in such a container. **3** the amount of liquid contained in a bath. **4** (*usually pl*) a place having baths or a swimming pool for public use. **5a** a vessel in which something is immersed to maintain it at a constant temperature, to process it photographically, etc., or to lubricate it. **5b** the liquid used in such a vessel. ◆ *vb* **6** *Brit.* to wash in a bath. [OE *bæth*]
Bath bun (bɑːθ) *n Brit.* a sweet bun containing spices and dried fruit. [C19: from *Bath,* city in England where orig. made]
Bath chair *n* a wheelchair for invalids.
bath cube *n* a cube of soluble scented material for use in a bath.
bathe ❶ (beɪð) *vb* **bathes, bathing, bathed. 1** (*intr*) to swim in a body of open water, esp. for pleasure. **2** (*tr*) to apply liquid to (skin, a wound, etc.) in order to cleanse or soothe. **3** to immerse or be immersed in a liquid. **4** *Chiefly US & Canad.* to wash in a bath. **5** (*tr; often passive*) to suffuse. ◆ *n* **6** *Brit.* a swim in a body of open water. [OE *bathian*]
▸'**bather** *n*
bathers ('beɪðəz) *pl n Austral.* a swimming costume.
bathhouse ('bɑːθˌhaʊs) *n* a building containing baths, esp. for public use.
bathing cap ('beɪðɪŋ) *n* a tight rubber cap worn by a swimmer to keep the hair dry.
bathing costume ❶ ('beɪðɪŋ) *n* another name for **swimming costume.**
bathing machine ('beɪðɪŋ) *n* a small hut, on wheels so that it could be pulled to the sea, used in the 18th and 19th centuries for bathers to change their clothes.
bathing suit ('beɪðɪŋ) *n* a garment worn for bathing, esp. an old-fashioned one that covers much of the body.
batho- *combining form.* a variant of **bathy-.**
batholith (ˌbæθəlɪθ) *or* **batholite** ('bæθəˌlaɪt) *n* a very large irregular-shaped mass of igneous rock, esp. granite, formed from an intrusion of magma at great depth, esp. one exposed after erosion of less resistant overlying rocks.
▸ˌ**batho'lithic** *or* **batholitic** (ˌbæθə'lɪtɪk) *adj*

THESAURUS

bass[1] *adj* **6** = **deep**, deep-toned, grave, low, low-pitched, resonant, sonorous
bastard *n* **1** *Informal, offensive* = **rogue**, blackguard, criminal, evildoer, knave (*arch.*), libertine, malefactor, miscreant, profligate, rapscallion, reprobate, scoundrel, villain, wretch **4** *Archaic or offensive* = **illegitimate child**, by-blow (*arch.*), love child, natural child ◆ *adj* **7** *Archaic or offensive* = **illegitimate**, baseborn, misbegotten **10** = **false**, adulterated, counterfeit, illegitimate, imperfect, impure, inferior, irregular, sham, spurious
bastardize *vb* **1** = **corrupt**, adulterate, cheapen, debase, defile, degrade, demean, devalue, distort, pervert
bastion *n* **1, 2** = **stronghold**, bulwark, citadel, defence, fastness, fortress **3** = **mainstay**, prop, rock, support, tower of strength
bat[1] *vb* **8** = **hit**, bang, punch, rap, smack, strike, swat, thump, wallop (*inf.*), whack
batch[1] *n* **1** = **group**, accumulation, aggregation, amount, assemblage, bunch, collection, crowd, lot, pack, quantity, set
bath *n* **2** = **wash**, ablution, cleansing, douche, douse, scrubbing, shower, soak, soaping, sponging, tub, washing ◆ *vb* **6** = **wash**, bathe, clean, douse, scrub down, shower, soak, soap, sponge, tub
bathe *vb* **1** = **swim 2, 4** = **wash**, cleanse, rinse **3** = **cover**, flood, immerse, steep, suffuse ◆ *n* **6** *Brit.* = **swim**, dip, dook (*Scot.*)
bathing costume *n* = **swimming costume**, bathing suit, bikini, swimsuit, trunks

Bath Oliver ('ɒlɪvə) *n Brit.* a kind of unsweetened biscuit [C19: after William *Oliver* (1695–1764), a physician at Bath]

bathometer (bə'θɒmɪtə) *n* an instrument for measuring the depth of water.
▸**bathometric** (ˌbæθə'mɛtrɪk) *adj* ▸**ba'thometry** *n*

bathos Ⓣ ('beɪθɒs) *n* **1** a sudden ludicrous descent from exalted to ordinary matters or style in speech or writing. **2** insincere or excessive pathos. [C18: from Gk: depth]
▸**ba'thetic** *adj*

bathrobe ('bɑːθˌrəʊb) *n* **1** a loose-fitting garment of towelling, for wear before or after a bath or swimming. **2** *US & Canad.* a dressing gown.

bathroom Ⓣ ('bɑːθˌruːm, -ˌrʊm) *n* **1** a room containing a bath or shower and usually a washbasin and lavatory. **2** *US & Canad.* another name for **lavatory**.

bath salts *pl n* soluble scented salts for use in a bath.

bathtub ('bɑːθˌtʌb) *n* a bath, esp. one not permanently fixed.

bathy- *or* **batho-** *combining form.* indicating depth: *bathysphere.* [from Gk *bathus* deep]

bathyscaph ('bæθɪˌskæf), **bathyscaphe** ('bæθɪˌskeɪf, -ˌskæf), *or* **bathyscape** ('bæθɪˌskæp) *n* a submersible vessel with an observation capsule underneath, capable of reaching ocean depths of over 10 000 metres. [C20: from BATHY- + Gk *skaphē* light boat]

bathysphere ('bæθɪˌsfɪə) *n* a strong steel deep-sea diving sphere, lowered by cable.

batik ('bætɪk) *n* **a** a process of printing fabric in which parts not to be dyed are covered by wax. **b** fabric printed in this way. [C19: via Malay from Javanese: painted]

batiste (bæ'tiːst) *n* a fine plain-weave cotton. [C17: from F, prob. after *Baptiste* of Cambrai, 13th-cent. F weaver, its reputed inventor]

batman ('bætmən) *n, pl* **batmen.** an officer's servant in the armed forces. [C18: from OF *bat, bast,* from Med. L *bastum* packsaddle]

baton Ⓣ ('bætən) *n* **1** a thin stick used by the conductor of an orchestra, choir, etc. **2** *Athletics.* a short bar carried by a competitor in a relay race and transferred to the next runner at the end of each stage. **3** a long stick with a knob on one end, carried, twirled, and thrown up and down by a drum major or majorette, esp. at the head of a parade. **4** a police truncheon (esp. in **baton charge**). **5** a staff or club carried as a symbol of authority. [C16: from F *bâton,* from LL *bastum* rod]

baton round *n* the official name for **plastic bullet.**

batrachian (bə'treɪkɪən) *n* **1** any amphibian, esp. a frog or toad. ◆ *adj* **2** of or relating to the frogs and toads. [C19: from NL *Batrachia,* from Gk *batrakhos* frog]

bats (bæts) *adj Inf.* mad or eccentric.

batsman ('bætsmən) *n, pl* **batsmen. 1** *Cricket, etc.* **1a** a person who bats or whose turn it is to bat. **1b** a player who specializes in batting. **2** a person on the ground who uses bats to guide the pilot of an aircraft when taxiing.

battalion Ⓣ (bə'tæljən) *n* **1** a military unit comprised of three or more companies or formations of similar size. **2** (*usually pl*) any large array. [C16: from F *bataillon,* from OIt., from *battaglia* company of soldiers, BATTLE]

batten[1] Ⓣ ('bætᵊn) *n* **1** a sawn strip of wood used in building to cover joints, support lathing, etc. **2** a long narrow board used for flooring. **3** a lath used for holding a tarpaulin along the side of a hatch on a ship. **4** *Theatre.* **4a** a row of lights. **4b** the bar supporting them. ◆ *vb* **5** (*tr*) to furnish or strengthen with battens. **6 batten down the hatches. 6a** to use battens in securing a tarpaulin over a hatch on a ship. **6b** to prepare for action, a crisis, etc. [C15: from F *bâton* stick; see BATON]

batten[2] Ⓣ ('bætᵊn) *vb* (*intr*) (usually foll. by *on*) to thrive, esp. at the expense of someone else. [C16: prob. from ON *batna* to improve]

batter[1] Ⓣ ('bætə) *vb* **1** to hit (someone or something) repeatedly using heavy blows, as with a club. **2** (*tr; often passive*) to damage or injure, as by blows, heavy wear, etc. **3** (*tr*) to subject (a person, esp. a close relative) to repeated physical violence. [C14: *bateren,* prob. from *batten* to BAT[1]]
▸**'batterer** *n* ▸**'battering** *n*

batter[2] ('bætə) *n* a mixture of flour, eggs, and milk, used to make cakes, pancakes, etc., and to coat certain foods before frying. [C15 *bater,* prob. from *bateren* to BATTER[1]]

batter[3] ('bætə) *n Baseball, etc.* a player who bats.

batter[4] ('bætə) *n* **1** the slope of the face of a wall that recedes gradually backwards and upwards. ◆ *vb* **2** (*intr*) to have such a slope. [C16 (vb: to incline): from ?]

battered[1] Ⓣ ('bætəd) *adj* subjected to persistent physical violence, esp. by a close relative living in the house: *a battered baby.*

battered[2] ('bætəd) *adj* coated in batter: *battered cod.*

battering ram *n* (esp. formerly) a large beam used to break down fortifications.

battery Ⓣ ('bætərɪ) *n, pl* **batteries. 1** two or more primary cells connected, usually in series, to provide a source of electric current. **2** another name for **accumulator** (sense 1). **3** a number of similar things occurring together: *a battery of questions.* **4** *Criminal law.* unlawful beating or wounding of a person or mere touching in a hostile or offensive manner. **5** a fortified structure on which artillery is mounted. **6** a group of guns, missile launchers, etc, operated as a single entity. **7** a small unit of artillery. **8** *Chiefly Brit.* **8a** a large group of cages for intensive rearing of poultry and other farm animals. **8b** (*as modifier*): *battery hens.* **9** *Baseball.* the pitcher and the catcher considered together. [C16: from OF *batterie* beating, from *battre* to beat, from L *battuere*]

batting ('bætɪŋ) *n* **1** cotton or woollen wadding used in quilts, etc. **2** the action of a person or team that hits with a bat.

battle Ⓣ ('bætᵊl) *n* **1** a fight between large armed forces; military or naval engagement. **2** conflict; struggle. **3 do, give,** *or* **join battle.** to engage in conflict or competition. ◆ *vb* **battles, battling, battled. 4** (when *intr,* often foll. by *against, for,* or *with*) to fight in or as if in military combat; contend (with): *shop stewards battling to improve conditions at work.* **5** to struggle: *he battled through the crowd.* **6** (*intr*) *Austral.* to scrape a living. [C13: from OF *bataile,* from LL *battālia* exercises performed by soldiers, from *battuere* to beat]
▸**'battler** *n*

battle-axe Ⓣ *n* **1** (formerly) a large broad-headed axe. **2** *Inf.* an argumentative domineering woman.

battle-axe block *n Austral.* a block of land behind another, with access from the street through a narrow drive.

battle cruiser *n* a high-speed warship of battleship size but with lighter armour.

battle cry Ⓣ *n* **1** a shout uttered by soldiers going into battle. **2** a slogan used to rally the supporters of a campaign, movement, etc.

battledore ('bætᵊlˌdɔː) *n* **1** Also called: **battledore and shuttlecock.** an ancient racket game. **2** a light racket used in this game. **3** (formerly) a wooden utensil used for beating clothes, in baking, etc. [C15 *batyldoure,* ?from OProvençal *batedor* beater, from OF *battre* to beat]

battledress ('bætᵊlˌdrɛs) *n* the ordinary uniform of a soldier.

battle fatigue *n Psychol.* mental disorder, characterized by anxiety and depression, caused by the stress of warfare. Also: **combat fatigue.**

battlefield Ⓣ ('bætᵊlˌfiːld) *or* **battleground** ('bætᵊlˌgraʊnd) *n* the place where a battle is fought.

battlement Ⓣ ('bætᵊlmənt) *n* a parapet or wall with indentations or embrasures, originally for shooting through. [C14: from OF *batailles,* pl. of *bataille* BATTLE]
▸**'battlemented** *adj*

battle royal *n* **1** a fight, esp. with fists or cudgels, involving more than two combatants; melee. **2** a long violent argument.

battleship Ⓣ ('bætᵊlˌʃɪp) *n* a heavily armoured warship of the largest type.

batty Ⓣ ('bætɪ) *adj* **battier, battiest.** *Sl.* **1** insane; crazy. **2** odd; eccentric. [C20: from BAT[2]]

batwoman ('bætwʊmən) *n, pl* **batwomen.** a female servant in any of the armed forces.

bauble Ⓣ ('bɔːbᵊl) *n* **1** a trinket of little value. **2** (formerly) a mock staff of office carried by a jester. [C14: from OF *baubel* plaything, from ?]

baud (bɔːd) *n* a unit used to measure the speed of electronic code transmissions. [after J. M. E. *Baudot* (1845-1903), F inventor]

bauera ('baʊərə) *n* a small evergreen Australian shrub with pink or pur-

THESAURUS

bathos *n* = **anticlimax**, letdown **2** = **mawkishness**, false pathos, sentimentality

bathroom *n* **1, 2** = **lavatory**, comfort station (*US*), convenience (*chiefly Brit.*), powder room, rest room, shower, toilet, washroom, water closet, WC

baton *n* **4** = **truncheon**, club **5** = **stick**, crook, mace, rod, sceptre, staff, wand

battalion *n* **1** = **army**, brigade, company, contingent, division, force, legion, regiment, squadron, team, troop **2** = **multitude**, horde, host, throng

batten[1] *vb* **6a batten down** = **fasten**, board up, clamp down, cover up, fasten down, fix, nail down, secure, tighten

batten[2] *vb, usually with* **on** = **thrive**, fatten, flourish, gain, grow, increase, prosper

batter[1] *vb* **1, 3** = **beat**, assault, bash (*inf.*), beat the living daylights out of, belabour, break, buffet, clobber (*sl.*), dash against, lambast(e), lash, pelt, pound, pummel, smash, smite, thrash, wallop (*inf.*) **2** = **damage**, bruise, crush, deface, demolish, destroy, disfigure, hurt, injure, mangle, mar, maul, ruin, shatter, shiver, total (*sl.*), trash (*sl.*)

battered[1] *adj* = **beaten**, beat-up (*inf.*), black-and-blue, bruised, injured

battery *n* **3** = **series**, chain, ring, sequence, set, suite **4** *Criminal law* = **beating**, assault, attack, mayhem, onslaught, physical violence, thumping **6, 7** = **artillery**, cannon, cannonry, guns

battle *n* **1** = **fight**, action, attack, combat, encounter, engagement, fray, hostilities, skirmish, war, warfare **2** = **conflict**, agitation, campaign, clash, contest, controversy, crusade, debate, disagreement, dispute, head-to-head, strife, struggle ◆ *vb* **4** = **struggle**, agitate, argue, clamour, combat, contend, contest, dispute, feud, fight, lock horns, strive, war
Antonyms *n* ≠ **fight, conflict:** accord, agreement, armistice, ceasefire, concord, entente, peace, suspension of hostilities, truce

battle-axe *n* **2** *Informal* = **harridan**, ballbreaker (*sl.*), disciplinarian, fury, scold, shrew, tartar, termagant, virago, vixen

battle cry *n* **1** = **war cry**, war whoop **2** = **slogan**, catchword, motto, watchword

battlefield *n* = **battleground**, combat zone, field, field of battle, front

battlement *n* = **rampart**, barbican, bartizan, bastion, breastwork, bulwark, crenellation, fortification, parapet

battleship *n* = **warship**, capital ship, gunboat, man-of-war, ship of the line

batty *adj* **1** = **crazy**, barmy (*sl.*), bats (*sl.*), bonkers, crackers (*Brit. sl.*), daft (*inf.*), insane, loony (*sl.*), loopy (*inf.*), lunatic, mad, nuts (*sl.*), off one's rocker (*sl.*), off one's trolley (*sl.*), out of one's mind, potty (*Brit. inf.*), round the twist (*Brit. sl.*), touched **2** = **eccentric**, crackpot (*inf.*), cranky (*inf.*), dotty (*sl., chiefly Brit.*), odd, oddball (*inf.*), off the rails, off-the-wall (*sl.*), outré, peculiar, queer (*inf.*)

bauble *n* **1** = **trinket**, bagatelle, gewgaw, gimple flowers. [C19: after Franz & Ferdinand *Bauer*, 19th-cent. Austrian botanical artists]

Bauhaus ('bau,haus) *n* a German school of functionalist architecture and applied arts founded in 1919. [G, lit.: building house]

bauhinia (bɔː'hɪnɪə, bəu-) *n* a climbing leguminous plant of tropical and warm regions, cultivated for ornament. [C18: NL, after Jean & Gaspard *Bauhin*, 16th-cent. F herbalists]

baulk (bɔːk; *usually for sense 1* bɔːlk) *n* **1** Also: **balk.** *Billiards.* the space between the baulk line and the bottom cushion. **2** *Archaeol.* a strip of earth left between excavation trenches for the study of the complete stratigraphy of a site. ◆ *vb, n* **3** a variant spelling of **balk.**

baulk line *or* **balk line** *n Billiards.* a straight line across a billiard table behind which the cue balls are placed at the start of a game. Also: **string line.**

baulky ('bɔːkɪ, 'bɔːlkɪ) *adj* a variant of **balky.**

bauxite ('bɔːksaɪt) *n* an amorphous claylike substance consisting of hydrated alumina with iron and other impurities: the chief source of alumina and aluminium and also used as an abrasive and catalyst. [C19: from F, from *(Les) Baux* in southern France, where orig. found]

bawd Ⓣ (bɔːd) *n Arch.* **1** a person who runs a brothel, esp. a woman. **2** a prostitute. [C14: from OF *baude,* fem. of *baud* merry]

bawdy Ⓣ ('bɔːdɪ) *adj* **bawdier, bawdiest. 1** (of language, plays, etc.) containing references to sex, esp. to be humorous. ◆ *n* **2** obscenity or eroticism, esp. in writing or drama.
▸ **'bawdily** *adv* ▸ **'bawdiness** *n* ▸ **bawdry** ('bɔːdrɪ) *n*

bawdyhouse ('bɔːdɪ,haus) *n* an archaic word for **brothel.**

bawl Ⓣ (bɔːl) *vb* **1** (*intr*) to utter long loud cries, as from pain or frustration; wail. **2** to shout loudly, as in anger. ◆ *n* **3** a loud shout or cry. [C15: imit.]
▸ **'bawler** *n* ▸ **'bawling** *n*

bawl out *vb* (*tr, adv*) *Inf.* to scold loudly.

bay[1] Ⓣ (beɪ) *n* **1** a wide semicircular indentation of a shoreline, esp. between two headlands. **2** an extension of lowland into hills that partly surround it. [C14: from OF *baie,* ?from OF *baer* to gape, from Med. L *batāre* to yawn]

bay[2] Ⓣ (beɪ) *n* **1** an alcove or recess in a wall. **2** any partly enclosed compartment. **3** See **bay window. 4** an area off a road in which vehicles may park or unload. **5** a compartment in an aircraft: *the bomb bay.* **6** *Naut.* a compartment in the forward part of a ship between decks, often used as the ship's hospital. **7** *Brit.* a tracked recess in the platform of a railway station, esp. one forming the terminus of a branch line. [C14: from OF *baee* gap, from *baer* to gape; see BAY[1]]

bay[3] Ⓣ (beɪ) *n* **1** a deep howl, esp. of a hound on the scent. **2 at bay. 2a** forced to turn and face attackers: *the dogs held the deer at bay.* **2b** at a distance. **3 bring to bay.** to force into a position from which retreat is impossible. ◆ *vb* **4** (*intr*) to howl (at) in deep prolonged tones. **5** (*tr*) to utter in a loud prolonged tone. **6** (*tr*) to hold at bay. [C13: from OF, imit.]

bay[4] (beɪ) *n* **1** a Mediterranean laurel. See **laurel** (sense 1). **2** any of several magnolias. See **sweet bay. 3** any of certain other trees or shrubs, esp. bayberry. **4** (*pl*) a wreath of bay leaves. [C14: from OF *baie* laurel berry, from L *bāca* berry]

bay[5] (beɪ) *n, adj* **1** (of) a reddish-brown colour. ◆ *n* **2** an animal of this colour. [C14: from OF *bai,* from L *badius*]

bayberry ('beɪbərɪ) *or* **bay** *n, pl* **bayberries. 1** any of several North American aromatic shrubs or small trees that bear grey waxy berries. **2** a tropical American tree that yields an oil used in making bay rum. **3** the fruit of any of these plants.

bay leaf *n* a leaf, usually dried, of the Mediterranean laurel, used in cooking to flavour soups and stews.

bayonet Ⓣ ('beɪənɪt) *n* **1** a blade for stabbing that can be attached to the muzzle of a firearm. **2** a type of fastening in which a cylindrical member is inserted into a socket against spring pressure and turned so that pins on its side engage in slots in the socket. ◆ *vb* **bayonets, bayoneting, bayoneted** *or* **bayonets, bayonetting, bayonetted. 3** (*tr*) to stab or kill with a bayonet. [C17: from F *baïonnette,* from *Bayonne,* a port in SW France, where it originated]

bayou ('baɪuː) *n* (in the southern US) a sluggish marshy tributary of a lake or river. [C18: from Louisiana F, from Amerind *bayuk*]

bay rum *n* an aromatic liquid, used in medicines and cosmetics, originally obtained by distilling the leaves of the bayberry tree with rum: now also synthesized.

bay window *n* a window projecting from a wall and forming an alcove of a room.

bazaar Ⓣ *or* **bazar** (bə'zɑː) *n* **1** (esp. in the Orient) a market area, esp. a street of small stalls. **2** a sale in aid of charity, esp. of second-hand or handmade articles. **3** a shop where a variety of goods is sold. [C16: from Persian *bāzār*]

bazooka (bə'zuːkə) *n* a portable tubular rocket-launcher, used by infantrymen as a short-range antitank weapon. [C20: after a comic pipe instrument]

BB *abbrev. for:* **1** Boys' Brigade. **2** (on British pencils, signifying degrees of softness of lead) double black.

BBC *abbrev. for* British Broadcasting Corporation.

bbl. *abbrev. for* barrel (container or measure).

BBQ *abbrev. for* barbecue.

BC *abbrev. for* British Columbia.

B.C. *or* **BC** *abbrev. for* (indicating years numbered back from the supposed year of the birth of Christ) before Christ.

> **USAGE NOTE** See at **A.D.**

BCE *abbrev. for:* **1** Before Common Era (used, esp. by non-Christians, in numbering years B.C.). **2** *Brit.* Board of Customs and Excise.

BCG *abbrev. for* Bacillus Calmette-Guérin (antituberculosis vaccine).

BCNZ *abbrev. for* Broadcasting Corporation of New Zealand.

B complex *n* short for **vitamin B complex.**

BD *abbrev. for* Bachelor of Divinity.

bdellium ('dɛlɪəm) *n* **1** any of several African or W Asian trees that yield a gum resin. **2** the aromatic gum resin produced by any of these trees. [C16: from L, from Gk *bdellion,* ? from Heb. *bĕdhōlah*]

BDS *abbrev. for* Bachelor of Dental Surgery.

be Ⓣ (biː; *unstressed* bɪ) *vb present sing 1st person* **am;** *2nd person* **are;** *3rd person* **is.** *present pl* **are.** *past sing 1st person* **was;** *2nd person* **were;** *3rd person* **was.** *past pl* **were.** *present participle* **being.** *past participle* **been.** (*intr*) **1** to have presence in perceived reality; exist; live: *I think, therefore I am.* **2** (*used in the perfect tenses only*) to pay a visit; go: *have you been to Spain?* **3** to take place: *my birthday was last Thursday.* **4** (*copula*) used as a linking verb between the subject of a sentence and its noun or adjective complement. In this case *be* expresses relationship of equivalence or identity (*John is a man; John is a musician*) or specifies an attribute (*honey is sweet; Susan is angry*). It is also used with an adverbial complement to indicate a relationship in space or time (*Bill is at the office; the party is on Saturday*). **5** (*takes a present participle*) forms the progressive present tense: *the man is running.* **6** (*takes a past participle*) forms the passive voice of all transitive verbs: *a good film is being shown on television tonight.* **7** (*takes an infinitive*) expresses intention, expectation, or obligation: *the president is to arrive at 9.30.* [OE *bēon*]

Be *the chemical symbol for* beryllium.

BE *abbrev. for:* **1** bill of exchange. **2** Bachelor of Education. **3** Bachelor of Engineering.

be- *prefix forming transitive verbs.* **1** (*from nouns*) to surround or cover: *befog.* **2** (*from nouns*) to affect completely: *bedazzle.* **3** (*from nouns*) to consider as or cause to be: *befriend.* **4** (*from nouns*) to provide or cover with: *bejewel.* **5** (*from verbs*) at, for, against, on, or over: *bewail; berate.* [OE *be-, bi-,* unstressed var. of *bī* BY]

beach Ⓣ (biːtʃ) *n* **1** an area of sand or shingle sloping down to a sea or lake, esp. the area between the high- and low-water marks on a seacoast. ◆ *vb* **2** to run or haul (a boat) onto a beach. [C16: perhaps rel. to OE *bæce* river]

beachcomber Ⓣ ('biːtʃ,kəumə) *n* **1** a person who searches shore debris for anything of worth. **2** a long high wave rolling onto a beach.

beachhead ('biːtʃ,hɛd) *n Mil.* an area on a beach that has been captured from the enemy and on which troops and equipment are landed.

beacon Ⓣ ('biːkən) *n* **1** a signal fire or light on a hill, tower, etc., esp. formerly as a warning of invasion. **2** a hill on which such fires were lit. **3** a lighthouse, signalling buoy, etc. **4** short for **radio beacon. 5** a radio or other signal marking a flight course in air navigation. **6** short for **Belisha beacon. 7** a person or thing that serves as a guide, inspiration, or warning. [OE *beacen* sign]

bead Ⓣ (biːd) *n* **1** a small pierced usually spherical piece of glass, wood, plastic, etc., which may be strung with others to form a necklace, etc. **2 tell one's beads.** to pray with a rosary. **3** a small drop of moisture. **4** a small bubble in or on a liquid. **5** a small metallic knob acting as the sight of a firearm. **6 to draw** *or* **hold a bead on.** to aim a rifle or pistol at. **7** *Archit., furniture.* a small convex moulding having a semicircular cross

THESAURUS

crack, kickshaw, knick-knack, plaything, toy, trifle

bawd *n* **1** = **madam,** brothel-keeper, pimp, procuress **2** = **prostitute,** whore, working girl (*facetious sl.*)

bawdy *adj* **1** = **rude,** blue, coarse, dirty, indecent, indelicate, lewd, libidinous, licentious, near the knuckle (*inf.*), obscene, prurient, ribald, risqué, salacious, smutty, suggestive, vulgar, X-rated (*inf.*)
Antonyms *adj* chaste, clean, decent, good, modest, moral, respectable, seemly, undefiled, upright, virtuous

bawl *vb* **1** = **cry,** blubber, sob, squall, wail, weep **2** = **shout,** bellow, call, clamour, halloo, howl, roar, vociferate, yell

bay[1] *n* **1** = **inlet,** bight, cove, gulf, natural harbour, sound

bay[2], 2 *n* = **recess,** alcove, compartment, embrasure, niche, nook, opening

bay[3] *n* **1** = **howl,** bark, bell, clamour, cry, growl, yelp **2a at bay** = **cornered,** caught, trapped

bayonet *vb* **3** = **stab,** impale, knife, run through, spear, stick, transfix

bazaar *n* **1** = **market,** exchange, marketplace, mart **2** = **fair,** bring-and-buy, fête, sale of work

be *vb* **1** = **exist,** be alive, breathe, inhabit, live **3** = **take place,** befall, come about, come to pass, happen, occur, transpire (*inf.*)

beach *n* **1** = **shore,** coast, lido, littoral, margin, sands, seaboard, seashore, seaside, shingle, strand, water's edge

beachcomber *n* **1** = **scavenger,** forager, loafer, scrounger, tramp, vagabond, vagrant, wanderer

beached *adj* **2** = **stranded,** abandoned, aground, ashore, deserted, grounded, high and dry, marooned, wrecked

beacon *n* **1** = **signal,** beam, bonfire, flare, rocket, sign, signal fire, smoke signal **3** = **lighthouse,** pharos, watchtower

bead *n* **1** = **pellet,** blob, dot, pill, spherule **3** = **drop,** droplet, globule **4** = **bubble**

section. ◆ *vb* **8** (*tr*) to decorate with beads. **9** to form into beads or drops. [OE *bed* prayer]
▸**'beaded** *adj*

beading ('bi:dɪŋ) *n* **1** another name for **bead** (sense 7). **2** Also called: **beadwork** ('bi:d,wɜ:k). a narrow strip of some material used for edging or ornamentation.

beadle ('bi:dᵊl) *n* **1** *Brit.* (formerly) a minor parish official who acted as an usher and kept order. **2** *Judaism.* a synagogue attendant. **3** *Scot.* a church official who attends the minister. **4** an official in certain British institutions. [OE *bydel*]
▸**'beadleship** *n*

beadsman *or* **bedesman** ('bi:dzmən) *n, pl* **beadsmen** *or* **bedesmen.** *Arch.* **1** a person who prays for another's soul, esp. one paid or fed for doing so. **2** a person kept in an almshouse.

beady ➊ ('bi:dɪ) *adj* **beadier, beadiest. 1** small, round, and glittering (esp. in **beady eyes**). **2** resembling or covered with beads.
▸**'beadiness** *n*

beagle ('bi:gᵊl) *n* **1** a small sturdy breed of hound. **2** *Arch.* a spy. ◆ *vb* **beagles, beagling, beagled. 3** (*intr*) to hunt with beagles. [C15: from ?]

beak[1] ➊ (bi:k) *n* **1** the projecting jaws of a bird, covered with a horny sheath. **2** any beaklike mouthpart in other animals. **3** *Sl.* a person's nose. **4** any projecting part, such as the pouring lip of a bucket. **5** *Naut.* another word for **ram** (sense 5). [C13: from OF *bec,* from L *beccus,* of Gaulish origin]
▸**beaked** *adj* ▸**'beaky** *adj*

beak[2] (bi:k) *n* a Brit. slang word for **judge, magistrate, headmaster,** or **schoolmaster.** [C19: orig. thieves' jargon]

beaker ('bi:kə) *n* **1** a cup usually having a wide mouth. **2** a cylindrical flat-bottomed container used in laboratories, usually made of glass and having a pouring lip. [C14: from ON *bikarr*]

Beaker folk ('bi:kə) *n* a prehistoric people inhabiting Europe and Britain during the second millennium B.C. [after beakers found among their remains]

be-all and end-all *n Inf.* the ultimate aim or justification.

beam ➊ (bi:m) *n* **1** a long thick piece of wood, metal, etc., esp. one used as a horizontal structural member. **2** the breadth of a ship or boat taken at its widest part. **3** a ray or column of light, as from a beacon. **4** a broad smile. **5** one of two cylindrical rollers on a loom, which hold the warp threads and the finished work. **6** the main stem of a deer's antler. **7** the central shaft of a plough to which all the main parts are attached. **8** a narrow unidirectional flow of electromagnetic radiation or particles: *an electron beam.* **9** the horizontal centrally pivoted bar in a balance. **10 beam in one's eye.** a fault or grave error greater in oneself than in another person. **11 broad in the beam.** *Inf.* having wide hips. **12 off (the) beam. 12a** not following a radio beam to maintain a course. **12b** *Inf.* mistaken or irrelevant. **13 on the beam. 13a** following a radio beam to maintain a course. **13b** *Inf.* correct, relevant, or appropriate. ◆ *vb* **14** to send out or radiate. **15** (*tr*) to divert or aim (a radio signal, light, etc.) in a certain direction: *to beam a programme to Tokyo.* **16** (*intr*) to smile broadly. [OE]
▸**'beaming** *adj*

beam-ends *pl n* **1 on her beam-ends.** (of a vessel) heeled over through an angle of 90°. **2 on one's beam-ends.** out of resources; destitute.

bean (bi:n) *n* **1** any of various leguminous plants producing edible seeds in pods. **2** any of various other plants whose seeds are produced in pods or podlike fruits. **3** the seed or pod of any of these plants. **4** any of various beanlike seeds, as coffee. **5** *US & Canad. sl.* another word for **head. 6 full of beans.** *Inf.* full of energy and vitality. **7 not have a bean.** *Sl.* to be without money. [OE *bēan*]

beanbag ('bi:n,bæg) *n* **1** a small cloth bag filled with dried beans and thrown in games. **2** a very large cushion filled with foam rubber or polystyrene granules and used as a seat.

bean counter *n Inf.* an accountant.

bean curd *n* another name for **tofu.**

beanfeast ('bi:n,fi:st) *n Brit. inf.* **1** an annual dinner given by employers to employees. **2** any festive or merry occasion.

beano ('bi:nəʊ) *n, pl* **beanos.** *Brit. sl.* a celebration, party, or other enjoyable time.

beanpole ('bi:n,pəʊl) *n* **1** a tall stick used to support bean plants. **2** *Sl.* a tall thin person.

bean sprout *n* the sprout of a newly germinated mung bean, eaten esp. in Chinese dishes.

beanstalk ('bi:n,stɔ:k) *n* the stem of a bean plant.

bear[1] ➊ (bɛə) *vb* **bears, bearing, bore, borne.** (*mainly tr*) **1** to support or hold up. **2** to bring: *to bear gifts.* **3** to accept or assume the responsibility of: *to bear an expense.* **4** (**born** in passive use except when followed by *by*) to give birth to: *to bear children.* **5** (*also intr*) to produce as by natural growth: *to bear fruit.* **6** to tolerate or endure. **7** to admit of; sustain: *his story does not bear scrutiny.* **8** to hold in the mind: *to bear a grudge.* **9** to show or be marked with: *he still bears the scars.* **10** to render or supply (esp. in **bear witness**). **11** to conduct (oneself, the body, etc.). **12** to have, be, or stand in (relation or comparison): *his account bears no relation to the facts.* **13** (*intr*) to move or lie in a specified direction. **14 bear a hand.** to give assistance. **15 bring to bear.** to bring into operation or effect. ◆ See also **bear down, bear on,** etc. [OE *beran*]

bear[2] (bɛə) *n, pl* **bears** *or* **bear. 1** a plantigrade mammal typically having a large head, a long shaggy coat, and strong claws. **2** any of various bearlike animals, such as the koala. **3** a clumsy, churlish, or ill-mannered person. **4** a teddy bear. **5** *Stock Exchange.* **5a** a speculator who sells in anticipation of falling prices to make a profit on repurchase. **5b** (*as modifier*): *a bear market.* Cf. **bull**[1] (sense 4). ◆ *vb* **bears, bearing, beared. 6** (*tr*) to lower or attempt to lower the price or prices of (a stock market or a security) by speculative selling. [OE *bera*]

Bear (bɛə) *n* **the. 1** the English name for either Ursa Major (Great Bear) or Ursa Minor (Little Bear). **2** an informal name for Russia.

bearable ➊ ('bɛərəbᵊl) *adj* endurable; tolerable.

bear-baiting *n* (formerly) an entertainment in which dogs attacked a chained bear.

beard ➊ (bɪəd) *n* **1** the hair growing on the lower parts of a man's face. **2** any similar growth in animals. **3** a tuft of long hairs in plants such as barley; awn. **4** a barb, as on a fish-hook. ◆ *vb* (*tr*) **5** to oppose boldly or impertinently. [OE *beard*]
▸**'bearded** *adj*

beardless ➊ ('bɪədlɪs) *adj* **1** without a beard. **2** too young to grow a beard; immature.

bear down ➊ *vb* (*intr, adv;* often foll. by *on* or *upon*) **1** to press or weigh down. **2** to approach in a determined or threatening manner.

bearer ➊ ('bɛərə) *n* **1** a person or thing that bears, presents, or upholds. **2** a person who presents a note or bill for payment. **3** (in Africa, India, etc., formerly) a native porter or servant. **4** (*modifier*) *Finance.* payable to the person in possession: *bearer bonds.*

bear garden *n* **1** (formerly) a place where bear-baiting took place. **2** a scene of tumult.

bear hug *n* **1** a wrestling hold in which the arms are locked tightly round an opponent's chest and arms. **2** any similar tight embrace. **3** *Commerce.* an approach to the board of one company by another to indicate that an offer is to be made for their shares.

bearing ➊ ('bɛərɪŋ) *n* **1** a support for a rotating or reciprocating mechanical part. **2** (foll. by *on* or *upon*) relevance (to): *it has no bearing on this problem.* **3** a person's general social conduct. **4** the act, period, or capability of producing fruit or young. **5** anything that carries weight or acts as a support. **6** the angular direction of a point or course measured from a known position. **7** (*usually pl*) the position, as of a ship, fixed with reference to two or more known points. **8** (*usually pl*) a sense of one's relative position; orientation (esp. in **lose, get,** *or* **take one's bearings**). **9** *Heraldry.* **9a** a device on a heraldic shield. **9b** another name for **coat of arms.**

bearing rein *n Chiefly Brit.* a rein from the bit to the saddle, designed to keep the horse's head in the desired position.

bearish ➊ ('bɛərɪʃ) *adj* **1** like a bear; rough; clumsy; churlish. **2** *Stock Exchange.* causing, expecting, or characterized by a fall in prices: *a bearish feel to the market.*
▸**'bearishness** *n*

bear on ➊ *vb* (*intr, prep*) **1** to be relevant to; relate to. **2** to be burdensome to or afflict.

THESAURUS

beady *adj* **1** = **bright**, gleaming, glinting, glittering, sharp, shining

beak[1] *n* **1, 2** = **bill**, mandible, neb (*arch. or dialect*), nib **3** *Slang* = **nose**, proboscis, snout

beam *n* **1** = **rafter**, girder, joist, plank, spar, support, timber **3** = **ray**, bar, emission, gleam, glimmer, glint, glow, radiation, shaft, streak, stream **4** = **smile**, grin ◆ *vb* **14** = **radiate**, emit, glare, gleam, glitter, glow, shine **15** = **send out**, broadcast, emit, transmit **16** = **smile**, grin

beaming *adj* **14** = **radiating**, beautiful, bright, brilliant, flashing, gleaming, glistening, glittering, radiant, scintillating, shining, sparkling **16** = **smiling**, cheerful, grinning, happy, joyful, sunny

bear[1] *vb* **1** = **support**, hold up, shoulder, sustain, uphold **2** = **carry**, bring, convey, hump (*Brit. sl.*), move, take, tote (*inf.*), transport **4, 5** = **produce**, beget, breed, bring forth, develop, engender, generate, give birth to, yield **6** = **tolerate**, abide, admit, allow, brook, endure, hack (*sl.*), permit, put up with (*inf.*), stomach, suffer, undergo **8** = **hold**, cherish, entertain, harbour, have, maintain, possess
Antonyms *vb* ≠ **support**: abandon, cease, desert, discontinue, drop, give up, leave, quit, relinquish ≠ **carry**: drop, put down, shed

bearable *adj* = **tolerable**, admissible, endurable, manageable, passable, sufferable, supportable, sustainable
Antonyms *adj* insufferable, insupportable, intolerable, oppressive, too much (*inf.*), unacceptable, unbearable, unendurable

beard *n* **1** = **whiskers**, bristles, five-o'clock shadow, stubble ◆ *vb* **5** = **confront**, brave, dare, defy, face, oppose, tackle

bearded *adj* **1** = **unshaven**, bewhiskered, bristly, bushy, hairy, hirsute, shaggy, stubbly, whiskered

beardless *adj* **1** = **clean-shaven**, barefaced, hairless, smooth, smooth-faced

bear down *vb* **1** = **press down**, burden, compress, encumber, push, strain, weigh down **2** = **approach**, advance on, attack, close in, converge on, move in

bearer *n* **2** = **payee**, beneficiary, consignee **3** = **carrier**, agent, conveyor, messenger, porter, runner, servant

bearing *n* **2** = **relevance**, application, connection, import, pertinence, reference, relation, significance **3** = **manner**, air, aspect, attitude, behaviour, carriage, demeanour, deportment, mien, posture **6, 7** = **position**, course, direction, point of compass **8** *usually plural* = **position**, aim, course, direction, location, orientation, situation, track, way, whereabouts
Antonyms *n* ≠ **relevance**: inappositeness, inappropriateness, inaptness, inconsequence, irrelevance, irrelevancy, non sequitur

bearish *adj* **1** = **gruff**, churlish, clumsy, rough, sullen, surly **2** *Stock Exchange* = **falling**, declining, slumping

bear on *vb* **1** = **be relevant to**, affect, appertain

bear out ➊ *vb (tr, adv)* to show to be true or truthful; confirm: *the witness will bear me out.*

bear raid *n* an attempt to force down the price of a security or commodity by sustained selling.

bearskin ('bɛəˌskɪn) *n* **1** the pelt of a bear, esp. when used as a rug. **2** a tall helmet of black fur worn by certain British Army regiments.

bear up ➊ *vb (intr, adv)* to endure cheerfully.

bear with ➊ *vb (intr, prep)* to be patient with.

beast ➊ (biːst) *n* **1** any animal other than man, esp. a large wild quadruped. **2** savage nature or characteristics: *the beast in man.* **3** a brutal, uncivilized, or filthy person. [C13: from OF *beste,* from L *bestia,* from ?]

beastly ➊ ('biːstlɪ) *adj* **beastlier, beastliest. 1** *Inf.* unpleasant; disagreeable. **2** *Obs.* of or like a beast; bestial. ◆ *adv* **3** *Inf.* (intensifier): *the weather is so beastly hot.*
▸**'beastliness** *n*

beast of burden *n* an animal, such as a donkey or ox, used for carrying loads.

beast of prey *n* any animal that hunts other animals for food.

beat ➊ (biːt) *vb* **beats, beating, beat; beaten** *or* **beat. 1** (when *intr,* often foll. by *against, on,* etc.) to strike with or as if with a series of violent blows. **2** *(tr)* to punish by striking; flog. **3** to move up and down; flap: *the bird beat its wings heavily.* **4** *(intr)* to throb rhythmically; pulsate. **5** *(tr;* sometimes foll. by *up) Cookery.* to stir or whisk vigorously. **6** *(tr;* sometimes foll. by *out)* to shape, thin, or flatten (metal) by repeated blows. **7** *(tr) Music.* to indicate (time) by one's hand, baton, etc., or by a metronome. **8** (when *tr,* sometimes foll. by *out)* to produce (a sound or signal) by or as if by striking a drum. **9** to overcome; defeat. **10** *(tr)* to form (a path, track, etc.) by repeatedly walking or riding over it. **11** *(tr)* to arrive, achieve, or finish before (someone or something). **12** *(tr;* often foll. by *back, down, off,* etc.) to drive, push, or thrust. **13** to scour (woodlands or undergrowth) so as to rouse game for shooting. **14** *(tr) Sl.* to puzzle or baffle: *it beats me.* **15** *(intr) Naut.* to steer a sailing vessel as close as possible to the direction from which the wind is blowing. **16 beat a retreat.** to withdraw in haste. **17 beat it.** *Sl. (often imperative)* to go away. **18 beat the bounds.** *Brit.* (formerly) to define the boundaries of a parish by making a procession around them and hitting the ground with rods. **19 can you beat it** *or* **that?** *Sl.* an expression of surprise. ◆ *n* **20** a stroke or blow. **21** the sound made by a stroke or blow. **22** a regular throb. **23a** an assigned or habitual round or route, as of a policeman. **23b** *(as modifier): beat police officers.* **24** the basic rhythmic unit in a piece of music. **25a** pop or rock music characterized by a heavy rhythmic beat. **25b** *(as modifier): a beat group.* **26** *Physics.* one of the regular pulses produced by combining two sounds or electrical signals that have similar frequencies. **27** *Prosody.* the accent or stress in a metrical foot. **28** *(modifier) (often cap.)* of, characterized by, or relating to the Beat Generation. ◆ *adj* **29** *(postpositive) Sl.* totally exhausted. ◆ See also **beat down, beat up.** [OE *bēatan*]
▸**'beatable** *adj*

beatbox ('biːtˌbɒks) *n* another name for **drum machine.**

beat down *vb (adv)* **1** *(tr) Inf.* to force or persuade (a seller) to accept a lower price. **2** *(intr)* (of the sun) to shine intensely.

beaten ➊ ('biːtᵊn) *adj* **1** defeated or baffled. **2** shaped or made thin by hammering: *beaten gold.* **3** much travelled; well trodden. **4 off the beaten track. 4a** in unfamiliar territory. **4b** out of the ordinary; unusual. **5** (of food) mixed by beating; whipped. **6** tired out; exhausted.

beater ('biːtə) *n* **1** a person who beats or hammers: *a panel beater.* **2** a device used for beating: *a carpet beater.* **3** a person who rouses wild game.

Beat Generation *n (functioning as sing or pl)* **1** members of the generation that came to maturity in the 1950s, whose rejection of the social and political systems of the West was expressed through contempt for regular work, possessions, traditional dress, etc. **2** a group of US writers, notably Jack Kerouac, Allen Ginsberg, and William Burroughs, who emerged in the 1950s.

beatific ➊ (ˌbiːəˈtɪfɪk) *adj* **1** displaying great happiness, calmness, etc. **2** of or conferring a state of celestial happiness. [C17: from LL *beātificus,* from L *beātus,* from *beāre* to bless + *facere* to make]
▸**ˌbea'tifically** *adv*

beatify (bɪ'ætɪˌfaɪ) *vb* **beatifies, beatifying, beatified.** *(tr)* **1** *RC Church.* (of the pope) to declare formally that (a deceased person) showed a heroic degree of holiness in life and is worthy of veneration: the first step towards canonization. **2** to make extremely happy. [C16: from OF *beatifier;* see BEATIFIC]
▸**beatification** (bɪˌætɪfɪ'keɪʃən) *n*

beating ➊ ('biːtɪŋ) *n* **1** a whipping or thrashing. **2** a defeat or setback. **3 take some** *or* **a lot of beating.** to be difficult to improve upon.

beatitude ➊ (bɪ'ætɪˌtjuːd) *n* **1** supreme blessedness or happiness. **2** an honorific title of the Eastern Christian Church, applied to those of patriarchal rank. [C15: from L *beātitūdō,* from *beātus* blessed; see BEATIFIC]

Beatitude (bɪ'ætɪˌtjuːd) *n Christianity.* any of eight sayings of Jesus in the Sermon on the Mount (Matthew 5:3–11) in which he declares that the poor, the meek, etc., will, in various ways, receive the blessings of heaven.

beatnik ('biːtnɪk) *n* **1** a member of the Beat Generation (sense 1). **2** *Inf.* any person with long hair and shabby clothes. [C20: from BEAT (n) + -NIK]

beat up ➊ *Inf.* ◆ *vb* **1** *(tr, adv)* to strike or kick repeatedly, so as to inflict severe physical damage. ◆ *adj* **beat-up. 2** worn-out; dilapidated.

beau ➊ (bəʊ) *n, pl* **beaux** (bəʊ, bəʊz) *or* **beaus** (bəʊz). **1** a man who is greatly concerned with his clothes and appearance; dandy. **2** *Chiefly US.* a boyfriend; sweetheart. [C17: from F, from OF *biau,* from L *bellus* handsome]

Beaufort scale ('bəʊfət) *n Meteorol.* an international scale of wind velocities from 0 (calm) to 12 (hurricane) (0 to 17 in the US). [C19: after Sir Francis *Beaufort* (1774–1857), Brit. admiral and hydrographer who devised it]

beau geste *French.* (bo ʒɛst) *n, pl* ***beaux gestes*** (bo ʒɛst). a noble or gracious gesture or act. [lit.: beautiful gesture]

beaujolais ('bəʊʒəˌleɪ) *n (sometimes cap.)* a popular fresh-tasting red or white wine from southern Burgundy in France.

beau monde ('bəʊ 'mɒnd) *n* the world of fashion and society. [C18: F, lit.: fine world]

beaut (bjuːt) *Sl., chiefly Austral. & NZ.* ◆ *n* **1** an outstanding person or thing. ◆ *adj, interj* **2** excellent.

beauteous ('bjuːtɪəs) *adj* a poetic word for **beautiful.**
▸**'beauteousness** *n*

beautician (bjuː'tɪʃən) *n* a person who works in or manages a beauty salon.

beautiful ➊ ('bjuːtɪfʊl) *adj* **1** possessing beauty; aesthetically pleasing. **2** highly enjoyable; very pleasant.
▸**'beautifully** *adv*

beautify ➊ ('bjuːtɪˌfaɪ) *vb* **beautifies, beautifying, beautified.** to make or become beautiful.
▸**beautification** (ˌbjuːtɪfɪ'keɪʃən) *n* ▸**'beautiˌfier** *n*

beauty ➊ ('bjuːtɪ) *n, pl* **beauties. 1** the combination of all the qualities of a person or thing that delight the senses and mind. **2** a very attractive woman. **3** *Inf.* an outstanding example of its kind. **4** *Inf.* an advanta-

THESAURUS

to, belong to, concern, involve, pertain to, refer to, relate to, touch upon

bear out *vb* = **support,** confirm, corroborate, endorse, justify, prove, substantiate, uphold, vindicate

bear up *vb* = **cope,** bear the brunt, carry on, endure, go through the mill, grin and bear it *(inf.),* keep one's chin up, persevere, suffer, take it on the chin *(inf.),* withstand

bear with *vb* = **be patient with,** make allowances for, put up with *(inf.),* suffer, tolerate, wait for

beast *n* **1** = **animal,** brute, creature **3** = **brute,** barbarian, fiend, ghoul, monster, ogre, sadist, savage, swine

beastly *adj* **1** *Informal* = **unpleasant,** awful, disagreeable, foul, horrid, mean, nasty, rotten, terrible **2** *Obsolete* = **brutal,** animal, barbarous, bestial, brutish, coarse, cruel, depraved, inhuman, monstrous, repulsive, sadistic, savage
Antonyms *adj* ≠ **unpleasant:** agreeable, fine, good, pleasant ≠ **brutal:** humane, sensitive

beat *vb* **1, 2** = **hit,** bang, batter, belt *(inf.),* break, bruise, buffet, cane, chin *(sl.),* clobber *(sl.),* cudgel, deck *(sl.),* drub, flog, knock, lash, pelt, pound, punch, strike, thrash, thwack, whip **3** = **flap,** flutter **4** = **throb,** palpitate, pound, pulsate, pulse, quake, quiver, shake, thump, tremble, vibrate **6** = **shape,** fashion, forge, form, hammer, model, work **9** = **defeat,** best, blow out of the water *(sl.),* clobber *(sl.),* conquer, knock spots off *(inf.),* lick *(inf.),* master, outdo, outstrip, overcome, overwhelm, surpass, vanquish, wipe the floor with *(inf.)* **17 beat it** *Slang* = **go away,** depart, exit, get lost *(inf.),* get on one's bike *(Brit. sl.),* hop it *(sl.),* leave, make tracks, scarper *(Brit. sl.),* scram *(inf.),* sling one's hook *(Brit. sl.),* vamoose *(sl., chiefly US)* ◆ *n* **20** = **blow,** belt *(inf.),* hit, lash, punch, shake, slap, strike, swing, thump **22** = **throb,** palpitation, pulsation, pulse **23a** = **route,** circuit, course, path, rounds, way **27** = **rhythm,** accent, cadence, ictus, measure *(Prosody),* metre, stress ◆ *adj* **29** *Slang* = **exhausted,** clapped out *(Austral. & NZ inf.),* fatigued, on one's last legs, tired, wearied, wiped out *(inf.),* worn out, zonked *(sl.)*

beaten *adj* **1** = **defeated,** baffled, cowed, disappointed, disheartened, frustrated, overcome, overwhelmed, thwarted, vanquished **2** = **shaped,** forged, formed, hammered, stamped, worked **3** = **well-trodden,** much travelled, trampled, trodden, well-used, worn **5** = **stirred,** blended, foamy, frothy, mixed, whipped, whisked

beatific *adj* **1** = **blissful,** blissed out, ecstatic, enraptured, exalted, glorious, joyful, rapt, rapturous, serene, sublime **2** = **divine,** blessed, heavenly

beating *n* **1** = **thrashing,** belting *(inf.),* caning, chastisement, corporal punishment, flogging, pasting *(sl.),* slapping, smacking, whipping **2** = **defeat,** conquest, downfall, overthrow, pasting *(sl.),* rout, ruin

beatitude *n* **1** = **blessedness,** beatification, bliss, ecstasy, exaltation, felicity, happiness, holy joy, saintliness

beat up *Informal vb* **1** = **assault,** attack, batter, clobber *(sl.),* do over *(Brit., Austral., & NZ sl.),* duff up *(Brit. sl.),* knock about *or* around, put the boot in *(sl.),* thrash, work over *(sl.)*

beau *n* **1** = **dandy,** coxcomb, fop, gallant, ladies' man, popinjay, swell *(inf.)* **2** *Chiefly U.S.* = **boyfriend,** admirer, escort, fancy man *(sl.),* fiancé, guy *(inf.),* lover, suitor, swain, sweetheart

beautiful *adj* **1** = **attractive,** alluring, appealing, charming, comely, delightful, drop-dead *(sl.),* exquisite, fair, fine, glamorous, good-looking, gorgeous, graceful, handsome, lovely, pleasing, radiant, ravishing, stunning *(inf.)*
Antonyms *adj* awful, bad, hideous, repulsive, terrible, ugly, unattractive, unpleasant, unsightly

beautify *vb* = **make beautiful,** adorn, array, bedeck, deck, decorate, embellish, enhance, festoon, garnish, gild, glamorize, grace, ornament

beauty *n* **1** = **attractiveness,** allure, bloom, charm, comeliness, elegance, exquisiteness, fairness, glamour, grace, handsomeness, loveliness, pulchritude, seemliness, symmetry **2** = **belle,** charmer, cracker *(sl.),* goddess, good-looker, humdinger *(sl.),* lovely *(sl.),* stunner *(inf.),* Venus **4** *Informal* = **advantage,** asset, atgeous feature: *one beauty of the job is the short hours.* ◆ *interj* **5** (NZ 'bju:dɪ). *Austral. & NZ sl.* an expression of approval or agreement. [C13: from OF *biauté,* from *biau* beautiful; see BEAU]

beauty queen *n* an attractive young woman, esp. one who has won a beauty contest.

beauty salon *or* **parlour** *n* an establishment providing services such as hairdressing, facial treatment, and massage.

beauty sleep *n Inf.* sleep, esp. sleep before midnight.

beauty spot *n* **1** a place of outstanding beauty. **2** a mole or other similar natural mark on the skin. **3** (esp. in the 18th century) a small dark-coloured patch or spot worn on a lady's face as an adornment.

beaux (bəʊ, bəʊz) *n* a plural of **beau.**

beaux-arts (bəʊ'zɑ:) *pl n* **1** another word for **fine art. 2** (*modifier*) relating to the classical decorative style, esp. that of the École des Beaux-Arts in Paris: *beaux-arts influences.* [F]

beaver[1] ❶ ('bi:və) *n* **1** a large amphibious rodent of Europe, Asia, and North America. It has soft brown fur, a broad flat hairless tail, and webbed hind feet, and constructs complex dams and houses (lodges) in rivers. **2** its fur. **3** a tall hat of beaver fur worn during the 19th century. **4** a woollen napped cloth resembling beaver fur. **5** *Obs.* a full beard. **6** a bearded man. **7** (*modifier*) made of beaver fur or similar material. ◆ *vb* **8** (*intr;* usually foll. by *away*) to work industriously or steadily. [OE *beofor*]

beaver[2] ('bi:və) *n* a movable piece on a medieval helmet used to protect the lower face. [C15: from OF *baviere,* from *baver* to dribble]

bebop ('bi:bɒp) *n* the full name for **bop** (sense 1). [C20: imit. of the rhythm]
▸**'bebopper** *n*

becalmed ❶ (bɪ'kɑ:md) *adj* (of a sailing boat or ship) motionless through lack of wind.

became (bɪ'keɪm) *vb* the past tense of **become.**

because ❶ (bɪ'kɒz, -'kəz) *conj* **1** (*subordinating*) on account of the fact that; since: *because it's so cold we'll go home.* **2 because of.** (*prep*) on account of: *I lost my job because of her.* [C14 *bi cause,* from *bi* BY + CAUSE]

> **USAGE NOTE** See at **reason.**

béchamel sauce (ˌbeɪʃə'mɛl) *n* a thick white sauce flavoured with onion and seasonings. [C18: after the Marquis of *Béchamel,* its F inventor]

bêche-de-mer (ˌbeʃdə'mɛə) *n, pl* **bêches-de-mer** (ˌbeʃdə'mɛə) *or* **bêche-de-mer.** another name for **trepang.** [C19: quasi-F, from earlier E *biche de mer,* from Port. *bicho do mar* worm of the sea]

Bechuana (be'tʃwɑ:nə; ˌbɛkju'ɑ:nə) *n, pl* **Bechuana** *or* **Bechuanas.** a former name for a Bantu of Botswana, a republic in southern Africa.

beck[1] (bɛk) *n* **1** a nod, wave, or other gesture. **2 at (someone's) beck and call.** subject to (someone's) slightest whim. [C14: short for *becnen* to BECKON]

beck[2] (bɛk) *n* (in N England) a stream. [OE *becc*]

beckon ❶ ('bɛkən) *vb* **1** to summon with a gesture of the hand or head. **2** to entice or lure. ◆ *n* **3** a summoning gesture. [OE *bīecnan,* from *bēacen* sign]
▸**'beckoner** *n* ▸**'beckoning** *adj, n*

becloud (bɪ'klaʊd) *vb* (*tr*) **1** to cover or obscure with a cloud. **2** to confuse or muddle.

become ❶ (bɪ'kʌm) *vb* **becomes, becoming, became, become.** (*mainly intr*) **1** (*copula*) to come to be; develop or grow into: *he became a monster.* **2** (foll. by *of; usually used in a question*) to happen (to): *what became of him?* **3** (*tr*) to suit: *that dress becomes you.* **4** (*tr*) to be appropriate; to befit: *it ill becomes you to complain.* [OE *becuman* to happen]

becoming ❶ (bɪ'kʌmɪŋ) *adj* suitable; appropriate.
▸**be'comingly** *adv* ▸**be'comingness** *n*

becquerel (ˌbɛkə'rɛl) *n* the SI unit of activity of a radioactive source. [after A.H. *Becquerel* (1852–1908), F physicist]

bed ❶ (bɛd) *n* **1** a piece of furniture on which to sleep. **2** the mattress and bedclothes: *an unmade bed.* **3** sleep or rest: *time for bed.* **4** any place in which a person or animal sleeps or rests. **5** *Med.* a unit of potential occupancy in a hospital or residential institution. **6** *Inf.* sexual intercourse. **7** a plot of ground in which plants are grown. **8** the bottom of a river, lake, or sea. **9** a part of this used for cultivation of a plant or animal: *oyster beds.* **10** any underlying structure or part. **11** a layer of rock, esp. sedimentary rock. **12 go to bed. 12a** (often foll. by *with*) to have sexual intercourse (with). **12b** *Journalism, printing.* (of a newspaper, etc.) to go to press; start printing. **13 in bed with.** *Inf.* cooperating closely with (another person, organization, government, etc.), esp. covertly. **14 put to bed.** *Journalism.* to finalize work on (a newspaper, etc.) so that it is ready to go to press. **15 take to one's bed.** to remain in bed, esp. because of illness. ◆ *vb* **beds, bedding, bedded. 16** (usually foll. by *down*) to go to or put into a place to sleep or rest. **17** (*tr*) to have sexual intercourse with. **18** (*tr*) to place firmly into position; embed. **19** *Geol.* to form or be arranged in a distinct layer; stratify. **20** (*tr;* often foll. by *out*) to plant in a bed of soil. [OE *bedd*]

BEd *abbrev. for* Bachelor of Education.

bed and board *n* sleeping accommodation and meals.

bed and breakfast *n Chiefly Brit.* **1** (in a hotel, boarding house, etc.) overnight accommodation and breakfast. **2** the selling of shares after hours one evening on a stock exchange and buying them back the next morning, in order to establish a loss for capital-gains tax purposes.

bedaub ❶ (bɪ'dɔ:b) *vb* (*tr*) **1** to smear all over with something thick, sticky, or dirty. **2** to ornament in a gaudy or vulgar fashion.

bedazzle ❶ (bɪ'dæz^əl) *vb* **bedazzles, bedazzling, bedazzled.** (*tr*) to dazzle or confuse, as with brilliance.
▸**be'dazzlement** *n*

bed bath *n* another name for **blanket bath.**

bedbug ('bɛdˌbʌg) *n* any of several bloodsucking wingless insects of temperate regions, infesting dirty houses.

bedchamber ('bɛdˌtʃeɪmbə) *n* an archaic word for **bedroom.**

bedclothes ❶ ('bɛdˌkləʊðz) *pl n* sheets, blankets, and other coverings for a bed.

beddable ('bɛdəb^əl) *adj* sexually attractive.

bedding ❶ ('bɛdɪŋ) *n* **1** bedclothes, sometimes considered with a mattress. **2** litter, such as straw, for animals. **3** a foundation, such as mortar under a brick. **4** the stratification of rocks.

bedding plant *n* an immature plant that may be planted out in a garden bed.

bedeck ❶ (bɪ'dɛk) *vb* (*tr*) to cover with decorations; adorn.

bedevil ❶ (bɪ'dɛv^əl) *vb* **bedevils, bedevilling, bedevilled** *or US* **bedevils, bedeviling, bedeviled.** (*tr*) **1** to harass or torment. **2** to throw into confusion. **3** to possess, as with a devil.
▸**be'devilment** *n*

bedew ❶ (bɪ'dju:) *vb* (*tr*) to wet as with dew.

bedfellow ('bɛdˌfɛləʊ) *n* **1** a person with whom one shares a bed. **2** a temporary ally or associate.

bedight (bɪ'daɪt) *Arch.* ◆ *vb* **bedights, bedighting, bedight** *or* **bedighted. 1** (*tr*) to array or adorn. ◆ *adj* **2** (*p.p.*) adorned or bedecked. [C14: from DIGHT]

bedim ❶ (bɪ'dɪm) *vb* **bedims, bedimming, bedimmed.** (*tr*) to make dim or obscure.

bedizen (bɪ'daɪz^ən, -'dɪz^ən) *vb* (*tr*) *Arch.* to dress or decorate gaudily or tastelessly. [C17: from BE- + obs. *dizen* to dress up, from ?]
▸**be'dizenment** *n*

bed jacket *n* a woman's short upper garment worn over a nightgown when sitting up in bed.

bedlam ❶ ('bɛdləm) *n* **1** a noisy confused situation. **2** *Arch.* a madhouse. [C13 *bedlem, bethlem,* from Hospital of St Mary of *Bethlehem* in London]

bed linen *n* sheets, pillowcases, etc., for a bed.

Bedouin *or* **Beduin** ('bɛduɪn) *n* **1** (*pl* **Bedouins, Bedouin** *or* **Beduins, Beduin**) a nomadic Arab tribesman of the deserts of Arabia, Jordan, and Syria. **2** a wanderer. ◆ *adj* **3** of or relating to the Bedouins. **4** wandering. [C14: from OF *beduin,* from Ar. *badāwi,* pl. of *badwi,* from *badw* desert]

bedpan ('bɛdˌpæn) *n* a vessel used by a bedridden patient to collect faeces and urine.

bedraggle ❶ (bɪ'dræg^əl) *vb* **bedraggles, bedraggling, bedraggled.** (*tr*) to make (hair, clothing, etc.) limp, untidy, or dirty, as with rain or mud.
▸**be'draggled** *adj*

THESAURUS

traction, benefit, blessing, boon, excellence, feature, good thing
Antonyms *n* ≠ **attractiveness:** repulsiveness, ugliness, unpleasantness, unseemliness ≠ **advantage:** detraction, disadvantage, flaw

beaver[1] *vb* **8** *usually with* **away** = **work,** exert oneself, graft (*inf.*), hammer away, keep one's nose to the grindstone, peg away, persevere, persist, plug away (*inf.*), slog

becalmed *adj* = **still,** motionless, settled, stranded, stuck

because *conj* **1** = **since,** as, in that **2** = **on account of,** by reason of, owing to, thanks to

beckon *vb* **1** = **gesture,** bid, gesticulate, motion, nod, signal, summon, wave at **2** = **lure,** allure, attract, call, coax, draw, entice, invite, pull, tempt

become *vb* **1** = **come to be,** alter to, be transformed into, change into, develop into, evolve into, grow into, mature into, metamorphose into, ripen into **3** = **suit,** embellish, enhance, fit, flatter, grace, harmonize, ornament, set off

becoming *adj* = **appropriate,** befitting, *comme il faut,* compatible, congruous, decent, decorous, fit, fitting, in keeping, meet (*arch.*), proper, seemly, suitable, worthy
Antonyms *adj* improper, inappropriate, unfit, unsuitable, unworthy

bed *n* **1** = **bedstead,** berth, bunk, cot, couch, divan, pallet **7** = **plot,** area, border, garden, patch, row, strip **10** = **bottom,** base, foundation, groundwork **11** = **substratum** ◆ *vb* **16** *usually foll. by* **down** = **sleep,** hit the hay, lie, retire, settle down, turn in (*inf.*) **18** = **fix,** base, embed, establish, found, implant, insert, settle, set up **20** = **plant**

bedaub *vb* **1** = **smear,** besmear, smirch, soil, spatter, splash, stain

bedazzle *vb* = **dazzle,** amaze, astound, bewilder, blind, captivate, confuse, daze, dumbfound, enchant, overwhelm, stagger, stun, sweep off one's feet

bedclothes *pl n* = **bedding,** bed linen, blankets, coverlets, covers, duvets, eiderdowns, pillowcases, pillows, quilts, sheets

bedding *n* **1** = **bedclothes,** bed linen, linen, sheets

bedeck *vb* = **decorate,** adorn, array, embellish, engarland, festoon, garnish, ornament, trim

bedevil *vb* **1** = **torment,** aggravate (*inf.*), annoy, harass, hassle (*inf.*), irk, irritate, pester, plague, torture, trouble, vex, worry **2** = **confuse,** confound

bedew *vb* = **sprinkle,** besprinkle, dampen, drench, moisten, shower, soak, spray, water, wet

bedim *vb* = **dim,** becloud, cloak, cloud, darken, obscure, overcast, shade, shadow

bedlam *n* **1** = **pandemonium,** chaos, clamour, commotion, confusion, furore, hubbub, hullabaloo, noise, tumult, turmoil, uproar

bedraggled *adj* = **messy,** dirty, dishevelled, disordered, drenched, dripping, muddied, muddy, sodden, soiled, stained, sullied, unkempt, untidy

bedridden Ⓣ (ˈbɛdˌrɪdᵊn) *adj* confined to bed because of illness, esp. for a long or indefinite period. [OE *bedreda*]
bedrock Ⓣ (ˈbɛdˌrɒk) *n* **1** the solid rock beneath the surface soil, etc. **2** basic principles or facts. **3** the lowest point, level, or layer.
bedroll (ˈbɛdˌrəʊl) *n* a portable roll of bedding.
bedroom (ˈbɛdˌruːm, -ˌrʊm) *n* **1** a room used for sleeping. **2** (*modifier*) containing references to sex: *a bedroom comedy*.
Beds (bɛdz) *abbrev. for* Bedfordshire.
bedside (ˈbɛdˌsaɪd) *n* **a** the space beside a bed, esp. a sickbed. **b** (*as modifier*): *a bedside lamp*.
bedsit (ˈbɛdˌsɪt) *n* a furnished sitting room containing sleeping accommodation. Also called: **bedsitting room, bedsitter.**
bedsore (ˈbɛdˌsɔː) *n* a chronic ulcer on the skin of a bedridden person, caused by prolonged pressure.
bedspread (ˈbɛdˌsprɛd) *n* a top cover on a bed.
bedstead (ˈbɛdˌstɛd) *n* the framework of a bed.
bedstraw (ˈbɛdˌstrɔː) *n* any of numerous plants which have small white or yellow flowers and prickly or hairy fruits: formerly used as straw for beds.
bedtime (ˈbɛdˌtaɪm) *n* **a** the time when one usually goes to bed. **b** (*as modifier*): *a bedtime story*.
bed-wetting *n* the act of urinating in bed.
bee[1] (biː) *n* **1** any of various four-winged insects that collect nectar and pollen and make honey and wax. **2 busy bee.** a person who is industrious or has many things to do. **3 have a bee in one's bonnet.** to be obsessed with an idea. [OE *bīo*]
bee[2] (biː) *n Chiefly US.* a social gathering for a specific purpose, as to carry out a communal task: *quilting bee*. [?from dialect *bean* neighbourly help, from OE *bēn* boon]
Beeb (biːb) *n* **the.** an informal name for the **BBC.**
beebread (ˈbiːˌbrɛd) *n* a mixture of pollen and nectar prepared by worker bees and fed to the larvae. Also called: **ambrosia.**
beech (biːtʃ) *n* **1** a European tree having smooth greyish bark. **2** a similar tree of temperate Australasia and South America. **3** the hard wood of either of these trees. **4** See **copper beech.** [OE *bēce*]
▸ **ˈbeechen** *or* **ˈbeechy** *adj*
beechnut (ˈbiːtʃˌnʌt) *n* the small brown triangular edible nut of the beech tree, collectively often termed **beech mast.**
bee-eater *n* any of various insectivorous birds of the Old World tropics and subtropics.
beef Ⓣ (biːf) *n* **1** the flesh of various bovine animals, esp. the cow, when killed for eating. **2** (*pl* **beeves**) an adult ox, etc., reared for its meat. **3** *Inf.* human flesh, esp. when muscular. **4** (*pl* **beefs**) *Sl.* a complaint. ◆ *vb* **5** (*intr*) *Sl.* to complain, esp. repeatedly. **6** (*tr;* often foll. by *up*) *Inf.* to strengthen; reinforce. [C13: from OF *boef*, from L *bōs* ox]
beefburger (ˈbiːfˌbɜːgə) *n* a flat fried cake of minced beef; hamburger.
beefcake (ˈbiːfˌkeɪk) *n Sl.* men displayed for their muscular bodies, esp. in photographs.
beefeater (ˈbiːfˌiːtə) *n* a nickname applied to the Yeomen of the Guard, and the Yeomen Warders at the Tower of London.
beef road *n Austral.* a road used for transporting cattle.
beefsteak (ˈbiːfˌsteɪk) *n* a lean piece of beef that can be grilled, fried, etc.
beef tomato *n* a very large fleshy variety of tomato. Also called: **beefsteak tomato.**
beef tea *n* a drink made by boiling pieces of lean beef.
beefy Ⓣ (ˈbiːfɪ) *adj* **beefier, beefiest. 1** like beef. **2** *Inf.* muscular; brawny.
▸ **ˈbeefiness** *n*
beehive Ⓣ (ˈbiːˌhaɪv) *n* **1** a man-made receptacle used to house a swarm of bees. **2** a dome-shaped structure. **3** a place where busy people are assembled. **4 the Beehive.** the dome-shaped building which houses Parliament in Wellington, New Zealand.
beekeeper (ˈbiːˌkiːpə) *n* a person who keeps bees for their honey.
▸ **ˈbeeˌkeeping** *n*
beeline (ˈbiːˌlaɪn) *n* the most direct route between two places (esp. in **make a beeline for**).
Beelzebub (bɪˈɛlzɪˌbʌb) *n* Satan or any devil. [OE *Belzebub*, ult. from Heb. *bá'al zebūb*, lit.: lord of flies]
bee moth *n* any of various moths whose larvae live in the nests of bees or wasps, feeding on nest materials and host larvae.
been (biːn, bɪn) *vb* the past participle of **be.**
beep (biːp) *n* **1** a short high-pitched sound, as made by a car horn or by electronic apparatus. ◆ *vb* **2** to make or cause to make such a noise. [C20: imit.]
▸ **ˈbeeper** *n*
beer Ⓣ (bɪə) *n* **1** an alcoholic drink brewed from malt, sugar, hops, and water. **2** a slightly fermented drink made from the roots or leaves of certain plants: *ginger beer*. **3** (*modifier*) relating to beer: *beer glass*. **4** (*modifier*) in which beer is drunk, esp. (of licensed premises) having a licence to sell beer but not spirits: *beer house; beer garden*. [OE *beor*]
beer and skittles *n* (*functioning as sing*) *Inf.* enjoyment or pleasure.
beer parlour *n Canad.* a licensed place in which beer is sold to the public.
beery (ˈbɪərɪ) *adj* **beerier, beeriest. 1** smelling or tasting of beer. **2** given to drinking beer.
▸ **ˈbeerily** *adv* ▸ **ˈbeeriness** *n*
bee's knees *n* **the** (*functioning as sing*) *Inf.* an excellent or ideally suitable person or thing.
beestings, biestings, *or US* **beastings** (ˈbiːstɪŋz) *n* (*functioning as sing*) the first milk secreted by a cow or similar animal after giving birth; colostrum. [OE *bȳsting*]
beeswax (ˈbiːzˌwæks) *n* **1** a wax secreted by honeybees for constructing honeycombs. **2** this wax after refining, used in polishes, etc.
beeswing (ˈbiːzˌwɪŋ) *n* a light filmy crust of tartar that forms in some wines after long keeping in the bottle.
beet (biːt) *n* **1** a plant of a genus widely cultivated in such varieties as the sugar beet, mangelwurzel, and beetroot. **2** the leaves of any of several varieties of this plant, cooked and eaten as a vegetable. **3 red beet.** the US name for **beetroot.** [OE *bēte*, from L *bēta*]
beetle[1] Ⓣ (ˈbiːtᵊl) *n* **1** an insect having biting mouthparts and forewings modified to form shell-like protective casings. **2** a game in which the players draw or assemble a beetle-shaped form. ◆ *vb* **beetles, beetling, beetled.** (*intr;* foll. by *along, off,* etc.) **3** *Inf.* to scuttle or scurry; hurry. [OE *bitela*]
beetle[2] (ˈbiːtᵊl) *n* **1** a heavy hand tool for pounding or beating. **2** a machine used to finish cloth by stamping it with wooden hammers. [OE *bīetel*, from *bēatan* to BEAT]
beetle[3] Ⓣ (ˈbiːtᵊl) *vb* **beetles, beetling, beetled. 1** (*intr*) to overhang; jut. ◆ *adj* **2** overhanging; prominent. [C14: ? rel. to BEETLE[1]]
▸ **ˈbeetling** *adj*
beetle-browed Ⓣ *adj* having bushy or overhanging eyebrows.
beetroot (ˈbiːtˌruːt) *n* a variety of the beet plant that has a bulbous dark red root that may be eaten as a vegetable, in salads, or pickled.
beet sugar *n* the sucrose obtained from sugar beet, identical in composition to cane sugar.
beeves (biːvz) *n* the plural of **beef** (sense 2).
BEF *abbrev. for* British Expeditionary Force, the British army that served in France 1939-40.
befall Ⓣ (bɪˈfɔːl) *vb* **befalls, befalling, befell, befallen.** *Arch. or literary.* **1** (*intr*) to take place. **2** (*tr*) to happen to. **3** (*intr;* usually foll. by *to*) to be due, as by right. [OE *befeallan;* see BE-, FALL]
befit Ⓣ (bɪˈfɪt) *vb* **befits, befitting, befitted.** (*tr*) to be appropriate to or suitable for. [C15: from BE- + FIT[1]]
▸ **beˈfitting** *adj* ▸ **beˈfittingly** *adv*
befog Ⓣ (bɪˈfɒg) *vb* **befogs, befogging, befogged.** (*tr*) **1** to surround with fog. **2** to make confused.
before Ⓣ (bɪˈfɔː) *conj* (*subordinating*) **1** earlier than the time when. **2** rather than: *he'll resign before he agrees to it*. ◆ *prep* **3** preceding in space or time; in front of; ahead of: *standing before the altar*. **4** in the presence of: *to be brought before a judge*. **5** in preference to: *to put friendship before money*. ◆ *adv* **6** at an earlier time; previously. **7** in front. [OE *beforan*]
beforehand Ⓣ (bɪˈfɔːˌhænd) *adj* (*postpositive*), *adv* early; in advance; in anticipation.
befoul (bɪˈfaʊl) *vb* (*tr*) to make dirty or foul.
befriend Ⓣ (bɪˈfrɛnd) *vb* (*tr*) to be a friend to; assist; favour.
befuddle Ⓣ (bɪˈfʌdᵊl) *vb* **befuddles, befuddling, befuddled.** (*tr*) **1** to confuse. **2** to make stupid with drink.
▸ **beˈfuddlement** *n*

THESAURUS

bedridden *adj* = **confined to bed**, confined, flat on one's back, incapacitated, laid up (*inf.*)
bedrock *n* **1** = **bottom**, bed, foundation, rock bottom, substratum, substructure **2** = **basics**, basis, core, essentials, fundamentals, nuts and bolts (*inf.*), roots
beef *n* **3** *Informal* = **flesh**, brawn, heftiness, muscle, physique, robustness, sinew, strength **4** *Slang* = **complaint**, criticism, dispute, grievance, gripe (*inf.*), grouch (*inf.*), grouse, grumble, objection, protest, protestation
beefy *adj* **2** *Informal* = **brawny**, bulky, burly, hulking, muscular, stalwart, stocky, strapping, sturdy, thickset
Antonyms *adj* feeble, frail, puny, scrawny, skinny, weak
beehive *n* **1** = **hive**, apiary, comb, honeycomb
beer *n* **1** = **ale**, amber fluid *or* nectar (*Austral. inf.*), brew, hop juice, swipes (*Brit. sl.*), wallop (*Brit. sl.*)
beetle-browed *adj* = **scowling**, frowning, glowering, lowering, pouting, sullen
beetling *adj* **1** = **overhanging**, hanging over, jutting, leaning over, pendent, projecting, prominent, protruding, sticking out, swelling over
befall *vb Archaic or literary* **1** = **happen**, chance, come to pass, ensue, fall, follow, materialize, occur, supervene, take place, transpire (*inf.*) **2** = **happen to**, betide
befit *vb* = **be appropriate**, become, be fitting, behoove (*US*), behove, be seemly, be suitable, suit
befitting *adj* = **appropriate**, apposite, becoming, fit, fitting, meet (*arch.*), proper, right, seemly, suitable
Antonyms *adj* improper, inappropriate, irrelevant, unbecoming, unfit, unsuitable, wrong
befog *vb* **2** = **make unclear**, blur, confuse, darken, fuzz, make hazy, make indistinct, make vague, muddle, muddy the waters, obfuscate, obscure
before *conj* **1** = **earlier than**, in advance of, prior to ◆ *prep* **3** = **ahead of**, in advance of, in front of **4** = **in the presence of**, in front of ◆ *adv* **6** = **previously**, ahead, earlier, formerly, in advance, sooner **7** = **in front**, ahead
Antonyms *prep* ≠ **ahead of, earlier than:** after, behind, following, succeeding ◆ *adv* ≠ **previously, in front:** after, afterwards, behind, later, subsequently, thereafter
beforehand *adv* = **in advance**, ahead of time, already, before, before now, earlier, early, in anticipation, previously, sooner
befriend *vb* = **help**, advise, aid, assist, back, benefit, encourage, favour, patronize, side with, stand by, support, sustain, uphold
befuddle *vb* **1** = **confuse**, baffle, bewilder, dis-

beg ⓣ (bɛg) *vb* **begs, begging, begged. 1** (when *intr*, often foll. by *for*) to solicit (for money, food, etc.), esp. in the street. **2** to ask formally, humbly, or earnestly: *I beg forgiveness; I beg to differ.* **3** (*intr*) (of a dog) to sit up with forepaws raised expectantly. **4 beg the question. 4a** to evade the issue. **4b** to put forward an argument that assumes the very point it is supposed to establish or that depends on some other questionable assumption. **4c** to suggest that a question needs to be asked: *the firm's success begs the question: why aren't more companies doing the same?* **5 go begging.** to be unwanted or unused. ◆ See also **beg off.** [C13: prob. from OE *bedecian*]

> **USAGE NOTE** The use of *beg the question* to mean that a question needs to be asked is considered by some people to be incorrect.

began (bɪˈgæn) *vb* the past tense of **begin.**

beget ⓣ (bɪˈgɛt) *vb* **begets, begetting, begot** *or* **begat; begotten** *or* **begot.** (*tr*) **1** to father. **2** to cause or create. [OE *begietan;* see BE-, GET]
▸**beˈgetter** *n*

beggar ⓣ (ˈbɛgə) *n* **1** a person who begs, esp. one who lives by begging. **2** a person who has no money or resources; pauper. **3** *Chiefly Brit.* a fellow: *lucky beggar!* ◆ *vb* (*tr*) **4** to be beyond the resources of (esp. in **beggar description**). **5** to impoverish.
▸**ˈbeggardom** *n*

beggarly ⓣ (ˈbɛgəlɪ) *adj* meanly inadequate; very poor.
▸**ˈbeggarliness** *n*

beggar-my-neighbour *n* a card game in which one player tries to win all the cards of the other player.

beggary ⓣ (ˈbɛgərɪ) *n* extreme poverty or need.

begin ⓣ (bɪˈgɪn) *vb* **begins, beginning, began, begun. 1** to start or cause to start (something or to do something). **2** to bring or come into being; arise or originate. **3** to start to say or speak. **4** (*with a negative*) to have the least capacity (to do something): *he couldn't begin to compete.* **5 to begin with.** in the first place. [OE *beginnan*]

beginner ⓣ (bɪˈgɪnə) *n* a person who has just started to do or learn something; novice.

beginning ⓣ (bɪˈgɪnɪŋ) *n* **1** a start; commencement. **2** (*often pl*) a first or early part or stage. **3** the place where or time when something starts. **4** an origin; source.

begird (bɪˈgɜːd) *vb* **begirds, begirding, begirt** *or* **begirded.** (*tr*) *Poetic.* **1** to surround; gird around. **2** to bind. [OE *begierdan;* see BE-, GIRD[1]]

beg off *vb* (*intr, adv*) to ask to be released from an engagement, obligation, etc.

begone (bɪˈgɒn) *sentence substitute.* go away! [C14: from BE (imperative) + GONE]

begonia (bɪˈgəʊnjə) *n* a plant of warm and tropical regions, having ornamental leaves and waxy flowers. [C18: NL, after Michel *Bégon* (1638–1710), F patron of science]

begorra (bɪˈgɔːrə) *interj* an emphatic exclamation, regarded as characteristic of Irishmen. [C19: from *by God!*]

begot (bɪˈgɒt) *vb* a past tense and past participle of **beget.**

begotten (bɪˈgɒtᵊn) *vb* a past participle of **beget.**

begrime (bɪˈgraɪm) *vb* **begrimes, begriming, begrimed.** (*tr*) to make dirty; soil.

begrudge ⓣ (bɪˈgrʌdʒ) *vb* **begrudges, begrudging, begrudged.** (*tr*) **1** to give, admit, or allow unwillingly or with a bad grace. **2** to envy (someone) the possession of (something).
▸**beˈgrudgingly** *adv*

beguile ⓣ (bɪˈgaɪl) *vb* **beguiles, beguiling, beguiled.** (*tr*) **1** to charm; fascinate. **2** to delude; influence by slyness. **3** (often foll. by *of* or *out of*) to cheat (someone) of. **4** to pass pleasantly; while away.
▸**beˈguilement** *n* ▸**beˈguiler** *n* ▸**beˈguiling** *adj* ▸**beˈguilingly** *adv*

beguine (bɪˈgiːn) *n* **1** a dance of South American origin in bolero rhythm. **2** a piece of music in the rhythm of this dance. [C20: from Louisiana F, from F *béguin* flirtation]

begum (ˈbeɪgəm) *n* (in certain Muslim countries) a woman of high rank. [C18: from Urdu *begam*, from Turkish *begim;* see BEY]

begun (bɪˈgʌn) *vb* the past participle of **begin.**

behalf ⓣ (bɪˈhɑːf) *n* interest, part, benefit, or respect (only in **on (someone's) behalf, on** *or US & Canad.* **in behalf of, in this** (*or* **that) behalf**). [OE *be halfe*, from *be* by + *halfe* side]

behave ⓣ (bɪˈheɪv) *vb* **behaves, behaving, behaved. 1** (*intr*) to act or function in a specified or usual way. **2** to conduct (oneself) in a specified way: *he behaved badly.* **3** to conduct (oneself) properly or as desired. [C15: see BE-, HAVE]

behaviour ⓣ *or US* **behavior** (bɪˈheɪvjə) *n* **1** manner of behaving. **2 on one's best behaviour.** behaving with careful good manners. **3** *Psychol.* the response of an organism to a stimulus. **4** the reaction or functioning of a machine, etc., under normal or specified circumstances. [C15: from BEHAVE; infl. by ME *havior*, from OF *havoir*, from L *habēre* to have]
▸**beˈhavioural** *or US* **beˈhavioral** *adj*

behavioural science *n* the scientific study of the behaviour of organisms.

behaviourism *or US* **behaviorism** (bɪˈheɪvjəˌrɪzəm) *n* a school of psychology that regards objective observation of the behaviour of organisms as the only valid subject for study.
▸**beˈhaviourist** *or US* **beˈhaviorist** *adj, n* ▸**beˌhaviourˈistic** *or US* **beˌhaviorˈistic** *adj*

behaviour therapy *n* any of various means of treating psychological disorders, such as aversion therapy, that depend on the patient systematically learning new behaviour.

behead ⓣ (bɪˈhɛd) *vb* (*tr*) to remove the head from. [OE *beheāfdian*, from BE- + *heafod* HEAD]

beheld (bɪˈhɛld) *vb* the past tense and past participle of **behold.**

behemoth (bɪˈhiːmɒθ) *n* **1** *Bible.* a gigantic beast described in Job 40:15. **2** a huge or monstrous person or thing. [C14: from Heb. *bĕhēmōth*, pl. of *bĕhēmāh* beast]

behest ⓣ (bɪˈhɛst) *n* an order or earnest request. [OE *behǣs*, from *behātan;* see BE-, HEST]

behind ⓣ (bɪˈhaɪnd) *prep* **1** in or to a position further back than. **2** in the past in relation to: *I've got the exams behind me now.* **3** late according to: *running behind schedule.* **4** concerning the circumstances surrounding: *the reasons behind his departure.* **5** supporting: *I'm right behind you in your application.* ◆ *adv* **6** in or to a position further back; following. **7** remaining after someone's departure: *he left his books behind.* **8** in debt;

THESAURUS

orient, muddle, puzzle **2** = **intoxicate**, daze, stupefy
Antonyms *vb* ≠ **confuse:** clarify, clear up, elucidate, explicate, illuminate, interpret, make clear, make plain, resolve, simplify, throw *or* shed light on

befuddled *adj* **1** = **confused**, at sea, dazed, fuddled, groggy (*inf.*), muddled **2** = **intoxicated**, inebriated, woozy (*inf.*)

beg *vb* **1** = **scrounge**, blag (*sl.*), cadge, call for alms, mooch (*sl.*), seek charity, solicit charity, sponge on, touch (someone) for (*sl.*) **2** = **implore**, beseech, crave, desire, entreat, importune, petition, plead, pray, request, solicit, supplicate **4a** *As in* **beg the question** = **dodge**, avoid, duck (*inf.*), equivocate, evade, fend off, flannel (*Brit. inf.*), hedge, shirk, sidestep
Antonyms *vb* ≠ **scrounge:** claim, demand, exact, extort, insist on ≠ **implore:** apportion, award, bestow, commit, confer, contribute, donate, give, grant, impart, present

beget *vb* **1** = **father**, breed, generate, get, procreate, propagate, sire **2** = **cause**, bring, bring about, create, effect, engender, give rise to, occasion, produce, result in

begetter *n* **1** = **father**, genitor, parent, procreator, sire **2** = **creator**, architect, author, founder, inventor, originator

beggar *n* **1** = **scrounger** (*inf.*), cadger, mendicant, sponger (*inf.*), supplicant **2** = **tramp**, bag lady (*chiefly US*), bankrupt, bum (*inf.*), down-and-out, pauper, starveling, vagrant ◆ *vb* **4** *As in* **beggar description** = **defy**, baffle, challenge, surpass

beggarly *adj* = **inadequate**, low, meagre, mean, miserly, niggardly, stingy

beggary *n* = **poverty**, bankruptcy, destitution, indigence, need, pauperism, vagrancy, want, wretchedness

begin *vb* **1** = **start**, commence, embark on, get the show on the road (*inf.*), inaugurate, initiate, instigate, institute, prepare, set about, set on foot **2** = **happen**, appear, arise, be born, come into being, come into existence, commence, crop up (*inf.*), dawn, emerge, originate, spring, start
Antonyms *vb* cease, complete, end, finish, stop, terminate

beginner *n* = **novice**, amateur, apprentice, cub, fledgling, freshman, greenhorn (*inf.*), initiate, learner, neophyte, recruit, starter, student, tenderfoot, trainee, tyro
Antonyms *n* authority, expert, master, old hand, old stager, old-timer, past master *or* past mistress, pro (*inf.*), professional, trouper, veteran

beginning *n* **1, 2** = **start**, birth, commencement, inauguration, inception, initiation, onset, opening, opening move, origin, outset, overture, preface, prelude, rise, rudiments, source, starting point **4** = **seed**, embryo, fount, fountainhead, germ, root
Antonyms *n* ≠ **start:** closing, completion, conclusion, end, ending, finish, termination

begrudge *vb* **1** = **resent**, be reluctant, be stingy, grudge **2** = **envy**, be jealous

begrudgingly *adv* **1** = **resentfully**, grudgingly, hesitantly, reluctantly, stingily, unenthusiastically, unwillingly, with bad grace, without enthusiasm
Antonyms *adv* enthusiastically, freely, generously, gladly, willingly, with good grace

beguile *vb* **1** = **charm**, amuse, cheer, delight, distract, divert, engross, entertain, occupy **2** = **fool**, befool, cheat, deceive, delude, dupe, hoodwink, impose on, mislead, take for a ride (*inf.*), trick
Antonyms *vb* ≠ **fool:** alarm, alert, enlighten, put right

beguiling *adj* **1** = **charming**, alluring, attractive, bewitching, captivating, diverting, enchanting, entertaining, enthralling, interesting, intriguing

behalf *n* = **benefit**, account, advantage, defence, good, interest, part, profit, sake, side, support

behave *vb* **1** = **act**, function, operate, perform, run, work **3** = **conduct oneself properly**, act correctly, keep one's nose clean, mind one's manners
Antonyms *vb* ≠ **conduct oneself properly:** act up (*inf.*), be bad, be insubordinate, be naughty, carry on (*inf.*), get up to mischief (*inf.*), misbehave, muck about (*Brit. sl.*)

behaviour *n* **1** = **conduct**, actions, bearing, carriage, comportment, demeanour, deportment, manner, manners, ways **4** = **action**, functioning, operation, performance

behead *vb* = **decapitate**, execute, guillotine, truncate

behest *n* = **command**, bidding, canon, charge, commandment, decree, dictate, direction, injunction, instruction, mandate, order, precept, wish

behind *prep* **1** = **after**, at the back of, at the heels of, at the rear of, following **4** = **causing**, at the bottom of, initiating, instigating, responsiin arrears: *to fall behind with payments.* ◆ *adj* **9** (*postpositive*) in a position further back. ◆ *n* **10** *Inf.* the buttocks. **11** *Australian Rules football.* a score of one point made by kicking the ball over the **behind line** between a goalpost and one of the smaller outer posts (**behind posts**). [OE *behindan*]

behindhand ⓣ (bɪˈhaɪnd,hænd) *adj* (*postpositive*), *adv* **1** remiss in fulfilling an obligation. **2** in arrears. **3** backward. **4** late.

behold ⓣ (bɪˈhəʊld) *vb* **beholds, beholding, beheld.** (often imperative) *Arch. or literary.* to look (at); observe. [OE *bihealdan*; see BE-, HOLD[1]]
▸**beˈholder** *n*

beholden ⓣ (bɪˈhəʊldᵊn) *adj* indebted; obliged. [OE *behealden*, p.p. of *behealdan* to BEHOLD]

behoof (bɪˈhuːf) *n, pl* **behooves.** *Rare.* advantage or profit. [OE *behōf*; see BEHOVE]

behove ⓣ (bɪˈhəʊv) *vb* **behoves, behoving, behoved.** (*tr; impersonal*) *Arch.* to be necessary or fitting for: *it behoves me to arrest you.* [OE *behōfian*]

beige ⓣ (beɪʒ) *n* **1a** a very light brown, sometimes with a yellowish tinge. **1b** (*as adj*): *beige gloves.* **2** a fabric made of undyed or unbleached wool. [C19: from OF, from ?]

being ⓣ (ˈbiːɪŋ) *n* **1** the state or fact of existing; existence. **2** essential nature; self. **3** something that exists or is thought to exist: *a being from outer space.* **4** a person; human being.

bejabers (bɪˈdʒeɪbəz) *or* **bejabbers** (bɪˈdʒæbəz) *interj* an exclamation of surprise, emphasis, etc., regarded as characteristic of Irishmen. [C19: from *by Jesus!*]

bejewel (bɪˈdʒuːəl) *vb* **bejewels, bejewelling, bejewelled** *or US* **bejewels, bejeweling, bejeweled.** (*tr*) to decorate as with jewels.

bel (bɛl) *n* a unit for comparing two power levels, equal to the logarithm to the base ten of the ratio of the two powers. [C20: after A. G. *Bell* (1847–1922), US scientist]

belabour ⓣ *or US* **belabor** (bɪˈleɪbə) *vb* (*tr*) **1** to beat severely; thrash. **2** to attack verbally.

Belarussian *or* **Belorussian** (ˌbjɛləˈrʌʃən, ˌbɛləʊˈrʌʃən) *adj* **1** of or relating to Belarus, a country in E Europe. **2** relating to, or characteristic of Belarus, its people, or their language. **3** the official language of Belarus. **4** a native or inhabitant of Belarus. ◆ Also called: **White Russian.**

belated ⓣ (bɪˈleɪtɪd) *adj* late or too late: *belated greetings.*
▸**beˈlatedly** *adv* ▸**beˈlatedness** *n*

belay *vb* (bɪˈleɪ) **belays, belaying, belayed. 1** *Naut.* to secure (a line) to a pin, cleat, or bitt. **2** (*usually imperative*) *Naut.* to stop. **3** (ˈbiːˌleɪ). *Mountaineering.* to secure (a climber) by means of a belay. ◆ *n* (ˈbiːlˌeɪ). **4** *Mountaineering.* the attachment of a climber to a mountain by securing a rope round a rock, piton, etc., to safeguard the party in the event of a fall. [OE *belecgan*]

belaying pin *n Naut.* a cylindrical metal or wooden pin used for belaying.

bel canto (ˈbɛl ˈkæntəʊ) *n Music.* a style of singing characterized by beauty of tone rather than dramatic power. [It., lit.: beautiful singing]

belch ⓣ (bɛltʃ) *vb* **1** (*usually intr*) to expel wind from the stomach noisily through the mouth. **2** to expel or be expelled forcefully from inside: *smoke belching from factory chimneys.* ◆ *n* **3** an act of belching. [OE *bialcan*]

beldam *or* **beldame** (ˈbɛldəm) *n Arch.* an old woman. [C15: from *bel*-grand (as in *grandmother*), from OF *bel* beautiful, + *dam* mother]

beleaguer ⓣ (bɪˈliːgə) *vb* (*tr*) **1** to lay siege to. **2** to harass. [C16: from BE- + obs. *leaguer* a siege]

belemnite (ˈbɛləmˌnaɪt) *n* **1** an extinct marine mollusc related to the cuttlefish. **2** its long pointed conical internal shell: a common fossil. [C17: from Gk *belemnon* dart]

belfry (ˈbɛlfrɪ) *n, pl* **belfries. 1** the part of a tower or steeple in which bells are hung. **2** a tower or steeple. [C13: from OF *berfrei*, of Gmc origin]

Belg. *or* **Bel.** *abbrev. for:* **1** Belgian. **2** Belgium.

Belgian (ˈbɛldʒən) *n* **1** a native or inhabitant of Belgium, a kingdom in NW Europe. ◆ *adj* **2** of or relating to Belgium, the Belgians, or their languages.

Belgian hare *n* a large red domestic rabbit.

Belial (ˈbiːlɪəl) *n* the devil or Satan. [C13: from Heb. *bəlīyya'al*, from *bəlīy* without + *ya'al* worth]

belie ⓣ (bɪˈlaɪ) *vb* **belies, belying, belied.** (*tr*) **1** to show to be untrue. **2** to misrepresent; disguise the nature of. **3** to fail to justify; disappoint. [OE *belēogan*; see BE-, LIE[1]]

belief ⓣ (bɪˈliːf) *n* **1** a principle, etc., accepted as true, esp. without proof. **2** opinion; conviction. **3** religious faith. **4** trust or confidence, as in a person's abilities, etc.

believe ⓣ (bɪˈliːv) *vb* **believes, believing, believed. 1** (*tr; may take a clause as object*) to accept (a statement or opinion) as true: *I believe God exists.* **2** (*tr*) to accept the statement or opinion of (a person) as true. **3** (*intr;* foll. by *in*) to be convinced of the truth or existence (of): *to believe in fairies.* **4** (*intr*) to have religious faith. **5** (when *tr*, *takes a clause as object*) to think, assume, or suppose. **6** (*tr*) to think that someone is able to do (a particular action): *I wouldn't have believed it of him.* [OE *beliefan*]
▸**beˈlievable** *adj* ▸**beˈliever** *n*

belike (bɪˈlaɪk) *adv Arch.* perhaps; maybe.

Belisha beacon (bəˈliːʃə) *n Brit.* a flashing orange globe on a post, indicating a pedestrian crossing on a road. [C20: after L. Hore-*Belisha* (1893–1957), Brit. politician]

belittle ⓣ (bɪˈlɪtᵊl) *vb* **belittles, belittling, belittled.** (*tr*) **1** to consider or speak of (something) as less important than it really is. **2** to make small; dwarf.
▸**beˈlittlement** *n* ▸**beˈlittler** *n*

bell[1] (bɛl) *n* **1** a hollow, usually metal, cup-shaped instrument that emits a ringing sound when struck. **2** the sound made by such an instrument, as for marking the beginning or end of a period of time. **3** an electrical device that rings or buzzes as a signal. **4** something shaped like a bell, as the tube of certain musical wind instruments, or the corolla of certain flowers. **5** *Naut.* a signal rung on a ship's bell to count the number of half-hour intervals during each of six four-hour watches reckoned from midnight. **6** *Brit. sl.* a telephone call **7 bell, book, and candle. 7a** instruments used formerly in excommunications and other ecclesiastical rites. **7b** *Inf.* the solemn ritual ratification of such acts. **8 ring a bell.** to sound familiar; recall something previously experienced. **9 sound as a bell.** in perfect condition. ◆ *vb* **10** to be or cause to be shaped like a bell. **11** (*tr*) to attach a bell or bells to. [OE *belle*]

bell[2] (bɛl) *n* **1** a bellowing or baying cry, esp. that of a stag in rut. ◆ *vb* **2** to utter (such a cry). [OE *bellan*]

belladonna (ˌbɛləˈdɒnə) *n* **1** either of two alkaloid drugs obtained from the leaves and roots of the deadly nightshade. **2** another name for **deadly nightshade.** [C16: from It., lit.: beautiful lady; supposed to refer to its use as a cosmetic]

bellbird (ˈbɛlˌbɜːd) *n* **1** any of several tropical American birds having a bell-like call. **2** either of two other birds with a bell-like call: an Australian flycatcher (**crested bellbird**) or a New Zealand honeyeater.

bell-bottoms *pl n* trousers that flare from the knee.
▸ˈ**bell-ˌbottomed** *adj*

bellboy (ˈbɛlˌbɔɪ) *n Chiefly US & Canad.* a porter or page in a hotel, club, etc. Also called: **bellhop.**

bell buoy *n* a navigational buoy with a bell which strikes when the waves move the buoy.

THESAURUS

ble for **5** = **supporting**, backing, for, in agreement, on the side of ◆ *adv* **6** = **after**, afterwards, following, in the wake (of), next, subsequently **8** = **overdue**, behindhand, in arrears, in debt ◆ *n* **10** *Informal* = **bottom**, arse (*taboo sl.*), ass (*US & Canad. taboo sl.*), bum (*Brit. sl.*), buns (*US sl.*), butt (*US & Canad. inf.*), buttocks, derrière (*euphemistic*), jacksy (*Brit. sl.*), posterior, rump, seat, tail (*inf.*)
Antonyms *adv* ≠ **after:** earlier than, in advance of, in front of, in the presence of, prior to ≠ **overdue:** ahead, earlier, formerly, in advance, previously, sooner

behindhand *adj* **1** = **late**, dilatory, remiss, slow **4** = **late**, behind time, tardy

behold *vb Archaic or literary* = **look at**, check, check out, consider, contemplate, discern, eye, observe, perceive, recce (*sl.*), regard, scan, survey, view, watch, witness

beholden *adj* = **indebted**, bound, grateful, obligated, obliged, owing, under obligation

behove *vb Archaic* = **be fitting**, be advisable, befit, be incumbent upon, be necessary, benefit, be obligatory, beseem, be wise

beige *n* **1** = **fawn**, biscuit, buff, *café au lait*, camel, cinnamon, coffee, cream, ecru, khaki, mushroom, neutral, oatmeal, sand, tan

being *n* **1** = **existence**, actuality, animation, life, living, reality **2** = **nature**, essence, soul, spirit, substance **3** = **creature**, animal, beast, body, living thing, mortal, thing **4** = **human being**, individual
Antonyms *n* ≠ **existence:** nihility, nonbeing, nonexistence, nothingness, nullity, oblivion

belabour *vb* **1** = **beat**, batter, clobber (*sl.*), flog, thrash, whip **2** = **attack**, berate, blast, castigate, censure, criticize, excoriate, flay, go for the jugular, lay into (*inf.*), put down, tear into (*inf.*)

belated *adj* = **late**, behindhand, behind time, delayed, late in the day, overdue, tardy

belch *vb* **1** = **burp** (*inf.*), eruct, eructate, hiccup **2** = **emit**, discharge, disgorge, erupt, give off, gush, spew forth, vent, vomit

beleaguered *adj* **1** = **besieged**, assailed, beset, blockaded, encompassed, hemmed in, surrounded **2** = **harassed**, aggravated (*inf.*), annoyed, badgered, hassled (*inf.*), persecuted, pestered, plagued, put upon, vexed

belie *vb* **1** = **disprove**, confute, contradict, deny, gainsay (*arch. or literary*), give the lie to, make a nonsense of, negate, rebut, repudiate **2** = **misrepresent**, conceal, deceive, disguise, falsify, gloss over, mislead

belief *n* **2** = **opinion**, assurance, confidence, conviction, feeling, impression, judgment, notion, persuasion, presumption, theory, view **3** = **faith**, credence, credo, creed, doctrine, dogma, ideology, principles, tenet **4** = **trust**, credit, reliance
Antonyms *n* ≠ **trust:** disbelief, distrust, doubt, dubiety, incredulity, mistrust, scepticism

believable *adj* **1, 2** = **credible**, acceptable, authentic, creditable, imaginable, likely, plausible, possible, probable, reliable, trustworthy
Antonyms *adj* cock-and-bull (*inf.*), doubtful, dubious, fabulous, implausible, incredible, questionable, unacceptable, unbelievable

believe *vb* **1, 2** = **accept**, be certain of, be convinced of, buy (*sl.*), count on, credit, depend on, have faith in, hold, place confidence in, presume true, rely on, swallow (*inf.*), swear by, take as gospel, take on board, trust **5** = **think**, assume, conjecture, consider, gather, guess (*inf., chiefly US & Canad.*), imagine, judge, maintain, postulate, presume, reckon, speculate, suppose
Antonyms *vb* ≠ **accept:** disbelieve, distrust, doubt, know, question

believer *n* **4** = **follower**, adherent, convert, devotee, disciple, proselyte, protagonist, supporter, upholder, zealot
Antonyms *n* agnostic, atheist, disbeliever, doubting Thomas, infidel, sceptic, unbeliever

belittle *vb* **1** = **disparage**, decry, denigrate, deprecate, depreciate, deride, derogate, detract, diminish, minimize, scoff at, scorn, sneer at, underestimate, underrate, undervalue

belle ❶ (bɛl) *n* **1** a beautiful woman. **2** the most attractive woman at a function, etc. (esp. in **belle of the ball**). [C17: from F, fem of BEAU]

belle époque *French.* (bɛl epɔk) *n* the period of comfortable well-established life before World War I. [lit.: fine period]

belles-lettres (*French* bɛlɛtrə) *n* (*functioning as sing*) literary works, esp. essays and poetry, valued for their aesthetic content. [C17: from F: fine letters]
▸**bel'letrist** *n*

bellflower ('bɛl,flauə) *n* another name for **campanula.**

bellfounder ('bɛl,faundə) *n* a foundry worker who casts bells.

bellicose ❶ ('bɛlɪ,kəus, -,kəuz) *adj* warlike; aggressive; ready to fight. [C15: from L *bellicōsus,* from *bellum* war]
▸**bellicosity** (,bɛlɪ'kɒsɪtɪ) *n*

belligerence ❶ (bɪ'lɪdʒərəns) *n* the act or quality of being belligerent or warlike; aggressiveness.

belligerency (bɪ'lɪdʒərənsɪ) *n* the state of being at war.

belligerent ❶ (bɪ'lɪdʒərənt) *adj* **1** marked by readiness to fight or argue; aggressive. **2** relating to or engaged in a war. ◆ *n* **3** a person or country engaged in war. [C16: from L *belliger,* from *bellum* war + *gerere* to wage]

bell jar *n* a bell-shaped glass cover to protect flower arrangements, etc., or to cover apparatus in experiments. Also called: **bell glass.**

bellman ('bɛlmən) *n, pl* **bellmen.** a man who rings a bell; (formerly) a town crier.

bell metal *n* an alloy of copper and tin, with some zinc and lead, used in casting bells.

bellow ❶ ('bɛləu) *vb* **1** (*intr*) to make a loud deep cry like that of a bull; roar. **2** to shout (something) unrestrainedly, as in anger or pain. ◆ *n* **3** the characteristic noise of a bull. **4** a loud deep sound, as of pain or anger. [C14: prob. from OE *bylgan*]

bellows ('bɛləuz) *n* (*functioning as sing or pl*) **1** Also: **pair of bellows.** an instrument consisting of an air chamber with flexible sides that is used to create a stream of air, as for producing a draught for a fire or for sounding organ pipes. **2** a flexible corrugated part, as that connecting the lens system of some cameras to the body. [C16: from pl of OE *belig* BELLY]

bell pull *n* a handle, rope, or cord pulled to operate a doorbell or servant's bell.

bell push *n* a button pressed to operate an electric bell.

bell-ringer *n* a person who rings church bells or musical handbells.
▸**'bell-,ringing** *n*

bells and whistles *pl n* additional features or accessories which are nonessential but very attractive. [C20: from the bells and whistles which used to decorate fairground organs]

bell tent *n* a cone-shaped tent having a single central supporting pole.

bellwether ('bɛl,wɛðə) *n* **1** a sheep that leads the herd, often bearing a bell. **2** a leader, esp. one followed blindly.

belly ❶ ('bɛlɪ) *n, pl* **bellies. 1** the lower or front part of the body of a vertebrate, containing the intestines and other organs; abdomen. **2** the stomach, esp. when regarded as the seat of gluttony. **3** a part that bulges deeply: *the belly of a sail.* **4** the inside or interior cavity of something. **5** the front, lower, or inner part of something. **6** the surface of a stringed musical instrument over which the strings are stretched. **7** *Austral. & NZ.* the wool from a sheep's belly. **8** *Arch.* the womb. **9 go belly up.** *Inf.* to die, fail, or come to an end. ◆ *vb* **bellies, bellying, bellied. 10** to swell out or cause to swell out; bulge. [OE *belig*]

bellyache ('bɛlɪ,eɪk) *n* **1** an informal term for **stomachache.** ◆ *vb* **bellyaches, bellyaching, bellyached. 2** (*intr*) *Sl.* to complain repeatedly.
▸**'belly,acher** *n*

bellyband ('bɛlɪ,bænd) *n* a strap around the belly of a draught animal, holding the shafts of a vehicle.

bellybutton ('bɛlɪ,bʌtᵊn) *n* an informal name for the **navel.** Also called: **tummy button.**

belly dance *n* **1** a sensuous dance of Middle Eastern origin, performed by women, with undulating movements of the abdomen. ◆ *vb* **belly-dance, belly-dances, belly-dancing, belly-danced. 2** (*intr*) to dance thus.
▸**belly dancer** *n*

belly flop *n* **1** a dive into water in which the body lands horizontally. ◆ *vb* **belly-flop, belly-flops, belly-flopping, belly-flopped. 2** (*intr*) to perform a belly flop.

bellyful ❶ ('bɛlɪ,ful) *n* **1** as much as one wants or can eat. **2** *Sl.* more than one can tolerate.

belly landing *n* the landing of an aircraft on its fuselage without use of its landing gear.

belly laugh *n* a loud deep hearty laugh.

belong ❶ (bɪ'lɒŋ) *vb* (*intr*) **1** (foll. by *to*) to be the property or possession (of). **2** (foll. by *to*) to be bound (to) by ties of affection, allegiance, etc. **3** (foll. by *to, under, with,* etc.) to be classified (with): *this plant belongs to the daisy family.* **4** (foll. by *to*) to be a part or adjunct (of). **5** to have a proper or usual place. **6** *Inf.* to be acceptable, esp. socially. [C14 *belongen,* from BE- (intensive) + *longen,* from OE *langian* to belong]

belonging ❶ (bɪ'lɒŋɪŋ) *n* secure relationship; affinity (esp. in **a sense of belonging**).

belongings ❶ (bɪ'lɒŋɪŋz) *pl n* (*sometimes sing*) the things that a person owns or has with him.

beloved ❶ (bɪ'lʌvɪd, -'lʌvd) *adj* **1** dearly loved. ◆ *n* **2** a person who is dearly loved.

below ❶ (bɪ'ləu) *prep* **1** at or to a position lower than; under. **2** less than. **3** south of. **4** downstream of. **5** unworthy of; beneath. ◆ *adv* **6** at or to a lower position. **7** at a later place (in something written). **8** *Arch.* on earth or in hell. [C14 *bilooghe,* from *bi* BY + *looghe* LOW[1]]

Bel Paese ('bɛl pɑː'eɪzɪ) *n* a mild creamy Italian cheese. [from It., lit.: beautiful country]

belt ❶ (bɛlt) *n* **1** a band of cloth, leather, etc., worn, usually around the waist, to support clothing, carry weapons, etc., or as decoration. **2** a belt worn to show rank (as by a knight), to mark expertise (as in judo), or awarded as a prize (as in boxing). **3** a narrow band, circle, or stripe, as of colour. **4** an area where a specific thing is found; zone: *a belt of high pressure.* **5** See **seat belt. 6** a band of flexible material between rotating shafts or pulleys to transfer motion or transmit goods: *a fan belt; a conveyer belt.* **7** *Inf.* a sharp blow. **8 below the belt. 8a** *Boxing.* below the waist. **8b** *Inf.* in an unscrupulous or cowardly way. **9 tighten one's belt.** to take measures to reduce expenditure. **10 under one's belt. 10a** in one's stomach. **10b** as part of one's experience: *he had a degree under his belt.* ◆ *vb* **11** (*tr*) to fasten or attach with or as if with a belt. **12** (*tr*) to hit with a belt. **13** (*tr*) *Sl.* to give a sharp blow; punch. **14** (*intr;* often foll. by *along*) *Sl.* to move very fast, esp. in a car. **15** (*tr*) *Rare.* to encircle. [OE, from L *balteus*]
▸**'belted** *adj*

belt-and-braces *adj* providing double security, in case one security measure should fail: *a belt-and-braces policy.*

Beltane ('bɛlteɪn, -tən) *n* an ancient Celtic festival with a sacrificial bonfire on May Day. [C15: from Scot. Gaelic *bealltainn*]

belter ('bɛltə) *n Sl.* **1** an event, person, quality, etc., that is admirable, outstanding, or thrilling: *a real belter of a match.* **2a** a rousing or spirited popular song that is sung loudly and enthusiastically. **2b** a person who sings popular songs in a loud and spirited manner.

belting ('bɛltɪŋ) *n* **1** material for belts. **2** belts collectively. **3** *Inf.* a beating.

belt man *n Austral. & NZ.* (formerly) the member of a beach life-saving team who swam out wearing a belt with a line attached.

belt out *vb* (*tr, adv*) *Inf.* to sing or emit sound loudly.

belt up *vb* (*adv*) **1** *Sl.* to stop talking: often imperative. **2** to fasten with a belt.

beluga (bɪ'luːgə) *n* **1** a large white sturgeon of the Black and Caspian Seas: a source of caviar and isinglass. **2** another name for **white whale.** [C18: from Russian *byeluga,* from *byely* white]

belvedere ('bɛlvɪ,dɪə, ,bɛlvɪ'dɪə) *n* a building, such as a summerhouse, sited to command a fine view. [C16: from It.: beautiful sight]

bemire (bɪ'maɪə) *vb* **bemires, bemiring, bemired.** (*tr*) **1** to soil as with mire. **2** (*usually passive*) to stick fast in mire.

bemoan ❶ (bɪ'məun) *vb* to mourn; lament (esp. in **bemoan one's fate**). [OE *bemǣnan;* see BE-, MOAN]

bemuse ❶ (bɪ'mjuːz) *vb* **bemuses, bemusing, bemused.** (*tr*) to confuse; bewilder.

THESAURUS

Antonyms *vb* boast about, elevate, exalt, magnify, praise, vaunt

belle *n* **1** = **beauty,** cracker (*inf.*), good-looker, looker (*inf.*), lovely, peach (*inf.*), stunner (*inf.*), Venus

bellicose *adj* = **aggressive,** antagonistic, belligerent, combative, defiant, hawkish, hostile, militaristic, provocative, pugnacious, quarrelsome, warlike, warloving, warmongering

bellicosity *n* = **aggression,** aggressiveness, antagonism, belligerence, combativeness, hostility, pugnacity, truculence, warlike nature

belligerence *n* = **aggressiveness,** animosity, antagonism, combativeness, hostility, pugnacity, unfriendliness

belligerent *adj* **1** = **aggressive,** antagonistic, argumentative, combative, contentious, hostile, pugnacious, quarrelsome, unfriendly **2** = **warring,** bellicose, warlike ◆ *n* **3** = **fighter,** combatant, warring nation

Antonyms *adj* ≠ **aggressive:** amicable, benign, conciliatory, friendly, harmonious, nonviolent, without hostility

bellow *n, vb* = **shout,** bawl, bell, call, clamour, cry, howl, roar, scream, shriek, yell

belly *n* **1** = **abdomen,** gut, insides (*inf.*), vitals **2** = **stomach,** breadbasket, corporation (*inf.*), gut, paunch, potbelly, tummy ◆ *vb* **10** = **swell out,** billow, bulge, fill, spread, swell

bellyful *n* **1, 2** = **surfeit,** enough, excess, glut, plateful, plenty, satiety, superabundance, too much

belong *vb* **1** *foll. by* **to** = **be the property of,** be at the disposal of, be held by, be owned by **2** *foll. by* **to** = **be a member of,** be affiliated to, be allied to, be associated with, be included in **4** *foll. by* **to** = **go with,** attach to, be connected with, be part of, fit, pertain to, relate to

belonging *n* = **relationship,** acceptance, affiliation, affinity, association, attachment, fellowship, inclusion, kinship, loyalty, rapport

belongings *pl n* = **possessions,** accoutrements, chattels, effects, gear, goods, paraphernalia, personal property, stuff, things

beloved *adj* **1** = **dear,** admired, adored, cherished, darling, dearest, loved, pet, precious, prized, revered, sweet, treasured, valued, worshipped

below *prep* **1** = **lesser,** inferior, subject, subordinate **2** = **less than,** lower than **5** = **unworthy of,** beneath ◆ *adv* **6** = **lower,** beneath, down, under, underneath

belt *n* **1** = **waistband,** band, cincture, cummerbund, girdle, girth, sash **4** = **zone,** area, district, layer, region, stretch, strip, tract **8b below the belt** *Informal* = **unfair,** cowardly, foul, not playing the game (*inf.*), unjust, unscrupulous, unsporting, unsportsmanlike

bemoan *vb* = **lament,** bewail, cry over spilt milk, deplore, express sorrow, grieve for, moan over, mourn, regret, rue, weep for

bemuse *vb* = **puzzle,** amaze, bewilder, confuse,

bemused 🅣 (bɪˈmjuːzd) *adj* preoccupied; lost in thought.

ben[1] (bɛn) *Scot.* ◆ *n* **1** an inner room in a cottage. ◆ *prep, adv* **2** in; within; inside. ◆ Cf. **but**[2]. [OE *binnan*, from BE- + *innan* inside]

ben[2] (bɛn) *n Scot., Irish.* a mountain peak: *Ben Lomond.* [C18: from Gaelic *beinn*, from *beann*]

bench 🅣 (bɛntʃ) *n* **1** a long seat for more than one person, usually lacking a back. **2** a plain stout worktable. **3 the bench.** (*sometimes cap.*) **3a** a judge or magistrate sitting in court. **3b** judges or magistrates collectively. **4** a ledge in a mine or quarry from which work is carried out. **5** (in a gymnasium) a low table, which may be inclined, used for various exercises. **6** a platform on which dogs, etc., are exhibited at shows. **7** *NZ.* a hollow formed by sheep on a hillside. ◆ *vb* (*tr*) **8** to provide with benches. **9** to exhibit (a dog, etc.) at a show. **10** *US & Canad., Sports.* to take (a player) out of a game, often for disciplinary reasons. [OE *benc*]

bencher (ˈbɛntʃə) *n* (*often pl*) *Brit.* **1** a member of the governing body of one of the Inns of Court. **2** See **backbencher.**

benchmark 🅣 (ˈbɛntʃˌmɑːk) *n* **1** a mark on a stone post or other permanent feature, used as a reference point in surveying. **2** a criterion by which to measure something; reference point.

bench press *n* a weight-training exercise in which a person lies on a bench and pushes a barbell upwards with both hands from chest level until the arms are straight, then lowers it again.

bench test *n* the critical evaluation of a new or repaired component, device, apparatus, etc., prior to installation to ensure that it is in perfect condition.

bench warrant *n* a warrant issued by a judge or court directing that an offender be apprehended.

bend[1] 🅣 (bɛnd) *vb* **bends, bending, bent. 1** to form or cause to form a curve. **2** to turn or cause to turn from a particular direction: *the road bends left.* **3** (*intr;* often foll. by *down,* etc.) to incline the body; stoop; bow. **4** to submit or cause to submit: *to bend before superior force.* **5** (*tr*) to turn or direct (one's eyes, steps, attention, etc.). **6** (*tr*) *Naut.* to attach or fasten, as a sail to a boom. **7 bend (someone's) ear.** to speak at length to an unwilling listener, esp. to voice one's troubles. **8 bend the rules.** *Inf.* to ignore rules or change them to suit one's own convenience. ◆ *n* **9** a curved part. **10** *Naut.* a knot in a line for joining it to another or to an object. **11** the act of bending. **12 round the bend.** *Brit. sl.* mad. [OE *bendan*]
▸ **ˈbendable** *adj* ▸ **ˈbendy** *adj*

bend[2] (bɛnd) *n Heraldry.* a diagonal line traversing a shield. [OE *bend* BAND[2]]

bender (ˈbɛndə) *n Inf.* **1** a drinking bout. **2** a makeshift shelter constructed by placing tarpaulin or plastic sheeting over bent saplings or woven branches.

bends (bɛndz) *pl n* (*functioning as sing or pl*) **the.** a nontechnical name for **decompression sickness.**

bend sinister *n Heraldry.* a diagonal line bisecting a shield from the top right to the bottom left, typically indicating a bastard line.

beneath 🅣 (bɪˈniːθ) *prep* **1** below, esp. if covered, protected, or obscured by. **2** not as great or good as would be demanded by: *beneath his dignity.* ◆ *adv* **3** below; underneath. [OE *beneothan*, from BE- + *neothan* low]

benedicite (ˌbɛnɪˈdaɪsɪtɪ) *n* (esp. in Christian religious orders) a blessing or grace. [C13: from L, from *benedīcere*, from *bene* well + *dīcere* to speak]

Benedictine *n* **1** (ˌbɛnɪˈdɪktɪn, -taɪn). a monk or nun who is a member of the order of Saint Benedict, founded about 540 A.D. **2** (ˌbɛnɪˈdɪktiːn). a greenish-yellow liqueur first made at the Benedictine monastery at Fécamp in France in about 1510. ◆ *adj* (ˌbɛnɪˈdɪktɪn, -taɪn). **3** of or relating to Saint Benedict or his order.

benediction 🅣 (ˌbɛnɪˈdɪkʃən) *n* **1** an invocation of divine blessing. **2** a Roman Catholic service in which the congregation is blessed with the sacrament. **3** the state of being blessed. [C15: from L *benedictio*, from *benedīcere* to bless; see BENEDICITE]
▸ **ˌbeneˈdictory** *adj*

Benedictus (ˌbɛnɪˈdɪktəs) *n* (*sometimes not cap.*) *Christianity.* **1** a canticle beginning *Benedictus qui venit in nomine Domini* in Latin and *Blessed is he that cometh in the name of the Lord* in English. **2** a canticle beginning *Benedictus Dominus Deus Israel* in Latin and *Blessed be the Lord God of Israel* in English.

benefaction 🅣 (ˌbɛnɪˈfækʃən) *n* **1** the act of doing good, esp. by giving a donation to charity. **2** the donation or help given. [C17: from LL *benefactiō*, from L *bene* well + *facere* to do]

benefactor 🅣 (ˈbɛnɪˌfæktə, ˌbɛnɪˈfæk-) *n* a person who supports or helps a person, institution, etc., esp. by giving money.
▸ **ˈbeneˌfactress** *fem n*

benefice 🅣 (ˈbɛnɪfɪs) *n* **1** *Christianity.* an endowed Church office yielding an income to its holder; a Church living. **2** the property or revenue attached to such an office. [C14: from OF, from L *beneficium* benefit, from *bene* well + *facere* to do]
▸ **ˈbeneficed** *adj*

beneficent 🅣 (bɪˈnɛfɪsᵊnt) *adj* charitable; generous. [C17: from L *beneficus;* see BENEFICE]
▸ **beˈneficence** *n*

beneficial 🅣 (ˌbɛnɪˈfɪʃəl) *adj* **1** (sometimes foll. by *to*) advantageous. **2** *Law.* entitling a person to receive the profits or proceeds of property. [C15: from LL *beneficiālis*, from L *beneficium* kindness]

beneficiary 🅣 (ˌbɛnɪˈfɪʃərɪ) *n, pl* **beneficiaries. 1** a person who gains or benefits. **2** *Law.* a person entitled to receive funds or other property under a trust, will, etc. **3** the holder of a benefice. **4** *NZ.* a person who receives government assistance: *social security beneficiary.* ◆ *adj* **5** of or relating to a benefice.

benefit 🅣 (ˈbɛnɪfɪt) *n* **1** something that improves or promotes. **2** advantage or sake. **3** (*sometimes pl*) a payment or series of payments made by an institution or government to a person who is ill, unemployed, etc. **4** a theatrical performance, sports event, etc., to raise money for a charity. ◆ *vb* **benefits, benefiting, benefited** *or US* **benefits, benefitting, benefitted. 5** to do or receive good; profit. [C14: from Anglo-F *benfet*, from L *benefactum*, from *bene facere* to do well]

benefit in kind *n* a non-pecuniary benefit, such as a company car or medical insurance, given to an employee.

benefit of clergy *n Christianity.* **1** sanction by the church: *marriage without benefit of clergy.* **2** (in the Middle Ages) a privilege that placed the clergy outside the jurisdiction of secular courts.

benefit society *n* a US term for **friendly society.**

benevolence 🅣 (bɪˈnɛvələns) *n* **1** inclination to do good; charity. **2** an act of kindness.

benevolent 🅣 (bɪˈnɛvələnt) *adj* **1** intending or showing goodwill; kindly; friendly. **2** doing good rather than making profit; charitable: *a benevolent organization.* [C15: from L *benevolēns*, from *bene* well + *velle* to wish]

BEng *abbrev. for* Bachelor of Engineering.

Bengali (bɛnˈgɔːlɪ, bɛŋ-) *n* **1** a member of a people living chiefly in Bangladesh (a republic in S Asia) and in West Bengal (in NE India). **2** Also called: **Bangla.** their language. ◆ *adj* **3** of or relating to Bengal, the Bengalis, or their language.

Bengal light (bɛnˈgɔːl, bɛŋ-) *n* a firework or flare that burns with a bright blue light, formerly used as a signal.

benighted 🅣 (bɪˈnaɪtɪd) *adj* **1** lacking cultural, moral, or intellectual enlightenment. **2** *Arch.* overtaken by night.
▸ **beˈnightedness** *n*

benign 🅣 (bɪˈnaɪn) *adj* **1** showing kindliness; genial. **2** (of soil, climate, etc.) mild; gentle. **3** favourable; propitious. **4** *Pathol.* (of a tumour,

THESAURUS

daze, flummox, muddle, nonplus, overwhelm, perplex, stun

bemused *adj* = **puzzled**, absent-minded, at sea, bewildered, confused, dazed, engrossed, flummoxed, fuddled, half-drunk, muddled, nonplussed, perplexed, preoccupied, stunned, stupefied, tipsy

bench *n* **1** = **seat**, form, pew, settle, stall **2** = **worktable**, board, counter, table, trestle table, workbench **3 the bench** = **court**, courtroom, judge, judges, judiciary, magistrate, magistrates, tribunal

benchmark *n* **2** = **reference point**, criterion, example, gauge, level, measure, model, norm, par, reference, standard, touchstone, yardstick

bend[1] *vb* **1** = **curve**, arc, arch, bow, buckle, contort, flex, twist, warp **2** = **turn**, deflect, diverge, swerve, veer **3** = **incline**, bow, crouch, lean, stoop **4** = **force**, compel, direct, influence, mould, persuade, shape, subdue, submit, sway, yield ◆ *n* **9** = **curve**, angle, arc, arch, bow, corner, crook, hook, loop, turn, twist, zigzag

beneath *prep* **1** = **under**, below, lower than, underneath **2** = **unworthy of**, below, inferior to, less than, unbefitting ◆ *adv* **3** = **underneath**, below, in a lower place

Antonyms *prep* ≠ **under**: above, atop, higher than, on top of, over, upon

benediction *n* **1** = **blessing**, benison, consecration, invocation, orison, prayer

benefaction *n* **1** = **charity**, beneficence, benevolence, generosity, largesse *or* largess, liberality, munificence, philanthropy **2** = **donation**, alms, bequest, boon, charity, contribution, endowment, gift, grant, gratuity, hand-out, largesse *or* largess, legacy, offering, present, stipend

benefactor *n* = **supporter**, angel (*inf.*), backer, contributor, donor, helper, patron, philanthropist, promoter, sponsor, subscriber, subsidizer, well-wisher

benefice *n* **1** *Christianity* = **office**, Church living, emolument, incumbency, prebend, preferment, sinecure, stipend

beneficence *n* = **generosity**, altruism, benevolence, charity, compassion, goodness, goodwill, helpfulness, kindness, largesse *or* largess, liberality, love, unselfishness, virtue

beneficent *adj* = **generous**, benevolent, benign, bounteous, bountiful, charitable, helpful, kind, liberal, munificent, princely

beneficial *adj* **1** = **helpful**, advantageous, benign, expedient, favourable, gainful, healthful, profitable, salubrious, salutary, serviceable, useful, valuable, wholesome

Antonyms *adj* detrimental, disadvantageous, harmful, pernicious, useless

beneficiary *n* **2** *Law* = **recipient**, assignee, heir, inheritor, legatee, payee, receiver, successor

benefit *n* **1** = **help**, advantage, aid, asset, assistance, avail, betterment, blessing, boon, favour, gain, good, interest, mileage (*inf.*), profit, use, utility ◆ *vb* **5** = **help**, advance, advantage, aid, ameliorate, assist, avail, better, enhance, further, improve, profit, promote, serve

Antonyms *n* ≠ **help**: damage, detriment, disadvantage, downside, harm, impairment, injury, loss ◆ *vb* ≠ **help**: damage, deprive, detract from, harm, impair, injure, worsen

benevolence *n* **1** = **kindness**, altruism, charity, compassion, fellow feeling, generosity, goodness, goodwill, humanity, kindheartedness, sympathy

Antonyms *n* ill will, malevolence, selfishness, stinginess, unkindness

benevolent *adj* **1** = **kind**, affable, altruistic, beneficent, benign, bounteous, bountiful, caring, charitable, compassionate, considerate, generous, humane, humanitarian, kind-hearted, liberal, philanthropic, tender-hearted, warm-hearted, well-disposed

benighted *adj* **1** = **uncivilized**, backward,

etc.) not malignant. [C14: from OF *benigne,* from L *benignus,* from *bene* well + *gignere* to produce]
▸**be'nignly** *adv*

benignant (bɪ'nɪgnənt) *adj* **1** kind; gracious. **2** a less common word for **benign** (senses 3, 4).
▸**be'nignancy** *n*

benignity (bɪ'nɪgnɪtɪ) *n, pl* **benignities. 1** the quality of being benign. **2** a kind or gracious act.

benison ('bɛnɪzᵊn, -sᵊn) *n Arch.* a blessing. [C13: from OF *beneison,* from L *benedictiō* BENEDICTION]

bent[1] ❶ (bɛnt) *adj* **1** not straight; curved. **2** (foll. by *on*) resolved (to); determined (to). **3** *Sl.* **3a** dishonest; corrupt. **3b** (of goods) stolen. **3c** crazy. **3d** sexually deviant. ◆ *n* **4** personal inclination or aptitude. **5** capacity of endurance (esp. in **to the top of one's bent**).

bent[2] (bɛnt) *n* **1** short for **bent grass. 2** *Arch.* any stiff grass or sedge. **3** *Arch. or dialect.* heath or moorland. [OE *bionot*]

bent grass *n* a perennial grass which has a spreading panicle of tiny flowers sometimes planted for hay or in lawns.

Benthamism ('bɛnθəm,ɪzəm) *n* the utilitarian philosophy of Jeremy Bentham (1748–1832), English philosopher and jurist, which holds that the ultimate goal of society should be to promote the greatest happiness of the greatest number.
▸**'Bentham,ite** *n, adj*

benthos ('bɛnθɒs) *n* the animals and plants living at the bottom of a sea or lake. [C19: from Gk: depth; rel. to *bathus* deep]
▸**'benthic** *adj*

bentonite ('bɛntə,naɪt) *n* a clay that swells as it absorbs water: used as a filler in various industries. [after Fort *Benton,* Montana, USA, where found]

bentwood ('bɛnt,wʊd) *n* **a** wood bent in moulds after being heated by steaming, used mainly for furniture. **b** *(as modifier): a bentwood chair.*

benumb ❶ (bɪ'nʌm) *vb (tr)* **1** to make numb or powerless; deaden, as by cold. **2** *(usually passive)* to stupefy (the mind, senses, will, etc.).

Benzedrine ('bɛnzɪ,driːn, -drɪn) *n* a trademark for **amphetamine.**

benzene ('bɛnziːn) *n* a colourless flammable poisonous liquid used in the manufacture of styrene, phenol, etc., as a solvent for fats, resins, etc., and as an insecticide. Formula: $C_6 H_6$.

benzene ring *n* the hexagonal ring of bonded carbon atoms in the benzene molecule.

benzine ('bɛnziːn, bɛn'ziːn) *or* **benzin** ('bɛnzɪn) *n* a volatile mixture of the lighter hydrocarbon constituents of petroleum.

benzo- *or* **benz-** *combining form.* **1** indicating a fused benzene ring. **2** indicating derivation from benzene or benzoic acid or the presence of phenyl groups. [from BENZOIN]

benzoate ('bɛnzəʊ,eɪt, -ɪt) *n* a salt or ester of benzoic acid.

benzocaine ('bɛnzəʊ,keɪn) *n* a white crystalline ester used as a local anaesthetic.

benzodiazepine (,bɛnzəʊdaɪ'eɪzə,piːn) *n* any of a group of chemical compounds that are used as minor tranquillizers, such as diazepam (Valium) and chlordiazepoxide (Librium). [C20: from BENZO- + DI-[1] + AZ(O)- + EP(OXY)- + -INE[2]]

benzoic (bɛn'zəʊɪk) *adj* of, containing, or derived from benzoic acid or benzoin.

benzoic acid *n* a white crystalline solid occurring in many natural resins, used in plasticizers and dyes and as a food preservative (**E210**).

benzoin ('bɛnzɔɪn, -zəʊɪn) *n* a gum resin containing benzoic acid, obtained from various tropical Asian trees and used in ointments, perfume, etc. [C16: from F *benjoin,* from OCatalan *benjui,* from Ar. *lubān jāwī,* lit.: frankincense of Java]

benzol *or* **benzole** ('bɛnzɒl) *n* **1** a crude form of benzene obtained from coal tar or coal gas and used as a fuel. **2** an obsolete name for **benzene.**

bequeath ❶ (bɪ'kwiːð, -'kwiːθ) *vb (tr)* **1** *Law.* to dispose of (property) by will. **2** to hand down; pass on. [OE *becwethan*]
▸**be'queathal** *n*

bequest ❶ (bɪ'kwɛst) *n* **1** the act of bequeathing. **2** something that is bequeathed. [C14: BE- + OE *-cwiss* degree]

berate ❶ (bɪ'reɪt) *vb* **berates, berating, berated.** *(tr)* to scold harshly.

Berber ('bɜːbə) *n* **1** a member of a Caucasoid Muslim people of N Africa. **2** the language of this people. ◆ *adj* **3** of or relating to this people or their language.

berberis ('bɜːbərɪs) *n* any of a genus of mainly N temperate shrubs. See **barberry.** [C19: from Med. L, from ?]

berceuse (*French* bɛrsøz) *n* **1** a lullaby. **2** an instrumental piece suggestive of this. [C19: from F: lullaby]

bereave ❶ (bɪ'riːv) *vb* **bereaves, bereaving, bereaved.** *(tr)* (usually foll. by *of*) to deprive (of) something or someone valued, esp. through death. [OE *bereafian*]
▸**be'reaved** *adj* ▸**be'reavement** *n*

bereft ❶ (bɪ'rɛft) *adj* (usually foll. by *of*) deprived; parted (from): *bereft of hope.*

beret ('bɛreɪ) *n* a round close-fitting brimless cap. [C19: from F *béret,* from OProvençal *berret*]

berg[1] (bɜːg) *n* short for **iceberg.**

berg[2] (bɜːg) *n* a South African word for **mountain.**

bergamot ('bɜːgə,mɒt) *n* **1** a small Asian tree having sour pear-shaped fruit. **2 essence of bergamot.** a fragrant essential oil extracted from the fruit rind of this plant, used in perfumery. **3** a Mediterranean mint that yields a similar oil. [C17: from F *bergamote,* from It. *bergamotta,* of Turkic origin]

bergie ('bɜːgiː) *n S. African inf.* a vagabond, esp. one living on the slopes of Table Mountain in SW South Africa. [from Afrik. *berg* mountain]

bergschrund ('bɛrkʃrʊnt) *n* a crevasse at the head of a glacier. [C19: G: mountain crack]

bergwind ('bɜːxvənt) *n* a hot dry wind in South Africa blowing from the plateau down to the coast.

beriberi (,bɛrɪ'bɛrɪ) *n* a disease, endemic in E and S Asia, caused by dietary deficiency of thiamine (vitamin B_1). [C19: from Sinhalese, by reduplication from *beri* weakness]

berk *or* **burk** (bɜːk) *n Brit. sl.* a stupid person; fool. [C20: shortened from *Berkeley* or *Berkshire Hunt,* rhyming slang for *cunt*]

berkelium (bɜː'kiːlɪəm, 'bɜːklɪəm) *n* a radioactive transuranic element produced by bombardment of americium. Symbol: Bk; atomic no.: 97; half-life of most stable isotope, ^{247}Bk: 1400 years. [C20: after *Berkeley,* California, where it was discovered]

Berks (bɑːks) *abbrev. for* Berkshire.

berley *or* **burley** ('bɜːlɪ) *Austral.* ◆ *n* **1** bait scattered on water to attract fish. **2** *Sl.* rubbish, nonsense. ◆ *vb (tr)* **3** to scatter (bait) on water. **4** to hurry (someone); urge on. [from ?]

berlin (bə'lɪn, 'bɜːlɪn) *n* **1** *(sometimes cap.)* Also called: **berlin wool.** a fine wool yarn used for tapestry work, etc. **2** a four-wheeled two-seated covered carriage, popular in the 18th century. [after *Berlin,* city in N Germany]

berm *or* **berme** (bɜːm) *n* **1** a narrow path or ledge as at the edge of a slope, road, or canal. **2** *Mil.* a man-made ridge of sand or earth, used as an obstacle to tanks. **3** *NZ.* the grass verge of a suburban street, usually kept mown. [C18: from F *berme,* from Du. *berm*]

Bermuda shorts (bə'mjuːdə) *pl n* shorts that come down to the knees. [after the *Bermudas,* islands in the NW Atlantic]

berretta (bɪ'rɛtə) *n* a variant spelling of **biretta.**

berry ('bɛrɪ) *n, pl* **berries. 1** any of various small edible fruits such as the blackberry and strawberry. **2** *Bot.* a fruit with two or more seeds and a fleshy pericarp, such as the grape or gooseberry. **3** any of various seeds or dried kernels, such as a coffee bean. **4** the egg of a lobster, crayfish, or similar animal. ◆ *vb* **berries, berrying, berried.** *(intr)* **5** to bear or produce berries. **6** to gather or look for berries. [OE *berie*]

berserk ❶ (bə'zɜːk, -'sɜːk) *adj* **1** frenziedly violent or destructive (esp. in **go berserk**). ◆ *n* **2** Also called: **berserker.** one of a class of ancient Norse warriors who fought frenziedly. [C19: Icelandic *berserkr,* from *björn* bear + *serkr* shirt]

berth ❶ (bɜːθ) *n* **1** a bed or bunk in a vessel or train. **2** *Naut.* a place assigned to a ship at a mooring. **3** *Naut.* sufficient room for a ship to manoeuvre. **4 give a wide berth to.** to keep clear of. **5** *Inf.* a job, esp. as a member of a ship's crew. ◆ *vb* **6** *(tr) Naut.* to assign a berth to (a vessel). **7** *Naut.* to dock (a vessel). **8** *(tr)* to provide with a sleeping place. **9** *(intr) Naut.* to pick up a mooring in an anchorage. [C17: prob. from BEAR[1] + -TH[1]]

THESAURUS

crude, ignorant, illiterate, primitive, uncultivated, unenlightened

benign *adj* **1 = kindly,** affable, amiable, complaisant, friendly, generous, genial, gracious, kind, liberal, obliging, sympathetic **3 = favourable,** advantageous, auspicious, beneficial, encouraging, good, lucky, propitious, salutary **4** *Pathol.* **= harmless,** curable, limited, remediable, slight, superficial
Antonyms *adj* ≠ **kindly:** bad, disobliging, harsh, hateful, inhumane, malicious, malign, severe, stern, unfavourable, unkind, unpleasant, unsympathetic ≠ **favourable:** bad, unfavourable, unlucky ≠ **harmless:** malignant

bent[1] *adj* **1 = curved,** angled, arched, bowed, crooked, hunched, stooped, twisted **2** *foll. by* **on = curved,** determined to, disposed to, fixed on, inclined to, insistent on, predisposed to, resolved on, set on ◆ *n* **4 = inclination,** ability, aptitude, bag (*sl.*), cup of tea, facility, faculty, flair, forte, knack, leaning, penchant, preference, proclivity, propensity, talent, tendency
Antonyms *adj* ≠ **curved:** aligned, erect, even, horizontal, in line, level, perpendicular, plumb, smooth, square, straight, true, upright, vertical

benumb *vb* **1 = paralyse,** anaesthetize, chill, deaden, freeze, numb **2 = stupefy,** shock, stun

benumbed *adj* **1 = paralysed,** anaesthetized, deadened, frozen, immobilized, insensible, insensitive, numb, unfeeling, unresponsive **2 = stupefied,** dazed, stunned

bequeath *vb* **1, 2 = leave,** bestow, commit, endow, entrust, give, grant, hand down, impart, leave to by will, pass on, transmit, will

bequest *n* **1 = bequeathal,** bestowal, endowment, gift, settlement **2 = legacy,** dower, endowment, estate, gift, heritage, inheritance, settlement, trust

berate *vb* **= scold,** bawl out (*inf.*), blast, castigate, censure, chew out (*US. & Canad. inf.*), chide, criticize, give a rocket (*Brit. & NZ. inf.*), harangue, rail at, rap over the knuckles, read the riot act, rebuke, reprimand, reproach, reprove, revile, slap on the wrist, slate (*inf., chiefly Brit.*), tear into (*inf.*), tear (someone) off a strip (*Brit. inf.*), tell off (*inf.*), upbraid, vituperate
Antonyms *vb* acclaim, admire, applaud, approve, cheer, commend, compliment, congratulate, extol, laud, praise, take one's hat off to

bereavement *n* **= loss,** affliction, death, deprivation, misfortune, tribulation

bereft *adj* **= deprived,** cut off, destitute, devoid, lacking, minus, parted from, robbed of, shorn, wanting

berserk *adj* **1 = crazy,** amok, ape, enraged, frantic, frenzied, insane, mad, maniacal, manic, raging, uncontrollable, violent, wild

berth *n* **1 = bunk,** bed, billet, cot (*Nautical*), hammock **2** *Nautical* **= anchorage,** dock, harbour, haven, pier, port, quay, slip, wharf **5** *Infor-*

bertha ('bɜːθə) *n* a wide deep collar, often of lace, usually to cover a low neckline. [C19: from F *berthe,* from *Berthe,* 8th-cent. Frankish queen]

beryl ('berɪl) *n* a green, blue, yellow, pink, or white hard mineral consisting of beryllium aluminium silicate in hexagonal crystalline form. Emerald and aquamarine are transparent varieties. [C13: from OF, from L, from Gk *bērullos*]
▸ **'beryline** *adj*

beryllium (be'rɪlɪəm) *n* a corrosion-resistant toxic silvery-white metallic element used mainly in X-ray windows and alloys. Symbol: Be; atomic no.: 4; atomic wt.: 9.012. [C19: from L, from Gk *bērullos*]

beseech ⓣ (bɪ'siːtʃ) *vb* **beseeches, beseeching, besought** *or* **beseeched.** (*tr*) to ask (someone) earnestly (to do something or for something); beg. [C12: see BE-, SEEK]

beseem (bɪ'siːm) *vb Arch.* to be suitable for or worthy of; befit.

beset ⓣ (bɪ'set) *vb* **besets, besetting, beset.** (*tr*) **1** (esp. of dangers or temptations) to trouble or harass constantly. **2** to surround or attack from all sides. **3** *Arch.* to cover with, esp. with jewels.

besetting ⓣ (bɪ'setɪŋ) *adj* tempting, harassing, or assailing (esp. in **besetting sin**).

beside ⓣ (bɪ'saɪd) *prep* **1** next to; at, by, or to the side of. **2** as compared with. **3** away from; wide of. **4** *Arch.* besides. **5 beside oneself.** (*postpositive;* often foll. by *with*) overwhelmed; overwrought: *beside oneself with grief.* ◆ *adv* **6** at, by, to, or along the side of something or someone. [OE *be sīdan;* see BY, SIDE]

besides ⓣ (bɪ'saɪdz) *prep* **1** apart from; even considering. ◆ *sentence connector.* **2** anyway; moreover. ◆ *adv* **3** as well.

besiege ⓣ (bɪ'siːdʒ) *vb* **besieges, besieging, besieged.** (*tr*) **1** to surround (a fortified area) with military forces to bring about its surrender. **2** to crowd round; hem in. **3** to overwhelm, as with requests.
▸ **be'sieger** *n*

besmear (bɪ'smɪə) *vb* (*tr*) **1** to smear over; daub. **2** to sully; defile (often in **besmear (a person's) reputation**).

besmirch ⓣ (bɪ'smɜːtʃ) *vb* (*tr*) **1** to make dirty; soil. **2** to reduce the brightness of. **3** to sully (often in **besmirch (a person's) name**).

besom[1] ('biːzəm) *n* a broom, esp. one made of a bundle of twigs tied to a handle. [OE *besma*]

besom[2] ('bɪzəm) *n Scot. & N English dialect.* a derogatory term for a **woman.** [?from OE *bysen* example; rel. to ON *bysn* wonder]

besotted ⓣ (bɪ'sɒtɪd) *adj* **1** stupefied with drink. **2** infatuated; doting. **3** foolish; muddled.

besought (bɪ'sɔːt) *vb* a past tense and past participle of **beseech.**

bespangle (bɪ'spæŋgᵊl) *vb* **bespangles, bespangling, bespangled.** (*tr*) to cover or adorn with or as if with spangles.

bespatter ⓣ (bɪ'spætə) *vb* (*tr*) **1** to splash, as with dirty water. **2** to defile; besmirch.

bespeak ⓣ (bɪ'spiːk) *vb* **bespeaks, bespeaking, bespoke; bespoken** *or* **bespoke.** (*tr*) **1** to engage or ask for in advance. **2** to indicate or suggest: *this act bespeaks kindness.* **3** *Poetic.* to address.

bespectacled (bɪ'spektəkᵊld) *adj* wearing spectacles.

bespoke (bɪ'spəʊk) *adj Chiefly Brit.* **1** (esp. of a suit, jacket, etc.) made to the customer's specifications. **2** making or selling such suits, jackets, etc.: *a bespoke tailor.*

besprinkle (bɪ'sprɪŋkᵊl) *vb* **besprinkles, besprinkling, besprinkled.** (*tr*) to sprinkle all over with liquid, powder, etc.

Bessemer process ('besɪmə) *n* (formerly) a process for producing steel by blowing air through molten pig iron in a **Bessemer converter** (a refractory-lined furnace): impurities are removed and the carbon content is controlled. [C19: after Sir Henry *Bessemer* (1813–98), E engineer]

best ⓣ (best) *adj* **1** the superlative of **good. 2** most excellent of a particular group, category, etc. **3** most suitable, desirable, etc. **4 the best part of.** most of. ◆ *adv* **5** the superlative of **well**[1]. **6** in a manner surpassing all others; most excellently, attractively, etc. ◆ *n* **7 the best.** the most outstanding or excellent person, thing, or group in a category. **8** the utmost effort. **9** a winning majority. **10** Also: **all the best.** best wishes. **11** a person's smartest outfit of clothing. **12 at best. 12a** in the most favourable interpretation. **12b** under the most favourable conditions. **13 for the best. 13a** for an ultimately good outcome. **13b** with good intentions. **14 get** *or* **have the best of.** to defeat or outwit. **15 give (someone) the best.** to concede (someone's) superiority. **16 make the best of.** to cope as well as possible with. ◆ *vb* **17** (*tr*) to gain the advantage over or defeat. [OE *betst*]

bestead (bɪ'sted) *Arch.* ◆ *vb* **besteads, besteading, besteaded; besteaded** *or* **bestead. 1** (*tr*) to help; avail. ◆ *adj also* **bested. 2** placed; situated. [C13: see BE-, STEAD]

bestial ⓣ ('bestɪəl) *adj* **1** brutal or savage. **2** sexually depraved. **3** lacking in refinement; brutish. **4** of or relating to a beast. [C14: from LL *bestiālis,* from L *bestia* BEAST]

bestiality ⓣ (ˌbestɪ'ælɪtɪ) *n, pl* **bestialities. 1** bestial behaviour. **2** sexual activity between a person and an animal.

bestialize *or* **bestialise** ('bestɪəˌlaɪz) *vb* **bestializes, bestializing, bestialized** *or* **bestialises, bestialising, bestialised.** (*tr*) to make bestial or brutal.

bestiary ('bestɪərɪ) *n, pl* **bestiaries.** a moralizing medieval collection of descriptions of real and mythical animals.

bestir ⓣ (bɪ'stɜː) *vb* **bestirs, bestirring, bestirred.** (*tr*) to cause (oneself) to become active; rouse.

best man *n* the male attendant of the bridegroom at a wedding.

bestow ⓣ (bɪ'stəʊ) *vb* (*tr*) **1** to present (a gift) or confer (an honour). **2** *Arch.* to apply (energy, resources, etc.). **3** *Arch.* to house (a person) or store (goods).
▸ **be'stowal** *n*

bestrew (bɪ'struː) *vb* **bestrews, bestrewing, bestrewed; bestrewn** *or* **bestrewed.** (*tr*) to scatter or lie scattered over (a surface).

bestride ⓣ (bɪ'straɪd) *vb* **bestrides, bestriding, bestrode** *or* (*Arch.*) **bestrid; bestridden** *or* (*Arch.*) **bestrid.** (*tr*) **1** to have or put a leg on either side of. **2** to extend across; span. **3** to stride over or across.

bestseller ⓣ (ˌbest'selə) *n* **1** a book or other product that has sold in great numbers. **2** the author of one or more such books, etc.
▸ **ˌbest'selling** *adj*

bet ⓣ (bet) *n* **1** an agreement between two parties that a sum of money or other stake will be paid by the loser to the party who correctly predicts the outcome of an event. **2** the stake risked. **3** the predicted result in such an agreement. **4** a person, event, etc., considered as likely to succeed or occur. **5** a course of action (esp. in **one's best bet**). **6** *Inf.* an opinion: *my bet is that you've been up to no good.* ◆ *vb* **bets, betting, bet** *or* **betted. 7** (when *intr* foll. by *on* or *against*) to make or place a bet with (a person or persons). **8** (*tr*) to stake (money, etc.) in a bet. **9** (*tr; may take a clause as object*) *Inf.* to predict (a certain outcome). **10 you bet.** *Inf.* of course; naturally. [C16: prob. short for ABET]

THESAURUS

mal = **job**, appointment, employment, living, position, post, situation ◆ *vb* **9** *Nautical* = **anchor**, dock, drop anchor, land, moor, tie up

beseech *vb* = **beg**, adjure, ask, call upon, crave, entreat, implore, importune, petition, plead, pray, solicit, sue, supplicate

beset *vb* **1** = **plague**, badger, bedevil, embarrass, entangle, harass, perplex, pester, trouble **2** = **attack**, assail, besiege, encircle, enclose, encompass, environ, hem in, surround

besetting *adj* = **troublesome**, habitual, harassing, inveterate, persistent, prevalent

beside *prep* **1** = **next to**, abreast of, adjacent to, alongside, at the side of, cheek by jowl, close to, near, nearby, neighbouring, next door to, overlooking **5 beside oneself** = **distraught**, apoplectic, at the end of one's tether, berserk, crazed, delirious, demented, deranged, desperate, frantic, frenzied, insane, mad, out of one's mind, unbalanced, uncontrolled, unhinged

besides *prep* **1** = **apart from**, barring, excepting, excluding, in addition to, other than, over and above, without ◆ *adv* **3** = **too**, also, as well, further, furthermore, in addition, into the bargain, moreover, otherwise, what's more

besiege *vb* **1** = **surround**, beleaguer, beset, blockade, confine, encircle, encompass, environ, hedge in, hem in, invest (*rare*), lay siege to, shut in **3** = **harass**, badger, bend someone's ear (*inf.*), bother, harry, hassle (*inf.*), hound, importune, nag, pester, plague, trouble

besmirch *vb* **1** = **soil**, daub, smear, smirch, stain **2** = **tarnish 3** = **sully**, defame, dishonour, slander, smear

besotted *adj* **1** = **drunk**, befuddled, bevvied (*dialect*), blitzed (*sl.*), blotto (*sl.*), Brahms and Liszt (*sl.*), intoxicated, legless (*inf.*), out of it (*sl.*), out to it (*Austral. & NZ sl.*), paralytic (*inf.*), pissed (*taboo sl.*), smashed (*sl.*), stupefied, wrecked (*sl.*) **2** = **infatuated**, doting, hypnotized, smitten, spellbound **3** = **muddled**, confused, foolish, witless

bespatter *vb* **1** = **splatter**, bedaub, befoul, begrime, besprinkle, muddy, smear, spatter **2** = **defile**, besmirch, dishonour, slander, sully

bespeak *vb* **1** = **order beforehand**, engage, prearrange **2** = **indicate**, betoken, denote, display, evidence, evince, exhibit, imply, proclaim, reveal, show, signify, suggest, testify to

best *adj* **1, 2** = **finest**, chief, first, first-class, first-rate, foremost, highest, leading, most excellent, outstanding, perfect, pre-eminent, principal, superlative, supreme, unsurpassed **3** = **most fitting**, advantageous, apt, correct, golden, most desirable, right ◆ *adv* **5** = **most highly**, extremely, greatly, most deeply, most fully **6** = **excellently**, advantageously, attractively, most fortunately ◆ *n* **7 the best** = **finest**, choice, cream, *crème de la crème,* elite, favourite, first, flower, pick, prime, top **8** = **utmost**, hardest, highest endeavour ◆ *vb* **17** = **defeat**, beat, blow out of the water (*sl.*), conquer, get the better of, lick (*inf.*), master, outclass, outdo, put in the shade (*inf.*), run rings around (*inf.*), surpass, tank (*sl.*), thrash, triumph over, trounce, wipe the floor with (*inf.*)

bestial *adj* **1** = **brutal**, barbaric, barbarous, beastlike, beastly, brutish, inhuman, savage **2** = **depraved**, carnal, degraded, gross, sensual, sordid, vile **4** = **animal**

bestiality *n* **1** = **brutality 2** = **zoophilia**, barbarity, beastliness, brutishness, carnality, cruelty, depravity, inhumanity, savagery

bestir *vb* = **get going**, activate, actuate, animate, awaken, exert, incite, motivate, rouse, set off, stimulate, stir up, trouble

bestow *vb* **1** = **present**, accord, allot, apportion, award, commit, confer, donate, endow, entrust, give, grant, hand out, honour with, impart, lavish, render to
Antonyms *vb* acquire, attain, come by, earn, gain, get, land, make, net, obtain, procure, secure

bestowal *n* **1** = **presentation**, allotment, award, bestowment, conferment, conferral, donation, endowment, gift, grant

bestride *vb* **1** = **straddle**, bestraddle **2** = **span**, bridge, extend across **3** = **step over**

bestseller *n* **1** = **success**, blockbuster, chart-topper (*inf.*), hit (*inf.*), number one, runaway success, smash (*inf.*), smash hit (*inf.*)
Antonyms *n* dud (*inf.*), failure, flop (*inf.*), turkey (*sl., chiefly US & Canad.*)

bestselling *adj* **1** = **successful**, chart-topping (*inf.*), highly successful, hit (*inf.*), number one, smash (*inf.*), smash-hit (*inf.*)

bet *n* **1** = **gamble**, ante, hazard, long shot, pledge, risk, speculation, stake, venture, wager ◆ *vb* **7, 8** = **gamble**, chance, hazard, pledge, punt (*chiefly Brit.*), put money on, risk, speculate, stake, venture, wager

beta ('bi:tə) *n* **1** the second letter in the Greek alphabet (Β or β). **2** the second in a group or series. [from Gk *bēta*, from Heb.; see BETH]
beta-blocker *n* any of a class of drugs, such as propranolol, that decrease the activity of the heart: used in the treatment of high blood pressure and angina.
betacarotene (ˌbi:tə'kærəˌti:n) *n* the most important form of the plant pigment carotene, which occurs in milk, vegetables, and other foods and, when eaten by man and animals, is converted in the body to vitamin A.
beta decay *n* the radioactive change in an atomic nucleus accompanying the emission of an electron.
betake (bɪ'teɪk) *vb* **betakes, betaking, betook, betaken.** (*tr*) **1 betake oneself.** to go; move. **2** *Arch.* to apply (oneself) to.
beta particle *n* a high-speed electron or positron emitted by a nucleus during radioactive decay or nuclear fission.
beta ray *n* a stream of beta particles.
beta rhythm *or* **wave** *n Physiol.* the normal electrical activity of the cerebral cortex.
beta stock *n* any of the second rank of active securities on the London stock exchange, of which there are about 500. Continuous display of prices by market makers is required but not immediate publication of transactions.
betatron ('bi:təˌtrɒn) *n* a type of particle accelerator for producing high-energy beams of electrons by magnetic induction.
betel ('bi:t^{ə}l) *n* an Asian climbing plant, the leaves of which are chewed by the peoples of SE Asia. [C16: from Port., from Malayalam *vettila*]
betel nut *n* the seed of the betel palm, chewed with betel leaves and lime by people in S and SE Asia as a digestive stimulant and narcotic.
betel palm *n* a tropical Asian feather palm.
bête noire **T** *French.* (bɛt nwar) *n, pl* ***bêtes noires*** (bɛt nwar). a person or thing that one particularly dislikes or dreads. [lit.: black beast]
beth (bɛt) *n* the second letter of the Hebrew alphabet. [from Heb. *bēth-*, *bayith* house]
bethink **T** (bɪ'θɪŋk) *vb* **bethinks, bethinking, bethought.** *Arch. or dialect.* **1** to cause (oneself) to consider or meditate. **2** (*tr*; often foll. by *of*) to remind (oneself).
betide **T** (bɪ'taɪd) *vb* **betides, betiding, betided.** to happen or happen to (often in **woe betide** (**someone**)). [C13: from BE- + obs. *tide* to happen]
betimes (bɪ'taɪmz) *adv Arch.* **1** in good time; early. **2** soon. [C14 *bitimes*; see BY, TIME]
betoken **T** (bɪ'təʊkən) *vb* (*tr*) **1** to indicate; signify. **2** to portend; augur.
betony ('bɛtənɪ) *n, pl* **betonies.** **1** a Eurasian plant with a spike of reddish-purple flowers, formerly used in medicine and dyeing. **2** any of several related plants. [C14: from OF, from L]
betray **T** (bɪ'treɪ) *vb* (*tr*) **1** to hand over or expose (one's nation, friend, etc.) treacherously to an enemy. **2** to disclose (a secret, confidence, etc.) treacherously. **3** to break (a promise) or be disloyal to (a person's trust). **4** to show signs of; indicate. **5** to reveal unintentionally: *his grin betrayed his satisfaction.* [C13: from BE- + *trayen*, from OF, from L *trādere* to hand over]
▸**be'trayal** *n* ▸**be'trayer** *n*
betroth (bɪ'trəʊð) *vb* (*tr*) *Arch.* to promise to marry or to give in marriage. [C14 *betreuthen*, from BE- + *treuthe* TROTH, TRUTH]
betrothal **T** (bɪ'trəʊðəl) *n* **1** engagement to be married. **2** a mutual promise to marry.
betrothed **T** (bɪ'trəʊðd) *adj* **1** engaged to be married: *he was betrothed to her.* ◆ *n* **2** the person to whom one is engaged; fiancé or fiancée.
better **T** ('bɛtə) *adj* **1** the comparative of **good.** **2** more excellent than others. **3** more suitable, advantageous, attractive, etc. **4** improved or fully recovered in health. **5 better off.** in more favourable circumstances, esp. financially. **6 the better part of.** a large part of. ◆ *adv* **7** the comparative of **well**[1]. **8** in a more excellent manner; more advantageously, attractively, etc. **9** in or to a greater degree or extent; more. **10 had better.** would be wise, sensible, etc., to: *I had better be off.* **11 think better of. 11a** to change one's mind about (a course of action, etc.) after reconsideration. **11b** to rate more highly. ◆ *n* **12 the better.** something that is the more excellent, useful, etc., of two such things. **13** (*usually pl*) a person who is superior, esp. in social standing or ability. **14 for the better.** by way of improvement. **15 get the better of.** to defeat, outwit, or surpass. ◆ *vb* **16** to make or become better. **17** (*tr*) to improve upon; surpass. [OE *betera*]
better half *n Humorous.* one's spouse.
betterment **T** ('bɛtəmənt) *n* **1** a change for the better; improvement. **2** *Property law.* an improvement effected on real property that enhances the value of the property.
betting shop *n* (in Britain) a licensed bookmaker's premises not on a racecourse.
between **T** (bɪ'twi:n) *prep* **1** at a point or in a region intermediate to two other points in space, times, degrees, etc. **2** in combination; together: *between them, they saved enough money to buy a car.* **3** confined or restricted to: *between you and me.* **4** indicating a reciprocal relation or comparison. **5** indicating two or more alternatives. ◆ *adv also* **in between. 6** between one specified thing and another. [OE *betwēonum*; see TWO, TWAIN]

> **USAGE NOTE** After *distribute* and words with a similar meaning, *among* should be used rather than *between*: *this enterprise issued shares which were distributed among its workers.*

betweentimes (bɪ'twi:nˌtaɪmz) *or* **betweenwhiles** *adv* between other activities; during intervals.
betwixt (bɪ'twɪkst) *prep, adv* **1** *Arch.* another word for **between. 2 betwixt and between.** in an intermediate or indecisive position. [OE *betwix*] [Hebrew, literally: married woman]
BeV (in the US) *abbrev. for* gigaelectronvolts (GeV). [C20: from *b(illion) e(lectron) v(olts)*]
bevatron ('bɛvəˌtrɒn) *n* a synchrotron used to accelerate protons. [C20: from BEV + -TRON]
bevel **T** ('bɛv^{ə}l) *n* **1** Also called: **cant.** a surface that meets another at an angle other than a right angle. ◆ *vb* **bevels, bevelling, bevelled** *or US* **bevels, beveling, beveled. 2** (*intr*) to be inclined; slope. **3** (*tr*) to cut a bevel on (a piece of timber, etc.). [C16: from OF, from *baer* to gape; see BAY[1]]
bevel gear *n* a gear having teeth cut into a conical surface. Two such gears mesh together to transmit power between two shafts at an angle.
bevel square *n* a tool with an adjustable arm that can be set to mark out an angle.
beverage **T** ('bɛvərɪdʒ, 'bɛvrɪdʒ) *n* any drink, usually other than water. [C13: from OF *bevrage*, from *beivre* to drink, from L *bibere*]
beverage room *n Canad.* another name for **beer parlour.**
bevvy ('bɛvɪ) *n, pl* **bevvies.** *Dialect.* **1** a drink, esp. an alcoholic one. **2** a session of drinking. [prob. from OF *bevee*, *buvee* drinking]
bevy **T** ('bɛvɪ) *n, pl* **bevies.** **1** a flock of quails. **2** a group, esp. of girls. [C15: from ?]
bewail **T** (bɪ'weɪl) *vb* to express great sorrow over (a person or thing); lament.
▸**be'wailer** *n*

THESAURUS

bête noire *n French* = **pet hate**, abomination, anathema, aversion, bane, bogey, bugaboo, bugbear, curse, devil, dread, nemesis, nightmare, scourge, thorn in the flesh *or* side
bethink *vb* **1** = **consider**, cogitate, ponder, reconsider, reflect, review, take thought **2** = **remind oneself**, recall, recollect, remember
betide *vb* = **happen**, bechance, befall, chance, come to pass, crop up (*inf.*), ensue, occur, overtake, supervene, take place, transpire (*inf.*)
betoken *vb* **1** = **indicate**, bespeak, declare, denote, evidence, manifest, mark, represent, signify, suggest, typify **2** = **portend**, augur, bode, presage, prognosticate, promise
betray *vb* **1, 3** = **be disloyal**, be treacherous, be unfaithful, break one's promise, double-cross (*inf.*), grass (*Brit. sl.*), grass up (*sl.*), inform on *or* against, sell down the river (*inf.*), sell out (*inf.*), shop (*sl., chiefly Brit.*), stab in the back **2** = **give away**, blurt out, disclose, divulge, evince, expose, lay bare, let slip, manifest, reveal, show, tell, tell on, uncover, unmask
betrayal *n* **1, 3** = **disloyalty**, deception, double-cross (*inf.*), double-dealing, duplicity, falseness, perfidy, sell-out (*inf.*), treachery, treason, trickery, unfaithfulness **2** = **giving away**, blurting out, disclosure, divulgence, revelation, telling
Antonyms *n* ≠ **disloyalty:** allegiance, constancy, devotion, faithfulness, fealty, fidelity, loyalty, steadfastness, trustiness, trustworthiness ≠ **giving away:** guarding, keeping, keeping secret, preserving, safeguarding
betrayer *n* **1** = **traitor**, apostate, conspirator, deceiver, renegade, snake in the grass
betrothal *n* **1, 2** = **engagement**, affiancing, betrothing, marriage compact, plight, promise, troth, vow
betrothed *adj* **1** = **engaged**, affianced, pledged, plighted, promised ◆ *n* **2** = **fiancé** *or* **fiancée**, husband- *or* bride-to-be, future husband *or* wife, intended, prospective spouse
better *adj* **1, 2** = **superior**, bigger, excelling, finer, greater, higher-quality, larger, streets ahead, surpassing, worthier **3** = **more desirable**, fitter, more appropriate, more fitting, more suitable, more useful, more valuable, preferable **4** = **well**, cured, fitter, fully recovered, healthier, improving, less ill, mending, more healthy, on the mend (*inf.*), progressing, recovering, stronger ◆ *adv* **7, 8** = **in a more excellent manner**, in a superior way, more advantageously, more attractively, more competently, more effectively **9** = **to a greater degree**, more completely, more thoroughly **11a think better of** = **change one's mind about**, decide against, go back on, have second thoughts about, reconsider, repent, think again, think twice about ◆ *n* **15 get the better of** = **defeat**, beat, best, get the upper hand, outdo, outsmart (*inf.*), outwit, prevail over, score off, surpass, triumph over, worst ◆ *vb* **16** = **improve**, advance, ameliorate, amend, correct, enhance, forward, further, meliorate, mend, promote, raise, rectify, reform **17** = **beat**, cap (*inf.*), clobber (*sl.*), exceed, excel, improve on *or* upon, knock spots off (*inf.*), lick (*inf.*), outdo, outstrip, put in the shade (*inf.*), run rings around (*inf.*), surpass, top
Antonyms *adj* ≠ **superior:** inferior, lesser, smaller, substandard, worse ≠ **well:** worse ◆ *adv* ≠ **in a more excellent manner:** worse ◆ *vb* ≠ **improve:** depress, devaluate, go downhill, impoverish, lessen, lower, weaken, worsen
betterment *n* **1** = **improvement**, amelioration, edification, melioration
between *prep* **1** = **amidst**, among, betwixt, in the middle of, mid
bevel *n* **1** = **slant**, angle, bezel, cant, chamfer, diagonal, mitre, oblique, slope ◆ *vb* **2** = **cut at an angle**, cant, chamfer, mitre
beverage *n* = **drink**, bevvy (*dialect*), draught, libation (*facetious*), liquid, liquor, potable, potation, refreshment
bevy *n* **1** = **flock**, covey, flight **2** = **group**, band, bunch (*inf.*), collection, company, crowd, gathering, pack, troupe
bewail *vb* = **lament**, bemoan, cry over, express

beware ❶ (bɪˈwɛə) *vb (usually used in the imperative or infinitive;* often foll. by *of)* to be cautious or wary (of); be on one's guard (against). [C13 *be war,* from BE (imperative) + *war* WARY]

bewilder ❶ (bɪˈwɪldə) *vb (tr)* to confuse utterly; puzzle. [C17: see BE-, WILDER]
▸**beˈwildering** *adj* ▸**beˈwilderingly** *adv* ▸**beˈwilderment** *n*

bewitch ❶ (bɪˈwɪtʃ) *vb (tr)* **1** to attract and fascinate. **2** to cast a spell over. [C13 *bewicchen;* see BE-, WITCH[1]]
▸**beˈwitching** *adj*

bewray (bɪˈreɪ) *vb (tr)* an obsolete word for **betray.** [C13: from BE- + OE *wrēgan* to accuse]

bey (beɪ) *n* **1** (in the Ottoman Empire) a title given to provincial governors. **2** (in modern Turkey) a title of address, corresponding to *Mr.* ◆ Also called: **beg.** [C16: Turkish: lord]

beyond ❶ (bɪˈjɒnd) *prep* **1** at or to a point on the other side of; at or to the further side of: *beyond those hills.* **2** outside the limits or scope of. ◆ *adv* **3** at or to the other or far side of something. **4** outside the limits of something. ◆ *n* **5 the beyond.** the unknown, esp. life after death in certain religious beliefs. [OE *begeondan;* see BY, YONDER]

bezel (ˈbɛzᵊl) *n* **1** the sloping face adjacent to the working edge of a cutting tool. **2** the upper oblique faces of a cut gem. **3** a grooved ring or part holding a gem, watch crystal, etc. **4** a retaining outer rim used in vehicle instruments such as tachometers and speedometers. **5** a small indicator light used in vehicle instrument panels. [C17: prob. from F *biseau*]

bezique (bɪˈziːk) *n* **1** a card game for two or more players using two packs with nothing below a seven. **2** (in this game) the queen of spades and jack of diamonds declared together. [C19: from F *bésigue,* from ?]

B/F *or* **b/f** *Book-keeping. abbrev. for* brought forward.

BFPO *abbrev. for* British Forces Post Office.

bhaji (ˈbɑːdʒɪ) *n, pl* **bhaji, bhajis,** *or* **bhajia** (ˈbɑːdʒɪə). an Indian savoury made of chopped vegetables mixed in a spiced batter and deep-fried. [Hindi *bhājī* fried vegetables]

bhang *or* **bang** (bæŋ) *n* a preparation of the leaves and flower tops of Indian hemp having psychoactive properties: much used in India. [C16: from Hindi *bhāng*]

bhangra (ˈbæŋgrə) *n* a type of Asian pop music that combines elements of traditional Punjabi music with Western pop. [C20: from Hindi]

bharal *or* **burhel** (ˈbʌrəl) *n* a wild Himalayan sheep with a bluish-grey coat. [Hindi]

bhindi (ˈbɪndɪ) *n* the okra as used in Indian cooking. [Hindi]

bhp *abbrev. for* brake horsepower.

BHP *Austral. abbrev. for* Broken Hill Proprietary.

Bi *the chemical symbol for* bismuth.

bi- *or sometimes before a vowel* **bin-** *combining form.* **1** two; having two: *bifocal.* **2** occurring every two; lasting for two: *biennial.* **3** on both sides, directions, etc.: *bilateral.* **4** occurring twice during: *biweekly.* **5a** denoting a compound containing two identical cyclic hydrocarbon systems: *biphenyl.* **5b** (rare in technical usage) indicating an acid salt of a dibasic acid: *sodium bicarbonate.* **5c** (not in technical usage) equivalent of **di-**[1] (sense 2). [from L, from *bis* TWICE]

biannual (baɪˈænjʊəl) *adj* occurring twice a year. Cf. **biennial.**
▸**biˈannually** *adv*

bias ❶ (ˈbaɪəs) *n* **1** mental tendency or inclination, esp. irrational preference or prejudice. **2** a diagonal line or cut across the weave of a fabric. **3** *Electronics.* the voltage applied to an electrode of a transistor or valve to establish suitable working conditions. **4** *Bowls.* **4a** a bulge or weight inside one side of a bowl. **4b** the curved course of such a bowl. **5** *Statistics.* a latent influence that disturbs an analysis. ◆ *adv* **6** obliquely; diagonally. ◆ *vb* **biases, biasing, biased** *or* **biasses, biassing, biassed. 7** *(tr; usually passive)* to cause to have a bias; prejudice; influence. [C16: from OF *biais*]
▸**ˈbiased** *or* **ˈbiassed** *adj*

bias binding *n* a strip of material cut on the bias, used for binding hems or for decoration.

biathlon (baɪˈæθlən, -lɒn) *n Sport.* a contest in which skiers with rifles shoot at four targets along a 20-kilometre (12.5-mile) cross-country course.

biaxial (baɪˈæksɪəl) *adj* (esp. of a crystal) having two axes.

bib (bɪb) *n* **1** a piece of cloth or plastic worn, esp. by babies, to protect their clothes while eating. **2** the upper front part of some aprons, dungarees, etc. **3** Also called: **pout, whiting pout.** a light brown European marine gadoid food fish with a barbel on its lower jaw. **4 stick one's bib in.** *Austral. inf.* to interfere. ◆ *vb* **bibs, bibbing, bibbed. 5** *Arch.* to drink (something). [C14 *bibben* to drink, prob. from L *bibere*]

Bib. *abbrev. for:* **1** Bible. **2** Biblical.

bib and tucker *n Inf.* an outfit of clothes.

bibcock (ˈbɪb,kɒk) *or* **bib** *n* a tap with a nozzle bent downwards fed from a horizontal pipe.

bibelot (ˈbɪbləʊ) *n* an attractive or curious trinket. [C19: from F, from OF *beubelet*]

bibl. *abbrev. for:* **1** bibliographical. **2** bibliography.

Bibl. *abbrev. for* Biblical.

Bible (ˈbaɪbᵊl) *n* **1a the.** the sacred writings of the Christian religion, comprising the Old and New Testaments. **1b** *(as modifier): a Bible reading.* **2** *(often not cap.)* the sacred writings of a religion. **3** *(usually not cap.)* a book regarded as authoritative. [C13: from OF, from Med. L *biblia* books, from Gk, dim. of *biblos* papyrus]

Bible Belt *n* those states of the S US where Protestant fundamentalism is dominant.

Bible-thumper *n Sl.* an enthusiastic or aggressive exponent of the Bible. Also: **Bible-basher.**
▸**ˈBible-ˌthumping** *n, adj*

biblical (ˈbɪblɪkᵊl) *adj* **1** of or referring to the Bible. **2** resembling the Bible in written style.

Biblicist (ˈbɪblɪsɪst) *or* **Biblist** *n* **1** a biblical scholar. **2** a person who takes the Bible literally.

biblio- *combining form.* indicating book or books: *bibliography.* [from Gk *biblion* book]

bibliography (ˌbɪblɪˈɒgrəfɪ) *n, pl* **bibliographies. 1** a list of books on a subject or by a particular author. **2** a list of sources used in a book, thesis, etc. **3a** the study of the history, classification, etc., of literary material. **3b** a work on this subject.
▸**ˌbibliˈographer** *n* ▸**bibliographic** (ˌbɪblɪəʊˈgræfɪk) *or* **ˌbiblioˈgraphical** *adj*

bibliomancy (ˈbɪblɪəʊˌmænsɪ) *n* prediction of the future by interpreting a passage chosen at random from a book, esp. the Bible.

bibliomania (ˌbɪblɪəʊˈmeɪnɪə) *n* extreme fondness for books.
▸**ˌbiblioˈmaniˌac** *n, adj*

bibliophile (ˈbɪblɪəˌfaɪl) *or* **bibliophil** (ˈbɪblɪəfɪl) *n* a person who collects or is fond of books.
▸**bibliophilism** (ˌbɪblɪˈɒfɪˌlɪzəm) *n* ▸**ˌbibliˈophily** *n*

bibliopole (ˈbɪblɪəʊˌpəʊl) *or* **bibliopolist** (ˌbɪblɪˈɒpəlɪst) *n* a dealer in books, esp. rare or decorative ones. [C18: from L, from Gk, from BIBLIO- + *pōlein* to sell]
▸**ˌbibliˈopoly** *n*

bibulous (ˈbɪbjʊləs) *adj* addicted to alcohol. [C17: from L *bibulus,* from *bibere* to drink]
▸**ˈbibulously** *adv* ▸**ˈbibulousness** *n*

bicameral (baɪˈkæmərəl) *adj* (of a legislature) consisting of two chambers. [C19: from BI- + L *camera* CHAMBER]
▸**biˈcameralˌism** *n*

bicarb (ˈbaɪkɑːb) *n* short for **bicarbonate of soda.**

bicarbonate (baɪˈkɑːbənɪt, -ˌneɪt) *n* a salt of carbonic acid.

bicarbonate of soda *n* sodium bicarbonate, esp. as medicine or a raising agent in baking.

bice (baɪs) *n* **1** Also called: **bice blue.** medium blue. **2** Also called: **bice green.** a yellowish green. [C14: from OF *bis* dark grey, from ?]

bicentenary (ˌbaɪsɛnˈtiːnərɪ) *or US* **bicentennial** (ˌbaɪsɛnˈtɛnɪəl) *adj* **1** marking a 200th anniversary. **2** occurring every 200 years. **3** lasting 200 years. ◆ *n, pl* **bicentenaries. 4** a 200th anniversary.

bicephalous (baɪˈsɛfələs) *adj* **1** *Biol.* having two heads. **2** crescent-shaped.

biceps (ˈbaɪsɛps) *n, pl* **biceps.** *Anat.* any muscle having two heads or origins, esp. the muscle that flexes the forearm. [C17: from L, from BI- + *caput* head]

bichloride (baɪˈklɔːraɪd) *n* another name for **dichloride.**

bichloride of mercury *n* another name for **mercuric chloride.**

bichromate (baɪˈkrəʊˌmeɪt, -mɪt) *n* another name for **dichromate.**

bicker ❶ (ˈbɪkə) *vb (intr)* **1** to argue over petty matters; squabble. **2** *Po-*

THESAURUS

sorrow, grieve for, keen, moan, mourn, wail, weep over

beware *vb* = **be careful,** avoid, be cautious, be wary, guard against, heed, look out, mind, refrain from, shun, steer clear of, take heed, watch out

bewilder *vb* = **confound,** baffle, befuddle, bemuse, confuse, daze, flummox, mix up, mystify, nonplus, perplex, puzzle, stun, stupefy

bewildered *adj* = **confused,** at a loss, at sea, baffled, bamboozled, disconcerted, flummoxed, mystified, nonplussed, perplexed, puzzled, speechless, startled, stunned, surprised, taken aback

bewildering *adj* = **confusing,** amazing, astonishing, astounding, baffling, mystifying, perplexing, puzzling, staggering, stunning, stupefying, surprising

bewitch *vb* **1** = **fascinate,** absorb, allure, attract, beguile, captivate, charm, enchant, enrapture, entrance, hypnotize, ravish, spellbind **2** = **enchant,** spellbind
Antonyms *vb* ≠ **fascinate:** disgust, give one the creeps *(inf.),* make one sick, offend, repel, repulse, sicken, turn off *(inf.)*

bewitched *adj* **1** = **enchanted,** charmed, entranced, fascinated, mesmerized **2** = **under a spell,** mesmerized, possessed, spellbound

beyond *prep* **1** = **past,** above, apart from, at a distance, away from, outwith *(Scot.),* over **2** = **exceeding,** out of reach of, superior to, surpassing

bias *n* **1** = **prejudice,** bent, bigotry, favouritism, inclination, intolerance, leaning, narrow-mindedness, nepotism, one-sidedness, partiality, penchant, predilection, predisposition, proclivity, proneness, propensity, tendency, turn, unfairness **2** = **slant,** angle, cross, diagonal line ◆ *vb* **7** = **prejudice,** distort, influence, predispose, slant, sway, twist, warp, weight
Antonyms *n* ≠ **prejudice:** equality, equity, fairness, impartiality, neutrality, objectivity, open-mindedness

biased *adj* **1** = **prejudiced,** distorted, embittered, jaundiced, one-sided, partial, predisposed, slanted, swayed, twisted, warped, weighted

bicker *vb* **1** = **quarrel,** argue, disagree, dispute, fight, row *(inf.),* scrap *(inf.),* spar, squabble, wrangle
Antonyms *vb* accord, acquiesce, agree, assent, concur, cooperate, get on, harmonize

etic. **2a** (esp. of a stream) to run quickly. **2b** to flicker; glitter. ◆ *n* **3** a squabble. [C13: from ?]
▸ **'bickerer** *n*

bicolour ('baɪˌkʌlə), **bicoloured** *or US* **bicolor, bicolored** *adj* two-coloured.

biconcave (baɪ'kɒnkeɪv, ˌbaɪkɒn'keɪv) *adj* (of a lens) having concave faces on both sides.

biconditional (ˌbaɪkən'dɪʃənᵊl) *n* **1** *Logic, maths.* a relation, taken as meaning *if and only if,* between two propositions which are either both true or both false and such that each implies the other. **2** *Logic.* a logical connective between two propositions whose truth table is true only if both propositions are true or both false. ◆ Also called (esp. sense 1): **equivalence.**

biconvex (baɪ'kɒnvɛks, ˌbaɪkɒn'vɛks) *adj* (of a lens) having convex faces on both sides.

bicuspid (baɪ'kʌspɪd) *or* **bicuspidate** (baɪ'kʌspɪˌdeɪt) *adj* **1** having two cusps or points. ◆ *n* **2** a bicuspid tooth; premolar.

bicycle ('baɪsɪkᵊl) *n* **1** a vehicle with a tubular metal frame mounted on two spoked wheels, one behind the other. The rider sits on a saddle, propels the vehicle by means of pedals, and steers with handlebars on the front wheel. Often shortened to **bike** (inf.), **cycle.** ◆ *vb* **bicycles, bicycling, bicycled. 2** (*intr*) to ride a bicycle.
▸ **'bicyclist** *or* **'bicycler** *n*

bicycle clip *n* one of a pair of clips worn around the ankles by cyclists to keep the trousers tight and out of the chain.

bid ❶ (bɪd) *vb* **bids, bidding, bad, bade,** *or* (esp. for senses 1, 2, 5, 6) **bid; bidden** *or* (esp. for senses 1, 2, 5, 6) **bid. 1** (often foll. by *for* or *against*) to offer (an amount) in attempting to buy something. **2** *Commerce.* to respond to an offer by a seller stating (the more favourable terms) on which one is willing to make a purchase. **3** (*tr*) to say (a greeting, etc.): *to bid farewell.* **4** to order; command: *do as you are bid!* **5** (*intr;* usually foll. by *for*) to attempt to attain power, etc. **6** *Bridge, etc.* to declare before play how many tricks one expects to make. **7 bid defiance.** to resist boldly. **8 bid fair.** to seem probable. ◆ *n* **9a** an offer of a specified amount. **9b** the price offered. **10a** the quoting by a seller of a price. **10b** the price quoted. **11** *Commerce.* **11a** a statement by a buyer, in response to an offer by a seller, of the more favourable terms that would be acceptable. **11b** the price or other terms so stated. **12** an attempt, esp. to attain power. **13** *Bridge.* **13a** the number of tricks a player undertakes to make. **13b** a player's turn to make a bid. ◆ See also **bid up.** [OE *biddan*]
▸ **'bidder** *n*

biddable ❶ ('bɪdəbᵊl) *adj* **1** having sufficient value to be bid on, as a hand at bridge. **2** docile; obedient.
▸ **'biddableness** *n*

bidding ❶ ('bɪdɪŋ) *n* **1** an order; command. **2** an invitation; summons. **3** bids or the act of making bids.

biddy[1] ('bɪdɪ) *n, pl* **biddies.** a dialect word for **chicken** or **hen.** [C17: ? imit. of calling chickens]

biddy[2] ('bɪdɪ) *n, pl* **biddies.** *Inf.* a woman, esp. an old gossipy one. [C18: from pet form of *Bridget*]

biddy-biddy ('bɪdɪˌbɪdɪ) *n, pl* **biddy-biddies. 1** a low-growing rosaceous plant of New Zealand, having prickly burs. **2** the burs of this plant. ◆ Also: **bidgee-widgee** ('bɪdʒɪˌwɪdʒɪ). [from Maori *piripiri*]

bide (baɪd) *vb* **bides, biding, bided** *or* **bode, bided. 1** (*intr*) *Arch. or dialect.* to continue in a certain place or state; stay. **2** (*tr*) *Arch. or dialect.* to tolerate; endure. **3 bide one's time.** to wait patiently for an opportunity. [OE *bīdan*]

bidentate (baɪ'dɛnˌteɪt) *adj* having two teeth or toothlike parts or processes.

bidet ('biːdeɪ) *n* a small low basin for washing the genital area. [C17: from F: small horse]

bid up *vb* (*adv*) to increase the market price of (a commodity) by making artificial bids.

biennial (baɪ'ɛnɪəl) *adj* **1** occurring every two years. **2** lasting two years. Cf. **biannual.** ◆ *n* **3** a plant that completes its life cycle in two years. **4** an event that takes place every two years.
▸ **bi'ennially** *adv*

bier (bɪə) *n* a platform or stand on which a corpse or a coffin containing a corpse rests before burial. [OE *bǣr;* rel. to *beran* to BEAR[1]]

biestings ('biːstɪŋz) *n* a variant spelling of **beestings.**

biff (bɪf) *Sl.* ◆ *n* **1** a blow with the fist. ◆ *vb* **2** (*tr*) to give (someone) such a blow. [C20: prob. imit.]

bifid ('baɪfɪd) *adj* divided into two lobes by a median cleft. [C17: from L, from BI- + *-fidus,* from *findere* to split]
▸ **bi'fidity** *n* ▸ **'bifidly** *adv*

bifocal (baɪ'fəʊkᵊl) *adj* **1** *Optics.* having two different focuses. **2** relating to a compound lens permitting near and distant vision.

bifocals (baɪ'fəʊkᵊlz) *pl n* a pair of spectacles with bifocal lenses.

BIFU (in Britain) *abbrev. for* Banking, Insurance and Finance Union.

bifurcate *vb* ('baɪfəˌkeɪt), **bifurcates, bifurcating, bifurcated. 1** to fork or divide into two branches. ◆ *adj* ('baɪfəˌkeɪt, -kɪt). **2** forked or divided into two branches. [C17: from Med. L, from L, from BI- + *furca* fork]
▸ **ˌbifur'cation** *n*

big ❶ (bɪg) *adj* **bigger, biggest. 1** of great or considerable size, height, weight, number, power, or capacity. **2** having great significance; important. **3** important through having power, influence, wealth, authority, etc. **4** *Inf.* considerable in extent or intensity (esp. in **in a big way**). **5a** elder: *my big brother.* **5b** grown-up. **6a** generous; magnanimous: *that's very big of you.* **6b** (*in combination*): *big-hearted.* **7** extravagant; boastful: *big talk.* **8 too big for one's boots** *or* **breeches.** conceited; unduly self-confident. **9** in an advanced stage of pregnancy (esp. in **big with child**). ◆ *adv Inf.* **10** boastfully; pretentiously (esp. in **talk big**). **11** in an exceptional way; well: *his talk went over big.* **12** on a grand scale (esp. in **think big**). ◆ See also **big up.** [C13: ?from ON]
▸ **'bigness** *n*

bigamy ('bɪgəmɪ) *n, pl* **bigamies.** the crime of marrying a person while still legally married to someone else. [C13: via F from Med. L; see BI-, -GAMY]
▸ **'bigamist** *n* ▸ **'bigamous** *adj*

Big Apple *n* **the.** *Inf.* New York City. [C20: prob. from US jazzmen's earlier use to mean any big, esp. northern, city; from ?]

Big Bang *n* the reorganization of the London Stock Exchange that took effect in October 1986 when operations became fully computerized, fixed commissions were abolished, and the functions of jobbers and brokers were merged.

big-bang theory *n* a cosmological theory postulating that all the matter of the universe was hurled in all directions by a cataclysmic explosion and that the universe is still expanding. Cf. **steady-state theory.**

Big Brother *n* a person, organization, etc., that exercises total dictatorial control. [C20: from George Orwell's novel *1984* (1949)]

big business *n* large commercial organizations collectively, esp. when considered as exploitative or socially harmful.

Big C *n* **the.** a euphemism for **cancer** (senses 1 and 2).

big deal *interj Sl.* an exclamation of scorn, derision, etc., used esp. to belittle a claim or offer.

big dipper *n* (in amusement parks) a narrow railway with open carriages that run swiftly over a route of sharp curves and steep inclines.

big end *n Brit.* the larger end of a connecting rod in an internal-combustion engine.

big game *n* large animals that are hunted or fished for sport.

big gun *n Inf.* an important person.

bighead ❶ ('bɪgˌhɛd) *n Inf.* a conceited person.
▸ **ˌbig'headed** *adj* ▸ **ˌbig'headedness** *n*

bighorn ('bɪgˌhɔːn) *n, pl* **bighorns** *or* **bighorn.** a large wild sheep inhabiting mountainous regions in North America.

bight (baɪt) *n* **1** a wide indentation of a shoreline, or the body of water bounded by such a curve. **2** the slack middle part or loop in a rope. [OE *byht;* see BOW[2]]

Big Mac (mæk) *n Trademark.* two hamburgers served with salad, dressing, and a pickle on a soft bread roll.

bigmouth ('bɪgˌmaʊθ) *n Sl.* a noisy, indiscreet, or boastful person.
▸ **'big-ˌmouthed** *adj*

big name *n Inf.* **a** a famous person. **b** (*as modifier*): *a big-name performer.*

big noise *n Brit. inf.* an important person.

bignonia (bɪg'nəʊnɪə) *n* a tropical American climbing shrub cultivated for its trumpet-shaped yellow or reddish flowers. [C19: from NL, after the Abbé Jean-Paul *Bignon* (1662–1743)]

big-note *vb* **big-notes, big-noting, big-noted.** (*tr*) *Austral. inf.* to boast about (oneself).

bigot ❶ ('bɪgət) *n* a person who is intolerant, esp. regarding religion,

THESAURUS

bid *vb* **1 = offer,** proffer, propose, submit, tender **3 = say,** call, greet, tell, wish **4 = tell,** ask, call, charge, command, desire, direct, enjoin, instruct, invite, order, require, solicit, summon ◆ *n* **9 = offer,** advance, amount, price, proposal, proposition, submission, sum, tender **12 = attempt,** crack (*inf.*), effort, endeavour, go (*inf.*), stab (*inf.*), try, venture

biddable *adj* **2 = obedient,** amenable, complaisant, cooperative, docile, teachable, tractable
Antonyms *adj* awkward, difficult, disobedient, intractable, petulant, querulous, refractory, unruly

bidding *n* **1 = order,** beck, beck and call, behest, call, charge, command, demand, direction, injunction, instruction **2 = invitation,** request, summons **3 = offers,** auction, offer, proposal, tender

big *adj* **1 = large,** bulky, burly, colossal, considerable, elephantine, enormous, extensive, gigantic, great, huge, hulking, humongous *or* humungous (*US sl.*), immense, mammoth, massive, ponderous, prodigious, sizable *or* sizeable, spacious, substantial, vast, voluminous **2, 3 = important,** big-time (*inf.*), eminent, influential, leading, main, major league (*inf.*), momentous, paramount, powerful, prime, principal, prominent, serious, significant, valuable, weighty **5b = grown-up,** adult, elder, grown, mature **6 = generous,** altruistic, benevolent, gracious, heroic, magnanimous, noble, princely, unselfish **7 = boastful,** arrogant, bragging, conceited, haughty, inflated, pompous, pretentious, proud
Antonyms *adj* ≠ **large:** diminutive, insignificant, little, mini, miniature, petite, pint-sized (*inf.*), pocket-sized, pygmy *or* pigmy, small, tiny, wee ≠ **important:** humble, ignoble, insignificant, minor, modest, ordinary, unimportant, unknown ≠ **grown-up:** immature, young

bighead *n Informal* = **boaster,** blowhard (*inf.*), braggadocio, braggart, egotist, know-all (*inf.*)

bigheaded *adj* = **boastful,** arrogant, bumptious, cocky, conceited, egotistic, full of oneself, immodest, overconfident, swollen-headed, too big for one's boots *or* breeches

bigot *n* = **fanatic,** dogmatist, persecutor, racist, sectarian, zealot

bigoted *adj* = **intolerant,** biased, dogmatic, illiberal, narrow-minded, obstinate, opinionated, prejudiced, sectarian, twisted, warped

politics, or race. [C16: from OF: name applied contemptuously to the Normans by the French, from ?]
►'**bigoted** *adj* ►'**bigotry** *n*

big shot *n Inf.* an important person.

Big Smoke *n* **the.** *Inf.* a large city, esp. London.

big stick *n Inf.* force or the threat of force.

big time *n Inf.* **a the.** the highest level of a profession, esp. entertainment. **b** (*as modifier*): *a big-time comedian.*
►'**big-'timer** *n*

big top *n Inf.* **1** the main tent of a circus. **2** the circus itself.

big up *vb* **bigs, bigging, bigged.** (*tr, adv*) *Sl., chiefly Caribbean.* to make important, prominent, or famous: *we'll do our best to big you up.*

bigwig Ⓣ ('bɪg,wɪg) *n Inf.* an important person.

bijou ('biːʒuː) *n, pl* **bijoux** (-ʒuːz). **1** something small and delicately worked. **2** (*modifier*) *Often ironic.* small but tasteful: *a bijou residence.* [C19: from F, from Breton *bizou* finger ring, from *biz* finger]

bijugate ('baɪdʒʊ,geɪt, baɪ'dʒuːgeɪt) *or* **bijugous** *adj* (of compound leaves) having two pairs of leaflets.

bike (baɪk) *n* **1** *Inf.* short for **bicycle** or **motorcycle. 2** *Sl.* a promiscuous woman. **3 get off one's bike.** *Austral. & NZ sl.* to lose one's self-control. ◆ *vb* **bikes, biking, biked. 4** (*intr*) *Inf.* to ride a cycle.

biker ('baɪkə) *n* a member of a motorcycle gang. Also called (Austral. and NZ): **bikie.**

biker jacket *n* a short, close-fitting leather jacket with zips and studs, often worn by motorcyclists.

bikini (bɪ'kiːnɪ) *n* a woman's very brief two-piece swimming costume. [C20: after the Pacific atoll of *Bikini*, from a comparison between obvious and powerful effect of the atom-bomb test and the effect (on men) of women wearing bikinis]

bilabial (baɪ'leɪbɪəl) *adj* **1** of or denoting a speech sound articulated using both lips: *(p) is a bilabial stop.* ◆ *n* **2** a bilabial speech sound.

bilabiate (baɪ'leɪbɪ,eɪt, -ɪt) *adj Bot.* divided into two lips: *the snapdragon has a bilabiate corolla.*

bilateral (baɪ'lætərəl) *adj* **1** having or involving two sides. **2** affecting or undertaken by two parties; mutual. **3** having identical sides or parts on each side of an axis; symmetrical.

bilateral symmetry *n* symmetry in one plane only. Cf. **radial symmetry.**

bilberry ('bɪlbərɪ) *n, pl* **bilberries. 1** any of several shrubs, such as the whortleberry, having edible blue or blackish berries. **2** the fruit of any of these plants. [C16: prob. of Scand. origin]

bilboes ('bɪlbəʊz) *pl n* a long iron bar with sliding shackles, for the ankles of a prisoner. [C16: ?from Bilbao, Spain]

Bildungsroman *German.* ('bɪldʊŋsromaːn) *n* a novel about a person's formative years.

bile Ⓣ (baɪl) *n* **1** a bitter greenish to golden brown alkaline fluid secreted by the liver and stored in the gall bladder. It aids digestion of fats. **2** a health disorder due to faulty secretion of bile. **3** irritability or peevishness. [C17: from F, from L *bīlis*]

bilge (bɪldʒ) *n* **1** *Naut.* the parts of a vessel's hull where the sides curve inwards to form the bottom. **2** (*often pl*) the parts of a vessel between the lowermost floorboards and the bottom. **3** Also called: **bilge water.** the dirty water that collects in a vessel's bilge. **4** *Inf.* silly rubbish; nonsense. **5** the widest part of a cask. ◆ *vb* **bilges, bilging, bilged. 6** (*intr*) *Naut.* (of a vessel) to take in water at the bilge. **7** (*tr*) *Naut.* to damage (a vessel) in the bilge. [C16: prob. var. of BULGE]

bilharzia (bɪl'hɑːtsɪə) *n* **1** another name for a **schistosome. 2** another name for **schistosomiasis.** [C19: NL, after Theodor *Bilharz* (1825–62), G parasitologist who discovered schistosomes]

bilharziasis (,bɪlhɑː'tsaɪəsɪs) *or* **bilharziosis** (bɪl,hɑːtsɪ'əʊsɪs) *n* another name for **schistosomiasis.**

biliary ('bɪlɪərɪ) *adj* of or relating to bile, to the ducts that convey bile, or to the gall bladder.

bilingual (baɪ'lɪŋgwəl) *adj* **1** able to speak two languages, esp. with fluency. **2** expressed in two languages. ◆ *n* **3** a bilingual person.
►**bi'lingual,ism** *n*

bilious Ⓣ ('bɪlɪəs) *adj* **1** of or relating to bile. **2** affected with or denoting any disorder related to secretion of bile. **3** *Inf.* bad-tempered; irritable. [C16: from L *bīliōsus* full of BILE]
►'**biliousness** *n*

bilk Ⓣ (bɪlk) *vb* (*tr*) **1** to balk; thwart. **2** (often foll. by *of*) to cheat or deceive, esp. to avoid making payment to. **3** to escape from; elude. ◆ *n* **4** a swindle or cheat. **5** a person who swindles or cheats. [C17: ? var. of BALK]
►'**bilker** *n*

bill[1] Ⓣ (bɪl) *n* **1** money owed for goods or services supplied. **2** a statement of money owed. **3** *Chiefly Brit.* such an account for food and drink in a restaurant, hotel, etc. **4** any list of items, events, etc., such as a theatre programme. **5** a statute in draft, before it becomes law. **6** a printed notice or advertisement. **7** *US & Canad.* a piece of paper money; note. **8** an obsolete name for **promissory note. 9** See **bill of exchange, bill of fare.** ◆ *vb* (*tr*) **10** to send or present an account for payment to (a person). **11** to enter (items, goods, etc.) on an account or statement. **12** to advertise by posters. **13** to schedule as a future programme. [C14: from Anglo-L *billa*, alteration of LL *bulla* document, BULL[3]]

bill[2] Ⓣ (bɪl) *n* **1** the projecting jaws of a bird, covered with a horny sheath; beak. **2** any beaklike mouthpart in other animals. **3** a narrow promontory. ◆ *vb* (*intr*) (esp. in **bill and coo**). **4** (of birds, esp. doves) to touch bills together. **5** (of lovers) to kiss and whisper amorously. [OE *bile*]

bill[3] (bɪl) *n* **1** a pike or halberd with a narrow hooked blade. **2** short for **billhook.** [OE *bill* sword]

billabong ('bɪlə,bɒŋ) *n Austral.* **1** a backwater channel that forms a lagoon or pool. **2** a branch of a river running to a dead end. [C19: from Abor., from *billa* river + *bong* dead]

billboard ('bɪl,bɔːd) *n Chiefly US & Canad.* another name for **hoarding.** [C19: from BILL[1] + BOARD]

billet[1] Ⓣ ('bɪlɪt) *n* **1** accommodation, esp. for a soldier, in civilian lodgings. **2** the official requisition for such lodgings. **3** a space or berth in a ship. **4** *Inf.* a job. ◆ *vb* **5** (*tr*) to assign a lodging to (a soldier). **6** to lodge or be lodged. [C15: from OF *billette*, from *bulle* a document; see BULL[3]]

billet[2] ('bɪlɪt) *n* **1** a chunk of wood, esp. for fuel. **2** a small bar of iron or steel. [C15: from OF *billette* a little log, from *bille* log]

billet-doux (,bɪlɪ'duː) *n, pl* **billets-doux** (,bɪlɪ'duːz). *Old-fashioned or jocular.* a love letter. [C17: from F, lit.: a sweet letter]

billhook ('bɪl,hʊk) *n* a tool with a curved blade terminating in a hook, used for pruning, chopping, etc. Also called: **bill.**

billiard ('bɪljəd) *n* (*modifier*) of or relating to billiards: *a billiard table; a billiard cue.*

billiards ('bɪljədz) *n* (*functioning as sing*) any of various games in which long cues are used to drive balls on a rectangular table covered with a smooth cloth and having raised cushioned edges. [C16: from OF *billard* curved stick, from *bille* log; see BILLET[2]]

billing ('bɪlɪŋ) *n* **1** *Theatre.* the relative importance of a performer or act as reflected in the prominence given in programmes, advertisements, etc. **2** *Chiefly US & Canad.* public notice or advertising.

billingsgate ('bɪlɪŋz,geɪt) *n* obscene or abusive language. [C17: after *Billingsgate*, a London fish market, notorious for such language]

Billings method ('bɪlɪŋz) *n* a natural method of birth control that involves examining the colour and viscosity of the cervical mucus to discover when ovulation is occurring. [C20: after Drs John and Evelyn *Billings*]

billion ('bɪljən) *n, pl* **billions** *or* **billion. 1** one thousand million: written as 1 000 000 000 or 10^9. **2** (formerly, in Britain) one million million: written as 1 000 000 000 000 or 10^{12}. US word: **trillion. 3** (*often pl*) any exceptionally large number. ◆ *determiner* **4** (preceded by *a* or a cardinal number) amounting to a billion. [C17: from F, from BI- + *-llion* as in *million*]
►'**billionth** *adj, n*

billionaire (,bɪljə'nɛə) *n* a person whose wealth exceeds a billion monetary units of his country.

bill of attainder *n* (formerly) a legislative act finding a person guilty without trial of treason or felony and declaring him attainted.

bill of exchange *n* (now chiefly in foreign transactions) a document, usually negotiable, instructing a third party to pay a stated sum at a designated future date or on demand.

bill of fare *n* another name for **menu.**

bill of health *n* **1** a certificate that attests to the health of a ship's company. **2 clean bill of health.** *Inf.* **2a** a good report of one's physical condition. **2b** a favourable account of a person's or a company's financial position.

THESAURUS

Antonyms *adj* broad-minded, equitable, open-minded, tolerant, unbiased, unbigoted, unprejudiced

bigotry *n* = **intolerance**, bias, discrimination, dogmatism, fanaticism, ignorance, injustice, mindlessness, narrow-mindedness, prejudice, provincialism, racialism, racism, sectarianism, sexism, unfairness
Antonyms *n* broad-mindedness, forbearance, open-mindedness, permissiveness, tolerance

bigwig *n Informal* = **important person**, big cheese (*sl., old-fashioned*), big gun (*inf.*), big hitter (*inf.*), big name, big noise (*inf.*), big shot (*inf.*), celeb (*inf.*), celebrity, dignitary, heavy hitter (*inf.*), heavyweight (*inf.*), mogul, notable, panjandrum, personage, somebody, V.I.P.
Antonyms *n* cipher, lightweight (*inf.*), nobody, nonentity, nothing, zero

bile *n* **3** = **bitterness**, anger, churlishness, ill humour, irascibility, irritability, nastiness, peevishness, rancour, spleen

bilious *adj* **2** = **sick**, liverish, nauseated, nauseous, out of sorts, queasy **3** *Informal* = **bad-tempered**, cantankerous, crabby, cross, crotchety, edgy, grouchy (*inf.*), grumpy, ill-humoured, ill-tempered, irritable, like a bear with a sore head, nasty, peevish, ratty (*Brit. & NZ inf.*), short-tempered, testy, tetchy, touchy

bilk *vb* **2** = **cheat**, bamboozle, con (*inf.*), cozen, deceive, defraud, do (*sl.*), fleece, pull a fast one on (*inf.*), rook (*sl.*), sell a pup, skin (*sl.*), stiff (*sl.*), swindle, trick

bill[1] *n* **1** = **charges 2, 3** = **charges**, account, invoice, reckoning, score, statement, tally **4** = **list**, agenda, card, catalogue, inventory, listing, programme, roster, schedule, syllabus **5** = **proposal**, measure, piece of legislation, projected law **6** = **advertisement**, broadsheet, bulletin, circular, handbill, handout, leaflet, notice, placard, playbill, poster ◆ *vb* **10, 11** = **charge**, debit, invoice **12** = **advertise**, announce, give advance notice of, post

bill[2] *n* **1, 2** = **beak**, mandible, neb (*arch. or dialect*), nib

billet[1] *n* **1** = **quarters**, accommodation, barracks, lodging ◆ *vb* **5** = **quarter**, accommodate, berth, station

bill of lading *n* (in foreign trade) a document containing full particulars of goods shipped.

bill of quantities *n* a document drawn up by a quantity surveyor providing details of the prices, dimensions, etc., of the materials required to build a large structure, such as a factory.

Bill of Rights *n* **1** an English statute of 1689 guaranteeing the rights and liberty of the individual subject. **2** the first ten amendments to the US Constitution which guarantee the liberty of the individual. **3** (*usually not caps.*) any charter of basic human rights.

bill of sale *n Law.* a deed transferring personal property.

billow ❶ ('bɪləʊ) *n* **1** a large sea wave. **2** a swelling or surging mass, as of smoke or sound. ◆ *vb* **3** to rise up, swell out, or cause to rise up or swell out. [C16: from ON *bylgja*]
▸**'billowing** *adj, n* ▸**'billowy** *adj* ▸**'billowiness** *n*

billposter ('bɪl,pəʊstə) *or* **billsticker** *n* a person who sticks advertising posters to walls, etc.
▸**'bill,posting** *or* **'bill,sticking** *n*

billy ('bɪlɪ) *or* **billycan** ('bɪlɪ,kæn) *n, pl* **billies** *or* **billycans. 1** a metal can or pot for boiling water, etc., over a campfire. **2** *Austral. & NZ.* (*as modifier*): *billy-tea.* **3 boil the billy.** *Austral. & NZ. inf.* to make tea. [C19: from Scot. *billypot* cooking vessel]

billy goat *n* a male goat.

bilobate (baɪ'ləʊ,beɪt) *or* **bilobed** ('baɪ,ləʊbd) *adj* divided into or having two lobes.

biltong ('bɪl,tɒŋ) *n S. African.* strips of meat dried and cured in the sun. [C19: Afrik., from Du. *bil* buttock + *tong* TONGUE]

BIM *abbrev. for* British Institute of Management.

bimanous ('bɪmənəs, baɪ'meɪ-) *adj* (of man and the higher primates) having two hands distinct in form and function from the feet. [C19: from NL, from BI- + L *manus* hand]

bimanual (,baɪ'mænjʊəl) *adj* using both hands.

bimbo ('bɪmbəʊ) *n, pl* **bimbos.** *Derog. sl.* **1** an attractive but empty-headed young person, esp. a woman. **2** a fellow; a foolish or stupid person. [C20: from It.: little child, perhaps via Polari]

bimetallic (,baɪmɪ'tælɪk) *adj* **1** consisting of two metals. **2** of or based on bimetallism.

bimetallic strip *n* strips of two metals that expand differently welded together for use in a thermostat.

bimetallism (baɪ'mɛtə,lɪzəm) *n* the use of two metals, esp. gold and silver, in fixed relative values as the standard of value and currency.
▸**bi'metallist** *n*

bimonthly (baɪ'mʌnθlɪ) *adj, adv* **1** every two months. **2** twice a month. ◆ *n, pl* **bimonthlies. 3** a periodical published every two months.

bimorph ('baɪmɔ:f) *or* **bimorph cell** *n Electron.* two piezoelectric crystals cemented together so that their movement converts electrical signals into mechanical energy or vice versa: used in record-player pick-ups and loudspeakers.

bin (bɪn) *n* **1** a large container for storing something in bulk, such as coal, grain, or bottled wine. **2** Also called: **bread bin.** a small container for bread. **3** Also called: **dustbin, rubbish bin.** a container for rubbish, etc. ◆ *vb* **bins, binning, binned.** (*tr*) **4** to store in a bin. **5** to put in a wastepaper bin. [OE *binne* basket]

binary ('baɪnərɪ) *adj* **1** composed of or involving two; dual. **2** *Maths, computing.* of or expressed in binary notation or binary code. **3** (of a compound or molecule) containing atoms of two different elements. ◆ *n, pl* **binaries. 4** something composed of two parts. **5** *Astron.* See **binary star.** [C16: from LL *bīnārius;* see BI-]

binary code *n Computing.* the representation of each one of a set of numbers, letters, etc., as a unique group of bits.

binary notation *or* **system** *n* a number system having a base of two, numbers being expressed by sequences of the digits 0 and 1: used in computing, as 0 and 1 can be represented electrically as *off* and *on.*

binary number *n* a number expressed in binary notation.

binary star *n* a double star system containing two associated stars revolving around a common centre of gravity in different orbits.

binary weapon *n* a chemical weapon containing two substances separately that mix to produce a lethal agent when the projectile is fired.

binate ('baɪ,neɪt) *adj Bot.* occurring in two parts or in pairs: *binate leaves.* [C19: from NL *bīnātus,* prob. from L *combīnātus* united]
▸**'bi,nately** *adv*

binaural (baɪ'nɔ:rəl, bɪn'ɔ:rəl) *adj* **1** relating to, having, or hearing with both ears. **2** employing two separate channels for recording or transmitting sound.

bind ❶ (baɪnd) *vb* **binds, binding, bound. 1** to make or become fast or secure with or as if with a tie or band. **2** (*tr;* often foll. by *up*) to encircle or enclose with a band: *to bind the hair.* **3** (*tr*) to place (someone) under obligation; oblige. **4** (*tr*) to impose legal obligations or duties upon (a person). **5** (*tr*) to make (a bargain, agreement, etc.) irrevocable; seal. **6** (*tr*) to restrain or confine with or as if with ties, as of responsibility or loyalty. **7** (*tr*) to place under certain constraints; govern. **8** (*tr;* often foll. by *up*) to bandage. **9** to cohere or cause to cohere: *egg binds fat and flour.* **10** to make or become compact, stiff, or hard: *frost binds the earth.* **11** (*tr*) to enclose and fasten (the pages of a book) between covers. **12** (*tr*) to provide (a garment, hem, etc.) with a border or edging. **13** (*tr;* sometimes foll. by *out* or *over*) to employ as an apprentice; indenture. **14** (*intr*) *Sl.* to complain. ◆ *n* **15** something that binds. **16** *Inf.* a difficult or annoying situation. **17** a situation in which freedom of action is restricted. ◆ See also **bind over.** [OE *bindan*]

binder ('baɪndə) *n* **1** a firm cover or folder for holding loose sheets of paper together. **2** a material used to bind separate particles together. **3** a person who binds books; bookbinder. **4** something used to fasten or tie, such as rope or twine. **5** Also called: **reaper binder.** *Obs.* a machine for cutting grain and binding it into sheaves. **6** an informal agreement giving insurance coverage pending formal issue of a policy.

bindery ('baɪndərɪ) *n, pl* **binderies.** a place in which books are bound.

bindi-eye ('bɪndɪ,aɪ) *n Austral.* **1** any of various small weedy Australian herbaceous plants with burlike fruits. **2** any bur or prickle. [C20: ?from Abor.]

binding ❶ ('baɪndɪŋ) *n* **1** anything that binds or fastens. **2** the covering within which the pages of a book are bound. **3** the tape used for binding hems, etc. ◆ *adj* **4** imposing an obligation or duty. **5** causing hindrance; restrictive.

bind over *vb* (*tr, adv*) to place (a person) under a legal obligation, such as one to keep the peace.

bindweed ('baɪnd,wi:d) *n* any of various plants that twine around a support. See also **convolvulus.**

bine (baɪn) *n* the climbing or twining stem of any of various plants, such as the woodbine. [C19: var. of BIND]

Binet-Simon scale ('bi:neɪ'saɪmən) *n Psychol.* a test used to determine the mental age of subjects. Also called: **Binet scale** *or* **test.** [C20: after Alfred *Binet* (1857–1911) + Théodore *Simon* (1873–1961), F psychologists]

binge ❶ (bɪndʒ) *Inf.* ◆ *n* **1** a bout of excessive drinking or eating. **2** excessive indulgence in anything. ◆ *vb* **binges, bingeing** *or* **binging, binged. 3** (*intr*) to indulge in a binge. [C19: prob. dial. *binge* to soak]

bingo ('bɪŋgəʊ) *n, pl* **bingos.** a gambling game, usually played with several people, in which random numbers are called out and the players cover the numbers on their individual cards. The first to cover a given arrangement of numbers is the winner. [C19: ?from *bing,* imit. of a bell ringing to mark the win]

binman ('bɪn,mæn, 'bɪnmən) *n, pl* **binmen.** *Inf.* another name for **dustman.**

binnacle ('bɪnək^{ə}l) *n* a housing for a ship's compass. [C17: changed from C15 *bitakle,* from Port. from LL *habitāculum* dwelling-place, from L *habitāre* to inhabit]

binocular (bɪ'nɒkjʊlə, baɪ-) *adj* involving, relating to, seeing with or intended for both eyes: *binocular vision.* [C18: from BI- + L *oculus* eye]

binoculars (bɪ'nɒkjʊləz, baɪ-) *pl n* an optical instrument for use with both eyes, consisting of two small telescopes joined together.

binomial (baɪ'nəʊmɪəl) *n* **1** a mathematical expression consisting of two terms, such as $3x + 2y$. **2** a two-part taxonomic name for an animal or plant indicating genus and species. ◆ *adj* **3** referring to two names or terms. [C16: from Med. L, from BI- + L *nōmen* name]
▸**bi'nomially** *adv*

binomial distribution *n* a statistical distribution giving the probability of obtaining a specified number of independent trials of an experiment, with a constant probability of success in each.

binomial theorem *n* a general mathematical formula that expresses any power of a binomial without multiplying out, as in $(x+a)^n = x^n + nx^{n-1}a + [n(n-1)/2]x^{n-2}a^2 \ldots + a^n$.

bint (bɪnt) *n Sl.* a derogatory term for **girl** or **woman.** [C19: from Ar., lit.: daughter]

binturong ('bɪntjʊ,rɒŋ, bɪn'tjʊərɒŋ) *n* a long-bodied short-legged arboreal SE Asian mammal having shaggy black hair. [from Malay]

bio- *or before a vowel* **bi-** *combining form.* **1** indicating or involving life or living organisms: *biogenesis.* **2** indicating a human life or career: *biography.* [from Gk *bios* life]

bioassay (,baɪəʊ'æseɪ) *n* **1** a method of determining the concentration or effect of a drug, etc., by comparing its effect on living organisms with that of a standard preparation. ◆ *vb* (*tr*) **2** to subject to a bioassay.

bioastronautics (,baɪəʊ,æstrə'nɔ:tɪks) *n* (*functioning as sing*) the study of the effects of space flight on living organisms.

bioastronomy (,baɪəʊə'strɒnəmɪ) *n* the branch of astronomy concerned with the search for life on other planets.

biochemical oxygen demand *n* a measure of the organic pollution of water; the number of milligrams of oxygen per litre of water absorbed in a given period. Abbrev.: **BOD**

THESAURUS

billow *n* **1** = **wave**, breaker, crest, roller, surge, swell, tide **2** = **surge**, cloud, deluge, flood, outpouring, rush, wave ◆ *vb* **3** = **surge**, balloon, belly, puff up, rise up, roll, swell

billowy *adj* **1** = **wavy**, rippling, undulating, waving **2** = **surging**, heaving, rolling, swelling, swirling

bind *vb* **1** = **tie**, attach, fasten, glue, hitch, lash, paste, rope, secure, stick, strap, tie up, truss, wrap **3, 4** = **oblige**, compel, constrain, force, necessitate, obligate, prescribe, require **6, 7** = **restrict**, confine, detain, hamper, hinder, restrain **8** = **bandage**, cover, dress, encase, swathe, wrap **12** = **edge**, border, finish, hem, trim ◆ *n* **16** *Informal* = **nuisance**, bore, difficulty, dilemma, drag (*inf.*), hot water (*inf.*), pain in the arse (*taboo sl.*), pain in the neck (*inf.*), predicament, quandary, spot (*inf.*), tight spot
Antonyms *vb* ≠ **tie**: free, loosen, release, unbind, undo, unfasten, untie

binding *adj* **4** = **compulsory**, conclusive, imperative, indissoluble, irrevocable, mandatory, necessary, obligatory, unalterable
Antonyms *adj* discretionary, free, noncompulsory, optional, uncompelled, unconstrained, unforced, voluntary

binge *n* **1** *Informal* = **bout**, beano, bender (*inf.*), blind (*sl.*), feast, fling, jag (*sl.*), orgy, spree

biochemistry (ˌbaɪəʊˈkɛmɪstrɪ) *n* the study of the chemical compounds, reactions, etc., in living organisms.
▸**biochemical** (ˌbaɪəʊˈkɛmɪkˈl) *adj* ▸**ˌbioˈchemist** *n*
biocide (ˈbaɪəˌsaɪd) *n* a chemical capable of killing living organisms.
▸**ˌbioˈcidal** *adj*
biocoenosis *or US* **biocenosis** (ˌbaɪəʊsɪˈnəʊsɪs) *n* the relationships between animals and plants subsisting together. [C19: NL from BIO- + Gk *koinōsis* sharing]
biodegradable (ˌbaɪəʊdɪˈgreɪdəbˈl) *adj* (of sewage, packaging, etc.) capable of being decomposed by bacteria or other biological means.
▸**biodegradability** (ˌbaɪəʊdɪˌgreɪdəˈbɪlɪtɪ) *n*
biodiversity (ˌbaɪəʊdaɪˈvɜːsɪtɪ) *n* the existence of a wide variety of plant and animal species in their natural environments, the maintaining of which is the aim of conservationists concerned about the indiscriminate destruction of rainforests and other habitats.
bioengineering (ˌbaɪəʊˌɛndʒɪˈnɪərɪŋ) *n* **1** the design and manufacture of aids, such as artificial limbs, to rectify defective body functions. **2** the design, manufacture, and maintenance of engineering equipment used in biosynthetic processes.
▸**ˌbioˌengiˈneer** *n*
bioethics (ˌbaɪəʊˈɛθɪks) *n* (*functioning as sing*) the study of ethical problems arising from scientific advances, esp. in biology and medicine.
biofeedback (ˌbaɪəʊˈfiːdˌbæk) *n Physiol., psychol.* the technique of recording and presenting (usually visually) the activity of an autonomic function, such as the rate of heartbeat, in order to teach control of it.
biofuel (ˈbaɪəʊˌfjuəl) *n* a substance of biological origin that is used as a fuel.
biog. *abbrev. for:* **1** biographical. **2** biography.
biogenesis (ˌbaɪəʊˈdʒɛnɪsɪs) *n* the principle that a living organism must originate from a parent organism similar to itself.
▸**ˌbiogeˈnetic** *or* **ˌbiogeˈnetical** *adj*
biogenic (ˌbaɪəʊˈdʒɛnɪk) *adj* produced or originating from a living organism.
biography ❶ (baɪˈɒgrəfɪ) *n, pl* **biographies.** **1** an account of a person's life by another. **2** such accounts collectively.
▸**biˈographer** *n* ▸**biographical** (ˌbaɪəˈgræfɪkˈl) *adj*
biol. *abbrev. for:* **1** biological. **2** biology.
biological (ˌbaɪəˈlɒdʒɪkˈl) *adj* **1** of or relating to biology. **2** (of a detergent) containing enzymes for removing stains of organic origin from items to be washed. ◆ *n* **3** (*usually pl*) a drug derived from a living organism.
biological clock *n* **1** an inherent periodicity in the physiological processes of living organisms that is independent of external periodicity. **2** the hypothetical mechanism responsible for this. ◆ See also **circadian.**
biological control *n* the control of destructive organisms by non-chemical means, such as introducing the natural enemy of a pest.
biological warfare *n* the use of living organisms or their toxic products to induce death or incapacity in humans.
biology (baɪˈɒlədʒɪ) *n* **1** the study of living organisms. **2** the animal and plant life of a particular region.
▸**biˈologist** *n*
bioluminescence (ˌbaɪəʊˌluːmɪˈnɛsəns) *n* the production of light by living organisms, such as the firefly.
▸**ˌbioˌlumiˈnescent** *adj*
biomass (ˈbaɪəʊˌmæs) *n* the total number of living organisms in a given area, expressed in terms of living or dry weight per unit area.
biomathematics (ˌbaɪəʊˌmæθəˈmætɪks, -ˌmæθˈmæt-) *n* (*functioning as sing*) the study of the application of mathematics to biology.
biomechanics (ˌbaɪəʊmɪˈkænɪks) *n* (*functioning as sing*) the study of the mechanics of the movement of living organisms.
biomedicine (ˌbaɪəʊˈmɛdɪsɪn) *n* **1** the medical and biological study of the effects of unusual environmental stress, esp. in connection with space travel. **2** the study of herbal remedies.
▸**ˌbioˈmedical** *adj*
biometry (baɪˈɒmɪtrɪ) *or* **biometrics** (ˌbaɪəˈmɛtrɪks) *n* (*functioning as sing*) the study of biological data by means of statistical analysis.
▸**ˌbioˈmetric** *adj*
bionic (baɪˈɒnɪk) *adj* **1** of or relating to bionics. **2** (in science fiction) having physiological functions augmented by electronic equipment.
bionics (baɪˈɒnɪks) *n* (*functioning as sing*) **1** the study of certain biological functions that are applicable to the development of electronic equipment designed to operate similarly. **2** the replacement of limbs or body parts by artificial limbs or parts that are electronically or mechanically powered.
bionomics (ˌbaɪəˈnɒmɪks) *n* (*functioning as sing*) a less common name for **ecology.** [C19: from BIO- + *nomics* on pattern of ECONOMICS]
▸**ˌbioˈnomic** *adj* ▸**bionomist** (baɪˈɒnəmɪst) *n*
biophysics (ˌbaɪəʊˈfɪzɪks) *n* (*functioning as sing*) the physics of biological processes and the application of the methods used in physics to biology.
▸**ˌbioˈphysical** *adj* ▸**ˌbioˈphysically** *adv* ▸**biophysicist** (ˌbaɪəʊˈfɪzɪsɪst) *n*
biopic (ˈbaɪəʊˌpɪk) *n Inf.* a film based on the life of a famous person. [C20: from *bio(graphical)* + *pic(ture)*]
biopsy (ˈbaɪɒpsɪ) *n, pl* **biopsies.** examination, esp. under a microscope, of tissue from a living body to determine the cause or extent of a disease. [C20: from BIO- + Gk *opsis* sight]
biorhythm (ˈbaɪəʊˌrɪðəm) *n* a cyclically recurring pattern of physiological states, believed by some to affect a person's physical, emotional, and mental states and behaviour.
bioscope (ˈbaɪəˌskəʊp) *n* **1** a kind of early film projector. **2** a South African word for **cinema.**
bioscopy (baɪˈɒskəpɪ) *n, pl* **bioscopies.** examination of a body to determine whether it is alive.
-biosis *n combining form.* indicating a specified mode of life. [NL, from Gk *biōsis;* see BIO-, -OSIS]
▸**-biotic** *adj combining form.*
biosphere (ˈbaɪəˌsfɪə) *n* the part of the earth's surface and atmosphere inhabited by living things.
biosynthesis (ˌbaɪəʊˈsɪnθɪsɪs) *n* the formation of complex compounds from simple substances by living organisms.
▸**biosynthetic** (ˌbaɪəʊsɪnˈθɛtɪk) *adj* ▸**ˌbiosynˈthetically** *adv*
biotech (ˈbaɪəʊˌtɛk) *n Inf.* short for **biotechnology.**
biotechnology (ˌbaɪəʊtɛkˈnɒlədʒɪ) *n* the use of microorganisms for beneficial effect, as in the processing of waste matter or (using genetic engineering) to produce antibiotics, hormones, vaccines, etc.
biotic (baɪˈɒtɪk) *adj* of or relating to living organisms. [C17: from Gk *biotikos,* from *bios* life]
biotin (ˈbaɪətɪn) *n* a vitamin of the B complex, abundant in egg yolk and liver. [C20: from Gk *biotē* life, way of life + -IN]
bipartisan (ˌbaɪpɑːtɪˈzæn, baɪˈpɑːtɪˌzæn) *adj* consisting of or supported by two political parties.
▸**ˌbipartiˈsanship** *n*
bipartite (baɪˈpɑːtaɪt) *adj* **1** consisting of or having two parts. **2** affecting or made by two parties. **3** *Bot.* (esp. of some leaves) divided into two parts almost to the base.
▸**biˈpartitely** *adv* ▸**bipartition** (ˌbaɪpɑːˈtɪʃən) *n*
biped (ˈbaɪpɛd) *n* **1** any animal with two feet. ◆ *adj also* **bipedal** (baɪˈpiːdˈl, -ˈpɛdˈl). **2** having two feet.
bipinnate (baɪˈpɪneɪt) *adj* (of compound leaves) having both the leaflets and the stems bearing them arranged pinnately.
▸**biˈpinnately** *adv*
biplane (ˈbaɪˌpleɪn) *n* a type of aeroplane having two sets of wings, one above the other.
bipolar (baɪˈpəʊlə) *adj* **1** having two poles: *a bipolar dynamo.* **2** of or relating to the North and South Poles. **3** having or characterized by two opposed opinions, etc. **4** (of a transistor) utilizing both majority and minority charge carriers.
▸**ˌbipoˈlarity** *n*
biprism (ˈbaɪˌprɪzəm) *n Physics.* a prism that has a highly obtuse angle to facilitate beam splitting.
biquadratic (ˌbaɪkwɒˈdrætɪk) *Maths.* ◆ *adj* **1** of or relating to the fourth power. ◆ *n* **2** a biquadratic equation, such as $x^4 + x + 6 = 0$.
biracial (baɪˈreɪʃəl) *adj* of or for members of two races.
▸**biˈracialism** *n*
birch (bɜːtʃ) *n* **1** any catkin-bearing tree or shrub having thin peeling bark. See also **silver birch.** **2** the hard close-grained wood of any of these trees. **3 the birch.** a bundle of birch twigs or a birch rod used, esp. formerly, for flogging offenders. ◆ *adj* **4** consisting or made of birch. ◆ *vb* **5** (*tr*) to flog with a birch. [OE *bierce*]
▸**ˈbirchen** *adj*
bird (bɜːd) *n* **1** any warm-blooded egg-laying vertebrate, characterized by a body covering of feathers and forelimbs modified as wings. **2** *Inf.* a person, as in **rare bird, odd bird, clever bird.** **3** *Sl., chiefly Brit.* a girl or young woman. **4** *Sl.* prison or a term in prison (esp. in **do bird**). **5 a bird in the hand.** something definite or certain. **6 birds of a feather.** people with the same characteristics, ideas, interests, etc. **7 get the bird.** *Inf.* **7a** to be fired or dismissed. **7b** (esp. of a public performer) to be hissed at. **8 kill two birds with one stone.** to accomplish two things with one action. **9 (strictly) for the birds.** *Inf.* deserving of disdain or contempt; not important. [OE *bridd,* from ?]
birdbath (ˈbɜːdˌbɑːθ) *n* a small basin or trough for birds to bathe in, usually in a garden.
bird-brained *adj Inf.* silly; stupid.
birdcage (ˈbɜːdˌkeɪdʒ) *n* **1** a wire or wicker cage for captive birds. **2** *Austral. & NZ.* an area on a racecourse where horses parade before a race. **3** *NZ inf.* a second-hand car dealer's yard.
bird call *n* **1** the characteristic call or song of a bird. **2** an imitation of this.
birdie (ˈbɜːdɪ) *n* **1** *Golf.* a score of one stroke under par for a hole. **2** *Inf.* a bird, esp. a small bird. ◆ *vb* **3** (*tr*) *Golf.* to play (a hole) in one stroke under par.
birdlime (ˈbɜːdˌlaɪm) *n* **1** a sticky substance smeared on twigs to catch small birds. ◆ *vb* **birdlimes, birdliming, birdlimed.** **2** (*tr*) to smear (twigs) with birdlime to catch (small birds).
bird-nesting *or* **birds'-nesting** *n* searching for birds' nests as a hobby, often to steal the eggs.
bird of paradise *n* **1** any of various songbirds of New Guinea and neighbouring regions, the males having brilliantly coloured plumage. **2 bird-of-paradise flower.** any of various plants native to tropical

THESAURUS

biography *n* **1** = **life story,** account, curriculum vitae, CV, life, life history, memoir, memoirs, profile, record southern Africa and South America that have purple bracts and large orange or yellow flowers resembling birds' heads.

bird of passage *n* **1** a bird that migrates seasonally. **2** a transient person.

bird of prey *n* a bird, such as a hawk or owl, that hunts other animals for food.

birdseed ('bɜːdˌsiːd) *n* a mixture of various kinds of seeds for feeding cagebirds.

bird's-eye *adj* **1a** seen or photographed from high above. **1b** summarizing (esp. in **bird's-eye view**). **2** having markings resembling birds' eyes.

bird's-foot *or* **bird-foot** *n, pl* **bird's-foots** *or* **bird-foots.** any of various plants whose flowers, leaves, or pods resemble a bird's foot or claw.

birdshot ('bɜːdˌʃɒt) *n* small pellets designed for shooting birds.

bird strike *n* a collision of an aircraft with a bird.

bird table *n* a table or platform in the open on which food for birds may be placed.

bird-watcher *n* a person who identifies and studies wild birds in their natural surroundings.
▸**'bird-ˌwatching** *n*

birefringence (ˌbaɪrɪ'frɪndʒəns) *n* another name for **double refraction.**
▸**ˌbire'fringent** *adj*

bireme ('baɪriːm) *n* an ancient galley having two banks of oars. [C17: from L, from BI- + *-rēmus* oar]

biretta *or* **berretta** (bɪ'rɛtə) *n RC Church.* a stiff square clerical cap. [C16: from It. *berretta,* from OProvençal, from LL *birrus* hooded cape]

birl (bɜːl) *vb* **1** *Scot.* to spin; twirl. **2** *US & Canad.* to cause (a floating log) to spin using the feet while standing on it, esp. as a sport among lumberjacks. ◆ *n* **3** a variant spelling of **burl**[2]. [C18: prob. imit. & infl. by WHIRL & HURL]

Biro ('baɪrəʊ) *n, pl* **Biros.** *Trademark, Brit.* a kind of ballpoint. [C20: after Laszlo Bíró (1900–85), its Hungarian inventor]

birth ❶ (bɜːθ) *n* **1** the process of bearing young; childbirth. **2** the act or fact of being born; nativity. **3** the coming into existence of something; origin. **4** ancestry; lineage: *of high birth.* **5** natural or inherited talent: *an artist by birth.* **6 give birth (to).** **6a** to bear (offspring). **6b** to produce or originate (an idea, plan, etc.). ◆ *vb* **7** *(tr) Rare.* to bear or bring forth (a child). [C12: from ON *byrth*]

birth certificate *n* an official form giving details of the time and place of a person's birth.

birth control *n* limitation of child-bearing by means of contraception.

birthday ('bɜːθˌdeɪ) *n* **1a** an anniversary of the day of one's birth. **1b** *(as modifier): birthday present.* **2** the day on which a person was born.

birthing centre ('bɜːθɪŋ) *n NZ.* a private maternity hospital.

birthmark ('bɜːθˌmɑːk) *n* a blemish on the skin formed before birth; naevus.

birth mother *n* the woman who gives birth to a child, regardless of whether she is the genetic mother or subsequently brings up the child.

birthplace ('bɜːθˌpleɪs) *n* the place where someone was born or where something originated.

birth rate *n* the ratio of live births in a specified area, group, etc., to population, usually expressed per 1000 population per year.

birthright ('bɜːθˌraɪt) *n* **1** privileges or possessions that a person has or is believed to be entitled to as soon as he is born. **2** the privileges or possessions of a first-born son. **3** inheritance.

birthstone ('bɜːθˌstəʊn) *n* a precious or semiprecious stone associated with a month or sign of the zodiac and thought to bring luck if worn by a person born in that month or under that sign.

biryani *or* **biriani** (ˌbɪrɪ'ɑːnɪ) *n* an Indian dish made with rice, highly flavoured and coloured, mixed with meat or fish. [from Urdu]

biscuit ('bɪskɪt) *n* **1** *Brit.* a small flat dry sweet or plain cake of many varieties. US and Canad. word: **cookie.** **2a** a pale brown or yellowish-grey colour. **2b** *(as adj): biscuit gloves.* **3** Also called: **bisque.** earthenware or porcelain that has been fired but not glazed. **4 take the biscuit.** *Brit.* to be regarded (by the speaker) as most surprising. [C14: from OF, from *(pain) bescuit* twice-cooked (bread), from *bes* twice + *cuire* to cook]

bise (biːz) *n* a cold dry northerly wind in Switzerland and parts of France and Italy. [C14: from OF, of Gmc origin]

bisect ❶ (baɪ'sɛkt) *vb* **1** *(tr) Maths.* to divide into two equal parts. **2** to cut or split into two. [C17: BI- + *-sect,* from L *secāre* to cut]
▸**bisection** (baɪ'sɛkʃən) *n*

bisector (baɪ'sɛktə) *n Maths.* a straight line or plane that bisects an angle, etc.

bisexual ❶ (baɪ'sɛksjʊəl) *adj* **1** sexually attracted by both men and women. **2** showing characteristics of both sexes. **3** of or relating to both sexes. ◆ *n* **4** a bisexual organism; a hermaphrodite. **5** a bisexual person.
▸**bisexuality** (ˌbaɪsɛksjʊ'ælɪtɪ) *n*

bishop ('bɪʃəp) *n* **1** a clergyman having spiritual and administrative powers over a diocese. See also **suffragan.** Related adj: **episcopal.** **2** a chesspiece, capable of moving diagonally. **3** mulled wine, usually port, spiced with oranges, cloves, etc. [OE *biscop,* from LL, from Gk *episkopos,* from EPI- + *skopos* watcher]

bishopric ❶ ('bɪʃəprɪk) *n* the see, diocese, or office of a bishop.

bismuth ('bɪzməθ) *n* a brittle pinkish-white crystalline metallic element. It is widely used in alloys; its compounds are used in medicines. Symbol: Bi; atomic no.: 83; atomic wt.: 208.98. [C17: from NL *bisemūtum,* from G *Wismut,* from ?]

bison ('baɪsən) *n, pl* **bison.** **1** Also called: **American bison, buffalo.** a member of the cattle tribe, formerly widely distributed over the prairies of W North America, with a massive head, shaggy forequarters, and a humped back. **2** Also called: **wisent, European bison.** a closely related and similar animal formerly widespread in Europe. [C14: from L *bisōn,* of Gmc origin]

bisque[1] (bɪsk) *n* a thick rich soup made from shellfish. [C17: from F]

bisque[2] (bɪsk) *n* **1a** a pink to yellowish tan colour. **1b** *(as adj): a bisque tablecloth.* **2** *Ceramics.* another name for **biscuit** (sense 3). [C20: shortened from BISCUIT]

bisque[3] (bɪsk) *n Tennis, golf, croquet.* an extra point, stroke, or turn allowed to an inferior player, usually taken when desired. [C17: from F, from ?]

bistable (ˌbaɪ'steɪbəl) *adj* **1** (of an electrical circuit switch, etc.) having two stable states. ◆ *n* **2** *Computing.* another name for **flip-flop** (sense 2).

bistort ('bɪstɔːt) *n* **1** Also called: **snakeweed.** a Eurasian plant having leaf stipules fused to form a tube around the stem and a spike of small pink flowers. **2** Also called: **snakeroot.** a related plant of W North America, with oval clusters of pink or white flowers. **3** any of several similar plants. [C16: from F, from L *bis* twice + *tortus* from *torquēre* to twist]

bistoury ('bɪstərɪ) *n, pl* **bistouries.** a long narrow-bladed surgical knife. [C15: from OF *bistorie* dagger, from ?]

bistre *or US* **bister** ('bɪstə) *n* **1** a transparent water-soluble brownish-yellow pigment made by boiling the soot of wood. **2a** a yellowish-brown to dark brown colour. **2b** *(as adj): bistre paint.* [C18: from F, from ?]

bistro ('biːstrəʊ) *n, pl* **bistros.** a small restaurant. [F: ?from Russian *bistro* fast]

bisulphate (baɪ'sʌlˌfeɪt) *n* a salt or ester of sulphuric acid containing the monovalent group $-HSO_4$ or the ion HSO_4^-. Systematic name: **hydrogensulphate.**

bisulphide (baɪ'sʌlfaɪd) *n* another name for **disulphide.**

bit[1] ❶ (bɪt) *n* **1** a small piece, portion, or quantity. **2** a short time or distance. **3** *US & Canad. inf.* the value of an eighth of a dollar: spoken of only in units of two: *two bits.* **4** any small coin. **5** short for **bit part.** **6 a bit.** rather; somewhat: *a bit dreary.* **7 a bit of.** **7a** rather: *a bit of a dope.* **7b** a considerable amount: *it takes quite a bit of time.* **8 bit by bit.** gradually. **9 do one's bit.** to make one's expected contribution. [OE *bite* action of biting; see BITE]

bit[2] ❶ (bɪt) *n* **1** a metal mouthpiece on a bridle for controlling a horse. **2** anything that restrains or curbs. **3** a cutting or drilling tool, part, or head in a brace, drill, etc. **4** the part of a key that engages the levers of a lock. **5** the mouthpiece of a smoker's pipe. ◆ *vb* **bits, bitting, bitted.** *(tr)* **6** to put a bit in the mouth of (a horse). **7** to restrain; curb. [OE *bita;* rel. to OE *bītan* to BITE]

bit[3] (bɪt) *vb* the past tense of **bite.**

bit[4] (bɪt) *n Maths, computing.* **1** a single digit of binary notation, represented either by 0 or by 1. **2** the smallest unit of information, indicating the presence or absence of a single feature. [C20: from B(INARY + DIG)IT]

bitch (bɪtʃ) *n* **1** a female dog or other female canine animal, such as a wolf. **2** *Sl., derog.* a malicious, spiteful, or coarse woman. **3** *Inf.* a difficult situation or problem. ◆ *vb Inf.* **4** *(intr)* to complain; grumble. **5** to behave (towards) in a spiteful manner. **6** *(tr; often foll. by up)* to botch; bungle. [OE *bicce*]

bitchin' ('bɪtʃɪn) *or* **bitching** ('bɪtʃɪŋ) *US sl.* ◆ *adj* **1** wonderful or excellent. ◆ *adv* **2** extremely: *bitchin' good.*

bitchy ❶ ('bɪtʃɪ) *adj* **bitchier, bitchiest.** *Sl.* of or like a bitch; malicious; snide.
▸**'bitchiness** *n*

bite ❶ (baɪt) *vb* **bites, biting, bit, bitten.** **1** to grip, cut off, or tear as with the teeth or jaws. **2** (of animals, insects, etc.) to injure by puncturing or tearing (the skin or flesh) with the teeth, fangs, etc. **3** *(tr)* to cut or

THESAURUS

birth *n* **1** = **childbirth**, delivery, nativity, parturition **3** = **beginning**, emergence, fountainhead, genesis, origin, rise, source **4** = **ancestry**, background, blood, breeding, derivation, descent, extraction, forebears, genealogy, line, lineage, nobility, noble extraction, parentage, pedigree, race, stock, strain
Antonyms *n* ≠ **childbirth**: death, demise, end, extinction, passing, passing away *or* on

bisect *vb* **1** = **halve**, cut in half **2** = **cut in two**, bifurcate, cross, cut across, divide in two, intersect, separate, split, split down the middle

bisexual *adj* **1** = **bi** *(sl.)*, AC/DC *(sl.)*, ambidextrous *(sl.)*, swinging both ways *(sl.)* **2** = **hermaphrodite**, androgyne, androgynous, epicene, gynandromorphic *or* gynandromorphous *(Entomology)*, gynandrous, hermaphroditic, monoclinous *(Botany)*

bishopric *n* = **diocese**, episcopacy, episcopate, primacy, see

bit[1] *n* **1** = **piece**, atom, chip, crumb, fragment, grain, iota, jot, mite, morsel, mouthful, part, remnant, scrap, segment, slice, small piece, speck, tittle, whit **2** = **little while**, instant, jiffy *(inf.)*, minute, moment, period, second, spell, tick *(Brit. inf.)*, time

bit[2] *n* **1** = **curb**, brake, check, restraint, snaffle

bitchy *adj Slang* = **spiteful**, backbiting, catty *(inf.)*, cruel, malicious, mean, nasty, rancorous, shrewish, snide, venomous, vicious, vindictive, vixenish
Antonyms *adj* charitable, generous, gracious, kindly, magnanimous, nice

bite *vb* **1, 2** = **tear**, champ, chew, clamp, crunch, crush, cut, gnaw, grip, hold, masticate, nibble, nip, pierce, pinch, rend, seize, snap, wound **4** =

penetrate, as with a knife. **4** (of corrosive material such as acid) to eat away or into. **5** to smart or cause to smart; sting. **6** (*intr*) *Angling.* (of a fish) to take or attempt to take the bait or lure. **7** to take firm hold (of) or act effectively (upon). **8** (*tr*) *Sl.* to annoy or worry: *what's biting her?* **9** (*tr;* often foll. by *for*) *Austral. & NZ sl.* to ask (for); scrounge from. **10 bite the dust. 10a** to fall down dead. **10b** to be rejected: *another good idea bites the dust.* ◆ *n* **11** the act of biting. **12** a thing or amount bitten off. **13** a wound, bruise, or sting inflicted by biting. **14** *Angling.* an attempt by a fish to take the bait or lure. **15** a light meal; snack. **16** a cutting, stinging, or smarting sensation. **17** *Dentistry.* the angle or manner of contact between the upper and lower teeth. **18 put the bite on.** *Sl.* to cadge or borrow from. [OE *bītan*]
▸ **'biter** *n*

biting Ⓣ ('baɪtɪŋ) *adj* **1** piercing; keen: *a biting wind.* **2** sarcastic; incisive.
▸ **'bitingly** *adv*

bitmap ('bɪt,mæp) *Computing.* ◆ *n* **1** a picture created on a visual display unit where each pixel corresponds to one or more bits in memory, the number of bits per pixel determining the number of available colours. ◆ *vb* **bitmaps, bitmapping, bitmapped. 2** (*tr*) to create a bitmap of.

bit part *n* a very small acting role with few lines to speak.

bitt (bɪt) *Naut.* ◆ *n* **1** one of a pair of strong posts on the deck of a ship for securing mooring and other lines. **2** another word for **bollard** (sense 1). ◆ *vb* **3** (*tr*) to secure (a line) by means of a bitt. [C14: prob. from ON]

bitten ('bɪtᵊn) *vb* the past participle of **bite.**

bitter Ⓣ ('bɪtə) *adj* **1** having or denoting an unpalatable harsh taste, as the peel of an orange. **2** showing or caused by strong unrelenting hostility or resentment. **3** difficult or unpleasant to accept or admit: *a bitter blow.* **4** cutting; sarcastic: *bitter words.* **5** bitingly cold: *a bitter night.* ◆ *adv* **6** very; extremely (esp. in **bitter cold**). ◆ *n* **7** a thing that is bitter. **8** *Brit.* beer with a slightly bitter taste. [OE *biter;* rel. to *bītan* to BITE]
▸ **'bitterly** *adv* ▸ **'bitterness** *n*

bitter end *n* **1** *Naut.* the end of a line, chain, or cable. **2 to the bitter end. 2a** until the finish of a task, etc., however unpleasant or difficult. **2b** until final defeat or death. [C19: ?from BITT]

bittern ('bɪtən) *n* a wading bird related and similar to the herons but with shorter legs and neck and a booming call. [C14: from OF *butor,* ?from L *būtiō* bittern + *taurus* bull]

bitters ('bɪtəz) *pl n* **1** bitter-tasting spirits of varying alcoholic content flavoured with plant extracts. **2** a similar liquid containing a bitter-tasting substance, used as a tonic.

bittersweet ('bɪtə,swiːt) *n* **1** any of several North American woody climbing plants having orange capsules that open to expose scarlet-coated seeds. **2** another name for **woody nightshade.** ◆ *adj* **3** tasting of or being a mixture of bitterness and sweetness. **4** pleasant but tinged with sadness.

bitty Ⓣ ('bɪtɪ) *adj* **bittier, bittiest. 1** lacking unity; disjointed. **2** containing bits, sediment, etc.
▸ **'bittiness** *n*

bitumen ('bɪtjʊmɪn) *n* **1** any of various viscous or solid impure mixtures of hydrocarbons that occur naturally in asphalt, tar, mineral waxes, etc.: used as a road surfacing and roofing material. **2 the bitumen.** *Austral. & NZ inf.* any road with a bitumen surface. [C15: from L *bitūmen*]
▸ **bituminous** (bɪ'tjuːmɪnəs) *adj*

bituminize *or* **bituminise** (bɪ'tjuːmɪ,naɪz) *vb* **bituminizes, bituminizing, bituminized** *or* **bituminises, bituminising, bituminised.** (*tr*) to treat with or convert into bitumen.

bituminous coal *n* a soft black coal that burns with a smoky yellow flame.

bivalent (baɪ'veɪlənt, 'bɪvə-) *adj* **1** *Chem.* another word for **divalent. 2** (of homologous chromosomes) associated together in pairs.
▸ **bi'valency** *n*

bivalve ('baɪ,vælv) *n* **1** a marine or freshwater mollusc, having a laterally compressed body, a shell consisting of two hinged valves, and gills for respiration. The group includes clams, cockles, oysters, and mussels. ◆ *adj* **2** of or relating to these molluscs. ◆ Also: **lamellibranch.**

bivouac ('bɪvʊ,æk, 'bɪvwæk) *n* **1** a temporary encampment, as used by soldiers, mountaineers, etc. ◆ *vb* **bivouacs, bivouacking, bivouacked. 2** (*intr*) to make such an encampment. [C18: from F *bivuac,* prob. from Swiss G *Beiwacht,* lit.: BY + WATCH]

biweekly (baɪ'wiːklɪ) *adj, adv* **1** every two weeks. **2** twice a week. See **bi-.** ◆ *n, pl* **biweeklies. 3** a periodical published every two weeks.

biyearly (baɪ'jɪəlɪ) *adj, adv* **1** every two years; biennial or biennially. **2** twice a year; biannual or biannually. See **bi-.**

biz (bɪz) *n Inf.* short for **business.**

bizarre Ⓣ (bɪ'zɑː) *adj* odd or unusual, esp. in an interesting or amusing way. [C17: from F, from It. *bizzarro* capricious, from ?]
▸ **bi'zarreness** *n*

bizzy ('bɪzɪ) *n, pl* **bizzies.** *Brit. sl., chiefly Liverpudlian.* a policeman. [C20: from BUSY]

bk *abbrev. for:* **1** bank. **2** book.

Bk *the chemical symbol for* berkelium.

bkg *abbrev. for* banking.

BL *abbrev. for:* **1** Bachelor of Law. **2** Bachelor of Letters. **3** Barrister-at-Law. **4** British Library.

B/L, b/l, *or* **b.l.** *pl* **Bs/L, bs/l,** *or* **bs.l.** *abbrev. for* bill of lading.

blab Ⓣ (blæb) *vb* **blabs, blabbing, blabbed. 1** to divulge (secrets, etc.) indiscreetly. **2** (*intr*) to chatter thoughtlessly; prattle. ◆ *n* **3** a less common word for **blabber.** [C14: of Gmc origin]

blabber Ⓣ ('blæbə) *n* **1** a person who blabs. **2** idle chatter. ◆ *vb* **3** (*intr*) to talk without thinking; chatter. [C15 *blabberen,* prob. imit.]

black Ⓣ (blæk) *adj* **1** of the colour of jet or carbon black, having no hue due to the absorption of all or nearly all incident light. **2** without light; completely dark. **3** without hope of alleviation; gloomy: *the future looked black.* **4** very dirty or soiled. **5** angry or resentful: *black looks.* **6** (of a play or other work) dealing with the unpleasant realities of life, esp. in a cynical or macabre manner: *black comedy.* **7** (of coffee or tea) without milk or cream. **8a** wicked or harmful: *a black lie.* **8b** (*in combination*): *black-hearted.* **9** *Brit.* (of goods, jobs, works, etc.) being subject to boycott by trade unionists. ◆ *n* **10** a black colour. **11** a dye or pigment of or producing this colour. **12** black clothing, worn esp. as a sign of mourning. **13** *Chess, draughts.* a black or dark-coloured piece or square. **14** complete darkness: *the black of the night.* **15 in the black.** in credit or without debt. ◆ *vb* **16** another word for **blacken. 17** (*tr*) to polish (shoes, etc.) with blacking. **18** (*tr*) *Brit., Austral., & NZ.* (of trade unionists) to organize a boycott of (specified goods, jobs, work, etc.). ◆ See also **blackout.** [OE *blæc*]
▸ **'blackness** *n*

Black (blæk) *n* **1** *Sometimes derog.* a member of a dark-skinned race, esp. someone of Negroid or Australoid origin. ◆ *adj* **2** of or relating to a Black person or Black people.

blackamoor ('blækə,mʊə, -,mɔː) *n Arch.* a Black person or other person with dark skin. [C16: see BLACK, MOOR]

black-and-blue *adj* **1** (of the skin) discoloured, as from a bruise. **2** feeling pain or soreness, as from a beating.

Black and Tans *pl n* **the.** a specially recruited armed force sent to Ireland in 1921 by the British Government to combat Sinn Féin. [named after the colour of their uniforms]

black-and-white *n* **1a** a photograph, picture, sketch, etc., in black, white, and shades of grey rather than in colour. **1b** (*as modifier*):

THESAURUS

eat into, burn, corrode, eat away, erode, wear away **5** = **eat into**, smart, sting, tingle **10a bite the dust** *Informal* = **die**, drop dead, expire, fall in battle, pass away, perish ◆ *n* **13** = **wound**, itch, nip, pinch, prick, smarting, sting, tooth marks **15** = **snack**, food, light meal, morsel, mouthful, piece, refreshment, taste

biting *adj* **1** = **piercing**, bitter, blighting, cold, cold as ice, cutting, freezing, harsh, nipping, penetrating, sharp **2** = **sarcastic**, caustic, cutting, incisive, mordacious, mordant, scathing, severe, sharp, stinging, trenchant, vitriolic, withering

bitter *adj* **1** = **sour**, acid, acrid, astringent, harsh, sharp, tart, unsweetened, vinegary **2** = **resentful**, acrimonious, begrudging, crabbed, embittered, hostile, morose, rancorous, sore, sour, sullen, with a chip on one's shoulder **3** = **grievous**, calamitous, cruel, dire, distressing, galling, gut-wrenching, harsh, heartbreaking, merciless, painful, poignant, ruthless, savage, vexatious **5** = **freezing**, biting, fierce, intense, severe, stinging
Antonyms *adj* ≠ **sour:** bland, mellow, mild, pleasant, sugary, sweet ≠ **resentful:** appreciative, friendly, gentle, grateful, happy, mellow, mild, pleasant, sweet, thankful ≠ **grievous:** fortunate, happy, pleasant ≠ **freezing:** balmy, gentle, mild, pleasant

bitterly *adv* **1** = **sourly**, acerbically, acidly, acridly, sharply, tartly **2** = **resentfully**, acrimoniously, grudgingly, irascibly, mordantly, sorely, sourly, sullenly, tartly, testily **3** = **grievously**, cruelly, distressingly, harshly, mercilessly, painfully, poignantly, ruthlessly, sadly, savagely, terribly **5** = **intensely**, bitingly, fiercely, severely

bitterness *n* **1** = **sourness**, acerbity, acidity, sharpness, tartness, vinegariness **2** = **resentment**, acrimony, animosity, asperity, chip on one's shoulder, grudge, hostility, pique, rancour, venom, virulence

bitty *adj* **1** = **disjointed**, disconnected, fragmentary, fragmented, incoherent, incomplete, jumbled, patchy, scrappy, sketchy
Antonyms *adj* all-embracing, coherent, complete, comprehensive, unified

bizarre *adj* = **strange**, abnormal, curious, eccentric, extraordinary, fantastic, freakish, grotesque, ludicrous, odd, oddball (*inf.*), off-beat, off-the-wall (*sl.*), outlandish, outré, peculiar, queer, ridiculous, rum (*Brit. sl.*), unusual, way-out (*inf.*), weird, zany
Antonyms *adj* common, customary, normal, ordinary, regular, routine, standard, typical

blab *vb* **1** = **tell**, blow the gaff (*Brit. sl.*), blow wide open (*sl.*), blurt out, disclose, divulge, give away, let slip, let the cat out of the bag, open one's mouth, reveal, spill one's guts (*sl.*), spill the beans (*inf.*), tell all, tell on

blabber *n* **1** = **gossip**, busybody, informer, rumour-monger, scandalmonger, talebearer, tattler, telltale ◆ *vb* **3** = **prattle**, blather, blether, chatter, gab (*inf.*), jabber, run off at the mouth

black *adj* **1, 2** = **dark**, coal-black, dusky, ebony, inky, jet, murky, pitch-black, pitchy, raven, sable, stygian **3** = **gloomy**, atrocious, depressing, dismal, distressing, doleful, foreboding, funereal, hopeless, horrible, lugubrious, mournful, ominous, sad, sombre **4** = **dirty**, dingy, filthy, grimy, grubby, soiled, sooty, stained **5** = **angry**, furious, hostile, menacing, resentful, sullen, threatening **8** = **wicked**, bad, evil, iniquitous, nefarious, villainous ◆ *n* **15 in the black** = **in credit**, in funds, solvent, without debt ◆ *vb* **18** = **boycott**, ban, bar, blacklist
Antonyms *adj* ≠ **dark:** bright, illuminated, light, lighted, lit, moonlit, sunny ≠ **gloomy:** cheerful, happy, warm ≠ **dirty:** clean, pure, white, whitish ≠ **angry:** amicable, cheerful, friendly, happy, pleased, warm ≠ **wicked:** good, honourable, moral, pure

black-and-white film. **2 in black and white. 2a** in print or writing. **2b** in extremes: *he always saw things in black and white.*

black art *n* **the.** another name for **black magic.**

black-backed gull *n* either of two common black-and-white European coastal gulls, **lesser black-backed gull** and **great black-backed gull.**

blackball ➊ ('blæk,bɔːl) *n* **1** a negative vote or veto. **2** a black wooden ball used to indicate disapproval or to veto in a vote. ◆ *vb (tr)* **3** to vote against. **4** to exclude (someone) from a group, profession, etc.; ostracize. [C18: from *black ball* used to veto]

black bean *n* an Australian leguminous tree: used in furniture manufacture. Also called: **Moreton Bay chestnut.**

black bear *n* **1 American black bear.** a bear inhabiting forests of North America. It is smaller and less ferocious than the brown bear. **2 Asiatic black bear.** a bear of central and E Asia, black with a pale V-shaped mark on the chest.

black belt *n Judo, karate, etc.* **a** a black belt worn by an instructor or expert. **b** a person entitled to wear this.

blackberry ('blækbərɪ) *n, pl* **blackberries. 1** Also called: **bramble.** any of several woody rosaceous plants that have thorny stems and black or purple edible berry-like fruits. **2** the fruit of any of these plants. ◆ *vb* **blackberries, blackberrying, blackberried. 3** *(intr)* to gather blackberries.

blackbird ('blæk,bɜːd) *n* **1** a common European thrush in which the male has black plumage and a yellow bill. **2** any of various American orioles having dark plumage. **3** (formerly) a person, esp. a South Sea Islander, who was kidnapped and sold as a slave, esp. in Australia. ◆ *vb* **4** *(tr)* (formerly) to kidnap and sell into slavery.

blackboard ('blæk,bɔːd) *n* a hard or rigid surface made of a smooth usually dark substance, used for writing or drawing on with chalk, esp. in teaching.

black body *n Physics.* a hypothetical body capable of absorbing all the electromagnetic radiation falling on it. Also called: **full radiator.**

black book *n* **1** a book containing the names of people to be punished, blacklisted, etc. **2 in someone's black books.** *Inf.* out of favour with someone.

black box *n* **1** a self-contained unit in an electronic or computer system whose circuitry need not be known to understand its function. **2** an informal name for **flight recorder.**

blackboy ('blæk,bɔɪ) *n* another name for **grass tree** (sense 1).

blackbuck ('blæk,bʌk) *n* an Indian antelope, the male of which has a dark back.

blackbutt ('blæk,bʌt) *n* any of various Australian eucalyptus trees having rough fibrous bark and hard wood used as timber.

blackcap ('blæk,kæp) *n* a brownish-grey Old World warbler, the male of which has a black crown.

blackcock ('blæk,kɒk) *n* the male of the black grouse.

blackcurrant (,blæk'kʌrənt) *n* **1** a N temperate shrub having red or white flowers and small edible black berries. **2** its fruit.

blackdamp ('blæk,dæmp) *n* air that is low in oxygen content and high in carbon dioxide as a result of an explosion in a mine. Also called: **chokedamp.**

Black Death *n* **the.** a form of bubonic plague pandemic in Europe and Asia during the 14th century. See **bubonic plague.**

black disc *n* a conventional black vinyl gramophone record as opposed to a compact disc.

black earth *n* another name for **chernozem.**

black economy *n* that portion of the income of a nation that remains illegally undeclared.

blacken ➊ ('blækən) *vb* **1** to make or become black or dirty. **2** *(tr)* to defame; slander (esp. in **blacken someone's name**).

black eye *n* bruising round the eye.

black-eyed Susan ('suːzᵊn) *n* any of several North American plants having flower heads of orange-yellow rays and brown-black centres.

blackface ('blæk,feɪs) *n* **1** a variety of sheep with a black face. **2** the make-up used by a White performer imitating a Black person.

blackfish ('blæk,fɪʃ) *n, pl* **blackfish** *or* **blackfishes. 1** any of various dark fishes, esp. a common edible Australian estuary fish. **2** a female salmon that has recently spawned. Cf. **redfish** (sense 1).

black flag *n* another name for the **Jolly Roger.**

blackfly ('blæk,flaɪ) *n, pl* **blackflies.** a black aphid that infests beans, sugar beet, and other plants. Also called: **bean aphid.**

Black Friar *n* a Dominican friar.

black grouse *n* **1** a large N European grouse, the male of which has a bluish-black plumage. **2** a related and similar species of W Asia.

blackguard ➊ ('blægɑːd, -gəd) *n* **1** an unprincipled contemptible person; scoundrel. ◆ *vb* **2** *(tr)* to ridicule or denounce with abusive language. **3** *(intr)* to behave like a blackguard. [C16: see BLACK, GUARD]
▸**'blackguardism** *n* ▸**'blackguardly** *adj*

blackhead ('blæk,hɛd) *n* **1** a black-tipped plug of fatty matter clogging a pore of the skin. **2** any of various birds with black plumage on the head.

black hole *n* **1a** *Astron.* a hypothetical region of space resulting from the gravitational collapse of a star and surrounded by a gravitational field so high that neither matter nor radiation could escape from it. **1b** a similar but much more massive region of space at the centre of a galaxy. **2** any place regarded as resembling a black hole in that items or information entering it cannot be retrieved.

black ice *n* a thin transparent layer of new ice on a road or similar surface.

blacking ('blækɪŋ) *n* any preparation for giving a black finish to shoes, metals, etc.

blackjack[1] ('blæk,dʒæk) *Chiefly US & Canad.* ◆ *n* **1** a truncheon of leather-covered lead with a flexible shaft. ◆ *vb (tr)* **2** to hit as with a blackjack. **3** to compel (a person) by threats. [C19: from BLACK + JACK (implement)]

blackjack[2] ('blæk,dʒæk) *n* pontoon or any similar card game. [C20: from BLACK + JACK (the knave)]

black knight *n Commerce.* a person or firm that makes an unwelcome takeover bid for a company. Cf. **grey knight, white knight.**

black lead (lɛd) *n* another name for **graphite.**

blackleg ('blæklɛg) *n* **1** Also called **scab.** *Brit.* a person who acts against the interests of a trade union, as by continuing to work during a strike or taking over a striker's job. ◆ *vb* **blacklegs, blacklegging, blacklegged. 2** *(intr) Brit.* to act against the interests of a trade union, esp. by refusing to join a strike.

black light *n* the invisible electromagnetic radiation in the ultraviolet and infrared regions of the spectrum.

blacklist ➊ ('blæk,lɪst) *n* **1** a list of persons or organizations under suspicion, or considered untrustworthy, disloyal, etc. ◆ *vb* **2** *(tr)* to put on a blacklist.

black magic ➊ *n* magic used for evil purposes.

blackmail ➊ ('blæk,meɪl) *n* **1** the act of attempting to obtain money by intimidation, as by threats to disclose discreditable information. **2** the exertion of pressure, esp. unfairly, in an attempt to influence someone. ◆ *vb (tr)* **3** to exact or attempt to exact (money or anything of value) from (a person) by threats or intimidation; extort. **4** to attempt to influence (a person), esp. by unfair pressure. [C16: from BLACK + OE *māl* terms]
▸**'black,mailer** *n*

Black Maria (mə'raɪə) *n* a police van for transporting prisoners.

black mark *n* an indication of disapproval, failure, etc.

black market *n* **1** any system in which goods or currencies are sold and bought illegally, esp. in violation of controls or rationing. **2** the place where such a system operates. ◆ *vb* **black-market. 3** to sell (goods) on the black market.
▸**black marketeer** *n*

black mass *n (sometimes caps.)* a blasphemous travesty of the Christian Mass, performed by practitioners of black magic.

black money *n* **1** that part of a nation's income that relates to its black economy. **2** any money that a person or organization acquires illegally, as by a means that involves tax evasion. **3** *US.* money to fund a government project that is concealed in the cost of some other project.

Black Muslim *n* (esp. in the US) a member of an Islamic political movement of Black people who seek to establish a new Black nation.

black nightshade *n* a common poisonous weed in cultivated land, having white flowers and black berry-like fruits.

blackout ➊ ('blækaʊt) *n* **1** the extinguishing or hiding of all artificial light, esp. in a city visible to an air attack. **2** a momentary loss of consciousness, vision, or memory. **3** a temporary electrical power failure or cut. **4** the suspension of broadcasting, as by a strike or for political reasons. ◆ *vb* **black out.** *(adv)* **5** *(tr)* to obliterate or extinguish (lights). **6** *(tr)* to create a blackout in (a city, etc.). **7** *(intr)* to lose vision, consciousness, or memory temporarily. **8** *(tr)* to stop (news, a television programme, etc.) from being broadcast.

black pepper *n* a pungent condiment made by grinding the dried unripe berries and husks of the pepper plant.

Black Power *n* a social, economic, and political movement of Black people, esp. in the US, to obtain equality with Whites.

THESAURUS

blackball *vb* **4** = **exclude**, ban, bar, blacklist, debar, drum out, expel, ostracize, oust, repudiate, snub

blacken *vb* **1** = **darken**, befoul, begrime, cloud, dirty, grow black, make black, smudge, soil **2** = **discredit**, bad-mouth (*sl., chiefly US & Canad.*), calumniate, decry, defame, denigrate, dishonour, knock (*inf.*), malign, rubbish (*inf.*), slag (off) (*sl.*), slander, smear, smirch, stain, sully, vilify

blackguard *n* **1** = **scoundrel**, bastard (*offens.*), blighter (*Brit. inf.*), bounder (*old-fashioned Brit. sl.*), miscreant, rascal, rogue, scumbag (*sl.*), shit (*taboo sl.*), son-of-a-bitch (*sl., chiefly US & Canad.*), swine, villain, wretch

blacklist *vb* **2** = **exclude**, ban, bar, blackball, boycott, debar, expel, ostracize, preclude, proscribe, reject, repudiate, snub, vote against

black magic *n* = **witchcraft**, black art, diabolism, necromancy, sorcery, voodoo, wizardry

blackmail *n* **1** = **extortion**, exaction, hush money (*sl.*), intimidation, milking, pay-off (*inf.*), protection (*inf.*), ransom, shakedown, threat ◆ *vb* **3** = **extort**, bleed (*inf.*), coerce, compel, demand, exact, force, hold to ransom, intimidate, milk, squeeze, threaten

blackness *n* **1, 2** = **darkness**, duskiness, gloom, inkiness, murkiness, swarthiness
Antonyms *n* brightness, brilliance, effulgence, incandescence, lambency, light, lightness, luminescence, luminosity, phosphorescence, radiance

blackout *n* **2** = **unconsciousness**, coma, faint, loss of consciousness, oblivion, swoon, syncope (*Pathology*) **3** = **power cut**, power failure **4** = **noncommunication**, censorship, radio silence, secrecy, suppression, withholding news ◆ *vb* **black out 5** = **darken**, conceal, cover, eclipse, shade **8** = **pass out**, collapse, faint, flake out, lose consciousness, swoon

black pudding *n* a kind of black sausage made from minced pork fat, pig's blood, and other ingredients. Also called: **blood pudding.**

Black Rod *n* (in Britain) an officer of the House of Lords and of the Order of the Garter, whose main duty is summoning the Commons at the opening and proroguing of Parliament.

black section *n* (in Britain) an unofficial group within the Labour Party in any constituency which represents the interests of local Black people.

black sheep ⓣ *n* a person who is regarded as a disgrace or failure by his family or peer group.

Blackshirt ('blæk,ʃɜːt) *n* (in Europe) a member of a fascist organization, esp. the Italian Fascist party before and during World War II.

blacksmith ('blæk,smɪθ) *n* an artisan who works iron with a furnace, anvil, hammer, etc. [C14: see BLACK, SMITH]

black snake *n* **1** any of several Old World black venomous snakes, esp. the **Australian black snake. 2** any of various dark nonvenomous snakes.

black spot *n* **1** a place on a road where accidents frequently occur. **2** any dangerous or difficult place. **3** a disease of roses that causes black blotches on the leaves.

black stump *n* **the.** *Austral.* an imaginary marker of the extent of civilization (esp. in **beyond the black stump**).

black tea *n* tea made from fermented tea leaves.

blackthorn ('blæk,θɔːn) *n* a thorny Eurasian shrub with black twigs, white flowers, and small sour plumlike fruits. Also called: **sloe.**

black tie *n* **1** a black bow tie worn with a dinner jacket. **2** (*modifier*) denoting an occasion when a dinner jacket should be worn.

blacktop ('blæk,tɒp) *n Chiefly US & Canad.* a bituminous mixture used for paving.

Black tracker *n Austral.* an Aboriginal tracker working for the police.

black velvet *n* a mixture of stout and champagne in equal proportions.

Black Watch *n* **the.** the Royal Highland Regiment in the British Army.

blackwater fever ('blæk,wɔːtə) *n* a rare and serious complication of malaria, characterized by massive destruction of red blood cells, producing dark red or blackish urine.

black widow *n* an American spider, the female of which is highly venomous, and commonly eats its mate.

Blackwood ('blæk,wʊd) *n Bridge.* a conventional bidding sequence of four and five no-trumps, which are requests to the partner to show aces and kings respectively. [C20: after E. F. *Blackwood,* its US inventor]

bladder ('blædə) *n* **1** *Anat.* a distensible membranous sac, usually containing liquid or gas, esp. the urinary bladder. **2** an inflatable part of something. **3** a hollow saclike part in certain plants, such as the bladderwrack. [OE *blǣdre*]
▸'**bladdery** *adj*

bladderwort ('blædə,wɜːt) *n* an aquatic plant some of whose leaves are modified as small bladders to trap minute aquatic animals.

bladderwrack ('blædə,ræk) *n* any of several seaweeds that grow in the intertidal regions of rocky shores and have branched brown fronds with air bladders.

blade (bleɪd) *n* **1** the part of a sharp weapon, tool, etc., that forms the cutting edge. **2** the thin flattish part of various tools, implements, etc., as of a propeller, turbine, etc. **3** the flattened expanded part of a leaf, sepal, or petal. **4** the long narrow leaf of a grass or related plant. **5** the striking surface of a bat, club, stick, or oar. **6** the metal runner on an ice skate. **7** the upper part of the tongue lying directly behind the tip. **8** *Arch.* a dashing or swaggering young man. **9** short for **shoulder blade. 10** a poetic word for a **sword** or **swordsman.** [OE *blæd*]
▸'**bladed** *adj*

blaeberry ('bleɪbərɪ) *n, pl* **blaeberries.** *Brit.* another name for **whortleberry** (senses 1, 2). [C15: from dialect *blae* bluish + BERRY]

blag (blæg) *Sl.* ◆ *n* **1** a robbery, esp. with violence. ◆ *vb* **blags, blagging, blagged.** (*tr*) **2** to obtain by wheedling or cadging: *she blagged free tickets from her mate.* **3** to snatch (wages, someone's handbag, etc.); steal. **4** to rob (esp. a bank or post office). [C19: from ?]
▸'**blagger** *n*

blah *or* **blah blah** (blɑː) *n Sl.* worthless or silly talk. [C20: imit.]

blain (bleɪn) *n* a blister, blotch, or sore on the skin. [OE *blegen*]

Blairite ('blɛəraɪt) *adj* **1** of or relating to the modernizing policies of Tony Blair, British prime minister from 1997. ◆ *n* **2** a supporter of the modernizing policies of Tony Blair.

blame ⓣ (bleɪm) *n* **1** responsibility for something that is wrong; culpability. **2** an expression of condemnation. ◆ *vb* **blames, blaming, blamed.** (*tr*) **3** (usually foll. by *for*) to attribute responsibility to: *I blame him for the failure.* **4** (usually foll. by *on*) to ascribe responsibility for (something) to: *I blame the failure on him.* **5** to find fault with. **6 be to blame.** to be at fault. [C12: from OF *blasmer,* ult. from LL *blasphēmāre* to blaspheme]
▸'**blamable** *or* '**blameable** *adj* ▸'**blamably** *or* '**blameably** *adv*

blameful ('bleɪmfʊl) *adj* deserving blame; guilty.
▸'**blamefully** *adv* ▸'**blamefulness** *n*

blameless ⓣ ('bleɪmlɪs) *adj* free from blame; innocent.
▸'**blamelessness** *n*

blameworthy ⓣ ('bleɪm,wɜːðɪ) *adj* deserving censure.
▸'**blame,worthiness** *n*

blanch ⓣ (blɑːntʃ) *vb* (*mainly tr*) **1** to remove colour from; whiten. **2** (*usually intr*) to become or cause to become pale, as with sickness or fear. **3** to prepare (meat, green vegetables, nuts, etc.) by plunging them in boiling water. **4** to cause (celery, chicory, etc.) to grow free of chlorophyll by the exclusion of sunlight. [C14: from OF *blanchir,* from *blanc* white; see BLANK]

blancmange (blə'mɒnʒ) *n* a jelly-like dessert of milk, stiffened usually with cornflour. [C14: from OF *blanc manger,* lit.: white food]

bland ⓣ (blænd) *adj* **1** devoid of distinctive or stimulating characteristics; uninteresting. **2** gentle and agreeable; suave. **3** mild and soothing. [C15: from L *blandus* flattering]
▸'**blandly** *adv* ▸'**blandness** *n*

blandish ('blændɪʃ) *vb* (*tr*) to seek to persuade or influence by mild flattery; coax. [C14: from OF *blandir,* from L *blandīrī*]

blandishments ⓣ ('blændɪʃmənts) *pl n* (*rarely sing*) flattery intended to coax or cajole.

blank ⓣ (blæŋk) *adj* **1** (of a writing surface) bearing no marks; not written on. **2** (of a form, etc.) with spaces left for details to be filled in. **3** without ornament or break. **4** not filled in; empty. **5** exhibiting no interest or expression: *a blank look.* **6** lacking understanding; confused: *he looked blank.* **7** absolute; complete: *blank rejection.* **8** devoid of ideas or inspiration: *his mind went blank.* ◆ *n* **9** an emptiness; void; blank space. **10** an empty space for writing in. **11** a printed form containing such empty spaces. **12** something characterized by incomprehension or confusion: *my mind went a complete blank.* **13** a mark, often a dash, in place of a word, esp. a taboo word. **14** short for **blank cartridge. 15** a piece of material prepared for stamping, punching, forging, or some other operation. **16 draw a blank.** to get no results from something. ◆ *vb* (*tr*) **17** (usually foll. by *out*) to cross out, blot, or obscure. [C15: from OF *blanc* white, of Gmc origin]
▸'**blankness** *n*

blank cartridge *n* a cartridge containing powder but no bullet.

blank cheque *n* **1** a cheque that has been signed but on which the amount payable has not been specified. **2** complete freedom of action.

blanket ⓣ ('blæŋkɪt) *n* **1** a large piece of thick cloth for use as a bed covering, animal covering, etc. **2** a concealing cover, as of smoke, leaves, or snow. **3** (*modifier*) applying to or covering a wide group or variety of people, conditions, situations, etc.: *blanket insurance against loss, injury, and theft.* **4** (**born**) **on the wrong side of the blanket.** *Inf.* illegitimate. **5 on the blanket.** *Irish.* (of an imprisoned terrorist) wearing only a blanket

THESAURUS

black sheep *n* = **disgrace**, dropout, ne'er-do-well, outcast, prodigal, renegade, reprobate

blamable *adj* **3-5** = **responsible**, answerable, at fault, blameworthy, culpable, deserving of censure, faulty, guilty, in the wrong, liable, reprehensible, reproachable, reprovable

blame *n* **1** = **responsibility**, accountability, accusation, culpability, fault, guilt, incrimination, liability, rap (*sl.*) **2** = **condemnation**, castigation, censure, charge, complaint, criticism, recrimination, reproach, reproof, stick (*sl.*) ◆ *vb* **3, 4** = **hold responsible**, accuse, point a *or* the finger at **5** = **criticize**, admonish, blast, censure, charge, chide, condemn, disapprove, express disapprobation, find fault with, lambast(e), put down, reprehend, reproach, reprove, tax, tear into (*inf.*), upbraid
Antonyms *n* ≠ **responsibility:** absolution, alibi, excuse, exoneration, vindication ≠ **condemnation:** acclaim, Brownie points, commendation, credit, honour, praise, tribute ◆ *vb* ≠ **hold responsible:** absolve, acquit, clear, excuse, exonerate, forgive, vindicate ≠ **criticize:** acclaim, approve of, commend, compliment, praise

blameless *adj* = **innocent**, above suspicion, clean, faultless, guiltless, immaculate, impeccable, in the clear, irreproachable, perfect, squeaky-clean, stainless, unblemished, unimpeachable, unoffending, unspotted, unsullied, untarnished, upright, virtuous
Antonyms *adj* at fault, censurable, culpable, guilty, reprovable, responsible, to blame

blameworthy *adj* = **reprehensible**, discreditable, disreputable, indefensible, inexcusable, iniquitous, reproachable, shameful

blanch *vb* **1** = **whiten**, bleach, fade **2** = **turn pale**, become *or* grow white, become pallid, blench, drain, pale

bland *adj* **1** = **dull**, boring, flat, humdrum, insipid, monotonous, tasteless, tedious, tiresome, undistinctive, unexciting, uninspiring, uninteresting, unstimulating, vanilla (*inf.*), vapid, weak **2** = **smooth**, affable, amiable, congenial, courteous, debonair, friendly, gentle, gracious, suave, unemotional, urbane
Antonyms *adj* ≠ **dull:** distinctive, exciting, inspiring, interesting, rousing, stimulating, turbulent, volatile

blandishments *pl n* = **flattery**, blarney, cajolery, coaxing, compliments, fawning, ingratiation, inveiglement, soft soap (*inf.*), soft words, sweet talk (*inf.*), wheedling

blank *adj* **1, 2, 4** = **unmarked**, bare, clean, clear, empty, plain, spotless, uncompleted, unfilled, void, white **5** = **expressionless**, deadpan, dull, empty, hollow, impassive, inane, lifeless, poker-faced (*inf.*), vacant, vacuous, vague **6** = **puzzled**, at a loss, at sea, bewildered, confounded, confused, disconcerted, dumbfounded, flummoxed, muddled, nonplussed, uncomprehending **7** = **absolute**, complete, out and out, outright, thorough, total, unqualified, utter ◆ *n* **8** = **empty space**, emptiness, gap, nothingness, space, tabula rasa, vacancy, vacuity, vacuum, void
Antonyms *adj* ≠ **unmarked:** completed, filled in, full, marked ≠ **expressionless:** alert, expressive, intelligent, interested, lively, thoughtful

blanket *n* **1** = **cover**, afghan, coverlet, rug **2** = **covering**, carpet, cloak, coat, coating, envelope, film, layer, mantle, sheet, wrapper, wrapping ◆ *modifier* **3** = **comprehensive**, across-the-board, all-inclusive, overall, sweeping, wide-ranging ◆ *vb* **6** = **cover**, cloak, cloud, instead of prison uniform, as a protest against not being recognized as a political prisoner. ◆ *vb* (*tr*) **6** to cover as with a blanket; overlie. **7** to cover a wide area; give blanket coverage. **8** (usually foll. by *out*) to obscure or suppress. [C13: from OF *blancquete,* from *blanc;* see BLANK]

blanket bath *n* an all-over wash given to a person confined to bed.

blanket bog *n* a very acid peat bog, low in nutrients, extending widely over a flat terrain, found in cold wet climates.

blanket stitch *n* a strong reinforcing stitch for the edges of blankets and other thick material.

blankety ('blæŋkɪtɪ) *adj, adv* a euphemism for any taboo word. [C20: from BLANK]

blank verse *n Prosody.* unrhymed verse, esp. in iambic pentameters.

blare ❶ (blɛə) *vb* **blares, blaring, blared. 1** to sound loudly and harshly. **2** to proclaim loudly and sensationally. ◆ *n* **3** a loud harsh noise. [C14: from MDu. *bleren;* imit.]

blarney ❶ ('blɑːnɪ) *n* **1** flattering talk. ◆ *vb* **2** to cajole with flattery; wheedle. [C19: after the *Blarney* Stone in SW Ireland, said to endow whoever kisses it with skill in flattery]

blasé ❶ ('blɑːzeɪ) *adj* **1** indifferent to something because of familiarity. **2** lacking enthusiasm; bored. [C19: from F, p.p. of *blaser* to cloy]

blaspheme ❶ (blæs'fiːm) *vb* **blasphemes, blaspheming, blasphemed. 1** (*tr*) to show contempt or disrespect for (God or sacred things), esp. in speech. **2** (*intr*) to utter profanities or curses. [C14: from LL, from Gk, from *blasphēmos* BLASPHEMOUS]

▸**blas'phemer** *n*

blasphemous ❶ ('blæsfɪməs) *adj* involving impiousness or gross irreverence towards God or something sacred. [C15: via LL, from Gk *blasphēmos* evil-speaking, from *blapsis* evil + *phēmē* speech]

blasphemy ❶ ('blæsfɪmɪ) *n, pl* **blasphemies. 1** blasphemous behaviour or language. **2** Also called: **blasphemous libel.** *Law.* the crime committed if a person insults, offends, or vilifies the deity, Christ, or the Christian religion.

blast ❶ (blɑːst) *n* **1** an explosion, as of dynamite. **2** the rapid movement of air away from the centre of an explosion; shock wave. **3** the charge used in a single explosion. **4** a sudden strong gust of wind or air. **5** a sudden loud sound, as of a trumpet. **6** a violent verbal outburst, as of criticism. **7** a forcible jet of air, esp. one used to intensify the heating effect of a furnace. **8** any of several diseases of plants and animals. **9** *US sl.* a very enjoyable or thrilling experience: *the party was a blast.* **10** (**at**) **full blast.** at maximum speed, volume, etc. ◆ *interj* **11** *Sl.* an exclamation of annoyance. ◆ *vb* **12** (*tr*) to destroy or blow up with explosives, shells, etc. **13** to make or cause to make a loud harsh noise. **14** to wither or cause to wither; blight or be blighted. **15** (*tr*) to criticize severely. [OE *blǣst*]

▸**'blaster** *n*

-blast *n combining form.* (in biology) indicating an embryonic cell or formative layer: *mesoblast.* [from Gk *blastos* bud]

blasted ❶ ('blɑːstɪd) *adj* **1** blighted or withered. ◆ *adj* (*prenominal*), *adv* **2** *Sl.* (intensifier): *a blasted idiot.*

blast furnace *n* a vertical cylindrical furnace for smelting into which a blast of preheated air is forced.

blasto- *combining form.* indicating an embryo or bud. [see BLAST]

blastoff ❶ ('blɑːst,ɒf) *n* **1** the launching of a rocket under its own power. **2** the time at which this occurs. ◆ *vb* **blast off. 3** (*adv; when tr, usually passive*) to be launched.

blastula ('blæstjʊlə) *n, pl* **blastulas** *or* **blastulae** (-liː). an early form of an animal embryo that develops a sphere of cells with a central cavity. Also called: **blastosphere.** [C19: NL from Gk, from dim. of *blastos* bud]

▸**'blastular** *adj*

blat (blæt) *n Sl.* a newspaper. [C20: from G *Blatt* leaf, sheet of paper]

blatant ❶ ('bleɪtᵊnt) *adj* **1** glaringly conspicuous or obvious: *a blatant lie.* **2** offensively noticeable; obtrusive. **3** offensively noisy. [C16: coined by Edmund Spenser (?1552–99), E poet, prob. infl. by L *blatīre* to babble]

▸**'blatancy** *n*

blather ('blæðə) *vb, n* a variant of **blether.**

blatherskite ('blæðə,skaɪt) *n* **1** a talkative silly person. **2** foolish talk; nonsense. [C17: from BLATHER + Scot. & N English dialect *skate* fellow]

blaxploitation (,blæksplɔɪ'teɪʃən) *n* exploitative use of stereotypical images of Black people in films, books, etc. [C20: from BLACK + EXPLOITATION]

blaze[1] ❶ (bleɪz) *n* **1** a strong fire or flame. **2** a very bright light or glare. **3** an outburst (of passion, acclaim, patriotism, etc.). **4** brilliance; brightness. ◆ *vb* **blazes, blazing, blazed.** (*intr*) **5** to burn fiercely. **6** to shine brightly. **7** (often foll. by *up*) to become stirred, as with anger or excitement. **8** (usually foll. by *away*) to shoot continuously. ◆ See also **blazes.** [OE *blæse*]

blaze[2] (bleɪz) *n* **1** a mark, usually indicating a path, made on a tree. **2** a light-coloured marking on the face of a domestic animal. ◆ *vb* **blazes, blazing, blazed.** (*tr*) **3** to mark (a tree, path, etc.) with a blaze. **4 blaze a trail.** to explore new territories, areas of knowledge, etc., so that others can follow. [C17: prob. from MLow G *bles* white marking]

blaze[3] (bleɪz) *vb* **blazes, blazing, blazed.** (*tr;* often foll. by *abroad*) to make widely known; proclaim. [C14: from MDu. *blāsen,* from OHG *blāsan*]

blazer ('bleɪzə) *n* a fairly lightweight jacket, often in the colours of a sports club, school, etc.

blazes ('bleɪzɪz) *pl n* **1** *Sl.* a euphemistic word for **hell. 2** *Inf.* (intensifier): *to run like blazes.*

blazon ❶ ('bleɪzᵊn) *vb* (*tr*) **1** (often foll. by *abroad*) to proclaim publicly. **2** *Heraldry.* to describe (heraldic arms) in proper terms. **3** to draw and colour (heraldic arms) conventionally. ◆ *n* **4** *Heraldry.* a conventional description or depiction of heraldic arms. [C13: from OF *blason* coat of arms]

▸**'blazoner** *n*

blazonry ('bleɪzənrɪ) *n, pl* **blazonries. 1** the art or process of describing heraldic arms in proper form. **2** heraldic arms collectively. **3** colourful or ostentatious display.

bldg *abbrev. for* building.

bleach ❶ (bliːtʃ) *vb* **1** to make or become white or colourless, as by exposure to sunlight, by the action of chemical agents, etc. ◆ *n* **2** a bleaching agent. **3** the act of bleaching. [OE *blǣcan*]

▸**'bleacher** *n*

bleaching powder *n* a white powder consisting of chlorinated calcium hydroxide. Also called: **chloride of lime, chlorinated lime.**

bleak[1] ❶ (bliːk) *adj* **1** exposed and barren. **2** cold and raw. **3** offering little hope; dismal: *a bleak future.* [OE *blāc* bright, pale]

▸**'bleakness** *n*

bleak[2] (bliːk) *n* any of various European cyprinid fishes occurring in slow-flowing rivers. [C15: prob. from ON *bleikja* white colour]

blear (blɪə) *Arch.* ◆ *vb* **1** (*tr*) to make (eyes or sight) dim as with tears; blur. ◆ *adj* **2** a less common word for **bleary.** [C13: *blere* to make dim]

bleary ❶ ('blɪərɪ) *adj* **blearier, bleariest. 1** (of eyes or vision) dimmed or blurred, as by tears or tiredness. **2** indistinct or unclear.

▸**'bleariness** *n*

THESAURUS

coat, eclipse, mask, surround **8** = **suppress**, conceal, hide, obscure

blankness *n* **5** = **indifference**, abstraction, obliviousness **8** = **vacancy**, fatuity, inanity, vacuity

blare *vb* **1** = **sound out**, blast, boom, clamour, clang, honk, hoot, peal, resound, roar, scream, toot, trumpet

blarney *n* **1** = **flattery**, blandishment, cajolery, coaxing, exaggeration, honeyed words, overpraise, soft soap (*inf.*), spiel, sweet talk (*inf.*), wheedling

blasé *adj* **1** = **jaded**, cloyed, glutted, satiated, surfeited **2** = **indifferent**, apathetic, bored, lukewarm, nonchalant, offhand, unconcerned, unexcited, uninterested, unmoved, weary, world-weary

Antonyms *adj* affected, caring, enthusiastic, excited, interested, responsive, stimulated

blaspheme *vb* **1** = **profane**, abuse, desecrate **2** = **swear**, curse, damn, execrate, revile

blasphemous *adj* **1** = **irreverent**, godless, impious, irreligious, profane, sacrilegious, ungodly

Antonyms *adj* devout, God-fearing, godly, pious, religious, respectful, reverent, reverential

blasphemy *n* **1** = **irreverence**, cursing, desecration, execration, impiety, impiousness, profanation, profaneness, profanity, sacrilege, swearing

blast *n* **1** = **explosion**, bang, blow-up, burst, crash, detonation, discharge, eruption, outburst, salvo, volley **4** = **gust**, gale, squall, storm, strong breeze, tempest **5** = **blare**, blow, clang, honk, peal, scream, toot, wail ◆ *vb* **12** = **blow up**, blow sky-high, break up, burst, demolish, destroy, explode, put paid to, ruin, shatter **14** = **blight**, kill, shrivel, wither **15** = **criticize**, attack, castigate, flay, lambast(e), put down, rail at, tear into (*inf.*)

blasted *adj* **1** = **ruined**, blighted, desolated, destroyed, devastated, ravaged, shattered, spoiled, wasted, withered

blastoff *n* **1** = **launch**, discharge, expulsion, firing, launching, liftoff, projection, shot

blatant *adj* **1, 2** = **obvious**, bald, brazen, conspicuous, flagrant, flaunting, glaring, naked, obtrusive, ostentatious, outright, overt, prominent, pronounced, sheer, unmitigated

Antonyms *adj* agreeable, cultured, dignified, hidden, inconspicuous, quiet, refined, soft, subtle, tasteful, unnoticeable, unobtrusive, well-mannered

blaze[1] *n* **1** = **fire**, bonfire, conflagration, flame, flames **2, 4** = **glare**, beam, brilliance, flare, flash, gleam, glitter, glow, light, radiance **3** = **outburst**, blast, burst, eruption, flare-up, fury, outbreak, rush, storm, torrent ◆ *vb* **5** = **burn**, fire, flame **6** = **shine**, beam, flare, flash, glare, gleam, glow **7** = **flare up**, boil, explode, fume, seethe

blazing *adj* **1** = **burning**, ablaze, afire, aflame, alight, fiery, flaming, on fire **2** = **shining**, aglow, brilliant, coruscating, flashing, gleaming, glowing, illuminated, incandescent, luminous, radiant, sparkling **7** = **furious**, angry, excited, fervent, frenzied, fuming, impassioned, incensed, passionate, raging, seething

blazon *vb* **1** = **proclaim**, broadcast, celebrate, flourish, make known, renown, trumpet

bleach *vb* **1** = **whiten**, blanch, etiolate, fade, grow pale, lighten, peroxide, wash out

bleached *adj* **1** = **whiten**, achromatic, etiolated, faded, lightened, peroxided, stonewashed, washed-out

bleak[1] *adj* **1** = **exposed**, bare, barren, desolate, gaunt, open, stark, unsheltered, weatherbeaten, windswept, windy **2** = **cold**, chilly, raw **3** = **dismal**, cheerless, comfortless, depressing, discouraging, disheartening, dreary, gloomy, grim, hopeless, joyless, sombre, unpromising

Antonyms *adj* ≠ **exposed:** protected, sheltered, shielded ≠ **dismal:** cheerful, cosy, encouraging, promising

bleary *adj* **1, 2** = **dim**, blurred, blurry, fogged, foggy, fuzzy, hazy, indistinct, misty

bleary-eyed *or* **blear-eyed** *adj* with eyes blurred, as with old age or after waking.

bleat (bliːt) *vb* **1** (*intr*) (of a sheep, goat, or calf) to utter its characteristic plaintive cry. **2** (*intr*) to speak with any similar sound. **3** to whine; whimper. ◆ *n* **4** the characteristic cry of sheep, goats, and calves. **5** any sound similar to this. **6** a weak complaint or whine. [OE *blǣtan*]
▸ **'bleater** *n* ▸ **'bleating** *n, adj*

bleb (blɛb) *n* **1** a fluid-filled blister on the skin. **2** a small air bubble. [C17: var. of BLOB]

bleed Ⓣ (bliːd) *vb* **bleeds, bleeding, bled** (blɛd). **1** (*intr*) to lose or emit blood. **2** (*tr*) to remove or draw blood from (a person or animal). **3** (*intr*) to be injured or die, as for a cause. **4** (of plants) to exude (sap or resin), esp. from a cut. **5** (*tr*) *Inf.* to obtain money, etc., from, esp. by extortion. **6** (*tr*) to draw liquid or gas from (a container or enclosed system): *to bleed the hydraulic brakes.* **7** (*intr*) (of dye or paint) to run or become mixed, as when wet. **8** to print or be printed so that text, illustrations, etc., run off the trimmed page. **9 one's heart bleeds.** used to express sympathetic grief, often ironically. [OE *blēdan*]

bleeder ('bliːdə) *n* **1** *Sl.* **1a** *Derog.* a despicable person. **1b** any person. **2** *Pathol.* a nontechnical name for a **haemophiliac.**

bleeding ('bliːdɪŋ) *adj, adv Brit. sl.* (intensifier): *a bleeding fool.*

bleeding heart *n* **1** any of several plants, esp. a widely cultivated Japanese species which has heart-shaped nodding pink flowers. **2** *Inf.* **2a** an excessively softhearted person. **2b** (*as modifier*): *bleeding-heart liberals.*

bleep (bliːp) *n* **1** a single short high-pitched signal made by an electronic apparatus; beep. **2** another word for **bleeper.** ◆ *vb* **3** (*intr*) to make such a noise. **4** (*tr*) to call (somebody) by means of a bleeper. [C20: imit.]

bleeper ('bliːpə) *n* a small portable radio receiver, carried esp. by doctors, that sounds a coded bleeping signal to call the carrier. Also called: **bleep.**

blemish Ⓣ ('blɛmɪʃ) *n* **1** a defect; flaw; stain. ◆ *vb* **2** (*tr*) to flaw the perfection of; spoil; tarnish. [C14: from OF *blemir* to make pale]

blench Ⓣ (blɛntʃ) *vb* (*intr*) to shy away, as in fear; quail. [OE *blencan* to deceive]

blend Ⓣ (blɛnd) *vb* **1** to mix or mingle (components) together thoroughly. **2** (*tr*) to mix (different grades or varieties of tea, whisky, etc.). **3** (*intr*) to look good together; harmonize. **4** (*intr*) (esp. of colours) to shade imperceptibly into each other. ◆ *n* **5** a mixture or type produced by blending. **6** the act of blending. **7** Also called: **portmanteau word.** a word formed by joining together the beginning and the end of two other words: *"brunch" is a blend of "breakfast" and "lunch."* [OE *blandan*]

blende (blɛnd) *n* **1** another name for **sphalerite. 2** any of several sulphide ores. [C17: G, from *blenden* to deceive, BLIND; so called because it is easily mistaken for galena]

blender ('blɛndə) *n* **1** a person or thing that blends. **2** Also called: **liquidizer.** a kitchen appliance with blades used for puréeing vegetables, blending liquids, etc.

blenny ('blɛnɪ) *n, pl* **blennies.** any of various small fishes of coastal waters having a tapering scaleless body, a long dorsal fin, and long raylike pelvic fins. [C18: from L, from Gk *blennos* slime]

blent (blɛnt) *vb Arch. or literary.* a past participle of **blend.**

blepharitis (ˌblɛfəˈraɪtɪs) *n* inflammation of the eyelids. [C19: from Gk *blephar(on)* eyelid + -ITIS]

blesbok *or* **blesbuck** ('blɛsˌbʌk) *n, pl* **blesboks, blesbok** *or* **blesbucks, blesbuck.** an antelope of southern Africa. The coat is reddish brown with a white blaze between the eyes; the horns are lyre-shaped. [C19: Afrik., from Du. *bles* BLAZE[2] + *bok* BUCK[1]]

bless Ⓣ (blɛs) *vb* **blesses, blessing, blessed** *or* **blest.** (*tr*) **1** to consecrate or render holy by means of a religious rite. **2** to give honour or glory to (a person or thing) as holy. **3** to call upon God to protect; give a benediction to. **4** to worship or adore (God). **5** (*often passive*) to grant happiness, health, or prosperity to. **6** (*usually passive*) to endow with a talent, beauty, etc. **7** *Rare.* to protect against evil or harm. **8 bless you!** (*interj*) **8a** a traditional phrase said to a person who has just sneezed. **8b** an exclamation of well-wishing or surprise. **9 bless me!** *or* **(God) bless my soul!** (*interj*) an exclamation of surprise. [OE *blǣdsian* to sprinkle with sacrificial blood]

blessed Ⓣ ('blɛsɪd, blɛst) *adj* **1** made holy; consecrated. **2** worthy of deep reverence or respect. **3** *RC Church.* (of a person) beatified by the pope. **4** characterized by happiness or good fortune. **5** bringing great happiness or good fortune. **6** a euphemistic word for **damned,** used in mild oaths: *I'm blessed if I know.*
▸ **'blessedly** *adv* ▸ **'blessedness** *n*

Blessed Sacrament *n Chiefly RC Church.* the consecrated elements of the Eucharist.

blessing Ⓣ ('blɛsɪŋ) *n* **1** the act of invoking divine protection or aid. **2** the words or ceremony used for this. **3** a short prayer before or after a meal; grace. **4** approval; good wishes. **5** the bestowal of a divine gift or favour. **6** a happy event.

blest (blɛst) *vb* a past tense and past participle of **bless.**

blether Ⓣ ('blɛðə) *Scot.* ◆ *vb* **1** (*intr*) to speak foolishly. ◆ *n* **2** foolish talk; nonsense. [C16: from ON *blathr* nonsense]

blew (bluː) *vb* the past tense of **blow**[1] and **blow**[3].

blight Ⓣ (blaɪt) *n* **1** any plant disease characterized by withering and shrivelling without rotting. **2** any factor that causes the symptoms of blight in plants. **3** a person or thing that mars or prevents growth. **4** an ugly urban district. ◆ *vb* **5** to cause or suffer a blight. **6** (*tr*) to frustrate or disappoint. **7** (*tr*) to spoil; destroy. [C17: ? rel. to OE *blǣce* rash]

blighter ('blaɪtə) *n Brit. inf.* **1** a fellow. **2** a despicable or irritating person or thing.

Blighty ('blaɪtɪ) *n* (*sometimes not cap.*) *Brit. sl.* (used esp. by troops serving abroad) **1** England; home. **2** (*pl* **Blighties**) Also called: **a blighty one.** (esp. in World War I) a wound that causes the recipient to be sent home to England. [C20: from Hindi *bilāyatī* foreign land, England, from Ar. *wilāyat* country]

blimey ('blaɪmɪ) *interj Brit. sl.* an exclamation of surprise or annoyance. [C19: short for *gorblimey* God blind me]

blimp[1] (blɪmp) *n* **1** a small nonrigid airship. **2** *Films.* a soundproof cover fixed over a camera during shooting. [C20: prob. from (*type*) *B-limp*]

blimp[2] (blɪmp) *n* (*often cap.*) *Chiefly Brit.* a person, esp. a military officer, who is stupidly complacent and reactionary. Also called: **Colonel Blimp.** [C20: from a character created by David Low (1891–1963), Brit. cartoonist, born NZ]
▸ **'blimpish** *adj*

blind Ⓣ (blaɪnd) *adj* **1a** unable to see; sightless. **1b** (*as collective n; preceded by the*): *the blind.* **2** (usually foll. by *to*) unable or unwilling to understand or discern. **3** not determined by reason: *blind hatred.* **4** acting or performed without control or preparation. **5** done without being able to see, relying on instruments for information. **6** hidden from sight: *a blind corner.* **7** closed at one end: *a blind alley.* **8** completely lacking awareness or consciousness: *a blind stupor.* **9** *Inf.* very drunk. **10** having no openings or outlets: *a blind wall.* **11** (intensifier): *not a blind bit of notice.* ◆ *adv* **12** without being able to see ahead or using only instruments: *to drive blind; flying blind.* **13** without adequate knowledge or information; carelessly: *to buy a house blind.* **14 bake blind.** to bake (an empty pastry case) by half filling with dried peas, crusts, etc., to keep it in shape. ◆ *vb* (*mainly tr*) **15** to deprive of sight permanently or temporarily. **16** to deprive of good sense, reason, or judgment. **17** to darken; conceal. **18** (foll. by *with*) to overwhelm by showing detailed knowledge: *to blind somebody with science.* ◆ *n* **19** (*modifier*) for or intended to help the blind: *a blind school.* **20** a shade for a window, usually on a roller. **21** any obstruction or hindrance to

THESAURUS

bleed *vb* **1** = **lose blood,** exude, flow, gush, ooze, run, seep, shed blood, spurt, trickle, weep **2** = **draw** *or* **take blood,** extract, leech, phlebotomize (*Medical*) **5** *Informal* = **extort,** drain, exhaust, fleece, milk, squeeze **6** = **drain,** extract

blemish *n* **1** = **mark,** blot, blotch, blur, defect, demerit, disfigurement, disgrace, dishonour, fault, flaw, imperfection, scar, smirch, smudge, speck, spot, stain, taint ◆ *vb* **2** = **mark,** blot, blotch, blur, damage, deface, disfigure, flaw, impair, injure, mar, smirch, smudge, spoil, spot, stain, sully, taint, tarnish
Antonyms *n* ≠ **mark:** enhancement, improvement, ornament, perfection, purity, refinement ◆ *vb* ≠ **mark:** correct, enhance, improve, perfect, purify, refine, restore

blench *vb* = **recoil,** cower, cringe, falter, flinch, hesitate, quail, quake, quiver, shrink, shudder, shy, start, wince

blend *vb* **1, 2** = **mix,** amalgamate, coalesce, combine, compound, fuse, intermix, meld, merge, mingle, synthesize, unite **3** = **go well,** complement, fit, go with, harmonize, suit ◆ *n* **5, 6** = **mixture,** alloy, amalgam, amalgamation, combination, composite, compound, concoction, fusion, meld, mix, synthesis, union

bless *vb* **1** = **sanctify,** anoint, consecrate, dedicate, exalt, hallow, invoke happiness on, ordain **2** = **praise,** extol, give thanks to, glorify, magnify, thank **6** = **endow,** bestow, favour, give, grace, grant, provide
Antonyms *vb* ≠ **sanctify:** anathematize, curse, damn, excommunicate, execrate, fulminate, imprecate ≠ **endow:** afflict, blight, burden, curse, destroy, doom, plague, scourge, torment, trouble, vex

blessed *adj* **1** = **holy,** adored, beatified, divine, hallowed, revered, sacred, sanctified **4** = **fortunate,** blissful, contented, endowed, favoured, glad, happy, jammy (*Brit. sl.*), joyful, joyous, lucky

blessedness *n* **1, 3** = **sanctity,** beatitude, heavenly joy, state of grace, *summum bonum* **4** = **happiness,** bliss, blissfulness, content, felicity, pleasure

blessing *n* **1-3** = **benediction,** benison, commendation, consecration, dedication, grace, invocation, thanksgiving **4** = **approval,** approbation, backing, concurrence, consent, favour, good wishes, leave, permission, regard, sanction, support **6** = **benefit,** advantage, boon, bounty, favour, gain, gift, godsend, good fortune, help, kindness, profit, service, windfall
Antonyms *n* ≠ **benediction:** condemnation, curse, malediction ≠ **approval:** disapproval, disfavour, objection, reproof ≠ **benefit:** damage, deprivation, disadvantage, drawback, harm, misfortune

blether *Scot.* **2** *n* = **jabbering,** blather, claptrap, drivel, gibberish, gobbledegook, jabber, moonshine, pap, twaddle

blight *n* **1, 2** = **disease,** canker, decay, fungus, infestation, mildew, pest, pestilence, rot **3** = **curse,** affliction, bane, contamination, corruption, evil, plague, pollution, scourge, woe ◆ *vb* **5** = **destroy,** blast, injure, nip in the bud, ruin, shrivel, taint with mildew, wither **6** = **frustrate,** dash, disappoint **7** = **spoil,** annihilate, crush, mar, nullify, put a damper on, ruin, undo, wreck
Antonyms *n* ≠ **curse:** benefaction, blessing, boon, bounty, favour, godsend, help, service

blind *adj* **1** = **sightless,** destitute of vision, eyeless, stone-blind, unseeing, unsighted, visionless **2** = **unaware of,** careless, heedless, ignorant, inattentive, inconsiderate, indifferent, injudicious, insensitive, neglectful, oblivious,

sight, light, or air. **22** a person, action, or thing that serves to deceive or conceal the truth. **23** Also: **blinder.** *Brit. sl.* a drunken binge. [OE *blind*]
▸ '**blindly** *adv* ▸ '**blindness** *n*

USAGE NOTE See at **disabled.**

blind alley *n* **1** an alley open at one end only; cul-de-sac. **2** *Inf.* a situation in which no further progress can be made.
blind date *n Inf.* a prearranged social meeting between a man and a woman who have not met before.
blinder ('blaɪndə) *n* **1** an outstanding performance in sport. **2** *Brit. sl.* another name for **blind** (sense 23).
blinders ('blaɪndəz) *pl n* the usual US & Canad. word for **blinkers.**
blindfold ('blaɪnd,fəʊld) *vb* (*tr*) **1** to prevent (a person or animal) from seeing by covering (the eyes). ◆ *n* **2** a piece of cloth, etc., used to cover the eyes. ◆ *adj, adv* **3** having the eyes covered with a cloth or bandage. **4** rash; inconsiderate. [changed (C16) through association with FOLD[1] from OE *blindfellian* to strike blind; see BLIND, FELL[2]]
blinding ❶ ('blaɪndɪŋ) *adj* **1** making one blind or as if blind. **2** most noticeable; brilliant or dazzling.
blind man's buff *n* a game in which a blindfolded person tries to catch and identify the other players. [C16: *buff*, ?from OF *buffe* a blow; see BUFFET[2]]
blind register *n* (in Britain) a list of those who are blind and are therefore entitled to financial and other benefits.
blindsight ('blaɪnd,saɪt) *n* the ability to respond to visual stimuli without having any conscious visual experience; it can occur after some forms of brain damage.
blind spot *n* **1** a small oval-shaped area of the retina, where the optic nerve enters, in which vision is not experienced. **2** a place or area where vision is obscured. **3** a subject about which a person is ignorant or prejudiced.
blind trust *n* a trust fund that manages the financial affairs of a person without informing him or her of any investments made, so that the beneficiary cannot be accused of using public office for private gain.
blindworm ('blaɪnd,wɜːm) *n* another name for **slowworm.**
blink ❶ (blɪŋk) *vb* **1** to close and immediately reopen (the eyes or an eye), usually involuntarily. **2** (*intr*) to look with the eyes partially closed. **3** to shine intermittently or unsteadily. **4** (*tr*; foll. by *away, from*, etc.) to clear the eyes of (dust, tears, etc.). **5** (when *tr*, usually foll. by *at*) to be surprised or amazed. **6** (when *intr*, foll. by *at*) to pretend not to know or see (a fault, injustice, etc.). ◆ *n* **7** the act or an instance of blinking. **8** a glance; glimpse. **9** short for **iceblink** (sense 1). **10 on the blink.** *Sl.* not working properly. [C14: var. of BLENCH]
blinker[1] ('blɪŋkə) *n* **1** a flashing light for sending messages, as a warning device, etc., such as a direction indicator on a road vehicle. **2** (*often pl*) a slang word for **eye**[1] (sense 1).
blinker[2] ('blɪŋkə) *vb* (*tr*) **1** to provide (a horse) with blinkers. **2** to obscure or be obscured with or as with blinkers.
▸ '**blinkered** *adj*
blinkers ('blɪŋkəz) *pl n* (*sometimes sing*) *Chiefly Brit.* leather sidepieces attached to a horse's bridle to prevent sideways vision.
blinking ('blɪŋkɪŋ) *adj, adv Inf.* (intensifier): *a blinking fool; a blinking good film.*
blip (blɪp) *n* **1** a repetitive sound, such as that produced by an electronic device. **2** Also called: **pip.** the spot of light on a radar screen indicating the position of an object. **3** a temporary irregularity recorded in the performance of something. ◆ *vb* **blips, blipping, blipped. 4** (*intr*) to produce a blip. [C20: imit.]
bliss ❶ (blɪs) *n* **1** perfect happiness; serene joy. **2** the ecstatic joy of heaven. [OE *blīths*; rel. to *blīthe* BLITHE]
blissful ❶ ('blɪsfʊl) *adj* **1** serenely joyful or glad. **2 blissful ignorance.** unawareness or inexperience of something unpleasant.
▸ '**blissfully** *adv* ▸ '**blissfulness** *n*
B list *n* **a** a category considered to be slightly below the most socially desirable. **b** (*as modifier*): *B-list celebrities.* ◆ Cf. **A list.**
blister ❶ ('blɪstə) *n* **1** a small bubble-like elevation of the skin filled with serum, produced as a reaction to a burn, mechanical irritation, etc. **2** a swelling containing air or liquid, as on a painted surface. **3** *NZ sl.* **3a** a rebuke. **3b** a summons to court. ◆ *vb* **4** to have or cause to have blisters. **5** (*tr*) to attack verbally with great scorn or sarcasm. [C13: from OF *blestre*]
▸ '**blistered** *adj*
blister pack *n* a type of pack for small goods, consisting of a transparent dome on a firm backing. Also called: **bubble pack.**
BLit *abbrev. for* Bachelor of Literature.
blithe ❶ (blaɪð) *adj* **1** very happy or cheerful; gay. **2** heedless; casual and indifferent. [OE *blīthe*]
▸ '**blithely** *adv* ▸ '**blitheness** *n*
blithering ('blɪðərɪŋ) *adj* **1** talking foolishly; jabbering. **2** *Inf.* stupid; foolish: *you blithering idiot.* [C19: var. of BLETHER + -ING[2]]
blithesome ('blaɪðsəm) *adj Literary.* cheery; merry.
BLitt *abbrev. for* Bachelor of Letters. [L *Baccalaureus Litterarum*]
blitz ❶ (blɪts) *n* **1** a violent and sustained attack, esp. with intensive aerial bombardment. **2** any sudden intensive attack or concerted effort. **3** *American football.* a defensive charge on the quarterback. ◆ *vb* **4** (*tr*) to attack suddenly and intensively. [C20: shortened from G *Blitzkrieg* lightning war]
Blitz (blɪts) *n* **the.** the systematic bombing of Britain in 1940–41 by the German Luftwaffe.
blitzkrieg ('blɪts,kriːg) *n* a swift intensive military attack designed to defeat the opposition quickly. [C20: from G: lightning war]
blizzard ❶ ('blɪzəd) *n* a strong cold wind accompanied by widespread heavy snowfall. [C19: from ?]
bloat ❶ (bləʊt) *vb* **1** to swell or cause to swell, as with a liquid or air. **2** to become or cause to be puffed up, as with conceit. **3** (*tr*) to cure (fish, esp. herring) by half drying in smoke. [C17: prob. rel. to ON *blautr* soaked]
▸ '**bloated** *adj*
bloater ('bləʊtə) *n* a herring that has been salted in brine, smoked, and cured.
blob ❶ (blɒb) *n* **1** a soft mass or drop. **2** a spot, dab, or blotch of colour, ink, etc. **3** an indistinct or shapeless form or object. [C15: ? imit.]
bloc ❶ (blɒk) *n* a group of people or countries combined by a common interest. [from F: BLOCK]
block ❶ (blɒk) *n* **1** a large solid piece of wood, stone, or other material usually having at least one face fairly flat. **2** such a piece on which particular tasks may be done, as chopping, cutting, or beheading. **3** Also called: **building block.** one of a set of wooden or plastic cubes as a child's toy. **4** a form on which things are shaped: *a wig block.* **5** *Sl.* a person's head. **6 do one's block.** *Austral. & NZ sl.* to become angry. **7** a dull, unemotional, or hardhearted person. **8** a large building of offices, flats, etc. **9a** a group of buildings in a city bounded by intersecting streets on each side. **9b** the area or distance between such intersecting streets. **10** *Austral. & NZ.* an area of land for a house, farm, etc. **11** *NZ.* an area of bush reserved by licence for a trapper or hunter. **12** a piece of wood, metal, or other material having a design in relief, used for printing. **13** *Austral. & NZ.* a log, usually of willow, fastened to a timber base and used in a wood-chopping competition. **14** a cas-

THESAURUS

thoughtless, unconscious of, uncritical, undiscerning, unmindful of, unobservant **3** = **unreasoning**, indiscriminate, prejudiced **4** = **unthinking**, hasty, impetuous, irrational, mindless, rash, reckless, senseless, uncontrollable, uncontrolled, violent, wild **6** = **hidden**, concealed, dim, obscured **7** = **dead-end**, closed, dark, leading nowhere, obstructed, without exit ◆ *n* **21, 22** = **cover**, camouflage, cloak, façade, feint, front, mask, masquerade, screen, smoke screen
Antonyms *adj* ≠ **sightless:** seeing, sighted ≠ **unaware of:** alive to, attentive, aware, concerned, conscious, discerning, heedful, knowledgeable, noticeable, observant ≠ **hidden:** obvious, open
blinding *adj* **2** = **bright**, bedazzling, blurring, brilliant, dazzling, flaming, glaring, intense
blindly *adv* **4** = **thoughtlessly**, aimlessly, carelessly, heedlessly, impulsively, inconsiderately, madly, passionately, purposelessly, recklessly, regardlessly, senselessly, wildly, wilfully
blink *vb* **1** = **wink**, bat, flutter, nictate, nictitate **2** = **peer**, glimpse, squint **3** = **flicker**, flash, gleam, glimmer, scintillate, shine, sparkle, twinkle, wink **6** = **turn a blind eye to**, condone, connive at, disregard, ignore, overlook, pass by ◆ *n* **10 on the blink** *Slang* = **not working (properly)**, faulty, malfunctioning, out of action, out of order, playing up
blinkered[2] *adj* **2** = **narrow-minded**, biased, constricted, discriminatory, hidebound, insular, narrow, one-sided, parochial, partial, prejudiced, restrictive, selective
Antonyms *adj* broad-minded, impartial, open-minded, unbiased, unprejudiced
bliss *n* **1** = **joy**, blissfulness, ecstasy, euphoria, felicity, gladness, happiness, rapture **2** = **heaven**, beatitude, blessedness, nirvana, paradise
Antonyms *n* ≠ **joy:** affliction, anguish, distress, grief, heartbreak, misery, mourning, regret, sadness, sorrow, unhappiness, woe, wretchedness
blissful *adj* **1** = **joyful**, cock-a-hoop, delighted, ecstatic, elated, enchanted, enraptured, euphoric, happy, heavenly (*inf.*), in ecstasies, joyous, over the moon (*inf.*), rapt, rapturous
blister *n* **1** = **sore**, abscess, blain, bleb, boil, bubble, canker, carbuncle, cyst, pimple, pustule, swelling, ulcer, welt, wen
blithe *adj* **1** = **happy**, animated, buoyant, carefree, cheerful, cheery, chirpy (*inf.*), debonair, gay, genial, gladsome, jaunty, light-hearted, merry, mirthful, sprightly, sunny, upbeat (*inf.*), vivacious **2** = **heedless**, careless, casual, indifferent, nonchalant, thoughtless, unconcerned, untroubled
Antonyms *adj* ≠ **happy:** dejected, depressed, gloomy, melancholy, morose, sad, unhappy ≠ **heedless:** concerned, preoccupied, thoughtful
blitz *n* **1, 2** = **attack**, assault, blitzkrieg, bombardment, campaign, offensive, onslaught, raid, strike
blizzard *n* = **snowstorm**, blast, gale, squall, storm, tempest
bloat *vb* **1** = **puff up**, balloon, blow up, dilate, distend, enlarge, expand, inflate, swell
Antonyms *vb* contract, deflate, shrink, shrivel, wither, wrinkle
bloated *adj* **1** = **puffed up**, blown-up, bulging, dilated, distended, enlarged, expanded, inflated, puffy, swollen, tumescent, tumid, turgid
Antonyms *adj* contracted, deflated, flaccid, shrivelled, shrunken, withered, wrinkled
blob *n* **1** = **drop**, ball, bead, bubble, droplet, glob, globule, lump, mass, pearl, pellet, pill **2** = **dab**
bloc *n* = **group**, alliance, axis, cabal, clique, coalition, combine, entente, faction, league, ring, schism, union, wing
block *n* **1** = **piece**, bar, brick, cake, chunk, cube, hunk, ingot, lump, mass, nugget, square **15** = **obstruction**, bar, barrier, blockage, hindrance, impediment, jam, obstacle, occlusion, stoppage ◆ *vb* **21** = **obstruct**, bung up (*inf.*), choke,

ing housing one or more freely rotating pulleys. See also **block and tackle. 15** an obstruction or hindrance. **16** *Pathol.* **16a** interference in the normal physiological functioning of an organ or part. **16b** See **heart block. 16c** See **nerve block. 17** *Psychol.* a short interruption of perceptual or thought processes. **18** obstruction of an opponent in a sport. **19a** a quantity handled or considered as a single unit. **19b** (*as modifier*): *a block booking.* **20** *Athletics.* short for **starting block.** ◆ *vb* (*mainly tr*) **21** (often foll. by *up*) to obstruct (a passage, channel, etc.) or prevent or impede the motion or flow of (something or someone) by introducing an obstacle: *to block the traffic; to block up a pipe.* **22** to impede, retard, or prevent (an action, procedure, etc.). **23** to stamp (a title, design, etc.) on (a book cover, etc.) esp. using gold leaf. **24** to shape by use of a block: *to block a hat.* **25** (*also intr*) *Sport.* to obstruct or impede movement by (an opponent). **26** to interrupt a physiological function, as by use of an anaesthetic. **27** (*also intr*) *Cricket.* to play (a ball) defensively. ◆ See also **block in, block out.** [C14: from OF *bloc*, from Du. *blok*]
▸**'blocker** *n*

blockade 🅣 (blɒ'keɪd) *n* **1** *Mil.* the interdiction of a nation's sea lines of communications, esp. of an individual port by the use of sea power. **2** something that prevents access or progress. **3** *Med.* the inhibition of the effect of a hormone or the action of a nerve by a drug. ◆ *vb* **blockades, blockading, blockaded.** (*tr*) **4** to impose a blockade on. **5** to obstruct the way to. [C17: from BLOCK + *-ade*, as in AMBUSCADE]
▸**block'ader** *n*

blockage 🅣 ('blɒkɪdʒ) *n* **1** the act of blocking or state of being blocked. **2** an object causing an obstruction.

block and tackle *n* a hoisting device in which a rope or chain is passed around a pair of blocks containing one or more pulleys.

blockboard ('blɒk,bɔːd) *n* a bonded board in which strips of soft wood are sandwiched between two layers of veneer.

blockbuster ('blɒk,bʌstə) *n Inf.* **1** a large bomb used to demolish extensive areas. **2** a very successful, effective, or forceful person, thing, etc. **3** a lavish film, show, novel, etc., that proves to be an outstanding popular success.

block diagram *n* **1** a diagram showing the interconnections between the parts of an industrial process. **2** *Computing.* a diagram showing the interconnections between electronic components or parts of a program.

blockhead 🅣 ('blɒk,hɛd) *n Derog.* a stupid person.
▸**'block,headed** *adj*

blockhouse ('blɒk,haʊs) *n* **1** (formerly) a wooden fortification with ports for defensive fire, observation, etc. **2** a concrete structure strengthened to give protection against enemy fire, with apertures to allow defensive gunfire. **3** a building constructed of logs or squared timber.

block in *vb* (*tr, adv*) to sketch or outline with little detail.

blockish ('blɒkɪʃ) *adj* lacking vivacity or imagination; stupid.
▸**'blockishly** *adv*

block letter *n* **1** *Printing.* a less common name for **sans serif. 2** Also called: **block capital.** a plain capital letter.

block out 🅣 *vb* (*tr, adv*) **1** to plan or describe (something) in a general fashion. **2** to prevent the entry or consideration of (something).

block release *n Brit.* the release of industrial trainees from work for study at a college for several weeks.

block vote *n Brit.* (at a trade-union conference) the system whereby each delegate's vote has a value in proportion to the number of people he represents.

bloke 🅣 (bləʊk) *n Brit. & Austral.* an informal word for **man.** [C19: from Shelta]

blokeish *or* **blokish** ('bləʊkɪʃ) *adj Brit. inf., sometimes derog.* denoting or exhibiting the characteristics believed typical of an ordinary man. Also: **blokey** ('bləʊkɪ).
▸**'blokeishness** *or* **'blokishness** *n*

blonde 🅣 *or* (*masc*) **blond** (blɒnd) *adj* **1** (of hair) of a light colour; fair. **2** (of people or a race) having fair hair, a light complexion, and, typically, blue or grey eyes. ◆ *n* **3** a person having light-coloured hair and skin. [C15: from OF *blond* (fem *blonde*), prob. of Gmc origin]
▸**'blondeness** *or* **'blondness** *n*

blood 🅣 (blʌd) *n* **1** a reddish fluid in vertebrates that is pumped by the heart through the arteries and veins. **2** a similar fluid in invertebrates. **3** bloodshed, esp. when resulting in murder. **4** life itself; lifeblood. **5** relationship through being of the same family, race, or kind; kinship. **6 flesh and blood. 6a** near kindred or kinship, esp. that between a parent and child. **6b** human nature (esp. in **it's more than flesh and blood can stand**). **7 in one's blood.** as a natural or inherited characteristic or talent. **8 the blood.** royal or noble descent: *a prince of the blood.* **9** temperament; disposition; temper. **10a** good or pure breeding; pedigree. **10b** (*as modifier*): *blood horses.* **11** people viewed as members of a group, esp. as an invigorating force (**new blood, young blood**). **12** *Chiefly Brit., rare.* a dashing young man. **13 in cold blood.** showing no passion; deliberately; ruthlessly. **14 make one's blood boil.** to cause to be angry or indignant. **15 make one's blood run cold.** to fill with horror. ◆ *vb* (*tr*) **16** *Hunting.* to cause (young hounds) to taste the blood of a freshly killed quarry. **17** to initiate (a person) to war or hunting. [OE *blōd*]

blood-and-thunder *adj* denoting or relating to a melodramatic adventure story.

blood bank *n* a place where whole blood or blood plasma is stored until required in transfusion.

blood bath *n* indiscriminate slaughter; a massacre.

blood brother *n* **1** a brother by birth. **2** a man or boy who has sworn to treat another as his brother, often in a ceremony in which their blood is mingled.

blood count *n* determination of the number of red and white blood corpuscles in a specific sample of blood.

bloodcurdling 🅣 ('blʌd,kɜːdlɪŋ) *adj* terrifying; horrifying.
▸**'blood,curdlingly** *adv*

blood donor *n* a person who gives his blood to be used for transfusion.

blood doping *n* the illegal practice of removing a quantity of blood from an athlete long before a race and reinjecting it shortly before a race, so boosting oxygenation of the blood.

blooded ('blʌdɪd) *adj* **1** (of horses, cattle, etc.) of good breeding. **2** (*in combination*) having blood or temperament as specified: *hot-blooded, cold-blooded, warm-blooded, red-blooded.*

blood group *n* any one of the various groups into which human blood is classified on the basis of its specific agglutinating properties. Also called: **blood type.**

blood heat *n* the normal temperature of the human body, 98.4°F. or 37°C.

bloodhound ('blʌd,haʊnd) *n* a large breed of hound, formerly used in tracking and police work.

bloodless 🅣 ('blʌdlɪs) *adj* **1** without blood. **2** conducted without violence (esp. in **bloodless revolution**). **3** anaemic-looking; pale. **4** lacking vitality; lifeless. **5** lacking in emotion; unfeeling.
▸**'bloodlessly** *adv* ▸**'bloodlessness** *n*

blood-letting ('blʌd,lɛtɪŋ) *n* **1** the therapeutic removal of blood. See also **phlebotomy. 2** bloodshed, esp. in a feud.

bloodline ('blʌd,laɪn) *n* all the members of a family group over generations, esp. regarding characteristics common to that group; pedigree.

blood money *n* **1** compensation paid to the relatives of a murdered person. **2** money paid to a hired murderer. **3** a reward for information about a criminal, esp. a murderer.

blood orange *n* a variety of orange all or part of the pulp of which is dark red when ripe.

blood poisoning *n* a nontechnical term for **septicaemia.**

blood pressure *n* the pressure exerted by the blood on the inner walls of the arteries, being relative to the elasticity and diameter of the vessels and the force of the heartbeat.

blood pudding *n* another name for **black pudding.**

blood relation *or* **relative** *n* a person related to another by birth, as distinct from one related by marriage.

bloodshed 🅣 ('blʌd,ʃɛd) *n* slaughter; killing.

bloodshot ('blʌd,ʃɒt) *adj* (of an eye) inflamed.

blood sport *n* any sport involving the killing of an animal, esp. hunting.

bloodstain ('blʌd,steɪn) *n* a dark discoloration caused by blood, esp. dried blood.
▸**'blood,stained** *adj*

bloodstock ('blʌd,stɒk) *n* thoroughbred horses.

bloodstone ('blʌd,stəʊn) *n* a dark green variety of chalcedony with red spots: used as a gemstone. Also called: **heliotrope.**

bloodstream ('blʌd,striːm) *n* the flow of blood through the vessels of a living body.

blood substitute *n* a mixture of plasma, albumin, and dextran used to replace lost blood or increase the blood volume.

bloodsucker ('blʌd,sʌkə) *n* **1** an animal that sucks blood, esp. a leech or mosquito. **2** *Inf.* a person or thing that preys upon another person, esp. by extorting money.
▸**'blood,sucking** *adj*

THESAURUS

clog, close, plug, stem the flow, stop up **22** = **stop**, arrest, bar, check, deter, halt, hinder, hobble, impede, obstruct, put a spoke in someone's wheel, throw a spanner in the works, thwart

Antonyms *vb* ≠ **obstruct:** clear, open, unblock, unclog ≠ **stop:** advance, aid, expedite, facilitate, foster, further, lend support to, promote, push, support

blockade *n* **1** = **barricade**, encirclement, siege **2** = **stoppage**, barrier, block, closure, hindrance, impediment, obstacle, obstruction, restriction

blockage *n* **1, 2** = **obstruction**, block, blocking, impediment, occlusion, stoppage, stopping up

blockhead *n* = **fool**, dimwit (*inf.*), dipstick (*Brit. sl.*), divvy (*Brit. sl.*), dolt, dork (*sl.*), dunce, fathead (*inf.*), idiot, ignoramus, jerk (*sl., chiefly US & Canad.*), nerd *or* nurd (*sl.*), nitwit, numbskull *or* numskull, pillock (*Brit. sl.*), plonker (*sl.*), prat (*sl.*), schmuck (*US sl.*), thickhead, twit (*inf., chiefly Brit.*)

block out *vb* **1** = **outline**, chart, map out, plan, sketch

bloke *n Informal* = **man**, chap, character (*inf.*), customer (*inf.*), fellow, guy (*inf.*), individual, person, punter (*inf.*)

blonde *adj* **1** = **fair**, fair-haired, fair-skinned, flaxen, golden-haired, light, light-coloured, light-complexioned, tow-headed

blood *n* **1** = **lifeblood**, gore, vital fluid **5** = **family**, ancestry, birth, consanguinity, descendants, descent, extraction, kindred, kinship, lineage, noble extraction, relations **9** = **feeling**, disposition, passion, spirit, temper

bloodcurdling *adj* = **terrifying**, appalling, chilling, dreadful, fearful, frightening, hair-raising, horrendous, horrifying, scaring, spine-chilling

bloodless *adj* **3** = **pale**, anaemic, ashen, chalky, colourless, like death warmed up (*inf.*), pallid, pasty, sallow, sickly, wan **4, 5** = **listless**, cold, languid, lifeless, passionless, spiritless, torpid, unemotional, unfeeling

bloodshed *n* = **killing**, blood bath,

blood sugar *n Med.* the glucose circulating in the blood: the normal fasting level is between 3·9 and 5·6 millimoles per litre.

bloodthirsty ❶ (ˈblʌdˌθɜːstɪ) *adj* **bloodthirstier, bloodthirstiest. 1** murderous; cruel. **2** taking pleasure in bloodshed or violence. **3** describing or depicting killing and violence; gruesome.
▸**ˈbloodˌthirstily** *adv* ▸**ˈbloodˌthirstiness** *n*

blood type *n* another name for **blood group.**

blood vessel *n* an artery, capillary, or vein.

bloodwood (ˈblʌdˌwʊd) *n* any of several species of Australian eucalyptus with red sap.

bloody ❶ (ˈblʌdɪ) *adj* **bloodier, bloodiest. 1** covered or stained with blood. **2** resembling or composed of blood. **3** marked by much killing and bloodshed: *a bloody war.* **4** cruel or murderous: *a bloody tyrant.* ◆ *adv, adj* **5** *Sl.* (intensifier): *a bloody fool.* ◆ *vb* **bloodies, bloodying, bloodied. 6** (*tr*) to stain with blood.
▸**ˈbloodily** *adv* ▸**ˈbloodiness** *n*

Bloody Mary (ˈmeərɪ) *n* **1** nickname of Mary I of England. **2** a drink consisting of tomato juice and vodka.

bloody-minded ❶ *adj Brit. inf.* deliberately obstructive and unhelpful.

bloom[1] ❶ (bluːm) *n* **1** a blossom on a flowering plant; a flower. **2** the state, time, or period when flowers open. **3** open flowers collectively. **4** a healthy, vigorous, or flourishing condition; prime. **5** youthful or healthy rosiness in the cheeks or face; glow. **6** a fine whitish coating on the surface of fruits, leaves, etc. **7** Also called: **chill.** a dull area on the surface of old gloss paint, lacquer, or varnish. **8** *Ecology.* a visible increase in the algal constituent of plankton, which may be due to excessive organic pollution. ◆ *vb* (*intr*) **9** (of flowers) to open; come into flower. **10** to bear flowers; blossom. **11** to flourish or grow. **12** to be in a healthy, glowing, or flourishing condition. [C13: of Gmc origin; cf. ON *blōm* flower]

bloom[2] (bluːm) *n* a rectangular mass of metal obtained by rolling or forging a cast ingot. [OE *blōma* lump of metal]

bloomer[1] (ˈbluːmə) *n* a plant that flowers, esp. in a specified way: *a night bloomer.*

bloomer[2] (ˈbluːmə) *n Brit. inf.* a stupid mistake; blunder. [C20: from BLOOMING]

bloomer[3] (ˈbluːmə) *n Brit.* a medium-sized loaf, glazed and notched on top. [C20: from ?]

bloomers (ˈbluːməz) *pl n* **1** *Inf.* women's baggy knickers. **2** (formerly) loose trousers gathered at the knee worn by women for cycling, etc. **3** *History.* loose trousers gathered at the ankle and worn under a shorter skirt. [after Amelia *Bloomer* (1818–94), US social reformer]

blooming (ˈbluːmɪŋ) *adv, adj Brit. inf.* (intensifier): *a blooming genius; blooming painful.* [C19: euphemistic for BLOODY]

blossom ❶ (ˈblɒsəm) *n* **1** the flower or flowers of a plant, esp. producing edible fruit. **2** the time or period of flowering. ◆ *vb* (*intr*) **3** (of plants) to come into flower. **4** to develop or come to a promising stage. [OE *blōstm*]
▸**ˈblossomy** *adj*

blot ❶ (blɒt) *n* **1** a stain or spot of ink, paint, dirt, etc. **2** something that spoils. **3** a blemish or stain on one's character or reputation. **4** *Austral. sl.* the anus. ◆ *vb* **blots, blotting, blotted. 5** (of ink, dye, etc.) to form spots or blobs on (a material) or (of a person) to cause such spots or blobs to form on (a material). **6** (*intr*) to stain or become stained or spotted. **7** (*tr*) to cause a blemish in or on; disgrace. **8** to soak up (excess ink, etc.) by using blotting paper. **9** (of blotting paper) to absorb (excess ink, etc.). **10** (*tr;* often foll. by *out*) **10a** to darken or hide completely; obscure; obliterate. **10b** to destroy; annihilate. [C14: prob. of Gmc origin]

blotch ❶ (blɒtʃ) *n* **1** an irregular spot or discoloration, esp. a dark and relatively large one. ◆ *vb* **2** to become or cause to become marked by such discoloration. [C17: prob. from BOTCH, infl. by BLOT]
▸**ˈblotchy** *adj*

blotter (ˈblɒtə) *n* something used to absorb excess ink, esp. a sheet of blotting paper.

blotting paper *n* a soft absorbent unsized paper, used esp. for soaking up surplus ink.

blotto (ˈblɒtəʊ) *adj Sl.* unconscious, esp. through drunkenness. [C20: from BLOT (vb)]

blouse (blaʊz) *n* **1** a woman's shirtlike garment. **2** a waist-length belted jacket worn by soldiers. ◆ *vb* **blouses, blousing, bloused. 3** to hang or make so as to hang in full loose folds. [C19: from F, from ?]

blouson (ˈbluːzɒn) *n* a tight-waisted jacket or top that blouses out. [C20: from F]

blow[1] ❶ (bləʊ) *vb* **blows, blowing, blew, blown. 1** (of a current of air, the wind, etc.) to be or cause to be in motion. **2** (*intr*) to move or be carried by or as if by wind. **3** to expel (air, cigarette smoke, etc.) through the mouth or nose. **4** to force or cause (air, dust, etc.) to move (into, in, over, etc.) by using an instrument or by expelling breath. **5** (*intr*) to breathe hard; pant. **6** (sometimes foll. by *up*) to inflate with air or the breath. **7** (*intr*) (of wind, a storm, etc.) to make a roaring sound. **8** to cause (a whistle, siren, etc.) to sound by forcing air into it or (of a whistle, etc.) to sound thus. **9** (*tr*) to force air from the lungs through (the nose) to clear out mucus. **10** (often foll. by *up, down, in,* etc.) to explode, break, or disintegrate completely. **11** *Electronics.* to burn out (a fuse, valve, etc.) because of excessive current or (of a fuse, valve, etc.) to burn out. **12** (*tr*) to wind (a horse) by making it run excessively. **13** to cause (a wind instrument) to sound by forcing one's breath into the mouthpiece or (of such an instrument) to sound in this way. **14** (*intr*) (of flies) to lay eggs (in). **15** to shape (glass, ornaments, etc.) by forcing air or gas through the material when molten. **16** (*tr*) *Sl.* to spend (money) freely. **17** (*tr*) *Sl.* to use (an opportunity) ineffectively. **18** *Sl.* to go suddenly away (from). **19** (*tr*) *Sl.* to expose or betray (a secret). **20** (p.p. **blowed**). *Inf.* another word for **damn. 21 blow hot and cold.** *Inf.* to vacillate. **22 blow one's top.** *Inf.* to lose one's temper. ◆ *n* **23** the act or an instance of blowing. **24** the sound produced by blowing. **25** a blast of air or wind. **26a** *Brit.* a slang name for **cannabis** (sense 2). **26b** *US* a slang name for **cocaine. 27** *Austral. sl.* a brief rest; a breather. ◆ See also **blow away, blow in,** etc. [OE *blāwan*]

blow[2] ❶ (bləʊ) *n* **1** a powerful or heavy stroke with the fist, a weapon, etc. **2 at one** *or* **a blow.** by or with only one action. **3** a sudden setback. **4 come to blows. 4a** to fight. **4b** to result in a fight. **5** an attacking action: *a blow for freedom.* **6** *Austral. & NZ.* a stroke of the shears in sheep-shearing. [C15: prob. of Gmc origin]

blow[3] (bləʊ) *vb* **blows, blowing, blew, blown. 1** (*intr*) (of a plant or flower) to blossom or open out. ◆ *n* **2** a mass of blossoms. **3** the state or period of blossoming. [OE *blōwan*]

blow away *vb* (*tr, adv*) *Sl., chiefly US.* **1** to kill (someone) by shooting. **2** to defeat decisively.

blow-by-blow *adj* (*prenominal*) explained in great detail: *a blow-by-blow account.*

blow-dry *vb* **blow-dries, blow-drying, blow-dried. 1** (*tr*) to style (the hair) while drying it with a hand-held hair dryer. ◆ *n* **2** this method of styling hair.

blower (ˈbləʊə) *n* **1** a mechanical device, such as a fan, that blows. **2** a low-pressure compressor, esp. in a furnace or internal-combustion engine. **3** an informal name for **telephone.**

blowfish (ˈbləʊˌfɪʃ) *n, pl* **blowfish** *or* **blowfishes.** a popular name for **puffer** (sense 2).

blowfly (ˈbləʊˌflaɪ) *n, pl* **blowflies.** any of various flies that lay their eggs in rotting meat, dung, carrion, and open wounds. Also called: **bluebottle.**

blowgun (ˈbləʊˌgʌn) *n* the US word for **blowpipe** (sense 1).

blowhard (ˈbləʊˌhɑːd) *Inf.* ◆ *n* **1** a boastful person. ◆ *adj* **2** blustering or boastful.

blowhole (ˈbləʊˌhəʊl) *n* **1** the nostril of whales, situated far back on the skull. **2** a hole in ice through which whales, seals, etc., breathe. **3** *Geol.* a hole in a cliff top leading to a sea cave through which air is forced by the action of the sea. **4a** a vent for air or gas. **4b** *NZ.* a hole emitting gas or steam in a volcanic region.

blow in *Inf.* ◆ *vb* **1** (*intr, adv*) to arrive or enter suddenly. ◆ *n* **blow-in. 2** *Austral.* a newcomer.

THESAURUS

blood-letting, butchery, carnage, gore, massacre, murder, slaughter, slaying

bloodthirsty *adj* **1, 2** = **cruel**, barbarous, brutal, cut-throat, ferocious, inhuman, murderous, ruthless, savage, vicious, warlike **3** = **gory**

bloody *adj* **1** = **bloodstained**, bleeding, blood-soaked, blood-spattered, gaping, raw, unstaunched **4** = **cruel**, ferocious, fierce, sanguinary, savage

bloody-minded *adj Brit. informal* = **difficult**, awkward, contrary, cussed (*inf.*), obstructive, perverse, uncooperative, unhelpful, unreasonable
Antonyms *adj* accommodating, cooperative, fair-minded, helpful, open-minded, reasonable

bloom[1] *n* **1** = **flower**, blossom, bud **2** = **blossoming**, efflorescence, opening (*of flowers*) **4** = **prime**, beauty, flourishing, health, heyday, perfection, vigour **5** = **glow**, blush, flush, freshness, lustre, radiance, rosiness ◆ *vb* **9, 10** = **blossom**, blow, bud, burgeon, open, sprout **11** = **flourish**, develop, fare well, grow, prosper, succeed, thrive, wax
Antonyms *n* ≠ **glow**: bloodlessness, paleness, pallor, wanness, whiteness ◆ *vb* ≠ **blossom, flourish**: decay, decline, die, droop, fade, fail, languish, perish, shrink, shrivel, wane, waste, wilt, wither

blossom *n* **1** = **flower**, bloom, bud, floret, flowers ◆ *vb* **3** = **flower**, bloom, burgeon **4** = **grow**, bloom, develop, flourish, mature, progress, prosper, thrive

blot *n* **1** = **spot**, blotch, mark, patch, smear, smudge, speck, splodge **2** = **stain**, blemish, blur, defect, fault, flaw, scar, spot, taint **3** = **disgrace**, blot on one's escutcheon, demerit, smirch ◆ *vb* **5, 6** = **stain**, bespatter, disfigure, mark, smudge, spoil, spot, tarnish **7** = **disgrace**, smirch, sully **8, 9** = **soak up**, absorb, dry, take up **10a** = **erase**, darken, destroy, eclipse, efface, obscure, shadow **10b** cancel, expunge

blotch *n, vb* = **mark**, blemish, blot, patch, scar, smirch, smudge, smutch, splash, splodge, spot, stain

blotchy *adj* = **spotty**, blemished, patchy, reddened, scurvy, uneven

blow[1] *vb* **1, 2** = **carry**, bear, buffet, drive, fling, flutter, move, sweep, waft, whirl, whisk **3** = **exhale**, breathe **5** = **pant**, puff **8** = **play**, blare, mouth, pipe, sound, toot, trumpet, vibrate **22 blow one's top** *Informal* = **lose one's temper**, blow up (*inf.*), do one's nut (*Brit. sl.*), explode, flip one's lid (*sl.*), fly into a temper, fly off the handle (*inf.*), go spare (*Brit. sl.*), have a fit (*inf.*), lose it (*inf.*), lose the plot (*inf.*), see red (*inf.*), throw a tantrum ◆ *n* **25** = **gust**, blast, draught, flurry, gale, puff, strong breeze, tempest, wind

blow[2] *n* **1** = **knock**, bang, bash (*inf.*), belt (*inf.*), buffet, clout (*inf.*), clump (*sl.*), punch, rap, slosh (*Brit. sl.*), smack, sock (*sl.*), stroke, thump, wallop (*inf.*), whack **3** = **setback**, affliction, bolt from the blue, bombshell, bummer (*sl.*), calamity, catastrophe, choker (*inf.*), comedown (*inf.*), disappointment, disaster, jolt, misfortune, re-

blow job *Taboo.* a slang term for **fellatio.**
blowlamp ('bləʊˌlæmp) *n* another name for **blowtorch.**
blown (bləʊn) *vb* the past participle of **blow**[1] and **blow**[3].
blow out ❶ *vb* (*adv*) **1** to extinguish (a flame, candle, etc.) or (of a flame, etc.) to become extinguished. **2** (*intr*) (of a tyre) to puncture suddenly, esp. at high speed. **3** (*intr*) (of a fuse) to melt suddenly. **4** (*tr; often reflexive*) to diminish or use up the energy of: *the storm blew itself out.* **5** (*intr*) (of an oil or gas well) to lose oil or gas in an uncontrolled manner. ◆ *n* **blowout. 6** the sudden melting of an electrical fuse. **7** a sudden burst in a tyre. **8** the uncontrolled escape of oil or gas from an oil or gas well. **9** *Sl.* a large filling meal or lavish entertainment.
blow over ❶ *vb* (*intr, adv*) **1** to cease or be finished: *the storm blew over.* **2** to be forgotten.
blowpipe ('bləʊˌpaɪp) *n* **1** a long tube from which pellets, poisoned darts, etc., are shot by blowing. **2** Also called: **blow tube.** a tube for blowing air or oxygen into a flame to intensify its heat. **3** a long narrow iron pipe used to gather molten glass and blow it into shape.
blowsy ❶ *or* **blowzy** ('blaʊzɪ) *adj* **blowsier, blowsiest** *or* **blowzier, blowziest. 1** (esp. of a woman) untidy in appearance; slovenly or sluttish. **2** (of a woman) ruddy in complexion. [C18: from dialect *blowze* beggar girl, from ?]
blow through *vb* (*intr, adv*) *Austral. inf.* to leave; make off.
blowtorch ('bləʊˌtɔːtʃ) *n* a small burner that produces a very hot flame, used to remove paint, melt soft metal, etc.
blow up ❶ *vb* (*adv*) **1** to explode or cause to explode. **2** (*tr*) to increase the importance of (something): *they blew the whole affair up.* **3** (*intr*) to arise: *we lived very quietly before this affair blew up.* **4** (*intr*) to come into existence with sudden force: *a storm had blown up.* **5** (*intr*) *Inf.* to lose one's temper (with a person). **6** (*tr*) *Inf.* to reprimand. **7** (*tr*) *Inf.* to enlarge the size of (a photograph). ◆ *n* **blow-up. 8** an explosion. **9** *Inf.* an enlarged photograph or part of a photograph. **10** *Inf.* a fit of temper.
blowy ('bləʊɪ) *adj* **blowier, blowiest.** another word for **windy** (sense 1).
blub (blʌb) *vb* **blubs, blubbing, blubbed.** *Brit.* a slang word for **blubber** (senses 1–3).
blubber ('blʌbə) *vb* **1** to sob without restraint. **2** to utter while sobbing. **3** (*tr*) to make (the face) wet and swollen by crying. ◆ *n* **4** the fatty tissue of aquatic mammals such as the whale. **5** *Inf.* flabby body fat. **6** the act or an instance of weeping without restraint. ◆ *adj* **7** (*often in combination*) swollen or fleshy: *blubber-faced.* [C12: ?from Low G *blubbern* to BUBBLE, imit.]
▸**'blubberer** *n* ▸**'blubbery** *adj*
bludge (blʌdʒ) *Austral. & NZ inf.* ◆ *vb* **bludges, bludging, bludged. 1** (when *intr*, often foll. by *on*) to scrounge from (someone). **2** (*intr*) to skive. ◆ *n* **3** a very easy task. [C19: back formation from *bludger* pimp, from BLUDGEON]
bludgeon ❶ ('blʌdʒən) *n* **1** a stout heavy club, typically thicker at one end. **2** a person, line of argument, etc., that is effective but unsubtle. ◆ *vb* (*tr*) **3** to hit as with a bludgeon. **4** (often foll. by *into*) to force; bully; coerce. [C18: from ?]
bludger ('blʌdʒə) *n Austral. & NZ inf.* **1** a person who scrounges. **2** a person who avoids work. **3** a person in authority regarded as ineffectual by those working under him.
blue ❶ (bluː) *n* **1** any of a group of colours, such as that of a clear unclouded sky or the deep sea. **2** a dye or pigment of any of these colours. **3** blue cloth or clothing: *dressed in blue.* **4** a sportsman who represents or has represented Oxford or Cambridge University and has the right to wear the university colour. **5** *Brit.* an informal name for **Tory. 6** any of numerous small blue-winged butterflies. **7** a blue substance used in laundering. **8** *Austral. & NZ sl.* an argument or fight: *he had a blue with a taxi driver.* **9** Also: **bluey.** *Austral. & NZ sl.* a court summons. **10** *Austral. & NZ inf.* a mistake; error. **11 out of the blue.** apparently from nowhere; unexpectedly. ◆ *adj* **bluer, bluest. 12** of the colour blue. **13** (of the flesh) having a purple tinge, as from cold or contusion. **14** depressed, moody, or unhappy. **15** indecent, titillating, or pornographic: *blue films.* ◆ *vb* **blues, blueing** *or* **bluing, blued. 16** to make, dye, or become blue. **17** (*tr*) to treat (laundry) with blue. **18** (*tr*) *Sl.* to spend extravagantly or wastefully; squander. ◆ See also **blues.** [C13: from OF *bleu*, of Gmc origin]
▸**'blueness** *n*
Blue (bluː) *or* **Bluey** ('bluːɪ) *n Austral. inf.* a person with red hair.
blue baby *n* a baby born with a bluish tinge to the skin because of lack of oxygen in the blood.
Bluebeard ('bluːˌbɪəd) *n* **1** a villain in European folk tales who marries several wives and murders them in turn. **2** a man who has had several wives.
bluebell ('bluːˌbɛl) *n* **1** Also called: **wild** *or* **wood hyacinth.** a European woodland plant having a one-sided cluster of blue bell-shaped flowers. **2** a Scottish name for **harebell. 3** any of various other plants with blue bell-shaped flowers.
blueberry ('bluːbərɪ, -brɪ) *n, pl* **blueberries. 1** Also called: **huckleberry.** any of several North American ericaceous shrubs that have blue-black edible berries with tiny seeds. See also **bilberry. 2** the fruit of any of these plants.
bluebird ('bluːˌbɜːd) *n* **1** a North American songbird of the thrush family having a blue or partly blue plumage. **2** any of various other birds having a blue plumage.
blue blood *n* royal or aristocratic descent. [C19: translation of Sp. *sangre azul*]
▸**ˌblue-'blooded** *adj*
bluebook ('bluːˌbʊk) *n* **1** (in Britain) a government publication bound in a stiff blue paper cover: usually the report of a royal commission or a committee. **2** (in Canada) an annual statement of government accounts.
bluebottle ('bluːˌbɒtᵊl) *n* **1** another name for the **blowfly. 2** any of various blue-flowered plants, esp. the cornflower. **3** *Brit.* an informal word for a **policeman. 4** *Austral. & NZ.* an informal name for **Portuguese man-of-war.**
blue button *n* a trainee market maker on the London stock exchange. [C20: from the *blue button* badge worn in the lapel]
blue cheese *n* cheese containing a blue mould, esp. Stilton, Roquefort, or Danish Blue.
blue chip *n* **1** a gambling chip with the highest value. **2** *Finance.* a stock considered reliable with respect to both dividend income and capital value. **3** (*modifier*) denoting something considered to be a valuable asset.
blue-collar *adj* of or designating manual industrial workers. Cf. **white-collar.**
blue-eyed boy *n Inf., chiefly Brit.* the favourite or darling of a person or group.
bluefish ('bluːˌfɪʃ) *n, pl* **bluefish** *or* **bluefishes. 1** Also called: **snapper.** a bluish marine food and game fish, related to the horse mackerel. **2** any of various other bluish fishes.
Blue Flag *n* an award given to a seaside resort that meets EU standards of cleanliness of beaches and purity of water in bathing areas.
blue fox *n* **1** a variety of the arctic fox that has a pale grey winter coat. **2** the fur of this animal.
blue funk *n Sl.* a state of great terror.
bluegrass ('bluːˌgrɑːs) *n* **1** any of several North American bluish-green grasses, esp. **Kentucky bluegrass,** grown for forage. **2** a type of folk music originating in Kentucky.
blue-green algae *pl n* the former name for **cyanobacteria.**
blue ground *n Mineralogy.* another name for **kimberlite.**
blue gum *n* a tall fast-growing widely cultivated Australian eucalyptus, having bluish aromatic leaves containing a medicinal oil, bark that peels off in shreds, and hard timber.
blue heeler *n Austral.* a type of dog with dark speckled markings: used for herding cattle.
bluejacket ('bluːˌdʒækɪt) *n* a sailor in the Navy.
blue jay *n* a common North American jay having bright blue plumage.
blue moon ❶ *n* **once in a blue moon.** *Inf.* very rarely; almost never.
blue mould *n* any fungus that forms a bluish mass on decaying food, leather, etc. Also called: **green mould.**
blue pencil *n* **1** deletion, alteration, or censorship of the contents of a book or other work. ◆ *vb* **blue-pencil, blue-pencils, blue-pencilling, blue-pencilled** *or US* **blue-pencils, blue-penciling, blue-penciled. 2** (*tr*) to alter or delete parts of (a book, film, etc.), esp. to censor.
blue peter *n* a signal flag of blue with a white square at the centre, displayed by a vessel about to leave port. [C19: from the name *Peter*]
blue pointer *n* a large shark of Australian coastal waters, having a blue back and pointed snout.
blueprint ❶ ('bluːˌprɪnt) *n* **1** Also called: **cyanotype.** a photographic

THESAURUS

verse, shock, sucker punch, upset, whammy (*inf., chiefly US*)
blow out *vb* **1** = **put out**, extinguish, snuff **2** = **burst**, erupt, explode, rupture, shatter ◆ *n* **blowout 7** = **burst**, break, flat, flat tyre, leak, puncture, rupture, tear **8** = **explosion**, blast, detonation, eruption **9** *Slang* = **binge** (*inf.*), beano (*Brit. sl.*), carousal, carouse, feast, hooley *or* hoolie (*chiefly Irish & NZ*), party, rave (*Brit. sl.*), rave-up (*Brit. sl.*), spree
blow over *vb* **1** = **finish**, cease, die down, disappear, end, pass, pass away, subside, vanish **2** = **be forgotten**
blowsy *adj* **1** = **slovenly**, bedraggled, dishevelled, frowzy, slatternly, sloppy, sluttish, tousled, unkempt, untidy **2** = **red-faced**, florid, ruddy
blow up *vb* **1** = **explode**, blast, blow sky-high, bomb, burst, detonate, dynamite, go off, rupture, shatter **2** = **exaggerate**, blow out of (all) proportion, enlarge, enlarge on, heighten, magnify, make a mountain out of a molehill, make a production out of, overstate **5** *Informal* = **lose one's temper**, become angry, become enraged, blow a fuse (*sl., chiefly US*), crack up (*inf.*), erupt, flip one's lid (*sl.*), fly off the handle (*inf.*), go ballistic (*sl., chiefly US*), go off the deep end (*inf.*), go up the wall (*sl.*), hit the roof (*inf.*), lose it (*inf.*), rage, see red (*inf.*)
bludgeon *n* **1** = **club**, cosh (*Brit.*), cudgel, shillelagh, truncheon ◆ *vb* **3** = **club**, beat, beat up, cosh (*Brit.*), cudgel, knock down, strike **4** = **bully**, browbeat, bulldoze (*inf.*), coerce, dragoon, force, hector, put the screws on, railroad (*inf.*), steamroller
blue *adj* **1** = **azure**, cerulean, cobalt, cyan, navy, sapphire, sky-coloured, ultramarine **14** = **depressed**, dejected, despondent, dismal, downcast, down-hearted, down in the dumps (*inf.*), down in the mouth, fed up, gloomy, glum, low, melancholy, sad, unhappy **15** = **smutty**, bawdy, dirty, indecent, lewd, naughty, near the knuckle (*inf.*), obscene, risqué, vulgar, X-rated (*inf.*)
Antonyms *adj* ≠ **depressed:** blithe, cheerful, cheery, chirpy (*inf.*), elated, genial, happy, jolly, merry, optimistic, sunny ≠ **smutty:** decent, respectable
blue moon *n* **once in a blue moon** *Informal* = **rarely**, almost never, hardly ever, very seldom
blueprint *n* **2** = **plan**, design, draft, layout, outline, pattern, pilot scheme, project, prototype, scheme, sketch

print of plans, technical drawings, etc., consisting of white lines on a blue background. **2** an original plan or prototype. ◆ *vb* **3** (*tr*) to make a blueprint of (a plan, etc.).

blue ribbon *n* **1** (in Britain) a badge of blue silk worn by members of the Order of the Garter. **2** a badge awarded as the first prize in a competition.

blues Ⓣ (bluːz) *pl n* (*sometimes functioning as sing*) **the. 1** a feeling of depression or deep unhappiness. **2** a type of folk song devised by Black Americans, usually employing a basic 12-bar chorus and frequent minor intervals.

blue-sky *n* (*modifier*) of or denoting theoretical research without regard to any future application of its result: *a blue-sky project.*

bluestocking (ˈbluːˌstɒkɪŋ) *n Usually disparaging.* a scholarly or intellectual woman. [from the blue worsted stockings worn by members of an 18th-cent. literary society]

bluestone (ˈbluːˌstəʊn) *n* **1** a blue-grey sandstone containing much clay, used for building and paving. **2** the blue crystalline form of copper sulphate.

bluetit (ˈbluːˌtɪt) *n* a common European tit having a blue crown, wings, and tail, yellow underparts, and a black-and-grey head.

blue whale *n* the largest mammal: a widely distributed bluish-grey whalebone whale, closely related and similar to the rorquals.

bluey (ˈbluːɪ) *n Austral. inf.* **1** a blanket. **2** a swagman's bundle. **3 hump (one's) bluey.** to carry one's bundle; tramp. **4** a variant of **blue** (sense 9). **5** a cattle dog. [(for senses 1, 2, 4) C19: from BLUE (on account of their colour) + -Y[2]]

Bluey (ˈbluːɪ) *n* a variant of **Blue.**

bluff[1] Ⓣ (blʌf) *vb* **1** to pretend to be confident about an uncertain issue in order to influence (someone). ◆ *n* **2** deliberate deception intended to create the impression of a stronger position than one actually has. **3 call someone's bluff.** to challenge someone to give proof of his claims. [C19: orig. US poker-playing term, from Du. *bluffen* to boast]
▸ **ˈbluffer** *n*

bluff[2] Ⓣ (blʌf) *n* **1** a steep promontory, bank, or cliff. **2** *Canad.* a clump of trees on the prairie; copse. ◆ *adj* **3** good-naturedly frank and hearty. **4** (of a bank, cliff, etc.) presenting a steep broad face. [C17 (in the sense: nearly perpendicular): ?from MDu. *blaf* broad]
▸ **ˈbluffly** *adv* ▸ **ˈbluffness** *n*

bluish *or* **blueish** (ˈbluːɪʃ) *adj* somewhat blue.

blunder Ⓣ (ˈblʌndə) *n* **1** a stupid or clumsy mistake. **2** a foolish tactless remark. ◆ *vb* (*mainly intr*) **3** to make stupid or clumsy mistakes. **4** to make foolish tactless remarks. **5** (often foll. by *about, into,* etc.) to act clumsily; stumble. **6** (*tr*) to mismanage; botch. [C14: of Scand. origin; cf. ON *blunda* to close one's eyes]
▸ **ˈblunderer** *n* ▸ **ˈblundering** *n, adj*

blunderbuss (ˈblʌndəˌbʌs) *n* an obsolete short musket with large bore and flared muzzle. [C17: changed (infl. by BLUNDER) from Du. *donderbus;* from *donder* THUNDER + obs. *bus* gun]

blunge (blʌndʒ) *vb* **blunges, blunging, blunged.** (*tr*) to mix (clay or a similar substance) with water in order to form a suspension for use in ceramics. [C19: prob. from BLEND + PLUNGE]
▸ **ˈblunger** *n*

blunt Ⓣ (blʌnt) *adj* **1** (esp. of a knife or blade) lacking sharpness or keenness; dull. **2** not having a sharp edge or point: *a blunt instrument.* **3** (of people, manner of speaking, etc.) straightforward and uncomplicated. ◆ *vb* (*tr*) **4** to make less sharp. **5** to diminish the sensitivity or perception of; make dull. [C12: prob. of Scand. origin]
▸ **ˈbluntly** *adv* ▸ **ˈbluntness** *n*

blur Ⓣ (blɜː) *vb* **blurs, blurring, blurred. 1** to make or become vague or less distinct. **2** to smear or smudge. **3** (*tr*) to make (the judgment, memory, or perception) less clear; dim. ◆ *n* **4** something vague, hazy, or indistinct. **5** a smear or smudge. [C16: ? var. of BLEAR]
▸ **blurred** *adj* ▸ **ˈblurry** *adj*

blurb (blɜːb) *n* a promotional description, as on the jackets of books. [C20: coined by G. Burgess (1866–1951), US humorist & illustrator]

blurt Ⓣ (blɜːt) *vb* (*tr;* often foll. by *out*) to utter suddenly and involuntarily. [C16: prob. imit.]

blush Ⓣ (blʌʃ) *vb* **1** (*intr*) to become suddenly red in the face from embarrassment, shame, modesty, or guilt; redden. **2** to make or become reddish or rosy. ◆ *n* **3** a sudden reddening of the face from embarrassment, shame, modesty, or guilt. **4** a rosy glow. **5** a cloudy area on the surface of freshly applied gloss paint. **6** another word for **rosé. 7 at first blush.** when first seen; as a first impression. [OE *blȳscan*]

blusher (ˈblʌʃə) *n* a cosmetic applied to the cheeks to give a rosy colour.

bluster Ⓣ (ˈblʌstə) *vb* **1** to speak or say loudly or boastfully. **2** to act in a bullying way. **3** (*tr;* foll. by *into*) to force or attempt to force (a person) into doing something by behaving thus. **4** (*intr*) (of the wind) to be noisy or gusty. ◆ *n* **5** boisterous talk or action; swagger. **6** empty threats or protests. **7** a strong wind; gale. [C15: prob. from MLow G *blüsteren* to storm, blow violently]
▸ **ˈblusterer** *n* ▸ **ˈblustery** *adj*

Blvd *abbrev. for* Boulevard.

BM *abbrev. for:* **1** Bachelor of Medicine. **2** *Surveying.* benchmark. **3** British Museum.

BMA *abbrev. for* British Medical Association.

BMC *abbrev. for* British Medical Council.

B-movie *n* a film originally made (esp. in the 1940s and 50s) as a supporting film, now often considered as a genre in its own right.

BMus *abbrev. for* Bachelor of Music.

BMX 1 *abbrev. for* bicycle motocross: stunt riding over an obstacle course on a bicycle. ◆ *n* **2** a bicycle designed for bicycle motocross.

Bn *abbrev. for:* **1** Baron. **2** Battalion.

BNFL *abbrev. for* British Nuclear Fuels Limited.

bo *or* **boh** (bəʊ) *interj* an exclamation to startle or surprise someone, esp. a child in a game.

BO *abbrev. for:* **1** *Inf.* body odour. **2** box office.

b.o. *abbrev. for:* **1** back order. **2** branch office. **3** broker's order. **4** buyer's option.

boa (ˈbəʊə) *n* **1** any of various large nonvenomous snakes of Central and South America and the Caribbean. They kill their prey by constriction. **2** a woman's long thin scarf, usually of feathers or fur. [C19: from NL, from L]

boa constrictor *n* a very large snake of tropical America and the Caribbean that kills its prey by constriction.

boar (bɔː) *n* **1** an uncastrated male pig. **2** See **wild boar.** [OE *bār*]

board Ⓣ (bɔːd) *n* **1** a long wide flat piece of sawn timber. **2a** a smaller flat piece of rigid material for a specific purpose: *ironing board.* **2b** (*in combination*): *breadboard.* **3** a person's meals, provided regularly for money. **4** *Arch.* a table, esp. when laden with food. **5a** (*sometimes functioning as pl*) a group of people who officially administer a company, trust, etc. **5b** (*as modifier*): *a board meeting.* **6** any other committee or council: *a board of interviewers.* **7** stiff cardboard or similar material, used for the outside covers of a book. **8** a flat thin rectangular sheet of composite material, such as plasterboard or chipboard. **9** *Chiefly US.* **9a** a list of stock-exchange prices. **9b** *Inf.* the stock exchange itself. **10** *Naut.* the side of a ship. **11** *Austral. & NZ.* the part of the floor of a sheep-shearing shed where the shearers work. **12** any of various por-

THESAURUS

blues *pl n* **1 = depression,** dejection, despondency, doldrums, dumps (*inf.*), gloom, gloominess, glumness, low spirits, melancholy, moodiness, the hump (*Brit. inf.*), unhappiness

bluff[1] *vb* **1 = deceive,** con, defraud, delude, fake, feign, humbug, lie, mislead, pretend, pull the wool over someone's eyes, sham ◆ *n* **2 = deception,** bluster, boast, braggadocio, bragging, bravado, deceit, fake, feint, fraud, humbug, idle boast, lie, mere show, pretence, sham, show, subterfuge

bluff[2] *n* **1 = precipice,** bank, cliff, crag, escarpment, headland, peak, promontory, ridge, scarp ◆ *adj* **3 = hearty,** abrupt, blunt, blustering, downright, frank, genial, good-natured, open, outspoken, plain-spoken **4 = steep,** abrupt, perpendicular, precipitous, sheer, towering
Antonyms *adj* ≠ **hearty:** delicate, diplomatic, discreet, judicious, sensitive, tactful, thoughtful

blunder *n* **1 = error,** fault, inaccuracy, mistake, oversight, slip, slip-up (*inf.*) **2 = mistake,** bloomer, boob (*Brit. sl.*), boo-boo (*inf.*), clanger (*inf.*), faux pas, gaffe, gaucherie, howler (*inf.*), impropriety, indiscretion ◆ *vb* **3 = make a mistake,** bodge (*inf.*), botch, bungle, err, slip up (*inf.*) **4 = put one's foot in it** (*inf.*), drop a brick (*Brit. inf.*), drop a clanger (*inf.*) **5 = stumble,** bumble, confuse, flounder, misjudge
Antonyms *n* ≠ **error:** accuracy, correctness ◆ *vb* ≠ **make a mistake:** be correct, be exact, get it right

blunt *adj* **1, 2 = dull,** dulled, edgeless, pointless, rounded, unsharpened **3 = forthright,** bluff, brusque, discourteous, downright, explicit, frank, impolite, outspoken, plain-spoken, rude, straightforward, straight from the shoulder, tactless, trenchant, uncivil, unpolished, upfront (*inf.*) ◆ *vb* **4 = dull 5 = deaden,** dampen, dull, numb, soften, take the edge off, water down, weaken
Antonyms *adj* ≠ **dull:** keen, pointed, sharp ≠ **forthright:** acute, courteous, diplomatic, keen, pointed, sensitive, sharp, subtle, tactful ◆ *vb* ≠ **dull:** sharpen ≠ **deaden:** animate, put an edge on, stimulate, vitalize

bluntness *n* **3 = forthrightness,** candour, frankness, ingenuousness, openness, outspokenness, plain speaking, truthfulness

blur *vb* **1 = make indistinct,** becloud, bedim, befog, blear, cloud, darken, dim, fog, make hazy, make vague, mask, obscure, soften **2 = smudge,** blot, smear, spot, stain ◆ *n* **4 = indistinctness,** blear, blurredness, cloudiness, confusion, dimness, fog, haze, obscurity **5 = smudge,** blot, smear, spot, stain

blurred *adj* **1 = indistinct,** bleary, blurry, dim, faint, foggy, fuzzy, hazy, ill-defined, lacking definition, misty, nebulous, out of focus, unclear, vague

blurt *vb, often foll. by* **out = exclaim,** babble, blab, blow the gaff (*Brit. sl.*), disclose, let the cat out of the bag, reveal, spill, spill one's guts (*sl.*), spill the beans (*inf.*), spout (*inf.*), tell all, utter suddenly

blush *vb* **1 = turn red,** colour, crimson, flush, go red (as a beetroot), redden, turn scarlet ◆ *n* **3 = flush,** colour, reddening, ruddiness **4 = glow,** pink tinge, rosiness, rosy tint
Antonyms *vb* ≠ **turn red:** blanch, blench, drain, fade, pale, turn pale, whiten

bluster *vb* **1 = boast,** blow one's own horn, blow one's own trumpet, brag, swagger, swell, vaunt **2, 3 = bully,** bulldoze, domineer, hector ◆ *n* **5 = hot air** (*inf.*), bluff, boasting, boisterousness, bombast, bragging, bravado, crowing, swagger, swaggering

blustery *adj* **4 = gusty,** blusterous, boisterous, inclement, squally, stormy, tempestuous, violent, wild, windy

board *n* **1 = plank,** panel, piece of timber, slat, timber **3 = meals,** daily meals, provisions, victuals **5a = directors,** advisers, advisory group, committee, conclave, council, directorate, panel, quango, trustees ◆ *vb* **16 = get on,** embark, embus, enplane, enter, entrain, mount **19 = lodge,** feed, room **20 = accommodate,** house, put up, quarter
Antonyms *vb* ≠ **get on:** alight, arrive, disembark, dismount, get off, go ashore, land

table surfaces specially designed for indoor games such as chess, backgammon, etc. **13 go by the board.** *Inf.* to be in disuse, neglected, or lost: *in these days courtesy goes by the board.* **14 on board.** on or in a ship, boat, aeroplane, or other vehicle. **15 the boards.** the stage. ◆ *vb* **16** to go aboard (a vessel, train, aircraft, or other vehicle). **17** to attack (a ship) by forcing one's way aboard. **18** (*tr;* often foll. by *up, in,* etc.) to cover or shut with boards. **19** (*intr*) to receive meals or meals and lodging in return for money. **20** (sometimes foll. by *out*) to arrange for (someone, esp. a child) to receive food and lodging away from home. **21** (in ice hockey and box lacrosse) to bodycheck an opponent against the boards. ◆ See also **boards.** [OE *bord*]

boarder ('bɔːdə) *n* **1** a pupil who lives at school during term time. **2** another word for **lodger. 3** a person who boards a ship, esp. in an attack.

boarding ('bɔːdɪŋ) *n* **1** a structure of boards. **2** timber boards collectively. **3a** the act of embarking on an aircraft, train, ship, etc. **3b** (*as modifier*): *a boarding pass.* **4** (in ice hockey and box lacrosse) an act of bodychecking an opponent against the boards.

boarding house *n* a private house in which accommodation and meals are provided for paying guests.

boarding school *n* a school providing living accommodation for some or all of its pupils.

Board of Trade *n* (in Britain) a part of the Department of Trade and Industry responsible for the supervision of commerce and the promotion of export trade.

boardroom ('bɔːd,ruːm, -,rʊm) *n* a room where the board of directors of a company meets.

boards (bɔːdz) *pl n* a wooden wall about one metre high forming the enclosure in which ice hockey or box lacrosse is played.

board school *n* (formerly) a school managed by a board of local ratepayers.

boardwalk ('bɔːd,wɔːk) *n US & Canad.* a promenade, esp. along a beach, usually made of planks.

boast Ⓣ (bəʊst) *vb* **1** (*intr;* sometimes foll. by *of* or *about*) to speak in excessively proud terms of one's possessions, skills, or superior qualities; brag. **2** (*tr*) to possess (something to be proud of): *the city boasts a fine cathedral.* ◆ *n* **3** a bragging statement. **4** a possession, attribute, etc., that is or may be bragged about. [C13: from ?]
▸'**boaster** *n* ▸'**boasting** *n, adj*

boastful Ⓣ ('bəʊstfʊl) *adj* tending to boast; characterized by boasting.
▸'**boastfully** *adv* ▸'**boastfulness** *n*

boat Ⓣ (bəʊt) *n* **1** a small vessel propelled by oars, paddle, sails, or motor. **2** (not in technical use) another word for **ship. 3** a container for gravy, sauce, etc. **4 burn one's boats.** See **burn**[1] (sense 13). **5 in the same boat.** sharing the same problems. **6 miss the boat.** to lose an opportunity. **7 rock the boat.** *Inf.* to cause a disturbance in the existing situation. ◆ *vb* **8** (*intr*) to travel or go in a boat, esp. as a form of recreation. **9** (*tr*) to transport or carry in a boat. [OE *bāt*]

boater ('bəʊtə) *n* a stiff straw hat with a straight brim and flat crown.

boathook ('bəʊt,hʊk) *n* a pole with a hook at one end, used aboard a vessel for fending off other vessels or for catching a mooring buoy.

boathouse ('bəʊt,haʊs) *n* a shelter by the edge of a river, lake, etc., for housing boats.

boatie ('bəʊtɪ) *n Austral. & NZ inf.* a boating enthusiast.

boating ('bəʊtɪŋ) *n* rowing, sailing, or cruising in boats as a form of recreation.

boatload ('bəʊt,ləʊd) *n* the amount of cargo or number of people held by a boat or ship.

boatman ('bəʊtmən) *n, pl* **boatmen.** a man who works on, hires out, or repairs a boat or boats.

boatswain, bosun, *or* **bo's'n** ('bəʊsᵊn) *n* a petty officer or a warrant officer who is responsible for the maintenance of a ship and its equipment. [OE *bātswegen;* see BOAT, SWAIN]

boat train *n* a train scheduled to take passengers to or from a particular ship.

bob[1] Ⓣ (bɒb) *vb* **bobs, bobbing, bobbed. 1** to move or cause to move up and down repeatedly, as while floating in water. **2** to move or cause to move with a short abrupt movement, as of the head. **3** (*intr;* usually foll. by *up*) to appear or emerge suddenly. **4** (*intr;* usually foll. by *for*) to attempt to get hold (of a floating or hanging object, esp. an apple) in the teeth as a game. ◆ *n* **5** a short abrupt movement, as of the head. [C14: from ?]

bob[2] (bɒb) *n* **1** a hairstyle for women and children in which the hair is cut short evenly all round the head. **2** a dangling or hanging object, such as the weight on a pendulum or on a plumb line. **3** short for **bobsleigh. 4** a docked tail, esp. of a horse. ◆ *vb* **bobs, bobbing, bobbed. 5** (*tr*) to cut (the hair) in a bob. **6** (*tr*) to cut short (something, esp. the tail of an animal); dock or crop. **7** (*intr*) to ride on a bobsleigh. [C14 *bobbe* bunch of flowers]

bob[3] (bɒb) *n, pl* **bob.** *Brit.* (formerly) an informal word for a **shilling.** [C19: from ?]

bobbejaan ('bɒbə,jɑːn) *n S. African.* **1** a baboon. **2** a large black spider. **3** a monkey wrench. [from Afrik., from MDu. *babiaen*]

bobbin ('bɒbɪn) *n* a spool or reel on which thread or yarn is wound. [C16: from OF *bobine,* from ?]

bobble ('bɒbᵊl) *n* **1** a short jerky motion, as of a cork floating on disturbed water; bobbing movement. **2** a tufted ball, usually for ornament, as on a knitted hat. ◆ *vb* **3** (*intr*) *Sport.* (of a ball) to bounce with a rapid, erratic motion due to an uneven playing surface. [C19: from BOB[1] (vb)]

bobby ('bɒbɪ) *n, pl* **bobbies.** *Inf.* a British policeman. [C19: from *Bobby,* after *Robert* Peel (1788–1850), who set up the Metropolitan Police Force in 1828]

bobby calf *n* an unweaned calf culled for slaughter.

bobby-dazzler *n Dialect.* anything outstanding, striking, or showy. [C19: expanded from *dazzler* something striking or attractive]

bobby pin *n US, Canad., Austral., & NZ.* a metal hairpin bent in order to hold the hair in place.

bobby socks *pl n* ankle-length socks worn by teenage girls, esp. in the US in the 1940s.

bobcat ('bɒb,kæt) *n* a North American feline mammal, closely related to but smaller than the lynx, having reddish-brown fur with dark spots or stripes, tufted ears, and a short tail. Also called: **bay lynx.** [C19: from BOB[2] + CAT[1]]

bobolink ('bɒbə,lɪŋk) *n* an American songbird, the male of which has a white back and black underparts. [C18: imit.]

bobotie (bʊ'bʊtɪ) *n* a South African dish consisting of curried mincemeat with a topping of beaten egg baked to a crust. [C19: from Afrik., prob. from Malay]

bobsleigh ('bɒb,sleɪ) *n* **1** a racing sledge for two or more people, with a steering mechanism enabling the driver to direct it down a steeply banked ice-covered run. ◆ *vb* **2** (*intr*) to ride on a bobsleigh. ◆ Also called (esp. US and Canad.): **bobsled** ('bɒb,sled). [C19: BOB[2] + SLEIGH]

bobstay ('bɒb,steɪ) *n* a strong stay between a bowsprit and the stem of a vessel for holding down the bowsprit. [C18: ?from BOB[1] + STAY[3]]

bobsy-die ('bɒbzɪ,daɪ) *n NZ inf.* fuss; confusion (esp. in **kick up bobsy-die**). [from C19 *Bob's a-dying*]

bobtail ('bɒb,teɪl) *n* **1** a docked or diminutive tail. **2** an animal with such a tail. ◆ *adj also* **bobtailed. 3** having the tail cut short. ◆ *vb* (*tr*) **4** to dock the tail of. **5** to cut short; curtail.

Boche (bɒʃ) *n Derog. sl.* (esp. in World Wars I and II) **1** a German, esp. a German soldier. **2 the.** (*usually functioning as pl*) Germans collectively, esp. German soldiers regarded as the enemy. [C20: from F, prob. shortened from *alboche* German, from *allemand* German + *caboche* pate]

bockedy ('bɒkədɪ) *adj Irish.* (of a structure, piece of furniture, etc.) unsteady. [from Irish Gaelic *bacaideach* limping]

bod (bɒd) *n Inf.* **1** a fellow; chap: *he's a queer bod.* **2** another word for **body** (sense 1). [C18: short for BODY]

BOD *abbrev. for:* biochemical oxygen demand.

bodacious (bəʊ'deɪʃəs) *adj Sl., chiefly US.* impressive or remarkable; excellent. [C19: from E dialect; blend of BOLD and AUDACIOUS]

bode[1] Ⓣ (bəʊd) *vb* **bodes, boding, boded. 1** to be an omen of (good or ill, esp. of ill); portend; presage. **2** (*tr*) *Arch.* to predict; foretell. [OE *bodian*]
▸'**bodement** *n*

bode[2] (bəʊd) *vb* a past tense of **bide.**

bodega (bəʊ'diːgə) *n* a shop selling wine and sometimes groceries, esp. in a Spanish-speaking country. [C19: from Sp., ult. from Gk *apothēkē* storehouse]

bodge (bɒdʒ) *vb* **bodges, bodging, bodged.** *Inf.* to make a mess of; botch. [C16: changed from BOTCH]

bodgie ('bɒdʒɪ) *Austral. & NZ sl.* ◆ *n* **1** an unruly or uncouth young man, esp. in the 1950s. ◆ *adj* **2** false, fraudulent. [C20: from BODGE]

Bodhisattva (,bəʊdɪ'sætvə, -wə, ,bɒd-) *n* (in Buddhism) a divine being worthy of nirvana who remains on the human plane to help men to salvation. [Sansk., from *bodhi* enlightenment + *sattva* essence]

bodice ('bɒdɪs) *n* **1** the upper part of a woman's dress, from the shoulder to the waist. **2** a tight-fitting corset worn laced over a blouse, or (formerly) as a woman's undergarment. [C16: orig. Scot. *bodies,* pl. of BODY]

bodice ripper *n Inf.* a romantic novel, usually on a historical theme, that involves some sex and violence.

-bodied *adj* (*in combination*) having a body or bodies as specified: *able-bodied; long-bodied.*

bodiless ('bɒdɪlɪs) *adj* having no body or substance; incorporeal or insubstantial.

THESAURUS

boast *vb* **1 = brag,** blow one's own trumpet, bluster, crow, exaggerate, puff, strut, swagger, talk big (*sl.*), vaunt **2 = possess,** be proud of, congratulate oneself on, exhibit, flatter oneself, pride oneself on, show off ◆ *n* **3 = brag,** avowal, gasconade (*rare*), rodomontade (*literary*), swank (*inf.*), vaunt **4 = source of pride,** gem, joy, pride, pride and joy, treasure

Antonyms *vb* ≠ **brag:** cover up, depreciate, disavow, disclaim ◆ *n* ≠ **brag:** disavowal, disclaimer

boastful *adj* **= bragging,** cocky, conceited, crowing, egotistical, full of oneself, puffed-up, swaggering, swanky (*inf.*), swollen-headed, vainglorious, vaunting

Antonyms *adj* deprecating, humble, modest, self-belittling, self-effacing, unassuming

boat *n* **1, 2 = vessel,** barge, barque, craft, ship **5 in the same boat = alike,** equal, even, on a par, on equal *or* even terms, on the same *or* equal footing, together **6 miss the boat = miss one's chance** *or* **opportunity,** be too late, blow one's chance (*inf.*), let slip, lose out, miss out **7 rock the boat** *Informal* **= cause trouble,** dissent, make waves (*inf.*), throw a spanner in the works, upset the apple cart

bob[1] *vb* **1 = duck,** bounce, hop, jerk, leap, nod, oscillate, quiver, skip, waggle, weave, wobble **3** *usually foll. by* **up = appear,** arise, emerge, materialize, pop up, rise, spring up, surface, turn up

bode[1] *vb* **1 = portend,** augur, be an omen of, betoken, forebode, foreshadow, presage, signify, threaten **2** *Archaic* **= foretell,** forewarn, predict, prophesy

bodily ❶ ('bɒdɪlɪ) *adj* **1** relating to or being a part of the human body. ◆ *adv* **2** by taking hold of the body: *he threw him bodily from the platform.* **3** in person; in the flesh.

bodkin ('bɒdkɪn) *n* **1** a blunt large-eyed needle. **2** *Arch.* a dagger. **3** *Arch.* a long ornamental hairpin. [C14: prob. of Celtic origin]

body ❶ ('bɒdɪ) *n, pl* **bodies. 1a** the entire physical structure of an animal or human being. Related adj: **corporeal. 1b** (*as modifier*): *body odour.* **2** the trunk or torso. **3** a dead human or animal; corpse. **4** the flesh as opposed to the spirit. **5** the largest or main part of anything: *the body of a vehicle; the body of a plant.* **6** a separate or distinct mass of water or land. **7** a number of individuals regarded as a single entity; group. **8** fullness in the appearance of the hair. **9** the characteristic full quality of certain wines. **10** firmness, esp. of cloth. **11a** the pigment contained in or added to paint, dye, etc. **11b** the opacity of a paint. **11c** (*as modifier*): *body colour.* **12** an informal or dialect word for a **person. 13** another word for **bodysuit** (sense 1). **14 keep body and soul together.** to manage to keep alive; survive. ◆ *vb* **bodies, bodying, bodied.** (*tr*) **15** (usually foll. by *forth*) to give a body or shape to. [OE *bodig*]

body blow *n* **1** *Boxing.* a blow to an opponent's body. **2** a severe disappointment or setback.

body building *n* the practice of exercises to make the muscles of the body conspicuous.

bodycheck ('bɒdɪ,tʃɛk) *Ice hockey, etc.* ◆ *n* **1** obstruction of another player. ◆ *vb* **2** (*tr*) to deliver a bodycheck to (an opponent).

body double *n Films.* a person who substitutes for a star for the filming of a scene that involves shots of the body rather than the face.

bodyguard ('bɒdɪ,gɑːd) *n* a person or group of people who escort and protect someone.

body horror *n* a genre of horror film in which the main feature is the graphically depicted destruction or degeneration of a human body or bodies.

body language *n* the nonverbal imparting of information by means of conscious or subconscious bodily gestures, posture, etc.

body-line *adj Cricket.* denoting or relating to fast bowling aimed at the batsman's body.

body politic *n* **the.** the people of a nation or the nation itself considered as a political entity.

body search *n* **1** a form of search by police, customs officials, etc., that involves examination of a prisoner's or suspect's bodily orifices. ◆ *vb* **body-search. 2** (*tr*) to search (a prisoner or suspect) in this manner.

body shop *n* a repair yard for vehicle bodywork.

body snatcher *n* (formerly) a person who robbed graves and sold the corpses for dissection.

body stocking *n* a one-piece undergarment for women, usually of nylon, covering the torso.

bodysuit ('bɒdɪ,suːt, -,sjuːt) *n* **1** a woman's close-fitting one-piece garment for the torso. Sometimes shortened to **body. 2** a one-piece undergarment for a baby.

body swerve *n* **1** *Sport.* (esp. in football games) the act or an instance of swerving past an opponent. **2** *Scot.* the act or an instance of avoiding (a situation considered unpleasant): *I think I'll give the meeting a body swerve.* ◆ *vb* **body-swerve, body-swerves, body-swerving, body-swerved. 3** *Sport.* (esp. in football games) to pass (an opponent) using a body swerve. **4** *Scot.* to avoid (a situation or person considered unpleasant).

body warmer *n* a sleeveless type of jerkin, usually quilted, worn as an outer garment.

bodywork ('bɒdɪ,wɜːk) *n* the external shell of a motor vehicle.

Boeotian (bɪ'əʊʃɪən) *adj* **1** of Boeotia, a region in ancient Greece. **2** dull or stupid. ◆ *n* **3** a person from Boeotia. **4** a dull or stupid person.

Boer (bʊə) *n* **a** a descendant of any of the Dutch or Huguenot colonists who settled in South Africa. **b** (*as modifier*): *a Boer farmer.* [C19: from Du. *Boer*; see BOOR]

boerbul ('bʊəbəl) *n S. African.* a crossbred mastiff used esp. as a watchdog. [from Afrik. *boerboel*, from *boel* large dog]

boeremusiek ('bʊərə,mœsɪk) *n S. African.* light music associated with the culture of the Afrikaners. [from Afrik. *boere* country, folk + *musiek* music]

boet (bʊt) *or* **boetie** *n S. African inf.* a friend. [from Afrik.: brother]

boffin ('bɒfɪn) *n Brit. inf.* a scientist, esp. one carrying out military research. [C20: from ?]

boffo ('bɒfəʊ) *adj Sl.* very good; highly successful. [C20: from ?]

Bofors gun ('bəʊfəz) *n* an automatic 40 mm anti-aircraft gun, one or more of which are controlled by a radar-operated computer system mounted on a lightweight vehicle. [C20: after the Swedish armament firm that developed it]

bog ❶ (bɒg) *n* **1** wet spongy ground consisting of decomposing vegetation. **2** an area of such ground. **3** a slang word for **lavatory.** [C13: from Gaelic *bogach* swamp, from *bog* soft]
▸ **'boggy** *adj* ▸ **'bogginess** *n*

bogan ('bəʊgən) *n Canad.* (esp. in the Maritime Provinces) a sluggish side stream. Also called: **logan, pokelogan.** [of Algonquian origin]

bogbean ('bɒg,biːn) *n* another name for **buckbean.**

bog down ❶ *vb* **bogs, bogging, bogged.** (*adv*; when *tr, often passive*) to impede or be impeded physically or mentally.

bogey ❶ *or* **bogy** ('bəʊgɪ) *n* **1** an evil or mischievous spirit. **2** something that worries or annoys. **3** *Golf.* **3a** a score of one stroke over par on a hole. Cf. **par** (sense 5). **3b** *Obs.* a standard score for a hole or course, regarded as one that a good player should make. **4** *Sl.* a piece of dried mucus discharged from the nose. [C19: prob. rel. to obs. *bug* an evil spirit and BOGLE]

bogeyman ('bəʊgɪ,mæn) *n, pl* **bogeymen.** a person, real or imaginary, used as a threat, esp. to children.

boggle ❶ ('bɒgᵊl) *vb* **boggles, boggling, boggled.** (*intr*; often foll. by *at*) **1** to be surprised, confused, or alarmed (esp. in **the mind boggles**). **2** to hesitate or be evasive when confronted with a problem. [C16: prob. var. of BOGLE]

bogie *or* **bogy** ('bəʊgɪ) *n* **1** an assembly of four or six wheels forming a pivoted support at either end of a railway coach. **2** *Chiefly Brit.* a small railway truck of short wheelbase, used for conveying coal, ores, etc. [C19: from ?]

bogle ('bəʊgᵊl, 'bɒg-) *n* a dialect or archaic word for **bogey** (sense 1). [C16: from Scot. *bogill*]

bog myrtle *n* another name for **sweet gale.**

bog oak *n* oak found preserved in peat bogs.

bog off *Brit. sl.* ◆ *interj* **1** go away! ◆ *vb* **bogs, bogging, bogged. 2** (*intr, adv*) to go away.

bogong ('bəʊ,gɒŋ) *or* **bugong** ('buː,gɒŋ) *n* an edible dark-coloured Australian noctuid moth.

bog-standard *adj Brit. & Irish sl.* completely ordinary; run-of-the-mill.

bogtrotter ('bɒg,trɒtə) *n* a derogatory term for an Irishman, esp. an Irish peasant.

bogus ❶ ('bəʊgəs) *adj* spurious or counterfeit; not genuine. [C19: from *bogus* apparatus for making counterfeit money]
▸ **'bogusly** *adv* ▸ **'bogusness** *n*

bogy ('bəʊgɪ) *n, pl* **bogies.** a variant spelling of **bogey** or **bogie.**

bohea (bəʊ'hiː) *n* a black Chinese tea, once regarded as the choicest, but now as an inferior grade. [C18: from Chinese *Wu-i Shan*, range of hills on which this tea was grown]

Bohemian ❶ (bəʊ'hiːmɪən) *n* **1** a native or inhabitant of Bohemia, a former kingdom; a Czech. **2** (*often not cap.*) a person, esp. an artist or writer, who lives an unconventional life. **3** the Czech language. ◆ *adj* **4** of, relating to, or characteristic of Bohemia, its people, or their language. **5** unconventional in appearance, behaviour, etc.

Bohemianism (bəʊ'hiːmɪə,nɪzəm) *n* unconventional behaviour or appearance, esp. of an artist.

bohrium ('bɔːrɪəm) *n* a transuranic element artificially produced in minute quantities by bombarding ^{204}Bi atoms with ^{54}Cr nuclei. Symbol: Bh; atomic no.: 107. Former names: **element 107, unnilheptium.** [C20: after Niels *Bohr* (1885–1962), Danish physicist]

boil[1] ❶ (bɔɪl) *vb* **1** to change or cause to change from a liquid to a vapour so rapidly that bubbles of vapour are formed in the liquid. **2** to reach or cause to reach boiling point. **3** to cook or be cooked by the process of boiling. **4** (*intr*) to bubble and be agitated like something boiling; seethe: *the ocean was boiling.* **5** (*intr*) to be extremely angry or indignant. ◆ *n* **6** the state or action of boiling. ◆ See also **boil away, boil down, boil over.** [C13: from OF, from L, from *bulla* a bubble]

boil[2] ❶ (bɔɪl) *n* a red painful swelling with a hard pus-filled core caused by bacterial infection of the skin. Technical name: **furuncle.** [OE *bȳle*]

THESAURUS

bodily *adj* **1 = physical**, actual, carnal, corporal, corporeal, fleshly, material, substantial, tangible

body *n* **1 = physique**, build, figure, form, frame, shape **2 = torso**, trunk **3 = corpse**, cadaver, carcass, dead body, relics, remains, stiff (*sl.*) **5 = main part**, bulk, essence, mass, material, matter, substance **7 = organization**, association, band, bloc, collection, company, confederation, congress, corporation, society **9 = consistency**, density, richness, substance **12 = person**, being, creature, human, human being, individual, mortal

bog *n* **1, 2 = marsh**, fen, marshland, mire, morass, moss (*Scot. & N English dialect*), peat bog, quagmire, slough, swamp, wetlands

bog down *vb* **= hold up**, delay, halt, impede, sink, slow down, slow up, stall, stick

bogey *n* **1 = spirit**, apparition, bogeyman, goblin, hobgoblin, imp, spectre, spook (*inf.*), sprite **2 = bugbear**, bête noire, bugaboo, nightmare

boggle *vb* **1 = be confused**, be alarmed, be surprised, be taken aback, shy, stagger, startle, take fright **2 = hesitate**, demur, dither, doubt, equivocate, falter, hang back, hover, jib, shilly-shally (*inf.*), shrink from, vacillate, waver

boggy *adj* **1 = marshy**, fenny, miry, muddy, oozy, quaggy, soft, spongy, swampy, waterlogged, yielding

bogus *adj* **= fake**, artificial, counterfeit, dummy, ersatz, false, forged, fraudulent, imitation, phoney *or* phony (*inf.*), pseudo (*inf.*), sham, spurious
Antonyms *adj* actual, authentic, genuine, real, true

Bohemian *n* **2** *often not cap.* **= nonconformist**, beatnik, dropout, hippy, iconoclast ◆ *adj* **5** *often not cap.* **= unconventional**, alternative, artistic, arty (*inf.*), avant-garde, eccentric, exotic, left bank, nonconformist, oddball (*inf.*), offbeat, off-the-wall (*sl.*), outré, unorthodox, way-out (*inf.*)
Antonyms *adj* ≠ **unconventional:** bourgeois, conservative, conventional, Pooterish, square (*inf.*), straight (*sl.*), straight-laced, stuffy

boil[1] *vb* **4 = bubble**, agitate, churn, effervesce, fizz, foam, froth, seethe **5 = be furious**, be angry, be indignant, blow a fuse (*sl., chiefly US*), crack up (*inf.*), fly off the handle (*inf.*), foam at the mouth (*inf.*), fulminate, fume, go ballistic (*sl., chiefly US*), go off the deep end (*inf.*), go up the wall (*sl.*), rage, rave, see red (*inf.*), storm, wig out (*sl.*)

boil[2] *n* **= pustule**, blain, blister, carbuncle, gathering, swelling, tumour, ulcer

boil away *vb* (*adv*) to cause (liquid) to evaporate completely by boiling or (of liquid) to evaporate completely.
boil down Ⓣ *vb* (*adv*) **1** to reduce or be reduced in quantity by boiling. **2 boil down to. 2a** (*intr*) to be the essential element in something. **2b** (*tr*) to summarize; reduce to essentials.
boiled shirt *n Inf.* a dress shirt with a stiff front.
boiler ('bɔɪlə) *n* **1** a closed vessel in which water is heated to supply steam or provide heat. **2** a domestic device to provide hot water, esp. for central heating. **3** a large tub for boiling laundry.
boilermaker ('bɔɪləˌmeɪkə) *n* a person who works with metal in heavy industry; plater or welder.
boilerplate ('bɔɪləˌpleɪt) *n* **1** a form of mild-steel plate used in the production of boiler shells. **2** a copy made with the intention of making other copies from it. **3** a set of instructions incorporated in several places in a computer program or a standard form of words used repeatedly in drafting contracts, guarantees, etc. **4** a draft contract that can be modified to cover various types of transaction.
boiler suit *n Brit.* a one-piece overall work garment.
boiling point *n* **1** the temperature at which a liquid boils at sea level. **2** *Inf.* the condition of being angered or highly excited.
boiling-water reactor *n* a nuclear reactor using water as coolant and moderator, steam being produced in the reactor itself. Abbrev.: **BWR.**
boil over *vb* (*adv*) **1** to overflow or cause to overflow while boiling. **2** (*intr*) to burst out in anger or excitement.
boisterous Ⓣ ('bɔɪstərəs, -strəs) *adj* **1** noisy and lively; unruly. **2** (of the wind, sea, etc.) stormy. [C13 *boistuous*, from ?]
▸**'boisterously** *adv* ▸**'boisterousness** *n*
bok choy ('bɒk 'tʃɔɪ) *n* a Chinese plant that is related to the cabbage and has edible stalks and leaves. Also called: **Chinese cabbage, Chinese leaf.** [from Chinese dialect, lit.: white vegetable]
bola ('bəʊlə) *or* **bolas** ('bəʊləs) *n, pl* **bolas** *or* **bolases.** a missile used by gauchos and Indians of South America, consisting of heavy balls on a cord. It is hurled at a running quarry, so as to entangle its legs. [Sp.: ball, from L *bulla* knob]
bold Ⓣ (bəʊld) *adj* **1** courageous, confident, and fearless; ready to take risks. **2** showing or requiring courage: *a bold plan.* **3** immodest or impudent: *she gave him a bold look.* **4** standing out distinctly; conspicuous: *a figure carved in bold relief.* **5** very steep: *the bold face of the cliff.* **6** imaginative in thought or expression. [OE *beald*]
▸**'boldly** *adv* ▸**'boldness** *n*
bold face *Printing.* ◆ *n* **1** a weight of type characterized by thick heavy lines, as the entry words in this dictionary. ◆ *adj* **boldface. 2** (of type) having this weight.
bole (bəʊl) *n* the trunk of a tree. [C14: from ON *bolr*]
bolero (bəˈlɛərəʊ) *n, pl* **boleros. 1** a Spanish dance, usually in triple time. **2** a piece of music for or in the rhythm of this dance. **3** (*also* 'bɒlərəʊ). a short open bodice-like jacket not reaching the waist. [C18: from Sp.]
boliviano (bəˌlɪvɪˈɑːnəʊ; *Spanish* boliˈβjano) **bolivianos** (-nəʊz; *Spanish* -nos). (until 1963 and from 1987) the standard monetary unit of Bolivia, equal to 100 centavos.
boll (bəʊl) *n* the fruit of such plants as flax and cotton, consisting of a rounded capsule containing the seeds. [C13: from Du. *bolle;* rel. to OE *bolla* BOWL[1]]
bollard ('bɒlɑːd, 'bɒləd) *n* **1** a strong wooden or metal post on a wharf, quay, etc., used for securing mooring lines. **2** *Brit.* a small post placed on a kerb or traffic island to make it conspicuous to motorists. [C14: ?from BOLE + -ARD]
bollocking ('bɒləkɪŋ) *n Sl.* a severe telling-off. [from *bollock* (vb) in the sense "to reprimand"]
bollocks ('bɒləks) *or* **ballocks** *Taboo sl.* ◆ *pl n* **1** another word for **testicles. 2** nonsense; rubbish. ◆ *interj* **3** an exclamation of annoyance, disbelief, etc. [OE *beallucas;* see BALL[1]]
boll weevil *n* a greyish weevil of the southern US and Mexico, whose larvae live in and destroy cotton bolls.
bologna sausage (bəˈləʊnjə) *n Chiefly US & Canad.* a large smoked sausage made of seasoned mixed meats. Also called: **baloney, boloney,** (esp. Brit.) **polony.**
bolometer (bəʊˈlɒmɪtə) *n* a sensitive instrument for measuring radiant energy. [C19: from Gk *bolē* ray of light, from *ballein* to throw + -METER]
▸**bolometric** (ˌbəʊləˈmɛtrɪk) *adj*
boloney (bəˈləʊnɪ) *n* **1** a variant of **baloney. 2** another name for **bologna sausage.**
Bolshevik ('bɒlʃɪvɪk) *n, pl* **Bolsheviks** *or* **Bolsheviki** (ˌbɒlʃɪˈviːkɪ). **1** (formerly) a Russian Communist. Cf. **Menshevik. 2** any Communist. **3** (*often not cap.*) *Inf. & derog.* any political radical, esp. a revolutionary. [C20: from Russian *Bol'shevik* majority, from *bol'shoi* great]
▸**'BolsheˌVism** *n* ▸**'Bolshevist** *adj, n*
bolshie *or* **bolshy** ('bɒlʃɪ) (*sometimes cap.*) *Brit. inf.* ◆ *adj* **1** difficult to manage; rebellious. **2** politically radical or left-wing. ◆ *n, pl* **bolshies. 3** *Derog.* any political radical. [C20: shortened from BOLSHEVIK]
bolster Ⓣ ('bəʊlstə) *vb* (*tr*) **1** (often foll. by *up*) to support or reinforce; strengthen: *to bolster morale.* **2** to prop up with a pillow or cushion. ◆ *n* **3** a long narrow pillow or cushion. **4** any pad or padded support. **5** a cold chisel used for cutting stone slabs, etc. [OE *bolster*]
bolt[1] Ⓣ (bəʊlt) *n* **1** a bar that can be slid into a socket to lock a door, gate, etc. **2** a bar or rod that forms part of a locking mechanism and is moved by a key or a knob. **3** a metal rod or pin that has a head and a screw thread to take a nut. **4** a sliding bar in a breech-loading firearm that ejects the empty cartridge, replaces it with a new one, and closes the breech. **5** a flash of lightning. **6** a sudden start or movement, esp. in order to escape. **7** a roll of something, such as cloth, wallpaper, etc. **8** an arrow, esp. for a crossbow. **9 a bolt from the blue.** a sudden, unexpected, and usually unwelcome event. **10 shoot one's bolt.** to exhaust one's efforts. ◆ *vb* **11** (*tr*) to secure or lock with or as with a bolt. **12** (*tr*) to eat hurriedly. **13** (*intr;* usually foll. by *from* or *out*) to move or jump suddenly: *he bolted from the chair.* **14** (*intr*) (esp. of a horse) to start hurriedly and run away without warning. **15** (*tr*) to roll (cloth, wallpaper, etc.) into bolts. **16** (*intr*) (of cultivated plants) to produce flowers and seeds prematurely. ◆ *adv* **17** stiffly, firmly, or rigidly (archaic except in **bolt upright**). [OE *bolt* arrow]
▸**'bolter** *n*
bolt[2] *or* **boult** (bəʊlt) *vb* (*tr*) **1** to pass (a powder, etc.) through a sieve. **2** to examine and separate. [C13: from OF *bulter,* prob. of Gmc origin]
▸**'bolter** *or* **'boulter** *n*
bolt hole *n* a place of escape from danger.
boltrope ('bəʊltˌrəʊp) *n Naut.* a rope sewn to the foot or luff of a sail to strengthen it.
bolus ('bəʊləs) *n, pl* **boluses. 1** a small round soft mass, esp. of chewed food. **2** a large pill or tablet used in veterinary and clinical medicine. [C17: from NL, from Gk *bōlos* clod, lump]
bomb Ⓣ (bɒm) *n* **1a** a hollow projectile containing explosive, incendiary, or other destructive substance. **1b** (*as modifier*): *bomb disposal; a bomb bay.* **1c** (*in combination*): *bombproof.* **2** an object in which an explosive device has been planted: *a car bomb; a letter bomb.* **3** a round mass of volcanic rock, solidified from molten lava that has been thrown into the air. **4** *Med.* a container for radioactive material, applied therapeutically to any part of the body: *a cobalt bomb.* **5** *Brit. sl.* a large sum of money. **6** *US & Canad. sl.* a disastrous failure: *the new play was a total bomb.* **7** *Austral. & NZ sl.* an old or dilapidated motorcar. **8** *American football.* a very long high pass. **9 like a bomb.** *Brit. & NZ inf.* with great speed or success; very well. **10 the bomb.** a hydrogen or an atomic bomb considered as the ultimate destructive weapon. ◆ *vb* **11** to attack with or as if with a bomb or bombs; drop bombs (on). **12** (*intr;* often foll. by *off, along,* etc.) *Inf.* to move or drive very quickly. **13** (*intr*) *US sl.* to fail disastrously. [C17: from F, from It., from L, from Gk *bombos,* imit.]
bombard Ⓣ *vb* (bɒmˈbɑːd). (*tr*) **1** to attack with concentrated artillery fire or bombs. **2** to attack with vigour and persistence. **3** to attack verbally, esp. with questions. **4** *Physics.* to direct high-energy particles or photons against (atoms, nuclei, etc.). ◆ *n* ('bɒmbɑːd). **5** an ancient type of cannon that threw stone balls. [C15: from OF, from *bombarde* stone-throwing cannon, prob. from L *bombus* booming sound; see BOMB]
▸**bom'bardment** *n*
bombardier (ˌbɒmbəˈdɪə) *n* **1** the member of a bomber aircrew responsible for aiming and releasing the bombs. **2** *Brit.* a noncommissioned

THESAURUS

boil down *vb* **1** = **reduce**, condense, decrease
boiling[1] *adj* **5** = **furious**, angry, choked, cross, enraged, fit to be tied (*sl.*), foaming at the mouth, fuming, incandescent, incensed, indignant, infuriated, on the warpath
boisterous *adj* **1** = **unruly**, bouncy, clamorous, disorderly, impetuous, loud, noisy, obstreperous, riotous, rollicking, rowdy, rumbustious, unrestrained, uproarious, vociferous, wild **2** = **stormy**, blustery, gusty, raging, rough, squally, tempestuous, tumultuous, turbulent
Antonyms *adj* ≠ **unruly:** calm, controlled, peaceful, quiet, restrained, self-controlled, subdued ≠ **stormy:** calm, peaceful, quiet
bold *adj* **1** = **fearless**, adventurous, audacious, brave, courageous, daring, dauntless, enterprising, gallant, gritty, heroic, intrepid, lion-hearted, valiant, valorous **3** = **impudent**, barefaced, brash, brazen, cheeky, confident, feisty (*inf., chiefly US & Canad.*), forward, fresh (*inf.*), insolent, in-your-face (*Brit. sl.*), pert, pushy (*inf.*), rude, sassy (*US inf.*), saucy, shameless **4** = **conspicuous**, bright, colourful, eye-catching, flashy, forceful, lively, loud, prominent, pronounced, salient, showy, spirited, striking, strong, vivid
Antonyms *adj* ≠ **fearless:** cowardly, faint-hearted, fearful, timid, timorous ≠ **impudent:** conservative, cool, courteous, meek, modest, polite, retiring, shy, tactful ≠ **conspicuous:** dull, ordinary, pale, soft, unimaginative
bolster *vb* **1** = **support**, aid, assist, augment, boost, brace, buoy up, buttress, give a leg up (*inf.*), help, hold up, maintain, reinforce, shore up, stay, strengthen **2** = **prop up**, cushion, pillow
bolt[1] *n* **1, 2** = **bar**, catch, fastener, latch, lock, sliding bar **3** = **pin**, peg, rivet, rod **6** = **dash**, bound, dart, escape, flight, rush, spring, sprint **8** = **arrow**, dart, missile, projectile, shaft, thunderbolt ◆ *vb* **11** = **lock**, bar, fasten, latch, secure **12** = **gobble**, cram, devour, gorge, gulp, guzzle, stuff, swallow whole, wolf **13** = **spring**, bound, jump, leap **14** = **run away**, abscond, dash, decamp, do a runner, escape, flee, fly, fly the coop (*US & Canad. inf.*), hurtle, make a break (for it), run, run for it, rush, skedaddle (*inf.*), sprint
bomb *n* **1** = **explosive**, bombshell, charge, device, grenade, mine, missile, projectile, rocket, shell, torpedo ◆ *vb* **11** = **blow up**, attack, blow sky-high, bombard, destroy, shell, strafe, torpedo
bombard *vb* **1** = **bomb**, assault, blast, blitz, cannonade, fire upon, open fire, pound, shell, strafe **2, 3** = **attack**, assail, barrage, batter, beset, besiege, harass, hound, pester
bombardment *n* **1** = **bombing**, assault, attack,

rank, below the rank of sergeant, in the Royal Artillery. [C16: from OF; see BOMBARD]

Bombardier (ˌbɒmbəˈdɪə) *n Canad. trademark.* a snow tractor, usually having caterpillar tracks at the rear and skis at the front. [C20: after J. A. *Bombardier*, Canadian inventor and manufacturer]

bombast ❶ (ˈbɒmbæst) *n* pompous and grandiloquent language. [C16: from OF, from Med. L *bombāx* cotton]
▸**bomˈbastic** *adj* ▸**bomˈbastically** *adv*

Bombay duck (bɒmˈbeɪ) *n* a fish that is eaten dried with curry dishes as a savoury. Also called: **bummalo.** [C19: changed from *bombil* through association with *Bombay*, port in W India]

bombazine *or* **bombasine** (ˌbɒmbəˈziːn, ˈbɒmbəˌziːn) *n* a twilled fabric, esp. one of silk and worsted, formerly worn dyed black for mourning. [C16: from OF, from L, from *bombyx* silk]

bomber (ˈbɒmə) *n* **1** a military aircraft designed to carry out bombing missions. **2** a person who plants bombs.

bomber jacket *n* a short jacket finishing at the waist with an elasticated band, usually having a zip front.

bombora (bɒmˈbɔːrə) *n Austral.* **1** a submerged reef. **2** a turbulent area of sea over such a reef. [from Abor.]

bombshell (ˈbɒmˌʃel) *n* **1** (esp. formerly) a bomb or artillery shell. **2** a shocking or unwelcome surprise.

bombsight (ˈbɒmˌsaɪt) *n* a mechanical or electronic device in an aircraft for aiming bombs.

bona fide ❶ (ˈbəʊnə ˈfaɪdɪ) *adj* **1** real or genuine: *a bona fide manuscript.* **2** undertaken in good faith: *a bona fide agreement.* [C16: from L]

bona fides (ˈbəʊnə ˈfaɪdiːz) *n Law.* good faith; honest intention. [L]

bonanza (bəˈnænzə) *n* **1** a source, usually sudden and unexpected, of luck or wealth. **2** *US & Canad.* a mine or vein rich in ore. [C19: from Sp., lit.: calm sea, hence, good luck, from Med. L, from L *bonus* good + *malacia* calm, from Gk *malakia* softness]

bonbon (ˈbɒnbɒn) *n* a sweet. [C19: from F, orig. a children's word from *bon* good]

bonce (bɒns) *n Brit. sl.* the head. [C19 (orig.: a large playing marble): from ?]

bond ❶ (bɒnd) *n* **1** something that binds, fastens, or holds together. **2** (*often pl*) something that brings or holds people together; tie: *a bond of friendship.* **3** (*pl*) something that restrains or imprisons; captivity or imprisonment. **4** a written or spoken agreement, esp. a promise. **5** *Finance.* a certificate of debt issued in order to raise funds. It is repayable with or without security at a specified future date. **6** *Law.* a written acknowledgment of an obligation to pay a sum or to perform a contract. **7** any of various arrangements of bricks or stones in a wall in which they overlap so as to provide strength. **8** **chemical bond.** a mutual attraction between two atoms resulting from a redistribution of their outer electrons, determining chemical properties; shown in some formulae by a dot (.) or score (—). **9** See **bond paper.** **10** **in bond.** *Commerce.* deposited in a bonded warehouse. ◆ *vb* (*mainly tr*) **11** (*also intr*) to hold or be held together, as by a rope or an adhesive; bind; connect. **12** (*intr*) to become emotionally attached. **13** to put or hold (goods) in bond. **14** *Law.* to place under bond. **15** *Finance.* to issue bonds on; mortgage. [C13: from ON *band;* see BAND[2]]

bondage ❶ (ˈbɒndɪdʒ) *n* **1** slavery or serfdom; servitude. **2** subjection to some influence or duty. **3** a sexual practice in which one participant is physically bound.

bonded (ˈbɒndɪd) *adj* **1** *Finance.* consisting of, secured by, or operating under a bond or bonds. **2** *Commerce.* deposited in a bonded warehouse.

bonded warehouse *n* a warehouse in which goods are deposited until duty is paid.

bondholder (ˈbɒndˌhəʊldə) *n* an owner of bonds issued by a company or other institution.

bonding (ˈbɒndɪŋ) *n* the process by which individuals become emotionally attached to one another.

bondmaid (ˈbɒndˌmeɪd) *n* an unmarried female serf or slave.

bond paper *n* a superior quality of strong white paper, used esp. for writing and typing.

bondservant (ˈbɒndˌsɜːvənt) *n* a serf or slave.

bondsman (ˈbɒndzmən) *n, pl* **bondsmen. 1** *Law.* a person bound by bond to act as surety for another. **2** another word for **bondservant.**

bond washing *n* a series of illegal deals in bonds made with the intention of avoiding taxation.

bone (bəʊn) *n* **1** any of the various structures that make up the skeleton in most vertebrates. **2** the porous rigid tissue of which these parts are made. **3** something consisting of bone or a bonelike substance. **4** (*pl*) the human skeleton or body. **5** a thin strip of whalebone, plastic, etc., used to stiffen corsets and brassieres. **6** (*pl*) the essentials (esp. in **the bare bones**). **7** (*pl*) dice. **8** **close** *or* **near to the bone.** **8a** risqué or indecent. **8b** in poverty; destitute. **9** **feel in one's bones.** to have an intuition of. **10** **have a bone to pick.** to have grounds for a quarrel. **11** **make no bones about.** **11a** to be direct and candid about. **11b** to have no scruples about. **12** **point the bone.** (often foll. by *at*) *Austral.* **12a** to wish bad luck (on). **12b** to cast a spell (on) in order to kill. ◆ *vb* **bones, boning, boned.** (*mainly tr*) **13** to remove the bones from (meat for cooking, etc.). **14** to stiffen (a corset, etc.) by inserting bones. **15** *Brit.* a slang word for **steal.** ◆ See also **bone up.** [OE *bān*]
▸ˈ**boneless** *adj*

bone ash *n* ash obtained when bones are burnt in air, consisting mainly of calcium phosphate.

bone china *n* porcelain containing bone ash.

bone-dry *adj Inf.* **a** completely dry: *a bone-dry well.* **b** (*postpositive*): *the well was bone dry.*

bonehead (ˈbəʊnˌhed) *n Sl.* a stupid or obstinate person.
▸ˈ**boneˌheaded** *adj*

bone idle *adj* very idle; extremely lazy.

bone marrow *n* See **marrow** (sense 1).

bone meal *n* dried and ground animal bones, used as a fertilizer or in stock feeds.

boner (ˈbəʊnə) *n Sl.* a blunder.

bonesetter (ˈbəʊnˌsetə) *n* a person who sets broken or dislocated bones, esp. one who has no formal medical qualifications.

boneshaker (ˈbəʊnˌʃeɪkə) *n* **1** an early type of bicycle having solid tyres and no springs. **2** *Sl.* any decrepit or rickety vehicle.

bone up *vb* (*adv; when intr,* usually foll. by *on*) *Inf.* to study intensively.

bonfire (ˈbɒnˌfaɪə) *n* a large outdoor fire. [C15: alteration (infl. by F *bon* good) of *bone-fire;* from the use of bones as fuel]

bong (bɒŋ) *n* **1** a deep reverberating sound, as of a large bell. ◆ *vb* **2** to make a deep reverberating sound. [C20: imit.]

bongo[1] (ˈbɒŋgəʊ) *n, pl* **bongo** *or* **bongos.** a rare spiral-horned antelope inhabiting forests of central Africa. The coat is bright red-brown with narrow vertical stripes. [of African origin]

bongo[2] (ˈbɒŋgəʊ) *n, pl* **bongos** *or* **bongoes.** a small bucket-shaped drum, usually one of a pair, played by beating with the fingers. [American Sp., prob. imit.]

bonhomie (ˈbɒnəmiː) *n* exuberant friendliness. [C18: from F, from *bon* good + *homme* man]

bonito (bəˈniːtəʊ) *n, pl* **bonitos.** any of various small tunny-like marine food fishes of warm Atlantic and Pacific waters. [C16: from Sp., from L *bonus* good]

bonk (bɒŋk) *vb Inf.* **1** (*tr*) to hit. **2** to have sexual intercourse (with). [C20: prob. imit.]
▸ˈ**bonking** *n*

bonkbuster (ˈbɒŋkˌbʌstə) *n Inf.* a novel characterized by graphic descriptions of the heroine's frequent sexual encounters. [C20: from BONK (sense 2) + (BLOCK)BUSTER]

bonkers (ˈbɒŋkəz) *adj Sl., chiefly Brit.* mad; crazy. [C20: from ?]

bon mot (*French* bɔ̃ mo) *n, pl* **bons mots** (bɔ̃ mo). a clever and fitting remark. [F, lit.: good word]

bonnet (ˈbɒnɪt) *n* **1** any of various hats worn, esp. formerly, by women and girls, and tied with ribbons under the chin. **2** (in Scotland) Also: **bunnet.** **2a** a soft cloth cap. **2b** (formerly) a flat brimless cap worn by men. **3** the hinged metal part of a motor vehicle body that provides access to the engine. US name: **hood.** **4** a cowl on a chimney. **5** *Naut.* a piece of sail laced to the foot of a foresail to give it greater area in light winds. **6** (in the US and Canada) a headdress of feathers worn by some tribes of American Indians. [C14: from OF *bonet,* from ?]

bonny ❶ (ˈbɒnɪ) *adj* **bonnier, bonniest.** **1** *Scot. & N English dialect.* beautiful or handsome: *a bonny lass.* **2** good or fine. **3** (esp. of babies) plump. [C15: from OF *bon* good, from L *bonus*]

bonsai (ˈbɒnsaɪ) *n, pl* **bonsai.** **1** the art of growing dwarfed ornamental varieties of trees or shrubs in small shallow pots or trays by selective pruning, etc. **2** a tree or shrub grown by this method. [C20: from Japanese, from *bon* bowl + *sai* to plant]

bontebok (ˈbɒntɪˌbʌk) *n, pl* **bonteboks** *or* **bontebok.** an antelope of southern Africa, having a deep reddish-brown coat with a white blaze, tail, and rump patch. [C18: Afrik. from *bont* pied + *bok* BUCK[1]]

bonus ❶ (ˈbəʊnəs) *n* **1** something given, paid, or received above what is due or expected. **2** *Chiefly Brit.* an extra dividend allotted to shareholders out of profits. **3** *Insurance, Brit.* a dividend, esp. a percentage of net profits, distributed to policyholders. [C18: from L *bonus* (adj) good]

bonus issue *n Brit.* a free issue of shares distributed among shareholders pro rata with their holdings.

bon vivant ❶ *French.* (bɔ̃ vivɑ̃) *n, pl* **bons vivants** (bɔ̃ vivɑ̃). a person who

THESAURUS

barrage, blitz, cannonade, fire, flak, fusillade, shelling, strafe

bombast *n* = **grandiloquence,** bluster, brag, braggadocio, extravagant boasting, grandiosity, hot air (*inf.*), magniloquence, pomposity, rant

bombastic *adj* = **grandiloquent,** declamatory, grandiose, high-flown, histrionic, inflated, magniloquent, pompous, ranting, turgid, verbose, windy, wordy

bona fide *adj* **1** = **genuine,** actual, authentic, honest, kosher (*inf.*), lawful, legal, legitimate, on the level (*inf.*), real, the real McCoy, true
Antonyms *adj* bogus, counterfeit, ersatz, fake, false, imitation, phoney *or* phony (*inf.*), sham

bond *n* **1** = **fastening,** band, binding, chain, cord, fetter, ligature, link, manacle, shackle, tie **2** = **tie,** affiliation, affinity, attachment, connection, link, relation, union **4** = **agreement,** compact, contract, covenant, guarantee, obligation, pledge, promise, word ◆ *vb* **11** = **hold together,** bind, connect, fasten, fix together, fuse, glue, gum, paste

bondage *n* **1** = **slavery,** enslavement, enthralment, serfdom, servitude, subjection, subjugation, thraldom, vassalage, yoke

bonny *adj* **1** *Scot. & N English dialect* = **beautiful,** comely, fair, handsome, lovely, pretty, sweet

bonus *n* **1** = **extra,** benefit, bounty, gift, gratuity, hand-out, icing on the cake, perk (*Brit. inf.*), plus, prize, reward **2** = **dividend,** commission, premium

bon vivant *n* = **gourmet,** bon viveur, epicure, epicurean, foodie, gastronome, hedonist, pleasure-seeker, voluptuary enjoys luxuries, esp. good food and drink. Also called (but not in French): **bon viveur** (ˌbɒn viːˈvɜː). [lit.: good-living (man)]

bon voyage (*French* bɔ̃ vwajaʒ) *sentence substitute.* a phrase used to wish a traveller a pleasant journey. [F, lit.: good journey]

bony ➊ (ˈbəʊnɪ) *adj* **bonier, boniest. 1** resembling or consisting of bone. **2** having many bones. **3** having prominent bones. **4** thin or emaciated.

bony fish *n* any of a class of fishes, including most of the extant species, having a skeleton of bone rather than cartilage.

bonze (bɒnz) *n* a Chinese or Japanese Buddhist priest or monk. [C16: from F, from Port. *bonzo,* from Japanese *bonsō,* from Sanskrit *bon* + *sō* priest or monk]

bonzer (ˈbɒnzə) *adj Austral & NZ sl., arch.* very good; excellent. [C20: ?from BONANZA]

boo (buː) *interj* **1** an exclamation uttered to startle or surprise someone, esp. a child. **2** a shout uttered to express disgust, dissatisfaction, or contempt. ◆ *vb* **boos, booing, booed. 3** to shout "boo" at (someone or something), esp. as an expression of disapproval.

boob (buːb) *Sl.* ◆ *n* **1** an ignorant or foolish person. **2** *Brit.* an embarrassing mistake; blunder. **3** a female breast. ◆ *vb* **4** *(intr) Brit.* to make a blunder. [C20: back formation from BOOBY]

boobialla (ˌbuːbɪˈælə) *n Austral.* **1** another name for **golden wattle** (sense 2). **2** any of various trees or shrubs of the genus *Myoporum.*

boo-boo *n, pl* **boo-boos.** an embarrassing mistake; blunder. [C20: ?from nursery talk]

boob tube *n Sl.* **1** a close-fitting strapless top, worn by women. **2** *Chiefly US & Canad.* a television receiver.

booby ➊ (ˈbuːbɪ) *n, pl* **boobies. 1** an ignorant or foolish person. **2** *Brit.* the losing player in a game. **3** any of several tropical marine birds related to the gannet. They have a straight stout bill and the plumage is white with darker markings. [C17: from Sp. *bobo,* from L *balbus* stammering]

booby prize *n* a mock prize given to the person having the lowest score.

booby trap *n* **1** a hidden explosive device primed in such a way as to be set off by an unsuspecting victim. **2** a trap for an unsuspecting person, esp. one intended as a practical joke. ◆ *vb* **booby-trap, booby-traps, booby-trapping, booby-trapped. 3** *(tr)* to set a booby trap in or on (a building or object) or for (a person).

boodle (ˈbuːdᵊl) *n Sl.* money or valuables, esp. when stolen, counterfeit, or used as a bribe. [C19: from Du. *boedel* possessions]

boogie (ˈbuːgɪ) *vb* **boogies, boogieing, boogied.** *(intr) Sl.* **1** to dance to pop music. **2** to make love. [C20: orig. African-American slang, ?from Bantu *mbugi* devilishly good]

boogie-woogie (ˈbʊgɪˈwʊgɪ, ˈbuːgɪˈwuːgɪ) *n* a style of piano jazz using a dotted bass pattern, usually with eight notes in a bar and the harmonies of the 12-bar blues. [C20: ? imit.]

boohai (buːˈhaɪ) *n* **up the boohai.** *NZ inf.* thoroughly lost. [from the remote township of *Puhoi*]

boohoo (ˌbuːˈhuː) *vb* **boohoos, boohooing, boohooed.** *(intr)* **1** to sob or pretend to sob noisily. ◆ *n, pl* **boohoos. 2** *(sometimes pl)* distressed or pretended sobbing. [C20: nursery talk]

book ➊ (bʊk) *n* **1** a number of printed or written pages bound together along one edge and usually protected by covers. **2a** a written work or composition, such as a novel, technical manual, or dictionary. **2b** *(as modifier): book reviews.* **2c** *(in combination): bookseller; bookshop; bookshelf.* **3** a number of blank or ruled sheets of paper bound together, used to record lessons, keep accounts, etc. **4** *(pl)* a record of the transactions of a business or society. **5** the libretto of an opera, musical, etc. **6** a major division of a written composition, as of a long novel or of the Bible. **7** a number of tickets, stamps, etc., fastened together along one edge. **8** a record of betting transactions. **9** (in card games) the number of tricks that must be taken by a side or player before any trick has a scoring value. **10** strict or rigid rules or standards (esp. in **by the book**). **11** a source of knowledge or authority: *the book of life.* **12 a closed book.** a person or subject that is unknown or beyond comprehension: *chemistry is a closed book to him.* **13 an open book.** a person or subject that is thoroughly understood. **14 bring to book.** to reprimand or require (someone) to give an explanation of his conduct. **15 close the books.** *Book-keeping.* to balance accounts in order to prepare a statement or report. **16 in someone's good** *(or* **bad) books.** regarded by someone with favour *(or* disfavour). **17 keep the books.** to keep written records of the finances of a business. **18 on the books. 18a** enrolled as a member. **18b** recorded. **19 the book.** *(sometimes cap.)* the Bible. **20 throw the book at. 20a** to charge with every relevant offence. **20b** to inflict the most severe punishment on. ◆ *vb* **21** to reserve (a place, passage, etc.) or engage the services of (a performer, driver, etc.) in advance. **22** *(tr)* to take the name and address of (a person guilty of a minor offence) with a view to bringing a prosecution. **23** *(tr)* (of a football referee) to take the name of (a player) who grossly infringes the rules. **24** *(tr) Arch.* to record in a book. ◆ See also **book in.** [OE *bōc;* see BEECH (its bark was used as a writing surface)]

bookbinder (ˈbʊkˌbaɪndə) *n* a person whose business is binding books.
▸ **ˈbookˌbinding** *n*

bookbindery (ˈbʊkˌbaɪndərɪ) *n, pl* **bookbinderies.** a place in which books are bound. Often shortened to **bindery.**

bookcase (ˈbʊkˌkeɪs) *n* a piece of furniture containing shelves for books.

book club *n* a club that sells books at low prices to members, usually by mail order.

book end *n* one of a pair of usually ornamental supports for holding a row of books upright.

Booker Prize (ˈbʊkə) *n* an annual prize for a work of British, Commonwealth, or Irish fiction of £20,000, awarded since 1969 by the Booker McConnell engineering company.

bookie (ˈbʊkɪ) *n Inf.* short for **bookmaker.**

book in *vb (adv)* **1** to reserve a room at a hotel. **2** *Chiefly Brit.* to register, esp. one's arrival at a hotel.

booking ➊ (ˈbʊkɪŋ) *n* **1** *Chiefly Brit.* a reservation, as of a table, room, or seat. **2** *Theatre.* an engagement of an actor or company.

bookish ➊ (ˈbʊkɪʃ) *adj* **1** fond of reading; studious. **2** consisting of or forming opinions through reading rather than experience; academic. **3** of or relating to books.
▸ **ˈbookishness** *n*

book-keeping *n* the skill or occupation of systematically recording business transactions.
▸ **ˈbook-ˌkeeper** *n*

book-learning *n* knowledge gained from books rather than from experience.

booklet ➊ (ˈbʊklɪt) *n* a thin book, esp. one having paper covers; pamphlet.

bookmaker (ˈbʊkˌmeɪkə) *n* a person who as an occupation accepts bets, esp. on horseraces, and pays out to winning betters.
▸ **ˈbookˌmaking** *n*

bookmark (ˈbʊkˌmɑːk) *n* **1** Also called: **bookmarker.** a strip of some material put between the pages of a book to mark a place. **2** *Computing.* an identifier put on a website that enables the user to return to it quickly and easily. ◆ *vb* **3** *(tr) Computing.* to identify and store (a website) so that one can return to it quickly and easily.

Book of Common Prayer *n* the official book of church services of the Church of England until 1980, when the Alternative Service Book was sanctioned.

bookplate (ˈbʊkˌpleɪt) *n* a label bearing the owner's name and a design, pasted into a book.

bookstall (ˈbʊkˌstɔːl) *n* a stall or stand where periodicals, newspapers, or books are sold.

book token *n Brit.* a gift token to be exchanged for books.

book value *n* **1** the value of an asset of a business according to its books. **2** the net capital value of an enterprise as shown by the excess of book assets over book liabilities.

bookworm (ˈbʊkˌwɜːm) *n* **1** a person devoted to reading. **2** any of various small insects that feed on the binding paste of books.

Boolean algebra (ˈbuːlɪən) *n* a system of symbolic logic devised to codify nonmathematical logical operations. It is used in computing. [C19: after George *Boole* (1815–64), E mathematician]

boom[1] ➊ (buːm) *vb* **1** to make a deep prolonged resonant sound. **2** to prosper or cause to prosper vigorously and rapidly: *business boomed.* ◆ *n* **3** a deep prolonged resonant sound. **4** a period of high economic growth. **5** any similar period of high activity. **6** the activity itself: *a baby boom.* [C15: ?from Du. *bommen,* imit.]

boom[2] (buːm) *n* **1** *Naut.* a spar to which a sail is fastened to control its position relative to the wind. **2** a pole carrying an overhead microphone and projected over a film or television set. **3** a barrier across a waterway, usually consisting of a chain of logs, to confine free-floating logs, protect a harbour from attack, etc. [C16: from Du. *boom* tree, BEAM]

boomer (ˈbuːmə) *n* **1** *Austral.* a large male kangaroo. **2** *Austral. & NZ inf.* anything exceptionally large.

boomerang ➊ (ˈbuːməˌræŋ) *n* **1** a curved flat wooden missile of native Australians, which can be made to return to the thrower. **2** an action or statement that recoils on its originator. ◆ *vb* **3** *(intr)* (of a plan, etc.)

THESAURUS

Antonyms *n* abstainer, ascetic, celibate, self-denier

bony *adj* **3** = **angular,** gangling **4** = **thin,** emaciated, gaunt, lanky, lean, rawboned, scrawny, skin and bone, skinny

booby *n* **1** = **fool,** berk *(Brit. sl.),* blockhead, dimwit, divvy *(Brit. sl.),* dork *(sl.),* duffer, dunce, fathead *(inf.),* idiot, muggins *(Brit. sl.),* numbskull *or* numskull, pillock *(Brit. sl.),* plonker *(sl.),* schmuck *(US sl.),* simpleton, twit *(inf., chiefly Brit.),* wally *(sl.)*

book *n* **1** = **work,** hardback, manual, paperback, publication, roll, scroll, textbook, title, tome, tract, volume **3** = **notebook,** album, diary, exercise book, jotter, pad ◆ *vb* **21** = **reserve,** arrange for, bill, charter, engage, line up, make reservations, organize, programme, schedule **24** *Archaic* = **record,** enter, insert, list, log, mark down, note, put down, register, write down

booking *n* **1** *Chiefly Brit.* = **reservation,** appointment, date **2** *Theatre* = **engagement,** commission, gig *(inf.)*

bookish *adj* **1** = **studious,** academic, donnish, erudite, intellectual, learned, literary, scholarly, well-read

booklet *n* = **brochure,** leaflet, pamphlet

boom[1] *vb* **1** = **bang,** blast, crash, explode, resound, reverberate, roar, roll, rumble, thunder **2** = **flourish,** develop, expand, gain, grow, increase, intensify, prosper, spurt, strengthen, succeed, swell, thrive ◆ *n* **3** = **bang,** blast, burst, clap, crash, explosion, roar, rumble, thunder **4, 5** = **expansion,** advance, boost, development, gain, growth, improvement, increase, jump, push, spurt, upsurge, upswing, upturn

Antonyms *vb* ≠ **flourish:** crash, fail, fall, slump ◆ *n* ≠ **expansion:** bust *(inf.),* collapse, crash, decline, depression, downturn, failure, hard times, recession, slump

boomerang *vb* **3** = **rebound,** backfire, come back, come home to roost, recoil, return, reverse, ricochet to recoil or return unexpectedly, causing harm to its originator. [C19: from Abor.]

boomslang ('bu:m,slæŋ) *n* a large greenish venomous arboreal snake of southern Africa. [C18: from Afrik., from *boom* tree + *slang* snake]

boon[1] ➊ (bu:n) *n* **1** something extremely useful, helpful, or beneficial; a blessing or benefit. **2** *Arch.* a favour; request. [C12: from ON *bōn* request]

boon[2] ➊ (bu:n) *adj* **1** close, special, or intimate (in **boon companion**). **2** *Arch.* jolly or convivial. [C14: from OF *bon*, from L *bonus* good]

boondocks ('bu:n,dɒks) *pl n* **the.** *US & Canad. sl.* **1** wild, desolate, or uninhabitable country. **2** a remote rural or provincial area. [C20: from Tagalog *bundok* mountain]

boong (bʊŋ) *n Austral. offens.* a Black person. [C20: from Abor.]

boongary (bu:n'gɛərɪ) *n, pl* **-ries.** a tree kangaroo of NE Queensland. [from Abor.]

boor ➊ (bʊə) *n* an ill-mannered, clumsy, or insensitive person. [OE *gebūr* dweller, farmer; see NEIGHBOUR]
▸**'boorish** *adj* ▸**'boorishly** *adv* ▸**'boorishness** *n*

boost ➊ (bu:st) *n* **1** encouragement, improvement, or help: *a boost to morale.* **2** an upward thrust or push. **3** an increase or rise. **4** the amount by which the induction pressure of a supercharged internal-combustion engine is increased. ◆ *vb (tr)* **5** to encourage, assist, or improve: *to boost morale.* **6** to lift by giving a push from below or behind. **7** to increase or raise: *to boost the voltage in an electrical circuit.* **8** to cause to rise; increase: *to boost sales.* **9** to advertise on a big scale. **10** to increase the induction pressure of (an internal-combustion engine); supercharge. [C19: from ?]

booster ('bu:stə) *n* **1** a person or thing that supports, assists, or increases power. **2** Also called: **launch vehicle.** the first stage of a multistage rocket. **3** a radio-frequency amplifier to strengthen signals. **4** another name for **supercharger. 5** short for **booster shot.**

booster shot *n Inf.* a supplementary injection of a vaccine given to maintain the immunization provided by an earlier dose.

boot[1] ➊ (bu:t) *n* **1** a strong outer covering for the foot; shoe that extends above the ankle, often to the knee. **2** *Brit.* an enclosed compartment of a car for holding luggage, etc., usually at the rear. US and Canad. name: **trunk. 3** an instrument of torture used to crush the foot and lower leg. **4** *Inf.* a kick: *he gave the door a boot.* **5 boots and all.** *Austral. & NZ inf.* making every effort. **6 die with one's boots on.** to die while still active. **7 lick the boots of.** to be servile towards. **8 put the boot in.** *Sl.* **8a** to kick a person, esp. when he is already down. **8b** to harass someone. **8c** to finish off (something) with unnecessary brutality. **9 the boot.** *Sl.* dismissal from employment; the sack. **10 the boot is on the other foot** *or* **leg.** the situation is or has now reversed. ◆ *vb (tr)* **11** to kick. **12** to equip with boots. **13** *Inf.* **13a** (often foll. by *out*) to eject forcibly. **13b** to dismiss from employment. **14** to bootstrap (a computer system). [C14 *bote*, from OF, from ?]

boot[2] (bu:t) *vb (usually impersonal)* **1** *Arch.* to be of advantage or use to (a person): *what boots it to complain?* ◆ *n* **2** *Obs.* an advantage. **3 to boot.** as well; in addition. [OE *bōt* compensation]

bootblack ('bu:t,blæk) *n* (esp. formerly) a person who shines boots and shoes.

boot camp *n* **1** *US sl.* a basic training camp for new recruits to the US Navy or Marine Corps. **2** a centre for juvenile offenders with a strict disciplinary regime, hard physical exercise, and community labour programmes.

bootee ('bu:ti:, bu:'ti:) *n* **1** a soft shoe for a baby, esp. a knitted one. **2** a boot for women and children, esp. an ankle-length one.

Boötes (bəʊ'əʊti:z) *n, Latin genitive* **Boötis** (bəʊ'əʊtɪs). a constellation in the N hemisphere containing the star Arcturus. [C17: via L from Gk: ploughman]

booth (bu:ð, bu:θ) *n, pl* **booths** (bu:ðz). **1** a stall, esp. a temporary one at a fair or market. **2** a small partially enclosed cubicle, such as one for telephoning (**telephone booth**) or for voting (**polling booth**). **3** two high-backed benches with a table between, used esp. in bars and restaurants. **4** (formerly) a temporary structure for shelter, dwelling, storage, etc. [C12: of Scand. origin]

bootjack ('bu:t,dʒæk) *n* a device that grips the heel of a boot to enable the foot to be withdrawn easily.

bootleg ➊ ('bu:t,lɛg) *vb* **bootlegs, bootlegging, bootlegged. 1** to make, carry, or sell (illicit goods, esp. alcohol). ◆ *n* **2** something made or sold illicitly, such as alcohol. **3** an illegally made copy of a CD, tape, etc. ◆ *adj* **4** produced, distributed, or sold illicitly. [C17: see BOOT[1], LEG; from smugglers carrying bottles of liquor concealed in their boots]
▸**'boot,legger** *n*

bootless ('bu:tlɪs) *adj* of little or no use; vain; fruitless. [OE *bōtlēas*, from *bōt* compensation]

bootlicker ➊ ('bu:t,lɪkə) *n Inf.* one who seeks favour by servile or ingratiating behaviour towards (someone, esp. in authority); toady.

bootstrap ('bu:t,stræp) *n* **1** a loop on a boot for pulling it on. **2 by one's (own) bootstraps.** by one's own efforts; unaided. **3a** a technique for loading the first few program instructions into a computer main store to enable the rest of the program to be introduced from an input device. **3b** *(as modifier)*: *a bootstrap loader.* **4** *Commerce.* an offer to purchase a controlling interest in a company, esp. with the intention of purchasing the remainder of the equity at a lower price. ◆ *vb* **bootstraps, bootstrapping, bootstrapped.** *(tr)* **5** to initiate (a computer system) by executing a bootstrap; boot.

booty ➊ ('bu:tɪ) *n, pl* **booties.** any valuable article or articles, esp. when obtained as plunder. [C15: from OF, from MLow G *buite* exchange]

booze ➊ (bu:z) *Inf.* ◆ *n* **1** alcoholic drink. **2** a drinking bout. ◆ *vb* **boozes, boozing, boozed. 3** *(usually intr)* to drink (alcohol), esp. in excess. [C13: from MDu. *būsen*]

boozer ➊ ('bu:zə) *n Inf.* **1** a person who is fond of drinking. **2** *Brit., Austral., & NZ.* a bar or pub.

booze-up ➊ *n Brit., Austral., & NZ sl.* a drinking spree.

boozy ('bu:zɪ) *adj* **boozier, booziest.** *Inf.* inclined to or involving excessive drinking of alcohol; drunken: *a boozy lecturer; a boozy party.*

bop (bɒp) *n* **1** a form of jazz originating in the 1940s, characterized by rhythmic and harmonic complexity and instrumental virtuosity. Originally called: **bebop.** ◆ *vb* **bops, bopping, bopped. 2** *(intr) Inf.* to dance to pop music. [C20: shortened from BEBOP]
▸**'bopper** *n*

bo-peep (,bəʊ'pi:p) *n* a game for very young children, in which one hides (esp. hiding one's face in one's hands) and reappears suddenly.

bora[1] ('bɔ:rə) *n (sometimes cap.)* a violent cold north wind blowing from the Adriatic. [C19: from It. dialect., from L *borēas* the north wind]

bora[2] ('bɔ:rə) *n* an initiation ceremony of native Australians, introducing youths to manhood. [from Abor.]

boracic (bə'ræsɪk) *adj* another word for **boric.**

borage ('bɒrɪdʒ, 'bʌrɪdʒ) *n* a Mediterranean plant with star-shaped blue flowers. The young leaves are sometimes used in salads. [C13: from OF, ?from Ar. *abū 'āraq*, lit.: father of sweat]

borate *n* ('bɔ:reɪt, -rɪt). **1** a salt or ester of boric acid. ◆ *vb* ('bɔ:reɪt), **borates, borating, borated. 2** *(tr)* to treat with borax, boric acid, or borate.

borax ('bɔ:ræks) *n, pl* **boraxes** *or* **boraces** (-rə,si:z). a soluble readily fusible white mineral in monoclinic crystalline form, occurring in alkaline soils and salt deposits. Formula: $Na_2B_4O_7.10H_2O$. [C14: from OF, from Med. L, from Ar., from Persian *būrah*]

borazon ('bɔ:rə,zɒn) *n* an extremely hard form of boron nitride. [C20: from BOR(ON) + AZO + -ON]

borborygmus (,bɔ:bə'rɪgməs) *n, pl* **borborygmi** (-maɪ). rumbling of the stomach. [C18: from Gk]

Bordeaux (bɔ:'dəʊ) *n* any of several red, white, or rosé wines produced around Bordeaux in SW France.

Bordeaux mixture *n Horticulture.* a fungicide consisting of a solution of equal quantities of copper sulphate and quicklime.

THESAURUS

booming *adj* **1 = loud**, bellowing, deafening, echoing, resonant, resounding, rich, sonorous, stentorian, thundering **2 = flourishing**, expanding, on the up and up (*Brit.*), prospering, thriving

boon[1] *n* **1 = benefit**, advantage, blessing, donation, gift, godsend, grant, gratuity, hand-out, manna from heaven, present, windfall

boon[2] *adj* **1 = intimate**, close, special

boor *n* **= lout**, barbarian, brute, bumpkin, churl, clodhopper (*inf.*), hayseed (*US & Canad. inf.*), hick (*inf., chiefly US & Canad.*), oaf, peasant, philistine, redneck (*US sl.*)

boorish *adj* **= loutish**, awkward, barbaric, bearish, churlish, clownish, coarse, crude, gross, hick (*inf., chiefly US & Canad.*), ill-bred, lubberly, oafish, rude, uncivilized, uncouth, uneducated, unrefined, vulgar
Antonyms *adj* cultured, gallant, genteel, polite, refined, sophisticated, urbane

boost *n* **1 = help**, encouragement, gee-up, hype, improvement, praise, promotion **2 = push**, heave, hoist, lift, raise, shove, thrust **3 = rise**, addition, expansion, improvement, increase, increment, jump ◆ *vb* **6 = raise**, elevate, heave, hoist, lift, push, shove, thrust **7, 8 = increase**, add to, amplify, develop, enlarge, expand, heighten, jack up, magnify, raise **9 = promote**, advance, advertise, assist, crack up (*inf.*), encourage, foster, further, gee up, hype, improve, inspire, plug (*inf.*), praise, support, sustain
Antonyms *n* ≠ **help:** condemnation, criticism, knock (*inf.*) ≠ **rise:** cut-back, decline, decrease, deterioration, fall, reduction ◆ *vb* ≠ **raise:** drop, let down, lower ≠ **increase:** cut, decrease, diminish, drop, lessen, lower, moderate, pare, reduce, scale down ≠ **promote:** condemn, criticize, hinder, hold back, knock (*inf.*)

boot[1] *vb* **11 = kick**, drive, drop-kick, knock, punt, put the boot in(to) (*sl.*), shove **13a** *Informal often with* **out = throw out**, eject, give the bum's rush (*sl.*), kick out, show one the door, throw out on one's ear (*inf.*) **13b** *Informal* **= sack** (*inf.*), dismiss, expel, give (someone) their marching orders, give the boot (*sl.*), give the bullet, give the heave *or* push (*inf.*), kick out, kiss off (*sl., chiefly US & Canad.*), oust, relegate

bootleg *adj* **4 = illicit**, black-market, contraband, illegal, outlawed, pirate, unauthorized, under-the-counter, under-the-table, unlicensed, unofficial
Antonyms *adj* authorized, legal, licensed, licit, official, on the level (*inf.*)

bootlicker *n Informal* **= toady**, crawler, fawner, flatterer, lackey, spaniel, sycophant, yes man

booty *n* **= plunder**, gains, haul, loot, pillage, prey, spoil, spoils, swag (*sl.*), takings, winnings

booze *Informal n* **1 = alcohol**, drink, firewater, grog (*inf., chiefly Austral. & NZ*), hooch *or* hootch (*inf., chiefly US & Canad.*), intoxicant, juice (*inf.*), liquor, spirits, strong drink, the bottle (*inf.*), the hard stuff (*inf.*) ◆ *vb* **3 = drink**, bevvy, carouse, drink like a fish, get drunk, get plastered, get soused, get tanked up (*inf.*), go on a binge *or* bender (*inf.*), hit the booze *or* bottle (*inf.*), imbibe, indulge, tipple, tope

boozer *n Informal* **1 = drinker**, alcoholic, drunk, drunkard, inebriate, lush (*sl.*), soak (*sl.*), sot, tippler, toper, wino (*inf.*) **2 = pub** (*inf., chiefly Brit.*), alehouse (*arch.*), bar, hostelry, inn, local (*Brit. inf.*), public house, roadhouse, taproom, tavern, watering hole (*facetious sl.*)

booze-up *n Brit., Austral., & NZ slang* **= drinking**

border ➊ ('bɔːdə) *n* **1** a band or margin around or along the edge of something. **2** the dividing line or frontier between political or geographic regions. **3** a region straddling such a boundary. **4** a design around the edge of something. **5** a long narrow strip of ground planted with flowers, shrubs, etc.: *a herbaceous border.* ◆ *vb* **6** (*tr*) to provide with a border. **7** (when *intr*, foll. by *on* or *upon*) **7a** to be adjacent (to); lie along the boundary (of). **7b** to be nearly the same (as); verge (on): *his stupidity borders on madness.* [C14: from OF, from *bort* side of a ship, of Gmc origin]

borderer ('bɔːdərə) *n* a person who lives in a border area.

borderland ('bɔːdə,lænd) *n* **1** land located on or near a frontier or boundary. **2** an indeterminate state or condition.

borderline ➊ ('bɔːdə,laɪn) *n* **1** a border; dividing line. **2** an indeterminate position between two conditions: *the borderline between friendship and love.* ◆ *adj* **3** on the edge of one category and verging on another: *a borderline failure in the exam.*

bore[1] ➊ (bɔː) *vb* **bores, boring, bored. 1** to produce (a hole) in (a material) by use of a drill, auger, or rotary cutting tool. **2** to increase the diameter of (a hole), as by turning. **3** (*tr*) to produce (a hole in the ground, tunnel, mine shaft, etc.) by digging, drilling, etc. **4** (*intr*) *Inf.* (of a horse or athlete in a race) to push other competitors out of the way. ◆ *n* **5** a hole or tunnel in the ground, esp. one drilled in search of minerals, oil, etc. **6** *Austral.* an artesian well. **7a** the hollow part of a tube or cylinder, esp. of a gun barrel. **7b** the diameter of such a hollow part; calibre. [OE *borian*]

bore[2] ➊ (bɔː) *vb* **bores, boring, bored. 1** (*tr*) to tire or make weary by being dull, repetitious, or uninteresting. ◆ *n* **2** a dull or repetitious person, activity, or state. [C18: from ?]
▸**bored** *adj* ▸**'boring** *adj*

bore[3] (bɔː) *n* a high steep-fronted wave moving up a narrow estuary, caused by the tide. [C17: from ON *bāra* wave, billow]

bore[4] (bɔː) *vb* the past tense of **bear**[1].

boreal ('bɔːrɪəl) *adj* of or relating to the north or the north wind. [C15: from L *boreās* the north wind]

Boreal ('bɔːrɪəl) *adj* of or denoting the coniferous forests in the north of the N hemisphere.

boredom ➊ ('bɔːdəm) *n* the state of being bored.

boree ('bɔːriː) *n Austral.* another name for **myall.** [from Abor.]

borer ('bɔːrə) *n* **1** a tool for boring holes. **2** any of various insects, insect larvae, molluscs, or crustaceans, that bore into plant material, esp. wood.

boric ('bɔːrɪk) *adj* of or containing boron. Also: **boracic.**

boric acid *n* a white soluble weakly acid crystalline solid used in the manufacture of heat-resistant glass and porcelain enamels, as a fireproofing material, and as a mild antiseptic. Formula: H_3BO_3. Also called: **orthoboric acid.** Systematic name: **trioxoboric(III) acid.**

borlotti bean (bɔː'lɒtɪ) *n* a variety of kidney bean with a pinkish-brown speckled skin that turns brown when cooked. [from It., plural of *borlotto* kidney bean]

born (bɔːn) *vb* **1** the past participle (in most passive uses) of **bear**[1] (sense 4). **2 not born yesterday.** not gullible or foolish. ◆ *adj* **3** possessing certain qualities from birth: *a born musician.* **4a** being at birth in a particular social status or other condition as specified: *ignobly born.* **4b** (*in combination*): *lowborn.* **5 in all one's born days.** *Inf.* so far in one's life.

> **USAGE NOTE** Care should be taken not to use *born* when *borne* is intended: *he had borne* (not *born*) *his ordeal with great courage; the following points should be borne in mind.*

born-again ('bɔːnə,gen) *adj* **1** having experienced conversion, esp. to evangelical Christianity. **2** showing the enthusiasm of one newly converted to any cause: *a born-again monetarist.* ◆ *n* **3** a person who shows fervent enthusiasm for a new-found cause, belief, etc.

borne (bɔːn) *vb* **1** the past participle of **bear**[1] (for all active uses of the verb; also for all passive uses except sense 4 unless foll. by *by*). **2 be borne in on** *or* **upon.** (of a fact, etc.) to be realized by (someone).

boron ('bɔːrɒn) *n* a very hard almost colourless crystalline metalloid element that in impure form exists as a brown amorphous powder. It occurs principally in borax and is used in hardening steel. Symbol: B; atomic no.: 5; atomic wt.: 10.81. [C19: from BOR(AX) + (CARB)ON]

boron carbide *n* a black extremely hard inert substance used as an abrasive and in control rods in nuclear reactors. Formula: B_4C.

boronia (bə'rəʊnɪə) *n* any aromatic shrub of the Australian genus *Boronia.*

boron nitride *n* a white inert crystalline solid, used as a refractory, high-temperature lubricant and insulator, and heat shield.

borosilicate glass (,bɔːrəʊ'sɪlɪkɪt, -,keɪt) *n* any of a range of heat- and chemical-resistant glasses, such as Pyrex, prepared by fusing together oxides of boron and silicon and, usually, a metal oxide.

borough ('bʌrə) *n* **1** a town, esp. (in Britain) one that forms the constituency of an MP or that was originally incorporated by royal charter. See also **burgh. 2** any of the 32 constituent divisions of Greater London. **3** any of the five constituent divisions of New York City. **4** (in the US) a self-governing incorporated municipality. [OE *burg*]

borrow ➊ ('bɒrəʊ) *vb* **1** to obtain or receive (something, such as money) on loan for temporary use, intending to give it, or something equivalent, back to the lender. **2** to adopt (ideas, words, etc.) from another source; appropriate. **3** *Not standard.* to lend. **4** (*intr*) *Golf.* to putt the ball uphill of the direct path to the hole: *make sure you borrow enough.* [OE *borgian*]
▸**'borrower** *n*

> **USAGE NOTE** The use of *off* after *borrow* was formerly considered incorrect, but is now acceptable in informal contexts.

borscht (bɔːʃt), **borsch** (bɔːʃ), *or* **borshch** (bɔːʃtʃ) *n* a Russian and Polish soup based on beetroot. [from Russian *borshch*]

borscht belt *n Inf., chiefly US.* a resort area of the Catskill Mountains in New York State, popular with Jewish holiday-makers; its hotels and nightclubs (the **borscht circuit**) are regarded as a training ground for entertainers.

borstal ('bɔːstəl) *n* **1** (formerly, in Britain) an establishment in which offenders aged 15 to 21 could be detained for corrective training. Since 1982 they have been replaced by **young offender institutions. 2** a similar establishment in Australia and New Zealand. [C20: after *Borstal*, village in Kent where the first institution was founded]

bort, boart (bɔːt), *or* **bortz** (bɔːts) *n* an inferior grade of diamond used for cutting and drilling or, in powdered form, as an industrial abrasive. [OE *gebrot* fragment]

borzoi ('bɔːzɔɪ) *n, pl* **borzois.** a tall fast-moving breed of dog with a long coat. Also called: **Russian wolfhound.** [C19: Russian, lit.: swift]

boscage *or* **boskage** ('bɒskɪdʒ) *n Literary.* a mass of trees and shrubs; thicket. [C14: from OF *bosc*, prob. of Gmc origin; see BUSH[1], -AGE]

bosh (bɒʃ) *n Inf.* empty or meaningless talk or opinions; nonsense. [C19: from Turkish *boş* empty]

bosk (bɒsk) *n Literary.* a small wood of bushes and small trees. [C13: var. of *busk* BUSH[1]]

bosky ('bɒskɪ) *adj* **boskier, boskiest.** *Literary.* containing or consisting of bushes or thickets.

bo's'n ('bəʊsᵊn) *n Naut.* a variant spelling of **boatswain.**

bosom ➊ ('bʊzəm) *n* **1** the chest or breast of a person, esp. the female breasts. **2** the part of a woman's dress, coat, etc., that covers the chest. **3** a protective centre or part: *the bosom of the family.* **4** the breast considered as the seat of emotions. **5** (*modifier*) very dear; intimate: *a bosom friend.* ◆ *vb* (*tr*) **6** to embrace. **7** to conceal or carry in the bosom. [OE *bōsm*]

bosomy ('bʊzəmɪ) *adj* (of a woman) having large breasts.

boson ('bəʊzɒn) *n* any of a group of elementary particles, such as a photon or pion, that has zero or integral spin and does not obey the Pauli exclusion principle. Cf. **fermion.** [C20: after S. N. *Bose* (1894–1974), Indian physicist]

boss[1] ➊ (bɒs) *Inf.* ◆ *n* **1** a person in charge of or employing others. **2** *Chiefly US.* a professional politician who controls a political organization, often using devious or illegal methods. ◆ *vb* (*tr*) **3** to employ, supervise, or be in charge of. **4** (usually foll. by *around* or *about*) to be domineering or overbearing towards (others). ◆ *adj* **5** *Sl.* excellent; fine: *a boss hand at carpentry; that's boss!* [C19: from Du. *baas* master]

THESAURUS

spree, bevvy (*dialect*), drink, session (*inf.*), wet (*inf.*)

border *n* **1** = **edge**, bound, boundary, bounds, brim, brink, confine, confines, flange, hem, limit, limits, lip, margin, pale, rim, skirt, verge **2** = **frontier**, borderline, boundary, line, march ◆ *vb* **6** = **edge**, bind, decorate, fringe, hem, rim, trim **7a** *foll. by* **on** = **adjoin**, abut, connect, contact, impinge, join, march, neighbour, touch, verge on **7b** *foll. by* **on** = **come close to**, approach, approximate, be like, be similar to, come near, echo, match, parallel, resemble

borderline *adj* **3** = **marginal**, ambivalent, doubtful, equivocal, indecisive, indefinite, indeterminate, inexact, unclassifiable

bore[1] *vb* **1** = **drill**, gouge out, penetrate, perforate, pierce **3** = **tunnel**, burrow, mine, sink ◆ *n* **5** = **hole**, borehole, drill hole, shaft, tunnel

bore[2] *vb* **1** = **tire**, annoy, be tedious, bother, exhaust, fatigue, jade, pall on, pester, send to sleep, trouble, vex, wear out, weary, worry ◆ *n* **2** = **nuisance**, bother, drag (*inf.*), dull person, pain (*inf.*), pain in the neck (*inf.*), pest, tiresome person, yawn (*inf.*)
Antonyms *vb* ≠ **tire:** amuse, divert, engross, excite, fascinate, hold the attention of, interest, stimulate

bored *adj* **1** = **fed up**, listless, tired, uninterested, wearied

boredom *n* = **tedium**, apathy, doldrums, dullness, ennui, flatness, irksomeness, monotony, sameness, tediousness, weariness, world-weariness
Antonyms *n* amusement, entertainment, excitement, interest, stimulation

boring *adj* **1** = **uninteresting**, dead, dull, flat, ho-hum (*inf.*), humdrum, insipid, mind-numbing, monotonous, old, repetitious, routine, stale, tedious, tiresome, tiring, unexciting, unvaried, wearisome

borrow *vb* **1** = **take on loan**, blag (*sl.*), cadge, mooch (*sl.*), scrounge (*inf.*), take and return, touch (someone) for (*sl.*), use temporarily **2** = **steal**, acquire, adopt, appropriate, copy, filch, imitate, obtain, pilfer, pirate, plagiarize, simulate, take, use, usurp
Antonyms *vb* ≠ **take on loan:** advance, give, lend, loan, provide, return, supply

bosom *n* **1** = **breast**, bust, chest **3** = **midst**, centre, circle, core, protection, shelter **4** = **feelings**, affections, emotions, heart, sentiments, soul, spirit, sympathies ◆ *modifier* **5** = **intimate**, boon, cherished, close, confidential, dear, very dear

boss[1] *n* **1** = **head**, administrator, chief, director, employer, executive, foreman, gaffer (*inf.*, *chiefly Brit.*), governor (*inf.*), kingpin, leader, manager, master, overseer, owner, superinten-

boss[2] ❶ (bɒs) *n* **1** a knob, stud, or other circular rounded protuberance, esp. an ornamental one on a vault, a ceiling, or a shield. **2** an area of increased thickness, usually cylindrical, that strengthens or provides room for a locating device on a shaft, hub of a wheel, etc. **3** a rounded mass of igneous rock. ◆ *vb (tr)* **4** to ornament with bosses; emboss. [C13: from OF *boce*; rel. to It. *bozza* metal knob, swelling]

bossa nova (ˈbɒsə ˈnəʊvə) *n* **1** a dance similar to the samba, originating in Brazil. **2** a piece of music composed for or in the rhythm of this dance. [C20: from Port., lit.: new voice]

bosset (ˈbɒsɪt) *n* either of the rudimentary antlers found in young deer. [C19: from F *bossette* a small protuberance, from *bosse* BOSS[2]]

bossy ❶ (ˈbɒsɪ) *adj* **bossier, bossiest.** *Inf.* domineering, overbearing, or authoritarian.
▸**ˈbossily** *adv* ▸**ˈbossiness** *n*

bosun (ˈbəʊsᵊn) *n Naut.* a variant spelling of **boatswain.**

bot[1] *or* **bott** (bɒt) *n* **1** the larva of a botfly, which typically develops inside the body of a horse, sheep, or man. **2** any similar larva. [C15: prob. from Low G; rel. to Du. *bot*, from ?]

bot[2] (bɒt) *Austral. inf.* ◆ *vb* **bots, botting, botted. 1** to scrounge or borrow. ◆ *n* **2** a scrounger. **3 on the bot (for).** wanting to scrounge. [C20: ?from BOTFLY, alluding to its bite; see BITE (sense 9)]

bot. *abbrev. for:* **1** botanical. **2** botany. **3** bottle.

botanical (bəˈtænɪkᵊl) *or* **botanic** *adj* **1** of or relating to botany or plants. ◆ *n* **2** any drug or pesticide that is made from parts of a plant. [C17: from Med. L, from Gk *botanē* plant, pasture]
▸**boˈtanically** *adv*

botanize *or* **botanise** (ˈbɒtəˌnaɪz) *vb* **botanizes, botanizing, botanized** *or* **botanises, botanising, botanised. 1** *(intr)* to collect or study plants. **2** *(tr)* to explore and study the plants in (an area or region).

botany (ˈbɒtənɪ) *n, pl* **botanies. 1** the study of plants, including their classification, structure, physiology, ecology, and economic importance. **2** the plant life of a particular region or time. **3** the biological characteristics of a particular group of plants. [C17: from BOTANICAL; cf. ASTRONOMY, ASTRONOMICAL]
▸**ˈbotanist** *n*

Botany wool *n* fine wool from merino sheep. [C19: from *Botany* Bay, Australia]

botch ❶ (bɒtʃ) *vb (tr; often foll. by up)* **1** to spoil through clumsiness or ineptitude. **2** to repair badly or clumsily. ◆ *n* **3** a badly done piece of work or repair (esp. in **make a botch of**). [C14: from ?]
▸**ˈbotcher** *n* ▸**ˈbotchy** *adj*

botfly (ˈbɒtˌflaɪ) *n, pl* **botflies.** any of various stout-bodied hairy dipterous flies, the larvae of which are parasites of man, sheep, and horses.

both (bəʊθ) *determiner* **1a** the two; two considered together: *both dogs were dirty.* **1b** *(as pron): both are to blame.* ◆ *conj* **2** *(coordinating)* used preceding words, phrases, or clauses joined by *and: both Ellen and Keith enjoyed the play; both new and exciting.* [C12: from ON *bāthir*]

bother ❶ (ˈbɒðə) *vb* **1** *(tr)* to give annoyance, pain, or trouble to. **2** *(tr)* to trouble (a person) by repeatedly disturbing; pester. **3** *(intr)* to take the time or trouble; concern oneself: *don't bother to come with me.* **4** *(tr)* to make (a person) alarmed or confused. ◆ *n* **5** a state of worry, trouble, or confusion. **6** a person or thing that causes fuss, trouble, or annoyance. **7** *Inf.* a disturbance or fight; trouble (esp. in **a spot of bother**). ◆ *interj* **8** *Chiefly Brit.* an exclamation of slight annoyance. [C18: ?from Irish Gaelic *bodhar* deaf, vexed]

botheration (ˌbɒðəˈreɪʃən) *n, interj Inf.* another word for **bother** (senses 5, 8).

bothersome ❶ (ˈbɒðəsəm) *adj* causing bother; troublesome.

bothy (ˈbɒθɪ) *n, pl* **bothies.** *Chiefly Scot.* **1** a cottage or hut. **2** a farmworker's summer quarters. [C18: ? rel. to BOOTH]

bo tree (bəʊ) *n* another name for the **peepul.** [C19: from Sinhalese, from Pali *bodhitaru* tree of wisdom]

bott (bɒt) *n* a variant spelling of **bot**[1].

bottle (ˈbɒtᵊl) *n* **1a** a vessel, often of glass and typically cylindrical with a narrow neck, for containing liquids. **1b** *(as modifier): a bottle rack.* **2** Also called: **bottleful.** the amount such a vessel will hold. **3** *Brit. sl.* courage; nerve; initiative. **4 the bottle.** *Inf.* drinking of alcohol, esp. to excess. ◆ *vb* **bottles, bottling, bottled.** *(tr)* **5** to put or place in a bottle or bottles. **6** to store (gas) in a portable container under pressure. ◆ See also **bottle out, bottle up.** [C14: from OF *botaille*, from Med. L *butticula*, from LL *buttis* cask]

bottle bank *n* a large container into which the public may throw glass bottles for recycling.

bottlebrush (ˈbɒtᵊlˌbrʌʃ) *n* **1** a cylindrical brush on a thin shaft, used for cleaning bottles. **2** Also called: **callistemon.** any of various Australian shrubs or trees having dense spikes of large red flowers with protruding brushlike stamens.

bottled (*or* **bottle**) **gas** *n* butane or propane liquefied under pressure in portable metal containers for use in camping stoves, blowtorches, etc.

bottle-feed *vb* **bottle-feeds, bottle-feeding, bottle-fed.** to feed (a baby) with milk from a bottle.

bottle glass *n* glass used for making bottles, consisting of a silicate of sodium, calcium, and aluminium.

bottle green *n, adj* (of) a dark green colour.

bottle-jack *n NZ.* a large jack used for heavy lifts.

bottleneck ❶ (ˈbɒtᵊlˌnɛk) *n* **1a** a narrow stretch of road or a junction at which traffic is or may be held up. **1b** the hold-up. **2** something that holds up progress.

bottlenose dolphin (ˈbɒtᵊlˌnəʊz) *n* a type of dolphin with a bottle-shaped snout.

bottle out *vb (intr, adv) Brit. sl.* to lose one's nerve.

bottle party *n* a party to which guests bring drink.

bottler (ˈbɒtᵊlə) *n Austral. & NZ inf.* an exceptional or outstanding person or thing.

bottle shop *n Austral. & NZ.* a shop selling alcohol in unopened containers for consumption elsewhere. Also called (Austral.): **bottle store.**

bottle tree *n* any of several Australian trees that have a bottle-shaped swollen trunk.

bottle up ❶ *vb (tr, adv)* **1** to restrain (powerful emotion). **2** to keep (an army or other force) contained or trapped.

bottom ❶ (ˈbɒtəm) *n* **1** the lowest, deepest, or farthest removed part of a thing: *the bottom of a hill.* **2** the least important or successful position: *the bottom of a class.* **3** the ground underneath a sea, lake, or river. **4** the inner depths of a person's true feelings (esp. in **from the bottom of one's heart**). **5** the underneath part of a thing. **6** *Naut.* the parts of a vessel's hull that are under water. **7** (in literary or commercial contexts) a boat or ship. **8** *(often pl) US & Canad.* the low land bordering a river. **9** (esp. of horses) staying power; stamina. **10** *Inf.* the buttocks. **11** importance, seriousness, or influence: *his views have weight and bottom.* **12 at bottom.** in reality; basically. **13 be at the bottom of.** to be the ultimate cause of. **14 get to the bottom of.** to discover the real truth about. ◆ *adj (prenominal)* **15** lowest or last. **16 bet** (*or* **put**) **one's bottom dollar on.** to be absolutely sure of. **17** of, relating to, or situated at the bottom. **18** fundamental; basic. ◆ *vb* **19** *(tr)* to provide (a chair, etc.) with a bottom or seat. **20** *(tr)* to discover the full facts or truth of; fathom. **21** (usually foll. by *on* or *upon*) to base or be founded (on an idea, etc.). [OE *botm*]

bottom drawer *n Brit.* a young woman's collection of linen, cutlery, etc., made in anticipation of marriage. US, Canad., and NZ equivalent: **hope chest.**

bottoming (ˈbɒtəmɪŋ) *n* the lowest level of foundation material for a road or other structure.

bottomless ❶ (ˈbɒtəmlɪs) *adj* **1** having no bottom. **2** unlimited; inexhaustible. **3** very deep.

bottom line *n* **1** the last line of a financial statement that shows the net profit or loss of a company or organization. **2** the conclusion or main point of a process, discussion, etc.

bottom out *vb (intr, adv)* to reach the lowest point and level out.

bottomry (ˈbɒtəmrɪ) *n, pl* **bottomries.** *Maritime law.* a contract whereby the owner of a ship borrows money to enable the vessel to complete the voyage and pledges the ship as security for the loan. [C16: from Du. *bodemerij*, from *bodem* BOTTOM (hull of a ship) + *-erij* -RY]

bottom-up processing *n* a processing technique, either in the brain or in a computer, in which incoming information is analysed in successive steps and later-stage processing does not affect processing in earlier stages.

botulism (ˈbɒtjʊˌlɪzəm) *n* severe, often fatal, poisoning resulting from

THESAURUS

dent, supervisor ◆ *vb* **3** = **be in charge,** administrate, call the shots, call the tune, command, control, direct, employ, manage, oversee, run, superintend, supervise, take charge **4** *usually foll. by* **around** *or* **about** = **domineer,** bully, dominate, oppress, order, overbear, push around (*sl.*), put upon, ride roughshod over, tyrannize

boss[2] *n* **1** = **stud,** knob, nub, nubble, point, protuberance, tip

bossy *adj Informal* = **domineering,** arrogant, authoritarian, autocratic, despotic, dictatorial, hectoring, high-handed, imperious, lordly, overbearing, tyrannical

botch *vb* **1** = **spoil,** blunder, bodge (*inf.*), bungle, butcher, cobble, cock up (*Brit. sl.*), make a pig's ear of (*inf.*), mar, mess up, mismanage, muff, screw up (*inf.*) ◆ *n* **3** = **mess,** blunder, bungle, bungling, cock-up (*Brit. sl.*), failure, hash, miscarriage, pig's breakfast (*inf.*), pig's ear (*inf.*)

bother *vb* **1** = **trouble,** annoy, concern, dismay, distress, disturb, gall, inconvenience, irritate, put out, upset, vex, worry **2** = **pester,** bend someone's ear (*inf.*), get on one's nerves (*inf.*), get on one's wick (*Brit. sl.*), harass, hassle (*inf.*), nag, nark (*Brit., Austral., & NZ sl.*), plague ◆ *n* **5** = **trouble,** aggravation, annoyance, difficulty, grief (*inf.*), hassle (*inf.*), inconvenience, irritation, strain, vexation, worry **6** = **nuisance,** pest, problem
Antonyms *vb* ≠ **trouble:** aid, assist, facilitate, further, help, relieve, succour, support ◆ *n* ≠ **trouble:** advantage, aid, benefit, comfort, convenience, help, service, use

bothersome *adj* = **troublesome,** aggravating, annoying, distressing, exasperating, inconvenient, irritating, tiresome, vexatious, vexing
Antonyms *adj* appropriate, beneficial, commodious, convenient, handy, helpful, serviceable, useful

bottleneck *n* = **hold-up,** block, blockage, impediment, jam, obstacle, obstruction

bottle up *vb* **1** = **suppress,** check, contain, curb, keep back, restrict, shut in

bottom *n* **1** = **lowest part,** base, basis, bed, deepest part, depths, floor, foot, foundation, groundwork, pedestal, support **5** = **underside,** lower side, sole, underneath **10** *Informal* = **buttocks,** arse (*taboo sl.*), ass (*US & Canad. taboo sl.*), backside, behind (*inf.*), bum (*Brit. sl.*), buns (*US sl.*), butt (*US & Canad. inf.*), derrière (*euphemistic*), jacksy (*Brit. sl.*), posterior, rear, rear end, rump, seat, tail (*inf.*) ◆ *adj* **15** = **lowest,** last **17** = **undermost,** base, basement, ground
Antonyms *n* ≠ **lowest part:** cover, crown, height, lid, peak, summit, surface, top ◆ *adj* ≠ **undermost:** higher, highest, top, upper

bottomless *adj* **2** = **unlimited,** boundless, fathomless, immeasurable, inexhaustible, infinite, unfathomable the potent bacterial toxin, **botulin,** produced in imperfectly preserved food, etc. [C19: from G *Botulismus,* lit.: sausage poisoning, from L *botulus* sausage]

bouclé ('bu:kleɪ) *n* **1** a curled or looped yarn or fabric giving a thick knobbly effect. ◆ *adj* **2** of or designating such a yarn or fabric. [C19: from F *bouclé* curly, from *boucle* a curl]

boudoir ('bu:dwɑ:, -dwɔ:) *n* a woman's bedroom or private sitting room. [C18: from F, lit.: room for sulking in, from *bouder* to sulk]

bouffant ('bu:fɔ:ŋ) *adj* **1** (of a hairstyle) having extra height and width through backcombing; puffed out. **2** (of sleeves, skirts, etc.) puffed out. [C20: from F, from *bouffer* to puff up]

bougainvillea (ˌbu:gən'vɪlɪə) *n* a tropical woody climbing plant having inconspicuous flowers surrounded by showy red or purple bracts. [C19: NL, after L. A. de *Bougainville* (1729–1811), F navigator]

bough (baʊ) *n* any of the main branches of a tree. [OE *bōg* arm, twig]

bought (bɔ:t) *vb* the past tense and past participle of **buy.**

bougie ('bu:ʒi:, bu:'ʒi:) *n Med.* a slender semiflexible instrument for inserting into body passages such as the rectum or urethra to introduce medication, etc. [C18: from F, orig. a wax candle from *Bougie* (Bujiya), Algeria]

bouillabaisse (ˌbu:jə'bɛs) *n* a rich stew or soup of fish and vegetables. [C19: from F, from Provençal *bouiabaisso,* lit.: boil down]

bouillon ('bu:jɒn) *n* a plain unclarified broth or stock. [C18: from F, from *bouillir* to BOIL[1]]

boulder ('bəʊldə) *n* a smooth rounded mass of rock that has been shaped by erosion. [C13: prob. from ON; cf. OSwedish *bulder* rumbling + *sten* STONE]

boulder clay *n* an unstratified glacial deposit consisting of fine clay, boulders, and pebbles.

boule ('bu:li:) *n* **1** the senate of an ancient Greek city-state. **2** the parliament in modern Greece. [C19: from Gk *boulē* senate]

boules *French.* (bul) *n* (*functioning as sing*) a game, popular in France, in which metal bowls are thrown to land as near as possible to a target ball. [pl. of *boule* BALL[1]: see BOWL[2]]

boulevard ('bu:lvɑ:, -vɑ:d) *n* a wide usually tree-lined road in a city. [C18: from F, from MDu. *bolwerc* BULWARK; so called because orig. often built on the ruins of an old rampart]

boulle, boule, *or* **buhl** (bu:l) *adj* **1** denoting or relating to a type of marquetry of patterned inlays of brass and tortoiseshell, etc. ◆ *n* **2** something ornamented with such marquetry. [C18: after A. C. *Boulle* (1642–1732), F cabinet-maker]

boult (bəʊlt) *vb* a variant spelling of **bolt**[2].

bounce ❶ (baʊns) *vb* **bounces, bouncing, bounced. 1** (*intr*) (of a ball, etc.) to rebound from an impact. **2** (*tr*) to cause (a ball, etc.) to hit a solid surface and spring back. **3** to move or cause to move suddenly, excitedly, or violently; spring. **4** *Sl.* (of a bank) to send (a cheque) back or (of a cheque) to be sent back by a bank to a payee unredeemed because of lack of funds in the drawer's account. **5** (*tr*) *Sl.* to force (a person) to leave a place or job; throw out; eject. ◆ *n* **6** the action of rebounding from an impact. **7** a leap; jump; bound. **8** the quality of being able to rebound; springiness. **9** *Inf.* vitality; vigour; resilience. **10** *Brit.* swagger or impudence. [C13: prob. imit.; cf. Low G *bunsen* to beat, Du. *bonken* to thump]

bounce back *vb* (*intr, adv*) to recover one's health, good spirits, confidence, etc., easily.

bouncer ('baʊnsə) *n Sl.* a man employed at a club, disco, etc., to eject drunks or troublemakers.

bouncing ❶ ('baʊnsɪŋ) *adj* (when *postpositive,* foll. by *with*) vigorous and robust (esp. in **a bouncing baby**).

bouncy ❶ ('baʊnsɪ) *adj* **bouncier, bounciest. 1** lively, exuberant, or self-confident. **2** having the capability or quality of bouncing: *a bouncy ball.* **3** responsive to bouncing; springy: *a bouncy bed.*

Bouncy Castle *n Trademark.* a large inflatable model, usually of a castle, on which children may bounce at fairs, etc.

bound[1] ❶ (baʊnd) *vb* **1** the past tense and past participle of **bind.** ◆ *adj* **2** in bonds or chains; tied as with a rope. **3** (*in combination*) restricted; confined: *housebound.* **4** (*postpositive;* foll. by an infinitive) destined; sure; certain: *it's bound to happen.* **5** (*postpositive;* often foll. by *by*) compelled or obliged. **6** *Rare.* constipated. **7** (of a book) secured within a cover or binding. **8** *Logic.* (of a variable) occurring within the scope of a quantifier. Cf. **free** (sense 18). **9 bound up with.** closely or inextricably linked with.

bound[2] ❶ (baʊnd) *vb* **1** to move forwards by leaps or jumps. **2** to bounce; spring away from an impact. ◆ *n* **3** a jump upwards or forwards. **4** a bounce, as of a ball. [C16: from OF *bond* a leap]

bound[3] ❶ (baʊnd) *vb* **1** (*tr*) to place restrictions on; limit. **2** (when *intr,* foll. by *on*) to form a boundary of. ◆ *n* **3** See **bounds.** [C13: from OF *bonde,* from Med. L *bodina*]

bound[4] (baʊnd) *adj* **a** (*postpositive;* often foll. by *for*) going or intending to go towards: *bound for Jamaica; homeward bound.* **b** (*in combination*): *northbound traffic.* [C13: from ON *buinn,* p.p. of *būa* to prepare]

boundary ❶ ('baʊndərɪ, -drɪ) *n, pl* **boundaries. 1** something that indicates the farthest limit, as of an area; border. **2** *Cricket.* **2a** the marked limit of the playing area. **2b** a stroke that hits the ball beyond this limit. **2c** the four or six runs scored with such a stroke.

boundary rider *n Austral.* an employee on a sheep or cattle station whose job is to maintain fences.

bounden ('baʊndən) *adj* morally obligatory (arch. except in **bounden duty**). [arch. p.p. of BIND]

bounder ('baʊndə) *n Old-fashioned Brit. sl.* a morally reprehensible person; cad.

boundless ❶ ('baʊndlɪs) *adj* unlimited; vast: *boundless energy.*
▸**'boundlessly** *adv*

bounds ❶ (baʊndz) *pl n* **1** (*sometimes sing*) a limit; boundary (esp. in **know no bounds**). **2** something that restrains or confines, esp. the standards of a society: *within the bounds of modesty.* ◆ See also **out of bounds.**

bounteous ('baʊntɪəs) *adj Literary.* **1** giving freely; generous. **2** plentiful; abundant.
▸**'bounteously** *adv* ▸**'bounteousness** *n*

bountiful ❶ ('baʊntɪfʊl) *adj* **1** plentiful; ample (esp. in **a bountiful supply**). **2** giving freely; generous.
▸**'bountifully** *adv*

bounty ❶ ('baʊntɪ) *n, pl* **bounties. 1** generosity; liberality. **2** a generous gift. **3** a payment made by a government, as, formerly, to a sailor on enlisting or to a soldier after a campaign. **4** any reward or premium. [C13 (in the sense: goodness): from OF, from L, from *bonus* good]

bouquet ❶ (bu:'keɪ) *n* **1** a bunch of flowers, esp. a large carefully arranged one. **2** the characteristic aroma or fragrance of a wine or liqueur. **3** a compliment or expression of praise. [C18: from F: thicket, from OF *bosc* forest]

bouquet garni ('bu:keɪ gɑ:'ni:) *n, pl* **bouquets garnis** ('bu:keɪz gɑ:'ni:). a bunch of herbs tied together and used for flavouring soups, stews, etc. [C19: from F, lit.: garnished bouquet]

bourbon ('bɜ:bən) *n* a whiskey distilled, chiefly in the US, from maize, esp. one containing at least 51 per cent maize. [C19: after *Bourbon* county, Kentucky, where it was first made]

bourdon ('bʊədən, 'bɔ:dən) *n* **1** a bass organ stop. **2** the drone of a bagpipe. [C14: from OF: drone (of a musical instrument), imit.]

bourgeois ❶ ('bʊəʒwɑ:) *Often disparaging.* ◆ *n, pl* **bourgeois. 1** a member of the middle class, esp. one regarded as being conservative and materialistic or capitalistic. **2** a mediocre, unimaginative, or materialistic person. ◆ *adj* **3** characteristic of, relating to, or comprising the middle class. **4** conservative or materialistic in outlook. **5** (in Marxist thought) dominated by capitalists or capitalist interests. [C16: from OF *borjois, burgeis* burgher, citizen; see BURGESS]
▸**bourgeoise** ('bʊəʒwɑ:z, bʊə'ʒwɑ:z) *fem n*

bourgeoisie (ˌbʊəʒwɑ:'zi:) *n* **the. 1** the middle classes. **2** (in Marxist thought) the capitalist ruling class. The bourgeoisie owns the means of production, through which it exploits the working class.

bourgeon ('bɜ:dʒən) *n, vb* a variant spelling of **burgeon.**

bourn[1] *or* **bourne** (bɔ:n) *n Arch.* **1** a destination; goal. **2** a boundary. [C16: from OF *borne;* see BOUND[3]]

bourn[2] (bɔ:n) *n Chiefly southern Brit.* a stream. [C16: from OF *bodne* limit; see BOUND[3]]

bourrée ('bʊəreɪ) *n* **1** a traditional French dance in fast duple time. **2** a piece of music in the rhythm of this dance. [C18: from F]

THESAURUS

bounce *vb* **1** = **rebound**, bob, bound, bump, jounce, jump, leap, recoil, resile, ricochet, spring, thump **5** *Slang* = **throw out**, boot out (*inf.*), eject, fire (*inf.*), kick out (*inf.*), oust, relegate ◆ *n* **8** = **springiness**, bound, elasticity, give, rebound, recoil, resilience, spring **9** *Informal* = **life**, animation, brio, dynamism, energy, go (*inf.*), liveliness, pep, vigour, vitality, vivacity, zip (*inf.*)

bouncing *adj* = **lively**, alive and kicking, blooming, bonny, fighting fit, fit as a fiddle (*inf.*), healthy, robust, thriving, vigorous

bouncy *adj* **1** = **lively**, bubbly, confident, ebullient, effervescent, enthusiastic, exuberant, full of beans (*inf.*), irrepressible, vivacious, zestful **3** = **springy**, elastic

Antonyms *adj* ≠ **lively:** dull, listless, unenthusiastic ≠ **springy:** flat, inelastic

bound[1] *adj* **2** = **tied**, cased, fastened, fixed, pinioned, secured, tied up **4** = **certain**, destined, doomed, fated, sure **5** = **obliged**, beholden, committed, compelled, constrained, duty-bound, forced, obligated, pledged, required

bound[2] *vb, n* **1, 3** = **leap**, bob, caper, frisk, gambol, hurdle, jump, lope, pounce, prance, skip, spring, vault ◆ *vb, n* **2, 4** = **bounce**

bound[3] *vb* **1, 2** = **limit**, circumscribe, confine, define, delimit, demarcate, encircle, enclose, hem in, restrain, restrict, surround

boundary *n* **1** = **limits**, barrier, border, borderline, bounds, brink, confines, edge, extremity, fringe, frontier, march, margin, pale, precinct, termination, verge

boundless *adj* = **unlimited**, endless, illimitable, immeasurable, immense, incalculable, inexhaustible, infinite, limitless, measureless, unbounded, unconfined, unending, untold, vast

Antonyms *adj* bounded, confined, limited, little, restricted, small

bounds *pl n* **1** = **boundary**, border, confine, edge, extremity, fringe, limit, line, march, margin, pale, periphery, rim, termination, verge

bountiful *adj* **1** = **plentiful**, abundant, ample, bounteous, copious, exuberant, lavish, luxuriant, plenteous, prolific **2** = **generous**, beneficent, bounteous, liberal, magnanimous, munificent, open-handed, princely, prodigal, unstinting

bounty *n* **1** = **generosity**, almsgiving, assistance, beneficence, benevolence, charity, kindness, largesse *or* largess, liberality, openhandedness, philanthropy **2** = **gift**, bonus, donation, grant, gratuity, largesse *or* largess, present **4** = **reward**, meed (*arch.*), premium, recompense

bouquet *n* **1** = **bunch of flowers**, boutonniere, buttonhole, corsage, garland, nosegay, posy, spray, wreath **2** = **aroma**, fragrance, perfume, redolence, savour, scent

bourgeois *adj* **3, 4** = **middle-class**, conven-

Bourse (buəs) *n* a stock exchange of continental Europe, esp. Paris. [C19: from F, lit.: purse, from Med. L *bursa*, ult. from Gk: leather]

boustrophedon (ˌbaʊstrəˈfiːdən) *adj* having alternate lines written from right to left and from left to right. [C17: from Gk, lit.: turning as in ploughing with oxen, from *bous* ox + *strephein* to turn]

bout ❶ (baʊt) *n* **1a** a period of time spent doing something, such as drinking. **1b** a period of illness. **2** a contest or fight, esp. a boxing or wrestling match. [C16: var. of obs. *bought* turn]

boutique (buːˈtiːk) *n* **1** a shop, esp. a small one selling fashionable clothes and other items. **2** (*modifier*) of or denoting a small specialized producer or business: *a boutique operation.* [C18: from F, ult. from Gk *apothēkē* storehouse]

boutonniere (ˌbuːtɒnɪˈɛə) *n* the US name for **buttonhole** (sense 2). [C19: from F: buttonhole]

bouzouki (buːˈzuːkɪ) *n* a Greek long-necked stringed musical instrument related to the mandolin. [C20: from Mod. Gk, ?from Turkish *büjük* large]

bovine ❶ (ˈbəʊvaɪn) *adj* **1** of or relating to cattle. **2** (of people) dull; sluggish; stolid. [C19: from LL *bovīnus*, from L *bōs* ox, cow]
▸ˈ**bovinely** *adv*

bovine somatotrophin *n* the full name for **BST** (sense 1).

bovine spongiform encephalopathy *n* the full name for **BSE**.

Bovril (ˈbɒvrɪl) *n Trademark.* a concentrated beef extract, used for flavouring, as a stock, etc.

bovver (ˈbɒvə) *n Brit. sl.* **a** rowdiness, esp. caused by gangs of teenage youths. **b** (*as modifier*): *a bovver boy.* [C20: sl. pronunciation of BOTHER]

bow[1] ❶ (baʊ) *vb* **1** to lower (one's head) or bend (one's knee or body) as a sign of respect, greeting, assent, or shame. **2** to bend or cause to bend. **3** (*intr;* usually foll. by *to* or *before*) to comply or accept: *bow to the inevitable.* **4** (*tr;* foll. by *in, out, to,* etc.) to usher (someone) in or out with bows and deference. **5** (*tr;* usually foll. by *down*) to bring (a person, nation, etc.) to a state of submission. **6 bow and scrape.** to behave in an excessively deferential or obsequious way. ◆ *n* **7** a lowering or inclination of the head or body as a mark of respect, greeting, or assent. **8 take a bow.** to acknowledge or receive applause or praise. ◆ See also **bow out.** [OE *būgan*]

bow[2] (bəʊ) *n* **1** a weapon for shooting arrows, consisting of an arch of flexible wood, plastic, etc., bent by a string fastened at each end. **2a** a long stick across which are stretched strands of horsehair, used for playing the strings of a violin, viola, cello, etc. **2b** a stroke with such a stick. **3a** a decorative interlacing of ribbon or other fabrics, usually having two loops and two loose ends. **3b** the knot forming such an interlacing. **4** something that is curved, bent, or arched. ◆ *vb* **5** to form or cause to form a curve or curves. **6** to make strokes of a bow across (violin strings). [OE *boga* arch, bow]

bow[3] ❶ (baʊ) *n* **1** *Chiefly Naut.* **1a** (*often pl*) the forward end or part of a vessel. **1b** (*as modifier*): *the bow mooring line.* **2** *Rowing.* the oarsman at the bow. [C15: prob. from Low G *boog*]

bow compass (bəʊ) *n Geom.* a compass in which the legs are joined by a flexible metal bow-shaped spring rather than a hinge.

bowdlerize ❶ *or* **bowdlerise** (ˈbaʊdləˌraɪz) *vb* **bowdlerizes, bowdlerizing, bowdlerized** *or* **bowdlerises, bowdlerising, bowdlerised.** (*tr*) to remove passages or words regarded as indecent from (a play, novel, etc.); expurgate. [C19: after Thomas *Bowdler* (1754–1825), E editor who expurgated Shakespeare]
▸ˌ**bowdleriˈzation** *or* ˌ**bowdleriˈsation** *n* ▸ˈ**bowdlerism** *n*

bowel ❶ (ˈbaʊəl) *n* **1** an intestine, esp. the large intestine in man. **2** (*pl*) innards; entrails. **3** (*pl*) the deep or innermost part (esp. in **the bowels of the earth**). [C13: from OF *bouel*, from L *botellus* a little sausage]

bowel movement *n* **1** the discharge of faeces; defecation. **2** the waste matter discharged; faeces.

bower[1] ❶ (ˈbaʊə) *n* **1** a shady leafy shelter or recess, as in a wood or garden; arbour. **2** *Literary.* a lady's bedroom or apartments; boudoir. [OE *būr* dwelling]

bower[2] (ˈbaʊə) *n Naut.* a vessel's bow anchor. [C18: from BOW[3] + -ER[1]]

bowerbird (ˈbaʊəˌbɜːd) *n* **1** any of various songbirds of Australia and New Guinea. The males build bower-like display grounds to attract the females. **2** *Inf., chiefly Austral.* a collector of unconsidered trifles. [C17: from Dutch *bouwerij*, from *bouwen* to farm + *erij* -ERY; see BOOR, BOER]

bowfin (ˈbəʊˌfɪn) *n* a primitive North American freshwater bony fish with an elongated body and a very long dorsal fin.

bowhead (ˈbəʊˌhɛd) *n* a large-mouthed arctic right whale. Also called: **Greenland whale.**

bowie knife (ˈbəʊɪ) *n* a stout hunting knife with a short hilt and a guard for the hand. [C19: after Jim *Bowie* (1796–1836), Texan adventurer]

bowl[1] ❶ (bəʊl) *n* **1** a round container open at the top, used for holding liquid, serving food, etc. **2** Also: **bowlful.** the amount a bowl will hold. **3** the rounded or hollow part of an object, esp. of a spoon or tobacco pipe. **4** any container shaped like a bowl, such as a sink or lavatory. **5** a bowl-shaped building or other structure, such as an amphitheatre. **6** *Chiefly US.* a bowl-shaped depression of the land surface. **7** *Literary.* a drinking cup. [OE *bolla*]

bowl[2] ❶ (bəʊl) *n* **1** a wooden ball used in the game of bowls, having one flattened side in order to make it run on a curved course. **2** a large heavy ball with holes for gripping, used in tenpin bowling. ◆ *vb* **3** to roll smoothly or cause to roll smoothly along the ground. **4** (*intr;* usually foll. by *along*) to move easily and rapidly, as in a car. **5** *Cricket.* **5a** to send (a ball) from one's hand towards the batsman. **5b** Also: **bowl out.** to dismiss (a batsman) by delivering a ball that breaks his wicket. **6** (*intr*) to play bowls or tenpin bowling. ◆ See also **bowl over, bowls.** [C15: from F *boule*, ult. from L *bulla* bubble]

bow legs (bəʊ) *pl n* a condition in which the legs curve outwards like a bow between the ankle and the thigh. Also called: **bandy legs.**
▸**bow-legged** (bəʊˈlɛgɪd, bəʊˈlɛgd) *adj*

bowler[1] (ˈbəʊlə) *n* **1** one who bowls in cricket. **2** a player at the game of bowls.

bowler[2] (ˈbəʊlə) *n* a stiff felt hat with a rounded crown and narrow curved brim. US and Canad. name: **derby.** [C19: after John *Bowler*, 19th-cent. London hatter]

bowline (ˈbəʊlɪn) *n Naut.* **1** a line for controlling the weather leech of a square sail when a vessel is close-hauled. **2** a knot used for securing a loop that will not slip at the end of a piece of rope. [C14: prob. from MLow G *bōlīne*, equivalent to BOW[3] + LINE[1]]

bowling (ˈbəʊlɪŋ) *n* **1** any of various games in which a heavy ball is rolled down a special alley at a group of wooden pins. **2** the game of bowls. **3** *Cricket.* the act of delivering the ball to the batsman.

bowling alley *n* **1a** a long narrow wooden lane down which the ball is rolled in tenpin bowling. **1b** a similar lane or alley for playing skittles. **2** a building having lanes for tenpin bowling.

bowling crease *n Cricket.* a line marked at the wicket, over which a bowler must not advance fully before delivering the ball.

bowling green *n* an area of closely mown turf on which the game of bowls is played.

bowl over *vb* (*tr, adv*) **1** *Inf.* to surprise (a person) greatly, esp. in a pleasant way; astound; amaze. **2** to knock down.

bowls (bəʊlz) *n* (*functioning as sing*) **1** a game played on a bowling green in which a small bowl (the jack) is pitched from a mark and two opponents take turns to roll biased wooden bowls as near the jack as possible. **2** skittles or tenpin bowling.

bowman (ˈbəʊmən) *n, pl* **bowmen.** *Arch.* an archer.

bow out ❶ (baʊ) *vb* (*adv; usually tr;* often foll. by *of*) to retire or withdraw gracefully.

bowser (ˈbaʊzə) *n* **1** a tanker containing fuel for aircraft, military vehicles, etc. **2** *Austral. & NZ obs.* a petrol pump at a filling station. [orig. a US proprietary name]

bowshot (ˈbəʊˌʃɒt) *n* the distance an arrow travels from the bow.

bowsprit (ˈbəʊsprɪt) *n Naut.* a spar projecting from the bow of a vessel, esp. a sailing vessel. [C13: from MLow G, from *bōch* BOW[3] + *sprēt* pole]

bowstring (ˈbəʊˌstrɪŋ) *n* the string of an archer's bow.

bow tie (bəʊ) *n* a man's tie tied in a bow, now chiefly in plain black for formal evening wear.

bow window (bəʊ) *n* a bay window in the shape of a curve.

bow-wow (ˈbaʊˌwaʊ, -ˈwaʊ) *n* **1** a child's word for **dog. 2** an imitation of the bark of a dog. ◆ *vb* **3** (*intr*) to bark or imitate a dog's bark.

bowyangs (ˈbəʊjæŋz) *pl n Austral. & NZ sl.* a pair of strings or straps worn around the trouser leg below the knee, orig. esp. by agricultural workers. [C19: from E dialect *bowy-yanks* leggings]

box[1] ❶ (bɒks) *n* **1** a receptacle or container made of wood, cardboard, etc., usually rectangular and having a removable or hinged lid. **2** Also called: **boxful.** the contents of such a receptacle. **3** (*often in combination*) any of various small cubicles, kiosks, or shelters: *a telephone box; a signal box.* **4** a separate compartment in a public place for a small group of people, as in a theatre. **5** an enclosure within a courtroom: *witness box.* **6** a compartment for a horse in a stable or a vehicle. **7** *Brit.* a small country house occupied by sportsmen when following a field sport, esp. shooting. **8a** a protective housing for machinery or mechanical parts. **8b** (*in combination*): *a gearbox.* **9** a shaped device of light tough material worn by sportsmen to protect the genitals, esp. in cricket. **10**

THESAURUS

tional, hidebound, materialistic, Pooterish, traditional

bout *n* **1 = period**, course, fit, round, run, session, spell, stint, stretch, term, time, turn **2 = fight**, battle, boxing match, competition, contest, encounter, engagement, head-to-head, match, set-to, struggle

bovine *adj* **2 = dull**, dense, dozy (*Brit. inf.*), slow, sluggish, stolid, stupid, thick

bow[1] *vb* **1 = bend**, bob, droop, genuflect, incline, make obeisance, nod, stoop **3 = give in**, accept, acquiesce, comply, concede, defer, kowtow, relent, submit, succumb, surrender, yield ◆ *n* **7 = bending**, bob, genuflexion, inclination, kowtow, nod, obeisance, salaam

bow[3] *n* **1** *Chiefly nautical* **= prow**, beak, fore, head, stem

bowdlerize *vb* **= censor**, blue-pencil, clean up, expurgate, mutilate, sanitize

bowed *adj* **2 = bent**, crooked, curved, hunched, inclined, lowered, stooped

Antonyms *adj* erect, straight, upright

bowels *pl n* **2 = guts**, entrails, innards (*inf.*), insides (*inf.*), intestines, viscera, vitals **3 = depths**, belly, core, deep, hold, inside, interior

bower[1] *n* **1 = arbour**, alcove, grotto, leafy shelter, shady recess, summerhouse

bowl[1] *n* **1 = basin**, dish, vessel

bowl[2] *vb* **3 = roll**, revolve, rotate, spin, trundle, whirl **5a = throw**, fling, hurl, pitch

bowl over *vb* **1** *Informal* **= surprise**, amaze, astonish, astound, dumbfound, stagger, startle, stun, sweep off one's feet **2 = knock down**, bring down, deck (*sl.*), fell, floor, overthrow, overturn

bow out *vb* **= give up**, abandon, back out, call it a day *or* night, cop out (*sl.*), get out, pull out, quit, resign, retire, step down (*inf.*), throw in the sponge, throw in the towel, withdraw

box[1] *n* **1 = container**, ark (*dialect*), carton, case, casket, chest, pack, package, portmanteau, receptacle, trunk ◆ *vb* **19 = pack**, package, wrap

a section of printed matter on a page, enclosed by lines, a border, etc. **11** a central agency to which mail is addressed and from which it is collected or redistributed: *a post-office box; a box number in a newspaper advertisement.* **12** short for **penalty box.** **13** the raised seat on which the driver sits in a horse-drawn coach. **14** *Austral. & NZ.* an accidental mixing of herds or flocks. **15** *Brit.* (esp. formerly) a present, esp. of money, given at Christmas to tradesmen, etc. **16** *Austral. taboo sl.* the female genitals. **17 out of the box.** *Austral. inf.* outstanding or excellent. **18 the box.** *Brit. inf.* television. ◆ *vb* **19** (*tr*) to put into a box. **20** (*tr;* usually foll. by *in* or *up*) to prevent from moving freely; confine. **21** (*tr;* foll. by *in*) *Printing.* to enclose (text) within a ruled frame. **22** *Austral. & NZ.* to mix (flocks or herds) or (of flocks) to become mixed accidentally. **23 box the compass.** *Naut.* to name the compass points in order. [OE *box*, from L *buxus*, from Gk *puxos* BOX[3]]
▸**'box,like** *adj*

box[2] ⓣ (bɒks) *vb* **1** (*tr*) to fight (an opponent) in a boxing match. **2** (*intr*) to engage in boxing. **3** (*tr*) to hit (a person) with the fist. ◆ *n* **4** a punch with the fist, esp. on the ear. [C14: from ?]

box[3] (bɒks) *n* **1** a slow-growing evergreen tree or shrub with small shiny leaves: used for hedges. **2** the wood of this tree. **3** any of several trees the timber or foliage of which resembles this tree, esp. various eucalyptus trees with rough bark. [OE, from L *buxus*, from Gk *puxus*]

box camera *n* a simple box-shaped camera having an elementary lens, shutter, and viewfinder.

box chronometer *n Naut.* a ship's chronometer, supported on gimbals in a wooden box.

boxer ⓣ ('bɒksə) *n* **1** a person who boxes; pugilist. **2** a medium-sized smooth-haired breed of dog with a short nose and a docked tail.

Boxer ('bɒksə) *n* a member of a nationalistic Chinese secret society that led an unsuccessful rebellion in 1900 against foreign interests in China. [C18: rough translation of Chinese *I Ho Ch'üan*, lit.: virtuous harmonious fist]

boxer shorts *pl n* men's underpants shaped like shorts but having a front opening. Also called: **boxers.**

box girder *n* a girder that is hollow and square or rectangular in shape.

boxing ⓣ ('bɒksɪŋ) *n* **a** the act, art, or profession of fighting with the fists. **b** (*as modifier*): *a boxing enthusiast.*

Boxing Day *n Brit.* the first day (traditionally and strictly, the first weekday) after Christmas, observed as a holiday. [C19: from the custom of giving Christmas boxes to tradesmen and staff on this day]

boxing glove *n* one of a pair of thickly padded mittens worn for boxing.

box junction *n* (in Britain) a road junction having yellow cross-hatching painted on the road surface. Vehicles may only enter the hatched area when their exit is clear.

box kite *n* a kite with a boxlike frame open at both ends.

box lacrosse *n Canad.* lacrosse played indoors. Also called: **boxla.**

box number *n* **1** the number of an individual pigeonhole at a newspaper to which replies to an advertisement may be addressed. **2** the number of an individual pigeonhole at a post office from which mail may be collected.

box office *n* **1** an office at a theatre, cinema, etc., where tickets are sold. **2a** the public appeal of an actor or production. **2b** (*as modifier*): *a box-office success.*

box pleat *n* a flat double pleat made by folding under the fabric on either side of it.

boxroom ('bɒks,ruːm, -,rʊm) *n* a small room or large cupboard in which boxes, cases, etc., may be stored.

box seat *n* **1** a seat in a theatre box. **2 in the box seat.** *Brit., Austral., & NZ.* in the best position.

box spanner *n* a spanner consisting of a steel cylinder with a hexagonal end that fits over a nut.

box spring *n* a coiled spring contained in a boxlike frame, used for mattresses, chairs, etc.

boxwood ('bɒks,wʊd) *n* **1** the hard close-grained yellow wood of the box tree, used to make tool handles, etc. **2** the box tree.

boxy ('bɒksɪ) *adj* squarish or chunky in style or appearance: *a boxy square-cut jacket.*

boy ⓣ (bɔɪ) *n* **1** a male child; lad; youth. **2** a man regarded as immature or inexperienced. **3 the boys.** *Inf.* a group of men, esp. a group of friends. **4** *S. African derog.* a Black male servant. **5 the boy.** *Irish inf.* the right tool for a particular task: *that's the boy to cut it.* ◆ *interj* **6** an exclamation of surprise, pleasure, contempt, etc. [C13 (in the sense: male servant; C14: young male): ?from Anglo-F *abuié* fettered (unattested), from L *boia* fetter]
▸**'boyish** *adj*

boycott ⓣ ('bɔɪkɒt) *vb* **1** (*tr*) to refuse to have dealings with (a person, organization, etc.) or refuse to buy (a product) as a protest or means of coercion. ◆ *n* **2** an instance or the use of boycotting. [C19: after Captain C. C. *Boycott* (1832–97), Irish land agent, a victim of such practices for refusing to reduce rents]

boyfriend ⓣ ('bɔɪ,frɛnd) *n* a male friend with whom a person is romantically or sexually involved; sweetheart or lover.

boyhood ('bɔɪhʊd) *n* the state or time of being a boy.

Boyle's law (bɔɪlz) *n* the principle that the pressure of a gas varies inversely with its volume at constant temperature. [C18: after Robert *Boyle* (1627–91), Irish scientist]

boyo ('bɔɪəʊ) *n Brit. inf.* a boy or young man: often used in direct address. [from Irish and Welsh]

boy racer *n Derog. sl.* **a** a young man who drives a car irresponsibly and at high speeds. **b** (*as modifier*): *boy-racer accessories.*

Boys' Brigade *n* (in Britain) an organization for boys, founded in 1883, with the aim of promoting discipline and self-respect.

boy scout *n* See **Scout.**

boysenberry ('bɔɪzᵊnbərɪ) *n, pl* **boysenberries. 1** a type of bramble: a hybrid of the loganberry and various blackberries and raspberries. **2** the large red edible fruit of this plant. [C20: after Rudolph *Boysen*, American botanist]

bp *abbrev. for:* **1** (of alcoholic density) below proof. **2** boiling point. **3** bishop. **4** Also: **B/P.** bills payable.

BP *abbrev. for:* **1** blood pressure. **2** British Pharmacopoeia.

bp. *abbrev. for:* **1** baptized. **2** birthplace.

B/P *or* **bp** *abbrev. for* bills payable.

BPC *abbrev. for* British Pharmaceutical Codex.

BPhil *abbrev. for* Bachelor of Philosophy.

bpi *abbrev. for* bits per inch (used of a computer tape).

bpm *abbrev. for* beats per minute: used in electronic dance music to indicate the tempo of a record.

BPR *abbrev. for* business process re-engineering.

b.pt. *abbrev. for* boiling point.

Bq *Physics. symbol for* becquerel.

br *abbrev. for* brother.

Br 1 *abbrev. for* (in a religious order) Brother. ◆ **2** *the chemical symbol for* bromine.

BR *abbrev. for* British Rail (British Railways).

br. *abbrev. for:* **1** branch. **2** bronze.

Br. *abbrev. for:* **1** Breton. **2** Britain. **3** British.

bra (brɑː) *n* a woman's undergarment for covering and supporting the breasts. [C20: from BRASSIERE]

braai (braɪ) *n* short for **braaivleis.**

braaivleis ('braɪ,fleɪs) *n S. African.* a barbecue. [from Afrik. *braai* grill + *vleis* meat]

brace ⓣ (breɪs) *n* **1** a hand tool for drilling holes, with a socket to hold the drill at one end and a cranked handle by which the tool can be turned. See also **brace and bit. 2** something that steadies, binds, or holds up another thing. **3** a structural member, such as a beam or prop, used to stiffen a framework. **4** a pair, esp. of game birds. **5** either of a pair of characters, { }, used for connecting lines of printing or writing. **6** Also called: **accolade.** a line or bracket connecting two or more staves of music. **7** (*often pl*) an appliance of metal bands and wires for correcting uneven alignment of teeth. **8** *Med.* any of various appliances for supporting the trunk or a limb. **9** See **braces.** ◆ *vb* **braces, bracing, braced.** (*mainly tr*) **10** to provide, strengthen, or fit with a brace. **11** to steady or prepare (oneself or something) as before an impact. **12** (*also intr*) to stimulate; freshen; invigorate: *sea air is bracing.* [C14: from OF, from L *bracchia* arms]

brace and bit *n* a hand tool for boring holes, consisting of a cranked handle into which a drilling bit is inserted.

bracelet ('breɪslɪt) *n* an ornamental chain worn around the arm or wrist. [C15: from OF, from L *bracchium* arm]

bracelets ('breɪslɪts) *pl n* a slang name for **handcuffs.**

bracer ('breɪsə) *n* **1** a person or thing that braces. **2** *Inf.* a tonic, esp. an alcoholic drink taken as a tonic.

braces ('breɪsɪz) *pl n Brit.* a pair of straps worn over the shoulders by men for holding up the trousers. US and Canad. word: **suspenders.**

brachial ('breɪkɪəl, 'bræk-) *adj* of or relating to the arm or to an armlike part or structure.

brachiate *adj* ('breɪkɪɪt, -,eɪt, 'bræk-). **1** *Bot.* having widely divergent paired branches. ◆ *vb* ('breɪkɪ,eɪt, 'bræk-), **brachiates, brachiating, brachiated. 2** (*intr*) (of some arboreal apes and monkeys) to swing by the arms from one hold to the next. [C19: from L *bracchiātus* with armlike branches]
▸**,brachi'ation** *n*

brachio- *or before a vowel* **brachi-** *combining form.* indicating a brachium: *brachiopod.*

brachiopod ('breɪkɪə,pɒd, 'bræk-) *n* any marine invertebrate animal

THESAURUS

20 *usually foll. by* **in** *or* **up** = **confine**, cage, contain, coop up, enclose, hem in, isolate, shut in, surround, trap

box[2] *vb* **1, 2** = **fight**, exchange blows, spar **3** = **punch**, belt (*inf.*), buffet, clout (*inf.*), cuff, deck (*sl.*), hit, lay one on (*sl.*), slap, sock (*sl.*), strike, thwack, wallop (*inf.*), whack ◆ *n* **4** = **punch**, belt (*inf.*), blow, buffet, clout (*inf.*), cuff, slap, stroke, thumping, wallop (*inf.*)

boxer *n* **1** = **fighter**, prizefighter, pugilist, sparrer, sparring partner

boxing *n* = **prizefighting**, fisticuffs, pugilism, sparring, the fight game (*inf.*), the ring

boy *n* **1** = **lad**, fellow, junior, schoolboy, stripling, youngster, youth

boycott *vb* **1** = **embargo**, ban, bar, black, blackball, blacklist, exclude, ostracize, outlaw, prohibit, proscribe, refrain from, refuse, reject, spurn
Antonyms *vb* accept, advocate, back, champion, defend, espouse, help, patronize, promote, support, welcome

boyfriend *n* = **sweetheart**, admirer, beau, date, follower, leman (*arch.*), lover, man, steady, suitor, swain, toy boy, young man

boyish *adj* **1, 2** = **youthful**, adolescent, childish, immature, juvenile, puerile, young

brace *n* **2, 3** = **support**, bolster, bracer, bracket, buttress, prop, reinforcement, stanchion, stay, strut, truss ◆ *vb* **10** = **support**, bandage, bind, bolster, buttress, fasten, fortify, hold up, prop, reinforce, shove, shove up, strap, strengthen, tie, tighten having a ciliated feeding organ and a shell consisting of dorsal and ventral valves. [C19: from NL *Brachiopoda;* see BRACHIUM, -POD]

brachiosaurus (ˌbreɪkɪə'sɔːrəs, ˌbræk-) *n* a dinosaur up to 30 metres long: the largest land animal ever known.

brachium ('breɪkɪəm, 'bræk-) *n, pl* **brachia** (-kɪə). **1** *Anat.* the arm, esp. the upper part. **2** a corresponding part in an animal. **3** *Biol.* a branching or armlike part. [C18: NL, from L *bracchium* arm]

brachy- *combining form.* indicating something short: *brachycephalic.* [from Gk *brakhus* short]

brachycephalic (ˌbrækɪsɪ'fælɪk) *adj* having a head nearly as broad from side to side as from front to back. Also: **brachycephalous** (ˌbrækɪ'sɛfələs).
▸ˌ**brachy'cephaly** *n*

bracing ➊ ('breɪsɪŋ) *adj* **1** refreshing; stimulating; invigorating. ◆ *n* **2** a system of braces used to strengthen or support.

bracken ('brækən) *n* **1** Also called: **brake.** any of various large coarse ferns having large fronds with spore cases along the undersides. **2** a clump of any of these ferns. [C14: from ON]

bracket ('brækɪt) *n* **1** an L-shaped or other support fixed to a wall to hold a shelf, etc. **2** one or more wall shelves carried on brackets. **3** *Archit.* a support projecting from the side of a wall or other structure. **4** Also called: **square bracket.** either of a pair of characters, [ ], used to enclose a section of writing or printing. **5** a general name for **parenthesis** (sense 2), **square bracket,** and **brace** (sense 5). **6** a group or category falling within certain defined limits: *the lower income bracket.* **7** the distance between two preliminary shots of artillery fire in range-finding. ◆ *vb* **brackets, bracketing, bracketed.** (*tr*) **8** to fix or support by means of brackets. **9** to put (written or printed matter) in brackets. **10** to couple or join (two lines of text, etc.) with a brace. **11** (often foll. by *with*) to group or class together. **12** to adjust (artillery fire) until the target is hit. [C16: from OF *braguette* codpiece, from OProvençal *braga,* from L *brāca* breeches]

brackish ➊ ('brækɪʃ) *adj* (of water) slightly briny or salty. [C16: from MDu. *brac* salty; see -ISH]
▸'**brackishness** *n*

bract (brækt) *n* a specialized leaf with a single flower or inflorescence growing in its axil. [C18: from L *bractea* thin metal plate, gold leaf, from ?]
▸'**bracteal** *adj* ▸**bracteate** ('bræktɪɪt) *adj*

bracteole ('bræktɪˌəʊl) *n* a secondary or small bract. Also called: **bractlet.** [C19: from NL *bracteola;* see BRACT]

brad (bræd) *n* a small tapered nail with a small head. [OE *brord* point, prick]

bradawl ('brædˌɔːl) *n* an awl used to pierce wood, leather, etc.

Bradshaw ('brædˌʃɔː) *n* a British railway timetable, published annually from 1839 to 1961. [C19: after its original publisher, George *Bradshaw* (1801–53)]

bradycardia (ˌbrædɪ'kɑːdɪə) *n Pathol.* an abnormally slow heartbeat. [C19: from Gk *bradus* slow + *kardia* heart]

brae (breɪ) *n Scot.* **1** a hill or hillside **2** (*pl*) an upland area. [C14 *bra;* rel to ON *brā* eyelash]

brag ➊ (bræg) *vb* **brags, bragging, bragged. 1** to speak arrogantly and boastfully. ◆ *n* **2** boastful talk or behaviour. **3** something boasted of. **4** a braggart; boaster. **5** a card game: an old form of poker. [C13: from ?]
▸'**bragger** *n*

braggadocio (ˌbrægə'dəʊtʃɪˌəʊ) *n, pl* **braggadocios. 1** vain empty boasting. **2** a person who boasts; braggart. [C16: from *Braggadocchio,* a boastful character in Spenser's *Faerie Queene;* prob. from BRAGGART + It. *-occhio* (augmentative suffix)]

braggart ➊ ('brægət) *n* **1** a person who boasts loudly or exaggeratedly; bragger. ◆ *adj* **2** boastful. [C16: see BRAG]

Brahma ('brɑːmə) *n* a Hindu god, the Creator. [from Sansk., from *brahman* praise]

Brahman ('brɑːmən) *n, pl* **Brahmans. 1** (*sometimes not cap.*) Also (esp. formerly): **Brahmin.** a member of the highest or priestly caste in the Hindu caste system. **2** another name for **Brahma.** [C14: from Sansk. *brahman* prayer]
▸**Brahmanic** (brɑː'mænɪk) *or* **Brah'manical** *adj*

Brahmanism ('brɑːməˌnɪzəm) *or* **Brahminism** *n* (*sometimes not cap.*) the religious and social system of orthodox Hinduism.
▸'**Brahmanist** *or* '**Brahminist** *n*

Brahmin ('brɑːmɪn) *n, pl* **Brahmin** *or* **Brahmins. 1** the older spelling of **Brahman** (a Hindu priest). **2** *US.* a highly intelligent or socially exclusive person.

braid ➊ (breɪd) *vb* (*tr*) **1** to interweave (hair, thread, etc.); plait. **2** to decorate with an ornamental trim or border. ◆ *n* **3** a length of hair, fabric, etc., that has been braided; plait. **4** narrow ornamental tape of woven silk, wool, etc. [OE *bregdan* to move suddenly, weave together]
▸'**braider** *n* ▸'**braiding** *n*

Braille (breɪl) *n* **1** a system of writing for the blind consisting of raised dots interpreted by touch. **2** any writing produced by this method. ◆ *vb* **3** (*tr*) to print or write using this method. [C19: after Louis *Braille* (1809–52), F inventor]

brain ➊ (breɪn) *n* **1** the soft convoluted mass of nervous tissue within the skull of vertebrates that is the controlling and coordinating centre of the nervous system and the seat of thought, memory, and emotion. Related adj: **cerebral. 2** (*often pl*) *Inf.* intellectual ability: *he's got brains.* **3** *Inf.* shrewdness or cunning. **4** *Inf.* an intellectual or intelligent person. **5** (*usually pl; functioning as sing*) *Inf.* a person who plans and organizes. **6** an electronic device, such as a computer, that performs similar functions to those of the human brain. **7 on the brain.** *Inf.* constantly in mind: *I had that song on the brain.* ◆ *vb* (*tr*) **8** to smash the skull of. **9** *Sl.* to hit hard on the head. [OE *brægen*]

brainchild ('breɪnˌtʃaɪld) *n, pl* **brainchildren.** *Inf.* an idea or plan produced by creative thought.

braindead ('breɪnˌdɛd) *adj* **1** having suffered brain death. **2** *Inf.* not using or showing intelligence; stupid.

brain death *n* irreversible cessation of respiration due to irreparable brain damage: widely considered as the criterion of death.

brain drain *n Inf.* the emigration of scientists, technologists, academics, etc.

brain fever *n* inflammation of the brain.

brainless ➊ ('breɪnlɪs) *adj* stupid or foolish.

brainpan ('breɪnˌpæn) *n Inf.* the skull.

brainstem ('breɪnˌstɛm) *n* the part of the brain that controls such reflex actions as breathing and is continuous with the spinal cord.

brainstorm ('breɪnˌstɔːm) *n* **1** a severe outburst of excitement, often as the result of a transitory disturbance of cerebral activity. **2** *Brit. inf.* a sudden mental aberration. **3** *US. & Canad. inf.* another word for **brainwave.**

brainstorming ('breɪnˌstɔːmɪŋ) *n* intensive discussion to solve problems or generate ideas.

brains trust *n* a group of knowledgeable people who discuss topics in public or on radio or television.

brain-teaser *or* **brain-twister** *n Inf.* a difficult problem.

brainwash ➊ ('breɪnˌwɒʃ) *vb* (*tr*) to effect a radical change in the ideas and beliefs of (a person), esp. by methods based on isolation, sleeplessness, etc.
▸'**brainˌwashing** *n*

brainwave ➊ ('breɪnˌweɪv) *n Inf.* a sudden idea or inspiration.

brain wave *n* any of the fluctuations of electrical potential in the brain.

brainy ➊ ('breɪnɪ) *adj* **brainier, brainiest.** *Inf.* clever; intelligent.
▸'**braininess** *n*

braise (breɪz) *vb* **braises, braising, braised.** to cook (meat, vegetables, etc.) by lightly browning in fat and then cooking slowly in a closed pan with a small amount of liquid. [C18: from F *braiser,* from OF *brese* live coals]

brak (bræk) *n S. African.* a crossbred dog; mongrel. [from Du. *brak* setter]

brake[1] ➊ (breɪk) *n* **1** (*often pl*) a device for slowing or stopping a vehicle, wheel, shaft, etc., or for keeping it stationary, esp. by means of friction. **2** a machine or tool for crushing or breaking flax or hemp to separate the fibres. **3** Also called: **brake harrow.** a heavy harrow for breaking up clods. **4** short for **shooting brake.** ◆ *vb* **brakes, braking, braked. 5** to slow down or cause to slow down, by or as if by using a brake. **6** (*tr*) to crush or break up using a brake. [C18: from MDu. *braeke;* rel. to *breken* to BREAK]
▸'**brakeless** *adj*

brake[2] (breɪk) *n* an area of dense undergrowth, shrubs, brushwood, etc.; thicket. [OE *bracu*]

brake[3] (breɪk) *n* another name for **bracken** (sense 1).

brake[4] (breɪk) *vb Arch., chiefly biblical.* a past tense of **break.**

brake-fade *n* a decrease in the efficiency of the braking system of a motor vehicle as a result of overheating of the brakes.

brake horsepower *n* the rate at which an engine does work, expressed in horsepower. It is measured by the resistance of an applied brake. Abbrev.: **bhp.**

THESAURUS

bracing *adj* **1** = **refreshing,** brisk, chilly, cool, crisp, energizing, exhilarating, fortifying, fresh, invigorating, lively, restorative, reviving, rousing, stimulating, tonic, vigorous
Antonyms *adj* debilitating, draining, enervating, exhausting, fatiguing, sapping, soporific, taxing, tiring, weakening

brackish *adj* = **salty,** bitter, briny, saline, salt, undrinkable
Antonyms *adj* clean, clear, fresh, pure, sweet, unpolluted

brag *vb* **1** = **boast,** blow one's own horn (*US & Canad.*), blow one's own trumpet, bluster, crow, swagger, talk big (*sl.*), vaunt

braggart *n* **1** = **boaster,** bigmouth (*sl.*), brag, braggadocio, bragger, show-off (*inf.*), swaggerer

braid *vb* **1** = **interweave,** entwine, interlace, intertwine, lace, plait, ravel, twine, weave

brain 2, 3 *often plural Informal* = **intelligence,** capacity, intellect, mind, nous (*Brit. sl.*), reason, sagacity, savvy (*sl.*), sense, shrewdness, smarts (*sl., chiefly US*), suss (*sl.*), understanding, wit **4** *Informal* = **intellectual,** bluestocking (*usually disparaging*), brainbox, egghead (*inf.*), genius, highbrow, intellect, mastermind, prodigy, pundit, sage, scholar

brainless *adj* = **stupid,** braindead (*inf.*), dead from the neck up (*inf.*), foolish, idiotic, inane, inept, mindless, senseless, thoughtless, unintelligent, witless

brainwashing *n* = **indoctrination,** alteration, conditioning, persuasion, re-education

brainwave *n* = **idea,** bright idea, stroke of genius, thought

brainy *adj Informal* = **intelligent,** bright, brilliant, clever, smart

brake[1] *n* **1** = **control,** check, constraint, curb, rein, restraint ◆ *vb* **5** = **slow,** check, decelerate, halt, moderate, reduce speed, slacken, stop

brake light *n* a red light or lights at the rear of a motor vehicle that light up when the brakes are applied.
brake lining *n* a renewable strip of asbestos riveted to a brake shoe.
brake pad *n* the flat metal casting, together with the attached friction material, in a disc brake.
brake shoe *n* **1** the curved metal casting to which the brake lining is riveted in a drum brake. **2** the curved metal casting together with the attached brake lining. ◆ Sometimes shortened (for both senses) to **shoe.**
brakesman ('breɪksmən) *n, pl* **brakesmen. 1** a pithead winch operator. **2** a brake operator on railway rolling stock.
brake van *n Railways, Brit.* the coach or vehicle from which the guard applies the brakes; guard's van.
bramble ('bræmbəl) *n* **1** any of various prickly rosaceous plants or shrubs, esp. the blackberry. **2** any of several similar and related shrubs, such as the dog rose. **3** *Scot. & N English.* a blackberry. [OE *brǣmbel*]
▸'**brambly** *adj*
brambling ('bræmblɪŋ) *n* a Eurasian finch with a speckled head and back and, in the male, a reddish-brown breast.
bran (bræn) *n* **1** husks of cereal grain separated from the flour. **2** food prepared from these husks. [C13: from OF, prob. of Gaulish origin]
branch ⓘ (brɑːntʃ) *n* **1** a secondary woody stem arising from the trunk or bough of a tree or the main stem of a shrub. **2** an offshoot or secondary part: *a branch of a deer's antlers.* **3a** a subdivision or subsidiary section of something larger or more complex: *branches of learning; branch of the family.* **3b** (*as modifier*): *a branch office.* **4** *US.* any small stream. ◆ *vb* **5** (*intr*) (of a tree or other plant) to produce or possess branches. **6** (*intr;* usually foll. by *from*) (of stems, roots, etc.) to grow and diverge (from another part). **7** to divide or be divided into subsidiaries or offshoots. **8** (*intr;* often foll. by *off*) to diverge from the main way, road, topic, etc. [C13: from OF *branche,* from LL *branca* paw, foot]
▸'**branch,like** *adj*
branchia ('bræŋkɪə) *n, pl* **branchiae** (-kɪ,iː). a gill in aquatic animals.
▸'**branchial** *or* '**branchiate** *adj*
branch out ⓘ *vb* (*intr, adv;* often foll. by *into*) to expand or extend one's interests.
brand ⓘ (brænd) *n* **1** a particular product or a characteristic that identifies a particular producer. **2** a particular kind or variety. **3** an identifying mark made, usually by burning, on the skin of animals or (formerly) slaves or criminals, esp. as a proof of ownership. **4** an iron heated and used for branding animals, etc. **5** a mark of disgrace or infamy; stigma. **6** a burning or burnt piece of wood, as in a fire. **7** *Arch. or poetic.* **7a** a flaming torch. **7b** a sword. **8** a fungal disease of garden plants characterized by brown spots on the leaves. ◆ *vb* (*tr*) **9** to label, burn, or mark with or as with a brand. **10** to place indelibly in the memory: *the scene was branded in their minds.* **11** to denounce; stigmatize: *they branded him a traitor.* [OE *brand-;* see BURN[1]]
▸'**brander** *n* ▸'**branding** *n*
brandish ⓘ ('brændɪʃ) *vb* **1** (*tr*) to wave or flourish (a weapon, etc.) in a triumphant, threatening, or ostentatious way. ◆ *n* **2** a threatening or defiant flourish. [C14: from OF *brandir,* of Gmc origin]
▸'**brandisher** *n*
brand leader *n* the most widely sold brand of a particular product.
brandling ('brændlɪŋ) *n* a small red earthworm, found in manure and used as bait by anglers. [C17: from BRAND (n) + -LING[1]]
brand name *n* the name used for a particular make of a commodity.
brand-new *adj* absolutely new. [C16: from BRAND (n) + NEW, likened to newly forged iron]
brandy ('brændɪ) *n, pl* **brandies. 1** an alcoholic spirit distilled from grape wine. **2** a distillation of wines made from other fruits: *plum brandy.* [C17: from earlier *brandewine,* from Du. *brandewijn* burnt (or distilled) wine]
brandy butter *n* butter and sugar creamed together with brandy and served with Christmas pudding, etc. Also called: **hard sauce.**
brandy snap *n* a crisp sweet biscuit, rolled into a cylinder and filled with whipped cream.
brant (brænt) *n, pl* **brants** *or* **brant.** another name (esp. US and Canad.) for **brent** (the goose).
bran tub *n Brit.* a tub containing bran in which small wrapped gifts are hidden.
brash[1] ⓘ (bræʃ) *adj* **1** tastelessly or offensively loud, showy, or bold. **2** hasty; rash. **3** impudent. [C19: ? infl. by RASH[1]]
▸'**brashly** *adv* ▸'**brashness** *n*
brash[2] (bræʃ) *n* loose rubbish, such as broken rock, hedge clippings, etc. [C18: from ?]
▸'**brashy** *adj*
brasier ('breɪzɪə) *n* a less common spelling of **brazier.**
brass ⓘ (brɑːs) *n* **1** an alloy of copper and zinc containing more than 50 per cent of copper. Cf. **bronze** (sense 1). **2** an object, ornament, or utensil made of brass. **3a** the large family of wind instruments including the trumpet, trombone, French horn, etc., made of brass. **3b** (*sometimes functioning as pl*) instruments of this family forming a section in an orchestra. **4** (*functioning as pl*) *Inf.* important or high-ranking officials, esp. military officers: *the top brass.* See also **brass hat. 5** *N English dialect.* money. **6** *Brit.* an engraved brass memorial tablet or plaque in a church. **7** *Inf.* bold self-confidence; cheek; nerve. **8** (*modifier*) of, consisting of, or relating to brass or brass instruments: *a brass ornament; a brass band.* [OE *bræs*]
brassard ('bræsɑːd) *or* **brassart** ('bræsət) *n* an identifying armband or badge. [C19: from F, from *bras* arm]
brass band *n* See **band**[1] (sense 2).
brasserie ('bræsərɪ) *n* **1** a bar in which drinks and often food are served. **2** a small and usually cheap restaurant. [C19: from F, from *brasser* to stir]
brass hat *n Brit. inf.* a top-ranking official, esp. a military officer. [C20: from the gold decoration on the caps of officers of high rank]
brassica ('bræsɪkə) *n* any plant of the genus *Brassica,* such as cabbage, rape, turnip, and mustard. [C19: from L: cabbage]
brassie *or* **brassy** ('bræsɪ, 'brɑː-) *n, pl* **brassies.** *Golf.* a former name for a club, a No. 2 wood, originally having a brass-plated sole.
brassiere ('bræsɪə, 'bræz-) *n* the full name for **bra.** [C20: from 17th-cent. F: bodice, from OF *braciere* a protector for the arm]
brass rubbing *n* **1** the taking of an impression of an engraved brass tablet or plaque by rubbing a paper placed over it with heelball, chalk, etc. **2** an impression made in this way.
brass tacks *pl n Inf.* basic realities; hard facts (esp. in **get down to brass tacks**).
brassy ⓘ ('brɑːsɪ) *adj* **brassier, brassiest. 1** insolent; brazen. **2** flashy; showy. **3** (of sound) harsh and strident. **4** like brass, esp. in colour. **5** decorated with or made of brass.
▸'**brassily** *adv* ▸'**brassiness** *n*
brat ⓘ (bræt) *n* a child, esp. one who is ill-mannered or unruly. [C16: ?from earlier *brat* rag, from OE *bratt* cloak]
▸'**bratty** *adj*
bratpack ('bræt,pæk) *n* **1** a group of precocious and successful young actors, writers, etc. **2** a group of ill-mannered young people.
▸'**brat,packer** *n*
brattice ('brætɪs) *n* **1** a partition of wood or treated cloth used to control ventilation in a mine. **2** *Medieval fortifications.* a fixed wooden tower or parapet. [C13: from OF *bretesche* wooden tower]
bravado ⓘ (brə'vɑːdəʊ) *n, pl* **bravadoes** *or* **bravados.** vaunted display of courage or self-confidence; swagger. [C16: from Sp. *bravada;* see BRAVE]
brave ⓘ (breɪv) *adj* **1a** having or displaying courage, resolution, or daring; not cowardly or timid. **1b** (*as collective n;* preceded by *the*): *the brave.* **2** fine; splendid: *a brave sight.* ◆ *n* **3** a warrior of a North American Indian tribe. ◆ *vb* **braves, braving, braved.** (*tr*) **4** to dare or defy: *to brave the odds.* **5** to confront with resolution or courage: *to brave the storm.* [C15: from F, from It. *bravo* courageous, wild, ? ult. from L *barbarus* BARBAROUS]
▸'**bravely** *adv* ▸'**braveness** *n* ▸'**bravery** *n*

THESAURUS

branch *n* **1, 2** = **bough**, arm, limb, offshoot, prong, ramification, shoot, spray, sprig **3** = **division**, chapter, department, local office, office, part, section, subdivision, subsection, wing
branch out *vb* = **expand**, add to, develop, diversify, enlarge, extend, increase, multiply, proliferate, ramify, spread out
brand *n* **1** = **label**, emblem, hallmark, logo, mark, marker, sign, stamp, symbol, trademark **2** = **kind**, cast, class, grade, make, quality, sort, species, type, variety **5** = **stigma**, blot, disgrace, infamy, mark, reproach, slur, smirch, stain, taint ◆ *vb* **9** = **mark**, burn, burn in, label, scar, stamp **11** = **stigmatize**, censure, denounce, discredit, disgrace, expose, mark
brandish *vb* **1** = **wave**, display, exhibit, flaunt, flourish, parade, raise, shake, swing, wield
brash[1] *adj* **3** = **bold**, brazen, cocky, forward, impertinent, impudent, insolent, pushy (*inf.*), rude
Antonyms *adj* polite, reserved, respectful, timid, uncertain
brass *n* **7** *Informal* = **nerve** (*inf.*), audacity, brass neck (*Brit. inf.*), cheek, chutzpah (*US & Canad. inf.*), effrontery, face (*inf.*), front, gall, impertinence, impudence, insolence, neck (*inf.*), presumption, rudeness, sassiness (*US inf.*)
brassy *adj* **1** = **brazen**, barefaced, bold, brash, forward, impudent, insolent, loud-mouthed, pert, pushy (*inf.*), saucy **2** = **flashy**, blatant, garish, gaudy, hard, jazzy (*inf.*), loud, obtrusive, showy, vulgar **3** = **strident**, blaring, cacophonous, dissonant, grating, harsh, jangling, jarring, loud, noisy, piercing, raucous, shrill
Antonyms *adj* ≠ **flashy:** discreet, low-key, modest, played down, quiet, restrained, subdued, toned down, understated
brat *n* = **youngster**, cub, guttersnipe, jackanapes, kid (*inf.*), puppy (*inf.*), rascal, spoilt child, urchin, whippersnapper
bravado *n* = **swagger**, bluster, boast, boastfulness, boasting, bombast, brag, braggadocio, swaggering, swashbuckling, vaunting
brave *adj* **1** = **courageous**, bold, daring, dauntless, fearless, gallant, gritty, heroic, intrepid, plucky, resolute, undaunted, valiant, valorous ◆ *vb* **4, 5** = **confront**, bear, beard, challenge, dare, defy, endure, face, face the music, stand up to, suffer, tackle, walk into the lion's den, withstand
Antonyms *adj* ≠ **courageous:** afraid, cowardly, craven, faint-hearted, fearful, frightened, scared, shrinking, timid ◆ *vb* ≠ **confront:** give in to, retreat from, surrender to
bravery *n* **1** = **courage**, balls (*taboo sl.*), ballsiness (*taboo sl.*), boldness, bravura, daring, dauntlessness, doughtiness, fearlessness, fortitude, gallantry, grit, guts (*inf.*), hardihood, hardiness, heroism, indomitability, intrepidity, mettle, pluck, pluckiness, spirit, spunk (*inf.*), valour

DICTIONARY

bravo ❶ *interj* **1** (brɑːˈvəʊ). well done! ◆ *n* **2** (brɑːˈvəʊ) *pl* **bravos.** a cry of "bravo." **3** (ˈbrɑːvəʊ) *pl* **bravoes** *or* **bravos.** a hired killer or assassin. [C18: from It.: splendid! see BRAVE]

bravura ❶ (brəˈvjʊərə, -ˈvʊərə) *n* **1** a display of boldness or daring. **2** *Music.* brilliance of execution. [C18: from It.: spirit, courage; see BRAVE]

braw (brɔː, brɑː) *adj Chiefly Scot.* fine or excellent, esp. in appearance or dress. [C16: Scot. var. of BRAVE]

brawl ❶ (brɔːl) *n* **1** a loud disagreement or fight. **2** *US sl.* an uproarious party. ◆ *vb* (*intr*) **3** to quarrel or fight noisily; squabble. **4** (esp. of water) to flow noisily. [C14: prob. rel. to Du. *brallen* to boast, behave aggressively]
▸ˈ**brawler** *n*

brawn ❶ (brɔːn) *n* **1** strong well-developed muscles. **2** physical strength, esp. as opposed to intelligence. **3** *Brit.* a seasoned jellied loaf made from the head of a pig or calf. [C14: from OF *braon* slice of meat, of Gmc origin]

brawny ❶ (ˈbrɔːnɪ) *adj* **brawnier, brawniest.** muscular and strong.
▸ˈ**brawniness** *n*

bray ❶ (breɪ) *vb* **1** (*intr*) (of a donkey) to utter its characteristic loud harsh sound; heehaw. **2** (*intr*) to make a similar sound, as in laughing. **3** (*tr*) to utter with a loud harsh sound. ◆ *n* **4** the loud harsh sound uttered by a donkey. **5** a similar loud cry or uproar. [C13: from OF *braire,* prob. of Celtic origin]

braze[1] (breɪz) *vb* **brazes, brazing, brazed.** (*tr*) **1** to decorate with or make of brass. **2** to make like brass, as in hardness. [OE *bræsen,* from *bræs* BRASS]

braze[2] (breɪz) *vb* **brazes, brazing, brazed.** (*tr*) to make a joint between (two metal surfaces) by fusing a layer of brass or high-melting solder between them. [C16: from OF: to burn, of Gmc origin; see BRAISE]
▸ˈ**brazer** *n*

brazen ❶ (ˈbreɪzᵊn) *adj* **1** shameless and bold. **2** made of or resembling brass. **3** having a ringing metallic sound. ◆ *vb* (*tr*) **4** (usually foll. by *out* or *through*) to face and overcome boldly or shamelessly. [OE *bræsen,* from *bræs* BRASS]
▸ˈ**brazenly** *adv* ▸ˈ**brazenness** *n*

brazier[1] *or* **brasier** (ˈbreɪzɪə) *n* a person engaged in brass-working or brass-founding. [C14: from OE *bræsian* to work in brass + -ER[1]]
▸ˈ**braziery** *n*

brazier[2] *or* **brasier** (ˈbreɪzɪə) *n* a portable metal receptacle for burning charcoal or coal. [C17: from F *brasier,* from *braise* live coals; see BRAISE]

brazil (brəˈzɪl) *n* **1** Also called: **brazil wood.** the red wood obtained from various tropical trees of America: used for cabinetwork. **2** the red or purple dye extracted from these woods. **3** short for **brazil nut.** [C14: from OSp., from *brasa* glowing coals, of Gmc origin; referring to the redness of the wood]

Brazilian (brəˈzɪlɪən) *adj* **1** of or relating to Brazil, a republic in South America. ◆ *n* **2** a native or inhabitant of Brazil.

brazil nut *n* **1** a tropical South American tree producing large globular capsules, each containing several closely packed triangular nuts. **2** the nut, having an edible oily kernel and a woody shell. ◆ Often shortened to **brazil.**

BRCS *abbrev. for* British Red Cross Society.

breach ❶ (briːtʃ) *n* **1** a crack, break, or rupture. **2** a breaking, infringement, or violation of a promise, obligation, etc. **3** any severance or separation. ◆ *vb* (*tr*) **4** to break through or make an opening, hole, or incursion in. **5** to break a promise, law, etc. [OE *bræc*]

breach of promise *n Law.* (formerly) failure to carry out one's promise to marry.

breach of the peace *n Law.* an offence against public order causing an unnecessary disturbance of the peace.

bread ❶ (brɛd) *n* **1** a food made from a dough of flour or meal mixed with water or milk, usually raised with yeast or baking powder and then baked. **2** necessary food; nourishment. **3** *Sl.* money. **4 cast one's bread upon the waters.** to do good without expectation of advantage or return. **5 know which side one's bread is buttered.** to know what to do in order to keep one's advantages. **6 take the bread out of (someone's) mouth.** to deprive of a livelihood. ◆ *vb* **7** (*tr*) to cover with bread-crumbs before cooking. [OE *brēad*]

bread and butter *Inf.* ◆ *n* **1** a means of support or subsistence; livelihood. ◆ *modifier.* **bread-and-butter. 2a** providing a basic means of subsistence. **2b** expressing gratitude, as for hospitality (esp. in **bread-and-butter letter**).

breadbasket (ˈbrɛd,bɑːskɪt) *n* **1** a basket for carrying bread or rolls. **2** *Sl.* stomach.

breadboard (ˈbrɛd,bɔːd) *n* **1** a wooden board on which bread is sliced. **2** an experimental arrangement of electronic circuits.

breadfruit (ˈbrɛd,fruːt) *n, pl* **breadfruits** *or* **breadfruit. 1** a tree of the Pacific Islands, having edible round, usually seedless, fruit. **2** the fruit, which is eaten baked or roasted and has a texture like bread.

breadline (ˈbrɛd,laɪn) *n* **1** a queue of people waiting for free food. **2 on the breadline.** impoverished; living at subsistence level.

breadth ❶ (brɛdθ, brɛtθ) *n* **1** the linear extent or measurement of something from side to side; width. **2** a piece of fabric, etc., having a standard or definite width. **3** distance, extent, size, or dimension. **4** openness and lack of restriction, esp. of viewpoint or interest; liberality. [C16: from obs. *brēde* (from OE *brǣdu,* from *brād* BROAD) + -TH[1]]

breadthways (ˈbrɛdθ,weɪz, ˈbrɛtθ-) *or esp. US* **breadthwise** (ˈbrɛdθ,waɪz, ˈbrɛtθ-) *adv* from side to side.

breadwinner (ˈbrɛd,wɪnə) *n* a person supporting a family with his or her earnings.

break ❶ (breɪk) *vb* **breaks, breaking, broke, broken. 1** to separate or become separated into two or more pieces. **2** to damage or become damaged so as to be inoperative: *my radio is broken.* **3** to crack or become cracked without separating. **4** to burst or cut the surface of (skin, etc.). **5** to discontinue or become discontinued: *to break a journey.* **6** to disperse or become dispersed: *the clouds broke.* **7** (*tr*) to fail to observe (an agreement, promise, law, etc.): *to break one's word.* **8** (foll. by *with*) to discontinue an association (with). **9** to disclose or be disclosed: *he broke the news gently.* **10** (*tr*) to fracture (a bone) in (a limb, etc.). **11** (*tr*) to divide (something complete or perfect): *to break a set of books.* **12** to bring or come to an end: *the summer weather broke at last.* **13** (*tr*) to bring to an end as by force: *to break a strike.* **14** (when *intr,* often foll. by *out*) to escape (from): *he broke out of jail.* **15** to weaken or overwhelm or be weakened or overwhelmed, as in spirit. **16** (*tr*) to cut through or penetrate: *a cry broke the silence.* **17** (*tr*) to improve on or surpass: *to break a record.* **18** (*tr;* often foll. by *in*) to accustom (a horse) to the bridle and saddle, to being ridden, etc. **19** (*tr;* often foll. by *of*) to cause (a person) to give up (a habit): *this cure will break you of smoking.* **20** (*tr*) to weaken the impact or force of: *this net will break his fall.* **21** (*tr*) to decipher: *to break a code.* **22** (*tr*) to lose the order of: *to break ranks.* **23** (*tr*) to reduce to poverty or the state of bankruptcy. **24** (when *intr,* foll. by *into*) to obtain, give, or receive smaller units in exchange for; change: *to break a pound note.* **25** (*tr*) *Chiefly mil.* to demote to a lower rank. **26** (*intr;* often foll. by *from* or *out of*) to proceed suddenly. **27** (*intr*) to come into being: *light broke over the mountains.* **28** (*intr;* foll. by *into* or *out into*) **28a** to burst into song, laughter, etc. **28b** to change to a faster pace. **29** (*tr*) to open with explosives: *to break a safe.* **30** (*intr*) (of waves) **30a** (often foll. by *against*) to strike violently. **30b** to collapse into foam or surf. **31** (*intr*) (of prices, esp. stock exchange quotations) to fall sharply. **32** (*intr*) to make a sudden effort, as in running, horse racing, etc. **33** (*intr*) *Cricket.* (of a ball) to change direction on bouncing. **34** (*intr*) *Snooker.* to scatter the balls at the start of a game. **35** (*intr*) *Boxing, wrestling.* (of

THESAURUS

Antonyms *n* cowardice, faint-heartedness, fearfulness, fright, timidity

bravo *n* **3** = **hired killer**, assassin, bandit, brigand, cut-throat, desperado, murderer, villain

bravura *n* **1** = **daring**, audacity, boldness, dash, panache, spirit **2** = **brilliance**, brio, display, élan, virtuosity

brawl *n* **1** = **fight**, affray, altercation, argument, battle, clash, disorder, dispute, donnybrook, fracas, fray, free-for-all (*inf.*), melee *or* mêlée, punch-up (*Brit. inf.*), quarrel, row (*inf.*), ruckus (*inf.*), rumpus, scrap (*inf.*), scrimmage, scuffle, shindig (*inf.*), shindy (*inf.*), skirmish, squabble, tumult, uproar, wrangle ◆ *vb* **3** = **fight**, altercate, argue, battle, dispute, go at it hammer and tongs, quarrel, row (*inf.*), scrap (*inf.*), scuffle, tussle, wrangle, wrestle

brawn *n* **1, 2** = **muscle**, beef (*inf.*), beefiness (*inf.*), brawniness, flesh, might, muscles, muscularity, power, robustness, strength, vigour

brawny *adj* = **muscular**, athletic, beefy (*inf.*), bulky, burly, fleshy, hardy, hefty, herculean, husky (*inf.*), lusty, powerful, robust, sinewy, stalwart, strapping, strong, sturdy, thewy, thickset, vigorous, well-built

Antonyms *adj* frail, scrawny, skinny, thin, undeveloped, weak, weakly, weedy (*inf.*), wimpish *or* wimpy (*inf.*)

bray *vb, n* **1, 4** = **heehaw**, bell, bellow, blare, cry, hoot, roar, screech, trumpet

brazen *adj* **1** = **bold**, audacious, barefaced, brash, brassy (*inf.*), defiant, forward, immodest, impudent, insolent, pert, pushy (*inf.*), saucy, shameless, unabashed, unashamed **2** = **brassy**, brass, bronze, metallic ◆ *vb* **4** *usually foll. by* **out** *or* **through** = **be unashamed**, be impenitent, confront, defy, outface, outstare, persevere

Antonyms *adj* ≠ **bold:** cautious, decorous, diffident, mannerly, modest, reserved, respectful, reticent, secret, shy, stealthy, timid

breach *n* **1** = **crack**, aperture, break, chasm, cleft, fissure, gap, hole, opening, rent, rift, rupture, split **2** = **nonobservance**, contravention, disobedience, infraction, infringement, noncompliance, offence, transgression, trespass, violation **3** = **disagreement**, alienation, difference, disaffection, dissension, division, estrangement, falling-out (*inf.*), parting of the ways, quarrel, schism, separation, severance, variance

Antonyms *n* ≠ **nonobservance:** adherence to, attention, compliance, discharge, fulfilment, heeding, honouring, observation, performance

bread *n* **2** = **food**, aliment, diet, fare, necessities, nourishment, nutriment, provisions, subsistence, sustenance, viands, victuals **3** *Slang* = **money**, brass (*N English dialect*), cash, dibs, dosh (*Brit. & Austral. sl.*), dough (*sl.*), finance, funds, necessary (*inf.*), needful (*inf.*), shekels (*inf.*), silver, spondulicks (*sl.*)

breadth *n* **1** = **width**, beam, broadness, latitude, span, spread, wideness **3** = **extent**, amplitude, area, compass, comprehensiveness, dimension, expanse, extensiveness, magnitude, measure, range, reach, scale, scope, size, space, spread, sweep, vastness **4** = **broad-mindedness**, freedom, latitude, liberality, openmindedness, openness, permissiveness

break *vb* **1** = **separate**, disintegrate, divide, fragment, part, rend, sever, shatter, shiver, smash, split, tear **2** = **damage**, demolish, destroy, total (*sl.*), trash (*sl.*) **3** = **crack**, burst, fracture, snap, splinter **7** = **disobey**, breach, contravene, disregard, infract (*Law*), infringe, renege on, transgress, violate **8** *foll. by* **with** = **separate from**, break away from, depart from, ditch, drop (*inf.*), jilt, part company, reject, renounce, repudiate **9** = **reveal**, announce, come out, disclose, divulge, impart, inform, let out, make public, proclaim, tell **12, 13** = **stop**, abandon, cut, discontinue, give up, interrupt, pause, rest, suspend **15** = **weaken**, cow, cripple, demoralize, dispirit, enervate, enfeeble, impair, incapacitate, subdue, tame, undermine **17** = **beat**, two fighters) to separate from a clinch. **36** (*intr*) (of the male voice) to undergo a change in register, quality, and range at puberty. **37** (*tr*) to open the breech of (certain firearms) by snapping the barrel away from the butt on its hinge. **38** (*tr*) to interrupt the flow of current in (an electrical circuit). **39** *Inf., chiefly US.* to become successful. **40 break camp.** to pack up and leave a camp. **41 break service.** *Tennis.* to win a game in which an opponent is serving. **42 break the bank.** to ruin financially or deplete the resources of a bank (as in gambling). **43 break the mould.** to make a change that breaks an established habit, pattern, etc. ◆ **44** the act or result of breaking; fracture. **45** a crack formed as the result of breaking. **46** a brief respite. **47** a sudden rush, esp. to escape: *to make a break for freedom.* **48** a breach in a relationship. **49** any sudden interruption in a continuous action. **50** *Brit.* a short period between classes at school. **51** *Inf.* a fortunate opportunity, esp. to prove oneself. **52** *Inf.* a piece of good or bad luck. **53** (esp. in a stock exchange) a sudden and substantial decline in prices. **54** *Billiards, snooker.* a series of successful shots during one turn. **55** *Billiards, snooker.* the opening shot that scatters the placed balls. **56** Also called: **service break, break of serve.** *Tennis.* the act or an instance of breaking an opponent's service. **57a** *Jazz.* a short usually improvised solo passage. **57b** an instrumental passage in a pop song. **58** a discontinuity in an electrical circuit. **59** access to a radio channel by a citizens' band radio operator. **60 break of day.** the dawn. ◆ *interj* **61** *Boxing, wrestling.* a command by a referee for two opponents to separate. ◆ See also **breakaway, break down,** etc. [OE *brecan*]

breakable ⓘ ('breɪkəbᵊl) *adj* **1** capable of being broken. ◆ *n* **2** (*usually pl*) a fragile easily broken article.

breakage ⓘ ('breɪkɪdʒ) *n* **1** the act or result of breaking. **2** the quantity or amount broken. **3** compensation or allowance for goods damaged while in use, transit, etc.

breakaway ⓘ ('breɪkəˌweɪ) *n* **1a** loss or withdrawal of a group of members from an association, club, etc. **1b** (*as modifier*): *a breakaway faction.* **2** *Austral.* a stampede of animals, esp. at the smell of water. ◆ *vb* **break away.** (*intr, adv*) **3** (often foll. by *from*) to leave hastily or escape. **4** to withdraw or secede.

break dance *n* **1** an acrobatic dance style of the 1980s. ◆ *vb* **break-dance, break-dances, break-dancing, break-danced.** (*intr*) **2** to perform a break dance.
▸**break dancer** *n* ▸**break dancing** *n*

break down ⓘ *vb* (*adv*) **1** (*intr*) to cease to function; become ineffective. **2** to yield or cause to yield, esp. to strong emotion or tears. **3** (*tr*) to crush or destroy. **4** (*intr*) to have a nervous breakdown. **5** to analyse or be subjected to analysis. **6** to separate or cause to separate into simpler chemical elements; decompose. **7 break it down.** *Austral. & NZ inf.* **7a** stop it. **7b** don't expect me to believe that; come off it. ◆ *n* **breakdown. 8** an act or instance of breaking down; collapse. **9** short for **nervous breakdown. 10** an analysis or classification of something into its component parts: *he prepared a breakdown of the report.* **11** a lively American country dance.

breaker ⓘ ('breɪkə) *n* **1** a person or thing that breaks something, such as a person or firm that breaks up old cars, etc. **2** a large wave with a white crest on the open sea or one that breaks into foam on the shore. **3** a citizens' band radio operator.

break even *vb* **1** (*intr, adv*) to attain a level of activity, as in commerce, or a point of operation, as in gambling, at which there is neither profit nor loss. ◆ *n* **breakeven. 2** *Accounting.* the level of commercial activity at which the total cost and total revenue of a business enterprise are equal.

breakfast ('brɛkfəst) *n* **1** the first meal of the day. **2** the food at this meal. ◆ *vb* **3** to eat or supply with breakfast. [C15: from BREAK + FAST[2]]
▸**'breakfaster** *n*

break in ⓘ *vb* (*adv*) **1** (sometimes foll. by *on*) to interrupt. **2** (*intr*) to enter a house, etc., illegally, esp. by force. **3** (*tr*) to accustom (a person or animal) to normal duties or practice. **4** (*tr*) to use or wear (shoes, new equipment, etc.) until comfortable or running smoothly. **5** *Austral.* to bring new land under cultivation. ◆ *n* **break-in. 6** the illegal entering of a building, esp. by thieves.

breaking and entering *n* (formerly) the gaining of unauthorized access to a building with intent to commit a crime.

breaking point *n* the point at which something or someone gives way under strain.

breakneck ⓘ ('breɪkˌnɛk) *adj* (*prenominal*) (of speed, pace, etc.) excessive and dangerous.

break off ⓘ *vb* **1** to sever or detach or be severed or detached. **2** (*adv*) to end (a relationship, association, etc.) or (of a relationship) to be ended. **3** (*intr, adv*) to stop abruptly: *he broke off in the middle of his speech.*

break out ⓘ *vb* (*intr, adv*) **1** to begin or arise suddenly. **2** to make an escape, esp. from prison. **3** (foll. by *in*) (of the skin) to erupt (in a rash, pimples, etc.). ◆ *n* **break-out. 4** an escape, esp. from prison or confinement.

break through ⓘ *vb* **1** (*intr*) to penetrate. **2** (*intr, adv*) to achieve success, make a discovery, etc., esp. after lengthy efforts. ◆ *n* **breakthrough. 3** a significant development or discovery, esp. in science. **4** the penetration of an enemy's defensive position.

breakthrough bleeding ('breɪkˌθruː) *n* vaginal bleeding that occurs other than at a menstrual period while a woman is using a low-dose oral contraceptive.

break up ⓘ *vb* (*adv*) **1** to separate or cause to separate. **2** to put an end to (a relationship) or (of a relationship) to come to an end. **3** to dissolve or cause to dissolve; disrupt or be disrupted: *the meeting broke up at noon.* **4** (*intr*) *Brit.* (of a school) to close for the holidays. **5** *Inf.* to lose or cause to lose control of the emotions. **6** *Sl.* to be or cause to be overcome with laughter. ◆ *n* **break-up. 7** a separation or disintegration. **8a** in the Canadian north, the breaking up of the ice on a body of water that marks the beginning of spring. **8b** this season.

break-up value *n Commerce.* **1** the value of an organization assuming that it will not continue to trade. **2** the value of a share in a company based only on the value of its assets.

breakwater ⓘ ('breɪkˌwɔːtə) *n* **1** Also called: **mole.** a massive wall built out into the sea to protect a shore or harbour from the force of waves. **2** another name for **groyne.**

bream[1] (briːm; *Austral.* brɪm) *or Austral.* **brim** (brɪm) *n, pl* **bream** *or* **brim. 1** any of several Eurasian freshwater cyprinid fishes having a deep compressed body covered with silvery scales. **2** short for **sea bream. 3** *Austral.* any of various marine fishes. [C14: from OF *bresme,* of Gmc origin]

bream[2] (briːm) *vb Naut.* (formerly) to clean debris from (the bottom of a vessel) by heating to soften the pitch. [C15: prob. from MDu. *bremme* broom; from burning broom as a source of heat]

breast ⓘ (brɛst) *n* **1** the front part of the body from the neck to the abdomen; chest. **2** either of the two soft fleshy milk-secreting glands on the chest in sexually mature human females. **3** a similar organ in certain other mammals. **4** anything that resembles a breast in shape or position: *the breast of the hill.* **5** a source of nourishment. **6** the source of human emotions. **7** the part of a garment that covers the breast. **8** a projection from the side of a wall, esp. that formed by a chimney. **9 beat one's breast.** to display guilt and remorse publicly or ostentatiously. **10 make a clean breast of.** to make a confession of. ◆ *vb* (*tr*) **11** to confront boldly; face: *breast the storm.* **12** to oppose with the breast or meet at breast level: *breasting the waves.* **13** to reach the summit of: *breasting the mountain top.* [OE *brēost*]

THESAURUS

better, cap (*inf.*), exceed, excel, go beyond, outdo, outstrip, surpass, top **20** = **reduce**, cushion, diminish, lessen, lighten, moderate, soften, weaken **23** = **ruin**, bankrupt, bust (*inf.*), degrade, demote, discharge, dismiss, humiliate, impoverish, make bankrupt, reduce **27** = **happen**, appear, burst out, come forth suddenly, emerge, erupt, occur **28a** *foll. by* **into** = **begin**, burst into, burst out, commence, give way to, launch into ◆ *n* **44** = **division**, breach, cleft, gap, gash, hole, opening, rent, rift, rupture, split, tear **45** = **crack**, fissure, fracture **46, 49** = **rest**, breather, breathing space, entr'acte, halt, hiatus, interlude, intermission, interruption, interval, let-up (*inf.*), lull, pause, recess, respite, suspension **48** = **breach**, alienation, disaffection, dispute, divergence, estrangement, rift, rupture, schism, separation, split **51** *Informal* = **stroke of luck**, advantage, chance, fortune, opening, opportunity
Antonyms *vb* ≠ **separate:** attach, bind, connect, fasten, join, repair, unite ≠ **disobey:** abide by, adhere to, conform, discharge, follow, obey, observe

breakable *adj* **1** = **fragile**, brittle, crumbly, delicate, flimsy, frail, frangible, friable
Antonyms *adj* durable, indestructible, infrangible, lasting, nonbreakable, resistant, rugged, shatterproof, solid, strong, toughened, unbreakable

breakage *n* **1** = **break**, breach, cleft, crack, cut, fissure, fracture, rent, rift, rupture, tear

breakaway *modifier* **1b** = **dissenting**, heretical, rebel, schismatic, seceding, secessionist ◆ *vb* **break away 3** = **flee**, decamp, escape, fly, hook it (*sl.*), make a break for it, make a run for it (*inf.*), make off, run away **4** = **break with**, detach, part company, secede, separate

break down *vb* **1** = **collapse**, come unstuck, conk out (*inf.*), fail, go kaput (*inf.*), go phut, seize up, stop, stop working **2, 4** = **be overcome**, crack up (*inf.*), go to pieces ◆ *n* **breakdown 8** = **collapse**, crackup (*inf.*), disintegration, disruption, failure, mishap, stoppage **10** = **analysis**, categorization, classification, detailed list, diagnosis, dissection, itemization

breaker *n* **2** = **wave**, billow, comber, roller, whitecap, white horse

break in *vb* **1** = **interrupt**, barge in, burst in, butt in, interfere, interject, interpose, intervene, intrude, put one's oar in, put one's two cents in (*US sl.*) **2** = **burgle**, break and enter, invade, rob **3** = **get used to**, accustom, condition, habituate, initiate, prepare, tame, train ◆ *n* **break-in 6** = **burglary**, breaking and entering, invasion, robbery

breakneck *adj* = **dangerous**, excessive, express, headlong, precipitate, rapid, rash, reckless

break off *vb* **1** = **detach**, divide, part, pull off, separate, sever, snap off, splinter **2, 3** = **stop**, cease, desist, discontinue, end, finish, halt, pause, suspend, terminate

break out *vb* **1** = **begin**, appear, arise, commence, emerge, happen, occur, set in, spring up, start **2** = **escape**, abscond, bolt, break loose, burst out, flee, get free **3** = **erupt**, burst out

break through *vb* **1** = **penetrate**, burst through, emerge, get past **2** = **succeed**, achieve, crack it (*inf.*), cut it, pass, shine forth ◆ *n* **breakthrough 3** = **development**, advance, discovery, find, finding, gain, improvement, invention, leap, progress, quantum leap, step forward

break up *vb* **1** = **separate**, dissolve, divide, divorce, end, part, scatter, sever, split **3** = **stop**, adjourn, disband, disperse, disrupt, end, suspend, terminate ◆ *n* **break-up 7** = **separation**, breakdown, breaking, crackup (*inf.*), disintegration, dispersal, dissolution, divorce, ending, parting, rift, split, splitting, termination, wind-up

breakwater *n* **1, 2** = **sea wall**, groyne, jetty, mole, spur

breast *n* **2, 3** = **bosom**, boob (*sl.*), bust, chest, front, teat, tit (*sl.*), udder **6** = **heart**, being, conscience, core, emotions, feelings, seat of the affections, sentiments, soul, thoughts

breastbone (ˈbrɛst,bəʊn) *n* the nontechnical name for **sternum.**

breast-feed *vb* **breast-feeds, breast-feeding, breast-fed.** to feed (a baby) with milk from the breast; suckle.

breastpin (ˈbrɛst,pɪn) *n* a brooch worn on the breast, esp. to close a garment.

breastplate (ˈbrɛst,pleɪt) *n* a piece of armour covering the chest.

breaststroke (ˈbrɛst,strəʊk) *n* a swimming stroke in which the arms are extended in front of the head and swept back on either side while the legs are drawn up beneath the body and thrust back together.

breastwork (ˈbrɛst,wɜːk) *n Fortifications.* a temporary defensive work, usually breast-high.

breath ⊙ (brɛθ) *n* **1** the intake and expulsion of air during respiration. **2** the air inhaled or exhaled during respiration. **3** a single respiration or inhalation of air, etc. **4** the vapour, heat, or odour of exhaled air. **5** a slight gust of air. **6** a short pause or rest. **7** a brief time. **8** a suggestion or slight evidence; suspicion: *a breath of scandal.* **9** a whisper or soft sound. **10** life, energy, or vitality: *the breath of new industry.* **11** *Phonetics.* the exhalation of air without vibration of the vocal cords, as in pronouncing fricatives such as (f) or (h) or stops such as (p) or (k). **12** **catch one's breath. 12a** to rest until breathing is normal, esp. after exertion. **12b** to stop breathing momentarily from excitement, fear, etc. **13 in the same breath.** done or said at the same time. **14 out of breath.** gasping for air after exertion. **15 save one's breath.** to refrain from useless talk. **16 take one's breath away.** to overwhelm with surprise, etc. **17 under** *or* **below one's breath.** in a quiet voice or whisper. [OE *brǣth*]

breathable (ˈbriːðəbᵊl) *adj* **1** (of air) fit to be breathed. **2** (of a material) allowing air to pass through so that perspiration can evaporate.

Breathalyser *or* **Breathalyzer** (ˈbrɛθə,laɪzə) *n Trademark.* a device for estimating the amount of alcohol in the breath: used in testing people suspected of driving under the influence of alcohol. [C20: BREATH + (AN)ALYSER]
▸ **ˈbreatha,lyse** *or* **ˈbreatha,lyze** *vb*

breathe ⊙ (briːð) *vb* **breathes, breathing, breathed. 1** to take in oxygen and give out carbon dioxide; respire. **2** (*intr*) to exist; be alive. **3** (*intr*) to rest to regain breath, composure, etc. **4** (*intr*) (esp. of air) to blow lightly. **5** (*intr*) *Machinery.* to take in air, esp. for combustion. **6** (*tr*) *Phonetics.* to articulate (a speech sound) without vibration of the vocal cords. **7** to exhale or emit: *the dragon breathed fire.* **8** (*tr*) to impart; instil: *to breathe confidence into the actors.* **9** (*tr*) to speak softly; whisper. **10** (*tr*) to permit to rest: *to breathe a horse.* **11** (*intr*) (of a material) to allow air to pass through so that perspiration can evaporate. **12 breathe again, freely,** *or* **easily.** to feel relief. **13 breathe one's last.** to die or be finished or defeated. [C13: from BREATH]

breather ⊙ (ˈbriːðə) *n* **1** *Inf.* a short pause for rest. **2** a person who breathes in a specified way: *a deep breather.* **3** a vent in a container to equalize internal and external pressure.

breathing (ˈbriːðɪŋ) *n* **1** the passage of air into and out of the lungs to supply the body with oxygen. **2** a single breath: *a breathing between words.* **3** *Phonetics.* **3a** expulsion of breath (**rough breathing**) or absence of such expulsion (**smooth breathing**) preceding the pronunciation of an initial vowel or rho in ancient Greek. **3b** either of two symbols indicating this.

breathless ⊙ (ˈbrɛθlɪs) *adj* **1** out of breath; gasping, etc. **2** holding one's breath or having it taken away by excitement, etc. **3** (esp. of the atmosphere) motionless and stifling. **4** *Rare.* lifeless; dead.
▸ **ˈbreathlessly** *adv* ▸ **ˈbreathlessness** *n*

breathtaking ⊙ (ˈbrɛθ,teɪkɪŋ) *adj* causing awe or excitement.
▸ **ˈbreath,takingly** *adv*

breath test *n Brit.* a chemical test of a driver's breath to determine the amount of alcohol he has consumed.

breathy (ˈbrɛθɪ) *adj* **breathier, breathiest. 1** (of the speaking voice) accompanied by an audible emission of breath. **2** (of the singing voice) lacking resonance.
▸ **ˈbreathily** *adv* ▸ **ˈbreathiness** *n*

breccia (ˈbrɛtʃɪə) *n* a rock consisting of angular fragments embedded in a finer matrix. [C18: from It.]
▸ **ˈbrecci,ated** *adj*

bred (brɛd) *vb* the past tense and past participle of **breed.**

breech ⊙ *n* (briːtʃ). **1** the buttocks; rump. **2** the lower part or bottom of something. **3** the part of a firearm behind the barrel or bore. ◆ *vb* (briːtʃ, brɪtʃ). (*tr*) **4** to fit (a gun) with a breech. **5** *Arch.* to clothe in breeches or any other clothing. [OE *brēc*, pl. of *brōc* leg covering]

> **USAGE NOTE** *Breech* is sometimes wrongly used as a verb where *breach* is meant: *the barrier/agreement was breached* (not *breeched*).

breechblock (ˈbriːtʃ,blɒk) *n* a metal block in breech-loading firearms that is withdrawn to insert the cartridge and replaced before firing.

breech delivery *n* birth of a baby with the feet or buttocks appearing first.

breeches (ˈbrɪtʃɪz, ˈbriː-) *pl n* **1** trousers extending to the knee or just below, worn for riding, etc. **2** *Inf. or dialect.* any trousers or pants, esp. extending to the knee.

breeches buoy *n* a ring-shaped life buoy with a support in the form of a pair of short breeches, in which a person is suspended for safe transfer from a ship.

breeching (ˈbrɪtʃɪŋ, ˈbriː-) *n* the strap of a harness that passes behind a horse's haunches.

breech-loader (ˈbriːtʃ,ləʊdə) *n* a firearm that is loaded at the breech.
▸ **ˈbreech-,loading** *adj*

breed ⊙ (briːd) *vb* **breeds, breeding, bred. 1** to bear (offspring). **2** (*tr*) to bring up; raise. **3** to produce or cause to produce by mating; propagate. **4** to produce new or improved strains of (domestic animals and plants). **5** to produce or be produced; generate: *to breed trouble.* ◆ *n* **6** a group of organisms within a species, esp. domestic animals, having clearly defined characteristics. **7** a lineage or race. **8** a kind, sort, or group. [OE *brēdan*, of Gmc origin; rel. to BROOD]

breeder (ˈbriːdə) *n* **1** a person who breeds plants or animals. **2** something that reproduces. **3** an animal kept for breeding purposes. **4** a source or cause: *a breeder of discontent.* **5** short for **breeder reactor.**

breeder reactor *n* a type of nuclear reactor that produces more fissionable material than it consumes.

breeding ⊙ (ˈbriːdɪŋ) *n* **1** the process of bearing offspring; reproduction. **2** the process of producing plants or animals by hybridization, inbreeding, or other methods of reproduction. **3** the result of good training, esp. the knowledge of correct social behaviour; refinement.

breeze[1] ⊙ (briːz) *n* **1** a gentle or light wind. **2** *Meteorol.* a wind of force two to six (4–31 mph) inclusive on the Beaufort scale. **3** *US & Canad. inf.* an easy task or state of ease. **4** *Inf., chiefly Brit.* a disturbance, esp. a lively quarrel. ◆ *vb* **breezes, breezing, breezed.** (*intr*) **5** to move quickly or casually: *he breezed into the room.* [C16: prob. from OSp. *briza* northeast wind]

breeze[2] (briːz) *n* ashes of coal, coke, or charcoal used to make breeze blocks. [C18: from F *braise* live coals; see BRAISE]

breeze block *n* a light building brick made from the ashes of coal, coke, etc., bonded together by cement.

breezeway (ˈbriːz,weɪ) *n* a roofed passageway connecting two buildings.

breezy ⊙ (ˈbriːzɪ) *adj* **breezier, breeziest. 1** fresh; windy. **2** casual or carefree; lively; light-hearted.
▸ **ˈbreezily** *adv* ▸ **ˈbreeziness** *n*

bremsstrahlung (ˈbrɛmz,ʃtrɑːlʊŋ) *n* the x-radiation produced when an electrically charged particle, such as an electron, is slowed down by the electric field of an atomic nucleus. [G: braking radiation]

Bren gun (brɛn) *n* an air-cooled gas-operated light machine gun: used by the British in World War II. [C20: after *Br(no)*, now in the Czech Republic, where it was first made and *En(field)*, England, where manufacture was continued]

brent goose (brɛnt) *n* a small goose that has a dark grey plumage and short neck and occurs in most northern coastal regions. Also called: **brent,** (esp. US and Canad.) **brant.** [C16: ? of Scand. origin]

THESAURUS

breath *n* **1 = respiration**, breathing, exhalation, gasp, gulp, inhalation, pant, wheeze **5 = gust**, faint breeze, flutter, puff, sigh, slight movement, waft, zephyr **6, 7 = rest**, break, breather, breathing-space, instant, moment, pause, respite, second **8 = suggestion**, hint, murmur, suspicion, undertone, whisper **10 = life**, animation, energy, existence, lifeblood, life force, vitality

breathe *vb* **1 = inhale and exhale**, draw in, gasp, gulp, pant, puff, respire, wheeze **8 = instil**, imbue, impart, infuse, inject, inspire, transfuse **9 = whisper**, articulate, express, murmur, say, sigh, utter, voice

breather *n* **1** *Informal* **= rest**, break, breathing space, breath of air, halt, pause, recess, respite

breathless *adj* **1 = out of breath**, choking, exhausted, gasping, gulping, out of whack (*inf.*), panting, short-winded, spent, wheezing, winded **2 = excited**, agog, anxious, astounded, avid, eager, flabbergasted (*inf.*), gobsmacked (*Brit. sl.*), on tenterhooks, open-mouthed, thunderstruck, with bated breath

breathtaking *adj* **= amazing**, astonishing, awe-inspiring, awesome, brilliant, dramatic, exciting, heart-stirring, impressive, magnificent, moving, overwhelming, sensational, striking, stunning (*inf.*), thrilling, wondrous (*arch. or literary*)

breech *n* **1 = buttocks**, arse, ass (*US & Canad. taboo sl.*), backside (*inf.*), behind (*inf.*), bum (*Brit. sl.*), buns (*US sl.*), butt (*US & Canad. inf.*), derrière (*euphemistic*), jacksy (*Brit. sl.*), posterior, rump, seat, tail (*inf.*)

breed *vb* **1 = reproduce**, bear, beget, bring forth, engender, generate, hatch, multiply, originate, procreate, produce, propagate **2 = bring up**, cultivate, develop, discipline, educate, foster, instruct, nourish, nurture, raise, rear **5 = produce**, arouse, bring about, cause, create, generate, give rise to, induce, make, occasion, originate, stir up ◆ *n* **6 = variety**, pedigree, race, species, stock, strain, type **7 = lineage**, class, extraction, family, ilk, line, pedigree, race, stock **8 = kind**, brand, sort, stamp, type, variety

breeding *n* **1 = reproduction**, nurture, raising, rearing, training, upbringing **2 = cultivation**, development **3 = refinement**, civility, conduct, courtesy, cultivation, culture, gentility, manners, polish, sophistication, urbanity

breeze[1] *n* **1 = light wind**, air, breath of wind, current of air, draught, flurry, gust, puff of air, waft, whiff, zephyr ◆ *vb* **5 = move briskly**, flit, glide, hurry, pass, sail, sally, sweep, trip

breezy *adj* **1 = windy**, airy, blowing, blowy, blusterous, blustery, fresh, gusty, squally **2 = carefree**, airy, animated, blithe, buoyant, casual, cheerful, chirpy (*inf.*), debonair, easy-going, free and easy, full of beans (*inf.*), genial, informal, jaunty, light, light-hearted, lively, sparkling, sparky, spirited, sprightly, sunny, upbeat (*inf.*), vivacious

Antonyms *adj* ≠ **windy:** calm, heavy, oppressive, windless ≠ **carefree:** calm, depressed, dull, heavy, lifeless, mournful, sad, serious

brethren (ˈbrɛðrɪn) *pl n Arch. except when referring to fellow members of a religion, society, etc.* a plural of **brother.**

Breton (ˈbrɛtᵊn) *adj* **1** of, relating to, or characteristic of Brittany, a region of NW France, its people, or their language. ◆ *n* **2** a native or inhabitant of Brittany. **3** the Celtic language of Brittany.

breve (briːv) *n* **1** an accent, ˘ , placed over a vowel to indicate that it is short or is pronounced in a specified way. **2** *Music.* a note, now rarely used, equivalent to two semibreves. **3** *RC Church.* a less common word for **brief** (papal letter). [C13: from Med. L, from L *brevis* short]

brevet (ˈbrɛvɪt) *n* **1** a document entitling a commissioned officer to hold temporarily a higher military rank without the appropriate pay and allowances. ◆ *vb* **brevets, brevetting, brevetted** *or* **brevets, breveting, breveted. 2** (*tr*) to promote by brevet. [C14: from OF, from *brief* letter; see BRIEF]
▸ ˈ**brevetcy** *n*

breviary (ˈbriːvjərɪ) *n, pl* **breviaries.** *RC Church.* a book of psalms, hymns, prayers, etc., to be recited daily by clerics and certain members of religious orders as part of the divine office. [C16: from L *breviārium* an abridged version, from *brevis* short]

brevity Ⓣ (ˈbrɛvɪtɪ) *n, pl* **brevities. 1** conciseness of expression; lack of verbosity. **2** a short duration; brief time. [C16: from L, from *brevis* BRIEF]

brew Ⓣ (bruː) *vb* **1** to make (beer, ale, etc.) from malt and other ingredients by steeping, boiling, and fermentation. **2** to prepare (a drink, such as tea) by boiling or infusing. **3** (*tr*) to devise or plan: *to brew a plot.* **4** (*intr*) to be in the process of being brewed. **5** (*intr*) to be impending or forming: *there's a storm brewing.* ◆ *n* **6** a beverage produced by brewing, esp. tea or beer. **7** an instance or time of brewing: *last year's brew.* **8** a mixture. [OE *brēowan*]
▸ ˈ**brewer** *n*

brewery (ˈbrʊərɪ) *n, pl* **breweries.** a place where beer, ale, etc., is brewed.

brewing (ˈbruːɪŋ) *n* a quantity of a beverage brewed at one time.

briar[1] *or* **brier** (ˈbraɪə) *n* **1** Also called: **tree heath.** a shrub of S Europe, having a hard woody root (briarroot). **2** a tobacco pipe made from the root of this plant. [C19: from F *bruyère* heath]
▸ ˈ**briary** *or* ˈ**briery** *adj*

briar[2] (ˈbraɪə) *n* a variant spelling of **brier**[1].

briarroot *or* **brierroot** (ˈbraɪəˌruːt) *n* the hard woody root of the briar, used for making tobacco pipes. Also called: **briarwood, brierwood.**

bribe Ⓣ (braɪb) *vb* **bribes, bribing, bribed. 1** to promise, offer, or give something, often illegally, to (a person) to procure services or gain influence. ◆ *n* **2** a reward, such as money or favour, given or offered for this purpose. **3** any persuasion or lure. [C14: from OF *briber* to beg, from ?]
▸ ˈ**bribery** *n*

bric-a-brac Ⓣ (ˈbrɪkəˌbræk) *n* miscellaneous small objects, esp. furniture and curios, kept because they are ornamental or rare. [C19: from F]

brick (brɪk) *n* **1a** a rectangular block of clay mixed with sand and fired in a kiln or baked by the sun, used in building construction. **1b** (*as modifier*): *a brick house.* **2** the material used to make such blocks. **3** any rectangular block: *a brick of ice.* **4** bricks collectively. **5** *Inf.* a reliable, trustworthy, or helpful person. **6** *Brit.* a child's building block. **7 drop a brick.** *Brit. inf.* to make a tactless or indiscreet remark. **8 like a ton of bricks.** *Inf.* with great force; severely. ◆ *vb* **9** (*tr; usually foll. by in, up, or over*) to construct, line, pave, fill, or wall up with bricks: *to brick up a window.* [C15: from OF *brique,* from MDu. *bricke*]
▸ ˈ**bricky** *adj*

brickbat (ˈbrɪkˌbæt) *n* **1** a piece of brick or similar material, esp. one used as a weapon. **2** blunt criticism. [C16: BRICK + BAT[1]]

brickie (ˈbrɪkɪ) *n Inf.* a bricklayer.

bricklayer (ˈbrɪkˌleɪə) *n* a person trained or skilled in laying bricks.
▸ ˈ**brickˌlaying** *n*

brick red *n, adj* (of) a reddish-brown colour.

brickwork (ˈbrɪkˌwɜːk) *n* **1** a structure built of bricks. **2** construction using bricks.

brickyard (ˈbrɪkˌjɑːd) *n* a place in which bricks are made, stored, or sold.

bricolage (ˈbrɪkəˌlɑːʒ; *French* brikɔlaʒ) *n Archit.* a jumbled effect produced by the close proximity of buildings from different periods or in different styles. [F: odd jobs, do-it-yourself]

bridal Ⓣ (ˈbraɪdᵊl) *adj* of or relating to a bride or a wedding; nuptial. [OE *brȳdealu,* lit.: "bride ale", that is, wedding feast]

bride (braɪd) *n* a woman who has just been or is about to be married. [OE *brȳd*]

bridegroom (ˈbraɪdˌgruːm, -ˌgrʊm) *n* a man who has just been or is about to be married. [C14: changed (through infl. of GROOM) from OE *brȳdguma,* from *brȳd* BRIDE + *guma* man]

bride price *or* **wealth** *n* (in some societies) money, property, or services given by a bridegroom to the kinsmen of his bride.

bridesmaid (ˈbraɪdzˌmeɪd) *n* a girl or young unmarried woman who attends a bride at her wedding.

bridge[1] Ⓣ (brɪdʒ) *n* **1** a structure that spans and provides a passage over a road, railway, river, or some other obstacle. **2** something that resembles this in shape or function. **3** the hard ridge at the upper part of the nose, formed by the underlying nasal bones. **4** the part of a pair of glasses that rests on the nose. **5** Also called: **bridgework.** a dental plate containing one or more artificial teeth that is secured to the surrounding natural teeth. **6** a platform from which a ship is piloted and navigated. **7** a piece of wood, usually fixed, supporting the strings of a violin, guitar, etc., and transmitting their vibrations to the sounding board. **8** Also called: **bridge passage.** a passage in a musical, literary, or dramatic work linking two or more important sections. **9** Also called: **bridge circuit.** *Electronics.* any of several networks across which a device is connected for measuring resistance, capacitance, etc. **10** *Computing.* a device that connects networks and sends packets between them. **11** *Billiards, snooker.* a support for a cue. **12 cross a bridge when (one) comes to it.** to deal with a problem only when it arises. ◆ *vb* **bridges, bridging, bridged.** (*tr*) **13** to build or provide a bridge over something; span: *to bridge a river.* **14** to connect or reduce the distance between: *let us bridge our differences.* [OE *brycg*]
▸ ˈ**bridgeable** *adj*

bridge[2] (brɪdʒ) *n* a card game for four players, based on whist, in which one hand (the dummy) is exposed and the trump suit decided by bidding between the players. See also **contract bridge, auction bridge.** [C19: from ?]

bridgehead (ˈbrɪdʒˌhɛd) *n* **1** *Mil.* an area of ground secured or to be taken on the enemy's side of an obstacle. **2** *Mil.* a fortified or defensive position at the end of a bridge nearest to the enemy. **3** an advantageous position gained for future expansion.

bridge roll *n* a soft bread roll in a long thin shape. [C20: from BRIDGE[2] or ? BRIDGE[1]]

bridgework (ˈbrɪdʒˌwɜːk) *n* a partial denture attached to the surrounding teeth.

bridging loan *n* a loan made to cover the period between two transactions, such as the buying of another house before the sale of the first is completed.

bridle Ⓣ (ˈbraɪdᵊl) *n* **1** a headgear for a horse, etc., consisting of a series of buckled straps and a metal mouthpiece (bit) by which the animal is controlled through the reins. **2** something that curbs or restrains; check. **3** a Y-shaped cable, rope, or chain, used for holding, towing, etc. ◆ *vb* **bridles, bridling, bridled. 4** (*tr*) to put a bridle on (a horse, mule, etc.). **5** (*tr*) to restrain; curb: *he bridled his rage.* **6** (*intr; often foll. by at*) to show anger, scorn, or indignation. [OE *brigdels*]

bridle path *n* a path suitable for riding or leading horses.

Brie (briː) *n* a soft creamy white cheese. [C19: F, after *Brie,* region in N France where it originated]

brief Ⓣ (briːf) *adj* **1** short in duration. **2** short in length or extent; scanty: *a brief bikini.* **3** abrupt in manner; brusque: *the professor was brief with me.* **4** terse or concise. ◆ *n* **5** a condensed statement or written synopsis; abstract. **6** *Law.* a document containing all the facts and points of law of a case by which a solicitor instructs a barrister to represent a client. **7** *RC Church.* a letter issuing from the Roman court written in modern characters, as contrasted with a papal bull; papal brief. **8** Also called: **briefing.** instructions. **9 hold a brief for.** to argue for; champion. **10 in brief.** in short; to sum up. ◆ *vb* (*tr*) **11** to prepare or in-

THESAURUS

brevity *n* **1** = **conciseness**, concision, condensation, crispness, curtness, economy, pithiness, succinctness, terseness **2** = **shortness**, briefness, ephemerality, impermanence, transience, transitoriness
Antonyms *n* ≠ **conciseness:** circuity, diffuseness, discursiveness, long-windedness, prolixity, rambling, redundancy, tautology, tediousness, verbiage, verboseness, verbosity, wordiness

brew *vb* **1, 2** = **make** (*beer*), boil, ferment, infuse (*tea*), prepare by fermentation, seethe, soak, steep, stew **3** = **devise**, breed, concoct, contrive, form, hatch, plan, plot, project, scheme, start, stir up **5** = **develop**, foment, gather ◆ *n* **6** = **drink**, beverage, blend, concoction, distillation, fermentation, infusion, liquor, preparation

bribe *vb* **1** = **buy off**, corrupt, get at, grease the palm of (*sl.*), pay off (*inf.*), reward, square, suborn ◆ *n* **2** = **inducement**, backhander, enticement, graft (*inf.*), hush money (*sl.*), incentive, kickback (*US*), pay-off (*inf.*), payola (*inf.*)

bribery *n* **1** = **buying off**, corruption, graft (*inf.*), inducement, palm-greasing (*sl.*), payola (*inf.*), protection, subornation

bric-a-brac *n* = **knick-knacks**, baubles, bibelots, curios, gewgaws, objects of virtu, *objets d'art*, ornaments, trinkets

bridal *adj* = **matrimonial**, bride's, conjugal, connubial, hymeneal, marital, marriage, nuptial, spousal, wedding

bridge[1] *n* **1** = **arch**, flyover, overpass, span, viaduct **2** = **link**, band, bond, connection, tie ◆ *vb* **13** = **connect**, arch over, attach, bind, couple, cross, cross over, extend across, go over, join, link, reach across, span, traverse, unite
Antonyms *vb* ≠ **connect:** cleave, come apart, disjoin, divide, keep apart, separate, sever, split, sunder, widen

bridle *n* **2** = **curb**, check, control, rein, restraint ◆ *vb* **5** = **curb**, check, constrain, control, govern, have in one's pocket, keep a tight rein on, keep in check, keep on a string, master, moderate, rein, repress, restrain, subdue **6** = **get angry**, be indignant, bristle, draw (oneself) up, get one's back up, raise one's hackles, rear up

brief *adj* **1** = **short**, ephemeral, fast, fleeting, hasty, little, momentary, quick, quickie (*inf.*), short-lived, swift, temporary, transitory **3** = **curt**, abrupt, blunt, brusque, sharp, short, surly **4** = **concise**, clipped, compendious, compressed, crisp, curt, laconic, limited, monosyllabic, pithy, short, succinct, terse, thumbnail, to the point ◆ *n* **5** = **summary**, abridgment, abstract, digest, epitome, outline, précis, sketch, synopsis **6** *Law* = **case**, argument, contention, data, defence, demonstration ◆ *vb* **11** = **inform**, advise, clue in, explain, fill in (*inf.*), gen up (*Brit. inf.*), give (someone) a rundown, give (someone) the gen (*Brit. inf.*), instruct, keep posted, prepare, prime, put (someone) in the picture (*inf.*)
Antonyms *adj* ≠ **short:** extensive, lengthy, long, protracted ≠ **concise:** circuitous, detailed, diffuse, lengthy, long, long-drawn-out, long-winded

struct by giving a summary of relevant facts. **12** to make a summary or synopsis of. **13** *English law.* **13a** to instruct (a barrister) by brief. **13b** to retain (a barrister) as counsel. [C14: from OF *bref,* from L *brevis*]
▸ **'briefly** *adv* ▸ **'briefness** *n*

briefcase ('bri:f,keɪs) *n* a flat portable case, often of leather, for carrying papers, books, etc.

briefing ➊ ('bri:fɪŋ) *n* **1** a meeting at which information and instructions are given. **2** the facts presented at such a meeting.

briefless ('bri:flɪs) *adj* (said of a barrister) without clients.

briefs (bri:fs) *pl n* men's underpants or women's pants without legs.

brier[1] *or* **briar** ('braɪə) *n* any of various thorny shrubs or other plants, such as the sweetbrier. [OE *brēr, brǣr,* from ?]
▸ **'briery** *or* **'briary** *adj*

brier[2] ('braɪə) *n* a variant spelling of **briar**[1].

brierroot ('braɪə,ru:t) *n* a variant spelling of **briarroot.** Also called: **brierwood.**

brig[1] (brɪg) *n* **1** *Naut.* a two-masted square-rigger. **2** *Chiefly US.* a prison, esp. in a navy ship. [C18: shortened from BRIGANTINE]

brig[2] (brɪg) *n* a Scot. and N English word for a **bridge**[1].

Brig. *abbrev. for* Brigadier.

brigade ➊ (brɪ'geɪd) *n* **1** a military formation smaller than a division and usually commanded by a brigadier. **2** a group of people organized for a certain task: *a rescue brigade.* ◆ *vb* **brigades, brigading, brigaded.** (*tr*) **3** to organize into a brigade. [C17: from OF, from OIt., from *brigare* to fight; see BRIGAND]

brigadier (,brɪgə'dɪə) *n* **1** an officer of the British Army or Royal Marines junior to a major general but senior to a colonel, usually commanding a brigade. **2** an equivalent rank in other armed forces. [C17: from F, from BRIGADE]

brigalow ('brɪgələʊ) *n Austral.* **a** any of various acacia trees, forming dense scrub. **b** (*as modifier*): *brigalow country.* [C19: from Abor.]

brigand ➊ ('brɪgənd) *n* a bandit, esp. a member of a gang operating in mountainous areas. [C14: from OF, from OIt. *brigante* fighter, from *briga* strife]
▸ **'brigandage** *or* **'brigandry** *n*

brigantine ('brɪgən,ti:n, -,taɪn) *n* a two-masted sailing ship, rigged square on the foremast and fore-and-aft on the mainmast. [C16: from OIt. *brigantino* pirate ship, from *brigante* BRIGAND]

bright ➊ (braɪt) *adj* **1** emitting or reflecting much light; shining. **2** (of colours) intense or vivid. **3** full of promise: *a bright future.* **4** full of animation; cheerful: *a bright face.* **5** *Inf.* quick-witted or clever: *a bright child.* **6** magnificent; glorious. **7** polished; glistening. **8** (of a liquid) translucent and clear. **9 bright and early.** very early in the morning. ◆ *adv* **10** brightly: *the fire was burning bright.* [OE *beorht*]
▸ **'brightly** *adv* ▸ **'brightness** *n*

brighten ➊ ('braɪtᵊn) *vb* **1** to make or become bright or brighter. **2** to make or become cheerful.

brightening agent *n* a compound applied to a textile to increase its brightness by the conversion of ultraviolet radiation to visible (blue) light, used in detergents.

Bright's disease (braɪts) *n* chronic inflammation of the kidneys; chronic nephritis. [C19: after Richard *Bright* (1789–1858), E physician]

brightwork ('braɪt,wɜ:k) *n* shiny metal trimmings or fittings on ships, cars, etc.

brill[1] (brɪl) *n, pl* **brill** *or* **brills.** a European flatfish similar to the turbot. [C15: prob. from Cornish *brȳthel* mackerel, from OCornish *brȳth* speckled]

brill[2] (brɪl) *adj Brit sl.* excellent or wonderful. [C20: shortened form of BRILLIANT]

brilliance ➊ ('brɪljəns) *or* **brilliancy** *n* **1** great brightness; radiance. **2** excellence or distinction in physical or mental ability; exceptional talent. **3** splendour; magnificence.

brilliant ➊ ('brɪljənt) *adj* **1** shining with light; sparkling. **2** (of a colour) reflecting a considerable amount of light; vivid. **3** outstanding; exceptional: *a brilliant success.* **4** splendid; magnificent: *a brilliant show.* **5** of outstanding intelligence or intellect: *a brilliant mind.* ◆ *n* **6** Also called: **brilliant cut. 6a** a cut for diamonds and other gemstones in the form of two many-faceted pyramids joined at their bases. **6b** a diamond of this cut. [C17: from F *brillant* shining, from It. *brillo* BERYL]
▸ **'brilliantly** *adv*

brilliantine ('brɪljən,ti:n) *n* a perfumed oil used to make the hair smooth and shiny. [C19: from F, from *brillant* shining]

brim ➊ (brɪm) *n* **1** the upper rim of a vessel: *the brim of a cup.* **2** a projecting rim or edge: *the brim of a hat.* **3** the brink or edge of something. ◆ *vb* **brims, brimming, brimmed. 4** to fill or be full to the brim: *eyes brimming with tears.* [C13: from MHG *brem*]
▸ **'brimless** *adj*

brimful ➊ *or* **brimfull** (,brɪm'fʊl) *adj* (*postpositive;* foll. by *of*) filled up to the brim (with).

brimstone ('brɪm,stəʊn) *n* **1** an obsolete name for **sulphur. 2** a common yellow butterfly of N temperate regions of the Old World. [OE *brynstān;* see BURN[1], STONE]

brindle ('brɪndᵊl) *n* **1** a brindled animal. **2** a brindled colouring. [C17: back formation from BRINDLED]

brindled ('brɪndᵊld) *adj* brown or grey streaked or patched with a darker colour: *a brindled dog.* [C17: changed from C15 *brended,* lit.: branded]

brine ➊ (braɪn) *n* **1** a strong solution of salt and water, used for salting and pickling meats, etc. **2** the sea or its water. ◆ *vb* **brines, brining, brined. 3** (*tr*) to soak in or treat with brine. [OE *brīne*]
▸ **'brinish** *adj*

bring ➊ (brɪŋ) *vb* **brings, bringing, brought.** (*tr*) **1** to carry, convey, or take (something or someone) to a designated place or person: *bring that book to me.* **2** to cause to happen or occur to (oneself or another): *to bring disrespect on oneself.* **3** to cause to happen as a consequence: *responsibility brings maturity.* **4** to cause to come to mind: *it brought back memories.* **5** to cause to be in a certain state, position, etc.: *the punch brought him to his knees.* **6** to force, persuade, or make (oneself): *I couldn't bring myself to do it.* **7** to sell for; fetch: *the painting brought 20 pounds.* **8** *Law.* **8a** to institute (proceedings, charges, etc.). **8b** to put (evidence, etc.) before a tribunal. **9 bring forth.** to give birth to. ◆ See also **bring about, bring down,** etc. [OE *bringan*]
▸ **'bringer** *n*

bring about ➊ *vb* (*tr, adv*) **1** to cause to happen. **2** to turn (a ship) around.

bring-and-buy sale *n Brit. & NZ.* an informal sale, often for charity, to

THESAURUS

briefing *n* **1 = meeting**, conference, preparation **2 = instructions**, directions, guidance, information, instruction, preamble, rundown

briefly *adv* **1 = momentarily**, briskly, cursorily, fleetingly, hastily, hurriedly, in passing, precisely, quickly, shortly, temporarily **4 = concisely**, in a few words, in a nutshell, in brief, in outline

brigade *n* **1, 2 = group**, band, body, camp, company, contingent, corps, crew, force, organization, outfit, party, squad, team, troop, unit

brigand *n* **= bandit**, desperado, footpad (*arch.*), freebooter, gangster, highwayman, marauder, outlaw, plunderer, robber, ruffian

bright *adj* **1 = shining**, beaming, blazing, brilliant, dazzling, effulgent, flashing, gleaming, glistening, glittering, glowing, illuminated, intense, lambent, luminous, lustrous, radiant, resplendent, scintillating, shimmering, sparkling, twinkling, vivid **3 = promising**, auspicious, encouraging, excellent, favourable, golden, good, hopeful, optimistic, palmy, propitious, prosperous, rosy **4 = cheerful**, chirpy (*inf.*), full of beans (*inf.*), gay, genial, glad, happy, jolly, joyful, joyous, light-hearted, lively, merry, sparky, upbeat (*inf.*), vivacious **5** *Informal* **= intelligent**, acute, astute, aware, brainy, brilliant, clear-headed, clever, ingenious, inventive, keen, quick, quick-witted, sharp, smart, wide-awake
Antonyms *adj* ≠ **intelligent:** dense, dim, dim-witted (*inf.*), dull, dumb (*inf.*), dumb-ass (*sl.*), foolish, idiotic, ignorant, retarded, simple, slow, stupid, thick, unintelligent, witless

brighten *vb* **1 = light up**, clear up, enliven, gleam, glow, illuminate, lighten, make brighter, shine **2 = cheer up**, become cheerful, buck up (*inf.*), buoy up, encourage, enliven, gladden, hearten, make happy, perk up
Antonyms *vb* ≠ **light up:** becloud, blacken, cloud over *or* up, dim, dull, obscure, overshadow, shade, shadow ≠ **cheer up:** become angry, become gloomy, blacken, cloud, deject, depress, dispirit, look black, sadden

brightness *n* **1 = shine**, brilliance, effulgence, glare, incandescence, intensity, light, luminosity, radiance, refulgence, resplendence, sparkle, splendour, vividness **5 = intelligence**, acuity, alertness, awareness, cleverness, quickness, sharpness, smartness, smarts (*sl., chiefly US.*)
Antonyms *n* ≠ **shine:** dimness, dullness

brilliance *n* **1 = brightness**, blaze, dazzle, effulgence, gleam, glitter, intensity, luminosity, lustre, radiance, refulgence, resplendence, sheen, sparkle, vividness **2 = cleverness**, acuity, aptitude, braininess, distinction, excellence, genius, giftedness, greatness, inventiveness, talent, wisdom **3 = splendour**, éclat, gilt, glamour, gorgeousness, grandeur, illustriousness, magnificence, pizzazz *or* pizazz (*inf.*)
Antonyms *n* ≠ **brightness:** darkness, dimness, dullness, obscurity, paleness ≠ **cleverness:** folly, idiocy, inanity, incompetence, ineptitude, silliness, simple-mindedness, stupidity

brilliant *adj* **1 = shining**, ablaze, bright, coruscating, dazzling, glittering, glossy, intense, luminous, lustrous, radiant, refulgent, resplendent, scintillating, sparkling **3, 4 = splendid**, celebrated, eminent, exceptional, famous, glorious, illustrious, magnificent, notable, outstanding, superb **5 = intelligent**, accomplished, acute, astute, brainy, clever, discerning, expert, gifted, intellectual, inventive, masterly, penetrating, profound, quick, talented
Antonyms *adj* ≠ **shining:** dark, dim, dull, gloomy, obscure ≠ **splendid:** dull, ordinary, run-of-the-mill, unaccomplished, unexceptional, untalented ≠ **intelligent:** dim, simple, slow, stupid

brim *n* **2, 3 = rim**, border, brink, circumference, edge, flange, lip, margin, skirt, verge ◆ *vb* **4 = be full**, fill, fill up, hold no more, overflow, run over, spill, well over

brimful *adj* **= full**, brimming, filled, flush, level with, overflowing, overfull, packed, running over

brine *n* **1 = salt water**, pickling solution, saline solution **2 = the sea**, sea water

bring *vb* **1 = take**, accompany, bear, carry, conduct, convey, deliver, escort, fetch, gather, guide, import, lead, transfer, transport, usher **2, 3 = cause**, contribute to, create, effect, engender, inflict, occasion, produce, result in, wreak **6 = make**, compel, convince, dispose, force, induce, influence, move, persuade, prevail on *or* upon, prompt, sway **7 = sell for**, command, earn, fetch, gross, net, produce, return, yield

bring about *vb* **1 = cause**, accomplish, achieve, bring to pass, compass, create, effect, effectuate, generate, give rise to, make happen, manage, occasion, produce, realize

which people bring items for sale and buy those that others have brought.
bring down ❶ *vb (tr, adv)* to cause to fall.
bring forward *vb (tr, adv)* **1** to present or introduce (a subject) for discussion. **2** *Book-keeping.* to transfer (a sum) to the top of the next page or column.
bring in ❶ *vb (tr, adv)* **1** to yield (income, profit, or cash). **2** to produce or return (a verdict). **3** to introduce (a legislative bill, etc.).
bring off ❶ *vb (tr, adv)* to succeed in achieving (something), esp. with difficulty.
bring out *vb (tr, adv)* **1** to produce or publish or have published. **2** to expose, reveal, or cause to be seen: *she brought out the best in me.* **3** (foll. by *in*) to cause (a person) to become covered (with spots, a rash, etc.). **4** *Brit.* to introduce (a girl) formally into society as a debutante.
bring over *vb (tr, adv)* to cause (a person) to change allegiances.
bring round *or* **around** *vb (tr, adv)* **1** to restore (a person) to consciousness, esp. after a faint. **2** to convince (another person, usually an opponent) of an opinion or point of view.
bring to *vb (tr, adv)* **1** to restore (a person) to consciousness. **2** to cause (a ship) to turn into the wind and reduce her headway.
bring up ❶ *vb (tr, adv)* **1** to care for and train (a child); rear. **2** to raise (a subject) for discussion; mention. **3** to vomit (food).
brinjal ('brɪndʒəl) *n* (in India and Africa) another name for the **aubergine.** [C17: from Port. *berinjela,* from Ar.]
brink ❶ (brɪŋk) *n* **1** the edge, border, or verge of a steep place. **2** the land at the edge of a body of water. **3** the verge of an event or state: *the brink of disaster.* [C13: from MDu. *brinc,* of Gmc origin]
brinkmanship ('brɪŋkmən,ʃɪp) *n* the art or practice of pressing a dangerous situation, esp. in international affairs, to the limit of safety and peace in order to win an advantage.
briny ('braɪnɪ) *adj* **brinier, briniest. 1** of or resembling brine; salty. ◆ *n* **2** (preceded by *the*) *Inf.* the sea.
▸ **'brininess** *n*
brio ❶ ('bri:əʊ) *n* liveliness or vigour; spirit. See also **con brio.** [C19: from It., of Celtic origin]
brioche ('bri:əʊʃ, -ɒʃ) *n* a soft roll made from a very light yeast dough. [C19: from Norman dialect, from *brier* to knead, of Gmc origin]
briquette *or* **briquet** (brɪ'ket) *n* a small brick made of compressed coal dust, sawdust, charcoal, etc., used for fuel. [C19: from F: a little brick, from *brique* BRICK]
brisk ❶ (brɪsk) *adj* **1** lively and quick; vigorous: *a brisk walk.* **2** invigorating or sharp: *brisk weather.* ◆ *vb* **3** (often foll. by *up*) to enliven; make or become brisk. [C16: prob. var. of BRUSQUE]
▸ **'briskly** *adv* ▸ **'briskness** *n*
brisket ('brɪskɪt) *n* **1** the breast of a four-legged animal. **2** the meat from this part, esp. of beef. [C14: prob. from ON]
brisling ('brɪslɪŋ) *n* another name for a **sprat.** [C20: from Norwegian; rel. to obs. Danish *bretling*]
bristle ❶ ('brɪs^əl) *n* **1** any short stiff hair of an animal or plant, such as on a pig's back. **2** something resembling these hairs: *toothbrush bristle.* ◆ *vb* **bristles, bristling, bristled. 3** (when *intr,* often foll. by *up*) to stand up or cause to stand up like bristles. **4** (*intr;* sometimes foll. by *up*) to show anger, indignation, etc.: *she bristled at the suggestion.* **5** (*intr*) to be thickly covered or set: *the target bristled with arrows.* [C13 *bristil, brustel,* from earlier *brust,* from OE *byrst*]
▸ **'bristly** *adj*
Bristol board ('brɪst^əl) *n* a heavy smooth cardboard of fine quality, used for drawing.
Bristol fashion *adv, adj (postpositive)* in good order; efficiently arranged.
bristols ('brɪst^əlz) *pl n Brit. sl.* a woman's breasts. [C20: short for *Bristol Cities,* rhyming slang for *titties*]
Brit (brɪt) *n Inf.* a British person.
Brit. *abbrev. for:* **1** Britain. **2** British.
Britannia (brɪ'tænɪə) *n* **1** a female warrior carrying a trident and wearing a helmet, personifying Great Britain or the British Empire. **2** (in the ancient Roman Empire) the S part of Great Britain. **3** short for **Britannia coin.**
Britannia coin *n* any of four British gold coins introduced in 1987 for investment purposes; their denominations are £100, £50, £25, and £10.
Britannia metal *n* an alloy of tin with antimony and copper: used for decorative purposes and for bearings.
Britannic (brɪ'tænɪk) *adj* of Britain; British (esp. in **His** *or* **Her Britannic Majesty**).
britches ('brɪtʃɪz) *pl n* a variant spelling of **breeches.**
Briticism ('brɪtɪ,sɪzəm) *n* a custom, linguistic usage, or other feature peculiar to Britain or its people. Also: **Britishism.**
British ('brɪtɪʃ) *adj* **1** of or denoting Britain, a country of W Europe, consisting of the island of Great Britain (comprising England, Scotland, and Wales) and part of the island of Ireland (Northern Ireland). **2** relating to, denoting, or characteristic of the inhabitants of Britain. **3** relating to or denoting the English language as spoken and written in Britain. **4** of or relating to the Commonwealth: *British subjects.* ◆ *n* **5 the British.** (*functioning as pl*) the natives or inhabitants of Britain.
▸ **'Britishness** *n*
British Council *n* an organization founded (1934) to extend the influence of British culture and education throughout the world.
Britisher ('brɪtɪʃə) *n* (not used by the British) **1** a native or inhabitant of Great Britain. **2** any British subject.
Britishism ('brɪtɪ,ʃɪzəm) *n* a variant of **Briticism.**
British Legion *n Brit.* an organization founded in 1921 to provide services and assistance for former members of the armed forces.
British thermal unit *n* a unit of heat in the fps system equal to the quantity of heat required to raise the temperature of 1 pound of water by 1°F. 1 British thermal unit is equivalent to 1055.06 joules. Abbrev.: **btu, BThU.**
Briton ❶ ('brɪt^ən) *n* **1** a native or inhabitant of Britain. **2** *History.* any of the early Celtic inhabitants of S Britain. [C13: from OF *Breton,* of Celtic origin]
Britpop ('brɪt,pɒp) *n* the characteristic pop music performed by some British bands of the mid 1990s.
brittle ❶ ('brɪt^əl) *adj* **1** easily cracked, snapped, or broken; fragile. **2** curt or irritable. **3** hard or sharp in quality. ◆ *n* **4** a crunchy sweet made with treacle and nuts: *peanut brittle.* [C14: ult. from OE *brēotan* to break]
▸ **'brittleness** *n*
brittle-star *n* an echinoderm occurring on the sea bottom and having long slender arms radiating from a small central disc.
bro. *abbrev. for* brother.
broach ❶ (brəʊtʃ) *vb (tr)* **1** to initiate (a topic) for discussion. **2** to tap or pierce (a container) to draw off (a liquid): *to broach a cask.* **3** to open in order to begin to use. ◆ *n* **4** a long tapered toothed cutting tool for enlarging holes. **5** a spit for roasting meat, etc. [C14: from OF *broche,* from L *brochus* projecting]
broad ❶ (brɔ:d) *adj* **1** having relatively great breadth or width. **2** of vast extent; spacious: *a broad plain.* **3** (*postpositive*) from one side to the other: *four miles broad.* **4** of great scope or potential: *that invention had broad applications.* **5** not detailed; general: *broad plans.* **6** clear and open; full (esp. in **broad daylight**). **7** obvious or plain: *broad hints.* **8** liberal; tolerant: *a broad political stance.* **9** widely spread; extensive: *broad support.* **10** vulgar; coarse; indecent: *a broad joke.* **11** (of a dialect or pronunciation) consisting of a large number of speech sounds characteristic of a particular geographic area: *a broad Yorkshire accent.* **12** *Finance.* denoting an assessment of liquidity as including notes and coin in circulation with the public, banks' till money and balances, most private-sector bank deposits, and sterling bank-deposit certificates: *broad money.* Cf. **narrow** (sense 7). **13** *Phonetics.* the long vowel in English words such as *father, half,* as represented in Received Pronuncia-

THESAURUS

bring down *vb* = **lower,** cut down, drop, fell, floor, lay low, level, pull down, shoot down, upset
bring in *vb* **1** = **produce,** accrue, bear, be worth, fetch, generate, gross, net, profit, realize, return, yield
bring off *vb* = **accomplish,** achieve, bring home the bacon (*inf.*), bring to pass, carry off, carry out, crack it (*inf.*), cut it (*inf.*), discharge, execute, perform, pull off, succeed
bring up *vb* **1** = **rear,** breed, develop, educate, form, nurture, raise, support, teach, train **2** = **mention,** advance, allude to, broach, introduce, move, propose, put forward, raise, submit
brink *n* **1-3** = **edge,** border, boundary, brim, fringe, frontier, limit, lip, margin, point, rim, skirt, threshold, verge
brio *n* = **energy,** animation, dash, élan, enthusiasm, get-up-and-go (*inf.*), gusto, liveliness, panache, pep, spirit, verve, vigour, vivacity, zest, zip (*inf.*)
brisk *adj* **1** = **lively,** active, agile, alert, animated, bustling, busy, energetic, nimble, no-nonsense, quick, sparky, speedy, sprightly, spry, vigorous, vivacious **2** = **invigorating,** biting, bracing, crisp, exhilarating, fresh, keen, nippy, refreshing, sharp, snappy, stimulating
Antonyms *adj* ≠ **lively:** heavy, lazy, lethargic, slow, sluggish, unenergetic ≠ **invigorating:** boring, dull, enervating, tiring, wearisome
briskly *adv* **1** = **quickly,** actively, apace, brusquely, coolly, decisively, efficiently, energetically, firmly, incisively, nimbly, posthaste, promptly, pronto (*inf.*), rapidly, readily, smartly, vigorously
bristle *n* **1** = **hair,** barb, prickle, spine, stubble, thorn, whisker ◆ *vb* **3** = **stand up,** prickle, rise, stand on end **4** = **be angry,** be infuriated, be maddened, bridle, flare up, get one's dander up (*sl.*), go ballistic (*sl., chiefly US*), rage, see red, seethe, spit (*inf.*), wig out (*sl.*) **5** = **be thick,** abound, be alive, crawl, hum, swarm, teem
bristly *adj* **1** = **hairy,** bearded, bewhiskered, prickly, rough, stubbly, unshaven, whiskered
Briton *n* **1** = **Brit** (*inf.*), Anglo-Saxon, Britisher, limey (*US & Canad. sl.*), pommy *or* pom (*Austral. & NZ sl.*)
brittle *adj* **1** = **fragile,** breakable, crisp, crumbling, crumbly, delicate, frail, frangible, friable, shatterable, shivery **2** = **tense,** curt, edgy, irritable, nervous, prim, stiff, stilted, wired (*sl.*)
Antonyms *adj* ≠ **fragile:** durable, elastic, flexible, infrangible, nonbreakable, resistant, rugged, shatterproof, strong, sturdy, toughened
broach *vb* **1** = **bring up,** approach, hint at, introduce, mention, open up, propose, raise the subject, speak of, suggest, talk of, touch on **2, 3** = **open,** crack, draw off, pierce, puncture, start, tap, uncork
broad *adj* **1, 2** = **wide,** ample, beamy (*of a ship*), capacious, expansive, extensive, generous, large, roomy, spacious, vast, voluminous, widespread **4, 5** = **general,** all-embracing, catholic, comprehensive, encyclopedic, far-reaching, global, inclusive, nonspecific, overarching, sweeping, undetailed, universal, unlimited, wide, wide-ranging **6** *As in* **broad daylight** = **clear,** full, obvious, open, plain, straightforward, undisguised **8** = **tolerant,** broad-minded, liberal, open, open-minded, permissive, progressive, unbiased **10** = **vulgar,** blue, coarse,

tion. ◆ *n* **14** the broad part of something. **15** *Sl., chiefly US & Canad.* **15a** a girl or woman. **15b** a prostitute. **16** See **Broads.** [OE *brād*]
► **'broadly** *adv*

B-road *n* a secondary road in Britain.

broad arrow *n* **1** a mark shaped like a broad arrowhead designating British government property and formerly used on prison clothing. **2** an arrow with a broad head.

broad bean *n* **1** an erect annual Eurasian bean plant cultivated for its large edible flattened seeds. **2** the seed of this plant.

broadcast Ⓣ ('brɔːdˌkɑːst) *vb* **broadcasts, broadcasting, broadcast** *or* **broadcasted. 1** to transmit (announcements or programmes) on radio or television. **2** (*intr*) to take part in a radio or television programme. **3** (*tr*) to make widely known throughout an area: *to broadcast news.* **4** (*tr*) to scatter (seed, etc.) over an area, esp. by hand. ◆ *n* **5a** a transmission or programme on radio or television. **5b** (*as modifier*): *a broadcast signal.* **6** the act of scattering seeds. ◆ *adj* **7** dispersed over a wide area. ◆ *adv* **8** far and wide.
► **'broadˌcaster** *n* ► **'broadˌcasting** *n*

Broad Church *n* **1** a party within the Church of England which favours a broad and liberal interpretation of Anglican doctrine. **2** (*usually not caps.*) a group which embraces a wide and varied number of views and opinions. ◆ *adj* **Broad-Church. 3** of or relating to this party in the Church of England.

broadcloth ('brɔːdˌklɒθ) *n* **1** fabric woven on a wide loom. **2** a closely woven fabric of wool, worsted, cotton, or rayon with lustrous finish, used for clothing.

broaden Ⓣ ('brɔːdᵊn) *vb* to make or become broad or broader; widen.

broad gauge *n* **1** a railway track with a greater distance between the lines than the standard gauge of 56½ inches (about 1·44 metres). ◆ *adj* **broad-gauge. 2** of or denoting a railway having this track.

broad-leaved *adj* denoting trees other than conifers; having broad rather than needle-shaped leaves.

broadloom ('brɔːdˌluːm) *n* (*modifier*) of or designating carpets woven on a wide loom.

broad-minded Ⓣ *adj* **1** tolerant of opposing viewpoints; not prejudiced; liberal. **2** not easily shocked by permissive sexual habits, pornography, etc.
► **ˌbroad-'mindedly** *adv* ► **ˌbroad-'mindedness** *n*

broadsheet ('brɔːdˌʃiːt) *n* **1** a newspaper having a large format, approximately 15 by 24 inches (38 by 61 centimetres). **2** another word for **broadside** (sense 4).

broadside Ⓣ ('brɔːdˌsaɪd) *n* **1** *Naut.* the entire side of a vessel. **2** *Naval.* **2a** all the armament fired from one side of a warship. **2b** the simultaneous discharge of such armament. **3** a strong or abusive verbal or written attack. **4** Also called: **broadside ballad.** a ballad or popular song printed on one side of a sheet of paper, esp. in 16th-century England. ◆ *adv* **5** with a broader side facing an object; sideways.

broad-spectrum *n* (*modifier*) effective against a wide variety of diseases or microorganisms: *a broad-spectrum antibiotic.*

broadsword ('brɔːdˌsɔːd) *n* a broad-bladed sword used for cutting rather than stabbing.

broadtail ('brɔːdˌteɪl) *n* **1** the highly valued black wavy fur obtained from the skins of newly born karakul lambs; caracul. **2** another name for **karakul.**

Broadway('brɔːdˌweɪ) *n* **1** a thoroughfare in New York City: the centre of the commercial theatre in the US. ◆ *adj* **2** of, relating to, or suitable for the commercial theatre, esp. on Broadway.

brocade (brəʊ'keɪd) *n* **1** a rich fabric woven with a raised design, often using gold or silver threads. ◆ *vb* **brocades, brocading, brocaded. 2** (*tr*) to weave with such a design. [C17: from Sp. *brocado,* from It. *broccato* embossed fabric, from L *brochus* projecting]

broccoli ('brɒkəlɪ) *n* **1** a cultivated variety of cabbage having branched greenish flower heads. **2** the flower head, eaten as a vegetable before the buds have opened. [C17: from It., pl of *broccolo* a little sprout, from *brocco* sprout]

broch (brɒk, brɒx) *n* (in Scotland) a prehistoric circular dry-stone tower large enough to serve as a fortified home. [C17: from ON *borg;* rel. to OE *burh* settlement, burgh]

brochette (brɒ'ʃɛt) *n* a skewer or small spit, used for holding pieces of meat, etc., while roasting or grilling. [C19: from OF *brochete* small pointed tool; see BROACH]

brochure Ⓣ ('brəʊʃjʊə, -ʃə) *n* a pamphlet or booklet, esp. one containing summarized or introductory information or advertising. [C18: from F, from *brocher* to stitch (a book)]

brock (brɒk) *n* a Brit. name for **badger** (sense 1). [OE *broc,* of Celtic origin]

brocket ('brɒkɪt) *n* a small deer of tropical America, having small unbranched antlers. [C15: from Anglo-F *broquet,* from *broque* horn]

broderie anglaise ('brəʊdərɪ: ɑːŋ'glɛz) *n* open embroidery on white cotton, fine linen, etc. [C19: from F: English embroidery]

Broederbond ('brʊdəˌbɔːnt, 'bruːdəˌbɒnt) *n* (in South Africa) a secret society of Afrikaner Nationalists. [Afrik.: band of brothers]

brogue[1] (brəʊg) *n* a broad gentle-sounding dialectal accent, esp. that used by the Irish in speaking English. [C18: from ?]

brogue[2] (brəʊg) *n* **1** a sturdy walking shoe, often with ornamental perforations. **2** an untanned shoe worn formerly in Ireland and Scotland. [C16: from Irish Gaelic *bróg* shoe]

broil[1] (brɔɪl) *vb* **1** the usual US and Canad. word for **grill** (sense 1). **2** to become or cause to become extremely hot. **3** (*intr*) to be furious. [C14: from OF *bruillir* to burn]

broil[2] (brɔɪl) *Arch.* ◆ *n* **1** a loud quarrel or disturbance; brawl. ◆ *vb* **2** (*intr*) to brawl; quarrel. [C16: from OF *brouiller* to mix]

broiler ('brɔɪlə) *n* **1** a young tender chicken suitable for roasting. **2** a pan, grate, etc., for broiling food. **3** a very hot day.

broke Ⓣ (brəʊk) *vb* **1** the past tense of **break.** ◆ *adj* **2** *Inf.* having no money; bankrupt. **3 go for broke.** *Sl.* to risk everything in a gambling or other venture.

broken Ⓣ ('brəʊkən) *vb* **1** the past participle of **break.** ◆ *adj* **2** fractured, smashed, or splintered: *a broken vase.* **3** interrupted; disturbed; disconnected: *broken sleep.* **4** intermittent or discontinuous: *broken sunshine.* **5** not functioning. **6** spoilt or ruined by divorce (esp. in **broken home, broken marriage**). **7** (of a trust, promise, contract, etc.) violated; infringed. **8** (of the speech of a foreigner) imperfect in grammar, vocabulary, and pronunciation: *broken English.* **9** Also: **broken-in.** made tame or disciplined by training. **10** exhausted or weakened, as through ill-health or misfortune. **11** irregular or rough; uneven: *broken ground.* **12** bankrupt. **13** (of colour) having a multicoloured decorative effect, as by stippling paint onto a surface.
► **'brokenly** *adv*

broken chord *n* another term for **arpeggio.**

broken-down Ⓣ *adj* **1** worn out, as by age or long use; dilapidated. **2** not in working order.

brokenhearted Ⓣ (ˌbrəʊkən'hɑːtɪd) *adj* overwhelmed by grief or disappointment.
► **ˌbroken'heartedly** *adv*

broken wind (wɪnd) *n* *Vet. science.* another name for **heaves.**
► **ˌbroken'winded** *adj*

broker Ⓣ ('brəʊkə) *n* **1** an agent who, acting on behalf of a principal, buys or sells goods, securities, etc.: *insurance broker.* **2** short for **stockbroker. 3** a person who deals in second-hand goods. [C14: from Anglo-F *brocour* broacher (of casks, hence, one who sells, agent), from OF *broquier* to tap a cask]

brokerage ('brəʊkərɪdʒ) *n* **1** commission charged by a broker. **2** a broker's business or office.

brolga ('brɒlgə) *n* a large grey Australian crane having a red-and-green head and a trumpeting call. Also called: **native companion.** [C19: from Abor.]

THESAURUS

gross, improper, indecent, indelicate, near the knuckle, unrefined
Antonyms *adj* ≠ **wide:** close, confined, constricted, cramped, limited, meagre, narrow, restricted, tight

broadcast *vb* **1 = transmit,** air, beam, cable, put on the air, radio, relay, show, televise **3 = make public,** advertise, announce, circulate, disseminate, proclaim, promulgate, publish, report, shout from the rooftops (*inf.*), spread ◆ *n* **5a = transmission,** programme, show, telecast

broaden *vb* **= expand,** augment, develop, enlarge, extend, fatten, increase, open up, spread, stretch, supplement, swell, widen
Antonyms *vb* circumscribe, constrain, diminish, narrow, reduce, restrict, simplify, tighten

broadly *adv* **1, 2 = widely,** expansively, extensively, far and wide, greatly, hugely, vastly **9 = generally,** commonly, for the most part, in general, in the main, largely, mainly, mostly, on the whole, predominantly, universally, widely
Antonyms *adv* ≠ **widely, generally:** exclusively, narrowly

broad-minded **1** *adj* **= tolerant,** catholic, cosmopolitan, flexible, free-thinking, indulgent, liberal, open-minded, permissive, responsive, unbiased, unbigoted, undogmatic, unprejudiced
Antonyms *adj* biased, bigoted, closed-minded, dogmatic, inflexible, intolerant, narrow-minded, prejudiced, uncharitable

broadside *n* **3 = attack,** abuse, assault, battering, bombardment, censure, criticism, denunciation, diatribe, stick (*sl.*), swipe

brochure *n* **= booklet,** advertisement, circular, folder, handbill, hand-out, leaflet, mailshot, pamphlet

broke *adj* **2** *Informal* **= penniless,** bankrupt, bust, cleaned out (*sl.*), dirt-poor (*inf.*), down and out, flat broke (*inf.*), impoverished, in queer street, insolvent, in the red, on one's uppers, penurious, ruined, short, skint (*Brit. sl.*), stony-broke (*Brit. sl.*), strapped for cash (*inf.*), without two pennies to rub together (*inf.*)
Antonyms *adj* affluent, comfortable, flush (*inf.*), in the money (*inf.*), prosperous, rich, solvent, wealthy, well-to-do

broken *adj* **2 = smashed,** burst, demolished, destroyed, fractured, fragmented, rent, ruptured, separated, severed, shattered, shivered **3, 4 = interrupted,** disconnected, discontinuous, disturbed, erratic, fragmentary, incomplete, intermittent, spasmodic **5 = not working,** defective, imperfect, kaput (*inf.*), not functioning, on its last legs, on the blink (*sl.*), out of order, ruined **7 = violated,** dishonoured, disobeyed, disregarded, forgotten, ignored, infringed, not kept, retracted, traduced, transgressed **8 = imperfect,** disjointed, halting, hesitating, stammering **10 = defeated,** beaten, browbeaten, crippled, crushed, demoralized, humbled, oppressed, overpowered, subdued, vanquished

broken-down *adj* **1 = dilapidated,** old, worn out **2 = not in working order,** collapsed, in disrepair, inoperative, kaput (*inf.*), not functioning, on the blink (*sl.*), out of commission, out of order

brokenhearted *adj* **= heartbroken,** choked, desolate, despairing, devastated, disappointed, disconsolate (*inf.*), grief-stricken, heart-sick, inconsolable, miserable, mournful, prostrated, sorrowful, wretched

broker *n* **1 = dealer,** agent, factor, go-between, intermediary, middleman, negotiator

brolly ('brɒlɪ) *n, pl* **brollies.** an informal Brit. name for **umbrella** (sense 1).

bromeliad (brəʊ'miːlɪ,æd) *n* any of a family of tropical American plants, typically epiphytes with a rosette of fleshy leaves, such as the pineapple and Spanish moss. [C19: from NL, after Olaf *Bromelius* (1639–1705), Swedish botanist]

bromide ('brəʊmaɪd) *n* **1** any salt of hydrobromic acid. **2** any compound containing a bromine atom. **3** a dose of sodium or potassium bromide given as a sedative. **4a** a platitude. **4b** a boring person.

bromide paper *n* a type of photographic paper coated with an emulsion of silver bromide.

bromine ('brəʊmiːn, -mɪn) *n* a pungent dark red volatile liquid element that occurs in brine and is used in the production of chemicals. Symbol: Br; atomic no.: 35; atomic wt.: 79.91. [C19: from F *brome* bromine, from Gk *brōmos* bad smell, from ?]

bronchi ('brɒŋkaɪ) *n* the plural of **bronchus.**

bronchial ('brɒŋkɪəl) *adj* of or relating to the bronchi or the bronchial tubes.
▸ **'bronchially** *adv*

bronchial tubes *pl n* the bronchi or their smaller divisions.

bronchiectasis (,brɒŋkɪ'ɛktəsɪs) *n* chronic dilation and usually infection of the bronchi. [C19: from BRONCHO- + Gk *ektasis* a stretching]

bronchiole ('brɒŋkɪ,əʊl) *n* any of the smallest bronchial tubes. [C19: from NL; see BRONCHUS]
▸ **,bronchi'olar** *adj*

bronchitis (brɒŋ'kaɪtɪs) *n* inflammation of the bronchial tubes, characterized by coughing, difficulty in breathing, etc.
▸ **bronchitic** (brɒŋ'kɪtɪk) *adj, n*

broncho- *or before a vowel* **bronch-** *combining form.* indicating or relating to the bronchi: *bronchitis.* [from Gk: BRONCHUS]

bronchodilator (,brɒŋkəʊdaɪ'leɪtə, -dɪ-) *n* any drug or other agent that causes dilation of the bronchial tubes by relaxing bronchial muscle: used, esp. in the form of aerosol sprays, for the relief of asthma and chronic bronchitis.

bronchopneumonia (,brɒŋkəʊnjuː'məʊnɪə) *n* inflammation of the lungs, starting in the bronchioles.

bronchoscope ('brɒŋkə,skəʊp) *n* an instrument for examining and providing access to the interior of the bronchial tubes.

bronchus ('brɒŋkəs) *n, pl* **bronchi.** either of the two main branches of the trachea. [C18: from NL, from Gk *bronkhos* windpipe]

bronco *or* **broncho** ('brɒŋkəʊ) *n, pl* **broncos** *or* **bronchos.** (in the US and Canada) a wild or partially tamed pony or mustang of the western plains. [C19: from Mexican Sp., from Sp.: rough, wild]

brontosaurus (,brɒntə'sɔːrəs) *or* **brontosaur** ('brɒntə,sɔː) *n* a very large herbivorous quadrupedal dinosaur, common in N America during late Jurassic times, having a long neck and long tail. [C19: from NL, from Gk *brontē* thunder + *sauros* lizard]

Bronx cheer (brɒŋks) *n Chiefly US.* a loud spluttering noise made with the lips and tongue and expressing derision or contempt; raspberry. [C20: from the *Bronx*, a borough of New York City]

bronze ❶ (brɒnz) *n* **1** any hard water-resistant alloy consisting of copper and smaller proportions of tin and sometimes zinc and lead. **2** a yellowish-brown colour or pigment. **3** a statue, medal, or other object made of bronze. Cf. **bronze** (sense 1). ◆ *adj* **4** made of or resembling bronze. **5** of a yellowish-brown colour. ◆ *vb* **bronzes, bronzing, bronzed. 6** (esp. of the skin) to make or become brown; tan. **7** (*tr*) to give the appearance of bronze to. [C18: from F, from It. *bronzo*]
▸ **'bronzy** *adj*

Bronze Age *n* **a** a technological stage between the Stone and Iron Ages, beginning in the Middle East about 4500 B.C. and lasting in Britain from about 2000 to 500 B.C., during which weapons and tools were made of bronze. **b** (*as modifier*): *a Bronze-Age tool.*

bronze medal *n* a medal awarded to a competitor who comes third in a contest or race.

bronzing ('brɒnzɪŋ) *n* **1** blue pigment producing a metallic lustre when ground into paint media at fairly high concentrations. **2** the application of a mixture of powdered metal or pigments of a metallic lustre to a surface.

brooch (brəʊtʃ) *n* an ornament with a hinged pin and catch, worn fastened to clothing. [C13: from OF *broche*; see BROACH]

brood ❶ (bruːd) *n* **1** a number of young animals, esp. birds, produced at one hatching. **2** all the offspring in one family: often used jokingly or contemptuously. **3** a group of a particular kind; breed. **4** (*modifier*) kept for breeding: *a brood mare.* ◆ *vb* **5** (of a bird) **5a** to sit on or hatch (eggs). **5b** (*tr*) to cover (young birds) protectively with the wings. **6** (when *intr*, often foll. by *on, over,* or *upon*) to ponder morbidly or persistently. [OE *brōd*]
▸ **'brooding** *n, adj*

brooder ('bruːdə) *n* **1** a structure, usually heated, used for rearing young chickens or other fowl. **2** a person or thing that broods.

broody ('bruːdɪ) *adj* **broodier, broodiest. 1** moody; introspective. **2** (of poultry) wishing to sit on or hatch eggs. **3** *Inf.* (of a woman) wishing to have a baby.
▸ **'broodiness** *n*

brook[1] ❶ (brʊk) *n* a natural freshwater stream smaller than a river. [OE *brōc*]

brook[2] ❶ (brʊk) *vb* (*tr*) (*usually used with a negative*) to bear; tolerate. [OE *brūcan*]

brooklet ('brʊklɪt) *n* a small brook.

brooklime ('brʊk,laɪm) *n* either of two blue-flowered trailing plants, *Veronica americana* of North America or *V. beccabunga* of Europe and Asia, growing in moist places. See also **speedwell.** [C16: from BROOK[1] + *-lemk*, from OE *hleomoce*]

brook trout *n* a North American trout, valued as a food and game fish.

broom (bruːm, brʊm) *n* **1** an implement for sweeping consisting of a long handle to which is attached either a brush of straw or twigs, bound together, or a solid head into which are set tufts of bristles or fibres. **2** any of various yellow-flowered Eurasian leguminous shrubs. **3 new broom.** a newly appointed official, etc., eager to make changes. ◆ *vb* **4** (*tr*) to sweep with a broom. [OE *brōm*]

broomrape ('bruːm,reɪp, 'brʊm-) *n* any of a genus of leafless fleshy parasitic plants growing on the roots of other plants, esp. on broom. [C16: adaptation & partial translation of Med. L *rāpum genistae* tuber (hence: root nodule) of Genista (a type of broom plant)]

broomstick ('bruːm,stɪk, 'brʊm-) *n* the long handle of a broom.

bros. *or* **Bros.** *abbrev. for* brothers.

brose (brəʊz) *n Scot.* a porridge made by adding a boiling liquid to meal, esp. oatmeal. [C13 *broys*, from OF *broez*, from *breu* broth, of Gmc origin]

broth (brɒθ) *n* **1** a soup made by boiling meat, fish, vegetables, etc., in water. **2** another name for **stock** (sense 19). [OE *broth*]

brothel ❶ ('brɒθəl) *n* **1** a house where men pay to have sexual intercourse with prostitutes. **2** *Austral. inf.* any untidy place. [C16: short for *brothel-house*, from C14 *brothel* useless person, from OE *brēothan* to deteriorate]

brother ❶ ('brʌðə) *n* **1** a male person having the same parents as another person. **2a** a male person belonging to the same group, profession, nationality, trade union, etc., as another or others; fellow member. **2b** (*as modifier*): *brother workers.* **3** comrade; friend: used as a form of address. **4** *Christianity.* a member of a male religious order. ◆ Related adj: **fraternal.** [OE *brōthor*]

brotherhood ❶ ('brʌðə,hʊd) *n* **1** the state of being related as a brother or brothers. **2** an association or fellowship, such as a trade union. **3** all persons engaged in a particular profession, trade, etc. **4** the belief, feeling, or hope that all men should treat one another as brothers.

brother-in-law *n, pl* **brothers-in-law. 1** the brother of one's wife or husband. **2** the husband of one's sister. **3** the husband of the sister of one's husband or wife.

brotherly ❶ ('brʌðəlɪ) *adj* of, resembling, or suitable to a brother, esp. in showing loyalty and affection; fraternal.
▸ **'brotherliness** *n*

brougham ('bruːəm, bruːm) *n* **1** a four-wheeled horse-drawn closed carriage having a raised open driver's seat in front. **2** *Obs.* a large car with an open compartment at the front for the driver. **3** *Obs.* an early electric car. [C19: after Lord *Brougham* (1778–1868)]

brought (brɔːt) *vb* the past tense and past participle of **bring.**

brouhaha ('bruːhɑːhɑː) *n* a loud confused noise; commotion; uproar. [F, imit.]

brow ❶ (braʊ) *n* **1** the part of the face from the eyes to the hairline; forehead. **2** short for **eyebrow. 3** the expression of the face; countenance: *a troubled brow.* **4** the jutting top of a hill, etc. [OE *brū*]

browbeat ❶ ('braʊ,biːt) *vb* **browbeats, browbeating, browbeat, browbeaten.** (*tr*) to discourage or frighten with threats or a domineering manner; intimidate.

brown ❶ (braʊn) *n* **1** any of various dark colours, such as those of

THESAURUS

bronze *adj* **5** = **reddish-brown**, brownish, chestnut, copper, copper-coloured, metallic brown, reddish-tan, rust, tan, yellowish-brown

bronzed *adj* **6** = **tanned**, brown, sunburnt, suntanned

brood *n* **1** = **offspring**, breed, chicks, children, clutch, family, hatch, infants, issue, litter, progeny, young ◆ *vb* **5a** = **incubate**, cover, hatch, set, sit upon **6** = **think upon**, agonize, dwell upon, eat one's heart out, fret, have a long face, meditate, mope, mull over, muse, obsess, ponder, repine, ruminate

brook[1] *n* = **stream**, beck, burn, gill (*dialect*), rill, rivulet, runnel (*literary*), streamlet, watercourse

brook[2] *vb* = **tolerate**, abide, accept, allow, bear, countenance, endure, hack (*sl.*), put up with, stand, stomach, suffer, support, swallow, thole (*dialect*), withstand

brothel *n* **1** = **whorehouse**, bawdy house (*arch.*), bordello, cathouse (*US sl.*), house of ill fame *or* ill repute, house of prostitution, knocking shop (*sl.*), red-light district

brother *n* **1** = **sibling**, blood brother, kin, kinsman, relation, relative **3** = **comrade**, associate, chum (*inf.*), cock (*Brit. inf.*), colleague, companion, compeer, confrère, fellow member, mate, pal (*inf.*), partner **4** *Christianity* = **monk**, cleric, friar, regular, religious

brotherhood *n* **1** = **fellowship**, brotherliness, camaraderie, companionship, comradeship, friendliness, kinship **2, 3** = **association**, alliance, clan, clique, community, coterie, fraternity, guild, league, order, society, union

brotherly *adj* = **kind**, affectionate, altruistic, amicable, benevolent, cordial, fraternal, friendly, neighbourly, philanthropic, sympathetic

brow *n* **3** = **forehead**, air, appearance, aspect, bearing, countenance, eyebrow, face, front, mien, temple **4** = **top**, brim, brink, crest, crown, edge, peak, rim, summit, tip, verge

browbeat *vb* = **bully**, badger, bulldoze (*inf.*), coerce, cow, domineer, dragoon, hector, intimidate, lord it over, oppress, overawe, overbear, ride roughshod over, threaten, tyrannize
Antonyms *vb* beguile, cajole, coax, entice, flatter, inveigle, lure, manoeuvre, seduce, sweet-talk (*inf.*), tempt, wheedle

brown *adj* **3** = **brunette**, auburn, bay, brick, bronze, bronzed, browned, chestnut, choco-

wood or earth. **2** a dye or pigment producing these colours. ◆ *adj* **3** of the colour brown. **4** (of bread) made from a flour that has not been bleached or bolted, such as wheatmeal or wholemeal flour. **5** deeply tanned or sunburnt. **6 in a brown study.** See **study** (sense 15). ◆ *vb* **7** to make (esp. food as a result of cooking) brown or (esp. of food) to become brown. [OE *brūn*]
▸**'brownish** *or* **'browny** *adj* ▸**'brownness** *n*

brown bear *n* a large ferocious brownish bear inhabiting temperate forests of North America, Europe, and Asia.

brown coal *n* another name for **lignite.**

brown dwarf *n* a type of celestial body midway in size between a large planet and a small star, thought to be one possible explanation of dark matter in the universe.

browned-off ⓣ *adj Inf.* thoroughly discouraged or disheartened; fed up.

brown fat *n* a dark form of adipose tissue that is readily converted into energy.

Brownian movement ('braʊnɪən) *n* random movement of microscopic particles suspended in a fluid, caused by bombardment of the particles by molecules of the fluid. [C19: after Robert *Brown* (1773–1858), Scot. botanist]

brownie ('braʊnɪ) *n* **1** (in folklore) an elf said to do helpful work at night, esp. household chores. **2** a small square nutty chocolate cake. [C16: dim. of BROWN (that is, a small brown man)]

Brownie Guide *or* **Brownie** ('braʊnɪ) *n* a member of the junior branch of the Guides.

Brownie point *n* a notional mark to one's credit for being seen to do the right thing. [C20: ?from the mistaken notion that Brownie Guides earn points for good deeds]

browning ('braʊnɪŋ) *n Brit.* a substance used to darken soups, gravies, etc.

brown paper *n* a kind of coarse unbleached paper used for wrapping.

brown rice *n* unpolished rice, in which the grains retain the outer yellowish-brown layer (bran).

Brown Shirt *n* **1** (in Nazi Germany) a storm trooper. **2** a member of any fascist party or group.

brownstone ('braʊn,stəʊn) *n US.* a reddish-brown iron-rich sandstone used for building.

brown sugar *n* sugar that is unrefined or only partially refined.

brown trout *n* a common brownish variety of the trout that occurs in the rivers of N Europe.

browse ⓣ (braʊz) *vb* **browses, browsing, browsed. 1** to look through (a book, articles for sale in a shop, etc.) in a casual leisurely manner. **2** *Computing.* to read hypertext, esp. on the World Wide Web. **3** (of deer, goats, etc.) to feed upon (vegetation) by continual nibbling. ◆ *n* **4** the act or an instance of browsing. **5** the young twigs, shoots, leaves, etc., on which certain animals feed. [C15: from F *broust, brost* bud, of Gmc origin]

browser ('braʊzə) *n* **1** a person or animal that browses. **2** *Computing.* a software package that enables a user to read hypertext, esp. on the World Wide Web.

BRS *abbrev. for* British Road Services.

Bruce (bru:s) *n Brit.* a jocular name for an Australian man.

brucellosis (,bru:sɪ'ləʊsɪs) *n* an infectious disease of cattle, goats, and pigs, caused by bacteria and transmittable to man. Also called: **undulant fever.** [C20: from NL *Brucella*, after Sir David *Bruce* (1855–1931), Australian bacteriologist & physician]

bruin ('bru:ɪn) *n* a name for a bear, used in children's tales, etc. [C17: from Du. *bruin* brown]

bruise ⓣ (bru:z) *vb* **bruises, bruising, bruised.** (*mainly tr*) **1** (*also intr*) to injure (tissues) without breaking the skin, usually with discoloration, or (of tissues) to be injured in this way. **2** to offend or injure (someone's feelings). **3** to damage the surface of (something). **4** to crush (food, etc.) by pounding. ◆ *n* **5** a bodily injury without a break in the skin, usually with discoloration; contusion. [OE *brȳsan*]

bruiser ⓣ ('bru:zə) *n Inf.* a strong tough person, esp. a boxer or a bully.

bruit (bru:t) *vb* **1** (*tr; often passive;* usually foll. by *about*) to report; rumour. ◆ *n* **2** *Arch.* **2a** a rumour. **2b** a loud outcry; clamour. [C15: via F from Med. L *brūgītus*, prob. from L *rugīre* to roar]

brumby ('brʌmbɪ) *n, pl* **brumbies.** *Austral.* **1** a wild horse, esp. one descended from runaway stock. **2** *Inf.* a wild or unruly person. [C19: from ?]

brume (bru:m) *n Poetic.* heavy mist or fog. [C19: from F: mist, winter, from L *brūma*, contracted from *brevissima diēs* the shortest day]

brunch (brʌntʃ) *n* a meal eaten late in the morning, combining breakfast with lunch. [C20: from BR(EAKFAST) + (L)UNCH]

brunette (bru:'nɛt) *n* **1** a girl or woman with dark brown hair. ◆ *adj* **2** dark brown: *brunette hair.* [C17: from F, fem of *brunet* dark, brownish, from *brun* brown]

brunt ⓣ (brʌnt) *n* the main force or shock of a blow, attack, etc. (esp. in **bear the brunt of**). [C14: from ?]

brush[1] ⓣ (brʌʃ) *n* **1** a device made of bristles, hairs, wires, etc., set into a firm back or handle: used to apply paint, clean or polish surfaces, groom the hair, etc. **2** the act or an instance of brushing. **3** a light stroke made in passing; graze. **4** a brief encounter or contact, esp. an unfriendly one; skirmish. **5** the bushy tail of a fox. **6** an electric conductor, esp. one made of carbon, that conveys current between stationary and rotating parts of a generator, motor, etc. ◆ *vb* **7** (*tr*) to clean, polish, scrub, paint, etc., with a brush. **8** (*tr*) to apply or remove with a brush or brushing movement. **9** (*tr*) to touch lightly and briefly. **10** (*intr*) to move so as to graze or touch something lightly. ◆ See also **brush aside, brush off, brush up.** [C14: from OF *broisse*, ?from *broce* BRUSH[2]]
▸**'brusher** *n*

brush[2] ⓣ (brʌʃ) *n* **1** a thick growth of shrubs and small trees; scrub. **2** land covered with scrub. **3** broken or cut branches or twigs; brushwood. **4** wooded sparsely populated country; backwoods. [C16 (dense undergrowth), C14 (cuttings of trees): from OF *broce*, from Vulgar L *bruscia* (unattested) brushwood]
▸**'brushy** *adj*

brush aside ⓣ *or* **away** *vb* (*tr, adv*) to dismiss without consideration; disregard.

brush discharge *n* a slightly luminous brushlike electrical discharge.

brushed (brʌʃt) *adj Textiles.* treated with a brushing process to raise the nap and give a softer and warmer finish: *brushed nylon.*

brushmark ('brʌʃ,mɑ:k) *n* the indented lines sometimes left by the bristles of a brush on a painted surface.

brush off ⓣ *Sl.* ◆ *vb* (*tr, adv*) **1** to dismiss and ignore (a person), esp. curtly. ◆ *n* **brushoff. 2** an abrupt dismissal or rejection.

brush turkey *n* any of several gallinaceous flightless birds of New Guinea and Australia, having a black plumage.

brush up ⓣ *vb* (*adv*) **1** (*tr;* often foll. by *on*) to refresh one's knowledge, skill, or memory of (a subject). **2** to make (a person or oneself) clean or neat as after a journey. ◆ *n* **brush-up. 3** *Brit.* the act or an instance of tidying one's appearance (esp. in **wash and brush-up**).

brushwood ('brʌʃ,wʊd) *n* **1** cut or broken-off tree branches, twigs, etc. **2** another word for **brush**[2] (sense 1).

brushwork ('brʌʃ,wɜ:k) *n* **1** a characteristic manner of applying paint with a brush: *Rembrandt's brushwork.* **2** work done with a brush.

brusque ⓣ (bru:sk, brʊsk) *adj* blunt or curt in manner or speech. [C17: from F, from It. *brusco* sour, rough, from Med. L *bruscus* butcher's broom]
▸**'brusquely** *adv* ▸**'brusqueness** *n*

Brussels carpet ('brʌsᵊlz) *n* a worsted carpet with a heavy pile formed by uncut loops of wool on a linen warp.

Brussels lace *n* a fine lace with a raised or appliqué design.

Brussels sprout *n* **1** a variety of cabbage, having a stout stem studded with budlike heads resembling tiny cabbages. **2** the head of this plant, eaten as a vegetable.

brut (bru:t) *adj* (of champagne or sparkling wine) very dry. [F, lit.: dry]

brutal ⓣ ('bru:tᵊl) *adj* **1** cruel; vicious; savage. **2** extremely honest or coarse in speech or manner. **3** harsh; severe; extreme: *brutal cold.*
▸**bru'tality** *n* ▸**'brutally** *adv*

brutalism ('bru:tə,lɪzəm) *n* an austere style of architecture character-

THESAURUS

late, coffee, dark, donkey brown, dun, dusky, fuscous, ginger, hazel, rust, sunburnt, tan, tanned, tawny, toasted, umber ◆ *vb* **7** = **fry,** cook, grill, sauté, seal, sear

browned-off *adj Informal* = **fed up,** cheesed off (*Brit. sl.*), discontented, discouraged, disgruntled, disheartened, pissed off (*taboo sl.*), sick as a parrot (*inf.*), weary

browse *vb* **1** = **skim,** dip into, examine cursorily, flip through, glance at, leaf through, look round, look through, peruse, scan, survey **3** = **graze,** crop, eat, feed, nibble, pasture

bruise *vb* **1** = **discolour,** blacken, blemish, contuse, deface, injure, mar, mark **2** = **hurt,** displease, grieve, injure, insult, offend, pain, sting, wound **4** = **crush,** pound, pulverize ◆ *n* **5** = **discoloration,** black-and-blue mark, black mark, blemish, contusion, injury, mark, swelling, trauma (*Pathology*)

bruiser *n Informal* = **tough,** bully, bully boy, gorilla (*inf.*), hard man, heavy (*sl.*), hoodlum, rough (*inf.*), roughneck (*sl.*), rowdy, ruffian, thug, tough guy

bruising *n* **5** = **discoloration,** contusion, ecchymosis, marking, swelling

brunt *n* = **full force,** burden, force, impact, pressure, shock, strain, stress, thrust, violence

brush[1] *n* **1** = **broom,** besom, sweeper **4** = **encounter,** clash, conflict, confrontation, fight, fracas, scrap (*inf.*), set-to (*inf.*), skirmish, slight engagement, spot of bother (*inf.*), tussle ◆ *vb* **7** = **clean,** buff, paint, polish, sweep, wash **9** = **touch,** caress, contact, flick, glance, graze, kiss, scrape, stroke, sweep

brush[2] *n* **1, 2** = **shrubs,** brushwood, bushes, copse, scrub, thicket, undergrowth, underwood

brush aside *vb* = **dismiss,** discount, disregard, have no time for, ignore, override, sweep aside

brush off *Slang vb* **1** = **ignore,** blank (*sl.*), cold-shoulder, cut, deny, disdain, dismiss, disown, disregard, put down, rebuff, refuse, reject, repudiate, scorn, send to Coventry, slight, snub, spurn ◆ *n* **brushoff 2** = **snub,** bum's rush (*sl.*), cold shoulder, cut, dismissal, go-by (*sl.*), kick in the teeth (*sl.*), knock-back, rebuff, refusal, rejection, repudiation, repulse, slight, the (old) heave-ho (*inf.*)

brush up *vb* **1** = **revise,** bone up (*inf.*), cram, go over, polish up, read up, refresh one's memory, relearn, study

brusque *adj* = **curt,** abrupt, blunt, discourteous, gruff, hasty, impolite, monosyllabic, sharp, short, surly, tart, terse, unmannerly
Antonyms *adj* accommodating, civil, courteous, gentle, patient, polite, well-mannered

brutal *adj* **1** = **cruel,** barbarous, bloodthirsty, ferocious, heartless, inhuman, merciless, pitiless, remorseless, ruthless, savage, uncivilized, vicious **2** = **harsh,** bearish, callous, gruff, impolite, insensitive, rough, rude, severe, uncivil, unfeeling, unmannerly
Antonyms *adj* ≠ **cruel:** civilized, gentle, humane, kind, merciful, soft-hearted ≠ **harsh:** polite, refined, sensitive

ized by emphasis on such structural materials as undressed concrete and unconcealed service pipes. Also called: **new brutalism.**
▸ '**brutalist** *n, adj*

brutalize ⓣ *or* **brutalise** ('bru:təˌlaɪz) *vb* **brutalizes, brutalizing, brutalized** *or* **brutalises, brutalising, brutalised. 1** to make or become brutal. **2** (*tr*) to treat brutally.
▸ ˌ**brutali'zation** *or* ˌ**brutali'sation** *n*

brute ⓣ (bru:t) *n* **1a** any animal except man; beast; lower animal. **1b** (*as modifier*): *brute nature.* **2** a brutal person. ◆ *adj* (*prenominal*) **3** wholly instinctive or physical (esp. in **brute strength, brute force**). **4** without reason or intelligence. **5** coarse and grossly sensual. [C15: from L *brūtus* heavy, irrational]

brutish ⓣ ('bru:tɪʃ) *adj* **1** of, relating to, or resembling a brute; animal. **2** coarse; cruel; stupid.
▸ '**brutishly** *adv* ▸ '**brutishness** *n*

bryology (braɪ'ɒlədʒɪ) *n* the branch of botany concerned with the study of bryophytes.
▸ **bryological** (ˌbraɪə'lɒdʒɪk^əl) *adj* ▸ **bry'ologist** *n*

bryony *or* **briony** ('braɪənɪ) *n, pl* **bryonies** *or* **brionies.** any of several herbaceous climbing plants of Europe and N Africa. [OE *bryōnia,* from L, from Gk *bruōnia*]

bryophyte ('braɪəˌfaɪt) *n* any plant of the phylum *Bryophyta,* esp. mosses and liverworts. [C19: from Gk *bruon* moss + -PHYTE]
▸ **bryophytic** (ˌbraɪə'fɪtɪk) *adj*

bryozoan (ˌbraɪə'zəʊən) *n* any aquatic invertebrate animal forming colonies of polyps each having a ciliated feeding organ. Popular name: **sea mat.** [C19: from Gk *bruon* moss + *zōion* animal]

Brythonic (brɪ'θɒnɪk) *n* **1** the S group of Celtic languages, consisting of Welsh, Cornish, and Breton. ◆ *adj* **2** of or relating to this group of languages. [C19: from Welsh; see BRITON]

bs *abbrev. for:* **1** balance sheet. **2** bill of sale.

BS *abbrev. for* British Standard(s).

BSc *abbrev. for* Bachelor of Science.

BSE *abbrev. for* bovine spongiform encephalopathy: a fatal slow-developing virus disease of cattle, affecting the nervous system. Informal name: **mad cow disease.**

BSI *abbrev. for* British Standards Institution.

B-side *n* the less important side of a gramophone record.

BST *abbrev. for:* **1** bovine somatotrophin: a growth hormone that can be used to increase milk production in dairy cattle. **2** British Summer Time.

Bt *abbrev. for* Baronet.

BT *abbrev. for* British Telecom. [C20: shortened from TELECOMMUNICATIONS]

btu *or* **BThU** *abbrev. for* British thermal unit. US abbrev.: **BTU.**

bu. *abbrev. for* bushel.

bubble ⓣ ('bʌb^əl) *n* **1** a thin film of liquid forming a hollow globule around air or a gas: *a soap bubble.* **2** a small globule of air or a gas in a liquid or a solid. **3** the sound made by a bubbling liquid. **4** something lacking substance, stability, or seriousness. **5** an unreliable scheme or enterprise. **6** a dome, esp. a transparent glass or plastic one. ◆ *vb* **bubbles, bubbling, bubbled. 7** to form or cause to form bubbles. **8** (*intr*) to move or flow with a gurgling sound. **9** (*intr;* often foll. by *over*) to overflow (with excitement, anger, etc.). [C14: prob. from ON; imit.]

bubble and squeak *n Brit. & Austral.* a dish of leftover boiled cabbage and potatoes fried together.

bubble bath *n* **1** a powder, liquid, or crystals used to scent, soften, and foam in bath water. **2** a bath to which such a substance has been added.

bubble car *n Brit.* (formerly) a small car with a transparent bubble-shaped top.

bubble chamber *n* a device that enables the tracks of ionizing particles to be photographed as a row of bubbles in a superheated liquid.

bubble gum *n* a type of chewing gum that can be blown into large bubbles.

bubble memory *n Computing.* a method of storing high volumes of data by using minute pockets of magnetism (bubbles) in a semiconducting material.

bubble point *n Chem.* the temperature at which bubbles just start to appear in a heated liquid mixture.

bubble wrap *n* a type of polythene wrapping containing many small air pockets, used as a protective covering when transporting breakable goods.

bubbly ⓣ ('bʌblɪ) *adj* **bubblier, bubbliest. 1** full of or resembling bubbles. **2** lively; animated; excited. ◆ *n* **3** *Inf.* champagne.

bubo ('bju:bəʊ) *n, pl* **buboes.** *Pathol.* inflammation and swelling of a lymph node, esp. in the armpit or groin. [C14: from Med. L *bubō,* from Gk *boubōn* groin]
▸ **bubonic** (bju:'bɒnɪk) *adj*

bubonic plague *n* an acute infectious febrile disease characterized by chills, prostration, delirium, and formation of buboes: caused by the bite of an infected rat flea.

buccal ('bʌk^əl) *adj* **1** of or relating to the cheek. **2** of or relating to the mouth; oral. [C19: from L *bucca* cheek]

buccaneer ⓣ (ˌbʌkə'nɪə) *n* **1** a pirate, esp. one who preyed on Spanish shipping in the Caribbean in the 17th and 18th centuries. ◆ *vb* (*intr*) **2** to be or act like a buccaneer. [C17: from *boucan,* dried meat taken on long voyages, from F *boucaner* to smoke meat]

buccinator ('bʌksɪˌneɪtə) *n* either of two flat cheek muscles used in chewing. [C17: from L, from *buccina* a trumpet]

buck[1] ⓣ (bʌk) *n* **1a** the male of various animals including the goat, hare, kangaroo, rabbit, and reindeer. **1b** (*as modifier*): *a buck antelope.* **2** *S. African.* an antelope or deer of either sex. **3** *Arch.* a robust spirited young man. **4** the act of bucking. ◆ *vb* **5** (*intr*) (of a horse or other animal) to jump vertically, with legs stiff and back arched. **6** (*tr*) (of a horse, etc.) to throw (its rider) by bucking. **7** (when *intr,* often foll. by *against* or *at*) *Chiefly US, Canad., & Austral. inf.* to resist or oppose obstinately. **8** (*tr; usually passive*) *Inf.* to cheer or encourage: *I was very bucked at passing the exam.* ◆ See also **buck up.** [OE *bucca* he-goat]
▸ '**bucker** *n*

buck[2] (bʌk) *n US, Canad., & Austral. inf.* a dollar. [C19: from ?]

buck[3] (bʌk) *n* **1** *Poker.* a marker in the jackpot to remind the winner of some obligation when his turn comes to deal. **2** **pass the buck.** *Inf.* to shift blame or responsibility onto another. [C19: prob. from *buckhorn knife,* placed before a player in poker to indicate that he was the next dealer]

buckbean ('bʌkˌbi:n) *n* a marsh plant with white or pink flowers. Also called: **bogbean.**

buckboard ('bʌkˌbɔ:d) *n US & Canad.* an open four-wheeled horse-drawn carriage with the seat attached to a flexible board between the front and rear axles.

bucket ('bʌkɪt) *n* **1** an open-topped roughly cylindrical container; pail. **2** Also called: **bucketful.** the amount a bucket will hold. **3** any of various bucket-like parts of a machine, such as the scoop on a mechanical shovel. **4** *Chiefly US.* a turbine rotor blade. **5** *Austral.* a small container for ice cream. **6** **kick the bucket.** *Sl.* to die. ◆ *vb* **buckets, bucketing, bucketed. 7** (*tr*) to carry in or put into a bucket. **8** (*intr;* often foll. by *down*) (of rain) to fall very heavily. **9** (*intr;* often foll. by *along*) *Chiefly Brit.* to travel or drive fast. **10** (*tr*) *Austral. sl.* to criticize severely. [C13: from Anglo-F *buket,* from OE *būc*]

bucket seat *n* a seat in a car, etc., having curved sides.

bucket shop *n* **1** an unregistered firm of stockbrokers that engages in fraudulent speculation. **2** *Chiefly Brit.* a firm specializing in cheap airline tickets.

buckeye ('bʌkˌaɪ) *n* any of several North American trees of the horse chestnut family having erect clusters of white or red flowers and prickly fruits.

buckhorn ('bʌkˌhɔ:n) *n* **a** horn from a buck, used for knife handles, etc. **b** (*as modifier*): *a buckhorn knife.*

buckjumper ('bʌkˌdʒʌmpə) *n Austral.* an untamed horse.

buckle ⓣ ('bʌk^əl) *n* **1** a clasp for fastening together two loose ends, esp. of a belt or strap, usually consisting of a frame with an attached movable prong. **2** an ornamental representation of a buckle, as on a shoe. **3** a kink, bulge, or other distortion. ◆ *vb* **buckles, buckling, buckled. 4** to fasten or be fastened with a buckle. **5** to bend or cause to bend out of shape. [C14: from OF, from L *buccula* a little cheek, hence, cheek strap of a helmet]

buckle down ⓣ *vb* (*intr, adv*) *Inf.* to apply oneself with determination.

buckler ('bʌklə) *n* **1** a small round shield worn on the forearm. **2** a means of protection; defence. [C13: from OF *bocler,* from *bocle* shield boss]

Buckley's chance ('bʌklɪz) *n Austral. & NZ sl.* no chance at all. Often shortened to **Buckley's.** [C19: from ?]

bucko ('bʌkəʊ) *n, pl* **buckoes.** *Irish.* a lively young fellow: often a term of address.

buckram ('bʌkrəm) *n* **a** cotton or linen cloth stiffened with size, etc.,

THESAURUS

brutality *n* **1** = **cruelty,** atrocity, barbarism, barbarity, bloodthirstiness, brutishness, ferocity, inhumanity, ruthlessness, savageness, savagery, viciousness

brutalize *vb* **1** = **dehumanize,** bestialize, degrade **2** = **terrorize,** barbarize, vandalize

brutally *adv* **1** = **cruelly,** barbarically, barbarously, brutishly, callously, ferociously, fiercely, hardheartedly, heartlessly, in cold blood, inhumanly, mercilessly, murderously, pitilessly, remorselessly, ruthlessly, savagely, unkindly, viciously

brute *n* **1** = **animal,** beast, creature, wild animal **2** = **savage,** barbarian, beast, devil, fiend, ghoul, monster, ogre, sadist, swine ◆ *adj* **3** = **physical,** bodily, carnal, fleshly **4** = **mindless,** instinctive, senseless, unthinking **5** = **coarse,** animal, bestial, depraved, gross, sensual

brutish *adj* **1** = **coarse,** boorish, crass, crude, gross, loutish, subhuman, swinish, uncouth, vulgar **2** = **stupid**

bubble *n* **1, 2** = **air ball,** bead, blister, blob, drop, droplet, globule, vesicle ◆ *vb* **7** = **foam,** boil, effervesce, fizz, froth, percolate, seethe, sparkle **8** = **gurgle,** babble, burble, murmur, purl, ripple, trickle, trill

bubbly *adj* **1** = **frothy,** carbonated, curly, effervescent, fizzy, foamy, lathery, sparkling, sudsy **2** = **lively,** alive and kicking, animated, bouncy, elated, excited, full of beans, happy, merry, sparky

buccaneer *n* **1** = **pirate,** corsair, freebooter, privateer, sea-rover

buck[1] *n* **3** *Archaic* = **gallant,** beau, blade, blood, coxcomb, dandy, fop, popinjay, spark ◆ *vb* **5** = **jump,** bound, jerk, leap, prance, spring, start, vault **6** = **throw,** dislodge, unseat

buckle *n* **1** = **fastener,** catch, clasp, clip, hasp **3** = **distortion,** bulge, contortion, kink, warp ◆ *vb* **4** = **fasten,** catch, clasp, close, hook, secure **5** = **distort,** bend, bulge, cave in, collapse, contort, crumple, fold, twist, warp

buckle down *vb Informal,* = **apply oneself,**

used in lining clothes, bookbinding, etc. **b** (*as modifier*): *a buckram cover.* [C14: from OF *boquerant*, ult. from *Bukhara*, Uzbekistan, once important for textiles]

Bucks (bʌks) *abbrev. for* Buckinghamshire.

buckshee (ˌbʌk'ʃiː) *adj Brit. sl.* without charge; free. [C20: from BAKSHEESH]

buckshot ('bʌkˌʃɒt) *n* lead shot of large size used in shotgun shells, esp. for hunting game.

buckskin ('bʌkˌskɪn) *n* **1** the skin of a male deer. **2a** a strong greyish-yellow suede leather, originally made from deerskin but now usually made from sheepskin. **2b** (*as modifier*): *buckskin boots.* **3** a stiffly starched cotton cloth. **4** a strong and heavy satin-woven woollen fabric.

buckthorn ('bʌkˌθɔːn) *n* any of several thorny small-flowered shrubs whose berries were formerly used as a purgative. [C16: from BUCK[1] (from the spiny branches resembling antlers) + THORN]

bucktooth ('bʌkˌtuːθ) *n, pl* **buckteeth.** *Derog.* a projecting upper front tooth. [C18: from BUCK[1] (deer) + TOOTH]

buck up Ⓣ *vb* (*adv*) *Inf.* **1** to make or cause to make haste. **2** to make or become more cheerful, confident, etc.

buckwheat ('bʌkˌwiːt) *n* **1** a cereal plant with fragrant white flowers, cultivated, esp. in the US, for its seeds. **2** the edible seeds of this plant, ground into flour or used as animal fodder. **3** the flour obtained from these seeds. [C16: from MDu. *boecweite*, from *boeke* BEECH + *weite* WHEAT, from the resemblance of the seeds to beechnuts]

buckyball ('bʌkɪˌbɔːl) *n Inf.* a ball-like polyhedral carbon molecule, of the type found in buckminsterfullerene and other fullerenes.

bucolic (bjuː'kɒlɪk) *adj also* **bucolical. 1** of the countryside or country life; rustic. **2** of or relating to shepherds; pastoral. ◆ *n* **3** (*sometimes pl*) a pastoral poem. [C16: from L, from Gk, from *boukolos* cowherd, from *bous* ox]
▸**bu'colically** *adv*

bud Ⓣ (bʌd) *n* **1** a swelling on a plant stem consisting of overlapping immature leaves or petals. **2a** a partially opened flower. **2b** (*in combination*): *rosebud.* **3** any small budlike outgrowth: *taste buds.* **4** something small or immature. **5** an asexually produced outgrowth in simple organisms such as yeasts that develops into a new individual. **6 nip in the bud.** to put an end to (an idea, movement, etc.) in its initial stages. ◆ *vb* **buds, budding, budded. 7** (*intr*) (of plants and some animals) to produce buds. **8** (*intr*) to begin to develop or grow. **9** (*tr*) *Horticulture.* to graft (a bud) from one plant onto another. [C14 *budde*, of Gmc origin]

Buddha ('bʊdə) *n* **the.** ?563–483 B.C., a title applied to Gautama Siddhartha, a religious teacher of N India regarded by his followers as the most recent rediscoverer of the path to enlightenment: the founder of Buddhism.

Buddhism ('bʊdɪzəm) *n* a religious teaching propagated by the Buddha and his followers, which declares that by destroying greed, hatred, and delusion, which are the causes of all suffering, man can attain perfect enlightenment.
▸**'Buddhist** *n, adj*

buddleia ('bʌdlɪə) *n* an ornamental shrub which has long spikes of mauve flowers. Also called: **butterfly bush.** [C19: after A. *Buddle* (died 1715), Brit. botanist]

buddy ('bʌdɪ) *n, pl* **buddies. 1** Also (as a term of address): **bud.** *Chiefly US & Canad.* an informal word for **friend. 2** a volunteer who visits and gives help and support to a person suffering from AIDS. ◆ *vb* **buddies, buddying, buddied. 3** (*intr*) to act as a buddy to a person suffering from AIDS. [C19: prob. baby-talk var. (US) of BROTHER]

buddy-buddy *adj Inf., chiefly US.* on very friendly or intimate terms.

buddy movie *or* **film** *n* a genre of film dealing with the relationship and adventures of two friends.

budge Ⓣ (bʌdʒ) *vb* **budges, budging, budged.** (*usually used with a negative*) **1** to move, however slightly. **2** to change or cause to change opinions, etc. [C16: from OF *bouger*, from L *bullīre* to boil]

budgerigar ('bʌdʒərɪˌgɑː) *n* a small green Australian parrot: a popular cagebird bred in many different-coloured varieties. [C19: from Abor., from *budgeri* good + *gar* cockatoo]

budget Ⓣ ('bʌdʒɪt) *n* **1** an itemized summary of expected income and expenditure over a specified period. **2** (*modifier*) economical; inexpensive: *budget meals for a family.* **3** the total amount of money allocated for a specific purpose during a specified period. ◆ *vb* **budgets, budgeting, budgeted. 4** (*tr*) to enter or provide for in a budget. **5** to plan the expenditure of (money, time, etc.). **6** (*intr*) to make a budget. [C15 (meaning: leather pouch, wallet): from OF *bougette*, dim. of *bouge*, from L *bulga*]
▸**'budgetary** *adj*

Budget ('bʌdʒɪt) *n* **the.** an estimate of British government expenditures and revenues and the financial plans for the ensuing fiscal year presented annually to the House of Commons by the Chancellor of the Exchequer.

budget account *n* **1** an account with a department store, etc., enabling a customer to make monthly payments to cover his past and future purchases. **2** a bank account that allows the holder credit to pay certain bills in return for regular deposits.

budget deficit *n* the amount by which government expenditure exceeds income from taxation, customs duties, etc., in any one fiscal year.

budgie ('bʌdʒɪ) *n Inf.* short for **budgerigar.**

buff[1] Ⓣ (bʌf) *n* **1a** a soft thick flexible undyed leather made chiefly from the skins of buffalo, oxen, and elk. **1b** (*as modifier*): *a buff coat.* **2a** a dull yellow or yellowish-brown colour. **2b** (*as adj*): *a buff envelope.* **3** Also called: **buffer. 3a** a cloth or pad of material used for polishing an object. **3b** a disc or wheel impregnated with a fine abrasive for polishing metals, etc. **4** *Inf.* one's bare skin (esp. in **in the buff**). ◆ *vb* **5** to clean or polish (a metal, floor, shoes, etc.) with a buff. **6** to remove the grain surface of (a leather). [C16: from OF, from OIt. *bufalo*, from LL *būfalus* BUFFALO]

buff[2] (bʌf) *n Arch.* a blow or buffet (now only in **blind man's buff**). [C15: back formation from BUFFET[2]]

buff[3] Ⓣ (bʌf) *n Inf.* an expert on or devotee of a given subject. [C20: orig. US: an enthusiastic fire-watcher, from the buff-coloured uniforms worn by volunteer firemen in New York City]

buffalo ('bʌfəˌləʊ) *n, pl* **buffaloes** *or* **buffalo. 1** a type of cattle, mostly found in game reserves in southern and eastern Africa and having upward-curving horns. **2** short for **water buffalo. 3** a US & Canad. name for **bison** (sense 1). [C16: from It. *bufalo*, ult. from Gk *bous* ox]

buffalo grass *n* **1** a short grass growing on the dry plains of the central US. **2** *Austral.* a grass, *Stenotaphrum americanum*, introduced from North America.

buffel grass ('bʌfᵊl) *n* (in Australia) any of various grasses used for grazing or fodder, originally introduced from Africa.

buffer[1] Ⓣ ('bʌfə) *n* **1** one of a pair of spring-loaded steel pads attached at both ends of railway vehicles and at the end of a railway track to reduce shock due to contact. **2** a person or thing that lessens shock or protects from damaging impact, circumstances, etc. **3** *Chem.* **3a** an ionic compound added to a solution to resist changes in its acidity or alkalinity and thus stabilize its pH. **3b** Also called: **buffer solution.** a solution containing such a compound. **4** *Computing.* a memory device for temporarily storing data. ◆ *vb* (*tr*) **5** *Chem.* to add a buffer to (a solution). **6** to insulate against or protect from shock. [C19: from BUFF[2]]

buffer[2] ('bʌfə) *n* **1** any device used to shine, polish, etc.; buff. **2** a person who uses such a device.

buffer[3] ('bʌfə) *n Brit. inf.* a stupid or bumbling man (esp. in **old buffer**). [C18: ?from ME *buffer* stammerer]

buffer state *n* a small and usually neutral state between two rival powers.

buffer stock *n Commerce.* a stock of a commodity built up by a government or trade organization with the object of using it to stabilize prices.

buffet[1] Ⓣ *n* **1** ('bʊfeɪ). a counter where light refreshments are served. **2** ('bʊfeɪ). **2a** a meal at which guests help themselves from a number of dishes. **2b** (*as modifier*): *a buffet lunch.* **3** ('bʌfɪt, 'bʊfeɪ). (formerly) a piece of furniture used for displaying plate, etc., and typically comprising cupboards and open shelves. [C18: from F]

buffet[2] Ⓣ ('bʌfɪt) *vb* **buffets, buffeting, buffeted. 1** (*tr*) to knock against or about; batter. **2** (*tr*) to hit, esp. with the fist; cuff. **3** to force (one's way), as through a crowd. **4** (*intr*) to struggle; battle. ◆ *n* **5** a blow, esp. with a fist or hand. **6** aerodynamic oscillation of an aircraft structure by separated flows. [C13: from OF *buffet* a light blow]

buffet car ('bʊfeɪ) *n Brit.* a railway coach where light refreshments are served.

buffeting ('bʌfɪtɪŋ) *n* response of an aircraft structure to buffet, esp. an irregular oscillation of the tail.

bufflehead ('bʌfᵊlˌhɛd) *n* a small North American diving duck: the male has black-and-white plumage and a fluffy head. [C17 *buffle*, from obs. *buffle* wild ox, referring to the duck's head]

buffo ('bʊfəʊ) *n, pl* **buffi** (-fɪ) *or* **buffos. 1** (in Italian opera of the 18th cen-

THESAURUS

exert oneself, launch into, pitch in, put one's shoulder to the wheel, set to

buck up *vb* **1** *Informal* = **hurry up**, get a move on, hasten, shake a leg, speed up **2** = **cheer up**, brighten, encourage, hearten, inspirit, perk up, rally, take heart

bud *n* **1** = **shoot**, embryo, germ, sprout ◆ *vb* **7** = **develop**, burgeon, burst forth, grow, pullulate, shoot, sprout

budding *adj* **8** = **developing**, beginning, burgeoning, embryonic, fledgling, flowering, germinal, growing, incipient, nascent, potential, promising

budge *vb* **1** = **move**, dislodge, give way, inch, propel, push, remove, roll, shift, slide, stir **2** = **change**, bend, convince, give way, influence, persuade, sway, yield

budget *n* **1** = **fiscal estimate**, finances, financial statement **3** = **allowance**, allocation, cost, funds, means, resources ◆ *vb* **4-6** = **plan**, allocate, apportion, cost, cost out, estimate, ration

buff[1] *adj* **2b** = **yellowish-brown**, sandy, straw, tan, yellowish ◆ *n* **4** *Informal* = **naked**, bare, buck naked (*sl.*), in one's birthday suit (*inf.*), in the altogether (*inf.*), in the bare scud (*sl.*), in the raw (*inf.*), nude, unclad, unclothed, with bare skin, without a stitch on (*inf.*) ◆ *vb* **5** = **polish**, brush, burnish, rub, shine, smooth

buff[3] *n Informal* = **expert**, addict, admirer, aficionado, connoisseur, devotee, enthusiast, fan, fiend (*inf.*), freak (*inf.*), grandmaster, hotshot (*inf.*), maven (*US*), whizz (*inf.*)

buffer[1] *n* **2** = **safeguard**, bulwark, cushion, fender, intermediary, screen, shield, shock absorber

buffet[1] *n* **1** = **snack bar**, brasserie, café, cafeteria, cold table, counter, cupboard, refreshment counter, salad bar, sideboard, smorgasbord

buffet[2] *vb* **1, 2** = **batter**, bang, beat, box, bump, clobber (*sl.*), cuff, flail, knock, lambast(e), pound, pummel, punch, rap, shove, slap, strike, thump, wallop (*inf.*) ◆ *n* **5** = **blow**, bang, box, bump, cuff, jolt, knock, push, rap, shove, slap, smack, thump, wallop (*inf.*)

tury) a comic part, esp. one for a bass. **2** Also called: **buffo bass, basso buffo.** a bass singer who performs such a part. [C18: from It. (adj): comic, from *buffo* (n) BUFFOON]

buffoon ❶ (bə'fu:n) *n* **1** a person who amuses others by ridiculous or odd behaviour, jokes, etc. **2** a foolish person. [C16: from F *bouffon,* from It. *buffone,* from Med. L *būfō,* from L: toad]
▸**buf'foonery** *n*

bug ❶ (bʌg) *n* **1** an insect having piercing and sucking mouthparts specialized as a beak. **2** *Chiefly US & Canad.* any insect. **3** *Inf.* **3a** a microorganism, esp. a bacterium, that produces disease. **3b** a disease, esp. a stomach infection, caused by a microorganism. **4** *Inf.* an obsessive idea, hobby, etc.; craze. **5** *Inf.* a person having such a craze. **6** (*often pl*) *Inf.* a fault, as in a machine. **7** *Inf.* a concealed microphone used for recording conversations, as in spying. ◆ *vb* **bugs, bugging, bugged.** *Inf.* **8** (*tr*) to irritate; bother. **9** (*tr*) to conceal a microphone in (a room, etc.). **10** (*intr*) *US.* (of eyes) to protrude. [C16: from ?]

bugaboo ('bʌgə,bu:) *n, pl* **bugaboos.** an imaginary source of fear; bugbear; bogey. [C18: prob. of Celtic origin; cf. Cornish *buccaboo* the devil]

bugbear ❶ ('bʌg,beə) *n* **1** a thing that causes obsessive anxiety. **2** (in English folklore) a goblin in the form of a bear. [C16: from obs. *bug* an evil spirit+ BEAR[2]]

bug-eyed *adj* having protruding eyes.

bugger ('bʌgə) *n* **1** a person who practises buggery. **2** *Taboo sl.* a person or thing considered to be contemptible, unpleasant, or difficult. **3** *Sl.* a humorous or affectionate term for a man or child: *a friendly little bugger.* **4 bugger all.** *Sl.* nothing. ◆ *vb* **5** to practise buggery (with). **6** (*tr*) *Sl., chiefly Brit.* to ruin, complicate, or frustrate. **7** (*tr*) *Sl.* to tire; weary. ◆ *interj* **8** *Taboo sl.* an exclamation of annoyance or disappointment. [C16: from OF *bougre,* from Med. L *Bulgarus* Bulgarian; from the condemnation of the Eastern Orthodox Bulgarians as heretics]

bugger about *or* **around** *vb* (*adv*) *Sl.* **1** (*intr*) to fool about and waste time. **2** (*tr*) to create difficulties or complications for (a person).

bugger off *vb* (*intr, adv*) *Taboo sl.* to go away; depart.

buggery ('bʌgərɪ) *n* anal intercourse between a man and another man, a woman, or an animal.

buggy[1] ('bʌgɪ) *n, pl* **buggies. 1** a light horse-drawn carriage having either four wheels (esp. in the US and Canada) or two wheels (esp. in Britain and India). **2** any small light cart or vehicle, such as a baby buggy. [C18: from ?]

buggy[2] ('bʌgɪ) *adj* **buggier, buggiest.** infested with bugs.

bugle[1] ('bju:gᵊl) *n* **1** *Music.* a brass instrument similar to the cornet but usually without valves: used for military fanfares, signal calls, etc. ◆ *vb* **bugles, bugling, bugled. 2** (*intr*) to play or sound (on) a bugle. [C14: short for *bugle horn* ox horn, from OF *bugle,* from L *būculus* young bullock, from *bōs* ox]
▸**'bugler** *n*

bugle[2] ('bju:gᵊl) *n* any of several Eurasian plants having small blue or white flowers. [C13: from LL *bugula,* from ?]

bugle[3] ('bju:gᵊl) *n* a tubular glass or plastic bead sewn onto clothes for decoration. [C16: from ?]

bugloss ('bju:glɒs) *n* any of various hairy Eurasian plants having clusters of blue flowers. [C15: from L, from Gk *bouglōssos* ox-tongued]

bugong ('bu:gɒŋ) *n* another name for **bogong.**

buhl (bu:l) *adj, n* a variant spelling of **boulle.**

build ❶ (bɪld) *vb* **builds, building, built. 1** to make, construct, or form by joining parts or materials: *to build a house.* **2** (*tr*) to order the building of: *the government builds most of our hospitals.* **3** (foll. by *on* or *upon*) to base; found: *his theory was not built on facts.* **4** (*tr*) to establish and develop: *it took ten years to build a business.* **5** (*tr*) to make in a particular way or for a particular purpose: *the car was not built for speed.* **6** (*intr;* often foll. by *up*) to increase in intensity. ◆ *n* **7** physical form, figure, or proportions: *a man with an athletic build.* [OE *byldan*]

builder ('bɪldə) *n* a person who builds, esp. one who contracts for and supervises the construction or repair of buildings.

building ❶ ('bɪldɪŋ) *n* **1** something built with a roof and walls. **2** the act, business, occupation, or art of building houses, boats, etc.

building society *n* a cooperative banking enterprise financed by deposits on which interest is paid and from which mortgage loans are advanced on homes and real property; many now offer a range of banking services.

build up ❶ *vb* (*adv*) **1** (*tr*) to construct gradually, systematically, and in stages. **2** to increase, accumulate, or strengthen, esp. by degrees: *the murmur built up to a roar.* **3** (*tr*) to improve the health or physique of (a person). **4** (*intr*) to prepare for or gradually approach a climax. ◆ *n* **build-up. 5** progressive increase in number, size, etc.: *the build-up of industry.* **6** a gradual approach to a climax. **7** extravagant publicity or praise, esp. in the form of a campaign. **8** *Mil.* the process of attaining the required strength of forces and equipment.

built (bɪlt) *vb* the past tense and past participle of **build.**

built-in ❶ *adj* **1** made or incorporated as an integral part: *a built-in cupboard.* **2** essential; inherent. ◆ *n* **3** *Austral.* a built-in cupboard.

built-in obsolescence *n* See **planned obsolescence.**

built-up *adj* **1** having many buildings (esp. in **built-up area**). **2** increased by the addition of parts: *built-up heels.*

bulb ❶ (bʌlb) *n* **1** a rounded organ of vegetative reproduction in plants such as the tulip and onion: a flattened stem bearing a central shoot surrounded by fleshy nutritive inner leaves and thin brown outer leaves. **2** a plant, such as a hyacinth or daffodil, that grows from a bulb. **3** See **light bulb. 4** any bulb-shaped thing. [C16: from L *bulbus,* from Gk *bolbos* onion]
▸**'bulbous** *adj*

bulbil ('bʌlbɪl) *n* **1** a small bulb produced from a parent bulb. **2** a bulb-like reproductive organ in a leaf axil of certain plants. **3** any small bulblike structure in an animal. [C19: from NL *bulbillus* BULB]

bulbul ('bʊlbʊl) *n* a songbird of tropical Africa and Asia having brown plumage and, in many species, a distinct crest. [C18: via Persian from Ar.]

Bulgarian (bʌl'geərɪən, bʊl-) *adj* **1** of or denoting Bulgaria, a country of SE Europe, on the Balkan Peninsula, its people, or their language. ◆ *n* **2** the official language of Bulgaria. **3** a native or inhabitant of Bulgaria.

bulge ❶ (bʌldʒ) *n* **1** a swelling or an outward curve. **2** a sudden increase in number, esp. of population. ◆ *vb* **bulges, bulging, bulged. 3** to swell outwards. [C13: from OF *bouge,* from L *bulga* bag, prob. of Gaulish origin]
▸**'bulging** *adj* ▸**'bulgy** *adj*

bulgur ('bʌlgə) *n* cracked wheat that has been hulled, steamed, and roasted so that it requires little or no cooking. [C20: from Ar. *burghul*]

bulimia (bju:'lɪmɪə) *n* **1** pathologically insatiable hunger. **2** Also called: **bulimia nervosa.** a disorder characterized by compulsive overeating followed by vomiting. [C17: from NL, from Gk *bous* ox + *limos* hunger]

bulk ❶ (bʌlk) *n* **1** volume, size, or magnitude, esp. when great. **2** the main part: *the bulk of the work is repetitious.* **3** a large body, esp. of a person. **4** the part of food which passes unabsorbed through the digestive system. **5 in bulk. 5a** in large quantities. **5b** (of a cargo, etc.) unpackaged. ◆ *vb* **6** to cohere or cause to cohere in a mass. **7 bulk large.** to be or seem important or prominent. [C15: from ON *bulki* cargo]

> **USAGE NOTE** The use of a plural noun after *bulk* was formerly considered incorrect, but is now acceptable.

bulk buying *n* the purchase of goods in large amounts, often at reduced prices.

bulkhead ('bʌlk,hɛd) *n* any upright wall-like partition in a ship, aircraft, etc. [C15: prob. from *bulk* projecting framework from ON *bálkr* +HEAD]

bulk modulus *n* a coefficient of elasticity of a substance equal to the ratio of the applied stress to the resulting fractional change in volume.

bulky ❶ ('bʌlkɪ) *adj* **bulkier, bulkiest.** very large and massive, esp. so as to be unwieldy.
▸**'bulkily** *adv* ▸**'bulkiness** *n*

THESAURUS

buffoon *n* **1** = **clown**, comedian, comic, droll, fool, harlequin, jester, joker, wag

buffoonery *n* **1** = **clowning**, drollery, jesting, nonsense, tomfoolery, waggishness

bug *n* **3** *Informal* = **illness**, disease, infection, lurgy (*inf.*), virus **4** *Informal* = **mania**, craze, fad, obsession, rage **6** = **fault**, blemish, catch, defect, error, failing, flaw, glitch, gremlin, imperfection, snarl-up (*inf., chiefly Brit.*), virus ◆ *vb* **8** *Informal* = **annoy**, aggravate (*inf.*), badger, be on one's back (*sl.*), bother, disturb, gall, get on one's nerves (*inf.*), get under one's skin (*inf.*), harass, hassle (*inf.*), irk, irritate, nark (*Brit., Austral., & NZ sl.*), needle (*inf.*), nettle, pester, piss one off (*taboo sl.*), plague, vex **9** = **tap**, eavesdrop, listen in, spy, wiretap

bugbear *n* **1** = **pet hate**, anathema, bane, bête noire, bogey, bogeyman, bugaboo, devil, dread, fiend, horror, nightmare

build *vb* **1** = **construct**, assemble, erect, fabricate, form, make, put up, raise **4** = **establish**, base, begin, constitute, formulate, found, inaugurate, initiate, institute, originate, set up, start **6** = **increase**, accelerate, amplify, augment, develop, enlarge, escalate, extend, improve, intensify, strengthen ◆ *n* **7** = **physique**, body, figure, form, frame, shape, structure
Antonyms *vb* ≠ **construct**: demolish, dismantle, tear down ≠ **establish**: end, finish, relinquish, suspend ≠ **increase**: contract, debilitate, decline, decrease, dilute, harm, impair, lower, reduce, sap, weaken

building *n* **1** = **structure**, domicile, dwelling, edifice, house, pile **2** = **construction**, architecture, erection, fabricating, raising

build up *vb* **2** = **increase**, add to, amplify, augment, develop, enhance, expand, extend, fortify, heighten, improve, intensify, reinforce, strengthen **4** = **hype**, advertise, boost, plug (*inf.*), promote, publicize, spotlight ◆ *n* **build-up 5** = **increase**, accumulation, development, enlargement, escalation, expansion, gain, growth **7** = **hype**, ballyhoo (*inf.*), plug (*inf.*), promotion, publicity, puff

built-in *adj* **2** = **integral**, essential, immanent, implicit, in-built, included, incorporated, inherent, inseparable, part and parcel of

bulbous *adj* **1, 4** = **bulging**, bloated, convex, rounded, swelling, swollen

bulge *n* **1** = **swelling**, bump, hump, lump, projection, protrusion, protuberance **2** = **increase**, boost, intensification, rise, surge ◆ *vb* **3** = **swell out**, bag, dilate, distend, enlarge, expand, project, protrude, puff out, sag, stand out, stick out, swell
Antonyms *n* ≠ **swelling**: bowl, cave, cavity, concavity, crater, dent, depression, hole, hollow, indentation, pit, trough

bulk *n* **1** = **size**, amplitude, bigness, dimensions, immensity, largeness, magnitude, massiveness, substance, volume, weight **2** = **main part**, better part, body, generality, lion's share, majority, major part, mass, most, nearly all, plurality, preponderance ◆ *vb* **7 bulk large** = **be important**, carry weight, dominate, loom, loom large, preponderate, stand out, threaten

bulky *adj* = **large**, big, colossal, cumbersome, elephantine, enormous, heavy, huge, hulking,

bull[1] (bʊl) *n* **1** any male bovine animal, esp. one that is sexually mature. Related adj: **taurine. 2** the male of various other animals including the elephant and whale. **3** a very large, strong, or aggressive person. **4** *Stock Exchange.* **4a** a speculator who buys in anticipation of rising prices in order to make a profit on resale. **4b** (*as modifier*): *a bull market.* Cf. **bear**[2] (sense 5). **5** *Chiefly Brit.* short for **bull's-eye** (senses 1, 2). **6** *Sl.* short for **bullshit. 7 a bull in a china shop.** a clumsy person. **8 take the bull by the horns.** to face and tackle a difficulty without shirking. ◆ *adj* **9** male; masculine: *a bull elephant.* **10** large; strong. [OE *bula*]

bull[2] (bʊl) *n* a ludicrously self-contradictory or inconsistent statement. [C17: from ?]

bull[3] (bʊl) *n* a formal document issued by the pope. [C13: from Med. L *bulla* seal attached to a bull, from L: round object]

Bull (bʊl) *n* **the.** the constellation Taurus, the second sign of the zodiac.

Bullamakanka (ˌbuːləməˈkæŋkə) *n Austral.* an imaginary very remote place.

bull bars *pl n* a large protective metal grille on the front of some vehicles, esp. four-wheel-drive vehicles.

bulldog (ˈbʊlˌdɒg) *n* a sturdy thickset breed of dog with an undershot jaw, broad head, and a muscular body.

bulldog clip *n* a clip for holding papers together, consisting of two T-shaped metal clamps held in place by a cylindrical spring.

bulldoze 🅣 (ˈbʊlˌdəʊz) *vb* **bulldozes, bulldozing, bulldozed.** (*tr*) **1** to move, demolish, flatten, etc., with a bulldozer. **2** *Inf.* to force; push. **3** *Inf.* to intimidate or coerce. [C19: prob. from BULL[1] + DOSE]

bulldozer (ˈbʊlˌdəʊzə) *n* **1** a powerful tractor fitted with caterpillar tracks and a blade at the front, used for moving earth, rocks, etc. **2** *Inf.* a person who bulldozes.

bull dust *n Austral.* **1** fine dust, as on roads in outback Australia. **2** *Sl.* nonsense.

bullet 🅣 (ˈbʊlɪt) *n* **1a** a small metallic missile enclosed in a cartridge, used as the projectile of a gun, rifle, etc. **1b** the entire cartridge. **2** something resembling a bullet, esp. in shape or effect. **3** *Stock Exchange.* a fixed interest security with a single maturity date. **4** *Commerce.* a security that offers a fixed interest and matures on a fixed date. **5** *Commerce.* **5a** the final repayment of a loan that repays the whole of the sum borrowed, as interim payments have been for interest only. **5b** (*as modifier*): *a bullet loan.* [C16: from F *boulette*, dim. of *boule* ball; see BOWL[2]]

bulletin 🅣 (ˈbʊlɪtɪn) *n* **1** an official statement on a matter of public interest. **2** a broadcast summary of the news. **3** a periodical publication of an association, etc. ◆ *vb* **4** (*tr*) to make known by bulletin. [C17: from F, from It., from *bulletta*, dim. of *bulla* papal edict, BULL[3]]

bulletin board *n* **1** the US and Canad. name for **notice board. 2** *Computing.* a facility on a computer network allowing any user to leave messages that can be read by any other user, and to download software and information to the user's own computer.

bulletproof (ˈbʊlɪtˌpruːf) *adj* **1** not penetrable by bullets. ◆ *vb* **2** (*tr*) to make bulletproof.

bulletwood (ˈbʊlɪtˌwʊd) *n* the tough durable wood of a tropical American tree, widely used for construction.

bullfight (ˈbʊlˌfaɪt) *n* a traditional Spanish, Portuguese, and Latin American spectacle in which a matador baits and usually kills a bull in an arena.
▸ **ˈbullˌfighter** *n* ▸ **ˈbullˌfighting** *n*

bullfinch (ˈbʊlˌfɪntʃ) *n* **1** a common European finch: the male has a bright red throat and breast. **2** any of various similar finches. [C14: see BULL[1], FINCH]

bullfrog (ˈbʊlˌfrɒg) *n* any of various large frogs having a loud deep croak, esp. the **American bullfrog.**

bullhead (ˈbʊlˌhɛd) *n* any of various small northern mainly marine fishes that have a large head covered with bony plates and spines.

bull-headed 🅣 *adj* blindly obstinate; stupid.
▸ **ˌbull-ˈheadedly** *adv* ▸ **ˌbull-ˈheadedness** *n*

bullhorn (ˈbʊlˌhɔːn) *n* the US and Canad. name for **loud-hailer.**

bullion (ˈbʊljən) *n* **1** gold or silver in mass. **2** gold or silver in the form of bars and ingots, suitable for further processing. [C14: from Anglo-F: mint, prob. from OF *bouillir* to boil, from L *bullīre*]

bullish (ˈbʊlɪʃ) *adj* **1** like a bull. **2** *Stock Exchange.* causing, expecting, or characterized by a rise in prices. **3** *Inf.* cheerful and optimistic.
▸ **ˈbullishness** *n*

bull-necked *adj* having a short thick neck.

bullock (ˈbʊlək) *n* **1** a gelded bull; steer. ◆ *vb* **2** (*intr*) *Austral. & NZ inf.* to work hard and long. [OE *bulluc*; see BULL[1], -OCK]

bullocky (ˈbʊlәkɪ) *n, pl* **bullockies.** *Austral. & NZ.* a bullock driver; teamster.

bullring (ˈbʊlˌrɪŋ) *n* an arena for bullfighting.

bullroarer (ˈbʊlˌrɔːrə) *n* a wooden slat attached to a thong that makes a roaring sound when the thong is whirled: used esp. by native Australians in religious rites.

bull's-eye *n* **1** the small central disc of a target, usually the highest valued area. **2** a shot hitting this. **3** *Inf.* something that exactly achieves its aim. **4** a small circular or oval window or opening. **5** a thick disc of glass set into a ship's deck, etc., to admit light. **6** the glass boss at the centre of a sheet of blown glass. **7a** a small thick plano-convex lens used as a condenser. **7b** a lamp containing such a lens. **8** a peppermint-flavoured boiled sweet.

bullshit (ˈbʊlˌʃɪt) *Taboo sl.* ◆ *n* **1** exaggerated or foolish talk; nonsense. **2** deceitful or pretentious talk. **3** (in the British Army) exaggerated zeal, esp. for ceremonial drill, cleaning, etc. Usually shortened to **bull.** ◆ *vb* **bullshits, bullshitting, bullshitted** *or* **bullshit. 4** (*intr*) to talk in an exaggerated or foolish manner. **5** (*tr*) to talk bullshit to.

bull terrier *n* a breed of terrier having a muscular body and thick neck, with a short smooth coat. See also **pit bull terrier, Staffordshire bull terrier.**

bully 🅣 (ˈbʊlɪ) *n, pl* **bullies. 1** a person who hurts, persecutes, or intimidates weaker people. **2** a small New Zealand freshwater fish. ◆ *vb* **bullies, bullying, bullied. 3** (when *tr*, often foll. by *into*) to hurt, intimidate, or persecute (a weaker or smaller person), esp. to make him do something. ◆ *adj* **4** dashing; jolly: *my bully boy.* **5** *Inf.* very good; fine. ◆ *interj* **6** Also: **bully for you, him,** etc. *Inf.* well done! bravo! [C16 (in the sense: sweetheart, hence fine fellow, hence swaggering coward): prob. from MDu. *boele* lover, from MHG *buole*]

bully beef *n* canned corned beef. Often shortened to **bully.** [C19 *bully*, anglicized version of F *bouilli*, from *boeuf bouilli* boiled beef]

bully-off *Hockey.* ◆ *n* **1** the method by which a game is restarted after a stoppage. Two opposing players stand with the ball between them and alternately strike their sticks together and against the ground three times before trying to hit the ball. ◆ *vb* **bully off. 2** (*intr, adv*) to restart play with a bully-off. ◆ Often shortened to **bully.** [C19: from ?]

bullyrag (ˈbʊlɪˌræg) *vb* **bullyrags, bullyragging, bullyragged.** (*tr*) to bully, esp. by means of cruel practical jokes. Also: **ballyrag.** [C18: from ?]

bulrush (ˈbʊlˌrʌʃ) *n* **1** a popular name for **reed mace. 2** a grasslike marsh plant used for making mats, chair seats, etc. **3** a biblical word for **papyrus** (the plant). [C15 *bulrish*, *bul-* ?from BULL[1] + *rish* RUSH[2]]

bulwark 🅣 (ˈbʊlwək) *n* **1** a wall or similar structure used as a fortification; rampart. **2** a person or thing acting as a defence. **3** (*often pl*) *Naut.* a solid vertical fencelike structure along the outward sides of a deck. **4** a breakwater or mole. ◆ *vb* **5** (*tr*) to defend or fortify with or as if with a bulwark. [C15: via Du. from MHG *bolwerk*, from *bol* plank, BOLE + *werk* WORK]

bum[1] (bʌm) *n Brit. sl.* the buttocks or anus. [C14: from ?]

bum[2] (bʌm) *Inf.* ◆ *n* **1** a disreputable loafer or idler. **2** a tramp; hobo. ◆ *vb* **bums, bumming, bummed. 3** (*tr*) to get by begging; cadge: *to bum a lift.* **4** (*intr*; often foll. by *around*) to live by begging or as a vagrant or loafer. **5** (*intr*; usually foll. by *around*) to spend time to no good purpose; loaf; idle. **6 bum (someone) off.** *US & Canad. sl.* to disappoint, annoy, or upset (someone). ◆ *adj* **7** (*prenominal*) of poor quality; useless. [C19: prob. shortened from earlier *bummer* a loafer, prob. from G *bummeln* to loaf]

bum bag *n* a small bag worn on a belt, round the waist.

bumbailiff (ˌbʌmˈbeɪlɪf) *n Brit. derog.* (formerly) an officer employed to collect debts and arrest debtors. [C17: from BUM[1] + *bailiff*, so called because he follows hard behind debtors]

bumble 🅣 (ˈbʌmbᵊl) *vb* **bumbles, bumbling, bumbled. 1** to speak or do in a clumsy, muddled, or inefficient way. **2** (*intr*) to proceed unsteadily. [C16: ? a blend of BUNGLE + STUMBLE]
▸ **ˈbumbler** *n* ▸ **ˈbumbling** *adj, n*

bumblebee (ˈbʌmbᵊlˌbiː) *or* **humblebee** *n* any large hairy social bee of temperate regions. [C16: from *bumble* to buzz + BEE[1]]

bumf *or* **bumph** (bʌmf) *n Brit.* **1** *Inf., derog.* official documents, forms, etc. **2** *Sl.* toilet paper. [C19: short for earlier *bumfodder*; see BUM[1]]

bummer (ˈbʌmə) *n Sl.* a disappointing or unpleasant experience.

bump 🅣 (bʌmp) *vb* **1** (when *intr*, usually foll. by *against* or *into*) to knock or strike with a jolt. **2** (*intr*; often foll. by *along*) to travel or proceed in jerks and jolts. **3** (*tr*) to hurt by knocking. **4** *Cricket.* to bowl (a ball) so that it bounces high on pitching or (of a ball) to bounce high when bowled. **5** (*tr*) *Inf.* to exclude (a ticket-holding passenger) from a

THESAURUS

immense, mammoth, massive, massy, ponderous, substantial, unmanageable, unwieldy, voluminous, weighty
Antonyms *adj* convenient, handy, manageable, neat, slim, small, wieldy

bulldoze *vb* **1** = **demolish,** flatten, level, raze **2** *Informal* = **push,** drive, force, propel, shove, thrust **3** *Informal* = **force,** browbeat, bully, coerce, cow, dragoon, hector, intimidate, put the screws on, railroad (*inf.*)

bullet *n* **1a** = **projectile,** ball, missile, pellet, shot, slug

bulletin *n* **1, 2** = **announcement,** account, communication, communiqué, dispatch, message, news flash, notification, report, statement

bull-headed *adj* = **stubborn,** headstrong, inflexible, mulish, obstinate, pig-headed, stiff-necked, stupid, tenacious, uncompromising, unyielding, wilful

bully *n* **1** = **persecutor,** browbeater, bully boy, coercer, intimidator, oppressor, ruffian, tormentor, tough ◆ *vb* **3** = **persecute,** bluster, browbeat, bulldoze (*inf.*), bullyrag, coerce, cow, domineer, hector, intimidate, oppress, overbear, push around (*sl.*), ride roughshod over, swagger, terrorize, tyrannize ◆ *interjection* **6** *Informal* = **well done,** bravo, capital, good, grand, great

bulwark *n* **1** = **fortification,** bastion, buttress, defence, embankment, outwork, partition, rampart, redoubt **2** = **defence,** buffer, guard, mainstay, safeguard, security, support

bumbler *n* **1** = **bungler,** blunderer, duffer (*inf.*), geek (*sl.*), klutz (*US & Canad. sl.*), lummox (*inf.*), muddler

bumbling *adj* **1** = **clumsy,** awkward, blundering, botching, bungling, incompetent, inefficient, inept, lumbering, maladroit, muddled
Antonyms *adj* able, brisk, capable, competent, efficient, equal, fit

bump *vb* **1** = **knock,** bang, collide (with), crash, hit, slam, smash into, strike **2** = **jerk,** bounce, jar, jolt, jostle, jounce, rattle, shake ◆ *n* **6, 7** = **knock,** bang, blow, collision, crash, hit, impact, jar, jolt, rap, shock, smash, thud, thump **9** =

flight as a result of overbooking. ◆ *n* **6** an impact; knock; jolt; collision. **7** a dull thud or other noise from an impact or collision. **8** the shock of a blow or collision. **9** a lump on the body caused by a blow. **10** a protuberance, as on a road surface. **11** any of the natural protuberances of the human skull, said by phrenologists to indicate underlying faculties and character. ◆ See also **bump into, bump off, bump up.** [C16: prob. imit.]

bumper[1] ('bʌmpə) *n* **1** a horizontal usually metal bar attached to the front or rear end of a car, lorry, etc., to protect against damage from impact. **2** *Cricket.* a ball bowled so that it bounces high on pitching; bouncer.

bumper[2] **T** ('bʌmpə) *n* **1** a glass, tankard, etc., filled to the brim, esp. as a toast. **2** an unusually large or fine example of something. ◆ *adj* **3** unusually large, fine, or abundant: *a bumper crop.* [C17 (in the sense: a brimming glass): prob. from *bump* (obs. vb) to bulge; see BUMP]

bumph (bʌmf) *n* a variant spelling of **bumf.**

bump into **T** *vb (intr, prep) Inf.* to meet by chance; encounter unexpectedly.

bumpkin **T** ('bʌmpkɪn) *n* an awkward simple rustic person (esp. in **country bumpkin**). [C16: ?from Du. *boomken* small tree, or from MDu. *boomekijn* small barrel]

bump off **T** *vb (tr, adv) Sl.* to murder; kill.

bumptious **T** ('bʌmpʃəs) *adj* offensively self-assertive or conceited. [C19: ?from BUMP + FRACTIOUS]
▸**'bumptiously** *adv* ▸**'bumptiousness** *n*

bump up *vb (tr, adv) Inf.* to raise or increase.

bumpy **T** ('bʌmpɪ) *adj* **bumpier, bumpiest. 1** having an uneven surface. **2** full of jolts; rough.
▸**'bumpily** *adv* ▸**'bumpiness** *n*

bun (bʌn) *n* **1** a small roll, similar to bread but usually containing sweetening, currants, etc. **2** any of various small round cakes. **3** a hairstyle in which long hair is gathered into a bun shape at the back of the head. [C14: from ?]

bunch **T** (bʌntʃ) *n* **1** a number of things growing, fastened, or grouped together: *a bunch of grapes; a bunch of keys.* **2** a collection; group: *a bunch of queries.* **3** *Inf.* a group or company: *a bunch of boys.* ◆ *vb* **4** (sometimes foll. by *up*) to group or be grouped into a bunch. [C14: from ?]

bunchy ('bʌntʃɪ) *adj* **bunchier, bunchiest. 1** composed of or resembling bunches. **2** bulging.

buncombe ('bʌŋkəm) *n* a variant spelling (esp. US) of **bunkum.**

bundle **T** ('bʌndᵊl) *n* **1** a number of things or a quantity of material gathered or loosely bound together: *a bundle of sticks.* Related adj: **fascicular. 2** something wrapped or tied for carrying; package. **3** *Sl.* a large sum of money. **4 go a bundle on.** *Sl.* to be extremely fond of. **5** *Biol.* a collection of strands of specialized tissue such as nerve fibres. **6** *Bot.* short for **vascular bundle. 7 drop one's bundle.** *Austral. & NZ sl.* to panic or give up hope. ◆ *vb* **bundles, bundling, bundled. 8** (*tr;* often foll. by *up*) to make into a bundle. **9** (foll. by *out, off, into,* etc.) to go or cause to go, esp. roughly or unceremoniously. **10** (*tr;* usually foll. by *into*) to push or throw, esp. quickly and untidily. **11** (*tr*) to give away (a relatively cheap product) when selling an expensive one to attract business: *software is often bundled with computers.* **12** (*intr*) to sleep or lie in one's clothes on the same bed as one's betrothed: formerly a custom in New England, Wales, and elsewhere. [C14: prob. from MDu. *bundel;* rel. to OE *bindele* bandage; see BIND, BOND]
▸**'bundler** *n*

bundle up **T** *vb (adv)* **1** to dress (somebody) warmly and snugly. **2** (*tr*) to make (something) into a bundle or bundles, esp. by tying.

bun fight *n Brit. sl.* **1** a tea party. **2** *Ironic.* an official function.

bung[1] (bʌŋ) *n* **1** a stopper, esp. of cork or rubber, for a cask, etc. **2** short for **bunghole.** ◆ *vb (tr)* **3** (often foll. by *up*) *Inf.* to close or seal with or as with a bung. **4** *Brit. sl.* to throw; sling. **5 bung it on.** *Austral. sl.* to behave in a pretentious manner. [C15: from MDu. *bonghe*]

bung[2] (bʌŋ) *adj Austral. & NZ inf.* **1** useless. **2 go bung. 2a** to fail or collapse. **2b** to die. [C19: from Abor.]

bungalow ('bʌŋgə,ləu) *n* a one-storey house, sometimes with an attic. [C17: from Hindi *banglā* (house) of the Bengal type]

bungee jumping *or* **bungy jumping** ('bʌndʒɪ) *n* a sport in which a participant jumps from a high bridge, building, etc., secured only by a rubber cord attached to the ankles. [C20: from *bungie,* slang for India rubber, of unknown origin]

bunghole ('bʌŋ,həul) *n* a hole in a cask, barrel, etc., through which liquid can be drained.

bungle **T** ('bʌŋgᵊl) *vb* **bungles, bungling, bungled. 1** (*tr*) to spoil (an operation) through clumsiness, incompetence, etc. ◆ *n* **2** a clumsy or unsuccessful performance. [C16: ? of Scand. origin]
▸**'bungler** *n* ▸**'bungling** *adj, n*

bunion ('bʌnjən) *n* an inflamed swelling of the first joint of the big toe. [C18: ?from obs. *bunny* a swelling, from ?]

bunk[1] (bʌŋk) *n* **1** a narrow shelflike bed fixed along a wall. **2** short for **bunk bed. 3** *Inf.* any place where one sleeps. ◆ *vb* **4** (*intr;* often foll. by *down*) to prepare to sleep: *he bunked down on the floor.* **5** (*intr*) to occupy a bunk or bed. [C19: prob. short for BUNKER]

bunk[2] (bʌŋk) *n Inf.* short for **bunkum** (sense 1).

bunk[3] **T** (bʌŋk) *n Brit. sl.* a hurried departure, usually under suspicious circumstances (esp. in **do a bunk**). [C19: ?from BUNK[1] (in the sense: to occupy a bunk, hence a hurried departure)]

bunk bed *n* one of a pair of beds constructed one above the other to save space.

bunker ('bʌŋkə) *n* **1** a large storage container or tank, as for coal. **2** Also called (esp. US and Canad.): **sand trap.** an obstacle on a golf course, usually a sand-filled hollow bordered by a ridge. **3** an underground shelter with a bank and embrasures for guns above ground. ◆ *vb* **4** (*tr*) *Golf.* **4a** to drive (the ball) into a bunker. **4b** (*passive*) to have one's ball trapped in a bunker. [C16 (in the sense: chest, box): from Scot. *bonkar,* from ?]

bunkhouse ('bʌŋk,haus) *n* (in the US and Canada) a building containing the sleeping quarters of workers on a ranch.

bunkum **T** *or* **buncombe** ('bʌŋkəm) *n* **1** empty talk; nonsense. **2** *Chiefly US.* empty or insincere speechmaking by a politician. [C19: after *Buncombe,* a county in North Carolina, alluded to in an inane speech by its Congressional representative Felix Walker (about 1820)]

bunny ('bʌnɪ) *n, pl* **bunnies. 1** Also called: **bunny rabbit.** a child's word for **rabbit** (sense 1). **2** Also called: **bunny girl.** a night-club hostess whose costume includes rabbit-like tail and ears. **3** *Austral. sl.* a mug; dupe. [C17: from Scot. Gaelic *bun* scut of a rabbit]

Bunsen burner ('bʌnsᵊn) *n* a gas burner consisting of a metal tube with an adjustable air valve at the base. [C19: after R. W. *Bunsen* (1811–99), G chemist]

bunting[1] ('bʌntɪŋ) *n* **1** a coarse, loosely woven cotton fabric used for flags, etc. **2** decorative flags, pennants, and streamers. [C18: from ?]

bunting[2] ('bʌntɪŋ) *n* any of numerous seed-eating songbirds of the Old World and North America having short stout bills. [C13: from ?]

buntline ('bʌntlɪn, -,laɪn) *n Naut.* one of several lines fastened to the foot of a square sail for hauling it up to the yard when furling. [C17: from *bunt* centre of a sail + LINE[1] (sense 11)]

bunya ('bʌnjə) *n* a tall dome-shaped Australian coniferous tree having edible cones (**bunya nuts**) and thickish flattened needles. Also called: **bunya-bunya.** [C19: from Abor.]

bunyip ('bʌnjɪp) *n Austral.* a legendary monster said to inhabit swamps and lagoons. [C19: from Abor.]

buoy **T** (bɔɪ; *US* 'buːɪ) *n* **1** a distinctively shaped and coloured float, anchored to the bottom, for designating moorings, navigable channels,

THESAURUS

lump, bulge, contusion, hump, knob, knot, node, nodule, protuberance, swelling

bumper[2] *adj* **3** = **exceptional,** abundant, bountiful, excellent, jumbo (*inf.*), massive, mega (*sl.*), prodigal, spanking (*inf.*), teeming, unusual, whacking (*inf., chiefly Brit.*), whopping (*inf.*)

bump into *vb Informal* = **meet,** chance upon, come across, encounter, happen upon, light upon, meet up with, run across, run into

bumpkin *n* = **yokel,** boor, clodhopper, clown, country bumpkin, hayseed (*US & Canad. inf.*), hick (*inf., chiefly US & Canad.*), hillbilly, lout, oaf, peasant, rustic

bump off *vb Slang* = **murder,** assassinate, blow away (*sl., chiefly US*), dispatch, do away with, do in (*sl.*), eliminate, finish off, kill, knock off (*sl.*), liquidate, remove, take out (*sl.*), wipe out (*inf.*)

bumptious *adj* = **cocky,** arrogant, boastful, brash, conceited, egotistic, forward, full of oneself, impudent, overbearing, overconfident, presumptuous, pushy (*inf.*), self-assertive, showy, swaggering, vainglorious, vaunting

bumpy *adj* **1** = **uneven,** irregular, knobby, lumpy, pitted, potholed, rough, rutted **2** = **rough,** bone-breaking, bouncy, choppy, jarring, jerky, jolting

bunch *n* **1, 2** = **number,** assortment, batch, bouquet, bundle, clump, cluster, collection, heap, lot, mass, parcel, pile, quantity, rick, sheaf, spray, stack, tuft **3** *Informal* = **group,** band, bevy, crew (*inf.*), crowd, flock, gang, gathering, knot, mob, multitude, party, posse (*inf.*), swarm, team, troop ◆ *vb* **4** = **group,** assemble, bundle, cluster, collect, congregate, cram together, crowd, flock, herd, huddle, mass, pack

bundle *n* **1** = **bunch,** accumulation, assortment, batch, collection, group, heap, mass, pile, quantity, rick, stack **2** = **package,** bag, bale, box, carton, crate, pack, packet, pallet, parcel, roll ◆ *vb* **8** = **package,** bale, bind, fasten, pack, palletize, tie, tie together, tie up, truss, wrap **9, 10** *with* **out, off, into,** etc. = **push,** hurry, hustle, rush, shove, throw, thrust

bundle up *vb* **1** = **wrap up,** clothe warmly, muffle up, swathe

bungle *vb* **1** = **mess up,** blow (*sl.*), blunder, bodge, botch, butcher, cock up (*Brit. sl.*), drop a brick *or* clanger (*inf.*), foul up, make a mess of, make a nonsense of (*inf.*), make a pig's ear of (*inf.*), mar, miscalculate, mismanage, muff, ruin, screw up (*inf.*), spoil
Antonyms *vb* accomplish, achieve, carry off, effect, fulfil, succeed, triumph

bungler *n* **1** = **incompetent,** blunderer, botcher, butcher, butterfingers (*inf.*), duffer (*inf.*), fumbler, lubber, muddler, muff

bungling *adj* **1** = **incompetent,** awkward, blundering, botching, cack-handed (*inf.*), clumsy, ham-fisted (*inf.*), ham-handed, inept, maladroit, unskilful

bunk[3] *vb* **do a bunk** *Brit. slang* = **run away,** abscond, beat it (*sl.*), bolt, clear out (*inf.*), cut and run (*inf.*), decamp, do a runner (*sl.*), flee, fly the coop (*US & Canad. inf.*), run for it (*inf.*), scram (*inf.*), skedaddle (*inf.*)

bunkum *n* **1** = **nonsense,** balderdash, balls (*taboo sl.*), baloney (*inf.*), bilge (*inf.*), bosh (*inf.*), bullshit (*taboo sl.*), cobblers (*Brit. taboo sl.*), crap (*sl.*), garbage (*inf.*), hogwash, hokum (*sl., chiefly US & Canad.*), hot air (*inf.*), piffle (*inf.*), poppycock (*inf.*), rot, rubbish, shit (*taboo sl.*), stuff and nonsense, tommyrot, tosh (*sl., chiefly Brit.*), trash, tripe (*inf.*), twaddle

buoy *n* **1** = **marker,** beacon, float, guide, signal ◆ *vb* **3 buoy up** = **encourage,** boost, cheer, or obstructions in a body of water. See also **life buoy.** ◆ *vb* **2** (*tr;* usually foll. by *up*) to prevent from sinking: *the life belt buoyed him up.* **3** (*tr;* usually foll. by *up*) to raise the spirits of; hearten. **4** (*tr*) *Naut.* to mark (a channel or obstruction) with a buoy or buoys. **5** (*intr*) to rise to the surface; float. [C13: prob. of Gmc origin]

buoyancy ❶ ('bɔɪənsɪ) *n* **1** the ability to float in a liquid or to rise in liquid, air, or other gas. **2** the tendency of a fluid to keep a body afloat. **3** the ability to recover quickly after setbacks; resilience. **4** cheerfulness.

buoyant ❶ ('bɔɪənt) *adj* **1** able to float in or rise to the surface of a liquid. **2** (of a liquid or gas) able to keep a body afloat. **3** cheerful or resilient. [C16: prob. from Sp. *boyante,* from *boyar* to float]

BUPA ('bu:pə) *n acronym for* The British United Provident Association Limited: a company which provides private medical insurance.

bupivacaine (bju:'pɪvə,keɪn) *n* a local anaesthetic of long duration, used for nerve blocks. [C20: ?from BU(TYL) + *pi*(*pecoloxylidide*) + *-vacaine,* from (NO)VOCAINE]

bur (bɜ:) *n* **1** a seed vessel or flower head having hooks or prickles. **2** any plant that produces burs. **3** a person or thing that clings like a bur. **4** a small surgical or dental drill. ◆ *vb* **burs, burring, burred. 5** (*tr*) to remove burs from. ◆ Also: **burr.** [C14: prob. from ON]

burble ('bɜ:bᵊl) *vb* **burbles, burbling, burbled. 1** to make or utter with a bubbling sound; gurgle. **2** (*intr;* often foll. by *away* or *on*) to talk quickly and excitedly. ◆ *n* **3** a bubbling or gurgling sound. **4** a flow of excited speech. [C14: prob. imit.]
▸**'burbler** *n*

burbot ('bɜ:bət) *n, pl* **burbots** *or* **burbot.** a freshwater gadoid food fish that has barbels around its mouth and occurs in Europe, Asia, and North America. [C14: from OF *bourbotte,* from *bourbeter* to wallow in mud, from *bourbe* mud]

burden[1] ❶ ('bɜ:dᵊn) *n* **1** something that is carried; load. **2** something that is exacting, oppressive, or difficult to bear. Related adj: **onerous. 3** *Naut.* **3a** the cargo capacity of a ship. **3b** the weight of a ship's cargo. ◆ *vb* (*tr*) **4** (sometimes foll. by *up*) to put or impose a burden on; load. **5** to weigh down; oppress. [OE *byrthen*]

burden[2] ('bɜ:dᵊn) *n* **1** a line of words recurring at the end of each verse of a song; chorus or refrain. **2** the theme of a speech, book, etc. **3** another word for **bourdon.** [C16: from OF *bourdon* bass horn, droning sound, imit.]

burden of proof *n Law.* the obligation to provide evidence that will convince the court or jury of the truth of one's contention.

burdensome ❶ ('bɜ:dᵊnsəm) *adj* hard to bear.

burdock ('bɜ:,dɒk) *n* a coarse weedy Eurasian plant having large heart-shaped leaves, tiny purple flowers surrounded by hooked bristles, and burlike fruits. [C16: from BUR + DOCK[4]]

bureau ❶ ('bjʊərəʊ) *n, pl* **bureaus** *or* **bureaux. 1** *Chiefly Brit.* a writing desk with pigeonholes, drawers, etc., against which the writing surface can be closed when not in use. **2** *US.* a chest of drawers. **3** an office or agency, esp. one providing services for the public. **4** a government department. [C17: from F, orig.: type of cloth used for covering desks, from OF *burel*]

bureaucracy ❶ (bjʊə'rɒkrəsɪ) *n, pl* **bureaucracies. 1** a system of administration based upon organization into bureaus, division of labour, a hierarchy of authority, etc. **2** government by such a system. **3** government or other officials collectively. **4** any administration in which action is impeded by unnecessary official procedures.

bureaucrat ❶ ('bjʊərə,kræt) *n* **1** an official in a bureaucracy. **2** an official who adheres to bureaucracy, esp. rigidly.
▸**,bureau'cratic** *adj* ▸**,bureau'cratically** *adv*

bureaucratize *or* **bureaucratise** (bjʊə'rɒkrə,taɪz) *vb* **bureaucratizes, bureaucratizing, bureaucratized** *or* **bureaucratises, bureaucratising, bureaucratised.** (*tr*) to administer by or transform into a bureaucracy.
▸**bu,reaucrati'zation** *or* **bu,reaucrati'sation** *n*

bureaux ('bjʊərəʊz) *n* a plural of **bureau.**

burette *or US* **buret** (bjʊ'rɛt) *n* a graduated glass tube with a stopcock on one end for dispensing and transferring known volumes of fluids, esp. liquids. [C15: from F, from OF *buire* ewer]

burg (bɜ:g) *n* **1** *History.* a fortified town. **2** *US inf.* a town or city. [C18 (in the sense: fortress): from OHG *burg*]

burgage ('bɜ:gɪdʒ) *n History.* **1** (in England) tenure of land or tenement in a town or city, which originally involved a fixed money rent. **2** (in Scotland) the tenure of land direct from the crown in Scottish royal burghs in return for watching and warding. [C14: from Med. L *burgāgium,* from OE *burg*]

burgeon *or* **bourgeon** ('bɜ:dʒən) *vb* **1** (often foll. by *forth* or *out*) (of a plant) to sprout (buds). **2** (*intr;* often foll. by *forth* or *out*) to develop or grow rapidly; flourish. [C13: from OF *burjon*]

burger ('bɜ:gə) *n Inf.* **a** short for **hamburger. b** (*in combination*): *a cheeseburger.*

burgess ('bɜ:dʒɪs) *n* **1** (in England) a citizen, freeman, or inhabitant of a borough. **2** *English history.* a Member of Parliament from a borough, corporate town, or university. [C13: from OF *burgeis;* see BOROUGH]

burgh ('bʌrə) *n* **1** (in Scotland until 1975) a town, esp. one incorporated by charter, that enjoyed a degree of self-government. **2** an archaic form of **borough.** [C14: Scot. form of BOROUGH]
▸**burghal** ('bɜ:gᵊl) *adj*

burgher ('bɜ:gə) *n* **1** a member of the trading or mercantile class of a medieval city. **2** a respectable citizen; bourgeois. **3** *Arch.* a citizen or inhabitant of a corporate town, esp on the Continent. **4** *S. African history.* a citizen of the Cape Colony or of one of the Transvaal and Free State republics. [C16: from G *Bürger* or Du. *burger* freeman of a BOROUGH]

burglar ❶ ('bɜ:glə) *n* a person who commits burglary; housebreaker. [C15: from Anglo-F, from Med. L *burglātor,* prob. from *burgāre* to thieve]

burglary ❶ ('bɜ:glərɪ) *n, pl* **burglaries.** the crime of entering a building as a trespasser to commit theft or another offence.
▸**burglarious** (bɜ:'glɛərɪəs) *adj*

burgle ('bɜ:gᵊl) *vb* **burgles, burgling, burgled.** to commit burglary upon (a house, etc.).

burgomaster ('bɜ:gə,mɑ:stə) *n* the chief magistrate of a town in Austria, Belgium, Germany, or the Netherlands; mayor. [C16: partial translation of Du. *burgemeester;* see BOROUGH, MASTER]

Burgundy ('bɜ:gəndɪ) *n, pl* **Burgundies. 1a** any red or white wine produced in the region of Burgundy, around Dijon. **1b** any heavy red table wine. **2** (*often not cap.*) a blackish-purple to purplish-red colour. [OE *byrgels* burial place, tomb; see BURY, -AL[2]]

burial ❶ ('bɛrɪəl) *n* the act of burying, esp. the interment of a dead body. [C17: from *Burgundy,* region of E France]

burial ground ❶ *n* a graveyard or cemetery.

burin ('bjʊərɪn) *n* **1** a chisel of tempered steel used for engraving metal, wood, or marble. **2** *Archaeol.* a prehistoric flint tool. [C17: from F, ?from It. *burino,* of Gmc origin]

burk (bɜ:k) *n* a variant spelling of **berk.**

burl[1] (bɜ:l) *n* **1** a small knot or lump in wool. **2** a roundish warty outgrowth from certain trees. ◆ *vb* **3** (*tr*) to remove the burls from (cloth). [C15: from OF *burle* tuft of wool, prob. ult. from LL *burra* shaggy cloth]

burl[2] *or* **birl** (bɜ:l) *n Inf.* **1** *Scot., Austral., & NZ.* an attempt; try (esp. in **give it a burl**). **2** *Austral, & NZ.* a ride in a car. [C20: ?from BIRL in Scots sense: to spin or turn]

burlap ('bɜ:læp) *n* a coarse fabric woven from jute, hemp, or the like. [C17: from *borel* coarse cloth, from OF *burel* (see BUREAU) + LAP[1]]

burlesque ❶ (bɜ:'lɛsk) *n* **1** an artistic work, esp. literary or dramatic, satirizing a subject by caricaturing it. **2** a ludicrous imitation or caricature. **3** Also: **burlesk.** *US. & Canad. theatre.* a bawdy comedy show of the late 19th and early 20th centuries: the striptease eventually became one of its chief elements. ◆ *adj* **4** of, relating to, or characteristic of a burlesque. ◆ *vb* **burlesques, burlesquing, burlesqued. 5** to represent or imitate (a person or thing) in a ludicrous way; caricature. [C17: from F, from It., from *burla* a jest, piece of nonsense]
▸**bur'lesquer** *n*

burley ('bɜ:lɪ) *n* a variant spelling of **berley.**

THESAURUS

cheer up, gee up, hearten, lift, raise, support, sustain

buoyancy *n* **1** = **lightness**, floatability, weightlessness **4** = **cheerfulness**, animation, bounce, cheeriness, good humour, high spirits, liveliness, pep, spiritedness, sunniness, zing (*inf.*)

buoyant *adj* **1** = **floating**, afloat, floatable, light, weightless **3** = **cheerful**, animated, blithe, bouncy, breezy, bright, carefree, chirpy (*inf.*), debonair, full of beans (*inf.*), genial, happy, jaunty, joyful, light-hearted, lively, peppy (*inf.*), sparky, sunny, upbeat (*inf.*), vivacious
Antonyms *adj* ≠ **cheerful:** cheerless, depressed, despairing, dull, forlorn, gloomy, glum, hopeless, melancholy, moody, morose, pessimistic, sad, sullen, unhappy

burden[1] *n* **1** = **load**, encumbrance, weight **2** = **trouble**, affliction, albatross, anxiety, care, clog, encumbrance, grievance, millstone, obstruction, onus, pigeon (*inf.*), responsibility, sorrow, strain, stress, trial, weight, worry **3** *Nautical* = **tonnage**, cargo, freight, lading ◆ *vb* **5** = **weigh down**, bother, encumber, handicap, load, oppress, overload, overwhelm, saddle with, strain, tax, worry

burdensome *adj* = **troublesome**, crushing, difficult, exacting, heavy, irksome, onerous, oppressive, taxing, trying, weighty

bureau *n* **1** *Chiefly Brit.* = **desk**, writing desk **3, 4** = **office**, agency, branch, department, division, service

bureaucracy *n* **1-3** = **government**, administration, authorities, civil service, corridors of power, directorate, ministry, officialdom, officials, the system **4** = **red tape**, officialdom, regulations

bureaucrat *n* **1** = **official**, apparatchik, civil servant, functionary, mandarin, minister, office-holder, officer, public servant

burglar *n* = **housebreaker**, cat burglar, picklock, robber, sneak thief, thief

burglary *n* = **breaking and entering**, break-in, housebreaking, larceny, robbery, stealing, theft, thieving

burial *n* = **interment**, burying, entombment, funeral, inhumation, obsequies

burial ground *n* = **graveyard**, cemetery, churchyard, necropolis

buried *adj* **1** = **interred**, coffined, consigned to the grave, entombed, laid to rest **3** = **hidden**, cloistered, concealed, private, sequestered, tucked away **5** = **engrossed**, caught up, committed, concentrating, devoted, immersed, intent, lost, occupied, preoccupied, rapt **6** = **forgotten**, covered, hidden, repressed, sunk in oblivion, suppressed

burlesque *n* **1, 2** = **parody**, caricature, mock, mockery, satire, send-up (*Brit. inf.*), spoof (*inf.*), takeoff (*inf.*), travesty ◆ *adj* **4** = **satirical**, caricatural, comic, farcical, ironical, ludicrous, mock, mock-heroic, mocking, parodic, travestying ◆ *vb* **5** = **satirize**, ape, caricature, exaggerate, imitate, lampoon, make a monkey out of, make fun of, mock, parody, ridicule, send up (*Brit. inf.*), spoof (*inf.*), take off (*inf.*), take the piss out of (*taboo sl.*), travesty

burly ⓣ ('bɜːlɪ) *adj* **burlier, burliest.** large and thick of build; sturdy. [C13: of Gmc origin]
▸**'burliness** *n*

Burmese (bɜː'miːz) *adj also* **Burman. 1** of or denoting Burma (now Myanmar), a country of SE Asia, or its inhabitants, their customs, etc. ◆ *n* **2** (*pl* **Burmese**) a native or inhabitant of Burma (Myanmar). **3** the language of the Burmese.

burn[1] ⓣ (bɜːn) *vb* **burns, burning, burnt** *or* **burned. 1** to undergo or cause to undergo combustion. **2** to destroy or be destroyed by fire. **3** (*tr*) to damage, injure, or mark by heat: *he burnt his hand; she was burnt by the sun.* **4** to die or put to death by fire. **5** (*intr*) to be or feel hot: *my forehead burns.* **6** to smart or cause to smart: *brandy burns one's throat.* **7** (*intr*) to feel strong emotion, esp. anger or passion. **8** (*tr*) to use for the purposes of light, heat, or power: *to burn coal.* **9** (*tr*) to form by or as if by fire: *to burn a hole.* **10** to char or become charred: *the potatoes are burning.* **11** (*tr*) to brand or cauterize. **12** to produce by or subject to heat as part of a process: *to burn charcoal.* **13 burn one's bridges** *or* **boats.** to commit oneself to a particular course of action with no possibility of turning back. **14 burn one's fingers.** to suffer from having meddled or interfered. ◆ *n* **15** an injury caused by exposure to heat, electrical, chemical, or radioactive agents. **16** a mark, e.g. on wood, caused by burning. **17** a controlled use of rocket propellant, esp. for a course correction. **18** a hot painful sensation in a muscle, experienced during vigorous exercise. **19** *Sl.* tobacco or a cigarette. ◆ See also **burn out.** [OE *beornan* (intr), *bærnan* (tr)]

burn[2] (bɜːn) *n Scot. & N English.* a small stream; brook. [OE *burna;* rel. to ON *brunnr* spring]

burner ('bɜːnə) *n* **1** the part of a stove, lamp, etc., that produces flame or heat. **2** an apparatus for burning something, as fuel or refuse.

burnet ('bɜːnɪt) *n* **1** a plant of the rose family which has purple-tinged green flowers and leaves. **2 burnet rose.** a very prickly Eurasian rose with white flowers and purplish-black fruits. **3** a moth with red-spotted dark green wings and antennae with enlarged tips. [C14: from OF *burnete,* var. of *brunete* BRUNETTE]

burning ⓣ ('bɜːnɪŋ) *adj* **1** intense; passionate. **2** urgent; crucial: *a burning problem.*

burning bush *n* **1** any of several shrubs or trees that have bright red fruits or seeds. **2** any of several plants with a bright red autumn foliage. **3** *Bible.* the bush that burned without being consumed, from which God spoke to Moses (Exodus 3:2–4).

burning glass *n* a convex lens for concentrating the sun's rays to produce fire.

burnish ⓣ ('bɜːnɪʃ) *vb* **1** to make or become shiny or smooth by friction; polish. ◆ *n* **2** a shiny finish; lustre. [C14 *burnischen,* from OF *brunir* to make brown, from *brun* BROWN]
▸**'burnisher** *n*

burnoose, burnous, *or* **burnouse** (bɜː'nuːs, -'nuːz) *n* a long circular cloak with a hood attached, worn esp. by Arabs. [C20: via F *burnous* from Ar. *burnus,* from Gk *birros* cloak]

burn out *vb* (*adv*) **1** to become or cause to become inoperative as a result of heat or friction: *the clutch burnt out.* **2** (*intr*) (of a rocket, jet engine, etc.) to cease functioning as a result of exhaustion of the fuel supply. **3** (*tr; usually passive*) to destroy by fire. **4** to become or cause to become exhausted through overwork or dissipation.

burnt (bɜːnt) *vb* **1** a past tense and past participle of **burn**[1]. ◆ *adj* **2** affected by or as if by burning; charred.

burnt offering *n* a sacrificial offering burnt, usually on an altar, to honour, propitiate, or supplicate a deity.

burnt sienna *n* **1** a reddish-brown pigment obtained by roasting raw sienna. ◆ *n, adj* **2** (of) a reddish-brown colour.

burnt umber *n* **1** a brown pigment obtained by heating umber. ◆ *n, adj* **2** (of) a dark brown colour.

burp (bɜːp) *n* **1** *Inf.* a belch. ◆ *vb* **2** (*intr*) *Inf.* to belch. **3** (*tr*) to cause (a baby) to burp. [C20: imit.]

burr[1] (bɜː) *n* **1** a small power-driven hand-operated rotary file, esp. for removing burrs or for machining recesses. **2** a rough edge left on a workpiece after cutting, drilling, etc. **3** a rough or irregular protuberance, such as a burl on a tree. **4** a variant spelling of **bur.** [C14: var. of BUR]

burr[2] (bɜː) *n* **1** an articulation of (r) characteristic of certain English dialects, esp. the uvular fricative trill of Northumberland or the retroflex *r* of the West of England. **2** a whirring sound. ◆ *vb* **3** to pronounce (words) with a burr. **4** (*intr*) to make a whirring sound. [C18: either special use of BUR (in the sense: rough sound) or imit.]

burrito (bə'riːtəʊ) *n, pl* **burritos.** *Mexican cookery.* a tortilla folded over a filling of minced beef, chicken, cheese, or beans. [C20: from Mexican Sp., from Sp.: literally, a young donkey]

burro ('bʊrəʊ) *n, pl* **burros.** a donkey, esp. one used as a pack animal. [C19: Sp., from Port., from *burrico*]

burrow ⓣ ('bʌrəʊ) *n* **1** a hole dug in the ground by a rabbit or other small animal. **2** a small snug place affording shelter or retreat. ◆ *vb* **3** to dig (a burrow) in, through, or under (ground). **4** (*intr; often foll. by through*) to move through by or as by digging. **5** (*intr*) to hide or live in a burrow. **6** (*intr*) to delve deeply: *he burrowed into his pockets.* **7** to hide (oneself). [C13: prob. var. of BOROUGH]
▸**'burrower** *n*

burry ('bɜːrɪ) *adj* **burrier, burriest. 1** full of or covered in burs. **2** resembling burs; prickly.

bursa ('bɜːsə) *n, pl* **bursae** (-siː) *or* **bursas. 1** *Anat.* a small fluid-filled sac that reduces friction, esp. at joints. **2** *Zool.* any saclike cavity or structure. [C19: from Med. L: bag, pouch, from Gk: skin, hide; see PURSE]
▸**'bursal** *adj*

bursar ('bɜːsə) *n* **1** a treasurer of a school, college, or university. **2** *Chiefly Scot. & NZ.* a student holding a bursary. [C13: from Med. L *bursārius* keeper of the purse, from *bursa* purse]

bursary ('bɜːsərɪ) *n, pl* **bursaries. 1** Also called: **'bursar,ship.** a scholarship awarded esp. in Scottish and New Zealand schools and universities. **2** *Brit.* the treasury of a college, etc.
▸**bursarial** (bɜː'sɛərɪəl) *adj*

bursitis (bɜː'saɪtɪs) *n* inflammation of a bursa.

burst ⓣ (bɜːst) *vb* **bursts, bursting, burst. 1** to break or cause to break open or apart suddenly and noisily; explode. **2** (*intr*) to come, go, etc., suddenly and forcibly: *he burst into the room.* **3** (*intr*) to be full to the point of breaking open. **4** (*intr*) to give vent (to) suddenly or loudly: *to burst into song.* **5** (*tr*) to cause or suffer the rupture of: *to burst a blood vessel.* ◆ *n* **6** a sudden breaking open; explosion. **7** a break; breach; rupture. **8** a sudden display or increase of effort; spurt: *a burst of speed.* **9** a sudden and violent emission, occurrence, or outbreak: *a burst of applause.* **10** a volley of fire from a weapon. [OE *berstan*]

burthen ('bɜːðən) *n, vb* an archaic word for **burden**[1].
▸**'burthensome** *adj*

burton ('bɜːtᵊn) *n* **go for a burton.** *Brit. sl.* **a** to be broken, useless, or lost. **b** to die. [C20: from ?]

bury ⓣ ('bɛrɪ) *vb* **buries, burying, buried.** (*tr*) **1** to place (a corpse) in a grave; inter. **2** to place in the earth and cover with soil. **3** to cover from sight; hide. **4** to embed; sink: *to bury a nail in plaster.* **5** to occupy (oneself) with deep concentration; engross: *to be buried in a book.* **6** to dismiss from the mind; abandon: *to bury old hatreds.* [OE *byrgan*]

bus (bʌs) *n, pl* **buses** *or* **busses. 1** a large motor vehicle designed to carry passengers between stopping places along a regular route. More formal name: **omnibus. 2** (*modifier*) of or relating to a bus or buses: *a bus driver; a bus station.* **3** *Inf.* a car or aircraft, esp. one that is old and shaky. **4** *Electronics, computing.* short for **busbar. 5** *Astronautics.* a platform in a space vehicle used for various experiments and processes. **6 miss the bus.** to miss an opportunity. ◆ *vb* **buses, busing, bused** *or* **busses, bussing, bussed. 7** to travel or transport by bus. **8** *Chiefly US & Canad.* to transport (children) by bus from one area to another in order to create racially integrated schools. [C19: short for OMNIBUS]

bus. *abbrev. for* business.

busbar ('bʌzˌbɑː) *n* **1** an electrical conductor usually used to make a common connection between several circuits. **2** a group of such electrical conductors maintained at a low voltage, used for carrying data in binary form between the various parts of a computer or its peripherals.

busby ('bʌzbɪ) *n, pl* **busbies. 1** a tall fur helmet worn by hussars. **2** (not in official usage) another name for **bearskin** (the hat). [C18: ?from a proper name]

bush[1] ⓣ (bʊʃ) *n* **1** a dense woody plant, smaller than a tree, with many branches arising from the lower part of the stem; shrub. **2** a dense cluster of such shrubs; thicket. **3** something resembling a bush, esp.

THESAURUS

burly *adj* = **brawny,** beefy (*inf.*), big, bulky, hefty, hulking, muscular, powerful, stocky, stout, strapping, strong, sturdy, thickset, well-built
Antonyms *adj* lean, puny, scraggy, scrawny, slight, spare, thin, weak, weedy (*inf.*), wimpish *or* wimpy (*inf.*)

burn[1] *vb* **1** = **be on fire,** be ablaze, blaze, flame, flare, flash, flicker, glow, go up in flames, smoke **3** = **set on fire,** brand, char, ignite, incinerate, kindle, light, parch, reduce to ashes, scorch, sear, shrivel, singe, toast, wither **6** = **sting,** bite, hurt, pain, smart, tingle **7** = **be passionate,** be angry, be aroused, be excited, be inflamed, blaze, desire, fume, seethe, simmer, smoulder, yearn

burning *adj* **1** = **intense,** ablaze, afire, all-consuming, ardent, eager, earnest, fervent, fervid, flaming, frantic, frenzied, impassioned, passionate, vehement, zealous **2** = **crucial,** acute, compelling, critical, essential, important, now or never, pressing, significant, urgent, vital
Antonyms *adj* ≠ **intense:** apathetic, calm, cool, faint, indifferent, mild, passive

burnish *vb* **1** = **polish,** brighten, buff, furbish, glaze, rub up, shine, smooth ◆ *n* **2** = **shine,** gloss, lustre, patina, polish, sheen
Antonyms *vb* ≠ **polish:** abrade, graze, scratch, scuff

burrow *n* **1** = **hole,** den, lair, retreat, shelter, tunnel ◆ *vb* **3** = **dig,** delve, excavate, hollow out, scoop out, tunnel

burst *vb* **1** = **explode,** blow up, break, crack, disintegrate, fly open, fragment, puncture, rend asunder, rupture, shatter, shiver, split, tear apart **2** = **rush,** barge, break, break out, erupt, gush forth, run, spout ◆ *n* **6** = **explosion,** bang, blast, blasting, blowout, blow-up, breach, break, crack, discharge, rupture, split **8, 9** = **rush,** eruption, fit, gush, gust, outbreak, outburst, outpouring, spate, spurt, surge, torrent

bury *vb* **1** = **inter,** consign to the grave, entomb, inearth, inhume, lay to rest, sepulchre **3** = **hide,** conceal, cover, cover up, draw a veil over, enshroud, secrete, shroud, stash (*inf.*), stow away **4** = **embed,** drive in, engulf, implant, sink, submerge **5** = **engross,** absorb, engage, immerse, interest, occupy
Antonyms *vb* ≠ **inter, hide:** bring to light, dig up, discover, disinter, dredge up, exhume, expose, find, reveal, turn up, uncover, unearth

bush[1] *n* **1, 2** = **shrub,** hedge, plant, shrubbery, thicket **4** = **the wild,** back country (*US*), backlands, backwoods, brush, scrub, scrubland, woodland in density: *a bush of hair.* **4** (often preceded by *the*) an uncultivated or sparsely settled area, covered with trees or shrubs, which can vary from open, shrubby country to dense rainforest. **5** a forested area; woodland. **6** *Canad.* Also called: **bush lot, woodlot.** an area on a farm on which timber is grown and cut. **7** (often preceded by *the*) *Inf.* the countryside, as opposed to the city: *out in the bush.* **8** *Obs.* a bunch of ivy hung as a vintner's sign in front of a tavern. **9 beat about the bush.** to avoid the point at issue; prevaricate. ◆ *adj* **10** *Austral. & NZ inf.* rough-and-ready. **11** *US & Canad. inf.* unprofessional, unpolished, or second-rate. **12 go bush.** *Inf.* **12a** *Austral. & NZ.* to abandon city amenities and live rough. **12b** *Austral.* to go into hiding. ◆ *vb* **13** (*intr*) to grow thick and bushy. **14** (*tr*) to cover, decorate, support, etc., with bushes. **15 bush it.** *Austral.* to camp out in the bush. [C13: of Gmc origin]

bush[2] (bʊʃ) *n* **1** a thin metal sleeve or tubular lining serving as a bearing. ◆ *vb* **2** to fit a bush to (a bearing, etc.). [C15: from MDu. *busse* box, bush; rel. to LL *buxis* BOX[1]]

bushbaby ('bʊʃˌbeɪbɪ) *n, pl* **bushbabies.** an agile nocturnal arboreal primate occurring in Africa south of the Sahara. It has large eyes and ears and a long tail. Also called: **galago.**

bushbuck ('bʊʃˌbʌk) *or* **boschbok** ('bɒʃˌbʌk) *n, pl* **bushbucks, bushbuck** *or* **boschboks, boschbok.** a small nocturnal spiral-horned antelope of the bush and tropical forest of Africa.

bush carpenter *n Austral. & NZ sl.* a rough-and-ready unskilled workman.

bushed (bʊʃt) *adj Inf.* **1** (*postpositive*) extremely tired; exhausted. **2** *Canad.* mentally disturbed from living in isolation. **3** *Austral. & NZ.* lost or bewildered, as in the bush.

bushel ('bʊʃəl) *n* **1** a British unit of dry or liquid measure equal to 8 Imperial gallons. 1 Imperial bushel is equivalent to 0.036 37 cubic metres. **2** a US unit of dry measure equal to 64 US pints. 1 US bushel is equivalent to 0.035 24 cubic metres. **3** a container with a capacity equal to either of these quantities. **4** *US inf.* a large amount. **5 hide one's light under a bushel.** to conceal one's abilities or good qualities. [C14: from OF *boissel*]

bushfire ('bʊʃˌfaɪə) *n* an uncontrolled fire in the bush; a scrub or forest fire.

bushfly ('bʊʃˌflaɪ) *n pl* **bushflies.** any of various small black dipterous flies of Australia that breed in faeces and dung.

bush house *n Chiefly Austral.* a shed or hut in the bush or a garden.

Bushido (ˌbuːʃɪ'dəʊ) *n* (*sometimes not cap.*) the feudal code of the Japanese samurai. [C19: from Japanese *bushi* warrior + *dō* way]

bushie ('bʊʃɪ) *n* a variant spelling of **bushy**[2].

bushing ('bʊʃɪŋ) *n* **1** another word for **bush**[2]. **2** an adaptor used to connect pipes of different sizes. **3** a layer of electrical insulation enabling a live conductor to pass through an earthed wall, etc.

bush jacket *or* **shirt** *n* a casual jacket or shirt having four patch pockets and a belt.

bush lawyer *n Austral. & NZ.* **1** a trailing plant with sharp hooks. **2** *Inf.* a person who gives legal opinions but is not qualified to do so.

bush line *n* an airline operating in the bush country of Canada's northern regions.

bushman ('bʊʃmən) *n, pl* **bushmen.** *Austral. & NZ.* a person who lives or travels in the bush, esp. one versed in bush lore.

Bushman ('bʊʃmən) *n, pl* **Bushmen.** a member of a hunting and gathering people of southern Africa. [C18: from Afrik. *boschjesman*]

bushmaster ('bʊʃˌmɑːstə) *n* a large greyish-brown highly venomous snake of tropical America.

bush pilot *n Canad.* a pilot who operates in the bush country.

bushranger ('bʊʃˌreɪndʒə) *n* **1** *Austral.* (formerly) an outlaw living in the bush. **2** *US.* a person who lives away from civilization.

bush tea *n* **1** a leguminous shrub of southern Africa. **2** a beverage prepared from the dried leaves of such a plant.

bush telegraph *n* a means of spreading rumour, gossip, etc.

bushveld ('bʊʃˌfelt) *n S. African.* bushy countryside. [from Afrik. *bosveld*]

bushwhack ('bʊʃˌwæk) *vb* **1** (*tr*) *US, Canad., & Austral.* to ambush. **2** (*intr*) *US, Canad., & Austral.* to cut or beat one's way through thick woods. **3** (*intr*) *US, Canad., & Austral.* to range or move around in woods or the bush. **4** (*intr*) *NZ.* to work in the bush. **5** (*intr*) *US & Canad.* to fight as a guerrilla in wild regions.

bushwhacker ('bʊʃˌwækə) *n* **1** *US, Canad., & Austral.* a person who travels around or lives in thinly populated woodlands. **2** *Austral. sl.* an unsophisticated person. **3** *NZ.* a person who works in the bush. **4** a Confederate guerrilla in the American Civil War. **5** *US.* any guerrilla.

bushy[1] ➊ ('bʊʃɪ) *adj* **bushier, bushiest. 1** covered or overgrown with bushes. **2** thick and shaggy.
▸**'bushily** *adv* ▸**'bushiness** *n*

bushy[2] *or* **bushie** ('bʊʃɪ) *n, pl* **bushies.** *Austral. inf.* **1** a person who lives in the bush. **2** an unsophisticated uncouth person.

business ➊ ('bɪznɪs) *n* **1** a trade or profession. **2** the purchase and sale of goods and services. **3** a commercial or industrial establishment. **4** commercial activity; dealings (esp. in **do business**). **5** volume of commercial activity: *business is poor today.* **6** commercial policy: *overcharging is bad business.* **7** proper or rightful concern or responsibility (often in **mind one's own business**). **8** a special task; assignment. **9** an affair; matter. **10** serious work or activity: *get down to business.* **11** a difficult or complicated matter. **12** *Theatre.* an incidental action performed by an actor for dramatic effect. **13 mean business.** to be in earnest. [OE *bisignis* solicitude, from *bisig* BUSY + *-nis* -NESS]

business college *n* a college providing courses in secretarial studies, business management, accounting, commerce, etc.

businesslike ➊ ('bɪznɪsˌlaɪk) *adj* efficient and methodical.

businessman ➊ ('bɪznɪsˌmæn, -mən) *or* (*fem*) **businesswoman** *n, pl* **businessmen** *or* **businesswomen.** a person engaged in commercial or industrial business, esp. as an owner or executive.

business park *n* an area specially designated and landscaped to accommodate offices, warehouses, etc.

business plan *n* a detailed plan setting out the objectives of a business, the strategy and tactics planned to achieve them, and the expected profits.

business process re-engineering *n* restructuring an organization by means of a reassessment of its core processes and predominant competencies. Abbrev.: **BPR.**

business school *n* an institution that offers courses in aspects of business, such as marketing, finance, and law, designed to train managers in industry and commerce to do their jobs effectively.

busk (bʌsk) *vb* (*intr*) *Brit.* to make money singing, playing an instrument, performing, or dancing in public places. [C20: ?from Sp. *buscar* to look for]
▸**'busker** *n*

buskin ('bʌskɪn) *n* **1** (formerly) a sandal-like covering for the foot and leg, reaching the calf. **2** a thick-soled laced half-boot worn esp. by actors of ancient Greece. **3** (usually preceded by *the*) *Chiefly literary.* tragic drama. [C16: ?from Sp. *borzeguí*; rel. to OF *bouzequin*]

busman's holiday ('bʌsmənz) *n Inf.* a holiday spent doing the same as one does at work. [C20: from a bus driver having a driving holiday]

buss (bʌs) *n, vb* an archaic or dialect word for **kiss.** [C16: prob. imit.]

bust[1] ➊ (bʌst) *n* **1** the chest of a human being, esp. a woman's bosom. **2** a sculpture of the head, shoulders, and upper chest of a person. [C17: from F, from It. *busto* a sculpture, from ?]

bust[2] ➊ (bʌst) *Inf.* ◆ *vb* **busts, busting, busted** *or* **bust. 1** to burst or break. **2** to make or become bankrupt. **3** (*tr*) (of the police) to raid, search, or arrest. **4** (*tr*) *US & Canad.* to demote, esp. in military rank. ◆ *n* **5** a raid, search, or arrest by the police. **6** *Chiefly US.* a punch. **7** *US & Canad.* a failure, esp. bankruptcy. **8** a drunken party. ◆ *adj* **9** broken. **10** bankrupt. **11 go bust.** to become bankrupt. [C19: from a dialect pronunciation of BURST]

bustard ('bʌstəd) *n* a large terrestrial bird inhabiting open regions of the Old World. It has long strong legs, a heavy body, a long neck, and speckled plumage. [C15: from OF *bistarde*, from L *avis tarda* slow bird]

bustier ('buːstɪeɪ) *n* a type of close-fitting usually strapless top worn by women.

bustle[1] ➊ ('bʌsᵊl) *vb* **bustles, bustling, bustled. 1** (when *intr*, often foll. by *about*) to hurry or cause to hurry with a great show of energy or activity. ◆ *n* **2** energetic and noisy activity. [C16: prob. from obs. *buskle* to make energetic preparation]
▸**'bustling** *adj*

bustle[2] ('bʌsᵊl) *n* a cushion or framework worn by women in the late 19th century at the back in order to expand the skirt. [C18: from ?]

bust-up *Inf.* ◆ *n* **1** a quarrel, esp. a serious one ending a friendship, etc. **2** *Brit.* a disturbance or brawl. ◆ *vb* **bust up** (*adv*) **3** (*intr*) to quarrel and part. **4** (*tr*) to disrupt (a meeting), esp. violently.

busy ➊ ('bɪzɪ) *adj* **busier, busiest. 1** actively or fully engaged; occupied. **2**

THESAURUS

bushy[1] *adj* **2** = **thick**, bristling, bristly, fluffy, fuzzy, luxuriant, rough, shaggy, spreading, stiff, unruly, wiry

busily *adv* **2** = **actively**, assiduously, briskly, carefully, diligently, earnestly, energetically, industriously, intently, purposefully, speedily, strenuously

business *n* **1** = **profession**, calling, career, craft, employment, function, job, line, métier, occupation, pursuit, trade, vocation, work **2** = **trade**, bargaining, commerce, dealings, industry, manufacturing, merchandising, selling, trading, transaction **3** = **establishment**, company, concern, corporation, enterprise, firm, organization, venture **7** = **concern**, assignment, duty, function, pigeon (*inf.*), responsibility, task **9** = **affair**, issue, matter, point, problem, question, subject, topic

businesslike *adj* = **efficient**, correct, matter-of-fact, methodical, orderly, organized, practical, professional, regular, routine, systematic, thorough, well-ordered, workaday
Antonyms *adj* careless, disorderly, disorganized, frivolous, impractical, inefficient, irregular, sloppy, unprofessional, unsystematic, untidy

businessman *n* = **executive**, capitalist, employer, entrepreneur, financier, industrialist, merchant, tradesman, tycoon

bust[1] *n* **1** = **bosom**, breast, chest, front, torso

bust[2] *Informal vb* **1** = **break**, burst, fracture, rupture **3** = **arrest**, catch, collar (*inf.*), cop (*sl.*), feel one's collar (*sl.*), lift (*sl.*), nab (*inf.*), nail (*inf.*), raid, search ◆ *n* **5** = **arrest**, capture, cop (*sl.*), raid, search, seizure ◆ *adj* **10** = **bankrupt**, broken, failed, insolvent, ruined

bustle[1] *vb* **1** = **hurry**, beetle, bestir, dash, flutter, fuss, hasten, rush, scamper, scramble, scurry, scuttle, stir, tear ◆ *n* **2** = **activity**, ado, agitation, commotion, excitement, flurry, fuss, haste, hurly-burly, hurry, pother, stir, to-do, tumult
Antonyms *vb* ≠ **hurry:** be indolent, idle, laze, lie around, loaf, loiter, loll, relax, rest, take it easy ◆ *n* ≠ **activity:** inaction, inactivity, quiet, quietness, stillness, tranquillity

bustling *adj* **1** = **busy**, active, astir, buzzing, crowded, energetic, eventful, full, humming, hustling, lively, rushing, stirring, swarming, teeming, thronged

busy *adj* **1** = **occupied**, active, assiduous, brisk, diligent, employed, engaged, engrossed, hard crowded with or characterized by activity. **3** *Chiefly US & Canad.* (of a room, telephone line, etc.) in use; engaged. **4** overcrowded with detail: *a busy painting.* **5** meddlesome; inquisitive. ◆ *vb* **busies, busying, busied. 6** (*tr*) to make or keep (someone, esp. oneself) busy. [OE *bisig*] ▸ **'busily** *adv* ▸ **'busyness** *n*

busybody ❶ ('bɪzɪˌbɒdɪ) *n, pl* **busybodies.** a meddlesome, prying, or officious person.

busy Lizzie ('lɪzɪ) *n* a flowering plant that has pink, red, or white flowers and is often grown as a pot plant.

but[1] ❶ (bʌt; *unstressed* bət) *conj* (*coordinating*) **1** contrary to expectation: *he cut his knee but didn't cry.* **2** in contrast; on the contrary: *I like opera but my husband doesn't.* **3** (*usually used after a negative*) other than: *we can't do anything but wait.* ◆ *conj* (*subordinating*) **4** (*usually used after a negative*) without it happening: *we never go out but it rains.* **5** (foll. by *that*) except that: *nothing is impossible but that we live forever.* **6** *Arch.* if not; unless. ◆ *prep* **7** except; save: *they saved all but one.* **8 but for.** were it not for: *but for you, we couldn't have managed.* ◆ *adv* **9** just; merely: *he was but a child.* **10** *Dialect & Austral.* though; however: *it's a rainy day; warm, but.* ◆ *n* **11** an objection (esp. in **ifs and buts**). [OE *būtan* without, outside, except, from *be* BY + *ūtan* OUT]

but[2] (bʌt) *n Scot.* the outer room of a two-roomed cottage. Cf. **ben**[1]. [C18: from *but* (adv) outside; see BUT[1]]

butadiene (ˌbjuːtə'daɪiːn) *n* a colourless flammable gas used mainly in the manufacture of synthetic rubbers. Formula: CH_2:CHCH:CH_2. Systematic name: **buta-1,3-diene.** [C20: from BUTA(NE) + DI-[1] + -ENE]

butane ('bjuːteɪn, bjuː'teɪn) *n* a colourless flammable gaseous alkane used mainly in the manufacture of rubber and fuels. Formula: C_4H_{10}. [C20: from BUT(YL) + -ANE]

butanoic acid (ˌbjuːtə'nəʊɪk) *n* a carboxylic acid that produces the smell in rancid butter. Formula: $CH_3(CH_2)_2COOH$. Also called: **butyric acid.** [C20: from BUTAN(E) + -OIC]

butanol ('bjuːtəˌnɒl) *n* a colourless substance existing in four isomeric forms. The three liquid isomers are used as solvents and in the manufacture of organic compounds. Formula: C_4H_9OH. Also called: **butyl alcohol.**

butanone ('bjuːtəˌnəʊn) *n* a colourless flammable liquid used as a resin solvent, and paint remover, and in lacquers, adhesives, etc. Formula: $CH_3COC_2H_5$.

butch (bʊtʃ) *Sl.* ◆ *adj* **1** (of a woman or man) markedly or aggressively masculine. ◆ *n* **2** a lesbian who is noticeably masculine. **3** a strong rugged man. [C18: back formation from BUTCHER]

butcher ❶ ('bʊtʃə) *n* **1** a retailer of meat. **2** a person who slaughters or dresses meat. **3** an indiscriminate or brutal murderer. ◆ *vb* (*tr*) **4** to slaughter or dress (animals) for meat. **5** to kill indiscriminately or brutally. **6** to make a mess of; botch. [C13: from OF *bouchier*, from *bouc* he-goat]

butcherbird ('bʊtʃəˌbɜːd) *n* **1** a shrike, esp. of the genus *Lanius.* **2** any of several Australian magpies that impale their prey on thorns.

butcher's-broom *n* an evergreen shrub with stiff prickle-tipped flattened green stems, formerly used for making brooms.

butchery ❶ ('bʊtʃərɪ) *n, pl* **butcheries. 1** the business of a butcher. **2** wanton and indiscriminate slaughter. **3** a slaughterhouse.

butler ('bʌtlə) *n* the male servant of a household in charge of the wines, table, etc.: usually the head servant. [C13: from OF, from *bouteille* BOTTLE]

butlery ('bʌtlərɪ) *n, pl* **butleries. 1** a butler's room. **2** another name for **buttery**[2].

butt[1] ❶ (bʌt) *n* **1** the thicker or blunt end of something, such as the end of the stock of a rifle. **2** the unused end of something, esp. of a cigarette; stub. **3** *Inf., chiefly US & Canad.* the buttocks. **4** *US.* a slang word for **cigarette. 5** *Building.* short for **butt joint.** [C15 (in the sense: thick end of something, buttock): rel. to OE *buttuc* end, ridge]

butt[2] ❶ (bʌt) *n* **1** a person or thing that is the target of ridicule, wit, etc. **2** *Shooting, archery.* **2a** a mound of earth behind the target that stops bullets or wide shots. **2b** the target itself. **2c** (*pl*) the target range. **3** a low barrier behind which sportsmen shoot game birds, esp. grouse. ◆ *vb* **4** (usually foll. by *on* or *against*) to lie or be placed end on to; abut. [C14 (in the sense: mark for archery practice): from OF *but*]

butt[3] ❶ (bʌt) *vb* **1** to strike or push (something) with the head or horns. **2** (*intr*) to project; jut. **3** (*intr;* foll. by *in* or *into*) to intrude, esp. into a conversation; interfere. ◆ *n* **4** a blow with the head or horns. [C12: from OF *boter*, of Gmc origin]

butt[4] ❶ (bʌt) *n* a large cask for storing wine or beer. [C14: from OF *botte*, from LL *buttis* cask]

butte (bjuːt) *n US & Canad.* an isolated steep flat-topped hill. [C19: F, from OF *bute* mound behind a target; see BUTT[2]]

butter ('bʌtə) *n* **1** an edible fatty whitish-yellow solid made from cream by churning. **2** any substance with a butter-like consistency, such as peanut butter. **3 look as if butter wouldn't melt in one's mouth.** to look innocent, although probably not so. ◆ *vb* (*tr*) **4** to put butter on or in. **5** to flatter. ◆ See also **butter up.** [OE *butere*, from L, from Gk *bouturon*, from *bous* cow + *turos* cheese]

butter bean *n* a variety of lima bean that has large pale flat edible seeds.

butterbur ('bʌtəˌbɜː) *n* a plant of the composite family with fragrant whitish or purple flowers, and large leaves formerly used to wrap butter.

buttercup ('bʌtəˌkʌp) *n* any of various yellow-flowered plants of the genus *Ranunculus* of Europe, Asia, and North America.

butterfat ('bʌtəˌfæt) *n* the fatty substance of milk from which butter is made, consisting of a mixture of glycerides.

butterfingers ('bʌtəˌfɪŋgəz) *n* (*functioning as sing*) *Inf.* a person who drops things inadvertently or fails to catch things. ▸ **'butterˌfingered** *adj*

butterfish ('bʌtəˌfɪʃ) *n, pl* **butterfish** *or* **butterfishes.** any of several species of fishes having a slippery skin.

butterflies ('bʌtəˌflaɪz) *pl n Inf.* tremors in the stomach region due to nervousness.

butterfly ('bʌtəˌflaɪ) *n, pl* **butterflies. 1** any diurnal insect that has a slender body with clubbed antennae and typically rests with the wings (often brightly coloured) closed over the back. **2** a person who never settles with one interest or occupation for long. **3** a swimming stroke in which the arms are plunged forward together in large circular movements. **4** *Commerce.* the simultaneous purchase and sale of traded call options, at different exercise prices or with different expiry dates, on a stock exchange or commodity market. [OE *buttorflēoge*]

butterfly collar *n* the Irish name for **wing collar.**

butterfly effect *n* the idea, used in chaos theory, that a very small difference in the initial state of a physical system can make a significant difference to the state at some later time. [C20: from the theory that a butterfly flapping its wings in one part of the world might ultimately cause a hurricane in another part of the world]

butterfly nut *n* another name for **wing nut.**

buttermilk ('bʌtəˌmɪlk) *n* the sourish liquid remaining after the butter has been separated from milk.

butter muslin *n* a fine loosely woven cotton material originally used for wrapping butter.

butternut ('bʌtəˌnʌt) *n* **1** *Austral. & NZ.* a type of small edible pumpkin. **2a** a walnut tree of North America. **2b** its oily edible nut.

butterscotch ('bʌtəˌskɒtʃ) *n* **1** a kind of hard brittle toffee made with butter, brown sugar, etc. **2** a flavouring made from these ingredients. [C19: ? first made in Scotland]

butter up ❶ *vb* (*tr, adv*) to flatter.

butterwort ('bʌtəˌwɜːt) *n* a plant that grows in wet places and has violet-blue spurred flowers and fleshy greasy glandular leaves on which insects are trapped and digested.

buttery[1] ('bʌtərɪ) *adj* containing, like, or coated with butter. ▸ **'butteriness** *n*

buttery[2] ('bʌtərɪ) *n, pl* **butteries. 1** a room for storing foods or wines. **2** *Brit.* (in some universities) a room in which food and drink are supplied or sold to students. [C14: from Anglo-F *boterie*, prob. from L *butta* cask, BUTT[4]]

butt joint *n* a joint between two plates, planks, etc., fastened end to end without overlapping or interlocking. Sometimes shortened to **butt.**

buttock ❶ ('bʌtək) *n* **1** either of the two large fleshy masses of thick muscular tissue that form the human rump. See also **gluteus.** Related adj: **gluteal. 2** the analogous part in some mammals. [C13: ?from OE *buttuc* round slope]

button ('bʌtᵊn) *n* **1** a disc or knob of plastic, wood, etc., attached to a garment, etc., usually for fastening two surfaces together by passing it through a buttonhole or loop. **2** a small round object, such as any of various sweets, decorations, or badges. **3** a small disc that completes an electric circuit when pushed, as one that operates a machine. **4**

THESAURUS

at work, industrious, in harness, on active service, on duty, persevering, rushed off one's feet, slaving, working **2** = **lively**, active, energetic, exacting, full, hectic, hustling, on the go (*inf.*), restless, strenuous, tireless, tiring ◆ *vb* **6** = **occupy**, absorb, employ, engage, engross, immerse, interest

Antonyms *adj* ≠ **occupied, lively:** idle, inactive, indolent, lackadaisical, lazy, off duty, relaxed, shiftless, slothful, unoccupied

busybody *n* = **nosy parker** (*inf.*), eavesdropper, gossip, intriguer, intruder, meddler, pry, scandalmonger, snoop, snooper, stirrer (*inf.*), troublemaker

but[1] *conj* **2** = **however**, further, moreover, nevertheless, on the contrary, on the other hand, still, yet ◆ *prep* **7** = **except**, bar, barring, excepting, excluding, notwithstanding, save, with the exception of ◆ *adv* **9** = **only**, just, merely, simply, singly, solely

butcher *n* **3** = **murderer**, destroyer, killer, slaughterer, slayer ◆ *vb* **4** = **slaughter**, carve, clean, cut, cut up, dress, joint, prepare **5** = **kill**, assassinate, cut down, destroy, exterminate, liquidate, massacre, put to the sword, slaughter, slay **6** = **mess up**, bodge (*inf.*), botch, destroy, mutilate, ruin, spoil, wreck

butchery *n* **2** = **slaughter**, blood bath, blood-letting, bloodshed, carnage, killing, massacre, mass murder, murder

butt[1] *n* **1** = **end**, haft, handle, hilt, shaft, shank, stock **2** = **stub**, base, end, fag end (*inf.*), foot, leftover, tail, tip

butt[2] *n* **1** = **target**, Aunt Sally, dupe, laughing stock, mark, object, point, subject, victim

butt[3] *vb, n* **1, 4** = **knock**, buck, buffet, bump, bunt, jab, poke, prod, punch, push, ram, shove, thrust ◆ *vb* **3** *foll. by* **in** *or* **into** = **interfere**, chip in (*inf.*), cut in, interrupt, intrude, meddle, put one's oar in, put one's two cents in (*US. sl.*), stick one's nose in

butt[4] *n* = **cask**, barrel, pipe

butter up *vb* = **flatter**, blarney, cajole, coax, fawn on *or* upon, kiss (someone's) ass (*US. sl.*), pander to, soft-soap, suck up to (*inf.*), wheedle

buttocks *pl n* **1, 2** = **bottom**, arse (*taboo sl.*), ass

Biol. any rounded knoblike part or organ, such as an unripe mushroom. **5** *Fencing.* the protective knob fixed to the point of a foil. **6** *Brit.* an object of no value (esp. in **not worth a button**). ◆ *vb* **7** to fasten with a button or buttons. **8** (*tr*) to provide with buttons. [C14: from OF *boton,* from *boter* to thrust, butt; see BUTT[3]]
▸**'buttoner** *n* ▸**'buttonless** *adj*

buttonhole ⓣ ('bʌtᵊnˌhəʊl) *n* **1** a slit in a garment, etc., through which a button is passed to fasten two surfaces together. **2** a flower or small bunch of flowers worn pinned to the lapel or in the buttonhole, esp. at weddings. US name: **boutonniere.** ◆ *vb* **buttonholes, buttonholing, buttonholed.** (*tr*) **3** to detain (a person) in conversation. **4** to make buttonholes in.

buttonhook ('bʌtᵊnˌhʊk) *n* a thin tapering hooked instrument formerly used for pulling buttons through the buttonholes of shoes.

button up *vb* (*tr, adv*) **1** to fasten (a garment) with a button or buttons. **2** *Inf.* to conclude (business) satisfactorily. **3 button up one's lip** *or* **mouth.** *Sl.* to be silent.

buttress ⓣ ('bʌtrɪs) *n* **1** Also called: **pier.** a construction, usually of brick or stone, built to support a wall. **2** any support or prop. **3** something shaped like a buttress, such as a projection from a mountainside. ◆ *vb* (*tr*) **4** to support (a wall) with a buttress. **5** to support or sustain. [C13: from OF *bouterez,* from *bouter* to thrust, BUTT[3]]

butty[1] ('bʌtɪ) *n, pl* **butties.** *Chiefly N English dialect.* a sandwich: *a jam butty.* [C19: from *buttered* (bread)]

butty[2] ('bʌtɪ) *n, pl* **butties.** *English dialect.* (esp. in mining parlance) a friend or workmate. [C19: ?from obs. *booty* sharing, from BOOT[2]]

butyl ('bjuːˌtaɪl, -tɪl) *n* (*modifier*) of or containing any of four isomeric forms of the group C_4H_9–: *butyl rubber.* [C19: from BUT(YRIC ACID) + -YL]

butyl alcohol *n* another name for **butanol.**

butyl rubber *n* a copolymer of isobutene and isoprene, used in tyres and as a waterproofing material.

butyric acid (bjuː'tɪrɪk) *n* another name for **butanoic acid.** [C19 *butyric,* from L *būtyrum* BUTTER]

buxom ⓣ ('bʌksəm) *adj* **1** (esp. of a woman) healthily plump, attractive, and vigorous. **2** (of a woman) full-bosomed. [C12: *buhsum* compliant, pliant, from OE *būgan* to bend, BOW[1]]
▸**'buxomness** *n*

buy ⓣ (baɪ) *vb* **buys, buying, bought.** (*mainly tr*) **1** to acquire by paying or promising to pay a sum of money; purchase. **2** to be capable of purchasing: *money can't buy love.* **3** to acquire by any exchange or sacrifice: *to buy time by equivocation.* **4** to bribe or corrupt; hire by or as by bribery. **5** *Sl.* to accept as true, practical, etc. **6** (*intr;* foll. by *into*) to purchase shares of (a company). ◆ *n* **7** a purchase (often in **good** or **bad buy**). ◆ See also **buy in, buy into,** etc. [OE *bycgan*]

> **USAGE NOTE** The use of *off* after *buy* as in *I bought this off my neighbour* was formerly considered incorrect, but is now acceptable in informal contexts.

buy-back *n Commerce.* the repurchase by a company of some or all of its shares from an investor, who acquired them by putting venture capital into the company when it was formed.

buyer ('baɪə) *n* **1** a person who buys; customer. **2** a person employed to buy merchandise, materials, etc., as for a shop or factory.

buy in *vb* (*adv*) **1** (*tr*) to buy back for the owner (an item in an auction) at or below the reserve price. **2** (*intr*) to purchase shares in a company. **3** (*tr*) Also: **buy into.** *US inf.* to pay money to secure a position or place for (someone, esp. oneself) in some organization, esp. a business or club. **4** to purchase (goods, etc.) in large quantities. ◆ *n* **buy-in. 5** the purchase of a company by a manager or group who does not work for that company.

buy into *vb* (*intr, prep*) **1** to agree with or accept as valid (an argument, theory, etc.). **2** *Austral. & NZ inf.* to get involved in (an argument, fight, etc.).

buy off *vb* (*tr, adv*) to pay (a person or group) to drop a charge, end opposition, etc.

buy out *vb* (*tr, adv*) **1** to purchase the ownership, controlling interest, shares, etc., of (a company, etc.). **2** to gain the release of (a person) from the armed forces by payment. **3** to pay (a person) to give up ownership of (property, etc.). ◆ *n* **buy-out. 4** the purchase of a company, esp. by its former management or staff. See also **leveraged buyout, management buyout.**

buy up *vb* (*tr, adv*) **1** to purchase all, or all that is available, of (something). **2** to purchase a controlling interest in (a company, etc.).

buzz ⓣ (bʌz) *n* **1** a rapidly vibrating humming sound, as of a bee. **2** a low sound, as of many voices in conversation. **3** a rumour; report; gossip. **4** *Inf.* a telephone call. **5** *Inf.* **5a** a pleasant sensation. **5b** a sense of excitement; kick. **6** (*modifier*) fashionable, trendy. ◆ *vb* **7** (*intr*) to make a vibrating sound like that of a prolonged *z.* **8** (*intr*) to talk or gossip with an air of excitement: *the town buzzed with the news.* **9** (*tr*) to utter or spread (a rumour). **10** (*intr;* often foll. by *about*) to move around quickly and busily. **11** (*tr*) to signal or summon with a buzzer. **12** (*tr*) *Inf.* to call by telephone. **13** (*tr*) *Inf.* to fly an aircraft very low over (an object). **14** (*tr*) (esp. of insects) to make a buzzing sound with (wings, etc.). [C16: imit.]

buzzard ('bʌzəd) *n* a diurnal bird of prey of the hawk family, typically having broad wings and tail and a soaring flight. [C13: from OF *buisard,* from L *būteō* hawk]

buzzer ('bʌzə) *n* **1** a device that produces a buzzing sound, esp. one similar to an electric bell. **2** *NZ.* a wood-planing machine.

buzz off *vb* (*intr, adv; often imperative*) *Inf., chiefly Brit.* to go away; leave; depart.

buzz word *n Inf.* a word, originally from a particular jargon, which becomes a popular vogue word. [C20: from ?]

BVM *abbrev. for* Beata Virgo Maria. [L: Blessed Virgin Mary]

bwana ('bwɑːnə) *n* (in E Africa) a master, often used as a form of address corresponding to *sir.* [Swahili, from Ar. *abūna* our father]

by ⓣ (baɪ) *prep* **1** used to indicate the agent after a passive verb: *seeds eaten by the birds.* **2** used to indicate the person responsible for a creative work: *this song is by Schubert.* **3** via; through: *enter by the back door.* **4** foll. by a gerund to indicate a means used: *he frightened her by hiding behind the door.* **5** beside; next to; near: *a tree by the house.* **6** passing the position of; past: *he drove by the old cottage.* **7** not later than; before: *return the books by Tuesday.* **8** used to indicate extent, after a comparative: *it is hotter by five degrees.* **9** (esp. in oaths) invoking the name of: *I swear by all the gods.* **10** multiplied by: *four by three equals twelve.* **11** during the passing of (esp. in **by day, by night**). **12** placed between measurements of the various dimensions of something: *a pane four inches by seven.* ◆ *adv* **13** near: *the house is close by.* **14** away; aside: *he put some money by each week.* **15** passing a point near something; past: *he drove by.* ◆ *n, pl* **byes. 16** a variant spelling of **bye**[1]. [OE *bī*]

by- *or* **bye-** *prefix* **1** near: *bystander.* **2** secondary or incidental: *by-election; by-product.* [from BY]

by and by ⓣ *adv* presently or eventually.

by and large *adv* in general; on the whole. [C17: orig. nautical: to the wind and off it]

bye[1] (baɪ) *n* **1** *Sport.* the situation in which a player or team wins a preliminary round by virtue of having no opponent. **2** *Golf.* one or more holes that are left unplayed after the match has been decided. **3** *Cricket.* a run scored off a ball not struck by the batsman. **4** something incidental or secondary. **5 by the bye.** incidentally; by the way. [C16: var. of BY]

bye[2] *or* **bye-bye** *sentence substitute. Brit. inf.* goodbye.

bye-byes *n* (*functioning as sing*) an informal word for **sleep,** used esp. to children (as in **go to bye-byes**).

by-election *or* **bye-election** *n* (in Great Britain and other countries of the Commonwealth) an election held during the life of a parliament to fill a vacant seat.

Byelorussian (ˌbjɛləʊ'rʌʃən) *adj* a variant spelling of **Belarussian.**

bygone ⓣ ('baɪˌgɒn) *adj* **1** (*usually prenominal*) past; former. ◆ *n* **2** (*often pl*) a past occurrence. **3** an artefact, implement, etc., of former domestic or industrial use. **4 let bygones be bygones.** to agree to forget past quarrels.

bylaw *or* **bye-law** ('baɪˌlɔː) *n* **1** a rule made by a local authority. **2** a regulation of a company, society, etc. [C13: prob. of Scand. origin; cf. ON *býr* dwelling, town]

by-line *n* **1** a line under the title of a newspaper or magazine article giving the author's name. **2** another word for **touchline.**

BYO(G) *n Austral. & NZ.* an unlicensed restaurant at which diners may drink their own wine, etc. [C20: from *bring your own* (*grog*)]

bypass ⓣ ('baɪˌpɑːs) *n* **1** a main road built to avoid a city or other congested area. **2** a means of redirecting the flow of a substance around

THESAURUS

(*US. & Canad. taboo sl.*), backside, behind (*inf.*), bum (*Brit. sl.*), buns (*US. sl.*), butt (*US. & Canad. inf.*), derrière (*euphemistic*), gluteus maximus (*Anatomy*), haunches, hindquarters, posterior, rear, rump, seat, tail (*inf.*)

buttonhole *vb* **3** = **detain**, accost, bore, catch, grab, importune, persuade importunately, take aside, waylay

buttress *n* **1, 2** = **support**, abutment, brace, mainstay, pier, prop, reinforcement, shore, stanchion, stay, strut ◆ *vb* **4, 5** = **support**, augment, back up, bolster, brace, prop, prop up, reinforce, shore, shore up, strengthen, sustain, uphold

buxom *adj* **1** = **plump**, ample, curvaceous, voluptuous, well-rounded **2** = **full-bosomed**, bosomy, busty

Antonyms *adj* ≠ **plump:** delicate, frail, slender, slight, slim, svelte, sylphlike, thin, trim

buy *vb* **1** = **purchase**, acquire, get, invest in, obtain, pay for, procure, score (*sl.*), shop for **4** = **bribe**, corrupt, fix (*inf.*), grease someone's palm (*sl.*), square, suborn ◆ *n* **6** = **purchase**, acquisition, bargain, deal

Antonyms *vb* ≠ **purchase:** auction, barter, retail, sell, vend

buzz *n* **1, 2** = **hum**, buzzing, drone, hiss, murmur, purr, ring, ringing, sibilation, whir, whisper **3** = **gossip**, dirt (*US sl.*), gen (*Brit. inf.*), hearsay, latest (*inf.*), news, report, rumour, scandal, scuttlebutt (*US sl.*), whisper, word ◆ *vb* **7** = **hum**, drone, fizzle, murmur, reverberate, ring, sibilate, whir, whisper, whizz **9** = **gossip**, chatter, natter, rumour, tattle

by *prep* **3** = **via**, by way of, over **4** = **through**, through the agency of, under the aegis of **5** = **near**, along, beside, close to, next to, past ◆ *adv* **13** = **near**, at hand, close, handy, in reach **14** = **past**, aside, away, to one side

by and by *adv* = **presently**, anon, before long, erelong, eventually, in a while, in the course of time, one day, shortly, soon

bygone *adj* **1** = **past**, ancient, antiquated, departed, erstwhile, extinct, former, gone by, lost, of old, of yore, olden, one-time, previous

Antonyms *adj* coming, forthcoming, future, prospective, to be, to come

bypass *vb* **5** = **go round**, avoid, body-swerve (*Scot.*), circumvent, depart from, detour round, deviate from, get round, give a wide berth to, pass round an appliance through which it would otherwise pass. **3** *Surgery*. **3a** the redirection of blood flow, either to avoid a diseased blood vessel or in order to perform heart surgery. See **coronary bypass. 3b** (*as modifier*): *bypass surgery*. **4** *Electronics*. an electrical circuit connected in parallel around one or more components, providing an alternative path for certain frequencies. ◆ *vb* (*tr*) **5** to go around or avoid (a city, obstruction, problem, etc.). **6** to cause (traffic, fluid, etc.) to go through a bypass. **7** to proceed without reference to (regulations, a superior, etc.); get round; avoid.

bypass engine *n* a gas turbine in which part of the compressor delivery bypasses the combustion zone, flowing directly into or around the exhaust to provide additional thrust.

bypath ('baɪˌpɑːθ) *n* a little-used path or track.

by-play *n* secondary action or talking carried on apart while the main action proceeds, esp. in a play.

by-product *n* **1** a secondary or incidental product of a manufacturing process. **2** a side effect.

byre ('baɪə) *n Brit.* a shelter for cows. [OE *bȳre*; rel. to *būr* hut, cottage]

byroad ('baɪˌrəʊd) *n* a secondary or side road.

Byronic (baɪ'rɒnɪk) *adj* of, like, or characteristic of Byron, his poetry, or his style. [C19: from Lord *Byron* (1788–1824), E poet]

byssinosis (ˌbɪsɪ'nəʊsɪs) *n* a lung disease caused by prolonged inhalation of fibre dust. [C19: from NL, from Gk *bussinos* of linen + -OSIS]

bystander ➊ ('baɪˌstændə) *n* a person present but not involved; onlooker; spectator.

byte (baɪt) *n Computing*. **1** a group of bits processed as one unit of data. **2** the storage space allocated to such a group of bits. **3** a subdivision of a word. [C20: prob. a blend of BIT[4] + BITE]

byway ('baɪˌweɪ) *n* **1** a secondary or side road, esp. in the country. **2** an area, field of study, etc., that is very obscure or of secondary importance.

byword ➊ ('baɪˌwɜːd) *n* **1** a person or thing regarded as a perfect or proverbial example of something: *their name is a byword for good service*. **2** an object of scorn or derision. **3** a common saying; proverb. [OE *bīwyrde*; see BY, WORD]

Byzantine (bɪ'zænˌtaɪn, -ˌtiːn, baɪ-; 'bɪzənˌtiːn, -ˌtaɪn) *adj* **1** of or relating to Byzantium, an ancient Greek city on the Bosphorus. **2** of or relating to the Byzantine Empire, the continuation of the Roman Empire in the East. **3** of, relating to, or characterizing the Orthodox Church. **4** of or relating to the highly coloured stylized form of religious art developed in the Byzantine Empire. **5** of or relating to the style of architecture developed in the Byzantine Empire, characterized by massive domes, rounded arches, spires and minarets, and mosaics. **6** (of attitudes, etc.) inflexible or complicated. ◆ *n* **7** an inhabitant of Byzantium.

▸**Byzantinism** (bɪ'zæntɑˌnɪzəm, -tiː-, baɪ-; 'bɪzəntiːˌnɪzəm, -taɪ-) *n*

Bz *or* **bz.** *abbrev. for* benzene.

THESAURUS

Antonyms *vb* abut, adjoin, come together, connect, converge, cross, intersect, join, link, meet, touch, unite

bystander *n* = **onlooker**, eyewitness, looker-on, observer, passer-by, spectator, viewer, watcher, witness

Antonyms *n* contributor, partaker, participant, party

byword *n* **3** = **saying**, adage, aphorism, apophthegm, dictum, epithet, gnome, maxim, motto, precept, proverb, saw, slogan

Cc

c *or* **C** (siː) *n, pl* **c's, C's,** *or* **Cs. 1** the third letter of the English alphabet. **2** a speech sound represented by this letter, usually either as in *cigar* or as in *case.* **3** the third in a series, esp. the third highest grade in an examination. **4** something shaped like a C.

c *symbol for:* **1** centi-. **2** *Maths.* constant. **3** cubic. **4** cycle. **5** specific heat capacity. **6** the speed of light and other types of electromagnetic radiation in free space.

C *symbol for:* **1** *Music.* **1a** the first degree of a major scale containing no sharps or flats (**C major**). **1b** the major or minor key having this note as its tonic. **1c** a time signature denoting four crotchet beats to the bar. See also **alla breve** (sense 2), **common time. 2** *Chem.* carbon. **3** *Biochem.* cytosine. **4** capacitance. **5** heat capacity. **6** cold (water). **7** *Physics.* compliance. **8** Celsius. **9** centigrade. **10** century: C20. **11** coulomb. **12** *the Roman numeral for* 100. ◆ *n* **13** a type of high-level computer programming language.

c. *abbrev. for:* **1** carat. **2** carbon (paper). **3** *Cricket.* caught. **4** cent(s). **5** century *or* centuries. **6** (*pl* **cc.**) chapter. **7** (used esp. preceding a date) circa: *c. 1800.* [L: about] **8** colt. **9** contralto. **10** copyright. **11** coulomb.

C. *abbrev. for:* **1** (on maps as part of name) Cape. **2** Catholic. **3** Celtic. **4** Conservative. **5** Corps.

c/- (in Australia) *abbrev. for* care for.

C1 (ˈsiːˈwʌn) *n* **a** a person whose job is supervisory or clerical, or who works in junior management. **b** (*as adj*): *a C1 worker.* ◆ See also **occupation groupings.**

C2 (ˈsiːˈtuː) *n* **a** a skilled manual worker, or a manual worker with responsibility for other people. **b** (*as adj*): *a C2 worker.* ◆ See also **occupation groupings.**

Ca *the chemical symbol for* calcium.

CA *abbrev. for:* **1** California. **2** Central America. **3** chartered accountant. **4** Civil Aviation. **5** (in Britain) Consumers' Association.

ca. *abbrev. for* circa. [L: about]

CAA (in Britain) *abbrev. for* Civil Aviation Authority.

Caaba (ˈkɑːbə) *n* a variant spelling of **Kaaba.**

cab Ⓣ (kæb) *n* **1a** a taxi. **1b** (*as modifier*): *a cab rank.* **2** the enclosed compartment of a lorry, crane, etc., from which it is driven. **3** (formerly) a horse-drawn vehicle used for public hire. [C19: from CABRIOLET]

cabal Ⓣ (kəˈbæl) *n* **1** a small group of intriguers, esp. one formed for political purposes. **2** a secret plot; conspiracy. **3** a clique. ◆ *vb* **cabals, caballing, caballed. 4** (*intr*) to form a cabal; plot. [C17: from F *cabale,* from Med. L *cabala*]

cabala (kəˈbɑːlə) *n* a variant spelling of **cabbala.**

caballero (ˌkæbəˈljɛərəʊ) *n, pl* **caballeros** (-rəʊz). a Spanish gentleman. [C19: from Sp.: gentleman, from LL *caballārius* rider, from *caballus* horse]

cabana (kəˈbɑːnə) *n Chiefly US.* a tent used as a dressing room by the sea. [from Sp. *cabaña:* CABIN]

cabaret (ˈkæbəˌreɪ) *n* **1** a floor show of dancing, singing, etc., at a nightclub or restaurant. **2** *Chiefly US.* a nightclub or restaurant providing such entertainment. [C17: from Norman F: tavern, prob. from LL *camera* an arched roof]

cabbage (ˈkæbɪdʒ) *n* **1** Also called: **cole.** any of various cultivated varieties of a plant of the genus *Brassica* having a short thick stalk and a large head of green or reddish edible leaves. See also **brassica. 2a** the head of a cabbage. **2b** the edible leaf bud of the cabbage palm. **3** *Inf.* a dull or unimaginative person. **4** *Inf.* a person who has no mental faculties and is dependent on others. [C14: from Norman F *caboche* head]

cabbage palm *n* **1** a West Indian palm whose leaf buds are eaten like cabbage. **2** a similar Brazilian palm.

cabbage rose *n* a rose with a round compact full-petalled head.

cabbage tree *n* **1** a tall palmlike ornamental New Zealand tree. **2** a tall palm tree of Eastern Australia.

cabbage white *n* a large white butterfly, the larvae of which feed on the leaves of cabbages and related vegetables.

cabbala, cabala, kabbala, *or* **kabala** Ⓣ (kəˈbɑːlə) *n* **1** an ancient Jewish mystical tradition. **2** any secret or occult doctrine. [C16: from Med. L, from Heb. *qabbālāh* tradition, from *qābal* to receive] ▸**cabbalism, cabalism, kabballism,** *or* **kabalism** (ˈkæbəˌlɪzəm) *n* ▸ˈ**cabbalist,** ˈ**cabalist,** ˈ**kabbalist,** *or* ˈ**kabalist** *n* ▸ˌ**cabbaˈlistic,** ˌ**cabaˈlistic,** ˌ**kabbaˈlistic,** *or* ˌ**kabaˈlistic** *adj*

cabbie *or* **cabby** (ˈkæbɪ) *n, pl* **cabbies.** *Inf.* a cab driver.

caber (ˈkeɪbə) *n Scot.* a heavy section of trimmed tree trunk thrown in competition at Highland games (**tossing the caber**). [C16: from Gaelic *cabar* pole]

Cabernet Sauvignon (ˈkæbəneɪ ˈsəʊvɪnjɒn; *French* kabɛrnɛ sovinɔ̃) *n* (*sometimes not caps.*) **1** a black grape grown in the Bordeaux area of France, Australia, California, Bulgaria, and elsewhere, used for making wine. **2** any of various red wines made from this grape. [F]

cabin Ⓣ (ˈkæbɪn) *n* **1** a small simple dwelling; hut. **2** a simple house providing accommodation for travellers or holiday-makers. **3** a room used as an office or living quarters in a ship. **4** a covered compartment used for shelter in a small boat. **5** *Brit.* another name for **signal box. 6a** the enclosed part of a light aircraft in which the pilot and passengers sit. **6b** the part of an aircraft for passengers or cargo. ◆ *vb* **7** (*tr*) to confine in a small space. [C14: from OF *cabane,* from OProvençal *cabana,* from LL *capanna* hut]

cabin boy *n* a boy who waits on the officers and passengers of a ship.

cabin cruiser *n* a power boat fitted with a cabin for pleasure cruising or racing.

cabinet Ⓣ (ˈkæbɪnɪt) *n* **1** a piece of furniture containing shelves, cupboards, or drawers for storage or display. **2** the outer case of a television, radio, etc. **3a** (*often cap.*) the executive and policy-making body of a country, consisting of senior government ministers. **3b** (*sometimes cap.*) an advisory council to a president, governor, etc. **3c** (*as modifier*): *a cabinet reshuffle.* **4a** a standard size of paper, 6 × 4 inches (15 × 10 cm), for mounted photographs. **4b** (*as modifier*): *a cabinet photograph.* **5** *Arch.* a private room. [C16: from OF, dim. of *cabine,* from ?]

cabinet-maker *n* a craftsman specializing in making fine furniture. ▸ˈ**cabinet-ˌmaking** *n*

cabinetwork (ˈkæbɪnɪtˌwɜːk) *n* **1** the making of furniture, esp. of fine quality. **2** an article made by a cabinet-maker.

cabin fever *n Canad.* acute depression resulting from being isolated or sharing cramped quarters in the wilderness.

cable (ˈkeɪbᵊl) *n* **1** a strong thick rope, usually of twisted hemp or steel wire. **2** *Naut.* an anchor chain or rope. **3a** a unit of distance in navigation, equal to one tenth of a sea mile (about 600 ft). **3b** Also called: **cable length, cable's length.** a unit of length in nautical use that has various values, including 100 fathoms (600 ft). **4** a wire or bundle of wires that conducts electricity: *a submarine cable.* **5** Also called: **cablegram.** a telegram sent abroad by submarine cable, telephone line, etc. **6** Also called: **cable stitch.** a knitting pattern resembling a twisted rope. ◆ *vb* **cables, cabling, cabled. 7** to send (a message) to (someone) by cable. **8** (*tr*) to fasten or provide with a cable or cables. **9** (*tr*) to supply (a place) with cable television. [C13: from OF, from LL *capulum* halter]

cable car *n* **1** a cabin suspended from and moved by an overhead cable in a mountain area. **2** the passenger car on a **cable railway,** drawn along by a strong cable operated by a motor.

cable television *n* a television service in which the subscriber's television is connected to the supplier by cable, enabling a much greater choice of channels to be provided.

cabochon (ˈkæbəˌʃɒn) *n* a smooth domed gem, polished but unfaceted. [C16: from OF, from *caboche* head]

caboodle (kəˈbuːdᵊl) *n Inf.* a lot, bunch, or group (esp. in **the whole caboodle**). [C19: prob. contraction of KIT[1] & BOODLE]

caboose (kəˈbuːs) *n* **1** *US inf.* short for **calaboose. 2** *Railways. US & Canad.* a guard's van. **3** *Naut.* **3a** a deckhouse for a galley aboard ship. **3b** *Chiefly Brit.* the galley itself. **4** *Canad.* **4a** a mobile bunkhouse used by lumbermen, etc. **4b** an insulated cabin on runners, equipped with a stove. [C18: from Du. *cabūse,* from ?]

cabotage (ˈkæbəˌtɑːʒ) *n* **1** *Naut.* coastal navigation or shipping. **2** reservation to a country's carriers of its internal traffic, esp. air traffic. [C19: from F, from *caboter* to sail near the coast, apparently from Sp. *cabo* CAPE[2]]

cabriole (ˈkæbrɪˌəʊl) *n* a type of curved furniture leg, popular in the first half of the 18th century. Also called: **cabriole leg.** [C18: from F, from *cabrioler* to caper; from its being based on the leg of a capering animal]

cabriolet (ˌkæbrɪəʊˈleɪ) *n* **1** a small two-wheeled horse-drawn carriage with two seats and a folding hood. **2** a type of motorcar with a folding top. [C18: from F, lit.: a little skip, from L, from *caper* goat; referring to the lightness of movement]

cacao (kəˈkɑːəʊ, -ˈkeɪəʊ) *n* **1** a small tropical American evergreen tree having reddish-brown seed pods from which cocoa and chocolate are prepared. **2 cacao bean.** the seed pod; cocoa bean. **3 cacao butter.** another name for **cocoa butter.** [C16: from Sp., from Nahuatl *cacauatl* cacao beans]

cachalot (ˈkæʃəˌlɒt) *n* another name for **sperm whale.** [C18: from F, from Port. *cachalote,* from ?]

cache Ⓣ (kæʃ) *n* **1** a hidden store of provisions, weapons, treasure, etc. **2** the place where such a store is hidden. **3** *Computing.* a small

THESAURUS

cab *n* **1a, 3 = taxi,** hackney, hackney carriage, minicab, taxicab

cabal *n* **1, 3 = clique,** camp, caucus, coalition, combination, conclave, confederacy, coterie, faction, junta, league, party, schism, set **2 = plot,** conspiracy, intrigue, machination, scheme

cabbalistic *adj* **2 = occult,** cryptic, dark, esoteric, fanciful, mysterious, mystic, mystical, obscure, secret

cabin *n* **1 = hut,** bothy, chalet, cot, cottage, crib, hovel, lodge, shack, shanty, shed **4 = room,** berth, compartment, deckhouse, quarters

cabinet *n* **1 = cupboard,** case, chiffonier, closet, commode, dresser, escritoire, locker **3a** *often cap.* **= council,** administration, assembly, counsellors, ministry

cache *n* **1, 2 = store,** accumulation, fund, garner, hiding place, hoard, nest egg, repository, high-speed memory that improves computer performance. ◆ *vb* **caches, caching, cached. 4** (*tr*) to store in a cache. [C19: from F, from *cacher* to hide]

cachepot ('kæʃ,pɒt, kæʃ'pəʊ) *n* an ornamental container for a flowerpot. [F: pot-hider]

cachet ('kæʃeɪ) *n* **1** an official seal on a document, letter, etc. **2** a distinguishing mark. **3** prestige; distinction. **4** *Philately.* a mark stamped by hand on mail for commemorative purposes. **5** a hollow wafer, formerly used for enclosing an unpleasant-tasting medicine. [C17: from OF, from *cacher* to hide]

cachexia (kə'kɛksɪə) *or* **cachexy** *n* a weakened condition of body or mind resulting from any debilitating disease. [C16: from LL, from Gk, from *kakos* bad + *hexis* condition]

cachinnate ('kækɪ,neɪt) *vb* **cachinnates, cachinnating, cachinnated.** (*intr*) to laugh loudly. [C19: from L *cacchināre*, prob. imit.]
▸**,cachin'nation** *n* ▸**,cachin'natory** *adj*

cachou ('kæʃuː, kæ'ʃuː) *n* **1** a lozenge eaten to sweeten the breath. **2** another name for **catechu.** [C18: via F from Port., from Malay *kāchu*]

cacique (kə'siːk) *or* **cazique** (kə'ziːk) *n* **1** an American Indian chief in a Spanish-speaking region. **2** (esp. in Spanish America) a local political boss. [C16: from Sp., of Amerind origin]

cack-handed (,kæk'hændɪd) *adj Inf.* **1** left-handed. **2** clumsy. [from dialect *cack* excrement]

cackle Ⓣ ('kæk^{ə}l) *vb* **cackles, cackling, cackled. 1** (*intr*) (esp. of a hen) to squawk with shrill broken notes. **2** (*intr*) to laugh or chatter raucously. **3** (*tr*) to utter in a cackling manner. ◆ *n* **4** the noise or act of cackling. **5** noisy chatter. **6 cut the cackle.** *Inf.* to be quiet. [C13: prob. from MLow G *kākelen*, imit.]

caco- *combining form.* bad, unpleasant, or incorrect: *cacophony.* [from Gk *kakos* bad]

cacodyl ('kækə,daɪl) *n* an oily poisonous liquid with a strong garlic smell; tetramethyldiarsine. [C19: from Gk, from *kakos* CACO- + *ozein* to smell + -YL]

cacoethes (,kækəʊ'iːθiːz) *n* an uncontrollable urge or desire: *a cacoethes for smoking.* [C16: from L *cacoēthes* malignant disease, from Gk, from *kakos* CACO- + *ēthos* character]

cacography (kæ'kɒgrəfɪ) *n* **1** bad handwriting. **2** incorrect spelling.
▸**cacographic** (,kækə'græfɪk) *adj*

cacophony Ⓣ (kə'kɒfənɪ) *n, pl* **cacophonies.** harsh discordant sound.
▸**ca'cophonous** *adj*

cactus ('kæktəs) *n, pl* **cactuses** *or* **cacti** (-taɪ). **1** any of a family of spiny succulent plants of the arid regions of America with swollen tough stems and leaves reduced to spines. **2 cactus dahlia.** a double-flowered variety of dahlia. [C17: from L: prickly plant, from Gk *kaktos* cardoon]
▸**cactaceous** (kæk'teɪʃəs) *adj*

cacuminal (kæ'kjuːmɪn^{ə}l) *Phonetics.* ◆ *adj* **1** denoting a consonant articulated with the tip of the tongue turned back towards the hard palate. ◆ *n* **2** a consonant articulated in this manner. [C19: from L *cacūmen* point]

cad Ⓣ (kæd) *n Brit. inf. old-fashioned.* a man who does not behave in a gentlemanly manner towards others. [C18: from CADDIE]
▸**'caddish** *adj*

CAD (kæd) *n acronym for* computer-aided design.

cadaver (kə'deɪvə, -'dɑːv-) *n Med.* a corpse. [C16: from L, from *cadere* to fall]
▸**cadaveric** (kə'dævərɪk) *adj*

cadaverous Ⓣ (kə'dævərəs) *adj* **1** of or like a corpse, esp. in being deathly pale. **2** thin and haggard.
▸**ca'daverousness** *n*

CADCAM ('kæd,kæm) *n acronym for* computer-aided design and manufacture.

caddie *or* **caddy** ('kædɪ) *Golf.* ◆ *n, pl* **caddies. 1** an attendant who carries clubs, etc., for a player. ◆ *vb* **caddies, caddying, caddied. 2** (*intr*) to act as a caddie. [C17 (C18 (Scot.): an errand-boy): from F CADET]

caddis fly *n* a small mothlike insect having two pairs of hairy wings and aquatic larvae (caddis worms). [C17: from ?]

caddis worm *or* **caddis** ('kædɪs) *n* the aquatic larva of a caddis fly, which constructs a protective case around itself made of silk, sand, stones, etc. Also called: **caseworm, strawworm.**

caddy[1] ('kædɪ) *n, pl* **caddies.** *Chiefly Brit.* a small container, esp. for tea. [C18: from Malay *kati*]

caddy[2] ('kædɪ) *n, pl* **caddies,** *vb* **caddies, caddying, caddied.** a variant spelling of **caddie.**

cadence Ⓣ ('keɪd^{ə}ns) *or* **cadency** *n, pl* **cadences** *or* **cadencies. 1** the beat or measure of something rhythmic. **2** a fall in the pitch of the voice, as at the end of a sentence. **3** intonation. **4** rhythm in verse or prose. **5** the close of a musical phrase. [C14: from OF, from OIt. *cadenza*, lit.: a falling, from L *cadere* to fall]

cadenza (kə'dɛnzə) *n* a virtuoso solo passage occurring near the end of a piece of music, formerly improvised by the soloist. [C19: from It.; see CADENCE]

cadet (kə'dɛt) *n* **1** a young person undergoing preliminary training, usually before full entry to the uniformed services, police, etc. **2** (in England and in France before 1789) a gentleman who entered the army to prepare for a commission. **3** a younger son. **4 cadet branch.** the family of a younger son. **5** (in New Zealand, formerly) a person learning sheep farming on a sheep station. [C17: from F, from dialect *capdet* captain, ult. from L *caput* head]
▸**ca'detship** *n*

cadge Ⓣ (kædʒ) *vb* **cadges, cadging, cadged. 1** to get (food, money, etc.) by sponging or begging. ◆ *n* **2** *Brit.* a person who cadges. [C17: from ?]
▸**'cadger** *n*

cadi *or* **kadi** ('kɑːdɪ, 'keɪdɪ) *n, pl* **cadis** *or* **kadis.** a judge in a Muslim community. [C16: from Ar. *qādī* judge]

Cadmean victory ('kædmɪən) *n* another name for **Pyrrhic victory.** [after *Cadmus*, in Gk myth., who sowed dragon's teeth from which sprang soldiers who fought among themselves]

cadmium ('kædmɪəm) *n* a malleable bluish-white metallic element that occurs in association with zinc ores. It is used in electroplating and alloys. Symbol: Cd; atomic no.: 48; atomic wt.: 112.4. [C19: from NL, from L *cadmia* zinc ore, CALAMINE: both calamine and cadmium are found in the ore]

cadmium yellow *n* an orange or yellow insoluble solid (cadmium sulphide) used as a pigment in paints, etc.

cadre ('kɑːdə) *n* **1** the nucleus of trained professional servicemen forming the basis for military expansion. **2** a group of activists, esp. in the Communist Party. **3** a basic unit or structure; nucleus. **4** a member of a cadre. [C19: from F, from It. *quadro*, from L *quadrum* square]

caduceus (kə'djuːsɪəs) *n, pl* **caducei** (-sɪ,aɪ). **1** *Classical myth.* a winged staff entwined with two serpents carried by Hermes (Mercury) as messenger of the gods. **2** an insignia resembling this staff used as an emblem of the medical profession. [C16: from L, from Doric Gk *karukeion*, from *karux* herald]

caducous (kə'djuːkəs) *adj Biol.* (of parts of a plant or animal) shed during the life of the organism. [C17: from L, from *cadere* to fall]

caecilian (siː'sɪlɪən) *n* a tropical limbless cylindrical amphibian resembling the earthworm and inhabiting moist soil. [C19: from L, from *caecus* blind]

caecum *or US* **cecum** ('siːkəm) *n, pl* **caeca** *or US* **ceca** (-kə). *Anat.* any structure that ends in a blind sac or pouch, esp. that at the beginning of the large intestine. [C18: short for L *intestinum caecum* blind intestine, translation of Gk *tuphlon enteron*]
▸**'caecal** *or US* **'cecal** *adj*

Caenozoic (,siːnə'zəʊɪk) *adj* a variant spelling of **Cenozoic.**

Caerphilly (kɛə'fɪlɪ) *n* a creamy white mild-flavoured cheese, orig. made in Caerphilly in SE Wales.

Caesar ('siːzə) **1** any Roman emperor. **2** (*sometimes not cap.*) any emperor, autocrat, or dictator. **3** a title of the Roman emperors from Augustus to Hadrian. [after Gaius Julius *Caesar* (100–44 B.C.), Roman general and statesman]

Caesarean, Caesarian, *or US* **Cesarean, Cesarian** (sɪ'zɛərɪən) *adj* **1** of or relating to any of the Caesars, esp. Julius Caesar. ◆ *n* **2** (*sometimes not cap.*) *Surgery.* **2a** a Caesarean section. **2b** (*as modifier*): *Caesarean operation.*

Caesarean section *n* surgical incision through the abdominal and uterine walls in order to deliver a baby. [C17: from the belief that Julius Caesar was so delivered, the name allegedly being derived from *caedere* to cut]

caesious *or US* **cesious** ('siːzɪəs) *adj Bot.* having a waxy bluish-grey coating. [C19: from L *caesius* bluish grey]

caesium *or US* **cesium** ('siːzɪəm) *n* a ductile silvery-white element of the alkali metal group. It is used in photocells and in an atomic clock (**caesium clock**) that uses the frequency of radiation from changing the spin of electrons. The radioisotope **caesium-137,** with a half-life of 30.2 years, is used in radiotherapy. Symbol: Cs; atomic no.: 55; atomic wt.: 132.905.

caesura (sɪ'zjʊərə) *n, pl* **caesuras** *or* **caesurae** (-riː). **1** (in modern prosody) a pause, esp. for sense, usually near the middle of a verse line. **2** (in classical prosody) a break between words within a metrical foot. [C16: from L, lit.: a cutting, from *caedere* to cut]
▸**cae'sural** *adj*

café Ⓣ ('kæfeɪ, 'kæfɪ) *n* **1** a small or inexpensive restaurant serving light

THESAURUS

reserve, stash (*inf.*), stockpile, storehouse, supply, treasury ◆ *vb* **4** = **store**, bury, conceal, hide, put away, secrete, stash (*inf.*)

cackle *vb* **1, 3** = **squawk**, babble, chatter, cluck, crow, gabble, gibber, jabber, prattle **2** = **laugh**, chuckle, giggle, snicker, snigger, titter

cacophonous *adj* = **discordant**, dissonant, grating, harsh, inharmonious, jarring, raucous, strident

cacophony *n* = **discord**, caterwauling, disharmony, dissonance, stridency

cad *n Old-fashioned, informal* = **scoundrel**, bounder (*old-fashioned Brit. sl.*), churl, cur, dastard (*arch.*), heel (*sl.*), knave, rat (*inf.*), rotter (*sl., chiefly Brit.*), scumbag (*sl.*)

cadaverous *adj* **1, 2** = **deathly**, ashen, blanched, bloodless, corpse-like, deathlike, emaciated, exsanguinous, gaunt, ghastly, haggard, hollow-eyed, like death warmed up (*inf.*), pale, pallid, wan

caddish *adj* = **ungentlemanly**, despicable, ill-bred, low, unmannerly

Antonyms *adj* gentlemanly, honourable, laudable, mannerly, pleasant, praiseworthy

cadence *n* **1** = **rhythm**, beat, lilt, measure (*Prosody*), metre, pulse, swing, tempo, throb **3** = **intonation**, accent, inflection, modulation

cadge *vb* **1** = **scrounge** (*inf.*), beg, freeload (*sl.*), sponge

cadger *n* **1** = **scrounger** (*inf.*), beggar, bloodsucker (*inf.*), freeloader, hanger-on, leech, parasite, sponger

café *n* **1** = **snack bar**, brasserie, cafeteria, coffee or easily prepared meals and refreshments. **2** *S. African.* a corner shop or grocer. [C19: from F: COFFEE]

café au lait *French.* (kafe o lɛ) *n* **1** coffee with milk. **2a** a light brown colour. **2b** (*as adj*): *café au lait brocade.*

café noir *French.* (kafe nwar) *n* black coffee.

cafeteria (ˌkæfɪˈtɪərɪə) *n* a self-service restaurant. [C20: from American Sp.: coffee shop]

caff (kæf) *n* a slang word for **café.**

caffeine *or* **caffein** (ˈkæfiːn) *n* a white crystalline bitter alkaloid responsible for the stimulant action of tea, coffee, and cocoa. [C19: from G *Kaffein,* from *Kaffee* COFFEE]

caftan (ˈkæfˌtæn, -ˌtɑːn) *n* a variant spelling of **kaftan.**

cage ❶ (keɪdʒ) *n* **1a** an enclosure, usually made with bars or wire, for keeping birds, monkeys, etc. **1b** (*in combination*): *cagebird.* **2** a thing or place that confines. **3** something resembling a cage in function or structure: *the rib cage.* **4** the enclosed platform of a lift, esp. as used in a mine. ◆ *vb* **cages, caging, caged. 5** (*tr*) to confine in or as in a cage. [C13: from OF, from L *cavea* enclosure, from *cavus* hollow]

cagey ❶ *or* **cagy** (ˈkeɪdʒɪ) *adj* **cagier, cagiest.** *Inf.* not frank; wary. [C20: from ?]

▸ˈ**caginess** *n*

cagoule (kəˈguːl) *n* a lightweight usually knee-length type of anorak. [C20: from F]

cahoots (kəˈhuːts) *pl n* (*sometimes sing*) *Inf.* **1** *US.* partnership; league. **2 in cahoots.** in collusion. [C19: from ?]

caiman (ˈkeɪmən) *n, pl* **caimans.** a variant spelling of **cayman.**

Cainozoic (ˌkaɪnəʊˈzəʊɪk, ˌkeɪ-) *adj* a variant spelling of **Cenozoic.**

caïque (kaɪˈiːk) *n* **1** a long rowing skiff used on the Bosporus. **2** a sailing vessel of the E Mediterranean with a square topsail. [C17: from F, from It. *caicco,* from Turkish *kayik*]

cairn (kɛən) *n* **1** a mound of stones erected as a memorial or marker. **2** Also called: **cairn terrier.** a small rough-haired breed of terrier orig. from Scotland. [C15: from Gaelic *carn*]

cairngorm (ˌkɛənˈgɔːm) *n* a smoky yellow or brown variety of quartz, used as a gemstone. Also called: **smoky quartz.** [C18: from *Cairn Gorm* (lit.: blue cairn), mountain in Scotland]

caisson (kəˈsuːn, ˈkeɪsᵊn) *n* **1** a watertight chamber open at the bottom and containing air under pressure, used to carry out construction work under water. **2** a watertight float filled with air, used to raise sunken ships. **3** a watertight structure placed across the entrance of a dry dock, etc., to exclude water. **4a** a box containing explosives formerly used as a mine. **4b** an ammunition chest. [C18: from F, assimilated to *caisse* CASE[2]]

caisson disease *n* another name for **decompression sickness.**

caitiff (ˈkeɪtɪf) *Arch. or poetic.* ◆ *n* **1** a cowardly or base person. ◆ *adj* **2** cowardly. [C13: from OF, from L *captīvus* CAPTIVE]

cajole ❶ (kəˈdʒəʊl) *vb* **cajoles, cajoling, cajoled.** to persuade (someone) by flattery to do what one wants; wheedle; coax. [C17: from F *cajoler* to coax, from ?]

▸**caˈjolement** *n* ▸**caˈjoler** *n* ▸**caˈjolery** *n*

cake ❶ (keɪk) *n* **1** a baked food, usually in loaf or layer form, made from a mixture of flour, sugar, and eggs. **2** a flat thin mass of bread, esp. unleavened bread. **3** a shaped mass of dough or other food: *a fish cake.* **4** a mass, slab, or crust of a solidified substance, as of soap. **5 go** *or* **sell like hot cakes.** *Inf.* to be sold very quickly. **6 have one's cake and eat it.** to enjoy both of two desirable but incompatible alternatives. **7 piece of cake.** *Inf.* something that is easily achieved or obtained. **8 take the cake.** *Inf.* to surpass all others, esp. in stupidity, folly, etc. **9** *Inf.* the whole of something that is to be shared or divided: *a larger slice of the cake.* ◆ *vb* **cakes, caking, caked. 10** (*tr*) to encrust: *the hull was caked with salt.* **11** to form or be formed into a hardened mass. [C13: from ON *kaka*]

cakewalk (ˈkeɪkˌwɔːk) *n* **1** a dance based on a march with intricate steps, orig. performed by African-Americans for the prize of a cake. **2** a piece of music for this dance. **3** *Inf.* an easy task.

CAL (kæl) *acronym for* computer-aided (*or* -assisted) learning.

cal. *abbrev. for:* **1** calendar. **2** calibre. **3** calorie (small).

Cal. *abbrev. for* Calorie (large).

calabash (ˈkæləˌbæʃ) *n* **1** Also called: **calabash tree.** a tropical American evergreen tree that produces large round gourds. **2** the gourd. **3** the dried hollow shell of a gourd used as the bowl of a tobacco pipe, a bottle, etc. **4 calabash nutmeg.** a tropical African shrub whose seeds can be used as nutmegs. [C17: from obs. F *calabasse,* from Sp., ?from Ar., from *qar'ah* gourd + *yābisah* dry]

calaboose (ˈkæləˌbuːs) *n US inf.* a prison. [C18: from Creole F, from Sp. *calabozo* dungeon, from ?]

calabrese (ˌkæləˈbreɪzɪ) *n* a variety of green sprouting broccoli. [C20: from It.: Calabrian]

calamander (ˈkæləˌmændə) *n* the hard black-and-brown striped wood of several trees of India and Sri Lanka, used in making furniture. See also **ebony** (sense 2). [C19: metathetic var. of *Coromandel,* coast in SE India]

calamine (ˈkæləˌmaɪn) *n* a pink powder consisting of zinc oxide and iron(III) oxide, used medicinally in the form of soothing lotions or ointments. [C17: from OF, from Med. L *calamīna,* from L *cadmīa;* see CADMIUM]

calamint (ˈkæləmɪnt) *n* an aromatic Eurasian plant having clusters of purple or pink flowers. [C14: from OF *calament,* from Med. L *calamentum,* from Gk *kalaminthē*]

calamitous ❶ (kəˈlæmɪtəs) *adj* causing, involving, or resulting in a calamity; disastrous.

calamity ❶ (kəˈlæmɪtɪ) *n, pl* **calamities. 1** a disaster or misfortune, esp. one causing distress or misery. **2** a state or feeling of deep distress or misery. [C15: from F *calamité,* from L *calamitās*]

calamus (ˈkæləməs) *n, pl* **calami** (-ˌmaɪ). **1** any of a genus of tropical Asian palms, some of which are a source of rattan and canes. **2** another name for **sweet flag. 3** *Ornithol.* a quill. [C14: from L, from Gk *kalamos* reed, stem]

calandria (kəˈlændrɪə) *n* a cylindrical vessel through which vertical tubes pass, esp. one forming part of a heat exchanger or nuclear reactor. [C20: arbitrarily named, from Sp., lit.: lark]

calash (kəˈlæʃ) *or* **calèche** *n* **1** a horse-drawn carriage with low wheels and a folding top. **2** a woman's folding hooped hood worn in the 18th century. [C17: from F, from G, from Czech *kolesa* wheels]

calcaneus (kælˈkeɪnɪəs) *or* **calcaneum** *n, pl* **calcanei** (-nɪˌaɪ). the largest tarsal bone, forming the heel in man. Nontechnical name: **heel bone.** [C19: from LL: heel, from L *calx* heel]

calcareous (kælˈkɛərɪəs) *adj* of, containing, or resembling calcium carbonate; chalky. [C17: from L *calcārius,* from *calx* lime]

calceolaria (ˌkælsɪəˈlɛərɪə) *n* a tropical American plant cultivated for its speckled slipper-shaped flowers. Also called: **slipperwort.** [C18: from L *calceolus* small shoe, from *calceus*]

calces (ˈkælsiːz) *n* a plural of **calx.**

calci- *or before a vowel* **calc-** *combining form.* indicating lime or calcium: *calcify.* [from L *calx, calc-* limestone]

calciferol (kælˈsɪfərɒl) *n* a fat-soluble steroid, found esp. in fish-liver oils and used in the treatment of rickets. Also called: **vitamin D_2.** [C20: from CALCIF(EROUS + ERGOST)EROL]

calciferous (kælˈsɪfərəs) *adj* producing salts of calcium, esp. calcium carbonate.

calcify (ˈkælsɪˌfaɪ) *vb* **calcifies, calcifying, calcified. 1** to convert or be converted into lime. **2** to harden or become hardened by impregnation with calcium salts.

▸ˌ**calcifiˈcation** *n*

calcine (ˈkælsaɪn, -sɪn) *vb* **calcines, calcining, calcined. 1** (*tr*) to heat (a substance) so that it is oxidized, is reduced, or loses water. **2** (*intr*) to oxidize as a result of heating. [C14: from Med. L *calcināre* to heat, from L *calx* lime]

▸**calcination** (ˌkælsɪˈneɪʃən) *n*

calcite (ˈkælsaɪt) *n* a colourless or white mineral consisting of crystalline calcium carbonate: the transparent variety is Iceland spar. Formula: $CaCO_3$.

calcium (ˈkælsɪəm) *n* a malleable silvery-white metallic element of the alkaline earth group, occurring esp. as forms of calcium carbonate. It is an essential constituent of bones and teeth. Symbol: Ca; atomic no.: 20; atomic wt.: 40.08. [C19: from NL, from L *calx* lime]

calcium antagonist *or* **blocker** *n* any drug that prevents the influx of calcium ions into cardiac and smooth muscle: used to treat high blood pressure and angina.

calcium carbide *n* a grey salt of calcium used in the production of acetylene. Formula: CaC_2. Sometimes shortened to **carbide.**

calcium carbonate *n* a white crystalline salt occurring in limestone, chalk, and pearl: used in the production of lime. Formula: $CaCO_3$.

calcium chloride *n* a white deliquescent salt occurring naturally in seawater and used in the de-icing of roads. Formula: $CaCl_2$.

calcium hydroxide *n* a white crystalline slightly soluble alkali with many uses, esp. in cement, water softening, and the neutralization of acid soils. Formula: $Ca(OH)_2$. Also called: **lime, slaked lime, caustic lime.**

calcium oxide *n* a white crystalline base used in the production of calcium hydroxide and in the manufacture of glass and steel. Formula: CaO. Also called: **lime, quicklime, calx.**

calcium phosphate *n* an insoluble nonacid calcium salt that occurs in bones and is the main constituent of bone ash. Formula: $Ca_3(PO_4)_2$

calcspar (ˈkælkˌspɑː) *n* another name for **calcite.** [C19: from Swedish *kalkspat,* from *kalk* lime (ult. from L *calx*) + *spat* SPAR[3]]

THESAURUS

bar, coffee shop, lunchroom, restaurant, tearoom

cage *n* **1a** = **enclosure**, corral (*US*), pen, pound ◆ *vb* **5** = **shut up**, confine, coop up, fence in, immure, impound, imprison, incarcerate, lock up, mew, pound, restrain

cagey *adj Informal* = **wary**, careful, cautious, chary, discreet, guarded, noncommittal, shrewd, wily

Antonyms *adj* careless, dull, imprudent, indiscreet, reckless, unthinking, unwary

cajole *vb* = **persuade**, beguile, coax, decoy, dupe, entice, entrap, flatter, inveigle, lure, manoeuvre, mislead, seduce, sweet-talk (*inf.*), tempt, wheedle

cake *n* **4** = **block**, bar, cube, loaf, lump, mass, slab ◆ *vb* **11** = **encrust**, bake, cement, coagulate, congeal, consolidate, dry, harden, inspissate (*arch.*), ossify, solidify, thicken

calamitous *adj* = **disastrous**, blighting, cataclysmic, catastrophic, deadly, devastating, dire, fatal, pernicious, ruinous, tragic, woeful

Antonyms *adj* advantageous, beneficial, favourable, fortunate, good, helpful

calamity *n* **1, 2** = **disaster**, adversity, affliction, cataclysm, catastrophe, distress, downfall, hardship, misadventure, mischance, misfortune, mishap, reverse, ruin, scourge, tragedy, trial, tribulation, woe, wretchedness

Antonyms *n* advantage, benefit, blessing, boon, good fortune, good luck, help

calculable ➊ ('kælkjʊləbᵊl) *adj* **1** that may be computed or estimated. **2** predictable.
▸ˌ**calcula'bility** *n* ▸'**calculably** *adv*

calculate ➊ ('kælkjʊˌleɪt) *vb* **calculates, calculating, calculated. 1** to solve (one or more problems) by a mathematical procedure. **2** (*tr; may take a clause as object*) to determine beforehand by judgment, etc.; estimate. **3** (*tr; usually passive*) to aim: *the car was calculated to appeal to women.* **4** (*intr; foll. by on or upon*) to rely. **5** (*tr; may take a clause as object*) *US dialect.* to suppose. [C16: from LL *calculāre*, from *calculus* pebble used as a counter]
▸**calculative** ('kælkjʊlətɪv) *adj*

calculated ➊ ('kælkjʊˌleɪtɪd) *adj* (*usually prenominal*) **1** undertaken after considering the likelihood of success or failure. **2** premeditated: *a calculated insult.*

calculating ➊ ('kælkjʊˌleɪtɪŋ) *adj* **1** selfishly scheming. **2** shrewd.
▸'**calcuˌlatingly** *adv*

calculation ➊ (ˌkælkjʊ'leɪʃən) *n* **1** the act, process, or result of calculating. **2** a forecast. **3** careful planning, esp. for selfish motives.

calculator ('kælkjʊˌleɪtə) *n* **1** a device for performing mathematical calculations, esp. an electronic device that can be held in the hand. **2** a person or thing that calculates. **3** a set of tables used as an aid to calculations.

calculous ('kælkjʊləs) *adj Pathol.* of or suffering from a calculus.

calculus ('kælkjʊləs) *n, pl* **calculuses. 1** a branch of mathematics, developed independently by Newton and Leibnitz. Both **differential calculus** and **integral calculus** are concerned with the effect on a function of an infinitesimal change in the independent variable. **2** any mathematical system of calculation involving the use of symbols. **3** (*pl* **calculi** (-ˌlaɪ)). *Pathol.* a stonelike concretion of minerals found in organs of the body. [C17: from L: pebble, from *calx* small stone, counter]

caldera (kæl'dɛərə) *n* a large basin-shaped crater at the top of a volcano, formed by the collapse of the cone. [C19: from Sp. *caldera*, lit.: CAULDRON]

caldron ('kɔːldrən) *n* a variant spelling of **cauldron.**

calèche (*French* kalɛʃ) *n* a variant of **calash.**

Caledonia (ˌkælɪ'dəʊnɪə) *n* the Roman name for **Scotland.**

Caledonian (ˌkælɪ'dəʊnɪən) *adj* **1** relating to Scotland. **2** of a period of mountain building in NW Europe in the Palaeozoic era. ◆ *n* **3** *Literary.* a native or inhabitant of Scotland.

calefacient (ˌkælɪ'feɪʃənt) *adj* **1** causing warmth. ◆ *n* **2** *Med.* an agent that warms, such as a mustard plaster. [C17: from L, from *calefacere* to heat]

calendar ('kælɪndə) *n* **1** a system for determining the beginning, length, and order of years and their divisions. **2** a table showing any such arrangement, esp. as applied to one or more successive years. **3** a list or schedule of pending court cases, appointments, etc. ◆ *vb* **calendars, calendaring, calendared. 4** (*tr*) to enter in a calendar; schedule. [C13: via Norman F from Med. L *kalendārium* account book, from *Kalendae* the CALENDS]
▸**calendrical** (kæ'lɛndrɪkᵊl) *or* **ca'lendric** *adj*

calendar month *n* See **month** (sense 1).

calendar year *n* See **year** (sense 1).

calender ('kælɪndə) *n* **1** a machine in which paper or cloth is smoothed by passing between rollers. ◆ *vb* **2** (*tr*) to subject (material) to such a process. [C17: from F *calandre*, from ?]

calends *or* **kalends** ('kælɪndz) *pl n* the first day of each month in the ancient Roman calendar. [C14: from L *kalendae*]

calendula (kæ'lɛndjʊlə) *n* any of a genus of Eurasian plants, esp. the pot marigold, having orange-and-yellow rayed flowers. [C19: from Med. L, from L *kalendae* CALENDS]

calf[1] (kɑːf) *n, pl* **calves. 1** the young of cattle, esp. domestic cattle. **2** the young of certain other mammals, such as the buffalo and whale. **3** a large piece of ice detached from an iceberg, etc. **4 kill the fatted calf.** to celebrate lavishly, esp. as a welcome. [OE *cealf*]

calf[2] (kɑːf) *n, pl* **calves.** the thick fleshy part of the back of the leg between the ankle and the knee. [C14: from ON *kalfi*]

calf love *n* temporary infatuation of an adolescent for a member of the opposite sex.

calf's-foot jelly *n* a jelly made from the stock of boiled calves' feet and flavourings.

calfskin ('kɑːfˌskɪn) *n* **1** the skin or hide of a calf. **2** Also called: **calf. 2a** fine leather made from this skin. **2b** (*as modifier*): *calfskin boots.*

Calgon ('kælgɒn) *n Trademark.* a chemical compound, sodium hexametaphosphate, with water-softening properties, used in detergents.

calibrate ➊ ('kælɪˌbreɪt) *vb* **calibrates, calibrating, calibrated.** (*tr*) **1** to measure the calibre of (a gun, etc.). **2** to mark (the scale of a measuring instrument) so that readings can be made in appropriate units. **3** to determine the accuracy of (a measuring instrument, etc.).
▸ˌ**cali'bration** *n* ▸'**caliˌbrator** *n*

calibre ➊ *or US* **caliber** ('kælɪbə) *n* **1** the diameter of a cylindrical body, esp. the internal diameter of a tube or the bore of a firearm. **2** the diameter of a shell or bullet. **3** ability; distinction. **4** personal character: *a man of high calibre.* [C16: from OF, from It. *calibro*, from Ar. *qālib* shoemaker's last]
▸'**calibred** *or US* '**calibered** *adj*

calices ('kælɪˌsiːz) *n* the plural of **calix.**

calico ('kælɪˌkəʊ) *n, pl* **calicoes** *or* **calicos. 1** a white or unbleached cotton fabric. **2** *Chiefly US.* a coarse printed cotton fabric. [C16: based on *Calicut*, town in India]

calif ('keɪlɪf, 'kæl-) *n* a variant spelling of **caliph.**

California poppy *n* a plant of the poppy family, native to the Pacific coast of North America, having yellow or orange flowers and finely dissected bluish-green leaves. Also called: **eschscholzia** *or* **eschscholtzia.**

californium (ˌkælɪ'fɔːnɪəm) *n* a transuranic element artificially produced from curium. Symbol: Cf; atomic no.: 98; half-life of most stable isotope, ^{251}Cf: 800 years (approx.). [C20: NL; discovered at the University of *California*]

calipash *or* **callipash** ('kælɪˌpæʃ) *n* the greenish glutinous edible part of the turtle found next to the upper shell. [C17: ? changed from Sp. *carapacho* CARAPACE]

calipee ('kælɪˌpiː) *n* the yellow glutinous edible part of the turtle found next to the lower shell. [C17: ? a var. of CALIPASH]

caliper ('kælɪpə) *n* the usual US spelling of **calliper.**

caliph, calif, *or* **khalif** ('keɪlɪf, 'kæl-) *n Islam.* the title of the successors of Mohammed as rulers of the Islamic world. [C14: from OF, from Ar. *khalīfa* successor]

caliphate, califate *or* **khalifate** ('keɪlɪˌfeɪt) *n* the office, jurisdiction, or reign of a caliph.

calisthenics (ˌkælɪs'θɛnɪks) *n* a variant spelling (esp. US) of **callisthenics.**

calix ('keɪlɪks, 'kæ-) *n, pl* **calices.** a cup; chalice. [C18: from L: CHALICE]

calk[1] (kɔːk) *vb* a variant spelling of **caulk.**

calk[2] (kɔːk) *or* **calkin** ('kɔːkɪn, 'kæl-) *n* **1** a metal projection on a horse's shoe to prevent slipping. ◆ *vb* (*tr*) **2** to provide with calks. [C17: from L *calx* heel]

call ➊ (kɔːl) *vb* **1** (often foll. by *out*) to speak or utter (words, sounds, etc.) loudly so as to attract attention: *he called out her name.* **2** (*tr*) to ask or order to come: *to call a policeman.* **3** (*intr;* sometimes foll. by *on*) to make a visit (to): *she called on him.* **4** (often foll. by *up*) to telephone (a person). **5** (*tr*) to summon to a specific office, profession, etc. **6** (of animals or birds) to utter (a characteristic sound or cry). **7** (*tr*) to summon (a bird or animal), as by imitating its cry. **8** (*tr*) to name or style: *they called the dog Rover.* **9** (*tr*) to designate: *they called him a coward.* **10** (*tr*) to regard in a specific way: *I call it a foolish waste of time.* **11** (*tr*) to attract (attention). **12** (*tr*) to read (a list, etc.) aloud to check for omissions or absentees. **13** (when *tr*, usually foll. by *for*) to give an order (for): *to call a strike.* **14** (*intr*) to try to predict the result of tossing a coin. **15** (*tr*) to awaken: *I was called early this morning.* **16** (*tr*) to cause to assemble. **17** (*tr*) *Sport.* (of an umpire, etc.) to pass judgment upon (a shot, etc.) with a call. **18** (*tr*) *Austral. & NZ.* to broadcast a commentary on (a horse race, etc.). **19** (*tr*) to demand repayment of (a loan, security, etc.). **20** (*tr*) *Brit.* to award (a student at an Inn of Court) the degree of barrister (esp. in **call to the bar**). **21** (*tr*) *Poker.* to demand that (a player) expose his hand, after equalling his bet. **22** (*intr*) *Bridge.* to make a bid. **23** (in square-dancing) to call out (instructions) to the dancers. **24** (*intr;* foll. by *for*) **24a** to require: *this problem calls for study.* **24b** to come or go (for) in order to fetch. **25** (*intr;* foll. by *on* or *upon*) to make an appeal or request (to): *they called upon him to reply.* **26 call into being.** to create. **27 call**

THESAURUS

calculable *adj* **1** = **computable,** appraisable, assessable, determinable, estimable (*rare*), gaugeable *or* gageable, judgeable, measurable, quantifiable, ratable *or* rateable

calculate *vb* **1, 2** = **work out,** adjust, compute, consider, count, determine, enumerate, estimate, figure, gauge, judge, rate, reckon, value, weigh **3** = **plan,** aim, design, intend

calculated *adj* **1, 2** = **deliberate,** considered, intended, intentional, planned, premeditated, purposeful
Antonyms *adj* haphazard, hasty, heedless, hurried, impetuous, impulsive, rash, spontaneous, unintentional, unplanned, unpremeditated

calculating *adj* **1, 2** = **scheming,** canny, cautious, contriving, crafty, cunning, designing, devious, Machiavellian, manipulative, politic, sharp, shrewd, sly
Antonyms *adj* blunt, direct, downright, frank, guileless, honest, open, outspoken, sincere, undesigning

calculation *n* **1, 2** = **working out,** answer, computation, estimate, estimation, figuring, forecast, judgment, reckoning, result **3** = **planning,** caution, circumspection, contrivance, deliberation, discretion, foresight, forethought, precaution

calibrate *vb* **1-3** = **measure,** gauge

calibre *n* **1** = **diameter,** bore, gauge, measure **3, 4** = **worth,** ability, capacity, distinction, endowment, faculty, force, gifts, merit, parts, quality, scope, stature, strength, talent

call *vb* **1, 15** = **cry,** announce, arouse, awaken, cry out, hail, halloo, proclaim, rouse, shout, waken, yell **3** *sometimes foll. by* **on** = **visit,** drop in on, look in on, look up, see **4** = **phone,** give (someone) a bell (*Brit. sl.*), ring up (*inf., chiefly Brit.*), telephone **8, 9** = **name,** christen, denominate, describe as, designate, dub, entitle, label, style, term **10** = **consider,** estimate, judge, regard, think **16** = **summon,** assemble, bid, collect, contact, convene, convoke, gather, invite, muster, rally **24a** *foll. by* **for** = **require,** demand, entail, involve, necessitate, need, occasion, suggest **24b** *foll. by* **for** = **fetch,** collect, pick up, uplift (*Scot.*) **25** *foll. by* **on** *or* **upon** = **request,** appeal to, ask, bid, call upon, entreat, invite, invoke, summon, supplicate ◆ *n* **29** = **cry,** hail, scream, shout, signal, whoop, yell **32-34** = **summons,** announcement, appeal, command, demand, invitation, notice, order, plea, request, supplication, visit **38, 39** = **need,** cause, claim, excuse, grounds, justification, occasion, reason, right, urge
Antonyms *vb* ≠ **cry:** be quiet, be silent, murmur, mutter, speak softly, whisper ≠ **summon:** call off, cancel, dismiss, disperse, excuse, release ◆ *n* ≠ **cry:** murmur, mutter, whisper ≠ **summons:** dismissal, release

someone's bluff. see **bluff**[1]. **28 call to mind.** to remember or cause to be remembered. ◆ *n* **29** a cry or shout. **30** the characteristic cry of a bird or animal. **31** a device, such as a whistle, intended to imitate the cry of a bird or animal. **32** a summons or invitation. **33** a summons or signal sounded on a horn, bugle, etc. **34** a short visit: *the doctor made six calls this morning.* **35** an inner urge to some task or profession; vocation. **36** allure or fascination, esp. of a place: *the call of the forest.* **37** need, demand, or occasion: *there is no call to shout.* **38** demand or claim (esp. in **the call of duty**). **39** *Theatre.* a notice to actors informing them of times of rehearsals. **40** a conversation or a request for a connection by telephone. **41** *Commerce.* **41a** a demand for repayment of a loan. **41b** (*as modifier*): *call money.* **42** *Finance.* a demand for redeemable bonds or shares to be presented for repayment. **43** *Poker.* a demand for a hand or hands to be exposed. **44** *Bridge.* a bid or a player's turn to bid. **45** *Sport.* a decision of an umpire or referee regarding a shot, pitch, etc. **46** *Austral.* a broadcast commentary on a horse race, etc. **47** Also called: **call option.** *Stock Exchange.* an option to buy a stated amount of securities at a specified price during a specified period. **48 on call. 48a** (of a loan, etc.) repayable on demand. **48b** available to be called for work outside normal working hours. **49 within call.** accessible. ◆ See also **call down, call forth,** etc. [OE *ceallian*]

calla ('kælə) *n* **1** Also called: **calla lily, arum lily.** a southern African plant which has a white funnel-shaped spathe enclosing a yellow spadix. **2** a plant that grows in wet places and has a white spathe and red berries. [C19: from NL, prob. from Gk *kalleia* wattles on a cock, prob. from *kallos* beauty]

Callanetics (ˌkælə'nɛtɪks) *n* (*functioning as sing*) *Trademark.* a system of exercise involving frequent repetition of small muscular movements and squeezes, designed to improve muscle tone. [C20: after *Callan* Pinckney (born 1939), its US inventor]

call bird *n Marketing.* a cheap article displayed in a shop to attract custom, in the hope of selling expensive items.

call box *n* a soundproof enclosure for a public telephone. Also called: **telephone kiosk.**

callboy ('kɔːlˌbɔɪ) *n* a person who notifies actors when it is time to go on stage.

call centre *n* an office where staff carry out an organization's telephone transactions.

call down *vb* (*tr, adv*) to request or invoke: *to call down God's anger.*

caller ('kɔːlə) *n* **1** a person or thing that calls, esp. a person who makes a brief visit. **2** *Austral.* a racing commentator.

call forth *vb* (*tr, adv*) to cause (something) to come into action or existence.

call girl *n* a prostitute with whom appointments are made by telephone.

calligraphy (kə'lɪgrəfɪ) *n* handwriting, esp. beautiful handwriting.
▸**cal'ligrapher** *or* **cal'ligraphist** *n* ▸**calligraphic** (ˌkælɪ'græfɪk) *adj*

call in *vb* (*adv*) **1** (*intr; often foll. by on*) to pay a visit, esp. a brief one: *call in if you are in the neighbourhood.* **2** (*tr*) to demand payment of: *to call in a loan.* **3** (*tr*) to take (something) out of circulation, because it is defective. **4** to summon to one's assistance: *to call in a specialist.*

calling ❶ ('kɔːlɪŋ) *n* **1** a strong inner urge to follow an occupation, etc.; vocation. **2** an occupation, profession, or trade.

calling card *n* the usual US and Canad. term for **visiting card.**

calliope (kə'laɪəpɪ) *n US & Canad.* a steam organ. [after CALLIOPE (lit.: beautiful-voiced)]

calliper *or US* **caliper** ('kælɪpə) *n* **1** (*often pl*) Also called: **calliper compasses.** an instrument for measuring internal or external dimensions, consisting of two steel legs hinged together. **2** Also called: **calliper splint.** *Med.* a metal splint for supporting the leg. ◆ *vb* **3** (*tr*) to measure with callipers. [C16: var. of CALIBRE]

calliper rule *n* a measuring instrument having two parallel jaws, one fixed and the other sliding.

callistemon (kə'lɪstəmən) *n* another name for **bottlebrush** (sense 1).

callisthenics *or* **calisthenics** (ˌkælɪs'θɛnɪks) *n* **1** (*functioning as pl*) light exercises designed to promote general fitness. **2** (*functioning as sing*) the practice of callisthenic exercises. [C19: from Gk *kalli-* beautiful + *sthenos* strength]
▸ˌ**callis'thenic** *or* ˌ**calis'thenic** *adj*

call loan *n* a loan that is repayable on demand. Also called: **demand loan.**

call off *vb* (*tr, adv*) **1** to cancel or abandon: *the game was called off.* **2** to order (an animal or person) to desist: *the man called off his dog.* **3** to stop (something).

callose ('kæləʊz, -ləʊs) *n* a carbohydrate, a polymer of glucose, found in plants.

callosity (kə'lɒsɪtɪ) *n, pl* **callosities. 1** hard-heartedness. **2** a callus.

callous ❶ ('kæləs) *adj* **1** insensitive. **2** (of skin) hardened and thickened. ◆ *vb* **3** *Pathol.* to make or become callous. [C16: from L *callōsus;* see CALLUS]
▸'**callously** *adv* ▸'**callousness** *n*

call out *vb* (*adv*) **1** to utter aloud, esp. loudly. **2** (*tr*) to summon: *call out the troops.* **3** (*tr*) to order (workers) to strike. **4** (*tr*) to challenge to a duel.

callow ❶ ('kæləʊ) *adj* lacking experience of life; immature. [OE *calu*]
▸'**callowness** *n*

call sign *n* a group of letters and numbers identifying a radio transmitting station.

call up *vb* (*tr, adv*) **1** to summon to report for active military service, as in time of war. **2** to recall (something); evoke. **3** to bring or summon (people, etc.) into action. **4** to telephone. ◆ *n* **call-up. 5a** a general order to report for military service. **5b** the number of men so summoned.

callus ('kæləs) *n, pl* **calluses. 1** Also called: **callosity.** an area of skin that is hard or thick, esp. on the sole of the foot. **2** an area of bony tissue formed during the healing of a fractured bone. **3** *Bot.* a mass of hard protective tissue produced in woody plants at the site of an injury. [C16: from L, var. of *callum* hardened skin]

calm ❶ (kɑːm) *adj* **1** still: *a calm sea.* **2** *Meteorol.* without wind, or with wind of less than 1 mph. **3** not disturbed, agitated, or excited. **4** tranquil; serene: *a calm voice.* ◆ *n* **5** an absence of disturbance or rough motion. **6** absence of wind. **7** tranquillity. ◆ *vb* **8** (often foll. by *down*) to make or become calm. [C14: from OF *calme,* from OIt., from LL *cauma* heat, hence a rest during the heat of the day, from Gk, from *kaiein* to burn]
▸'**calmly** *adv* ▸'**calmness** *n*

calmative ('kælmətɪv, 'kɑːmə-) *adj* (of a remedy or agent) sedative.

caló (kə'ləʊ; *Spanish* ka'lo) *n* a form of Mexican Spanish incorporating many slang terms and English words: spoken esp. by Mexican Americans in the SW US.

calomel ('kæləˌmɛl, -məl) *n* a colourless tasteless powder consisting chiefly of mercurous chloride, used medicinally, esp. as a cathartic. [C17: ?from NL *calomelas* (unattested), lit.: beautiful black, from Gk *kalos* beautiful + *melas* black]

Calor Gas ('kælə) *n Trademark.* butane gas liquefied under pressure in portable containers for domestic use.

caloric (kə'lɒrɪk) *adj* **1** of or concerned with heat or calories. ◆ *n* **2** *Obs.* a hypothetical elastic fluid, the embodiment of heat.

calorie *or* **calory** ('kælərɪ) *n, pl* **calories.** a unit of heat, equal to 4.1868 joules (**International Table calorie**): formerly defined as the quantity of heat required to raise the temperature of 1 gram of water by 1°C. Abbrev.: **cal.** Also called: **small calorie.** [C19: from F, from L *calor* heat]

Calorie ('kælərɪ) *n* **1** Also called: **kilogram calorie, large calorie.** a unit of heat, equal to one thousand calories. Abbrev.: **Cal. 2** the amount of a specific food capable of producing one thousand calories of energy.

calorific (ˌkælə'rɪfɪk) *adj* of, concerning, or generating heat.
▸ˌ**calo'rifically** *adv*

calorific value *n* the quantity of heat produced by the complete combustion of a given mass of a fuel.

calorimeter (ˌkælə'rɪmɪtə) *n* an apparatus for measuring amounts of heat, esp. to find calorific values, etc.
▸**calorimetric** (ˌkælərɪ'mɛtrɪk) *adj* ▸ˌ**calo'rimetry** *n*

calorize *or* **calorise** ('kæləˌraɪz) *vb* **calorizes, calorizing, calorized** *or* **calorises, calorising, calorised.** (*tr*) to coat (a ferrous metal) by spraying with aluminium powder and then heating.

calque (kælk) *n* another word for **loan translation.** [C20: from F: a tracing, from L *calcāre* to tread]

calumet ('kæljʊˌmɛt) *n* the peace pipe. [C18: from Canad. F, from F: straw, from LL *calamellus* a little reed, from L: CALAMUS]

THESAURUS

calling *n* **1, 2** = **profession**, business, career, employment, life's work, line, métier, mission, occupation, province, pursuit, trade, vocation, walk of life, work

callous *adj* **1** = **heartless**, apathetic, case-hardened, cold, hard-bitten, hard-boiled (*inf.*), hardened, hardhearted, harsh, indifferent, indurated (*rare*), insensate, insensible, insensitive, inured, obdurate, soulless, thick-skinned, torpid, uncaring, unfeeling, unresponsive, unsusceptible, unsympathetic
Antonyms *adj* caring, compassionate, considerate, gentle, sensitive, soft, sympathetic, tender, understanding

callously *adv* **1** = **heartlessly**, apathetically, brutally, coldly, hardheartedly, harshly, indifferently, insensately, insensibly, insensitively, obdurately, soullessly, torpidly, unfeelingly

callousness *n* **1** = **heartlessness**, apathy, coldness, hardheartedness, hardness, harshness, indifference, induration (*rare*), insensateness, insensibility, insensibleness, insensitivity, inuredness *or* enuredness, obduracy, obdurateness, soullessness, torpidity, unfeelingness

callow *adj* = **inexperienced**, green, guileless, immature, jejune, juvenile, naive, puerile, raw, unfledged, unsophisticated, untried

callowness *n* = **inexperience**, greenness, guilelessness, immaturity, innocence, jejuneness, jejunity, juvenileness, naïveté *or* naivety, puerility, rawness, unsophisticatedness, unsophistication

calm *adj* **1** = **still**, balmy, halcyon, mild, pacific, peaceful, placid, quiet, restful, serene, smooth, tranquil, windless **3** = **cool**, as cool as a cucumber, collected, composed, dispassionate, equable, impassive, imperturbable, keeping one's cool, relaxed, sedate, self-possessed, undisturbed, unemotional, unexcitable, unexcited, unfazed (*inf.*), unflappable (*inf.*), unmoved, unruffled ◆ *n* **7** = **peacefulness**, calmness, hush, peace, quiet, repose, serenity, stillness ◆ *vb* **8** = **quieten**, hush, mollify, placate, relax, soothe
Antonyms *adj* ≠ **still**: rough, stormy, wild ≠ **cool**: agitated, aroused, discomposed, disturbed, emotional, excited, fierce, frantic, heated, perturbed, shaken, troubled, worried ◆ *n* ≠ **peacefulness**: agitation, disturbance, wildness ◆ *vb* ≠ **quieten**: aggravate, agitate, arouse, disturb, excite, irritate, stir

calmly *adv* **3, 4** = **coolly**, casually, collectedly, composedly, dispassionately, equably, impassively, imperturbably, nonchalantly, placidly, relaxedly, sedately, self-possessedly, serenely, tranquilly, unflappably, unflinchingly

calmness *n* **1** = **peacefulness**, calm, hush, motionlessness, peace, placidity, quiet, repose, restfulness, serenity, smoothness, stillness, tranquillity **3** = **coolness**, composure, cool (*sl.*), dispassion, equanimity, impassivity, imperturbability, poise, sang-froid, self-possession

calumniate (kəˈlʌmnɪˌeɪt) *vb* **calumniates, calumniating, calumniated.** (*tr*) to slander.
▸**caˌlumniˈation** *n* ▸**caˈlumniˌator** *n*

calumny ⓣ (ˈkæləmnɪ) *n, pl* **calumnies. 1** the malicious utterance of false charges or misrepresentation. **2** such a false charge or misrepresentation. [C15: from L *calumnia* deception, slander]
▸**calumnious** (kəˈlʌmnɪəs) *or* **caˈlumniatory** *adj*

Calvados (ˈkælvəˌdɒs) *n* an apple brandy distilled from cider in Calvados, a region in Normandy, France.

Calvary (ˈkælvərɪ) *n* the place just outside the walls of Jerusalem where Jesus was crucified. Also called: **Golgotha.** [from LL *Calvāria,* translation of Gk *kranion* skull, translation of Aramaic *gulgulta* Golgotha]

calve (kɑːv) *vb* **calves, calving, calved. 1** to give birth to (a calf). **2** (of a glacier or iceberg) to release (masses of ice) in breaking up.

calves (kɑːvz) *n* the plural of **calf**[1] and **calf**[2].

Calvin cycle *n Bot.* a series of reactions, occurring during photosynthesis, in which glucose is synthesized from carbon dioxide. [C20: named after M. *Calvin* (1911–97), US chemist who elucidated it]

Calvinism (ˈkælvɪˌnɪzəm) *n* the theological system of Calvin, 16th-century French theologian, and his followers, characterized by emphasis on predestination and justification by faith.
▸**ˈCalvinist** *n, adj* ▸**ˌCalvinˈistic** *or* **ˌCalvinˈistical** *adj*

calx (kælks) *n, pl* **calxes** *or* **calces. 1** the powdery metallic oxide formed when an ore or mineral is roasted. **2** calcium oxide. **3** *Anat.* the heel. [C15: from L: lime, from Gk *khalix* pebble]

calypso (kəˈlɪpsəʊ) *n, pl* **calypsos.** a popular type of satirical West Indian ballad, esp. from Trinidad, usually extemporized to a syncopated accompaniment. [C20: from *Calypso,* sea nymph in Gk myth]

calyx (ˈkeɪlɪks, ˈkælɪks) *n, pl* **calyxes** *or* **calyces** (ˈkælɪˌsiːz, ˈkeɪlɪ-). **1** the sepals of a flower collectively that protect the developing flower bud. **2** any cup-shaped cavity or structure. [C17: from L, from Gk *kalux* shell, from *kaluptein* to cover]

calzone (kælˈtsəʊnɪ) *n* a dish of Italian origin consisting of pizza dough folded over a filling of cheese and tomatoes, herbs, ham, etc. [C20: It., lit.: trouser leg, from *calzoni* trousers]

cam (kæm) *n* a slider or roller attached to a moving shaft to give a particular type of motion to a part in contact with it. [C16: from Du. *kam* comb]

CAM (kæm) *acronym for* computer-aided manufacture.

camaraderie ⓣ (ˌkæməˈrɑːdərɪ) *n* a spirit of familiarity and trust existing between friends. [C19: from F, from *camarade* COMRADE]

camarilla (ˌkæməˈrɪlə) *n* a group of confidential advisers, esp. formerly, to the Spanish kings. [C19: from Sp., lit.: a little room]

camber (ˈkæmbə) *n* **1** a slight upward curve to the centre of the surface of a road, ship's deck, etc. **2** another name for **bank**[2] (sense 8). **3** an outward inclination of the front wheels of a road vehicle so that they are slightly closer together at the bottom. **4** aerofoil curvature expressed by the ratio of the maximum height of the aerofoil mean line to its chord. ◆ *vb* **5** to form or be formed with a surface that curves upwards to its centre. [C17: from OF *cambre* curved, from L *camurus*]

cambium (ˈkæmbɪəm) *n, pl* **cambiums** *or* **cambia** (-bɪə). *Bot.* a layer of cells that increases the girth of stems and roots. [C17: from Med. L: exchange, from LL *cambiāre* to exchange]
▸**ˈcambial** *adj*

Cambodian (kæmˈbəʊdɪən) *adj* **1** of or relating to Cambodia, in SE Asia, or its people. ◆ *n* **2** a native or inhabitant of Cambodia.

Cambrian (ˈkæmbrɪən) *adj* **1** of or formed in the first 100 million years of the Palaeozoic era. **2** of or relating to Wales. ◆ *n* **3 the.** the Cambrian period or rock system. **4** a Welshman.

cambric (ˈkeɪmbrɪk) *n* a fine white linen fabric. [C16: from Flemish *Kamerijk* Cambrai, town in N France]

Cambs *abbrev. for* Cambridgeshire.

camcorder (ˈkæmˌkɔːdə) *n* a video camera and recorder combined in a portable unit.

came (keɪm) *vb* the past tense of **come.**

camel (ˈkæməl) *n* **1** either of two cud-chewing, humped mammals (see **Arabian camel, Bactrian camel**) that are adapted for surviving long periods without food or water in desert regions. **2** a float attached to a vessel to increase its buoyancy. **3a** a fawn colour. **3b** (*as adj*): *a camel coat.* [OE, from L, from Gk *kamēlos,* of Semitic origin]

cameleer (ˌkæmɪˈlɪə) *n* a camel driver.

camel hair *or* **camel's hair** *n* **1** the hair of the camel, used in rugs, etc. **2a** soft cloth made of or containing this hair or a substitute, usually tan in colour. **2b** (*as modifier*): *a camelhair coat.* **3a** the hair of the squirrel's tail, used for paintbrushes. **3b** (*as modifier*): *a camelhair brush.*

camellia (kəˈmiːlɪə) *n* any of a genus of ornamental shrubs having glossy evergreen leaves and showy white, pink, or red flowers. Also called: **japonica.** [C18: NL, after Georg Josef *Kamel* (1661–1706), Moravian Jesuit missionary]

camelopard (ˈkæmɪləˌpɑːd, kəˈmɛl-) *n* an obsolete word for **giraffe.** [C14: from Med. L, from Gk, from *kamēlos* CAMEL + *pardalis* LEOPARD, because the giraffe was thought to have a head like a camel's and spots like a leopard's]

Camembert (ˈkæməmˌbɛə) *n* a soft creamy cheese. [F, from *Camembert,* a village in Normandy]

cameo (ˈkæmɪˌəʊ) *n, pl* **cameos. 1** a medallion, as on a brooch or ring, with a profile head carved in relief. **2** an engraving upon a gem or other stone so that the background is of a different colour from the raised design. **3** a stone with such an engraving. **4a** a brief dramatic scene played by a well-known actor or actress in a film or television play. **4b** (*as modifier*): *a cameo performance.* **5** a short literary work. [C15: from It. *cammeo,* from ?]

camera (ˈkæmərə) *n* **1** an optical device consisting of a lens system set in a light-proof construction inside which a light-sensitive film or plate can be positioned. **2** *Television.* the equipment used to convert the optical image of a scene into the corresponding electrical signals. **3** (*pl* **camerae** (-əˌriː)). a judge's private room. **4 in camera. 4a** *Law.* relating to a hearing from which members of the public are excluded. **4b** in private. [C18: from L: vault, from Gk *kamara*]

cameraman (ˈkæmərəˌmæn) *n, pl* **cameramen.** a person who operates a film or television camera.

camera obscura (ɒbˈskjʊərə) *n* a darkened chamber with an aperture, in which images of outside objects are projected onto a flat surface. [NL: dark chamber]

camiknickers (ˈkæmɪˌnɪkəz) *pl n* women's knickers attached to a camisole top.

camisole (ˈkæmɪˌsəʊl) *n* **1** a woman's underbodice with shoulder straps, originally designed as a cover for a corset. **2** a woman's short negligee. [C19: from F, from Provençal *camisola,* from *camisa* shirt, from LL *camīsia*]

camomile *or* **chamomile** (ˈkæməˌmaɪl) *n* **1** any of a genus of aromatic plants whose finely dissected leaves and daisy-like flowers are used medicinally. **2** any plant of a related genus as **German** or **wild camomile. 3 camomile tea.** a herbal beverage made from the fragrant leaves and flowers of any of these plants. [C14: from OF, from Med. L, from Gk *khamaimēlon* lit., earth-apple (referring to the scent of the flowers)]

camouflage ⓣ (ˈkæməˌflɑːʒ) *n* **1** the exploitation of natural surroundings or artificial aids to conceal or disguise the presence of military units, etc. **2** (*modifier*) (of fabric or clothing) having a design of irregular patches, in dull colours (such as browns and greens), as used in military camouflage. **3** the means by which animals escape the notice of predators. **4** a device or expedient designed to conceal or deceive. ◆ *vb* **camouflages, camouflaging, camouflaged. 5** (*tr*) to conceal by camouflage. [C20: from F, from *camoufler,* from It. *camuffare* to disguise, from ?]

camp[1] ⓣ (kæmp) *n* **1** a place where tents, cabins, etc., are erected for the use of military troops, etc. **2** tents, cabins, etc., used as temporary lodgings by holiday-makers, Scouts, Gypsies, etc. **3** the group of people living in such lodgings. **4** a group supporting a given doctrine: *the socialist camp.* **5** (*modifier*) suitable for use in temporary quarters, on holiday, etc.: *a camp bed.* **6** *S. African.* a field or pasture. **7** *Austral.* a place where sheep or cattle gather to rest. ◆ *vb* (*intr*) **8** (often foll. by *down*) to establish or set up a camp. **9** (often foll. by *out*) to live temporarily in or as if in a tent. [C16: from OF, ult. from L *campus* field]
▸**ˈcamping** *n*

camp[2] ⓣ (kæmp) *Inf.* ◆ *adj* **1** effeminate; affected. **2** homosexual. **3** consciously artificial, vulgar, or mannered. ◆ *vb* **4** (*tr*) to perform or invest with a camp quality. **5 camp it up. 5a** to overact. **5b** to flaunt one's homosexuality. [C20: from ?]
▸**ˈcampy** *adj*

campaign ⓣ (kæmˈpeɪn) *n* **1** a series of coordinated activities, such as public speaking, designed to achieve a social, political, or commercial goal: *a presidential campaign.* **2** *Mil.* a number of operations aimed at achieving a single objective. ◆ *vb* **3** (*intr;* often foll. by *for*) to conduct, serve in, or go on a campaign. [C17: from F *campagne* open country, from It., from LL, from L *campus* field]
▸**camˈpaigner** *n*

campanile (ˌkæmpəˈniːlɪ) *n* (esp. in Italy) a bell tower, not usually attached to another building. [C17: from It., from *campana* bell]

campanology (ˌkæmpəˈnɒlədʒɪ) *n* the art or skill of ringing bells. [C19: from NL, from LL *campāna* bell]
▸**campanological** (ˌkæmpənəˈlɒdʒɪkəl) *adj* ▸**ˌcampaˈnologist** *or* **ˌcampaˈnologer** *n*

campanula (kæmˈpænjʊlə) *n* any of a genus of N temperate plants having blue or white bell-shaped flowers. Also called: **bellflower.** [C17: from NL: a little bell, from LL *campāna* bell]

camp drafting *n Austral.* a competitive test of horsemen's skill in drafting cattle.

THESAURUS

calumny *n* **1** = **slander,** abuse, aspersion, backbiting, calumniation, defamation, denigration, derogation, detraction, evil-speaking, insult, libel, lying, misrepresentation, obloquy, revilement, smear, stigma, vilification, vituperation

camaraderie *n* = **comradeship,** brotherhood, brotherliness, companionability, companionship, esprit de corps, fellowship, fraternization, good-fellowship, togetherness

camouflage *n* **1, 4** = **disguise,** blind, cloak, concealment, cover, deceptive markings, false appearance, front, guise, mask, masquerade, mimicry, protective colouring, screen, subterfuge ◆ *vb* **5** = **disguise,** cloak, conceal, cover, hide, mask, obfuscate, obscure, screen, veil
Antonyms *vb* ≠ **disguise:** bare, display, exhibit, expose, reveal, show, uncover, unmask, unveil

camp[1] *n* **1** = **camp site,** bivouac, camping ground, cantonment (*Military*), encampment, tents

camp[2] *adj* **1, 3** *Informal* = **effeminate,** affected, artificial, camped up, campy (*inf.*), mannered, ostentatious, poncy (*sl.*), posturing

campaign *n* **1, 2** = **operation,** attack, crusade, drive, expedition, jihad (*rare*), movement, offensive, push

campaigner *n* **1** = **demonstrator,** activist, crusader

camper ('kæmpə) *n* **1** a person who lives or temporarily stays in a tent, cabin, etc. **2** *US & Canad.* a vehicle equipped for camping out.
camp follower *n* **1** any civilian, esp. a prostitute, who unofficially provides services to military personnel. **2** a nonmember who is sympathetic to a particular group, theory, etc.
camphor ('kæmfə) *n* a whitish crystalline aromatic ketone obtained from the wood of an Asian or Australian laurel (**camphor tree**): used in medicine as a liniment. [C15: from OF *camphre,* from Med. L *camphora,* from Ar. *kāfūr,* from Malay *kāpūr* chalk]
▸**camphoric** (kæm'fɒrɪk) *adj*
camphorate ('kæmfə,reɪt) *vb* **camphorates, camphorating, camphorated.** (*tr*) to apply, treat with, or impregnate with camphor.
camphor ball *n* another name for **mothball** (sense 1).
camphor ice *n* an ointment consisting of camphor, white wax, spermaceti, and castor oil, used to treat skin ailments, esp. chapped skin.
camphor wood *n Austral.* a popular name for any of several trees with pungent smelling wood.
campion ('kæmpɪən) *n* any of various plants related to the pink, having red, pink, or white flowers. [C16: prob. from *campion,* obs. var. of CHAMPION]
camp oven *n Austral. & NZ.* a heavy metal pot or box with a lid, used for baking over an open fire.
camp pie *n Austral.* tinned meat.
camp site *n* an area on which holiday-makers may pitch a tent, etc. Also called: **camping site.**
campus ('kæmpəs) *n, pl* **campuses. 1** the grounds and buildings of a university. **2** *Chiefly US.* the outside area of a college, etc. [C18: from L: field]
campylobacter ('kæmpɪləʊ,bæktə) *n* a rod-shaped bacterium that causes infections in animals and man; a common cause of gastroenteritis. [from Gk *kampulos* bent + BACTER(IUM)]
camshaft ('kæm,ʃɑːft) *n* a shaft having one or more cams attached to it.
can[1] (kæn; *unstressed* kən) *vb, past* **could.** (takes an infinitive without *to* or an implied infinitive) used as an auxiliary: **1** to indicate ability, skill, or fitness to perform a task: *I can run.* **2** to indicate permission or the right to something: *can I have a drink?* **3** to indicate knowledge of how to do something: *he can speak three languages.* **4** to indicate the possibility, opportunity, or likelihood: *my trainer says I can win the race.* [OE *cunnan*]

> **USAGE NOTE** See at **may**[1].

can[2] (kæn) *n* **1** a container, esp. for liquids, usually of thin metal: *a petrol can.* **2** a tin (metal container): *a beer can.* **3** Also: **canful.** the contents of a can or the amount a can will hold. **4** a slang word for **prison. 5** *US & Canad.* a slang word for **toilet. 6** a shallow cylindrical metal container used for storing and handling film. **7 can of worms.** *Inf.* a complicated problem. **8 in the can. 8a** (of a film, piece of music, etc.) having been recorded, edited, etc. **8b** *Inf.* agreed: *the contract is in the can.* ◆ *vb* **cans, canning, canned. 9** to put (food, etc.) into a can or cans. [OE *canne*]
▸**'canner** *n*
Can. *abbrev. for:* **1** Canada. **2** Canadian.
Canaan ('keɪnən) *n* an ancient region between the River Jordan and the Mediterranean: the Promised Land of the Israelites.
Canaanite ('keɪnə,naɪt) *n* a member of an ancient Semitic people who occupied the land of Canaan before the Israelite conquest.
Canada balsam *n* **1** a yellow transparent resin obtained from the balsam fir. Because its refractive index is similar to that of glass, it is used as a mounting medium for microscope specimens. **2** another name for **balsam fir.**
Canada Day *n* (in Canada) July 1, the anniversary of the day in 1867 when Canada received dominion status: a public holiday.
Canada goose *n* a large common greyish-brown North American goose with a black neck and head and a white throat patch.
Canada jay *n* a grey crestless jay, notorious in northern parts of N America for its stealing. Also called: **camp robber, whisky-jack.**
Canadian (kə'neɪdɪən) *adj* **1** of or relating to Canada or its people. ◆ *n* **2** a native, citizen, or inhabitant of Canada.
Canadiana (kə,neɪdɪ'ɑːnə; *Canad.* -'ænə) *n* objects, such as books, furniture, and antiques, relating to Canadian history and culture.
Canadian football *n* a game like American football played on a grass pitch between teams of 12 players.
Canadianism (kə'neɪdɪə,nɪzəm) *n* **1** the Canadian national character or spirit. **2** a linguistic usage, custom, or other feature peculiar to Canada, its people, or their culture.
Canadianize *or* **Canadianise** (kə'neɪdɪə,naɪz) *vb* **Canadianizes, Canadianizing, Canadianized** *or* **Canadianises, Canadianising, Canadianised.** to make or become Canadian by changing customs, ownership, character, content, etc.
Canadian Shield *n* the wide area of Precambrian rock extending over most of E and central Canada: rich in minerals. Also called: **Laurentian Shield.**
Canadien (*French* kanadjẽ; *English* kə,nædɪ'ɛn) *or* (*fem*) **Canadienne** (*French* kanadjɛn; *English* kə,nædɪ'ɛn) *n* a French Canadian.
canaille *French.* (kanɑj) *n* the masses; mob; rabble. [C17: from F, from It. *canaglia* pack of dogs]
canakin ('kænɪkɪn) *n* a variant spelling of **cannikin.**
canal ⓣ (kə'næl) *n* **1** an artificial waterway constructed for navigation, irrigation, etc. **2** any of various passages or ducts: *the alimentary canal.* **3** any of various intercellular spaces in plants. **4** *Astron.* any of the indistinct surface features of Mars orig. thought to be a network of channels. ◆ *vb* **canals, canalling, canalled** *or US* **canals, canaling, canaled.** (*tr*) **5** to dig a canal through. **6** to provide with a canal or canals. [C15 (in the sense: pipe, tube): from L *canālis* channel, from *canna* reed]
canal boat *n* a long narrow boat used on canals, esp. for carrying freight.
canaliculus (,kænə'lɪkjʊləs) *n, pl* **canaliculi** (-,laɪ). a small channel or groove, as in some bones. [C16: from L: a little channel, from *canālis* CANAL]
▸**,cana'licular** *or* **,cana'liculate** *adj*
canalize *or* **canalise** ('kænə,laɪz) *vb* **canalizes, canalizing, canalized** *or* **canalises, canalising, canalised.** (*tr*) **1** to provide with or convert into a canal or canals. **2** to give a particular direction to or provide an outlet for.
▸**,canali'zation** *or* **,canali'sation** *n*
canal ray *n Physics.* a stream of positive ions produced in a discharge tube by allowing them to pass through holes in the cathode.
canapé ('kænəpɪ, -,peɪ) *n* a small piece of bread, toast, etc., spread with a savoury topping. [C19: from F: sofa]
canard (kæ'nɑːd) *n* **1** a false report; rumour or hoax. **2** an aircraft in which the tailplane is mounted in front of the wing. [C19: from F: a duck, from OF *caner* to quack, imit.]
canary (kə'neərɪ) *n, pl* **canaries. 1** a small finch of the Canary Islands and Azores: a popular cagebird noted for its singing. **2 canary yellow. 2a** a light yellow. **2b** (*as adj*): *a canary-yellow car.* **3** a sweet wine similar to Madeira. **4** *Arch.* a sweet wine from the Canary Islands. [C16: from OSp. *canario* of or from the Canary Islands]
canasta (kə'næstə) *n* **1** a card game for two to six players who seek to amass points by declaring sets of cards. **2** Also called: **meld.** a declared set in this game, containing seven or more like cards. [C20: from Sp.: basket (because two packs of cards are required), from L *canistrum;* see CANISTER]
canaster ('kænəstə) *n* coarsely broken dried tobacco leaves. [C19: (meaning: basket in which tobacco was packed): from Sp.; see CANISTER]
cancan ('kæn,kæn) *n* a high-kicking dance performed by a female chorus, originating in the music halls of 19th-century Paris. [C19: from F, from ?]
cancel ⓣ ('kænsᵊl) *vb* **cancels, cancelling, cancelled** *or US* **cancels, canceling, canceled.** (*mainly tr*) **1** to order (something already arranged, such as a meeting or event) to be postponed indefinitely; call off. **2** to revoke or annul: *the order was cancelled.* **3** to delete (writing, numbers, etc.); cross out. **4** to mark (a cheque, stamp, etc.) with an official stamp to prevent further use. **5** (*also intr; usually foll. by out*) to counterbalance: *his generosity cancelled out his past unkindness.* **6** *Maths.* to eliminate (numbers or terms) as common factors from both the numerator and denominator of a fraction or as equal terms from opposite sides of an equation. ◆ *n* **7** a new leaf or section of a book replacing one containing errors, or one that has been omitted. **8** a cancellation. **9** *Music.* a US word for **natural** (sense 16). [C14: from OF *canceller,* from Med. L, from LL: to make like a lattice, from L *cancellī* lattice]
▸**'canceller** *or US* **'canceler** *n*
cancellate ('kænsɪ,leɪt) *or* **cancellated** *adj* **1** *Anat.* having a spongy internal structure: *cancellate bones.* **2** *Bot.* forming a network. [C17: from L *cancellāre* to make like a lattice]
cancellation ⓣ (,kænsɪ'leɪʃən) *n* **1** the fact or an instance of cancelling. **2** something that has been cancelled, such as a theatre ticket: *we have a cancellation in the stalls.* **3** the marks made by cancelling.
cancer ⓣ ('kænsə) *n* **1** any type of malignant growth or tumour, caused by abnormal and uncontrolled cell division. **2** the condition resulting from this. **3** an evil influence that spreads dangerously. [C14: from L: crab, a creeping tumour]
▸**'cancerous** *adj*
Cancer ('kænsə) *n, Latin genitive* **Cancri** ('kæŋkriː). **1** *Astron.* Also called: the **Crab.** a small N constellation. **2** *Astrol.* the fourth sign of the zodiac. The sun is in this sign between about June 21 and July 22. **3 tropic of Cancer.** See **tropic** (sense 1).
cancerophobia (,kænsərəʊ'fəʊbɪə) *n* a morbid dread of being afflicted by cancer.
cancroid ('kæŋkrɔɪd) *adj* **1** resembling a cancerous growth. **2** resembling a crab. ◆ *n* **3** a skin cancer.

THESAURUS

canal *n* **1, 2** = **waterway,** channel, conduit, duct, passage, watercourse
cancel *vb* **1-3** = **call off,** abolish, abort, abrogate, annul, blot out, countermand, cross out, delete, do away with, efface, eliminate, erase, expunge, obliterate, obviate, quash, repeal, repudiate, rescind, revoke **5** *usually foll. by* **out** = **make up for,** balance out, compensate for, counterbalance, neutralize, nullify, obviate, offset, redeem
cancellation *n* **1** = **abandonment,** abandoning, abolition, annulment, deletion, elimination, quashing, repeal, revocation
cancer *n* **1-3** = **growth,** blight, canker, carcinoma (*Pathology*), corruption, evil, malignancy, pestilence, rot, sickness, tumour

candela (kænˈdiːlə, -ˈdeɪlə) *n* the basic SI unit of luminous intensity; the intensity, in a perpendicular direction, of a surface of 1/600 000 square metre of a black body at the temperature of freezing platinum under a pressure of 101 325 newtons per square metre. Symbol: cd [C20: from L: CANDLE]

candelabrum (ˌkændɪˈlɑːbrəm) *or* **candelabra** *n, pl* **candelabra** (-brə), **candelabrums,** *or* **candelabras.** a large branched candleholder or holder for overhead lights. [C19: from L, from *candēla* CANDLE]

candescent (kænˈdesᵊnt) *adj Rare.* glowing or starting to glow with heat. [C19: from L, from *candēre* to be white, shine]
▸**canˈdescence** *n*

c & f *abbrev. for* cost and freight.

C & G *abbrev. for* City and Guilds.

candid Ⓣ (ˈkændɪd) *adj* **1** frank and outspoken. **2** without partiality; unbiased. **3** unposed or informal: *a candid photograph.* [C17: from L, from *candēre* to be white]
▸**ˈcandidly** *adv* ▸**ˈcandidness** *n*

candida (ˈkændɪdə) *n* any of a genus of yeastlike parasitic fungi, esp. one that causes thrush (**candidiasis**).

candidate Ⓣ (ˈkændɪˌdeɪt) *n* **1** a person seeking or nominated for election to a position of authority or selection for a job, etc. **2** a person taking an examination or test. **3** a person or thing regarded as suitable or likely for a particular fate or position. [C17: from L *candidātus* clothed in white (because the candidate wore a white toga), from *candidus* white]
▸**candidacy** (ˈkændɪdəsɪ) *or* **candidature** (ˈkændɪdətʃə) *n*

candid camera *n* a small camera that may be used to take informal photographs of people.

candied (ˈkændɪd) *adj* impregnated or encrusted with or as if with sugar: *candied peel.*

candle (ˈkændᵊl) *n* **1** a cylindrical piece of wax, tallow, or other fatty substance surrounding a wick, which is burned to produce light. **2** *Physics.* another name for **candela. 3 burn the candle at both ends.** to exhaust oneself by doing too much, esp. by being up late and getting up early to work. **4 not hold a candle to.** *Inf.* to be inferior or contemptible in comparison with. **5 not worth the candle.** *Inf.* not worth the price or trouble entailed. ◆ *vb* **candles, candling, candled. 6** (*tr*) to examine (eggs) for freshness or the likelihood of being hatched by viewing them against a bright light. [OE *candel,* from L *candēla,* from *candēre* to glitter]
▸**ˈcandler** *n*

candleberry (ˈkændᵊlbərɪ) *n, pl* **candleberries.** another name for **wax myrtle.**

candlelight (ˈkændᵊlˌlaɪt) *n* **1a** the light from a candle or candles. **1b** (*as modifier*): *a candlelight dinner.* **2** dusk; evening.

Candlemas (ˈkændᵊlməs) *n Christianity.* Feb. 2, the Feast of the Purification of the Virgin Mary and the presentation of Christ in the Temple.

candlenut (ˈkændᵊlˌnʌt) *n* **1** a tree of tropical Asia and Polynesia. **2** the nut of this tree, which yields an oil used in paints. In their native regions the nuts are burned as candles.

candlepower (ˈkændᵊlˌpaʊə) *n* the luminous intensity of a source of light in a given direction: now expressed in candelas.

candlestick (ˈkændᵊlˌstɪk) *or* **candleholder** (ˈkændᵊlˌhəʊldə) *n* a holder, usually ornamental, with a spike or socket for a candle.

candlewick (ˈkændᵊlˌwɪk) *n* **1** unbleached cotton or muslin into which loops of yarn are hooked and then cut to give a tufted pattern. **2** (*modifier*) being or made of candlewick fabric.

C & M *abbrev. for* care and maintenance.

can-do *adj* confident and resourceful in the face of challenges: *a can-do attitude.*

candour Ⓣ *or US* **candor** (ˈkændə) *n* **1** the quality of being open and honest; frankness. **2** fairness; impartiality. [C17: from L *candor,* from *candēre* to be white]

C & W *abbrev. for* country and western.

candy (ˈkændɪ) *n, pl* **candies. 1** *Chiefly US. & Canad.* sweets, chocolate, etc. ◆ *vb* **candies, candying, candied. 2** to cause (sugar, etc.) to become crystalline or (of sugar) to become crystalline. **3** (*tr*) to preserve (fruit peel, ginger, etc.) by boiling in sugar. **4** (*tr*) to cover with any crystalline substance, such as ice or sugar. [C18: from OF *sucre candi* candied sugar, from Ar. *qandi* candied, from *qand* cane sugar]

candyfloss (ˈkændɪˌflɒs) *n Brit.* a very light fluffy confection made from coloured spun sugar, usually held on a stick. US and Canad. name: **cotton candy.** Austral. name: **fairyfloss.**

candy-striped *adj* (esp. of clothing fabric) having narrow coloured stripes on a white background.
▸**candy stripe** *n*

candytuft (ˈkændɪˌtʌft) *n* either of two species of *Iberis* having clusters of white, red, or purplish flowers. [C17: *Candy,* obs. var. of *Candia* (former name of city in Crete) + TUFT]

cane (keɪn) *n* **1a** the long jointed pithy or hollow flexible stem of the bamboo, rattan, or any similar plant. **1b** any plant having such a stem. **2a** strips of such stems, woven or interlaced to make wickerwork, etc. **2b** (*as modifier*): *a cane chair.* **3** the woody stem of a reed, blackberry, or loganberry. **4** a flexible rod with which to administer a beating. **5** a slender rod used as a walking stick. **6** See **sugar cane.** ◆ *vb* **canes, caning, caned.** (*tr*) **7** to whip or beat with or as if with a cane. **8** to make or repair with cane. **9** *Inf.* to defeat: *we got well caned in the match.* [C14: from OF, from L *canna,* from Gk *kanna,* of Semitic origin]
▸**ˈcaner** *n*

canebrake (ˈkeɪnˌbreɪk) *n US.* a thicket of canes.

cane sugar *n* **1** the sucrose obtained from sugar cane. **2** another name for **sucrose.**

cangue *or* **cang** (kæŋ) *n* (formerly in China) a large wooden collar worn by petty criminals as a punishment. [C18: from F, from Port. *canga* yoke]

canikin (ˈkænɪkɪn) *n* a variant spelling of **cannikin.**

canine (ˈkeɪnaɪn, ˈkæn-) *adj* **1** of or resembling a dog. **2** of or belonging to the Canidae, a family of mammals, including dogs, wolves, and foxes, typically having a bushy tail, erect ears, and a long muzzle. **3** of or relating to any of the four teeth, two in each jaw, situated between the incisors and the premolars. ◆ *n* **4** any animal of the family Canidae. **5** a canine tooth. [C17: from L *canīnus,* from *canis* dog]

caning (ˈkeɪnɪŋ) *n Inf.* a severe defeat or punishment.

Canis Major (ˈkeɪnɪs) *n, Latin genitive* **Canis Majoris** (məˈdʒɔːrɪs). a S constellation containing Sirius, the brightest star in the sky. Also called: the **Great Dog.** [L: the greater dog]

Canis Minor *n, Latin genitive* **Canis Minoris** (maɪˈnɔːrɪs). a small N constellation. Also called: the **Little Dog.** [L: the lesser dog]

canister (ˈkænɪstə) *n* **1** a container, usually made of metal, in which dry food, such as tea or coffee, is stored. **2** (formerly) **2a** a type of shrapnel shell for firing from a cannon. **2b** Also called: **canister shot.** the shot or shrapnel packed inside this. [C17: from L *canistrum* basket woven from reeds, from Gk, from *kanna* reed]

canker Ⓣ (ˈkæŋkə) *n* **1** an ulceration, esp. of the lips. **2** *Vet. science.* **2a** a disease of horses in which the horn of the hoofs becomes spongy. **2b** an ulcerative disease of the lining of the external ear, esp. in dogs and cats. **2c** ulceration or abscess of the mouth, eyelids, ears, or cloaca of birds. **3** an open wound in the stem of a tree or shrub. **4** something evil that spreads and corrupts. ◆ *vb* **5** to infect or become infected with or as if with canker. [OE *cancer,* from L *cancer* cancerous sore]
▸**ˈcankerous** *adj*

cankerworm (ˈkæŋkəˌwɜːm) *n* the larva of either of two moths, which feed on and destroy fruit and shade trees in North America.

canna (ˈkænə) *n* any of a genus of tropical plants having broad leaves and red or yellow showy flowers. [C17: from NL CANE]

cannabis (ˈkænəbɪs) *n* **1** another name for **hemp** (the plant), esp. Indian hemp. **2** the drug obtained from the dried leaves and flowers of the hemp plant, which is smoked or chewed for its psychoactive properties. See also **hashish, marijuana. 3 cannabis resin.** a poisonous resin obtained from the hemp plant. [C18: from L, from Gk *kannabis*]

canned (kænd) *adj* **1** preserved and stored in airtight cans or tins. **2** *Inf.* prepared or recorded in advance: *canned music.* **3** *Sl.* drunk.

cannel coal *or* **cannel** (ˈkænᵊl) *n* a dull coal burning with a smoky luminous flame. [C16: from N English dialect *cannel* candle]

cannelloni *or* **canneloni** (ˌkænɪˈləʊnɪ) *pl n* tubular pieces of pasta filled with meat or cheese. [It., pl of *cannellone,* from *cannello* stalk]

cannery (ˈkænərɪ) *n, pl* **canneries.** a place where foods are canned.

cannibal (ˈkænɪbᵊl) *n* **1** a person who eats the flesh of other human beings. **2** an animal that feeds on the flesh of others of its kind. [C16: from Sp. *Canibales,* the name used by Columbus to designate the Caribs of Cuba and Haiti]
▸**ˈcannibaˌlism** *n*

cannibalize *or* **cannibalise** (ˈkænɪbəˌlaɪz) *vb* **cannibalizes, cannibalizing, cannibalized** *or* **cannibalises, cannibalising, cannibalised.** (*tr*) to use (serviceable parts from one machine or vehicle) to repair another.
▸**ˌcannibaliˈzation** *or* **ˌcannibaliˈsation** *n*

cannikin, canakin, *or* **canikin** (ˈkænɪkɪn) *n* a small can, esp. one used as a drinking vessel. [C16: from MDu. *kanneken;* see CAN[2], -KIN]

canning (ˈkænɪŋ) *n* the process or business of sealing food in cans or tins to preserve it.

cannon Ⓣ (ˈkænən) *n, pl* **cannons** *or* **cannon. 1** an automatic aircraft gun. **2** *History.* a heavy artillery piece consisting of a metal tube mounted on a carriage. **3** a heavy tube or drum, esp. one that can rotate freely. **4** See **cannon bone. 5** *Billiards.* a shot in which the cue ball is caused to contact one object ball after another. Usual US and Canad. word:

THESAURUS

candid *adj* **1, 2 = honest,** blunt, downright, fair, forthright, frank, free, guileless, impartial, ingenuous, just, open, outspoken, plain, round, sincere, straightforward, truthful, unbiased, unequivocal, unprejudiced, upfront (*inf.*) **3 = informal,** impromptu, uncontrived, unposed
Antonyms *adj* ≠ **honest:** biased, complimentary, diplomatic, flattering, kind, subtle

candidate *n* **1-3 = contender,** applicant, aspirant, claimant, competitor, contestant, entrant, nominee, possibility, runner, suitor

candour *n* **1, 2 = honesty,** artlessness, directness, fairness, forthrightness, frankness, guilelessness, impartiality, ingenuousness, naïveté, openness, outspokenness, simplicity, sincerity, straightforwardness, truthfulness, unequivocalness
Antonyms *n* bias, cunning, deceit, diplomacy, dishonesty, flattery, insincerity, prejudice, subtlety

canker *n* **1, 3, 4 = disease,** bane, blight, blister, cancer, corrosion, corruption, infection, lesion, rot, scourge, sore, ulcer ◆ *vb* **5 = rot,** blight, consume, corrode, corrupt, embitter, envenom, inflict, poison, pollute, rust, waste away

canniness *n* **1 = shrewdness,** acuteness, artfulness, astuteness, carefulness, cautiousness, circumspection, judiciousness, knowingness, perspicaciousness, perspicacity, prudence, sagacity, sageness, sharpness, subtlety, wariness, wisdom, worldliness

cannon *n* **1, 2 = gun,** artillery piece, big gun, field gun, mortar

carom. ◆ *vb* **6** (*intr*) to rebound; collide (*with* into). **7** (*intr*) *Billiards.* to make a cannon. [C16: from OF *canon,* from It. *cannone* cannon, from *canna* tube]

cannonade (ˌkænəˈneɪd) *n* **1** an intense and continuous artillery bombardment. ◆ *vb* **cannonades, cannonading, cannonaded. 2** to attack (a target) with cannon.

cannonball (ˈkænənˌbɔːl) *n* **1** a projectile fired from a cannon: usually a solid round metal shot. ◆ *vb* (*intr*) **2** (often foll. by *along,* etc.) to rush along. ◆ *adj* **3** very fast or powerful.

cannon bone *n* a bone in the legs of horses and other hoofed animals consisting of greatly elongated fused metatarsals or metacarpals.

cannoneer (ˌkænəˈnɪə) *n* (formerly) a soldier who served and fired a cannon; artilleryman.

cannon fodder *n* men regarded as expendable in war because they are part of a huge army.

cannot (ˈkænɒt, kæˈnɒt) an auxiliary verb expressing incapacity, inability, withholding permission, etc.; can not.

cannula *or* **canula** (ˈkænjʊlə) *n, pl* **cannulas, cannulae** (-ˌliː), *or* **canulas, canulae** (-ˌliː). *Surgery.* a narrow tube for draining fluid from or introducing medication into the body. [C17: from L: a small reed, from *canna* a reed]

canny Ⓣ (ˈkænɪ) *adj* **cannier, canniest. 1** shrewd, esp. in business. **2** *Scot. & NE English dialect.* good or nice: used as a general term of approval. **3** *Scot.* lucky or fortunate. [C16: from CAN[1] (in the sense: to know how) + -Y[1]]
▸ˈ**cannily** *adv* ▸ˈ**canniness** *n*

canoe (kəˈnuː) *n* **1** a light narrow open boat, propelled by one or more paddles. ◆ *vb* **canoes, canoeing, canoed. 2** to go in or transport by canoe. [C16: from Sp. *canoa,* of Carib origin]
▸**caˈnoeist** *n*

canon[1] Ⓣ (ˈkænən) *n* **1** *Christianity.* a Church decree enacted to regulate morals or religious practices. **2** (*often pl*) a general rule or standard, as of judgment, morals, etc. **3** (*often pl*) a principle or criterion applied in a branch of learning or art. **4** *RC Church.* the list of the canonized saints. **5** *RC Church.* Also called: **Eucharistic Prayer.** the prayer in the Mass in which the Host is consecrated. **6** a list of writings, esp. sacred writings, recognized as genuine. **7** a piece of music in which an extended melody in one part is imitated successively in one or more other parts. **8** a list of the works of an author that are accepted as authentic. [OE, from L, from Gk *kanōn* rule, rod for measuring]

canon[2] (ˈkænən) *n* **1** one of several priests on the permanent staff of a cathedral, who are responsible for organizing services, maintaining the fabric, etc. **2** *RC Church.* Also called: **canon regular.** a member of either of two religious orders living communally as monks but performing clerical duties. [C13: from Anglo-F, from LL *canonicus* one living under a rule, from CANON[1]]

canonical (kəˈnɒnɪkᵊl) *or* **canonic** *adj* **1** included in a canon of sacred or other officially recognized writings. **2** in conformity with canon law. **3** accepted; authoritative. **4** *Music.* in the form of a canon. **5** of or relating to a cathedral chapter. **6** of a canon (clergyman).
▸**caˈnonically** *adv*

canonical hour *n* **1** *RC Church.* one of the seven prayer times appointed for each day by canon law. **2** *Church of England.* any time at which marriages may lawfully be celebrated.

canonicals (kəˈnɒnɪkᵊlz) *pl n* the vestments worn by clergy when officiating.

canonicity (ˌkænəˈnɪsɪtɪ) *n* the fact or quality of being canonical.

canonist (ˈkænənɪst) *n* a specialist in canon law.

canonize *or* **canonise** (ˈkænəˌnaɪz) *vb* **canonizes, canonizing, canonized** *or* **canonises, canonising, canonised.** (*tr*) **1** *RC Church.* to declare (a person) to be a saint. **2** to regard as a saint. **3** to sanction by canon law.
▸ˌ**canoniˈzation** *or* ˌ**canoniˈsation** *n*

canon law *n* the codified body of laws enacted by the supreme authorities of a Christian Church.

canonry (ˈkænənrɪ) *n, pl* **canonries. 1** the office, benefice, or status of a canon. **2** canons collectively. [C15: from CANON[2] + -RY]

canoodle (kəˈnuːdᵊl) *vb* **canoodles, canoodling, canoodled.** (*intr;* often by *with*) *Sl.* to kiss and cuddle. [C19: from ?]

Canopic jar, urn, *or* **vase** (kəˈnəʊpɪk) *n* (in ancient Egypt) one of four containers for holding the entrails of a mummy. [C19: from *Canopus,* a port in ancient Egypt]

canopy Ⓣ (ˈkænəpɪ) *n, pl* **canopies. 1** an ornamental awning above a throne, bed, person, etc. **2** a rooflike covering over an altar, niche, etc. **3** a roofed structure serving as a sheltered passageway. **4** a large or wide covering: *the sky was a grey canopy.* **5** the hemisphere that forms the supporting surface of a parachute. **6** the transparent cover of an aircraft cockpit. **7** the highest level of foliage in a forest, formed by the crowns of the trees. ◆ *vb* **canopies, canopying, canopied. 8** (*tr*) to cover with or as with a canopy. [C14: from Med. L *canōpeum* mosquito net, from L, from Gk *kōnōpeion* bed with protective net]

canst (kænst) *vb Arch.* the form of **can**[1] used with the pronoun *thou* or its relative form.

cant[1] Ⓣ (kænt) *n* **1** insincere talk, esp. concerning religion or morals. **2** phrases that have become meaningless through repetition. **3** specialized vocabulary of a particular group, such as thieves, journalists, or lawyers. ◆ *vb* **4** (*intr*) to speak in or use cant. [C16: prob. via Norman F *canter* to sing, from L *cantāre;* used disparagingly, from the 12th cent., of chanting in religious services]
▸ˈ**cantingly** *adv*

cant[2] Ⓣ (kænt) *n* **1** inclination from a vertical or horizontal plane. **2** a sudden movement that tilts or turns something. **3** the angle or tilt thus caused. **4** a corner or outer angle. **5** an oblique or slanting surface, edge, or line. ◆ *vb* (*tr*) **6** to tip, tilt, or overturn. **7** to set in an oblique position. **8** another word for **bevel** (sense 1). ◆ *adj* **9** oblique; slanting. **10** having flat surfaces. [C14 (in the sense: edge): ?from L *canthus* iron hoop round a wheel, from ?]

can't (kɑːnt) *contraction of* cannot.

Cantab. (ˈkæntæb) *abbrev. for* Cantabrigiensis. [L: of Cambridge]

cantabile (kænˈtɑːbɪlɪ) *Music.* ◆ *adj, adv* **1** (to be performed) flowingly and melodiously. ◆ *n* **2** a piece or passage performed in this way. [It., from LL, from L *cantāre* to sing]

Cantabrigian (ˌkæntəˈbrɪdʒɪən) *adj* **1** of or characteristic of Cambridge or Cambridge University. ◆ *n* **2** a member or graduate of Cambridge University. **3** an inhabitant or native of Cambridge. [C17: from Med. L *Cantabrigia*]

cantaloupe *or* **cantaloup** (ˈkæntəˌluːp) *n* **1** a cultivated variety of muskmelon with ribbed warty rind and orange flesh. **2** any of several other muskmelons. [C18: from F, from *Cantaluppi,* near Rome, where first cultivated in Europe]

cantankerous Ⓣ (kænˈtæŋkərəs) *adj* quarrelsome; irascible. [C18: ?from C14 (obs.) *conteckour* a contentious person, from Anglo-F *contek* strife, from ?]
▸**canˈtankerously** *adv* ▸**canˈtankerousness** *n*

cantata (kænˈtɑːtə) *n* a musical setting of a text, esp. a religious text, consisting of arias, duets, and choruses. [C18: from It., from *cantare* to sing, from L]

canteen (kænˈtiːn) *n* **1** a restaurant attached to a factory, school, etc., providing meals for large numbers. **2a** a small shop that provides a limited range of items to a military unit. **2b** a recreation centre for military personnel. **3** a temporary or mobile stand at which food is provided. **4a** a box in which a set of cutlery is laid out. **4b** the cutlery itself. **5** a flask for carrying water or other liquids. [C18: from F, from It. *cantina* wine cellar, from *canto* corner, from L *canthus* iron hoop encircling chariot wheel]

canter Ⓣ (ˈkæntə) *n* **1** a gait of horses, etc., between a trot and a gallop in speed. **2 at a canter.** easily; without effort. ◆ *vb* **3** to move or cause to move at a canter. [C18: short for *Canterbury trot,* the supposed pace at which pilgrims rode to Canterbury]

Canterbury bell (ˈkæntəbərɪ) *n* a biennial European plant related to the campanula and widely cultivated for its blue, violet, or white flowers.

cantharides (kænˈθærɪˌdiːz) *pl n, sing* **cantharis** (ˈkænθərɪs). a diuretic and urogenital stimulant prepared from the dried bodies of Spanish fly. Also called: **Spanish fly.** [C15: from L, pl of *cantharis,* from Gk *kantharis* Spanish fly]

cant hook *or* **dog** *n Forestry.* a wooden pole with a blunt steel tip and an adjustable hook at one end, used for handling logs.

canthus (ˈkænθəs) *n, pl* **canthi** (-ˌθaɪ). the inner or outer corner of the eye, formed by the natural junction of the eyelids. [C17: from NL, from L: iron tyre]

canticle (ˈkæntɪkᵊl) *n* a nonmetrical hymn, derived from the Bible and used in the liturgy of certain Christian churches. [C13: from L *canticulum,* dim. of *canticus* a song, from *canere* to sing]

cantilena (ˌkæntɪˈleɪnə) *n* a smooth flowing style in the writing of vocal music. [C18: It.]

cantilever (ˈkæntɪˌliːvə) *n* **1** a beam, girder, or structural framework that is fixed at one end only. **2** a part of a beam or a structure projecting outwards beyond its support. [C17: ?from CANT[2] + LEVER]

cantilever bridge *n* a bridge having spans that are constructed as cantilevers.

cantillate (ˈkæntɪˌleɪt) *vb* **cantillates, cantillating, cantillated. 1** to chant (passages of the Hebrew Scriptures) according to the traditional Jewish melody. **2** to intone or chant. [C19: from LL *cantillāre* to sing softly, from L *cantāre* to sing]
▸ˌ**cantilˈlation** *n*

THESAURUS

canny *adj* **1** = **shrewd,** acute, artful, astute, careful, cautious, circumspect, clever, judicious, knowing, on the ball (*inf.*), perspicacious, prudent, sagacious, sharp, subtle, wise, worldly-wise
Antonyms *adj* bumbling, inept, lumpen (*inf.*), obtuse, unskilled

canon *n* **2, 3** = **rule,** criterion, dictate, formula, precept, principle, regulation, standard, statute, yardstick **8** = **list,** catalogue, roll

canopy *n* **1-4** = **awning,** baldachin, covering, shade, sunshade, tester

cant[1] *n* **1** = **hypocrisy,** affected piety, humbug, insincerity, lip service, pious platitudes, pretence, pretentiousness, sanctimoniousness, sham holiness **3** = **jargon,** argot, lingo, patter, slang, vernacular

cant[2] *vb* **1, 3, 5** = **tilt,** angle, bevel, incline, rise, slant, slope

cantankerous *adj* = **bad-tempered,** captious, choleric, contrary, crabby, cranky (*US, Canad., & Irish informal*), crotchety (*inf.*), crusty, difficult, disagreeable, grouchy (*inf.*), grumpy, ill-humoured, irascible, irritable, liverish, peevish, perverse, quarrelsome, ratty (*Brit. & NZ inf.*), testy, tetchy, waspish
Antonyms *adj* agreeable, amiable, breezy, cheerful, complaisant, congenial, genial, good-natured, happy, kindly, merry, placid, pleasant, vivacious

canter *n* **1** = **jog,** amble, dogtrot, easy gait, lope ◆ *vb* **3** = **jog,** amble, lope

cantle ('kæntᵊl) *n* **1** the back part of a saddle that slopes upwards. **2** a broken-off piece. [C14: from OF *cantel*, from *cant* corner]

canto ('kæntəʊ) *n, pl* **cantos.** a main division of a long poem. [C16: from It.: song, from L, from *canere* to sing]

canto fermo ('kæntəʊ 'fɜːməʊ) *or* **cantus firmus** ('kæntəs 'fɜːməs) *n* **1** a melody that is the basis to which other parts are added in polyphonic music. **2** the traditional Church plainchant as prescribed by use and regulation. [It., from Med L: fixed song]

canton *n* **1** ('kæntɒn, kæn'tɒn). a political division of Switzerland. **2** ('kæntən). *Heraldry.* a small square charge on a shield, usually in the top left corner. ◆ *vb* **3** (kæn'tɒn). (*tr*) to divide into cantons. **4** (kən'tuːn). (esp. formerly) to allocate accommodation to (military personnel, etc.). [C16: from OF: corner, from It., from *canto* corner, from L *canthus* iron rim]
▸**'cantonal** *adj*

Cantonese (,kæntə'niːz) *n* **1** the Chinese language spoken in the city of Canton, Guangdong and Guanxi provinces, Hong Kong, and elsewhere inside and outside China. **2** (*pl* **Cantonese**) a native or inhabitant of Canton city or Guangdong province. ◆ *adj* **3** of or relating to Canton or Guangdong or the Chinese language spoken there.

cantonment (kən'tuːnmənt) *n Mil.* (esp. formerly) **1** a large training camp. **2** the winter quarters of a campaigning army. **3** *History.* a permanent military camp in British India.

cantor ('kæntɔː) *n* **1** *Judaism.* a man employed to lead synagogue services. **2** *Christianity.* the leader of the singing in a church choir. [C16: from L: singer, from *canere* to sing]

cantorial (kæn'tɔːrɪəl) *adj* **1** of a precentor. **2** (of part of a choir) on the same side of a cathedral, etc., as the precentor.

cantoris (kæn'tɔːrɪs) *adj* (in antiphonal music) to be sung by the cantorial side of a choir. Cf. **decani.** [L: genitive of *cantor* precentor]

Cantuar. ('kæntjʊ,ɑː) *abbrev. for* Cantuariensis. [L: (Archbishop) of Canterbury]

Canuck (kə'nʌk) *n, adj US & Canad. inf.* Canadian. [C19: from ?]

canvas ('kænvəs) *n* **1a** a heavy cloth made of cotton, hemp, or jute, used for sails, tents, etc. **1b** (*as modifier*): *a canvas bag.* **2a** a piece of canvas, etc., on which a painting is done, usually in oils. **2b** an oil painting. **3** a tent or tents collectively. **4** *Naut.* the sails of a vessel collectively. **5** any coarse loosely woven cloth on which tapestry, etc., is done. **6** (preceded by *the*) the floor of a boxing or wrestling ring. **7** *Rowing.* the covered part at either end of a racing boat: *to win by a canvas.* **8 under canvas. 8a** in tents. **8b** *Naut.* with sails unfurled. [C14: from Norman F *canevas*, ult. from L *cannabis* hemp]

canvasback ('kænvəs,bæk) *n, pl* **canvasbacks** *or* **canvasback.** a North American diving duck, the male of which has a reddish-brown head.

canvass Ⓣ ('kænvəs) *vb* **1** to solicit votes, orders, etc., (from). **2** to determine the opinions of (voters before an election, etc.), esp. by conducting a survey. **3** to investigate (something) thoroughly, esp. by discussion. **4** *Chiefly US.* to inspect (votes) to determine their validity. ◆ *n* **5** a solicitation of opinions, votes, etc. [C16: prob. from obs. sense of CANVAS (to toss someone in a canvas sheet, hence, to criticize)]
▸**'canvasser** *n*

canyon Ⓣ *or* **cañon** ('kænjən) *n* a gorge or ravine, esp. in North America, usually formed by a river. [C19: from Sp., from *caña* tube, from L *canna* cane]

canzonetta (,kænzə'nɛtə) *or* **canzonet** (,kænzə'nɛt) *n* a short, lively song, typically of the 16th to 18th centuries. [C16: It.: dim. of *canzone*, from L *canere* to sing]

caoutchouc ('kaʊtʃʊk) *n* another name for **rubber**[1] (sense 1). [C18: from F, from obs. Sp., from Quechua]

cap Ⓣ (kæp) *n* **1** a covering for the head, esp. a small close-fitting one. **2** such a covering serving to identify the wearer's rank, occupation, etc.: *a nurse's cap.* **3** something that protects or covers: *lens cap.* **4** an uppermost surface or part: *the cap of a wave.* **5a** See **percussion cap. 5b** a small amount of explosive enclosed in paper and used in a toy gun. **6** *Sport, chiefly Brit.* **6a** an emblematic hat or beret given to someone chosen for a representative team. **6b** a player chosen for such a team. **7** any part like a cap in shape. **8** *Bot.* the pileus of a mushroom or toadstool. **9** *Hunting.* money contributed to the funds of a hunt by a follower who is neither a subscriber nor a farmer, in return for a day's hunting. **10** *Anat.* **10a** the natural enamel covering a tooth. **10b** an artificial protective covering for a tooth. **11** Also: **Dutch cap, diaphragm.** a contraceptive membrane placed over the mouth of the cervix. **12** an upper financial limit. **13** a mortarboard worn at an academic ceremony (esp. in **cap and gown**). **14** *Meteorol.* **14a** the cloud covering the peak of a mountain. **14b** the transient top of detached clouds above an increasing cumulus. **15 set one's cap at.** (of a woman) to be determined to win as a husband or lover. **16 cap in hand.** humbly, as when asking a favour. ◆ *vb* **caps, capping, capped.** (*tr*) **17** to cover, as with a cap: *snow capped the mountain tops.* **18** *Inf.* to outdo; excel. **19 cap it all.** to provide the finishing touch. **20** *Sport, Brit.* to select (a player) for a representative team. **21** to seal off (an oil or gas well). **22** to impose an upper limit on the level of increase of (a tax): *charge-cap.* **23** *Chiefly Scot. & NZ.* to award a degree to. [OE *cæppe*, from LL *cappa* hood, ?from L *caput* head]

CAP *abbrev. for:* Common Agricultural Policy: (in the EU) the system for supporting farm incomes by maintaining agricultural prices at agreed levels.

cap. *abbrev. for:* **1** capacity. **2** capital. **3** capitalize. **4** capital letter.

capability Ⓣ (,keɪpə'bɪlɪtɪ) *n, pl* **capabilities. 1** the quality of being capable; ability. **2** the quality of being susceptible to the use or treatment indicated: *the capability of a metal to be fused.* **3** (*usually pl*) potential aptitude.

capable Ⓣ ('keɪpəbᵊl) *adj* **1** having ability; competent. **2** (*postpositive;* foll. by *of*) able or having the skill (to do something): *she is capable of hard work.* **3** (*postpositive;* foll. by *of*) having the temperament or inclination (to do something): *he seemed capable of murder.* [C16: from F, from LL *capābilis* able to take in, from L *capere* to take]
▸**'capableness** *n* ▸**'capably** *adv*

capacious Ⓣ (kə'peɪʃəs) *adj* capable of holding much; roomy. [C17: from L, from *capere* to take]
▸**ca'paciously** *adv* ▸**ca'paciousness** *n*

capacitance (kə'pæsɪtəns) *n* **1** the property of a system that enables it to store electric charge. **2** a measure of this, equal to the charge that must be added to such a system to raise its electrical potential by one unit. Former name: **capacity.** [C20: from CAPACIT(Y) + -ANCE]
▸**ca'pacitive** *adj*

capacitor (kə'pæsɪtə) *n* a device for accumulating electric charge, usually consisting of two conducting surfaces separated by a dielectric. Former name: **condenser.**

capacity Ⓣ (kə'pæsɪtɪ) *n, pl* **capacities. 1** the ability or power to contain, absorb, or hold. **2** the amount that can be contained: *a capacity of six gallons.* **3a** the maximum amount something can contain or absorb (esp. in **filled to capacity**). **3b** (*as modifier*): *a capacity crowd.* **4** the ability to understand or learn: *he has a great capacity for Greek.* **5** the ability to do or produce: *the factory's output was not at capacity.* **6** a specified position or function. **7** a measure of the electrical output of a piece of apparatus such as a generator or accumulator. **8** *Electronics.* a former name for **capacitance. 9** *Computing.* **9a** the number of words or characters that can be stored in a storage device. **9b** the range of numbers that can be processed in a register. **10** legal competence: *the capacity to make a will.* [C15: from OF *capacite*, from L, from *capāx* spacious, from *capere* to take]

cap and bells *n* the traditional garb of a court jester, including a cap with bells.

cap-a-pie (,kæpə'piː) *adv* (dressed, armed, etc.) from head to foot. [C16: from OF]

caparison (kə'pærɪsᵊn) *n* **1** a decorated covering for a horse. **2** rich or elaborate clothing and ornaments. ◆ *vb* **3** (*tr*) to put a caparison on. [C16: via obs. F from OSp. *caparazón* saddlecloth, prob. from *capa* CAPE[1]]

cape[1] (keɪp) *n* a sleeveless garment like a cloak but usually shorter. [C16: from F, from Provençal *capa*, from LL *cappa;* see CAP]

cape[2] Ⓣ (keɪp) *n* a headland or promontory. [C14: from OF *cap*, from OProvençal, from L *caput* head]

Cape Coloured *n* (in South Africa) another name for a **Coloured** (sense 2).

Cape doctor *n S. African inf.* a strong fresh SE wind blowing in the vicinity of Cape Town, esp. in the summer.

Cape Dutch *n* **1** (in South Africa) a distinctive style in furniture or buildings. **2** an obsolete name for **Afrikaans.**

Cape gooseberry *n* another name for **strawberry tomato.**

capelin ('kæpəlɪn) *or* **caplin** ('kæplɪn) *n* a small marine food fish of northern and Arctic seas. [C17: from F *capelan*, from OProvençal, lit.: chaplain]

capellmeister *or* **kapellmeister** (kæ'pɛl,maɪstə) *n* a person in charge

THESAURUS

canvass *vb* **1** = **campaign**, electioneer, solicit, solicit votes **2, 3** = **poll**, analyse, examine, fly a kite, inspect, investigate, scan, scrutinize, sift, study, ventilate ◆ *n* **5** = **poll**, examination, investigation, scrutiny, survey, tally

canyon *n* = **gorge**, coulee (*US*), gulch (*US*), gulf, gully, ravine, valley

cap *vb* **18** *Informal* = **beat**, better, clobber (*sl.*), complete, cover, crown, eclipse, exceed, excel, finish, lick (*inf.*), outdo, outstrip, overtop, put in the shade, run rings around (*inf.*), surpass, top, transcend

capability *n* **1** = **ability**, capacity, competence, facility, faculty, means, potential, potentiality, power, proficiency, qualification(s), wherewithal
Antonyms *n* inability, incompetence, inefficiency, ineptitude, powerlessness

capable *adj* **1, 2** = **able**, accomplished, adapted, adept, adequate, apt, clever, competent, efficient, experienced, fitted, gifted, intelligent, masterly, proficient, qualified, skilful, suited, susceptible, talented
Antonyms *adj* incapable, incompetent, ineffective, inept, inexpert, unqualified, unskilled

capacious *adj* = **spacious**, ample, broad, comfortable, commodious, comprehensive, expansive, extended, extensive, generous, liberal, roomy, sizable *or* sizeable, substantial, vast, voluminous, wide
Antonyms *adj* confined, constricted, cramped, enclosed, incommodious, insubstantial, limited, narrow, poky, restricted, small, tight, tiny, uncomfortable, ungenerous

capaciousness *n* = **spaciousness**, ampleness, commodiousness, roominess, sizableness *or* sizeableness

capacity *n* **1** = **size**, amplitude, compass, dimensions, extent, magnitude, range, room, scope, space, volume **4** = **ability**, aptitude, aptness, brains, capability, cleverness, competence, competency, efficiency, facility, faculty, forte, genius, gift, intelligence, power, readiness, strength **6** = **function**, appointment, office, position, post, province, role, service, sphere

cape[2] *n* = **headland**, chersonese (*poetic*), head, ness (*arch.*), peninsula, point, promontory of an orchestra, esp. in an 18th-century princely household. [from G, from *Kapelle* chapel + *Meister* MASTER]

Cape pigeon *n* a kind of petrel common in S Africa.

caper[1] **T** ('keɪpə) *n* **1** a playful skip or leap. **2** a high-spirited escapade. **3 cut a caper** *or* **capers.** to skip, leap, or frolic. **4** *US & Canad. sl.* a crime. ◆ *vb* **5** (*intr*) to leap or dance about in a light-hearted manner. [C16: prob. from CAPRIOLE]

caper[2] ('keɪpə) *n* **1** a spiny trailing Mediterranean shrub with edible flower buds. **2** its pickled flower buds, used in sauces. [C15: from earlier *capers, capres* (assumed to be pl), from L, from Gk *kapparis*]

capercaillie *or* **capercailzie** (ˌkæpəˈkeɪljɪ) *n* a large European woodland grouse having a black plumage. [C16: from Scot. Gaelic *capull coille* horse of the woods]

Cape sparrow *n* a sparrow very common in southern Africa. Also called (esp. S. African): **mossie.**

capias (ˈkeɪpɪˌæs, ˈkæp-) *n Law.* a writ directing a sheriff or other officer to arrest a named person. [C15: from L, lit.: you must take, from *capere*]

capillarity (ˌkæpɪˈlærɪtɪ) *n* a phenomenon caused by surface tension and resulting in the elevation or depression of the surface of a liquid in contact with a solid. Also called: **capillary action.**

capillary (kəˈpɪlərɪ) *adj* **1** resembling a hair; slender. **2** (of tubes) having a fine bore. **3** *Anat.* of the delicate thin-walled blood vessels that interconnect between the arterioles and the venules. **4** *Physics.* of or relating to capillarity. ◆ *n, pl* **capillaries. 5** *Anat.* any of the capillary blood vessels. [C17: from L *capillāris,* from *capillus* hair]

capital[1] **T** ('kæpɪtᵊl) *n* **1a** the seat of government of a country. **1b** (*as modifier*): *a capital city.* **2** material wealth owned by an individual or business enterprise. **3** wealth available for or capable of use in the production of further wealth, as by industrial investment. **4 make capital (out) of.** to get advantage from. **5** (*sometimes cap.*) the capitalist class or their interests: *capital versus labour.* **6** *Accounting.* **6a** the ownership interests of a business as represented by the excess of assets over liabilities. **6b** the nominal value of the issued shares. **7** any assets or resources. **8a** a capital letter. Abbrev.: **cap. 8b** (*as modifier*): *capital B.* ◆ *adj* **9** (*prenominal*) *Law.* involving or punishable by death: *a capital offence.* **10** very serious: *a capital error.* **11** primary, chief, or principal: *our capital concern.* **12** of, relating to, or designating the large letter used chiefly as the initial letter in personal names and place names and often for abbreviations and acronyms. See also **upper case. 13** *Chiefly Brit.* excellent; first-rate: *a capital idea.* [C13: from L *capitālis* (adj) concerning the head, from *caput* head]

capital[2] ('kæpɪtᵊl) *n* the upper part of a column or pier that supports the entablature. [C14: from OF, from LL *capitellum,* dim. of *caput* head]

capital account *n* **1** *Econ.* that part of a balance of payments composed of movements of capital. **2** *Accounting.* a financial statement showing the net value of a company at a specified date.

capital expenditure *n* expenditure to increase fixed assets.

capital gain *n* the amount by which the selling price of a financial asset exceeds its cost.

capital gains tax *n* a tax on the profit made from sale of an asset.

capital goods *pl n Econ.* goods that are themselves utilized in the production of other goods.

capitalism **T** ('kæpɪtəˌlɪzəm) *n* an economic system based on the private ownership of the means of production, distribution, and exchange. Also called: **free enterprise, private enterprise.** Cf. **socialism** (sense 1).

capitalist ('kæpɪtəlɪst) *n* **1** a person who owns capital, esp. capital invested in a business. **2** *Politics.* a supporter of capitalism. ◆ *adj* **3** relating to capital, capitalists, or capitalism.
▸ˌ**capital'istic** *adj*

capitalization *or* **capitalisation** (ˌkæpɪtəlaɪˈzeɪʃən) *n* **1a** the act of capitalizing. **1b** the sum so derived. **2** *Accounting.* the par value of the total share capital issued by a company. **3** the act of estimating the present value of future payments, etc.

capitalize **T** *or* **capitalise** ('kæpɪtəˌlaɪz) *vb* **capitalizes, capitalizing, capitalized** *or* **capitalises, capitalising, capitalised.** (*mainly tr*) **1** (*intr;* foll. by *on*) to take advantage (of). **2** to write or print (text) in capital letters. **3** to convert (debt or earnings) into capital stock. **4** to authorize (a business enterprise) to issue a specified amount of capital stock. **5** to provide with capital. **6** *Accounting.* to treat (expenditures) as assets. **7a** to estimate the present value of (a periodical income). **7b** to compute the present value of (a business) from actual or potential earnings.

capitally ('kæpɪtəlɪ) *adv Chiefly Brit.* in an excellent manner; admirably.

capital punishment *n* the punishment of death for a crime; death penalty.

capital ship *n* one of the largest and most heavily armed ships in a naval fleet.

capital stock *n* **1** the par value of the total share capital that a company is authorized to issue. **2** the total physical capital existing in an economy at any moment of time.

capital transfer tax *n* (in Britain) a tax payable from 1974 to 1986 on the cumulative total of gifts of money or property made during the donor's lifetime or after his death. It was replaced by inheritance tax.

capitation (ˌkæpɪˈteɪʃən) *n* **1** a tax levied on the basis of a fixed amount per head. **2 capitation grant.** a grant of money given to every person who qualifies under certain conditions. [C17: from LL, from L *caput* head]

Capitol ('kæpɪtᵊl) *n* **1** the temple on the Capitoline. **2 the.** the main building of the US Congress. [C14: from Latin *Capitōlium,* from *caput* head]

capitulate **T** (kəˈpɪtjʊˌleɪt) *vb* **capitulates, capitulating, capitulated.** (*intr*) to surrender, esp. under agreed conditions. [C16 (meaning: to draw up in order): from Med. L *capitulare* to draw up under heads, from *capitulum* CHAPTER]
▸**ca'pituˌlator** *n*

capitulation **T** (kəˌpɪtjʊˈleɪʃən) *n* **1** the act of capitulating. **2** a document containing terms of surrender. **3** a statement summarizing the main divisions of a subject.
▸**ca'pitulatory** *adj*

capitulum (kəˈpɪtjʊləm) *n, pl* **capitula** (-lə). an inflorescence in the form of a disc, the youngest at the centre. It occurs in the daisy and related plants. [C18: from L, lit.: a little head, from *caput* head]

capo ('kæpəʊ) *n, pl* **capos.** a device fitted across all the strings of a guitar, lute, etc., so as to raise the pitch of each string simultaneously. Also called: **capo tasto** ('tæstəʊ). [from It. *capo tasto* head stop]

capon ('keɪpən) *n* a castrated cock fowl fattened for eating. [OE *capun,* from L *cāpō* capon]
▸ˈ**caponˌize** *or* ˈ**caponˌise** *vb*

capote (kəˈpəʊt) *n* a long cloak or soldier's coat, usually with a hood. [C19: from F: cloak, from *cape*]

capping ('kæpɪŋ) *n Scot. & NZ.* **a** the act of conferring an academic degree. **b** (*as modifier*): *Capping Day.*

cappuccino (ˌkæpʊˈtʃiːnəʊ) *n, pl* **cappuccinos.** coffee with steamed milk, usually sprinkled with powdered chocolate. [It.: CAPUCHIN]

capriccio (kəˈprɪtʃɪˌəʊ) *or* **caprice** *n, pl* **capriccios, capricci** (-ˈpriːtʃɪ), *or* **caprices.** *Music.* a lively piece of irregular musical form. [C17: from It.: CAPRICE]

capriccioso (kəˌprɪtʃɪˈəʊzəʊ) *adv Music.* to be played in a free and lively style. [It.: from *capriccio* CAPRICE]

caprice **T** (kəˈpriːs) *n* **1** a sudden change of attitude, behaviour, etc. **2** a tendency to such changes. **3** another word for **capriccio.** [C17: from F, from It. *capriccio* a shiver, caprice, from *capo* head + *riccio* lit.: hedgehog]

capricious **T** (kəˈprɪʃəs) *adj* characterized by or liable to sudden unpredictable changes in attitude or behaviour.
▸**ca'priciously** *adv*

Capricorn ('kæprɪˌkɔːn) *n* **1** *Astrol.* Also called: the **Goat, Capricornus.** the tenth sign of the zodiac. The sun is in this sign between about Dec. 22 and Jan. 19. **2** *Astron.* a S constellation. **3 tropic of Capricorn.** See **tropic** (sense 1). [C14: from L *Capricornus,* from *caper* goat + *cornū* horn]

caprine ('kæpraɪn) *adj* of or resembling a goat. [C17: from L *caprīnus,* from *caper* goat]

capriole ('kæprɪˌəʊl) *n* **1** *Dressage.* a high upward but not forward leap made by a horse with all four feet off the ground. ◆ *vb* **caprioles, caprioling, caprioled. 2** (*intr*) to perform a capriole. [C16: from F, from OIt., from *capriolo* roebuck, from L *capreolus, caper* goat]

caps. *abbrev. for:* **1** capital letters. **2** capsule.

capsicum ('kæpsɪkəm) *n* **1** any of a genus of tropical American plants related to the potato, having mild or pungent seeds enclosed in a bell-shaped fruit. **2** the fruit of any of these plants, used as a vegetable or ground to produce a condiment. ◆ See also **pepper** (sense 4). [C18: from NL, from L *capsa* box]

capsid[1] ('kæpsɪd) *n* a bug related to the water bug that feeds on plant tissues, causing damage to crops. [C19: from NL *Capsus* (genus)]

capsid[2] ('kæpsɪd) *n* the outer protein coat of a mature virus. [C20: from F *capside,* from L *capsa* box]

THESAURUS

caper[1] *n* **1, 2** = **escapade**, antic, dido (*inf.*), gambol, high jinks, hop, jape, jest, jump, lark (*inf.*), leap, mischief, practical joke, prank, revel, shenanigan (*inf.*), sport, stunt ◆ *vb* **5** = **dance**, bounce, bound, cavort, cut a rug, frisk, frolic, gambol, hop, jump, leap, romp, skip, spring, trip

capital[1] *n* **2,3** = **money**, assets, cash, finance, finances, financing, funds, investment(s), means, principal, property, resources, stock, wealth, wherewithal ◆ *adj* **11** = **principal**, cardinal, central, chief, controlling, essential, foremost, important, leading, main, major, overruling, paramount, pre-eminent, primary, prime, prominent, vital **13** *Old-fashioned* = **first-rate**, excellent, fine, first, prime, splendid, sterling, superb, world-class

capitalism *n* = **private enterprise**, free enterprise, laissez faire *or* laisser faire, private ownership

capitalize *vb* **1** *foll. by* **on** = **take advantage of**, benefit from, cash in on (*inf.*), exploit, gain from, make the most of, profit from

capitulate *vb* = **give in**, cave in (*inf.*), come to terms, give up, relent, submit, succumb, surrender, yield
Antonyms *vb* beat, conquer, crush, defeat, get the better of, lick (*inf.*), overcome, overpower, subdue, subjugate, vanquish

capitulation *n* **1** = **surrender**, accedence, cave-in (*inf.*), submission, yielding

caprice *n* **1, 2** = **whim**, changeableness, fad, fancy, fickleness, fitfulness, freak, humour, impulse, inconstancy, notion, quirk, vagary, whimsy

capricious *adj* = **unpredictable**, changeful, crotchety (*inf.*), erratic, fanciful, fickle, fitful, freakish, impulsive, inconsistent, inconstant, mercurial, odd, queer, quirky, variable, wayward, whimsical
Antonyms *adj* certain, consistent, constant, decisive, determined, firm, immovable, resolute, responsible, stable, unchangeable, unwavering

capsize ➊ (kæp'saɪz) *vb* **capsizes, capsizing, capsized.** to overturn accidentally; upset. [C18: from ?]
▸**cap'sizal** *n*

capstan ('kæpstən) *n* **1** a machine with a drum equipped with a ratchet, used for hauling in heavy ropes, etc. **2** the rotating shaft in a tape recorder that pulls the tape past the head. [C14: from OProvençal *cabestan,* from L *capistrum* a halter, from *capere* to seize]

capstan lathe *n* a lathe for repetitive work, having a rotatable turret to hold tools for successive operations. Also called: **turret lathe.**

capstone ('kæp,stəun) *n* another word for **copestone** (sense 2).

capsule ➊ ('kæpsju:l) *n* **1** a soluble case of gelatine enclosing a dose of medicine. **2** a thin metal cap, seal, or cover. **3** *Bot.* **3a** a dry fruit that liberates its seeds by splitting, as in the violet, or through pores, as in the poppy. **3b** the spore-producing organ of mosses and liverworts. **4** *Anat.* a membranous envelope surrounding any of certain organs or parts. **5** See **space capsule. 6** an aeroplane cockpit that can be ejected in a flight emergency, complete with crew, instruments, etc. **7** (*modifier*) in a highly concise form: *a capsule summary.* [C17: from F, from L *capsula,* dim. of *capsa* box]
▸**'capsu,late** *adj*

capsulize *or* **capsulise** ('kæpsjʊ,laɪz) *vb* **capsulizes, capsulizing, capsulized** *or* **capsulises, capsulising, capsulised.** (*tr*) **1** to state (information, etc.) in a highly condensed form. **2** to enclose in a capsule.

Capt. *abbrev. for* Captain.

captain ➊ ('kæptɪn) *n* **1** the person in charge of a vessel. **2** an officer of the navy who holds a rank junior to a rear admiral. **3** an officer of the army, certain air forces, and the marines who holds a rank junior to a major. **4** the officer in command of a civil aircraft. **5** the leader of a team in games. **6** a person in command over a group, organization, etc.: *a captain of industry.* **7** *US.* a policeman in charge of a precinct. **8** *US & Canad.* (formerly) a head waiter. ◆ *vb* **9** (*tr*) to be captain of. [C14: from OF, from LL *capitāneus* chief, from L *caput* head]
▸**'captaincy** *or* **'captainship** *n*

Captain Cooker ('kukə) *n NZ.* a wild pig. [from Captain James *Cook* (1728–79), E navigator, who first released pigs in the New Zealand bush]

caption ('kæpʃən) *n* **1** a title, brief explanation, or comment accompanying an illustration. **2** a heading or title of a chapter, article, etc. **3** graphic material used in television presentation. **4** another name for **subtitle** (sense 2). **5** the formal heading of a legal document. ◆ *vb* **6** to provide with a caption or captions. [C14 (meaning: seizure): from L *captiō* a seizing, from *capere* to take]

captious ➊ ('kæpʃəs) *adj* apt to make trivial criticisms. [C14 (meaning: catching in error): from L *captiōsus,* from *captiō* a seizing]
▸**'captiously** *adv* ▸**'captiousness** *n*

captivate ➊ ('kæptɪ,veɪt) *vb* **captivates, captivating, captivated.** (*tr*) to hold the attention of by fascinating; enchant. [C16: from LL *captivāre,* from *captīvus* CAPTIVE]
▸**'capti,vating** *adj* ▸**,capti'vation** *n*

captive ➊ ('kæptɪv) *n* **1** a person or animal that is confined or restrained. **2** a person whose behaviour is dominated by some emotion: *a captive of love.* ◆ *adj* **3** held as prisoner. **4** held under restriction or control; confined. **5** captivated. **6** unable to avoid speeches, advertisements, etc.: *a captive audience.* [C14: from L *captīvus,* from *capere* to take]

captivity ➊ (kæp'tɪvɪtɪ) *n, pl* **captivities. 1** imprisonment. **2** the period of imprisonment.

captor ➊ ('kæptə) *n* a person or animal that holds another captive. [C17: from L, from *capere* to take]

capture ➊ ('kæptʃə) *vb* **captures, capturing, captured.** (*tr*) **1** to take prisoner or gain control over: *to capture a town.* **2** (in a game) to win possession of: *to capture a pawn in chess.* **3** to succeed in representing (something elusive): *the artist captured her likeness.* **4** *Physics.* (of an atom, etc.) to acquire (an additional particle). **5** to insert or transfer (data) into a computer. ◆ *n* **6** the act of taking by force. **7** the person or thing captured. **8** *Physics.* a process by which an atom, etc., acquires an additional particle. **9** *Geog.* the process by which the headwaters of one river are diverted into another. **10** *Computing.* the collection of data for processing. [C16: from L *captūra* a catching, that which is caught, from *capere* to take]
▸**'capturer** *n*

capuchin ('kæpjutʃɪn, -juʃɪn) *n* **1** an agile intelligent S American monkey having a cowl of thick hair on the top of the head. **2** a woman's hooded cloak. **3** (*sometimes cap.*) a variety of domestic fancy pigeon. [C16: from F, from It., from *cappuccio* hood]

Capuchin ('kæpjutʃɪn, -juʃɪn) *n* **1** a friar belonging to a branch of the Franciscan Order founded in 1525. ◆ *adj* **2** of or relating to this order. [C16: from F, from It. *cappuccio* hood]

capybara (,kæpɪ'bɑ:rə) *n* the largest rodent, resembling a guinea pig and native to Central and South America. [C18: from Port. *capibara,* from Tupi]

car ➊ (kɑ:) *n* **1a** Also called: **motorcar, automobile.** a self-propelled road vehicle designed to carry passengers, that is powered by an internal-combustion engine. **1b** (*as modifier*): *car coat.* **2** a conveyance for passengers, freight, etc., such as a cable car or the carrier of an airship or balloon. **3** *Brit.* a railway vehicle for passengers only. **4** *Chiefly US. & Canad.* a railway carriage or van. **5** a poetic word for **chariot.** [C14: from Anglo-F *carre,* ult. rel. to L *carra, carrum* two-wheeled wagon, prob. of Celtic origin]

CAR *abbrev. for* compound annual return.

carabineer *or* **carabinier** (,kærəbɪ'nɪə) *n* variants of **carbineer.**

carabiner (,kærə'bi:nə) *n* a variant of **karabiner.**

caracal ('kærə,kæl) *n* **1** a lynxlike feline mammal inhabiting deserts of N Africa and S Asia, having a smooth coat of reddish fur. **2** this fur. [C18: from F, from Turkish *kara kūlāk,* lit.: black ear]

caracara (,kɑ:rə'kɑ:rə) *n* a large carrion-eating bird of prey of Central and South America, having long legs. [C19: from Sp. or Port., from Tupi; imit.]

caracole ('kærə,kəul) *or* **caracol** ('kærə,kɒl) *Dressage.* ◆ *n* **1** a half turn to the right or left. ◆ *vb* **caracoles, caracoling, caracoled** *or* **caracols, caracoling, caracoled.** (*intr*) **2** to execute a half turn. [C17: from F, from Sp. *caracol* snail, spiral staircase]

caracul ('kærə,kʌl) *n* **1** Also called: **Persian lamb.** the black loosely curled fur obtained from the skins of newly born lambs of the karakul sheep. **2** a variant spelling of **karakul.**

carafe ➊ (kə'ræf, -'rɑ:f) *n* an open-topped glass container for serving water or wine at table [C18: from F, from It., from Sp., from Ar. *gharrāfah* vessel]

carageen ('kærə,gi:n) *n* a variant spelling of **carrageen.**

carambola (,kærəm'bəulə) *n* the yellow edible star-shaped fruit of a Brazilian tree, cultivated in the tropics, esp. SE Asia. Also called: **star fruit.** [Sp., from Port.]

caramel ('kærəməl) *n* **1** burnt sugar, used for colouring and flavouring food. **2** a chewy sweet made from sugar, milk, etc. [C18: from F, from Sp. *caramelo,* from ?]

caramelize *or* **caramelise** ('kærəmə,laɪz) *vb* **caramelizes, caramelizing, caramelized** *or* **caramelises, caramelising, caramelised.** to convert or be converted into caramel.

carapace ('kærə,peɪs) *n* the thick hard shield that covers part of the body of crabs, tortoises, etc. [C19: from F, from Sp. *carapacho,* from ?]

carat ('kærət) *n* **1** a measure of the weight of precious stones, esp. diamonds, now standardized as 0.20 grams. **2** Usual US and Canad. spelling: **karat.** a measure of the gold in an alloy, expressed as the number of parts of gold in 24 parts of the alloy. [C16: from OF, from Med. L, from Ar. *qīrāt* weight of four grains, from Gk, from *keras* horn]

caravan ('kærə,væn) *n* **1a** a large enclosed vehicle capable of being pulled by a car and equipped to be lived in. US and Canad. name: **trailer. 1b** (*as modifier*): *a caravan site.* **2** (esp. in some parts of Asia and Africa) a company of traders or other travellers journeying together. **3** a large covered vehicle, esp. a gaily coloured one used by Gypsies, circuses, etc. ◆ *vb* **caravans, caravanning, caravanned. 4** (*intr*) *Brit.* to travel or have a holiday in a caravan. [C16: from It. *caravana,* from Persian *kārwān*]

caravanserai (,kærə'vænsə,raɪ) *or* **caravansary** (,kærə'vænsərɪ) *n, pl* **caravanserais** *or* **caravansaries.** (in some Eastern countries) a large inn enclosing a courtyard, providing accommodation for caravans. [C16: from Persian *kārwānsarāī* caravan inn]

caravel ('kærə,vɛl) *or* **carvel** *n* a two- or three-masted sailing ship used by the Spanish and Portuguese in the 15th and 16th centuries. [C16: from Port. *caravela,* dim. of *caravo* ship, ult. from Gk *karabos* crab]

caraway ('kærə,weɪ) *n* **1** an umbelliferous Eurasian plant having finely divided leaves and clusters of small whitish flowers. **2 caraway seed.**

THESAURUS

capsize *vb* = **overturn**, invert, keel over, tip over, turn over, turn turtle, upset

capsule *n* **1** = **pill**, bolus, lozenge, tablet, troche (*Medical*) **3** *Botany* = **pod**, case, pericarp (*Botany*), receptacle, seed case, sheath, shell, vessel

captain *n* **1, 4, 6** = **leader**, boss, chief, chieftain, commander, head, master, number one (*inf.*), officer, (senior) pilot, skipper, torchbearer

captious *adj* = **fault-finding**, carping, cavilling, censorious, critical, deprecating, disparaging, hypercritical, nagging, nit-picking (*inf.*)

captivate *vb* = **charm**, absorb, allure, attract, beguile, bewitch, dazzle, enamour, enchant, enrapture, enslave, ensnare, enthral, entrance, fascinate, hypnotize, infatuate, lure, mesmerize, ravish, seduce, sweep off one's feet, win

Antonyms *vb* alienate, disenchant, disgust, repel, repulse

captivation *n* = **fascination**, absorption, allurement, attraction, beguilement, enchantment, enslavement, ensnarement, enthralment, entrancement, hypnotization *or* hypnotisation, infatuation, mesmerization *or* mesmerisation, ravishment, seduction, tantalization *or* tantalisation

captive *n* **1** = **prisoner**, bondservant, convict, detainee, hostage, internee, prisoner of war, slave ◆ *adj* **3, 4** = **confined**, caged, enslaved, ensnared, imprisoned, incarcerated, locked up, penned, restricted, subjugated

captivity *n* **1** = **confinement**, bondage, custody, detention, durance (*arch.*), duress, enthralment, imprisonment, incarceration, internment, restraint, servitude, slavery, thraldom, vassalage

captor *n* = **capturer**, confiner, custodian, detainer, enslaver, ensnarer, imprisoner, incarcerator, jailer *or* gaoler

capture *vb* **1** = **catch**, apprehend, arrest, bag, collar (*inf.*), feel one's collar (*sl.*), lift (*sl.*), nab (*inf.*), nail (*inf.*), secure, seize, take, take into custody, take prisoner ◆ *n* **6** = **catching**, apprehension, arrest, imprisonment, seizure, taking, taking captive, trapping

Antonyms *vb* ≠ **catch:** free, let go, let out, liberate, release, set free, turn loose

car *n* **1** = **vehicle**, auto (*US*), automobile, jalopy (*inf.*), machine, motor, motorcar, wheels (*inf.*) **4** *US & Canad.* = **(railway) carriage**, buffet car, cable car, coach, dining car, sleeping car, van

carafe *n* = **jug**, decanter, flagon, flask, pitcher

the pungent aromatic fruit of this plant, used in cooking. [C14: prob. from Med. L *carvi*, from Ar. *karawyā*, from Gk *karon*]

carb (kɑːb) *n Inf.* short for **carburettor.**

carbaryl ('kɑːbərɪl) *n* an organic compound of the carbamate group: used as an insecticide, esp. to treat head lice.

carbide ('kɑːbaɪd) *n* **1** a binary compound of carbon with a metal. **2** See **calcium carbide.**

carbine ('kɑːbaɪn) *n* **1** a light automatic or semiautomatic rifle. **2** a light short-barrelled rifle formerly used by cavalry. [C17: from F *carabine*, from OF *carabin* carabineer]

carbineer (ˌkɑːbɪ'nɪə), **carabineer,** *or* **carabinier** (ˌkærəbɪ'nɪə) *n* (formerly) a soldier equipped with a carbine.

carbo- *or before a vowel* **carb-** *combining form.* carbon: *carbohydrate; carbonate.*

carbocyclic (ˌkɑːbəʊ'saɪklɪk) *adj* (of a chemical compound) containing a closed ring of carbon atoms.

carbohydrate (ˌkɑːbəʊ'haɪdreɪt) *n* any of a large group of organic compounds, including sugars and starch, that contain carbon, hydrogen, and oxygen, with the general formula $C_m(H_2O)_n$: a source of food and energy for animals.

carbolic acid (kɑː'bɒlɪk) *n* another name for **phenol,** esp. when used as a disinfectant. [C19: from CARBO- + -OL[1] + -IC]

carbon ('kɑːbᵊn) *n* **1a** a nonmetallic element existing in three crystalline forms: graphite, diamond, and buckminsterfullerene: occurring in all organic compounds. The isotope **carbon-12** is the standard for atomic wt.; **carbon-14** is used in radiocarbon dating and as a tracer. Symbol: C; atomic no.: 6; atomic wt.: 12.011 15. **1b** (*as modifier*): *a carbon compound.* **2** short for **carbon paper** or **carbon copy. 3** a carbon electrode used in a carbon-arc light. **4** a rod or plate, made of carbon, used in some types of battery. [C18: from F, from L *carbō* charcoal]

carbon-14 dating *n* another name for **carbon dating.**

carbonaceous (ˌkɑːbə'neɪʃəs) *adj* of, resembling, or containing carbon.

carbonade (ˌkɑːbə'neɪd, -'nɑːd) *n* beef and onions stewed in beer. [C20: F]

carbonado (ˌkɑːbə'neɪdəʊ) *n, pl* **carbonados** *or* **carbonadoes.** an inferior variety of diamond used in industry. Also called: **black diamond.** [Port., lit.: carbonated]

carbon arc *n* an electric arc between two carbon electrodes or between a carbon electrode and materials to be welded.

carbonate *n* ('kɑːbəˌneɪt, -nɪt). **1** a salt or ester of carbonic acid. ◆ *vb* ('kɑːbəˌneɪt), **carbonates, carbonating, carbonated. 2** to turn into a carbonate. **3** (*tr*) to treat with carbon dioxide, as in the manufacture of soft drinks. [C18: from F, from *carbone* CARBON]

carbon black *n* a finely divided form of carbon produced by incomplete combustion of natural gas or petroleum: used in pigments and ink.

carbon brush *n* a small spring-loaded block of carbon used to convey current between the stationary and moving parts of an electric generator, motor, etc.

carbon copy *n* **1** a duplicate copy of writing, typewriting, or drawing obtained by using carbon paper. **2** *Inf.* a person or thing that is identical to another.

carbon dating *n* a technique for determining the age of organic materials, such as wood, based on their content of the radioisotope ^{14}C acquired from the atmosphere when they formed part of a living plant.

carbon dioxide *n* a colourless odourless incombustible gas present in the atmosphere and formed during respiration, etc.: used in fire extinguishers, and as dry ice for refrigeration. Formula: CO_2. Also called: **carbonic-acid gas.**

carbonette (ˌkɑːbə'nɛt) *n NZ.* a ball of compressed coal dust used as fuel.

carbon fibre *n* a thread of pure carbon used because of its lightness and strength at high temperatures for reinforcing resins, ceramics, and metals, and for fishing rods.

carbonic (kɑː'bɒnɪk) *adj* (of a compound) containing carbon, esp. tetravalent carbon.

carbonic acid *n* a weak acid formed when carbon dioxide combines with water. Formula: H_2CO_3.

carboniferous (ˌkɑːbə'nɪfərəs) *adj* yielding coal or carbon.

Carboniferous (ˌkɑːbə'nɪfərəs) *adj* **1** of, denoting, or formed in the fifth period of the Palaeozoic era during which coal measures were formed. ◆ *n* **2 the.** the Carboniferous period or rock system divided into the **Upper Carboniferous** period and the **Lower Carboniferous** period.

carbonize *or* **carbonise** ('kɑːbəˌnaɪz) *vb* **carbonizes, carbonizing, carbonized** *or* **carbonises, carbonising, carbonised. 1** to turn or be turned into carbon as a result of heating, fossilization, chemical treatment, etc. **2** (*tr*) to coat (a substance) with carbon.
▸ˌ**carboni'zation** *or* ˌ**carboni'sation** *n*

carbon monoxide *n* a colourless odourless poisonous gas formed when carbon compounds burn in insufficient air. Formula: CO.

carbon paper *n* a thin sheet of paper coated on one side with a dark waxy pigment, often containing carbon, that is transferred by pressure onto the copying surface below.

carbon tax *n* a tax on the emissions caused by the burning of coal, gas, and oil, aimed at reducing the production of greenhouse gases.

carbon tetrachloride *n* a colourless volatile nonflammable liquid made from chlorine and used as a solvent, cleaning fluid, and insecticide. Formula: CCl_4. Systematic name: **tetrachloromethane.**

car-boot sale *n* a sale of goods from car boots in a site hired for the occasion.

Carborundum (ˌkɑːbə'rʌndəm) *n Trademark.* any of various abrasive materials, esp. one consisting of silicon carbide.

carboxyl group *or* **radical** (kɑː'bɒksaɪl) *n* the monovalent group -COOH: the functional group in organic acids. [C19 *carboxyl*, from CARBO- + OXY-[2] + -YL]

carboxylic acid (ˌkɑːbɒk'sɪlɪk) *n* any of a class of organic acids containing the carboxyl group. See also **fatty acid.**

carboy ('kɑːˌbɔɪ) *n* a large bottle, usually protected by a basket or box, used for containing corrosive liquids. [C18: from Persian *qarāba*]

carbuncle ('kɑːˌbʌŋkᵊl) *n* **1** an extensive skin eruption, similar to a boil, with several openings. **2** a rounded gemstone, esp. a garnet cut without facets. [C13: from L *carbunculus*, dim. of *carbō* coal]
▸**carbuncular** (kɑː'bʌŋkjʊlə) *adj*

carburation (ˌkɑːbjʊ'reɪʃən) *n* the process of mixing a hydrocarbon fuel with air to make an explosive mixture for an internal-combustion engine.

carburet ('kɑːbjʊˌrɛt, ˌkɑːbjʊ'rɛt) *vb* **carburets, carburetting, carburetted** *or US* **carburets, carbureting, carbureted.** (*tr*) to combine or mix (a gas, etc.) with carbon or carbon compounds. [C18: from CARB(ON) + -URET]

carburettor, carburetter (ˌkɑːbə'rɛtə, 'kɑːbəˌrɛtə), *or US & Canad.* **carburetor** ('kɑːbəˌreɪtə) *n* a device used in some petrol engines for mixing atomized petrol with air, and regulating the intake of the mixture into the engine.

carcajou ('kɑːkəˌdʒuː, -kəˌʒuː) *n* a North American name for **wolverine.** [C18: from Canad. F, from Algonquian *karkajou*]

carcass ⓣ *or* **carcase** ('kɑːkəs) *n* **1** the dead body of an animal, esp. one that has been slaughtered for food. **2** *Inf., usually facetious or derog.* a person's body. **3** the skeleton or framework of a structure. **4** the remains of anything when its life or vitality is gone. [C14: from OF *carcasse*, from ?]

carcinogen (kɑː'sɪnədʒən) *n Pathol.* any substance that produces cancer. [C20: from Gk *karkinos* CANCER + -GEN]
▸ˌ**carcino'genic** *adj*

carcinogenesis (ˌkɑːsɪnəʊ'dʒɛnɪsɪs) *n Pathol.* the development of cancerous cells from normal ones.

carcinoma (ˌkɑːsɪ'nəʊmə) *n, pl* **carcinomas** *or* **carcinomata** (-mətə). *Pathol.* any malignant tumour derived from epithelial tissue. [C18: from L, from Gk, from *karkinos* CANCER]

card[1] (kɑːd) *n* **1** a piece of stiff paper or thin cardboard, usually rectangular, with varied uses, as for bearing a written notice for display, etc. **2** such a card used for identification, reference, proof of membership, etc.: *identity card.* **3** such a card used for sending greetings, messages, or invitations: *birthday card.* **4a** one of a set of small pieces of cardboard, marked with figures, symbols, etc., used for playing games or for fortune-telling. See also **playing card. 4b** (*as modifier*): *a card game.* **5** short for **cheque card** or **credit card. 6** *Inf.* a witty or eccentric person. **7** See **compass card. 8** Also called: **racecard.** *Horse racing.* a daily programme of all the races at a meeting. **9 a card up one's sleeve.** a thing or action used in order to gain an advantage, esp. one kept in reserve until needed. ◆ See also **cards.** [C15: from OF *carte*, from L *charta* leaf of papyrus, from Gk *khartēs*, prob. of Egyptian origin]

card[2] (kɑːd) *vb* **1** (*tr*) to comb out and clean (fibres of wool or cotton) before spinning. ◆ *n* **2** (formerly) a machine or comblike tool for carding fabrics or for raising the nap on cloth. [C15: from OF *carde* card, teasel, from L *carduus* thistle]
▸'**carder** *n* ▸'**carding** *n*

cardamom ('kɑːdəməm) *or* **cardamon** ('kɑːdəmən) *n* **1** a tropical Asian plant that has large hairy leaves. **2** the seeds of this plant, used esp. as a spice or condiment. [C15: from L, from Gk, from *kardamon* cress + *amōmon* an Indian spice]

cardboard ('kɑːdˌbɔːd) *n* **1a** a thin stiff board made from paper pulp. **1b** (*as modifier*): *cardboard boxes.* ◆ *adj* **2** (*prenominal*) without substance.

cardboard city *n Inf.* an area of a city in which homeless people sleep rough, often in cardboard boxes.

card-carrying *adj* being an official member of an organization: *a card-carrying Communist.*

cardiac ('kɑːdɪˌæk) *adj* **1** of or relating to the heart. **2** of or relating to the portion of the stomach connected to the oesophagus. ◆ *n* **3** a person with a heart disorder. [C17: from L *cardiacus*, from Gk, from *kardia* heart]

cardiac arrest *n* failure of the pumping action of the heart, resulting in loss of consciousness and absence of pulse and breathing: a medical emergency requiring immediate resuscitative treatment.

cardie *or* **cardy** ('kɑːdɪ) *n, pl* **cardies.** *Inf.* short for **cardigan.**

cardigan ('kɑːdɪgən) *n* a knitted jacket or sweater with buttons up the front. [C19: after 7th Earl of *Cardigan* (1797–1868)]

cardinal ⓣ ('kɑːdɪnᵊl) *n* **1** *RC Church.* any of the members of the Sacred College who elect the pope and act as his chief counsellors. **2** Also called: **cardinal red.** a deep red colour. **3** See **cardinal number. 4** Also called (US): **redbird.** a crested North American bunting, the male of which has a bright red plumage. **5** a woman's hooded shoulder cape

THESAURUS

carcass *n* **1-4** = **body,** cadaver (*Medical*), corpse, corse (*arch.*), dead body, framework, hulk, remains, shell, skeleton

cardinal *adj* **6** = **principal,** capital, central, chief, essential, first, foremost, fundamental, greatest, highest, important, key, leading, main, paramount, pre-eminent, primary, prime
Antonyms *adj* dispensable, inessential, least important, lowest, secondary, subordinate

worn in the 17th and 18th centuries. ◆ *adj* 6 (*usually prenominal*) fundamentally important; principal. 7 of a deep red. [C13: from L *cardinālis*, lit.: relating to a hinge, from *cardō* hinge]
▸'**cardinally** *adv*

cardinalate ('kɑːdɪnᵊˌleɪt) *or* **cardinalship** *n* **1** the rank, office, or term of office of a cardinal. **2** the cardinals collectively.

cardinal flower *n* a lobelia of E North America that has brilliant scarlet flowers.

cardinal number *or* **numeral** *n* a number denoting quantity but not order in a group. Sometimes shortened to **cardinal.** Cf. **ordinal number.**

cardinal points *pl n* the four main points of the compass: north, south, east, and west.

cardinal virtues *pl n* the most important moral qualities, traditionally justice, prudence, temperance, and fortitude.

cardinal vowels *pl n* a set of theoretical vowel sounds, based on the shape of the mouth needed to articulate them, that can be used to classify the vowel sounds of any speaker in any language.

card index *or* **file** *n* **1** an index in which each item is separately listed on systematically arranged cards. ◆ *vb* **card-index** *or* **card-file, card-indexes, card-indexing, card-indexed** *or* **card-files, card-filing, card-filed.** (*tr*) **2** to make such an index of (a book, etc.).

cardio- *or before a vowel* **cardi-** *combining form.* heart: *cardiogram.* [from Gk *kardia* heart]

cardiocentesis (ˌkɑːdɪəʊsɛnˈtiːsɪs) *n Med.* surgical puncture of the heart.

cardiogram ('kɑːdɪəʊˌgræm) *n* short for **electrocardiogram.** See **electrocardiograph.**

cardiograph ('kɑːdɪəʊˌgrɑːf) *n* **1** an instrument for recording heart movements. **2** short for **electrocardiograph.**
▸**cardiographer** (ˌkɑːdɪˈɒgrəfə) *n* ▸ˌ**cardi'ography** *n*

cardiology (ˌkɑːdɪˈɒlədʒɪ) *n* the branch of medical science concerned with the heart and its diseases.
▸ˌ**cardi'ologist** *n*

cardioplegia (ˌkɑːdɪəʊˈpliːdʒə) *n Med.* deliberate arrest of the action of the heart, as by hypothermia or the injection of chemicals, to enable complex heart surgery to be carried out.

cardiopulmonary resuscitation (ˌkɑːdɪəʊˈpʌlmənərɪ, -ˈpʊl-) *n* an emergency measure to revive a patient whose heart has stopped beating, in which compressions applied with the hands to the patient's chest are alternated with mouth-to-mouth respiration. Abbrev.: **CPR.**

cardiovascular (ˌkɑːdɪəʊˈvæskjʊlə) *adj* of or relating to the heart and the blood vessels.

cardoon (kɑːˈduːn) *n* a thistle-like relative of the artichoke with an edible leafstalk. [C17: from F, from L *carduus* thistle, artichoke]

cardphone ('kɑːdfəʊn) *n* a public telephone operated by the insertion of a phonecard instead of coins.

card punch *n* a device, no longer widely used, controlled by a computer, for transferring information from the central processing unit onto punched cards which can then be read by a **card reader.**

card reader *n* a device, no longer widely used, for reading information on a punched card and transferring it to a computer or storage device.

cards (kɑːdz) *n* **1** (*usually functioning as sing*) **1a** any game played with cards, esp. playing cards. **1b** the playing of such a game. **2** an employee's tax and national insurance documents or information held by the employer. **3 ask for** *or* **get one's cards.** to ask or be told to terminate one's employment. **4 on the cards.** possible. **5 play one's cards (right).** to manoeuvre (cleverly). **6 put** *or* **lay one's cards on the table.** to declare one's intentions, etc.

cardsharp ('kɑːdˌʃɑːp) *or* **cardsharper** *n* a professional card player who cheats.

card vote *n Brit.* a vote by delegates, esp. at a trade-union conference, in which each delegate's vote counts as a vote by all his constituents.

care ⓣ (kɛə) *vb* **cares, caring, cared. 1** (when *tr*, *may take a clause as object*) to be troubled or concerned: *he is dying, and she doesn't care.* **2** (*intr;* foll. by *for* or *about*) to have regard or consideration (for): *he cares more for his hobby than his job.* **3** (*intr;* foll. by *for*) to have a desire or taste (for): *would you care for tea?* **4** (*intr;* foll. by *for*) to provide physical needs, help, or comfort (for). **5** (*tr*) to agree or like (to do something): *would you care to sit down?* **6 for all I care** *or* **I couldn't care less.** I am completely indifferent. ◆ *n* **7** careful or serious attention: *he does his work with care.* **8** protective or supervisory control: *in the care of a doctor.* **9** (*often pl*) trouble; worry. **10** an object of or cause for concern. **11** caution: *handle with care.* **12 care of.** at the address of: written on envelopes. Usual abbrev.: **c/o. 13 in** (*or* **into**) **care.** *Brit.* made the legal responsibility of a local authority by order of a court. [OE *cearu* (n), *cearian* (vb), of Gmc origin]
▸'**carer** *n*

CARE (kɛə) *n acronym for:* **1** Cooperative for American Relief Everywhere. **2** communicated authenticity, regard, empathy: the three qualities believed to be essential in the therapist practising client-centred therapy.

care and maintenance *n Commerce.* the state of a building, ship, machinery, etc., that is not in current use although it is kept in good condition to enable it to be brought into service quickly if there is a demand for it. Abbrev.: **C & M.**

careen (kəˈriːn) *vb* **1** to sway or cause to sway over to one side. **2** (*tr*) *Naut.* to cause (a vessel) to keel over to one side, esp. in order to clean its bottom. **3** (*intr*) *Naut.* (of a vessel) to keel over to one side. [C17: from F, from It., from L *carīna* keel]
▸**ca'reenage** *n*

career ⓣ (kəˈrɪə) *n* **1** a path through life or history. **2a** a profession or occupation chosen as one's life's work. **2b** (*as modifier*): *a career diplomat.* **3** a course or path, esp. a headlong one. ◆ *vb* **4** (*intr*) to rush in an uncontrolled way. [C16: from F, from LL *carrāria* carriage road, from L *carrus* two-wheeled wagon]

career girl *or* **woman** *n* a woman, often unmarried, who follows a profession.

careerist (kəˈrɪərɪst) *n* a person who seeks to advance his career by any possible means.

carefree ⓣ ('kɛəˌfriː) *adj* without worry or responsibility.
▸'**care,freeness** *n*

careful ⓣ ('kɛəfʊl) *adj* **1** cautious in attitude or action. **2** painstaking in one's work; exact and thorough. **3** (*usually postpositive;* foll. by *of, in,* or *about*) solicitous; protective. **4** *Brit.* mean or miserly.
▸'**carefully** *adv* ▸'**carefulness** *n*

careless ⓣ ('kɛəlɪs) *adj* **1** done with or acting with insufficient attention. **2** (often foll. by *in, of,* or *about*) unconcerned in attitude or action. **3** (*usually prenominal*) carefree. **4** (*usually prenominal*) unstudied: *careless elegance.*
▸'**carelessly** *adv* ▸'**carelessness** *n*

caress ⓣ (kəˈrɛs) *n* **1** a gentle touch or embrace, esp. one given to show affection. ◆ *vb* **2** (*tr*) to touch or stroke gently with or as with affection. [C17: from F, from It., from L *cārus* dear]

caret ('kærɪt) *n* a symbol (‸) used to indicate the place in written or printed matter at which something is to be inserted. [C17: from L, lit.: there is missing, from *carēre* to lack]

caretaker ⓣ ('kɛəˌteɪkə) *n* **1** a person who looks after a place or thing, esp. in the owner's absence. **2** (*modifier*) interim: *a caretaker government.*

careworn ⓣ ('kɛəˌwɔːn) *adj* showing signs of care, stress, worry, etc.: *a careworn face.*

cargo ⓣ ('kɑːgəʊ) *n, pl* **cargoes** *or esp. US* **cargos. 1a** goods carried by a ship, aircraft, or other vehicle; freight. **1b** (*as modifier*): *a cargo vessel.* **2** any load: *a cargo of new arrivals.* [C17: from Sp.: from *cargar* to load, from LL, from L *carrus* CAR]

Carib ('kærɪb) *n* **1** (*pl* **Caribs** *or* **Carib**) a member of a group of American Indian peoples of NE South America and the Lesser Antilles. **2** the

THESAURUS

care *vb* **1 = be concerned**, be bothered, be interested, mind **2, 3** *foll. by* **for = like**, be fond of, desire, enjoy, find congenial, love, prize, take to, want **4** *foll. by* **for = look after**, attend, foster, mind, minister to, nurse, protect, provide for, tend, watch over ◆ *n* **7, 11 = caution**, attention, carefulness, circumspection, consideration, direction, forethought, heed, management, meticulousness, pains, prudence, regard, vigilance, watchfulness **8 = protection**, charge, control, custody, guardianship, keeping, management, ministration, supervision, ward **9, 10 = worry**, affliction, anxiety, burden, concern, disquiet, hardship, interest, perplexity, pressure, responsibility, solicitude, stress, tribulation, trouble, vexation, woe
Antonyms *n* ≠ **caution:** abandon, carelessness, heedlessness, inattention, indifference, laxity, laxness, neglect, negligence, unconcern ≠ **worry:** pleasure, relaxation

career *n* **2a = occupation**, calling, employment, life's work, livelihood, pursuit, vocation **3 = progress**, course, passage, path, procedure, race, walk ◆ *vb* **4 = rush**, barrel (along) (*inf.*, *chiefly US & Canad.*), bolt, burn rubber (*inf.*), dash, hurtle, race, speed, tear

carefree *adj* **= untroubled**, airy, blithe, breezy, buoyant, careless, cheerful, cheery, chirpy (*inf.*), easy-going, halcyon, happy, happy-go-lucky, insouciant, jaunty, light-hearted, lightsome (*arch.*), radiant, sunny
Antonyms *adj* blue, careworn, cheerless, dejected, depressed, desolate, despondent, down, down in the dumps (*inf.*), gloomy, low, melancholy, miserable, sad, unhappy, worried

careful *adj* **1 = cautious**, accurate, attentive, chary, circumspect, conscientious, discreet, fastidious, heedful, painstaking, precise, prudent, punctilious, scrupulous, thoughtful, thrifty **2 = thorough**, conscientious, meticulous, painstaking, particular, precise
Antonyms *adj* abandoned, careless, casual, inaccurate, inattentive, inexact, neglectful, negligent, reckless, remiss, slovenly, thoughtless, unconcerned, untroubled

careless *adj* **1 = slapdash**, cavalier, inaccurate, irresponsible, lackadaisical, neglectful, offhand, slipshod, sloppy (*inf.*) **2 = negligent**, absent-minded, cursory, forgetful, hasty, heedless, incautious, inconsiderate, indiscreet, perfunctory, regardless, remiss, thoughtless, unconcerned, unguarded, unmindful, unthinking **4 = nonchalant**, artless, casual, unstudied
Antonyms *adj* ≠ **slapdash:** accurate, careful, neat, orderly, painstaking, tidy ≠ **negligent:** alert, anxious, attentive, careful, cautious, concerned, correct, on the ball (*inf.*), wary, watchful

carelessness *n* **1, 2 = negligence**, inaccuracy, inattention, inconsiderateness, indiscretion, irresponsibility, laxity, laxness, neglect, omission, remissness, slackness, sloppiness (*inf.*), thoughtlessness

caress *n* **1 = stroke**, cuddle, embrace, fondling, hug, kiss, pat ◆ *vb* **2 = stroke**, cuddle, embrace, fondle, hug, kiss, neck (*inf.*), nuzzle, pet

caretaker *n* **1 = warden**, concierge, curator, custodian, janitor, keeper, porter, superintendent, watchman ◆ *modifier* **2 = temporary**, holding, interim, short-term

careworn *adj* **= stressed**, heavy-laden, overburdened

cargo *n* **1a, 2 = load**, baggage, consignment, contents, freight, goods, lading, merchandise, shipment, tonnage, ware family of languages spoken by these peoples. [C16: from Sp. *Caribe*, from Amerind]

Caribbean (ˌkærɪˈbiːən) *adj* **1** of the Caribbean Sea and its islands. **2** of the Carib or any of their languages. ◆ *n* **3** the Caribbean Sea. **4** a member of any of the peoples inhabiting the islands of the Caribbean Sea, such as a West Indian or a Carib.

caribou (ˈkærɪˌbuː) *n, pl* **caribou** *or* **caribous.** a large North American reindeer. [C18: from Canad. F, of Algonquian origin]

caricature ⓣ (ˈkærɪkəˌtjʊə) *n* **1** a pictorial, written, or acted representation of a person, which exaggerates his characteristic traits for comic effect. **2** an inadequate or inaccurate imitation. ◆ *vb* **caricatures, caricaturing, caricatured. 3** (*tr*) to represent in caricature or produce a caricature of. [C18: from It. *caricatura* a distortion, from *caricare* to load, exaggerate]
▸ˈ**caricaˌturist** *n*

CARICOM (ˈkærɪˌkɒm) *n acronym for* Caribbean Community and Common Market.

caries (ˈkɛəriːz) *n, pl* **caries.** progressive decay of a bone or a tooth. [C17: from L: decay]

carillon (kəˈrɪljən) *n Music.* **1** a set of bells usually hung in a tower. **2** a tune played on such bells. **3** a mixture stop on an organ giving the effect of a bell. [C18: from F: set of bells, from OF *quarregnon*, ult. from L *quattuor* four]

carina (kəˈriːnə, -ˈraɪ-) *n, pl* **carinae** (-niː) *or* **carinas.** a keel-like part or ridge, as in the breastbone of birds or the fused lower petals of a leguminous flower. [C18: from L: keel]

carinate (ˈkærɪˌneɪt) *or* **carinated** *adj Biol.* having a keel or ridge. [C17: from L *carīnāre*, from *carīna* keel]

caring ⓣ (ˈkɛərɪŋ) *adj* **1** showing care and compassion: *a caring attitude.* **2** of or relating to professional social or medical care: *nursing is a caring job.* ◆ *n* **3** the practice of providing care.

carioca (ˌkærɪˈəʊkə) *n* **1** a Brazilian dance similar to the samba. **2** a piece of music for this dance. [C19: from Brazilian Port.]

cariogenic (ˌkɛərɪəʊˈdʒɛnɪk) *adj* (of a substance) producing caries of the teeth.

cariole *or* **carriole** (ˈkærɪˌəʊl) *n* **1** a small open two-wheeled horse-drawn vehicle. **2** a covered cart. [C19: from F, ult. from L *carrus*; see CAR]

carious (ˈkɛərɪəs) *or* **cariose** (ˈkɛərɪˌəʊz) *adj* (of teeth or bone) affected with caries; decayed.

carl *or* **carle** (kɑːl) *n Arch. or Scot.* another word for **churl.** [OE, from ON *karl*]

Carlovingian (ˌkɑːləʊˈvɪndʒɪən) *adj, n History.* a variant of **Carolingian.**

carmagnole (ˌkɑːmənˈjəʊl) *n* **1** a dance and song popular during the French Revolution. **2** the costume worn by many French Revolutionaries. [C18: from F, prob. after *Carmagnola*, Italy]

Carmelite (ˈkɑːməˌlaɪt) *n RC Church.* **1** a member of an order of mendicant friars founded about 1154. **2** a member of a corresponding order of nuns founded in 1452, noted for its austere rule. ◆ *adj* **3** of or relating to either of these orders. [C14: from F, after Mount *Carmel*, in Palestine, where the order was founded]

carminative (ˈkɑːmɪnətɪv) *adj* **1** able to relieve flatulence. ◆ *n* **2** a carminative drug. [C15: from F, from L *carmināre* to card wool]

carmine (ˈkɑːmaɪn) *n* **1a** a vivid red colour. **1b** (*as adj*): *carmine paint.* **2** a pigment of this colour obtained from cochineal. [C18: from Med. L *carmīnus*, from Ar. *qirmiz* KERMES]

carnage ⓣ (ˈkɑːnɪdʒ) *n* extensive slaughter. [C16: from F, from It., from Med. L, from L *carō* flesh]

carnal ⓣ (ˈkɑːnᵊl) *adj* relating to the appetites and passions of the body. [C15: from LL, from L *carō* flesh]
▸**carˈnality** *n* ▸ˈ**carnally** *adv*

carnal knowledge *n Chiefly law.* sexual intercourse.

carnation (kɑːˈneɪʃən) *n* **1** Also called: **clove pink.** a Eurasian plant cultivated in many varieties for its white, pink, or red flowers, which have a fragrant scent of cloves. **2** the flower of this plant. **3a** a pink or reddish-pink colour. **3b** (*as adj*): *a carnation dress.* [C16: from F: flesh colour, from LL, from L *carō* flesh]

carnauba (kɑːˈnaʊbə) *n* **1** Also called: **wax palm.** a Brazilian fan palm. **2** Also called: **carnauba wax.** the wax obtained from the young leaves of this tree. [from Brazilian Port., prob. of Tupi origin]

carnelian (kɑːˈniːljən) *n* a reddish-yellow translucent variety of chalcedony, used as a gemstone. [C17: var. of *cornelian*, from OF, from ?]

carnet (ˈkɑːneɪ) *n* **1** a customs licence authorizing the temporary importation of a motor vehicle. **2** an official document permitting motorists to cross certain frontiers. [F: notebook, from OF, ult. from L *quaternī* four at a time]

carnival ⓣ (ˈkɑːnɪvᵊl) *n* **1a** a festive period marked by merrymaking, etc.: esp. in some Roman Catholic countries, the period just before Lent. **1b** (*as modifier*): *a carnival atmosphere.* **2** a travelling fair having sideshows, rides, etc. **3** a show or display arranged as an amusement. **4** *Austral.* a sports meeting. [C16: from It., from OIt. *carnelevare* a removing of meat (referring to the Lenten fast)]

carnivore (ˈkɑːnɪˌvɔː) *n* **1** any of an order of mammals having large pointed canine teeth specialized for eating flesh. The order includes cats, dogs, bears, and weasels. **2** any other animal or any plant that feeds on animals. **3** *Inf.* an aggressively ambitious person. [C19: prob. back formation from CARNIVOROUS]

carnivorous (kɑːˈnɪvərəs) *adj* **1** (esp. of animals) feeding on flesh. **2** (of plants such as the pitcher plant and sundew) able to trap and digest insects. **3** of or relating to the carnivores. **4** *Inf.* aggressively ambitious or reactionary. [C17: from L, from *carō* flesh + *vorāre* to consume]
▸**carˈnivorousness** *n*

carob (ˈkærəb) *n* **1** an evergreen Mediterranean tree with compound leaves and edible pods. **2** the long blackish sugary pod of this tree, used for animal fodder and sometimes for human food. [C16: from OF, from Med. L *carrūbium*, from Ar. *al kharrūbah*]

carol ⓣ (ˈkærəl) *n* **1** a joyful hymn or religious song, esp. one (a **Christmas carol**) celebrating the birth of Christ. ◆ *vb* **carols, carolling, carolled** *or US* **carols, caroling, caroled. 2** (*intr*) to sing carols at Christmas. **3** to sing (something) in a joyful manner. [C13: from OF, from ?]

Caroline (ˈkærəˌlaɪn) *or* **Carolean** (ˌkærəˈliːən) *adj* characteristic of or relating to Charles I or Charles II (kings of England, Scotland, and Ireland), the society over which they ruled, or their government. Also called: **Carolinian.**

Carolingian (ˌkærəˈlɪndʒɪən) *adj* **1** of or relating to the Frankish dynasty founded by Pepin the Short which ruled in France from 751–987 A.D. and in Germany until 911 A.D. ◆ *n* **2** a member of the dynasty of the Carolingian Franks. ◆ Also: **Carlovingian, Carolinian.**

Carolinian (ˌkærəˈlɪnɪən) *adj, n* a variant of **Caroline** or **Carolingian.**

carom (ˈkærəm) *n Billiards.* another word (esp. US & Canad.) for **cannon** (sense 5). [C18: from earlier *carambole* (taken as *carom ball*), from Sp. *carambola* a CARAMBOLA]

carotene (ˈkærəˌtiːn) *or* **carotin** (ˈkærətɪn) *n* any of four orange-red isomers of a hydrocarbon present in many plants and converted to vitamin A in the liver. [C19 *carotin*, from L *carōta* CARROT]

carotenoid *or* **carotinoid** (kəˈrɒtɪˌnɔɪd) *n* any of a group of red or yellow pigments, including carotenes, found in plants and certain animal tissues.

carotid (kəˈrɒtɪd) *n* **1** either of the two principal arteries that supply blood to the head and neck. ◆ *adj* **2** of either of these arteries. [C17: from F, from Gk, from *karoun* to stupefy; so named because pressure on them produced unconsciousness]

carousal (kəˈraʊzᵊl) *n* a merry drinking party.

carouse ⓣ (kəˈraʊz) *vb* **carouses, carousing, caroused. 1** (*intr*) to have a merry drinking spree. ◆ *n* **2** another word for **carousal.** [C16: via F *carrousser* from G (*trinken*) *gar aus* (to drink) right out]
▸**caˈrouser** *n*

carousel (ˌkærəˈsɛl, -ˈzɛl) *n* **1** a circular tray in which slides for a projector are held in slots from which they can be released in turn. **2** a revolving luggage conveyor, as at an airport. **3** *US and Canad.* a merry-go-round. **4** *History.* a tournament in which horsemen took part in races. [C17: from F, from It. *carosello*, from ?]

carp[1] (kɑːp) *n, pl* **carp** *or* **carps. 1** a freshwater food fish having one long dorsal fin, and two barbels on each side of the mouth. **2** a cyprinid. [C14: from OF *carpe*, of Gmc origin]

carp[2] ⓣ (kɑːp) *vb* (*intr*; often foll. by *at*) to complain or find fault. [C13: from ON *karpa* to boast]
▸ˈ**carper** *n* ▸ˈ**carping** *adj, n*

-carp *n combining form.* (in botany) fruit or a reproductive structure that develops into a particular part of the fruit: *epicarp.* [from NL *-carpium*, from Gk *-karpion*, from *karpos* fruit]

carpal (ˈkɑːpᵊl) *n* **a** any bone of the wrist. **b** (*as modifier*): *carpal bones.* [C18: from NL *carpālis*, from Gk *karpos* wrist]

car park *n* an area or building reserved for parking cars. Usual US and Canad. term: **parking lot.**

carpe diem *Latin.* (ˈkɑːpɪ ˈdiːɛm) *sentence substitute.* enjoy the pleasures of the moment, without concern for the future. [lit.: seize the day!]

carpel (ˈkɑːpᵊl) *n* the female reproductive organ of flowering plants,

THESAURUS

caricature *n* **1** = **parody**, burlesque, cartoon, distortion, farce, lampoon, mimicry, pasquinade, satire, send-up (*Brit. inf.*), takeoff (*inf.*), travesty ◆ *vb* **3** = **parody**, burlesque, distort, lampoon, mimic, mock, ridicule, satirize, send up (*Brit. inf.*), take off (*inf.*)

caring *adj* **1** = **compassionate**, considerate, kindly, loving, receptive, responsive, sensitive, soft, softhearted, sympathetic, tender, tenderhearted, touchy-feely (*inf.*), warm, warmhearted

carnage *n* = **slaughter**, blood bath, bloodshed, butchery, havoc, holocaust, massacre, mass murder, murder, shambles

carnal *adj* = **sexual**, amorous, animal, erotic, fleshly, impure, lascivious, lecherous, lewd, libidinous, licentious, lustful, prurient, randy (*inf., chiefly Brit.*), raunchy (*sl.*), salacious, sensual, sensuous, sexy (*inf.*), steamy (*inf.*), unchaste, voluptuous, wanton

carnality *n* = **lust**, bestiality, corporeality, fleshliness, lechery, lustfulness, prurience, salaciousness, sensuality, voluptuousness, worldliness

carnival *n* **1** = **festival**, celebration, fair, fête, fiesta, gala, holiday, jamboree, jubilee, Mardi Gras, merrymaking, revelry

carol *n* **1** = **song**, canticle, canzonet, chorus, ditty, hymn, lay, noel, strain

carouse *vb* **1** = **drink**, bend the elbow (*inf.*), bevvy (*dialect*), booze (*inf.*), imbibe, make merry, quaff, roister, wassail

carp[2] *vb, often foll. by* **at** = **find fault**, beef (*sl.*), cavil, censure, complain, criticize, knock (*inf.*), nag, pick holes, quibble, reproach

Antonyms *vb* admire, applaud, approve, commend, compliment, extol, laud (*literary*), pay tribute to, praise, sing the praises of, speak highly of

consisting of an ovary, style, and stigma. [C19: from NL *carpellum*, from Gk *karpos* fruit]
▸'**carpellary** *adj*

carpenter ❶ ('kɑːpɪntə) *n* **1** a person skilled in woodwork, esp. in buildings, ships, etc. ◆ *vb* **2** (*intr*) to do the work of a carpenter. **3** (*tr*) to make or fit together by or as if by carpentry. [C14: from Anglo-F, from L, from *carpentum* wagon]

carpentry ('kɑːpɪntrɪ) *n* **1** the art or technique of working wood. **2** the work produced by a carpenter; woodwork.

carpet ('kɑːpɪt) *n* **1** a heavy fabric for covering floors. **2** a covering like a carpet: *a carpet of leaves*. **3 on the carpet.** *Inf.* **3a** before authority to be reproved. **3b** under consideration. ◆ *vb* **carpets, carpeting, carpeted.** (*tr*) **4** to cover with or as if with a carpet. **5** *Inf.* to reprimand. [C14: from OF, from OIt., from LL *carpeta*, from L *carpere* to pluck, card]

carpetbag ('kɑːpɪtˌbæg) *n* a travelling bag originally made of carpeting.

carpetbagger ('kɑːpɪtˌbægə) *n* **1** a politician who seeks public office in a locality where he has no real connections. **2** *Brit.* a person who makes a short-term investment in a mutual savings or life-assurance organization in order to benefit from free shares issued following the organization's conversion to a public limited company.

carpet beetle *or US* **carpet bug** *n* any of various beetles, the larvae of which feed on carpets, furnishing fabrics, etc.

carpet bombing *n* systematic intensive bombing of an area.

carpeting ('kɑːpɪtɪŋ) *n* carpet material or carpets in general.

carpet slipper *n* one of a pair of slippers, originally one made with woollen uppers resembling carpeting.

carpet snake *or* **python** *n* a large nonvenomous Australian snake having a carpet-like pattern on its back.

carpet-sweeper *n* a household device with a revolving brush for sweeping carpets.

car phone *n* a telephone that operates by cellular radio for use in a car.

carpo- *combining form.* (in botany) indicating fruit or a seed. [from Gk *karpos* fruit]

carport ('kɑːˌpɔːt) *n* a shelter for a car usually consisting of a roof built out from the side of a building and supported by posts.

-carpous *or* **-carpic** *adj combining form.* (in botany) indicating a certain kind or number of fruit: *apocarpous*. [from NL, from Gk *karpos* fruit]

carpus ('kɑːpəs) *n, pl* **carpi** (-paɪ). **1** the technical name for **wrist. 2** the eight small bones of the human wrist. [C17: NL, from Gk *karpos*]

carrack ('kærək) *n* a galleon sailed in the Mediterranean as a merchantman in the 15th and 16th centuries. [C14: from OF *caraque*, from OSp. *carraca*, from Ar. *qarāqīr* merchant ships]

carrageen, carragheen, *or* **carageen** ('kærəˌgiːn) *n* an edible red seaweed of North America and N Europe. Also called: **Irish moss.** [C19: from *Carragheen*, near Waterford, Ireland]

carrageenan, carragheenan, *or* **carageenan** (ˌkærə'giːnən) *n* a carbohydrate extracted from carrageen, used to make a beverage, medicine, and jelly, and as an emulsifying and gelling agent (**E407**) in various processed desserts and drinks.

carrel *or* **carrell** ('kærəl) *n* a small individual study room or private desk, often in a library. [C20: from obs. *carrel* study area, var. of CAROL]

carriage ❶ ('kærɪdʒ) *n* **1** *Brit.* a railway coach for passengers. **2** the manner in which a person holds and moves his head and body. **3** a four-wheeled horse-drawn vehicle for persons. **4** the moving part of a machine that bears another part: *a typewriter carriage*. **5** ('kærɪdʒ, 'kærɪɪdʒ). **5a** the act of conveying. **5b** the charge made for conveying (esp. in **carriage forward,** when the charge is to be paid by the receiver, and **carriage paid**). [C14: from OF *cariage*, from *carier* to CARRY]

carriage clock *n* a portable clock, usually in a rectangular case, originally used by travellers.

carriage trade *n* trade from the wealthy part of society.

carriageway ('kærɪdʒˌweɪ) *n Brit.* the part of a road along which traffic passes in a single line moving in one direction only: *a dual carriageway*.

carrier ('kærɪə) *n* **1** a person, thing, or organization employed to carry goods, etc. **2** a mechanism by which something is carried or moved, such as a device for transmitting rotation from the faceplate of a lathe to the workpiece. **3** *Pathol.* another name for **vector** (sense 3). **4** *Pathol.* a person or animal that, without having any symptoms of a disease, is capable of transmitting it to others. **5** Also called: **charge carrier.** *Physics.* an electron or hole that carries the charge in a conductor or semiconductor. **6** short for **carrier wave. 7** *Chem.* **7a** an inert substance used to absorb a dyestuff, transport a sample through a gas chromatography column, contain a radioisotope for radioactive tracing, etc. **7b** a substance used to support a catalyst. **8** See **aircraft carrier.**

carrier bag *n Brit.* a large paper or plastic bag for carrying shopping, etc.

carrier pigeon *n* any homing pigeon, esp. one used for carrying messages.

carrier wave *n Radio.* a wave modulated in amplitude, frequency, or phase in order to carry a signal in radio transmission, etc.

carriole ('kærɪˌəʊl) *n* a variant spelling of **cariole.**

carrion ('kærɪən) *n* **1** dead and rotting flesh. **2** (*modifier*) eating carrion. **3** something rotten. [C13: from Anglo-F *caroine*, ult. from L *carō* flesh]

carrion crow *n* a common predatory and scavenging European crow similar to the rook but having a pure black bill.

carrot ('kærət) *n* **1** an umbelliferous plant with finely divided leaves. **2** the long tapering orange root of this plant, eaten as a vegetable. **3a** something offered as a lure or incentive. **3b carrot and stick.** reward and punishment as methods of persuasion. [C16: from OF *carotte*, from LL *carōta*, from Gk *karōton*]

carroty ('kærətɪ) *adj* **1** of a reddish or yellowish-orange colour. **2** having red hair.

carrousel (ˌkærə'sɛl, -'zɛl) *n* a variant spelling of **carousel.**

carry ❶ ('kærɪ) *vb* **carries, carrying, carried.** (*mainly tr*) **1** (*also intr*) to take or bear (something) from one place to another. **2** to transfer for consideration: *he carried his complaints to her superior*. **3** to have on one's person: *he carries a watch*. **4** (*also intr*) to be transmitted or serve as a medium for transmitting: *sound carries over water*. **5** to bear or be able to bear the weight, pressure, or responsibility of: *her efforts carry the whole production*. **6** to have as an attribute or result: *this crime carries a heavy penalty*. **7** to bring or communicate: *to carry news*. **8** (*also intr*) to be pregnant with (young). **9** to bear (the head, body, etc.) in a specified manner: *she carried her head high*. **10** to conduct or bear (oneself) in a specified manner: *she carried herself well*. **11** to continue or extend: *the war was carried into enemy territory*. **12** to cause to move or go: *desire for riches carried him to the city*. **13** to influence, esp. by emotional appeal: *his words carried the crowd*. **14** to secure the passage of (a bill, motion, etc.). **15** to win (an election). **16** to obtain victory for (a candidate). **17** *Chiefly US.* to win a majority of votes in (a district, etc.): *the candidate carried 40 states*. **18** to capture: *our troops carried the town*. **19** (of communications media) to include as the content: *this newspaper carries no book reviews*. **20** Also (esp. US): **carry over.** *Book-keeping.* to transfer (an item) to another account, esp. to transfer to the following year's account: *to carry a loss*. **21** *Maths.* to transfer (a number) from one column of figures to the next. **22** (of a shop, trader, etc.) to keep in stock: *to carry confectionery*. **23** to support (a musical part or melody) against the other parts. **24** (*intr*) (of a ball, projectile, etc.) to travel through the air or reach a specified point: *his first drive carried to the green*. **25** *Inf.* to imbibe (alcoholic drink) without showing ill effects. **26** (*intr*) *Sl.* to have drugs on one's person. **27 carry all before (one).** to win unanimous support or approval for (oneself). **28 carry the can (for).** *Inf.* to take responsibility for some misdemeanour, etc. (on behalf of). **29 carry the day.** to be successful. ◆ *n, pl* **carries. 30** the act of carrying. **31** *US & Canad.* a portion of land over which a boat must be portaged. **32** the range of a firearm or its projectile. **33** *Golf.* the distance from where the ball is struck to where it first touches the ground. ◆ See also **carry away, carry forward,** etc. [C14 *carien*, from OF *carier* to move by vehicle, from *car*, from L *carrum* transport wagon]

carryall ('kærɪˌɔːl) *n* the usual US and Canad. name for a **holdall.**

carry away *vb* (*tr, adv*) **1** to remove forcefully. **2** (*usually passive*) to cause (a person) to lose self-control. **3** (*usually passive*) to delight: *he was carried away by the music*.

carrycot ('kærɪˌkɒt) *n* a light cot with handles, similar to but smaller than the body of a pram.

carry forward *vb* (*tr, adv*) **1** *Book-keeping.* to transfer (a balance) to the next column, etc. **2** *Tax accounting.* to apply (a legally permitted credit, esp. an operating loss) to the taxable income of following years. ◆ Also: **carry over.**

carrying-on *n, pl* **carryings-on.** *Inf.* **1** unconventional behaviour. **2** excited or flirtatious behaviour.

carry off *vb* (*tr, adv*) **1** to remove forcefully. **2** to win. **3** to handle (a situation) successfully: *he carried off the introductions well*. **4** to cause to die: *he was carried off by pneumonia*.

carry on ❶ *vb* (*adv*) **1** (*intr*) to continue or persevere. **2** (*tr*) to conduct: *to carry on a business*. **3** (*intr*; often foll. by *with*) *Inf.* to have an affair. **4** (*intr*) *Inf.* to cause a fuss or commotion. ◆ *n* **carry-on. 5** *Inf., chiefly Brit.* a fuss.

carry out ❶ *vb* (*tr, adv*) **1** to perform or cause to be implemented: *I wish he could afford to carry out his plan*. **2** to accomplish. ◆ *n* **carry-out.** *Chiefly Scot.* **3** alcohol bought at an off-licence, etc., for consumption elsewhere. **4a** a shop which sells hot cooked food for consumption away from the premises. **4b** (*as modifier*): *a carry-out shop*.

THESAURUS

carpenter *n* **1** = **joiner**, cabinet-maker, woodworker

carping[2] *adj* = **fault-finding**, captious, cavilling, critical, grouchy (*inf.*), hard to please, hypercritical, nagging, nit-picking (*inf.*), on someone's back (*inf.*), picky (*inf.*), reproachful

carriage *n* **1, 3** = **vehicle**, cab, coach, conveyance **2** = **bearing**, air, behaviour, comportment, conduct, demeanour, deportment, gait, manner, mien, posture, presence **5a** = **transportation**, carrying, conveyance, conveying, delivery, freight, transport

carry *vb* **1** = **transport**, bear, bring, conduct, convey, fetch, haul, hump, lift, lug, move, relay, take, tote (*inf.*), transfer, transmit **5** = **support**, bear, bolster, hold up, maintain, shoulder, stand, suffer, sustain, underpin, uphold **7, 19, 22** = **include**, broadcast, communicate, display, disseminate, give, offer, publish, release, stock **14, 15, 18** = **win**, accomplish, capture, effect, gain, secure

carry on *vb* **1** = **continue**, endure, keep going, last, maintain, perpetuate, persevere, persist **2** = **run**, administer, manage, operate **4** *Informal* = **make a fuss**, create (*sl.*), misbehave, raise Cain ◆ *n* **carry-on 5** *Informal, chiefly Brit.* = **fuss**, commotion, disturbance, fracas, hubbub, racket, rumpus, shindy (*inf.*), tumult

carry out *vb* **1, 2** = **perform**, accomplish, achieve, carry through, consummate, discharge, effect, execute, fulfil, implement, realize

carry over *vb (tr, adv)* **1** to postpone or defer. **2** *Book-keeping, tax accounting.* another term for **carry forward.** ◆ *n* **carry-over. 3** something left over for future use, esp. goods to be sold. **4** *Book-keeping.* a sum or balance carried forward.

carry through *vb (tr, adv)* **1** to bring to completion. **2** to enable to endure (hardship, trouble, etc.); support.

carse (kɑːs) *n Scot.* a riverside area of flat fertile alluvium. [C14: from ?]

carsick ('kɑːˌsɪk) *adj* nauseated from riding in a car or other vehicle.
▸**'carˌsickness** *n*

cart (kɑːt) *n* **1** a heavy open vehicle, usually having two wheels and drawn by horses. **2** a light open horse-drawn vehicle for business or pleasure. **3** any small vehicle drawn or pushed by hand, such as a trolley. **4 in the cart. 4a** in an awkward situation. **4b** in the lurch. **5 put the cart before the horse.** to reverse the usual order of things. ◆ *vb* **6** *(usually tr)* to use or draw a cart to convey (goods, etc.). **7** *(tr)* to carry with effort: *to cart wood home.* [C13: from ON *kartr*]
▸**'carter** *n*

cartage ('kɑːtɪdʒ) *n* the process or cost of carting.

carte blanche ('kɑːt 'blɑːntʃ) *n, pl* **cartes blanches** ('kɑːts 'blɑːntʃ). complete discretion or authority: *the government gave their negotiator carte blanche.* [C18: from F: blank paper]

cartel (kɑː'tɛl) *n* **1** Also called: **trust.** a collusive association of independent enterprises formed to monopolize production and distribution of a product or service. **2** *Politics.* an alliance of parties to further common aims. [C20: from G *Kartell,* from F, from It. *cartello* public notice, dim. of *carta* CARD[1]]

Cartesian (kɑː'tiːzɪən) *adj* **1** of or relating to the works of Descartes, 17th-century French philosopher and mathematician. **2** of or used in Descartes' mathematical system.
▸**Car'tesianˌism** *n*

Cartesian coordinates *pl n* a system of coordinates that defines the location of a point in space in terms of its perpendicular distance from each of a set of mutually perpendicular axes.

carthorse ('kɑːtˌhɔːs) *n* a large heavily built horse kept for pulling carts or carriages.

Carthusian (kɑː'θjuːzɪən) *RC Church.* ◆ *n* **1** a member of a monastic order founded by Saint Bruno in 1084 near Grenoble, France. ◆ *adj* **2** of or relating to this order: *a Carthusian monastery.* [C14: from Med. L, from L *Carthusia* Chartreuse, near Grenoble]

cartilage ('kɑːtɪlɪdʒ) *n* a tough elastic tissue composing most of the embryonic skeleton of vertebrates. In the adults of higher vertebrates it is mostly converted into bone. Nontechnical name: **gristle.** [C16: from L *cartilāgō*]
▸**cartilaginous** (ˌkɑːtɪ'lædʒɪnəs) *adj*

cartilaginous fish *n* any of a class of fish including the sharks and rays, having a skeleton composed entirely of cartilage.

cartload ('kɑːtˌləud) *n* the amount a cart can hold.

cart off, away, *or* **out** *vb (tr, adv) Inf.* to carry or remove brusquely or by force.

cartogram ('kɑːtəˌgræm) *n* a map showing statistical information in diagrammatic form. [C20: from F *cartogramme,* from *carte* map, CHART]

cartography (kɑː'tɒgrəfɪ) *n* the art, technique, or practice of compiling or drawing maps or charts. [C19: from F *cartographie,* from *carte* map, CHART]
▸**car'tographer** *n* ▸**cartographic** (ˌkɑːtə'græfɪk) *or* **ˌcarto'graphical** *adj*

carton ❶ ('kɑːtᵊn) *n* **1** a cardboard box for containing goods. **2** a container of waxed paper in which liquids, such as milk, are sold. [C19: from F, from It. *cartone* pasteboard, from *carta* CARD[1]]

cartoon ❶ (kɑː'tuːn) *n* **1** a humorous or satirical drawing, esp. one in a newspaper or magazine. **2** Also called: **comic strip.** a sequence of drawings in a newspaper, magazine, etc. **3** See **animated cartoon. 4** a full-size preparatory sketch for a fresco, tapestry, mosaic, etc. [C17: from It. *cartone* pasteboard]
▸**car'toonist** *n*

cartouche *or* **cartouch** (kɑː'tuːʃ) *n* **1** a carved or cast ornamental tablet or panel in the form of a scroll. **2** an oblong figure enclosing characters expressing royal or divine names in Egyptian hieroglyphics. [C17: from F: scroll, cartridge, from It., from *carta* paper]

cartridge ❶ ('kɑːtrɪdʒ) *n* **1** a metal casing containing an explosive charge and often a bullet, for a rifle or other small arms. **2** a stylus unit of a record player, either containing a piezoelectric crystal (**crystal cartridge**) or an induction coil that moves in the field of a permanent magnet (**magnetic cartridge**). **3** an enclosed container of magnetic tape, photographic film, ink, etc., for insertion into a tape deck, camera, pen, etc. **4** *Computing.* a removable unit in a computer, such as an integrated circuit, containing software. [C16: from earlier *cartage,* var. of CARTOUCHE (cartridge)]

cartridge belt *n* a belt with pockets for cartridge clips or loops for cartridges.

cartridge clip *n* a metallic container holding cartridges for an automatic firearm.

cartridge paper *n* **1** an uncoated type of drawing or printing paper. **2** a heavy paper used in making cartridges or as drawing or printing paper.

cartwheel ('kɑːtˌwiːl) *n* **1** the wheel of a cart, usually having wooden spokes. **2** an acrobatic movement in which the body makes a revolution supported on the hands with legs outstretched.

caruncle ('kærəŋkᵊl, kə'rʌŋ-) *n* **1** a fleshy outgrowth on the heads of certain birds, such as a cock's comb. **2** an outgrowth near the hilum on the seeds of some plants. [C17: from obs. F *caruncule,* from L *caruncula* a small piece of flesh, from *carō* flesh]
▸**caruncular** (kə'rʌŋkjʊlə) *or* **ca'runculous** *adj*

carve ❶ (kɑːv) *vb* **carves, carving, carved. 1** *(tr)* to cut or chip in order to form something: *to carve wood.* **2** to form (something) by cutting or chipping: *to carve statues.* **3** to slice (meat) into pieces. ◆ See also **carve out, carve up.** [OE *ceorfan*]

carvel ('kɑːvᵊl) *n* another word for **caravel.**

carvel-built *adj* (of a vessel) having a hull with planks made flush at the seams. Cf. **clinker-built.**

carven ('kɑːvᵊn) *vb* an archaic or literary past participle of **carve.**

carve out *vb (tr, adv) Inf.* to make or create (a career): *he carved out his own future.*

carver ('kɑːvə) *n* **1** a carving knife. **2** *(pl)* a large matched knife and fork for carving meat. **3** *Brit.* a chair having arms that forms part of a set of dining chairs.

carvery ('kɑːvərɪ) *n, pl* **carveries.** an eating establishment at which customers pay a set price for unrestricted helpings from a variety of meats, salads, etc.

carve up *vb (tr, adv)* **1** to cut (something) into pieces. **2** to divide (land, etc.). ◆ *n* **carve-up. 3** *Inf.* an act or instance of dishonestly prearranging the result of a competition. **4** *Sl.* the distribution of something.

carving ❶ ('kɑːvɪŋ) *n* a figure or design produced by carving stone, wood, etc.

carving knife *n* a long-bladed knife for carving cooked meat for serving.

caryatid (ˌkærɪ'ætɪd) *n, pl* **caryatids** *or* **caryatides** (-ɪˌdiːz). a column, used to support an entablature, in the form of a draped female figure. [C16: from L, from Gk *Karuatides* priestesses of Artemis at *Karuai* (Caryae), in Laconia]

Casanova (ˌkæsə'nəuvə) *n* any man noted for his amorous adventures. [after Giovanni *Casanova,* (1725–98), It. adventurer]

casbah ('kæzbɑː) *n (sometimes cap.)* a variant spelling of **kasbah.**

cascade ❶ (kæs'keɪd) *n* **1** a waterfall or series of waterfalls over rocks. **2** something resembling this, such as folds of lace. **3** a consecutive sequence of chemical or physical processes. **4** a series of stages or devices in which each operates the next in turn. ◆ *vb* **cascades, cascading, cascaded. 5** *(intr)* to flow or fall in or like a cascade. [C17: from F, from It., ult. from L *cadere* to fall]

cascara (kæs'kɑːrə) *n* **1** Also called: **cascara sagrada.** the dried bark of the cascara buckthorn, used as a laxative and stimulant. **2** Also called: **cascara buckthorn.** a shrub or small tree of NW North America. [C19: from Sp.: bark]

case[1] ❶ (keɪs) *n* **1** a single instance or example of something. **2** an instance of disease, injury, etc. **3** a question or matter for discussion. **4** a specific condition or state of affairs; situation. **5** a set of arguments supporting a particular action, cause, etc. **6a** a person attended or served by a doctor, social worker, solicitor, etc. **6b** *(as modifier): a case study.* **7a** an action or suit at law: *he has a good case.* **7b** the evidence offered in court to support a claim. **8** *Grammar.* **8a** a set of grammatical categories of nouns, pronouns, and adjectives indicating the relation of the noun, adjective, or pronoun to other words in the sentence. **8b** any one of these categories: *the dative case.* **9** *Inf.* an eccentric. **10 in any case.** *(adv)* no matter what. **11 in case.** *(adv)* **11a** in order to allow for eventualities. **11b** *(conj)* in order to allow for the possibility that: *take your coat in case it rains.* **12 in case of.** *(prep)* in the event of. **13 in no case.** *(adv)* under no circumstances. [OE *casus* (grammatical) case, associated also with OF *cas* a happening; both from L *cāsus,* a befalling, from *cadere* to fall]

case[2] ❶ (keɪs) *n* **1a** a container, such as a box or chest. **1b** *(in combination): suitcase.* **2** an outer cover, esp. for a watch. **3** a receptacle and its contents: *a case of ammunition.* **4** *Archit.* another word for **casing** (sense 3). **5** a cover ready to be fastened to a book to form its binding. **6** *Printing.* a tray in which a compositor keeps individual metal types of a particular size and style. Cases were originally used in pairs, one (the **upper case**) for capitals, the other (the **lower case**) for small letters.

THESAURUS

carton *n* **1, 2 = box,** case, container, pack, package, packet

cartoon *n* **1, 2 = drawing,** caricature, comic strip, lampoon, parody, satire, sketch, takeoff *(inf.)* **3 = animation,** animated cartoon, animated film

cartridge *n* **1 = shell,** charge, round **3 = container,** capsule, case, cassette, cylinder, magazine

carve *vb* **1, 2 = cut,** chip, chisel, divide, engrave, etch, fashion, form, grave *(arch.),* hack, hew, incise, indent, inscribe, mould, sculpt, sculpture, slash, slice, whittle

carving *n* **= sculpture,** engraving, etching, inscription

cascade *n* **1 = waterfall,** avalanche, cataract, deluge, downpour, falls, flood, fountain, outpouring, shower, torrent ◆ *vb* **5 = flow,** descend, fall, flood, gush, overflow, pitch, plunge, pour, spill, surge, teem, tumble

case[1] *n* **1 = instance,** example, illustration, occasion, occurrence, specimen **4 = situation,** circumstance(s), condition, context, contingency, dilemma, event, plight, position, predicament, state **7a** *Law* **= lawsuit,** action, cause, dispute, proceedings, process, suit, trial

case[2] *n* **1 = container,** box, cabinet, canister, capsule, carton, cartridge, casket, chest, compact, crate, holder, receptacle, suitcase, tray, trunk **2 = covering,** capsule, casing, cover, enve-

◆ *vb* **cases, casing, cased.** (*tr*) **7** to put into or cover with a case. **8** *Sl.* to inspect carefully (esp. a place to be robbed). [C13: from OF *casse,* from L, from *capere* to take, hold]

casebook ('keɪsˌbʊk) *n* a book in which records of legal or medical cases are kept.

case-harden *vb* (*tr*) **1** *Metallurgy.* to form a hard surface layer of high carbon content on (a steel component). **2** to make callous: *experience case-hardened the judge.*

case history *n* a record of a person's background, medical history, etc.

casein ('keɪsɪɪn, -si:n) *n* a protein, precipitated from milk by the action of rennin, forming the basis of cheese. [C19: from L *cāseus* cheese + -IN]

case law *n* law established by following judicial decisions given in earlier cases. Cf. **statute law.**

caseload ('keɪsˌləʊd) *n* the number of cases constituting the work of a doctor, solicitor, social worker, etc., over a specified period.

casemate ('keɪsˌmeɪt) *n* an armoured compartment in a ship or fortification in which guns are mounted. [C16: from F, from It. *casamatta,* ?from Gk *khasmata* apertures]

casement ('keɪsmənt) *n* **1** a window frame that is hinged on one side. **2** a window containing frames hinged at the side. **3** a poetic word for **window.** [C15: prob. from OF *encassement* frame, from *encasser* to encase, from *casse* framework]

caseous ('keɪsɪəs) *adj* of or like cheese. [C17: from L *cāseus* CHEESE]

casern *or* **caserne** (kə'zɜ:n) *n* (formerly) a billet or accommodation for soldiers in a town. [C17: from F *caserne,* from OProvençal *cazerna* group of four men, ult. from L *quattuor* four]

casework ('keɪsˌwɜ:k) *n* social work based on close study of the personal histories and circumstances of individuals and families.
▸**'caseˌworker** *n*

cash[1] ➊ (kæʃ) *n* **1** banknotes and coins, esp. when readily available. **2** immediate payment for goods or services (esp. in **cash down**). **3** (*modifier*) of, for, or paid by cash: *a cash transaction.* ◆ *vb* **4** (*tr*) to obtain or pay ready money for. ◆ See also **cash in, cash up.** [C16: from OIt. *cassa* money box, from L *capsa* CASE[2]]
▸**'cashable** *adj*

cash[2] (kæʃ) *n, pl* **cash.** any of various Chinese or Indian coins of low value. [C16: from Port. *caixa,* from Tamil *kāsu,* from Sansk. *karsa* weight of gold]

cash-and-carry *adj, adv* **1** sold or operated on a basis of cash payment for merchandise that is not delivered but removed by the purchaser. ◆ *n, pl* **cash-and-carries. 2** a wholesale store, esp. for groceries, that operates on this basis. **3** an operation on a commodities futures market in which spot goods are purchased for cash and sold at a profit on a futures contract, after paying interest and storage charges.

cash-book *n Book-keeping.* a journal in which all receipts and disbursements are recorded.

cash card *n* a plastic card issued by a bank or building society enabling the holder to obtain cash from a cash dispenser.

cash cow *n* a product, acquisition, etc., that produces a steady flow of cash, esp. one with a well-known brand name commanding a high market share.

cash crop *n* a crop grown for sale rather than for subsistence.

cash desk *n* a counter or till in a shop where purchases are paid for.

cash discount *n* a discount granted to a purchaser who pays before a stipulated date.

cash dispenser *n* a computerized device outside a bank that supplies cash when the user inserts his cash card and keys in his identification number. Also called: **automated teller machine.**

cashew ('kæʃu:, kæ'ʃu:) *n* **1** a tropical American evergreen tree, bearing kidney-shaped nuts. **2** Also called: **cashew nut.** the edible nut of this tree. [C18: from Port. *cajú,* from Tupi *acajú*]

cash flow *n* **1** the movement of money into and out of a business. **2** a document that records or predicts this movement.

cashier[1] ➊ (kæ'ʃɪə) *n* **1** a person responsible for receiving payments for goods, services, etc., as in a shop. **2** an employee of a bank responsible for receiving deposits, cashing cheques, etc.: bank clerk. **3** any person responsible for handling cash in a business. [C16: from Du. or F, from *casse* money chest]

cashier[2] ➊ (kæ'ʃɪə) *vb* (*tr*) to dismiss with dishonour, esp. from the armed forces. [C16: from MDu., from OF, from L *quassāre* to QUASH]

cash in *vb* (*adv*) **1** (*tr*) to give (something) in exchange. **2** (*intr;* often foll. by *on*) *Inf.* **2a** to profit (from). **2b** to take advantage (of).

cashmere *or* **kashmir** ('kæʃmɪə) *n* **1** a fine soft wool from goats of the Kashmir area. **2a** cloth or knitted material made from this or similar wool. **2b** (*as modifier*): *a cashmere sweater.*

cash on delivery *n* a service entailing cash payment to the carrier on delivery of merchandise. Abbrev.: **COD.**

cash point *n* **1** any retail outlet at which goods are bought for cash. **2** a cash dispenser.

cash register *n* a till with a keyboard that operates a mechanism for displaying and adding the amounts of cash received in individual sales.

cash up *vb* (*intr, adv*) *Brit.* (of cashiers, shopkeepers, etc.) to add up the money taken, esp. at the end of a working day.

casing ➊ ('keɪsɪŋ) *n* **1** a protective case or cover. **2** material for a case or cover. **3** Also called: **case.** a frame containing a door or window.

casino (kə'si:nəʊ) *n, pl* **casinos. 1** a public building or room in which gaming takes place. **2** a variant spelling of **cassino.** [C18: from It., dim. of *casa* house, from L]

cask ➊ (kɑ:sk) *n* **1** a strong wooden barrel used mainly to hold alcoholic drink: *a wine cask.* **2** any barrel. **3** the quantity contained in a cask. **4** *Austral.* a lightweight cardboard container used to hold and serve wine. [C15: from Sp. *casco* helmet]

casket ➊ ('kɑ:skɪt) *n* **1** a small box or chest for valuables, esp. jewels. **2** *Chiefly US.* another word for **coffin** (sense 1). [C15: prob. from OF *cassette* little box]

casque (kæsk) *n Zool.* a helmet or a helmet-like structure, as on the bill of most hornbills. [C17: from F, from Sp. *casco*]
▸**casqued** *adj*

Cassandra (kə'sændrə) *n* **1** *Greek myth.* a daughter of Priam and Hecuba, endowed with the gift of prophecy but fated never to be believed. **2** anyone whose prophecies of doom are unheeded.

cassava (kə'sɑ:və) *n* **1** Also called: **manioc.** any of various tropical plants, esp. the widely cultivated American species (**bitter cassava, sweet cassava**). **2** a starch derived from the root of this plant: a source of tapioca. [C16: from Sp. *cazabe* cassava bread, from Taino *caçábi*]

casserole ('kæsəˌrəʊl) *n* **1** a covered dish of earthenware, glass, etc., in which food is cooked and served. **2** any food cooked and served in such a dish: *chicken casserole.* ◆ *vb* **casseroles, casseroling, casseroled. 3** to cook or be cooked in a casserole. [C18: from F, from OF *casse* ladle, from OProvençal, from LL *cattia* dipper, from Gk *kuathion,* dim. of *kuathos* cup]

cassette (kæ'sɛt) *n* **1a** a plastic container for magnetic tape, inserted into a tape deck to be played or used. **1b** (*as modifier*): *a cassette recorder.* **2** *Photog.* another term for **cartridge** (sense 3). **3** the injection of genes from one species into the fertilized egg of another species. [C18: from F: little box]

cassia ('kæsɪə) *n* **1** any of a genus of tropical plants whose pods yield **cassia pulp,** a mild laxative. See also **senna. 2** a lauraceous tree of tropical Asia. **3 cassia bark.** the cinnamon-like bark of this tree, used as a spice. [OE, from L *casia,* from Gk *kasia,* of Semitic origin]

cassino *or* **casino** (kə'si:nəʊ) *n* a card game for two to four players in which players pair cards with those exposed on the table.

Cassiopeia (ˌkæsɪə'pi:ə) *n, Latin genitive* **Cassiopeiae** (ˌkæsɪə'pi:i:). a very conspicuous W-shaped constellation near the Pole Star.

cassis (kɑ:'si:s) *n* a blackcurrant cordial. [C19: from F]

cassiterite (kə'sɪtəˌraɪt) *n* a hard heavy brownish-black mineral, the chief ore of tin. Formula: SnO_2. Also called: **tinstone.** [C19: from Gk *kassiteros* tin]

cassock ('kæsək) *n* an ankle-length garment, usually black, worn by Christian priests. [C16: from OF, from It. *casacca* a long coat, from ?]

cassowary ('kæsəˌweərɪ) *n, pl* **cassowaries.** a large flightless bird inhabiting forests in NE Australia, New Guinea, and adjacent islands, having a horny head crest, black plumage, and brightly coloured neck. [C17: from Malay *kěsuari*]

cast ➊ (kɑ:st) *vb* **casts, casting, cast.** (*mainly tr*) **1** to throw or expel with force. **2** to throw off or away: *she cast her clothes to the ground.* **3** to reject: *he cast the idea from his mind.* **4** to shed or drop: *the horse cast a shoe.* **5** to cause to appear: *to cast a shadow.* **6** to express (doubts, etc.) or cause (them) to be felt. **7** to direct (a glance, etc.): *cast your eye over this.* **8** to place, esp. violently: *he was cast into prison.* **9** (*also intr*) *Angling.* to throw (a line) into the water. **10** to draw or choose (lots). **11** to give or deposit (a vote). **12** to select (actors) to play parts in (a play, etc.). **13a** to shape (molten metal, glass, etc.) by pouring into a mould. **13b** to make (an object) by such a process. **14** (*also intr;* often foll. by *up*) to compute (figures or a total). **15** *Astrol.* to draw on (a horoscope) details concerning the positions of the planets in the signs of the zodiac at a particular time for interpretation. **16** to contrive (esp. in **cast a spell**). **17** to formulate: *he cast his work in the form of a chart.* **18** (*also intr*) to twist or cause to twist. **19** (*intr*) (of birds of prey) to eject from the crop and bill a pellet consisting of the indigestible parts of birds or animals previously eaten. **20** *Printing.* to stereotype or electrotype. **21 be cast.** *NZ.* (of sheep) to have fallen and been unable to rise. ◆ *n* **22** the act of casting or throwing. **23a** Also called: **casting.** something that is shed, dropped, or egested, such as the coil of earth left by an earthworm. **23b** another name for **pellet** (sense 4). **24** the distance an object is or

THESAURUS

lope, folder, integument, jacket, sheath, shell, wrapper, wrapping

cash[1] *n* **1, 2** = **money,** banknotes, brass (*N English dialect*), bread, bullion, change, coin, coinage, currency, dibs (*sl.*), dosh (*Brit. & Austral. sl.*), dough (*sl.*), funds, necessary (*inf.*), needful (*inf.*), notes, payment, ready (*inf.*), ready money, resources, rhino (*Brit. sl.*), shekels (*inf.*), silver, specie, spondulicks (*sl.*), tin (*sl.*), wherewithal

cashier[1] *n* = **1–3 teller,** accountant, bank clerk, banker, bursar, clerk, purser, treasurer

cashier[2] *vb* = **dismiss,** break, cast off, discard, discharge, drum out, expel, give the boot to (*sl.*)

casing *n* **1** = **covering,** cover, integument, shell

cask *n* **2** = **barrel,** cylinder, drum

casket *n* **1** = **box,** ark, case, chest, coffer, coffret, jewel box, kist (*Scot. & Northern English dialect*)

cast *vb* **1** = **throw,** chuck (*inf.*), drive, drop, fling, hurl, impel, launch, lob, pitch, project, shed, shy, sling, thrust, toss **12** = **choose,** allot, appoint, assign, name, pick, select **13** = **form,** found, model, mould, set, shape ◆ *n* **22** = **throw,** fling, lob, thrust, toss **28a** = **actors,** characters, company, dramatis personae, players, troupe **30** = **type,** air, appearance, complexion, demeanour, look, manner, mien, semblance, shade, stamp, style, tinge, tone, turn may be thrown. **25a** a throw at dice. **25b** the resulting number shown. **26** *Angling.* the act or an instance of casting a line. **27** the wide sweep made by a sheepdog to get behind a flock of sheep or by a hunting dog in search of a scent. **28a** the actors in a play collectively. **28b** (*as modifier*): *a cast list.* **29a** an object made of metal, glass, etc., that has been shaped in a molten state by being poured or pressed into a mould. **29b** the mould used to shape such an object. **30** form or appearance. **31** a sort, kind, or style. **32** a fixed twist or defect, esp. in the eye. **33** a distortion of shape. **34** *Surgery.* a rigid encircling casing, often made of plaster of Paris (**plaster cast**), for immobilizing broken bones while they heal. **35** a slight tinge or trace, as of colour. **36** fortune or stroke of fate. ◆ See also **cast about, castaway,** etc. [C13: from ON *kasta*]

cast about *or* **around** *vb* (*intr, adv*) to make a mental or visual search: *to cast about for a plot.*

castanets (ˌkæstəˈnɛts) *pl n* curved pieces of hollow wood, usually held between the fingers and thumb and made to click together: used esp. by Spanish dancers. [C17 *castanet,* from Sp. *castañeta,* dim. of *castaña* CHESTNUT]

castaway (ˈkɑːstəˌweɪ) *n* **1** a person who has been shipwrecked. ◆ *adj* (*prenominal*) **2** shipwrecked. **3** thrown away or rejected. ◆ *vb* **cast away. 4** (*tr, adv; often passive*) to cause (a ship, person, etc.) to be shipwrecked.

cast back *vb* (*adv*) to turn (the mind) to the past.

cast down Ⓣ *vb* (*tr, adv*) to make (a person) discouraged or dejected.

caste Ⓣ (kɑːst) *n* **1a** any of the four major hereditary classes, namely the **Brahman, Kshatriya, Vaisya,** and **Sudra,** into which Hindu society is divided. **1b** Also called: **caste system.** the system or basis of such classes. **2** any social class or system based on such distinctions as heredity, rank, wealth, etc. **3** the position conferred by such a system. **4** **lose caste.** *Inf.* to lose one's social position. **5** *Entomol.* any of various types of individual, such as the worker, in social insects. [C16: from Port. *casta* race, from *casto* pure, chaste, from L *castus*]

castellan (ˈkæstɪlən) *n Rare.* a keeper or governor of a castle. Also called: **chatelain.** [C14: from L *castellānus,* from *castellum* CASTLE]

castellated (ˈkæstɪˌleɪtɪd) *adj* **1** having turrets and battlements, like a castle. **2** having indentations similar to battlements: *a castellated nut.* [C17: from Med. L *castellātus,* from *castellāre* to fortify as a CASTLE]
▸ˌ**castelˈlation** *n*

caster (ˈkɑːstə) *n* **1** a person or thing that casts. **2** a bottle with a perforated top for sprinkling sugar, etc. **3** a small swivelled wheel fixed to a piece of furniture to enable it to be moved easily in any direction. ◆ Also (for senses 2, 3): **castor.**

caster sugar (ˈkɑːstə) *n* finely ground white sugar.

castigate Ⓣ (ˈkæstɪˌgeɪt) *vb* **castigates, castigating, castigated.** (*tr*) to rebuke or criticize in a severe manner. [C17: from L *castīgāre* to correct, from *castum* pure + *agere* to compel (to be)]
▸ˌ**castiˈgation** *n* ▸ˈ**castiˌgator** *n*

Castile soap (kæsˈtiːl) *n* a hard soap made from olive oil and sodium hydroxide.

Castilian (kæˈstɪljən) *n* **1** the Spanish dialect of Castile; the standard form of European Spanish. **2** a native or inhabitant of Castile. ◆ *adj* **3** denoting or of Castile, its inhabitants, or the standard form of European Spanish.

casting (ˈkɑːstɪŋ) *n* **1** an object that has been cast, esp. in metal from a mould. **2** the process of transferring molten steel to a mould. **3** the choosing of actors for a production. **4** *Zool.* another word for **cast** (sense 23) or **pellet** (sense 4).

casting couch *n Inf.* a couch on which a casting director is said to seduce girls seeking a part in a film or play.

casting vote *n* the deciding vote used by the presiding officer of an assembly when votes cast on both sides are equal in number.

cast iron Ⓣ *n* **1** iron containing so much carbon that it cannot be wrought and must be cast into shape. ◆ *adj* **cast-iron. 2** made of cast iron. **3** rigid or unyielding: *a cast-iron decision.*

castle Ⓣ (ˈkɑːsᵊl) *n* **1** a fortified building or set of buildings as in medieval Europe. **2** any fortified place or structure. **3** a large magnificent house, esp. when the present or former home of a nobleman or prince. **4** *Chess.* another name for **rook**[2]. ◆ *vb* **castles, castling, castled. 5** *Chess.* to move (the king) two squares laterally on the first rank and place the nearest rook on the square passed over by the king. [C11: from L *castellum,* dim. of *castrum* fort]

castle in the air *or* **in Spain** *n* a hope or desire unlikely to be realized; daydream.

cast-off Ⓣ *adj* **1** (*prenominal*) abandoned: *cast-off shoes.* ◆ *n* **castoff. 2** a person or thing that has been discarded or abandoned. **3** *Printing.* an estimate of the amount of space that a piece of copy will occupy. ◆ *vb* **cast off.** (*adv*) **4** to remove (mooring lines) that hold (a vessel) to a dock. **5** to knot (a row of stitches, esp. the final row) in finishing off knitted or woven material. **6** *Printing.* to estimate the amount of space that will be taken up by (a book, piece of copy, etc.).

cast on *vb* (*adv*) to form (the first row of stitches) in knitting and weaving.

castor[1] (ˈkɑːstə) *n* **1** the aromatic secretion of a beaver, used in perfumery and medicine. **2** the fur of the beaver. **3** a hat made of beaver or similar fur. [C14: from L, from Gk *kastōr* beaver]

castor[2] (ˈkɑːstə) *n* a variant spelling of **caster** (senses 2, 3).

castor oil *n* an oil obtained from the seeds of the castor-oil plant and used as a lubricant and cathartic.

castor-oil plant *n* a tall Indian plant cultivated for its poisonous seeds, from which castor oil is extracted.

castrate Ⓣ (kæˈstreɪt) *vb* **castrates, castrating, castrated.** (*tr*) **1** to remove the testicles of. **2** to deprive of vigour, masculinity, etc. **3** to remove the ovaries of; spay. [C17: from L *castrāre* to emasculate, geld]
▸**casˈtration** *n*

castrato (kæˈstrɑːtəʊ) *n, pl* **castrati** (-tɪ) *or* **castratos.** (in 17th- and 18th-century opera, etc.) a male singer whose testicles were removed before puberty, allowing the retention of a soprano or alto voice. [C18: from It., from L *castrātus* castrated]

cast steel *n* steel containing varying amounts of carbon, manganese, etc., that is cast into shape rather than wrought.

cast stone *n Building trades.* a building component, such as a block or lintel, made from cast concrete with a facing that resembles natural stone.

casual Ⓣ (ˈkæʒjʊəl) *adj* **1** happening by accident or chance. **2** offhand: *a casual remark.* **3** shallow or superficial: *a casual affair.* **4** being or seeming unconcerned or apathetic: *he assumed a casual attitude.* **5** (esp. of dress) for informal wear: *a casual coat.* **6** occasional or irregular: *a casual labourer.* ◆ *n* **7** (*usually pl*) an informal article of clothing or footwear. **8** an occasional worker. **9** (*usually pl*) a young man dressed in expensive casual clothes who goes to football matches in order to start fights. [C14: from LL *cāsuālis* happening by chance, from L *cāsus* event, from *cadere* to fall]
▸ˈ**casually** *adv* ▸ˈ**casualness** *n*

casualization *or* **casualisation** (ˌkæʒjʊəlaɪˈzeɪʃən) *n* the altering of working practices so that regular workers are re-employed on a casual or short-term basis.

casualty Ⓣ (ˈkæʒjʊəltɪ) *n, pl* **casualties. 1** a serviceman who is killed, wounded, captured, or missing as a result of enemy action. **2** a person who is injured or killed in an accident. **3** the hospital department treating victims of accidents. **4** anything that is lost, damaged, or destroyed as the result of an accident, etc.

casuarina (ˌkæzjʊəˈriːnə) *n* any of a genus of trees of Australia and the East Indies, having jointed leafless branchlets. [C19: from NL, from Malay *kĕsuari* CASSOWARY, referring to the resemblance of the branches to the feathers of the cassowary]

casuist (ˈkæzjʊɪst) *n* **1** a person, esp. a theologian, who attempts to resolve moral dilemmas by the application of general rules and the careful distinction of special cases. **2** a sophist. [C17: from F, from Sp. *casuista,* from L *cāsus* CASE[1]]
▸ˌ**casuˈistic** *or* ˌ**casuˈistical** *adj*

casuistry (ˈkæzjʊɪstrɪ) *n, pl* **casuistries. 1** *Philosophy.* the resolution of particular moral dilemmas, esp. those arising from conflicting general moral rules, by the careful distinction of the cases to which these rules apply. **2** reasoning that is specious or oversubtle.

cat[1] Ⓣ (kæt) *n* **1** Also called: **domestic cat.** a small domesticated feline mammal having thick soft fur and occurring in many breeds in which the colour of the fur varies greatly: kept as a pet or to catch rats and mice. **2** Also called: **big cat.** any of the larger felines, such as a lion or tiger. **3** any wild feline mammal such as the lynx or serval, resembling the domestic cat. **4** *Inf.* a woman who gossips maliciously. **5** *Sl.* a man. **6** *Naut.* a heavy tackle for hoisting an anchor to the cathead. **7** *Austral. sl.* a coward. **8** short for **catboat. 9** *Inf.* short for **caterpillar** (the vehicle). **10** short for **cat-o'-nine-tails. 11 a bag of cats.** *Irish inf.* a

THESAURUS

cast down *vb* = **discourage**, deject, depress, desolate, dishearten, dispirit

caste *n* **2** = **class**, estate, grade, lineage, order, race, rank, social order, species, station, status, stratum

castigate *vb* = **reprimand**, bawl out, beat, berate, blast, cane, carpet (*inf.*), censure, chasten, chastise, correct, criticize, discipline, dress down (*inf.*), excoriate, flail, flay, flog, give a rocket (*Brit. & NZ inf.*), haul over the coals (*inf.*), lambast(e), lash, put down, rap over the knuckles, read the riot act, rebuke, scold, scourge, slap on the wrist, slate (*inf., chiefly Brit.*), tear into (*inf.*), tear (someone) off a strip (*Brit. inf.*), whip

castigation *n* = **reprimand**, bawling-out (*inf.*), beating, blast, caning, censure, chastisement, condemnation, correction, criticism, discipline, dressing down (*inf.*), excoriation, flogging, put-down, whipping

cast iron *adj* **cast-iron 3** = **certain**, copper-bottomed, definite, established, fixed, guaranteed, idiot-proof, settled

castle *n* **2, 3** = **fortress**, chateau, citadel, donjon, fastness, keep, mansion, palace, peel, stronghold, tower

cast-off *adj* **1** = **unwanted**, discarded, rejected, scrapped, surplus to requirements, unneeded, useless ◆ *n* **castoff 2** = **reject**, discard, failure, outcast, second

castrate *vb* **1, 2** = **neuter**, emasculate, geld, unman

casual *adj* **1, 6** = **chance**, accidental, contingent, fortuitous, hit-and-miss *or* hit-or-miss (*inf.*), incidental, irregular, occasional, random, serendipitous, uncertain, unexpected, unforeseen, unintentional, unpremeditated **2, 4** = **careless**, apathetic, blasé, cursory, indifferent, informal, insouciant, lackadaisical, nonchalant, offhand, perfunctory, relaxed, unconcerned **5** = **informal**, non-dressy, sporty
Antonyms *adj* ≠ **chance:** arranged, deliberate, expected, fixed, foreseen, intentional, planned, premeditated ≠ **careless:** committed, concerned, direct, enthusiastic, passionate, serious ≠ **informal:** ceremonial, dressy, formal

casualty *n* **2** = **victim**, death, fatality, loss, sufferer, wounded

cat[1] *n* **1** = **feline**, gib, grimalkin, kitty (*inf.*), moggy (*sl.*), mouser, puss (*inf.*), pussy (*inf.*), tabby

bad-tempered person: *she's a real bag of cats this morning.* **12 fight like Kilkenny cats.** to fight until both parties are destroyed. **13 let the cat out of the bag.** to disclose a secret, often by mistake. **14 like a cat on a hot tin roof** *or* **on hot bricks.** in an uneasy or agitated state. **15 put, set, etc., the cat among the pigeons.** to introduce some violently disturbing new element. **16 rain cats and dogs.** to rain very heavily. ◆ *vb* **cats, catting, catted. 17** *(tr) Naut.* to hoist (an anchor) to the cathead. **18** *(intr) Sl.* to vomit. [OE *catte,* from L *cattus*]
▸**'cat,like** *adj* ▸**'cattish** *adj*

cat[2] (kæt) *adj* short for **catalytic**: *a cat cracker.*

CAT *abbrev. for* computer-assisted trading.

cat. *abbrev. for:* **1** catalogue. **2** catamaran.

cata-, kata-, *before an aspirate* **cath-,** *or before a vowel* **cat-** *prefix* **1** down; downwards; lower in position: *catadromous.* **2** indicating reversal, opposition, degeneration, etc.: *catatonia.* [from Gk *kata-,* from *kata.* In compound words borrowed from Gk *kata-* means: down, away, off, against, according to, and thoroughly]

catabolism *or* **katabolism** (kəˈtæbəˌlɪzəm) *n* a metabolic process in which complex molecules are broken down into simple ones with the release of energy; destructive metabolism. [C19: from Gk *katabolē* a throwing down, from *kata-* down + *ballein* to throw]
▸**catabolic** *or* **katabolic** (ˌkætəˈbɒlɪk) *adj*

catachresis (ˌkætəˈkriːsɪs) *n* the incorrect use of words, as *luxuriant* for *luxurious.* [C16: from L, from Gk *katakhrēsis* a misusing, from *khrēsthai* to use]
▸**catachrestic** (ˌkætəˈkrestɪk) *adj*

cataclysm **T** (ˈkætəˌklɪzəm) *n* **1** a violent upheaval, esp. of a political, military, or social nature. **2** a disastrous flood. [C17: via F from L, from Gk, from *katakluzein* to flood, from *kluzein* to wash]
▸**ˌcataˈclysmic** *or* **ˌcataˈclysmal** *adj* ▸**ˌcataˈclysmically** *adv*

catacomb **T** (ˈkætəˌkəʊm) *n* **1** *(usually pl)* an underground burial place, esp. in Rome, consisting of tunnels with niches leading off them for tombs. **2** a series of underground tunnels or caves. [OE *catacumbe,* from LL *catacumbas* (sing), name of the cemetery under the Basilica of St Sebastian, near Rome; from ?]

catadioptric (ˌkætədaɪˈɒptrɪk) *adj* involving a combination of reflecting and refracting components: *a catadioptric telescope.* [C18: from CATA- + DIOPTRIC(S)]

catadromous (kəˈtædrəməs) *adj* (of fishes such as the eel) migrating down rivers to the sea in order to breed. Cf. **anadromous.** [C19: from Gk, from *kata-* down + *dromos,* from *dremein* to run]

catafalque (ˈkætəˌfælk) *n* a temporary raised platform on which a body lies in state before or during a funeral. [C17: from F, from It. *catafalco,* from ?]

Catalan (ˈkætəˌlæn) *n* **1** a language of Catalonia, a region of NE Spain, closely related to Spanish and Provençal. **2** a native or inhabitant of Catalonia. ◆ *adj* **3** denoting or characteristic of Catalonia, its inhabitants, or their language.

catalepsy (ˈkætəˌlepsɪ) *n* a state of prolonged rigid posture, occurring for example in schizophrenia. [C16: from LL *catalēpsis,* from Gk *katalēpsis,* lit.: a seizing, from *kata-* down + *lambanein* to grasp]
▸**ˌcataˈleptic** *adj*

catalogue **T** *or US* **catalog** (ˈkætəˌlɒg) *n* **1** a complete, usually alphabetical, list of items. **2** a book, usually illustrated, containing details of items for sale. **3** a list of all the books of a library. **4** *US and Canad.* a publication issued by a university, college, etc., listing courses offered, regulations, services, etc. ◆ *vb* **catalogues, cataloguing, catalogued** *or US* **catalogs, cataloging, cataloged. 5** to compile a catalogue of (a library, etc.). **6** to add (books, items, etc.) to an existing catalogue. [C15: from LL *catalogus,* from Gk, from *katalegein* to list, from *kata-* completely + *legein* to collect]
▸**ˈcataˌloguer** *n*

catalpa (kəˈtælpə) *n* any of a genus of trees of North America and Asia, having large leaves, bell-shaped whitish flowers, and long slender pods. [C18: NL, from Carolina Creek *kutuhlpa,* lit.: winged head]

catalyse *or US* **catalyze** (ˈkætəˌlaɪz) *vb* **catalyses, catalysing, catalysed** *or US* **catalyzes, catalyzing, catalyzed.** *(tr)* to influence (a chemical reaction) by catalysis.

catalysis (kəˈtælɪsɪs) *n, pl* **catalyses** (-ˌsiːz). acceleration of a chemical reaction by the action of a catalyst. [C17: from NL, from Gk, from *kataluein* to dissolve]
▸**catalytic** (ˌkætəˈlɪtɪk) *adj*

catalyst (ˈkætəlɪst) *n* **1** a substance that increases the rate of a chemical reaction without itself suffering any permanent chemical change. **2** a person or thing that causes a change.

catalytic converter *n* a device using three-way catalysts to reduce the poisonous products of combustion (mainly oxides of nitrogen, carbon monoxide, and unburnt hydrocarbons) from the exhaust of motor vehicles.

catalytic cracker *n* a unit in an oil refinery in which mineral oils with high boiling points are converted to fuels with lower boiling points by a catalytic process.

catamaran (ˌkætəməˈræn) *n* **1** a vessel, usually a sailing vessel, with twin hulls held parallel by a rigid framework. **2** a primitive raft made of logs lashed together. **3** *Inf.* a quarrelsome woman. [C17: from Tamil *kattumaram* tied timber]

catamite (ˈkætəˌmaɪt) *n* a boy kept for homosexual purposes. [C16: from L *Catamitus,* var. of *Ganymēdēs* Ganymede, cupbearer to the gods in Gk myth]

catamount (ˈkætəˌmaʊnt) *or* **catamountain** *n* any of various felines, such as the puma or lynx. [C17: short for *cat of the mountain*]

catananche (kætənˈæŋkɪ) *n* any herb of the genus *Catananche,* having blue or yellow flowers. [C18: NL, from L, from Gk *kata* down + *anagkē* compulsion (from its use by ancient Greeks as a philtre)]

cataplexy (ˈkætəˌpleksɪ) *n* **1** sudden temporary paralysis, brought on by severe shock. **2** a state assumed by animals while shamming death. [C19: from Gk *kataplēxis* amazement, from *kataplēssein,* from *kata-* down + *plēssein* to strike]
▸**ˌcataˈplectic** *adj*

catapult **T** (ˈkætəˌpʌlt) *n* **1** a Y-shaped implement with a loop of elastic fastened to the ends of the prongs, used mainly by children for shooting stones, etc. US and Canad. name: **slingshot. 2** a war engine used formerly for hurling stones, etc. **3** a device installed in warships to launch aircraft. ◆ *vb* **4** *(tr)* to shoot forth from or as if from a catapult. **5** (foll. by *over, into,* etc.) to move precipitately. [C16: from L, from Gk *katapeltēs,* from *kata-* down + *pallein* to hurl]

cataract **T** (ˈkætəˌrækt) *n* **1** a large waterfall or rapids. **2** a downpour. **3** *Pathol.* **3a** partial or total opacity of the lens of the eye. **3b** the opaque area. [C15: from L, from Gk, from *katarassein* to dash down, from *arassein* to strike]

catarrh (kəˈtɑː) *n* inflammation of a mucous membrane with increased production of mucus, esp. affecting the nose and throat. [C16: via F from LL, from Gk, from *katarrhein* to flow down, from *kata-* down + *rhein* to flow]
▸**caˈtarrhal** *adj*

catarrhine (ˈkætəˌraɪn) *adj* **1** (of apes and Old World monkeys) having the nostrils set close together and opening to the front of the face. ◆ *n* **2** an animal with this characteristic. [C19: ult. from Gk *katarrhin* having a hooked nose, from *kata-* down + *rhis* nose]

catastrophe **T** (kəˈtæstrəfɪ) *n* **1** a sudden, extensive disaster or misfortune. **2** the denouement of a play. **3** a final decisive event, usually causing a disastrous end. [C16: from Gk, from *katastrephein* to overturn, from *strephein* to turn]
▸**catastrophic** (ˌkætəˈstrɒfɪk) *adj* ▸**ˌcataˈstrophically** *adv*

catastrophism (kəˈtæstrəˌfɪzəm) *n* **1** a former doctrine that the earth was formed by sudden divine acts rather than by evolutionary processes. **2** a modern doctrine that the evolutionary processes shaping the earth have in the past been supplemented by the effects of huge natural catastrophes.

catatonia (ˌkætəˈtəʊnɪə) *n* a form of schizophrenia characterized by stupor, with outbreaks of excitement. [C20: NL, from G *Katatonie,* from CATA- + Gk *tonos* tension]
▸**catatonic** (ˌkætəˈtɒnɪk) *adj, n*

catbird (ˈkætˌbɜːd) *n* **1** any of several North American songbirds whose call resembles the mewing of a cat. **2** any of several Australian bowerbirds having a catlike call.

catboat (ˈkætˌbəʊt) *n* a sailing vessel with a single mast, set well forward, and a large sail. Shortened form: **cat.**

cat burglar *n* a burglar who enters buildings by climbing through upper windows, etc.

catcall **T** (ˈkætˌkɔːl) *n* **1** a shrill whistle or cry expressing disapproval, as at a public meeting, etc. ◆ *vb* **2** to utter such a call (at).

catch **T** (kætʃ) *vb* **catches, catching, caught. 1** *(tr)* to take hold of so as to retain or restrain. **2** *(tr)* to take or capture, esp. after pursuit. **3** *(tr)* to ensnare or deceive. **4** *(tr)* to surprise or detect in an act: *he caught the dog rifling the larder.* **5** *(tr)* to reach with a blow: *the stone caught him on the side of the head.* **6** *(tr)* to overtake or reach in time to board. **7** *(tr)* to

THESAURUS

cataclysm *n* **1** = **disaster**, calamity, catastrophe, collapse, convulsion, debacle, upheaval

cataclysmic *adj* **1** = **disastrous**, calamitous, catastrophic, convulsionary

catacomb *n* **1** *usually pl* = **vault**, crypt, ossuary, tomb

catalogue *n* **1** = **list**, directory, gazetteer, index, inventory, record, register, roll, roster, schedule ◆ *vb* **5** = **list**, accession, alphabetize, classify, file, index, inventory, register, tabulate

catapult *n* **1** = **sling**, ballista, slingshot (*US*), trebuchet ◆ *vb* **4** = **shoot**, heave, hurl, hurtle, pitch, plunge, propel, toss

cataract *n* **1, 2** = **waterfall**, cascade, deluge, downpour, falls, Niagara, rapids, torrent **3** *Pathology* = **opacity** (*of the eye*)

catastrophe *n* **1** = **disaster**, adversity, affliction, blow, bummer (*sl.*), calamity, cataclysm, deep water, devastation, failure, fiasco, ill, meltdown (*inf.*), mischance, misfortune, mishap, reverse, tragedy, trial, trouble, whammy (*inf., chiefly US*)

catastrophic *adj* **1** = **disastrous**, calamitous, cataclysmic, devastating, tragic

catcall *n* **1** = **jeer**, boo, gibe, hiss, raspberry, whistle ◆ *vb* **2** = **jeer**, boo, deride, gibe, give the bird to, hiss, whistle

catch *vb* **1** = **seize**, clutch, get, grab, grasp, grip, lay hold of, snatch, take **2** = **capture**, apprehend, arrest, ensnare, entangle, entrap, feel one's collar (*sl.*), lift (*sl.*), nab (*inf.*), nail (*inf.*), snare, trap **4** = **discover**, catch in the act, detect, expose, find out, surprise, take unawares, unmask **8** = **contract**, develop, get, go down with, incur, succumb to, suffer from **12, 13** = **make out**, apprehend, comprehend, discern, feel, follow, get, grasp, hear, perceive, recognize, sense, take in, twig (*Brit. informal*) **14** = **attract**, bewitch, captivate, capture, charm, delight, enchant, enrapture, fascinate ◆ *n* **22** = **fastener**, bolt, clasp, clip, hasp, hook, hook and eye, latch, sneck (*dialect, chiefly Scot. & N. English*), snib (*Scot.*) **27a** *Informal* = **drawback**, disadvan-

see or hear; attend. **8** (*tr*) to be infected with: *to catch a cold.* **9** to hook or entangle or become hooked or entangled. **10** to fasten or be fastened with or as if with a latch or other device. **11** (*tr*) to attract: *she tried to catch his eye.* **12** (*tr*) to comprehend: *I didn't catch his meaning.* **13** (*tr*) to hear accurately: *I didn't catch what you said.* **14** (*tr*) to captivate or charm. **15** (*tr*) to reproduce accurately: *the painter managed to catch his model's beauty.* **16** (*tr*) to hold back or restrain: *he caught his breath in surprise.* **17** (*intr*) to become alight: *the fire won't catch.* **18** (*tr*) *Cricket.* to dismiss (a batsman) by intercepting and holding a ball struck by him before it touches the ground. **19** (*intr; often foll. by at*) **19a** to grasp or attempt to grasp. **19b** to take advantage (of): *he caught at the chance.* **20** **catch it.** *Inf.* to be scolded or reprimanded. ◆ *n* **21** the act of catching or grasping. **22** a device that catches and fastens, such as a latch. **23** anything that is caught. **24** the amount or number caught. **25** *Inf.* an eligible matrimonial prospect. **26** a check or break in the voice. **27** *Inf.* **27a** a concealed, unexpected, or unforeseen drawback. **27b** (*as modifier*): *a catch question.* **28** *Cricket.* the catching of a ball struck by a batsman before it touches the ground, resulting in him being out. **29** *Music.* a type of round having a humorous text that is often indecent or bawdy and hard to articulate. ◆ See also **catch on, catch out, catch up.** [C13 *cacchen* to pursue, from OF *cachier,* from L *captāre* to snatch, from *capere* to seize]
▸ **'catchable** *adj*

catch-22 *n* a situation in which a person is frustrated by a set of circumstances that preclude any attempt to escape from them. [C20: from the title of a novel (1961) by J. Heller]

catch-as-catch-can *n* a style of wrestling in which trips, holds below the waist, etc., are allowed.

catchfly ('kætʃˌflaɪ) *n, pl* **catchflies.** any of various plants that have sticky calyxes and stems on which insects are sometimes trapped.

catching ⓣ ('kætʃɪŋ) *adj* **1** infectious. **2** attractive; captivating.

catching pen *n Austral. & NZ.* a pen adjacent to a shearer's stand containing the sheep ready for shearing.

catchment ('kætʃmənt) *n* **1** the act of catching or collecting water. **2** a structure in which water is collected. **3** the water so collected. **4** *Brit.* the intake of a school from one catchment area.

catchment area *n* **1** the area of land bounded by watersheds draining into a river, basin, or reservoir. **2** the area from which people are allocated to a particular school, hospital, etc.

catch on ⓣ *vb* (*intr, adv*) *Inf.* **1** to become popular or fashionable. **2** to understand.

catch out *vb* (*tr, adv*) *Inf., chiefly Brit.* to trap (a person), esp. in an error.

catchpenny ('kætʃˌpɛnɪ) *adj* (*prenominal*) designed to have instant appeal, esp. in order to sell quickly: *catchpenny ornaments.*

catch phrase *n* a well-known frequently used phrase, esp. one associated with a particular group, etc.

catch up *vb* (*adv*) **1** (*tr*) to seize and take up (something) quickly. **2** (when *intr,* often foll. by *with*) to reach or pass (someone or something): *he caught him up.* **3** (*intr;* usually foll. by *on* or *with*) to make up for lost ground or deal with a backlog. **4** (*tr; often passive*) to absorb or involve: *she was caught up in her reading.* **5** (*tr*) to raise by or as if by fastening.

catchweight ('kætʃˌweɪt) *adj Wrestling.* of or relating to a contest in which normal weight categories have been waived by agreement.

catchword ⓣ ('kætʃˌwɜːd) *n* **1** a word or phrase made temporarily popular; slogan. **2** a word printed as a running head in a book. **3** *Theatre.* an actor's cue to speak or enter. **4** the first word of a page repeated at the bottom of the page preceding.

catchy ⓣ ('kætʃɪ) *adj* **catchier, catchiest. 1** (of a tune, etc.) pleasant and easily remembered. **2** deceptive: *a catchy question.* **3** irregular: *a catchy breeze.*

cat cracker *n* an informal name for **catalytic cracker.**

catechetical (ˌkætɪ'kɛtɪkᵊl) *or* **catechetic** *adj* of or relating to teaching by question and answer.
▸ **ˌcate'chetically** *adv*

catechism ('kætɪˌkɪzəm) *n* instruction by a series of questions and answers, esp. a book containing such instruction on the religious doctrine of a Christian Church. [C16: from LL, ult. from Gk *katēkhizein* to CATECHIZE]
▸ **ˌcate'chismal** *adj*

catechize ⓣ *or* **catechise** ('kætɪˌkaɪz) *vb* **catechizes, catechizing, catechized** *or* **catechises, catechising, catechised.** (*tr*) **1** to teach or examine by means of questions and answers. **2** to give oral instruction in Christianity, esp. by using a catechism. **3** to put questions to (someone). [C15: from LL, from Gk *katēkhizein,* from *katēkhein* to instruct orally, from *kata-* down + *ēkhein* to sound]
▸ **'catechist, 'cateˌchizer** *or* **'cateˌchiser** *n*

catechu ('kætɪˌtʃuː) *or* **cachou** *n* an astringent resinous substance obtained from certain tropical plants, and used in medicine, tanning, and dyeing. [C17: prob. from Malay *kachu*]

catechumen (ˌkætɪ'kjuːmɛn) *n Christianity.* a person, esp. in the early Church, undergoing instruction prior to baptism. [C15: via OF, from LL, from Gk *katēkhoumenos* one being instructed verbally]

categorial (ˌkætɪ'gɔːrɪəl) *adj* **1** of or relating to a category. **2** *Logic.* (of a statement) consisting of a subject, S, and a predicate, P, each of which denote a class, as in: *all S are P.*

categorical ⓣ (ˌkætɪ'gɒrɪkᵊl) *or* **categoric** *adj* **1** unqualified; unconditional: *a categorical statement.* **2** relating to or included in a category. **3** another word for **categorial** (sense 2).
▸ **ˌcate'gorically** *adv*

categorize *or* **categorise** ('kætɪgəˌraɪz) *vb* **categorizes, categorizing, categorized** *or* **categorises, categorising, categorised.** (*tr*) to place in a category.
▸ **ˌcategori'zation** *or* **ˌcategori'sation** *n*

category ⓣ ('kætɪgərɪ) *n, pl* **categories. 1** a class or group of things, people, etc., possessing some quality or qualities in common. **2** *Metaphysics.* one of the most basic classes into which objects and concepts can be analysed. **3a** (in the philosophy of Aristotle) any one of ten most fundamental modes of being, such as quantity, quality, and substance. **3b** (in the philosophy of Kant) one of twelve concepts required by human beings to interpret the empirical world. [C15: from LL, from Gk *katēgoria,* from *kategorein* to accuse, assert]

catena (kə'tiːnə) *n, pl* **catenae** (-niː). a connected series, esp. of patristic comments on the Bible. [C17: from L: chain]

catenaccio (*Italian* kate'nattʃo) *n Soccer.* an extremely defensive style of play. [C20: from L *catena* chain]

catenary (kə'tiːnərɪ) *n, pl* **catenaries. 1** the curve formed by a heavy uniform flexible cord hanging freely from two points. **2** the hanging cable between pylons along a railway track, from which the trolley wire is suspended. ◆ *adj* **3** of, resembling, relating to, or constructed using a catenary or suspended chain. [C18: from L *catēnārius* relating to a chain]

catenate ('kætɪˌneɪt) *vb* **catenates, catenating, catenated.** *Biol.* to arrange or be arranged in a series of chains or rings. [C17: from L *catēnāre* to bind with chains]
▸ **ˌcate'nation** *n*

cater ⓣ ('keɪtə) *vb* **1** (*intr;* foll. by *for* or *to*) to provide what is required or desired (for). **2** (when *intr,* foll. by *for*) to provide food, services, etc. (for): *we cater for parties.* [C16: from earlier *catour* purchaser, var. of *acatour,* from Anglo-Norman *acater* to buy]
▸ **'catering** *n*

cater-cornered ('kætəˌkɔːnəd) *adj, adv US & Canad. inf.* diagonal. Also: **catty-cornered, kitty-cornered.** [C16: from dialect *cater* (adv) diagonally, from obs. *cater* (n) four-spot of dice, from OF *quatre* four, from L *quattuor*]

caterer ('keɪtərə) *n* one who as a profession provides food for large social events, etc.

caterpillar ('kætəˌpɪlə) *n* **1** the wormlike larva of butterflies and moths, having numerous pairs of legs and powerful biting jaws. **2** *Trademark.* an endless track, driven by sprockets or wheels, used to propel a heavy vehicle. **3** *Trademark.* a vehicle, such as a tractor, tank, etc., driven by such tracks. [C15 *catyrpel,* prob. from OF *catepelose,* lit.: hairy cat]

caterwaul ⓣ ('kætəˌwɔːl) *vb* (*intr*) **1** to make a yowling noise, as a cat on heat. ◆ *n* **2** a yell made by or sounding like a cat on heat. [C14: imit.]

catfish ('kætˌfɪʃ) *n, pl* **catfish** *or* **catfishes. 1** any of numerous mainly freshwater fishes having whisker-like barbels around the mouth. **2** another name for **wolffish.**

cat flap *or* **door** *n* a small flap or door in a larger door through which a cat can pass.

catgut ('kætˌgʌt) *n* a strong cord made from the dried intestines of sheep and other animals that is used for stringing certain musical instruments and sports rackets.

Cath. *abbrev. for:* **1** Cathedral. **2** Catholic.

cath- *prefix* a variant of **cata-** before an aspirate: *cathode.*

Cathar ('kæθə) *or* **Catharist** ('kæθərɪst) *n, pl* **Cathars, Cathari** (-ərɪ) *or* **Catharists.** a member of a Christian sect in Provence in the 12th and 13th centuries who believed the material world was evil and only the spiritual was good. [from Med. L, from Gk *katharoi* the pure]
▸ **'Catharˌism** *n*

catharsis ⓣ (kə'θɑːsɪs) *n, pl* **catharses** (-siːz). **1** the purging or purification of the emotions through the evocation of pity and fear, as in tragedy. **2** *Psychoanal.* the bringing of repressed ideas or experiences into consciousness, thus relieving tensions. **3** purgation, esp. of

THESAURUS

tage, fly in the ointment, hitch, snag, stumbling block, trap, trick
Antonyms *vb* ≠ **seize:** drop, free, give up, liberate, loose, release ≠ **contract:** avert, avoid, escape, ward off ≠ **attract:** alienate, bore, disenchant, disgust, fail to interest, repel ◆ *n* ≠ **drawback:** advantage, benefit, bonus, boon, reward

catching *adj* **1** = **infectious**, communicable, contagious, infective, transferable, transmittable
Antonyms *adj* incommunicable, non-catching, non-contagious, non-infectious, non-transmittable

catch on *vb* **2** *Informal* = **understand**, comprehend, find out, get the picture, grasp, see, see the light of day, see through, twig (*Brit. inf.*)

catchword *n* **1** = **slogan**, byword, motto, password, refrain, watchword

catchy *adj* **1** = **memorable**, captivating, haunting, popular

catechize *vb* **1, 3** = **question**, cross-examine, drill, examine, grill (*inf.*), interrogate

categorical *adj* **1** = **absolute**, direct, downright, emphatic, explicit, express, positive, unambiguous, unconditional, unequivocal, unqualified, unreserved
Antonyms *adj* conditional, hesitant, indefinite, qualified, questionable, uncertain, vague

category *n* **1** = **class**, classification, department, division, grade, grouping, head, heading, list, order, rank, section, sort, type

cater *vb* **1, 2** = **provide**, furnish, outfit, provision, purvey, supply, victual

caterwaul *vb* **1** = **yowl**, bawl, howl, scream, screech, shriek, squall, wail

catharsis *n* **1, 3** = **release**, abreaction, cleansing, lustration, purgation, purging, purification the bowels. [C19: NL, from Gk *katharsis*, from *kathairein* to purge, purify]

cathartic (kə'θɑːtɪk) *adj* **1** purgative. **2** effecting catharsis. ◆ *n* **3** a purgative drug or agent.
▸**ca'thartically** *adv*

Cathay (kæ'θeɪ) *n* a literary or archaic name for **China.** [C14: from Med. L *Cataya*]

cathead ('kæt,hɛd) *n* a fitting at the bow of a vessel for securing the anchor when raised.

cathedral (kə'θiːdrəl) *n* **a** the principal church of a diocese, containing the bishop's official throne. **b** (*as modifier*): *a cathedral city.* [C13: from LL (*ecclesia*) *cathedrālis* cathedral (church), from Gk *kathedra* seat]

Catherine wheel (kæθrɪn) *n* **1** a firework which rotates, producing coloured flame. **2** a circular window having ribs radiating from the centre. [C16: after St *Catherine* of Alexandria, martyred on a spiked wheel, 307 A.D.]

catheter ('kæθɪtə) *n Med.* a long slender flexible tube for inserting into a bodily cavity for introducing or withdrawing fluid. [C17: from LL, from Gk *kathetēr*, from *kathienai* to insert]

catheterize *or* **catheterise** ('kæθɪtə,raɪz) *vb* **catheterizes, catheterizing, catheterized** *or* **catheterises, catheterising, catheterised.** (*tr*) to insert a catheter into.

cathexis (kə'θɛksɪs) *n, pl* **cathexes** (-'θɛksiːz). *Psychoanal.* concentration of psychic energy on a single goal. [C20: from NL, from Gk *kathexis*, from *katekhein* to hold fast]

cathode ('kæθəʊd) *n* **1** the negative electrode in an electrolytic cell. **2** the negatively charged electron source in an electronic valve. **3** the positive terminal of a primary cell. ◆ Cf. **anode.** [C19: from Gk *kathodos* a descent, from *kata-* down + *hodos* way]
▸**cathodal** (kæ'θəʊdᵊl) *or* **cathodic** (kæ'θɒdɪk, -'θəʊ-) *adj*

cathode rays *pl n* a stream of electrons emitted from the surface of a cathode in a vacuum tube.

cathode-ray tube *n* a vacuum tube in which a beam of electrons is focused onto a fluorescent screen to give a visible spot of light. The device is used in television receivers, visual display units, etc.

catholic ❶ ('kæθəlɪk, 'kæθlɪk) *adj* **1** universal; relating to all men. **2** broad-minded; liberal. [C14: from L, from Gk *katholikos* universal, from *kata-* according to + *holos* whole]
▸**catholically** *or* **catholicly** (kə'θɒlɪklɪ) *adv*

Catholic ('kæθəlɪk, 'kæθlɪk) *Christianity.* ◆ *adj* **1** denoting or relating to the entire body of Christians, esp. to the Church before separation into the Eastern and Western Churches. **2** denoting or relating to the Latin or Western Church after this separation. **3** denoting or relating to the Roman Catholic Church. ◆ *n* **4** a member of the Roman Catholic Church.

Catholicism (kə'θɒlɪ,sɪzəm) *n* **1** short for **Roman Catholicism. 2** the beliefs, practices, etc., of any Catholic Church.

catholicity (,kæθə'lɪsɪtɪ) *n* **1** a wide range of interests, tastes, etc. **2** comprehensiveness.

catholicize *or* **catholicise** (kə'θɒlɪ,saɪz) *vb* **catholicizes, catholicizing, catholicized** *or* **catholicises, catholicising, catholicised. 1** to make or become catholic. **2** (*often cap.*) to convert to or become converted to Catholicism.

cation ('kæt,aɪən) *n* a positively charged ion; an ion that is attracted to the cathode during electrolysis. Cf. **anion.** [C19: from CATA- + ION]
▸**cationic** (,kætaɪ'ɒnɪk) *adj*

catkin ('kætkɪn) *n* an inflorescence consisting of a hanging spike of much reduced flowers of either sex: occurs in birch, hazel, etc. [C16: from obs. Du. *katteken* kitten]

cat litter *n* absorbent material used to line a receptacle in which a domestic cat can urinate and defecate.

catmint ('kæt,mɪnt) *n* a Eurasian plant having spikes of purple-spotted white flowers and scented leaves of which cats are fond. Also called: **catnip.**

catnap ❶ ('kæt,næp) *n* **1** a short sleep or doze. ◆ *vb* **catnaps, catnapping, catnapped. 2** (*intr*) to sleep or doze for a short time or intermittently.

cat-o'-nine-tails *n, pl* **cat-o'-nine-tails.** a rope whip consisting of nine knotted thongs, used formerly to flog prisoners. Often shortened to **cat.**

CATS (kæts) *n acronym for* credit accumulation transfer scheme: a scheme enabling school-leavers and others to acquire transferable certificates for relevant work experience and study towards a recognized qualification.

CAT scanner (kæt) *n* former name for **CT scanner.** [C20: from Computerized Axial Tomography]

cat's cradle *n* a game played by making patterns with a loop of string between the fingers.

cat's-eye *n* any of a group of gemstones that reflect a streak of light when cut in a rounded unfaceted shape.

Catseye ('kætsaɪ) *n Trademark, Brit.* a glass reflector set into a small fixture, placed at intervals along roads to indicate traffic lanes at night.

cat's-paw *n* **1** a person used by another as a tool; dupe. **2** a pattern of ripples on the surface of water caused by a light wind. [(sense 1) C18: so called from the tale of the monkey who used a cat's paw to draw chestnuts out of a fire]

catsup ('kætsəp) *n* a variant spelling (esp. US) of **ketchup.**

cat's whisker *n* a pointed wire formerly used to make contact with the crystal in a crystal radio receiver.

cat's whiskers *or* **cat's pyjamas** *n* **the.** *Sl.* a person or thing that is excellent or superior.

cattery ('kætərɪ) *n, pl* **catteries.** a place where cats are bred or looked after.

cattle ❶ ('kætᵊl) *n* (*functioning as pl*) **1** bovid mammals of the tribe *Bovini* (bovines). **2** Also called: **domestic cattle.** any domesticated bovine mammals. [C13: from OF *chatel* CHATTEL]

cattle-cake *n* concentrated food for cattle in the form of cakes.

cattle-grid *n* a grid of metal bars covering a hole dug in a roadway intended to prevent the passage of livestock while allowing vehicles, etc., to pass unhindered.

cattleman ('kætᵊlmən) *n, pl* **cattlemen. 1** a person who breeds, rears, or tends cattle. **2** *Chiefly US & Canad.* a person who rears cattle on a large scale.

cattle market *n* **1** a place in which cattle are bought and sold. **2** *Brit. sl.* a situation or place in which women are on display and judged solely by their appearance.

cattle-stop *n* the New Zealand name for a **cattle-grid.**

catty ❶ ('kætɪ) *or* **cattish** *adj* **cattier, cattiest. 1** *Inf.* spiteful: *a catty remark.* **2** of or resembling a cat.
▸**'cattily** *or* **'cattishly** *adv* ▸**'cattiness** *or* **'cattishness** *n*

CATV *abbrev. for* community antenna television.

catwalk ('kæt,wɔːk) *n* **1** a narrow ramp extending from the stage into the audience in a theatre etc., esp. as used by models in a fashion show. **2** a narrow pathway over the stage of a theatre, along a bridge, etc.

Caucasian (kɔː'keɪzɪən) *adj* **1** another word for **Caucasoid. 2** of or relating to Caucasia or the Caucasus in the SW Soviet Union. ◆ *n* **3** a member of the Caucasoid race; a White person. **4** a native or inhabitant of Caucasia or the Caucasus.

Caucasoid ('kɔːkə,zɔɪd) *adj* **1** denoting or belonging to the light-complexioned racial group of mankind, which includes the peoples indigenous to Europe, N Africa, SW Asia, and the Indian subcontinent. ◆ *n* **2** a member of this racial group.

caucus ❶ ('kɔːkəs) *n, pl* **caucuses. 1** *Chiefly US & Canad.* a closed meeting of the members of one party in a legislative chamber, etc., to coordinate policy, choose candidates, etc. **2** *Chiefly US.* a local meeting of party members. **3** *Brit.* a group or faction within a larger group, esp. a political party, who discuss tactics, choose candidates, etc. **4** *NZ.* a formal meeting of all MPs of one party. **5** *Austral.* a group of MPs from one party who meet to discuss tactics, etc. ◆ *vb* **6** (*intr*) to hold a caucus. [C18: prob. of Algonquian origin]

caudal ('kɔːdᵊl) *adj* **1** *Anat.* of the posterior part of the body. **2** *Zool.* resembling or in the position of the tail. [C17: from NL, from L *cauda* tail]
▸**'caudally** *adv*

caudal fin *n* the tail fin of fishes and some other aquatic vertebrates, used for propulsion.

caudate ('kɔːdeɪt) *or* **caudated** *adj* having a tail or a tail-like appendage. [C17: from NL *caudātus*, from L *cauda* tail]
▸**cau'dation** *n*

caudillo (kɔː'diːljəʊ) *n, pl* **caudillos** (-ljəʊz). (in Spanish-speaking countries) a military or political leader. [Sp., from LL *capitellum*, dim. of L *caput* head]

caudle ('kɔːdᵊl) *n* a hot spiced wine drink made with gruel, formerly used medicinally. [C13: from OF *caudel*, from Med. L, from L *calidus* warm]

caught (kɔːt) *vb* the past tense and past participle of **catch.**

caul (kɔːl) *n Anat.* a portion of the amniotic sac sometimes covering a child's head at birth. [C13: from OF *cale*, back formation from *calotte* close-fitting cap, of Gmc origin]

cauldron *or* **caldron** ('kɔːldrən) *n* a large pot used for boiling, esp. one with handles. [C13: from Anglo-F, from L *caldārium* hot bath, from *calidus* warm]

cauliflower ('kɒlɪ,flaʊə) *n* **1** a variety of cabbage having a large edible head of crowded white flowers on a very short thick stem. **2** the flower head of this plant, used as a vegetable. [C16: from It. *caoli fiori*, lit.: cabbage flowers]

cauliflower ear *n* permanent swelling and distortion of the external ear as the result of ruptures of the blood vessels: usually caused by blows received in boxing.

caulk *or* **calk** (kɔːk) *vb* **1** to stop up (cracks, crevices, etc.) with a filler. **2** *Naut.* to pack (the seams) between the planks of the bottom of (a ves-

THESAURUS

catholic *adj* **1, 2** = **wide,** all-embracing, all-inclusive, broad-minded, charitable, comprehensive, eclectic, ecumenical, general, global, liberal, tolerant, unbigoted, universal, unsectarian, whole, world-wide
Antonyms *adj* bigoted, exclusive, illiberal, limited, narrow-minded, parochial, sectarian

catnap *n* **1** = **doze,** forty winks (*inf.*), kip (*Brit. sl.*), nap, siesta, sleep, snooze ◆ *vb* **2** = **doze,** drowse, kip (*Brit. sl.*), nap, snooze, take forty winks (*inf.*)

cattiness *n* **1** *Informal* = **spitefulness,** bitchiness, ill-naturedness, malevolence, maliciousness, meanness, rancorousness, shrewishness, snideness, venomousness, virulence

cattle *pl n* **2** = **cows,** beasts, bovines, kine (*arch.*), livestock, stock

catty *adj* **1** = **spiteful,** backbiting, bitchy (*inf.*), ill-natured, malevolent, malicious, mean, rancorous, shrewish, snide, venomous
Antonyms *adj* benevolent, charitable, compassionate, considerate, generous, kind, pleasant

caucus *n* **1-5** = **meeting,** assembly, conclave, congress, convention, get-together (*inf.*), parley, session sel) with waterproof material to prevent leakage. [C15: from OF *cauquer* to press down, from L *calcāre* to trample, from *calx* heel]

causal ('kɔːzᵊl) *adj* **1** acting as or being a cause. **2** stating, involving, or implying a cause: *the causal part of the argument.*
▸**'causally** *adv*

causality (kɔː'zælɪtɪ) *n, pl* **causalities. 1a** the relationship of cause and effect. **1b** the principle that nothing can happen without being caused. **2** causal agency or quality.

causation (kɔː'zeɪʃən) *n* **1** the production of an effect by a cause. **2** the relationship of cause and effect.
▸**cau'sational** *adj*

causative ('kɔːzətɪv) *adj* **1** *Grammar.* relating to a form or class of verbs, such as *persuade,* that express causation. **2** (*often postpositive* and foll. by *of*) producing an effect. ◆ *n* **3** the causative form or class of verbs.
▸**'causatively** *adv*

cause ❶ (kɔːz) *n* **1** a person, thing, event, state, or action that produces an effect. **2** grounds for action; justification: *she had good cause to shout like that.* **3** the ideals, etc., of a group or movement: *the Communist cause.* **4** the welfare or interests of a person or group in a dispute: *they fought for the miners' cause.* **5a** a ground for legal action; matter giving rise to a lawsuit. **5b** the lawsuit itself. **6** *Arch.* a subject of debate or discussion. **7 make common cause with.** to join with (a person, group, etc.) for a common objective. ◆ *vb* **causes, causing, caused. 8** (*tr*) to be the cause of; bring about. [C13: from L *causa* cause, reason, motive]
▸**'causeless** *adj*

cause célèbre ('kɔːz sə'lɛbrə) *n, pl* **causes célèbres** ('kɔːz sə'lɛbrəz). a famous lawsuit, trial, or controversy. [C19: from F: famous case]

causerie ('kəʊzərɪ) *n* an informal talk or conversational piece of writing. [C19: from F, from *causer* to chat]

causeway ('kɔːzˌweɪ) *n* **1** a raised path or road crossing water, marshland, etc. **2** a paved footpath. [C15 *cauciwey* (from *cauci* + WAY); *cauci* paved road, from Med. L, from L *calx* limestone]

caustic ❶ ('kɔːstɪk) *adj* **1** capable of burning or corroding by chemical action: *caustic soda.* **2** sarcastic; cutting: *a caustic reply.* ◆ *n* **3** Also called: **caustic surface.** a surface that envelops the light rays reflected or refracted by a curved surface. **4** Also called: **caustic curve.** a curve formed by the intersection of a caustic surface with a plane. **5** *Chem.* a caustic substance, esp. an alkali. [C14: from L, from Gk *kaustikos,* from *kaiein* to burn]
▸**'caustically** *adv* ▸**causticity** (kɔː'stɪsɪtɪ) *n*

caustic potash *n* another name for **potassium hydroxide.**

caustic soda *n* another name for **sodium hydroxide.**

cauterize *or* **cauterise** ('kɔːtəˌraɪz) *vb* **cauterizes, cauterizing, cauterized** *or* **cauterises, cauterising, cauterised.** (*tr*) (esp. in the treatment of a wound) to burn or sear (body tissue) with a hot iron or caustic agent. [C14: from OF, from LL, from *cautērium* branding iron, from Gk *kautērion,* from *kaiein* to burn]
▸**ˌcauteri'zation** *or* **ˌcauteri'sation** *n*

cautery ('kɔːtərɪ) *n, pl* **cauteries. 1** the coagulation of blood or destruction of body tissue by cauterizing. **2** an instrument or agent for cauterizing. [C14: from OF *cautère,* from L *cautērium*]

caution ❶ ('kɔːʃən) *n* **1** care, forethought, or prudence, esp. in the face of danger. **2** something intended or serving as a warning. **3** *Law, chiefly Brit.* a formal warning given to a person suspected of an offence that his words will be taken down and may be used in evidence. **4** *Inf.* an amusing or surprising person or thing. ◆ *vb* **5** (*tr*) to warn (a person) to be careful. **6** (*tr*) *Law, chiefly Brit.* to give a caution to (a person). **7** (*intr*) to warn, urge, or advise: *he cautioned against optimism.* [C13: from OF, from L *cautiō,* from *cavēre* to beware]

cautionary ('kɔːʃənərɪ) *adj* serving as a warning; intended to warn: *a cautionary tale.*

cautious ❶ ('kɔːʃəs) *adj* showing or having caution.
▸**'cautiously** *adv* ▸**'cautiousness** *n*

cavalcade ❶ (ˌkævəl'keɪd) *n* **1** a procession of people on horseback, in cars, etc. **2** any procession. [C16: from F, from It., from *cavalcare* to ride on horseback, from LL, from *caballus* horse]

cavalier ❶ (ˌkævə'lɪə) *adj* **1** supercilious; offhand. ◆ *n* **2** a courtly gentleman, esp. one acting as a lady's escort. **3** *Arch.* a horseman, esp. one who is armed. [C16: from It., from OProvençal, from LL *caballārius* rider, from *caballus* horse, from ?]
▸**ˌcava'lierly** *adv*

Cavalier (ˌkævə'lɪə) *n* a supporter of Charles I during the English Civil War.

cavalry ❶ ('kævəlrɪ) *n, pl* **cavalries. 1** (esp. formerly) the part of an army composed of mounted troops. **2** the armoured element of a modern army. **3** (*as modifier*): *a cavalry unit.* [C16: from F *cavallerie,* from It., from *cavaliere* horseman]
▸**'cavalryman** *n*

cavatina (ˌkævə'tiːnə) *n, pl* **cavatine** (-nɪ). **1** a simple solo song. **2** an instrumental composition reminiscent of this. [C19: from It.]

cave[1] ❶ (keɪv) *n* **1** an underground hollow with access from the ground surface or from the sea. **2** *Brit. history.* a secession or a group seceding from a political party on some issue. **3** (*modifier*) living in caves. ◆ *vb* **caves, caving, caved. 4** (*tr*) to hollow out. [C13: from OF, from L *cava,* pl. of *cavum* cavity, from *cavus* hollow]

cave[2] ('keɪvɪ) *Brit. school sl.* ◆ *n* **1** lookout: *keep cave.* ◆ *sentence substitute.* **2** watch out! [from L *cavē* beware!]

caveat ❶ ('keɪvɪˌæt, 'kæv-) *n* **1** *Law.* a formal notice requesting the court not to take a certain action without warning the person lodging the caveat. **2** a caution. [C16: from L, lit.: let him beware]

caveat emptor ('ɛmptɔː) *n* the principle that the buyer must bear the risk for the quality of goods purchased. [L: let the buyer beware]

cave in *vb* (*intr, adv*) **1** to collapse; subside. **2** *Inf.* to yield completely, esp. under pressure. ◆ *n* **cave-in. 3** the sudden collapse of a roof, piece of ground, etc. **4** the site of such a collapse, as at a mine or tunnel.

cavel ('keɪvᵊl) *n NZ.* a drawing of lots among miners for an easy and profitable place at the coalface. [C19: from E dialect *cavel* to cast lots, apportion]

caveman ('keɪvˌmæn) *n, pl* **cavemen. 1** a man of the Palaeolithic age; cave dweller. **2** *Inf.* a man who is primitive or brutal in behaviour, etc.

cavendish ('kævəndɪʃ) *n* tobacco that has been sweetened and pressed into moulds to form bars. [C19: ?from the name of the first maker]

cavern ❶ ('kævᵊn) *n* **1** a cave, esp. when large. ◆ *vb* (*tr*) **2** to shut in or as if in a cavern. **3** to hollow out. [C14: from OF *caverne,* from L *caverna,* from *cavus* hollow]

cavernous ❶ ('kævənəs) *adj* **1** suggestive of a cavern in vastness, etc.: *cavernous eyes.* **2** filled with small cavities. **3** (of rocks) containing caverns.

caviar *or* **caviare** ('kævɪˌɑː, ˌkævɪ'ɑː) *n* the salted roe of sturgeon, usually served as an hors d'oeuvre. [C16: from earlier *cavery,* from OIt. *caviari,* pl. of *caviaro* caviar, from Turkish *havyār*]

cavil ❶ ('kævɪl) *vb* **cavils, cavilling, cavilled** *or US* **cavils, caviling, caviled. 1** (*intr;* foll. by *at* or *about*) to raise annoying petty objections. ◆ *n* **2** a trifling objection. [C16: from OF, from L *cavillārī* to jeer, from *cavilla* raillery]
▸**'caviller** *n*

caving ('keɪvɪŋ) *n* the sport of climbing in and exploring caves.
▸**'caver** *n*

cavity ❶ ('kævɪtɪ) *n, pl* **cavities. 1** a hollow space. **2** *Dentistry.* a decayed area on a tooth. **3** any empty or hollow space within the body. [C16: from F, from LL *cavitās,* from L *cavus* hollow]

cavity wall *n* a wall that consists of two separate walls with an airspace between them.

cavort ❶ (kə'vɔːt) *vb* (*intr*) to prance; caper. [C19: ?from CURVET]
▸**ca'vorter** *n*

cavy ('keɪvɪ) *n, pl* **cavies.** a small South American rodent having a thickset body and very small tail. See also **guinea pig.** [C18: from NL *Cavia,* from Carib *cabiai*]

caw (kɔː) *n* **1** the cry of a crow, rook, or raven. ◆ *vb* **2** (*intr*) to make this cry. [C16: imit.]

cay (keɪ, kiː) *n* a small low island or bank composed of sand and coral fragments. [C18: from Sp. *cayo,* prob. from OF *quai* QUAY]

cayenne pepper (keɪ'ɛn) *n* a very hot red condiment made from the

THESAURUS

cause *n* **1 = origin**, agent, beginning, creator, genesis, mainspring, maker, originator, prime mover, producer, root, source, spring **2 = reason**, account, agency, aim, basis, consideration, end, grounds, incentive, inducement, justification, motivation, motive, object, purpose, the why and wherefore **3 = aim**, attempt, belief, conviction, enterprise, ideal, movement, principle, purpose, undertaking ◆ *vb* **8 = produce**, begin, bring about, compel, create, effect, engender, generate, give rise to, incite, induce, lead to, motivate, occasion, precipitate, provoke, result in
Antonyms *n* ≠ **origin:** consequence, effect, end, outcome, result ◆ *vb* ≠ **produce:** deter, foil, inhibit, prevent, stop

caustic *adj* **1 = burning**, acrid, astringent, biting, corroding, corrosive, keen, mordant, vitriolic **2 = sarcastic**, acrimonious, cutting, mordacious, pungent, scathing, severe, stinging, trenchant, virulent, vitriolic
Antonyms *adj* ≠ **sarcastic:** agreeable, bland, gentle, kind, loving, mild, pleasant, pleasing, soft, soothing, sweet, temperate

caution *n* **1 = care**, alertness, belt and braces, carefulness, circumspection, deliberation, discretion, forethought, heed, heedfulness, prudence, vigilance, watchfulness **2 = warning**, admonition, advice, counsel, injunction ◆ *vb* **5-7 = warn**, admonish, advise, tip off, urge
Antonyms *n* ≠ **care:** carelessness, daring, imprudence, rashness, recklessness ◆ *vb* ≠ **warn:** dare

cautious *adj* **= careful**, alert, belt-and-braces, cagey (*inf.*), chary, circumspect, discreet, guarded, heedful, judicious, keeping a weather eye on, on one's toes, prudent, tentative, vigilant, wary, watchful
Antonyms *adj* adventurous, bold, careless, daring, foolhardy, heedless, impetuous, inattentive, incautious, indiscreet, madcap, rash, reckless, unguarded, unheedful, venturesome, venturous

cautiously *adv* **= carefully**, alertly, cagily (*inf.*), circumspectly, discreetly, guardedly, heedfully, judiciously, mindfully, prudently, tentatively, vigilantly, warily, watchfully

cavalcade *n* **2 = parade**, array, march-past, procession, spectacle, train

cavalier *adj* **1 = haughty**, arrogant, condescending, curt, disdainful, insolent, lofty, lordly, offhand, scornful, supercilious ◆ *n* **2 = gentleman**, beau, blade (*arch.*), escort, gallant **3 = knight**, chevalier, equestrian, horseman

cavalry *n* **1 = horsemen**, horse, mounted troops
Antonyms *n* foot soldiers, infantrymen

cave[1] *n* **1 = hollow**, cavern, cavity, den, grotto

caveat *n* **2 = warning**, admonition, caution

cavern *n* **1 = cave**, hollow, pothole

cavernous *adj* **1 = deep**, concave, hollow, sunken, yawning

cavil *vb* **1 = find fault**, beef (*sl.*), carp, censure, complain, hypercriticize, kvetch (*US sl.*), object, quibble

cavity *n* **1 = hollow**, crater, dent, gap, hole, pit

cavort *vb* **= caper**, caracole, frisk, frolic, gambol, prance, romp, sport dried seeds of various capsicums. Often shortened to **cayenne.** Also called: **red pepper.** [C18: ult. from Tupi *quiynha*]

cayman or **caiman** ('keɪmən) *n, pl* **caymans** *or* **caimans.** a tropical American crocodilian similar to alligators but with a more heavily armoured belly. [C16: from Sp. *caimán*, from Carib *cayman*]

CB *abbrev. for:* **1** Citizens' Band. **2** Companion of the (Order of the) Bath (a Brit. title). **3** County Borough.

CBC *abbrev. for* Canadian Broadcasting Corporation.

CBE *abbrev. for* Commander of the (Order of the) British Empire.

CBI *abbrev. for:* **1** *US.* Central Bureau of Investigation. **2** Confederation of British Industry.

CBT *abbrev. for* computer-based training.

cc *or* **c.c.** *abbrev. for:* **1** carbon copy *or* copies. **2** cubic centimetre(s).

CC *abbrev. for:* **1** City Council. **2** County Council. **3** Cricket Club.

cc. *abbrev. for* chapters.

c.c.c. *abbrev. for* cwmni cyfyngedig cyhoeddus; a public limited company in Wales.

C clef *n Music.* a symbol (𝄡), placed at the beginning of the staff, establishing the position of middle C: see **alto clef, soprano clef, tenor clef.**

CCTV *abbrev. for* closed-circuit television.

CCW *abbrev. for* Curriculum Council for Wales.

cd *symbol for* candela.

Cd *the chemical symbol for* cadmium.

CD *abbrev. for:* **1** compact disc. **2** Civil Defence (Corps). **3** Corps Diplomatique (Diplomatic Corps). **4** Conference on Disarmament: a United Nations standing conference, held in Geneva, to negotiate a global ban on chemical weapons.

CDE *abbrev. for:* compact disc erasable: a compact disc that can be used to record and rerecord. Cf. **CDR.**

CDI *abbrev. for* compact disc interactive.

Cdn *abbrev. for* Canadian.

cDNA *abbrev. for* complementary DNA.

CD player *n* a device for playing compact discs. In full: **compact-disc player.**

Cdr *Mil. abbrev. for* Commander.

CDR *abbrev. for* compact disc recordable: a compact disc that can be used to record only once. Cf. **CDE.**

CD-ROM (ˌsiːdiːˈrɒm) *abbrev. for* compact disc read only memory; a compact disc used for storing written information to be displayed on a visual-display unit.

CDT *abbrev. for:* **1** *US & Canad.* Central Daylight Time. **2** Craft, Design, and Technology: a subject on the GCSE syllabus, related to the National Curriculum.

CDV *abbrev. for* compact disc video.

CD-video *n* a compact-disc player that, when connected to a television and hi-fi, produces high-quality stereo sound and synchronized pictures from a disc resembling a compact audio disc. In full **compact-disc video.**

Ce *the chemical symbol for* cerium.

CE *abbrev. for:* **1** Church of England. **2** civil engineer. **3** Common Era.

cease ❶ (siːs) *vb* **ceases, ceasing, ceased. 1** (when *tr*, may take a gerund or an infinitive as object) to bring or come to an end. ◆ *n* **2 without cease.** without stopping. [C14: from OF, from L *cessāre*, frequentative of *cēdere* to yield]

ceasefire ('siːsˌfaɪə) *Chiefly mil.* ◆ *n* **1** a period of truce, esp. one that is temporary. ◆ *sentence substitute, n* **2** the order to stop firing.

ceaseless ❶ ('siːslɪs) *adj* without stop or pause; incessant.
▸ **'ceaselessly** *adv*

cecum ('siːkəm) *n, pl* **ceca** (-kə). *US.* a variant spelling of **caecum.**
▸ **'cecal** *adj*

cedar ('siːdə) *n* **1** any of a genus of Old World coniferous trees having needle-like evergreen leaves, and erect barrel-shaped cones. See also **cedar of Lebanon, deodar. 2** any of various other conifers, such as the red cedars and white cedars. **3** the wood of any of these trees. ◆ *adj* **4** made of the wood of a cedar tree. [C13: from OF, from L *cedrus*, from Gk *kedros*]

cedar of Lebanon ('lɛbənən) *n* a cedar of SW Asia with level spreading branches and fragrant wood.

cede ❶ (siːd) *vb* **cedes, ceding, ceded. 1** (when *intr*, often foll. by *to*) to transfer, make over, or surrender (something, esp. territory or legal rights). **2** (*tr*) to allow or concede (a point in an argument, etc.). [C17: from L *cēdere* to yield]
▸ **'ceder** *n*

cedilla (sɪ'dɪlə) *n* a character (¸) placed underneath a *c* before *a, o,* or *u,* esp. in French, Portuguese, or Catalan, denoting that it is to be pronounced (s), not (k). [C16: from Sp.: little *z*, from *ceda* zed, from LL *zeta*]

Ceefax ('siːfæks) *n Trademark.* the BBC Teletext service. See **Teletext.**

CEGB (in Britain) *abbrev. for* Central Electricity Generating Board.

ceil (siːl) *vb* (*tr*) **1** to line (a ceiling) with plaster, etc. **2** to provide with a ceiling. [C15 *celen*, ? back formation from CEILING]

ceilidh ('keɪlɪ) *n* (esp. in Scotland and Ireland) an informal social gathering with singing, dancing, and storytelling. [C19: from Gaelic]

ceiling ('siːlɪŋ) *n* **1** the inner upper surface of a room. **2** an upper limit, such as one set by regulation on prices or wages. **3** the upper altitude to which an aircraft can climb measured under specified conditions. **4** *Meteorol.* the highest level in the atmosphere from which the earth's surface is visible at a particular time, usually the base of a cloud layer. [C14: from ?]

celadon ('sɛləˌdɒn) *n* **1** a type of porcelain having a greyish-green glaze: mainly Chinese. **2a** a pale greyish-green colour. **2b** (*as adj*): *a celadon jar.* [C18: from F, from the name of the shepherd hero of *L'Astrée* (1610), a romance by Honoré d'Urfé]

celandine ('sɛlənˌdaɪn) *n* either of two unrelated plants, **greater celandine** or **lesser celandine,** with yellow flowers. [C13: earlier *celydon*, from L, from Gk *khelidōn* swallow; the plant's season was believed to parallel the migration of swallows]

-cele *n combining form.* tumour or hernia: *hydrocele.* [from Gk *kēlē* tumour]

celeb (sɪ'lɛb) *n Inf.* a celebrity.

celebrant ('sɛlɪbrənt) *n* a person participating in a religious ceremony, esp. at the Eucharist.

celebrate ❶ ('sɛlɪˌbreɪt) *vb* **celebrates, celebrating, celebrated. 1** to rejoice in or have special festivities to mark (a happy day, event, etc.). **2** (*tr*) to observe (a birthday, anniversary, etc.). **3** (*tr*) to perform (a solemn or religious ceremony), esp. to officiate at (Mass). **4** (*tr*) to praise publicly; proclaim. [C15: from L, from *celeber* numerous, renowned]
▸ ˌ**cele'bration** *n* ▸ **'celeˌbrator** *n* ▸ **'celeˌbratory** *adj*

celebrated ❶ ('sɛlɪˌbreɪtɪd) *adj* (*usually prenominal*) famous: *a celebrated pianist.*

celebrity ❶ (sɪ'lɛbrɪtɪ) *n, pl* **celebrities. 1** a famous person. **2** fame or notoriety.

celeriac (sɪ'lɛrɪˌæk) *n* a variety of celery with a large turnip-like root, used as a vegetable. [C18: from CELERY + *-ac*, from ?]

celerity (sɪ'lɛrɪtɪ) *n* rapidity; swiftness; speed. [C15: from OF *celerite*, from L *celeritās*, from *celer* swift]

celery ('sɛlərɪ) *n* **1** an umbelliferous Eurasian plant whose blanched leafstalks are used in salads or cooked as a vegetable. **2 wild celery.** a related and similar plant. [C17: from F *céleri*, from It. (Lombardy) dialect *selleri* (pl), from Gk *selinon* parsley]

celesta (sɪ'lɛstə) *or* **celeste** (sɪ'lɛst) *n Music.* a keyboard percussion instrument consisting of a set of steel plates of graduated length that are struck with key-operated hammers. [C19: from F, Latinized var. of *céleste* heavenly]

celestial ❶ (sɪ'lɛstɪəl) *adj* **1** heavenly; divine: *celestial peace.* **2** of or relating to the sky: *celestial bodies.* **3** of or connected with the celestial sphere: *celestial pole.* [C14: from Med. L, from L *caelestis*, from *caelum* heaven]
▸ **ce'lestially** *adv*

celestial equator *n* the great circle lying on the celestial sphere the plane of which is perpendicular to the line joining the north and south celestial poles. Also called: **equinoctial, equinoctial circle.**

celestial mechanics *n* the study of the motion of celestial bodies under the influence of gravitational fields.

celestial sphere *n* an imaginary sphere of infinitely large radius enclosing the universe so that all celestial bodies appear to be projected onto its surface.

celiac ('siːlɪˌæk) *adj Anat.* the usual US spelling of **coeliac.**

celibate ❶ ('sɛlɪbɪt) *n* **1** a person who is unmarried, esp. one who has taken a religious vow of chastity. ◆ *adj* **2** abstaining from sexual in-

THESAURUS

cease *vb* **1 = stop**, break off, bring *or* come to an end, conclude, culminate, desist, die away, discontinue, end, fail, finish, halt, leave off, refrain, stay, terminate
Antonyms *vb* begin, commence, continue, initiate, start

ceaseless *adj* **= continual**, constant, continuous, endless, eternal, everlasting, incessant, indefatigable, interminable, never-ending, nonstop, perennial, perpetual, unending, unremitting, untiring
Antonyms *adj* broken, erratic, intermittent, irregular, occasional, periodic, spasmodic, sporadic

cede *vb* **1, 2 = surrender**, abandon, abdicate, allow, concede, convey, grant, hand over, make over, relinquish, renounce, resign, step down (*inf.*), transfer, yield

celebrate *vb* **1, 2 = rejoice**, commemorate, drink to, keep, kill the fatted calf, observe, put the flags out, toast **3 = perform**, bless, honour, reverence, solemnize **4 = praise**, commend, crack up (*inf.*), eulogize, exalt, extol, glorify, honour, laud, proclaim, publicize

celebrated *adj* **= well-known**, acclaimed, distinguished, eminent, famed, famous, glorious, illustrious, lionized, notable, outstanding, popular, pre-eminent, prominent, renowned, revered
Antonyms *adj* dishonoured, forgotten, insignificant, obscure, trivial, unacclaimed, undistinguished, unknown, unnotable, unpopular

celebration *n* **1 = party**, beano (*Brit. sl.*), carousal, -fest (*in combination*), festival, festivity, gala, hooley *or* hoolie (*chiefly Irish & N.Z.*), jollification, jubilee, junketing, merrymaking, rave (*Brit. sl.*), rave-up (*Brit. sl.*), red-letter day, revelry **2, 3 = performance**, anniversary, commemoration, honouring, observance, remembrance, solemnization

celebrity *n* **1 = personality**, big name, big shot (*inf.*), bigwig (*inf.*), celeb (*inf.*), dignitary, face (*inf.*), lion, luminary, megastar (*inf.*), name, personage, star, superstar, V.I.P. **2 = fame**, distinction, éclat, glory, honour, notability, popularity, pre-eminence, prestige, prominence, renown, reputation, repute, stardom
Antonyms *n* ≠ **personality:** has-been, nobody, unknown ≠ **fame:** obscurity

celestial *adj* **1 = heavenly**, angelic, astral, divine, elysian, empyrean (*poetic*), eternal, ethereal, godlike, immortal, seraphic, spiritual, sublime, supernatural

celibacy *n* **2, 3 = chastity**, continence, purity, singleness, virginity

tercourse. **3** unmarried. [C17: from L, from *caelebs* unmarried, from ?]
▸**ˈcelibacy** *n*

cell ❶ (sɛl) *n* **1** a small simple room, as in a prison, convent, etc. **2** any small compartment: *the cells of a honeycomb.* **3** *Biol.* the smallest unit of an organism that is able to function independently. It consists of a nucleus, containing the genetic material, surrounded by the cytoplasm. **4** *Biol.* any small cavity, such as the cavity containing pollen in an anther. **5** a device for converting chemical energy into electrical energy, usually consisting of a container with two electrodes immersed in an electrolyte. See also **dry cell, fuel cell. 6** In full: **electrolytic cell.** a device in which electrolysis occurs. **7** a small religious house dependent upon a larger one. **8** a small group of persons operating as a nucleus of a larger organization: *Communist cell.* **9** the geographical area served by an individual transmitter in a cellular-radio network. [C12: from Med. L *cella* monk's cell, from L: room, storeroom]

cellar (ˈsɛlə) *n* **1** an underground room, or storey of a building, usually used for storage. **2** a place where wine is stored. **3** a stock of bottled wines. ◆ *vb* **4** *(tr)* to store in a cellar. [C13: from Anglo-F, from L *cellārium* foodstore, from *cella* cell]

cellarage (ˈsɛlərɪdʒ) *n* **1** an area of a cellar. **2** a charge for storing goods in a cellar, etc.

cellarer (ˈsɛlərə) *n* a monastic official responsible for food, drink, etc.

cellaret (ˌsɛləˈrɛt) *n* a cabinet or sideboard with compartments for holding wine bottles.

cell line *n Biol.* a cell culture derived from a single cell and thus of invariable genetic make-up.

Cellnet (ˈsɛlˌnɛt) *n Trademark.* a British Telecom mobile phone.

cello (ˈtʃɛləʊ) *n, pl* **cellos.** *Music.* a bowed stringed instrument of the violin family. It has four strings, is held between the knees, and has a metal spike at the lower end, which acts as a support. Full name: **violoncello.**
▸**ˈcellist** *n*

Cellophane (ˈsɛləˌfeɪn) *n Trademark.* a flexible thin transparent sheeting made from wood pulp and used as a moisture-proof wrapping. [C20: from CELLULOSE + -PHANE]

cellphone (ˈsɛlˌfəʊn) *n* a portable telephone operated by cellular radio. In full: **cellular telephone.**

cellular (ˈsɛljʊlə) *adj* **1** of, relating to, or composed of a cell or cells. **2** having cells or small cavities; porous. **3** divided into a network of cells. **4** *Textiles.* woven with an open texture: *a cellular blanket.* **5** designed for or involving cellular radio.

cellular radio *n* radio communication based on a network of transmitters each serving a small area known as a cell: used esp. in car phones in which the receiver switches frequencies automatically as it passes from one cell to another.

cellule (ˈsɛljuːl) *n* a very small cell. [C17: from L *cellula,* dim. of *cella* CELL]

cellulite (ˈsɛljʊˌlaɪt) *n* subcutaneous fat alleged to resist dieting.

cellulitis (ˌsɛljʊˈlaɪtɪs) *n* inflammation of body tissue, with fever, pain, and swelling. [C19: from L *cellula* CELLULE + -ITIS]

celluloid (ˈsɛljʊˌlɔɪd) *n* **1** a flammable material consisting of cellulose nitrate and camphor: used in sheets, rods, etc. **2a** a cellulose derivative used for coating film. **2b** cinema film.

cellulose (ˈsɛljʊˌləʊz, -ˌləʊs) *n* a substance which is the main constituent of plant cell walls and used in making paper, rayon, and film. [C18: from F *cellule* cell (see CELLULE) + -OSE[2]]

cellulose acetate *n* nonflammable material used in the manufacture of film, dopes, lacquers, and artificial fibres.

cellulose nitrate *n* cellulose treated with nitric and sulphuric acids, used in plastics, lacquers, and explosives. See also **guncotton.**

Celsius (ˈsɛlsɪəs) *adj* denoting a measurement on the Celsius scale. Symbol: C [C18: after Anders *Celsius* (1701–44), Swedish astronomer who invented it]

Celsius scale *n* a scale of temperature in which 0° represents the melting point of ice and 100° represents the boiling point of water. See also **centigrade.** Cf. **Fahrenheit scale.**

celt (sɛlt) *n Archaeol.* a stone or metal axelike instrument. [C18: from LL *celtes* chisel, from ?]

Celt (kɛlt, sɛlt) *or* **Kelt** *n* **1** a person who speaks a Celtic language. **2** a member of an Indo-European people who in pre-Roman times inhabited Britain, Gaul, and Spain.

Celtic (ˈkɛltɪk, ˈsɛl-) *or* **Keltic** *n* **1** a branch of the Indo-European family of languages that includes Gaelic, Welsh, and Breton. Modern Celtic is divided into the Brythonic (southern) and Goidelic (northern) groups. ◆ *adj* **2** of, relating to, or characteristic of the Celts or the Celtic languages.
▸**Celticism** (ˈkɛltɪˌsɪzəm, ˈsɛl-) *or* **ˈKeltiˌcism** *n*

Celtic cross *n* a Latin cross with a broad ring surrounding the point of intersection.

cembalo (ˈtʃɛmbələʊ) *n, pl* **cembali** (-lɪ) *or* **cembalos.** another word for **harpsichord.** [C19: from It. *clavicembalo* from Med. L *clāvis* key + *cymbalum* CYMBAL]

cement ❶ (sɪˈmɛnt) *n* **1** a fine grey powder made of a mixture of limestone and clay, used with water and sand to make mortar, or with water, sand, and aggregate, to make concrete. **2** a binder, glue, or adhesive. **3** something that unites or joins. **4** *Dentistry.* any of various materials used in filling teeth. **5** another word for **cementum.** ◆ *vb (tr)* **6** to join, bind, or glue together with or as if with cement. **7** to coat or cover with cement. [C13: from OF, from L *caementum* stone from the quarry, from *caedere* to hew]

cementum (sɪˈmɛntəm) *n* a thin bonelike tissue that covers the dentine in the root of a tooth. [C19: NL, from L: CEMENT]

cemetery ❶ (ˈsɛmɪtrɪ) *n, pl* **cemeteries.** a place where the dead are buried, esp. one not attached to a church. [C14: from LL, from Gk *koimētērion,* from *koiman* to put to sleep]

-cene *n and adj combining form.* denoting a recent geological period. [from Gk *kainos* new]

cenobite (ˈsiːnəʊˌbaɪt) *n* a variant spelling of **coenobite.**

cenotaph (ˈsɛnəˌtɑːf) *n* a monument honouring a dead person or persons buried elsewhere. [C17: from L, from Gk, from *kenos* empty + *taphos* tomb]

Cenotaph (ˈsɛnəˌtɑːf) *n* **the.** the monument in Whitehall, London, honouring the dead of both World Wars: designed by Sir Edwin Lutyens: erected in 1920.

Cenozoic, Caenozoic (ˌsiːnəʊˈzəʊɪk), *or* **Cainozoic** *adj* **1** of, denoting, or relating to the most recent geological era characterized by the development and increase of the mammals. ◆ *n* **2 the.** the Cenozoic era. [C19: from Gk *kainos* recent + *zōikos,* from *zōion* animal]

censer (ˈsɛnsə) *n* a container for burning incense. Also called: **thurible.**

censor ❶ (ˈsɛnsə) *n* **1** a person authorized to examine publications, films, letters, etc., in order to suppress in whole or part those considered obscene, politically unacceptable, etc. **2** any person who controls or suppresses the behaviour of others, usually on moral grounds. **3** (in republican Rome) either of two senior magistrates elected to keep the list of citizens up to date, and supervise public morals. **4** *Psychoanal.* the postulated factor responsible for regulating the translation of ideas and desires from the unconscious to the conscious mind. ◆ *vb (tr)* **5** to ban or cut portions of (a film, letter, etc.). **6** to act as a censor of (behaviour, etc.). [C16: from L, from *cēnsēre* to consider]
▸**censorial** (sɛnˈsɔːrɪəl) *adj*

censorious ❶ (sɛnˈsɔːrɪəs) *adj* harshly critical; fault-finding.
▸**cenˈsoriously** *adv*

censorship ❶ (ˈsɛnsəˌʃɪp) *n* **1** a policy or programme of censoring. **2** the act or system of censoring.

censure ❶ (ˈsɛnʃə) *n* **1** severe disapproval. ◆ *vb* **censures, censuring, censured.** **2** to criticize (someone or something) severely. [C14: from L *censūra,* from *cēnsēre*: see CENSOR]
▸**ˈcensurable** *adj*

census (ˈsɛnsəs) *n, pl* **censuses. 1** an official periodic count of a population including such information as sex, age, occupation, etc. **2** any official count: *a traffic census.* **3** (in ancient Rome) a registration of the population and a property evaluation for taxation. [C17: from L, from *cēnsēre* to assess]

cent (sɛnt) *n* a monetary unit of Australia, Barbados, Canada, Cyprus, Dominica, Estonia, Ethiopia, Fiji, Grenada, Guyana, Jamaica, Kenya, Malaysia, New Zealand, Singapore, South Africa, Tanzania, Trinidad and Tobago, Uganda, the United States, etc. It is worth one hundredth of their respective standard units. [C16: from L *centēsimus* hundredth, from *centum* hundred]

cent. *abbrev. for:* **1** centigrade. **2** central. **3** century.

centaur (ˈsɛntɔː) *n Greek myth.* one of a race of creatures with the head, arms, and torso of a man, and the lower body and legs of a horse. [C14: from L, from Gk *kentauros,* from ?]

centaurea (sɛntɔːˈrɪə, sɛnˈtɔːrɪə) *n* any plant of the genus *Centaurea* which includes the cornflower and knapweed. [C19: ult. from Gk *Kentauros* the Centaur; see CENTAURY]

centaury (ˈsɛntɔːrɪ) *n, pl* **centauries. 1** any of a genus of Eurasian plants having purplish-pink flowers and formerly believed to have medicinal properties. **2** another name for **centaurea.** [C14: ult. from Gk *Kentauros* the Centaur; from the legend that Chiron the Centaur divulged its healing properties]

centavo (sɛnˈtɑːvəʊ) *n, pl* **centavos.** a monetary unit of Argentina, Brazil, Colombia, Ecuador, El Salvador, Mexico, Nicaragua, the Phil-

THESAURUS

cell *n* **1** = **room,** cavity, chamber, compartment, cubicle, dungeon, stall **8** = **unit,** caucus, core, coterie, group, nucleus

cement *n* **2** = **mortar,** adhesive, binder, glue, gum, paste, plaster, sealant ◆ *vb* **6** = **stick together,** attach, bind, bond, cohere, combine, glue, gum, join, plaster, seal, solder, unite, weld

cemetery *n* = **graveyard,** burial ground, churchyard, God's acre, necropolis

censor *vb* **5** = **cut,** blue-pencil, bowdlerize, expurgate

censorious *adj* = **critical,** captious, carping, cavilling, condemnatory, disapproving, disparaging, fault-finding, hypercritical, scathing, severe

censorship *n* **2** = **expurgation,** blue pencil, bowdlerization *or* bowdlerisation, purgation, sanitization *or* sanitisation

censure *n* **1** = **disapproval,** blame, castigation, condemnation, criticism, dressing down (*inf.*), obloquy, rebuke, remonstrance, reprehension, reprimand, reproach, reproof, stick (*sl.*), stricture ◆ *vb* **2** = **criticize,** abuse, bawl out (*inf.*), berate, blame, blast, carpet (*inf.*), castigate, chide, condemn, denounce, excoriate, give (someone) a rocket (*Brit. & NZ. inf.*), lambast(e), put down, rap over the knuckles, read the riot act, rebuke, reprehend, reprimand, reproach, reprove, scold, slap on the wrist, slate (*inf., chiefly US.*), tear into (*inf.*), tear (someone) off a strip (*Brit. inf.*), upbraid
Antonyms *n* ≠ **disapproval:** approval, commendation, compliment, encouragement ◆ *vb* ≠ **criticize:** applaud, commend, compliment, laud (*literary*)

ippines, Portugal, etc. It is worth one hundredth of their respective standard units. [Sp.: one hundredth part]

centenarian (ˌsɛntɪˈnɛərɪən) *n* **1** a person who is at least 100 years old. ◆ *adj* **2** being at least 100 years old. **3** of or relating to a centenarian.

centenary (sɛnˈtiːnərɪ) *adj* **1** of or relating to a period of 100 years. **2** occurring once every 100 years. ◆ *n, pl* **centenaries. 3** a 100th anniversary or its celebration. [C17: from L, from *centēnī* a hundred each, from *centum* hundred]

centennial (sɛnˈtɛnɪəl) *adj* **1** relating to or completing a period of 100 years. **2** occurring every 100 years. ◆ *n* **3** *US & Canad.* another name for **centenary.** [C18: from L *centum* hundred, on the model of BIENNIAL]

center (ˈsɛntə) *n, vb* the US spelling of **centre.**

centesimal (sɛnˈtɛsɪməl) *n* **1** hundredth. ◆ *adj* **2** relating to division into hundredths. [C17: from L, from *centum* hundred]
▸**cenˈtesimally** *adv*

centesimo (sɛnˈtɛsɪˌməʊ) *n, pl* **centesimos** *or* **centesimi.** a monetary unit of Italy, Panama, Uruguay, etc. It is worth one hundredth of their respective standard units. [C19: from Sp. & It., from L, from *centum* hundred]

centi- *or before a vowel* **cent-** *prefix* **1** denoting one hundredth: *centimetre.* Symbol: c **2** *Rare.* denoting a hundred: *centipede.* [from F, from L *centum* hundred]

centiare (ˈsɛntɪˌɛə) *or* **centare** (ˈsɛntɛə) *n* a unit of area equal to one square metre. [F, from CENTI- + *are* from L *ārea*]

centigrade (ˈsɛntɪˌgreɪd) *adj* **1** a former name for **Celsius.** ◆ *n* **2** a unit of angle equal to one hundredth of a grade.

> **USAGE NOTE** Although still used in meteorology, *centigrade,* when indicating the Celsius scale of temperature, is now usually avoided because of its possible confusion with the hundredth part of a grade.

centigram *or* **centigramme** (ˈsɛntɪˌgræm) *n* one hundredth of a gram.

centilitre *or US* **centiliter** (ˈsɛntɪˌliːtə) *n* one hundredth of a litre.

centime (ˈsɒnˌtiːm; *French* sɑ̃tim) *n* a monetary unit of Algeria, Belgium, the Central African Republic, France, Guinea, Haiti, Liechtenstein, Luxembourg, Mali, Switzerland, Togo, etc. It is worth one hundredth of their respective standard units. [C18: from F, from OF, from L, from *centum* hundred]

centimetre *or US* **centimeter** (ˈsɛntɪˌmiːtə) *n* one hundredth of a metre.

centimetre-gram-second *n* See **cgs units.**

céntimo (ˈsɛntɪˌməʊ) *n, pl* **céntimos.** a monetary unit of Costa Rica, Peru, Spain, Venezuela, etc. It is worth one hundredth of their respective standard currency units. [from Sp.; see CENTIME]

centipede (ˈsɛntɪˌpiːd) *n* a carnivorous arthropod having a body of between 15 and 190 segments, each bearing one pair of legs.

cento (ˈsɛntəʊ) *n, pl* **centos.** a piece of writing, esp. a poem, composed of quotations from other authors. [C17: from L, lit.: patchwork garment]

CENTO (ˈsɛntəʊ) *n acronym for* Central Treaty Organization; an organization for military and economic cooperation formed in 1959 by the UK, Iran, Pakistan, and Turkey: disbanded 1979.

central ❶ (ˈsɛntrəl) *adj* **1** in, at, of, from, containing, or forming the centre of something: *the central street in a city.* **2** main, principal, or chief: *the central cause of a problem.*
▸**centrality** (sɛnˈtrælɪtɪ) *n* ▸**ˈcentrally** *adv*

central bank *n* a national bank that does business mainly with a government and with other banks: it regulates the volume of credit.

central heating *n* a system for heating the rooms of a building by means of radiators or air vents connected to a central source of heat.

centralism (ˈsɛntrəˌlɪzəm) *n* the principle or act of bringing something under central control.
▸**ˈcentralist** *n, adj*

centralize ❶ *or* **centralise** (ˈsɛntrəˌlaɪz) *vb* **centralizes, centralizing, centralized** *or* **centralises, centralising, centralised. 1** to draw or move (something) to or towards a centre. **2** to bring or come under central, esp. governmental, control.
▸**ˌcentraliˈzation** *or* **ˌcentraliˈsation** *n*

central limit theorem *n Statistics.* the fundamental result that the sum of independent identically distributed random variables with finite variance approaches a normally distributed random variable as their number increases.

central locking *n* a system by which all the doors of a motor vehicle can be locked simultaneously.

central nervous system *n* the mass of nerve tissue that controls and coordinates the activities of an animal. In vertebrates it consists of the brain and spinal cord.

central processing unit *n* the part of a computer that performs logical and arithmetical operations on the data. Abbrev.: **CPU.**

central reserve *or* **reservation** *n Brit. & Austral.* the strip, often covered with grass, that separates the two sides of a motorway or dual carriageway.

central tendency *n Statistics.* the tendency of the values of a random variable to cluster around the mean, median, and mode.

centre ❶ *or US* **center** (ˈsɛntə) *n* **1** *Geom.* **1a** the midpoint of any line or figure, esp. the point within a circle or sphere that is equidistant from any point on the circumference or surface. **1b** the point within a body through which a specified force may be considered to act, such as the centre of gravity. **2** the point, axis, or pivot about which a body rotates. **3** a point, area, or part that is approximately in the middle of a larger area or volume. **4** a place at which some specified activity is concentrated: *a shopping centre.* **5** a person or thing that is a focus of interest. **6** a place of activity or influence: *a centre of power.* **7** a person, group, or thing in the middle. **8** (*usually cap.*) *Politics.* a political party or group favouring moderation. **9** a bar with a conical point upon which a workpiece or part may be turned or ground. **10** *Football, hockey, etc.* **10a** a player who plays in the middle of the forward line. **10b** an instance of passing the ball from a wing to the middle of the field, etc. ◆ *vb* **centres, centring, centred** *or US* **centers, centering, centered. 11** to move towards, mark, put, or be at a centre. **12** (*tr*) to focus or bring together: *to centre one's thoughts.* **13** (*intr;* often foll. by *on*) to have as a main theme: *the novel centred on crime.* **14** (*intr;* foll. by *on* or *round*) to have as a centre. **15** (*tr*) *Football, hockey, etc.* to pass (the ball) into the middle of the field or court. [C14: from L *centrum* the stationary point of a compass, from Gk *kentron* needle, from *kentein* to prick]

centre bit *n* a drilling bit with a central point and two side cutters.

centreboard (ˈsɛntəˌbɔːd) *n* a supplementary keel for a sailing vessel.

centrefold *or US* **centerfold** (ˈsɛntəˌfəʊld) *n* **1** a large coloured illustration folded so that it forms the central spread of a magazine. **2a** a photograph of a nude or nearly nude woman (or man) in a magazine on such a spread. **2b** the subject of such a photograph.

centre forward *n Soccer, hockey, etc.* the central forward in the attack.

centre half *or* **centre back** *n Soccer.* a defender who plays in the middle of the defence.

centre of gravity *n* the point through which the resultant of the gravitational forces on a body always acts.

centre pass *n Hockey.* a push or hit made in any direction to start the game or restart the game after a goal has been scored.

centrepiece ❶ (ˈsɛntəˌpiːs) *n* an object used as the centre of something, esp. for decoration.

centre spread *n* **1** the pair of two facing pages in the middle of a magazine, newspaper, etc. **2a** a photograph of a nude or nearly nude woman (or man) in a magazine on such pages. **2b** the subject of such a photograph.

centri- *combining form.* a variant of **centro-.**

centric (ˈsɛntrɪk) *or* **centrical** *adj* **1** being central or having a centre. **2** relating to a nerve centre.
▸**centricity** (sɛnˈtrɪsɪtɪ) *n*

-centric *suffix forming adjectives.* having a centre as specified: *heliocentric.* [abstracted from ECCENTRIC, CONCENTRIC, etc.]

centrifugal ❶ (sɛnˈtrɪfjʊgᵊl, ˈsɛntrɪˌfjuːgᵊl) *adj* **1** acting, moving, or tending to move away from a centre. Cf. **centripetal. 2** of, concerned with, or operated by centrifugal force: *centrifugal pump.* [C18: from NL, from CENTRI- + L *fugere* to flee]
▸**cenˈtrifugally** *adv*

centrifugal force *n* a fictitious force that can be thought of as acting outwards on any body that rotates or moves along a curved path.

centrifuge (ˈsɛntrɪˌfjuːdʒ) *n* **1** any of various rotating machines that separate liquids from solids or other liquids by the action of centrifugal force. **2** any of various rotating devices for subjecting human beings or animals to varying accelerations. ◆ *vb* **centrifuges, centrifuging, centrifuged. 3** (*tr*) to subject to the action of a centrifuge.
▸**centrifugation** (ˌsɛntrɪfjʊˈgeɪʃən) *n*

centring (ˈsɛntrɪŋ) *or US* **centering** (ˈsɛntərɪŋ) *n* a temporary structure, esp. one made of timber, used to support an arch during construction.

centripetal (sɛnˈtrɪpɪtᵊl, ˈsɛntrɪˌpiːtᵊl) *adj* **1** acting, moving, or tending to move towards a centre. Cf. **centrifugal. 2** of, concerned with, or operated by centripetal force. [C17: from NL *centripetus* seeking the centre]
▸**cenˈtripetally** *adv*

centripetal force *n* a force that acts inwards on any body that rotates or moves along a curved path.

centrist (ˈsɛntrɪst) *n* a person holding moderate political views.
▸**ˈcentrism** *n*

centro-, centri-, *or before a vowel* **centr-** *combining form.* denoting a centre: *centrosome; centrist.* [from Gk *kentron* CENTRE]

centrosome (ˈsɛntrəˌsəʊm) *n* a small protoplasmic body found near the cell nucleus.

centuplicate *vb* (sɛnˈtjuːplɪˌkeɪt), **centuplicates, centuplicating, centuplicated. 1** (*tr*) to increase 100 times. ◆ *adj* (sɛnˈtjuːplɪkɪt). **2** increased a hundredfold. ◆ *n* (sɛnˈtjuːplɪkɪt). **3** one hundredfold.

THESAURUS

central *adj* **1** = **middle,** inner, interior, mean, median, mid **2** = **main,** chief, essential, focal, fundamental, key, primary, principal
Antonyms *adj* ≠ **middle:** exterior, outer, outermost ≠ **main:** minor, secondary, subordinate, subsidiary

centralize *vb* **2** = **unify,** amalgamate, compact, concentrate, concentre, condense, converge, incorporate, rationalize, streamline

centre *n* **1-7** = **middle,** bull's-eye, core, crux, focus, heart, hub, kernel, mid (*arch.*), midpoint, nucleus, pivot ◆ *vb* **11, 12** = **focus,** cluster, concentrate, converge, revolve
Antonyms *n* ≠ **middle:** border, boundary, brim, circumference, edge, fringe, limit, lip, margin, perimeter, periphery, rim

centrepiece *n* = **focus,** cynosure, epergne, highlight, hub, star

centrifugal *adj* **1** = **radiating,** diffusive, divergent, diverging, efferent, radial

◆ Also **centuple** ('sɛntjʊp°l). [C17: from LL, from *centuplex* hundred-fold, from L *centum* hundred + *-plex* -fold]
centurion (sɛn'tjʊərɪən) *n* the officer commanding a Roman century. [C14: from L *centuriō,* from *centuria* CENTURY]
century ('sɛntʃərɪ) *n, pl* **centuries. 1** a period of 100 years. **2** one of the successive periods of 100 years dated before or after an epoch or event, esp. the birth of Christ. **3** a score or grouping of 100: *to score a century in cricket.* **4** (in ancient Rome) a unit of foot soldiers, originally consisting of 100 men. **5** (in ancient Rome) a division of the people for purposes of voting. [C16: from L *centuria,* from *centum* hundred]
cep (sɛp) *n* an edible woodland fungus with a brown shining cap and a rich nutty flavour. [C19: from F, from Gascon dialect *cep,* from L *cippus* stake]
cephalic (sɪ'fælɪk) *adj* **1** of or relating to the head. **2** situated in, on, or near the head.
-cephalic *or* **-cephalous** *adj combining form.* indicating skull or head; -headed: *brachycephalic.* [from Gk *-kephalos*]
▸**-cephaly** *or* **-cephalism** *n combining form*
cephalic index *n* the ratio of the greatest width of the human head to its greatest length, multiplied by 100.
cephalo- *or before a vowel* **cephal-** *combining form.* indicating the head: *cephalopod.* [via L from Gk, from *kephalē* head]
cephalopod ('sɛfələˌpɒd) *n* any of various marine molluscs, characterized by well-developed head and eyes and a ring of sucker-bearing tentacles, including the octopuses, squids, and cuttlefish.
▸ˌ**cepha'lopodan** *adj, n*
cephalothorax (ˌsɛfələʊ'θɔːræks) *n, pl* **cephalothoraxes** *or* **cephalothoraces** (-rəˌsiːz). the anterior part of many crustaceans and some other arthropods consisting of a united head and thorax.
-cephalus *n combining form.* denoting a cephalic abnormality: *hydrocephalus.* [NL *-cephalus;* see -CEPHALIC]
Cepheid variable ('siːfɪɪd) *n Astron.* any of a class of variable stars with regular cycles of variations in luminosity, which are used for measuring distances.
ceramic (sɪ'ræmɪk) *n* **1** a hard brittle material made by firing clay and similar substances. **2** an object made from such a material. ◆ *adj* **3** of or made from a ceramic. **4** of or relating to ceramics: *ceramic arts.* [C19: from Gk, from *keramos* potter's clay]
ceramic hob *n* (on an electric cooker) a flat ceramic cooking surface having heating elements fitted on the underside.
ceramic oxide *n* a compound of oxygen with nonorganic material: recently discovered to act as a high-temperature superconductor.
ceramics (sɪ'ræmɪks) *n* (*functioning as sing*) the art and techniques of producing articles of clay, porcelain, etc.
▸**ceramist** ('sɛrəmɪst) *n*
cere (sɪə) *n* a soft waxy swelling, containing the nostrils, at the base of the upper beak, as in the parrot. [C15: from OF *cire* wax, from L *cēra*]
cereal ('sɪərɪəl) *n* **1** any grass that produces an edible grain, such as oat, wheat, rice, maize, and millet. **2** the grain produced by such a plant. **3** any food made from this grain, esp. breakfast food. **4** (*modifier*) of or relating to any of these plants or their products. [C19: from L *cereālis* concerning agriculture]
cerebellum (ˌsɛrɪ'bɛləm) *n, pl* **cerebellums** *or* **cerebella** (-lə). one of the major divisions of the vertebrate brain whose function is coordination of voluntary movements. [C16: from L, dim. of CEREBRUM]
▸ˌ**cere'bellar** *adj*
cerebral ('sɛrɪbrəl; *US also* sə'riːbrəl) *adj* **1** of or relating to the cerebrum or to the entire brain. **2** involving intelligence rather than emotions or instinct. **3** *Phonetics.* another word for **cacuminal.**
▸**'cerebrally** *adv*
cerebral haemorrhage *n* bleeding from an artery in the brain, which in severe cases causes a stroke.
cerebral palsy *n* a nonprogressive impairment of muscular function and weakness of the limbs, caused by lack of oxygen to the brain immediately after birth, brain injury during birth, or viral infection.
cerebrate ('sɛrɪˌbreɪt) *vb* **cerebrates, cerebrating, cerebrated.** (*intr*) *Usually facetious.* to use the mind; think; ponder; consider.
▸ˌ**cere'bration** *n*
cerebro- *or before a vowel* **cerebr-** *combining form.* indicating the brain: *cerebrospinal.* [from CEREBRUM]
cerebrospinal (ˌsɛrɪbrəʊ'spaɪn°l) *adj* of or relating to the brain and spinal cord: *cerebrospinal fluid.*
cerebrovascular (ˌsɛrɪbrəʊ'væskjʊlə) *adj* of or relating to the blood vessels and the blood supply of the brain.
cerebrum ('sɛrɪbrəm) *n, pl* **cerebrums** *or* **cerebra** (-brə). **1** the anterior portion of the brain of vertebrates, consisting of two lateral hemispheres: the dominant part of the brain in man, associated with intellectual function, emotion, and personality. **2** the brain considered as a whole. [C17: from L: the brain]
▸**'cerebric** *adj*
cerecloth ('sɪəˌklɒθ) *n* waxed waterproof cloth of a kind formerly used as a shroud. [C15: from earlier *cered cloth,* from L *cērāre* to wax]
cerement ('sɪəmənt) *n* **1** cerecloth. **2** any burial clothes. [C17: from F, from *cirer* to wax]
ceremonial ❶ (ˌsɛrɪ'məʊnɪəl) *adj* **1** involving or relating to ceremony or ritual. ◆ *n* **2** the observance of formality, esp. in etiquette. **3** a plan for formal observances; ritual. **4** *Christianity.* **4a** the prescribed order of rites and ceremonies. **4b** a book containing this.
▸ˌ**cere'monialism** *n* ▸ˌ**cere'monialist** *n* ▸ˌ**cere'monially** *adv*
ceremonious ❶ (ˌsɛrɪ'məʊnɪəs) *adj* **1** especially or excessively polite or formal. **2** involving formalities.
▸ˌ**cere'moniously** *adv*
ceremony ❶ ('sɛrɪmənɪ) *n, pl* **ceremonies. 1** a formal act or ritual, often set by custom or tradition, performed in observation of an event or anniversary. **2** a religious rite or series of rites. **3** a courteous gesture or act: *the ceremony of toasting the Queen.* **4** ceremonial observances or gestures collectively. **5 stand on ceremony.** to insist on or act with excessive formality. [C14: from Med. L, from L *caerimōnia* what is sacred]
cerise (sə'riːz, -'riːs) *n, adj* (of) a moderate to dark red colour. [C19: from F: CHERRY]
cerium ('sɪərɪəm) *n* a malleable ductile steel-grey element of the lanthanide series of metals, used in lighter flints. Symbol: Ce; atomic no.: 58; atomic wt.: 140.12. [C19: NL, from *Ceres* (the asteroid) + -IUM]
CERN (sɜːn) *n acronym for* Conseil Européen pour la Recherche Nucléaire; an organization of European states with a centre in Geneva, for research in high-energy particle physics, now called the European Laboratory for Particle Physics.
cerography (sɪə'rɒgrəfɪ) *n* the art of engraving on a waxed plate on which a printing surface is created by electrotyping.
ceroplastic (ˌsɪərəʊ'plæstɪk) *adj* **1** relating to wax modelling. **2** modelled in wax.
cert (sɜːt) *n Inf.* something that is a certainty, esp. a horse that is certain to win a race.
cert. *abbrev. for:* **1** certificate. **2** certification. **3** certified.
certain ❶ ('sɜːt°n) *adj* **1** (*postpositive*) positive and confident about the truth of something; convinced: *I am certain that he wrote a book.* **2** (*usually postpositive*) definitely known: *it is certain that they were on the bus.* **3** (*usually postpositive*) sure; bound: *he was certain to fail.* **4** fixed: *the date is already certain for the invasion.* **5** reliable: *his judgment is certain.* **6** moderate or minimum: *to a certain extent.* **7 for certain.** without a doubt. ◆ *determiner* **8a** known but not specified or named: *certain people.* **8b** (*as pron; functioning as pl*): *certain of the members have not paid.* **9** named but not known: *he had written to a certain Mrs Smith.* [C13: from OF, from L *certus* sure, from *cernere* to decide]
certainly ❶ ('sɜːt°nlɪ) *adv* **1** without doubt: *he certainly rides very well.* ◆ *sentence substitute.* **2** by all means; definitely.
certainty ❶ ('sɜːt°ntɪ) *n, pl* **certainties. 1** the condition of being certain. **2** something established as inevitable. **3 for a certainty.** without doubt.
CertEd (in Britain) *abbrev. for* Certificate in Education.
certes ('sɜːtɪz) *adv Arch.* with certainty; truly. [C13: from OF, ult. from L *certus* CERTAIN]
certificate ❶ *n* (sə'tɪfɪkɪt). **1** an official document attesting the truth of the facts stated, as of birth, death, completion of an academic course, ownership of shares, etc. ◆ *vb* (sə'tɪfɪˌkeɪt), **certificates, certificating, certificated. 2** (*tr*) to authorize by or present with an official document. [C15: from OF, from *certifier* to CERTIFY]
▸**cer'tificatory** *adj*
Certificate of Secondary Education *n* the full name for **CSE.**
certification (ˌsɜːtɪfɪ'keɪʃən) *n* **1** the act of certifying or state of being certified. **2** *Law.* a document attesting the truth of a fact or statement.
certified ('sɜːtɪˌfaɪd) *adj* **1** holding or guaranteed by a certificate. **2** endorsed or guaranteed: *a certified cheque.* **3** (of a person) declared legally insane.
certified accountant *n* (in Britain) a member of the Chartered Association of Certified Accountants, who is authorized to audit company accounts. Cf. **chartered accountant.**
certify ❶ ('sɜːtɪˌfaɪ) *vb* **certifies, certifying, certified. 1** to confirm or attest (to), usually in writing. **2** (*tr*) to endorse or guarantee that certain re-

THESAURUS

ceremonial *adj* **1** = **ritual,** formal, liturgical, ritualistic, solemn, stately ◆ *n* **3** = **ritual,** ceremony, formality, rite, solemnity
Antonyms *adj* ≠ **ritual:** casual, informal, relaxed, simple
ceremonious *adj* **1** = **formal,** civil, courteous, courtly, deferential, dignified, exact, precise, punctilious, ritual, solemn, starchy (*inf.*), stately, stiff
ceremony *n* **1, 2** = **ritual,** commemoration, function, observance, parade, rite, service, show, solemnities **4** = **formality,** ceremonial, decorum, etiquette, form, formal courtesy, niceties, pomp, propriety, protocol
certain *adj* **1** = **sure,** assured, confident, convinced, positive, satisfied **2** = **known,** ascertained, conclusive, incontrovertible, indubitable, irrefutable, plain, true, undeniable, undoubted, unequivocal, unmistakable, valid **3** = **inevitable,** bound, definite, destined, fated, ineluctable, inescapable, inexorable, sure **4** = **fixed,** decided, definite, established, settled
Antonyms *adj* disputable, doubtful, dubious, equivocal, fallible, indefinite, questionable, uncertain, unconvinced, undecided, unlikely, unreliable, unsettled, unsure
certainly *adv* **1** = **definitely,** absolutely, assuredly, come hell or high water, decidedly, doubtlessly, indisputably, indubitably, irrefutably, positively, surely, truly, undeniably, undoubtedly, unequivocally, unquestionably, without doubt, without question
certainty *n* **1** = **sureness,** assurance, authoritativeness, certitude, confidence, conviction, faith, indubitableness, inevitability, positiveness, trust, validity **2** = **fact,** banker, reality, sure thing (*inf.*), surety, truth
Antonyms *n* ≠ **sureness:** disbelief, doubt, indecision, qualm, scepticism, uncertainty, unsureness
certificate *n* **1** = **document,** authorization, credential(s), diploma, licence, testimonial, voucher, warrant
certify *vb* **1-3** = **confirm,** ascertain, assure, attest, authenticate, aver, avow, corroborate, de-

quired standards have been met. **3** to give reliable information or assurances: *he certified that it was Walter's handwriting.* **4** (*tr*) to declare legally insane. [C14: from OF, from Med. L, from L *certus* CERTAIN + *facere* to make]
▸'**certi,fiable** *adj*

certiorari (ˌsɜːtɪɔːˈreəraɪ) *n Law.* an order of a superior court directing that a record of proceedings in a lower court be sent up for review. [C15: from legal L: to be informed]

certitude ❶ (ˈsɜːtɪˌtjuːd) *n* confidence; certainty. [C15: from Church L *certitūdō*, from L *certus* CERTAIN]

cerulean (sɪˈruːlɪən) *n, adj* (of) a deep blue colour. [C17: from L *caeruleus*, prob. from *caelum* sky]

cerumen (sɪˈruːmɛn) *n* the soft brownish-yellow wax secreted by glands in the external ear. Nontechnical name: **earwax.** [C18: from NL, from L *cēra* wax + ALBUMEN]
▸**ceˈruminous** *adj*

cervelat (ˈsɜːvəˌlæt, -ˌlɑː) *n* a smoked sausage made from pork and beef. [C17: via obs. F from It. *cervellata*]

cervical (səˈvaɪkᵊl, ˈsɜːvɪkᵊl) *adj* of or relating to the neck or cervix. [C17: from NL, from L *cervīx* neck]

cervical smear *n Med.* a smear taken from the neck (cervix) of the uterus for detection of cancer. See also **Pap test** *or* **smear.**

cervine (ˈsɜːvaɪn) *adj* resembling or relating to a deer. [C19: from L *cervīnus*, from *cervus* a deer]

cervix (ˈsɜːvɪks) *n, pl* **cervixes** *or* **cervices** (səˈvaɪsiːz). **1** the technical name for **neck. 2** any necklike part, esp. the lower part of the uterus that extends into the vagina. [C18: from L]

cesium (ˈsiːzɪəm) *n* the usual US spelling of **caesium.**

cess[1] (sɛs) *n Brit.* any of several special taxes, such as a land tax in Scotland. [C16: short for ASSESSMENT]

cess[2] (sɛs) *n* an Irish slang word for **luck** (esp. in **bad cess to you!**). [C19: prob. from CESS[1]]

cessation ❶ (sɛˈseɪʃən) *n* a ceasing or stopping; pause: *temporary cessation of hostilities.* [C14: from L, from *cessāre* to be idle, from *cēdere* to yield]

cession (ˈsɛʃən) *n* **1** the act of ceding. **2** something that is ceded, esp. land or territory. [C14: from L *cessiō*, from *cēdere* to yield]

cessionary (ˈsɛʃənərɪ) *n, pl* **cessionaries.** *Law.* a person to whom something is transferred.

cesspool (ˈsɛsˌpuːl) *or* **cesspit** (ˈsɛsˌpɪt) *n* **1** Also called: **sink, sump.** a covered cistern, etc., for collecting and storing sewage or waste water. **2** a filthy or corrupt place: *a cesspool of iniquity.* [C17: ? changed from earlier *cesperalle*, from OF *souspirail* vent, air, from *soupirer* to sigh]

cestoid (ˈsɛstɔɪd) *adj* (esp. of tapeworms and similar animals) ribbon-like in form.

cesura (sɪˈzjʊərə) *n, pl* **cesuras** *or* **cesurae** (-riː). *Prosody.* a variant spelling of **caesura.**

cetacean (sɪˈteɪʃən) *adj also* **cetaceous. 1** of or belonging to an order of aquatic placental mammals having no hind limbs and a blowhole for breathing: includes toothed whales (dolphins, porpoises, etc.) and whalebone whales (rorquals, etc.). ◆ *n* **2** a whale. [C19: from NL, ult. from L *cētus* whale, from Gk *kētos*]

cetane (ˈsiːteɪn) *n* a colourless insoluble liquid hydrocarbon used in the determination of the cetane number of diesel fuel. Also called: **hexadecane.** [C19: from L *cētus* whale + -ANE]

cetane number *n* a measure of the quality of a diesel fuel expressed as the percentage of cetane. Also called: **cetane rating.** Cf. **octane number.**

cetrimide (ˈsɛtrɪˌmaɪd) *n* an ammonium compound used as a detergent and, having powerful antiseptic properties, for sterilizing surgical instruments, cleaning wounds, etc.

Cf *the chemical symbol for* californium.

CF *abbrev. for* Canadian Forces.

cf. *abbrev. for:* **1** (in bookbinding, etc.) calfskin. **2** compare. [L: *confer*]

CFB *abbrev. for* Canadian Forces Base.

CFC *abbrev. for* chlorofluorocarbon.

CFL *abbrev. for* Canadian Football League.

CFS *abbrev. for* chronic fatigue syndrome.

cg *abbrev. for* centigram.

CGBR *abbrev. for* Central Government Borrowing Requirement.

cgs units *pl n* a metric system of units based on the centimetre, gram, and second. For scientific and technical purposes these units have been replaced by SI units.

CGT *abbrev. for* Capital Gains Tax.

CH 1 *abbrev. for* Companion of Honour (a Brit. title). **2** *international car registration for* Switzerland. [from F *Confédération Helvétique*]

ch. *abbrev. for:* **1** chain (unit of measure). **2** chapter. **3** *Chess.* check. **4** chief. **5** church.

Chablis (ˈʃæblɪ) *n* (*sometimes not cap.*) a dry white wine made around Chablis, France.

cha-cha-cha (ˌtʃɑːtʃɑːˈtʃɑː) *or* **cha-cha** *n* **1** a modern ballroom dance from Latin America with small steps and swaying hip movements. **2** a piece of music composed for this dance. ◆ *vb* (*intr*) **3** to perform this dance. [C20: from American (Cuban) Sp.]

chaconne (ʃəˈkɒn) *n* **1** a musical form consisting of a set of continuous variations upon a ground bass. **2** *Arch.* a dance in slow triple time probably originating in Spain. [C17: from F, from Sp. *chacona*]

chafe ❶ (tʃeɪf) *vb* **chafes, chafing, chafed. 1** to make or become sore or worn by rubbing. **2** (*tr*) to warm (the hands, etc.) by rubbing. **3** to irritate or be irritated or impatient. **4** (*intr; often foll. by on, against, etc.*) to rub. ◆ *n* **5** a soreness or irritation caused by friction. [C14: from OF *chaufer* to warm, ult. from L, from *calēre* to be warm + *facere* to make]

chafer (ˈtʃeɪfə) *n* any of various beetles, such as the cockchafer. [OE *ceafor*]

chaff[1] ❶ (tʃɑːf) *n* **1** the mass of husks, etc., separated from the seeds during threshing. **2** finely cut straw and hay used to feed cattle. **3** something of little worth; rubbish: *to separate the wheat from the chaff.* **4** thin strips of metallic foil released into the earth's atmosphere to deflect radar signals and prevent detection. [OE *ceaf*]
▸ˈ**chaffy** *adj*

chaff[2] ❶ (tʃɑːf) *n* **1** light-hearted teasing or joking; banter. ◆ *vb* **2** to tease good-naturedly. [C19: prob. slang var. of CHAFE]
▸ˈ**chaffer** *n*

chaffer (ˈtʃæfə) *vb* **1** (*intr*) to haggle or bargain. **2** to chatter, talk, or say idly. ◆ *n* **3** haggling or bargaining. [C13 *chaffare*, from *chep* bargain + *fare* journey]
▸ˈ**chafferer** *n*

chaffinch (ˈtʃæfɪntʃ) *n* a European finch with black-and-white wings and, in the male, a reddish body and blue-grey head. [OE *ceaffinc*, from *ceaf* CHAFF[1] + *finc* FINCH]

chafing dish *n* a vessel with a heating apparatus beneath it, for cooking or keeping food warm at the table.

chagrin ❶ (ˈʃægrɪn) *n* **1** a feeling of annoyance or mortification. ◆ *vb* **2** to embarrass and annoy. [C17: from F *chagrin, chagriner*, from ?]

chain ❶ (tʃeɪn) *n* **1** a flexible length of metal links, used for confining, connecting, etc., or in jewellery. **2** (*usually pl*) anything that confines or restrains: *the chains of poverty.* **3** (*usually pl*) a set of metal links that fit over the tyre of a motor vehicle to reduce skidding on an icy surface. **4** a series of related or connected facts, events, etc. **5a** a number of establishments such as hotels, shops, etc., having the same owner or management. **5b** (*as modifier*): *a chain store.* **6** Also called: **Gunter's chain.** a unit of length equal to 22 yards. **7** Also called: **engineer's chain.** a unit of length equal to 100 feet. **8** Also called: **nautical chain.** a unit of length equal to 15 feet. **9** *Chem.* two or more atoms or groups bonded together so that the resulting molecule, ion, or radical resembles a chain. **10** *Geog.* a series of natural features, esp. mountain ranges. ◆ *vb* **11** (*tr; often foll. by up*) to confine, tie, or make fast with or as if with a chain. [C13: from OF, ult. from L; see CATENA]

chain gang *n US.* a group of convicted prisoners chained together.

chain letter *n* a letter, often with a request for and promise of money, that is sent to many people who add to or recopy it and send it on.

chain mail *n* **a** another term for **mail**[2] (sense 1). **b** (*as modifier*): *a chain-mail hood.*

chain printer *n* a line printer in which the type is on a continuous chain.

chain reaction *n* **1** a process in which a neutron colliding with an atomic nucleus causes fission and the ejection of one or more other neutrons. **2** a chemical reaction in which the product of one step is a reactant in the following step. **3** a series of events, each of which precipitates the next.
▸ˌ**chain-reˈact** *vb* (*intr*)

chain saw *n* a motor-driven saw in which the cutting teeth form links in a continuous chain.

chain-smoke *vb* **chain-smokes, chain-smoking, chain-smoked.** to smoke (cigarettes, etc.) continually, esp. lighting one from the preceding one.
▸**chain smoker** *n*

chain stitch *n* **1** a looped embroidery stitch resembling the links of a chain. ◆ *vb* **chain-stitch. 2** to sew (something) with this stitch.

chainwheel (ˈtʃeɪnˌwiːl) *n* (esp. on a bicycle) a toothed wheel that transmits drive via the chain.

chair (tʃɛə) *n* **1** a seat with a back on which one person sits, typically

THESAURUS

clare, endorse, guarantee, notify, show, testify, validate, verify, vouch, witness

certitude *n* = **certainty**, assurance, confidence, conviction

cessation *n* = **ceasing**, abeyance, arrest, break, discontinuance, ending, entr'acte, halt, halting, hiatus, intermission, interruption, interval, let-up (*inf.*), pause, recess, remission, respite, rest, standstill, stay, stoppage, suspension, termination, time off

chafe *vb* **1** = **rub**, abrade, rasp, scrape, scratch **3** = **be annoyed**, be angry, be exasperated, be impatient, be incensed, be inflamed, be irritated, be narked (*Brit., Austral., & NZ sl.*), be offended, be ruffled, be vexed, fret, fume, rage, worry

chaff[1] *n* **1, 3** = **waste**, dregs, glumes, hulls, husks, refuse, remains, rubbish, trash

chaff[2] *n* **1** = **teasing**, badinage, banter, joking, josh (*sl., chiefly US & Canad.*), persiflage, raillery ◆ *vb* **2** = **tease**, banter, deride, jeer, josh (*sl., chiefly US & Canad.*), mock, rib (*inf.*), ridicule, scoff, take the piss out of (*taboo sl.*), taunt

chagrin *n* **1** = **annoyance**, discomfiture, discomposure, displeasure, disquiet, dissatisfaction, embarrassment, fretfulness, humiliation, ill-humour, irritation, mortification, peevishness, spleen, vexation ◆ *vb* **2** = **annoy**, discomfit, discompose, displease, disquiet, dissatisfy, embarrass, humiliate, irk, irritate, mortify, peeve, vex

chain *n* **2** *usually plural* = **link**, bond, coupling, fetter, manacle, shackle, union **4** = **series**, concatenation, progression, sequence, set, string, succession, train ◆ *vb* **11** = **bind**, confine, enhaving four legs and often having arms. **2** an official position of authority. **3** the chairman of a debate or meeting: *the speaker addressed the chair.* **4** a professorship. **5** *Railways.* an iron or steel cradle bolted to a sleeper in which the rail is locked. **6** short for **sedan chair. 7 take the chair.** to preside as chairman for a meeting, etc. **8 the chair.** *Inf.* the electric chair. ◆ *vb (tr)* **9** to preside over (a meeting). **10** *Brit.* to carry aloft in a sitting position after a triumph. **11** to provide with a chair of office. **12** to install in a chair. [C13: from OF, from L *cathedra,* from Gk *kathedra,* from *kata-* down + *hedra* seat]

chairlift ('tʃɛəˌlɪft) *n* a series of chairs suspended from a power-driven cable for conveying people, esp. skiers, up a mountain.

chairman ❶ ('tʃɛəmən) *n, pl* **chairmen.** a person who presides over a company's board of directors, a committee, a debate, etc. Also: **chair, chairperson,** *or (fem)* **chairwoman.**

USAGE NOTE *Chairman* can seem inappropriate when applied to a woman, while *chairwoman* can be offensive. *Chair* and *chairperson* can be applied to either a man or a woman; *chair* is generally preferred to *chairperson.*

chaise (ʃeɪz) *n* **1** a light open horse-drawn carriage, esp. one with two wheels. **2** short for **post chaise** and **chaise longue.** [C18: from F, var. of OF *chaiere* CHAIR]

chaise longue ('ʃeɪz 'lɒŋ) *n, pl* **chaise longues** *or* **chaises longues** ('ʃeɪz 'lɒŋ). a long low chair with a back and single armrest. [C19: from F: long chair]

chakra ('tʃækrə, 'tʃʌkrə) *n* (in yoga) any of the seven major energy centres in the human body. [C19: from Sansk. *cakra* wheel, circle]

chalaza (kə'leɪzə) *n, pl* **chalazas** *or* **chalazae** (-ziː). one of a pair of spiral threads holding the yolk of a bird's egg in position. [C18: NL, from Gk: hailstone]

chalcedony (kæl'sɛdənɪ) *n, pl* **chalcedonies.** a form of quartz with crystals arranged in parallel fibres: a gemstone. [C15: from LL, from Gk *khalkēdōn* a precious stone, ? after *Khalkēdōn* Chalcedon, town in Asia Minor]
▸**chalcedonic** (ˌkælsɪ'dɒnɪk) *adj*

chalcolithic (ˌkælkə'lɪθɪk) *adj Archaeol.* of or relating to the period in which both stone and bronze tools were used. [C19: from Gk *khalkos* copper + *lithos* stone]

chalcopyrite (ˌkælkə'paɪraɪt) *n* a common ore of copper, a crystalline sulphide of copper and iron. Formula: $CuFeS_2$. Also called: **copper pyrites.**

chaldron ('tʃɔːldrən) *n* a unit of capacity equal to 36 bushels. [C17: from OF *chauderon* CAULDRON]

chalet ('ʃæleɪ) *n* **1** a type of wooden house of Swiss origin, with wide projecting eaves. **2** a similar house used as a ski lodge, etc. [C19: from F (Swiss dialect)]

chalice ('tʃælɪs) *n* **1** *Poetic.* a drinking cup; goblet. **2** *Christianity.* a gold or silver cup containing the wine at Mass. **3** a cup-shaped flower. [C13: from OF, from L *calix* cup]

chalk (tʃɔːk) *n* **1** a soft fine-grained white sedimentary rock consisting of nearly pure calcium carbonate, containing minute fossil fragments of marine organisms. **2** a piece of chalk, or substance like chalk, often coloured, used for writing and drawing on blackboards. **3 as alike** (*or* **different**) **as chalk and cheese.** *Inf.* totally different in essentials. **4 by a long chalk.** *Brit. inf.* by far. **5 not by a long chalk.** *Brit. inf.* by no means. **6** *(modifier)* made of chalk. ◆ *vb* **7** to draw or mark (something) with chalk. **8** *(tr)* to mark, rub, or whiten with or as with chalk. [OE *cealc,* from L *calx* limestone, from Gk *khalix* pebble]
▸**'chalk,like** *adj* ▸**'chalky** *adj* ▸**'chalkiness** *n*

chalk out *vb (tr, adv)* to outline (a plan, scheme, etc.); sketch.

chalkpit ('tʃɔːkˌpɪt) *n* a quarry for chalk.

chalk up ❶ *vb (tr, adv) Inf.* **1** to score or register (something). **2** to credit (money) to an account, etc. (esp. in **chalk it up**).

challenge ❶ ('tʃælɪndʒ) *vb* **challenges, challenging, challenged.** *(mainly tr)* **1** to invite or summon (someone to do something, esp. to take part in a contest). **2** *(also intr)* to call (something) into question. **3** to make demands on; stimulate: *the job challenges his ingenuity.* **4** to order (a person) to halt and be identified. **5** *Law.* to make formal objection to (a juror or jury). **6** to lay claim to (attention, etc.). **7** to inject (an experimental animal immunized with a test substance) with disease microorganisms to test for immunity to the disease. ◆ *n* **8** a call to engage in a fight, argument, or contest. **9** a questioning of a statement or fact. **10** a demanding or stimulating situation, career, etc. **11** a demand by a sentry, etc., for identification or a password. **12** *Law.* a formal objection to a person selected to serve on a jury or to the whole body of jurors. [C13: from OF *chalenge,* from L *calumnia* CALUMNY]
▸**'challengeable** *adj* ▸**'challenger** *n* ▸**'challenging** *adj*

challis ('ʃælɪ, -lɪs) *or* **challie** ('ʃælɪ) *n* a lightweight fabric of wool, cotton, etc., usually with a printed design. [C19: prob. from a surname]

chalybeate (kə'lɪbɪɪt) *adj* containing or impregnated with iron salts. [C17: from NL *chalybēātus,* ult. from Gk *khalups* iron]

chamber ❶ ('tʃeɪmbə) *n* **1** a meeting hall, esp. one used for a legislative or judicial assembly. **2** a reception room in an official residence, palace, etc. **3** *Arch. or poetic.* a room in a private house, esp. a bedroom. **4a** a legislative, judicial, or administrative assembly. **4b** any of the houses of a legislature. **5** an enclosed space; compartment; cavity. **6** an enclosure for a cartridge in the cylinder of a revolver or for a shell in the breech of a cannon. **7** short for **chamber pot. 8** *(modifier)* of, relating to, or suitable for chamber music: *a chamber concert.* **9** *(modifier)* on a small, quasi-domestic scale. ◆ See also **chambers.** [C13: from OF, from LL *camera* room, L: vault, from Gk *kamara*]

chamberlain ('tʃeɪmbəlɪn) *n* **1** an officer who manages the household of a king. **2** the steward of a nobleman or landowner. **3** the treasurer of a municipal corporation. [C13: from OF *chamberlayn,* of Frankish origin]

chambermaid ('tʃeɪmbəˌmeɪd) *n* a woman employed to clean bedrooms, esp. in hotels.

chamber music *n* music for performance by a small group of instrumentalists.

chamber of commerce *n (sometimes cap.)* an organization composed mainly of local businessmen to promote, regulate, and protect their interests.

chamber orchestra *n* a small orchestra of about 25 players, used for the authentic performance of baroque and early classical music as well as modern music.

chamber pot *n* a vessel for urine, used in bedrooms.

chambers ('tʃeɪmbəz) *pl n* **1** a judge's room for hearing private cases not taken in open court. **2** (in England) the set of rooms occupied by barristers where clients are interviewed.

chambray ('ʃæmbreɪ) *n* a smooth light fabric of cotton, linen, etc., with white weft and a coloured warp. [C19: after *Cambrai;* see CAMBRIC]

chameleon (kə'miːlɪən) *n* **1** a lizard of Africa and Madagascar, having long slender legs, a prehensile tail and tongue, and the ability to change colour. **2** a changeable or fickle person. [C14: from L, from Gk *khamaileōn,* from *khamai* on the ground + *leōn* LION]
▸**chameleonic** (kəˌmiːlɪ'ɒnɪk) *adj*

chamfer ('tʃæmfə) *n* **1** a narrow flat surface at the corner of a beam, post, etc. ◆ *vb (tr)* **2** to cut such a surface on (a beam, etc.). [C16: back formation from *chamfering,* from OF, from *chant* edge (see CANT[2]) + *fraindre* to break, from L *frangere*]

chamois ('ʃæmɪ; *for senses 1 and 4* 'ʃæmwɑː) *n, pl* **chamois. 1** a sure-footed goat antelope of Europe and SW Asia, having vertical horns with backward-pointing tips. **2** a soft suede leather formerly made from this animal, now obtained from the skins of sheep and goats. **3** Also called: **chamois leather, shammy (leather), chammy (leather).** a piece of such leather or similar material used for polishing, etc. **4a** a greyish-yellow colour. **4b** *(as adj)*: *a chamois stamp.* ◆ *vb (tr)* **5** to dress (leather or skin) like chamois. **6** to polish with a chamois. [C16: from OF, from LL *camox,* from ?]

chamomile ('kæməˌmaɪl) *n* a variant spelling of **camomile.**

champ[1] (tʃæmp) *vb* **1** to munch (food) noisily like a horse. **2** (when *intr,* often foll. by *on, at,* etc.) to bite (something) nervously or impatiently. **3 champ** (*or* **chafe**) **at the bit.** *Inf.* to be impatient to start work, a journey, etc. ◆ *n* **4** the act or noise of champing. [C16: prob. imit.]

champ[2] (tʃæmp) *n Inf.* short for **champion.**

champagne (ʃæm'peɪn) *n* **1** *(sometimes cap.)* a white sparkling wine produced around Reims and Épernay, France. **2** (loosely) any effervescent white wine. **3a** a pale tawny colour. **3b** *(as adj)*: *champagne tights.* **4** *(modifier)* denoting a luxurious lifestyle: *a champagne capitalist.* [from *Champagne,* a region of NE France]

champagne socialist *n* a professed socialist who enjoys an extravagant lifestyle.

champers ('ʃæmpəz) *n (functioning as sing) Sl.* champagne.

champerty ('tʃæmpətɪ) *n, pl* **champerties.** *Law.* (formerly) an illegal bargain between a party to litigation and an outsider whereby the latter agrees to pay for the action and thereby share in any proceeds recovered. [C14: from Anglo-F *champartie,* from OF *champart* share of produce, from *champ* field + *part* share]

champion ❶ ('tʃæmpɪən) *n* **1a** a person, plant, or animal that has defeated all others in a competition: *a chess champion.* **1b** *(as modifier): a champion team; a champion marrow.* **2** a person who defends a person or cause: *champion of the underprivileged.* **3** (formerly) a knight who did battle for another, esp. a king or queen. ◆ *adj* **4** *N English dialect.* excellent. ◆ *adv* **5** *N English dialect.* very well. ◆ *vb (tr)* **6** to support: *we*

THESAURUS

slave, fetter, gyve (*arch.*), handcuff, manacle, restrain, shackle, tether, trammel, unite

chairman *n* = **director**, chairperson, chairwoman, master of ceremonies, president, presider, speaker, spokesman, toastmaster

chalk up *vb Informal* **1** = **score**, accumulate, achieve, attain, credit, enter, gain, log, mark, record, register, tally, win

challenge *vb* **1-6** = **test**, accost, arouse, beard, brave, call out, call (someone's) bluff, claim, confront, dare, defy, demand, dispute, face off (*sl.*), impugn, investigate, object to, provoke, question, require, stimulate, summon, tackle, tax, throw down the gauntlet, try ◆ *n* **8, 9** = **test**, confrontation, dare, defiance, face-off (*sl.*), interrogation, provocation, question, summons to contest, trial, ultimatum

chamber *n* **1-3, 5** = **room**, apartment, bedroom, cavity, compartment, cubicle, enclosure, hall, hollow **4a** = **council**, assembly, legislative body, legislature

champion *n* **1** = **winner**, challenger, conqueror, hero, nonpareil, title holder, victor, warrior **2** = **defender**, backer, guardian, patron, protector, upholder, vindicator ◆ *vb* **6** = **support**, advocate, back, commend, defend, encourage, espouse, fight for, promote, stick up for (*inf.*), uphold *champion the cause of liberty.* [C13: from OF, from LL *campiō*, from L *campus* field]

championship (ˈtʃæmpɪənˌʃɪp) *n* **1** (*sometimes pl*) any of various contests held to determine a champion. **2** the title of being a champion. **3** support for a cause, person, etc.

champlevé *French.* (ʃɑ̃lve) *adj* **1** of a process of enamelling by which grooves are cut into a metal base and filled with enamel colours. ♦ *n* **2** an object enamelled by this process. [C19: from *champ* field (level surface) + *levé* raised]

Chanc. *abbrev. for:* **1** Chancellor. **2** Chancery.

chance Ⓣ (tʃɑːns) *n* **1a** the unknown and unpredictable element that causes an event to result in a certain way rather than another, spoken of as a real force. **1b** (*as modifier*): *a chance meeting.* Related adj: **fortuitous.** **2** fortune; luck; fate. **3** an opportunity or occasion. **4** a risk; gamble. **5** the extent to which an event is likely to occur; probability. **6** an unpredicted event, esp. a fortunate one. **7 by chance.** accidentally: *he slipped by chance.* **8 on the (off) chance.** acting on the (remote) possibility. ♦ *vb* **chances, chancing, chanced. 9** (*tr*) to risk; hazard. **10** (*intr*) to happen by chance: *I chanced to catch sight of her.* **11 chance on** (*or* **upon**). to come upon by accident. **12 chance one's arm.** to attempt to do something although the chance of success may be slight. [C13: from OF, from *cheoir* to occur, from L *cadere*]
▸ˈ**chanceful** *adj*

chancel (ˈtʃɑːnsəl) *n* the part of a church containing the altar, sanctuary, and choir. [C14: from OF, from L *cancellī* (pl) lattice]

chancellery *or* **chancellory** (ˈtʃɑːnsələrɪ) *n, pl* **chancelleries** *or* **chancellories. 1** the building or room occupied by a chancellor's office. **2** the position or office of a chancellor. **3** *US.* the office of an embassy or legation. [C14: from Anglo-F *chancellerie*, from OF *chancelier* CHANCELLOR]

chancellor (ˈtʃɑːnsələ) *n* **1** the head of the government in several European countries. **2** *US.* the president of a university. **3** *Brit. & Canad.* the honorary head of a university. Cf. **vice chancellor. 4** *Christianity.* a clergyman acting as the law officer of a bishop. [C11: from Anglo-F *chanceler*, from LL *cancellārius* porter, from L *cancellī* lattice]
▸ˈ**chancellor,ship** *n*

Chancellor of the Exchequer *n Brit.* the cabinet minister responsible for finance.

chance-medley *n Law.* a sudden quarrel in which one party kills another. [C15: from Anglo-F *chance medlee* mixed chance]

chancer (ˈtʃɑːnsə) *n Sl.* an unscrupulous or dishonest opportunist. [C19: from CHANCE + -ER[1]]

chancery (ˈtʃɑːnsərɪ) *n, pl* **chanceries.** (*usually cap.*) **1** Also called: **Chancery Division.** (in England) the Lord Chancellor's court, now a division of the High Court of Justice. **2** Also called: **court of chancery.** (in the US) a court of equity. **3** *Brit.* the political section or offices of an embassy or legation. **4** another name for **chancellery. 5** a court of public records. **6** *Christianity.* a diocesan office under the supervision of a bishop's chancellor. **7 in chancery. 7a** *Law.* (of a suit) pending in a court of equity. **7b** in an awkward situation. [C14: shortened from CHANCELLERY]

chancre (ˈʃæŋkə) *n Pathol.* a small hard growth, which is the first sign of syphilis. [C16: from F, from L: CANCER]
▸ˈ**chancrous** *adj*

chancroid (ˈʃæŋkrɔɪd) *n* **1** a soft venereal ulcer, esp. of the male genitals. ♦ *adj* **2** relating to or resembling a chancroid or chancre.

chancy Ⓣ *or* **chancey** (ˈtʃɑːnsɪ) *adj* **chancier, chanciest.** *Inf.* uncertain; risky.

chandelier (ˌʃændɪˈlɪə) *n* an ornamental hanging light with branches and holders for several candles or bulbs. [C17: from F: candleholder, from L CANDELABRUM]

chandler (ˈtʃɑːndlə) *n* **1** a dealer in a specified trade or merchandise: *ship's chandler.* **2** a person who makes or sells candles. [C14: from OF *chandelier* one who makes or deals in candles, from *chandelle* CANDLE]
▸ˈ**chandlery** *n*

Chandrasekhar limit *n Astron.* the upper limit to the mass of a white dwarf, equal to 1.44 solar masses. A star with greater mass will continue to collapse to form a neutron star. [C20: named after S. *Chandrasekhar* (1910–95), US astronomer who calculated it]

change Ⓣ (tʃeɪndʒ) *vb* **changes, changing, changed. 1** to make or become different; alter. **2** (*tr*) to replace with or exchange for another: *to change one's name.* **3** (sometimes foll. by *to* or *into*) to transform or convert or be transformed or converted. **4** to give and receive (something) in return: *to change places.* **5** (*tr*) to give or receive (money) in exchange for the equivalent sum in a smaller denomination or different currency. **6** (*tr*) to remove or replace the coverings of: *to change a baby.* **7** (when *intr*, may be foll. by *into* or *out of*) to put on other clothes. **8** to operate (the gear lever of a motor vehicle): *to change gear.* **9** to alight from (one bus, train, etc.) and board another. ♦ *n* **10** the act or fact of changing or being changed. **11** a variation or modification. **12** the substitution of one thing for another. **13** anything that is or may be substituted for something else. **14** variety or novelty (esp. in **for a change**). **15** a different set, esp. of clothes. **16** money given or received in return for its equivalent in a larger denomination or in a different currency. **17** the balance of money when the amount tendered is larger than the amount due. **18** coins of a small denomination. **19** (*often cap.*) *Arch.* a place where merchants meet to transact business. **20** the act of passing from one state or phase to another. **21** the transition from one phase of the moon to the next. **22** the order in which a peal of bells may be rung. **23 get no change out of (someone).** *Sl.* not to be successful in attempts to exploit (someone). **24 ring the changes.** to vary the manner or performance of an action that is often repeated. ♦ See also **change down, changeover, change up.** [C13: from OF, from L *cambīre* to exchange, barter]
▸ˈ**changeful** *adj* ▸ˈ**changeless** *adj* ▸ˈ**changer** *n*

changeable Ⓣ (ˈtʃeɪndʒəbᵊl) *adj* **1** able to change or be changed: *changeable weather.* **2** varying in colour as when viewed from different angles.
▸ˌ**changeaˈbility** *n* ▸ˈ**changeably** *adv*

change down *vb* (*intr, adv*) to select a lower gear when driving.

changeling (ˈtʃeɪndʒlɪŋ) *n* a child believed to have been exchanged by fairies for the parents' true child.

change of life *n* a nontechnical name for **menopause.**

changeover (ˈtʃeɪndʒˌəʊvə) *n* **1** an alteration or complete reversal from one method, system, or product to another. **2** a reversal of a situation, attitude, etc. **3** *Sport.* the act of transferring to or being relieved by a team-mate in a relay race, as by handing over a baton, etc. ♦ *vb* **change over.** (*adv*) **4** to adopt (a different position or attitude): *the driver and navigator changed over.*

change-ringing *n* the art of bell-ringing in which a set of bells is rung in an established order which is then changed.

change up *vb* (*intr, adv*) to select a higher gear when driving.

channel Ⓣ (ˈtʃænᵊl) *n* **1** a broad strait connecting two areas of sea. **2** the bed or course of a river, stream, or canal. **3** a navigable course through a body of water. **4** (*often pl*) a means or agency of access, communication, etc.: *through official channels.* **5** a course into which something can be directed or moved. **6** *Electronics.* **6a** a band of radio frequencies assigned for a particular purpose, esp. the broadcasting of a television signal. **6b** a path for an electrical signal: *a stereo set has two channels.* **7** a tubular passage for fluids. **8** a groove, as in the shaft of a column. **9** *Computing.* **9a** a path along which data can be transmitted. **9b** one of the lines along the length of a paper tape on which information can be stored in the form of punched holes. ♦ *vb* **channels, channelling, channelled** *or US* **channels, channeling, channeled. 10** to make or cut channels in (something). **11** (*tr*) to guide into or convey through a channel or channels: *information was channelled through to them.* **12** to serve as a medium through whom the spirit of (a person of a former age) allegedly communicates with the living. **13** (*tr*) to form a groove or flute in (a column, etc.). [C13: from OF, from L *canālis* pipe, groove, conduit]

Channel (ˈtʃænᵊl) *n* **the.** the English Channel, between England and France.

channel-hop *vb* **channel-hops, channel-hopping, channel-hopped.** (*intr*) to change television channels repeatedly using a remote control device.

chanson de geste *French.* (ʃɑ̃sɔ̃ də ʒɛst) *n* one of a genre of Old French epic poems, the most famous of which is the *Chanson de Roland.* [lit.: song of exploits]

chant Ⓣ (tʃɑːnt) *n* **1** a simple song. **2** a short simple melody in which

THESAURUS

chance *n* **1a, 2** = **luck**, accident, casualty, coincidence, contingency, destiny, fate, fortuity, fortune, misfortune, peril, providence ♦ *modifier* **1b** = **accidental**, casual, contingent, fortuitous, inadvertent, incidental, random, serendipitous, unforeseeable, unforeseen, unintentional, unlooked-for ♦ *n* **3** = **opportunity**, occasion, opening, scope, time, window **4** = **risk**, gamble, hazard, jeopardy, speculation, uncertainty **5** = **probability**, liability, likelihood, odds, possibility, prospect ♦ *vb* **9** = **risk**, endanger, gamble, go out on a limb, hazard, jeopardize, skate on thin ice, stake, try, venture, wager **10** = **happen**, befall, betide, come about, come to pass, fall out, occur
Antonyms *n* ≠ **probability**: certainty, design, impossibility, improbability, intention, surety, unlikelihood ♦ *modifier* ≠ **accidental**: arranged, deliberate, designed, expected, foreseen, intentional, planned

chancy *adj Informal* = **risky**, dangerous, dicey (*inf., chiefly Brit.*), dodgy (*Brit., Austral., & NZ sl.*), hazardous, perilous, problematical, speculative, uncertain
Antonyms *adj* certain, reliable, safe, secure, sound, stable, sure

change *vb* **1, 3** = **alter**, convert, diversify, fluctuate, metamorphose, moderate, modify, mutate, reform, remodel, reorganize, restyle, shift, transform, transmute, vacillate, vary, veer **2** = **exchange**, alternate, barter, convert, displace, interchange, remove, replace, substitute, swap, trade, transmit ♦ *n* **10** = **alteration**, difference, innovation, metamorphosis, modification, mutation, permutation, revolution, transformation, transition, transmutation, vicissitude **12** = **exchange**, conversion, interchange, substitution, swap, trade **14** = **variety**, break (*inf.*), departure, diversion, novelty, variation, whole new ball game (*inf.*)
Antonyms *vb* ≠ **alter**: hold, keep, remain, stay ♦ *n* ≠ **alteration, variety**: constancy, invariability, monotony, permanence, stability, uniformity

changeable *adj* **1** = **variable**, capricious, changeful, chequered, erratic, fickle, fitful, fluid, inconstant, irregular, kaleidoscopic, mercurial, mobile, mutable, protean, shifting, temperamental, uncertain, uneven, unpredictable, unreliable, unsettled, unstable, unsteady, vacillating, versatile, volatile, wavering, whimsical
Antonyms *adj* constant, invariable, irreversible, regular, reliable, stable, steady, unchangeable

changeless *adj* **10, 11** = **unchanging**, abiding, consistent, constant, eternal, everlasting, fixed, immovable, immutable, permanent, perpetual, regular, reliable, resolute, settled, stationary, steadfast, steady, unalterable, uniform, unvarying

channel *n* **4, 5** = **route**, approach, artery, avenue, course, means, medium, path, way **7, 8** = **passage**, canal, chamber, conduit, duct, fluting, furrow, groove, gutter, main, route, strait ♦ *vb* **11** = **direct**, conduct, convey, guide, transmit

chant *n* **1-3** = **song**, carol, chorus, melody,

several words or syllables are assigned to one note. **3** a psalm or canticle performed by using such a melody. **4** a rhythmic or repetitious slogan, usually spoken or sung, as by sports supporters, etc. ◆ *vb* **5** to sing or recite (a psalm, etc.) as a chant. **6** to intone (a slogan). [C14: from OF *chanter* to sing, from L *cantāre*, frequentative of *canere* to sing] ▸**'chanting** *n, adj*
chanter ('tʃɑːntə) *n* the pipe on a set of bagpipes on which the melody is played.
chanterelle (ˌtʃæntə'rɛl) *n* any of a genus of fungi having an edible yellow funnel-shaped mushroom. [C18: from F, from L *cantharus* drinking vessel, from Gk *kantharos*]
chanteuse (*French* ʃɑ̃tøz) *n* a female singer, esp. in a nightclub or cabaret. [F: singer]
chanticleer (ˌtʃæntɪ'klɪə) *n* a name for a cock, used esp. in fables. [C13: from OF, from *chanter cler* to sing clearly]
chantry ('tʃɑːntrɪ) *n, pl* **chantries.** *Christianity.* **1** an endowment for the singing of Masses for the soul of the founder. **2** a chapel or altar so endowed. [C14: from OF, from *chanter* to sing; see CHANT]
chanty ('ʃæntɪ, 'tʃæn-) *n, pl* **chanties.** a variant of **shanty**².
Chanukah *or* **Hanukkah** ('hɑːnəkə, -nʊˌkɑː) *n* the eight-day Jewish festival of lights commemorating the rededication of the temple by Judas Maccabaeus in 165 B.C. Also called: **Feast of Dedication, Feast of Lights.** [from Heb., lit.: a dedication]
chaology (keɪ'ɒlədʒɪ) *n* the study of chaos theory.
▸**cha'ologist** *n*
chaos ➊ ('keɪɒs) *n* **1** (*usually cap.*) the disordered formless matter supposed to have existed before the ordered universe. **2** complete disorder; utter confusion. [C15: from L, from Gk *khaos*]
▸**chaotic** (keɪ'ɒtɪk) *adj* ▸**cha'otically** *adv*
chaos theory *n* a theory, applied in various branches of science, that apparently random phenomena have underlying order.
chap¹ (tʃæp) *vb* **chaps, chapping, chapped. 1** (of the skin) to make or become raw and cracked, esp. by exposure to cold. ◆ *n* **2** (*usually pl*) a cracked patch on the skin. [C14: prob. of Gmc origin]
chap² ➊ (tʃæp) *n Inf.* a man or boy; fellow. [C16 (in the sense: buyer): shortened from CHAPMAN]
chap³ (tʃɒp, tʃæp) *n* a less common word for **chop**³.
chaparejos *or* **chaparajos** (ˌʃæpə'reɪəʊs) *pl n* another name for **chaps.** [from Mexican Sp.]
chaparral (ˌtʃæpə'ræl, ˌʃæp-) *n* (in the southwestern US) a dense growth of shrubs and trees. [C19: from Sp., from *chaparra* evergreen oak]
chapati *or* **chapatti** (tʃə'pætɪ, -'pɑːtɪ) *n, pl* **chapati, chapatis, chapaties** *or* **chapatti, chapattis, chapatties.** (in Indian cookery) a flat unleavened bread resembling a pancake. [from Hindi]
chapbook ('tʃæpˌbʊk) *n* a book of popular ballads, stories, etc., formerly sold by chapmen.
chapel ('tʃæpᵊl) *n* **1** a place of Christian worship, esp. with a separate altar, in a church or cathedral. **2** a similar place of worship in a large house or institution, such as a college. **3** a church subordinate to a parish church. **4** (in Britain) **4a** a Nonconformist place of worship. **4b** Nonconformist religious practices or doctrine. **5a** the members of a trade union in a newspaper office, printing house, etc. **5b** a meeting of these members. [C13: from OF, from LL *cappella*, dim. of *cappa* cloak (see CAP); orig. the sanctuary where the cloak of St Martin was kept]
chaperon ➊ *or* **chaperone** ('ʃæpəˌrəʊn) *n* **1** (esp. formerly) an older or married woman who accompanies or supervises a young unmarried woman on social occasions. ◆ *vb* **chaperons, chaperoning, chaperoned** *or* **chaperones, chaperoning, chaperoned. 2** to act as a chaperon to. [C14: from OF, from *chape* hood; see CAP]
▸**'chaperˌonage** *n*
chapfallen ('tʃæpˌfɔːlən) *or* **chopfallen** *adj* dejected; downhearted. [C16: from CHOPS + FALLEN]
chaplain ('tʃæplɪn) *n* a Christian clergyman attached to a chapel of an institution or ministering to a military body, etc. [C12: from OF, from LL, from *cappella* CHAPEL]
▸**'chaplaincy** *n*
chaplet ➊ ('tʃæplɪt) *n* **1** an ornamental wreath of flowers worn on the head. **2** a string of beads. **3** *RC Church.* **3a** a string of prayer beads constituting one third of the rosary. **3b** the prayers counted on this string. **4** a narrow moulding in the form of a string of beads; astragal. [C14: from OF, from *chapel* hat]
▸**'chapleted** *adj*
chapman ('tʃæpmən) *n, pl* **chapmen.** *Arch.* a trader, esp. an itinerant pedlar. [OE *cēapman*, from *cēap* buying and selling]
chappie ('tʃæpɪ) *n Inf.* another word for **chap**².
chaps (tʃæps, ʃæps) *pl n* leather overleggings without a seat, worn by cowboys. Also called: **chaparajos, chaparejos.** [C19: shortened from CHAPAREJOS]
chapter ➊ ('tʃæptə) *n* **1** a division of a written work. **2** a sequence of events: *a chapter of disasters.* **3** a period in a life, history, etc. **4** a numbered reference to that part of a Parliamentary session which relates to a specified Act of Parliament. **5** a branch of some societies, clubs, etc. **6** the collective body or a meeting of the canons of a cathedral or of the members of a monastic or knightly order. **7 chapter and verse.** exact authority for an action or statement. ◆ *vb* **8** (*tr*) to divide into chapters. [C13: from OF *chapitre*, from L *capitulum*, lit.: little head, hence, section of writing, from *caput* head]
chapterhouse ('tʃæptəˌhaʊs) *n* **1** the building in which a chapter meets. See **chapter** (sense 6). **2** *US.* the meeting place of a college fraternity or sorority.
char¹ ➊ (tʃɑː) *vb* **chars, charring, charred. 1** to burn or be burned partially; scorch. **2** (*tr*) to reduce (wood) to charcoal by partial combustion. [C17: short for CHARCOAL]
char² *or* **charr** (tʃɑː) *n, pl* **char, chars** *or* **charr, charrs.** any of various troutlike fishes occurring in cold lakes and northern seas. [C17: from ?]
char³ (tʃɑː) *n* **1** *Inf.* short for **charwoman.** ◆ *vb* **chars, charring, charred. 2** (*intr*) *Brit. inf.* to do cleaning as a job. [C18: from OE *cęrran*]
char⁴ (tʃɑː) *n Brit.* a slang word for **tea.** [from Chinese *ch'a*]
charabanc ('ʃærəˌbæŋ) *n Brit.* a coach, esp. for sightseeing. [C19: from F: wagon with seats]
character ➊ ('kærɪktə) *n* **1** the combination of traits and qualities distinguishing the individual nature of a person or thing. **2** one such distinguishing quality; characteristic. **3** moral force: *a man of character.* **4a** reputation, esp. a good reputation. **4b** (*as modifier*): *character assassination.* **5** a person represented in a play, film, story, etc.; role. **6** an outstanding person: *one of the great characters of the century.* **7** *Inf.* an odd, eccentric, or unusual person: *he's quite a character.* **8** an informal word for **person:** *a shady character.* **9** a symbol used in a writing system, such as a letter of the alphabet. **10** Also called: **sort.** *Printing.* any single letter, numeral, etc., cast as a type. **11** *Computing.* any letter, numeral, etc., which can be represented uniquely by a binary pattern. **12** a style of writing or printing. **13** *Genetics.* any structure, function, attribute, etc., in an organism that is determined by a gene or group of genes. **14** a short prose sketch of a distinctive type of person. **15 in** (*or* **out of**) **character.** typical (*or* not typical) of the apparent character of a person. [C14: from L: distinguishing mark, from Gk *kharaktēr* engraver's tool]
▸**'characterful** *adj* ▸**'characterless** *adj*
character actor *n* an actor who specializes in playing odd or eccentric characters.
character assassination *n* the act of deliberately attempting to destroy a person's reputation by defamatory remarks.
characteristic ➊ (ˌkærɪktə'rɪstɪk) *n* **1** a distinguishing quality, attribute, or trait. **2** *Maths.* **2a** the integral part of a common logarithm: *the characteristic of 2.4771 is 2.* **2b** another name for **exponent** (sense 4). ◆ *adj* **3** indicative of a distinctive quality, etc.; typical.
▸ˌ**character'istically** *adv*
characterize ➊ *or* **characterise** ('kærɪktəˌraɪz) *vb* **characterizes, characterizing, characterized** *or* **characterises, characterising, characterised.** (*tr*) **1** to be a characteristic of. **2** to distinguish or mark as a characteristic. **3** to describe or portray the character of.
▸ˌ**characteri'zation** *or* ˌ**characteri'sation** *n*
charade ➊ (ʃə'rɑːd) *n* **1** an act in the game of charades. **2** *Chiefly Brit.* an absurd act; travesty.
charades (ʃə'rɑːdz) *n* (*functioning as sing*) a parlour game in which one team acts out each syllable of a word, the other team having to guess the word. [C18: from F, from Provençal *charrado* chat, from *charra* chatter]
charcoal ('tʃɑːˌkəʊl) *n* **1** a black amorphous form of carbon made by heating wood or other organic matter in the absence of air. **2** a stick of this for drawing. **3** a drawing done in charcoal. **4** Also: **charcoal grey. 4a** a dark grey colour. **4b** (*as adj*): *a charcoal suit.* ◆ *vb* **5** (*tr*) to write, draw, or blacken with charcoal. [C14: from *char* (from ?) + COAL]

THESAURUS

psalm ◆ *vb* **5** = **sing**, carol, chorus, croon, descant, intone, recite, warble
chaos *n* **2** = **disorder**, anarchy, bedlam, confusion, disorganization, entropy, lawlessness, mayhem, pandemonium, tumult
Antonyms *n* neatness, orderliness, organization, tidiness
chaotic *adj* **2** = **disordered**, anarchic, confused, deranged, disorganized, lawless, purposeless, rampageous, riotous, topsy-turvy, tumultuous, uncontrolled
chap² *n Informal* = **fellow**, bloke (*Brit. inf.*), character, cove, customer (*inf.*), dude (*US & Canad. inf.*), guy (*inf.*), individual, man, person, sort, type
chaperon *n* **1** = **escort**, companion, duenna, governess ◆ *vb* **2** = **escort**, accompany, attend, protect, safeguard, shepherd, watch over
chaplet *n* **1** = **garland**, bouquet, coronal, wreath
chapter *n* **1, 3** = **section**, clause, division, episode, part, period, phase, stage, topic
char¹ *vb* **1** = **scorch**, carbonize, cauterize, sear, singe
character *n* **1** = **nature**, attributes, bent, calibre, cast, complexion, constitution, disposition, individuality, kidney, make-up, marked traits, personality, quality, temper, temperament, type **3, 4a** = **reputation**, honour, integrity, rectitude, strength, uprightness **5** = **role**, part, persona, portrayal **7** = **eccentric**, card (*inf.*), nut (*sl.*), oddball (*inf.*), odd bod (*inf.*), oddity, original, queer fish (*Brit. inf.*) **8** *Informal* = **person**, fellow, guy (*inf.*), individual, sort, type **9** = **symbol**, cipher, device, emblem, figure, hieroglyph, letter, logo, mark, rune, sign, type
characteristic *n* **1** = **feature**, attribute, faculty, idiosyncrasy, mark, peculiarity, property, quality, quirk, trait ◆ *adj* **3** = **typical**, distinctive, distinguishing, idiosyncratic, individual, peculiar, representative, singular, special, specific, symbolic, symptomatic
Antonyms *adj* ≠ **typical**: rare, uncharacteristic, unrepresentative, unusual
characterize *vb* **1-3** = **identify**, brand, distinguish, indicate, inform, mark, represent, stamp, typify
charade *n* **2** = **pretence**, fake, farce, pantomime, parody, travesty
charge *vb* **3** = **accuse**, arraign, blame, im-

charcuterie (ʃɑːˈkuːtəri:) *n* **1** cooked cold meats. **2** a shop selling cooked cold meats. [F]

chard (tʃɑːd) *n* a variety of beet with large succulent leaves and thick stalks, used as a vegetable. Also called: **Swiss chard.** [C17: prob. from F *carde*, ult. from L *carduus* thistle]

Chardonnay (ˈʃɑːdəˌneɪ) *n* (*sometimes not cap.*) **1** a white grape grown in the Burgundy region of France, Australia, California, New Zealand and elsewhere, used for making wine. **2** any of various white wines made from this grape. [F]

charge ➊ (tʃɑːdʒ) *vb* **charges, charging, charged. 1** to set or demand (a price). **2** (*tr*) to enter a debit against a person or his account. **3** (*tr*) to accuse or impute a fault to (a person, etc.), as formally in a court of law. **4** (*tr*) to command; place a burden upon or assign responsibility to: *I was charged to take the message to headquarters.* **5** to make a rush at or sudden attack upon (a person or thing). **6** (*tr*) to fill (a receptacle) with the proper quantity. **7** (often foll. by *up*) to cause (an accumulator, capacitor, etc.) to take or store electricity or (of an accumulator) to have electricity fed into it. **8** to fill or be filled with matter by dispersion, solution, or absorption: *to charge water with carbon dioxide.* **9** (*tr*) to fill or suffuse with feeling, emotion, etc.: *the atmosphere was charged with excitement.* **10** (*tr*) *Law.* (of a judge) to address (a jury) authoritatively. **11** (*tr*) to load (a firearm). **12** (*tr*) *Heraldry.* to paint (a shield, banner, etc.) with a charge. ◆ *n* **13** a price charged for some article or service; cost. **14** a financial liability, such as a tax. **15** a debt or a book entry recording it. **16** an accusation or allegation, such as a formal accusation of a crime in law. **17a** an onrush, attack, or assault. **17b** the call to such an attack in battle. **18** custody or guardianship. **19** a person or thing committed to someone's care. **20a** a cartridge or shell. **20b** the explosive required to discharge a firearm. **20c** an amount of explosive to be detonated at any one time. **21** the quantity of anything that a receptacle is intended to hold. **22** *Physics.* **22a** the attribute of matter responsible for all electrical phenomena, existing in two forms: *negative charge; positive charge.* **22b** an excess or deficiency of electrons in a system. **22c** a quantity of electricity determined by the product of an electric current and the time for which it flows, measured in coulombs. **22d** the total amount of electricity stored in a capacitor or an accumulator. **23** a load or burden. **24** a duty or responsibility; control. **25** a command, injunction, or order. **26** *Heraldry.* a design depicted on heraldic arms. **27 in charge.** in command. **28 in charge of. 28a** having responsibility for. **28b** *US.* under the care of. [C13: from OF *chargier* to load, from LL *carricāre*; see CARRY]

chargeable (ˈtʃɑːdʒəbᵊl) *adj* **1** liable to be charged. **2** liable to result in a legal charge.

chargeable asset *n* any asset that can give rise to assessment for capital gains tax on its disposal. Exempt assets include principal private residences, cars, investments held in a personal equity plan, and government securities.

charge account *n* another term for **credit account.**

charge-cap (ˈtʃɑːdʒˌkæp) *vb* **charge-caps, charge-capping, charge-capped.** (*tr*) (in Britain) to impose on (a local authority) an upper limit on the community charge it may levy.
▸**ˈcharge-ˌcapping** *n*

charge card *n* a card issued by a chain store, shop, or organization, that enables customers to obtain goods and services for which they pay at a later date.

charge carrier *n* an electron, hole, or ion that transports the electric charge in an electric current.

chargé d'affaires (ˈʃɑːʒeɪ dæˈfɛə) *n, pl* **chargés d'affaires** (ˈʃɑːʒeɪ, -ʒeɪz). **1** the temporary head of a diplomatic mission in the absence of the ambassador or minister. **2** the head of a diplomatic mission of the lowest level. [C18: from F: (one) charged with affairs]

charge hand *n Brit.* a workman whose grade of responsibility is just below that of a foreman.

charge nurse *n Brit.* a nurse in charge of a ward in a hospital. Male equivalent of **sister.**

charger[1] (ˈtʃɑːdʒə) *n* **1** a person or thing that charges. **2** a horse formerly ridden into battle. **3** a device for charging an accumulator.

charger[2] (ˈtʃɑːdʒə) *n Antiques.* a large dish. [C14 *chargeour*, from *chargen* to CHARGE]

charge sheet *n Brit.* a document on which a police officer enters details of the charge against a prisoner and the court in which he will appear.

char-grilled *adj* (of food) grilled over charcoal.

charily (ˈtʃɛərɪlɪ) *adv* **1** cautiously; carefully. **2** sparingly.

chariness (ˈtʃɛərɪnɪs) *n* the state of being chary.

chariot (ˈtʃærɪət) *n* **1** a two-wheeled horse-drawn vehicle used in ancient wars, races, etc. **2** a light four-wheeled horse-drawn ceremonial carriage. **3** *Poetic.* any stately vehicle. [C14: from OF, augmentative of *char* CAR]

charioteer (ˌtʃærɪəˈtɪə) *n* the driver of a chariot.

charisma ➊ (kəˈrɪzmə) *or* **charism** (ˈkærɪzəm) *n* **1** a special personal quality or power making an individual capable of influencing or inspiring people. **2** a quality inherent in a thing, such as a particular type of car, which inspires great enthusiasm and devotion. **3** *Christianity.* a divinely bestowed power or talent. [C17: from Church L, from Gk *kharisma*, from *kharis* grace, favour]
▸**charismatic** (ˌkærɪzˈmætɪk) *adj*

charismatic movement *n Christianity.* any of various groups, within existing denominations, emphasizing the charismatic gifts of speaking in tongues, healing, etc.

charitable ➊ (ˈtʃærɪtəbᵊl) *adj* **1** generous in giving to the needy. **2** kind or lenient in one's attitude towards others. **3** of or for charity.
▸**ˈcharitableness** *n* ▸**ˈcharitably** *adv*

charitable trust *n* a trust set up for the benefit of a charity that complies with the regulations of the Charity Commissioners to enable it to be exempt from paying income tax.

charity ➊ (ˈtʃærɪtɪ) *n, pl* **charities. 1a** the giving of help, money, food, etc., to those in need. **1b** (*as modifier*): *a charity show.* **2** an institution or organization set up to provide help, money, etc., to those in need. **3** the help, money, etc., given to the needy; alms. **4** a kindly attitude towards people. **5** love of one's fellow men. [C13: from OF, from L *cāritās* affection, from *cārus* dear]

charivari (ˌʃɑːrɪˈvɑːrɪ), **shivaree,** *or esp. US.* **chivaree** *n* **1** a discordant mock serenade to newlyweds, made with pans, kettles, etc. **2** a confused noise; din. [C17: from F, from LL, from Gk *karēbaria*, from *karē* head + *barus* heavy]

charlady (ˈtʃɑːˌleɪdɪ) *n, pl* **charladies.** another name for **charwoman.**

charlatan ➊ (ˈʃɑːlətᵊn) *n* someone who professes expertise, esp. in medicine, that he does not have; quack. [C17: from F, from It., from *ciarlare* to chatter]
▸**ˈcharlatanˌism** *or* **ˈcharlatanry** *n*

Charles's Wain (weɪn) *n* another name for the **Plough.** [OE *Carles wægn*, from *Carl* Charlemagne + *wægn* WAIN]

charleston (ˈtʃɑːlstən) *n* a fast rhythmic dance of the 1920s, characterized by kicking and by twisting of the legs from the knee down. [named after *Charleston*, South Carolina]

charley horse (ˈtʃɑːlɪ) *n US & Canad. inf.* cramp following strenuous athletic exercise. [C19: from ?]

charlie (ˈtʃɑːlɪ) *n Brit. inf.* a silly person; fool.

charlock (ˈtʃɑːlɒk) *n* a weedy Eurasian plant with hairy stems and foliage and yellow flowers. Also called: **wild mustard.** [OE *cerlic*, from ?]

charlotte (ˈʃɑːlət) *n* **1** a dessert made with fruit and layers or a casing of bread or cake crumbs, sponge cake, etc.: *apple charlotte.* **2** short for **charlotte russe.** [C19: from F, from the name *Charlotte*]

charlotte russe (ruːs) *n* a cold dessert made with sponge fingers enclosing a mixture of cream, custard, etc. [F.: Russian charlotte]

charm ➊ (tʃɑːm) *n* **1** the quality of pleasing, fascinating, or attracting people. **2** a pleasing or attractive feature. **3** a small object worn for supposed magical powers; amulet. **4** a trinket worn on a bracelet. **5** a magic spell. **6** a formula used in casting such a spell. **7** *Physics.* a property of certain elementary particles, used to explain some scattering experiments. **8 like a charm.** perfectly; successfully. ◆ *vb* **9** to attract or fascinate; delight greatly. **10** to cast a magic spell on. **11** to protect, influence, or heal, supposedly by magic. **12** (*tr*) to influence or obtain by personal charm. [C13: from OF, from L *carmen* song]
▸**ˈcharmer** *n*

THESAURUS

peach, incriminate, indict, involve **4** *Formal* = **command**, bid, commit, demand, enjoin, entrust, exhort, instruct, order, require **5** = **attack**, assail, assault, rush, stampede, storm **6** = **fill**, instil, lade, load, suffuse ◆ *n* **13** = **price**, amount, cost, damage (*inf.*), expenditure, expense, outlay, payment, rate, toll **16** = **accusation**, allegation, imputation, indictment **17a** = **attack**, assault, onset, onslaught, rush, sortie, stampede **18, 24** = **care**, custody, duty, office, responsibility, safekeeping, trust **19, 23** = **ward**, burden, concern **25** = **instruction**, canon, command, demand, dictate, direction, exhortation, injunction, mandate, order, precept

Antonyms *vb* ≠ **accuse:** absolve, acquit, clear, exonerate, pardon ≠ **attack:** back off, retreat, withdraw ◆ *n* ≠ **accusation:** absolution, acquittal, clearance, exoneration, pardon, reprieve ≠ **attack:** retreat, withdrawal

charisma *n* **1** = **charm**, allure, attraction, lure, magnetism, personality

charismatic *adj* **1** = **charming**, alluring, attractive, enticing, influential, magnetic

charitable *adj* **1** = **generous**, beneficent, benevolent, bountiful, eleemosynary, kind, lavish, liberal, philanthropic **2** = **kind**, broad-minded, considerate, favourable, forgiving, gracious, humane, indulgent, lenient, magnanimous, sympathetic, tolerant, understanding

Antonyms *adj* ≠ **generous:** mean, stingy, ungenerous ≠ **kind:** inconsiderate, mean, strict, uncharitable, unforgiving, unkind, unsympathetic

charity *n* **1** = **donations**, alms-giving, assistance, benefaction, contributions, endowment, fund, gift, hand-out, help, largesse *or* largess, philanthropy, relief **4, 5** = **kindness**, affection, Agape, altruism, benevolence, benignity, bountifulness, bounty, compassion, fellow feeling, generosity, goodness, goodwill, humanity, indulgence, love, pity, tenderheartedness

Antonyms *n* ≠ **donations:** meanness, miserliness, selfishness, stinginess ≠ **kindness:** hatred, ill will, intolerance, malice

charlatan *n* = **fraud**, cheat, con man (*inf.*), fake, fraudster, impostor, mountebank, phoney *or* phony (*inf.*), pretender, quack, sham, swindler

charm *n* **1** = **attraction**, allure, allurement, appeal, desirability, fascination, magnetism **3** = **talisman**, amulet, fetish, good-luck piece, lucky piece, trinket **5** = **spell**, enchantment, magic, sorcery ◆ *vb* **9** = **attract**, absorb, allure, beguile, bewitch, cajole, captivate, delight, enamour, enchant, enrapture, entrance, fascinate, mesmerize, please, ravish, win, win over

charming ❶ ('tʃɑːmɪŋ) *adj* delightful; pleasant; attractive.
▸**'charmingly** *adv*

charm offensive *n* a concentrated attempt to gain favour or respectability by conspicuously cooperative and obliging behaviour.

charnel ('tʃɑːnᵊl) *n* **1** short for **charnel house.** ◆ *adj* **2** ghastly; sepulchral; deathly. [C14: from OF: burial place, from L *carnālis* fleshly, CARNAL]

charnel house *n* (esp. formerly) a building or vault where corpses or bones are deposited.

Charon ('kɛərən) *n Greek myth.* the ferryman who brought the dead across the rivers Styx or Acheron to Hades.

chart ❶ (tʃɑːt) *n* **1** a map designed to aid navigation by sea or air. **2** an outline map, esp. one on which weather information is plotted. **3** a sheet giving graphical, tabular, or diagrammatical information. **4 the charts.** *Inf.* the lists produced weekly of the bestselling pop singles and albums or the most popular videos. ◆ *vb* **5** (*tr*) to make a chart of. **6** (*tr*) to plot or outline the course of. **7** (*intr*) (of a record) to appear in the charts. [C16: from L, from Gk *khartēs* papyrus]
▸**'chartless** *adj*

charter ❶ ('tʃɑːtə) *n* **1** a formal document from the sovereign or state incorporating a city, bank, college, etc., and specifying its purposes and rights. **2** (*sometimes cap.*) a formal document granting or demanding certain rights or liberties. **3** a document issued by a society or an organization authorizing the establishment of a local branch or chapter. **4** a special privilege or exemption. **5** (*often cap.*) the fundamental principles of an organization; constitution. **6a** the hire or lease of transportation. **6b** (*as modifier*): *a charter flight.* ◆ *vb* (*tr*) **7** to lease or hire by charter. **8** to hire (a vehicle, etc.). **9** to grant a charter to (a group or person). [C13: from OF, from L *chartula,* dim. of *charta* leaf of papyrus; see CHART]
▸**'charterer** *n*

chartered accountant *n* (in Britain) an accountant who has passed the examinations of the Institute of Chartered Accountants.

chartered bank *n Canad.* a privately owned bank that has been incorporated by Parliament to operate in the commercial banking system.

chartered librarian *n* (in Britain) a librarian who has obtained a qualification from the Library Association in addition to a degree or diploma in librarianship.

chartered surveyor *n* (in Britain) a member of the Royal Institution of Chartered Surveyors.

Chartism ('tʃɑːtɪzəm) *n English history.* a movement (1838-48) to achieve certain political reforms, demand for which was embodied in charters presented to Parliament.
▸**'Chartist** *n, adj*

chartreuse (ʃɑː'trɜːz; *French* ʃartrøz) *n* **1** either of two liqueurs, green or yellow, made from herbs. **2a** a yellowish-green colour. **2b** (*as adj*): *a chartreuse dress.* [C19: from F, after *La Grande Chartreuse,* monastery near Grenoble, where the liqueur is produced]

charwoman ('tʃɑː,wʊmən) *n, pl* **charwomen.** *Brit.* a woman who is hired to clean a house.

chary ❶ ('tʃɛərɪ) *adj* **charier, chariest. 1** wary; careful. **2** choosy; finicky. **3** shy. **4** sparing; mean. [OE *cearig;* rel. to *caru* CARE]

Charybdis (kə'rɪbdɪs) *n* a ship-devouring monster in classical mythology, identified with a whirlpool off the coast of Sicily. Cf. **Scylla.**

chase[1] ❶ (tʃeɪs) *vb* **chases, chasing, chased. 1** to follow or run after (a person, animal, or goal) persistently or quickly. **2** (*tr; often foll. by out, away,* or *off*) to force to run (away); drive (out). **3** (*tr*) *Inf.* to court (a member of the opposite sex) in an unsubtle manner. **4** (*tr; often foll. by up*) *Inf.* to pursue persistently and energetically in order to obtain results, information, etc. **5** (*intr*) *Inf.* to hurry; rush. ◆ *n* **6** the act of chasing; pursuit. **7** any quarry that is pursued. **8** *Brit.* an unenclosed area of land where wild animals are preserved to be hunted. **9** *Brit.* the right to hunt a particular quarry over the land of others. **10 the chase.** the act or sport of hunting. **11** short for **steeplechase. 12 give chase.** to pursue (a person, animal, or thing) actively. [C13: from OF *chacier,* from Vulgar L *captiāre* (unattested), from L, from *capere* to take; see CATCH]

chase[2] (tʃeɪs) *n* **1** *Letterpress printing.* a rectangular steel frame into which metal type and blocks are locked for printing. **2** the part of a gun barrel from the trunnions to the muzzle. **3** a groove or channel, esp. to take a pipe, cable, etc. ◆ *vb* **chases, chasing, chased.** (*tr*) **4** Also: **chamfer.** to cut a groove, furrow, or flute in (a surface, column, etc.). [C17: prob. from F *châsse* frame, from OF *chas* enclosure, from LL *capsus* pen for animals; both from L *capsa* CASE[2]]

chase[3] (tʃeɪs) *vb* **chases, chasing, chased.** (*tr*) to ornament (metal) by engraving or embossing. Also: **enchase.** [C14: from OF *enchasser* ENCHASE]

chaser ('tʃeɪsə) *n* **1** a person or thing that chases. **2** a drink drunk after another of a different kind, as beer after spirits.

chasm ❶ ('kæzəm) *n* **1** a deep cleft in the ground; abyss. **2** a break in continuity; gap. **3** a wide difference in interests, feelings, etc. [C17: from L, from Gk *khasma;* rel. to *khainein* to gape]
▸**chasmal** ('kæzməl) *or* **'chasmic** *adj*

chasseur (ʃæ'sɜː) *n* **1** *French Army.* a member of a unit specially trained for swift deployment. **2** a uniformed attendant. ◆ *adj* **3** (*often postpositive*) designating or cooked in a sauce consisting of white wine and mushrooms. [C18: from F: huntsman]

Chassid *or* **Hassid** ('hæsɪd) *n pl* **Chassidim** *or* **Hassidim** ('hæsɪ,diːm, -dɪm). **1** a sect of Jewish mystics founded in Poland about 1750, characterized by religious zeal and a spirit of prayer, joy, and charity. **2** a Jewish sect of the 2nd century B.C., formed to combat Hellenistic influences.
▸**Chassidic** *or* **Hassidic** (hə'sɪdɪk) *adj*

chassis ❶ ('ʃæsɪ) *n, pl* **chassis** (-sɪz). **1** the steel frame, wheels, and mechanical parts of a motor vehicle. **2** *Electronics.* a mounting for the circuit components of an electrical or electronic device, such as a radio or television. **3** the landing gear of an aircraft. **4** the frame on which a cannon carriage moves. [C17 (meaning: window frame): from F *châssis,* from Vulgar L *capsicum* (unattested), ult. from L *capsa* CASE[2]]

chaste ❶ (tʃeɪst) *adj* **1** not having experienced sexual intercourse; virginal. **2** abstaining from unlawful sexual intercourse. **3** abstaining from all sexual intercourse. **4** (of conduct, speech, etc.) pure; decent; modest. **5** (of style) simple; restrained. [C13: from OF, from L *castus* pure]
▸**'chastely** *adv* ▸**'chasteness** *n*

chasten ❶ ('tʃeɪsᵊn) *vb* (*tr*) **1** to bring to submission; subdue. **2** to discipline or correct by punishment. **3** to moderate; restrain. [C16: from OF, from L *castigāre;* see CASTIGATE]
▸**'chastener** *n*

chastise ❶ (tʃæs'taɪz) *vb* **chastises, chastising, chastised.** (*tr*) **1** to punish, esp. by beating. **2** to scold severely. [C14 *chastisen,* irregularly from *chastien* to CHASTEN]
▸**chastisement** ('tʃæstɪzmənt, tʃæs'taɪz-) *n* ▸**chas'tiser** *n*

chastity ❶ ('tʃæstɪtɪ) *n* **1** the state of being chaste; purity. **2** abstention from sexual intercourse; virginity or celibacy. [C13: from OF, from L, from *castus* CHASTE]

chasuble ('tʃæzjubᵊl) *n Christianity.* a long sleeveless outer vestment worn by a priest when celebrating Mass. [C13: from F, from LL *casubla* garment with a hood]

chat ❶ (tʃæt) *n* **1** informal conversation or talk in an easy familiar manner. **2** an Old World songbird of the thrush family, having a harsh chattering cry. **3** any of various North American warblers. **4** any of various Australian wrens. ◆ *vb* **chats, chatting, chatted. 5** (*intr*) to talk in an easy familiar way. ◆ See also **chat up.** [C16: short for CHATTER]

chateau *or* **château** ('ʃætəʊ) *n, pl* **chateaux** (-təʊ, -təʊz), **chateaus** *or* **châteaux, châteaus. 1** a country house or castle, esp. in France. **2** (in the name of a wine) estate or vineyard. [C18: from F, from OF, from L *castellum* CASTLE]

Chateaubriand (*French* ʃatobrijɑ̃) *n* a thick steak cut from the fillet of beef. [C19: after F. R. *Chateaubriand* (1768–1848), F writer & statesman]

chatelaine ('ʃætə,leɪn) *n* **1** (esp. formerly) the mistress of a castle or large household. **2** a chain or clasp worn at the waist by women in the

THESAURUS

Antonyms *n* ≠ **attraction:** repulsiveness, unattractiveness ◆ *vb* ≠ **attract:** alienate, repel, repulse

charming *adj* = **attractive,** appealing, bewitching, captivating, cute, delectable, delightful, engaging, eye-catching, fetching, irresistible, likable *or* likeable, lovely, pleasant, pleasing, seductive, winning, winsome
Antonyms *adj* disgusting, horrid, repulsive, unappealing, unattractive, unlikable *or* unlikeable, unpleasant, unpleasing

chart *n* **1-3** = **table,** blueprint, diagram, graph, map, plan, tabulation ◆ *vb* **5, 6** = **plot,** delineate, draft, graph, map out, outline, shape, sketch

charter *n* **1-4** = **document,** bond, concession, contract, deed, franchise, indenture, licence, permit, prerogative, privilege, right ◆ *vb* **7** = **hire,** commission, employ, lease, rent **9** = **authorize,** sanction

chary *adj* **1** = **wary,** careful, cautious, circumspect, guarded, heedful, leery (*sl.*), prudent, reluctant, scrupulous, slow, suspicious, uneasy **4** = **mean,** careful (*Brit.*), frugal, niggardly, parsimonious, stingy, thrifty

chase *vb* **1** = **pursue,** course, follow, hunt, run after, track **2** *often foll. by* **out, away,** *or* **off** = **drive away,** drive, expel, hound, put to flight ◆ *n* **6** = **pursuit,** hunt, hunting, race

chasm *n* **1-3** = **gulf,** abyss, alienation, breach, cavity, cleft, crack, crater, crevasse, fissure, gap, gorge, hiatus, hollow, opening, ravine, rent, rift, split, void

chassis *n* **1** = **frame,** anatomy, bodywork, framework, fuselage, skeleton, substructure

chaste *adj* **1, 4, 5** = **pure,** austere, decent, decorous, elegant, immaculate, incorrupt, innocent, modest, moral, neat, quiet, refined, restrained, simple, unaffected, uncontaminated, undefiled, unsullied, vestal, virginal, virtuous, wholesome
Antonyms *adj* blemished, corrupt, dirty, dishonourable, immoral, impure, promiscuous, self-indulgent, tainted, unchaste, unclean, unrestrained, wanton

chasten *vb* **1-3** = **subdue,** afflict, castigate, chastise, correct, cow, curb, discipline, humble, humiliate, put in one's place, repress, soften, tame

chastise *vb* **1** *Old-fashioned* = **beat,** flog, lash, lick (*inf.*), punish, scourge, whip **2** = **scold,** berate, castigate, censure, correct, discipline, upbraid
Antonyms *vb* ≠ **beat:** caress, cuddle, embrace, fondle, hug ≠ **scold:** commend, compliment, congratulate, praise, reward

chastity *n* **1, 2** = **purity,** celibacy, continence, innocence, maidenhood, modesty, virginity, virtue
Antonyms *n* debauchery, immorality, lewdness, licentiousness, profligacy, promiscuity, wantonness

chat *n* **1** = **talk,** chatter, chinwag (*Brit. inf.*), confab (*inf.*), conversation, gossip, heart-to-heart, natter, schmooze (*sl.*), tête-à-tête ◆ *vb* **5** = **talk,** chatter, chew the rag *or* fat (*sl.*), gossip, jaw (*sl.*), natter, rabbit (on) (*Brit. inf.*), schmooze (*sl.*), shoot the breeze

16th to the 19th centuries, with handkerchief, keys, etc., attached. [from F, from OF, ult. from L *castellum* CASTLE]

chatline ('tʃæt,laɪn) *n* a telephone service enabling callers to join in general conversation with each other.

chat show *n Brit.* a television or radio show in which guests are interviewed informally.

chattel ('tʃætᵊl) *n* **1** (*often pl*) *Property law.* **1a chattel personal.** an item of movable personal property, such as furniture, etc. **1b chattel real.** an interest in land less than a freehold. **2 goods and chattels.** personal property. [C13: from OF *chatel* personal property, from Med. L *capitāle* wealth]

chatter ❶ ('tʃætə) *vb* **1** to speak (about unimportant matters) rapidly and incessantly. **2** (*intr*) (of birds, monkeys, etc.) to make rapid repetitive high-pitched noises. **3** (*intr*) (of the teeth) to click together rapidly through cold or fear. **4** (*intr*) to make rapid intermittent contact with a component, as in machining. ◆ *n* **5** idle or foolish talk; gossip. **6** the high-pitched repetitive noise made by a bird, monkey, etc. **7** the rattling of objects, such as parts of a machine. [C13: imit.]
▸ **'chatterer** *n*

chatterbox ❶ ('tʃætə,bɒks) *n Inf.* a person who talks constantly, esp. about trivial matters.

chattering classes *n Inf., often derog.* (usually preceded by *the*) those members of the educated sections of society who enjoy talking about politics, society, culture, etc.

chatty ❶ ('tʃætɪ) *adj* **chattier, chattiest. 1** full of trivial conversation; talkative. **2** informal and friendly; gossipy.
▸ **'chattily** *adv* ▸ **'chattiness** *n*

chat up *vb* (*tr, adv*) *Brit. inf.* **1** to talk flirtatiously to (someone) with a view to starting a romantic or sexual relationship. **2** to talk persuasively to (a person), esp. with an ulterior motive.

chauffeur ('ʃəʊfə, ʃəʊ'fɜː) *n* **1** a person employed to drive a car. ◆ *vb* **2** to act as driver for (a person, etc.): *he chauffeured me to the stadium.* [C20: from F, lit.: stoker, from *chauffer* to heat]
▸ **chauffeuse** (ʃəʊ'fɜːz) *fem n*

chaunt (tʃɔːnt) *n* a less common variant of **chant.**
▸ **'chaunter** *n*

chauvinism ('ʃəʊvɪ,nɪzəm) *n* **1** aggressive or fanatical patriotism; jingoism. **2** enthusiastic devotion to a cause. **3** smug irrational belief in the superiority of one's own race, party, sex, etc.: *male chauvinism.* [C19: from F, after Nicolas *Chauvin,* F soldier under Napoleon, noted for his unthinking patriotism]
▸ **'chauvinist** *n, adj* ▸ **,chauvin'istic** *adj* ▸ **,chauvin'istically** *adv*

cheap ❶ (tʃiːp) *adj* **1** costing relatively little; inexpensive; of good value. **2** charging low prices: *a cheap hairdresser.* **3** of poor quality; shoddy: *cheap furniture.* **4** worth relatively little: *promises are cheap.* **5** not worthy of respect; vulgar. **6** ashamed; embarrassed: *to feel cheap.* **7** stingy; miserly. **8** *Inf.* mean; despicable: *a cheap liar.* ◆ *n* **9 on the cheap.** *Brit. inf.* at a low cost. ◆ *adv* **10** at very little cost. [OE *ceap* barter, bargain, price, property]
▸ **'cheaply** *adv* ▸ **'cheapness** *n*

cheapen ❶ ('tʃiːpᵊn) *vb* **1** to make or become lower in reputation, quality, etc. **2** to make or become cheap or cheaper.
▸ **'cheapener** *n*

cheap-jack *Inf.* ◆ *n* **1** a person who sells cheap and shoddy goods. ◆ *adj* **2** shoddy or inferior. [C19: from CHEAP + JACK]

cheapo ('tʃiːpəʊ) *adj Inf.* very cheap and possibly shoddy.

cheapskate ('tʃiːp,skeɪt) *n Inf.* a miserly person.

cheat ❶ (tʃiːt) *vb* **1** to deceive or practise deceit, esp. for one's own gain; trick or swindle (someone). **2** (*intr*) to obtain unfair advantage by trickery, as in a game of cards. **3** (*tr*) to escape or avoid (something unpleasant) by luck or cunning: *to cheat death.* **4** (when *intr,* usually foll. by *on*) *Inf.* to be sexually unfaithful to (one's wife, husband, or lover). ◆ *n* **5** a person who cheats. **6** a deliberately dishonest transaction, esp. for gain; fraud. **7** *Inf.* sham. **8** *Law.* the obtaining of another's property by fraudulent means. [C14: short for ESCHEAT]
▸ **'cheater** *n*

check ❶ (tʃɛk) *vb* **1** to pause or cause to pause, esp. abruptly. **2** (*tr*) to restrain or control: *to check one's tears.* **3** (*tr*) to slow the growth or progress of; retard. **4** (*tr*) to rebuke or rebuff. **5** (when *intr,* often foll. by *on* or *up on*) to examine, investigate, or make an inquiry into (facts, a product, etc.) for accuracy, quality, or progress. **6** (*tr*) *Chiefly US & Canad.* to mark off so as to indicate approval, correctness, or preference. **7** (*intr;* often foll. by *with*) *Chiefly US & Canad.* to correspond or agree: *this report checks with the other.* **8** (*tr*) *Chiefly US, Canad., & NZ.* to leave in or accept (property) for temporary custody. **9** *Chess.* to place (an opponent's king) in check. **10** (*tr*) to mark with a pattern of squares or crossed lines. **11** to crack or cause to crack. **12** (*tr*) *Ice hockey.* to impede (an opponent). **13** (*intr*) *Hunting.* (of hounds) to pause while relocating a lost scent. ◆ *n* **14** a break in progress; stoppage. **15** a restraint or rebuff. **16** a person or thing that restrains, halts, etc. **17** a control, esp. a rapid or informal one, to ensure accuracy, progress, etc. **18** a means or standard to ensure against fraud or error. **19** the US word for **tick**[1] (senses 3, 6). **20** the US spelling of **cheque. 21** *US & Canad.* the bill in a restaurant. **22** *Chiefly US & Canad.* a tag used to identify property deposited for custody. **23** a pattern of squares or crossed lines. **24** a single square in such a pattern. **25** fabric with a pattern of squares or crossed lines. **26** *Chess.* the state or position of a king under direct attack. **27** a small crack, as one that occurs in timber during drying. **28** a chip or counter used in some card and gambling games. **29** *Hunting.* a pause by the hounds owing to loss of the scent. **30** *Ice hockey.* the act of impeding an opponent with one's body or stick. **31 in check.** under control or restraint. ◆ *sentence substitute.* **32** *Chess.* a call made to an opponent indicating that his king is in check. **33** *Chiefly US & Canad.* an expression of agreement. ◆ See also **check in, check out, checkup.** [C14: from OF *eschec* a check at chess, via Ar. from Persian *shāh* the king]
▸ **'checkable** *adj*

checked (tʃɛkt) *adj* having a pattern of squares.

checker[1] ('tʃɛkə) *n, vb* **1** the usual US spelling of **chequer.** ◆ *n* **2** *Textiles.* the US spelling of **chequer** (sense 2). **3** the US and Canad. name for **draughtsman** (sense 3).

checker[2] ('tʃɛkə) *n Chiefly US.* **1** a cashier, esp. in a supermarket. **2** an attendant in a cloakroom, left-luggage office, etc.

checkerboard ('tʃɛkə,bɔːd) *n* the US and Canad. name for a **draughtboard.**

checkers ('tʃɛkəz) *n* (*functioning as sing*) the US and Canad. name for **draughts.**

check in *vb* (*adv*) **1** (*intr*) to record one's arrival, as at a hotel or for work; sign in or report. **2** (*tr*) to register the arrival of (passengers, etc.). ◆ *n* **check-in. 3** the formal registration of arrival, as at an airport or a hotel. **4** the place where one registers arrival at an airport, etc.

check list *n* a list of items, names, etc., to be referred to for identification or verification.

checkmate ('tʃɛk,meɪt) *n* **1** *Chess.* **1a** the winning position in which an opponent's king is under attack and unable to escape. **1b** the move by which this position is achieved. **2** utter defeat. ◆ *vb* **checkmates, checkmating, checkmated.** (*tr*) **3** *Chess.* to place (an opponent's king) in checkmate. **4** to thwart or render powerless. ◆ *sentence substitute.* **5** *Chess.* a call made when placing an opponent's king in checkmate. [C14: from OF, from Ar. *shāh māt* the king is dead; see CHECK]

check out *vb* (*adv*) **1** (*intr*) to pay the bill and depart, esp. from a hotel. **2** (*intr*) to depart from a place; record one's departure from work. **3** (*tr*) to investigate or prove to be in order after investigation: *the police checked out all the statements.* **4** (*tr*) *Inf.* to have a look at; inspect: *check out the wally in the pink shirt.* ◆ *n* **checkout. 5** the latest time for vacating a room in a hotel, etc. **6** a counter, esp. in a supermarket, where customers pay.

THESAURUS

chatter *vb* **1** = **prattle**, babble, blather, chat, gab (*inf.*), gossip, jabber, natter, prate, rabbit (on) (*Brit. inf.*), schmooze (*sl.*), tattle ◆ *n* **5** = **prattle**, babble, blather, chat, gab (*inf.*), gossip, jabber, natter, rabbit (*Brit. informal*), tattle, twaddle

chatterbox *Informal n* = **chatterer**, babbler, blather *or* blether (*Scot.*), gossip, jabberer, natterer, prater, prattler, tattler, tattletale (*Chiefly US & Canad.*), twaddler

chatty *adj* **1, 2** = **talkative**, colloquial, familiar, friendly, gossipy, informal, newsy (*inf.*)
Antonyms *adj* aloof, cold, distant, formal, hostile, quiet, reserved, shy, silent, standoffish, taciturn, timid, unfriendly, unsociable

cheap *adj* **1** = **inexpensive**, bargain, cheapo (*inf.*), cut-price, economical, economy, keen, low-cost, low-priced, reasonable, reduced, sale **3** = **inferior**, bush-league (*Austral. & NZ inf.*), common, crappy (*sl.*), dime-a-dozen (*inf.*), low-rent (*inf., chiefly US*), paltry, piss-poor (*US taboo sl.*), poor, poxy (*sl.*), second-rate, shoddy, tatty, tawdry, two a penny, two-bit (*US & Canad. sl.*), worthless **5, 8** *Informal* = **despicable**, base, contemptible, low, mean, scurvy, sordid, vulgar
Antonyms *adj* ≠ **inexpensive:** costly, dear, expensive, pricey (*inf.*), steep ≠ **inferior:** admirable, decent, elegant, good, high-class, superior, tasteful, valuable ≠ **despicable:** admirable, charitable, decent, generous, good, honourable

cheapen *vb* **1** = **degrade**, belittle, debase, demean, denigrate, depreciate, derogate, devalue, discredit, disparage, lower

cheapness *n* **1** = **inexpensiveness**, affordability, reasonableness **3** = **inferiority**, commonness, crappiness, paltriness, poorness, shoddiness, tattiness, tawdriness, valuelessness, worthlessness

cheat *vb* **1** = **deceive**, bamboozle (*inf.*), beguile, bilk, con (*inf.*), cozen, defraud, diddle (*inf.*), do (*inf.*), double-cross (*inf.*), dupe, finagle (*inf.*), fleece, fool, hoax, hoodwink, kid (*inf.*), mislead, pull a fast one on (*inf.*), rip off (*sl.*), sting (*inf.*), stitch up (*sl.*), swindle, take for a ride (*inf.*), take in (*inf.*), trick ◆ *n* **5** = **deceiver**, charlatan, cheater, chiseller (*inf.*), con man (*inf.*), dodger, double-crosser (*inf.*), fraudster, impostor, knave (*arch.*), rogue, shark, sharper, swindler, trickster **6** = **deception**, artifice, deceit, fraud, imposture, rip-off (*sl.*), scam (*sl.*), sting (*inf.*), swindle, trickery

check *vb* **2, 3** = **stop**, arrest, bar, bridle, control, curb, delay, halt, hinder, hobble, impede, inhibit, limit, nip in the bud, obstruct, pause, put a spoke in someone's wheel, rein, repress, restrain, retard, stem the flow, thwart **5** = **examine**, check out (*inf.*), compare, confirm, inquire into, inspect, investigate, look at, look over, make sure, monitor, note, probe, research, scrutinize, study, test, tick, verify, vet, work over ◆ *n* **14** = **stoppage**, constraint, control, curb, damper, hindrance, impediment, inhibition, limitation, obstacle, obstruction, rein, restraint **15** = **setback**, blow, disappointment, frustration, rejection, reverse, whammy (*inf., chiefly US*) **17** = **examination**, inspection, investigation, once-over (*inf.*), research, scrutiny, test
Antonyms *vb* ≠ **stop:** accelerate, advance, begin, encourage, further, give free rein, help, release, start ≠ **examine:** disregard, ignore, neglect, overlook, pass over, pay no attention to

checkpoint ('tʃɛk,pɔɪnt) *n* a place, as at a frontier, where vehicles or travellers are stopped for official identification, inspection, etc.

checkup ('tʃɛk,ʌp) *n* **1** an examination to see if something is in order. **2** *Med.* a medical examination, esp. one taken at regular intervals. ◆ *vb* **check up. 3** (*intr, adv; sometimes foll. by on*) to investigate or make an inquiry into (a person's character, evidence, etc.).

Cheddar ('tʃɛdə) *n* (*sometimes not cap.*) any of several types of smooth hard yellow or whitish cheese. [C17: from *Cheddar*, village in Somerset, where it was orig. made]

cheek ❶ (tʃiːk) *n* **1** either side of the face, esp. that part below the eye. **2** *Inf.* impudence; effrontery. **3** (*often pl*) *Inf.* either side of the buttocks. **4** (*often pl*) a side of a door jamb. **5** one of the jaws of a vice. **6 cheek by jowl.** close together; intimately linked. **7 turn the other cheek.** to be submissive and refuse to retaliate. ◆ *vb* **8** (*tr*) *Inf.* to speak or behave disrespectfully to. [OE *ceace*]

cheekbone ('tʃiːk,bəʊn) *n* the nontechnical name for **zygomatic bone.**

cheeky ❶ ('tʃiːkɪ) *adj* **cheekier, cheekiest.** disrespectful in speech or behaviour; impudent.
▸**'cheekily** *adv* ▸**'cheekiness** *n*

cheep (tʃiːp) *n* **1** the short weak high-pitched cry of a young bird; chirp. ◆ *vb* **2** (*intr*) (of young birds) to utter such sounds.
▸**'cheeper** *n*

cheer ❶ (tʃɪə) *vb* **1** (usually foll. by *up*) to make or become happy or hopeful; comfort or be comforted. **2** to applaud with shouts. **3** (when *tr*, sometimes foll. by *on*) to encourage (a team, etc.) with shouts. ◆ *n* **4** a shout or cry of approval, encouragement, etc., often using **hurrah! 5 three cheers.** three shouts of hurrah given in unison to honour someone or celebrate something. **6** happiness; good spirits. **7** state of mind; spirits (archaic, except in **be of good cheer, with good cheer**). **8** *Arch.* provisions for a feast; fare. [C13 (in the sense: face, welcoming aspect): from OF *chere*, from LL *cara* face, from Gk *kara* head]

cheerful ❶ ('tʃɪəfʊl) *adj* **1** having a happy disposition; in good spirits. **2** pleasantly bright: *a cheerful room.* **3** ungrudging: *cheerful help.*
▸**'cheerfully** *adv* ▸**'cheerfulness** *n*

cheerio (,tʃɪərɪ'əʊ) *Inf.* ◆ *sentence substitute. Chiefly Brit.* **1** a farewell greeting. **2** a drinking toast. ◆ *n, pl* **cheerios. 3** *NZ.* a type of small sausage.

cheerleader ('tʃɪə,liːdə) *n US & Canad.* a person who leads a crowd in cheers, esp. at sports events.

cheerless ❶ ('tʃɪəlɪs) *adj* dreary or gloomy.
▸**'cheerlessly** *adv* ▸**'cheerlessness** *n*

cheers (tʃɪəz) *sentence substitute. Inf., chiefly Brit.* **1** a drinking toast. **2** goodbye! cheerio! **3** thanks!

cheery ❶ ('tʃɪərɪ) *adj* **cheerier, cheeriest.** showing or inspiring cheerfulness.
▸**'cheerily** *adv* ▸**'cheeriness** *n*

cheese (tʃiːz) *n* **1** the curd of milk separated from the whey and variously prepared as a food. **2** a mass or cake of this substance. **3** any of various substances of similar consistency, etc.: *lemon cheese.* **4** *Sl.* an important person (esp. in **big cheese**). [OE *cēse*, from L *cāseus* cheese]

cheeseburger ('tʃiːz,bɜːgə) *n* a hamburger cooked with a slice of cheese on top of it.

cheesecake ('tʃiːz,keɪk) *n* **1** a rich tart filled with cheese, esp. cream cheese, cream, sugar, etc. **2** *Sl.* women displayed for their sex appeal, as in photographs in magazines or films.

cheesecloth ('tʃiːz,klɒθ) *n* a loosely woven cotton cloth formerly used for wrapping cheese.

cheesed off *adj* (*usually postpositive*) *Brit. sl.* bored, disgusted, or angry. [C20: from ?]

cheeseparing ('tʃiːz,pɛərɪŋ) *adj* **1** penny-pinching. ◆ *n* **2a** a paring of cheese rind. **2b** anything similarly worthless. **3** stinginess.

cheesy ('tʃiːzɪ) *adj* **cheesier, cheesiest. 1** like cheese in flavour, smell, or consistency. **2** *Inf.* (of a smile) broad but possibly insincere: *a big cheesy grin.* **3** *Inf.* banal or trite; in poor taste.
▸**'cheesiness** *n*

cheetah *or* **chetah** ('tʃiːtə) *n* a large feline of Africa and SW Asia: the swiftest mammal, having very long legs, and a black-spotted coat. [C18: from Hindi *cītā*, from Sansk. *citra* speckled]

chef (ʃɛf) *n* a cook, esp. the principal cook in a restaurant. [C19: from F, from OF *chief* head, CHIEF]

chef-d'œuvre *French.* (ʃɛdœvrə) *n, pl* ***chefs-d'œuvre*** (ʃɛdœvrə). a masterpiece.

chela[1] ('kiːlə) *n, pl* **chelae** (-liː). a large pincer-like claw of such arthropods as the crab and scorpion. [C17: NL, from Gk *khēlē* claw]

chela[2] ('tʃeɪlə) *n Hinduism.* a disciple of a religious teacher. [C19: from Hindi *celā*, from Sansk. *ceta* servant, slave]

chelate ('kiːleɪt) *n* **1** *Chem.* a chemical compound whose molecules contain a closed ring of atoms of which one is a metal atom. ◆ *adj* **2** *Zool.* of or possessing chelae. **3** *Chem.* of a chelate. ◆ *vb* **chelates, chelating, chelated. 4** (*intr*) *Chem.* to form a chelate. [C20: from CHELA[1]]
▸**che'lation** *n*

chelicera (kɪ'lɪsərə) *n, pl* **chelicerae** (-ə,riː). one of a pair of appendages on the head of spiders and other arachnids: often modified as food-catching claws. [C19: from NL, from Gk *khēle* claw + *keras* horn]

cheloid ('kiːlɔɪd) *n Pathol.* a variant spelling of **keloid.**
▸**che'loidal** *adj*

chelonian (kɪ'ləʊnɪən) *n* **1** any reptile of the order *Chelonia*, including the tortoises and turtles, in which most of the body is enclosed in a bony capsule. ◆ *adj* **2** of or belonging to the *Chelonia.* [C19: from NL, from Gk *khelōnē* tortoise]

Chelsea Pensioner ('tʃɛlsɪ) *n* an inhabitant of the Chelsea Royal Hospital in SW London, a home for old and infirm soldiers.

chem. *abbrev. for:* **1** chemical. **2** chemist. **3** chemistry.

chem- *combining form.* a variant of **chemo-** before a vowel.

chemical ❶ ('kɛmɪkᵊl) *n* **1** any substance used in or resulting from a reaction involving changes to atoms or molecules. ◆ *adj* **2** of or used in chemistry. **3** of, made from, or using chemicals: *chemical fertilizer.*
▸**'chemically** *adv*

chemical engineering *n* the branch of engineering concerned with the design and manufacture of the plant used in industrial chemical processes.
▸**chemical engineer** *n*

chemical warfare *n* warfare using asphyxiating or nerve gases, poisons, defoliants, etc.

chemiluminescence (,kɛmɪ,luːmɪ'nɛsəns) *n* the phenomenon in which a chemical reaction leads to the emission of light without incandescence.
▸**,chemi,lumi'nescent** *adj*

chemin de fer (ʃə'mæn də 'fɛə) *n* a gambling game, a variation of baccarat. [F: railway, referring to the fast tempo of the game]

chemise (ʃə'miːz) *n* **1** an unwaisted loose-fitting dress hanging straight from the shoulders. **2** a loose shirtlike undergarment. ◆ Also called: **shift.** [C14: from OF: shirt, from LL *camisa*]

chemist ❶ ('kɛmɪst) *n* **1** *Brit.* a shop selling medicines, cosmetics, etc. **2** *Brit.* a qualified dispenser of prescribed medicines. **3** a person studying, trained in, or engaged in chemistry. [C16: from earlier *chimist*, from NL, shortened from Med. L *alchimista* ALCHEMIST]

chemistry ('kɛmɪstrɪ) *n, pl* **chemistries. 1** the branch of physical science concerned with the composition, properties, and reactions of substances. **2** the composition, properties, and reactions of a particular substance. **3** the nature and effects of any complex phenomenon: *the chemistry of humour.* [C17: from earlier *chimistrie*, from *chimist* CHEMIST]

chemo-, chemi-, *or before a vowel* **chem-** *combining form.* indicating that chemicals or chemical reactions are involved: *chemotherapy.* [NL, from LGk *khēmeia*; see ALCHEMY]

chemoreceptor (,kiːməʊrɪ'sɛptə) *or* **chemoceptor** *n* a sensory receptor in a biological cell membrane to which an external molecule binds to generate a smell or taste sensation.

chemosynthesis (,kiːməʊ'sɪnθɪsɪs) *n* the formation of organic material by some bacteria using energy from simple chemical reactions.

chemotherapy (,kiːməʊ'θɛrəpɪ) *n* treatment of disease, esp. cancer, by means of chemical agents. Cf. **radiotherapy.**
▸**,chemo'therapist** *n*

chemurgy ('kɛmɜːdʒɪ) *n* the branch of chemistry concerned with the industrial use of organic raw materials, esp. of agricultural origin.
▸**chem'urgic** *or* **chem'urgical** *adj*

THESAURUS

cheek *n* **2** *Informal* = **impudence**, audacity, brass neck (*Brit. inf.*), brazenness, chutzpah (*US & Canad. informal*), disrespect, effrontery, face (*inf.*), front, gall (*inf.*), impertinence, insolence, lip (*sl.*), neck (*inf.*), nerve, sassiness (*US inf.*), sauce (*inf.*), temerity

cheeky *adj* = **impudent**, audacious, disrespectful, forward, fresh (*inf.*), impertinent, insolent, insulting, pert, sassy (*US inf.*), saucy
Antonyms *adj* civil, complaisant, courteous, decorous, deferential, mannerly, polite, respectful, well-behaved, well-mannered

cheer *vb* **1** *usually foll. by* **up** = **cheer up**, animate, brighten, buck up (*inf.*), buoy up, comfort, console, elate, elevate, encourage, enliven, exhilarate, gee up, gladden, hearten, incite, inspirit, jolly along (*inf.*), perk up, rally, solace, take heart, uplift, warm **2** = **applaud**, acclaim, clap, hail, hurrah ◆ *n* **4** = **applause**, acclamation, ovation, plaudits **6** = **cheerfulness**, animation, buoyancy, comfort, gaiety, gladness, glee, hopefulness, joy, liveliness, merriment, merry-making, mirth, optimism, solace
Antonyms ≠ cheer up: darken, depress, discourage, dishearten, sadden *vb* **≠ applaud:** blow a raspberry, boo, hiss, jeer, ridicule

cheerful *adj* **1** = **happy**, animated, blithe, bright, buoyant, cheery, chirpy (*inf.*), contented, enlivening, enthusiastic, gay, genial, glad, hearty, jaunty, jolly, joyful, light-hearted, merry, optimistic, pleasant, sparkling, sprightly, sunny, upbeat (*inf.*)
Antonyms *adj* cheerless, dejected, depressed, depressing, despondent, dismal, down, downcast, down in the dumps (*inf.*), dull, gloomy, lifeless, low, melancholy, miserable, morose, pensive, sad, unhappy, unpleasant

cheerfulness *n* **1** = **happiness**, buoyancy, exuberance, gaiety, geniality, gladness, good cheer, good humour, high spirits, jauntiness, joyousness, light-heartedness

cheerless *adj* = **gloomy**, austere, bleak, comfortless, dark, dejected, depressed, desolate, despondent, disconsolate, dismal, dolorous, drab, dreary, dull, forlorn, funereal, grim, joyless, melancholy, miserable, mournful, sad, sombre, sorrowful, sullen, unhappy, woebegone, woeful
Antonyms *adj* cheerful, cheery, elated, happy, jolly, joyful, light-hearted, merry

cheery *adj* = **cheerful**, breezy, carefree, chirpy (*inf.*), full of beans (*inf.*), genial, good-humoured, happy, jovial, lively, pleasant, sunny, upbeat (*inf.*)

chemical *n* **1** = **compound**, drug, potion, substance, synthetic

chemist *n* **2** = **pharmacist**, apothecary, dispenser

chenille (ʃəˈniːl) *n* **1** a thick soft tufty silk or worsted velvet cord or yarn used in embroidery and for trimmings, etc. **2** a fabric of such yarn. **3** a carpet of such fabric. [C18: from F, lit.: hairy caterpillar, from L *canicula,* dim. of *canis* dog]
cheongsam (ˈtʃɒŋˈsæm) *n* a straight dress with a stand-up collar and a slit in one side of the skirt, worn by Chinese women. [from Chinese *ch'ang shan* long jacket]
cheque *or US* **check** (tʃɛk) *n* **1** a bill of exchange drawn on a bank by the holder of a current account. **2** *Austral. & NZ.* the total sum of money received for contract work or a crop. **3** *Austral. & NZ.* wages. [C18: from CHECK, in the sense: means of verification]
cheque account *n* an account at a bank or a building society upon which cheques can be drawn.
chequebook *or US* **checkbook** (ˈtʃɛkˌbʊk) *n* a book of detachable blank cheques issued by a bank or building society to holders of cheque accounts.
chequebook journalism *n* the practice of securing exclusive rights to material for newspaper stories by paying a high price, regardless of any moral implications.
cheque card *n* a card issued by a bank or building society, guaranteeing payment of a customer's cheques up to a stated value.
chequer *or US* **checker** (ˈtʃɛkə) *n* **1** any of the marbles, pegs, or other pieces used in the game of Chinese chequers. **2a** a pattern of squares. **2b** one of the squares in such a pattern. ◆ *vb (tr)* **3** to make irregular in colour or character; variegate. **4** to mark off with alternating squares of colour. ◆ See also **chequers.** [C13: chessboard, from Anglo-F *escheker,* from *eschec* CHECK]
chequered *or esp. US* **checkered** (ˈtʃɛkəd) *adj* marked by fluctuations of fortune (esp. in **a chequered career**).
chequers (ˈtʃɛkəz) *n (functioning as sing)* another name for **draughts.**
cherish ◘ (ˈtʃɛrɪʃ) *vb (tr)* **1** to feel or show great tenderness or care for. **2** to cling fondly to (a hope, idea, etc.); nurse: *to cherish ambitions.* [C14: from OF, from *cher* dear, from L *cārus*]
chernozem (ˈtʃɜːnəʊˌzɛm) *n* a rich black soil found in temperate semiarid regions, such as the grasslands of Russia. [from Russian *chernaya zemlya* black earth]
Cherokee (ˈtʃɛrəˌkiː) *n* **1** (*pl* **Cherokees** *or* **Cherokee**) a member of a North American Indian people formerly living in the Appalachian Mountains. **2** the Iroquois language of this people.
cheroot (ʃəˈruːt) *n* a cigar with both ends cut off squarely. [C17: from Tamil *curuttu* curl, roll]
cherry (ˈtʃɛrɪ) *n, pl* **cherries. 1** any of several trees of the genus *Prunus,* having a small fleshy rounded fruit containing a hard stone. **2** the fruit or wood of any of these trees. **3** any of various unrelated plants, such as the ground cherry and Jerusalem cherry. **4a** a bright red colour; cerise. **4b** (*as adj*): *a cherry coat.* **5** *Taboo sl.* virginity or the hymen as its symbol. [C14: back formation from OE *ciris* (mistakenly thought to be pl), ult. from LL *ceresia,* ?from L *cerasus* cherry tree, from Gk *kerasios*]
cherry tomato *n* a miniature tomato not much bigger than a cherry.
chert (tʃɜːt) *n* an impure black or grey microcrystalline variety of quartz that resembles flint. [C17: from ?]
▸ **ˈcherty** *adj*
cherub ◘ (ˈtʃɛrəb) *n, pl* **cherubs** *or (for sense 1)* **cherubim** (ˈtʃɛrəbɪm, -ʊbɪm). **1** a member of the second order of angels, often represented as a winged child. **2** an innocent or sweet child. [OE, from Heb. *kĕrūbh*]
▸ **cherubic** (tʃəˈruːbɪk) *or* **cheˈrubical** *adj* ▸ **cheˈrubically** *adv*
chervil (ˈtʃɜːvɪl) *n* an aromatic umbelliferous Eurasian plant with small white flowers and aniseed-flavoured leaves used as herbs in soups and salads. [OE *cerfelle,* from L, from Gk, from *khairein* to enjoy + *phullon* leaf]
Cheshire cheese *n* a mild-flavoured cheese with a crumbly texture, originally made in Cheshire.
chess (tʃɛs) *n* a game of skill for two players using a chessboard on which chessmen are moved. The object is to checkmate the opponent's king. [C13: from OF *esches,* pl. of *eschec* CHECK]
chessboard (ˈtʃɛsˌbɔːd) *n* a square board divided into 64 squares of two alternating colours, used for playing chess or draughts.
chessman (ˈtʃɛsˌmæn, -mən) *n, pl* **chessmen.** any of the pieces and pawns used in a game of chess. [C17: from *chessmen,* from ME *chessemeyne* chess company]
chest ◘ (tʃɛst) *n* **1a** the front part of the trunk from the neck to the belly. Related adj: **pectoral. 1b** (*as modifier*): *a chest cold.* **2 get (something) off one's chest.** *Inf.* to unburden oneself of troubles, worries, etc., by talking about them. **3** a box used for storage or shipping: *a tea chest.* [OE *cest,* from L, from Gk *kistē* box]
▸ **ˈchested** *adj*
chesterfield (ˈtʃɛstəˌfiːld) *n* **1** a man's overcoat, usually with a velvet collar. **2** a large tightly stuffed sofa, with straight upholstered arms of the same height as the back. [C19: after a 19th-cent. Earl of *Chesterfield*]
chestnut (ˈtʃɛsˌnʌt) *n* **1** a N temperate tree such as the **sweet** or **Spanish chestnut,** which produces flowers in long catkins and nuts in a prickly bur. Cf. **horse chestnut. 2** the edible nut of any of these trees. **3** the hard wood of any of these trees, used in making furniture, etc. **4a** a reddish-brown colour. **4b** (*as adj*): *chestnut hair.* **5** a horse of a golden-brown colour. **6** *Inf.* an old or stale joke. [C16: from earlier *chesten nut: chesten,* from OF, from L, from Gk *kastanea*]
chest of drawers *n* a piece of furniture consisting of a set of drawers in a frame.
chesty (ˈtʃɛstɪ) *adj* **chestier, chestiest.** *Inf.* **1** *Brit.* suffering from or symptomatic of chest disease: *a chesty cough.* **2** having a large well-developed chest or bosom.
▸ **ˈchestiness** *n*
cheval glass (ʃəˈvæl) *n* a full-length mirror mounted so as to swivel within a frame. [C19: from F *cheval* support (lit.: horse)]
chevalier (ˌʃɛˈvælɪə) *n* **1** a member of certain orders of merit, such as the French Legion of Honour. **2** the lowest title of rank in the old French nobility. **3** an archaic word for **knight. 4** a chivalrous man; gallant. [C14: from OF, from Med. L *caballārius* horseman, CAVALIER]
Cheviot (ˈtʃiːvɪət, ˈtʃɛv-) *n* **1** a large British breed of sheep reared for its wool. **2** (*often not cap.*) a rough twill-weave woollen suiting fabric. [from *Cheviot* Hills on borders of England and Scotland]
chèvre (ˈʃɛvrə) *n* any cheese made from goats' milk. [C20: from F, lit.: goat]
chevron (ˈʃɛvrən) *n* **1** *Mil.* a badge or insignia consisting of one or more V-shaped stripes to indicate a noncommissioned rank or length of service. **2** *Heraldry.* an inverted V-shaped charge on a shield. **3** (*usually pl*) a pattern of horizontal black and white V-shapes on a road sign indicating a sharp bend. **4** any V-shaped pattern or device. [C14: from OF, ult. from L *caper* goat; cf. L *capreoli* pair of rafters (lit.: little goats)]
chevrotain (ˈʃɛvrəˌteɪn, -tɪn) *n* a small timid ruminant mammal of S and SE Asia. Also called: **mouse deer.** [C18: from F, from OF *chevrot* kid, from *chèvre* goat, ult. from L *caper* goat]
chevy (ˈtʃɛvɪ) *n, vb* a variant spelling of **chivy.**
chew ◘ (tʃuː) *vb* **1** to work the jaws and teeth in order to grind (food); masticate. **2** to bite repeatedly: *she chewed her nails anxiously.* **3** (*intr*) to use chewing tobacco. **4 chew the fat** *or* **rag.** *Sl.* **4a** to argue over a point. **4b** to talk idly; gossip. ◆ *n* **5** the act of chewing. **6** something that is chewed. [OE *ceowan*]
▸ **ˈchewable** *adj* ▸ **ˈchewer** *n*
chewing gum *n* a preparation for chewing, usually made of flavoured and sweetened chicle or such substitutes as polyvinyl acetate.
chew over ◘ *vb (tr, adv)* to consider carefully.
chewy ◘ (ˈtʃuːɪ) *adj* **chewier, chewiest.** of a consistency requiring chewing.
chez *French.* (ʃe) *prep* **1** at the home of. **2** with, among, or in the manner of.
chi[1] (kaɪ) *n* the 22nd letter of the Greek alphabet (Χ, χ).
chi[2] *or* **ch'i** *or* **qi** (tʃiː) *n* (*sometimes cap.*) (in Oriental medicine, martial arts, etc.) vital energy believed to circulate round the body in currents. [Chinese, lit.: energy]
chiack *or* **chyack** (ˈtʃaɪæk) *Austral inf.* ◆ *vb (tr)* **1** to tease or banter. ◆ *n* **2** good-humoured banter. [C19: from *chi-hike,* a shout of greeting]
chianti (kɪˈæntɪ) *n* (*sometimes cap.*) a dry red wine produced in Tuscany, Italy.
chiaroscuro (kɪˌɑːrəˈskʊərəʊ) *n, pl* **chiaroscuros. 1** the artistic distribution of light and dark masses in a picture. **2** monochrome painting using light and dark only. [C17: from It., from *chiaro* CLEAR + *oscuro* OBSCURE]
chiasma (kaɪˈæzmə) *n, pl* **chiasmas, chiasmata** (-mətə) **1** *Cytology.* the cross-shaped connection produced by the crossing over of pairing chromosomes during meiosis. **2** *Anat.* the crossing over of two parts or structures. [C19: from Gk *khiasma,* from *khi* CHI[1]]
chiasmus (kaɪˈæzməs) *n, pl* **chiasmi** (-maɪ). *Rhetoric.* reversal of word order in the second of two parallel phrases: *he came in triumph and in defeat departs.* [NL from Gk: see CHIASMA]
▸ **chiastic** (kaɪˈæstɪk) *adj*
chic ◘ (ʃiːk, ʃɪk) *adj* **1** (esp. of fashionable clothes, women, etc.) stylish or elegant. ◆ *n* **2** stylishness, esp. in dress; modishness; fashionable good taste. [C19: from F, from ?]
▸ **ˈchicly** *adv*
chicane (ʃɪˈkeɪn) *n* **1** a bridge or whist hand without trumps. **2** *Motor racing.* a short section of sharp narrow bends formed by barriers placed on a motor-racing circuit. **3** a less common word for **chicanery.** ◆ *vb* **chicanes, chicaning, chicaned. 4** (*tr*) to deceive or trick by chicanery. **5** (*intr*) to use tricks or chicanery. [C17: from F *chicaner* to quibble, from ?]
▸ **chiˈcaner** *n*
chicanery ◘ (ʃɪˈkeɪnərɪ) *n, pl* **chicaneries. 1** verbal deception or trickery, dishonest or sharp practice. **2** a trick, deception, or quibble.

THESAURUS

cherish *vb* **1 = care for,** comfort, cosset, hold dear, love, nourish, nurse, shelter, support, treasure **2 = cling to,** cleave to, encourage, entertain, foster, harbour, hold dear, nurture, prize, sustain, treasure
Antonyms *vb* abandon, desert, despise, disdain, dislike, forsake, hate, neglect
cherubic *adj* **1, 2 = angelic,** adorable, heavenly, innocent, lovable, seraphic, sweet
chest *n* **3 = box,** ark (*dialect*), case, casket, coffer, crate, kist (*Scot. & N English dialect*), strongbox, trunk
chew *vb* **1 = bite,** champ, chomp, crunch, gnaw, grind, masticate, munch
chew over *vb* **= consider,** deliberate upon, meditate, mull (over), muse on, ponder, reflect upon, ruminate, weigh
chewy *adj* **= tough,** as tough as old boots, fibrous, leathery
chic *adj* **1 = stylish,** elegant, fashionable, modish, sexy, smart, trendy (*Brit. informal*), up-to-date, urbane
Antonyms *adj* dinosaur, inelegant, naff (*Brit. sl.*), old-fashioned, outmoded, out-of-date, passé, shabby, unfashionable
chicanery *n* **1 = trickery,** artifice, cheating,

chicano (tʃɪ'kɑːnəʊ) *n, pl* **chicanos.** *US.* an American citizen of Mexican origin. [C20: from Sp. *mejicano* Mexican]
chichi ('ʃiː,ʃiː) *adj* **1** affectedly pretty or stylish. ◆ *n* **2** the quality of being affectedly pretty or stylish. [C20: from F]
chick (tʃɪk) *n* **1** the young of a bird, esp. of a domestic fowl. **2** *Sl.* a girl or young woman, esp. an attractive one. **3** a young child: used as a term of endearment. [C14: short for CHICKEN]
chickadee ('tʃɪkə,diː) *n* any of various small North American songbirds, typically having grey-and-black plumage. [C19: imit.]
chicken ('tʃɪkɪn) *n* **1** a domestic fowl bred for its flesh or eggs. **2** the flesh of such a bird used for food. **3** any of various similar birds, such as a prairie chicken. **4** *Sl.* a cowardly person. **5** *Sl.* a young inexperienced person. **6** *Inf.* any of various, often dangerous, games or challenges in which the object is to make one's opponent lose his nerve. **7** **count one's chickens before they are hatched.** to be over-optimistic in acting on expectations which are not yet fulfilled. ◆ *adj* **8** *Sl.* easily scared; cowardly; timid. [OE *ciecen*]
chicken feed *n Sl.* a trifling amount of money.
chicken-hearted *or* **chicken-livered** *adj* easily frightened; cowardly.
chicken out *vb (intr, adv) Inf.* to fail to do something through fear or lack of conviction.
chickenpox ('tʃɪkɪn,pɒks) *n* a highly communicable viral disease most commonly affecting children, characterized by slight fever and the eruption of a rash.
chicken wire *n* wire netting with a hexagonal mesh.
chickpea ('tʃɪk,piː) *n* **1** a bushy leguminous plant, cultivated for its edible pealike seeds. **2** the seed of this plant. [C16 *ciche peasen,* from *ciche* (from F, from L *cicer* chickpea) + *peasen;* see PEA]
chickweed ('tʃɪk,wiːd) *n* any of various plants of the pink family, esp. a common garden weed with small white flowers.
chicle ('tʃɪkəl) *n* a gumlike substance obtained from the sapodilla; the main ingredient of chewing gum. [from Sp., from Nahuatl *chictli*]
chicory ('tʃɪkərɪ) *n, pl* **chicories. 1** a blue-flowered plant, cultivated for its leaves, which are used in salads, and for its roots. **2** the root of this plant, roasted, dried, and used as a coffee substitute. ◆ Cf. **endive.** [C15: from OF, from L *cichorium,* from Gk *kikhōrion*]
chide **T** (tʃaɪd) *vb* **chides, chiding, chided** *or* **chid** (tʃɪd); **chided, chid** *or* **chidden** ('tʃɪdən). **1** to rebuke or scold. **2** *(tr)* to goad into action. [OE *cīdan*]
▸'**chider** *n* ▸'**chidingly** *adv*
chief **T** (tʃiːf) *n* **1** the head or leader of a group or body of people. **2** *Heraldry.* the upper third of a shield. **3** **in chief.** primarily; especially. ◆ *adj* **4** *(prenominal)* **4a** most important; principal. **4b** highest in rank or authority. ◆ *adv* **5** *Arch.* principally. [C13: from OF, from L *caput* head]
chief executive *n* the person with overall responsibility for the efficient running of a company, organization, etc.
chief justice *n* **1** (in any of several Commonwealth countries) the judge presiding over a supreme court. **2** (in the US) the presiding judge of a court composed of a number of members. ◆ See also **Lord Chief Justice.**
chiefly **T** ('tʃiːflɪ) *adv* **1** especially or essentially; above all. **2** in general; mainly; mostly. ◆ *adj* **3** of or relating to a chief or chieftain.
Chief of Staff *n* **1** the senior staff officer under the commander of a major military formation or organization. **2** the senior officer of each service of the armed forces.
chief petty officer *n* the senior naval rank for personnel without commissioned or warrant rank.
chieftain ('tʃiːftən, -tɪn) *n* the head or leader of a tribe or clan. [C14: from OF, from LL *capitāneus* commander; see CAPTAIN]
▸'**chieftaincy** *or* '**chieftain,ship** *n*
chief technician *n* a noncommissioned officer in the Royal Air Force, junior to a flight sergeant.
chiffchaff ('tʃɪf,tʃæf) *n* a common European warbler with a yellowish-brown plumage. [C18: imit.]
chiffon (ʃɪ'fɒn, 'ʃɪfɒn) *n* **1** a fine almost transparent fabric of silk, nylon, etc. **2** *(often pl) Now rare.* feminine finery. ◆ *adj* **3** made of chiffon. **4** (of soufflés, pies, cakes, etc.) having a very light fluffy texture. [C18: from F, from *chiffe* rag]
chiffonier *or* **chiffonnier** (,ʃɪfə'nɪə) *n* **1** a tall, elegant chest of drawers. **2** a wide low open-fronted cabinet. [C19: from F, from *chiffon* rag]
chigetai (,tʃɪgɪ'taɪ) *n* a variety of the Asiatic wild ass of Mongolia. Also spelled: **dziggetai.** [from Mongolian *tchikhitei* long-eared, from *tchikhi* ear]
chigger ('tʃɪgə) *n* **1** *US & Canad.* the parasitic larva of a mite, which causes intense itching. **2** another name for **chigoe.**
chignon ('ʃiːnjɒn) *n* an arrangement of long hair in a roll or knot at the back of the head. [C18: from F, from OF *chaignon* link, from *chaine* CHAIN; infl. also by OF *tignon* coil of hair]
chigoe ('tʃɪgəʊ) *n* **1** a tropical flea, the female of which burrows into the skin of its host, which includes man. **2** another name for **chigger.** [C17: from Carib *chigo*]
Chihuahua (tʃɪ'wɑːwɑː, -wə) *n* a breed of tiny dog originally from Mexico, having short hair and protruding eyes. [after *Chihuahua,* state in Mexico]
chilblain ('tʃɪl,bleɪn) *n (usually pl)* an inflammation of the fingers or toes, caused by exposure to cold. [C16: from CHILL (n) + BLAIN]
▸'**chil,blained** *adj*
child **T** (tʃaɪld) *n, pl* **children. 1a** a boy or girl between birth and puberty. **1b** *(as modifier): child labour.* **2** a baby or infant. **3** an unborn baby. **4** **with child.** an old-fashioned term for **pregnant. 5** a human offspring; a son or daughter. Related adj: **filial. 6** a childish or immature person. **7** a member of a family or tribe; descendant: *a child of Israel.* **8** a person or thing regarded as the product of an influence or environment: *a child of nature.* [OE *cild*]
▸'**childless** *adj* ▸'**childlessness** *n*
child abuse *n* physical, sexual, or emotional ill-treatment of a child by its parents or other adults responsible for its welfare.
child-bearing *n* **a** the act or process of carrying and giving birth to a child. **b** *(as modifier): of child-bearing age.*
childbed ('tʃaɪld,bɛd) *n* (often preceded by *in*) the condition of giving birth to a child.
child benefit *n* (in Britain and New Zealand) a regular government payment to parents of children up to a certain age.
childbirth **T** ('tʃaɪld,bɜːθ) *n* the act of giving birth to a child.
childcare ('tʃaɪld,kɛə) *n Brit.* **1** care provided for children without homes (or with a seriously disturbed home life) by a local authority. **2** care and supervision of children whose parents are working, provided by a childminder or local authority.
child endowment *n* (in Australia) a social security payment for dependent children.
childhood **T** ('tʃaɪldhʊd) *n* the condition of being a child; the period of life before puberty.
childish **T** ('tʃaɪldɪʃ) *adj* **1** in the manner of or suitable to a child. **2** foolish or petty: *childish fears.*
▸'**childishly** *adv* ▸'**childishness** *n*
childlike **T** ('tʃaɪld,laɪk) *adj* like or befitting a child, as in being innocent, trustful, etc.
childminder ('tʃaɪld,maɪndə) *n* a person who looks after children, esp. those whose parents are working.
children ('tʃɪldrən) *n* the plural of **child.**
Children of Israel *pl n* the Jewish people or nation.
child-resistant *adj* (of packaging etc., esp. of drugs) designed to be difficult for children to open or tamper with. Also: **child-proof.**
child's play *n Inf.* something easy to do.
chile ('tʃɪlɪ) *n* a variant spelling of **chilli.**
Chilean ('tʃɪlɪən) *adj* **1** of or relating to Chile, a republic in South America. ◆ *n* **2** a native or inhabitant of Chile.
Chile pine *n* another name for the **monkey puzzle.**
Chile saltpetre *or* **nitre** *n* a naturally occurring form of sodium nitrate.
chiliad ('kɪlɪ,æd) *n* **1** a group of one thousand. **2** one thousand years. [C16: from Gk, from *khilioi* a thousand]
chill **T** (tʃɪl) *n* **1** a moderate coldness. **2** a sensation of coldness resulting from a cold or damp environment, or from a sudden emotional reaction. **3** a feverish cold. **4** a check on enthusiasm or joy. ◆ *adj* **5** another word for **chilly.** ◆ *vb* **6** to make or become cold. **7** *(tr)* to cool or freeze (food, drinks, etc.). **8** *(tr)* **8a** to depress (enthusiasm, etc.). **8b** to discourage. **9** *(intr) Sl., chiefly US.* to relax; calm oneself. ◆ See also **chill out.** [OE *ciele*]
▸'**chilling** *adj* ▸'**chillingly** *adv* ▸'**chillness** *n*
chiller ('tʃɪlə) *n* **1** short for **spine-chiller. 2** *NZ.* a refrigerated storage area for meat.

THESAURUS

chicane, deception, deviousness, dodge, double-dealing, duplicity, intrigue, sharp practice, skulduggery (*inf.*), sophistry, stratagems, subterfuge, underhandedness, wiles, wire-pulling (*chiefly US*)

chide *vb* **1** = **scold**, admonish, bawl out (*inf.*), berate, blame, blast, carpet (*inf.*), censure, check, criticize, find fault, give (someone) a rocket (*Brit. & NZ inf.*), lambast(e), lecture, put down, rap over the knuckles, read the riot act, rebuke, reprehend, reprimand, reproach, reprove, slap on the wrist, tear into (*inf.*), tear (someone) off a strip (*Brit. inf.*), tell off (*inf.*), tick off (*inf.*), upbraid

chief *n* **1** = **head**, boss (*inf.*), captain, chieftain, commander, director, governor, leader, lord, manager, master, principal, ringleader, ruler, superintendent, superior, suzerain, torchbearer ◆ *adj* **4** = **primary**, big-time (*inf.*), capital, cardinal, central, especial, essential, foremost, grand, highest, key, leading, main, major league (*inf.*), most important, outstanding, paramount, predominant, pre-eminent, premier, prevailing, prime, principal, superior, supreme, uppermost, vital
Antonyms *n* ≠ **head:** follower, subject, subordinate ◆ *adj* ≠ **primary:** least, minor, subordinate, subsidiary

chiefly *adv* **1** = **especially**, above all, essentially, primarily, principally **2** = **mainly**, in general, in the main, largely, mostly, on the whole, predominantly, usually

child *n* **1, 2** = **youngster**, ankle-biter (*Austral. sl.*), babe, babe in arms, baby, bairn (*Scot.*), brat, chit, descendant, infant, issue, juvenile, kid (*inf.*), little one, minor, nipper (*inf.*), nursling, offspring, progeny, rug rat (*sl.*), sprog (*sl.*), suckling, toddler, tot, wean (*Scot.*)

childbirth *n* = **child-bearing**, accouchement, confinement, delivery, labour, lying-in, parturition, travail

childhood *n* = **youth**, boyhood *or* girlhood, immaturity, infancy, minority, schooldays

childish *adj* **1, 2** = **immature**, boyish *or* girlish, foolish, frivolous, infantile, juvenile, puerile, silly, simple, trifling, weak, young
Antonyms *adj* adult, grown-up, manly *or* womanly, mature, sensible, sophisticated

childlike *adj* = **innocent**, artless, credulous, guileless, ingenuous, naive, simple, trustful, trusting, unfeigned

chill *n* **1** = **cold**, bite, coldness, coolness, crispness, frigidity, nip, rawness, sharpness ◆ *vb* **7** =

chilli *or* **chili** ('tʃɪlɪ) *n, pl* **chillies** *or* **chilies.** the small red hot-tasting pod of a type of capsicum used for flavouring sauces, etc. [C17: from Sp., from Nahuatl *chilli*]

chilli con carne ('tʃɪlɪ kɒn 'kɑːnɪ) *n* a highly seasoned Mexican dish of meat, onions, beans, and chilli powder. [from Sp.: chilli with meat]

chilli dog *n US.* a frankfurter garnished with chilli con carne, served in a roll.

chilli powder *n* ground chilli blended with other spices.

chilli sauce *n* a highly seasoned sauce made of tomatoes cooked with chilli and other spices.

chill out *Inf.* ◆ *vb* **1** (*intr, adv*) to relax, esp. after energetic dancing at a rave. ◆ *adj* **chill-out. 2** suitable for relaxation after energetic dancing: *a chill-out area; chill-out music.*

chilly ❶ ('tʃɪlɪ) *adj* **chillier, chilliest. 1** causing or feeling cool or moderately cold. **2** without warmth; unfriendly. **3** (of people) sensitive to cold.
▸**'chilliness** *n*

chilly bin *n NZ inf.* a portable insulated container with provision for packing food and drink in ice.

Chiltern Hundreds ('tʃɪltən) *pl n* (in Britain) short for **Stewardship of the Chiltern Hundreds;** a nominal office that an MP applies for in order to resign his seat.

chime[1] ❶ (tʃaɪm) *n* **1** an individual bell or the sound it makes when struck. **2** (*often pl*) the machinery employed to sound a bell in this way. **3** Also called: **bell.** a percussion instrument consisting of a set of vertical metal tubes of graduated length, suspended in a frame and struck with a hammer. **4** agreement; concord. ◆ *vb* **chimes, chiming, chimed. 5a** to sound (a bell) or (of a bell) to be sounded by a clapper or hammer. **5b** to produce (music or sounds) by chiming. **6** (*tr*) to indicate or show (time or the hours) by chiming. **7** (*intr; foll. by with*) to agree or harmonize. [C13: prob. shortened from earlier *chymbe bell,* ult. from L *cymbalum* CYMBAL]
▸**'chimer** *n*

chime[2], **chimb** (tʃaɪm), *or* **chine** *n* the projecting rim of a cask or barrel. [OE *cimb-*]

chime in *vb* (*intr, adv*) *Inf.* **1** to join in or interrupt (a conversation), esp. repeatedly and unwelcomely. **2** to voice agreement.

chimera ❶ *or* **chimaera** (kaɪ'mɪərə, kɪ-) *n* **1** a wild and unrealistic dream or notion. **2** (*often cap.*) *Greek myth.* a fire-breathing monster with the head of a lion, body of a goat, and tail of a serpent. **3** a fabulous beast made up of parts taken from various animals. **4** *Biol.* an organism consisting of at least two genetically different kinds of tissue as a result of mutation, grafting, etc. [C16: from L, from Gk *khimaira* she-goat]

chimerical (kaɪ'merɪk°l, kɪ-) *or* **chimeric** *adj* **1** wildly fanciful; imaginary. **2** given to or indulging in fantasies.
▸**chi'merically** *adv*

chimney ('tʃɪmnɪ) *n* **1** a vertical structure of brick, masonry, or steel that carries smoke or steam away from a fire, engine, etc. **2** another name for **flue** (sense 1). **3** short for **chimney stack. 4** an open-ended glass tube fitting around the flame of an oil or gas lamp in order to exclude draughts. **5** *Brit.* a fireplace, esp. an old and large one. **6** the vent of a volcano. **7** *Mountaineering.* a vertical fissure large enough for a person's body to enter. [C14: from OF *cheminée,* from LL *camīnāta,* from L *camīnus* furnace, from Gk *kaminos* oven]

chimney breast *n* the wall or walls that surround the base of a chimney or fireplace.

chimneypot ('tʃɪmnɪˌpɒt) *n* a short pipe on the top of a chimney.

chimney stack *n* the part of a chimney that rises above the roof of a building.

chimney sweep *or* **sweeper** *n* a person who cleans soot from chimneys.

chimp (tʃɪmp) *n Inf.* short for **chimpanzee.**

chimpanzee (ˌtʃɪmpæn'ziː) *n* a gregarious and intelligent anthropoid ape, inhabiting forests in central W Africa. [C18: from Central African dialect]

chin (tʃɪn) *n* **1** the protruding part of the lower jaw. **2** the front part of the face below the lips. **3 keep one's chin up.** *Inf.* to keep cheerful under difficult circumstances. **4 take it on the chin.** *Inf.* to face squarely up to a defeat, adversity, etc. ◆ *vb* **chins, chinning, chinned. 5** *Gymnastics.* to raise one's chin to (a horizontal bar, etc.) when hanging by the arms. [OE *cinn*]

Chin. *abbrev. for:* **1** China. **2** Chinese.

china ❶ ('tʃaɪnə) *n* **1** ceramic ware of a type originally from China. **2** any porcelain or similar ware. **3** cups, saucers, etc., collectively. **4** (*modifier*) made of china. [C16 *chiny,* from Persian *chīnī*]

china clay *n* another name for **kaolin.**

Chinagraph ('tʃaɪnəˌgrɑːf) *n Trademark.* a coloured pencil used for writing on china, glass, etc.

Chinaman ('tʃaɪnəmən) *n, pl* **Chinamen. 1** *Arch. or derog.* a native or inhabitant of China. **2** (*often not cap.*) *Cricket.* a ball bowled by a left-handed bowler to a right-handed batsman that spins from off to leg.

china stone *n* **1** a type of kaolinized granitic rock containing unaltered plagioclase. **2** any of certain limestones having a very fine grain and smooth texture.

Chinatown ('tʃaɪnəˌtaʊn) *n* a quarter of any city or town outside China with a predominantly Chinese population.

chinaware ('tʃaɪnəˌweə) *n* articles made of china, esp. those made for domestic use.

chincherinchee (ˌtʃɪntʃərɪn'tʃiː, -'rɪntʃɪ) *n* a bulbous South African liliaceous plant having long spikes of white or yellow long-lasting flowers. [from ?]

chinchilla (tʃɪn'tʃɪlə) *n* **1** a small gregarious rodent inhabiting mountainous regions of South America. It is bred in captivity for its soft silvery grey fur. **2** the highly valued fur of this animal. **3** a thick napped woollen cloth used for coats. [C17: from Sp., ?from Aymara]

chin-chin *sentence substitute. Inf.* a greeting or toast. [C18: from Chinese (Peking) *ch'ing-ch'ing,* please-please]

Chindit ('tʃɪndɪt) *n* a member of the Allied forces fighting behind the Japanese lines in Burma (1943–45). [C20: from Burmese *chinthé* a fabulous lion]

chine[1] (tʃaɪn) *n* **1** the backbone. **2** the backbone of an animal with adjoining meat, cut for cooking. **3** a ridge or crest of land. ◆ *vb* **chines, chining, chined. 4** (*tr*) to cut (meat) along or across the backbone. [C14: from OF *eschine,* of Gmc origin; see SHIN]

chine[2] (tʃaɪn) *n S English dialect.* a deep fissure in the wall of a cliff. [OE *cīnan* to crack]

Chinese (tʃaɪ'niːz) *adj* **1** of, relating to, or characteristic of China, its people, or their languages. ◆ *n* **2** (*pl* **Chinese**) a native or inhabitant of China or a descendant of one. **3** any of the languages of China.

Chinese cabbage *n* **1** a Chinese plant that is related to the cabbage and has crisp edible leaves growing in a loose cylindrical head. **2** another name for **bok choy.**

Chinese chequers *n* (*functioning as sing*) a board game played with marbles or pegs.

Chinese gooseberry *n* another name for **kiwi fruit.**

Chinese lantern *n* **1** a collapsible lantern made of thin coloured paper. **2** an Asian plant, cultivated for its attractive orange-red inflated calyx.

Chinese leaf *n* another name for **bok choy.**

Chinese puzzle *n* **1** an intricate puzzle, esp. one consisting of boxes within boxes. **2** a complicated problem.

Chinese wall *n* (esp. in financial institutions) a notional barrier between departments in the same company in order to avoid conflicts of interest between them.

chink[1] ❶ (tʃɪŋk) *n* **1** a small narrow opening, such as a fissure or crack. **2 chink in one's armour.** a small but fatal weakness. [C16: ? var. of earlier *chine,* from OE *cine* crack]

chink[2] (tʃɪŋk) *vb* **1** to make or cause to make a light ringing sound, as by the striking of glasses or coins. ◆ *n* **2** such a sound. [C16: imit.]

chinless wonder ('tʃɪnlɪs) *n Brit. inf.* a person, esp. upper-class, lacking strength of character.

chinoiserie (ʃiːnˌwɑːzə'riː, -'wɑːzərɪ) *n* **1** a style of decorative or fine art based on imitations of Chinese motifs. **2** an object or objects in this style. [F, from *chinois* CHINESE; see -ERY]

chinook (tʃɪ'nuːk, -'nʊk) *n* **1** a warm dry southwesterly wind blowing down the eastern slopes of the Rocky Mountains. **2** a warm moist wind blowing onto the Washington and Oregon coasts from the sea. [C19: from Amerind]

Chinook (tʃɪ'nuːk, -'nʊk) *n* **1** (*pl* **Chinook** *or* **Chinooks**) a North American Indian people of the Pacific coast near the Columbia River. **2** the language of this people.

Chinook Jargon *n* a pidgin language containing elements of North American Indian languages, English, and French: formerly used among fur traders and Indians on the NW coast of North America.

Chinook salmon *n* a Pacific salmon valued as a food fish.

chinos ('tʃiːnəʊz) *pl n* trousers made of a durable cotton twill cloth. [C20: from *chino,* the cloth, from ?]

chintz (tʃɪnts) *n* a printed, patterned cotton fabric, with glazed finish. [C17: from Hindi *chīnt,* from Sansk. *citra* gaily-coloured]

chintzy ('tʃɪntsɪ) *adj* **chintzier, chintziest. 1** of, resembling, or covered with chintz. **2** *Brit. inf.* typical of the décor associated with the use of chintz soft furnishings.

chinwag ('tʃɪnˌwæg) *n Brit. inf.* a chat.

chip ❶ (tʃɪp) *n* **1** a small piece removed by chopping, cutting, or breaking. **2** a mark left after a small piece has been broken off something. **3** (in some games) a counter used to represent money. **4** a thin strip of potato fried in deep fat. **5** the US, Canad. and Austral. name for **crisp** (sense 10). **6** *Sport.* a shot, kick, etc., lofted into the air, and travelling only a short distance. **7** *Electronics.* Also called: **microchip.** a tiny wafer of semiconductor material, such as silicon, processed to form a type

THESAURUS

cool, congeal, freeze, refrigerate **8 = dishearten,** dampen, deject, depress, discourage, dismay

chilly *adj* **1 = cool,** brisk, cold, crisp, fresh, nippy, parky (*Brit. inf.*), penetrating, sharp, wintry **2 = unfriendly,** aloof, cold as ice, cool, distant, frigid, hostile, stony, ungenial, unresponsive, unsympathetic, unwelcoming
Antonyms *adj* ≠ **cool:** balmy, hot, mild, scorching, sunny, sweltering, warm ≠ **unfriendly:** affable, chummy (*inf.*), congenial, cordial, friendly, responsive, sociable, sympathetic, warm, welcoming

chime *vb* **5a = ring,** boom, clang, dong, jingle, peal, sound, tinkle, toll

chimera *n* **1, 3 = illusion,** bogy, delusion, dream, fantasy, figment, hallucination, ignis fatuus, monster, monstrosity, snare, spectre, will-o'-the-wisp

china *n* **2, 3 = pottery,** ceramics, crockery, porcelain, service, tableware, ware

chink[1] *n* **1 = opening,** aperture, cleft, crack, cranny, crevice, cut, fissure, flaw, gap, rift

chip *n* **1, 2 = scratch,** dent, flake, flaw, fragment, nick, notch, paring, scrap, shard, shavof integrated circuit or component such as a transistor. **8** a thin strip of wood or straw used for making woven hats, baskets, etc. **9** *NZ.* a container for soft fruit, made of thin sheets of wood; punnet. **10 chip off the old block.** *Inf.* a person who resembles one of his or her parents in behaviour. **11 have a chip on one's shoulder.** *Inf.* to be aggressive or bear a grudge. **12 have had one's chips.** *Brit. inf.* to be defeated, condemned to die, killed, etc. **13 when the chips are down.** *Inf.* at a time of crisis. ◆ *vb* **chips, chipping, chipped. 14** to break small pieces from or become broken off in small pieces: *will the paint chip?* **15** (*tr*) to break or cut into small pieces: *to chip ice.* **16** (*tr*) to shape by chipping. **17** *Austral.* to dig or weed (a crop) with a hoe. **18** *Sport.* to strike or kick (a ball) in a high arc. [OE *cipp* (n), *cippian* (vb), from ?]

chip-based *adj* using or incorporating microchips in electronic equipment.

chipboard ('tʃɪpˌbɔːd) *n* a thin rigid sheet made of compressed wood chips.

chip heater *n Austral. & NZ.* a domestic water heater that burns chips of wood.

chip in ❶ *vb* (*adv*) *Inf.* **1** to contribute (money, time, etc.) to a cause or fund. **2** (*intr*) to interpose a remark or interrupt with a remark.

chipmunk ('tʃɪpˌmʌŋk) *n* a burrowing rodent of North America and Asia, typically having black-striped yellowish fur and cheek pouches for storing food. [C19: of Algonquian origin]

chipolata (ˌtʃɪpə'lɑːtə) *n Chiefly Brit.* a small sausage. [via F from It., from *cipolla* onion]

Chippendale ('tʃɪpᵊnˌdeɪl) *adj* (of furniture) designed by, made by, or in the style of Thomas Chippendale (?1718–79), characterized by the use of Chinese and Gothic motifs, cabriole legs, and massive carving.

chipper ('tʃɪpə) *adj Inf.* **1** cheerful; lively. **2** smartly dressed.

chippy[1] ('tʃɪpɪ) *n, pl* **chippies. 1** *Brit. inf.* a fish-and-chip shop. **2** *NZ.* a potato crisp.

chippy[2] ('tʃɪpɪ) *adj* **chippier, chippiest.** *Inf.* resentful or oversensitive about being perceived as inferior: *a chippy miner's son.* [C20: from CHIP (sense 11)]
▸ **'chippiness** *n*

chip shot *n Golf.* a short approach shot to the green, esp. one that is lofted.

chiral ('kaɪrəl) *adj* relating to chirality. [C20: from CHIRO- + -AL[1]]

chirality (kaɪ'rælɪtɪ) *n* right- or left-handedness in an asymmetric molecule.

chiro- *or* **cheiro-** *combining form.* of or by means of the hand: *chiromancy; chiropractic.* [via L from Gk *kheir* hand]

chirography (kaɪ'rɒgrəfɪ) *n* another name for **calligraphy.**
▸ **chi'rographer** *n* ▸ **chirographic** (ˌkaɪrə'græfɪk) *or* **ˌchiro'graphical** *adj*

chiromancy ('kaɪrəˌmænsɪ) *n* another word for **palmistry.**
▸ **'chiroˌmancer** *n*

chiropody (kɪ'rɒpədɪ) *n* the treatment of the feet, esp. corns, verrucas, etc.
▸ **chi'ropodist** *n*

chiropractic (ˌkaɪrə'præktɪk) *n* a system of treating bodily disorders by manipulation of the spine and other parts. [C20: from CHIRO- + Gk *praktikos* PRACTICAL]
▸ **'chiroˌpractor** *n*

chirp ❶ (tʃɜːp) *vb* (*intr*) **1** (esp. of some birds and insects) to make a short high-pitched sound. **2** to speak in a lively fashion. ◆ *n* **3** a chirping sound. [C15 (as *chirpinge,* gerund): imit.]
▸ **'chirper** *n*

chirpy ❶ ('tʃɜːpɪ) *adj* **chirpier, chirpiest.** *Inf.* cheerful; lively.
▸ **'chirpily** *adv* ▸ **'chirpiness** *n*

chirr *or* **churr** (tʃɜː) *vb* **1** (*intr*) (esp. of certain insects, such as crickets) to make a shrill trilled sound. ◆ *n* **2** such a sound. [C17: imit.]

chirrup ('tʃɪrəp) *vb* (*intr*) **1** (esp. of some birds) to chirp repeatedly. **2** to make clucking sounds with the lips. ◆ *n* **3** such a sound. [C16: var. of CHIRP]
▸ **'chirruper** *n* ▸ **'chirrupy** *adj*

chisel ('tʃɪzᵊl) *n* **1a** a hand tool for working wood, consisting of a flat steel blade with a handle. **1b** a similar tool without a handle for working stone or metal. ◆ *vb* **chisels, chiselling, chiselled** *or US* **chisels, chiseling, chiseled. 2** to carve (wood, stone, metal, etc.) or form (an engraving, statue, etc.) with or as with a chisel. **3** *Sl.* to cheat or obtain by cheating. [C14: via OF, from Vulgar L *cīsellus* (unattested), from L *caesus* cut]

chiseller ('tʃɪzᵊlə) *n* **1** a person who uses a chisel. **2** *Inf.* a cheat. **3** *Dublin sl.* a child.

chi-square distribution *n Statistics.* a continuous single-parameter distribution used esp. to measure goodness of fit and to test hypotheses.

chi-square test *n Statistics.* a test derived from the chi-square distribution to compare the goodness of fit of theoretical and observed frequency distributions.

chit[1] (tʃɪt) *n* **1** a voucher for a sum of money owed, esp. for food or drink. **2** Also called: **chitty.** *Chiefly Brit.* **2a** a note or memorandum. **2b** a requisition or receipt. [C18: from earlier *chitty,* from Hindi *cittha* note, from Sansk. *citra* marked]

chit[2] (tʃɪt) *n Facetious or derog.* a pert, impudent, or self-confident girl or child. [C14 (in the sense: young of an animal, kitten): from ?]

chital ('tʃiːtᵊl) *n* another name for **axis**[2] (the deer). [from Hindi]

chitchat ('tʃɪtˌtʃæt) *n* **1** gossip. ◆ *vb* **chitchats, chitchatting, chitchatted. 2** (*intr*) to gossip.

chitin ('kaɪtɪn) *n* a polysaccharide that is the principal component of the exoskeletons of arthropods and of the bodies of fungi. [C19: from F, from Gk *khitōn* CHITON + -IN]
▸ **'chitinous** *adj*

chiton ('kaɪtᵊn, -tɒn) *n* **1** (in ancient Greece) a loose woollen tunic worn by men and women. **2** any small primitive marine mollusc having an elongated body covered with eight overlapping shell plates. [C19: from Gk *khitōn* coat of mail]

chitterlings ('tʃɪtəlɪŋz) *or* **chitlings** ('tʃɪtlɪŋz) *pl n* (*sometimes sing*) the intestines of a pig or other animal prepared as a dish. [C13: from ?]

chiv (tʃɪv, ʃɪv) *or* **shiv** (ʃɪv) *Sl.* ◆ *n* **1** a knife. ◆ *vb* **chivs, chivving, chivved** *or* **shivs, shivving, shivved. 2** to stab (someone). [C17: ?from Romany *chiv* blade]

chivalrous ❶ ('ʃɪvəlrəs) *adj* **1** gallant; courteous. **2** involving chivalry. [C14: from OF, from CHEVALIER]
▸ **'chivalrously** *adv* ▸ **'chivalrousness** *n*

chivalry ❶ ('ʃɪvəlrɪ) *n, pl* **chivalries. 1** the combination of qualities expected of an ideal knight, esp. courage, honour, justice, and a readiness to help the weak. **2** courteous behaviour, esp. towards women. **3** the medieval system and principles of knighthood. **4** knights, noblemen, etc., collectively. [C13: from OF *chevalerie,* from CHEVALIER]
▸ **'chivalric** *adj*

chive (tʃaɪv) *n* a small Eurasian purple-flowered alliaceous plant, whose long slender hollow leaves are used in cooking. Also called: **chives.** [C14: from OF *cive,* ult. from L *caepa* onion]

chivy ❶, **chivvy** ('tʃɪvɪ), *or* **chevy** *Brit.* ◆ *vb* **chivies, chivying, chivied, chivvies, chivvying, chivvied,** *or* **chevies, chevying, chevied. 1** (*tr*) to harass or nag. **2** (*tr*) to hunt. **3** (*intr*) to run about. ◆ *n, pl* **chivies, chivvies,** *or* **chevies. 4** a hunt. **5** *Obs.* a hunting cry. [C19: var. of *chevy,* prob. from *Chevy Chase,* title of a Scottish border ballad]

chlamydia (klə'mɪdɪə) *n* any of a genus of virus-like bacteria responsible for such diseases as trachoma, psittacosis, and some sexually transmitted diseases. [C20: NL, from Gk *khlamus* mantle + -IA]

chloral ('klɔːrəl) *n* **1** a colourless oily liquid with a pungent odour, made from chlorine and acetaldehyde and used in preparing chloral hydrate and DDT. Formula: CCl_3CHO. **2** short for **chloral hydrate.**

chloral hydrate *n* a colourless crystalline soluble solid produced by the reaction of chloral with water and used as a sedative and hypnotic. Formula: $CCl_3C(OH)_3$.

chloramphenicol (ˌklɔːræm'fɛnɪˌkɒl) *n* a broad-spectrum antibiotic used esp. in treating typhoid fever and rickettsial infections. [C20: from CHLORO- + AM(IDE)- + PHE(NO)- + NI(TRO)- + (GLY)COL]

chlorate ('klɔːreɪt, -rɪt) *n* any salt of chloric acid, containing the monovalent ion ClO_3^-.

chlordane ('klɔːdeɪn) *or* **chlordan** *n* a white insoluble toxic solid used as an insecticide. [C20: from CHLORO- + (IN)D(OLE + -ENE) + -ANE]

chlorhexidine (klɔː'hɛksɪdiːn) *n* an antiseptic compound used in skin cleansers, mouthwashes, etc. [C20: from CHLOR(O)- + HEX(ANE) + -I(DE) + (AM)INE]

chloric ('klɔːrɪk) *adj* of or containing chlorine in the pentavalent state.

chloric acid *n* a strong acid with a pungent smell, known only in solution and in the form of chlorate salts. Formula: $HClO_3$.

chloride ('klɔːraɪd) *n* **1** any salt of hydrochloric acid, containing the chloride ion Cl^-. **2** any compound containing a chlorine atom, such as methyl chloride (chloromethane), CH_3Cl.

chloride of lime *or* **chlorinated lime** *n* another name for **bleaching powder.**

chlorinate ('klɔːrɪˌneɪt) *vb* **chlorinates, chlorinating, chlorinated.** (*tr*) **1** to combine or treat (a substance) with chlorine. **2** to disinfect (water) with chlorine.
▸ **ˌchlorin'ation** *n* ▸ **'chlorinˌator** *n*

chlorine ('klɔːriːn) *or* **chlorin** ('klɔːrɪn) *n* a toxic pungent greenish-yellow gas of the halogen group; occurring only in the combined state, mainly in common salt: used in the manufacture of many organic chemicals, in water purification, and as a disinfectant and bleaching agent. Symbol: Cl; atomic no.: 17; atomic wt.: 35.453. [C19 (coined by Sir Humphrey Davy): from CHLORO- + -INE[2], referring to its colour]

chlorite[1] ('klɔːraɪt) *n* any of a group of green soft secondary minerals

THESAURUS

ing, sliver, wafer ◆ *vb* **14** = **nick**, chisel, damage, gash, whittle

chip in *vb* **1, 2** *Informal* = **contribute**, donate, go Dutch (*inf.*), interpose, interrupt, pay, subscribe

chirp *vb* **1** = **chirrup**, cheep, peep, pipe, tweet, twitter, warble

chirpy *adj Informal* = **cheerful**, animated, blithe, bright, buoyant, enlivening, enthusiastic, full of beans (*inf.*), happy, in high spirits, jaunty, jolly, light-hearted, lively, radiant, sparkling, sprightly, sunny

chivalrous *adj* **1** = **courteous**, bold, brave, courageous, courtly, gallant, gentlemanly, heroic, high-minded, honourable, intrepid, knightly, magnanimous, true, valiant
Antonyms *adj* boorish, cowardly, dishonourable, disloyal, rude, uncourtly, ungallant, unmannerly

chivalry *n* **1-3** = **courtesy**, courage, courtliness, gallantry, gentlemanliness, knight-errantry, knighthood, politeness

chivy *vb Brit.* **1** = **nag**, annoy, badger, bend someone's ear (*inf.*), breathe down someone's neck (*inf.*), bug (*inf.*), harass, hassle (*inf.*), hound, pester, plague, pressure (*inf.*), prod, torment

consisting of the hydrated silicates of aluminium, iron, and magnesium. [C18: from L, from Gk, from *khlōros* greenish yellow]
▸**chloritic** (klɔːˈrɪtɪk) *adj*
chlorite[2] (ˈklɔːraɪt) *n* any salt of chlorous acid.
chloro- *or before a vowel* **chlor-** *combining form.* **1** indicating the colour green: *chlorophyll.* **2** chlorine: *chloroform.*
chlorofluorocarbon (ˌklɔːrəˌfluərəʊˈkɑːbᵊn) *n Chem.* any of various gaseous compounds of carbon, hydrogen, chlorine, and fluorine, used as refrigerants, aerosol propellants, solvents, and in foam: some cause a breakdown of ozone in the earth's atmosphere.
chloroform (ˈklɔːrəˌfɔːm) *n* a heavy volatile liquid with a sweet taste and odour, used as a solvent and cleansing agent and in refrigerants: formerly used as an inhalation anaesthetic. Formula: $CHCl_3$. Systematic name: **trichloromethane.** [C19: from CHLORO- + *formyl* from FORMIC]
Chloromycetin (ˌklɔːrəumaɪˈsiːtɪn) *n Trademark.* a brand of **chloramphenicol.**
chlorophyll *or US* **chlorophyl** (ˈklɔːrəfɪl) *n* the green pigment of plants, occurring in chloroplasts, that traps the energy of sunlight for photosynthesis: used as a colouring agent (**E140**) in medicines and food.
▸ˈ**chloroˌphylloid** *adj* ▸ˌ**chloroˈphyllous** *adj*
chloroplast (ˈklɔːrəʊˌplæst) *n* a plastid containing chlorophyll and other pigments, occurring in plants that carry out photosynthesis.
chlorosis (klɔːˈrəʊsɪs) *n* **1** Also called: **greensickness.** *Pathol.* a once-common iron-deficiency disease of adolescent girls, characterized by greenish-yellow skin colour, weakness, and palpitation. **2** *Bot.* a deficiency of chlorophyll in green plants caused by mineral deficiency, lack of light, disease, etc., the leaves appearing uncharacteristically pale. [C17: from CHLORO- + -OSIS]
▸**chlorotic** (klɔːˈrɒtɪk) *adj*
chlorous (ˈklɔːrəs) *adj* **1** of or containing chlorine in the trivalent state. **2** of or containing chlorous acid.
chlorous acid *n* an unstable acid that is a strong oxidizing agent. Formula: $HClO_2$.
chlorpromazine (klɔːˈprɒməˌziːn) *n* a drug used as a sedative and tranquillizer. [C20: from CHLORO- + PRO(PYL + A)M(INE) + AZINE]
chlortetracycline (klɔːˌtɛtrəˈsaɪkliːn) *n* an antibiotic used in treating many bacterial and rickettsial infections and some viral infections.
chock (tʃɒk) *n* **1** a block or wedge of wood used to prevent the sliding or rolling of a heavy object. **2** *Naut.* **2a** a ringlike device with an opening at the top through which a rope is placed. **2b** a cradle-like support for a boat, barrel, etc. ◆ *vb (tr)* **3** (*usually foll. by up*) *Brit.* to cram full. **4** to fit with or secure by a chock. **5** to support (a boat, barrel, etc.) on chocks. ◆ *adv* **6** as closely or tightly as possible: *chock against the wall.* [C17: from ?; ? rel. to OF *çoche* log]
chock-a-block *adj, adv* **1** filled to capacity; in a crammed state. **2** *Naut.* with the blocks brought close together, as when a tackle is pulled as tight as possible.
chocker (ˈtʃɒkə) *adj* **1** *Austral. & NZ inf.* full up; packed. **2** *Brit. sl.* irritated; fed up. [C20: from CHOCK-A-BLOCK]
chock-full *or* **choke-full** *adj* (*postpositive*) completely full. [C17 *choke-full;* see CHOKE, FULL[1]]
choco *or* **chocko** (ˈtʃɒkəʊ) *n, pl* **chocos** *or* **chockos.** *Austral. sl.* a conscript or militiaman. [from *chocolate soldier*]
chocolate (ˈtʃɒkəlɪt, ˈtʃɒklɪt, -lət) *n* **1** a food preparation made from roasted ground cacao seeds, usually sweetened and flavoured. **2** a drink or sweetmeat made from this. **3a** a deep brown colour. **3b** (*as adj*): *a chocolate carpet.* [C17: from Sp., from Aztec *xocolatl,* from *xococ* sour + *atl* water]
▸ˈ**chocolaty** *adj*
chocolate-box *n* (*modifier*) *Inf.* sentimentally pretty or appealing.
Choctaw (ˈtʃɒktɔː) *n* **1** (*pl* **-taws** *or* **-taw**) a member of a N American people originally of Alabama. **2** their language. [C18: from Choctaw *Chahta*]
choice ➊ (tʃɔɪs) *n* **1** the act or an instance of choosing or selecting. **2** the opportunity or power of choosing. **3** a person or thing chosen or that may be chosen: *he was a possible choice.* **4** an alternative action or possibility: *what choice did I have?* **5** a supply from which to select. ◆ *adj* **6** of superior quality; excellent: *choice wine.* **7** carefully chosen, appropriate: *a few choice words will do the trick.* **8** vulgar or rude: *choice language.* [C13: from OF, from *choisir* to CHOOSE]
▸ˈ**choicely** *adv* ▸ˈ**choiceness** *n*
choir (ˈkwaɪə) *n* **1** an organized group of singers, esp. for singing in church services. **2** the part of a cathedral, abbey, or church in front of the altar and used by the choir and clergy. **3** a number of instruments of the same family playing together: *a brass choir.* **4** Also called: **choir organ.** one of the manuals on an organ controlling a set of soft sweet-toned pipes. [C13 *quer,* from OF *cuer,* from L CHORUS]
choirboy (ˈkwaɪəˌbɔɪ) *n* a young boy who sings the treble part in a church choir.
choir school *n* (in Britain) a school attached to a cathedral, college, etc., offering general education to boys whose singing ability is good.
choke ➊ (tʃəʊk) *vb* **chokes, choking, choked. 1** (*tr*) to hinder or stop the breathing of (a person or animal), esp. by constricting the windpipe or by asphyxiation. **2** (*intr*) to have trouble or fail in breathing, swallowing, or speaking. **3** (*tr*) to block or clog up (a passage, pipe, street, etc.). **4** (*tr*) to retard the growth or action of: *the weeds are choking my plants.* **5** (*tr*) to enrich the petrol-air mixture by reducing the air supply to (a carburettor, petrol engine, etc.). ◆ *n* **6** the act or sound of choking. **7** a device in the carburettor of a petrol engine that enriches the petrol-air mixture by reducing the air supply. **8** any mechanism for reducing the flow of a fluid in a pipe, tube, etc. **9** Also called: **choke coil.** *Electronics.* an inductor having a relatively high impedance, used to prevent the passage of high frequencies or to smooth the output of a rectifier. [OE *ācēocian*]
▸ˈ**choky** *or* ˈ**chokey** *adj*
choke back *or* **down** *vb (tr, adv)* to suppress (anger, tears, etc.).
choke chain *n* a collar and lead for a dog so designed that if the dog drags on the lead the collar tightens round its neck.
choked (tʃəʊkt) *adj Brit. inf.* annoyed or disappointed.
choker (ˈtʃəʊkə) *n* **1** a woman's high collar. **2** any neckband or necklace worn tightly around the throat. **3** a high clerical collar; stock. **4** a person who chokes. **5** something that causes a person to choke.
choke up *vb (tr, adv)* **1** to block (a drain, pipe, etc.) completely. **2** *Inf.* (*usually passive*) to overcome (a person) with emotion.
chokey *or* **choky** (ˈtʃəʊkɪ) *n Brit. sl.* prison. [C17: from Anglo-Indian, from Hindi *caukī* a lockup]
choko (ˈtʃəʊkəʊ) *n, pl* **chokos.** *Austral. & NZ.* the cucumber-like fruit of a tropical American vine: eaten as a vegetable in the Caribbean, Australia, and New Zealand. [C18: from Brazilian Indian]
cholangiography (kəˌlændʒɪˈɒgrəfɪ) *n* radiographic examination of the bile ducts after the introduction into them of a contrast medium.
chole- *or before a vowel* **chol-** *combining form.* bile or gall: *cholesterol.* [from Gk *kholē*]
choler (ˈkɒlə) *n* **1** anger or ill humour. **2** *Arch.* one of the four bodily humours; yellow bile. [C14: from OF, from Med. L, from L: jaundice, CHOLERA]
cholera (ˈkɒlərə) *n* an acute intestinal infection characterized by severe diarrhoea, cramp, etc.: caused by ingestion of water or food contaminated with the bacterium *Vibrio comma.* [C14: from L, from Gk *kholera* jaundice, from *kholē* bile]
▸**choleraic** (ˌkɒləˈreɪɪk) *adj*
choleric (ˈkɒlərɪk) *adj* **1** bad-tempered. **2** *Obs.* bilious or causing biliousness.
▸ˈ**cholerically** *adv*
cholesterol (kəˈlɛstəˌrɒl) *or* **cholesterin** (kəˈlɛstərɪn) *n* a sterol found in all animal tissues, blood, bile, and animal fats. A high level of cholesterol is implicated in some cases of atherosclerosis. [C19: from CHOLE- + Gk *stereos* solid]
choline (ˈkəʊliːn, -ɪn, ˈkɒl-) *n* a colourless viscous soluble alkaline substance present in animal tissues, esp. as a constituent of lecithin. [C19: from CHOLE- + -INE[2]]
chomp (tʃɒmp) *or* **chump** *vb* **1** to chew (food) noisily; champ. ◆ *n* **2** the act or sound of chewing in this manner. [var. of CHAMP[1]]
Chondokyo (ˌtʃɒndəʊˈkjəʊ) *n* an indigenous religion of Korea, incorporating elements of Buddhism, Confucianism, Christianity, and shamanism. Former name: **Tongchak.** [C20: from Korean: Religion of the Heavenly Way]
chondrite (ˈkɒndraɪt) *n* a stony meteorite consisting mainly of silicate minerals in small spherical masses.
choof off (tʃʊf) *vb (intr, adv) Austral. sl.* to go away; make off.
chook (tʃʊk) *n Inf., chiefly Austral. & NZ.* a hen or chicken. Also called: **chookie.**
choose ➊ (tʃuːz) *vb* **chooses, choosing, chose, chosen. 1** to select (a person, thing, course of action, etc.) from a number of alternatives. **2** (*tr; takes a clause as object or an infinitive*) to consider it desirable or proper: *I don't choose to read that book.* **3** (*intr*) to like; please: *you may stand if you choose.* [OE *ceosan*]
▸ˈ**chooser** *n*
choosy ➊ (ˈtʃuːzɪ) *adj* **choosier, choosiest.** *Inf.* particular in making a choice; difficult to please.
chop[1] ➊ (tʃɒp) *vb* **chops, chopping, chopped. 1** (often foll. by *down* or *off*) to cut (something) with a blow from an axe or other sharp tool. **2** (*tr;* often foll. by *up*) to cut into pieces. **3** (*tr*) *Brit. inf.* to dispense with or reduce. **4** (*intr*) to move quickly or violently. **5** *Tennis, cricket, etc.* to hit (a ball) sharply downwards. **6** *Boxing, karate, etc.* to punch or strike (an opponent) with a short sharp blow. ◆ *n* **7** a cutting blow. **8** the act or an instance of chopping. **9** a piece chopped off. **10** a slice of mutton, lamb, or pork, generally including a rib. **11** *Austral. & NZ sl.* a share (esp. in **get** *or* **hop in for one's chop**). **12** *Austral. & NZ.* a competition of skill and speed in chopping logs. **13** *Sport.* a sharp downward blow or stroke. **14 not much chop.** *Austral. & NZ inf.* not much good; poor. **15 the chop.** *Brit. & Austral. sl.* dismissal from employment. [C16: var. of CHAP[1]]

THESAURUS

choice *n* **1-4** = **option**, alternative, discrimination, election, pick, preference, say **5** = **selection**, range, variety ◆ *adj* **6** = **best**, elect, elite, excellent, exclusive, exquisite, hand-picked, nice, precious, prime, prize, rare, select, special, superior, uncommon, unusual, valuable

choke *vb* **1** = **strangle**, asphyxiate, gag, overpower, smother, stifle, suffocate, suppress, throttle **3** = **block**, bar, bung, clog, close, congest, constrict, dam, obstruct, occlude, stop

choose *vb* **1, 3** = **pick**, adopt, cherry-pick, cull, designate, desire, elect, espouse, fix on, opt for, predestine, prefer, see fit, select, settle upon, single out, take, wish
Antonyms *vb* decline, dismiss, exclude, forgo, leave, refuse, reject, throw aside

choosy *adj Informal* = **fussy**, discriminating, exacting, faddy, fastidious, finicky, particular, picky (*inf.*), selective
Antonyms *adj* easy (*inf.*), easy to please, indiscriminate, undemanding, unselective

chop[1] *vb* **1** = **cut**, axe, cleave, fell, hack, hew, lop, sever, shear, slash, truncate **2** *often foll. by up* = **cut up**, cube, dice, divide, fragment, mince

chop[2] (tʃɒp) *vb* **chops, chopping, chopped. 1** (*intr*) to change direction suddenly; vacillate (esp. in **chop and change**). **2 chop logic.** use excessively subtle or involved argument. [OE *ceapian* to barter]

chop[3] (tʃɒp) *n* a design stamped on goods as a trademark, esp. in the Far East. [C17: from Hindi *chhāp*]

chop chop *adv* pidgin English for **quickly.** [C19: from Chinese dialect]

chophouse ('tʃɒpˌhaus) *n* a restaurant specializing in steaks, grills, chops, etc.

chopper ('tʃɒpə) *n* **1** *Chiefly Brit.* a small hand axe. **2** a butcher's cleaver. **3** a person or thing that cuts or chops. **4** an informal name for a **helicopter. 5** a device for periodically interrupting an electric current or beam of radiation to produce a pulsed current or beam. **6** a type of bicycle or motorcycle with very high handlebars. **7** *NZ.* a child's bicycle. **8** *Sl., chiefly US.* a sub-machine-gun.

choppy ❶ ('tʃɒpɪ) *adj* **choppier, choppiest.** (of the sea, weather, etc.) fairly rough.
▸ **'choppily** *adv* ▸ **'choppiness** *n*

chops (tʃɒps) *pl n* **1** the jaws or cheeks; jowls. **2** the mouth. **3 lick one's chops.** *Inf.* to anticipate with pleasure. [C16: from ?]

chopsticks ('tʃɒpstɪks) *pl n* a pair of thin sticks, of ivory, wood, etc., used for eating Chinese or other East Asian food. [C17: from pidgin E, from *chop* quick, from Chinese dialect + STICK[1]]

chop suey ('suːɪ) *n* a Chinese-style dish originating in the US, consisting of meat, bean sprouts, etc., served with rice. [C19: from Chinese *tsap sui* odds and ends]

choral ('kɔːrəl) *adj* relating to, sung by, or designed for a chorus or choir.
▸ **'chorally** *adv*

chorale *or* **choral** (kɒ'rɑːl) *n* **1** a slow stately hymn tune. **2** *Chiefly US.* a choir or chorus. [C19: from G *Choralgesang,* translation of L *cantus chorālis* choral song]

chord[1] (kɔːd) *n* **1** *Maths.* a straight line connecting two points on a curve or curved surface. **2** *Engineering.* one of the principal members of a truss, esp. one that lies along the top or the bottom. **3** *Anat.* a variant spelling of **cord. 4** an emotional response, esp. one of sympathy: *the story struck the right chord.* [C16: from L, from Gk *khordē* gut, string; see CORD]

chord[2] (kɔːd) *n* **1** the simultaneous sounding of a group of musical notes, usually three or more in number. ◆ *vb* **2** (*tr*) to provide (a melodic line) with chords. [C15: short for ACCORD; spelling infl. by CHORD[1]]
▸ **'chordal** *adj*

chordate ('kɔːdeɪt) *n* **1** an animal with a backbone or notochord. ◆ *adj* **2** of or relating to the chordates. [C19: from Med. L *chordata:* see CHORD[1] & -ATE[1]]

chore ❶ (tʃɔː) *n* **1** a routine task, esp. a domestic one. **2** a boring task. [C19: from ME *chare,* from OE *cierr* a job]

-chore *n combining form.* (in botany) indicating a plant that is distributed by a certain means: *anemochore.* [from Gk *khōrein* to move]
▸ **-chorous** *or* **-choric** *adj combining form.*

chorea (kɒ'rɪə) *n* a disorder of the central nervous system characterized by uncontrollable irregular jerky movements. See **Huntington's disease, Sydenham's chorea.** [C19: from NL, from L: dance, from Gk *khoreia;* see CHORUS]

choreograph ('kɒrɪəˌgrɑːf) *vb* (*tr*) to compose the steps and dances for (a ballet, etc.)

choreography (ˌkɒrɪ'ɒgrəfɪ) *or* **choregraphy** (kɒ'regrəfɪ) *n* **1** the composition of dance steps and sequences for ballet and stage and film dancing. **2** the steps and sequences of a ballet or dance. **3** the notation representing such steps. **4** the art of dancing. [C18: from Gk *khoreia* dance + -GRAPHY]
▸ **ˌchore'ographer** *or* **cho'regrapher** *n* ▸ **choreographic** (ˌkɒrɪə'græfɪk) *or* **choregraphic** (ˌkɒrə'græfɪk) *adj* ▸ **ˌchoreo'graphically** *or* **ˌchore'graphically** *adv*

choric ('kɒrɪk) *adj* of, like, or for a chorus, esp. of singing, dancing, or the speaking of verse.

chorion ('kɔːrɪən) *n* the outer membrane surrounding an embryo. [C16: from Gk *khorion* afterbirth]
▸ **chorionic** (ˌkɔːrɪ'ɒnɪk) *adj*

chorionic gonadotrophin *n* a hormone, secreted by the placenta in mammals, that promotes the secretion of progesterone. See **HCG.**

chorionic villus sampling *n* a method of diagnosing genetic disorders early in pregnancy by the removal by catheter through the cervix of a tiny sample of tissue from the chorionic villi. Abbrev.: **CVS.**

chorister ('kɒrɪstə) *n* a singer in a choir, esp. a choirboy. [C14: from Med. L *chorista*]

choroid ('kɔːrɔɪd) *or* **chorioid** ('kɔːrɪˌɔɪd) *adj* **1** resembling the chorion, esp. in being vascular. ◆ *n* **2** the vascular membrane of the eyeball between the sclera and the retina. [C18: from Gk *khoroeidēs,* erroneously for *khorioeidēs,* from CHORION]

chortle ❶ ('tʃɔːtᵊl) *vb* **chortles, chortling, chortled. 1** (*intr*) to chuckle gleefully. ◆ *n* **2** a gleeful chuckle. [C19: coined (1871) by Lewis Carroll; prob. a blend of CHUCKLE + SNORT]
▸ **'chortler** *n*

chorus ❶ ('kɔːrəs) *n, pl* **choruses. 1** a large choir of singers or a piece of music composed for such a choir. **2** a body of singers or dancers who perform together. **3** a section of a song in which a soloist is joined by a group of singers, esp. in a recurring refrain. **4** an intermediate section of a pop song, blues, etc., as distinct from the verse. **5** *Jazz.* any of a series of variations on a theme. **6** (in ancient Greece) **6a** a lyric poem sung by a group of dancers, originally as a religious rite. **6b** an ode or series of odes sung by a group of actors. **6c** the actors who sang the chorus and commented on the action of the play. **7a** (esp. in Elizabethan drama) the actor who spoke the prologue, etc. **7b** the part spoken by this actor. **8** a group of people or animals producing words or sounds simultaneously. **9** any speech, song, or utterance produced by a group of people or animals simultaneously: *the dawn chorus.* **10 in chorus.** in unison. ◆ *vb* **11** to speak, sing, or utter (words, sounds, etc.) in unison. [C16: from L, from Gk *khoros*]

chorus girl *n* a girl who dances or sings in the chorus of a musical comedy, revue, etc.

chose (tʃəuz) *vb* the past tense of **choose.**

chosen ('tʃəuzᵊn) *vb* **1** the past participle of **choose.** ◆ *adj* **2** selected, esp. for some special quality.

chough (tʃʌf) *n* a large black passerine bird of parts of Europe, Asia, and Africa, with a long downward-curving red bill: family Corvidae (crows). [C14: from ?]

choux pastry (ʃuː) *n* a very light pastry made with eggs, used for éclairs, etc. [partial translation of F *pâte choux* cabbage dough]

chow (tʃau) *n* **1** *Inf.* food. **2** short for **chow-chow** (sense 1).

chow-chow *n* **1** a thick-coated breed of dog with a curled tail, originally from China. Often shortened to **chow. 2** a Chinese preserve of ginger, orange peel, etc., in syrup. **3** a mixed vegetable pickle. [C19: from pidgin E, prob. based on Chinese *cha* miscellaneous]

chowder ('tʃaudə) *n Chiefly US & Canad.* a thick soup or stew containing clams or fish. [C18: from F *chaudière* kettle, from LL *caldāria; see* CAULDRON]

chow mein (meɪn) *n* a Chinese-American dish, consisting of mushrooms, meat, shrimps, etc., served with fried noodles. [from Chinese *ch'ao mien* fried noodles]

Chr. *abbrev. for:* **1** Christ. **2** Christian.

chrism *or* **chrisom** ('krɪzəm) *n* a mixture of olive oil and balsam used for sacramental anointing in the Greek Orthodox and Roman Catholic Churches. [OE, from Med. L, from Gk, from *khriein* to anoint]
▸ **chrismal** ('krɪzməl) *adj*

Christ (kraɪst) *n* **1** Jesus of Nazareth (Jesus Christ), regarded by Christians as fulfilling Old Testament prophecies of the Messiah. **2** the Messiah or anointed one of God as the subject of Old Testament prophecies. **3** an image or picture of Christ. ◆ *interj* **4** *Taboo sl.* an oath expressing anger, etc. ◆ See also **Jesus.** [OE *Crīst,* from L *Chrīstus,* from Gk *khristos* anointed one (from *khriein* to anoint), translating Heb. *māshīah* MESSIAH]
▸ **'Christly** *adj*

Christadelphian (ˌkrɪstə'delfɪən) *n* **1** a member of a Christian millenarian sect founded in the US about 1848, holding that only the just will enter eternal life, and that the ignorant and unconverted will not be raised from the dead. ◆ *adj* **2** of or relating to this body or its beliefs and practices. [C19: from LGk *khristadelphos, khristos* CHRIST + *adelpos* brother]

christen ❶ ('krɪsᵊn) *vb* (*tr*) **1** to give a Christian name to in baptism as a sign of incorporation into a Christian Church. **2** another word for **baptize. 3** to give a name to anything, esp. with some ceremony. **4** *Inf.* to use for the first time. [OE *cristnian,* from *Crīst* CHRIST]
▸ **'christening** *n*

Christendom ('krɪsᵊndəm) *n* the collective body of Christians throughout the world.

Christian ('krɪstʃən) *n* **1a** a person who believes in and follows Jesus Christ. **1b** a member of a Christian Church or denomination. **2** *Inf.* a person who possesses Christian virtues. ◆ *adj* **3** of, relating to, or derived from Jesus Christ, his teachings, example, or followers. **4** (*sometimes not cap.*) exhibiting kindness or goodness.
▸ **'christianly** *adj, adv*

Christian Democrat *n* a member or supporter of any of various right-of-centre political parties in Europe and Latin America that combine moderate conservatism with historical links to the Christian Church.
▸ **Christian Democracy** *n* ▸ **Christian Democratic** *adj*

Christian Era *n* the period beginning with the year of Christ's birth.

Christianity (ˌkrɪstɪ'ænɪtɪ) *n* **1** the Christian religion. **2** Christian beliefs or practices. **3** a less common word for **Christendom.**

Christianize *or* **Christianise** ('krɪstʃəˌnaɪz) *vb* **Christianizes, Christianizing, Christianized** *or* **Christianises, Christianising, Christianised.** (*tr*) **1** to make Christian or convert to Christianity. **2** to imbue with Christian principles, spirit, or outlook.
▸ **ˌChristiani'zation** *or* **ˌChristiani'sation** *n* ▸ **'Christianˌizer** *or* **'Christianˌiser** *n*

Christian name *n* a personal name formally given to Christians at christening: loosely used to mean any person's first name.

THESAURUS

◆ *n* **15 the chop** *Slang, chiefly Brit.* = **the sack** (*inf.*), dismissal, one's cards, sacking (*inf.*), termination, the axe (*inf.*), the boot (*sl.*), the (old) heave-ho (*inf.*), the order of the boot (*sl.*)

choppy *adj* = **rough,** blustery, broken, ruffled, squally, tempestuous

Antonyms *adj* calm, smooth, windless

chore *n* **1, 2** = **task,** burden, duty, errand, fag (*inf.*), job, no picnic

chortle *vb, n* **1, 2** = **chuckle,** cackle, crow, guffaw

chorus *n* **1** = **choir,** choristers, ensemble, singers, vocalists **3** = **refrain,** burden, response, strain **10** = **unison,** accord, concert, harmony

christen *vb* **2** = **baptize 3** = **name,** call, designate, dub, style, term, title

Christian Science *n* the religious system of the Church of Christ, Scientist, founded by Mary Baker Eddy (1879), emphasizing spiritual regeneration and healing through prayer alone.
▸**Christian Scientist** *n*

Christingle (ˌkrɪsˈtɪŋgl) *n* (in Britain) a Christian service for children held shortly before Christmas, in which each child is given a decorated fruit with a lighted candle in it. [C20: from CHRIST(MAS) + INGLE]

Christlike (ˈkraɪstˌlaɪk) *adj* resembling the spirit of Jesus Christ.
▸**ˈChristˌlikeness** *n*

Christmas ➊ (ˈkrɪsməs) *n* **1a** the annual commemoration by Christians of the birth of Jesus Christ, on Dec. 25. **1b** Also called: **Christmas Day.** Dec. 25, observed as a day of secular celebrations when gifts and greetings are exchanged. **1c** (*as modifier*): *Christmas celebrations.* **2** Also called: **Christmastide.** the season of Christmas extending from Dec. 24 (Christmas Eve) to Jan. 6 (the festival of the Epiphany or Twelfth Night). [OE *Crīstes mæsse* MASS OF CHRIST]
▸**ˈChristmassy** *adj*

Christmas box *n* a tip or present given at Christmas, esp. to postmen, tradesmen, etc.

Christmas Eve *n* the evening or the whole day before Christmas Day.

Christmas pudding *n Brit.* a rich steamed pudding containing suet, dried fruit, spices, etc. Also called: **plum pudding.**

Christmas rose *n* an evergreen plant of S Europe and W Asia with white or pinkish winter-blooming flowers. Also called: **hellebore, winter rose.**

Christmastide (ˈkrɪsməsˌtaɪd) *n* another name for **Christmas** (sense 2).

Christmas tree *n* **1** an evergreen tree or an imitation of one, decorated as part of Christmas celebrations. **2** Also called: **Christmas bush.** *Austral.* any of various trees or shrubs flowering at Christmas and used for decoration. **3** *NZ.* another name for the **pohutukawa.**

Christy *or* **Christie** (ˈkrɪstɪ) *n, pl* **Christies.** *Skiing.* a turn in which the body is swung sharply round with the skis parallel: used for stopping or changing direction quickly. [C20: from *Christiania*, former name of Oslo]

chroma (ˈkrəʊmə) *n* the attribute of a colour that enables an observer to judge how much chromatic colour it contains. See also **saturation** (sense 4). [C19: from Gk *khrōma* colour]

chromate (ˈkrəʊmeɪt) *n* any salt or ester of chromic acid.

chromatic (krəˈmætɪk) *adj* **1** of, relating to, or characterized by a colour or colours. **2** *Music.* **2a** involving the sharpening or flattening of notes or the use of such notes in chords and harmonic progressions. **2b** of or relating to the chromatic scale or an instrument capable of producing it. [C17: from Gk, from *khrōma* colour]
▸**chroˈmatically** *adv* ▸**chroˈmaticism** *n* ▸**chromaticity** (ˌkrəʊməˈtɪsɪtɪ) *n*

chromatic aberration *n* a defect in a lens system in which different wavelengths of light are focused at different distances because they are refracted through different angles. It produces a blurred image with coloured fringes.

chromatics (krəʊˈmætɪks) *n* (*functioning as sing*) the science of colour.

chromatic scale *n* a twelve-note scale including all the semitones of the octave.

chromatin (ˈkrəʊmətɪn) *n* the part of the nucleus that consists of DNA, RNA, and proteins, forms the chromosomes, and stains with basic dyes.

chromato- *or before a vowel* **chromat-** *combining form.* **1** indicating colour or coloured: *chromatophore.* **2** indicating chromatin: *chromatolysis.* [from Gk *khrōma, khrōmat-* colour]

chromatography (ˌkrəʊməˈtɒgrəfɪ) *n* the technique of separating and analysing the components of a mixture of liquids or gases by selective adsorption.

chrome (krəʊm) *n* **1a** another word for **chromium,** esp. when present in a pigment or dye. **1b** (*as modifier*): *a chrome dye.* **2** anything plated with chromium. **3** a pigment or dye that contains chromium. ◆ *vb* **chromes, chroming, chromed. 4** to plate or be plated with chromium. **5** to treat or be treated with a chromium compound, as in dyeing or tanning. [C19: via F from Gk *khrōma* colour]

-chrome *n and adj combining form.* colour, coloured, or pigment: *monochrome.* [from Gk *khrōma* colour]

chrome dioxide *n* another name for **chromium dioxide.**

chromel (ˈkrəʊmel) *n* a nickel-based alloy containing about 10 per cent chromium, used in heating elements. [C20: from CHRO(MIUM) + ME(TA)L]

chrome steel *n* any of various hard rust-resistant steels containing chromium.

chrome yellow *n* any yellow pigment consisting of lead chromate.

chromic (ˈkrəʊmɪk) *adj* **1** of or containing chromium in the trivalent state. **2** of or derived from chromic acid.

chromic acid *n* an unstable dibasic oxidizing acid known only in solution and as chromate salts. Formula: H_2CrO_4.

chromite (ˈkrəʊmaɪt) *n* a brownish-black mineral consisting of a ferrous chromic oxide in crystalline form: the only commercial source of chromium. Formula: $FeCr_2O_4$.

chromium (ˈkrəʊmɪəm) *n* a hard grey metallic element, used in steel alloys and electroplating to increase hardness and corrosion-resistance. Symbol: Cr; atomic no.: 24; atomic wt.: 51.996. [C19: from NL, from F: CHROME]

chromium dioxide *n* a chemical compound used as a magnetic coating on cassette tapes; chromium(IV) oxide. Formula: CrO_2. Also called (*not in technical usage*): **chrome dioxide.**

chromium steel *n* another name for **chrome steel.**

chromo (ˈkrəʊməʊ) *n, pl* **chromos.** short for **chromolithograph.**

chromo- *or before a vowel* **chrom-** *combining form.* **1** indicating colour, coloured, or pigment: *chromogen.* **2** indicating chromium: *chromyl.* [from Gk *khrōma* colour]

chromolithograph (ˌkrəʊməʊˈlɪθəˌgrɑːf) *n* a picture produced by chromolithography.

chromolithography (ˌkrəʊməʊlɪˈθɒgrəfɪ) *n* the process of making coloured prints by lithography.
▸ˌ**chromoliˈthographer** *n* ▸**chromolithographic** (ˌkrəʊməʊlɪθəˈgræfɪk) *adj*

chromosome (ˈkrəʊməˌsəʊm) *n* any of the microscopic rod-shaped structures that appear in a cell nucleus during cell division, consisting of nucleoprotein arranged into units (genes) that are responsible for the transmission of hereditary characteristics.
▸ˌ**chromoˈsomal** *adj*

chromosome map *n* a graphic representation of the positions of genes on chromosomes, obtained by observation of stained chromosomes or by determining the degree of linkage between genes. See also **genetic map.**
▸**chromosome mapping** *n*

chromosphere (ˈkrəʊməˌsfɪə) *n* a gaseous layer of the sun's atmosphere extending from the photosphere to the corona.
▸**chromospheric** (ˌkrəʊməˈsferɪk) *adj*

chromous (ˈkrəʊməs) *adj* of or containing chromium in the divalent state.

chron. *or* **chronol.** *abbrev. for:* **1** chronological. **2** chronology.

Chron. *Bible. abbrev. for* Chronicles.

chronic ➊ (ˈkrɒnɪk) *adj* **1** continuing for a long time; constantly recurring. **2** (of a disease) developing slowly, or of long duration. Cf. **acute** (sense 7). **3** inveterate; habitual: *a chronic smoker.* **4** *Inf.* **4a** very bad: *the play was chronic.* **4b** very serious: *he left her in a chronic condition.* [C15: from L, from Gk, from *khronos* time]
▸**ˈchronically** *adv* ▸**chronicity** (krɒˈnɪsɪtɪ) *n*

chronicle ➊ (ˈkrɒnɪkᵊl) *n* **1** a record or register of events in chronological order. ◆ *vb* **chronicles, chronicling, chronicled. 2** (*tr*) to record in or as if in a chronicle. [C14: from Anglo-F, via L *chronica* (pl), from Gk *khronika* annals; see CHRONIC]
▸**ˈchronicler** *n*

chrono- *or before a vowel* **chron-** *combining form.* time: *chronology.* [from Gk *khronos* time]

chronograph (ˈkrɒnəˌgrɑːf, ˈkrəʊnə-) *n* **1** an accurate instrument for recording small intervals of time. **2** any timepiece, esp. a wristwatch designed for maximum accuracy.
▸**chronographic** (ˌkrɒnəˈgræfɪk) *adj*

chronological ➊ (ˌkrɒnəˈlɒdʒɪkᵊl, ˌkrəʊ-) *or* **chronologic** *adj* **1** (esp. of a sequence of events) arranged in order of occurrence. **2** relating to or in accordance with chronology.
▸ˌ**chronoˈlogically** *adv*

chronology (krəˈnɒlədʒɪ) *n, pl* **chronologies. 1** the determination of the proper sequence of past events. **2** the arrangement of dates, events, etc., in order of occurrence. **3** a table of events arranged in order of occurrence.
▸**chroˈnologist** *n*

chronometer (krəˈnɒmɪtə) *n* a timepiece designed to be accurate in all conditions of temperature, pressure, etc., used esp. at sea.
▸**chronometric** (ˌkrɒnəˈmetrɪk) *or* ˌ**chronoˈmetrical** *adj* ▸ˌ**chronoˈmetrically** *adv*

chronometry (krəˈnɒmɪtrɪ) *n* the science of measuring time with extreme accuracy.

chronon (ˈkrəʊnɒn) *n* a unit of time equal to the time that a photon would take to traverse the diameter of an electron: about 10^{-24} seconds.

chrysalid (ˈkrɪsəlɪd) *n* **1** another name for **chrysalis.** ◆ *adj* **2** of or relating to a chrysalis.

chrysalis (ˈkrɪsəlɪs) *n, pl* **chrysalises** *or* **chrysalides** (krɪˈsælɪˌdiːz). **1** the pupa of a moth or butterfly, in a case or cocoon. **2** anything in the process of developing. [C17: from L, from Gk *khrusallis,* from *khrusos* gold]

chrysanthemum (krɪˈsænθəməm) *n* **1** any of various widely cultivated plants of the composite family, having brightly coloured showy flower heads in autumn. **2** any other plant of the genus *Chrysanthemum,* such as the oxeye daisy. [C16: from L: marigold, from Gk, from *khrusos* gold + *anthemon* flower]

chryselephantine (ˌkrɪselɪˈfæntɪn) *adj* (of ancient Greek statues, etc.)

THESAURUS

Christmas *n* **2** = **festive season,** Noel, Xmas (*inf.*), Yule (*arch.*), Yuletide (*arch.*)

chronic *adj* **3** = **habitual,** confirmed, deep-rooted, deep-seated, incessant, incurable, ineradicable, ingrained, inveterate, persistent **4a** *Informal* = **dreadful,** abysmal, appalling, atrocious, awful

Antonyms *adj* ≠ **habitual:** infrequent, occasional, temporary

chronicle *n* **1** = **record,** account, annals, diary, history, journal, narrative, register, story ◆ *vb* **2** = **record,** enter, narrate, put on record, recount, register, relate, report, set down, tell

chronicler *n* **2** = **recorder,** annalist, diarist, historian, historiographer, narrator, reporter, scribe

chronological *adj* **1** = **in order,** consecutive, historical, in sequence, ordered, progressive, sequential

Antonyms *adj* haphazard, intermittent, irregular, out-of-order, random made of or overlaid with gold and ivory. [C19: from Gk, from *khrusos* gold + *elephas* ivory]

chrysoberyl (ˈkrɪsəˌberɪl) *n* a rare very hard greenish-yellow mineral consisting of beryllium aluminate: used as a gemstone. Formula: $BeAl_2O_4$. [C17: from L, from Gk, from *khrusos* gold + *bērullos* beryl]

chrysolite (ˈkrɪsəˌlaɪt) *n* a brown or yellowish-green olivine: used as a gemstone. [C14 *crisolite*, from OF, from L, from Gk, from *khrusos* gold + *lithos* stone]

chrysoprase (ˈkrɪsəˌpreɪz) *n* an apple-green variety of chalcedony: used as a gemstone. [C13 *crisopace*, from OF, from L, from Gk, from *khrusos* gold + *prason* leek]

chthonian (ˈθəunɪən) *or* **chthonic** (ˈθɒnɪk) *adj* of or relating to the underworld. [C19: from Gk *khthonios* in or under the earth, from *khthōn* earth]

chub (tʃʌb) *n, pl* **chub** *or* **chubs. 1** a common European freshwater cyprinid game fish, having a cylindrical dark greenish body. **2** any of various North American fishes, esp. certain whitefishes and minnows. [C15: from ?]

chubby Ⓣ (ˈtʃʌbɪ) *adj* **chubbier, chubbiest.** (esp. of the human form) plump. [C17: ?from CHUB]
▸ˈ**chubbiness** *n*

chuck[1] Ⓣ (tʃʌk) *vb* (*mainly tr*) **1** *Inf.* to throw. **2** to pat affectionately, esp. under the chin. **3** *Inf.* (sometimes foll. by *in* or *up*) to give up; reject: *he chucked up his job.* ◆ *n* **4** a throw or toss. **5** a pat under the chin. **6 the chuck.** *Inf.* dismissal. ◆ See also **chuck in, chuck off, chuck out.** [C16: from ?]

chuck[2] (tʃʌk) *n* **1** Also called: **chuck steak.** a cut of beef from the neck to the shoulder blade. **2** a device that holds a workpiece in a lathe or tool in a drill. [C17: var. of CHOCK]

chuck[3] (tʃʌk) *n W Canad.* **1** a large body of water. **2** In full: **saltchuck.** the sea. [C19: from Chinook Jargon, of Amerind origin, from *chauk*]

chuck in *vb* (*adv*) **1** (*tr*) *Brit inf.* to abandon or give up: *to chuck in a hopeless attempt.* **2** (*intr*) *Austral. inf.* to contribute to the cost of something.

chuckle Ⓣ (ˈtʃʌkᵊl) *vb* **chuckles, chuckling, chuckled.** (*intr*) **1** to laugh softly or to oneself. **2** (of animals, esp. hens) to make a clucking sound. ◆ *n* **3** a partly suppressed laugh. [C16: prob. from *chuck* cluck + *-le*]

chucklehead (ˈtʃʌkᵊlˌhɛd) *n Inf.* a stupid person; dolt.

chuck off *vb* (*intr, adv;* often foll. by *at*) *Austral. & NZ inf.* to abuse or make fun of.

chuck out *vb* (*tr, adv;* often foll. by *of*) *Inf.* to eject forcibly (from); throw out (of).

chuff[1] (tʃʌf) *n* **1** a puffing sound as of a steam engine. ◆ *vb* **2** (*intr*) to move while emitting such sounds. [C20: imit.]

chuff[2] (tʃʌf) *vb* (*tr; usually passive*) *Brit. sl.* to please or delight: *he was chuffed by his pay rise.* [prob. from *chuff* (adj) pleased, happy]

chug (tʃʌg) *n* **1** a short dull sound, such as that made by an engine. ◆ *vb* **chugs, chugging, chugged. 2** (*intr*) (of an engine, etc.) to operate while making such sounds. [C19: imit.]

chukar (tʃʌˈkɑː) *n* a common Indian partridge having a red bill and black-barred sandy plumage. [from Hindi *cakor*, from Sansk. *cakora*, prob. imit.]

chukka *or US* **chukker** (ˈtʃʌkə) *n Polo.* a period of continuous play, generally lasting 7½ minutes. [C20: from Hindi *cakkar*, from Sansk. *cakra* wheel]

chukka boot (ˈtʃʌkə) *or* **chukka** *n* an ankle-high boot worn for playing polo. [C19: from CHUKKA]

chum Ⓣ (tʃʌm) *n* **1** *Inf.* a close friend. ◆ *vb* **chums, chumming, chummed. 2** (*intr;* usually foll. by *up with*) to be or become an intimate friend (of). [C17 (meaning: a person sharing rooms with another): prob. shortened from *chamber fellow*]

chummy Ⓣ (ˈtʃʌmɪ) *adj* **chummier, chummiest.** *Inf.* friendly.
▸ˈ**chummily** *adv* ▸ˈ**chumminess** *n*

chump (tʃʌmp) *n* **1** *Inf.* a stupid person. **2** a thick heavy block of wood. **3** the thick blunt end of anything, esp. of a piece of meat. **4** *Brit. sl.* the head (esp. in **off one's chump**). [C18: ? a blend of CHUNK + LUMP[1]]

chunder (ˈtʃʌndə) *Sl., chiefly Austral.* ◆ *vb* (*intr*) **1** to vomit. ◆ *n* **2** vomit. [C20: from ?]

chunk Ⓣ (tʃʌŋk) *n* **1** a thick solid piece, as of meat, wood, etc. **2** a considerable amount. [C17: var. of CHUCK[2]]

chunky Ⓣ (ˈtʃʌŋkɪ) *adj* **chunkier, chunkiest. 1** thick and short. **2** containing thick pieces. **3** *Chiefly Brit.* (of clothes, esp. knitwear) made of thick bulky material.
▸ˈ**chunkiness** *n*

Chunnel (ˈtʃʌnᵊl) *n* an informal name for **Channel Tunnel.** [C20: from CH(ANNEL) + T(UNNEL)]

chunter (ˈtʃʌntə) *vb* (*intr;* often foll. by *on*) *Brit. inf.* to mutter or grumble incessantly in a meaningless fashion. [C16: prob. imit.]

church Ⓣ (tʃɜːtʃ) *n* **1** a building for public worship, esp. Christian worship. **2** an occasion of public worship. **3** the clergy as distinguished from the laity. **4** (*usually cap.*) institutionalized forms of religion as a political or social force: *conflict between Church and State.* **5** (*usually cap.*) the collective body of all Christians. **6** (*often cap.*) a particular Christian denomination or group. **7** (*often cap.*) the Christian religion. ◆ Related adj: **ecclesiastical.** ◆ *vb* (*tr*) **8** *Church of England.* to bring (someone, esp. a woman after childbirth) to church for special ceremonies. [OE *cirice*, from LGk, from Gk *kuriakon* (*dōma*) the Lord's (house), from *kurios* master, from *kuros* power]

Church Army *n* a voluntary Anglican organization founded to assist the parish clergy.

Church Commissioners *pl n Brit.* a group of representatives of Church and State that administers the property of the Church of England.

churchgoer (ˈtʃɜːtʃˌgəuə) *n* a person who attends church regularly.
▸ˈ**churchˌgoing** *adj, n*

churchly (ˈtʃɜːtʃlɪ) *adj* appropriate to or associated with the church.
▸ˈ**churchliness** *n*

churchman (ˈtʃɜːtʃmən) *n, pl* **churchmen. 1** a clergyman. **2** a male member of a church.

Church of Christ, Scientist *n* See **Christian Science.**

Church of England *n* the reformed established state Church in England, with the Sovereign as its temporal head.

Church of Jesus Christ of Latter-Day Saints *n* See **Mormon** (sense 1).

churchwarden (ˌtʃɜːtʃˈwɔːdᵊn) *n* **1** *Church of England, Episcopal Church.* one of two assistants of a parish priest who administer the secular affairs of the church. **2** a long-stemmed tobacco pipe made of clay.

churchwoman (ˈtʃɜːtʃˌwumən) *n, pl* **churchwomen.** a female member of a church.

churchyard (ˈtʃɜːtʃˌjɑːd) *n* the grounds round a church, used as a graveyard.

churinga (tʃəˈrɪŋgə) *n, pl* **churinga** *or* **churingas.** a sacred amulet of the native Australians. [from Abor.]

churl Ⓣ (tʃɜːl) *n* **1** a surly ill-bred person. **2** *Arch.* a farm labourer. **3** *Arch.* a miserly person. [OE *ceorl*]
▸ˈ**churlish** *adj*

churn Ⓣ (tʃɜːn) *n* **1** *Brit.* a large container for milk. **2** a vessel or machine in which cream or whole milk is vigorously agitated to produce butter. ◆ *vb* **3a** to agitate (milk or cream) to make butter. **3b** to make (butter) by this process. **4** (sometimes foll. by *up*) to move or cause to move with agitation. **5** (of a bank, broker, etc.) to encourage an investor or policyholder to change investments, endowment policies, etc., to increase commissions at the client's expense. **6** (of a government) to pay benefits to a wide category of people and claw it back by taxation from the well off. **7** to promote the turnover of existing subscribers leasing, and new subscribers joining, a cable television system. [OE *ciern*]
▸ˈ**churner** *n*

churn out *vb* (*tr, adv*) *Inf.* **1** to produce (something) at a rapid rate: *to churn out ideas.* **2** to perform (something) mechanically: *to churn out a song.*

churr (tʃɜː) *vb, n* a variant spelling of **chirr.**

chute[1] Ⓣ (juːt) *n* **1** an inclined channel or vertical passage down which water, parcels, coal, etc., may be dropped. **2** a steep slope, used as a slide as for toboggans. **3** a slide into a swimming pool. **4** a rapid or waterfall. [C19: from OF *cheoite*, fem. p.p. of *cheoir* to fall, from L *cadere*; in some senses, var. spelling of SHOOT]

chute[2] (juːt) *n, vb* **chutes, chuting, chuted.** *Inf.* short for **parachute.**
▸ˈ**chutist** *n*

chutney (ˈtʃʌtnɪ) *n* a pickle of Indian origin, made from fruit, vinegar, spices, sugar, etc.: *mango chutney.* [C19: from Hindi *catnī*, from ?]

chutzpah (ˈxutspə) *n US & Canad. inf.* shameless audacity; impudence. [C20: from Yiddish]

chyack (ˈtʃaɪæk) *vb, n* a variant spelling of **chiack.**

chyle (kaɪl) *n* a milky fluid composed of lymph and emulsified fat globules, formed in the small intestine during digestion. [C17: from LL, from Gk *khulos* juice]
▸**chylaceous** (kaɪˈleɪʃəs) *or* ˈ**chylous** *adj*

chyme (kaɪm) *n* the thick fluid mass of partially digested food that leaves the stomach. [C17: from LL, from Gk *khumos* juice]
▸ˈ**chymous** *adj*

THESAURUS

chubby *adj* = **plump**, buxom, flabby, fleshy, podgy, portly, roly-poly, rotund, round, stout, tubby
Antonyms *adj* lean, skinny, slender, slight, slim, sylphlike, thin

chuck[1] *vb* **1** *Informal* = **throw**, cast, discard, fling, heave, hurl, pitch, shy, sling, toss

chuckle *vb* **1** = **laugh**, chortle, crow, exult, giggle, snigger, titter

chum *n* **1** *Informal* = **friend**, cock (*Brit. inf.*), companion, comrade, crony, mate (*inf.*), pal (*inf.*)

chummy *adj Informal* = **friendly**, affectionate, buddy-buddy (*sl., chiefly U.S. & Canad.*), close, intimate, matey *or* maty (*Brit. inf.*), pally (*inf.*), palsy-walsy (*inf.*), thick (*inf.*)

chunk *n* **1, 2** = **piece**, block, dollop (*inf.*), hunk, lump, mass, nugget, portion, slab, wad, wodge (*Brit. inf.*)

chunky *adj* **1** = **thickset**, beefy (*inf.*), dumpy, stocky, stubby

church *n* **1** = **chapel**, basilica, cathedral, house of God, kirk (*Scot.*), minster, place of worship, procathedral, tabernacle, temple

churl *n* **1** = **boor**, lout, oaf **2** *Archaic* = **peasant**, bumpkin, clodhopper (*inf.*), clown, hick (*inf., chiefly US & Canad.*), hillbilly, rustic, yokel

churlish *adj* **1** = **boorish**, brusque, crabbed, harsh, ill-tempered, impolite, loutish, morose, oafish, rude, sullen, surly, uncivil, uncouth, unmannerly, vulgar
Antonyms *adj* agreeable, amiable, civil, courteous, cultivated, good-tempered, mannerly, noble, pleasant, polite, well-bred

churn *vb* **4** *sometimes foll. by* **up** = **stir up**, agitate, beat, boil, convulse, foam, froth, seethe, swirl, toss

chute[1] *n* **1** = **slope**, channel, gutter, incline, ramp, runway, slide, trough

chypre *French.* (ʃiprə) *n* a perfume made from sandalwood. [lit.: Cyprus, ? where it originated]

Ci *symbol for* curie.

CI *abbrev. for* Channel Islands.

CIA *abbrev. for* Central Intelligence Agency; a federal US bureau created in 1947 to coordinate and conduct espionage and intelligence activities.

ciabatta (tʃə'bætə) *n* a type of open-textured bread made with olive oil. [C20: from It., lit.: slipper]

CIB *abbrev. for* Criminal Investigation Branch (of the New Zealand and Australian police).

ciborium (sɪ'bɔːrɪəm) *n, pl* **ciboria** (-rɪə). *Christianity.* **1** a goblet-shaped lidded vessel used to hold consecrated wafers in Holy Communion. **2** a canopy fixed over an altar. [C17: from Med. L, from L, from Gk *kibōrion* cup-shaped seed vessel of the Egyptian lotus]

cicada (sɪ'kɑːdə) *or* **cicala** *n, pl* **cicadas, cicadae** (-diː) *or* **cicale** (-leɪ). any large broad insect, most common in warm regions, having membranous wings: the males produce a high-pitched drone by vibration of a pair of drumlike abdominal organs. [C19: from L]

cicatrix ('sɪkətrɪks) *n, pl* **cicatrices** (ˌsɪkə'traɪsiːz). **1** the tissue that forms in a wound during healing; scar. **2** a scar on a plant indicating the former point of attachment of a part, esp. a leaf. [C17: from L: scar, from ?]
▸**cicatricial** (ˌsɪkə'trɪʃəl) *adj*

cicatrize *or* **cicatrise** ('sɪkəˌtraɪz) *vb* **cicatrizes, cicatrizing, cicatrized** *or* **cicatrises, cicatrising, cicatrised.** (of a wound or defect in tissue) to be closed by scar formation; heal.
▸ˌ**cicatri'zation** *or* ˌ**cicatri'sation** *n*

cicely ('sɪsəlɪ) *n, pl* **cicelies.** short for **sweet cicely.** [C16: from L *seselis,* from Gk, from ?]

cicerone (ˌsɪsə'rəʊnɪ, ˌtʃɪtʃ-) *n, pl* **cicerones** *or* **ciceroni** (-nɪ). a person who conducts and informs sightseers. [C18: from It.: antiquarian scholar, guide, after *Cicero* (106–43 B.C.), Roman orator and writer]

CID (in Britain) *abbrev. for* Criminal Investigation Department; the detective division of a police force.

-cide *n combining form.* **1** indicating a person or thing that kills: *insecticide.* **2** indicating a killing; murder: *homicide.* [from L *-cīda* (agent), *-cīdium* (act), from *caedere* to kill]
▸**-cidal** *adj combining form.*

cider *or* **cyder** ('saɪdə) *n* **1** an alcoholic drink made from the fermented juice of apples. **2** Also called: **sweet cider.** *US & Canad.* an unfermented drink made from apple juice. [C14: from OF, via Med. L, from LGk *sikera* strong drink, from Heb. *shēkhār*]

c.i.f. *or* **CIF** *abbrev. for* cost, insurance, and freight (included in the price quoted).

c.i.f.c.i. *abbrev. for* cost, insurance, freight, commission, and interest (included in the price quoted).

cig (sɪg) *or* **ciggy** ('sɪgɪ) *n, pl* **cigs** *or* **ciggies.** *Inf.* a cigarette.

cigar (sɪ'gɑː) *n* a cylindrical roll of cured tobacco leaves, for smoking. [C18: from Sp. *cigarro*]

cigarette ❶ *or US (sometimes)* **cigaret** (ˌsɪgə'rɛt) *n* a short tightly rolled cylinder of tobacco, wrapped in thin paper for smoking. [C19: from F, lit.: a little CIGAR]

cigarette card *n* a small picture card, formerly given away with cigarettes, now collected as a hobby.

cigarillo (ˌsɪgə'rɪləʊ) *n, pl* **cigarillos.** a small cigar, often only slightly larger than a cigarette.

ciliary ('sɪlɪərɪ) *adj* of or relating to cilia.

ciliary body *n* the part of the eye that joins the choroid to the iris.

cilium ('sɪlɪəm) *n, pl* **cilia** ('sɪlɪə). **1** any of the short threads projecting from the surface of a cell, organism, etc., whose rhythmic beating causes movement. **2** the technical name for **eyelash.** [C18: NL, from L: (lower) eyelid, eyelash]
▸**ciliate** ('sɪlɪɪt, -eɪt) *or* '**ciliˌated** *adj*

C in C *or* **C.-in-C.** *Mil. abbrev. for* Commander in Chief.

cinch (sɪntʃ) *n* **1** *Sl.* an easy task. **2** *Sl.* a certainty. **3** a US and Canad. name for **girth** (sense 2). **4** *US inf.* a firm grip. ◆ *vb* **5** (often foll. by *up*) *US & Canad.* to fasten a girth around (a horse). **6** (*tr*) *Inf.* to make sure of. **7** (*tr*) *Inf., chiefly US.* to get a firm grip on. [C19: from Sp., from L, from *cingere* to encircle]

cinchona (sɪŋ'kəʊnə) *n* **1** any tree or shrub of the South American genus *Cinchona,* having medicinal bark. **2** the dried bark of any of these trees, which yields quinine. **3** any of the drugs derived from cinchona bark. [C18: NL, after the Countess of *Chinchón* (1576–1639), vicereine of Peru]
▸**cinchonic** (sɪŋ'kɒnɪk) *adj*

cincture ('sɪŋktʃə) *n* something that encircles, esp. a belt or girdle. [C16: from L, from *cingere* to gird]

cinder ('sɪndə) *n* **1** a piece of incombustible material left after the combustion of coal, coke, etc.; clinker. **2** a piece of charred material that burns without flames; ember. **3** any solid waste from smelting or refining. **4** (*pl*) fragments of volcanic lava; scoriae. [OE *sinder*]
▸'**cindery** *adj*

Cinderella (ˌsɪndə'rɛlə) *n* **1** a girl who achieves fame after being obscure. **2** a poor, neglected, or unsuccessful person or thing. [C19: after *Cinderella,* the heroine of a fairy tale]

cine- *combining form.* indicating motion picture or cinema: *cine camera; cinephotography.*

cineaste ('sɪnɪˌæst) *n* an enthusiast for films. [C20: F]

cinema ❶ ('sɪnɪmə) *n* **1** *Chiefly Brit.* a place designed for the exhibition of films. **2 the cinema. 2a** the art or business of making films. **2b** films collectively. [C19 (earlier spelling: *kinema*): shortened from CINEMATOGRAPH]
▸**cinematic** (ˌsɪnɪ'mætɪk) *adj* ▸ˌ**cine'matically** *adv*

cinematograph (ˌsɪnɪ'mætəˌgrɑːf) *Chiefly Brit.* ◆ *n* **1** a combined camera, printer, and projector. ◆ *vb* **2** to take (pictures) with a film camera. [C19 (earlier spelling: *kinematograph*): from Gk *kinēma* motion + -GRAPH]
▸**cinematographer** (ˌsɪnɪmə'tɒgrəfə) *n* ▸**cinematographic** (ˌsɪnɪˌmætə'græfɪk) *adj* ▸ˌ**cineˌmato'graphically** *adv* ▸ˌ**cinema'tography** *n*

cinéma vérité (*French* sinema verite) *n* films characterized by subjects, actions, etc., that have the appearance of real life. [F, lit.: truth cinema]

cineraria (ˌsɪnə'rɛərɪə) *n* a plant of the Canary Islands, widely cultivated for its blue, purple, red, or variegated daisy-like flowers. [C16: from NL, from L, from *cinis* ashes; from its downy leaves]

cinerarium (ˌsɪnə'rɛərɪəm) *n, pl* **cineraria** (-'rɛərɪə). a place for keeping the ashes of the dead after cremation. [C19: from L, from *cinerārius* relating to ashes]
▸**cinerary** ('sɪnərərɪ) *adj*

cinerator ('sɪnəˌreɪtə) *n Chiefly US.* a furnace for cremating corpses.
▸ˌ**cine'ration** *n*

cinnabar ('sɪnəˌbɑː) *n* **1** a heavy red mineral consisting of mercury(II) sulphide: the chief ore of mercury. Formula: HgS. **2** the red form of mercury(II) sulphide, esp. when used as a pigment. **3a** a bright red; vermilion. **3b** (*as adj*): *a cinnabar tint.* **4** a large red-and-black European moth. [C15: from OF, from L, from Gk *kinnabari,* of Oriental origin]

cinnamon ('sɪnəmən) *n* **1** a tropical Asian tree, having aromatic yellowish-brown bark. **2** the spice obtained from the bark of this tree, used for flavouring food and drink. **3a** a light yellowish brown. **3b** (*as adj*): *a cinnamon coat.* [C15: from OF, via L & Gk, from Heb. *qinnamown*]

cinque (sɪŋk) *n* the number five in cards, dice, etc. [C14: from OF *cinq* five]

cinquecento (ˌtʃɪŋkwɪ'tʃɛntəʊ) *n* the 16th century, esp. in reference to Italian art, architecture, or literature. [C18: It., shortened from *milcinquecento* 1500]

cinquefoil ('sɪŋkˌfɔɪl) *n* **1** any plant of the N temperate rosaceous genus *Potentilla,* typically having five-lobed compound leaves. **2** an ornamental carving in the form of five arcs arranged in a circle and separated by cusps. [C13 *sink foil,* from OF, from L *quinquefolium* plant with five leaves]

Cinque Ports (sɪŋk) *pl n* an association of ports on the SE coast of England, which from late Anglo-Saxon times until 1685 provided ships for the king's service in return for the profits of justice in their courts.

cipher ❶ *or* **cypher** ('saɪfə) *n* **1** a method of secret writing using substitution of letters according to a key. **2** a secret message. **3** the key to a secret message. **4** an obsolete name for **zero** (sense 1). **5** any of the Arabic numerals or the Arabic system of numbering. **6** a person or thing of no importance; nonentity. **7** a design consisting of interwoven letters; monogram. ◆ *vb* **8** to put (a message) into secret writing. **9** *Rare.* to perform (a calculation) arithmetically. [C14: from OF *cifre* zero, from Med. L, from Ar. *sifr* zero]

circa ❶ ('sɜːkə) *prep* (used with a date) at the approximate time of: *circa 1182* B.C. Abbrev.: **c, ca.** [L: about]

circadian (sɜː'keɪdɪən) *adj* of or relating to biological processes that occur regularly at 24-hour intervals. See also **biological clock.** [C20: from L *circa* about + *diēs* day]

circle ❶ ('sɜːkᵊl) *n* **1** a closed plane curve every point of which is equidistant from a given fixed point, the centre. **2** the figure enclosed by such a curve. **3** *Theatre.* the section of seats above the main level of the auditorium, usually comprising the dress circle and the upper circle. **4** something formed or arranged in the shape of a circle. **5** a group of people sharing an interest, activity, upbringing, etc.; set: *golf circles; a family circle.* **6** a domain or area of activity, interest, or influence. **7** a circuit. **8** a process or chain of events or parts that forms a connected whole; cycle. **9** a parallel of latitude. See also **great circle, small circle. 10** one of a number of Neolithic or Bronze Age rings of standing stones, such as Stonehenge. **11 come full circle.** to arrive back at one's starting point. See also **vicious circle.** ◆ *vb* **circles, circling, circled. 12** to move in

THESAURUS

cigarette *n* = **fag** (*Brit. slang*), cancer stick (*sl.*), ciggy (*inf.*), coffin nail (*sl.*), gasper (*sl.*), smoke

cinema *n* **2 the cinema** = **films**, big screen (*inf.*), flicks (*sl.*), motion pictures, movies, pictures

cipher *n* **1** = **code**, cryptograph **4** *Obsolete* = **zero**, nil, nothing, nought **5** = **symbol**, character, digit, figure, number, numeral **6** = **nobody**, nonentity **7** = **monogram**, device, logo, mark

circa *adv* = **approximately**, about, around, in the region of, roughly

circle *n* **1, 4** = **ring**, band, circumference, coil, cordon, cycle, disc, globe, lap, loop, orb, perimeter, periphery, revolution, round, sphere, turn **5** = **group**, assembly, class, clique, club, company, coterie, crowd, fellowship, fraternity, order, school, set, society **6, 7** = **area**, bounds, circuit, compass, domain, enclosure, field, orbit, province, range, realm, region, scene, sphere ◆ *vb* **12, 13** = **go round**, belt, circumnavigate, circumscribe, coil, compass, curve, encircle, enclose, encompass, envelop, enwreath, gird, hem in, pivot, revolve, ring, rotate, surround, tour, wheel, whirl

a circle (around). **13** (*tr*) to enclose in a circle; encircle. [C14: from L *circulus*, from *circus* ring, circle]
▸'**circler** *n*

circlet ('sɜːklɪt) *n* a small circle or ring, esp. a circular ornament worn on the head. [C15: from OF *cerclet* a little CIRCLE]

circuit ➊ ('sɜːkɪt) *n* **1a** a complete route or course, esp. one that is curved or circular or that lies around an object. **1b** the area enclosed within such a route. **2** the act of following such a route: *we made three circuits of the course.* **3a** a complete path through which an electric current can flow. **3b** (*as modifier*): *a circuit diagram.* **4a** a periodical journey around an area, as made by judges, salesmen, etc. **4b** the places visited on such a journey. **4c** the persons making such a journey. **5** an administrative division of the Methodist Church comprising a number of neighbouring churches. **6** a number of theatres, cinemas, etc., under one management. **7** *Sport.* **7a** a series of tournaments in which the same players regularly take part: *the international tennis circuit.* **7b** (usually preceded by *the*) the contestants who take part in such a series. **8** *Chiefly Brit.* a motor-racing track, usually of irregular shape. ◆ *vb* **9** to make or travel in a circuit around (something). [C14: from L *circuitus*, from *circum* around + *īre* to go]
▸'**circuital** *adj*

circuit breaker *n* a device that under abnormal conditions, such as a short circuit, stops the flow of current in an electrical circuit.

circuitous ➊ (sə'kjuːɪtəs) *adj* indirect and lengthy; roundabout: *a circuitous route.*
▸**cir'cuitously** *adv* ▸**cir'cuitousness** *n*

circuitry ('sɜːkɪtrɪ) *n* **1** the design of an electrical circuit. **2** the system of circuits used in an electronic device.

circuity (sə'kjuːɪtɪ) *n, pl* **circuities.** (of speech, reasoning, etc.) a roundabout or devious quality.

circular ➊ ('sɜːkjʊlə) *adj* **1** of, involving, resembling, or shaped like a circle. **2** circuitous. **3** (of arguments) futile because the truth of the premises cannot be established independently of the conclusion. **4** travelling or occurring in a cycle. **5** (of letters, announcements, etc.) intended for general distribution. ◆ *n* **6** a printed advertisement or notice for mass distribution.
▸**circularity** (ˌsɜːkjʊ'lærɪtɪ) *n* ▸'**circularly** *adv*

circular breathing *n* a technique for sustaining a phrase on a wind instrument, using the cheeks to force air out of the mouth while breathing in through the nose.

circularize *or* **circularise** ('sɜːkjʊləˌraɪz) *vb* **circularizes, circularizing, circularized** *or* **circularises, circularising, circularised.** (*tr*) **1** to distribute circulars to. **2** to canvass or petition (people), as for support, votes, etc., by distributing letters, etc. **3** to make circular.
▸ˌ**circulari'zation** *or* ˌ**circulari'sation** *n*

circular saw *n* a power-driven saw in which a circular disc with a toothed edge is rotated at high speed.

circulate ➊ ('sɜːkjʊˌleɪt) *vb* **circulates, circulating, circulated. 1** to send, go, or pass from place to place or person to person: *don't circulate the news.* **2** to distribute or be distributed over a wide area. **3** to move or cause to move through a circuit, system, etc., returning to the starting point: *blood circulates through the body.* **4** to move in a circle. [C15: from L *circulārī*, from *circulus* CIRCLE]
▸'**circulative** *adj* ▸'**circuˌlator** *n* ▸'**circulatory** *adj*

circulating library *n* **1** another word (esp. US) for **lending library. 2** a small library circulated in turn to a group of institutions.

circulation ➊ (ˌsɜːkjʊ'leɪʃən) *n* **1** the transport of oxygenated blood through the arteries, and the return of oxygen-depleted blood through the veins to the heart, where the cycle is renewed. **2** the flow of sap through a plant. **3** any movement through a closed circuit. **4** the spreading or transmission of something to a wider group of people or area. **5** (of air and water) free movement within an area or volume. **6a** the distribution of newspapers, magazines, etc. **6b** the number of copies of an issue that are distributed. **7 in circulation. 7a** (of currency) serving as a medium of exchange. **7b** (of people) active in a social or business context.

circulatory system *n Anat., zool.* the system concerned with the transport of blood and lymph, consisting of the heart, blood vessels, lymph vessels, etc.

circum- *prefix* around; surrounding; on all sides: *circumlocution; circumpolar.* [from L *circum* around, from *circus* circle]

circumambient (ˌsɜːkəm'æmbɪənt) *adj* surrounding. [C17: from LL, from L CIRCUM- + *ambīre* to go round]
▸ˌ**circum'ambience** *or* ˌ**circum'ambiency** *n*

circumambulate (ˌsɜːkəm'æmbjʊˌleɪt) *vb* **circumambulates, circumambulating, circumambulated. 1** to walk around (something). **2** (*intr*) to avoid the point. [C17: from LL, from L CIRCUM- + *ambulāre* to walk]
▸ˌ**circumˌambu'lation** *n*

circumcise ('sɜːkəmˌsaɪz) *vb* **circumcises, circumcising, circumcised.** (*tr*) **1** to remove the foreskin of (a male). **2** to incise surgically the skin over the clitoris of (a female). **3** to remove the clitoris of (a female). **4** to perform such an operation as a religious rite on (someone). [C13: from L from CIRCUM- + *caedere* to cut]
▸**circumcision** (ˌsɜːkəm'sɪʒən) *n*

circumference ➊ (sə'kʌmfərəns) *n* **1** the boundary of a specific area or figure, esp. of a circle. **2** the length of a closed geometric curve, esp. of a circle. [C14: from OF, from L from CIRCUM- + *ferre* to bear]
▸**circumferential** (səˌkʌmfə'renʃəl) *adj* ▸**cirˌcumfer'entially** *adv*

circumflex ('sɜːkəmˌfleks) *n* **1** a mark (^) placed over a vowel to show that it is pronounced with rising and falling pitch, as in ancient Greek, or as a long vowel, as in French. ◆ *adj* **2** (of nerves, arteries, etc.) bending or curving around. [C16: from L, from CIRCUM- + *flectere* to bend]
▸ˌ**circum'flexion** *n*

circumfuse (ˌsɜːkəm'fjuːz) *vb* **circumfuses, circumfusing, circumfused.** (*tr*) **1** to pour or spread (a liquid, powder, etc.) around. **2** to surround with a substance, such as a liquid. [C16: from L *circumfūsus*, from CIRCUM- + *fundere* to pour]
▸**circumfusion** (ˌsɜːkəm'fjuːʒən) *n*

circumlocution ➊ (ˌsɜːkəmlə'kjuːʃən) *n* **1** an indirect way of expressing something. **2** an indirect expression.
▸**circumlocutory** (ˌsɜːkəm'lɒkjətərɪ, -trɪ) *adj*

circumnavigate (ˌsɜːkəm'nævɪˌgeɪt) *vb* **circumnavigates, circumnavigating, circumnavigated.** (*tr*) to sail or fly completely around.
▸ˌ**circumˌnavi'gation** *n* ▸ˌ**circum'naviˌgator** *n*

circumscribe ➊ (ˌsɜːkəm'skraɪb, 'sɜːkəmˌskraɪb) *vb* **circumscribes, circumscribing, circumscribed.** (*tr*) **1** to restrict within limits. **2** to mark or set the bounds of. **3** to draw a geometric construction around (another construction) so that the two are in contact but do not intersect. **4** to draw a line round. [C15: from L from CIRCUM- + *scrībere* to write]
▸ˌ**circum'scribable** *adj* ▸ˌ**circum'scriber** *n* ▸**circumscription** (ˌsɜːkəm'skrɪpʃən) *n*

circumspect ➊ ('sɜːkəmˌspekt) *adj* cautious, prudent, or discreet. [C15: from L, from CIRCUM- + *specere* to look]
▸ˌ**circum'spection** *n* ▸'**circumˌspectly** *adv*

circumstance ➊ ('sɜːkəmstəns) *n* **1** (*usually pl*) a condition of time, place, etc., that accompanies or influences an event or condition. **2** an incident or occurrence, esp. a chance one. **3** accessory information or detail. **4** formal display or ceremony (archaic except in **pomp and circumstance**). **5 under** *or* **in no circumstances.** in no case; never. **6 under the circumstances.** because of conditions; this being the case. ◆ *vb* **circumstances, circumstancing, circumstanced.** (*tr*) **7** to place in a particular condition or situation. [C13: from OF, from L *circumstantia*, from CIRCUM- + *stāre* to stand]

circumstantial ➊ (ˌsɜːkəm'stænʃəl) *adj* **1** of or dependent on circumstances. **2** fully detailed. **3** incidental.
▸ˌ**circumˌstanti'ality** *n* ▸ˌ**circum'stantially** *adv*

circumstantial evidence *n* indirect evidence that tends to establish a conclusion by inference.

circumstantiate (ˌsɜːkəm'stænʃɪˌeɪt) *vb* **circumstantiates, circumstantiating, circumstantiated.** (*tr*) to support by giving particulars.
▸ˌ**circumˌstanti'ation** *n*

circumvallate (ˌsɜːkəm'væleɪt) *vb* **circumvallates, circumvallating, circumvallated.** (*tr*) to surround with a defensive fortification. [C19: from L, from CIRCUM- + *vallum* rampart]
▸ˌ**circumval'lation** *n*

circumvent ➊ (ˌsɜːkəm'vent) *vb* (*tr*) **1** to evade or go around. **2** to out-

THESAURUS

circuit *n* **1** = **range**, area, boundary, bounding line, bounds, circumference, compass, district, journey, lap, limit, orbit, pale, perambulation, region, revolution, round, route, tour, track, tract

circuitous *adj* = **indirect**, ambagious (*arch.*), devious, labyrinthine, meandering, oblique, rambling, roundabout, tortuous, winding
Antonyms *adj* as the crow flies, direct, straight, undeviating, unswerving

circuitousness *n* = **indirectness**, deviousness, obliqueness, rambling, roundaboutness, tortuousness

circular *adj* **1** = **round**, annular, discoid, globelike, orbicular, ring-shaped, rotund, spherical **2** = **orbital**, circuitous, cyclical ◆ *n* **6** = **advertisement**, notice

circulate *vb* **2** = **spread**, broadcast, diffuse, disseminate, distribute, issue, make known, promulgate, propagate, publicize, publish **3** = **flow**, gyrate, radiate, revolve, rotate

circulation *n* **1** = **bloodstream 3** = **flow**, circling, motion, rotation **4** = **distribution**, currency, dissemination, spread, transmission, vogue

circumference *n* **1** = **boundary**, ambit, border, bounds, circuit, edge, extremity, fringe, limits, outline, pale, perimeter, periphery, rim, verge

circumlocution *n* **1** = **indirectness**, beating about the bush (*inf.*), diffuseness, discursiveness, euphemism, periphrasis, prolixity, redundancy, wordiness

circumscribe *vb Formal* **1, 2, 4** = **restrict**, bound, confine, define, delimit, delineate, demarcate, encircle, enclose, encompass, environ, hem in, limit, mark off, restrain, straiten, surround

circumspect *adj* = **cautious**, attentive, canny, careful, deliberate, discreet, discriminating, guarded, heedful, judicious, observant, politic, prudent, sagacious, sage, vigilant, wary, watchful
Antonyms *adj* bold, careless, daring, foolhardy, heedless, imprudent, rash, venturous

circumspection *n* = **caution**, canniness, care, chariness, deliberation, discretion, keeping one's head down, prudence, wariness

circumstance *n* **1, 2** = **event**, accident, condition, contingency, detail, element, fact, factor, happening, incident, item, occurrence, particular, position, respect, situation

circumstantial *adj* **1, 3** = **conjectural**, contingent, founded on circumstances, hearsay, incidental, indirect, inferential, presumptive, provisional **2** = **detailed**, particular, specific

circumvent *vb* **1** = **evade**, bypass, elude, side-

wit. **3** to encircle (an enemy) so as to intercept or capture. [C15: from L, from CIRCUM- + *venīre* to come]
▸ˌ**circum'vention** *n*

circus ('sɜːkəs) *n, pl* **circuses. 1** a travelling company of entertainers such as acrobats, clowns, trapeze artists, and trained animals. **2** a public performance given by such a company. **3** an arena, usually tented, in which such a performance is held. **4** a travelling group of professional sportsmen: *a cricket circus.* **5** (in ancient Rome) **5a** an open-air stadium, usually oval or oblong, for chariot races or public games. **5b** the games themselves. **6** *Brit.* **6a** an open place, usually circular, where several streets converge. **6b** (*cap. when part of a name*): *Piccadilly Circus.* **7** *Inf.* noisy or rowdy behaviour. **8** *Inf.* a group of people travelling together and putting on a display. [C16: from L, from Gk *kirkos* ring]

ciré ('sɪəreɪ) *adj* **1** (of fabric) treated with a heat or wax process to make it smooth. ◆ *n* **2** such a surface on a fabric. **3** a fabric having such a surface. [C20: F, from L *cēra* wax]

cirque (sɜːk) *n* a steep-sided semicircular or crescent-shaped depression found in mountainous regions. [C17: from F, from L *circus* ring]

cirrhosis (sɪ'rəʊsɪs) *n* any of various chronic progressive diseases of the liver, characterized by death of liver cells, irreversible fibrosis, etc. [C19: NL, from Gk *kirrhos* orange-coloured + -OSIS; referring to the appearance of the diseased liver]
▸**cirrhotic** (sɪ'rɒtɪk) *adj*

cirripede ('sɪrɪˌpiːd) *or* **cirriped** ('sɪrɪˌpɛd) *n* **1** any marine crustacean of the subclass *Cirripedia*, including the barnacles. ◆ *adj* **2** of, relating to, or belonging to the *Cirripedia.*

cirrocumulus (ˌsɪrəʊ'kjuːmjʊləs) *n, pl* **cirrocumuli** (-ˌlaɪ). a high cloud of ice crystals grouped into small separate globular masses.

cirrostratus (ˌsɪrəʊ'strɑːtəs) *n, pl* **cirrostrati** (-taɪ). a uniform layer of cloud above about 6000 metres.

cirrus ('sɪrəs) *n, pl* **cirri** (-raɪ). **1** a thin wispy fibrous cloud at high altitudes, composed of ice particles. **2** a plant tendril or similar part. **3a** a slender tentacle or filament in barnacles and other marine invertebrates. **3b** any of various hairlike structures in other animals. [C18: from L: curl]

CIS *abbrev. for* Commonwealth of Independent States.

cis- *prefix* on this side of, as in **cismontane** on this side of the mountains. Often retains the original Latin sense of 'side nearest Rome', as in **cispadane** on this (the southern) side of the Po. [from L]

cisalpine (sɪs'ælpaɪn) *adj* on this (the southern) side of the Alps, as viewed from Rome.

cisco ('sɪskəʊ) *n, pl* **ciscoes** *or* **ciscos.** any of various whitefish, esp. the lake herring of cold deep lakes of North America. [C19: short for Canad. F *ciscoette,* of Algonquian origin]

cislunar (sɪs'luːnə) *adj* of or relating to the space between the earth and the moon.

cisplatin (sɪs'plætɪn) *n* a cytotoxic drug that acts by preventing DNA replication and hence cell divisions, used in the treatment of tumours of the ovary and testis. [C20: from CIS- + PLATIN(UM)]

cissing ('sɪsɪŋ) *n Building trades.* the appearance of pinholes, craters, etc., in paintwork due to poor adhesion of the paint to the surface.

cissy ('sɪsɪ) *n, pl* **-sies.** a variant spelling of **sissy.**

cist[1] (sɪst) *n* a wooden box for holding ritual objects used in ancient Rome and Greece. [C19: from L *cista* box, from Gk *kistē*]

cist[2] (sɪst) *or* **kist** *n* a box-shaped burial chamber made from stone slabs or a hollowed tree trunk. [C19: from Welsh: chest, from L; see CIST[1]]

Cistercian (sɪ'stɜːʃən) *n* **1** Also called: **White Monk.** a member of a Christian order of monks and nuns founded in 1098, which follows an especially strict form of the Benedictine rule. ◆ *adj* **2** of or relating to this order. [C17: from F, from Med. L, from *Cistercium* (modern *Cîteaux*), original home of the order]

cistern ➊ ('sɪstən) *n* **1** a tank for the storage of water, esp. on or within the roof of a house or connected to a WC. **2** an underground reservoir for the storage of a liquid, esp. rainwater. **3** Also called: **cisterna.** *Anat.* a sac or partially enclosed space containing body fluid. [C13: from OF, from L *cisterna* underground tank, from *cista* box]

cistus ('sɪstəs) *n* any plant of the genus *Cistus.* See **rockrose.** [C16: NL, from Gk *kistos*]

citadel ➊ ('sɪtədᵊl, -ˌdɛl) *n* **1** a stronghold within or close to a city. **2** any strongly fortified building or place of safety; refuge. [C16: from OF, from OIt. *cittadella* a little city, from L *cīvitās*]

citation ➊ (saɪ'teɪʃən) *n* **1** the quoting of a book or author. **2** a passage or source cited. **3a** an official commendation or award, esp. for bravery or outstanding service. **3b** a formal public statement of this. **4** *Law.* **4a** an official summons to appear in court. **4b** the document containing such a summons.
▸**citatory** ('saɪtətərɪ) *adj*

cite ➊ (saɪt) *vb* **cites, citing, cited.** (*tr*) **1** to quote or refer to (a passage, book, or author). **2** to mention or commend (a soldier, etc.) for outstanding bravery or meritorious action. **3** to summon to appear before a court of law. **4** to enumerate: *he cited the king's virtues.* [C15: from OF *citer* to summon, ult. from L *ciēre* to excite]
▸'**citable** *or* '**citeable** *adj*

cithara ('sɪθərə) *or* **kithara** ('kɪθərə) *n* a stringed musical instrument of ancient Greece, similar to the lyre. [C18: from Gk *kithara*]

cither ('sɪθə) *or* **cithern** ('sɪθən) *n* a variant spelling of **cittern.** [C17: from L, from Gk *kithara*]

citified *or* **cityfied** ('sɪtɪˌfaɪd) *adj Often derog.* having the customs, manners, or dress of city people.

citizen ➊ ('sɪtɪzᵊn) *n* **1** a native registered or naturalized member of a state, nation, or other political community. **2** an inhabitant of a city or town. **3** a civilian, as opposed to a soldier, public official, etc. [C14: from Anglo-F *citesein,* from OF *citeien,* from *cité* CITY]

citizenry ('sɪtɪzənrɪ) *n, pl* **citizenries.** citizens collectively.

Citizens' Band *n* a range of radio frequencies assigned officially for use by the public for private communication. Abbrev.: **CB**

Citizens' Charter *n* (in Britain) a government document setting out standards of service for various public and private sector companies.

citizenship ('sɪtɪzənʃɪp) *n* **1** the condition or status of a citizen, with its rights and duties. **2** a person's conduct as a citizen.

citrate ('sɪtreɪt, -rɪt; 'saɪtreɪt) *n* any salt or ester of citric acid. [C18: from CITR(US) + -ATE[1]]

citric ('sɪtrɪk) *adj* of or derived from citrus fruits or citric acid.

citric acid *n* a water-soluble weak tribasic acid found in many fruits, esp. citrus fruits, and used in pharmaceuticals and as a flavouring (**E330**). Formula: $CH_2(COOH)C(OH)(COOH)CH_2COOH$.

citrine ('sɪtrɪn) *n* **1** a brownish-yellow variety of quartz: a gemstone; false topaz. **2a** the yellow colour of a lemon. **2b** (*as adj*): *citrine hair.*

citron ('sɪtrən) *n* **1** a small Asian tree, having lemon-like fruit with a thick aromatic rind. **2** the fruit of this tree. **3** the rind of this fruit candied and used for decoration and flavouring of foods. [C16: from OF, from L *citrus* citrus tree]

citronella (ˌsɪtrə'nɛlə) *n* **1** a tropical Asian grass with bluish-green lemon-scented leaves. **2** Also called: **citronella oil.** the yellow aromatic oil obtained from this grass, used in insect repellents, soaps, perfumes, etc. [C19: NL, from F, from *citron* lemon]

citrus ('sɪtrəs) *n, pl* **citruses. 1** any tree or shrub of the tropical and subtropical genus *Citrus,* which includes the orange, lemon, and lime. ◆ *adj also* **citrous. 2** of or relating to the genus *Citrus* or to the fruits of plants of this genus. [C19: from L: citrus tree]

cittern ('sɪtɜːn), **cither,** *or* **cithern** *n* a medieval stringed instrument resembling a lute but having wire strings and a flat back. [C16: ? a blend of CITHER + GITTERN]

city ➊ ('sɪtɪ) *n, pl* **cities. 1** any large town or populous place. **2** (in Britain) a town that has received this title from the Crown: usually the seat of a bishop. **3** (in the US) an incorporated urban centre with its own government and administration established by state charter. **4** (in Canada) a similar urban municipality incorporated by the provincial government. **5** the people of a city collectively. **6** (*modifier*) in or characteristic of a city: *city habits.* ◆ Related adjs.: **civic, urban, municipal.** [C13: from OF *cité,* from L *cīvitās* state, from *cīvis* citizen]

City ('sɪtɪ) *n* **the. 1** the area in central London in which the United Kingdom's major financial business is transacted. **2** the various financial institutions located in this area.

City and Guilds Institute *n* (in Britain) an examining body for technical and craft skills.

city chambers *n* (*functioning as sing*) (in Scotland) the municipal buildings of a city; town hall.

City Code *n* (in Britain) short for **City Code on Takeovers and Mergers:** a code laid down in 1968 (later modified) to control takeovers and mergers.

city desk *n* the editorial section of a newspaper dealing in Britain with financial news, in the US and Canada with local news.

city editor *n* (on a newspaper) **1** *Brit.* the editor in charge of financial and commercial news. **2** *US & Canad.* the editor in charge of local news.

city father *n* a person who is active or prominent in the public affairs of a city.

cityscape ('sɪtɪˌskeɪp) *n* an urban landscape; view of a city.

city-state *n Ancient history.* a state consisting of a sovereign city and its dependencies.

city technology college *n* (in Britain) a type of senior secondary school specializing in technological subjects, set up in inner-city areas with funding from industry as well as the government.

civet ('sɪvɪt) *n* **1** a catlike mammal of Africa and S Asia, typically having spotted fur and secreting a powerfully smelling fluid from anal glands. **2** the yellowish fatty secretion of such an animal, used as a fixative in the manufacture of perfumes. **3** the fur of such an animal. [C16: from OF, from It., from Ar. *zabād* civet perfume]

civic ➊ ('sɪvɪk) *adj* of or relating to a city, citizens, or citizenship. [C16: from L, from *cīvis* citizen]
▸'**civically** *adv*

THESAURUS

step, steer clear of **2 = outwit,** beguile, deceive, dupe, ensnare, entrap, hoodwink, mislead, outflank, outgeneral, overreach, thwart, trick

circumvention *n* **1 = evasion,** dodging **2 = trickery,** chicanery, deceit, deception, duplicity, fraud, guile, imposition, imposture, wiles

cistern *n* **1, 2 = tank,** basin, reservoir, sink, vat

citadel *n* **1 = fortress,** bastion, fastness, fortification, keep, stronghold, tower

citation *n* **2 = quotation,** commendation, excerpt, illustration, passage, quote, reference, source **3a = commendation,** award, mention

cite *vb* **1 = quote,** adduce, advance, allude to, enumerate, evidence, extract, mention, name, specify **3 = summon,** call, subpoena

citizen *n* **2 = inhabitant,** burgess, burgher, denizen, dweller, freeman, ratepayer, resident, subject, townsman

city *n* **1 = town,** conurbation, megalopolis, metropolis, municipality ◆ *modifier* **6 = urban,** civic, metropolitan, municipal

civic *adj* **= public,** borough, communal, community, local, municipal

civic centre *n Brit.* the public buildings of a town, including recreational facilities and offices of local administration.
civics ('sɪvɪks) *n* (*functioning as sing*) the study of the rights and responsibilities of citizenship.
civies ('sɪvɪz) *pl n Inf.* a variant spelling of **civvies**. See **civvy** (sense 2).
civil ❶ ('sɪvᵊl) *adj* **1** of the ordinary life of citizens as distinguished from military, legal, or ecclesiastical affairs. **2** of or relating to the citizen as an individual: *civil rights.* **3** of or occurring within the state or between citizens: *civil strife.* **4** polite or courteous: *a civil manner.* **5** of or in accordance with Roman law. [C14: from OF, from L *cīvīlis,* from *cīvis* citizen]
▸**'civilly** *adv*
civil defence *n* the organizing of civilians to deal with enemy attacks.
civil disobedience *n* a refusal to obey laws, pay taxes, etc.: a nonviolent means of protesting.
civil engineer *n* a person qualified to design and construct public works, such as roads, bridges, harbours, etc.
▸**civil engineering** *n*
civilian (sɪ'vɪljən) *n* **a** a person whose occupation is civil or nonmilitary. **b** (*as modifier*): *civilian life.* [C14 (orig.: a practitioner of civil law): from *civile* (from L *jūs cīvīle* civil law) + -IAN]
civility ❶ (sɪ'vɪlɪtɪ) *n, pl* **civilities. 1** politeness or courtesy. **2** (*often pl*) an act of politeness.
civilization ❶ *or* **civilisation** (ˌsɪvɪlaɪ'zeɪʃən) *n* **1** a human society that has a complex cultural, political, and legal organization; an advanced state in social development. **2** the peoples or nations collectively who have achieved such a state. **3** the total culture and way of life of a particular people, nation, region, or period. **4** the process of bringing or achieving civilization. **5** intellectual, cultural, and moral refinement. **6** cities or populated areas, as contrasted with sparsely inhabited areas, deserts, etc.
civilize ❶ *or* **civilise** ('sɪvɪˌlaɪz) *vb* **civilizes, civilizing, civilized** *or* **civilises, civilising, civilised.** (*tr*) **1** to bring out of savagery or barbarism into a state characteristic of civilization. **2** to refine, educate, or enlighten.
▸**'civiˌlizable** *or* **'civiˌlisable** *adj* ▸**'civiˌlized** *or* **'civiˌlised** *adj*
civil law *n* **1** the law of a state relating to private and civilian affairs. **2** the body of law in ancient Rome, esp. as applicable to private citizens. **3** law based on the Roman system as distinguished from common law and canon law.
civil liberty *n* the right of an individual to certain freedoms of speech and action.
civil list *n* (in Britain) the annuities voted by Parliament for the support of the royal household and the royal family.
civil marriage *n Law.* a marriage performed by an official other than a clergyman.
civil rights *pl n* **1** the personal rights of the individual citizen. **2** (*modifier*) of, relating to, or promoting equality in social, economic, and political rights.
civil servant *n* a member of the civil service.
civil service *n* **1** the service responsible for the public administration of the government of a country. It excludes the legislative, judicial, and military branches. **2** the members of the civil service collectively.
civil war *n* war between parties or factions within the same nation.
Civil War *n* **1** *English history.* the conflict between Charles I and the Parliamentarians resulting from disputes over their respective prerogatives. Parliament gained decisive victories at Marston Moor in 1644 and Naseby in 1645, and Charles was executed in 1649. **2** *US history.* the war fought from 1861 to 1865 between the North and the South, sparked off by Lincoln's election as president but with deep-rooted political and economic causes, exacerbated by the slavery issue. The advantages of the North in terms of population, finance, and communications brought about the South's eventual surrender at Appomattox.
civvy ('sɪvɪ) *n, pl* **civvies.** *Sl.* **1** a civilian. **2** (*pl*) Also: **civies.** civilian dress as opposed to uniform. **3 civvy street.** civilian life.
CJ *abbrev. for* Chief Justice.
CJA (in Britain) *abbrev. for* Criminal Justice Act.
CJD *abbrev. for* Creutzfeldt-Jakob disease.
Cl *the chemical symbol for* chlorine.
clachan (*Gaelic* 'klaxən; *English* 'klæ-) *n Scot. & Irish dialect.* a small village; hamlet. [C15: from Scot. Gaelic: prob. from *clach* stone]
clack (klæk) *vb* **1** to make or cause to make a sound like that of two pieces of wood hitting each other. **2** (*intr*) to jabber. ◆ *n* **3** a short sharp sound. **4** chatter. **5** Also called: **clack valve.** a simple nonreturn valve using a hinged flap or a ball. [C13: prob. from ON *klaka* to twitter, imit.]
▸**'clacker** *n*
clad[1] ❶ (klæd) *vb* a past tense and past participle of **clothe.** [OE *clāthode* clothed, from *clāthian* to CLOTHE]
clad[2] (klæd) *vb* **clads, cladding, clad.** (*tr*) to bond a metal to (another metal), esp. to form a protective coating. [C14: special use of CLAD[1]]
cladding ('klædɪŋ) *n* **1** the process of protecting one metal by bonding a second metal to its surface. **2** the protective coating so bonded to metal. **3** the material used for the outside facing of a building, etc.
clade (kleɪd) *n Biol.* a group of organisms considered as having evolved from a common ancestor. [C20: from Gk *klados* branch, shoot]
cladistics (klə'dɪstɪks) *n* (*functioning as sing*) a method of grouping animals by measurable likenesses or homologues. [C20: NL from Gk *klados* branch, shoot]
▸**cladism** ('klædɪzəm) *n* ▸**cladist** ('klædɪst) *n*
claim ❶ (kleɪm) *vb* (*mainly tr*) **1** to demand as being due or as one's property; assert one's title or right to: *he claimed the record.* **2** (*takes a clause as object or an infinitive*) to assert as a fact; maintain against denial: *he claimed to be telling the truth.* **3** to call for or need; deserve: *this problem claims our attention.* **4** to take: *the accident claimed four lives.* ◆ *n* **5** an assertion of a right; a demand for something as due. **6** an assertion of something as true, real, or factual. **7** a right or just title to something; basis for demand: *a claim to fame.* **8** anything that is claimed, such as a piece of land staked out by a miner. **9a** a demand for payment in connection with an insurance policy, etc. **9b** the sum of money demanded. [C13: from OF *claimer* to call, from L *clāmāre* to shout]
▸**'claimable** *adj* ▸**'claimant** *or* **'claimer** *n*
clairvoyance (klɛə'vɔɪəns) *n* **1** the alleged power of perceiving things beyond the natural range of the senses. **2** keen intuitive understanding. [C19: from F: clear-seeing, from *clair* clear + *voyance,* from *voir* to see]
clairvoyant ❶ (klɛə'vɔɪənt) *adj* **1** of or possessing clairvoyance. **2** having great insight. ◆ *n* **3** a person claiming to have the power to foretell future events.
▸**clair'voyantly** *adv*
clam (klæm) *n* **1** any of various burrowing bivalve molluscs. **2** the edible flesh of such a mollusc. **3** *Inf.* a reticent person. ◆ *vb* **clams, clamming, clammed. 4** (*intr*) *Chiefly US.* to gather clams. ◆ See also **clam up.** [C16: from earlier *clamshell,* that is, shell that clamps]
clamant ('kleɪmənt) *adj* **1** noisy. **2** calling urgently. [C17: from L, from *clāmāre* to shout]
clamber ❶ ('klæmbə) *vb* **1** (usually foll. by *up, over,* etc.) to climb (something) awkwardly, esp. by using both hands and feet. ◆ *n* **2** a climb performed in this manner. [C15: prob. var. of CLIMB]
▸**'clamberer** *n*
clammy ❶ ('klæmɪ) *adj* **clammier, clammiest. 1** unpleasantly sticky; moist. **2** (of the weather) close; humid. [C14: from OE *clǣman* to smear]
▸**'clammily** *adv* ▸**'clamminess** *n*
clamour ❶ *or US* **clamor** ('klæmə) *n* **1** a loud persistent outcry. **2** a vehement expression of collective feeling or outrage: *a clamour against higher prices.* **3** a loud and persistent noise: *the clamour of traffic.* ◆ *vb* **4** (*intr; often foll. by for or against*) to make a loud noise or outcry; make a public demand. **5** (*tr*) to move or force by outcry. [C14: from OF, from L, from *clāmāre* to cry out]
▸**'clamorous** *adj* ▸**'clamorously** *adv* ▸**'clamorousness** *n*
clamp[1] ❶ (klæmp) *n* **1** a mechanical device with movable jaws with which an object can be secured to a bench or with which two objects may be secured together. **2** See **wheel clamp.** ◆ *vb* (*tr*) **3** to fix or fasten with or as if with a clamp **4** to immobilize (a car) by means of a wheel

THESAURUS

civil *adj* **1** = **civic**, domestic, home, interior, municipal, political **4** = **polite**, accommodating, affable, civilized, complaisant, courteous, courtly, obliging, polished, refined, urbane, well-bred, well-mannered
Antonyms *adj* ≠ **civic:** military, religious, state ≠ **polite:** discourteous, ill-mannered, impolite, rude, uncivil, unfriendly, ungracious, unpleasant
civility *n* **1** = **politeness**, affability, amiability, breeding, complaisance, cordiality, courteousness, courtesy, good manners, graciousness, politesse, tact, urbanity
civilization *n* **1** = **society**, community, nation, people, polity **3** = **customs**, mores, way of life **4, 5** = **culture**, advancement, cultivation, development, education, enlightenment, progress, refinement, sophistication
civilize *vb* **2** = **cultivate**, educate, enlighten, humanize, improve, polish, refine, sophisticate, tame
civilized *adj* **2** = **cultured**, educated, enlightened, humane, polite, sophisticated, tolerant, urbane
Antonyms *adj* barbarous, ignorant, naive, primitive, simple, uncivilized, uncultivated, uncultured, undeveloped, uneducated, unenlightened, unsophisticated, untutored, wild
clad[1] *adj* = **dressed**, accoutred, apparelled, arrayed, attired, clothed, covered, decked out, draped, fitted out, invested, rigged out (*inf.*)
claim *vb* **1, 2** = **assert**, allege, challenge, exact, hold, insist, maintain, profess, uphold **3** = **demand**, ask, call for, insist, need, require **4** = **take**, collect, pick up ◆ *n* **5, 6** = **demand**, affirmation, allegation, application, call, petition, pretension, privilege, protestation, request, requirement **7** = **right**, title
claimant *n* **1** = **applicant**, petitioner, pretender, suppliant, supplicant
clairvoyant *adj* **1** = **psychic**, extrasensory, fey, oracular, prescient, prophetic, second-sighted, sibylline, telepathic, vatic, visionary ◆ *n* **3** = **psychic**, augur, diviner, fortune-teller, haruspex, oracle, prophet, prophetess, seer, sibyl, soothsayer, telepath, telepathist, visionary
clamber *vb* **1** = **climb**, claw, scale, scrabble, scramble, shin
clamminess *n* **1, 2** = **moistness**, airlessness, closeness, dampness, dankness, drizzliness, heaviness, humidity, humidness, mugginess, oppressiveness, pastiness, sliminess, stickiness, stuffiness, sultriness, sweatiness, thickness
clammy *adj* **1, 2** = **moist**, close, damp, dank, drizzly, pasty, slimy, sticky, sweating, sweaty
clamorous *adj* **1-3** = **noisy**, blaring, deafening, insistent, loud, lusty, riotous, strident, tumultuous, uproarious, vehement, vociferous
clamour *n* **1** = **noise**, agitation, babel, blare, brouhaha, commotion, din, exclamation, hubbub, hullabaloo, outcry, racket, shout, shouting, uproar, vociferation
clamp[1] *n* **1** = **vice**, bracket, fastener, grip, press

clamp. 5 to inflict or impose forcefully: *they clamped a curfew on the town.* [C14: from Du. or Low G *klamp*]

clamp[2] (klæmp) *n* 1 a mound of a harvested root crop, covered with straw and earth to protect it from winter weather. ◆ *vb* 2 (*tr*) to enclose (a harvested root crop) in a mound. [C16: from MDu. *klamp* heap]

clamp down *vb* (*intr, adv;* often foll. by *on*) 1 to behave repressively; attempt to suppress something regarded as undesirable. ◆ *n* **clampdown.** 2 a sudden restrictive measure.

clam up *vb* (*intr, adv*) *Inf.* to keep or become silent or withhold information.

clan ❶ (klæn) *n* 1 a group of people interrelated by ancestry or marriage. 2 a group of families with a common surname and a common ancestor, esp. among the Scots and the Irish. 3 a group of people united by common characteristics, aims, or interests. [C14: from Scot. Gaelic *clann* family, descendants, from L *planta* sprout]

clandestine ❶ (klæn'dɛstɪn) *adj* secret and concealed, often for illicit reasons; furtive. [C16: from L, from *clam* secretly]
▸**clan'destinely** *adv*

clang ❶ (klæŋ) *vb* 1 to make or cause to make a loud resounding noise, as metal when struck. 2 (*intr*) to move or operate making such a sound. ◆ *n* 3 a resounding metallic noise. 4 the harsh cry of certain birds. [C16: from L *clangere*]

clanger ('klæŋə) *n* 1 *Inf.* a conspicuous mistake (esp. in **drop a clanger**). 2 something that clangs or causes a clang. [C20: from CLANG]

clangour *or US* **clangor** ('klæŋgə, 'klæŋə) *n* 1 a loud resonant often-repeated noise. 2 an uproar. ◆ *vb* 3 (*intr*) to make or produce a loud resonant noise.
▸**'clangorous** *adj* ▸**'clangorously** *adv*

clank (klæŋk) *n* 1 an abrupt harsh metallic sound. ◆ *vb* 2 to make or cause to make such a sound. 3 (*intr*) to move or operate making such a sound. [C17: imit.]
▸**'clankingly** *adv*

clannish ❶ ('klænɪʃ) *adj* 1 of or characteristic of a clan. 2 tending to associate closely within a group to the exclusion of outsiders; cliquish.
▸**'clannishly** *adv* ▸**'clannishness** *n*

clansman ('klænzmən) *or* (*fem*) **clanswoman** *n, pl* **clansmen** *or* **clanswomen.** a person belonging to a clan.

clap[1] ❶ (klæp) *vb* **claps, clapping, clapped.** 1 to make or cause to make a sharp abrupt sound, as of two nonmetallic objects struck together. 2 to applaud (someone or something) by striking the palms of the hands together sharply. 3 (*tr*) to strike (a person) lightly with an open hand, in greeting, etc. 4 (*tr*) to place or put quickly or forcibly: *they clapped him into jail.* 5 (of certain birds) to flap (the wings) noisily. 6 (*intr;* foll. by *up* or *together*) to contrive or put together hastily. 7 **clap eyes on.** *Inf.* to catch sight of. 8 **clap hold of.** *Inf.* to grasp suddenly or forcibly. ◆ *n* 9 the sharp abrupt sound produced by striking the hands together. 10 the act of clapping, esp. in applause. 11 a sudden sharp sound, esp. of thunder. 12 a light blow. 13 *Arch.* a sudden action or mishap. [OE *clæppan;* imit.]

clap[2] (klæp) *n* (usually preceded by *the*) a slang word for **gonorrhoea.** [C16: from OF *clapoir* venereal sore, from *clapier* brothel, from ?]

clapboard ('klæp,bɔːd, 'klæbəd) *n* 1 a long thin timber board, used esp. in the US and Canada in wood-frame construction by lapping each board over the one below. ◆ *vb* 2 (*tr*) to cover with such boards. [C16: partial translation of Low G *klappholt,* from *klappen* to crack + *holt* wood]

clapped out *adj* (**clapped-out** *when prenominal*). *Inf.* 1 *Brit., Austral. & NZ.* worn out; dilapidated. 2 *Austral. & NZ.* extremely tired; exhausted.

clapper ('klæpə) *n* 1 a person or thing that claps. 2 Also called: **tongue.** a small piece of metal suspended within a bell that causes it to sound when made to strike against its side. 3 **go (run, move) like the clappers.** *Brit. inf.* to move extremely fast.

clapperboard ('klæpə,bɔːd) *n* a pair of hinged boards clapped together during film shooting to aid in synchronizing sound and picture prints.

claptrap ❶ ('klæp,træp) *n Inf.* 1 contrived but foolish talk. 2 insincere and pretentious talk: *politicians' claptrap.* [C18: from CLAP[1] + TRAP[1]]

claque (klæk) *n* 1 a group of people hired to applaud. 2 a group of fawning admirers. [C19: from F, from *claquer* to clap, imit.]

claret ('klærət) *n* 1 a red wine, esp. one from the Bordeaux district of France. 2a a purplish-red colour. 2b (*as adj*): *a claret football strip.* [C14: from OF (*vin*) *claret* clear (wine), from Med. L *clārātum,* from L *clārus* clear]

clarify ❶ ('klærɪ,faɪ) *vb* **clarifies, clarifying, clarified.** 1 to make or become clear or easy to understand. 2 to make or become free of impurities. 3 to make (fat, butter, etc.) clear by heating, etc., or (of fat, etc.) to become clear as a result of such a process. [C14: from OF, from LL, from L *clārus* clear + *facere* to make]
▸,**clarifi'cation** *n* ▸**'clari,fier** *n*

clarinet (,klærɪ'net) *n Music.* 1 a keyed woodwind instrument with a cylindrical bore and a single reed. 2 an orchestral musician who plays the clarinet. [C18: from F, prob. from It., from *clarino* trumpet]
▸,**clari'nettist** *or US sometimes* ,**clari'netist** *n*

clarion ('klærɪən) *n* 1 a stop of trumpet quality on an organ. 2 an obsolete, high-pitched, small-bore trumpet. 3 the sound of such an instrument or any similar sound. ◆ *adj* 4 (*prenominal*) clear and ringing; inspiring: *a clarion call to action.* ◆ *vb* 5 to proclaim loudly. [C14: from Med. L *clāriō* trumpet, from L *clārus* clear]

clarity ❶ ('klærɪtɪ) *n* 1 clearness, as of expression. 2 clearness, as of water. [C16: from L *clāritās,* from *clārus* clear]

clarkia ('klɑːkɪə) *n* any North American plant of the genus *Clarkia:* cultivated for their red, purple, or pink flowers. [C19: NL, after William *Clark* (1770–1838), American explorer]

clary ('klɛərɪ) *n, pl* **claries.** any of several European plants having aromatic leaves and blue flowers. [C14: from earlier *sclarreye,* from Med. L *sclareia,* from ?]

-clase *n combining form.* (in mineralogy) indicating a particular type of cleavage: *plagioclase.* [via F from Gk *klasis* a breaking]

clash ❶ (klæʃ) *vb* 1 to make or cause to make a loud harsh sound, esp. by striking together. 2 (*intr*) to be incompatible. 3 (*intr*) to engage together in conflict. 4 (*intr*) (of dates or events) to coincide. 5 (*intr*) (of colours) to look inharmonious together. ◆ *n* 6 a loud harsh noise. 7 a collision or conflict. [C16: imit.]
▸**'clasher** *n*

clasp ❶ (klɑːsp) *n* 1 a fastening, such as a catch or hook, for holding things together. 2 a firm grasp or embrace. 3 *Mil.* a bar on a medal ribbon, to indicate either a second award or the battle, campaign, or reason for its award. ◆ *vb* (*tr*) 4 to hold in a firm grasp. 5 to grasp firmly with the hand. 6 to fasten together with or as if with a clasp. [C14: from ?]
▸**'clasper** *n*

claspers ('klɑːspəz) *pl n Zool.* 1 a paired organ of male insects, used to clasp the female during copulation. 2 a paired organ of male sharks and related fish, used to assist the transfer of spermatozoa into the body of the female during copulation.

clasp knife *n* a large knife with one or more blades or other devices folding into the handle.

class ❶ (klɑːs) *n* 1 a collection or division of people or things sharing a common characteristic. 2 a group of persons sharing a similar social and economic position. 3a the pattern of divisions that exist within a society on the basis of rank, economic status, etc. 3b (*as modifier*): *the class struggle; class distinctions.* 4a a group of pupils or students who are taught together. 4b a meeting of a group of students for tuition. 5 *US.* a group of students who graduated in a specified year: *the class of '53.* 6 (*in combination and as modifier*) *Brit.* a grade of attainment in a university honours degree: *second-class honours.* 7 one of several standards of accommodation in public transport. 8 *Inf.* excellence or elegance, esp. in dress, design, or behaviour. 9 *Biol.* any of the taxonomic groups into which a phylum is divided and which contains one or more orders. 10 *Maths.* another name for **set**[2] (sense 3). 11 **in a class of its own** *or* **in a class by oneself.** unequalled; unparalleled. ◆ *vb* 12 to

THESAURUS

◆ *vb* 3 = **fasten**, brace, clinch, fix, impose, make fast, secure

clan *n* 1-3 = **family**, band, brotherhood, clique, coterie, faction, fraternity, gens, group, house, order, race, schism, sect, sept, set, society, sodality, tribe

clandestine *adj* = **secret**, cloak-and-dagger, closet, concealed, covert, fraudulent, furtive, hidden, private, sly, stealthy, surreptitious, underground, underhand, under-the-counter

clang *vb* 1 = **ring**, bong, chime, clank, clash, jangle, resound, reverberate, toll ◆ *n* 3 = **ringing**, clangour, ding-dong, knell, reverberation

clannish *adj* 2 = **cliquish**, exclusive, insular, narrow, sectarian, select, unfriendly

clannishness *n* 2 = **cliquishness**, exclusiveness, exclusivity, insularity, narrowness, sectarianism, selectness, unfriendliness

clap[1] *vb* 1 = **strike**, bang, pat, punch, slap, thrust, thwack, wallop (*inf.*), whack 2 = **applaud**, acclaim, cheer, give (someone) a big hand

Antonyms *vb* ≠ **applaud**: blow a raspberry, boo, catcall, hiss, jeer

claptrap *n Informal* 1, 2 = **nonsense**, affectation, blarney, bombast, bosh (*inf.*), bullshit (*taboo sl.*), bunk (*inf.*), bunkum *or* buncombe (*chiefly US*), cobblers (*Brit. taboo sl.*), crap (*sl.*), drivel, eyewash (*inf.*), flannel (*Brit. inf.*), garbage (*inf.*), guff (*sl.*), hogwash, hot air (*inf.*), humbug, insincerity, moonshine, pap, piffle (*inf.*), poppycock (*inf.*), rot, rubbish, tommyrot, tosh (*sl., chiefly Brit.*), trash, tripe (*inf.*), twaddle

clarification *n* 1 = **explanation**, elucidation, exposition, illumination, interpretation, simplification

clarify *vb* 1 = **explain**, clear the air, clear up, elucidate, explicate, illuminate, interpret, make plain, resolve, simplify, throw *or* shed light on 2 = **refine**, cleanse, purify

clarity *n* 1 = **clearness**, comprehensibility, definition, explicitness, intelligibility, limpidity, lucidity, obviousness, precision, simplicity, transparency

Antonyms *n* cloudiness, complexity, complication, dullness, haziness, imprecision, intricacy, murkiness, obscurity

clash *vb* 1 = **crash**, bang, clang, clank, clatter, jangle, jar, rattle 3 = **conflict**, cross swords, feud, grapple, lock horns, quarrel, war, wrangle ◆ *n* 7 = **conflict**, brush, collision, confrontation, difference of opinion, disagreement, fight, showdown (*inf.*)

clasp *n* 1 = **fastening**, brooch, buckle, catch, clip, fastener, grip, hasp, hook, pin, press stud, snap 2 = **grasp**, embrace, grip, hold, hug ◆ *vb* 4, 5 = **grasp**, attack, clutch, embrace, enfold, grapple, grip, hold, hug, press, seize, squeeze 6 = **fasten**, concatenate, connect

class *n* 1, 2 = **group**, caste, category, classification, collection, denomination, department, division, genre, genus, grade, grouping, kind, league, order, rank, set, sort, species, sphere, stamp, status, type, value ◆ *vb* 12 = **classify**, have or assign a place within a group, grade, or class. [C17: from L *classis* class, rank, fleet]

class. *abbrev. for:* **1** classic(al). **2** classification. **3** classified.

class-conscious *adj* aware of belonging to a particular social rank.
▸ˌ**class-'consciousness** *n*

classic ❶ ('klæsɪk) *adj* **1** of the highest class, esp. in art or literature. **2** serving as a standard or model of its kind. **3** adhering to an established set of principles in the arts or sciences: *a classic proof.* **4** characterized by simplicity, balance, regularity, and purity of form; classical. **5** of lasting interest or significance. **6** continuously in fashion because of its simple style: *a classic dress.* ◆ *n* **7** an author, artist, or work of art of the highest excellence. **8** a creation or work considered as definitive. **9** *Horse racing.* any of the five principal races for three-year-old horses in Britain, namely the One Thousand Guineas, Two Thousand Guineas, Derby, Oaks, and Saint Leger. [C17: from L *classicus* of the first rank, from *classis* division, rank, class]

classical ❶ ('klæsɪkᵊl) *adj* **1** of, relating to, or characteristic of the ancient Greeks and Romans or their civilization. **2** designating, following, or influenced by the art or culture of ancient Greece or Rome: *classical architecture.* **3** *Music.* **3a** of, relating to, or denoting any music or its period of composition marked by stability of form, intellectualism, and restraint. Cf. **romantic** (sense 5). **3b** accepted as a standard: *the classical suite.* **3c** denoting serious art music in general. Cf. **pop**². **4** denoting or relating to a style in any of the arts characterized by emotional restraint and conservatism: *a classical style of painting.* **5** (of an education) based on the humanities and the study of Latin and Greek. **6** *Physics.* not involving the quantum theory or the theory of relativity: *classical mechanics.*
▸ˌ**classi'cality** *or* '**classicalness** *n* ▸'**classically** *adv*

Classical school *n* economic theory based on the works of Adam Smith and David Ricardo, which explains the creation of wealth and advocates free trade.

classic car *n Chiefly Brit.* a car that is more than twenty five years old. Cf. **veteran car, vintage car.**

classicism ('klæsɪˌsɪzəm) *or* **classicalism** ('klæsɪkəˌlɪzəm) *n* **1** a style based on the study of Greek and Roman models, characterized by emotional restraint and regularity of form; the antithesis of romanticism. **2** knowledge of the culture of ancient Greece and Rome. **3a** a Greek or Latin expression. **3b** an expression in a modern language that is modelled on a Greek or Latin form.
▸'**classicist** *n*

classicize *or* **classicise** ('klæsɪˌsaɪz) *vb* **classicizes, classicizing, classicized** *or* **classicises, classicising, classicised. 1** (*tr*) to make classic. **2** (*intr*) to imitate classical style.

classics ('klæsɪks) *n* **1 the.** a body of literature regarded as great or lasting, esp. that of ancient Greece or Rome. **2 the.** the ancient Greek and Latin languages. **3** (*functioning as sing*) ancient Greek and Roman culture as a subject for academic study.

classification ❶ (ˌklæsɪfɪ'keɪʃən) *n* **1** systematic placement in categories. **2** one of the divisions in a system of classifying. **3** *Biol.* **3a** the placing of animals and plants in a series of increasingly specialized groups because of similarities in structure, origin, etc., that indicate a common relationship. **3b** the study of the principles and practice of this process; taxonomy. [C18: from F; see CLASS, -IFY, -ATION]
▸'**classificatory** *adj*

classified ('klæsɪˌfaɪd) *adj* **1** arranged according to some system of classification. **2** *Government.* (of information) not available to people outside a restricted group, esp. for reasons of national security. **3** *US & Canad. inf.* (of information) closely concealed or secret. **4** (of advertisements in newspapers, etc.) arranged according to type. **5** *Brit.* (of newspapers) containing sports results. **6** (of British roads) having a number in the national road system.

classify ❶ ('klæsɪˌfaɪ) *vb* **classifies, classifying, classified.** (*tr*) **1** to arrange or order by classes; categorize. **2** *Government.* to declare (information, documents, etc.) of possible aid to an enemy and therefore not available to people outside a restricted group. [C18: back formation from CLASSIFICATION]
▸'**classiˌfiable** *adj* ▸'**classiˌfier** *n*

class interval *n Statistics.* one of the intervals into which the range of a variable of a distribution is divided, esp. one of the divisions of the base line of a bar chart or histogram.

classless ('klɑːslɪs) *adj* **1** not belonging to a class. **2** characterized by the absence of economic and social distinctions.
▸'**classlessness** *n*

class list *n* (in Britain) a list categorizing students according to the class of honours they have obtained in their degree examination.

classmate ('klɑːsˌmeɪt) *n* a friend or contemporary of the same class in a school.

classroom ('klɑːsˌruːm, -ˌrʊm) *n* a room in which classes are conducted, esp. in a school.

class struggle *n* **the.** *Marxism.* the continual conflict between the capitalist and working classes for economic and political power.

classy ❶ ('klɑːsɪ) *adj* **classier, classiest.** *Sl.* elegant; stylish.
▸'**classiness** *n*

clatter ('klætə) *vb* **1** to make or cause to make a rattling noise, esp. as a result of movement. **2** (*intr*) to chatter. ◆ *n* **3** a rattling sound or noise. **4** a noisy commotion, such as loud chatter. [OE *clatrung* clattering (gerund)]
▸'**clatterer** *n* ▸'**clatteringly** *adv*

clause ❶ (klɔːz) *n* **1** *Grammar.* a group of words, consisting of a subject and a predicate including a finite verb, that does not necessarily constitute a sentence. Cf. **phrase.** See also **main clause, subordinate clause. 2** a section of a legal document such as a contract, will, or draft statute. [C13: from OF, from Med. L *clausa* a closing (of a rhetorical period), from L, from *claudere* to close]
▸'**clausal** *adj*

claustrophobia (ˌklɔːstrə'fəʊbɪə, ˌklɒs-) *n* an abnormal fear of being in a confined space. [C19: NL from L *claustrum* CLOISTER + -PHOBIA]
▸'**claustroˌphobe** *n* ▸ˌ**claustro'phobic** *adj*

clavate ('kleɪveɪt, -vɪt) *or* **claviform** ('klævɪˌfɔːm) *adj Biol.* shaped like a club. [C19: from L *clāva* club]
▸'**clavately** *adv*

clave¹ (kleɪv, klɑːv) *n Music.* one of a pair of hardwood sticks struck together to make a hollow sound, esp. to mark the beat in Latin-Ameriian dance music. [C20: from American Sp., from L *clavis* key]

clave² (kleɪv) *vb Arch.* a past tense of **cleave.**

clavichord ('klævɪˌkɔːd) *n* a keyboard instrument consisting of a number of thin wire strings struck from below by brass tangents. [C15: from Med. L, from L *clāvis* key + *chorda* CHORD¹]

clavicle ('klævɪkᵊl) *n* **1** either of the two bones connecting the shoulder blades with the upper part of the breastbone. Nontechnical name: **collarbone. 2** the corresponding structure in other vertebrates. [C17: from Med. L *clāvicula,* from L *clāvis* key]
▸**clavicular** (klə'vɪkjʊlə) *adj*

clavier (klə'vɪə, 'klævɪə) *n* **a** any keyboard instrument. **b** the keyboard itself. [C18: from F: keyboard, from L *clāvis* key]

claw ❶ (klɔː) *n* **1** a curved pointed horny process on the end of each digit in birds, some reptiles, and certain mammals. **2** a corresponding structure in some invertebrates, such as the pincer of a crab. **3** a part or member like a claw in function or appearance. ◆ *vb* **4** to scrape, tear, or dig (something or someone) with claws, etc. **5** (*tr*) to create by scratching as with claws: *to claw an opening.* [OE *clawu*]
▸'**clawer** *n*

claw back *vb* (*tr, adv*) **1** to get back (something) with difficulty. **2** to recover (a sum of money), esp. by taxation or a penalty. ◆ *n* **clawback. 3** the recovery of a sum of money, esp. by taxation or a penalty. **4** the sum so recovered.

claw hammer *n* a hammer with a cleft at one end of the head for extracting nails.

clay (kleɪ) *n* **1** a very fine-grained material that occurs as sedimentary rocks, soils, and other deposits. It becomes plastic when moist but hardens on heating and is used in the manufacture of bricks, ceramics, etc. **2** earth or mud. **3** *Poetic.* the material of the human body. [OE *clǣg*]
▸'**clayey,** '**clayish,** *or* '**clayˌlike** *adj*

claymore ('kleɪˌmɔː) *n* a large two-edged broadsword used formerly by Scottish Highlanders. [C18: from Gaelic *claidheamh mōr* great sword]

clay pigeon *n* a disc of baked clay hurled into the air from a machine as a target to be shot at.

clay road *n NZ.* an unmetalled road in a rural area.

CLC *abbrev. for* Canadian Labour Congress.

-cle *suffix forming nouns.* indicating smallness: *cubicle; particle.* [via OF from L *-culus.* See -CULE]

clean ❶ (kliːn) *adj* **1** without dirt or other impurities; unsoiled. **2** without anything in it or on it: *a clean page.* **3** recently washed; fresh. **4** without extraneous or foreign materials. **5** without defect, difficulties, or problems. **6** (of a nuclear weapon) producing little or no radio-

THESAURUS

brand, categorize, codify, designate, grade, group, label, rank, rate

classic *adj* **1** = **best**, consummate, finest, first-rate, masterly, world-class **2** = **definitive**, archetypal, exemplary, ideal, master, model, paradigmatic, quintessential, standard **3** = **typical**, characteristic, regular, standard, time-honoured, usual **5** = **lasting**, abiding, ageless, deathless, enduring, immortal, undying ◆ *n* **7**, **8** = **standard**, exemplar, masterpiece, masterwork, model, paradigm, prototype
Antonyms *adj* ≠ **best**: inferior, modern, poor, second-rate, terrible

classical *adj* **1** = **Greek**, Attic, Augustan, Grecian, Hellenic, Latin, Roman **4** = **pure**, chaste, elegant, harmonious, refined, restrained, symmetrical, understated, well-proportioned

classification *n* **1** = **categorization**, analysis, arrangement, cataloguing, codification, grading, sorting, taxonomy

classify *vb* **1** = **categorize**, arrange, catalogue, codify, dispose, distribute, file, grade, pigeonhole, rank, sort, systematize, tabulate

classy *adj Informal* = **high-class**, elegant, exclusive, high-toned, posh (*inf., chiefly Brit.*), ritzy (*sl.*), select, stylish, superior, swanky (*inf.*), swish (*inf., chiefly Brit.*), top-drawer, up-market, urbane

clause *n* **2** = **section**, article, chapter, condition, heading, item, paragraph, part, passage, point, provision, proviso, rider, specification, stipulation

claw *n* **1**, **2** = **nail**, nipper, pincer, talon, tentacle, unguis ◆ *vb* **4** = **scratch**, dig, graze, lacerate, mangle, maul, rip, scrabble, scrape, tear

clean *adj* **1**, **3** = **pure**, faultless, flawless, fresh, hygienic, immaculate, impeccable, laundered, sanitary, spotless, squeaky-clean, unblemished, unsoiled, unspotted, unstained, unsullied, washed **1**, **4** = **hygienic**, antiseptic, clarified, decontaminated, natural, purified, sterile, sterilized, unadulterated, uncontaminated, unpolluted **8** = **moral**, chaste, decent, exemplary, good, honourable, impeccable, innocent, pure, respectable, undefiled, upright, virtuous **10** = **complete**, conclusive, decisive,

active fallout or contamination. **7** (of a wound, etc.) having no pus or other sign of infection. **8** pure; morally sound. **9** without objectionable language or obscenity. **10** thorough or complete: *a clean break.* **11** dexterous or adroit: *a clean throw.* **12** *Sport.* played fairly and without fouls. **13** simple in design: *a ship's clean lines.* **14** *Aeronautics.* causing little turbulence; streamlined. **15** honourable or respectable. **16** habitually neat. **17** (esp. of a driving licence) showing or having no record of offences. **18** *Sl.* **18a** innocent; not guilty. **18b** not carrying illegal drugs, weapons, etc. ◆ *vb* **19** to make or become free of dirt, filth, etc.: *the stove cleans easily.* **20** (*tr*) to remove in making clean: *to clean marks off the wall.* **21** (*tr*) to prepare (fish, poultry, etc.) for cooking: *to clean a chicken.* ◆ *adv* **22** in a clean way; cleanly. **23** *Not standard.* (intensifier): *clean forgotten.* **24 come clean.** *Inf.* to make a revelation or confession. ◆ *n* **25** the act or an instance of cleaning: *he gave his shoes a clean.* **26 clean sweep.** See **sweep** (sense 28). ◆ See also **clean out, clean up.** [OE *clǣne*]
▸**'cleanable** *adj* ▸**'cleanness** *n*

clean-cut Ⓣ *adj* **1** clearly outlined; neat: *clean-cut lines of a ship.* **2** definite.

cleaner ('kliːnə) *n* **1** a person, device, chemical agent, etc., that removes dirt, as from clothes or carpets. **2** (*usually pl*) a shop, etc., that provides a dry-cleaning service. **3 take (a person) to the cleaners.** *Inf.* to rob or defraud (a person).

cleanly Ⓣ ('kliːnlɪ) *adv* **1** in a fair manner. **2** easily or smoothly. ◆ *adj* ('klɛnlɪ), **cleanlier, cleanliest. 3** habitually clean or neat.
▸**cleanlily** ('klɛnlɪlɪ) *adv* ▸**cleanliness** ('klɛnlɪnɪs) *n*

clean out *vb* (*tr, adv*) **1** (foll. by *of* or *from*) to remove (something) (from or away from). **2** *Sl.* to leave (someone) with no money. **3** *Inf.* to exhaust (stocks, goods, etc.) completely.

cleanse Ⓣ (klɛnz) *vb* **cleanses, cleansing, cleansed.** (*tr*) **1** to remove dirt, filth, etc., from. **2** to remove guilt from. **3** *Arch.* to cure. [OE *clǣnsian*; see CLEAN]

cleanser Ⓣ ('klɛnzə) *n* a cleansing agent.

clean-shaven *adj* (of men) having the facial hair shaved off.

clean up *vb* (*adv*) **1** to rid (something) of dirt, filth, or other impurities. **2** to make (someone or something) orderly or presentable. **3** (*tr*) to rid (a place) of undesirable people or conditions. **4** *Inf., chiefly US & Canad.* to make (a great profit). ◆ *n* **cleanup. 5** the process of cleaning up. **6** *Inf., chiefly US.* a great profit.

clear Ⓣ (klɪə) *adj* **1** free from darkness or obscurity; bright. **2** (of weather) free from dullness or clouds. **3** transparent. **4** even and pure in tone or colour. **5** without blemish: *a clear skin.* **6** easy to see or hear; distinct. **7** free from doubt or confusion. **8** (*postpositive*) certain in the mind; sure: *are you clear?* **9** (*in combination*) perceptive, alert: *clear-headed.* **10** evident or obvious: *it is clear that he won't come now.* **11** (of sounds or the voice) not harsh or hoarse. **12** serene; calm. **13** without qualification; complete: *a clear victory.* **14** free of suspicion, guilt, or blame: *a clear conscience.* **15** free of obstruction; open: *a clear passage.* **16** free from debt or obligation. **17** (of money, profits, etc.) without deduction; net. **18** emptied of freight or cargo. **19** *Showjumping.* (of a round) ridden without any points being lost. ◆ *adv* **20** in a clear or distinct manner. **21** completely or utterly. **22** (*postpositive;* often foll. by *of*) not in contact (with); free: *stand clear of the gates.* ◆ *n* **23** a clear space. **24 in the clear. 24a** free of suspicion, guilt, or blame. **24b** *Sport.* able to receive a pass without being tackled. ◆ *vb* **25** to make or become free from darkness, obscurity, etc. **26** (*intr*) **26a** (of the weather) to become free from dullness, fog, rain, etc. **26b** (of mist, fog, etc.) to disappear. **27** (*tr*) to free from impurity or blemish. **28** (*tr*) to free from doubt or confusion. **29** (*tr*) to rid of objects, obstructions, etc. **30** (*tr*) to make or form (a path, way, etc.) by removing obstructions. **31** (*tr*) to free or remove (a person or thing) from something, as of suspicion, blame, or guilt. **32** (*tr*) to move or pass by or over without contact: *he cleared the wall easily.* **33** (*tr*) to rid (the throat) of phlegm. **34** (*tr*) to make or gain (money) as profit. **35** (*tr;* often foll. by *off*) to discharge or settle (a debt). **36** (*tr*) to free (a debtor) from obligation. **37** (*intr*) (of a cheque) to pass through one's bank and be charged against one's account. **38** *Banking.* to settle accounts by exchanging (commercial documents) in a clearing house. **39** to permit (ships, aircraft, cargo, passengers, etc.) to unload, disembark, depart, etc., or (of ships, etc.) to be permitted to unload, etc. **40** to obtain or give (clearance). **41** (*tr*) to obtain clearance from. **42** (*tr*) to permit (a person, company, etc.) to see or handle classified information. **43** (*tr*) *Mil., etc.* to decode (a message, etc.). **44** (*tr*) *Computing.* to remove data from a storage device and revert to zero. **45 clear the air.** to dispel tension, confusion, etc., by settling misunderstandings, etc. ◆ See also **clear away, clear off,** etc. [C13: *clere,* from OF *cler,* from L *clārus* clear]
▸**'clearer** *n* ▸**'clearly** *adv* ▸**'clearness** *n*

clearance Ⓣ ('klɪərəns) *n* **1a** the process or an instance of clearing: *slum clearance.* **1b** (*as modifier*): *a clearance order.* **2** space between two parts in motion or in relative motion. **3** permission for an aircraft, ship, passengers, etc., to proceed. **4** official permission to have access to secret information, projects, areas, etc. **5** *Banking.* the exchange of commercial documents drawn on the members of a clearing house. **6a** the disposal of merchandise at reduced prices. **6b** (*as modifier*): *a clearance sale.* **7** the act of clearing an area of land by mass eviction: *the Highland Clearances.*

clear away *vb* (*adv*) to remove (objects) from (the table) after a meal.

clear-cut Ⓣ *adj* (**clear cut** *when postpositive*). **1** definite; not vague: *a clear-cut proposal.* **2** clearly outlined.

clearing Ⓣ ('klɪərɪŋ) *n* an area with few or no trees or shrubs in wooded or overgrown land.

clearing bank *n* (in Britain) any bank that makes use of the central clearing house in London.

clearing house *n* **1** *Banking.* an institution where cheques and other commercial papers drawn on member banks are cancelled against each other so that only net balances are payable. **2** a central agency for the collection and distribution of information or materials.

clear off *vb* (*intr, adv*) *Inf.* to go away: often used imperatively.

clear out Ⓣ *vb* (*adv*) **1** (*intr*) *Inf.* to go away: often used imperatively. **2** (*tr*) to remove and sort the contents of (a room, etc.). **3** (*tr*) *Sl.* to leave (someone) with no money. **4** (*tr*) *Sl.* to exhaust (stocks, goods, etc.) completely.

clearstory ('klɪə,stɔːrɪ) *n* a variant of **clerestory.**

clear up Ⓣ *vb* (*adv*) **1** (*tr*) to explain or solve (a mystery, misunderstanding, etc.). **2** to put (a place or thing that is disordered) in order. **3** (*intr*) (of the weather) to become brighter.

clearway ('klɪə,weɪ) *n* **1** *Brit.* a stretch of road on which motorists may stop only in an emergency. **2** an area at the end of a runway over which an aircraft taking off makes its initial climb.

cleat (kliːt) *n* **1** a wedge-shaped block attached to a structure to act as a support. **2** a device consisting of two hornlike prongs projecting horizontally in opposite directions from a central base, used for securing lines on vessels, wharves, etc. ◆ *vb* (*tr*) **3** to supply or support with a cleat or cleats. **4** to secure (a line) on a cleat. [C14: of Gmc origin]

cleavage ('kliːvɪdʒ) *n* **1** *Inf.* the separation between a woman's breasts, esp. as revealed by a low-cut dress. **2** a division or split. **3** (of crystals)

THESAURUS

entire, final, perfect, thorough, total, unimpaired, whole **13** = **neat**, delicate, elegant, graceful, simple, tidy, trim, uncluttered ◆ *vb* **19** = **cleanse**, bath, deodorize, disinfect, do up, dust, launder, lave, mop, purge, purify, rinse, sanitize, scour, scrub, sponge, swab, sweep, vacuum, wash, wipe **24 come clean** *Informal* = **confess**, acknowledge, admit, come out of the closet, cough up (*sl.*), get (something) off one's chest (*inf.*), make a clean breast of, own up, reveal, sing (*sl., chiefly US*), spill one's guts (*sl.*)
Antonyms *adj* ≠ **pure:** dirty, filthy, mucky, scuzzy (*sl., chiefly US*), soiled, sullied, unwashed ≠ **hygienic:** adulterated, contaminated, infected, polluted ≠ **moral:** dishonourable, immoral, impure, indecent, unchaste ≠ **neat:** chaotic, disorderly, disorganized, higgledy-piggledy (*inf.*), shambolic (*inf.*), untidy ◆ *vb* ≠ **cleanse:** adulterate, defile, dirty, infect, mess up, pollute, soil, stain

clean-cut *adj* **1, 2** = **clear**, chiselled, definite, etched, neat, outlined, sharp, trim, well-defined

cleanliness *n* **3** = **cleanness**, asepsis, freshness, immaculacy, immaculateness, neatness, purity, sanitariness, spotlessness, stainlessness, sterility, tidiness, unspottedness, whiteness

cleanse *vb* **1** = **clean**, clear, lustrate, purge, purify, rinse, scour, scrub, wash

cleanser *n* = **detergent**, disinfectant, purifier, scourer, soap, soap powder, solvent

clear *adj* **2** = **bright**, cloudless, fair, fine, halcyon, light, luminous, shining, sunny, unclouded, undimmed **3** = **transparent**, crystalline, glassy, limpid, pellucid, see-through, translucent **6, 7, 10** = **obvious**, apparent, articulate, audible, blatant, bold, coherent, comprehensible, conspicuous, cut-and-dried (*inf.*), definite, distinct, evident, explicit, express, incontrovertible, intelligible, lucid, manifest, palpable, patent, perceptible, plain, pronounced, recognizable, unambiguous, unequivocal, unmistakable, unquestionable **8** = **certain**, convinced, decided, definite, positive, resolved, satisfied, sure **13** = **unobstructed**, empty, free, open, smooth, unhampered, unhindered, unimpeded, unlimited **14** = **unblemished**, clean, guiltless, immaculate, innocent, pure, sinless, stainless, undefiled, untarnished, untroubled ◆ *vb* **26** = **brighten**, break up, clarify, lighten **27** = **clean**, cleanse, erase, purify, refine, sweep away, tidy (up), wipe **29** = **unblock**, disengage, disentangle, extricate, free, loosen, open, rid, unclog, unload, unpack **31** = **absolve**, acquit, excuse, exonerate, justify, vindicate **32** = **pass over**, jump, leap, miss, vault **34** = **gain**, acquire, earn, make, reap, secure
Antonyms *adj* ≠ **bright:** cloudy, dark, dull, foggy, hazy, misty, murky, overcast, stormy ≠ **transparent:** cloudy, muddy, non-translucent, non-transparent, opaque, turbid ≠ **obvious:** ambiguous, confused, doubtful, equivocal, hidden, inarticulate, inaudible, incoherent, indistinct, inexplicit, obscured, unrecognizable ≠ **unobstructed:** barricaded, blocked, closed, engaged, hampered, impeded, obstructed ◆ *vb* ≠ **absolve:** accuse, blame, charge, condemn, convict, find guilty

clearance *n* **2** = **space**, allowance, gap, headroom, margin **3, 4** = **permission**, authorization, blank cheque, consent, endorsement, go-ahead, green light, leave, O.K. *or* okay (*inf.*), sanction **7** = **evacuation**, depopulation, emptying, eviction, removal, unpeopling, withdrawal

clear-cut *adj* **1** = **straightforward**, black-and-white, cut-and-dried (*inf.*), definite, explicit, plain, precise, specific, unambiguous, unequivocal

clearing *n* = **glade**, dell

clearly *adv* **10** = **obviously**, beyond doubt, distinctly, evidently, incontestably, incontrovertibly, markedly, openly, overtly, undeniably, undoubtedly

clearness *n* **1, 3** = **clarity**, audibility, brightness, coherence, distinctness, glassiness, intelligibility, lucidity, luminosity, transparency

clear out *vb* **1** *Informal* = **go away**, beat it (*sl.*), decamp, depart, hook it (*sl.*), leave, make oneself scarce, make tracks, pack one's bags (*inf.*), retire, slope off, take oneself off, withdraw **2** = **get rid of**, empty, exhaust, sort, tidy up

clear up *vb* **1** = **solve**, answer, clarify, elucidate, explain, resolve, straighten out, unravel **2** = **tidy (up)**, order, rearrange the act of splitting or the tendency to split along definite planes so as to yield smooth surfaces. 4 Also called: **segmentation.** (in animals) the repeated division of a fertilized ovum into a solid ball of cells. 5 the breaking of a chemical bond in a molecule to give smaller molecules or radicals. 6 *Geol.* the natural splitting of certain rocks, such as slates, into thin plates.

cleave[1] ⓣ (kliːv) *vb* **cleaves, cleaving; cleft, cleaved,** *or* **clove; cleft, cleaved,** *or* **cloven. 1** to split or cause to split, esp. along a natural weakness. **2** (*tr*) to make by or as if by cutting: *to cleave a path.* **3** (when *intr,* foll. by *through*) to penetrate or traverse. [OE *clēofan*]
▸**'cleavable** *adj*

cleave[2] ⓣ (kliːv) *vb* **cleaves, cleaving, cleaved.** (*intr;* foll. by *to*) to cling or adhere. [OE *cleofian*]

cleaver ('kliːvə) *n* a heavy knife or long-bladed hatchet, esp. one used by butchers.

cleavers ('kliːvəz) *n* (*functioning as sing*) a Eurasian plant, having small white flowers and prickly stems and fruits. Also called: **goosegrass, hairif.** [OE *clīfe;* see CLEAVE[2]]

clef (klɛf) *n* one of several symbols placed on the left-hand side beginning of each stave indicating the pitch of the music written after it. [C16: from F: key, clef, from L *clāvis*]

cleft ⓣ (klɛft) *vb* **1** a past tense and past participle of **cleave**[1]. ◆ *n* **2** a fissure or crevice. **3** an indentation or split in something, such as the chin, palate, etc. ◆ *adj* **4** split; divided. [OE *geclyft* (n); see CLEAVE[1]]

cleft palate *n* a congenital crack or fissure in the midline of the hard palate, often associated with a harelip.

cleg (klɛg) *n* another name for a **horsefly.** [C15: from ON *kleggi*]

clematis ('klɛmətɪs, klə'meɪtɪs) *n* any N temperate climbing plant of the genus *Clematis.* Many species are cultivated for their large colourful flowers. [C16: from L, from Gk, from *klēma* vine twig]

clemency ⓣ ('klɛmənsɪ) *n, pl* **clemencies. 1** mercy or leniency. **2** mildness, esp. of the weather. [C15: from L, from *clēmēns* gentle]

clement ⓣ ('klɛmənt) *adj* **1** merciful. **2** (of the weather) mild. [C15: from L *clēmēns* mild]

clementine ('klɛmən,tiːn, -,taɪn) *n* a citrus fruit thought to be either a variety of tangerine or a hybrid between a tangerine and sweet orange. [C20: from F *clémentine*]

clench (klɛntʃ) *vb* (*tr*) **1** to close or squeeze together (the teeth, a fist, etc.) tightly. **2** to grasp or grip firmly. ◆ *n* **3** a firm grasp or grip. **4** a device that grasps or grips. ◆ *n, vb* **5** another word for **clinch.** [OE *beclencan*]

Cleopatra's Needle *n* either of two Egyptian obelisks, originally set up at Heliopolis about 1500 B.C.: one was moved to the Thames Embankment, London, in 1878, the other to Central Park, New York, in 1880.

clepsydra ('klɛpsɪdrə) *n, pl* **clepsydras** *or* **clepsydrae** (-,driː). an ancient device for measuring time by the flow of water or mercury through a small aperture. Also called: **water clock.** [C17: from L, from Gk, from *kleptein* to steal + *hudōr* water]

cleptomania (,klɛptəʊ'meɪnɪə) *n* a variant spelling of **kleptomania.**

clerestory *or* **clearstory** ('klɪə,stɔːrɪ) *n, pl* **clerestories** *or* **clearstories. 1** a row of windows in the upper part of the wall of a church that divides the nave from the aisle. **2** the part of the wall in which these windows are set. [C15: from CLEAR + STOREY]
▸**'clere,storied** *or* **'clear,storied** *adj*

clergy ⓣ ('klɜːdʒɪ) *n, pl* **clergies.** the collective body of men and women ordained as religious ministers, esp. of the Christian Church. [C13: from OF; see CLERK]

clergyman ⓣ ('klɜːdʒɪmən) *n, pl* **clergymen.** a member of the clergy.

cleric ('klɛrɪk) *n* a member of the clergy. [C17: from Church L *clēricus* priest, CLERK]

clerical ⓣ ('klɛrɪkᵊl) *adj* **1** relating to or associated with the clergy: *clerical dress.* **2** of or relating to office clerks or their work: *a clerical error.* **3** supporting or advocating clericalism.
▸**'clerically** *adv*

clerical collar *n* a stiff white collar with no opening at the front that buttons at the back of the neck; the distinctive mark of the clergy in certain Churches. Informal name: **dog collar.**

clericalism ('klɛrɪkᵊ,lɪzəm) *n* **1** a policy of upholding the power of the clergy. **2** the power of the clergy.
▸**'clericalist** *n*

clericals ('klɛrɪkᵊlz) *pl n* the distinctive dress of a clergyman.

clerihew ('klɛrɪ,hjuː) *n* a form of comic or satiric verse, consisting of two couplets of metrically irregular lines, containing the name of a well-known person. [C20: after E. *Clerihew* Bentley (1875–1956), E writer who invented it]

clerk (klɑːk; *US & Canad.* klɜːrk) *n* **1** a worker, esp. in an office, who keeps records, files, etc. **2** an employee of a court, legislature, board, corporation, etc., who keeps records and accounts, etc.: *a town clerk.* **3** Also called: **clerk in holy orders.** a cleric. **4** *US & Canad.* short for **salesclerk. 5** Also called: **desk clerk.** *US & Canad.* a hotel receptionist. **6** *Arch.* a scholar. ◆ *vb* **7** (*intr*) to serve as a clerk. [OE *clerc,* from Church L *clēricus,* from Gk *klērikos* cleric, from *klēros* heritage]
▸**'clerkess** *fem n* (*chiefly Scot.*) ▸**'clerkish** *adj* ▸**'clerkship** *n*

clerk of works *n* an employee who supervises building work in progress.

clever ⓣ ('klɛvə) *adj* **1** displaying sharp intelligence or mental alertness. **2** adroit or dexterous, esp. with the hands. **3** smart in a superficial way. **4** *Brit. inf.* sly; cunning. [C13 *cliver* (in the sense: quick to seize, adroit), from ?]
▸**'cleverly** *adv* ▸**'cleverness** *n*

clevis ('klɛvɪs) *n* the U-shaped component of a shackle. [C16: rel. to CLEAVE[1]]

clew (kluː) *n* **1** a ball of thread, yarn, or twine. **2** *Naut.* either of the lower corners of a square sail or the after lower corner of a fore-and-aft sail. ◆ *vb* **3** (*tr*) to coil into a ball. [OE *cliewen* (vb)]

clianthus (klɪ'ænθəs) *n* a leguminous plant of Australia and New Zealand with ornamental clusters of slender flowers. [C19: NL, prob. from Gk *klei-, kleos* glory + *anthos* flower]

cliché ⓣ ('kliːʃeɪ) *n* **1** a word or expression that has lost much of its force through overexposure. **2** an idea, action, or habit that has become trite from overuse. **3** *Printing, chiefly Brit.* a stereotype or electrotype plate. [C19: from F, from *clicher* to stereotype; imit.]
▸**'clichéd** *or* **'cliché'd** *adj*

click ⓣ (klɪk) *n* **1** a short light often metallic sound. **2** the locking member of a ratchet mechanism, such as a pawl or detent. **3** *Phonetics.* any of various stop consonants that are produced by the suction of air into the mouth. ◆ *vb* **4** to make or cause to make a clicking sound: *to click one's heels.* **5** (usually foll. by *on*) *Computing.* to press and release (a button on a mouse) or to select (a particular function) by pressing and releasing a button on a mouse. **6** (*intr*) *Sl.* to be a great success: *that idea really clicked.* **7** (*intr*) *Inf.* to become suddenly clear: *it finally clicked.* **8** (*intr*) *Sl.* to get on well: *they clicked from their first meeting.* [C17: imit.]
▸**'clicker** *n*

client ⓣ ('klaɪənt) *n* **1** a person, company, etc., that seeks the advice of a professional man or woman. **2** a customer. **3** a person for whom a social worker, etc., is responsible. **4** *Computing.* a program or work station that requests data or information from a server. [C14: from L *cliēns* retainer, dependent]
▸**cliental** (klaɪ'ɛntᵊl) *adj*

clientele ⓣ (,kliːɒn'tɛl) *or* **clientage** ('klaɪəntɪdʒ) *n* customers or clients collectively. [C16: from L, from *cliēns* CLIENT]

cliff ⓣ (klɪf) *n* a steep high rock face, esp. one that runs along the seashore. [OE *clif*]
▸**'cliffy** *adj*

cliffhanger ('klɪf,hæŋə) *n* **1a** a situation of imminent disaster usually occurring at the end of each episode of a serialized film. **1b** the serialized film itself. **2** a situation that is dramatic or uncertain.
▸**'cliff,hanging** *adj*

climacteric (klaɪ'mæktərɪk, ,klaɪmæk'tɛrɪk) *n* **1** a critical event or period. **2** another name for **menopause. 3** the period in the life of a man corresponding to the menopause, chiefly characterized by diminished sexual activity. ◆ *adj also* **climacterical** (,klaɪmæk'tɛrɪkᵊl). **4** in-

THESAURUS

cleave[1] *vb* **1** = **split,** crack, dissever, disunite, divide, hew, open, part, rend, rive, sever, slice, sunder, tear asunder

cleave[2] *vb* = **stick,** abide by, adhere, agree, attach, be devoted to, be true, cling, cohere, hold, remain, stand by

cleft *n* **2** = **opening,** breach, break, chasm, chink, crack, cranny, crevice, fissure, fracture, gap, rent, rift ◆ *adj* **4** = **split,** cloven, parted, rent, riven, ruptured, separated, sundered, torn

clemency *n* **1** = **mercy,** compassion, forbearance, forgiveness, humanity, indulgence, kindness, leniency, mercifulness, mildness, moderation, pity, quarter, soft-heartedness, tenderness

clement *adj* **1** = **merciful,** compassionate, forbearing, forgiving, gentle, humane, indulgent, kind, kind-hearted, lenient, mild, soft-hearted, tender **2** = **mild,** balmy, calm, fair, fine, temperate

clergy *n* = **priesthood,** churchmen, clergymen, clerics, ecclesiastics, first estate, holy orders, ministry, the cloth

clergyman *n* = **minister,** chaplain, churchman, cleric, curate, divine, father, man of God, man of the cloth, padre, parson, pastor, priest, rabbi, rector, reverend (*inf.*), vicar

clerical *adj* **1** = **ecclesiastical,** pastoral, priestly, sacerdotal **2** = **office,** book-keeping, clerkish, clerkly, secretarial, stenographic

clever *adj* **1-4** = **intelligent,** able, adroit, apt, astute, brainy (*inf.*), bright, canny, capable, cunning, deep, dexterous, discerning, expert, gifted, ingenious, inventive, keen, knowing, knowledgeable, quick, quick-witted, rational, resourceful, sagacious, sensible, shrewd, skilful, smart, talented, witty
Antonyms *adj* awkward, boring, clumsy, dense, dull, dumb (*inf.*), ham-fisted (*inf.*), inept, inexpert, maladroit, slow, stupid, thick, unaccomplished, unimaginative, witless

cleverness *n* **1-4** = **intelligence,** ability, adroitness, astuteness, brains, brightness, canniness, dexterity, flair, gift, gumption (*Brit. inf.*), ingenuity, nous (*Brit. sl.*), quickness, quick wits, resourcefulness, sagacity, sense, sharpness, shrewdness, smartness, suss (*sl.*), talent, wit

cliché *n* **1** = **platitude,** banality, bromide, chestnut (*inf.*), commonplace, hackneyed phrase, old saw, stereotype, truism

click *n, vb* **1, 4** = **snap,** beat, clack, tick **7** *Informal* = **become clear,** come home (to), fall into place, make sense **8** *Slang* = **get on,** be compatible, be on the same wavelength, feel a rapport, get on like a house on fire (*inf.*), go over, hit it off (*inf.*), make a hit, succeed, take to each other

client *n* **1-3** = **customer,** applicant, buyer, consumer, dependant, habitué, patient, patron, protégé, shopper

clientele *n* = **customers,** business, clients, following, market, patronage, regulars, trade

cliff *n* = **rock face,** bluff, crag, escarpment, face, overhang, precipice, scar, scarp volving a crucial event or period. [C16: from L, from Gk, from *klimakter* rung of a ladder from *klimax* ladder]

climactic ❶ (klaɪˈmæktɪk) *or* **climactical** *adj* consisting of, involving, or causing a climax.
▸**cliˈmactically** *adv*

> **USAGE NOTE** See at **climate.**

climate ❶ (ˈklaɪmɪt) *n* **1** the long-term prevalent weather conditions of an area, determined by latitude, altitude, etc. **2** an area having a particular kind of climate. **3** a prevailing trend: *the political climate.* [C14: from LL, from Gk *klima* inclination, region]
▸**climatic** (klaɪˈmætɪk), **cliˈmatical,** *or* **ˈclimatal** *adj* ▸**cliˈmatically** *adv*

> **USAGE NOTE** *Climatic* is sometimes wrongly used where *climactic* is meant. *Climatic* is properly used to talk about things relating to climate; *climactic* is used to describe something which forms a climax.

climatic zone *n* any of the eight principal zones, roughly demarcated by lines of latitude, into which the earth can be divided on the basis of climate.

climatology (ˌklaɪməˈtɒlədʒɪ) *n* the study of climates.
▸**climatologic** (ˌklaɪmətəˈlɒdʒɪk) *or* ˌ**climatoˈlogical** *adj* ▸ˌ**climaˈtologist** *n*

climax ❶ (ˈklaɪmæks) *n* **1** the most intense or highest point of an experience or of a series of events: *the party was the climax of the week.* **2** a decisive moment in a dramatic or other work. **3** a rhetorical device by which a series of sentences, clauses, or phrases are arranged in order of increasing intensity. **4** *Ecology.* the stage in the development of a community during which it remains stable under the prevailing environmental conditions. **5** another word for **orgasm.** ◆ *vb* **6** to reach or bring to a climax. [C16: from LL, from Gk *klimax* ladder]

climb ❶ (klaɪm) *vb* (*mainly intr*) **1** (*also tr; often foll. by up*) to go up or ascend (stairs, a mountain, etc.). **2** (often foll. by *along*) to progress with difficulty: *to climb along a ledge.* **3** to rise to a higher point or intensity: *the temperature climbed.* **4** to incline or slope upwards: *the road began to climb.* **5** to ascend in social position. **6** (of plants) to grow upwards by twining, using tendrils or suckers, etc. **7** *Inf.* (foll. by *into*) to put (on) or get (into). **8** to be a climber or mountaineer. ◆ *n* **9** the act or an instance of climbing. **10** a place or thing to be climbed, esp. a route in mountaineering. [OE *climban*]
▸**ˈclimbable** *adj*

climb down ❶ *vb* (*intr, adv*) **1** to descend. **2** (often foll. by *from*) to retreat (from an opinion, position, etc.). ◆ *n* **climb-down. 3** a retreat from an opinion, etc.

climber (ˈklaɪmə) *n* **1** a person or thing that climbs, esp. a mountaineer. **2** a plant that grows upwards by twining or clinging with tendrils and suckers. **3** *Chiefly Brit.* short for **social climber.**

clime (klaɪm) *n Poetic.* a region or its climate. [C16: from LL *clima;* see CLIMATE]

clinch ❶ (klɪntʃ) *vb* **1** (*tr*) to secure (a driven nail), by bending the protruding point over. **2** (*tr*) to hold together in such a manner. **3** (*tr*) to settle (something, such as an argument, bargain, etc.) in a definite way. **4** (*tr*) *Naut.* to fasten by means of a clinch. **5** (*intr*) to engage in a clinch, as in boxing or wrestling. ◆ *n* **6** the act of clinching. **7a** a nail with its point bent over. **7b** the part of such a nail, etc., that has been bent over. **8** *Boxing, wrestling, etc.* an act or an instance in which one or both competitors hold on to the other to avoid punches, regain wind, etc. **9** *Sl.* a lovers' embrace. **10** *Naut.* a loop or eye formed in a line. ◆ Also (for senses 1, 2, 4, 7, 8, 10): **clench.** [C16: var. of CLENCH]

clincher (ˈklɪntʃə) *n* **1** *Inf.* something decisive, such as fact, score, etc. **2** a person or thing that clinches.

cline (klaɪn) *n* the range of variation of form within a species. [C20: from Gk *klinein* to lean]
▸**ˈclinal** *adj*

-cline *n combining form.* indicating a slope: *anticline.* [back formation from INCLINE]
▸**-clinal** *adj combining form.*

cling ❶ (klɪŋ) *vb* **clings, clinging, clung.** (*intr*) **1** (often foll. by *to*) to hold fast or adhere closely (to something), as by gripping or sticking. **2** (foll. by *together*) to remain in contact (with each other). **3** to be or remain physically or emotionally close. ◆ *n* **4** short for **clingstone.** [OE *clingan*]
▸**ˈclinging** *adj* ▸**ˈclingingly** *adv* ▸**ˈclingy** *adj* ▸**ˈclinginess** *or* **ˈclingingness** *n*

clingfilm (ˈklɪŋˌfɪlm) *n* a thin polythene material having the power to adhere closely: used for wrapping food.

clingstone (ˈklɪŋˌstəʊn) *n* **a** a fruit, such as certain peaches, in which the flesh adheres to the stone. **b** (*as modifier*): *a clingstone peach.*

clinic (ˈklɪnɪk) *n* **1** a place in which outpatients are given medical treatment or advice. **2** a similar place staffed by specialist physicians or surgeons: *eye clinic.* **3** *Brit.* a private hospital or nursing home. **4** the teaching of medicine to students at the bedside. **5** *Chiefly US & Canad.* a group or centre that offers advice or instruction. [C17: from L *clīnicus* one on a sickbed, from Gk, from *klinē* bed]

clinical ❶ (ˈklɪnɪkᵊl) *adj* **1** of or relating to a clinic. **2** of or relating to the observation and treatment of patients directly: *clinical medicine.* **3** scientifically detached; strictly objective: *a clinical attitude to life.* **4** plain, simple, and usually unattractive.
▸**ˈclinically** *adv*

clinical thermometer *n* a thermometer for determining the temperature of the body.

clinician (klɪˈnɪʃən) *n* a physician, psychiatrist, etc., who specializes in clinical work as opposed to one engaged in experimental studies.

clink[1] (klɪŋk) *vb* **1** to make or cause to make a light and sharply ringing sound. ◆ *n* **2** such a sound. [C14: ?from MDu. *klinken*]

clink[2] (klɪŋk) *n* a slang word for **prison.** [C16: after *Clink,* a prison in Southwark, London]

clinker (ˈklɪŋkə) *n* **1** the ash and partially fused residues from a coal-fired furnace or fire. **2** a partially vitrified brick or mass of brick. **3** *Sl., chiefly US.* something of poor quality, such as a film. ◆ *vb* **4** (*intr*) to form clinker. [C17: from Du. *klinker* a type of brick, from *klinken* to CLINK[1]]

clinker-built *or* **clincher-built** *adj* (of a boat or ship) having a hull constructed with each plank overlapping that below. [C18 *clinker* a nailing together, prob. from CLINCH]

clinometer (klaɪˈnɒmɪtə) *n* an instrument used in surveying for measuring an angle of inclination.
▸**clinometric** (ˌklaɪnəˈmetrɪk) *or* ˌ**clinoˈmetrical** *adj* ▸**cliˈnometry** *n*

Clio (ˈklaɪəʊ) *n Greek myth.* the Muse of history. [C19: from L, from Gk *Kleiō,* from *kleein* to celebrate]

clip[1] ❶ (klɪp) *vb* **clips, clipping, clipped.** (*mainly tr*) **1** (*also intr*) to cut or trim with scissors or shears, esp. in order to shorten or remove a part. **2** *Brit.* to punch (a hole) in something, esp. a ticket. **3** to curtail. **4** to move a short section from (a film, etc.). **5** to shorten (a word). **6** *Inf.* to strike with a sharp, often slanting, blow. **7** *Sl.* to obtain (money) by deception or cheating. ◆ *n* **8** the act or process of clipping. **9** something clipped off. **10** a short extract from a film, etc. **11** *Inf.* a sharp, often slanting, blow. **12** *Inf.* speed: *a rapid clip.* **13** *Austral. & NZ.* the total quantity of wool shorn, as in one season, etc. **14** another word for **clipped form.** [C12: from ON *klippa* to cut]

clip[2] ❶ (klɪp) *n* **1** any of various small implements used to hold loose articles together or to attach one article to another. **2** an article of jewellery that can be clipped onto a dress, hat, etc. **3** short for **paperclip** or **cartridge clip.** ◆ *vb* **clips, clipping, clipped.** (*tr*) **4** to hold together tightly, as with a clip. [OE *clyppan* to embrace]

clipboard (ˈklɪpˌbɔːd) *n* **1** a portable writing board with a clip at the top for holding paper. **2** *Computing.* a temporary storage area in desktop publishing and other programs where text or graphics are held when cut or copied.

clip joint *n Sl.* a place, such as a nightclub or restaurant, in which customers are overcharged.

clipped (klɪpt) *adj* (of speech or tone of voice) abrupt, terse, and distinct.

clipped form *n* a shortened form of a word.

clipper (ˈklɪpə) *n* **1** any fast sailing ship. **2** a person or thing that cuts or clips.

clippers (ˈklɪpəz) *or* **clips** *pl n* **1** a hand tool for clipping fingernails, veneers, etc. **2** a hairdresser's tool for cutting short hair.

clippie (ˈklɪpɪ) *n Brit. inf.* a bus conductress.

clipping ❶ (ˈklɪpɪŋ) *n* **1** something cut out, esp. an article from a newspaper; cutting. **2** the distortion of an audio or visual signal in which the tops of peaks with a high amplitude are cut off, caused by, for example, overloading of amplifier circuits.

clique ❶ (kliːk, klɪk) *n* a small exclusive group of friends or associates. [C18: from F, ?from OF: latch, from *cliquer* to click]
▸**ˈcliquey** *or* **ˈcliquy** *adj* ▸**ˈcliquish** *adj* ▸**ˈcliquishly** *adv* ▸**ˈcliquishness** *n*

clitoridectomy (ˌklɪtərɪˈdektəmɪ) *n* surgical removal of the clitoris: a form of female circumcision, esp. practised as a religious or ethnic rite.

clitoris (ˈklɪtərɪs, ˈklaɪ-) *n* a part of the female genitalia consisting of a

THESAURUS

climactic *adj* = **crucial**, climactical, critical, decisive, paramount, peak

climate *n* **1** = **weather**, clime, country, region, temperature **3** = **trend**, ambience, disposition, feeling, mood, temper, tendency

climax *n* **1** = **culmination**, acme, apogee, crest, head, height, highlight, high point, high spot (*inf.*), *ne plus ultra*, pay-off (*inf.*), peak, summit, top, zenith ◆ *vb* **6** = **culminate**, come to a head, peak

climb *vb* = **ascend**, clamber, mount, rise, scale, shin up, soar, top

climb down *vb* **1** = **descend**, dismount **2** = **back down**, eat crow (*US inf.*), eat one's words, retract, retreat

clinch *vb* **1, 2** = **secure**, bolt, clamp, fasten, fix, make fast, nail, rivet **3** = **settle**, assure, cap, conclude, confirm, decide, determine, seal, secure, set the seal on, sew up (*inf.*), tip the balance, verify

cling *vb* **1** = **stick**, adhere, attach to, be true to, clasp, cleave to, clutch, embrace, fasten, grasp, grip, hug, twine round

clinical *adj* **3** = **unemotional**, analytic, antiseptic, cold, detached, disinterested, dispassionate, emotionless, impersonal, objective, scientific

clip[1] *vb* **1** = **trim**, crop, curtail, cut, cut short, dock, pare, prune, shear, shorten, snip ◆ *n, vb* **6** *Informal* = **smack**, belt (*inf.*), box, clout (*inf.*), cuff, knock, punch, skelp (*dialect*), strike, thump, wallop (*inf.*), whack ◆ *n* **12** *Informal* = **speed**, gallop, lick (*inf.*), rate, velocity

clip[2] *vb* = **attach**, fasten, fix, hold, pin, staple

clipping *n* **1** = **cutting**, excerpt, extract, piece

clique *n* = **group**, cabal, circle, clan, coterie, crew (*inf.*), crowd, faction, gang, mob, pack, posse (*inf.*), schism, set

small elongated highly sensitive erectile organ at the front of the vulva. [C17: from NL, from Gk *kleitoris*]
▸**'clitoral** *adj*

Cllr *abbrev. for* Councillor.

cloaca (kləʊ'eɪkə) *n, pl* **cloacae** (-kiː). **1** a cavity in most vertebrates, except higher mammals, and certain invertebrates, into which the alimentary canal and the genital and urinary ducts open. **2** a sewer. [C18: from L: sewer]
▸**clo'acal** *adj*

cloak ❶ (kləʊk) *n* **1** a wraplike outer garment fastened at the throat and falling straight from the shoulders. **2** something that covers or conceals. ◆ *vb* (*tr*) **3** to cover with or as if with a cloak. **4** to hide or disguise. [C13: from OF *cloque*, from Med. L *clocca* cloak, bell]

cloak-and-dagger *n* (*modifier*) characteristic of or concerned with intrigue and espionage.

cloakroom ('kləʊk,ruːm, -rʊm) *n* **1** a room in which hats, coats, etc., may be temporarily deposited. **2** *Brit.* a euphemistic word for **toilet.**

clobber[1] ❶ ('klɒbə) *vb* (*tr*) *Sl.* **1** to batter. **2** to defeat utterly. **3** to criticize severely. [C20: from ?]

clobber[2] ❶ ('klɒbə) *n Brit. sl.* personal belongings, such as clothes. [C19: from ?]

clobbering machine *n NZ inf.* pressure to conform with accepted standards.

cloche (klɒʃ) *n* **1** a bell-shaped cover used to protect young plants. **2** a woman's close-fitting hat. [C19: from F: bell, from Med. L *clocca*]

clock[1] (klɒk) *n* **1** a timepiece having mechanically or electrically driven pointers that move constantly over a dial showing the numbers of the hours. Cf. **watch** (sense 7). **2** any clocklike device for recording or measuring, such as a taximeter or pressure gauge. **3** the downy head of a dandelion that has gone to seed. **4** short for **time clock. 5** (usually preceded by *the*) an informal word for **speedometer** or **mileometer. 6** *Brit.* a slang word for **face. 7 around** *or* **round the clock.** all day and all night. ◆ *vb* (*tr*) **8** *Brit., Austral., & NZ sl.* to strike, esp. on the face or head. **9** to record time as with a stopwatch, esp. in the calculation of speed. **10** *Inf.* to turn back the mileometer on (a car) illegally so that its mileage appears less. [C14: from MDu. *clocke* clock, from Med. L *clocca* bell, ult. of Celtic origin]

clock[2] (klɒk) *n* an ornamental design on the side of a stocking. [C16: see CLOCK[1]]

clock off *or* **out** *vb* (*intr, adv*) to depart from work, esp. when it involves registering the time of departure on a card.

clock on *or* **in** *vb* (*intr, adv*) to arrive at work, esp. when it involves registering the time of arrival on a card.

clock up *vb* (*tr, adv*) to record or register: *this car has clocked up 80 000 miles.*

clock-watcher *n* an employee who frequently checks the time in anticipation of a break or of the end of the working day.

clockwise ('klɒk,waɪz) *adv, adj* in the direction that the hands of a clock rotate; from top to bottom towards the right when seen from the front.

clockwork ('klɒk,wɜːk) *n* **1** the mechanism of a clock. **2** any similar mechanism, as in a wind-up toy. **3 like clockwork.** with complete regularity and precision; smoothly.

clod ❶ (klɒd) *n* **1** a lump of earth or clay. **2** earth, esp. when heavy or in hard lumps. **3** Also called: **clod poll, clodpate.** a dull or stupid person. [OE *clod-* (occurring in compound words) lump]
▸**'cloddy** *adj* ▸**'cloddish** *adj* ▸**'cloddishly** *adv* ▸**'cloddishness** *n*

clodhopper ❶ ('klɒd,hɒpə) *n Inf.* **1** a clumsy person; lout. **2** (*usually pl*) a large heavy shoe.

clog ❶ (klɒg) *vb* **clogs, clogging, clogged. 1** to obstruct or become obstructed with thick or sticky matter. **2** (*tr*) to encumber; hinder; impede. **3** (*intr*) to adhere or stick in a mass. ◆ *n* **4a** any of various wooden or wooden-soled shoes. **4b** (*as modifier*): *clog dance.* **5** a heavy block, esp. of wood, fastened to the leg of a person or animal to impede motion. **6** something that impedes motion or action; hindrance. [C14 (in the sense: block of wood): from ?]
▸**'cloggy** *adj*

cloisonné (klwɑː'zɒneɪ) *n* **1a** a design made by filling in with coloured enamel an outline of flattened wire. **1b** the method of doing this. ◆ *adj* **2** of or made by cloisonné. [C19: from F, from *cloisonner* to divide into compartments, ult. from L *claudere* to close]

cloister ❶ ('klɔɪstə) *n* **1** a covered walk, usually around a quadrangle in a religious institution, having an open colonnade on the inside. **2** (*sometimes pl*) a place of religious seclusion, such as a monastery. **3** life in a monastery or convent. ◆ *vb* **4** (*tr*) to confine or seclude in or as if in a monastery. [C13: from OF *cloistre*, from Med. L *claustrum* monastic cell, from L *claudere* to close]
▸**'cloistered** *adj* ▸**'cloistral** *adj*

clomb (kləʊm) *vb Arch.* a past tense and past participle of **climb.**

clomp (klɒmp) *n, vb* a less common word for **clump** (senses 2, 7).

clone (kləʊn) *n* **1** a group of organisms or cells of the same genetic constitution that are descended from a common ancestor by asexual reproduction, as by cuttings, grafting, etc. **2** Also called: **gene clone.** a segment of DNA that has been isolated and replicated by laboratory manipulation. **3** *Inf.* a person or thing that closely resembles another. **4** *Sl.* **4a** a mobile phone that has been given the electronic identity of an existing mobile phone, so that calls made on it are charged to the owner of that phone. **4b** any similar object, such as a credit card, that has been given the electronic identity of another device, usually in order to commit theft. ◆ *vb* **clones, cloning, cloned. 5** to produce or cause to produce a clone. **6** *Inf.* to produce near copies of (a person or thing). **7** (*tr*) *Sl.* to give (a mobile phone, etc.) the electronic identity of an existing mobile phone (or other device), so that calls, purchases, etc. made with it are charged to the original owner. [C20: from Gk *klōn* twig, shoot]
▸**'cloning** *n*

clonk (klɒŋk) *vb* **1** (*intr*) to make a loud dull thud. **2** (*tr*) *Inf.* to hit. ◆ *n* **3** a loud thud. [C20: imit.]

clonus ('kləʊnəs) *n* a type of convulsion characterized by rapid contraction and relaxation of a muscle. [C19: from NL, from Gk *klonos* turmoil]
▸**clonic** ('klɒnɪk) *adj* ▸**clonicity** (klɒ'nɪsɪtɪ) *n*

clop (klɒp) *vb* **clops, clopping, clopped. 1** (*intr*) to make or move along with a sound as of a horse's hooves striking the ground. ◆ *n* **2** a sound of this nature. [C20: imit.]

close[1] ❶ (kləʊs) *adj* **1** near in space or time; in proximity. **2** having the parts near together; dense: *a close formation.* **3** near to the surface; short: *a close haircut.* **4** near in relationship: *a close relative.* **5** intimate: *a close friend.* **6** almost equal: *a close contest.* **7** not deviating or varying greatly from a model or standard: *a close resemblance; a close translation.* **8** careful, strict, or searching: *a close study.* **9** confined or enclosed. **10** shut or shut tight. **11** oppressive, heavy, or airless: *a close atmosphere.* **12** strictly guarded: *a close prisoner.* **13** neat or tight in fit. **14** secretive or reticent. **15** miserly; not generous, esp. with money. **16** (of money or credit) hard to obtain. **17** restricted as to public admission or membership. **18** hidden or secluded. **19** Also: **closed.** restricted or prohibited as to the type of game or fish able to be taken. ◆ *adv* **20** closely; tightly. **21** near or in proximity. **22 close to the wind.** *Naut.* sailing as nearly as possible towards the direction from which the wind is blowing. See also **wind**[1] (sense 23). [C13: from OF *clos*, from L *clausus*, from *claudere* to close]
▸**'closely** *adv* ▸**'closeness** *n*

close[2] ❶ (kləʊz) *vb* **closes, closing, closed. 1** to put or be put in such a position as to cover an opening; shut: *the door closed behind him.* **2** (*tr*) to bar, obstruct, or fill up (an entrance, a hole, etc.): *to close a road.* **3** to bring the parts or edges of (a wound, etc.) together or (of a wound, etc.) to be brought together. **4** (*intr; foll. by on, over, etc.*) to take hold: *his hand closed over the money.* **5** to bring or be brought to an end; terminate. **6** (of agreements, deals, etc.) to complete or be completed successfully. **7** to cease or cause to cease to render service: *the shop closed at six.* **8** (*intr*) *Stock Exchange.* to have a value at the end of a day's trading, as specified: *steels closed two points down.* **9** (*tr*) *Arch.* to enclose or shut in. ◆ *n* **10** the act of closing. **11** the end or conclusion: *the close of the day.* **12** (kləʊs). *Brit.* a courtyard or quadrangle enclosed by buildings or an entry leading to such a courtyard. **13** (kləʊs). *Brit.* (*cap. when part of a street name*) a small quiet residential road: *Hillside Close.* **14** (kləʊs). the precincts of a cathedral or similar building. **15** (kləʊs). *Scot.* the entry from the street to a tenement building. ◆ See also

THESAURUS

cloak *n* **1** = **cape**, coat, mantle, wrap **2** = **cover**, blind, front, mask, pretext, shield ◆ *vb* **3, 4** = **cover**, camouflage, conceal, disguise, hide, mask, obscure, screen, veil

clobber[1] *vb* **1** *Informal* = **batter**, assault, bash (*inf.*), beat, beat up (*inf.*), belabour, duff up (*inf.*), lambast(e), lash, pound, pummel, rough up (*inf.*), smash, thrash, wallop (*inf.*)

clobber[2] *n Brit. informal* = **belongings**, accoutrements, effects, gear, possessions

clod *n* **1** = **lump**, block, chunk, clump, hunk, mass, piece

clodhopper *n* **1** *Informal* = **oaf**, booby, boor, bumpkin, clown, galoot, loon (*inf.*), lout, yokel

clog *vb* **1, 2** = **obstruct**, block, bung, burden, congest, dam up, hamper, hinder, impede, jam, occlude, shackle, stop up

cloistered *adj* **4** = **sheltered**, cloistral, confined, hermitic, insulated, protected, reclusive, restricted, secluded, sequestered, shielded, shut off, withdrawn
Antonyms *adj* extrovert, genial, gregarious, outgoing, public, sociable, social

close[1] *adj* **1** = **near**, adjacent, adjoining, approaching, at hand, cheek by jowl, handy, hard by, imminent, impending, just round the corner, nearby, neighbouring, nigh, proximate, upcoming, within sniffing distance, within striking distance (*inf.*) **2** = **compact**, congested, cramped, cropped, crowded, dense, impenetrable, jam-packed, packed, short, solid, thick, tight **5** = **intimate**, attached, confidential, dear, devoted, familiar, inseparable, loving **7** = **accurate**, conscientious, exact, faithful, literal, precise, strict **8** = **careful**, alert, assiduous, attentive, concentrated, detailed, dogged, earnest, fixed, intense, intent, keen, minute, painstaking, rigorous, searching, thorough **11** = **stifling**, airless, confined, frowsty, fuggy, heavy, humid, muggy, oppressive, stale, stuffy, suffocating, sweltering, thick, unventilated **14** = **secretive**, hidden, private, reticent, retired, secluded, secret, taciturn, uncommunicative, unforthcoming **15** = **mean**, illiberal, mingy (*Brit. inf.*), miserly, near, niggardly, parsimonious, penurious, stingy, tight-fisted, ungenerous
Antonyms *adj* ≠ **near**: distant, far, far away, far off, future, outlying, remote ≠ **compact**: dispersed, empty, free, loose, penetrable, porous, uncongested, uncrowded ≠ **intimate**: alienated, aloof, chilly, cold, cool, distant, indifferent, standoffish, unfriendly ≠ **stifling**: airy, fresh, refreshing, roomy, spacious ≠ **mean**: charitable, extravagant, generous, lavish, liberal, magnanimous, unstinting

close[2] *vb* **1, 2** = **shut**, bar, block, bung, choke, clog, confine, cork, fill, lock, obstruct, plug, seal, secure, shut up, stop up **3** = **connect**, come together, couple, fuse, grapple, join, unite **5** =

close down, close in, etc. [C13: from OF *clos,* from L *clausus,* from *claudere* to close]
▸ **ˈcloser** *n*

close company *n* a company that is controlled by its directors or by five or fewer participants.

closed ❶ (kləʊzd) *adj* **1** blocked against entry; shut. **2** restricted; exclusive. **3** not open to question or debate. **4** (of a hunting season, etc.) close. **5** *Maths.* **5a** (of a curve or surface) completely enclosing an area or volume. **5b** (of a set) having members that can be produced by a specific operation on other members of the same set. **6** *Phonetics.* denoting a syllable that ends in a consonant. **7** not open to public entry or membership: *a closed society.*

closed chain *n Chem.* another name for **ring**[1] (sense 17).

closed circuit *n* a complete electrical circuit through which current can flow.

closed-circuit television *n* a television system in which signals are transmitted from the television camera to the receivers by cables or telephone links.

close down (kləʊz) *vb* (*adv*) **1** to cease or cause to cease operations. **2** (*tr*) *Soccer.* to deny (an opposing player) space to run with the ball or to make or receive a pass. ◆ *n* **close-down. 3** a closure or stoppage, esp. in a factory. **4** *Brit. radio, television.* the end of a period of broadcasting, esp. late at night.

closed shop *n* (formerly) an industrial establishment in which there exists a contract between a trade union and the employer permitting the employment of the union's members only.

close-fisted (ˌkləʊsˈfɪstɪd) *adj* very careful with money; mean.
▸ **ˌclose-ˈfistedness** *n*

close harmony (kləʊs) *n* a type of singing in which all the parts except the bass lie close together.

close-hauled (ˌkləʊsˈhɔːld) *adj Naut.* with the sails flat, so as to sail as close to the wind as possible.

close in (kləʊz) *vb* (*intr, adv*) **1** (of days) to become shorter with the approach of winter. **2** (foll. by *on* or *upon*) to advance (on) so as to encircle or surround.

close out (kləʊz) *vb* (*adv*) to terminate (a client's or other account) usually by sale of securities to realize cash.

close punctuation (kləʊs) *n* punctuation in which many commas, full stops, etc., are used. Cf. **open punctuation.**

close quarters (kləʊs) *pl n* **1** a narrow cramped space or position. **2 at close quarters. 2a** engaged in hand-to-hand combat. **2b** in close proximity; very near together.

close season (kləʊs) *or* **closed season** *n* **1** the period of the year when it is prohibited to kill certain game or fish. **2** *Sport.* the period of the year when there is no domestic competition.

close shave (kləʊs) *n Inf.* a narrow escape.

closet ❶ (ˈklɒzɪt) *n* **1** a small cupboard or recess. **2** a small private room. **3** short for **water closet. 4** (*modifier*) private or secret. ◆ *vb* **closets, closeting, closeted. 5** (*tr*) to shut up or confine in a small private room, esp. for conference or meditation. [C14: from OF, from *clos* enclosure; see CLOSE[1]]

close-up (ˈkləʊsˌʌp) *n* **1** a photograph or film or television shot taken at close range. **2** a detailed or intimate view or examination. ◆ *vb* **close up** (kləʊz). (*adv*) **3** to shut entirely. **4** (*intr*) to draw together: *the ranks closed up.* **5** (*intr*) (of wounds) to heal completely.

close with (kləʊz) *vb* (*intr, prep*) to engage in battle with (an enemy).

closure ❶ (ˈkləʊʒə) *n* **1** the act of closing or the state of being closed. **2** an end or conclusion. **3** something that closes or shuts, such as a cap or seal for a container. **4** Also called: **gag.** (in a deliberative body) a procedure by which debate may be halted and an immediate vote taken. ◆ *vb* **closures, closuring, closured. 5** (*tr*) (in a deliberative body) to end (debate) by closure. [C14: from OF, from LL, from L *claudere* to close]

clot ❶ (klɒt) *n* **1** a soft thick lump or mass. **2** *Brit. inf.* a stupid person; fool. ◆ *vb* **clots, clotting, clotted. 3** to form or cause to form into a soft thick lump or lumps. [OE *clott,* of Gmc origin]

cloth ❶ (klɒθ) *n, pl* **cloths** (klɒθs, klɒðz). **1a** a fabric formed by weaving, felting or knitting wool, cotton, etc. **1b** (*as modifier*): *a cloth bag.* **2** a piece of such fabric used for a particular purpose, as for a dishcloth. **3** (usually preceded by *the*) the clergy. [OE *clāth*]

clothe ❶ (kləʊð) *vb* **clothes, clothing, clothed** *or* **clad.** (*tr*) **1** to dress or attire (a person). **2** to provide with clothing. **3** to conceal or disguise. **4** to endow or invest. [OE *clāthian,* from *clāth* cloth]

clothes ❶ (kləʊðz) *pl n* **1** articles of dress. **2** *Chiefly Brit.* short for **bedclothes.** [OE *clāthas,* pl. of *clāth* cloth]

clotheshorse (ˈkləʊðzˌhɔːs) *n* **1** a frame on which to hang laundry for drying or airing. **2** *Inf.* an excessively fashionable person.

clothesline (ˈkləʊðzˌlaɪn) *n* a piece of rope or wire on which clean washing is hung to dry.

clothes peg *n* a small wooden or plastic clip for attaching washing to a clothesline.

clothes pole *n* a post to which a clothesline is attached. Also called: **clothes post.**

clothes-press *n* a piece of furniture for storing clothes, usually containing wide drawers.

clothes prop *n* a long wooden pole with a forked end used to raise a line of washing to enable it to catch the breeze.

clothier (ˈkləʊðɪə) *n* a person who makes, sells, or deals in clothes or cloth.

clothing ❶ (ˈkləʊðɪŋ) *n* **1** garments collectively. **2** something that covers or clothes.

Clotho (ˈkləʊθəʊ) *n Greek myth.* one of the three Fates, spinner of the thread of life. [L, from Gk *Klōtho,* one who spins, from *klōthein* to spin]

cloth of gold *n* cloth woven from silk threads interspersed with gold.

clotted cream *n Brit.* a thick cream made from scalded milk, esp. in SW England.

clotting factor *n* any one of a group of substances, including factor VIII, the presence of which in the blood is essential for blood clotting to occur. Also called: **coagulation factor.**

cloture (ˈkləʊtʃə) *n* **1** closure in the US Senate. ◆ *vb* **clotures, cloturing, clotured. 2** (*tr*) to end (debate) by cloture. [C19: from F *clôture,* from OF CLOSURE]

cloud ❶ (klaʊd) *n* **1** a mass of water or ice particles visible in the sky. **2** any collection of particles visible in the air, esp. of smoke or dust. **3** a large number of insects or other small animals in flight. **4** something that darkens, threatens, or carries gloom. **5** *Jewellery.* a cloudlike blemish in a transparent stone. **6 in the clouds.** not in contact with reality. **7 on cloud nine.** *Inf.* elated; very happy. **8 under a cloud. 8a** under reproach or suspicion. **8b** in a state of gloom or bad temper. ◆ *vb* **9** (when *intr,* often foll. by *over* or *up*) to make or become cloudy, overcast, or indistinct. **10** (*tr*) to make obscure; darken. **11** to make or become gloomy or depressed. **12** (*tr*) to place under or render liable to suspicion or disgrace. **13** to render (liquids) milky or dull or (of liquids) to become milky or dull. [C13 (in the sense: a mass of vapour): from OE *clūd* rock, hill]
▸ **ˈcloudless** *adj* ▸ **ˈcloudlessly** *adv* ▸ **ˈcloudlessness** *n*

cloudburst (ˈklaʊdˌbɜːst) *n* a heavy downpour.

cloud chamber *n Physics.* an apparatus for detecting high-energy particles by observing their tracks through a chamber containing a supersaturated vapour.

cloud-cuckoo-land *n* a realm of fantasy, dreams, or impractical notions.

THESAURUS

end, axe (*inf.*), cease, complete, conclude, culminate, discontinue, finish, mothball, shut down, terminate, wind up ◆ *n* **11** = **end,** cessation, completion, conclusion, culmination, denouement, ending, finale, finish, run-in, termination

Antonyms *vb* ≠ **shut:** clear, free, open, release, unblock, unclog, uncork, unstop, widen ≠ **connect:** disconnect, disjoin, disunite, divide, part, separate, split, uncouple ≠ **end:** begin, commence, initiate, open, start

closed *adj* **1** = **shut,** fastened, locked, out of business, out of service, sealed **2** = **exclusive,** restricted **3** = **finished,** concluded, decided, ended, over, resolved, settled, terminated

Antonyms *adj* ≠ **shut:** ajar, open, unclosed, unfastened, unlocked, unsealed

closeness *n* **1** = **nearness,** adjacency, handiness, imminence, imminentness, impendence, impendency, proximity **2** = **compactness,** crowdedness, denseness, impenetrability, impenetrableness, snugness, solidness, thickness, tightness **5** = **intimacy,** confidentiality, confidentialness, dearness, devotedness, familiarness, inseparability, intimateness, lovingness **7** = **accuracy,** exactness, faithfulness, literality, literalness, preciseness, strictness **8** = **carefulness,** alertness, assiduousness, attentiveness, doggedness, earnestness, fixedness, intensiveness, intentness, keenness, minuteness, painstakingness, rigorousness, searchingness, thoroughness **11** = **stuffiness,** airlessness, confinedness, frowstiness, heaviness, humidity, humidness, mugginess, oppressiveness, staleness, sultriness, thickness **14** = **secretiveness,** reticence, secludedness, taciturnity, uncommunicativeness **15** = **meanness,** illiberality, illiberalness, minginess (*Brit. inf.*), miserliness, niggardliness, parsimony, penuriousness, stinginess

closet *n* **1** = **cupboard,** cabinet, cubbyhole, cubicle, recess ◆ *modifier* **4** = **secret,** concealed, covert, hidden, private

closure *n* **1** = **closing,** cessation, conclusion, end, finish, stoppage **3** = **plug,** bung, cap, lid, seal, stopper **4** = **guillotine,** cloture

clot *n* **1** = **lump,** clotting, coagulation, curdling, embolism, embolus, gob, mass, occlusion, thrombus **2** *Brit. informal* = **idiot,** ass, berk (*Brit. sl.*), buffoon, charlie (*Brit. inf.*), coot, divvy (*Brit. sl.*), dolt, dope (*inf.*), dork (*sl.*), dunderhead, fathead (*inf.*), fool, nincompoop, nit (*inf.*), nitwit (*inf.*), numbskull *or* numskull, pillock (*Brit. sl.*), plank (*Brit. sl.*), plonker (*sl.*), schmuck (*US slang*), wally (*sl.*) ◆ *vb* **3** = **congeal,** coagulate, coalesce, curdle, jell, thicken

cloth *n* **1a** = **fabric,** dry goods, material, stuff, textiles

clothe *vb* **1** = **dress,** accoutre, apparel, array, attire, bedizen (*arch.*), caparison, cover, deck, doll up (*sl.*), drape, endow, enwrap, equip, fit out, garb, get ready, habit, invest, outfit, rig, robe, swathe

Antonyms *vb* disrobe, divest, expose, strip, strip off, unclothe, uncover, undress

clothes *pl n* **1** = **clothing,** apparel, attire, clobber (*Brit. slang*), costume, dress, duds (*inf.*), ensemble, garb, garments, gear (*inf.*), get-up (*inf.*), glad rags (*inf.*), habits, outfit, raiment (*arch. or poetic*), rigout (*inf.*), threads (*sl.*), togs (*inf.*), vestments, vesture, wardrobe, wear

clothing *n* **1** = **clothes,** apparel, attire, clobber (*Brit. slang*), costume, dress, duds (*inf.*), ensemble, garb, garments, gear (*inf.*), get-up (*inf.*), glad rags (*inf.*), habits, outfit, raiment (*arch. or poetic*), rigout (*inf.*), threads (*sl.*), togs (*inf.*), vestments, vesture, wardrobe, wear

cloud *n* **2** = **mist,** billow, darkness, fog, gloom, haze, murk, nebula, nebulosity, obscurity, vapour **3** = **dense mass,** crowd, flock, horde, host, multitude, shower, swarm, throng ◆ *vb* **9** = **obscure,** becloud, darken, dim, eclipse, obfuscate, overcast, overshadow, shade, shadow,

cloudy ❶ ('klaʊdɪ) *adj* **cloudier, cloudiest. 1** covered with cloud or clouds. **2** of or like clouds. **3** streaked or mottled like a cloud. **4** opaque or muddy. **5** obscure or unclear. **6** troubled or gloomy.
▸'**cloudily** *adv* ▸'**cloudiness** *n*

clough (klʌf) *n Dialect.* a ravine. [OE *clōh*]

clout ❶ (klaʊt) *n* **1** *Inf.* a blow with the hand or a hard object. **2** power or influence, esp. political. **3** Also called: **clout nail.** a short, flat-headed nail. **4** *Dialect.* **4a** a piece of cloth: *a dish clout.* **4b** a garment. ◆ *vb* (*tr*) **5** *Inf.* to give a hard blow to, esp. with the hand. [OE *clūt* piece of metal or cloth, *clūtian* to patch (C14: to strike with the hand)]

clove[1] (kləʊv) *n* **1** a tropical evergreen tree of the myrtle family. **2** the dried unopened flower buds of this tree, used as a pungent fragrant spice. [C14: from OF, lit.: nail of clove, *clou* from L *clāvus* nail + *girofle* clove tree]

clove[2] (kləʊv) *n* any of the segments of a compound bulb that arise from the axils of the scales of a large bulb. [OE *clufu* bulb; see CLEAVE[1]]

clove[3] (kləʊv) *vb* a past tense of **cleave**[1].

clove hitch *n* a knot or hitch used for securing a rope to a spar, post, or larger rope.

cloven ❶ ('kləʊvᵊn) *vb* **1** a past participle of **cleave**[1]. ◆ *adj* **2** split; cleft; divided.

cloven hoof *or* **foot** *n* **1** the divided hoof of a pig, goat, cow, deer, or related animal. **2** the mark or symbol of Satan.
▸ˌ**cloven-'hoofed** *or* ˌ**cloven-'footed** *adj*

clove oil *n* a volatile pale-yellow aromatic oil obtained from clove flowers, formerly much used in confectionery, dentistry, and microscopy. Also called: **oil of cloves.**

clover ('kləʊvə) *n* **1** a leguminous fodder plant having trifoliate leaves and dense flower heads. **2** any of various similar or related plants. **3 in clover.** *Inf.* in a state of ease or luxury. [OE *clāfre*]

cloverleaf ('kləʊvəˌliːf) *n, pl* **cloverleaves. 1** an arrangement of connecting roads, resembling a four-leaf clover in form, that joins two intersecting main roads. **2** (*modifier*) in the shape or pattern of a leaf of clover.

clown ❶ (klaʊn) *n* **1** a comic entertainer, usually grotesquely costumed and made up, appearing in the circus. **2** a person who acts in a comic or buffoon-like manner. **3** a clumsy rude person; boor. **4** *Arch.* a countryman or rustic. ◆ *vb* (*intr*) **5** to perform as a clown. **6** to play jokes or tricks. **7** to act foolishly. [C16: ?from Low G]
▸'**clownery** *n* ▸'**clownish** *adj* ▸'**clownishly** *adv* ▸'**clownishness** *n*

cloy ❶ (klɔɪ) *vb* to make weary or cause weariness through an excess of something initially pleasurable or sweet. [C14 (orig.: to nail, hence, to obstruct): from earlier *acloyen,* from OF, from Med. L *inclavāre,* from L, from *clāvus* a nail]
▸'**cloyingly** *adv*

cloze test (kləʊz) *n* a test of the ability to comprehend text in which the reader has to supply the missing words that have been removed from the text. [altered from *close* to complete a pattern (in Gestalt theory)]

club ❶ (klʌb) *n* **1** a stout stick, usually with one end thicker than the other, esp. one used as a weapon. **2** a stick or bat used to strike the ball in various sports, esp. golf. See **golf club. 3** short for **Indian club. 4** a group or association of people with common aims or interests. **5** the room, building, or facilities used by such a group. **6** a building in which elected, fee-paying members go to meet, dine, read, etc. **7** a commercial establishment in which people can drink and dance; disco. See also **nightclub. 8** *Chiefly Brit.* an organization, esp. in a shop, set up as a means of saving. **9** *Brit.* an informal word for **friendly society. 10a** the black trefoil symbol on a playing card. **10b** a card with one or more of these symbols or (*when pl*) the suit of cards so marked. **11 in the club.** *Brit. sl.* pregnant. ◆ *vb* **clubs, clubbing, clubbed. 12** (*tr*) to beat with or as if with a club. **13** (often foll. by *together*) to gather or become gathered into a group. **14** (often foll. by *together*) to unite or combine (resources, efforts, etc.) for a common purpose. [C13: from ON *klubba,* rel. to CLUMP]
▸'**clubbing** *n*

clubbed (klʌbd) *adj* having a thickened end, like a club.

clubber ('klʌbə) *n* a person who regularly frequents nightclubs and similar establishments.

club class *n* **1** a class of air travel that is less luxurious than first class but more luxurious than economy class. ◆ *adj* **club-class. 2** of or relating to this class of travel.

club foot *n* **1** a congenital deformity of the foot, esp. one in which the foot is twisted so that most of the weight rests on the heel. Technical name: **talipes. 2** a foot so deformed.
▸ˌ**club-'footed** *adj*

clubhouse ('klʌbˌhaʊs) *n* the premises of a sports or other club, esp. a golf club.

clubman ('klʌbmən) *or* (*fem*) **clubwoman** *n, pl* **clubmen** *or* **clubwomen.** a person who is an enthusiastic member of a club or clubs.

club root *n* a fungal disease of cabbages and related plants, in which the roots become thickened and distorted.

cluck (klʌk) *n* **1** the low clicking sound made by a hen or any similar sound. ◆ *vb* **2** (*intr*) (of a hen) to make a clicking sound. **3** (*tr*) to call or express (a feeling) by making a similar sound. [C17: imit.]

clucky ('klʌkɪ) *adj Austral. inf.* **1** wanting to have a baby. **2** excessively protective towards children.

clue ❶ (kluː) *n* **1** something that helps to solve a problem or unravel a mystery. **2 not have a clue. 2a** to be completely baffled. **2b** to be ignorant or incompetent. ◆ *vb* **clues, cluing, clued. 3** (*tr;* usually foll. by *in* or *up*) to provide with helpful information. [C15: var. of CLEW]

clued-up *adj Inf.* shrewd; well-informed.

clueless ❶ ('kluːlɪs) *adj Sl.* helpless; stupid.

clump ❶ (klʌmp) *n* **1** a cluster, as of trees or plants. **2** a dull heavy tread or any similar sound. **3** an irregular mass. **4** an inactive mass of microorganisms, esp. a mass of bacteria produced as a result of agglutination. **5** an extra sole on a shoe. **6** *Sl.* a blow. ◆ *vb* **7** (*intr*) to walk or tread heavily. **8** to gather or be gathered into clumps, clusters, clots, etc. **9** to cause (bacteria, blood cells, etc.) to collect together or (of bacteria, etc.) to collect together. **10** (*tr*) *Sl.* to punch (someone). [OE *clympe*]
▸'**clumpy** *adj*

clumsy ❶ ('klʌmzɪ) *adj* **clumsier, clumsiest. 1** lacking in skill or physical coordination. **2** awkwardly constructed or contrived. [C16 (in obs. sense: benumbed with cold; hence, awkward): ?from C13 dialect *clumse* to benumb, prob. of Scand. origin]
▸'**clumsily** *adv* ▸'**clumsiness** *n*

clung (klʌŋ) *vb* the past tense and past participle of **cling.**

clunk (klʌŋk) *n* **1** a blow or the sound of a blow. **2** a dull metallic sound. ◆ *vb* **3** to make or cause to make such a sound. [C19: imit.]

clunky ('klʌŋkɪ) *adj* **clunkier, clunkiest. 1** making a clunking noise. **2** clumsy or inelegant: *clunky ankle-strap shoes.* **3** awkward or unsophisticated: *then you guffaw at clunky dialogue.*

cluster ❶ ('klʌstə) *n* **1** a number of things growing, fastened, or occurring close together. **2** a number of persons or things grouped together. ◆ *vb* **3** to gather or be gathered in clusters. [OE *clyster*]
▸'**clustered** *adj* ▸'**clustery** *adj*

clutch[1] ❶ (klʌtʃ) *vb* **1** (*tr*) to seize with or as if with hands or claws. **2** (*tr*) to grasp or hold firmly. **3** (*intr;* usually foll. by *at*) to attempt to get hold or possession (of). ◆ *n* **4** a device that enables two revolving shafts to be joined or disconnected, esp. one that transmits the drive from the engine to the gearbox in a vehicle. **5** a device for holding fast. **6** a firm grasp. **7** a hand, claw, or talon in the act of clutching: *in the clutches of a bear.* **8** (*often pl*) power or control: *in the clutches of the Mafia.* [OE *clyccan*]

clutch[2] (klʌtʃ) *n* **1** a hatch of eggs laid by a particular bird or laid in a

THESAURUS

veil **10** = **confuse,** disorient, distort, impair, muddle, muddy the waters

cloudy *adj* **1** = **dull,** dark, dim, dismal, dusky, gloomy, leaden, louring *or* lowering, nebulous, obscure, overcast, sombre, sullen, sunless **4** = **opaque,** emulsified, muddy, murky **5** = **confused,** blurred, hazy, indistinct, unclear
Antonyms *adj* ≠ **dull:** bright, clear, fair, sunny, uncloudy ≠ **confused:** clear, distinct, obvious, plain

clout *Informal n* **2** = **influence,** *Informal n* **2** = **influence,** authority, bottom, power, prestige, pull, standing, weight ◆ *vb* **5** = **hit,** box, chin (*sl.*), clobber (*sl.*), cuff, deck (*sl.*), lay one on (*sl.*), punch, skelp (*dialect*), sock (*sl.*), strike, thump, tonk (*inf.*), wallop (*inf.*), wham

cloven *adj* **2** = **split,** bisected, cleft, divided

clown *n* **1** = **comedian,** buffoon, comic, dolt, fool, harlequin, jester, joker, merry-andrew, mountebank, pierrot, prankster, punchinello **3, 4** = **boor,** clodhopper (*inf.*), hind (*obs.*), peasant, swain (*arch.*), yahoo, yokel ◆ *vb* **7** = **play the fool,** act the fool, act the goat, jest, mess about, piss about *or* around (*taboo slang*), play the goat

clownish *adj* **1** = **comic,** foolish, galumphing (*inf.*), nonsensical, slapstick, zany **3** = **boorish,** awkward, churlish, clumsy, ill-bred, rough, rude, rustic, uncivil, ungainly, vulgar

cloy *vb* = **sicken,** disgust, glut, gorge, nauseate, sate, satiate, surfeit, weary

club *n* **1** = **stick,** bat, bludgeon, cosh (*Brit.*), cudgel, truncheon **4** = **association,** circle, clique, company, fraternity, group, guild, lodge, order, set, society, sodality, union ◆ *vb* **12** = **beat,** bash, baste, batter, bludgeon, clobber (*sl.*), clout (*inf.*), cosh (*Brit.*), hammer, pommel (*rare*), pummel, strike

clue *n* **1** = **indication,** evidence, hint, inkling, intimation, lead, pointer, sign, suggestion, suspicion, tip, tip-off, trace

clueless *adj* = **stupid,** dense, dim, dopey, dozy (*Brit. inf.*), dull, dumb (*inf.*), half-witted, moronic, naive, simple, simple-minded, slow, slow on the uptake (*inf.*), thick, unintelligent, witless

clump *n* **1** = **cluster,** bunch, bundle, group, mass, shock ◆ *vb* **7** = **stomp,** bumble, clomp, lumber, plod, stamp, stump, thud, thump, tramp

clumsiness *n* **1** = **awkwardness,** accident-proneness, gaucheness, gawkiness, gracelessness, heaviness, heavy-handedness, inelegance, inelegancy, ineptitude, ineptness, inexpertness, lumberingness, maladroitness, ponderosity, ponderousness, uncouthness, ungainliness, unskilfulness
Antonyms *n* adeptness, adroitness, agility, deftness, dexterity, dexterousness *or* dextrousness, expertise, finesse, grace, gracefulness, handiness, nimbleness, proficiency, skill

clumsy *adj* **1, 2** = **awkward,** accident-prone, blundering, bumbling, bungling, butterfingered (*inf.*), cack-handed (*inf.*), clunky (*inf.*), gauche, gawky, ham-fisted (*inf.*), ham-handed (*inf.*), heavy, ill-shaped, inept, inexpert, klutzy (*US. & Canad. sl.*), like a bull in a china shop, lumbering, maladroit, ponderous, uncoordinated, uncouth, ungainly, unhandy, unskilful, unwieldy
Antonyms *adj* adept, adroit, competent, deft, dexterous, expert, graceful, handy, proficient, skilful

cluster *n* **1, 2** = **gathering,** assemblage, batch, bunch, clump, collection, group, knot ◆ *vb* **3** = **gather,** assemble, bunch, collect, flock, group

clutch[1] *vb* **1, 2** = **seize,** catch, clasp, cling to, embrace, fasten, grab, grapple, grasp, grip, snatch ◆ *n* **8** *often pl* = **power,** claws, control, single nest. 2 a brood of chickens. 3 *Inf.* a group or cluster. ◆ *vb* 4 (*tr*) to hatch (chickens). [C17 (N English dialect) *cletch,* from ON *klekja* to hatch]

clutter ❶ ('klʌtə) *vb* 1 (*usually tr;* often foll. by *up*) to strew or amass (objects) in a disorderly manner. 2 (*intr*) to move about in a bustling manner. ◆ *n* 3 a disordered heap or mass of objects. 4 a state of disorder. 5 unwanted echoes that confuse the observation of signals on a radar screen. [C15 *clotter,* from *clotteren* to CLOT]

Clydesdale ('klaɪdzˌdeɪl) *n* a heavy powerful breed of carthorse, originally from Scotland.

clypeus ('klɪpɪəs) *n, pl* **clypei** ('klɪpɪˌaɪ). a cuticular plate on the head of some insects. [C19: from NL, from L *clipeus* round shield]
▸'**clypeal** *adj* ▸**clypeate** ('klɪpɪˌeɪt) *adj*

cm *symbol for* centimetre.

Cm *the chemical symbol for* curium.

Cmdr *Mil. abbrev. for* Commander.

CMEA *abbrev. for* Council for Mutual Economic Assistance. See **Comecon.**

CMG *abbrev. for* Companion of St Michael and St George (a Brit. title).

CMOS ('siːmɒs) *adj Computing. acronym for* complementary metal oxide silicon: *CMOS memory.*

CMV *abbrev. for* cytomegalovirus.

CNAA *abbrev. for* Council for National Academic Awards.

CNAR *abbrev. for* compound net annual rate.

CND *Chiefly Brit. abbrev. for* Campaign for Nuclear Disarmament.

Co *the chemical symbol for* cobalt.

CO *abbrev. for:* 1 Commanding Officer. 2 conscientious objector.

Co. *or* **co.** *abbrev. for:* 1 (esp. in names of business organizations) Company. 2 **and co.** (kəʊ) *Inf.* and the rest of them: *Harold and co.*

Co. *abbrev. for* County.

co- *prefix* 1 together; joint or jointly; mutual or mutually: *coproduction.* 2 indicating partnership or equality: *cofounder; copilot.* 3 to the same or a similar degree: *coextend.* 4 (in mathematics and astronomy) of the complement of an angle: *cosecant.* [from L, reduced form of COM-]

c/o *abbrev. for:* 1 care of. 2 *Book-keeping.* carried over.

coach ❶ (kəʊtʃ) *n* 1 a large vehicle for several passengers, used for transport over long distances, sightseeing, etc. 2 a large four-wheeled enclosed carriage, usually horse-drawn. 3 a railway carriage. 4 a trainer or instructor: *a drama coach.* 5 a tutor who prepares students for examinations. ◆ *vb* 6 to give tuition or instruction to (a pupil). 7 (*tr*) to transport in a bus or coach. [C16: from F *coche,* from Hungarian *kocsi szekér* wagon of Kocs, village in Hungary where coaches were first made]
▸'**coacher** *n*

coach-built *adj* (of a vehicle) having specially built bodywork.
▸'**coach-ˌbuilder** *n*

coachman ('kəʊtʃmən) *n, pl* **coachmen.** the driver of a coach or carriage.

coachwork ('kəʊtʃˌwɜːk) *n* 1 the design and manufacture of car bodies. 2 the body of a car.

coadjutor (kəʊ'ædʒʊtə) *n* 1 a bishop appointed as assistant to a diocesan bishop. 2 *Rare.* an assistant. [C15: via OF from L *co-* together + *adjūtor* helper, from *adjūtāre* to assist]

coagulate ❶ *vb* (kəʊ'ægjʊˌleɪt), **coagulates, coagulating, coagulated.** 1 to cause (a fluid, such as blood) to change into a soft semisolid mass or (of such a fluid) to change into such a mass; clot; curdle. ◆ *n* (kəʊ'ægjʊlɪt, -ˌleɪt). 2 the solid or semisolid substance produced by coagulation. [C16: from L *coāgulāre,* from *coāgulum* rennet, from *cōgere* to drive together]
▸**co'agulant** *or* **co'aguˌlator** *n* ▸**coˌagu'lation** *n* ▸**coagulative** (kəʊ'ægjʊlətɪv) *adj*

coagulation factor *n Med.* another name for **clotting factor.**

coal (kəʊl) *n* 1a a compact black or dark brown carbonaceous rock consisting of layers of partially decomposed vegetation deposited in the Carboniferous period: a fuel and a source of coke, coal gas, and coal tar. 1b (*as modifier*): *coal cellar; coal mine; coal dust.* 2 one or more lumps of coal. 3 short for **charcoal.** 4 **coals to Newcastle.** something supplied where it is already plentiful. ◆ *vb* 5 to take in, provide with, or turn into coal. [OE *col*]
▸'**coaly** *adj*

coaler ('kəʊlə) *n* a ship, train, etc., used to carry or supply coal.

coalesce ❶ (ˌkəʊə'lɛs) *vb* **coalesces, coalescing, coalesced.** (*intr*) to unite or come together in one body or mass; merge; fuse; blend. [C16: from L CO- + *alēscere* to increase, from *alere* to nourish]
▸ˌ**coa'lescence** *n* ▸ˌ**coa'lescent** *adj*

coalface ('kəʊlˌfeɪs) *n* the exposed seam of coal in a mine.

coalfield ('kəʊlˌfiːld) *n* an area rich in deposits of coal.

coalfish ('kəʊlˌfɪʃ) *n, pl* **coalfish** *or* **coalfishes.** a dark-coloured gadoid food fish occurring in northern seas. Also called (Brit.): **saithe, coley.**

coal gas *n* a mixture of gases produced by the distillation of bituminous coal and used for heating and lighting.

coalition ❶ (ˌkəʊə'lɪʃən) *n* 1a an alliance between groups or parties, esp. for some temporary and specific reason. 1b (*as modifier*): *a coalition government.* 2 a fusion or merging into one body or mass. [C17: from Med. L *coalitiō,* from L *coalēscere* to COALESCE]
▸ˌ**coa'litionist** *n*

Coal Measures *pl n* **the.** a series of coal-bearing rocks formed in the upper Carboniferous period.

coal miner's lung *n* an informal name for **anthracosis.**

coal scuttle *n* a container to supply coal to a domestic fire.

coal tar *n* a black tar, produced by the distillation of bituminous coal, that can be further distilled to yield benzene, toluene, etc.

coal tit *n* a small European songbird having a black head with a white patch on the nape.

coaming ('kəʊmɪŋ) *n* a raised frame round a ship's hatchway for keeping out water. [C17: from ?]

coarse ❶ (kɔːs) *adj* 1 rough in texture, structure, etc.; not fine: *coarse sand.* 2 lacking refinement or taste; indelicate; vulgar: *coarse jokes.* 3 of inferior quality. 4 (of a metal) not refined. [C14: from ?]
▸'**coarsely** *adv* ▸'**coarseness** *n*

coarse fish *n* a freshwater fish that is not of the salmon family.
▸**coarse fishing** *n*

coarsen ❶ ('kɔːsᵊn) *vb* to make or become coarse.

coast ❶ (kəʊst) *n* 1 the line or zone where the land meets the sea. Related adj: **littoral.** 2 *Brit.* the seaside. 3 *US.* 3a a slope down which a sledge may slide. 3b the act or an instance of sliding down a slope. 4 **the coast is clear.** *Inf.* the obstacles or dangers are gone. ◆ *vb* 5 to move or cause to move by momentum or force of gravity. 6 (*intr*) to proceed without great effort: *to coast to victory.* 7 to sail along (a coast). [C13: from OF *coste,* from L *costa* side, rib]
▸'**coastal** *adj*

coaster ('kəʊstə) *n* 1 *Brit.* a vessel engaged in coastal commerce. 2 a small tray for holding a decanter, wine bottle, etc. 3 a person or thing that coasts. 4 a protective mat for glasses. 5 *US.* short for **roller coaster.**

Coaster ('kəʊstə) *n NZ.* a person from the West Coast of the South Island, New Zealand.

coastguard ('kəʊstˌgɑːd) *n* 1 a maritime force which aids shipping, saves lives at sea, prevents smuggling, etc. 2 Also called: **coastguardsman.** a member of such a force.

coastline ('kəʊstˌlaɪn) *n* the outline of a coast.

coat ❶ (kəʊt) *n* 1 an outdoor garment with sleeves, covering the body from the shoulders to waist, knees, or feet. 2 any similar garment, esp. one forming the top to a suit. 3 a layer that covers or conceals a surface: *a coat of dust.* 4 the hair, wool, or fur of an animal. ◆ *vb* (*tr*) 5 (often foll. by *with*) to cover (with) a layer or covering. 6 to provide with a coat. [C16: from OF *cote,* of Gmc origin]

coat hanger *n* a curved piece of wood, wire, etc., with a hook, used to hang up clothes.

coati (kəʊ'ɑːtɪ), **coati-mondi,** *or* **coati-mundi** (kəʊˌɑːtɪ'mʌndɪ) *n, pl* **coatis, coati-mondis,** *or* **coati-mundis.** an omnivorous mammal of Central and South America, related to but larger than the raccoons, having a long flexible snout and a brindled coat. [C17: from Port., from Tupi, lit.: belt-nosed, from *cua* belt + *tim* nose]

coating ❶ ('kəʊtɪŋ) *n* 1 a layer or film spread over a surface. 2 fabric suitable for coats.

coat of arms *n* the heraldic bearings of a person, family, or corporation.

coat of mail *n* a protective garment made of linked metal rings or overlapping metal plates.

coat-tail *n* the long tapering tails at the back of a man's tailed coat.

coauthor (kəʊ'ɔːθə) *n* 1 a person who shares the writing of a book, etc., with another. ◆ *vb* 2 (*tr*) to be the joint author of (a book, etc.).

coax ❶ (kəʊks) *vb* 1 to seek to manipulate or persuade (someone) by

THESAURUS

custody, grasp, grip, hands, keeping, possession, sway

clutter *vb* 1 *often foll. by* **up** = **litter**, scatter, strew ◆ *n* 4 = **untidiness**, confusion, disarray, disorder, hotchpotch, jumble, litter, mess, muddle
Antonyms *vb* ≠ **litter:** arrange, order, organize, straighten, tidy ◆ *n* ≠ **untidiness:** neatness, order, organization, tidiness

coach *n* 1 = **bus**, car, carriage, charabanc, vehicle 4 = **instructor**, handler, teacher, trainer, tutor ◆ *vb* 6 = **instruct**, cram, drill, exercise, prepare, train, tutor

coagulate *vb* 1 = **congeal**, clot, curdle, jell, thicken

coalesce *vb* = **blend**, amalgamate, cohere, combine, come together, commingle, commix, consolidate, fraternize, fuse, incorporate, integrate, meld, merge, mix, unite

coalition *n* 2 = **alliance**, affiliation, amalgam, amalgamation, association, bloc, combination, compact, confederacy, confederation, conjunction, fusion, integration, league, merger, union

coarse *adj* 1 = **rough**, coarse-grained, crude, homespun, impure, rough-hewn, unfinished, unpolished, unprocessed, unpurified, unrefined 2 = **vulgar**, bawdy, boorish, brutish, coarse-grained, earthy, foul-mouthed, gruff, immodest, impolite, improper, impure, indecent, indelicate, loutish, mean, offensive, raunchy (*sl.*), ribald, rough, rude, smutty, uncivil
Antonyms *adj* ≠ **rough:** fine-grained, polished, purified, refined, smooth, soft ≠ **vulgar:** civilized, cultured, fine, genteel, inoffensive, pleasant, polished, polite, proper, refined, sophisticated, urbane, well-bred, well-mannered

coarsen *vb* = **roughen**, anaesthetize, blunt, callous, deaden, desensitize, dull, harden, indurate

coarseness *n* 1 = **roughness**, crudity, unevenness 3 = **vulgarity**, bawdiness, boorishness, crudity, earthiness, indelicacy, offensiveness, poor taste, ribaldry, roughness, smut, smuttiness, uncouthness

coast *n* 1, 2 = **shore**, beach, border, coastline, littoral, seaboard, seaside, strand ◆ *vb* 5 = **cruise**, drift, freewheel, get by, glide, sail, taxi

coat *n* 3 = **layer**, coating, covering, overlay 4 = **fur**, fleece, hair, hide, pelt, skin, wool ◆ *vb* 5 = **cover**, apply, Artex, plaster, smear, spread

coating *n* 1 = **layer**, blanket, coat, covering, dusting, film, finish, glaze, lamination, membrane, patina, sheet, skin, varnish, veneer

coax *vb* 1 = **persuade**, allure, beguile, cajole, decoy, entice, flatter, inveigle, prevail upon,

tenderness, flattery, pleading, etc. **2** (*tr*) to obtain by persistent coaxing. **3** (*tr*) to work on (something) carefully and patiently so as to make it function as desired: *he coaxed the engine into starting.* [C16: verb formed from obs. noun *cokes* fool, from ?]
▸'**coaxer** *n* ▸'**coaxingly** *adv*

coaxial (kəʊ'æksɪəl) *or* **coaxal** (kəʊ'æksᵊl) *adj* **1** having or mounted on a common axis. **2** *Geom.* (of a set of circles) having the same radical axis. **3** *Electronics.* formed from, using, or connected to a coaxial cable.

coaxial cable *n* a cable consisting of an inner insulated core of stranded or solid wire surrounded by an outer insulated flexible wire braid, used esp. as a transmission line for radio-frequency signals. Often shortened to **coax** ('kəʊæks).

cob (kɒb) *n* **1** a male swan. **2** a thickset type of riding and draught horse. **3** short for **corncob** or **cobnut.** **4** *Brit.* another name for **hazel** (sense 1). **5** a small rounded lump or heap of coal, ore, etc. **6** *Brit. & NZ.* a building material consisting of a mixture of clay and chopped straw. **7** *Brit.* a round loaf of bread. [C15: from ?]

cobalt ('kəʊbɔːlt) *n* a brittle hard silvery-white element that is a ferromagnetic metal: used in alloys. The radioisotope **cobalt-60** is used in radiotherapy and as a tracer. Symbol: Co; atomic no.: 27; atomic wt.: 58.933. [C17: G *Kobalt,* from MHG *kobolt* goblin; from the miners' belief that goblins placed it in the silver ore]

cobalt blue *n* **1** any greenish-blue pigment containing cobalt aluminate. **2a** a deep blue colour. **2b** (*as adj*): *a cobalt-blue car.*

cobalt bomb *n* **1** a cobalt-60 device used in radiotherapy. **2** a nuclear weapon consisting of a hydrogen bomb encased in cobalt, which releases large quantities of radioactive cobalt-60 into the atmosphere.

cobber ('kɒbə) *n Austral. arch. & NZ.* a friend; mate: used as a term of address to males. [C19: from E dialect *cob* to take a liking to someone]

cobble[1] ('kɒbᵊl) *n* **1** short for **cobblestone.** ◆ *vb* **cobbles, cobbling, cobbled.** **2** (*tr*) to pave (a road, etc.) with cobblestones. [C15 (in *cobblestone*): from COB]

cobble[2] ❶ ('kɒbᵊl) *vb* **cobbles, cobbling, cobbled.** (*tr*) **1** to make or mend (shoes). **2** to put together clumsily. [C15: back formation from COBBLER[1]]

cobbler[1] ('kɒblə) *n* a person who makes or mends shoes. [C13 (as surname): from ?]

cobbler[2] ('kɒblə) *n* **1** a sweetened iced drink, usually made from fruit and wine. **2** *Chiefly US.* a hot dessert made of fruit covered with a rich cakelike crust. [C19: (for sense 1) ? shortened from *cobbler's punch*]

cobblers ('kɒbləz) *pl n Brit. taboo sl.* **1** another word for **testicles.** **2** (**a load of old**) **cobblers.** rubbish; nonsense. [C20: from rhyming sl. *cobblers' awls* balls]

cobblestone ('kɒbᵊlˌstəʊn) *n* a rounded stone used for paving. Sometimes shortened to **cobble.**

cobelligerent (ˌkəʊbɪ'lɪdʒərənt) *n* a country fighting in a war on the side of another country.

cobnut ('kɒbˌnʌt) *or* **cob** *n* other names for a **hazelnut.** [C16: from earlier *cobylle nut*]

COBOL *or* **Cobol** ('kəʊˌbɒl) *n* a high-level computer programming language designed for general commercial use. [C20: *co(mmon) b(usiness) o(riented) l(anguage)*]

cobra ('kəʊbrə) *n* any of several highly venomous snakes of tropical Africa and Asia. When alarmed they spread the skin of the neck region into a hood. [C19: from Port. *cobra* (*de capello*) snake (with a hood), from L *colubra* snake]

cobweb ('kɒbˌweb) *n* **1** a web spun by certain spiders. **2** a single thread of such a web. **3** something like a cobweb, as in its flimsiness or ability to trap. [C14: *cob,* from OE (*ātor*)*coppe* spider]
▸'**cobˌwebbed** *adj* ▸'**cobˌwebby** *adj*

cobwebs ('kɒbˌwebz) *pl n* **1** mustiness, confusion, or obscurity. **2** *Inf.* stickiness of the eyelids experienced upon first awakening.

coca ('kəʊkə) *n* either of two shrubs, native to the Andes, the dried leaves of which contain cocaine and are chewed for their stimulating effects. [C17: from Sp., from Quechuan *kúka*]

Coca-Cola (ˌkəʊkə'kəʊlə) *n* **1** *Trademark.* a carbonated soft drink flavoured with coca leaves, cola nuts, caramel, etc. **2** (*modifier*) denoting the spread of American culture and values to other parts of the world: *Coca-Cola generation.*

cocaine *or* **cocain** (kə'keɪn) *n* an addictive narcotic drug derived from coca leaves or synthesized, used medicinally as a topical anaesthetic. [C19: from COCA + -INE[1]]

coccus ('kɒkəs) *n, pl* **cocci** (-kaɪ, -ksaɪ). any spherical or nearly spherical bacterium, such as a staphylococcus. [C18: from NL, from Gk *kokkos* berry, grain]
▸'**coccoid** *or* '**coccal** *adj*

coccyx ('kɒksɪks) *n, pl* **coccyges** (kɒk'saɪdʒiːz). a small triangular bone at the end of the spinal column in man and some apes. [C17: from NL, from Gk *kokkux* cuckoo, imit.; from its likeness to a cuckoo's beak]
▸**coccygeal** (kɒk'sɪdʒɪəl) *adj*

cochineal (ˌkɒtʃɪ'niːl, 'kɒtʃɪˌniːl) *n* **1** a Mexican insect that feeds on cacti. **2** a crimson substance obtained from the crushed bodies of these insects, used for colouring food and for dyeing. **3** the colour of this dye. [C16: from OSp. *cochinilla,* from L *coccineus* scarlet-coloured, from Gk *kokkos* kermes berry]

cochlea ('kɒklɪə) *n, pl* **cochleae** (-lɪˌiː). the spiral tube that forms part of the internal ear, converting sound vibrations into nerve impulses. [C16: from L: snail, spiral, from Gk *kokhlias*]
▸'**cochlear** *adj*

cochlear implant ('kɒklɪə) *n* a device that stimulates the acoustic nerve in the inner ear in order to produce some form of hearing in people who are deaf from inner ear disease.

cochleate ('kɒklɪˌeɪt, -lɪɪt) *or* **cochleated** *adj Biol.* shaped like a snail's shell.

cock[1] ❶ (kɒk) *n* **1** the male of the domestic fowl. **2a** any other male bird. **2b** the male of certain other animals, such as the lobster. **2c** (*as modifier*): *a cock sparrow.* **3** short for **stopcock** or **weathercock.** **4** a taboo slang word for **penis.** **5a** the hammer of a firearm. **5b** its position when the firearm is ready to be discharged. **6** *Brit. inf.* a friend, mate, or fellow. **7** a jaunty or significant tilting upwards: *a cock of the head.* ◆ *vb* **8** (*tr*) to set the firing pin, hammer, or breech block of (a firearm) so that a pull on the trigger will release it and thus fire the weapon. **9** (*tr; sometimes foll. by up*) to raise in an alert or jaunty manner. **10** (*intr*) to stick or stand up conspicuously. ◆ See also **cockup.** [OE *cocc,* ult. imit.]

cock[2] (kɒk) *n* **1** a small, cone-shaped heap of hay, straw, etc. ◆ *vb* **2** (*tr*) to stack (hay, etc.) in such heaps. [C14: ? of Scand. origin]

cockabully (ˌkɒkə'bʊlɪ) *n, pl* **cockabullies.** any of several small freshwater fish of New Zealand. [Maori *kokopu*]

cockade (kɒ'keɪd) *n* a feather or ribbon worn on military headwear. [C18: changed from earlier *cockard,* from F, from *coq* COCK[1]]
▸**cock'aded** *adj*

cock-a-doodle-doo (ˌkɒkəˌduːdᵊl'duː) *interj* an imitation or representation of a cock crowing.

cock-a-hoop *adj* (*usually postpositive*) **1** in very high spirits. **2** boastful. **3** askew; confused. [C16: ?from *set the cock a hoop*: to put a cock on a *hoop,* a full measure of grain]

cockalorum (ˌkɒkə'lɔːrəm) *n* **1** a self-important little man. **2** bragging talk. [C18: from COCK[1] + *-alorum,* var. of L genitive pl ending; ? intended to suggest: the cock of all cocks]

cockamamie (ˌkɒkə'meɪmɪ) *adj Sl., chiefly US.* ridiculous or nonsensical: *a cockamamie story.* [C20: in an earlier sense: a paper transfer, prob. from DECALCOMANIA]

cock-and-bull story *n Inf.* an obviously improbable story, esp. one used as an excuse.

cockatoo (ˌkɒkə'tuː, 'kɒkəˌtuː) *n, pl* **cockatoos.** **1** any of a genus of parrots having an erectile crest and light-coloured plumage. **2** *Austral. & NZ.* a small farmer or settler. **3** *Austral. inf.* a lookout during some illegal activity. [C17: from Du., from Malay *kakatua*]

cockatrice ('kɒkətrɪs, -ˌtraɪs) *n* **1** a legendary monster, part snake and part cock, that could kill with a glance. **2** another name for **basilisk** (sense 1). [C14: from OF, ult. from L *calcāre* to tread, from *calx* heel]

cockboat ('kɒkˌbəʊt) *or* **cockleboat** *n* a ship's small boat. [C15 *cokbote,* ? ult. from LL *caudica* dugout canoe, from L *caudex* tree trunk]

cockchafer ('kɒkˌtʃeɪfə) *n* any of various Old World beetles, whose larvae feed on crops and grasses. Also called: **May beetle, May bug.** [C18: from COCK[1] + CHAFER]

cockcrow ('kɒkˌkrəʊ) *n* daybreak.

cocked hat *n* **1** a hat with brims turned up and caught together in order to give two points (bicorn) or three points (tricorn). **2 knock into a cocked hat.** *Sl.* to outdo or defeat.

cockerel ('kɒkərəl, 'kɒkrəl) *n* a young domestic cock, less than a year old. [C15: dim. of COCK[1]]

cocker spaniel ('kɒkə) *n* a small compact breed of spaniel. [C19: from *cocking* hunting woodcocks]

cockeyed ❶ ('kɒkˌaɪd) *adj Inf.* **1** afflicted with strabismus or squint. **2** physically or logically abnormal, absurd, etc.; crooked; askew: *cockeyed ideas.* **3** drunk.

cockfight ('kɒkˌfaɪt) *n* a fight between two gamecocks fitted with sharp metal spurs.
▸'**cockˌfighting** *n*

cockhorse (ˌkɒk'hɔːs) *n* another name for **rocking horse** or **hobbyhorse.**

cockieleekie, cockyleeky, *or* **cock-a-leekie** ('kɒkə'liːkɪ) *n Scot.* a soup made from a fowl boiled with leeks.

cockle[1] ('kɒkᵊl) *n* **1** any edible sand-burrowing bivalve mollusc of Europe, typically having a rounded shell with radiating ribs. **2** any of certain similar or related molluscs. **3** short for **cockleshell** (sense 1). **4** a wrinkle or puckering. **5** one's deepest feelings (esp. in **warm the cockles of one's heart**). ◆ *vb* **cockles, cockling, cockled.** **6** to contract or cause to contract into wrinkles. [C14: from OF *coquille* shell, from L *conchȳlium* shellfish, from Gk *konkhulē* mussel; see CONCH]

cockle[2] ('kɒkᵊl) *n* any of several plants, esp. the corn cockle, that grow as weeds in cornfields.

cockleshell ('kɒkᵊlˌʃel) *n* **1** the shell of the cockle. **2** any of the shells of certain other molluscs. **3** any small light boat.

cockney ('kɒknɪ) (*often cap.*) ◆ *n* **1** a native of London, esp. of the East End, speaking a characteristic dialect of English. Traditionally defined as someone born within the sound of the bells of St Mary-le-Bow church. **2** the urban dialect of London or its East End. ◆ *adj* **3** characteristic of cockneys or their dialect of English. [C14:

THESAURUS

soft-soap (*inf.*), soothe, sweet-talk (*inf.*), talk into, twist (someone's) arm, wheedle
Antonyms *vb* browbeat, bully, coerce, force, harass, intimidate, pressurize, threaten

cobble[2] *vb* **1, 2 = patch,** botch, bungle, clout, mend, tinker

cock1 *n* **1 = cockerel,** chanticleer, rooster ◆ *vb* **9, 10 = raise,** perk up, prick, stand up

cockeyed *adj Informal* **1 = crooked,** askew, asymmetrical, awry, lopsided, skewwhiff (*Brit. inf.*), squint (*inf.*) **2 = absurd,** crazy, ludicrous, nonsensical, preposterous

from *cokeney*, lit.: cock's egg, later applied contemptuously to townsmen, from *cokene*, genitive pl of *cok* COCK[1] + *ey* EGG[1]]
▸'**cockneyish** *adj* ▸'**cockney,ism** *n*
cock of the walk *n Inf.* a person who asserts himself in a strutting pompous way.
cockpit ('kɒk,pɪt) *n* **1** the compartment in a small aircraft in which the pilot, crew, and sometimes the passengers sit. Cf. **flight deck** (sense 1). **2** the driver's compartment in a racing car. **3** *Naut.* an enclosed or recessed area towards the stern of a small vessel from which it is steered. **4** the site of numerous battles or campaigns. **5** an enclosure used for cockfights.
cockroach ('kɒk,rəʊtʃ) *n* an insect having an oval flattened body with long antennae and biting mouthparts: a household pest. [C17: from Sp. *cucaracha*, from ?]
cockscomb *or* **coxcomb** ('kɒks,kəʊm) *n* **1** the comb of a domestic cock. **2** a garden plant with yellow, crimson, or purple feathery plumelike flowers in a broad spike resembling the comb of a cock. **3** *Inf.* a conceited dandy.
cockshy ('kɒk,ʃaɪ) *n, pl* **cockshies.** *Brit.* **1** a target aimed at in throwing games. **2** the throw itself. ◆ Often shortened to **shy.** [C18: from shying at a cock, the prize for the person who hit it]
cocksure ❶ (,kɒk'ʃʊə, -'ʃɔː) *adj* overconfident; arrogant. [C16: from ?]
▸,**cock'sureness** *n*
cocktail ❶ ('kɒk,teɪl) *n* **1a** any mixed drink with a spirit base. **1b** (*as modifier*): *the cocktail hour.* **2** an appetizer of seafood, mixed fruits, etc. **3** any combination of diverse elements, esp. one considered potent. **4** (*modifier*) appropriate for formal occasions: *a cocktail dress.* [C19: from ?]
cockup ('kɒk,ʌp) *n* **1** *Brit. sl.* something done badly. ◆ *vb* **cock up.** (*tr, adv*) **2** (of an animal) to raise (its ears etc.), esp. in an alert manner. **3** *Brit. sl.* to botch.
cocky[1] ❶ ('kɒkɪ) *adj* **cockier, cockiest.** excessively proud of oneself.
▸'**cockily** *adv* ▸'**cockiness** *n*
cocky[2] ('kɒkɪ) *n, pl* **cockies.** *Austral. & NZ inf.* short for **cockatoo** (sense 2).
coco ('kəʊkəʊ) *n, pl* **cocos.** short for **coconut** or **coconut palm.** [C16: from Port. *coco* grimace; from the likeness of the three holes of the nut to a face]
cocoa ('kəʊkəʊ) *or* **cacao** *n* **1** a powder made from cocoa beans after they have been roasted and ground. **2** a hot or cold drink made from cocoa and milk or water. **3a** a light to moderate brown colour. **3b** (*as adj*): *cocoa paint.* [C18: altered from CACAO]
cocoa bean *n* the seed of the cacao.
cocoa butter *n* a yellowish-white waxy solid that is obtained from cocoa beans and used for confectionery, soap, etc.
coconut *or* **cocoanut** ('kəʊkə,nʌt) *n* **1** the fruit of the coconut palm, consisting of a thick fibrous oval husk inside which is a thin hard shell enclosing edible white meat. The hollow centre is filled with a milky fluid (**coconut milk**). **2** the meat of the coconut, often shredded and used in cakes, curries, etc. [C18: see COCO]
coconut matting *n* a form of coarse matting made from the fibrous husk of the coconut.
coconut oil *n* the oil obtained from the meat of the coconut and used for making soap, etc.
coconut palm *n* a tall palm tree, widely planted throughout the tropics, having coconuts as fruits. Also called: **coco palm, coconut tree.**
cocoon ❶ (kə'kuːn) *n* **1** a silky protective envelope secreted by silkworms and certain other insect larvae, in which the pupae develop. **2** a protective spray covering used as a seal on machinery. **3** a cosy warm covering. ◆ *vb* **4** (*tr*) to wrap in a cocoon. [C17: from F, from Provençal *coucoun* eggshell, from *coco* shell]
cocopan ('kəʊkəʊ,pæn) *n* (in South Africa) a small wagon running on narrow-gauge railway lines used in mines. Also called: **hopper.** [C20: from Zulu *'ngkumbana* short truck]
cocotte (kəʊ'kɒt, kə-) *n* **1** a small fireproof dish in which individual portions of food are cooked and served. **2** a prostitute or promiscuous woman. [C19: from F, from fem of *coq* COCK[1]]
cod[1] (kɒd) *n, pl* **cod** *or* **cods.** **1** any of the gadoid food fishes which occur in the North Atlantic and have a long body with three rounded dorsal fins. **2** any of various Australian fishes of fresh or salt water, such as the Murray cod or the red cod. [C13: prob. of Gmc origin]
cod[2] (kɒd) *n* **1** *Brit. & US dialect.* a pod or husk. **2** *Taboo.* an obsolete word for **scrotum.** [OE *codd* husk, bag]
cod[3] (kɒd) *Brit. sl.* ◆ *vb* **cods, codding, codded.** (*tr*) **1** to make fun of; tease. **2** to play a trick on; befool. ◆ *n* **3** a hoax or trick. [C19: ?from earlier *cod* a fool]
COD *abbrev. for:* **1** cash on delivery. **2** (in the US) collect on delivery.
coda ('kəʊdə) *n* **1** *Music.* the final passage of a musical structure. **2** a concluding part of a literary work that rounds off the main work but is independent of it. [C18: from It.: tail, from L *cauda*]
cod-act *vb* (*intr*) *Irish inf.* to play tricks; fool. [from COD[3] + ACT]
coddle ❶ ('kɒd[ə]l) *vb* **coddles, coddling, coddled.** (*tr*) **1** to treat with indulgence. **2** to cook (something, esp. eggs) in water just below the boiling point. [C16: from ?; ? rel. to CAUDLE]
▸'**coddler** *n*
code ❶ (kəʊd) *n* **1** a system of letters or symbols, by which information can be communicated secretly, briefly, etc.: *binary code; Morse code.* See also **genetic code.** **2** a message in code. **3** a symbol used in a code. **4** a conventionalized set of principles or rules: *a code of behaviour.* **5** a system of letters or digits used for identification purposes. ◆ *vb* **codes, coding, coded.** (*tr*) **6** to translate or arrange into a code. [C14: from F, from L *cōdex* book, CODEX]
▸'**coder** *n*
codeine ('kəʊdiːn) *n* a white crystalline alkaloid prepared mainly from morphine. It is used as an analgesic, a sedative, and to relieve coughing. [C19: from Gk *kōdeia* head of a poppy, from *kōos* hollow place + -INE[2]]
codex ('kəʊdɛks) *n, pl* **codices** ('kəʊdɪ,siːz, 'kɒdɪ-). **1** a volume of manuscripts of an ancient text. **2** *Obs.* a legal code. [C16: from L: tree trunk, wooden block, book]
codfish ('kɒd,fɪʃ) *n, pl* **codfish** *or* **codfishes.** a cod.
codger ('kɒdʒə) *n Inf.* a man, esp. an old or eccentric one: often in **old codger.** [C18: prob. var. of CADGER]
codicil ('kɒdɪsɪl) *n* **1** *Law.* a supplement modifying a will or revoking some provision of it. **2** an additional provision; appendix. [C15: from LL dim. of CODEX]
▸,**codi'cillary** *adj*
codify ❶ ('kəʊdɪ,faɪ, 'kɒ-) *vb* **codifies, codifying, codified.** (*tr*) to organize or collect together (laws, rules, procedures, etc.) into a system or code.
▸'**codi,fier** *n* ▸,**codifi'cation** *n*
codling[1] ('kɒdlɪŋ) *or* **codlin** ('kɒdlɪn) *n* **1** any of several varieties of long tapering apples. **2** any unripe apple. [C15 *querdlyng*, from ?]
codling[2] ('kɒdlɪŋ) *n* a codfish, esp. a young one.
cod-liver oil *n* an oil extracted from the livers of cod and related fish, rich in vitamins A and D.
codology (kɒd'ɒlədʒɪ) *n Irish inf.* the art or practice of bluffing or deception.
codpiece ('kɒd,piːs) *n* a bag covering the male genitals, attached to breeches: worn in the 15th and 16th centuries. [C15: from COD[2] + PIECE]
codswallop ('kɒdz,wɒləp) *n Brit. sl.* nonsense. [C20: from ?]
co-ed (,kəʊ'ɛd) *adj* **1** coeducational. ◆ *n* **2** *US.* a female student in a coeducational college or university. **3** *Brit.* a school or college providing coeducation.
coeducation (,kəʊɛdjʊ'keɪʃən) *n* instruction in schools, colleges, etc., attended by both sexes.
▸,**coedu'cational** *adj* ▸,**coedu'cationally** *adv*
coefficient (,kəʊɪ'fɪʃənt) *n* **1** *Maths.* a numerical or constant factor in an algebraic term: *the coefficient of the term 3xyz is 3.* **2** *Physics.* a number that is the value of a given substance under specified conditions. [C17: from NL, from L *co-* together + *efficere* to EFFECT]
coefficient of variation *n Statistics.* a measure of the relative variation of distributions independent of the units of measurement; the standard deviation divided by the mean, sometimes expressed as a percentage.
coel- *prefix* indicating a cavity within a body or a hollow organ or part: *coelacanth; coelenterate.* [NL, from Gk *koilos* hollow]
coelacanth ('siːlə,kænθ) *n* a primitive marine bony fish, having fleshy limblike pectoral fins: thought to be extinct until a living specimen was discovered in 1938. [C19: from NL, from COEL- + Gk *akanthos* spine]
coelenterate (sɪ'lɛntə,reɪt, -rɪt) *n* any of various invertebrates having a saclike body with a single opening (mouth), such as jellyfishes, sea anemones, and corals. [C19: from NL *Coelenterata*, hollow-intestined (creatures)]
coeliac *or US* **celiac** ('siːlɪ,æk) *adj* of the abdomen. [C17: from L, from Gk, from *koilia* belly]
coeliac disease *n* an illness, esp. of children, in which the lining of the small intestine is sensitive to gluten in the diet, causing an impairment of food absorption.
coelom *or esp. US* **celom** ('siːləʊm, -ləm) *n* the body cavity of many multicellular animals, containing the digestive tract and other visceral organs. [C19: from Gk, from *koilos* hollow]
▸**coelomic** *or esp. US* **celomic** (sɪ'lɒmɪk) *adj*
coeno- *or before a vowel* **coen-** *combining form.* common: *coenobite.* [NL, from Gk *koinos*]
coenobite *or* **cenobite** ('siːnəʊ,baɪt) *n* a member of a religious order following a communal rule of life. [C17: from OF or ecclesiastical L, from Gk *koinobion* convent, from *koinos* common + *bios* life]
▸**coenobitic** (,siːnəʊ'bɪtɪk), ,**coeno'bitical** *or* ,**ceno'bitic,** ,**ceno'bitical** *adj*
coenzyme (kəʊ'ɛnzaɪm) *n Biochem.* a nonprotein organic molecule

THESAURUS

cockiness *n* = **overconfidence**, arrogance, bigheadedness, brashness, bumptiousness, cocksureness, conceit, conceitedness, confidence, egotism, lordliness, presumptuousness, self-assurance, vanity
cocksure *adj* = **overconfident**, arrogant, brash, bumptious, cocky, full of oneself, hubristic, presumptuous
cocktail *n* **3** = **mixture**, amalgamation, blend, combination, mix
cocky[1] *adj* = **overconfident**, arrogant, brash, cocksure, conceited, egotistical, full of oneself, lordly, swaggering, swollen-headed, vain
Antonyms *adj* hesitant, lacking confidence, modest, self-effacing, uncertain, unsure
cocoon *vb* **4** = **wrap**, cushion, envelop, insulate, pad, protect, swaddle, swathe
coddle *vb* **1** = **pamper**, baby, cosset, humour, indulge, mollycoddle, nurse, pet, spoil, wet-nurse (*inf.*)
code *n* **1** = **cipher**, cryptograph **4** = **principles**, canon, convention, custom, ethics, etiquette, manners, maxim, regulations, rules, system
codify *vb* = **organize**, catalogue, classify, collect, condense, digest, summarize, systematize, tabulate

that forms a complex with certain enzymes and is essential for their activity.

coequal (kəʊ'iːkwəl) *adj* **1** of the same size, rank, etc. ◆ *n* **2** a person or thing equal with another.
▸**coequality** (ˌkəʊɪ'kwɒlɪtɪ) *n*

coerce ➊ (kəʊ'ɜːs) *vb* **coerces, coercing, coerced.** (*tr*) to compel or restrain by force or authority without regard to individual wishes or desires. [C17: from L, from *co-* together + *arcēre* to enclose]
▸**co'ercer** *n* ▸**co'ercible** *adj*

coercion ➊ (kəʊ'ɜːʃən) *n* **1** the act or power of coercing. **2** government by force.
▸**coercive** (kəʊ'ɜːsɪv) *adj* ▸**co'ercively** *adv*

coeval (kəʊ'iːvᵊl) *adj* **1** of or belonging to the same age or generation. ◆ *n* **2** a contemporary. [C17: from LL, from L *co-* + *aevum* age]
▸**coevality** (ˌkəʊɪ'vælɪtɪ) *n* ▸**co'evally** *adv*

coexecutor (ˌkəʊɪg'zɛkjʊtə) *n Law.* a person acting jointly with another or others as executor.

coexist (ˌkəʊɪg'zɪst) *vb* (*intr*) **1** to exist together at the same time or in the same place. **2** to exist together in peace.
▸ˌ**coex'istence** *n* ▸ˌ**coex'istent** *adj*

coextend (ˌkəʊɪk'stɛnd) *vb* to extend or cause to extend equally in space or time.
▸ˌ**coex'tension** *n* ▸ˌ**coex'tensive** *adj*

C of C *abbrev. for* Chamber of Commerce.

C of E *abbrev. for* Church of England.

coffee ('kɒfɪ) *n* **1a** a drink consisting of an infusion of the roasted and ground seeds of the coffee tree. **1b** (*as modifier*): *coffee grounds.* **2** Also called: **coffee beans.** the beanlike seeds of the coffee tree, used to make this beverage. **3** the tree yielding these seeds. **4a** a light brown colour. **4b** (*as adj*): *a coffee carpet.* [C16: from It. *caffè*, from Turkish *kahve*, from Ar. *qahwah* coffee, wine]

coffee bar *n* a café; snack bar.

coffee cup *n* a small cup for serving coffee.

coffee house *n* a place where coffee is served, esp. one that was a fashionable meeting place in 18th-century London.

coffee mill *n* a machine for grinding roasted coffee beans.

coffeepot ('kɒfɪˌpɒt) *n* a pot in which coffee is brewed or served.

coffee shop *n* a shop where coffee is sold or drunk.

coffee table *n* a low table on which coffee may be served.

coffee-table book *n* a book, usually glossily illustrated, designed chiefly to be looked at, rather than read.

coffer ➊ ('kɒfə) *n* **1** a chest, esp. for storing valuables. **2** (*usually pl*) a store of money. **3** an ornamental sunken panel in a ceiling, dome, etc. **4** a watertight box or chamber. **5** short for **cofferdam.** ◆ *vb* (*tr*) **6** to store, as in a coffer. **7** to decorate (a ceiling, dome, etc.) with coffers. [C13: from OF *coffre*, from L, from Gk *kophinos* basket]

cofferdam ('kɒfəˌdæm) *n* **1** a watertight structure that encloses an area under water, pumped dry to enable construction work to be carried out. **2** (on a ship) a compartment separating two bulkheads, as for insulation or to serve as a barrier against the escape of gas, etc. ◆ Often shortened to **coffer.**

coffin ('kɒfɪn) *n* **1** a box in which a corpse is buried or cremated. **2** the bony part of a horse's foot. ◆ *vb* **3** (*tr*) to place in or as in a coffin. [C14: from OF *cofin*, from L *cophinus* basket]

coffin nail *n* a slang term for **cigarette.**

coffle ('kɒfᵊl) *n* a line of slaves, beasts, etc., fastened together. [C18: from Ar. *qāfilah* caravan]

C of S *abbrev. for* Church of Scotland.

cog[1] (kɒg) *n* **1** any of the teeth or projections on the rim of a gearwheel. **2** a gearwheel, esp. a small one. **3** a person or thing playing a small part in a large organization or process. [C13: of Scand. origin]

cog[2] (kɒg) *n* **1** a tenon that projects from the end of a timber beam for fitting into a mortise. ◆ *vb* **cogs, cogging, cogged.** **2** (*tr*) to join (pieces of wood) with cogs. [C19: from ?]

cogent ➊ ('kəʊdʒənt) *adj* compelling belief or assent; forcefully convincing. [C17: from L *cōgent-*, *cōgēns*, from *co-* together + *agere* to drive]
▸'**cogency** *n* ▸'**cogently** *adv*

cogitate ➊ ('kɒdʒɪˌteɪt) *vb* **cogitates, cogitating, cogitated.** to think deeply about (a problem, possibility, etc.); ponder. [C16: from L, from *co-* (intensive) + *agitāre* to turn over]
▸ˌ**cogi'tation** *n* ▸'**cogitative** *adj* ▸'**cogiˌtator** *n*

Cognac ('kɒnjæk) *n* (*sometimes not cap.*) a high-quality grape brandy, distilled near Cognac in SW France.

cognate ➊ ('kɒgneɪt) *adj* **1** akin; related: *cognate languages.* **2** related by blood or descended from a common maternal ancestor. ◆ *n* **3** something that is cognate with something else. [C17: from L, from *co-* same + *gnātus* born, var. of *nātus*, p.p. of *nāscī* to be born]
▸'**cognately** *adv* ▸'**cognateness** *n* ▸**cog'nation** *n*

cognition ➊ (kɒg'nɪʃən) *n* **1** the mental act or process by which knowledge is acquired, including perception, intuition, and reasoning. **2** the knowledge that results from such an act or process. [C15: from L, from *co-* (intensive) + *nōscere* to learn]
▸**cog'nitional** *adj* ▸'**cognitive** *adj*

cognitive therapy *n Psychol.* a form of psychotherapy in which the patient is encouraged to change the way he sees the world and himself: used particularly to treat depression.

cognizable *or* **cognisable** ('kɒgnɪzəbᵊl, 'kɒnɪ-) *adj* **1** perceptible. **2** *Law.* susceptible to the jurisdiction of a court.

cognizance *or* **cognisance** ('kɒgnɪzəns, 'kɒnɪ-) *n* **1** knowledge; acknowledgment. **2 take cognizance of.** to take notice of; acknowledge, esp. officially. **3** the range or scope of knowledge or perception. **4** *Law.* the right of a court to hear and determine a cause or matter. **5** *Heraldry.* a distinguishing badge or bearing. [C14: from OF, from L *cognōscere* to learn; see COGNITION]

cognizant *or* **cognisant** ('kɒgnɪzənt, 'kɒnɪ-) *adj* (usually foll. by *of*) aware; having knowledge.

cognomen (kɒg'nəʊmɛn) *n, pl* **cognomens** *or* **cognomina** (-'nɒmɪnə, -'nəʊ-). (originally) an ancient Roman's third name or nickname, which later became his family name. [C19: from L: additional name, from *co-* together + *nōmen* name]
▸**cognominal** (kɒg'nɒmɪnᵊl, -'nəʊ-) *adj*

cognoscenti (ˌkɒnjəʊ'ʃɛntɪ, ˌkɒgnəʊ-) *or* **conoscenti** (ˌkɒnəʊ'ʃɛntɪ) *pl n, sing* **cognoscente** *or* **conoscente** (-tiː). (*sometimes sing*) people with informed appreciation of a particular field, esp. in the fine arts; connoisseurs. [C18: from obs. It., from L *cognōscere* to learn]

cogwheel ('kɒgˌwiːl) *n* another name for **gearwheel.**

cohab ('kəʊˌhæb) *n* a sexual partner with whom one lives but to whom one is not married. [C20: a shortened form of *cohabitee*; see COHABIT]

cohabit (kəʊ'hæbɪt) *vb* (*intr*) to live together as husband and wife, esp. without being married. [C16: from L *co-* together + *habitāre* to live]
▸ˌ**cohabi'tee, co'habitant,** *or* **co'habiter** *n*

cohabitation (kəʊˌhæbɪ'teɪʃən) *n* **1** the state or condition of living together as husband and wife without being married. **2** (of political parties) the state or condition of cooperating for specific purposes without forming a coalition.

coheir (kəʊ'ɛə) *n* a person who inherits jointly with others.
▸**co'heiress** *fem n*

cohere ➊ (kəʊ'hɪə) *vb* **coheres, cohering, cohered.** (*intr*) **1** to hold or stick firmly together. **2** to be connected logically; be consistent. **3** *Physics.* to be held together by the action of molecular forces. [C16: from L *co-* together + *haerēre* to cling]

coherence ➊ (kəʊ'hɪərəns) *or* **coherency** *n* **1** logical or natural connection or consistency. **2** another word for **cohesion** (sense 1).

coherent ➊ (kəʊ'hɪərənt) *adj* **1** capable of intelligible speech. **2** logical; consistent and orderly. **3** cohering or sticking together. **4** *Physics.* (of two or more waves) having the same phase or a fixed phase difference: *coherent light.*
▸**co'herently** *adv*

cohesion (kəʊ'hiːʒən) *n* **1** the act or state of cohering; tendency to unite. **2** *Physics.* the force that holds together the atoms or molecules in a solid or liquid, as distinguished from adhesion. **3** *Bot.* the fusion in some plants of flower parts, such as petals, that are usually separate. [C17: from L *cohaesus*, p.p. of *cohaerēre* to COHERE]
▸**co'hesive** *adj*

coho ('kəʊhəʊ) *n, pl* **coho** *or* **cohos.** a Pacific salmon. Also called: **silver salmon.** [from ?]

cohort ➊ ('kəʊhɔːt) *n* **1** one of the ten units of an ancient Roman Legion. **2** any band of warriors or associates: *the cohorts of Satan.* **3** *Chiefly US.* an associate or follower. [C15: from L *cohors* yard, company of soldiers]

COHSE ('kəʊzɪ) *n* (formerly, in Britain) *acronym for* Confederation of Health Service Employees.

COI (in Britain) *abbrev. for* Central Office of Information.

THESAURUS

coerce *vb* = **force,** browbeat, bulldoze (*inf.*), bully, compel, constrain, dragoon, drive, intimidate, press-gang, pressurize, railroad (*inf.*), twist (someone's) arm (*inf.*)

coercion *n* **1** = **force,** browbeating, bullying, compulsion, constraint, duress, intimidation, pressure, strong-arm tactics (*inf.*), threats

coffer *n* **1** = **chest,** ark (*dialect*), case, casket, kist (*Scot. & N English dialect*), repository, strongbox, treasure chest, treasury **2** *usually plu* = **funds,** assets, capital, finances, means, reserves, treasury, vaults

cogency *n* = **conviction,** force, potency, power, strength

cogent *adj* = **convincing,** compelling, compulsive, conclusive, effective, forceful, forcible, influential, irresistible, potent, powerful, strong, urgent, weighty

cogitate *vb* = **think,** consider, contemplate, deliberate, meditate, mull over, muse, ponder, reflect, ruminate

cogitation *n* = **thought,** consideration, contemplation, deliberation, meditation, reflection, rumination

cognate *adj* **1** = **related,** affiliated, akin, alike, allied, analogous, associated, connected, kindred, similar

cognition *n* **2** = **perception,** apprehension, awareness, comprehension, discernment, insight, intelligence, reasoning, understanding

cohere *vb* **1** = **stick together,** adhere, bind, cling, coalesce, combine, consolidate, fuse, glue, hold, unite **2** = **be consistent,** agree, be connected, be logical, correspond, hang together, harmonize, hold good, hold water, square

coherence *n* **1** = **consistency,** agreement, concordance, congruity, connection, consonance, correspondence, rationality, union, unity

coherent *adj* **1** = **intelligible,** articulate, comprehensible **2** = **consistent,** logical, lucid, meaningful, orderly, organized, rational, reasoned, systematic
Antonyms *adj* ≠ **intelligible:** incomprehensible, unintelligible ≠ **consistent:** confusing, disjointed, illogical, inconsistent, meaningless, rambling, vague

cohort *n* **2** = **company,** band, contingent, legion, regiment, squadron, troop **3** *Chiefly U.S.* =

coif (kɔɪf) *n* **1** a close-fitting cap worn under a veil in the Middle Ages. **2** a leather cap worn under a chain-mail hood. **3** (kwɑːf). a less common word for **coiffure** (sense 1). ◆ *vb* **coifs, coiffing, coiffed.** (*tr*) **4** to cover with or as if with a coif. **5** (kwɑːf). to arrange (the hair). [C14: from OF *coiffe,* from LL *cofea* helmet, cap, from ?]

coiffeur (kwɑːˈfɜː) *n* a hairdresser.
▸**coiffeuse** (kwɑːˈfɜːz) *fem n*

coiffure (kwɑːˈfjʊə) *n* **1** a hairstyle. **2** an obsolete word for **headdress.** ◆ *vb* **coiffures, coiffuring, coiffured. 3** (*tr*) to dress or arrange (the hair).

coign of vantage (kɔɪn) *n* an advantageous position for observation or action.

coil[1] Ⓣ (kɔɪl) *vb* **1** to wind or gather (ropes, hair, etc.) into loops or (of ropes, hair, etc.) to be formed in such loops. **2** (*intr*) to move in a winding course. ◆ *n* **3** something wound in a connected series of loops. **4** a single loop of such a series. **5** an arrangement of pipes in a spiral or loop, as in a condenser. **6** an electrical conductor wound into the form of a spiral, to provide inductance or a magnetic field. **7** an intrauterine contraceptive device in the shape of a coil. **8** the transformer in a petrol engine that supplies the high voltage to the sparking plugs. [C16: from OF *coillir* to collect together; see CULL]

coil[2] (kɔɪl) *n* the troubles of the world (in Shakespeare's phrase **this mortal coil**). [C16: from ?]

coin Ⓣ (kɔɪn) *n* **1** a metal disc or piece used as money. **2** metal currency, as opposed to paper currency, etc. **3** *Archit.* a variant spelling of **quoin. 4 pay (a person) back in (his) own coin.** to treat (a person) in the way that he has treated others. ◆ *vb* (*tr*) **5** to make or stamp (coins). **6** to make into a coin. **7** to fabricate or invent (words, etc.). **8** *Inf.* to make (money) rapidly (esp. in **coin it in**). [C14: from OF: stamping die, from L *cuneus* wedge]

coinage (ˈkɔɪnɪdʒ) *n* **1** coins collectively. **2** the act of striking coins. **3** the currency of a country. **4** the act of inventing something, esp. a word or phrase. **5** a newly invented word, phrase, usage, etc.

coincide Ⓣ (ˌkəʊɪnˈsaɪd) *vb* **coincides, coinciding, coincided.** (*intr*) **1** to occur or exist simultaneously. **2** to be identical in nature, character, etc. **3** to agree. [C18: from Med. L, from L *co-* together + *incidere* to occur, befall, from *cadere* to fall]

coincidence Ⓣ (kəʊˈɪnsɪdəns) *n* **1** a chance occurrence of events remarkable either for being simultaneous or for apparently being connected. **2** the fact, condition, or state of coinciding. **3** (*modifier*) *Electronics.* of or relating to a circuit that produces an output pulse only when both its input terminals receive pulses within a specified interval: *coincidence gate.*

coincident Ⓣ (kəʊˈɪnsɪdənt) *adj* **1** having the same position in space or time. **2** (usually *postpositive* and foll. by *with*) in exact agreement.
▸**coˌinciˈdental** *adj* ▸**coˌinciˈdentally** *adv*

coin-op (ˈkɔɪnˌɒp) *n* a launderette or other installation in which the machines are operated by the insertion of coins.
▸**ˈcoin-ˌoperˌated** *adj*

Cointreau (ˈkwɑːntrəʊ) *n Trademark.* a colourless liqueur with orange flavouring.

coir (ˈkɔɪə) *n* the fibre from the husk of the coconut, used in making rope and matting. [C16: from Malayalam *kāyar* rope, from *kāyaru* to be twisted]

coitus Ⓣ (ˈkəʊɪtəs) *or* **coition** (kəʊˈɪʃən) *n* a technical term for **sexual intercourse.** [C18: from L, from *coīre* to meet, from *īre* to go]
▸**ˈcoital** *adj*

coke[1] (kəʊk) *n* **1** a solid-fuel product produced by distillation of coal to drive off its volatile constituents: used as a fuel. **2** the layer formed in the cylinders of a car engine by incomplete combustion of the fuel. ◆ *vb* **cokes, coking, coked. 3** to become or convert into coke. [C17: prob. var. of C14 N English dialect *colk* core, from ?]

coke[2] (kəʊk) *n Sl.* short for **cocaine.**

Coke (kəʊk) *n Trademark.* short for **Coca-Cola.**

col (kɒl) *n* **1** Also called: **saddle.** the lowest point of a ridge connecting two mountain peaks. **2** *Meteorol.* a low-pressure region between two anticyclones. [C19: from F: neck, col, from L *collum* neck]

Col. *abbrev. for:* **1** Colombia(n). **2** Colonel. **3** *Bible.* Colossians.

Col. *abbrev. for:* **1** Colombia(n). **2** Colonel. **3** *Bible.* Colossians.

col- *prefix* a variant of **com-** before *l: collateral.*

cola *or* **kola** (ˈkəʊlə) *n* **1** either of two trees widely cultivated in tropical regions for their seeds (see **cola nut**). **2** a sweet carbonated drink flavoured with cola nuts. [C18: from *kola,* prob. var. of W African *kolo* nut]

colander (ˈkɒləndə, ˈkʌl-) *or* **cullender** *n* a pan with a perforated bottom for straining or rinsing foods. [C14 *colyndore,* prob. from OProvençal *colador,* from LL, from L *cōlum* sieve]

cola nut *n* any of the seeds of the cola tree, which contain caffeine and theobromine and are used medicinally and in soft drinks.

colchicine (ˈkɒltʃɪˌsiːn, -sɪn, ˈkɒlkɪ-) *n* a pale yellow crystalline alkaloid extracted from seeds or corms of the autumn crocus and used in the treatment of gout. [C19: from COLCHICUM + -INE[2]]

colchicum (ˈkɒltʃɪkəm, ˈkɒlkɪ-) *n* **1** any Eurasian plant of the lily family, such as the autumn crocus. **2** the dried seeds or corms of the autumn crocus. [C16: from L, from Gk, from *kolkhikos* of *Colchis,* ancient country on the Black Sea]

cold Ⓣ (kəʊld) *adj* **1** having relatively little warmth; of a rather low temperature: *cold weather; cold hands.* **2** without proper warmth: *this meal is cold.* **3** lacking in affection or enthusiasm: *a cold manner.* **4** not affected by emotion: *cold logic.* **5** dead. **6** sexually unresponsive or frigid. **7** lacking in freshness: *a cold scent; cold news.* **8** chilling to the spirit; depressing. **9** (of a colour) having violet, blue, or green predominating; giving no sensation of warmth. **10** *Sl.* unconscious. **11** *Inf.* (of a seeker) far from the object of a search. **12** denoting the contacting of potential customers, voters, etc., without previously approaching them in order to establish their interest: *cold mailing.* **13 cold comfort.** little or no comfort. **14 leave (someone) cold.** *Inf.* to fail to excite: *the performance left me cold.* **15 throw cold water on.** *Inf.* to be unenthusiastic about or discourage. ◆ *n* **16** the absence of heat regarded as a positive force: *the cold took away our breath.* **17** the sensation caused by loss or lack of heat. **18 (out) in the cold.** *Inf.* neglected; ignored. **19** an acute viral infection of the upper respiratory passages characterized by discharge of watery mucus from the nose, sneezing, etc. **20 catch a cold.** *Inf.* to make a financial loss. ◆ *adv* **21** *Inf.* without preparation: *he played his part cold.* [OE *ceald*]
▸**ˈcoldish** *adj* ▸**ˈcoldly** *adv* ▸**ˈcoldness** *n*

cold-blooded Ⓣ *adj* **1** having or showing a lack of feeling or pity. **2** *Inf.* particularly sensitive to cold. **3** (of all animals except birds and mammals) having a body temperature that varies with that of the surroundings. Technical name: **poikilothermic.**
▸**ˌcold-ˈbloodedly** *adv* ▸**ˌcold-ˈbloodedness** *n*

cold cathode *n Electronics.* a cathode from which electrons are emitted at an ambient temperature.

cold chisel *n* a toughened steel chisel.

cold cream *n* an emulsion of water and fat used for softening and cleansing the skin.

cold cuts *pl n* cooked meats sliced and served cold.

cold feet *n Inf.* loss or lack of confidence.

cold frame *n* an unheated wooden frame with a glass top, used to protect young plants.

cold front *n Meteorol.* the boundary line between a warm air mass and the cold air pushing it from beneath and behind as it moves.

cold-hearted Ⓣ *adj* lacking in feeling or warmth; unkind.
▸**ˌcold-ˈheartedly** *adv* ▸**ˌcold-ˈheartedness** *n*

cold-rolled *adj* (of metal sheets, etc.) having been rolled without heating, producing a smooth surface finish.

cold shoulder *Inf.* ◆ *n* **1** (often preceded by *the*) a show of indifference; a slight. ◆ *vb* **cold-shoulder.** (*tr*) **2** to treat with indifference.

cold sore *n* a cluster of blisters at the margin of the lips: a form of herpes simplex.

cold start *n Computing.* the reloading of a program or operating system.

cold storage *n* **1** the storage of things in an artificially cooled place for preservation. **2** *Inf.* a state of temporary suspension: *to put an idea into cold storage.*

THESAURUS

supporter, accomplice, assistant, associate, comrade, follower, henchman, mate, myrmidon, partner, protagonist, sidekick (*sl.*)

coil[1] *vb* **1, 2 = wind**, convolute, curl, entwine, loop, snake, spiral, twine, twist, wreathe, writhe

coin *n* **2 = money**, cash, change, copper, dosh (*Brit. & Austral. sl.*), silver, specie ◆ *vb* **7 = invent**, conceive, create, fabricate, forge, formulate, frame, make up, mint, mould, originate, think up

coincide *vb* **1 = occur simultaneously**, be concurrent, coexist, synchronize **3 = agree**, accord, concur, correspond, harmonize, match, square, tally
Antonyms *vb* ≠ **agree:** be inconsistent, be unlike, contradict, differ, disagree, diverge, divide, part, separate

coincidence *n* **1 = chance**, accident, eventuality, fluke, fortuity, happy accident, luck, stroke of luck **2 = coinciding**, concomitance, concurrence, conjunction, correlation, correspondence, synchronism

coincident *adj* **1 = coinciding**, concomitant, concurring, consonant, contemporaneous, coordinate, correspondent, synchronous

coincidental *adj* **1 = coinciding**, coincident, concomitant, concurrent, simultaneous, synchronous

coitus *n* **= sexual intercourse**, coition, congress, copulation, coupling, mating, nookie (*sl.*), rumpy-pumpy (*sl.*), the other (*inf.*), union

cold *adj* **1 = chilly**, arctic, biting, bitter, bleak, chilled, cool, freezing, frigid, frosty, frozen, gelid, harsh, icy, inclement, parky (*Brit. inf.*), raw, wintry **3 = unfriendly**, aloof, apathetic, cold-blooded, dead, distant, frigid, glacial, indifferent, inhospitable, lukewarm, passionless, phlegmatic, reserved, spiritless, standoffish, stony, undemonstrative, unfeeling, unmoved, unresponsive, unsympathetic ◆ *n* **16, 17 = coldness**, chill, chilliness, frigidity, frostiness, iciness
Antonyms *adj* ≠ **chilly:** balmy, heated, hot, mild, sunny, warm ≠ **unfriendly:** alive, animated, caring, compassionate, demonstrative, emotional, friendly, loving, open, passionate, responsive, spirited, sympathetic, warm

cold-blooded *adj* **1 = callous**, barbarous, brutal, cruel, dispassionate, heartless, inhuman, merciless, pitiless, ruthless, savage, steely, stony-hearted, unemotional, unfeeling, unmoved
Antonyms *adj* caring, charitable, civilized, concerned, emotional, feeling, friendly, humane, involved, kind, kind-hearted, merciful, open, passionate, sensitive, warm

cold-hearted *adj* **= heartless**, callous, detached, frigid, hardhearted, harsh, indifferent, inhuman, insensitive, stony-hearted, uncaring, unfeeling, unkind, unsympathetic

cold-heartedness *n* **= heartlessness**, callousness, chilliness, coldness, detachment, flintiness, frigidity, frigidness, hardheartedness, harshness, indifference, inhumanity, insensi-

cold sweat *n Inf.* a bodily reaction to fear or nervousness, characterized by chill and moist skin.

cold turkey *n Sl.* **1** a method of curing drug addiction by abrupt withdrawal of all doses. **2** the withdrawal symptoms, esp. nausea and shivering, brought on by this method.

cold war *n* a state of political hostility and military tension between two countries or power blocs, involving propaganda, threats, etc., esp. that between the American and Soviet blocs after World War II (the **Cold War**).

cold wave *n* **1** *Meteorol.* a sudden spell of low temperatures over a wide area. **2** *Hairdressing.* a permanent wave made by chemical agents applied at normal temperatures.

cole (kəʊl) *n* any of various plants such as the cabbage and rape. Also called: **colewort.** [OE *cāl,* from L *caulis* cabbage]

coleopter (ˌkɒlɪˈɒptə) *n Aeronautics.* an aircraft that has an annular wing with the fuselage and engine on the centre line.

coleopteran (ˌkɒlɪˈɒptərən) *n also* **coleopteron. 1** any of the order of insects in which the forewings are modified to form shell-like protective elytra. It includes the beetles and weevils. ◆ *adj also* **coleopterous. 2** of, relating to, or belonging to this order. [C18: from NL, from Gk, from *koleon* sheath + *pteron* wing]

coleslaw (ˈkəʊlˌslɔː) *n* a salad of shredded cabbage, mayonnaise, carrots, onions, etc. [C19: from Du. *koolsla,* from *koolsalade,* lit.: cabbage salad]

colestipol (kəˈlɛstɪˌpɒl) *n* a drug that reduces the level of cholesterol in the blood: used to prevent atherosclerosis.

coletit (ˈkəʊltɪt) *n* another name for **coal tit.**

coleus (ˈkəʊlɪəs) *n, pl* **coleuses.** any plant of the Old World genus *Coleus:* cultivated for their variegated leaves. [C19: from NL, from Gk, var. of *koleon* sheath]

coley (ˈkəʊlɪ, ˈkɒlɪ) *n Brit.* any of various edible fishes, esp. the coalfish.

colic (ˈkɒlɪk) *n* a condition characterized by acute spasmodic abdominal pain, esp. that caused by inflammation, distention, etc., of the gastrointestinal tract. [C15: from OF, from LL, from Gk *kōlon,* var. of *kolon* COLON[2]]
▸ **ˈcolicky** *adj*

coliform bacteria (ˈkɒlɪfɔːm) *pl n* a large group of bacteria that inhabit the intestinal tract of man.

coliseum (ˌkɒlɪˈsɪəm) *or* **colosseum** (ˌkɒləˈsɪəm) *n* a large building, such as a stadium, used for entertainments, sports, etc. [C18: from Med. L, var. of *Colosseum,* amphitheatre in Rome]

colitis (kɒˈlaɪtɪs) *n* inflammation of the colon.

collaborate Ⓣ (kəˈlæbəˌreɪt) *vb* **collaborates, collaborating, collaborated.** (*intr*) **1** (often foll. by *on, with,* etc.) to work with another or others on a joint project. **2** to cooperate as a traitor, esp. with an enemy occupying one's own country. [C19: from LL, from L *com-* together + *labōrāre* to work]
▸ **colˌlaboˈration** *n* ▸ **colˈlaborative** *adj* ▸ **colˈlaboˌrator** *n*

collage (kəˈlɑːʒ, kɒ-) *n* **1** an art form in which compositions are made out of pieces of paper, cloth, photographs, etc., pasted on a dry ground. **2** a composition made in this way. **3** any work, such as a piece of music, created by combining unrelated styles. [C20: F, from *colle* glue, from Gk *kolla*]
▸ **colˈlagist** *n*

collagen (ˈkɒlədʒən) *n* a fibrous protein of connective tissue and bones that yields gelatine on boiling. [C19: from Gk *kolla* glue + -GEN]

collapsar (kɒˈlæpsɑː) *n Astron.* another name for **black hole.**

collapse Ⓣ (kəˈlæps) *vb* **collapses, collapsing, collapsed. 1** (*intr*) to fall down or cave in suddenly: *the whole building collapsed.* **2** (*intr*) to fail completely. **3** (*intr*) to break down or fall down from lack of strength. **4** to fold (furniture, etc.) compactly or (of furniture, etc.) to be designed to fold compactly. ◆ *n* **5** the act or instance of suddenly falling down, caving in, or crumbling. **6** a sudden failure or breakdown. [C18: from L, from *collābī* to fall in ruins, from *lābī* to fall]
▸ **colˈlapsible** *or* **colˈlapsable** *adj* ▸ **colˌlapsiˈbility** *n*

collar Ⓣ (ˈkɒlə) *n* **1** the part of a garment around the neck and shoulders, often detachable or folded over. **2** any band, necklace, garland, etc., encircling the neck. **3** a band or chain of leather, rope, or metal placed around an animal's neck. **4** *Biol.* a marking resembling a collar, such as that found around the necks of some birds. **5** a section of a shaft or rod having a locally increased diameter to provide a bearing seat or a locating ring. **6** a cut of meat, esp. bacon, taken from around the neck of an animal. ◆ *vb* (*tr*) **7** to put a collar on; furnish with a collar. **8** to seize by the collar. **9** *Inf.* to seize; arrest; detain. [C13: from L *collāre* neckband, from *collum* neck]

collarbone (ˈkɒləˌbəʊn) *n* the nontechnical name for **clavicle.**

collard (ˈkɒləd) *n* a variety of the cabbage, having a crown of edible leaves. See also **kale.** [C18: var. of *colewort,* from COLE + WORT]

collate Ⓣ (kɒˈleɪt, kə-) *vb* **collates, collating, collated.** (*tr*) **1** to examine and compare (texts, statements, etc.) in order to note points of agreement and disagreement. **2** to check the number and order of (the pages of a book). **3** *Bookbinding.* **3a** to check the sequence of (the sections of a book) after gathering. **3b** a nontechnical word for **gather** (sense 8). **4** (often foll. by *to*) *Christianity.* to appoint (an incumbent) to a benefice. [C16: from L, from *com-* together + *lātus,* p.p. of *ferre* to bring]
▸ **colˈlator** *n*

collateral Ⓣ (kɒˈlætərəl, kə-) *n* **1a** security pledged for the repayment of a loan. **1b** (*as modifier*): *a collateral loan.* **2** a person, animal, or plant descended from the same ancestor as another but through a different line. ◆ *adj* **3** situated or running side by side. **4** descended from a common ancestor but through different lines. **5** serving to support or corroborate. [C14: from Med. L, from L *com-* together + *laterālis* of the side, from *latus* side]
▸ **colˈlaterally** *adv*

collateral damage *n Mil.* unintentional damage to civil property and civilian casualties, caused by military operations.

collation (kɒˈleɪʃən, kə-) *n* **1** the act or process of collating. **2** a description of the technical features of a book. **3** *RC Church.* a light meal permitted on fast days. **4** any light informal meal.

colleague Ⓣ (ˈkɒliːg) *n* a fellow worker or member of a staff, department, profession, etc. [C16: from F, from L *collēga,* from *com-* together + *lēgāre* to choose]

collect[1] Ⓣ (kəˈlɛkt) *vb* **1** to gather together or be gathered together. **2** to accumulate (stamps, books, etc.) as a hobby or for study. **3** (*tr*) to call for or receive payment of (taxes, dues, etc.). **4** (*tr*) to regain control of (oneself, one's emotions, etc.) as after a shock or surprise: *he collected his wits.* **5** (*tr*) to fetch: *collect your own post.* **6** (*intr;* sometimes foll. by *on*) *Sl.* to receive large sums of money. **7** (*tr*) *Austral. & NZ inf.* to collide with; be hit by. ◆ *adv, adj* **8** *US.* (of telephone calls, etc.) on a reverse-charge basis. [C16: from L, from *com-* together + *legere* to gather]

collect[2] (ˈkɒlɛkt) *n Christianity.* a short Church prayer in Communion and other services. [C13: from Med. L *collecta* (from *ōrātiō ad collēctam* prayer at the assembly), from L *colligere* to COLLECT[1]]

collectable *or* **collectible** (kəˈlɛktəbᵊl) *adj* **1** (of antiques) of interest to a collector. ◆ *n* **2** (*often pl*) any object regarded as being of interest to a collector.

collected Ⓣ (kəˈlɛktɪd) *adj* **1** in full control of one's faculties; composed. **2** assembled in totality or brought together into one volume or a set of volumes: *the collected works of Dickens.*
▸ **colˈlectedly** *adv* ▸ **colˈlectedness** *n*

collection Ⓣ (kəˈlɛkʃən) *n* **1** the act or process of collecting. **2** a number of things collected or assembled together. **3** something gathered into a mass or pile; accumulation: *a collection of rubbish.* **4** a sum of money collected or solicited, as in church. **5** removal, esp. regular removal of letters from a postbox. **6** (*often pl*) (at Oxford University) a college examination or an oral report by a tutor.

collective Ⓣ (kəˈlɛktɪv) *adj* **1** formed or assembled by collection. **2** forming a whole or aggregate. **3** of, done by, or characteristic of individuals acting in cooperation. ◆ *n* **4a** a cooperative enterprise or unit, such as a collective farm. **4b** the members of such a cooperative. **5** short for **collective noun.**
▸ **colˈlectively** *adv* ▸ **colˈlectiveness** *n* ▸ **ˌcollecˈtivity** *n*

collective bargaining *n* negotiation between a trade union and an employer or an employers' organization on the incomes and working conditions of the employees.

THESAURUS

tiveness, insensitivity, mercilessness, pitilessness, steeliness, stony-heartedness, unfeelingness, unkindness, unresponsiveness

collaborate *vb* **1** = **work together**, cooperate, coproduce, join forces, participate, play ball (*inf.*), team up **2** = **conspire**, collude, cooperate, fraternize

collaboration *n* **1** = **teamwork**, alliance, association, concert, cooperation, partnership

collaborator *n* **1** = **co-worker**, associate, colleague, confederate, partner, team-mate **2** = **traitor**, collaborationist, fraternizer, quisling, turncoat

collapse *vb* **1** = **fall down**, cave in, crumple, fall, fall apart at the seams, give way, subside **2** = **fail**, come to nothing, fold, founder, go belly-up (*inf.*) **3** = **faint**, break down, crack up ◆ *n* **5** = **falling down**, cave-in, disintegration, falling apart, ruin, subsidence **6** = **failure**, breakdown, downfall, exhaustion, faint, flop, prostration, slump

collar *vb* **9** *Informal* = **seize**, apprehend, appropriate, arrest, capture, catch, catch in the act, grab, lay hands on, nab (*inf.*), nail (*inf.*)

collate *vb* **1** = **collect**, adduce, analogize, compare, compose, gather (*Printing*)

collateral *n* **1a** = **security**, assurance, deposit, guarantee, pledge, surety ◆ *adj* **3** = **concurrent**, not lineal, parallel **4** = **related 5** = **secondary**, ancillary, auxiliary, confirmatory, corroborative, subordinate, supporting

colleague *n* = **fellow worker**, aider, ally, assistant, associate, auxiliary, coadjutor (*rare*), collaborator, companion, comrade, confederate, confrère, helper, partner, team-mate, workmate

collect[1] *vb* **1** = **assemble**, cluster, congregate, convene, converge, flock together, rally **2** = **gather**, accumulate, aggregate, amass, assemble, heap, hoard, save, stockpile **6** = **obtain**, acquire, muster, raise, secure, solicit

Antonyms *vb* ≠ **gather:** disperse, distribute, scatter, spread, strew

collected *adj* **1** = **calm**, as cool as a cucumber, composed, confident, cool, keeping one's cool, placid, poised, sedate, self-controlled, self-possessed, serene, together (*sl.*), unfazed (*inf.*), unperturbable, unperturbed, unruffled

Antonyms *adj* agitated, distressed, emotional, excitable, irritable, nervous, perturbed, ruffled, shaky, troubled, twitchy (*inf.*), unpoised, unsteady

collection *n* **2, 3** = **accumulation**, anthology, compilation, congeries, heap, hoard, mass, pile, set, stockpile, store **4** = **contribution**, alms, offering, offertory

collective *adj* **2, 3** = **combined**, aggregate, common, composite, concerted, cooperative, corporate, cumulative, joint, shared, unified, united

Antonyms *adj* divided, individual, piecemeal, split, uncombined, uncooperative

collective noun *n* a noun that is singular in form but that refers to a group of people or things.

> **USAGE NOTE** Collective nouns are usually used with singular verbs: *the family is on holiday; General Motors is mounting a big sales campaign.* In British usage, however, plural verbs are sometimes employed in this context, esp. where reference is being made to a collection of individual objects or people rather than to the group as a unit: *the family are all on holiday.* Care should be taken that the same collective noun is not treated as both singular and plural in the same sentence: *the family is well and sends its best wishes* or *the family are all well and send their best wishes,* but not *the family is well and send their best wishes.*

collective ownership *n* ownership by a group for the benefit of members of that group.
collective unconscious *n* (in Jungian psychological theory) a part of the unconscious mind incorporating patterns of memories, instincts, and experiences common to all mankind.
collectivism (kə'lɛktɪˌvɪzəm) *n* the principle of ownership of the means of production by the state or the people.
▸**col'lectivist** *n* ▸**colˌlectiv'istic** *adj*
collectivize *or* **collectivise** (kə'lɛktɪˌvaɪz) *vb* **collectivizes, collectivizing, collectivized** *or* **collectivises, collectivising, collectivised.** (*tr*) to organize according to the principles of collectivism.
▸**colˌlectivi'zation** *or* **colˌlectivi'sation** *n*
collector ❶ (kə'lɛktə) *n* **1** a person or thing that collects. **2** a person employed to collect debts, rents, etc. **3** a person who collects objects as a hobby. **4** (in India, formerly) the head of a district administration. **5** *Electronics.* the region in a transistor into which charge carriers flow from the base.
colleen ('kɒliːn, kɒ'liːn) *n* an Irish word for **girl.** [C19: from Irish Gaelic *cailīn*]
college ('kɒlɪdʒ) *n* **1** an institution of higher education; part of a university. **2** a school or an institution providing specialized courses: *a college of music.* **3** the buildings in which a college is housed. **4** the staff and students of a college. **5** an organized body of persons with specific rights and duties: *an electoral college.* **6** a body organized within a particular profession, concerned with regulating standards. **7** *Brit.* a name given to some secondary schools. [C14: from L, from *collēga;* see COLLEAGUE]
College of Cardinals *n RC Church.* the collective body of cardinals having the function of electing and advising the pope.
college of education *n Brit.* a professional training college for teachers.
collegian (kə'liːdʒɪən) *n* a member of a college.
collegiate (kə'liːdʒɪɪt) *adj* **1** Also: **col'legial.** of or relating to a college or college students. **2** (of a university) composed of various colleges of equal standing.
collegiate church *n* **1** *RC Church, Church of England.* a church that has an endowed chapter of canons and prebendaries attached to it but that is not a cathedral. **2** *US Protestantism.* one of a group of churches presided over by a body of pastors. **3** *Scot. Protestantism.* a church served by two or more ministers.
col legno ('kɒl 'lɛgnəʊ, 'leɪnjəʊ) *adv Music.* to be played (on a stringed instrument) with the back of the bow. [It.: with the wood]
Colles' fracture ('kɒlɪs) *n* a fracture of the radius just above the wrist with backward and outward displacement of the hand. [C19: after Abraham *Colles* (d. 1843), Irish surgeon]
collet ('kɒlɪt) *n* **1** (in a jewellery setting) a band or coronet-shaped claw that holds an individual stone. **2** *Mechanical engineering.* an externally tapered sleeve made in two or more segments and used to grip a shaft passed through its centre. **3** *Horology.* a small metal collar that supports the inner end of the hairspring. [C16: from OF: a little collar, from *col,* from L *collum* neck]
collide ❶ (kə'laɪd) *vb* **collides, colliding, collided.** (*intr*) **1** to crash together with a violent impact. **2** to conflict; clash; disagree. [C17: from L, from *com-* together + *laedere* to strike]
collider (kə'laɪdə) *n Physics.* a particle accelerator in which beams of particles are made to collide.
collie ('kɒlɪ) *n* any of several silky-coated breeds of dog developed for herding sheep and cattle. [C17: Scot., prob. from earlier *colie* black from *cole* coal]
collier ('kɒlɪə) *n Chiefly Brit.* **1** a coal miner. **2a** a ship designed to transport coal. **2b** a member of its crew. [C14: from COAL + -IER]
colliery ('kɒljərɪ) *n, pl* **collieries.** *Chiefly Brit.* a coal mine.
collimate ('kɒlɪˌmeɪt) *vb* **collimates, collimating, collimated.** (*tr*) **1** to adjust the line of sight of (an optical instrument). **2** to use a collimator on (a beam of radiation). **3** to make parallel or bring into line. [C17: from NL *collimāre,* erroneously for L *collīneāre* to aim, from *com-* (intensive) + *līneāre,* from *līnea* line]
▸ˌ**colli'mation** *n*
collimator ('kɒlɪˌmeɪtə) *n* **1** a small telescope attached to a larger optical instrument as an aid in fixing its line of sight. **2** an optical system of lenses and slits producing a nondivergent beam of light. **3** any device for limiting the size and angle of spread of a beam of radiation or particles.
collinear (kɒ'lɪnɪə) *adj* lying on the same straight line.
▸**collinearity** (ˌkɒlɪnɪ'ærɪtɪ) *n*
collins ('kɒlɪnz) *n* (*functioning as sing*) an iced drink made with gin, vodka, rum, etc., mixed with fruit juice, soda water, and sugar. [C20: prob. from the name *Collins*]
collision ❶ (kə'lɪʒən) *n* **1** a violent impact of moving objects; crash. **2** the conflict of opposed ideas, wishes, attitudes, etc. [C15: from LL, from L *collīdere* to COLLIDE]
collocate ('kɒləˌkeɪt) *vb* **collocates, collocating, collocated.** (*tr*) to group or place together in some system or order. [C16: from L, from *com-* together + *locāre* to place]
▸ˌ**collo'cation** *n*
collocutor ('kɒləˌkjuːtə) *n* a person who talks or engages in conversation with another.
collodion (kə'ləʊdɪən) *or* **collodium** (kə'ləʊdɪəm) *n* a syrupy liquid that consists of a solution of pyroxylin in ether and alcohol: used in medicine and in the manufacture of photographic plates, lacquers, etc. [C19: from NL, from Gk *kollōdēs* glutinous, from *kolla* glue]
collogue (kɒ'ləʊg) *vb* **collogues, colloguing, collogued.** (*intr;* usually foll. by *with*) to confer confidentially; conspire. [C16: ?from obs. *colleague* (vb) to conspire, infl. by L *colloquī* to talk with]
colloid ('kɒlɔɪd) *n* **1** a mixture having particles of one component suspended in a continuous phase of another component. The mixture has properties between those of a solution and a fine suspension. **2** *Physiol.* a gelatinous substance of the thyroid follicles that holds the hormonal secretions of the thyroid gland. [C19: from Gk *kolla* glue + -OID]
▸**col'loidal** *adj*
collop ('kɒləp) *n Dialect.* **1** a slice of meat. **2** a small piece of anything. [C14: of Scand. origin]
colloq. *abbrev. for* colloquial(ly).
colloquial ❶ (kə'ləʊkwɪəl) *adj* **1** of or relating to conversation. **2** denoting or characterized by informal or conversational idiom or vocabulary.
▸**col'loquially** *adv* ▸**col'loquialness** *n*
colloquialism (kə'ləʊkwɪəˌlɪzəm) *n* **1** a word or phrase appropriate to conversation and other informal situations. **2** the use of colloquial words and phrases.
colloquium (kə'ləʊkwɪəm) *n, pl* **colloquiums** *or* **colloquia** (-kwɪə). **1** a gathering for discussion. **2** an academic seminar. [C17: from L: COLLOQUY]
colloquy ('kɒləkwɪ) *n, pl* **colloquies. 1** a formal conversation or conference. **2** an informal conference on religious or theological matters. [C16: from L *colloquium,* from *com-* together + *loquī* to speak]
▸'**colloquist** *n*
collotype ('kɒləʊˌtaɪp) *n* **1** a method of lithographic printing (usually of high-quality reproductions) from a plate of hardened gelatine. **2** a print so made.
collude ❶ (kə'luːd) *vb* **colludes, colluding, colluded.** (*intr*) to conspire together, esp. in planning a fraud. [C16: from L, from *com-* together + *lūdere* to play]
▸**col'luder** *n*
collusion ❶ (kə'luːʒən) *n* **1** secret agreement for a fraudulent purpose; conspiracy. **2** a secret agreement between opponents at law for some improper purpose. [C14: from L, from *collūdere* to COLLUDE]
▸**col'lusive** *adj*
collywobbles ('kɒlɪˌwɒbᵊlz) *pl n* (usually preceded by *the*) *Sl.* **1** an upset stomach. **2** an intense feeling of nervousness. [C19: prob. from NL *cholera morbus,* infl. through folk etymology by COLIC and WOBBLE]
colobus ('kɒləbəs) *n* any leaf-eating arboreal Old World monkey of W and central Africa, having long silky fur and reduced or absent thumbs. [C19: NL, from Gk *kolobos* cut short; referring to its thumb]
cologarithm (kəʊ'lɒgəˌrɪðəm) *n* the logarithm of the reciprocal of a number; the negative value of the logarithm: *the cologarithm of 4 is log ¼.* Abbrev.: **colog.**
cologne (kə'ləʊn) *n* a perfumed liquid or solid made of fragrant essential oils and alcohol. Also called: **Cologne water, eau de cologne.** [C18: *Cologne water* from Cologne, where it was first manufactured]
colon[1] ('kəʊlən) *n, pl* **colons. 1** the punctuation mark : , usually preceding an explanation or an example, a list, or an extended quotation. **2** this mark used for certain other purposes, such as when a ratio is given in figures, as in *5:3.* [C16: from L, from Gk *kōlon* limb, clause]
colon[2] ('kəʊlən) *n, pl* **colons** *or* **cola** (-lə). the part of the large intestine between the caecum and the rectum. [C16: from L: large intestine, from Gk *kolon*]
▸**colonic** (kə'lɒnɪk) *adj*
colón (kəʊ'ləʊn; *Spanish* ko'lon) *n, pl* **colons** *or* **colones** (*Spanish* -'lones). **1** the standard monetary unit of Costa Rica, divided into 100 céntimos.

THESAURUS

collector *n* **1** = **gatherer**, acquirer, amasser, hoarder, saver, stockpiler
collide *vb* **1** = **crash**, clash, come into collision, meet head-on **2** = **conflict**, clash
collision *n* **1** = **crash**, accident, bump, impact, pile-up (*inf.*), prang (*inf.*), smash **2** = **conflict**, clash, clashing, confrontation, encounter, opposition, skirmish
colloquial *adj* **2** = **informal**, conversational, demotic, everyday, familiar, idiomatic, vernacular
collude *vb* = **conspire**, abet, be in cahoots (*inf.*), collaborate, complot, connive, contrive, intrigue, machinate, plot, scheme
collusion *n* **1** = **conspiracy**, cahoots (*inf.*), complicity, connivance, craft, deceit, fraudulent artifice, intrigue, secret understanding

2 the standard monetary unit of El Salvador, divided into 100 centavos. [C19: American Sp., from Sp., after Cristóbal *Colón* Christopher Columbus]

colonel ('kɜːnᵊl) *n* an officer of land or air forces junior to a brigadier but senior to a lieutenant colonel. [C16: via OF, from OIt. *colonnello* column of soldiers, from *colonna* COLUMN]
▸**'colonelcy** *or* **'colonelship** *n*

colonial (kə'ləʊnɪəl) *adj* **1** of, characteristic of, relating to, possessing, or inhabiting a colony or colonies. **2** (*often cap.*) characteristic of or relating to the 13 British colonies that became the United States of America (1776). **3** (*often cap.*) of or relating to the colonies of the British Empire. **4** denoting or having the style of Neoclassical architecture used in the British colonies in America in the 17th and 18th centuries. **5** of or relating to the period of Australian history before federation (1901). **6** (of animals and plants) having become established in a community in a new environment. ◆ *n* **7** a native of a colony.
▸**co'lonially** *adv*

colonial goose *n NZ.* an old-fashioned name for stuffed roast mutton.

colonialism (kə'ləʊnɪə,lɪzəm) *n* the policy and practice of a power in extending control over weaker peoples or areas. Also called: **imperialism.**
▸**co'lonialist** *n, adj*

Colonies ('kɒlənɪz) *pl n* **the. 1** *Brit.* the subject territories formerly in the British Empire. **2** *US history.* the 13 states forming the original United States of America when they declared their independence (1776).

colonist ❶ ('kɒlənɪst) *n* **1** a person who settles or colonizes an area. **2** an inhabitant of a colony.

colonize ❶ *or* **colonise** ('kɒlə,naɪz) *vb* **colonizes, colonizing, colonized** *or* **colonises, colonising, colonised. 1** to send colonists to or establish a colony in (an area). **2** to settle in (an area) as colonists. **3** (*tr*) to transform (a community, etc.) into a colony. **4** (of plants and animals) to become established in (a new environment).
▸**,coloni'zation** *or* **,coloni'sation** *n* ▸**'colo,nizer** *or* **'colo,niser** *n*

colonnade ❶ (,kɒlə'neɪd) *n* **1** a set of evenly spaced columns. **2** a row of regularly spaced trees. [C18: from F, from *colonne* COLUMN; on the model of It. *colonnato*]
▸**,colon'naded** *adj*

colony ❶ ('kɒlənɪ) *n, pl* **colonies. 1** a body of people who settle in a country distant from their homeland but maintain ties with it. **2** the community formed by such settlers. **3** a subject territory occupied by a settlement from the ruling state. **4a** a community of people who form a national, racial, or cultural minority concentrated in a particular place: *an artists' colony.* **4b** the area itself. **5** *Zool.* a group of the same type of animal or plant living or growing together. **6** *Bacteriol.* a group of bacteria, fungi, etc., derived from one or a few spores, esp. when grown on a culture medium. [C16: from L, from *colere* to cultivate, inhabit]

colony-stimulating factor *n Immunol.* any of a number of substances, secreted by the bone marrow, that stimulate the formation of blood cells. Synthetic forms are being tested for their ability to reduce the toxic effects of chemotherapy. Abbrev.: **CSF.**

colophon ('kɒlə,fɒn, -fən) *n* **1** a publisher's emblem on a book. **2** (formerly) an inscription at the end of a book showing the title, printer, date, etc. [C17: via LL, from Gk *kolophōn* a finishing stroke]

colophony (kɒ'lɒfənɪ) *n* another name for **rosin** (sense 1). [C14: from L: resin from Colophon, town in Lydia]

color ('kʌlə) *n, vb* the US spelling of **colour.**

Colorado beetle (,kɒlə'rɑːdəʊ) *n* a black-and-yellow beetle that is a serious pest of potatoes, feeding on the leaves. [from *Colorado*, state of central US]

colorant ('kʌlərənt) *n* any substance that imparts colour, such as a pigment, dye, or ink.

coloration *or* **colouration** (,kʌlə'reɪʃən) *n* **1** arrangement of colour; colouring. **2** the colouring or markings of insects, birds, etc.

coloratura (,kɒlərə'tʊərə) *n Music.* **1** (in 18th- and 19th-century arias) a florid virtuoso passage. **2** Also called: **coloratura soprano.** a soprano who specializes in such music. [C19: from obs. It., lit.: colouring.]

colorific (,kʌlə'rɪfɪk) *adj* producing, imparting, or relating to colour.

colorimeter (,kʌlə'rɪmɪtə) *n* apparatus for measuring the quality of a colour by comparison with standard colours or combinations of colours.
▸**colorimetric** (,kʌlərɪ'metrɪk) *adj* ▸**,color'imetry** *n*

colossal ❶ (kə'lɒsᵊl) *adj* **1** of immense size; huge; gigantic. **2** (in figure sculpture) approximately twice life-size. **3** *Archit.* of the order of columns that extend more than one storey in a façade.
▸**co'lossally** *adv*

colossus (kə'lɒsəs) *n, pl* **colossi** (-saɪ) *or* **colossuses.** something very large, esp. a statue. [C14: from L, from Gk *kolossos*]

Colossus of Rhodes *n* a giant bronze statue of Apollo built on Rhodes in about 292–280 B.C.; destroyed by an earthquake in 225 B.C.; one of the Seven Wonders of the World.

colostomy (kə'lɒstəmɪ) *n, pl* **colostomies.** the surgical formation of an opening from the colon onto the surface of the body, which functions as an anus.

colostrum (kə'lɒstrəm) *n* the thin milky secretion from the nipples that precedes and follows true lactation. [C16: from L, from ?]

colotomy (kə'lɒtəmɪ) *n, pl* **colotomies.** a colonic incision. [C19: COLON[2] + -TOMY]

colour ❶ *or US* **color** ('kʌlə) *n* **1a** an attribute of things that results from the light they reflect or emit in so far as this causes a visual sensation that depends on its wavelengths. **1b** the aspect of visual perception by which an observer recognizes this attribute. **1c** the quality of the light producing this visual perception. **2** Also called: **chromatic colour. 2a** a colour, such as red or green, that possesses hue, as opposed to achromatic colours such as white or black. **2b** (*as modifier*): *colour television.* **3** a substance, such as a dye or paint, that imparts colour. **4a** the skin complexion of a person, esp. as determined by his race. **4b** (*as modifier*): *colour prejudice.* **5** the use of all the hues in painting as distinct from composition, form, and light and shade. **6** the quantity and quality of ink used in a printing process. **7** the distinctive tone of a musical sound. **8** vividness or authenticity: *period colour.* **9** semblance or pretext: *under colour of.* **10** *Physics.* one of three characteristics of quarks, designated red, blue, or green, but having only a remote formal relationship with the physical sensation. ◆ *vb* **11** (*tr*) to apply colour to (something). **12** (*tr*) to give a convincing appearance to: *to colour an alibi.* **13** (*tr*) to influence or distort: *anger coloured her judgment.* **14** (*intr*; often foll. by *up*) to become red in the face, esp. when embarrassed or annoyed. ◆ See also **colours.** [C13 from OF *colour* from L *color* tint, hue]

colourable ('kʌlərəbᵊl) *adj* **1** capable of being coloured. **2** appearing to be true; plausible. **3** pretended; feigned.

colour bar *n* discrimination against people of a different race, esp. as practised by Whites against Blacks.

colour-blind *adj* of or relating to any defect in the normal ability to distinguish certain colours.
▸**colour blindness** *n*

colour code *n* a system of easily distinguishable colours, as for the identification of electrical wires or resistors.

coloured ('kʌləd) *adj* **1** possessing colour. **2** having a strong element of fiction or fantasy; distorted (esp. in **highly coloured**).

Coloured ('kʌləd) *n* **1** an individual who is not a White person, esp. a Black person. **2** Also called: **Cape Coloured.** (in South Africa) a person of racially mixed parentage or descent. ◆ *adj* **3a** (in South Africa) designating or relating to a person or people of racially mixed descent. **3b** designating or relating to a person or people who are not White.

> **USAGE NOTE** The use of *Coloured* to refer to people is now generally considered to be offensive.

colourfast ('kʌlə,fɑːst) *adj* (of a fabric) having a colour that does not run or change when washed or worn.
▸**'colour,fastness** *n*

colourful ❶ ('kʌləfʊl) *adj* **1** having intense colour or richly varied colours. **2** vivid, rich, or distinctive in character.
▸**'colourfully** *adv*

colour guard *n* a military guard in a parade, ceremony, etc., that carries and escorts the flag.

colouring ('kʌlərɪŋ) *n* **1** the process or art of applying colour. **2** anything used to give colour, such as paint. **3** appearance with regard to shade and colour. **4** arrangements of colours, as in the markings of birds. **5** the colour of a person's complexion. **6** a false or misleading appearance.

colourist ('kʌlərɪst) *n* a person who uses colour, esp. an artist.

colourize, colourise, *or US* **colorize** ('kʌlə,raɪz) *vb* **colourizes, colourizing, colourized** *or* **colourises, colourising, colourised** *or US* **colorizes,**

THESAURUS

colonist *n* **1** = **settler**, colonial, colonizer, frontiersman, homesteader (*US*), immigrant, pioneer, planter

colonize *vb* **1, 2** = **settle**, open up, people, pioneer, populate, put down roots

colonnade *n* **1** = **cloisters**, arcade, covered walk, peristyle, portico

colony *n* **3** = **settlement**, community, dependency, dominion, outpost, possession, province, satellite state, territory

colossal *adj* **1** = **huge**, Brobdingnagian, elephantine, enormous, gargantuan, gigantic, ginormous (*inf.*), herculean, humongous *or* humungous (*US sl.*), immense, mammoth, massive, monstrous, monumental, mountainous, prodigious, stellar (*inf.*), titanic, vast
Antonyms *adj* average, diminutive, little, miniature, minute, ordinary, pygmy *or* pigmy, slight, small, tiny, weak, wee

colour *n* **3** = **hue**, colorant, coloration, complexion, dye, paint, pigment, pigmentation, shade, tincture, tinge, tint **9** = **pretext**, appearance, disguise, excuse, façade, false show, guise, plea, pretence, semblance ◆ *vb* **11** = **paint**, colourwash, dye, stain, tinge, tint **13** = **misrepresent**, disguise, distort, embroider, exaggerate, falsify, garble, gloss over, pervert, prejudice, slant, taint **14** = **blush**, burn, crimson, flush, go as red as a beetroot, go crimson, redden

colourful *adj* **1** = **bright**, brilliant, Day-glo (*Trademark*), intense, jazzy (*inf.*), kaleidoscopic, motley, multicoloured, psychedelic, rich, variegated, vibrant, vivid **2** = **interesting**, characterful, distinctive, graphic, lively, picturesque, rich, stimulating, unusual, vivid
Antonyms *adj* ≠ **bright:** colourless, dark, drab, dreary, dull, faded, pale, washed out ≠ **interesting:** boring, characterless, dull, flat, lifeless, monotonous, unexciting, uninteresting, unvaried

colorizing, colorized. (*tr*) to add colour electronically to (an old black-and-white film).
▸ **ˌcolouriˈzation, ˌcolouriˈsation** *or US* **ˌcoloriˈzation** *n*

colourless ❶ (ˈkʌləlɪs) *adj* **1** without colour. **2** lacking in interest: *a colourless individual.* **3** grey or pallid in tone or hue. **4** without prejudice; neutral.
▸ **ˈcolourlessly** *adv*

colours ❶ (ˈkʌləz) *pl n* **1a** the flag that indicates nationality. **1b** *Mil.* the ceremony of hoisting or lowering the colours. **2** a pair of silk flags borne by a military unit and showing its crest and battle honours. **3** true nature or character (esp. in **show one's colours**). **4** a distinguishing badge or flag. **5** *Sport, Brit.* a badge or other symbol denoting membership of a team, esp. at a school or college. **6 nail one's colours to the mast. 6a** to commit oneself publicly and irrevocably to some party, course of action, etc. **6b** to refuse to admit defeat.

colour sergeant *n* a sergeant who carries the regimental, battalion, or national colours.

colour supplement *n Brit.* an illustrated magazine accompanying a newspaper.

colourway (ˈkʌləˌweɪ) *n* one of several different combinations of colours in which a given pattern is printed on fabrics or wallpapers, etc.

colposcope (ˈkɒlpəˌskəʊp) *n* an instrument for examining the cervix. [C20: from Gk *kolpos* womb + -SCOPE]

colt (kəʊlt) *n* **1** a male horse or pony under the age of four. **2** *Sport.* **2a** a young and inexperienced player. **2b** a member of a junior team. [OE *colt* young ass]

colter (ˈkəʊltə) *n* a variant spelling (esp. US) of **coulter.**

coltish ❶ (ˈkəʊltɪʃ) *adj* **1** inexperienced; unruly. **2** playful and lively.
▸ **ˈcoltishness** *n*

coltsfoot (ˈkəʊltsˌfʊt) *n, pl* **coltsfoots.** a European plant with yellow daisy-like flowers and heart-shaped leaves: a common weed.

colubrine (ˈkɒljʊˌbraɪn) *adj* **1** of or resembling a snake. **2** of or belonging to the Colubrinae, a subfamily of harmless snakes. [C16: from L *colubrīnus,* from *coluber* snake]

columbine (ˈkɒləmˌbaɪn) *n* any plant of the genus *Aquilegia,* having flowers with five spurred petals. Also called: **aquilegia.** [C13: from Med. L *columbīna herba* dovelike plant]

Columbine (ˈkɒləmˌbaɪn) *n* the sweetheart of Harlequin in English pantomime.

column ❶ (ˈkɒləm) *n* **1** an upright pillar usually having a cylindrical shaft, a base, and a capital. **2a** a form or structure in the shape of a column: *a column of air.* **2b** a monument. **3** a line, as of people in a queue. **4** *Mil.* a narrow formation in which individuals or units follow one behind the other. **5** *Journalism.* **5a** any of two or more vertical sections of type on a printed page, esp. on a newspaper page. **5b** a regular feature in a paper: *the fashion column.* **6** a vertical array of numbers. [C15: from L *columna,* from *columen* top, peak]
▸ **columnar** (kəˈlʌmnə) *adj* ▸ **ˈcolumned** *adj*

column inch *n* a unit of measurement for advertising space, one inch deep and one column wide.

columnist ❶ (ˈkɒləmnɪst, -əmɪst) *n* a journalist who writes a regular feature in a newspaper.

colure (kəˈlʊə, ˈkəʊlʊə) *n* either of two great circles on the celestial sphere, one passing through the poles and the equinoxes, the other through the poles and the solstices. [C16: from LL, from Gk *kolourai,* dock-tailed, from *kolos* docked + *oura* tail (because the lower portion is not visible)]

colza (ˈkɒlzə) *n* another name for **rape**[2]. [C18: via F (Walloon) from Du., from *kool* cabbage, COLE + *zaad* SEED]

COM (kɒm) *n* direct conversion of computer output to microfiche or film. [C20: *C(omputer) O(utput on) M(icrofilm)*]

Com. *abbrev. for:* **1** Commander. **2** Committee. **3** Commodore. **4** Communist.

com- *or* **con-** *prefix* together; with; jointly: *commingle.* [from L *com-;* rel. to *cum* with. In compound words of L origin, *com-* becomes *col-* and *cor-* before *l* and *r, co-* before *gn, h,* and most vowels, and *con-* before consonants other than *b, p,* and *m*]

coma[1] ❶ (ˈkəʊmə) *n, pl* **comas.** a state of unconsciousness from which a person cannot be aroused, caused by injury, narcotics, poisons, etc. [C17: from medical L, from Gk *kōma* heavy sleep]

coma[2] (ˈkəʊmə) *n, pl* **comae** (-miː). **1** *Astron.* the luminous cloud surrounding the nucleus in the head of a comet. **2** *Bot.* **2a** a tuft of hairs attached to the seed coat of some seeds. **2b** the terminal crown of leaves of palms and moss stems. [C17: from L: hair of the head, from Gk *komē*]

comanche (kəˈmæntʃɪ) *n* **1** (*pl* **comanches** *or* **comanche**) a member of a North American Indian people formerly inhabiting the W plains of the US. **2** the language of this people.

comatose ❶ (ˈkəʊməˌtəʊs) *adj* **1** in a state of coma. **2** torpid; lethargic.

comb ❶ (kəʊm) *n* **1** a toothed device for disentangling or arranging hair. **2** a tool or machine that cleans and straightens wool, cotton, etc. **3** *Austral. & NZ.* the fixed cutter on a sheep-shearing machine. **4** anything resembling a comb in form or function. **5** the fleshy serrated outgrowth on the heads of certain birds, esp. the domestic fowl. **6** a honeycomb. ◆ *vb* **7** (*tr*) to use a comb on. **8** (when *tr,* often foll. by *through*) to search with great care: *the police combed the woods.* ◆ **See also comb out.** [OE *camb*]

combat ❶ *n* (ˈkɒmbæt, -bət, ˈkʌm-). **1** a fight, conflict, or struggle. **2a** an action fought between two military forces. **2b** (*as modifier*): *a combat jacket.* **3 single combat.** a duel. ◆ *vb* (kəmˈbæt; ˈkɒmbæt, ˈkʌm-). **-bats, -bating, -bated. 4** (*tr*) to fight. **5** (*intr;* often foll. by *with* or *against*) to struggle or strive (against): *to combat against disease.* [C16: from F, from OF *combattre,* from Vulgar L *combattere* (unattested), from L *com-* with + *battuere* to beat]

combatant ❶ (ˈkɒmbətᵊnt, ˈkʌm-) *n* **1** a person or group engaged in or prepared for a fight. ◆ *adj* **2** engaged in or ready for combat.

combat fatigue *n* another term for **battle fatigue.**

combative ❶ (ˈkɒmbətɪv, ˈkʌm-) *adj* eager or ready to fight, argue, etc.
▸ **ˈcombativeness** *n*

combe *or* **comb** (kuːm) *n* variant spellings of **coomb.**

comber (ˈkəʊmə) *n* **1** a person, tool, or machine that combs wool, flax, etc. **2** a long curling wave; roller.

combination ❶ (ˌkɒmbɪˈneɪʃən) *n* **1** the act of combining or state of being combined. **2** a union of separate parts, qualities, etc. **3** an alliance of people or parties. **4** the set of numbers that opens a combination lock. **5** *Brit.* a motorcycle with a sidecar attached. **6** *Maths.* an arrangement of the numbers, terms, etc., of a set into specified groups without regard to order in the group. **7** the chemical reaction of two or more compounds, usually to form one other compound. **8** *Chess.* a tactical manoeuvre involving a sequence of moves and more than one piece.
▸ **ˌcombiˈnational** *adj*

combination lock *n* a type of lock that can only be opened when a set of dials is turned to show a specific sequence of numbers.

combinations (ˌkɒmbɪˈneɪʃənz) *pl n Brit.* a one-piece undergarment with long sleeves and legs. Often shortened to **combs** or **coms.**

combine ❶ *vb* (kəmˈbaɪn), **combines, combining, combined. 1** to join together. **2** to unite or cause to unite to form a chemical compound. ◆ *n* (ˈkɒmbaɪn). **3** short for **combine harvester. 4** an association of enterprises, esp. in order to gain a monopoly of a market. **5** an association of related bodies, such as business corporations or sports clubs, for a common purpose. [C15: from LL *combīnāre,* from L *com-* together + *bīnī* two by two]
▸ **comˈbinable** *adj* ▸ **comˌbinaˈbility** *n* ▸ **combinative** (ˈkɒmbɪˌneɪtɪv) *or* **combinatory** (ˈkɒmbɪˌneɪtərɪ) *adj*

combine harvester (ˈkɒmbaɪn) *n* a machine that simultaneously cuts, threshes, and cleans a standing crop of grain.

combings (ˈkəʊmɪŋz) *pl n* **1** the loose hair removed by combing. **2** the unwanted fibres removed in combing cotton, etc.

combining form *n* a linguistic element that occurs only as part of a compound word, such as *anthropo-* in *anthropology* and *anthropomorph.*

THESAURUS

colourless *adj* **1, 3** = **drab,** achromatic, achromic, anaemic, ashen, bleached, faded, neutral, sickly, wan, washed out **2** = **uninteresting,** characterless, dreary, dull, insipid, lacklustre, tame, unmemorable, vacuous, vapid
Antonyms *adj* ≠ **drab:** blooming, flushed, glowing, healthy, radiant, robust, ruddy ≠ **uninteresting:** animated, bright, colourful, compelling, distinctive, exciting, interesting, unusual

colours *pl n* **1a** = **flag,** banner, emblem, ensign, standard **3** *As in* **show one's colours** = **nature,** aspect, breed, character, identity, stamp, strain

coltish *adj* **2** = **frisky,** frolicsome, lively, playful, romping, skittish, sportive

column *n* **1** = **pillar,** caryatid, obelisk, pilaster, post, shaft, support, upright **3** = **line,** cavalcade, file, list, procession, queue, rank, row, string, train

columnist *n* = **journalist,** correspondent, critic, editor, gossip columnist, journo (*sl.*), reporter, reviewer

coma[1] *n* = **unconsciousness,** insensibility, lethargy, oblivion, somnolence, stupor, torpor, trance

comatose *adj* **1, 2** = **unconscious,** drugged, insensible, lethargic, somnolent, stupefied, torpid

comb *vb* **7** = **untangle,** arrange, curry, dress, groom, tease **8** = **search,** forage, go through with a fine-tooth comb, hunt, rake, ransack, rummage, scour, screen, sift, sweep

combat *n* **1** = **fight,** action, battle, conflict, contest, encounter, engagement, skirmish, struggle, war, warfare ◆ *vb* **4, 5** = **fight,** battle, contend, contest, cope, defy, do battle with, engage, oppose, resist, strive, struggle, withstand
Antonyms *n* ≠ **fight:** agreement, armistice, peace, surrender, truce ◆ *vb* ≠ **fight:** accept, acquiesce, declare a truce, give up, make peace, support, surrender

combatant *n* **1** = **fighter,** adversary, antagonist, belligerent, contender, enemy, fighting man, gladiator, opponent, serviceman, soldier, warrior ◆ *adj* **2** = **fighting,** battling, belligerent, combative, conflicting, contending, opposing, warring

combative *adj* = **aggressive,** antagonistic, bellicose, belligerent, contentious, militant, pugnacious, quarrelsome, truculent, warlike
Antonyms *adj* nonaggressive, nonbelligerent, nonviolent, pacific, pacifist, peaceable, peaceful, peace-loving

combination *n* **2** = **mixture,** amalgam, amalgamation, blend, coalescence, composite, connection, meld, mix **3** = **association,** alliance, cabal, cartel, coalition, combine, compound, confederacy, confederation, consortium, conspiracy, federation, merger, syndicate, unification, union

combine *vb* **1** = **join together,** amalgamate, associate, bind, blend, bond, compound, connect, cooperate, fuse, incorporate, integrate, link, marry, meld, merge, mix, pool, put together, synthesize, unify, unite
Antonyms *vb* detach, dissociate, dissolve, disunite, divide, part, separate, sever

DICTIONARY

combo ('kɒmbəʊ) *n, pl* **combos.** **1** a small group of jazz musicians. **2** *Inf.* any combination.

comb out *vb (tr, adv)* **1** to remove (tangles) from (the hair) with a comb. **2** to remove for a purpose. **3** to examine systematically.

combustible ❶ (kəm'bʌstɪbᵊl) *adj* **1** capable of igniting and burning. **2** easily annoyed; excitable. ◆ *n* **3** a combustible substance.
▸**com,busti'bility** *or* **com'bustibleness** *n*

combustion (kəm'bʌstʃən) *n* **1** the process of burning. **2** any process in which a substance reacts to produce a significant rise in temperature and the emission of light. **3** a process in which a compound reacts slowly with oxygen to produce little heat and no light. [C15: from OF, from L *combūrere* to burn up]
▸**com'bustive** *n, adj*

combustion chamber *n* an enclosed space in which combustion takes place, such as the space above the piston in the cylinder head of an internal-combustion engine.

combustor (kəm'bʌstə) *n* the combustion system of a jet engine or ramjet.

Comdr *Mil. abbrev. for* Commander.

Comdt *Mil. abbrev. for* Commandant.

come ❶ (kʌm) *vb* **comes, coming, came, come.** *(mainly intr)* **1** to move towards a specified person or place. **2** to arrive by movement or by making progress. **3** to become perceptible: *light came into the sky.* **4** to occur: *Christmas comes but once a year.* **5** to happen as a result: *no good will come of this.* **6** to be derived: *good may come of evil.* **7** to occur to the mind: *the truth suddenly came to me.* **8** to reach: *she comes up to my shoulder.* **9** to be produced: *that dress comes in red.* **10** to arrive at or be brought into a particular state: *you will soon come to grief.* **11** (foll. by *from*) to be or have been a resident or native (of): *I come from London.* **12** to become: *your wishes will come true.* **13** *(tr; takes an infinitive)* to be given awareness: *I came to realize its value.* **14** *Taboo sl.* to have an orgasm. **15** *(tr) Brit. inf.* to play the part of: *don't come the fine gentleman with me.* **16** *(tr) Brit. inf.* to cause or produce: *don't come that nonsense.* **17** *(subjunctive use): come next August, he will be fifty years old:* when next August arrives. **18 as ... as they come.** the most characteristic example of a type. **19 come again?** *Inf.* what did you say? **20 come good.** to recover and perform well after a setback or poor start. **21 come to light.** to be revealed. **22 come to light with.** *Austral. & NZ inf.* to find or produce. ◆ *interj* **23** an exclamation expressing annoyance, etc.: *come now!* ◆ See also **come about, come across,** etc. [OE *cuman*]

come about ❶ *vb (intr, adv)* **1** to take place; happen. **2** *Naut.* to change tacks.

come across ❶ *vb (intr)* **1** *(prep)* to meet or find by accident. **2** *(adv)* to communicate the intended meaning or impression. **3** (often foll. by *with*) to provide what is expected.

come at ❶ *vb (intr, prep)* **1** to discover (facts, the truth, etc.). **2** to attack: *he came at me with an axe.* **3** *(usually used with a negative) Austral. sl.* to agree to do (something).

comeback ❶ ('kʌm,bæk) *n Inf.* **1** a return to a former position, status, etc. **2** a response, esp. recriminatory. **3** a quick retort. ◆ *vb* **come back.** *(intr, adv)* **4** to return, esp. to the memory. **5** to become fashionable again. **6 come back to (someone).** (of something forgotten) to return to (someone's) memory.

come between ❶ *vb (intr, prep)* to cause the estrangement or separation of (two people).

come by ❶ *vb (intr, prep)* to find or obtain, esp. accidentally: *do you ever come by any old books?*

Comecon ('kɒmɪ,kɒn) *n* (formerly) an association of Soviet-oriented Communist nations, founded in 1949 to coordinate economic development, etc.: disbanded in 1991. [C20: *Co(uncil for) M(utual) Econ(omic Aid)*]

comedian ❶ (kə'mi:dɪən) *n* **1** an entertainer who specializes in jokes, comic skits, etc. **2** an actor in comedy. **3** an amusing person: sometimes used ironically.

comedienne (kə,mi:dɪ'ɛn) *n* a female comedian.

comedo ('kɒmɪ,dəʊ) *n, pl* **comedos** *or* **comedones** (,kɒmɪ'dəʊni:z). *Pathol.* the technical name for **blackhead.** [C19: from NL, from L: glutton]

comedown ❶ ('kʌm,daʊn) *n* **1** a decline in status or prosperity. **2** *Inf.* a disappointment. ◆ *vb* **come down.** *(intr, adv)* **3** to come to a place regarded as lower. **4** to lose status, etc. (esp. in **come down in the world**). **5** (of prices) to become lower. **6** to reach a decision: *the report came down in favour of a pay increase.* **7** (often foll. by *to*) to be handed down by tradition or inheritance. **8** *Brit.* to leave university. **9** (foll. by *with*) to succumb (to illness). **10** (foll. by *on*) to rebuke harshly. **11** (foll. by *to*) to amount in essence (to): *it comes down to two choices.*

comedy ❶ ('kɒmɪdɪ) *n, pl* **comedies.** **1** a dramatic or other work of light and amusing character. **2** the genre of drama represented by works of this type. **3** (in classical literature) a play in which the main characters triumph over adversity. **4** the humorous aspect of life or of events. **5** an amusing event or sequence of events. **6** humour: *the comedy of Chaplin.* [C14: from OF, from L, from Gk *kōmōidia*, from *kōmos* village festival + *aeidein* to sing]
▸**comedic** (kə'mi:dɪk) *adj*

comedy of manners *n* a comedy dealing with the way of life and foibles of a social group.

come forward ❶ *vb (intr, adv)* **1** to offer one's services; volunteer. **2** to present oneself.

come-hither *adj (usually prenominal) Inf.* alluring; seductive: *a come-hither look.*

come in ❶ *vb (intr, mainly adv)* **1** to enter. **2** to prove to be: *it came in useful.* **3** to become fashionable or seasonable. **4** *Cricket.* to begin an innings. **5** to finish a race (in a certain position). **6** to be received: *news is coming in of a big fire in Glasgow.* **7** (of money) to be received as income. **8** to play a role: *where do I come in?* **9** (foll. by *for*) to be the object of: *the Chancellor came in for a lot of criticism.*

come into *vb (intr, prep)* **1** to enter. **2** to inherit.

comely ❶ ('kʌmlɪ) *adj* **comelier, comeliest.** **1** good-looking; attractive. **2** *Arch.* suitable; fitting. [OE *cȳmlīc* beautiful]
▸**'comeliness** *n*

come of *vb (intr, prep)* **1** to be descended from. **2** to result from: *nothing came of it.*

come off ❶ *vb (intr, mainly adv)* **1** *(also prep)* to fall (from). **2** to become detached. **3** *(prep)* to be removed from (a price, tax, etc.): *will anything come off income tax in the budget?* **4** *(copula)* to emerge from or as if from a contest: *he came off the winner.* **5** *Inf.* to happen. **6** *Inf.* to have the intended effect: *his jokes did not come off.* **7** *Taboo sl.* to have an orgasm.

come on ❶ *vb (intr, mainly adv)* **1** (of power, water, etc.) to start running or functioning. **2** to progress: *my plants are coming on nicely.* **3** to advance, esp. in battle. **4** to begin: *she felt a cold coming on.* **5** to make an entrance on stage. **6 come on!** **6a** hurry up! **6b** cheer up! pull yourself together! **6c** make an effort! **6d** don't exaggerate! stick to the facts! **7** to attempt to give a specified impression: *he came on like a hard man.* **8 come on strong.** to make a forceful or exaggerated impression. **9 come on to.** *Inf.* to make sexual advances to. ◆ *n* **come-on. 10.** anything that serves as a lure or enticement.

come out ❶ *vb (intr, adv)* **1** to be made public or revealed: *the news of her death came out last week.* **2** to make a debut in society. **3** Also: **come out of the closet. 3a** to declare openly that one is a homosexual. **3b** to reveal or declare any practice or habit formerly concealed. **4** *Chiefly Brit.* to go on strike. **5** to declare oneself: *the government came out in favour of scrapping the project.* **6** to be shown clearly: *you came out very well in the*

THESAURUS

combustible *adj* **1 = flammable**, explosive, incendiary, inflammable

come *vb* **1, 2 = move towards**, advance, appear, approach, arrive, become, draw near, enter, happen, materialize, move, near, occur, originate, show up *(inf.)*, turn out, turn up *(inf.)* **3 = arrive**, appear, attain, enter, materialize, reach, show up *(inf.)*, turn up *(inf.)* **4 = happen**, fall, occur, take place **6 = result**, arise, emanate, emerge, end up, flow, issue, originate, turn out **8 = reach**, extend **9 = be available**, be made, be offered, be on offer, be produced

come about *vb* **1 = happen**, arise, befall, come to pass, occur, result, take place, transpire *(inf.)*

come across *vb* **1 = find**, bump into *(inf.)*, chance upon, discover, encounter, happen upon, hit upon, light upon, meet, notice, stumble upon, unearth

come at *vb* **2 = attack**, assail, assault, charge, fall upon, fly at, go for, light into, rush, rush at

comeback *Informal n* **1 = return**, rally, rebound, recovery, resurgence, revival, triumph **2 = response**, rejoinder, reply, retaliation, retort, riposte ◆ *vb* **come back 4 = return**, reappear, recur, re-enter

come between *vb* **= separate**, alienate, divide, estrange, interfere, meddle, part, set at odds

come by *vb* **= get**, acquire, land, lay hold of, obtain, procure, score *(sl.)*, secure, take possession of, win

comedian *n* **1, 3 = comic**, card *(inf.)*, clown, funny man, humorist, jester, joker, laugh *(inf.)*, wag, wit

comedown *n* **1 = decline**, deflation, demotion, reverse **2** *Informal* **= disappointment**, anticlimax, blow, humiliation, letdown, whammy *(inf., chiefly U.S.)* ◆ *vb* **come down 3 = descend**, go downhill **4 = decline**, degenerate, deteriorate, fall, go to pot *(inf.)*, reduce, worsen **6 = decide**, choose, favour, recommend **9** *foll. by* **with = catch**, ail, be stricken with, contract, fall ill, fall victim to, get, sicken, take, take sick **10** *foll. by* **on = reprimand**, bawl out *(inf.)*, blast, carpet *(inf.)*, criticize, dress down *(inf.)*, jump on *(inf.)*, lambast(e), put down, rap over the knuckles, read the riot act, rebuke, tear into *(inf.)*, tear (someone) off a strip *(Brit. inf.)* **11** *foll. by* **to = amount to**, boil down to, end up as, result in

comedy *n* **1, 4-6 = humour**, chaffing, drollery, facetiousness, farce, fun, hilarity, jesting, joking, light entertainment, sitcom *(inf.)*, slapstick, wisecracking, witticisms
Antonyms *n* high drama, melancholy, melodrama, opera, sadness, seriousness, serious play, soap opera, solemnity, tragedy

come forward *vb* **1, 2 = volunteer**, offer one's services, present or proffer oneself

come in *vb* **1 = enter**, appear, arrive, cross the threshold, show up *(inf.)* **5 = finish**, reach **9** *foll. by* **for = receive**, acquire, bear the brunt of, endure, get, suffer

comely *adj* **1** *Old-fashioned* **= good-looking**, attractive, beautiful, becoming, blooming, bonny, buxom, cute, fair, graceful, handsome, lovely, pleasing, pretty, wholesome, winsome **2** *Archaic* **= proper**, decent, decorous, fit, fitting, seemly, suitable
Antonyms *adj* ≠ **good-looking:** disagreeable, distasteful, faded, homely, mumsy, plain, repulsive, ugly, unattractive, unpleasant ≠ **proper:** improper, indecorous, unbecoming, unfitting, unnatural, unseemly

come off *vb* **5** *Informal* **= happen**, go off, occur, succeed, take place, transpire *(inf.)*

come on *vb* **2, 3 = progress**, advance, develop, improve, make headway, proceed **4 = begin**, appear, take place

come out *vb* **1 = be revealed**, appear, be announced, be divulged, be issued, be published, be released, be reported **10** *foll. by* **with = say,**

photos. **7** to yield a satisfactory solution: *these sums just won't come out.* **8** to be published: *the paper comes out on Fridays.* **9** (foll. by *in*) to become covered (with). **10** (foll. by *with*) to declare openly: *you can rely on him to come out with the facts.*

come over *vb* (*intr, adv*) **1** to communicate the intended meaning or impression: *he came over very well.* **2** to change allegiances. **3** *Inf.* to feel a particular sensation: *I came over funny.*

comer ('kʌmə) *n* **1** (*in combination*) a person who comes: *all-comers; newcomers.* **2** *Inf.* a potential success.

come round ❶ *vb* (*intr, adv*) **1** to be restored to consciousness. **2** to modify one's opinion.

comestible (kə'mɛstɪbᵊl) *n* (*usually pl*) food. [C15: from LL *comestibilis*, from *comedere* to eat up]

comet ('kɒmɪt) *n* a celestial body that travels around the sun, usually in a highly elliptical orbit: thought to consist of a frozen nucleus, part of which vaporizes on approaching the sun to form a long luminous tail. [C13: from OF, from L, from Gk *komētēs* long-haired]
▸**'cometary** *or* **cometic** (kɒ'mɛtɪk) *adj*

come through ❶ *vb* (*intr*) **1** (*adv*) to emerge successfully. **2** (*prep*) to survive (an illness, etc.).

come to *vb* (*intr*) **1** (*adv* or *prep and reflexive*) to regain consciousness. **2** (*adv*) *Naut.* to slow a vessel or bring her to a stop. **3** (*prep*) to amount to (a sum of money). **4** (*prep*) to arrive at: *what is the world coming to?*

come up ❶ *vb* (*intr, adv*) **1** to come to a place regarded as higher. **2** (of the sun) to rise. **3** to present itself: *that question will come up again.* **4** *Brit.* to begin a term at a university. **5** to appear from out of the ground: *my beans have come up early.* **6** *Inf.* to win: *have your premium bonds ever come up?* **7 come up against.** to come into conflict with. **8 come up to.** to meet a standard. **9 come up with.** to produce.

come upon *vb* (*intr, prep*) to meet or encounter unexpectedly.

comeuppance ❶ (ˌkʌm'ʌpəns) *n Inf.* just retribution. [C19: from *come up* (in the sense): to appear before a court]

comfit ('kʌmfɪt, 'kɒm-) *n* a sugar-coated sweet containing a nut or seed. [C15: from OF, from L *confectum* something prepared]

comfort ❶ ('kʌmfət) *n* **1** a state of ease or well-being. **2** relief from affliction, grief, etc. **3** a person, thing, or event that brings solace or ease. **4** (*usually pl*) something that affords physical ease and relaxation. ◆ *vb* (*tr*) **5** to soothe; cheer. **6** to bring physical ease to. [C13: from OF *confort*, from LL *confortāre* to strengthen, from L *con-* (intensive) + *fortis* strong]
▸**'comforting** *adj* ▸**'comfortless** *adj*

comfortable ❶ ('kʌmftəbᵊl) *adj* **1** giving comfort. **2** at ease. **3** free from affliction or pain. **4** (of a person or situation) relaxing. **5** *Inf.* having adequate income. **6** *Inf.* (of income, etc.) adequate to provide comfort.
▸**'comfortably** *adv*

comforter ('kʌmfətə) *n* **1** a person or thing that comforts. **2** *Chiefly Brit.* a woollen scarf. **3** a baby's dummy. **4** *US.* a quilted bed covering.

Comforter ('kʌmfətə) *n Christianity.* an epithet of the Holy Spirit. [C14: translation of L *consolātor*, representing Gk *paraklētos* advocate]

comfrey ('kʌmfrɪ) *n* a hairy Eurasian plant having blue, purplish-pink, or white flowers. [C15: from OF *cunfirie*, from L *conferva* water plant]

comfy ('kʌmfɪ) *adj* **comfier, comfiest.** *Inf.* short for **comfortable.**

comic ❶ ('kɒmɪk) *adj* **1** of, characterized by, or characteristic of comedy. **2** (*prenominal*) acting in or composing comedy: *a comic writer.* **3** humorous; funny. ◆ *n* **4** a person who is comic; comedian. **5** a book or magazine containing comic strips. [C16: from L *cōmicus*, from Gk *kōmikos*]

comical ❶ ('kɒmɪkᵊl) *adj* **1** causing laughter. **2** ludicrous; laughable.
▸**'comically** *adv*

comic opera *n* a play largely set to music, employing comic effects or situations.

comic strip *n* a sequence of drawings in a newspaper, magazine, etc., relating a humorous story or an adventure.

coming ❶ ('kʌmɪŋ) *adj* **1** (*prenominal*) (of time, events, etc.) approaching or next. **2** promising (esp. in **up and coming**). **3** of future importance: *this is the coming thing.* **4 have it coming to one.** *Inf.* to deserve what one is about to suffer. ◆ *n* **5** arrival or approach.

Comintern *or* **Komintern** ('kɒmɪnˌtɜːn) *n* short for **Communist International;** an international Communist organization founded by Lenin in 1919 and dissolved in 1943; it degenerated under Stalin into an instrument of Soviet politics. Also called: **Third International.**

comity ('kɒmɪtɪ) *n, pl* **comities. 1** mutual civility; courtesy. **2** short for **comity of nations.** [C16: from L *cōmitās*, from *cōmis* affable]

comity of nations *n* the friendly recognition accorded by one nation to the laws and usages of another.

comm. *abbrev. for:* **1** commerce. **2** commercial. **3** committee. **4** commonwealth.

comma ('kɒmə) *n* **1** the punctuation mark , indicating a slight pause and used where there is a listing of items or to separate a nonrestrictive clause from a main clause. **2** *Music.* a minute difference in pitch. [C16: from L, from Gk *komma* clause, from *koptein* to cut]

comma bacillus *n* a comma-shaped bacterium that causes cholera in man.

command ❶ (kə'mɑːnd) *vb* **1** (when *tr*, may take a clause as object or an infinitive) to order or compel. **2** to have or be in control or authority over. **3** (*tr*) to receive as due: *his nature commands respect.* **4** to dominate (a view, etc.) as from a height. ◆ *n* **5** an order. **6** the act of commanding. **7** the right to command. **8** the exercise of the power to command. **9** knowledge; control: *a command of French.* **10** *Chiefly mil.* the jurisdiction of a commander. **11** a military unit or units commanding a specific function, as in the RAF. **12** *Brit.* **12a** an invitation from the monarch. **12b** (*as modifier*): *a command performance.* **13** *Computing.* a word or phrase that can be selected from a menu or typed after a prompt in order to carry out an action. [C13: from OF *commander*, from L *com-* (intensive) + *mandāre* to enjoin]

commandant ('kɒmənˌdænt, -ˌdɑːnt) *n* an officer commanding a group or establishment.

command economy *n* an economy in which business activities and the allocation of resources are determined by government order rather than market forces. Also called: **planned economy.**

commandeer ❶ (ˌkɒmən'dɪə) *vb* (*tr*) **1** to seize for public or military use. **2** to seize arbitrarily. [C19: from Afrik. *kommandeer*, from F *commander* to COMMAND]

commander ❶ (kə'mɑːndə) *n* **1** an officer in command of a military formation or operation. **2** a naval commissioned rank junior to captain but senior to lieutenant commander. **3** the second in command of larger British warships. **4** someone who holds authority. **5** a high-ranking member of some knightly orders. **6** an officer responsible for a district of the Metropolitan Police in London.
▸**com'manderˌship** *n*

commander in chief *n, pl* **commanders in chief.** the officer holding supreme command of the forces in an area or operation.

THESAURUS

acknowledge, come clean, declare, disclose, divulge, lay open, own, own up

come round *vb* **1 = regain consciousness,** come to, rally, recover, revive **2 = change one's opinion,** accede, acquiesce, allow, concede, grant, mellow, relent, yield

come through *vb* **1 = accomplish,** achieve, make the grade (*inf.*), prevail, succeed, triumph **2 = survive,** endure, weather the storm, withstand

come up *vb* **3 = happen,** arise, crop up, occur, rise, spring up, turn up **8 come up to = compare with,** admit of comparison with, approach, equal, match, measure up to, meet, resemble, rival, stand *or* bear comparison with **9 come up with = produce,** advance, create, discover, furnish, offer, present, propose, provide, submit, suggest

comeuppance *n Informal* **= punishment,** chastening, deserts, due reward, dues, merit, recompense, requital, retribution

comfort *n* **1 = luxury,** cosiness, creature comforts, ease, opulence, snugness, wellbeing **2 = relief,** aid, alleviation, cheer, compensation, consolation, ease, encouragement, enjoyment, help, satisfaction, succour, support ◆ *vb* **5, 6 = console,** alleviate, assuage, cheer, commiserate with, ease, encourage, enliven, gladden, hearten, inspirit, invigorate, reassure, refresh, relieve, solace, soothe, strengthen
Antonyms *n* ≠ **relief:** aggravation, annoyance, discouragement, displeasure, hassle (*inf.*), inconvenience, irritation ◆ *vb* ≠ **console:** aggravate (*inf.*), agitate, annoy, bother, depress, discomfort, distress, excite, hassle (*inf.*), irk, irritate, rile, ruffle, sadden, trouble

comfortable *adj* **1, 4 = pleasant,** agreeable, convenient, cosy, delightful, easy, enjoyable, homely, relaxing, restful **2 = happy,** at ease, at home, contented, gratified, relaxed, serene **5** *Informal* **= well-off,** affluent, in clover (*inf.*), prosperous, well-to-do
Antonyms *adj* ≠ **pleasant:** inadequate, uncomfortable, unpleasant ≠ **happy:** distressed, disturbed, ill at ease, like a fish out of water, miserable, nervous, on tenterhooks, tense, troubled, uncomfortable, uneasy

comforting *adj* **5 = consoling,** cheering, consolatory, encouraging, heart-warming, inspiriting, reassuring, soothing
Antonyms *adj* alarming, dismaying, disturbing, perplexing, upsetting, worrying

comfortless *adj* **1 = cheerless,** bleak, cold, desolate, dismal, dreary **2 = inconsolable,** disconsolate, forlorn, miserable, sick at heart, woebegone, wretched

comic *adj* **3 = funny,** amusing, comical, droll, facetious, farcical, humorous, jocular, joking, light, rich, waggish, witty ◆ *n* **4 = comedian,** buffoon, clown, funny man, humorist, jester, joculator *or* (*fem.*) joculatrix, wag, wit
Antonyms *adj* ≠ **funny:** depressing, melancholy, pathetic, sad, serious, solemn, touching, tragic

comical *adj* **1, 2 = funny,** absurd, amusing, comic, diverting, droll, entertaining, farcical, hilarious, humorous, laughable, ludicrous, priceless, ridiculous, risible, side-splitting, silly, whimsical, zany

coming *adj* **1 = approaching,** at hand, due, en route, forthcoming, future, imminent, impending, in store, in the wind, just round the corner, near, next, nigh, on the cards, upcoming **2 = up-and-coming,** aspiring, future, promising ◆ *n* **5 = arrival,** accession, advent, approach

command *vb* **1 = order,** bid, charge, compel, demand, direct, enjoin, require **2 = have authority over,** administer, call the shots, call the tune, control, dominate, govern, handle, head, lead, manage, reign over, rule, supervise, sway ◆ *n* **5 = order,** behest, bidding, canon, commandment, decree, demand, direction, directive, edict, fiat, injunction, instruction, mandate, precept, requirement, ultimatum **7, 8 = authority,** charge, control, direction, domination, dominion, government, grasp, management, mastery, power, rule, supervision, sway, upper hand
Antonyms *vb* ≠ **order:** appeal (to), ask, beg, beseech, plead, request, supplicate ≠ **have authority over:** be inferior, be subordinate, follow

commandeer *vb* **1, 2 = seize,** appropriate, confiscate, expropriate, hijack, requisition, sequester, sequestrate, usurp

commander *n* **1, 4 = officer,** boss, captain, chief, C in C, C.O., commander-in-chief, commanding officer, director, head, leader, ruler

commanding ❶ (kəˈmɑːndɪŋ) *adj (usually prenominal)* **1** being in command. **2** having the air of authority: *a commanding voice.* **3** (of a situation) exerting control. **4** (of a viewpoint, etc.) overlooking; advantageous.
▸**comˈmandingly** *adv*

commanding officer *n* an officer in command of a military unit.

command language *n Computing.* the language used to access a computer system.

commandment (kəˈmɑːndmənt) *n* **1** a divine command, esp. one of the Ten Commandments of the Old Testament. **2** *Literary.* any command.

command module *n* the module used as the living quarters in an Apollo spacecraft and functioning as the splashdown vehicle.

commando (kəˈmɑːndəʊ) *n, pl* **commandos** *or* **commandoes. 1a** an amphibious military unit trained for raiding. **1b** a member of such a unit. **2** the basic unit of the Royal Marine Corps. **3** (originally) an armed force raised by Boers during the Boer War. **4** (*modifier*) denoting or relating to commandos: *a commando unit.* [C19: from Afrik. *kommando,* from Du. *commando* command]

command paper *n* (in Britain) a government document that is presented to Parliament, in theory by royal command.

command post *n Mil.* the position from which a commander exercises command.

commedia dell'arte (*Italian* kɔmˈmeːdia delˈlarte) *n* a form of popular improvised comedy in Italy during the 16th to 18th centuries, with stock characters such as Punchinello, Harlequin, and Columbine. [It., lit.: comedy of art]

comme il faut *French.* (kɔm il fo) correct or correctly.

commemorate ❶ (kəˈmɛməˌreɪt) *vb* **commemorates, commemorating, commemorated.** (*tr*) to honour or keep alive the memory of. [C16: from L *commemorāre,* from *com-* (intensive) + *memorāre* to remind]
▸**comˌmemoˈration** *n* ▸**comˈmemorative** *adj* ▸**comˈmemoˌrator** *n*

commence ❶ (kəˈmɛns) *vb* **commences, commencing, commenced.** to begin; come or cause to come into being, operation, etc. [C14: from OF *comencer,* from Vulgar L *cominitiāre* (unattested), from L *com-* (intensive) + *initiāre* to begin]

commencement ❶ (kəˈmɛnsmənt) *n* **1** the beginning; start. **2** *US.* a ceremony for the conferment of academic degrees. **3** *US & Canad.* a ceremony for the presentation of awards at secondary schools.

commend ❶ (kəˈmɛnd) *vb* (*tr*) **1** to represent as being worthy of regard, confidence, etc.; recommend. **2** to give in charge; entrust. **3** to praise. **4** to give the regards of: *commend me to your aunt.* [C14: from L *commendāre,* from *com-* (intensive) + *mandāre* to entrust]
▸**comˈmendable** *adj* ▸**comˈmendably** *adv* ▸**comˈmendatory** *adj*

commendation ❶ (ˌkɒmɛnˈdeɪʃən) *n* **1** the act of commending; praise. **2** *US.* an award.

commensal (kəˈmɛnsəl) *adj* **1** (of two different species of plant or animal) living in close association without being interdependent. See also **inquiline** (sense 1). **2** *Rare.* of or relating to eating together, esp. at the same table. ◆ *n* **3** a commensal plant or animal. **4** *Rare.* a companion at table. [C14: from Med. L *commensālis,* from L *com-* together + *mensa* table]
▸**comˈmensalism** *n* ▸**commensality** (ˌkɒmɛnˈsælɪtɪ) *n*

commensurable (kəˈmɛnsərəbəl, -ʃə-) *adj* **1** *Maths.* **1a** having a common factor. **1b** having units of the same dimensions and being related by whole numbers. **2** proportionate.
▸**comˌmensuraˈbility** *n* ▸**comˈmensurably** *adv*

commensurate ❶ (kəˈmɛnsərɪt, -ʃə-) *adj* **1** having the same extent or duration. **2** corresponding in degree, amount, or size; proportionate. **3** commensurable. [C17: from LL *commēnsūrātus,* from L *com-* same + *mēnsurāre* to MEASURE]
▸**comˈmensurately** *adv*

comment ❶ (ˈkɒmɛnt) *n* **1** a remark, criticism, or observation. **2** talk or gossip. **3** a note explaining or criticizing a passage in a text. **4** explanatory or critical matter added to a text. ◆ *vb* **5** (when *intr,* often foll. by *on;* when *tr,* takes a clause as object) to remark or express an opinion. **6** (*intr*) to write notes explaining or criticizing a text. [C15: from L *commentum* invention, from *comminiscī* to contrive]
▸**ˈcommenter** *n*

commentary ❶ (ˈkɒməntərɪ) *n, pl* **commentaries. 1** an explanatory series of notes. **2** a spoken accompaniment to a broadcast, film, etc. **3** an explanatory treatise on a text. **4** (*usually pl*) a personal record of events: *the commentaries of Caesar.*

commentate (ˈkɒmənˌteɪt) *vb* **commentates, commentating, commentated. 1** (*intr*) to serve as a commentator. **2** (*tr*) *US.* to make a commentary on.

> **USAGE NOTE** The verb *commentate,* derived from *commentator,* is sometimes used as a synonym for *comment on* or *provide a commentary for.* It is not yet fully accepted as standard, though widespread in sports reporting and journalism.

commentator ❶ (ˈkɒmənˌteɪtə) *n* **1** a person who provides a spoken commentary for a broadcast, film, etc., esp. of a sporting event. **2** a person who writes notes on a text, etc.

commerce ❶ (ˈkɒmɜːs) *n* **1** the activity embracing all forms of the purchase and sale of goods and services. **2** social relations. **3** *Arch.* sexual intercourse. [C16: from L *commercium,* from *commercārī,* from *mercārī* to trade, from *merx* merchandise]

commercial ❶ (kəˈmɜːʃəl) *adj* **1** of or engaged in commerce. **2** sponsored or paid for by an advertiser: *commercial television.* **3** having profit as the main aim: *commercial music.* **4** (of chemicals, etc.) unrefined and produced in bulk for use in industry. ◆ *n* **5** a commercially sponsored advertisement on radio or television.
▸**commerciality** (kəˌmɜːʃɪˈælɪtɪ) *n* ▸**comˈmercially** *adv*

commercial art *n* graphic art for commercial uses such as advertising, packaging, etc.

commercial bank *n* a bank primarily engaged in making short-term loans from funds deposited in current accounts.

commercial break *n* an interruption in a radio or television programme for the broadcasting of advertisements.

commercialism (kəˈmɜːʃəˌlɪzəm) *n* **1** the spirit, principles, or procedure of commerce. **2** exclusive or inappropriate emphasis on profit.

commercialize *or* **commercialise** (kəˈmɜːʃəˌlaɪz) *vb* **commercializes, commercializing, commercialized** *or* **commercialises, commercialising, commercialised.** (*tr*) **1** to make commercial. **2** to exploit for profit, esp. at the expense of quality.
▸**comˌmercialiˈzation** *or* **comˌmercialiˈsation** *n*

commercial paper *n* a short-term negotiable document, such as a bill of exchange, calling for the transference of a specified sum of money at a designated date.

commercial traveller *n* another name for a **travelling salesman.**

commercial vehicle *n* a vehicle for carrying goods or (less commonly) passengers.

commie *or* **commy** (ˈkɒmɪ) *n, pl* **commies,** *adj Inf. & derog.* short for **communist.**

commination (ˌkɒmɪˈneɪʃən) *n* **1** the act of threatening punishment or vengeance. **2** *Church of England.* a recital of prayers, including a list of God's judgments against sinners, in the office for Ash Wednesday. [C15: from L *comminātiō,* from *com-* (intensive) + *minārī* to threaten]
▸**comminatory** (ˈkɒmɪnətərɪ) *adj*

commingle (kɒˈmɪŋgᵊl) *vb* **commingles, commingling, commingled.** to mix or be mixed.

comminute (ˈkɒmɪˌnjuːt) *vb* **comminutes, comminuting, comminuted. 1** to break (a bone) into small fragments. **2** to divide (property) into small lots. [C17: from L *comminuere,* from *com-* (intensive) + *minuere* to reduce]
▸ˌ**commiˈnution** *n*

commis (ˈkɒmɪs, ˈkɒmɪ) *n, pl* **commis. 1** an agent or deputy. ◆ *adj* **2** (of a

THESAURUS

commanding *adj* **1** = **controlling,** advantageous, decisive, dominant, dominating, superior **2** = **authoritative,** assertive, autocratic, compelling, forceful, imposing, impressive, peremptory
Antonyms *adj* ≠ **authoritative:** retiring, shrinking, shy, submissive, timid, unassertive, unimposing, weak

commemorate *vb* = **remember,** celebrate, honour, immortalize, keep, memorialize, observe, pay tribute to, recognize, salute, solemnize
Antonyms *vb* disregard, forget, ignore, omit, overlook, pass over, take no notice of

commemoration *n* = **remembrance,** ceremony, honouring, memorial service, observance, tribute

commemorative *adj* = **memorial,** celebratory, dedicatory, in honour, in memory, in remembrance

commence *vb* = **begin,** embark on, enter upon, get the show on the road (*inf.*), inaugurate, initiate, open, originate, start
Antonyms *vb* bring *or* come to an end, cease, complete, conclude, desist, end, finish, halt, stop, terminate, wind up

commencement *n* **1** = **beginning,** birth, dawn, embarkation, inauguration, inception, initiation, launch, onset, opening, origin, outset, square one (*inf.*), start

commend *vb* **1, 3** = **praise,** acclaim, applaud, approve, compliment, crack up (*inf.*), eulogize, extol, recommend, speak highly of **2** = **entrust,** commit, confide, consign, deliver, hand over, yield
Antonyms *vb* ≠ **praise:** attack, blast, censure, condemn, criticize, denounce, disapprove, knock (*inf.*), lambast(e), put down, slam, tear into (*inf.*) ≠ **entrust:** hold back, keep, keep back, retain, withdraw, withhold

commendable *adj* **3** = **praiseworthy,** admirable, creditable, deserving, estimable, exemplary, laudable, meritorious, worthy

commendation *n* **1, 3** = **praise,** acclaim, acclamation, approbation, approval, Brownie points, credit, encomium, encouragement, good opinion, panegyric, recommendation

commensurate *adj* **1, 2** = **proportionate,** adequate, appropriate, coextensive, comparable, compatible, consistent, corresponding, due, equivalent, fit, fitting, in accord, sufficient

comment *n* **1** = **remark,** animadversion, observation, statement **3, 4** = **note,** annotation, commentary, criticism, elucidation, explanation, exposition, illustration ◆ *vb* **5** = **remark,** animadvert, interpose, mention, note, observe, opine, point out, say, utter **6** = **annotate,** criticize, elucidate, explain, interpret

commentary *n* **2** = **narration,** description, voice-over **3** = **notes,** analysis, critique, exegesis, explanation, review, treatise

commentator *n* **1** = **reporter,** commenter, special correspondent, sportscaster **2** = **critic,** annotator, expositor, interpreter, scholiast

commerce *n* **1** = **trade,** business, dealing, exchange, merchandising, traffic **2** *Literary* = **relations,** communication, dealings, intercourse, socializing

commercial *adj* **1** = **mercantile,** business, profit-making, sales, trade, trading waiter or chef) apprentice. [C16 (meaning: deputy): from F, from *commettre* to employ]

commiserate ⓣ (kəˈmɪzəˌreɪt) *vb* **commiserates, commiserating, commiserated.** (when *intr*, usually foll. by *with*) to feel or express sympathy or compassion (for). [C17: from L *commiserārī*, from *com-* together + *miserārī* to bewail]
▸**comˌmiserˈation** *n* ▸**comˈmiserˌator** *n*

commissar (ˈkɒmɪˌsɑː, ˌkɒmɪˈsɑː) *n* (in the former Soviet Union) **1** an official of the Communist Party responsible for political education. **2** (before 1946) the head of a government department. [C20: from Russian *kommissar*]

commissariat (ˌkɒmɪˈsɛərɪət) *n* **1** (in the former Soviet Union) a government department before 1946. **2** a military department in charge of food supplies, etc. [C17: from NL *commissāriātus*, from Med. L *commissārius* COMMISSARY]

commissary (ˈkɒmɪsərɪ) *n, pl* **commissaries. 1** *US.* a shop supplying food or equipment, as in a military camp. **2** *US army.* an officer responsible for supplies. **3** *US.* a restaurant in a film studio. **4** a representative or deputy, esp. of a bishop. [C14: from Med. L *commissārius* official in charge, from L *committere* to COMMIT]
▸**commissarial** (ˌkɒmɪˈsɛərɪəl) *adj*

commission ⓣ (kəˈmɪʃən) *n* **1** a duty committed to a person or group to perform. **2** authority to perform certain duties. **3** a document granting such authority. **4** *Mil.* **4a** a document conferring a rank on an officer. **4b** the rank granted. **5** a group charged with certain duties: *a commission of inquiry.* **6** a government board empowered to exercise administrative, judicial, or legislative authority. See also **Royal Commission. 7a** the authority given to a person or organization to act as an agent to a principal in commercial transactions. **7b** the fee allotted to an agent for services rendered. **8** the state of being charged with specific responsibilities. **9** the act of committing a sin, crime, etc. **10** good working condition or (esp. of a ship) active service (esp. in **in commission, out of commission**). ◆ *vb* (*mainly tr*) **11** to grant authority to. **12** *Mil.* to confer a rank on. **13** to equip and test (a ship) for active service. **14** to place an order for (something): *to commission a portrait.* **15** to make or become operative or operable: *the plant is due to commission next year.* [C14: from OF, from L *commissiō* a bringing together, from *committere* to COMMIT]

commissionaire (kəˌmɪʃəˈnɛə) *n Chiefly Brit.* a uniformed doorman at a hotel, theatre, etc. [C18: from F, from COMMISSION]

commissioned officer *n* a military officer holding a commission, such as Second Lieutenant in the British Army, Acting Sub-Lieutenant in the Royal Navy, Pilot Officer in the Royal Air Force, and officers of all ranks senior to these.

commissioner (kəˈmɪʃənə) *n* **1** a person endowed with certain powers. **2** any of several types of civil servant. **3** a member of a commission.
▸**comˈmissionerˌship** *n*

commissioner for oaths *n* a solicitor authorized to authenticate oaths on sworn statements.

commit ⓣ (kəˈmɪt) *vb* **commits, committing, committed.** (*tr*) **1** to hand over, as for safekeeping; entrust. **2 commit to memory.** to memorize. **3** to take into custody: *to commit someone to prison.* **4** (*usually passive*) to pledge or align (oneself), as to a particular cause: *a committed radical.* **5** to order (forces) into action. **6** to perform (a crime, error, etc.). **7** to surrender, esp. for destruction: *she committed the letter to the fire.* **8** to refer (a bill, etc.) to a committee. [C14: from L *committere* to join, from *com-* together + *mittere* to send]
▸**comˈmittable** *adj* ▸**comˈmitter** *n*

commitment ⓣ (kəˈmɪtmənt) *n* **1** the act of committing or pledging. **2** the state of being committed or pledged. **3** an obligation, promise, etc., that restricts freedom of action. **4** Also called (esp. formerly): **mittimus.** *Law.* a written order of a court directing that a person be imprisoned. **5** a future financial obligation or contingent liability. ◆ Also called (esp. for sense 4): **committal** (kəˈmɪtᵊl).

committee ⓣ *n* **1** (kəˈmɪtɪ). a group of people appointed to perform a specified service or function. **2** (ˌkɒmɪˈtiː). (formerly) a person to whom the care of a mentally incompetent person or his property was entrusted by a court. [C15: from *committen* to entrust + -EE]

committeeman (kəˈmɪtɪmən, -ˌmæn) *n, pl* **committeemen.** *Chiefly US.* a member of one or more committees.
▸**comˈmitteeˌwoman** *fem n*

Committee of the Whole House *n* (in Britain) an informal sitting of the House of Commons to discuss and amend a bill.

commode (kəˈməʊd) *n* **1** a piece of furniture, usually highly ornamented, containing drawers or shelves. **2** a bedside table with a cabinet for a chamber pot or washbasin. **3** a chair with a hinged flap concealing a chamber pot. [C17: from F, from L *commodus* COMMODIOUS]

commodious ⓣ (kəˈməʊdɪəs) *adj* **1** roomy; spacious. **2** *Arch.* convenient. [C15: from Med. L, from L *commodus* convenient, from *com-* with + *modus* measure]
▸**comˈmodiousness** *n*

commodity (kəˈmɒdɪtɪ) *n, pl* **commodities. 1** an article of commerce. **2** something of use or profit. **3** *Econ.* an exchangeable unit of economic wealth, such as a primary product. [C14: from OF *commodité*, from L *commoditās* suitability; see COMMODIOUS]

commodo (kəˈməʊdəʊ) *adv* a variant spelling of **comodo.**

commodore (ˈkɒməˌdɔː) *n* **1** *Brit.* a naval rank junior to rear admiral and senior to captain. **2** the captain of a shipping line. **3** the officer in command of a merchant convoy. **4** the titular head of a yacht club. [C17: prob. from Du. *commandeur*, from F, from OF *commander* to COMMAND]

common ⓣ (ˈkɒmən) *adj* **1** belonging to two or more people: *common property.* **2** belonging to members of one or more communities; public: *a common culture.* **3** of ordinary standard; average. **4** prevailing; widespread: *common opinion.* **5** frequently encountered; ordinary: *a common brand of soap.* **6** notorious: *a common nuisance.* **7** *Derog.* considered by the speaker to be low-class, vulgar, or coarse. **8** (*prenominal*) having no special distinction: *the common man.* **9** *Maths.* having a specified relationship with a group of numbers or quantities: *common denominator.* **10** *Prosody.* (of a syllable) able to be long or short. **11** *Grammar.* (in certain languages) denoting or belonging to a gender of nouns that includes both masculine and feminine referents. **12 common or garden.** *Inf.* ordinary; unexceptional. ◆ *n* **13** a tract of open public land. **14** *Law.* the right to go onto someone else's property and remove natural products, as by pasturing cattle (esp. in **right of common**). **15** *Christianity.* **15a** a form of the proper of the Mass used on festivals that have no special proper of their own. **15b** the ordinary of the Mass. **16 in common.** mutually held or used. ◆ See also **commons.** [C13: from OF *commun*, from L *commūnis* general]
▸**ˈcommonly** *adv* ▸**ˈcommonness** *n*

commonage (ˈkɒmənɪdʒ) *n* **1** *Chiefly law.* **1a** the use of something, esp. a pasture, in common with others. **1b** the right to such use. **2** the state of being held in common. **3** another word for **commonalty** (sense 1).

commonality (ˌkɒməˈnælɪtɪ) *n, pl* **commonalities. 1** the fact of being common. **2** another word for **commonalty** (sense 1).

commonalty (ˈkɒmənəltɪ) *n, pl* **commonalties. 1** the ordinary people as distinct from those with rank or title. **2** the members of an incorporated society. [C13: from OF *comunalte*, from *comunal* communal]

common carrier *n* a person or firm engaged in the business of transporting goods or passengers.

common chord *n Music.* a chord consisting of the keynote, a major or minor third, and a perfect fifth.

common cold *n* a mild viral infection of the upper respiratory tract, characterized by sneezing, coughing, etc.

commoner (ˈkɒmənə) *n* **1** a person who does not belong to the nobility. **2** a person who has a right in or over common land. **3** *Brit.* a student at a university who is not on a scholarship.

common fraction *n* another name for **simple fraction.**

common knowledge *n* something widely or generally known.

common law *n* **1** the body of law based on judicial decisions and custom, as distinct from statute law. **2** (*modifier*) of or denoting a marriage that is deemed to exist after a man and a woman have cohabited for a number of years: *common-law marriage; common-law wife; common-law husband.*

Common Market *n* **the.** an informal name for the European Economic Community (now the **European Union**) and its policies of greater eco-

THESAURUS

commiserate *vb* = **sympathize**, compassionate (*arch.*), condole, console, feel for, pity

commiseration *n* = **sympathy**, compassion, condolence, consolation, fellow feeling, pity

commission *n* **1, 2** = **duty**, appointment, authority, charge, employment, errand, function, mandate, mission, task, trust, warrant **5** = **committee**, board, body of commissioners, commissioners, delegation, deputation, representatives **7b** = **fee**, allowance, brokerage, compensation, cut, percentage, rake-off (*sl.*), royalties ◆ *vb* **11** = **appoint**, authorize, contract, delegate, depute, empower, engage, nominate, order, select, send

commit *vb* **1** = **give**, commend, confide, consign, deliver, deposit, engage, entrust, hand over **3** = **put in custody**, confine, imprison **4** = **pledge**, align, bind, compromise, endanger, make liable, obligate, rank **6** = **do**, carry out, enact, execute, perform, perpetrate
Antonyms *vb* ≠ **give:** receive, withhold ≠ **put in custody:** free, let out, release, set free ≠ **pledge:** disavow, vacillate, waver ≠ **do:** omit

commitment *n* **1** = **pledge**, assurance, guarantee, promise, undertaking, vow, word **2** = **dedication**, adherence, devotion, involvement, loyalty **3** = **responsibility**, duty, engagement, liability, obligation, tie
Antonyms *n* ≠ **dedication:** indecisiveness, vacillation, wavering ≠ **pledge:** disavowal, negation

committee *n* **1** = **group**, commission, delegation, deputation, panel, subcommittee

commodious *adj* **1** = **roomy**, ample, capacious, comfortable, expansive, extensive, large, loose, spacious

common *adj* **1, 2** = **collective**, communal, community, popular, public, social **3, 5** = **average**, a dime a dozen, bog-standard (*Brit. & Irish slang*), commonplace, conventional, customary, daily, everyday, familiar, frequent, general, habitual, humdrum, obscure, ordinary, plain, regular, routine, run-of-the-mill, simple, standard, stock, usual, vanilla (*sl.*), workaday **4** = **popular**, accepted, general, prevailing, prevalent, universal, widespread **7** = **vulgar**, coarse, inferior, low, plebeian, undistinguished
Antonyms *adj* ≠ **average:** abnormal, famous, formal, important, infrequent, noble, outstanding, rare, scarce, sophisticated, strange, superior, uncommon, unknown, unusual ≠ **collective:** personal, private ≠ **vulgar:** cultured, distinguished, gentle, refined, sensitive

commonness *n* **3, 5** = **usualness**, commonplaceness, conventionality, customariness, familiarness, generalness, habitualness, humdrumness, ordinariness, plainness, regularity, simpleness **7** = **vulgarity**, baseness, coarseness, inferiority, lowness
Antonyms *n* ≠ **usualness:** abnormality, extraordinariness, rarity, strangeness, uncommonness, unfamiliarness, uniqueness

nomic cooperation between member states. See also **European Community.**

common noun *n Grammar.* a noun that refers to each member of a whole class sharing the features connoted by the noun, as for example *orange* and *drum*. Cf. **proper noun.**

commonplace ❶ ('kɒmən,pleɪs) *adj* **1** ordinary; everyday. **2** dull; trite: *commonplace prose.* ◆ *n* **3** a platitude; truism. **4** a passage in a book marked for inclusion in a commonplace book, etc. **5** an ordinary thing. [C16: translation of L *locus commūnis* argument of wide application]
▸'**common,placeness** *n*

commonplace book *n* a notebook in which quotations, poems, etc., that catch the owner's attention are entered.

common room *n Chiefly Brit.* a sitting room in schools, colleges, etc.

commons ('kɒmənz) *n* **1** (*functioning as pl*) the lower classes as contrasted with the ruling or noble classes of society. **2** (*functioning as sing*) *Brit.* a hall for dining, recreation, etc., usually attached to a college, etc. **3** (*usually functioning as pl*) *Brit.* food or rations (esp. in **short commons**).

Commons ('kɒmənz) *n* **the.** See **House of Commons.**

common sense ❶ *n* **1** sound practical sense. ◆ *adj* **common-sense;** *also* **common-sensical. 2** inspired by or displaying this.

common time *n Music.* a time signature indicating four crotchet beats to the bar; four-four time. Symbol: **C**

commonweal ('kɒmən,wi:l) *n Arch.* **1** the public good. **2** another name for **commonwealth.**

commonwealth ('kɒmən,wɛlθ) *n* **1** the people of a state or nation viewed politically; body politic. **2** a state in which the people possess sovereignty; republic. **3** a group of persons united by some common interest.

Commonwealth ('kɒmən,wɛlθ) *n* **the. 1** Official name: **the Commonwealth of Nations.** an association of sovereign states, most of which are or at some time were ruled by Britain. **2** the republic that existed in Britain from 1649 to 1660. **3** the official designation of Australia, four states of the US, and Puerto Rico.

Commonwealth Day *n* the anniversary of Queen Victoria's birth, May 24, celebrated (now on the second Monday in March) in many parts of the Commonwealth. Former name: **Empire Day.**

commotion ❶ (kə'məʊʃən) *n* **1** violent disturbance; upheaval. **2** political insurrection. **3** a confused noise; din. [C15: from L *commōtiō*, from *commovēre*, from *com-* (intensive) + *movēre* to MOVE]

communal ❶ ('kɒmjun°l) *adj* **1** belonging to a community as a whole. **2** of a commune or a religious community.
▸**communality** (,kɒmju'nælɪtɪ) *n* ▸'**communally** *adv*

communalism ('kɒmjunə,lɪzəm) *n* **1** a system or theory of government in which the state is seen as a loose federation of self-governing communities. **2** the practice or advocacy of communal living or ownership.
▸'**communalist** *n* ▸,**communal'istic** *adj*

communalize *or* **communalise** ('kɒmjunə,laɪz) *vb* **communalizes, communalizing, communalized** *or* **communalises, communalising, communalised.** (*tr*) to render (something) the property of a commune or community.
▸,**communali'zation** *or* ,**communali'sation** *n*

communautaire *French.* (kɔmynotɛr) *adj* supporting the principles of the European Union. [lit.: community (as modifier)]

commune[1] *vb* (kə'mju:n), **communes, communing, communed.** (*intr*; usually foll. by *with*) **1** to talk intimately. **2** to experience strong emotion (for): *to commune with nature.* ◆ *n* ('kɒmju:n). **3** intimate conversation; communion. [C13: from OF *comuner* to hold in common, from *comun* COMMON]

commune[2] ❶ ('kɒmju:n) *n* **1** a group of families or individuals living together and sharing possessions and responsibilities. **2** any small group of people having common interests or responsibilities. **3** the smallest administrative unit in Belgium, France, Italy, and Switzerland. **4** a medieval town enjoying a large degree of autonomy. [C18: from F, from Med. L *commūnia*, from L: things held in common]

Commune ('kɒmju:n) *n French history.* **1** See **Paris Commune. 2** a committee that governed Paris during the French Revolution: suppressed 1794.

communicable ❶ (kə'mju:nɪkəb°l) *adj* **1** capable of being communicated. **2** (of a disease) capable of being passed on readily.
▸**com,munica'bility** *n* ▸**com'municably** *adv*

communicant (kə'mju:nɪkənt) *n* **1** *Christianity.* a person who receives Communion. **2** a person who communicates or informs.

communicate ❶ (kə'mju:nɪ,keɪt) *vb* **communicates, communicating, communicated. 1** to impart (knowledge) or exchange (thoughts) by speech, writing, gestures, etc. **2** (*tr*; usually foll. by *to*) to transmit (to): *the dog communicated his fear to the other animals.* **3** (*intr*) to have a sympathetic mutual understanding. **4** (*intr*; usually foll. by *with*) to make or have a connecting passage: *the kitchen communicates with the dining room.* **5** (*tr*) to transmit (a disease). **6** (*intr*) *Christianity.* to receive Communion. [C16: from L *commūnicāre* to share, from *commūnis* COMMON]
▸**com'muni,cator** *n* ▸**com'municatory** *adj*

communication ❶ (kə,mju:nɪ'keɪʃən) *n* **1** the imparting or exchange of information, ideas, or feelings. **2** something communicated, such as a message. **3** (*usually pl; sometimes functioning as sing*) the study of ways in which human beings communicate. **4** a connecting route or link. **5** (*pl*) *Mil.* the system of routes by which forces, supplies, etc., are moved within an area of operations.

communication cord *n Brit.* a cord or chain in a train which may be pulled by a passenger to stop the train in an emergency.

communications satellite *n* an artificial satellite used to relay radio, television, and telephone signals around the earth's surface, usually in geostationary orbit.

communicative ❶ (kə'mju:nɪkətɪv) *adj* **1** inclined or able to communicate readily; talkative. **2** of or relating to communication.

communion ❶ (kə'mju:njən) *n* **1** an exchange of thoughts, emotions, etc. **2** sharing in common; participation. **3** (foll. by *with*) strong feelings (for): *communion with nature.* **4** a religious group or denomination having common beliefs and practices. **5** spiritual union. [C14: from L *commūniō*, from *commūnis* COMMON]

Communion ❶ (kə'mju:njən) *n Christianity.* **1** the act of participating in the Eucharist. **2** the celebration of the Eucharist. **3** the consecrated elements of the Eucharist. ◆ Also called: **Holy Communion.**

communiqué ❶ (kə'mju:nɪ,keɪ) *n* an official communication or announcement, esp. to the press or public. [C19: from F]

communism ❶ ('kɒmju,nɪzəm) *n* **1** advocacy of a classless society in which private ownership has been abolished and the means of production belong to the community. **2** any movement or doctrine aimed at achieving such a society. **3** (*usually cap.*) a political movement based upon the writings of Marx that considers history in terms of class conflict and revolutionary struggle. **4** (*usually cap.*) a system of government established by a ruling Communist Party, esp. in the former Soviet Union. **5** communal living. [C19: from F *communisme*, from *commun* COMMON]

communist ❶ ('kɒmjunɪst) *n* **1** a supporter of communism. **2** (*often cap.*) a supporter of a Communist movement or state. **3** (*often cap.*) a member of a Communist party. **4** (*often cap.*) *Chiefly US.* any person

THESAURUS

commonplace *adj* **1, 2** = **everyday**, banal, common, customary, dime-a-dozen (*inf.*), humdrum, mundane, obvious, ordinary, pedestrian, run-of-the-mill, stale, threadbare, trite, uninteresting, vanilla (*sl.*), widespread, worn out ◆ *n* **3** = **cliché**, banality, platitude, truism
Antonyms *adj* ≠ **everyday:** exciting, extraordinary, ground-breaking, infrequent, interesting, left-field (*inf.*), new, novel, original, rare, strange, uncommon, unfamiliar, unique, unusual

common sense *n* **1** = **good sense**, gumption (*Brit. inf.*), horse sense, level-headedness, mother wit, native intelligence, nous (*Brit. slang*), practicality, prudence, reasonableness, sound judgment, soundness, wit ◆ *adj* **common-sense 2** = **sensible**, astute, down-to-earth, hard-headed, judicious, level-headed, matter-of-fact, practical, realistic, reasonable, sane, shrewd, sound
Antonyms *adj* airy-fairy (*inf.*), daft (*inf.*), foolish, impractical, irrational, unrealistic, unreasonable, unthinking, unwise

commotion *n* **1** = **disturbance**, ado, agitation, brouhaha, bustle, disorder, excitement, ferment, furore, fuss, hubbub, hue and cry, hullabaloo, hurly-burly, perturbation, racket, riot, rumpus, to-do, tumult, turmoil, upheaval, uproar

communal *adj* **1** = **public**, collective, communistic, community, general, joint, neighbourhood, shared
Antonyms *adj* exclusive, individual, personal, private, single, unshared

commune[2] *n* **1, 2** = **community**, collective, co-operative, kibbutz

commune *vb* **1** *usually foll. by* **with** = **talk to**, communicate with, confer with, confide in, converse with, discourse with, discuss with, parley with

communicable *adj* **2** = **infectious**, catching, contagious, taking, transferable, transmittable

communicate *vb* **1, 2** = **make known**, acquaint, announce, be in contact, be in touch, connect, convey, correspond, declare, disclose, disseminate, divulge, impart, inform, pass on, phone, proclaim, publish, report, reveal, ring up (*inf., chiefly Brit.*), signify, spread, transmit, unfold
Antonyms *vb* conceal, cover up, hold back, hush up, keep back, keep secret, keep under wraps, repress, sit on (*inf.*), suppress, whitewash (*inf.*), withhold

communication *n* **1** = **passing on**, connection, contact, conversation, correspondence, dissemination, intercourse, link, transmission **2** = **message**, announcement, disclosure, dispatch, information, intelligence, news, report, statement, word **3** *usually plu* = **information technology**, media, publicity, public relations, telecommunications **5** *pl* = **transport**, routes, travel

communicative *adj* **1** = **talkative**, candid, chatty, conversable, expansive, forthcoming, frank, informative, loquacious, open, outgoing, unreserved, voluble
Antonyms *adj* quiet, reserved, reticent, secretive, taciturn, uncommunicative, uninformative, untalkative

communion *n* **1-3** = **closeness**, accord, affinity, agreement, communing, concord, consensus, converse, fellowship, harmony, intercourse, participation, rapport, sympathy, togetherness, unity

Communion *n Church* **2** = **Eucharist**, Lord's Supper, Mass, Sacrament

communiqué *n* = **announcement**, bulletin, dispatch, news flash, official communication, report

communism *n, usually cap.* **3, 4** = **socialism**, Bolshevism, collectivism, Eurocommunism, Maoism, Marxism, Marxism-Leninism, Stalinism, state socialism, Titoism, Trotskyism

communist *n, often cap.* **2-4** = **socialist**, Bolshevik, collectivist, Marxist, Red (*inf.*)

holding left-wing views, esp. when considered subversive. **5** a person who practises communal living. ◆ *adj* **6** of, favouring, or relating to communism.
▸ **ˌcommuˈnistic** *adj*

community 🅣 (kəˈmjuːnɪtɪ) *n, pl* **communities. 1a** the people living in one locality. **1b** the locality in which they live. **1c** (*as modifier*): *community spirit.* **2** a group of people having cultural, religious, or other characteristics in common: *the Protestant community.* **3** a group of nations having certain interests in common. **4** the public; society. **5** common ownership. **6** similarity or agreement: *community of interests.* **7** (in Wales and Scotland) the smallest unit of local government. **8** *Ecology.* a group of interdependent plants and animals inhabiting the same region. [C14: from L *commūnitās,* from *commūnis* COMMON]

community centre *n* a building used by a community for social gatherings, etc.

community charge *n* (formerly in Britain) a flat-rate charge paid by each adult in a community to their local authority in place of rates. Also called: **poll tax.**

community chest *n US.* a fund raised by voluntary contribution for local welfare activities.

community council *n* (in Scotland and Wales) an independent voluntary local body set up to attend to local interests and organize community activities.

community education *n* the provision of a wide range of educational and special-interest courses and activities by a local authority.

community home *n* (in Britain) **1** a home provided by a local authority for children who cannot remain with their parents. **2** a boarding school for young offenders.

community medicine *n* the branch of medicine concerned with evaluating and providing for the health needs of populations, esp. through monitoring and preventive measures.

community policing *n* the assigning of the same one or two policemen to a particular area so that they become familiar with the residents and they with them, as a way of reducing crime.

community service *n* work undertaken for the community by an offender without pay, by the order of a court.

communize *or* **communise** (ˈkɒmjuˌnaɪz) *vb* **communizes, communizing, communized** *or* **communises, communising, communised.** (*tr*) (*sometimes cap.*) **1** to make (property) public; nationalize. **2** to make (a person or country) communist.
▸ **ˌcommuniˈzation** *or* **ˌcommuniˈsation** *n*

commutate (ˈkɒmjuˌteɪt) *vb* **commutates, commutating, commutated.** (*tr*) **1** to reverse the direction of (an electric current). **2** to convert (an alternating current) into a direct current.

commutation (ˌkɒmjuˈteɪʃən) *n* **1** a substitution or exchange. **2** the replacement of one method of payment by another. **3** the reduction in severity of a penalty imposed by law. **4** the process of commutating an electric current.

commutative (kəˈmjuːtətɪv, ˈkɒmjuˌteɪtɪv) *adj* **1** relating to or involving substitution. **2** *Maths, logic.* **2a** giving the same result irrespective of the order of the arguments; thus addition is commutative but subtraction is not. **2b** relating to this property: *the commutative law of addition.*

commutator (ˈkɒmjuˌteɪtə) *n* **1** a device used to reverse the direction of flow of an electric current. **2** the segmented metal cylinder or disc of an electric motor, generator, etc., used to make electrical contact with the rotating coils.

commute 🅣 (kəˈmjuːt) *vb* **commutes, commuting, commuted. 1** (*intr*) to travel some distance regularly between one's home and one's place of work. **2** (*tr*) to substitute. **3** (*tr*) *Law.* to reduce (a sentence) to one less severe. **4** to pay (an annuity, etc.) at one time, instead of in instalments. **5** to change: *to commute base metal into gold.* [C17: from L *commūtāre,* from *com-* mutually + *mūtāre* to change]
▸ **comˈmutable** *adj* ▸ **comˌmutaˈbility** *n*

commuter 🅣 (kəˈmjuːtə) *n* a person who travels to work over an appreciable distance, usually from the suburbs to the centre of a city.

comodo *or* **commodo** (kəˈməudəu) *adv Music.* in a convenient tempo. [It.: comfortable, from L *commodus* convenient: see COMMODIOUS]

comose (ˈkəuməus, kəuˈməus) *adj Bot.* having tufts of hair; hairy. Also: **comate.** [C18: from L *comōsus* hairy]

comp (kɒmp) *Inf.* ◆ *n* **1** a compositor. **2** an accompaniment. **3** a competition. ◆ *vb* **4** (*intr*) to work as a compositor in the printing industry. **5** to play an accompaniment (to).

comp. *abbrev. for:* **1** companion. **2** comparative. **3** compare. **4** compiled. **5** composer. **6** composition. **7** compositor. **8** compound. **9** comprehensive. **10** comprising.

compact[1] 🅣 *adj* (kəmˈpækt). **1** closely packed together. **2** neatly fitted into a restricted space. **3** concise; brief. **4** well constructed; solid; firm. **5** (foll. by *of*) composed (of). ◆ *vb* (kəmˈpækt). (*tr*) **6** to pack closely together; compress. **7** (foll. by *of*) to form by pressing together: *sediment compacted of three types of clay.* **8** *Metallurgy.* to compress (a metal powder) to form a stable product suitable for sintering. ◆ *n* (ˈkɒmpækt). **9** a small flat case containing a mirror, face powder, and powder puff, designed to be carried in a woman's handbag. **10** *US & Canad.* a small and economical car. [C16: from L *compactus,* from *compingere,* from *com-* together + *pangere* to fasten]
▸ **comˈpactly** *adv* ▸ **comˈpactness** *n*

compact[2] 🅣 (ˈkɒmpækt) *n* an official contract or agreement. [C16: from L *compactum,* from *compacīscī,* from *com-* together + *pacīscī* to contract]

compact disc (ˈkɒmpækt) *n* a small digital audio disc on which sound is recorded as a series of metallic pits enclosed in PVC and read by an optical laser system. Also called: **compact audio disc.** Abbrev.: **CD, CAD.**

compact video disc *n* a compact laser disc that plays both pictures and sound.

compages (kəmˈpeɪdʒiːz) *n* (*functioning as sing*) a structure or framework. [C17: from L: from *com-* together + *pangēre* to fasten]

companion[1] 🅣 (kəmˈpænjən) *n* **1** a person who is an associate of another or others; comrade. **2** (esp. formerly) an employee, usually a woman, who provides company for an employer. **3a** one of a pair. **3b** (*as modifier*): *a companion volume.* **4** a guidebook or handbook. **5** a member of the lowest rank of certain orders of knighthood. **6** *Astron.* the fainter of the two components of a double star. ◆ *vb* **7** (*tr*) to accompany. [C13: from LL *compāniō,* lit.: one who eats bread with another, from L *com-* with + *pānis* bread]
▸ **comˈpanionˌship** *n*

companion[2] (kəmˈpænjən) *n Naut.* a raised frame on an upper deck with windows to give light to the deck below. [C18: from Du. *kompanje* quarterdeck, from OF *compagne,* from OIt. *compagna* pantry, ? ult. from L *pānis* bread]

companionable 🅣 (kəmˈpænjənəbᵊl) *adj* sociable.
▸ **comˈpanionableness** *n* ▸ **comˈpanionably** *adv*

companionate (kəmˈpænjənɪt) *adj* **1** resembling, appropriate to, or acting as a companion. **2** harmoniously suited.

companionway (kəmˈpænjənˌweɪ) *n* a ladder from one deck to another in a ship.

company 🅣 (ˈkʌmpənɪ) *n, pl* **companies. 1** a number of people gathered together; assembly. **2** the fact of being with someone; companionship: *I enjoy her company.* **3** a guest or guests. **4** a business enterprise. **5** the members of an enterprise not specifically mentioned in the enterprise's title. Abbrev.: **Co., co. 6** a group of actors. **7** a small unit of troops. **8** the officers and crew of a ship. **9** a unit of Guides. **10** *English history.* a medieval guild. **11 keep company. 11a** to accompany (someone). **11b** (esp. of lovers) to spend time together. ◆ *vb* **companies, companying, companied. 12** *Arch.* to associate (with someone). [C13: from OF *compaignie,* from LL *compāniō;* see COMPANION[1]]

company doctor *n* **1** a businessman or accountant who specializes in turning ailing companies into profitable enterprises. **2** a physician employed by a company to look after its staff and to advise on health matters.

company sergeant major *n Mil.* the senior noncommissioned officer in a company.

company town *n US & Canad.* a town built by a company for its employees.

compar. *abbrev. for* comparative.

comparable 🅣 (ˈkɒmpərəbᵊl) *adj* **1** worthy of comparison. **2** able to be compared (with).
▸ **ˌcomparaˈbility** *or* **ˈcomparableness** *n*

THESAURUS

community *n* **1-4 = society,** association, body politic, brotherhood, commonwealth, company, district, general public, locality, people, populace, population, public, residents, state

commute *vb* **2 = substitute,** barter, exchange, interchange, switch, trade **3** *Law* **= reduce,** alleviate, curtail, mitigate, modify, remit, shorten, soften

commuter *n* **= daily traveller,** straphanger (*inf.*), suburbanite

compact[1] *adj* **1 = closely packed,** compressed, condensed, dense, firm, impenetrable, impermeable, pressed together, solid, thick **3 = brief,** compendious, concise, epigrammatic, laconic, pithy, pointed, succinct, terse, to the point ◆ *vb* **6 = pack closely,** compress, condense, cram, stuff, tamp
Antonyms *adj* ≠ **closely packed:** dispersed, large, loose, roomy, scattered, spacious, sprawling ≠ **brief:** circumlocutory, garrulous, lengthy, long-winded, prolix, rambling, verbose, wordy ◆ *vb* ≠ **pack closely:** disperse, loosen, separate

compact[2] *n* **= agreement,** alliance, arrangement, bargain, bond, concordat, contract, covenant, deal, entente, pact, stipulation, treaty, understanding

companion[1] *n* **1 = friend,** accomplice, ally, associate, buddy (*inf.*), colleague, comrade, confederate, consort, crony, gossip (*arch.*), homeboy (*sl., chiefly US*), mate (*inf.*), partner **2 = escort,** aide, assistant, attendant, chaperon, duenna, squire **3a = mate,** complement, counterpart, fellow, match, twin

companionable *adj* **= friendly,** affable, congenial, conversable, convivial, cordial, familiar, genial, gregarious, neighbourly, outgoing, sociable

companionship *n* **1 = fellowship,** amity, camaraderie, company, comradeship, conviviality, esprit de corps, fraternity, friendship, rapport, togetherness

company *n* **1 = group,** assemblage, assembly, band, bevy, body, camp, circle, collection, community, concourse, convention, coterie, crew, crowd, ensemble, gathering, league, party, set, throng, troop, troupe, turnout **2 = companionship,** fellowship, presence, society **3 = guests,** callers, party, visitors **4 = business,** association, concern, corporation, establishment, firm, house, partnership, syndicate

comparable *adj* **1 = on a par,** a match for, as good as, commensurate, equal, equivalent, in a class with, proportionate, tantamount **2 = similar,** akin, alike, analogous, cognate, corresponding, cut from the same cloth, of a piece, related

comparative 🅣 (kəmˈpærətɪv) *adj* **1** denoting or involving comparison: *comparative literature.* **2** relative: *a comparative loss of prestige.* **3** *Grammar.* denoting the form of an adjective that indicates that the quality denoted is possessed to a greater extent. In English the comparative is marked by the suffix *-er* or the word *more.* ◆ *n* **4** the comparative form of an adjective.
▸**comˈparatively** *adv* ▸**comˈparativeness** *n*

comparative advertising *n* the usual US term for **knocking copy.**

compare 🅣 (kəmˈpɛə) *vb* **compares, comparing, compared. 1** (*tr;* foll. by *to*) to regard as similar; liken: *the general has been compared to Napoleon.* **2** (*tr*) to examine in order to observe resemblances or differences: *to compare rum and gin.* **3** (*intr;* usually foll. by *with*) to be the same or similar: *gin compares with rum in alcoholic content.* **4** (*intr*) to bear a specified relation when examined: *this car compares badly with the other.* **5** (*tr*) *Grammar.* to give the positive, comparative, and superlative forms of (an adjective). **6 compare notes.** to exchange opinions. ◆ *n* **7** comparison (esp. in **beyond compare**). [C15: from OF, from L *comparāre,* from *compar,* from *com-* together + *par* equal]

comparison 🅣 (kəmˈpærɪsᵊn) *n* **1** the act of comparing. **2** the state of being compared. **3** likeness: *there was no comparison between them.* **4** a rhetorical device involving comparison, such as a simile. **5** Also called: **degrees of comparison.** *Grammar.* the listing of the positive, comparative, and superlative forms of an adjective or adverb. **6 bear** *or* **stand comparison (with).** to be sufficiently similar to be compared with (something else), esp. favourably.

compartment 🅣 (kəmˈpɑːtmənt) *n* **1** one of the sections into which an area, esp. an enclosed space, is partitioned. **2** any separate section: *a compartment of the mind.* **3** a small storage space. [C16: from F *compartiment,* ult. from LL *compartīrī* to share]
▸**compartmental** (ˌkɒmpɑːtˈmentᵊl) *adj* ▸ˌ**compartˈmentally** *adv*

compartmentalize 🅣 *or* **compartmentalise** (ˌkɒmpɑːtˈmentᵊˌlaɪz) *vb* **compartmentalizes, compartmentalizing, compartmentalized** *or* **compartmentalises, compartmentalising, compartmentalised.** (*usually tr*) to put into categories, etc., esp. to an excessive degree.
▸ˌ**compartˌmentaliˈzation** *or* ˌ**compartˌmentaliˈsation** *n*

compass 🅣 (ˈkʌmpəs) *n* **1** Also called: **magnetic compass.** an instrument for finding direction, having a magnetized needle which points to magnetic north. **2** (*often pl*) Also called: **pair of compasses.** an instrument used for drawing circles, measuring distances, etc., that consists of two arms, joined at one end. **3** limits or range: *within the compass of education.* **4** *Music.* the interval between the lowest and highest note attainable. ◆ *vb* (*tr*) **5** to surround; hem in. **6** to grasp mentally. **7** to achieve; accomplish. **8** *Obs.* to plot. [C13: from OF *compas,* from Vulgar L *compassāre* (unattested) to pace out, ult. from L *passus* step]
▸ˈ**compassable** *adj*

compass card *n* a compass in the form of a card that rotates so that "0°" or "North" points to magnetic north.

compassion 🅣 (kəmˈpæʃən) *n* a feeling of distress and pity for the suffering or misfortune of another. [C14: from OF, from LL *compassiō,* from L *com-* with + *patī* to suffer]

compassionate 🅣 (kəmˈpæʃənɪt) *adj* showing or having compassion.
▸**comˈpassionately** *adv*

compassionate leave *n* leave granted on the grounds of bereavement, family illness, etc.

compassion fatigue *n* the inability to react sympathetically to a crisis, disaster, etc., because of overexposure to previous crises, disasters, etc.

compass rose *n* a circle or decorative device printed on a map or chart showing the points of the compass.

compass saw *n* a hand saw with a narrow tapered blade for making a curved cut.

compatible 🅣 (kəmˈpætɪbᵊl) *adj* **1** (usually foll. by *with*) able to exist together harmoniously. **2** (usually foll. by *with*) consistent: *her deeds were not compatible with her ideology.* **3** (of pieces of machinery, etc.) capable of being used together without modification or adaptation. [C15: from Med. L *compatibilis,* from LL *compatī;* see COMPASSION]
▸**comˌpatiˈbility** *n* ▸**comˈpatibly** *adv*

compatriot 🅣 (kəmˈpætrɪət) *n* a fellow countryman. [C17: from F *compatriote,* from LL; see PATRIOT]
▸**comˌpatriˈotic** *adj*

compeer (ˈkɒmpɪə) *n* **1** a person of equal rank, status, or ability. **2** a comrade. [C13: from OF *comper,* from Med. L *compater* godfather]

compel 🅣 (kəmˈpɛl) *vb* **compels, compelling, compelled.** (*tr*) **1** to cause (someone) by force (to be or do something). **2** to obtain by force; exact: *to compel obedience.* [C14: from L *compellere,* from *com-* together + *pellere* to drive]
▸**comˈpellable** *adj*

compelling 🅣 (kəmˈpɛlɪŋ) *adj* **1** arousing or denoting strong interest, esp. admiring interest. **2** (of an argument, evidence, etc.) convincing.

compendious 🅣 (kəmˈpɛndɪəs) *adj* stating the essentials of a subject in a concise form.
▸**comˈpendiously** *adv* ▸**comˈpendiousness** *n*

compendium 🅣 (kəmˈpɛndɪəm) *n, pl* **compendiums** *or* **compendia** (-dɪə). **1** *Brit.* a book containing a collection of useful hints. **2** *Brit.* a selection, esp. of different games in one container. **3** a summary. [C16: from L: a saving, lit.: something weighed]

compensate 🅣 (ˈkɒmpɛnˌseɪt) *vb* **compensates, compensating, compensated. 1** to make amends to (someone), esp. for loss or injury. **2** (*tr*) to serve as compensation or damages for (injury, loss, etc.). **3** to counterbalance the effects of (a force, weight, etc.) so as to produce equilibrium. **4** (*intr*) to attempt to conceal one's shortcomings by the exaggerated exhibition of qualities regarded as desirable. [C17: from L *compēnsāre,* from *pendere* to weigh]
▸**compensatory** (ˈkɒmpɛnˌseɪtərɪ, kəmˈpɛnsətərɪ) *or* **compensative** (ˈkɒmpɛnˌseɪtɪv, kəmˈpɛnsə-) *adj*

compensation 🅣 (ˌkɒmpɛnˈseɪʃən) *n* **1** the act of making amends for something. **2** something given as reparation for loss, injury, etc. **3** the attempt to conceal one's shortcomings by the exaggerated exhibition of qualities regarded as desirable.
▸ˌ**compenˈsational** *adj*

comper (ˈkɒmpə) *n Inf.* a person who regularly enters competitions in newspapers, magazines, etc., esp. competitions offering consumer goods as prizes. [C20: COMP(ETITION) + -ER[1]]
▸ˈ**comping** *n*

compere (ˈkɒmpɛə) *Brit.* ◆ *n* **1** a master of ceremonies who introduces cabaret, television acts, etc. ◆ *vb* **comperes, compering, compered. 2** to act as a compere (for). [C20: from F, lit.: godfather]

compete 🅣 (kəmˈpiːt) *vb* **competes, competing, competed.** (*intr;* often foll. by *with*) to contend (against) for profit, an award, etc. [C17: from LL *competere,* from L, from *com-* together + *petere* to seek]

competence 🅣 (ˈkɒmpɪtəns) *or* **competency** *n* **1** the condition of being capable; ability. **2** a sufficient income to live on. **3** the state of being legally competent or qualified.

THESAURUS

Antonyms *adj* different, dissimilar, incommensurable, incomparable, unequal

comparative *adj* **2** = **relative**, approximate, by comparison, qualified

compare *vb* **1** *foll. by* **to** = **liken to**, correlate to, equate to, identify with, mention in the same breath as, parallel, resemble **2** = **weigh**, balance, collate, contrast, juxtapose, set against **3** *usually with* **with** = **be on a par with**, approach, approximate to, bear comparison, be in the same class as, be the equal of, come up to, compete with, equal, hold a candle to, match, vie

comparison *n* **1** = **contrast**, collation, distinction, juxtaposition **3** = **similarity**, analogy, comparability, correlation, likeness, resemblance

compartment *n* **1, 3** = **section**, alcove, bay, berth, booth, carrel, carriage, cell, chamber, cubbyhole, cubicle, locker, niche, pigeonhole **2** = **category**, area, department, division, section, subdivision

compartmentalize *vb* = **categorize** *or* **categorise**, classify, pigeonhole, sectionalize *or* sectionalise

compass *n* **3** = **range**, area, bound, boundary, circle, circuit, circumference, enclosure, extent, field, limit, reach, realm, round, scope, sphere, stretch, zone ◆ *vb* **5** = **surround**, beset, besiege, blockade, circumscribe, encircle, enclose, encompass, environ, hem in, invest (*rare*)

compassion *n* = **sympathy**, charity, clemency, commiseration, compunction, condolence, fellow feeling, heart, humanity, kindness, mercy, pity, quarter, ruth (*arch.*), soft-heartedness, sorrow, tender-heartedness, tenderness, understanding

Antonyms *n* apathy, cold-heartedness, indifference, mercilessness, unconcern

compassionate *adj* = **sympathetic**, benevolent, charitable, humane, humanitarian, indulgent, kind-hearted, kindly, lenient, merciful, pitying, tender, tender-hearted, understanding

Antonyms *adj* callous, harsh, heartless, inhumane, pitiless, uncaring, unfeeling, unmerciful, unsympathetic

compatibility *n* **1** = **harmony**, affinity, agreement, amity, concord, congeniality, empathy, like-mindedness, rapport, single-mindedness, sympathy

compatible *adj* **1, 2** = **harmonious**, accordant, adaptable, agreeable, congenial, congruent, congruous, consistent, consonant, in harmony, in keeping, like-minded, reconcilable, suitable

Antonyms *adj* contradictory, inappropriate, inapt, incompatible, unfitting, unharmonious, unsuitable

compatriot *n* = **fellow countryman**, countryman, fellow citizen

compel *vb* **1, 2** = **force**, bulldoze (*inf.*), coerce, constrain, dragoon, drive, enforce, exact, hustle (*sl.*), impel, make, necessitate, oblige, railroad (*inf.*), restrain, squeeze, urge

compelling *adj* **1** = **fascinating**, enchanting, enthralling, gripping, hypnotic, irresistible, mesmeric, spellbinding **2** = **convincing**, cogent, conclusive, forceful, irrefutable, powerful, telling, weighty

Antonyms *adj* ≠ **fascinating:** boring, dull, humdrum, monotonous, ordinary, repetitious, tiresome, uneventful, uninteresting, wearisome

compendious *adj* = **concise**, abbreviated, abridged, brief, comprehensive, condensed, contracted, short, succinct, summarized, summary, synoptic

compendium *n* **1** = **collection**, compilation, digest **3** = **summary**, abbreviation, abridgment, abstract, capsule, epitome, outline, précis, synopsis

compensate *vb* **1** = **recompense**, atone, indemnify, make amends, make good, make restitution, refund, reimburse, remunerate, repay, requite, reward, satisfy **2** = **cancel (out)**, balance, counteract, counterbalance, countervail, make up for, offset, redress

compensation *n* **1, 2** = **recompense**, amends, atonement, damages, indemnification, indemnity, meed (*arch.*), offset, payment, reimbursement, remuneration, reparation, requital, restitution, reward, satisfaction

compete *vb* = **contend**, be in the running, challenge, contest, emulate, fight, pit oneself against, rival, strive, struggle, vie

competence *n* **1** = **ability**, adequacy, appropriateness, capability, capacity, competency, craft, expertise, fitness, proficiency, skill, suitability

Antonyms *n* inability, inadequacy, incompetence

competent ❶ (ˈkɒmpɪtənt) *adj* **1** having sufficient skill, knowledge, etc.; capable. **2** suitable or sufficient for the purpose: *a competent answer.* **3** *Law.* (of a witness, etc.) qualified to testify, etc. [C14: from L *competēns,* from *competere;* see COMPETE]
▸ˈ**competently** *adv*

competition ❶ (ˌkɒmpɪˈtɪʃən) *n* **1** the act of competing. **2** a contest in which a winner is selected from among two or more entrants. **3** a series of games, sports events, etc. **4** the opposition offered by competitors. **5** competitors offering opposition.

competitive ❶ (kəmˈpɛtɪtɪv) *adj* **1** involving rivalry: *competitive sports.* **2** sufficiently low in price or high in quality to be successful against commercial rivals. **3** characterized by an urge to compete: *a competitive personality.*
▸**comˈpetitiveness** *n*

competitor ❶ (kəmˈpɛtɪtə) *n* a person, group, team, firm, etc., that vies or competes; rival.

compile ❶ (kəmˈpaɪl) *vb* **compiles, compiling, compiled.** (*tr*) **1** to make or compose from other sources: *to compile a list of names.* **2** to collect for a book, hobby, etc. **3** *Computing.* to create (a set of machine instructions) from a high-level programming language, using a compiler. [C14: from L *compīlāre,* from *com-* together + *pīlāre* to thrust down, pack]
▸**compilation** (ˌkɒmpɪˈleɪʃən) *n*

compiler (kəmˈpaɪlə) *n* **1** a person who compiles something. **2** a computer program by which a high-level programming language is converted into machine language that can be acted upon by a computer. Cf. **assembler.**

complacency ❶ (kəmˈpleɪsənsɪ) *or* **complacence** *n* extreme self-satisfaction; smugness.

complacent ❶ (kəmˈpleɪsᵊnt) *adj* extremely self-satisfied. [C17: from L *complacēns* very pleasing, from *complacēre,* from *com-* (intensive) + *placēre* to please]
▸**comˈplacently** *adv*

complain ❶ (kəmˈpleɪn) *vb* (*intr*) **1** to express resentment, displeasure, etc.; grumble. **2** (foll. by *of*) to state the presence of pain, illness, etc.: *she complained of a headache.* [C14: from OF *complaindre,* from Vulgar L *complangere* (unattested), from L *com-* (intensive) + *plangere* to bewail]
▸**comˈplainer** *n* ▸**comˈplainingly** *adv*

complainant (kəmˈpleɪnənt) *n Law.* a plaintiff.

complaint ❶ (kəmˈpleɪnt) *n* **1** the act of complaining. **2** a cause for complaining; grievance. **3** a mild ailment.

complaisant ❶ (kəmˈpleɪzᵊnt) *adj* showing a desire to comply or oblige; polite. [C17: from F *complaire,* from L *complacēre* to please greatly; cf. COMPLACENT]
▸**comˈplaisance** *n*

complement ❶ *n* (ˈkɒmplɪmənt). **1** a person or thing that completes something. **2** a complete amount, number, etc. (often in **full complement**). **3** the officers and crew needed to man a ship. **4** *Grammar.* a word, phrase, or clause that completes the meaning of the predicate, as *an idiot* in *He is an idiot* or *that he would be early* in *I hoped that he would be early.* **5** *Maths.* the angle that when added to a specified angle produces a right angle. **6** *Logic.* the class of all the things that are not members of a given class. **7** *Immunol.* a group of proteins in the blood serum that, when activated by antibodies, destroys alien cells, such as bacteria. ◆ *vb* (ˈkɒmplɪˌmɛnt). **8** (*tr*) to complete or form a complement to. [C14: from L *complēmentum,* from *complēre,* from *com-* (intensive) + *plēre* to fill]
▸ˌ**complemenˈtation** *n*

> **USAGE NOTE** Avoid confusion with **compliment.**

complementary ❶ (ˌkɒmplɪˈmɛntərɪ) *adj* **1** forming a complement. **2** forming a satisfactory or balanced whole. **3** involving or using the treatments and techniques of alternative (complementary) medicine.
▸ˌ**compleˈmentarily** *adv* ▸ˌ**compleˈmentariness** *n*

complementary angle *n* either of two angles whose sum is 90°. Cf. **supplementary angle.**

complementary colour *n* one of any pair of colours, such as yellow and blue, that give white or grey when mixed in the correct proportions.

complementary DNA *n* a form of DNA artificially synthesized from a messenger RNA template and used in genetic engineering to produce gene clones. Abbrev.: **cDNA.**

complementary medicine *n* another name for **alternative medicine.**

complete ❶ (kəmˈpliːt) *adj* **1** having every necessary part; entire. **2** finished. **3** (*prenominal*) thorough: *he is a complete rogue.* **4** perfect in quality or kind: *he is a complete scholar.* **5** (of a logical system) constituted such that a contradiction or inconsistency arises on the addition of an axiom that cannot be deduced from the axioms of the system. **6** *Arch.* skilled; accomplished. ◆ *vb* **completes, completing, completed.** (*tr*) **7** to make perfect. **8** to finish. **9** (in land law) to pay any outstanding balance on a contract for the conveyance of land in exchange for the title deeds, so that the ownership of the land changes hands. **10** *American football.* (of a quarterback) to make a forward pass successfully. [C14: from L *complētus,* p.p. of *complēre* to fill up; see COMPLEMENT]
▸**comˈpletely** *adv* ▸**comˈpleteness** *n* ▸**comˈpletion** *n*

completist (kəmˈpliːtɪst) *n* a person who collects objects or memorabilia obsessively.

complex ❶ (ˈkɒmplɛks) *adj* **1** made up of interconnected parts. **2** (of thoughts, writing, etc.) intricate. **3** *Maths.* **3a** of or involving complex numbers. **3b** consisting of a real and an imaginary part, either of which can be zero. ◆ *n* **4** a whole made up of related parts: *a building complex.* **5** *Psychoanal.* a group of emotional impulses that have been banished from the conscious mind but continue to influence a person's behaviour. **6** *Inf.* an obsession: *he's got a complex about cats.* **7** any chemical compound in which one molecule is linked to another by a coordinate bond. [C17: from L *complexus,* from *complectī,* from *com-* together + *plectere* to braid]
▸ˈ**complexness** *n*

> **USAGE NOTE** *Complex* is sometimes wrongly used where *complicated* is meant. *Complex* is properly used to say only that something consists of several parts. It should not be used to say that, because something consists of many parts, it is difficult to understand or analyse.

THESAURUS

competent *adj* **1, 2 = able,** adapted, adequate, appropriate, capable, clever, endowed, equal, fit, pertinent, proficient, qualified, sufficient, suitable
Antonyms *adj* cowboy (*inf.*), inadequate, incapable, incompetent, inexperienced, inexpert, undependable, unqualified, unskilled

competition *n* **1 = rivalry,** contention, contest, emulation, one-upmanship (*inf.*), opposition, strife, struggle **2, 3 = contest,** championship, event, head-to-head, puzzle, quiz, tournament **5 = opposition,** challengers, field, rivals

competitive *adj* **1 = cut-throat,** aggressive, antagonistic, at odds, dog-eat-dog, opposing, rival, vying **3 = ambitious,** combative

competitor *n* **= contestant,** adversary, antagonist, challenger, competition, emulator, opponent, opposition, rival

compilation *n* **1, 2 = collection,** accumulation, anthology, assemblage, assortment, treasury

compile *vb* **1 = put together,** accumulate, amass, anthologize, collect, cull, garner, gather, marshal, organize

complacency *n* **= self-satisfaction,** contentment, gratification, pleasure, satisfaction, smugness

complacent *adj* **= self-satisfied,** contented, gratified, pleased, pleased with oneself, resting on one's laurels, satisfied, self-assured, self-contented, self-righteous, serene, smug, unconcerned
Antonyms *adj* discontent, dissatisfied, insecure, troubled, uneasy, unsatisfied

complain *vb* **1 = find fault,** beef (*sl.*), bellyache (*sl.*), bemoan, bewail, bleat, carp, deplore, fuss, grieve, gripe (*inf.*), groan, grouch (*inf.*), grouse, growl, grumble, kvetch (*US sl.*), lament, moan, whine, whinge (*inf.*)

complaint *n* **1, 2 = criticism,** accusation, annoyance, beef (*sl.*), bitch (*sl.*), charge, dissatisfaction, fault-finding, grievance, gripe (*inf.*), grouch (*inf.*), grouse, grumble, lament, moan, plaint, protest, remonstrance, trouble, wail **3 = illness,** affliction, ailment, disease, disorder, indisposition, malady, sickness, upset

complaisance *n* **= obligingness,** accommodativeness, acquiescence, agreeableness, compliance, deference

complaisant *adj* **= obliging,** accommodating, amiable, compliant, conciliatory, deferential, polite, solicitous

complement *n* **1 = completion,** companion, consummation, correlative, counterpart, finishing touch, rounding-off, supplement **2 = total,** aggregate, capacity, entirety, quota, totality, wholeness ◆ *vb* **8 = complete,** cap (*inf.*), crown, round off, set off

complementary *adj* **1, 2 = completing,** companion, correlative, corresponding, fellow, interdependent, interrelating, matched, reciprocal
Antonyms *adj* contradictory, different, incompatible, incongruous, uncomplementary

complete *adj* **1 = entire,** all, faultless, full, intact, integral, plenary, unabridged, unbroken, undivided, unimpaired, whole **2 = finished,** accomplished, achieved, concluded, ended **3, 4 = total,** absolute, consummate, deep-dyed (*usually derogatory*), dyed-in-the-wool, outright, perfect, thorough, thoroughgoing, utter ◆ *vb* **8 = finish,** accomplish, achieve, cap, close, conclude, crown, discharge, do, end, execute, fill in, finalize, fulfil, perfect, perform, put the tin lid on, realize, round off, settle, terminate, wrap up (*inf.*)
Antonyms *adj* ≠ **entire:** deficient, imperfect, incomplete, spoilt ≠ **finished:** inconclusive, unaccomplished, unfinished, unsettled ≠ **total:** partial ◆ *vb* ≠ **finish:** begin, commence, initiate, mar, spoil, start

completely *adv* **3, 4 = totally,** absolutely, a hundred per cent, altogether, down to the ground, en masse, entirely, every inch, from A to Z, from beginning to end, fully, heart and soul, hook, line and sinker, in full, *in toto,* lock, stock and barrel, one hundred per cent, perfectly, quite, root and branch, solidly, thoroughly, utterly, wholly

completion *n* **2 = finishing,** accomplishment, attainment, bitter end, close, conclusion, consummation, culmination, end, expiration, finalization, fruition, fulfilment, realization

complex *adj* **1 = compound,** composite, compounded, heterogeneous, manifold, multifarious, multiple **2 = complicated,** circuitous, convoluted, Daedalian (*literary*), elaborate, intricate, involved, knotty, labyrinthine, mingled, mixed, tangled, tortuous ◆ *n* **4 = structure,** aggregate, composite, network, organization, scheme, synthesis, system **6** *Informal* **= obsession,** fixation, fixed idea, *idée fixe,* phobia, preoccupation
Antonyms *adj* ≠ **complicated:** clear, easy,

complex fraction *n Maths.* a fraction in which the numerator or denominator or both contain fractions. Also called: **compound fraction.**
complexion ◑ (kəm'plɛkʃən) *n* **1** the colour and general appearance of a person's skin, esp. of the face. **2** aspect or nature: *the general complexion of a nation's finances.* **3** *Obs.* temperament. [C14: from L *complexiō* a combination, from *complectī* to embrace; see COMPLEX]
▸**com'plexional** *adj*
complexioned (kəm'plɛkʃənd) *adj* of a specified complexion: *light-complexioned.*
complexity ◑ (kəm'plɛksɪtɪ) *n, pl* **complexities. 1** the state or quality of being intricate or complex. **2** something intricate or complex; complication.
complex number *n* any number of the form $a + bi$, where a and b are real numbers and $i = \sqrt{-1}$.
complex sentence *n Grammar.* a sentence containing at least one main clause and one subordinate clause.
compliance ◑ (kəm'plaɪəns) *or* **compliancy** *n* **1** acquiescence. **2** a disposition to yield to others. **3** a measure of the ability of a mechanical system to respond to an applied vibrating force.
compliance officer *or* **lawyer** *n* a specialist, usually a lawyer, employed by a financial group operating in a variety of fields and for multiple clients to ensure that no conflict of interest arises and that all obligations and regulations are complied with.
compliant ◑ (kəm'plaɪənt) *adj* complying, obliging, or yielding.
▸**com'pliantly** *adv*
complicate ◑ *vb* ('kɒmplɪˌkeɪt), **complicates, complicating, complicated. 1** to make or become complex, etc. ◆ *adj* ('kɒmplɪkɪt). **2** *Biol.* folded on itself: *a complicate leaf.* [C17: from L *complicāre* to fold together]
complicated ◑ ('kɒmplɪˌkeɪtɪd) *adj* made up of intricate parts or aspects that are difficult to understand or analyse.
▸**'compliˌcatedly** *adv*
complication ◑ (ˌkɒmplɪ'keɪʃən) *n* **1** a condition, event, etc., that is complex or confused. **2** the act of complicating. **3** an event or condition that complicates or frustrates: *her coming was a serious complication.* **4** a disease arising as a consequence of another.
complicity ◑ (kəm'plɪsɪtɪ) *n, pl* **complicities. 1** the fact of being an accomplice, esp. in a criminal act. **2** a less common word for **complexity.**
compliment ◑ *n* ('kɒmplɪmənt). **1** a remark or act expressing respect, admiration, etc. **2** (*usually pl*) a greeting of respect or regard. ◆ *vb* ('kɒmplɪˌmɛnt). (*tr*) **3** to express admiration for; congratulate. **4** to express or show regard for, esp. by a gift. [C17: from F, from It. *complimento,* from Sp. *cumplimiento,* from *cumplir* to complete]

> **USAGE NOTE** Avoid confusion with **complement.**

complimentary ◑ (ˌkɒmplɪ'mɛntərɪ) *adj* **1** conveying a compliment. **2** flattering. **3** given free, esp. as a courtesy or for publicity purposes.
▸**ˌcompli'mentarily** *adv*
compline ('kɒmplɪn, -plaɪn) *or* **complin** ('kɒmplɪn) *n RC Church.* the last of the seven canonical hours of the divine office. [C13: from OF *complie,* from Med. L *hōra complēta,* lit.: the completed hour]
comply ◑ (kəm'plaɪ) *vb* **complies, complying, complied.** (*intr*) (usually foll. by *with*) to act in accordance with rules, wishes, etc.; be obedient (to). [C17: from It. *complire,* from Sp. *cumplir* to complete]
compo ('kɒmpəʊ) *n, pl* **compos. 1** a mixture of materials, such as mortar, plaster, etc. **2** *Austral. & NZ inf.* compensation, esp. for injury or loss of work. ◆ *adj* **3** *Mil.* intended to last for several days: *a compo pack.* [short for *composition, compensation, composite*]
component ◑ (kəm'pəʊnənt) *n* **1** a constituent part or aspect of something more complex. **2** any electrical device that has distinct electrical characteristics and may be connected to other devices to form a circuit. **3** *Maths.* one of a set of two or more vectors whose resultant is a given vector. **4** See **phase rule.** ◆ *adj* **5** forming or functioning as a part or aspect; constituent. [C17: from L *compōnere* to put together]
▸**componential** (ˌkɒmpə'nɛnʃəl) *adj*
comport ◑ (kəm'pɔːt) *vb* **1** (*tr*) to conduct or bear (oneself) in a specified way. **2** (*intr;* foll. by *with*) to agree (with). [C16: from L *comportāre* collect, from *com-* together + *portāre* to carry]
▸**com'portment** *n*
compose ◑ (kəm'pəʊz) *vb* **composes, composing, composed.** (*mainly tr*) **1** to put together or make up. **2** to be the component elements of. **3** to create (a musical or literary work). **4** (*intr*) to write music. **5** to calm (someone, esp. oneself); make quiet. **6** to adjust or settle (a quarrel, etc.). **7** to order the elements of (a painting, sculpture, etc.); design. **8** *Printing.* to set up (type). [C15: from OF *composer,* from L *compōnere* to put in place]
composed ◑ (kəm'pəʊzd) *adj* (of people) calm; tranquil.
▸**composedly** (kəm'pəʊzɪdlɪ) *adv*
composer (kəm'pəʊzə) *n* **1** a person who composes music. **2** a person or machine that composes anything, esp. type for printing.
composite ◑ *adj* ('kɒmpəzɪt). **1** composed of separate parts; compound. **2** of or belonging to the plant family Compositae. **3** *Maths.* capable of being factorized: *a composite function.* **4** (*sometimes cap.*) denoting one of the five classical orders of architecture: characterized by a combination of the Ionic and Corinthian styles. ◆ *n* ('kɒmpəzɪt). **5** something composed of separate parts; compound. **6** any plant of the family Compositae, having flower heads composed of many small flowers (e.g. dandelion, daisy). **7** a material, such as reinforced concrete, made of two or more distinct materials. **8** a proposal that has been composited. ◆ *vb* ('kɒmpəˌzaɪt), **composites, compositing, composited.** (*tr*) **9** to merge related motions from local branches (of a political party, trade union, etc.) so as to produce a manageable number of proposals for discussion at national level. [C16: from L *compositus* well arranged, from *compōnere* to arrange]
▸**'compositely** *adv* ▸**'compositeness** *n*
composite school *n E. Canad.* a secondary school offering both academic and nonacademic courses.
composition ◑ (ˌkɒmpə'zɪʃən) *n* **1** the act of putting together or making up by combining parts. **2** something formed in this manner; a mixture. **3** the parts of which something is composed; constitution. **4**

THESAURUS

easy-peasy (*sl.*), elementary, obvious, simple, straightforward, uncomplicated
complexion *n* **1** = **skin**, colour, colouring, hue, pigmentation, skin tone **2** = **nature**, appearance, aspect, cast, character, countenance, disposition, guise, light, look, make-up, stamp
complexity *n* **1** = **complication**, convolution, elaboration, entanglement, intricacy, involvement, multiplicity, ramification
compliance *n* **1, 2** = **obedience**, acquiescence, agreement, assent, complaisance, concession, concurrence, conformity, consent, deference, observance, passivity, submission, submissiveness, yielding
Antonyms *n* defiance, disobedience, noncompliance, nonconformity, opposition, refusal, resistance, revolt
compliant *adj* = **obedient**, accepting, accommodating, accordant, acquiescent, agreeable, assentient, complaisant, concessive, concurrent, conformable, conformist, consentient, co-operative, deferential, obliging, passive, submissive, willing, yielding
complicate *vb* **1** = **make difficult**, confuse, embroil, entangle, interweave, involve, make intricate, muddle, ravel, snarl up
Antonyms *vb* clarify, clear up, disentangle, elucidate, explain, facilitate, simplify, spell out, unsnarl
complicated *adj* = **difficult**, complex, convoluted, elaborate, interlaced, intricate, involved, labyrinthine, perplexing, problematic, puzzling, troublesome
Antonyms *adj* ≠ **difficult**: clear, easy, easy-peasy (*sl.*), simple, straightforward, uncomplicated, undemanding, understandable, uninvolved, user-friendly
complication *n* **1** = **complexity**, combination, confusion, entanglement, intricacy, mixture, web **3** = **problem**, aggravation, difficulty, drawback, embarrassment, factor, obstacle, snag
complicity *n* **1** = **collusion**, abetment, collaboration, concurrence, connivance
compliment *n* **1** = **praise**, admiration, bouquet, commendation, congratulations, courtesy, eulogy, favour, flattery, honour, tribute **2** *usually plu* = **greetings**, good wishes, regards, remembrances, respects, salutation ◆ *vb* **3** = **praise**, commend, congratulate, crack up (*inf.*), extol, felicitate, flatter, laud, pat on the back, pay tribute to, salute, sing the praises of, speak highly of, wish joy to
Antonyms *n* ≠ **praise**: complaint, condemnation, criticism, disparagement, insult, reproach ◆ *vb* ≠ **praise**: blast, condemn, criticize, decry, disparage, insult, lambast(e), put down, reprehend, reproach, tear into (*inf.*)
complimentary *adj* **2** = **flattering**, appreciative, approving, commendatory, congratulatory, eulogistic, laudatory, panegyrical **3** = **free**, courtesy, donated, free of charge, gratis, gratuitous, honorary, on the house
Antonyms *adj* ≠ **flattering**: abusive, critical, disparaging, fault-finding, insulting, scathing, uncomplimentary, unflattering
comply *vb* = **obey**, abide by, accede, accord, acquiesce, adhere to, agree to, conform to, consent to, defer, discharge, follow, fulfil, observe, perform, play ball (*inf.*), respect, satisfy, submit, toe the line, yield
Antonyms *vb* break, defy, disobey, disregard, fight, ignore, oppose, refuse to obey, reject, repudiate, resist, spurn, violate
component *n* **1** = **part**, constituent, element, ingredient, item, piece, unit ◆ *adj* **5** = **constituent**, composing, inherent, intrinsic
comport *vb Formal* **1** = **behave**, acquit, act, bear, carry, conduct, demean **2** *foll. by* **with** = **suit**, accord with, agree with, be appropriate to, coincide with, correspond with, fit, harmonize with, square with, tally with
compose *vb* **1** = **put together**, build, compound, comprise, constitute, construct, fashion, form, make, make up **3, 4** = **create**, contrive, devise, frame, imagine, indite, invent, produce, write **5** = **calm**, appease, assuage, collect, control, pacify, placate, quell, quiet, soothe, still, tranquillize **6** = **arrange**, adjust, reconcile, regulate, resolve, settle
Antonyms *vb* ≠ **put together**: bulldoze, demolish, destroy, dismantle, obliterate, raze ≠ **calm**: agitate, disturb, excite, perturb, trouble, unsettle, upset
composed *adj* = **calm**, as cool as a cucumber, at ease, collected, confident, cool, imperturbable, keeping one's cool, laid-back (*inf.*), level-headed, poised, relaxed, sedate, self-controlled, self-possessed, serene, together (*sl.*), tranquil, unfazed (*inf.*), unflappable, unruffled, unworried
Antonyms *adj* agitated, anxious, disturbed, excited, hot and bothered (*inf.*), nervous, ruffled, twitchy (*inf.*), uncontrolled, uneasy, unpoised, upset
composite *adj* **1** = **compound**, blended, combined, complex, conglomerate, mixed, synthesized ◆ *n* **5** = **compound**, amalgam, blend, conglomerate, fusion, meld, synthesis
composition *n* **1** = **creation**, compilation, fashioning, formation, formulation, invention, making, mixture, production, putting together **2** = **design**, arrangement, configuration, consti-

a work of music, art, or literature. **5** the harmonious arrangement of the parts of a work of art in relation to each other. **6** a piece of writing undertaken as an academic exercise; an essay. **7** *Printing.* the act or technique of setting up type. **8** a settlement by mutual consent, esp. a legal agreement whereby the creditors agree to accept partial payment of a debt in full settlement. [C14: from OF, from L *compositus;* see COMPOSITE, -ION]

compositor (kəm'pɒzɪtə) *n Printing.* a person who sets and corrects type.

compos mentis *Latin.* ('kɒmpəs 'mentɪs) *adj* (*postpositive*) of sound mind; sane.

compost 🅣 ('kɒmpɒst) *n* **1** a mixture of organic residues such as decomposed vegetation, manure, etc., used as a fertilizer. **2** a mixture, as of sand, peat, and charcoal, in which plants are grown, esp. in pots. **3** *Rare.* a mixture. ◆ *vb* (*tr*) **4** to make (vegetable matter) into compost. **5** to fertilize with compost. [C14: from OF *compost,* from L *compositus* put together]

composure 🅣 (kəm'pəʊʒə) *n* calmness, esp. of the mind; tranquillity; serenity.

compote ('kɒmpəʊt) *n* a dish of fruit stewed with sugar or in a syrup. [C17: from F *composte,* from L *compositus* put in place]

compound[1] 🅣 *n* ('kɒmpaʊnd). **1** a substance that contains atoms of two or more chemical elements held together by chemical bonds. **2** any combination of two or more parts, aspects, etc. **3** a word formed from two existing words or combining forms. ◆ *vb* (kəm'paʊnd). (*mainly tr*) **4** to combine so as to create a compound. **5** to make by combining parts, aspects, etc.: *to compound a new plastic.* **6** to intensify by an added element: *his anxiety was compounded by her crying.* **7** (*also intr*) to come to an agreement in (a dispute, etc.) or to settle (a debt, etc.) for less than what is owed; compromise. **8** *Law.* to agree not to prosecute in return for a consideration: *to compound a crime.* ◆ *adj* ('kɒmpaʊnd). **9** composed of two or more parts, elements, etc. **10** (of a word) consisting of elements that are also words or combining forms. **11** *Grammar.* (of tense, mood, etc.) formed by using an auxiliary verb in addition to the main verb. **12** *Music.* **12a** denoting a time in which the number of beats per bar is a multiple of three: *six-four is an example of compound time.* **12b** (of an interval) greater than an octave. **13** (of a steam engine, etc.) having multiple stages in which the steam or working fluid from one stage is used in a subsequent stage. **14** (of a piston engine) having a supercharger powered by a turbine in the exhaust stream. [C14: from earlier *compounen,* from OF *compondre* to set in order, from L *compōnere*]
▸**com'poundable** *adj*

compound[2] ('kɒmpaʊnd) *n* **1** (esp. formerly in South Africa) an enclosure, esp. on the mines, containing the living quarters for Black workers. **2** any similar enclosure, such as a camp for prisoners of war. [C17: from Malay *kampong* village]

compound eye *n* the convex eye of insects and some crustaceans, consisting of numerous separate light-sensitive units (ommatidia).

compound fraction *n* another name for **complex fraction.**

compound fracture *n* a fracture in which the broken bone pierces the skin.

compound interest *n* interest calculated on both the principal and its accrued interest.

compound leaf *n* a leaf consisting of two or more leaflets borne on the same leafstalk.

compound number *n* a quantity expressed in two or more different but related units: *3 hours 10 seconds is a compound number.*

compound sentence *n* a sentence containing at least two coordinate clauses.

compound time *n* See **compound**[1] (sense 12).

comprehend 🅣 (ˌkɒmprɪ'hɛnd) *vb* **1** to understand. **2** (*tr*) to comprise; include. [C14: from L *comprehendere,* from *prehendere* to seize]

comprehensible 🅣 (ˌkɒmprɪ'hɛnsəbᵊl) *adj* capable of being comprehended.
▸ˌ**compreˌhensi'bility** *n* ▸ˌ**compre'hensibly** *adv*

comprehension 🅣 (ˌkɒmprɪ'hɛnʃən) *n* **1** the act or capacity of understanding. **2** the state of including; comprehensiveness.

comprehensive 🅣 (ˌkɒmprɪ'hɛnsɪv) *adj* **1** of broad scope or content. **2** (of a car insurance policy) providing protection against most risks, including third-party liability, fire, theft, and damage. **3** of or being a comprehensive school. ◆ *n* **4** short for **comprehensive school.**
▸ˌ**compre'hensively** *adv* ▸ˌ**compre'hensiveness** *n*

comprehensive school *n Chiefly Brit.* a secondary school for children of all abilities from the same district.

compress 🅣 *vb* (kəm'prɛs). **1** (*tr*) to squeeze together; condense. ◆ *n* ('kɒmprɛs). **2** a cloth or gauze pad applied firmly to some part of the body to relieve discomfort, reduce fever, etc. [C14: from LL *compressāre,* from L *comprimere,* from *premere* to press]
▸**com'pressible** *adj* ▸**com'pressive** *adj*

compressed air *n* air at a higher pressure than atmospheric pressure: used esp. as a source of power for machines.

compressibility (kəmˌprɛsɪ'bɪlɪtɪ) *n* **1** the ability to be compressed. **2** *Physics.* the reciprocal of the bulk modulus; the ratio of volume strain to stress at constant temperature. Symbol: *k*

compression 🅣 (kəm'prɛʃən) *n* **1** the act of compressing or the condition of being compressed. **2** an increase in pressure of the charge in an engine or compressor obtained by reducing its volume.

compressor (kəm'prɛsə) *n* **1** any device that compresses a gas. **2** the part of a gas turbine that compresses the air before it enters the combustion chambers. **3** any muscle that causes compression. **4** an electronic device for reducing the variation in signal amplitude in a transmission system.

comprise 🅣 (kəm'praɪz) *vb* **comprises, comprising, comprised.** (*tr*) **1** to be made up of. **2** to constitute the whole of; consist of: *her singing comprised the entertainment.* [C15: from F *compris* included, from *comprendre* to COMPREHEND]
▸**com'prisable** *adj*

> **USAGE NOTE** The use of *of* after *comprise* should be avoided: *the library comprises* (not *comprises of*) *500,000 books and manuscripts.*

compromise 🅣 ('kɒmprəˌmaɪz) *n* **1** settlement of a dispute by concessions on both or all sides. **2** the terms of such a settlement. **3** something midway between different things. ◆ *vb* **compromises, compromising, compromised. 4** to settle (a dispute) by making concessions. **5** (*tr*) to expose (oneself or another) to disrepute. [C15: from OF *compromis,* from L, from *comprōmittere,* from *prōmittere* to promise]
▸'**comproˌmiser** *n* ▸'**comproˌmisingly** *adv*

compte rendu *French.* (kɔ̃t rɑ̃dy) *n, pl* ***comptes rendus*** (kɔ̃t rɑ̃dy). **1** a review or notice. **2** an account. [lit.: account rendered]

comptroller (kən'trəʊlə) *n* a variant spelling of **controller** (sense 2), esp. as a title of any of various financial executives.

compulsion 🅣 (kəm'pʌlʃən) *n* **1** the act of compelling or the state of being compelled. **2** something that compels. **3** *Psychiatry.* an inner

THESAURUS

tution, form, formation, layout, make-up, organization, structure **5** = **arrangement**, balance, concord, consonance, harmony, placing, proportion, symmetry **6** = **essay**, creation, exercise, literary work, opus, piece, study, treatise, work, writing

compost *n* **1** = **organic fertilizer**, humus, mulch

composure *n* = **calmness**, aplomb, calm, collectedness, cool (*sl.*), coolness, dignity, ease, equanimity, imperturbability, placidity, poise, sang-froid, sedateness, self-assurance, self-possession, serenity, tranquillity
Antonyms *n* agitation, discomposure, excitability, impatience, nervousness, perturbation, uneasiness

compound[1] *n* **2** = **combination**, alloy, amalgam, blend, composite, composition, conglomerate, fusion, medley, meld, mixture, synthesis ◆ *vb* **5** = **combine**, amalgamate, blend, coalesce, concoct, fuse, intermingle, meld, mingle, mix, synthesize, unite **6** = **intensify**, add insult to injury, add to, aggravate, augment, complicate, exacerbate, heighten, magnify, worsen **7** = **settle**, adjust, arrange, compose ◆ *adj* **9** = **complex**, composite, conglomerate, intricate, multiple, not simple
Antonyms *n* ≠ **combination:** element ◆ *vb* ≠ **combine:** divide, part, segregate ≠ **intensify:** decrease, lessen, minimize, moderate, modify ◆ *adj* ≠ **complex:** pure, simple, single, unmixed

comprehend *vb* **1** = **understand**, apprehend, assimilate, conceive, discern, fathom, get the hang of (*inf.*), get the picture, grasp, know, make out, perceive, see, see the light of day, take in **2** = **include**, comprise, contain, embody, embrace, enclose, encompass, involve, take in
Antonyms *vb* ≠ **understand:** be at cross-purposes, get (it) wrong, get one's lines crossed, get the wrong end of the stick, misapprehend, misconceive, misconstrue, misinterpret, miss the point of, mistake, misunderstand, pervert

comprehensibility *n* = **intelligibility**, apprehensibility, clarity, clearness, conceivability, conceivableness, explicitness, intelligibleness, plainness, user-friendliness

comprehensible *adj* = **understandable**, clear, coherent, conceivable, explicit, graspable, intelligible, plain, user-friendly

comprehension *n* **1** = **understanding**, conception, discernment, grasp, intelligence, judgment, knowledge, perception, realization, sense **2** = **inclusion**, compass, domain, field, limits, province, range, reach, scope
Antonyms *n* ≠ **understanding:** incomprehension, misapprehension, misunderstanding, unawareness

comprehensive *adj* **1** = **broad**, all-embracing, all-inclusive, blanket, catholic, complete, encyclopedic, exhaustive, extensive, full, inclusive, overarching, sweeping, thorough, umbrella, wide
Antonyms *adj* incomplete, limited, narrow, restricted, specialized, specific

compress *vb* **1** = **squeeze**, abbreviate, compact, concentrate, condense, constrict, contract, cram, crowd, crush, knit, press, pucker, shorten, squash, summarize, wedge

compression *n* **1** = **squeezing**, condensation, consolidation, constriction, crushing, pressure, wedging

comprise *vb* **1** = **be composed of**, comprehend, consist of, contain, embrace, encompass, include, take in **2** = **make up**, compose, constitute, form

compromise *n* **1** = **give-and-take**, accommodation, accord, adjustment, agreement, concession, half measures, middle ground, settlement, trade-off ◆ *vb* **4** = **meet halfway**, adjust, agree, arbitrate, compose, compound, concede, give and take, go fifty-fifty (*inf.*), settle, strike a balance **5** = **weaken**, discredit, dishonour, embarrass, endanger, expose, hazard, imperil, implicate, jeopardize, prejudice
Antonyms *n* ≠ **give-and-take:** contention, controversy, difference, disagreement, dispute, quarrel ◆ *vb* ≠ **meet halfway:** argue, contest, differ, disagree ≠ **weaken:** assure, boost, enhance, support

compulsion *n* **2** = **force**, coercion, constraint, demand, duress, obligation, pressure, urgency drive that causes a person to perform actions, often repetitive, against his or her will. See also **obsession.** [C15: from OF, from L *compellere* to COMPEL]

compulsive ❶ (kəmˈpʌlsɪv) *adj* relating to or involving compulsion.
▸**comˈpulsively** *adv*

compulsory ❶ (kəmˈpʌlsərɪ) *adj* **1** required by regulations or laws; obligatory. **2** involving or employing compulsion; compelling; essential.
▸**comˈpulsorily** *adv* ▸**comˈpulsoriness** *n*

compulsory purchase *n* purchase of a property by a local authority or government department for public use or development, regardless of whether or not the owner wishes to sell.

compunction ❶ (kəmˈpʌŋkʃən) *n* a feeling of remorse, guilt, or regret. [C14: from Church L *compunctiō*, from L *compungere* to sting]
▸**comˈpunctious** *adj* ▸**comˈpunctiously** *adv*

computation (ˌkɒmpjʊˈteɪʃən) *n* a calculation involving numbers or quantities.
▸ˌ**compuˈtational** *adj*

compute ❶ (kəmˈpjuːt) *vb* **computes, computing, computed.** to calculate (an answer, result, etc.), often with the aid of a computer. [C17: from L *computāre*, from *putāre* to think]
▸**comˈputable** *adj* ▸**comˌputaˈbility** *n*

computed tomography *n Med.* another name (esp. US) for **computerized tomography.**

computer (kəmˈpjuːtə) *n* **1a** a device, usually electronic, that processes data according to a set of instructions. The **digital computer** stores data in discrete units and performs operations at very high speed. The **analog computer** has no memory and is slower than the digital computer but has a continuous rather than a discrete input. **1b** (*as modifier*): *computer technology.* **2** a person who computes or calculates.

computer-aided design *n* the use of computer techniques in designing products, esp. involving the use of computer graphics. Abbrev.: **CAD.**

computer-aided engineering *n* the use of computers to automate manufacturing processes. Abbrev.: **CAE.**

computer architecture *n* the structure, behaviour, and design of computing.

computerate (kəmˈpjuːtərɪt) *adj* able to use computing. [C20: COMPUTER + -ATE[1], by analogy with *literate*]

computer dating *n* the use of computers by dating agencies to match their clients.

computer game *n* any of various games, recorded on cassette or disc for use in a home computer, that are played by manipulating a mouse, joystick or the keys on the keyboard of a computer in response to the graphics on the screen.

computer graphics *n* (*functioning as sing*) the use of a computer to produce and manipulate pictorial images on a video screen, as in animation techniques or the production of audiovisual aids.

computerize *or* **computerise** (kəmˈpjuːtəˌraɪz) *vb* **computerizes, computerizing, computerized** *or* **computerises, computerising, computerised. 1** (*tr*) to cause (certain operations) to be performed by a computer, esp. as a replacement for human labour. **2** (*intr*) to install a computer. **3** (*tr*) to control or perform (operations) by means of a computer. **4** (*tr*) to process or store (information) by or in a computer.
▸**comˌputeriˈzation** *or* **comˌputeriˈsation** *n*

computerized tomography *n Med.* a radiological technique that produces images of cross sections through a patient's body. Also called (esp. US): **computed tomography.** Abbrev.: **CT.** See also **CT scanner.**

computer language *n* another term for **programming language.**

computer science *n* the study of computers and their application.

comrade ❶ (ˈkɒmreɪd, -rɪd) *n* **1** a companion. **2** a fellow member of a political party, esp. a fellow Communist. [C16: from F *camarade*, from Sp. *camarada* group of soldiers sharing a billet, from *cámara* room, from L]
▸ˈ**comradely** *adj* ▸ˈ**comradeˌship** *n*

Comsat (ˈkɒmsæt) *n Trademark.* short for **communications satellite.**

con[1] ❶ (kɒn) *Inf.* ◆ *n* **1a** short for **confidence trick. 1b** (*as modifier*): *con man.* ◆ *vb* **cons, conning, conned. 2** (*tr*) to swindle or defraud. [C19: from CONFIDENCE]

con[2] (kɒn) *n* (*usually pl*) an argument or vote against a proposal, motion, etc. See also **pros and cons.** [from L *contrā* against]

con[3] *or esp. US* **conn** (kɒn) *vb* **cons** *or esp. US* **conns, conning, conned.** (*tr*) *Naut.* to direct the steering of (a vessel). [C17 *cun*, from earlier *condien* to guide, from OF *conduire*, from L *condūcere*; see CONDUCT]

con[4] (kɒn) *vb* **cons, conning, conned.** (*tr*) *Arch.* to study attentively or learn. [C15: var. of CAN[1] in the sense: to come to know]

con[5] (kɒn) *prep Music.* with. [It.]

con. *abbrev. for:* **1** concerto. **2** conclusion. **3** connection. **4** consolidated. **5** continued.

con- *prefix* a variant of **com-.**

con amore (kɒn æˈmɔːrɪ) *adj, adv Music.* (to be performed) lovingly. [C19: from It.: with love]

con brio (kɒn ˈbriːəʊ) *adj, adv Music.* (to be performed) with liveliness or spirit. [It.: with energy]

concatenate (kɒnˈkætɪˌneɪt) *vb* **concatenates, concatenating, concatenated.** (*tr*) to link or join together, esp. in a chain or series. [C16: from LL *concatēnāre*, from L *com-* together + *catēna* CHAIN]
▸ˌ**concateˈnation** *n*

concave ❶ (ˈkɒnkeɪv, kɒnˈkeɪv) *adj* **1** curving inwards; having the shape of a section of the interior of a sphere, paraboloid, etc.: *a concave lens.* ◆ *vb* **2** (*tr*) to make concave. [C15: from L *concavus* arched, from *cavus* hollow]
▸ˈ**concavely** *adv* ▸ˈ**concaveness** *n*

concavity (kɒnˈkævɪtɪ) *n, pl* **concavities. 1** the state of being concave. **2** a concave surface or thing.

concavo-concave (kɒnˌkeɪvəʊkɒnˈkeɪv) *adj* (esp. of a lens) having both sides concave.

concavo-convex *adj* **1** having one side concave and the other side convex. **2** (of a lens) having a concave face with greater curvature than the convex face.

conceal ❶ (kənˈsiːl) *vb* (*tr*) **1** to keep from discovery; hide. **2** to keep secret. [C14: from OF *conceler*, from L *concēlāre*, from *com-* (intensive) + *cēlāre* to hide]
▸**conˈcealer** *n* ▸**conˈcealment** *n*

concede ❶ (kənˈsiːd) *vb* **concedes, conceding, conceded. 1** (when *tr, may take a clause as object*) to admit or acknowledge (something) as true or correct. **2** to yield or allow (something, such as a right). **3** (*tr*) to admit as certain in outcome: *to concede an election.* [C17: from L *concēdere*, from *cēdere* to give way]
▸**conˈceder** *n*

conceit ❶ (kənˈsiːt) *n* **1** a high, often exaggerated, opinion of oneself or one's accomplishments. **2** *Literary.* an elaborate image or far-fetched comparison. **3** *Arch.* **3a** a witty expression. **3b** fancy; imagination. **3c** an idea. ◆ *vb* (*tr*) **4** *Obs.* to think. [C14: from CONCEIVE]

conceited ❶ (kənˈsiːtɪd) *adj* having an exaggerated opinion of oneself or one's accomplishments.
▸**conˈceitedly** *adv* ▸**conˈceitedness** *n*

conceivable ❶ (kənˈsiːvəbᵊl) *adj* capable of being understood, believed, or imagined; possible.
▸**conˌceivaˈbility** *n* ▸**conˈceivably** *adv*

conceive ❶ (kənˈsiːv) *vb* **conceives, conceiving, conceived. 1** (when *intr*, foll. by *of*; when *tr, often takes a clause as object*) to have an idea (of); imagine; think. **2** (*tr; takes a clause as object or an infinitive*) to believe. **3**

THESAURUS

3 = **urge**, drive, necessity, need, obsession, preoccupation

compulsive *adj* = **irresistible**, besetting, compelling, driving, neurotic, obsessive, overwhelming, uncontrollable, urgent

compulsory *adj* **1** = **obligatory**, binding, *de rigueur*, forced, imperative, mandatory, required, requisite
Antonyms *adj* discretionary, elective, non-obligatory, non-requisite, optional, unimperative, unnecessary, voluntary

compunction *n* = **guilt**, contrition, misgiving, penitence, qualm, regret, reluctance, remorse, repentance, sorrow, stab *or* sting of conscience

compute *vb* = **calculate**, add up, cast up, cipher, count, enumerate, estimate, figure, figure out, measure, rate, reckon, sum, tally, total

comrade *n* **1** = **companion**, ally, associate, colleague, compatriot, compeer, confederate, co-worker, crony, fellow, friend, mate (*inf.*), partner

comradely *adj* **1** = **friendly**, associatory, fraternal

comradeship *n* **1** = **fellowship**, alliance, association, camaraderie, companionship, fraternity, membership, partnership, sodality

con *Informal n* **1a** = **swindle**, bluff, canard, deception, fraud, scam, sting (*inf.*), trick ◆ *vb* **2** = **swindle**, bilk, cheat, cozen, deceive, defraud, diddle (*inf.*), double-cross (*inf.*), dupe, gull (*arch.*), hoax, hoodwink, humbug, inveigle, kid (*inf.*), mislead, pull a fast one on (*inf.*), rip off (*sl.*), sting (*inf.*), trick

concave *adj* **1** = **hollow**, cupped, depressed, excavated, hollowed, incurved, indented, scooped, sunken
Antonyms *adj* bulging, convex, curving, protuberant, rounded

conceal *vb* **1, 2** = **hide**, bury, camouflage, cover, disguise, dissemble, draw a veil over, keep dark, keep secret, keep under one's hat, mask, obscure, screen, secrete, shelter, stash (*inf.*)
Antonyms *vb* disclose, display, divulge, expose, lay bare, reveal, show, uncover, unmask, unveil

concealed *adj* **1, 2** = **hidden**, covered, covert, inconspicuous, masked, obscured, screened, secret, secreted, tucked away, under wraps, unseen

concealment *n* **1, 2** = **hiding**, camouflage, cover, disguise, hideaway, hide-out, secrecy
Antonyms *n* disclosure, display, exposure, give-away, leak, revelation, showing, uncovering

concede *vb* **1** = **admit**, accept, acknowledge, allow, confess, grant, own **3** = **give up**, cede, hand over, relinquish, surrender, yield
Antonyms *vb* ≠ **admit:** contest, deny, disclaim, dispute, protest, refute, reject ≠ **give up:** beat, conquer, defeat, fight to the bitter end, make a stand

conceit *n* **1** = **self-importance**, amour-propre, arrogance, complacency, egotism, narcissism, pride, self-love, swagger, vainglory, vanity **3** *Archaic* = **fancy**, belief, fantasy, idea, image, imagination, judgment, notion, opinion, quip, thought, vagary, whim, whimsy

conceited *adj* = **self-important**, arrogant, bigheaded, cocky, egotistical, full of oneself, immodest, narcissistic, overweening, puffed up, stuck up (*inf.*), swollen-headed, too big for one's boots *or* breeches, vain, vainglorious
Antonyms *adj* humble, modest, self-effacing, unassuming

conceivable *adj* = **imaginable**, believable, credible, possible, thinkable
Antonyms *adj* inconceivable, incredible, unbelievable, unimaginable, unthinkable

conceive *vb* **1, 2** = **imagine**, appreciate, apprehend, believe, comprehend, envisage, fancy, get the picture, grasp, realize, suppose, think, (*tr*) to develop: *she conceived a passion for music.* **4** to become pregnant with (a child). **5** (*tr*) *Rare.* to express in words. [C13: from OF *conceivre*, from L *concipere* to take in, from *capere* to take]

concelebrate (kən'selɪˌbreɪt) *vb* **concelebrates, concelebrating, concelebrated.** *Christianity.* to celebrate (the Eucharist or Mass) jointly with one or more other priests. [C16: from L *concelebrāre*]
►**conˌcele'bration** *n*

concentrate ❶ ('kɒnsənˌtreɪt) *vb* **concentrates, concentrating, concentrated. 1** to come or cause to come to a single purpose or aim: *to concentrate one's hopes on winning.* **2** to make or become denser or purer by the removal of certain elements. **3** (*intr*; often foll. by *on*) to think intensely (about). ◆ *n* **4** a concentrated material or solution. [C17: back formation from CONCENTRATION, ult. from L *com-* same + *centrum* CENTRE]
►**'concenˌtrative** *adj* ►**'concenˌtrator** *n*

concentration ❶ (ˌkɒnsən'treɪʃən) *n* **1** intense mental application. **2** the act of concentrating. **3** something that is concentrated. **4** the strength of a solution, esp. the amount of dissolved substance in a given volume of solvent. **5** *Mil.* **5a** the act of bringing together military forces. **5b** the application of fire from a number of weapons against a target.

concentration camp *n* a guarded prison camp for nonmilitary prisoners, esp. one in Nazi Germany.

concentre *or US* **concenter** (kən'sentə) *vb* **concentres, concentring, concentred** *or US* **concenters, concentering, concentered.** to converge or cause to converge on a common centre; concentrate. [C16: from F *concentrer*]

concentric (kən'sentrɪk) *adj* having a common centre: *concentric circles.* [C14: from Med. L *concentricus*, from L *com-* same + *centrum* CENTRE]
►**con'centrically** *adv*

concept ❶ ('kɒnsept) *n* **1** an idea, esp. an abstract idea: *the concepts of biology.* **2** *Philosophy.* a general idea that corresponds to some class of entities and consists of the essential features of the class. **3** a new idea; invention. **4** (*modifier*) (of a product, esp. a car) created to demonstrate the technical skills and imagination of the designers, and not for mass production or sale. [C16: from L *conceptum*, from *concipere* to CONCEIVE]

conception ❶ (kən'sepʃən) *n* **1** something conceived; notion, idea, or plan. **2** the description under which someone considers something: *a strange conception of freedom.* **3** the fertilization of an ovum by a sperm in the Fallopian tube followed by implantation in the womb. **4** origin or beginning. [C13: from L *conceptiō*, from *concipere* to CONCEIVE]
►**con'ceptional** *or* **con'ceptive** *adj*

conceptual (kən'septjuəl) *adj* of or characterized by concepts.
►**con'ceptually** *adv*

conceptualize *or* **conceptualise** (kən'septjuəˌlaɪz) *vb* **conceptualizes, conceptualizing, conceptualized** *or* **conceptualises, conceptualising, conceptualised.** to form (a concept or concepts) out of observations, experience, data, etc.
►**conˌceptuali'zation** *or* **conˌceptuali'sation** *n*

concern ❶ (kən'sɜːn) *vb* (*tr*) **1** to relate to; affect. **2** (usually foll. by *with* or *in*) to involve or interest (oneself): *he concerns himself with other people's affairs.* ◆ *n* **3** something that affects a person; affair; business. **4** regard or interest: *he felt a strong concern for her.* **5** anxiety or solicitude. **6** important relation: *his news has great concern for us.* **7** a commercial company. **8** *Inf.* a material thing, esp. one of which one has a low opinion. [C15: from LL *concernere*, from L *com-* together + *cernere* to sift]

concerned ❶ (kən'sɜːnd) *adj* **1** (*postpositive*) interested, guilty, or involved: *I shall find the boy concerned and punish him.* **2** worried or solicitous.
►**concernedly** (kən'sɜːnɪdlɪ) *adv*

concerning ❶ (kən'sɜːnɪŋ) *prep* **1** about; regarding. ◆ *adj* **2** worrying or troublesome.

concernment (kən'sɜːnmənt) *n Rare.* affair or business; concern.

concert ❶ *n* ('kɒnsɜːt). **1a** a performance of music by players or singers that does not involve theatrical staging. **1b** (*as modifier*): *a concert version of an opera.* **2** agreement in design, plan, or action. **3 in concert. 3a** acting with a common purpose. **3b** (of musicians, etc.) performing live. ◆ *vb* (kən'sɜːt). **4** to arrange or contrive (a plan) by mutual agreement. [C16: from F *concerter* to bring into agreement, from It., from LL *concertāre* to work together, from L *certāre* to contend]

concertante (ˌkɒntʃə'tæntɪ) *adj Music.* characterized by contrasting alternating tutti and solo passages. [It.: from *concertare* to perform a CONCERT]

concerted ❶ (kən'sɜːtɪd) *adj* **1** mutually contrived, planned, or arranged; combined: *a concerted effort.* **2** *Music.* arranged in parts for a group of singers or players.

concert grand *n* a grand piano of the largest size.

concertina (ˌkɒnsə'tiːnə) *n* **1** a hexagonal musical instrument similar to the accordion, in which metallic reeds are vibrated by air from a set of bellows operated by the player's hands. ◆ *vb* **concertinas, concertinaing, concertinaed. 2** (*intr*) to collapse or fold up like the bellows of a concertina. [C19: CONCERT + *-ina*]
►**ˌconcer'tinist** *n*

concertino (ˌkɒntʃə'tiːnəʊ) *n, pl* **concertini** (-nɪ). *Music.* **1** the solo group in a concerto grosso. **2** a short concerto. [It.: a little CONCERTO]

concertmaster ('kɒnsətˌmɑːstə) *n* a US and Canad. word for **leader** (of an orchestra).

concerto (kən'tʃeətəʊ) *n, pl* **concertos** *or* **concerti** (-tɪ). a composition for an orchestra and one or more soloists. [C18: from It.: CONCERT]

concerto grosso ('grɒsəʊ) *n, pl* **concerti grossi** ('grɒsɪ) *or* **concerto grossos.** a composition for an orchestra and a group of soloists. [It., lit.: big concerto]

concert party *n* **1** a musical entertainment popular in the early 20th century, esp. one at a British seaside resort. **2** *Stock Exchange inf.* a group of individuals or companies who secretly agree together to purchase shares separately in a particular company which they plan to amalgamate later into a single holding: a malpractice which is illegal in some countries.

concert pitch *n* **1** the frequency of 440 hertz assigned to the A above middle C. **2** *Inf.* a state of extreme readiness.

concession ❶ (kən'seʃən) *n* **1** the act of yielding or conceding. **2** something conceded. **3** *Brit.* a reduction in the usual price of a ticket granted to a special group of customers: *a student concession.* **4** any grant of rights, land, or property by a government, local authority, corporation, or individual. **5** the right, esp. an exclusive right, to market a particular product in a given area. **6** *Canad.* **6a** a land subdivision in a township survey. **6b** another name for a **concession road.** [C16: from L *concēssiō*, from *concēdere* to CONCEDE]
►**con'cessible** *adj* ►**con'cessive** *adj*

concessionaire (kənˌseʃə'neə), **concessioner** (kən'seʃənə), *or* **concessionary** *n* someone who holds or operates a concession.

concessionary (kən'seʃənərɪ) *adj* **1** of, granted, or obtained by a concession. ◆ *n, pl* **concessionaries. 2** another word for **concessionaire.**

concession road *n Canad.* one of a series of roads separating concessions in a township.

conch (kɒŋk, kɒntʃ) *n, pl* **conchs** (kɒŋks) *or* **conches** ('kɒntʃɪz). **1** any of various tropical marine gastropod molluscs characterized by a large brightly coloured spiral shell. **2** the shell of such a mollusc, used as a trumpet. [C16: from L *concha*, from Gk *konkhē* shellfish]

conchie *or* **conchy** ('kɒntʃɪ) *n, pl* **conchies.** *Inf.* short for **conscientious objector.**

conchology (kɒŋ'kɒlədʒɪ) *n* the study of mollusc shells.
►**con'chologist** *n*

concierge (ˌkɒnsɪ'eəʒ) *n* (esp. in France) a caretaker of a block of flats, hotel, etc., esp. one who lives on the premises. [C17: from F, ult. from L *conservus*, from *servus* slave]

conciliar (kən'sɪlɪə) *adj* of, from, or by means of a council, esp. an ecclesiastical one.

conciliate ❶ (kən'sɪlɪˌeɪt) *vb* **conciliates, conciliating, conciliated.** (*tr*) **1** to overcome the hostility of; win over. **2** to gain (favour, regard, etc.), esp. by making friendly overtures. [C16: from L *conciliāre* to bring together, from *concilium* COUNCIL]
►**con'ciliable** *adj* ►**con'ciliˌator** *n*

THESAURUS

understand **3** = **think up**, contrive, create, design, develop, devise, form, formulate, produce, project, purpose **4** = **become pregnant**, become impregnated

concentrate *vb* **1, 3** = **focus one's attention on**, be engrossed in, consider closely, give all one's attention to, put one's mind to, rack one's brains
Antonyms *vb* disregard, let one's mind wander, lose concentration, pay no attention to, pay no heed to

concentration *n* **1** = **single-mindedness**, absorption, application, heed
Antonyms *n* absent-mindedness, disregard, distraction, inattention

concept *n* **1** = **idea**, abstraction, conception, conceptualization, hypothesis, image, impression, notion, theory, view

conception *n* **1** = **idea**, concept, design, image, notion, plan **2** = **understanding**, appreciation, clue, comprehension, impression, inkling, perception, picture **3** = **impregnation**, fertilization, germination, insemination **4** = **origin**, beginning, birth, formation, inception, initiation, invention, launching, outset

concern *vb* **1** = **be relevant to**, affect, apply to, bear on, interest, involve, pertain to, regard, touch ◆ *n* **3** = **business**, affair, charge, department, field, interest, involvement, job, matter, mission, occupation, pigeon (*inf.*), responsibility, task, transaction **5** = **worry**, anxiety, apprehension, attention, burden, care, consideration, disquiet, disquietude, distress, heed, responsibility, solicitude **6** = **importance**, bearing, interest, reference, relation, relevance **7** = **business**, company, corporation, enterprise, establishment, firm, house, organization

concerned *adj* **1** = **involved**, active, implicated, interested, mixed up, privy to **2** = **worried**, anxious, attentive, bothered, caring, distressed, disturbed, exercised, interested, solicitous, troubled, uneasy, upset
Antonyms *adj* aloof, carefree, detached, indifferent, neglectful, unconcerned, uninterested, untroubled, without a care

concerning *prep* **1** = **regarding**, about, apropos of, as regards, as to, in the matter of, on the subject of, re, relating to, respecting, touching, with reference to

concert *n* **2** = **agreement**, accord, concord, concordance, harmony, unanimity, union, unison **3a in concert** = **together**, concertedly, in collaboration, in league, in unison, jointly, shoulder to shoulder, unanimously

concerted *adj* **1** = **coordinated**, agreed upon, collaborative, combined, joint, planned, prearranged, united
Antonyms *adj* disunited, separate, uncontrived, uncooperative, unplanned

concession *n* **1** = **conceding**, acknowledgment, admission, assent, confession, surrender, yielding **2** = **grant**, adjustment, allowance, boon, compromise, indulgence, permit, privilege, sop

conciliate *vb* **1, 2** = **pacify**, appease, clear the

conciliation ⓘ (kən,sɪlɪ'eɪʃən) *n* **1** the act or process of conciliating. **2** a method of helping the parties in a dispute to reach agreement, esp. divorcing or separating couples to part amicably.

conciliatory ⓘ (kən'sɪljətərɪ) *or* **conciliative** (kən'sɪljətɪv) *adj* intended to placate or reconcile.
▸**con'ciliatorily** *adv*

concise ⓘ (kən'saɪs) *adj* brief and to the point. [C16: from L *concīsus* cut short, from *concīdere,* from *caedere* to cut, strike down]
▸**con'cisely** *adv* ▸**con'ciseness** *or* **concision** (kən'sɪʒən) *n*

conclave ⓘ ('kɒnkleɪv) *n* **1** a secret meeting. **2** *RC Church.* **2a** the closed apartments where the college of cardinals elects a new pope. **2b** a meeting of the college of cardinals for this purpose. [C14: from Med. L *conclāve,* from L: place that may be locked, from *clāvis* key]

conclude ⓘ (kən'klu:d) *vb* **concludes, concluding, concluded.** (*mainly tr*) **1** (*also intr*) to come or cause to come to an end. **2** (*takes a clause as object*) to decide by reasoning; deduce: *the judge concluded that the witness had told the truth.* **3** to settle: *to conclude a treaty.* **4** *Obs.* to confine. [C14: from L *conclūdere,* from *claudere* to close]

conclusion ⓘ (kən'klu:ʒən) *n* **1** end or termination. **2** the last main division of a speech, essay, etc. **3** outcome or result (esp. in **a foregone conclusion**). **4** a final decision or judgment (esp. in **come to a conclusion**). **5** *Logic.* **5a** a statement that purports to follow from another or others (the **premises**) by means of an argument. **5b** a statement that does validly follow from given premises. **6** *Law.* **6a** an admission or statement binding on the party making it; estoppel. **6b** the close of a pleading or of a conveyance. **7 in conclusion.** lastly; to sum up. **8 jump to conclusions.** to come to a conclusion prematurely, without sufficient thought or on incomplete evidence. [C14: via OF from L; see CONCLUDE, -ION]

conclusive ⓘ (kən'klu:sɪv) *adj* **1** putting an end to doubt; decisive; final. **2** approaching or involving an end.
▸**con'clusively** *adv*

concoct ⓘ (kən'kɒkt) *vb* (*tr*) **1** to make by combining different ingredients. **2** to invent; make up; contrive. [C16: from L *concoctus* cooked together, from *coquere* to cook]
▸**con'cocter** *or* **con'coctor** *n* ▸**con'coction** *n*

concomitance (kən'kɒmɪtəns) *n* **1** existence together. **2** *Christianity.* the doctrine that the body and blood of Christ are present in the Eucharist.

concomitant (kən'kɒmɪtənt) *adj* **1** existing or occurring together. ◆ *n* **2** a concomitant act, person, etc. [C17: from LL *concomitārī* to accompany, from *com-* with + *comes* companion]

concord ⓘ ('kɒnkɔ:d) *n* **1** agreement or harmony. **2** a treaty establishing peaceful relations between nations. **3** *Music.* a combination of musical notes, esp. one containing a series of consonant intervals. **4** *Grammar.* another word for **agreement** (sense 6). [C13: from OF *concorde,* from L *concordia,* from *com-* same + *cor* heart]

concordance (kən'kɔ:dᵊns) *n* **1** a state of harmony. **2** a book that indexes the principal words in a literary work, often with the immediate context and an account of the meaning. **3** an index produced by computer or machine.

concordant (kən'kɔ:dᵊnt) *adj* being in agreement; harmonious.
▸**con'cordantly** *adv*

concordat (kɒn'kɔ:dæt) *n* a pact or treaty, esp. one between the Vatican and another state concerning the interests of religion in that state. [C17: via F, from Med. L *concordātum,* from L: something agreed; see CONCORD]

concourse ⓘ ('kɒnkɔ:s) *n* **1** a crowd; throng. **2** a coming together; confluence. **3** a large open space for the gathering of people in a public place. [C14: from OF *concours,* ult. from L *concurrere* to run together]

concrete ⓘ ('kɒnkri:t) *n* **1** a construction material made of cement, sand, stone and water that hardens to a stonelike mass. ◆ *adj* **2** relating to a particular instance; specific as opposed to general. **3** relating to things capable of being perceived by the senses, as opposed to abstractions. **4** formed by the coalescence of particles; condensed; solid. ◆ *vb* **concretes, concreting, concreted. 5** (*tr*) to construct in or cover with concrete. **6** (kən'kri:t). to become or cause to become solid; coalesce. [C14: from L *concrētus,* from *concrēscere* to grow together]
▸**'concretely** *adv* ▸**'concreteness** *n*

concrete music *n* music consisting of an electronically modified montage of tape-recorded sounds.

concrete noun *n* a noun that refers to a material object.

concrete poetry *n* poetry in which the visual form of the poem is used to convey meaning.

concretion (kən'kri:ʃən) *n* **1** the act of growing together; coalescence. **2** a solidified mass. **3** something made real, tangible, or specific. **4** a rounded or irregular mineral mass different in composition from the sedimentary rock that surrounds it. **5** *Pathol.* another word for **calculus.**
▸**con'cretionary** *adj*

concretize *or* **concretise** ('kɒnkrɪ,taɪz) *vb* **concretizes, concretizing, concretized** *or* **concretises, concretising, concretised.** (*tr*) to render concrete; make real or specific.

concubine ⓘ ('kɒŋkjʊ,baɪn, 'kɒn-) *n* **1** (in polygamous societies) a secondary wife. **2** a woman who cohabits with a man, esp. (formerly) the mistress of a king, nobleman, etc. [C13: from OF, from L *concubīna,* from *concumbere* to lie together]
▸**concubinage** (kɒn'kju:bɪnɪdʒ) *n* ▸**con'cubinary** *adj*

concupiscence (kən'kju:pɪsəns) *n* strong desire, esp. sexual desire. [C14: from Church L *concupiscentia,* from L *concupiscere* to covet]
▸**con'cupiscent** *adj*

concur ⓘ (kən'kɜ:) *vb* **concurs, concurring, concurred.** (*intr*) **1** to agree; be in accord. **2** to combine or cooperate. **3** to occur simultaneously; coincide. [C15: from L *concurrere* to run together]

concurrence ⓘ (kən'kʌrəns) *n* **1** the act of concurring. **2** agreement; accord. **3** cooperation or combination. **4** simultaneous occurrence.

concurrent ⓘ (kən'kʌrənt) *adj* **1** taking place at the same time or in the same location. **2** cooperating. **3** meeting at, approaching, or having a common point: *concurrent lines.* **4** in agreement; harmonious.
▸**con'currently** *adv*

concurrent engineering *n* a method of designing and marketing new products in which development stages are run in parallel rather than in series, to reduce lead times and costs. Also called: **interactive engineering.**

concuss (kən'kʌs) *vb* (*tr*) **1** to injure (the brain) by a violent blow, fall, etc. **2** to shake violently. [C16: from L *concussus,* from *concutere* to disturb greatly, from *quatere* to shake]

concussion ⓘ (kən'kʌʃən) *n* **1** a jarring of the brain, caused by a blow or a fall, usually resulting in loss of consciousness. **2** any violent shaking.

condemn ⓘ (kən'dɛm) *vb* (*tr*) **1** to express strong disapproval of. **2** to pronounce judicial sentence on. **3** to demonstrate the guilt of: *his secretive behaviour condemned him.* **4** to judge or pronounce unfit for use.

THESAURUS

air, disarm, mediate, mollify, placate, pour oil on troubled waters, propitiate, reconcile, restore harmony, soothe, win over

conciliation *n* **1** = **pacification**, appeasement, disarming, mollification, placation, propitiation, reconciliation, soothing

conciliatory *adj* = **pacifying**, appeasing, disarming, irenic, mollifying, pacific, peaceable, placatory, propitiative

concise *adj* = **brief**, compact, compendious, compressed, condensed, epigrammatic, in a nutshell, laconic, pithy, short, succinct, summary, synoptic, terse, to the point
Antonyms *adj* diffuse, discursive, garrulous, lengthy, long-winded, prolix, rambling, verbose, wordy

conciseness *n* = **brevity**, briefness, compactness, compendiousness, compression, laconicism, pithiness, shortness, succinctness, summariness, synoptic, terseness
Antonyms *n* diffuseness, discursiveness, garrulity, garrulousness, lengthiness, long-windedness, prolixity, verboseness, verbosity, wordiness

conclave *n* **1** = **secret** *or* **private meeting**, assembly, cabinet, conference, congress, council, parley, session

conclude *vb* **1** = **end**, bring down the curtain, cease, close, come to an end, complete, draw to a close, finish, round off, terminate, wind up **2** = **decide**, assume, clinch, deduce, determine, establish, fix, gather, infer, judge, reckon (*inf.*), resolve, settle, sum up, suppose, surmise, work out **3** = **accomplish**, bring about, carry out, effect, pull off
Antonyms *vb* ≠ **end:** begin, commence, extend, initiate, open, protract, start

conclusion *n* **1** = **end**, bitter end, close, completion, ending, finale, finish, result, termination **3** = **outcome**, consequence, culmination, end result, issue, result, sequel, upshot **4** = **decision**, agreement, conviction, deduction, inference, judgment, opinion, resolution, settlement, verdict **7 in conclusion** = **finally**, in closing, lastly, to sum up

conclusive *adj* **1** = **decisive**, clinching, convincing, definite, definitive, final, irrefutable, ultimate, unanswerable, unarguable
Antonyms *adj* contestable, disputable, doubtful, dubious, impeachable, inconclusive, indecisive, indefinite, questionable, refutable, unconvincing, vague

concoct *vb* **1, 2** = **make up**, brew, contrive, cook up, design, devise, fabricate, formulate, hatch, invent, manufacture, mature, plot, prepare, project, think up, trump up

concoction *n* **1, 2** = **mixture**, blend, brew, combination, compound, contrivance, creation, preparation

concord *n* **1** = **harmony**, accord, agreement, amity, concert, consensus, consonance, friendship, good understanding, goodwill, peace, rapport, unanimity, unison **2** = **treaty**, agreement, compact, concordat, convention, entente, protocol

concourse *n* **1, 2** = **crowd**, assemblage, assembly, collection, confluence, convergence, crush, gathering, meeting, multitude, rout (*arch.*), throng **3** = **gathering** *or* **meeting place**, entrance, foyer, hall, lounge, rallying point

concrete *n* **1** = **cement** (*not in technical usage*), concretion ◆ *adj* **2** = **specific**, definite, explicit **3** = **real**, actual, factual, material, sensible, substantial, tangible
Antonyms *adj* ≠ **specific:** indefinite, unspecified, vague ≠ **real:** abstract, immaterial, insubstantial, intangible, notional, theoretical

concubine *n* **2** = **mistress**, courtesan, kept woman, leman (*arch.*), odalisque, paramour

concur *vb* **1-3** = **agree**, accede, accord, acquiesce, approve, assent, buy into (*inf.*), coincide, combine, consent, cooperate, harmonize, join

concurrent *adj* **1** = **simultaneous**, coexisting, coincident, concerted, concomitant, contemporaneous, synchronous **3** = **converging**, confluent, convergent, uniting **4** = **in agreement**, agreeing, at one, compatible, consentient, consistent, cooperating, harmonious, in rapport, like-minded, of the same mind

concussion *n* **1, 2** = **shaking**, clash, collision, crash, impact, jarring, jolt, jolting, shock

condemn *vb* **1** = **disapprove**, blame, censure, criticize, damn, denounce, excoriate, reprehend, reproach, reprobate, reprove, upbraid **2** = **sentence**, convict, damn, doom, pass sentence on, proscribe
Antonyms *vb* ≠ **disapprove:** acclaim, applaud, approve, commend, compliment, condone, praise ≠ **sentence:** acquit, free, liberate

5 to force into a particular state: *his disposition condemned him to boredom.* [C13: from OF *condempner,* from L *condemnāre,* from *damnāre* to condemn]
▸**condemnable** (kən'dɛmnəbᵊl) *adj* ▸ˌ**condem'nation** *n* ▸**condemnatory** (kən'dɛmnətərɪ) *adj*

condensate (kən'dɛnseɪt) *n* a substance formed by condensation.

condensation ⓣ (ˌkɒndɛn'seɪʃən) *n* **1** the act or process of condensing, or the state of being condensed. **2** anything that has condensed from a vapour, esp. on a window. **3** *Chem.* a type of reaction in which two organic molecules combine to form a larger molecule as well as a simple molecule such as water, etc. **4** an abridged version of a book.
▸ˌ**conden'sational** *adj*

condensation trail *n* another name for **vapour trail.**

condense ⓣ (kən'dɛns) *vb* **condenses, condensing, condensed. 1** (*tr*) to increase the density of; compress. **2** to reduce or be reduced in volume or size. **3** to change or cause to change from a gaseous to a liquid or solid state. **4** *Chem.* to undergo or cause to undergo condensation. [C15: from L *condēnsāre,* from *dēnsāre* to make thick, from *dēnsus* DENSE]
▸**con'densable** *or* **con'densible** *adj*

condensed matter *n Physics.* **a** crystalline and amorphous solids and liquids, including liquid crystals, glasses, polymers, and gels. **b** (*as modifier*): *condensed-matter physics.*

condensed milk *n* milk reduced by evaporation to a thick concentration, with sugar added.

condenser (kən'dɛnsə) *n* **1a** an apparatus for reducing gases to their liquid or solid form by the abstraction of heat. **1b** a device for abstracting heat, as in a refrigeration unit. **2** a lens that concentrates light. **3** another name for **capacitor. 4** a person or device that condenses.

condescend ⓣ (ˌkɒndɪ'sɛnd) *vb* (*intr*) **1** to act graciously towards another or others regarded as being on a lower level; behave patronizingly. **2** to do something that one regards as below one's dignity. [C14: from Church L *condēscendere,* from L *dēscendere* to DESCEND]
▸ˌ**conde'scending** *adj* ▸ˌ**conde'scendingly** *adv* ▸ˌ**conde'scension** *n*

condign (kən'daɪn) *adj* (esp. of a punishment) fitting; deserved. [C15: from OF *condigne,* from L *condignus,* from *dignus* worthy]
▸**con'dignly** *adv*

condiment ('kɒndɪmənt) *n* any spice or sauce such as salt, pepper, mustard, etc. [C15: from L *condīmentum* seasoning, from *condīre* to pickle]

condition ⓣ (kən'dɪʃən) *n* **1** a particular state of being or existence: *the human condition.* **2** something that limits or restricts; a qualification. **3** (*pl*) circumstances: *conditions were right for a takeover.* **4** state of physical fitness, esp. good health: *out of condition.* **5** an ailment: *a heart condition.* **6** something indispensable: *your happiness is a condition of mine.* **7** something required as part of an agreement; term: *the conditions of the lease are set out.* **8** *Law.* **8a** a provision in a will, contract, etc., that makes some right or liability contingent upon the happening of some event. **8b** the event itself. **9** *Logic.* a statement whose truth is either required for the truth of a given statement (a **necessary condition**) or sufficient to guarantee the truth of the given statement (a **sufficient condition**). **10** rank, status, or position. **11 on condition that.** (*conj*) provided that. ◆ *vb* (*mainly tr*) **12** *Psychol.* **12a** to alter the response of (a person or animal) to a particular stimulus or situation. **12b** to establish a conditioned response in. **13** to put into a fit condition. **14** to improve the condition of (one's hair) by use of special cosmetics. **15** to accustom or inure. **16** to subject to a condition. [C14: from L *conditiō,* from *condīcere* to discuss, from *con-* together + *dīcere* to say]
▸**con'ditioner** *n* ▸**con'ditioning** *n, adj*

conditional ⓣ (kən'dɪʃənᵊl) *adj* **1** depending on other factors. **2** *Grammar.* expressing a condition on which something else is contingent: *"If he comes" is a conditional clause in the sentence "If he comes I shall go".* **3** *Logic.* Also called: **hypothetical.** (of a proposition) consisting of two component propositions associated by the words *if...then* so that the proposition is false only when the antecedent is true and the consequent false. ◆ *n* **4** a conditional verb form, clause, sentence, etc.
▸**con**ˌ**dition'ality** *n* ▸**con'ditionally** *adv*

conditional access *n* the distortion of television programme transmissions so that only authorized subscribers with suitable decoding apparatus may have access to them.

conditioned response *n Psychol.* a response that is transferred from the second to the first of a pair of stimuli. A well-known Pavlovian example is salivation by a dog when it hears a bell ring, because food has always been presented when the bell has been rung previously. Also called (esp. formerly): **conditioned reflex.**

condo ('kɒndəʊ) *n, pl* **condos.** *US & Canad. inf.* a condominium building or apartment.

condole ⓣ (kən'dəʊl) *vb* **condoles, condoling, condoled.** (*intr;* foll. by *with*) to express sympathy with someone in grief, pain, etc. [C16: from Church L *condolēre,* from L *com-* together + *dolēre* to grieve]
▸**con'dolence** *n*

condom ⓣ ('kɒndɒm, 'kɒndəm) *n* a rubber sheath worn on the penis or in the vagina during sexual intercourse to prevent conception or infection. [C18: from ?]

condominium (ˌkɒndə'mɪnɪəm) *n, pl* **condominiums. 1** joint rule or sovereignty. **2** a country ruled by two or more foreign powers. **3** *US & Canad.* **3a** an apartment building in which each apartment is individually owned and the common areas are jointly owned. **3b** an apartment in such a building. Sometimes shortened to **condo.** [C18: from NL, from L *com-* together + *dominium* ownership]

condone ⓣ (kən'dəʊn) *vb* **condones, condoning, condoned.** (*tr*) **1** to overlook or forgive (an offence, etc.). **2** *Law.* (esp. of a spouse) to pardon or overlook (an offence, usually adultery). [C19: from L *condōnāre,* from *com-* (intensive) + *dōnāre* to donate]
▸**condonation** (ˌkɒndəʊ'neɪʃən) *n* ▸**con'doner** *n*

condor ('kɒndɔː) *n* either of two very large rare New World vultures, the **Andean condor,** which has black plumage with white around the neck, and the **California condor,** which is nearly extinct. [C17: from Sp. *cóndor,* from Quechuan *kuntur*]

condottiere (ˌkɒndɒ'tjɛərɪ) *n, pl* **condottieri** (-riː). a commander or soldier in a professional mercenary company in Europe from the 13th to the 16th centuries. [C18: from It., from *condotto* leadership, from *condurre* to lead, from L *condūcere*]

conduce (kən'djuːs) *vb* **conduces, conducing, conduced.** (*intr;* foll. by *to*) to lead or contribute (to a result). [C15: from L *condūcere,* from *com-* together + *dūcere* to lead]

conducive ⓣ (kən'djuːsɪv) *adj* (when *postpositive,* foll. by *to*) contributing, leading, or tending.

conduct ⓣ *n* ('kɒndʌkt). **1** behaviour. **2** the way of managing a business, affair, etc.; handling. **3** *Rare.* the act of leading. ◆ *vb* (kən'dʌkt). **4** (*tr*) to accompany and guide (people, a party, etc.) (esp. in **conducted tour**). **5** (*tr*) to direct (affairs, business, etc.); control. **6** (*tr*) to carry out; organize: *conduct a survey.* **7** (*tr*) to behave (oneself). **8** to control (an orchestra, etc.) by the movements of the hands or a baton. **9** to transmit (heat, electricity, etc.). [C15: from Med. L *conductus* escorted, from L, from *condūcere* to CONDUCE]
▸**con'ductible** *adj* ▸**con**ˌ**ducti'bility** *n*

conductance (kən'dʌktəns) *n* the ability of a system to conduct electricity, measured by the ratio of the current flowing through the system to the potential difference across it. Symbol: G

THESAURUS

condemnation *n* **1 = disapproval,** blame, censure, denouncement, denunciation, reproach, reprobation, reproof, stricture **2 = sentence,** conviction, damnation, doom, judgment, proscription

condemnatory *adj* **1 = disapproving,** accusatory, accusing, censorious, critical, damnatory, denunciatory, proscriptive, reprobative, scathing

condensation *n* **1 = concentration,** compression, consolidation, crystallization, curtailment, reduction **2 = distillation,** condensate, deliquescence, liquefaction, precipitate, precipitation **4 = abridgment,** contraction, digest, précis, synopsis

condense *vb* **1, 3 = concentrate,** boil down, coagulate, decoct, precipitate (*Chemistry*), reduce, solidify, thicken **2 = abridge,** abbreviate, compact, compress, concentrate, contract, curtail, encapsulate, epitomize, précis, shorten, summarize
Antonyms *vb* **≠ concentrate:** dilute, make thinner, thin (out), water down, weaken **≠ abridge:** elaborate, enlarge, expand, expatiate, increase, lengthen, pad out, spin out

condescend *vb* **1 = patronize,** talk down to **2 = lower oneself,** bend, come down off one's high horse (*inf.*), deign, humble *or* demean oneself, see fit, stoop, submit, unbend (*inf.*), vouchsafe

condescending *adj* **1 = patronizing,** disdainful, lofty, lordly, on one's high horse (*inf.*), snobbish, snooty (*inf.*), supercilious, superior, toffee-nosed (*sl., chiefly Brit.*)

condescension *n* **1 = patronizing attitude,** airs, disdain, haughtiness, loftiness, lordliness, superciliousness, superiority

condition *n* **1 = state,** case, circumstances, lie of the land, plight, position, predicament, shape, situation, state of affairs, *status quo* **2 = requirement,** arrangement, article, demand, limitation, modification, prerequisite, provision, proviso, qualification, requisite, restriction, rider, rule, stipulation, terms **3** *pl* **= circumstances,** environment, milieu, situation, surroundings, way of life **4 = health,** fettle, fitness, kilter, order, shape, state of health, trim **5 = ailment,** complaint, infirmity, malady, problem, weakness ◆ *vb* **13, 15 = accustom,** adapt, educate, equip, habituate, inure, make ready, prepare, ready, tone up, train, work out

conditional *adj* **1 = dependent,** contingent, limited, provisional, qualified, subject to, with reservations
Antonyms *adj* absolute, categorical, unconditional, unrestricted

conditioning *n* **13, 15 = accustoming,** familiarization, grooming, hardening, inurement, preparation, readying, reorientation, seasoning, training ◆ *adj* **13 = toning,** astringent

condolence *n* **= sympathy,** commiseration, compassion, consolation, fellow feeling, pity

condom *n* **= sheath,** flunky (*sl.*), French letter (*sl.*), French tickler (*sl.*), rubber (*US sl.*), rubber johnny (*Brit. sl.*), scumbag (*US sl.*)

condone *vb* **1 = overlook,** disregard, excuse, forgive, let pass, look the other way, make allowance for, pardon, turn a blind eye to, wink at
Antonyms *vb* censure, condemn, denounce, disapprove, punish

conducive *adj* **= leading,** calculated to produce, contributive, contributory, favourable, helpful, productive, promotive, tending

conduct *n* **1 = behaviour,** attitude, bearing, carriage, comportment, demeanour, deportment, manners, mien (*literary*), ways **2 = management,** administration, control, direction, guidance, handling, leadership, organization, running, supervision ◆ *vb* **4 = accompany,** attend, chair, convey, escort, guide, lead, pilot, steer, usher **5, 6 = carry out,** administer, control, direct, govern, handle, manage, organize, preside over, regulate, run, supervise **7 = behave,** acquit, act, carry, comport, deport

conducting tissue *n Bot.* another name for **vascular tissue.**

conduction (kənˈdʌkʃən) *n* **1** the transfer of energy by a medium without bulk movement of the medium itself. Cf. **convection** (sense 1). **2** the transmission of an impulse along a nerve fibre. **3** the act of conveying or conducting, as through a pipe. **4** *Physics.* another name for **conductivity** (sense 1).
▸**conˈductional** *adj*

conductive (kənˈdʌktɪv) *adj* of, denoting, or having the property of conduction.

conductive education *n* an educational system, developed in Hungary, in which teachers (**conductors**) teach children and adults with motor disorders to function independently, by guiding them to attain their own goals in their own way.

conductivity (ˌkɒndʌkˈtɪvɪtɪ) *n, pl* **conductivities. 1** the property of transmitting heat, electricity, or sound. **2** a measure of the ability of a substance to conduct electricity. Symbol: κ

conductivity water *n* water that has a conductivity of less than 0.043 $\times 10^{-6}$ S cm^{-1}.

conductor (kənˈdʌktə) *n* **1** an official on a bus who collects fares. **2** a person who conducts an orchestra, choir, etc. **3** a person who leads or guides. **4** *US & Canad.* a railway official in charge of a train. **5** a substance, body, or system that conducts electricity, heat, etc. **6** See **lightning conductor.**
▸**conˈductorship** *n* ▸**conductress** (kənˈdʌktrɪs) *fem n*

conduit ❶ (ˈkɒndɪt, -djʊɪt) *n* **1** a pipe or channel for carrying a fluid. **2** a rigid tube for carrying electrical cables. **3** an agency or means of access, communication, etc. [C14: from OF, from Med. L *conductus* channel, from L *condūcere* to lead]

condyle (ˈkɒndɪl) *n* the rounded projection on the articulating end of a bone. [C17: from L *condylus*, from Gk *kondulos*]
▸**ˈcondylar** *adj*

cone (kəʊn) *n* **1** a geometric solid consisting of a plane base bounded by a closed curve, usually a circle or an ellipse, every point of which is joined to a fixed point lying outside the plane of the base. **2** anything that tapers from a circular section to a point, such as a wafer shell used to contain ice cream. **3a** the reproductive body of conifers and related plants, made up of overlapping scales. **3b** a similar structure in horsetails, club mosses, etc. **4** a small cone used as a temporary traffic marker on roads. **5** any one of the cone-shaped cells in the retina of the eye, sensitive to colour and bright light. ◆ *vb* **cones, coning, coned. 6** (*tr*) to shape like a cone. [C16: from L *cōnus*, from Gk *kōnus* pine cone, geometrical cone]

cone off *vb* (*tr, adv*) *Brit.* to close (one carriageway of a motorway) by placing warning cones across it.

coney (ˈkəʊnɪ) *n* a variant spelling of **cony.**

confab ❶ (ˈkɒnfæb) *Inf.* ◆ *n* **1** a conversation. ◆ *vb* **confabs, confabbing, confabbed. 2** (*intr*) to converse.

confabulate (kənˈfæbjʊˌleɪt) *vb* **confabulates, confabulating, confabulated.** (*intr*) **1** to talk together; chat. **2** *Psychiatry.* to replace the gaps left by a disorder of the memory with imaginary remembered experiences consistently believed to be true. [C17: from L *confābulārī*, from *fābulārī* to talk, from *fābula* a story]
▸**conˌfabuˈlation** *n*

confect (kənˈfɛkt) *vb* (*tr*) **1** to prepare by combining ingredients. **2** to make; construct. [C16: from L *confectus* prepared, from *conficere*, from *com-* (intensive) + *facere* to make]

confection (kənˈfɛkʃən) *n* **1** the act of compounding or mixing. **2** any sweet preparation, such as a preserve or a sweet. **3** *Old-fashioned.* an elaborate article of clothing, esp. for women. [C14: from OF, from L *confectiō* a preparing, from *conficere;* see CONFECT]

confectioner (kənˈfɛkʃənə) *n* a person who makes or sells sweets or confections.

confectionery (kənˈfɛkʃənərɪ) *n, pl* **confectioneries. 1** sweets and other confections collectively. **2** the art or business of a confectioner.

confederacy ❶ (kənˈfɛdərəsɪ) *n, pl* **confederacies. 1** a union of states, etc.; alliance; league. **2** a combination of groups or individuals for unlawful purposes. [C14: from OF *confederacie*, from LL *confoederātiō* agreement]
▸**conˈfederal** *adj*

confederate ❶ *n* (kənˈfɛdərɪt). **1** a nation, state, or individual that is part of a confederacy. **2** someone who is part of a conspiracy. ◆ *adj* (kənˈfɛdərɪt). **3** united; allied. ◆ *vb* (kənˈfɛdəˌreɪt), **confederates, confederating, confederated. 4** to form into or become part of a confederacy [C14: from LL *confoederātus*, from *confoederāre* to unite by a league]

Confederate (kənˈfɛdərɪt) *adj* **1** of or supporting the Confederate States of America, which seceded from the Union in 1861. ◆ *n* **2** a supporter of the Confederate States.

confederation (kənˌfɛdəˈreɪʃən) *n* **1** the act of confederating or the state of being confederated. **2** a loose alliance of political units. **3** (esp. in Canada) another name for a **federation.**
▸**conˌfederˈationist** *n*

confer ❶ (kənˈfɜː) *vb* **confers, conferring, conferred. 1** (*tr;* foll. by *on* or *upon*) to grant or bestow (an honour, gift, etc.). **2** (*intr*) to consult together. [C16: from L *conferre*, from *com-* together + *ferre* to bring]
▸**conˈferment** *or* **conˈferral** *n* ▸**conˈferrable** *adj*

conferee *or* **conferree** (ˌkɒnfɜːˈriː) *n* **1** a person who takes part in a conference. **2** a person on whom an honour or gift is conferred.

conference ❶ (ˈkɒnfərəns) *n* **1** a meeting for consultation or discussion, esp. one with a formal agenda. **2** an assembly of the clergy or of clergy and laity of any of certain Protestant Churches acting as representatives of their denomination. **3** *Sport, US & Canad.* a league or division of clubs or teams. [C16: from Med. L *conferentia*, from L *conferre* to bring together]
▸**conferential** (ˌkɒnfəˈrɛnʃəl) *adj*

conference call *n* a special telephone facility by which three or more people using conventional or cellular phones can be linked up to speak to one another.

conferencing (ˈkɒnfərənsɪŋ) *n* the practice of holding a conference, esp. by means of a telephone service. See **conference call.**

confess ❶ (kənˈfɛs) *vb* (when *tr, may take a clause as object*) **1** (when *intr*, often foll. by *to*) to make an admission (of faults, crimes, etc.). **2** (*tr*) to admit to be true; concede. **3** *Christianity.* to declare (one's sins) to God or to a priest as his representative, so as to obtain pardon and absolution. [C14: from OF *confesser*, from LL, from L *confessus* confessed, from *confitērī* to admit]

confessedly (kənˈfɛsɪdlɪ) *adv* (*sentence modifier*) by admission or confession; avowedly.

confession ❶ (kənˈfɛʃən) *n* **1** the act of confessing. **2** something confessed. **3** an acknowledgment, esp. of one's faults or crimes. **4** *Christianity.* the act of a penitent accusing himself of his sins. **5 confession of faith.** a formal public avowal of religious beliefs. **6** a religious sect united by common beliefs.
▸**conˈfessionary** *adj*

confessional (kənˈfɛʃənᵊl) *adj* **1** of or suited to a confession. ◆ *n* **2** *Christianity.* a small stall where a priest hears confessions.

confessor (kənˈfɛsə) *n* **1** *Christianity.* a priest who hears confessions and sometimes acts as a spiritual counsellor. **2** *History.* a person who bears witness to his Christian religious faith by the holiness of his life, but does not suffer martyrdom. **3** a person who makes a confession.

confetti (kənˈfɛtɪ) *n* small pieces of coloured paper thrown on festive occasions, esp. at weddings. [C19: from It., pl of *confetto*, orig., a bonbon]

confidant ❶ *or* (*fem*) **confidante** (ˌkɒnfɪˈdænt, ˈkɒnfɪˌdænt) *n* a person to whom private matters are confided. [C17: from F *confident*, from It. *confidente*, n. use of adj: trustworthy]

confide ❶ (kənˈfaɪd) *vb* **confides, confiding, confided. 1** (usually foll. by *in;* when *tr, may take a clause as object*) to disclose (secret or personal matters) in confidence (to). **2** (*intr;* foll. by *in*) to have complete trust. **3** (*tr*) to entrust into another's keeping. [C15: from L *confidere*, from *fidere* to trust]
▸**conˈfider** *n*

confidence ❶ (ˈkɒnfɪdəns) *n* **1** trust in a person or thing. **2** belief in one's own abilities; self-assurance. **3** trust or a trustful relationship: *take me into your confidence.* **4** something confided; secret. **5 in confidence.** as a secret.

confidence trick *or US & Canad.* **confidence game** *n* a swindle involving money in which the victim's trust is won by the swindler.

confident ❶ (ˈkɒnfɪdənt) *adj* **1** (*postpositive;* foll. by *of*) having or show-

THESAURUS

conduit *n* **1** = **passage**, canal, channel, duct, main, pipe, tube

confab *n* **1** *Informal* = **conversation**, chat, chinwag (*Brit. inf.*), confabulation (*formal*), discussion, gossip, natter, powwow, session, talk

confederacy *n* **1, 2** = **union**, alliance, bund, coalition, compact, confederation, conspiracy, covenant, federation, league

confederate *n* **1, 2** = **associate**, abettor, accessory, accomplice, ally, colleague, partner ◆ *adj* **3** = **allied**, associated, combined, federal, federated, in alliance ◆ *vb* **4** = **unite**, ally, amalgamate, associate, band together, combine, federate, merge

confer *vb* **1** = **grant**, accord, award, bestow, give, hand out, present, vouchsafe **2** = **discuss**, consult, converse, deliberate, discourse, parley, talk

conference *n* **1** = **meeting**, colloquium, congress, consultation, convention, convocation, discussion, forum, seminar, symposium, teach-in

confess *vb* **1, 2** = **admit**, acknowledge, allow, blurt out, come clean (*inf.*), come out of the closet, concede, confide, disclose, divulge, get (something) off one's chest (*inf.*), grant, make a clean breast of, own, own up, recognize, sing (*sl., chiefly U.S.*), spill one's guts (*sl.*)
Antonyms *vb* button one's lips, conceal, cover, deny, hide, hush up, keep mum, keep secret, keep under wraps, repudiate, suppress, withhold

confession *n* **1** = **admission**, acknowledgment, avowal, disclosure, divulgence, exposure, revelation, unbosoming

confidant *n* = **close friend**, alter ego, bosom friend, crony, familiar, intimate

confide *vb* **1** = **tell**, admit, breathe, confess, disclose, divulge, impart, reveal, whisper **3** *Formal* = **entrust**, commend, commit, consign

confidence *n* **1** = **trust**, belief, credence, dependence, faith, reliance **2** = **self-assurance**, aplomb, assurance, boldness, courage, firmness, nerve, self-possession, self-reliance **5 in confidence** = **in secrecy**, between you and me (and the gatepost), confidentially, privately
Antonyms *n* ≠ **trust:** disbelief, distrust, doubt, misgiving, mistrust ≠ **self-assurance:** apprehension, fear, self-doubt, shyness, uncertainty

confident *adj* **1** = **certain**, convinced, counting on, positive, satisfied, secure, sure **2** = **self-assured**, assured, bold, can-do (*inf.*), dauntless, fearless, self-reliant
Antonyms *adj* ≠ **certain:** doubtful, dubious, not sure, tentative, uncertain, unconvinced, unsure ≠ **self-assured:** afraid, hesitant, insecure, jittery,

ing certainty; sure: *confident of success.* **2** sure of oneself. **3** presumptuous. [C16: from L *confidens,* from *confidere* to have complete trust in]
►**'confidently** *adv*

confidential ❶ (ˌkɒnfɪ'dɛnʃəl) *adj* **1** spoken or given in confidence; private. **2** entrusted with another's secret affairs: *a confidential secretary.* **3** suggestive of intimacy: *a confidential approach.*
►**ˌconfiˌdenti'ality** *n* ►**ˌconfi'dentially** *adv*

confiding (kən'faɪdɪŋ) *adj* unsuspicious; trustful.
►**con'fidingly** *adv* ►**con'fidingness** *n*

configuration ❶ (kənˌfɪgjʊ'reɪʃən) *n* **1** the arrangement of the parts of something. **2** the external form or outline achieved by such an arrangement. **3** *Psychol.* the unit or pattern in perception studied by Gestalt psychologists. [C16: from LL *configūrātiō,* from *configūrāre* to model on something, from *figūrāre* to shape, fashion]
►**conˌfigu'rational** *or* **con'figurative** *adj*

confine ❶ *vb* (kən'faɪn), **confines, confining, confined.** (*tr*) **1** to keep within bounds; limit; restrict. **2** to restrict the free movement of: *arthritis confined him to bed.* ◆ *n* ('kɒnfaɪn). **3** (*often pl*) a limit; boundary. [C16: from Med. L *confīnāre,* from L *confinis* adjacent, from *finis* boundary]
►**con'finer** *n*

confined ❶ (kən'faɪnd) *adj* **1** enclosed; limited. **2** in childbed; undergoing childbirth.

confinement ❶ (kən'faɪnmənt) *n* **1** the act of confining or the state of being confined. **2** the period of the birth of a child.

confirm ❶ (kən'fɜːm) *vb* (*tr*) **1** (*may take a clause as object*) to prove to be true or valid; corroborate. **2** (*may take a clause as object*) to assert for a further time, so as to make more definite: *he confirmed that he would appear in court.* **3** to strengthen: *his story confirmed my doubts.* **4** to make valid by a formal act; ratify. **5** to administer the rite of confirmation to. [C13: from OF *confermer,* from L *confirmāre,* from *firmus* FIRM[1]]
►**con'firmatory** *or* **con'firmative** *adj*

confirmation ❶ (ˌkɒnfə'meɪʃən) *n* **1** the act of confirming. **2** something that confirms. **3** a rite in several Christian churches that confirms a baptized person in his faith and admits him to full participation in the church.

confirmed ❶ (kən'fɜːmd) *adj* **1** (*prenominal*) long-established in a habit, way of life, etc. **2** having received the rite of confirmation.

confiscate ❶ ('kɒnfɪˌskeɪt) *vb* **confiscates, confiscating, confiscated.** (*tr*) **1** to seize (property), esp. for public use and esp. by way of a penalty. ◆ *adj* **2** confiscated; forfeit. [C16: from L *confiscāre* to seize for the public treasury, from *fiscus* treasury]
►**ˌconfis'cation** *n* ►**'confisˌcator** *n* ►**confiscatory** (kən'fɪskətərɪ) *adj*

Confiteor (kən'fɪtɪˌɔː) *n RC Church.* a prayer consisting of a general confession of sinfulness and an entreaty for forgiveness. [C13: from L: I confess]

conflagration ❶ (ˌkɒnflə'greɪʃən) *n* a large destructive fire. [C16: from L *conflagrātiō,* from *conflagrāre,* from *com-* (intensive) + *flagrāre* to burn]

conflate (kən'fleɪt) *vb* **conflates, conflating, conflated.** (*tr*) to combine or blend (two things, esp. two versions of a text) so as to form a whole. [C16: from L *conflāre* to blow together, from *flāre* to blow]
►**con'flation** *n*

conflict ❶ *n* ('kɒnflɪkt). **1** a struggle between opposing forces; battle. **2** opposition between ideas, interests, etc.; controversy. **3** *Psychol.* opposition between two simultaneous but incompatible wishes or drives, sometimes leading to emotional tension. ◆ *vb* (kən'flɪkt). (*intr*) **4** to come into opposition; clash. **5** to fight. [C15: from L *conflictus,* from *conflīgere* to combat, from *flīgere* to strike]
►**con'flicting** *adj* ►**con'flictingly** *adv* ►**con'fliction** *n*

confluence ('kɒnfluəns) *or* **conflux** ('kɒnflʌks) *n* **1** a flowing together, esp. of rivers. **2** a gathering.
►**'confluent** *adj*

conform ❶ (kən'fɔːm) *vb* **1** (*intr;* usually foll. by *to*) to comply in actions, behaviour, etc., with accepted standards. **2** (*intr;* usually foll. by *with*) to be in accordance: *he conforms with my idea of a teacher.* **3** to make or become similar. **4** (*intr*) to comply with the practices of an established church, esp. the Church of England. [C14: from OF *conformer,* from L *confirmāre* to strengthen, from *firmāre* to make firm]
►**con'former** *n* ►**con'formist** *n, adj*

conformable (kən'fɔːməbᵊl) *adj* **1** corresponding in character; similar. **2** obedient; submissive. **3** (foll. by *to*) consistent (with). **4** (of rock strata) lying in a parallel arrangement so that their original relative positions have remained undisturbed.
►**conˌforma'bility** *n* ►**con'formably** *adv*

conformal (kən'fɔːməl) *adj* (of a map projection) maintaining true shape over a small area and scale in every direction. [C17: from LL *conformālis,* from L *com-* same + *forma* shape]

conformation ❶ (ˌkɒnfɔː'meɪʃən) *n* **1** the general shape of an object; configuration. **2** the arrangement of the parts of an object. **3** *Chem.* the three-dimensional arrangement of the atoms in a molecule.

conformity ❶ (kən'fɔːmɪtɪ) *or* **conformance** *n, pl* **conformities** *or* **conformances. 1** compliance in actions, behaviour, etc., with certain accepted standards. **2** likeness; congruity; agreement. **3** compliance with the practices of an established church.

confound ❶ (kən'faʊnd) *vb* (*tr*) **1** to astound; bewilder. **2** to confuse. **3** to treat mistakenly as similar to or identical with. **4** (kɒn'faʊnd). to curse (usually in **confound it!**). **5** to contradict or refute (an argument, etc.). **6** to rout or defeat (an enemy). [C13: from OF *confondre,* from L *confundere* to mingle, pour together]
►**con'founder** *n*

confounded (kən'faʊndɪd) *adj* **1** bewildered; confused. **2** (*prenominal*) *Inf.* execrable; damned.
►**con'foundedly** *adv*

confraternity (ˌkɒnfrə'tɜːnɪtɪ) *n, pl* **confraternities.** a group of men united for some particular purpose, esp. Christian laymen organized for religious or charitable service; brotherhood. [C15: from Med. L *confrāternitās,* ult. from L *frāter* brother]

confrère ('kɒnfreə) *n* a fellow member of a profession, etc. [C15: from OF, from Med. L *confrāter*]

confront ❶ (kən'frʌnt) *vb* (*tr*) **1** (usually foll. by *with*) to present (with something), esp. in order to accuse or criticize. **2** to face boldly; oppose in hostility. **3** to be face to face with. [C16: from Med. L *confrontārī,* from *frons* forehead]
►**confrontation** (ˌkɒnfrʌn'teɪʃən) *n* ►**ˌconfron'tational** *adj*

Confucian (kən'fjuːʃən) *adj* **1** of or relating to the doctrines of Confucius (551–479 B.C.), Chinese philosopher. ◆ *n* **2** a follower of Confucius.

Confucianism (kən'fjuːʃəˌnɪzəm) *n* the ethical system of Confucius

THESAURUS

lacking confidence, mousy, nervous, scared, self-doubting, unsure

confidential *adj* **1** = **secret**, classified, hush-hush (*inf.*), intimate, off the record, private, privy **2** = **trusted**, faithful, familiar, trustworthy, trusty

confidentially *adv* **1** = **in secret**, behind closed doors, between ourselves, in camera, in confidence, personally, privately, sub rosa

configuration *n* **1, 2** = **arrangement**, cast, conformation, contour, figure, form, outline, shape

confine *vb* **1** = **restrict**, bind, bound, cage, circumscribe, clip someone's wings, enclose, hem in, hold back, immure, imprison, incarcerate, intern, keep, limit, repress, restrain, shut up, straiten ◆ *n* **3** *often pl* = **limits**, boundaries, bounds, circumference, edge, pale, precincts

confined *adj* **1** = **restricted**, enclosed, limited **2** = **in childbirth**, in childbed, lying-in

confinement *n* **1** = **imprisonment**, custody, detention, incarceration, internment, porridge (*sl.*) **2** = **childbirth**, *accouchement*, childbed, labour, lying-in, parturition, time, travail

confirm *vb* **1** = **prove**, approve, authenticate, bear out, corroborate, endorse, ratify, sanction, substantiate, validate, verify **3** = **strengthen**, assure, buttress, clinch, establish, fix, fortify, reinforce, settle

confirmation *n* **1** = **proof**, authentication, corroboration, evidence, substantiation, testimony, validation, verification **2** = **sanction**, acceptance, agreement, approval, assent, endorsement, ratification
Antonyms *n* ≠ **proof**: contradiction, denial, disavowal, repudiation ≠ **sanction**: annulment, cancellation, disapproval, refusal, rejection

confirmed *adj* **1** = **long-established**, chronic, dyed-in-the-wool, habitual, hardened, ingrained, inured, inveterate, rooted, seasoned

confiscate *vb* **1** = **seize**, appropriate, commandeer, expropriate, impound, sequester, sequestrate
Antonyms *vb* free, give, give back, hand back, release, restore, return

confiscation *n* **1** = **seizure**, appropriation, expropriation, forfeiture, impounding, sequestration, takeover

conflagration *n* = **fire**, blaze, holocaust, inferno, wildfire

conflict *n* **1** = **battle**, clash, collision, combat, contention, contest, encounter, engagement, fight, fracas, head-to-head, set-to (*inf.*), strife, war, warfare **2** = **opposition**, antagonism, bad blood, difference, disagreement, discord, dissension, divided loyalties, friction, hostility, interference, strife, variance ◆ *vb* **4, 5** = **be incompatible**, be at variance, clash, collide, combat, contend, contest, differ, disagree, fight, interfere, strive, struggle
Antonyms *n* ≠ **battle, opposition**: accord, agreement, harmony, peace, treaty, truce ◆ *vb* ≠ **be incompatible**: agree, coincide, harmonize, reconcile

conflicting *adj* **4** = **incompatible**, antagonistic, clashing, contradictory, contrary, discordant, inconsistent, opposed, opposing, paradoxical
Antonyms *adj* accordant, agreeing, compatible, congruous, consistent, harmonious, similar, unopposing

conform *vb* **1** = **comply**, adapt, adjust, fall in with, follow, follow the crowd, obey, run with the pack, toe the line, yield **2, 3** = **agree**, accord, assimilate, correspond, harmonize, match, square, suit, tally

conformation *n* **1, 2** = **shape**, anatomy, arrangement, build, configuration, form, framework, outline, structure

conformist *n* **1** = **traditionalist**, Babbitt (*US.*), conventionalist, stick-in-the-mud (*inf.*), yes man

conformity *n* **1** = **compliance**, allegiance, Babbittry (*US.*), conventionality, observance, orthodoxy, traditionalism **2** = **likeness**, affinity, agreement, conformance, congruity, consonance, correspondence, harmony, resemblance, similarity

confound *vb* **1** = **bewilder**, amaze, astonish, astound, baffle, be all Greek to (*inf.*), boggle the mind, confuse, dumbfound, flabbergast (*inf.*), flummox, mix up, mystify, nonplus, perplex, startle, surprise **5** = **destroy**, annihilate, contradict, demolish, explode, make a nonsense of, overthrow, overwhelm, refute, ruin

confront *vb* **2, 3** = **face**, accost, beard, brave, bring face to face with, call out, challenge, defy, encounter, face off (*sl.*), face the music, face up to, oppose, stand up to, tackle, walk into the lion's den
Antonyms *vb* avoid, body-swerve (*Scot.*), circumvent, dodge, evade, flee, give a wide berth to, keep *or* steer clear of, sidestep

confrontation *n* **2, 3** = **conflict**, contest, crisis, encounter, face-off (*sl.*), fight, head-to-head, set-to (*inf.*), showdown (*inf.*)

emphasizing moral order, the virtue of China's ancient rules, and gentlemanly education.
▸**Con'fucianist** *n*

confuse ❶ (kən'fju:z) *vb* **confuses, confusing, confused.** (*tr*) **1** to bewilder; perplex. **2** to mix up (things, ideas, etc.). **3** to make unclear: *he confused his talk with irrelevant details.* **4** to mistake (one thing) for another. **5** to disconcert; embarrass. **6** to cause to become disordered: *the enemy ranks were confused by gas.* [C18: back formation from *confused,* from L *confūsus,* from *confundere* to pour together]
▸**con'fusable** *adj* ▸**confusedly** (kən'fju:zɪdlɪ, -'fju:zd-) *adv* ▸**con'fusing** *adj* ▸**con'fusingly** *adv*

confusion ❶ (kən'fju:ʒən) *n* **1** the act of confusing or the state of being confused. **2** disorder. **3** bewilderment; perplexity. **4** lack of clarity. **5** embarrassment; abashment.

confute (kən'fju:t) *vb* **confutes, confuting, confuted.** (*tr*) to prove (a person or thing) wrong, invalid, or mistaken; disprove. [C16: from L *confūtāre* to check, silence]
▸**con'futable** *adj* ▸**confutation** (ˌkɒnfju'teɪʃən) *n*

conga ('kɒŋgə) *n* **1** a Latin American dance of three steps and a kick to each bar, performed by a number of people in single file. **2** Also called: **conga drum.** a large tubular bass drum played with the hands. ◆ *vb* **congas, congaing, congaed. 3** (*intr*) to perform this dance. [C20: from American Sp., fem of *congo* belonging to the *Congo*]

congé ('kɒnʒeɪ) *n* **1** permission to depart or dismissal, esp. when formal. **2** a farewell. [C16: from OF *congié,* from L *commeātus* leave of absence, from *meāre* to go]

congeal ❶ (kən'dʒi:l) *vb* **1** to change or cause to change from a soft or fluid state to a firm state. **2** to form or cause to form into a coagulated mass; jell. [C14: from OF *congeler,* from L *congelāre,* from *com-* together + *gelāre* to freeze]
▸**con'gealable** *adj* ▸**con'gealment** *n*

congelation (ˌkɒndʒɪ'leɪʃən) *n* **1** the process of congealing. **2** something formed by this process.

congener (kən'dʒi:nə, 'kɒndʒɪnə) *n* a member of a class, group, or other category, esp. any animal of a specified genus. [C18: from L, from *com-* same + *genus* kind]

congenial ❶ (kən'dʒi:njəl) *adj* **1** friendly, pleasant, or agreeable: *a congenial atmosphere to work in.* **2** having a similar disposition, tastes, etc.; compatible. [C17: from CON- (same) + GENIAL[1]]
▸**congeniality** (kənˌdʒi:nɪ'ælɪtɪ) *n*

congenital ❶ (kən'dʒɛnɪtᵊl) *adj* **1** denoting any nonhereditary condition, esp. an abnormal condition, existing at birth: *congenital blindness.* **2** *Inf.* complete, as if from birth: *a congenital idiot.* [C18: from L *congenitus,* from *genitus* born, from *gignere* to bear]
▸**con'genitally** *adv*

conger ('kɒŋgə) *n* a large marine eel occurring in temperate and tropical coastal waters. [C14: from OF *congre,* from L *conger,* from Gk *gongros*]

congeries (kɒn'dʒɪəri:z) *n* (*functioning as sing or pl*) a collection; mass; heap. [C17: from L, from *congerere* to pile up, from *gerere* to carry]

congest ❶ (kən'dʒɛst) *vb* **1** to crowd or become crowded to excess; overfill. **2** to clog (an organ) with blood or (of an organ) to become clogged with blood. **3** (*tr; usually passive*) to block (the nose) with mucus. [C16: from L *congestus,* from *congerere;* see CONGERIES]
▸**con'gestion** *n*

conglomerate ❶ *n* (kən'glɒmərɪt). **1** a thing composed of heterogeneous elements. **2** any coarse-grained sedimentary rock consisting of rounded fragments of rock embedded in a finer matrix. **3** a large corporation consisting of a group of companies dealing in widely diversified goods, services, etc. ◆ *vb* (kən'glɒməˌreɪt), **conglomerates, conglomerating, conglomerated. 4** to form into a mass. ◆ *adj* (kən'glɒmərɪt). **5** made up of heterogeneous elements. **6** (of sedimentary rocks) consisting of rounded fragments within a finer matrix. [C16: from L *conglomerāre* to roll up, from *glomerāre* to wind into a ball, from *glomus* ball of thread]
▸**conˌglomer'ation** *n*

congrats (kən'græts) *pl n, sentence substitute.* informal shortened form of **congratulations.**

congratulate ❶ (kən'grætjuˌleɪt) *vb* **congratulates, congratulating, congratulated.** (*tr*) **1** (usually foll. by *on*) to communicate pleasure, approval, or praise to; compliment. **2** (often foll. by *on*) to consider (oneself) clever or fortunate (as a result of): *she congratulated herself on her tact.* **3** *Obs.* to greet; salute. [C16: from L *congrātulārī,* from *grātulārī* to rejoice, from *grātus* pleasing]
▸**conˌgratu'lation** *n* ▸**con'gratulatory** *or* **con'gratulative** *adj*

congratulations ❶ (kənˌgrætju'leɪʃənz) *pl n, sentence substitute.* expressions of pleasure or joy on another's success, good fortune, etc.

congregate ❶ ('kɒŋgrɪˌgeɪt) *vb* **congregates, congregating, congregated.** to collect together in a body or crowd; assemble. [C15: from L *congregāre* to collect into a flock, from *grex* flock]

congregation ❶ (ˌkɒŋgrɪ'geɪʃən) *n* **1** a group of persons gathered for worship, prayer, etc., esp. in a church. **2** the act of congregating together. **3** a group collected together; assemblage. **4** the group of persons habitually attending a given church, chapel, etc. **5** *RC Church.* **5a** a society of persons who follow a common rule of life but who are bound only by simple vows. **5b** an administrative subdivision of the papal curia. **6** *Chiefly Brit.* an assembly of senior members of a university.

congregational (ˌkɒŋgrɪ'geɪʃənᵊl) *adj* **1** of or relating to a congregation. **2** (*usually cap.*) of or denoting Congregationalism.

Congregationalism (ˌkɒŋgrɪ'geɪʃənəˌlɪzəm) *n* a system of Christian doctrines and ecclesiastical government in which each congregation is self-governing.
▸**ˌCongre'gationalist** *adj, n*

congress ❶ ('kɒŋgrɛs) *n* **1** a meeting or conference, esp. of representatives of sovereign states. **2** a national legislative assembly. **3** a society or association. [C16: from L *congressus,* from *congredī,* from *com-* together + *gradī* to walk]

Congress ('kɒŋgrɛs) *n* **1** the bicameral federal legislature of the US, consisting of the House of Representatives and the Senate. **2** Also called: **Congress Party.** (in India) a major political party.
▸**Con'gressional** *adj*

congressional (kən'grɛʃənᵊl) *adj* of or relating to a congress.
▸**con'gressionalist** *n*

Congressman ('kɒŋgrɛsmən) *or* (*fem*) **Congresswoman** *n, pl* **Congressmen** *or* **Congresswomen.** (in the US) a member of Congress, esp. of the House of Representatives.

congruence ❶ ('kɒŋgruəns) *or* **congruency** *n* **1** the quality or state of corresponding, agreeing, or being congruent. **2** *Maths.* the relationship between two integers, *x* and *y*, such that their difference, with re-

THESAURUS

confuse *vb* **1** = **bewilder,** baffle, be all Greek to (*inf.*), bemuse, darken, faze, flummox, muddy the waters, mystify, nonplus, obscure, perplex, puzzle **2** = **mix up,** blend, confound, disarrange, disorder, intermingle, involve, jumble, mingle, mistake, muddle, ravel, snarl up (*inf.*), tangle **5** = **disconcert,** abash, addle, demoralize, discomfit, discompose, discountenance, disorient, embarrass, fluster, mortify, nonplus, rattle (*inf.*), shame, throw into disorder, throw off balance, unnerve, upset

confused *adj* **1** = **bewildered,** at a loss, at sea, at sixes and sevens, baffled, dazed, discombobulated (*inf., chiefly US & Canad.*), disorganized, disorientated, flummoxed, muddled, muzzy (*US inf.*), nonplussed, not knowing if one is coming or going, not with it (*inf.*), perplexed, puzzled, taken aback, thrown off balance, upset **2** = **disordered,** at sixes and sevens, chaotic, disarranged, disarrayed, disorderly, disorganized, higgledy-piggledy (*inf.*), hugger-mugger (*arch.*), in disarray, jumbled, mistaken, misunderstood, mixed up, out of order, topsy-turvy, untidy
Antonyms *adj* ≠ **bewildered:** aware, enlightened, informed, on the ball (*inf.*), with it (*inf.*) ≠ **disordered:** arranged, in order, ordered, orderly, organized, tidy

confusing *adj* **1** = **bewildering,** ambiguous, baffling, clear as mud (*inf.*), complicated, contradictory, disconcerting, inconsistent, misleading, muddling, perplexing, puzzling, unclear
Antonyms *adj* clear, definite, explicit, plain, simple, straightforward, uncomplicated, understandable

confusion *n* **1, 3** = **bewilderment,** befuddlement, bemusement, disorientation, mystification, perplexity, puzzlement **2** = **disorder,** bustle, chaos, clutter, commotion, disarrangement, disarray, disorganization, hodgepodge (*US*), hotchpotch, jumble, mess, muddle, pig's breakfast (*inf.*), shambles, state, tangle, turmoil, untidiness, upheaval **5** = **disconcertion,** abashment, chagrin, demoralization, discomfiture, distraction, embarrassment, fluster, mind-fuck (*taboo sl.*), perturbation
Antonyms *n* ≠ **bewilderment:** clarification, enlightenment, explanation, solution ≠ **disorder:** arrangement, neatness, order, organization, tidiness

congeal *vb* **1, 2** = **thicken,** benumb, clot, coagulate, condense, curdle, freeze, gelatinize, harden, jell, set, solidify, stiffen

congenial *adj* **1** = **pleasant,** affable, agreeable, companionable, complaisant, favourable, friendly, genial, kindly, pleasing **2** = **compatible,** adapted, fit, kindred, like-minded, suitable, sympathetic, well-suited

congenital *adj* **1** = **inborn,** constitutional, immanent, inbred, inherent, innate, natural **2** *Informal* = **complete,** deep-dyed (*usually derogatory*), inveterate, thorough, utter

congested *adj* **1** = **overcrowded,** crowded, teeming **2** = **clogged,** blocked-up, crammed, jammed, overfilled, overflowing, packed, stuffed, stuffed-up
Antonyms *adj* ≠ **overcrowded:** empty, half-full, uncrowded ≠ **clogged:** clear, free, uncongested, unhampered, unhindered, unimpeded, unobstructed

congestion *n* **1** = **overcrowding,** crowding **2** = **clogging,** bottleneck, jam, mass, snarl-up (*inf., chiefly Brit.*), surfeit

conglomerate *n* **3** = **corporation,** agglomerate, aggregate, multinational ◆ *vb* **4** = **amass,** accumulate, agglomerate, aggregate, cluster, coalesce, snowball ◆ *adj* **5** = **amassed,** clustered, composite, heterogeneous, massed

conglomeration *n* **4** = **mass,** accumulation, aggregation, assortment, combination, composite, hotchpotch, medley, miscellany, mishmash, potpourri

congratulate *vb* **1** = **compliment,** felicitate, pat on the back, wish joy to

congratulations *pl n, sentence substitute* = **good wishes,** best wishes, compliments, felicitations, greetings, pat on the back

congregate *vb* = **come together,** assemble, collect, concentrate, convene, converge, convoke, flock, forgather, gather, mass, meet, muster, rally, rendezvous, throng
Antonyms *vb* break up, dispel, disperse, dissipate, part, scatter, separate, split up

congregation *n* **1, 3, 4** = **assembly,** brethren, crowd, fellowship, flock, host, laity, multitude, parish, parishioners, throng

congress *n* **1, 2** = **meeting,** assembly, chamber of deputies, conclave, conference, convention, convocation, council, delegates, diet, house, legislative assembly, legislature, parliament, quango, representatives

congruence *n* **1** = **correspondence,** accord,

spect to another integer called the modulus, *n*, is a multiple of the modulus.

congruent ➊ (ˈkɒŋgrʊənt) *adj* **1** agreeing; corresponding. **2** having identical shapes so that all parts correspond: *congruent triangles*. **3** of or concerning two integers related by a congruence. [C15: from L *congruere* to agree]

congruous ➊ (ˈkɒŋgrʊəs) *adj* **1** corresponding or agreeing. **2** appropriate. [C16: from L *congruus*; see CONGRUENT]
▸**congruity** (kənˈgruːɪtɪ) *n*

conic ➊ (ˈkɒnɪk) *adj also* **conical**. **1a** having the shape of a cone. **1b** of a cone. ◆ *n* **2** another name for **conic section**.
▸**ˈconically** *adv*

conics (ˈkɒnɪks) *n* (*functioning as sing*) the geometry of the parabola, ellipse, and hyperbola.

conic section *n* one of a group of curves formed by the intersection of a plane and a right circular cone. It is either a circle, ellipse, parabola, or hyperbola.

conidium (kəʊˈnɪdɪəm) *n, pl* **conidia** (-ˈnɪdɪə). an asexual spore formed at the tip of a specialized hypha in fungi such as *Penicillium*. [C19: from NL, from Gk *konis* dust + -IUM]

conifer (ˈkəʊnɪfə, ˈkɒn-) *n* any tree or shrub of the phylum *Coniferophyta*, typically bearing cones and evergreen leaves. The group includes the pines, spruces, firs, larches, etc. [C19: from L, from *cōnus* CONE + *ferre* to bear]
▸**coˈniferous** *adj*

conj. *abbrev. for:* **1** conjugation. **2** conjunction.

conjectural ➊ (kənˈdʒɛktʃərəl) *adj* involving or inclined to conjecture.
▸**conˈjecturally** *adv*

conjecture ➊ (kənˈdʒɛktʃə) *n* **1** the formation of conclusions from incomplete evidence; guess. **2** the conclusion so formed. ◆ *vb* **conjectures, conjecturing, conjectured. 3** to infer or arrive at (an opinion, conclusion, etc.) from incomplete evidence. [C14: from L *conjectūra*, from *conjicere* to throw together, from *jacere* to throw]
▸**conˈjecturable** *adj*

conjoin (kənˈdʒɔɪn) *vb* to join or become joined. [C14: from OF *conjoindre*, from L *conjungere*, from *jungere* to JOIN]
▸**conˈjoiner** *n*

conjoined twins *pl n* the technical name for **Siamese twins**.

conjoint (kənˈdʒɔɪnt) *adj* united, joint, or associated.
▸**conˈjointly** *adv*

conjugal ➊ (ˈkɒndʒʊgᵊl) *adj* of or relating to marriage or the relationship between husband and wife: *conjugal rights*. [C16: from L *conjugālis*, from *conjunx* wife or husband]
▸**conjugality** (ˌkɒndʒʊˈgælɪtɪ) *n* ▸**ˈconjugally** *adv*

conjugate *vb* (ˈkɒndʒʊˌgeɪt), **conjugates, conjugating, conjugated. 1** (*tr*) *Grammar.* to state or set out the conjugation of (a verb). **2** (*intr*) (of a verb) to undergo inflection according to a specific set of rules. **3** (*intr*) *Biol.* to undergo conjugation. **4** (*tr*) *Obs.* to join together, esp. in marriage. ◆ *adj* (ˈkɒndʒʊgɪt, -ˌgeɪt). **5** joined together in pairs. **6** *Maths.* **6a** (of two angles) having a sum of 360°. **6b** (of two complex numbers) differing only in the sign of the imaginary part as 4 + 3i and 4 – 3i. **7** *Chem.* of the state of equilibrium in which two liquids can exist as separate phases that are both solutions. **8** *Chem.* (of acids and bases) related by loss or gain of a proton. **9** (of a compound leaf) having one pair of leaflets. **10** (of words) cognate; related in origin. ◆ *n* (ˈkɒndʒʊgɪt). **11** one of a pair or set of conjugate substances, values, quantities, words, etc. [C15: from L *conjugāre*, from *com-* together + *jugāre* to connect, from *jugum* a yoke]
▸**ˈconjuˌgative** *adj* ▸**ˈconjuˌgator** *n*

conjugation (ˌkɒndʒʊˈgeɪʃən) *n* **1** *Grammar.* **1a** inflection of a verb for person, number, tense, voice, mood, etc. **1b** the complete set of the inflections of a given verb. **2** a joining. **3** a type of sexual reproduction in ciliate protozoans involving the temporary union of two individuals and the subsequent migration and fusion of the gametic nuclei. **4** the union of gametes, as in some fungi. **5** the pairing of chromosomes in the early phase of a meiotic division. **6** *Chem.* the existence of alternating double or triple bonds in a chemical compound, with consequent electron delocalization over part of the molecule.
▸**ˌconjuˈgational** *adj*

conjunct (ˈkɒndʒʌŋkt, kənˈdʒʌŋkt) *n Logic.* one of the propositions or formulas in a conjunction.

conjunction ➊ (kənˈdʒʌŋkʃən) *n* **1** the act of joining together; union. **2** simultaneous occurrence of events; coincidence. **3** any word or group of words, other than a relative pronoun, that connects words, phrases, or clauses; for example *and* and *while*. **4** *Astron.* **4a** the position of a planet when it is in line with the sun as seen from the earth. **4b** the apparent proximity or coincidence of two celestial bodies on the celestial sphere. **5** *Logic.* **5a** the operator that forms a compound sentence from two given sentences, and corresponds to the English *and*. **5b** a sentence so formed: it is true only when both the component sentences are true. **5c** the relation between such sentences.
▸**conˈjunctional** *adj*

conjunctiva (ˌkɒndʒʌŋkˈtaɪvə) *n, pl* **conjunctivas** *or* **conjunctivae** (-viː). the delicate mucous membrane that covers the eyeball and the under surface of the eyelid. [C16: from NL *membrāna conjunctīva* the conjunctive membrane]
▸**ˌconjuncˈtival** *adj*

conjunctive (kənˈdʒʌŋktɪv) *adj* **1** joining; connective. **2** joined. **3** of or relating to conjunctions. ◆ *n* **4** a less common word for **conjunction** (sense 3). [C15: from LL *conjunctīvus*, from L *conjungere* to CONJOIN]

conjunctivitis (kənˌdʒʌŋktɪˈvaɪtɪs) *n* inflammation of the conjunctiva.

conjuncture ➊ (kənˈdʒʌŋktʃə) *n* a combination of events, esp. a critical one.

conjuration (ˌkɒndʒʊˈreɪʃən) *n* **1** a magic spell; incantation. **2** a less common word for **conjuring**. **3** *Arch.* supplication; entreaty.

conjure ➊ (ˈkʌndʒə) *vb* **conjures, conjuring, conjured. 1** (*intr*) to practise conjuring. **2** (*intr*) to call upon supposed supernatural forces by spells and incantations. **3** (kənˈdʒʊə). (*tr*) to appeal earnestly to: *I conjure you to help me*. **4** **a name to conjure with. 4a** a person thought to have great power or influence. **4b** any name that excites the imagination. [C13: from OF *conjurer* to plot, from L *conjūrāre* to swear together]

conjure up ➊ *vb* (*tr, adv*) **1** to present to the mind; evoke or imagine: *he conjured up a picture of his childhood*. **2** to call up or command (a spirit or devil) by an incantation.

conjuring ➊ (ˈkʌndʒərɪŋ) *n* **1** the performance of tricks that appear to defy natural laws. ◆ *adj* **2** denoting or of such tricks or entertainment.

conjuror ➊ *or* **conjurer** (ˈkʌndʒərə) *n* **1** a person who practises conjuring, esp. for people's entertainment. **2** a sorcerer.

conk (kɒŋk) *Sl.* ◆ *vb* **1** to strike (someone) a blow, esp. on the head or nose. ◆ *n* **2** a punch or blow, esp. on the head or nose. **3** the head or nose. [C19: prob. changed from CONCH]

conker (ˈkɒŋkə) *n* an informal name for the **horse chestnut** (sense 2).

conkers (ˈkɒŋkəz) *n* (*functioning as sing*) *Brit.* a game in which a player swings a horse chestnut (conker), threaded onto a string, against that of another player to try to break it. [C19: from dialect *conker* snail shell, orig. used in the game]

conk out *vb* (*intr, adv*) *Inf.* **1** (of machines, cars, etc.) to fail suddenly. **2** to tire suddenly or collapse. [C20: from ?]

con man *n Inf.* a person who swindles another by means of a confidence trick. More formal term: **confidence man**.

con moto (kɒn ˈməʊtəʊ) *adj, adv Music.* (to be performed) in a brisk or lively manner. [It., lit.: with movement]

conn (kɒn) *vb, n* a variant spelling (esp. US) of **con**[3].

connate (ˈkɒneɪt) *adj* **1** existing from birth; congenital or innate. **2** allied in nature or origin. **3** *Biol.* (of similar parts or organs) closely joined or united by growth. **4** *Geol.* (of fluids) produced at the same time as the rocks surrounding them: *connate water*. [C17: from LL *connātus* born at the same time]

connect ➊ (kəˈnɛkt) *vb* **1** to link or be linked. **2** (*tr*) to associate: *I connect him with my childhood*. **3** (*tr*) to establish telephone communications with or between. **4** (*intr*) to be meaningful or meaningfully related. **5** (*intr*) (of two public vehicles, such as trains or buses) to have the arrival of one timed to occur just before the departure of the other, for the convenient transfer of passengers. **6** (*intr*) *Inf.* to hit, punch, kick, etc., solidly. [C17: from L *connectere* to bind together, from *nectere* to tie]
▸**conˈnectible** *or* **conˈnectable** *adj* ▸**conˈnector** *or* **conˈnecter** *n*

connecting rod *n* **1** a rod or bar for transmitting motion, esp. one that connects a rotating part to a reciprocating part. **2** such a rod that connects the piston to the crankshaft in an internal-combustion engine.

connection ➊ *or* **connexion** (kəˈnɛkʃən) *n* **1** the act of connecting; union. **2** something that connects or relates; link or bond. **3** a relationship or association. **4** logical sequence in thought or expression;

THESAURUS

agreement, coincidence, compatibility, concurrence, conformity, congruity, consistency, harmony, identity

congruent *adj* **1** = **corresponding**, according, agreeing, coinciding, compatible, concurrent, conforming, congruous, consistent, identical

congruous *adj* **1** = **corresponding**, agreeing, compatible, concordant, congruent, consistent, consonant, correspondent **2** = **appropriate**, apt, becoming, fit, meet, seemly, suitable

conic 1a *adj* = **cone-shaped**, conoid, funnel-shaped, pointed, pyramidal, tapered, tapering

conjectural *adj* = **speculative**, academic, hypothetical, supposed, suppositional, surmised, tentative, theoretical

conjecture *n* **1, 2** = **guess**, assumption, conclusion, fancy, guesstimate (*inf.*), guesswork, hypothesis, inference, notion, presumption, shot in the dark, speculation, supposition, surmise, theorizing, theory ◆ *vb* **3** = **guess**, assume, fancy, hypothesize, imagine, infer, speculate, suppose, surmise, suspect, theorize

conjugal *adj* = **marital**, bridal, connubial, hymeneal, married, matrimonial, nuptial, spousal, wedded

conjunction *n* **1, 2** = **joining**, association, coincidence, combination, concurrence, juxtaposition, union

conjuncture *n* = **crucial point**, combination, concurrence, connection, crisis, crossroads, emergency, exigency, juncture, pass, predicament, stage, turning point

conjure *vb* **1** = **perform tricks**, juggle **2** = **summon up**, bewitch, call upon, cast a spell, charm, enchant, invoke, raise, rouse **3** *Formal* = **appeal to**, adjure, beg, beseech, crave, entreat, implore, importune, pray, supplicate

conjure up *vb* **1** = **bring to mind**, contrive, create, evoke, produce as if by magic, recall, recollect

conjuring *n* **1** = **magic**, juggling, sorcery, thaumaturgy (*rare*), wizardry

conjuror *n* **1, 2** = **magician**, illusionist, miracle-worker, sorcerer, thaumaturge (*rare*), wizard

connect *vb* **1, 2** = **link**, affix, ally, associate, attach, cohere, combine, couple, fasten, join, relate, unite

Antonyms *vb* detach, disconnect, dissociate, divide, part, separate, sever, unfasten

connection *n* **1** = **link**, alliance, association, attachment, coupling, fastening, junction, tie,

coherence. **5** the relation of a word or phrase to its context: *in this connection the word has no political significance.* **6** (*often pl*) an acquaintance, esp. one who is influential. **7** a relative, esp. if distant and related by marriage. **8a** an opportunity to transfer from one train, bus, etc., to another. **8b** the vehicle scheduled to provide such an opportunity. **9** a link, usually a wire or metallic strip, between two components in an electric circuit. **10** a communications link, esp. by telephone. **11** *Sl.* a supplier of illegal drugs, such as heroin. **12** *Rare.* sexual intercourse.
▸**con'nectional** *or* **con'nexional** *adj*

connective (kə'nɛktɪv) *adj* **1** connecting. ◆ *n* **2** a thing that connects. **3** *Grammar, logic.* **3a** any word that connects phrases, clauses, or individual words. **3b** a symbol used in a formal language in the construction of compound sentences, corresponding to terms such as *or, and,* etc., in ordinary speech. **4** *Bot.* the tissue of a stamen that connects the two lobes of the anther.

connective tissue *n* an animal tissue that supports organs, fills the spaces between them, and forms tendons and ligaments.

conning tower ('kɒnɪŋ) *n* **1** a superstructure of a submarine, used as the bridge when the vessel is on the surface. **2** the armoured pilot house of a warship. [C19: see CON[3]]

connivance ❶ (kə'naɪvəns) *n* **1** the act or fact of conniving. **2** *Law.* the tacit encouragement of or assent to another's wrongdoing.

connive ❶ (kə'naɪv) *vb* **connives, conniving, connived.** (*intr*) **1** to plot together; conspire. **2** (foll. by *at*) *Law.* to give assent or encouragement (to the commission of a wrong). [C17: from F *conniver,* from L *connīvēre* to blink, hence, leave uncensured]
▸**con'niver** *n*

connoisseur ❶ (ˌkɒnɪ'sɜː) *n* a person with special knowledge or appreciation of a field, esp. in the arts. [C18: from F, from OF *conoiseor,* from *connoistre* to know, from L *cognōscere*]
▸ˌ**connois'seurship** *n*

connotation ❶ (ˌkɒnə'teɪʃən) *n* **1** an association or idea suggested by a word or phrase. **2** the act of connoting. **3** *Logic.* the characteristic or set of characteristics that determines to which object the common name properly applies. Also, in traditional logic, **intension.**
▸**connotative** ('kɒnəˌteɪtɪv, kə'nəʊtə-) *or* **con'notive** *adj*

connote ❶ (kɒ'nəʊt) *vb* **connotes, connoting, connoted.** (*tr; often takes a clause as object*) **1** (of a word, phrase, etc.) to imply or suggest (associations or ideas) other than the literal meaning: *the word "maiden" connotes modesty.* **2** to involve as a consequence or condition. [C17: from Med. L *connotāre,* from L *notāre* to mark, note, from *nota* sign, note]

connubial ❶ (kə'njuːbɪəl) *adj* of or relating to marriage: *connubial bliss.* [C17: from L *cōnūbiālis,* from *cōnūbium* marriage]
▸**conˌnubi'ality** *n*

conoid ('kəʊnɔɪd) *n* **1** a cone-shaped object. ◆ *adj also* **conoidal** (kəʊ'nɔɪdᵊl). **2** cone-shaped. [C17: from Gk *kōnoeidēs,* from *kōnos* CONE]
▸**co'noidally** *adv*

conquer ❶ ('kɒŋkə) *vb* **1** to overcome (an enemy, army, etc.); defeat. **2** to overcome (an obstacle, desire, etc.); surmount. **3** (*tr*) to gain possession or control of as by force or war; win. [C13: from OF *conquerre,* from Vulgar L *conquērere* (unattested) to obtain, from L *conquīrere* to search for, from *quaerere* to seek]
▸**'conquerable** *adj* ▸**'conquering** *adj* ▸**'conqueror** *n*

Conqueror ('kɒŋkərə) *n* **the.** epithet of William I, duke of Normandy, and king of England (1066–87).

conquest ❶ ('kɒnkwɛst) *n* **1** the act of conquering or the state of having been conquered; victory. **2** a person, thing, etc., that has been conquered. **3** a person, whose compliance, love, etc., has been won. [C13: from OF *conqueste,* from Vulgar L *conquēsta* (unattested), from L *conquīsīta,* fem. p.p. of *conquīrere;* see CONQUER]

Conquest ('kɒnkwɛst) *n* **the.** See **Norman Conquest.**

conquistador (kɒn'kwɪstəˌdɔː) *n, pl* **conquistadors** *or* **conquistadores** (kɒnˌkwɪstə'dɔːrɛs). an adventurer or conqueror, esp. one of the Spanish conquerors of the New World in the 16th century. [C19: from Sp., from *conquistar* to conquer]

cons. *abbrev. for:* **1** consecrated. **2** consigned. **3** consignment. **4** consolidated. **5** consonant. **6** constitutional. **7** construction.

Cons. *abbrev. for* Conservative.

consanguinity (ˌkɒnsæŋ'gwɪnɪtɪ) *n* **1** relationship by blood; kinship. **2** close affinity or connection. [C14: see CON-, SANGUINE]
▸ˌ**consan'guineous** *or* **con'sanguine** *adj*

conscience ❶ ('kɒnʃəns) *n* **1** the sense of right and wrong that governs a person's thoughts and actions. **2** conscientiousness; diligence. **3** a feeling of guilt or anxiety: *he has a conscience about his unkind action.* **4 in (all) conscience. 4a** with regard to truth and justice. **4b** certainly. **5 on one's conscience.** causing feelings of guilt or remorse. [C13: from OF, from L *conscientia* knowledge, from *conscīre* to know; see CONSCIOUS]

conscience clause *n* a clause in a law or contract exempting persons with moral scruples.

conscience money *n* money paid voluntarily to compensate for dishonesty, esp. for taxes formerly evaded.

conscience-stricken ❶ *adj* feeling anxious or guilty. Also: **conscience-smitten.**

conscientious ❶ (ˌkɒnʃɪ'ɛnʃəs) *adj* **1** involving or taking great care; painstaking. **2** governed by or done according to conscience.
▸ˌ**consci'entiously** *adv* ▸ˌ**consci'entiousness** *n*

conscientious objector *n* a person who refuses to serve in the armed forces on the grounds of conscience.

conscious ❶ ('kɒnʃəs) *adj* **1** alert and awake. **2** aware of one's surroundings, one's own motivations and thoughts, etc. **3a** aware (of) and giving value and emphasis (to a particular fact): *I am conscious of your great kindness to me.* **3b** (*in combination*): *clothes-conscious.* **4** deliberate or intended: *a conscious effort; conscious rudeness.* **5a** denoting a part of the human mind that is aware of a person's self, environment, and mental activity and that to a certain extent determines his choices of action. **5b** (*as n*): *the conscious is only a small part of the mind.* [C17: from L *conscius* sharing knowledge, from *com-* with + *scīre* to know]
▸**'consciously** *adv* ▸**'consciousness** *n*

consciousness raising *n* **a** the process of developing awareness in a person or group of a situation regarded as wrong or unjust, with the aim of producing active participation in changing it. **b** (*as modifier*): *a consciousness-raising group.*

conscript *n* ('kɒnskrɪpt). **1a** a person who is enrolled for compulsory military service. **1b** (*as modifier*): *a conscript army.* ◆ *vb* (kən'skrɪpt). **2** (*tr*) to enrol (youths, civilians, etc.) for compulsory military service. [C15: from L *conscrīptus,* p.p. of *conscrībere* to enrol, from *scrībere* to write]

conscription (kən'skrɪpʃən) *n* compulsory military service.

consecrate ❶ ('kɒnsɪˌkreɪt) *vb* **consecrates, consecrating, consecrated.** (*tr*) **1** to make or declare sacred or holy. **2** to dedicate (one's life, time, etc.) to a specific purpose. **3** *Christianity.* to sanctify (bread and wine) for the Eucharist to be received as the body and blood of Christ. **4** to cause to be respected or revered: *time has consecrated this custom.* [C15: from L *consecrāre,* from *com-* (intensive) + *sacrāre* to devote, from *sacer* sacred]
▸ˌ**conse'cration** *n* ▸**'conseˌcrator** *n* ▸**'conseˌcratory** *adj*

Consecration (ˌkɒnsɪ'kreɪʃən) *n RC Church.* the part of the Mass after the sermon during which the bread and wine are believed to change into the Body and Blood of Christ.

consecutive ❶ (kən'sɛkjʊtɪv) *adj* **1** (of a narrative, account, etc.) fol-

THESAURUS

union **2** = **association**, affiliation, affinity, bond, commerce, communication, correlation, correspondence, intercourse, interrelation, liaison, link, marriage, nexus, relation, relationship, relevance, tie-in **5** = **context**, frame of reference, reference **6** = **contact**, acquaintance, ally, associate, friend, sponsor **7** = **relative**, kin, kindred, kinsman, kith, relation

connivance *n* **1, 2** = **collusion**, abetment, abetting, complicity, conspiring, tacit consent

connive *vb* **1** = **conspire**, cabal, collude, cook up (*inf.*), intrigue, plot, scheme **2 connive at** = **turn a blind eye to**, abet, aid, be an accessory to, be a party to, be in collusion with, blink at, disregard, lend oneself to, let pass, look the other way, overlook, pass by, shut one's eyes to, wink at

connoisseur *n* = **expert**, aficionado, appreciator, arbiter, authority, buff (*inf.*), cognoscente, devotee, judge, maven (*US*), savant, specialist, whiz (*inf.*)

connotation *n* **1** = **implication**, association, colouring, nuance, significance, suggestion, undertone

connote *vb* **1** = **imply**, betoken, hint at, indicate, intimate, involve, signify, suggest

connubial *adj Formal* = **marital**, conjugal, married, matrimonial, nuptial, wedded

conquer *vb* **1, 2** = **defeat**, beat, bring to their knees, checkmate, clobber (*sl.*), crush, discomfit, get the better of, humble, lick (*inf.*), make mincemeat of (*inf.*), master, overcome, overpower, overthrow, prevail, put in their place, quell, rout, stuff (*sl.*), subdue, subjugate, succeed, surmount, triumph, undo, vanquish **3** = **seize**, acquire, annex, obtain, occupy, overrun, win
Antonyms *vb* ≠ **defeat:** be defeated, capitulate, give in, give up, lose, quit, submit, surrender, throw in the towel, yield

conqueror *n* **1** = **winner**, champion, conquistador, defeater, hero, lord, master, subjugator, vanquisher, victor

conquest *n* **1** = **defeat**, acquisition, annexation, appropriation, coup, discomfiture, invasion, mastery, occupation, overthrow, pasting (*sl.*), rout, subjection, subjugation, takeover, triumph, vanquishment, victory **2, 3** = **catch**, acquisition, adherent, admirer, fan, feather in one's cap, follower, prize, supporter, worshipper

conscience *n* **1** = **principles**, moral sense, scruples, sense of right and wrong, still small voice **4 in all conscience** = **in fairness**, assuredly, certainly, fairly, honestly, in truth, rightly, truly

conscience-stricken *adj* = **guilty**, ashamed, compunctious, contrite, disturbed, penitent, remorseful, repentant, sorry, troubled

conscientious *adj* **1** = **thorough**, careful, diligent, exact, faithful, having one's nose to the grindstone, meticulous, painstaking, particular, punctilious **2** = **honourable**, high-minded, high-principled, honest, incorruptible, just, moral, responsible, scrupulous, straightforward, strict, upright
Antonyms *adj* ≠ **thorough:** careless, irresponsible, negligent, remiss, slack, thoughtless, unconscientious, unreliable, untrustworthy ≠ **honourable:** unprincipled, unscrupulous

conscious *adj* **1** = **aware**, alert, alive to, awake, clued-up (*inf.*), cognizant, percipient, responsive, sensible, sentient, wise to (*sl.*) **4** = **deliberate**, calculated, intentional, knowing, premeditated, rational, reasoning, reflective, responsible, self-conscious, studied, wilful
Antonyms *adj* ≠ **aware:** ignorant, insensible, oblivious, unaware, unconscious ≠ **deliberate:** accidental, uncalculated, unintended, unintentional, unplanned, unpremeditated, unwitting

consciousness *n* **1** = **awareness**, apprehension, knowledge, realization, recognition, sensibility

consecrate *vb* **1, 2** = **sanctify**, dedicate, devote, exalt, hallow, ordain, set apart, venerate

consecutive *adj* **1-3** = **successive**, chronological, following, in sequence, in turn, run-

lowing chronological sequence. **2** following one another without interruption; successive. **3** characterized by logical sequence. **4** *Grammar.* expressing consequence or result: *consecutive clauses.* **5** *Music.* another word for **parallel** (sense 3). [C17: from F *consécutif,* from L *consecūtus,* from *consequī* to pursue]
▸**con'secutively** *adv* ▸**con'secutiveness** *n*

consensual (kən'sɛnsjuəl) *adj* **1** *Law.* (of a contract, etc.) existing by consent. **2** (of reflex actions of the body) responding to stimulation of another part.
▸**con'sensually** *adv*

consensus 🅣 (kən'sɛnsəs) *n* general or widespread agreement (esp. in **consensus of opinion**). [C19: from L, from *consentīre;* see CONSENT]

> **USAGE NOTE** Since *consensus* refers to a collective opinion, the words *of opinion* in the phrase *consensus of opinion* are redundant and should therefore be avoided.

consent 🅣 (kən'sɛnt) *vb* **1** to give assent or permission; agree. ◆ *n* **2** acquiescence to or acceptance of something done or planned by another. **3** harmony in opinion; agreement (esp. in **with one consent**). [C13: from OF *consentir,* from L *consentīre* to agree, from *sentīre* to feel]
▸**con'senting** *adj*

consequence 🅣 ('kɒnsɪkwəns) *n* **1** a result or effect. **2** an unpleasant result (esp. in **take the consequences**). **3** an inference reached by reasoning; conclusion. **4** significance or importance: *it's of no consequence; a man of consequence.* **5 in consequence.** as a result.

consequent 🅣 ('kɒnsɪkwənt) *adj* **1** following as an effect. **2** following as a logical conclusion. **3** (of a river) flowing in the direction of the original slope of the land. ◆ *n* **4** something that follows something else, esp. as a result. **5** *Logic.* the resultant clause in a conditional sentence. [C15: from L *consequēns* following closely, from *consequī* to pursue]

> **USAGE NOTE** See at **consequential.**

consequential 🅣 (ˌkɒnsɪ'kwɛnʃəl) *adj* **1** important or significant. **2** self-important. **3** following as a consequence, esp. indirectly: *consequential loss.*
▸ˌ**conseˌquenti'ality** *n* ▸ˌ**conse'quentially** *adv*

> **USAGE NOTE** Although both *consequential* and *consequent* can refer to something which happens as the result of something else, *consequent* is more common in this sense in modern English: *the new measures were put into effect, and the consequent protest led to the dismissal of those responsible.*

consequently 🅣 ('kɒnsɪkwəntlɪ) *adv, sentence connector.* as a result or effect; therefore; hence.

conservancy (kən'sɜːvənsɪ) *n, pl* **conservancies. 1** (in Britain) a court or commission with jurisdiction over a river, port, area of countryside, etc. **2** another word for **conservation** (sense 2).

conservation 🅣 (ˌkɒnsə'veɪʃən) *n* **1** the act of conserving or keeping from change, loss, injury, etc. **2a** protection, preservation, and careful management of natural resources. **2b** (*as modifier*): *a conservation area.* **3** *Physics, etc.* the preservation of a specified aspect or value of a system, as in **conservation of charge, conservation of momentum, conservation of parity.**
▸ˌ**conser'vational** *adj* ▸ˌ**conser'vationist** *n*

conservation of energy *n* the principle that the total energy of any isolated system is constant and independent of any changes occurring within the system.

conservation of mass *n* the principle that the total mass of any isolated system is constant and is independent of any chemical and physical changes taking place within the system.

conservatism (kən'sɜːvəˌtɪzəm) *n* **1** opposition to change and innovation. **2** a political philosophy advocating the preservation of the best of the established order in society.

conservative 🅣 (kən'sɜːvətɪv) *adj* **1** favouring the preservation of established customs, values, etc., and opposing innovation. **2** of conservatism. **3** moderate or cautious: *a conservative estimate.* **4** conventional in style: *a conservative suit.* **5** *Med.* (of treatment) designed to alleviate symptoms. Cf. **radical** (sense 4). ◆ *n* **6** a person who is reluctant to change or consider new ideas; conformist. **7** a supporter of conservatism.
▸**con'servatively** *adv* ▸**con'servativeness** *n*

Conservative 🅣 (kən'sɜːvətɪv) ◆ *adj* **1** (in Britain and elsewhere) of, supporting, or relating to a Conservative Party. **2** (in Canada) of, supporting, or relating to the Progressive Conservative Party. **3** of, relating to, or characterizing Conservative Judaism. ◆ *n* **4** a supporter or member of a Conservative Party, or, (in Canada) of the Progressive Conservative Party.

Conservative Judaism *n* a movement rejecting extreme change and advocating moderate relaxations of traditional Jewish law.

Conservative Party *n* **1** (in Britain) the major right-wing party, which developed from the Tories in the 1830s. It encourages property owning and free enterprise. **2** (in Canada) short for Progressive Conservative Party. **3** (in other countries) any of various political parties generally opposing change.

conservatoire (kən'sɜːvəˌtwɑː) *n* an institution or school for instruction in music. Also called: **conservatory.** [C18: from F: CONSERVATORY]

conservator ('kɒnsəˌveɪtə, kən'sɜːvə-) *n* a custodian, guardian, or protector.

conservatorium (kənˌsɜːvə'tɔːrɪəm) *n Austral.* the usual term for **conservatoire.**

conservatory 🅣 (kən'sɜːvətrɪ) *n, pl* **conservatories. 1** a greenhouse, esp. one attached to a house. **2** another word for **conservatoire.**

conserve *vb* (kən'sɜːv), **conserves, conserving, conserved.** (*tr*) **1** to keep or protect from harm, decay, loss, etc. **2** to preserve (a foodstuff, esp. fruit) with sugar. ◆ *n* ('kɒnsɜːv, kən'sɜːv). **3** a preparation similar to jam but usually containing whole pieces of fruit. [(vb) C14: from L *conservāre* to keep safe, from *servāre* to save; (n) C14: from Med. L *conserva,* from L *conservāre*]

consider 🅣 (kən'sɪdə) *vb* (*mainly tr*) **1** (*also intr*) to think carefully about (a problem, decision, etc.). **2** (*may take a clause as object*) to judge; deem: *I consider him a fool.* **3** to have regard for: *consider your mother's feelings.* **4** to look at: *he considered her face.* **5** (*may take a clause as object*) to bear in mind: *when buying a car consider this make.* **6** to describe or discuss. [C14: from L *consīderāre* to inspect closely]

considerable 🅣 (kən'sɪdərəbᵊl) *adj* **1** large enough to reckon with: *a considerable quantity.* **2** a lot of; much: *he had considerable courage.* **3** worthy of respect: *a considerable man in the scientific world.*
▸**con'siderably** *adv*

considerate 🅣 (kən'sɪdərɪt) *adj* **1** thoughtful towards other people; kind. **2** *Rare.* carefully thought out; considered.
▸**con'siderately** *adv*

consideration 🅣 (kənˌsɪdə'reɪʃən) *n* **1** deliberation; contemplation. **2 take into consideration.** to bear in mind; consider. **3 under consideration.** being currently discussed. **4** a fact to be taken into account when making a judgment or decision. **5** thoughtfulness for other people; kindness. **6** payment for a service. **7** thought resulting from delibera-

THESAURUS

ning, sequential, seriatim, succeeding, uninterrupted

consensus *n* = **agreement**, assent, common consent, concord, concurrence, general agreement, harmony, unanimity, unity

consent *vb* **1** = **agree**, accede, acquiesce, allow, approve, assent, comply, concede, concur, permit, play ball (*inf.*), yield ◆ *n* **2** = **agreement**, acquiescence, approval, assent, compliance, concession, concurrence, go-ahead (*inf.*), green light, O.K. *or* okay (*inf.*), permission, sanction
Antonyms *vb* ≠ **agree:** decline, demur, disagree, disapprove, dissent, refuse, resist ◆ *n* ≠ **agreement:** disagreement, disapproval, dissent, refusal, unwillingness

consequence *n* **1** = **result**, effect, end, end result, event, issue, outcome, repercussion, sequel, upshot **4** = **importance**, account, concern, distinction, eminence, import, interest, moment, note, portent, rank, significance, standing, status, value, weight **5 in consequence** = **as a result**, because, following

consequent *adj* **1, 2** = **following**, ensuing, resultant, resulting, sequential, subsequent, successive

consequential *adj* **1** = **important**, eventful, far-reaching, grave, momentous, serious, significant, weighty **2** = **arrogant**, bumptious, conceited, inflated, pompous, pretentious, self-important, supercilious, vainglorious **3** = **resultant**, consequent, indirect

consequently *adv* = **as a result**, accordingly, ergo, hence, necessarily, subsequently, therefore, thus

conservation *n* **1** = **protection**, custody, economy, guardianship, husbandry, maintenance, preservation, safeguarding, safekeeping, saving, upkeep

conservative *adj* **1, 3** = **traditional**, cautious, conventional, die-hard, guarded, hidebound, middle-of-the-road, moderate, quiet, reactionary, sober ◆ *n* **6** = **traditionalist**, die-hard, middle-of-the-roader, moderate, reactionary, stick-in-the-mud (*inf.*)
Antonyms *adj* ≠ **traditional:** imaginative, innovative, liberal, progressive, radical ◆ *n* ≠ **traditionalist:** changer, innovator, progressive, radical

Conservative *adj* **1** = **Tory**, right-wing ◆ *n* **4** = **Tory**, right-winger

conservatory *n* **1** = **greenhouse**, glasshouse, hothouse

consider *vb* **1** = **think about**, chew over, cogitate, consult, contemplate, deliberate, discuss, examine, eye up, meditate, mull over, muse, ponder, reflect, revolve, ruminate, study, turn over in one's mind, weigh, work over **2** = **think**, believe, deem, hold to be, judge, rate, regard as **5** = **bear in mind**, care for, keep in view, make allowance for, reckon with, regard, remember, respect, take into account

considerable *adj* **1, 2** = **large**, abundant, ample, appreciable, comfortable, goodly, great, lavish, marked, much, noticeable, plentiful, reasonable, sizable *or* sizeable, substantial, tidy, tolerable **3** = **important**, distinguished, influential, notable, noteworthy, renowned, significant, venerable
Antonyms *adj* ≠ **large:** insignificant, insubstantial, meagre, paltry, small ≠ **important:** insignificant, ordinary, unimportant, unremarkable

considerably *adv* **1, 2** = **greatly**, appreciably, markedly, noticeably, remarkably, seriously (*inf.*), significantly, substantially, very much

considerate *adj* **1** = **thoughtful**, attentive, charitable, circumspect, concerned, discreet, forbearing, kind, kindly, mindful, obliging, patient, tactful, unselfish
Antonyms *adj* heedless, inconsiderate, selfish, thoughtless

consideration *n* **1** = **thought**, analysis, attention; opinion. **8** *Law.* the promise, object, etc., given by one party to persuade another to enter into a contract. **9** esteem. **10 in consideration of. 10a** because of. **10b** in return for.

considered (kən'sɪdəd) *adj* **1** presented or thought out with care: *a considered opinion.* **2** (*qualified by a preceding adverb*) esteemed: *highly considered.*

considering Ⓣ (kən'sɪdərɪŋ) *prep* **1** in view of. ◆ *adv* **2** *Inf.* all in all; taking into account the circumstances: *it's not bad considering.* ◆ *conj* **3** (*subordinating*) in view of the fact that.

consign Ⓣ (kən'saɪn) *vb* (*mainly tr*) **1** to give into the care or charge of; entrust. **2** to commit irrevocably: *he consigned the papers to the flames.* **3** to commit: *to consign someone to jail.* **4** to address or deliver (goods): *it was consigned to his London address.* [C15: from OF *consigner,* from L *consignāre* to put one's seal to, sign, from *signum* mark]
▸**con'signable** *adj* ▸**ˌconsign'ee** *n* ▸**con'signor** *or* **con'signer** *n*

consignment Ⓣ (kən'saɪnmənt) *n* **1** the act of consigning; commitment. **2** a shipment of goods consigned. **3 on consignment.** for payment by the consignee after sale.

consist Ⓣ (kən'sɪst) *vb* (*intr*) **1** (foll. by *of* or *in*) to be composed (of). **2** (foll. by *in* or *of*) to have its existence (in): *his religion consists only in going to church.* **3** to be consistent; accord. [C16: from L *consistere* to stand firm, from *sistere* to stand]

consistency Ⓣ (kən'sɪstənsɪ) *or* **consistence** *n, pl* **consistencies** *or* **consistences. 1** agreement or accordance. **2** degree of viscosity or firmness. **3** the state or quality of holding or sticking together and retaining shape. **4** conformity with previous attitudes, behaviour, practice, etc.

consistent Ⓣ (kən'sɪstənt) *adj* **1** (usually foll. by *with*) showing consistency or harmony. **2** steady; even: *consistent growth.* **3** *Logic.* (of a logical system) constituted so that the propositions deduced from different axioms of the system do not contradict each other.
▸**con'sistently** *adv*

consistory (kən'sɪstərɪ) *n, pl* **consistories. 1** *Church of England.* the court of a diocese (other than Canterbury) administering ecclesiastical law. **2** *RC Church.* an assembly of the cardinals and the pope. **3** (in certain Reformed Churches) the governing body of a local congregation. **4** *Arch.* a council. [C14: from OF, from Med. L *consistōrium* ecclesiastical tribunal, ult. from L *consistere* to stand still]
▸**consistorial** (ˌkɒnsɪ'stɔːrɪəl) *adj*

consolation Ⓣ (ˌkɒnsə'leɪʃən) *n* **1** the act of consoling or state of being consoled. **2** a person or thing that is a comfort in a time of grief, disappointment, etc.
▸**consolatory** (kən'sɒlətərɪ) *adj*

consolation prize *n* a prize given to console a loser of a game.

console[1] Ⓣ (kən'səʊl) *vb* **consoles, consoling, consoled.** to serve as a comfort to (someone) in disappointment, sadness, etc. [C17: from L *consōlārī,* from *sōlārī* to comfort]
▸**con'solable** *adj* ▸**con'soler** *n* ▸**con'solingly** *adv*

console[2] ('kɒnsəʊl) *n* **1** an ornamental bracket used to support a wall fixture, etc. **2** the part of an organ comprising the manuals, pedals, stops, etc. **3** a unit on which the controls of an electronic system are mounted. **4** a cabinet for a television, etc., designed to stand on the floor. **5** See **console table.** [C18: from F, from OF *consolateur* one that provides support; see CONSOLE[1]]

console table *n* a table with one or more curved legs of bracket-like construction, designed to stand against a wall.

consolidate Ⓣ (kən'sɒlɪˌdeɪt) *vb* **consolidates, consolidating, consolidated. 1** to form or cause to form into a whole. **2** to make or become stronger or more stable. **3** *Mil.* to strengthen one's control over (a situation, area, etc.). [C16: from L *consolidāre* to make firm, from *solidus* strong]
▸**conˌsoli'dation** *n* ▸**con'soliˌdator** *n*

consolidated fund *n Brit.* a fund maintained from tax revenue to meet standing charges, esp. national debt interest.

consols ('kɒnsɒlz, kən'sɒlz) *pl n* irredeemable British government securities carrying annual interest. [short for *consolidated stock*]

consommé (kən'sɒmeɪ) *n* a clear soup made from meat stock. [C19: from F, from *consommer* to use up]

consonance ('kɒnsənəns) *n* **1** agreement, harmony, or accord. **2** *Prosody.* similarity between consonants, but not between vowels, as between the *s* and *t* sounds in *sweet silent thought.* **3** *Music.* a combination of notes which can sound together without harshness.

consonant ('kɒnsənənt) *n* **1** a speech sound or letter of the alphabet other than a vowel. ◆ *adj* **2** (*postpositive;* foll. by *with* or *to*) consistent; in agreement. **3** harmonious. **4** *Music.* characterized by the presence of a consonance. [C14: from L *consonāns,* from *consonāre* to sound at the same time, from *sonāre* to sound]
▸**'consonantly** *adv*

consonantal (ˌkɒnsə'næntᵊl) *adj* relating to, functioning as, or characterized by consonants.

consort Ⓣ *vb* (kən'sɔːt). (*intr*) **1** (usually foll. by *with*) to keep company (with undesirable people); associate. **2** to harmonize. ◆ *n* ('kɒnsɔːt). **3** (esp. formerly) a small group of instruments, either of the same type (**a whole consort**) or of different types (**a broken consort**). **4** the husband or wife of a reigning monarch. **5** a husband or wife. **6** a ship that escorts another. [C15: from OF, from L *consors* partner, from *sors* lot, portion]

consortium (kən'sɔːtɪəm) *n, pl* **consortia** (-tɪə). **1** an association of financiers, companies, etc., esp. for a particular purpose. **2** *Law.* the right of husband or wife to the company and affection of the other. [C19: from L: partnership; see CONSORT]

conspectus (kən'spɛktəs) *n* **1** an overall view; survey. **2** a summary; résumé. [C19: from L: a viewing, from *conspicere,* from *specere* to look]

conspicuous Ⓣ (kən'spɪkjʊəs) *adj* **1** clearly visible. **2** attracting attention because of a striking feature: *conspicuous stupidity.* [C16: from L *conspicuus,* from *conspicere* to perceive; see CONSPECTUS]
▸**con'spicuously** *adv* ▸**con'spicuousness** *n*

conspiracy Ⓣ (kən'spɪrəsɪ) *n, pl* **conspiracies. 1** a secret plan to carry out an illegal or harmful act, esp. with political motivation; plot. **2** the act of making such plans in secret.
▸**con'spirator** *n* ▸**conˌspira'torial** *adj*

conspiracy theory *n* the belief that the government or a covert organization is responsible for an unusual or unexplained event.

conspire Ⓣ (kən'spaɪə) *vb* **conspires, conspiring, conspired.** (when *intr,* sometimes foll. by *against*) **1** to plan (a crime) together in secret. **2** (*intr*) to act together as if by design: *the elements conspired to spoil our picnic.* [C14: from OF, from L *conspīrāre* to plot together, lit.: to breathe together, from *spīrāre* to breathe]

con spirito (kɒn 'spɪrɪtəʊ) *adj, adv Music.* (to be performed) in a spirited or lively manner. [It.: with spirit]

constable ('kʌnstəbᵊl, 'kɒn-) *n* **1** (in Britain, Australia, New Zealand, Canada, etc.) a police officer of the lowest rank. **2** any of various officers of the peace, esp. one who arrests offenders, serves writs, etc. **3** the keeper of a royal castle. **4** (in medieval Europe) the chief military officer and functionary of a royal household. **5** an officer of a hundred in medieval England. [C13: from OF, from LL *comes stabulī* officer in charge of the stable]
▸**'constableˌship** *n*

THESAURUS

tion, cogitation, contemplation, deliberation, discussion, examination, perusal, reflection, regard, review, scrutiny, study **2 take into consideration = bear in mind**, make allowance for, take into account, weigh **4 = factor**, concern, issue, point **5 = thoughtfulness**, concern, considerateness, friendliness, kindliness, kindness, respect, solicitude, tact **6 = payment**, fee, perquisite, recompense, remuneration, reward, tip

considering *prep* **1 = taking into account**, in the light of, in view of ◆ *adv* **2** *Informal* **= all things considered**, all in all

consign *vb* **1 = hand over**, commend to, commit, deposit with, entrust, relegate **4 = deliver**, convey, ship (*cargo*), transfer, transmit

consignment *n* **1 = handing over**, assignment, committal, entrusting, relegation **2 = shipment**, batch, delivery, goods

consist *vb* **1** *foll. by* **of** *or* **in = be made up of**, amount to, be composed of, comprise, contain, embody, include, incorporate, involve **2** *foll. by* **in** *or* **of = lie in**, be expressed by, be found *or* contained in, inhere in, reside in

consistency *n* **1 = agreement**, accordance, coherence, compatibility, congruity, correspondence, harmony **2 = texture**, compactness, density, firmness, thickness, viscosity **4 = constancy**, evenness, regularity, steadfastness, steadiness, uniformity

consistent *adj* **1 = agreeing**, accordant, all of a piece, coherent, compatible, congruous, consonant, harmonious, logical **2 = unchanging**, constant, dependable, persistent, regular, steady, true to type, undeviating
Antonyms *adj* ≠ **agreeing:** contradictory, contrary, discordant, incompatible, incongruous, inconsistent, inharmonious ≠ **unchanging:** changing, deviating, erratic, inconsistent, irregular

consolation *n* **1 = comfort**, alleviation, assuagement, cheer, ease, easement, encouragement, help, relief, solace, succour, support

console[1] *vb* **= comfort**, assuage, calm, cheer, encourage, express sympathy for, relieve, solace, soothe
Antonyms *vb* aggravate (*inf.*), agitate, annoy, discomfort, distress, hassle (*inf.*), hurt, sadden, torment, trouble, upset

consolidate *vb* **1 = combine**, amalgamate, cement, compact, condense, conjoin, federate, fuse, harden, join, solidify, thicken, unite **2 = strengthen**, fortify, reinforce, secure, stabilize

consolidation *n* **1 = combination**, alliance, amalgamation, association, compression, condensation, federation, fusion **2 = strengthening**, fortification, reinforcement

consort *vb* **1 = associate**, fraternize, go around with, hang about, around *or* out with, hang with (*inf., chiefly US*), keep company, mingle, mix **2 = agree**, accord, be consistent, correspond, harmonize, square, tally ◆ *n* **5 = spouse**, companion, husband, partner, significant other (*US inf.*), wife

conspicuous *adj* **1 = obvious**, apparent, blatant, clear, discernible, easily seen, evident, manifest, noticeable, patent, perceptible, salient, visible **2 = noteworthy**, celebrated, distinguished, eminent, famous, illustrious, notable, outstanding, prominent, remarkable, salient, signal, striking
Antonyms *adj* ≠ **obvious:** concealed, hidden, imperceptible, inconspicuous, indiscernible, invisible, obscure, unnoticeable ≠ **noteworthy:** humble, inconspicuous, insignificant, ordinary, unacclaimed, undistinguished, unmemorable, unnotable

conspiracy *n* **1, 2 = plot**, cabal, collusion, confederacy, frame-up (*sl.*), intrigue, league, machination, scheme, treason

conspirator *n* **1 = plotter**, cabalist, conspirer, intriguer, schemer, traitor

conspire *vb* **1 = plot**, cabal, confederate, contrive, devise, hatch treason, intrigue, machinate, manoeuvre, plan, scheme **2 = work together**, combine, concur, conduce, contribute, cooperate, tend

constabulary (kən'stæbjulərɪ) *Chiefly Brit.* ◆ *n, pl* **constabularies. 1** the police force of a town or district. ◆ *adj* **2** of or relating to constables.

constant ➊ ('kɒnstənt) *adj* **1** unchanging. **2** incessant: *constant interruptions.* **3** resolute; loyal. ◆ *n* **4** something that is unchanging. **5** a specific quantity that is invariable: *the velocity of light is a constant.* **6a** *Maths.* a symbol representing an unspecified number that remains invariable throughout a particular series of operations. **6b** *Physics.* a quantity or property that is considered invariable throughout a particular series of experiments. [C14: from OF, from L *constāns,* from *constāre* to be steadfast, from *stāre* to stand]
▸**'constancy** *n* ▸**'constantly** *adv*

constellate ('kɒnstɪ,leɪt) *vb* **constellates, constellating, constellated.** to form into clusters in or as if in constellations.

constellation (,kɒnstɪ'leɪʃən) *n* **1** any of the 88 groups of stars as seen from the earth, many of which were named by the ancient Greeks after animals, objects, or mythological persons. **2** a gathering of brilliant people or things. **3** *Psychoanalysis.* a group of ideas felt to be related. [C14: from LL *constellātiō,* from L *com-* together + *stella* star]
▸**constellatory** (kən'stelətərɪ) *adj*

consternate ('kɒnstə,neɪt) *vb* **consternates, consternating, consternated.** (*tr; usually passive*) to fill with anxiety, dismay, dread, or confusion. [C17: from L *consternāre,* from *sternere* to lay low]

consternation ➊ (,kɒnstə'neɪʃən) *n* a feeling of anxiety, dismay, dread, or confusion.

constipate ('kɒnstɪ,peɪt) *vb* **constipates, constipating, constipated.** (*tr*) to cause constipation in. [C16: from L *constīpāre* to press closely together]
▸**'consti,pated** *adj*

constipation (,kɒnstɪ'peɪʃən) *n* infrequent or difficult evacuation of the bowels.

constituency (kən'stɪtjuənsɪ) *n, pl* **constituencies. 1** the whole body of voters who elect one representative to a legislature or all the residents represented by one deputy. **2** a district that sends one representative to a legislature.

constituent ➊ (kən'stɪtjuənt) *adj* (*prenominal*) **1** forming part of a whole; component. **2** having the power to frame a constitution or to constitute a government: *constituent assembly.* ◆ *n* **3** a component part; ingredient. **4** a resident of a constituency, esp. one entitled to vote. **5** *Chiefly law.* a person who appoints another to act for him. [C17: from L *constituēns,* from *constituere* to establish, CONSTITUTE]
▸**con'stituently** *adv*

constitute ➊ ('kɒnstɪ,tju:t) *vb* **constitutes, constituting, constituted.** (*tr*) **1** to form; compose: *the people who constitute a jury.* **2** to appoint to an office: *a legally constituted officer.* **3** to set up (an institution) formally; found. **4** *Law.* to give legal form to (a court, assembly, etc.). [C15: from L *constituere,* from *com-* (intensive) + *statuere* to place]
▸**'consti,tutor** *n*

constitution ➊ (,kɒnstɪ'tju:ʃən) *n* **1** the act of constituting or state of being constituted. **2** physical make-up; structure. **3** the fundamental principles on which a state is governed, esp. when considered as embodying the rights of the subjects. **4** (*often cap.*) (in certain countries, esp. the US and Australia) a statute embodying such principles. **5** a person's state of health. **6** a person's temperament.

constitutional ➊ (,kɒnstɪ'tju:ʃən°l) *adj* **1** of a constitution. **2** authorized by or subject to a constitution: *constitutional monarchy.* **3** inherent in the nature of a person or thing: *a constitutional weakness.* **4** beneficial to one's physical wellbeing. ◆ *n* **5** a regular walk taken for the benefit of one's health.
▸**,consti,tution'ality** *n* ▸**,consti'tutionally** *adv*

constitutionalism (,kɒnstɪ'tju:ʃənə,lɪzəm) *n* **1** the principles or system of government in accord with a constitution. **2** adherence to or advocacy of such a system.
▸**,consti'tutionalist** *n*

constitutive ('kɒnstɪ,tju:tɪv) *adj* **1** having power to enact or establish. **2** another word for **constituent** (sense 1).
▸**'consti,tutively** *adv*

constrain ➊ (kən'streɪn) *vb* (*tr*) **1** to compel, esp. by circumstances, etc. **2** to restrain as by force. [C14: from OF, from L *constringere* to bind together]
▸**con'strainer** *n*

constrained ➊ (kən'streɪnd) *adj* embarrassed, unnatural, or forced: *a constrained smile.*

constraint ➊ (kən'streɪnt) *n* **1** compulsion or restraint. **2** repression of natural feelings. **3** a forced unnatural manner. **4** something that serves to constrain; restrictive condition.

constrict ➊ (kən'strɪkt) *vb* (*tr*) **1** to make smaller or narrower, esp. by contracting at one place. **2** to hold in or inhibit; limit. [C18: from L *constrictus,* from *constringere* to tie up together]

constriction ➊ (kən'strɪkʃən) *n* **1** a feeling of tightness in some part of the body, such as the chest. **2** the act of constricting or condition of being constricted. **3** something that is constricted.
▸**con'strictive** *adj*

constrictor (kən'strɪktə) *n* **1** any of various nonvenomous snakes, such as the boas, that coil around and squeeze their prey to kill it. **2** any muscle that constricts; sphincter.

construct ➊ *vb* (kən'strʌkt). (*tr*) **1** to put together substances or parts systematically; build; assemble. **2** to frame mentally (an argument, sentence, etc.). **3** *Geom.* to draw (a line, angle, or figure) so that certain requirements are satisfied. ◆ *n* ('kɒnstrʌkt). **4** something formulated or built systematically. **5** a complex idea resulting from a synthesis of simpler ideas. [C17: from L *constructus,* from *construere* to build, from *struere* to arrange, erect]
▸**con'structor** *or* **con'structer** *n*

construction ➊ (kən'strʌkʃən) *n* **1** the act of constructing or manner in which a thing is constructed. **2** a structure. **3a** the business or work of building dwellings, offices, etc. **3b** (*as modifier*): *a construction site.* **4** an interpretation: *they put a sympathetic construction on her behaviour.* **5** *Grammar.* a group of words that make up one of the constituents into which a sentence may be analysed; a phrase or clause. **6** an abstract work of art in three dimensions.
▸**con'structional** *adj* ▸**con'structionally** *adv*

constructive ➊ (kən'strʌktɪv) *adj* **1** serving to improve; positive: *constructive criticism.* **2** *Law.* deduced by inference; not expressed. **3** another word for **structural.**
▸**con'structively** *adv*

constructivism (kən'strʌktɪ,vɪzəm) *n* a movement in abstract art evolved after World War I, which explored the use of movement and machine-age materials in sculpture.
▸**con'structivist** *adj, n*

construe ➊ (kən'stru:) *vb* **construes, construing, construed.** (*mainly tr*) **1** to interpret the meaning of (something): *you can construe that in different ways.* **2** (*may take a clause as object*) to infer; deduce. **3** to analyse the grammatical structure of; parse (esp. a Latin or Greek text as a prelimi-

THESAURUS

constancy *n* **2 = steadiness**, firmness, fixedness, permanence, perseverance, regularity, stability, steadfastness, tenacity, uniformity **3 = faithfulness**, devotion, fidelity

constant *adj* **1 = unchanging**, continual, even, firm, fixed, habitual, immovable, immutable, invariable, permanent, perpetual, regular, stable, steadfast, steady, unalterable, unbroken, uniform, unvarying **2 = continuous**, ceaseless, continual, endless, eternal, everlasting, incessant, interminable, never-ending, nonstop, perpetual, persistent, relentless, sustained, uninterrupted, unrelenting, unremitting **3 = faithful**, attached, dependable, devoted, loyal, stalwart, staunch, tried-and-true, true, trustworthy, trusty, unfailing
Antonyms *adj* ≠ **unchanging:** changeable, changing, deviating, uneven, unstable, variable ≠ **continuous:** erratic, inconstant, intermittent, irregular, occasional, random, unsustained ≠ **faithful:** disloyal, fickle, irresolute, undependable

constantly *adv* **2 = continuously**, all the time, always, aye (*Scot.*), continually, endlessly, everlastingly, incessantly, interminably, invariably, morning, noon and night, night and day, nonstop, perpetually, persistently, relentlessly
Antonyms *adv* (every) now and then, every so often, from time to time, intermittently, irregularly, now and again, occasionally, off and on, periodically, sometimes

consternation *n* **= dismay**, alarm, amazement, anxiety, awe, bewilderment, confusion, distress, dread, fear, fright, horror, panic, shock, terror, trepidation

constituent *adj* **1 = component**, basic, elemental, essential, integral ◆ *n* **3 = component**, element, essential, factor, ingredient, part, principle, unit **4 = voter**, elector

constitute *vb* **1 = make up**, compose, comprise, create, enact, establish, fix, form, found, make, set up **2 = set up**, appoint, authorize, commission, delegate, depute, empower, name, nominate, ordain

constitution *n* **1 = establishment**, composition, formation, organization **2 = structure**, composition, form, make-up, nature **5, 6 = health**, build, character, disposition, physique, temper, temperament

constitutional *adj* **2 = statutory**, chartered, vested **3 = inherent**, congenital, immanent, inborn, intrinsic, organic ◆ *n* **5 = walk**, airing, stroll, turn

constrain *vb* **1 = force**, bind, coerce, compel, drive, impel, necessitate, oblige, pressure, pressurize, urge **2 = restrict**, chain, check, confine, constrict, curb, hem in, rein, restrain, straiten

constrained *adj* **= forced**, embarrassed, guarded, inhibited, reserved, reticent, subdued, unnatural

constraint *n* **1 = restriction**, check, coercion, compulsion, curb, damper, deterrent, force, hindrance, limitation, necessity, pressure, rein, restraint **2 = repression**, bashfulness, diffidence, embarrassment, inhibition, reservation, restraint, timidity

constrict *vb* **1, 2 = squeeze**, choke, compress, contract, cramp, inhibit, limit, narrow, pinch, restrict, shrink, strangle, strangulate, tighten

constriction *n* **1, 2 = tightness**, blockage, compression, constraint, cramp, impediment, limitation, narrowing, pressure, reduction, restriction, squeezing, stenosis (*Pathology*), stricture

construct *vb* **1 = build**, assemble, compose, create, design, elevate, engineer, erect, establish, fabricate, fashion, form, formulate, found, frame, make, manufacture, organize, put together, put up, raise, set up, shape
Antonyms *vb* bulldoze, demolish, destroy, devastate, dismantle, flatten, knock down, level, pull down, raze, tear down

construction *n* **1 = building**, assembly, composition, creation, edifice, erection, fabrication, formation **2 = structure**, composition, fabric, figure, form, shape **4** *Formal* **= interpretation**, explanation, inference, reading, rendering, take (*inf., chiefly US*)

constructive *adj* **1 = helpful**, positive, practical, productive, useful, valuable
Antonyms *adj* destructive, futile, ineffective, limp-wristed, negative, unhelpful, unproductive, useless, vain, worthless

construe *vb* **1, 2 = interpret**, deduce, explain, expound, read, read between the lines, render,

nary to translation). **4** to combine words syntactically. **5** (*also intr*) *Old-fashioned.* to translate literally, esp. aloud. [C14: from L *construere*; see CONSTRUCT]
▸**con'struable** *adj*

consubstantial (ˌkɒnsəb'stænʃəl) *adj Christian theol.* (esp. of the three persons of the Trinity) regarded as identical in essence though different in aspect. [C15: from Church L, from L *com-* COM- + *substantia* SUBSTANCE]
▸**ˌconsubˌstanti'ality** *n*

consubstantiation (ˌkɒnsəbˌstænʃɪ'eɪʃən) *n Christian theol.* (in the Lutheran branch of Protestantism) the doctrine that after the consecration of the Eucharist the substance of the body and blood of Christ coexists within the substance of the consecrated bread and wine. Cf. **transubstantiation.**

consuetude ('kɒnswɪˌtju:d) *n* an established custom or usage, esp. one having legal force. [C14: from L *consuētūdō*, from *consuēscere*, from CON- + *suēscere* to be wont]

consul ('kɒns^{ə}l) *n* **1** an official appointed by a sovereign state to protect its commercial interests and aid its citizens in a foreign city. **2** (in ancient Rome) either of two annually elected magistrates who jointly exercised the highest authority in the republic. **3** (in France from 1799 to 1804) any of the three chief magistrates of the First Republic. [C14: from L, from *consulere* to CONSULT]
▸**consular** ('kɒnsjʊlə) *adj* ▸**'consulˌship** *n*

consulate ('kɒnsjʊlɪt) *n* **1** the premises of a consul. **2** government by consuls. **3** the office or period of office of a consul. **4** (*often cap.*) **4a** the government of France by the three consuls from 1799 to 1804. **4b** this period. **5** (*often cap.*) the consular government of the Roman republic.

consul general *n, pl* **consuls general.** a consul of the highest grade, usually stationed in a city of considerable commercial importance.

consult ❶ (kən'sʌlt) *vb* **1** (when *intr*, often foll. by *with*) to ask advice from (someone). **2** (*tr*) to refer to for information: *to consult a map.* **3** (*tr*) to have regard for (a person's feelings, interests, etc.); consider. [C17: from F, from L *consultāre*, from *consulere* to consult]

consultant ❶ (kən'sʌlt^{ə}nt) *n* **1a** a specialist physician who is asked to confirm a diagnosis. **1b** a physician or surgeon holding the highest appointment in a particular branch of medicine or surgery in a hospital. **2** a specialist who gives expert advice or information. **3** a person who asks advice in a consultation.
▸**con'sultancy** *n*

consultation ❶ (ˌkɒns^{ə}l'teɪʃən) *n* **1** the act of consulting. **2** a conference for discussion or the seeking of advice.
▸**consultative** (kən'sʌltətɪv) *adj*

consulting (kən'sʌltɪŋ) *adj* (*prenominal*) acting in an advisory capacity on professional matters: *a consulting engineer.*

consulting room *n* a room in which a doctor sees his patients.

consume ❶ (kən'sju:m) *vb* **consumes, consuming, consumed. 1** (*tr*) to eat or drink. **2** (*tr; often passive*) to obsess. **3** (*tr*) to use up; expend. **4** to destroy or be destroyed by: *fire consumed the forest.* **5** (*tr*) to waste. **6** (*passive*) to waste away. [C14: from L *consūmere*, from *com-* (intensive) + *sūmere* to take up]
▸**con'sumable** *adj* ▸**con'suming** *adj*

consumedly (kən'sju:mɪdlɪ) *adv Old-fashioned.* (intensifier): *consumedly fascinating.*

consumer ❶ (kən'sju:mə) *n* **1** a person who purchases goods and services for his own personal needs. Cf. **producer** (sense 6). **2** a person or thing that consumes.

consumer durable *n* a manufactured product that has a relatively long useful life, such as a car or a television.

consumer goods *pl n* goods that satisfy personal needs rather than those required for the production of other goods or services.

consumerism (kən'sju:məˌrɪzəm) *n* **1** protection of the interests of consumers. **2** advocacy of a high rate of consumption as a basis for a sound economy.
▸**con'sumerist** *n, adj*

consumer terrorism *n* the practice of introducing dangerous substances to foodstuffs or other consumer products, esp. to extort money from the manufacturers.

consummate ❶ *vb* ('kɒnsəˌmeɪt), **consummates, consummating, consummated.** (*tr*) **1** to bring to completion; fulfil. **2** to complete (a marriage) legally by sexual intercourse. ◆ *adj* (kən'sʌmɪt, 'kɒnsəmɪt). **3** supremely skilled: *a consummate artist.* **4** (*prenominal*) (intensifier): *a consummate fool.* [C15: from L *consummāre* to complete, from *summus* utmost]
▸**con'summately** *adv* ▸**ˌconsum'mation** *n*

consumption ❶ (kən'sʌmpʃən) *n* **1** the act of consuming or the state of being consumed, esp. by eating, burning, etc. **2** *Econ.* expenditure on goods and services for final personal use. **3** the quantity consumed. **4** a wasting away of the tissues of the body, esp. in tuberculosis of the lungs. [C14: from L *consumptiō*, from *consūmere* to CONSUME]

consumptive (kən'sʌmptɪv) *adj* **1** causing consumption; wasteful; destructive. **2** relating to or affected with tuberculosis of the lungs. ◆ *n* **3** *Pathol.* a person who suffers from consumption.
▸**con'sumptively** *adv* ▸**con'sumptiveness** *n*

cont. *abbrev. for:* **1** contents. **2** continued.

contact ❶ *n* ('kɒntækt). **1** the act or state of touching. **2** the state or fact of communication (esp. in **in contact, make contact**). **3a** a junction of electrical conductors. **3b** the part of the conductors that makes the junction. **3c** the part of an electrical device to which such connections are made. **4** an acquaintance, esp. one who might be useful in business, etc. **5** any person who has been exposed to a contagious disease. **6** (*modifier*) caused by touching the causative agent: *contact dermatitis.* **7** (*modifier*) denoting a herbicide or insecticide that kills on contact. **8** (*modifier*) of or maintaining contact. **9** (*modifier*) requiring or involving (physical) contact: *a contact sport.* ◆ *vb* ('kɒntækt, kən'tækt). **10** (when *intr*, often foll. by *with*) to put, come, or be in association, touch, or communication. [C17: from L *contactus*, from *contingere* to touch on all sides, from *tangere* to touch]
▸**contactual** (kɒn'tæktjʊəl) *adj*

contact lens *n* a thin convex lens, usually of plastic, which floats on the layer of tears in front of the cornea to correct defects of vision.

contact print *n* a photographic print made by exposing the printing paper through a negative placed directly on to it.

contagion ❶ (kən'teɪdʒən) *n* **1** the transmission of disease from one person to another by contact. **2** a contagious disease. **3** a corrupting influence that tends to spread. **4** the spreading of an emotional or mental state among a number of people: *the contagion of mirth.* [C14: from L *contāgiō* infection, from *contingere*; see CONTACT]

contagious ❶ (kən'teɪdʒəs) *adj* **1** (of a disease) capable of being passed on by direct contact with a diseased individual or by handling his clothing, etc. **2** (of an organism) harbouring the causative agent of a transmissible disease. **3** causing or likely to cause the same reaction in several people: *her laughter was contagious.*

contain ❶ (kən'teɪn) *vb* (*tr*) **1** to hold or be capable of holding: *this contains five pints.* **2** to restrain (feelings, behaviour, etc.). **3** to consist of: *the book contains three sections.* **4** *Mil.* to prevent (enemy forces) from operating beyond a certain area. **5** to be a multiple of, leaving no remainder: *6 contains 2 and 3.* [C13: from OF, from L *continēre*, from *com-* together + *tenēre* to hold]
▸**con'tainable** *adj*

container ❶ (kən'teɪnə) *n* **1** an object used for or capable of holding, esp. for transport or storage. **2a** a large cargo-carrying standard-sized container that can be loaded from one mode of transport to another. **2b** (*as modifier*): *a container ship.*

containerize *or* **containerise** (kən'teɪnəˌraɪz) *vb* **containerizes, containerizing, containerized** *or* **containerises, containerising, containerised.**

THESAURUS

take **3** = **parse**, analyse **5** *Old-fashioned* = **translate**

consult *vb* **1, 2** = **ask**, ask advice of, commune, compare notes, confer, consider, debate, deliberate, interrogate, pick (someone's) brains, question, refer to, take counsel, turn to **3** = **consider**, have regard for, regard, respect, take account of, take into consideration

consultant *n* **2** = **specialist**, adviser, authority

consultation *n* **2** = **seminar**, appointment, conference, council, deliberation, dialogue, discussion, examination, hearing, interview, meeting, session

consume *vb* **1** = **eat**, devour, eat up, gobble (up), guzzle, polish off (*inf.*), put away, swallow **2** *often passive* = **obsess**, absorb, devour, dominate, eat up, engross, monopolize, preoccupy **3, 5** = **use up**, absorb, deplete, dissipate, drain, eat up, employ, exhaust, expend, finish up, fritter away, lavish, lessen, spend, squander, use, utilize, vanish, waste, wear out **4** = **destroy**, annihilate, decay, demolish, devastate, lay waste, ravage

consumer *n* **1** = **buyer**, customer, purchaser, shopper, user

consuming *adj* **2** = **overwhelming**, absorbing, compelling, devouring, engrossing, excruciating, gripping, immoderate, tormenting

consummate *vb* **1** = **complete**, accomplish, achieve, carry out, compass, conclude, crown, effectuate, end, finish, fulfil, perfect, perform, put the tin lid on ◆ *adj* **3** = **skilled**, accomplished, matchless, perfect, polished, practised, superb, supreme **4** = **complete**, absolute, conspicuous, deep-dyed (*usually derogatory*), extreme, supreme, total, transcendent, ultimate, unqualified, utter

Antonyms *vb* ≠ **complete:** begin, commence, conceive, get under way, inaugurate, initiate, originate, start

consummation *n* **1** = **completion**, achievement, culmination, end, fulfilment, perfection, realization

consumption *n* **1** = **using up**, consuming, decay, decrease, depletion, destruction, diminution, dissipation, drain, exhaustion, expenditure, loss, use, utilization, waste **4** *Old-fashioned* = **tuberculosis**, atrophy, emaciation, phthisis, T.B.

contact *n* **1** = **touch**, approximation, contiguity, junction, juxtaposition, union **2** = **communication**, association, connection **4** = **acquaintance**, connection ◆ *vb* **10** = **get** *or* **be in touch with**, approach, call, communicate with, get hold of, phone, reach, ring (up) (*inf., chiefly Brit.*), speak to, write to

contagion *n* **1, 4** = **spread**, communication, passage, transference, transmittal **2** = **contamination**, corruption, infection, pestilence, plague, pollution, taint

contagious *adj* **1** = **infectious**, catching, communicable, epidemic, epizootic (*Veterinary medicine*), pestiferous, pestilential, spreading, taking (*inf.*), transmissible

contain *vb* **1** = **hold**, accommodate, enclose, have capacity for, incorporate, seat **2** = **restrain**, control, curb, hold back, hold in, keep a tight rein on, repress, stifle **3** = **include**, comprehend, comprise, consist of, embody, embrace, involve

container *n* **1** = **holder**, receptacle, repository, vessel

(*tr*) **1** to convey (cargo) in standard-sized containers. **2** to adapt (a port or transportation system) to the use of standard-sized containers.
▸**con,taineri'zation** *or* **con,taineri'sation** *n*

containment (kən'teɪnmənt) *n* the act of containing, esp. of restraining the power of a hostile country or the operations of a hostile military force.

contaminate ⓣ (kən'tæmɪ,neɪt) *vb* **contaminates, contaminating, contaminated.** (*tr*) **1** to make impure; pollute. **2** to make radioactive by the addition of radioactive material. [C15: from L *contamināre* to defile]
▸**con'taminable** *adj* ▸**con'taminant** *n* ▸**con,tami'nation** *n* ▸**con'tami,nator** *n*

contango (kən'tæŋgəʊ) *n, pl* **contangos. 1** (formerly, on the London Stock Exchange) postponement of payment for and delivery of stock from one account day to the next. **2** the fee paid for such a postponement. ◆ Also called: **carry-over, continuation.** Cf. **backwardation.** [C19: apparently an arbitrary coinage]

conte *French.* (kɔ̃t) *n* a tale or short story.

contemn (kən'tɛm) *vb* (*tr*) *Formal.* to regard with contempt; scorn. [C15: from L *contemnere,* from *temnere* to slight]
▸**contemner** (kən'tɛmnə, -'tɛmə) *n*

contemplate ⓣ ('kɒntɛm,pleɪt) *vb* **contemplates, contemplating, contemplated.** (*mainly tr*) **1** to think about intently and at length. **2** (*intr*) to think intently and at length, esp. for spiritual reasons; meditate. **3** to look at thoughtfully. **4** to have in mind as a possibility. [C16: from L *contemplāre,* from *templum* TEMPLE[1]]
▸**,contem'plation** *n* ▸**'contem,plator** *n*

contemplative ⓣ ('kɒntɛm,pleɪtɪv, -təm-; kən'tɛmplə-) *adj* **1** denoting, concerned with, or inclined to contemplation; meditative. ◆ *n* **2** a person dedicated to religious contemplation.

contemporaneous (kən,tɛmpə'reɪnɪəs) *adj* existing, beginning, or occurring in the same period of time.
▸**contemporaneity** (kən,tɛmpərə'niːɪtɪ) *or* **con,tempo'raneousness** *n*

contemporary ⓣ (kən'tɛmprərɪ) *adj* **1** living or occurring in the same period. **2** existing or occurring at the present time. **3** conforming to modern ideas in style, fashion, etc. **4** having approximately the same age as one another. ◆ *n, pl* **contemporaries. 5** a person living at the same time or of approximately the same age as another. **6** something that is contemporary. [C17: from Med. L *contemporārius,* from L *com-* together + *temporārius* relating to time, from *tempus* time]
▸**con'temporarily** *adv* ▸**con'temporariness** *n*

> **USAGE NOTE** Since *contemporary* can mean either of the same period or of the present period, it is best to avoid this word where ambiguity might arise, as in *a production of* Othello *in contemporary dress. Modern dress* or *Elizabethan dress* should be used in this example to avoid ambiguity.

contemporize *or* **contemporise** (kən'tɛmpə,raɪz) *vb* **contemporizes, contemporizing, contemporized** *or* **contemporises, contemporising, contemporised.** to be or make contemporary.

contempt ⓣ (kən'tɛmpt) *n* **1** the feeling of a person towards a person or thing that he considers despicable; scorn. **2** the state of being scorned; disgrace (esp. in **hold in contempt**). **3** wilful disregard of the authority of a court of law or legislative body: *contempt of court.* [C14: from L *contemptus,* from *contemnere* to CONTEMN]

contemptible ⓣ (kən'tɛmptɪb[ə]l) *adj* deserving or worthy of contempt.
▸**con,tempti'bility** *or* **con'temptibleness** *n* ▸**con'temptibly** *adv*

contemptuous ⓣ (kən'tɛmptjʊəs) *adj* (when *predicative,* often foll. by *of*) showing or feeling contempt; disdainful.
▸**con'temptuously** *adv*

contend ⓣ (kən'tɛnd) *vb* **1** (*intr;* often foll. by *with*) to struggle in rivalry, battle, etc.; vie. **2** to argue earnestly. **3** (*tr; may take a clause as object*) to assert. [C15: from L *contendere* to strive, from *com-* with + *tendere* to stretch]
▸**con'tender** *n*

content[1] ⓣ ('kɒntɛnt) *n* **1** (*often pl*) everything inside a container. **2** (*usually pl*) **2a** the chapters or divisions of a book. **2b** a list of these printed at the front of a book. **3** the meaning or significance of a work of art, as distinguished from its style or form. **4** all that is contained or dealt with in a piece of writing, etc.; substance. **5** the capacity or size of a thing. **6** the proportion of a substance contained in an alloy, mixture, etc.: *the lead content of petrol.* [C15: from L *contentus* contained, from *continēre* to CONTAIN]

content[2] ⓣ (kən'tɛnt) *adj* (*postpositive*) **1** satisfied with things as they are. **2** assenting to or willing to accept circumstances, a proposed course of action, etc. ◆ *vb* **3** (*tr*) to make (oneself or another person) satisfied. ◆ *n* **4** peace of mind. [C14: from OF, from L *contentus* contented, having restrained desires, from *continēre* to restrain]
▸**con'tentment** *n*

contented ⓣ (kən'tɛntɪd) *adj* accepting one's situation or life with equanimity and satisfaction.
▸**con'tentedly** *adv* ▸**con'tentedness** *n*

contention ⓣ (kən'tɛnʃən) *n* **1** a struggling between opponents; competition. **2** a point of dispute (esp. in **bone of contention**). **3** a point asserted in argument. [C14: from L *contentiō,* from *contendere* to CONTEND]

contentious ⓣ (kən'tɛnʃəs) *adj* **1** tending to quarrel. **2** causing or characterized by dispute; controversial.
▸**con'tentiousness** *n*

conterminous (kən'tɜːmɪnəs) *or* **coterminous** (kəʊ'tɜːmɪnəs) *adj* **1** enclosed within a common boundary. **2** without a break or interruption. [C17: from L *conterminus,* from CON- + *terminus* boundary]

contest ⓣ *n* ('kɒntɛst). **1** a formal game or match in which people, teams, etc., compete. **2** a struggle for victory between opposing forces. ◆ *vb* (kən'tɛst). **3** (*tr*) to try to disprove; call in question. **4** (when *intr,* foll. by *with* or *against*) to dispute or contend (with): *to con-*

THESAURUS

contaminate *vb* **1** = **pollute**, adulterate, befoul, corrupt, defile, deprave, infect, smirch, soil, stain, sully, taint, tarnish, vitiate
Antonyms *vb* clean, cleanse, decontaminate, deodorize, disinfect, fumigate, purify, sanitize, sterilize

contamination *n* **1** = **pollution**, adulteration, contagion, corruption, decay, defilement, dirtying, filth, foulness, impurity, infection, poisoning, rottenness, taint

contemplate *vb* **1** = **think about**, brood over, consider, deliberate, meditate, meditate on, mull over, muse over, observe, ponder, reflect upon, revolve *or* turn over in one's mind, ruminate (upon) **3** = **look at**, behold, check out (*inf.*), examine, eye, eye up, gaze at, inspect, recce (*sl.*), regard, scrutinize, stare at, study, survey, view, weigh **4** = **consider**, aspire to, design, envisage, expect, foresee, have in view *or* in mind, intend, mean, plan, propose, think of

contemplation *n* **1** = **thought**, cogitation, consideration, deliberation, meditation, musing, pondering, reflection, reverie, rumination **3** = **looking at**, examination, gazing at, inspection, observation, recce (*sl.*), scrutiny, survey, viewing

contemplative *adj* **1** = **thoughtful**, deep *or* lost in thought, in a brown study, intent, introspective, meditative, musing, pensive, rapt, reflective, ruminative

contemporary *adj* **1, 2** = **coexisting**, coetaneous (*rare*), coeval, coexistent, concurrent, contemporaneous, synchronous **3** = **modern**, à la mode, current, happening (*inf.*), in fashion, latest, newfangled, present, present-day, recent, trendy (*Brit. inf.*), ultramodern, up-to-date, up-to-the-minute, with it (*inf.*) ◆ *n* **5** = **peer**, compeer, fellow
Antonyms *adj* ≠ **modern**: antecedent, antique, early, obsolete, old, old-fashioned, out-of-date, passé

contempt *n* **1** = **scorn**, condescension, contumely, derision, despite (*arch.*), disdain, disregard, disrespect, mockery, neglect, slight
Antonyms *n* admiration, esteem, honour, liking, regard, respect

contemptible *adj* = **despicable**, abject, base, cheap, degenerate, detestable, ignominious, low, low-down (*inf.*), mean, measly, paltry, pitiful, scurvy, shabby, shameful, vile, worthless
Antonyms *adj* admirable, attractive, honourable, laudable, pleasant, praiseworthy

contemptuous *adj* = **scornful**, arrogant, cavalier, condescending, contumelious, derisive, disdainful, haughty, high and mighty, insolent, insulting, on one's high horse (*inf.*), sneering, supercilious, withering
Antonyms *adj* civil, courteous, deferential, gracious, humble, mannerly, obsequious, polite, respectful

contend *vb* **1** = **compete**, clash, contest, cope, emulate, fight, grapple, jostle, litigate, skirmish, strive, struggle, vie **3** = **argue**, affirm, allege, assert, aver, avow, debate, dispute, hold, maintain

contender *n* **1** = **competitor**, contestant, rival, vier

content[1] *n* **1** *often pl* = **constituents**, elements, ingredients, load **2a** *usually pl* = **chapters**, divisions, subject matter, subjects, themes, topics **4** = **meaning**, burden, essence, gist, ideas, matter, significance, substance, text, thoughts **5** = **amount**, capacity, load, measure, size, volume

content[2] *adj* **1, 2** = **satisfied**, agreeable, at ease, comfortable, contented, fulfilled, willing to accept ◆ *vb* **3** = **satisfy**, appease, delight, gladden, gratify, humour, indulge, mollify, placate, please, reconcile, sate, suffice ◆ *n* **4** = **satisfaction**, comfort, contentment, ease, gratification, peace, peace of mind, pleasure

contented *adj* = **satisfied**, at ease, at peace, cheerful, comfortable, complacent, content, glad, gratified, happy, pleased, serene, thankful
Antonyms *adj* annoyed, discontented, displeased, dissatisfied, pissed off (*taboo sl.*), troubled, uncomfortable, uneasy

contention *n* **1, 2** = **dispute**, bone of contention, competition, contest, disagreement, discord, dissension, enmity, feuding, hostility, rivalry, row, strife, struggle, wrangling **3** = **assertion**, affirmation, allegation, argument, asseveration, belief, claim, declaration, ground, idea, maintaining, opinion, position, profession, stand, thesis, view

contentious *adj* **1** = **argumentative**, bickering, cantankerous, captious, cavilling, combative, cross, disputatious, factious, litigious, peevish, perverse, pugnacious, quarrelsome, querulous, wrangling

contentment *n* **1** = **satisfaction**, comfort, complacency, content, contentedness, ease, equanimity, fulfilment, gladness, gratification, happiness, peace, pleasure, repletion, serenity
Antonyms *n* discomfort, discontent, discontentment, displeasure, dissatisfaction, uneasiness, unhappiness

contest *n* **1** = **competition**, game, head-to-head, match, tournament, trial **2** = **struggle**, affray, altercation, battle, combat, conflict, controversy, debate, discord, dispute, encounter, fight, shock ◆ *vb* **3** = **dispute**, argue, call in *or* into question, challenge, debate, doubt, litigate, object to, oppose, question **4** = **compete**, contend, fight, fight over, strive, vie

test an election. [C16: from L *contestārī* to introduce a lawsuit, from *testis* witness]
▸**con'testable** *adj* ▸**con'tester** *n*

contestant ➊ (kən'tɛstənt) *n* a person who takes part in a contest; competitor.

context ➊ ('kɒntɛkst) *n* **1** the parts of a piece of writing, speech, etc., that precede and follow a word or passage and contribute to its full meaning: *it is unfair to quote out of context.* **2** the circumstances that are relevant to an event, fact, etc. [C15: from L *contextus* a putting together, from *contexere*, from *com-* together + *texere* to weave]
▸**con'textual** *adj*

contiguous (kən'tɪgjʊəs) *adj* **1** touching along the side or boundary; in contact. **2** neighbouring. **3** preceding or following in time. [C17: from L *contiguus*, from *contingere* to touch; see CONTACT]
▸**con'tiguously** *adv*

continent[1] ('kɒntɪnənt) *n* **1** one of the earth's large land masses (Asia, Australia, Africa, Europe, North and South America, and Antarctica). **2** *Obs.* **2a** mainland. **2b** a continuous extent of land. [C16: from the L phrase *terra continens* continuous land]
▸**continental** (,kɒntɪ'nɛntᵊl) *adj* ▸**,conti'nentally** *adv*

continent[2] ➊ ('kɒntɪnənt) *adj* **1** able to control urination and defecation. **2** exercising self-restraint, esp. from sexual activity; chaste. [C14: from L *continēre*; see CONTAIN]
▸**'continence** *n*

Continental (,kɒntɪ'nɛntᵊl) *adj* **1** of or characteristic of Europe, excluding the British Isles. **2** of or relating to the 13 original British North American colonies during the War of American Independence. ◆ *n* **3** (*sometimes not cap.*) an inhabitant of Europe, excluding the British Isles. **4** a regular soldier of the rebel army during the War of American Independence.

continental breakfast *n* a light breakfast of coffee and rolls.

continental climate *n* a climate characterized by hot summers, cold winters, and little rainfall, typical of the interior of a continent.

continental drift *n Geol.* the theory that the earth's continents move gradually over the surface of the planet on a substratum of magma.

continental quilt *n Brit.* a quilt, stuffed with down or a synthetic material, used as a bed cover in place of the top sheet and blankets. Also called: **duvet**, (Austral.) **doona.**

continental shelf *n* the sea bed surrounding a continent at depths of up to about 200 metres (100 fathoms), at the edge of which the **continental slope** drops steeply.

contingency ➊ (kən'tɪndʒənsɪ) *or* **contingence** (kən'tɪndʒəns) *n, pl* **contingencies** *or* **contingences. 1a** a possible but not very likely future event or condition. **1b** (*as modifier*): *a contingency plan.* **2** something dependent on a possible future event. **3** a fact, event, etc., incidental to something else. **4** *Logic.* the state of being contingent. **5** uncertainty. **6** *Statistics.* **6a** the degree of association between theoretical and observed common frequencies of two graded or classified variables. **6b** (*as modifier*): *a contingency table.*

contingent ➊ (kən'tɪndʒənt) *adj* **1** (when *postpositive*, often foll. by *on* or *upon*) dependent on events, conditions, etc., not yet known; conditional. **2** *Logic.* (of a proposition) true under certain conditions, false under others; not logically necessary. **3** happening by chance; accidental. **4** uncertain. ◆ *n* **5** a part of a military force, parade, etc. **6** a group distinguished by common interests, etc., that is part of a larger group. **7** a chance occurrence. [C14: from L *contingere* to touch, befall]

continual ➊ (kən'tɪnjʊəl) *adj* **1** recurring frequently, esp. at regular intervals. **2** occurring without interruption; continuous in time. [C14: from OF *continuel*, from L *continuus* uninterrupted, from *continēre* to CONTAIN]
▸**con'tinually** *adv*

> **USAGE NOTE** See at **continuous.**

continuance ➊ (kən'tɪnjʊəns) *n* **1** the act of continuing. **2** the duration of an action, etc. **3** *US.* the adjournment of a legal proceeding.

continuant (kən'tɪnjʊənt) *Phonetics.* ◆ *n* **1** a speech sound, such as (l), (r), (f), or (s), in which the closure of the vocal tract is incomplete, allowing the continuous passage of the breath. ◆ *adj* **2** relating to or denoting a continuant.

continuation ➊ (kən,tɪnjʊ'eɪʃən) *n* **1** a part or thing added, esp. to a book or play; sequel. **2** a renewal of an interrupted action, process, etc.; resumption. **3** the act of continuing; prolongation. **4** another word for **contango.**

continue ➊ (kən'tɪnjuː) *vb* **continues, continuing, continued. 1** (when *tr*, may take an infinitive) to remain or cause to remain in a particular condition or place. **2** (when *tr*, may take an infinitive) to carry on uninterruptedly (a course of action): *he continued running.* **3** (when *tr*, may take an infinitive) to resume after an interruption: *we'll continue after lunch.* **4** to prolong or be prolonged: *continue the chord until it meets the tangent.* **5** (*tr*) *Law, chiefly Scots.* to adjourn (legal proceedings). [C14: from OF *continuer*, from L *continuāre* to join together]

continuity ➊ (,kɒntɪ'njuːɪtɪ) *n, pl* **continuities. 1** logical sequence. **2** a continuous or connected whole. **3** the comprehensive script or scenario of detail in a film or broadcast. **4** the continuous projection of a film.

continuity girl *or* **man** *n* a woman or man whose job is to ensure continuity and consistency in successive shots of a film.

continuo (kən'tɪnjʊəʊ) *n, pl* **continuos. 1** *Music.* **1a** a shortened form of **basso continuo** (see **thorough bass**). **1b** (*as modifier*): *a continuo accompaniment.* **2** the thorough-bass part as played on a keyboard instrument. [It., lit.: continuous]

continuous ➊ (kən'tɪnjʊəs) *adj* **1** unceasing: *a continuous noise.* **2** in an unbroken series or pattern. **3** *Statistics.* (of a variable) having a continuum of possible values so that its distribution requires integration rather than summation to determine its cumulative probability. **4** *Grammar.* another word for **progressive** (sense 7). [C17: from L *continuus*, from *continēre* to CONTAIN]
▸**con'tinuously** *adv*

> **USAGE NOTE** Both *continual* and *continuous* can be used to say that something continues without interruption, but only *continual* can correctly be used to say that something keeps happening repeatedly.

continuous assessment *n* the assessment of a pupil's progress throughout a course of study rather than exclusively by examination at the end of it.

continuous creation *n* the theory that matter is created continuously in the universe. See **steady-state theory.**

continuum (kən'tɪnjʊəm) *n, pl* **continua** (-'tɪnjʊə) *or* **continuums.** a continuous series or whole, no part of which is perceptibly different from the adjacent parts. [C17: from L, neuter of *continuus* CONTINUOUS]

contort ➊ (kən'tɔːt) *vb* to twist or bend out of place or shape. [C15: from L *contortus* intricate, from *contorquēre* to whirl around, from *torquēre* to twist]
▸**con'tortion** *n* ▸**con'tortive** *adj*

contortionist (kən'tɔːʃənɪst) *n* **1** a performer who contorts his body for the entertainment of others. **2** a person who twists or warps meaning.

contour ➊ ('kɒntʊə) *n* **1** the outline of a mass of land, figure, or body; a defining line. **2a** See **contour line. 2b** (*as modifier*): *a contour map.* **3** (*often pl*) the shape of a curving form: *the contours of her body were full and round.* ◆ *vb* (*tr*) **4** to shape so as to form the contour of something. **5** to mark contour lines on. **6** to construct (a road, railway, etc.) to follow the outline of the land. [C17: from F, from It. *contorno*, from *contornare* to sketch, from *tornare* to TURN]

contour line *n* a line on a map or chart joining points of equal height or depth.

THESAURUS

contestant *n* = **competitor**, aspirant, candidate, contender, entrant, participant, player

context *n* **2** = **frame of reference**, ambience, background, conditions, connection, framework, relation, situation

continence *n* **2** = **self-restraint**, abstinence, asceticism, celibacy, chastity, moderation, self-control, temperance

continent[2] *adj* **2** = **self-restrained**, abstemious, abstinent, ascetic, austere, celibate, chaste, sober

contingency *n* **1a** = **possibility**, accident, chance, emergency, event, eventuality, fortuity, happening, incident, juncture, uncertainty

contingent *adj* **1** *often foll. by* **on** *or* **upon** = **dependent on**, conditional on, controlled by, subject to **3, 4** = **chance**, accidental, casual, fortuitous, haphazard, random, uncertain ◆ *n* **6** = **group**, batch, body, bunch, deputation, detachment, mission, quota, section, set

continual *adj* **1, 2** = **constant**, continuous, endless, eternal, everlasting, frequent, incessant, interminable, oft-repeated, perpetual, recurrent, regular, repeated, repetitive, unceasing, uninterrupted, unremitting
Antonyms *adj* broken, ceasing, erratic, fluctuating, fragmentary, infrequent, intermittent, interrupted, irregular, occasional, periodic, spasmodic, sporadic, terminable

continually *adv* **1, 2** = **constantly**, all the time, always, aye (*Scot.*), endlessly, eternally, everlastingly, forever, incessantly, interminably, nonstop, persistently, repeatedly

continuance *n* **1, 2** = **duration**, continuation, period, protraction, term

continuation *n* **1** = **addition**, extension, furtherance, postscript, sequel, supplement **3** = **continuing**, maintenance, perpetuation, prolongation, resumption

continue *vb* **1** = **remain**, abide, carry on, endure, last, live on, persist, rest, stay, stay on, survive **2** = **keep on**, carry on, go on, keep at, keep one's hand in, keep the ball rolling, keep up, maintain, persevere, persist in, prolong, pursue, stick at, stick to, sustain **3** = **resume**, carry on, pick up where one left off, proceed, recommence, return to, take up **4** = **go on**, draw out, extend, lengthen, project, prolong, reach
Antonyms *vb* ≠ **remain:** abdicate, leave, quit, resign, retire, step down ≠ **keep on, resume:** break off, call it a day, cease, discontinue, give up, leave off, pack in (*Brit. informal*), quit, stop

continuing *adj* **2** = **lasting**, enduring, in progress, ongoing, sustained

continuity *n* **1, 2** = **sequence**, cohesion, connection, flow, interrelationship, progression, succession, whole

continuous *adj* **1, 2** = **constant**, connected, continued, extended, prolonged, unbroken, unceasing, undivided, uninterrupted
Antonyms *adj* broken, disconnected, ending, inconstant, intermittent, interrupted, occasional, passing, severed, spasmodic

contort *vb* = **twist**, convolute, deform, distort, gnarl, knot, misshape, warp, wrench, writhe

contortion *n* = **twist**, bend, convolution, deformity, distortion, gnarl, knot, tortuosity, warp

contour ploughing *n* ploughing along the contours of the land to minimize erosion.

Contra ('kɒntrə) *n* a member of a US-backed guerrilla army, founded in 1979, whose aim was to overthrow the Sandinista government in Nicaragua.

contra- *prefix* **1** against; contrary; opposing; contrasting: *contraceptive*. **2** (in music) pitched below: *contrabass*. [from L, from *contrā* against]

contraband ➊ ('kɒntrə,bænd) *n* **1a** goods that are prohibited by law from being exported or imported. **1b** illegally imported or exported goods. **2** illegal traffic in such goods; smuggling. **3** Also called: **contraband of war.** goods that a neutral country may not supply to a belligerent. ◆ *adj* **4** (of goods) **4a** forbidden by law from being imported or exported. **4b** illegally imported or exported. [C16: from Sp. *contrabanda*, from It., from Med. L, from CONTRA- + *bannum* ban]
▸'**contra,bandist** *n*

contrabass (,kɒntrə'beɪs) *n* **1** another name for **double bass.** ◆ *adj* **2** denoting the instrument of a family that is lower than the bass.

contrabassoon (,kɒntrəbə'su:n) *n* the largest instrument in the oboe family, pitched an octave below the bassoon; double bassoon.

contraception (,kɒntrə'sɛpʃən) *n* the intentional prevention of conception by artificial or natural means. [C19: from CONTRA- + CONCEPTION]
▸,**contra'ceptive** *adj, n*

contract ➊ *vb* (kən'trækt). **1** to make or become smaller, narrower, shorter, etc. **2** ('kɒntrækt). (when *intr*, sometimes foll. by *for;* when *tr*, may take an infinitive) to enter into an agreement with (a person, company, etc.) to deliver (goods or services) or to do (something) on mutually agreed terms. **3** to draw or be drawn together. **4** (*tr*) to incur or become affected by (a disease, debt, etc.). **5** (*tr*) to shorten (a word or phrase) by the omission of letters or syllables, usually indicated in writing by an apostrophe. **6** (*tr*) to wrinkle (the brow or a muscle). **7** (*tr*) to arrange (a marriage) for; betroth. ◆ *n* ('kɒntrækt). **8** a formal agreement between two or more parties. **9** a document that states the terms of such an agreement. **10** the branch of law treating of contracts. **11** marriage considered as a formal agreement. **12** See **contract bridge.** **13** *Bridge.* **13a** the highest bid, which determines trumps and the number of tricks one side must make. **13b** the number and suit of these tricks. **14** *Sl.* **14a** a criminal agreement to kill a particular person in return for an agreed sum of money. **14b** (*as modifier*): *a contract killing.* [C16: from L *contractus* agreement, from *contrahere* to draw together, from *trahere* to draw]
▸**con'tractible** *adj*

contract bridge ('kɒntrækt) *n* the most common variety of bridge, in which the declarer receives points counting towards game and rubber only for tricks he bids as well as makes. Cf. **auction bridge.**

contractile (kən'træktaɪl) *adj* having the power to contract or to cause contraction.

contraction ➊ (kən'trækʃən) *n* **1** an instance of contracting or the state of being contracted. **2** a shortening of a word or group of words, often marked by an apostrophe: *I've come* for *I have come.*
▸**con'tractive** *adj*

contractor (kən'træktə) *n* **1** a person or firm that contracts to supply materials or labour, esp. for building. **2** something that contracts.

contract out ('kɒntrækt) *vb* (*intr, adv*) *Brit.* to agree not to participate in something, esp. the state pension scheme.

contractual (kən'træktjʊəl) *adj* of the nature of or assured by a contract.

contradance ('kɒntrə,dɑ:ns) *n* a courtly Continental version of the English country dance.

contradict ➊ (,kɒntrə'dɪkt) *vb* **1** (*tr*) to affirm the opposite of (a statement, etc.). **2** (*tr*) to declare (a statement, etc.) to be false or incorrect; deny. **3** (*tr*) to be inconsistent with: *the facts contradicted his theory.* **4** (*intr*) to be at variance; be in contradiction. [C16: from L *contrādīcere*, from CONTRA- + *dīcere* to speak]
▸,**contra'dictable** *adj* ▸,**contra'dictor** *n*

contradiction ➊ (,kɒntrə'dɪkʃən) *n* **1** opposition; denial. **2** a declaration of the opposite. **3** a statement that is at variance with itself (often in **a contradiction in terms**). **4** conflict or inconsistency, as between events, qualities, etc. **5** a person or thing containing conflicting qualities. **6** *Logic.* a statement that is false under all circumstances; necessary falsehood.

contradictory ➊ (,kɒntrə'dɪktərɪ) *adj* **1** inconsistent; incompatible. **2** given to argument and contention: *a contradictory person.* **3** *Logic.* (of a pair of statements) unable both to be true or both to be false under the same circumstances.
▸,**contra'dictorily** *adv* ▸,**contra'dictoriness** *n*

contradistinction (,kɒntrədɪ'stɪŋkʃən) *n* a distinction made by contrasting different qualities.
▸,**contradis'tinctive** *adj*

contraflow ('kɒntrə,fləʊ) *n Brit.* two-way traffic on one carriageway of a motorway.

contrail ('kɒntreɪl) *n* another name for **vapour trail.** [C20: from CON(DENSATION) + TRAIL]

contralto (kən'træltəʊ) *n, pl* **contraltos** *or* **contralti** (-tɪ). **1** the lowest female voice: in the context of a choir often shortened to **alto. 2** a singer with such a voice. ◆ *adj* **3** of or denoting a contralto: *the contralto part.* [C18: from It.; see CONTRA-, ALTO]

contraposition (,kɒntrəpə'zɪʃən) *n* **1** the act of placing opposite or against. **2** *Logic.* the conclusion drawn from a subject-predicate proposition by negating its terms and changing their order.

contraption ➊ (kən'træpʃən) *n Inf., often facetious or derog.* a device or contrivance, esp. one considered strange, unnecessarily intricate, or improvised. [C19: ?from CON(TRIVANCE) + TRAP[1] + (INVEN)TION]

contrapuntal (,kɒntrə'pʌntᵊl) *adj Music.* characterized by counterpoint. [C19: from It. *contrappunto*]
▸,**contra'puntally** *adv* ▸,**contra'puntist** *or* ,**contra'puntalist** *n*

contrariety (,kɒntrə'raɪətɪ) *n, pl* **contrarieties. 1** opposition between one thing and another; disagreement. **2** an instance of such opposition; inconsistency; discrepancy.

contrariwise ('kɒntrərɪ,waɪz) *adv* **1** from a contrasting point of view. **2** in the reverse way. **3** (kən'treərɪ,waɪz). in a contrary manner.

contrary ➊ ('kɒntrərɪ) *adj* **1** opposed in nature, position, etc.: *contrary ideas.* **2** (kən'treərɪ). perverse; obstinate. **3** (esp. of wind) adverse; unfavourable. **4** (of plant parts) situated at right angles to each other. **5** *Logic.* (of a pair of propositions) related so they cannot both be true, although they may both be false. ◆ *n, pl* **contraries. 6** the exact opposite (esp. in **to the contrary**). **7 on the contrary.** quite the reverse. **8** either of two exactly opposite objects, facts, or qualities. ◆ *adv* (usually foll. by *to*) **9** in an opposite or unexpected way: *contrary to usual belief.* **10** in conflict (with): *contrary to nature.* [C14: from L *contrārius* opposite, from *contrā* against]
▸**con'trarily** *adv* ▸**con'trariness** *n*

contrast ➊ *vb* (kən'trɑ:st). **1** (often foll. by *with*) to distinguish or be distinguished by comparison of unlike or opposite qualities. ◆ *n* ('kɒntrɑ:st). **2** distinction by comparison of opposite or dissimilar things, qualities, etc. (esp. in **by contrast, in contrast to** *or* **with**). **3** a person or thing showing differences when compared with another. **4** the effect of the juxtaposition of different colours, tones, etc. **5** the extent to which adjacent areas of an optical image, esp. on a television screen or in a photograph, differ in brightness. [C16: (n): via F from It., from *contrastare* (vb), from L *contra-* against + *stare* to stand]
▸**con'trasting** *adj* ▸**con'trastive** *adj*

contrast medium *n Med.* a radiopaque substance, such as barium sulphate, used to increase the contrast of an image in radiography.

contravene ➊ (,kɒntrə'vi:n) *vb* **contravenes, contravening, contravened.** (*tr*) **1** to come into conflict with or infringe (rules, laws, etc.). **2** to dispute or contradict (a statement, proposition, etc.). [C16: from LL *contrāvenīre*, from L CONTRA- + *venīre* to come]
▸,**contra'vener** *n* ▸**contravention** (,kɒntrə'vɛnʃən) *n*

THESAURUS

contour *n* **1, 3** = **outline**, curve, figure, form, lines, profile, relief, shape, silhouette

contraband *n* **2** = **smuggling**, black-marketing, bootlegging, moonshine (*US*), rum-running, trafficking ◆ *adj* **4** = **smuggled**, banned, black-market, bootleg, bootlegged, forbidden, hot, illegal, illicit, interdicted, prohibited, unlawful

contract *vb* **1** = **shorten**, abbreviate, abridge, compress, condense, confine, constrict, curtail, diminish, dwindle, epitomize, knit, lessen, narrow, pucker, purse, reduce, shrink, shrivel, tighten, wither, wrinkle **2** = **agree**, arrange, bargain, clinch, close, come to terms, commit oneself, covenant, engage, enter into, negotiate, pledge, shake hands, stipulate **4** = **catch**, acquire, be afflicted with, develop, get, go down with, incur ◆ *n* **8** = **agreement**, arrangement, bargain, bond, commission, commitment, compact, concordat, convention, covenant, deal (*inf.*), engagement, pact, settlement, stipulation, treaty, understanding
Antonyms *vb* ≠ **shorten:** broaden, develop, distend, enlarge, expand, grow, increase, inflate, multiply, spread, stretch, swell, widen ≠ **agree:** decline, disagree, refuse, turn down ≠ **catch:** avert, avoid, escape, ward off

contraction *n* **1** = **shortening**, abbreviation, compression, constriction, diminution, drawing in, elision, narrowing, reduction, shrinkage, shrivelling, tensing, tightening

contradict *vb* **1-4** = **deny**, be at variance with, belie, challenge, contravene, controvert, counter, counteract, dispute, fly in the face of, gainsay (*arch. or literary*), impugn, make a nonsense of, negate, oppose, rebut
Antonyms *vb* affirm, agree, authenticate, confirm, defend, endorse, support, verify

contradiction *n* **4** = **denial**, conflict, confutation, contravention, incongruity, inconsistency, negation, opposite

contradictory *adj* **1** = **inconsistent**, antagonistic, antithetical, conflicting, contrary, discrepant, incompatible, irreconcilable, opposed, opposite, paradoxical, repugnant

contraption *n Informal* = **device**, apparatus, contrivance, gadget, instrument, mechanism, rig, waldo

contrary *adj* **1** = **opposed**, adverse, antagonistic, clashing, contradictory, counter, discordant, hostile, inconsistent, inimical, opposite, paradoxical **2** = **perverse**, awkward, balky, cantankerous, cussed (*inf.*), difficult, disobliging, froward (*arch.*), intractable, obstinate, stroppy (*Brit. sl.*), thrawn (*N English dialect*), unaccommodating, wayward, wilful ◆ *n* **7 on the contrary** = **quite the opposite** *or* **reverse**, conversely, in contrast, not at all, on the other hand **8** = **opposite**, antithesis, converse, reverse
Antonyms *adj* ≠ **opposed:** accordant, congruous, consistent, harmonious, in agreement, parallel, unopposed ≠ **perverse:** accommodating, agreeable, amiable, cooperative, eager to please, helpful, obliging, tractable, willing

contrast *vb* **1** = **differentiate**, compare, differ, distinguish, oppose, set in opposition, set off ◆ *n* **2** = **difference**, comparison, contrariety, differentiation, disparity, dissimilarity, distinction, divergence, foil, opposition

contravene *vb* **1** *Formal* = **break**, disobey, go against, infringe, transgress, violate **2** = **conflict with**, contradict, counteract, cross, go against, hinder, interfere, oppose, refute, thwart

contravention *n* **1** = **breach**, disobedience,

contretemps ('kɒntrəˌtɑːn) *n, pl* **contretemps.** **1** an awkward or difficult situation or mishap. **2** a small disagreement that is rather embarrassing. [C17: from F, from *contre* against + *temps* time]

contribute ❶ (kən'trɪbjuːt) *vb* **contributes, contributing, contributed.** (often foll. by *to*) **1** to give (support, money, etc.) for a common purpose or fund. **2** to supply (ideas, opinions, etc.). **3** (*intr*) to be partly responsible (for): *drink contributed to the accident.* **4** to write (articles, etc.) for a publication. [C16: from L *contribuere* to collect, from *tribuere* to grant]
▸**con'tributable** *adj* ▸**con'tributive** *adj* ▸**con'tributor** *n*

contribution ❶ (ˌkɒntrɪ'bjuːʃən) *n* **1** the act of contributing. **2** something contributed, such as money. **3** an article, etc., contributed to a newspaper or other publication. **4** *Arch.* a levy.

contributory (kən'trɪbjʊtərɪ, -trɪ) *adj* **1** (often foll. by *to*) being partly responsible: *a contributory factor.* **2** giving to a common purpose or fund. **3** of or designating an insurance or pension scheme in which the premiums are paid partly by the employer and partly by the employees who benefit from it. ◆ *n, pl* **contributories.** **4** a person or thing that contributes. **5** *Company law.* a member or former member of a company liable to contribute to the assets on the winding-up of the company.

contrite ❶ (kən'traɪt, 'kɒntraɪt) *adj* **1** full of guilt or regret; remorseful. **2** arising from a sense of shame or guilt: *contrite promises.* [C14: from L *contrītus* worn out, from *conterere* to bruise, from *terere* to grind]
▸**con'tritely** *adv* ▸**con'triteness** *or* **contrition** (kən'trɪʃən) *n*

contrivance ❶ (kən'traɪvəns) *n* **1** something contrived, esp. an ingenious device; contraption. **2** inventive skill or ability. **3** an artificial rather than natural arrangement of details, parts, etc. **4** an elaborate or deceitful plan; stratagem.

contrive ❶ (kən'traɪv) *vb* **contrives, contriving, contrived.** **1** (*tr*) to manage (something or to do something), esp. by a trick: *he contrived to make them meet.* **2** (*tr*) to think up or adapt ingeniously: *he contrived a new mast for the boat.* **3** to plot or scheme. [C14: from OF *controver,* from LL *contropāre* to represent by figures of speech, compare]
▸**con'triver** *n*

contrived ❶ (kən'traɪvd) *adj* obviously planned; artificial; forced; unnatural.

control ❶ (kən'trəʊl) *vb* **controls, controlling, controlled.** (*tr*) **1** to command, direct, or rule. **2** to check, limit, or restrain: *to control one's emotions.* **3** to regulate or operate (a machine). **4** to verify (a scientific experiment) by conducting a parallel experiment in which the variable being investigated is held constant or is compared with a standard. **5a** to regulate (financial affairs). **5b** to examine (financial accounts). **6** to restrict or regulate the authorized supply of (certain substances, such as drugs). ◆ *n* **7** power to direct: *under control.* **8** a curb; check: *a frontier control.* **9** (*often pl*) a mechanism for operating a car, aircraft, etc. **10a** a standard of comparison used in a statistical analysis, etc. **10b** (*as modifier*): *a control group.* **11a** a device that regulates the operation of a machine. **11b** (*as modifier*): *control room.* [C15: from OF *conteroller* to regulate, from *contrerolle* duplicate register, from *contre-* COUNTER- + *rolle* ROLL]
▸**con'trollable** *adj* ▸**conˌtrolla'bility** *n* ▸**con'trollably** *adv*

control experiment *n* an experiment designed to check or correct the results of another experiment by removing the variable or variables operating in that other experiment.

controller (kən'trəʊlə) *n* **1** a person who directs. **2** Also called: **comptroller.** a business executive or government officer responsible for financial planning, control, etc. **3** the equipment concerned with controlling the operation of an electrical device.
▸**con'trollerˌship** *n*

controlling interest *n* a quantity of shares in a business that is sufficient to ensure control over its direction.

control tower *n* a tower at an airport from which air traffic is controlled.

controversy ❶ ('kɒntrəˌvɜːsɪ, kən'trɒvəsɪ) *n, pl* **controversies.** dispute, argument, or debate, esp. one concerning a matter about which there is strong disagreement and esp. one carried on in public or in the press. [C14: from L *contrōversia,* from *contrōversus,* from CONTRA- + *vertere* to turn]
▸**controversial** (ˌkɒntrə'vɜːʃəl) *adj* ▸ˌ**contro'versialˌism** *n* ▸ˌ**contro'versialist** *n*

controvert ('kɒntrəˌvɜːt, ˌkɒntrə'vɜːt) *vb* (*tr*) **1** to deny, refute, or oppose (argument or opinion). **2** to argue about. [C17: from L *contrōversus;* see CONTROVERSY]
▸ˌ**contro'vertible** *adj*

contumacious (ˌkɒntjʊ'meɪʃəs) *adj* stubbornly resistant to authority.
▸ˌ**contu'maciously** *adv*

contumacy ('kɒntjʊməsɪ) *n, pl* **contumacies.** obstinate and wilful resistance to authority, esp. refusal to comply with a court order. [C14: from L *contumācia,* from *contumāx* obstinate]

contumely ('kɒntjʊmɪlɪ) *n, pl* **contumelies.** **1** scornful or insulting language or behaviour. **2** a humiliating insult. [C14: from L *contumēlia,* from *tumēre* to swell, as with wrath]
▸**contumelious** (ˌkɒntjʊ'miːlɪəs) *adj* ▸ˌ**contu'meliously** *adv*

contuse ❶ (kən'tjuːz) *vb* **contuses, contusing, contused.** (*tr*) to injure (the body) without breaking the skin; bruise. [C15: from L *contūsus* bruised, from *contundere* to grind, from *tundere* to beat]
▸**con'tusion** *n*

conundrum ❶ (kə'nʌndrəm) *n* **1** a riddle, esp. one whose answer makes a play on words. **2** a puzzling question or problem. [C16: from ?]

conurbation (ˌkɒnɜː'beɪʃən) *n* a large densely populated urban sprawl formed by the growth and coalescence of individual towns or cities. [C20: from CON- + *-urbation,* from L *urbs* city]

convalesce ❶ (ˌkɒnvə'lɛs) *vb* **convalesces, convalescing, convalesced.** (*intr*) to recover from illness, injury, or the aftereffects of a surgical operation. [C15: from L *convalēscere,* from *com-* (intensive) + *valēscere* to grow strong]

convalescence ❶ (ˌkɒnvə'lɛsəns) *n* **1** gradual return to health after illness, injury, or an operation. **2** the period during which such recovery occurs.
▸ˌ**conva'lescent** *n, adj*

convection (kən'vɛkʃən) *n* **1** a process of heat transfer through a gas or liquid by bulk motion of hotter material into a cooler region. Cf. **conduction** (sense 1). **2** *Meteorol.* the process by which masses of relatively warm air are raised into the atmosphere, often cooling and forming clouds, with compensatory downward movements of cooler air. [C19: from LL *convectiō,* from L *convehere* to bring together, from *vehere* to carry]
▸**con'vectional** *adj* ▸**con'vective** *adj*

convector (kən'vɛktə) *n* a space-heating device from which heat is transferred to the surrounding air by convection.

convene ❶ (kən'viːn) *vb* **convenes, convening, convened.** **1** to gather, call together or summon, esp. for a formal meeting. **2** (*tr*) to order to appear before a court of law, judge, tribunal, etc. [C15: from L *convenīre* to assemble, from *venīre* to come]
▸**con'venable** *adj*

convener *or* **convenor** (kən'viːnə) *n* **1** a person who convenes or chairs a meeting, committee, etc., esp. one who is specifically elected to do so: *a convener of shop stewards.* **2** the chairman and civic head of certain Scottish councils. Cf. **provost** (sense 2).
▸**con'venership** *or* **con'venorship** *n*

convenience ❶ (kən'viːnɪəns) *n* **1** the quality of being suitable or op-

THESAURUS

infraction, infringement, transgression, trespass, violation **2 = conflict**, contradiction, counteraction, disputation, hindrance, impugnation, interference, rebuttal, refutation

contribute *vb* **1, 2 = give**, add, afford, bestow, chip in (*inf.*), donate, furnish, provide, subscribe, supply **3 = be partly responsible for**, be conducive to, be instrumental in, conduce to, help, lead to, tend to

contribution *n* **2 = gift**, addition, bestowal, donation, grant, input, offering, stipend, subscription

contributor *n* **1 = giver**, backer, bestower, conferrer, donor, patron, subscriber, supporter **4 = writer**, correspondent, freelance, freelancer, journalist, journo, reporter

contrite *adj* **1 = sorry**, chastened, conscience-stricken, humble, in sackcloth and ashes, penitent, regretful, remorseful, repentant, sorrowful

contriteness *n* **1 = regret**, compunction, humiliation, penitence, remorse, repentance, self-reproach, sorrow

contrivance *n* **1 = device**, apparatus, appliance, contraption, equipment, gadget, gear, implement, instrument, invention, machine, mechanism **4 = plan**, artifice, design, dodge, expedient, fabrication, formation, intrigue, inventiveness, machination, measure, plot, project, ruse, scheme, stratagem, trick

contrive *vb* **1, 3 = bring about**, arrange, effect, hit upon, manage, manoeuvre, plan, plot, scheme, succeed **2 = devise**, concoct, construct, create, design, engineer, fabricate, frame, improvise, invent, manufacture, wangle (*inf.*)

contrived *adj* **= forced**, artificial, elaborate, laboured, overdone, planned, recherché, strained, unnatural
Antonyms *adj* genuine, natural, relaxed, spontaneous, unaffected, unconstrained, unfeigned, unforced, unpretentious

control *vb* **1 = have power over**, administer, boss (*inf.*), call the shots, call the tune, command, conduct, direct, dominate, govern, handle, have charge of, have (someone) in one's pocket, hold the purse strings, keep a tight rein on, keep on a string, lead, manage, manipulate, oversee, pilot, reign over, rule, steer, superintend, supervise **2 = restrain**, bridle, check, constrain, contain, curb, hold back, limit, master, rein in, repress, subdue ◆ *n* **7 = power**, authority, charge, command, direction, discipline, government, guidance, jurisdiction, management, mastery, oversight, rule, superintendence, supervision, supremacy **8 = restraint**, brake, check, curb, limitation, regulation **9** *often pl* **= instruments**, console, control panel, dash, dashboard, dials

controversial *adj* **= disputed**, at issue, contended, contentious, controvertible, debatable, disputable, open to question, polemic, under discussion

controversy *n* **= argument**, altercation, contention, debate, discussion, dispute, dissension, polemic, quarrel, row, squabble, strife, wrangle, wrangling

contusion *n Formal* **= bruise**, discoloration, injury, knock, swelling, trauma (*Pathology*)

conundrum *n* **1, 2 = puzzle**, brain-teaser, enigma, poser, problem, riddle, teaser

convalesce *vb* **= recover**, improve, rally, recuperate, rehabilitate, rest

convalescence *n* **1 = recovery**, improvement, recuperation, rehabilitation, return to health

convalescent *adj* **1 = recovering**, getting better, improving, mending, on the mend, recuperating

convene *vb* **1 = gather**, assemble, bring together, call, come together, congregate, convoke, meet, muster, rally, summon

convenience *n* **1 = usefulness**, accessibility, advantage, appropriateness, availability, bene-

portune. **2** a convenient time or situation. **3** **at your convenience.** at a time suitable to you. **4** usefulness, comfort, or facility. **5** an object that is useful, esp. a labour-saving device. **6** *Euphemistic, chiefly Brit.* a lavatory, esp. a public one. **7** **make a convenience of.** to take advantage of; impose upon.

convenience food *n* food that needs little preparation, especially food that has been pre-prepared and preserved for long-term storage.

convenience store *n* a shop that has long opening hours, caters to local tastes, and is conveniently situated.

convenient ⓘ (kən'viːnɪənt) *adj* **1** suitable; opportune. **2** easy to use. **3** close by; handy. [C14: from L *conveniēns*, from *convenīre* to be in accord with, from *venīre* to come]
▸**con'veniently** *adv*

convent ⓘ ('kɒnvənt) *n* **1** a building inhabited by a religious community, usually of nuns. **2** the religious community inhabiting such a building. **3** Also called: **convent school.** a school in which the teachers are nuns. [C13: from OF, from L *conventus* meeting, from *convenīre*; see CONVENE]

conventicle (kən'ventɪk^ə^l) *n* **1** a secret or unauthorized assembly for worship. **2** a small meeting house or chapel, esp. of Dissenters. [C14: from L *conventiculum*, from *conventus*; see CONVENT]

convention ⓘ (kən'venʃən) *n* **1** a large formal assembly of a group with common interests, such as a trade union. **2** *US politics.* an assembly of delegates of one party to select candidates for office. **3** an international agreement second only to a treaty in formality. **4** any agreement or contract. **5** the established view of what is thought to be proper behaviour, good taste, etc. **6** an accepted rule, usage, etc.: *a convention used by printers.* **7** *Bridge.* a bid or play not to be taken at its face value, which one's partner can interpret according to a prearranged bidding system. [C15: from L *conventiō* an assembling]

conventional ⓘ (kən'venʃən^ə^l) *adj* **1** following the accepted customs and proprieties, esp. in a way that lacks originality. **2** established by accepted usage or general agreement. **3** of a convention or assembly. **4** *Visual arts.* conventionalized. **5** (of weapons, warfare, etc.) not nuclear.
▸**con'ventionalism** *n* ▸**con'ventionally** *adv*

conventionality (kən,venʃə'nælɪtɪ) *n, pl* **conventionalities. 1** the quality of being conventional. **2** (*often pl*) something conventional.

conventionalize *or* **conventionalise** (kən'venʃənə,laɪz) *vb* **conventionalizes, conventionalizing, conventionalized** *or* **conventionalises, conventionalising, conventionalised.** (*tr*) **1** to make conventional. **2** to simplify or stylize (a design, decorative device, etc.).
▸**con,ventionali'zation** *or* **con,ventionali'sation** *n*

conventual (kən'ventjuəl) *adj* **1** of, belonging to, or characteristic of a convent. ◆ *n* **2** a member of a convent.
▸**con'ventually** *adv*

converge ⓘ (kən'vɜːdʒ) *vb* **converges, converging, converged. 1** to move or cause to move towards the same point. **2** to meet or join. **3** (*intr*) (of opinions, effects, etc.) to tend towards a common conclusion or result. **4** (*intr*) *Maths.* (of an infinite series) to approach a finite limit as the number of terms increases. **5** (*intr*) (of animals and plants) to undergo convergence. [C17: from LL *convergere*, from L *com-* together + *vergere* to incline]
▸**con'vergent** *adj*

convergence ⓘ (kən'vɜːdʒəns) *n* **1** Also: **convergency.** the act, degree, or a point of converging. **2** Also called: **convergent evolution.** the evolutionary development of a superficial resemblance between unrelated animals that occupy a similar environment, as in the evolution of wings in birds and bats.

convergent thinking *n Psychol.* analytical, usually deductive, thinking in which ideas are examined for their logical validity or in which a set of rules is followed, for example in arithmetic.

conversable (kən'vɜːsəb^ə^l) *adj* **1** easy or pleasant to talk to. **2** able or inclined to talk.

conversant ⓘ (kən'vɜːs^ə^nt) *adj* (*usually postpositive* and foll. by *with*) experienced (in), familiar (with), or acquainted (with).
▸**con'versance** *or* **con'versancy** *n* ▸**con'versantly** *adv*

conversation ⓘ (,kɒnvə'seɪʃən) *n* the interchange through speech of information, ideas, etc.; spoken communication.

conversational ⓘ (,kɒnvə'seɪʃən^ə^l) *adj* **1** of, using, or in the manner of conversation. **2** inclined to conversation; conversable.
▸**,conver'sationalist** *n* ▸**,conver'sationally** *adv*

conversation piece *n* **1** something, esp. an unusual object, that provokes conversation. **2** (esp. in 18th-century Britain) a group portrait in a landscape or domestic setting.

converse[1] ⓘ *vb* (kən'vɜːs), **converses, conversing, conversed.** (*intr*; often foll. by *with*) **1** to engage in conversation (with). **2** to commune spiritually (with). ◆ *n* ('kɒnvɜːs). **3** conversation (often in **hold converse with**). [C16: from OF *converser*, from L *conversārī* to keep company with, from *conversāre* to turn constantly, from *vertere* to turn]
▸**con'verser** *n*

converse[2] ⓘ ('kɒnvɜːs) *adj* **1** (*prenominal*) reversed; opposite; contrary. ◆ *n* **2** something that is opposite or contrary. **3** *Logic.* a categorial proposition obtained from another by the transposition of the subject and predicate, as *no bad man is bald* from *no bald man is bad.* [C16: from L *conversus* turned around; see CONVERSE[1]]
▸**con'versely** *adv*

conversion ⓘ (kən'vɜːʃən) *n* **1a** a change or adaptation in form, character, or function. **1b** something changed in one of these respects. **2** a change to another belief, as in a change of religion. **3** alteration to the structure or fittings of a building undergoing a change in function or legal status. **4** *Maths.* a change in the units or form of a number or expression: *the conversion of miles to kilometres.* **5** *Rugby.* a score made after a try by kicking the ball over the crossbar from a place kick. **6** *Physics.* a change of fertile material to fissile material in a reactor. **7** an alteration to a car engine to improve its performance. [C14: from L *conversiō* a turning around; see CONVERT]

conversion disorder *n* a psychological disorder in which severe physical symptoms like blindness or paralysis appear with no apparent physical cause.

convert ⓘ *vb* (kən'vɜːt). (*mainly tr*) **1** to change or adapt the form, character, or function of. **2** to cause (someone) to change in opinion, belief, etc. **3** (*intr*) to admit of being changed (into): *the table converts into a tray.* **4** (*also intr*) to change or be changed into another state: *to convert water into ice.* **5** *Law.* to assume unlawful proprietary rights over (personal property). **6** (*also intr*) *Rugby.* to make a conversion after (a try). **7** *Logic.* to transpose the subject and predicate of (a proposition). **8** to change (a value or measurement) from one system of units to another. **9** to exchange (a security or bond) for something of equivalent value. ◆ *n* ('kɒnvɜːt). **10** a person who has been converted to another belief, religion, etc. [C13: from OF, from L *convertere* to turn around, alter, from *vertere* to turn]

converter *or* **convertor** (kən'vɜːtə) *n* **1** a person or thing that converts. **2** *Physics.* **2a** a device for converting alternating current to direct current or vice versa. **2b** a device for converting a signal from one frequency to another. **3** a vessel in which molten metal is refined, using a blast of air or oxygen. **4** *Computing.* a device for converting one form of coded information to another, such as an analogue-to-digital converter.

converter reactor *n* a nuclear reactor for converting one fuel into another, esp. fertile material into fissionable material.

convertible ⓘ (kən'vɜːtɪb^ə^l) *adj* **1** capable of being converted. **2** (of a car) having a folding or removable roof. **3** *Finance.* **3a** (of a currency) freely exchangeable into other currencies. **3b** (of a paper currency)

THESAURUS

fit, fitness, handiness, opportuneness, serviceability, suitability, utility **2** = **suitable time**, chance, leisure, opportunity, spare moment, spare time **5** = **appliance**, amenity, comfort, facility, help, labour-saving device
Antonyms *n* ≠ **usefulness:** inconvenience, uselessness

convenient *adj* **1** = **useful**, adapted, appropriate, beneficial, commodious, fit, fitted, handy, helpful, labour-saving, opportune, seasonable, serviceable, suitable, suited, timely, well-timed **3** = **nearby**, accessible, at hand, available, close at hand, handy, just round the corner, within reach
Antonyms *adj* ≠ **useful:** awkward, inconvenient, unsuitable, useless ≠ **nearby:** distant, inaccessible, inconvenient, out-of-the-way

convent *n* **1, 2** = **nunnery**, religious community

convention *n* **1** = **assembly**, conference, congress, convocation, council, delegates, meeting, representatives **3, 4** = **agreement**, bargain, compact, concordat, contract, pact, protocol, stipulation, treaty **5** = **custom**, code, etiquette, formality, practice, propriety, protocol, tradition, usage

conventional *adj* **1** = **unoriginal**, banal, bourgeois, commonplace, hackneyed, hidebound, pedestrian, Pooterish, prosaic, routine, run-of-the-mill, stereotyped, vanilla (*sl.*) **2** = **ordinary**, accepted, bog-standard (*Brit. & Irish slang*), common, correct, customary, decorous, expected, formal, habitual, normal, orthodox, prevailing, prevalent, proper, regular, ritual, standard, traditional, usual, wonted
Antonyms *adj* ≠ **ordinary:** abnormal, left-field (*inf.*), off-the-wall (*sl.*), uncommon, unconventional, unorthodox

converge *vb* **1, 2** = **come together**, coincide, combine, concentrate, focus, gather, join, meet, merge, mingle

convergence *n* **1** = **meeting**, approach, blending, coincidence, concentration, concurrence, confluence, conflux, conjunction, junction, merging, mingling

conversant *adj, foll. by* **with** = **experienced in**, acquainted with, *au fait* with, familiar with, knowledgeable about, practised in, proficient in, skilled in, versed in, well-informed about, well up in (*inf.*)

conversation *n* = **talk**, chat, chinwag (*Brit. inf.*), colloquy, communication, communion, confab (*inf.*), confabulation, conference, converse, dialogue, discourse, discussion, exchange, gossip, intercourse, powwow, tête-à-tête

conversational *adj* **1, 2** = **chatty**, colloquial, communicative, informal

converse[1] *vb* **1** = **talk**, chat, commune, confer, discourse, exchange views ◆ *n* **3** = **talk**, chat, communication, conference, conversation, dialogue

converse[2] *adj* **1** = **opposite**, contrary, counter, reverse, reversed, transposed ◆ *n* **2** = **opposite**, antithesis, contrary, obverse, other side of the coin, reverse

conversion *n* **1a** = **change**, metamorphosis, transfiguration, transformation, transmogrification (*jocular*), transmutation **2** = **reformation**, change of heart, proselytization, rebirth, regeneration **3** = **adaptation**, alteration, modification, reconstruction, remodelling, reorganization

convert *vb* **1** = **adapt**, apply, appropriate, customize, modify, remodel, reorganize, restyle, revise **2** = **reform**, baptize, bring to God, convince, proselytize, regenerate, save **3** = **change**, alter, interchange, metamorphose, transform, transmogrify (*jocular*), transmute, transpose, turn ◆ *n* **10** = **neophyte**, catechumen, disciple, proselyte

convertible *adj* **1** = **adaptable**, adjustable, exchangeable, interchangeable

exchangeable on demand for precious metal to an equivalent value. **3c** (of a bond, debenture, etc.) able to be exchanged for a share on a specified date at a specified price. ◆ *n* **4** a car with a folding or removable roof. **5** any convertible document or currency.
▸**con,verti'bility** *n* ▸**con'vertibly** *adv*

convex ❶ ('kɒnvɛks, kɒn'vɛks) *adj* **1** curving outwards. **2** having one or two surfaces curved or ground in the shape of a section of the exterior of a sphere, ellipsoid, etc.: *a convex lens.* [C16: from L *convexus* vaulted, rounded]
▸**con'vexity** *n* ▸**'convexly** *adv*

convexo-concave (kən,vɛksəukɒn'keɪv) *adj* **1** having one side convex and the other side concave. **2** (of a lens) having a convex face with greater curvature than the concave face.

convexo-convex *adj* (esp. of a lens) having both sides convex; biconvex.

convey ❶ (kən'veɪ) *vb* (*tr*) **1** to take, carry, or transport from one place to another. **2** to communicate (a message, information, etc.). **3** (of a channel, path, etc.) to conduct or transfer. **4** *Law.* to transfer (the title to property). [C13: from OF *conveier,* from Med. L *conviāre* to escort, from L *com-* with + *via* way]
▸**con'veyable** *adj*

conveyance ❶ (kən'veɪəns) *n* **1** the act of conveying. **2** a means of transport. **3** *Law.* **3a** a transfer of the legal title to property. **3b** the document effecting such a transfer.
▸**con'veyancer** *n* ▸**con'veyancing** *n*

conveyor *or* **conveyer** (kən'veɪə) *n* **1** a person or thing that conveys. **2** short for **conveyor belt.**

conveyor belt *n* a flexible endless strip of fabric or linked plates driven by rollers and used to transport objects, esp. in a factory.

convict ❶ *vb* (kən'vɪkt). (*tr*) **1** to pronounce (someone) guilty of an offence. ◆ *n* ('kɒnvɪkt). **2** a person found guilty of an offence against the law. **3** a person serving a prison sentence. [C14: from L *convictus* convicted, from *convincere* to prove guilty, CONVINCE]

conviction ❶ (kən'vɪkʃən) *n* **1** the state of being convinced. **2** a firmly held belief, opinion, etc. **3** the act of convincing. **4** the act of convicting or the state of being convicted. **5 carry conviction.** to be convincing.
▸**con'victional** *adj* ▸**con'victive** *adj*

convince ❶ (kən'vɪns) *vb* **convinces, convincing, convinced.** (*tr*) (*may take a clause as object*) to make (someone) agree, understand, or realize the truth or validity of something; persuade. [C16: from L *convincere* to demonstrate incontrovertibly, from *com-* (intensive) + *vincere* to overcome]
▸**con'vincer** *n* ▸**con'vincible** *adj* ▸**con'vincing** *adj* ▸**con'vincingly** *adv*

> **USAGE NOTE** The use of *convince* to talk about persuading someone to do something is considered by many British speakers to be wrong or unacceptable.

convivial ❶ (kən'vɪvɪəl) *adj* sociable; jovial or festive: *a convivial atmosphere.* [C17: from LL *convīviālis,* from L *convīvium,* a living together, banquet, from *vīvere* to live]
▸**con,vivi'ality** *n*

convocation ❶ (,kɒnvə'keɪʃən) *n* **1** a large formal assembly. **2** the act of convoking or state of being convoked. **3** *Church of England.* either of the synods of the provinces of Canterbury or York. **4** *Episcopal Church.* an assembly of the clergy and part of the laity of a diocese. **5** (*sometimes cap.*) (in some British universities) a legislative assembly. **6** (in Australia and New Zealand) the graduate membership of a university.
▸**,convo'cational** *adj*

convoke ❶ (kən'vəuk) *vb* **convokes, convoking, convoked.** (*tr*) to call (a meeting, assembly, etc.) together; summon. [C16: from L *convocāre,* from *vocāre* to call]
▸**con'voker** *n*

convolute ('kɒnvə,lu:t) *vb* **convolutes, convoluting, convoluted.** (*tr*) **1** to form into a twisted, coiled, or rolled shape. ◆ *adj* **2** *Bot.* rolled longitudinally upon itself: *a convolute petal.* [C18: from L *convolūtus,* from *convolvere* to roll together, from *volvere* to turn]

convoluted ('kɒnvə,lu:tɪd) *adj* **1** (esp. of meaning, style, etc.) difficult to comprehend; involved. **2** coiled.
▸**'convo,lutedly** *adv*

convolution ❶ (,kɒnvə'lu:ʃən) *n* **1** a turn, twist, or coil. **2** an intricate or confused matter or condition. **3** any of the numerous convex folds of the surface of the brain.
▸**,convo'lutional** *or* **,convo'lutionary** *adj*

convolve (kən'vɒlv) *vb* **convolves, convolving, convolved.** to wind or roll together; coil; twist. [C16: from L *convolvere;* see CONVOLUTE]

convolvulus (kən'vɒlvjuləs) *n, pl* **convolvuluses** *or* **convolvuli** (-,laɪ). a twining herbaceous plant having funnel-shaped flowers and triangular leaves. [C16: from L: bindweed; see CONVOLUTE]

convoy ❶ ('kɒnvɔɪ) *n* **1** a group of merchant ships with an escort of warships. **2** a group of land vehicles assembled to travel together. **3** the act of travelling or escorting by convoy (esp. in **in convoy**). ◆ *vb* **4** (*tr*) to escort while in transit. [C14: from OF *convoier* to CONVEY]

convulse ❶ (kən'vʌls) *vb* **convulses, convulsing, convulsed. 1** (*tr*) to shake or agitate violently. **2** (*tr*) to cause (muscles) to undergo violent spasms or contractions. **3** (*intr; often foll. by with*) *Inf.* to shake or be overcome (with violent emotion, esp. laughter). **4** (*tr*) to disrupt the normal running of (a country, etc.): *student riots have convulsed India.* [C17: from L *convulsus,* from *convellere,* from *vellere* to pluck, pull]
▸**con'vulsive** *adj* ▸**con'vulsively** *adv*

convulsion ❶ (kən'vʌlʃən) *n* **1** a violent involuntary muscular contraction. **2** a violent upheaval, esp. a social one. **3** (*usually pl*) *Inf.* uncontrollable laughter: *I was in convulsions.*

cony *or* **coney** ('kəunɪ) *n, pl* **conies** *or* **coneys. 1** a rabbit or fur made from the skin of a rabbit. **2** (in the Bible) another name for the **hyrax.** [C13: back formation from *conies,* from OF *conis,* pl. of *conil,* from L *cunīculus* rabbit]

coo (ku:) *vb* **coos, cooing, cooed. 1** (*intr*) (of doves, pigeons, etc.) to make a characteristic soft throaty call. **2** (*tr*) to speak in a soft murmur. **3** (*intr*) to murmur lovingly (esp. in **bill and coo**). ◆ *n* **4** the sound of cooing. ◆ *interj* **5** *Brit. sl.* an exclamation of surprise, awe, etc.
▸**'cooing** *adj, n* ▸**'cooingly** *adv*

cooee *or* **cooey** ('ku:i:) *interj* **1** a call used to attract attention, esp. a long loud high-pitched call on two notes. ◆ *vb* **cooees, cooeeing, cooeed** *or* **cooeys, cooeying, cooeyed. 2** (*intr*) to utter this call. ◆ *n* **3** *Austral. & NZ inf.* calling distance (esp. in **within (a) cooee (of)**). [C19: from Abor.]

cook (kuk) *vb* **1** to prepare (food) by the action of heat, or (of food) to become ready for eating through such a process. Related adj: **culinary. 2** to subject or be subjected to intense heat: *the town cooked in the sun.* **3** (*tr*) *Sl.* to alter or falsify (figures, accounts, etc.): *to cook the books.* **4** (*tr*) *Sl.* to spoil (something). **5** (*intr*) *Sl.* to happen (esp. in **what's cooking?**). ◆ *n* **6** a person who prepares food for eating. ◆ See also **cook up.** [OE *cōc* (n), from L *coquus* a cook, from *coquere* to cook]
▸**'cookable** *adj*

cook-chill *n* a method of food preparation used by caterers, in which cooked dishes are chilled rapidly and reheated as required.

cooker ('kukə) *n* **1** an apparatus heated by gas, electricity, oil, or solid fuel, for cooking food. **2** *Brit.* another name for **cooking apple.**

cookery ('kukərɪ) *n* **1** the art, study, or practice of cooking. **2** *US.* a place for cooking.

cookery book *or* **cookbook** ('kuk,buk) *n* a book containing recipes.

cook-general *n, pl* **cooks-general.** *Brit.* (formerly, esp. in the 1920s and 30s) a domestic servant who did cooking and housework.

cookie *or* **cooky** ('kukɪ) *n, pl* **cookies. 1** the US and Canad. word for **biscuit. 2** *Inf.* a person: *smart cookie.* **3 that's the way the cookie crumbles.** *Inf.* matters are inevitably so. [C18: from Du. *koekje,* dim. of *koek* cake]

cooking apple *n* any large sour apple used in cooking.

cook shop *n* **1** *Brit.* a shop that sells cookery equipment. **2** *US.* a restaurant.

Cook's tour (kuks) *n Inf.* a rapid but extensive tour or survey of anything. [C19: after Thomas *Cook* (1808–92), E travel agent]

cook up ❶ *vb* (*tr, adv*) **1** *Inf.* to concoct or invent (a story, alibi, etc.). **2** to prepare (a meal), esp. quickly. **3** *Sl.* to prepare (a drug) for use by heating, as by dissolving heroin in a spoon.

THESAURUS

convex *adj* **1** = **rounded**, bulging, gibbous, outcurved, protuberant
Antonyms *adj* concave, cupped, depressed, excavated, hollowed, indented, sunken

convey *vb* **1** = **carry**, bear, bring, conduct, fetch, forward, grant, guide, move, send, support, transmit, transport **2** = **communicate**, disclose, impart, make known, relate, reveal, tell **4** *Law* = **transfer**, bequeath, cede, deliver, demise, devolve, grant, lease, will

conveyance *n* **1** = **transportation**, carriage, movement, transfer, transference, transmission, transport **2** *Old-fashioned* = **vehicle**, transport

convict *vb* **1** = **find guilty**, condemn, imprison, pronounce guilty, sentence ◆ *n* **2, 3** = **prisoner**, con (*sl.*), criminal, culprit, felon, jailbird, lag (*sl.*), malefactor, villain

conviction *n* **1** = **confidence**, assurance, certainty, certitude, earnestness, fervour, firmness, reliance **2** = **belief**, creed, faith, opinion, persuasion, principle, tenet, view

convince *vb* = **persuade**, assure, bring round, gain the confidence of, prevail upon, prove to, satisfy, sway, win over

convincing *adj* = **persuasive**, cogent, conclusive, credible, impressive, incontrovertible, likely, plausible, powerful, probable, telling, verisimilar
Antonyms *adj* beyond belief, cock-and-bull (*inf.*), dubious, far-fetched, implausible, improbable, inconclusive, incredible, unconvincing, unlikely

convivial *adj* = **sociable**, back-slapping, cheerful, festive, friendly, fun-loving, gay, genial, hearty, hilarious, jolly, jovial, lively, merry, mirthful

conviviality *n* = **sociability**, bonhomie, cheer, cordiality, festivity, gaiety, geniality, good fellowship, jollification, jollity, joviality, liveliness, merrymaking, mirth

convocation *n* **1** *Formal* = **meeting**, assemblage, assembly, conclave, concourse, congregation, congress, convention, council, diet, synod

convoke *vb Formal* = **call together**, assemble, collect, convene, gather, muster, summon

convolution *n* **1** = **twist**, coil, coiling, complexity, contortion, curlicue, helix, intricacy, involution, loop, sinuosity, sinuousness, spiral, tortuousness, undulation, winding

convoy *vb* **4** = **escort**, accompany, attend, guard, pilot, protect, shepherd, usher

convulse *vb* **1** = **shake**, agitate, churn up, derange, disorder, disturb, shatter, twist, work

convulsion *n* **1** = **spasm**, contortion, contraction, cramp, fit, paroxysm, seizure, throe (*rare*), tremor **2** = **upheaval**, agitation, commotion, disturbance, furore, shaking, tumult, turbulence

convulsive *adj* **1** = **jerky**, churning, fitful, paroxysmal, spasmodic, sporadic, violent

cook up *vb* **1** *Informal* = **invent**, concoct, con-

cool ⓘ (ku:l) *adj* **1** moderately cold: *a cool day.* **2** comfortably free of heat: *a cool room.* **3** calm: *a cool head.* **4** lacking in enthusiasm, cordiality, etc.: *a cool welcome.* **5** calmly impudent. **6** *Inf.* (of sums of money, etc.) without exaggeration; actual: *a cool ten thousand.* **7** (of a colour) having violet, blue, or green predominating; cold. **8** (of jazz) economical and rhythmically relaxed. **9** *Inf.* sophisticated or elegant; unruffled. **10** *Inf., chiefly US & Canad.* marvellous. ◆ *n* **11** coolness: *the cool of the evening.* **12** *Sl.* calmness; composure (esp. in **keep** *or* **lose one's cool**). **13** *Sl.* unruffled elegance or sophistication. ◆ *vb* **14** (usually foll. by *down* or *off*) to make or become cooler. **15** (usually foll. by *down* or *off*) to lessen the intensity of (anger or excitement) or (of anger or excitement) to become less intense; calm down. **16** **cool it.** (*usually imperative*) *Sl.* to calm down. [OE *cōl*]
▸**'coolly** *adv* ▸**'coolness** *n*

coolant ('ku:lənt) *n* **1** a fluid used to cool a system or to transfer heat from one part of it to another. **2** a liquid used to lubricate and cool the workpiece and cutting tool during machining.

cool bag *or* **box** *n* an insulated container for keeping food cool.

cool-down *n* another name for **warm-down.**

cool drink *n S. African.* a soft drink.

cooler ('ku:lə) *n* **1** a container, vessel, or apparatus for cooling, such as a heat exchanger. **2** a slang word for **prison. 3** a drink consisting of wine, fruit juice, and carbonated water.

coolibah *or* **coolabah** ('ku:lə,bɑ:) *n* an Australian eucalyptus that grows along rivers and has smooth bark and long narrow leaves. [from Abor.]

coolie *or* **cooly** ('ku:lɪ) *n, pl* **coolies.** an unskilled Oriental labourer. [C17: from Hindi *kulī*]

cooling-off period *n* **1** a period during which the contending sides to a dispute reconsider their options before taking further action. **2** *Brit.* a period, often 14 days, that begins when a sale contract or life-assurance policy is received by a member of the public, during which the contract or policy can be cancelled without loss.

cooling tower *n* a tall, hollow structure, designed to permit free passage of air, inside which hot water trickles down, becoming cool as it does so: the water is normally reused as part of an industrial process.

coomb, combe, coombe, *or* **comb** (ku:m) *n* **1** *Chiefly southern English.* a short valley or deep hollow. **2** *Chiefly northern English.* another name for a **cirque.** [OE *cumb*]

coon (ku:n) *n* **1** *Inf.* short for **raccoon. 2** *Offens. sl.* a Black or a native Australian. **3** *S. African offens.* a person of mixed race.

coonskin ('ku:n,skɪn) *n* **1** the pelt of a raccoon. **2** a raccoon cap with the tail hanging at the back. **3** *US.* an overcoat made of raccoon.

coop[1] ⓘ (ku:p) *n* **1** a cage or small enclosure for poultry or small animals. **2** a small narrow place of confinement, esp. a prison cell. **3** a wicker basket for catching fish. ◆ *vb* **4** (*tr;* often foll. by *up* or *in*) to confine in a restricted area. [C15: prob. from MLow G *kūpe* basket]

coop[2] *or* **co-op** ('kəʊ,ɒp) *n* a cooperative society or a shop run by a cooperative society.

cooper ('ku:pə) *n* **1** a person skilled in making and repairing barrels, casks, etc. ◆ *vb* **2** (*tr*) to make or mend (barrels, casks, etc.). [C13: from MDu. *cūper* or MLow G *kūper;* see COOP[1]]

cooperage ('ku:pərɪdʒ) *n* **1** Also called: **coopery.** the craft, place of work, or products of a cooper. **2** the labour fee charged by a cooper.

cooperate ⓘ *or* **co-operate** (kəʊ'ɒpə,reɪt) *vb* **cooperates, cooperating, cooperated** *or* **co-operates, co-operating, co-operated.** (*intr*) **1** to work or act together. **2** to be of assistance or be willing to assist. **3** *Econ.* to engage in economic cooperation. [C17: from LL *cooperārī* to combine, from L *operārī* to work]
▸**co'oper,ator** *or* **co-'oper,ator** *n*

cooperation ⓘ *or* **co-operation** (kəʊ,ɒpə'reɪʃən) *n* **1** joint operation or action. **2** assistance or willingness to assist. **3** *Econ.* the combination of consumers, workers, etc., in activities usually embracing production, distribution, or trade.
▸**co,oper'ationist** *or* **co-,oper'ationist** *n*

cooperative ⓘ *or* **co-operative** (kəʊ'ɒpərətɪv, -'ɒprə-) *adj* **1** willing to cooperate; helpful. **2** acting in conjunction with others; cooperating. **3a** (of an enterprise, farm, etc.) owned collectively and managed for joint economic benefit. **3b** (of an economy) based on collective ownership and cooperative use of the means of production and distribution. ◆ *n* **4** a cooperative organization, such as a farm.

cooperative society *n* a commercial enterprise owned and managed by and for the benefit of customers or workers.

coopt ⓘ *or* **co-opt** (kəʊ'ɒpt) *vb* (*tr*) to add (someone) to a committee, board, etc., by the agreement of the existing members. [C17: from L *cooptāre,* from *optāre* to choose]
▸**co'option, co-'option** *or* **,coop'tation, ,co-op'tation** *n*

coordinate ⓘ *or* **co-ordinate** *vb* (kəʊ'ɔ:dɪ,neɪt), **coordinates, coordinating, coordinated** *or* **co-ordinates, co-ordinating, co-ordinated. 1** (*tr*) to integrate (diverse elements) in a harmonious operation. **2** to place (things) in the same class, or (of things) to be placed in the same class, etc. **3** (*intr*) to work together harmoniously. **4** (*intr*) to take or be in the form of a harmonious order. ◆ *n* (kəʊ'ɔ:dɪnɪt). **5** *Maths.* any of a set of numbers that defines the location of a point with reference to a system of axes. **6** a person or thing equal in rank, type, etc. ◆ *adj* (kəʊ'ɔ:dɪnɪt). **7** of or involving coordination. **8** of the same rank, type, etc. **9** of or involving the use of coordinates: *coordinate geometry.* **10** *Chem.* denoting a type of covalent bond in which both the shared electrons are provided by one of the atoms.
▸**co'ordinative** *or* **co-'ordinative** *adj* ▸**co'ordi,nator** *or* **co-'ordi,nator** *n*

coordinate clause *n* one of two or more clauses in a sentence having the same status and introduced by coordinating conjunctions.

coordinates (kəʊ'ɔ:dɪnɪts) *pl n* clothes of matching or harmonious colours and design, suitable for wearing together.

coordinating conjunction *n* a conjunction that introduces coordinate clauses, such as *and, but,* and *or.*

coordination *or* **co-ordination** (kəʊ,ɔ:dɪ'neɪʃən) *n* balanced and effective interaction of movement, actions, etc. [C17: from LL *coordinātiō,* from L *ordinātiō* an arranging]

coot (ku:t) *n* **1** an aquatic bird of Europe and Asia, having dark plumage, and a white bill with a frontal shield: family Rallidae (rails, etc.). **2** a foolish person, esp. an old man. [C14: prob. from Low G]

cootie ('ku:tɪ) *n US & NZ.* a slang name for the body louse. [C20: from Maori & ? (for US) Malay *kutu* louse]

cop[1] (kɒp) *Sl.* ◆ *n* **1** another name for **policeman. 2** *Brit.* an arrest (esp. in **a fair cop**). ◆ *vb* **cops, copping, copped.** (*tr*) **3** to catch. **4** to steal. **5** to suffer (a punishment): *you'll cop a clout if you do that!* **6** **cop it sweet.** *Austral. sl.* **6a** to accept a punishment without complaint. **6b** to have good fortune. **7** **cop this!** just look at this! ◆ See also **cop out.** [C18: (vb) ?from obs. *cap* to arrest, from OF *caper* to seize]

cop[2] (kɒp) *n* **1** a conical roll of thread wound on a spindle. **2** *Now chiefly dialect.* the top or crest, as of a hill. [OE *cop, copp* top, summit]

cop[3] (kɒp) *n Brit. sl.* (*usually used with a negative*) value: *not much cop.* [C19: n use of COP[1]]

copal ('kəʊpəl, -pæl) *n* a hard aromatic resin obtained from various tropical trees and used in making varnishes and lacquers. [C16: from Sp., from Nahuatl *copalli*]

copartner (kəʊ'pɑ:tnə) *n* a partner or associate, esp. an equal partner in business.
▸**co'partnership** *n*

THESAURUS

trive, devise, dream up, fabricate, improvise, manufacture, plot, prepare, scheme, trump up

cool *adj* **1** = **cold**, chilled, chilling, chilly, coldish, nippy, refreshing **3** = **calm**, collected, composed, deliberate, dispassionate, imperturbable, laid-back (*inf.*), level-headed, placid, quiet, relaxed, sedate, self-controlled, self-possessed, serene, together (*sl.*), unemotional, unexcited, unfazed (*inf.*), unruffled **4** = **unfriendly**, aloof, apathetic, distant, frigid, incurious, indifferent, lukewarm, offhand, reserved, standoffish, uncommunicative, unconcerned, unenthusiastic, uninterested, unresponsive, unwelcoming **5** = **impudent**, audacious, bold, brazen, cheeky, impertinent, presumptuous, shameless **9** *Informal* = **sophisticated**, cosmopolitan, elegant, urbane ◆ *n* **12** *Slang* = **calmness**, composure, control, poise, self-control, self-discipline, self-possession, temper ◆ *vb* **14** = **chill**, cool off, freeze, lose heat, refrigerate **15** = **calm (down)**, abate, allay, assuage, dampen, lessen, moderate, quiet, temper
Antonyms *adj* ≠ **cold:** lukewarm, moderately hot, sunny, tepid, warm ≠ **calm:** agitated, delirious, excited, impassioned, nervous, overwrought, perturbed, tense, troubled, twitchy (*inf.*) ≠ **unfriendly:** amiable, chummy (*inf.*), cordial, friendly, outgoing, receptive, responsive, sociable, warm ◆ *vb* ≠ **chill:** heat, reheat, take the chill off, thaw, warm (up)

coolness *n* **1** = **coldness**, chilliness, freshness, nippiness **3** = **calmness**, collectedness, composedness, composure, control, deliberateness, dispassionateness, imperturbability, levelheadedness, placidity, placidness, quietness, sedateness, self-control, self-discipline, self-possession **4** = **unfriendliness**, aloofness, apathy, distantness, frigidity, frigidness, frostiness, impassiveness, impassivity, incuriosity, incuriousness, indifference, lukewarmness, offhandedness, poise, remoteness, reservedness, standoffishness, uncommunicativeness, unconcernedness, uninterestedness, unresponsiveness **5** = **impudence**, audaciousness, audacity, boldness, brazenness, cheekiness, impertinence, insolence, presumptuousness, shamelessness **9** *Informal* = **sophistication**, elegance, urbanity
Antonyms *n* ≠ **coldness:** sunniness, tepidness, warmness ≠ **calmness:** agitation, deliriousness, discomposure, disconcertedness, excitedness, impassionedness, nervousness, perturbation, tenseness, twitchiness (*inf.*) ≠ **unfriendliness:** affability, amiability, amiableness, chumminess (*inf.*), cordiality, friendliness, geniality, receptiveness, receptivity, responsiveness, sociability, sociableness, warmth

coop[1] *n* **1** = **pen**, box, cage, corral (*chiefly U.S. & Canad.*), enclosure, hutch, pound ◆ *vb* **4 coop up** = **confine**, cage, immure, impound, imprison, pen, pound, shut up

cooperate *vb* **1** = **work together**, collaborate, combine, concur, conduce, conspire, coordinate, join forces, pool resources, pull together **2** = **help**, abet, aid, assist, contribute, go along with, lend a helping hand, pitch in, play ball (*inf.*)
Antonyms *vb* ≠ **work together, help:** conflict, contend with, fight, hamper, hamstring, hinder, impede, obstruct, oppose, prevent, put the mockers on (*inf.*), resist, struggle against, stymie, thwart

cooperation *n* **1** = **teamwork**, collaboration, combined effort, concert, concurrence, esprit de corps, give-and-take, unity **2** = **help**, assistance, helpfulness, participation, responsiveness
Antonyms *n* ≠ **teamwork, help:** discord, dissension, hindrance, opposition, rivalry

cooperative *adj* **1** = **helpful**, accommodating, obliging, onside (*inf.*), responsive, supportive **2** = **shared**, coactive, collective, combined, concerted, coordinated, joint, unified, united

coopt *vb* = **appoint**, choose, elect

coordinate *vb* **1** = **bring together**, correlate, harmonize, integrate, match, mesh, organize,

cope[1] ❶ (kəup) *vb* **copes, coping, coped.** (*intr*) **1** (foll. by *with*) to contend (against). **2** to deal successfully (with); manage: *she coped well with the problem.* [C14: from OF *coper* to strike, cut, from *coup* blow]

cope[2] (kəup) *n* **1** a large ceremonial cloak worn at liturgical functions by priests of certain Christian sects. **2** any covering shaped like a cope. ◆ *vb* **copes, coping, coped. 3** (*tr*) to dress (someone) in a cope. [OE *cāp*, from Med. L *cāpa*, from LL *cappa* hooded cloak]

cope[3] (kəup) *vb* **copes, coping, coped.** (*tr*) **1** to provide (a wall, etc.) with a coping. ◆ *n* **2** another name for **coping.** [C17: prob. from F *couper* to cut]

copeck ('kəupɛk) *n* a variant spelling of **kopeck.**

Copenhagen interpretation (ˌkəupən'heɪgən, -'hɑː-; 'kəupənˌheɪ-, -ˌhɑː-) *n* an interpretation of quantum mechanics developed by Niels Bohr (1885–1962) and his colleagues at the University of Copenhagen, based on the concept of wave–particle duality and the idea that the observation influences the result of an experiment.

copepod ('kəupɪˌpɒd) *n* a minute marine or freshwater crustacean, an important constituent of plankton. [C19: from NL *copepoda*, from Gk *kōpē* oar + *pous* foot]

coper ('kəupə) *n* a horse dealer. [C17 (a dealer): from dialect *cope* to buy, barter, from Low G]

Copernican system (kə'pɜːnɪkən) *n* the theory published in 1543 by Copernicus (1473–1543), Polish astronomer, which stated that the earth and the planets rotated round the sun.

copestone ('kəupˌstəun) *n* **1** Also called: **coping stone.** a stone used to form a coping. **2** the stone at the top of a building, wall, etc.

copier ('kɒpɪə) *n* a person or device that copies.

copilot ('kəuˌpaɪlət) *n* a second or relief pilot of an aircraft.

coping ('kəupɪŋ) *n* the sloping top course of a wall, usually made of masonry or brick.

coping saw *n* a handsaw with a U-shaped frame used for cutting curves in a material too thick for a fret saw.

copious ❶ ('kəupɪəs) *adj* **1** abundant; extensive. **2** having an abundant supply. **3** full of words, ideas, etc.; profuse. [C14: from L *cōpiōsus*, from *cōpia* abundance]
▸'**copiously** *adv* ▸'**copiousness** *n*

coplanar (kəu'pleɪnə) *adj* lying in the same plane: *coplanar lines.*
▸ˌ**copla'narity** *n*

copolymer (kəu'pɒlɪmə) *n* a chemical compound of high molecular weight formed by uniting the molecules of two or more different compounds (monomers).

cop out ❶ *Sl.* ◆ *vb* **1** (*intr, adv*) to fail to assume responsibility or fail to perform. ◆ *n* **cop-out. 2** a way or an instance of avoiding responsibility or commitment. [C20: prob. from COP[1]]

copper[1] ('kɒpə) *n* **1** a malleable reddish metallic element occurring as the free metal, copper glance, and copper pyrites: used in such alloys as brass and bronze. Symbol: Cu; atomic no.: 29; atomic wt.: 63.54. Related adjs.: **cupric, cuprous. 2a** the reddish-brown colour of copper. **2b** (*as adj*) *copper hair.* **3** *Inf.* any copper or bronze coin. **4** *Chiefly Brit.* a large vessel, formerly of copper, used for boiling or washing. **5** any of various small widely distributed butterflies having reddish-brown wings. ◆ *vb* **6** (*tr*) to coat or cover with copper. [OE *coper*, from L *Cyprium aes* Cyprian metal, from Gk *Kupris* Cyprus]

copper[2] ('kɒpə) *n* a slang word for **policeman.** Often shortened to **cop.** [C19: from COP[1] (vb)]

copperas ('kɒpərəs) *n* a less common name for **ferrous sulphate.** [C14 *coperose*, via OF from Med. L *cuperosa*, ? orig. in *aqua cuprosa* copper water]

copper beech *n* a cultivated variety of European beech that has reddish leaves.

copper-bottomed *adj* reliable, esp. financially reliable. [from the practice of coating bottom of ships with copper to prevent the timbers rotting]

copper-fasten *vb* (*tr*) *Irish.* to make (a bargain or agreement) binding.

copperhead ('kɒpəˌhɛd) *n* **1** a venomous pit viper of the US, with a reddish-brown head. **2** a venomous marsh snake of Australia, with a reddish band behind the head.

copperplate ('kɒpəˌpleɪt) *n* **1** a polished copper plate on which a design has been etched or engraved. **2** a print taken from such a plate. **3** a fine handwriting based upon that used on copperplate engravings.

copper pyrites ('paɪraɪts) *n* (*functioning as sing*) another name for **chalcopyrite.**

coppersmith ('kɒpəˌsmɪθ) *n* a person who works in copper.

copper sulphate *n* a copper salt found naturally and made by the action of sulphuric acid on copper oxide: used as a mordant, in electroplating, and in plant sprays. Formula: $CuSO_4$.

coppice ('kɒpɪs) *n* **1** a dense growth of small trees or bushes, esp. one regularly trimmed back so that a continual supply of small poles and firewood is obtained. ◆ *vb* **coppices, coppicing, coppiced. 2** (*tr*) to trim back (trees or bushes) to form a coppice. [C14: from OF *copeiz*]
▸'**coppiced** *adj*

copra ('kɒprə) *n* the dried, oil-yielding kernel of the coconut. [C16: from Port., from Malayalam *koppara* coconut]

copro- *or before a vowel* **copr-** *combining form.* indicating dung or obscenity, as in **cop'rology** *n* preoccupation with excrement, **cop'rophagous** *adj* feeding on dung. [from Gk *kopros* dung]

copse (kɒps) *n* another word for **coppice** (sense 1). [C16: from COPPICE]

Copt (kɒpt) *n* **1** a member of the Coptic Church. **2** an Egyptian descended from the ancient Egyptians. [C17: from Ar., from Coptic *kyptios* Egyptian, from Gk *Aiguptios*, from *Aiguptos* Egypt]

Coptic ('kɒptɪk) *n* **1** an Afro-Asiatic language, written in the Greek alphabet but descended from ancient Egyptian. Extinct as a spoken language, it survives in the Coptic Church. ◆ *adj* **2** of this language. **3** of the Copts.

Coptic Church *n* the ancient Christian Church of Egypt.

copula ('kɒpjulə) *n, pl* **copulas** *or* **copulae** (-ˌliː). **1** a verb, such as *be, seem,* or *taste,* that is used to identify or link the subject with the complement of a sentence, as in *he became king, sugar tastes sweet.* **2** anything that serves as a link. [C17: from L: bond, from *co-* together + *apere* to fasten]
▸'**copular** *adj*

copulate ❶ ('kɒpjuˌleɪt) *vb* **copulates, copulating, copulated.** (*intr*) to perform sexual intercourse. [C17: from L *copulāre* to join together; see COPULA]
▸ˌ**copu'lation** *n* ▸'**copulatory** *adj*

copulative ('kɒpjulətɪv) *adj* **1** serving to join or unite. **2** of copulation. **3** *Grammar.* (of a verb) having the nature of a copula.

copy ❶ ('kɒpɪ) *n, pl* **copies. 1** an imitation or reproduction of an original. **2** a single specimen of something that occurs in a multiple edition, such as a book. **3a** matter to be reproduced in print. **3b** written matter or text as distinct from graphic material in books, etc. **4** the words used to present a promotional message in an advertisement. **5** *Journalism, inf.* suitable material for an article: *disasters are always good copy.* **6** *Arch.* a model to be copied, esp. an example of penmanship. ◆ *vb* **copies, copying, copied. 7** (when *tr,* often foll. by *out*) to make a copy (of). **8** (*tr*) to imitate as a model. **9** to imitate unfairly. [C14: from Med. L *cōpia* an imitation, from L: abundance]

copybook ('kɒpɪˌbuk) *n* **1** a book of specimens, esp. of penmanship, for imitation. **2** *Chiefly US.* a book for or containing documents. **3 blot one's copybook.** *Inf.* to spoil one's reputation by a mistake or indiscretion. **4** (*modifier*) trite or unoriginal.

copycat ('kɒpɪˌkæt) *n Inf.* **a** a person, esp. a child, who imitates or copies another. **b** (*as modifier*): *copycat murders.*

copyhold ('kɒpɪˌhəuld) *n Law.* (formerly) a tenure less than freehold of land in England evidenced by a copy of the Court roll.

copyist ('kɒpɪɪst) *n* **1** a person who makes written copies. **2** a person who imitates.

copyreader ('kɒpɪˌriːdə) *n US.* a person who edits and prepares newspaper copy for publication; subeditor.

copyright ('kɒpɪˌraɪt) *n* **1** the exclusive right to produce copies and to control an original literary, musical, or artistic work, granted by law for a specified number of years. ◆ *adj* **2** (of a work, etc.) subject to copyright. ◆ *vb* **3** (*tr*) to take out a copyright on.

copy typist *n* a typist whose job is to type from written or typed drafts rather than dictation.

copywriter ('kɒpɪˌraɪtə) *n* a person employed to write advertising copy.
▸'**copyˌwriting** *n*

coquet ❶ (kəu'kɛt, kɒ-) *vb* **coquets, coquetting, coquetted.** (*intr*) **1** to behave flirtatiously. **2** to dally or trifle. [C17: from F: a gallant, lit.: a little cock, from *coq* cock]
▸'**coquetry** *n*

coquette ❶ (kəu'kɛt, kɒ-) *n* **1** a woman who flirts. **2** any hummingbird of the genus *Lophornis.* [C17: from F, fem of COQUET]
▸**co'quettish** *adj* ▸**co'quettishness** *n*

THESAURUS

relate, synchronize, systematize ◆ *adj* **8** = **equivalent**, coequal, correlative, correspondent, equal, parallel, tantamount

cope[1] *vb* **1** *foll. by* **with** = **deal with**, contend with, dispatch, encounter, grapple with, handle, struggle with, tangle with, tussle with, weather, wrestle with **2** = **manage**, carry on, get by, hold one's own, make out (*inf.*), make the grade, rise to the occasion, struggle through, survive

copious *adj* **1-3** = **abundant**, ample, bounteous, bountiful, extensive, exuberant, full, generous, lavish, liberal, luxuriant, overflowing, plenteous, plentiful, profuse, rich, superabundant

copiousness *n* **1-3** = **abundance**, amplitude, bountifulness, bounty, cornucopia, exuberance, fullness, horn of plenty, lavishness, luxuriance, plentifulness, plenty, richness, superabundance

cop out *Slang* ◆ **vb 1** = **avoid**, abandon, desert, dodge, quit, renege, renounce, revoke, skip, skive (*Brit. sl.*), withdraw ◆ *n* **cop-out 2** = **dodge**, alibi, fraud, pretence, pretext

copulate *vb* = **have intercourse**, bonk (*inf.*), fuck (*taboo sl.*), have sex, hump (*taboo sl.*), screw (*taboo sl.*), shag (*taboo sl., chiefly Brit.*)

copulation *n* = **sexual intercourse**, carnal knowledge, coition, coitus, congress, coupling, intimacy, legover (*sl.*), love, lovemaking, mating, nookie (*sl.*), rumpy-pumpy (*sl.*), sex, sex act, the other (*inf.*), venery (*arch.*)

copy *n* **1** = **reproduction**, archetype, carbon copy, counterfeit, duplicate, facsimile, fake, fax, forgery, image, imitation, likeness, model, pattern, photocopy, Photostat (*Trademark*), print, replica, replication, representation, transcription, Xerox (*Trademark*) ◆ *vb* **7** = **reproduce**, counterfeit, duplicate, photocopy, Photostat (*Trademark*), replicate, transcribe, Xerox (*Trademark*) **8** = **imitate**, act like, ape, behave like, echo, emulate, follow, follow suit, follow the example of, mimic, mirror, parrot, repeat, simulate

Antonyms *n* ≠ **reproduction:** model, original, pattern, prototype, the real thing ◆ *vb* ≠ **reproduce:** create, originate

coquetry *n* **1, 2** = **flirtation**, dalliance, wantonness

coquettish *adj* **1** = **flirtatious**, amorous, arch,

Cor. *Bible. abbrev. for* Corinthians.
coracle ('kɒrəkᵊl) *n* a small roundish boat made of waterproofed hides stretched over a wicker frame. [C16: from Welsh *corwgl*]
coracoid ('kɒrəˌkɔɪd) *n* a paired ventral bone of the pectoral girdle in vertebrates. In mammals it is reduced to a peg (the **coracoid process**) on the scapula. [C18: from NL *coracoīdēs*, from Gk *korakoeidēs* like a raven, from *korax* raven]
coral ('kɒrəl) *n* **1** any of a class of marine colonial coelenterates having a calcareous, horny, or soft skeleton. **2a** the calcareous or horny material forming the skeleton of certain of these animals. **2b** (*as modifier*): *a coral reef.* **3** a rocklike aggregation of certain of these animals or their skeletons, forming an island or reef. **4a** something made of coral. **4b** (*as modifier*): *a coral necklace.* **5a** a yellowish-pink colour. **5b** (*as adj*): *coral lipstick.* **6** the roe of a lobster or crab, which becomes pink when cooked. [C14: from OF, from L *corāllium*, from Gk *korallion*, prob. of Semitic origin]
coral reef *n* a marine reef consisting of coral consolidated into limestone.
coralroot ('kɒrəlˌruːt) *n* a N temperate leafless orchid with branched roots resembling coral.
coral snake *n* **1** a venomous snake of tropical and subtropical America, marked with red, black, yellow, and white transverse bands. **2** any of various other brightly coloured snakes of Africa and SE Asia.
cor anglais ('kɔːr 'ɑːŋgleɪ) *n, pl* **cors anglais** ('kɔːz 'ɑːŋgleɪ). *Music.* a woodwind instrument, the alto of the oboe family. Also called: **English horn.** [C19: from F: English horn]
corbel ('kɔːbᵊl) *Archit.* ◆ *n* **1** a bracket, usually of stone or brick. ◆ *vb* **corbels, corbelling, corbelled** *or US* **corbels, corbeling, corbeled. 2** (*tr*) to lay (a stone) so that it forms a corbel. [C15: from OF, lit.: a little raven, from Med. L *corvellus*, from L *corvus* raven]
corbie ('kɔːbɪ) *n* a Scot. name for **raven**[1] (sense 1) or **crow**[1] (sense 1). [C15: from OF *corbin*, from L *corvīnus* CORVINE]
corbie-step *or* **corbel step** *n Archit.* any of a set of steps on the top of a gable. Also called: **crow step.**
cord ➊ (kɔːd) *n* **1** string or thin rope made of twisted strands. **2** a length of woven or twisted strands of silk, etc., used as a belt, etc. **3** a ribbed fabric, esp. corduroy. **4** the US and Canad. name for **flex** (sense 1). **5** *Anat.* any part resembling a rope: *the spinal cord.* **6** a unit for measuring cut wood, equal to 128 cubic feet. ◆ *vb* (*tr*) **7** to bind or furnish with a cord or cords. ◆ See also **cords.** [C13: from OF *corde*, from L *chorda*, from Gk *khordē*]
▸**'cordˌlike** *adj*
cordage ('kɔːdɪdʒ) *n* **1** *Naut.* the lines and rigging of a vessel. **2** an amount of wood measured in cords.
cordate ('kɔːdeɪt) *adj* heart-shaped.
corded ('kɔːdɪd) *adj* **1** bound or fastened with cord. **2** (of a fabric) ribbed. **3** (of muscles) standing out like cords.
cordial ➊ ('kɔːdɪəl) *adj* **1** warm and friendly: *a cordial greeting.* **2** stimulating. ◆ *n* **3** a drink with a fruit base: *lime cordial.* **4** another word for **liqueur.** [C14: from Med. L *cordiālis*, from L *cor* heart]
▸**'cordially** *adv*
cordiality ➊ (ˌkɔːdɪ'ælɪtɪ) *n, pl* **cordialities.** warmth of feeling.
cordillera (ˌkɔːdɪl'jɛərə) *n* a series of parallel ranges of mountains, esp. in the northwestern US. [C18: from Sp., from *cordilla*, lit.: a little cord]
cordite ('kɔːdaɪt) *n* any of various explosive materials containing cellulose nitrate, sometimes mixed with nitroglycerine. [C19: from CORD + -ITE[1], from its stringy appearance]
cordless ('kɔːdlɪs) *adj* (of an electrical device) operated by an internal battery so that no connection to mains supply is needed.
cordless telephone *n* a portable battery-powered telephone with a short-range radio link to a fixed base unit.
cordon ➊ ('kɔːdᵊn) *n* **1** a chain of police, soldiers, ships, etc., stationed around an area. **2** a ribbon worn as insignia of honour. **3** a cord or ribbon worn as an ornament. **4** *Archit.* another name for **string course. 5** *Horticulture.* a fruit tree consisting of a single stem bearing fruiting spurs, produced by cutting back all lateral branches. ◆ *vb* **6** (*tr; often foll. by off*) to put or form a cordon (around); close (off). [C16: from OF, lit.: a little cord, from *corde* CORD]
cordon bleu (*French* kɔrdɔ̃ blø) *n* **1** *French history.* the sky-blue ribbon worn by members of the highest order of knighthood under the Bourbon monarchy. **2** any very high distinction. ◆ *adj* **3** of or denoting food prepared to a very high standard. [F, lit.: blue ribbon]
cordon sanitaire *French.* (kɔrdɔ̃ sanitɛr) *n* **1** a guarded line isolating an infected area. **2** a line of buffer states shielding a country. [C19: lit.: sanitary line]
cordovan ('kɔːdəvᵊn) *n* a fine leather now made mainly from horsehide. [C16: from Sp. *cordobán* of Córdoba, city in Spain]
cords (kɔːdz) *pl n* trousers made of corduroy.
corduroy ('kɔːdəˌrɔɪ, ˌkɔːdə'rɔɪ) *n* a heavy cotton pile fabric with lengthways ribs. [C18: ?from the proper name *Corderoy*]
corduroys (ˌkɔːdə'rɔɪz, 'kɔːdəˌrɔɪz) *pl n* trousers or breeches of corduroy.
cordwainer ('kɔːdˌweɪnə) *n Arch.* a shoemaker or worker in leather. [C12: *cordwaner*, from OF, from OSp. *cordován* CORDOVAN]
cordwood ('kɔːdˌwʊd) *n* wood that has been cut into lengths of four feet so that it can be stacked in cords.
core ➊ (kɔː) *n* **1** the central part of certain fleshy fruits, such as the apple, consisting of the seeds. **2** the central or essential part of something: *the core of the argument.* **3** a piece of magnetic material, such as soft iron, inside an electromagnet or transformer. **4** *Geol.* the central part of the earth. **5** a cylindrical sample of rock, soil, etc., obtained by the use of a hollow drill. **6** *Physics.* the region of a nuclear reactor in which the reaction takes place. **7** *Computing.* **7a** a ferrite ring formerly used in a computer memory to store one bit of information. **7b** (*as modifier*): *core memory.* **8** *Archaeol.* a stone or flint from which flakes have been removed. **9** *Physics.* the nucleus together with all complete electron shells of an atom. ◆ *vb* **cores, coring, cored. 10** (*tr*) to remove the core from (fruit). [C14: from ?]
coreligionist (ˌkəʊrɪ'lɪdʒənɪst) *n* an adherent of the same religion as another.
coreopsis (ˌkɒrɪ'ɒpsɪs) *n* a plant of America and Africa, with yellow, brown, or yellow-and-red daisy-like flowers. [C18: from NL, from Gk *koris* bedbug + -OPSIS; so called from the appearance of the seed]
co-respondent (ˌkəʊrɪ'spɒndənt) *n Law.* a person cited in divorce proceedings, alleged to have committed adultery with the respondent.
core subjects *pl n Brit. education.* three foundation subjects (English, mathematics, and science) that are compulsory throughout each key stage in the National Curriculum.
core time *n* See **flexitime.**
corf (kɔːf) *n, pl* **corves.** *Brit.* a wagon or basket used formerly in mines. [C14: from MDu. *corf* or MLow G *korf*, prob. from L *corbis* basket]
corgi ('kɔːgɪ) *n* either of two short-legged sturdy breeds of dog, the Cardigan and the Pembroke. [C20: from Welsh, from *cor* dwarf + *ci* dog]
coriander (ˌkɒrɪ'ændə) *n* a European umbelliferous plant, cultivated for its aromatic seeds and leaves, used in flavouring foods. [C14: from OF *coriandre*, from L *coriandrum*, from Gk *koriannon*, from ?]
Corinthian (kə'rɪnθɪən) *adj* **1** of Corinth, a port in S Greece. **2** denoting one of the five classical orders of architecture: characterized by a bell-shaped capital having carved ornaments based on acanthus leaves. **3** *Obs.* given to luxury; dissolute. ◆ *n* **4** a native or inhabitant of Corinth.
Coriolis force (ˌkɒrɪ'əʊlɪs) *n* a hypothetical force postulated to explain a deflection in the path of a body moving relative to the earth: it is due to the earth's rotation and is to the left in the S hemisphere and to the right in the N hemisphere. [C19: after Gaspard G. *Coriolis* (1792–1843), F civil engineer]
corium ('kɔːrɪəm) *n, pl* **coria** (-rɪə). the deep inner layer of the skin, beneath the epidermis, containing connective tissue, blood vessels, and fat. Also called: **derma, dermis.** [C19: from L: rind, skin]
cork (kɔːk) *n* **1** the thick light porous outer bark of the cork oak. **2** a piece of cork used as a stopper. **3** an angling float. **4** Also called: **phellem.** *Bot.* a protective layer of dead impermeable cells on the outside of the stems and roots of woody plants. Related adj: **suberose.** ◆ *adj* **5** made of cork. ◆ *vb* (*tr*) **6** to stop up (a bottle, etc.) with or as with a cork. **7** (often foll. by *up*) to restrain. **8** to black (the face, hands, etc.) with burnt cork. [C14: prob. from Ar. *qurq*, from L *cortex* bark]
▸**'corkˌlike** *adj*
corkage ('kɔːkɪdʒ) *n* a charge made at a restaurant for serving wine, etc., bought off the premises.
corked (kɔːkt) *adj* tainted through having a cork containing excess tannin.
corker ('kɔːkə) *n Old-fashioned sl.* **1** something or somebody striking or outstanding. **2** an irrefutable remark that puts an end to discussion.
cork oak *n* an evergreen Mediterranean oak whose porous bark yields cork.
corkscrew ('kɔːkˌskruː) *n* **1** a device for drawing corks from bottles, typically consisting of a pointed metal spiral attached to a handle or screw mechanism. **2** (*modifier*) resembling a corkscrew in shape. ◆ *vb* **3** to move or cause to move in a spiral or zigzag course.
corm (kɔːm) *n* an organ of vegetative reproduction in plants such as the crocus, consisting of a globular stem base swollen with food and surrounded by papery scale leaves. [C19: from NL *cormus*, from Gk *kormos* tree trunk from which the branches have been lopped]
cormorant ('kɔːmərənt) *n* an aquatic bird having a dark plumage, a long neck and body, and a slender hooked beak. [C13: from OF *cormareng*, from *corp* raven + *-mareng* of the sea]
corn[1] (kɔːn) *n* **1** *Brit.* **1a** any of various cereal plants, esp. the predominant crop of a region, such as wheat in England and oats in Scotland. **1b** the seeds of such plants, esp. after harvesting. **1c** a single seed of such plants; a grain. **2** the usual US, Canad., Austral., and NZ name for **maize. 3** *Sl.* an idea, song, etc., regarded as banal or sentimental. ◆ *vb* (*tr*) **4a** to preserve in brine. **4b** to salt. [OE *corn*]

THESAURUS

come-hither (*inf.*), coy, dallying, flighty, flirty, inviting, teasing
cord *n* **1** = **rope**, line, string, twine
cordial *adj* **1** = **warm**, affable, affectionate, agreeable, cheerful, congenial, earnest, friendly, genial, heartfelt, hearty, sociable, warm-hearted, welcoming, wholehearted
Antonyms *adj* aloof, cold, distant, formal, frigid, reserved, unfriendly, ungracious
cordiality *n* = **warmth**, affability, amiability, friendliness, geniality, heartiness, sincerity, wholeheartedness
cordon *n* **1** = **chain**, barrier, line, ring ◆ *vb* **6** *foll. by* **off** = **surround**, close off, encircle, enclose, fence off, isolate, picket, separate
core *n* **1, 2** = **centre**, crux, essence, gist, heart, kernel, nub, nucleus, pith

corn[2] (kɔːn) *n* **1** a hardening of the skin, esp. of the toes, caused by pressure. **2 tread on (someone's) corns.** *Brit. inf.* to offend or hurt (someone) by touching on a sensitive subject. [C15: from OF *corne* horn, from L *cornū*]

corn borer *n* the larva of a moth native to Europe: in E North America a serious pest of maize.

corn bread *n Chiefly US.* bread made from maize meal. Also called: **Indian bread.**

corn bunting *n* a heavily built European songbird with a streaked brown plumage.

corncob (ˈkɔːnˌkɒb) *n* the core of an ear of maize, to which kernels are attached.

corncob pipe *n* a pipe with a bowl made from a dried corncob.

corncockle (ˈkɔːnˌkɒkᵊl) *n* a European plant that has reddish-purple flowers and grows in cornfields and by roadsides.

corncrake (ˈkɔːnˌkreɪk) *n* a common Eurasian rail with a buff speckled plumage and reddish wings.

corn dolly *n* a decorative figure made by plaiting straw.

cornea (ˈkɔːnɪə) *n, pl* **corneas** *or* **corneae** (-nɪˌiː). the convex transparent membrane that forms the anterior covering of the eyeball. [C14: from Med. L *cornea tēla* horny web, from L *cornū* HORN]
▸ **ˈcorneal** *adj*

corned (kɔːnd) *adj* (esp. of beef) cooked and then preserved or pickled in salt or brine.

cornel (ˈkɔːnᵊl) *n* any shrub of the genus *Cornus*, such as the dogwood. [C16: prob. from MLow G *kornelle*, ult. from L *cornus*]

cornelian (kɔːˈniːlɪən) *n* a variant spelling of **carnelian.**

corner ❶ (ˈkɔːnə) *n* **1** the place or angle formed by the meeting of two converging lines or surfaces. **2** a projecting angle of a solid object. **3** the place where two streets meet. **4** any small, secluded, or private place. **5** a dangerous position from which escape is difficult: *a tight corner.* **6** any region, esp. a remote place. **7** something used to protect or mark a corner, as of the hard cover of a book. **8** *Commerce.* a monopoly over the supply of a commodity so that its market price can be controlled. **9** *Soccer, hockey, etc.* a free kick or shot from the corner of the field, taken against a defending team when the ball goes out of play over their goal line after last touching one of their players. **10** either of two opposite angles of a boxing ring in which the opponents take their rests. **11 cut corners.** to take the shortest or easiest way, esp. at the expense of high standards. **12 turn the corner.** to pass the critical point (in an illness, etc.). **13** (*modifier*) on a corner: *a corner shop.* ◆ *vb* **14** (*tr*) to manoeuvre (a person or animal) into a position from which escape is difficult or impossible. **15** (*tr*) **15a** to acquire enough of (a commodity) to attain control of the market. **15b** Also: **engross.** to attain control of (a market) in such a manner. **16** (*intr*) (of vehicles, etc.) to turn a corner. **17** (*intr*) (in soccer, etc.) to take a corner. [C13: from OF *corniere*, from L *cornū* point, HORN]

cornerback (ˈkɔːnəˌbæk) *n American football.* a defensive back.

cornerstone ❶ (ˈkɔːnəˌstəʊn) *n* **1** a stone at the corner of a wall, uniting two intersecting walls. **2** a stone placed at the corner of a building during a ceremony to mark the start of construction. **3** a person or thing of prime importance: *the cornerstone of the whole argument.*

cornerwise (ˈkɔːnəˌwaɪz) *or* **cornerways** (ˈkɔːnəˌweɪz) *adv, adj* with a corner in front; diagonally.

cornet (ˈkɔːnɪt) *n* **1** a three-valved brass instrument of the trumpet family. **2** a person who plays the cornet. **3** a cone-shaped paper container for sweets, etc. **4** *Brit.* a cone-shaped wafer container for ice cream. **5** (formerly) the lowest rank of commissioned cavalry officer in the British Army. **6** the large white headdress of some nuns. [C14: from OF, from L *cornū* HORN]
▸ **corˈnetist** *or* **corˈnettist** *n*

corn exchange *n* a building where corn is bought and sold.

cornfield (ˈkɔːnˌfiːld) *n* a field planted with cereal crops.

cornflakes (ˈkɔːnˌfleɪks) *pl n* a breakfast cereal made from toasted maize.

cornflour (ˈkɔːnˌflaʊə) *n* a fine maize flour, used for thickening sauces. US and Canad. name: **cornstarch.**

cornflower (ˈkɔːnˌflaʊə) *n* a herbaceous plant, with blue, purple, pink, or white flowers, formerly a common weed in cornfields.

cornice (ˈkɔːnɪs) *n* **1** *Archit.* **1a** the top projecting mouldings of an entablature. **1b** a continuous horizontal projecting course or moulding at the top of a wall, building, etc. **2** an overhanging ledge of snow. [C16: from OF, from It., ?from L *cornix* crow, but infl. also by L *corōnis* decorative flourish]

corniche (ˈkɔːnɪʃ) *n* a coastal road, esp. one built into the face of a cliff. [C19: from *corniche road;* see CORNICE]

Cornish (ˈkɔːnɪʃ) *adj* **1** of Cornwall or its inhabitants. ◆ *n* **2** a former language of Cornwall: extinct by 1800. **3 the.** (*functioning as pl*) the natives or inhabitants of Cornwall.
▸ **ˈCornishman** *n*

Cornish pasty (ˈpæstɪ) *n Cookery.* a pastry case with a filling of meat and vegetables.

corn meal *n* meal made from maize. Also called: **Indian meal.**

corn salad *n* a plant which often grows in cornfields and whose leaves are sometimes used in salads. Also called: **lamb's lettuce.**

cornstarch (ˈkɔːnˌstɑːtʃ) *n* the US and Canad. name for **cornflour.**

cornucopia (ˌkɔːnjʊˈkəʊpɪə) *n* **1** a representation of a horn in painting, sculpture, etc., overflowing with fruit, vegetables, etc.; horn of plenty. **2** a great abundance. **3** a horn-shaped container. [C16: from LL, from L *cornū cōpiae* horn of plenty]
▸ **ˌcornuˈcopian** *adj*

corn whisky *n* whisky made from maize.

corny ❶ (ˈkɔːnɪ) *adj* **cornier, corniest.** *Sl.* **1** trite or banal. **2** sentimental or mawkish. **3** abounding in corn. [C16 (C20 in the sense banal): from CORN[1] + -Y[1]]

corolla (kəˈrɒlə) *n* the petals of a flower collectively, forming an inner floral envelope. [C17: dim. of L *corōna* crown]

corollary ❶ (kəˈrɒlərɪ) *n, pl* **corollaries. 1** a proposition that follows directly from the proof of another proposition. **2** an obvious deduction. **3** a natural consequence. [C14: from L *corollārium* money paid for a garland, from L *corolla* garland]

corona (kəˈrəʊnə) *n, pl* **coronas** *or* **coronae** (-niː). **1** a circle of light around a luminous body, usually the moon. **2** Also called: **aureole.** the outermost region of the sun's atmosphere, visible as a faint halo during a solar eclipse. **3** *Archit.* the flat vertical face of a cornice. **4** a circular chandelier. **5** *Bot.* **5a** the trumpet-shaped part of the corolla of daffodils and similar plants. **5b** a crown of leafy outgrowths from inside the petals of some flowers. **6** *Anat.* a crownlike structure. **7** a long cigar with blunt ends. **8** *Physics.* an electrical discharge appearing around the surface of a charged conductor. [C16: from L: crown]

coronach (ˈkɒrənəx) *n Scot. & Irish.* a dirge or lamentation for the dead. [C16: from Scot. Gaelic *corranach*]

coronary (ˈkɒrənərɪ) *adj* **1** *Anat.* designating blood vessels, nerves, ligaments, etc., that encircle a part or structure. ◆ *n, pl* **coronaries. 2** short for **coronary thrombosis.** [C17: from L *corōnārius* belonging to a wreath or crown]

coronary artery *n* either of the two arteries branching from the aorta and supplying blood to the heart.

coronary bypass *n* the surgical bypass of a narrowed or blocked coronary artery by grafting a section of a healthy blood vessel taken from another part of the patient's body.

coronary heart disease *n* any heart disorder caused by disease of the coronary arteries.

coronary thrombosis *n* a condition of interrupted blood flow to the heart due to a blood clot in a coronary artery.

coronation (ˌkɒrəˈneɪʃən) *n* the act or ceremony of crowning a monarch. [C14: from OF, from *coroner* to crown, from L *corōnāre*]

coroner (ˈkɒrənə) *n* a public official responsible for the investigation of violent, sudden, or suspicious deaths. [C14: from Anglo-F *corouner*, from OF *corone* CROWN]
▸ **ˈcoronerˌship** *n*

coronet (ˈkɒrənɪt) *n* **1** any small crown, esp. one worn by princes or peers. **2** a woman's jewelled circlet for the head. **3** the margin between the skin of a horse's pastern and the horn of the hoof. **4** the knob at the base of a deer's antler. [C15: from OF *coronete*]

coroutine (ˈkəʊruːˌtiːn) *n Computing.* a section of a computer program similar to but differing from a subroutine in that it can be left and re-entered at any point.

corp. *abbrev. for:* **1** corporation. **2** corporal.

corporal[1] ❶ (ˈkɔːpərəl, ˈkɔːprəl) *adj* of or relating to the body. [C14: from L *corporālis*, from *corpus* body]
▸ **ˌcorpoˈrality** *n* ▸ **ˈcorporally** *adv*

corporal[2] (ˈkɔːpərəl) *n* **1** a noncommissioned officer junior to a sergeant in the army, air force, or marines. **2** (in the Royal Navy) a petty officer who assists the master-at-arms. [C16: from OF, via It., from L *caput* head; ? also infl. in OF by *corps* body (of men)]

corporal[3] (ˈkɔːpərəl) *or* **corporale** (ˌkɔːpəˈreɪlɪ) *n* a white linen cloth on which the bread and wine are placed during the Eucharist. [C14: from Med. L *corporāle pallium* eucharistic altar cloth, from L *corporālis*, from *corpus* body (of Christ)]

Corporal of Horse *n* a noncommissioned rank in the British Army, above that of sergeant and below that of staff sergeant.

corporal punishment *n* punishment of a physical nature, such as caning.

corporate ❶ (ˈkɔːpərɪt) *adj* **1** forming a corporation; incorporated. **2** of a corporation or corporations: *corporate finance.* **3** of or belonging to a united group; joint. [C15: from L *corporātus*, from *corpus* body]
▸ **ˈcorporatism** *n*

corporate advertising *n* advertising designed to publicize or create a favourable image of a company rather than a particular product.

THESAURUS

corner *n* **1 = angle**, bend, crook, joint **4 = space**, cavity, cranny, hideaway, hide-out, hidey-hole (*inf.*), hole, niche, nook, recess, retreat **5 = tight spot**, hole (*inf.*), hot water (*inf.*), pickle (*inf.*), predicament, spot (*inf.*) ◆ *vb* **14 = trap**, bring to bay, run to earth **15 = monopolize**, dominate, engross, hog

cornerstone *n* **1 = quoin 3 = basis**, bedrock, key, premise, starting point

corny *adj Slang* **1, 2 = unoriginal**, banal, commonplace, dull, feeble, hackneyed, maudlin, mawkish, old-fashioned, old hat, sentimental, stale, stereotyped, trite

corollary *n* **2 = deduction**, conclusion, induction, inference **3 = consequence**, result, sequel, upshot

corporal[1] *adj* **= bodily**, anatomical, carnal, corporeal (*arch.*), fleshly, material, physical, somatic

corporate *adj* **3 = collective**, allied, collaborative, combined, communal, joint, merged, pooled, shared, united

corporate anorexia *n* a malaise of a business organization resulting from making too many creative people redundant in a cost-cutting exercise.

corporate culture *n* the distinctive ethos of an organization that influences the level of formality, loyalty, and general behaviour of its employees.

corporate identity *or* **image** *n* the way an organization is presented to or perceived by its members and the public.

corporate raider *n Finance.* a person or organization that acquires a substantial holding of the shares of a company in order to take it over or to force its management to act in a desired way.

corporate venturing *n Finance.* the provision of venture capital by one company for another in order to obtain information about the company requiring capital or as a step towards acquiring it.

corporation Ⓣ (ˌkɔːpəˈreɪʃən) *n* **1** a group of people authorized by law to act as an individual and having its own powers, duties, and liabilities. **2** Also called: **municipal corporation.** the municipal authorities of a city or town. **3** a group of people acting as one body. **4** See **public corporation. 5** *Inf.* a large paunch.
▸ˈ**corporative** *adj*

corporation tax *n* a British tax on the profits of a company or other incorporated body.

corporeal Ⓣ (kɔːˈpɔːrɪəl) *adj* **1** of the nature of the physical body; not spiritual. **2** of a material nature; physical. [C17: from L *corporeus*, from *corpus* body]
▸**cor,poreˈality** *or* **corporeity** (ˌkɔːpəˈriːɪtɪ) *n* ▸**corˈporeally** *adv*

corps Ⓣ (kɔː) *n, pl* **corps** (kɔːz). **1** a military formation that comprises two or more divisions. **2** a military body with a specific function: *medical corps.* **3** a body of people associated together: *the diplomatic corps.* [C18: from F, from L *corpus* body]

corps de ballet (ˈkɔː də ˈbæleɪ) *n* the members of a ballet company who dance together in a group.

corps diplomatique (ˌdɪpləʊmæˈtiːk) *n* another name for **diplomatic corps.**

corpse Ⓣ (kɔːps) *n* a dead body, esp. of a human being. [C14: from OF *corps*, from L *corpus*]

corpulent Ⓣ (ˈkɔːpjʊlənt) *adj* physically bulky; fat. [C14: from L *corpulentus*]
▸ˈ**corpulence** *n*

cor pulmonale (ˌkɔː ˌpʌlməˈnɑːlɪ) *n* pulmonary heart disease: a serious heart condition in which there is enlargement and failure of the right ventricle resulting from lung disease. [NL]

corpus Ⓣ (ˈkɔːpəs) *n, pl* **corpora** (-pərə). **1** a body of writings, esp. by a single author or on a specific topic: *the corpus of Dickens' works.* **2** the main body or substance of something. **3** *Anat.* **3a** any distinct mass or body. **3b** the main part of an organ or structure. **4** *Obs.* a corpse. [C14: from L: body]

Corpus Christi (ˈkrɪstɪ) *n Chiefly RC Church.* a festival in honour of the Eucharist, observed on the Thursday after Trinity Sunday. [C14: from L: body of Christ]

corpuscle (ˈkɔːpʌsᵊl) *n* **1** any cell or similar minute body that is suspended in a fluid, esp. any of the **red blood corpuscles** (see **erythrocyte**) or **white blood corpuscles** (see **leucocyte**). **2** Also: **corpuscule** (kɔːˈpʌskjuːl). any minute particle. [C17: from L *corpusculum* a little body, from *corpus* body]
▸**corpuscular** (kɔːˈpʌskjʊlə) *adj*

corpuscular theory *n* the theory, originally proposed by Newton, that light consists of a stream of particles. Cf. **wave theory.**

corpus delicti (dɪˈlɪktaɪ) *n Law.* the body of facts that constitute an offence. [NL, lit.: the body of the crime]

corpus juris (ˈdʒʊərɪs) *n* a body of law, esp. of a nation or state. [from LL, lit.: a body of law]

corpus luteum (ˈluːtɪəm) *n, pl* **corpora lutea** (ˈluːtɪə). a mass of tissue that forms in a Graafian follicle following release of an ovum. [NL, lit.: yellow body]

corral Ⓣ (kɒˈrɑːl) *n* **1** *Chiefly US & Canad.* an enclosure for cattle or horses. **2** *Chiefly US.* (formerly) a defensive enclosure formed by a ring of covered wagons. ◆ *vb* **corrals, corralling, corralled.** (*tr*) *US & Canad.* **3** to drive into a corral. **4** *Inf.* to capture. [C16: from Sp., ult. from L *currere* to run]

corrasion (kəˈreɪʒən) *n* erosion of a rock surface by rock fragments transported over it by water, wind, or ice. [C17: from L *corrādere* to scrape together]

correa (ˈkɒrɪə, kəˈriːə) *n* an Australian evergreen shrub with large showy tubular flowers. [C19: after Jose Francesco *Correa* da Serra (1750-1823), Portuguese botanist]

correct Ⓣ (kəˈrɛkt) *vb* (*tr*) **1** to make free from errors. **2** to indicate the errors in. **3** to rebuke or punish in order to improve: *to stand corrected.* **4** to rectify (a malfunction, ailment, etc.). **5** to adjust or make conform, esp. to a standard. ◆ *adj* **6** true; accurate: *the correct version.* **7** in conformity with accepted standards: *correct behaviour.* [C14: from L *corrigere* to make straight, from *com-* (intensive) + *regere* to rule]
▸**corˈrectly** *adv* ▸**corˈrectness** *n*

correction Ⓣ (kəˈrɛkʃən) *n* **1** the act of correcting. **2** something substituted for an error; an improvement. **3** a reproof. **4** a quantity added to or subtracted from a scientific calculation or observation to increase its accuracy.
▸**corˈrectional** *adj*

corrective Ⓣ (kəˈrɛktɪv) *adj* **1** tending or intended to correct. ◆ *n* **2** something that tends or is intended to correct.

correlate Ⓣ (ˈkɒrɪˌleɪt) *vb* **correlates, correlating, correlated. 1** to place or be placed in a complementary or reciprocal relationship. **2** (*tr*) to establish or show a correlation between. ◆ *n* **3** either of two things mutually related.

correlation Ⓣ (ˌkɒrɪˈleɪʃən) *n* **1** a mutual relationship between two or more things. **2** the act of correlating or the state of being correlated. **3** *Statistics.* the extent of correspondence between the ordering of two variables. [C16: from Med. L *correlātiō*, from *com-* together + *relātiō* RELATION]
▸ˌ**correˈlational** *adj*

correlation coefficient *n Statistics.* a statistic measuring the degree of correlation between two variables.

correlative (kɒˈrɛlətɪv) *adj* **1** in complementary or reciprocal relationship; corresponding. **2** denoting words, usually conjunctions, occurring together though not adjacently in certain grammatical constructions, as *neither* and *nor.* ◆ *n* **3** either of two things that are correlative. **4** a correlative word.
▸**corˈrelatively** *adv* ▸**cor,relaˈtivity** *n*

correspond Ⓣ (ˌkɒrɪˈspɒnd) *vb* (*intr*) **1** (usually foll. by *with* or *to*) to be consistent or compatible (with); tally (with). **2** (usually foll. by *to*) to be similar in character or function. **3** (usually foll. by *with*) to communicate by letter. [C16: from Med. L *correspondēre*, from L *respondēre* to RESPOND]
▸ˌ**correˈsponding** *adj* ▸ˌ**correˈspondingly** *adv*

USAGE NOTE See at **similar.**

correspondence Ⓣ (ˌkɒrɪˈspɒndəns) *n* **1** the condition of agreeing or corresponding. **2** similarity. **3** agreement or conformity. **4a** communication by letters. **4b** the letters so exchanged.

correspondence school *n* an educational institution that offers tuition (**correspondence courses**) by post.

correspondent Ⓣ (ˌkɒrɪˈspɒndənt) *n* **1** a person who communicates

THESAURUS

corporation *n* **1, 3** = **business**, association, corporate body, society **2** = **town council**, civic authorities, council, municipal authorities **5** *Informal* = **paunch**, beer belly (*inf.*), middle-age spread (*inf.*), pod, pot, potbelly, spare tyre (*Brit. sl.*), spread (*inf.*)

corporeal *adj* **1, 2** = **physical**, bodily, fleshy, human, material, mortal, substantial

corps *n* **1-3** = **team**, band, body, company, contingent, crew, detachment, division, regiment, squad, squadron, troop, unit

corpse *n* = **body**, cadaver, carcass, remains, stiff (*sl.*)

corpulence *n* = **fatness**, beef, blubber, burliness, *embonpoint*, fleshiness, obesity, plumpness, portliness, rotundity, stoutness, tubbiness

corpulent *adj* = **fat**, beefy (*inf.*), bulky, burly, fattish, fleshy, large, lusty, obese, overweight, plump, portly, roly-poly, rotund, stout, tubby, well-padded
Antonyms *adj* anorexic, bony, emaciated, gaunt, scrawny, skin and bones (*inf.*), skinny, slim, thin, thin as a rake, underweight

corpus *n* **1** = **collection**, body, compilation, complete works, entirety, *oeuvre*, whole

corral *U.S. & Canad.* ◆ *n* **1** = **enclosure**, confine, coop, fold, pen, yard ◆ *vb* **3** = **enclose**, cage, confine, coop up, fence in, impound, mew, pen in

correct *vb* **1** = **rectify**, adjust, amend, cure, emend, improve, redress, reform, regulate, remedy, right, set the record straight **3** = **punish**, admonish, chasten, chastise, chide, discipline, rebuke, reprimand, reprove ◆ *adj* **6** = **true**, accurate, equitable, exact, faultless, flawless, just, O.K. *or* okay (*inf.*), on the right lines, precise, regular, right, strict **7** = **proper**, acceptable, appropriate, diplomatic, fitting, kosher (*inf.*), O.K. *or* okay (*inf.*), seemly, standard
Antonyms *vb* ≠ **rectify:** damage, harm, impair, ruin, spoil ≠ **punish:** compliment, excuse, praise ◆ *adj* ≠ **true:** false, inaccurate, incorrect, untrue, wrong ≠ **proper:** improper, inappropriate, unacceptable, unfitting, unsuitable

correction *n* **1, 2** = **rectification**, adjustment, alteration, amendment, emendation, improvement, modification, righting **3** = **punishment**, admonition, castigation, chastisement, discipline, reformation, reproof

corrective *adj* **1** = **disciplinary**, penal, punitive, reformatory

correctly *adv* **6** = **rightly**, accurately, aright, perfectly, precisely, properly, right

correctness *n* **6** = **truth**, accuracy, exactitude, exactness, faultlessness, fidelity, preciseness, precision, regularity **7** = **decorum**, *bon ton*, civility, good breeding, propriety, seemliness

correlate *vb* **1, 2** = **correspond**, associate, compare, connect, coordinate, equate, interact, parallel, tie in

correlation *n* **1** = **correspondence**, alternation, equivalence, interaction, interchange, interdependence, interrelationship, reciprocity

correspond *vb* **1** *usually foll. by* **with** *or* **to** = **be consistent**, accord, agree, be related, coincide, complement, conform, correlate, dovetail, fit, harmonize, match, square, tally **3** = **communicate**, exchange letters, keep in touch, write
Antonyms *vb* ≠ **be consistent:** be at variance, be dissimilar, be inconsistent, belie, be unlike, differ, disagree, diverge, vary

correspondence *n* **1-3** = **relation**, agreement, analogy, coincidence, comparability, comparison, concurrence, conformity, congruity, correlation, fitness, harmony, match, similarity **4** = **letters**, communication, mail, post, writing

correspondent *n* **1** = **letter writer**, pen friend *or* pal **2** = **reporter**, contributor, gazetteer (*arch.*), journalist, journo (*sl.*), special correspondent ◆ *adj* **4** = **corresponding**, analogous, by letter. **2** a person employed by a newspaper, etc., to report on a special subject or from a foreign country. **3** a person or firm that has regular business relations with another, esp. one abroad. ◆ *adj* **4** similar or analogous.

corrida (ko'rriða) *n* the Spanish word for **bullfight**. [Sp., from *corrida de toros*, lit.: a running of bulls]

corridor ❶ ('kɒrɪˌdɔː) *n* **1** a passage connecting parts of a building. **2** a strip of land or airspace that affords access, either from a landlocked country to the sea or from a state to an exclave. **3** a passageway connecting the compartments of a railway coach. **4** a flight path that affords safe access for intruding aircraft. **5** the path that a spacecraft must follow when re-entering the atmosphere, above which lift is insufficient and below which heating effects are excessive. **6 corridors of power.** the higher echelons of government, the Civil Service, etc., considered as the location of power and influence. [C16: from OF, from OIt. *corridore*, lit.: place for running]

corrie ('kɒrɪ) *n* **1** (in Scotland) a circular hollow on a hillside. **2** *Geol.* another name for **cirque**. [C18: from Gaelic *coire* cauldron]

corrigendum (ˌkɒrɪ'dʒɛndəm) *n, pl* **corrigenda** (-də). **1** an error to be corrected. **2** (*sometimes pl*) Also called: **erratum.** a slip of paper inserted into a book after printing, listing corrections. [C19: from L: that which is to be corrected]

corrigible ('kɒrɪdʒɪbᵊl) *adj* **1** capable of being corrected. **2** submissive. [C15: from OF, from Med. L *corrigibilis*, from L *corrigere* to CORRECT]

corroborate ❶ (kə'rɒbəˌreɪt) *vb* **corroborates, corroborating, corroborated.** (*tr*) to confirm or support (facts, opinions, etc.), esp. by providing fresh evidence. [C16: from L *corrōborāre*, from *rōborāre* to make strong, from *rōbur* strength]
▸**corˌrobo'ration** *n* ▸**corroborative** (kə'rɒbərətɪv) *or* **cor'roboratory** *adj* ▸**cor'roboˌrator** *n*

corroboree (kə'rɒbərɪ) *n Austral.* **1** a native assembly of sacred, festive, or warlike character. **2** *Inf.* any noisy gathering. [C19: from Abor.]

corrode ❶ (kə'rəʊd) *vb* **corrodes, corroding, corroded. 1** to eat away or be eaten away, esp. as in the oxidation or rusting of a metal. **2** (*tr*) to destroy gradually: *his jealousy corroded his happiness.* [C14: from L *corrōdere* to gnaw to pieces, from *rōdere* to gnaw]
▸**cor'rodible** *adj*

corrosion (kə'rəʊʒən) *n* **1** a process in which a solid, esp. a metal, is eaten away and changed by a chemical action, as in the oxidation of iron. **2** slow deterioration by being eaten or worn away. **3** the product of corrosion.

corrosive ❶ (kə'rəʊsɪv) *adj* **1** tending to eat away or consume. ◆ *n* **2** a corrosive substance, such as a strong acid.
▸**cor'rosively** *adv* ▸**cor'rosiveness** *n*

corrosive sublimate *n* another name for **mercuric chloride.**

corrugate ('kɒrʊˌgeɪt) *vb* **corrugates, corrugating, corrugated.** (*usually tr*) to fold or be folded into alternate furrows and ridges. [C18: from L *corrūgāre*, from *rūga* a wrinkle]
▸**'corruˌgated** *adj* ▸**ˌcorru'gation** *n*

corrugated iron *n* a thin sheet of iron or steel, formed with alternating ridges and troughs.

corrupt ❶ (kə'rʌpt) *adj* **1** open to or involving bribery or other dishonest practices: *a corrupt official; corrupt practices.* **2** morally depraved. **3** putrid or rotten. **4** (of a text or manuscript) made meaningless or different in meaning by scribal errors or alterations. **5** (of computer programs or data) containing errors. ◆ *vb* **6** to become or cause to become dishonest or disloyal. **7** (*tr*) to deprave. **8** (*tr*) to infect or contaminate. **9** (*tr*) to cause to become rotten. **10** (*tr*) to alter (a text, etc.) from the original. **11** (*tr*) *Computing.* to introduce errors into (data or a program). [C14: from L *corruptus* spoiled, from *corrumpere* to ruin, from *rumpere* to break]
▸**cor'rupter** *or* **cor'ruptor** *n* ▸**cor'ruptly** *adv* ▸**cor'ruptness** *n*

corruptible (kə'rʌptɪbᵊl) *adj* capable of being corrupted.
▸**cor'ruptibly** *adv*

corruption ❶ (kə'rʌpʃən) *n* **1** the act of corrupting or state of being corrupt. **2** depravity. **3** dishonesty, esp. bribery. **4** decay. **5** alteration, as of a manuscript. **6** an altered form of a word.

corsage (kɔː'sɑːʒ) *n* **1** a small bunch of flowers worn pinned to the lapel, bosom, etc. **2** the bodice of a dress. [C15: from OF, from *cors* body, from L *corpus*]

corsair ('kɔːsɛə) *n* **1** a pirate. **2** a privateer, esp. of the Barbary Coast, the Mediterranean coast of N Africa. [C15: from OF *corsaire*, from Med. L *cursārius*, from L *cursus* a running]

corse (kɔːs) *n* an archaic word for **corpse.**

corselet ('kɔːslɪt) *n* **1** Also spelt: **corslet.** a piece of armour for the top part of the body. **2** a one-piece foundation garment. [C15: from OF, from *cors* bodice, from L *corpus* body]

corset ❶ ('kɔːsɪt) *n* **1a** a stiffened, elasticated, or laced foundation garment, worn esp. by women. **1b** a similar garment worn because of injury, weakness, etc., by either sex. **2** *Inf.* a restriction or limitation, esp. government control of bank lending. ◆ *vb* **3** (*tr*) to dress or enclose in, or as in, a corset. [C14: from OF, lit.: a little bodice]
▸**corsetière** (ˌkɔːsɛtɪ'ɛə) *n* ▸**'corsetry** *n*

cortege ❶ *or* **cortège** (kɔː'teɪʒ) *n* **1** a formal procession, esp. a funeral procession. **2** a train of attendants; retinue. [C17: from F, from It. *corteggio*, from *corteggiare* to attend]

cortex ('kɔːtɛks) *n, pl* **cortices** (-tɪˌsiːz). **1** *Anat.* the outer layer of any organ or part, such as the grey matter in the brain that covers the cerebrum (**cerebral cortex**). **2** *Bot.* **2a** the tissue in plant stems and roots between the vascular bundles and the epidermis. **2b** the outer layer of a part such as the bark of a stem. [C17: from L: bark, outer layer]
▸**cortical** ('kɔːtɪkᵊl) *adj*

corticate ('kɔːtɪkɪt, -ˌkeɪt) *or* **corticated** *adj* (of plants, seeds, etc.) having a bark, husk, or rind. [C19: from L *corticātus*]

cortisone ('kɔːtɪˌzəʊn) *n* a steroid hormone, the synthetic form of which has been used in treating rheumatoid arthritis, allergic and skin diseases, leukaemia, etc. [C20: from *corticosterone*, a hormone]

corundum (kə'rʌndəm) *n* a hard mineral consisting of aluminium oxide: used as an abrasive. Precious varieties include ruby and white sapphire. Formula: Al_2O_3. [C18: from Tamil *kuruntam*; rel. to Sansk. *kuruvinda* ruby]

coruscate ('kɒrəˌskeɪt) *vb* **coruscates, coruscating, coruscated.** (*intr*) to emit flashes of light; sparkle. [C18: from L *coruscāre* to flash]
▸**ˌcorus'cation** *n*

corvée ('kɔːveɪ) *n* **1** *European history.* a day's unpaid labour owed by a feudal vassal to his lord. **2** the practice or an instance of forced labour. [C14: from OF, from LL *corrogāta* contribution, from L *corrogāre* to collect, from *rogāre* to ask]

corvette (kɔː'vɛt) *n* a lightly armed escort warship. [C17: from OF, ?from MDu. *corf*]

corvine ('kɔːvaɪn) *adj* **1** of or resembling a crow. **2** of the passerine bird family Corvidae, which includes the crows, ravens, rooks, jackdaws, magpies, and jays. [C17: from L *corvīnus*, from *corvus* a raven]

Corybant ('kɒrɪˌbænt) *n, pl* **Corybants** *or* **Corybantes** (ˌkɒrɪ'bæntiːz). *Classical myth.* a wild attendant of the goddess Cybele. [C14: from L *Corybās*, from Gk *Korubas*]
▸**ˌCory'bantic** *adj*

corymb ('kɒrɪmb, -rɪm) *n* an inflorescence in the form of a flat-topped flower cluster with the oldest flowers at the periphery. [C18: from L *corymbus*, from Gk *korumbos* cluster]

coryza (kə'raɪzə) *n* acute inflammation of the mucous membrane of the nose, with discharge of mucus; a head cold. [C17: from LL: catarrh, from Gk *koruza*]

cos[1] *or* **cos lettuce** (kɒs) *n* a variety of lettuce with a long slender head and crisp leaves. Usual US and Canad. name: **romaine.** [C17: after *Kos*, the Aegean island of its origin]

cos[2] (kɒz) *abbrev. for* cosine.

Cosa Nostra ('kəʊzə 'nɒstrə) *n* the branch of the Mafia that operates in the US. [It.: our thing]

cosec ('kəʊsɛk) *abbrev. for* cosecant.

THESAURUS

comparable, like, of a piece, parallel, reciprocal, similar

corresponding *adj* **2** = **related**, analogous, answering, complementary, correlative, correspondent, equivalent, identical, interrelated, matching, reciprocal, similar, synonymous

corridor *n* **1** = **passage**, aisle, alley, hallway, passageway

corroborate *vb* = **support**, authenticate, back up, bear out, confirm, document, endorse, establish, ratify, substantiate, sustain, validate
Antonyms *vb* contradict, disprove, invalidate, negate, rebut, refute

corroboration *n* = **support**, authentication, certification, circumstantiation, confirmation, documentation, endorsement, establishment, fortification, ratification, substantiation, sustainment, validation

corrode *vb* **1, 2** = **eat away**, canker, consume, corrupt, deteriorate, erode, gnaw, impair, oxidize, rust, waste, wear away

corrosive *adj* **1** = **corroding**, acrid, biting, caustic, consuming, erosive, virulent, vitriolic, wasting, wearing

corrupt *adj* **1** = **dishonest**, bent (*sl.*), bribable, crooked (*inf.*), fraudulent, rotten, shady (*inf.*), unethical, unprincipled, unscrupulous, venal **2** = **depraved**, abandoned, debased, defiled, degenerate, demoralized, dishonoured, dissolute, profligate, vicious **3** = **contaminated**, adulterated, decayed, defiled, infected, polluted, putrescent, putrid, rotten, tainted **4** = **distorted**, altered, doctored, falsified ◆ *vb* **6** = **bribe**, buy off, entice, fix (*inf.*), grease (someone's) palm (*sl.*), lure, square, suborn **7** = **deprave**, debauch, demoralize, pervert, subvert **8, 9** = **contaminate**, adulterate, debase, defile, infect, putrefy, spoil, taint, vitiate **10** = **distort**, doctor, tamper with
Antonyms *adj* ≠ **dishonest, depraved:** ethical, honest, honourable, moral, noble, principled, righteous, scrupulous, straight, upright, virtuous ◆ *vb* ≠ **deprave:** correct, reform ≠ **contaminate:** purify

corrupted *adj* **6, 7** = **depraved**, abandoned, debased, debauched, defiled, degenerate, demoralized, dishonoured, perverted, profligate, reprobate, warped **8, 9** = **contaminated**, adulterated, decayed, defiled, dirtied, infected, polluted, putrefied, rotten, soiled, spoiled, stained, sullied, tainted, tarnished, vitiated **10** = **distorted**, altered, doctored, falsified

corruption *n* **2** = **depravity**, baseness, decadence, degeneration, degradation, evil, immorality, impurity, iniquity, perversion, profligacy, sinfulness, turpitude, vice, viciousness, wickedness **3** = **dishonesty**, breach of trust, bribery, bribing, crookedness (*inf.*), demoralization, extortion, fiddling (*inf.*), fraud, fraudulency, graft (*inf.*), jobbery, profiteering, shadiness, shady dealings (*inf.*), unscrupulousness, venality **4** = **rotting**, adulteration, debasement, decay, defilement, foulness, infection, pollution, putrefaction, putrescence, rot, rottenness **5** = **distortion**, doctoring, falsification

corset *n* **1a** = **girdle**, belt, bodice, corselet, foundation garment, panty girdle, stays (*rare*)

cortege *n* **1, 2** = **procession**, cavalcade, entourage, retinue, suite, train

cosecant (kəʊˈsiːkənt) *n* (of an angle) a trigonometric function that in a right-angled triangle is the ratio of the length of the hypotenuse to that of the opposite side.

coset (ˈkəʊˌsɛt) *n Maths.* a set that produces a specified larger set when added to another set.

cosh[1] (kɒʃ) *Brit.* ◆ *n* **1** a blunt weapon, often made of hard rubber; bludgeon. **2** an attack with such a weapon. ◆ *vb* **3** to hit with such a weapon, esp. on the head. [C19: from Romany *kosh*]

cosh[2] (kɒʃ, kɒsˈeɪtʃ) *n* hyperbolic cosine. [C19: from COS(INE) + H(YPERBOLIC)]

cosignatory (kəʊˈsɪɡnətərɪ, -trɪ) *n, pl* **cosignatories. 1** a person, country, etc., that signs a document jointly with others. ◆ *adj* **2** signing jointly.

cosine (ˈkəʊˌsaɪn) *n* (of an angle) a trigonometric function that in a right-angled triangle is the ratio of the length of the adjacent side to that of the hypotenuse. [C17: from NL *cosinus;* see CO-, SINE[1]]

cosmetic ➊ (kɒzˈmɛtɪk) *n* **1** any preparation applied to the body, esp. the face, with the intention of beautifying it. ◆ *adj* **2** serving or designed to beautify the body, esp. the face. **3** having no other function than to beautify: *cosmetic illustrations in a book.* [C17: from Gk *kosmētikos,* from *kosmein* to arrange, from *kosmos* order]
▸**cosˈmetically** *adv*

cosmic ➊ (ˈkɒzmɪk) *adj* **1** of or relating to the whole universe: *cosmic laws.* **2** occurring or originating in outer space, esp. as opposed to the vicinity of the earth: *cosmic rays.* **3** immeasurably extended; vast.
▸**ˈcosmically** *adv*

cosmic dust *n* fine particles of solid matter occurring throughout interstellar space and often collecting into clouds of extremely low density.

cosmic rays *pl n* radiation consisting of atomic nuclei, esp. protons, of very high energy, that reach the earth from outer space. Also called: **cosmic radiation.**

cosmic string *n* any of a number of linear defects in space-time postulated in certain theories of cosmology to exist in the universe as a consequence of the big bang.

cosmo- *or before a vowel* **cosm-** *combining form.* indicating the world or universe: *cosmology; cosmonaut.* [from Gk: COSMOS]

cosmogony (kɒzˈmɒɡənɪ) *n, pl* **cosmogonies.** the study of the origin and development of the universe or of a particular system in the universe, such as the solar system. [C17: from Gk *kosmogonia,* from COSMO- + *gonos* creation]
▸**cosmogonic** (ˌkɒzməˈɡɒnɪk) *or* ˌ**cosmoˈgonical** *adj* ▸**cosˈmogonist** *n*

cosmography (kɒzˈmɒɡrəfɪ) *n* **1** a representation of the world or the universe. **2** the science dealing with the whole order of nature.
▸**cosˈmographer** *n* ▸**cosmographic** (ˌkɒzməˈɡræfɪk) *or* ˌ**cosmoˈgraphical** *adj*

cosmological principle *n Astron.* the theory that the universe is uniform, homogenous, and isotropic, and therefore appears the same from any position.

cosmology (kɒzˈmɒlədʒɪ) *n* **1** the study of the origin and nature of the universe. **2** a particular account of the origin or structure of the universe.
▸**cosmological** (ˌkɒzməˈlɒdʒɪkᵊl) *or* ˌ**cosmoˈlogic** *adj* ▸**cosˈmologist** *n*

cosmonaut ➊ (ˈkɒzməˌnɔːt) *n* an astronaut, esp. in the former Soviet Union. [C20: from Russian *kosmonavt,* from COSMO- + Gk *nautēs* sailor]

cosmopolitan ➊ (ˌkɒzməˈpɒlɪtᵊn) *n* **1** a person who has lived and travelled in many countries, esp. one who is free of national prejudices. ◆ *adj* **2** familiar with many parts of the world. **3** sophisticated or urbane. **4** composed of people or elements from all parts of the world or from many different spheres. [C17: from F, ult. from Gk *kosmopolitēs,* from *kosmo-* COSMO- + *politēs* citizen]
▸ˌ**cosmoˈpolitanism** *n*

cosmopolite (kɒzˈmɒpəˌlaɪt) *n* **1** a less common word for **cosmopolitan** (sense 1). **2** an animal or plant that occurs in most parts of the world.
▸**cosˈmopolitˌism** *n*

cosmos ➊ (ˈkɒzmɒs) *n* **1** the universe considered as an ordered system. **2** any ordered system. **3** (*pl* **cosmos** *or* **cosmoses**) any tropical American plant of the genus *Cosmos* cultivated as garden plants for their brightly coloured flowers. [C17: from Gk *kosmos* order]

Cosmos (ˈkɒzmɒs) *n Astronautics.* any of various types of Soviet satellite, including Cosmos 1 (launched 1962) and nearly 2000 subsequent satellites.

Cossack (ˈkɒsæk) *n* **1** (formerly) any of the free warrior-peasants of chiefly East Slavonic descent who served as cavalry under the tsars. ◆ *adj* **2** of, relating to, or characteristic of the Cossacks: *a Cossack dance.* [C16: from Russian *kazak* vagabond, of Turkic origin]

cosset ➊ (ˈkɒsɪt) *vb* **cossets, cosseting, cosseted. 1** (*tr*) to pamper; pet. ◆ *n* **2** any pet animal, esp. a lamb. [C16: from ?]

cost ➊ (kɒst) *n* **1** the price paid or required for acquiring, producing, or maintaining something, measured in money, time, or energy; outlay. **2** suffering or sacrifice: *I know to my cost.* **3a** the amount paid for a commodity by its seller: *to sell at cost.* **3b** (*as modifier*): *the cost price.* **4** (*pl*) *Law.* the expenses of judicial proceedings. **5 at all costs.** regardless of sacrifice involved. **6 at the cost of.** at the expense of losing. ◆ *vb* **costs, costing, cost. 7** (*tr*) to be obtained or obtainable in exchange for: *the ride cost one pound.* **8** to cause or require the loss or sacrifice (of): *the accident cost him dearly.* **9** (*p.t. & p.p.* **costed**) to estimate the cost of (a product, process, etc.) for the purposes of pricing, budgeting, control, etc. [C13: from OF (n), from *coster* to cost, from L *constāre* to stand at, cost, from *stāre* to stand]

costa (ˈkɒstə) *n, pl* **costae** (-tiː). **1** the technical name for **rib**[1] (sense 1). **2** a riblike part. [C19: from L: rib, side]
▸**ˈcostal** *adj*

cost accounting *n* the recording and controlling of all the expenditures of an enterprise in order to facilitate control of separate activities. Also called: **management accounting.**
▸**cost accountant** *n*

cost-benefit *adj* denoting or relating to a method of assessing a project that takes into account its costs and its benefits to society as well as the revenue it generates: *a cost-benefit analysis; the project was assessed on a cost-benefit basis.*

cost-effective *adj* providing adequate financial return in relation to outlay.
▸ˌ**cost-efˈfectiveness** *n*

costermonger (ˈkɒstəˌmʌŋɡə) *or* **coster** *n Brit., rare.* a person who sells fruit, vegetables, etc., from a barrow. [C16: from *costard* a kind of apple + MONGER]

costive (ˈkɒstɪv) *adj* **1** constipated. **2** niggardly. [C14: from OF *costivé,* from L *constipātus;* see CONSTIPATE]
▸**ˈcostiveness** *n*

costly ➊ (ˈkɒstlɪ) *adj* **costlier, costliest. 1** expensive. **2** entailing great loss or sacrifice: *a costly victory.* **3** splendid; lavish.
▸**ˈcostliness** *n*

cost of living *n* **a** the basic cost of the food, clothing, shelter, and fuel necessary to maintain life, esp. at a standard of living regarded as basic. **b** (*as modifier*): *the cost-of-living index.*

cost-plus *n* a method of establishing a selling price in which an agreed percentage is added to the cost price to cover profit.

costume ➊ (ˈkɒstjuːm) *n* **1** a style of dressing, including all the clothes, accessories, etc., worn at one time, as in a particular country or period. **2** *Old-fashioned.* a woman's suit. **3** a set of clothes, esp. unusual or period clothes: *a jester's costume.* **4** short for **swimming costume.** ◆ *vb* **costumes, costuming, costumed.** (*tr*) **5** to furnish the costumes for (a show, film, etc.). **6** to dress (someone) in a costume. [C18: from F, from It.: dress, habit, CUSTOM]

costumier (kɒˈstjuːmɪə) *or* **costumer** *n* a person or firm that makes or supplies theatrical or fancy costumes.

cosy ➊ *or US* **cozy** (ˈkəʊzɪ) *adj* **cosier, cosiest** *or US* **cozier, coziest. 1** warm and snug. **2** intimate; friendly. ◆ *n, pl* **cosies** *or US* **cozies. 3** a cover for keeping things warm: *egg cosy.* [C18: from Scot., from ?]
▸**ˈcosily** *or US* **ˈcozily** *adv* ▸**ˈcosiness** *or US* **ˈcoziness** *n*

cot[1] (kɒt) *n* **1** a child's boxlike bed, usually incorporating vertical bars. **2** a portable bed. **3** a light bedstead. **4** *Naut.* a hammock-like bed. [C17: from Hindi *khāt* bedstead]

cot[2] (kɒt) *n* **1** *Literary or arch.* a small cottage. **2** Also called: **cote. 2a** a small shelter, esp. one for pigeons, sheep, etc. **2b** (*in combination*): *dovecot.* [OE *cot*]

cot[3] (kɒt) *abbrev. for* cotangent.

cotangent (kəʊˈtændʒənt) *n* (of an angle) a trigonometric function that in a right-angled triangle is the ratio of the length of the adjacent side to that of the opposite side.

COTC *abbrev. for* Canadian Officers Training Corps.

cot death *n* the unexplained sudden death of an infant during sleep. Technical name: **sudden infant death syndrome.**

cote (kəʊt) *or* **cot** *n* **1** a small shelter for pigeons, sheep, etc. **2** (*in combination*): *dovecote.* [OE *cote*]

THESAURUS

cosmetic *adj* **3** = **beautifying,** nonessential, superficial, surface, touching-up

cosmic *adj* **1** = **universal,** stellar **3** = **vast,** grandiose, huge, immense, infinite, limitless, measureless

cosmonaut *n* = **astronaut,** spaceman, space pilot

cosmopolitan *n* **1** = **man** *or* **woman of the world,** cosmopolite, jet-setter, sophisticate ◆ *adj* **2, 3** = **sophisticated,** broad-minded, catholic, open-minded, universal, urbane, well-travelled, worldly, worldly-wise
Antonyms *adj* ≠ **sophisticated:** hidebound, illiberal, insular, limited, narrow-minded, parochial, provincial, restricted, rustic, unsophisticated

cosmos *n* **1** = **universe,** creation, macrocosm, world **2** = **order,** harmony, structure

cosset *vb* **1** = **pamper,** baby, coddle, cosher (*Irish*), mollycoddle, pet, wrap up in cotton wool (*inf.*)

cost *n* **1** = **price,** amount, charge, damage (*inf.*), expenditure, expense, figure, outlay, payment, rate, worth **2** = **loss,** damage, deprivation, detriment, expense, harm, hurt, injury, penalty, sacrifice, suffering **5 at all costs** = **no matter what,** at any price, regardless, without fail ◆ *vb* **7** = **sell at,** come to, command a price of, set (someone) back (*inf.*) **8** = **lose,** do disservice to, harm, hurt, injure, necessitate

costly *adj* **1** = **expensive,** dear, excessive, exorbitant, extortionate, highly-priced, steep (*inf.*), stiff, valuable **2** = **damaging,** catastrophic, deleterious, disastrous, harmful, loss-making, ruinous, sacrificial **3** = **splendid,** gorgeous, lavish, luxurious, opulent, precious, priceless, rich, sumptuous
Antonyms *adj* ≠ **expensive:** cheap, cheapo (*inf.*), dirt-cheap, economical, fair, inexpensive, low-priced, reasonable, reduced

costume *n* **1, 3** = **outfit,** apparel, attire, clothing, dress, ensemble, garb, get-up (*inf.*), livery, national dress, robes, uniform

cosy *adj* **1** = **snug,** comfortable, comfy (*inf.*), cuddled up, homely, secure, sheltered, snuggled down, tucked up, warm

coterie ❶ ('kəʊtərɪ) *n* a small exclusive group of people with common interests; clique. [C18: from F, from OF: association of tenants, from *cotier* (unattested) cottager]
coterminous (kəʊ'tɜːmɪnəs) *or* **conterminous** *adj* **1** having a common boundary. **2** coextensive or coincident in range, time, etc.
coth (kɒθ, 'kɒt'eɪtʃ) *n* hyperbolic cotangent. [C20: from COT(ANGENT) + H(YPERBOLIC)]
cotillion *or* **cotillon** (kə'tɪljən, kəʊ-) *n* **1** a French formation dance of the 18th century. **2** *US.* a quadrille. **3** *US.* a formal ball. [C18: from F *cotillon* dance, from OF: petticoat]
cotinga (kə'tɪŋgə) *n* a tropical American passerine bird having a broad slightly hooked bill.
cotoneaster (kə,təʊnɪ'æstə) *n* any Old World shrub of the rosaceous genus *Cotoneaster:* cultivated for their ornamental flowers and red or black berries. [C18: from NL, from L *cotōneum* QUINCE]
cotta ('kɒtə) *n RC Church.* a short form of surplice. [C19: from It.: tunic]
cottage ❶ ('kɒtɪdʒ) *n* a small simple house, esp. in a rural area. [C14: from COT[2]]
cottage cheese *n* a mild loose soft white cheese made from skimmed milk curds.
cottage hospital *n Brit.* a small rural hospital.
cottage industry *n* an industry in which employees work in their own homes, often using their own equipment.
cottage pie *n Brit.* another term for **shepherd's pie.**
cottager ('kɒtɪdʒə) *n* **1** a person who lives in a cottage. **2** a rural labourer.
cottaging ('kɒtɪdʒɪŋ) *n Brit. sl.* homosexual activity between men in a public lavatory.
cotter[1] ('kɒtə) *n Machinery.* **1** any part, such as a pin, wedge, key, etc., that is used to secure two other parts so that relative motion between them is prevented. **2** short for **cotter pin.** [C14: shortened from *cotterel,* from ?]
cotter[2] ('kɒtə) *n* **1** *English history.* a villein in late Anglo-Saxon and early Norman times occupying a cottage and land in return for labour. **2** Also called: **cottar.** a peasant occupying a cottage and land in the Scottish Highlands. [C14: from Med. L *cotārius,* from ME *cote* COT[2]]
cotter pin *n Machinery.* a split pin secured, after passing through holes in the parts to be attached, by spreading the ends.
cotton ('kɒtᵊn) *n* **1** any of various herbaceous plants and shrubs cultivated in warm climates for the fibre surrounding the seeds and the oil within the seeds. **2** the soft white downy fibre of these plants, used to manufacture textiles. **3** cotton plants collectively, as a cultivated crop. **4** a cloth or thread made from cotton fibres. [C14: from OF *coton,* from Ar. *qutn*]
▸ **'cottony** *adj*
cotton bud *n* a small stick with a cotton-wool tip used for cleaning the ears, applying make-up, etc.
cotton grass *n* any of various N temperate and arctic grasslike bog plants whose clusters of long silky hairs resemble cotton tufts.
cotton on *vb* (*intr, adv;* often foll. by *to*) *Inf.* to perceive the meaning (of).
cotton-picking *adj US & Canad. sl.* (intensifier qualifying something undesirable): *you cotton-picking layabout!*
cottonseed ('kɒtᵊn,siːd) *n, pl* **cottonseeds** *or* **cottonseed.** the seed of the cotton plant: a source of oil and fodder.
cotton wool *n* **1** *Chiefly Brit.* bleached and sterilized cotton from which the impurities, such as the seeds, have been removed. Usual US term: **absorbent cotton. 2** cotton in the natural state. **3** *Brit. inf.* a state of pampered comfort and protection.
cotyledon (,kɒtɪ'liːdᵊn) *n* a simple embryonic leaf in seed-bearing plants, which, in some species, forms the first green leaf after germination. [C16: from L: a plant, navelwort, from Gk *kotulēdōn,* from *kotulē* cup, hollow]
▸ **,coty'ledonous** *adj* ▸ **,coty'ledonal** *adj*
coucal ('kuːkæl) *n* any ground-living bird of the genus *Centropus* of Africa, S Asia, and Australia. [C19: from F, ?from *couc(ou)* cuckoo + *al(ouette)* lark]
couch ❶ (kaʊtʃ) *n* **1** a piece of upholstered furniture, usually having a back and armrests, for seating more than one person. **2** a bed, esp. one used in the daytime by the patients of a doctor or a psychoanalyst. ◆ *vb* **3** (*tr*) to express in a particular style of language: *couched in an archaic style.* **4** (when *tr, usually reflexive or passive*) to lie down or cause to lie down for or as for sleep. **5** (*intr*) *Arch.* to crouch. **6** (*intr*) *Arch.* to lie in ambush; lurk. **7** (*tr*) *Surgery.* to remove (a cataract) by downward displacement of the lens of the eye. **8** (*tr*) *Arch.* to lower (a lance) into a horizontal position. [C14: from OF *couche* a bed, lair, from *coucher* to lay down, from L *collocāre* to arrange, from *locāre* to place]
couchant ('kaʊtʃənt) *adj* (*usually postpositive*) *Heraldry.* in a lying position: *a lion couchant.* [C15: from F: lying]
couchette (kuː'ʃɛt) *n* a bed or berth in a railway carriage, esp. one converted from seats. [C20: from F, dim. of *couche* bed]
couch grass (kaʊtʃ, kuːtʃ) *n* a grass with a yellowish-white creeping underground stem by which it spreads quickly: a troublesome weed. Also called: **twitch grass, quitch grass.**
couch potato *n Sl., chiefly US.* a lazy person whose recreation consists chiefly of watching television.
cougar ('kuːgə) *n* another name for **puma.** [C18: from F *couguar,* from Port., from Tupi]
cough ❶ (kɒf) *vb* **1** (*intr*) to expel air abruptly and explosively through the partially closed vocal chords. **2** (*intr*) to make a sound similar to this. **3** (*tr*) to utter or express with a cough or coughs. ◆ *n* **4** an act or sound of coughing. **5** a condition of the lungs or throat which causes frequent coughing. [OE *cohhetten*]
▸ **'cougher** *n*
cough drop *n* a lozenge to relieve a cough.
cough mixture *n* any medicine that relieves coughing.
cough up ❶ *vb* (*adv*) **1** *Inf.* to surrender (money, information, etc.), esp. reluctantly. **2** (*tr*) to bring into the mouth or eject (phlegm, food, etc.) by coughing.
could (kʊd) *vb* (takes an infinitive without *to* or an implied infinitive) used as an auxiliary: **1** to make the past tense of **can**[1]. **2** to make the subjunctive mood of **can**[1], esp. used in polite requests or in conditional sentences: *could I see you tonight?* **3** to indicate suggestion of a course of action: *you could take the car if it's raining.* **4** (often foll. by *well*) to indicate a possibility: *he could well be a spy.* [OE *cūthe*]
couldn't ('kʊdᵊnt) *contraction of* could not.
couldst (kʊdst) *vb Arch.* the form of **could** used with the pronoun *thou* or its relative form.
coulee ('kuːleɪ, -lɪ) *n* **1a** a flow of molten lava. **1b** such lava when solidified. **2** *Western US & Canad.* a steep-sided ravine. [C19: from Canad. F *coulée* a flow, from F, from *couler* to flow, from L *cōlāre* to sift]
coulis ('kuːliː) *n* a thin purée of vegetables, fruit, etc., usually served as a sauce. [C20: F, lit.: purée]
coulomb ('kuːlɒm) *n* the derived SI unit of electric charge; the quantity of electricity transported in one second by a current of 1 ampere. Symbol: C [C19: after C.A. de *Coulomb* (1736–1806), F physicist]
coulter ('kəʊltə) *n* a blade or sharp-edged disc attached to a plough so that it cuts through the soil vertically in advance of the ploughshare. Also (esp. US): **colter.** [OE *culter,* from L: ploughshare, knife]
coumarin *or* **cumarin** ('kuːmərɪn) *n* a white vanilla-scented crystalline ester, used in perfumes and flavouring. [C19: from F, from *coumarou* tonka-bean tree, from Sp., from Tupi]
council ❶ ('kaʊnsəl) *n* **1** an assembly of people meeting for discussion, consultation, etc. **2a** a body of people elected or appointed to serve in an administrative, legislative, or advisory capacity: *a student council.* **2b** short for **legislative council. 3** (*sometimes cap.;* often preceded by *the*) *Brit.* the local governing authority of a town, county, etc. **4** *Austral.* an administrative or legislative assembly, esp. the upper house of a state parliament in Australia. **5** a meeting of a council. **6** (*modifier*) of, provided for, or used by a local council: *a council chamber; council offices.* **7** (*modifier*) *Brit.* provided by a local council, esp. (of housing) at a subsidized rent: *a council house; a council estate; a council school.* **8** *Christianity.* an assembly of bishops, etc., convened for regulating matters of doctrine or discipline. [C12: from OF *concile,* from L *concilium* assembly, from *com-* together + *calāre* to call]

USAGE NOTE Avoid confusion with **counsel.**

council area *n* any of the 32 unitary authorities into which Scotland was divided for administrative purposes in 1996.
councillor *or US* **councilor** ('kaʊnsələ) *n* a member of a council.

USAGE NOTE Avoid confusion with **counsellor.**

councilman ('kaʊnsəlmən) *n, pl* **councilmen.** *Chiefly US.* a councillor.
council tax *n* (in Britain) a tax based on the relative value of property levied to fund local council services.
counsel ❶ ('kaʊnsəl) *n* **1** advice or guidance on conduct, behaviour, etc. **2** discussion; consultation: *to take counsel with a friend.* **3** a person whose advice is sought. **4** a barrister or group of barristers engaged in conducting cases in court and advising on legal matters. **5** *Christianity.* any of the **counsels of perfection,** namely poverty, chastity, and obedience. **6** **counsel of perfection.** excellent but unrealizable advice. **7** private opinions (esp. in **keep one's own counsel**). **8** *Arch.* wisdom; prudence. ◆ *vb* **counsels, counselling, counselled** *or US* **counsels, counseling, counseled. 9** (*tr*) to give advice or guidance to. **10** (*tr; often takes a clause as object*) to recommend; urge. **11** (*intr*) *Arch.* to take counsel; consult.

THESAURUS

coterie *n* = **clique,** cabal, camp, circle, gang, group, outfit (*inf.*), posse (*inf.*), set
cottage *n* = **cabin,** but-and-ben (*Scot.*), chalet, cot, hut, lodge, shack
couch *n* **1, 2** = **sofa,** bed, chaise longue, chesterfield, day bed, divan, ottoman, settee ◆ *vb* **3** = **express,** frame, phrase, set forth, utter, word
cough *vb* **1, 2** = **clear one's throat,** bark, hack, hawk, hem ◆ *n* **4** = **frog** *or* **tickle in one's throat,** bark, hack
cough up *vb* **1** *Informal* = **give up,** deliver, fork out, hand over, shell out (*inf.*), surrender
council *n* **1, 2** = **governing body,** assembly, board, cabinet, chamber, committee, conclave, conference, congress, convention, convocation, diet, house, ministry, panel, parliament, quango, synod
counsel *n* **1, 2** = **advice,** admonition, caution, consideration, consultation, deliberation, direction, forethought, guidance, information, recommendation, suggestion, warning **4** = **legal adviser,** advocate, attorney, barrister, lawyer, solicitor ◆ *vb* **9, 10** = **advise,** admonish, advocate, caution, exhort, instruct, prescribe, recommend, urge, warn

[C13: from OF *counseil*, from L *consilium* deliberating body; rel. to CONSULT]

USAGE NOTE Avoid confusion with **council**.

counselling *or US* **counseling** ('kaʊnsəlɪŋ) *n* systematic guidance offered by social workers, doctors, etc., in which a person's problems are discussed and advice is given.

counsellor *or US* **counselor** ('kaʊnsələ) *n* **1** a person who gives counsel; adviser. **2** Also called: **counselor-at-law**. *US*. a lawyer, esp. one who conducts cases in court. **3** a senior diplomatic officer.

USAGE NOTE Avoid confusion with **councillor**.

count[1] ⓣ (kaʊnt) *vb* **1** to add up or check (each unit in a collection) in order to ascertain the sum: *count your change*. **2** (*tr*) to recite numbers in ascending order up to and including. **3** (*tr; often foll. by in*) to take into account or include: *we must count him in*. **4 not counting**. excluding. **5** (*tr*) to consider; deem: *count yourself lucky*. **6** (*intr*) to have importance: *this picture counts as a rarity*. **7** (*intr*) *Music*. to keep time by counting beats. ◆ *n* **8** the act of counting. **9** the number reached by counting; sum: *a blood count*. **10** *Law*. a paragraph in an indictment containing a separate charge. **11 keep** *or* **lose count**. to keep or fail to keep an accurate record of items, events, etc. **12** *Boxing, wrestling*. the act of telling off a number of seconds by the referee, as when a boxer has been knocked down by his opponent. **13 out for the count**. *Boxing*. knocked out and unable to continue after a count of ten by the referee. ◆ See also **count against, countdown**, etc. [C14: from Anglo-F *counter*, from OF *conter*, from L *computāre* to calculate]
▸ **'countable** *adj*

count[2] (kaʊnt) *n* **1** a nobleman in any of various European countries having a rank corresponding to that of a British earl. **2** any of various officials in the late Roman Empire and in the early Middle Ages. [C16: from OF *conte*, from L *comes* associate, from COM- with + *īre* to go]

count against *vb* (*intr, prep*) to have influence to the disadvantage of.

countdown ('kaʊnt,daʊn) *n* **1** the act of counting backwards to time a critical operation exactly, such as the launching of a rocket. ◆ *vb* **count down**. (*intr, adv*) **2** to count thus.

countenance ⓣ ('kaʊntɪnəns) *n* **1** the face, esp. when considered as expressing a person's character or mood. **2** support or encouragement; sanction. **3** composure; self-control (esp. in **keep** *or* **lose one's countenance**). ◆ *vb* **countenances, countenancing, countenanced**. (*tr*) **4** to support or encourage; sanction. **5** to tolerate; endure. [C13: from OF *contenance* mien, behaviour, from L *continentia* restraint, control; see CONTAIN]

counter[1] ('kaʊntə) *n* **1** a horizontal surface, as in a shop or bank, over which business is transacted. **2** (in some cafeterias) a long table on which food is served. **3a** a small flat disc of wood, metal, or plastic, used in various board games. **3b** a similar disc or token used as an imitation coin. **4** a person or thing that may be used or manipulated. **5 under the counter**. (**under-the-counter** *when prenominal*) (of the sale of goods) clandestine or illegal. **6 over the counter**. (**over-the-counter** *when prenominal*) (of security transactions) through a broker rather than on a stock exchange. [C14: from OF *comptouer*, ult. from L *computāre* to COMPUTE]

counter[2] ('kaʊntə) *n* **1** a person who counts. **2** an apparatus that records the number of occurrences of events. [C14: from OF *conteor*, from L *computātor*; see COUNT[1]]

counter[3] ⓣ ('kaʊntə) *adv* **1** in a contrary direction or manner. **2** in a wrong or reverse direction. **3 run counter to**. to have a contrary effect or action to. ◆ *adj* **4** opposing; opposite; contrary. ◆ *n* **5** something that is contrary or opposite to some other thing. **6** an act, effect, or force that opposes another. **7** a return attack, such as a blow in boxing. **8** *Fencing*. a parry in which the foils move in a circular fashion. **9** the portion of the stern of a boat or ship that overhangs the water aft of the rudder. **10** a piece of leather forming the back of a shoe. ◆ *vb* **11** to say or do (something) in retaliation or response. **12** (*tr*) to move, act, or perform in a manner or direction opposite to (a person or thing). **13** to return the attack of (an opponent). [C15: from OF *contre*, from L *contrā* against]

counter- *prefix* **1** against; opposite; contrary: *counterattack*. **2** complementary; corresponding: *counterfoil*. **3** duplicate or substitute: *counterfeit*. [via OF from L *contrā* against, opposite; see CONTRA-]

counteract ⓣ (,kaʊntər'ækt) *vb* (*tr*) to oppose or neutralize by contrary action; check.
▸ **,counter'action** *n* ▸ **,counter'active** *adj*

counterattack ('kaʊntərə,tæk) *n* **1** an attack in response to an attack. ◆ *vb* **2** to make a counterattack (against).

counterbalance ⓣ *n* ('kaʊntə,bæləns). **1** a weight or force that balances or offsets another. ◆ *vb* (,kaʊntə'bæləns), **counterbalances, counterbalancing, counterbalanced**. (*tr*) **2** Also: **counterweigh**. to act as a counterbalance to. ◆ Also: **counterpoise**.

counterblast ('kaʊntə,blɑːst) *n* an aggressive response to a verbal attack.

countercheck *n* ('kaʊntə,tʃek). **1** a check or restraint, esp. one that acts in opposition to another. **2** a double check, as for accuracy. ◆ *vb* (,kaʊntə'tʃek). (*tr*) **3** to oppose by counteraction. **4** to double-check.

counterclaim ('kaʊntə,kleɪm) *Chiefly law*. ◆ *n* **1** a claim set up in opposition to another. ◆ *vb* **2** to set up (a claim) in opposition to another claim.
▸ **,counter'claimant** *n*

counterclockwise (,kaʊntə'klɒk,waɪz) *adv, adj* the US and Canad. equivalent of **anticlockwise**.

counterculture ('kaʊntə,kʌltʃə) *n* an alternative culture, deliberately at variance with the social norm.

counterespionage (,kaʊntər'ɛspɪə,nɑːʒ) *n* activities to counteract enemy espionage.

counterfeit ⓣ ('kaʊntəfɪt) *adj* **1** made in imitation of something genuine with the intent to deceive or defraud; forged. **2** simulated; sham: *counterfeit affection*. ◆ *n* **3** an imitation designed to deceive or defraud. ◆ *vb* **4** (*tr*) to make a fraudulent imitation of. **5** (*intr*) to make counterfeits. **6** to feign; simulate. [C13: from OF *contrefait*, from *contrefaire* to copy, from *contre-* COUNTER- + *faire* to make]
▸ **'counterfeiter** *n*

counterfoil ('kaʊntə,fɔɪl) *n Brit*. the part of a cheque, receipt, etc., retained as a record. Also called (esp. in the US and Canada): **stub**.

counterforce ('kaʊntə,fɔːs) *n* (*modifier*) denoting military strategy based on retaliation against attacking forces.

counterinsurgency (,kaʊntərɪn'sɜːdʒənsɪ) *n* action taken by a government against rebels, guerrillas, etc.

counterintelligence (,kaʊntərɪn'telɪdʒəns) *n* activities designed to frustrate enemy espionage.

counterintuitive *adj Chiefly US*. (of an idea, proposal, etc.) seemingly contrary to common sense.

counterirritant (,kaʊntər'ɪrɪtᵊnt) *n* **1** an agent that causes a superficial irritation of the skin and thereby relieves inflammation of deep structures. ◆ *adj* **2** producing a counterirritation.
▸ **,counter,irri'tation** *n*

countermand ⓣ *vb* (,kaʊntə'mɑːnd). (*tr*) **1** to revoke or cancel (a command, order, etc.). **2** to order (forces, etc.) to retreat; recall. ◆ *n* ('kaʊntə,mɑːnd). **3** a command revoking another. [C15: from OF *contremander*, from *contre-* COUNTER- + *mander* to command, from L *mandāre*]

countermarch ('kaʊntə,mɑːtʃ) *Chiefly mil*. ◆ *vb* **1** to march back or cause to march back or in the opposite direction. ◆ *n* **2** the act or an instance of countermarching.

countermeasure ('kaʊntə,mɛʒə) *n* action taken to oppose, neutralize, or retaliate against some other action.

countermove ('kaʊntə,muːv) *n* **1** an opposing move. ◆ *vb* **countermoves, countermoving, countermoved**. **2** to make or do (something) as an opposing move.
▸ **'counter,movement** *n*

counteroffensive ('kaʊntərə,fɛnsɪv) *n* a series of attacks by a defending force against an attacking enemy.

counteroffer ('kaʊntər,ɒfə) *n* a response to a bid in which a seller amends his original offer, making it more favourable to the buyer.

counterpane ⓣ ('kaʊntə,peɪn) *n* another word for **bedspread**. [C17: from obs. *counterpoint* (infl. by *pane* coverlet), changed from OF *coutepointe* quilt, from Med. L *culcita puncta* quilted mattress]

counterpart ⓣ ('kaʊntə,pɑːt) *n* **1** a person or thing identical to or closely resembling another. **2** one of two parts that complement or

THESAURUS

count[1] *vb* **1** = **add (up)**, calculate, cast up, check, compute, enumerate, estimate, number, reckon, score, tally, tot up **3** = **take into account** *or* **consideration**, include, number among **5** = **consider**, deem, esteem, impute, judge, look upon, rate, regard, think **6** = **matter**, be important, carry weight, cut any ice (*inf*.), enter into consideration, rate, signify, tell, weigh ◆ *n* **8, 9** = **calculation**, computation, enumeration, numbering, poll, reckoning, sum, tally

countenance *n* **1** *Literary* = **face**, appearance, aspect, expression, features, look, mien, physiognomy, visage **2** = **support**, aid, approval, assistance, backing, endorsement, favour, sanction ◆ *vb* **4** = **support**, abet, aid, approve, back, champion, commend, condone, encourage, endorse, help, sanction **5** = **tolerate**, brook, endure, hack (*sl*.), put up with (*inf*.), stand for (*inf*.)

counter[3] *adv* **1** = **opposite to**, against, at variance with, contrarily, contrariwise, conversely, in defiance of, versus ◆ *adj* **4** = **opposing**, adverse, against, conflicting, contradictory, contrary, contrasting, obverse, opposed, opposite ◆ *vb* **11** = **retaliate**, answer, hit back, meet, obviate, offset, oppose, parry, resist, respond, return, ward off
Antonyms *adv* ≠ **opposite to**: in agreement, parallel ◆ *adj* ≠ **opposing**: accordant, parallel, similar ◆ *vb* ≠ **retaliate**: accept, cave in (*inf*.), give in, surrender, take, yield

counteract *vb* = **act against**, annul, check, contravene, counterbalance, countervail, cross, defeat, foil, frustrate, hinder, invalidate, negate, neutralize, obviate, offset, oppose, resist, thwart

counterbalance *vb* **2** = **offset**, balance, compensate, counterpoise, countervail, make up for, set off

counterfeit *adj* **1, 2** = **fake**, bogus, copied, ersatz, false, feigned, forged, fraudulent, imitation, phoney *or* phony (*inf*.), pseud *or* pseudo (*inf*.), sham, simulated, spurious, suppositious ◆ *n* **3** = **fake**, copy, forgery, fraud, imitation, phoney *or* phony (*inf*.), reproduction, sham ◆ *vb* **3-6** = **fake**, copy, fabricate, feign, forge, imitate, impersonate, pretend, sham, simulate
Antonyms *adj* ≠ **fake**: authentic, genuine, good, original, real, the real thing

countermand *vb* **1** = **cancel**, annul, override, repeal, rescind, retract, reverse, revoke

counterpane *n* = **bedspread**, bed cover, cover, coverlet, doona (*Austral*.), quilt

counterpart *n* **2** = **opposite number**, comple-

correspond to each other. **3** a duplicate, esp. of a legal document; copy.
counterparty ('kaʊntə,pɑːtɪ) *n* a person who is a party to a contract.
counterplot ('kaʊntə,plɒt) *n* **1** a plot designed to frustrate another plot. ◆ *vb* **counterplots, counterplotting, counterplotted. 2** (*tr*) to oppose with a counterplot.
counterpoint ('kaʊntə,pɔɪnt) *n* **1** the technique involving the simultaneous sounding of two or more parts or melodies. **2** a melody or part combined with another melody or part. **3** the musical texture resulting from the simultaneous sounding of two or more melodies or parts. ◆ *vb* **4** (*tr*) to set in contrast. ◆ Related adj: **contrapuntal.** [C15: from OF *contrepoint,* from *contre-* COUNTER- + *point* dot, note in musical notation, i.e. an accompaniment set against the notes of a melody]
counterpoise ('kaʊntə,pɔɪz) *n* **1** a force, influence, etc., that counterbalances another. **2** a state of balance; equilibrium. **3** a weight that balances another. ◆ *vb* **counterpoises, counterpoising, counterpoised.** (*tr*) **4** to oppose with something of equal effect, weight, or force; offset. **5** to bring into equilibrium.
counterproductive (,kaʊntəprə'dʌktɪv) *adj* tending to hinder the achievement of an aim; having effects contrary to those intended.
counterproposal ('kaʊntəprə,pəʊzᵊl) *n* a proposal offered as an alternative to a previous proposal.
Counter-Reformation (,kaʊntə,rɛfə'meɪʃən) *n* the reform movement of the Roman Catholic Church in the 16th and early 17th centuries considered as a reaction to the Reformation.
counter-revolution (,kaʊntə,rɛvə'luːʃən) *n* a revolution opposed to a previous revolution.
▸ **,counter-,revo'lutionist** *n* ▸ **counter-,revo'lutionary** *n, adj*
countershaft ('kaʊntə,ʃɑːft) *n* an intermediate shaft driven by a main shaft, esp. in a gear train.
countersign *vb* ('kaʊntə,saɪn, ,kaʊntə'saɪn). **1** (*tr*) to sign (a document already signed by another). ◆ *n* ('kaʊntə,saɪn). **2** Also called: **countersignature.** the signature so written. **3** a secret sign given in response to another sign. **4** *Chiefly mil.* a password.
countersink ('kaʊntə,sɪŋk) *vb* **countersinks, countersinking, countersank, countersunk.** (*tr*) **1** to enlarge the upper part of (a hole) in timber, metal, etc., so that the head of a bolt or screw can be sunk below the surface. **2** to drive (a screw) or sink (a bolt) into such a hole. ◆ *n* **3** Also called: **countersink bit.** a tool for countersinking. **4** a countersunk hole.
countertenor (,kaʊntə'tɛnə) *n* **1** an adult male voice with an alto range. **2** a singer with such a voice.
countervail (,kaʊntə'veɪl, 'kaʊntə,veɪl) *vb* **1** (when *intr,* usually foll. by *against*) to act or act against with equal power or force. **2** (*tr*) to make up for; compensate; offset. [C14: from OF *contrevaloir,* from L *contrā valēre,* from *contrā* against + *valēre* to be strong]
countervailing duty *n* an extra import duty imposed by a country on certain imports, esp. to prevent dumping or to counteract subsidies in the exporting country.
counterweigh (,kaʊntə'weɪ) *vb* another word for **counterbalance** (sense 2).
counterweight ('kaʊntə,weɪt) *n* a counterbalancing weight, influence, or force.
countess ('kaʊntɪs) *n* **1** the wife or widow of a count or earl. **2** a woman of the rank of count or earl.
counting house *n Rare, chiefly Brit.* a room or building used by the accountants of a business.
countless ➊ ('kaʊntlɪs) *adj* innumerable; myriad.
count noun *n* a noun that can be qualified by the indefinite article and may be used in the plural, as *telephone* and *thing* but not *airs and graces* or *bravery.* Cf. **mass noun.**
count on ➊ *vb* (*intr, prep*) to rely or depend on.
count out ➊ *vb* (*tr, adv*) **1** *Inf.* to leave out; exclude. **2** (of a boxing referee) to judge (a floored boxer) to have failed to recover within the specified time.
count palatine *n, pl* **counts palatine.** *History.* **1** (in the Holy Roman Empire) a count who exercised royal authority in his own domain. **2** (in England and Ireland) the lord of a county palatine.
countrified ➊ *or* **countryfied** ('kʌntrɪ,faɪd) *adj* in the style, manners, etc., of the country; rural.
country ➊ ('kʌntrɪ) *n, pl* **countries. 1** a territory distinguished by its people, culture, geography, etc. **2** an area of land distinguished by its political autonomy; state. **3** the people of a territory or state. **4a** the part of the land that is away from cities or industrial areas; rural districts. **4b** (*as modifier*): *country cottage.* Related adjs.: **pastoral, rural. 5** short for **country music. 6 across country.** not keeping to roads, etc. **7 go** *or* **appeal to the country.** *Chiefly Brit.* to dissolve Parliament and hold an election. **8 up country.** away from the coast or the capital. **9** one's native land or nation of citizenship. [C13: from OF *contrée,* from Med. L *contrāta,* lit.: that which lies opposite, from L *contrā* opposite]
country and western *n* another name for **country music.**
country club *n* a club in the country, having sporting and social facilities.
country dance *n* a type of folk dance in which couples face one another in a line.
country house *n* a large house in the country, esp. belonging to a wealthy family.
countryman ➊ ('kʌntrɪmən) *n, pl* **countrymen. 1** a person who lives in the country. **2** a person from a particular country or from one's own country.
▸ **'country,woman** *fem n*
country music *n* a type of 20th-century popular music based on White folk music of the southeastern US.
country park *n Brit.* an area of countryside set aside for public recreation.
country seat *n* a large estate or property in the country.
countryside ➊ ('kʌntrɪ,saɪd) *n* a rural area or its population.
county ➊ ('kaʊntɪ) *n, pl* **counties. 1a** any of various administrative, political, judicial, or geographic subdivisions of certain English-speaking countries or states. **1b** (*as modifier*): *county cricket.* ◆ *adj* **2** *Brit. inf.* upper class; of or like the landed gentry. [C14: from OF *conté* land belonging to a count, from LL *comes* COUNT[2]]
county borough *n* **1** (in England from 1888 to 1974 and in Wales from 1888 to 1974 and from 1996) a borough administered independently of any higher tier of local government. **2** (in the Republic of Ireland) a borough governed by an elected council that constitutes an all-purpose authority.
county palatine *n, pl* **counties palatine. 1** the lands of a count palatine. **2** (in England and Ireland) a county in which the earl (or other lord) exercised many royal powers, esp. judicial authority.
county town *n* the town in which a county's affairs are or were administered.
coup ➊ (kuː) *n* **1** a brilliant and successful stroke or action. **2** short for **coup d'état.** [C18: from F: blow, from L *colaphus* blow with the fist, from Gk *kolaphos*]
coup de grâce ➊ *French.* (ku də grɑs) *n, pl* **coups de grâce** (ku də grɑs). **1** a mortal or finishing blow, esp. one delivered as an act of mercy to a sufferer. **2** a final or decisive stroke. [lit.: blow of mercy]
coup d'état ➊ ('kuː deɪ'tɑː) *n, pl* **coups d'état** ('kuːz deɪ'tɑː). a sudden violent or illegal seizure of government. [F, lit.: stroke of state]
coupe (kuːp) *n* **1** a dessert of fruit and ice cream. **2** a dish or stemmed glass bowl designed for this dessert. [C19: from F: goblet, CUP]
coupé ('kuːpeɪ) *n* **1** a four-seater car with a sloping back, and usually two doors. **2** a four-wheeled horse-drawn carriage with two seats inside and one outside for the driver. [C19: from F *carrosse coupé,* lit.: cut-off carriage]
couple ➊ ('kʌpᵊl) *n* **1** two people who regularly associate with each other or live together: *an engaged couple.* **2** (*functioning as sing or pl*) two people considered as a pair, for or as if for dancing, games, etc. **3** a pair of equal and opposite parallel forces that have a tendency to produce rotation. **4** a connector or link between two members, such as a tie connecting a pair of rafters in a roof. **5 a couple of.** (*functioning as sing or pl*) **5a** a combination of two; a pair of: *a couple of men.* **5b** *Inf.* a small number of; a few: *a couple of days.* ◆ *pron* **6** (usually preceded by *a; functioning as sing or pl*) two; a pair: *give him a couple.* ◆ *vb* **couples, coupling, coupled. 7** (*tr*) to connect (two things) together or to connect (one thing) to (another): *to couple railway carriages.* **8** to form or be formed into a pair or pairs. **9** to associate, put, or connect together. **10**

THESAURUS

ment, correlative, equal, fellow, match, mate, supplement, tally, twin **3 = copy,** duplicate
countless *adj* = **innumerable,** endless, immeasurable, incalculable, infinite, legion, limitless, measureless, multitudinous, myriad, numberless, uncounted, untold
Antonyms *adj* finite, limited, restricted
count on *vb* = **depend on,** bank on, believe (in), lean on, pin one's faith on, reckon on, rely on, take for granted, take on trust, trust
count out *vb Informal* = **leave out,** disregard, except, exclude, leave out of account, pass over
countrified *adj* = **rural,** agrestic, Arcadian, bucolic, cracker-barrel, homespun, idyllic, pastoral, picturesque, provincial, rustic
country *n* **1 = territory,** land, part, region, terrain **2 = nation,** commonwealth, kingdom, people, realm, sovereign state, state **3 = people,** citizenry, citizens, community, electors, grass roots, inhabitants, nation, populace, public, society, voters **4a = countryside,** backlands (*US*), backwoods, farmland, green belt, outback (*Austral. & NZ*), provinces, rural areas, sticks (*inf.*), the back of beyond, wide open spaces (*inf.*) ◆ *modifier* **4b = rural,** agrarian, agrestic, Arcadian, bucolic, georgic (*literary*), landed, pastoral, provincial, rustic ◆ *n* **9 = native land,** fatherland, homeland, motherland, nationality, *patria*
Antonyms *n* ≠ **countryside:** city, metropolis, town ◆ *modifier* ≠ **rural:** city, cosmopolitan, sophisticated, urban, urbane
countryman *n* **1 = yokel,** bumpkin, country dweller, farmer, hayseed (*US & Canad. inf.*), hick (*inf., chiefly US & Canad.*), husbandman, peasant, provincial, rustic, swain **2 = compatriot,** fellow citizen
countryside *n* = **country,** farmland, green belt, outback (*Austral. & NZ*), outdoors, panorama, sticks (*inf.*), view, wide open spaces (*inf.*)
county *n* **1a = province,** shire ◆ *adj* **2** *Informal* = **upper-class,** green-wellie, huntin', shootin', and fishin' (*inf.*), plummy (*inf.*), tweedy, upper-crust (*inf.*)
coup *n* **1 = masterstroke,** accomplishment, action, deed, exploit, feat, manoeuvre, stratagem, stroke, stroke of genius, stunt, *tour de force*
coup de grâce *n* **1 = final blow,** comeuppance (*sl.*), deathblow, kill, knockout blow, mercy stroke, mortal blow, quietus
coup d'état *n* = **overthrow,** coup, palace revolution, putsch, rebellion, seizure of power, takeover
couple *n* **5a = pair,** brace, duo, item, span (*of horses or oxen*), twain (*arch.*), two, twosome ◆ *vb* **7 = link,** buckle, clasp, conjoin, connect, hitch, join, marry, pair, unite, wed, yoke

(*intr*) to have sexual intercourse. [C13: from OF: a pair, from L *cōpula* a bond; see COPULA]

coupledom ('kʌpəldəm) *n* the state of living as a couple.

coupler ('kʌplə) *n Music.* a device on an organ or harpsichord connecting two keys, two manuals, etc., so that both may be played at once.

couplet ('kʌplɪt) *n* two successive lines of verse, usually rhymed and of the same metre. [C16: from F, lit.: a little pair; see COUPLE]

coupling ('kʌplɪŋ) *n* **1** a mechanical device that connects two things. **2** a device for connecting railway cars or trucks together.

coupon Ⓣ ('ku:pɒn) *n* **1a** a detachable part of a ticket or advertisement entitling the holder to a discount, free gift, etc. **1b** a detachable slip usable as a commercial order form. **1c** a voucher given away with certain goods, a certain number of which are exchangeable for goods offered by the manufacturers. **2** one of a number of detachable certificates attached to a bond, the surrender of which entitles the bearer to receive interest payments. **3** *Brit.* a detachable entry form for any of certain competitions, esp. football pools. [C19: from F, from OF *colpon* piece cut off, from *colper* to cut, var. of *couper*]

courage Ⓣ ('kʌrɪdʒ) *n* **1** the power or quality of dealing with or facing danger, fear, pain, etc. **2 the courage of one's convictions.** the confidence to act in accordance with one's beliefs. [C13: from OF *corage*, from *cuer* heart, from L *cor*]

courageous Ⓣ (kə'reɪdʒəs) *adj* possessing or expressing courage. ►**cou'rageously** *adv* ►**cou'rageousness** *n*

courante (kʊ'rɑ:nt) *n Music.* **1** an old dance in quick triple time. **2** a movement of a (mostly) 16th- to 18th-century suite based on this. [C16: from F, lit.: running, from *courir* to run, from L *currere*]

courbaril ('kʊəbərɪl) *n* a tropical American leguminous tree: its wood is a useful timber and its gum is a source of copal. Also called: **West Indian locust.** [C18: from Amerind]

coureur de bois (*French* kurœr də bwa) *n, pl* **coureurs de bois** (kurœr də bwa). *Canad. history.* a French Canadian woodsman or Métis who traded with Indians for furs. [Canad. F: trapper (lit.: wood-runner)]

courgette (kʊə'ʒɛt) *n* a small variety of vegetable marrow. US, Canad., and Austral. name: **zucchini.** [from F, dim. of *courge* marrow, gourd]

courier Ⓣ ('kʊərɪə) *n* **1** a special messenger, esp. one carrying diplomatic correspondence. **2** a person employed to collect and deliver parcels, packages, etc. **3** a person who makes arrangements for or accompanies a group of travellers on a journey or tour. ◆ *vb* **4** (*tr*) to send (a parcel, letter, etc.) by courier. [C16: from OF *courrier*, from OIt. *correre* to run, from L *currere*]

course Ⓣ (kɔ:s) *n* **1** a continuous progression in time or space; onward movement. **2** a route or direction followed. **3** the path or channel along which something moves: *the course of a river.* **4** an area or stretch of land or water on which a sport is played or a race is run: *a golf course.* **5** a period of time; duration: *in the course of the next hour.* **6** the usual order of and time required for a sequence of events; regular procedure: *the illness ran its course.* **7** a mode of conduct or action: *if you follow that course, you will fail.* **8** a connected series of events, actions, etc. **9a** a prescribed number of lessons, lectures, etc., in an educational curriculum. **9b** the material covered in such a curriculum. **10** a regimen prescribed for a specific period of time: *a course of treatment.* **11** a part of a meal served at one time. **12** a continuous, usually horizontal, layer of building material, such as a row of bricks, tiles, etc. **13 as a matter of course.** as a natural or normal consequence, mode of action, or event. **14 in course of.** in the process of. **15 in due course.** at some future time, esp. the natural or appropriate time. **16 of course. 16a** (*adv*) as expected; naturally. **16b** (*sentence substitute*) certainly; definitely. **17 the course of nature.** the ordinary course of events. ◆ *vb* **courses, coursing, coursed. 18** (*intr*) to run, race, or flow. **19** to cause (hounds) to hunt by sight rather than scent or (of hounds) to hunt (a quarry) thus. [C13: from OF *cours*, from L *cursus* a running, from *currere* to run]

courser[1] ('kɔ:sə) *n* **1** a person who courses hounds or dogs, esp. greyhounds. **2** a hound or dog trained for coursing.

courser[2] ('kɔ:sə) *n Literary.* a swift horse; steed. [C13: from OF *coursier*, from *cours* COURSE]

coursework ('kɔ:sˌwɜ:k) *n* written or oral work completed by a student within a given period, which is assessed as part of an educational course.

coursing ('kɔ:sɪŋ) *n* **1** hunting with hounds or dogs that follow their quarry by sight. **2** a sport in which hounds are matched against one another in pairs for the hunting of hares by sight.

court Ⓣ (kɔ:t) *n* **1** an area of ground wholly or partly surrounded by walls or buildings. **2** *Brit.* **2a** a block of flats. **2b** a mansion or country house. **2c** a short street, sometimes closed at one end. **3a** the residence, retinues, or household of a sovereign or nobleman. **3b** (*as modifier*): *a court ball.* **4** a sovereign or prince and his retinue, advisers, etc. **5** any formal assembly held by a sovereign or nobleman. **6** homage, flattering attention, or amorous approaches (esp. in **pay court to someone**). **7** *Law.* **7a** a tribunal having power to adjudicate in civil, criminal, military, or ecclesiastical matters. **7b** the regular sitting of such a judicial tribunal. **7c** the room or building in which such a tribunal sits. **8a** a marked outdoor or enclosed area used for any of various ball games, such as tennis, squash, etc. **8b** a marked section of such an area. **9 go to court.** to take legal action. **10 hold court.** to preside over admirers, attendants, etc. **11 out of court.** without a trial or legal case. **12 the ball is in your court.** you are obliged to make the next move. ◆ *vb* **13** to attempt to gain the love of; woo. **14** (*tr*) to pay attention to (someone) in order to gain favour. **15** (*tr*) to try to obtain (fame, honour, etc.). **16** (*tr*) to invite, usually foolishly, as by taking risks. [C12: from OF, from L *cohors* COHORT]

court-bouillon (kʊət'bu:jɒn) *n* a stock made from root vegetables, water, and wine or vinegar, used primarily for poaching fish. [from F, from *court* short, + *bouillon* broth, from *bouillir* to BOIL[1]]

court card *n* (in a pack of playing cards) a king, queen, or jack of any suit. [C17: altered from earlier *coat-card*, from the decorative coats worn by the figures depicted]

court circular *n* a daily report of the activities, engagements, etc., of the sovereign, published in a national newspaper.

Courtelle (kɔ:'tɛl) *n Trademark.* a synthetic acrylic fibre resembling wool.

courteous Ⓣ ('kɜ:tɪəs) *adj* polite and considerate in manner. [C13 *corteis*, lit.: with courtly manners, from OF; see COURT] ►**'courteously** *adv* ►**'courteousness** *n*

courtesan Ⓣ *or* **courtezan** (ˌkɔ:tɪ'zæn) *n* (esp. formerly) a prostitute, or the mistress of a man of rank. [C16: from OF *courtisane*, from It. *cortigiana* female courtier, from *corte* COURT]

courtesy Ⓣ ('kɜ:tɪsɪ) *n, pl* **courtesies. 1** politeness; good manners. **2** a courteous gesture or remark. **3** favour or consent (esp. in **(by) courtesy of**). **4** common consent as opposed to right (esp. in **by courtesy**). [C13 *curteisie*, from OF, from *corteis* COURTEOUS]

courtesy light *n* the interior light in a motor vehicle.

courtesy title *n* any of several titles having no legal significance, such as those borne by the children of peers.

courthouse ('kɔ:tˌhaʊs) *n* a public building in which courts of law are held.

courtier Ⓣ ('kɔ:tɪə) *n* **1** an attendant at a court. **2** a person who seeks favour in an ingratiating manner. [C13: from Anglo-F *courteour* (unattested), from OF *corteier* to attend at court]

courtly Ⓣ ('kɔ:tlɪ) *adj* **courtlier, courtliest. 1** of or suitable for a royal court. **2** refined in manner. **3** ingratiating. ►**'courtliness** *n*

court martial *n, pl* **court martials** *or* **courts martial. 1** a military court that tries persons subject to military law. ◆ *vb* **court-martial, court-martials,**

THESAURUS

coupon *n* **1** = **slip**, card, certificate, detachable portion, ticket, token, voucher

courage *n* **1** = **bravery**, balls (*taboo sl.*), ballsiness (*taboo sl.*), boldness, bottle (*Brit. sl.*), daring, dauntlessness, fearlessness, firmness, fortitude, gallantry, grit, guts (*inf.*), hardihood, heroism, intrepidity, lion-heartedness, mettle, nerve, pluck, resolution, spunk (*inf.*), valour
Antonyms *n* cowardice, cravenness, faint-heartedness, fear, timidity

courageous *adj* = **brave**, audacious, ballsy (*taboo sl.*), bold, daring, dauntless, fearless, gallant, gritty, hardy, heroic, indomitable, intrepid, lion-hearted, plucky, resolute, stalwart, stouthearted, valiant, valorous
Antonyms *adj* chicken (*sl.*), chicken-hearted, cowardly, craven, dastardly, faint-hearted, gutless (*inf.*), lily-livered, pusillanimous, scared, spineless, timid, timorous, yellow (*inf.*)

courier *n* **1, 2** = **messenger**, bearer, carrier, emissary, envoy, herald, pursuivant (*Historical*), runner **3** = **guide**, representative

course *n* **1** = **progression**, advance, advancement, continuity, development, flow, furtherance, march, movement, order, progress, sequence, succession, tenor, unfolding **2** = **route**, channel, direction, line, orbit, passage, path, road, tack, track, trail, trajectory, way **4** = **racecourse**, cinder track, circuit, lap, race, round **5** = **period**, duration, lapse, passage, passing, sweep, term, time **7, 10** = **procedure**, behaviour, conduct, manner, method, mode, plan, policy, programme, regimen **9a** = **classes**, course of study, curriculum, lectures, programme, schedule, studies **15 in due course** = **in time**, eventually, finally, in the course of time, in the end, sooner or later **16 of course** = **naturally**, certainly, definitely, indubitably, needless to say, obviously, undoubtedly, without a doubt ◆ *vb* **18** = **run**, dash, flow, gush, move apace, race, scud, scurry, speed, stream, surge, tumble **19** = **hunt**, chase, follow, pursue

court *n* **1** = **courtyard**, cloister, piazza, plaza, quad (*inf.*), quadrangle, square, yard **3a** = **palace**, hall, manor **4** = **royal household**, attendants, cortege, entourage, retinue, suite, train **7** = **law court**, bar, bench, court of justice, seat of judgment, tribunal ◆ *vb* **13** = **woo**, chase, date, go (out) with, go steady with, keep company with, make love to, pay court to, pay one's addresses to, pursue, run after, serenade, set one's cap at, sue (*arch.*), take out, walk out with **14** = **cultivate**, curry favour with, fawn upon, flatter, pander to, seek, solicit **15, 16** = **invite**, attract, bring about, incite, prompt, provoke, seek

courteous *adj* = **polite**, affable, attentive, ceremonious, civil, courtly, elegant, gallant, gracious, mannerly, polished, refined, respectful, urbane, well-bred, well-mannered
Antonyms *adj* discourteous, disrespectful, ill-mannered, impolite, insolent, rude, uncivil, ungracious, unkind

courtesan *n History* = **mistress**, call girl, demi-mondaine, *fille de joie*, harlot, hetaera, kept woman, paramour, prostitute, scarlet woman, whore, working girl (*facetious slang*)

courtesy *n* **1** = **politeness**, affability, civility, courteousness, courtliness, elegance, gallantness, gallantry, good breeding, good manners, grace, graciousness, polish, urbanity **3** = **favour**, benevolence, consent, consideration, generosity, indulgence, kindness

courtier *n* **1** = **attendant**, follower, henchman, liegeman, pursuivant (*Historical*), squire, train-bearer

courtliness *n* **2** = **ceremony**, affability, breeding, chivalrousness, correctness, courtesy, decorum, elegance, formality, gallantry, gentility, graciousness, politeness, politesse, propriety, refinement, stateliness, urbanity

courtly *adj* **2** = **ceremonious**, affable, aristocratic, chivalrous, civil, decorous, dignified, ele-

court-martialling, court-martialled *or US* **court-martials, court-martialing, court-martialed. 2** *(tr)* to try by court martial.

Court of Appeal *n* a court that hears appeals from the High Court and from the county and crown courts.

Court of St James's *n* the official name of the royal court of Britain.

court plaster *n* a plaster, composed of isinglass on silk, formerly used to cover superficial wounds. [C18: so called because formerly used by court ladies for beauty spots]

courtroom ('kɔːtˌruːm, -ˌrum) *n* a room in which the sittings of a law court are held.

courtship ❶ ('kɔːtʃɪp) *n* **1** the act, period, or art of seeking the love of someone with intent to marry. **2** the seeking or soliciting of favours.

court shoe *n* a low-cut shoe for women, without any laces or straps.

courtyard ❶ ('kɔːtˌjɑːd) *n* an open area of ground surrounded by walls or buildings; court.

couscous ('kuːskuːs) *n* a spicy dish, originating in North Africa, consisting of steamed semolina served with a meat stew. [C17: via F from Ar. *kouskous*, from *kaskasa* to pound until fine]

cousin ('kʌzᵊn) *n* **1** Also called: **first cousin, cousin-german, full cousin.** the child of one's aunt or uncle. **2** a relative descended from one of one's common ancestors. **3** a title used by a sovereign when addressing another sovereign or a nobleman. [C13: from OF *cosin*, from L *consōbrīnus*, from *sōbrīnus* cousin on the mother's side]
▸**'cousinˌhood** *or* **'cousinˌship** *n* ▸**'cousinly** *adj, adv*

couture (kuːˈtʊə) *n* **a** high-fashion designing and dressmaking. **b** *(as modifier)*: *couture clothes.* [from F: sewing, from OF *cousture* seam, from L *consuere* to stitch together]

couturier (kuːˈtʊərɪˌeɪ) *n* a person who designs, makes, and sells fashion clothes for women. [from F: dressmaker; see COUTURE]
▸**couturière** (kuːˌtuːrɪˈɛə) *fem n*

couvade (kuːˈvɑːd) *n Anthropol.* the custom in certain cultures of treating the husband of a woman giving birth as if he were bearing the child. [C19: from F, from *couver* to hatch, from L *cubāre* to lie down]

covalency (kəʊˈveɪlənsɪ) *or US* **covalence** *n* **1** the formation and nature of covalent bonds, that is, chemical bonds involving the sharing of electrons between atoms in a molecule. **2** the number of covalent bonds that a particular atom can make with other atoms in forming a molecule.
▸**coˈvalent** *adj* ▸**coˈvalently** *adv*

cove[1] ❶ (kəʊv) *n* **1** a small bay or inlet. **2** a narrow cavern in the side of a cliff, mountain, etc. **3** Also called: **coving.** *Archit.* a concave curved surface between the wall and ceiling of a room. [OE *cofa*]

cove[2] ❶ (kəʊv) *n Sl., Brit. old-fashioned & Austral.* a fellow; chap. [C16: prob. from Romany *kova* thing, person]

coven ('kʌvᵊn) *n* a meeting of witches. [C16: prob. from OF *covin* group, ult. from L *convenīre* to come together]

covenant ❶ ('kʌvənənt) *n* **1** a binding agreement; contract. **2** *Law.* an agreement in writing under seal, as to pay a stated annual sum to a charity. **3** *Bible.* God's promise to the Israelites and their commitment to worship him alone. ◆ *vb* **4** to agree to a covenant (concerning). [C13: from OF, from *covenir* to agree, from L *convenīre* to come together, make an agreement; see CONVENE]
▸**covenantal** (ˌkʌvəˈnæntᵊl) *adj* ▸**'covenantor** *or* **'covenanter** *n*

Covenanter ('kʌvənəntə, ˌkʌvəˈnæntə) *n Scot. history.* a person upholding either of two 17th-century covenants to establish and defend Presbyterianism.

Coventry ('kɒvəntrɪ) *n* **send to Coventry.** to ostracize or ignore. [after *Coventry*, a city in England, in the W Midlands]

cover ❶ ('kʌvə) *vb (mainly tr)* **1** to place or spread something over so as to protect or conceal. **2** to provide with a covering; clothe. **3** to put a garment, esp. a hat, on (the body or head). **4** to extend over or lie thickly on the surface of: *snow covered the fields.* **5** to bring upon (oneself); invest (oneself) as if with a covering: *covered with shame.* **6** (sometimes foll. by *up*) to act as a screen or concealment for; hide from view. **7** *Mil.* to protect (an individual, formation, or place) by taking up a position from which fire may be returned if those being protected are fired upon. **8** *(also intr,* sometimes foll. by *for)* to assume responsibility for (a person or thing). **9** *(intr;* foll. by *for* or *up for)* to provide an alibi (for). **10** to have as one's territory: *this salesman covers your area.* **11** to travel over. **12** to have or place in the aim and within the range of (a firearm). **13** to include or deal with. **14** (of an asset or income) to be sufficient to meet (a liability or expense). **15a** to insure against loss, risk, etc. **15b** to provide for (loss, risk, etc.) by insurance. **16** to deposit (an equivalent stake) in a bet. **17** to act as reporter or photographer on (a news event, etc.) for a newspaper or magazine: *to cover sports events.* **18** *Music.* to record a cover version of. **19** *Sport.* to guard or protect (an opponent, team-mate, or area). **20** (of a male animal, esp. a horse) to copulate with (a female animal). ◆ *n* **21** anything that covers, spreads over, protects, or conceals. **22a** a blanket used on a bed for warmth. **22b** another word for **bedspread. 23** a pretext, disguise, or false identity: *the thief sold brushes as a cover.* **24** an envelope or package for sending through the post: *under plain cover.* **25a** an individual table setting, esp. in a restaurant. **25b** *(as modifier)*: *a cover charge.* **26** Also called: **cover version.** a version by a different artist of a previously recorded musical item. **27** *Cricket.* **27a** *(often pl)* the area more or less at right angles to the pitch on the off side and usually about halfway to the boundary. **27b** *(as modifier)*: *a cover drive.* **28** *Philately.* an entire envelope that has been postmarked. **29 break cover.** to come out from a shelter or hiding place. **30 take cover.** to make for a place of safety or shelter. **31 under cover.** protected, concealed, or in secret. ◆ See also **cover-up.** [C13: from OF *covrir*, from L *cooperīre* to cover completely, from *operīre* to cover over]
▸**'coverable** *adj* ▸**'coverer** *n*

coverage ❶ ('kʌvərɪdʒ) *n* **1** the amount or extent to which something is covered. **2** *Journalism.* the amount and quality of reporting or analysis given to a particular subject or event. **3** the extent of the protection provided by insurance.

cover crop *n* a crop planted between main crops to prevent leaching or soil erosion or to provide green manure.

covered wagon *n US & Canad.* a large horse-drawn wagon with an arched canvas top, used formerly for prairie travel.

cover girl *n* a glamorous girl whose picture appears on the cover of a magazine.

covering letter *n* an accompanying letter sent as an explanation, introduction, or record.

coverlet ('kʌvəlɪt) *n* another word for **bedspread.**

cover note *n Brit.* a certificate issued by an insurance company stating that a policy is operative: used as a temporary measure between the commencement of cover and the issue of the policy.

cover point *n Cricket.* **a** a fielding position in the covers. **b** a fielder in this position.

cover slip *n* a very thin piece of glass placed over a specimen on a glass slide that is to be examined under a microscope.

covert ❶ ('kʌvət) *adj* **1** concealed or secret. ◆ *n* **2** a shelter or disguise. **3** a thicket or woodland providing shelter for game. **4** short for **covert cloth. 5** *Ornithol.* Also called: **tectrix.** any of the small feathers on the wings and tail of a bird that surround the bases of the larger feathers. [C14: from OF: covered, from *covrir* to COVER]
▸**'covertly** *adv*

covert cloth *n* a twill-weave cotton or worsted suiting fabric.

coverture ('kʌvətʃə) *n Rare.* shelter, concealment, or disguise. [C13: from OF, from *covert* covered; see COVERT]

cover-up ❶ *n* **1** concealment or attempted concealment of a mistake, crime, etc. ◆ *vb* **cover up.** *(adv)* **2** *(tr)* to cover completely. **3** (when *intr*, often foll. by *for*) to attempt to conceal (a mistake or crime).

cover version *n* another name for **cover** (sense 26).

covet ❶ ('kʌvɪt) *vb* **covets, coveting, coveted.** *(tr)* to wish, long, or crave for (something, esp. the property of another person). [C13: from OF *coveitier*, from *coveitié* eager desire, ult. from L *cupiditās* CUPIDITY]
▸**'covetable** *adj*

covetous ❶ ('kʌvɪtəs) *adj (usually postpositive* and foll. by *of)* jealously

THESAURUS

gant, flattering, formal, gallant, highbred, lordly, obliging, polished, refined, stately, urbane

courtship *n* **1** = **wooing**, courting, engagement, keeping company, pursuit, romance, suit

courtyard *n* = **yard**, area, enclosure, peristyle, playground, quad, quadrangle

cove[1] *n* **1** = **bay**, anchorage, bayou, creek, firth *or* frith *(Scot.)*, inlet, sound

cove[2] *n Old-fashioned slang* = **fellow**, bloke *(Brit. inf.)*, chap, character, customer, type

covenant *n* **1** = **promise**, agreement, arrangement, bargain, commitment, compact, concordat, contract, convention, pact, pledge, stipulation, treaty, trust **2** *Law* = **deed**, bond ◆ *vb* **4** = **promise**, agree, bargain, contract, engage, pledge, shake hands, stipulate, undertake

cover *vb* **1** = **overlay**, canopy, coat, daub, encase, envelop, layer, mantle, overspread **3** = **clothe**, dress, envelop, invest, put on, wrap **4** = **submerge**, engulf, flood, overrun, wash over **6** = **conceal**, camouflage, cloak, cover up, curtain, disguise, eclipse, enshroud, hide, hood, house, mask, obscure, screen, secrete, shade, shroud, veil **7** = **protect**, defend, guard, reinforce, shelter, shield, watch over **8** *sometimes foll. by* **for** = **stand in for**, double for, fill in for, hold the fort, relieve, substitute, take over, take the rap for *(sl.)* **11** = **travel over**, cross, pass through *or* over, range, traverse **13** = **deal with**, comprehend, comprise, consider, contain, embody, embrace, encompass, examine, include, incorporate, involve, provide for, refer to, survey, take account of **15** = **make up for**, balance, compensate, counterbalance, insure, make good, offset **17** = **report**, describe, detail, investigate, narrate, recount, relate, tell of, write up ◆ *n* **21** = **covering**, awning, binding, canopy, cap, case, clothing, coating, dress, envelope, jacket, lid, sheath, top, wrapper **23** = **disguise**, cloak, cover-up, façade, front, mask, pretence, pretext, screen, smoke screen, veil, window-dressing

Antonyms *vb* ≠ **conceal:** exhibit, expose, reveal, show, unclothe, uncover, unmask, unwrap ≠ **deal with:** exclude, omit ◆ *n* ≠ **covering:** base, bottom

coverage *n* **2** = **reporting**, analysis, description, reportage, treatment

covert *adj* **1** = **secret**, clandestine, concealed, disguised, dissembled, hidden, private, sly, stealthy, surreptitious, underhand, unsuspected, veiled ◆ *n* **3** = **thicket**, brush *(arch.)*, bushes, coppice, shrubbery, undergrowth, underwood

cover-up *n* **1** = **concealment**, complicity, conspiracy, front, smoke screen, whitewash *(inf.)* ◆ *vb* **cover up 3** = **conceal**, cover one's tracks, draw a veil over, feign ignorance, hide, hush up, keep dark, keep secret, keep silent about, keep under one's hat *(inf.)*, repress, stonewall, suppress, sweep under the carpet, whitewash *(inf.)*

covet *vb* = **long for**, aspire to, begrudge, crave, desire, envy, fancy *(inf.)*, hanker after, have one's eye on, lust after, set one's heart on, thirst for, would give one's eyeteeth for, yearn for

covetous *adj* = **envious**, acquisitive, avari-

eager for the possession of something (esp. the property of another person).
▸'**covetously** *adv* ▸'**covetousness** *n*

covey ⓣ ('kʌvɪ) *n* **1** a small flock of grouse or partridge. **2** a small group, as of people. [C14: from OF *covee*, from *cover* to sit on, hatch]

cow[1] (kaʊ) *n* **1** the mature female of any species of cattle, esp. domesticated cattle. **2** the mature female of various other mammals, such as the elephant, whale, and seal. **3** (not in technical use) any domestic species of cattle. **4** *Inf.* a disagreeable woman. **5** *Austral. & NZ sl.* something objectionable (esp. in **a fair cow**). [OE *cū*]

cow[2] ⓣ (kaʊ) *vb* (*tr*) to frighten or overawe, as with threats. [C17: from ON *kūga* to oppress]

coward ⓣ ('kaʊəd) *n* a person who shrinks from or avoids danger, pain, or difficulty. [C13: from OF *cuard*, from *coue* tail, from L *cauda*; ? suggestive of a frightened animal with its tail between its legs]

cowardice ⓣ ('kaʊədɪs) *n* lack of courage in facing danger, pain, or difficulty.

cowardly ⓣ ('kaʊədlɪ) *adj* of or characteristic of a coward; lacking courage.
▸'**cowardliness** *n*

cowbell ('kaʊˌbɛl) *n* a bell hung around a cow's neck so that the cow can be easily located.

cowberry ('kaʊbərɪ, -brɪ) *n, pl* **cowberries. 1** a creeping evergreen shrub of N temperate and arctic regions, with pink or red flowers and edible slightly acid berries. **2** the berry of this plant.

cowbird ('kaʊˌbɜːd) *n* any of various American orioles, having dark plumage and a short bill.

cowboy ⓣ ('kaʊˌbɔɪ) *n* **1** Also called: **cowhand.** a hired man who herds and tends cattle, usually on horseback, esp. in the western US. **2** a conventional character of Wild West folklore, films, etc., esp. one involved in fighting Indians. **3** *Inf.* an irresponsible or unscrupulous operator in business, etc.
▸'**cowˌgirl** *fem n*

cowcatcher ('kaʊˌkætʃə) *n* a metal frame on the front of a locomotive to clear the track of animals or other obstructions.

cow-cocky *n, pl* **cow-cockies.** *Austral. & NZ.* a one-man dairy farmer.

cower ⓣ ('kaʊə) *vb* (*intr*) to crouch or cringe, as in fear. [C13: from MLow G *kūren* to lie in wait; rel. to Swedish *kura*]

cowherd ('kaʊˌhɜːd) *n* a person employed to tend cattle.

cowhide ('kaʊˌhaɪd) *n* **1** the hide of a cow. **2** the leather made from such a hide.

cowl (kaʊl) *n* **1** a hood, esp. a loose one. **2** the hooded habit of a monk. **3** a cover fitted to a chimney to increase ventilation and prevent draughts. **4** the part of a car body that supports the windscreen and the bonnet. ◆ *vb* (*tr*) **5** to cover or provide with a cowl. [OE *cugele*, from LL *cucullа* cowl, from L *cucullus* hood]

cowlick ('kaʊˌlɪk) *n* a tuft of hair over the forehead.

cowling ('kaʊlɪŋ) *n* a streamlined metal covering, esp. around an aircraft engine.

cowman ('kaʊmən) *n, pl* **cowmen. 1** *Brit.* another name for **cowherd. 2** *US & Canad.* a man who owns cattle; rancher.

co-worker *n* a fellow worker; associate.

cow parsley *n* a common Eurasian umbelliferous hedgerow plant having umbrella-shaped clusters of white flowers.

cowpat ('kaʊˌpæt) *n* a single dropping of cow dung.

cowpea ('kaʊˌpiː) *n* **1** a leguminous tropical climbing plant producing pods containing edible pealike seeds. **2** the seed of this plant.

cowpox ('kaʊˌpɒks) *n* a contagious viral disease of cows characterized by vesicles, esp. on the teats and udder. Inoculation of humans with this virus provides temporary immunity to smallpox.

cowpuncher ('kaʊˌpʌntʃə) *or* **cowpoke** ('kaʊˌpəʊk) *n US & Canad.* an informal word for **cowboy.**

cowrie *or* **cowry** ('kaʊrɪ) *n, pl* **cowries. 1** any marine gastropod mollusc of a mostly tropical family having a glossy brightly marked shell. **2** the shell of any of these molluscs, esp. the money cowrie, used as money in parts of Africa and S Asia. [C17: from Hindi *kaurī*, from Sansk. *kaparda*]

cowslip ('kaʊˌslɪp) *n* **1** a primrose native to temperate regions of the Old World, having yellow flowers. **2** *US & Canad.* another name for **marsh marigold.** [OE *cūslyppe*; see COW[1], SLIP[3]]

cox (kɒks) *n* **1** a coxswain. ◆ *vb* **2** to act as coxswain of (a boat).
▸'**coxless** *adj*

coxa ('kɒksə) *n, pl* **coxae** ('kɒksiː). **1** a technical name for the hipbone or hip joint. **2** the basal segment of the leg of an insect. [C18: from L: hip]
▸'**coxal** *adj*

coxalgia (kɒk'sældʒɪə) *n* **1** pain in the hip joint. **2** disease of the hip joint causing pain. [C19: from COXA + -ALGIA]
▸**cox'algic** *adj*

coxcomb ('kɒksˌkəʊm) *n* **1** a variant spelling of **cockscomb. 2** *Obs.* the cap, resembling a cock's comb, worn by a jester.
▸'**coxˌcombry** *n*

coxswain ('kɒksən, -ˌsweɪn) *n* **1** (usually shortened to **cox** in competitive rowing) the helmsman of a lifeboat, racing shell, etc. **2** the senior petty officer on a small naval craft. ◆ Also called: **cockswain.** [C15: from *cock* a ship's boat + SWAIN]

coy ⓣ (kɔɪ) *adj* **1** affectedly demure, esp. in a playful or provocative manner. **2** shy; modest. **3** evasive, esp. in an annoying way. [C14: from OF *coi* reserved, from L *quiētus* QUIET]
▸'**coyly** *adv* ▸'**coyness** *n*

Coy. *Mil. abbrev. for* company.

coyote ('kɔɪəʊt, kɔɪ'əʊtɪ; *esp. US.* 'kaɪəʊt, kaɪ'əʊtɪ) *n, pl* **coyotes** *or* **coyote.** a predatory canine mammal of the deserts and prairies of North America. Also called: **prairie wolf.** [C19: from Mexican Sp., from Nahuatl *coyotl*]

coypu ('kɔɪpuː) *n, pl* **coypus** *or* **coypu. 1** an aquatic South American rodent, naturalized in Europe. It resembles a small beaver and is bred for its fur. **2** the fur of this animal. ◆ Also called: **nutria.** [C18: from American Sp. *coipú*, from Amerind *kóypu*]

coz (kʌz) *n* an archaic word for **cousin.**

cozen ('kʌzᵊn) *vb* to cheat or trick (someone). [C16: cant term ? rel. to COUSIN]
▸'**cozenage** *n*

cozy ('kəʊzɪ) *adj, n* the usual US spelling of **cosy.**

CP *abbrev. for:* **1** Canadian Pacific Ltd. **2** Common Prayer. **3** Communist Party.

cp. *abbrev. for* compare.

CPAG *abbrev. for* Child Poverty Action Group.

cpd *abbrev. for* compound.

cpi *abbrev. for* characters per inch.

Cpl *abbrev. for* Corporal.

CPO *abbrev. for* Chief Petty Officer.

CPR *abbrev. for* cardiopulmonary resuscitation.

cps *abbrev. for:* **1** *Physics.* cycles per second. **2** *Computing.* characters per second.

CPS (in England and Wales) *abbrev. for* Crown Prosecution Service.

CPSA *abbrev. for* Civil and Public Services Association.

CPVE (in Britain) *abbrev. for* Certificate of Pre-vocational Education: a certificate awarded for completion of a broad-based course of study offered as a less advanced alternative to traditional school-leaving qualifications.

CQ a symbol transmitted by an amateur radio operator requesting communication with any other amateur radio operator.

Cr 1 *abbrev. for* Councillor. **2** *the chemical symbol for* chromium.

cr. *abbrev. for:* **1** credit. **2** creditor.

crab[1] (kræb) *n* **1** any chiefly marine decapod crustacean having a broad flattened carapace covering the cephalothorax, beneath which is folded the abdomen. The first pair of limbs are pincers. **2** any of various similar or related arthropods. **3** short for **crab louse. 4** a mechanical lifting device, esp. the travelling hoist of a gantry crane. **5 catch a crab.** *Rowing.* to make a stroke in which the oar either misses the water or digs too deeply, causing the rower to fall backwards. ◆ *vb* **crabs, crabbing, crabbed. 6** (*intr*) to hunt or catch crabs. [OE *crabba*]

crab[2] (kræb) *Inf.* ◆ *vb* **crabs, crabbing, crabbed. 1** (*intr*) to find fault; grumble. ◆ *n* **2** an irritable person. [C16: prob. back formation from CRABBED]

crab[3] (kræb) *n* short for **crab apple.** [C15: ? of Scand. origin; cf. Swedish *skrabbe* crab apple]

Crab (kræb) *n* **the.** the constellation Cancer, the fourth sign of the zodiac.

crab apple *n* **1** any of several rosaceous trees that have white, pink, or red flowers and small sour apple-like fruits. **2** the fruit of any of these trees, used to make jam.

crabbed ⓣ ('kræbɪd) *adj* **1** surly; irritable; perverse. **2** (esp. of handwrit-

THESAURUS

cious, close-fisted, grasping, greedy, jealous, mercenary, rapacious, yearning

covey *n* = **flock**, bevy, brood, cluster, flight, group, nye *or* nide (*of pheasants*)

cow[2] *vb* = **intimidate**, awe, browbeat, bully, daunt, dishearten, dismay, frighten, overawe, psych out (*inf.*), scare, subdue, terrorize, unnerve

coward *n* = **wimp** (*inf.*), chicken (*sl.*), craven, dastard (*arch.*), faint-heart, poltroon, recreant, renegade, scaredy-cat (*inf.*), yellow-belly (*sl.*)

cowardice *n* = **faint-heartedness**, cravenness, dastardliness, fearfulness, pusillanimity, recreance *or* recreancy (*arch.*), softness, spinelessness, timorousness, weakness

cowardly *adj* = **faint-hearted**, boneless, chicken (*sl.*), chicken-hearted, craven, dastardly, fearful, gutless (*inf.*), lily-livered, pusillanimous, recreant (*arch.*), scared, shrinking, soft, spineless, timorous, weak, weak-kneed (*inf.*), white-livered, yellow (*inf.*)
Antonyms *adj* audacious, bold, brave, courageous, daring, dauntless, doughty, intrepid, plucky, valiant

cowboy *n* **1** = **cowhand**, broncobuster (*US.*), buckaroo (*US.*), cattleman, drover, gaucho (*S. Amer.*), herder, herdsman, rancher, ranchero (*US.*), stockman, wrangler (*US.*)

cower *vb* = **cringe**, crouch, draw back, fawn, flinch, grovel, quail, shrink, skulk, sneak, tremble, truckle

coy *adj* **1-3** = **shy**, arch, backward, bashful, coquettish, demure, evasive, flirtatious, kittenish, modest, overmodest, prudish, reserved, retiring, self-effacing, shrinking, skittish, timid
Antonyms *adj* bold, brash, brass-necked (*Brit. informal*), brassy (*inf.*), brazen, flip (*inf.*), forward, impertinent, impudent, pert, pushy (*inf.*), saucy, shameless

coyness *n* **1-3** = **shyness**, affectation, archness, backwardness, bashfulness, coquettishness, demureness, diffidence, evasiveness, modesty, primness, prissiness (*inf.*), prudery, prudishness, reserve, shrinking, skittishness, timidity

crabbed *adj* **1** = **bad-tempered**, acrid, acrimonious, captious, churlish, cross, cynical, difficult, fretful, harsh, ill-tempered, irritable, morose, perverse, petulant, prickly, ratty (*Brit. & N.Z. in-*

ing) cramped and hard to decipher. 3 *Rare.* abstruse. [C13: prob. from CRAB[1] (from its wayward gait), infl. by CRAB (APPLE) (from its tartness)] ▸**'crabbedly** *adv* ▸**'crabbedness** *n*

crabby ● ('kræbɪ) *adj* **crabbier, crabbiest.** bad-tempered.

crab louse *n* a parasitic louse that infests the pubic region in man.

crabwise ('kræbˌwaɪz) *adj, adv* (of motion) sideways; like a crab.

crack ● (kræk) *vb* **1** to break or cause to break without complete separation of the parts. **2** to break or cause to break with a sudden sharp sound; snap. **3** to make or cause to make a sudden sharp sound: *to crack a whip.* **4** to cause (the voice) to change tone or become harsh or (of the voice) to change tone, esp. to a higher register; break. **5** *Inf.* to fail or cause to fail. **6** to yield or cause to yield. **7** (*tr*) to hit with a forceful or resounding blow. **8** (*tr*) to break into or force open: *to crack a safe.* **9** (*tr*) to solve or decipher (a code, problem, etc.). **10** (*tr*) *Inf.* to tell (a joke, etc.). **11** to break (a molecule) into smaller molecules or radicals by the action of heat, as in the distillation of petroleum. **12** (*tr*) to open (a bottle) for drinking. **13** (*intr*) *Scot. & N English dialect.* to chat; gossip. **14** (*tr*) *Inf.* to achieve (esp. in **crack it**). **15 crack a smile.** *Inf.* to break into a smile. **16 crack hardy** *or* **hearty.** *Austral. & NZ inf.* to disguise one's discomfort, etc.; put on a bold front. ◆ *n* **17** a sudden sharp noise. **18** a break or fracture without complete separation of the two parts. **19** a narrow opening or fissure. **20** *Inf.* a resounding blow. **21** a physical or mental defect; flaw. **22** a moment or specific instant: *the crack of day.* **23** a broken or cracked tone of voice, as a boy's during puberty. **24** (often foll. by *at*) *Inf.* an attempt; opportunity to try. **25** *Sl.* a gibe; wisecrack; joke. **26** *Sl.* a person that excels. **27** *Scot. & N English dialect.* a talk; chat. **28** *Sl.* a concentrated highly addictive form of cocaine made into pellets or powder and smoked. **29** *Inf., chiefly Irish.* fun; informal entertainment. **30 a fair crack of the whip.** *Inf.* a fair chance or opportunity. **31 crack of doom.** doomsday; the end of the world; the Day of Judgment. ◆ *adj* **32** (*prenominal*) *Sl.* first-class; excellent: *a crack shot.* ◆ See also **crack down, crack up.** [OE *cracian*]

crackbrained ● ('krækˌbreɪnd) *adj* insane, idiotic, or crazy.

crack down ● *vb* (*intr, adv;* often foll. by *on*) **1** to take severe measures (against); become stricter (with). ◆ *n* **crackdown. 2** severe or repressive measures.

cracked ● (krækt) *adj* **1** damaged by cracking. **2** *Inf.* crazy.

cracked wheat *n* whole wheat cracked between rollers so that it will cook more quickly.

cracker ('krækə) *n* **1** a decorated cardboard tube that emits a bang when pulled apart, releasing a toy, a joke, or a paper hat. **2** short for **firecracker. 3** a thin crisp biscuit, usually unsweetened. **4** a person or thing that cracks. **5** *Brit., Austral., & NZ sl.* a thing or person of notable qualities or abilities. **6** See **catalytic cracker.**

crackerjack ('krækəˌdʒæk) *Inf.* ◆ *adj* **1** excellent. ◆ *n* **2** a person or thing of exceptional quality or ability. [C20: changed from CRACK (first-class) + JACK (man)]

crackers ('krækəz) *adj* (*postpositive*) *Brit.* a slang word for **insane.**

crackhead ('krækˌhɛd) *n Sl.* a person addicted to the drug crack.

cracking ('krækɪŋ) *adj* **1** (*prenominal*) *Inf.* fast; vigorous (esp. in **a cracking pace**). **2 get cracking.** *Inf.* to start doing something quickly or with increased speed. ◆ *adv, adj* **3** *Brit. inf.* first-class; excellent. ◆ *n* **4** the process in which molecules are cracked, esp. the oil-refining process in which heavy oils are broken down into hydrocarbons of lower molecular weight by heat or catalysis.

crackjaw ('krækˌdʒɔː) *Inf.* ◆ *adj* **1** difficult to pronounce. ◆ *n* **2** a word or phrase that is difficult to pronounce.

crackle ('krækᵊl) *vb* **crackles, crackling, crackled. 1** to make or cause to make a series of slight sharp noises, as of paper being crushed. **2** (*tr*) to decorate (porcelain or pottery) by causing fine cracks to appear in the glaze. **3** (*intr*) to abound in vivacity or energy. ◆ *n* **4** the act or sound of crackling. **5** intentional crazing in the glaze of porcelain or pottery. **6** Also called: **crackleware.** porcelain or pottery so decorated. ▸**'crackly** *adj*

crackling ('kræklɪŋ) *n* the crisp browned skin of roast pork.

crackpot ('krækˌpɒt) *Inf.* ◆ *n* **1** an eccentric person; crank. ◆ *adj* **2** eccentric; crazy.

crack up ● *vb* (*adv*) **1** (*intr*) to break into pieces. **2** (*intr*) *Inf.* to undergo a physical or mental breakdown. **3** (*tr*) *Inf.* to present or report, esp. in glowing terms: *it's not all it's cracked up to be.* **4** *Inf., chiefly US & Canad.* to laugh or cause to laugh uncontrollably. ◆ *n* **crackup. 5** *Inf.* a physical or mental breakdown.

-cracy *n combining form.* indicating a type of government or rule: *plutocracy; mobocracy.* See also **-crat.** [from Gk *-kratia,* from *kratos* power]

cradle ● ('kreɪdᵊl) *n* **1** a baby's bed, often with rockers. **2** a place where something originates. **3** a frame, rest, or trolley made to support a piece of equipment, aircraft, ship, etc. **4** a platform or trolley in which workmen are suspended on the side of a building or ship. **5** *Agriculture.* **5a** a framework of several wooden fingers attached to a scythe to gather the grain into bunches as it is cut. **5b** a scythe with such a cradle. **6** Also called: **rocker.** a boxlike apparatus for washing rocks, sand, etc., containing gold or gemstones. **7 rob the cradle.** *Inf.* to take for a lover, husband, or wife a person much younger than oneself. ◆ *vb* **cradles, cradling, cradled.** (*tr*) **8** to rock or place in or as if in a cradle; hold tenderly. **9** to nurture in or bring up from infancy. **10** to wash (soil bearing gold, etc.) in a cradle. [OE *cradol*]

cradle snatcher *n Inf.* another name for **baby snatcher** (sense 2).

cradlesong ('kreɪdᵊlˌsɒŋ) *n* a lullaby.

craft ● (krɑːft) *n* **1** skill or ability. **2** skill in deception and trickery. **3** an occupation or trade requiring special skill, esp. manual dexterity. **4a** the members of such a trade, regarded collectively. **4b** (*as modifier*): *a craft union.* **5** a single vessel, aircraft, or spacecraft. **6** (*functioning as pl*) ships, boats, aircraft, or spacecraft collectively. ◆ *vb* **7** (*tr*) to make or fashion with skill, esp. by hand. [OE *cræft* skill, strength]

craftsman ● ('krɑːftsmən) *n, pl* **craftsmen. 1** a member of a skilled trade; someone who practises a craft; artisan. **2** an artist skilled in an art or craft. ▸**'craftsmanˌship** *n*

crafty ● ('krɑːftɪ) *adj* **craftier, craftiest. 1** skilled in deception; shrewd; cunning. **2** *Arch.* skilful. ▸**'craftily** *adv* ▸**'craftiness** *n*

crag ● (kræg) *n* a steep rugged rock or peak. [C13: of Celtic origin]

craggy ● ('krægɪ) *or US* **cragged** ('krægɪd) *adj* **craggier, craggiest. 1** having many crags. **2** (of the face) rugged; rocklike. ▸**'cragginess** *n*

crake (kreɪk) *n Zool.* any of several rails of the Old World, such as the corncrake. [C14: from ON *krāka* crow or *krākr* raven, imit.]

cram ● (kræm) *vb* **crams, cramming, crammed. 1** (*tr*) to force more (people, material, etc.) into (a room, container, etc.) than it can hold; stuff. **2** to eat or cause to eat more than necessary. **3** *Inf.* to study or cause to study (facts, etc.), esp. for an examination, by hastily memorizing. ◆ *n* **4** the act or condition of cramming. **5** a crush. [OE *crammian*]

crambo ('kræmbəʊ) *n* a word game in which one team says a rhyme or rhyming line for a word or line given by the other team. [C17: from earlier *crambe,* prob. from L *crambē repetīta* cabbage repeated, hence an old story]

THESAURUS

formal), sour, splenetic, surly, tart, testy, tetchy, tough, trying **2** = **unreadable**, awkward, cramped, hieroglyphical, illegible, indecipherable, laboured, squeezed

crabby *adj* = **bad-tempered**, acid, cross, crotchety (*inf.*), grouchy (*inf.*), ill-humoured, irritable, prickly, ratty (*Brit. & NZ inf.*), snappish, snappy, sour, surly, testy, tetchy

crack *vb* **1** = **break**, burst, chip, chop, cleave, crackle, craze, fracture, rive, snap, splinter, split **2** = **snap**, burst, crash, detonate, explode, pop, ring **7** *Informal* = **hit**, buffet, clip (*inf.*), clout (*inf.*), cuff, slap, smack, thump, wallop (*inf.*), whack **9** = **solve**, decipher, fathom, get the answer to, work out ◆ *n* **17** = **snap**, burst, clap, crash, explosion, pop, report **19** = **break**, breach, chink, chip, cleft, cranny, crevice, fissure, fracture, gap, interstice, rift **20** *Informal* = **blow**, buffet, clip (*inf.*), clout (*inf.*), cuff, slap, smack, thump, wallop (*inf.*), whack **24** *Informal* = **attempt**, go (*inf.*), opportunity, shot, stab (*inf.*), try **25** *Informal* = **joke**, dig, funny remark, gag (*inf.*), insult, jibe, quip, smart-alecky remark, wisecrack, witticism ◆ *adj* **32** *Slang* = **first-class**, ace, choice, elite, excellent, first-rate, hand-picked, superior, world-class

crackbrained *adj* = **crazy** (*inf.*), cracked (*sl.*), crackers (*Brit. sl.*), crackpot, idiotic, insane, loopy (*inf.*), lunatic, off one's rocker (*sl.*), off one's trolley (*sl.*), out of one's mind, out to lunch (*inf.*)

crackdown *n* **2** = **suppression**, clampdown, crushing, repression

cracked *adj* **1** = **broken**, chipped, crazed, damaged, defective, faulty, fissured, flawed, imperfect, split **2** *Informal* = **crazy** (*inf.*), batty, crackbrained, crackpot (*inf.*), doolally (*sl.*), eccentric, insane, loony (*sl.*), loopy (*inf.*), nuts (*sl.*), nutty (*sl.*), off one's head *or* nut (*sl.*), off one's trolley (*sl.*), out of one's mind, outré, out to lunch (*inf.*), touched

crack up *vb* **1** *Informal* = **have a breakdown**, break down, collapse, come apart at the seams (*inf.*), flip one's lid (*sl.*), freak out (*inf.*), go crazy (*inf.*), go off one's head (*sl.*), go off the deep end (*inf.*), go out of one's mind, go to pieces, throw a wobbly (*sl.*)

cradle *n* **1** = **crib**, bassinet, cot, Moses basket **2** = **birthplace**, beginning, fount, fountainhead, origin, source, spring, wellspring ◆ *vb* **8** = **hold**, lull, nestle, nurse, rock, support

craft *n* **1** = **skill**, ability, aptitude, art, artistry, cleverness, dexterity, expertise, expertness, ingenuity, knack, know-how (*inf.*), technique, workmanship **2** = **cunning**, artfulness, artifice, contrivance, craftiness, deceit, duplicity, guile, ruse, scheme, shrewdness, stratagem, subterfuge, subtlety, trickery, wiles **3** = **occupation**, business, calling, employment, handicraft, handiwork, line, pursuit, trade, vocation, work **5** = **vessel**, aircraft, barque, boat, plane, ship, spacecraft

craftiness *n* **1** = **cunning**, artfulness, astuteness, canniness, deviousness, duplicity, foxiness, guile, shrewdness, slyness, subtlety, trickiness, wiliness

craftsman *n* **1, 2** = **skilled worker**, artificer, artisan, maker, master, smith, technician, wright

craftsmanship *n* **1** = **workmanship**, artistry, expertise, mastery, technique

crafty *adj* **1** = **cunning**, artful, astute, calculating, canny, deceitful, designing, devious, duplicitous, foxy, fraudulent, guileful, insidious, knowing, scheming, sharp, shrewd, sly, subtle, tricksy, tricky, wily
Antonyms *adj* as green as grass, candid, ethical, frank, honest, ingenuous, innocent, naive, open, simple, wet behind the ears

crag *n* = **rock**, aiguille, bluff, peak, pinnacle, tor

craggy *adj* **1** = **rocky**, broken, cragged, jagged, jaggy (*Scot.*), precipitous, rock-bound, rough, rugged, stony, uneven

cram *vb* **1** = **stuff**, compact, compress, crowd, crush, fill to overflowing, force, jam, overcrowd, overfill, pack, pack in, press, ram, shove, squeeze **2** = **overeat**, glut, gorge, gormandize, guzzle, overfeed, pig out (*sl.*), put *or* pack away, satiate, stuff **3** = **study**, bone up (*inf.*), con, grind, mug up, revise, swot, swot up

crammer ('kræmə) *n* a person or school that prepares pupils for an examination.

cramp[1] ➊ (kræmp) *n* **1** a painful involuntary contraction of a muscle, typically caused by overexertion, heat, or chill. **2** temporary partial paralysis of a muscle group: *writer's cramp.* **3** (*usually pl in the US and Canada*) severe abdominal pain. ◆ *vb* **4** (*tr*) to affect with or as if with a cramp. [C14: from OF *crampe,* of Gmc origin]

cramp[2] ➊ (kræmp) *n* **1** Also called: **cramp iron.** a strip of metal with its ends bent at right angles, used to bind masonry. **2** a device for holding pieces of wood while they are glued; clamp. **3** something that confines or restricts. ◆ *vb* (*tr*) **4** to hold with a cramp. **5** to confine or restrict. **6 cramp (someone's) style.** *Inf.* to prevent (a person) from using his abilities or acting freely and confidently. [C15: from MDu. *crampe* cramp, hook, of Gmc origin]

cramped ➊ (kræmpt) *adj* **1** closed in; restricted. **2** (esp. of handwriting) small and irregular.

crampon ('kræmpən) *or* **crampoon** (kræm'pu:n) *n* **1** one of a pair of pivoted steel levers used to lift heavy objects; grappling iron. **2** (*often pl*) one of a pair of frames each with 10 or 12 metal spikes, strapped to boots for climbing or walking on ice or snow. [C15: from F, from MDu. *crampe* hook; see CRAMP[2]]

cran (kræn) *n* a unit of capacity used for fresh herring, equal to 37.5 gallons. [C18: from ?]

cranberry ('krænbərɪ, -brɪ) *n, pl* **cranberries. 1** any of several trailing shrubs that bear sour edible red berries. **2** the berry of this plant. [C17: from Low G *kraanbere,* from *kraan* CRANE + *bere* BERRY]

crane (kreɪn) *n* **1** a large long-necked long-legged wading bird inhabiting marshes and plains in most parts of the world. **2** (not in ornithological use) any similar bird, such as a heron. **3** a device for lifting and moving heavy objects, typically consisting of a pivoted boom rotating about a vertical axis with lifting gear suspended from the end of the boom. ◆ *vb* **cranes, craning, craned. 4** (*tr*) to lift or move (an object) by or as if by a crane. **5** to stretch out (esp. the neck), as to see over other people's heads. [OE *cran*]

crane fly *n* a dipterous fly having long legs, slender wings, and a narrow body. Also called (Brit.): **daddy-longlegs.**

cranesbill ('kreɪnz,bɪl) *n* any of various plants of the genus *Geranium,* having pink or purple flowers and long slender beaked fruits.

cranial ('kreɪnɪəl) *adj* of or relating to the skull.
▸**'cranially** *adv*

cranial index *n* the ratio of the greatest length to the greatest width of the cranium, multiplied by 100.

cranial nerve *n* any of the 12 paired nerves that have their origin in the brain.

craniate ('kreɪnɪɪt, -,eɪt) *adj* **1** having a skull or cranium. ◆ *adj, n* **2** another word for **vertebrate.**

cranio- *or before a vowel* **crani-** *combining form.* indicating the cranium or cranial.

craniology (,kreɪnɪ'ɒlədʒɪ) *n* the branch of science concerned with the shape and size of the human skull.
▸**craniological** (,kreɪnɪə'lɒdʒɪk°l) *adj* ▸**,cranio'logically** *adv* ▸**,crani'ologist** *n*

craniometry (,kreɪnɪ'ɒmɪtrɪ) *n* the study and measurement of skulls.
▸**craniometric** (,kreɪnɪə'metrɪk) *or* **,cranio'metrical** *adj* ▸**,cranio'metrically** *adv* ▸**,crani'ometrist** *n*

craniotomy (,kreɪnɪ'ɒtəmɪ) *n, pl* **craniotomies. 1** surgical incision into the skull. **2** surgical crushing of a fetal skull to extract a dead fetus.

cranium ('kreɪnɪəm) *n, pl* **craniums** *or* **crania** (-nɪə). **1** the skull of a vertebrate. **2** the part of the skull that encloses the brain. [C16: from Med. L *crānium* skull, from Gk *kranion*]

crank ➊ (kræŋk) *n* **1** a device for communicating or converting motion, consisting of an arm projecting from a shaft, often with a second member attached to it parallel to the shaft. **2** Also called: **crank handle, starting handle.** a handle incorporating a crank, used to start an engine or motor. **3** *Inf.* **3a** an eccentric or odd person. **3b** *US, Canad., Austral., NZ, & Irish.* a bad-tempered person. ◆ *vb* (*tr*) **4** to rotate (a shaft) by means of a crank. **5** to start (an engine, motor, etc.) by means of a crank handle. [OE *cranc*]

crankcase ('kræŋk,keɪs) *n* the metal housing that encloses the crankshaft, connecting rods, etc., in an internal-combustion engine.

crankpin ('kræŋk,pɪn) *n* a short cylindrical surface fitted between two arms of a crank parallel to the main shaft of the crankshaft.

crankshaft ('kræŋk,ʃɑ:ft) *n* a shaft having one or more cranks, to which the connecting rods are attached.

crank up *vb* (*adv*) *Sl.* **1** (*tr*) to increase (loudness, output, etc.): *he cranked up his pace.* **2** (*tr*) to set in motion or invigorate: *news editors have to crank up tired reporters.* **3** (*intr*) to inject a narcotic drug.

cranky ➊ ('kræŋkɪ) *adj* **crankier, crankiest. 1** *Inf.* eccentric. **2** *Inf.* fussy and bad-tempered. **3** shaky; out of order.
▸**'crankily** *adv* ▸**'crankiness** *n*

crannog ('krænəg) *n* an ancient Celtic lake or bog dwelling. [C19: from Irish Gaelic *crannóg,* from OIrish *crann* tree]

cranny ➊ ('krænɪ) *n, pl* **crannies.** a narrow opening, as in a wall or rock face; chink; crevice (esp. in **every nook and cranny**). [C15: from OF *cran* notch, fissure; cf. CRENEL]
▸**'crannied** *adj*

crap[1] (kræp) *n* **1** a losing throw in the game of craps. **2** another name for **craps.** [C20: back formation from CRAPS]

crap[2] (kræp) *Sl.* ◆ *n* **1** nonsense. **2** rubbish. **3** a taboo word for **faeces.** ◆ *vb* **craps, crapping, crapped. 4** (*intr*) a taboo word for **defecate.** [C15 *crappe* chaff, from MDu., prob. from *crappen* to break off]

crape (kreɪp) *n* **1** a variant spelling of **crepe. 2** crepe, esp. when used for mourning clothes. **3** a band of black crepe worn in mourning.

crap out *vb* (*intr, adv*) *Sl.* **1** *US.* to make a losing throw in craps. **2** *US.* to fail; withdraw. **3** to fail to attempt something through fear.

craps (kræps) *n* (*usually functioning as sing*) **1** a gambling game using two dice. **2 shoot craps.** to play this game. [C19: prob. from *crabs* lowest throw at dice, pl of CRAB[1]]
▸**'crap,shooter** *n*

crapulent ('kræpjʊlənt) *or* **crapulous** ('kræpjʊləs) *adj* **1** given to or resulting from intemperance. **2** suffering from intemperance; drunken. [C18: from LL *crāpulentus* drunk, from L *crāpula,* from Gk *kraipalē* drunkenness, headache resulting therefrom]
▸**'crapulence** *n*

crash[1] ➊ (kræʃ) *vb* **1** to make or cause to make a loud noise as of solid objects smashing or clattering. **2** to fall or cause to fall with force, breaking in pieces with a loud noise. **3** (*intr*) to break or smash in pieces with a loud noise. **4** (*intr*) to collapse or fail suddenly. **5** to cause (an aircraft) to land violently resulting in severe damage or (of an aircraft) to land in this way. **6** to cause (a car, etc.) to collide with another car or other object or (of two or more cars) to be involved in a collision. **7** to move or cause to move violently or noisily. **8** (*intr*) (of a computer system or program) to fail suddenly because of a malfunction. **9** *Brit. inf.* short for **gate-crash.** ◆ *n* **10** an act or instance of breaking and falling to pieces. **11** a sudden loud noise. **12** a collision, as between vehicles. **13** a sudden descent of an aircraft as a result of which it hits land or water. **14** the sudden collapse of a business, stock exchange, etc. **15** (*modifier*) requiring or using intensive effort and all possible resources in order to accomplish something quickly: *a crash course.* [C14: prob. from *crasen* to smash, shatter + *dasshen* to strike violently, DASH[1]; see CRAZE]

crash[2] (kræʃ) *n* a coarse cotton or linen cloth. [C19: from Russian *krashenina* coloured linen]

crash barrier *n* a barrier erected along the centre of a motorway, around a racetrack, etc., for safety purposes.

crash dive *n* **1** a sudden steep dive from the surface by a submarine. ◆ *vb* **crash-dive, crash-dives, crash-diving, crash-dived. 2** (*intr*) (usually of an aircraft) to descend steeply and rapidly, before hitting the ground. **3** to perform or cause to perform a crash dive.

crash helmet *n* a padded helmet worn for motorcycling, flying, etc., to protect the head.

crashing ('kræʃɪŋ) *adj* (*prenominal*) *Inf.* (intensifier) (esp. in **a crashing bore**).

crash-land *vb* to land (an aircraft) causing some damage to it or (of an aircraft) to land in this way.
▸**'crash-,landing** *n*

crash team *n* a medical team with special equipment able to be mobilized quickly to treat cardiac arrest.

crass ➊ (kræs) *adj* **1** stupid; gross. **2** *Rare.* thick or coarse. [C16: from L *crassus* thick, dense, gross]
▸**'crassly** *adv* ▸**'crassness** *or* **'crassi,tude** *n*

THESAURUS

cramp[1] *n* **1** = **spasm**, ache, contraction, convulsion, crick, pain, pang, shooting pain, stiffness, stitch, twinge

cramp[2] *vb* **5** = **restrict**, check, circumscribe, clip someone's wings, clog, confine, constrain, encumber, hamper, hamstring, handicap, hinder, impede, inhibit, obstruct, shackle, stymie, thwart

cramped *adj* **1** = **closed in**, awkward, circumscribed, confined, congested, crowded, hemmed in, jammed in, narrow, overcrowded, packed, restricted, squeezed, uncomfortable **2** = **small**, crabbed, indecipherable, irregular
Antonyms *adj* ≠ **closed in**: capacious, commodious, large, open, roomy, sizable *or* sizeable, spacious, uncongested, uncrowded

crank *n* **3a** *Informal* = **eccentric**, case (*inf.*), character (*inf.*), freak (*inf.*), kook (*US & Canad. inf.*), nut (*sl.*), oddball (*inf.*), odd fish (*inf.*), queer fish (*Brit. inf.*), rum customer (*Brit. sl.*), weirdo *or* weirdie (*inf.*)

cranky *adj* **1** *Informal* = **eccentric**, bizarre, capricious, erratic, freaky (*sl.*), funny (*inf.*), idiosyncratic, odd, oddball (*inf.*), off-the-wall (*sl.*), outré, peculiar, queer, quirky, rum (*Brit. sl.*), strange, wacky (*sl.*)

cranny *n* = **crevice**, breach, chink, cleft, crack, fissure, gap, hole, interstice, nook, opening, rift

crash[1] *vb* **2** = **hurtle**, come a cropper (*inf.*), dash, fall, fall headlong, give way, lurch, overbalance, pitch, plunge, precipitate oneself, sprawl, topple **3** = **smash**, break, break up, dash to pieces, disintegrate, fracture, fragment, shatter, shiver, splinter **4** = **collapse**, be ruined, fail, fold, fold up, go belly up (*inf.*), go broke (*inf.*), go bust (*inf.*), go to the wall, go under, smash **5, 6** = **collide**, bang, bump (into), crash-land (*an aircraft*), drive into, have an accident, hit, hurtle into, plough into, run together, wreck ◆ *n* **11** = **smash**, bang, boom, clang, clash, clatter, clattering, din, racket, smashing, thunder **12** = **collision**, accident, bump, jar, jolt, pile-up (*inf.*), prang (*inf.*), smash, smash-up, thud, thump, wreck **14** = **collapse**, bankruptcy, debacle, depression, downfall, failure, ruin, smash ◆ *modifier* **15** = **intensive**, emergency, immediate, round-the-clock, speeded-up, telescoped, urgent

crass *adj* **1** = **insensitive**, asinine, blundering, boorish, bovine, coarse, dense, doltish, gross, indelicate, lumpish, oafish, obtuse, stupid, unrefined, witless
Antonyms *adj* brainy (*inf.*), bright, clever, elegant,

-crat *n combining form.* indicating a person who takes part in or is a member of a form of government or class. [from Gk *-kratēs*, from *-kratia* -CRACY]
▸**-cratic** *or* **-cratical** *adj combining form.*

crate ⓘ (kreɪt) *n* **1** a fairly large container, usually made of wooden slats or wickerwork, used for packing, storing, or transporting goods. **2** *Sl.* an old car, aeroplane, etc. ◆ *vb* **crates, crating, crated. 3** *(tr)* to pack or place in a crate. [C16: from L *crātis* wickerwork, hurdle]
▸**'crater** *n* ▸**'crateful** *n*

crater ⓘ ('kreɪtə) *n* **1** the bowl-shaped opening in a volcano or a geyser. **2** a similar depression formed by the impact of a meteorite or exploding bomb. **3** any of the roughly circular or polygonal walled formations on the moon and some planets. **4** a large open bowl with two handles, used for mixing wines, esp. in ancient Greece. ◆ *vb* **5** to make or form craters in (a surface, such as the ground). [C17: from L: mixing bowl, crater, from Gk *kratēr*, from *kerannunai* to mix]
▸**'crater-ˌlike** *adj* ▸**'craterous** *adj*

cravat (krə'væt) *n* a scarf worn round the neck instead of a tie, esp. by men. [C17: from F *cravate*, from Serbo-Croat *Hrvat* Croat; so called because worn by Croats in the French army during the Thirty Years' War]

crave ⓘ (kreɪv) *vb* **craves, craving, craved. 1** (when *intr*, foll. by *for* or *after*) to desire intensely; long (for). **2** *(tr)* to need greatly or urgently. **3** *(tr)* to beg or plead for. [OE *crafian*]
▸**'craver** *n* ▸**'craving** *n*

craven ⓘ ('kreɪvᵊn) *adj* **1** cowardly. ◆ *n* **2** a coward. [C13 *cravant*, prob. from OF *crevant* bursting, from *crever* to burst, die, from L *crepāre* to burst, crack]
▸**'cravenly** *adv* ▸**'cravenness** *n*

craw (krɔː) *n* **1** a less common word for **crop** (sense 6). **2** the stomach of an animal. **3 stick in one's craw.** *Inf.* to be difficult, or against one's conscience, for one to accept, utter, etc. [C14: rel. to MHG *krage*, MDu. *crāghe* neck, Icelandic *kragi* collar]

crawfish ('krɔːˌfɪʃ) *n, pl* **crawfish** *or* **crawfishes.** a variant of **crayfish** (esp. sense 2).

crawl[1] ⓘ (krɔːl) *vb (intr)* **1** to move slowly, either by dragging the body along the ground or on the hands and knees. **2** to proceed very slowly or laboriously. **3** to act in a servile manner; fawn. **4** to be or feel as if overrun by something unpleasant, esp. crawling creatures: *the pile of refuse crawled with insects.* **5** (of insects, worms, snakes, etc.) to move with the body close to the ground. **6** to swim the crawl. ◆ *n* **7** a slow creeping pace or motion. **8** *Swimming.* a stroke in which the feet are kicked like paddles while each arm in turn reaches forward and pulls back through the water. [C14: prob. from ON *krafla* to creep]
▸**'crawler** *n* ▸**'crawlingly** *adv*

crawl[2] (krɔːl) *n* an enclosure in shallow, coastal water for fish, lobsters, etc. [C17: from Du. KRAAL]

crawler lane *n* a lane on an uphill section of a motorway reserved for slow vehicles.

crawling ('krɔːlɪŋ) *n* a defect in freshly applied paint or varnish characterized by bare patches and ridging.

crawly ('krɔːlɪ) *adj* **crawlier, crawliest.** *Inf.* feeling or causing a sensation like creatures crawling on one's skin.

crayfish ('kreɪˌfɪʃ) *or esp. US* **crawfish** *n, pl* **crayfish** *or* **crayfishes. 1** a freshwater decapod crustacean resembling a small lobster. **2** any of various similar crustaceans, esp. the spiny lobster. [C14: *cray*, by folk etymology, from OF *crevice* crab, from OHG *krebiz* + fish]

crayon ('kreɪən, -ɒn) *n* **1** a small stick or pencil of charcoal, wax, clay, or chalk mixed with coloured pigment. **2** a drawing made with crayons. ◆ *vb* **3** to draw or colour with crayons. [C17: from F, from *craie*, from L *crēta* chalk]
▸**'crayonist** *n*

craze ⓘ (kreɪz) *n* **1** a short-lived fashion. **2** a wild or exaggerated enthusiasm. ◆ *vb* **crazes, crazing, crazed. 3** to make or become mad. **4** *Ceramics, metallurgy.* to develop or cause to develop fine cracks. [C14 (in the sense: to break, shatter): prob. from ON]

crazy ⓘ ('kreɪzɪ) *adj* **crazier, craziest. 1** *Inf.* insane. **2** fantastic; strange; ridiculous. **3** *(postpositive;* foll. by *about* or *over) Inf.* extremely fond (of).
▸**'crazily** *adv* ▸**'craziness** *n*

crazy paving *n Brit.* a form of paving, as for a path, made of irregular slabs of stone.

creak ⓘ (kriːk) *vb* **1** to make or cause to make a harsh squeaking sound. **2** *(intr)* to make such sounds while moving: *the old car creaked along.* ◆ *n* **3** a harsh squeaking sound. [C14: var. of CROAK, imit.]
▸**'creaky** *adj* ▸**'creakily** *adv* ▸**'creakiness** *n* ▸**'creakingly** *adv*

cream ⓘ (kriːm) *n* **1a** the fatty part of milk, which rises to the top. **1b** *(as modifier): cream buns.* **2** anything resembling cream in consistency. **3** the best one or most essential part of something; pick. **4** a soup containing cream or milk: *cream of chicken soup.* **5** any of various foods resembling or containing cream. **6a** a yellowish-white colour. **6b** *(as adj): cream wallpaper.* ◆ *vb (tr)* **7** to skim or otherwise separate the cream from (milk). **8** to beat (foodstuffs) to a light creamy consistency. **9** to add or apply cream or any creamlike substance to. **10** (sometimes foll. by *off*) to take away the best part of. **11** to prepare or cook (vegetables, chicken, etc.) with cream or milk. [C14: from OF *cresme*, from LL *crāmum* cream, of Celtic origin; infl. by Church L *chrisma* unction, CHRISM]
▸**'creamˌlike** *adj*

cream cheese *n* a smooth soft white cheese made from soured cream or milk.

cream cracker *n Brit.* a crisp unsweetened biscuit, often eaten with cheese.

creamer ('kriːmə) *n* **1** a vessel or device for separating cream from milk. **2** a powdered substitute for cream, used in coffee. **3** *Now chiefly US & Canad.* a small jug or pitcher for serving cream.

creamery ('kriːmərɪ) *n, pl* **creameries. 1** an establishment where milk and cream are made into butter and cheese. **2** a place where dairy products are sold.

cream of tartar *n* potassium hydrogen tartrate, esp. when used in baking powders.

cream puff *n* a shell of light pastry with a custard or cream filling.

cream soda *n* a soft drink flavoured with vanilla.

cream tea *n* afternoon tea including bread or scones served with clotted cream and jam.

creamy ⓘ ('kriːmɪ) *adj* **creamier, creamiest. 1** resembling cream in colour, taste, or consistency. **2** containing cream.
▸**'creaminess** *n*

crease ⓘ (kriːs) *n* **1** a line or mark produced by folding, pressing, or wrinkling. **2** a wrinkle or furrow, esp. on the face. **3** *Cricket.* any of four lines near each wicket marking positions for the bowler or batsman. See also **bowling crease, popping crease, return crease.** ◆ *vb* **creases, creas-**

THESAURUS

intelligent, polished, refined, sensitive, sharp, smart

crassness *n* **1** = **insensitivity**, asininity, boorishness, coarseness, denseness, doltishness, grossness, indelicacy, oafishness, stupidity, tactlessness, vulgarity

crate *n* **1** = **container**, box, case, packing case, tea chest ◆ *vb* **3** = **box**, case, encase, enclose, pack, pack up

crater *n* **2** = **hollow**, depression, dip, shell hole

crave *vb* **1, 2** = **long for**, be dying for, cry out for (*inf.*), desire, eat one's heart out over, fancy (*inf.*), hanker after, hope for, hunger after, lust after, need, pant for, pine for, require, set one's heart on, sigh for, thirst for, want, would give one's eyeteeth for, yearn for **3** *Informal* = **beg**, ask, beseech, entreat, implore, petition, plead for, pray for, seek, solicit, supplicate

craven *adj* **1** = **cowardly**, abject, chicken-hearted, dastardly, fearful, lily-livered, mean-spirited, pusillanimous, scared, timorous, weak, yellow (*inf.*) ◆ *n* **2** = **coward**, caitiff (*arch.*), dastard (*arch.*), poltroon, recreant (*arch.*), renegade, yellow-belly (*sl.*)

craving *n* **1** = **longing**, ache, appetite, cacoethes, desire, hankering, hope, hunger, lust, thirst, urge, yearning, yen (*inf.*)

craw *n* **2** = **throat**, crop, gizzard, gullet, maw, stomach

crawl[1] *vb* **1, 2** = **creep**, advance slowly, drag, go on all fours, inch, move at a snail's pace, move on hands and knees, pull *or* drag oneself along, slither, worm one's way, wriggle, writhe **3** = **grovel**, abase oneself, brown-nose, creep, cringe, fawn, kiss ass (*US. & Canad. taboo slang*), lick someone's boots (*sl.*), pander to, suck up to someone (*sl.*), toady, truckle **4** = **be full of**, be alive, be lousy, be overrun (*sl.*), swarm, teem
Antonyms *vb* ≠ **creep:** dart, dash, fly, hasten, hurry, race, run, rush, sprint, step on it (*inf.*), walk

craze *n* **1, 2** = **fad**, enthusiasm, fashion, infatuation, mania, mode, novelty, passion, preoccupation, rage, the latest (*inf.*), thing, trend, vogue ◆ *vb* **3** = **drive mad**, bewilder, confuse, dement, derange, distemper, enrage, infatuate, inflame, madden, make insane, send crazy *or* berserk, unbalance, unhinge, unsettle

crazy *adj* **1** = **insane**, barking (*sl.*), barmy (*sl.*), batty (*sl.*), berserk, bonkers (*sl., chiefly Brit.*), cracked (*sl.*), crazed, cuckoo (*inf.*), daft (*inf.*), delirious, demented, deranged, doolally (*sl.*), idiotic, loopy (*inf.*), lunatic, mad, mad as a hatter, maniacal, mental (*sl.*), not right in the head, not the full shilling (*inf.*), nuts (*sl.*), nutty (*sl.*), off one's head (*sl.*), off one's trolley (*sl.*), of unsound mind, out of one's mind, out to lunch (*inf.*), potty (*Brit. inf.*), touched, unbalanced, unhinged **2** = **ridiculous**, absurd, bird-brained (*inf.*), bizarre, derisory, eccentric, fantastic, fatuous, foolhardy, foolish, half-baked (*inf.*), idiotic, ill-conceived, impracticable, imprudent, inane, inappropriate, irresponsible, ludicrous, nonsensical, odd, oddball, outrageous, peculiar, potty (*Brit. inf.*), preposterous, puerile, quixotic, senseless, short-sighted, silly, strange, unrealistic, unwise, unworkable, weird, wild **3** *foll. by* **about** *or* **over** = **fanatical**, ablaze, ardent, devoted, eager, enamoured, enthusiastic, hysterical, infatuated, into (*inf.*), mad, passionate, smitten, very keen, wild (*inf.*), zealous
Antonyms *adj* ≠ **insane:** all there (*inf.*), *compos mentis*, down-to-earth, in one's right mind, intelligent, mentally sound, practical, prudent, rational, reasonable, sane, sensible, smart, wise ≠ **ridiculous:** appropriate, brilliant, conventional, feasible, orthodox, possible, practicable, prudent, realistic, responsible, sensible, wise, workable ≠ **fanatical:** cool, indifferent, uncaring, unenthusiastic, uninterested

creak *vb* **1** = **squeak**, grate, grind, groan, rasp, scrape, scratch, screech, squeal

creaky *adj* **1** = **squeaky**, creaking, grating, rasping, raspy, rusty, squeaking, unoiled

cream *n* **2** = **lotion**, cosmetic, emulsion, essence, liniment, oil, ointment, paste, salve, unguent **3** = **best**, *crème de la crème*, elite, flower, pick, prime ◆ *adj* **6b** = **off-white**, yellowish-white

creamy *adj* **1** = **smooth**, buttery, creamed, lush, milky, oily, rich, soft, velvety

crease *n* **1** = **line**, bulge, corrugation, fold, groove, overlap, pucker, ridge, ruck, tuck, wrinkle ◆ *vb* **4** = **wrinkle**, corrugate, crimp, crinkle, crumple, double up, fold, pucker, ridge, ruck up, rumple, screw up

ing, creased. **4** to make or become wrinkled or furrowed. **5** (*tr*) to graze with a bullet. [C15: from earlier *crēst;* prob. rel. to OF *cresté* wrinkled]
▸'**creaser** *n* ▸'**creasy** *adj*

create ⓘ (kriː'eɪt) *vb* **creates, creating, created. 1** (*tr*) to cause to come into existence. **2** (*tr*) to invest with a new honour, office, or title; appoint. **3** (*tr*) to be the cause of. **4** (*tr*) to act (a role) in the first production of a play. **5** (*intr*) *Brit. sl.* to make a fuss or uproar. [C14 *creat* created, from L *creātus,* from *creāre* to produce, make]

creatine ('kriːəˌtiːn, -tɪn) *n* an important compound involved in many biochemical reactions and present in many types of living cells. [C19: from Gk *kreas* flesh + -INE[2]]

creation ⓘ (kriː'eɪʃən) *n* **1** the act or process of creating. **2** the fact of being created or produced. **3** something brought into existence or created. **4** the whole universe.

Creation (kriː'eɪʃən) *n Christianity.* **1** (often preceded by *the*) God's act of bringing the universe into being. **2** the universe as thus brought into being by God.

creative ⓘ (kriː'eɪtɪv) *adj* **1** having the ability to create. **2** characterized by originality of thought; having or showing imagination. **3** designed to or tending to stimulate the imagination. **4** characterized by sophisticated bending of the rules or conventions: *creative accounting.*
▸**cre'atively** *adv* ▸**cre'ativeness** *n* ▸ˌ**crea'tivity** *n*

creator ⓘ (kriː'eɪtə) *n* a person or thing that creates; originator.
▸**cre'atorship** *n*

Creator (kriː'eɪtə) *n* (usually preceded by *the*) an epithet of God.

creature ⓘ ('kriːtʃə) *n* **1** a living being, esp. an animal. **2** something that has been created, whether animate or inanimate. **3** a human being; person: used as a term of scorn, pity, or endearment. **4** a person who is dependent upon another; tool. [C13: from Church L *creātūra,* from L *creāre* to create]
▸'**creatural** *or* '**creaturely** *adj*

crèche (krɛʃ, kreɪʃ) *n* **1** *Chiefly Brit.* **1a** a day nursery for very young children. **1b** a supervised play area provided for young children for short periods. **2** a tableau of Christ's Nativity. [C19: from OF: manger, crib, ult. of Gmc origin]

cred (krɛd) *n Sl.* short for **credibility** (esp. in **street cred**).

credence ⓘ ('kriːdᵊns) *n* **1** acceptance or belief, esp. with regard to the evidence of others. **2** something supporting a claim to belief; credential (esp. in **letters of credence**). **3** short for **credence table.** [C14: from Med. L *crēdentia* trust, credit, from L *crēdere* to believe]

credence table *n Christianity.* a small table on which the Eucharistic bread and wine are placed.

credential ⓘ (krɪ'dɛnʃəl) *n* **1** something that entitles a person to confidence, authority, etc. **2** (*pl*) a letter or certificate giving evidence of the bearer's identity or competence. [C16: from Med. L *crēdentia* credit, trust; see CREDENCE]

credenza (krɪ'dɛnzə) *n* another name for **credence table.** [It.: see CREDENCE]

credibility gap *n* a disparity between claims or statements made and the evident facts of the situation or circumstances to which they relate.

credible ⓘ ('krɛdɪbᵊl) *adj* **1** capable of being believed. **2** trustworthy or reliable: *the latest claim is the only one to involve a credible witness.* [C14: from L *crēdibilis,* from L *crēdere* to believe]
▸'**credibleness** *or* ˌ**credi'bility** *n* ▸'**credibly** *adv*

credit ⓘ ('krɛdɪt) *n* **1** commendation or approval, as for an act or quality. **2** a person or thing serving as a source of good influence, repute, etc. **3** influence or reputation coming from the good opinion of others. **4** belief in the truth, reliability, quality, etc., of someone or something. **5** a sum of money or equivalent purchasing power, available for a person's use. **6a** the positive balance in a person's bank account. **6b** the sum of money that a bank makes available to a client in excess of any deposit. **7a** the practice of permitting a buyer to receive goods or services before payment. **7b** the time permitted for paying for such goods or services. **8** reputation for solvency and probity, inducing confidence among creditors. **9** *Accounting.* **9a** acknowledgment of an income, liability, or capital item by entry on the right-hand side of an account. **9b** the right-hand side of an account. **9c** an entry on this side. **9d** the total of such entries. **9e** (*as modifier*): *credit entries.* **10** *Education.* **10a** a distinction awarded to an examination candidate obtaining good marks. **10b** a section of an examination syllabus satisfactorily completed. **11 on credit.** with payment to be made at a future date. ◆ *vb* **credits, crediting, credited.** (*tr*) **12** (foll. by *with*) to ascribe (to); give credit (for). **13** to accept as true; believe. **14** to do credit to. **15** *Accounting.* **15a** to enter (an item) as a credit in an account. **15b** to acknowledge (a payer) by making such an entry. ◆ See also **credits.** [C16: from OF *crédit,* from It. *credito,* from L *crēditum* loan, from *crēdere* to believe]

creditable ⓘ ('krɛdɪtəbᵊl) *adj* deserving credit, honour, etc.; praiseworthy.
▸'**creditableness** *or* ˌ**credita'bility** *n* ▸'**creditably** *adv*

credit account *n Brit.* a credit system by means of which customers may obtain goods and services before payment.

credit card *n* a card issued by banks, businesses, etc., enabling the holder to obtain goods and services on credit.

Creditiste (ˌkrɛdɪ'tiːst) *Canad.* ◆ *adj* **1** of, supporting, or relating to the Social Credit Rally of Quebec. ◆ *n* **2** a supporter or member of this organization.

creditor ('krɛdɪtə) *n* a person or commercial enterprise to whom money is owed.

credit rating *n* an evaluation of the creditworthiness of an individual or business.

credits ('krɛdɪts) *pl n* a list of those responsible for the production of a film or a television programme.

credit transfer *n* a method of settling a debt by transferring money through a bank or post office, esp. for those who do not have cheque accounts.

creditworthy ('krɛdɪtˌwɜːðɪ) *adj* (of an individual or business) adjudged as meriting credit on the basis of earning power, previous record of debt repayment, etc.
▸'**creditˌworthiness** *n*

credo ('kriːdəʊ, 'kreɪ-) *n, pl* **credos.** any formal statement of beliefs, principles, or opinions.

Credo ('kriːdəʊ, 'kreɪ-) *n, pl* **Credos. 1** the Apostles' or Nicene Creed. **2** a musical setting of the Creed. [C12: from L, lit.: I believe; first word of the Apostles' and Nicene Creeds]

credulity ⓘ (krɪ'djuːlɪtɪ) *n* disposition to believe something on little evidence; gullibility.

credulous ⓘ ('krɛdjʊləs) *adj* **1** tending to believe something on little evidence. **2** arising from or characterized by credulity: *credulous beliefs.* [C16: from L *crēdulus,* from *crēdere* to believe]
▸'**credulously** *adv* ▸'**credulousness** *n*

Cree (kriː) *n* **1** (*pl* **Cree** *or* **Crees**) a member of a N American Indian people living in Ontario, Saskatchewan, and Manitoba. **2** the language of this people.

creed ⓘ (kriːd) *n* **1** a concise, formal statement of the essential articles of Christian belief, such as the Apostles' Creed or the Nicene Creed. **2**

THESAURUS

create *vb* **1 = make,** beget, bring into being *or* existence, coin, compose, concoct, design, develop, devise, dream up (*inf.*), form, formulate, generate, give birth to, give life to, hatch, initiate, invent, originate, produce, spawn **2 = appoint,** constitute, establish, found, install, invest, set up **3 = cause,** bring about, lead to, occasion
Antonyms *vb* ≠ **make:** annihilate, demolish, destroy

creation *n* **1 = making,** conception, constitution, development, establishment, formation, foundation, generation, genesis, inception, institution, laying down, origination, procreation, production, setting up, siring **3 = invention,** achievement, brainchild (*inf.*), *chef-d'oeuvre,* concept, concoction, handiwork, magnum opus, *pièce de résistance,* production **4 = universe,** all living things, cosmos, life, living world, natural world, nature, world

creative *adj* **2 = imaginative,** artistic, clever, fertile, gifted, ingenious, inspired, inventive, original, productive, stimulating, visionary

creativity *n* **2 = imagination,** cleverness, fecundity, fertility, imaginativeness, ingenuity, inspiration, inventiveness, originality, productivity, talent

creator *n* **= maker,** architect, author, begetter, designer, father, framer, initiator, inventor, originator, prime mover

creature *n* **1 = living thing,** animal, beast, being, brute, critter (*US dialect*), dumb animal, lower animal, quadruped **3 = person,** body, character, fellow, human being, individual, man, mortal, soul, wight (*arch.*), woman **4 = minion,** cohort (*chiefly US*), dependant, hanger-on, hireling, instrument (*inf.*), lackey, puppet, retainer, tool, wretch

credence *n* **1 = belief,** acceptance, assurance, certainty, confidence, credit, dependence, faith, reliance, trust

credential *n* **2** *pl* **= certification,** attestation, authorization, card, deed, diploma, docket, document, letter of recommendation *or* introduction, letters of credence, licence, missive, papers, passport, recommendation, reference(s), testament, testimonial, title, voucher, warrant

credibility *n* **1, 2 = believability,** believableness, integrity, plausibility, reliability, tenability, trustworthiness

credible *adj* **1 = believable,** conceivable, imaginable, likely, plausible, possible, probable, reasonable, supposable, tenable, thinkable, verisimilar **2 = reliable,** dependable, honest, sincere, trustworthy, trusty
Antonyms *adj* ≠ **believable:** doubtful, implausible, inconceivable, incredible, questionable, unbelievable, unlikely ≠ **reliable:** dishonest, insincere, not dependable, unreliable, untrustworthy

credit *n* **1 = praise,** acclaim, acknowledgment, approval, Brownie points, commendation, fame, glory, honour, kudos, merit, recognition, thanks, tribute **2 = source of satisfaction** *or* **pride,** feather in one's cap, honour **3 = prestige,** character, clout (*inf.*), esteem, estimation, good name, influence, position, regard, reputation, repute, standing, status **4 = belief,** confidence, credence, faith, reliance, trust **11 on credit = on account,** by deferred payment, by instalments, on hire-purchase, on (the) H.P., on the slate (*inf.*), on tick (*inf.*) ◆ *vb* **12** *foll. by* **with = attribute to,** accredit to, ascribe to, assign to, chalk up to (*inf.*), impute to, refer to **13 = believe,** accept, bank on, buy (*sl.*), depend on, fall for, have faith in, rely on, swallow (*inf.*), trust

creditable *adj* **= praiseworthy,** admirable, commendable, deserving, estimable, exemplary, honourable, laudable, meritorious, reputable, respectable, worthy

credulity *n* **= gullibility,** blind faith, credulousness, naïveté, silliness, simplicity, stupidity

credulous *adj* **1 = gullible,** as green as grass, born yesterday (*inf.*), dupable, green, naive, overtrusting, trustful, uncritical, unsuspecting, unsuspicious, wet behind the ears (*inf.*)
Antonyms *adj* cynical, incredulous, sceptical, suspecting, unbelieving, wary

creed *n* **2 = belief,** articles of faith, canon, catechism, confession, credo, doctrine, dogma,

any statement or system of beliefs or principles. [OE *crēda,* from L *crēdo* I believe]
▸'**creedal** *or* '**credal** *adj*

creek ⓣ (kri:k) *n* **1** *Chiefly Brit.* a narrow inlet or bay, esp. of the sea. **2** *US, Canad., Austral., & NZ.* a small stream or tributary. **3 up the creek.** *Sl.* in trouble; in a difficult position. [C13: from ON *kriki* nook; rel. to MDu. *krēke* creek, inlet]

Creek (kri:k) *n* **1** (*pl* **Creek** *or* **Creeks**) a member of a confederacy of N American Indian tribes formerly living in Georgia and Alabama. **2** any of their languages.

creel (kri:l) *n* **1** a wickerwork basket, esp. one used to hold fish. **2** a wickerwork trap for catching lobsters, etc. [C15: from Scot., from ?]

creep ⓣ (kri:p) *vb* **creeps, creeping, crept.** (*intr*) **1** to crawl with the body near to or touching the ground. **2** to move slowly, quietly, or cautiously. **3** to act in a servile way; fawn; cringe. **4** to move or slip out of place, as from pressure or wear. **5** (of plants) to grow along the ground or over rocks. **6** to develop gradually: *creeping unrest.* **7** to have the sensation of something crawling over the skin. ◆ *n* **8** the act of creeping or a creeping movement. **9** *Sl.* a person considered to be obnoxious or servile. **10** *Geol.* the gradual downward movement of loose rock material, soil, etc., on a slope. [OE *crēopan*]

creeper ⓣ ('kri:pə) *n* **1** a person or animal that creeps. **2** a plant, such as the ivy, that grows by creeping. **3** the US and Canad. name for the **tree creeper. 4** a hooked instrument for dragging deep water. **5** *Inf.* a shoe with a soft sole.

creeps (kri:ps) *pl n* (preceded by *the*) *Inf.* a feeling of fear, repulsion, disgust, etc.

creepy ⓣ ('kri:pɪ) *adj* **creepiest. 1** *Inf.* having or causing a sensation of repulsion or fear, as of creatures crawling on the skin. **2** creeping; slow-moving.
▸'**creepily** *adv* ▸'**creepiness** *n*

creepy-crawly *Brit. inf.* ◆ *n, pl* **creepy-crawlies. 1** a small crawling creature. ◆ *adj* **2** feeling or causing a sensation as of creatures crawling on one's skin.

cremate (krɪ'meɪt) *vb* **cremates, cremating, cremated.** (*tr*) to burn up (something, esp. a corpse) and reduce to ash. [C19: from L *cremāre*]
▸**cre'mation** *n* ▸**cre'mator** *n* ▸**crematory** ('krɛmətərɪ, -trɪ) *adj*

crematorium (ˌkrɛmə'tɔ:rɪəm) *n, pl* **crematoriums** *or* **crematoria** (-rɪə). a building in which corpses are cremated. Also called (esp. US): **crematory.**

crème (krɛm, kri:m, kreɪm; *French* krɛm) *n* **1** cream. **2** any of various sweet liqueurs: *crème de moka.* ◆ *adj* **3** (of a liqueur) rich and sweet.

crème de la crème *French.* (krɛm də la krɛm) *n* the very best. [lit.: cream of the cream]

crème de menthe ('krɛm də 'mɛnθ, 'mɪnt; 'kri:m, 'kreɪm) *n* a liqueur flavoured with peppermint. [F, lit.: cream of mint]

crème fraîche ('krɛm 'frɛʃ) *n* thickened and slightly fermented cream. [F, lit.: fresh cream]

crenate ('kri:neɪt) *or* **crenated** *adj* having a scalloped margin, as certain leaves. [C18: from NL *crēnātus,* from Med. L, prob. from LL *crēna* a notch]
▸'**crenately** *adv* ▸**crenation** (krɪ'neɪʃən) *n*

crenel ('krɛnᵊl) *or* **crenelle** (krɪ'nɛl) *n* any of a set of openings formed in the top of a wall or parapet and having slanting sides, as in a battlement. [C15: from OF, lit.: a little notch, from *cren* notch, from LL *crēna*]

crenellate *or US* **crenelate** ('krɛnɪˌleɪt) *vb* **crenellates, crenellating, crenellated** *or US* **crenelates, crenelating, crenelated.** (*tr*) to supply with battlements. [C19: from OF *creneler,* from CRENEL]
▸'**crenelˌlated** *or US* '**crenelˌated** *adj* ▸ˌ**crenel'lation** *or US* ˌ**crenel'ation** *n*

creole ('kri:əʊl) *n* **1** a language that has its origin in extended contact between two language communities, one of which is European. ◆ *adj* **2** of or relating to creole. **3** (of a sauce or dish) containing or cooked with tomatoes, green peppers, onions, etc. [C17: via F & Sp., prob. from Port. *crioulo* slave born in one's household, prob. from *criar* to bring up, from L *creāre* to CREATE]

Creole ('kri:əʊl) *n* **1** (*sometimes not cap.*) (in the Caribbean and Latin America) **1a** a native-born person of European ancestry. **1b** a native-born person of mixed European and African ancestry who speaks a creole. **2** (in Louisiana and other Gulf States of the US) a native-born person of French ancestry. **3** the French Creole spoken in Louisiana. ◆ *adj* **4** of or relating to any of these peoples.

creosol ('kri:əˌsɒl) *n* a colourless or pale yellow insoluble oily liquid with a smoky odour and a burning taste. [C19: from CREOS(OTE) + -OL[1]]

creosote ('krɪəˌsəʊt) *n* **1** a colourless or pale yellow liquid with a burning taste and penetrating odour distilled from wood tar. It is used as an antiseptic. **2** a thick dark liquid mixture prepared from coal tar: used as a preservative for wood. ◆ *vb* **creosotes, creosoting, creosoted. 3** to treat (wood) with creosote. [C19: from Gk *kreas* flesh + *sōtēr* preserver, from *sōzein* to keep safe]
▸**creosotic** (ˌkrɪə'sɒtɪk) *adj*

crepe *or* **crape** (kreɪp) *n* **1a** a light cotton, silk, or other fabric with a fine ridged or crinkled surface. **1b** (*as modifier*): *a crepe dress.* **2** a black armband originally made of this, worn as a sign of mourning. **3** a very thin pancake, often folded around a filling. **4** short for **crepe paper** or **crepe rubber.** [C19: from F *crêpe,* from L *crispus* curled, uneven, wrinkled]

crepe de Chine (kreɪp də ʃi:n) *n* a very thin crepe of silk or a similar light fabric. [C19: from F: Chinese crepe]

crepe paper *n* thin crinkled coloured paper, resembling crepe and used for decorations.

creperie ('krɛpərɪ, 'kreɪp-) *n* an eating establishment that specializes in pancakes.

crepe rubber *n* a type of rubber in the form of colourless or pale yellow crinkled sheets: used for the soles of shoes.

crêpe suzette (kreɪp su:'zɛt) *n, pl* **crêpes suzettes.** (*sometimes pl*) an orange-flavoured pancake flambéed in a liqueur or brandy.

crepitate ('krɛpɪˌteɪt) *vb* **crepitates, crepitating, crepitated.** (*intr*) to make a rattling or crackling sound. [C17: from L *crepitāre*]
▸'**crepitant** *adj* ▸ˌ**crepi'tation** *n*

crepitus ('krɛpɪtəs) *n* **1** a crackling chest sound heard in pneumonia, etc. **2** the grating sound of two ends of a broken bone rubbing together. ◆ Also called: **crepitation.** [C19: from L, from *crepāre* to crack, creak]

crept (krɛpt) *vb* the past tense and past participle of **creep.**

crepuscular (krɪ'pʌskjʊlə) *adj* **1** of or like twilight; dim. **2** (of certain creatures) active at twilight or just before dawn. [C17: from L *crepusculum* dusk, from *creper* dark]

crepy *or* **crepey** ('kreɪpɪ) *adj* **crepier, crepiest.** (esp. of the skin) having a dry wrinkled appearance.

Cres. *abbrev. for* Crescent.

crescendo (krɪ'ʃɛndəʊ) *n, pl* **crescendos** *or* **crescendi** (-dɪ). **1** *Music.* **1a** a gradual increase in loudness or the musical direction or symbol indicating this. Abbrev.: **cresc.** Symbol: < **1b** (*as modifier*): *a crescendo passage.* **2** any similar gradual increase in loudness. **3** a peak of noise or intensity: *the cheers reached a crescendo.* ◆ *vb* **crescendos, crescendoing, crescendoed. 4** (*intr*) to increase in loudness or force. ◆ *adv* **5** with a crescendo. [C18: from It., lit.: increasing, from *crescere* to grow, from L]

crescent ⓣ ('krɛsᵊnt, -zᵊnt) *n* **1** the curved shape of the moon in its first or last quarter. **2** any shape or object resembling this. **3** *Chiefly Brit.* a crescent-shaped street. **4** (*often cap.* and preceded by *the*) **4a** the emblem of Islam or Turkey. **4b** Islamic or Turkish power. ◆ *adj* **5** *Arch. or poetic.* increasing or growing. [C14: from L *crescēns* increasing, from *crescere* to grow]

cresol ('kri:sɒl) *n* an aromatic compound found in coal tar and creosote and used in making synthetic resins and as an antiseptic and disinfectant. Formula: $C_6H_4(CH_3)OH$. Systematic name: **methylphenol.**

cress (krɛs) *n* any of various plants having pungent-tasting leaves often used in salads and as a garnish. [OE *cressa*]

cresset ('krɛsɪt) *n History.* a metal basket mounted on a pole in which oil or pitch was burned for illumination. [C14: from OF *craisset,* from *craisse* GREASE]

crest ⓣ (krɛst) *n* **1** a tuft or growth of feathers, fur, or skin along the top of the heads of some birds, reptiles, and other animals. **2** something resembling or suggesting this. **3** the top, highest point, or highest stage of something. **4** an ornamental piece, such as a plume, on top of a helmet. **5** *Heraldry.* a symbol of a family or office, borne in addition to a coat of arms and used in medieval times to decorate the helmet. ◆ *vb* **6** (*intr*) to come or rise to a high point. **7** (*tr*) to lie at the top of; cap. **8** (*tr*) to reach the top of (a hill, wave, etc.). [C14: from OF *creste,* from L *crista*]
▸'**crested** *adj* ▸'**crestless** *adj*

crestfallen ⓣ ('krɛstˌfɔ:lən) *adj* dejected or disheartened.
▸'**crestˌfallenly** *adv*

cretaceous (krɪ'teɪʃəs) *adj* consisting of or resembling chalk. [C17: from L *crētāceus,* from *crēta,* lit.: Cretan earth, that is, chalk]

THESAURUS

persuasion, principles, profession (*of faith*), tenet

creek *n* **1** = **inlet**, bay, bight, cove, firth *or* frith (*Scot.*) **2** *US, Canad., Austral., & N.Z.* = **stream**, bayou, brook, rivulet, runnel, streamlet, tributary, watercourse

creep *vb* **1** = **crawl**, crawl on all fours, glide, insinuate, slither, squirm, worm, wriggle, writhe **2** = **sneak**, approach unnoticed, crawl, dawdle, edge, inch, proceed at a snail's pace, skulk, slink, steal, tiptoe **3** = **grovel**, bootlick (*inf.*), brown-nose (*taboo sl.*), cower, cringe, fawn, kiss (someone's) ass (*US & Canad. taboo sl.*), kowtow, pander to, scrape, suck up to (*inf.*), toady, truckle ◆ *n* **9** *Slang* = **bootlicker** (*inf.*), ass-kisser (*US & Canad. taboo sl.*), brown-noser (*taboo sl.*), crawler (*sl.*), sneak, sycophant, toady

creeper *n* **2** = **climbing plant**, climber, rambler, runner, trailing plant, vine (*chiefly US*)

creepy *adj* **1** *Informal* = **disturbing**, awful, direful, disgusting, eerie, forbidding, frightening, ghoulish, goose-pimply (*inf.*), gruesome, hair-raising, horrible, macabre, menacing, nightmarish, ominous, scary (*inf.*), sinister, terrifying, threatening, unpleasant, weird

crescent *n* **1** = **meniscus**, half-moon, new moon, old moon, sickle, sickle-shape ◆ *adj* **5** *Archaic* = **waxing**, growing, increasing

crest *n* **1** = **tuft**, aigrette, caruncle (*Zoology*), cockscomb, comb, crown, mane, panache, plume, tassel, topknot **3** = **top**, apex, crown, head, height, highest point, peak, pinnacle, ridge, summit **5** = **emblem**, badge, bearings, charge, device, insignia, symbol

crestfallen *adj* = **disappointed**, chapfallen, choked, dejected, depressed, despondent, disconsolate, discouraged, disheartened, downcast, downhearted, sick as a parrot (*inf.*)
Antonyms *adj* cock-a-hoop, elated, encouraged,

Cretaceous (krɪˈteɪʃəs) *adj* **1** of, denoting, or formed in the last period of the Mesozoic era, during which chalk deposits were formed. ◆ *n* **2 the.** the Cretaceous period or rock system.

Cretan (ˈkriːtən) *adj* **1** of or relating to the island of Crete in the W Mediterranean. **2** of the inhabitants of Crete. ◆ *n* **3** a native or inhabitant of Crete.

cretin (ˈkrɛtɪn) *n* **1** a person afflicted with cretinism. **2** a person considered to be extremely stupid. [C18: from F *crétin,* from Swiss F *crestin,* from L *Chrīstiānus* Christian, alluding to the humanity of such people, despite their handicaps]
▸ **ˈcretinous** *adj*

cretinism (ˈkrɛtɪˌnɪzəm) *n* a condition arising from a deficiency of thyroid hormone, present from birth, characterized by dwarfism and mental retardation. See also **myxoedema.**

cretonne (krɛˈtɒn, ˈkrɛtɒn) *n* a heavy cotton or linen fabric with a printed design, used for furnishing. [C19: from F, from *Creton* Norman village where it originated]

Creutzfeldt-Jakob disease (ˈkrɔɪtsfelt ˈjaːkɒp) *n* a fatal slow-developing disease that affects the central nervous system, characterized by mental deterioration and loss of coordination of the limbs. It is thought to be caused by an abnormal prion protein in the brain. [C20: after Hans G. *Creutzfeldt* (1885–1964) and Alfons *Jakob* (1884–1931), German physicians]

crevasse ⓣ (krɪˈvæs) *n* **1** a deep crack or fissure, esp. in the ice of a glacier. **2** *US.* a break in a river embankment. ◆ *vb* **crevasses, crevassing, crevassed. 3** (*tr*) *US.* to make a break or fissure in (a dyke, wall, etc.). [C19: from F: CREVICE]

crevice ⓣ (ˈkrɛvɪs) *n* a narrow fissure or crack; split; cleft. [C14: from OF *crevace,* from *crever* to burst, from L *crepāre* to crack]

crew[1] ⓣ (kruː) *n* (*sometimes functioning as pl*) **1** the men who man a ship, boat, aircraft, etc. **2** *Naut.* a group of people assigned to a particular job or type of work. **3** *Inf.* a gang, company, or crowd. ◆ *vb* **4** to serve on (a ship) as a member of the crew. [C15 *crue* (military) reinforcement, from OF *creue* augmentation, from OF *creistre* to increase, from L *crescere*]

crew[2] (kruː) *vb Arch.* a past tense of **crow**[2].

crew cut *n* a closely cropped haircut for men. [C20: from the style of haircut worn by the boat crews at Harvard and Yale Universities]

crewel (ˈkruːɪl) *n* a loosely twisted worsted yarn, used in fancy work and embroidery. [C15: from ?]
▸ **ˈcrewelist** *n* ▸ **ˈcrewelˌwork** *n*

crew neck *n* a plain round neckline in sweaters.
▸ **ˈcrew-ˌneck** *or* **ˈcrew-ˌnecked** *adj*

crib ⓣ (krɪb) *n* **1** a child's bed with slatted wooden sides; cot. **2** a cattle stall or pen. **3** a fodder rack or manger. **4** a small crude cottage or room. **5** *NZ.* a weekend cottage: term is South Island usage only. **6** any small confined space. **7** a representation of the manger in which the infant Jesus was laid at birth. **8** *Inf.* a theft, esp. of another's writing or thoughts. **9** *Inf., chiefly Brit.* a translation of a foreign text or a list of answers used by students, often illicitly, as an aid in lessons, examinations, etc. **10** short for **cribbage. 11** *Cribbage.* the discard pile. **12** Also called: **cribwork.** a framework of heavy timbers used in the construction of foundations, mines, etc. ◆ *vb* **cribs, cribbing, cribbed. 13** (*tr*) to put or enclose in or as if in a crib; furnish with a crib. **14** (*tr*) *Inf.* to steal (another's writings or thoughts). **15** (*intr*) *Inf.* to copy either from a crib or from someone else during a lesson or examination. **16** (*intr*) *Inf.* to grumble. [OE *cribb*]
▸ **ˈcribber** *n*

cribbage (ˈkrɪbɪdʒ) *n* a game of cards for two to four, in which players try to win a set number of points before their opponents. [C17: from ?]

cribbage board *n* a board, with pegs and holes, used for scoring at cribbage.

crib-biting *n* a harmful habit of horses in which the animal leans on the manger or seizes it with the teeth and swallows a gulp of air.

crick ⓣ (krɪk) *Inf.* ◆ *n* **1** a painful muscle spasm or cramp, esp. in the neck or back. ◆ *vb* **2** (*tr*) to cause a crick in. [C15: from ?]

cricket[1] (ˈkrɪkɪt) *n* an insect having long antennae and, in the males, the ability to produce a chirping sound by rubbing together the leathery forewings. [C14: from OF *criquet,* from *criquer* to creak, imit.]

cricket[2] (ˈkrɪkɪt) *n* **1a** a game played by two teams of eleven players on a field with a wicket at either end of a 22-yard pitch, the object being for one side to score runs by hitting a hard leather-covered ball with a bat while the other side tries to dismiss them by bowling, catching, running them out, etc. **1b** (*as modifier*): *a cricket bat.* **2 not cricket.** *Inf.* not fair play. ◆ *vb* (*intr*) **3** to play cricket. [C16: from OF *criquet* goalpost, wicket, from ?]
▸ **ˈcricketer** *n*

cricoid (ˈkraɪkɔɪd) *adj* **1** of or relating to the ring-shaped lowermost cartilage of the larynx. ◆ *n* **2** this cartilage. [C18: from NL *cricoīdes,* from Gk *krikoeidēs* ring-shaped, from *krikos* ring]

cri de coeur (kriː də kɜː) *n, pl* **cris de coeur.** (kriː də kɜː). a heartfelt or impassioned appeal. [C20: altered from F *cri du coeur*]

crier (ˈkraɪə) *n* **1** a person or animal that cries. **2** (formerly) an official who made public announcements, esp. in a town or court.

crime ⓣ (kraɪm) *n* **1** an act or omission prohibited and punished by law. **2** unlawful acts in general. **3** an evil act. **4** *Inf.* something to be regretted. [C14: from OF, from L *crīmen* verdict, accusation, crime]

criminal ⓣ (ˈkrɪmɪnᵊl) *n* **1** a person charged with and convicted of crime. **2** a person who commits crimes for a living. ◆ *adj* **3** of, involving, or guilty of crime. **4** (*prenominal*) of or relating to crime or its punishment. **5** *Inf.* senseless or deplorable. [C15: from LL *crīminālis;* see CRIME, -AL[1]]
▸ **ˈcriminally** *adv* ▸ **ˌcrimiˈnality** *n*

criminal conversation *n* another term for **adultery.**

criminalize *or* **criminalise** (ˈkrɪmɪnəˌlaɪz) *vb* **criminalizes, criminalizing, criminalized** *or* **criminalises, criminalising, criminalised.** (*tr*) to declare (an action or activity) criminal.
▸ **ˌcriminaliˈzation** *or* **ˌcriminaliˈsation** *n*

criminal law *n* the body of law dealing with offences and offenders.

criminology (ˌkrɪmɪˈnɒlədʒɪ) *n* the scientific study of crime. [C19: from L *crimin-* CRIME, + -LOGY]
▸ **criminological** (ˌkrɪmɪnəˈlɒdʒɪkᵊl) *or* **ˌcriminoˈlogic** *adj* ▸ **ˌcriminoˈlogically** *adv* ▸ **ˌcrimiˈnologist** *n*

crimp (krɪmp) *vb* (*tr*) **1** to fold or press into ridges. **2** to fold and pinch together (something, such as two pieces of metal). **3** to curl or wave (the hair) tightly, esp. with curling tongs. **4** *Inf., chiefly US.* to hinder. ◆ *n* **5** the act or result of folding or pressing together or into ridges. **6** a tight wave or curl in the hair. [OE *crympan;* rel. to *crump* bent; see CRAMP]
▸ **ˈcrimper** *n* ▸ **ˈcrimpy** *adj*

Crimplene (ˈkrɪmpliːn) *n Trademark.* a synthetic material similar to Terylene, characterized by its crease-resistance.

crimson (ˈkrɪmzən) *n* **1a** a deep or vivid red colour. **1b** (*as adj*): *a crimson rose.* ◆ *vb* **2** to make or become crimson. **3** (*intr*) to blush. [C14: from OSp. *cremesin,* from Ar. *qirmizi* red of the kermes, from *qirmiz* KERMES]
▸ **ˈcrimsonness** *n*

cringe ⓣ (krɪndʒ) *vb* **cringes, cringing, cringed.** (*intr*) **1** to shrink or flinch, esp. in fear or servility. **2** to behave in a servile or timid way. **3** *Inf.* to experience a sudden feeling of embarrassment or distaste. ◆ *n* **4** the act of cringing. **5 the cultural cringe.** *Austral.* subservience to overseas cultural standards. [OE *cringan* to yield in battle]
▸ **ˈcringer** *n*

cringle (ˈkrɪŋgᵊl) *n* an eyelet at the edge of a sail. [C17: from Low G *Kringel* small ring]

crinkle ⓣ (ˈkrɪŋkᵊl) *vb* **crinkles, crinkling, crinkled. 1** to form or cause to form wrinkles, twists, or folds. **2** to make or cause to make a rustling noise. ◆ *n* **3** a wrinkle, twist, or fold. **4** a rustling noise. [OE *crincan* to bend, give way]

crinkly ⓣ (ˈkrɪŋklɪ) *adj* **1** wrinkled; crinkled. ◆ *n, pl* **crinklies. 2** *Sl.* an old person.

crinoid (ˈkraɪnɔɪd, ˈkrɪn-) *n* **1** a primitive echinoderm having delicate feathery arms radiating from a central disc. ◆ *adj* **2** of, relating to, or belonging to the *Crinoidea.* **3** shaped like a lily. [C19: from Gk *krinoeidēs* lily-like]
▸ **criˈnoidal** *adj*

crinoline (ˈkrɪnᵊlɪn) *n* **1** a stiff fabric, originally of horsehair and linen

THESAURUS

exuberant, happy, in seventh heaven, joyful, on cloud nine (*inf.*), over the moon (*inf.*)

crevasse *n* **1** = **crack,** abyss, bergschrund, chasm, cleft, fissure

crevice *n* = **gap,** chink, cleft, crack, cranny, fissure, fracture, hole, interstice, opening, rent, rift, slit, split

crew[1] *n* **1** = **(ship's) company,** hands, (ship's) complement **2** = **team,** company, corps, gang, party, posse, squad, working party **3** *Informal* = **crowd,** assemblage, band, bunch (*inf.*), camp, company, gang, herd, horde, lot, mob, pack, posse (*inf.*), set, swarm, troop

crib *n* **1** = **cradle,** bassinet, bed, cot **2, 3** = **manger,** bin, box, bunker, rack, stall **9** *Informal* = **translation,** key, trot (*US sl.*) ◆ *vb* **13** = **confine,** box up, cage, coop, coop up, enclose, fence, imprison, limit, pen, rail, restrict, shut in **14, 15** *Informal* = **copy,** cheat, pass off as one's own work, pilfer, pirate, plagiarize, purloin, steal

crick *Informal n* **1** = **spasm,** convulsion, cramp, twinge ◆ *vb* **2** = **rick,** jar, wrench

crime *n* **1** = **offence,** atrocity, fault, felony, job (*inf.*), malfeasance, misdeed, misdemeanour, outrage, transgression, trespass, unlawful act, violation, wrong **3** = **lawbreaking,** corruption, delinquency, guilt, illegality, iniquity, malefaction, misconduct, sin, unrighteousness, vice, villainy, wickedness, wrong, wrongdoing

criminal *n* **1, 2** = **lawbreaker,** con (*sl.*), con man (*inf.*), convict, crook, culprit, delinquent, evildoer, felon, jailbird, lag (*sl.*), malefactor, offender, sinner, transgressor, villain ◆ *adj* **3** = **unlawful,** bent (*sl.*), corrupt, crooked (*inf.*), culpable, felonious, illegal, illicit, immoral, indictable, iniquitous, lawless, nefarious, peccant, under-the-table, unrighteous, vicious, villainous, wicked, wrong **5** *Informal* = **disgraceful,** deplorable, foolish, preposterous, ridiculous, scandalous, senseless

Antonyms *adj* ≠ **unlawful:** commendable, honest, honourable, innocent, law-abiding, lawful, legal, right

criminality *n* **3** = **illegality,** corruption, culpability, delinquency, depravity, guiltiness, sinfulness, turpitude, villainy, wickedness

cringe *vb* **1** = **shrink,** blench, cower, dodge, draw back, duck, flinch, quail, quiver, recoil, shy, start, tremble, wince **2** = **grovel,** bend, bootlick (*inf.*), bow, brown-nose (*taboo sl.*), crawl, creep, crouch, fawn, kiss ass (*US & Canad. taboo sl.*), kneel, kowtow, pander to, sneak, stoop, toady, truckle

crinkle *n, vb* **1** = **crease,** cockle, crimp, crimple, crumple, curl, fold, pucker, ruffle, rumple, scallop, twist, wrinkle **2** = **rustle,** crackle, hiss, swish, whisper

crinkly *adj* **1** = **wrinkled,** buckled, cockled, creased, curly, fluted, frizzy, furrowed, gathered, kinky, knit, puckered, ruffled, scalloped used in lining garments. **2** a petticoat stiffened with this, worn to distend skirts, esp. in the mid-19th century. **3** a framework of steel hoops worn for the same purpose. [C19: from F, from It. *crinolino,* from *crino* horsehair, from L *crīnis* hair + *lino* flax, from L *līnum*]

cripple ⓘ ('krɪpᵊl) *n* **1** a person who is lame. **2** a person who is or seems disabled or deficient in some way: *a mental cripple.* ◆ *vb* **cripples, crippling, crippled. 3** (*tr*) to make a cripple of; disable. [OE *crypel; rel.* to *crēopan* to creep]
▸'**crippler** *n*

crisis ⓘ ('kraɪsɪs) *n, pl* **crises** (-si:z). **1** a crucial stage or turning point, esp. in a sequence of events or a disease. **2** an unstable period, esp. one of extreme trouble or danger. **3** *Pathol.* a sudden change in the course of a disease. [C15: from L: decision, from Gk *krisis,* from *krinein* to decide]

crisp ⓘ (krɪsp) *adj* **1** dry and brittle. **2** fresh and firm. **3** invigorating or bracing: *a crisp breeze.* **4** clear; sharp: *crisp reasoning.* **5** lively or stimulating. **6** clean and orderly. **7** concise and pithy. **8** wrinkled or curly: *crisp hair.* ◆ *vb* **9** to make or become crisp. ◆ *n* **10** *Brit.* a very thin slice of potato fried and eaten cold as a snack. **11** something that is crisp. [OE, from L *crispus* curled, uneven, wrinkled]
▸'**crisply** *adv* ▸'**crispness** *n*

crispbread ('krɪsp,brɛd) *n* a thin dry biscuit made of wheat or rye.

crisper ('krɪspə) *n* a compartment in a refrigerator for storing salads, vegetables, etc., in order to keep them fresh.

crispy ('krɪspɪ) *adj* **crispier, crispiest. 1** crisp. **2** having waves or curls.
▸'**crispiness** *n*

crisscross ('krɪs,krɒs) *vb* **1** to move or cause to move in a crosswise pattern. **2** to mark with or consist of a pattern of crossing lines. ◆ *adj* **3** (esp. of lines) crossing one another in different directions. ◆ *n* **4** a pattern made of crossing lines. ◆ *adv* **5** in a crosswise manner or pattern.

crit. *abbrev. for:* **1** *Med.* critical. **2** criticism.

criterion ⓘ (kraɪ'tɪərɪən) *n, pl* **criteria** (-rɪə) *or* **criterions.** a standard by which something can be judged or decided. [C17: from Gk *kritērion,* from *kritēs* judge, from *krinein* to decide]

> **USAGE NOTE** *Criteria,* the plural of *criterion,* is not acceptable as a singular noun: *this criterion is not valid; these criteria are not valid.*

critic ⓘ ('krɪtɪk) *n* **1** a person who judges something. **2** a professional judge of art, music, literature, etc. **3** a person who often finds fault and criticizes. [C16: from L *criticus,* from Gk *kritikos* capable of judging, from *kritēs* judge; see CRITERION]

critical ⓘ ('krɪtɪkᵊl) *adj* **1** containing or making severe or negative judgments. **2** containing analytical evaluations. **3** of a critic or criticism. **4** of or forming a crisis; crucial. **5** urgently needed. **6** *Inf.* so seriously injured or ill as to be in danger of dying. **7** *Physics.* of, denoting, or concerned with a state in which the properties of a system undergo an abrupt change. **8 go critical.** (of a nuclear power station or reactor) to reach a state in which a nuclear-fission chain reaction becomes self-sustaining.
▸,**criti'cality** *n* ▸'**critically** *adv* ▸'**criticalness** *n*

critical mass *n* the minimum mass of fissionable material that can sustain a nuclear chain reaction.

critical path analysis *n* a technique for planning projects with reference to the critical path, which is the sequence of stages requiring the longest time.

critical temperature *n* the temperature of a substance in its critical state. A gas can only be liquefied at temperatures below this.

criticism ⓘ ('krɪtɪ,sɪzəm) *n* **1** the act or an instance of making an unfavourable or severe judgment, comment, etc. **2** the analysis or evaluation of a work of art, literature, etc. **3** the occupation of a critic. **4** a work that sets out to evaluate or analyse.

criticize ⓘ *or* **criticise** ('krɪtɪ,saɪz) *vb* **criticizes, criticizing, criticized** *or* **criticises, criticising, criticised. 1** to judge (something) with disapproval; censure. **2** to evaluate or analyse (something).
▸'**criti,cizable** *or* '**criti,cisable** *adj* ▸'**criti,cizer** *or* '**criti,ciser** *n*

critique ⓘ (krɪ'ti:k) *n* **1** a critical essay or commentary. **2** the act or art of criticizing. [C17: from F, from Gk *kritikē,* from *kritikos* able to discern]

croak ⓘ (krəʊk) *vb* **1** (*intr*) (of frogs, crows, etc.) to make a low, hoarse cry. **2** to utter (something) in this manner. **3** (*intr*) to grumble or be pessimistic. **4** *Sl.* **4a** (*intr*) to die. **4b** (*tr*) to kill. ◆ *n* **5** a low hoarse utterance or sound. [OE *crācettan*]
▸'**croaky** *adj* ▸'**croakiness** *n*

croaker ('krəʊkə) *n* **1** an animal, bird, etc., that croaks. **2** a grumbling person.

Croat ('krəʊæt) *n* **1a** a native or inhabitant of Croatia, a country in SE Europe. **1b** a speaker of Croatian. ◆ *n, adj* **2** another word for **Croatian.**

Croatian (krəʊ'eɪʃən) *adj* **1** of or relating to Croatia, its people, or their language. ◆ *n* **2** the official language of Croatia, a dialect of Serbo-Croat. **3a** a native or inhabitant of Croatia. **3b** a speaker of Croatian.

croc (krɒk) *n* short for **crocodile** (senses 1 and 2).

crochet ('krəʊʃeɪ, -ʃɪ) *vb* **crochets, crocheting** (-ʃeɪɪŋ, -ʃɪɪŋ), **crocheted** (-ʃeɪd, -ʃɪd). **1** to make (a piece of needlework, a garment, etc.) by looping and intertwining thread with a hooked needle (**crochet hook**). ◆ *n* **2** work made by crocheting. [C19: from F *crochet,* dim. of *croc* hook, prob. of Scand. origin]
▸'**crocheter** *n*

crock[1] (krɒk) *n* **1** an earthen pot, jar, etc. **2** a piece of broken earthenware. [OE *crocc* pot]

crock[2] (krɒk) *Sl., chiefly Brit.* ◆ *n* **1** a person or thing that is old or decrepit (esp. in **old crock**). ◆ *vb* **2** to become or cause to become weak or disabled. [C15: orig. Scot.; rel. to Norwegian *krake* unhealthy animal, Du. *kraak* decrepit person or animal]

crockery ('krɒkərɪ) *n* china dishes, earthen vessels, etc., collectively.

crocket ('krɒkɪt) *n* a carved ornament in the form of a curled leaf or cusp, used in Gothic architecture. [C17: from Anglo-F *croket* a little hook, from *croc* hook, of Scand. origin]

crocodile ('krɒkə,daɪl) *n* **1** a large tropical reptile having a broad head, tapering snout, massive jaws, and a thick outer covering of bony plates. **2a** leather made from the skin of any of these animals. **2b** (*as modifier*): *crocodile shoes.* **3** *Brit. inf.* a line of people, esp. schoolchildren walking two by two. [C13: via OF, from L *crocodīlus,* from Gk *krokodeilos* lizard, ult. from *krokē* pebble + *drilos* worm; referring to its basking on shingle]

crocodile clip *n* a clasp with serrated interlocking edges used for making electrical connections, etc.

crocodile tears *pl n* an insincere show of grief; false tears. [from the belief that crocodiles wept over their prey to allure further victims]

crocodilian (,krɒkə'dɪlɪən) *n* **1** any large predatory reptile of the order *Crocodilia,* which includes the crocodiles, alligators, and caymans. ◆ *adj* **2** of, relating to, or belonging to the *Crocodilia.* **3** of, relating to, or resembling a crocodile.

crocus ('krəʊkəs) *n, pl* **crocuses.** any plant of the iridaceous genus *Crocus,* having white, yellow, or purple flowers. [C17: from NL, from L *crocus,* from Gk *krokos* saffron]

Croesus ('kri:səs) *n* any very rich man. [after *Croesus* (died ?546 BC) the last king of Lydia, noted for his great wealth]

croft (krɒft) *n Brit.* a small enclosed plot of land, adjoining a house, worked by the occupier and his family, esp. in Scotland. [OE *croft*]
▸'**crofter** *n* ▸'**crofting** *adj, n*

croissant ('krwʌsɒŋ) *n* a flaky crescent-shaped bread roll. [F, lit.: crescent]

THESAURUS

cripple *vb* **3** = **disable**, debilitate, enfeeble, hamstring, incapacitate, lame, maim, mutilate, paralyse, weaken

crisis *n* **1** = **critical point**, climacteric, climax, confrontation, crunch (*inf.*), crux, culmination, height, moment of truth, point of no return, turning point **2** = **emergency**, catastrophe, critical situation, deep water, dilemma, dire straits, disaster, exigency, extremity, meltdown (*inf.*), mess, panic stations (*inf.*), pass, plight, predicament, quandary, strait, trouble

crisp *adj* **1, 2** = **firm**, brittle, crispy, crumbly, crunchy, fresh, unwilted **3** = **bracing**, brisk, fresh, invigorating, refreshing **4** = **brief**, brusque, clear, incisive, pithy, short, succinct, tart, terse **6** = **clean**, clean-cut, neat, orderly, smart, snappy, spruce, tidy, trig (*arch. or dialect*), trim, well-groomed, well-pressed
Antonyms *adj* ≠ **firm:** drooping, droopy, flaccid, floppy, limp, soft, wilted, withered ≠ **bracing:** balmy, clement, mild, pleasant, warm

criterion *n* = **standard**, bench mark, canon, gauge, measure, norm, par, principle, proof, rule, test, touchstone, yardstick

critic *n* **1, 2** = **judge**, analyst, arbiter, authority, commentator, connoisseur, expert, expositor, pundit, reviewer **3** = **fault-finder**, attacker, carper, caviller, censor, censurer, detractor, knocker (*inf.*), Momus, reviler, vilifier

critical *adj* **1** = **disparaging**, captious, carping, cavilling, censorious, derogatory, disapproving, fault-finding, nagging, niggling, nit-picking (*inf.*), on someone's back (*inf.*), scathing **2** = **analytical**, accurate, diagnostic, discerning, discriminating, fastidious, judicious, penetrating, perceptive, precise **4, 5** = **crucial**, all-important, dangerous, deciding, decisive, grave, hairy (*sl.*), high-priority, momentous, now or never, perilous, pivotal, precarious, pressing, psychological, risky, serious, urgent, vital
Antonyms *adj* ≠ **crucial:** safe, secure, settled, unimportant ≠ **disparaging:** appreciative, approving, complimentary, uncritical ≠ **analytical:** undiscriminating

criticism *n* **1** = **fault-finding**, animadversion, bad press, brickbats (*inf.*), censure, character assassination, critical remarks, denigration, disapproval, disparagement, flak (*inf.*), knocking (*inf.*), panning (*inf.*), slagging (*sl.*), slam (*sl.*), slating (*inf.*), stick (*sl.*), stricture **4** = **analysis**, appraisal, appreciation, assessment, comment, commentary, critique, elucidation, evaluation, judgment, notice, review

criticize *vb* **1** = **find fault with**, animadvert on *or* upon, blast, carp, censure, condemn, disapprove of, disparage, excoriate, give (someone *or* something) a bad press, have a go (at) (*inf.*), knock (*inf.*), lambast(e), nag at, pan (*inf.*), pass strictures upon, pick holes in, pick to pieces, put down, slam (*sl.*), slate (*inf.*), tear into (*inf.*) **2** = **analyse**, appraise, assess, comment upon, evaluate, give an opinion, judge, pass judgment on, review
Antonyms *vb* ≠ **find fault with:** commend, compliment, extol, laud (*literary*), praise

critique *n* **1** = **essay**, analysis, appraisal, assessment, commentary, examination, review, treatise

croak *vb* **2** = **squawk**, caw, gasp, grunt, utter *or* speak harshly, utter *or* speak huskily, utter *or* speak throatily, wheeze **4a** *Slang* = **die**, buy it (*US sl.*), expire, kick it (*sl.*), kick the bucket (*inf.*), pass away, peg it (*inf.*), perish, pop one's clogs (*inf.*)

Croix de Guerre *French.* (krwa də gɛr) *n* a French military decoration awarded for gallantry in battle: established 1915. [lit.: cross of war]
Cro-Magnon man (ˈkrəʊˈmænjɒn, -ˈmægnɒn) *n* an early type of modern man, *Homo sapiens,* who lived in Europe during late Palaeolithic times. [C19: after the cave (Cro-Magnon), Dordogne, France, where the remains were first found]
cromlech (ˈkrɒmlɛk) *n* **1** a circle of prehistoric standing stones. **2** (no longer in technical usage) a megalithic chamber tomb or dolmen. [C17: from Welsh, from *crom,* fem. of *crwm* bent, arched + *llech* flat stone]
crone ❶ (krəʊn) *n* a witchlike old woman. [C14: from OF *carogne* carrion, ult. from L *caro* flesh]
cronk (krɒŋk) *adj Austral. sl.* **1** unfit; unsound. **2** dishonest. [C19: ?from G *krank* ill]
crony ❶ (ˈkrəʊnɪ) *n, pl* **cronies.** a friend or companion. [C17: student sl. (Cambridge), from Gk *khronios* of long duration, from *khronos* time]
cronyism (ˈkrəʊnɪˌɪzəm) *n* the practice of appointing friends to high-level posts, esp. political posts, regardless of their suitability.
crook ❶ (krʊk) *n* **1** a curved or hooked thing. **2** a staff with a hooked end, such as a bishop's crosier or shepherd's staff. **3** a turn or curve; bend. **4** *Inf.* a dishonest person, esp. a swindler or thief. ◆ *vb* **5** to bend or curve or cause to bend or curve. ◆ *adj* **6** *Austral. & NZ sl.* **6a** ill. **6b** of poor quality. **6c** unpleasant; bad. **7 go (off) crook.** *Austral. & NZ sl.* to lose one's temper. **8 go crook at** *or* **on.** *Austral. & NZ sl.* to rebuke or upbraid. [C12: from ON *krokr* hook]
crooked ❶ (ˈkrʊkɪd) *adj* **1** bent, angled or winding. **2** set at an angle; not straight. **3** deformed or contorted. **4** *Inf.* dishonest or illegal. **5 crooked on.** (*also* krʊkt) *Austral. inf.* hostile or averse to.
▸**ˈcrookedly** *adv* ▸**ˈcrookedness** *n*
croon ❶ (kruːn) *vb* **1** to sing or speak in a soft low tone. ◆ *n* **2** a soft low singing or humming. [C14: via MDu. *crōnen* to groan]
▸**ˈcrooner** *n*
crop ❶ (krɒp) *n* **1** the produce of cultivated plants, esp. cereals, vegetables, and fruit. **2a** the amount of such produce in any particular season. **2b** the yield of some other farm produce: *the lamb crop.* **3** a group of products, thoughts, people, etc., appearing at one time or in one season. **4** the stock of a thonged whip. **5** short for **riding crop. 6** a pouchlike part of the oesophagus of birds, in which food is stored or partially digested before passing on to the gizzard. **7** a short cropped hairstyle. **8** a notch in or a piece cut out of the ear of an animal. **9** the act of cropping. ◆ *vb* **crops, cropping, cropped.** (*mainly tr*) **10** to cut (hair, grass, etc.) very short. **11** to cut and collect (mature produce) from the land or plant on which it has been grown. **12** to clip part of (the ear or ears) of (an animal), esp. as a means of identification. **13** (of herbivorous animals) to graze on (grass or similar vegetation). ◆ See also **crop out, crop up.** [OE *cropp*]
crop-dusting *n* the spreading of fungicide, etc., on crops in the form of dust, often from an aircraft.
crop-eared *adj* having the ears or hair cut short.
crop out *vb* (*intr, adv*) (of a formation of rock strata) to appear or be exposed at the surface.
cropper (ˈkrɒpə) *n* **1** a person who cultivates or harvests a crop. **2 come a cropper.** *Inf.* **2a** to fall heavily. **2b** to fail completely.
crop rotation *n* the system of growing a sequence of different crops on the same ground so as to maintain or increase its fertility.
crop up ❶ *vb* (*intr, adv*) *Inf.* to occur or appear, esp. unexpectedly.
croquet (ˈkrəʊkeɪ, -kɪ) *n* a game for two to four players who hit a wooden ball through iron hoops with mallets in order to hit a peg. [C19: ?from F dialect, var. of CROCHET (little hook)]
croquette (krəʊˈkɛt, krɒ-) *n* a savoury cake of minced meat, fish, etc., fried in breadcrumbs. [C18: from F, from *croquer* to crunch, imit.]
crosier *or* **crozier** (ˈkrəʊʒə) *n* a staff surmounted by a crook or cross, carried by bishops as a symbol of pastoral office. [C14: from OF *crossier* staff bearer, from *crosse* pastoral staff]
cross ❶ (krɒs) *n* **1** a structure or symbol consisting of two intersecting lines or pieces at right angles to one another. **2** a wooden structure used as a means of execution, consisting of an upright post with a transverse piece to which people were nailed or tied. **3** a representation of the Cross used as an emblem of Christianity or as a reminder of Christ's death. **4** any mark or shape consisting of two intersecting lines, esp. such a symbol (×) used as a signature, error mark, etc. **5** a sign representing the Cross made either by tracing a figure in the air or by touching the forehead, breast, and either shoulder in turn. **6** any variation of the Christian symbol, such as a Maltese or Greek cross. **7** a cruciform emblem awarded to indicate membership of an order or as a decoration for distinguished service. **8** (*sometimes cap.*) Christianity or Christendom, esp. as contrasted with non-Christian religions. **9** the place in a town or village where a cross has been set up. **10** *Biol.* **10a** the process of crossing; hybridization. **10b** an individual produced as a result of this process. **11** a mixture of two qualities or types. **12** an opposition, hindrance, or misfortune; affliction (esp. in **bear one's cross**). **13** *Boxing.* a straight punch delivered from the side, esp. with the right hand. **14** *Football.* the act or an instance of passing the ball from a wing to the middle of the field. ◆ *vb* **15** (sometimes foll. by *over*) to move or go across (something); traverse or intersect. **16a** to meet and pass. **16b** (of each of two letters in the post) to be dispatched before receipt of the other. **17** (*tr;* usually foll. by *out, off,* or *through*) to cancel with a cross or with lines; delete. **18** (*tr*) to place or put in a form resembling a cross: *to cross one's legs.* **19** (*tr*) to mark with a cross or crosses. **20** (*tr*) *Brit.* to draw two parallel lines across the face of (a cheque) and so make it payable only into a bank account. **21** (*tr*) **21a** to trace the form of the Cross upon (someone or something) in token of blessing. **21b** to make the sign of the Cross upon (oneself). **22** (*intr*) (of telephone lines) to interfere with each other so that several callers are connected together at one time. **23** to cause fertilization between (plants or animals of different breeds, races, varieties, etc.). **24** (*tr*) to oppose the wishes or plans of; thwart. **25** *Football.* to pass (the ball) from a wing to the middle of the field. **26 cross one's fingers.** to fold one finger across another in the hope of bringing good luck. **27 cross one's heart.** to promise or pledge, esp. by making the sign of a cross over one's heart. **28 cross one's mind.** to occur to one briefly or suddenly. **29 cross the path (of).** to meet or thwart (someone). **30 cross swords.** to argue or fight. ◆ *adj* **31** angry; ill-humoured; vexed. **32** lying or placed across; transverse: *a cross timber.* **33** involving interchange; reciprocal. **34** contrary or unfavourable. **35** another word for **crossbred.** [OE *cros,* from OIrish *cross* (unattested), from L *crux;* see CRUX]
▸**ˈcrossly** *adv* ▸**ˈcrossness** *n*
Cross (krɒs) *n* **the. 1** the cross on which Jesus Christ was crucified. **2** the Crucifixion of Jesus.
cross- *combining form.* **1** indicating action from one individual, group, etc., to another: *cross-cultural; cross-fertilize; cross-refer.* **2** indicating movement, position, etc., across something: *crosscurrent; crosstalk.* **3** indicating a crosslike figure or intersection: *crossbones.* [from CROSS (in various senses)]
crossbar (ˈkrɒsˌbɑː) *n* **1** a horizontal bar, line, stripe, etc. **2** a horizontal beam across a pair of goalposts. **3** the horizontal bar on a man's bicycle.
crossbeam (ˈkrɒsˌbiːm) *n* a beam that spans from one support to another.

THESAURUS

crone *n* = **old woman,** beldam (*arch.*), gammer, hag, old bag (*derogatory slang*), old bat (*sl.*), witch
crony *n* = **friend,** accomplice, ally, associate, buddy (*inf.*), china (*Brit. sl.*), chum (*inf.*), cock, colleague, companion, comrade, gossip (*arch.*), mate (*inf.*), pal (*inf.*), sidekick (*sl.*)
crook *n* **4** *Informal* = **criminal,** cheat, chiseller (*inf.*), fraudster, knave (*arch.*), lag (*sl.*), racketeer, robber, rogue, shark, swindler, thief, villain ◆ *vb* **5** = **bend,** angle, bow, curve, flex, hook
crooked *adj* **1, 3** = **bent,** anfractuous, bowed, crippled, curved, deformed, deviating, disfigured, distorted, hooked, irregular, meandering, misshapen, out of shape, tortuous, twisted, twisting, warped, winding, zigzag **2** = **at an angle,** angled, askew, asymmetric, awry, lopsided, off-centre, skewwhiff (*Brit. inf.*), slanted, slanting, squint, tilted, to one side, uneven, unsymmetrical **4** *Informal* = **dishonest,** bent (*sl.*), corrupt, crafty, criminal, deceitful, dishonourable, dubious, fraudulent, illegal, knavish, nefarious, questionable, shady (*inf.*), shifty, treacherous, underhand, under-the-table, unlawful, unprincipled, unscrupulous
Antonyms *adj* ≠ **bent:** flat, straight ≠ **dishonest:** ethical, fair, honest, honourable, lawful, legal, straight, upright
crookedness *n* **1, 3** = **distortedness,** anfractuosity, contortedness, curvedness, deformedness, deviance, disfigurement, hookedness, irregularity, tortuousness, zigzaggedness **2** = **unevenness,** asymmetry, lopsidedness **4** = **dishonesty,** corruptness, craftiness, criminality, deceitfulness, dishonourableness, dubiousness, fraudulence, fraudulency, illegality, improbity, knavishness, nefariousness, questionability, questionableness, shadiness (*inf.*), shiftiness, treacherousness, underhandedness, unlawfulness, unprincipledness, unscrupulosity, unscrupulousness
Antonyms *n* ≠ **distortedness:** flatness, levelness, straightness ≠ **dishonesty:** ethicality, ethicalness, fairness, honesty, honourableness, lawfulness, legality, straightness, trustworthiness, uprightness
croon *vb* **1** = **sing,** breathe, hum, purr, warble
crop *n* **2a** = **produce,** fruits, gathering, harvest, reaping, season's growth, vintage, yield ◆ *vb* **10** = **cut,** clip, curtail, dock, lop, mow, pare, prune, reduce, shear, shorten, snip, top, trim **11** = **harvest,** bring home, bring in, collect, garner, gather, mow, pick, reap **13** = **graze,** browse, nibble
crop up *vb Informal* = **happen,** appear, arise, emerge, occur, spring up, turn up
cross *n* **3, 4** = **crucifix,** rood **10b** = **crossbreed,** cur, hybrid, mongrel, mutt (*sl.*) **11** = **mixture,** amalgam, blend, combination **12** = **trouble,** affliction, burden, grief, load, misery, misfortune, trial, tribulation, woe, worry ◆ *vb* **15** = **go across,** bridge, crisscross, cut across, extend over, ford, intersect, intertwine, lace, lie athwart of, meet, move across, pass over, ply, span, traverse, zigzag **17** *usually foll. by* **out, off,** *or* **through** = **strike off** *or* **out,** blue-pencil, cancel, delete, eliminate, score off *or* out **23** = **interbreed,** blend, crossbreed, cross-fertilize, cross-pollinate, hybridize, intercross, mix, mongrelize **24** = **oppose,** block, deny, foil, frustrate, hinder, impede, interfere, obstruct, resist, thwart **30 cross swords** = **fight,** argue, come to blows, dispute, spar, wrangle ◆ *adj* **31** = **angry,** annoyed, cantankerous, captious, choked, churlish, crotchety (*inf.*), crusty, disagreeable, fractious, fretful, grouchy (*inf.*), grumpy, hacked (off) (*US sl.*), ill-humoured, ill-tempered, in a bad mood, irascible, irritable, liverish, peeved (*inf.*), peevish, petulant, pissed off (*taboo sl.*), put out, querulous, ratty (*Brit. & NZ inf.*), short, snappish, snappy, splenetic, sullen, surly, testy, tetchy, vexed, waspish **32** = **transverse,** crosswise, diagonal, intersecting, oblique **33** = **reciprocal,** opposite **34** = **opposing,** adverse, contrary, opposed, unfavourable
Antonyms *adj* ≠ **angry:** affable, agreeable, calm, cheerful, civil, congenial, even-tempered, genial, good-humoured, good-natured, nice, placid, pleasant, sweet

cross-bench *n* (*usually pl*) *Brit.* a seat in Parliament occupied by a neutral or independent member.
▸**'cross-,bencher** *n*

crossbill ('krɒs,bɪl) *n* any of various widely distributed finches that occur in coniferous woods and have a bill with crossed tips.

crossbones ('krɒs,bəʊnz) *pl n* See **skull and crossbones.**

crossbow ('krɒs,bəʊ) *n* a type of medieval bow fixed transversely on a stock grooved to direct a square-headed arrow.
▸**'cross,bowman** *n*

crossbred ('krɒs,brɛd) *adj* **1** (of plants or animals) produced as a result of crossbreeding. ◆ *n* **2** a crossbred plant or animal.

crossbreed ('krɒs,bri:d) *vb* **crossbreeds, crossbreeding, crossbred. 1** Also: **interbreed.** to breed (animals or plants) using parents of different races, varieties, breeds, etc. ◆ *n* **2** the offspring produced by such a breeding.

crosscheck (,krɒs'tʃɛk) *vb* **1** to verify (a fact, report, etc.) by considering conflicting opinions or consulting other sources. ◆ *n* **2** the act or an instance of crosschecking.

cross-country *adj, adv* **1** by way of fields, etc., as opposed to roads. **2** across a country. ◆ *n* **3** a long race held over open ground.

crosscurrent ('krɒs,kʌrənt) *n* **1** a current flowing across another current. **2** a conflicting tendency moving counter to the usual trend.

cross-curricular *adj Brit. education.* denoting or relating to an approach to a topic that includes contributions from several different disciplines and viewpoints.

crosscut ('krɒs,kʌt) *adj* **1** cut at right angles or obliquely to the major axis. ◆ *n* **2** a transverse cut or course. **3** *Mining.* a tunnel through a vein of ore or from the shaft to a vein. ◆ *vb* **crosscuts, crosscutting, crosscut. 4** to cut across.

crosscut saw *n* a saw for cutting timber across the grain.

crosse (krɒs) *n* a light staff with a triangular frame to which a network is attached, used in playing lacrosse. [F, from OF *croce* CROSIER]

cross-examine Ⓣ *vb* **cross-examines, cross-examining, cross-examined.** (*tr*) **1** *Law.* to examine (a witness for the opposing side), as in attempting to discredit his testimony. **2** to examine closely or relentlessly.
▸**'cross-ex,ami'nation** *n* ▸**,cross-ex'aminer** *n*

cross-eye *n* a turning inwards towards the nose of one or both eyes, caused by abnormal alignment.
▸**'cross-,eyed** *adj*

cross-fertilize *vb* **cross-fertilizes, cross-fertilizing, cross-fertilized. 1** to fertilize by fusion of male and female gametes from different individuals of the same species. **2** a non-technical term for **cross-pollinate.**
▸**'cross-,fertili'zation** *n*

crossfire ('krɒs,faɪə) *n* **1** *Mil., etc.* converging fire from one or more positions. **2** a lively exchange of ideas, opinions, etc.

cross-grained Ⓣ *adj* **1** (of timber) having the fibres arranged irregularly or across the axis of the piece. **2** perverse, cantankerous, or stubborn.

crosshatch ('krɒs,hætʃ) *vb Drawing.* to shade or hatch with two or more sets of parallel lines that cross one another.

crossing ('krɒsɪŋ) *n* **1** the place where one thing crosses another. **2** a place where a street, railway, etc., may be crossed. **3** the act or an instance of travelling across something, esp. the sea. **4** the act or process of crossbreeding.

crossing over *n Genetics.* the interchange of sections between pairing chromosomes during meiosis that produces variations in inherited characteristics by rearranging genes.

cross-legged ('krɒs'lɛgɪd, -'lɛgd) *adj* standing or sitting with one leg crossed over the other.

cross-match *vb Immunol.* to test the compatibility of (a donor's and recipient's blood) by checking that the red cells of each do not agglutinate in the other's serum.

crossover ('krɒs,əʊvə) *n* **1** a place at which a crossing is made. **2** *Railways.* a point of transfer between two main lines. **3** short for **crossover network. 4** *Genetics.* another term for **crossing over. 5** a recording, book, or other product that becomes popular in a genre other than its own. ◆ *adj* **6** (of music, fashion, art, etc.) combining two distinct styles. **7** (of a performer, writer, recording, book, etc.) having become popular in more than one genre.

crossover network *n Electronics.* an arrangement in a loudspeaker system that separates the signal into two or more frequency bands for feeding into different speakers.

crosspatch Ⓣ ('krɒs,pætʃ) *n Inf.* a bad-tempered person. [C18: from CROSS + obs. *patch* fool]

crosspiece ('krɒs,pi:s) *n* a transverse beam, joist, etc.

cross-ply *adj* (of a motor tyre) having the fabric cords in the outer casing running diagonally to stiffen the sidewalls.

cross-pollinate *vb* **cross-pollinates, cross-pollinating, cross-pollinated.** to transfer pollen from the anthers of one flower to the stigma of another.
▸**,cross-polli'nation** *n*

cross-purpose *n* **1** a contrary aim or purpose. **2 at cross-purposes.** conflicting; opposed; disagreeing.

cross-question *vb* **1** to cross-examine. ◆ *n* **2** a question asked in cross-examination.

cross-refer *vb* to refer from one part of something, esp. a book, to another.

cross-reference *n* **1** a reference within a text to another part of the text. ◆ *vb* **cross-references, cross-referencing, cross-referenced. 2** to cross-refer.

crossroad ('krɒs,rəʊd) *n US & Canad.* **1** a road that crosses another road. **2** Also called: **crossway.** a road that crosses from one main road to another.

crossroads ('krɒs,rəʊdz) *n* (*functioning as sing*) **1** the point at which two or more roads cross each other. **2** the point at which an important choice has to be made (esp. in **at the crossroads**).

crossruff ('krɒs,rʌf) *Bridge, whist.* ◆ *n* **1** the alternate trumping of each other's leads by two partners, or by declarer and dummy. ◆ *vb* **2** (*intr*) to trump alternately in this way.

cross section *n* **1** *Maths.* a plane surface formed by cutting across a solid, esp. perpendicular to its longest axis. **2** a section cut off in this way. **3** the act of cutting anything in this way. **4** a random sample, esp. one regarded as representative.
▸**,cross-'sectional** *adj*

cross-stitch *n* **1** an embroidery stitch made by two stitches forming a cross. **2** embroidery worked with this stitch. ◆ *vb* **3** to embroider (a piece of needlework) with cross-stitch.

crosstalk ('krɒs,tɔ:k) *n* **1** unwanted signals in one channel of a communications system as a result of a transfer of energy from other channels. **2** *Brit.* rapid or witty talk.

cross training *n* training in two or more sports to improve performance, esp. in one's main sport.

crosstree ('krɒs,tri:) *n Naut.* either of a pair of wooden or metal braces on the head of a mast to support the topmast, etc.

crosswise Ⓣ ('krɒs,waɪz) *or* **crossways** ('krɒs,weɪz) *adj, adv* **1** across; transversely. **2** in the shape of a cross.

crossword puzzle ('krɒs,wɜ:d) *n* a puzzle in which the solver guesses words suggested by numbered clues and writes them into a grid to form a vertical and horizontal pattern.

crotch Ⓣ (krɒtʃ) *n* **1** Also called (Brit.): **crutch. 1a** the angle formed by the legs where they join the human trunk. **1b** the human genital area. **1c** the corresponding part of a pair of trousers, pants, etc. **2** a forked region formed by the junction of two members. **3** a forked pole or stick. [C16: prob. var. of CRUTCH]
▸**crotched** *adj*

crotchet ('krɒtʃɪt) *n* **1** *Music.* Also called (US and Canad.): **quarter note.** a note having the time value of a quarter of a semibreve. **2** a perverse notion. [C14: from OF *crochet,* lit.: little hook, from *croche* hook; see CROCKET]

crotchety Ⓣ ('krɒtʃɪtɪ) *adj* **1** *Inf.* irritable; contrary. **2** full of crotchets.
▸**'crotchetiness** *n*

croton ('krəʊtᵊn) *n* **1** any shrub or tree of the chiefly tropical genus *Croton,* esp. *C. tiglium,* the seeds of which yield croton oil, formerly used as a purgative. **2** any of various tropical plants of the related genus *Codiaeum.* [C18: from NL, from Gk *krotōn* tick, castor-oil plant (whose berries resemble ticks)]

crouch Ⓣ (kraʊtʃ) *vb* (*intr*) **1** to bend low with the limbs pulled up close together, esp. (of an animal) in readiness to pounce. **2** to cringe, as in humility or fear. ◆ *n* **3** the act of stooping or bending. [C14: ?from OF *crochir* to become bent like a hook, from *croche* hook]

croup[1] (kru:p) *n* a throat condition, occurring usually in children, characterized by a hoarse cough and laboured breathing, resulting from inflammation of the larynx. [C16 *croup* to cry hoarsely, prob. imit.]
▸**'croupous** *or* **'croupy** *adj*

croup[2] (kru:p) *n* the hindquarters, esp. of a horse. [C13: from OF *croupe;* rel. to G *Kruppe*]

croupier ('kru:pɪə) *n* a person who deals cards, collects bets, etc., at a gaming table. [C18: lit.: one who rides behind another, from F *croupe* CROUP[2]]

crouton ('kru:tɒn) *n* a small piece of fried or toasted bread, usually served in soup. [F: dim. of *croûte* CRUST]

crow[1] (krəʊ) *n* **1** any large gregarious songbird of the genus *Corvus* of Europe and Asia, such as the raven, rook, and jackdaw. All have a heavy bill, glossy black plumage, and rounded wings. **2** any of various similar birds. **3** *Sl.* an old or ugly woman. **4 as the crow flies.** as directly as possible. **5 eat crow.** *US & Canad. inf.* to be forced to do something humiliating. **6 stone the crows.** (*interj*) *Brit. & Austral. sl.* an expression of surprise, dismay, etc. [OE *crāwa*]

crow[2] Ⓣ (krəʊ) *vb* (*intr*) **1** (p.t. **crowed** *or* **crew**) to utter a shrill squawking sound, as a cock. **2** (often foll. by *over*) to boast one's superiority. **3**

THESAURUS

cross-examine *vb* **2** = **question,** catechize, grill (*inf.*), interrogate, pump, quiz

cross-grained *adj* **2** = **difficult,** awkward, cantankerous, crabby, disobliging, ill-natured, morose, peevish, perverse, refractory, shrewish, stubborn, truculent, wayward

crosspatch *n Informal* = **grump** (*inf.*), bear, crank (*US, Canad., & Irish inf.*), curmudgeon, scold, shrew, sourpuss (*inf.*)

crosswise *adv* **1** = **across,** aslant, at an angle, athwart, at right angles, awry, crisscross, diagonally, from side to side, on the bias, over, sideways, transversely

crotch *n* **1a, 1b** = **groin,** crutch

crotchety *adj* **1** *Informal* = **bad-tempered,** awkward, cantankerous, contrary, crabby, cross, crusty, curmudgeonly, difficult, disagreeable, fractious, grumpy, irritable, liverish, obstreperous, peevish, ratty (*Brit. & NZ inf.*), surly, testy, tetchy

crouch *vb* **1** = **bend down,** bow, duck, hunch, kneel, squat, stoop

crow[2] *vb* **2** = **gloat,** blow one's own trumpet,

(esp. of babies) to utter cries of pleasure. ◆ *n* **4** an act or instance of crowing. [OE *crāwan;* rel. to OHG *krāen,* Du. *kraaien*]
▸'**crowingly** *adv*

crowbar ('krəʊ,bɑː) *n* a heavy iron lever with one end forged into a wedge shape.

crowd ❶ (kraʊd) *n* **1** a large number of things or people gathered or considered together. **2** a particular group of people, esp. considered as a set: *the crowd from the office.* **3** (preceded by *the*) the common people; the masses. ◆ *vb* **4** (*intr*) to gather together in large numbers; throng. **5** (*tr*) to press together into a confined space. **6** (*tr*) to fill to excess; fill by pushing into. **7** (*tr*) *Inf.* to urge or harass by urging. [OE *crūdan*]
▸'**crowded** *adj* ▸'**crowdedness** *n*

crowfoot ('krəʊ,fʊt) *n, pl* **crowfoots.** any of several plants that have yellow or white flowers and divided leaves resembling the foot of a crow.

crown ❶ (kraʊn) *n* **1** an ornamental headdress denoting sovereignty, usually made of gold embedded with precious stones. **2** a wreath or garland for the head, awarded as a sign of victory, success, honour, etc. **3** (*sometimes cap.*) monarchy or kingship. **4** an award, distinction, or title, given as an honour to reward merit, victory, etc. **5** anything resembling or symbolizing a crown. **6a** a coin worth five shillings (25 pence). **6b** a coin worth £5. **6c** any of several continental coins, such as the krona or krone, with a name meaning *crown.* **7** the top or summit of something: *crown of a hill.* **8** the centre part of a road, esp. when it is cambered. **9** the outstanding quality, achievement, state, etc.: *the crown of his achievements.* **10a** the enamel-covered part of a tooth above the gum. **10b artificial crown.** a substitute crown, usually of gold, porcelain, or acrylic resin, fitted over a decayed or broken tooth. **11** the part of an anchor where the arms are joined to the shank. ◆ *vb* (*tr*) **12** to put a crown on the head of, symbolically vesting with royal title, powers, etc. **13** to place a crown, wreath, garland, etc., on the head of. **14** to place something on or over the head or top of. **15** to confer a title, dignity, or reward upon. **16** to form the summit or topmost part of. **17** to cap or put the finishing touch to (a series of events): *to crown it all it rained, too.* **18** *Draughts.* to promote (a draught) to a king by placing another draught on top of it. **19** to attach a crown to (a tooth). **20** *Sl.* to hit over the head. [C12: from OF *corone,* from L *corōna* wreath, crown, from Gk *korōnē* crown, something curved]

Crown ❶ (kraʊn) *n* (*sometimes not cap.;* usually preceded by *the*) **1** the sovereignty or realm of a monarch. **2a** the government of a monarchy. **2b** (*as modifier*): *Crown property.*

crown colony *n* a British colony whose administration is controlled by the Crown.

crown court *n English law.* a court of criminal jurisdiction holding sessions in towns throughout England and Wales.

Crown Derby *n* **1** a type of porcelain manufactured at Derby from 1784–1848. **2** *Trademark.* shortened form of Royal Crown Derby.

crown glass *n* **1** another name for **optical crown. 2** an old form of window glass made by blowing a globe and spinning it until it forms a flat disc.

crown green *n* a type of bowling green in which the sides are lower than the middle.

crowning ('kraʊnɪŋ) *n Obstetrics.* the stage of labour at which the infant's head is passing through the vaginal opening.

crown jewels *pl n* the jewellery, including the regalia, used by a sovereign on a state occasion.

Crown Office *n* (in Britain) an administrative office of the Queen's Bench Division of the High Court, where actions are entered for trial.

crown prince *n* the male heir to a sovereign throne.

crown princess *n* **1** the wife of a crown prince. **2** the female heir to a sovereign throne.

Crown Prosecution Service *n* (in England and Wales) an independent prosecuting body, established in 1986, that decides whether cases brought by the police should go to the courts: headed by the Director of Public Prosecutions. Cf. **procurator fiscal.** Abbrev.: **CPS.**

crown wheel *n* **1** *Horology.* a wheel that has one set of teeth at right angles to another. **2** the larger of two wheels in a bevel gear.

crow's-foot *n, pl* **crow's-feet.** (*often pl*) a wrinkle at the outer corner of the eye.

crow's-nest *n* a lookout platform high up on a ship's mast.

crow step *n* another term for **corbie-step.**

crozier ('krəʊʒə) *n* a variant spelling of **crosier.**

CRT *abbrev. for:* **1** cathode-ray tube. **2** (in Britain) composite rate tax: a system of paying interest to savers by which a rate of tax for a period is determined in advance and interest is paid net of tax which is deducted at source.

crucial ❶ ('kruːʃəl) *adj* **1** involving a final or supremely important decision or event; decisive; critical. **2** *Inf.* very important. **3** *Sl.* very good. [C18: from F, from L *crux* CROSS]
▸'**crucially** *adv*

crucible ('kruːsɪbᵊl) *n* **1** a vessel in which substances are heated to high temperatures. **2** the hearth at the bottom of a metallurgical furnace in which the metal collects. **3** a severe trial or test. [C15 *corusible,* from Med. L *crūcibulum* night lamp, crucible, from ?]

crucifix ('kruːsɪfɪks) *n* a cross or image of a cross with a figure of Christ upon it. [C13: from Church L *crucifixus* the crucified Christ, from *crucifigere* to CRUCIFY]

crucifixion (,kruːsɪ'fɪkʃən) *n* a method of putting to death by nailing or binding to a cross, normally by the hands and feet.

Crucifixion (,kruːsɪ'fɪkʃən) *n* **1** (usually preceded by *the*) the crucifying of Christ. **2** a picture or representation of this.

cruciform ('kruːsɪ,fɔːm) *adj* shaped like a cross. [C17: from L *crux* cross + -FORM]
▸'**cruci,formly** *adv*

crucify ❶ ('kruːsɪ,faɪ) *vb* **crucifies, crucifying, crucified.** (*tr*) **1** to put to death by crucifixion. **2** *Sl.* to defeat, ridicule, etc., totally. **3** to treat very cruelly; torment. [C13: from OF *crucifier,* from LL *crucifigere* to crucify, to fasten to a cross, from L *crux* cross + *figere* to fasten]
▸'**cruci,fier** *n*

crud (krʌd) *n* **1** *Sl.* a sticky substance, esp. when dirty and encrusted. **2** *Sl.* something or someone that is worthless, disgusting, or contemptible. **3** an undesirable residue, esp. one inside a nuclear reactor. [C14: earlier form of CURD]
▸'**cruddy** *adj*

crude ❶ (kruːd) *adj* **1** lacking taste, tact, or refinement; vulgar. **2** in a natural or unrefined state. **3** lacking care, knowledge, or skill. **4** (*prenominal*) stark; blunt. ◆ *n* **5** short for **crude oil.** [C14: from L *crūdus* bloody, raw; rel. to L *cruor* blood]
▸'**crudely** *adv* ▸'**crudity** *or* '**crudeness** *n*

crude oil *n* unrefined petroleum.

crudités (,kruːdɪ'teɪ) *pl n* a selection of raw vegetables, served as an hors d'oeuvre. [C20: from F, pl of *crudité,* lit.: rawness]

cruel ❶ ('kruːəl) *adj* **1** causing or inflicting pain without pity. **2** causing pain or suffering. ◆ *vb* **cruels, cruelling, cruelled** *or US* **cruels, crueling, crueled.** (*tr*) **3 cruel someone's pitch.** *Austral. sl.* to ruin someone's chances. [C13: from OF, from L *crūdēlis,* from *crūdus* raw, bloody]
▸'**cruelly** *adv* ▸'**cruelness** *n*

cruelty ❶ ('kruːəltɪ) *n, pl* **cruelties. 1** deliberate infliction of pain or suffering. **2** the quality or characteristic of being cruel. **3** a cruel action. **4** *Law.* conduct that causes danger to life or limb or a threat to bodily or mental health.

THESAURUS

bluster, boast, brag, drool, exult, flourish, glory in, strut, swagger, triumph, vaunt

crowd *n* **1** = **multitude,** army, assembly, bevy, company, concourse, flock, herd, horde, host, mass, mob, pack, press, rabble, swarm, throng, troupe **2** = **group,** bunch (*inf.*), circle, clique, lot, set **3** *preceded by* **the** = **masses,** hoi polloi, mob, people, populace, proletariat, public, rabble, rank and file, riffraff, vulgar herd ◆ *vb* **4** = **flock,** cluster, congregate, cram, foregather, gather, huddle, mass, muster, press, push, stream, surge, swarm, throng **5** = **squeeze,** bundle, congest, cram, pack, pile

crowded *adj* **5** = **packed,** busy, congested, cramped, crushed, full, huddled, jam-packed, mobbed, overflowing, populous, swarming, teeming, thronged

crown *n* **1** = **coronet,** chaplet, circlet, coronal (*poetic*), diadem, tiara **2** = **laurel wreath,** bays, distinction, garland, honour, kudos, laurels, prize, trophy, wreath **7** = **high point,** acme, apex, crest, head, perfection, pinnacle, summit, tip, top, ultimate, zenith ◆ *vb* **15** = **honour,** adorn, dignify, festoon, invest, reward **17** = **cap,** be the climax *or* culmination of, complete, consummate, finish, fulfil, perfect, put the finishing touch to, put the tin lid on, round off, surmount, terminate, top **20** *Slang* = **strike,** belt (*inf.*), biff (*sl.*), box, cuff, hit over the head, punch

Crown *n* **1** = **monarch,** emperor *or* empress, king *or* queen, *rex,* ruler, sovereign **2** = **monarchy,** royalty, sovereignty

crucial *adj* **1** = **critical,** central, decisive, pivotal, psychological, searching, testing, trying **2** *Informal* = **vital,** essential, high-priority, important, momentous, now or never, pressing, urgent

crucify *vb* **2** *Slang* = **pan** (*inf.*), lampoon, ridicule, tear to pieces, wipe the floor with (*inf.*) **3** = **torment,** harrow, persecute, rack, torture

crude *adj* **1** = **vulgar,** boorish, coarse, crass, dirty, gross, indecent, lewd, obscene, smutty, tactless, tasteless, uncouth, X-rated (*inf.*) **2** = **unrefined,** natural, raw, unmilled, unpolished, unprepared, unprocessed **3** = **primitive,** clumsy, makeshift, rough, rough-and-ready, rough-hewn, rude, rudimentary, simple, sketchy, undeveloped, unfinished, unformed, unpolished
Antonyms *adj* ≠ **vulgar:** genteel, polished, refined, subtle, tasteful ≠ **unrefined:** fine, fine-grained, polished, prepared, processed, refined

crudely *adv* **1, 4** = **vulgarly,** bluntly, clumsily, coarsely, impolitely, indecently, pulling no punches (*inf.*), roughly, rudely, sketchily, tastelessly

crudity *n* **1** = **vulgarity,** coarseness, crudeness, impropriety, indecency, indelicacy, lewdness, loudness, lowness, obscenity, obtrusiveness, smuttiness **3** = **roughness,** clumsiness, crudeness, primitiveness, rudeness

cruel *adj* **1, 2** = **brutal,** atrocious, barbarous, bitter, bloodthirsty, brutish, callous, cold-blooded, depraved, excruciating, fell (*arch.*), ferocious, fierce, flinty, grim, hard, hard-hearted, harsh, heartless, hellish, implacable, inclement, inexorable, inhuman, inhumane, malevolent, merciless, murderous, painful, pitiless, poignant, ravening, raw, relentless, remorseless, ruthless, sadistic, sanguinary, savage, severe, spiteful, stony-hearted, unfeeling, unkind, unnatural, unrelenting, vengeful, vicious
Antonyms *adj* benevolent, caring, compassionate, gentle, humane, kind, merciful, sympathetic, warm-hearted

cruelly *adv* **1, 2** = **brutally,** barbarously, brutishly, callously, ferociously, fiercely, heartlessly, in cold blood, mercilessly, pitilessly, sadistically, savagely, spitefully, unmercifully, viciously

cruelty *n* **1** = **brutality,** barbarity, bestiality, bloodthirstiness, brutishness, callousness, depravity, ferocity, fiendishness, hardheartedness, harshness, heartlessness, inhumanity, mercilessness, murderousness, ruthlessness, sa-

cruelty-free *adj* (of a cosmetic or other product) developed without being tested on animals.

cruet ('kru:ɪt) *n* **1** a small container for holding pepper, salt, vinegar, oil, etc., at table. **2** a set of such containers, esp. on a stand. [C13: from Anglo-F, dim. of OF *crue* flask, of Gmc origin]

cruise ❶ (kru:z) *vb* **cruises, cruising, cruised. 1** (*intr*) to make a trip by sea for pleasure, usually calling at a number of ports. **2** to sail or travel over (a body of water) for pleasure. **3** (*intr*) to search for enemy vessels in a warship. **4** (*intr*) (of a vehicle, aircraft, or vessel) to travel at a moderate and efficient speed. ◆ *n* **5** an act or instance of cruising, esp. a trip by sea. [C17: from Du. *kruisen* to cross, from *cruis* CROSS]

cruise control *n* a system in a road vehicle that automatically maintains a selected speed until cancelled.

cruise missile *n* a low-flying subsonic missile that is guided throughout its flight.

cruiser ('kru:zə) *n* **1** a high-speed, long-range warship armed with medium-calibre weapons. **2** Also called: **cabin cruiser.** a pleasure boat, esp. one that is power-driven and has a cabin. **3** any person or thing that cruises.

cruiserweight ('kru:zə,weɪt) *n Boxing.* another term (esp. Brit.) for **light heavyweight.**

crumb ❶ (krʌm) *n* **1** a small fragment of bread, cake, or other baked foods. **2** a small piece or bit. **3** the soft inner part of bread. **4** *Sl.* a contemptible person. ◆ *vb* **5** (*tr*) to prepare or cover (food) with breadcrumbs. **6** to break into small fragments. [OE *cruma*]

crumble ❶ ('krʌmb^{ə}l) *vb* **crumbles, crumbling, crumbled. 1** to break or be broken into crumbs or fragments. **2** (*intr*) to fall apart or away. ◆ *n* **3** *Brit., Austral., & NZ.* a baked pudding consisting of a crumbly mixture of flour, fat, and sugar over stewed fruit: *apple crumble.* [C16: var. of *crimble,* of Gmc origin]

crumbly ❶ ('krʌmblɪ) *adj* **crumblier, crumbliest. 1** easily crumbled or crumbling. ◆ *n, pl* **crumblies. 2** *Brit. sl.* an older person.
▸**'crumbliness** *n*

crumby ('krʌmɪ) *adj* **crumbier, crumbiest. 1** full of or littered with crumbs. **2** soft, like the inside of bread. **3** a variant spelling of **crummy.**

crummy ❶ ('krʌmɪ) *adj* **crummier, crummiest.** *Sl.* **1** of little value; contemptible. **2** unwell or depressed: *to feel crummy.* [C19: var. spelling of CRUMBY]

crumpet ('krʌmpɪt) *n Chiefly Brit.* **1** a light soft yeast cake, eaten toasted and buttered. **2** *Sl.* women collectively. [C17: from ?]

crumple ❶ ('krʌmp^{ə}l) *vb* **crumples, crumpling, crumpled. 1** (when *intr,* often foll. by *up*) to collapse or cause to collapse. **2** (when *tr,* often foll. by *up*) to crush or cause to be crushed so as to form wrinkles or creases. ◆ *n* **3** a loose crease or wrinkle. [C16: from obs. *crump* to bend]
▸**'crumply** *adj*

crumple zones *pl n* parts of a motor vehicle, at the front and the rear, that are designed to crumple in a collision, thereby absorbing part of the energy of the impact.

crunch ❶ (krʌntʃ) *vb* **1** to bite or chew with a crushing or crackling sound. **2** to make or cause to make a crisp or brittle sound. ◆ *n* **3** the sound or act of crunching. **4 the crunch.** *Inf.* the critical moment or situation. ◆ *adj* **5** *Inf.* critical; decisive: *crunch time.* [C19: changed (through infl. of MUNCH) from earlier *craunch,* imit.]
▸**'crunchy** *adj* ▸**'crunchily** *adv* ▸**'crunchiness** *n*

crupper ('krʌpə) *n* **1** a strap from the back of a saddle that passes under a horse's tail. **2** the horse's rump. [C13: from OF *crupiere,* from *crupe* CROUP^{2}]

crusade ❶ (kru:'seɪd) *n* **1** (*often cap.*) any of the military expeditions undertaken in the 11th, 12th, and 13th centuries by the Christian powers of Europe to recapture the Holy Land from the Muslims. **2** (formerly) any holy war. **3** a vigorous and dedicated action or movement in favour of a cause. ◆ *vb* **crusades, crusading, crusaded.** (*intr*) **4** to campaign vigorously for something. **5** to go on a crusade. [C16: from earlier *croisade,* from OF *crois* cross, from L *crux;* infl. also by Sp. *cruzada,* from *cruzar* to take up the cross]
▸**cru'sader** *n*

cruse (kru:z) *n* a small earthenware container used, esp. formerly, for liquids. [OE *crūse*]

crush ❶ (krʌʃ) *vb* (*mainly tr*) **1** to press, mash, or squeeze so as to injure, break, crease, etc. **2** to break or grind into small particles. **3** to put down or subdue, esp. by force. **4** to extract (juice, water, etc.) by pressing. **5** to oppress harshly. **6** to hug or clasp tightly. **7** to defeat or humiliate utterly, as in argument or by a cruel remark. **8** (*intr*) to crowd; throng. **9** (*intr*) to become injured, broken, or distorted by pressure. ◆ *n* **10** a dense crowd, esp. at a social occasion. **11** the act of crushing; pressure. **12** a drink or pulp prepared by or as if by crushing fruit: *orange crush.* **13** *Inf.* **13a** an infatuation: *she had a crush on him.* **13b** the person with whom one is infatuated. [C14: from OF *croissir,* of Gmc origin]
▸**'crushable** *adj* ▸**'crusher** *n*

crush barrier *n* a barrier erected to separate sections of large crowds.

crust ❶ (krʌst) *n* **1a** the hard outer part of bread. **1b** a piece of bread consisting mainly of this. **2** the baked shell of a pie, tart, etc. **3** any hard or stiff outer covering or surface: *a crust of ice.* **4** the solid outer shell of the earth. **5** the dry covering of a skin sore or lesion; scab. **6** *Sl.* impertinence. **7** *Brit., Austral., & NZ sl.* a living (esp. in **earn a crust**). ◆ *vb* **8** to cover with or acquire a crust. **9** to form or be formed into a crust. [C14: from L *crūsta* hard surface, rind, shell]

crustacean (krʌ'steɪʃən) *n* **1** any arthropod of the mainly aquatic class *Crustacea,* typically having a carapace and including the lobsters, crabs, woodlice, and water fleas. ◆ *adj also* **crustaceous. 2** of, relating to, or belonging to the *Crustacea.* [C19: from NL *crūstāceus* hard-shelled, from L *crūsta* shell]

crustal ('krʌst^{ə}l) *adj* of or relating to the earth's crust.

crusty ❶ ('krʌstɪ) *adj* **crustier, crustiest. 1** having or characterized by a crust. **2** having a rude or harsh character or exterior.
▸**'crustily** *adv* ▸**'crustiness** *n*

crutch (krʌtʃ) *n* **1** a long staff having a rest for the armpit, for supporting the weight of the body. **2** something that supports, helps, or sustains. **3** *Brit.* another word for **crotch** (sense 1). ◆ *vb* **4** (*tr*) to support or sustain (a person or thing) as with a crutch. **5** *Austral. & NZ.* to clip (wool) from the hindquarters of a sheep. [OE *crycc*]

crutchings ('krʌtʃɪŋz) *pl n Austral. & NZ.* wool clipped from a sheep's hindquarters.

crux ❶ (krʌks) *n, pl* **cruxes** *or* **cruces** ('kru:si:z). **1** a vital or decisive stage, point, etc. (often in **the crux of the matter**). **2** a baffling problem or difficulty. [C18: from L: cross]

cruzado (kru:'zeɪdəʊ) *n, pl* **cruzadoes** *or* **cruzados** (-dəʊz). a former standard monetary unit of Brazil. [C16: lit., marked with a cross, from *cruzar* to bear a cross; see CRUSADE]

cruzeiro (kru:'zeərəʊ) *n, pl* **cruzeiros** (-rəʊz). a former standard monetary unit of Brazil. [Port.: from *cruz* CROSS]

cry ❶ (kraɪ) *vb* **cries, crying, cried. 1** (*intr*) to utter inarticulate sounds, esp. when weeping; sob. **2** (*intr*) to shed tears; weep. **3** (*intr;* usually foll. by *out*) to scream or shout in pain, terror, etc. **4** (*tr;* often foll. by *out*) to utter or shout (words of appeal, exclamation, fear, etc.). **5** (*intr;* often foll. by *out*) (of animals, birds, etc.) to utter loud characteristic sounds. **6** (*tr*) to hawk or sell by public announcement: *to cry newspapers.* **7** to announce (something) publicly or in the streets. **8** (*intr;* foll. by *for*) to clamour or beg. **9 cry for the moon.** to desire the unattainable.

THESAURUS

dism, savagery, severity, spite, spitefulness, venom, viciousness

cruise *vb* **1, 2** = **sail**, coast, voyage **4** = **travel along**, coast, drift, keep a steady pace ◆ *n* **5** = **sail**, boat trip, sea trip, voyage

crumb *n* **2** = **bit**, atom, fragment, grain, mite, morsel, particle, scrap, shred, sliver, snippet, *soupçon*, speck

crumble *vb* **1** = **crush**, bruise, crumb, fragment, granulate, grind, pound, powder, pulverize, triturate **2** = **disintegrate**, break down, break up, collapse, come to dust, decay, decompose, degenerate, deteriorate, fall apart, go to pieces, go to wrack and ruin, moulder, perish, tumble down

crumbling *adj* **2** = **disintegrating**, collapsing, decaying, decomposing, deteriorating, eroding, mouldering

crumbly *adj* **1** = **brittle**, brashy, friable, powdery, rotted, short (*of pastry*)

crummy *adj* **1** *Slang* = **second-rate**, bush-league (*Austral. & NZ inf.*), cheap, contemptible, crappy (*sl.*), dime-a-dozen (*inf.*), duff (*Brit. informal*), inferior, lousy (*sl.*), low-rent (*inf., chiefly U.S.*), piss-poor (*taboo sl.*), poor, poxy (*sl.*), rotten (*inf.*), rubbishy, shitty (*taboo sl.*), shoddy, third-rate, tinhorn (*US sl.*), trashy, two-bit (*US & Canad. sl.*), useless, worthless

crumple *vb* **1** = **collapse**, break down, cave in, fall, give way, go to pieces **2** = **crush**, crease, pucker, rumple, screw up, wrinkle

crumpled *adj* **2** = **crushed**, creased, puckered, ruffled, rumpled, shrivelled, wrinkled

crunch *vb* **1** = **chomp**, champ, chew noisily, grind, masticate, munch ◆ *n* **4 the crunch** *Informal* = **critical point**, crisis, crux, emergency, hour of decision, moment of truth, test

crusade *n* **2, 3** = **campaign**, cause, drive, holy war, jihad, movement, push

crusader *n* **4** = **campaigner**, advocate, champion, reformer

crush *vb* **1, 2** = **squash**, break, bruise, comminute, compress, contuse, crease, crumble, crumple, crunch, mash, pound, press, pulverize, rumple, smash, squeeze, wrinkle **3** = **overcome**, conquer, extinguish, overpower, overwhelm, put down, quell, stamp out, subdue, vanquish **6** = **squeeze**, embrace, enfold, hug, press **7** = **humiliate**, abash, browbeat, chagrin, dispose of, mortify, put down (*sl.*), quash, shame ◆ *n* **10** = **crowd**, huddle, jam, party

crust *n* **3** = **layer**, caking, coat, coating, concretion, covering, film, incrustation, outside, scab, shell, skin, surface

crusty *adj* **1** = **crispy**, brittle, crisp, friable, hard, short, well-baked, well-done **2** = **irritable**, brusque, cantankerous, captious, choleric, crabby, cross, curt, gruff, ill-humoured, peevish, prickly, ratty (*Brit. & NZ inf.*), short, short-tempered, snappish, snarling, splenetic, surly, testy, tetchy, touchy

crux *n* **1** = **crucial point**, core, decisive point, essence, heart, nub

cry *vb* **1, 2** = **weep**, bawl, bewail, blubber, boohoo, greet (*Scot. or arch.*), howl one's eyes out, keen, lament, mewl, pule, shed tears, snivel, sob, wail, whimper, whine, whinge (*inf.*), yowl **3** = **shout**, bawl, bell, bellow, call, call out, ejaculate, exclaim, hail, halloo, holler (*inf.*), howl, roar, scream, screech, shriek, sing out, vociferate, whoop, yell **7** = **announce**, advertise, bark (*inf.*), broadcast, bruit, hawk, noise, proclaim, promulgate, publish, shout from the rooftops (*inf.*), trumpet **8** = **beg**, beseech, clamour, entreat, implore, plead, pray ◆ *n* **11** = **weeping**, bawling, blubbering, crying, greet (*Scot. or arch.*), howl, keening, lament, lamentation, plaint (*arch.*), snivel, snivelling, sob, sobbing, sorrowing, wailing, weep **11** = **shout**, bawl, bell, yellow, call, ejaculation, exclamation, holler (*inf.*), hoot, howl, outcry, roar, scream, screech, shriek, squawk, whoop, yell, yelp, yoohoo

Antonyms *vb* ≠ **weep:** chortle, chuckle, giggle, laugh, snicker, snigger, twitter ≠ **shout:** drone, mumble, murmur, mutter, speak in hushed tones, speak softly, utter indistinctly, whisper

10 cry one's eyes *or* **heart out.** to weep bitterly. ◆ *n, pl* **cries. 11** the act or sound of crying; a shout, scream, or wail. **12** the characteristic utterance of an animal or bird. **13** a fit of weeping. **14** *Hunting.* the baying of a pack of hounds hunting their quarry by scent. **15 a far cry. 15a** a long way. **15b** something very different. **16 in full cry.** (esp. of a pack of hounds) in hot pursuit of a quarry. ◆ See also **cry down, cry off,** etc. [C13: from OF *crier,* from L *quirītāre* to call for help]

crybaby ('kraɪ,beɪbɪ) *n, pl* **crybabies.** a person, esp. a child, given to frequent crying or complaint.

cry down ❶ *vb (tr, adv)* to belittle; disparage.

crying ('kraɪɪŋ) *adj (prenominal)* notorious; lamentable (esp. in **crying shame**).

cryo- *combining form.* cold or freezing: *cryogenics.* [from Gk *kruos* icy cold, frost]

cryobiology (,kraɪəubaɪ'ɒlədʒɪ) *n* the biology of the effects of very low temperatures on organisms.
▸**,cryobi'ologist** *n*

cry off ❶ *vb (intr) Inf.* to withdraw from or cancel (an agreement or arrangement).

cryogen ('kraɪədʒən) *n* a substance used to produce low temperatures; a freezing mixture.

cryogenics (,kraɪə'dʒenɪks) *n (functioning as sing)* the branch of physics concerned with very low temperatures and the phenomena occurring at these temperatures.
▸**,cryo'genic** *adj*

cryolite ('kraɪə,laɪt) *n* a white or colourless fluoride of sodium and aluminium: used in the production of aluminium, glass, and enamel. Formula: Na_3AlF_6.

cryonics (kraɪ'ɒnɪks) *n (functioning as sing)* the practice of freezing a human corpse in the hope of restoring it to life later.

cryoprecipitate (,kraɪəuprɪ'sɪpɪtɪt) *n* a precipitate obtained by controlled thawing of a previously frozen substance. Factor VIII, for treating haemophilia, is often obtained as a cryoprecipitate from frozen blood.

cryostat ('kraɪə,stæt) *n* an apparatus for maintaining a constant low temperature.

cryosurgery (,kraɪəu'sɜːdʒərɪ) *n* surgery involving quick freezing for therapeutic benefit.

cry out *vb (intr, adv)* **1** to scream or shout aloud, esp. in pain, terror, etc. **2** (often foll. by *for*) *Inf.* to demand in an obvious manner.

crypt ❶ (krɪpt) *n* a vault or underground chamber, esp. beneath a church, often used as a chapel, burial place, etc. [C18: from L *crypta,* from Gk *kruptē* vault, secret place, ult. from *kruptein* to hide]

cryptanalysis (,krɪptə'nælɪsɪs) *n* the study of codes and ciphers; cryptography. [C20: from CRYPTO- + ANALYSIS]
▸**cryptanalytic** (,krɪptænə'lɪtɪk) *adj* ▸**crypt'analyst** *n*

cryptic ❶ ('krɪptɪk) *adj* **1** hidden; secret. **2** esoteric or obscure in meaning. **3** (of coloration) effecting camouflage or concealment. [C17: from LL *crypticus,* from Gk *kruptikos,* from *kruptos* concealed; see CRYPT]
▸**'cryptically** *adv*

crypto- *or before a vowel* **crypt-** *combining form.* secret, hidden, or concealed. [NL, from Gk *kruptos* hidden, from *kruptein* to hide]

cryptocrystalline (,krɪptəu'krɪstəlaɪn) *adj* (of rocks) composed of crystals visible only under a polarizing microscope.

cryptogam ('krɪptəu,gæm) *n* (in former plant classification schemes) any organism that does not produce seeds, including algae, fungi, mosses, and ferns. [C19: from NL *Cryptogamia,* from CRYPTO- + Gk *gamos* marriage]
▸**,crypto'gamic** *or* **cryptogamous** (krɪp'tɒgəməs) *adj*

cryptograph ('krɪptəu,grɑːf) *n* **1** something written in code or cipher. **2** a code using secret symbols (**cryptograms**).

cryptography (krɪp'tɒgrəfɪ) *n* the science or study of analysing and deciphering codes, ciphers, etc. Also called: **cryptanalysis.**
▸**cryp'tographer** *or* **cryp'tographist** *n* ▸**cryptographic** (,krɪptə'græfɪk) *or* **,crypto'graphical** *adj* ▸**,crypto'graphically** *adv*

crystal ('krɪst°l) *n* **1** a solid, such as quartz, with a regular shape in which plane faces intersect at definite angles. **2** a single grain of a crystalline substance. **3** anything resembling a crystal, such as a piece of cut glass. **4a** a highly transparent and brilliant type of glass. **4b** *(as modifier): a crystal chandelier.* **5** something made of or resembling crystal. **6** crystal glass articles collectively. **7** *Electronics.* **7a** a crystalline element used in certain electronic devices as a detector, oscillator, etc. **7b** *(as modifier): crystal pick-up.* **8** a transparent cover for the face of a watch. **9** *(modifier)* of or relating to a crystal or the regular atomic arrangement of crystals: *crystal structure.* ◆ *adj* **10** resembling crystal; transparent: *crystal water.* [OE *cristalla,* from L *crystallum,* from Gk *krustallos* ice, crystal, from *krustainein* to freeze]

crystal ball *n* the glass globe used in crystal gazing.

crystal class *n Crystallography.* any of 32 possible types of crystals, classified according to their rotational symmetry about axes through a point. Also called: **point group.**

crystal detector *n Electronics.* a demodulator, used esp. in early radio receivers, incorporating a semiconductor crystal.

crystal gazing *n* **1** the act of staring into a crystal ball supposedly in order to arouse visual perceptions of the future, etc. **2** the act of trying to foresee or predict.
▸**crystal gazer** *n*

crystal healing *n* (in alternative therapy) the use of the supposed power of crystals to affect the human energy field.

crystal lattice *n* the regular array of points about which the atoms, ions, or molecules composing a crystal are centred.

crystalline ('krɪstə,laɪn) *adj* **1** having the characteristics or structure of crystals. **2** consisting of or containing crystals. **3** made of or like crystal; transparent; clear.

crystalline lens *n* a biconvex transparent elastic lens in the eye.

crystallize ❶ *or* **crystallise** ('krɪstə,laɪz) *vb* **crystallizes, crystallizing, crystallized** *or* **crystallises, crystallising, crystallised. 1** to form or cause to form crystals; assume or cause to assume a crystalline form or structure. **2** to coat or become coated with sugar. **3** to give a definite form or expression to (an idea, argument, etc.) or (of an idea, argument, etc.) to assume a definite form.
▸**'crystal,lizable** *or* **'crystal,lisable** *adj* ▸**,crystalli'zation** *or* **,crystalli'sation** *n*

crystallo- *or before a vowel* **crystall-** *combining form.* crystal: *crystallography.*

crystallography (,krɪstə'lɒgrəfɪ) *n* the science of crystal structure.
▸**,crystal'lographer** *n* ▸**crystallographic** (,krɪstələu'græfɪk) *adj*

crystalloid ('krɪstə,lɔɪd) *adj* **1** resembling or having the properties of a crystal. ◆ *n* **2** a substance that in solution can pass through a semipermeable membrane.

Crystal Palace *n* a building of glass and iron designed by Joseph Paxton to house the Great Exhibition of 1851. Erected in Hyde Park, London, it was moved to Sydenham (1852–53): destroyed by fire in 1936.

crystal set *n* an early form of radio receiver having a crystal detector.

cry up *vb (tr, adv)* to praise highly; extol.

Cs *the chemical symbol for* caesium.

CS *abbrev. for:* **1** Also: **cs.** capital stock. **2** chartered surveyor. **3** Christian Science. **4** Civil Service. **5** Also: **cs.** Court of Session.

CSA (in Britain) *abbrev. for* Child Support Agency.

csc *abbrev. for* cosecant.

CSC *abbrev. for* Civil Service Commission.

CSE (in Britain) *abbrev. for* Certificate of Secondary Education; a former examination the first grade pass of which was an equivalent to a GCE O level.

CSEU *abbrev. for* Confederation of Shipbuilding and Engineering Unions.

CSF *abbrev. for:* **1** cerebrospinal fluid. **2** *Immunol.* colony-stimulating factor.

CS gas *n* a gas causing tears, salivation, and painful breathing, used in civil disturbances. [C20: from the surname initials of its US inventors, Ben Carson and Roger Staughton]

CSIRO (in Australia) *abbrev. for* Commonwealth Scientific and Industrial Research Organization.

CSM (in Britain) *abbrev. for* Company Sergeant-Major.

C-spanner *n* a sickle-shaped spanner having a projection at the end of the curve, used for turning large narrow nuts that have an indentation into which the projection on the spanner fits.

CST (in the US and Canada) *abbrev. for* Central Standard Time.

CSU *abbrev. for* Civil Service Union.

ct *abbrev. for:* **1** carat. **2** cent. **3** court.

CTC (in Britain) *abbrev. for* city technology college.

ctenophore ('tenə,fɔː, 'tiːnə-) *n* any marine invertebrate of the phylum *Ctenophora,* whose body bears eight rows of fused cilia, for locomotion. [C19: from NL *ctenophorus,* from Gk *kteno-, kteis* comb + -PHORE]

ctn *abbrev. for* cotangent.

CT scanner *n* computerized tomography scanner: an X-ray machine that can produce multiple cross-sectional images of the soft tissues (**CT scans**). Former name: **CAT scanner.**

CTT *abbrev. for* Capital Transfer Tax.

CTV *abbrev. for* Canadian Television (Network Limited).

Cu *the chemical symbol for* copper. [from LL *cuprum*]

cu. *abbrev. for* cubic.

cub ❶ (kʌb) *n* **1** the young of certain animals, such as the lion, bear, etc. **2** a young or inexperienced person. ◆ *vb* **cubs, cubbing, cubbed. 3** to give birth to (cubs). [C16: ?from ON *kubbi* young seal]
▸**'cubbish** *adj*

Cub (kʌb) *n* short for **Cub Scout.**

Cuban ('kjuːbən) *adj* **1** of or relating to Cuba, a republic and the largest island in the Caribbean. ◆ *n* **2** a native or inhabitant of Cuba.

cubby ('kʌbɪ) *n, pl* **cubbies.** *Austral.* a small room or enclosed area, esp. one used as a child's play area. Also: **cubbyhole, cubby-house.**

THESAURUS

cry down *vb* = **run down,** asperse, bad-mouth *(sl., chiefly U.S. & Canad.),* belittle, decry, denigrate, disparage, knock *(inf.),* rubbish *(inf.),* slag (off) *(sl.)*

cry off *vb Informal* = **back out,** beg off, cop out *(sl.),* excuse oneself, quit, withdraw, withdraw from

crypt *n* = **vault,** catacomb, ossuary, tomb, undercroft

cryptic *adj* **1, 2** = **mysterious,** abstruse, ambiguous, apocryphal, arcane, cabbalistic, coded, dark, Delphic, enigmatic, equivocal, esoteric, hidden, obscure, occult, oracular, perplexing, puzzling, recondite, secret, vague, veiled

crystallize *vb* **1, 3** = **form,** appear, coalesce, harden, materialize, take shape

cub *n* **1** = **young,** offspring, whelp **2** = **youngster,** babe *(inf.),* beginner, fledgling, greenhorn *(inf.),* lad, learner, puppy, recruit, tenderfoot, trainee, whippersnapper

cubbyhole ❶ ('kʌbɪˌhəʊl) *n* a small enclosed space or room. [C19: from dialect *cub* cattle pen]

cube (kju:b) *n* **1** a solid having six plane square faces in which the angle between two adjacent sides is a right angle. **2** the product of three equal factors. **3** something in the form of a cube. ◆ *vb* **cubes, cubing, cubed. 4** to raise (a number or quantity) to the third power. **5** (*tr*) to make, shape, or cut (something) into cubes. [C16: from L *cubus* die, cube, from Gk *kubos*]
▸**'cuber** *n*

cubeb ('kju:bɛb) *n* **1** a SE Asian treelike climbing plant. **2** its spicy fruit, dried and used as a stimulant and diuretic and sometimes smoked in cigarettes. [C14: from OF *cubebe,* from Med. L *cubēba,* from Ar. *kubābah*]

cube root *n* the number or quantity whose cube is a given number or quantity: 2 is the cube root of 8 (usually written $\sqrt[3]{8}$ or $8^{1/3}$).

cubic ('kju:bɪk) *adj* **1** having the shape of a cube. **2a** having three dimensions. **2b** denoting or relating to a linear measure that is raised to the third power: *a cubic metre.* **3** *Maths.* of, relating to, or containing a variable to the third power or a term in which the sum of the exponents of the variables is three.
▸**'cubical** *adj*

cubicle ('kju:bɪkᵊl) *n* an enclosed compartment, screened for privacy, as in a dormitory, shower, etc. [C15: from L *cubiculum,* from *cubāre* to lie down]

cubic measure *n* a system of units for the measurement of volumes.

cubiform ('kju:bɪˌfɔ:m) *adj* having the shape of a cube.

cubism ('kju:bɪzəm) *n* (*often cap.*) a French school of art, initiated in 1907 by Picasso and Braque, which amalgamated viewpoints of natural forms into a multifaceted surface of geometrical planes.
▸**'cubist** *adj, n* ▸**cu'bistic** *adj*

cubit ('kju:bɪt) *n* an ancient measure of length based on the length of the forearm. [C14: from L *cubitum* elbow, cubit]

cuboid ('kju:bɔɪd) *adj also* **cuboidal** (kju:'bɔɪdᵊl). **1** shaped like a cube; cubic. **2** of or denoting the cuboid bone. ◆ *n* **3** the cubelike bone of the foot. **4** *Maths.* a geometric solid whose six faces are rectangles.

Cub Scout *or* **Cub** *n* a member of the junior branch of the Scout Association.

cucking stool ('kʌkɪŋ) *n History.* a stool to which suspected witches, scolds, etc., were tied and pelted or ducked into water. [C13 *cucking stol,* lit.: defecating chair, from *cukken* to defecate]

cuckold ('kʌkəld) *n* **1** a man whose wife has committed adultery. ◆ *vb* **2** (*tr*) to make a cuckold of. [C13 *cukeweld,* from OF *cucuault,* from *cucu* CUCKOO; ? an allusion to cuckoos that lay eggs in the nests of other birds]
▸**'cuckoldry** *n*

cuckoo ('kʊku:) *n, pl* **cuckoos. 1** any bird of the family Cuculidae, having pointed wings and a long tail. Many species, including the **European cuckoo,** lay their eggs in the nests of other birds and have a two-note call. **2** *Inf.* an insane or foolish person. ◆ *adj* **3** *Inf.* insane or foolish. ◆ *interj* **4** an imitation or representation of the call of a cuckoo. ◆ *vb* **cuckoos, cuckooing, cuckooed. 5** (*intr*) to make the sound imitated by the word *cuckoo.* [C13: from OF *cucu,* imit.]

cuckoo clock *n* a clock in which a mechanical cuckoo pops out with a sound like a cuckoo's call when the clock strikes.

cuckoopint ('kʊku:ˌpaɪnt, -ˌpɪnt) *n* a European plant with arrow-shaped leaves, a spathe marked with purple, a pale purple spadix, and scarlet berries. Also called: **lords-and-ladies.**

cuckoo spit *n* a white frothy mass on the stems and leaves of many plants, produced by froghopper larvae.

cucumber ('kju:ˌkʌmbə) *n* **1** a creeping plant cultivated in many forms for its edible fruit. **2** the cylindrical fruit of this plant, which has hard thin green rind and white crisp flesh. [C14: from L *cucumis,* from ?]

cucurbit (kju:'kɜ:bɪt) *n* any of a family of creeping flowering plants that includes the pumpkin, cucumber, and gourds. [C14: from OF, from L *cucurbita* gourd, cup]
▸**cuˌcurbi'taceous** *adj*

cud (kʌd) *n* **1** partially digested food regurgitated from the first stomach of ruminants to the mouth for a second chewing. **2 chew the cud.** to reflect or think over something. [OE *cudu,* from *cwidu* what has been chewed]

cuddle ❶ ('kʌdᵊl) *vb* **cuddles, cuddling, cuddled. 1** to hold close or (of two people, etc.) to hold each other close, as for affection or warmth; hug. **2** (*intr;* foll. by *up*) to curl or snuggle up into a comfortable or warm position. ◆ *n* **3** a close embrace, esp. when prolonged. [C18: from ?]
▸**'cuddlesome** *adj* ▸**'cuddly** *adj*

cuddy ('kʌdɪ) *n, pl* **cuddies.** a small cabin in a boat. [C17: ?from Du. *kajute*]

cudgel ❶ ('kʌdʒəl) *n* **1** a short stout stick used as a weapon. **2 take up the cudgels.** (often foll. by *for* or *on behalf of*) to join in a dispute, esp. to defend oneself or another. ◆ *vb* **cudgels, cudgelling, cudgelled** *or US* **cudgels, cudgeling, cudgeled. 3** (*tr*) to strike with a cudgel. **4 cudgel one's brains.** to think hard. [OE *cycgel*]

cudgerie ('kʌdʒərɪ) *n Austral.* any of various large rainforest trees, such as the pink poplar or blush cudgerie, with pink wood. [from Abor.]

cudweed ('kʌdˌwi:d) *n* any of various temperate woolly plants having clusters of whitish or yellow button-like flowers.

cue[1] ❶ (kju:) *n* **1a** (in the theatre, films, music, etc.) anything that serves as a signal to an actor, musician, etc., to follow with specific lines or action. **1b on cue.** at the right moment. **2** a signal or reminder to do something. ◆ *vb* **cues, cueing, cued. 3** (*tr*) to give a cue or cues to (an actor). **4** (usually foll. by *in* or *into*) to signal (to something or somebody) at a specific moment in a musical or dramatic performance. [C16: prob. from name of the letter *q,* used in an actor's script to represent L *quando* when]

cue[2] (kju:) *n* **1** *Billiards, etc.* a long tapered shaft used to drive the balls. **2** hair caught at the back forming a tail or braid. ◆ *vb* **cues, cueing, cued. 3** to drive (a ball) with a cue. [C18: var. of QUEUE]

cue ball *n Billiards, etc.* the ball struck by the cue, as distinguished from the object balls.

cuesta ('kwɛstə) *n* a long low ridge with a steep scarp slope and a gentle back slope. [Sp.: shoulder, from L *costa* side, rib]

cuff[1] ❶ (kʌf) *n* **1** the end of a sleeve, sometimes turned back. **2** the part of a glove that extends past the wrist. **3** the US, Canad., and Austral. name for **turn-up** (sense 4). **4 off the cuff.** *Inf.* improvised; extemporary. [C14 *cuffe* glove, from ?]

cuff[2] ❶ (kʌf) *vb* **1** (*tr*) to strike with an open hand. ◆ *n* **2** a blow of this kind. [C16: from ?]

cuff link *n* one of a pair of linked buttons, used to join the buttonholes on the cuffs of a shirt.

cui bono *Latin.* (kwi: 'bəʊnəʊ) for whose benefit? for what purpose?

cuirass (kwɪ'ræs) *n* **1** a piece of armour covering the chest and back. ◆ *vb* **2** (*tr*) to equip with a cuirass. [C15: from F *cuirasse,* from LL *coriacea,* from *coriaceus* made of leather]

cuirassier (ˌkwɪərə'sɪə) *n* a mounted soldier, esp. of the 16th century, who wore a cuirass.

Cuisenaire rod (ˌkwɪzə'nɛə) *n Trademark.* one of a set of rods of various colours and lengths representing different numbers, used to teach arithmetic to young children. [C20: after Emil-Georges *Cuisenaire* (?1891–1976), Belgian educationalist]

cuisine (kwɪ'zi:n) *n* **1** a style or manner of cooking: *French cuisine.* **2** the food prepared by a restaurant, household, etc. [C18: from F, lit.: kitchen, from LL *coquīna,* from L *coquere* to cook]

cuisse (kwɪs) *or* **cuish** (kwɪʃ) *n* a piece of armour for the thigh. [C15: back formation from *cuisses* (pl), from OF *cuisseaux,* from *cuisse* thigh]

cul-de-sac ❶ ('kʌldəˌsæk, 'kʊl-) *n, pl* **culs-de-sac** *or* **cul-de-sacs. 1** a road with one end blocked off; dead end. **2** an inescapable position. [C18: from F, lit.: bottom of the bag]

-cule *suffix forming nouns.* indicating smallness. [from L *-culus,* dim. suffix]

culex ('kju:lɛks) *n, pl* **culices** (-lɪˌsi:z). any mosquito of the genus *Culex,* such as *C. pipiens,* the common mosquito. [C15: from L: midge, gnat]

culinary ('kʌlɪnərɪ) *adj* of, relating to, or used in the kitchen or in cookery. [C17: from L *culīnārius,* from *culīna* kitchen]
▸**'culinarily** *adv*

cull ❶ (kʌl) *vb* (*tr*) **1** to choose or gather the best or required examples of. **2** to take out (an animal, esp. an inferior one) from a herd or group. **3** to reduce the size of (a herd, etc.) by killing a proportion of its members. **4** to gather (flowers, fruit, etc.). ◆ *n* **5** the act or product of culling. **6** an inferior animal taken from a herd or group. [C15: from OF *coillir* to pick, from L *colligere;* see COLLECT[1]]
▸**'culler** *n*

culm[1] (kʌlm) *n Mining.* **1** coal-mine waste. **2** inferior anthracite. [C14: prob. rel. to COAL]

culm[2] (kʌlm) *n* the hollow jointed stem of a grass or sedge. [C17: from L *culmus* stalk; see HAULM]

culminate ❶ ('kʌlmɪˌneɪt) *vb* **culminates, culminating, culminated. 1** (when *intr,* usually foll. by *in*) to reach or bring to a final or climactic stage. **2** (*intr*) (of a celestial body) to cross the meridian. [C17: from LL *culmināre* to reach the highest point, from L *culmen* top]
▸**'culminant** *adj*

culmination ❶ (ˌkʌlmɪ'neɪʃən) *n* **1** the final or highest point. **2** the act of culminating. **3** *Astron.* the highest or lowest altitude attained by a heavenly body as it crosses the meridian.

THESAURUS

cubbyhole *n* = **compartment,** den, hideaway, hole, niche, pigeonhole, recess, slot, snug

cuddle *vb* **1** = **hug,** bill and coo, canoodle (*sl.*), clasp, cosset, embrace, fondle, nestle, pet, snuggle

cudgel *n* **1** = **club,** bastinado, baton, bludgeon, cosh (*Brit.*), shillelagh, stick, truncheon ◆ *vb* **3** = **beat,** bang, baste, batter, bludgeon, cane, cosh (*Brit.*), drub, maul, pound, pummel, thrash, thump, thwack

cue[1] *n* **1a, 2** = **signal,** catchword, hint, key, nod, prompting, reminder, sign, suggestion

cuff[1] *n* **4 off the cuff** *Informal* = **impromptu,** ad lib, extempore, improvised, offhand, off the top of one's head, on the spur of the moment, spontaneous, spontaneously, unrehearsed

cuff[2] *vb* **1** = **smack,** bat (*inf.*), beat, belt (*inf.*), biff (*sl.*), box, buffet, clap, clobber (*sl.*), clout (*inf.*), hit, knock, lambast(e), pummel, punch, slap, thump, whack ◆ *n* **2** = **smack,** belt (*inf.*), biff (*sl.*), blow, box, buffet, clout (*inf.*), knock, punch, rap, slap, thump, whack

cul-de-sac *n* **1** = **dead end,** blind alley

cull *vb* **1, 3** = **choose,** cherry-pick, pick, pluck, select, sift, thin, thin out, winnow **4** = **gather,** amass, collect, glean, pick up

culminate *vb* **1** = **end up,** climax, close, come to a climax, come to a head, conclude, end, finish, rise to a crescendo, terminate, wind up

culmination *n* **1** = **climax,** acme, apex, apogee, completion, conclusion, consummation, crown, crowning touch, finale, height, *ne plus ultra,* peak, perfection, pinnacle, punch line, summit, top, zenith

culottes (kjuːˈlɒts) *pl n* women's flared trousers cut to look like a skirt. [C20: from F, lit.: breeches, from *cul* bottom]

culpable ➊ (ˈkʌlpəbᵊl) *adj* deserving censure; blameworthy. [C14: from OF *coupable*, from L *culpābilis*, from *culpāre* to blame, from *culpa* fault]
▸ **ˌculpaˈbility** *n* ▸ **ˈculpably** *adv*

culpable homicide *n Scots Law.* manslaughter.

culprit ➊ (ˈkʌlprɪt) *n* **1** *Law.* a person awaiting trial. **2** the person responsible for a particular offence, misdeed, etc. [C17: from Anglo-F *cul-*, short for *culpable* guilty + *prit* ready, indicating that the prosecution was ready to prove the guilt of the one charged]

cult ➊ (kʌlt) *n* **1** a specific system of religious worship. **2** a sect devoted to such a system. **3** a quasi-religious organization using devious psychological techniques to gain and control adherents. **4** intense interest in and devotion to a person, idea, or activity. **5** the person, idea, etc., arousing such devotion. **6** something regarded as fashionable or significant by a particular group; craze. **7** (*modifier*) of, relating to, or characteristic of a cult or cults: *a cult figure; a cult show.* [C17: from L *cultus* cultivation, refinement, from *colere* to till]
▸ **ˈcultism** *n* ▸ **ˈcultist** *n*

cultic (ˈkʌltɪk) *adj* of or relating to a religious cult.

cultish (ˈkʌltɪʃ) *or* **culty** (ˈkʌltɪ) *adj* intended to appeal to a small group of fashionable people.

cultivable (ˈkʌltɪvəbᵊl) *or* **cultivatable** (ˈkʌltɪˌveɪtəbᵊl) *adj* (of land) capable of being cultivated. [C17: from F, from OF *cultiver* to CULTIVATE]
▸ **ˌcultivaˈbility** *n*

cultivar (ˈkʌltɪˌvɑː) *n* a variety of a plant produced from a natural species and maintained by cultivation. [C20: from CULTI(VATED) + VAR(IETY)]

cultivate ➊ (ˈkʌltɪˌveɪt) *vb* **cultivates, cultivating, cultivated.** (*tr*) **1** to prepare (land or soil) for the growth of crops. **2** to plant, tend, harvest, or improve (plants). **3** to break up (land or soil) with a cultivator or hoe. **4** to improve (the mind, body, etc.) as by study, education, or labour. **5** to give special attention to: *to cultivate a friendship.* [C17: from Med. L *cultivāre* to till, from *cultīvus* cultivable, from L *cultus* cultivated, from *colere* to till, toil over]
▸ **ˈcultiˌvated** *adj*

cultivation ➊ (ˌkʌltɪˈveɪʃən) *n* **1** *Agriculture.* **1a** the cultivating of crops or plants. **1b** the preparation of ground to promote their growth. **2** development, esp. through education, training, etc. **3** culture or sophistication.

cultivator (ˈkʌltɪˌveɪtə) *n* **1** a farm implement used to break up soil and remove weeds. **2** a person or thing that cultivates.

cultural ➊ (ˈkʌltʃərəl) *adj* **1** of or relating to artistic or social pursuits or events considered valuable or enlightened. **2** of or relating to a culture. **3** obtained by specialized breeding.

culture ➊ (ˈkʌltʃə) *n* **1** the total of the inherited ideas, beliefs, values, and knowledge, which constitute the shared bases of social action. **2** the total range of activities and ideas of a people. **3** a particular civilization at a particular period. **4** the artistic and social pursuits, expression, and tastes valued by a society or class. **5** the enlightenment or refinement resulting from these pursuits. **6** the cultivation of plants to improve stock or to produce new ones. **7** the rearing and breeding of animals, esp. with a view to improving the strain. **8** the act or practice of tilling or cultivating the soil. **9** *Biol.* **9a** the experimental growth of microorganisms in a nutrient substance. **9b** a group of microorganisms grown in this way. ◆ *vb* **cultures, culturing, cultured.** (*tr*) **10** to cultivate (plants or animals). **11** to grow (microorganisms) in a culture medium. [C15: from OF, from L *cultūra* a cultivating, from *colere* to till; see CULT]
▸ **ˈculturist** *n*

cultured ➊ (ˈkʌltʃəd) *adj* **1** showing or having good taste, manners, and education. **2** artificially grown or synthesized: *cultured pearls.* **3** treated by a culture of microorganisms.

cultured pearl *n* a pearl induced to grow in the shell of an oyster or clam, by the insertion of a small object.

culture shock *n Sociol.* the feelings of isolation, rejection, etc., experienced when one culture is brought into sudden contact with another.

culture vulture *n Inf.* a person considered to be excessively, and often pretentiously, interested in the arts.

cultus (ˈkʌltəs) *n, pl* **cultuses** *or* **culti** (-taɪ). another word for **cult** (sense 1). [C17: from L: a toiling over something, refinement, CULT]

culverin (ˈkʌlvərɪn) *n* **1** a medium-to-heavy cannon used during the 15th, 16th, and 17th centuries. **2** a medieval musket. [C15: from OF *coulevrine*, from *couleuvre*, from L *colubər* serpent]

culvert ➊ (ˈkʌlvət) *n* **1** a drain or covered channel that crosses under a road, railway, etc. **2** a channel for an electric cable. [C18: from ?]

cum (kʌm) *prep* used between nouns to designate a combined nature: *a kitchen-cum-dining room.* [L: with, together with]

cumber (ˈkʌmbə) *vb* (*tr*) **1** to obstruct or hinder. **2** *Obs.* to inconvenience. [C13: prob. from OF *combrer* to impede, prevent, from *combre* barrier; see ENCUMBER]

cumbersome ➊ (ˈkʌmbəsəm) *or* **cumbrous** (ˈkʌmbrəs) *adj* **1** awkward because of size, weight, or shape. **2** difficult because of extent or complexity: *cumbersome accounts.* [C14: *cumber*, short for ENCUMBER + -SOME[1]]
▸ **ˈcumbersomeness** *or* **ˈcumbrousness** *n*

cumin *or* **cummin** (ˈkʌmɪn) *n* **1** an umbelliferous Mediterranean plant with small white or pink flowers. **2** the aromatic seeds (collectively) of this plant, used as a condiment and a flavouring. [C12: from OF, from L *cumīnum*, from Gk *kuminon*, of Semitic origin]

cummerbund (ˈkʌməˌbʌnd) *n* a wide sash worn round the waist, esp. with a dinner jacket. [C17: from Hindi *kamarband*, from Persian, from *kamar* loins, waist + *band* band]

cum new *adv, adj* (of shares, etc.) with the right to take up any scrip issue or rights issue. Cf. **ex new.**

cumquat (ˈkʌmkwɒt) *n* a variant spelling of **kumquat.**

cumulate *vb* (ˈkjuːmjʊˌleɪt), **cumulates, cumulating, cumulated. 1** to accumulate. **2** (*tr*) to combine (two or more sequences) into one. ◆ *adj* (ˈkjuːmjʊlɪt). **3** heaped up. [C16: from L *cumulāre* from *cumulus* heap]
▸ **ˌcumuˈlation** *n*

cumulative ➊ (ˈkjuːmjʊlətɪv) *adj* **1** growing in quantity, strength, or effect by successive additions. **2** (of dividends or interest) intended to be accumulated. **3** *Statistics.* **3a** (of a frequency) including all values of a variable either below or above a specified value. **3b** (of error) tending to increase as the sample size is increased.
▸ **ˈcumulatively** *adv* ▸ **ˈcumulativeness** *n*

cumulonimbus (ˌkjuːmjʊləʊˈnɪmbəs) *n, pl* **cumulonimbi** (-baɪ) *or* **cumulonimbuses.** *Meteorol.* a cumulus cloud of great vertical extent, the bottom being dark-coloured, indicating rain or hail.

cumulus (ˈkjuːmjʊləs) *n, pl* **cumuli** (-ˌlaɪ). a bulbous or billowing white or dark grey cloud. [C17: from L: mass]
▸ **ˈcumulous** *adj*

cuneate (ˈkjuːnɪɪt, -ˌeɪt) *adj* wedge-shaped. [C19: from L *cuneāre* to make wedge-shaped, from *cuneus* a wedge]
▸ **ˈcuneately** *adv* ▸ **ˈcuneal** *adj*

cuneiform (ˈkjuːnɪˌfɔːm) *adj* **1** Also: **cuneal.** wedge-shaped. **2** of, relating to, or denoting the wedge-shaped characters in several ancient languages of Mesopotamia and Persia. **3** of or relating to a tablet in which this script is employed. ◆ *n* **4** cuneiform characters. [C17: prob. from OF *cunéiforme*, from L *cuneus* wedge]

cunjevoi (ˈkʌndʒɪˌvɔɪ) *n Austral.* **1** an arum of tropical Asia and Australia, cultivated for its edible rhizome. **2** a sea squirt. Often shortened to **cunjie, cunjy.** [C19: from Abor.]

cunnilingus (ˌkʌnɪˈlɪŋgəs) *or* **cunnilinctus** (ˌkʌnɪˈlɪŋktəs) *n* a sexual activity in which the female genitalia are stimulated by the partner's

THESAURUS

culpability *n* = **blameworthiness,** answerability, blame, fault, guilt, liability, responsibility

culpable *adj* = **blameworthy,** answerable, at fault, blamable, censurable, found wanting, guilty, in the wrong, liable, reprehensible, sinful, to blame, wrong
Antonyms *adj* blameless, clean (*sl.*), guiltless, innocent, in the clear, not guilty, squeaky-clean

culprit *n* **2** = **offender,** criminal, delinquent, evildoer, felon, guilty party, malefactor, miscreant, person responsible, rascal, sinner, transgressor, villain, wrongdoer

cult *n* **1, 2** = **sect,** body, church, clique, denomination, faction, faith, following, party, religion, school **4** = **devotion,** admiration, craze, idolization, reverence, veneration, worship

cultivate *vb* **1, 2** = **farm,** bring under cultivation, fertilize, harvest, plant, plough, prepare, tend, till, work **3** = **develop,** ameliorate, better, bring on, cherish, civilize, discipline, elevate, enrich, foster, improve, polish, promote, refine, train **5** = **encourage,** aid, devote oneself to, forward, foster, further, help, patronize, promote, pursue, support

cultivated *adj* **4** = **well-educated,** accomplished, advanced, civilized, cultured, developed, discerning, discriminating, educated, enlightened, erudite, genteel, polished, refined, sophisticated, urbane, versed, well-bred

cultivation *n* **1** = **farming,** agronomy, gardening, husbandry, planting, ploughing, tillage, tilling, working **2** = **development,** advancement, advocacy, encouragement, enhancement, fostering, furtherance, help, nurture, patronage, promotion, support **3** = **refinement,** breeding, civility, civilization, culture, discernment, discrimination, education, enlightenment, gentility, good taste, learning, letters, manners, polish, sophistication, taste

cultural *adj* **1** = **artistic,** broadening, civilizing, developmental, edifying, educational, educative, elevating, enlightening, enriching, humane, humanizing, liberal, liberalizing

culture *n* **1-4** = **civilization,** customs, lifestyle, mores, society, stage of development, the arts, way of life **5** = **refinement,** accomplishment, breeding, education, elevation, enlightenment, erudition, gentility, good taste, improvement, polish, politeness, sophistication, urbanity **6-8** = **farming,** agriculture, agronomy, cultivation, husbandry

cultured *adj* **1** = **refined,** accomplished, advanced, educated, enlightened, erudite, genteel, highbrow, knowledgeable, polished, scholarly, sophisticated, urbane, versed, well-bred, well-informed, well-read
Antonyms *adj* coarse, common, inelegant, uncultivated, uneducated, unpolished, unrefined, vulgar

culvert *n* **1** = **drain,** channel, conduit, gutter, watercourse

cumbersome *adj* **1** = **awkward,** bulky, burdensome, clumsy, clunky (*inf.*), cumbrous, embarrassing, heavy, hefty (*inf.*), incommodious, inconvenient, oppressive, unmanageable, unwieldy, weighty
Antonyms *adj* compact, convenient, easy to use, handy, manageable, practical, serviceable, wieldy

cumulative *adj* **1** = **collective,** accruing, accumulative, aggregate, amassed, heaped, increasing, snowballing lips and tongue. Cf. **fellatio.** [C19: from NL, from L *cunnus* vulva + *lingere* to lick]

cunning ❶ ('kʌnɪŋ) *adj* **1** crafty and shrewd, esp. in deception. **2** made with or showing skill; ingenious. ◆ *n* **3** craftiness, esp. in deceiving. **4** skill or ingenuity. [OE *cunnende;* rel. to *cunnan* to know (see CAN[1])]
▸**'cunningly** *adv* ▸**'cunningness** *n*

cunt (kʌnt) *n Taboo.* **1** the female genitals. **2** *Offens. sl.* a woman considered sexually. **3** *Offens. sl.* a mean or obnoxious person. [C13: of Gmc origin; rel. to ON *kunta,* MLow G *kunte*]

cup ❶ (kʌp) *n* **1** a small open container, usually having one handle, used for drinking from. **2** the contents of such a container. **3** Also called: **teacup, cupful.** a unit of capacity used in cooking. **4** something resembling a cup. **5** either of two cup-shaped parts of a brassiere. **6** a cup-shaped trophy awarded as a prize. **7** *Brit.* **7a** a sporting contest in which a cup is awarded to the winner. **7b** (*as modifier*): *a cup competition.* **8** a mixed drink with one ingredient as a base: *claret cup.* **9** *Golf.* the hole or metal container in the hole on a green. **10** the chalice or the consecrated wine used in the Eucharist. **11** one's lot in life. **12 in one's cups.** drunk. **13 one's cup of tea.** *Inf.* one's chosen or preferred thing, task, company, etc. ◆ *vb* **cups, cupping, cupped.** (*tr*) **14** to form (something, such as the hands) into the shape of a cup. **15** to put into or as if into a cup. **16** to draw blood to the surface of the body of (a person) by cupping. [OE *cuppe,* from LL *cuppa* cup, alteration of L *cūpa* cask]

cupbearer ('kʌpˌbeərə) *n* an attendant who fills and serves wine cups, as in a royal household.

cupboard ❶ ('kʌbəd) *n* a piece of furniture or a recessed area of a room, with a door concealing storage space.

cupboard love *n* a show of love inspired only by some selfish or greedy motive.

cupcake ('kʌpˌkeɪk) *n* a small cake baked in a cup-shaped foil or paper case.

cupel ('kjuːpᵊl, kjuˈpɛl) *n* **1** a refractory pot in which gold or silver is refined. **2** a small bowl in which gold and silver are recovered during assaying. ◆ *vb* **cupels, cupelling, cupelled** *or US* **cupels, cupeling, cupeled. 3** (*tr*) to refine (gold or silver) using a cupel. [C17: from F *coupelle,* dim. of *coupe* CUP]
▸ˌ**cupel'lation** *n*

Cup Final *n* **1** (often preceded by *the*) the annual final of the FA or Scottish Cup soccer competition. **2** (*often not cap.*) the final of any cup competition.

Cupid ('kjuːpɪd) *n* **1** the Roman god of love, represented as a winged boy with a bow and arrow. Greek counterpart: **Eros. 2** (*not cap.*) any similar figure. [C14: from L *Cupīdō,* from *cupīdō* desire, from *cupidus* desirous; see CUPIDITY]

cupidity (kjuːˈpɪdɪtɪ) *n* strong desire, esp. for wealth; greed. [C15: from L *cupiditās,* from *cupidus* eagerly desiring, from *cupere* to long for]

cupola ('kjuːpələ) *n* **1** a roof or ceiling in the form of a dome. **2** a small structure, usually domed, on the top of a roof or dome. **3** a protective dome for a gun on a warship. **4** a furnace in which iron is remelted. [C16: from It., from LL *cūpula* a small cask, from L *cūpa* tub]
▸**'cupoˌlated** *adj*

cuppa *or* **cupper** ('kʌpə) *n Brit. inf.* a cup of tea.

cupping ('kʌpɪŋ) *n Med.* formerly, the use of an evacuated glass cup to draw blood to the surface of the skin for blood-letting.

cupreous ('kjuːprɪəs) *adj* **1** of, containing, or resembling copper. **2** of the colour of copper. [C17: from LL *cupreus,* from *cuprum* COPPER[1]]

cupressus (kəˈprɛsəs) *n* any evergreen tree of the genus *Cupressus.*

cupric ('kjuːprɪk) *adj* of or containing copper in the divalent state. [C18: from LL *cuprum* copper]

cupriferous (kjuːˈprɪfərəs) *adj* (of a substance such as an ore) containing or yielding copper.

cupro-, cupri-, *or before a vowel* **cupr-** *combining form.* indicating copper. [from L *cuprum*]

cupronickel (ˌkjuːprəʊˈnɪkᵊl) *n* any copper alloy containing up to 40 per cent nickel: used in coins, condenser tubes, etc.

cuprous ('kjuːprəs) *adj* of or containing copper in the monovalent state.

cup tie *n Sport.* an eliminating match or round between two teams in a cup competition.

cupule ('kjuːpjuːl) *n Biol.* a cup-shaped part or structure. [C19: from LL *cūpula;* see CUPOLA]

cur ❶ (kɜː) *n* **1** any vicious dog, esp. a mongrel. **2** a despicable or cowardly person. [C13: from *kurdogge;* prob. rel. to ON *kurra* to growl]

curable ('kjʊərəbᵊl) *adj* capable of being cured.
▸ˌ**cura'bility** *or* **'curableness** *n*

curaçao (ˌkjʊərəˈsəʊ) *n* an orange-flavoured liqueur originally made in Curaçao, a Caribbean island.

curacy ('kjʊərəsɪ) *n, pl* **curacies.** the office or position of a curate.

curare *or* **curari** (kjʊˈrɑːrɪ) *n* **1** black resin obtained from certain tropical South American trees, which causes muscular paralysis: used medicinally as a muscle relaxant and by South American Indians as an arrow poison. **2** any of various trees from which this resin is obtained. [C18: from Port. & Sp., from Carib *kurari*]

curassow ('kjʊərəˌsəʊ) *n* any of various ground-nesting birds of S North, Central, and South America, having long legs and tail and a crest of curled feathers. [C17: anglicized from *Curaçao,* Caribbean island]

curate ('kjʊərɪt) *n* **1** a clergyman appointed to assist a parish priest. **2** *Irish.* an assistant barman. [C14: from Med. L *cūrātus,* from *cūra* spiritual oversight, CURE]

curate's egg *n* something that has good and bad parts. [C20: derived from a cartoon in *Punch* (Nov., 1895) in which a timid curate, who has been served a bad egg while breakfasting with his bishop, says that parts of the egg are excellent]

curative ❶ ('kjʊərətɪv) *adj* **1** able or tending to cure. ◆ *n* **2** anything able to heal or cure.
▸**'curatively** *adv* ▸**'curativeness** *n*

curator (kjʊəˈreɪtə) *n* the administrative head of a museum, art gallery, etc. [C14: from L: one who cares, from *cūrāre* to care for, from *cūra* care]
▸**curatorial** (ˌkjʊərəˈtɔːrɪəl) *adj* ▸**cu'ratorˌship** *n*

curb ❶ (kɜːb) *n* **1** something that restrains or holds back. **2** any enclosing framework, such as a wall around the top of a well. **3** Also called: **curb bit.** a horse's bit with an attached chain or strap, which checks the horse. ◆ *vb* (*tr*) **4** to control with or as if with a curb; restrain. ◆ See also **kerb.** [C15: from OF *courbe* curved piece of wood or metal, from L *curvus* curved]

curcuma ('kɜːkjʊmə) *n* any tropical Asian tuberous plant of the genus *Curcuma,* such as *C. longa,* which is the source of turmeric. [C17: from NL, from Ar. *kurkum* turmeric]

curd (kɜːd) *n* **1** (*often pl*) a substance formed from the coagulation of milk, used in making cheese or eaten as a food. **2** something similar in consistency. ◆ *vb* **3** to turn into or become curd. [C15: from earlier *crud,* from ?]
▸**'curdy** *adj*

curdle ❶ ('kɜːdᵊl) *vb* **curdles, curdling, curdled. 1** to turn or cause to turn into curd. **2 curdle someone's blood.** to fill someone with fear. [C16 (*crudled,* p.p.): from CURD]

cure ❶ (kjʊə) *vb* **cures, curing, cured. 1** (*tr*) to get rid of (an ailment or problem); heal. **2** (*tr*) to restore to health or good condition. **3** (*intr*) to bring about a cure. **4** (*tr*) to preserve (meat, fish, etc.) by salting, smoking, etc. **5** (*tr*) **5a** to treat or finish (a substance) by chemical or physical means. **5b** to vulcanize (rubber). **6** (*tr*) to assist the hardening of (concrete, mortar, etc.) by keeping it moist. ◆ *n* **7** a return to health. **8** any course of medical therapy, esp. one proved effective. **9** a means of restoring health or improving a situation, etc. **10** the spiritual and pastoral charge of a parish. **11** a process or method of preserving meat, fish, etc. [(n) C13: from OF, from L *cūra* care; in ecclesiastical sense, from Med. L *cūra* spiritual charge; (vb) C14: from OF *curer,* from L *cūrāre* to attend to, heal, from *cūra* care]
▸**'cureless** *adj* ▸**'curer** *n*

curé ('kjʊəreɪ) *n* a parish priest in France. [F, from Med. L *cūrātus;* see CURATE]

cure-all ❶ *n* something reputed to cure all ailments.

curettage (ˌkjʊərɪˈtɑːʒ, kjʊəˈrɛtɪdʒ) *or* **curettement** (kjʊəˈrɛtmənt) *n* the process of using a curette. See also **D and C.**

curette *or* **curet** (kjʊəˈrɛt) *n* **1** a surgical instrument for removing dead tissue, growths, etc., from the walls of body cavities. ◆ *vb* **curettes** *or* **curets, curetting, curetted. 2** (*tr*) to scrape or clean with such an instrument. [C18: from F *curette,* from *curer* to heal, make clean; see CURE]

curfew ('kɜːfjuː) *n* **1** an official regulation setting restrictions on movement, esp. after a specific time at night. **2** the time set as a deadline by such a regulation. **3** (in medieval Europe) **3a** the ringing of a bell to prompt people to extinguish fires and lights. **3b** the time at which the

THESAURUS

cunning *adj* **1 = crafty,** artful, astute, canny, devious, foxy, guileful, knowing, Machiavellian, sharp, shifty, shrewd, sly, subtle, tricky, wily **2 = skilful,** adroit, deft, dexterous, imaginative, ingenious ◆ *n* **3 = craftiness,** artfulness, astuteness, deceitfulness, deviousness, foxiness, guile, shrewdness, slyness, trickery, wiliness **4 = skill,** ability, adroitness, art, artifice, cleverness, craft, deftness, dexterity, finesse, ingenuity, subtlety
Antonyms *adj* ≠ **crafty:** artless, dull, ethical, frank, honest, ingenuous ≠ **skilful:** maladroit ◆ *n* ≠ **craftiness:** candour, ingenuousness, sincerity ≠ **skill:** clumsiness

cup *n* **1 = mug,** beaker, bowl, cannikin, chalice, demitasse, goblet, teacup **6 = trophy**

cupboard *n* **= cabinet,** ambry, closet, locker, press

cur *n* **1 = mongrel,** canine, hound, mutt (*sl.*), stray **2 = scoundrel,** bad egg (*old-fashioned inf.*), bastard, blackguard, coward, good-for-nothing, heel (*sl.*), rat (*inf.*), rotter (*sl., chiefly Brit.*), scumbag (*sl.*), shit (*taboo slang*), son-of-a-bitch (*sl., chiefly U.S. & Canad.*), villain, wretch

curative *adj* **1 = restorative,** alleviative, corrective, healing, healthful, health-giving, medicinal, remedial, salutary, therapeutic, tonic

curb *n* **1 = restraint,** brake, bridle, check, control, deterrent, limitation, rein ◆ *vb* **4 = restrain,** bite back, bridle, check, constrain, contain, control, hinder, impede, inhibit, keep a tight rein on, moderate, muzzle, repress, restrict, retard, stem the flow, subdue, suppress

curdle *vb* **1 = congeal,** clot, coagulate, condense, curd, solidify, thicken, turn sour
Antonyms *vb* deliquesce, dissolve, liquefy, melt, soften, thaw

cure *vb* **1, 2 = make better,** alleviate, correct, ease, heal, help, mend, rehabilitate, relieve, remedy, restore, restore to health **4 = preserve,** dry, kipper, pickle, salt, smoke ◆ *n* **7-9 = remedy,** alleviation, antidote, corrective, healing, medicine, nostrum, panacea, recovery, restorative, specific, treatment

cure-all *n* **= panacea,** catholicon, elixir, *elixir vitae,* nostrum curfew bell was rung. **3c** the bell itself. [C13: from OF *cuevrefeu,* lit.: cover the fire]

curia ('kjʊərɪə) *n, pl* **curiae** (-rɪˌiː). **1** (*sometimes cap.*) the papal court and government of the Roman Catholic Church. **2** (in the Middle Ages) a court held in the king's name. [C16: from L, from OL *coviria* (unattested), from CO- + *vir* man]
▸**'curial** *adj*

curie ('kjʊərɪ, -riː) *n* a unit of radioactivity equal to 3.7×10^{10} disintegrations per second. [C20: after Pierre *Curie* (1859–1906), F physicist and chemist]

curio ⓘ ('kjʊərɪˌəʊ) *n, pl* **curios.** a small article valued as a collector's item, esp. something unusual. [C19: shortened from CURIOSITY]

curiosity ⓘ (ˌkjʊərɪ'ɒsɪtɪ) *n, pl* **curiosities. 1** an eager desire to know; inquisitiveness. **2** the quality of being curious; strangeness. **3** something strange or fascinating.

curious ⓘ ('kjʊərɪəs) *adj* **1** eager to learn; inquisitive. **2** overinquisitive; prying. **3** interesting because of oddness or novelty. [C14: from L *cūriōsus* taking pains over something, from *cūra* care]
▸**'curiously** *adv* ▸**'curiousness** *n*

curium ('kjʊərɪəm) *n* a silvery-white metallic transuranic element artificially produced from plutonium. Symbol: Cm; at. no.: 96; half-life of most stable isotope, ^{247}Cm: 1.6×10^7 years. [C20: NL, after Pierre and Marie *Curie*, F physicists and chemists]

curl ⓘ (kɜːl) *vb* **1** (*intr*) (esp. of hair) to grow into curves or ringlets. **2** (*tr;* sometimes foll. by *up*) to twist or roll (esp. hair) into coils or ringlets. **3** (often foll. by *up*) to become or cause to become spiral-shaped or curved. **4** (*intr*) to move in a curving or twisting manner. **5** (*intr*) to play the game of curling. **6 curl one's lip.** to show contempt, as by raising a corner of the lip. ◆ *n* **7** a curve or coil of hair. **8** a curved or spiral shape or mark. **9** the act of curling or state of being curled. ◆ See also **curl up.** [C14: prob. from MDu. *crullen* to curl]

curler ('kɜːlə) *n* **1** any of various pins, clasps, or rollers used to curl or wave hair. **2** a person or thing that curls. **3** a person who plays curling.

curlew ('kɜːljuː) *n* any of certain large shore birds of Europe and Asia. They have a long downward-curving bill and occur in northern and arctic regions. [C14: from OF *corlieu,* ? imit.]

curlicue ('kɜːlɪˌkjuː) *n* an intricate ornamental curl or twist. [C19: from CURLY + CUE[2]]

curling ('kɜːlɪŋ) *n* a game played on ice, esp. in Scotland, in which heavy stones with handles (**curling stones**) are slid towards a target (**tee**).

curling tongs *pl n* a metal scissor-like device that is heated, so that strands of hair may be twined around it in order to form curls. Also called: **curling iron, curling irons, curling pins.**

curl up *vb* (*adv*) **1** (*intr*) to adopt a reclining position with the legs close to the body and the back rounded. **2** to become or cause to become spiral-shaped or curved. **3** (*intr*) to retire to a quiet cosy setting: *to curl up with a good novel.* **4** *Brit. inf.* to be or cause to be embarrassed or disgusted (esp. in **curl up and die**).

curly ⓘ ('kɜːlɪ) *adj* **curlier, curliest. 1** tending to curl; curling. **2** having curls. **3** (of timber) having waves in the grain.
▸**'curliness** *n*

curmudgeon ⓘ (kɜː'mʌdʒən) *n* a surly or miserly person. [C16: from ?]
▸**cur'mudgeonly** *adj*

currach *or* **curragh** *Gaelic.* ('kʌrəx, 'kʌrə) *n* a Scottish or Irish name for **coracle.** [C15: from Irish Gaelic *currach;* Cf. CORACLE]

currajong ('kʌrəˌdʒɒŋ) *n* a variant spelling of **kurrajong.**

currant ('kʌrənt) *n* **1** a small dried seedless grape of the Mediterranean region. **2** any of several mainly N temperate shrubs, esp. redcurrant and blackcurrant. **3** the small acid fruit of any of these plants. [C16: shortened from *rayson of Corannte* raisin of Corinth]

currawong ('kʌrəˌwɒŋ) *n* any Australian crowlike songbird of the genus *Strepera,* having black, grey, and white plumage. Also called: **bell-magpie.** [from Abor.]

currency ⓘ ('kʌrənsɪ) *n, pl* **currencies. 1** a metal or paper medium of exchange in current use in a particular country. **2** general acceptance or circulation; prevalence. **3** the period of time during which something is valid, accepted, or in force. ◆ *adj* **4** *Austral. inf.* native-born as distinct from immigrant: *a currency lad.* [C17: from Med. L *currentia,* lit.: a flowing, from L *currere* to run, flow]

current ⓘ ('kʌrənt) *adj* **1** of the immediate present; in progress. **2** most recent; up-to-date. **3** commonly known, practised, or accepted. **4** circulating and valid at present: *current coins.* ◆ *n* **5** (esp. of water or air) a steady, usually natural, flow. **6** a mass of air, body of water, etc., that has a steady flow in a particular direction. **7** the rate of flow of such a mass. **8** *Physics.* **8a** a flow of electric charge through a conductor. **8b** the rate of flow of this charge. **9** a general trend or drift: *currents of opinion.* [C13: from OF *corant,* lit.: running, from *corre* to run, from L *currere*]
▸**'currently** *adv* ▸**'currentness** *n*

current account *n* an account at a bank or building society against which cheques may be drawn at any time.

current-cost accounting *n* a method of accounting that values assets at their current replacement cost rather than their original cost. It is often used in times of high inflation. Cf. **historical-cost accounting.**

curricle ('kʌrɪkᵊl) *n* a two-wheeled open carriage drawn by two horses side by side. [C18: from L *curriculum* from *currus* chariot, from *currere* to run]

curriculum (kə'rɪkjʊləm) *n, pl* **curricula** (-lə) *or* **curriculums. 1** a course of study in one subject at a school or college. **2** a list of all the courses of study offered by a school or college. **3** any programme or plan of activities. [C19: from L: course, from *currere* to run]
▸**cur'ricular** *adj*

curriculum vitae (kə'rɪkjʊləm 'viːtaɪ, 'vaɪtiː) *n, pl* **curricula vitae** (kə'rɪkjʊlə). an outline of a person's educational and professional history, usually prepared for job applications. [L, lit.: the course of one's life]

currish ('kɜːrɪʃ) *adj* of or like a cur; rude or bad-tempered.
▸**'currishly** *adv* ▸**'currishness** *n*

curry[1] ('kʌrɪ) *n, pl* **curries. 1** a spicy dish of oriental, esp. Indian, origin that usually consists of meat or fish prepared in a hot piquant sauce. **2** curry seasoning or sauce. **3 give someone curry.** *Austral. sl.* to assault (a person) verbally or physically. ◆ *vb* **curries, currying, curried. 4** (*tr*) to prepare (food) with curry powder or sauce. [C16: from Tamil *kari* sauce, relish]

curry[2] ('kʌrɪ) *vb* **curries, currying, curried. 1** to beat vigorously, as in order to clean. **2** to dress and finish (leather) after it has been tanned. **3** to groom (a horse). **4 curry favour.** to ingratiate oneself, esp. with superiors. [C13: from OF *correer* to make ready]

currycomb ('kʌrɪˌkəʊm) *n* a square comb used for grooming horses.

curry powder *n* a mixture of finely ground pungent spices, such as turmeric, cumin, coriander, ginger, etc., used in making curries.

curse ⓘ (kɜːs) *n* **1** a profane or obscene expression of anger, disgust, surprise, etc.; oath. **2** an appeal to a supernatural power for harm to come to a specific person, group, etc. **3** harm resulting from an appeal to a supernatural power. **4** something that brings or causes great trouble or harm. **5** (preceded by *the*) *Inf.* menstruation or a menstrual period. ◆ *vb* **curses, cursing, cursed** *or* (*Arch.*) **curst. 6** (*intr*) to utter obscenities or oaths. **7** (*tr*) to abuse (someone) with obscenities or oaths. **8** (*tr*) to invoke supernatural powers to bring harm to (someone or something). **9** (*tr*) to bring harm upon. [OE *cursian* to curse, from *curs* a curse]
▸**'curser** *n*

cursed ⓘ ('kɜːsɪd, kɜːst) *or* **curst** *adj* **1** under a curse. **2** deserving to be cursed; detestable; hateful.
▸**'cursedly** *adv* ▸**'cursedness** *n*

cursive ('kɜːsɪv) *adj* **1** of or relating to handwriting in which letters are joined in a flowing style. **2** *Printing.* of or relating to typefaces that re-

THESAURUS

curio *n* = **collector's item**, antique, bibelot, bygone, knick-knack, *objet d'art*, trinket

curiosity *n* **1** = **inquisitiveness**, interest, nosiness (*inf.*), prying, snooping (*inf.*) **3** = **oddity**, celebrity, freak, marvel, novelty, phenomenon, rarity, sight, spectacle, wonder

curious *adj* **1** = **inquiring**, inquisitive, interested, puzzled, questioning, searching **2** = **inquisitive**, meddling, nosy (*inf.*), peeping, peering, prying, snoopy (*inf.*) **3** = **unusual**, bizarre, exotic, extraordinary, marvellous, mysterious, novel, odd, peculiar, puzzling, quaint, queer, rare, rum (*Brit. slang*), singular, strange, unconventional, unexpected, unique, unorthodox, wonderful
Antonyms *adj* ≠ **inquiring:** incurious, indifferent, uninquisitive, uninterested ≠ **unusual:** common, everyday, familiar, ordinary

curl *vb* **1-4** = **twirl**, bend, coil, convolute, corkscrew, crimp, crinkle, crisp, curve, entwine, frizz, loop, meander, ripple, spiral, turn, twine, twist, wind, wreathe, writhe ◆ *n* **7, 8** = **twist**, coil, curlicue, kink, ringlet, spiral, whorl

curly *adj* **1, 2** = **curling**, corkscrew, crimped, crimpy, crinkly, crisp, curled, frizzy, fuzzy, kinky, permed, spiralled, waved, wavy, winding

curmudgeon *n* = **grump** (*inf.*), bear, bellyacher (*sl.*), churl, crosspatch (*inf.*), grouch, grouser, grumbler, malcontent, sourpuss (*inf.*)

currency *n* **1** = **money**, bills, coinage, coins, dosh (*Brit. & Austral. sl.*), medium of exchange, notes **2** = **acceptance**, circulation, exposure, popularity, prevalence, publicity, transmission, vogue

current *adj* **1, 3** = **prevalent**, accepted, circulating, common, customary, general, going around, in circulation, in progress, in the air, in the news, ongoing, popular, prevailing, rife, topical, widespread **2** = **present**, contemporary, fashionable, happening (*inf.*), in, in fashion, in vogue, now (*inf.*), present-day, trendy (*Brit. inf.*), up-to-date, up-to-the-minute ◆ *n* **5, 6** = **flow**, course, draught, jet, progression, river, stream, tide, tideway, undertow **9** = **mood**, atmosphere, drift, feeling, inclination, tendency, trend, undercurrent, vibes (*sl.*)
Antonyms *adj* ≠ **present:** archaic, obsolete, old-fashioned, outmoded, out-of-date, passé, past

curse *n* **1** = **oath**, blasphemy, expletive, obscenity, swearing, swearword **2** = **denunciation**, anathema, ban, evil eye, excommunication, execration, hoodoo (*inf.*), imprecation, jinx, malediction, malison (*arch.*) **4** = **affliction**, bane, burden, calamity, cross, disaster, evil, hardship, misfortune, ordeal, plague, scourge, torment, tribulation, trouble, vexation ◆ *vb* **6** = **swear**, be foul-mouthed, blaspheme, cuss (*inf.*), take the Lord's name in vain, turn the air blue (*inf.*), use bad language **8** = **damn**, accurse, anathematize, excommunicate, execrate, fulminate, imprecate **9** = **afflict**, blight, burden, destroy, doom, plague, scourge, torment, trouble, vex

cursed *adj* **1** = **damned**, accursed, bedevilled, blighted, cast out, confounded, doomed, excommunicate, execrable, fey (*Scot.*), foredoomed, ill-fated, star-crossed, unholy, unsanctified, villainous **2** = **hateful**, abominable, damnable, detestable, devilish, fell (*arch.*), fiendish, infamous, infernal, loathsome, odious, pernicious, pestilential, vile

semble handwriting. ◆ *n* **3** a cursive letter or printing type. [C18: from Med. L *cursīvus* running, ult. from L *currere* to run]
▸**'cursively** *adv*

cursor ('kɜːsə) *n* **1** the sliding part of a measuring instrument, esp. on a slide rule. **2** any of various means, typically a flashing bar or underline, of identifying a particular position on a computer screen.

cursorial (kɜː'sɔːrɪəl) *adj Zool.* adapted for running: *a cursorial skeleton; cursorial birds.*

cursory ❶ ('kɜːsərɪ) *adj* hasty and usually superficial; quick. [C17: from LL *cursōrius* of running, from L *cursus* a course, from *currere* to run]
▸**'cursorily** *adv* ▸**'cursoriness** *n*

curst (kɜːst) *vb* **1** *Arch.* a past tense and past participle of **curse**. ◆ *adj* **2** a variant of **cursed**.

curt ❶ (kɜːt) *adj* **1** rudely blunt and brief. **2** short or concise. [C17: from L *curtus* cut short, mutilated]
▸**'curtly** *adv* ▸**'curtness** *n*

curtail ❶ (kɜː'teɪl) *vb* (*tr*) to cut short; abridge. [C16: changed (through infl. of TAIL[1]) from obs. *curtal* to dock]
▸**cur'tailer** *n* ▸**cur'tailment** *n*

curtain ❶ ('kɜːtᵊn) *n* **1** a piece of material that can be drawn across an opening or window, to shut out light or to provide privacy. **2** a barrier to vision, access, or communication. **3** a hanging cloth or similar barrier for concealing all or part of a theatre stage from the audience. **4** (often preceded by *the*) the end of a scene of a play, opera, etc., marked by the fall or closing of the curtain. **5** the rise or opening of the curtain at the start of a performance. ◆ *vb* **6** (*tr;* sometimes foll. by *off*) to shut off or conceal as with a curtain. **7** (*tr*) to provide (a window, etc.) with curtains. [C13: from OF *courtine,* from LL *cortīna* enclosed place, curtain, prob. from L *cohors* courtyard]

curtain call *n* the appearance of performers at the end of a theatrical performance to acknowledge applause.

curtain lecture *n* a scolding or rebuke given in private, esp. by a wife to her husband. [alluding to the curtained beds where such rebukes were once given]

curtain-raiser *n* **1** *Theatre.* a short dramatic piece presented before the main play. **2** any preliminary event.

curtains ('kɜːtᵊnz) *pl n Inf.* death or ruin: the end.

curtain wall *n* a non-load-bearing external wall attached to a framed structure.

curtsy *or* **curtsey** ('kɜːtsɪ) *n, pl* **curtsies** *or* **curtseys. 1** a formal gesture of greeting and respect made by women, in which the knees are bent and the head slightly bowed. ◆ *vb* **curtsies, curtsying, curtsied** *or* **curtseys, curtseying, curtseyed. 2** (*intr*) to make a curtsy. [C16: var. of COURTESY]

curvaceous ❶ (kɜː'veɪʃəs) *adj Inf.* (of a woman) having a well-rounded body.

curvature ❶ ('kɜːvətʃə) *n* **1** something curved or a curved part of a thing. **2** any curving of a bodily part. **3** the act of curving or the state or degree of being curved or bent.

curve ❶ (kɜːv) *n* **1** a continuously bending line that has no straight parts. **2** something that curves or is curved. **3** the act or extent of curving; curvature. **4** *Maths.* a system of points whose coordinates satisfy a given equation. **5** a line representing data on a graph. ◆ *vb* **curves, curving, curved. 6** to take or cause to take the shape or path of a curve; bend. [C15: from L *curvāre* to bend, from *curvus* crooked]
▸**'curvedness** *n* ▸**'curvy** *adj*

curvet (kɜː'vɛt) *n* **1** *Dressage.* a low leap with all four feet off the ground. ◆ *vb* **curvets, curvetting, curvetted** *or* **curvets, curveting, curveted. 2** *Dressage.* to make or cause to make such a leap. **3** (*intr*) to prance or frisk about. [C16: from OIt. *corvetta,* from OF *courbette,* from *courber* to bend, from L *curvāre*]

curvilinear (ˌkɜːvɪ'lɪnɪə) *or* **curvilineal** *adj* consisting of, bounded by, or characterized by a curved line.

cuscus ('kʌskʌs) *n, pl* **cuscuses.** any of several large nocturnal phalangers of N Australia, New Guinea, and adjacent islands, having dense fur, prehensile tails, large eyes, and a yellow nose. [C17: NL, prob. from a native name in New Guinea]

cusec ('kjuːsɛk) *n* a unit of flow equal to 1 cubic foot per second. [C20: from *cu(bic foot per) sec(ond)*]

cushat ('kʌʃət) *n* another name for **wood pigeon.** [OE *cūscote;* ? rel. to *sceōtan* to shoot]

cushion ❶ ('kʊʃən) *n* **1** a bag filled with a yielding substance, used for sitting on, leaning against, etc. **2** something resembling a cushion in function or appearance, esp. one to support or pad or to absorb shock. **3** the resilient felt-covered rim of a billiard table. ◆ *vb* (*tr*) **4** to place on or as on a cushion. **5** to provide with cushions. **6** to protect. **7** to lessen or suppress the effects of. **8** to provide with a means of absorbing shock. [C14: from OF *coussin,* from L *culcita* mattress]
▸**'cushiony** *adj*

cushion plant *n* a type of low-growing plant having many closely spaced short upright shoots, typical of alpine and arctic habitats.

Cushitic (kʊ'ʃɪtɪk) *n* **1** a group of languages of Somalia, Ethiopia, and adjacent regions. ◆ *adj* **2** of or relating to this group of languages.

cushy ❶ ('kʊʃɪ) *adj* **cushier, cushiest.** *Inf.* easy; comfortable. [C20: from Hindi *khush* pleasant, from Persian *khōsh*]

CUSO ('kjuːsəʊ) *n acronym for* Canadian University Services Overseas; an organization that sends students to work as volunteers in developing countries.

cusp (kʌsp) *n* **1** any of the small elevations on the grinding or chewing surface of a tooth. **2** any of the triangular flaps of a heart valve. **3** a point or pointed end. **4** *Geom.* a point at which two arcs of a curve intersect and at which the two tangents are coincident. **5** *Archit.* a carving at the meeting place of two arcs. **6** *Astron.* either of the points of a crescent moon. **7** *Astrol.* any division between houses or signs of the zodiac. [C16: from L *cuspis* point, pointed end]
▸**'cuspate** *adj*

cuspid ('kʌspɪd) *n* a tooth having one point; canine tooth.

cuspidate ('kʌspɪˌdeɪt), **cuspidated,** *or* **cuspidal** ('kʌspɪdᵊl) *adj* **1** having a cusp or cusps. **2** (esp. of leaves) narrowing to a point. [C17: from L *cuspidāre* to make pointed, from *cuspis* a point]

cuspidor ('kʌspɪˌdɔː) *n* another name (esp. US) for **spittoon.** [C18: from Port., from *cuspir* to spit, from L *conspuere,* from *spuere* to spit]

cuss (kʌs) *Inf.* ◆ *n* **1** a curse; an oath. **2** a person or animal, esp. an annoying one. ◆ *vb* **3** another word for **curse** (senses 6, 7).

cussed ('kʌsɪd) *adj Inf.* **1** another word for **cursed. 2** obstinate. **3** annoying: *a cussed nuisance.*
▸**'cussedly** *adv* ▸**'cussedness** *n*

custard ('kʌstəd) *n* **1** a baked sweetened mixture of eggs and milk. **2** a sauce made of milk and sugar and thickened with cornflour. [C15: alteration of ME *crustade* kind of pie]

custard apple *n* **1** a West Indian tree. **2** its large heart-shaped fruit, which has a fleshy edible pulp.

custard pie *n* **a** a flat, open pie filled with real or artificial custard, as thrown in slapstick comedy. **b** (*as modifier*): *custard-pie humour.*

custodian ❶ (kʌ'stəʊdɪən) *n* **1** a person who has custody, as of a prisoner, ward, etc. **2** a keeper of an art collection, etc.
▸**cus'todianˌship** *n*

custody ❶ ('kʌstədɪ) *n, pl* **custodies. 1** the act of keeping safe or guarding. **2** the state of being held by the police; arrest. [C15: from L *custōdia,* from *custōs* guard, defender]
▸**custodial** (kʌ'stəʊdɪəl) *adj*

custom ❶ ('kʌstəm) *n* **1** a usual or habitual practice; typical mode of behaviour. **2** the long-established habits or traditions of a society collectively; convention. **3a** a practice which by long-established usage has come to have the force of law. **3b** such practices collectively (esp. in **custom and practice**). **4** habitual patronage, esp. of a shop or business. **5** the customers of a shop or business collectively. ◆ *adj* **6** made to the specifications of an individual customer. ◆ See also **customs.** [C12: from OF *costume,* from L *consuētūdō,* from *consuēscere* to grow accustomed to]

customary ❶ ('kʌstəmərɪ, -təmrɪ) *adj* **1** in accordance with custom or habitual practice; usual. **2** *Law.* **2a** founded upon long-continued practices and usage. **2b** (of land) held by custom. ◆ *n, pl* **customaries. 3** a statement in writing of customary laws and practices.
▸**'customarily** *adv* ▸**'customariness** *n*

custom-built *adj* (of cars, houses, etc.) made according to the specifications of an individual buyer.

THESAURUS

cursory *adj* = **brief**, careless, casual, desultory, hasty, hurried, offhand, passing, perfunctory, rapid, slapdash, slight, summary, superficial

curt *adj* **1, 2** = **short**, abrupt, blunt, brief, brusque, concise, gruff, monosyllabic, offhand, pithy, rude, sharp, snappish, succinct, summary, tart, terse, unceremonious, uncivil, ungracious

curtail *vb* = **cut short**, abbreviate, abridge, contract, cut, cut back, decrease, diminish, dock, lessen, lop, pare down, reduce, retrench, shorten, trim, truncate

curtailment *n* = **cutting short**, abbreviation, abridgment, contraction, cutback, cutting, docking, retrenchment, truncation

curtain *n* **1** = **hanging**, drape (*chiefly US*) ◆ *vb* **6** = **conceal**, drape, hide, screen, shroud, shut off, shutter, veil

curvaceous *adj Informal* = **shapely**, bosomy, buxom, comely, curvy, voluptuous, well-rounded, well-stacked (*Brit. sl.*)

curvature *n* **3** = **curving**, arching, bend, curve, deflection, flexure, incurvation

curve *n* **2** = **bend**, arc, camber, curvature, half-moon, loop, trajectory, turn ◆ *vb* **6** = **bend**, arc, arch, bow, coil, hook, inflect, spiral, swerve, turn, twist, wind

cushion *n* **1** = **pillow**, beanbag, bolster, hassock, headrest, pad, scatter cushion, squab ◆ *vb* **6, 7** = **soften**, bolster, buttress, cradle, dampen, deaden, muffle, pillow, protect, stifle, support, suppress

cushy *adj Informal* = **easy**, comfortable, jammy (*Brit. sl.*), soft, undemanding

custodian *n* **1, 2** = **keeper**, caretaker, curator, guardian, overseer, protector, superintendent, warden, warder, watchdog, watchman

custody *n* **1** = **safekeeping**, aegis, auspices, care, charge, custodianship, guardianship, keeping, observation, preservation, protection, supervision, trusteeship, tutelage, ward, watch **2** = **imprisonment**, arrest, confinement, detention, durance (*arch.*), duress, incarceration

custom *n* **1** = **habit**, habitude (*rare*), manner, matter of course, mode, practice, procedure, routine, way, wont **2** = **tradition**, convention, etiquette, fashion, form, formality, observance, observation, policy, practice, praxis, ritual, rule, style, unwritten law, usage, use **4** = **customers**, patronage, trade

customarily *adv* **1** = **usually**, as a rule, commonly, generally, habitually, in the ordinary way, normally, ordinarily, regularly, traditionally

customary *adj* **1** = **usual**, accepted, accustomed, acknowledged, bog-standard (*Brit. & Irish sl.*), common, confirmed, conventional, established, everyday, familiar, fashionable, general, habitual, normal, ordinary, popular, regular, routine, traditional, wonted
Antonyms *adj* exceptional, infrequent, irregular, occasional, rare, uncommon, unusual

customer ❶ (ˈkʌstəmə) *n* **1** a person who buys. **2** *Inf.* a person with whom one has dealings.

custom house *n* a government office, esp. at a port, where customs are collected and ships cleared for entry.

customize *or* **customise** (ˈkʌstəˌmaɪz) *vb* **customizes, customizing, customized** *or* **customises, customising, customised.** (*tr*) to make (something) according to a customer's individual requirements.

custom-made *adj* (of suits, dresses, etc.) made according to the specifications of an individual buyer.

customs ❶ (ˈkʌstəmz) *n* (*functioning as sing or pl*) **1** duty on imports or exports. **2** the government department responsible for the collection of these duties. **3** the part of a port, airport, etc., where baggage and freight are examined for dutiable goods and contraband.

cut ❶ (kʌt) *vb* **cuts, cutting, cut. 1** to open up or incise (a person or thing) with a sharp edge or instrument. **2** (of a sharp instrument) to penetrate or incise (a person or thing). **3** to divide or be divided with or as if with a sharp instrument. **4** (*intr*) to use an instrument that cuts. **5** (*tr*) to trim or prune by or as if by clipping. **6** (*tr*) to reap or mow (a crop, grass, etc.). **7** (*tr; sometimes foll. by out*) to make, form, or shape by cutting. **8** (*tr*) to hollow or dig out; excavate. **9** to strike (an object) sharply. **10** *Cricket.* to hit (the ball) to the off side with a roughly horizontal bat. **11** to hurt the feelings of (a person). **12** (*tr*) *Inf.* to refuse to recognize; snub. **13** (*tr*) *Inf.* to absent oneself from, esp. without permission or in haste: *to cut a class.* **14** (*tr*) to abridge or shorten. **15** (*tr; often foll. by down*) to lower, reduce, or curtail. **16** (*tr*) to dilute or weaken: *to cut whisky with water.* **17** (*tr*) to dissolve or break up: *to cut fat.* **18** (when *intr*, foll. by *across* or *through*) to cross or traverse. **19** (*intr*) to make a sharp or sudden change in direction; veer. **20** to grow (teeth) through the gums or (of teeth) to appear through the gums. **21** (*intr*) *Films.* **21a** to call a halt to a shooting sequence. **21b** (foll. by *to*) to move quickly to another scene. **22** *Films.* to edit (film). **23** to switch off (a light, car engine, etc.). **24** (*tr*) to make (a record or tape of a song, performance, etc.). **25** *Cards.* **25a** to divide (the pack) at random into two parts after shuffling. **25b** (*intr*) to pick cards from a spread pack to decide dealer, partners, etc. **26** (*tr*) (of a tool) to bite into (an object). **27 cut a dash.** to make a stylish impression. **28 cut (a person) dead.** *Inf.* to ignore (a person) completely. **29 cut a (good, poor, etc.) figure.** to appear or behave in a specified manner. **30 cut and run.** *Inf.* to make a rapid escape. **31 cut both ways. 31a** to have both good and bad effects. **31b** to affect both sides, as two parties in an argument, etc. **32 cut it fine.** *Inf.* to allow little margin of time, space etc. **33 cut loose.** to free or become freed from restraint, custody, anchorage, etc. **34 cut no ice.** *Inf.* to fail to make an impression. **35 cut one's teeth on.** *Inf.* **35a** to use at an early age or stage. **35b** to practise on. ◆ *adj* **36** detached, divided, or separated by cutting. **37** made, shaped, or fashioned by cutting. **38** reduced or diminished as by cutting: *cut prices.* **39** weakened or diluted. **40** *Brit.* a slang word for **drunk:** *half cut.* **41 cut and dried.** *Inf.* settled or arranged in advance. ◆ *n* **42** the act of cutting. **43** a stroke or incision made by cutting; gash. **44** a piece or part cut off: *a cut of meat.* **45** the edge of anything cut or sliced. **46** a passage, channel, path, etc., cut or hollowed out. **47** an omission or deletion, esp. in a text, film, or play. **48** a reduction in price, salary, etc. **49** a decrease in government finance in a particular department or area. **50** *Inf.* a portion or share. **51** *Inf.* a straw, slip of paper, etc., used in drawing lots. **52** the manner or style in which a thing, esp. a garment, is cut. **53a** *Irish inf.* a person's general appearance: *I didn't like the cut of him.* **53b** *Irish derog.* a dirty or untidy condition: *look at the cut of your shoes.* **54** a direct route; short cut. **55** the US name for **block** (sense 13). **56** *Cricket.* a stroke made with the bat in a roughly horizontal position. **57** *Films.* an immediate transition from one shot to the next. **58** words or an action that hurt another person's feelings. **59** a refusal to recognize an acquaintance; snub. **60** *Brit.* a stretch of water, esp. a canal. **61 a cut above.** *Inf.* superior to; better than. ◆ See also **cut across, cutback,** etc. [C13: prob. from ON]

cut across *vb* (*intr, prep*) **1** to be contrary to ordinary procedure or limitations. **2** to cross or traverse, making a shorter route.

cut and paste *n* a technique used in word processing by which a section of text can be moved within a document.

cutaneous (kjuːˈteɪnɪəs) *adj* of or relating to the skin. [C16: from NL *cutāneus,* from L *cutis* skin]

cutaway (ˈkʌtəˌweɪ) *n* **1** a man's coat cut diagonally from the front waist to the back of the knees. **2a** a drawing or model of a machine, engine, etc., in which part of the casing is omitted to reveal the workings. **2b** (*as modifier*): *a cutaway model.* **3** *Films, television.* a shot separate from the main action of a scene.

cutback ❶ (ˈkʌtˌbæk) *n* **1** a decrease or reduction. ◆ *vb* **cut back** (*adv*) **2** (*tr*) to shorten by cutting off the end. **3** (when *intr*, foll. by *on*) to reduce or make a reduction (in).

cut down ❶ *vb* (*adv*) **1** (*tr*) to fell. **2** (when *intr*, often foll. by *on*) to reduce or make a reduction (in). **3** (*tr*) to remake (an old garment) in order to make a smaller one. **4** (*tr*) to kill. **5 cut (a person) down to size.** to reduce in importance or decrease the conceit of (a person).

cute ❶ (kjuːt) *adj* **1** appealing or attractive, esp. in a pretty way. **2** *Inf.* affecting cleverness or prettiness. **3** clever; shrewd. [C18 (in the sense: clever): shortened from ACUTE]
▸ **ˈcutely** *adv* ▸ **ˈcuteness** *n*

cut glass *n* **1a** glass, esp. bowls, vases, etc., decorated by facet-cutting or grinding. **1b** (*as modifier*): *a cut-glass vase.* **2** (*modifier*) (of an accent) upper-class; refined.

cuticle (ˈkjuːtɪkᵊl) *n* **1** dead skin, esp. round the base of a fingernail or toenail. **2** another name for **epidermis. 3** the protective layer that covers the epidermis of higher plants. **4** the protective layer covering the epidermis of many invertebrates. [C17: from L *cutīcula* dim. of *cutis* skin]
▸ **cuticular** (kjuːˈtɪkjʊlə) *adj*

cut in ❶ *vb* (*adv*) **1** (*intr; often foll. by on*) Also: **cut into.** to break in or interrupt. **2** (*intr*) to interrupt a dancing couple to dance with one of them. **3** (*intr*) (of a driver, motor vehicle, etc.) to draw in front of another vehicle leaving too little space. **4** (*tr*) *Inf.* to allow to have a share. **5** (*intr*) to take the place of a person in a card game.

cutis (ˈkjuːtɪs) *n, pl* **cutes** (-tiːz) *or* **cutises.** *Anat.* a technical name for the **skin.** [C17: from L: skin]

cutlass (ˈkʌtləs) *n* a curved, one-edged sword formerly used by sailors. [C16: from F *coutelas,* from *coutel* knife, ult. from L *culter* knife]

cutler (ˈkʌtlə) *n* a person who makes or sells cutlery. [C14: from F *coutelier,* ult. from L *culter* knife]

cutlery (ˈkʌtlərɪ) *n* **1** implements used for eating, such as knives, forks, and spoons. **2** instruments used for cutting. **3** the art or business of a cutler.

cutlet (ˈkʌtlɪt) *n* **1** a piece of meat taken esp. from the best end of neck of lamb, pork, etc. **2** a flat croquette of minced chicken, lobster, etc. [C18: from OF *costelette,* lit.: a little rib, from *coste* rib, from L *costa*]

cut off ❶ *vb* (*tr, adv*) **1** to remove by cutting. **2** to intercept or interrupt something, esp. a telephone conversation. **3** to discontinue the supply of. **4** to bring to an end. **5** to deprive of rights; disinherit: *cut off without a penny.* **6** to sever or separate. **7** to occupy a position so as to prevent or obstruct (a retreat or escape). ◆ *n* **cutoff. 8a** the act of cutting off; limit or termination. **8b** (*as modifier*): *the cutoff point.* **9** *Chiefly US.* a short cut. **10** a device to terminate the flow of a fluid in a pipe or duct.

cut out ❶ *vb* (*adv*) **1** (*tr*) to delete or remove. **2** (*tr*) to shape or form by cutting. **3** (*tr; usually passive*) to suit or equip for: *you're not cut out for this job.* **4** (*intr*) (of an engine, etc.) to cease to operate suddenly. **5** (*intr*) (of an electrical device) to switch off, usually automatically. **6** (*tr*) *Inf.* to oust and supplant (a rival). **7** (*intr*) (of a person) to be excluded from a card game. **8** (*tr*) *Inf.* to cease doing something, esp. something undesirable (esp. in **cut it out**). **9** (*tr*) *Soccer.* to intercept (a pass). **10** (*tr*) to separate (cattle) from a herd. **11** (*intr*) *Austral.* to end or finish: *the road cuts out at the creek.* **12 have one's work cut out.** to have as much work as one can manage. ◆ *n* **cutout. 13** something that has been or is intended to be cut out from something else. **14** a device that switches off or interrupts an electric circuit, esp. as a safety device. **15** *Austral. sl.* the end of shearing.

THESAURUS

customer *n* **1** = **client**, buyer, consumer, habitué, patron, prospect, purchaser, regular (*inf.*), shopper

customs *n* **1** = **duty**, import charges, tariff, tax, toll

cut *vb* **2** = **penetrate**, chop, cleave, divide, gash, incise, lacerate, lance, nick, notch, pierce, score, sever, slash, slice, slit, wound **3** = **divide**, bisect, carve, cleave, cross, dissect, interrupt, intersect, part, segment, sever, slice, split, sunder **5** = **trim**, clip, dock, fell, gather, hack, harvest, hew, lop, mow, pare, prune, reap, saw down, shave, snip **7** = **shape**, carve, chip, chisel, chop, engrave, fashion, form, inscribe, saw, sculpt, sculpture, whittle **11** = **hurt**, grieve, insult, pain, put down, sting, wound **12** *Informal* = **ignore**, avoid, cold-shoulder, freeze (someone) out (*inf.*), look straight through (someone), send to Coventry, slight, snub, spurn, turn one's back on **14** = **abridge**, abbreviate, condense, curtail, delete, edit out, excise, precis, shorten **15** = **reduce**, contract, cut back, decrease, diminish, downsize, ease up on, lower, rationalize, slash, slim (down) ◆ *adj* **41 cut and dried** *Informal* = **prearranged**, automatic, fixed, organized, predetermined, settled, sorted out (*inf.*) ◆ *n* **43** = **incision**, gash, graze, groove, laceration, nick, rent, rip, slash, slit, snip, stroke, wound **48, 49** = **reduction**, cutback, decrease, decrement, diminution, economy, fall, lowering, saving **50** *Informal* = **share**, chop (*sl.*), division, kickback (*chiefly US*), percentage, piece, portion, rake-off (*sl.*), section, slice **52** = **style**, configuration, fashion, form, look, mode, shape **61 a cut above** *Informal* = **superior to**, better than, higher than, more capable than, more competent than, more efficient than, more reliable than, more trustworthy than, more useful than

Antonyms *vb* ≠ **ignore:** accept gladly, embrace, greet, hail, receive, welcome with open arms ≠ **abridge, reduce:** add to, augment, enlarge, expand, extend, fill out, increase

cutback *n* **1** = **reduction**, cut, decrease, economy, lessening, retrenchment ◆ *vb* **cut back 2** = **trim**, prune, shorten **3** = **reduce**, check, curb, decrease, downsize, draw *or* pull in one's horns (*inf.*), economize, lessen, lower, retrench, slash

cut down *vb* **1** = **fell**, hew, level, lop, raze **2** = **reduce**, decrease, lessen, lower **4** = **kill**, blow away (*sl., chiefly US*), dispatch, massacre, mow down, slaughter, slay (*arch.*), take out (*sl.*) **5 cut (a person) down to size** = **make (a person) look small**, abash, humiliate, take the wind out of (a person's) sails

cute *adj* **1** = **appealing**, attractive, charming, delightful, engaging, lovable, sweet, winning, winsome

cut in *vb* **1** = **interrupt**, break in, butt in, interpose, intervene, intrude, move in (*inf.*)

cut off *vb* **2, 3** = **interrupt**, disconnect, intercept, intersect **4** = **halt**, bring to an end, discontinue, obstruct, suspend **5** = **disinherit**, disown, renounce **6** = **separate**, isolate, sever

cut out *vb* **1** = **stop**, cease, delete, extract, give up, kick (*inf.*), refrain from, remove, sever **6** *Informal* = **exclude**, displace, eliminate, oust, supersede, supplant

cut-price ➊ *or esp. US* **cut-rate** *adj* **1** available at prices or rates below the standard price or rate. **2** (*prenominal*) offering goods or services at prices below the standard price.
cutpurse ➊ ('kʌt,pɜːs) *n* an archaic word for **pickpocket.**
cutter ('kʌtə) *n* **1** a person or thing that cuts, esp. a person who cuts cloth for clothing. **2** a sailing boat with its mast stepped further aft than that of a sloop. **3** a ship's boat, powered by oars or sail, for carrying passengers or light cargo. **4** a small lightly armed boat, as used in the enforcement of customs regulations.
cut-throat ➊ ('kʌt,θrəut) *n* **1** a person who cuts throats; murderer. **2** Also called: **cut-throat razor, straight razor.** *Brit.* a razor with a long blade that usually folds into the handle. ◆ *adj* **3** bloodthirsty or murderous; cruel. **4** fierce or relentless in competition: *cut-throat prices.* **5** (of some games) played by three people: *cut-throat poker.*
cutting ➊ ('kʌtɪŋ) *n* **1** a piece cut off from something. **2** *Horticulture.* **2a** a method of propagation in which a part of a plant is induced to form its own roots. **2b** a part separated for this purpose. **3** Also called (esp. US and Canad.): **clipping.** an article, photograph, etc., cut from a publication. **4** the editing process of a film. **5** an excavation in a piece of high land for a road, railway, etc. **6** *Irish inf.* sharp-wittedness: *there is no cutting in him.* ◆ *adj* **7** designed for or adapted to cutting; sharp. **8** keen; piercing. **9** tending to hurt the feelings: *a cutting remark.*
▸ **'cuttingly** *adv*
cutting compound *n Engineering.* a mixture, such as oil, water, and soap, used for cooling drills and other cutting tools.
cutting edge *n* the leading position in any field; forefront: *on the cutting edge of space technology.*
cuttlebone ('kʌtᵊl,bəun) *n* the internal calcareous shell of the cuttlefish, used as a mineral supplement to the diet of cagebirds and as a polishing agent. [C16: OE *cudele* + BONE]
cuttlefish ('kʌtᵊl,fɪʃ) *n, pl* **cuttlefish** *or* **cuttlefishes.** a cephalopod mollusc which occurs near the bottom of inshore waters and has a broad flattened body. Sometimes shortened to **cuttle.**
cut up ➊ *vb* (*tr, adv*) **1** to cut into pieces. **2** to inflict injuries on. **3** (*usually passive*) *Inf.* to affect the feelings of deeply. **4** *Inf.* to subject to severe criticism. **5** *Inf.* (of a driver) to overtake or pull in front of (another driver) in a dangerous manner. **6 cut up rough.** *Brit. inf.* to become angry or bad-tempered. ◆ *n* **cut-up. 7** *Inf., chiefly US.* a joker or prankster.
cutwater ('kʌt,wɔːtə) *n* the forward part of the stem of a vessel, which cuts through the water.
cutworm ('kʌt,wɜːm) *n* the caterpillar of various noctuid moths, which is a pest of young crop plants in North America.
cuvée (kuː'veɪ) *n* an individual batch or blend of wine. [C19: from F, lit.: put in a cask, from *cuve* cask]
CV *abbrev. for* curriculum vitae.
CVS *abbrev. for* chorionic villus sampling.
Cwlth *abbrev. for* Commonwealth.
cwm (kuːm) *n* **1** (in Wales) a valley. **2** *Geol.* another name for **cirque.**
c.w.o. *or* **CWO** *abbrev. for* cash with order.
CWS *abbrev. for* Cooperative Wholesale Society.
cwt *abbrev. for* hundredweight. [*c*, from the L numeral *C* one hundred (*centum*)]
CWU (in Britain) *abbrev. for* Communication Workers Union.
-cy *suffix.* **1** indicating state, quality, or condition: *plutocracy; lunacy.* **2** rank or office: *captaincy.* [via OF from L *-cia, -tia,* Gk *-kia, -tia,* abstract noun suffixes]
cyan ('saɪæn, 'saɪən) *n* **1** a green-blue colour. ◆ *adj* **2** of this colour. [C19: from Gk *kuanos* dark blue]
cyanate ('saɪə,neɪt) *n* any salt or ester of cyanic acid.
cyanic (saɪ'ænɪk) *adj* **1** of or containing cyanogen. **2** blue.
cyanic acid *n* a colourless poisonous volatile liquid acid. Formula: HOCN.
cyanide ('saɪə,naɪd) *or* **cyanid** ('saɪənɪd) *n* any salt of hydrocyanic acid. Cyanides are extremely poisonous.
▸ **,cyani'dation** *n*
cyanite ('saɪə,naɪt) *n* a grey, green, or blue mineral consisting of aluminium silicate in crystalline form.
▸ **cyanitic** (,saɪə'nɪtɪk) *adj*
cyano- *or before a vowel* **cyan-** *combining form.* **1** blue or dark blue. **2** indicating cyanogen. **3** indicating cyanide. [from Gk *kuanos* (adj) dark blue, (n) dark blue enamel, lapis lazuli]
cyanobacteria (,saɪənəubæk'tɪərɪə) *pl n, sing* **cyanobacterium** (-rɪəm). a group of bacteria (phylum *Cyanobacteria*) containing a blue photosynthetic pigment and formerly regarded as algae. Former name: **blue-green algae.**
cyanocobalamin (,saɪənəukəu'bæləmɪn) *n* vitamin B_{12}, a complex crystalline compound of cobalt and cyanide, lack of which leads to pernicious anaemia. [C20: from CYANO- + COBAL(T) + (VIT)AMIN]
cyanogen (saɪ'ænədʒɪn) *n* an extremely poisonous colourless flammable gas. Formula: $(CN)_2$. [C19: from F *cyanogène;* see CYANO-, -GEN; so named because it is one of the constituents of Prussian blue]
cyanosis (,saɪə'nəusɪs) *n Pathol.* a bluish-purple discoloration of skin and mucous membranes usually resulting from a deficiency of oxygen in the blood.
▸ **cyanotic** (,saɪə'nɒtɪk) *adj*
cyber- *combining form.* indicating computers: *cyberphobia.* [C20: back formation from CYBERNETICS]
cybercafé ('saɪbə,kæfɪ, -,kæfeɪ) *n* a café with computer equipment that gives public access to the Internet.
cybernate ('saɪbə,neɪt) *vb* **cybernates, cybernating, cybernated.** to control with a servomechanism or to be controlled by a servomechanism. [C20: from CYBER(NETICS) + -ATE[1]]
▸ **,cyber'nation** *n*
cybernetics (,saɪbə'netɪks) *n* (*functioning as sing*) the branch of science concerned with control systems and comparisons between man-made and biological systems. [C20: from Gk *kubernētēs* steersman, from *kubernan* to steer]
▸ **,cyber'netic** *adj* ▸ **,cyber'neticist** *n*
cyberpet ('saɪbə,pɛt) *n* an electronic toy that simulates the activities of a pet, requiring the owner to feed, discipline, and entertain it.
cyberphobia (,saɪbə'fəubɪə) *n* an irrational fear of computing.
▸ **,cyber'phobic** *adj*
cyberpunk ('saɪbə,pʌŋk) *n* **1** a genre of science fiction that features rebellious computer hackers and is set in a society integrated by computer networks. **2** a writer of cyberpunk.
cyberspace ('saɪbə,speɪs) *n* all of the data stored in a large computer or network represented as a three-dimensional model through which a virtual-reality user can move.
cycad ('saɪkæd) *n* a tropical or subtropical plant, having an unbranched stem with fernlike leaves crowded at the top. [C19: from NL *Cycas* name of genus, from Gk *kukas,* scribe's error for *koïkas,* from *koïx* a kind of palm]
▸ **,cyca'daceous** *adj*
cyclamate ('saɪklə,meɪt, 'sɪkləmeɪt) *n* any of certain compounds formerly used as food additives and sugar substitutes. [C20: *cycl(ohexyl-sulph)amate*]
cyclamen ('sɪkləmən, -,mɛn) *n* **1** any Old World plant of the genus *Cyclamen,* having white, pink, or red flowers, with reflexed petals. ◆ *adj* **2** of a dark reddish-purple colour. [C16: from Med. L, from L *cyclamīnos,* from Gk *kuklaminos,* prob. from *kuklos* circle, referring to the bulblike roots]
cycle ➊ ('saɪkᵊl) *n* **1** a recurring period of time in which certain events or phenomena occur and reach completion. **2** a completed series of events that follows or is followed by another series of similar events occurring in the same sequence. **3** the time taken or needed for one such series. **4** a vast period of time; age; aeon. **5** a group of poems or prose narratives about a central figure or event: *the Arthurian cycle.* **6** short for **bicycle, motorcycle,** etc. **7** a recurrent series of events or processes in plants and animals: *a life cycle.* **8** one of a series of repeated changes in the magnitude of a periodically varying quantity, such as current or voltage. ◆ *vb* **cycles, cycling, cycled. 9** (*tr*) to process through a cycle or system. **10** (*intr*) to move in or pass through cycles. **11** to travel by or ride a bicycle or tricycle. [C14: from LL *cyclus,* from Gk *kuklos* cycle, circle, ring, wheel]
cyclic ('saɪklɪk, 'sɪklɪk) *or* **cyclical** *adj* **1** recurring or revolving in cycles. **2** (of an organic compound) containing a closed saturated or unsaturated ring of atoms. **3** *Bot.* **3a** arranged in whorls: *cyclic petals.* **3b** having parts arranged in this way: *cyclic flowers.*
▸ **'cyclically** *adv*
cycling shorts *pl n* tight-fitting shorts reaching partway to the knee for cycling, sport, etc.
cyclist ('saɪklɪst) *or US* **cycler** *n* a person who rides or travels by bicycle, motorcycle, etc.
cyclo- *or before a vowel* **cycl-** *combining form.* **1** indicating a circle or ring: *cyclotron.* **2** denoting a cyclic compound: *cyclopropane.* [from Gk *kuklos* CYCLE]
cyclogiro ('saɪkləu,dʒaɪrəu) *n, pl* **cyclogiros.** *Aeronautics.* an aircraft lifted and propelled by pivoted blades rotating parallel to roughly horizontal transverse axes.
cyclohexanone (,saɪkləu'hɛksə,nəun) *n* a colourless liquid used as a solvent for cellulose lacquers. Formula: $C_6H_{10}O$.
cycloid ('saɪklɔɪd) *adj* **1** resembling a circle. ◆ *n* **2** *Geom.* the curve described by a point on the circumference of a circle as the circle rolls along a straight line.
▸ **cy'cloidal** *adj*
cyclometer (saɪ'klɒmɪtə) *n* a device that records the number of revolutions made by a wheel and hence the distance travelled.

THESAURUS

cut-price *adj* **1, 2 = cheap,** bargain, cheapo (*inf.*), cut-rate (*chiefly US*), reduced, sale
cutpurse *n* **= pickpocket,** mugger (*inf.*), robber, thief
cut-throat *n* **1 = murderer,** assassin, bravo, butcher, executioner, heavy (*sl.*), hit man (*sl.*), homicide, killer, liquidator, slayer (*arch.*), thug ◆ *adj* **3 = murderous,** barbarous, bloodthirsty, bloody, cruel, death-dealing, ferocious, homicidal, savage, thuggish, violent **4 = competitive,** dog-eat-dog, fierce, relentless, ruthless, unprincipled
cutting *adj* **8 = piercing,** biting, bitter, chilling, keen, numbing, penetrating, raw, sharp, stinging **9 = hurtful,** acid, acrimonious, barbed, bitter, caustic, malicious, mordacious, pointed, sarcastic, sardonic, scathing, severe, trenchant, vitriolic, wounding
Antonyms *adj* ≠ **piercing:** balmy, pleasant, soothing ≠ **hurtful:** consoling, flattering, kind, mild
cut up *vb* **1 = chop,** carve, dice, divide, mince, slice **2 = slash,** injure, knife, lacerate, wound
cycle *n* **1, 4 = era,** aeon, age, circle, period, phase, revolution, rotation, round (*of years*)

cyclone ⓣ ('saɪkləʊn) *n* **1** another name for **depression** (sense 6). **2** a violent tropical storm; hurricane. ◆ *adj* **3** *Austral. & NZ trademark.* (of fencing) made of interlaced wire and metal. [C19: from Gk *kuklōn* a turning around, from *kuklos* wheel]
▸**cyclonic** (saɪ'klɒnɪk) *adj* ▸**cy'clonically** *adv*

Cyclopean (ˌsaɪkləʊ'piːən, saɪ'kləʊpɪən) *adj* **1** of, relating to, or resembling the Cyclops. **2** denoting or having the kind of masonry used in preclassical Greek architecture, characterized by large undressed blocks of stone.

cyclopedia *or* **cyclopaedia** (ˌsaɪkləʊ'piːdɪə) *n* a less common word for **encyclopedia.**

cyclopentadiene (ˌsaɪkləʊˌpentə'daɪiːn) *n* a colourless liquid unsaturated cyclic hydrocarbon obtained in the cracking of petroleum hydrocarbons and the distillation of coal tar: used in the manufacture of plastics and insecticides. Formula: C_5H_6.

cyclophosphamide (ˌsaɪkləʊ'fɒsfəˌmaɪd) *n* a cytotoxic drug used in the treatment of leukaemia and lymphoma. [C20: from CYCLO- + PHOSPH(ORUS) + AMIDE]

cyclopropane (ˌsaɪkləʊ'prəʊpeɪn) *n* a colourless gaseous hydrocarbon, used as an anaesthetic. Formula: C_3H_6.

Cyclops ('saɪklɒps) *n, pl* **Cyclopes** (saɪ'kləʊpiːz) *or* **Cyclopses.** *Classical myth.* one of a race of giants having a single eye in the middle of the forehead. [C15: from L *Cyclōps,* from Gk *Kuklōps,* lit.: round eye, from *kuklos* circle + *ōps* eye]

cyclorama (ˌsaɪkləʊ'rɑːmə) *n* **1** a large picture on the interior wall of a cylindrical room, designed to appear in natural perspective to a spectator. **2** *Theatre.* a curtain or wall curving along the back of a stage, usually painted to represent the sky. [C19: CYCLO- + Gk *horama* view, sight, on the model of *panorama*]
▸**cycloramic** (ˌsaɪkləʊ'ræmɪk) *adj*

cyclosporin-A (ˌsaɪkləʊ'spɔːrɪn-) *n* a drug extracted from a fungus and used in transplant surgery to suppress the body's immune mechanisms, and so prevent rejection of an organ.

cyclostome ('saɪkləˌstəʊm, 'sɪk-) *n* any primitive aquatic jawless vertebrate, such as the lamprey, having a round sucking mouth.
▸**cyclostomate** (saɪ'klɒstəmɪt, -ˌmeɪt) *or* **cyclostomatous** (ˌsaɪkləʊ'stɒmətəs, -'stəʊmə-, ˌsɪk-) *adj*

cyclostyle ('saɪkləˌstaɪl) *n* **1** a kind of pen with a small toothed wheel, used for cutting holes in a specially prepared stencil. **2** an office duplicator using such a stencil. ◆ *vb* **cyclostyles, cyclostyling, cyclostyled. 3** (*tr*) to print using such a stencil.
▸**'cycloˌstyled** *adj*

cyclothymia (ˌsaɪkləʊ'θaɪmɪə) *n Psychiatry.* a condition characterized by alternating periods of excitement and depression. [from CYCLO- + Gk *thumos,* cast of mind + -IA]
▸**ˌcyclo'thymic** *adj*

cyclotron ('saɪkləˌtrɒn) *n* a type of particle accelerator in which the particles spiral under the effect of a strong vertical magnetic field.

cyder ('saɪdə) *n* a variant spelling of **cider.**

cygnet ('sɪgnɪt) *n* a young swan. [C15 *sygnett,* from OF *cygne* swan, from L *cygnus,* from Gk *kuknos*]

cylinder ('sɪlɪndə) *n* **1** a solid consisting of two parallel planes bounded by identical closed curves, usually circles, that are interconnected at every point by a set of parallel lines, usually perpendicular to the planes. **2** a surface formed by a line moving round a closed plane curve at a fixed angle to it. **3** any object shaped like a cylinder. **4** the chamber in a reciprocating internal-combustion engine, pump, or compressor within which the piston moves. The cylinders are housed in the metal **cylinder block,** which is topped by the **cylinder head. 5** the rotating mechanism of a revolver, containing cartridge chambers. **6** *Printing.* any of the rotating drums on a printing press. **7** Also called: **cylinder seal.** an ancient cylindrical seal found in the Middle East and Balkans. [C16: from L *cylindrus,* from Gk *kulindros* a roller, from *kulindein* to roll]
▸**'cylinder-ˌlike** *adj*

cylindrical (sɪ'lɪndrɪkᵊl) *or* **cylindric** *adj* of, shaped like, or characteristic of a cylinder.
▸**cyˌlindri'cality** *n* ▸**cy'lindrically** *adv*

cymbal ('sɪmbᵊl) *n* a percussion instrument consisting of a thin circular piece of brass, which vibrates when clashed together with another cymbal or struck with a stick. [OE *cymbala,* from L *cymbalum,* from Gk *kumbalon,* from *kumbē* something hollow]
▸**'cymbalist** *n*

cyme (saɪm) *n* an inflorescence in which the first flower is the terminal bud of the main stem and subsequent flowers develop as terminal buds of lateral stems. [C18: from L *cȳma* cabbage sprout, from Gk *kuma* anything swollen]
▸**cymiferous** (saɪ'mɪfərəs) *adj* ▸**cymose** ('saɪməʊs, -məʊz, saɪ'məʊs) *adj*

Cymric *or* **Kymric** ('kɪmrɪk) *n* **1** the Welsh language. **2** the Brythonic group of Celtic languages. ◆ *adj* **3** of or relating to the Cymry, any of their languages, Wales, or the Welsh.

Cymry *or* **Kymry** ('kɪmrɪ) *n* **the.** (*functioning as pl*) **1** the Brythonic Celts, comprising the present-day Welsh, Cornish, and Bretons. **2** the Welsh people. [Welsh: the Welsh]

cynic ⓣ ('sɪnɪk) *n* **1** a person who believes the worst about people or the outcome of events. ◆ *adj* **2** a less common word for **cynical.** [C16: via L from Gk *Kunikos,* from *kuōn* dog]

Cynic ('sɪnɪk) *n* a member of an ancient Greek sect that scorned worldly things.

cynical ⓣ ('sɪnɪkᵊl) *adj* **1** believing the worst of others, esp. that all acts are selfish. **2** sarcastic; mocking. **3** showing contempt for accepted standards, esp. of honesty or morality.
▸**'cynically** *adv* ▸**'cynicalness** *n*

cynicism ⓣ ('sɪnɪˌsɪzəm) *n* **1** the attitude or beliefs of a cynic. **2** a cynical action, idea, etc.

Cynicism ('sɪnɪˌsɪzəm) *n* the doctrines of the Cynics.

cynosure ('sɪnəˌzjʊə, -ʃʊə) *n* **1** a person or thing that attracts notice. **2** something that serves as a guide. [C16: from L *Cynosūra* the constellation of Ursa Minor, from Gk *Kunosoura,* from *kuōn* dog + *oura* tail]

cypher ('saɪfə) *n, vb* a variant spelling of **cipher.**

cypress ('saɪprəs) *n* **1** any coniferous tree of a N temperate genus having dark green scalelike leaves and rounded cones. **2** any of several similar and related trees. **3** the wood of any of these trees. **4** cypress branches used as a symbol of mourning. [OE *cypresse,* from L *cyparissus,* from Gk *kuparissos;* rel. to L *cupressus*]

cypress pine *n* any coniferous tree of an Australian genus yielding valuable timber.

cyprinid (sɪ'praɪnɪd, 'sɪprɪnɪd) *n* **1** any teleost fish of the mainly freshwater family Cyprinidae, typically having toothless jaws and including the carp, tench, and dace. ◆ *adj* **2** of, relating to, or belonging to the Cyprinidae. **3** resembling a carp; cyprinoid. [C19: from NL *Cyprīnidae,* from L *cyprīnus* carp, from Gk *kuprinos*]

cyprinoid ('sɪprɪˌnɔɪd, sɪ'praɪnɔɪd) *adj* **1** of or relating to the Cyprinoidea, a large suborder of teleost fishes including the cyprinids, electric eels, and loaches. **2** of, relating to, or resembling the carp. ◆ *n* **3** any fish belonging to the Cyprinoidea. [C19: from L *cyprīnus* carp]

Cypriot ('sɪprɪət) *or* **Cypriote** ('sɪprɪˌəʊt) *n* **1** a native or inhabitant of Cyprus, an island in the E Mediterranean. **2** the dialect of Greek spoken in Cyprus. ◆ *adj* **3** denoting or relating to Cyprus, its inhabitants, or dialects.

cypripedium (ˌsɪprɪ'piːdɪəm) *n* any orchid of a genus having large flowers with an inflated pouchlike lip. See also **lady's-slipper.** [C18: from NL, from L *Cypria* the Cyprian, that is, Venus + *pēs* foot (that is, Venus' slipper)]

Cyrenaic (ˌsaɪrə'neɪɪk, ˌsɪrə-) *adj* **1** of or relating to the ancient Greek city of Cyrene in N Africa. **2** of or relating to the philosophical school founded by Aristippus in Cyrene that held pleasure to be the highest good. ◆ *n* **3** a follower of the Cyrenaica school of philosophy.

Cyrillic (sɪ'rɪlɪk) *adj* **1** denoting or relating to the alphabet said to have been devised by Saint Cyril, for Slavonic languages: now used primarily for Russian and Bulgarian. ◆ *n* **2** this alphabet.

cyst ⓣ (sɪst) *n* **1** *Pathol.* any abnormal membranous sac or blister-like pouch containing fluid or semisolid material. **2** *Anat.* any normal sac in the body. **3** a protective membrane enclosing a cell, larva, or organism. [C18: from NL *cystis,* from Gk *kustis* pouch, bag, bladder]

-cyst *n combining form.* indicating a bladder or sac: *otocyst.* [from Gk *kustis* bladder]

cystectomy (sɪ'stɛktəmɪ) *n, pl* **cystectomies. 1** surgical removal of the gall bladder or part of the urinary bladder. **2** surgical removal of a cyst.

cystic ('sɪstɪk) *adj* **1** of, relating to, or resembling a cyst. **2** having or enclosed within a cyst; encysted. **3** relating to the gall bladder or urinary bladder.

cysticercus (ˌsɪstɪ'sɜːkəs) *n, pl* **cysticerci** (-saɪ). an encysted larval form of many tapeworms, consisting of a head inverted in a fluid-filled bladder. [C19: from NL, from Gk *kustis* pouch, bladder + *kerkos* tail]

cystic fibrosis *n* an inheritable disease of the exocrine glands, controlled by a recessive gene: affected children inherit defective alleles from both parents. It is characterized by chronic infection of the respiratory tract and by pancreatic insufficiency.

cystitis (sɪ'staɪtɪs) *n* inflammation of the urinary bladder.

cysto- *or before a vowel* **cyst-** *combining form.* indicating a cyst or bladder: *cystoscope.*

cystoid ('sɪstɔɪd) *adj* **1** resembling a cyst or bladder. ◆ *n* **2** a tissue mass that resembles a cyst but lacks an outer membrane.

cystoscope ('sɪstəˌskəʊp) *n* a slender tubular medical instrument for examining the interior of the urethra and urinary bladder.
▸**cystoscopic** (ˌsɪstə'skɒpɪk) *adj* ▸**cystoscopy** (sɪs'tɒskəpɪ) *n*

-cyte *n combining form.* indicating a cell. [from NL *-cyta,* from Gk *kutos* vessel]

cyto- *combining form.* indicating a cell: *cytoplasm.* [from Gk *kutos* vessel]

cytogenetics (ˌsaɪtəʊdʒɪ'nɛtɪks) *n* (*functioning as sing*) the branch of ge-

THESAURUS

cyclone *n* **2** = **typhoon,** hurricane, storm, tempest, tornado, twister (*US. inf.*), whirlwind

cynic *n* **1** = **sceptic,** doubter, misanthrope, misanthropist, pessimist, scoffer

cynical *adj* **1-3** = **sceptical,** contemptuous, derisive, distrustful, ironic, misanthropic, misanthropical, mocking, mordacious, pessimistic, sarcastic, sardonic, scoffing, scornful, sneering, unbelieving
Antonyms *adj* credulous, green, gullible, hopeful, optimistic, trustful, trusting, unsceptical, unsuspecting

cynicism *n* **1** = **scepticism,** disbelief, doubt, misanthropy, pessimism, sarcasm, sardonicism

cyst *n* **1-3** = **sac,** bleb, blister, growth, vesicle, wen

netics that correlates the structure of chromosomes with heredity and variation.
▸ **ˌcytogeˈnetic** *adj*

cytokinin (ˌsaɪtəʊˈkaɪnɪn) *n* any of a group of plant hormones that promote cell division and retard ageing. Also called: **kinin.**

cytology (saɪˈtɒlədʒɪ) *n* **1** the study of plant and animal cells. **2** the detailed structure of a tissue as revealed by microscopic examination.
▸ **cytological** (ˌsaɪtəˈlɒdʒɪkˈl) *adj* ▸ **ˌcytoˈlogically** *adv* ▸ **cyˈtologist** *n*

cytomegalovirus (ˌsaɪtəʊˌmɛgələʊˈvaɪrəs) *n* a virus that may cause serious disease in patients whose immune systems are compromised and the birth of handicapped children to pregnant women infected with it. Abbrev.: **CMV.**

cytoplasm (ˈsaɪtəʊˌplæzəm) *n* the protoplasm of a cell excluding the nucleus.
▸ **ˌcytoˈplasmic** *adj*

cytosine (ˈsaɪtəsɪn) *n* a white crystalline base occurring in nucleic acids. **[**C19: from CYTO- + -OSE[2] + -INE[2]**]**

cytotoxic (ˌsaɪtəʊˈtɒksɪk) *adj* destructive to cells, esp. to cancer cells: *cytotoxic drugs.*
▸ **cytotoxicity** (ˌsaɪtəʊtɒkˈsɪsɪtɪ) *n*

cytotoxin (ˌsaɪtəʊˈtɒksɪn) *n* any substance that is poisonous to living cells.

czar (zɑː) *n* a variant spelling (esp. US) of **tsar.**
▸ **ˈczardom** *n* ▸ **ˈCzarevitch, czaˈrevna, czaˈrina, ˈczarism, ˈczarist:** see **ts-** spellings.

czardas (ˈtʃɑːdæʃ) *n* **1** a Hungarian national dance of alternating slow and fast sections. **2** music for this dance. **[**from Hungarian *csárdás***]**

Czech (tʃɛk) *adj* **1a** of, relating to, or characteristic of the Czech Republic, its people, or their language. **1b** of, relating to, or characteristic of Bohemia and Moravia, their people, or their language. **1c** (loosely) of, relating to, or characteristic of the former Czechoslovakia or its people. ◆ *n* **2** the official languages of the Czech Republic, belonging to the West Slavonic branch of the Indo-European family. Czech is closely related to Slovak; they are mutually intelligible. **3a** a native or inhabitant of the Czech Republic. **3b** a native or inhabitant of Bohemia or Moravia. **3c** (loosely) a native, inhabitant, or citizen of the former Czechoslovakia. **[**C19: from Polish, from Czech *Čech***]**

Czechoslovak (ˌtʃɛkəʊˈsləʊvæk) *or* **Czechoslovakian** (ˌtʃɛkəʊsləʊˈvækɪən) *adj* **1** of or relating to the former Czechoslovakia, its peoples, or languages. ◆ *n* **2** (loosely) either of the two languages of the former Czechoslovakia: Czech or Slovak.

Dd

d *or* **D** (diː) *n, pl* **d's, D's,** *or* **Ds. 1** the fourth letter of the modern English alphabet. **2** a speech sound represented by this letter.

d *symbol for Physics.* density.

D *symbol for:* **1** *Music.* **1a** the second note of the scale of C major. **1b** the major or minor key having this note as its tonic. **2** *Chem.* deuterium. **3a** a semiskilled or unskilled manual worker, or a trainee or apprentice to a skilled worker. **3b** (*as modifier*): *D worker.* ◆ See also **occupation groupings.** ◆ **4.** *the Roman numeral for* 500.

2,4-D *n* a synthetic auxin widely used as a weedkiller; 2,4-dichlorophenoxyacetic acid.

d. *abbrev. for:* **1** date. **2** daughter. **3** degree. **4** delete. **5** *Brit. currency before decimalization.* penny *or* pennies. [L *denarius* or *denarii*] **6** depart(s). **7** diameter. **8** died. **9** dose.

D. *abbrev. for:* **1** *US.* Democrat(ic). **2** Department. **3** Deus. [L: God] **4** *Optics.* dioptre. **5** Director. **6** Dominus. [L: Lord] **7** Dutch.

'd *contraction for* would *or* had: *I'd; you'd.*

DA *abbrev. for:* **1** (in the US) District Attorney. **2** Diploma of Art. **3** duck's arse (hairstyle). **4** drug addict.

dab[1] Ⓣ (dæb) *vb* **dabs, dabbing, dabbed. 1** to touch or pat lightly and quickly. **2** (*tr*) to daub with short tapping strokes: *to dab the wall with paint.* **3** (*tr*) to apply (paint, cream, etc.) with short tapping strokes. ◆ *n* **4** a small amount, esp. of something soft or moist. **5** a light stroke or tap, as with the hand. **6** (*often pl*) *Chiefly Brit.* a slang word for **fingerprint.** [C14: imit.]
▸**'dabber** *n*

dab[2] (dæb) *n* **1** a small common European flatfish covered with rough toothed scales. **2** any of various other small flatfish. [C15: from Anglo-F *dabbe,* from ?]

dabble Ⓣ ('dæbᵊl) *vb* **dabbles, dabbling, dabbled. 1** to dip, move, or splash (the fingers, feet, etc.) in a liquid. **2** (*intr;* usually foll. by *in, with,* or *at*) to deal (with) or work (at) frivolously or superficially. **3** (*tr*) to splash or smear. [C16: prob. from Du. *dabbelen*]
▸**'dabbler** *n*

dabchick ('dæbˌtʃɪk) *n* any of several small grebes. [C16: prob. from OE *dop* to dive + CHICK]

dab hand Ⓣ *n Brit. inf.* a person who is particularly skilled at something: *a dab hand at chess.* [?from DAB[1]]

da capo (dɑː 'kɑːpəʊ) *adj, adv Music.* to be repeated from the beginning. [C18: from It., lit.: from the head]

dace (deɪs) *n, pl* **dace** *or* **daces. 1** a European freshwater fish of the carp family. **2** any of various similar fishes. [C15: from OF *dars* DART]

dacha *or* **datcha** ('dætʃə) *n* a country house or cottage in Russia. [from Russian: a giving, gift]

dachshund ('dæksˌhʊnd, 'dæʃənd) *n* a long-bodied short-legged breed of dog. [C19: from G, from *Dachs* badger + *Hund* dog]

dacoit (də'kɔɪt) *n* (in India and Myanmar) a member of a gang of armed robbers. [C19: from Hindi *dakait,* from *dākā* robbery]

Dacron ('deɪkrɒn, 'dæk-) *n* the US name (trademark) for **Terylene.**

dactyl ('dæktɪl) *n Prosody.* a metrical foot of three syllables, one long followed by two short (–⏑⏑) [C14: via L from Gk *daktulos* finger, comparing the finger's three joints to the three syllables]

dactylic (dæk'tɪlɪk) *adj* **1** of, relating to, or having a dactyl: *dactylic verse.* ◆ *n* **2** a variant of **dactyl.**
▸**dac'tylically** *adv*

dad (dæd) *n* an informal word for **father.** [C16: childish word]

Dada ('dɑːdɑː) *or* **Dadaism** ('dɑːdɑːˌɪzəm) *n* a nihilistic artistic movement of the early 20th century, founded on principles of irrationality, incongruity, and irreverence towards accepted aesthetic criteria. [C20: from F, from children's word for hobbyhorse]
▸**'Dadaist** *n, adj* ▸**ˌDada'istic** *adj*

daddy ('dædɪ) *n, pl* **daddies. 1** an informal word for **father. 2 the daddy.** *Sl., chiefly US, Canad., & Austral.* the supreme or finest example.

daddy-longlegs *n* **1** *Brit., Austral., & NZ.* an informal name for **crane fly. 2** *US, Canad., Austral., & NZ.* an informal name for **harvestman** (sense 2).

dado ('deɪdəʊ) *n, pl* **dadoes** *or* **dados. 1** the lower part of an interior wall that is decorated differently from the upper part. **2** *Archit.* the part of a pedestal between the base and the cornice. ◆ *vb* **3** (*tr*) to provide with a dado. [C17: from It.: die, die-shaped pedestal]

daemon ('diːmən) *or* **daimon** *n* **1** a demigod. **2** the guardian spirit of a place or person. **3** a variant spelling of **demon** (sense 3).
▸**daemonic** (diː'mɒnɪk) *adj*

daff (dæf) *n Inf.* short for **daffodil.**

daffodil ('dæfədɪl) *n* **1** Also called: **Lent lily.** a widely cultivated Eurasian plant, *Narcissus pseudonarcissus,* having spring-blooming yellow nodding flowers. **2** any other plant of the genus *Narcissus.* **3a** a brilliant yellow colour. **3b** (*as adj*): *daffodil paint.* **4** a daffodil as a national emblem of Wales. [C14: from Med. L *affodillus,* var. of L *asphodelus* ASPHODEL]

daffy ('dæfɪ) *adj* **daffier, daffiest.** *Inf.* another word for **daft** (senses 1, 2). [C19: from obs. *daff* fool]

daft Ⓣ (dɑːft) *adj Chiefly Brit.* **1** *Inf.* foolish, simple, or stupid. **2** a slang word for **insane. 3** (*postpositive;* foll. by *about*) *Inf.* extremely fond (of). **4** *Sl.* frivolous; giddy. [OE *gedæfte* gentle, foolish]
▸**'daftness** *n*

daftie ('dɑːftɪ) *n Inf.* a daft person.

dag[1] (dæg) *n* **1** short for **daglock.** ◆ *vb* **dags, dagging, dagged. 2** to cut the daglock away from (a sheep). [C18: from ?]
▸**'dagger** *n*

dag[2] (dæg) *n Austral. & NZ inf.* **1** a character; eccentric. **2** a person who is untidily dressed. **3** a person with a good sense of humour. [back formation from DAGGY]

dagga ('daxə, 'dɑːgə) *n S. African inf.* a local name for marijuana. [C19: from Afrik., from Khoikhoi *dagab*]

dagger Ⓣ ('dægə) *n* **1** a short stabbing weapon with a pointed blade. **2** Also called: **obelisk.** a character (†) used in printing to indicate a cross reference. **3 at daggers drawn.** in a state of open hostility. **4 look daggers.** to glare with hostility; scowl. [C14: from ?]

daggy ('dægɪ) *adj* **daggier, daggiest.** *Austral. & NZ inf.* untidy; dishevelled. [from DAG[1]]

daglock ('dægˌlɒk) *n* a dung-caked lock of wool around the hindquarters of a sheep. [C17: see DAG[1], LOCK[2]]

dago ('deɪgəʊ) *n, pl* **dagos** *or* **dagoes.** *Derog.* a foreigner, esp. a Spaniard or Portuguese. [C19: from *Diego,* a common Sp. name]

daguerreotype (də'gerəʊˌtaɪp) *n* **1** one of the earliest photographic processes, in which the image was produced on iodine-sensitized silver and developed in mercury vapour. **2** a photograph formed by this process. [C19: after L. *Daguerre* (1789–1851), F inventor]
▸**da'guerreoˌtypy** *n*

dahlia ('deɪljə) *n* **1** any herbaceous perennial plant of the Mexican genus *Dahlia,* having showy flowers and tuberous roots. **2** the flower or root of any of these plants. [C19: after Anders *Dahl,* 18th-cent. Swedish botanist]

Dáil Éireann ('dɑːl 'eːrɪn) *or* **Dáil** *n* (in the Republic of Ireland) the lower chamber of parliament. [from Irish *dáil* assembly + *Éireann* of Eire]

daily Ⓣ ('deɪlɪ) *adj* **1** of or occurring every day or every weekday. ◆ *n, pl* **dailies. 2** a daily newspaper. **3** *Brit.* a charwoman. ◆ *adv* **4** every day. **5** constantly; often. [OE *dæglīc*]

daimon ('daɪmɒn) *n* a variant spelling of **daemon** or **demon** (sense 3).
▸**dai'monic** *adj*

daimyo bond ('daɪmjəʊ) *n* a bearer bond issued in Japan and the eurobond market by the World Bank. [from Japanese, from Ancient Chinese]

dainty Ⓣ ('deɪntɪ) *adj* **daintier, daintiest. 1** delicate or elegant. **2** choice; delicious: *a dainty morsel.* **3** excessively genteel; fastidious. ◆ *n, pl* **dainties. 4** a choice piece of food; delicacy. [C13: from OF *deintié,* from L *dignitās* DIGNITY]
▸**'daintily** *adv*

daiquiri ('daɪkɪrɪ, 'dæk-) *n, pl* **daiquiris.** an iced drink containing rum, lime juice, and sugar. [C20: after *Daiquiri,* town in Cuba]

THESAURUS

dab[1] *vb* **1** = **pat,** blot, daub, stipple, swab, tap, touch, wipe ◆ *n* **4** = **spot,** bit, dollop (*inf.*), drop, fleck, pat, smidgen *or* smidgin (*inf., chiefly US & Canad.*), smudge, speck **5** = **pat,** flick, peck, smudge, stroke, tap, touch

dabble *vb* **1** = **splash,** dip, guddle, moisten, paddle, spatter, sprinkle, wet **2** = **play at,** dally, dip into, potter, tinker, trifle (with)

dabbler *n* **2** = **amateur,** dilettante, potterer, tinkerer, trifler

dab hand *n Brit. inf.* = **expert,** ace, adept, buff (*inf.*), dabster (*dialect*), hotshot (*inf.*), maven (*US*), past master, whizz (*inf.*), wizard

daft *adj inf., chiefly Brit.* **1** = **foolish,** absurd, asinine, crackpot (*inf.*), crazy, doolally (*sl.*), dopey, dumb-ass (*sl.*), giddy, goofy (*inf.*), idiotic, inane, loopy (*inf.*), off one's head (*inf.*), off one's trolley (*sl.*), out to lunch (*inf.*), scatty (*Brit. inf.*), silly, simple, stupid, up the pole (*inf.*), witless **2** = **crazy,** barking (*sl.*), barking mad (*sl.*), crackers (*Brit. sl.*), demented, deranged, insane, lunatic, mental (*sl.*), not right in the head, not the full shilling (*inf.*), nuts (*sl.*), nutty (*sl.*), round the bend (*Brit. sl.*), touched, unhinged **3 daft about** = **enthusiastic,** besotted, crazy (*inf.*), doting, dotty (*sl., chiefly Brit.*), infatuated by, mad, nuts (*sl.*), nutty (*inf.*), potty (*Brit. inf.*), sweet on

daftness *n* **1, 2** *inf., chiefly Brit.* = **foolishness,** absurdity, asininity, brainlessness, craziness, dottiness (*sl., chiefly Brit.*), fatuity, fatuousness, folly, foolhardiness, idiocy, inanity, insanity, lunacy, madness, nonsense, scattiness (*Brit. inf.*), senselessness, silliness, stupidity, tomfoolery, witlessness
Antonyms *n* common sense, intelligence, judgment, reason, sanity, sense, wisdom

dagger *n* **1** = **knife,** bayonet, dirk, poniard, skean, stiletto **3 at daggers drawn** = **on bad terms,** at enmity, at loggerheads, at odds, at war, up in arms **4 look daggers** = **glare,** frown, glower, look black, lour *or* lower, scowl

daily *adj* **1** = **everyday,** circadian, diurnal, quotidian ◆ *adv* **3, 4** = **every day,** constantly, day after day, day by day, often, once a day, per diem, regularly

dainty *adj* **1** = **delicate,** charming, elegant, exquisite, fine, graceful, neat, petite, pretty **2** = **delectable,** choice, delicious, palatable, sa-

dairy ('dɛərɪ) *n, pl* **dairies. 1** a company that supplies milk and milk products. **2** a room or building where milk and cream are stored or made into butter and cheese. **3a** (*modifier*) of, relating to, or containing milk and milk products. **3b** (*in combination*): *a dairymaid.* **4a** a general shop, selling provisions, esp. milk and milk products. **4b** *NZ.* a shop that remains open outside normal trading hours. [C13 *daierie,* from OE *dǣge* servant girl, one who kneads bread]

dairying ('dɛərɪɪŋ) *n* the business of producing, processing, and selling dairy products.

dairyman ('dɛərɪmən) *n, pl* **dairymen.** a man who works in a dairy.

dais ➊ ('deɪɪs, deɪs) *n* a raised platform, usually at one end of a hall, used by speakers, etc. [C13: from OF *deis,* from L *discus* DISCUS]

daisy ('deɪzɪ) *n, pl* **daisies. 1** a small low-growing European plant having flower heads with a yellow centre and pinkish-white outer rays. **2** any of various other composite plants having conspicuous ray flowers. **3** *Sl.* an excellent person or thing. **4 pushing up the daisies.** dead and buried. [OE *dægesēge* day's eye]

▸ **'daisied** *adj*

daisy chain *n* a garland made, esp. by children, by threading daisies together.

daisycutter ('deɪzɪˌkʌtə) *n Cricket.* a ball bowled so that it rolls along the ground.

daisywheel ('deɪzɪˌwiːl) *n Computing.* a component of a computer printer shaped like a wheel with many spokes that prints using a disk with characters around the circumference. Also called: **printwheel.**

daks (dæks) *pl n Austral. inf.* trousers. [C20: from trade name *Daks*]

dal (dɑːl) *n* **1** split grain, a common foodstuff in India; pulse. **2** a variant spelling of **dhal.**

Dalai Lama ('dælaɪ 'lɑːmə) *n* **1** (until 1959) the chief lama and ruler of Tibet. **2** the 14th holder of this office (1940), who fled to India (1959). [from Mongolian *dalai* ocean; see LAMA]

dale ➊ (deɪl) *n* an open valley. [OE *dæl*]

Dalek ('dɑːlɛk) *n* a fictional robot-like creation that is aggressive, mobile, and produces rasping staccato speech. [C20: from a children's television series, *Dr Who*]

dalesman ('deɪlzmən) *n, pl* **dalesmen.** a person living in a dale, esp. in the dales of N England.

dalles ('dæləs, dælz) *pl n Canad.* a stretch of river between high rock walls, with rapids and dangerous currents. [from Canad. F.: sink; see DALE]

dalliance ➊ ('dælɪəns) *n* waste of time in frivolous action or in dawdling.

dally ➊ ('dælɪ) *vb* **dallies, dallying, dallied.** (*intr*) **1** to waste time idly; dawdle. **2** (usually foll. by *with*) to deal frivolously; trifle: *to dally with someone's affections.* [C14: from Anglo-F *dalier* to gossip, from ?]

Dalmatian (dæl'meɪʃən) *n* **1** a large breed of dog having a short smooth white coat with black or brown spots. **2** a native or inhabitant of Dalmatia, a region of W Croatia. ◆ *adj* **3** of Dalmatia or its inhabitants.

dalmatic (dæl'mætɪk) *n* a wide-sleeved tunic-like vestment open at the sides, worn by deacons and bishops, and by a king at his coronation. [C15: from LL *dalmatica* (*vestis*) Dalmatian (robe) (orig. made of Dalmatian wool)]

dal segno ('dæl 'sɛnjəʊ) *adj, adv Music.* to be repeated from the point marked with a sign to the word *fine.* [It., lit.: from the sign]

dalton ('dɔːltən) *n* another name for **atomic mass unit.** [C20: after J. *Dalton* (1766–1844), E scientist]

daltonism ('dɔːltəˌnɪzəm) *n* colour blindness, esp. the confusion of red and green. [C19: from F *daltonisme,* after J. *Dalton*]

Dalton's atomic theory *n Chem.* the theory that matter consists of indivisible particles called atoms and that atoms of a given element are all identical and can neither be created nor destroyed. [C19: after J. *Dalton*]

dam[1] ➊ (dæm) *n* **1** a barrier of concrete, earth, etc., built across a river to create a body of water. **2** a reservoir of water created by such a barrier. **3** something that resembles or functions as a dam. ◆ *vb* **dams, damming, dammed. 4** (*tr;* often foll. by *up*) to restrict by a dam. [C12: prob. from MLow G]

dam[2] (dæm) *n* the female parent of an animal, esp. of domestic livestock. [C13: var. of DAME]

damage ➊ ('dæmɪdʒ) *n* **1** injury or harm impairing the function or condition of a person or thing. **2** loss of something desirable. **3** *Inf.* cost; expense. ◆ *vb* **damages, damaging, damaged. 4** (*tr*) to cause damage to. **5** (*intr*) to suffer damage. [C14: from OF, from L *damnum* injury, loss]

▸ **'damaging** *adj*

damages ➊ ('dæmɪdʒɪz) *pl n Law.* money to be paid as compensation for injury, loss, etc.

damascene ('dæməˌsiːn) *vb* **damascenes, damascening, damascened. 1** (*tr*) to ornament (metal, esp. steel) by etching or by inlaying other metals, usually gold or silver. ◆ *n* **2** a design or article produced by this process. ◆ *adj* **3** of or relating to this process. [C14: from L *damascēnus* of Damascus]

Damascene ('dæməˌsiːn) *adj* **1** of Damascus, the capital of Syria. ◆ *n* **2** a native or inhabitant of Damascus.

Damascus steel (də'mɑːskəs, -'mæs-) *or* **damask steel** *n History.* a hard flexible steel with wavy markings, used for sword blades.

damask ('dæməsk) *n* **1a** a reversible fabric, usually silk or linen, with a pattern woven into it. It is used for table linen, curtains, etc. **1b** table linen made from this. **1c** (*as modifier*): *a damask tablecloth.* **2** short for **Damascus steel. 3** the wavy markings on such steel. **4a** the greyish-pink colour of the damask rose. **4b** (*as adj*): *damask wallpaper.* ◆ *vb* **5** (*tr*) another word for **damascene.** [C14: from Med. L *damascus,* from Damascus, where fabric orig. made]

damask rose *n* a rose with fragrant flowers, which are used to make the perfume attar. [C16: from Med. L *rosa damascēna* rose of Damascus]

dame ➊ (deɪm) *n* **1** (formerly) a woman of rank or dignity; lady. **2** *Arch., chiefly Brit.* an elderly woman. **3** *Sl., chiefly US & Canad.* a woman. **4** *Brit.* the role of a comic old woman in a pantomime, usually played by a man. [C13: from OF, from L *domina* lady, mistress of household]

Dame (deɪm) *n* (in Britain) **1** the title of a woman who has been awarded the Order of the British Empire or any of certain other orders of chivalry. **2** the title of the wife of a knight or baronet.

dame school *n* (formerly) a small school, offering basic education, usually run by an elderly woman in her own home.

damn ➊ (dæm) *interj* **1** *Sl.* an exclamation of annoyance. **2** *Inf.* an exclamation of surprise or pleasure. ◆ *adj* **3** (*prenominal*) *Sl.* deserving damnation. ◆ *adv, adj* (*prenominal*) **4** *Sl.* (intensifier): *a damn good pianist.* ◆ *adv* **5 damn all.** *Sl.* absolutely nothing. ◆ *vb* (*mainly tr*) **6** to condemn as bad, worthless, etc. **7** to curse. **8** to condemn to eternal damnation. **9** (*often passive*) to doom to ruin. **10** (*also intr*) to prove (someone) guilty: *damning evidence.* **11 damn with faint praise.** to praise so unenthusiastically that the effect is condemnation. ◆ *n* **12** *Sl.* something of negligible value (esp. in **not worth a damn**). **13 not give a damn.** *Inf.* not care. [C13: from OF *dampner,* from L *damnāre,* from *damnum* loss, injury]

damnable ➊ ('dæmnəbᵊl) *adj* **1** execrable; detestable. **2** liable to or deserving damnation.

▸ **'damnableness** *or* **ˌdamna'bility** *n*

damnably ➊ ('dæmnəblɪ) *adv* **1** in a detestable manner. **2** (intensifier): *it was damnably unfair.*

damnation ➊ (dæm'neɪʃən) *n* **1** the act of damning or state of being damned. ◆ *interj* **2** an exclamation of anger, disappointment, etc.

THESAURUS

voury, tasty, tender, toothsome **3** = **particular,** choosy, fastidious, finical, finicky, fussy, mincing, nice, picky (*inf.*), refined, scrupulous ◆ *n* **4** = **delicacy,** *bonne bouche,* fancy, sweetmeat, titbit

Antonyms *adj* ≠ **delicate:** awkward, clumsy, coarse, gauche, inelegant, maladroit, uncouth, ungainly

dais *n* = **platform,** estrade, podium, rostrum, stage

dale *n* = **valley,** bottom, coomb, dell, dingle, glen, strath (*Scot.*), vale

dalliance *n* = **dawdling,** dabbling, delay, dilly-dallying (*inf.*), frittering, frivolling (*inf.*), idling, loafing, loitering, playing, pottering, procrastination, toying, trifling

dally *vb* **1** *Old-fashioned* = **waste time,** dawdle, delay, dilly-dally (*inf.*), drag one's feet *or* heels, fool (about *or* around), fritter away, hang about, linger, loiter, procrastinate, tarry, while away **2 dally with** = **flirt,** caress, fondle, fool (about *or* around), frivol (*inf.*), lead on, play, play fast and loose (*inf.*), tamper, tease, toy, trifle

Antonyms *vb* ≠ **waste time:** hasten, hurry (up), make haste, push forward *or* on, run, step on it (*inf.*)

dam[1] *n* **1** = **barrier,** barrage, embankment, hindrance, obstruction, wall ◆ *vb* **4** = **block up,** barricade, block, check, choke, confine, hold back, hold in, obstruct, restrict

damage *n* **1** = **harm,** destruction, detriment, devastation, hurt, impairment, injury, loss, mischief, mutilation, suffering **3** *inf.* = **cost,** bill, charge, expense, total ◆ *vb* **4** = **harm,** deface, hurt, impair, incapacitate, injure, mar, mutilate, play (merry) hell with (*inf.*), ruin, spoil, tamper with, undo, weaken, wreck

Antonyms *vb* ≠ **harm:** better, fix, improve, mend, repair ◆ *n* ≠ **harm:** gain, improvement, reparation

damages *pl n Law* = **compensation,** fine, indemnity, reimbursement, reparation, satisfaction

damaging *adj* **4** = **harmful,** deleterious, detrimental, disadvantageous, hurtful, injurious, prejudicial, ruinous

Antonyms *adj* advantageous, favourable, healthful, helpful, profitable, salutary, useful, valuable, wholesome

dame *n* **1** = **noblewoman,** baroness, dowager, *grande dame,* lady, matron (*arch.*), peeress

damn *vb* **6** = **criticize,** blast, castigate, censure, condemn, denounce, denunciate, excoriate, inveigh against, lambast(e), pan (*inf.*), put down, slam (*sl.*), slate (*inf.*), tear into (*inf.*) **7** = **curse,** abuse, anathematize, blaspheme, execrate, imprecate, revile, swear **8** = **sentence,** condemn, doom ◆ *n* **13 not give a damn** *inf.* = **not care,** be indifferent, not care a brass farthing, not care a jot, not care a whit, not give a hoot, not give a tinker's curse *or* damn (*sl.*), not give two hoots, not mind

Antonyms *vb* ≠ **criticize:** acclaim, admire, applaud, approve, cheer, compliment, congratulate, extol, honour, laud, praise, take one's hat off to ≠ **curse:** adore, bless, exalt, glorify, magnify (*arch.*), pay homage to

damnable *adj* **1** = **detestable,** abominable, accursed, atrocious, culpable, cursed, despicable, execrable, hateful, horrible, offensive, wicked

Antonyms *adj* admirable, commendable, creditable, excellent, exemplary, fine, honourable, laudable, meritorious, praiseworthy, worthy

damnably *adv* **1** = **detestably,** abominably, accursedly, atrociously, despicably, disgracefully, execrably, hatefully, horribly, offensively, reprehensibly, wickedly

Antonyms *adv* admirably, commendably, creditably, excellently, honourably, laudably, worthily

damnation *n* **1** *Theology* = **condemnation,** anathema, ban, consigning to perdition,

damnatory ('dæmnətərɪ) *adj* threatening or occasioning condemnation.

damned ❶ (dæmd) *adj* **1a** condemned to hell. **1b** (*as collective n*; preceded by *the*): *the damned*. ◆ *adv, adj Sl.* **2** (intensifier): *a damned good try*. **3** used to indicate amazement, disavowal, or refusal (as in **damned if I care**).

damnedest ❶ ('dæmdɪst) *n Inf.* utmost; best (esp. in the phrases **do** or **try one's damnedest**).

damnify ('dæmnɪˌfaɪ) *vb* **damnifies, damnifying, damnified.** (*tr*) *Law.* to cause loss or damage to (a person); injure. [C16: from OF *damnifier*, ult. from L *damnum* harm, + *facere* to make]
▸ˌ**damnifi'cation** *n*

damoiselle, damosel, *or* **damozel** (ˌdæmə'zɛl) *n* archaic variants of **damsel.**

damp ❶ (dæmp) *adj* **1** slightly wet. ◆ *n* **2** slight wetness; moisture. **3** rank air or poisonous gas, esp. in a mine. **4** a discouragement; damper. ◆ *vb* (*tr*) **5** to make slightly wet. **6** (often foll. by *down*) to stifle or deaden: *to damp one's ardour*. **7** (often foll. by *down*) to reduce the flow of air to (a fire) to make it burn more slowly. **8** *Physics.* to reduce the amplitude of (an oscillation or wave). **9** *Music.* to muffle (the sound of an instrument). [C14: from MLow G *damp* steam]
▸'**dampness** *n*

dampcourse ('dæmpˌkɔːs) *n* a layer of impervious material in a wall, to stop moisture rising. Also called: **damp-proof course.**

dampen ❶ ('dæmpən) *vb* **1** to make or become damp. **2** (*tr*) to stifle; deaden.
▸'**dampener** *n*

damper ❶ ('dæmpə) *n* **1** a person, event, or circumstance that depresses or discourages. **2 put a damper on.** to produce a depressing or stultifying effect on. **3** a movable plate to regulate the draught in a stove or furnace flue. **4** a device to reduce electronic, mechanical, acoustic, or aerodynamic oscillations in a system. **5** the pad in a piano or harpsichord that deadens the vibration of each string as its key is released. **6** *Chiefly Austral. & NZ.* any of various unleavened loaves and scones, typically cooked on an open fire.

damping off *n* any of various diseases of plants caused by fungi in conditions of excessive moisture.

damp-proof *Building trades.* ◆ *vb* **1** to protect against the incursion of damp by adding a dampcourse or by coating with a moisture-resistant preparation. ◆ *adj* **2** protected against damp or causing protection against damp: *a damp-proof course.*

damsel ('dæmzᵊl) *n Arch. or poetic.* a young unmarried woman; maiden. [C13: from OF *damoisele*, from Vulgar L *domnicella* (unattested) young lady, from L *domina* mistress]

damselfly ('dæmzᵊlˌflaɪ) *n, pl* **damselflies.** any of various insects similar to dragonflies but usually resting with the wings closed over the back.

damson ('dæmzən) *n* **1** a small tree cultivated for its blue-black edible plumlike fruit. **2** the fruit of this tree. [C14: from L *prūnum damascēnum* Damascus plum]

dan (dæn) *n Judo, karate, etc.* **1** any one of the 10 black-belt grades of proficiency. **2** a competitor entitled to dan grading. [Japanese]

Dan. *abbrev. for:* **1** *Bible.* Daniel. **2** Danish.

dance ❶ (dɑːns) *vb* **dances, dancing, danced. 1** (*intr*) to move the feet and body rhythmically, esp. in time to music. **2** (*tr*) to perform (a particular dance). **3** (*intr*) to skip or leap. **4** to move or cause to move in a rhythmic way. **5 dance attendance on (someone).** to attend (someone) solicitously or obsequiously. ◆ *n* **6** a series of rhythmic steps and movements, usually in time to music. **7** an act of dancing. **8a** a social meeting arranged for dancing. **8b** (*as modifier*): *a dance hall*. **9** a piece of music in the rhythm of a particular dance form. **10** dancelike movements. **11 lead (someone) a dance.** *Brit. inf.* to cause (someone) continued worry and exasperation. [C13: from OF *dancier*]
▸'**danceable** *adj* ▸'**dancer** *n* ▸'**dancing** *n, adj*

dance floor *n* **a** an area of floor in a disco, etc., where patrons may dance. **b** (*as modifier*): *dancefloor music.*

dance of death *n* a medieval representation of a dance in which people are led off to their graves, by a personification of death. Also called (French): **danse macabre.**

D and C *n Med.* dilation (of the cervix) and curettage (of the uterus).

dandelion ('dændɪˌlaɪən) *n* **1** a plant native to Europe and Asia and naturalized as a weed in North America, having yellow rayed flowers and deeply notched leaves. **2** any of several similar plants. [C15: from OF *dent de lion*, lit.: tooth of a lion, referring to its leaves]

dander ('dændə) *n* **1** small particles of hair or feathers. **2 get one's** (*or* **someone's**) **dander up.** *Inf.* to become (*or* cause to become) annoyed or angry. [C19: from DANDRUFF]

dandify ('dændɪˌfaɪ) *vb* **dandifies, dandifying, dandified.** (*tr*) to dress like or cause to resemble a dandy.

dandle ❶ ('dændᵊl) *vb* **dandles, dandling, dandled.** (*tr*) **1** to move (a young child) up and down (on the knee or in the arms). **2** to pet; fondle. [C16: from ?]
▸'**dandler** *n*

dandruff ('dændrəf) *n* loose scales of dry dead skin shed from the scalp. [C16: *dand-* from ? + *-ruff*, prob. from ME *roufe* scab, from ON *hrūfa*]

dandy ❶ ('dændɪ) *n, pl* **dandies. 1** a man greatly concerned with smartness of dress. ◆ *adj* **dandier, dandiest. 2** *Inf.* good or fine. [C18: ? short for *jack-a-dandy*]
▸'**dandyish** *adj*

dandy-brush *n* a stiff brush used for grooming a horse.

dandy roll *or* **roller** *n* a roller used in the manufacture of paper to produce watermarks.

Dane (deɪn) *n* **1** a native, citizen, or inhabitant of Denmark. **2** any of the Vikings who invaded England from the late 8th to the 11th century A.D.

Danegeld ('deɪnˌgɛld) *or* **Danegelt** ('deɪnˌgɛlt) *n* the tax levied in Anglo-Saxon England to provide protection money for or to finance forces to oppose Viking invaders. [C11: from *Dan* Dane + *geld* tribute; see YIELD]

Danelaw ('deɪnˌlɔː) *n* the parts of Anglo-Saxon England in which Danish law and custom were observed. [OE *Dena lagu* Danes' law]

danger ❶ ('deɪndʒə) *n* **1** the state of being vulnerable to injury, loss, or evil; risk. **2** a person or thing that may cause injury, pain, etc. **3 in danger of.** liable to. **4 on the danger list.** critically ill in hospital. [C13 *daunger* power, hence power to inflict injury, from OF *dongier* from L *dominium* ownership]
▸'**dangerless** *adj*

danger money *n* extra money paid to compensate for the risks involved in certain dangerous jobs.

dangerous ❶ ('deɪndʒərəs) *adj* causing danger; perilous.
▸'**dangerously** *adv*

dangle ❶ ('dæŋgᵊl) *vb* **dangles, dangling, dangled. 1** to hang or cause to hang freely: *his legs dangled over the wall*. **2** (*tr*) to display as an enticement. [C16: ?from Danish *dangle*, prob. imit.]
▸'**dangler** *n*

Danish ('deɪnɪʃ) *adj* **1** of Denmark, its people, or their language. ◆ *n* **2** the official language of Denmark.

Danish blue *n* a strong-tasting white cheese with blue veins.

Danish pastry *n* a rich puff pastry filled with apple, almond paste, icing, etc.

dank ❶ (dæŋk) *adj* (esp. of cellars, caves, etc.) unpleasantly damp and chilly. [C14: prob. from ON]
▸'**dankly** *adv* ▸'**dankness** *n*

danseur *French.* (dɑ̃sœr) *or* (*fem*) ***danseuse*** (dɑ̃søz) *n* a ballet dancer.

dap (dæp) *vb* **daps, dapping, dapped. 1** *Angling.* to fly-fish so that the fly bobs on and off the water. **2** (*intr*) to dip lightly into water. **3** to bounce or cause to bounce. [C17: imit.]

daphne ('dæfnɪ) *n* any of various Eurasian ornamental shrubs with shiny evergreen leaves and clusters of small bell-shaped flowers. [via L from Gk: laurel]

daphnia ('dæfnɪə) *n* any of several waterfleas having a rounded body

THESAURUS

damning, denunciation, doom, excommunication, objurgation, proscription, sending to hell

damned *adj* **1a** = **doomed**, accursed, anathematized, condemned, infernal, lost, reprobate, unhappy

damnedest *n inf.* = **best**, hardest, utmost

damp *adj* **1** = **moist**, clammy, dank, dewy, dripping, drizzly, humid, misty, muggy, sodden, soggy, sopping, vaporous, wet ◆ *n* **2** = **moisture**, clamminess, dampness, dankness, dew, drizzle, fog, humidity, mist, mugginess, vapour ◆ *vb* **5** = **moisten**, dampen, wet **6 damp down** = **curb**, allay, check, chill, cool, dash, deaden, deject, depress, diminish, discourage, dispirit, dull, inhibit, moderate, pour cold water on, reduce, restrain, stifle
Antonyms *adj* ≠ **moist:** arid, dry, watertight ◆ *n* ≠ **moisture:** aridity, dryness ◆ *vb* ≠ **curb:** encourage, gee up, hearten, inspire

dampen *vb* **1** = **reduce**, check, dash, deaden, depress, deter, dishearten, dismay, dull, lessen, moderate, muffle, restrain, smother, stifle **2** = **moisten**, bedew, besprinkle, make damp, spray, wet

damper *n* **2** *As in* **put a damper on** = **discouragement**, chill, cloud, cold water (*inf.*), curb, gloom, hindrance, killjoy, pall, restraint, wet blanket (*inf.*)

dampness *n* **1** = **moistness**, clamminess, damp, dankness, humidity, moisture, mugginess, sogginess, wetness
Antonyms *n* aridity, aridness, dryness

dance *vb* **1** = **prance**, bob up and down, caper, cut a rug (*inf.*), frolic, gambol, hop, jig, rock, skip, spin, sway, swing, trip, whirl ◆ *n* **8a** = **ball**, dancing party, disco, discotheque, hop (*inf.*), knees-up (*Brit. inf.*), social

dancer *n* **1** = **ballerina**, Terpsichorean

dandle *vb* **1, 2** = **rock**, amuse, bounce, caress, cradle, cuddle, dance, fondle, give a knee ride, pet, toss, toy (with)

dandy *n* **1** = **fop**, beau, blade (*arch.*), blood (*rare*), buck (*arch.*), coxcomb, dude (*US & Canad. inf.*), exquisite (*obs.*), macaroni (*obs.*), man about town, peacock, popinjay, swell (*inf.*), toff (*Brit. sl.*) ◆ *adj* **2** *inf.* = **excellent**, capital, fine, first-rate, great, splendid

danger *n* **1** = **peril**, endangerment, hazard, insecurity, jeopardy, menace, pitfall, precariousness, risk, threat, venture, vulnerability

dangerous *adj* = **perilous**, alarming, breakneck, chancy (*inf.*), exposed, hairy, hazardous, insecure, menacing, nasty, parlous (*arch.*), precarious, risky, threatening, treacherous, ugly, unchancy (*Scot.*), unsafe, vulnerable
Antonyms *adj* harmless, innocuous, O.K. *or* okay (*inf.*), out of danger, out of harm's way, protected, safe, safe and sound, secure

dangerously *adv* = **perilously**, alarmingly, carelessly, daringly, desperately, harmfully, hazardously, precariously, recklessly, riskily, unsafely, unsecurely

dangle *vb* **1** = **hang**, depend, flap, hang down, sway, swing, trail **2** = **wave**, brandish, entice, flaunt, flourish, lure, tantalize, tempt

dangling *adj* **1** = **hanging**, disconnected, drooping, loose, swaying, swinging, trailing, unconnected

dank *adj* = **damp**, chilly, clammy, dewy, dripping, moist, slimy, soggy enclosed in a transparent shell. [C19: prob. from *Daphne*, a nymph in Gk mythology]

dapper ❶ ('dæpə) *adj* **1** neat in dress and bearing. **2** small and nimble. [C15: from MDu.: active, nimble]
▸ **'dapperly** *adv* ▸ **'dapperness** *n*

dapple ❶ ('dæpᵊl) *vb* **dapples, dappling, dappled. 1** to mark or become marked with spots of a different colour; mottle. ◆ *n* **2** mottled or spotted markings. **3** a dappled horse, etc. ◆ *adj* **4** marked with dapples or spots. [C14: from ?]

dapple-grey *n* a horse with a grey coat having spots of darker colour.

darbies ('dɑːbɪz) *pl n Brit.* a slang term for **handcuffs.** [C16: ?from *Father Derby's* (or *Darby's*) *bonds,* a rigid agreement between a usurer and his client]

Darby and Joan ('dɑːbɪ; dʒəʊn) *n* **1** an ideal elderly married couple living in domestic harmony. **2 Darby and Joan Club.** a club for elderly people. [C18: couple in 18th-cent. English ballad]

dare ❶ (dɛə) *vb* **dares, daring, dared. 1** (*tr*) to challenge (a person to do something) as proof of courage. **2** (can take an infinitive with or without *to*) to be courageous enough to try (to do something). **3** (*tr*) *Rare.* to oppose without fear; defy. **4 I dare say. 4a** (it is) quite possible (that). **4b** probably. ◆ *n* **5** a challenge to do something as proof of courage. **6** something done in response to such a challenge. [OE *durran*]
▸ **'darer** *n*

> **USAGE NOTE** When used negatively or interrogatively, *dare* does not usually add *-s: he dare not come; dare she come?* When used negatively in the past tense, however, *dare* usually adds *-d: he dared not come.*

daredevil ❶ ('dɛəˌdevᵊl) *n* **1** a recklessly bold person. ◆ *adj* **2** reckless; daring; bold.
▸ **'dareˌdevilry** *or* **'dareˌdeviltry** *n*

daring ❶ ('dɛərɪŋ) *adj* **1** bold or adventurous. ◆ *n* **2** courage in taking risks; boldness.

Darjeeling (dɑː'dʒiːlɪŋ) *n* a high-quality black tea grown in the mountains around Darjeeling, a town in NE India.

dark ❶ (dɑːk) *adj* **1** having little or no light. **2** (of a colour) reflecting or transmitting little light: *dark brown.* **3** (of complexion, hair colour, etc.) not fair; swarthy; brunette. **4** gloomy or dismal. **5** sinister; evil: *a dark purpose.* **6** sullen or angry. **7** ignorant or unenlightened: *a dark period in our history.* **8** secret or mysterious. ◆ *n* **9** absence of light; darkness. **10** night or nightfall. **11** a dark place. **12** a state of ignorance (esp. **in the dark**). [OE *deorc*]
▸ **'darkish** *adj* ▸ **'darkly** *adv* ▸ **'darkness** *n*

Dark Ages *pl n European history.* the period from about the late 5th century A.D. to about 1000 A.D., once considered an unenlightened period.

Dark Continent *n* **the.** a term for Africa when it was relatively unexplored by Europeans.

darken ❶ ('dɑːkən) *vb* **1** to make or become dark or darker. **2** to make or become gloomy, angry, or sad. **3 darken (someone's) door.** (*usually used with a negative*) to visit someone: *never darken my door again!*
▸ **'darkener** *n*

dark horse *n* **1** a competitor in a race or contest about whom little is known. **2** a person who reveals little about himself, esp. one who has unexpected talents. **3** *US politics.* a candidate who is unexpectedly nominated or elected.

dark lantern *n* a lantern having a sliding shutter or panel to dim or hide the light.

darkling ('dɑːklɪŋ) *adv, adj Poetic.* in the dark or night. [C15: from DARK + -LING[2]]

dark matter *n Astron.* matter known to make up a substantial part of the mass of the universe, but not detectable by its absorption or emission of electromagnetic radiation.

darkroom ('dɑːkˌruːm, -ˌrʊm) *n* a room in which photographs are processed in darkness or safe light.

darksome ('dɑːksəm) *adj Literary.* dark or darkish.

dark star *n* an invisible star known to exist only from observation of its radio, infrared, or other spectrum or of its gravitational effect.

darling ❶ ('dɑːlɪŋ) *n* **1** a person very much loved. **2** a favourite. ◆ *adj* (*prenominal*) **3** beloved. **4** much admired; pleasing: *a darling hat.* [OE *dēorling;* see DEAR, -LING[1]]

darn[1] ❶ (dɑːn) *vb* **1** to mend (a hole or a garment) with a series of crossing or interwoven stitches. ◆ *n* **2** a patch of darned work on a garment. [C16: prob. from F (dialect) *darner*]
▸ **'darner** *n*

darn[2] (dɑːn) *interj, adj, adv, n* a euphemistic word for **damn** (senses 1–5, 12, 13).

darnel ('dɑːnᵊl) *n* any of several grasses that grow as weeds in grain fields in Europe and Asia. [C14: prob. rel. to F (dialect) *darnelle,* from ?]

darning ('dɑːnɪŋ) *n* **1** the act of mending a hole using interwoven stitches. **2** garments needing to be darned.

darning needle *n* a long needle with a large eye used for darning.

dart ❶ (dɑːt) *n* **1** a small narrow pointed missile that is thrown or shot, as in the game of darts. **2** a sudden quick movement. **3** *Zool.* a slender pointed structure, as in snails for aiding copulation. **4** a tapered tuck made in dressmaking. ◆ *vb* **5** to move or throw swiftly and suddenly; shoot. [C14: from OF, of Gmc origin]
▸ **'darting** *adj*

dartboard ('dɑːtˌbɔːd) *n* a circular piece of wood, cork, etc., used as the target in the game of darts.

darter ('dɑːtə) *n* **1** Also called: **anhinga, snakebird.** any of various aquatic birds of tropical and subtropical inland waters, having a long slender neck and bill. **2** any of various small brightly coloured North American freshwater fish.

darts (dɑːts) *n* (*functioning as sing*) any of various competitive games in which darts are thrown at a dartboard.

Darwinian (dɑː'wɪnɪən) *adj* **1** of or relating to Charles Darwin (1809–92), English naturalist, or his theory of evolution. ◆ *n* **2** a person who accepts, supports, or uses this theory.

Darwinism ('dɑːwɪˌnɪzəm) *or* **Darwinian theory** *n* the theory of the origin of animal and plant species by evolution through a process of natural selection.
▸ **'Darwinist** *n, adj*

dash[1] ❶ (dæʃ) *vb* (*mainly tr*) **1** to hurl; crash: *he dashed the cup to the floor.* **2** to mix: *white paint dashed with blue.* **3** (*intr*) to move hastily or recklessly; rush. **4** (usually foll. by *off* or *down*) to write (down) or finish (off) hastily. **5** to frustrate: *his hopes were dashed.* **6** to daunt (someone); discourage. ◆ *n* **7** a sudden quick movement. **8** a small admixture:

THESAURUS

dapper *adj* **1 = neat,** active, brisk, chic, natty (*inf.*), nice, nimble, smart, soigné *or* soignée, spruce, spry, stylish, trig (*arch. or dialect*), trim, well-groomed, well turned out
Antonyms *adj* blowsy, disarrayed, dishevelled, dowdy, frowzy, ill-groomed, rumpled, slobby (*inf.*), sloppy (*inf.*), slovenly, unkempt, untidy

dapple *vb* **1 = mottle,** bespeckle, dot, fleck, freckle, speckle, spot, stipple

dappled *adj* **1 = mottled,** brindled, checkered, flecked, freckled, piebald, pied, speckled, spotted, stippled, variegated

dare *vb* **1 = challenge,** defy, goad, provoke, taunt, throw down the gauntlet **2 = risk,** brave, endanger, gamble, hazard, make bold, presume, skate on thin ice, stake, venture ◆ *n* **5 = challenge,** defiance, provocation, taunt

daredevil *n* **1 = adventurer,** adrenalin junky, desperado, exhibitionist, hot dog (*chiefly US*), madcap, show-off (*inf.*), stunt man ◆ *adj* **2 = daring,** adventurous, audacious, bold, death-defying, madcap, reckless

daredevilry *n* **= daring,** adventure, adventurousness, boldness, derring-do (*arch.*), fearlessness, foolhardiness, intrepidity, rashness, recklessness, temerity

daring *adj* **1 = brave,** adventurous, audacious, ballsy (*taboo sl.*), bold, daredevil, fearless, game (*inf.*), have-a-go (*inf.*), impulsive, intrepid, plucky, rash, reckless, valiant, venturesome ◆ *n* **2 = bravery,** audacity, balls (*taboo sl.*), ballsiness (*taboo sl.*), boldness, bottle (*Brit. sl.*), courage, derring-do (*arch.*), face (*inf.*), fearlessness, grit, guts (*inf.*), intrepidity, nerve (*inf.*), pluck, rashness, spirit, spunk (*inf.*), temerity
Antonyms *adj* ≠ **brave:** anxious, careful, cautious, cowardly, faint-hearted, fearful, timid, uncourageous, wary ◆ *n* ≠ **bravery:** anxiety, caution, cowardice, fear, timidity

dark *adj* **1 = dim,** cloudy, darksome (*literary*), dingy, indistinct, murky, overcast, pitch-black, pitchy, shadowy, shady, sunless, unlit **3 = brunette,** black, dark-skinned, dusky, ebony, sable, swarthy **4 = gloomy,** bleak, cheerless, dismal, doleful, drab, grim, joyless, morbid, morose, mournful, sad, sombre **5 = evil,** atrocious, damnable, foul, hellish, horrible, infamous, infernal, nefarious, satanic, sinful, sinister, vile, wicked **6 = angry,** dour, forbidding, frowning, glowering, glum, ominous, scowling, sulky, sullen, threatening **8 = secret,** abstruse, arcane, concealed, cryptic, deep, Delphic, enigmatic, hidden, mysterious, mystic, obscure, occult, puzzling, recondite ◆ *n* **9 = darkness,** dimness, dusk, gloom, murk, murkiness, obscurity, semi- darkness **10 = night,** evening, nightfall, night-time, twilight
Antonyms *adj* ≠ **brunette:** blond, blonde, fair, fair-haired, flaxen-haired, light, light-complexioned, towheaded ≠ **gloomy:** bright, cheerful, clear, genial, glad, hopeful, pleasant, sunny

darken *vb* **1 = make dark,** becloud, blacken, cloud up *or* over, deepen, dim, eclipse, make darker, make dim, obscure, overshadow, shade, shadow **2 = become gloomy,** become angry, blacken, cast a pall over, cloud, deject, depress, dispirit, grow troubled, look black, sadden
Antonyms *vb* ≠ **make dark:** brighten, clear up, enliven, gleam, glow, illuminate, lighten, light up, make bright, shine ≠ **become gloomy:** become cheerful, cheer, encourage, gladden, hearten, make happy, perk up

darkness *n* **1 = dark,** blackness, dimness, dusk, duskiness, gloom, murk, murkiness, nightfall, obscurity, shade, shadiness, shadows **8 = secrecy,** blindness, concealment, ignorance, mystery, privacy, unawareness

darling *n* **1 = beloved,** dear, dearest, love, sweetheart, truelove **2 = favourite,** apple of one's eye, blue-eyed boy, fair-haired boy (*US*), pet, spoilt child ◆ *adj* **3 = beloved,** adored, cherished, dear, precious, treasured **4 = adorable,** attractive, captivating, charming, cute, enchanting, lovely, sweet

darn[1] *vb* **1 = mend,** cobble up, patch, repair, sew up, stitch ◆ *n* **2 = mend,** invisible repair, patch, reinforcement

dart *vb* **5 = dash,** bound, flash, flit, fly, race, run, rush, scoot, shoot, spring, sprint, start, tear, whistle, whizz **5 = throw,** cast, fling, hurl, launch, propel, send, shoot, sling

dash[1] *vb* **1 = throw,** cast, fling, hurl, slam, sling **1 = crash,** break, destroy, shatter, shiver, smash, splinter **3 = rush,** barrel (along) (*inf., chiefly US & Canad.*), bolt, bound, burn rubber (*inf.*), dart, fly, haste, hasten, hurry, race, run, speed, spring, sprint, tear **5 = frustrate,** blight, foil, ruin, spoil, thwart, undo **6 = disappoint,** abash, chagrin, confound, dampen, discomfort, dis-

coffee with a dash of cream. **9** a violent stroke or blow. **10** the sound of splashing or smashing. **11** panache; style: *he rides with dash.* **12** Also called: **rule.** the punctuation mark –, used to indicate a sudden change of subject or to enclose a parenthetical remark. **13** the symbol (–) used, in combination with the symbol *dot* (•), in the written representation of Morse and other telegraphic codes. **14** *Athletics.* another word (esp. US and Canad.) for **sprint.** [ME *daschen, dassen,* ?from ON]

dash[2] (dæʃ) *interj Inf.* a euphemistic word for **damn** (senses 1, 2).

dashboard ('dæʃ,bɔːd) *n* **1** Also called (Brit.): **fascia.** the instrument panel in a car, boat, or aircraft. **2** *Obs.* a board at the side of a carriage or boat to protect against splashing.

dasher ('dæʃə) *n* **1** one that dashes. **2** *Canad.* the ledge along the top of the boards of an ice hockey rink.

dashiki (dɑː'ʃiːkɪ) *n* a large loose-fitting upper garment worn esp. by Blacks in the US, Africa, and the Caribbean. [C20: of W African origin]

dashing ❶ ('dæʃɪŋ) *adj* **1** spirited; lively: *a dashing young man.* **2** stylish; showy.

dashlight ('dæʃ,laɪt) *n* a light that illuminates the dashboard of a car, esp. at night.

Dassehra ('dæsεəræ) *n* an annual Hindu festival celebrated on the 10th lunar day of Navaratri; images of the goddess Durga are immersed in water.

dassie ('dæsɪ) *n* another name for a **hyrax,** esp. the rock hyrax. [C19: from Afrik.]

dastardly ❶ ('dæstədlɪ) *adj* mean and cowardly. [C15 *dastard* (in the sense: dullard): prob. from ON *dæstr* exhausted, out of breath]
▸ **'dastardliness** *n*

dasyure ('dæsɪ,jʊə) *n* **1** any of several small carnivorous marsupials of Australia, New Guinea, and adjacent islands. **2** the ursine dasyure. See **Tasmanian devil.** [C19: from NL, from Gk *dasus* shaggy + *oura* tail]

DAT *abbrev. for* digital audio tape.

dat. *abbrev. for* dative.

data ❶ ('deɪtə, 'dɑːtə) *pl n* **1** a series of observations, measurements, or facts; information. **2** Also called: **information.** *Computing.* the information operated on by a computer program. [C17: from L, lit.: (things) given, from *dare* to give]

> **USAGE NOTE** Although now often used as a singular noun, *data* is properly a plural.

database ('deɪtə,beɪs) *n* **1** Also called: **data bank.** a store of a large amount of information, esp. in a form that can be handled by a computer. **2** *Inf.* any large store of information: *a database of knowledge.*

data capture *n* any process for converting information into a form that can be handled by a computer.

data pen *n* a device for reading or scanning magnetically coded data on labels, packets, etc.

data processing *n* **a** a sequence of operations performed on data, esp. by a computer, in order to extract information, reorder files, etc. **b** (*as modifier*): *a data-processing centre.*

data protection *n* (in Britain) safeguards for individuals relating to personal data stored on a computer.

data set *n Computing.* another name for **file**[1] (sense 6).

date[1] ❶ (deɪt) *n* **1** a specified day of the month. **2** the particular day or year of an event. **3** an inscription on a coin, letter, etc., stating when it was made or written. **4a** an appointment for a particular time, esp. with a person of the opposite sex. **4b** the person with whom the appointment is made. **5** the present moment; now (esp. in **to date, up to date**). ◆ *vb* **dates, dating, dated. 6** (*tr*) to mark (a letter, coin, etc.) with the day, month, or year. **7** (*tr*) to assign a date of occurrence or creation to. **8** (*intr; foll. by from or back to*) to have originated (at a specified time). **9** (*tr*) to reveal the age of: *that dress dates her.* **10** to make or become old-fashioned: *some good films hardly date at all.* **11** *Inf., chiefly US & Canad.* **11a** to be a boyfriend or girlfriend of (someone of the opposite sex). **11b** to accompany (a member of the opposite sex) on a date. [C14: from OF, from L *dare* to give, as in *epistula data Romae* letter handed over at Rome]
▸ **'datable** *or* **'dateable** *adj*

> **USAGE NOTE** See at **year.**

date[2] (deɪt) *n* **1** the fruit of the date palm, having sweet edible flesh and a single large woody seed. **2** short for **date palm.** [C13: from OF, from L, from Gk *daktulos* finger]

dated ❶ ('deɪtɪd) *adj* **1** unfashionable; outmoded. **2** (of a security) having a fixed date for redemption.

dateless ('deɪtlɪs) *adj* likely to remain fashionable, good, or interesting regardless of age.

dateline ('deɪt,laɪn) *n Journalism.* the date and location of a story, placed at the top of an article.

date line *n* (*often caps.*) short for **International Date Line.**

date palm *n* a tall feather palm grown in tropical regions for its sweet edible fruit.

date rape *n* **1** the act or an instance of a man raping a woman while they are on a date together. **2** an act of sexual intercourse regarded as tantamount to rape, esp. if the woman was encouraged to drink excessively or was subjected to undue pressure.

date stamp *n* **1** an adjustable rubber stamp for recording the date. **2** an inked impression made by this.

dating ('deɪtɪŋ) *n* any of several techniques, such as radioactive dating, dendrochronology, or varve dating, for establishing the age of rocks, palaeontological or archaeological specimens, etc.

dating agency *n* an agency that provides introductions to people seeking a companion with similar interests.

dative ('deɪtɪv) *Grammar.* ◆ *adj* **1** denoting a case of nouns, pronouns, and adjectives used to express the indirect object, to identify the recipients, and for other purposes. ◆ *n* **2a** the dative case. **2b** a word or speech element in this case. [C15: from L *datīvus,* from *dare* to give]
▸ **datival** (deɪ'taɪvᵊl) *adj* ▸ **'datively** *adv*

datum ('deɪtəm, 'dɑːtəm) *n, pl* **data. 1** a single piece of information; fact. **2** a proposition taken as unquestionable, often in order to construct some theoretical framework upon it. See also **sense datum.** [C17: from L: something given; see DATA]

datura (də'tjʊərə) *n* any of various chiefly Indian plants and shrubs with large trumpet-shaped flowers. [C16: from NL, from Hindi]

daub ❶ (dɔːb) *vb* **1** (*tr*) to smear or spread (paint, mud, etc.), esp. carelessly. **2** (*tr*) to cover or coat (with paint, plaster, etc.) carelessly. **3** to paint (a picture) clumsily or badly. ◆ *n* **4** an unskilful or crude painting. **5** something daubed on, esp. as a wall covering. **6** a smear (of paint, mud, etc.). [C14: from OF *dauber* to paint, whitewash, from L *dealbāre,* from *albāre* to whiten]
▸ **'dauber** *n*

daughter ('dɔːtə) *n* **1** a female offspring; a girl or woman in relation to her parents. **2** a female descendant. **3** a female from a certain country, etc., or one closely connected with a certain environment, etc.: *a daughter of the church.* ◆ (*modifier*) **4** *Biol.* denoting a cell or unicellular organism produced by the division of one of its own kind. **5** *Physics.* (of a nuclide) formed from another nuclide by radioactive decay. [OE *dohtor*]
▸ **'daughterhood** *n* ▸ **'daughterless** *adj* ▸ **'daughterly** *adj*

daughter-in-law *n, pl* **daughters-in-law.** the wife of one's son.

daunt ❶ (dɔːnt) *vb* (*tr; often passive*) **1** to intimidate. **2** to dishearten. [C13: from OF *danter,* changed from *donter* to conquer, from L *domitāre* to tame]
▸ **'daunting** *adj* ▸ **'dauntingly** *adv*

dauntless ❶ ('dɔːntlɪs) *adj* bold; fearless; intrepid.
▸ **'dauntlessly** *adv* ▸ **'dauntlessness** *n*

dauphin ('dɔːfɪn; *French* dofɛ̃) *n* (1349–1830) the title of the eldest son of the king of France. [C15: from OF: orig. a family name]

THESAURUS

courage ◆ *n* **7** = **rush,** bolt, dart, haste, onset, race, run, sortie, sprint, spurt **8** = **little,** bit, drop, flavour, hint, pinch, smack, *soupçon,* sprinkling, suggestion, tinge, touch **11** = **style,** brio, élan, flair, flourish, panache, spirit, verve, vigour, vivacity
Antonyms *vb* ≠ **rush:** crawl, dawdle, walk ≠ **frustrate:** enhance, improve ◆ *n* ≠ **little:** lot, much

dashing *adj* **1** = **bold,** daring, debonair, exuberant, gallant, lively, plucky, spirited, swashbuckling **2** = **stylish,** dapper, dazzling, elegant, flamboyant, jaunty, showy, smart, sporty, swish (*inf., chiefly Brit.*), urbane
Antonyms *adj* ≠ **bold:** boring, dreary, dull, lacklustre, stolid, unexciting, uninteresting

dastardly *adj Old-fashioned* = **despicable,** abject, base, caitiff (*arch.*), contemptible, cowardly, craven, faint-hearted, low, mean, niddering (*arch.*), recreant (*arch.*), sneaking, sneaky, spiritless, underhand, vile, weak-kneed (*inf.*)

data *n* **1** = **information,** details, documents, dope (*inf.*), facts, figures, info (*inf.*), input, materials, statistics

date[1] *n* **1, 2** = **day,** time, year **4a** = **appointment,** assignation, engagement, meeting, rendezvous, tryst **4b** = **partner,** escort, friend, steady (*inf.*) ◆ *vb* **7** = **put a date on,** assign a date to, determine the date of, fix the period of **8 date from** *or* date back to = **come from,** bear a date of, belong to, exist from, originate in **10** = **become old-fashioned,** be dated, obsolesce, show one's age

dated *adj* **1** = **old-fashioned,** antiquated, archaic, *démodé,* obsolete, old hat, out, outdated, outmoded, out of date, out of the ark (*inf.*), passé, unfashionable, untrendy (*Brit. inf.*)
Antonyms *adj* à la mode, all the rage, chic, cool (*inf.*), current, hip (*sl.*), in vogue, latest, modern, modish, popular, stylish, trendy (*Brit. inf.*), up-to-date

daub *vb* **1** = **stain,** bedaub, begrime, besmear, blur, deface, dirty, grime, smirch, smudge, spatter, splatter, sully **2** = **smear,** coat, cover, paint, plaster, slap on (*inf.*) ◆ *n* **6** = **smear,** blot, blotch, smirch, splodge, splotch, spot, stain

daunt *vb* **1** = **intimidate,** alarm, appal, cow, dismay, frighten, frighten off, overawe, scare, subdue, terrify **2** = **discourage,** deter, dishearten, dispirit, put off, shake
Antonyms *vb* cheer, comfort, encourage, hearten, inspire, inspirit, reassure, spur, support

daunted *adj* **1, 2** = **intimidated,** alarmed, cowed, demoralized, deterred, discouraged, disillusioned, dismayed, dispirited, downcast, frightened, hesitant, overcome, put off, unnerved

daunting *adj* **1, 2** = **intimidating,** alarming, awesome, demoralizing, disconcerting, discouraging, disheartening, frightening, off-putting (*Brit. inf.*), unnerving
Antonyms *adj* cheering, comforting, encouraging, heartening, reassuring

dauntless *adj* = **fearless,** bold, brave, courageous, daring, doughty, gallant, gritty, heroic, indomitable, intrepid, lion-hearted, resolute,

dauphine ('dɔːfiːn; *French* dofin) *or* **dauphiness** ('dɔːfɪnɪs) *n French history.* the wife of a dauphin.

davenport ('dævən,pɔːt) *n* **1** *Chiefly Brit.* a tall narrow writing desk with drawers. **2** *US & Canad.* a large sofa, esp. one convertible into a bed. [C19: sense 1 supposedly after Captain *Davenport,* who commissioned the first ones]

davit ('dævɪt, 'deɪ-) *n* a cranelike device, usually one of a pair, fitted with a tackle for suspending or lowering equipment, esp. a lifeboat. [C14: from Anglo-F *daviot,* dim. of *Davi* David]

Davy Jones *n* **1** Also called: **Davy Jones's locker.** the ocean's bottom, esp. when regarded as the grave of those lost or buried at sea. **2** the spirit of the sea. [C18: from ?]

Davy lamp *n* See **safety lamp.** [C19: after Sir H. *Davy* (1778–1829), E chemist]

daw (dɔː) *n* an archaic, dialect, or poetic name for a **jackdaw.** [C15: rel. to OHG *taha*]

dawdle ❶ ('dɔːdᵊl) *vb* **dawdles, dawdling, dawdled. 1** (*intr*) to be slow or lag behind. **2** (when *tr,* often foll. by *away*) to waste (time); trifle. [C17: from ?]
▸**'dawdler** *n*

dawn ❶ (dɔːn) *n* **1** daybreak. Related adj: **auroral. 2** the sky when light first appears in the morning. **3** the beginning of something. ◆ *vb* (*intr*) **4** to begin to grow light after the night. **5** to begin to develop or appear. **6** (usually foll. by *on* or *upon*) to begin to become apparent (to). [OE *dagian* to dawn]
▸**'dawn,like** *adj*

dawn chorus *n* the singing of large numbers of birds at dawn.

dawn raid *n Stock Exchange.* an unexpected attempt to acquire a substantial proportion of a company's shares at the start of a day's trading as a preliminary to a takeover bid.

day ❶ (deɪ) *n* **1** Also called: **civil day.** the period of time, the **calendar day,** of 24 hours' duration reckoned from one midnight to the next. **2a** the period of light between sunrise and sunset. **2b** (*as modifier*): *the day shift.* **3** the part of a day occupied with regular activity, esp. work. **4** (*sometimes pl*) a period or point in time: *in days gone by; any day now.* **5** the period of time, the **sidereal day,** during which the earth makes one complete revolution on its axis relative to a particular star. **6** the period of time, the **solar day,** during which the earth makes one complete revolution on its axis relative to the sun. **7** the period of time taken by a specified planet to make one complete rotation on its axis: *the Martian day.* **8** (*often cap.*) a day designated for a special observance: *Christmas Day.* **9** a time of success, recognition, etc.: *his day will come.* **10** a struggle or issue at hand: *the day is lost.* **11 all in a day's work.** part of one's normal activity. **12 at the end of the day.** in the final reckoning. **13 call it a day.** to stop work or other activity. **14 day after day.** without respite; relentlessly. **15 day by day.** gradually or progressively. **16 day in, day out.** every day and all day long. **17 day of rest.** the Sabbath; Sunday. **18 every dog has his day.** one's luck will come. **19 in this day and age.** nowadays. **20 that will be the day. 20a** that is most unlikely to happen. **20b** I look forward to that. ◆ Related adj: **diurnal.** ◆ See also **days.** [OE *dæg*]

Dayak ('daɪæk) *n, pl* **Dayaks** *or* **Dayak.** a variant spelling of **Dyak.**

day bed *n* a narrow bed intended for use as a seat and as a bed.

daybook ('deɪ,bʊk) *n Book-keeping.* a book in which the transactions of each day are recorded as they occur.

dayboy ('deɪ,bɔɪ) *n Brit.* a boy who attends a boarding school daily, but returns home each evening.
▸**'daygirl** *fem n*

daybreak ❶ ('deɪ,breɪk) *n* the time in the morning when light first appears; dawn; sunrise.

daycare ('deɪ,kɛə) *n Brit. social welfare.* **1** occupation, treatment, or supervision during the working day for people who might be at risk if left on their own. **2** welfare services provided by a local authority, health service, etc., during the day.

daycentre ('deɪ,sɛntə) *or* **day centre** *n Social welfare.* (in Britain) **1** a building used for daycare or other welfare services. **2** the enterprise itself, including staff, users, and organization.

daydream ❶ ('deɪ,driːm) *n* **1** a pleasant dreamlike fantasy indulged in while awake. **2** a pleasant scheme or wish that is unlikely to be fulfilled. ◆ *vb* **3** (*intr*) to indulge in idle fantasy.
▸**'day,dreamer** *n* ▸**'day,dreamy** *adj*

Day-Glo *n Trademark.* **a** a brand of fluorescent colouring materials, as of paint. **b** (*as modifier*): *Day-Glo colours.*

day labourer *n* an unskilled worker hired and paid by the day.

daylight ❶ ('deɪ,laɪt) *n* **1** light from the sun. **2** daytime. **3** daybreak. **4 see daylight. 4a** to understand something previously obscure. **4b** to realize that the end of a difficult task is approaching.

daylight robbery *n Inf.* blatant overcharging.

daylights ('deɪ,laɪts) *pl n* consciousness or wits (esp. in **scare, knock,** or **beat the (living) daylights out of someone**).

daylight-saving time *n* time set usually one hour ahead of the local standard time, widely adopted in the summer to provide extra daylight in the evening.

daylong ('deɪ,lɒŋ) *adj, adv* lasting the entire day; all day.

day release *n Brit.* a system whereby workers are released for part-time education without loss of pay.

day return *n* a reduced fare for a journey (by train, etc.) travelling both ways in one day.

day room *n* a communal living room in a residential institution such as a hospital.

days (deɪz) *adv Inf.* during the day, esp. regularly: *he works days.*

day school *n* **1** a private school taking day students only. **2** a school giving instruction during the daytime.

daytime ('deɪ,taɪm) *n* the time between dawn and dusk.

day-to-day ❶ *adj* routine; everyday.

day trip *n* a journey made to and from a place within one day.
▸**'day-,tripper** *n*

daze ❶ (deɪz) *vb* **dazes, dazing, dazed.** (*tr*) **1** to stun, esp. by a blow or shock. **2** to bewilder or amaze. ◆ *n* **3** a state of stunned confusion or shock (esp. in **in a daze**). [C14: from ON *dasa-,* as in *dasast* to grow weary]

dazzle ❶ ('dæzᵊl) *vb* **dazzles, dazzling, dazzled. 1** (*usually tr*) to blind or be blinded partially and temporarily by sudden excessive light. **2** (*tr*) to amaze, as with brilliance. ◆ *n* **3** bright light that dazzles. **4** bewilderment caused by glamour, brilliance, etc.: *the dazzle of fame.* [C15: from DAZE]
▸**'dazzler** *n* ▸**'dazzling** *adj* ▸**'dazzlingly** *adv*

dazzle gun *n* a weapon consisting of a laser gun used to dazzle enemy pilots.

dB *or* **db** *symbol for* decibel *or* decibels.

DBE *abbrev. for* Dame (Commander of the Order) of the British Empire (a Brit. title).

DBMS *abbrev. for* database management system.

DBS *abbrev. for* direct broadcasting by satellite.

dbx *or* **DBX** *n Trademark. Electronics.* a noise-reduction system that works across the full frequency spectrum.

DC *abbrev. for:* **1** *Music.* da capo. **2** direct current. Cf. **AC. 3** Also: **D.C.** District of Columbia.

DCB *abbrev. for* Dame Commander of the Order of the Bath (a Brit. title).

DCC *abbrev. for* digital compact cassette.

DCM *Brit. mil. abbrev. for* Distinguished Conduct Medal.

DD *abbrev. for:* **1** Doctor of Divinity. **2** Also: **dd.** direct debit.

THESAURUS

stouthearted, undaunted, unflinching, valiant, valorous

dawdle *vb* **1, 2** = **waste time**, dally, delay, dilly-dally (*inf.*), drag one's feet *or* heels, fritter away, hang about, idle, lag, loaf, loiter, potter, trail
Antonyms *vb* fly, get a move on (*inf.*), hasten, hurry, lose no time, make haste, rush, scoot, step on it (*inf.*)

dawdler *n* **1** = **slowcoach** (*Brit. inf.*), laggard, lingerer, loiterer, slowpoke (*US & Canad. inf.*), snail, tortoise

dawn *n* **1** = **daybreak**, aurora (*poetic*), cockcrow, crack of dawn, dawning, daylight, dayspring (*poetic*), morning, sunrise, sunup **3** = **beginning**, advent, birth, dawning, emergence, genesis, inception, onset, origin, outset, rise, start, unfolding ◆ *vb* **4** = **grow light**, break, brighten, gleam, glimmer, lighten **5** = **begin**, appear, develop, emerge, initiate, open, originate, rise, unfold **6 dawn on** *or* **upon** = **hit**, become apparent, come into one's head, come to mind, cross one's mind, flash across one's mind, occur, register (*inf.*), strike

day *n* **1** = **twenty-four hours 2a** = **daytime**, daylight, daylight hours **3** = **working day 4** = **point in time**, date, particular day, set time, time **9** = **time**, age, ascendancy, epoch, era, height, heyday, period, prime, zenith **13 call it a day** *inf.* = **stop**, end, finish, knock off (*inf.*), leave off, pack it in (*sl.*), pack up (*inf.*), shut up shop **14 day after day** = **continually**, monotonously, persistently, regularly, relentlessly **15 day by day** = **gradually**, daily, progressively, steadily

daybreak *n* = **dawn**, break of day, cockcrow, crack of dawn, dayspring (*poetic*), first light, morning, sunrise, sunup

daydream *n* **1, 2** = **fantasy**, castle in the air *or* in Spain, dream, fancy, figment of the imagination, fond hope, imagining, pipe dream, reverie, wish ◆ *vb* **3** = **fantasize**, dream, envision, fancy, hallucinate, imagine, muse, stargaze

daydreamer *n* **1, 2** = **fantasizer**, castle-builder, dreamer, pipe dreamer, visionary, Walter Mitty, wishful thinker, woolgatherer

daylight *n* **1** = **sunlight**, light of day, sunshine **2** = **daytime**, broad day, daylight hours

day-to-day *adj* = **everyday**, accustomed, customary, habitual, quotidian, regular, routine, run-of-the-mill, usual, wonted

daze *vb* **1** = **stun**, benumb, numb, paralyse, shock, stupefy **2** = **confuse**, amaze, astonish, astound, befog, bewilder, blind, dazzle, dumbfound, flabbergast (*inf.*), flummox, nonplus, perplex, stagger, startle, surprise ◆ *n* **3** = **shock**, bewilderment, confusion, distraction, mindfuck (*taboo sl.*), stupor, trance, trancelike state

dazed *adj* **1, 2** = **shocked**, at sea, baffled, bemused, bewildered, confused, disorientated, dizzy, dopey (*sl.*), flabbergasted (*inf.*), flummoxed, fuddled, groggy (*inf.*), light-headed, muddled, nonplussed, numbed, perplexed, punch-drunk, staggered, stunned, stupefied, woozy (*inf.*)

dazzle *vb* **1** = **blind**, bedazzle, blur, confuse, daze **2** = **impress**, amaze, astonish, awe, bowl over (*inf.*), fascinate, hypnotize, overawe, overpower, overwhelm, strike dumb, stupefy, take one's breath away

dazzling *adj* **2** = **splendid**, brilliant, divine, drop-dead (*sl.*), glittering, glorious, radiant, ravishing, scintillating, sensational (*inf.*), shining, sparkling, stunning, sublime, superb, virtuoso
Antonyms *adj* dull, ordinary, tedious, unexceptional, unexciting, uninspiring, uninteresting, unmemorable, unremarkable, vanilla (*sl.*)

dead *adj* **1** = **deceased**, defunct, departed, ex-

D-day *n* the day selected for the start of some operation, esp. of the Allied invasion of Europe on June 6, 1944. [C20: from *D(ay)-day*]

DDR *abbrev. for* Deutsche Demokratische Republik (the former East Germany; GDR).

DDS *or* **DDSc** *abbrev. for* Doctor of Dental Surgery *or* Science.

DDT *n* dichlorodiphenyltrichloroethane; a colourless odourless substance used as an insecticide. It is now banned in the UK.

de- *prefix forming verbs and verbal derivatives.* **1** removal of or from something: *deforest; dethrone.* **2** reversal of something: *decode; desegregate.* **3** departure from: *decamp.* [from L, from *dē* (prep) from, away from, out of, etc. In compound words of Latin origin, *de-* also means away, away from (*decease*); down (*degrade*); reversal (*detect*); removal (*defoliate*); and is used intensively (*devote*) and pejoratively (*detest*)]

deacon ('di:kən) *n Christianity.* **1** (in the Roman Catholic and other episcopal churches) an ordained minister ranking immediately below a priest. **2** (in some other churches) a lay official who assists the minister, esp. in secular affairs. [OE, ult. from Gk *diakonos* servant] ▸**'deaconate** *n* ▸**'deacon,ship** *n*

deaconess ('di:kənɪs) *n Christianity.* (in the early church and in some modern Churches) a female member of the laity with duties similar to those of a deacon.

deactivate (di:'æktɪ,veɪt) *vb* **deactivates, deactivating, deactivated. 1** (*tr*) to make (a bomb, etc.) harmless or inoperative. **2** (*intr*) to become less radioactive.
▸**de'acti,vator** *n*

dead Ⓣ (dɛd) *adj* **1a** no longer alive. **1b** (*as collective n; preceded by the*): *the dead.* **2** not endowed with life; inanimate. **3** no longer in use, effective, or relevant: *a dead issue; a dead language.* **4** unresponsive or unaware. **5** lacking in freshness or vitality. **6** devoid of physical sensation; numb. **7** resembling death: *a dead sleep.* **8** no longer burning or hot: *dead coals.* **9** (of flowers or foliage) withered; faded. **10** (*prenominal*) (intensifier): *a dead stop.* **11** *Inf.* very tired. **12** *Electronics.* **12a** drained of electric charge. **12b** not connected to a source of potential difference or electric charge. **13** lacking acoustic reverberation: *a dead sound.* **14** *Sport.* (of a ball, etc.) out of play. **15** accurate; precise (esp. in **a dead shot**). **16** lacking resilience or bounce: *a dead ball.* **17** not yielding a return: *dead capital.* **18** (of colours) not glossy or bright. **19** stagnant: *dead air.* **20** *Mil.* shielded from view, as by a geographic feature. **21 dead from the neck up.** *Inf.* stupid. **22 dead to the world.** *Inf.* unaware of one's surroundings, esp. asleep or drunk. ◆ *n* **23** a period during which coldness, darkness, etc. is at its most intense: *the dead of winter.* ◆ *adv* **24** (intensifier): *dead easy; stop dead.* **25 dead on.** exactly right. [OE *dēad*]
▸**'deadness** *n*

dead-and-alive *adj Brit.* (of a place, activity, or person) dull; uninteresting.

dead-ball line *n Rugby.* a line behind the goal line beyond which the ball is out of play.

deadbeat Ⓣ ('dɛd,bi:t) *n* **1** *Inf.* a lazy or socially undesirable person. **2** a high grade escapement used in pendulum clocks. **3** (*modifier*) without recoil.

dead beat *adj Inf.* very tired; exhausted.

dead-cat bounce *n Stock Exchange inf.* a temporary recovery in prices following a substantial fall as a result of speculators buying stocks they have already sold rather than as a result of a genuine reversal of the downward trend.

dead centre *n* **1** the exact top or bottom of the piston stroke in a reciprocating engine or pump. **2** a rod mounted in the tailstock of a lathe to support a workpiece. ◆ Also called: **dead point.**

dead duck *n Sl.* a person or thing doomed to death, failure, etc., esp. because of a mistake.

deaden Ⓣ ('dɛdᵊn) *vb* **1** to make or become less sensitive, intense, lively, etc. **2** (*tr*) to make acoustically less resonant.
▸**'deadening** *adj*

dead end *n* **1** a cul-de-sac. **2** a situation in which further progress is impossible.

deadeye ('dɛd,aɪ) *n* **1** *Naut.* either of a pair of disclike wooden blocks, supported by straps in grooves around them, between which a line is rove so as to draw them together to tighten a shroud. **2** *Inf., chiefly US.* an expert marksman.

deadfall ('dɛd,fɔ:l) *n* a trap in which a heavy weight falls to crush the prey.

deadhead ('dɛd,hɛd) *n* **1** a person who uses a free ticket, as for the theatre, etc. **2** a train, etc., travelling empty. **3** *US & Canad.* a dull person. **4** *US & Canad.* a totally or partially submerged log floating in a lake, etc. ◆ *vb* **5** (*intr*) *US & Canad.* to drive an empty bus, train, etc. **6** (*tr*) to remove dead flower heads.

Dead Heart *n* (usually preceded by *the*) *Austral.* the remote interior of Australia. [C20: from *The Dead Heart of Australia* (1906) by J. W. Gregory (1864–1932), British geologist]

dead heat *n* **a** a race or contest in which two or more participants tie for first place. **b** a tie between two or more contestants in any position.

dead leg *n Inf.* temporary loss of sensation in the leg, caused by a blow to a muscle.

dead letter *n* **1** a law or ordinance that is no longer enforced. **2** a letter that cannot be delivered or returned because it lacks adequate directions.

deadlight ('dɛd,laɪt) *n* **1** *Naut.* **1a** a bull's-eye to admit light to a cabin. **1b** a shutter for sealing off a porthole or cabin window. **2** a skylight designed not to be opened.

deadline Ⓣ ('dɛd,laɪn) *n* a time limit for any activity.

deadlock Ⓣ ('dɛd,lɒk) *n* **1** a state of affairs in which further action between two opposing forces is impossible. **2** a tie between opponents. **3** a lock having a bolt that can be opened only with a key. ◆ *vb* **4** to bring or come to a deadlock.

dead loss *n* **1** a complete loss for which no compensation is paid. **2** *Inf.* a useless person or thing.

deadly Ⓣ ('dɛdlɪ) *adj* **deadlier, deadliest. 1** likely to cause death. **2** *Inf.* extremely boring. ◆ *adv, adj* **3** like death in appearance or certainty.

deadly nightshade *n* a poisonous Eurasian plant having purple bell-shaped flowers and black berries. Also called: **belladonna, dwale.**

deadly sins *pl n* the sins of pride, covetousness, lust, envy, gluttony, anger, and sloth.

dead man's handle *or* **pedal** *n* a safety switch on a piece of machinery that allows operation only while depressed by the operator.

dead march *n* a piece of solemn funeral music played to accompany a procession.

dead-nettle *n* any of several Eurasian plants having leaves resembling nettles but lacking stinging hairs.

deadpan Ⓣ ('dɛd,pæn) *adj, adv* with a deliberately emotionless face or manner.

dead reckoning *n* a method of establishing one's position using the distance and direction travelled rather than astronomical observations.

dead set *adv* **1** absolutely: *he is dead set against going to Spain.* ◆ *n* **2** the motionless position of a dog when pointing towards game. ◆ *adj* **3** (of a hunting dog) in this position.

dead soldier *or* **marine** *n Inf.* an empty beer or spirit bottle.

dead time *n Electronics.* the time immediately following a stimulus, during which an electrical device, component, etc. is insensitive to a further stimulus.

dead weight *n* **1** a heavy weight or load. **2** an oppressive burden. **3** the difference between the loaded and the unloaded weights of a ship. **4** the intrinsic invariable weight of a structure, such as a bridge.

deadwood ('dɛd,wʊd) *n* **1** dead trees or branches. **2** *Inf.* a useless person; encumbrance.

deaf Ⓣ (dɛf) *adj* **1a** partially or totally unable to hear. **1b** (*as collective n; preceded by the*): *the deaf.* **2** refusing to heed. [OE *dēaf*]
▸**'deafness** *n*

USAGE NOTE See at **disabled.**

deaf aid *n* another name for **hearing aid.**

deaf-and-dumb *Offens.* ◆ *adj* **1** unable to hear or speak. ◆ *n* **2** a deaf-mute person.

deafblind ('dɛf,blaɪnd) *adj* **a** unable to hear or ssee. **b** (*as collective n; preceded by the*): *the deafblind.*

USAGE NOTE See at **disabled.**

THESAURUS

tinct, gone, late, passed away, perished, pushing up (the) daisies **2** = **inanimate**, lifeless **3** = **not working**, barren, inactive, inoperative, obsolete, stagnant, sterile, still, unemployed, unprofitable, useless **5** = **spiritless**, apathetic, callous, cold, dull, frigid, glassy, glazed, indifferent, lukewarm, torpid, unresponsive, wooden **6** = **numb**, inert, paralysed **10** = **total**, absolute, complete, downright, entire, outright, thorough, unqualified, utter **11** *inf.* = **exhausted**, dead beat (*inf.*), spent, tired, worn out ◆ *n* **23** = **middle**, depth, midst ◆ *adv* **24** *inf.* = **exactly**, absolutely, completely, directly, entirely, totally

Antonyms *adj* ≠ **deceased:** alive, alive and kicking, animate, existing, living ≠ **inanimate:** animated, lively, responsive ≠ **not working:** active, alive, effective, in use, operative, productive, working ≠ **spiritless:** active, alive, alive and kicking, animated, full of beans (*inf.*), lively, vivacious

deadbeat *n* **1** *Inf., chiefly US & Canad.* = **layabout**, bum (*inf.*), cadger, drone, freeloader, good-for-nothing, idler, loafer, lounger, parasite, scrounger (*inf.*), skiver (*Brit. sl.*), slacker (*inf.*), sponge (*inf.*), sponger (*inf.*), waster, wastrel

deaden *vb* **1, 2** = **reduce**, abate, alleviate, anaesthetize, benumb, blunt, check, cushion, damp, dampen, diminish, dull, hush, impair, lessen, muffle, mute, numb, paralyse, quieten, smother, stifle, suppress, weaken

deadline *n* = **time limit**, cutoff point, limit, target date

deadlock *n* **1, 2** = **impasse**, cessation, dead heat, draw, full stop, gridlock, halt, stalemate, standoff, standstill, tie

deadly *adj* **1** = **lethal**, baleful, baneful, dangerous, death-dealing, deathly, destructive, fatal, malignant, mortal, noxious, pernicious, poisonous, venomous **2** *Informal* = **boring**, as dry as dust, dull, ho-hum (*inf.*), mind-numbing, monotonous, tedious, tiresome, uninteresting, wearisome **3** = **deathly**, ashen, deathlike, ghastly, ghostly, pallid, wan, white

deadpan *adj* = **expressionless**, blank, empty, impassive, inexpressive, inscrutable, poker-faced, straight-faced

deaf *adj* **1** = **hard of hearing**, stone deaf, without hearing **2** = **oblivious**, indifferent, unconcerned, unhearing, unmoved

deafen ➊ ('dɛfᵊn) *vb* (*tr*) to make deaf, esp. momentarily, as by a loud noise.
▸ **'deafening** *adj* ▸ **'deafeningly** *adv*

deaf-mute *n* **1** a person who is unable to hear or speak. See also **mute** (sense 7). ◆ *adj* **2** unable to hear or speak. [C19: translation of F *sourd-muet*]

deal[1] ➊ (di:l) *vb* **deals, dealing, dealt. 1** (*intr;* foll. by *in*) to engage in commercially: *to deal in upholstery.* **2** (often foll. by *out*) to apportion or distribute. **3** (*tr*) to give (a blow, etc.) to (someone); inflict. **4** (*intr*) *Sl.* to sell any illegal drug. ◆ *n* **5** *Inf.* a bargain, transaction, or agreement. **6** a particular type of treatment received, esp. as the result of an agreement: *a fair deal.* **7** an indefinite amount (esp. in **good** *or* **great deal**). **8** *Cards.* **8a** the process of distributing the cards. **8b** a player's turn to do this. **8c** a single round in a card game. **9 big deal.** *Sl.* an important person, event, or matter: often used sarcastically. ◆ See also **deal with.** [OE *dǣlan,* from *dǣl* a part; cf. OHG *teil* a part, ON *deild* a share]

deal[2] (di:l) *n* **1** a plank of softwood timber, such as fir or pine, or such planks collectively. **2** the sawn wood of various coniferous trees. ◆ *adj* **3** of fir or pine. [C14: from MLow G *dele* plank]

dealer ➊ ('di:lə) *n* **1** a person or firm engaged in commercial purchase and sale; trader: *a car dealer.* **2** *Cards.* the person who distributes the cards. **3** *Sl.* a person who sells illegal drugs.

dealings ➊ ('di:lɪŋz) *pl n* (*sometimes sing*) transactions or business relations.

dealt (dɛlt) *vb* the past tense and past participle of **deal**[1].

deal with ➊ *vb* (*tr, adv*) **1** to take action on: *to deal with each problem in turn.* **2** to punish: *the headmaster will deal with the culprit.* **3** to treat or be concerned with: *the book deals with architecture.* **4** to conduct onself (towards others), esp. with regard to fairness. **5** to do business with.

dean (di:n) *n* **1** the chief administrative official of a college or university faculty. **2** (at Oxford and Cambridge universities) a college fellow with responsibility for undergraduate discipline. **3** *Chiefly Church of England.* the head of a chapter of canons and administrator of a cathedral or collegiate church. **4** *RC Church.* the cardinal bishop senior by consecration and head of the college of cardinals. Related adj: **decanal.** See also **rural dean.** [C14: from OF *deien,* from LL *decānus* one set over ten persons, from L *decem* ten]

deanery ('di:nərɪ) *n, pl* **deaneries. 1** the office or residence of a dean. **2** the group of parishes presided over by a rural dean.

dear ➊ (dɪə) *adj* **1** beloved; precious. **2** used in conventional forms of address, as in *Dear Sir.* **3** (*postpositive;* foll. by *to*) important; close. **4a** highly priced. **4b** charging high prices. **5** appealing. **6 for dear life.** with extreme vigour or desperation. ◆ *interj* **7** used in exclamations of surprise or dismay, such as *Oh dear!* ◆ *n* **8** Also: **dearest.** (*often used in direct address*) someone regarded with affection and tenderness. ◆ *adv* **9** dearly. [OE *dēore*]
▸ **'dearness** *n*

dearly ➊ ('dɪəlɪ) *adv* **1** very much. **2** affectionately. **3** at a great cost.

dearth ➊ (dɜ:θ) *n* an inadequate amount, esp. of food; scarcity. [C13 *derthe,* from *dēr* DEAR]

deary *or* **dearie** ('dɪərɪ) *n* **1** (*pl* **dearies**) *Inf.* a term of affection: now often sarcastic or facetious. **2 deary** *or* **dearie me!** an exclamation of surprise or dismay.

death ➊ (dɛθ) *n* **1** the permanent end of all functions of life in an organism. **2** an instance of this: *his death ended an era.* **3** a murder or killing. **4** termination or destruction. **5** a state of affairs or an experience considered as terrible as death. **6** a cause or source of death. **7** (*usually cap.*) a personification of death, usually a skeleton or an old man holding a scythe. **8 at death's door.** likely to die soon. **9 catch one's death (of cold).** *Inf.* to contract a severe cold. **10 do to death. 10a** to kill. **10b** to overuse. **11 in at the death. 11a** present when a hunted animal is killed. **11b** present at the finish or climax. **12 like death warmed up.** *Inf.* very ill. **13 like grim death.** as if afraid of one's life. **14 put to death.** to kill deliberately or execute. **15 to death. 15a** until dead. **15b** very much. ◆ Related adjs.: **fatal, lethal, mortal.** [OE *dēath*]

death adder *n* a venomous thick-bodied Australian snake.

deathbed ('dɛθ,bɛd) *n* the bed in which a person is about to die.

deathblow ➊ ('dɛθ,bləʊ) *n* a thing or event that destroys life or hope, esp. suddenly.

death camp *n* a concentration camp in which the conditions are so brutal that few prisoners survive, or one to which prisoners are sent for execution.

death cap *or* **angel** *n* a poisonous woodland fungus with white gills and a cuplike structure at the base of the stalk.

death certificate *n* a legal document issued by a qualified medical practitioner certifying the death of a person and stating the cause if known.

death duty *n* a tax on property inheritances, in Britain replaced by capital transfer tax in 1975 and since 1986 by inheritance tax. Also called: **estate duty.**

death futures *pl n* life insurance policies of terminally ill people that are bought speculatively for a lump sum by a company, enabling it to collect the proceeds of the policies when the ill people die.

death knell *or* **bell** *n* **1** something that heralds death or destruction. **2** a bell rung to announce a death.

deathless ➊ ('dɛθlɪs) *adj* immortal, esp. because of greatness; everlasting.
▸ **'deathlessness** *n*

deathly ➊ ('dɛθlɪ) *adj* **1** deadly. **2** resembling death: *a deathly quiet.*

death mask *n* a cast of a dead person's face.

death rate *n* the ratio of deaths in a specified area, group, etc., to the population of that area, group, etc. Also called: **mortality rate.**

death rattle *n* a low-pitched gurgling sound sometimes made by a dying person.

death's-head *n* a human skull or a representation of one.

death's-head moth *n* a European hawk moth having markings resembling a human skull on its upper thorax.

death star *n* a weapon consisting of a flat star-shaped piece of metal with sharpened points that is thrown at an opponent. Also called: **throwing star.**

deathtrap ('dɛθ,træp) *n* a building, vehicle, etc., that is considered very unsafe.

death warrant *n* **1** the official authorization for carrying out a sentence of death. **2 sign one's (own) death warrant.** to cause one's own destruction.

deathwatch ('dɛθ,wɒtʃ) *n* **1** a vigil held beside a dying or dead person. **2 deathwatch beetle.** a beetle whose woodboring larvae are a serious pest. The adult produces a tapping sound that was once supposed to presage death.

death wish *n* (in Freudian psychology) the desire for self-annihilation.

deb (dɛb) *n Inf.* short for **debutante.**

debacle ➊ (deɪ'bɑ:kᵊl, dɪ-) *n* **1** a sudden disastrous collapse or defeat; rout. **2** the breaking up of ice in a river, often causing flooding. **3** a violent rush of water carrying along debris. [C19: from F, from OF *desbacler* to unbolt]

debag (di:'bæg) *vb* **debags, debagging, debagged.** (*tr*) *Brit. sl.* to remove the trousers from (someone) by force.

debar ➊ (dɪ'bɑ:) *vb* **debars, debarring, debarred.** (*tr;* usually foll. by *from*) to exclude from a place, a right, etc.; bar.
▸ **de'barment** *n*

> **USAGE NOTE** See at **disbar.**

THESAURUS

deafen *vb* = **make deaf**, din, drown out, split *or* burst the eardrums

deafening *adj* = **ear-piercing**, booming, dinning, ear-splitting, intense, overpowering, piercing, resounding, ringing, thunderous

deal[1] *vb* **1** = **sell**, bargain, buy and sell, do business, negotiate, stock, trade, traffic **2** = **distribute**, allot, apportion, assign, bestow, dispense, divide, dole out, give, mete out, reward, share ◆ *n* **1** *Informal* = **agreement**, arrangement, bargain, contract, pact, transaction, understanding **7** = **amount**, degree, distribution, extent, portion, quantity, share, transaction **8** = **hand**, cut and shuffle, distribution, round, single game

dealer *n* **1** = **trader**, chandler, marketer, merchandiser, merchant, purveyor, supplier, tradesman, wholesaler

dealings *pl n* = **business**, business relations, commerce, trade, traffic, transactions, truck

deal with *vb* **1** = **handle**, attend to, come to grips with, cope with, get to grips with, manage, oversee, see to, take care of, treat **3** = **be concerned with**, consider, treat of **4** = **behave towards**, act towards, conduct oneself towards

dear *adj* **1** = **beloved**, cherished, close, darling, esteemed, familiar, favourite, intimate, precious, prized, respected, treasured **4** = **expensive**, at a premium, costly, high-priced, overpriced, pricey (*inf.*) **6 for dear life** = **desperately**, for all one is worth, intensely, quickly, urgently, vigorously ◆ *n* **8** = **beloved**, angel, darling, loved one, precious, treasure ◆ *adv* **9** = **dearly**, at a heavy cost, at a high price, at great cost
Antonyms *adj* ≠ **beloved:** disliked, hated ≠ **expensive:** cheap, common, inexpensive, worthless

dearly *adv* **1** = **very much**, extremely, greatly, profoundly **3** = **at great cost**, at a heavy cost, at a high price, dear

dearth *n* = **scarcity**, absence, deficiency, exiguousness, famine, inadequacy, insufficiency, lack, need, paucity, poverty, scantiness, shortage, sparsity, want

death *n* **1** = **dying**, bereavement, cessation, curtains (*inf.*), decease, demise, departure, dissolution, end, exit, expiration, loss, passing, quietus, release **4** = **destruction**, annihilation, downfall, ending, eradication, extermination, extinction, finish, grave, obliteration, ruin, ruination, undoing **7** *sometimes capital* = **grim reaper**, Dark Angel
Antonyms *n* ≠ **dying:** birth ≠ **destruction:** beginning, emergence, genesis, growth, origin, rise, source

deathblow *n* = **finishing stroke**, clincher (*inf.*), *coup de grâce*, kill, knockout blow *or* punch, lethal *or* mortal blow, quietus

deathless *adj* = **eternal**, everlasting, immortal, imperishable, incorruptible, timeless, undying
Antonyms *adj* corporeal, earthly, ephemeral, human, mortal, passing, temporal, transient, transitory

deathly *adj* **1** = **fatal**, deadly, extreme, intense, mortal, terrible **2** = **deathlike**, cadaverous, gaunt, ghastly, grim, haggard, like death warmed up (*inf.*), pale, pallid, wan

debacle *n* **1** = **disaster**, catastrophe, collapse, defeat, devastation, downfall, fiasco, havoc, overthrow, reversal, rout, ruin, ruination

debar *vb* = **bar**, black, blackball, deny, exclude, hinder, interdict, keep out, obstruct, preclude, prevent, prohibit, refuse admission to, restrain, segregate, shut out, stop

debark[1] (dɪˈbɑːk) *vb* another word for **disembark.** [C17: from F *débarquer,* from *dé-* DIS-[1] + *barque* BARQUE]
▸**debarkation** (ˌdiːbɑːˈkeɪʃən) *n*

debark[2] (diːˈbɑːk) *vb* (*tr*) to remove the bark from (a tree). [C18: from DE-+ BARK[2]]

debase ⓘ (dɪˈbeɪs) *vb* **debases, debasing, debased.** (*tr*) to lower in quality, character, or value; adulterate. [C16: see DE-, BASE[2]]
▸**deˈbasement** *n* ▸**deˈbaser** *n*

debate ⓘ (dɪˈbeɪt) *n* **1** a formal discussion, as in a legislative body, in which opposing arguments are put forward. **2** discussion or dispute. **3** the formal presentation and opposition of a specific motion, followed by a vote. ◆ *vb* **debates, debating, debated. 4** to discuss (a motion, etc.), esp. in a formal assembly. **5** to deliberate upon (something). [C13: from OF *debatre* to discuss, argue, from L *battuere*]
▸**deˈbatable** *adj* ▸**deˈbater** *n*

debauch ⓘ (dɪˈbɔːtʃ) *vb* **1** (when *tr, usually passive*) to lead into a life of depraved self-indulgence. **2** (*tr*) to seduce (a woman). ◆ *n* **3** an instance or period of extreme dissipation. [C16: from OF *desbaucher* to corrupt, lit.: to shape (timber) roughly, from *bauch* beam, of Gmc origin]
▸**deˈbaucher** *n* ▸**deˈbauchery** *n*

debauchee (ˌdɛbɔːˈtʃiː) *n* a man who leads a life of promiscuity and self-indulgence.

debenture (dɪˈbɛntʃə) *n* **1** a long-term bond, bearing fixed interest and usually unsecured, issued by a company or governmental agency. **2** a certificate acknowledging a debt. **3** a customs certificate providing for a refund of excise or import duty. [C15: from L *dēbentur mihi* there are owed to me, from *dēbēre*]
▸**deˈbentured** *adj*

debenture stock *n* shares issued by a company, which guarantee a fixed return at regular intervals.

debilitate ⓘ (dɪˈbɪlɪˌteɪt) *vb* **debilitates, debilitating, debilitated.** (*tr*) to make feeble; weaken. [C16: from L, from *dēbilis* weak]
▸**deˌbiliˈtation** *n* ▸**deˈbilitative** *adj*

debility ⓘ (dɪˈbɪlɪtɪ) *n, pl* **debilities.** weakness or infirmity.

debit (ˈdɛbɪt) *n* **1a** acknowledgment of a sum owing by entry on the left side of an account. **1b** the left side of an account. **1c** an entry on this side. **1d** the total of such entries. **1e** (*as modifier*): *a debit balance.* ◆ *vb* **debits, debiting, debited. 2** (*tr*) **2a** to record (an item) as a debit in an account. **2b** to charge (a person or his account) with a debt. [C15: from L *dēbitum* DEBT]

debit card *n* a card issued by a bank or building society enabling customers to pay for goods or services by inserting it into a computer-controlled device at the place of sale, which is connected through the telephone network to the bank or building society.

debonair ⓘ *or* **debonnaire** (ˌdɛbəˈnɛə) *adj* **1** suave and refined. **2** carefree; light-hearted. **3** courteous and cheerful. [C13: from OF, from *de bon aire* having a good disposition]
▸ˌ**deboˈnairly** *adv* ▸ˌ**deboˈnairness** *n*

debouch (dɪˈbaʊtʃ) *vb* (*intr*) **1** (esp. of troops) to move into a more open space. **2** (of a river, glacier, etc.) to flow into a larger area or body. [C18: from F *déboucher,* from *dé-* DIS-[1] + *bouche* mouth]
▸**deˈbouchment** *n*

Debrett (dəˈbrɛt) *n* a list, considered exclusive, of the British aristocracy. In full: **Debrett's Peerage.** [C19: after J. *Debrett* (c 1750-1822), London publisher who first issued it]

debrief ⓘ (diːˈbriːf) *vb* (*tr*) to elicit a report from (a soldier, diplomat, etc.) after a mission or event.
▸**deˈbriefing** *n*

debris ⓘ *or* **débris** (ˈdeɪbrɪ, ˈdɛbrɪ) *n* **1** fragments of something destroyed or broken; rubble. **2** a collection of loose material derived from rocks, or an accumulation of animal or vegetable matter. [C18: from F, from obs. *debrisier* to break into pieces, of Celtic origin]

debt ⓘ (dɛt) *n* **1** something owed, such as money, goods, or services. **2 bad debt.** a debt that has little prospect of being paid. **3** an obligation to pay or perform something. **4** the state of owing something, or of being under an obligation (esp. in **in debt, in (someone's) debt**). [C13: from OF *dette,* from L *dēbitum,* from *dēbēre* to owe, from DE- + *habēre* to have]

debt collector *n* a person employed to collect debts for creditors.

debt of honour *n* a debt that is morally but not legally binding.

debtor ⓘ (ˈdɛtə) *n* a person or commercial enterprise that owes a financial obligation.

debt swap *n* See **swap** (sense 4).

debud (diːˈbʌd) *vb* **debuds, debudding, debudded.** another word for **disbud.**

debug (diːˈbʌg) *vb* **debugs, debugging, debugged.** (*tr*) *Inf.* **1** to locate and remove concealed microphones from (a room, etc.). **2** to locate and remove defects in (a device, system, plan, etc.). **3** to remove insects from. [C20: from DE- + BUG]

debunk ⓘ (diːˈbʌŋk) *vb* (*tr*) *Inf.* to expose the pretensions or falseness of, esp. by ridicule. [C20: from DE- + BUNK[2]]
▸**deˈbunker** *n*

debus (diːˈbʌs) *vb* **debuses, debusing, debused** *or* **debusses, debussing, debussed.** to unload (goods, etc.) or (esp. of troops) to alight from a bus.

debut ⓘ (ˈdeɪbjuː, ˈdɛbjuː) *n* **1a** the first public appearance of an actor, musician, etc. **1b** (*as modifier*): *debut album.* **2** the presentation of a debutante. [C18: from F, from OF *desbuter* to play first, from *des-* DE- + *but* goal, target]

debutante (ˈdɛbjʊˌtɑːnt, -ˌtænt) *n* **1** a young upper-class woman who is formally presented to society. **2** a young woman regarded as being upper-class, wealthy, and frivolous. [C19: from F, from *débuter* to lead off in a game, make one's first appearance; see DEBUT]

dec. *abbrev. for:* **1** deceased. **2** decimal. **3** decimetre. **4** declaration. **5** declension. **6** declination. **7** decrease. **8** *Music.* decrescendo.

Dec. *abbrev. for* December.

deca-, deka- *or before a vowel* **dec-, dek-** *prefix* denoting ten: *decagon.* In conjunction with scientific units the symbol **da** is used. [from Gk *deka*]

decade (ˈdɛkeɪd, dɪˈkeɪd) *n* **1** a period of ten years. **2** a group of ten. [C15: from OF, from LL, from Gk, from *deka* ten]
▸**deˈcadal** *adj*

decadence ⓘ (ˈdɛkədəns) *or* **decadency** *n* **1** deterioration, esp. of morality or culture. **2** the state reached through such a process. **3** (*often cap.*) the period or style associated with the 19th-century decadents. [C16: from F, from Med. L *dēcadentia,* lit.: a falling away; see DECAY]

decadent ⓘ (ˈdɛkədənt) *adj* **1** characterized by decline, as in being self-indulgent or morally corrupt. **2** belonging to a period of decline in artistic standards. ◆ *n* **3** a decadent person. **4** (*often cap.*) one of a group of French and English writers of the late 19th century whose works were characterized by refinement of style and a tendency toward the artificial and abnormal.

decaf (ˈdiːkæf) *Inf.* ◆ *n* **1** decaffeinated coffee. ◆ *adj* **2** decaffeinated.

decaffeinate (dɪˈkæfɪˌneɪt) *vb* **decaffeinates, decaffeinating, decaffeinated.** (*tr*) to remove all or part of the caffeine from (coffee, tea, etc.).

decagon (ˈdɛkəˌgɒn) *n* a polygon having ten sides.
▸**decagonal** (dɪˈkægənᵊl) *adj*

THESAURUS

debase *vb* = **degrade**, abase, cheapen, demean, devalue, disgrace, dishonour, drag down, humble, humiliate, lower, reduce, shame = **contaminate**, adulterate, bastardize, corrupt, defile, depreciate, impair, pollute, taint, vitiate
Antonyms *vb* ≠ **degrade:** elevate, enhance, exalt, improve, uplift ≠ **contaminate:** purify

debased *adj* = **degraded**, abandoned, base, corrupt, debauched, depraved, devalued, fallen, low, perverted, sordid, vile = **contaminated**, adulterated, depreciated, impure, lowered, mixed, polluted, reduced
Antonyms *adj* ≠ **degraded:** chaste, decent, ethical, good, honourable, incorruptible, innocent, moral, pure, upright, virtuous ≠ **contaminated:** pure

debasement *n* **1** = **degradation**, abasement, baseness, corruption, depravation, devaluation, perversion **1** = **contamination**, adulteration, depreciation, pollution, reduction

debatable *adj* **4, 5** = **doubtful**, arguable, borderline, controversial, disputable, dubious, iffy (*inf.*), in dispute, moot, open to question, problematical, questionable, uncertain, undecided, unsettled

debate *n* **1** = **consideration**, cogitation, deliberation, meditation, reflection **2** = **discussion**, altercation, argument, contention, controversy, disputation, dispute, polemic, row ◆ *vb* **4** = **discuss**, argue, contend, contest, controvert, dispute, question, wrangle **5** = **consider**, cogitate, deliberate, meditate upon, mull over, ponder, reflect, revolve, ruminate, weigh

debauched *adj* **1** = **corrupt**, abandoned, debased, degenerate, degraded, depraved, dissipated, dissolute, immoral, licentious, perverted, profligate, sleazy, wanton

debauchery *n* **3** = **depravity**, carousal, dissipation, dissoluteness, excess, gluttony, incontinence, indulgence, intemperance, lewdness, licentiousness, lust, orgy, overindulgence, revel

debilitate *vb* = **weaken**, devitalize, enervate, enfeeble, exhaust, incapacitate, prostrate, relax, sap, undermine, wear out
Antonyms *vb* animate, brighten, energize, enliven, excite, fire, invigorate, pep up, perk up, rouse, stimulate, vitalize, wake up

debilitating *adj* = **weakening**, devitalizing, draining, enervating, enfeebling, exhausting, fatiguing, incapacitating, sapping, tiring, wearing, wearisome
Antonyms *adj* animating, energizing, enlivening, exciting, invigorating, rousing, stimulating, vitalizing

debility *n* = **weakness**, decrepitude, enervation, enfeeblement, exhaustion, faintness, feebleness, frailty, incapacity, infirmity, languor, malaise, sickliness

debonair *adj* **1-3** = **elegant**, affable, buoyant, charming, cheerful, courteous, dashing, jaunty, light-hearted, refined, smooth, sprightly, suave, urbane, well-bred

debrief *vb* = **interrogate**, cross-examine, examine, probe, question, quiz

debris *n* **1, 2** = **remains**, bits, brash, detritus, dross, fragments, litter, pieces, rubbish, rubble, ruins, waste, wreck, wreckage

debt *n* **1** = **debit**, arrears, bill, claim, commitment, due, duty, liability, obligation, score **4 in debt** = **owing**, accountable, beholden, in arrears, in hock (*inf., chiefly US*), in the red (*inf.*), liable, responsible

debtor *n* = **borrower**, defaulter, insolvent, mortgagor

debunk *vb Informal* = **expose**, cut down to size, deflate, disparage, lampoon, mock, puncture, ridicule, show up

debut *n* **1a** = **introduction**, beginning, bow, coming out, entrance, first appearance, inauguration, initiation, launching, presentation

decadence *n* **1, 2** = **degeneration**, corruption, debasement, decay, decline, deterioration, dissipation, dissolution, fall, perversion, retrogression

decadent *adj* **1** = **degenerate**, abandoned, corrupt, debased, debauched, decaying, declining, degraded, depraved, dissolute, immoral, self-indulgent
Antonyms *adj* decent, ethical, good, high-minded, honourable, incorruptible, moral, principled, proper, upright, upstanding, virtuous

decahedron (ˌdɛkəˈhiːdrən) *n* a solid figure having ten plane faces.
▸ˌ**decaˈhedral** *adj*

decal (dɪˈkæl, ˈdiːkæl) *n* **1** short for **decalcomania.** ◆ *vb* **decals, decalling, decalled** *or US* **decals, decaling, decaled. 2** to transfer (a design, etc.) by decalcomania.

decalcify (diːˈkælsɪˌfaɪ) *vb* **decalcifies, decalcifying, decalcified.** (*tr*) to remove calcium or lime from (bones, etc.).
▸**deˈcalciˌfier** *n*

decalcomania (dɪˌkælkəˈmeɪnɪə) *n* **1** the process of transferring a design from prepared paper onto another surface, such as glass or paper. **2** a design so transferred. [C19: from F, from *décalquer*, from *de-* DE- + *calquer* to trace + *-manie* -MANIA]

decalitre *or US* **decaliter** (ˈdɛkəˌliːtə) *n* a metric measure of volume equivalent to 10 litres.

Decalogue (ˈdɛkəˌlɒg) *n* another name for the **Ten Commandments.** [C14: from Church L *decalogus*, from Gk, from *deka* ten + *logos* word]

decametre *or US* **decameter** (ˈdɛkəˌmiːtə) *n* a metric measure of length equivalent to 10 metres.

decamp ⓘ (dɪˈkæmp) *vb* (*intr*) **1** to leave a camp; break camp. **2** to depart secretly or suddenly; abscond.
▸**deˈcampment** *n*

decanal (dɪˈkeɪnᵊl) *adj* **1** of a dean or deanery. **2** on the same side of a cathedral, etc., as the dean; on the S side of the choir. [C18: from Med. L *decānālis*, *decānus* DEAN]

decani (dɪˈkeɪnaɪ) *adj, adv Music.* to be sung by the decanal side of a choir. Cf. **cantoris.** [L: genitive of *decānus*]

decant ⓘ (dɪˈkænt) *vb* **1** to pour (a liquid, such as wine) from one container to another, esp. without disturbing any sediment. **2** (*tr*) to rehouse (people) while their homes are being rebuilt or refurbished. [C17: from Med. L *dēcanthāre*, from *canthus* spout, rim]

decanter (dɪˈkæntə) *n* a stoppered bottle, into which a drink is poured for serving.

decapitate ⓘ (dɪˈkæpɪˌteɪt) *vb* **decapitates, decapitating, decapitated.** (*tr*) to behead. [C17: from LL *dēcapitāre*, from L DE- + *caput* head]
▸**deˌcapiˈtation** *n* ▸**deˈcapiˌtator** *n*

decapod (ˈdɛkəˌpɒd) *n* **1** any crustacean having five pairs of walking limbs, as a crab, lobster, shrimp, etc. **2** any cephalopod mollusc having eight short tentacles and two longer ones, as a squid or cuttlefish.
▸**decapodal** (dɪˈkæpədᵊl), **deˈcapodan,** *or* **deˈcapodous** *adj*

decarbonate (diːˈkɑːbəˌneɪt) *vb* **decarbonates, decarbonating, decarbonated.** (*tr*) to remove carbon dioxide from.
▸**deˌcarbonˈation** *n* ▸**deˈcarbonˌator** *n*

decarbonize *or* **decarbonise** (diːˈkɑːbəˌnaɪz) *vb* **decarbonizes, decarbonizing, decarbonized** *or* **decarbonises, decarbonising, decarbonised.** (*tr*) to remove carbon from (an internal-combustion engine, etc.). Also: **decoke, decarburize.**
▸**deˌcarboniˈzation** *or* **deˌcarboniˈsation** *n* ▸**deˈcarbonˌizer** *or* **deˈcarbonˌiser** *n*

decarboxylase (ˌdiːkɑːˈbɒksɪˌleɪz) *n* an enzyme that catalyses the removal of carbon dioxide from a compound.

decastyle (ˈdɛkəˌstaɪl) *n Archit.* a portico consisting of ten columns.

decasyllable (ˈdɛkəˌsɪləbᵊl) *n* a word or line of verse consisting of ten syllables.
▸**decasyllabic** (ˌdɛkəsɪˈlæbɪk) *adj*

decathlon (dɪˈkæθlɒn) *n* an athletic contest in which each athlete competes in ten different events. [C20: from DECA- + Gk *athlon* contest, prize; see ATHLETE]
▸**deˈcathlete** *n*

decay ⓘ (dɪˈkeɪ) *vb* **1** to decline or cause to decline gradually in health, prosperity, excellence, etc.; deteriorate. **2** to rot or cause to rot; decompose. **3** (*intr*) Also: **disintegrate.** *Physics.* **3a** (of an atomic nucleus) to undergo radioactive disintegration. **3b** (of an elementary particle) to transform into two or more different elementary particles. **4** (*intr*) *Physics.* (of a stored charge, magnetic flux, etc.) to decrease gradually when the source of energy has been removed. ◆ *n* **5** the process of decline, as in health, mentality, etc. **6** the state brought about by this process. **7** decomposition. **8** rotten or decayed matter. **9** *Physics.* **9a** See **radioactive decay. 9b** a spontaneous transformation of an elementary particle into two or more different particles. **10** *Physics.* a gradual decrease of a stored charge, current, etc., when the source of energy has been removed. [C15: from OF *decaïr*, from LL *dēcadere*, lit.: to fall away, from L *cadere* to fall]
▸**deˈcayable** *adj*

decease ⓘ (dɪˈsiːs) *n* **1** a more formal word for **death.** ◆ *vb* **deceases, deceasing, deceased. 2** (*intr*) a more formal word for **die**[1]. [C14 (n): from OF, from L *dēcēdere* to depart]

deceased ⓘ (dɪˈsiːst) *adj* **a** a more formal word for **dead** (sense 1). **b** (*as n; preceded by the*): *the deceased.*

deceit ⓘ (dɪˈsiːt) *n* **1** the act or practice of deceiving. **2** a statement, act, or device intended to mislead; fraud; trick. **3** a tendency to deceive. [C13: from OF, from *deceivre* to DECEIVE]

deceitful ⓘ (dɪˈsiːtfʊl) *adj* full of deceit.

deceive ⓘ (dɪˈsiːv) *vb* **deceives, deceiving, deceived.** (*tr*) **1** to mislead by deliberate misrepresentation or lies. **2** to delude (oneself). **3** to be unfaithful to (one's sexual partner). **4** *Arch.* to disappoint. [C13: from OF *deceivre*, from L *dēcipere* to ensnare, cheat, from *capere* to take]
▸**deˈceivable** *adj* ▸**deˈceiver** *n*

decelerate ⓘ (diːˈsɛləˌreɪt) *vb* **decelerates, decelerating, decelerated.** to slow down or cause to slow down. [C19: from DE- + (AC)CELERATE]
▸**deˌcelerˈation** *n* ▸**deˈcelerˌator** *n*

December (dɪˈsɛmbə) *n* the twelfth month of the year, consisting of 31 days. [C13: from OF, from L: the tenth month (the Roman year orig. began with March), from *decem* ten]

decencies (ˈdiːsᵊnsɪz) *pl n* **1 the.** those things that are considered necessary for a decent life. **2** another word for **proprieties,** see **propriety** (sense 3).

decency ⓘ (ˈdiːsᵊnsɪ) *n, pl* **decencies. 1** conformity to the prevailing standards of propriety, morality, modesty, etc. **2** the quality of being decent.

decennial (dɪˈsɛnɪəl) *adj* **1** lasting for ten years. **2** occurring every ten years. ◆ *n* **3** a tenth anniversary.
▸**deˈcennially** *adv*

decent ⓘ (ˈdiːsᵊnt) *adj* **1** polite or respectable. **2** proper and suitable; fitting. **3** conforming to conventions of sexual behaviour; not indecent. **4** free of oaths, blasphemy, etc. **5** good or adequate: *a decent wage.* **6** *Inf.* kind; generous. **7** *Inf.* sufficiently clothed to be seen by other people: *are you decent?* [C16: from L *decēns* suitable, from *decēre* to be fitting]
▸**ˈdecently** *adv*

decentralize *or* **decentralise** (diːˈsɛntrəˌlaɪz) *vb* **decentralizes, decentralizing, decentralized** *or* **decentralises, decentralising, decentralised. 1** to reorganize into smaller more autonomous units. **2** to disperse (a concentration, as of industry or population).
▸**deˈcentralist** *n, adj* ▸**deˌcentraliˈzation** *or* **deˌcentraliˈsation** *n*

deception ⓘ (dɪˈsɛpʃən) *n* **1** the act of deceiving or the state of being deceived. **2** something that deceives; trick.

THESAURUS

decamp *vb* **1** *Military* = **strike camp,** break up camp, evacuate, march off, move off, vacate **2** = **make off,** abscond, bolt, desert, do a bunk (*Brit. sl.*), do a runner (*sl.*), escape, flee, flit (*inf.*), fly, fly the coop (*US & Canad. inf.*), hightail (*inf., chiefly US*), hook it (*sl.*), run away, scarper (*Brit. sl.*), skedaddle (*inf.*), sneak off, steal away, take a powder (*US & Canad. sl.*), take it on the lam (*US & Canad. sl.*)

decant *vb* **1** = **pour out,** drain, draw off, tap

decapitate *vb* = **behead,** execute, guillotine

decay *vb* **1** = **decline,** atrophy, break down, crumble, degenerate, deteriorate, disintegrate, dissolve, dwindle, moulder, shrivel, sink, spoil, wane, waste away, wear away, wither **2** = **rot,** corrode, decompose, mortify, perish, putrefy ◆ *n* **5** = **decline,** atrophy, collapse, decadence, degeneracy, degeneration, deterioration, dying, fading, failing, wasting, withering **7** = **rot,** caries, cariosity, decomposition, gangrene, mortification, perishing, putrefaction, putrescence, putridity, rotting
Antonyms *vb* ≠ **decline:** expand, flourish, flower, grow, increase ◆ *n* ≠ **decline:** growth

decayed *adj* **1, 2** = **rotten,** bad, carious, carrion, corroded, decomposed, perished, putrefied, putrid, rank, spoiled, wasted, withered

decaying 1, 2 *adj* = **rotting,** crumbling, deteriorating, disintegrating, gangrenous, perishing, putrefacient, wasting away, wearing away

decease *n Formal* **1** = **death,** demise, departure, dissolution, dying, release

deceased *adj* **a** = **dead,** defunct, departed, expired, finished, former, gone, late, lifeless, lost, pushing up daisies

deceit *n* **1** = **dishonesty,** artifice, cheating, chicanery, craftiness, cunning, deceitfulness, deception, dissimulation, double-dealing, duplicity, fraud, fraudulence, guile, hypocrisy, imposition, lying, pretence, slyness, treachery, trickery, underhandedness **2** = **lie,** artifice, blind, cheat, chicanery, deception, duplicity, fake, feint, fraud, imposture, misrepresentation, pretence, ruse, scam (*sl.*), sham, shift, sting (*inf.*), stratagem, subterfuge, swindle, trick, wile
Antonyms *n* ≠ **dishonesty:** candour, frankness, honesty, openness, sincerity, truthfulness

deceitful *adj* = **dishonest,** counterfeit, crafty, deceiving, deceptive, designing, disingenuous, double-dealing, duplicitous, fallacious, false, fraudulent, guileful, hypocritical, illusory, insincere, knavish (*arch.*), sneaky, treacherous, tricky, two-faced, underhand, untrustworthy

deceive *vb* **1** = **take in** (*inf.*), bamboozle (*inf.*), beguile, betray, cheat, con, cozen, delude, disappoint, double-cross (*inf.*), dupe, ensnare, entrap, fool, hoax, hoodwink, impose upon, kid (*inf.*), lead (someone) on (*inf.*), mislead, outwit, pull a fast one (*sl.*), pull the wool over (someone's) eyes, stiff (*sl.*), sting (*inf.*), swindle, take for a ride (*inf.*), trick

deceiver *n* **1** = **liar,** betrayer, charlatan, cheat, chiseller (*inf.*), con man (*inf.*), cozener, crook (*inf.*), deluder, dissembler, double-dealer, fake, fraud, fraudster, hypocrite, impostor, inveigler, mountebank, pretender, sharper, snake in the grass, swindler, trickster

decelerate *vb* = **slow down** *or* **up,** brake, check, put the brakes on, reduce speed, slow
Antonyms *vb* accelerate, pick up speed, quicken, speed up

decency *n* **1, 2** = **respectability,** appropriateness, civility, correctness, courtesy, decorum, etiquette, fitness, good form, good manners, modesty, propriety, seemliness

decent *adj* **2** = **proper,** appropriate, becoming, befitting, comely, *comme il faut,* fit, fitting, seemly, suitable **3** = **respectable,** chaste, decorous, delicate, modest, nice, polite, presentable, proper, pure **5** = **satisfactory,** acceptable, adequate, ample, average, competent, fair, passable, reasonable, sufficient, tolerable **6** *Informal* = **kind,** accommodating, courteous, friendly, generous, gracious, helpful, obliging, thoughtful
Antonyms *adj* ≠ **satisfactory:** clumsy, inept, unsatisfactory ≠ **proper:** awkward, immodest, improper, incorrect, indecent, unseemly, unsuitable ≠ **kind:** awkward, discourteous

deception *n* **1** = **trickery,** craftiness, cunning,

deceptive ➊ (dɪˈsɛptɪv) *adj* likely or designed to deceive; misleading.
▸**deˈceptively** *adv* ▸**deˈceptiveness** *n*

deci- *prefix* denoting one tenth: *decimetre.* Symbol: d [from F *déci-*, from L *decimus* tenth]

decibel (ˈdɛsɪˌbɛl) *n* **1** a unit for comparing two currents, voltages, or power levels, equal to one tenth of a bel. **2** a similar unit for measuring the intensity of a sound. Abbrev.: **dB.**

decide ➊ (dɪˈsaɪd) *vb* **decides, deciding, decided. 1** (*may take a clause or an infinitive as object;* when *intr,* sometimes foll. by *on* or *about*) to reach a decision: *decide what you want; he decided to go.* **2** (*tr*) to cause to reach a decision. **3** (*tr*) to determine or settle (a contest or question). **4** (*tr*) to influence decisively the outcome of (a contest or question). **5** (*intr;* foll. by *for* or *against*) to pronounce a formal verdict. [C14: from OF, from L *dēcīdere,* lit.: to cut off, from *caedere* to cut]
▸**deˈcidable** *adj*

decided ➊ (dɪˈsaɪdɪd) *adj* (*prenominal*) **1** unmistakable. **2** determined; resolute: *a girl of decided character.*
▸**deˈcidedly** *adv*

decider (dɪˈsaɪdə) *n* the point, goal, game, etc., that determines who wins a match or championship.

deciduous (dɪˈsɪdjʊəs) *adj* **1** (of trees and shrubs) shedding all leaves annually at the end of the growing season. Cf. **evergreen. 2** (of antlers, teeth, etc.) being shed at the end of a period of growth. [C17: from L: falling off, from *dēcidere* to fall down, from *cadere* to fall]
▸**deˈciduousness** *n*

decilitre *or US* **deciliter** (ˈdɛsɪˌliːtə) *n* a metric measure of volume equivalent to one tenth of a litre.

decillion (dɪˈsɪljən) *n* **1** (in Britain, France, and Germany) the number represented as one followed by 60 zeros (10^{60}). **2** (in the US and Canada) the number represented as one followed by 33 zeros (10^{33}). [C19: from L *decem* ten + *-illion* as in *million*]
▸**deˈcillionth** *adj*

decimal (ˈdɛsɪməl) *n* **1** Also called: **decimal fraction.** a fraction that has an unwritten denominator of a power of ten. It is indicated by a decimal point to the left of the numerator: *.2=2/10.* **2** any number used in the decimal system. ◆ *adj* **3a** relating to or using powers of ten. **3b** of the base ten. **4** (*prenominal*) expressed as a decimal. [C17: from Med. L *decimālis* of tithes, from L *decima* a tenth]
▸ˈ**decimally** *adv*

decimal classification *n* another term for **Dewey Decimal System.**

decimal currency *n* a system of currency in which the monetary units are parts or powers of ten.

decimalize *or* **decimalise** (ˈdɛsɪməˌlaɪz) *vb* **decimalizes, decimalizing, decimalized** *or* **decimalises, decimalising, decimalised.** to change (a system, number, etc.) to the decimal system.
▸ˌ**decimaliˈzation** *or* ˌ**decimaliˈsation** *n*

decimal place *n* **1** the position of a digit after the decimal point. **2** the number of digits to the right of the decimal point.

decimal point *n* a full stop or a raised full stop placed between the integral and fractional parts of a number in the decimal system.

> **USAGE NOTE** Conventions relating to the use of the decimal point are confused. The IX General Conference on Weights and Measures resolved in 1948 that the decimal point should be a point on the line or a comma, but not a centre dot. It also resolved that figures could be grouped in threes about the decimal point, but that no point or comma should be used for this purpose. These conventions are adopted in this dictionary. However, the Decimal Currency Board recommended that for sums of money the centre dot should be used as the decimal point and that the comma should be used as the thousand marker. Moreover, in some countries the position is reversed, the comma being used as the decimal point and the dot as the thousand marker.

decimal system *n* **1** the number system in general use, having a base of ten, in which numbers are expressed by combinations of the ten digits 0 to 9. **2** a system of measurement in which the multiple and submultiple units are related to a basic unit by powers of ten.

decimate ➊ (ˈdɛsɪˌmeɪt) *vb* **decimates, decimating, decimated.** (*tr*) **1** to destroy or kill a large proportion of. **2** (esp. in the ancient Roman army) to kill every tenth man of (a mutinous section). [C17: from L *decimāre,* from *decem* ten]
▸ˌ**deciˈmation** *n* ▸ˈ**deciˌmator** *n*

> **USAGE NOTE** One talks about the whole of something being *decimated,* not a part: *disease decimated the population,* not *disease decimated most of the population.*

decimetre *or US* **decimeter** (ˈdɛsɪˌmiːtə) *n* one tenth of a metre. Symbol: **dm.**

decipher ➊ (dɪˈsaɪfə) *vb* (*tr*) **1** to determine the meaning of (something obscure or illegible). **2** to convert from code into plain text; decode.
▸**deˈcipherable** *adj* ▸**deˈcipherment** *n*

decision ➊ (dɪˈsɪʒən) *n* **1** a judgment, conclusion, or resolution reached or given; verdict. **2** the act of making up one's mind. **3** firmness of purpose or character; determination. [C15: from OF, from L *dēcīsiō,* lit.: a cutting off; see DECIDE]

decision tree *n* a treelike diagram illustrating the choices available to a decision maker, each possible decision and its estimated outcome being shown as a separate branch of the tree.

decisive ➊ (dɪˈsaɪsɪv) *adj* **1** influential; conclusive. **2** characterized by the ability to make decisions, esp. quickly; resolute.
▸**deˈcisively** *adv* ▸**deˈcisiveness** *n*

deck ➊ (dɛk) *n* **1** *Naut.* any of various platforms built into a vessel. **2** a similar platform, as in a bus. **3a** the horizontal platform that supports the turntable and pick-up of a record player. **3b** See **tape deck. 4** *Chiefly US.* a pack of playing cards. **5** *Computing.* a collection of punched cards relevant to a particular program. **6 clear the decks.** *Inf.* to prepare for action, as by removing obstacles. **7 hit the deck.** *Inf.* **7a** to fall to the ground, esp. to avoid injury. **7b** to prepare for action. **7c** to get out of bed. ◆ *vb* (*tr*) **8** (often foll. by *out*) to dress or decorate. **9** to build a deck on (a vessel). **10** *Sl.* to knock (someone) to the floor or ground. [C15: from MDu. *dec* a covering]

deck-access *adj* (of a block of flats) having a continuous balcony at each level onto which the front door of each flat opens.

deck chair *n* a folding chair consisting of a wooden frame suspending a length of canvas.

-decker *adj* (*in combination*) having a certain specified number of levels or layers: *a double-decker bus.*

deck hand *n* **1** a seaman assigned duties on the deck of a ship. **2** (in Britain) a seaman who has seen sea duty for at least one year. **3** a helper aboard a yacht.

deckle *or* **deckel** (ˈdɛkᵊl) *n* **1** a frame used to contain pulp on the mould in the making of handmade paper. **2** a strap on a paper-making machine that fixes the width of the paper. [C19: from G *Deckel* lid, from *decken* to cover]

deckle edge *n* **1** the rough edge of paper made using a deckle, often left as ornamentation. **2** an imitation of this.
▸ˈ**deckle-ˈedged** *adj*

declaim ➊ (dɪˈkleɪm) *vb* **1** to make (a speech, etc.) loudly and in a rhetorical manner. **2** to speak lines from (a play, poem, etc.) with studied

THESAURUS

deceit, deceitfulness, deceptiveness, dissimulation, duplicity, fraud, fraudulence, guile, hypocrisy, imposition, insincerity, legerdemain, treachery **2 = trick,** artifice, bluff, canard, cheat, decoy, feint, fraud, hoax, hokum (*sl., chiefly US. & Canad.*), illusion, imposture, leg-pull (*Brit. inf.*), lie, pork pie, porky (*Brit. sl.*), ruse, sham, snare, snow job (*sl., chiefly US. & Canad.*), stratagem, subterfuge, wile
Antonyms *n* ≠ **trickery:** artlessness, candour, fidelity, frankness, honesty, openness, scrupulousness, straightforwardness, trustworthiness, truthfulness

deceptive *adj* **= misleading,** ambiguous, deceitful, delusive, dishonest, fake, fallacious, false, fraudulent, illusory, mock, specious, spurious, unreliable

decide *vb* **1-5 = reach** *or* **come to a decision,** adjudge, adjudicate, choose, come to a conclusion, commit oneself, conclude, decree, determine, elect, end, make a decision, make up one's mind, purpose, resolve, settle, tip the balance
Antonyms *vb* be indecisive, be unable to decide, blow hot and cold (*inf.*), dither (*chiefly Brit.*), falter, fluctuate, hesitate, hum and haw, seesaw, shillyshally (*inf.*), swither (*Scot.*), vacillate

decided *adj* **1 = definite,** absolute, categorical, certain, clear-cut, distinct, express, indisputable, positive, pronounced, unambiguous, undeniable, undisputed, unequivocal, unquestionable **2 = determined,** assertive, decisive, deliberate, emphatic, firm, resolute, strong-willed, unfaltering, unhesitating
Antonyms *adj* ≠ **definite:** doubtful, dubious, questionable, undetermined ≠ **determined:** hesitant, indecisive, irresolute, undetermined, weak

decidedly *adv* **1 = definitely,** absolutely, certainly, clearly, decisively, distinctly, downright, positively, unequivocally, unmistakably

deciding *adj* **4 = determining,** chief, conclusive, critical, crucial, decisive, influential, prime, principal, significant

decimate *vb* **1 = devastate,** destroy, lay waste, ravage, wreak havoc on

decipher *vb* **1, 2 = figure out** (*inf.*), construe, crack, decode, deduce, explain, interpret, make out, read, reveal, solve, suss (out) (*sl.*), understand, unfold, unravel

decision *n* **1 = judgment,** arbitration, conclusion, finding, outcome, resolution, result, ruling, sentence, settlement, verdict **3 = decisiveness,** determination, firmness, purpose, purposefulness, resoluteness, resolution, resolve, strength of mind *or* will

decisive *adj* **1 = crucial,** absolute, conclusive, critical, definite, definitive, fateful, final, influential, momentous, positive, significant **2 = resolute,** decided, determined, firm, forceful, incisive, strong-minded, trenchant
Antonyms *adj* ≠ **crucial:** doubtful, indecisive, uncertain, undecided ≠ **resolute:** hesitant, hesitating, indecisive, in two minds (*inf.*), irresolute, pussy-footing (*inf.*), uncertain, undecided, vacillating

deck *vb* **8 = decorate,** adorn, apparel (*arch.*), array, attire, beautify, bedeck, bedight (*arch.*), bedizen (*arch.*), clothe, dress, embellish, engarland, festoon, garland, grace, ornament, trim **8 deck up** *or* **out = dress up,** doll up (*sl.*), get ready, prettify, pretty up, prink, rig out, tog up *or* out, trick out

declaim *vb* **1, 2 = orate,** harangue, hold forth, lecture, perorate, proclaim, rant, recite, speak, spiel (*inf.*) **3 declaim against = protest against,** attack, decry, denounce, inveigh, rail

eloquence. **3** (*intr; foll. by against*) to protest (against) loudly and publicly. [C14: from L *dēclāmāre*, from *clāmāre* to call out]
▸**de'claimer** *n* ▸**declamatory** (dɪ'klæmətərɪ) *adj*

declamation ◑ (ˌdɛklə'meɪʃən) *n* **1** a rhetorical or emotional speech, made esp. in order to protest; tirade. **2** a speech, verse, etc., that is or can be spoken. **3** the act or art of declaiming.

declaration ◑ (ˌdɛklə'reɪʃən) *n* **1** an explicit or emphatic statement. **2** a formal statement or announcement. **3** the act of declaring. **4** the ruling of a judge or court on a question of law. **5** *Law.* an unsworn statement of a witness admissible in evidence under certain conditions. **6** *Cricket.* the voluntary closure of an innings before all ten wickets have fallen. **7** *Contract bridge.* the final contract. **8** a statement or inventory of goods, etc., submitted for tax assessment.

declarative ◑ (dɪ'klærətɪv) *or* **declaratory** (dɪ'klærətərɪ, -trɪ) *adj* making or having the nature of a declaration.
▸**de'claratively** *or* **de'claratorily** *adv*

declare ◑ (dɪ'klɛə) *vb* **declares, declaring, declared.** (*mainly tr*) **1** (*may take a clause as object*) to make clearly known or announce officially: *war was declared.* **2** to state officially that (a person, fact, etc.) is as specified: *he declared him fit.* **3** (*may take a clause as object*) to state emphatically; assert. **4** to show, reveal, or manifest. **5** (*intr; often foll. by for or against*) to make known one's choice or opinion. **6** to make a statement of (dutiable goods, etc.). **7** (*also intr*) *Cards.* **7a** to display (cards) on the table so as to add to one's score. **7b** to decide (the trump suit) by making the winning bid. **8** (*intr*) *Cricket.* to close an innings voluntarily before all ten wickets have fallen. **9** to authorize payment of (a dividend). [C14: from L *dēclārāre* to make clear, from *clārus* clear]
▸**de'clarable** *adj* ▸**de'clarer** *n*

declassify (diː'klæsɪˌfaɪ) *vb* **declassifies, declassifying, declassified.** (*tr*) to release (a document or information) from the security list.
▸**deˌclassifi'cation** *n*

declension ◑ (dɪ'klɛnʃən) *n* **1** *Grammar.* **1a** inflection of nouns, pronouns, or adjectives for case, number, and gender. **1b** the complete set of the inflections of such a word. **2** a decline or deviation. **3** a downward slope. [C15: from L *dēclīnātiō*, lit.: a bending aside, hence variation; see DECLINE]
▸**de'clensional** *adj*

declination (ˌdɛklɪ'neɪʃən) *n* **1** *Astron.* the angular distance of a star, planet, etc., north or south from the celestial equator. Symbol: δ. **2** the angle made by a compass needle with the direction of the geographical north pole. **3** a refusal, esp. a courteous or formal one.
▸ˌ**decli'national** *adj*

decline ◑ (dɪ'klaɪn) *vb* **declines, declining, declined. 1** to refuse to do or accept (something), esp. politely. **2** (*intr*) to grow smaller; diminish. **3** to slope or cause to slope downwards. **4** (*intr*) to deteriorate gradually. **5** *Grammar.* to list the inflections of (a noun, adjective, or pronoun), or (of a noun, adjective, or pronoun) to be inflected for number, case, or gender. ◆ *n* **6** gradual deterioration or loss. **7** a movement downward; diminution. **8** a downward slope. **9** *Arch.* any slowly progressive disease, such as tuberculosis. [C14: from OF *decliner*, from L *dēclīnāre* to bend away, inflect grammatically]
▸**de'clinable** *adj* ▸**de'cliner** *n*

declivity (dɪ'klɪvɪtɪ) *n, pl* **declivities.** a downward slope, esp. of the ground. [C17: from L *dēclīvitās*, from DE- + *clīvus* a slope, hill]
▸**de'clivitous** *adj*

declutch (dɪ'klʌtʃ) *vb* (*intr*) to disengage the clutch of a motor vehicle.

decoct (dɪ'kɒkt) *vb* to extract the essence or active principle from (a medicinal or similar substance) by boiling. [C15: see DECOCTION]

decoction (dɪ'kɒkʃən) *n* **1** *Pharmacol.* the extraction of the water-soluble substances of a drug or medicinal plants by boiling. **2** the liquor resulting from this. [C14: from OF, from LL, from *dēcoquere* to boil down, from *coquere* to cook]

decode ◑ (diː'kəʊd) *vb* **decodes, decoding, decoded.** to convert from code into ordinary language.
▸**de'coder** *n*

decoke (diː'kəʊk) *vb* **decokes, decoking, decoked.** (*tr*) another word for **decarbonize.**

décolletage (ˌdeɪkɒl'tɑːʒ) *n* a low-cut dress or neckline. [C19: from F; see DÉCOLLETÉ]

décolleté (deɪ'kɒlteɪ) *adj* **1** (of a woman's garment) low-cut. **2** wearing a low-cut garment. ◆ *n* **3** a low-cut neckline. [C19: from F *décolleter* to cut out the neck (of a dress), from *collet* collar]

decolonize *or* **decolonise** (diː'kɒləˌnaɪz) *vb* **decolonizes, decolonizing, decolonized** *or* **decolonises, decolonising, decolonised.** (*tr*) to grant independence to (a colony).
▸**deˌcoloni'zation** *or* ▸**deˌcoloni'sation** *n*

decolour (diː'kʌlə), **decolorize,** *or* **decolorise** *vb* **decolorizes, decolorizing, decolorized** *or* **decolorises, decolorising, decolorised.** (*tr*) to deprive of colour.
▸**deˌcolori'zation** *or* **deˌcolori'sation** *n*

decommission (ˌdiːkə'mɪʃən) *vb* (*tr*) to dismantle or remove from service (a nuclear reactor, weapon, ship, etc. which is no longer required).

decompose ◑ (ˌdiːkəm'pəʊz) *vb* **decomposes, decomposing, decomposed. 1** to break down or be broken down into constituent elements by bacterial or fungal action; rot. **2** *Chem.* to break down or cause to break down into simpler chemical compounds. **3** to break up or separate into constituent parts.
▸**decomposition** (ˌdiːkɒmpə'zɪʃən) *n*

decomposer (ˌdiːkəm'pəʊzə) *n* a person or thing that causes decomposition, esp. any of the organisms, such as bacteria, that do so in an ecosystem.

decompress (ˌdiːkəm'prɛs) *vb* **1** to relieve or be relieved of pressure. **2** to return (a diver, etc.) to a condition of normal atmospheric pressure or to be returned to such a condition.
▸ˌ**decom'pression** *n*

decompression chamber *n* a chamber in which the pressure of air can be varied slowly for returning people safely from abnormal pressures to atmospheric pressure.

decompression sickness *or* **illness** *n* a disorder characterized by severe pain, cramp, and difficulty in breathing, caused by a sudden and sustained decrease in atmospheric pressure.

decongestant (ˌdiːkən'dʒɛstənt) *adj* **1** relieving congestion, esp. nasal congestion. ◆ *n* **2** a decongestant drug.

deconsecrate (diː'kɒnsɪˌkreɪt) *vb* **deconsecrates, deconsecrating, deconsecrated.** (*tr*) to transfer (a church, etc.) to secular use.
▸**deˌconse'cration** *n*

deconstruct (ˌdiːkən'strʌkt) *vb* (*tr*) **1** to apply the theories of deconstruction to (a text, film, etc.). **2** to expose or dismantle the existing structure in (a system, organization, etc.).

deconstruction (ˌdiːkən'strʌkʃən) *n* a technique of literary analysis that regards meaning as resulting from the differences between words rather than their reference to the things they stand for.

decontaminate ◑ (ˌdiːkən'tæmɪˌneɪt) *vb* **decontaminates, decontaminating, decontaminated.** (*tr*) to render harmless by the removal or neutralization of poisons, radioactivity, etc.
▸ˌ**deconˌtami'nation** *n*

decontrol (ˌdiːkən'trəʊl) *vb* **decontrols, decontrolling, decontrolled.** (*tr*) to free of restraints or controls, esp. government controls: *to decontrol prices.*

décor ◑ *or* **decor** ('deɪkɔː) *n* **1** a style or scheme of interior decoration, furnishings, etc., as in a room or house. **2** stage decoration; scenery. [C19: from F, from *décorer* to DECORATE]

decorate ◑ ('dɛkəˌreɪt) *vb* **decorates, decorating, decorated. 1** (*tr*) to ornament; adorn. **2** to paint or wallpaper. **3** (*tr*) to confer a mark of distinction, esp. a medal, upon. [C16: from L *decorāre*, from *decus* adornment]
▸'**decorative** *adj*

Decorated style *n* a 14th-century style of English architecture characterized by geometrical tracery and floral decoration.

decoration ◑ (ˌdɛkə'reɪʃən) *n* **1** an addition that renders something

THESAURUS

declamation *n* **1, 2 = oration,** address, harangue, lecture, rant, recitation, speech, tirade

declamatory *adj* **1, 2 = rhetorical,** bombastic, discursive, fustian, grandiloquent, high-flown, incoherent, inflated, magniloquent, orotund, pompous, stagy, stilted, theatrical, turgid

declaration *n* **1 = statement,** acknowledgment, affirmation, assertion, attestation, averment, avowal, deposition, disclosure, protestation, revelation, testimony **2 = announcement,** edict, manifesto, notification, proclamation, profession, promulgation, pronouncement, pronunciamento

declarative *adj* **= affirmative,** definite, demonstrative, enunciatory, explanatory, expository, expressive, positive

declare *vb* **1, 3 = state,** affirm, announce, assert, asseverate, attest, aver, avow, certify, claim, confirm, maintain, notify, proclaim, profess, pronounce, swear, testify, utter, validate **4 = make known,** confess, convey, disclose, manifest, reveal, show

declension *n* **1, 2 = inflection,** variation

decline *vb* **1 = refuse,** abstain, avoid, deny, forgo, reject, say 'no', send one's regrets, turn down **2 = lessen,** decrease, diminish, drop, dwindle, ebb, fade, fail, fall, fall off, flag, shrink, sink, wane **3 = slope,** descend, dip, sink, slant **4 = deteriorate,** decay, degenerate, droop, languish, pine, weaken, worsen ◆ *n* **6 = deterioration,** decay, decrepitude, degeneration, enfeeblement, failing, senility, weakening, worsening **7 = lessening,** abatement, diminution, downturn, drop, dwindling, falling off, recession, slump **8 = slope,** declivity, hill, incline **9** *Archaic* **= consumption,** phthisis, tuberculosis
Antonyms *vb* ≠ **lessen:** increase, rise ≠ **deteriorate:** improve ≠ **refuse:** accept, agree, consent ◆ *n* ≠ **lessening:** rise, upswing ≠ **deterioration:** improvement

decode *vb* **= decipher,** crack, decrypt, descramble, interpret, solve, unscramble, work out
Antonyms *vb* encipher, encode, encrypt, scramble

decompose *vb* **1 = rot,** break up, crumble, decay, fall apart, fester, putrefy, spoil **2, 3 = break down,** analyse, atomize, break up, decompound, disintegrate, dissect, dissolve, distil, separate

decomposition *n* **1 = rot,** corruption, decay, putrefaction, putrescence, putridity **2, 3 = breakdown,** atomization, disintegration, dissolution, division

decontaminate *vb* **= sterilize,** clean, cleanse, deodorize, disinfect, disinfest, fumigate, make safe, purify, sanitize
Antonyms *vb* contaminate, infect, infest, poison, pollute

décor *n* **1 = decoration,** colour scheme, furnishing style, ornamentation

decorate *vb* **1 = adorn,** beautify, bedeck, deck, embellish, engarland, enrich, festoon, grace, ornament, trim **2 = do up** (*inf.*), colour, furbish, paint, paper, renovate, wallpaper **3 = pin a medal on,** cite, confer an honour on *or* upon

decoration *n* **1 = ornament,** arabesque, bauble, cartouch(e), curlicue, falderal, festoon, flounce, flourish, frill, furbelow, garnish, scroll, more attractive or ornate. **2** the act or art of decorating. **3** a medal, etc., conferred as a mark of honour.

decorator ('dɛkəˌreɪtə) *n* **1** *Brit.* a person whose profession is the painting and wallpapering of buildings or their interiors. **2** a person who decorates.

decorous ⓣ ('dɛkərəs) *adj* characterized by propriety in manners, conduct, etc. [C17: from L, from *decor* elegance]
▸'**decorously** *adv* ▸'**decorousness** *n*

decorum ⓣ (dɪ'kɔːrəm) *n* **1** propriety, esp. in behaviour or conduct. **2** a requirement of correct behaviour in polite society. [C16: from L: propriety]

decoupage (ˌdeɪkuː'pɑːʒ) *n* the decoration of a surface with cutout shapes or illustrations. [C20: from F, from *découper*, from DE- + *couper* to cut]

decoy ⓣ *n* ('diːkɔɪ, dɪ'kɔɪ). **1** a person or thing used to lure someone into danger. **2** *Mil.* something designed to deceive an enemy. **3** a bird or animal, or an image of one, used to lure game into a trap or within shooting range. **4** a place into which game can be lured for capture. **5** *Canad.* another word for **deke** (sense 2). ◆ *vb* (dɪ'kɔɪ). **6** to lure or be lured by or as if by means of a decoy. **7** (*tr*) *Canad.* another word for **deke** (sense 1). [C17: prob. from Du. *de kooi*, lit.: the cage, from L *cavea* CAGE]

decrease ⓣ *vb* (dɪ'kriːs). **decreases, decreasing, decreased. 1** to diminish or cause to diminish in size, strength, etc. ◆ *n* ('diːkriːs, dɪ'kriːs). **2** a diminution; reduction. **3** the amount by which something has been diminished. [C14: from OF, from L *dēcrescere* to grow less, from DE- + *crescere* to grow]
▸**de'creasing** *adj* ▸**de'creasingly** *adv*

decree ⓣ (dɪ'kriː) *n* **1** an edict, law, etc., made by someone in authority. **2** an order or judgment of a court. ◆ *vb* **decrees, decreeing, decreed. 3** to order, adjudge, or ordain by decree. [C14: from OF, from L *dēcrētum* ordinance, from *dēcrētus* decided, p.p. of *dēcernere*]

decree absolute *n* the final decree in divorce proceedings, which leaves the parties free to remarry.

decree nisi ('naɪsaɪ) *n* a provisional decree, esp. in divorce proceedings, which will later be made absolute unless cause is shown why it should not.

decrement ('dɛkrɪmənt) *n* **1** the act of decreasing; diminution. **2** *Maths.* a negative increment. **3** *Physics.* a measure of the damping of an oscillator or oscillation, expressed by the ratio of amplitudes in successive cycles. [C17: from L *dēcrēmentum*, from *dēcrescere* to DECREASE]

decrepit ⓣ (dɪ'krɛpɪt) *adj* **1** enfeebled by old age; infirm. **2** broken down or worn out by hard or long use; dilapidated. [C15: from L *dēcrepitus*, from *crepāre* to creak]
▸**de'crepiˌtude** *n*

decrescendo (ˌdiːkrɪ'ʃɛndəʊ) *n, adj* another word for **diminuendo**. [It., from *decrescere* to DECREASE]

decrescent (dɪ'krɛsənt) *adj* (esp. of the moon) decreasing; waning. [C17: from L *dēcrescēns* growing less; see DECREASE]
▸**de'crescence** *n*

decretal (dɪ'kriːtᵊl) *n* **1** *RC Church.* a papal decree; edict on doctrine or church law. ◆ *adj* **2** of or relating to a decree. [C15: from OF, from LL *dēcrētālis*; see DECREE]

decriminalize *or* **decriminalise** (diː'krɪmɪnᵊˌlaɪz) *vb* **decriminalizes, decriminalizing, decriminalized** *or* **decriminalises, decriminalising, decriminalised.** (*tr*) to remove (an action) from the legal category of criminal offence: *to decriminalize the possession of marijuana.*

decry ⓣ (dɪ'kraɪ) *vb* **decries, decrying, decried.** (*tr*) **1** to express open disapproval of; disparage. **2** to depreciate by proclamation: *to decry obsolete coinage.* [C17: from OF *descrier*, from *des-* DIS-[1] + *crier* to CRY]

decumbent (dɪ'kʌmbənt) *adj* **1** lying down. **2** *Bot.* (of stems) lying flat with the tip growing upwards. [C17: from L, present participle of *dēcumbere* to lie down]
▸**de'cumbency** *n*

dedicate ⓣ ('dɛdɪˌkeɪt) *vb* **dedicates, dedicating, dedicated.** (*tr*) **1** (often foll. by *to*) to devote (oneself, one's time, etc.) wholly to a special purpose or cause. **2** (foll. by *to*) to address a book, performance, etc., to a person, cause, etc., as a token of affection or respect. **3** (foll. by *to*) to request or play (a record) on radio for another person as a greeting. **4** to assign or allocate to a particular project, function, etc. **5** to set apart for a deity or for sacred uses. [C15: from L *dēdicāre* to announce, from *dicāre* to make known]
▸'**dediˌcator** *n* ▸**dedicatory** ('dɛdɪˌkeɪtərɪ, 'dɛdɪkətərɪ) *or* '**dediˌcative** *adj*

dedicated ⓣ ('dɛdɪˌkeɪtɪd) *adj* **1** devoted to a particular purpose or cause. **2** assigned or allocated to a particular project, function, etc.: *a dedicated transmission line.* **3** *Computing.* designed to fulfil one function.

dedication ⓣ (ˌdɛdɪ'keɪʃən) *n* **1** the act of dedicating or being dedicated. **2** an inscription prefixed to a book, etc., dedicating it to a person or thing. **3** wholehearted devotion, esp. to a career, ideal, etc.
▸ˌ**dedi'cational** *adj*

deduce ⓣ (dɪ'djuːs) *vb* **deduces, deducing, deduced.** (*tr*) **1** (*may take a clause as object*) to reach (a conclusion) by reasoning; conclude (that); infer. **2** *Arch.* to trace the origin or derivation of. [C15: from L *dēdūcere* to lead away, derive, from DE- + *dūcere* to lead]
▸**de'ducible** *adj*

deduct ⓣ (dɪ'dʌkt) *vb* (*tr*) to take away or subtract (a number, quantity, part, etc.). [C15: from L *dēductus*, p.p. of *dēdūcere* to DEDUCE]

deductible (dɪ'dʌktɪbᵊl) *adj* **1** capable of being deducted. **2** *US.* short for **tax-deductible**. ◆ *n* **3** *Insurance.* the US name for **excess** (sense 5).

deduction ⓣ (dɪ'dʌkʃən) *n* **1** the act or process of deducting or subtracting. **2** something that is or may be deducted. **3** *Logic.* **3a** a process of reasoning by which a specific conclusion necessarily follows from a set of general premises. **3b** a logical conclusion reached by this process.
▸**de'ductive** *adj*

deed ⓣ (diːd) *n* **1** something that is done or performed; act. **2** a notable achievement. **3** action as opposed to words. **4** *Law.* a legal document signed, witnessed, and delivered to effect a conveyance or transfer of property or to create a legal contract. ◆ *vb* **5** (*tr*) *US.* to convey or transfer (property) by deed. [OE *dēd*]

deed box *n* a strong box in which deeds and other documents are kept.

deed poll *n Law.* a deed made by one party only, esp. one by which a person changes his name.

deejay ('diːˌdʒeɪ) *n* an informal name for **disc jockey**. [C20: from the initials DJ (disc jockey)]

THESAURUS

spangle, trimmings, trinket **2** = **adornment**, beautification, elaboration, embellishment, enrichment, garnishing, ornamentation, trimming **3** = **medal**, award, badge, colours, emblem, garter, order, ribbon, star

decorative *adj* **1** = **ornamental**, adorning, arty-crafty, beautifying, enhancing, fancy, nonfunctional, pretty

decorous *adj* = **proper**, appropriate, becoming, befitting, comely, *comme il faut*, correct, decent, dignified, fit, fitting, mannerly, polite, refined, sedate, seemly, staid, suitable, well-behaved
Antonyms *adj* inapposite, inappropriate, malapropos, out of keeping, unbefitting, undignified, unseemly

decorum *n* **1, 2** = **propriety**, behaviour, breeding, courtliness, decency, deportment, dignity, etiquette, gentility, good grace, good manners, gravity, politeness, politesse, protocol, punctilio, respectability, seemliness
Antonyms *n* bad manners, churlishness, impoliteness, impropriety, indecorum, rudeness, unseemliness

decoy *n* **1** = **lure**, attraction, bait, ensnarement, enticement, inducement, pretence, trap ◆ *vb* **6** = **lure**, allure, bait, deceive, ensnare, entice, entrap, inveigle, seduce, tempt

decrease *vb* **1** = **lessen**, abate, contract, curtail, cut down, decline, diminish, drop, dwindle, ease, fall off, lower, peter out, reduce, shrink, slacken, subside, wane ◆ *n* **2** = **lessening**, abatement, contraction, cutback, decline, diminution, downturn, dwindling, ebb, falling off, loss, reduction, shrinkage, subsidence
Antonyms *vb* ≠ **lessen**: enlarge, expand, extend, increase ◆ *n* ≠ **lessening**: expansion, extension, growth

decreasingly *adv* **1** = **less and less**, at a declining rate, diminishingly, ever less, to a lesser or smaller extent
Antonyms *adv* ever more, increasingly, more and more, to a greater extent

decree *n* **1, 2** = **law**, act, canon, command, demand, dictum, edict, enactment, mandate, order, ordinance, precept, proclamation, regulation, ruling, statute ◆ *vb* **3** = **order**, command, decide, demand, determine, dictate, enact, establish, lay down, ordain, prescribe, proclaim, pronounce, rule

decrepit *adj* **1** = **weak**, aged, crippled, debilitated, doddering, effete, feeble, frail, incapacitated, infirm, past it, superannuated, wasted **2** = **worn-out**, antiquated, battered, beat-up (*inf.*), broken-down, deteriorated, dilapidated, ramshackle, rickety, run-down, tumbledown, weather-beaten

decrepitude *n* **1** = **weakness**, debility, dotage, eld (*arch.*), feebleness, incapacity, infirmity, invalidity, old age, senility, wasting **2** = **dilapidation**, decay, degeneration, deterioration

decry *vb* **1** = **condemn**, abuse, asperse, belittle, blame, blast, censure, criticize, cry down, denigrate, denounce, depreciate, derogate, detract, devalue, discredit, disparage, excoriate, lambast(e), put down, rail against, run down, tear into (*inf.*), traduce, underestimate, underrate, undervalue

dedicate *vb* **1** = **devote**, commit, give over to, pledge, surrender **2** = **inscribe**, address, assign, offer **5** = **consecrate**, bless, hallow, sanctify, set apart

dedicated *adj* **1** = **devoted**, committed, enthusiastic, given over to, purposeful, single-minded, sworn, wholehearted, zealous
Antonyms *adj* indifferent, uncaring, uncommitted, unconcerned, uninterested, unresponsive

dedication *n* **2** = **inscription**, address, message **3** = **devotion**, adherence, allegiance, commitment, devotedness, faithfulness, loyalty, single-mindedness, wholeheartedness
Antonyms *n* ≠ **devotion**: apathy, coolness, indifference, insensibility, torpor, unconcern, uninterestedness

deduce *vb* **1** = **conclude**, derive, draw, gather, glean, infer, put two and two together, read between the lines, reason, take to mean, understand

deducible *adj* **1** = **inferable**, derivable, to be inferred, traceable

deduct *vb* = **subtract**, decrease by, knock off, reduce by, remove, take away, take from, take off, take out, withdraw
Antonyms *vb* add, add to, enlarge

deduction *n* **1** = **subtraction**, abatement, allowance, decrease, deduction, diminution, discount, reduction, withdrawal **3b** = **conclusion**, assumption, consequence, corollary, finding, inference, reasoning, result

deed *n* **1** = **action**, achievement, act, exploit, fact, feat, performance, reality, truth **4** *Law* =

deem ⓘ (diːm) *vb* (*tr*) to judge or consider. [OE *dēman*]

de-emphasize *or* **de-emphasise** (diːˈɛmfəˌsaɪz) *vb* **de-emphasizes, de-emphasizing, de-emphasized** *or* **de-emphasises, de-emphasising, de-emphasised.** (*tr*) to remove emphasis from.

deemster (ˈdiːmstə) *n* the title of one of the two justices in the Isle of Man. Also called: **dempster.**

de-energize *or* **de-energise** (diːˈɛnədʒaɪz) *vb* **de-energizes, de-energizing, de-energized** *or* **de-energises, de-energising, de-energised.** (*tr*) *Electrical engineering.* to disconnect (an electrical circuit) from its source.
▸**de-ˌenergiˈzation** *or* **de-ˌenergiˈsation** *n*

deep ⓘ (diːp) *adj* **1** extending or situated far down from a surface: *a deep pool.* **2** extending or situated far inwards, backwards, or sideways. **3** *Cricket.* far from the pitch: *the deep field.* **4** (*postpositive*) of a specified dimension downwards, inwards, or backwards: *six feet deep.* **5** coming from or penetrating to a great depth. **6** difficult to understand; abstruse. **7** intellectually demanding: *a deep discussion.* **8** of great intensity: *deep trouble.* **9** (*postpositive;* foll. by *in*) absorbed (by); immersed (in): *deep in study.* **10** very cunning; devious. **11** mysterious: *a deep secret.* **12** (of a colour) having an intense or dark hue. **13** low in pitch: *a deep voice.* **14 go off the deep end.** *Inf.* **14a** to lose one's temper; react angrily. **14b** *Chiefly US.* to act rashly. **15 in deep water.** *Inf.* in a tricky position or in trouble. ◆ *n* **16** any deep place on land or under water. **17 the deep. 17a** a poetic term for the **ocean. 17b** *Cricket.* the area of the field relatively far from the pitch. **18** the most profound, intense, or central part: *the deep of winter.* **19** a vast extent, as of space or time. ◆ *adv* **20** far on in time; late: *they worked deep into the night.* **21** profoundly or intensely. **22 deep down.** *Inf.* in reality, esp. as opposed to appearance. [OE *dēop*]
▸**ˈdeeply** *adv* ▸**ˈdeepness** *n*

deep-discount bond *n* a fixed-interest security that pays little or no interest but is issued at a substantial discount to its redemption value, thus largely substituting capital gain for income.

deepen ⓘ (ˈdiːpᵊn) *vb* to make or become deep, deeper, or more intense.
▸**ˈdeepener** *n*

deepfreeze (ˌdiːpˈfriːz) *n* **1** another name for **freezer. 2** storage in a freezer. **3** *Inf.* a state of suspended activity. ◆ *vb* **deep-freeze, deep-freezes, deep-freezing, deep-froze, deep-frozen. 4** (*tr*) to freeze (food) or keep (food) in a freezer.

deep-fry *vb* **deep-fries, deep-frying, deep-fried.** to cook (fish, etc.) in sufficient hot fat to cover the food.

deep-laid *adj* (of a plot or plan) carefully worked out and kept secret.

deep-rooted ⓘ *or* **deep-seated** *adj* (of ideas, beliefs, etc.) firmly fixed or held; ingrained.

deep-sea *n* (*modifier*) of, found in, or characteristic of the deep parts of the sea.

deep-set *adj* (esp. of eyes) deeply set.

deep space *n* any region of outer space beyond the system of the earth and moon.

deep structure *n Generative grammar.* a representation of a sentence at a level where logical or grammatical relations are made explicit. Cf. **surface structure.**

deer (dɪə) *n, pl* **deer** *or* **deers.** any of a family of hoofed, ruminant mammals including reindeer, elk, and roe deer, typically having antlers in the male. Related adj: **cervine.** [OE *dēor* beast]

deer lick *n* a naturally or artificially salty area of ground where deer come to lick the salt.

deerskin (ˈdɪəˌskɪn) *n* **a** the hide of a deer. **b** (*as modifier*): *a deerskin jacket.*

deerstalker (ˈdɪəˌstɔːkə) *n* **1** a person who stalks deer, esp. in order to shoot them. **2** a hat, peaked in front and behind, with earflaps usually tied together on the top.
▸**ˈdeerˌstalking** *adj, n*

de-escalate ⓘ (diːˈɛskəˌleɪt) *vb* **de-escalates, de-escalating, de-escalated.** to reduce the level or intensity of (a crisis, etc.) or (of a crisis, etc.) to decrease in level or intensity.
▸**de-ˌescaˈlation** *n*

def (dɛf) *adj Sl.* very good. [C20: ?from *definitive*]

def. *abbrev. for:* **1** defective. **2** defence. **3** defendant. **4** deferred. **5** definite. **6** definition.

deface ⓘ (dɪˈfeɪs) *vb* **defaces, defacing, defaced.** (*tr*) to spoil or mar the surface or appearance of; disfigure.
▸**deˈfaceable** *adj* ▸**deˈfacement** *n* ▸**deˈfacer** *n*

de facto ⓘ (deɪ ˈfæktəʊ) *adv* **1** in fact. ◆ *adj* **2** existing in fact, whether legally recognized or not: *a de facto regime.* Cf. **de jure.** ◆ *n, pl* **de factos. 3** *Austral. & NZ.* a de facto wife or husband. [C17: L]

defalcate (ˈdiːfælˌkeɪt) *vb* **defalcates, defalcating, defalcated.** (*intr*) *Law.* to misuse or misappropriate property or funds entrusted to one. [C15: from Med. L *dēfalcāre* to cut off, from L DE- + *falx* sickle]
▸**ˈdefalˌcator** *n*

defame ⓘ (dɪˈfeɪm) *vb* **defames, defaming, defamed.** (*tr*) to attack the good name or reputation of; slander; libel. [C14: from OF, from L, from *diffāmāre* to spread by unfavourable report, from *fāma* FAME]
▸**defamation** (ˌdɛfəˈmeɪʃən) *n* ▸**defamatory** (dɪˈfæmətərɪ) *adj*

default ⓘ (dɪˈfɔːlt) *n* **1** a failure to act, esp. a failure to meet a financial obligation or to appear in a court of law at a time specified. **2** absence or lack. **3 by default.** in the absence of opposition or a better alternative: *he became prime minister by default.* **4 in default of.** through or in the lack or absence of. **5 judgment by** *or* **in default.** *Law.* a judgment in the plaintiff's favour when the defendant fails to plead or to appear. **6** (*also* ˈdiːfɔːlt). *Computing.* **6a** the preset selection of an option offered by a system, which will always be followed except when explicitly altered. **6b** (*as modifier*): *default setting.* ◆ *vb* **7** (*intr;* often foll. by *on* or *in*) to fail to make payment when due. **8** (*intr*) to fail to fulfil an obligation. **9** *Law.* to lose (a case) by failure to appear in court. [C13: from OF *defaute,* from *defaillir* to fail, from Vulgar L *dēfallīre* (unattested) to be lacking]

defaulter ⓘ (dɪˈfɔːltə) *n* **1** a person who defaults. **2** *Chiefly Brit.* a person, esp. a soldier, who has broken the disciplinary code of his service.

defeat ⓘ (dɪˈfiːt) *vb* (*tr*) **1** to overcome; win a victory over. **2** to thwart or frustrate. **3** *Law.* to render null and void. ◆ *n* **4** a defeating or being defeated. [C14: from OF, from *desfaire* to undo, ruin, from *des-* DIS-[1] + *faire* to do, from L *facere*]

defeatism (dɪˈfiːtɪzəm) *n* a ready acceptance or expectation of defeat.
▸**deˈfeatist** *n, adj*

THESAURUS

document, contract, indenture, instrument, title, title deed, transaction

deem *vb* = **consider**, account, believe, conceive, esteem, estimate, hold, imagine, judge, reckon, regard, suppose, think

deep *adj* **1** = **wide**, abyssal, bottomless, broad, far, profound, unfathomable, yawning **6** = **mysterious**, abstract, abstruse, arcane, esoteric, hidden, obscure, recondite, secret **7** = **wise**, acute, discerning, learned, penetrating, sagacious **8** = **intense**, extreme, grave, great, profound, serious (*inf.*), unqualified **9** = **absorbed**, engrossed, immersed, lost, preoccupied, rapt **10** = **cunning**, artful, astute, canny, designing, devious, insidious, knowing, scheming, shrewd **12** = **dark**, intense, rich, strong, vivid **13** = **low**, bass, booming, full-toned, low-pitched, resonant, sonorous ◆ *n* **17 the deep** *Poetic* = **ocean**, briny (*inf.*), high seas, main, sea **18** = **middle**, culmination, dead, mid point ◆ *adv* **20** = **far into**, deeply, far down, late
Antonyms *adj* ≠ **wide:** shallow ≠ **mysterious:** shallow ≠ **intense:** shallow, superficial ≠ **wise:** simple ≠ **cunning:** shallow, simple ≠ **dark:** light, pale ≠ **low:** high, sharp

deepen *vb* = **intensify**, grow, increase, magnify, reinforce, strengthen

deeply *adv* **21** = **thoroughly**, completely, gravely, profoundly, seriously, severely, to the core, to the heart, to the quick **21** = **intensely**, acutely, affectingly, distressingly, feelingly, mournfully, movingly, passionately, sadly

deep-rooted *adj* = **fixed**, confirmed, dyed-in-the-wool, entrenched, ineradicable, ingrained, inveterate, rooted, settled, subconscious, unconscious
Antonyms *adj* eradicable, exterior, external, on the surface, peripheral, shallow, skin-deep, slight, superficial, surface

de-escalate *vb* = **reduce**, check, contain, curb, damp down, decrease, defuse, diminish, lessen, limit, minimize, take the heat *or* sting out
Antonyms *vb* escalate, heighten, increase, intensify, magnify

deface *vb* = **vandalize**, blemish, damage, deform, destroy, disfigure, impair, injure, mar, mutilate, obliterate, spoil, sully, tarnish, total (*sl.*), trash (*sl.*)

defacement *n* = **vandalism**, blemish, damage, destruction, disfigurement, distortion, impairment, injury, mutilation

de facto *adv* **1** = **in fact**, actually, in effect, in reality, really ◆ *adj* **2** = **actual**, existing, real

defamation *n* = **slander**, aspersion, calumny, character assassination, denigration, disparagement, libel, obloquy, opprobrium, scandal, slur, smear, traducement, vilification

defamatory *adj* = **slanderous**, abusive, calumnious, contumelious, denigrating, derogatory, disparaging, injurious, insulting, libellous, vilifying, vituperative

defame *vb* = **slander**, asperse, bad-mouth (*sl., chiefly US & Canad.*), belie, besmirch, blacken, calumniate, cast a slur on, cast aspersions on, denigrate, detract, discredit, disgrace, dishonour, disparage, knock (*inf.*), libel, malign, rubbish (*inf.*), slag (off) (*sl.*), smear, speak evil of, stigmatize, traduce, vilify, vituperate

default *n* **2** = **failure**, absence, defect, deficiency, dereliction, evasion, fault, lack, lapse, neglect, nonpayment, omission, want ◆ *vb* **7, 8** = **fail**, bilk, defraud, dodge, evade, levant (*Brit.*), neglect, rat (*inf.*), swindle, welsh (*sl.*)

defaulter *n* **7, 8** = **nonpayer**, delinquent, embezzler, levanter (*Brit.*), offender, peculator, welsher (*sl.*)

defeat *vb* **1** = **beat**, blow out of the water (*sl.*), clobber (*sl.*), conquer, crush, lick (*inf.*), make mincemeat of (*inf.*), master, outplay, overpower, overthrow, overwhelm, pip at the post, quell, repulse, rout, run rings around (*inf.*), stuff (*sl.*), subdue, subjugate, tank (*sl.*), trounce, undo, vanquish, wipe the floor with (*inf.*), worst **2** = **frustrate**, baffle, balk, confound, disappoint, discomfit, foil, get the better of, ruin, thwart ◆ *n* **4** = **conquest**, beating, debacle, overthrow, pasting (*sl.*), repulse, rout, trouncing, vanquishment **4** = **frustration**, disappointment, discomfiture, failure, rebuff, repulse, reverse, setback, thwarting
Antonyms *vb* ≠ **beat:** bow, cave in (*inf.*), lose, submit, succumb, surrender, yield ◆ *n* ≠ **conquest:** success, triumph, victory

defeated *adj* **1, 2** = **beaten**, balked, bested, checkmated, conquered, crushed, licked (*inf.*), overcome, overpowered, overwhelmed, routed, thrashed, thwarted, trounced, vanquished, worsted
Antonyms *adj* conquering, dominant, glorious, successful, triumphal, triumphant, undefeated, victorious, winning

defeatist *n* = **pessimist**, prophet of doom, quitter, submitter, yielder ◆ *adj* = **pessimistic**

defecate ⓘ (ˈdɛfɪˌkeɪt) *vb* **defecates, defecating, defecated. 1** (*intr*) to discharge waste from the body through the anus. **2** (*tr*) to remove impurities from. [C16: from L *dēfaecāre* to cleanse from dregs, from DE- + *faex* dregs]
▸**ˌdefeˈcation** *n* ▸**ˈdefeˌcator** *n*

defect ⓘ *n* (ˈdiːfɛkt). **1** a lack of something necessary for completeness; deficiency. **2** an imperfection or blemish. ◆ *vb* (dɪˈfɛkt). **3** (*intr*) to desert one's country, cause, etc., esp. in order to join the opposing forces. [C15: from L, from *dēficere* to forsake, fail]
▸**deˈfector** *n*

defection ⓘ (dɪˈfɛkʃən) *n* **1** abandonment of duty, allegiance, principles, etc. **2** a shortcoming.

defective ⓘ (dɪˈfɛktɪv) *adj* **1** having a defect or flaw; imperfect. **2** (of a person) below the usual standard or level, esp. in intelligence. **3** *Grammar.* lacking the full range of inflections characteristic of its form class.
▸**deˈfectiveness** *n*

defence ⓘ *or US* **defense** (dɪˈfɛns) *n* **1** resistance against danger or attack. **2** a person or thing that provides such resistance. **3** a plea, essay, etc., in support of something. **4** a country's military measures or resources. **5** *Law.* a defendant's denial of the truth of the allegations or charge against him. **6** *Law.* the defendant and his legal advisers collectively. **7** *Sport.* **7a** the action of protecting oneself or part of the playing area against an opponent's attacks. **7b** (usually preceded by *the*) the players in a team whose function is to do this. **8** *American football.* (usually preceded by *the*) **8a** the team that does not have possession of the ball. **8b** the members of a team that play in such circumstances. **9** (*pl*) fortifications. [C13: from OF, from LL *dēfensum*, p.p. of *dēfendere* to DEFEND]
▸**deˈfenceless** *or US* **deˈfenseless** *adj*

defence mechanism *n* **1** *Psychoanalysis.* an unconscious mental process designed to reduce anxiety or shame. **2** *Physiol.* the protective response of the body against disease.

defend ⓘ (dɪˈfɛnd) *vb* **1** (*tr*) to protect from harm or danger. **2** (*tr*) to support in the face of criticism, esp. by argument. **3** to represent (a defendant) in court. **4** *Sport.* to guard (one's goal, etc.) against attack. **5** (*tr*) to protect (a title, etc.) against a challenge. [C13: from OF, from L *dēfendere* to ward off, from DE- + *-fendere* to strike]
▸**deˈfender** *n*

defendant ⓘ (dɪˈfɛndənt) *n* **1** a person against whom an action or claim is brought in a court of law. Cf. **plaintiff.** ◆ *adj* **2** defending.

defenestration (diːˌfɛnɪˈstreɪʃən) *n* the act of throwing someone out of a window. [C17: from NL *dēfenestrātiō*, from L DE- + *fenestra* window]

defensible ⓘ (dɪˈfɛnsɪbᵊl) *adj* capable of being defended, as in war, an argument, etc.
▸**deˌfensiˈbility** *or* **deˈfensibleness** *n*

defensive ⓘ (dɪˈfɛnsɪv) *adj* **1** intended for defence. **2** rejecting criticisms of oneself. ◆ *n* **3** a position of defence. **4 on the defensive.** in a position of defence, as in being ready to reject criticism.
▸**deˈfensively** *adv*

defer[1] ⓘ (dɪˈfɜː) *vb* **defers, deferring, deferred.** (*tr*) to delay until a future time; postpone. [C14: from OF *differer* to be different, postpone; see DIFFER]
▸**deˈferment** *or* **deˈferral** *n* ▸**deˈferrer** *n*

defer[2] ⓘ (dɪˈfɜː) *vb* **defers, deferring, deferred.** (*intr;* foll. by *to*) to yield to or comply with the wishes or judgments (of). [C15: from L *dēferre*, lit.: to bear down, from DE- + *ferre* to bear]

deference ⓘ (ˈdɛfərəns) *n* **1** compliance with the wishes of another. **2** courteous regard; respect. [C17: from F *déférence;* see DEFER[2]]

deferent[1] (ˈdɛfərənt) *adj* another word for **deferential.**

deferent[2] (ˈdɛfərənt) *adj* (esp. of a nerve or duct) conveying an impulse, fluid, etc., down or away; efferent. [C17: from L *dēferre;* see DEFER[2]]

deferential ⓘ (ˌdɛfəˈrɛnʃəl) *adj* showing deference; respectful.
▸**ˌdeferˈentially** *adv*

defiance ⓘ (dɪˈfaɪəns) *n* **1** open or bold resistance to authority, opposition, or power. **2** a challenge.
▸**deˈfiant** *adj*

defibrillation (dɪˌfaɪbrɪˈleɪʃən) *n Med.* the application of an electric current to the heart to restore normal contractions after a heart attack caused by fibrillation.

defibrillator (dɪˈfaɪbrɪˌleɪtə) *n Med.* an apparatus for stopping fibrillation of the heart by application of an electric current.

deficiency ⓘ (dɪˈfɪʃənsɪ) *n, pl* **deficiencies. 1** the state or quality of being deficient. **2** a lack or insufficiency; shortage. **3** a deficit. **4** *Biol.* the absence of a gene or a region of a chromosome normally present.

deficiency disease *n* **1** *Med.* any condition, such as pellagra, beriberi, or scurvy, produced by a lack of vitamins or other essential substances. **2** *Bot.* any disease caused by lack of essential minerals.

deficient ⓘ (dɪˈfɪʃənt) *adj* **1** lacking some essential; incomplete; defective. **2** inadequate in quantity or supply; insufficient. [C16: from L *dēficiēns* lacking, from *dēficere* to fall short]
▸**deˈficiently** *adv*

deficit ⓘ (ˈdɛfɪsɪt, dɪˈfɪsɪt) *n* **1** the amount by which an actual sum is lower than that expected or required. **2a** an excess of liabilities over assets. **2b** an excess of expenditures over revenues. [C18: from L, lit.: there is lacking, from *dēficere*]

deficit financing *n* government spending in excess of revenues so that a budget deficit is incurred, which is financed by borrowing.

defile[1] ⓘ (dɪˈfaɪl) *vb* **defiles, defiling, defiled.** (*tr*) **1** to make foul or dirty; pollute. **2** to taint; corrupt. **3** to damage or sully (someone's reputation, etc.). **4** to make unfit for ceremonial use. **5** to violate the chastity

THESAURUS

defecate *vb* **1** = **excrete**, crap, egest, empty, evacuate (*Physiology*), move, open the bowels, pass a motion, shit (*taboo sl.*), void excrement

defecation *n* **1** = **excretion**, egestion, elimination, emptying *or* opening of the bowels, evacuation (*Physiology*), excrement, motion, movement, voiding excrement

defect *n* **1** = **deficiency**, absence, default, frailty, inadequacy, lack, shortcoming, weakness **2** = **imperfection**, blemish, blotch, error, failing, fault, flaw, foible, mistake, spot, taint, want ◆ *vb* **3** = **desert**, abandon, apostatize, break faith, change sides, go over, rebel, revolt, tergiversate, walk out on (*inf.*)

defection *n* **1** = **desertion**, abandonment, apostasy, backsliding, dereliction, rebellion, revolt

defective *adj* **1** = **faulty**, broken, deficient, flawed, imperfect, inadequate, incomplete, insufficient, not working, on the blink (*sl.*), out of order, scant, short **2** = **abnormal**, mentally deficient, retarded, subnormal
Antonyms *adj* ≠ **faulty:** adequate, intact, perfect, whole, working ≠ **abnormal:** normal

defector *n* **3** = **deserter**, apostate, rat (*inf.*), recreant (*arch.*), renegade, runagate (*arch.*), tergiversator, turncoat

defence *n* **1** = **protection**, armament, cover, deterrence, guard, immunity, resistance, safeguard, security, shelter **2** = **shield**, barricade, bastion, buckler, bulwark, buttress, fastness, fortification, rampart **3** = **argument**, apologia, apology, excuse, exoneration, explanation, extenuation, justification, plea, vindication **5** *Law* = **plea**, alibi, case, declaration, denial, pleading, rebuttal, testimony

defenceless *adj* **1, 2** = **helpless**, endangered, exposed, naked, powerless, unarmed, unguarded, unprotected, vulnerable, wide open
Antonyms *adj* free from harm, guarded, out of harm's way, protected, safe, safe and sound, secure

defend *vb* **1** = **protect**, cover, fortify, guard, keep safe, preserve, safeguard, screen, secure, shelter, shield, ward off, watch over **2** = **support**, assert, champion, endorse, espouse, justify, maintain, plead, speak up for, stand by, stand up for, stick up for (*inf.*), sustain, uphold, vindicate

defendant *n* **1** = **the accused**, appellant, defence, litigant, offender, prisoner at the bar, respondent

defender *n* **1** = **protector**, bodyguard, escort, guard **2** = **supporter**, advocate, champion, patron, sponsor, vindicator

defensible *adj* = **secure**, holdable, impregnable, safe, unassailable = **justifiable**, pardonable, permissible, plausible, tenable, valid, vindicable
Antonyms *adj* ≠ **justifiable:** faulty, inexcusable, insupportable, unforgivable, unjustifiable, unpardonable, untenable, wrong

defensive *adj* **1** = **on guard**, averting, defending, on the defensive, opposing, protective, safeguarding, uptight (*inf.*), watchful, withstanding

defensively *adv* **1** = **in self-defence**, at bay, in defence, on guard, on the defensive, suspiciously

defer[1] *vb* = **postpone**, adjourn, delay, hold over, procrastinate, prorogue, protract, put off, put on ice (*inf.*), put on the back burner (*inf.*), set aside, shelve, suspend, table, take a rain check on (*US & Canad. inf.*)

defer[2] *vb* = **comply**, accede, bow, capitulate, give in, give way to, respect, submit, yield

deference *n* **1** = **obedience**, acquiescence, capitulation, complaisance, compliance, obeisance, submission, yielding **2** = **respect**, attention, civility, consideration, courtesy, esteem, homage, honour, obeisance, politeness, regard, reverence, thoughtfulness, veneration
Antonyms *n* ≠ **respect:** contempt, discourtesy, dishonour, disregard, disrespect, impertinence, impoliteness, impudence, incivility, insolence, irreverence, lack of respect, rudeness ≠ **obedience:** disobedience, insubordination, non-compliance, nonobservance, revolt

deferential *adj* = **respectful**, civil, complaisant, considerate, courteous, dutiful, ingratiating, obedient, obeisant, obsequious, polite, regardful, reverential, submissive

deferment *n* = **postponement**, adjournment, delay, moratorium, putting off, stay, suspension

defiance *n* **1, 2** = **resistance**, challenge, confrontation, contempt, contumacy, disobedience, disregard, insolence, insubordination, opposition, provocation, rebelliousness, recalcitrance, spite
Antonyms *n* accordance, acquiescence, compliance, deference, obedience, observance, regard, respect, subservience

defiant *adj* **1, 2** = **resisting**, aggressive, audacious, bold, challenging, contumacious, daring, disobedient, insolent, insubordinate, mutinous, provocative, rebellious, recalcitrant, refractory, truculent
Antonyms *adj* cowardly, meek, obedient, respectful, submissive

deficiency *n* **1** = **resisting**, frailty, imperfection, weakness **2, 3** = **lack**, absence, dearth, deficit, inadequacy, insufficiency, scantiness, scarcity, shortage
Antonyms *n* ≠ **lack:** abundance, adequacy, sufficiency, superfluity, surfeit

deficient *adj* **1** = **unsatisfactory**, defective, faulty, flawed, impaired, imperfect, incomplete, inferior, weak **2** = **lacking**, exiguous, inadequate, insufficient, meagre, pathetic, scant, scanty, scarce, short, skimpy, wanting

deficit *n* **1** = **shortfall**, arrears, default, deficiency, loss, shortage

defile[1] *vb* **1, 2** = **dirty**, befoul, contaminate, corrupt, make foul, pollute, smear, smirch, soil, taint, tarnish, vitiate **3** = **degrade**, besmirch, de-

of. [C14: from earlier *defoilen,* from OF *defouler* to trample underfoot, abuse, from DE- + *fouler* to tread upon; see FULL[2]]
▸**de'filement** *n*

defile[2] Ⓣ ('di:faɪl, dɪ'faɪl) *n* **1** a narrow pass or gorge. **2** a single file of soldiers, etc. ◆ *vb* **defiles, defiling, defiled. 3** (*intr*) to march in single file. [C17: from F, from *défiler* to file off, from *filer* to march in a column, from OF, from L *fīlum* thread]

define Ⓣ (dɪ'faɪn) *vb* **defines, defining, defined.** (*tr*) **1** to state precisely the meaning of (words, terms, etc.). **2** to describe the nature, properties, or essential qualities of. **3** to determine the boundary or extent of. **4** (*often passive*) to delineate the form or outline of: *the shape of the tree was clearly defined by the light behind it.* **5** to fix with precision; specify. [C14: from OF: to determine, from L *dēfīnīre* to set bounds to, from *fīnīre* to FINISH]
▸**de'finable** *adj* ▸**de'finer** *n*

definite Ⓣ ('dɛfɪnɪt) *adj* **1** clearly defined; exact. **2** having precise limits or boundaries. **3** known for certain. [C15: from L *dēfīnītus* limited, distinct; see DEFINE]
▸**'definiteness** *n*

> **USAGE NOTE** *Definite* and *definitive* should be carefully distinguished. *Definite* indicates precision and firmness, as in *a definite decision. Definitive* includes these senses but also indicates conclusiveness. *A definite answer* indicates a clear and firm answer to a particular question; *a definitive answer* implies an authoritative resolution of a complex question.

definite article *n Grammar.* a determiner that expresses specificity of reference, such as *the* in English. Cf. **indefinite article.**

definite integral *n* See **integral.**

definitely Ⓣ ('dɛfɪnɪtlɪ) *adv* **1** in a definite manner. **2** (*sentence modifier*) certainly: *he said he was coming, definitely.* ◆ *sentence substitute.* **3** unquestionably.

definition Ⓣ (,dɛfɪ'nɪʃən) *n* **1** a formal and concise statement of the meaning of a word, phrase, etc. **2** the act of defining. **3** specification of the essential properties of something. **4** the act of making clear or definite. **5** the state of being clearly defined. **6** a measure of the clarity of an optical, photographic, or television image as characterized by its sharpness and contrast.

definitive Ⓣ (dɪ'fɪnɪtɪv) *adj* **1** serving to decide or settle finally. **2** most reliable or authoritative. **3** serving to define or outline. **4** *Zool.* fully developed. **5** (of postage stamps) permanently on sale. ◆ *n* **6** *Grammar.* a word indicating specificity of reference.
▸**de'finitively** *adv*

deflate Ⓣ (di:'fleɪt) *vb* **deflates, deflating, deflated. 1** to collapse through the release of gas. **2** (*tr*) to take away the self-esteem or conceit from. **3** (*tr*) to take away the enthusiasm or excitement from. **4** *Econ.* to cause deflation of (an economy, the money supply, etc.). [C19: from DE- + (IN)FLATE]
▸**de'flator** *n*

deflation (di:'fleɪʃən) *n* **1** the act of deflating or the state of being deflated. **2** *Econ.* a reduction in spending and economic activity resulting in lower levels of output, employment, investment, trade, profits, and prices. **3** the removal of loose rock material, etc., by wind.
▸**de'flationary** *adj* ▸**de'flationist** *n, adj*

deflect Ⓣ (dɪ'flɛkt) *vb* to turn or cause to turn aside from a course. [C17: from L *dēflectere,* from *flectere* to bend]
▸**de'flector** *n*

deflection Ⓣ *or* **deflexion** (dɪ'flɛkʃən) *n* **1** a deflecting or being deflected. **2** the amount of deviation. **3** the change in direction of a light beam as it crosses a boundary between two media with different refractive indexes. **4** a deviation of the indicator of a measuring instrument from its zero position.
▸**de'flective** *adj*

deflocculate (di:'flɒkjʊ,leɪt) *vb* **deflocculates, deflocculating, deflocculated.** (*tr*) to cause (an aggregate) to separate into particles.
▸**de,floccu'lation** *n* ▸**de'flocculant** *n*

deflower Ⓣ (di:'flaʊə) *vb* (*tr*) **1** to deprive (esp. a woman) of virginity. **2** to despoil of beauty, innocence, etc. **3** to rob or despoil of flowers.
▸**,deflo'ration** *n*

defoliant (di:'fəʊlɪənt) *n* a chemical sprayed or dusted onto trees to cause their leaves to fall, esp. to remove cover from an enemy in warfare.

defoliate (di:'fəʊlɪ,eɪt) *vb* **defoliates, defoliating, defoliated.** to deprive (a plant) of its leaves. [C18: from Med. L *dēfoliāre,* from L DE- + *folium* leaf]
▸**de,foli'ation** *n*

deforest (di:'fɒrɪst) *vb* (*tr*) to clear of trees. Also: **disforest.**
▸**de,fores'tation** *n*

deform Ⓣ (dɪ'fɔ:m) *vb* **1** to make or become misshapen or distorted. **2** (*tr*) to mar the beauty of; disfigure. **3** (*tr*) to subject or be subjected to a stress that causes a change of dimensions. [C15: from L *dēformāre,* from DE- + *forma* shape, beauty]
▸**de'formable** *adj* ▸**,defor'mation** *n*

deformed Ⓣ (dɪ'fɔ:md) *adj* **1** disfigured or misshapen. **2** morally perverted; warped.

deformity Ⓣ (dɪ'fɔ:mɪtɪ) *n, pl* **deformities. 1** a deformed condition. **2** *Pathol.* a distortion of an organ or part. **3** a deformed person or thing. **4** a defect, esp. of the mind or morals; depravity.

defraud Ⓣ (dɪ'frɔ:d) *vb* (*tr*) to take away or withhold money, rights, property, etc., from (a person) by fraud; swindle.
▸**de'frauder** *n*

defray Ⓣ (dɪ'freɪ) *vb* (*tr*) to provide money for (costs, expenses, etc.); pay. [C16: from OF *deffroier* to pay expenses, from *de-* DIS-[1] + *frai* expenditure]
▸**de'frayable** *adj* ▸**de'frayal** *or* **de'frayment** *n*

defrock (di:'frɒk) *vb* (*tr*) to deprive (a person in holy orders) of ecclesiastical status; unfrock.

defrost Ⓣ (di:'frɒst) *vb* **1** to make or become free of frost or ice. **2** to thaw, esp. through removal from a deepfreeze.

defroster (di:'frɒstə) *n* a device by which a de-icing process, as of a refrigerator, is accelerated.

deft Ⓣ (dɛft) *adj* quick and neat in movement; nimble; dexterous. [C13 (in the sense: gentle): see DAFT]
▸**'deftly** *adv* ▸**'deftness** *n*

THESAURUS

base, disgrace, dishonour, smirch, stain, sully **4** = **desecrate**, profane, treat sacrilegiously **5** = **violate**, abuse, deflower, molest, rape, ravish, seduce

defile[2] *n* **1** = **gorge**, gully, pass, passage, ravine, way through

defiled *adj* **3** = **unclean**, besmirched, dirtied, impure, polluted, spoilt, tainted **4** = **desecrated**, profaned **5** = **dishonoured**, ravished, violated
Antonyms *adj* ≠ **unclean:** clean, immaculate, spotless, uncontaminated, uncorrupted, undefiled, unstained, unsullied, untainted ≠ **dishonoured:** chaste, innocent

defilement *n* **1-3** = **contamination**, corruption, pollution, sullying **4** = **desecration**, profanation **5** = **violation**, debasement, degradation, depravity, disgrace

definable *adj* **1-5** = **specific**, apparent, definite, describable, determinable, explicable, perceptible

define *vb* **2** = **describe**, characterize, designate, detail, determine, explain, expound, interpret, specify, spell out **3** = **mark out**, bound, circumscribe, delimit, delineate, demarcate, limit, outline

definite *adj* **1** = **clear**, black-and-white, clear-cut, clearly defined, cut-and-dried (*inf.*), determined, exact, explicit, express, fixed, marked, obvious, particular, precise, specific **3** = **certain**, assured, decided, guaranteed, positive, settled, sure
Antonyms *adj* ≠ **clear:** confused, fuzzy, general, hazy, ill-defined, imprecise, indefinite, indeterminate, indistinct, inexact, loose, obscure, unclear, undetermined, vague ≠ **certain:** uncertain, undecided

definitely *adv* **1-3** = **certainly**, absolutely, beyond any doubt, categorically, clearly, come hell or high water (*inf.*), decidedly, easily, far and away, finally, indubitably, needless to say, obviously, plainly, positively, surely, undeniably, unequivocally, unmistakably, unquestionably, without doubt, without fail, without question

definition *n* **1-3** = **explanation**, clarification, elucidation, exposition, statement of meaning **4** = **description**, delimitation, delineation, demarcation, determination, fixing, outlining, settling **6** = **sharpness**, clarity, contrast, distinctness, focus, precision

definitive *adj* **1** = **final**, absolute, complete, conclusive, decisive **2** = **authoritative**, exhaustive, mother of all (*inf.*), perfect, reliable, ultimate

deflate *vb* **1** = **collapse**, contract, empty, exhaust, flatten, puncture, shrink, void **2, 3** = **humiliate**, chasten, dash, debunk (*inf.*), disconcert, dispirit, humble, mortify, put down (*sl.*), squash, take the wind out of (someone's) sails **4** *Economics* = **reduce**, decrease, depreciate, depress, devalue, diminish
Antonyms *vb* ≠ **collapse:** aerate, balloon, bloat, blow up, dilate, distend, enlarge, expand, increase, inflate, puff up *or* out, pump up, swell ≠ **humiliate:** boost, expand, increase, inflate

deflect *vb* = **turn aside**, bend, deviate, diverge, glance off, ricochet, shy, sidetrack, slew, swerve, turn, twist, veer, wind

deflection *n* = **deviation**, aberration, bend, declination, divergence, drift, refraction, swerve, turning aside, veer

deflower *vb Literary* **1** = **ravish**, assault, force, molest, rape, ruin, seduce, violate

deform *vb* **1** = **distort**, buckle, contort, gnarl, malform, mangle, misshape, twist, warp **2** = **disfigure**, cripple, deface, injure, maim, mar, mutilate, ruin, spoil

deformation *n* **1** = **distortion**, contortion, disfiguration, malformation, misshapenness, warping

deformed *adj* **1** = **distorted**, bent, blemished, crooked, disfigured, malformed, mangled, misshapen, twisted, warped

deformity *n* **1** = **abnormality**, defect, disfigurement, malformation

defraud *vb* = **cheat**, beguile, bilk, con (*inf.*), cozen, delude, diddle (*inf.*), do (*sl.*), dupe, embezzle, fleece, gull (*arch.*), gyp (*sl.*), outwit, pilfer, pull a fast one on (*inf.*), rip off (*sl.*), rob, rook (*sl.*), skin (*sl.*), stiff (*sl.*), stitch up (*sl.*), swindle, trick

defray *vb* = **pay**, clear, cover, discharge, foot the bill, liquidate, meet, settle

defrayal *n* = **payment**, clearance, discharge, liquidation, settlement

defrost *vb* **1, 2** = **thaw**, de-ice, unfreeze
Antonyms *vb* freeze (up), frost, ice over *or* up

deft *adj* = **skilful**, able, adept, adroit, agile, clever, dexterous, expert, handy, neat, nimble, proficient
Antonyms *adj* awkward, bumbling, cack-handed (*inf.*), clumsy, gauche, inept, maladroit, unskilful

deftness *n* = **skill**, ability, adeptness, adroitness, agility, cleverness, competence, coordination, dexterity, expertise, facility, finesse, neatness, nimbleness, proficiency, touch
Antonyms *n* awkwardness, cack-handedness

defunct Ⓣ (dɪ'fʌŋkt) *adj* **1** no longer living; dead or extinct. **2** no longer operative or valid. [C16: from L *dēfungī* to discharge (one's obligations), die; see DE-, FUNCTION]
▸**de'functness** *n*

defuse Ⓣ *or US* (*sometimes*) **defuze** (diː'fjuːz) *vb* **defuses, defusing, defused** *or US* (*sometimes*) **defuzes, defuzing, defuzed.** (*tr*) **1** to remove the triggering device of (a bomb, etc.). **2** to remove the cause of tension from (a crisis, etc.).

USAGE NOTE Avoid confusion with **diffuse.**

defy Ⓣ (dɪ'faɪ) *vb* **defies, defying, defied.** (*tr*) **1** to resist openly and boldly. **2** to elude, esp. in a baffling way. **3** *Formal.* to challenge (someone to do something); dare. **4** *Arch.* to invite to do battle or combat. [C14: from OF *desfier*, from *des-* DE- + *fier* to trust, from L *fīdere*]
▸**de'fier** *n*

deg. *abbrev. for* degree.

degauss (diː'gaʊs) *vb* (*tr*) to neutralize by producing an opposing magnetic field.
▸**de'gausser** *n*

degeneracy Ⓣ (dɪ'dʒɛnərəsɪ) *n, pl* **degeneracies. 1** the act or state of being degenerate. **2** the process of becoming degenerate.

degenerate Ⓣ *vb* (dɪ'dʒɛnəˌreɪt). **degenerates, degenerating, degenerated.** (*intr*) **1** to become degenerate. **2** *Biol.* (of organisms or their parts) to become less specialized or functionally useless. ◆ *adj* (dɪ'dʒɛnərɪt). **3** having declined or deteriorated to a lower mental, moral, or physical level; degraded; corrupt. ◆ *n* (dɪ'dʒɛnərɪt). **4** a degenerate person. [C15: from L, from *dēgener* departing from its kind, ignoble, from DE- + *genus* race]
▸**de'generately** *adv* ▸**de'generateness** *n* ▸**de'generative** *adj*

degenerate matter *n Astrophysics.* the highly compressed state of a star's matter when its atoms virtually touch in the final stage of its evolution into a white dwarf.

degeneration Ⓣ (dɪˌdʒɛnə'reɪʃən) *n* **1** the process of degenerating. **2** the state of being degenerate. **3** *Biol.* the loss of specialization, function, or structure by organisms and their parts. **4** impairment or loss of the function and structure of cells or tissues, as by disease or injury. **5** *Electronics.* negative feedback of a signal.

degradable (dɪ'greɪdəb^{ə}l) *adj* **1** capable of being decomposed chemically or biologically. **2** capable of being degraded.

degradation Ⓣ (ˌdɛgrə'deɪʃən) *n* **1** a degrading or being degraded. **2** a state of degeneration or squalor. **3** some act, constraint, etc., that is degrading. **4** the wearing down of the surface of rocks, cliffs, etc., by erosion. **5** *Chem.* a breakdown of a molecule into atoms or smaller molecules. **6** *Physics.* an irreversible process in which the energy available to do work is decreased. **7** *RC Church.* the permanent unfrocking of a priest.

degrade Ⓣ (dɪ'greɪd) *vb* **degrades, degrading, degraded. 1** (*tr*) to reduce in worth, character, etc.; disgrace. **2** (diː'greɪd) (*tr*) to reduce in rank or status; demote. **3** (*tr*) to reduce in strength, quality, etc. **4** to reduce or be reduced by erosion or down-cutting, as a land surface or bed of a river. **5** *Chem.* to decompose into atoms or smaller molecules. [C14: from LL *dēgradāre*, from L DE- + *gradus* rank, degree]
▸**de'grader** *n*

degrading Ⓣ (dɪ'greɪdɪŋ) *adj* causing humiliation; debasing.
▸**de'gradingly** *adv*

degree Ⓣ (dɪ'griː) *n* **1** a stage in a scale of relative amount or intensity: *a high degree of competence.* **2** an academic award conferred by a university or college on successful completion of a course or as an honorary distinction (**honorary degree**). **3** any of three categories of seriousness of a burn. **4** (in the US) any of the categories into which a crime is divided according to its seriousness. **5** *Genealogy.* a step in a line of descent. **6** *Grammar.* any of the forms of an adjective used to indicate relative amount or intensity: in English they are *positive, comparative,* and *superlative.* **7** *Music.* any note of a diatonic scale relative to the other notes in that scale. **8** a unit of temperature on a specified scale. Symbol: °. See also **Celsius scale, Fahrenheit scale. 9** a measure of angle equal to one three-hundred-and-sixtieth of the angle traced by one complete revolution of a line about one of its ends. Symbol: °. **10** a unit of latitude or longitude used to define points on the earth's surface. Symbol: °. **11** a unit on any of several scales of measurement, as for specific gravity. Symbol: °. **12** *Maths.* **12a** the highest power or the sum of the powers of any term in a polynomial or by itself: $x^4 + x + 3$ *and* xyz^2 *are of the fourth degree.* **12b** the greatest power of the highest order derivative in a differential equation. **13** *Obs.* a step; rung. **14** *Arch.* a stage in social status or rank. **15 by degrees.** little by little; gradually. **16 one degree under.** *Inf.* off colour; ill. **17 to a degree.** somewhat; rather. [C13: from OF *degre*, from L DE- + *gradus* step]

degree of freedom *n* **1** *Chem.* the least number of independently variable properties needed to determine the state of a system. See also **phase rule. 2** one of the independent components of motion (translation, vibration, and rotation) of an atom or molecule.

dehisce (dɪ'hɪs) *vb* **dehisces, dehiscing, dehisced.** (*intr*) (of fruits, anthers, etc.) to burst open spontaneously, releasing seeds, pollen, etc. [C17: from L *dēhiscere* to split open, from DE- + *hiscere* to yawn, gape]
▸**de'hiscent** *adj*

dehorn (diː'hɔːn) *vb* (*tr*) to remove the horns of (cattle, sheep, or goats).

dehumanize *or* **dehumanise** (diː'hjuːməˌnaɪz) *vb* **dehumanizes, dehumanizing, dehumanized** *or* **dehumanises, dehumanising, dehumanised.** (*tr*) **1** to deprive of human qualities. **2** to render mechanical, artificial, or routine.
▸**deˌhumani'zation** *or* **deˌhumani'sation** *n*

dehumidify (ˌdiːhjuː'mɪdɪˌfaɪ) *vb* **dehumidifies, dehumidifying, dehumidified.** (*tr*) to remove water from (the air, etc.)
▸ˌ**dehuˌmidifi'cation** *n* ▸ˌ**dehu'midiˌfier** *n*

dehydrate Ⓣ (diː'haɪdreɪt, ˌdiːhaɪ'dreɪt) *vb* **dehydrates, dehydrating, dehydrated. 1** to lose or cause to lose water. **2** to lose or deprive of water, as the body or tissues.
▸ˌ**dehy'dration** *n* ▸**de'hydrator** *n*

dehydrogenate (diː'haɪdrədʒəˌneɪt), **dehydrogenize,** *or* **dehydrogenise** (diː'haɪdrədʒəˌnaɪz) *vb* **dehydrogenates, dehydrogenating, dehydrogenated, dehydrogenizes, dehydrogenizing, dehydrogenized** *or* **dehydrogenises, dehydrogenising, dehydrogenised.** (*tr*) to remove hydrogen from.
▸**deˌhydroge'nation, deˌhydrogeni'zation,** *or* **deˌhydrogeni'sation** *n*

de-ice (diː'aɪs) *vb* **de-ices, de-icing, de-iced.** to free or be freed of ice.

de-icer (diː'aɪsə) *n* **1** a mechanical or thermal device designed to melt or stop the formation of ice on an aircraft. **2** a substance used for this purpose, esp. an aerosol that can be sprayed on car windscreens to remove ice or frost.

deictic ('daɪktɪk) *adj* **1** *Logic.* proving by direct argument. Cf. **elenctic** (see **elenchus**). ◆ *n* **2** another word for **indexical** (sense 2). [C17: from Gk *deiktikos* concerning proof, from *deiknunai* to show]

deify Ⓣ ('diːɪˌfaɪ, 'deɪɪ-) *vb* **deifies, deifying, deified.** (*tr*) **1** to exalt to the position of a god or personify as a god. **2** to accord divine honour or worship to. [C14: from OF, from LL *deificāre*, from L *deus* god + *facere* to make]
▸ˌ**deifi'cation** *n* ▸**'deiˌfier** *n*

deign Ⓣ (deɪn) *vb* **1** (*intr*) to think it fit or worthy of oneself (to do something); condescend. **2** (*tr*) *Arch.* to vouchsafe. [C13: from OF, from L *dignārī* to consider worthy, from *dignus*]

deindividuation (diːˌɪndɪˌvɪdjʊ'eɪʃən) *n Psychol.* the loss of a person's sense of individuality and responsibility.

de-industrialization *or* **de-industrialisation** (diːɪndʌstrɪəlaɪ'zeɪʃən) *n* a decline in importance of a country's manufacturing industry.

de-ionize *or* **de-ionise** (diː'aɪəˌnaɪz) *vb* **de-ionizes, de-ionizing, de-ionized**

THESAURUS

(*inf.*), clumsiness, ham-fistedness (*inf.*), incompetence, ineptitude

defunct *adj* **1 = dead**, deceased, departed, extinct, gone **2 = obsolete**, a dead letter, bygone, expired, inoperative, invalid, nonexistent, not functioning, out of commission

defuse *vb* **1 = deactivate**, disable, disarm, make safe **2 = calm**, contain, cool, damp down, settle, smooth, stabilize, take the heat *or* sting out
Antonyms *vb* ≠ **deactivate:** activate, arm ≠ **calm:** aggravate, escalate, exacerbate, inflame, intensify, magnify, make worse, worsen

defy *vb* **1 = resist**, beard, brave, confront, contemn, despise, disobey, disregard, face, flout, hurl defiance at, scorn, slight, spurn **2 = foil**, baffle, call (someone's) bluff, defeat, elude, frustrate, repel, repulse, thwart, withstand **3** *Formal* **= challenge**, dare, provoke

degeneracy *n* **1 = depravity**, corruption, decadence, degradation, dissoluteness, immorality, inferiority, meanness, poorness, turpitude **2 = worsening**, debasement, decay, decline, decrease, depravation, deterioration

degenerate *vb* **1 = worsen**, decay, decline, decrease, deteriorate, fall off, go to pot, lapse, regress, retrogress, rot, sink, slip ◆ *adj* **3 = depraved**, base, corrupt, debased, debauched, decadent, degenerated, degraded, deteriorated, dissolute, fallen, immoral, low, mean, perverted

degeneration *n* **1, 2 = deterioration**, debasement, decline, degeneracy, descent, dissipation, dissolution, regression

degradation *n* **1 = deterioration**, abasement, debasement, decadence, decline, degeneracy, degeneration, demotion, derogation, downgrading, perversion **2 = disgrace**, discredit, dishonour, humiliation, ignominy, mortification, shame

degrade *vb* **1 = demean**, cheapen, corrupt, debase, discredit, disgrace, dishonour, humble, humiliate, impair, injure, pervert, shame, vitiate **2 = demote**, break, cashier, depose, downgrade, lower, reduce to inferior rank **3 = adulterate**, dilute, doctor, mix, thin, water, water down, weaken
Antonyms *vb* ≠ **demean:** dignify, enhance, ennoble, honour, improve ≠ **demote:** elevate, promote, raise

degraded *adj* **1 = disgraced**, abandoned, base, corrupt, debased, debauched, decadent, depraved, despicable, disreputable, dissolute, low, mean, profligate, sordid, vicious, vile

degrading *adj* **= demeaning**, cheapening, contemptible, debasing, disgraceful, dishonourable, humiliating, infra dig (*inf.*), lowering, shameful, undignified, unworthy

degree *n* **1 = stage**, division, extent, gradation, grade, interval, limit, mark, measure, notch, point, rung, scale, step, unit **1 = rank**, class, grade, level, order, position, standing, station, status **1 = extent**, ambit, calibre, intensity, level, measure, proportion, quality, quantity, range, rate, ratio, scale, scope, severity, standard **15 by degrees = little by little**, bit by bit, gently, gradually, imperceptibly, inch by inch, slowly, step by step

dehydrate *vb* **1 = dry**, desiccate, drain, evaporate, exsiccate, parch

deification *n* **1, 2 = worship**, apotheosis, elevation, ennoblement, exaltation, glorification, idolization

deify *vb* **1, 2 = worship**, apotheosize, elevate, ennoble, enthrone, exalt, extol, glorify, idealize, idolize, immortalize, venerate

deign *vb* **1 = condescend**, consent, deem worthy, lower oneself, see fit, stoop, think fit

or **de-ionises, de-ionising, de-ionised.** (*tr*) to remove ions from (water, etc.), esp. by ion exchange.
▸**de,ioni'zation** *or* **de,ioni'sation** *n*

deism ('di:ɪzəm, 'deɪ-) *n* belief in the existence of God based on natural reason, without revelation. Cf. **theism.** [C17: from F *déisme,* from L *deus* god]
▸**'deist** *n, adj* ▸**de'istic** *or* **de'istical** *adj* ▸**de'istically** *adv*

deity ❶ ('di:ɪtɪ, 'deɪ-) *n, pl* **deities. 1** a god or goddess. **2** the state of being divine; godhead. **3** the rank of a god. **4** the nature or character of God. [C14: from OF, from LL *deitās,* from L *deus* god]

Deity ('di:ɪtɪ, 'deɪ-) *n* **the.** God.

déjà vu ('deɪʒæ 'vu:) *n* the experience of perceiving a new situation as if it had occurred before. [from F, lit.: already seen]

deject ❶ (dɪ'dʒɛkt) *vb* (*tr*) to have a depressing effect on; dispirit; dishearten. [C15: from L *dēicere* to cast down, from DE- + *iacere* to throw]

dejected ❶ (dɪ'dʒɛktɪd) *adj* miserable; despondent; downhearted.
▸**de'jectedly** *adv*

dejection ❶ (dɪ'dʒɛkʃən) *n* **1** lowness of spirits; depression. **2a** faecal matter. **2b** defecation.

de jure ❶ (deɪ 'dʒʊəreɪ) *adv* according to law; by right; legally. Cf. **de facto.** [L]

deka- *or* **dek-** *combining form.* variants of **deca-**.

deke (di:k) *Canad. sl.* ◆ *vb* **dekes, deking, deked. 1** (*tr*) (in ice hockey or box lacrosse) to draw a defending player out of position by faking a shot or movement. ◆ *n* **2** such a shot or movement. ◆ Also: **decoy.** [C20: from DECOY]

dekko ('dɛkəʊ) *n, pl* **dekkos.** *Brit. sl.* a look; glance. [C19: from Hindi *dekho!* look! from *dekhnā* to see]

del (dɛl) *n Maths.* the differential operator $\boldsymbol{i}(\partial/\partial x) + \boldsymbol{j}(\partial/\partial y) + \boldsymbol{k}(\partial/\partial z)$, where ***i, j,*** and ***k*** are unit vectors in the *x, y,* and *z* directions. Symbol: ∇ Also called: **nabla.**

del. *abbrev. for* delegate.

Del. *abbrev. for* Delaware.

Delaware ('dɛlə,wɛə) *n* **1** (*pl* **Delawares** *or* **Delaware**) a member of a North American Indian people formerly living near the Delaware River. **2** the language of this people.

delay ❶ (dɪ'leɪ) *vb* **1** (*tr*) to put off to a later time; defer. **2** (*tr*) to slow up or cause to be late. **3** (*intr*) to be irresolute or put off doing something. **4** (*intr*) to linger; dawdle. ◆ *n* **5** a delaying or being delayed. **6** the interval between one event and another. [C13: from OF, from *des-* off + *laier* to leave, from L *laxāre* to loosen]
▸**de'layer** *n*

delayed action *or* **delay action** *n* a device for operating a mechanism, such as a camera shutter, a short time after setting.

delayed drop *n Aeronautics.* a parachute descent in which the opening of the parachute is delayed for a predetermined time.

delayering (di:'leɪərɪŋ) *n* the process of pruning the administrative structure of a large organization by reducing the number of tiers in its hierarchy.

dele ('di:lɪ) *n, pl* **deles. 1** a sign (δ) indicating that typeset matter is to be deleted. ◆ *vb* **deles, deleing, deled. 2** (*tr*) to mark (matter to be deleted) with a dele. [C18: from L: delete (imperative), from *dēlēre* to destroy, obliterate]

delectable ❶ (dɪ'lɛktəbᵊl) *adj* highly enjoyable, esp. pleasing to the taste; delightful. [C14: from L *dēlectābilis,* from *dēlectāre* to DELIGHT]
▸**de'lectableness** *or* **de,lecta'bility** *n*

delectation ❶ (,di:lɛk'teɪʃən) *n* pleasure; enjoyment.

delegate ❶ *n* ('dɛlɪ,geɪt, -gɪt). **1** a person chosen to act for another or others, esp. at a conference or meeting. ◆ *vb* ('dɛlɪ,geɪt), **delegates, delegating, delegated. 2** to give (duties, powers, etc.) to another as representative; depute. **3** (*tr*) to authorize (a person) as representative. [C14: from L *dēlēgāre* to send on a mission, from *lēgāre* to send, depute]
▸**'delegable** *adj*

delegation ❶ (,dɛlɪ'geɪʃən) *n* **1** a person or group chosen to represent another or others. **2** a delegating or being delegated.

delete ❶ (dɪ'li:t) *vb* **deletes, deleting, deleted.** (*tr*) to remove (something printed or written); erase; strike out. [C17: from L *dēlēre* to destroy, obliterate]
▸**de'letion** *n*

deleterious (,dɛlɪ'tɪərɪəs) *adj* harmful; injurious; hurtful. [C17: from NL, from Gk *dēlētērios,* from *dēleisthai* to hurt]
▸**,dele'teriousness** *n*

Delft (dɛlft) *n* tin-glazed earthenware that originated in Delft, a town in the SW Netherlands, typically having blue decoration on a white ground. Also called: **delftware.**

deli ('dɛlɪ) *n, pl* **delis.** an informal word for **delicatessen.**

deliberate ❶ *adj* (dɪ'lɪbərɪt). **1** carefully thought out in advance; intentional. **2** careful or unhurried: *a deliberate pace.* ◆ *vb* (dɪ'lɪbə,reɪt). **deliberates, deliberating, deliberated. 3** to consider (something) deeply; think over. [C15: from L *dēlīberāre,* from *lībrāre* to weigh, from *lībra* scales]
▸**de'liberately** *adv* ▸**de'liberateness** *n* ▸**de'liber,ator** *n*

deliberation ❶ (dɪ,lɪbə'reɪʃən) *n* **1** careful consideration. **2** (*often pl*) formal discussion, as of a committee. **3** care or absence of hurry.

deliberative (dɪ'lɪbərətɪv) *adj* **1** of or for deliberating: *a deliberative assembly.* **2** characterized by deliberation.
▸**de'liberatively** *adv* ▸**de'liberativeness** *n*

delicacy ❶ ('dɛlɪkəsɪ) *n, pl* **delicacies. 1** fine or subtle quality, character, construction, etc. **2** fragile or graceful beauty. **3** something that is considered choice to eat, such as caviar. **4** fragile construction or constitution. **5** refinement of feeling, manner, or appreciation. **6** fussy or squeamish refinement, esp. in matters of taste, propriety, etc. **7** need for tactful or sensitive handling. **8** sensitivity of response, as of an instrument.

delicate ❶ ('dɛlɪkɪt) *adj* **1** fine or subtle in quality, character, construction, etc. **2** having a soft or fragile beauty. **3** (of colour, tone, taste, etc.) pleasantly subtle. **4** easily damaged or injured; fragile. **5** precise or sensitive in action: *a delicate mechanism.* **6** requiring tact. **7** showing regard for the feelings of others. **8** excessively refined; squeamish. [C14: from L *dēlicātus* affording pleasure, from *dēliciae* (pl) delight, pleasure]
▸**'delicately** *adv* ▸**'delicateness** *n*

THESAURUS

deity *n* **1, 2 = god,** celestial being, divine being, divinity, goddess, godhead, idol, immortal, supreme being

deject *vb* **= depress,** cast down, dampen, daunt, demoralize, discourage, dishearten, dismay, dispirit

dejected *adj* **= downhearted,** blue, cast down, crestfallen, depressed, despondent, disconsolate, disheartened, dismal, doleful, down, downcast, down in the dumps (*inf.*), gloomy, glum, low, low-spirited, melancholy, miserable, morose, sad, sick as a parrot (*inf.*), woebegone, wretched
Antonyms *adj* blithe, cheerful, chirpy (*inf.*), encouraged, genial, happy, joyous, light-hearted, upbeat (*inf.*)

dejection *n* **1 = low spirits,** blues, depression, despair, despondency, doldrums, downheartedness, dumps (*inf.*), gloom, gloominess, heavy-heartedness, melancholy, sadness, sorrow, the hump (*Brit. inf.*), unhappiness

de jure *adv* **= legally,** according to the law, by right, rightfully

delay *vb* **1 = put off,** beat about the bush, defer, hold over, play for time, postpone, procrastinate, prolong, protract, put on the back burner (*inf.*), shelve, stall, suspend, table, take a rain check on (*US & Canad. inf.*), temporize **2 = hold up,** arrest, bog down, check, detain, halt, hinder, hold back, impede, obstruct, retard, set back, slow up, stop, throw a spanner in the works **4 = drag one's feet** *or* **heels** (*inf.*), dawdle, dilly-dally (*inf.*), drag, lag, linger, loiter, tarry ◆ *n* **5 = putting off,** deferment, postponement, procrastination, stay, suspension **6 = hold-up,** check, detention, hindrance, impediment, interruption, interval, obstruction, setback, stoppage, wait
Antonyms *vb* ≠ **hold up:** accelerate, advance, dispatch, expedite, facilitate, forward, hasten, hurry, precipitate, press, promote, quicken, rush, speed (up), urge

delaying *adj* **2 = hindering,** halting, moratory, obstructive, retardant **3 = procrastinating,** temporizing **4 = dawdling,** dallying, dilatory, lingering, slow, tardy, tarrying
Antonyms *adj* ≠ **procrastinating, dawdling:** expeditious, hasty, precipitate, prompt, urgent

delectable *adj* **= delicious,** adorable, agreeable, appetizing, charming, dainty, delightful, enjoyable, enticing, gratifying, inviting, luscious, lush, pleasant, pleasurable, satisfying, scrumptious (*inf.*), tasty, toothsome, yummy (*sl.*)
Antonyms *adj* awful, disagreeable, disgusting, distasteful, dreadful, horrible, horrid, nasty, offensive, terrible, unappetizing, unpleasant, yucky *or* yukky (*sl.*)

delectation *n Formal* **= enjoyment,** amusement, delight, diversion, entertainment, gratification, happiness, jollies (*sl.*), pleasure, refreshment, relish, satisfaction

delegate *n* **1 = representative,** agent, ambassador, commissioner, deputy, envoy, legate, vicar ◆ *vb* **2 = entrust,** assign, consign, devolve, give, hand over, pass on, relegate, transfer **3 = appoint,** accredit, authorize, commission, designate, empower, mandate

delegation *n* **1 = deputation,** commission, contingent, embassy, envoys, legation, mission **2 = devolution,** assignment, commissioning, committal, deputizing, entrustment, relegation

delete *vb* **= remove,** blot out, blue-pencil, cancel, cross out, cut out, dele, edit, edit out, efface, erase, excise, expunge, obliterate, rub out, strike out

deliberate *adj* **1 = intentional,** calculated, conscious, considered, designed, planned, prearranged, premeditated, purposeful, studied, thoughtful, wilful **2 = unhurried,** careful, cautious, circumspect, heedful, measured, methodical, ponderous, prudent, slow, thoughtful, wary ◆ *vb* **3 = consider,** cogitate, consult, debate, discuss, meditate, mull over, ponder, reflect, think, weigh
Antonyms *adj* ≠ **intentional:** accidental, inadvertent, unconscious, unintended, unpremeditated, unthinking ≠ **unhurried:** fast, haphazard, hasty, heedless, hurried, impetuous, impulsive, rash

deliberately *adv* **1 = intentionally,** by design, calculatingly, consciously, determinedly, emphatically, in cold blood, knowingly, on purpose, pointedly, resolutely, studiously, wilfully, wittingly

deliberation *n* **1 = consideration,** calculation, care, carefulness, caution, circumspection, cogitation, coolness, forethought, meditation, prudence, purpose, reflection, speculation, study, thought, wariness **2 = discussion,** conference, consultation, debate

delicacy *n* **1 = fineness,** accuracy, daintiness, elegance, exquisiteness, lightness, nicety, precision, subtlety **3 = treat,** *bonne bouche,* dainty, luxury, relish, savoury, titbit **4 = fragility,** debility, flimsiness, frailness, frailty, infirmity, slenderness, tenderness, weakness **5 = fastidiousness,** discrimination, finesse, purity, refinement, sensibility, taste **7 = sensitivity,** sensitiveness, tact

delicate *adj* **1 = fine,** accurate, deft, detailed, elegant, exquisite, graceful, minute, precise, skilled, subtle **3 = soft,** faint, muted, pastel, subdued, subtle **4 = fragile,** flimsy, frail, slender,

delicatessen (ˌdɛlɪkəˈtesᵊn) *n* **1** a shop selling various foods, esp. unusual or imported foods, already cooked or prepared. **2** such foods. [C19: from G *Delikatessen*, lit.: delicacies, from F *délicatesse*]

delicious ❶ (dɪˈlɪʃəs) *adj* **1** very appealing, esp. to taste or smell. **2** extremely enjoyable. [C13: from OF, from LL *dēliciōsus*, from L *dēliciae* delights, from *dēlicere* to entice; see DELIGHT]
▸**deˈliciously** *adv* ▸**deˈliciousness** *n*

delight ❶ (dɪˈlaɪt) *vb* **1** (*tr*) to please greatly. **2** (*intr;* foll. by *in*) to take great pleasure (in). ◆ *n* **3** extreme pleasure. **4** something that causes this. [C13: from OF, from *deleitier* to please, from L *dēlectāre*, from *dēlicere* to allure, from DE- + *lacere* to entice]
▸**deˈlighted** *adj* ▸**deˈlightedly** *adv*

delightful ❶ (dɪˈlaɪtful) *adj* giving great delight; very pleasing, beautiful, charming, etc.
▸**deˈlightfully** *adv* ▸**deˈlightfulness** *n*

Delilah (dɪˈlaɪlə) *n* **1** Samson's Philistine mistress, who betrayed him (Judges 16). **2** a voluptuous and treacherous woman; temptress.

delimit ❶ (di:ˈlɪmɪt) *or* **delimitate** *vb* **delimits, delimiting, delimited** *or* **delimitates, delimitating, delimitated.** (*tr*) to mark or prescribe the limits or boundaries of.
▸**deˌlimiˈtation** *n* ▸**deˈlimitative** *adj*

delineate ❶ (dɪˈlɪnɪˌeɪt) *vb* **delineates, delineating, delineated.** (*tr*) **1** to trace the outline of. **2** to represent pictorially; depict. **3** to portray in words; describe. [C16: from L *dēlīneāre* to sketch out, from *līnea* LINE[1]]
▸**deˌlineˈation** *n* ▸**deˈlineative** *adj*

delinquency ❶ (dɪˈlɪŋkwənsɪ) *n, pl* **delinquencies. 1** an offence or misdeed, esp. one committed by a young person. See **juvenile delinquency. 2** failure or negligence in duty or obligation. **3** a delinquent nature or delinquent behaviour. [C17: from LL *dēlinquentia* fault, offence, from L *dēlinquere* to transgress, from DE- + *linquere* to forsake]

delinquent ❶ (dɪˈlɪŋkwənt) *n* **1** someone, esp. a young person, guilty of delinquency. ◆ *adj* **2** guilty of an offence or misdeed. **3** failing in or neglectful of duty or obligation. [C17: from L *dēlinquēns* offending; see DELINQUENCY]

deliquesce (ˌdɛlɪˈkwɛs) *vb* **deliquesces, deliquescing, deliquesced.** (*intr*) (esp. of certain salts) to dissolve gradually in water absorbed from the air. [C18: from L *dēliquēscere*, from DE- + *liquēscere* to melt, from *liquēre* to be liquid]
▸ˌ**deliˈquescence** *n* ▸ˌ**deliˈquescent** *adj*

delirious ❶ (dɪˈlɪrɪəs) *adj* **1** affected with delirium. **2** wildly excited, esp. with joy or enthusiasm.
▸**deˈliriously** *adv*

delirium ❶ (dɪˈlɪrɪəm) *n, pl* **deliriums** *or* **deliria** (-ˈlɪrɪə). **1** a state of excitement and mental confusion, often accompanied by hallucinations, caused by high fever, poisoning, brain injury, etc. **2** violent excitement or emotion; frenzy. [C16: from L: madness, from *dēlīrāre*, lit.: to swerve from a furrow, hence be crazy, from DE- + *līra* furrow]

delirium tremens (ˈtrɛmɛnz, ˈtri:-) *n* a severe psychotic condition occurring in some persons with chronic alcoholism, characterized by delirium, tremor, anxiety, and vivid hallucinations. Abbrevs.: **DT's** (informal), **dt.** [C19: NL, lit.: trembling delirium]

deliver ❶ (dɪˈlɪvə) *vb* (*mainly tr*) **1** to carry to a destination, esp. to distribute (goods, mail, etc.) to several places. **2** (often foll. by *over* or *up*) to hand over or transfer. **3** (often foll. by *from*) to release or rescue (from captivity, harm, etc.). **4** (*also intr*) **4a** to aid in the birth of (offspring). **4b** to give birth to (offspring). **4c** (usually foll. by *of*) to aid (a female) in the birth (of offspring). **4d** (*passive;* foll. by *of*) to give birth (to offspring). **5** to present (a speech, idea, etc.). **6** to utter: *to deliver a cry of exultation.* **7** to discharge or release (something, such as a blow or shot) suddenly. **8** (*intr*) *Inf.* Also: **deliver the goods.** to produce something promised or expected. **9** *Chiefly US.* to cause (voters, etc.) to support a given candidate, cause, etc. **10 deliver oneself of.** to speak with deliberation or at length. [C13: from OF, from LL *dēlīberāre* to set free, from L DE- + *līberāre* to free]
▸**deˈliverable** *adj* ▸**deˈliverer** *n*

deliverance ❶ (dɪˈlɪvərəns) *n* **1** a formal expression of opinion. **2** rescue from moral corruption or evil; salvation.

delivery ❶ (dɪˈlɪvərɪ) *n, pl* **deliveries. 1a** the act of delivering or distributing goods, mail, etc. **1b** something that is delivered. **2** the act of giving birth to a child. **3** manner or style of utterance, esp. in public speaking: *the chairman had a clear delivery.* **4** the act of giving or transferring or the state of being given or transferred. **5** a rescuing or being rescued; liberation. **6** *Sport.* the act or manner of bowling or throwing a ball. **7** the handing over of property, a deed, etc.

dell (dɛl) *n* a small, esp. wooded hollow. [OE]

delouse (di:ˈlaus, -ˈlauz) *vb* **delouses, delousing, deloused.** (*tr*) to rid (a person or animal) of lice as a sanitary measure.

Delphic (ˈdɛlfɪk) *or* **Delphian** *adj* **1** of or relating to the ancient Greek city of Delphi or its oracle or temple. **2** obscure or ambiguous.

delphinium (dɛlˈfɪnɪəm) *n, pl* **delphiniums** *or* **delphinia** (-ɪə). a plant with spikes of blue, pink, or white spurred flowers. See also **larkspur.** [C17: NL, from Gk *delphinion* larkspur, from *delphis* dolphin, referring to the shape of the nectary]

delta (ˈdɛltə) *n* **1** the fourth letter in the Greek alphabet (Δ or δ). **2** (*cap. when part of name*) the flat alluvial area at the mouth of some rivers where the mainstream splits up into several distributaries. **3** *Maths.* a finite increment in a variable. [C16: via L from Gk, of Semitic origin]
▸**deltaic** (dɛlˈteɪɪk) *or* ˈ**deltic** *adj*

delta connection *n* a connection used in a three-phase electrical system in which three elements in series form a triangle, the supply being input and output at the three junctions.

delta particle *n Physics* a very short-lived type of hyperon.

delta ray *n* a particle, esp. an electron, ejected from matter by ionizing radiation.

delta rhythm *or* **wave** *n Physiol.* the normal electrical activity of the cerebral cortex during deep sleep. See also **brain wave.**

delta stock *n* any of the fourth rank of active securities on the London stock exchange. Market makers need not display prices of these securities continuously.

delta wing *n* a triangular swept-back aircraft wing.

deltiology (ˌdɛltɪˈɒlədʒɪ) *n* the collection and study of postcards. [C20: from Gk *deltion*, dim. of *deltos* a writing tablet + -LOGY]
▸ˌ**deltiˈologist** *n*

deltoid (ˈdɛltɔɪd) *n* a thick muscle of the shoulder that acts to raise the arm. [C18: from Gk *deltoeidēs* triangular, from DELTA]

delude ❶ (dɪˈlu:d) *vb* **deludes, deluding, deluded.** (*tr*) to deceive; mislead; beguile. [C15: from L *dēlūdere* to mock, play false, from DE- + *lūdere* to play]
▸**deˈludable** *adj* ▸**deˈluder** *n*

deluge ❶ (ˈdɛlju:dʒ) *n* **1** a great flood of water. **2** torrential rain. **3** an overwhelming rush or number. ◆ *vb* **deluges, deluging, deluged.** (*tr*) **4** to

THESAURUS

slight, tender, weak **7** = **considerate**, diplomatic, discreet, sensitive, tactful **8** = **fastidious**, careful, critical, discriminating, nice, prudish, pure, refined, scrupulous, squeamish
Antonyms *adj* ≠ **fine:** coarse, crude, indelicate, unrefined ≠ **subtle:** harsh, strong ≠ **soft:** bright, harsh, rough ≠ **considerate:** harsh, inconsiderate, indelicate, insensitive, rough ≠ **fastidious:** careless, crude, rough

delicately *adv* **1** = **finely**, carefully, daintily, deftly, elegantly, exquisitely, gracefully, lightly, precisely, skilfully, softly, subtly **6** = **tactfully**, diplomatically, sensitively

delicious *adj* **1** = **delectable**, ambrosial, appetizing, choice, dainty, luscious, mouthwatering, nectareous, palatable, savoury, scrumptious (*inf.*), tasty, toothsome, yummy (*sl.*) **2** = **delightful**, agreeable, charming, enjoyable, entertaining, exquisite, pleasant, pleasing
Antonyms *adj* ≠ **delectable:** disagreeable, distasteful, unpleasant

delight *n* **1** = **pleasure**, ecstasy, enjoyment, felicity, gladness, glee, gratification, happiness, jollies (*sl.*), joy, rapture, transport ◆ *vb* **1** = **please**, amuse, charm, cheer, divert, enchant, gratify, ravish, rejoice, satisfy, thrill **2 delight in** = **take pleasure in**, appreciate, enjoy, feast on, glory in, indulge in, like, love, luxuriate in, relish, revel in, savour
Antonyms *n* ≠ **pleasure:** disapprobation, disfavour, dislike, displeasure, dissatisfaction, distaste ◆ *vb* ≠ **please:** disgust, displease, dissatisfy, gall, irk, offend, upset, vex

delighted *adj* **1** = **pleased**, blissed out, captivated, charmed, cock-a-hoop, ecstatic, elated, enchanted, gladdened, happy, in seventh heaven, joyous, jubilant, overjoyed, over the moon (*inf.*), rapt, sent, thrilled

delightful *adj* = **pleasant**, agreeable, amusing, captivating, charming, congenial, delectable, enchanting, engaging, enjoyable, entertaining, fascinating, gratifying, heavenly, pleasing, pleasurable, rapturous, ravishing, thrilling
Antonyms *adj* disagreeable, displeasing, distasteful, horrid, nasty, unpleasant

delimit *vb* = **define**, bound, demarcate, determine, fix, mark (out)

delineate *vb* **1-3** = **outline**, characterize, chart, contour, depict, describe, design, draw, figure, map out, paint, picture, portray, render, sketch, trace

delineation *n* **1-3** = **outline**, account, chart, depiction, description, design, diagram, drawing, picture, portrait, portrayal, representation, tracing

delinquency *n* **1** = **crime**, fault, misbehaviour, misconduct, misdeed, misdemeanour, offence, wrongdoing

delinquent *n* **1** = **criminal**, culprit, defaulter, juvenile delinquent, lawbreaker, malefactor, miscreant, offender, villain, wrongdoer, young offender

delirious *adj* **1** = **mad**, crazy, demented, deranged, incoherent, insane, light-headed, raving, unhinged **2** = **ecstatic**, beside oneself, blissed out, carried away, excited, frantic, frenzied, hysterical, sent, wild
Antonyms *adj* calm, clear-headed, coherent, *compos mentis*, in one's right mind, lucid, rational, sane, sensible

delirium *n* **1** = **madness**, aberration, derangement, hallucination, insanity, lunacy, raving **2** = **frenzy**, ecstasy, fever, fury, hysteria, passion, rage

deliver *vb* **1** = **carry**, bear, bring, cart, convey, distribute, transport **2** = **hand over**, cede, commit, give up, grant, make over, relinquish, resign, surrender, transfer, turn over, yield **3** = **release**, acquit, discharge, emancipate, free, liberate, loose, ransom, redeem, rescue, save **5** = **give**, announce, declare, give forth, present, proclaim, pronounce, publish, read, utter **7** = **strike**, administer, aim, deal, direct, give, inflict, launch, throw

deliverance *n* **2** = **release**, emancipation, escape, liberation, ransom, redemption, rescue, salvation

delivery *n* **1a** = **handing over**, consignment, conveyance, dispatch, distribution, surrender, transfer, transmission, transmittal **2** = **childbirth**, confinement, labour, parturition **3** = **speech**, articulation, elocution, enunciation, intonation, utterance **5** = **release**, deliverance, escape, liberation, rescue

delude *vb* = **deceive**, bamboozle (*inf.*), beguile, cheat, con (*inf.*), cozen, dupe, fool, gull (*arch.*), hoax, hoodwink, impose on, kid (*inf.*), lead up the garden path (*inf.*), misguide, mislead, pull the wool over someone's eyes, take for a ride (*inf.*), take in (*inf.*), trick

deluge *n* **1, 2** = **flood**, cataclysm, downpour, inundation, overflowing, spate, torrent **3** = **rush**, flood. **5** to overwhelm; inundate. [C14: from OF, from L *dīluvium,* from *dīluere* to wash away, drench, from *di-* DIS-[1] + *-luere,* from *lavere* to wash]

Deluge (ˈdɛljuːdʒ) *n* **the.** another name for the **Flood.**

delusion Ⓣ (dɪˈluːʒən) *n* **1** a mistaken idea, belief, etc. **2** *Psychiatry.* a belief held in the face of evidence to the contrary, that is resistant to all reason. **3** a deluding or being deluded.
▸**deˈlusional** *adj* ▸**deˈlusive** *adj* ▸**delusory** (dɪˈluːsərɪ) *adj*

de luxe Ⓣ (də ˈlʌks, ˈlʊks) *adj* **1** rich or sumptuous; superior in quality: *the de luxe model of a car.* ◆ *adv* **2** *Chiefly US.* in a luxurious manner. [C19: from F, lit.: of luxury]

delve Ⓣ (dɛlv) *vb* **delves, delving, delved.** (*mainly intr;* often foll. by *in* or *into*) **1** to research deeply or intensively (for information, etc.). **2** to search or rummage. **3** to dig or burrow deeply. **4** (*also tr*) *Arch. or Brit. dialect.* to dig. [OE *delfan*]
▸**ˈdelver** *n*

Dem. (in the US) *abbrev. for* Democrat(ic).

demagnetize *or* **demagnetise** (diːˈmægnəˌtaɪz) *vb* **demagnetizes, demagnetizing, demagnetized** *or* **demagnetises, demagnetising, demagnetised.** to remove or lose magnetic properties. Also: **degauss.**
▸**deˌmagnetiˈzation** *or* **deˌmagnetiˈsation** *n* ▸**deˈmagnetˌizer** *or* **deˈmagnetˌiser** *n*

demagogue Ⓣ *or US* (*sometimes*) **demagog** (ˈdɛməˌgɒg) *n* **1** a political agitator who appeals with crude oratory to the prejudice and passions of the mob. **2** (esp. in the ancient world) any popular political leader or orator. [C17: from Gk *dēmagōgos* people's leader, from *dēmos* people + *agein* to lead]
▸ˌ**demaˈgogic** *adj* ▸ˌ**demaˈgoguery** *n*

demagogy (ˈdɛməˌgɒgɪ) *n, pl* **demagogies. 1** demagoguery. **2** rule by a demagogue or by demagogues. **3** a group of demagogues.

demand Ⓣ (dɪˈmɑːnd) *vb* (*tr; may take a clause as object or an infinitive*) **1** to request peremptorily or urgently. **2** to require as just, urgent, etc.: *the situation demands attention.* **3** to claim as a right; exact. **4** *Law.* to make a formal legal claim to (property). ◆ *n* **5** an urgent or peremptory requirement or request. **6** something that requires special effort or sacrifice. **7** the act of demanding something or the thing demanded. **8** an insistent question. **9** *Econ.* **9a** willingness and ability to purchase goods and services. **9b** the amount of a commodity that consumers are willing and able to purchase at a specified price. Cf. **supply**[1] (sense 9). **10** *Law.* a formal legal claim, esp. to real property. **11 in demand.** sought after. **12 on demand.** as soon as requested. [C13: from Anglo-F, from Med. L *dēmandāre,* from L: to commit to, from DE- + *mandāre* to command, entrust]
▸**deˈmandable** *adj* ▸**deˈmander** *n*

demand feeding *n* the practice of feeding a baby whenever it is hungry, rather than at set intervals.

demanding Ⓣ (dɪˈmɑːndɪŋ) *adj* requiring great patience, skill, etc.: *a demanding job.*

demarcate Ⓣ (ˈdiːmɑːˌkeɪt) *vb* **demarcates, demarcating, demarcated.** (*tr*) **1** to mark the boundaries, limits, etc., of. **2** to separate; distinguish.
▸**ˈdemarˌcator** *n*

demarcation Ⓣ *or* **demarkation** (ˌdiːmɑːˈkeɪʃən) *n* **1** the act of establishing limits or boundaries. **2** a limit or boundary. **3a** a strict separation of the kinds of work performed by members of different trade unions. **3b** (*as modifier*): *demarcation dispute.* **4** separation or distinction (as in **line of demarcation**). [C18: from Sp. *demarcar* to appoint the boundaries of, from *marcar* to mark, from It., of Gmc origin]

démarche *French.* (demarʃ) *n* a move, step, or manoeuvre, esp. in diplomatic affairs. [C17: lit.: walk, gait, from OF *demarcher* to tread, trample]

dematerialize *or* **dematerialise** (diːməˈtɪərɪəˌlaɪz) *vb* **dematerializes, dematerializing, dematerialized** *or* **dematerialises, dematerialising, dematerialised.** (*intr*) **1** to cease to have material existence, as in science fiction or spiritualism. **2** to vanish.
▸**demaˌterialiˈzation** *or* **demaˌterialiˈsation** *n*

deme (diːm) *n* **1** (in ancient Attica) a geographical unit of local government. **2** *Biol.* a group of individuals within a species that possess particular characteristics of cytology, genetics, etc. [C19: from Gk *dēmos* district in local government, the populace]

demean[1] Ⓣ (dɪˈmiːn) *vb* (*tr*) to lower (oneself) in dignity, status, or character; humble; debase. [C17: see DE-, MEAN[2]]

demean[2] (dɪˈmiːn) *vb* (*tr*) *Rare.* to behave or conduct (oneself). [C13: from OF, from DE- + *mener* to lead, from L *mināre* to drive (animals), from *minārī* to use threats]

demeanour Ⓣ *or US* **demeanor** (dɪˈmiːnə) *n* **1** the way a person behaves towards others. **2** bearing or mien. [C15: see DEMEAN[2]]

dement (dɪˈmɛnt) *vb* **1** (*intr*) to deteriorate mentally, esp. because of old age. **2** (*tr*) *Rare.* to drive mad; make insane. [C16: from LL *dēmentāre* to drive mad, from L DE- + *mēns* mind]

demented Ⓣ (dɪˈmɛntɪd) *adj* mad; insane.
▸**deˈmentedly** *adv* ▸**deˈmentedness** *n*

dementia (dɪˈmɛnʃə, -ʃɪə) *n* a state of serious mental deterioration, of organic or functional origin. [C19: from L: madness; see DEMENT]

dementia praecox (ˈpriːkɒks) *n* a former name for **schizophrenia.** [C19: NL, lit.: premature dementia]

demerara (ˌdɛməˈrɛərə, -ˈrɑːrə) *n* brown crystallized cane sugar from the Caribbean. [C19: after *Demerara,* a region of Guyana]

demerit (diːˈmɛrɪt) *n* **1** something that deserves censure. **2** *US & Canad.* a mark given against a student, etc., for failure or misconduct. **3** a fault. [C14 (orig.: worth, desert, ult.: something worthy of blame): from L *dēmerērī* to deserve]
▸**deˌmeriˈtorious** *adj*

demersal (dɪˈmɜːsᵊl) *adj* living or occurring in deep water or on the bottom of a sea or lake. [C19: from L *dēmersus* submerged (from *mergere* to dip) + -AL[1]]

demesne (dɪˈmeɪn, -ˈmiːn) *n* **1** land surrounding a house or manor. **2** *Property law.* the possession and use of one's own property or land. **3** realm; domain. **4** a region or district. [C14: from OF *demeine;* see DOMAIN]

demi- *prefix* **1** half: *demirelief.* **2** of less than full size, status, or rank: *demigod.* [via F from Med. L, from L *dīmidius* half, from *dis-* apart + *medius* middle]

demigod (ˈdɛmɪˌgɒd) *n* **1a** a being who is part mortal, part god. **1b** a lesser deity. **2** a person with godlike attributes. [C16: translation of L *sēmideus*]
▸**ˈdemiˌgoddess** *fem n*

demijohn (ˈdɛmɪˌdʒɒn) *n* a large bottle with a short narrow neck, often encased in wickerwork. [C18: prob. from F *dame-jeanne,* from *dame* lady + *Jeanne* Jane]

demilitarize *or* **demilitarise** (diːˈmɪlɪtəˌraɪz) *vb* **demilitarizes, demilitarizing, demilitarized** *or* **demilitarises, demilitarising, demilitarised.** (*tr*) **1** to remove and prohibit any military presence or function in (an area): *demilitarized zone.* **2** to free of military character, purpose, etc.
▸**deˌmilitariˈzation** *or* **deˌmilitariˈsation** *n*

demimondaine (ˌdɛmɪˈmɒndeɪn) *n* a woman of the demimonde. [C19: from F]

demimonde (ˌdɛmɪˈmɒnd) *n* **1** (esp. in the 19th century) those women considered to be outside respectable society, esp. on account of sexual promiscuity. **2** any group considered to be not wholly respectable. [C19: from F, lit.: half-world]

demise Ⓣ (dɪˈmaɪz) *n* **1** failure or termination. **2** a euphemistic or formal word for **death. 3** *Property law.* a transfer of an estate by lease or on the death of the owner. **4** the transfer of sovereignty to a successor upon the death, abdication, etc., of a ruler (esp. in **demise of the crown**).

THESAURUS

avalanche, barrage, flood, spate, torrent ◆ *vb* **4** = **flood,** douse, drench, drown, inundate, soak, submerge, swamp **5** = **overwhelm,** engulf, inundate, overload, overrun, swamp

delusion *n* **1-3** = **misconception,** deception, error, fallacy, false impression, fancy, hallucination, illusion, misapprehension, misbelief, mistake, phantasm, self-deception

delusive *adj* **1** = **deceptive,** chimerical, fallacious, illusive, illusory, misleading, specious, spurious

delusory 1 *adj* = **deceptive,** deluded, erroneous, fallacious, false, fictitious, illusory, imaginary, imagined, misguided, mistaken, unfounded
Antonyms *adj* actual, authentic, genuine, real, true

de luxe *adj* **1** = **luxurious,** choice, costly, elegant, exclusive, expensive, gorgeous, grand, opulent, palatial, plush (*inf.*), rich, select, special, splendid, splendiferous (*facetious*), sumptuous, superior

delve *vb* **1-3** = **research,** burrow, dig into, examine, explore, ferret out, forage, investigate, look into, probe, ransack, rummage, search, unearth

demagogue *n* **1** = **agitator,** firebrand, haranguer, rabble-rouser, soapbox orator

demand *vb* **1** = **request,** ask, challenge, inquire, interrogate, question **2** = **require,** call for, cry out for, entail, involve, necessitate, need, take, want **3** = **claim,** exact, expect, insist on, order ◆ *n* **5** = **request,** bidding, charge, inquiry, interrogation, order, question, requisition **9a** = **need,** call, claim, market, necessity, requirement, want **11 in demand** = **sought after,** fashionable, in vogue, like gold dust, needed, popular, requested
Antonyms *vb* ≠ **require, claim:** come up with, contribute, furnish, give, grant, produce, provide, supply, yield

demanding *adj* = **difficult,** challenging, exacting, exhausting, exigent, hard, taxing, tough, trying, wearing
Antonyms *adj* ≠ **difficult:** a piece of cake (*inf.*), child's play (*inf.*), easy, easy-peasy (*sl.*), effortless, facile, no bother, painless, simple, straightforward, uncomplicated, undemanding

demarcate *vb* **1, 2** = **delimit,** define, determine, differentiate, distinguish between, fix, mark, separate

demarcation *n* **1** = **delimitation,** differentiation, distinction, division, separation **2** = **limit,** bound, boundary, confine, enclosure, margin, pale

demean[1] *vb* = **lower,** abase, debase, degrade, descend, humble, stoop

demeaning *adj* = **humiliating,** beneath one's dignity, cheapening, contemptible, debasing, degrading, disgraceful, dishonourable, infra dig (*inf.*), shameful, undignified, unworthy

demeanour *n* **1, 2** = **behaviour,** air, bearing, carriage, comportment, conduct, deportment, manner, mien

demented *adj* = **mad,** barking (*sl.*), barking mad, crackbrained, crackpot (*inf.*), crazed, crazy, daft (*inf.*), deranged, distraught, doolally (*sl.*), dotty (*sl., chiefly Brit.*), foolish, frenzied, idiotic, insane, loopy (*inf.*), lunatic, maniacal, manic, *non compos mentis,* not the full shilling (*inf.*), off one's trolley (*sl.*), out to lunch (*inf.*), unbalanced, unhinged, up the pole (*inf.*)
Antonyms *adj* all there (*inf.*), *compos mentis,* in one's right mind, lucid, mentally sound, normal, of sound mind, rational, reasonable, sensible, sound

demise *n* **1** = **failure,** collapse, dissolution, downfall, end, fall, ruin, termination **2** *Euphemistic* = **death,** decease, departure, expiration **3** *Property law* = **death,** alienation, conveyance,

◆ *vb* **demises, demising, demised.** 5 to transfer or be transferred by inheritance, will, or succession. 6 (*tr*) *Property law.* to transfer for a limited period; lease. 7 (*tr*) to transfer (sovereignty, a title, etc.) [C16: from OF, fem of *demis* dismissed, from *demettre* to send away, from L *dīmittere*]
▶**de'misable** *adj*

demi-sec (ˌdɛmɪ'sɛk) *adj* (of wine) medium-dry. [C20: from F, from *demi* half + *sec* dry]

demisemiquaver ('dɛmɪˌsɛmɪˌkweɪvə) *n Music.* a note having the time value of one thirty-second of a semibreve. Usual US and Canad. name: **thirty-second note.**

demist (diː'mɪst) *vb* to free or become free of condensation.
▶**de'mister** *n*

demitasse ('dɛmɪˌtæs) *n* 1 a small cup used to serve coffee, esp. after a meal. 2 the coffee itself. [C19: F, lit.: half-cup]

demiurge ('dɛmɪˌɜːdʒ) *n* 1 (in the philosophy of Plato) the creator of the universe. 2 (in Gnostic philosophy) the creator of the universe, supernatural but subordinate to the Supreme Being. [C17: from Church L, from Gk *dēmiourgos* skilled workman, lit.: one who works for the people, from *dēmos* people + *ergon* work]
▶ˌ**demi'urgic** *or* ˌ**demi'urgical** *adj*

demiveg ('dɛmɪˌvɛdʒ) *Inf.* ◆ *n* 1 a person who eats poultry and fish, but no red meat. ◆ *adj* 2 denoting a person who eats poultry and fish, but no red meat. [C20: from DEMI- + VEG(ETARIAN)]

demo ('dɛməʊ) *n, pl* **demos.** *Inf.* 1 short for **demonstration** (sense 4). 2 a demonstration record or tape.

demo- *or before a vowel* **dem-** *combining form.* indicating people or population: *demography.* [from Gk *dēmos*]

demob *Brit. inf.* ◆ *vb* (diː'mɒb), **demobs, demobbing, demobbed.** 1 to demobilize. ◆ *n* ('diːmɒb). 2 demobilization.

demobilize ⓣ *or* **demobilise** (diː'məʊbɪˌlaɪz) *vb* **demobilizes, demobilizing, demobilized** *or* **demobilises, demobilising, demobilised.** to disband, as troops, etc.
▶**deˌmobili'zation** *or* **deˌmobili'sation** *n*

Demochristian (ˌdɛməʊ'krɪstjən) *n* an informal name for a **Christian Democrat.**

democracy ⓣ (dɪ'mɒkrəsɪ) *n, pl* **democracies.** 1 government by the people or their elected representatives. 2 a political or social unit governed ultimately by all its members. 3 the practice or spirit of social equality. 4 a social condition of classlessness and equality. [C16: from F, from LL, from Gk *dēmokratia* government by the people]

democrat ('dɛməˌkræt) *n* 1 an advocate of democracy. 2 a member or supporter of a democratic party or movement.

Democrat ('dɛməˌkræt) *n* (in the US) a member or supporter of the Democratic Party.
▶ˌ**Demo'cratic** *adj*

democratic ⓣ (ˌdɛmə'krætɪk) *adj* 1 of or relating to the principles of democracy. 2 upholding democracy or the interests of the common people. 3 popular with or for the benefit of all.
▶ˌ**demo'cratically** *adv*

democratic centralism *n* the Leninist principle that policy should be decided centrally by officials, who are nominally democratically elected.

democratize *or* **democratise** (dɪ'mɒkrəˌtaɪz) *vb* **democratizes, democratizing, democratized** *or* **democratises, democratising, democratised.** (*tr*) to make democratic.
▶**deˌmocrati'zation** *or* **deˌmocrati'sation** *n*

démodé *French.* (demɔde) *adj* outmoded. [F, from *dé-* out of + *mode* fashion]

demodulate (diː'mɒdjʊˌleɪt) *vb* **demodulates, demodulating, demodulated.** to carry out demodulation on.
▶**de'moduˌlator** *n*

demodulation (ˌdiːmɒdjʊ'leɪʃən) *n Electronics.* the act or process by which an output wave or signal is obtained having the characteristics of the original modulating wave or signal; the reverse of modulation.

demographic timebomb *n Chiefly Brit.* a predicted shortage of school-leavers and consequently of available workers, caused by an earlier drop in the birth rate.

demography (dɪ'mɒgrəfɪ) *n* the scientific study of human populations, esp. of their size, distribution, etc. [C19: from F, from Gk *dēmos* the populace; see -GRAPHY]
▶**de'mographer** *n* ▶**demographic** (ˌdiːmə'græfɪk, ˌdɛmə-) *adj*

demoiselle (dəmwɑː'zɛl) *n* 1 a small crane of central Asia, N Africa, and SE Europe, having a grey plumage with black breast feathers and white ear tufts. 2 a less common name for a **damselfly.** 3 a literary word for **damsel.** [C16: from F: young woman; see DAMSEL]

demolish ⓣ (dɪ'mɒlɪʃ) *vb* (*tr*) 1 to tear down or break up (buildings, etc.). 2 to put an end to (an argument, etc.). 3 *Facetious.* to eat up. [C16: from F, from L *dēmōlīrī* to throw down, from DE- + *mōlīrī* to construct, from *mōles* mass]
▶**de'molisher** *n*

demolition ⓣ (ˌdɛmə'lɪʃən, ˌdiː-) *n* 1 a demolishing or being demolished. 2 *Chiefly mil.* destruction by explosives.
▶ˌ**demo'litionist** *n, adj*

demon ⓣ ('diːmən) *n* 1 an evil spirit or devil. 2 a person, obsession, etc., thought of as evil or cruel. 3 Also called: **daemon, daimon.** an attendant or ministering spirit; genius: *the demon of inspiration.* 4a a person extremely skilful in or devoted to a given activity, esp. a sport: *a demon at cycling.* 4b (*as modifier*): *a demon cyclist.* 5 a variant spelling of **daemon** (senses 1, 2). 6 *Austral. & NZ sl.* a detective or policeman, esp. one in plain clothes. [C15: from L *daemōn* (evil) spirit, from Gk *daimōn* spirit, deity, fate]
▶**demonic** (dɪ'mɒnɪk) *adj*

demonetize *or* **demonetise** (diː'mʌnɪˌtaɪz) *vb* **demonetizes, demonetizing, demonetized** *or* **demonetises, demonetising, demonetised.** (*tr*) 1 to deprive (a metal) of its capacity as a monetary standard. 2 to withdraw from use as currency.
▶**deˌmoneti'zation** *or* **deˌmoneti'sation** *n*

demoniac (dɪ'məʊnɪˌæk) *adj also* **demoniacal** (ˌdiːmə'naɪəkᵊl). 1 of or like a demon. 2 suggesting inner possession or inspiration. 3 frantic; frenzied. ◆ *n* 4 a person possessed by a demon.
▶ˌ**demo'niacally** *adv*

demonism ('diːməˌnɪzəm) *n* 1 belief in the existence and power of demons. 2 another name for **demonology** (sense 1).
▶'**demonist** *n*

demonolatry (ˌdiːmə'nɒlətrɪ) *n* the worship of demons. [C17: see DEMON, -LATRY]

demonology (ˌdiːmə'nɒlədʒɪ) *n* 1 Also called: **demonism.** the study of demons or demonic beliefs. 2 a set of people or things that are disliked or feared: *Adolf Hitler's place in contemporary demonology.*
▶ˌ**demon'ologist** *n*

demonstrable ⓣ ('dɛmənstrəbᵊl, dɪ'mɒn-) *adj* able to be demonstrated or proved.
▶ˌ**demonstra'bility** *n* ▶'**demonstrably** *adv*

demonstrate ⓣ ('dɛmənˌstreɪt) *vb* **demonstrates, demonstrating, demonstrated.** 1 (*tr*) to show or prove, esp. by reasoning, evidence, etc. 2 (*tr*) to evince; reveal the existence of. 3 (*tr*) to explain by experiment, example, etc. 4 (*tr*) to display and explain the workings of (a machine, product, etc.). 5 (*intr*) to manifest support, protest, etc., by public parades or rallies. 6 (*intr*) to be employed as a demonstrator of machinery, etc. 7 (*intr*) *Mil.* to make a show of force. [C16: from L *dēmonstrāre* to point out, from *monstrāre* to show]

demonstration ⓣ (ˌdɛmən'streɪʃən) *n* 1 the act of demonstrating. 2 proof or evidence leading to proof. 3 an explanation, illustration, or experiment showing how something works. 4 Also: **demo.** a manifestation of support or protest by public rallies, parades, etc. 5 a manifestation of emotion. 6 a show of military force.
▶ˌ**demon'strational** *adj* ▶ˌ**demon'strationist** *n*

demonstration model *n* a nearly new product, such as a car, that has been used to demonstrate its performance by a dealer and is offered at a discount.

demonstrative ⓣ (dɪ'mɒnstrətɪv) *adj* 1 tending to express one's feelings easily or unreservedly. 2 (*postpositive; foll. by of*) serving as proof; indicative. 3 involving or characterized by demonstration. 4 conclusive. 5 *Grammar.* denoting or belonging to a class of determiners used to point out the individual referent or referents intended, such as *this*

THESAURUS

transfer, transmission ◆ *vb* 5 = **transfer**, bequeath, convey, grant, leave, will

demobilize *vb* = **discharge**, deactivate, decommission, demob (*Brit. inf.*), disband, release
Antonyms *vb* call up, conscript, draft (*US.*), enlist, enrol, mobilize, muster, recruit

democracy *n* 1, 2 = **self-government**, commonwealth, government by the people, representative government, republic

democratic *adj* 1-3 = **self-governing**, autonomous, egalitarian, popular, populist, representative, republican

demolish *vb* 1 = **knock down**, bulldoze, destroy, dismantle, flatten, level, overthrow, pulverize, raze, ruin, tear down, total (*sl.*), trash (*sl.*) 2 = **defeat**, annihilate, blow out of the water (*sl.*), destroy, lick (*inf.*), master, overthrow, overturn, stuff (*sl.*), tank (*sl.*), undo, wipe the floor with (*inf.*), wreck 3 *Facetious* = **devour**, consume, eat, gobble up, put away
Antonyms *vb* ≠ **knock down**: build, construct, create, repair, restore, strengthen

demolition *n* 1 = **knocking down**, bulldozing, destruction, explosion, levelling, razing, tearing down, wrecking

demon *n* 1 = **evil spirit**, devil, fiend, ghoul, goblin, malignant spirit 2 = **monster**, devil, fiend, ghoul, rogue, villain 4a = **wizard**, ace (*inf.*), addict, fanatic, fiend, master

demonic *adj* 1 = **devilish**, diabolic, diabolical, fiendish, hellish, infernal, satanic 2 = **frenzied**, crazed, frantic, frenetic, furious, hectic, like one possessed, mad, maniacal, manic

demonstrable *adj* = **provable**, attestable, axiomatic, certain, evident, evincible, incontrovertible, indubitable, irrefutable, obvious, palpable, positive, self-evident, undeniable, unmistakable, verifiable

demonstrate *vb* 1 = **prove**, display, establish, evidence, evince, exhibit, indicate, manifest, show, testify to 3 = **show how**, describe, explain, illustrate, make clear, teach 5 = **march**, parade, picket, protest, rally

demonstration *n* 2 = **proof**, affirmation, confirmation, display, evidence, exhibition, expression, illustration, manifestation, substantiation, testimony, validation 3 = **explanation**, description, exposition, presentation, test, trial 4 = **march**, mass lobby, parade, picket, protest, rally, sit-in

demonstrative *adj* 1 = **open**, affectionate, effusive, emotional, expansive, expressive, gushing, loving, unreserved, unrestrained 3 = **indicative**, evincive, explanatory, expository, illustrative, symptomatic
Antonyms *adj* ≠ **open**: aloof, cold, contained, distant, formal, impassive, reserved, restrained, stiff, unaffectionate, undemonstrative, unemotional, unresponsive

demoralization *n* 1 = **lowering** *or* **loss of morale**, agitation, crushing, devitalization, dis-

and *those.* Cf. **interrogative, relative.** ◆ *n* **6** *Grammar.* a demonstrative word.
▸**de'monstratively** *adv* ▸**de'monstrativeness** *n*

demonstrator ('dɛmənˌstreɪtə) *n* **1** a person who demonstrates equipment, machines, products, etc. **2** a person who demonstrates in a public demonstration.

demoralize ❶ *or* **demoralise** (dɪ'mɒrəˌlaɪz) *vb* **demoralizes, demoralizing, demoralized** *or* **demoralises, demoralising, demoralised.** (*tr*) **1** to undermine the morale of; dishearten. **2** to corrupt. **3** to throw into confusion.
▸**deˌmorali'zation** *or* **deˌmorali'sation** *n*

demote ❶ (dɪ'məʊt) *vb* **demotes, demoting, demoted.** (*tr*) to lower in rank or position; relegate. [C19: from DE- + (PRO)MOTE]
▸**de'motion** *n*

demotic (dɪ'mɒtɪk) *adj* **1** of or relating to the common people; popular. **2** of or relating to a simplified form of hieroglyphics used in ancient Egypt. Cf. **hieratic.** ◆ *n* **3** the demotic script of ancient Egypt. [C19: from Gk *dēmotikos* of the people, from *dēmotēs* a man of the people, commoner]
▸**de'motist** *n*

dempster ('dɛmpstə) *n* a variant spelling of **deemster.**

demulcent (dɪ'mʌlsᵊnt) *adj* **1** soothing. ◆ *n* **2** a drug or agent that soothes irritation. [C18: from L *dēmulcēre,* from DE- + *mulcēre* to stroke]

demur ❶ (dɪ'mɜː) *vb* **demurs, demurring, demurred.** (*intr*) **1** to show reluctance. **2** *Law.* to raise an objection by entering a demurrer. ◆ *n also* **demurral** (dɪ'mʌrəl). **3** the act of demurring. **4** an objection raised. [C13: from OF, from L *dēmorārī,* from *morārī* to delay]
▸**de'murrable** *adj*

demure ❶ (dɪ'mjʊə) *adj* **1** sedate; decorous; reserved. **2** affectedly modest or prim; coy. [C14: ?from OF *demorer* to delay, linger; ? infl. by *meur* ripe, MATURE]
▸**de'murely** *adv* ▸**de'mureness** *n*

demurrage (dɪ'mʌrɪdʒ) *n* **1** the delaying of a ship, etc., caused by the charterer's failure to load, unload, etc., before the time of scheduled departure. **2** the extra charge required for such delay. [C14: from OF *demorage, demourage;* see DEMUR]

demurrer (dɪ'mʌrə) *n* **1** *Law.* a pleading that admits an opponent's point but denies that it is relevant or valid. **2** any objection raised.

demutualize *or* **demutualise** (diː'mjuːtjʊəˌlaɪz) *vb* **demutualizes, demutualizing, demutualized** *or* **demutualises, demutualising, demutualised.** (*intr*) (of a mutual savings or life-assurance organization) to convert to a public limited company.
▸**ˌdemutuali'zation** *or* **ˌdemutuali'sation** *n*

demy (dɪ'maɪ) *n, pl* **demies. 1** a size of printing paper, 17½ by 22½ inches (444.5 × 571.5 mm). **2** a size of writing paper, 15½ by 20 inches (Brit.) (393.7 × 508 mm) or 16 by 21 inches (US) (406.4 × 533.4 mm). [C16: see DEMI-]

demystify (diː'mɪstɪˌfaɪ) *vb* **demystifies, demystifying, demystified.** (*tr*) to remove the mystery from.
▸**deˌmystifi'cation** *n*

demythologize *or* **demythologise** (ˌdiːmɪ'θɒləˌdʒaɪz) *vb* **demythologizes, demythologizing, demythologized** *or* **demythologises, demythologising, demythologised.** (*tr*) **1** to eliminate mythical elements from (a piece of writing, esp. the Bible). **2** to restate (a religious message) in rational terms.

den ❶ (dɛn) *n* **1** the habitat or retreat of a wild animal; lair. **2** a small or secluded room in a home, often used for carrying on a hobby. **3** a squalid room or retreat. **4** a site or haunt: *a den of vice.* **5** *Scot.* a small wooded valley. ◆ *vb* **dens, denning, denned. 6** (*intr*) to live in or as if in a den. [OE *denn*]

Den. *abbrev. for* Denmark.

denar (dɪ'nɑː) *n* the standard monetary unit of (the Former Yugoslav Republic of) Macedonia.

denarius (dɪ'nɛərɪəs) *n, pl* **denarii** (-'nɛərɪˌaɪ). **1** a silver coin of ancient Rome, often called a penny in translation. **2** a gold coin worth 25 silver denarii. [C16: from L: coin orig. equal to ten asses, from *dēnārius* (adj) containing ten, from *decem* ten]

denary ('diːnərɪ) *adj* **1** calculated by tens; decimal. **2** containing ten parts; tenfold. [C16: from L *dēnārius;* see DENARIUS]

denationalize *or* **denationalise** (diː'næʃənᵊˌlaɪz) *vb* **denationalizes, denationalizing, denationalized** *or* **denationalises, denationalising, denationalised. 1** to transfer (an industry, etc.) from public to private ownership. **2** to deprive of national character or nationality.
▸**deˌnationali'zation** *or* **deˌnationali'sation** *n*

denaturalize *or* **denaturalise** (diː'nætʃrəˌlaɪz) *vb* **denaturalizes, denaturalizing, denaturalized** *or* **denaturalises, denaturalising, denaturalised.** (*tr*) **1** to deprive of nationality. **2** to make unnatural.
▸**deˌnaturali'zation** *or* **deˌnaturali'sation** *n*

denature (diː'neɪtʃə) *or* **denaturize, denaturise** (diː'neɪtʃəˌraɪz) *vb* **denatures, denaturing, denatured** *or* **denaturizes, denaturizing, denaturized; denaturises, denaturising, denaturised.** (*tr*) **1** to change the nature of. **2** to change the properties of (a protein), as by the action of acid or heat. **3** to render (something, such as alcohol) unfit for consumption by adding nauseous substances. **4** to render (fissile material) unfit for use in nuclear weapons by addition of an isotope.
▸**de'naturant** *n* ▸**deˌnatur'ation** *n*

dendrite ('dɛndraɪt) *n* **1** Also called: **dendron.** any of the branched extensions of a nerve cell, which conduct impulses towards the cell body. **2** a branching mosslike crystalline structure in some rocks and minerals. **3** a crystal that has branched during growth. [C18: from Gk *dendritēs* relating to a tree]
▸**dendritic** (dɛn'drɪtɪk) *adj*

dendro-, dendri-, *or before a vowel* **dendr-** *combining form.* tree: *dendrochronology.* [NL, from Gk, from *dendron* tree]

dendrochronology (ˌdɛndrəʊkrə'nɒlədʒɪ) *n* the study of the annual rings of trees, used esp. to date past events.

dendrology (dɛn'drɒlədʒɪ) *n* the branch of botany that is concerned with the natural history of trees.
▸**dendrological** (ˌdɛndrə'lɒdʒɪkᵊl) *or* **ˌdendro'logic** *adj* ▸**den'drologist** *n*

dene[1] *or* **dean** (diːn) *n Brit.* a narrow wooded valley. [OE *denu* valley]

dene[2] *or* **dean** (diːn) *n Dialect, chiefly southern English.* a sandy stretch of land or dune near the sea. [C13: prob. rel. to OE *dūn* hill]

denervate ('dɛnəˌveɪt) *vb* **denervates, denervating, denervated.** (*tr*) to deprive (a tissue or organ) of its nerve supply.
▸**ˌdener'vation** *n*

dengue ('dɛŋgɪ) *or* **dandy** ('dændɪ) *n* an acute viral disease transmitted by mosquitoes, characterized by headache, fever, pains in the joints, and skin rash. [C19: from Sp., prob. of African origin]

deniable (dɪ'naɪəbᵊl) *adj* able to be denied; questionable.
▸**de'niably** *adv*

denial ❶ (dɪ'naɪəl) *n* **1** a refusal to agree or comply with a statement. **2** the rejection of the truth of a proposition, doctrine, etc. **3** a rejection of a request. **4** a refusal to acknowledge; disavowal. **5** a psychological process by which painful truths are not admitted into an individual's consciousness. **6** abstinence; self-denial.

denier[1] *n* **1** ('dɛnɪˌeɪ, 'dɛnjə). a unit of weight used to measure the fineness of silk and man-made fibres, esp. when woven into women's tights, etc. **2** (də'njeɪ, -'nɪə). any of several former European coins of various denominations. [C15: from OF: coin, from L *dēnārius* DENARIUS]

denier[2] (dɪ'naɪə) *n* a person who denies.

denigrate ❶ ('dɛnɪˌgreɪt) *vb* **denigrates, denigrating, denigrated.** (*tr*) to belittle or disparage the character of; defame. [C16: from L *dēnigrāre* to make very black, from *nigrāre,* from *niger* black]
▸**ˌdeni'gration** *n* ▸**'deniˌgrator** *n*

denim ('dɛnɪm) *n* **1** a hard-wearing twill-weave cotton fabric used for trousers, work clothes, etc. **2** a similar lighter fabric used in upholstery. [C17: from F (*serge*) *de Nîmes* (serge) of Nîmes, in S France]

denims ('dɛnɪmz) *pl n* jeans or overalls made of denim.

denizen ❶ ('dɛnɪzən) *n* **1** an inhabitant; resident. **2** *Brit.* an individual permanently resident in a foreign country where he enjoys certain rights of citizenship. **3** a plant or animal established in a place to which it is not native. **4** a naturalized foreign word. [C15: from Anglo-F *denisein,* from OF *denzein,* from *denz* within, from L *de intus* from within]

THESAURUS

comfiture, enervation, panic, perturbation, trepidation, unmanning, weakening

demoralize *vb* **1 = dishearten,** cripple, daunt, deject, depress, disconcert, discourage, dispirit, enfeeble, psych out (*inf.*), rattle (*inf.*), sap, shake, undermine, unnerve, weaken
Antonyms *vb* boost, cheer, egg on, encourage, gee up, hearten, spur

demoralized *adj* **1 = disheartened,** broken, crushed, depressed, discouraged, dispirited, downcast, sick as a parrot (*inf.*), subdued, unmanned, unnerved, weakened

demoralizing *adj* **1 = disheartening,** crushing, dampening, daunting, depressing, disappointing, discouraging, dispiriting
Antonyms *adj* cheering, comforting, encouraging, heartening, reassuring

demote *vb* **= downgrade,** declass, degrade, disrate (*Naval*), kick downstairs (*sl.*), lower in rank, relegate

Antonyms *vb* advance, elevate, kick upstairs (*inf.*), prefer, promote, raise, upgrade

demur *vb* **1 = object,** balk, cavil, disagree, dispute, doubt, hesitate, pause, protest, refuse, take exception, waver

demure *adj* **1 = shy,** decorous, diffident, grave, modest, reserved, reticent, retiring, sedate, sober, staid, unassuming **2 = coy,** affected, bashful, niminy-piminy, priggish, prim, prissy (*inf.*), prudish, strait-laced
Antonyms *adj* brash, brazen, forward, immodest, impudent, shameless

den *n* **1 = lair,** cave, cavern, haunt, hide-out, hole, shelter **2 = study,** cloister, cubbyhole, hideaway, retreat, sanctuary, sanctum, snuggery

denial *n* **1 = negation,** adjuration, contradiction, disavowal, disclaimer, dismissal, dissent, renunciation, repudiation, retraction **3 = refusal,** prohibition, rebuff, rejection, repulse, veto

Antonyms *n* ≠ **negation:** acknowledgment, admission, affirmation, avowal, confession, declaration, disclosure, divulgence, profession, revelation

denigrate *vb* **= disparage,** asperse, bad-mouth (*sl., chiefly US & Canad.*), belittle, besmirch, blacken, calumniate, decry, defame, impugn, knock (*inf.*), malign, revile, rubbish (*inf.*), run down, slag (off) (*sl.*), slander, vilify
Antonyms *vb* acclaim, admire, approve, cheer, compliment, eulogize, extol, honour, laud, praise, take one's hat off to

denigration *n* **= disparagement,** aspersion, backbiting, defamation, detraction, obloquy, scandal, scurrility, slander, vilification

denizen *n* **1 = inhabitant,** citizen, dweller, occupant, resident

denominate ⓘ *vb* (dɪˈnɒmɪˌneɪt). **denominates, denominating, denominated.** **1** (*tr*) to give a specific name to; designate. ◆ *adj* (dɪˈnɒmɪnɪt, -ˌneɪt). **2** *Maths.* (of a number) representing a multiple of a unit of measurement: *4 is the denominate number in 4 miles.* [C16: from L *denōminare* from DE- (intensive) + *nōminare* to name]

denomination ⓘ (dɪˌnɒmɪˈneɪʃən) *n* **1** a group having a distinctive interpretation of a religious faith and usually its own organization. **2** a grade or unit in a series of designations of value, weight, measure, etc. **3** a name given to a class or group; classification. **4** the act of giving a name. **5** a name; designation.
▸**deˌnomiˈnational** *adj*

denominative (dɪˈnɒmɪnətɪv) *adj* **1** giving or constituting a name. **2** *Grammar.* **2a** formed from or having the same form as a noun. **2b** (*as n*): *the verb "to mushroom" is a denominative.*

denominator (dɪˈnɒmɪˌneɪtə) *n* the divisor of a fraction, as 8 in ⅞. Cf. **numerator.**

denotation ⓘ (ˌdiːnəʊˈteɪʃən) *n* **1** a denoting; indication. **2** a particular meaning given by a sign or symbol. **3** specific meaning as distinguished from suggestive meaning and associations. **4** *Logic.* another word for **extension** (sense 10).

denote ⓘ (dɪˈnəʊt) *vb* **denotes, denoting, denoted.** (*tr; may take a clause as object*) **1** to be a sign of; designate. **2** (of words, phrases, etc.) to have as a literal or obvious meaning. [C16: from L *dēnotāre* to mark, from *notāre* to mark, NOTE]
▸**deˈnotative** *adj*

denouement ⓘ (deɪˈnuːmɒn) *or* **dénouement** (*French* denumɑ̃) *n* **1** the clarification or resolution of a plot in a play or other work. **2** final outcome; solution. [C18: from F, lit.: an untying, from OF *desnoer,* from *des-* DE- + *noer* to tie, from L *nōdus* a knot]

denounce ⓘ (dɪˈnaʊns) *vb* **denounces, denouncing, denounced.** (*tr*) **1** to condemn openly or vehemently. **2** to give information against; accuse. **3** to announce formally the termination of (a treaty, etc.). [C13: from OF *denoncier,* from L *dēnuntiāre* to make an official proclamation, threaten, from DE- + *nuntiāre* to announce]
▸**deˈnouncement** *n* ▸**deˈnouncer** *n*

de novo *Latin.* (diː ˈnəʊvəʊ) *adv* from the beginning; anew.

dense ⓘ (dɛns) *adj* **1** thickly crowded or closely set. **2** thick; impenetrable. **3** *Physics.* having a high density. **4** stupid; dull. **5** (of a photographic negative) having many dark or exposed areas. [C15: from L *densus* thick]
▸**ˈdensely** *adv* ▸**ˈdenseness** *n*

densimeter (dɛnˈsɪmɪtə) *n Physics.* any instrument for measuring density.
▸**densimetric** (ˌdɛnsɪˈmɛtrɪk) *adj* ▸**denˈsimetry** *n*

density ⓘ (ˈdɛnsɪtɪ) *n, pl* **densities.** **1** the degree to which something is filled or occupied: *high density of building in towns.* **2** stupidity. **3** a measure of the compactness of a substance, expressed as its mass per unit volume. Symbol: ρ. See also **relative density.** **4** a measure of a physical quantity per unit of length, area, or volume. **5** *Physics, photog.* a measure of the extent to which a substance or surface transmits or reflects light.

dent ⓘ (dɛnt) *n* **1** a hollow in a surface, as one made by pressure or a blow. **2** an appreciable effect, esp. of lessening: *a dent in our resources.* ◆ *vb* (*tr*) **3** to make a dent in. [C13 (in the sense: a stroke, blow): var. of DINT]

dental (ˈdentᵊl) *adj* **1** of or relating to the teeth or dentistry. **2** *Phonetics.* pronounced with the tip of the tongue touching the backs of the upper teeth, as for *t* in French *tout.* ◆ *n* **3** *Phonetics.* a dental consonant. [C16: from Med. L *dentālis,* from L *dens* tooth]

dental floss *n* a waxed thread used to remove food particles from between the teeth.

dental plaque *n* a filmy deposit on the surface of a tooth consisting of a mixture of mucus, bacteria, food, etc.

dental surgeon *n* another name for **dentist.**

dentate (ˈdenteɪt) *adj* **1** having teeth or toothlike processes. **2** (of leaves) having a toothed margin. [C19: from L *dentātus*]
▸**ˈdentately** *adv*

denti- *or before a vowel* **dent-** *combining form.* indicating a tooth: *dentine.* [from L *dens, dent-*]

denticulate (dɛnˈtɪkjʊlɪt, -ˌleɪt) *adj* **1** *Biol.* very finely toothed: *denticulate leaves.* **2** *Arch.* having dentils. [C17: from L *denticulātus* having small teeth]

dentifrice (ˈdɛntɪfrɪs) *n* any substance, esp. paste or powder, for use in cleaning the teeth. [C16: from L *dentifricium,* from *dent-, dens* tooth + *fricāre* to rub]

dentil (ˈdɛntɪl) *n* one of a set of small square or rectangular blocks evenly spaced to form an ornamental row. [C17: from F, from obs. *dentille* a little tooth, from *dent* tooth]

dentine (ˈdɛntiːn) *or* **dentin** (ˈdɛntɪn) *n* the calcified tissue comprising the bulk of a tooth. [C19: from DENTI- + -IN]
▸**ˈdentinal** *adj*

dentist (ˈdɛntɪst) *n* a person qualified to practise dentistry. [C18: from F *dentiste,* from *dent* tooth]

dentistry (ˈdɛntɪstrɪ) *n* the branch of medical science concerned with the diagnosis and treatment of disorders of the teeth and gums.

dentition (dɛnˈtɪʃən) *n* **1** the arrangement, type, and number of the teeth in a particular species. **2** the time or process of teething. [C17: from L *dentītiō* a teething]

denture (ˈdɛntʃə) *n* (*usually pl*) **1** a partial or full set of artificial teeth. **2** *Rare.* a set of natural teeth. [C19: from F, from *dent* tooth + -URE]

denuclearize *or* **denuclearise** (dɪˈnjuːklɪəˌraɪz) *vb* **denuclearizes, denuclearizing, denuclearized** *or* **denuclearises, denuclearising, denuclearised.** (*tr*) to deprive (a state, etc.) of nuclear weapons.
▸**deˌnucleariˈzation** *or* **deˌnucleariˈsation** *n*

denudate (ˈdɛnjʊˌdeɪt, dɪˈnjuːdeɪt) *vb* **denudates, denudating, denudated.** **1** a less common word for **denude.** ◆ *adj* **2** denuded.

denude ⓘ (dɪˈnjuːd) *vb* **denudes, denuding, denuded.** (*tr*) **1** to make bare; strip. **2** to expose (rock) by the erosion of the layers above.
▸**denudation** (ˌdɛnjuˈdeɪʃən) *n*

denumerable (dɪˈnjuːmərəbᵊl) *adj Maths.* capable of being put into a one-to-one correspondence with the positive integers; countable.
▸**deˈnumerably** *adv*

denunciate ⓘ (dɪˈnʌnsɪˌeɪt) *vb* **denunciates, denunciating, denunciated.** (*tr*) to condemn; denounce. [C16: from L *dēnuntiāre;* see DENOUNCE]
▸**deˈnunciˌator** *n* ▸**deˈnunciatory** *adj*

denunciation ⓘ (dɪˌnʌnsɪˈeɪʃən) *n* **1** open condemnation; denouncing. **2** *Law, obsolete.* a charge or accusation of crime made before a public prosecutor or tribunal. **3** a formal announcement of the termination of a treaty.

Denver boot *n* a slang name for **wheel clamp.** [C20: from *Denver,* Colorado, where the device was first used]

deny ⓘ (dɪˈnaɪ) *vb* **denies, denying, denied.** (*tr*) **1** to declare (a statement, etc.) to be untrue. **2** to reject as false. **3** to withhold. **4** to refuse to fulfil the expectations of: *it is hard to deny a child.* **5** to refuse to acknowledge; disown. **6** to refuse (oneself) things desired. [C13: from OF *denier,* from L *dēnegāre,* from *negāre*]

deodar (ˈdiːəʊˌdɑː) *n* **1** a Himalayan cedar with drooping branches. **2** the durable fragrant highly valued wood of this tree. [C19: from Hindi, from Sansk. *devadāru,* lit.: wood of the gods]

deodorant ⓘ (diːˈəʊdərənt) *n* **1** a substance applied to the body to suppress or mask the odour of perspiration. **2** any substance for destroying or masking odours.

deodorize ⓘ *or* **deodorise** (diːˈəʊdəˌraɪz) *vb* **deodorizes, deodorizing, deodorized** *or* **deodorises, deodorising, deodorised.** (*tr*) to remove, disguise, or absorb the odour of, esp. when unpleasant.
▸**deˌodoriˈzation** *or* **deˌodoriˈsation** *n* ▸**deˈodorˌizer** *or* **deˈodorˌiser** *n*

deontic (diːˈɒntɪk) *adj Logic.* **a** of such ethical concepts as obligation and permissibility. **b** designating the branch of logic that deals with the formalization of these concepts. [C19: from Gk *deon* duty, from impersonal *dei* it behoves, it is binding]
▸**ˌdeonˈtology** *n*

deoxidize *or* **deoxidise** (diːˈɒksɪˌdaɪz) *vb* **deoxidizes, deoxidizing, deoxidized** *or* **deoxidises, deoxidising, deoxidised.** **1** (*tr*) to remove oxygen

THESAURUS

denominate *vb* **1** = **name**, call, christen, designate, dub, entitle, phrase, style, term

denomination *n* **1** = **religious group**, belief, communion, creed, persuasion, school, sect **2** = **unit**, grade, size, value **3** = **classification**, body, category, class, group **5** = **name**, appellation, designation, label, style, term, title

denotation *n* **1** = **indication**, designation, meaning, signification, specification

denote *vb* **1** = **indicate**, betoken, designate, express, imply, import, mark, mean, show, signify, typify

denouement *n* **1, 2** = **outcome**, climax, conclusion, culmination, finale, resolution, solution, termination, upshot

denounce *vb* **1, 2** = **condemn**, accuse, arraign, attack, brand, castigate, censure, declaim against, decry, denunciate, excoriate, impugn, point a *or* the finger at, proscribe, revile, stigmatize, vilify

dense *adj* **1, 2** = **thick**, close, close-knit, compact, compressed, condensed, heavy, impenetrable, opaque, solid, substantial, thickset **4** *Informal* = **stupid**, blockish, braindead (*inf.*), crass, dead from the neck up (*inf.*), dozy (*Brit. inf.*), dull, dumb (*inf.*), obtuse, slow, slow-witted, stolid, thick, thick-witted
Antonyms *adj* ≠ **thick:** light, scattered, sparse, thin, transparent ≠ **stupid:** alert, bright, clever, intelligent, quick

density *n* **1** = **tightness**, body, bulk, closeness, compactness, consistency, crowdedness, denseness, impenetrability, mass, solidity, thickness **2** *Informal* = **stupidity**, crassness, dullness, obtuseness, slowness, stolidity, thickness

dent *n* **1** = **hollow**, chip, concavity, crater, depression, dimple, dip, impression, indentation, pit ◆ *vb* **3** = **make a dent in**, depress, dint, gouge, hollow, imprint, make concave, press in, push in

denude *vb* **1** = **strip**, bare, divest, expose, lay bare, uncover

denunciate *vb* = **condemn**, castigate, curse, damn, denounce, stigmatize, vituperate

denunciation *n* **1** = **condemnation**, accusation, castigation, censure, character assassination, criticism, denouncement, fulmination, incrimination, invective, obloquy, stick (*sl.*), stigmatization

denunciatory *adj* = **condemnatory**, accusatory, censorious, comminatory, fulminatory, incriminatory, recriminatory, reproachful

deny *vb* **1, 2** = **contradict**, disagree with, disprove, gainsay (*arch. or literary*), oppose, rebuff, rebut, refute **3** = **refuse**, begrudge, decline, disallow, forbid, negate, reject, turn down, veto, withhold **5** = **renounce**, abjure, disavow, discard, disclaim, disown, recant, renege, repudiate, retract, revoke
Antonyms *vb* ≠ **contradict:** accept, acknowledge, admit, affirm, agree, allow, concede, confirm, recognize, take on board ≠ **refuse:** accept, grant, let, permit, receive

deodorant *n* **1, 2** = **antiperspirant**, air freshener, deodorizer, disinfectant, fumigant

deodorize *vb* = **purify**, aerate, disinfect, freshen, fumigate, refresh, ventilate

atoms from (a compound, molecule, etc.). **2** another word for **reduce** (sense 12).
▸**de,oxidi'zation** *or* **de,oxidi'sation** *n* ▸**de'oxi,dizer** *or* **de'oxi,diser** *n*

deoxygenate (diːˈɒksɪdʒɪˌneɪt) *or* **deoxygenize, deoxygenise** (diːˈɒksɪdʒɪˌnaɪz) *vb* **deoxygenates, deoxygenating, deoxygenated** *or* **deoxygenizes, deoxygenizing, deoxygenized; deoxygenises, deoxygenising, deoxygenised.** (*tr*) to remove oxygen from.
▸**de,oxygen'ation** *n*

deoxyribonuclease (diːˈɒksɪˌraɪbəʊˈnjuːklɪeɪz) *n* the full name for **DNAase.**

deoxyribonucleic acid (diːˌɒksɪˌraɪbəʊnjuːˈkleɪɪk) *or* **desoxyribonucleic acid** *n* the full name for **DNA.**

dep. *abbrev. for:* **1** department. **2** departure. **3** deposed. **4** deposit. **5** depot. **6** deputy.

depart ➊ (dɪˈpɑːt) *vb* (*mainly intr*) **1** to leave. **2** to set forth. **3** (usually foll. by *from*) to differ; vary: *to depart from normal procedure.* **4** (*tr*) to quit (arch., except in **depart this life**). [C13: from OF *departir,* from DE- + *partir* to go away, divide, from L *partīrī* to divide, distribute, from *pars* a part]

departed ➊ (dɪˈpɑːtɪd) *adj Euphemistic.* **a** dead. **b** (*as sing or collective n;* preceded by *the*): *the departed.*

department ➊ (dɪˈpɑːtmənt) *n* **1** a specialized division of a large concern, such as a business, store, or university. **2** a major subdivision of the administration of a government. **3** a branch of learning. **4** an administrative division in several countries, such as France. **5** *Inf.* a specialized sphere of skill or activity: *wine-making is my wife's department.* [C18: from F *département,* from *départir* to divide; see DEPART]
▸**departmental** (ˌdiːpɑːtˈmɛntᵊl) *adj*

departmentalize *or* **departmentalise** (ˌdiːpɑːtˈmɛntᵊˌlaɪz) *vb* **departmentalizes, departmentalizing, departmentalized** *or* **departmentalises, departmentalising, departmentalised.** (*tr*) to organize into departments, esp. excessively.
▸**ˌdepart,mentali'zation** *or* **ˌdepart,mentali'sation** *n*

department store *n* a large shop divided into departments selling a great many kinds of goods.

departure ➊ (dɪˈpɑːtʃə) *n* **1** the act or an instance of departing. **2** a variation from previous custom. **3** a course of action, venture, etc.: *selling is a new departure for him.* **4** *Naut.* the net distance travelled due east or west by a vessel. **5** a euphemistic word for **death.**

depend ➊ (dɪˈpɛnd) *vb* (*intr*) **1** (foll. by *on* or *upon*) to put trust (in); rely (on). **2** (usually foll. by *on* or *upon*) to be influenced or determined (by): *it all depends on you.* **3** (foll. by *on* or *upon*) to rely (on) for income, support, etc. **4** (foll. by *from*) *Rare.* to hang down. **5** to be undecided. [C15: from OF, from L *dēpendēre* to hang from, from DE- + *pendēre*]

dependable ➊ (dɪˈpɛndəbᵊl) *adj* able to be depended on; reliable.
▸**de,penda'bility** *or* **de'pendableness** *n* ▸**de'pendably** *adv*

dependant ➊ (dɪˈpɛndənt) *n* a person who depends on another person, organization, etc., for support, aid, or sustenance, esp. financial support.

> **USAGE NOTE** Avoid confusion with **dependent.**

dependence ➊ *or US* (*sometimes*) **dependance** (dɪˈpɛndəns) *n* **1** the state or fact of being dependent, esp. for support or help. **2** reliance; trust; confidence.

dependency ➊ *or US* (*sometimes*) **dependancy** (dɪˈpɛndənsɪ) *n, pl* **dependencies** *or US (sometimes)* **dependancies. 1** a territory subject to a state on which it does not border. **2** a dependent or subordinate person or thing. **3** *Psychol.* overreliance on another person or on a drug, etc. **4** another word for **dependence.**

dependent ➊ *or US* (*sometimes*) **dependant** (dɪˈpɛndənt) *adj* **1** depending on a person or thing for aid, support, etc. **2** (*postpositive;* foll. by *on* or *upon*) influenced or conditioned (by); contingent (on). **3** subordinate; subject. **4** *Obs.* hanging down. ◆ *n* **5** a variant spelling (esp. US) of **dependant.**
▸**de'pendently** *adv*

> **USAGE NOTE** Avoid confusion with **dependant.**

dependent clause *n Grammar.* another term for **subordinate clause.**

dependent variable *n* a variable in a mathematical equation or statement whose value depends on that taken on by the independent variable.

depersonalize *or* **depersonalise** (dɪˈpɜːsnᵊˌlaɪz) *vb* **depersonalizes, depersonalizing, depersonalized** *or* **depersonalises, depersonalising, depersonalised.** (*tr*) **1** to deprive (a person, organization, etc.) of individual or personal qualities. **2** to cause (someone) to lose his sense of identity.
▸**de,personali'zation** *or* **de,personali'sation** *n*

depict ➊ (dɪˈpɪkt) *vb* (*tr*) **1** to represent by drawing, sculpture, painting, etc.; delineate; portray. **2** to represent in words; describe. [C17: from L *dēpingere,* from *pingere* to paint]
▸**de'picter** *or* **de'pictor** *n* ▸**de'piction** *n* ▸**de'pictive** *adj*

depilate (ˈdɛpɪˌleɪt) *vb* **depilates, depilating, depilated.** (*tr*) to remove the hair from. [C16: from L *dēpilāre,* from *pilāre* to make bald, from *pilus* hair]
▸**ˌdepi'lation** *n* ▸**'depi,lator** *n*

depilatory (dɪˈpɪlətərɪ, -trɪ) *adj* **1** able or serving to remove hair. ◆ *n, pl* **depilatories. 2** a chemical used to remove hair from the body.

deplane (diːˈpleɪn) *vb* **deplanes, deplaning, deplaned.** (*intr*) *Chiefly US. & Canad.* to disembark from an aeroplane. [C20: from DE- + PLANE[1]]

deplete ➊ (dɪˈpliːt) *vb* **depletes, depleting, depleted.** (*tr*) **1** to use up (supplies, money, etc.); exhaust. **2** to empty entirely or partially. [C19: from L *dēplēre* to empty out, from DE- + *plēre* to fill]
▸**de'pletion** *n*

depletion layer *n* a region at the interface between dissimilar zones of conductivity in a semiconductor, in which there are few charge carriers.

deplorable ➊ (dɪˈplɔːrəbᵊl) *adj* **1** lamentable. **2** worthy of censure or reproach; very bad.
▸**de'plorably** *adv*

deplore ➊ (dɪˈplɔː) *vb* **deplores, deploring, deplored.** (*tr*) **1** to express or feel sorrow about. **2** to express or feel strong disapproval of; censure. [C16: from OF, from L *dēplōrāre* to weep bitterly, from *plōrāre* to weep]
▸**de'ploringly** *adv*

deploy ➊ (dɪˈplɔɪ) *vb Chiefly mil.* **1** to adopt or cause to adopt a battle formation. **2** (*tr*) to redistribute (forces) to or within a given area. [C18: from F, from L *displicāre* to unfold; see DISPLAY]
▸**de'ployment** *n*

THESAURUS

depart *vb* **1, 2** = **leave**, absent (oneself), decamp, disappear, escape, exit, go, go away, hook it (*sl.*), make tracks, migrate, pack one's bags (*inf.*), quit, remove, retire, retreat, set forth, slope off, start out, take (one's) leave, vanish, withdraw **3** = **deviate**, differ, digress, diverge, stray, swerve, turn aside, vary, veer
Antonyms *vb* ≠ **leave:** arrive, remain, show up (*inf.*), stay, turn up

departed *adj* **a** *Euphemistic* = **dead**, deceased, expired, late

department *n* **1** = **section**, branch, bureau, division, office, station, subdivision, unit **2** = **region**, district, division, province, sector **5** *Informal* = **speciality**, area, domain, function, line, province, realm, responsibility, sphere

departure *n* **1** = **leaving**, exit, exodus, going, going away, leave-taking, removal, retirement, withdrawal **2** = **divergence**, abandonment, branching off, deviation, digression, variation, veering **3** = **shift**, branching out, change, difference, innovation, novelty, whole new ball game (*inf.*)
Antonyms *n* ≠ **leaving:** advent, appearance, arrival, coming, entrance, return

depend *vb* **1** = **trust in**, bank on, build upon, calculate on, confide in, count on, lean on, reckon on, rely upon, turn to **2** = **be determined by**, be based on, be contingent on, be subject to, be subordinate to, hang on, hinge on, rest on, revolve around

dependable *adj* = **reliable**, faithful, reputable, responsible, staunch, steady, sure, trustworthy, trusty, unfailing
Antonyms *adj* irresponsible, undependable, unreliable, unstable, untrustworthy

dependant *n* = **relative**, child, client, cohort (*chiefly US.*), hanger-on, henchman, minion, minor, protégé, retainer, subordinate, vassal

dependence *n* **1** = **overreliance**, addiction, attachment, helplessness, need, subordination, subservience, vulnerability, weakness **2** = **reliance**, assurance, belief, confidence, expectation, faith, hope, trust

dependency *n Psychology* **3** = **overreliance**, addiction, attachment, helplessness, need, vulnerability, weakness

dependent *adj* **1** = **reliant**, counting on, defenceless, helpless, immature, relying on, vulnerable, weak **2 dependent on** *or* **upon** = **determined by**, conditional on, contingent on, depending on, influenced by, liable to, relative to, subject to
Antonyms *adj* ≠ **reliant:** autarkic, autonomous, independent, self-determining, self-governing, self-reliant

depict *vb* **1** = **draw**, delineate, illustrate, limn, outline, paint, picture, portray, render, reproduce, sculpt, sketch **2** = **describe**, characterize, detail, narrate, outline, represent, sketch

depiction *n* **1, 2** = **representation**, delineation, description, drawing, illustration, image, likeness, outline, picture, portrayal, sketch

deplete *vb* **1, 2** = **use up**, bankrupt, consume, decrease, drain, empty, evacuate, exhaust, expend, impoverish, lessen, milk, reduce
Antonyms *vb* add to, augment, enhance, expand, increase, raise, step up (*inf.*), swell

depleted *adj* **1, 2** = **used (up)**, consumed, decreased, depreciated, devoid of, drained, effete, emptied, exhausted, lessened, out of, reduced, short of, spent, wasted, weakened, worn out

depletion *n* **1, 2** = **using up**, attenuation, consumption, decrease, deficiency, diminution, drain, dwindling, exhaustion, expenditure, lessening, lowering, reduction

deplorable *adj* **1** = **terrible**, calamitous, dire, disastrous, distressing, grievous, heartbreaking, lamentable, melancholy, miserable, pitiable, regrettable, sad, unfortunate, wretched **2** = **disgraceful**, blameworthy, dishonourable, disreputable, execrable, opprobrious, reprehensible, scandalous, shameful
Antonyms *adj* ≠ **terrible:** A1 *or* A-one (*inf.*), bad (*sl.*), bodacious (*sl., chiefly US.*), brilliant, excellent, fantastic, great (*inf.*), marvellous, outstanding, super (*inf.*), superb ≠ **disgraceful:** admirable, laudable, notable, praiseworthy

deplore *vb* **1** = **lament**, bemoan, bewail, grieve for, mourn, regret, rue, sorrow over **2** = **disapprove of**, abhor, censure, condemn, denounce, deprecate, excoriate, object to, take a dim view of

deploy *vb* **2** = **position**, arrange, dispose, extend, redistribute, set out, set up, spread out, station, use, utilize

depolarize *or* **depolarise** (diːˈpəʊləˌraɪz) *vb* **depolarizes, depolarizing, depolarized** *or* **depolarises, depolarising, depolarised.** to undergo or cause to undergo a loss of polarity or polarization.
▸**deˌpolariˈzation** *or* **deˌpolariˈsation** *n*

deponent (dɪˈpəʊnənt) *adj* **1** *Grammar.* (of a verb, esp. in Latin) having the inflectional endings of a passive verb but the meaning of an active verb. ◆ *n* **2** *Grammar.* a deponent verb. **3** *Law.* a person who makes an affidavit or a deposition. [C16: from L *dēpōnēns* putting aside, putting down, from *dēpōnere*]

depopulate (dɪˈpɒpjʊˌleɪt) *vb* **depopulates, depopulating, depopulated.** to be or cause to be reduced in population.
▸**deˌpopuˈlation** *n*

deport ❶ (dɪˈpɔːt) *vb* (*tr*) **1** to remove forcibly from a country; expel. **2** to conduct, hold, or behave (oneself) in a specified manner. [C15: from F, from L *dēportāre* to carry away, banish, from DE- + *portāre* to carry]
▸**deˈportable** *adj*

deportation ❶ (ˌdiːpɔːˈteɪʃən) *n* the act of expelling someone from a country.

deportee (ˌdiːpɔːˈtiː) *n* a person deported or awaiting deportation.

deportment ❶ (dɪˈpɔːtmənt) *n* the manner in which a person behaves, esp. in physical bearing: *military deportment.* [C17: from F, from OF *deporter* to conduct (oneself); see DEPORT]

depose ❶ (dɪˈpəʊz) *vb* **deposes, deposing, deposed. 1** (*tr*) to remove from an office or position of power. **2** *Law.* to testify or give (evidence, etc.) on oath. [C13: from OF: to put away, put down, from LL *dēpōnere* to depose from office, from L: to put aside]

deposit ❶ (dɪˈpɒzɪt) *vb* (*tr*) **1** to put or set down, esp. carefully; place. **2** to entrust for safekeeping. **3** to place (money) in a bank or similar institution to earn interest or for safekeeping. **4** to give (money) in part payment or as security. **5** to lay down naturally: *the river deposits silt.* ◆ *n* **6a** an instance of entrusting money or valuables to a bank or similar institution. **6b** the money or valuables so entrusted. **7** money given in part payment or as security. **8** an accumulation of sediments, minerals, coal, etc. **9** any deposited material, such as a sediment. **10** a depository or storehouse. **11 on deposit.** payable as the first instalment, as when buying on hire-purchase. [C17: from Med. L *dēpositāre,* from L *dēpositus* put down]

deposit account *n Brit.* a bank account that earns interest and usually requires notice of withdrawal.

depositary ❶ (dɪˈpɒzɪtərɪ, -trɪ) *n, pl* **depositaries. 1** a person or group to whom something is entrusted for safety. **2** a variant spelling of **depository.**

deposition ❶ (ˌdɛpəˈzɪʃən) *n* **1** *Law.* **1a** the giving of testimony on oath. **1b** the testimony given. **1c** the sworn statement of a witness used in court in his absence. **2** the act or an instance of deposing. **3** the act or an instance of depositing. **4** something deposited. [C14: from LL *dēpositiō* a laying down, disposal, burying, testimony]

depositor (dɪˈpɒzɪtə) *n* a person who places or has money on deposit, esp. in a bank.

depository ❶ (dɪˈpɒzɪtərɪ, -trɪ) *n, pl* **depositories. 1** a store for furniture, valuables, etc.; repository. **2** a variant spelling of **depositary.** [C17 (in the sense: place of a deposit): from Med. L *dēpositōrium;* C18 (in the sense: depositary): see DEPOSIT, -ORY[1]]

depot ❶ (ˈdɛpəʊ; *US & Canad.* ˈdiːpəʊ) *n* **1** a storehouse or warehouse. **2** *Mil.* **2a** a store for supplies. **2b** a training and holding centre for recruits and replacements. **3** *Chiefly Brit.* a building used for the storage and servicing of buses or railway engines. **4** *US & Canad.* a bus or railway station. [C18: from F *dépôt,* from L *dēpositum* a deposit, trust]

deprave ❶ (dɪˈpreɪv) *vb* **depraves, depraving, depraved.** (*tr*) to make morally bad; corrupt. [C14: from L *dēprāvāre* to distort, corrupt, from DE- + *prāvus* crooked]
▸**depravation** (ˌdɛprəˈveɪʃən) *n* ▸**deˈpraved** *adj*

depravity ❶ (dɪˈprævɪtɪ) *n, pl* **depravities.** the state or an instance of moral corruption.

deprecate ❶ (ˈdɛprɪˌkeɪt) *vb* **deprecates, deprecating, deprecated.** (*tr*) **1** to express disapproval of; protest against. **2** to depreciate; belittle. [C17: from L *dēprecārī* to avert, ward off by entreaty, from DE- + *precārī* to PRAY]
▸**ˈdepreˌcating** *adj* ▸**ˈdepreˌcatingly** *adv* ▸**ˌdepreˈcation** *n* ▸**ˈdeprecative** *adj* ▸**ˈdepreˌcator** *n*

USAGE NOTE Avoid confusion with **depreciate.**

deprecatory ❶ (ˈdɛprɪkətərɪ) *adj* **1** expressing disapproval; protesting. **2** expressing apology; apologetic.
▸**ˈdeprecatorily** *adv*

depreciate ❶ (dɪˈpriːʃɪˌeɪt) *vb* **depreciates, depreciating, depreciated. 1** to reduce or decline in value or price. **2** (*tr*) to lessen the value of by derision, criticism, etc. [C15: from LL *dēpretiāre* to lower the price of, from L DE- + *pretium* PRICE]
▸**deˈpreciˌatingly** *adv* ▸**depreciatory** (dɪˈpriːʃɪətərɪ) *or* **deˈpreciative** *adj*

USAGE NOTE Avoid confusion with **deprecate.**

depreciation ❶ (dɪˌpriːʃɪˈeɪʃən) *n* **1** *Accounting.* **1a** the reduction in value of a fixed asset due to use, obsolescence, etc. **1b** the amount deducted from gross profit to allow for this. **2** the act or an instance of depreciating or belittling. **3** a decrease in the exchange value of a currency brought about by excess supply of that currency under conditions of fluctuating exchange rates.

depredation ❶ (ˌdɛprɪˈdeɪʃən) *n* the act or an instance of plundering; pillage. [C15: from LL *dēpraedārī* to ravage]

depress ❶ (dɪˈprɛs) *vb* (*tr*) **1** to lower in spirits; make gloomy. **2** to weaken the force, or energy of. **3** to lower prices of. **4** to press or push down. [C14: from OF *depresser,* from L *dēprimere* from DE- + *premere* to PRESS[1]]
▸**deˈpressing** *adj* ▸**deˈpressingly** *adv*

depressant (dɪˈprɛsᵊnt) *adj* **1** *Med.* able to reduce nervous or functional activity. **2** causing gloom; depressing. ◆ *n* **3** a depressant drug.

depressed ❶ (dɪˈprɛst) *adj* **1** low in spirits; downcast. **2** lower than the surrounding surface. **3** pressed down or flattened. **4** Also: **distressed.** characterized by economic hardship, such as unemployment: *a depressed area.* **5** lowered in force, intensity, or amount. **6** *Bot., zool.* flattened.

THESAURUS

deployment *n* **2 = position**, arrangement, disposition, organization, setup, spread, stationing, use, utilization

deport *vb* **1 = expel**, banish, exile, expatriate, extradite, oust **2 deport oneself = behave**, acquit oneself, act, bear oneself, carry oneself, comport oneself, conduct oneself, hold oneself

deportation *n* **= expulsion**, banishment, eviction, exile, expatriation, extradition, transportation

deportment *n* **= bearing**, air, appearance, aspect, behaviour, carriage, cast, comportment, conduct, demeanour, manner, mien, posture, stance

depose *vb* **1 = remove from office**, break, cashier, degrade, demote, dethrone, dismiss, displace, downgrade, oust **2** *Law* **= testify**, avouch, declare, make a deposition

deposit *vb* **1 = put**, drop, lay, locate, place, precipitate, settle, sit down **3 = store**, amass, bank, consign, entrust, hoard, lodge, save ◆ *n* **7 = down payment**, instalment, money (*in bank*), part payment, pledge, retainer, security, stake, warranty **8 = sediment**, accumulation, alluvium, deposition, dregs, lees, precipitate, silt

depositary *n* **1 = trustee**, fiduciary (*Law*), guardian, steward

deposition *n* **1** *Law* **= sworn statement**, affidavit, declaration, evidence, testimony **2 = removal**, dethronement, dismissal, displacement, ousting

depository *n* **1 = storehouse**, depot, repository, safe-deposit box, store, warehouse

depot *n* **1 = storehouse**, depository, repository, warehouse **2a** *Military* **= arsenal**, dump **4** *Chiefly U.S. & Canad.* **= bus station**, garage, terminus

deprave *vb* **= corrupt**, brutalize, debase, debauch, degrade, demoralize, lead astray, pervert, seduce, subvert, vitiate

depraved *adj* **= corrupt**, abandoned, debased, debauched, degenerate, degraded, dissolute, evil, immoral, lascivious, lewd, licentious, perverted, profligate, shameless, sinful, sink, vicious, vile, wicked
Antonyms *adj* chaste, decent, ethical, good, honourable, innocent, moral, principled, proper, pure, upright, virtuous, wholesome

depravity *n* **= corruption**, baseness, contamination, criminality, debasement, debauchery, degeneracy, depravation, evil, immorality, iniquity, profligacy, sinfulness, turpitude, vice, viciousness, vitiation, wickedness

deprecate *vb* **1 = disapprove of**, condemn, deplore, frown on, object to, protest against, take exception to **2 = disapprove of**, belittle, denigrate, depreciate, detract, disparage

deprecatory *adj* **1 = disapproving**, censuring, condemnatory, opprobrious, reproachful **2 = apologetic**, contrite, penitent, regretful, remorseful, rueful

depreciate *vb* **1 = decrease**, deflate, devaluate, devalue, lessen, lose value, lower, reduce **2 = disparage**, belittle, decry, denigrate, deride, detract, look down on, ridicule, run down, scorn, sneer at, traduce, underestimate, underrate, undervalue
Antonyms *vb* ≠ **decrease:** add to, appreciate, augment, enhance, enlarge, expand, grow, increase, rise ≠ **disparage:** admire, appreciate, cherish, esteem, like, prize, rate highly, regard, respect, value

depreciation *n* **1a, 3 = devaluation**, drop, fall, slump **2 = disparagement**, belittlement, denigration, deprecation, derogation, detraction, pejoration

depredation *n* **= plunder**, desolation, despoiling, destruction, devastation, harrying, laying waste, marauding, pillage, ransacking, rapine, ravaging, robbery, spoliation, theft

depress *vb* **1 = sadden**, cast down, chill, damp, daunt, deject, desolate, discourage, dishearten, dispirit, make despondent, oppress, weigh down **3 = lower**, cheapen, depreciate, devaluate, devalue, diminish, downgrade, impair, lessen, reduce **4 = press down**, flatten, level, lower, push down
Antonyms *vb* ≠ **sadden:** cheer, elate, hearten, heighten, increase, lift, raise, strengthen, uplift ≠ **lower:** heighten, increase, raise, strengthen

depressed *adj* **1 = low-spirited**, blue, crestfallen, dejected, despondent, discouraged, dispirited, down, downcast, downhearted, down in the dumps (*inf.*), fed up, glum, low, melancholy, moody, morose, pessimistic, sad, unhappy **2 = sunken**, concave, hollow, indented, recessed, set back **4 = poverty-stricken**, deprived, destitute, disadvantaged, distressed, grey, needy, poor, run-down **5 = lowered**, cheapened, depreciated, devalued, impaired, weakened

depressing *adj* **1 = bleak**, black, daunting, dejecting, depressive, discouraging, disheartening, dismal, dispiriting, distressing, dreary,

depression ⓣ (dɪˈprɛʃən) *n* **1** a depressing or being depressed. **2** a sunken place. **3** a mental disorder characterized by feelings of gloom and inadequacy. **4** *Pathol.* an abnormal lowering of the rate of any physiological activity or function. **5** an economic condition characterized by unemployment, low investment, etc.; slump. **6** Also called: **cyclone, low.** *Meteorol.* a body of moving air below normal atmospheric pressure, which often brings rain. **7** (esp. in surveying and astronomy) the angular distance of an object below the horizontal plane.

Depression (dɪˈprɛʃən) *n* (usually preceded by *the*) the worldwide economic depression of the early 1930s, when there was mass unemployment.

depressive (dɪˈprɛsɪv) *adj* **1** tending to depress. **2** *Psychol.* tending to be subject to periods of depression.
▸**deˈpressively** *adv*

depressor (dɪˈprɛsə) *n* **1** a person or thing that depresses. **2** any muscle that draws down a part. **3** *Med.* an instrument used to press down or aside an organ or part.

depressurize *or* **depressurise** (dɪˈprɛʃəˌraɪz) *vb* **depressurizes, depressurizing, depressurized** *or* **depressurises, depressurising, depressurised.** (*tr*) to reduce the pressure of a gas inside (an enclosed space), as in an aircraft cabin.
▸**deˌpressuriˈzation** *or* **deˌpressuriˈsation** *n*

deprive ⓣ (dɪˈpraɪv) *vb* **deprives, depriving, deprived.** (*tr*) **1** (foll. by *of*) to prevent from possessing or enjoying; dispossess (of). **2** *Arch.* to depose; demote. [C14: from OF, from Med. L *dēprīvāre*, from L DE- + *prīvāre* to deprive of]
▸**deˈprival** *n* ▸**deprivation** (ˌdɛprɪˈveɪʃən) *n*

deprived ⓣ (dɪˈpraɪvd) *adj* lacking adequate food, shelter, education, etc.: *deprived inner-city areas.*

dept *abbrev. for* department.

depth ⓣ (dɛpθ) *n* **1** the distance downwards, backwards, or inwards. **2** the quality of being deep; deepness. **3** intensity of emotion. **4** profundity of moral character; sagacity; integrity. **5** complexity or abstruseness, as of thought. **6** intensity, as of silence, colour, etc. **7** lowness of pitch. **8** (*often pl*) a deep, inner, or remote part, such as an inaccessible region of a country. **9** (*often pl*) the most intense or severe part: *the depths of winter.* **10** (*usually pl*) a low moral state. **11** (*often pl*) a vast space or abyss. **12 beyond** *or* **out of one's depth. 12a** in water deeper than one is tall. **12b** beyond the range of one's competence or understanding. [C14: from *dep* DEEP + -TH[1]]

depth charge *or* **bomb** *n* a bomb used to attack submarines that explodes at a preset depth of water.

depth gauge *n* a device attached to a drill bit to prevent the hole from exceeding a predetermined depth.

depth of field *n* the range of distance in front of and behind an object focused by an optical instrument, such as a camera or microscope, within which other objects will also appear sharply defined in the resulting image.

depth psychology *n Psychol.* the study of unconscious motives and attitudes.

depuration (ˌdɛpjʊˈreɪʃən) *n* the act or process of eliminating impurities; self-purification. [C17: from F or Med. L, ult. from L *pūrus* pure]

deputation ⓣ (ˌdɛpjʊˈteɪʃən) *n* **1** the act of appointing a person or body of people to represent others. **2** a person or body of people so appointed; delegation.

depute ⓣ *vb* (dɪˈpjuːt), **deputes, deputing, deputed.** (*tr*) **1** to appoint as an agent. **2** to assign (authority, duties, etc.) to a deputy. ◆ *n* (ˈdɛpjuːt). **3** *Scot.* **3a** a deputy. **3b** (*as modifier, usually postpositive*): *a sheriff-depute.* [C15: from OF, from LL *dēputāre* to assign, allot, from L DE- + *putāre* to think, consider]

deputize ⓣ *or* **deputise** (ˈdɛpjʊˌtaɪz) *vb* **deputizes, deputizing, deputized** *or* **deputises, deputising, deputised.** to appoint or act as deputy.

deputy ⓣ (ˈdɛpjʊtɪ) *n, pl* **deputies. 1a** a person appointed to act on behalf of or represent another. **1b** (*as modifier*): *the deputy chairman.* **2** a member of a legislative assembly in various countries, such as France. [C16: from OF, from *deputer* to appoint; see DEPUTE]

der. *abbrev. for:* **1** derivation. **2** derivative.

deracinate (dɪˈræsɪˌneɪt) *vb* **deracinates, deracinating, deracinated.** (*tr*) to pull up by or as if by the roots; uproot. [C16: from OF *desraciner*, from *des-* DIS-[1] + *racine* root, from LL, from L *rādīx* a root]
▸**deˌraciˈnation** *n*

derail (dɪˈreɪl) *vb* to go or cause to go off the rails, as a train, tram, etc.
▸**deˈrailment** *n*

derange ⓣ (dɪˈreɪndʒ) *vb* **deranges, deranging, deranged.** (*tr*) **1** to throw into disorder; disarrange. **2** to disturb the action of. **3** to make insane. [C18: from OF *desrengier*, from des- DIS-[1] + *reng* row, order]
▸**deˈrangement** *n*

derby (ˈdɜːrbɪ) *n, pl* **derbies.** the US and Canad. name for **bowler**[2].

Derby (ˈdɑːbɪ; *US* ˈdɜːrbɪ) *n, pl* **Derbies. 1 the.** an annual horse race run at Epsom Downs, Surrey, since 1780. **2** (*usually not cap.*) any of various other horse races. **3 local derby.** a football match between two teams from the same area. [C18: after the twelfth Earl of *Derby* (died 1834), who founded the race in 1780]

derecognize *or* **derecognise** (diːˈrɛkəgˌnaɪz) *vb* **derecognizes, derecognizing, derecognized** *or* **derecognises, derecognising, derecognised.** (*tr*) to cease to recognize (a trade union) as having special negotiating rights within a company or industry.
▸**ˌderecogˈnition** *n*

deregulate (diːˈrɛgjʊˌleɪt) *vb* **deregulates, deregulating, deregulated.** (*tr*) to remove regulations from.
▸**deˌreguˈlation** *n*

derelict ⓣ (ˈdɛrɪlɪkt) *adj* **1** deserted or abandoned, as by an owner, occupant, etc. **2** falling into ruins. **3** neglectful of duty; remiss. ◆ *n* **4** a social outcast or vagrant. **5** property deserted or abandoned by an owner, occupant, etc. **6** a vessel abandoned at sea. **7** a person who is neglectful of duty. [C17: from L, from *dērelinquere* to abandon, from DE- + *relinquere* to leave]

dereliction ⓣ (ˌdɛrɪˈlɪkʃən) *n* **1** conscious or wilful neglect (esp. in **dereliction of duty**). **2** an abandoning or being abandoned. **3** *Law.* accretion of dry land gained by the gradual receding of the sea.

derestrict (ˌdiːrɪˈstrɪkt) *vb* (*tr*) to render or leave free from restriction, esp. a road from speed limits.
▸**ˌdereˈstriction** *n*

deride ⓣ (dɪˈraɪd) *vb* **derides, deriding, derided.** (*tr*) to speak of or treat with contempt or ridicule; scoff at. [C16: from L *dērīdēre* to laugh to scorn, from DE- + *rīdēre* to laugh, smile]
▸**deˈrider** *n* ▸**deˈridingly** *adv*

de rigueur ⓣ *French.* (də rigœr) *adj* required by etiquette or fashion. [lit.: of strictness]

derision ⓣ (dɪˈrɪʒən) *n* the act of deriding; mockery; scorn. [C15: from LL *dērīsiō*, from L *dērīsus*; see DERIDE]
▸**deˈrisible** *adj*

THESAURUS

funereal, gloomy, harrowing, heartbreaking, hopeless, melancholy, sad, saddening, sombre

depression *n* **2** = **hollow**, bowl, cavity, concavity, dent, dimple, dip, excavation, impression, indentation, pit, sag, sink, valley **3** = **low spirits**, dejection, despair, despondency, dolefulness, downheartedness, dumps (*inf.*), gloominess, hopelessness, melancholia, melancholy, sadness, the blues, the hump (*Brit. inf.*) **5** = **recession**, dullness, economic decline, hard *or* bad times, inactivity, lowness, slump, stagnation

deprivation *n* **1** = **want**, destitution, detriment, disadvantage, distress, hardship, need, privation

deprive *vb* **1** = **withhold**, bereave, despoil, dispossess, divest, expropriate, rob, strip, wrest

deprived *adj* = **poor**, bereft, denuded, destitute, disadvantaged, down at heel, forlorn, in need, in want, lacking, necessitous, needy
Antonyms *adj* born with a silver spoon in one's mouth, favoured, fortunate, golden, happy, having a charmed life, lucky, prosperous, sitting pretty (*inf.*), successful, well-off

depth *n* **2** = **deepness**, drop, extent, measure, profoundness, profundity **4** = **profoundness**, astuteness, discernment, insight, penetration, profundity, sagacity, wisdom **5** = **complexity**, abstruseness, obscurity, reconditeness **6** = **intensity**, richness, strength **11** *often plural* = **deepest part**, abyss, bowels of the earth, furthest part, innermost part, middle, midst, most intense part, remotest part
Antonyms *n* ≠ **deepness:** apex, apogee, crest, crown, height, peak, pinnacle, summit, top, vertex, zenith ≠ **profoundness:** emptiness, lack of depth *or* substance, superficiality, triviality

deputation *n* **1** = **appointment**, assignment, commission, designation, nomination **2** = **delegation**, commission, delegates, deputies, embassy, envoys, legation

depute *vb* **1** = **appoint**, accredit, authorize, charge, commission, delegate, empower, entrust, mandate

deputize *vb* = **appoint**, commission, delegate, depute = **stand in for**, act for, take the place of, understudy

deputy *n* **1a** = **substitute**, agent, ambassador, commissioner, delegate, legate, lieutenant, number two, nuncio, proxy, representative, second-in-command, surrogate, vicegerent ◆ *modifier* **1b** = **assistant**, depute (*Scot.*), subordinate

derange *vb* **1** = **disorder**, confound, confuse, disarrange, disarray, discompose, disconcert, displace, disturb, ruffle, unsettle, upset **3** = **drive mad**, craze, dement (*rare*), madden, make insane, unbalance, unhinge

deranged *adj* **3** = **mad**, barking (*sl.*), barking mad (*sl.*), berserk, crackpot (*inf.*), crazed, crazy, delirious, demented, distracted, doolally (*sl.*), frantic, frenzied, insane, irrational, loopy (*inf.*), lunatic, maddened, not the full shilling (*inf.*), off one's trolley (*sl.*), out to lunch (*inf.*), unbalanced, unhinged, up the pole (*inf.*)
Antonyms *adj* all there (*inf.*), calm, *compos mentis*, in one's right mind, lucid, mentally sound, normal, of sound mind

derangement *n* **1, 2** = **disorder**, confusion, disarrangement, disarray, disturbance, irregularity, jumble, muddle **3** = **madness**, aberration, alienation, delirium, dementia, hallucination, insanity, loss of reason, lunacy, mania

derelict *adj* **1, 2** = **abandoned**, deserted, dilapidated, discarded, forsaken, neglected, ruined **3** = **negligent**, careless, irresponsible, lax, remiss, slack ◆ *n* **4** = **tramp**, bag lady, bum (*inf.*), down-and-out, good-for-nothing, ne'er-do-well, outcast, vagrant, wastrel

dereliction *n* **1** = **negligence**, delinquency, evasion, failure, faithlessness, fault, neglect, nonperformance, remissness **2** = **abandonment**, abdication, desertion, forsaking, relinquishment, renunciation

deride *vb* = **mock**, chaff, contemn, detract, disdain, disparage, flout, gibe, insult, jeer, knock (*inf.*), pooh-pooh, ridicule, scoff, scorn, sneer, take the piss out of (*taboo sl.*), taunt

de rigueur *adj* = **necessary**, *comme il faut*, conventional, correct, decent, decorous, done, fitting, proper, required, right, the done thing

derision *n* = **mockery**, contempt, contumely, denigration, disdain, disparagement, disrespect, insult, laughter, raillery, ridicule, satire, scoffing, scorn, sneering

derisive ➊ (dɪˈraɪsɪv) *adj* characterized by derision; mocking; scornful. ▸**deˈrisively** *adv* ▸**deˈrisiveness** *n*

derisory ➊ (dɪˈraɪsərɪ) *adj* **1** subject to or worthy of derision. **2** another word for **derisive.**

deriv. *abbrev. for:* **1** derivation. **2** derivative. **3** derived.

derivation ➊ (ˌdɛrɪˈveɪʃən) *n* **1** a deriving or being derived. **2** the origin or descent of something, such as a word. **3** something derived; a derivative. **4a** the process of deducing a mathematical theorem, formula, etc., as a necessary consequence of a set of accepted statements. **4b** this sequence of statements. ▸ˌ**deriˈvational** *adj*

derivative ➊ (dɪˈrɪvətɪv) *adj* **1** derived. **2** based on other sources; not original. ◆ *n* **3** a term, idea, etc., that is based on or derived from another in the same class. **4** a word derived from another word. **5** *Chem.* a compound that is formed from, or can be regarded as formed from, a structurally related compound. **6** *Maths.* **6a** Also called: **differential coefficient, first derivative.** the change of a function, f(*x*), with respect to an infinitesimally small change in the independent variable, *x*. **6b** the rate of change of one quantity with respect to another. **7** *Finance.* a financial instrument, such as a futures contract or option, the price of which is largely determined by the commodity, currency, share price, interest rate, etc., to which it is linked. ▸**deˈrivatively** *adv*

derive ➊ (dɪˈraɪv) *vb* **derives, deriving, derived. 1** (usually foll. by *from*) to draw or be drawn (from) in source or origin. **2** (*tr*) to obtain by reasoning; deduce; infer. **3** (*tr*) to trace the source or development of. **4** (usually foll. by *from*) to produce or be produced (from) by a chemical reaction. [C14: from OF: to spring from, from L *dērīvāre* to draw off, from DE- + *rīvus* a stream] ▸**deˈrivable** *adj* ▸**deˈriver** *n*

derived unit *n* a unit of measurement obtained by multiplication or division of the base units of a system without the introduction of numerical factors.

-derm *n combining form.* indicating skin: *endoderm.* [via F from Gk *derma* skin]

derma (ˈdɜːmə) *n* another name for **corium.** Also: **derm.** [C18: NL, from Gk: skin]

dermal (ˈdeːməl) *adj* of or relating to the skin.

dermatitis (ˌdɜːməˈtaɪtɪs) *n* inflammation of the skin.

dermato-, derma- *or before a vowel* **dermat-, derm-** *combining form.* indicating skin: *dermatitis.* [from Gk *derma* skin]

dermatology (ˌdɜːməˈtɒlədʒɪ) *n* the branch of medicine concerned with the skin and its diseases. ▸**dermatological** (ˌdɜːmətəˈlɒdʒɪkˈl) *adj* ▸ˌ**dermaˈtologist** *n*

dermis (ˈdɜːmɪs) *n* another name for **corium.** [C19: NL, from EPIDERMIS] ▸ˈ**dermic** *adj*

dernier cri *French.* (dɛrnje kri) *n* **le** (lə). the latest fashion; the last word. [lit.: last cry]

derogate (ˈdɛrəˌgeɪt) *vb* **derogates, derogating, derogated. 1** (*intr;* foll. by *from*) to cause to seem inferior; detract. **2** (*intr;* foll. by *from*) to deviate in standard or quality. **3** (*tr*) to cause to seem inferior, etc.; disparage. **4** (*tr*) to curtail the application of (a law or regulation). [C15: from L *dērogāre* to repeal some part of a law, modify it, from DE- + *rogāre* to ask, propose a law] ▸ˌ**deroˈgation** *n* ▸**derogative** (dɪˈrɒgətɪv) *adj*

derogatory ➊ (dɪˈrɒgətərɪ) *adj* tending or intended to detract, disparage, or belittle; intentionally offensive. ▸**deˈrogatorily** *adv*

derrick (ˈdɛrɪk) *n* **1** a simple crane having lifting tackle slung from a boom. **2** the framework erected over an oil well to enable drill tubes to be raised and lowered. [C17 (in the sense: gallows): from *Derrick*, celebrated hangman at Tyburn, London]

derrière (ˌdɛrɪˈɛə) *n* a euphemistic word for **buttocks.** [C18: lit.: behind (prep), from OF *deriere*, from L *dē retrō* from the back]

derring-do (ˈdɛrɪŋˈduː) *n Arch. or literary.* boldness or bold action. [C16: from ME *durring don* daring to do, from *durren* to dare + *don* to do]

deringer *or* **deringer** (ˈdɛrɪndʒə) *n* a short-barrelled pocket pistol of large calibre. [C19: after Henry *Deringer*, US gunsmith, who invented it]

derris (ˈdɛrɪs) *n* **1** an East Indian woody climbing plant. **2** an insecticide made from its powdered roots. [C19: NL, from Gk: covering, leather, from *deros* skin, hide, from *derein* to skin]

derv (dɜːv) *n* a Brit. name for **diesel oil** when used for road transport. [C20: from *d(iesel) e(ngine) r(oad) v(ehicle)*]

dervish (ˈdɜːvɪʃ) *n* a member of any of various Muslim orders of ascetics, some of which (**whirling dervishes**) are noted for a frenzied, ecstatic, whirling dance. [C16: from Turkish, from Persian *darvīsh* mendicant monk]

DES (in Britain) *abbrev. for* (the former) Department of Education and Science.

desalination (diːˌsælɪˈneɪʃən) *or* **desalinization, desalinisation** *n* the process of removing salt, esp. from sea water.

descale (ˌdiːˈskeɪl) *vb* **descales, descaling, descaled.** (*tr*) to remove the hard deposit formed by chemicals in water from (a kettle, pipe, etc.).

descant ➊ (ˈdɛskænt) *n* **1** Also called: **discant.** a decorative counterpoint added above a basic melody. **2** a comment or discourse. ◆ *adj* **3** Also: **discant.** of the highest member in common use in a family of musical instruments: *a descant recorder.* ◆ *vb* (*intr*) **4** Also: **discant.** (often foll. by *on* or *upon*) to perform a descant. **5** (often foll. by *on* or *upon*) to discourse or make comments. **6** *Arch.* to sing sweetly. [C14: from OF, from Med. L *discanthus*, from L DIS-[1] + *cantus* song] ▸**desˈcanter** *n*

descend ➊ (dɪˈsɛnd) *vb* (*mainly intr*) **1** (*also tr*) to move down (a slope, staircase, etc.). **2** to lead or extend down; slope. **3** to move to a lower level, pitch, etc.; fall. **4** (often foll. by *from*) to be connected by a blood relationship (to a dead or extinct individual, species, etc.). **5** to be inherited. **6** to sink or come down in morals or behaviour. **7** (often foll. by *on* or *upon*) to arrive or attack in a sudden or overwhelming way. **8** (of the sun, moon, etc.) to move towards the horizon. [C13: from OF, from L *dēscendere*, from DE- + *scandere* to climb] ▸**desˈcendable** *or* **desˈcendible** *adj*

descendant ➊ (dɪˈsɛndənt) *n* **1** a person, animal, or plant when described as descended from an individual, race, species, etc. **2** something that derives from an earlier form. ◆ *adj* **3** a variant spelling of **descendent.**

descendent (dɪˈsɛndənt) *adj* descending.

descender (dɪˈsɛndə) *n* **1** *Printing.* the part of certain lower-case letters, such as j, p, or y, that extends below the body of the letter. **2** a person or thing that descends.

descent ➊ (dɪˈsɛnt) *n* **1** the act of descending. **2** a downward slope. **3** a path or way leading downwards. **4** derivation from an ancestor; lineage. **5** a generation in a particular lineage. **6** a decline or degeneration. **7** a movement or passage in degree or state from higher to lower. **8** (often foll. by *on*) a sudden and overwhelming arrival or attack. **9** *Property law.* (formerly) the transmission of real property to the heir.

deschool (ˌdiːˈskuːl) *vb* (*tr*) to separate education from the institution of school and operate through the pupil's life experience as opposed to a set curriculum.

describe ➊ (dɪˈskraɪb) *vb* **describes, describing, described.** (*tr*) **1** to give an account or representation of in words. **2** to pronounce or label. **3** to draw a line or figure, such as a circle. [C15: from L *dēscrībere* to copy off, write out, from DE- + *scrībere* to write] ▸**deˈscribable** *adj* ▸**deˈscriber** *n*

description ➊ (dɪˈskrɪpʃən) *n* **1** a statement or account that describes. **2** the act, process, or technique of describing. **3** sort or variety: *reptiles of every description.*

descriptive ➊ (dɪˈskrɪptɪv) *adj* **1** characterized by or containing description. **2** *Grammar.* (of an adjective) serving to describe the referent of the noun modified, as for example the adjective *brown* as con-

THESAURUS

derisive *adj* = **mocking**, contemptuous, jeering, ridiculing, scoffing, scornful, taunting

derisory *adj* **1** = **ridiculous**, contemptible, insulting, laughable, ludicrous, outrageous, preposterous

derivation *n* **1** = **obtaining**, acquiring, deriving, extraction, getting **2** = **origin**, ancestry, basis, beginning, descent, etymology, foundation, genealogy, root, source

derivative *adj* **2** = **unoriginal**, copied, imitative, plagiaristic, plagiarized, rehashed, secondary, second-hand, uninventive ◆ *n* **3** = **by-product**, derivation, descendant, offshoot, outgrowth, spin-off
Antonyms *adj* ≠ **unoriginal:** archetypal, authentic, first-hand, genuine, master, original, prototypical, seminal

derive *vb* **1** *foll. by* **from** = **come from**, arise from, descend from, emanate from, flow from, issue from, originate from, proceed from, spring from, stem from **2** = **obtain**, collect, deduce, draw, elicit, extract, follow, gain, gather, get, glean, infer, procure, receive, trace

derogatory *adj* = **disparaging**, belittling, damaging, defamatory, depreciative, detracting, discreditable, dishonouring, injurious, offensive, slighting, uncomplimentary, unfavourable, unflattering
Antonyms *adj* appreciative, complimentary, flattering, fulsome, laudatory

descant *n* **1** = **counterpoint**, decoration, melody, song, tune

descend *vb* **1, 3** = **move down**, alight, dismount, drop, fall, go down, plummet, plunge, sink, subside, tumble **2** = **slope**, dip, gravitate, incline, slant **4** *often foll. by* **from** = **originate**, be handed down, be passed down, derive, issue, proceed, spring **6** = **lower oneself**, abase oneself, condescend, degenerate, deteriorate, stoop **7 descend on** = **attack**, arrive, assail, assault, come in force, invade, pounce, raid, swoop
Antonyms *vb* ≠ **move down:** ascend, climb, go up, mount, rise, scale, soar

descendant *n* **1** = **successor**, child, daughter, heir, inheritor, issue, offspring, progeny, scion, son
Antonyms *n* ancestor, antecedent, forebear, forefather, forerunner, precursor, predecessor, progenitor

descent *n* **1** = **coming down**, drop, fall, plunge, swoop **2** = **slope**, declination, declivity, dip, drop, incline, slant **4** = **ancestry**, extraction, family tree, genealogy, heredity, lineage, origin, parentage **6** = **decline**, debasement, decadence, degeneration, degradation, deterioration

describe *vb* **1** = **relate**, characterize, define, depict, detail, explain, express, illustrate, narrate, portray, recount, report, specify, tell **3** = **trace**, delineate, draw, mark out, outline

description *n* **1** = **account**, characterization, delineation, depiction, detail, explanation, narration, narrative, portrayal, report, representation, sketch **3** = **kind**, brand, breed, category, class, genre, genus, ilk, kidney, order, sort, species, type, variety

descriptive *adj* **1** = **graphic**, circumstantial,

trasted with *my*. **3** relating to description or classification rather than explanation or prescription.
▸**de'scriptively** *adv* ▸**de'scriptiveness** *n*

descry (dɪ'skraɪ) *vb* **descries, descrying, descried.** (*tr*) **1** to catch sight of. **2** to discover by looking carefully. [C14: from OF *descrier* to proclaim, DECRY]

desecrate ➊ ('dɛsɪˌkreɪt) *vb* **desecrates, desecrating, desecrated.** (*tr*) **1** to violate the sacred character of (an object or place) by destructive, blasphemous, or sacrilegious action. **2** to deconsecrate. [C17: from DE- + CONSECRATE]
▸**'deseˌcrator** *or* **'deseˌcrater** *n* ▸ˌ**dese'cration** *n*

desegregate (diː'sɛgrɪˌgeɪt) *vb* **desegregates, desegregating, desegregated.** to end racial segregation in (a school or other public institution).
▸ˌ**desegre'gation** *n*

deselect (ˌdiːsɪ'lɛkt) *vb* (*tr*) *Brit. politics*. (of a constituency organization) to refuse to select (an existing MP) for re-election.
▸ˌ**dese'lection** *n*

desensitize *or* **desensitise** (diː'sɛnsɪˌtaɪz) *vb* **desensitizes, desensitizing, desensitized** *or* **desensitises, desensitising, desensitised.** (*tr*) to render less sensitive or insensitive: *the patient was desensitized to the allergen*.
▸**deˌsensiti'zation** *or* **deˌsensiti'sation** *n* ▸**de'sensiˌtizer** *or* **de'sensiˌtiser** *n*

desert[1] ➊ ('dɛzət) *n* **1** a region that is devoid or almost devoid of vegetation, esp. because of low rainfall. **2** an uncultivated uninhabited region. **3** a place which lacks some desirable feature or quality: *a cultural desert*. **4** (*modifier*) of, relating to, or like a desert. [C13: from OF, from Church L *dēsertum*, from L *dēserere* to abandon, lit.: to sever one's links with, from DE- + *serere* to bind together]

desert[2] ➊ (dɪ'zɜːt) *vb* **1** (*tr*) to abandon (a person, place, etc.) without intending to return, esp. in violation of a promise or obligation. **2** *Mil.* to abscond from (a post or duty) with no intention of returning. **3** (*tr*) to fail (someone) in time of need. [C15: from F *déserter*, from LL *dēsertāre*, from L *dēserere* to forsake; see DESERT[1]]
▸**de'serted** *adj* ▸**de'serter** *n*

desert[3] ➊ (dɪ'zɜːt) *n* **1** (*often pl*) just reward or punishment. **2** the state of deserving a reward or punishment. [C13: from OF *deserte*, from *deservir* to DESERVE]

desert boots *pl n* ankle-high boots, often of suede, with laces and soft soles.

desertification (dɪˌzɜːtɪfɪ'keɪʃən) *n* the transformation of fertile land into an arid or semiarid region as a result of intensive farming, soil erosion, etc.

desertion ➊ (dɪ'zɜːʃən) *n* **1** a deserting or being deserted. **2** *Law.* wilful abandonment, esp. of one's spouse or children.

desert island *n* a small remote tropical island.

desert pea *n* an Australian trailing leguminous plant with scarlet flowers.

desert rat *n* **1** a jerboa inhabiting the deserts of N Africa. **2** *Brit. inf.* a soldier who served in North Africa with the British 7th Armoured Division in 1941–42.

deserve ➊ (dɪ'zɜːv) *vb* **deserves, deserving, deserved.** **1** (*tr*) to be entitled to or worthy of; merit. **2** (*intr*; foll. by *of*) *Obs.* to be worthy. [C13: from OF *deservir*, from L *dēservīre* to serve devotedly, from DE- + *servīre* to SERVE]

deserved ➊ (dɪ'zɜːvd) *adj* rightfully earned; justified; warranted.
▸**deservedly** (dɪ'zɜːvɪdlɪ) *adv* ▸**deservedness** (dɪ'zɜːvɪdnɪs) *n*

deserving ➊ (dɪ'zɜːvɪŋ) *adj* (often *postpositive* and foll. by *of*) worthy, esp. of praise or reward.
▸**de'servingly** *adv* ▸**de'servingness** *n*

deshabille (ˌdeɪzæ'biːl) *or* **dishabille** *n* the state of being partly or carelessly dressed. [C17: from F *déshabillé*, from *dés* DIS-[1] + *habiller* to dress]

desiccant ('dɛsɪkənt) *adj* **1** drying. ◆ *n* **2** a substance that absorbs water and is used to remove moisture. [C17: from L *dēsiccāns* drying up; see DESICCATE]

desiccate ➊ ('dɛsɪˌkeɪt) *vb* **desiccates, desiccating, desiccated.** **1** (*tr*) to remove most of the water from; dehydrate. **2** (*tr*) to preserve (food) by removing moisture; dry. **3** (*intr*) to become dried up. [C16: from L *dēsiccāre* to dry up, from DE- + *siccāre*, from *siccus* dry]
▸**'desicˌcated** *adj* ▸ˌ**desic'cation** *n*

desiderate (dɪ'zɪdəˌreɪt) *vb* **desiderates, desiderating, desiderated.** (*tr*) to feel the lack of or need for; miss. [C17: from L *dēsīderāre*, from DE- + *sīdus* star; see DESIRE]
▸**deˌsider'ation** *n*

desideratum (dɪˌzɪdə'rɑːtəm) *n, pl* **desiderata** (-tə). something lacked and wanted. [C17: from L; see DESIDERATE]

design ➊ (dɪ'zaɪn) *vb* **1** to work out the structure or form of (something), as by making a sketch or plans. **2** to plan and make (something) artistically or skilfully. **3** (*tr*) to invent. **4** (*tr*) to intend, as for a specific purpose; plan. ◆ *n* **5** a plan or preliminary drawing. **6** the arrangement, elements, or features of an artistic or decorative work: *the design of the desk is Chippendale*. **7** a finished artistic or decorative creation. **8** the art of designing. **9** a plan or project. **10** an intention; purpose. **11** (*often pl*; often foll. by *on* or *against*) a plot, often to gain possession of (something) by illegitimate means. [C16: from L *dēsignāre* to mark out, describe, from DE- + *signāre*, from *signum* a mark]
▸**de'signable** *adj*

designate ➊ *vb* ('dɛzɪgˌneɪt). **designates, designating, designated.** (*tr*) **1** to indicate or specify. **2** to give a name to; style; entitle. **3** to select or name for an office or duty; appoint. ◆ *adj* ('dɛzɪgnɪt, -ˌneɪt). **4** (*immediately postpositive*) appointed, but not yet in office: *a minister designate*. [C15: from L *dēsignātus* marked out, defined; see DESIGN]
▸**'desigˌnator** *n*

designation ➊ (ˌdɛzɪg'neɪʃən) *n* **1** something that designates, such as a name. **2** the act of designating or the fact of being designated.

designedly ➊ (dɪ'zaɪnɪdlɪ) *adv* by intention or design; on purpose.

designer ➊ (dɪ'zaɪnə) *n* **1** a person who devises and executes designs, as for clothes, machines, etc. **2** (*modifier*) designed by and bearing the label of a well-known fashion designer: *designer jeans*. **3** (*modifier*) (of things, ideas, etc.) fashionably trendy: *designer stubble*. **4** (*modifier*) (of cells, chemicals, etc.) designed or produced to perform a specific function or combat a specific problem: *designer insecticide*. **5** a person who devises plots; intriguer.

designer drug *n* **1** *Med.* a synthetic antibiotic designed to be effective against a particular bacterium. **2** a synthetic drug that has the same properties as an illegal narcotic or hallucinogen but can be manufactured legally.

designing ➊ (dɪ'zaɪnɪŋ) *adj* artful and scheming.

desirable ➊ (dɪ'zaɪərəb°l) *adj* **1** worthy of desire: *a desirable residence*. **2** arousing desire, esp. sexual desire; attractive.
▸**deˌsira'bility** *or* **de'sirableness** *n* ▸**de'sirably** *adv*

THESAURUS

depictive, detailed, explanatory, expressive, illustrative, pictorial, picturesque, vivid

desecrate *vb* **1** = **commit sacrilege**, abuse, blaspheme, contaminate, defile, despoil, dishonour, pervert, pollute, profane, violate
Antonyms *vb* esteem, exalt, glorify, hallow, prize, respect, revere, value, venerate, worship

desecration *n* **1** = **sacrilege**, blasphemy, debasement, defilement, impiety, profanation, violation

desert[1] *n* **1, 2** = **wilderness**, solitude, waste, wasteland, wilds ◆ *modifier* **4** = **barren**, arid, bare, desolate, infertile, lonely, solitary, uncultivated, uninhabited, unproductive, untilled, waste, wild

desert[2] *vb* **1-3** = **abandon**, abscond, betray, decamp, defect, forsake, give up, go over the hill (*Military sl.*), jilt, leave, leave high and dry, leave (someone) in the lurch, leave stranded, maroon, quit, rat (on) (*inf.*), relinquish, renounce, resign, run out on (*inf.*), strand, throw over, vacate, walk out on (*inf.*)
Antonyms *vb* be a source of strength to, look after, maintain, provide for, succour, sustain, take care of

desert[3] *n* **1** *often plural* = **due**, comeuppance, guerdon (*poetic*), meed (*arch.*), payment, punishment, recompense, requital, retribution, return, reward, right

deserted *adj* **1** = **abandoned**, bereft, cast off, derelict, desolate, empty, forlorn, forsaken, godforsaken, isolated, left in the lurch, left stranded, lonely, neglected, solitary, unfriended, unoccupied, vacant

deserter *n* **1, 2** = **defector**, absconder, apostate, escapee, fugitive, rat (*inf.*), renegade, runaway, traitor, truant

desertion *n* **1, 2** = **abandonment**, absconding, apostasy, betrayal, defection, departure, dereliction, escape, evasion, flight, forsaking, relinquishment, truancy

deserve *vb* **1** = **merit**, be entitled to, be worthy of, earn, gain, justify, procure, rate, warrant, win

deserved *adj* = **well-earned**, appropriate, condign, due, earned, fair, fitting, just, justifiable, justified, meet (*arch.*), merited, proper, right, rightful, suitable, warranted

deservedly *adv* = **by rights**, according to one's due, appropriately, condignly, duly, fairly, fittingly, justifiably, justly, properly, rightfully, rightly
Antonyms *adv* inappropriately, undeservedly, unduly, unfairly, unfittingly, unjustifiably, unjustly, unwarrantedly, wrongfully, wrongly

deserving *adj* = **worthy**, commendable, estimable, laudable, meritorious, praiseworthy, righteous
Antonyms *adj* not deserving of, not good enough, not worth, undeserving, unworthy

desiccate *vb* **1** = **dry**, dehydrate, drain, evaporate, exsiccate, parch

desiccated *adj* **2** = **dried**, dehydrated, dry, powdered

design *vb* **1** = **plan**, delineate, describe, draft, draw, outline, sketch, trace **2, 3** = **create**, conceive, fabricate, fashion, invent, originate, think up **4** = **intend**, aim, contrive, destine, devise, make, mean, plan, project, propose, purpose, scheme, tailor ◆ *n* **5** = **plan**, blueprint, delineation, draft, drawing, model, outline, scheme, sketch **6** = **arrangement**, configuration, construction, figure, form, motif, organization, pattern, shape, style **10** = **intention**, aim, end, goal, intent, meaning, object, objective, point, purport, purpose, target, view

designate *vb* **1** = **specify**, characterize, define, denote, describe, earmark, indicate, pinpoint, show, stipulate **2** = **name**, call, christen, dub, entitle, label, nominate, style, term **3** = **appoint**, allot, assign, choose, delegate, depute, nominate, select

designation *n* **1** = **name**, denomination, description, epithet, label, mark, title **2** = **appointment**, classification, delegation, indication, selection, specification

designedly *adv* = **intentionally**, by design, calculatedly, deliberately, knowingly, on purpose, purposely, studiously, wilfully, wittingly

designer *n* **1** = **creator**, architect, artificer, couturier, deviser, inventor, originator, planner, stylist

designing *adj* = **scheming**, artful, astute, conniving, conspiring, crafty, crooked (*inf.*), cunning, deceitful, devious, intriguing, Machiavellian, plotting, sharp, shrewd, sly, treacherous, tricky, unscrupulous, wily

desirability *n* **1** = **worth**, advantage, benefit, merit, profit, usefulness, value

desirable *adj* **1** = **agreeable**, advantageous, advisable, beneficial, covetable, eligible, enviable, good, pleasing, preferable, profitable, to

desire Ⓣ (dɪˈzaɪə) *vb* **desires, desiring, desired.** (*tr*) **1** to wish or long for; crave. **2** to request; ask for. ◆ *n* **3** a wish or longing. **4** an expressed wish; request. **5** sexual appetite. **6** a person or thing that is desired. [C13: from OF, from L *dēsīderāre* to desire earnestly; see DESIDERATE]
▸**deˈsirer** *n*

desirous Ⓣ (dɪˈzaɪərəs) *adj* (usually *postpositive* and foll. by *of*) having or expressing desire (for).

desist Ⓣ (dɪˈzɪst) *vb* (*intr*; often foll. by *from*) to cease, as from an action; stop or abstain. [C15: from OF, from L *dēsistere* to leave off, stand apart, from DE- + *sistere* to stand, halt]

desk (dɛsk) *n* **1** a piece of furniture with a writing surface and usually drawers or other compartments. **2** a service counter or table in a public building, such as a hotel. **3** a support for the book from which services are read in a church. **4** the editorial section of a newspaper, etc., responsible for a particular subject: *the news desk*. **5** a music stand shared by two orchestral players. [C14: from Med. L *desca* table, from L *discus* disc, dish]

desk-bound *adj* obliged by one's occupation to work sitting at a desk.

desk editor *n* (in a publishing house) an editor responsible for the preparation and checking of manuscripts for printing.

deskill (diːˈskɪl) *vb* (*tr*) **1** to mechanize or computerize (a job) so that little skill is required to do it. **2** to deprive (employees) of the opportunity for skilled work.

desktop (ˈdɛskˌtɒp) *n* (*modifier*) denoting a computer system, esp. for word processing, that is small enough to use at a desk.

desktop publishing *n* a means of publishing reports, advertising material, etc., to near-typeset quality using a desktop computer and a laser printer. Abbrev.: **DTP**.

desman (ˈdɛsmən) *n, pl* **desmans.** either of two molelike amphibious mammals, the Russian desman or the Pyrenean desman, with dense fur and webbed feet. [C18: from Swedish *desmansråtta*, from *desman* musk + *råtta* rat]

desolate Ⓣ *adj* (ˈdɛsəlɪt). **1** uninhabited; deserted. **2** made uninhabitable; laid waste; devastated. **3** without friends, hope, or encouragement. **4** dismal; depressing. ◆ *vb* (ˈdɛsəˌleɪt), **desolates, desolating, desolated.** (*tr*) **5** to deprive of inhabitants; depopulate. **6** to lay waste; devastate. **7** to make wretched or forlorn. **8** to forsake or abandon. [C14: from L *dēsōlāre* to leave alone, from DE- + *sōlāre* to make lonely, lay waste, from *sōlus* alone]
▸ˈ**desoˌlater** *or* ˈ**desoˌlator** *n* ▸ˈ**desolately** *adv* ▸ˈ**desolateness** *n*

desolation Ⓣ (ˌdɛsəˈleɪʃən) *n* **1** a desolating or being desolated; ruin or devastation. **2** solitary misery; wretchedness. **3** a desolate region.

despair Ⓣ (dɪˈspɛə) *vb* **1** (*intr*; often foll. by *of*) to lose or give up hope: *I despair of his coming*. ◆ *n* **2** total loss of hope. **3** a person or thing that causes hopelessness or for which there is no hope. [C14: from OF *despoir* hopelessness, from *desperer* to despair, from L *dēspērāre*, from DE- + *spērāre* to hope]

despairing Ⓣ (dɪˈspɛərɪŋ) *adj* hopeless, despondent; feeling or showing despair.
▸**deˈspairingly** *adv*

despatch Ⓣ (dɪˈspætʃ) *vb* (*tr*), *n* a less common spelling of **dispatch**.
▸**desˈpatcher** *n*

desperado Ⓣ (ˌdɛspəˈrɑːdəʊ) *n, pl* **desperadoes** *or* **desperados.** a reckless or desperate person, esp. one ready to commit any violent illegal act. [C17: prob. pseudo-Spanish var. of obs. *desperate* (n)]

desperate Ⓣ (ˈdɛspərɪt, -prɪt) *adj* **1** careless of danger, as from despair. **2** (of an act) reckless; risky. **3** used or undertaken as a last resort. **4** critical; very grave: *in desperate need*. **5** (often *postpositive* and foll. by *for*) in distress and having a great need or desire. **6** moved by or showing despair. [C15: from L *dēspērāre* to have no hope; see DESPAIR]
▸ˈ**desperately** *adv* ▸ˈ**desperateness** *n*

desperation Ⓣ (ˌdɛspəˈreɪʃən) *n* **1** desperate recklessness. **2** the state of being desperate.

despicable Ⓣ (ˈdɛspɪkəbᵊl, dɪˈspɪk-) *adj* worthy of being despised; contemptible; mean. [C16: from LL *dēspicābilis*, from *dēspicārī* to disdain; cf. DESPISE]
▸ˈ**despicably** *adv*

despise Ⓣ (dɪˈspaɪz) *vb* **despises, despising, despised.** (*tr*) to look down on with contempt; scorn: *he despises flattery*. [C13: from OF *despire*, from L *dēspicere* to look down, from DE- + *specere* to look]
▸**deˈspiser** *n*

despite Ⓣ (dɪˈspaɪt) *prep* **1** in spite of; undeterred by. ◆ *n* **2** *Arch.* contempt; insult. **3 in despite of.** (*prep*) *Rare.* in spite of. [C13: from OF *despit*, from L *dēspectus* contempt; see DESPISE]

despoil Ⓣ (dɪˈspɔɪl) *vb* (*tr*) to deprive by force; plunder; loot. [C13: from OF, from L *dēspoliāre*, from DE- + *spoliāre* to rob (esp. of clothing)]
▸**deˈspoiler** *n* ▸**deˈspoilment** *n*

despoliation (dɪˌspəʊlɪˈeɪʃən) *n* **1** plunder or pillage. **2** the state of being despoiled.

despond (dɪˈspɒnd) *vb* (*intr*) **1** to become disheartened; despair. ◆ *n* **2** *Arch.* despondency. [C17: from L *dēspondēre* to promise, make over to, yield, lose heart, from DE- + *spondēre* to promise]
▸**deˈspondingly** *adv*

despondent Ⓣ (dɪˈspɒndənt) *adj* downcast or disheartened; dejected.
▸**deˈspondence** *or* **deˈspondency** *n* ▸**deˈspondently** *adv*

despot Ⓣ (ˈdɛspɒt) *n* **1** an absolute or tyrannical ruler. **2** any person in power who acts tyrannically. [C16: from Med. L *despota*, from Gk *despotēs* lord, master]
▸**despotic** (dɛsˈpɒtɪk) *or* **desˈpotical** *adj* ▸**desˈpotically** *adv*

THESAURUS

die for (*inf.*), worthwhile **2** = **attractive**, adorable, alluring, fascinating, fetching, glamorous, seductive, sexy (*inf.*)
Antonyms *adj* ≠ **agreeable:** disagreeable, distasteful, unacceptable, unappealing, unattractive, undesirable, unpleasant, unpopular ≠ **attractive:** unappealing, unattractive, undesirable, unsexy (*inf.*)

desire *vb* **1** = **want**, aspire to, covet, crave, desiderate, fancy, hanker after, hope for, long for, set one's heart on, thirst for, wish for, yearn for **2** = **request**, ask, entreat, importune, petition, solicit ◆ *n* **3** = **wish**, ache, appetite, aspiration, craving, hankering, hope, longing, need, thirst, want, yearning, yen (*inf.*) **4** = **request**, appeal, entreaty, importunity, petition, solicitation, supplication **5** = **lust**, appetite, concupiscence, lasciviousness, lechery, libido, lustfulness, passion

desirous *adj* = **wishing**, ambitious, anxious, aspiring, avid, craving, desiring, eager, hopeful, hoping, keen, longing, ready, willing, yearning
Antonyms *adj* averse, disinclined, grudging, indisposed, loath, opposed, reluctant, unenthusiastic, unwilling

desist *vb* = **stop**, abstain, belay (*Nautical*), break off, cease, discontinue, end, forbear, give over (*inf.*), give up, have done with, kick (*inf.*), leave off, pause, refrain from, remit, suspend

desolate *adj* **1** = **uninhabited**, bare, barren, bleak, desert, dreary, godforsaken, ruined, solitary, unfrequented, waste, wild **3** = **miserable**, abandoned, bereft, cheerless, comfortless, companionless, dejected, depressing, despondent, disconsolate, dismal, downcast, down in the dumps (*inf.*), forlorn, forsaken, gloomy, lonely, melancholy, wretched ◆ *vb* **5, 6** = **lay waste**, depopulate, despoil, destroy, devastate, lay low, pillage, plunder, ravage, ruin **7** = **deject**, daunt, depress, discourage, dishearten, dismay, distress, grieve
Antonyms *adj* ≠ **uninhabited:** inhabited, populous ≠ **miserable:** cheerful, happy, joyous, lighthearted ◆ *vb* ≠ **lay waste:** develop ≠ **deject:** cheer, encourage, hearten, nourish

desolation *n* **1** = **ruin**, destruction, devastation, havoc, ravages, ruination **2** = **misery**, anguish, dejection, despair, distress, gloom, gloominess, melancholy, sadness, unhappiness, woe, wretchedness

despair *vb* **1** = **lose hope**, despond, give up, lose heart ◆ *n* **2** = **despondency**, anguish, dejection, depression, desperation, disheartenment, gloom, hopelessness, melancholy, misery, wretchedness **3** = **hardship**, burden, cross, ordeal, pain, trial, tribulation

despairing *adj* = **hopeless**, anxious, at the end of one's tether, broken-hearted, dejected, depressed, desperate, despondent, disconsolate, dismal, downcast, down in the dumps (*inf.*), frantic, grief-stricken, inconsolable, melancholy, miserable, suicidal, wretched

despatch *see* **dispatch**

desperado *n* = **criminal**, bandit, cut-throat, gangster, gunman, heavy (*sl.*), hoodlum (*chiefly US*), lawbreaker, mugger (*inf.*), outlaw, ruffian, thug, villain

desperate *adj* **2** = **reckless**, audacious, dangerous, daring, death-defying, determined, foolhardy, frantic, furious, hasty, hazardous, headstrong, impetuous, madcap, precipitate, rash, risky, violent, wild **4** = **grave**, acute, critical, dire, drastic, extreme, great, urgent, very grave **6** = **hopeless**, at the end of one's tether, despairing, despondent, forlorn, inconsolable, irrecoverable, irremediable, irretrievable, wretched

desperately *adv* **4** = **gravely**, badly, dangerously, perilously, seriously, severely **6** = **hopelessly**, appallingly, fearfully, frightfully, shockingly

desperation *n* **1** = **recklessness**, defiance, foolhardiness, frenzy, heedlessness, impetuosity, madness, rashness **2** = **misery**, agony, anguish, anxiety, despair, despondency, distraction, heartache, hopelessness, pain, sorrow, torture, trouble, unhappiness, worry

despicable *adj* = **contemptible**, abject, base, beyond contempt, cheap, degrading, detestable, disgraceful, disreputable, hateful, ignominious, infamous, low, mean, pitiful, reprehensible, scurvy, shameful, sordid, vile, worthless, wretched
Antonyms *adj* admirable, estimable, ethical, exemplary, good, honest, honourable, moral, noble, praiseworthy, righteous, upright, virtuous, worthy

despise *vb* = **look down on**, abhor, contemn, deride, detest, disdain, disregard, flout, have a down on (*inf.*), loathe, neglect, revile, scorn, slight, spurn, undervalue
Antonyms *vb* admire, adore, be fond of, be keen on, cherish, dig (*sl.*), esteem, fancy (*inf.*), love, relish, revel in, take to

despite *prep* **1** = **in spite of**, against, even with, in contempt of, in defiance of, in the face of, in the teeth of, notwithstanding, regardless of, undeterred by

despoil *vb Formal* = **plunder**, denude, deprive, destroy, devastate, dispossess, divest, loot, pillage, ravage, rifle, rob, strip, total (*sl.*), trash (*sl.*), vandalize, wreak havoc upon, wreck

despondency *n* = **dejection**, depression, despair, desperation, disconsolateness, discouragement, dispiritedness, downheartedness, gloom, hopelessness, low spirits, melancholy, misery, sadness, the hump (*Brit. inf.*), wretchedness

despondent *adj* = **dejected**, blue, depressed, despairing, disconsolate, discouraged, disheartened, dismal, dispirited, doleful, down, downcast, downhearted, down in the dumps (*inf.*), gloomy, glum, hopeless, in despair, low, low-spirited, melancholy, miserable, morose, sad, sick as a parrot (*inf.*), sorrowful, woebegone, wretched
Antonyms *adj* buoyant, cheerful, cheery, chirpy (*inf.*), genial, glad, happy, hopeful, joyful, lighthearted, optimistic, upbeat (*inf.*)

despot *n* **1, 2** = **tyrant**, autocrat, dictator, monocrat, oppressor

despotism ❶ ('dɛspəˌtɪzəm) *n* **1** the rule of a despot; absolute or tyrannical government. **2** arbitrary or tyrannical authority or behaviour.

des res ('dɛz 'rɛz) *n* (in estate agents' jargon) a desirable residence.

dessert ❶ (dɪ'zɜːt) *n* **1** the sweet, usually last course of a meal. **2** *Chiefly Brit.* (esp. formerly) fruit, dates, nuts, etc., served at the end of a meal. [C17: from F, from *desservir* to clear a table, from *des-* DIS-[1] + *servir* to SERVE]

dessertspoon (dɪ'zɜːtˌspuːn) *n* a spoon intermediate in size between a tablespoon and a teaspoon.

destination ❶ (ˌdɛstɪ'neɪʃən) *n* **1** the predetermined end of a journey. **2** the end or purpose for which something is created or a person is destined.

destine ❶ ('dɛstɪn) *vb* **destines, destining, destined.** (*tr*) to set apart (for a certain purpose or person); intend; design. [C14: from OF, from L *dēstināre* to appoint, from DE- + *-stināre,* from *stāre* to stand]

destined ❶ ('dɛstɪnd) *adj* (*postpositive*) **1** foreordained; meant. **2** (usually foll. by *for*) heading (towards a specific destination).

destiny ❶ ('dɛstɪnɪ) *n, pl* **destinies. 1** the future destined for a person or thing. **2** the predetermined or inevitable course of events. **3** the power that predetermines the course of events. [C14: from OF, from *destiner* to DESTINE]

destitute ❶ ('dɛstɪˌtjuːt) *adj* **1** lacking the means of subsistence; totally impoverished. **2** (*postpositive;* foll. by *of*) completely lacking: *destitute of words.* [C14: from L, from *dēstituere* to leave alone, from *statuere* to place]

destitution ❶ (ˌdɛstɪ'tjuːʃən) *n* the state of being destitute; utter poverty.

destrier ('dɛstrɪə) *n Arch.* a warhorse. [C13: from OF, from *destre* right hand, from L *dextra;* from the fact that a squire led a knight's horse with his right hand]

destroy ❶ (dɪ'strɔɪ) *vb* (*mainly tr*) **1** to ruin; spoil. **2** to tear down or demolish. **3** to put an end to. **4** to kill or annihilate. **5** to crush or defeat. **6** (*intr*) to be destructive or cause destruction. [C13: from OF, from L *dēstruere* to pull down, from DE- + *struere* to pile up, build]

destroyer (dɪ'strɔɪə) *n* **1** a small fast lightly armoured but heavily armed warship. **2** a person or thing that destroys.

destruct (dɪ'strʌkt) *vb* **1** to destroy (one's own missile, etc.) for safety. **2** (*intr*) (of a missile, etc.) to be destroyed, for safety, by those controlling it. ◆ *n* **3** the act of destructing. ◆ *adj* **4** designed to be capable of destroying itself or the object containing it: *destruct mechanism.*

destructible (dɪ'strʌktɪbᵊl) *adj* capable of being or liable to be destroyed.

destruction ❶ (dɪ'strʌkʃən) *n* **1** the act of destroying or state of being destroyed; demolition. **2** a cause of ruin or means of destroying. [C14: from L *dēstructiō* a pulling down; see DESTROY]

destructive ❶ (dɪ'strʌktɪv) *adj* **1** (often *postpositive* and foll. by *of* or *to*) causing or tending to cause the destruction (of). **2** intended to discredit, esp. without positive suggestions or help; negative: *destructive criticism.*
▸**de'structively** *adv* ▸**de'structiveness** *n*

destructive distillation *n* the decomposition of a complex substance, such as wood or coal, by heating it in the absence of air and collecting the volatile products.

destructor (dɪ'strʌktə) *n* **1** a furnace or incinerator for the disposal of refuse. **2** a device used to blow up a defective missile.

desuetude (dɪ'sjuːɪˌtjuːd, 'dɛswɪˌtjuːd) *n Formal.* the condition of not being in use or practice; disuse. [C15: from L, from *dēsuescere* to lay aside a habit, from DE- + *suescere* to grow accustomed]

desulphurize *or* **desulphurise** (diː'sʌlfjʊˌraɪz) *vb* **desulphurizes, desulphurizing, desulphurized** *or* **desulphurises, desulphurising, desulphurised.** to free or become free from sulphur.

desultory ❶ ('dɛsəltərɪ, -trɪ) *adj* **1** passing from one thing to another, esp. in a fitful way; unmethodical; disconnected. **2** random or incidental: *a desultory thought.* [C16: from L: relating to one who vaults or jumps, hence superficial, from *dēsilīre* to jump down, from DE- + *salīre*]
▸**'desultorily** *adv* ▸**'desultoriness** *n*

Det. *abbrev. for* Detective.

detach ❶ (dɪ'tætʃ) *vb* (*tr*) **1** to disengage and separate or remove; unfasten; disconnect. **2** *Mil.* to separate (a small unit) from a larger, esp. for a special assignment. [C17: from OF *destachier,* from *des-* DIS-[1] + *atachier* to ATTACH]
▸**de'tachable** *adj* ▸**deˌtacha'bility** *n*

detached ❶ (dɪ'tætʃt) *adj* **1** disconnected or standing apart; not attached: *a detached house.* **2** showing no bias or emotional involvement. **3** *Ophthalmol.* (of the retina) separated from the choroid layer of the eyeball to which it is normally attached, resulting in loss of vision in the affected part.

detachment ❶ (dɪ'tætʃmənt) *n* **1** indifference; aloofness. **2** freedom from self-interest or bias; disinterest. **3** the act of detaching something. **4** the condition of being detached; disconnection. **5** *Mil.* **5a** the separation of a small unit from its main body. **5b** the unit so detached.

detail ❶ ('diːteɪl) *n* **1** an item that is considered separately; particular. **2** an item that is unimportant: *passengers' comfort was regarded as a detail.* **3** treatment of particulars: *this essay includes too much detail.* **4** items collectively; particulars. **5** a small section or element in a painting, building, statue, etc., esp. when considered in isolation. **6** *Mil.* **6a** the act of assigning personnel for a specific duty. **6b** the personnel selected. **6c** the duty. **7 in detail.** including all or most particulars or items thoroughly. ◆ *vb* (*tr*) **8** to list or relate fully. **9** *Mil.* to select (personnel) for a specific duty. [C17: from F, from OF *detailler* to cut in pieces, from *de-* DIS-[1] + *tailler* to cut]

detailed ❶ ('diːteɪld) *adj* having many details or giving careful attention to details.

detain ❶ (dɪ'teɪn) *vb* (*tr*) **1** to delay; hold back. **2** to confine or hold in custody. [C15: from OF, from L *dētinēre* to hold off, keep back, from DE- + *tenēre* to hold]
▸**de'tainable** *adj* ▸**detainee** (ˌdiːteɪ'niː) *n* ▸**de'tainment** *n*

detect ❶ (dɪ'tɛkt) *vb* (*tr*) **1** to perceive or notice. **2** to discover the existence or presence of (esp. something likely to elude observation). **3**

THESAURUS

despotic *adj* **1, 2** = **tyrannical**, absolute, arbitrary, arrogant, authoritarian, autocratic, dictatorial, domineering, imperious, monocratic, oppressive, unconstitutional

despotism *n* **1, 2** = **tyranny**, absolutism, autarchy, autocracy, dictatorship, monocracy, oppression, totalitarianism

dessert *n* **1, 2** = **pudding**, afters (*Brit. inf.*), last course, second course, sweet, sweet course

destination *n* **1** = **journey's end**, harbour, haven, landing-place, resting-place, station, stop, terminus **2** = **objective**, aim, ambition, design, end, goal, intention, object, purpose, target

destine *vb* = **fate**, allot, appoint, assign, consecrate, decree, design, devote, doom, earmark, intend, mark out, ordain, predetermine, preordain, purpose, reserve

destined *adj* **1** = **fated**, bound, certain, designed, doomed, foreordained, ineluctable, inescapable, inevitable, intended, meant, ordained, predestined, unavoidable **2** = **bound for**, assigned, booked, directed, en route, heading for, on the road to, routed, scheduled

destiny *n* **1–3** = **fate**, cup, divine decree, doom, fortune, karma, kismet, lot, portion

destitute *adj* **1** = **penniless**, dirt-poor (*inf.*), distressed, down and out, flat broke (*inf.*), impecunious, impoverished, indigent, in queer street (*inf.*), insolvent, moneyless, necessitous, needy, on one's uppers, on the breadline (*inf.*), on the rocks, penurious, poor, poverty-stricken, short, without two pennies to rub together (*inf.*) **2** = **lacking**, bereft of, deficient in, depleted, deprived of, devoid of, drained, empty of, in need of, wanting, without

destitution *n* = **pennilessness**, beggary, dire straits, distress, impecuniousness, indigence, neediness, pauperism, penury, privation, utter poverty, want
Antonyms *n* affluence, fortune, good fortune, life of luxury, luxury, plenty, prosperity, riches, wealth

destroy *vb* = **ruin**, annihilate, blow sky-high, blow to bits, break down, crush, demolish, desolate, devastate, dismantle, dispatch, eradicate, extinguish, extirpate, gut, kill, put paid to, ravage, raze, shatter, slay, smash, torpedo, total (*sl.*), trash (*sl.*), waste, wipe out, wreck

destruction *n* **1** = **ruin**, annihilation, crushing, demolition, devastation, downfall, end, eradication, extermination, extinction, havoc, liquidation, massacre, overthrow, overwhelming, ruination, shattering, slaughter, undoing, wreckage, wrecking

destructive *adj* **1** = **damaging**, baleful, baneful, calamitous, cataclysmic, catastrophic, deadly, deleterious, detrimental, devastating, fatal, harmful, hurtful, injurious, lethal, maleficent, noxious, pernicious, ruinous **2** = **negative**, adverse, antagonistic, contrary, derogatory, discouraging, discrediting, disparaging, hostile, invalidating, opposed, undermining, vicious

desultory *adj* **1, 2** = **random**, aimless, capricious, cursory, disconnected, discursive, disorderly, erratic, fitful, haphazard, inconsistent, inconstant, inexact, irregular, loose, maundering, off and on, rambling, roving, spasmodic, unmethodical, unsettled, unsystematic, vague

detach *vb* **1** = **separate**, cut off, disconnect, disengage, disentangle, disjoin, disunite, divide, free, isolate, loosen, remove, segregate, sever, tear off, unbridle, uncouple, unfasten, unhitch
Antonyms *vb* attach, bind, connect, fasten

detached *adj* **1** = **separate**, disconnected, discrete, disjoined, divided, free, loosened, severed, unconnected **2** = **uninvolved**, aloof, disinterested, dispassionate, impartial, impersonal, neutral, objective, reserved, unbiased, uncommitted, unprejudiced
Antonyms *adj* ≠ **uninvolved**: biased, concerned, interested, involved, partisan, prejudiced

detachment *n* **1** = **indifference**, aloofness, coolness, nonchalance, remoteness, unconcern **2** = **impartiality**, disinterestedness, fairness, neutrality, nonpartisanship, objectivity **4** = **separation**, disconnection, disengagement, disjoining, severing **5b** *Military* = **unit**, body, detail, force, party, patrol, squad, task force

detail *n* **1** = **point**, aspect, component, count, element, fact, factor, feature, item, particular, respect, specific, technicality **2** = **fine point**, minutiae, nicety, part, particular, triviality **6b** *Military* = **party**, assignment, body, detachment, duty, fatigue, force, squad **7 in detail** = **comprehensively**, exhaustively, inside out, item by item, point by point, thoroughly ◆ *vb* **8** = **list**, catalogue, delineate, depict, describe, enumerate, individualize, itemize, narrate, particularize, portray, recite, recount, rehearse, relate, specify, tabulate **9** = **appoint**, allocate, assign, charge, commission, delegate, detach, send

detailed *adj* = **comprehensive**, blow-by-blow, circumstantial, elaborate, exact, exhaustive, full, intricate, itemized, meticulous, minute, particular, particularized, specific, thorough
Antonyms *adj* brief, compact, concise, condensed, limited, pithy, short, slight, succinct, summary, superficial, terse

detain *vb* **1** = **delay**, check, hinder, hold up, impede, keep, keep back, retard, slow up (*or* down), stay, stop **2** = **hold**, arrest, confine, intern, restrain

detect *vb* **1** = **notice**, ascertain, catch, descry, distinguish, identify, note, observe, perceive,

Obs. to discover, or reveal (a crime, criminal, etc.). **4** to extract information from (an electromagnetic wave). [C15: from L *dētectus,* from *dētegere* to uncover, from DE- + *tegere* to cover]
▸**de'tectable** *or* **de'tectible** *adj*

detection Ⓣ (dɪ'tɛkʃən) *n* **1** the act of discovering or the fact of being discovered. **2** the act or process of extracting information, esp. at audio or video frequencies, from an electromagnetic wave; demodulation.

detective Ⓣ (dɪ'tɛktɪv) *n* **1a** a police officer who investigates crimes. **1b** See **private detective. 1c** *(as modifier): a detective story.* ◆ *adj* **2** of or for detection.

detector (dɪ'tɛktə) *n* **1** a person or thing that detects. **2** any mechanical sensing device. **3** *Electronics.* a device used in the detection of radio signals.

detent (dɪ'tɛnt) *n* the locking piece of a mechanism, often spring-loaded to check the movement of a wheel in only one direction. [C17: from OF *destente* a loosening, trigger; see DÉTENTE]

détente (deɪ'tɑːnt; *French* detɑ̃t) *n* the relaxing or easing of tension, esp. between nations. [F, lit.: a loosening, from OF *destendre* to release, from *tendre* to stretch]

detention Ⓣ (dɪ'tɛnʃən) *n* **1** a detaining or being detained. **2a** custody or confinement, esp. of a suspect awaiting trial. **2b** *(as modifier): a detention order.* **3** a form of punishment in which a pupil is detained after school. [C16: from L *dētentiō* a keeping back; see DETAIN]

detention centre *n* (formerly) a place in which young persons could be detained for short periods by order of a court.

deter Ⓣ (dɪ'tɜː) *vb* **deters, deterring, deterred.** *(tr)* to discourage (from acting) or prevent (from occurring), usually by instilling fear, doubt, or anxiety. [C16: from L *dēterrēre,* from DE- + *terrēre* to frighten]
▸**de'terment** *n*

deterge (dɪ'tɜːdʒ) *vb* **deterges, deterging, deterged.** *(tr)* to cleanse: *to deterge a wound.* [C17: from L *dētergēre* to wipe away, from DE- + *tergēre* to wipe]

detergent Ⓣ (dɪ'tɜːdʒənt) *n* **1** a cleansing agent, esp. a chemical such as an alkyl sulphonate, widely used in industry, laundering, etc. ◆ *adj* **2** having cleansing power. [C17: from L *dētergēns* wiping off; see DETERGE]

deteriorate Ⓣ (dɪ'tɪərɪəˌreɪt) *vb* **deteriorates, deteriorating, deteriorated. 1** to make or become worse; depreciate. **2** *(intr)* to wear away or disintegrate. [C16: from LL *dēteriōrāre,* from L *dēterior* worse]
▸**deˌterio'ration** *n* ▸**de'teriorative** *adj*

determinacy (dɪ'tɜːmɪnəsɪ) *n* **1** the quality of being defined or fixed. **2** the condition of being predicted or deduced.

determinant (dɪ'tɜːmɪnənt) *adj* **1** serving to determine. ◆ *n* **2** a factor that influences or determines. **3** *Maths.* a square array of elements that represents the sum of certain products of these elements, used to solve simultaneous equations, in vector studies, etc.

determinate Ⓣ (dɪ'tɜːmɪnɪt) *adj* **1** definitely limited, defined, or fixed. **2** determined. **3** able to be predicted or deduced. **4** *Bot.* having the main and branch stems ending in flowers.
▸**de'terminateness** *n*

determination Ⓣ (dɪˌtɜːmɪ'neɪʃən) *n* **1** the act of making a decision. **2** the condition of being determined; resoluteness. **3** an ending of an argument by the decision of an authority. **4** the act of fixing the quality, limit, position, etc., of something. **5** a decision or opinion reached. **6** a resolute movement towards some object or end. **7** *Law.* the termination of an estate or interest. **8** *Law.* the decision reached by a court of justice on a disputed matter.

determinative (dɪ'tɜːmɪnətɪv) *adj* **1** serving to settle or determine; deciding. ◆ *n* **2** a factor, circumstance, etc., that settles or determines.
▸**de'terminatively** *adv* ▸**de'terminativeness** *n*

determine Ⓣ (dɪ'tɜːmɪn) *vb* **determines, determining, determined. 1** to settle or decide (an argument, question, etc.) conclusively. **2** *(tr)* to conclude, esp. after observation or consideration. **3** *(tr)* to influence; give direction to. **4** *(tr)* to fix in scope, variety, etc.: *the river determined the edge of the property.* **5** to make or cause to make a decision. **6** *(tr) Logic.* to define or limit (a notion) by adding or requiring certain features or characteristics. **7** *(tr) Geom.* to fix or specify the position or form of. **8** *Chiefly law.* to come or bring to an end, as an estate. [C14: from OF, from L *dēterminăre* to set boundaries to, from DE- + *termināre* to limit]
▸**de'terminable** *adj*

determined Ⓣ (dɪ'tɜːmɪnd) *adj* of unwavering mind; resolute; firm.
▸**de'terminedly** *adv*

determiner (dɪ'tɜːmɪnə) *n* **1** a word, such as a number, article, or personal pronoun, that determines (limits) the meaning of a noun phrase, e.g. *their* in 'their black cat'. **2** a person or thing that determines.

determinism (dɪ'tɜːmɪˌnɪzəm) *n* the philosophical doctrine that all events, including human actions, are fully determined by preceding events, and so freedom of choice is illusory. Also called: **necessitarianism.** Cf. **free will.**
▸**de'terminist** *n, adj* ▸**deˌtermin'istic** *adj*

deterrent Ⓣ (dɪ'tɛrənt) *n* **1** something that deters. **2** a weapon, esp. nuclear, held by one state, etc., to deter attack by another. ◆ *adj* **3** tending or used to deter. [C19: from L *dēterrēns* hindering; see DETER]
▸**de'terrence** *n*

detest Ⓣ (dɪ'tɛst) *vb (tr)* to dislike intensely; loathe. [C16: from L *dētestārī* to curse (while invoking a god as witness), from DE- + *testārī,* from *testis* a witness]
▸**de'tester** *n*

detestable Ⓣ (dɪ'tɛstəbᵊl) *adj* being or deserving to be abhorred or detested.
▸**deˌtesta'bility** *or* **de'testableness** *n* ▸**de'testably** *adv*

detestation Ⓣ (ˌdiːtɛs'teɪʃən) *n* **1** intense hatred; abhorrence. **2** a person or thing that is detested.

dethrone Ⓣ (dɪ'θrəʊn) *vb* **dethrones, dethroning, dethroned.** *(tr)* to remove from a throne or deprive of any high position or title.
▸**de'thronement** *n* ▸**de'throner** *n*

detonate Ⓣ ('dɛtəˌneɪt) *vb* **detonates, detonating, detonated.** to cause (a bomb, mine, etc.) to explode or (of a bomb, mine, etc.) to explode. [C18: from L *dētonāre* to thunder down, from DE- + *tonāre* to THUNDER]
▸**ˌdeto'nation** *n*

detonator ('dɛtəˌneɪtə) *n* **1** a small amount of explosive, as in a percussion cap, used to initiate a larger explosion. **2** a device, such as an electrical generator, used to set off an explosion from a distance. **3** an explosive.

detour Ⓣ ('diːtʊə) *n* **1** a deviation from a direct route or course of action. ◆ *vb* **2** to deviate or cause to deviate from a direct route or

THESAURUS

recognize, scent, spot **2** = **discover**, catch, disclose, expose, find, reveal, track down, uncover, unmask

detection *n* **1** = **discovery**, exposé, exposure, ferreting out, revelation, tracking down, uncovering, unearthing, unmasking

detective *n* **1a, 1b** = **investigator**, bizzy, C.I.D. man, constable, cop (*sl.*), copper (*sl.*), dick (*sl., chiefly US*), gumshoe (*US sl.*), private eye, private investigator, sleuth (*inf.*), tec (*sl.*)

detention *n* **1, 2a** = **imprisonment**, confinement, custody, delay, hindrance, holding back, incarceration, keeping in, porridge (*sl.*), quarantine, restraint, withholding
Antonyms *n* acquittal, discharge, emancipation, freedom, liberation, liberty, release

deter *vb* = **discourage**, caution, check, damp, daunt, debar, dissuade, frighten, hinder, inhibit from, intimidate, prevent, prohibit, put off, restrain, stop, talk out of

detergent *n* **1** = **cleaner**, cleanser ◆ *adj* **2** = **cleansing**, abstergent, cleaning, purifying

deteriorate *vb* **1** = **decline**, corrupt, debase, degenerate, degrade, deprave, depreciate, go downhill (*inf.*), go to pot, go to the dogs (*inf.*), impair, injure, lower, slump, spoil, worsen **2** = **disintegrate**, be the worse for wear (*inf.*), break down, crumble, decay, decline, decompose, ebb, fade, fall apart, lapse, retrogress, weaken, wear away
Antonyms *vb* ≠ **decline:** advance, ameliorate, get better, improve

deterioration *n* **1** = **decline**, debasement, degeneration, degradation, depreciation, descent, downturn, drop, fall, retrogression, slump, vitiation, worsening **2** = **disintegration**, atrophy, corrosion, dilapidation, lapse, meltdown (*inf.*)

determinable *adj* **2** = **ascertainable**, answerable, assessable, definable, describable, discoverable

determinate *adj* **1, 2** = **definite**, absolute, certain, conclusive, decided, decisive, defined, definitive, determined, distinct, established, explicit, express, fixed, limited, positive, precise, quantified, settled, specified

determination *n* **2** = **resolution**, backbone, constancy, conviction, dedication, doggedness, drive, firmness, fortitude, indomitability, perseverance, persistence, resoluteness, resolve, single-mindedness, steadfastness, tenacity, willpower **5** = **decision**, conclusion, judgment, purpose, resolve, result, settlement, solution, verdict
Antonyms *n* ≠ **resolution:** doubt, hesitancy, hesitation, indecision, instability, irresolution, vacillation

determine *vb* **1** = **settle**, arbitrate, conclude, decide, end, finish, fix upon, ordain, regulate, terminate **2** = **find out**, ascertain, certify, check, detect, discover, establish, learn, verify, work out **3** = **affect**, condition, control, decide, dictate, direct, govern, impel, impose, incline, induce, influence, lead, modify, regulate, rule, shape **5** = **decide**, choose, elect, establish, fix, make up one's mind, purpose, resolve

determined *adj* = **resolute**, bent on, constant, dogged, firm, fixed, immovable, intent, persevering, persistent, purposeful, set on, single-minded, stalwart, steadfast, strong-minded, strong-willed, tenacious, unflinching, unwavering

determining *adj* **1** = **deciding**, conclusive, critical, crucial, decisive, definitive, essential, final, important, settling

deterrent *n* **1** = **discouragement**, check, curb, defensive measures, determent, disincentive, hindrance, impediment, obstacle, restraint
Antonyms *n* bait, carrot (*inf.*), enticement, incentive, inducement, lure, motivation, spur, stimulus

detest *vb* = **hate**, abhor, abominate, despise, dislike intensely, execrate, feel aversion towards, feel disgust towards, feel hostility towards, feel repugnance towards, loathe, recoil from
Antonyms *vb* adore, cherish, dig (*sl.*), dote on, love, relish

detestable *adj* = **hateful**, abhorred, abominable, accursed, despicable, disgusting, execrable, heinous, loathsome, obnoxious, obscene, odious, offensive, repugnant, repulsive, revolting, shocking, vile, yucky *or* yukky (*sl.*)

detestation *n* **1** = **hatred**, abhorrence, abomination, animosity, animus, antipathy, aversion, disgust, dislike, execration, hostility, loathing, odium, repugnance, revulsion

dethrone *vb* = **depose**, oust, uncrown, unseat

detonate *vb* = **explode**, blast, blow up, discharge, fulminate, set off, touch off, trigger

detonation *n* = **explosion**, bang, blast, blow-up, boom, discharge, fulmination, report

detour *n* **1** = **diversion**, bypass, byway, circuitous route, deviation, indirect course, roundabout way course of action. [C18: from F, from OF *destorner* to divert, turn away, from *des-* DE- + *torner* to TURN]

detox ('diːˌtɒks) *Inf.* ◆ *n* **1** treatment designed to rid the body of poisonous substances, esp. alcohol and drugs. ◆ *vb* (*intr*) **2** to undergo treatment to rid the body of poisonous substances, esp. alcohol and drugs.

detoxification centre *n* a place that specializes in the treatment of alcoholism or drug addiction.

detoxify (diːˈtɒksɪˌfaɪ) *vb* **detoxifies, detoxifying, detoxified.** (*tr*) **1** to remove poison from. **2** to treat (a person) for alcoholism or drug dependency.
▸**deˌtoxifiˈcation** *n*

detract ⓣ (dɪˈtrækt) *vb* **1** (when *intr*, usually foll. by *from*) to take away a part (of); diminish: *her anger detracts from her beauty.* **2** (*tr*) to distract or divert. **3** (*tr*) *Obs.* to belittle or disparage. [C15: from L *dētractus*, from *dētrahere* to pull away, disparage, from DE- + *trahere* to drag]
▸**deˈtractive** *adj* ▸**deˈtractor** *n* ▸**deˈtraction** *n*

> **USAGE NOTE** *Detract* is sometimes wrongly used where *distract* is meant: *a noise distracted* (not *detracted*) *my attention.*

detrain (diːˈtreɪn) *vb* to leave or cause to leave a railway train.
▸**deˈtrainment** *n*

detriment ⓣ (ˈdetrɪmənt) *n* **1** disadvantage or damage. **2** a cause of disadvantage or damage. [C15: from L *dētrīmentum*, a rubbing off, hence damage, from *dēterere*, from DE- + *terere* to rub]

detrimental ⓣ (ˌdetrɪˈmentᵊl) *adj* (when *postpositive*, foll. by *to*) harmful; injurious.

detritus ⓣ (dɪˈtraɪtəs) *n* **1** a loose mass of stones, silt, etc., worn away from rocks. **2** the organic debris formed from the decay of organisms. [C18: from F, from L: a rubbing away; see DETRIMENT]
▸**deˈtrital** *adj*

de trop *French.* (də tro) *adj* (*postpositive*) not wanted; in the way. [lit.: of too much]

detumescence (ˌdiːtjuˈmesəns) *n* the subsidence of a swelling. [C17: from L *dētumescere* to cease swelling, from DE- + *tumescere*, from *tumēre* to swell]

deuce[1] (djuːs) *n* **1a** a playing card or dice with two spots. **1b** a throw of two in dice. **2** *Tennis, etc.* a tied score that requires one player to gain two successive points to win the game. [C15: from OF *deus* two, from L *duos*, from *duo* two]

deuce[2] (djuːs) *Inf.* ◆ *interj* **1** an expression of annoyance or frustration. ◆ *n* **2 the deuce.** (intensifier) used in such phrases as **what the deuce, where the deuce,** etc. [C17: prob. special use of DEUCE[1] (in the sense: lowest throw at dice)]

deuced (ˈdjuːsɪd, djuːst) *Brit. inf.* ◆ *adj* **1** (intensifier) confounded: *he's a deuced idiot.* ◆ *adv* **2** (intensifier): *deuced good luck.*

Deus *Latin.* (ˈdeɪʊs) *n* God. [rel. to Gk *Zeus*]

deus ex machina *Latin.* (ˈdeɪʊs eks ˈmækɪnə) *n* **1** (in ancient Greek and Roman drama) a god introduced into a play to resolve the plot. **2** any unlikely device serving this purpose. [lit.: god out of a machine]

Deut. *Bible. abbrev. for* Deuteronomy.

deuteride (ˈdjuːtəˌraɪd) *n* a compound of deuterium and another element.

deuterium (djuːˈtɪərɪəm) *n* a stable isotope of hydrogen, occurring in natural hydrogen and in heavy water. Symbol: D or ^{2}H; atomic no.: 1; atomic wt.: 2.014. [C20: NL; see DEUTERO-, -IUM; from the fact that it is the second heaviest hydrogen isotope]

deuterium oxide *n* the compound D_2O; water in which the normal hydrogen atoms are replaced by deuterium atoms. See also **heavy water.**

deutero-, deuto- *or before a vowel* **deuter-, deut-** *combining form.* second or secondary: *deuterium.* [from Gk *deuteros* second]

deuteron (ˈdjuːtəˌrɒn) *n* the nucleus of a deuterium atom.

Deutschmark (ˈdɔɪtʃˌmɑːk) *or* **Deutsche Mark** (ˈdɔɪtʃə) *n* the standard monetary unit of Germany.

deutzia (ˈdjuːtsɪə, ˈdɔɪtsɪə) *n* any of various shrubs with white, pink, or purplish flowers in early summer. [C19: NL, after J. *Deutz*, 18th-cent. Du. patron of botany]

devalue (diːˈvæljuː) *or* **devaluate** (diːˈvæljuːˌeɪt) *vb* **devalues, devaluing, devalued** *or* **devaluates, devaluating, devaluated. 1** to reduce (a currency) or (of a currency) be reduced in exchange value. **2** (*tr*) to reduce the value of.
▸**deˌvaluˈation** *n*

Devanagari (ˌdeɪvəˈnɑːgərɪ) *n* a syllabic script in which Sanskrit, Hindi, and other modern languages of India are written. [C18: from Sansk.: alphabet of the gods]

devastate ⓣ (ˈdevəˌsteɪt) *vb* **devastates, devastating, devastated.** (*tr*) **1** to lay waste or make desolate; ravage; destroy. **2** to confound or overwhelm. [C17: from L *dēvastāre*, from DE- + *vastāre* to ravage; rel. to *vastus* waste, empty]
▸ˌ**devasˈtation** *n* ▸ˈ**devasˌtator** *n*

develop ⓣ (dɪˈveləp) *vb* **1** to come or bring to a later or more advanced or expanded stage; grow or cause to grow gradually. **2** (*tr*) to work out in detail. **3** to disclose or unfold (thoughts, a plot, etc.) gradually or (of thoughts, etc.) to be gradually disclosed or unfolded. **4** to come or bring into existence: *he developed a new faith in God.* **5** (*intr*) to follow as a result of something; ensue: *a row developed after her remarks.* **6** (*tr*) to contract (a disease or illness). **7** (*tr*) to improve the value or change the use of (land). **8** to exploit or make available the natural resources of (a country or region). **9** (*tr*) *Photog.* to treat (exposed film, plate, or paper) with chemical solutions in order to produce a visible image. **10** *Biol.* to progress or cause to progress from simple to complex stages in the growth of an individual or the evolution of a species. **11** (*tr*) to elaborate upon (a musical theme) by varying the melody, key, etc. **12** (*tr*) *Maths.* to expand (a function or expression) in the form of a series. **13** (*tr*) *Geom.* to project or roll out (a surface) onto a plane without stretching or shrinking any element. **14** *Chess.* to bring (a piece) into play from its initial position on the back rank. [C19: from OF *desveloper* to unwrap, from *des-* DIS-[1] + *veloper* to wrap; see ENVELOP]
▸**deˈvelopable** *adj*

developer (dɪˈveləpə) *n* **1** a person or thing that develops something, esp. a person who develops property. **2** Also called: **developing agent.** *Photog.* a chemical used to convert the latent image recorded in the emulsion of a film or paper into a visible image.

developing country *n* a poor or non-industrial country that is seeking to develop its resources by industrialization.

development ⓣ (dɪˈveləpmənt) *n* **1** the act or process of growing or developing. **2** the product of developing. **3** a fact or event, esp. one that changes a situation. **4** an area of land that has been developed. **5** the section of a movement, usually in sonata form, in which the basic musical themes are developed. **6** *Chess.* the process of developing pieces.
▸**deˌvelopˈmental** *adj*

developmental disorder *n Psychiatry.* any condition, such as autism or dyslexia, that appears in childhood and is characterized by delay in the development of one or more psychological functions, such as language skill.

development area *n* (in Britain) an area which has experienced economic depression because of the decline of its main industry or industries, and which is given government assistance to establish new industry.

deviance (ˈdiːvɪəns) *n* **1** Also called: **deviancy.** the act or state of being deviant. **2** *Statistics.* a measure of the degree of fit of a statistical model compared to that of a more complete model.

deviant ⓣ (ˈdiːvɪənt) *adj* **1** deviating, as from what is considered acceptable behaviour. ◆ *n* **2** a person whose behaviour, esp. sexual behaviour, deviates from what is considered to be acceptable.

deviate ⓣ *vb* (ˈdiːvɪˌeɪt) **deviates, deviating, deviated. 1** (*usually intr*) to differ or cause to differ, as in belief or thought. **2** (*usually intr*) to turn aside or cause to turn aside. **3** (*intr*) *Psychol.* to depart from an accepted standard. ◆ *n, adj* (ˈdiːvɪɪt). **4** another word for **deviant.** [C17: from LL *dēviāre* to turn aside from the direct road, from DE- + *via* road]
▸ˈ**deviˌator** *n* ▸ˈ**deviatory** *adj*

THESAURUS

detract *vb* **1** = **lessen,** derogate, devaluate, diminish, lower, reduce, take away from **2** = **divert,** deflect, distract, shift
Antonyms *vb* ≠ **lessen:** add to, augment, boost, complement, enhance, improve, reinforce, strengthen

detraction *n* **3** = **disparagement,** abuse, aspersion, belittlement, calumny, defamation, denigration, deprecation, innuendo, insinuation, misrepresentation, muckraking, running down, scandalmongering, scurrility, slander, traducement, vituperation

detractor *n* **3** = **slanderer,** backbiter, belittler, defamer, denigrator, disparager, muckraker, scandalmonger, traducer

detriment *n* **1** = **damage,** disadvantage, disservice, harm, hurt, impairment, injury, loss, mischief, prejudice

detrimental *adj* = **damaging,** adverse, baleful, deleterious, destructive, disadvantageous, harmful, inimical, injurious, mischievous, pernicious, prejudicial, unfavourable
Antonyms *adj* advantageous, beneficial, efficacious, favourable, good, helpful, salutary

detritus *n* **1, 2** = **debris,** fragments, litter, remains, rubbish, waste

devastate *vb* **1** = **destroy,** demolish, desolate, despoil, lay waste, level, pillage, plunder, ravage, raze, ruin, sack, spoil, total (*sl.*), trash (*sl.*), waste, wreck **2** = **overwhelm,** chagrin, confound, discomfit, discompose, disconcert, floor (*inf.*), nonplus, overpower, take aback

devastating *adj* **2** = **overwhelming,** caustic, cutting, effective, incisive, keen, mordant, overpowering, ravishing, sardonic, satirical, savage, stunning, trenchant, vitriolic, withering

devastation *n* **1** = **destruction,** demolition, depredation, desolation, havoc, pillage, plunder, ravages, ruin, ruination, spoliation

develop *vb* **1** = **advance,** blossom, cultivate, evolve, flourish, foster, grow, mature, progress, promote, prosper, ripen **2** = **expand,** amplify, augment, broaden, dilate upon, elaborate, enlarge, unfold, work out **4** = **form,** acquire, begin, breed, commence, contract, establish, generate, invent, originate, pick up, start **5** = **result,** be a direct result of, break out, come about, ensue, follow, happen

development *n* **1** = **growth,** advance, advancement, evolution, expansion, improvement, increase, maturity, progress, progression, spread, unfolding, unravelling **3** = **event,** change, circumstance, happening, incident, issue, occurrence, outcome, phenomenon, result, situation, turn of events, upshot

deviant *adj* **1** = **perverted,** aberrant, abnormal, bent, deviate, devious, freaky (*sl.*), heretical, kinky (*sl.*), perverse, queer (*inf., derogatory*), sick (*inf.*), twisted, warped, wayward ◆ *n* **2** = **pervert,** deviate, freak, misfit, odd type, queer (*inf., derogatory*), sicko (*inf.*)
Antonyms *adj* ≠ **perverted:** conventional, normal, orthodox, straight, straightforward

deviate *vb* **2** = **differ,** avert, bend, deflect, depart, digress, diverge, drift, err, meander, part,

deviation ➊ (ˌdiːvɪˈeɪʃən) *n* **1** an act or result of deviating. **2** *Statistics.* the difference between an observed value in a series of such values and their arithmetic mean. **3** the error of a compass due to local magnetic disturbances.

device ➊ (dɪˈvaɪs) *n* **1** a machine or tool used for a specific task. **2** *Euphemistic.* a bomb. **3** a plan, esp. a clever or evil one; trick. **4** any ornamental pattern or picture, as in embroidery. **5** computer hardware designed for a specific function. **6** a design or figure, used as a heraldic sign, emblem, etc. **7** a particular pattern of words, figures of speech, etc., used in literature to produce an effect on the reader. **8 leave (someone) to his own devices.** to leave (someone) alone to do as he wishes. [C13: from OF *devis* purpose, contrivance & *devise* difference, intention, from *deviser* to divide, control; see DEVISE]

devil ➊ (ˈdɛvᵊl) *n* **1** (*often cap.*) *Theol.* the chief spirit of evil and enemy of God, often depicted as a human figure with horns, cloven hoofs, and tail. **2** any subordinate evil spirit. **3** a person or animal regarded as wicked or ill-natured. **4** a person or animal regarded as unfortunate or wretched. **5** a person or animal regarded as daring, mischievous, or energetic. **6** *Inf.* something difficult or annoying. **7** *Christian Science.* an error, lie, or false belief. **8** (in Malaysia) a ghost. **9** a portable furnace or brazier. **10** any of various mechanical devices, such as a machine for making wooden screws or a rag-tearing machine. **11** See **printer's devil. 12** *Law.* (in England) a junior barrister who does work for another in order to gain experience, usually for a half fee. **13** *Meteorol.* a small whirlwind in arid areas that raises dust or sand in a column. **14 between the devil and the deep blue sea.** between equally undesirable alternatives. **15 devil of 15a** *Inf.* (intensifier): *a devil of a fine horse.* **16 give the devil his due.** to acknowledge the talent or success of an unpleasant person. **17 go to the devil. 17a** to fail or become dissipated. **17b** (*interj*) used to express annoyance with the person causing it. **18 (let) the devil take the hindmost.** look after oneself and leave others to their fate. **19 talk** (*or* **speak**) **of the devil!** used when an absent person who has been the subject of conversation appears. **20 the devil!** (intensifier): **20a** used in **what the devil, where the devil,** etc. **20b** an exclamation of anger, surprise, disgust, etc. **21 the devil to pay.** trouble to be faced as a consequence of an action. ◆ *vb* **devils, devilling, devilled** *or US* **devils, deviling, deviled. 22** (*tr*) to prepare (food) by coating with a highly flavoured spiced paste or mixture of condiments before cooking. **23** (*tr*) to tear (rags) with a devil. **24** (*intr*) to serve as a printer's devil. **25** (*intr*) *Chiefly Brit.* to do hackwork, esp. for a lawyer or author. **26** (*tr*) *US inf.* to harass, vex, etc. [OE *dēofol*, from L *diabolus*, from Gk *diabolos* enemy, accuser, slanderer]

devilfish (ˈdɛvᵊlˌfɪʃ) *n, pl* **devilfish** *or* **devilfishes. 1** Also called: **devil ray.** another name for **manta** (the fish). **2** another name for **octopus.**

devilish ➊ (ˈdɛvəlɪʃ) *adj* **1** of, resembling, or befitting a devil; diabolic; fiendish. ◆ *adv, adj* **2** *Inf.* (intensifier): *devilish good food.*
▸ˈ**devilishly** *adv* ▸ˈ**devilishness** *n*

devil-may-care ➊ *adj* careless or reckless; happy-go-lucky: *a devil-may-care attitude.*

devilment ➊ (ˈdɛvᵊlmənt) *n* devilish or mischievous conduct.

devilry ➊ (ˈdɛvᵊlrɪ) *or* **deviltry** *n, pl* **devilries** *or* **deviltries. 1** reckless or malicious fun or mischief. **2** wickedness. **3** black magic or other forms of diabolism. [C18: from F *diablerie*, from *diable* DEVIL]

devil's advocate *n* **1** a person who advocates an opposing or unpopular view, often for the sake of argument. **2** *RC Church.* the official appointed to put the case against the beatification or canonization of a candidate. [translation of NL *advocātus diabolī*]

devil's coach-horse *n* a large black beetle with large jaws and ferocious habits.

devil's food cake *n Chiefly US & Canad.* a rich chocolate cake.

devious ➊ (ˈdiːvɪəs) *adj* **1** not sincere or candid; deceitful. **2** (of a route or course of action) rambling; indirect. **3** going astray; erring. [C16: from L *dēvius* lying to one side of the road, from DE- + *via* road]
▸ˈ**deviously** *adv* ▸ˈ**deviousness** *n*

devise ➊ (dɪˈvaɪz) *vb* **devises, devising, devised. 1** to work out or plan (something) in one's mind. **2** (*tr*) *Law.* to dispose of (real property) by will. ◆ *n Law.* **3** a disposition of property by will. **4** a will or clause in a will disposing of real property. [C15: from OF *deviser* to divide, apportion, intend, from L *dīvidere* to DIVIDE]
▸**deˈviser** *n*

devitalize *or* **devitalise** (diːˈvaɪtəˌlaɪz) *vb* **devitalizes, devitalizing, devitalized** *or* **devitalises, devitalising, devitalised.** (*tr*) to lower or destroy the vitality of; make weak or lifeless.
▸**deˌvitaliˈzation** *or* **deˌvitaliˈsation** *n*

devoid ➊ (dɪˈvɔɪd) *adj* (*postpositive; foll. by of*) destitute or void (of); free (from). [C15: orig. p.p. of *devoid* (*vb*) to remove, from OF *devoider* from DE- + *voider* to void]

devoirs (dəˈvwɑː) *pl n* (*sometimes sing*) compliments or respects. [C13: from OF: duty, from *devoir* to be obliged to, owe, from L *dēbēre*]

devolution ➊ (ˌdiːvəˈluːʃən) *n* **1** a devolving. **2** a passing onwards or downwards from one stage to another. **3** a transfer of authority from a central government to regional governments. [C16: from Med. L *dēvolūtiō* a rolling down, from L *dēvolvere*; see DEVOLVE]
▸ˌ**devoˈlutionary** *adj* ▸ˌ**devoˈlutionist** *n, adj*

devolve ➊ (dɪˈvɒlv) *vb* **devolves, devolving, devolved. 1** (foll. by *on, upon, to,* etc.) to pass or cause to pass to a successor or substitute, as duties, power, etc. **2** (*intr*; foll. by *on* or *upon*) *Law.* (of an estate, etc.) to pass to another by operation of law. [C15: from L *dēvolvere* to roll down, fall into, from DE- + *volvere* to roll]
▸**deˈvolvement** *n*

Devonian (dəˈvəʊnɪən) *adj* **1** of, denoting, or formed in the fourth period of the Palaeozoic era, between the Silurian and Carboniferous periods. **2** of or relating to Devon. ◆ *n* **3 the.** the Devonian period or rock system.

Devonshire split (ˈdɛvᵊnʃə) *n* a kind of yeast bun split open and served with cream or jam.

devoré (dəvɒˈreɪ) *n* a velvet fabric with a raised pattern created by disintegrating some of the pile with chemicals. [from F, p.p. of *dévorer* to devour]

devote ➊ (dɪˈvəʊt) *vb* **devotes, devoting, devoted.** (*tr*) to apply or dedicate (oneself, money, etc.) to some pursuit, cause, etc. [C16: from L *dēvōtus* devoted, solemnly promised, from *dēvovēre* to vow; see DE-, VOW]

devoted ➊ (dɪˈvəʊtɪd) *adj* **1** feeling or demonstrating loyalty or devotion; devout. **2** (*postpositive; foll. by to*) dedicated or consecrated.
▸**deˈvotedly** *adv* ▸**deˈvotedness** *n*

devotee ➊ (ˌdɛvəˈtiː) *n* **1** a person ardently enthusiastic about something, such as a sport or pastime. **2** a zealous follower of a religion.

devotion ➊ (dɪˈvəʊʃən) *n* **1** (often foll. by *to*) strong attachment (to) or affection (for a cause, person, etc.) marked by dedicated loyalty. **2** religious zeal; piety. **3** (*often pl*) religious observance or prayers.
▸**deˈvotional** *adj*

devour ➊ (dɪˈvaʊə) *vb* (*tr*) **1** to eat up greedily or voraciously. **2** to waste or destroy; consume. **3** to consume greedily or avidly with the senses

THESAURUS

stray, swerve, turn, turn aside, vary, veer, wander

deviation *n* **1 = departure**, aberration, alteration, change, deflection, digression, discrepancy, disparity, divergence, fluctuation, inconsistency, irregularity, shift, variance, variation

device *n* **1 = gadget**, apparatus, appliance, contraption, contrivance, gimmick, gizmo *or* gismo (*sl., chiefly US & Canad.*), implement, instrument, invention, machine, tool, utensil, waldo **3 = ploy**, artifice, design, dodge, expedient, gambit, improvisation, manoeuvre, plan, project, purpose, ruse, scheme, shift, stratagem, strategy, stunt, trick, wile **4 = emblem**, badge, colophon, crest, design, figure, insignia, logo, motif, motto, symbol, token

devil *n* **1 the Devil = Satan**, Apollyon, archfiend, Beelzebub, Belial, deil, demon, Deuce, Evil One, fiend, Foul Fiend, Lord of the Flies, Lucifer, Mephisto, Mephistopheles, Old Gentleman (*inf.*), Old Harry (*inf.*), Old Nick (*inf.*), Old One, Old Scratch (*inf.*), Prince of Darkness, Tempter, Wicked One **3 = brute**, beast, demon, fiend, ghoul, monster, ogre, rogue, savage, terror, villain **4 = person**, beggar, creature, thing, unfortunate, wretch **5 = scamp**, imp, monkey (*inf.*), pickle (*Brit. inf.*), rascal, rogue, scoundrel

devilish *adj* **1 = fiendish**, accursed, atrocious, damnable, detestable, diabolic, diabolical, execrable, hellish, infernal, satanic, wicked

devil-may-care *adj* **= happy-go-lucky**, careless, casual, easy-going, flippant, heedless, insouciant, nonchalant, reckless, swaggering, swashbuckling, unconcerned

devilment *n* **= mischief**, devilry, knavery, mischievousness, naughtiness, rascality, roguery, roguishness

devilry *n* **1 = mischief**, devilment, jiggery-pokery (*inf., chiefly Brit.*), knavery, mischievousness, monkey-business (*inf.*), rascality, roguery **2 = wickedness**, cruelty, evil, malevolence, malice, vice, viciousness, villainy **3 = sorcery**, black magic, diablerie, diabolism

devious *adj* **1 = sly**, calculating, crooked (*inf.*), deceitful, dishonest, double-dealing, evasive, indirect, insidious, insincere, not straightforward, scheming, surreptitious, treacherous, tricky, underhand, wily **2 = indirect**, circuitous, confusing, crooked, deviating, erratic, excursive, misleading, rambling, roundabout, tortuous, wandering
Antonyms *adj* ≠ **sly:** blunt, candid, direct, downright, forthright, frank, honest, straight, straightforward ≠ **indirect:** blunt, direct, downright, forthright, straight, straightforward, undeviating, unswerving

devise *vb* **= work out**, arrange, conceive, concoct, construct, contrive, design, dream up, form, formulate, frame, imagine, invent, plan, plot, prepare, project, scheme, think up

devoid *adj* **= lacking**, barren, bereft, deficient, denuded, destitute, empty, free from, sans (*arch.*), vacant, void, wanting, without

devolution *n* **1-3 = decentralization**, delegation

devolve *vb* **1 = fall upon** *or* **to**, be transferred, commission, consign, delegate, depute, entrust, rest with, transfer **2** *Law* **= be handed down**, alienate, convey

devote *vb* **= dedicate**, allot, apply, appropriate, assign, commit, concern oneself, consecrate, enshrine, give, occupy oneself, pledge, reserve, set apart

devoted *adj* **1 = dedicated**, ardent, caring, committed, concerned, constant, devout, faithful, fond, loving, loyal, staunch, steadfast, true
Antonyms *adj* disloyal, inconstant, indifferent, uncommitted, undedicated, unfaithful

devotee *n* **1, 2 = enthusiast**, addict, adherent, admirer, aficionado, buff (*inf.*), disciple, fan, fanatic, follower, supporter, votary

devotion *n* **1 = dedication**, adherence, affection, allegiance, ardour, commitment, consecration, constancy, earnestness, faithfulness, fervour, fidelity, fondness, intensity, love, loyalty, passion, zeal **2 = devoutness**, adoration, godliness, holiness, piety, prayer, religiousness, reverence, sanctity, spirituality, worship **3** *often plural* **= prayers**, church service, divine office, religious observance
Antonyms *n* ≠ **dedication:** carelessness, disregard, inattention, indifference, laxity, laxness, neglect, thoughtlessness ≠ **devoutness:** derision, disrespect, impiety, irreverence

devotional *adj* **2 = religious**, devout, holy, pious, reverential, sacred, solemn, spiritual

devour *vb* **1 = eat**, bolt, consume, cram, dispatch, gobble, gorge, gulp, guzzle, pig out on

or mind. **4** to engulf or absorb. [C14: from OF, from L *dēvorāre* to gulp down, from DE- + *vorāre;* see VORACIOUS]
▸de'vourer *n* ▸de'vouring *adj*

devout ❶ (dɪ'vaʊt) *adj* **1** deeply religious; reverent. **2** sincere; earnest; heartfelt. [C13: from OF *devot,* from LL *dēvōtus,* from L: faithful; see DEVOTE]
▸de'voutly *adv* ▸de'voutness *n*

dew (djuː) *n* **1** drops of water condensed on a cool surface, esp. at night, from vapour in the air. **2** something like this, esp. in freshness: *the dew of youth.* **3** small drops of moisture, such as tears. ◆ *vb* **4** (*tr*) to moisten with or as with dew. [OE *dēaw*]

dewberry ('djuːbərɪ, -brɪ) *n, pl* **dewberries. 1** any trailing bramble having blue-black fruits. **2** the fruit of any such plant.

dewclaw ('djuːˌklɔː) *n* **1** a nonfunctional claw in dogs. **2** an analogous rudimentary hoof in deer, goats, etc.
▸'dewˌclawed *adj*

dewdrop ('djuːˌdrɒp) *n* a drop of dew.

Dewey Decimal System ('djuːɪ) *n* a system of library book classification with ten main subject classes. Also called: **decimal classification.** [C19: after Melvil *Dewey* (1851–1931), US educator]

dewlap ('djuːˌlæp) *n* **1** a loose fold of skin hanging from beneath the throat in cattle, dogs, etc. **2** loose skin on an elderly person's throat. [C14 *dewlappe,* from DEW (prob. from an earlier form of different meaning) + LAP[1] (from OE *læppa* hanging flap), ?from ON]

DEW line (djuː) *n acronym for* distant early warning line, a network of radar stations situated mainly in Arctic regions of North America.

dew point *n* the temperature at which dew begins to form.

dew pond *n* a shallow pond, usually man-made, that is kept full by dew and mist.

dewy ('djuːɪ) *adj* **dewier, dewiest. 1** moist with or as with dew. **2** of or resembling dew. **3** *Poetic.* suggesting, falling, or refreshing like dew: *dewy sleep.*
▸'dewily *adv* ▸'dewiness *n*

dexter ('dɛkstə) *adj* **1** *Arch.* of or located on the right side. **2** (*usually postpositive*) *Heraldry.* of, on, or starting from the right side of a shield from the bearer's point of view and therefore on the spectator's left. ◆ Cf. **sinister.** [C16: from L; cf. Gk *dexios* on the right hand]

dexterity ❶ (dɛk'stɛrɪtɪ) *n* **1** physical, esp. manual, skill or nimbleness. **2** mental skill or adroitness. [C16: from L *dexteritās* aptness, readiness; see DEXTER]

dexterous ❶ ('dɛkstrəs) *adj* possessing or done with dexterity.
▸'dexterously *adv* ▸'dexterousness *n*

dextral ('dɛkstrəl) *adj* **1** of or located on the right side, esp. of the body. **2** of a person who prefers to use his right foot, hand, or eye; right-handed. **3** (of shells) coiling in an anticlockwise direction from the apex.
▸dextrality (dɛk'strælɪtɪ) *n* ▸'dextrally *adv*

dextran ('dɛkstrən) *n Biochem.* a chainlike polymer of glucose produced by the action of bacteria on sucrose: used as a substitute for plasma in blood transfusions. [C19: from DEXTRO- + -AN]

dextrin ('dɛkstrɪn) *or* **dextrine** ('dɛkstrɪn, -triːn) *n* any of a group of sticky substances obtained from starch: used as thickening agents in foods and as gums. [C19: from F *dextrine;* see DEXTRO-, -IN]

dextro- *or before a vowel* **dextr-** *combining form.* on or towards the right: *dextrorotation.* [from L, from *dexter* on the right side]

dextrorotation (ˌdɛkstrəʊrəʊ'teɪʃən) *n* a rotation to the right; clockwise rotation, esp. of the plane of polarization of plane-polarized light. Cf. **laevorotation.**
▸dextrorotatory (ˌdɛkstrəʊ'rəʊtətərɪ, -trɪ) *or* ˌdextro'rotary *adj*

dextrorse ('dɛkstrɔːs) *or* **dextrorsal** (dɛk'strɔːsəl) *adj* (of some climbing plants) growing upwards in a spiral from left to right or anticlockwise. [C19: from L *dextrorsum* towards the right, from DEXTRO- + *vorsus,* var. of *versus,* from *vertere* to turn]
▸'dextrorsely *adv*

dextrose ('dɛkstrəʊz, -trəʊs) *n* a glucose occurring widely in fruit, honey, and in the blood and tissue of animals. Formula: $C_6H_{12}O_6$. Also called: **grape sugar, dextroglucose.**

dextrous ('dɛkstrəs) *adj* a variant spelling of **dexterous.**
▸'dextrously *adv* ▸'dextrousness *n*

DF *abbrev. for* Defender of the Faith.

D/F *or* **DF** *Telecomm.* ◆ *abbrev. for:* **1** direction finder. **2** direction finding.

DFC *abbrev. for* Distinguished Flying Cross.

DfEE (in Britain) *abbrev. for* Department for Education and Employment.

DFM *abbrev. for* Distinguished Flying Medal.

dg *symbol for* decigram.

DH (in Britain) *abbrev. for* Department of Health.

dhal, dal, *or* **dholl** (dɑːl) *n* **1** a tropical African and Asian shrub cultivated for its nutritious pealike seeds. **2** the seed of this shrub. **3** a curry made from lentils or other pulses. [C17: from Hindi, from Sansk. *dal* to split]

dharma ('dɑːmə) *n* **1** *Hinduism.* social custom regarded as a religious and moral duty. **2** *Hinduism.* **2a** the essential principle of the cosmos; natural law. **2b** conduct that conforms with this. **3** *Buddhism.* ideal truth. [Sansk.: habit, usage, law]

dhobi ('dəʊbɪ) *n, pl* **dhobis.** (in India, E Africa, etc.) a washerman. [C19: from Hindi, from *dhōb* washing]

dhoti ('dəʊtɪ), **dhooti, dhootie,** *or* **dhuti** ('duːtɪ) *n, pl* **dhotis.** a long loincloth worn by men in India. [C17: from Hindi]

dhow (daʊ) *n* a lateen-rigged coastal Arab sailing vessel. [C19: from Ar.]

DHSS (formerly, in Britain) *abbrev. for* Department of Health and Social Security.

DI *abbrev. for* donor insemination.

di. *or* **dia.** *abbrev. for* diameter.

di-[1] *prefix* **1** twice; two; double: *dicotyledon.* **2a** containing two specified atoms or groups of atoms: *carbon dioxide.* **2b** a nontechnical equivalent of **bi-** (sense 5). [via L from Gk, from *dis* twice, double, rel. to *duo* two. Cf. BI-]

di-[2] *combining form.* a variant of **dia-** before a vowel: *dioptre.*

dia- *or* **di-** *prefix* **1** through or during: *diachronic.* **2** across: *diactinic.* **3** apart: *diacritic.* [from Gk *dia* through, between, across, by]

diabetes (ˌdaɪə'biːtɪs, -tiːz) *n* any of various disorders, esp. diabetes mellitus, characterized by excessive thirst and excretion of an abnormally large amount of urine. [C16: from L: siphon, from Gk, lit.: a passing through]

diabetes mellitus (mə'laɪtəs) *n* a form of diabetes, caused by a deficiency of insulin, in which the body is unable to metabolize sugars. [C18: NL, lit.: honey-sweet diabetes]

diabetic (ˌdaɪə'bɛtɪk) *adj* **1** of, relating to, or having diabetes. **2** for the use of diabetics. ◆ *n* **3** a person who has diabetes.

diablerie (dɪ'ɑːblərɪ) *n* **1** magic or witchcraft connected with devils. **2** esoteric knowledge of devils. **3** devilry; mischief. [C18: from OF, from *diable* devil, from L *diabolus;* see DEVIL]

diabolic ❶ (ˌdaɪə'bɒlɪk) *adj* **1** of the devil; satanic. **2** extremely cruel or wicked; fiendish. **3** very difficult or unpleasant. [C14: from LL, from Gk *diabolikos,* from *diabolos* DEVIL]
▸ˌdia'bolically *adv* ▸ˌdia'bolicalness *n*

diabolical ❶ (ˌdaɪə'bɒlɪkəl) *adj Inf.* **1** excruciatingly bad. **2** (intensifier): *a diabolical liberty.*
▸ˌdia'bolically *adv* ▸ˌdia'bolicalness *n*

diabolism (daɪ'æbəˌlɪzəm) *n* **1a** witchcraft or sorcery. **1b** worship of devils or beliefs concerning them. **2** character or conduct that is devilish.
▸di'abolist *n*

diabolo (dɪ'æbəˌləʊ) *n, pl* **diabolos. 1** a game in which one throws and catches a top on a cord fastened to two sticks. **2** the top used in this. [C20: from It., lit.: devil]

diachronic (ˌdaɪə'krɒnɪk) *adj* of, relating to, or studying the development of a phenomenon through time; historical. Cf. **synchronic.** [C19: from DIA- + Gk *khronos* time]

diacidic (ˌdaɪə'sɪdɪk) *adj* (of a base) capable of neutralizing two protons with one of its molecules. Also: **diacid.**

diaconal (daɪ'ækənəl) *adj* of or associated with a deacon or the diaconate. [C17: from LL *diāconālis,* from *diāconus* DEACON]

diaconate (daɪ'ækənɪt, -ˌneɪt) *n* the office, sacramental status, or period of office of a deacon. [C17: from LL *diāconātus;* see DEACON]

diacritic (ˌdaɪə'krɪtɪk) *n* **1** a sign placed above or below a character or letter to indicate that it has a different phonetic value, is stressed, or for some other reason. ◆ *adj* **2** another word for **diacritical.** [C17: from Gk *diakritikos* serving to distinguish, from *diakrinein,* from DIA- + *krinein* to separate]

diacritical (ˌdaɪə'krɪtɪkəl) *adj* **1** of or relating to a diacritic. **2** showing up a distinction.

diadem ❶ ('daɪəˌdɛm) *n* **1** a royal crown, esp. a light jewelled circlet. **2** royal dignity or power. [C13: from L, from Gk: fillet, royal headdress, from *diadein,* from DIA- + *dein* to bind]

diaeresis *or* **dieresis** (daɪ'ɛrɪsɪs) *n, pl* **diaereses** *or* **diereses** (-ˌsiːz). **1** the mark ¨ placed over the second of two adjacent vowels to indicate that

THESAURUS

(*sl.*), polish off (*inf.*), stuff, swallow, wolf **2** = **destroy,** annihilate, consume, ravage, spend, waste, wipe out **3** = **enjoy,** absorb, appreciate, be engrossed by, be preoccupied, delight in, drink in, feast on, go through, read compulsively *or* voraciously, relish, revel in, take in

devouring *adj* **3** = **overwhelming,** consuming, excessive, flaming, insatiable, intense, passionate, powerful

devout *adj* **1** = **religious,** godly, holy, orthodox, pious, prayerful, pure, reverent, saintly **2** = **sincere,** ardent, deep, devoted, earnest, fervent, genuine, heartfelt, intense, passionate, profound, serious, zealous

Antonyms *adj* ≠ **religious:** impious, irreligious, irreverent, sacrilegious ≠ **sincere:** indifferent, passive

devoutly *adv* **2** = **with all one's heart,** fervently, heart and soul, profoundly, sincerely

dexterity *n* **1** = **skill,** adroitness, artistry, craft, deftness, effortlessness, expertise, facility, finesse, handiness, knack, mastery, neatness, nimbleness, proficiency, smoothness, touch **2** = **cleverness,** ability, address, adroitness, aptitude, aptness, art, expertness, ingenuity, readiness, skilfulness, tact

Antonyms *n* clumsiness, gaucheness, inability, incapacity, incompetence, ineptitude, uselessness

dexterous *adj* = **skilful,** able, active, acute, adept, adroit, agile, apt, clever, deft, expert, handy, ingenious, masterly, neat, nimble, nimble-fingered, proficient, prompt, quick

diabolic *adj* **1** = **satanic,** demoniac, demonic, devilish, fiendish, hellish, infernal **2** = **wicked,** atrocious, cruel, evil, fiendish, monstrous, nefarious, vicious, villainous

diabolical *adj Informal* = **dreadful,** abysmal, appalling, atrocious, damnable, difficult, disastrous, excruciating, fiendish, from hell (*inf.*), hellacious (*US sl.*), hellish, nasty, outrageous, shocking, terrible, tricky, unpleasant, vile

diadem *n* **1** = **coronet,** circlet, crown, tiara

it is to be pronounced separately, as in some spellings of *coöperate, naïve,* etc. **2** this mark used for any other purpose, such as to indicate a special pronunciation for a particular vowel. **3** a pause in a line of verse when the end of a foot coincides with the end of a word. [C17: from L, from Gk: a division, from *diairein,* from DIA- + *hairein* to take; cf. HERESY]
▸**diaeretic** *or* **dieretic** (ˌdaɪəˈrɛtɪk) *adj*

diag. *abbrev. for* diagram.

diagnose ➊ (ˈdaɪəgˌnəʊz) *vb* **diagnoses, diagnosing, diagnosed. 1** to determine by diagnosis. **2** (*tr*) to examine (a person or thing), as for a disease.
▸ˌ**diag'nosable** *adj*

diagnosis ➊ (ˌdaɪəgˈnəʊsɪs) *n, pl* **diagnoses** (-siːz). **1a** the identification of diseases from the examination of symptoms. **1b** an opinion so reached. **2a** thorough analysis of facts or problems in order to gain understanding. **2b** an opinion reached through such analysis. [C17: NL, from Gk: a distinguishing, from *diagignōskein,* from *gignōskein* to perceive, KNOW]
▸**diagnostic** (ˌdaɪəgˈnɒstɪk) *adj*

diagonal ➊ (daɪˈægənᵊl) *adj* **1** *Maths.* connecting any two vertices that in a polygon are not adjacent and in a polyhedron are not in the same face. **2** slanting; oblique. **3** marked with slanting lines or patterns. ◆ *n* **4** a diagonal line, plane, or pattern. **5** something put, set, or drawn obliquely. [C16: from L, from Gk *diagōnios,* from DIA- + *gōnia* angle]
▸**di'agonally** *adv*

diagram ➊ (ˈdaɪəˌgræm) *n* **1** a sketch or plan demonstrating the form or workings of something. **2** *Maths.* a pictorial representation of a quantity or of a relationship. ◆ *vb* **diagrams, diagramming, diagrammed** *or US* **diagrams, diagraming, diagramed. 3** to show in or as if in a diagram. [C17: from L, from Gk, from *diagraphein,* from *graphein* to write]
▸**diagrammatic** (ˌdaɪəgrəˈmætɪk) *adj*

dial (ˈdaɪəl) *n* **1** the face of a watch, clock, etc., marked with divisions representing units of time. **2** the graduated disc of various measuring instruments. **3a** the control on a radio or television set used to change the station or channel. **3b** the panel on a radio on which the frequency, wavelength, or station is indicated. **4** a numbered disc on a telephone that is rotated a set distance for each digit of a number being called. **5** *Brit.* a slang word for **face.** ◆ *vb* **dials, dialling, dialled** *or US* **dials, dialing, dialed. 6** to try to establish a telephone connection with (a subscriber) by operating the dial or buttons on a telephone. **7** (*tr*) to indicate, measure, or operate with a dial. [C14: from Med. L *diālis* daily, from L *diēs* day]
▸**'dialler** *or US* **'dialer** *n*

dial. *abbrev. for* dialect(al).

dialect ➊ (ˈdaɪəˌlɛkt) *n* **a** a form of a language spoken in a particular geographical area or by members of a particular social class or occupational group, distinguished by its vocabulary, grammar, and pronunciation. **b** a form of a language that is considered inferior. [C16: from L, from Gk *dialektos* speech, dialect, discourse, from *dialegesthai* to converse, from *legein* to talk, speak]
▸ˌ**dia'lectal** *adj*

dialectic ➊ (ˌdaɪəˈlɛktɪk) *n* **1** disputation or debate, esp. when intended to resolve differences between two views. **2** logical argumentation. **3** a variant of **dialectics** (sense 1). **4** *Philosophy.* an interpretive method used by Hegel in which contradictions are resolved at a higher level of truth (synthesis). ◆ *adj* **5** of or relating to logical disputation. [C17: from L, from Gk *dialektikē* (*tekhnē*) (the art) of argument; see DIALECT]
▸ˌ**dialec'tician** *n*

dialectical (ˌdaɪəˈlɛktɪkᵊl) *adj* of or relating to dialectic or dialectics.
▸ˌ**dia'lectically** *adv*

dialectical materialism *n* the economic, political, and philosophical system of Marx and Engels that combines traditional materialism and Hegelian dialectic.

dialectics (ˌdaɪəˈlɛktɪks) *n* (*functioning as pl or* (*sometimes*) *sing*) **1** the study of reasoning. **2** a particular methodology or system. **3** the application of the Hegelian dialectic or the rationale of dialectical materialism.

dialling code *n* a sequence of numbers which is dialled for connection with another exchange before an individual subscriber's telephone number is dialled.

dialling tone *or US & Canad.* **dial tone** *n* a continuous sound, either purring or high-pitched, heard over a telephone indicating that a number can be dialled.

dialogue ➊ *or US* (*often*) **dialog** (ˈdaɪəˌlɒg) *n* **1** conversation between two or more people. **2** an exchange of opinions; discussion. **3** the lines spoken by characters in drama or fiction. **4** a passage of conversation in a literary or dramatic work. **5** a literary composition in the form of a dialogue. **6** a political discussion between representatives of two nations or groups. [C13: from OF, from L, from Gk, from *dialegesthai;* see DIALECT]

dialyse *or US* **dialyze** (ˈdaɪəˌlaɪz) *vb* **dialyses, dialysing, dialysed** *or US* **dialyzes, dialyzing, dialyzed.** (*tr*) to separate by dialysis.
▸ˌ**dialy'sation** *or US* ˌ**dialy'zation** *n*

dialyser *or US* **dialyzer** (ˈdaɪəˌlaɪzə) *n* a machine that performs dialysis, esp. one that removes impurities from the blood of patients with malfunctioning kidneys; kidney machine.

dialysis (daɪˈælɪsɪs) *n, pl* **dialyses** (-ˌsiːz). **1** the separation of small molecules from large molecules and colloids in a solution by the selective diffusion of the small molecules through a semipermeable membrane. **2** *Med.* the filtering of blood through a semipermeable membrane to remove waste products. [C16: from LL: a separation, from Gk *dialusis,* from *dialuein* to tear apart, dissolve, from *luein* to loosen]
▸**dialytic** (ˌdaɪəˈlɪtɪk) *adj*

diam. *abbrev. for* diameter.

diamagnetic (ˌdaɪəmægˈnɛtɪk) *adj* of, exhibiting, or concerned with diamagnetism.

diamagnetism (ˌdaɪəˈmægnɪˌtɪzəm) *n* the phenomenon exhibited by substances that have a relative permeability less than unity and a negative susceptibility; caused by the orbital motion of electrons in the atoms of the material.

diamanté (ˌdaɪəˈmæntɪ) *adj* **1** decorated with glittering ornaments, such as sequins. ◆ *n* **2** a fabric so covered. [C20: from F, from *diamanter* to adorn with diamonds]

diameter (daɪˈæmɪtə) *n* **1a** a straight line connecting the centre of a circle, sphere, etc. with two points on the perimeter or surface. **1b** the length of such a line. **2** the thickness of something, esp. with circular cross section. [C14: from Med. L, from Gk: diameter, diagonal, from DIA- + *metron* measure]

diametric ➊ (ˌdaɪəˈmɛtrɪk) *or* **diametrical** *adj* **1** Also: **diametral.** of, related to, or along a diameter. **2** completely opposed.

diametrically ➊ (ˌdaɪəˈmɛtrɪkəlɪ) *adv* completely; utterly (esp. in **diametrically opposed**).

diamond (ˈdaɪəmənd) *n* **1a** a usually colourless exceptionally hard form of carbon in cubic crystalline form. It is used as a precious stone and for industrial cutting or abrading. **1b** (*as modifier*): *a diamond ring.* **2** *Geom.* a figure having four sides of equal length forming two acute angles and two obtuse angles; rhombus. **3a** a red lozenge-shaped symbol on a playing card. **3b** a card with one or more of these symbols or (*when pl*) the suit of cards so marked. **4** *Baseball.* **4a** the whole playing field. **4b** the square formed by the four bases. ◆ *vb* **5** (*tr*) to decorate with or as with diamonds. [C13: from OF *diamant,* from Med. L *diamas,* from L *adamas* the hardest iron or steel, diamond; see ADAMANT]
▸**diamantine** (ˌdaɪəˈmæntaɪn) *adj*

diamond anniversary *n* a 60th, or occasionally 75th, anniversary.

diamondback (ˈdaɪəməndˌbæk) *n* **1** Also called: **diamondback terrapin** *or* **turtle.** any edible North American terrapin having diamond-shaped markings on the shell. **2** a large North American rattlesnake having diamond-shaped markings.

diamond wedding *n* the 60th, or occasionally the 75th, anniversary of a marriage.

diamorphine (ˌdaɪəˈmɔːfiːn) *n* a technical name for **heroin.**

dianthus (daɪˈænθəs) *n, pl* **dianthuses.** any Eurasian plant of the widely cultivated genus *Dianthus,* such as the carnation, pink, and sweet william. [C19: NL, from Gk DI-[1] + *anthos* flower]

diapason (ˌdaɪəˈpeɪzᵊn) *n Music.* **1** either of two stops (**open** and **stopped diapason**) found throughout the compass of a pipe organ that give it its characteristic tone colour. **2** the compass of an instrument or voice. **3a** a standard pitch used for tuning. **3b** a tuning fork or pitch pipe. **4** (in classical Greece) an octave. [C14: from L: the whole octave, from Gk: (*hē*) *dia pasōn* (*khordōn sumphōnia*) (concord) through all (the notes)]

diapause (ˈdaɪəˌpɔːz) *n* a period of suspended development and growth accompanied by decreased metabolism in insects and some other animals. [C19: from Gk *diapausis* pause, from *diapauein* to pause, bring to an end, from DIA- + *pauein* to stop]

diaper (ˈdaɪəpə) *n* **1** the US and Canad. word for **nappy**[1]. **2a** a fabric having a pattern of a small repeating design, esp. diamonds. **2b** such a pattern, used as decoration. ◆ *vb* **3** (*tr*) to decorate with such a pat-

THESAURUS

diagnose *vb* **1** = **identify,** analyse, determine, distinguish, interpret, investigate, pinpoint, pronounce, put one's finger on, recognize

diagnosis *n* **1a, 2a** = **examination,** analysis, investigation, scrutiny **1b, 2b** = **opinion,** conclusion, interpretation, pronouncement

diagnostic *adj* **1, 2** = **symptomatic,** demonstrative, distinctive, distinguishing, idiosyncratic, indicative, particular, peculiar, recognizable

diagonal *adj* **2** = **slanting,** angled, catercornered (*US inf.*), cornerways, cross, crossways, crosswise, oblique

diagonally *adv* **2** = **aslant,** at an angle, cornerwise, crosswise, obliquely, on the bias, on the cross

diagram *n* **1** = **plan,** chart, drawing, figure, graph, layout, outline, representation, sketch

dialect *n* = **language,** accent, brogue, idiom, jargon, lingo (*inf.*), localism, patois, pronunciation, provincialism, speech, tongue, vernacular

dialectal *n* = **regional,** dialect, idiomatic, local, nonstandard, restricted, vernacular

dialectic *n* **1, 2** = **debate,** argumentation, contention, discussion, disputation, logic, polemics, ratiocination, reasoning ◆ *adj* **5** = **logical,** analytic, argumentative, dialectical, polemical, rational, rationalistic

dialogue *n* **1, 2** = **conversation,** colloquy, communication, confabulation, conference, converse, discourse, discussion, duologue, exchange, interlocution **3** = **lines,** conversation, script, spoken part

diametric *adj* **2** = **opposed,** antipodal, antithetical, conflicting, contrary, contrasting, counter, opposite, poles apart

diametrically *adv* = **completely,** absolutely, entirely, totally, utterly tern. [C14: from OF *diaspre*, from Med. L *diasprus* made of diaper, from Med. Gk *diaspros* pure white, from DIA- + *aspros* white, shining]

diaphanous ❶ (daɪˈæfənəs) *adj* (usually of fabrics) fine and translucent. [C17: from Med. L, from Gk *diaphanēs* transparent, from DIA- + *phainein* to show]
▸**diˈaphanously** *adv*

diaphoresis (ˌdaɪəfəˈriːsɪs) *n* perspiration, esp. when perceptible and excessive. [C17: via LL from Gk, from *diaphorein* to disperse by perspiration, from DIA- + *phorein* to carry]

diaphoretic (ˌdaɪəfəˈretɪk) *adj* **1** relating to or causing perspiration. ◆ *n* **2** a diaphoretic drug.

diaphragm (ˈdaɪəˌfræm) *n* **1** *Anat.* any separating membrane, esp. the muscular partition that separates the abdominal and thoracic cavities in mammals. **2** another name for **cap** (sense 11). **3** any thin dividing membrane. **4** Also called: **stop.** a device to control the amount of light entering an optical instrument, such as a camera. **5** a thin vibrating disc used to convert sound signals to electrical signals or vice versa in telephones, etc. [C17: from LL, from Gk, from DIA- + *phragma* fence]
▸**diaphragmatic** (ˌdaɪəfrægˈmætɪk) *adj*

diapositive (ˌdaɪəˈpɒzɪtɪv) *n* a positive transparency; slide.

diarist (ˈdaɪərɪst) *n* a person who writes a diary, esp. one that is subsequently published.

diarrhoea ❶ *or esp. US* **diarrhea** (ˌdaɪəˈrɪə) *n* frequent and copious discharge of abnormally liquid faeces. [C16: from LL, from Gk, from *diarrhein*, from DIA- + *rhein* to flow]
▸ˌ**diarˈrhoeal**, ˌ**diarˈrhoeic** *or esp. US* ˌ**diarˈrheal**, ˌ**diarˈrheic** *adj*

diary ❶ (ˈdaɪərɪ) *n, pl* **diaries. 1** a personal record of daily events, appointments, observations, etc. **2** a book for this. [C16: from L *diārium* daily allocation of food or money, journal, from *diēs* day]

Diaspora (daɪˈæspərə) *n* **1a** the dispersion of the Jews after the Babylonian and Roman conquests of Palestine. **1b** the Jewish people and communities outside Israel. **2** (*often not cap.*) a dispersion, as of people originally belonging to one nation. [C19: from Gk: a scattering, from *diaspeirein*, from DIA- + *speirein* to scatter, sow]

diastalsis (ˌdaɪəˈstælsɪs) *n, pl* **diastalses** (-siːz). *Physiol.* a downward wave of contraction occurring in the intestine during digestion. [C20: NL, from DIA- + (PERI)STALSIS]
▸ˌ**diaˈstaltic** *adj*

diastase (ˈdaɪəˌsteɪs, -ˌsteɪz) *n* any of a group of enzymes that hydrolyse starch to maltose. They are present in germinated barley and in the pancreas. [C19: from F, from Gk *diastasis* a separation]
▸ˌ**diaˈstasic** *adj*

diastole (daɪˈæstəlɪ) *n* the dilation of the chambers of the heart that follows each contraction, during which they refill with blood. Cf. **systole.** [C16: via LL from Gk, from *diastellein* to expand, from DIA- + *stellein* to place, bring together, make ready]
▸**diastolic** (ˌdaɪəˈstɒlɪk) *adj*

diastrophism (daɪˈæstrəˌfɪzəm) *n* the process of movement of the earth's crust that gives rise to mountains, continents, and other large-scale features. [C19: from Gk *diastrophē* a twisting; see DIA-, STROPHE]
▸**diastrophic** (ˌdaɪəˈstrɒfɪk) *adj*

diathermancy (ˌdaɪəˈθɜːmənsɪ) *n, pl* **diathermancies.** the property of transmitting infrared radiation. [C19: from F, from DIA- + Gk *thermansis* heating, from *thermos* hot]
▸ˌ**diaˈthermanous** *adj*

diathermy (ˈdaɪəˌθɜːmɪ) *or* **diathermia** (ˌdaɪəˈθɜːmɪə) *n* local heating of the body tissues with an electric current for medical purposes. [C20: from NL, from DIA- + Gk *thermē* heat]

diatom (ˈdaɪətəm) *n* a microscopic unicellular alga having a cell wall impregnated with silica. [C19: from NL, from Gk *diatomos* cut in two, from DIA- + *temnein* to cut]

diatomaceous (ˌdaɪətəˈmeɪʃəs) *adj* of or containing diatoms or their fossil remains.

diatomic (ˌdaɪəˈtɒmɪk) *adj* (of a compound or molecule) containing two atoms.

diatomite (daɪˈætəˌmaɪt) *n* a soft whitish rock consisting of the siliceous remains of diatoms.

diatonic (ˌdaɪəˈtɒnɪk) *adj* **1** of, relating to, or based upon any scale of five tones and two semitones produced by playing the white keys of a keyboard instrument. **2** not involving the sharpening or flattening of the notes of the major or minor scale nor the use of such notes as modified by accidentals. [C16: from LL, from Gk, from *diatonos* extending, from DIA- + *teinein* to stretch]

diatonic scale *n Music.* the major and minor scales, made up of both tones and semitones.

diatribe ❶ (ˈdaɪəˌtraɪb) *n* a bitter or violent criticism or attack. [C16: from L *diatriba* learned debate, from Gk *diatribē* discourse, pastime, from *diatribein* to while away, from DIA- + *tribein* to rub]

diazepam (daɪˈæzəˌpæm) *n* a chemical compound used as a tranquillizer and muscle relaxant. [C20: from DI-[1] + *azo-* + *ep(oxide)* + *-am*]

diazo (daɪˈeɪzəʊ) *adj* **1** of, consisting of, or containing the divalent group, =N:N, or the divalent group, -N:N-. **2** of the reproduction of documents using the bleaching action of ultraviolet radiation on diazonium salts. ◆ *n, pl* **diazos** *or* **diazoes. 3** a document produced by this method.

diazonium (ˌdaɪəˈzəʊnɪəm) *n* (modifier) of, consisting of, or containing the group ArN:N–, where Ar is an aryl group: *a diazonium salt.*

dibasic (daɪˈbeɪsɪk) *adj* **1** (of an acid) containing two acidic hydrogen atoms. **2** (of a salt) derived by replacing two acidic hydrogen atoms.
▸**dibasicity** (ˌdaɪbeɪˈsɪsɪtɪ) *n*

dibble (ˈdɪbᵊl) *n* **1** Also: **dibber.** a small hand tool used to make holes in the ground for bulbs, seeds, or roots. ◆ *vb* **dibbles, dibbling, dibbled. 2** to make a hole in (the ground) with a dibble. **3** to plant (seeds, etc.) with a dibble. [C15: from ?]

dibs (dɪbz) *pl n* **1** another word for **jacks. 2** *Sl.* money. **3** (foll. by *on*) *Inf.* rights (to) or claims (on): used mainly by children. [C18: from *dibstones* game played with knucklebones or pebbles, prob. from *dib* to tap]

dice (daɪs) *pl n* **1** cubes of wood, plastic, etc., each of whose sides has a different number of spots (1 to 6), used in games of chance. **2** (*functioning as sing*) Also called: **die.** one of these cubes. **3** small cubes as of vegetables, meat, etc. **4 no dice.** *Sl., chiefly US & Canad.* an expression of refusal. ◆ *vb* **dices, dicing, diced. 5** to cut (food, etc.) into small cubes. **6** (*intr*) to gamble or play with dice. **7** (*intr*) to take a chance or risk (esp. in **dice with death**). **8** (*tr*) *Austral. inf.* to abandon or reject. [C14: pl of DIE[2]]
▸ˈ**dicer** *n*

dicey ❶ (ˈdaɪsɪ) *adj* **dicier, diciest.** *Inf., chiefly Brit.* difficult or dangerous; risky; tricky.

dichloride (daɪˈklɔːraɪd) *n* a compound in which two atoms of chlorine are combined with another atom or group. Also called: **bichloride.**

dichlorodiphenyltrichloroethane (daɪˌklɔːrəʊdaɪˌfiːnaɪltraɪˌklɔːrəʊˈiːθeɪn) *n* the full name for **DDT.**

dichloromethane (daɪˌklɔːrəʊˈmiːθeɪn) *n* a noxious colourless liquid widely used as a solvent, e.g. in paint strippers. Formula: CH_2Cl_2. Traditional name: **methylene dichloride.**

dichotomy ❶ (daɪˈkɒtəmɪ) *n, pl* **dichotomies. 1** division into two parts or classifications, esp. when they are sharply distinguished or opposed. **2** *Bot.* a simple method of branching by repeated division into two equal parts.
▸**diˈchotomous** *adj*

> **USAGE NOTE** *Dichotomy* should always refer to a division of some kind into two groups. It is sometimes used to refer to a puzzling situation which seems to involve a contradiction, but this use is generally thought to be incorrect.

dichroism (ˈdaɪkrəʊˌɪzəm) *n* a property of a uniaxial crystal of showing a difference in colour when viewed along two different axes (in transmitted white light). Also called: **dichromaticism.** See also **pleochroism.**
▸**diˈchroic** *adj*

dichromate (daɪˈkrəʊmeɪt) *n* any salt or ester of dichromic acid. Also called: **bichromate.**

dichromatic (ˌdaɪkrəʊˈmætɪk) *adj* **1** Also: **dichroic.** having two colours. **2** (of animal species) having two different colour varieties. **3** able to perceive only two colours (and mixes of them).
▸**dichromatism** (daɪˈkrəʊməˌtɪzəm) *n*

dichromic (daɪˈkrəʊmɪk) *adj* of or involving only two colours; dichromatic.

dick (dɪk) *n Sl.* **1** *Brit.* a fellow or person. **2 clever dick.** *Brit.* an opinionated person; know-all. **3** a taboo word for **penis.** [C16 (meaning: fellow): from *Dick*, familiar form of *Richard*, applied to any fellow, lad, etc.; hence, C19: penis]

dickens (ˈdɪkɪnz) *n Inf.* a euphemistic word for **devil** (used as intensifier in **what the dickens**). [C16: from the name *Dickens*]

Dickensian (dɪˈkenzɪən) *adj* **1** of Charles Dickens (1812–70), English novelist, or his novels. **2a** denoting poverty, distress, and exploitation as depicted in the novels of Dickens. **2b** grotesquely comic, as some of the characters of Dickens.

dicker (ˈdɪkə) *vb* **1** to trade (goods) by bargaining; barter. ◆ *n* **2** a petty bargain or barter. [C12: ult. from L *decuria* company of ten, from *decem* ten]

dickhead (ˈdɪkˌhed) *n Sl.* a stupid or despicable man or boy. [C20: from DICK (in the sense: penis) + HEAD]

dicky[1] *or* **dickey** (ˈdɪkɪ) *n, pl* **dickies** *or* **dickeys. 1** a false blouse or shirt front. **2** Also called: **dicky bow.** *Brit.* a bow tie. **3** Also called: **dicky-bird, dickeybird.** a child's word for a bird. **4** a folding outside seat at the rear of some early cars. [C18 (in the sense: shirt front): from *Dickey*, dim. of *Dick* (name)]

dicky[2] *or* **dickey** ❶ (ˈdɪkɪ) *adj* **dickier, dickiest.** *Brit. inf.* shaky, unsteady,

THESAURUS

diaphanous *n* = **fine,** chiffon, clear, cobwebby, delicate, filmy, gauzy, gossamer, light, pellucid, see-through, sheer, thin, translucent, transparent

diarrhoea *n* = **the runs,** dysentery, gippy tummy, holiday tummy, looseness, Montezuma's revenge (*inf.*), Spanish tummy, the skits (*inf.*), the skitters (*inf.*), the trots (*inf.*)

diary *n* **1, 2** = **journal,** appointment book, chronicle, daily record, day-to-day account, engagement book, Filofax (*Trademark*)

diatribe *n* = **tirade,** abuse, castigation, criticism, denunciation, disputation, harangue, invective, philippic, reviling, stream of abuse, stricture, verbal onslaught, vituperation

dicey *adj Informal, chiefly Brit.* = **dangerous,** chancy (*inf.*), difficult, hairy (*sl.*), risky, ticklish, tricky

dichotomy *n* **1** = **division,** bisection, disjunction, divorce, separation, split (in two)

dicky[2] *adj Brit. informal* = **weak,** fluttery, queer, shaky, unreliable, unsound, unsteady or unreliable: *I feel a bit dicky today.* [C18: ?from *as queer as Dick's hatband* feeling ill]

dicLinous ('daɪklɪnəs) *adj* (of flowering plants) unisexual. Cf. **monoclinous.**
▸ **'diclinism** *n*

dicotyledon (ˌdaɪkɒtɪ'liːdᵊn) *n* a flowering plant having two embryonic seed leaves.
▸ **ˌdicoty'ledonous** *adj*

dict. *abbrev. for:* **1** dictation. **2** dictator. **3** dictionary.

dicta ('dɪktə) *n* a plural of **dictum.**

Dictaphone ('dɪktəˌfəʊn) *n Trademark.* a tape recorder designed for recording dictation for subsequent typing.

dictate ➊ *vb* (dɪk'teɪt), **dictates, dictating, dictated. 1** to say (letters, speeches, etc.) aloud for mechanical recording or verbatim transcription by another person. **2** *(tr)* to prescribe (commands, etc.) authoritatively. **3** *(intr)* to seek to impose one's will on others. ◆ *n* ('dɪkteɪt). **4** an authoritative command. **5** a guiding principle: *the dictates of reason.* [C17: from L *dictāre* to say repeatedly, order, from *dīcere* to say]

dictation (dɪk'teɪʃən) *n* **1** the act of dictating material to be recorded or taken down in writing. **2** the material dictated. **3** authoritative commands or the act of giving them.

dictator ➊ (dɪk'teɪtə) *n* **1a** a ruler who is not effectively restricted by a constitution, laws, etc. **1b** an absolute, esp. tyrannical, ruler. **2** (in ancient Rome) a person appointed during a crisis to exercise supreme authority. **3** a person who makes pronouncements, which are regarded as authoritative. **4** a person who behaves in an authoritarian or tyrannical manner.

dictatorial ➊ (ˌdɪktə'tɔːrɪəl) *adj* **1** of or characteristic of a dictator. **2** tending to dictate; tyrannical; overbearing.
▸ **ˌdicta'torially** *adv*

dictatorship ➊ (dɪk'teɪtəˌʃɪp) *n* **1** the rank, office, or period of rule of a dictator. **2** government by a dictator. **3** a country ruled by a dictator. **4** absolute power or authority.

diction ➊ ('dɪkʃən) *n* **1** the choice of words in writing or speech. **2** the manner of enunciating words and sounds. [C15: from L *dictiō* a saying, mode of expression, from *dīcere* to speak, say]

dictionary ➊ ('dɪkʃənərɪ) *n, pl* **dictionaries. 1a** a book that consists of an alphabetical list of words with their meanings, parts of speech, pronunciations, etymologies, etc. **1b** a similar book giving equivalent words in two or more languages. **2** a reference book listing words or terms and giving information about a particular subject or activity. **3** a collection of information or examples with the entries alphabetically arranged: *a dictionary of quotations.* [C16: from Med. L *dictiōnārium* collection of words, from LL *dictiō* word; see DICTION]

dictum ➊ ('dɪktəm) *n, pl* **dictums** *or* **dicta. 1** a formal or authoritative statement; pronouncement. **2** a popular saying or maxim. **3** *Law.* See **obiter dictum.** [C16: from L, from *dīcere* to say]

did (dɪd) *vb* the past tense of **do**[1].

didactic ➊ (dɪ'dæktɪk) *adj* **1** intended to instruct, esp. excessively. **2** morally instructive. **3** (of works of art or literature) containing a political or moral message to which aesthetic considerations are subordinated. [C17: from Gk *didaktikos* skilled in teaching, from *didaskein*]
▸ **di'dactically** *adv* ▸ **di'dacticism** *n*

didactics (dɪ'dæktɪks) *n (functioning as sing)* the art or science of teaching.

diddle ('dɪdᵊl) *vb* **diddles, diddling, diddled.** *(tr) Inf.* to cheat or swindle. [C19: back formation from Jeremy *Diddler*, a scrounger in J. Kenney's farce *Raising the Wind* (1803)]
▸ **'diddler** *n*

didgeridoo (ˌdɪdʒərɪ'duː) *n Music.* a native deep-toned Australian wind instrument. [C20: imit.]

didn't ('dɪdᵊnt) *contraction of* did not.

dido ('daɪdəʊ) *n, pl* **didos** *or* **didoes.** *(usually pl) Inf.* an antic; prank; trick. [C19: from ?]

didst (dɪdst) *vb Arch.* (used with *thou*) a form of the past tense of **do**[1].

didymium (daɪ'dɪmɪəm) *n* a mixture of the metallic rare earths neodymium and praseodymium, once thought to be an element. [C19: from NL, from Gk *didumos* twin + -IUM]

die[1] ➊ (daɪ) *vb* **dies, dying, died.** *(mainly intr)* **1** (of an organism, organs, etc.) to cease all biological activity permanently. **2** (of something inanimate) to cease to exist. **3** (often foll. by *away, down,* or *out*) to lose strength, power, or energy, esp. by degrees. **4** (often foll. by *away* or *down*) to become calm; subside. **5** to stop functioning: *the engine died.* **6** to languish, as with love, longing, etc. **7** (usually foll. by *of*) *Inf.* to be nearly overcome (with laughter, boredom, etc.). **8** *Christianity.* to lack spiritual life within the soul. **9** *(tr)* to suffer (a death of a specified kind): *he died a saintly death.* **10 be dying.** (foll. by *for* or an infinitive) to be eager or desperate (for something or to do something). **11 die hard.** to cease to exist after a struggle: *old habits die hard.* **12 die in harness.** to die while still working or active. **13 never say die.** *Inf.* never give up. ◆ See also **die down, die out.** [OE *dīegan*, prob. of Scand. origin]

> **USAGE NOTE** It was formerly considered incorrect to use the preposition *from* after *die*, but *of* and *from* are now both acceptable: *he died of/from his injuries.*

die[2] (daɪ) *n* **1a** a shaped block used to cut or form metal in a drop forge, press, etc. **1b** a tool with a conical hole through which wires, etc. are drawn to reduce their diameter. **2** an internally-threaded tool for cutting external threads. **3** a casting mould. **4** *Archit.* the dado of a pedestal, usually cubic. **5** another name for **dice** (sense 2). **6 the die is cast.** the irrevocable decision has been taken. [C13 *dee*, from OF *de*, ?from Vulgar L *datum* (unattested) a piece in games, from L *dare* to give, play]

die-cast *vb* **die-casts, die-casting, die-cast.** *(tr)* to shape or form (an object) by introducing molten metal or plastic into a reusable mould, esp. under pressure.
▸ **'die-ˌcasting** *n*

die down *vb (intr, adv)* **1** (of plants) to wither above ground, leaving only the root alive during the winter. **2** to lose strength or power, esp. by degrees. **3** to become calm.

die-hard ➊ *n* **1** a person who resists change or who holds onto an untenable position. **2** *(modifier)* obstinately resistant to change.

dieldrin ('diːldrɪn) *n* a crystalline substance, consisting of a chlorinated derivative of naphthalene: a contact insecticide the use of which is now restricted. [C20: from *Diel(s-Al)d(e)r (reaction)* + -IN; Diels & Alder were G chemists]

dielectric (ˌdaɪɪ'lɛktrɪk) *n* **1** a substance that can sustain an electric field. **2** a substance of very low electrical conductivity; insulator. ◆ *adj* **3** concerned with or having the properties of a dielectric. [from DIA- + ELECTRIC]
▸ **ˌdie'lectrically** *adv*

diene ('daɪiːn) *n Chem.* a hydrocarbon that contains two carbon-to-carbon double bonds in its molecules. [from DI-[1] + -ENE]

die out *or* **off** *vb (intr, adv)* **1** to die one after another until few or none are left. **2** to become extinct, esp. after a period of gradual decline.

dieresis (daɪ'ɛrɪsɪs) *n, pl* **diereses** (-ˌsiːz). a variant spelling of **diaeresis.**

diesel ('diːzᵊl) *n* **1** See **diesel engine. 2** a ship, locomotive, lorry, etc., driven by a diesel engine. **3** *Inf.* short for **diesel oil** (*or* **fuel**). [after R. *Diesel* (1858–1913), G engineer]

diesel-electric *n* **1** a locomotive fitted with a diesel engine driving an electric generator that feeds electric traction motors. ◆ *adj* **2** of or relating to such a locomotive or system.

diesel engine *or* **motor** *n* a type of internal-combustion engine in which atomized fuel oil is ignited by compression alone.

diesel oil *or* **fuel** *n* a fuel obtained from petroleum distillation that is used in diesel engines. Also called (Brit.): **derv.**

Dies Irae *Latin.* ('diːeɪz 'ɪəraɪ) *n* **1** a Latin hymn of the 13th century, describing the Last Judgment. It is used in the Mass for the dead. **2** a musical setting of this. [lit.: day of wrath]

diesis ('daɪɪsɪs) *n, pl* **dieses** (-ˌsiːz). *Printing.* another name for **double dagger.** [C16: via L from Gk: a quarter tone, lit.: a sending through, from *diienai;* the double dagger was orig. used in musical notation]

diestock ('daɪˌstɒk) *n* the device holding the dies used to cut an external screw thread.

diet[1] ➊ ('daɪət) *n* **1** a specific allowance or selection of food, esp. prescribed to control weight or for health reasons: *a salt-free diet.* **2** the

THESAURUS

dictate *vb* **1** = **speak**, read out, say, transmit, utter **2** = **order**, command, decree, demand, direct, enjoin, establish, impose, lay down, lay down the law, ordain, prescribe, pronounce ◆ *n* **4** = **command**, behest, bidding, decree, demand, direction, edict, fiat, injunction, mandate, order, ordinance, requirement, statute, ultimatum, word **5** = **principle**, canon, code, dictum, law, precept, rule

dictator *n* = **absolute ruler**, autocrat, despot, oppressor, tyrant

dictatorial *adj* **1** = **absolute**, arbitrary, autocratic, despotic, totalitarian, tyrannical, unlimited, unrestricted **2** = **domineering**, authoritarian, bossy *(inf.)*, dogmatical, imperious, iron-handed, magisterial, oppressive, overbearing
Antonyms *adj* ≠ **absolute:** constitutional, democratic, egalitarian, restricted ≠ **domineering:** humble, servile, suppliant, tolerant

dictatorship *n* **2, 4** = **absolute rule**, absolutism, authoritarianism, autocracy, despotism, reign of terror, totalitarianism, tyranny

diction *n* **2** = **pronunciation**, articulation, delivery, elocution, enunciation, fluency, inflection, intonation, speech

dictionary *n* **1** = **wordbook**, concordance, encyclopedia, glossary, lexicon, vocabulary

dictum *n* **1** = **decree**, canon, command, demand, dictate, edict, fiat, order, pronouncement, statement **2** = **saying**, adage, axiom, gnome, maxim, precept, proverb, saw

didactic *adj* **1, 2** = **instructive**, edifying, educational, enlightening, homiletic, moral, moralizing, pedagogic, pedantic, preceptive

die[1] *vb* **1** = **pass away**, breathe one's last, buy it *(US. sl.)*, buy the farm *(US. sl.)*, check out *(US. sl.)*, croak *(sl.)*, decease, depart, expire, finish, give up the ghost, go belly-up *(sl.)*, hop the twig *(sl.)*, kick it *(sl.)*, kick the bucket *(sl.)*, peg it *(inf.)*, peg out *(inf.)*, perish, pop one's clogs *(inf.)*, snuff it *(sl.)* **3** = **dwindle**, decay, decline, disappear, ebb, end, fade, lapse, pass, sink, subside, vanish, wane, wilt, wither **5** = **stop**, break down, fade out *or* away, fail, fizzle out, halt, lose power, peter out, run down **7** *foll. by* **of** *Informal* = **be overcome with**, collapse with, succumb to **10 be dying** *foll. by* **for** = **long for**, ache for, be eager for, desire, hunger for, languish for, pine for, set one's heart on, swoon over, yearn for
Antonyms *vb* ≠ **pass away:** be born, begin, come to life, exist, live, survive ≠ **dwindle, stop:** flourish, grow, increase

die-hard *n* **1** = **reactionary**, fanatic, intransigent, old fogey, stick-in-the-mud *(inf.)*, ultraconservative, zealot ◆ *modifier* **2** = **reactionary**, dyed-in-the-wool, immovable, inflexible, intransigent, ultraconservative, uncompromising, unreconstructed *(chiefly US)*

diet[1] *n* **1** = **regime**, abstinence, dietary, fast, regimen **2** = **food**, aliment, comestibles, commons, edibles, fare, nourishment, nutriment, provi-

food and drink that a person or animal regularly consumes. **3** regular activities or occupations. ◆ *vb* **4** (*usually intr*) to follow or cause to follow a dietary regimen. [C13: from OF *diete*, from L *diaeta*, from Gk *diaita* mode of living, from *diaitan* to direct one's own life]
▸**'dieter** *n*

diet[2] ⓣ ('daɪət) *n* **1** (*sometimes cap.*) a legislative assembly in various countries. **2** (*sometimes cap.*) the assembly of the estates of the Holy Roman Empire. **3** *Scots Law.* a single session of a court. [C15: from Med. L *diēta* public meeting, prob. from L *diaeta* DIET[1] but associated with L *diēs* day]

dietary ('daɪətərɪ, -trɪ) *adj* **1** of or relating to a diet. ◆ *n, pl* **dietaries. 2** a regulated diet. **3** a system of dieting.

dietary fibre *n* fibrous substances in fruits and vegetables, such as the structural polymers of cell walls, which aid digestion. Also called: **roughage.**

dietetic (ˌdaɪɪ'tɛtɪk) *or* **dietetical** *adj* **1** denoting or relating to diet. **2** prepared for special dietary requirements.
▸**ˌdie'tetically** *adv*

dietetics (ˌdaɪɪ'tɛtɪks) *n* (*functioning as sing*) the scientific study and regulation of food intake and preparation.

diethylene glycol *n* a colourless soluble liquid used as an antifreeze and solvent.

dietitian *or* **dietician** (ˌdaɪɪ'tɪʃən) *n* a person who specializes in dietetics.

differ ⓣ ('dɪfə) *vb* (*intr*) **1** (often foll. by *from*) to be dissimilar in quality, nature, or degree (to); vary (from). **2** (often foll. by *from* or *with*) to disagree (with). **3** *Dialect.* to quarrel or dispute. [C14: from L *differre*, to scatter, put off, be different, from *dis-* apart + *ferre* to bear]

difference ⓣ ('dɪfərəns) *n* **1** the state or quality of being unlike. **2** a specific instance of being unlike. **3** a distinguishing mark or feature. **4** a significant change. **5** a disagreement or argument. **6** a degree of distinctness, as between two people or things. **7** Also called: **remainder.** the result of the subtraction of one number, quantity, etc., from another. **8** *Maths.* (of two sets) the set of members of the first that are not members of the second. **9** *Heraldry.* an addition to the arms of a family to represent a younger branch. **10 make a difference. 10a** to have an effect. **10b** to treat differently. **11 split the difference. 11a** to compromise. **11b** to divide a remainder equally. **12 with a difference.** with some distinguishing quality, good or bad.

different ⓣ ('dɪfərənt) *adj* **1** partly or completely unlike. **2** not identical or the same; other. **3** unusual.
▸**'differently** *adv* ▸**'differentness** *n*

> **USAGE NOTE** The constructions *different from, different to,* and *different than* are all found in the works of writers of English during the past. Nowadays, however, the most widely acceptable preposition to use after *different* is *from. Different to* is common in British English, but is considered by some people to be incorrect, or less acceptable. *Different than* is a standard construction in American English, and has the advantage of conciseness when a clause or phrase follows, as in *this result is only slightly different than in the US.* As, however, this idiom is not regarded as totally acceptable in British usage, it is preferable either to use *different from: this result is only slightly different from that obtained in the US* or to rephrase the sentence: *this result differs only slightly from that in the US.*

differentia (ˌdɪfə'rɛnʃɪə) *n, pl* **differentiae** (-ʃɪˌiː). *Logic.* a feature by which two subclasses of the same class of named objects can be distinguished. [C19: from L: diversity]

differential ⓣ (ˌdɪfə'rɛnʃəl) *adj* **1** of, relating to, or using a difference. **2** constituting a difference; distinguishing. **3** *Maths.* involving one or more derivatives or differentials. **4** *Physics, engineering.* relating to, operating on, or based on the difference between two opposing effects, motions, forces, etc. ◆ *n* **5** a factor that differentiates between two comparable things. **6** *Maths.* **6a** an increment in a given function, expressed as the product of the derivative of that function and the corresponding increment in the independent variable. **6b** an increment in a given function of two or more variables, $f(x_1, x_2, \ldots x_n)$, expressed as the sum of the products of each partial derivative and the increment in the corresponding variable. **7** See **differential gear. 8** *Chiefly Brit.* the difference between rates of pay for different types of labour, esp. when forming a pay structure within an industry. **9** (in commerce) a difference in rates, esp. between comparable services.
▸**ˌdiffer'entially** *adv*

differential calculus *n* the branch of calculus concerned with the study, evaluation, and use of derivatives and differentials.

differential equation *n* an equation containing differentials or derivatives of a function of one independent variable.

differential gear *n* the epicyclic gear mounted in the driving axle of a road vehicle that permits one driving wheel to rotate faster than the other, as when cornering.

differential operator *n* the mathematical operator del, ∇, used in vector analysis.

differentiate ⓣ (ˌdɪfə'rɛnʃɪˌeɪt) *vb* **differentiates, differentiating, differentiated. 1** (*tr*) to serve to distinguish between. **2** (when *intr*, often foll. by *between*) to perceive, show, or make a difference (in or between); discriminate. **3** (*intr*) to become dissimilar or distinct. **4** *Maths.* to perform a differentiation on (a quantity, expression, etc.). **5** (*intr*) (of unspecialized cells, etc.) to change during development to more specialized forms.
▸**ˌdiffer'entiˌator** *n*

differentiation (ˌdɪfəˌrɛnʃɪ'eɪʃən) *n* **1** the act, process, or result of differentiating. **2** *Maths.* an operation used in calculus in which the derivative of a function or variable is determined.

difficult ⓣ ('dɪfɪkᵊlt) *adj* **1** not easy to do; requiring effort. **2** not easy to understand or solve. **3** troublesome: *a difficult child.* **4** not easily convinced, pleased, or satisfied. **5** full of hardships or trials. [C14: back formation from DIFFICULTY]
▸**'difficultly** *adv*

difficulty ⓣ ('dɪfɪkᵊltɪ) *n, pl* **difficulties. 1** the state or quality of being difficult. **2** a task, problem, etc., that is hard to deal with. **3** (*often pl*) a troublesome or embarrassing situation, esp. a financial one. **4** a disagreement. **5** (*often pl*) an objection or obstacle. **6** a trouble or source of trouble; worry. **7** lack of ease; awkwardness. [C14: from L *difficultās*, from *difficilis*, from *dis-* not + *facilis* easy]

diffident ⓣ ('dɪfɪdənt) *adj* lacking self-confidence; shy. [C15: from L *diffidere*, from *dis-* not + *fidere* to trust]
▸**'diffidence** *n* ▸**'diffidently** *adv*

diffract (dɪ'frækt) *vb* to undergo or cause to undergo diffraction.
▸**dif'fractive** *adj* ▸**dif'fractively** *adv* ▸**dif'fractiveness** *n*

diffraction (dɪ'frækʃən) *n* **1** *Physics.* a deviation in the direction of a wave at the edge of an obstacle in its path. **2** any phenomenon caused by diffraction, such as the formation of light and dark fringes by the

THESAURUS

sions, rations, subsistence, sustenance, viands, victuals ◆ *vb* **4** = **slim**, abstain, eat sparingly, fast, lose weight
Antonyms *vb* ≠ **slim:** get fat, glut, gobble, gormandize, guzzle, indulge, overindulge, pig out (*sl.*), stuff oneself

diet[2] *n* = **council**, chamber, congress, convention, legislative assembly, legislature, meeting, parliament, sitting

dieter *n* = **slimmer**, calorie counter, faster, reducer, weight watcher

differ *vb* **1** = **be dissimilar**, be distinct, contradict, contrast, depart from, diverge, run counter to, stand apart, vary **2** = **disagree**, clash, contend, debate, demur, dispute, dissent, oppose, take exception, take issue
Antonyms *vb* ≠ **be dissimilar:** accord, coincide, harmonize ≠ **disagree:** accord, acquiesce, agree, assent, concur, cooperate

difference *n* **1** = **dissimilarity**, alteration, change, contrast, deviation, differentiation, discrepancy, disparity, distinction, distinctness, divergence, diversity, unlikeness, variation, variety **3** = **distinction**, exception, idiosyncrasy, particularity, peculiarity, singularity **5** = **disagreement**, argument, clash, conflict, contention, contrariety, contretemps, controversy, debate, discordance, dispute, quarrel, row, set-to (*inf.*), strife, tiff, wrangle **7** = **remainder**, balance, rest, result
Antonyms *n* ≠ **dissimilarity:** affinity, comparability, conformity, congruence, likeness, relation, resemblance, sameness, similarity, similitude ≠ **disagreement:** agreement, concordance

different *adj* **1** = **unlike**, altered, at odds, at variance, changed, clashing, contrasting, deviating, discrepant, disparate, dissimilar, divergent, diverse, inconsistent, opposed, streets apart **2** = **other**, another, discrete, distinct, individual, separate **3** = **unusual**, another story, atypical, bizarre, distinctive, extraordinary, left-field (*inf.*), out of the ordinary, peculiar, rare, singular, something else, special, strange, uncommon, unconventional, unique

differential *adj* **2** = **distinctive**, diacritical, discriminative, distinguishing ◆ *n* **5** = **difference**, amount of difference, discrepancy, disparity

differentiate *vb* **1** = **distinguish**, contrast, discern, discriminate, make a distinction, mark off, separate, set off *or* apart, tell apart

differently *adv* **1** = **otherwise**, contrastingly, in another way, in contrary fashion
Antonyms *adv* ≠ **otherwise:** in like manner, in the same way, likewise, similarly

difficult *adj* **1** = **hard**, arduous, burdensome, demanding, formidable, laborious, like getting blood out of a stone, no picnic (*inf.*), onerous, painful, strenuous, toilsome, uphill, wearisome **2** = **problematical**, abstract, abstruse, baffling, complex, complicated, delicate, enigmatical, intricate, involved, knotty, obscure, perplexing, thorny, ticklish **4** = **troublesome**, demanding, fastidious, fractious, fussy, hard to please, intractable, obstreperous, perverse, refractory, rigid, tiresome, trying, unaccommodating, unamenable, unmanageable **5** = **tough**, dark, full of hardship, grim, hard, straitened, trying
Antonyms *adj* ≠ **hard:** easy, easy-peasy (*sl.*), light, manageable, obvious, plain, simple, straightforward, uncomplicated ≠ **troublesome:** accommodating, amenable, cooperative, pleasant ≠ **tough:** easy, pleasant

difficulty *n* **1** = **laboriousness**, arduousness, awkwardness, hardship, labour, pain, painfulness, strain, strenuousness, tribulation **3** = **predicament**, deep water, dilemma, distress, embarrassment, fix (*inf.*), hot water (*inf.*), jam (*inf.*), mess, perplexity, pickle (*inf.*), plight, quandary, spot (*inf.*), straits, tight spot, trial, trouble **5** = **problem**, complication, hassle (*inf.*), hazard, hindrance, hurdle, impediment, objection, obstacle, opposition, pitfall, protest, snag, stumbling block

diffidence *n* = **shyness**, backwardness, bashfulness, constraint, doubt, fear, hesitancy, hesitation, humility, insecurity, lack of self-confidence, meekness, modesty, reluctance, reserve, self-consciousness, sheepishness, timidity, timidness, timorousness, unassertiveness
Antonyms *n* assurance, boldness, confidence, courage, firmness, self-confidence, self-possession

diffident *adj* = **shy**, backward, bashful, constrained, distrustful, doubtful, hesitant, insecure, meek, modest, reluctant, reserved, self-

passage of light through a small aperture. [C17: from NL *diffractiō* a breaking to pieces, from L *diffringere* to shatter, from *dis-* apart + *frangere* to break]

diffuse ❶ *vb* (dɪ'fju:z), **diffuses, diffusing, diffused. 1** to spread in all directions. **2** to undergo or cause to undergo diffusion. **3** to scatter; disperse. ◆ *adj* (dɪ'fju:s). **4** spread out over a wide area. **5** lacking conciseness. **6** characterized by diffusion. [C15: from L *diffūsus* spread abroad, from *diffundere* to pour forth, from *dis-* away + *fundere* to pour]
▸**diffusely** (dɪ'fju:slɪ) *adv* ▸**dif'fuseness** *n* ▸**diffusible** (dɪ'fju:zɪbᵊl) *adj*

USAGE NOTE Avoid confusion with **defuse.**

diffuser *or* **diffusor** (dɪ'fju:zə) *n* **1** a person or thing that diffuses. **2** a part of a lighting fixture, as a translucent covering, used to scatter the light and prevent glare. **3** a cone, wedge, or baffle placed in front of the diaphragm of a loudspeaker to diffuse the sound waves. **4** a duct, esp. in a wind tunnel or jet engine, that reduces the speed and increases the pressure of the air or fluid. **5** *Photog.* a light-scattering medium, such as a screen of fine fabric, used to reduce the sharpness of shadows and thus soften the lighting. **6** a device attached to a hair dryer that diffuses the warm air as it comes out.

diffusion ❶ (dɪ'fju:ʒən) *n* **1** a diffusing or being diffused; dispersion. **2** verbosity. **3** *Physics.* **3a** the random thermal motion of atoms, molecules, etc., in gases, liquids, and some solids. **3b** the transfer of atoms or molecules by their random motion from one part of a medium to another. **4** *Physics.* the transmission or reflection of electromagnetic radiation, esp. light, in which the radiation is scattered in many directions. **5** *Anthropol.* the transmission of social institutions, skills, and myths from one culture to another.

diffusionism (dɪ'fju:ʒən,ɪzəm) *n Anthropol.* the theory that diffusion is responsible for the similarities between different cultures.
▸**dif'fusionist** *n, adj*

diffusive (dɪ'fju:sɪv) *adj* characterized by diffusion.
▸**dif'fusively** *adv* ▸**dif'fusiveness** *n*

dig ❶ (dɪg) *vb* **digs, digging, dug. 1** (when *tr,* often foll. by *up*) to cut into, break up, and turn over or remove (earth, etc.), esp. with a spade. **2** to excavate (a hole, tunnel, etc.) by digging, usually with an implement or (of animals) with claws, etc. **3** (often foll. by *through*) to make or force (one's way): *he dug his way through the crowd.* **4** (*tr;* often foll. by *out* or *up*) to obtain by digging. **5** (*tr;* often foll. by *out* or *up*) to find by effort or searching: *to dig out facts.* **6** (*tr;* foll. by *in* or *into*) to thrust or jab. **7** (*tr;* foll. by *in* or *into*) to mix (compost, etc.) with soil by digging. **8** (*intr;* foll. by *in* or *into*) *Inf.* to begin vigorously to do something. **9** (*tr*) *Inf.* to like, understand, or appreciate. **10** (*intr*) *US sl.* to work hard, esp. for an examination. ◆ *n* **11** the act of digging. **12** a thrust or poke. **13** a cutting remark. **14** *Inf.* an archaeological excavation. **15** *Austral. & NZ inf.* short for **digger** (sense 4). ◆ See also **dig in.** [C13 *diggen,* from ?]

digest ❶ *vb* (dɪ'dʒest, daɪ-). **1** to subject (food) to a process of digestion. **2** (*tr*) to assimilate mentally. **3** *Chem.* to soften or disintegrate by the action of heat, moisture, or chemicals. **4** (*tr*) to arrange in a methodical order; classify. **5** (*tr*) to reduce to a summary. ◆ *n* ('daɪdʒest). **6** a comprehensive and systematic compilation of information or material, often condensed. **7** a magazine, periodical, etc., that summarizes news. **8** a compilation of rules of law. [C14: from LL *dīgesta* writings grouped under various heads, from L *dīgerere* to divide, from *di-* apart + *gerere* to bear]

Digest ('daɪdʒest) *n Roman law.* the books of law compiled by order of Justinian in the sixth century A.D.

digestible (dɪ'dʒestɪbᵊl, daɪ-) *adj* capable of being digested.
▸**di,gesti'bility** *n*

digestion ❶ (dɪ'dʒestʃən, daɪ-) *n* **1** the act or process in living organisms of breaking down food into easily absorbed substances by the action of enzymes, etc. **2** mental assimilation, esp. of ideas. **3** the decomposition of sewage by bacteria. **4** *Chem.* the treatment of material with heat, solvents, etc., to cause decomposition. [C14: from OF, from L *digestiō* a dissolving, digestion]
▸**di'gestional** *adj*

digestive (dɪ'dʒestɪv, daɪ-) *or* **digestant** (daɪ'dʒestənt) *adj* **1** relating to, aiding, or subjecting to digestion. ◆ *n* **2** any substance that aids digestion.
▸**di'gestively** *adv*

digestive biscuit *n* a round semisweet biscuit made from wholemeal flour.

digger ('dɪgə) *n* **1** a person, animal, or machine that digs. **2** a miner. **3** a tool or machine used for excavation. **4** (*sometimes cap.*) *Austral. & NZ inf.* an Australian or New Zealander, esp. a soldier: often used as a friendly term of address.

diggings ('dɪgɪŋz) *pl n* **1** (*functioning as pl*) material that has been dug out. **2** (*functioning as sing or pl*) a place where mining has taken place. **3** (*functioning as pl*) *Brit. inf.* a less common name for **digs.**

dight (daɪt) *vb* **dights, dighting, dight** *or* **dighted.** (*tr*) *Arch.* to adorn or equip, as for battle. [OE *dihtan* to compose, from L *dictāre* to DICTATE]

dig in ❶ *vb* (*adv*) **1** *Mil.* to dig foxholes, trenches, etc. **2** *Inf.* to entrench (oneself). **3** (*intr*) *Inf.* to defend a position firmly, as in an argument. **4** (*intr*) *Inf.* to begin to eat vigorously: *don't wait, just dig in.* **5 dig one's heels in.** *Inf.* to refuse to move or be persuaded.

digit ❶ ('dɪdʒɪt) *n* **1** a finger or toe. **2** any of the ten Arabic numerals from 0 to 9. [C15: from L *digitus* toe, finger]

digital ('dɪdʒɪtᵊl) *adj* **1** of, resembling, or possessing a digit or digits. **2** performed with the fingers. **3** representing data as a series of numerical values. **4** displaying information as numbers rather than by a pointer moving over a dial. ◆ *n* **5** *Music.* a key on a piano, harpsichord, etc.
▸**'digitally** *adv*

digital audio tape *n* magnetic tape on which sound is recorded digitally, giving high-fidelity reproduction. Abbrev.: **DAT.**

digital camera *n* a camera that produces digital images, which can be stored on a computer, displayed on a screen, and printed.

digital clock *or* **watch** *n* a clock or watch in which the time is indicated by digits rather than by hands on a dial.

digital compact cassette *n* a magnetic tape cassette on which sound can be recorded in digital format. Abbrev.: **DCC.**

digital computer *n* an electronic computer in which the input is discrete, consisting of numbers, letters, etc. that are represented internally in binary notation.

digitalin (,dɪdʒɪ'teɪlɪn) *n* a poisonous glycoside extracted from digitalis and used in treating heart disease. [C19: from DIGITAL(IS) + -IN]

digitalis (,dɪdʒɪ'teɪlɪs) *n* **1** any of a genus of Eurasian plants such as the foxglove, having long spikes of bell-shaped flowers. **2** a drug prepared from the dried leaves of the foxglove: used medicinally as a heart stimulant. [C17: from NL, from L: relating to a finger; based on G *Fingerhut* foxglove, lit.: finger-hat]

digitalize *or* **digitalise** ('dɪdʒɪtə,laɪz) *vb* **digitalizes, digitalizing, digitalized** *or* **digitalises, digitalising, digitalised.** (*tr*) another word for **digitize.**

digital mapping *n* a method of preparing maps in which the data is stored in a computer for ease of access and updating.
▸**digital map** *n*

digital recording *n* a sound recording process that converts audio or analogue signals into a series of pulses that correspond to the voltage level.

digital television *n* television in which the picture information is transmitted in digital form and decoded at the receiver.

digital video *n* video output based on digital rather than analogue signals.

digitate ('dɪdʒɪ,teɪt) *or* **digitated** *adj* **1** (of leaves) having the leaflets in the form of a spread hand. **2** (of animals) having digits.
▸**'digi,tately** *adv* ▸**,digi'tation** *n*

digitigrade ('dɪdʒɪtɪ,greɪd) *adj* **1** (of dogs, cats, horses, etc.) walking so that only the toes touch the ground. ◆ *n* **2** a digitigrade animal.

digitize *or* **digitise** ('dɪdʒɪ,taɪz) *vb* **digitizes, digitizing, digitized** *or* **digitises, digitising, digitised.** (*tr*) to transcribe (data) into a digital form for processing by a computer.
▸**,digiti'zation** *or* **,digiti'sation** *n* ▸**'digi,tizer** *or* **'digi,tiser** *n*

dignified ❶ ('dɪgnɪ,faɪd) *adj* characterized by dignity of manner or appearance; stately; noble.
▸**'digni,fiedly** *adv* ▸**'digni,fiedness** *n*

dignify ❶ ('dɪgnɪ,faɪ) *vb* **dignifies, dignifying, dignified.** (*tr*) **1** to invest with honour or dignity. **2** to add distinction to. **3** to add a semblance of

THESAURUS

conscious, self-effacing, sheepish, shrinking, suspicious, timid, timorous, unassertive, unassuming, unobtrusive, unsure, withdrawn

diffuse *vb* **1-3** = **spread,** circulate, dispel, dispense, disperse, disseminate, dissipate, distribute, propagate, scatter ◆ *adj* **4** = **spread out,** dispersed, scattered, unconcentrated **5** = **rambling,** circumlocutory, copious, diffusive, digressive, discursive, long-winded, loose, maundering, meandering, prolix, vague, verbose, waffling (*inf.*), wordy
Antonyms *adj* ≠ **spread out:** concentrated ≠ **rambling:** apposite, brief, compendious, concise, succinct, terse, to the point

diffusion *n* **1** = **spread,** circulation, dispersal, dispersion, dissemination, dissipation, distribution, expansion, propaganda, propagation, scattering **2** = **rambling,** circuitousness, diffuseness, digressiveness, discursiveness, longwindedness, prolixity, verbiage, verbosity, wandering, wordiness

dig *vb* **1, 2** = **excavate,** break up, burrow, delve, gouge, grub, hoe, hollow out, mine, penetrate, pierce, quarry, scoop, till, tunnel, turn over **4** *with* **out** *or* **up** = **find,** bring to light, come across, come up with, discover, expose, extricate, retrieve, root (*inf.*), rootle, uncover, unearth, uproot **5** = **investigate,** delve, dig down, go into, probe, research, search **6** = **poke,** drive, jab, prod, punch, thrust **9** *Informal* = **like,** appreciate, enjoy, follow, groove (*dated sl.*), understand ◆ *n* **12** = **poke,** jab, prod, punch, thrust **13** = **cutting remark,** barb, crack, gibe, insult, jeer, quip, sneer, taunt, wisecrack (*inf.*)

digest *vb* **1** = **ingest,** absorb, assimilate, concoct, dissolve, incorporate, macerate **2** = **take in,** absorb, assimilate, con, consider, contemplate, grasp, master, meditate, ponder, study, understand ◆ *n* **6** = **summary,** abridgment, abstract, compendium, condensation, epitome, précis, résumé, synopsis

digestion *n* **1** = **ingestion,** absorption, assimilation, conversion, incorporation, transformation

dig in *vb* **1-3** = **entrench,** defend, establish, fortify, maintain *Informal* **4** = **start eating,** begin, fall to, set about, tuck in (*inf.*)

digit *n* **1** = **finger,** toe **2** = **number,** figure, numeral

dignified *adj* = **distinguished,** august, decorous, exalted, formal, grave, honourable, imposing, lofty, lordly, noble, reserved, solemn, stately, upright
Antonyms *adj* crass, inelegant, unbecoming, undignified, unseemly, vulgar

dignify *vb* **1, 2** = **distinguish,** adorn, advance, dignity to, esp. by the use of a pretentious name or title. [C15: from OF *dignifier*, from LL *dignificāre*, from L *dignus* worthy + *facere* to make]

dignitary ➊ ('dɪgnɪtərɪ) *n, pl* **dignitaries.** a person of high official position or rank.

dignity ➊ ('dɪgnɪtɪ) *n, pl* **dignities. 1** a formal, stately, or grave bearing. **2** the state or quality of being worthy of honour. **3** relative importance; rank. **4** sense of self-importance (often in **stand** (*or* **be**) **on one's dignity, beneath one's dignity**). **5** high rank, esp. in government or the church. [C13: from OF *dignite*, from L *dignitās* merit, from *dignus* worthy]

digoxin (daɪ'dʒɒksɪn) *n* a glycoside extracted from digitalis leaves and used in the treatment of heart failure.

digraph ('daɪgrɑːf) *n* a combination of two letters used to represent a single sound such as *gh* in *tough*.
▸**digraphic** (daɪ'græfɪk) *adj*

digress ➊ (daɪ'gres) *vb* (*intr*) **1** to depart from the main subject in speech or writing. **2** to wander from one's path. [C16: from L *dīgressus* turned aside, from *dīgredī*, from *dis-* apart + *gradī* to go]
▸**di'gresser** *n* ▸**di'gression** *n*

digressive (daɪ'gresɪv) *adj* characterized by digression or tending to digress.
▸**di'gressively** *adv* ▸**di'gressiveness** *n*

digs ➊ (dɪgz) *pl n Brit. inf.* lodgings. [C19: from DIGGINGS, ? referring to where one *digs* or works, but see also DIG IN]

dihedral (daɪ'hiːdrəl) *adj* **1** having or formed by two intersecting planes. ◆ *n* **2** Also called: **dihedron, dihedral angle.** the figure formed by two intersecting planes. **3** the upward inclination of an aircraft wing in relation to the lateral axis.

dik-dik ('dɪkˌdɪk) *n* any of several small antelopes inhabiting semiarid regions of Africa. [C19: E African, prob. imit.]

dike (daɪk) *n, vb* **dikes, diking, diked.** a variant spelling of **dyke**[1].

diktat ('dɪktɑːt) *n* **1** a decree or settlement imposed, esp. by a ruler or a victorious nation. **2** a dogmatic statement. [from G: dictation, from L *dictātum*, from *dictāre* to DICTATE]

dilapidate ➊ (dɪ'læpɪˌdeɪt) *vb* **dilapidates, dilapidating, dilapidated.** to fall or cause to fall into ruin. [C16: from L *dīlapidāre* to waste, from *dis-* apart + *lapidāre* to stone, from *lapis* stone]
▸**diˌlapi'dation** *n*

dilapidated ➊ (dɪ'læpɪˌdeɪtɪd) *adj* falling to pieces or in a state of disrepair; shabby.

dilate ➊ (daɪ'leɪt, dɪ-) *vb* **dilates, dilating, dilated. 1** to make or become wider or larger. **2** (*intr*; often foll. by *on* or *upon*) to speak or write at length. [C14: from L *dīlātāre* to spread out, from *dis-* apart + *lātus* wide]
▸**di'latable** *adj* ▸**diˌlata'bility** *n* ▸**di'lation** *or* **dilatation** (ˌdaɪlə'teɪʃən) *n*
▸**dilative** (daɪ'leɪtɪv) *adj*

dilatory ➊ ('dɪlətərɪ, -trɪ) *adj* **1** tending to delay or waste time. **2** intended to waste time or defer action. [C15: from LL *dīlātōrius* inclined to delay, from *differre* to postpone; see DIFFER]
▸**'dilatorily** *adv* ▸**'dilatoriness** *n*

dildo *or* **dildoe** ('dɪldəʊ) *n, pl* **dildos** *or* **dildoes.** an object used as a substitute for an erect penis. [C16: from ?]

dilemma ➊ (dɪ'lemə, daɪ-) *n* **1** a situation necessitating a choice between two equally undesirable alternatives. **2** a problem that seems incapable of a solution. **3** *Logic.* a type of argument which forces the maintainer of a proposition to accept one of two conclusions each of which contradicts the original assertion. **4 on the horns of a dilemma. 4a** faced with the choice between two equally unpalatable alternatives. **4b** in an awkward situation. [C16: via L from Gk, from DI-[1] + *lēmma* proposition, from *lambanein* to grasp]
▸**dilemmatic** (ˌdɪlɪ'mætɪk) *adj*

> **USAGE NOTE** The use of *dilemma* to refer to a problem that seems incapable of a solution is considered by some people to be incorrect.

dilettante ➊ (ˌdɪlɪ'tɑːntɪ) *n, pl* **dilettantes** *or* **dilettanti** (-'tɑːntɪ). **1** a person whose interest in a subject is superficial rather than professional. **2** a person who loves the arts. ◆ *adj* **3** of or characteristic of a dilettante. [C18: from It., from *dilettare* to delight, from L *dēlectāre*]
▸**ˌdilet'tantish** *or* **ˌdilet'tanteish** *adj* ▸**ˌdilet'tantism** *or* **ˌdilet'tanteism** *n*

diligence[1] ➊ ('dɪlɪdʒəns) *n* **1** steady and careful application. **2** proper attention or care. [C14: from L *dīligentia* care]

diligence[2] ('dɪlɪdʒəns) *n History.* a stagecoach. [C18: from F, shortened from *carosse de diligence*, lit.: coach of speed]

diligent ➊ ('dɪlɪdʒənt) *adj* **1** careful and persevering in carrying out tasks or duties. **2** carried out with care and perseverance: *diligent work.* [C14: from OF, from L *dīligere* to value, from *dis-* apart + *legere* to read]
▸**'diligently** *adv*

dill[1] (dɪl) *n* **1** an aromatic Eurasian plant with umbrella-shaped clusters of yellow flowers. **2** the leaves or fruits of this plant, used for flavouring and in medicine. [OE *dile*]

dill[2] (dɪl) *n Austral. & NZ sl.* a fool. [C20: from DILLY[2]]

dill pickle *n* a pickled cucumber flavoured with dill.

dilly[1] ('dɪlɪ) *n, pl* **dillies.** *Sl., chiefly US & Canad.* a person or thing that is remarkable. [C20: ?from girl's name *Dilly*]

dilly[2] ('dɪlɪ) *adj* **dillier, dilliest.** *Austral. sl.* silly. [C20: from E dialect, ?from SILLY]

dilly bag *n Austral.* a small bag, esp., formerly, one made of plaited grass, etc., often used for carrying food. [from Abor. *dilly* small bag or basket]

dilly-dally ➊ (ˌdɪlɪ'dælɪ) *vb* **dilly-dallies, dilly-dallying, dilly-dallied.** (*intr*) *Inf.* to loiter or vacillate. [C17: by reduplication from DALLY]

dilute ➊ (daɪ'luːt) *vb* **dilutes, diluting, diluted. 1** to make or become less concentrated, esp. by adding water or a thinner. **2** to make or become weaker in force, effect, etc. ◆ *adj* **3** *Chem.* **3a** (of a solution, etc.) having a low concentration. **3b** (of a substance) present in solution, esp. a weak solution in water: *dilute acetic acid.* [C16: from L *dīluere*, from *dis-* apart + *-luere*, from *lavāre* to wash]
▸**di'luter** *n*

dilution (daɪ'luːʃən) *n* **1** the act of diluting or state of being diluted. **2** a diluted solution.

diluvial (daɪ'luːvɪəl, dɪ-) *or* **diluvian** *adj* of or connected with a deluge, esp. with the great Flood described in Genesis. [C17: from LL *dīluviālis*, from L *dīluere* to wash away; see DILUTE]

dim ➊ (dɪm) *adj* **dimmer, dimmest. 1** badly illuminated. **2** not clearly seen; faint. **3** having weak or indistinct vision. **4** mentally dull. **5** not clear in the mind; obscure: *a dim memory.* **6** lacking in brightness or

THESAURUS

aggrandize, elevate, ennoble, exalt, glorify, grace, honour, promote, raise

dignitary *n* = **public figure**, bigwig (*inf.*), celeb (*inf.*), high-up (*inf.*), notability, notable, personage, pillar of society, pillar of the church, pillar of the state, V.I.P., worthy

dignity *n* **1** = **decorum**, courtliness, grandeur, gravity, hauteur, loftiness, majesty, nobility, propriety, solemnity, stateliness **3** = **honour**, elevation, eminence, excellence, glory, greatness, importance, nobleness, rank, respectability, standing, station, status **4** = **self-importance**, *amour-propre*, pride, self-esteem, self-possession, self-regard, self-respect

digress *vb* **1** = **wander**, be diffuse, depart, deviate, diverge, drift, expatiate, get off the point *or* subject, go off at a tangent, meander, ramble, stray, turn aside

digression *n* **1** = **departure**, apostrophe, aside, detour, deviation, divergence, diversion, footnote, obiter dictum, parenthesis, straying, wandering

digs *pl n Brit. informal* = **lodgings**, accommodation, quarters, rooms

dilapidated *adj* = **ruined**, battered, beat-up, broken-down, crumbling, decayed, decaying, decrepit, fallen in, falling apart, gone to rack and ruin, in ruins, neglected, ramshackle, rickety, ruinous, run-down, shabby, shaky, tumbledown, uncared for, worn-out

dilapidation *n* = **ruin**, collapse, decay, demolition, destruction, deterioration, disintegration, disrepair, dissolution, downfall, waste, wear and tear

dilate *vb* **1** = **enlarge**, broaden, distend, expand, extend, puff out, stretch, swell, widen **2** = **expand**, amplify, be profuse, be prolix, descant, detail, develop, dwell on, enlarge, expatiate, expound, spin out
Antonyms *vb* ≠ **enlarge:** compress, constrict, contract, narrow, shrink

dilation *n* **1** = **enlargement**, broadening, dilatation, distension, expansion, extension, increase, spread

dilatory *adj* **1, 2** = **time-wasting**, backward, behindhand, dallying, delaying, laggard, lingering, loitering, procrastinating, putting off, slack, slow, sluggish, snail-like, tardy, tarrying
Antonyms *adj* on-the-ball (*inf.*), prompt, punctual, sharp (*inf.*)

dilemma *n* **2** = **predicament**, difficulty, embarrassment, fix (*inf.*), how-do-you-do (*inf.*), jam (*inf.*), mess, perplexity, pickle (*inf.*), plight, problem, puzzle, quandary, spot (*inf.*), strait, tight corner *or* spot **4a on the horns of a dilemma** = **between the devil and the deep blue sea**, between a rock and a hard place (*inf.*), between Scylla and Charybdis

dilettante *n* **1** = **amateur**, aesthete, dabbler, nonprofessional, trifler

diligence[1] *n* **1, 2** = **application**, activity, assiduity, assiduousness, attention, attentiveness, care, constancy, earnestness, heedfulness, industry, intentness, laboriousness, perseverance, sedulousness

diligent *adj* **1, 2** = **hard-working**, active, assiduous, attentive, busy, careful, conscientious, constant, earnest, indefatigable, industrious, laborious, painstaking, persevering, persistent, sedulous, studious, tireless
Antonyms *adj* careless, dilatory, good-for-nothing, inconstant, indifferent, lazy

dilly-dally *vb Informal* = **dawdle**, dally, delay, dither (*chiefly Brit.*), falter, fluctuate, hesitate, hover, hum and haw, linger, loiter, potter, procrastinate, shillyshally (*inf.*), trifle, vacillate, waver

dilute *vb* **1** = **water down**, adulterate, cut, make thinner, thin (out), weaken **2** = **reduce**, attenuate, decrease, diffuse, diminish, lessen, mitigate, temper, weaken
Antonyms *vb* ≠ **water down:** concentrate, condense, strengthen, thicken ≠ **reduce:** intensify, strengthen

diluted *adj* **1, 2** = **watered down**, adulterated, cut, dilute, thinned, watery, weak, weakened, wishy-washy (*inf.*)

dim *adj* **1** = **poorly lit**, caliginous (*arch.*), cloudy, dark, darkish, dusky, grey, overcast, shadowy, tenebrous, unilluminated **2** = **unclear**, bleary, blurred, faint, fuzzy, ill-defined, indistinct, obscured, shadowy **4** *Informal* = **stupid**, braindead (*inf.*), dense, doltish, dozy (*Brit. inf.*), dull, dumb (*inf.*), obtuse, slow, slow on the uptake (*inf.*), thick **5** = **obscure**, confused, hazy, imperfect, indistinct, intangible, remote, shadowy, vague **6** = **dull**, dingy, feeble, lacklustre, muted, opaque, pale, sullied, tarnished, weak **7 take a dim view** = **disapprove**, be displeased, be sceptical, look askance, reject, suspect, take exception, view with disfavour ◆ *vb* **8** = **dull**, bedim, blur, cloud, darken, fade, lower, obscure, tarnish, turn down
Antonyms *adj* ≠ **poorly lit:** bright, clear, cloudless, fair, limpid, pleasant, sunny, unclouded ≠ **un-**

lustre. 7 unfavourable, gloomy or disapproving (esp. in **take a dim view**). ◆ *vb* **dims, dimming, dimmed.** 8 to become or cause to become dim. 9 (*tr*) to cause to seem less bright. 10 the US and Canad. word for **dip** (sense 5). [OE *dimm*]
▸'**dimly** *adv* ▸'**dimness** *n*

dim. *abbrev. for:* 1 dimension. 2 Also: **dimin.** *Music.* diminuendo. 3 Also: **dimin.** diminutive.

dime (daɪm) *n* 1 a coin of the US and Canada, worth one tenth of a dollar or ten cents. 2 **a dime a dozen.** very cheap or common. [C14: from OF *disme,* from L *decimus* tenth, from *decem* ten]

dimenhydrinate (ˌdaɪmenˈhaɪdrɪˌneɪt) *n* a crystalline substance, used as an antihistamine and for the prevention of nausea, esp. in travel sickness. [from DI-[1] + ME(THYL) + (AMI)N(E) + (*diphen*)*hydr*(*am*)*in*(*e*) + -ATE[1]]

dime novel *n US.* (formerly) a cheap melodramatic novel, usually in paperback.

dimension ❶ (dɪˈmenʃən) *n* 1 (*often pl*) a measurement of the size of something in a particular direction, such as the length, width, height, or diameter. 2 (*often pl*) scope; size; extent. 3 aspect: *a new dimension to politics.* 4 *Maths.* the number of coordinates required to locate a point in space. ◆ *vb* 5 (*tr*) *Chiefly US.* to cut to or mark with specified dimensions. [C14: from OF, from L *dīmensiō* an extent, from *dīmētīrī* to measure out, from *mētīrī*]
▸**di'mensional** *adj* ▸**di'mensionless** *adj*

dimer (ˈdaɪmə) *n Chem.* a compound the molecule of which is formed by the linking of two identical molecules. [C20: from DI-[1] + -MER]
▸**dimeric** (daɪˈmerɪk) *adj*

dimerize *or* **dimerise** (ˈdaɪməˌraɪz) *vb* **dimerizes, dimerizing, dimerized** *or* **dimerises, dimerising, dimerised.** to react or cause to react to form a dimer.
▸ˌ**dimeri'zation** *or* ˌ**dimeri'sation** *n*

dimeter (ˈdɪmɪtə) *n Prosody.* a line of verse consisting of two metrical feet or a verse written in this metre.

dimethylformamide (daɪˌmiːθaɪlˈfɔːməˌmaɪd) *n* a colourless liquid widely used as a solvent and sometimes as a catalyst. Formula: $(CH_3)_2NCHO$. Abbrev.: **DMF.**

dimethylsulphoxide (daɪˌmiːθaɪlsʌlˈfɒksaɪd) *n* a liquid used as a solvent and in medicine to improve the penetration of drugs applied to the skin. Abbrev.: **DMSO.**

diminish ❶ (dɪˈmɪnɪʃ) *vb* 1 to make or become smaller, fewer, or less. 2 (*tr*) *Archit.* to cause to taper. 3 (*tr*) *Music.* to decrease (a minor or perfect interval) by a semitone. 4 to reduce in authority, status, etc. [C15: blend of *diminuen* to lessen (from L *dēminuere,* from *minuere*) + archaic *minish* to lessen]
▸**di'minishable** *adj*

diminished (dɪˈmɪnɪʃt) *adj* 1 reduced or lessened; made smaller. 2 *Music.* denoting any minor or perfect interval reduced by a semitone.

diminished responsibility *n Law.* a plea under which mental derangement is submitted as demonstrating lack of criminal responsibility.

diminishing returns *pl n Econ.* progressively smaller increases in output resulting from equal increases in production.

diminuendo (dɪˌmɪnjʊˈendəʊ) *Music.* ◆ *n, pl* **diminuendos.** 1a a gradual decrease in loudness. Symbol: 5 1b a musical passage affected by a diminuendo. ◆ *adj* 2 gradually decreasing in loudness. 3 with a diminuendo. [C18: from It., from *diminuire* to DIMINISH]

diminution ❶ (ˌdɪmɪˈnjuːʃən) *n* 1 reduction; decrease. 2 *Music.* the presentation of the subject of a fugue, etc., in which the note values are reduced in length. [C14: from L *dēminūtiō;* see DIMINISH]

diminutive ❶ (dɪˈmɪnjʊtɪv) *adj* 1 very small; tiny. 2 *Grammar.* 2a denoting an affix added to a word to convey the meaning *small* or *unimportant* or to express affection. 2b denoting a word formed by the addition of a diminutive affix. ◆ *n* 3 *Grammar.* a diminutive word or affix. 4 a tiny person or thing.
▸**di'minutively** *adv* ▸**di'minutiveness** *n*

dimissory (dɪˈmɪsərɪ) *adj* 1 granting permission to be ordained: *a bishop's dimissory letter.* 2 granting permission to depart.

dimity (ˈdɪmɪtɪ) *n, pl* **dimities.** a light strong cotton fabric with woven stripes or squares. [C15: from Med. L *dimitum,* from Gk *dimiton,* from DI-[1] + *mitos* thread of the warp]

dimmer (ˈdɪmə) *n* 1 a device for dimming an electric light. 2 (*often pl*) *US.* 2a a dipped headlight on a road vehicle. 2b a parking light on a car.

dimorphism (daɪˈmɔːfɪzəm) *n* 1 the occurrence within a plant of two distinct forms of any part. 2 the occurrence in an animal species of two distinct types of individual. 3 a property of certain substances that enables them to exist in two distinct crystalline forms.
▸**di'morphic** *or* **di'morphous** *adj*

dimple (ˈdɪmpᵊl) *n* 1 a small natural dent, esp. on the cheeks or chin. 2 any slight depression in a surface. ◆ *vb* **dimples, dimpling, dimpled.** 3 to make or become dimpled. 4 (*intr*) to produce dimples by smiling. [C13 *dympull*]
▸'**dimply** *adj*

dim sum (ˌdɪm ˈsʌm) *n* a Chinese appetizer of steamed dumplings containing various fillings. [Cantonese]

dimwit ❶ (ˈdɪmˌwɪt) *n Inf.* a stupid or silly person.
▸ˌ**dim-'witted** *adj* ▸ˌ**dim-'wittedness** *n*

din ❶ (dɪn) *n* 1 a loud discordant confused noise. ◆ *vb* **dins, dinning, dinned.** 2 (*tr; usually foll. by into*) to instil by constant repetition. 3 (*tr*) to subject to a din. 4 (*intr*) to make a din. [OE *dynn*]

DIN *n* 1 a formerly used logarithmic expression of the speed of a photographic film, plate, etc.; high-speed films have high numbers. 2 a system of standard plugs, sockets, etc. formerly used for interconnecting domestic audio and video equipment. [C20: from G *D*(*eutsche*) *I*(*ndustrie*) *N*(*ormen*) German Industry Standards]

dinar (ˈdiːnɑː) *n* the standard monetary unit of Algeria, Bahrain, Bosnia-Herzegovina, Iraq, Jordan, Kuwait, Libya, Sudan, Tunisia, and Yugoslavia. [C17: from Ar., from LGk *dēnarion,* from L *dēnārius* DENARIUS]

dine ❶ (daɪn) *vb* **dines, dining, dined.** 1 (*intr*) to eat dinner. 2 (*intr; often foll. by on, off,* or *upon*) to make one's meal (of): *the guests dined upon roast beef.* 3 (*tr*) *Inf.* to entertain to dinner (esp. in **wine and dine someone**). [C13: from OF *disner,* from Vulgar L *disjējūnāre* (unattested), from *dis-* not + LL *jējūnāre* to fast]

dine out *vb* (*intr, adv*) 1 to dine away from home. 2 (foll. by *on*) to have dinner at the expense of someone else mainly for the sake of one's conversation about (a subject or story).

diner (ˈdaɪnə) *n* 1 a person eating a meal, esp. in a restaurant. 2 *Chiefly US & Canad.* a small cheap restaurant. 3 a fashionable bar, or a section of one, where food is served.

dinette (daɪˈnet) *n* an alcove or small area for use as a dining room.

ding (dɪŋ) *vb* 1 to ring, esp. with tedious repetition. 2 (*tr*) another word for **din** (sense 2). ◆ *n* 3 an imitation of the sound of a bell. [C13: prob. imit., but infl. by DIN + RING[2]]

dingbat (ˈdɪŋˌbæt) *n Austral. sl.* a crazy or stupid person.

dingbats (ˈdɪŋˌbæts) *pl n Austral. & NZ sl.* an attack of nervousness, irritation, or loathing: *he had the dingbats.*

ding-dong *n* 1 the sound of a bell or bells. 2 an imitation of the sound of a bell. 3a a violent exchange of blows or words. 3b (*as modifier*): *a ding-dong battle.* ◆ *adj* 4 sounding or ringing repeatedly. [C16: imit.; see DING]

dinges (ˈdɪŋəs) *n S. African inf.* a jocular word for something whose name is unknown or forgotten; thingumabob. [from Afrik., from Du. *dinges* thing]

dinghy (ˈdɪŋɪ, ˈdɪŋgɪ) *n, pl* **dinghies.** any small boat, powered by sail, oars, or outboard motor. Also (esp. formerly): **dingy, dingey.** [C19: from Hindi or Bengali *dingi*]

dingle ❶ (ˈdɪŋgᵊl) *n* a small wooded dell. [C13: from ?]

dingo (ˈdɪŋgəʊ) *n, pl* **dingoes.** a wild dog of Australia, having a yellowish-brown coat and resembling a wolf. [C18: from Abor.]

dingy ❶ (ˈdɪndʒɪ) *adj* **dingier, dingiest.** 1 lacking light or brightness; drab. 2 dirty; discoloured. [C18: perhaps from an earlier dialect word rel. to OE *dynge* dung]
▸'**dingily** *adv* ▸'**dinginess** *n*

dining car *n* a railway coach in which meals are served at tables. Also called: **restaurant car.**

dining room *n* a room where meals are eaten.

dinitrogen oxide (daɪˈnaɪtrədʒən) *n* the systematic name for **nitrous oxide.**

dinkie (ˈdɪŋkɪ) *n* 1 an affluent married childless person. ◆ *adj* 2 designed for or appealing to dinkies. [C20: from *d*(*ouble*) *i*(*ncome*) *n*(*o*) *k*(*ids*) + -IE]

THESAURUS

clear: bright, brilliant, clear, distinct, limpid, palpable ≠ **stupid:** acute, astute, aware, brainy, bright, clever, intelligent, keen, quick-witted, sharp, smart

dimension *n* 1, 2 *often plural* = **measurement**, amplitude, bulk, capacity, extent, proportions, size, volume

diminish *vb* 1 = **decrease**, abate, contract, curtail, cut, downsize, lessen, lower, reduce, retrench, shrink, taper, weaken 4 = **belittle**, cheapen, demean, depreciate, devalue
Antonyms *vb* ≠ **decrease:** amplify, augment, enhance, enlarge, expand, grow, heighten, increase

diminution *n* 1 = **decrease**, abatement, contraction, curtailment, cut, cutback, decay, decline, deduction, lessening, reduction, retrenchment, weakening

diminutive *adj* 1 = **small**, bantam, Lilliputian, little, midget, mini, miniature, minute, petite, pocket(-sized), pygmy *or* pigmy, teensy-weensy, teeny-weeny, tiny, undersized, wee
Antonyms *adj* big, colossal, enormous, giant, gigantic, great, immense, jumbo (*inf.*), king-size, massive (*inf.*)

dimwit *n Informal* = **idiot**, blockhead, bonehead (*sl.*), booby, dullard, dumb-ass (*sl.*), dunce, dunderhead, fathead (*inf.*), gobshite (*Irish taboo sl.*), ignoramus, lamebrain (*inf.*), nitwit (*inf.*), numbskull *or* numskull

dim-witted *adj Informal* = **stupid**, braindead (*inf.*), dense, dim, doltish, dopey (*inf.*), dozy (*Brit. inf.*), dull, dumb (*inf.*), dumb-ass (*sl.*), obtuse, slow, slow on the uptake, thick (*inf.*), thick-skulled, unperceptive
Antonyms *adj* alert, astute, bright, clever, keen, perceptive, quick on the uptake, quick-witted, sharp, shrewd, smart

din *n* 1 = **noise**, babel, clamour, clangour, clash, clatter, commotion, crash, hubbub, hullabaloo, outcry, pandemonium, racket, row, shout, uproar ◆ *vb* 2 *usually foll. by* **into** = **instil**, drum into, go on at, hammer into, inculcate, instruct, teach
Antonyms *n* ≠ **noise:** calm, calmness, hush, peace, quiet, quietness, silence, tranquillity

dine *vb* 1 = **eat**, banquet, chow down (*sl.*), feast, lunch, sup 2 **dine on** *or* **off** = **eat**, consume, feed on

dingle *n* = **dell**, dale, glen, hollow, vale, valley

dingy *adj* 1 = **dull**, bedimmed, colourless, dark, dim, drab, dreary, dusky, faded, gloomy, murky, obscure, sombre 2 = **discoloured**, dirty, grimy, seedy, shabby, soiled, tacky (*inf.*)

dinkum ('dɪŋkəm) *adj Austral. & NZ inf.* **1** genuine or right: *a fair dinkum offer.* **2 dinkum oil.** the truth. [C19: from E dialect: work, from ?]

dinky ⓣ ('dɪŋkɪ) *adj* **dinkier, dinkiest.** *Inf.* **1** *Brit.* small and neat; dainty. **2** *US.* inconsequential; insignificant. [C18: from Scot. & N English dialect *dink* neat, neatly dressed]

dinky-di ('dɪŋkɪ'daɪ) *adj Austral. inf.* typical: *dinky-di Pom idleness.* [C20: var. of DINKUM]

dinner ⓣ ('dɪnə) *n* **1** a meal taken in the evening. **2** a meal taken at midday, esp. when it is the main meal of the day; lunch. **3** a formal meal or banquet in honour of someone or something. **4** (*as modifier*): *dinner table; dinner hour.* [C13: from OF *disner;* see DINE]

dinner dance *n* a formal dinner followed by dancing.

dinner jacket *n* a man's semiformal evening jacket without tails, usually black. US and Canad. name: **tuxedo.**

dinner service *n* a set of matching plates, dishes, etc., suitable for serving a meal.

dinosaur ('daɪnəˌsɔː) *n* **1** any of a large order of extinct reptiles many of which were of gigantic size and abundant in the Mesozoic era. **2** a person or thing that is considered to be out of date. [C19: from NL *dinosaurus,* from Gk *deinos* fearful + *sauros* lizard]
▸ˌ**dino'saurian** *adj*

dint ⓣ (dɪnt) *n* **1 by dint of.** by means or use of: *by dint of hard work.* **2** *Arch.* a blow or a mark made by a blow. ◆ *vb* **3** (*tr*) to mark with dints. [OE *dynt*]

dioc. *abbrev. for:* **1** diocesan. **2** diocese.

diocesan (daɪ'ɒsɪsᵊn) *adj* **1** of or relating to a diocese. ◆ *n* **2** the bishop of a diocese.

diocese ⓣ ('daɪəsɪs) *n* the district under the jurisdiction of a bishop. [C14: from OF, from LL *diocēsis,* from Gk *dioikēsis* administration, from *dioikein* to manage a household, from *oikos* house]

diode ('daɪəʊd) *n* **1** a semiconductor device used in circuits for converting alternating current to direct current. **2** the earliest type of electronic valve having two electrodes between which a current can flow only in one direction. [C20: from DI-[1] + -ODE[2]]

dioecious (daɪ'iːʃəs) *adj* (of plants) having the male and female reproductive organs on separate plants. [C18: from NL *Dioecia* name of class, from DI-[1] + Gk *oikia* house]

Dionysian (ˌdaɪə'nɪzɪən) *adj* **1** of or relating to Dionysus, the Greek god of wine and revelry. **2** (*often not cap.*) wild or orgiastic.

Diophantine equation (ˌdaɪəʊ'fæntaɪn) *n* (in number theory) an equation in more than one variable, for which integral solutions are sought. [from *Diophantus,* 3rd century A.D., Gk mathematician]

dioptre *or US* **diopter** (daɪ'ɒptə) *n* a unit for measuring the refractive power of a lens: the reciprocal of the focal length of the lens expressed in metres. [C16: from L *dioptra* optical instrument, from Gk, from *dia-* through + *opsesthai* to see]
▸**di'optral** *adj*

dioptrics (daɪ'ɒptrɪks) *n* (*functioning as sing*) the branch of geometrical optics concerned with the formation of images by lenses. [C20: from DIOPTRE + -ICS]

diorama (ˌdaɪə'rɑːmə) *n* **1** a miniature three-dimensional scene, in which models of figures are seen against a background. **2** a picture made up of illuminated translucent curtains, viewed through an aperture. **3** a museum display, as of an animal, of a specimen in its natural setting. [C19: from F, from Gk *dia-* through + *horama* view, from *horan* to see]
▸**dioramic** (ˌdaɪə'ræmɪk) *adj*

dioxide (daɪ'ɒksaɪd) *n* any oxide containing two oxygen atoms per molecule, both of which are bonded to an atom of another element.

dioxin (daɪ'ɒksɪn) *n* any of various chemical by-products of the manufacture of certain herbicides and bactericides, esp. the extremely toxic tetrachlorodibenzoparadioxin (TCDD).

dip ⓣ (dɪp) *vb* **dips, dipping, dipped. 1** to plunge or be plunged quickly or briefly into a liquid, esp. to wet or coat. **2** (*intr*) to undergo a slight decline, esp. temporarily: *sales dipped in November.* **3** (*intr*) to slope downwards. **4** (*intr*) to sink quickly. **5** (*tr*) to switch (car headlights) from the main to the lower beam. US and Canad. word: **dim. 6** (*tr*) **6a** to immerse (sheep, etc.) briefly in a chemical to rid them of or prevent infestation by insects, etc. **6b** to immerse (grain, vegetables, or wood) in a preservative liquid. **7** (*tr*) to dye by immersing in a liquid. **8** (*tr*) to baptize (someone) by immersion. **9** (*tr*) to plate or galvanize (a metal, etc.) by immersion in an electrolyte or electrolytic cell. **10** (*tr*) to scoop up a liquid or something from a liquid in the hands or in a container. **11** to lower or be lowered briefly. **12** (*tr*) to make (a candle) by plunging the wick into melted wax. **13** (*intr*) to plunge a container, the hands, etc., into something, esp. to obtain an object. **14** (*intr*) (of an aircraft) to drop suddenly and then regain height. ◆ *n* **15** the act of dipping or state of being dipped. **16** a brief swim in water. **17a** any liquid chemical in which sheep, etc. are dipped. **17b** any liquid preservative into which objects are dipped. **18** a dye into which fabric is immersed. **19** a depression, esp. in a landscape. **20** something taken up by dipping. **21** a container used for dipping; dipper. **22** a momentary sinking down. **23** the angle of slope of rock strata, etc., from the horizontal plane. **24** the angle between the direction of the earth's magnetic field and the plane of the horizon; the angle that a magnetic needle free to swing in a vertical plane makes with the horizontal. **25** a creamy savoury mixture into which pieces of food are dipped before being eaten. **26** *Surveying.* the angular distance of the horizon below the plane of observation. **27** a candle made by plunging a wick into wax. **28** a momentary loss of altitude when flying. ◆ See also **dip into.** [OE *dyppan*]

dip. *or* **Dip.** *abbrev. for* diploma.

DipAD *abbrev. for* Diploma in Art and Design.

DipEd (in Britain) *abbrev. for* Diploma in Education.

diphtheria (dɪp'θɪərɪə) *n* an acute contagious disease caused by a bacillus, producing fever, severe prostration, and difficulty in breathing and swallowing as the result of swelling of the throat and the formation of a false membrane. [C19: NL, from F *diphthérie,* from Gk *diphthera* leather; from the nature of the membrane]
▸**diph'therial, diphtheritic** (ˌdɪpθə'rɪtɪk), *or* **diphtheric** (dɪp'θɛrɪk) *adj*

diphthong ('dɪfθɒŋ) *n* **1** a vowel sound, occupying a single syllable, during the articulation of which the tongue moves continuously from one position to another, as in the pronunciation of *a* in *late.* **2** a digraph or ligature representing a composite vowel such as this, as *ae* in *Caesar.* [C15: from LL *diphthongus,* from Gk *diphthongos,* from DI-[1] + *phthongos* sound]
▸**diph'thongal** *adj*

diphthongize *or* **diphthongise** ('dɪfθɒŋˌaɪz) *vb* **diphthongizes, diphthongizing, diphthongized** *or* **diphthongises, diphthongising, diphthongised.** (*often passive*) to make (a simple vowel) into a diphthong.
▸ˌ**diphthongi'zation** *or* ˌ**diphthongi'sation** *n*

dip into ⓣ *vb* (*intr, prep*) **1** to draw upon: *he dipped into his savings.* **2** to dabble (in); play at. **3** to read passages at random from (a book, newspaper, etc.).

diplodocus (ˌdɪpləʊ'dəʊkəs, dɪ'plɒdəkəs) *n, pl* **diplodocuses.** a herbivorous dinosaur characterized by a very long neck and tail and a total body length of 27 metres. [C19: from NL, from Gk *diplo-,* (from *diploos,* from DI-[1] + *-ploos* -fold) + *dokos* beam]

diploid ('dɪplɔɪd) *adj* **1** *Biol.* (of cells or organisms) having paired homologous chromosomes so that twice the haploid number is present. **2** double or twofold. ◆ *n* **3** a diploid cell or organism.
▸**dip'loidic** *adj*

diploma (dɪ'pləʊmə) *n* **1** a document conferring a qualification, recording success in examinations or successful completion of a course of study. **2** an official document that confers an honour or privilege. [C17: from L: official letter or document, lit.: letter folded double, from Gk]

diplomacy ⓣ (dɪ'pləʊməsɪ) *n, pl* **diplomacies. 1** the conduct of the relations of one state with another by peaceful means. **2** skill in the management of international relations. **3** tact, skill, or cunning in dealing with people. [C18: from F *diplomatie,* from *diplomatique* DIPLOMATIC]

diplomat ⓣ ('dɪpləˌmæt) *n* **1** an official such as an ambassador, engaged in diplomacy. **2** a person who deals with people tactfully or skilfully. ◆ Also called: **diplomatist** (dɪ'pləʊmətɪst).

diplomatic ⓣ (ˌdɪplə'mætɪk) *adj* **1** of or relating to diplomacy or diplomats. **2** skilled in negotiating, esp. between states or people. **3** tactful in dealing with people. [C18: from F *diplomatique* concerning the documents of diplomacy, from NL *diplōmaticus;* see DIPLOMA]
▸ˌ**diplo'matically** *adv*

diplomatic bag *n* a container or bag in which official mail is sent, free from customs inspection, to and from an embassy or consulate.

diplomatic corps *or* **body** *n* the entire body of diplomats accredited to a given state.

diplomatic immunity *n* the immunity from local jurisdiction and exemption from taxation in the country to which they are accredited afforded to diplomats.

Diplomatic Service *n* **1** (in Britain) the division of the Civil Service which provides diplomats to represent the UK abroad. **2** (*not caps.*) the equivalent institution of any other country.

dipole ('daɪˌpəʊl) *n* **1** two equal but opposite electric charges or magnetic poles separated by a small distance. **2** a molecule in which the centre of positive charge does not coincide with the centre of nega-

THESAURUS

dinky *adj* **1** *Brit. informal* = **cute,** dainty, mini, miniature, natty (*inf.*), neat, petite, small, trim

dinner *n* **1, 3** = **meal,** banquet, beanfeast (*Brit. inf.*), blowout (*sl.*), collation, feast, main meal, refection, repast, spread (*inf.*)

dint *n* **1** *As in* **by dint of** = **means,** force, power, use, virtue

diocese *n* = **bishopric,** see

dip *vb* **1** = **plunge,** bathe, douse, duck, dunk, immerse, rinse, souse **3** = **slope,** decline, descend, disappear, droop, drop (down), fade, fall, lower, sag, set, sink, slump, subside, tilt ◆ *n* **15** = **plunge,** douche, drenching, ducking, immersion, soaking **16** = **bathe,** dive, plunge, swim **17b** = **mixture,** concoction, dilution, infusion, preparation, solution, suspension **19** = **hollow,** basin, concavity, depression, hole, incline, slope **22** = **drop,** decline, fall, lowering, sag, slip, slump

dip into *vb* **1** = **draw upon,** reach into **2, 3** = **sample,** browse, dabble, glance at, peruse, play at, run over, skim, try

diplomacy *n* **1** = **statesmanship,** international negotiation, statecraft **2** = **tact,** artfulness, craft, delicacy, discretion, finesse, savoir-faire, skill, subtlety

Antonyms *n* ≠ **tact:** awkwardness, clumsiness, ineptness, tactlessness, thoughtlessness

diplomat *n* **2** = **negotiator,** conciliator, go-between, mediator, moderator, politician, public relations expert, tactician

diplomatic *adj* **3** = **tactful,** adept, discreet, polite, politic, prudent, sensitive, subtle

Antonyms *adj* impolitic, insensitive, rude, tactless, thoughtless, undiplomatic, unsubtle

tive charge. **3** a directional aerial consisting of two metal rods with a connecting wire fixed between them in the form of a T.
▸**di'polar** *adj*

dipole moment *n Chem.* a measure of the polarity in a chemical bond or molecule, equal to the product of one charge and the distance between the charges. Symbol: μ

dipper ('dɪpə) *n* **1** a ladle used for dipping. **2** Also called: **water ouzel.** any of a genus of aquatic songbirds that inhabit fast-flowing streams. **3** a person or thing that dips. **4** *Arch.* an Anabaptist. ◆ See also **big dipper.**

dippy ('dɪpɪ) *adj* **dippier, dippiest.** *Sl.* odd, eccentric, or crazy. [C20: from ?]

dipsomania (ˌdɪpsəʊ'meɪnɪə) *n* a compulsive desire to drink alcoholic beverages. [C19: NL, from Gk *dipsa* thirst + -MANIA]
▸ˌ**dipso'maniac** *n, adj*

dipstick ('dɪpˌstɪk) *n* **1** a graduated rod or strip dipped into a container to indicate the fluid level. **2** *Brit. sl.* a fool.

dip switch *n* a device for dipping car headlights.

dipteran ('dɪptərən) *or* **dipteron** ('dɪptəˌrɒn) *n* **1** any dipterous insect. ◆ *adj* **2** another word for **dipterous** (sense 1).

dipterous ('dɪptərəs) *adj* **1** Also: **dipteran.** of a large order of insects having a single pair of wings and sucking or piercing mouthparts. The group includes flies, mosquitoes, and midges. **2** *Bot.* having two winglike parts. [C18: from Gk *dipteros* two-winged]

diptych ('dɪptɪk) *n* **1** a pair of hinged wooden tablets with waxed surfaces for writing. **2** a painting or carving on two hinged panels. [C17: from Gk *diptukhos* folded together, from DI-[1] + *ptukhos* fold]

dire **T** ('daɪə) *adj* (*usually prenominal*) **1** Also: **direful.** disastrous; fearful. **2** desperate; urgent: *a dire need.* **3** foreboding disaster; ominous. [C16: from L *dīrus* ominous]
▸'**direly** *adv* ▸'**direness** *n*

direct **T** (dɪ'rɛkt, daɪ-) *vb* (*mainly tr*) **1** to conduct or control the affairs of. **2** (*also intr*) to give commands or orders with authority to (a person or group). **3** to tell or show (someone) the way to a place. **4** to aim, point, or cause to move towards a goal. **5** to address (a letter, etc.). **6** to address (remarks, etc.). **7** (*also intr*) **7a** to provide guidance to (actors, cameramen, etc.) in a play or film. **7b** to supervise the making or staging of (a film or play). **8** (*also intr*) to conduct (a piece of music or musicians), usually while performing oneself. ◆ *adj* **9** without delay or evasion; straightforward. **10** without turning aside; shortest; straight: *a direct route.* **11** without intervening persons or agencies: *a direct link.* **12** honest; frank. **13** (*usually prenominal*) precise; exact: *a direct quotation.* **14** diametrical: *the direct opposite.* **15** in an unbroken line of descent: *a direct descendant.* **16** (of government, decisions, etc.) by or from the electorate rather than through representatives. **17** *Logic, maths.* (of a proof) progressing from the premises to the conclusion, rather than eliminating the possibility of the falsehood of the conclusion. Cf. **indirect proof. 18** *Astron.* moving from west to east. Cf. **retrograde. 19** of or relating to direct current. **20** *Music.* (of an interval or chord) in root position; not inverted. ◆ *adv* **21** directly; straight. [C14: from L *dīrectus,* from *dīrigere* to guide, from *dis-* apart + *regere* to rule]
▸**di'rectness** *n*

direct access *n* a method of reading data from a computer file without reading through the file from the beginning.

direct action *n* action such as strikes or civil disobedience employed to obtain demands from an employer, government, etc.

direct current *n* a continuous electric current that flows in one direction only.

direct debit *n* an order given to a bank or building society by a holder of an account, instructing it to pay to a specified person or organization any sum demanded by that person or organization. Cf. **standing order.**

direct-grant school *n* (in Britain, formerly) a school financed by endowment, fees, and a state grant conditional upon admittance of a percentage of nonpaying pupils.

direction **T** (dɪ'rɛkʃən, daɪ-) *n* **1** the act of directing or the state of being directed. **2** management, control, or guidance. **3** the work of a stage or film director. **4** the course or line along which a person or thing moves, points, or lies. **5** the place towards which a person or thing is directed. **6** a line of action; course. **7** the name and address on a letter, parcel, etc. **8** *Music.* the process of conducting an orchestra, choir, etc. **9** *Music.* an instruction to indicate tempo, dynamics, mood, etc.

directional (dɪ'rɛkʃənᵊl, daɪ-) *adj* **1** of or relating to a spatial direction. **2** *Electronics.* **2a** having or relating to an increased sensitivity to radio waves, nuclear particles, etc., coming from a particular direction. **2b** (of an aerial) transmitting or receiving radio waves more effectively in some directions than in others. **3** *Physics, electronics.* concentrated in, following, or producing motion in a particular direction.
▸**diˌrection'ality** *n*

directional drilling *n* a method of drilling for oil in which the well is not drilled vertically, as when a number of wells are to be drilled from a single platform. Also called: **deviated drilling.**

direction finder *n* a device to determine the direction of incoming radio signals, used esp. as a navigation aid.

directions **T** (dɪ'rɛkʃənz, daɪ-) *pl n* (*sometimes sing*) instructions for doing something or for reaching a place.

directive **T** (dɪ'rɛktɪv, daɪ-) *n* **1** an instruction; order. ◆ *adj* **2** tending to direct; directing. **3** indicating direction.

directly **T** (dɪ'rɛktlɪ, daɪ-) *adv* **1** in a direct manner. **2** at once; without delay. **3** (foll. by *before* or *after*) immediately; just. ◆ *conj* **4** (*subordinating*) as soon as.

direct marketing *n* selling goods directly to consumers rather than through retailers, as by mail order, telephone selling, etc. Also called: **direct selling.**

direct object *n Grammar.* a noun, pronoun, or noun phrase whose referent receives the direct action of a verb. For example, *a book* in *They bought Anne a book.*

directoire (dɪ'rɛktwɑː) *adj* (of ladies' knickers) knee-length, with elastic at waist and knees. [C19: after fashions of the period of the French *Directoire* Directorate (1795–99)]

director **T** (dɪ'rɛktə, daɪ-) *n* **1** a person or thing that directs, controls, or regulates. **2** a member of the governing board of a business concern. **3** a person who directs the affairs of an institution, trust, etc. **4** the person responsible for the artistic and technical aspects of the making of a film or television programme or the staging of a play. Cf. **producer** (sense 3). **5** *Music.* another word (esp. US) for **conductor.**
▸ˌ**direc'torial** *adj* ▸ˌ**di'rectorˌship** *n* ▸**di'rectress** *fem n*

directorate (dɪ'rɛktərɪt, daɪ-) *n* **1** a board of directors. **2** Also: **directorship.** the position of director.

director-general *n, pl* **directors-general.** the head of a large organization such as the CBI or BBC.

Director of Public Prosecutions *n* (in Britain) an official who, as head of the Crown Prosecution Service, is responsible for conducting all criminal prosecutions initiated by the police. Abbrev.: **DPP.**

director's chair *n* a light wooden folding chair with arm rests and a canvas seat and back, as used by film directors.

directory (dɪ'rɛktərɪ, -trɪ; daɪ-) *n, pl* **directories. 1** a book listing names, addresses, telephone numbers, etc., of individuals or firms. **2** a book giving directions. **3** a book containing the rules to be observed in the forms of worship used in churches. **4** a directorate. **5** *Computing.* an area of a disk, Winchester disk, or floppy disk that contains the names and locations of files currently held on that disk. ◆ *adj* **6** directing.

Directory (dɪ'rɛktərɪ, -trɪ; daɪ-) *n* **the.** *History.* the body of five directors in power in France from 1795 until their overthrow by Napoleon in 1799. Also called: **French Directory.**

direct primary *n US government.* a primary in which voters directly select the candidates who will run for office.

direct selling *n* another name for **direct marketing.**

direct speech *or esp. US* **direct discourse** *n* the reporting of what someone has said or written by quoting his exact words.

direct tax *n* a tax paid by the person or organization on which it is levied.

dirge **T** (dɜːdʒ) *n* **1** a chant of lamentation for the dead. **2** the funeral service in its solemn or sung forms. **3** any mourning song or melody. [C13: from L *dīrigē* direct (imperative), opening word of antiphon used in the office of the dead]
▸'**dirgeful** *adj*

THESAURUS

dire *adj* **1 = disastrous,** alarming, appalling, awful, calamitous, cataclysmic, catastrophic, cruel, horrible, horrid, ruinous, terrible, woeful **2 = desperate,** critical, crucial, crying, drastic, exigent, extreme, now or never, pressing, urgent **3 = grim,** dismal, dreadful, fearful, gloomy, ominous, portentous

direct *vb* **1 = control,** administer, advise, call the shots, call the tune, conduct, dispose, govern, guide, handle, lead, manage, mastermind, oversee, preside over, regulate, rule, run, superintend, supervise **2 = order,** bid, charge, command, demand, dictate, enjoin, instruct **3 = guide,** indicate, lead, point in the direction of, point the way, show **5 = address,** label, mail, route, send, superscribe **6 = aim,** address, cast, fix, focus, intend, level, mean, point, train, turn ◆ *adj* **10 = straight,** nonstop, not crooked, shortest, through, unbroken, undeviating, uninterrupted **11 = first-hand,** face-to-face, head-on, immediate, personal **12 = straightforward,** candid, downright, frank, honest, man-to-man, matter-of-fact, open, outspoken, plain-spoken, round, sincere, straight, upfront (*inf.*)
Antonyms *adj* ≠ **straight:** circuitous, crooked, indirect ≠ **first-hand:** indirect, mediated ≠ **straightforward:** circuitous, crooked, devious, indirect, sly, subtle ≠ **explicit:** ambiguous, circuitous, indirect

direction *n* **2 = management,** administration, charge, command, control, government, guidance, leadership, order, oversight, superintendence, supervision **4 = way,** aim, bearing, course, line, path, road, route, track

directions *pl n* **= instructions,** briefing, guidance, guidelines, indication, plan, recommendation, regulations

directive *n* **1 = order,** canon, charge, command, decree, dictate, edict, fiat, imperative, injunction, instruction, mandate, notice, ordinance, regulation, ruling

directly *adv* **1 = straight,** by the shortest route, exactly, in a beeline, precisely, unswervingly, without deviation **1 = honestly,** candidly, face-to-face, in person, openly, overtly, personally, plainly, point-blank, straightforwardly, truthfully, unequivocally, without prevarication **2 = at once,** as soon as possible, dead, due, forthwith, immediately, in a second, instantaneously, instantly, posthaste, presently, promptly, pronto (*inf.*), quickly, right away, soon, speedily, straightaway

directness *n* **12 = honesty,** bluntness, candour, forthrightness, frankness, outspokenness, plain speaking, sincerity, straightforwardness

director *n* **1-4 = controller,** administrator, boss (*inf.*), chairman, chief, executive, governor, head, leader, manager, organizer, principal, producer, supervisor

dirge *n* **1, 3 = lament,** coronach (*Scot. & Irish*),

dirham (ˈdɪəræm) *n* **1** the standard monetary unit of Morocco and the United Arab Emirates. **2** a monetary unit of Kuwait, Libya, Qatar, and Tunisia. **3** any of various N African coins. [C18: from Ar., from L: DRACHMA]

dirigible (ˈdɪrɪdʒɪbᵊl) *adj* **1** able to be steered or directed. ◆ *n* **2** another name for **airship**. [C16: from L *dīrigere* to DIRECT]
▸ ˌ**dirigiˈbility** *n*

dirigisme (diːriːˈʒiːzəm) *n* control by the state of economic and social matters. [C20: from F]
▸ **diriˈgiste** *adj*

dirk (dɜːk) *n* **1** a dagger, esp. as formerly worn by Scottish Highlanders. ◆ *vb* **2** (*tr*) to stab with a dirk. [C16: from Scot. *durk*, ?from G *Dolch* dagger]

dirndl (ˈdɜːndᵊl) *n* **1** a woman's dress with a full gathered skirt and fitted bodice; originating from Tyrolean peasant wear. **2** a gathered skirt of this kind. [G (Bavarian and Austrian): from *Dirndlkleid*, from *Dirndl* little girl + *Kleid* dress]

dirt Ⓣ (dɜːt) *n* **1** any unclean substance, such as mud, etc.; filth. **2** loose earth; soil. **3a** packed earth, gravel, cinders, etc., used to make a racetrack. **3b** (*as modifier*): *a dirt track*. **4** *Mining*. the gravel or soil from which minerals are extracted. **5** a person or thing regarded as worthless. **6** obscene or indecent speech or writing. **7** *Sl*. gossip; scandalous information. **8** moral corruption. **9 do (someone) dirt.** *Sl*. to do something vicious to (someone). **10 eat dirt.** *Sl*. to accept insult without complaining. [C13: from ON *drit* excrement]

dirt-cheap *adj, adv Inf*. at an extremely low price.

dirty Ⓣ (ˈdɜːtɪ) *adj* **dirtier, dirtiest. 1** covered or marked with dirt; filthy. **2a** obscene: *dirty books*. **2b** sexually clandestine: *a dirty weekend*. **3** causing one to become grimy: *a dirty job*. **4** (of a colour) not clear and bright. **5** unfair; dishonest. **6** mean; nasty: *a dirty cheat*. **7** scandalous; unkind. **8** revealing dislike or anger. **9** (of weather) rainy or squally; stormy. **10** (of a nuclear weapon) producing a large quantity of radioactive fallout. **11 dirty linen.** *Inf*. intimate secrets, esp. those that might give rise to gossip. **12 dirty work.** unpleasant or illicit activity. ◆ *n* **13 do the dirty on.** *Inf*. to behave meanly towards. ◆ *vb* **dirties, dirtying, dirtied. 14** to make or become dirty; stain; soil.
▸ ˈ**dirtily** *adv* ▸ ˈ**dirtiness** *n*

dis (dɪs) *vb* a variant spelling of **diss**.

dis-[1] *prefix* **1** indicating reversal: *disconnect*. **2** indicating negation, lack, or deprivation: *dissimilar; disgrace*. **3** indicating removal or release: *disembowel*. **4** expressing intensive force: *dissever*. [from L *dis-* apart; in some cases, via OF *des-*. In compound words of L origin, *dis-* becomes *dif-* before *f*, and *di-* before some consonants]

dis-[2] *combining form*. a variant of **di-**[1] before *s*: *dissyllable*.

disability Ⓣ (ˌdɪsəˈbɪlɪtɪ) *n, pl* **disabilities. 1** the condition of being physically or mentally impaired. **2** something that disables; handicap. **3** lack of necessary intelligence, strength, etc. **4** an incapacity in the eyes of the law to enter into certain transactions.

disable Ⓣ (dɪsˈeɪbᵊl) *vb* **disables, disabling, disabled.** (*tr*) **1** to make ineffective, unfit, or incapable, as by crippling. **2** to make or pronounce legally incapable. **3** to switch off (an electronic device).
▸ **disˈablement** *n*

disabled Ⓣ (dɪˈseɪbᵊld) *adj* **a** lacking one or more physical powers, such as the ability to walk or to coordinate one's movements. **b** (*as collective n; preceded by the*): *the disabled*. See usage note below.

> **USAGE NOTE** The use of *the disabled, the blind*, etc. can be offensive and should be avoided. Instead one should talk about *disabled people, blind people*, etc.

disabuse Ⓣ (ˌdɪsəˈbjuːz) *vb* **disabuses, disabusing, disabused.** (*tr; usually foll. by of*) to rid of a mistaken idea; set right.

disadvantage Ⓣ (ˌdɪsədˈvɑːntɪdʒ) *n* **1** an unfavourable circumstance, thing, person, etc. **2** injury, loss, or detriment. **3** an unfavourable situation (esp. in **at a disadvantage**). ◆ *vb* **disadvantages, disadvantaging, disadvantaged. 4** (*tr*) to put at a disadvantage; handicap.

disadvantaged Ⓣ (ˌdɪsədˈvɑːntɪdʒd) *adj* socially or economically deprived or discriminated against.

disadvantageous Ⓣ (ˌdɪsædvɑːnˈteɪdʒəs, dɪsˌædvənˈteɪdʒəs) *adj* unfavourable; detrimental.
▸ ˌ**disadvanˈtageously** *adv* ▸ ˌ**disadvanˈtageousness** *n*

disaffect Ⓣ (ˌdɪsəˈfɛkt) *vb* (*tr; often passive*) to cause to lose loyalty or affection; alienate.
▸ ˌ**disafˈfectedly** *adv* ▸ ˌ**disafˈfection** *n*

disaffiliate (ˌdɪsəˈfɪlɪˌeɪt) *vb* **disaffiliates, disaffiliating, disaffiliated.** to sever an affiliation (with).
▸ ˌ**disafˌfiliˈation** *n*

disafforest (ˌdɪsəˈfɒrɪst) *vb* (*tr*) *Law*. to reduce (land) from the status of a forest to the state of ordinary ground.
▸ ˌ**disafˌforesˈtation** *n*

disaggregate (dɪsˈægrɪˌgeɪt) *vb* **disaggregates, disaggregating, disaggregated. 1** to separate from a group or mass. **2** to divide into parts.
▸ ˌ**disaggreˈgation** *n*

disagree Ⓣ (ˌdɪsəˈgriː) *vb* **disagrees, disagreeing, disagreed.** (*intr; often foll. by with*) **1** to dissent in opinion or dispute (about an idea, fact, etc.). **2** to fail to correspond; conflict. **3** to be unacceptable (to) or unfavourable (for): *curry disagrees with me*. **4** to be opposed (to).

disagreeable Ⓣ (ˌdɪsəˈgriːəbᵊl) *adj* **1** not likable; bad-tempered, esp. disobliging, etc. **2** not to one's liking; unpleasant.
▸ ˌ**disaˈgreeableness** *n* ▸ ˌ**disaˈgreeably** *adv*

disagreement Ⓣ (ˌdɪsəˈgriːmənt) *n* **1** refusal or failure to agree. **2** a failure to correspond. **3** an argument or dispute.

disallow Ⓣ (ˌdɪsəˈlaʊ) *vb* (*tr*) **1** to reject as untrue or invalid. **2** to cancel.
▸ ˌ**disalˈlowable** *adj* ▸ ˌ**disalˈlowance** *n*

disappear Ⓣ (ˌdɪsəˈpɪə) *vb* **1** (*intr*) to cease to be visible; vanish. **2** (*intr*) to go away or become lost, esp. without explanation. **3** (*intr*) to cease to exist; become extinct or lost. **4** (*tr*) (esp. in South and Central

THESAURUS

dead march, elegy, funeral song, requiem, threnody

dirt *n* **1 = filth**, crap (*sl.*), crud (*sl.*), dust, excrement, grime, grot (*sl.*), impurity, mire, muck, mud, shit (*taboo sl.*), slime, slob (*Irish*), smudge, stain, tarnish **2 = soil**, clay, earth, loam **6 = obscenity**, indecency, pornography, sleaze, smut

dirty *adj* **1 = filthy**, begrimed, foul, grimy, grotty (*sl.*), grubby, grungy (*sl., chiefly US*), messy, mucky, muddy, nasty, polluted, scuzzy (*sl., chiefly US*), soiled, sullied, unclean **2a = obscene**, blue, indecent, off-colour, pornographic, risqué, salacious, sleazy, smutty, vulgar, X-rated (*inf.*) **4 = dark**, clouded, dull, miry, muddy, not clear **5 = dishonest**, corrupt, crooked, fraudulent, illegal, treacherous, unfair, unscrupulous, unsporting **6 = despicable**, base, beggarly, contemptible, cowardly, ignominious, low, low-down (*inf.*), mean, nasty, scurvy, shabby, sordid, squalid, vile **9 = stormy**, gusty, louring *or* lowering, rainy, squally ◆ *vb* **14 = soil**, begrime, blacken, defile, foul, mess up, muddy, pollute, smear, smirch, smudge, spoil, stain, sully
Antonyms *adj* ≠ **filthy:** clean, pure ≠ **dishonest:** decent, honest, moral, reputable, respectable, upright ≠ **obscene:** clean, decent ≠ **stormy:** pleasant ◆ *vb* ≠ **soil:** clean, tidy up

disability *n* **1, 2 = handicap**, affliction, ailment, complaint, defect, disablement, disorder, impairment, infirmity, malady **4 = incapacity**, disqualification, impotency, inability, incompetency, unfitness, weakness

disable *vb* **1 = handicap**, cripple, damage, debilitate, enfeeble, hamstring, immobilize, impair, incapacitate, paralyse, prostrate, put out of action, render *hors de combat*, render inoperative, unfit, unman, weaken **2 = disqualify**, disenable, invalidate, render *or* declare incapable

disabled *adj* **a = handicapped**, bedridden, crippled, incapacitated, infirm, lame, maimed, mangled, mutilated, paralysed, weak, weakened, wrecked
Antonyms *adj* able-bodied, fit, hale, healthy, hearty, robust, sound, strong, sturdy

disabuse *vb* **= enlighten**, correct, free from error, open the eyes of, set right, set straight, shatter (someone's) illusions, undeceive

disadvantage *n* **1 = drawback**, burden, downside, flaw, fly in the ointment (*inf.*), handicap, hardship, hindrance, impediment, inconvenience, liability, minus (*inf.*), nuisance, privation, snag, trouble, weakness, weak point **2 = harm**, damage, detriment, disservice, hurt, injury, loss, prejudice **3 at a disadvantage = vulnerable**, boxed in, cornered, handicapped, in a corner, with one's hands tied behind one's back
Antonyms *n* ≠ **harm, drawback:** advantage, aid, benefit, convenience, gain, help, merit, profit

disadvantaged *adj* **= deprived**, discriminated against, handicapped, impoverished, struggling, underprivileged

disadvantageous *adj* **= unfavourable**, adverse, damaging, deleterious, detrimental, harmful, hurtful, ill-timed, inconvenient, inexpedient, injurious, inopportune, prejudicial

disaffected *adj* **= alienated**, antagonistic, discontented, disloyal, dissatisfied, estranged, hostile, mutinous, rebellious, seditious, uncompliant, unsubmissive

disaffection *n* **= alienation**, animosity, antagonism, antipathy, aversion, breach, disagreement, discontent, dislike, disloyalty, dissatisfaction, estrangement, hostility, ill will, repugnance, resentment, unfriendliness

disagree *vb* **1 = differ (in opinion)**, argue, be at sixes and sevens, bicker, clash, contend, contest, cross swords, debate, dispute, dissent, fall out (*inf.*), have words (*inf.*), object, oppose, quarrel, take issue with, wrangle **2 = conflict**, be discordant, be dissimilar, contradict, counter, depart, deviate, differ, diverge, run counter to, vary **3 = make ill**, be injurious, bother, discomfort, distress, hurt, nauseate, sicken, trouble, upset
Antonyms *vb* ≠ **differ (in opinion):** agree, concur, get on (together) ≠ **conflict:** accord, coincide, harmonize

disagreeable *adj* **1 = ill-natured**, bad-tempered, brusque, churlish, contrary, cross, difficult, disobliging, irritable, nasty, peevish, ratty (*Brit. & NZ inf.*), rude, surly, tetchy, unfriendly, ungracious, unlikable *or* unlikeable, unpleasant **2 = nasty**, disgusting, displeasing, distasteful, horrid, objectionable, obnoxious, offensive, repellent, repugnant, repulsive, uninviting, unpalatable, unpleasant, unsavoury, yucky *or* yukky (*sl.*)
Antonyms *adj* ≠ **nasty:** agreeable, delightful, enjoyable, lovely, nice, pleasant ≠ **ill-natured:** agreeable, congenial, delightful, friendly, good-natured, lovely, nice, pleasant

disagreement *n* **3 = argument**, altercation, clash, conflict, debate, difference, discord, dispute, dissent, division, falling out, misunderstanding, quarrel, row, squabble, strife, tiff, wrangle
Antonyms *n* ≠ **argument:** accord, agreement, assent, consensus, unison, unity

disallow *vb* **1 = reject**, abjure, disavow, disclaim, dismiss, disown, rebuff, refuse, repudiate **2 = cancel**, ban, boycott, embargo, forbid, prohibit, proscribe, veto

disappear *vb* **1 = vanish**, be lost to view, drop out of sight, ebb, evanesce, fade away, pass, recede, vanish off the face of the earth, wane **2 =**

America) to arrest secretly and presumably imprison or kill (a member of an opposing political group).
▸ˌ**disap'pearance** *n*

disapplication (ˌdɪsæplɪˈkeɪʃən) *n Brit. education.* a provision for exempting schools or individuals from the requirements of the National Curriculum in special circumstances.

disappoint ⓣ (ˌdɪsəˈpɔɪnt) *vb* (*tr*) **1** to fail to meet the expectations, hopes, etc. of; let down. **2** to prevent the fulfilment of (a plan, etc.); frustrate. [C15 (orig. meaning: to remove from office): from OF *desapointier;* see DIS-[1], APPOINT]
▸ˌ**disap'pointed** *adj* ▸ˌ**disap'pointing** *adj* ▸ˌ**disap'pointingly** *adv*

disappointment ⓣ (ˌdɪsəˈpɔɪntmənt) *n* **1** a disappointing or being disappointed. **2** a person or thing that disappoints.

disapprobation ⓣ (ˌdɪsæprəʊˈbeɪʃən) *n* moral or social disapproval.

disapproval ⓣ (ˌdɪsəˈpruːvəl) *n* the act or a state or feeling of disapproving; censure.

disapprove ⓣ (ˌdɪsəˈpruːv) *vb* **disapproves, disapproving, disapproved. 1** (*intr;* often foll. by *of*) to consider wrong, bad, etc. **2** (*tr*) to withhold approval from.
▸ˌ**disap'proving** *adj* ▸ˌ**disap'provingly** *adv*

disarm ⓣ (dɪsˈɑːm) *vb* **1** (*tr*) to remove defensive or offensive capability from (a country, army, etc.). **2** (*tr*) to deprive of weapons. **3** (*tr*) to win the confidence or affection of. **4** (*intr*) (of a nation, etc.) to decrease the size and capability of one's armed forces. **5** (*intr*) to lay down weapons.
▸**dis'armer** *n*

disarmament ⓣ (dɪsˈɑːməmənt) *n* **1** the reduction of fighting capability, as by a nation. **2** a disarming or being disarmed.

disarming ⓣ (dɪsˈɑːmɪŋ) *adj* tending to neutralize hostility, suspicion, etc.
▸**dis'armingly** *adv*

disarrange ⓣ (ˌdɪsəˈreɪndʒ) *vb* **disarranges, disarranging, disarranged.** (*tr*) to throw into disorder.
▸ˌ**disar'rangement** *n*

disarray ⓣ (ˌdɪsəˈreɪ) *n* **1** confusion, dismay, and lack of discipline. **2** (esp. of clothing) disorderliness; untidiness. ◆ *vb* (*tr*) **3** to throw into confusion. **4** *Arch.* to undress.

disassemble ⓣ (ˌdɪsəˈsɛmbəl) *vb* **disassembles, disassembling, disassembled.** (*tr*) to take apart (a piece of machinery, etc.); dismantle.

disassembler (ˌdɪsəˈsɛmblə) *n Computing.* a computer program that translates machine code into assembly language.

disassociate (ˌdɪsəˈsəʊʃɪˌeɪt, -sɪ-) *vb* **disassociates, disassociating, disassociated.** a less common word for **dissociate.**
▸**disasˌsoci'ation** *n*

disaster ⓣ (dɪˈzɑːstə) *n* **1** an occurrence that causes great distress or destruction. **2** a thing, project, etc., that fails or has been ruined. [C16 (orig. in the sense: malevolent astral influence): from It. *disastro,* from *dis-* (pejorative) + *astro* star, ult. from Gk *astron*]
▸**dis'astrous** *adj*

disavow ⓣ (ˌdɪsəˈvaʊ) *vb* (*tr*) to deny knowledge of, connection with, or responsibility for.
▸ˌ**disa'vowal** *n* ▸**disavowedly** (ˌdɪsəˈvaʊɪdlɪ) *adv*

disband ⓣ (dɪsˈbænd) *vb* to cease to function or cause to stop functioning, as a unit, group, etc.
▸**dis'bandment** *n*

disbar (dɪsˈbɑː) *vb* **disbars, disbarring, disbarred.** (*tr*) *Law.* to deprive of the status of barrister; expel from the Bar.
▸**dis'barment** *n*

> **USAGE NOTE** *Disbar* is sometimes wrongly used where *debar* is meant: *he was debarred* (not *disbarred*) *from attending meetings.*

disbelief ⓣ (ˌdɪsbɪˈliːf) *n* refusal or reluctance to believe.

disbelieve ⓣ (ˌdɪsbɪˈliːv) *vb* **disbelieves, disbelieving, disbelieved. 1** (*tr*) to reject as false or lying. **2** (*intr;* usually foll. by *in*) to have no faith (in).
▸ˌ**disbe'liever** *n* ▸ˌ**disbe'lieving** *adj*

disbud (dɪsˈbʌd) *or* **debud** (diːˈbʌd) *vb* **disbuds, disbudding, disbudded** *or* **debuds, debudding, debudded. 1** to remove superfluous buds from (a plant). **2** *Vet. science.* to remove the horn buds of (calves, lambs, and kids).

disburden ⓣ (dɪsˈbɜːdən) *vb* **1** to remove a load from. **2** (*tr*) to relieve (one's mind, etc.) of a distressing worry.

disburse ⓣ (dɪsˈbɜːs) *vb* **disburses, disbursing, disbursed.** (*tr*) to pay out. [C16: from OF *desborser,* from *des-* DIS-[1] + *borser* to obtain money, from *borse* bag, from LL *bursa*]
▸**dis'bursable** *adj* ▸**dis'bursement** *n* ▸**dis'burser** *n*

> **USAGE NOTE** *Disburse* is sometimes wrongly used where *disperse* is meant: *the police used a water cannon to disperse* (not *disburse*) *the crowd.*

disc ⓣ (dɪsk) *n* **1** a flat circular plate. **2** something resembling this. **3** a gramophone record. **4** *Anat.* any approximately circular flat structure in the body, esp. an intervertebral disc. **5** the flat receptacle of composite flowers, such as the daisy. **6a** Also called: **parking disc.** a marker or device for display in a parked vehicle showing the time of arrival or the latest permitted time of departure or both. **6b** (*as modifier*): *disc parking.* **7** *Computing.* a variant spelling of **disk.** [C18: from L *discus* DISCUS]
▸**'discal** *adj*

disc. *abbrev. for:* **1** discount. **2** discovered.

THESAURUS

flee, abscond, depart, escape, fly, go, retire, withdraw **3 = cease,** cease to be known, cease to exist, die out, dissolve, end, evaporate, expire, fade, leave no trace, melt away, pass away, perish, vanish
Antonyms *vb* appear, arrive, materialize, reappear

disappearance *n* **2 = vanishing,** departure, desertion, disappearing, disappearing trick, eclipse, evanescence, evaporation, fading, flight, going, loss, melting, passing, vanishing point

disappoint *vb* **1 = let down,** chagrin, dash, deceive, delude, disenchant, disgruntle, dishearten, disillusion, dismay, dissatisfy, fail, sadden, vex **2 = frustrate,** baffle, balk, defeat, disconcert, foil, hamper, hinder, thwart

disappointed *adj* **1, 2 = let down,** balked, cast down, choked, depressed, despondent, discontented, discouraged, disenchanted, disgruntled, disillusioned, dissatisfied, distressed, downhearted, foiled, frustrated, saddened, thwarted, upset
Antonyms *adj* content, contented, fulfilled, happy, pleased, satisfied

disappointing *adj* **1 = unsatisfactory,** depressing, disagreeable, disconcerting, discouraging, failing, inadequate, inferior, insufficient, lame, not much cop (*Brit. sl.*), pathetic, sad, second-rate, sorry, unexpected, unhappy, unworthy, upsetting

disappointment *n* **1 = frustration,** chagrin, discontent, discouragement, disenchantment, disillusionment, displeasure, dissatisfaction, distress, failure, ill-success, mortification, regret, unfulfilment **2 = letdown,** blow, calamity, choker (*inf.*), disaster, failure, fiasco, miscarriage, misfortune, setback, washout (*inf.*), whammy (*inf., chiefly US*)

disapprobation *n* **= disapproval,** blame, censure, condemnation, disfavour, dislike, displeasure, dissatisfaction, reproof, stricture

disapproval *n* **= displeasure,** censure, condemnation, criticism, denunciation, deprecation, disapprobation, dissatisfaction, objection, reproach, stick (*sl.*)

disapprove *vb* **1 = condemn,** blame, censure, deplore, deprecate, discountenance, dislike, find unacceptable, frown on, have a down on (*inf.*), look down one's nose at (*inf.*), object to, raise an *or* one's eyebrow, reject, take a dim view of, take exception to **2 = turn down,** disallow, reject, set aside, spurn, veto
Antonyms *vb* ≠ **condemn:** applaud, approve, commend, compliment (*inf.*), like ≠ **turn down:** endorse, give the go-ahead (to), O.K. *or* okay (*inf.*)

disapproving *adj* **1 = critical,** censorious, condemnatory, denunciatory, deprecatory, disapprobatory, discouraging, disparaging, frowning, reproachful
Antonyms *adj* approbatory, approving, commendatory, encouraging

disarm *vb* **1, 2 = render defenceless,** disable, unarm **3 = win over,** persuade, set at ease **4 = demilitarize,** deactivate, demobilize, disband

disarmament *n* **1 = arms reduction,** arms limitation, de-escalation, demilitarization, demobilization

disarming *adj* **= charming,** irresistible, likable *or* likeable, persuasive, winning

disarrange *vb* **= disorder,** confuse, derange, discompose, disorganize, disturb, jumble (up), mess (up), scatter, shake (up), shuffle, unsettle, untidy

disarray *n* **1 = confusion,** discomposure, disharmony, dismay, disorder, disorderliness, disorganization, disunity, indiscipline, unruliness, upset **2 = untidiness,** chaos, clutter, dishevelment, hodgepodge (*US*), hotchpotch, jumble, mess, mix-up, muddle, pig's breakfast (*inf.*), shambles, state, tangle
Antonyms *n* arrangement, harmony, method, neatness, order, orderliness, organization, pattern, plan, regularity, symmetry, system, tidiness

disassemble *vb* **= take apart,** deconstruct, dismantle, dismount, knock down, strike, take down

disaster *n* **1 = catastrophe,** accident, act of God, adversity, blow, bummer (*sl.*), calamity, cataclysm, misadventure, mischance, misfortune, mishap, reverse, ruin, ruination, stroke, tragedy, trouble, whammy (*inf., chiefly US*)

disastrous *adj* **1 = terrible,** adverse, calamitous, cataclysmal, cataclysmic, catastrophic, destructive, detrimental, devastating, dire, dreadful, fatal, hapless, harmful, ill-fated, ill-starred, ruinous, tragic, unfortunate, unlucky, unpropitious, untoward

disavow *vb* **= deny,** abjure, contradict, disclaim, disown, forswear, gainsay (*arch. or literary*), rebut, reject, repudiate, retract

disavowal *n* **= denial,** abjuration, contradiction, disclaimer, gainsaying (*arch. or literary*), recantation, rejection, renunciation, repudiation, retraction

disband *vb* **= break up,** demobilize, dismiss, disperse, dissolve, go (their) separate ways, let go, part company, scatter, send home, separate

disbelief *n* **= scepticism,** distrust, doubt, dubiety, incredulity, mistrust, unbelief
Antonyms *n* belief, credence, credulity, faith, trust

disbelieve *vb* **1 = doubt,** discount, discredit, give no credence to, mistrust, not accept, not buy (*sl.*), not credit, not swallow (*inf.*), reject, repudiate, scoff at, suspect

disbeliever *n* **2 = sceptic,** agnostic, atheist, doubter, doubting Thomas, questioner, scoffer
Antonyms *n* adherent, believer, devotee, disciple, follower, proselyte, supporter, upholder, zealot

disburden *vb* **1, 2 = relieve,** alleviate, diminish, discharge, disencumber, ease, free, lighten, take a load off one's mind, unburden, unload

disburse *vb* **= pay out,** expend, fork out (*sl.*), lay out, shell out (*inf.*), spend

disbursement *n* **= payment,** disposal, expenditure, outlay, spending

disc *n* **1, 2 = circle,** discus, plate, saucer **3 = record,** gramophone record, phonograph record (*US & Canad.*), platter (*US sl.*), vinyl

discard ➊ *vb* (dɪs'kɑːd). **1** (*tr*) to get rid of as useless or undesirable. **2** *Cards.* to throw out (a card or cards) from one's hand. **3** *Cards.* to play (a card not of the suit led nor a trump) when unable to follow suit. ◆ *n* ('dɪskɑːd). **4** a person or thing that has been cast aside. **5** *Cards.* a discarded card. **6** the act of discarding.

disc brake *n* a type of brake in which two pads rub against a flat disc attached to the wheel hub when the brake is applied.

discern ➊ (dɪ'sɜːn) *vb* **1** (*tr*) to recognize or perceive clearly. **2** to recognize or perceive (differences). [C14: from OF *discerner*, from L *discernere* to divide, from DIS-[1] apart + *cernere* to separate]
▸**dis'cernible** *adj* ▸**dis'cernibly** *adv*

discerning ➊ (dɪ'sɜːnɪŋ) *adj* having or showing good taste or judgment; discriminating.

discernment ➊ (dɪ'sɜːnmənt) *n* keen perception or judgment.

disc flower *or* **floret** *n* any of the small tubular flowers at the centre of the flower head of certain composite plants, such as the daisy.

discharge ➊ *vb* (dɪs'tʃɑːdʒ). **discharges, discharging, discharged. 1** (*tr*) to release or allow to go. **2** (*tr*) to dismiss from or relieve of duty, employment, etc. **3** to fire or be fired, as a gun. **4** to pour forth or cause to pour forth: *the boil discharges pus.* **5** (*tr*) to remove (the cargo) from (a boat, etc.); unload. **6** (*tr*) to perform the duties of or meet the demands of (an office, obligation, etc.). **7** (*tr*) to relieve (oneself) of (a responsibility, debt, etc.). **8** (*intr*) *Physics.* **8a** to lose or remove electric charge. **8b** to form an arc, spark, or corona in a gas. **8c** to take or supply electrical current from a cell or battery. **9** (*tr*) *Law.* to release (a prisoner from custody, etc.). ◆ *n* ('dɪstʃɑːdʒ, dɪs'tʃɑːdʒ). **10** a person or thing that is discharged. **11a** dismissal or release from an office, job, institution, etc. **11b** the document certifying such release. **12** the fulfilment of an obligation or release from a responsibility or liability. **13** the act of removing a load, as of cargo. **14** a pouring forth of a fluid; emission. **15a** the act of firing a projectile. **15b** the volley, bullet, etc., fired. **16** *Law.* **16a** a release, as of a person held under legal restraint. **16b** an annulment, as of a court order. **17** *Physics.* **17a** the act or process of removing or losing charge. **17b** a conduction of electricity through a gas by the formation and movement of electrons and ions in an applied electric field.
▸**dis'chargeable** *adj* ▸**dis'charger** *n*

discharge tube *n Electronics.* an electrical device in which current flow is by electrons and ions in an ionized gas, as in a fluorescent light or neon tube.

disc harrow *n* a harrow with sharp-edged discs used to cut clods on the surface of the soil or to cover seed after planting.

disciple ➊ (dɪ'saɪpᵊl) *n* **1** a follower of the doctrines of a teacher or a school of thought. **2** one of the personal followers of Christ (including his 12 apostles) during his earthly life. [OE *discipul*, from L *discipulus* pupil, from *discere* to learn]
▸**dis'ciple,ship** *n* ▸**discipular** (dɪ'sɪpjʊlə) *adj*

disciplinarian ➊ (,dɪsɪplɪ'nɛərɪən) *n* a person who imposes or advocates strict discipline.

disciplinary ('dɪsɪ,plɪnərɪ) *adj* **1** of, promoting, or used for discipline; corrective. **2** relating to a branch of learning.

discipline ➊ ('dɪsɪplɪn) *n* **1** training or conditions imposed for the improvement of physical powers, self-control, etc. **2** systematic training in obedience. **3** the state of improved behaviour, etc., resulting from such training. **4** punishment or chastisement. **5** a system of rules for behaviour, etc. **6** a branch of learning or instruction. **7** the laws governing members of a Church. ◆ *vb* **disciplines, disciplining, disciplined.** (*tr*) **8** to improve or attempt to improve the behaviour, orderliness, etc., of by training, conditions, or rules. **9** to punish or correct. [C13: from L *disciplīna* teaching, from *discipulus* DISCIPLE]
▸**'disci,plinable** *adj* ▸**disciplinal** (,dɪsɪ'plaɪnᵊl) *adj* ▸**'disci,pliner** *n*

disc jockey *n* a person who announces and plays recorded music, esp. pop music, on a radio programme, etc.

disclaim ➊ (dɪs'kleɪm) *vb* **1** (*tr*) to deny or renounce (any claim, connection, etc.). **2** (*tr*) to deny the validity or authority of. **3** *Law.* to renounce or repudiate (a legal claim or right).

disclaimer ➊ (dɪs'kleɪmə) *n* a repudiation or denial.

disclose ➊ (dɪs'kləʊz) *vb* **discloses, disclosing, disclosed.** (*tr*) **1** to make known. **2** to allow to be seen.
▸**dis'closer** *n*

disclosure ➊ (dɪs'kləʊʒə) *n* **1** something that is disclosed. **2** the act of disclosing; revelation.

disco ('dɪskəʊ) *n, pl* **discos. 1a** an occasion at which people dance to pop records. **1b** (*as modifier*): *disco music.* **2** a nightclub or other public place where such dances are held. **3** mobile equipment for providing music for a disco. [C20: from DISCOTHEQUE]

discobolus (dɪs'kɒbələs) *n, pl* **discoboli** (-,laɪ). a discus thrower. [C18: from L, from Gk, from *diskos* DISCUS + *-bolos*, from *ballein* to throw]

discography (dɪs'kɒgrəfɪ) *n* a classified list of gramophone records.
▸**dis'cographer** *n*

discoid ('dɪskɔɪd) *adj also* **discoidal. 1** like a disc. ◆ *n* **2** a disclike object.

discolour ➊ *or US* **discolor** (dɪs'kʌlə) *vb* to change in colour; fade or stain.
▸**dis,color'ation** *or* **dis,colour'ation** *n*

discombobulate (,dɪskəm'bɒbjʊ,leɪt) *vb* **discombobulates, discombobulating, discombobulated.** (*tr*) *Inf., chiefly US & Canad.* to throw into confusion. [C20: prob. a whimsical alteration of DISCOMPOSE or DISCOMFIT]

discomfit ➊ (dɪs'kʌmfɪt) *vb* (*tr*) **1** to make uneasy or confused. **2** to frustrate the plans or purpose of. **3** *Arch.* to defeat. [C14: from OF *desconfire* to destroy, from *des-* (indicating reversal) + *confire* to make, from L *conficere* to produce]
▸**dis'comfiture** *n*

discomfort ➊ (dɪs'kʌmfət) *n* **1** an inconvenience, distress, or mild pain. **2** something that disturbs or deprives of ease. ◆ *vb* **3** (*tr*) to make uncomfortable or uneasy.

THESAURUS

discard *vb* **1 = get rid of**, abandon, axe (*inf.*), cast aside, chuck (*inf.*), dispense with, dispose of, ditch (*sl.*), drop, dump (*inf.*), jettison, junk (*inf.*), reject, relinquish, remove, repudiate, scrap, shed, throw away *or* out
Antonyms *vb* hang *or* hold on to, hold back, keep, reserve, retain, save

discern *vb* **1 = see**, behold, catch sight of, descry, discover, espy, make out, notice, observe, perceive, recognize, suss (out) (*sl.*) **2 = distinguish**, detect, determine, differentiate, discriminate, judge, make a distinction, pick out

discernible *adj* **1, 2 = perceptible**, apparent, appreciable, detectable, discoverable, distinct, distinguishable, noticeable, observable, obvious, plain, recognizable, visible

discerning *adj* **= discriminating**, acute, astute, clear-sighted, critical, ingenious, intelligent, judicious, knowing, penetrating, perceptive, percipient, perspicacious, piercing, sagacious, sensitive, sharp, shrewd, subtle, wise

discernment *n* **= judgment**, acumen, acuteness, astuteness, awareness, clear-sightedness, cleverness, discrimination, ingenuity, insight, intelligence, keenness, penetration, perception, perceptiveness, percipience, perspicacity, sagacity, sharpness, shrewdness, understanding

discharge *vb* **1 = release**, absolve, acquit, allow to go, clear, exonerate, free, liberate, pardon, set free **2 = dismiss**, cashier, discard, eject, expel, fire (*inf.*), give (someone) the boot (*sl.*), give (someone) the sack (*inf.*), oust, remove, sack (*inf.*) **3 = fire**, detonate, explode, let loose (*inf.*), let off, set off, shoot **4 = pour forth**, disembogue, dispense, emit, empty, excrete, exude, give off, gush, leak, ooze, release, void **5 = off-load**, disburden, lighten, remove, unburden, unload **6 = carry out**, accomplish, do, execute, fulfil, observe, perform **7 = pay**, clear, honour, meet, relieve, satisfy, settle, square up ◆ *n* **11a = dismissal**, congé, demobilization, ejection, the boot (*sl.*), the (old) heave-ho (*inf.*), the order of the boot (*sl.*), the sack (*inf.*) **11a = release**, acquittal, clearance, exoneration, liberation, pardon, remittance **12 = carrying out**, accomplishment, achievement, execution, fulfilment, observance, performance **13 = unloading**, disburdening, emptying, unburdening **14 = emission**, emptying, excretion, flow, ooze, pus, secretion, seepage, suppuration, vent, voiding **15 = firing**, blast, burst, detonation, discharging, explosion, fusillade, report, salvo, shot, volley

disciple *n* **1 = follower**, adherent, apostle, believer, catechumen, convert, devotee, learner, partisan, proselyte, pupil, student, supporter, votary
Antonyms *n* guru, leader, master, swami, teacher

disciplinarian *n* **= authoritarian**, despot, drill sergeant, hard master, martinet, stickler, strict teacher, taskmaster, tyrant

discipline *n* **1 = training**, drill, exercise, method, practice, regimen, regulation **3 = self-control**, conduct, control, orderliness, regulation, restraint, strictness **4 = punishment**, castigation, chastisement, correction **6 = field of study**, area, branch of knowledge, course, curriculum, speciality, subject ◆ *vb* **8 = train**, break in, bring up, check, control, drill, educate, exercise, form, govern, instruct, inure, prepare, regulate, restrain **9 = punish**, bring to book, castigate, chasten, chastise, correct, penalize, reprimand, reprove

disclaim *vb* **1-3 = deny**, abandon, abjure, abnegate, decline, disaffirm, disallow, disavow, disown, forswear, rebut, reject, renege, renounce, repudiate, retract

disclaimer *n* **= denial**, abjuration, contradiction, disavowal, rejection, renunciation, repudiation, retraction

disclose *vb* **1 = make known**, blow wide open (*sl.*), broadcast, communicate, confess, divulge, get off one's chest (*inf.*), impart, leak, let slip, make public, out (*inf.*), publish, relate, reveal, spill one's guts about (*sl.*), spill the beans about (*inf.*), tell, unveil, utter **2 = show**, bring to light, discover, exhibit, expose, lay bare, reveal, take the wraps off, uncover, unveil
Antonyms *vb* conceal, cover, dissemble, hide, keep dark, keep secret, mask, obscure, secrete, veil

disclosure *n* **1, 2 = revelation**, acknowledgment, admission, announcement, broadcast, confession, declaration, discovery, divulgence, exposé, exposure, leak, publication, uncovering

discoloration *n* **= stain**, blemish, blot, blotch, mark, patch, smirch, splotch, spot

discolour *vb* **= stain**, fade, mar, mark, rust, soil, streak, tarnish, tinge

discoloured *adj* **= stained**, besmirched, blotched, etiolated, faded, foxed, pale, tainted, tarnished, wan, washed out

discomfit *vb* **1 = embarrass**, abash, confound, confuse, demoralize, discompose, disconcert, faze, flurry, fluster, perplex, perturb, rattle (*inf.*), ruffle, take aback, take the wind out of someone's sails, unnerve, unsettle, worry **2 = frustrate**, baffle, balk, beat, checkmate, defeat, foil, outwit, overcome, thwart, trump, worst

discomfiture *n* **1 = embarrassment**, abashment, chagrin, confusion, demoralization, discomposure, humiliation, shame, unease **2 = frustration**, beating, defeat, disappointment, failure, overthrow, rout, ruin, undoing

discomfort *n* **1 = pain**, ache, hurt, irritation, malaise, soreness **2 = uneasiness**, annoyance, disquiet, distress, gall, hardship, inquietude, ir-

discommode ⊕ (ˌdɪskəˈməʊd) *vb* **discommodes, discommoding, discommoded.** (*tr*) to cause inconvenience to; disturb.
▸ˌ**discomˈmodious** *adj*

discompose ⊕ (ˌdɪskəmˈpəʊz) *vb* **discomposes, discomposing, discomposed.** (*tr*) **1** to disturb the composure of; disconcert. **2** *Now rare.* to disarrange.
▸ˌ**discomˈposure** *n*

disconcert ⊕ (ˌdɪskənˈsɜːt) *vb* (*tr*) **1** to disturb the composure of. **2** to frustrate or upset.
▸ˌ**disconˈcerted** *adj* ▸ˌ**disconˈcerting** *adj* ▸ˌ**disconˈcertion** *n*

disconformity (ˌdɪskənˈfɔːmɪtɪ) *n, pl* **disconformities. 1** lack of conformity; discrepancy. **2** the junction between two parallel series of stratified rocks.

disconnect ⊕ (ˌdɪskəˈnɛkt) *vb* (*tr*) to undo or break the connection of or between (something, as a plug and a socket).
▸ˌ**disconˈnection** *n*

disconnected ⊕ (ˌdɪskəˈnɛktɪd) *adj* **1** not rationally connected; confused or incoherent. **2** not connected or joined.

disconsolate ⊕ (dɪsˈkɒnsəlɪt) *adj* **1** sad beyond comfort; inconsolable. **2** disappointed; dejected. [C14: from Med. L *disconsōlātus,* from DIS-[1] + *consōlātus* comforted]
▸**disˈconsolately** *adv* ▸**disˈconsolateness** *or* **disˌconsoˈlation** *n*

discontent ⊕ (ˌdɪskənˈtɛnt) *n* **1** Also called: **discontentment.** lack of contentment, as with one's condition or lot in life. ◆ *vb* **2** (*tr*) to make dissatisfied.
▸ˌ**disconˈtented** *adj* ▸ˌ**disconˈtentedness** *n*

discontinue ⊕ (ˌdɪskənˈtɪnjuː) *vb* **discontinues, discontinuing, discontinued. 1** to come or bring to an end; interrupt or be interrupted; stop. **2** (*tr*) *Law.* to terminate or abandon (an action, suit, etc.).
▸ˌ**disconˈtinuance** *n* ▸ˌ**disconˌtinuˈation** *n*

discontinuity ⊕ (ˌdɪskɒntɪˈnjuːɪtɪ, dɪsˌkɒntɪ-) *n, pl* **discontinuities. 1** lack of rational connection or cohesion. **2** a break or interruption.

discontinuous ⊕ (ˌdɪskənˈtɪnjʊəs) *adj* characterized by interruptions or breaks; intermittent.
▸ˌ**disconˈtinuously** *adv* ▸ˌ**disconˈtinuousness** *n*

discord ⊕ *n* (ˈdɪskɔːd). **1** lack of agreement or harmony. **2** harsh confused mingling of sounds. **3** a combination of musical notes, esp. one containing one or more dissonant intervals. ◆ *vb* (dɪsˈkɔːd). **4** (*intr*) to disagree; clash. [C13: from OF *descort,* from *descorder* to disagree, from L *discordāre,* from *discors* at variance, from DIS-[1] + *cor* heart]

discordant ⊕ (dɪsˈkɔːdᵊnt) *adj* **1** at variance; disagreeing. **2** harsh in sound; inharmonious.
▸**disˈcordance** *n* ▸**disˈcordantly** *adv*

discotheque (ˈdɪskəˌtɛk) *n* the full term for **disco.** [C20: from F *discothèque,* from Gk *diskos* disc + *-o-* + Gk *thēkē* case]

discount ⊕ *vb* (dɪsˈkaʊnt, ˈdɪskaʊnt). (*mainly tr*) **1** to leave out of account as being unreliable, prejudiced, or irrelevant. **2** to anticipate and make allowance for. **3a** to deduct (an amount or percentage) from the price, cost, etc. **3b** to reduce (the regular price, etc.) by a percentage or amount. **4** to sell or offer for sale at a reduced price. **5** to buy or sell (a bill of exchange, etc.) before maturity, with a deduction for interest. **6** (*also intr*) to loan money on (a negotiable instrument) with a deduction for interest. ◆ *n* (ˈdɪskaʊnt). **7** a deduction from the full amount of a price or debt. See also **cash discount, trade discount. 8** Also called: **discount rate. 8a** the amount of interest deducted in the purchase or sale of or the loan of money on unmatured negotiable instruments. **8b** the rate of interest deducted. **9** (in the issue of shares) a percentage deducted from the par value to give a reduced amount payable by subscribers. **10** a discounting. **11 at a discount. 11a** below the regular price. **11b** held in low regard. **12** (*modifier*) offering or selling at reduced prices: *a discount shop.*
▸**disˈcountable** *adj* ▸**ˈdiscounter** *n*

discounted cash flow *n* the cash flow of an organization taking into account the future values of benefits and assets in addition to their present values.

discountenance (dɪsˈkaʊntɪnəns) *vb* **discountenances, discountenancing, discountenanced.** (*tr*) **1** to make ashamed or confused. **2** to disapprove of. ◆ *n* **3** disapproval.

discount house *n* **1** *Chiefly Brit.* a financial organization engaged in discounting bills of exchange, etc., on a large scale. **2** Also called: **discount store.** *Chiefly US.* a shop offering for sale most of its merchandise at prices below the recommended prices.

discount market *n* the part of the money market consisting of banks, discount houses, and brokers on which bills are discounted.

discourage ⊕ (dɪsˈkʌrɪdʒ) *vb* **discourages, discouraging, discouraged.** (*tr*) **1** to deprive of the will to persist in something. **2** to inhibit; prevent: *this solution discourages rust.* **3** to oppose by expressing disapproval.
▸**disˈcouragement** *n* ▸**disˈcouragingly** *adv*

discourse ⊕ *n* (ˈdɪskɔːs, dɪsˈkɔːs). **1** verbal communication; talk; conversation. **2** a formal treatment of a subject in speech or writing. **3** a

THESAURUS

ritation, nuisance, trouble, unpleasantness, vexation ◆ *vb* **3 = make uncomfortable,** discomfit, discompose, disquiet, distress, disturb, embarrass
Antonyms *n* ≠ **pain:** comfort, ease ≠ **uneasiness:** ease, reassurance, solace ◆ *vb* ≠ **make uncomfortable:** alleviate, assuage, comfort, ease, reassure, solace, soothe

discommode *vb* **= inconvenience,** annoy, bother, burden, disquiet, disturb, harass, hassle, incommode, molest, put out, trouble

discompose *vb* **1 = disturb,** agitate, annoy, bewilder, confuse, discomfit, disconcert, displease, embarrass, faze, flurry, fluster, fret, hassle (*inf.*), irritate, nettle, perplex, perturb, provoke, rattle (*inf.*), ruffle, unnerve, unsettle, upset, vex, worry

discomposure *n* **1 = disturbance,** agitation, anxiety, confusion, discomfiture, disquiet, disquietude, distraction, embarrassment, fluster, inquietude, malaise, nervousness, perturbation, trepidation, uneasiness

disconcert *vb* **1 = disturb,** abash, agitate, bewilder, discompose, faze, flummox, flurry, fluster, nonplus, perplex, perturb, put out of countenance, rattle (*inf.*), ruffle, shake up (*inf.*), take aback, throw off balance, trouble, unbalance, unnerve, unsettle, upset, worry **2 = frustrate,** baffle, balk, confuse, defeat, disarrange, hinder, put off, thwart, undo

disconcerted *adj* **1, 2 = disturbed,** annoyed, at sea, bewildered, caught off balance, confused, distracted, embarrassed, fazed, flummoxed, flurried, flustered, mixed-up, nonplussed, out of countenance, perturbed, rattled (*inf.*), ruffled, shook up (*inf.*), taken aback, thrown (*inf.*), troubled, unsettled, upset, worried

disconcerting *adj* **1, 2 = disturbing,** alarming, awkward, baffling, bewildering, bothersome, confusing, dismaying, distracting, embarrassing, off-putting (*Brit. inf.*), perplexing, upsetting

disconnect *vb* **= cut off,** detach, disengage, divide, part, separate, sever, take apart, uncouple

disconnected *adj* **1 = illogical,** confused, disjointed, garbled, incoherent, irrational, jumbled, mixed-up, rambling, uncoordinated, unintelligible, wandering

disconnection *n* **= cutting off,** cessation, cut-off, discontinuation, discontinuity, interruption, separation, severance, stoppage, suspension

disconsolate *adj* **1, 2 = inconsolable,** crushed, dejected, desolate, despairing, dismal, down in the dumps (*inf.*), forlorn, gloomy, grief-stricken, heartbroken, hopeless, low, melancholy, miserable, sad, unhappy, woeful, wretched

discontent *n* **1 = dissatisfaction,** discontentment, displeasure, envy, fretfulness, regret, restlessness, uneasiness, unhappiness, vexation

discontented *adj* **2 = dissatisfied,** brassed off (*Brit. sl.*), cheesed off, complaining, disaffected, disgruntled, displeased, exasperated, fed up, fretful, miserable, pissed off (*taboo sl.*), unhappy, vexed, with a chip on one's shoulder (*inf.*)
Antonyms *adj* cheerful, content, contented, happy, pleased, satisfied

discontinuance *n* **1 = stopping,** adjournment, cessation, discontinuation, disjunction, intermission, interruption, separation, stop, stoppage, suspension, termination

discontinue *vb* **1 = stop,** abandon, axe (*inf.*), belay (*Nautical*), break off, cease, drop, end, finish, give up, halt, interrupt, kick (*inf.*), leave off, pause, pull the plug on, put an end to, quit, refrain from, suspend, terminate, throw in the sponge, throw in the towel

discontinued *adj* **1 = stopped,** abandoned, ended, finished, given up *or* over, halted, no longer made, terminated

discontinuity *n* **1, 2 = disconnectedness,** disconnection, disjointedness, disruption, disunion, incoherence, interruption, lack of coherence, lack of unity

discontinuous *adj* **= intermittent,** broken, disconnected, fitful, interrupted, irregular, spasmodic

discord *n* **1 = disagreement,** clashing, conflict, contention, difference, discordance, dispute, dissension, disunity, division, friction, incompatibility, lack of concord, opposition, row, rupture, strife, variance, wrangling **2 = disharmony,** cacophony, din, dissonance, harshness, jangle, jarring, racket, tumult
Antonyms *n* ≠ **disagreement:** accord, agreement, concord, friendship, harmony, peace, understanding, unison, unity ≠ **disharmony:** concord, euphony, harmony, melody, tunefulness, unison

discordant *adj* **1 = disagreeing,** at odds, clashing, conflicting, contradictory, contrary, different, divergent, incompatible, incongruous, inconsistent, opposite **2 = inharmonious,** cacophonous, dissonant, grating, harsh, jangling, jarring, shrill, strident, unmelodious

discount *vb* **1 = leave out,** brush off (*sl.*), disbelieve, disregard, ignore, overlook, pass over **3, 4 = deduct,** lower, mark down, rebate, reduce, take off ◆ *n* **7 = deduction,** abatement, allowance, concession, cut, cut price, drawback, percentage (*inf.*), rebate, reduction

discourage *vb* **1 = dishearten,** abash, awe, cast down, cow, damp, dampen, dash, daunt, deject, demoralize, depress, dismay, dispirit, frighten, intimidate, overawe, psych out (*inf.*), put a damper on, scare, unman, unnerve **2 = prevent,** check, curb, deter, hinder, inhibit **3 = put off,** check, curb, deprecate, deter, discountenance, disfavour, dissuade, divert from, hinder, inhibit, prevent, restrain, talk out of, throw cold water on (*inf.*)
Antonyms *vb* ≠ **dishearten:** embolden, encourage, gee up, hearten, inspire ≠ **put off:** bid, countenance, encourage, urge

discouraged *adj* **1 = put off,** crestfallen, dashed, daunted, deterred, disheartened, dismayed, dispirited, downcast, down in the mouth, glum, pessimistic, sick as a parrot (*inf.*)

discouragement *n* **1 = loss of confidence,** cold feet (*inf.*), dejection, depression, despair, despondency, disappointment, discomfiture, dismay, downheartedness, hopelessness, low spirits, pessimism **2 = deterrent,** constraint, curb, damper, disincentive, hindrance, impediment, obstacle, opposition, rebuff, restraint, setback

discouraging *adj* **1 = disheartening,** dampening, daunting, depressing, disappointing, dispiriting, off-putting (*Brit. inf.*), unfavourable, unpropitious

discourse *n* **1 = conversation,** chat, communication, converse, dialogue, discussion, seminar, unit of text used by linguists for the analysis of linguistic phenomena that range over more than one sentence. **4** *Arch.* the ability to reason. ◆ *vb* (dɪsˈkɔːs), **discourses, discoursing, discoursed. 5** (*intr;* often foll. by *on* or *upon*) to speak or write (about) formally. **6** (*intr*) to hold a discussion. **7** (*tr*) *Arch.* to give forth (music). [C14: from Med. L *discursus* argument, from L: a running to and fro, from *discurrere,* from DIS-[1] + *currere* to run]

discourteous ❶ (dɪsˈkɜːtɪəs) *adj* showing bad manners; impolite; rude. ▸**disˈcourteously** *adv* ▸**disˈcourteousness** *n*

discourtesy ❶ (dɪsˈkɜːtɪsɪ) *n, pl* **discourtesies. 1** bad manners; rudeness. **2** a rude remark or act.

discover ❶ (dɪˈskʌvə) *vb* (*tr; may take a clause as object*) **1** to be the first to find or find out about. **2** to learn about for the first time; realize. **3** to find after study or search. **4** to reveal or make known. ▸**disˈcoverable** *adj* ▸**disˈcoverer** *n*

discovery ❶ (dɪˈskʌvərɪ) *n, pl* **discoveries. 1** the act, process, or an instance of discovering. **2** a person, place, or thing that has been discovered. **3** *Law.* the compulsory disclosure by a party to an action of relevant documents in his possession.

discredit ❶ (dɪsˈkrɛdɪt) *vb* (*tr*) **1** to damage the reputation of. **2** to cause to be disbelieved or distrusted. **3** to reject as untrue. ◆ *n* **4** something that causes disgrace. **5** damage to a reputation. **6** lack of belief or confidence.

discreditable ❶ (dɪsˈkrɛdɪtəbᵊl) *adj* tending to bring discredit; shameful or unworthy.

discreet ❶ (dɪˈskriːt) *adj* **1** careful to avoid embarrassment, esp. by keeping confidences secret; tactful. **2** unobtrusive. [C14: from OF *discret,* from Med. L *discrētus,* from L *discernere* to DISCERN] ▸**disˈcreetly** *adv* ▸**disˈcreetness** *n*

> **USAGE NOTE** Avoid confusion with **discrete.**

discrepancy ❶ (dɪˈskrɛpənsɪ) *n, pl* **discrepancies.** a conflict or variation, as between facts, figures, or claims. [C15: from L *discrepāns,* from *discrepāre* to differ in sound, from DIS-[1] + *crepāre* to be noisy] ▸**disˈcrepant** *adj*

> **USAGE NOTE** *Discrepancy* is sometimes wrongly used where *disparity* is meant. A *discrepancy* exists between things which ought to be the same; it can be small but is usually significant. A *disparity* is a large difference between measurable things such as age, rank, or wages.

discrete ❶ (dɪsˈkriːt) *adj* **1** separate or distinct. **2** consisting of distinct or separate parts. [C14: from L *discrētus* separated; see DISCREET] ▸**disˈcretely** *adv* ▸**disˈcreteness** *n*

> **USAGE NOTE** Avoid confusion with **discreet.**

discretion ❶ (dɪˈskrɛʃən) *n* **1** the quality of behaving so as to avoid social embarrassment or distress. **2** freedom or authority to make judgments and to act as one sees fit (esp. in **at one's own discretion, at the discretion of**). **3 age** *or* **years of discretion.** the age at which a person is thought able to manage his own affairs.

discretionary ❶ (dɪˈskrɛʃənərɪ, -ənrɪ) *or* **discretional** *adj* having or using the ability to decide at one's own discretion: *discretionary powers.*

discretionary trust *n* a trust in which the beneficiaries' shares are not fixed in the trust deed but are left to the discretion of other persons, often the trustees.

discriminate ❶ *vb* (dɪˈskrɪmɪˌneɪt). **discriminates, discriminating, discriminated. 1** (*intr;* usually foll. by *in favour of* or *against*) to single out a particular person, group, etc., for special favour or, esp., disfavour. **2** (when *intr,* foll. by *between* or *among*) to recognize or understand the difference (between); distinguish. **3** (*intr*) to constitute or mark a difference. **4** (*intr*) to be discerning in matters of taste. ◆ *adj* (dɪˈskrɪmɪnɪt). **5** showing or marked by discrimination. [C17: from L *discrīmināre* to divide, from *discrīmen* a separation, from *discernere* to DISCERN] ▸**disˈcriminately** *adv*

discriminating ❶ (dɪˈskrɪmɪˌneɪtɪŋ) *adj* **1** able to see fine distinctions and differences. **2** discerning in matters of taste. **3** (of a tariff, import duty, etc.) levied at differential rates.

discrimination ❶ (dɪˌskrɪmɪˈneɪʃən) *n* **1** unfair treatment of a person, racial group, minority, etc.; action based on prejudice. **2** subtle appreciation in matters of taste. **3** the ability to see fine distinctions and differences.

discriminatory ❶ (dɪˈskrɪmɪnətərɪ, -trɪ) *or* **discriminative** (dɪˈskrɪmɪnətɪv) *adj* **1** based on or showing prejudice; biased. **2** capable of making fine distinctions.

discursive (dɪˈskɜːsɪv) *adj* **1** passing from one topic to another; digressive. **2** *Philosophy.* of or relating to knowledge obtained by reason and argument rather than intuition. [C16: from Med. L *discursīvus,* from LL *discursus* DISCOURSE] ▸**disˈcursively** *adv* ▸**disˈcursiveness** *n*

discus (ˈdɪskəs) *n, pl* **discuses** *or* **disci** (ˈdɪskaɪ). **1** (originally) a circular stone or plate used in throwing competitions by the ancient Greeks. **2** *Field sports.* a similar disc-shaped object with a heavy middle, thrown by athletes. **3** (preceded by *the*) the event or sport of throwing the discus. [C17: from L, from Gk *diskos,* from *dikein* to throw]

discuss ❶ (dɪˈskʌs) *vb* (*tr*) **1** to have a conversation about; consider by talking over. **2** to treat (a subject) in speech or writing. [C14: from LL *discussus* examined, from *discutere,* from L: to dash to pieces, from DIS-[1] + *quatere* to shake] ▸**disˈcussant** *or* **disˈcusser** *n* ▸**disˈcussible** *or* **disˈcussable** *adj*

discussion ❶ (dɪˈskʌʃən) *n* the examination or consideration of a matter in speech or writing.

disdain ❶ (dɪsˈdeɪn) *n* **1** a feeling or show of superiority and dislike; contempt; scorn. ◆ *vb* **2** (*tr; may take an infinitive*) to refuse or reject

THESAURUS

speech, talk **2** = **speech**, address, disquisition, dissertation, essay, homily, lecture, oration, sermon, talk, treatise ◆ *vb* **5, 6** = **hold forth**, confer, converse, debate, declaim, discuss, expatiate, speak, talk

discourteous *adj* = **rude**, abrupt, bad-mannered, boorish, brusque, curt, disrespectful, ill-bred, ill-mannered, impolite, insolent, offhand, uncivil, uncourteous, ungentlemanly, ungracious, unmannerly
Antonyms *adj* civil, courteous, courtly, gracious, mannerly, polite, respectful, well-mannered

discourtesy *n* **1** = **rudeness**, bad manners, disrespectfulness, ill-breeding, impertinence, impoliteness, incivility, insolence, ungraciousness, unmannerliness **2** = **insult**, affront, cold shoulder, kick in the teeth (*sl.*), rebuff, slight, snub

discover *vb* **1** = **find**, bring to light, come across, come upon, dig up, light upon, locate, turn up, uncover, unearth **2** = **find out**, ascertain, descry, detect, determine, discern, disclose, espy, get wise to (*inf.*), learn, notice, perceive, realize, recognize, reveal, see, spot, suss (out) (*sl.*), turn up, uncover

discoverer *n* **1** = **inventor**, author, explorer, founder, initiator, originator, pioneer

discovery *n* **1** = **finding**, ascertainment, detection, disclosure, espial, exploration, introduction, locating, location, origination, revelation, uncovering

discredit *vb* **1** = **disgrace**, blame, bring into disrepute, censure, defame, degrade, detract from, dishonour, disparage, reproach, slander, slur, smear, vilify **2** = **doubt**, challenge, deny, disbelieve, discount, dispute, distrust, mistrust, question ◆ *n* **5** = **disgrace**, aspersion, censure, dishonour, disrepute, ignominy, ill-repute, imputation, odium, reproach, scandal, shame, slur, smear, stigma **6** = **doubt**, distrust, mistrust, question, scepticism, suspicion
Antonyms *vb* ≠ **disgrace:** acclaim, applaud, commend, honour, laud, pay tribute to, praise ◆ *n* ≠ **disgrace:** acclaim, acknowledgment, approval, commendation, credit, honour, merit, praise

discreditable *adj* = **disgraceful**, blameworthy, degrading, dishonourable, humiliating, ignominious, improper, infamous, reprehensible, scandalous, shameful, unprincipled, unworthy

discredited *adj* **2, 3** = **debunked**, discarded, exploded, exposed, obsolete, outworn, refuted, rejected

discreet *adj* **1** = **tactful**, careful, cautious, circumspect, considerate, diplomatic, discerning, guarded, judicious, politic, prudent, reserved, sagacious, sensible, wary
Antonyms *adj* incautious, indiscreet, injudicious, rash, tactless, undiplomatic, unthinking, unwise

discrepancy *n* = **disagreement**, conflict, contradiction, contrariety, difference, discordance, disparity, dissimilarity, dissonance, divergence, incongruity, inconsistency, variance, variation

discrete *adj* **1** = **separate**, detached, disconnected, discontinuous, distinct, individual, unattached

discretion *n* **1** = **tact**, acumen, care, carefulness, caution, circumspection, consideration, diplomacy, discernment, good sense, heedfulness, judgment, judiciousness, maturity, prudence, sagacity, wariness **2** = **choice**, disposition, inclination, liking, mind, option, pleasure, predilection, preference, responsibility, volition, will, wish
Antonyms *n* ≠ **tact:** carelessness, indiscretion, insensitivity, rashness, tactlessness, thoughtlessness

discretionary *adj* = **optional**, arbitrary, elective, nonmandatory, open, open to choice, unrestricted

discriminate *vb* **1** = **show prejudice**, disfavour, favour, show bias, single out, treat as inferior, treat differently, victimize **2, 4** = **differentiate**, assess, discern, distinguish, draw a distinction, evaluate, segregate, separate, separate the wheat from the chaff, sift, tell the difference

discriminating *adj* **1, 2** = **discerning**, acute, astute, critical, cultivated, fastidious, keen, particular, refined, selective, sensitive, tasteful
Antonyms *adj* careless, desultory, general, hit or miss (*inf.*), indiscriminate, random, undiscriminating, unselective, unsystematic

discrimination *n* **1** = **prejudice**, bias, bigotry, favouritism, inequity, intolerance, unfairness **2** = **discernment**, acumen, acuteness, clearness, insight, judgment, keenness, penetration, perception, refinement, sagacity, subtlety, taste

discriminatory *adj* **1** = **prejudiced**, biased, favouring, inequitable, one-sided, partial, partisan, preferential, prejudicial, unjust, weighted **2** = **discerning**, analytical, astute, differentiating, discriminating, perceptive, perspicacious

discuss *vb* **1** = **talk about**, argue, confer, consider, consult with, converse, debate, deliberate, examine, exchange views on, get together, go into, reason about, review, sift, thrash out, ventilate, weigh up the pros and cons

discussion *n* = **talk**, analysis, argument, colloquy, confabulation, conference, consideration, consultation, conversation, debate, deliberation, dialogue, discourse, examination, exchange, review, scrutiny, seminar, symposium

disdain *n* **1** = **contempt**, arrogance, contumely,

with disdain. [C13 *dedeyne*, from OF *desdeign*, from *desdeigner* to reject as unworthy, from L *dēdignārī*; see DIS-[1], DEIGN]
▸**dis'dainful** *adj*

disease ➊ (dɪ'zi:z) *n* **1** any impairment of normal physiological function affecting an organism, esp. a change caused by infection, stress, etc., producing characteristic symptoms; illness or sickness in general. **2** a corresponding condition in plants. **3** any condition likened to this. [C14: from OF *desaise*; see DIS-[1], EASE]
▸**dis'eased** *adj*

diseconomy (ˌdɪsɪ'kɒnəmɪ) *n Econ.* disadvantage, such as lower efficiency or higher costs, resulting from the scale on which an enterprise operates.

disembark ➊ (ˌdɪsɪm'bɑ:k) *vb* to land or cause to land from a ship, aircraft, etc.
▸**disembarkation** (dɪsˌembɑ:'keɪʃən) *n*

disembarrass (ˌdɪsɪm'bærəs) *vb (tr)* **1** to free from embarrassment, entanglement, etc. **2** to relieve or rid of something burdensome.

disembodied ➊ (ˌdɪsɪm'bɒdɪd) *adj* **1** lacking a body or freed from the body. **2** lacking in substance or any firm relation to reality.

disembody (ˌdɪsɪm'bɒdɪ) *vb* **disembodies, disembodying, disembodied.** *(tr)* to free from the body or from physical form.
▸ˌ**disem'bodiment** *n*

disembogue (ˌdɪsɪm'bəʊg) *vb* **disembogues, disemboguing, disembogued. 1** (of a river, stream, etc.) to discharge (water) at the mouth. **2** *(intr)* to flow out. [C16: from Sp. *desembocar*, from *des-* DIS-[1] + *embocar* to put into the mouth]
▸ˌ**disem'boguement** *n*

disembowel ➊ (ˌdɪsɪm'baʊəl) *vb* **disembowels, disembowelling, disembowelled** *or US* **disembowels, disemboweling, disemboweled.** *(tr)* to remove the entrails of.
▸ˌ**disem'bowelment** *n*

disempower (ˌdɪsɪm'paʊə) *vb (tr)* to deprive (a person) of power or authority.
▸ˌ**disem'powerment** *n*

disenchant ➊ (ˌdɪsɪn'tʃɑ:nt) *vb (tr)* to free from or as if from an enchantment; disillusion.
▸ˌ**disen'chantingly** *adv* ▸ˌ**disen'chantment** *n*

disencumber ➊ (ˌdɪsɪn'kʌmbə) *vb (tr)* to free from encumbrances.
▸ˌ**disen'cumberment** *n*

disenfranchise (ˌdɪsɪn'fræntʃaɪz) *or* **disfranchise** *vb* **disenfranchises, disenfranchising, disenfranchised** *or* **disfranchises, disfranchising, disfranchised.** *(tr)* **1** to deprive (a person) of the right to vote or other rights of citizenship. **2** to deprive (a place) of the right to send representatives to an elected body. **3** to deprive (a person, place, etc.) of any franchise or right.
▸**disenfranchisement** (ˌdɪsɪn'fræntʃɪzmənt) *or* **dis'franchisement** *n*

disengage ➊ (ˌdɪsɪn'geɪdʒ) *vb* **disengages, disengaging, disengaged. 1** to release or become released from a connection, obligation, etc. **2** *Mil.* to withdraw (forces) from close action. **3** *Fencing.* to move (one's blade) from one side of an opponent's blade to another in a circular motion.
▸ˌ**disen'gaged** *adj* ▸ˌ**disen'gagement** *n*

disentangle ➊ (ˌdɪsɪn'tæŋgᵊl) *vb* **disentangles, disentangling, disentangled. 1** to release or become free from entanglement or confusion. **2** *(tr)* to unravel or work out.
▸ˌ**disen'tanglement** *n*

disequilibrium (ˌdɪsi:kwɪ'lɪbrɪəm) *n* a loss or absence of equilibrium, esp. in an economy.

disestablish (ˌdɪsɪ'stæblɪʃ) *vb (tr)* to deprive (a church, custom, institution, etc.) of established status.
▸ˌ**dises'tablishment** *n*

disesteem (ˌdɪsɪ'sti:m) *vb* **1** *(tr)* to think little of. ◆ *n* **2** lack of esteem.

disfavour ➊ *or US* **disfavor** (dɪs'feɪvə) *n* **1** disapproval or dislike. **2** the state of being disapproved of or disliked. **3** an unkind act. ◆ *vb* **4** *(tr)* to treat with disapproval or dislike.

disfigure ➊ (dɪs'fɪgə) *vb* **disfigures, disfiguring, disfigured.** *(tr)* **1** to spoil the appearance or shape of; deface. **2** to mar the effect or quality of.
▸**dis'figurement** *n*

disforest (dɪs'fɒrɪst) *vb (tr)* **1** another word for **deforest. 2** *English law.* a less common word for **disafforest.**
▸**disˌfores'tation** *n*

disfranchise (dɪs'fræntʃaɪz) *vb* another word for **disenfranchise.**

disgorge ➊ (dɪs'gɔ:dʒ) *vb* **disgorges, disgorging, disgorged. 1** to throw out (food, etc.) from the throat or stomach; vomit. **2** to discharge or empty of (contents). **3** *(tr)* to yield up unwillingly.
▸**dis'gorgement** *n*

disgrace ➊ (dɪs'greɪs) *n* **1** a condition of shame, loss of reputation, or dishonour. **2** a shameful person or thing. **3** exclusion from confidence or trust: *he is in disgrace with his father.* ◆ *vb* **disgraces, disgracing, disgraced.** *(tr)* **4** to bring shame upon. **5** to treat or cause to be treated with disfavour.

disgraceful ➊ (dɪs'greɪsfʊl) *adj* shameful; scandalous.
▸**dis'gracefully** *adv*

disgruntle ➊ (dɪs'grʌntᵊl) *vb* **disgruntles, disgruntling, disgruntled.** *(tr)* to make sulky or discontented. [C17: DIS-[1] + obs. *gruntle* to complain]
▸**dis'gruntled** *adj* ▸**dis'gruntlement** *n*

disguise ➊ (dɪs'gaɪz) *vb* **disguises, disguising, disguised. 1** to modify the appearance or manner in order to conceal the identity of (someone or something). **2** *(tr)* to misrepresent in order to obscure the actual nature or meaning. ◆ *n* **3** a mask, costume, or manner that disguises. **4** a disguising or being disguised. [C14: from OF *desguisier*, from *des-* DIS-[1] + *guise* manner]
▸**dis'guised** *adj*

disgust ➊ (dɪs'gʌst) *vb (tr)* **1** to sicken or fill with loathing. **2** to offend the moral sense of. ◆ *n* **3** a great loathing or distaste. **4 in disgust.** as a

THESAURUS

derision, dislike, haughtiness, hauteur, indifference, scorn, sneering, snobbishness, superciliousness ◆ *vb* **2** = **scorn**, belittle, contemn, deride, despise, disregard, look down on, look down one's nose at (*inf.*), misprize, pooh-pooh, reject, slight, sneer at, spurn, undervalue

disdainful *adj* = **contemptuous**, aloof, arrogant, derisive, haughty, high and mighty (*inf.*), hoity-toity (*inf.*), insolent, looking down one's nose (at), on one's high horse (*inf.*), proud, scornful, sneering, supercilious, superior, turning up one's nose (at)

disease *n* **1** = **illness**, affliction, ailment, complaint, condition, disorder, ill health, indisposition, infection, infirmity, lurgy (*inf.*), malady, sickness, upset **3** = **malady**, blight, cancer, canker, contagion, contamination, disorder, plague

diseased *adj* **1** = **sick**, ailing, infected, rotten, sickly, tainted, unhealthy, unsound, unwell, unwholesome

disembark *vb* = **land**, alight, arrive, get off, go ashore, step out of

disembodied *adj* **1, 2** = **bodiless**, ghostly, immaterial, incorporeal, intangible, phantom, spectral, spiritual, unbodied

disembowel *vb* = **eviscerate**, draw, gut, paunch

disenchant *vb* = **disillusion**, break the spell, bring (someone) down to earth, destroy (someone's) illusions, disabuse, open (someone's) eyes, undeceive

disenchanted *adj* = **disillusioned**, blasé, cynical, disappointed, indifferent, jaundiced, let down, out of love, sick of, soured, undeceived

disenchantment *n* = **disillusionment**, disappointment, disillusion, revulsion, rude awakening

disencumber *vb* = **unburden**, disburden, discharge, disembarrass, disembroil, extricate, lighten, unhamper, unload

disengage *vb* **1** = **detach**, disconnect, disentangle, disjoin, disunite, divide, ease, extricate, free, liberate, loosen, release, separate, set free, unbridle, undo, unloose, untie, withdraw

disengaged *adj* **1** = **unconnected**, apart, detached, free, loose, out of gear, released, separate, unattached, uncoupled

disengagement *n* **1** = **disconnection**, detachment, disentanglement, division, separation, withdrawal

disentangle *vb* **1** = **untangle**, detach, disconnect, disengage, extricate, free, loose, separate, sever, unfold, unravel, unsnarl, untwist **2** = **sort out**, clarify, clear (up), resolve, simplify, work out

disfavour *n* **1** = **disapproval**, disapprobation, dislike, displeasure

disfigure *vb* **1** = **damage**, blemish, deface, deform, disfeature, distort, injure, maim, make ugly, mar, mutilate, scar

disfigurement *n* **1** = **damage**, blemish, defacement, defect, deformity, distortion, impairment, injury, mutilation, scar, spot, stain, trauma (*Pathology*)

disgorge *vb* **1** = **vomit**, barf (*US sl.*), belch, blow lunch (*US sl.*), chuck (up) (*sl., chiefly US*), chunder (*sl., chiefly Austral.*), discharge, do a technicolour yawn (*sl.*), eject, empty, expel, lose one's lunch (*US sl.*), regurgitate, spew, spit up, spout, throw up, toss one's cookies (*US sl.*) **3** = **give up**, cede, relinquish, renounce, resign, surrender, yield

disgrace *n* **1** = **shame**, baseness, degradation, dishonour, disrepute, ignominy, infamy, odium, opprobrium **3** = **discredit**, contempt, disesteem, disfavour, obloquy ◆ *vb* **4** = **bring shame upon**, abase, defame, degrade, discredit, disfavour, dishonour, disparage, humiliate, reproach, shame, slur, stain, stigmatize, sully, taint

Antonyms *n* ≠ **shame:** credit, esteem, favour, grace, honour, repute ◆ *vb* ≠ **bring shame upon:** credit, grace, honour

disgraced *adj* **4** = **shamed**, branded, degraded, discredited, dishonoured, humiliated, in disgrace, in the doghouse (*inf.*), mortified, stigmatized, under a cloud

disgraceful *adj* = **shameful**, blameworthy, contemptible, degrading, detestable, discreditable, dishonourable, disreputable, ignominious, infamous, low, mean, opprobrious, scandalous, shocking, unworthy

disgruntled *adj* = **discontented**, annoyed, cheesed off (*Brit. sl.*), displeased, dissatisfied, grumpy, hacked (off) (*US sl.*), huffy, irritated, malcontent, peeved, peevish, petulant, pissed off (*taboo sl.*), put out, sulky, sullen, testy, vexed

disguise *vb* **1** = **hide**, camouflage, cloak, conceal, cover, mask, screen, secrete, shroud, veil **2** = **misrepresent**, deceive, dissemble, dissimulate, fake, falsify, fudge, gloss over ◆ *n* **3** = **costume**, camouflage, cloak, cover, get-up (*inf.*), mask, screen, veil **4** = **façade**, deception, dissimulation, front, pretence, semblance, trickery, veneer

disguised *adj* **1** = **in disguise**, camouflaged, cloaked, covert, fake, false, feigned, incognito, masked, pretend, undercover, unrecognizable

disgust *vb* **1, 2** = **sicken**, cause aversion, displease, fill with loathing, gross out (*US. sl.*), nauseate, offend, outrage, put off, repel, revolt, turn one's stomach ◆ *n* **3** = **loathing**, abhorrence, abomination, antipathy, aversion, detestation, dislike, distaste, hatefulness, hatred, nausea, odium, repugnance, repulsion, revulsion

Antonyms *n* ≠ **loathing:** liking, love, pleasure, satisfaction, taste ◆ *vb* ≠ **sicken:** delight, impress, please

result of disgust. [C16: from OF *desgouster*, from *des-* DIS-[1] + *gouster* to taste, from L *gustus* taste]
▸**dis'gustedly** *adv* ▸**dis'gustedness** *n*

dish ❶ (dɪʃ) *n* **1** a container used for holding or serving food, esp. an open shallow container. **2** the food in a dish. **3** a particular kind of food. **4** Also called: **dishful.** the amount contained in a dish. **5** something resembling a dish. **6** a concavity. **7** short for **dish aerial. 8** *Inf.* an attractive person. ◆ *vb (tr)* **9** to put into a dish. **10** to make concave. **11** *Brit. inf.* to ruin or spoil. ◆ See also **dish out, dish up.** [OE *disc*, from L *discus* quoit]
▸**'dish,like** *adj*

dishabille (ˌdɪsæ'biːl) *n* a variant of **deshabille.**

dish aerial *n* a microwave aerial, used esp. in radar, radio telescopes, and satellite broadcasting (**satellite dish aerial**), consisting of a parabolic reflector. Formal name: **parabolic aerial.** ◆ Also called: **dish antenna.** Often shortened to **dish.**

disharmony ❶ (dɪs'hɑːmənɪ) *n, pl* **disharmonies. 1** lack of accord or harmony. **2** a situation, circumstance, etc., that is inharmonious.
▸**disharmonious** (ˌdɪshɑː'məʊnɪəs) *adj*

dishcloth ('dɪʃˌklɒθ) *n* a cloth or rag for washing or drying dishes.

dishearten ❶ (dɪs'hɑːtᵊn) *vb (tr)* to weaken or destroy the hope, courage, enthusiasm, etc., of.
▸**dis'hearteningly** *adv* ▸**dis'heartenment** *n*

dished (dɪʃt) *adj* **1** shaped like a dish. **2** (of wheels) closer to one another at the bottom than at the top. **3** *Inf.* exhausted or defeated.

dishevel (dɪ'ʃɛvᵊl) *vb* **dishevels, dishevelling, dishevelled** *or US* **dishevels, disheveling, disheveled.** to disarrange (the hair or clothes) of (someone). [C15: back formation from DISHEVELLED]
▸**di'shevelment** *n*

dishevelled ❶ *or US* **disheveled** (dɪ'ʃɛvᵊld) *adj* **1** (esp. of hair) hanging loosely. **2** unkempt; untidy. [C15 *dischevelee*, from OF *deschevelé*, from *des-* DIS-[1] + *chevel* hair, from L *capillus*]

dishonest ❶ (dɪs'ɒnɪst) *adj* not honest or fair; deceiving or fraudulent.
▸**dis'honestly** *adv*

dishonesty ❶ (dɪs'ɒnɪstɪ) *n, pl* **dishonesties. 1** lack of honesty. **2** a deceiving act or statement.

dishonour ❶ *or US* **dishonor** (dɪs'ɒnə) *vb (tr)* **1** to treat with disrespect. **2** to fail or refuse to pay (a cheque, etc.). **3** to cause the disgrace of (a woman) by seduction or rape. ◆ *n* **4** a lack of honour or respect. **5** a state of shame or disgrace. **6** a person or thing that causes a loss of honour. **7** an insult; affront. **8** refusal or failure to accept or pay a commercial paper.

dishonourable ❶ *or US* **dishonorable** (dɪs'ɒnərəbᵊl) *adj* **1** characterized by or causing dishonour or discredit. **2** having little or no integrity; unprincipled.
▸**dis'honourableness** *or US* **dis'honorableness** *n* ▸**dis'honourably** *or US* **dis'honorably** *adv*

dish out ❶ *vb (tr, adv)* **1** *Inf.* to distribute. **2 dish it out.** to inflict punishment.

dishtowel ('dɪʃˌtaʊəl) *n* another name (esp. Scot., US and Canad.) for a **tea towel.**

dish up ❶ *vb (adv)* **1** to serve (a meal, food, etc.). **2** *(tr) Inf.* to prepare or present, esp. in an attractive manner.

dishwasher ('dɪʃˌwɒʃə) *n* **1** a machine for washing dishes, etc. **2** a person who washes dishes, etc.

dishwater ('dɪʃˌwɔːtə) *n* **1** water in which dishes have been washed. **2** something resembling this.

dishy ('dɪʃɪ) *adj* **dishier, dishiest.** *Inf., chiefly Brit.* good-looking or attractive.

disillusion ❶ (ˌdɪsɪ'luːʒən) *vb* **1** *(tr)* to destroy the ideals, illusions, or false ideas of. ◆ *n also* **disillusionment. 2** the act of disillusioning or the state of being disillusioned.

disincentive ❶ (ˌdɪsɪn'sɛntɪv) *n* **1** something that acts as a deterrent. ◆ *adj* **2** acting as a deterrent: *a disincentive effect on productivity.*

disincline ❶ (ˌdɪsɪn'klaɪn) *vb* **disinclines, disinclining, disinclined.** to make or be unwilling, reluctant, or averse.
▸**disinclination** (ˌdɪsɪnklɪ'neɪʃən) *n*

disinfect ❶ (ˌdɪsɪn'fɛkt) *vb (tr)* to rid of microorganisms potentially harmful to man, esp. by chemical means.
▸**ˌdisin'fection** *n*

disinfectant ❶ (ˌdɪsɪn'fɛktənt) *n* an agent that destroys or inhibits the activity of microorganisms that cause disease.

disinfest (ˌdɪsɪn'fɛst) *vb (tr)* to rid of vermin.
▸**ˌdisinfes'tation** *n*

disinflation (ˌdɪsɪn'fleɪʃən) *n Econ.* a reduction or stabilization of the general price level intended to improve the balance of payments without incurring reductions in output, employment, etc.

disinformation (ˌdɪsɪnfə'meɪʃən) *n* false information intended to deceive or mislead.

disingenuous (ˌdɪsɪn'dʒenjuəs) *adj* not sincere; lacking candour.
▸**ˌdisin'genuously** *adv* ▸**ˌdisin'genuousness** *n*

disinherit ❶ (ˌdɪsɪn'hɛrɪt) *vb (tr)* **1** *Law.* to deprive (an heir or next of kin) of inheritance or right to inherit. **2** to deprive of a right or heritage.
▸**ˌdisin'heritance** *n*

disintegrate ❶ (dɪs'ɪntɪˌgreɪt) *vb* **disintegrates, disintegrating, disintegrated. 1** to break or be broken into fragments or parts; shatter. **2** to lose or cause to lose cohesion. **3** *(intr)* to lose judgment or control. **4** *Physics.* **4a** to induce or undergo nuclear fission. **4b** another word for **decay** (sense 3).
▸**disˌinte'gration** *n* ▸**dis'inteˌgrator** *n*

disinter ❶ (ˌdɪsɪn'tɜː) *vb* **disinters, disinterring, disinterred.** *(tr)* **1** to remove or dig up; exhume. **2** to bring to light; expose.
▸**ˌdisin'terment** *n*

disinterest ❶ (dɪs'ɪntrɪst, -tərɪst) *n* **1** freedom from bias or involvement. **2** lack of interest.

disinterested ❶ (dɪs'ɪntrɪstɪd, -tərɪs-) *adj* **1** free from bias or partiality; objective. **2** not interested.
▸**dis'interestedly** *adv* ▸**dis'interestedness** *n*

> **USAGE NOTE** Many people consider that the use of *disinterested* to mean not interested is incorrect and *uninterested* should be used.

THESAURUS

disgusted *adj* **1, 2** = **sickened**, appalled, nauseated, offended, outraged, repelled, repulsed, scandalized, sick and tired of (*inf.*), sick of (*inf.*)

disgusting *adj* **1, 2** = **sickening**, abominable, cringe-making (*Brit. inf.*), detestable, distasteful, foul, gross, grotty (*sl.*), hateful, loathsome, nasty, nauseating, nauseous, noisome, objectionable, obnoxious, odious, offensive, repellent, repugnant, revolting, shameless, stinking, vile, vulgar, yucky *or* yukky (*sl.*)

dish *n* **1** = **bowl**, plate, platter, salver **2** = **food**, fare, recipe ◆ *vb* **11** *Brit. informal* = **ruin**, finish, muck up, spoil, torpedo, wreck

disharmony *n* **1, 2** = **discord**, clash, conflict, disaccord, discordance, dissonance, friction, inharmoniousness

dishearten *vb* = **discourage**, cast down, crush, damp, dampen, dash, daunt, deject, depress, deter, dismay, dispirit, put a damper on
Antonyms *vb* buck up (*inf.*), cheer up, encourage, gee up, hearten, lift, perk up, rally

disheartened *adj* = **discouraged**, choked, crestfallen, crushed, daunted, dejected, depressed, disappointed, dismayed, dispirited, downcast, downhearted, sick as a parrot (*inf.*)

dishevelled *adj* = **untidy**, bedraggled, blowsy, disarranged, disarrayed, disordered, frowzy, hanging loose, messy, ruffled, rumpled, tousled, uncombed, unkempt
Antonyms *adj* chic, dapper, neat, smart, soigné *or* soignée, spick-and-span, spruce, tidy, trim, well-groomed

dishonest *adj* = **deceitful**, bent (*sl.*), cheating, corrupt, crafty, crooked (*inf.*), deceiving, deceptive, designing, disreputable, double-dealing, false, fraudulent, guileful, knavish (*arch.*), lying, mendacious, perfidious, shady (*inf.*), swindling, treacherous, unfair, unprincipled, unscrupulous, untrustworthy, untruthful
Antonyms *adj* honest, honourable, law-abiding, lawful, principled, true, trustworthy, upright

dishonesty *n* **1** = **deceit**, cheating, chicanery, corruption, craft, criminality, crookedness, duplicity, falsehood, falsity, fraud, fraudulence, graft (*inf.*), improbity, mendacity, perfidy, sharp practice, stealing, treachery, trickery, unscrupulousness, wiliness

dishonour *vb* **1** = **disgrace**, abase, blacken, corrupt, debase, debauch, defame, degrade, discredit, shame, sully **3** = **seduce**, defile, deflower, pollute, rape, ravish ◆ *n* **5** = **disgrace**, abasement, degradation, discredit, disfavour, disrepute, ignominy, infamy, obloquy, odium, opprobrium, reproach, scandal, shame **7** = **insult**, abuse, affront, discourtesy, indignity, offence, outrage, sacrilege, slight
Antonyms *vb* ≠ **disgrace:** esteem, exalt, respect, revere, worship ◆ *n* ≠ **disgrace:** decency, goodness, honour, integrity, morality, principles, rectitude

dishonourable *adj* **1** = **shameful**, base, contemptible, despicable, discreditable, disgraceful, ignoble, ignominious, infamous, not cricket (*inf.*), scandalous **2** = **untrustworthy**, blackguardly, corrupt, disreputable, shameless, treacherous, unprincipled, unscrupulous

dish out *vb* **1** *Informal* = **distribute**, allocate, dole out, hand out **2 dish it out** = **mete out**, inflict

dish up *vb* = **serve**, hand out, ladle, prepare, present, produce, scoop, spoon

disillusion *vb* **1** = **shatter one's illusions**, break the spell, bring down to earth, disabuse, disenchant, open the eyes of, undeceive

disillusioned *adj* **1** = **disenchanted**, disabused, disappointed, enlightened, indifferent, out of love, sadder and wiser, undeceived

disillusionment *n* **2** = **disenchantment**, disappointment, disillusion, enlightenment, lost innocence, rude awakening

disincentive *n* **1** = **discouragement**, damper, determent, deterrent, dissuasion, impediment

disinclination *n* = **reluctance**, alienation, antipathy, aversion, demur, dislike, hesitance, lack of desire, lack of enthusiasm, loathness, objection, opposition, repugnance, resistance, unwillingness

disinclined *adj* = **reluctant**, antipathetic, averse, balking, hesitating, indisposed, loath, not in the mood, opposed, resistant, unwilling

disinfect *vb* = **sterilize**, clean, cleanse, decontaminate, deodorize, fumigate, purify, sanitize
Antonyms *vb* contaminate, defile, infect, poison, pollute, taint

disinfectant *n* = **antiseptic**, germicide, sanitizer, sterilizer

disinherit *vb Law* **1** = **cut off**, cut off without a penny, disown, dispossess, oust, repudiate

disintegrate *vb* **1-3** = **break up**, break apart, crumble, disunite, fall apart, fall to pieces, go to pieces, go to seed, reduce to fragments, separate, shatter, splinter

disinter *vb* **1** = **dig up**, disentomb, exhume, unearth **2** = **expose**, bring to light, disclose, discover, uncover, unearth

disinterest *n* **1** = **impartiality**, candidness, detachment, disinterestedness, dispassionateness, equity, fairness, justice, neutrality, unbiasedness

disinterested *adj* **1** = **impartial**, candid, detached, dispassionate, equitable, even-handed,

disintermediation (dɪsˌɪntəˌmiːdɪˈeɪʃən) *n Finance.* the elimination of such financial intermediaries as banks and brokers in transactions between principals, often as a result of deregulation and the use of computing.

disinvest (dɪsɪnˈvɛst) *vb Econ.* **1** (usually foll. by *in*) to remove investment (from). **2** (*intr*) to reduce the capital stock of an economy or enterprise, as by not replacing obsolete machinery.
▸ **ˌdisinˈvestment** *n*

disjoin (dɪsˈdʒɔɪn) *vb* to disconnect or become disconnected; separate.
▸**disˈjoinable** *adj*

disjoint (dɪsˈdʒɔɪnt) *vb* **1** to take apart or come apart at the joints. **2** (*tr*) to disunite or disjoin. **3** to dislocate or become dislocated. **4** (*tr; usually passive*) to end the unity, sequence, or coherence of.

disjointed ⓣ (dɪsˈdʒɔɪntɪd) *adj* **1** having no coherence; disconnected. **2** separated at the joint. **3** dislocated.
▸**disˈjointedly** *adv*

disjunct (ˈdɪsdʒʌŋkt) *n Logic.* one of the propositions in a disjunction.

disjunction (dɪsˈdʒʌŋkʃən) *n* **1** Also called: **disjuncture.** a disconnecting or being disconnected; separation. **2** *Logic.* **2a** the operator that forms a compound sentence from two given sentences and corresponds to the English *or.* **2b** the relation between such sentences.

disjunctive (dɪsˈdʒʌŋktɪv) *adj* **1** serving to disconnect or separate. **2** *Grammar.* denoting a word, esp. a conjunction, that serves to express opposition or contrast: *but* in *She was poor but she was honest.* **3** *Logic.* relating to, characterized by, or containing disjunction. ◆ *n* **4** *Grammar.* a disjunctive word, esp. a conjunction. **5** *Logic.* a disjunctive proposition.
▸**disˈjunctively** *adv*

disk (dɪsk) *n* **1** a variant spelling (esp. US and Canad.) of **disc. 2** Also called: **magnetic disk, hard disk.** *Computing.* a direct-access storage device consisting of a stack of plates coated with a magnetic layer, the whole assembly rotating rapidly as a single unit.

disk drive *n Computing.* the controller and mechanism for reading and writing data on computer disks.

diskette (dɪsˈkɛt) *n* another name for **floppy disk.**

disk operating system *n* an operating system used on a computer system with one or more disk drives. Often shortened to: **DOS.**

dislike ⓣ (dɪsˈlaɪk) *vb* **dislikes, disliking, disliked. 1** (*tr*) to consider unpleasant or disagreeable. ◆ *n* **2** a feeling of aversion or antipathy.
▸**disˈlikable** *or* **disˈlikeable** *adj*

dislocate ⓣ (ˈdɪsləˌkeɪt) *vb* **dislocates, dislocating, dislocated.** (*tr*) **1** to disrupt or shift out of place. **2** to displace from its normal position, esp. a bone from its joint.

dislocation ⓣ (ˌdɪsləˈkeɪʃən) *n* **1** a displacing or being displaced. **2** the state or condition of being dislocated.

dislodge ⓣ (dɪsˈlɒdʒ) *vb* **dislodges, dislodging, dislodged.** to remove from or leave a lodging place, hiding place, or previously fixed position.
▸**disˈlodgment** *or* **disˈlodgement** *n*

disloyal ⓣ (dɪsˈlɔɪəl) *adj* not loyal or faithful; deserting one's allegiance.
▸**disˈloyally** *adv*

disloyalty ⓣ (dɪsˈlɔɪəltɪ) *n, pl* **disloyalties.** the condition or an instance of being unfaithful or disloyal.

dismal ⓣ (ˈdɪzməl) *adj* **1** causing gloom or depression. **2** causing dismay or terror. **3** of poor quality or a low standard; feeble. [C13: from *dismal* (n) list of 24 unlucky days in the year, from Med. L *diēs malī,* from L *diēs* day + *malus* bad]
▸**ˈdismally** *adv* ▸**ˈdismalness** *n*

dismantle ⓣ (dɪsˈmæntᵊl) *vb* **dismantles, dismantling, dismantled.** (*tr*) **1** to take apart. **2** to demolish or raze. **3** to strip of covering. [C17: from OF *desmanteler* to remove a cloak from]
▸**disˈmantlement** *n*

dismast (dɪsˈmɑːst) *vb* (*tr*) to break off the mast or masts of (a sailing vessel).

dismay ⓣ (dɪsˈmeɪ) *vb* (*tr*) **1** to fill with apprehension or alarm. **2** to fill with depression or discouragement. ◆ *n* **3** consternation or agitation. [C13: from OF *desmaiier* (unattested), from *des-* DIS-[1] + *esmayer* to frighten, ult. of Gmc origin]
▸**disˈmaying** *adj*

dismember ⓣ (dɪsˈmɛmbə) *vb* (*tr*) **1** to remove the limbs or members of. **2** to cut to pieces. **3** to divide or partition (something, such as an empire).
▸**disˈmemberment** *n*

dismiss ⓣ (dɪsˈmɪs) *vb* (*tr*) **1** to remove or discharge from employment or service. **2** to send away or allow to go. **3** to dispel from one's mind; discard. **4** to cease to consider (a subject). **5** to decline further hearing to (a claim or action). **6** *Cricket.* to bowl out a side for a particular number of runs. [C15: from Med. L *dismissus* sent away, from *dīmittere,* from *dī-* DIS-[1] + *mittere* to send]
▸**disˈmissal** *n* ▸**disˈmissible** *adj* ▸**disˈmissive** *adj*

dismount ⓣ (dɪsˈmaʊnt) *vb* **1** to get off a horse, bicycle, etc. **2** (*tr*) to disassemble or remove from a mounting. ◆ *n* **3** the act of dismounting.

Disneyfication (ˌdɪznɪfɪˈkeɪʃən) *n Derog.* the process by which historical places, local customs, etc. are transformed into trivial entertainment for tourists: *the Disneyfication of Britain's heritage.* [C20: from the *Disneyland* amusement park in California]
▸**ˌDisneyˈfy** *vb* (*tr*).

disobedience ⓣ (ˌdɪsəˈbiːdɪəns) *n* lack of obedience.

disobedient ⓣ (ˌdɪsəˈbiːdɪənt) *adj* not obedient; neglecting or refusing to obey.
▸**ˌdisoˈbediently** *adv*

disobey ⓣ (ˌdɪsəˈbeɪ) *vb* to neglect or refuse to obey (someone, an order, etc.).
▸**ˌdisoˈbeyer** *n*

disoblige ⓣ (ˌdɪsəˈblaɪdʒ) *vb* **disobliges, disobliging, disobliged.** (*tr*) **1** to disregard the desires of. **2** to slight; insult. **3** *Inf.* to cause trouble or inconvenience to.
▸**ˌdisoˈbliging** *adj*

disorder ⓣ (dɪsˈɔːdə) *n* **1** a lack of order; confusion. **2** a disturbance of public order. **3** an upset of health; ailment. **4** a deviation from the

THESAURUS

free from self-interest, impersonal, neutral, objective, outside, unbiased, uninvolved, unprejudiced, unselfish
Antonyms *adj* biased, involved, partial, prejudiced, selfish

disjointed *adj* **1** = **incoherent**, aimless, confused, disconnected, disordered, fitful, loose, rambling, spasmodic, unconnected **3** = **disconnected**, dislocated, displaced, disunited, divided, separated, split

dislike *vb* **1** = **be averse to**, abhor, abominate, despise, detest, disapprove, disfavour, disrelish, hate, have a down on (*inf.*), have no taste *or* stomach for, loathe, not be able to bear *or* abide *or* stand, object to, scorn, shun, take a dim view of ◆ *n* **2** = **aversion**, animosity, animus, antagonism, antipathy, detestation, disapprobation, disapproval, disgust, disinclination, displeasure, distaste, enmity, hatred, hostility, loathing, odium, repugnance
Antonyms *vb* ≠ **be averse to:** esteem, favour, like ◆ *n* ≠ **aversion:** admiration, attraction, delight, esteem, inclination, liking

dislocate *vb* **1** = **shift**, disorder, displace, disrupt, disturb, misplace **2** = **put out of joint**, disarticulate, disconnect, disengage, disjoint, disunite, luxate, unhinge

dislocation *n* **1** = **shift**, disarray, disorder, disorganization, disruption, disturbance, misplacement **2** = **putting out of joint**, disarticulation, disconnection, disengagement, luxation (*Medical*), unhinging

dislodge *vb* = **displace**, dig out, disentangle, disturb, eject, extricate, force out, knock loose, oust, remove, uproot

disloyal *adj* = **treacherous**, apostate, disaffected, faithless, false, perfidious, seditious, subversive, traitorous, treasonable, two-faced, unfaithful, unpatriotic, untrustworthy
Antonyms *adj* constant, dependable, dutiful, faithful, loyal, steadfast, true, trustworthy, trusty

disloyalty *n* = **treachery**, betrayal of trust, breach of trust, breaking of faith, deceitfulness, double-dealing, falseness, falsity, inconstancy, infidelity, perfidy, Punic faith, treason, unfaithfulness

dismal *adj* **1** = **gloomy**, black, bleak, cheerless, dark, depressing, despondent, discouraging, dolorous, dreary, forlorn, funereal, lonesome, louring *or* lowering, lugubrious, melancholy, sad, sombre, sorrowful, wretched
Antonyms *adj* bright, cheerful, cheery, glad, happy, joyful, light-hearted, sunny

dismantle *vb* **1-3** = **take apart**, demolish, disassemble, dismount, raze, strike, strip, take to pieces, unrig

dismay *vb* **1** = **alarm**, affright, appal, distress, fill with consternation, frighten, horrify, paralyse, scare, terrify, unnerve **2** = **disappoint**, daunt, discourage, dishearten, disillusion, dispirit, put off ◆ *n* **3** = **alarm**, agitation, anxiety, apprehension, consternation, distress, dread, fear, fright, horror, panic, terror, trepidation

dismember *vb* **1, 2** = **cut into pieces**, amputate, anatomize, disjoint, dislocate, dissect, divide, mutilate, rend, sever

dismiss *vb* **1** = **sack** (*inf.*), axe (*inf.*), cashier, discharge, fire (*inf.*), give notice to, give (someone) their marching orders, give the boot to (*sl.*), give the bullet to (*Brit. sl.*), kiss off (*sl., chiefly US & Canad.*), lay off, oust, remove, send packing (*inf.*) **2** = **let go**, disband, disperse, dissolve, free, release, send away **3, 4** = **put out of one's mind**, banish, discard, dispel, disregard, drop, lay aside, pooh-pooh, reject, relegate, repudiate, set aside, shelve, spurn

dismissal *n* **1** = **the sack** (*inf.*), discharge, expulsion, kiss-off (*sl., chiefly US & Canad.*), marching orders (*inf.*), notice, one's books *or* cards, removal, the boot (*sl.*), the bum's rush (*sl.*), the (old) heave-ho (*inf.*), the order of the boot (*sl.*), the push (*sl.*) **2** = **permission to go**, adjournment, congé, end, freedom to depart, release

dismount *vb* **1** = **get off**, alight, descend, get down, light

disobedience *n* = **defiance**, indiscipline, infraction, insubordination, mutiny, noncompliance, nonobservance, recalcitrance, revolt, unruliness, waywardness

disobedient *adj* = **defiant**, contrary, contumacious, disorderly, froward (*arch.*), insubordinate, intractable, mischievous, naughty, noncompliant, nonobservant, obstreperous, refractory, undisciplined, unruly, wayward, wilful
Antonyms *adj* biddable, compliant, dutiful, manageable, obedient, submissive, well-behaved

disobey *vb* = **refuse to obey**, contravene, defy, dig one's heels in, disregard, flout, go counter to, ignore, infringe, overstep, rebel, resist, transgress, violate

disoblige *vb* **2** = **offend**, affront, displease, insult, slight **3** = **inconvenience**, annoy, bother, discommode, disturb, put out, trouble, upset

disobliging *adj* **3** = **unhelpful**, awkward, bloody-minded (*Brit. inf.*), cussed (*inf.*), disagreeable, discourteous, ill-disposed, rude, unaccommodating, uncivil, uncooperative, unobliging, unpleasant

disorder *n* **1** = **untidiness**, chaos, clutter, confusion, derangement, disarray, disorderliness, normal system or order. ◆ *vb (tr)* **5** to upset the order of. **6** to disturb the health or mind of.

disorderly ❶ (dɪs'ɔːdəlɪ) *adj* **1** untidy; irregular. **2** uncontrolled; unruly. **3** *Law.* violating public peace or order.
▸**dis'orderliness** *n*

disorderly house *n Law.* an establishment in which unruly behaviour habitually occurs, esp. a brothel or a gaming house.

disorganize ❶ *or* **disorganise** (dɪs'ɔːgəˌnaɪz) *vb* **disorganizes, disorganizing, disorganized** *or* **disorganises, disorganising, disorganised.** *(tr)* to disrupt the arrangement, system, or unity of.
▸**disˌorgani'zation** *or* **disˌorgani'sation** *n*

disorientate ❶ (dɪs'ɔːrɪenˌteɪt) *or* **disorient** *vb* **disorientates, disorientating, disorientated** *or* **disorients, disorienting, disoriented.** *(tr)* **1** to cause (someone) to lose his bearings. **2** to perplex; confuse.
▸**disˌorien'tation** *n*

disown ❶ (dɪs'əʊn) *vb (tr)* to deny any connection with; refuse to acknowledge.
▸**dis'owner** *n*

disparage ❶ (dɪ'spærɪdʒ) *vb* **disparages, disparaging, disparaged.** *(tr)* **1** to speak contemptuously of; belittle. **2** to damage the reputation of. [C14: from OF *desparagier,* from *des-* DIS-[1] + *parage* equality, from L *par* equal]
▸**dis'paragement** *n* ▸**dis'paraging** *adj*

disparate ❶ ('dɪspərɪt) *adj* **1** utterly different or distinct in kind. ◆ *n* **2** *(pl)* unlike things or people. [C16: from L *disparāre* to divide, from DIS-[1] + *parāre* to prepare; also infl. by L *dispar* unequal]
▸**'disparately** *adv* ▸**'disparateness** *n*

disparity ❶ (dɪ'spærɪtɪ) *n, pl* **disparities.** **1** inequality or difference, as in age, rank, wages, etc. **2** dissimilarity.

USAGE NOTE See at **discrepancy.**

dispassionate ❶ (dɪs'pæʃənɪt) *adj* devoid of or uninfluenced by emotion or prejudice; objective; impartial.
▸**dis'passionately** *adv*

dispatch ❶ *or* **despatch** (dɪ'spætʃ) *vb (tr)* **1** to send off promptly, as to a destination or to perform a task. **2** to discharge or complete (a duty, etc.) promptly. **3** *Inf.* to eat up quickly. **4** to murder or execute. ◆ *n* **5** the act of sending off a letter, messenger, etc. **6** prompt action or speed (often in **with dispatch**). **7** an official communication or report, sent in haste. **8** a report sent to a newspaper, etc., by a correspondent. **9** murder or execution. [C16: from It. *dispacciare,* from Provençal *despachar,* from OF *despeechier* to set free, from *des-* DIS-[1] + *-peechier,* ult. from L *pedica* a fetter]
▸**dis'patcher** *n*

dispatch box *n* a case or box used to hold valuables or documents, esp. official state documents.

dispatch case *n* a case used for carrying papers, documents, books, etc.

dispatch rider *n* a horseman or motorcyclist who carries dispatches.

dispel ❶ (dɪ'spel) *vb* **dispels, dispelling, dispelled.** *(tr)* to disperse or drive away. [C17: from L *dispellere,* from DIS-[1] + *pellere* to drive]
▸**dis'peller** *n*

dispensable ❶ (dɪ'spensəb°l) *adj* **1** not essential; expendable. **2** (of a law, vow, etc.) able to be relaxed.
▸**disˌpensa'bility** *n*

dispensary (dɪ'spensərɪ) *n, pl* **dispensaries.** a place where medicine, etc., is dispensed.

dispensation ❶ (ˌdɪspen'seɪʃən) *n* **1** the act of distributing or dispensing. **2** something distributed or dispensed. **3** a system or plan of administering or dispensing. **4** *Chiefly RC Church.* permission to dispense with an obligation of church law. **5** any exemption from an obligation. **6a** the ordering of life and events by God. **6b** a religious system or code of prescriptions for life and conduct regarded as of divine origin.
▸**ˌdispen'sational** *adj*

dispensatory (dɪ'spensətərɪ, -trɪ) *n, pl* **dispensatories.** a book listing the composition, preparation, and application of various drugs.

dispense ❶ (dɪ'spens) *vb* **dispenses, dispensing, dispensed.** **1** *(tr)* to give out or distribute in portions. **2** *(tr)* to prepare and distribute (medicine), esp. on prescription. **3** *(tr)* to administer (the law, etc.). **4** *(intr;* foll. by *with)* to do away (with) or manage (without). **5** to grant a dispensation to. **6** to exempt or excuse from a rule or obligation. [C14: from Med. L *dispensāre* to pardon, from L *dispendere* to weigh out, from DIS-[1] + *pendere*]

USAGE NOTE *Dispense with* is sometimes wrongly used where *dispose of* is meant: *the task can be disposed of* (not *dispensed with*) *quickly and easily.*

dispenser (dɪ'spensə) *n* **1** a device that automatically dispenses a single item or a measured quantity. **2** a person or thing that dispenses.

dispensing optician *n* See **optician.**

THESAURUS

disorganization, hodgepodge (*US*), hotchpotch, irregularity, jumble, mess, muddle, pig's breakfast (*inf.*), shambles, state **2** = **disturbance**, brawl, clamour, commotion, fight, fracas, hubbub, hullabaloo, quarrel, riot, rumpus, scrimmage, shindig (*inf.*), shindy (*inf.*), tumult, turbulence, turmoil, unrest, unruliness, upheaval, uproar **3** = **illness**, affliction, ailment, complaint, disease, indisposition, malady, sickness ◆ *vb* **5** = **disorganize**, clutter, confound, confuse, derange, disarrange, discompose, disturb, jumble, make hay of, mess up, mix up, muddle, scatter, unsettle, upset

disordered *adj* **5** = **untidy**, all over the place, confused, deranged, disarranged, disarrayed, dislocated, disorganized, displaced, higgledy-piggledy (*inf.*), in a mess, in confusion, jumbled, misplaced, muddled, out of kilter, out of place

disorderly *adj* **1** = **untidy**, chaotic, confused, disorganized, higgledy-piggledy (*inf.*), indiscriminate, irregular, jumbled, messy, shambolic (*inf.*), unsystematic **2** = **unruly**, boisterous, disruptive, indisciplined, lawless, obstreperous, rebellious, refractory, riotous, rowdy, stormy, tumultuous, turbulent, ungovernable, unlawful, unmanageable
Antonyms *adj* ≠ **untidy:** arranged, neat, orderly, organized, tidy

disorganization *n* = **disorder**, chaos, confusion, derangement, disarray, disjointedness, disruption, incoherence, unconnectedness

disorganize *vb* = **disrupt**, break up, confuse, convulse, derange, destroy, disarrange, discompose, disorder, disturb, jumble, make a shambles of, muddle, turn topsy-turvy, unsettle, upset

disorganized *adj* = **muddled**, chaotic, confused, disordered, haphazard, jumbled, off the rails, shuffled, unmethodical, unorganized, unsystematic

disorientate *vb* **1, 2** = **confuse**, cause to lose one's bearings, dislocate, mislead, perplex, upset

disorientated *adj* **1, 2** = **confused**, adrift, all at sea, astray, bewildered, lost, mixed up, not adjusted, off-beam, off-course, out of joint, perplexed, unbalanced, unhinged, unsettled, unstable

disown *vb* = **deny**, abandon, abnegate, cast off, disallow, disavow, disclaim, rebut, refuse to acknowledge *or* recognize, reject, renounce, repudiate, retract

disparage *vb* **1, 2** = **run down**, asperse, bad-mouth (*sl., chiefly US & Canad.*), belittle, blast, criticize, decry, defame, degrade, denigrate, deprecate, depreciate, deride, derogate, detract from, discredit, disdain, dismiss, knock (*inf.*), lambast(e), malign, minimize, put down, ridicule, rubbish (*inf.*), scorn, slag (off) (*sl.*), slander, tear into (*inf.*), traduce, underestimate, underrate, undervalue, vilify

disparagement *n* **1, 2** = **contempt**, aspersion, belittlement, condemnation, contumely, criticism, debasement, degradation, denigration, denunciation, depreciation, derision, derogation, detraction, discredit, disdain, impairment, lessening, prejudice, reproach, ridicule, scorn, slander, underestimation

disparaging *adj* **1, 2** = **contemptuous**, abusive, belittling, contumelious, critical, damaging, defamatory, deprecatory, derisive, derogatory, disdainful, dismissive, fault-finding, insulting, libellous, malign, offensive, scathing, scornful, slanderous, slighting, uncomplimentary, unfavourable, unflattering
Antonyms *adj* appreciative, approving, commendatory, complimentary, favourable, flattering, laudatory

disparate *adj* **1** = **different**, at odds, at variance, contrary, contrasting, discordant, discrepant, dissimilar, distinct, diverse, unlike

disparity *n* **1, 2** = **difference**, discrepancy, disproportion, dissimilarity, dissimilitude, distinction, gap, imbalance, incongruity, inequality, unevenness, unlikeness

dispassionate *adj* = **unemotional**, calm, collected, composed, cool, imperturbable, moderate, quiet, serene, sober, temperate, unexcitable, unexcited, unfazed (*inf.*), unmoved, unruffled = **objective**, candid, detached, disinterested, fair, impartial, impersonal, indifferent, neutral, unbiased, uninvolved, unprejudiced
Antonyms *adj* ≠ **unemotional:** ablaze, ardent, emotional, excited, fervent, impassioned, intense, passionate ≠ **objective:** biased, concerned, interested, involved, partial, prejudiced

dispatch *vb* **1** = **send**, accelerate, consign, dismiss, express, forward, hasten, hurry, quicken, remit, transmit **2** = **carry out**, conclude, discharge, dispose of, expedite, finish, make short work of (*inf.*), perform, settle **4** = **murder**, assassinate, blow away (*sl., chiefly US*), bump off (*sl.*), butcher, eliminate (*sl.*), execute, finish off, kill, put an end to, slaughter, slay, take out (*sl.*) ◆ *n* **6** *As in* **with dispatch** = **promptness**, alacrity, celerity, expedition, haste, precipitateness, promptitude, quickness, rapidity, speed, swiftness **7, 8** = **message**, account, bulletin, communication, communiqué, document, instruction, item, letter, missive, news, piece, report, story

dispel *vb* = **drive away**, allay, banish, chase away, dismiss, disperse, dissipate, eliminate, expel, resolve, rout, scatter

dispensable *adj* **1** = **expendable**, disposable, inessential, needless, nonessential, superfluous, unnecessary, unrequired, useless
Antonyms *adj* crucial, essential, important, indispensable, necessary, requisite, vital

dispensation *n* **1** = **distribution**, allotment, appointment, apportionment, bestowal, conferment, consignment, dealing out, disbursement, endowment, supplying **5** = **exemption**, exception, immunity, indulgence, licence, permission, privilege, relaxation, relief, remission, reprieve

dispense *vb* **1** = **distribute**, allocate, allot, apportion, assign, deal out, disburse, dole out, mete out, share **2** = **prepare**, measure, mix, supply **3** = **administer**, apply, carry out, direct, discharge, enforce, execute, implement, operate, undertake **4 dispense with** = **do away with**, abolish, abstain from, brush aside, cancel, dispose of, disregard, do without, forgo, get rid of, give up, ignore, omit, pass over, relinquish, render needless, shake off, waive **6** = **exempt**, except,

dispersal ❶ (dɪˈspɜːsᵊl) *n* **1** a dispersing or being dispersed. **2** the spread of animals, plants, or seeds to new areas.

dispersant (dɪsˈpɜːsənt) *n* a liquid or gas used to disperse small particles or droplets, as in an aerosol.

disperse ❶ (dɪˈspɜːs) *vb* **disperses, dispersing, dispersed. 1** to scatter; distribute over a wide area. **2** to dissipate. **3** to leave or cause to leave a gathering. **4** to separate or be separated by dispersion. **5** (*tr*) to spread (news, etc.). **6** to separate (particles) throughout a solid, liquid, or gas. ◆ *adj* **7** of or consisting of the particles in a colloid or suspension: *disperse phase*. [C14: from L *dispersus*, from *dispergere* to scatter widely, from DI-[2] + *spargere* to strew]
▸**disˈperser** *n*

USAGE NOTE See at **disburse.**

dispersion (dɪˈspɜːʃən) *n* **1** another word for **dispersal. 2** *Physics.* **2a** the separation of electromagnetic radiation into constituents of different wavelengths. **2b** a measure of the ability of a substance to separate by refraction. **3** *Statistics.* the degree to which values of a frequency distribution are scattered around some central point, usually the arithmetic mean or median. **4** *Chem.* a system containing particles dispersed in a solid, liquid, or gas. **5** *Ecology.* the distribution pattern of a population of animals or plants.

dispirit ❶ (dɪˈspɪrɪt) *vb* (*tr*) to lower the spirit of; make downhearted; discourage.
▸**disˈpirited** *adj* ▸**disˈpiritedness** *n* ▸**disˈpiriting** *adj*

displace ❶ (dɪsˈpleɪs) *vb* **displaces, displacing, displaced.** (*tr*) **1** to move from the usual or correct location. **2** to remove from office or employment. **3** to occupy the place of; replace; supplant.

displaced person *n* a person forced from his or her home or country, esp. by war or revolution.

displacement (dɪsˈpleɪsmənt) *n* **1** a displacing or being displaced. **2** the weight or volume displaced by a body in a fluid. **3** *Psychoanal.* the transferring of emotional feelings from their original object to one that disguises their real nature. **4** *Maths.* the distance measured in a particular direction from a reference point. Symbol: *s*

displacement activity *n Psychol.* behaviour that occurs typically when there is a conflict of motives and that has no relevance to either motive: e.g. head scratching.

display ❶ (dɪˈspleɪ) *vb* **1** (*tr*) to show or make visible. **2** (*tr*) to put out to be seen; exhibit. **3** (*tr*) to disclose; reveal. **4** (*tr*) to flaunt in an ostentatious way. **5** (*tr*) to spread out; unfold. **6** (*tr*) to give prominence to. **7** (*intr*) *Zool.* to engage in a display. ◆ *n* **8** an exhibiting or displaying; show. **9** something exhibited or displayed. **10** an ostentatious exhibition. **11** an arrangement of certain typefaces to give prominence to headings, etc. **12** *Electronics.* **12a** a device capable of representing information visually, as on a cathode-ray tube screen. **12b** the information so presented. **13** *Zool.* a pattern of behaviour by which the animal attracts attention while it is courting the female, defending its territory, etc. **14** (*modifier*) designating typefaces that give prominence to the words they are used to set. [C14: from Anglo-F *despleier* to unfold, from LL *displicāre* to scatter, from DIS-[1] + *plicāre* to fold]
▸**disˈplayer** *n*

displease ❶ (dɪsˈpliːz) *vb* **displeases, displeasing, displeased.** to annoy, offend, or cause displeasure to (someone).
▸**disˈpleasing** *adj* ▸**disˈpleasingly** *adv*

displeasure ❶ (dɪsˈplɛʒə) *n* **1** the condition of being displeased. **2** *Arch.* **2a** pain. **2b** an act or cause of offence.

disport (dɪˈspɔːt) *vb* **1** (*tr*) to indulge (oneself) in pleasure. **2** (*intr*) to frolic or gambol. ◆ *n* **3** *Arch.* amusement. [C14: from Anglo-F *desporter*, from *des-* DIS-[1] + *porter* to carry]

disposable ❶ (dɪˈspəʊzəbᵊl) *adj* **1** designed for disposal after use: *disposable cups*. **2** available for use if needed: *disposable assets*. ◆ *n* **3** something, such as a baby's nappy, that is designed for disposal. **4** (*pl*) short for **disposable goods.**
▸**dis,posaˈbility** *or* **disˈposableness** *n*

disposable goods *pl n* consumer goods that are used up a short time after purchase, including perishables, newspapers, clothes, etc. Also called: **disposables.**

disposable income *n* **1** the money a person has available to spend after paying taxes, pension contributions, etc. **2** the total amount of money that the individuals in a community, country, etc., have available to buy consumer goods.

disposal ❶ (dɪˈspəʊzᵊl) *n* **1** the act or means of getting rid of something. **2** arrangement in a particular order. **3** a specific method of tending to matters, as in business. **4** the act or process of transferring something to or providing something for another. **5** the power or opportunity to make use of someone or something (esp. in **at one's disposal**).

dispose ❶ (dɪˈspəʊz) *vb* **disposes, disposing, disposed. 1** (*intr*; foll. by *of*) **1a** to deal with or settle. **1b** to give, sell, or transfer to another. **1c** to throw out or away. **1d** to consume, esp. hurriedly. **1e** to kill. **2** to arrange or settle (matters). **3** (*tr*) to make willing or receptive. **4** (*tr*) to place in a certain order. **5** (*tr*; often foll. by *to*) to accustom or condition. [C14: from OF *disposer*, from L *dispōnere* to set in different places, from DIS-[1] + *pōnere* to place]
▸**disˈposer** *n*

disposed ❶ (dɪˈspəʊzd) *adj* **a** having an inclination as specified (towards something). **b** (*in combination*): *well-disposed.*

disposition ❶ (ˌdɪspəˈzɪʃən) *n* **1** a person's usual temperament or frame of mind. **2** a tendency, inclination, or habit. **3** another word for **disposal** (senses 2–5). **4** *Arch.* manner of placing or arranging.

dispossess ❶ (ˌdɪspəˈzɛs) *vb* (*tr*) to take away possession of something, esp. property; expel.
▸ˌ**disposˈsession** *n* ▸ˌ**disposˈsessor** *n*

dispraise (dɪsˈpreɪz) *vb* **dispraises, dispraising, dispraised. 1** (*tr*) to express disapproval or condemnation of. ◆ *n* **2** the disapproval, etc., expressed.
▸**disˈpraiser** *n*

disproof (dɪsˈpruːf) *n* **1** facts that disprove something. **2** the act of disproving.

disproportion ❶ (ˌdɪsprəˈpɔːʃən) *n* **1** lack of proportion or equality. **2** an instance of disparity or inequality. ◆ *vb* **3** (*tr*) to cause to become exaggerated or unequal.
▸ˌ**disproˈportional** *adj*

disproportionate ❶ (ˌdɪsprəˈpɔːʃənɪt) *adj* out of proportion; unequal.
▸ˌ**disproˈportionately** *adv* ▸ˌ**disproˈportionateness** *n*

THESAURUS

excuse, exonerate, let off (*inf.*), release, relieve, reprieve

dispersal *n* **1** = **scattering**, broadcast, circulation, diffusion, dissemination, dissipation, distribution, spread

disperse *vb* **1** = **scatter**, broadcast, circulate, diffuse, disseminate, dissipate, distribute, spread, strew **4** = **break up**, disappear, disband, dismiss, dispel, dissolve, rout, scatter, send off, separate, vanish
Antonyms *vb* amass, assemble, collect, concentrate, congregate, convene, gather, muster, pool

dispirit *vb* = **dishearten**, cast down, damp, dampen, dash, deject, depress, deter, discourage, disincline, sadden

dispirited *adj* = **disheartened**, crestfallen, dejected, depressed, despondent, discouraged, down, downcast, gloomy, glum, in the doldrums, low, morose, sad, sick as a parrot (*inf.*)

dispiriting *adj* = **disheartening**, crushing, dampening, daunting, demoralizing, depressing, disappointing, discouraging, saddening, sickening
Antonyms *adj* cheering, comforting, encouraging, heartening, reassuring

displace *vb* **1** = **move**, derange, disarrange, disturb, misplace, shift, transpose **2** = **dismiss**, cashier, depose, discard, discharge, fire (*inf.*), remove, sack (*inf.*) **3** = **replace**, crowd out, oust, succeed, supersede, supplant, take the place of

display *vb* **1-3** = **show**, betray, demonstrate, disclose, evidence, evince, exhibit, expose, manifest, open, open to view, present, reveal, take the wraps off, unveil **4** = **show off**, boast, flash (*inf.*), flaunt, flourish, parade, vaunt **5** = **spread out**, expand, extend, model, open out, stretch out, unfold, unfurl ◆ *n* **9** = **exhibition**, array, demonstration, exposition, exposure, manifestation, presentation, revelation, show **10** = **show**, flourish, ostentation, pageant, parade, pomp, spectacle
Antonyms *vb* ≠ **show:** conceal, cover, hide, keep dark, keep secret, mask, secrete, veil

displease *vb* = **annoy**, aggravate (*inf.*), anger, disgust, dissatisfy, exasperate, gall, hassle (*inf.*), incense, irk, irritate, nark (*Brit., Austral., & NZ sl.*), nettle, offend, pique, piss one off (*taboo sl.*), provoke, put one's back up, put out, rile, upset, vex

displeasure *n* **1** = **annoyance**, anger, disapprobation, disapproval, disfavour, disgruntlement, dislike, dissatisfaction, distaste, indignation, irritation, offence, pique, resentment, vexation, wrath
Antonyms *n* approval, endorsement, pleasure, satisfaction

disposable *adj* **1** = **throwaway**, biodegradable, compostable, decomposable, nonreturnable, paper **2** = **available**, at one's service, consumable, expendable, free for use, spendable

disposal *n* **1** = **throwing away**, clearance, discarding, dumping (*inf.*), ejection, jettisoning, parting with, relinquishment, removal, riddance, scrapping **2** = **arrangement**, array, dispensation, disposition, distribution, grouping, placing, position **5 at one's disposal** = **available**, at one's service, consumable, expendable, free for use, spendable

dispose *vb* **1a** *foll. by* **of** = **deal with**, decide, determine, end, finish with, settle **1b** *foll. by* **of** = **give**, bestow, make over, part with, sell, transfer **1c** *foll. by* **of** = **get rid of**, bin (*inf.*), chuck (*inf.*), destroy, discard, dump (*inf.*), get shot of, jettison, junk (*inf.*), scrap, throw out *or* away, unload **3** = **lead**, actuate, adapt, bias, condition, incline, induce, influence, motivate, move, predispose, prompt, tempt

disposed *adj* **a** = **inclined**, apt, given, liable, likely, of a mind to, predisposed, prone, ready, subject, tending towards

disposition *n* **1** = **character**, constitution, make-up, nature, spirit, temper, temperament **2** = **tendency**, bent, bias, habit, inclination, leaning, predisposition, proclivity, proneness, propensity, readiness **3** = **arrangement**, adjustment, classification, direction, disposal, distribution, grouping, management, ordering, organization, placement, regulation

dispossess *vb* = **expel**, deprive, dislodge, divest, drive out, eject, evict, oust, strip, take away, turn out

dispossessed *adj* = **expelled**, destitute, evicted, exiled, homeless, landless

disproportion *n* **1** = **inequality**, asymmetry, discrepancy, disparity, imbalance, inadequacy, insufficiency, lopsidedness, unevenness, unsuitableness
Antonyms *n* balance, congruity, harmony, proportion, symmetry

disproportionate *adj* = **unequal**, excessive,

disprove ◑ (dɪsˈpruːv) *vb* **disproves, disproving, disproved.** (*tr*) to show (an assertion, claim, etc.) to be incorrect.
▸**disˈprovable** *adj* ▸**disˈproval** *n*

disputable ◑ (dɪˈspjuːtəbᵊl, ˈdɪspjʊtə-) *adj* capable of being argued; debatable.
▸**disˌputaˈbility** *or* **disˈputableness** *n* ▸**disˈputably** *adv*

disputant ◑ (dɪˈspjuːtᵊnt, ˈdɪspjutənt) *n* **1** a person who argues; contestant. ◆ *adj* **2** engaged in argument.

disputation (ˌdɪspjuˈteɪʃən) *n* **1** the act or an instance of arguing. **2** a formal academic debate on a thesis. **3** an obsolete word for **conversation.**

disputatious (ˌdɪspjuˈteɪʃəs) *or* **disputative** (dɪˈspjuːtətɪv) *adj* inclined to argument.
▸ˌ**dispuˈtatiousness** *or* **disˈputativeness** *n*

dispute ◑ *vb* (dɪˈspjuːt) **disputes, disputing, disputed. 1** to argue, debate, or quarrel about (something). **2** (*tr; may take a clause as object*) to doubt the validity, etc., of. **3** (*tr*) to seek to win; contest for. **4** (*tr*) to struggle against; resist. ◆ *n* (dɪˈspjuːt, ˈdɪspjuːt). **5** an argument or quarrel. **6** *Rare.* a fight. [C13: from LL *disputāre* to contend verbally, from L: to discuss, from DIS-[1] + *putāre* to think]
▸**disˈputer** *n*

disqualify ◑ (dɪsˈkwɒlɪˌfaɪ) *vb* **disqualifies, disqualifying, disqualified.** (*tr*) **1** to make unfit or unqualified. **2** to make ineligible, as for entry to an examination. **3** to debar from a contest. **4** to deprive of rights, powers, or privileges.
▸**disˌqualifiˈcation** *n*

disquiet ◑ (dɪsˈkwaɪət) *n* **1** a feeling or condition of anxiety or uneasiness. ◆ *vb* **2** (*tr*) to make anxious or upset.
▸**disˈquieting** *adj*

disquietude (dɪsˈkwaɪɪˌtjuːd) *n* a feeling or state of anxiety or uneasiness.

disquisition (ˌdɪskwɪˈzɪʃən) *n* a formal examination of a subject. [C17: from L *disquīsītiō,* from *disquīrere* to make an investigation, from DIS-[1] + *quaerere* to seek]
▸ˌ**disquiˈsitional** *adj*

disregard ◑ (ˌdɪsrɪˈgɑːd) *vb* (*tr*) **1** to give little or no attention to; ignore. **2** to treat as unworthy of consideration or respect. ◆ *n* **3** lack of attention or respect.
▸ˌ**disreˈgardful** *adj*

disremember (ˌdɪsrɪˈmɛmbə) *vb Inf., chiefly US.* to fail to recall.

disrepair ◑ (ˌdɪsrɪˈpɛə) *n* the condition of being worn out or in poor working order; a condition requiring repairs.

disreputable ◑ (dɪsˈrɛpjʊtəbᵊl) *adj* **1** having or causing a lack of repute. **2** disordered in appearance.
▸**disˈreputably** *adv*

disrepute ◑ (ˌdɪsrɪˈpjuːt) *n* a loss or lack of credit or repute.

disrespect ◑ (ˌdɪsrɪˈspɛkt) *n* contempt; rudeness; lack of respect.
▸ˌ**disreˈspectful** *adj*

disrobe ◑ (dɪsˈrəʊb) *vb* **disrobes, disrobing, disrobed. 1** to undress. **2** (*tr*) to divest of authority, etc.
▸**disˈrobement** *n*

disrupt ◑ (dɪsˈrʌpt) *vb* **1** (*tr*) to throw into turmoil or disorder. **2** (*tr*) to interrupt the progress of. **3** to break or split apart. [C17: from L *disruptus* burst asunder, from *dīrumpere* to dash to pieces, from DIS-[1] + *rumpere* to burst]
▸**disˈrupter** *or* **disˈruptor** *n* ▸**disˈruption** *n*

disruptive ◑ (dɪsˈrʌptɪv) *adj* involving, causing, or tending to cause disruption.

diss *or* **dis** (dɪs) *vb* **disses, dissing, dissed.** *Sl., chiefly US.* to treat (someone) with contempt. [C20: orig. US Black rap slang, short for DISRESPECT]

dissatisfy ◑ (dɪsˈsætɪsˌfaɪ) *vb* **dissatisfies, dissatisfying, dissatisfied.** (*tr*) to fail to satisfy; disappoint.
▸ˌ**dissatisˈfaction** *n* ▸ˌ**dissatisˈfactory** *adj*

dissect ◑ (dɪˈsɛkt, daɪ-) *vb* **1** to cut open and examine the structure of (a dead animal or plant). **2** (*tr*) to examine critically and minutely. [C17: from L *dissecāre,* from DIS-[1] + *secāre* to cut]
▸**disˈsection** *n* ▸**disˈsector** *n*

dissected (dɪˈsɛktɪd, daɪ-) *adj* **1** *Bot.* in the form of narrow lobes or segments. **2** *Geol.* cut by erosion into hills and valleys.

disselboom (ˈdɪsᵊlˌbuːm) *n S. African.* the single shaft of a wagon, esp. an ox wagon. [from Du. *dissel* shaft + *boom* beam]

dissemble ◑ (dɪˈsɛmbᵊl) *vb* **dissembles, dissembling, dissembled. 1** to conceal (one's real motives, emotions, etc.) by pretence. **2** (*tr*) to pretend; simulate. [C15: from earlier *dissimulen,* from L *dissimulāre;* prob. infl. by obs. *semble* to resemble]
▸**disˈsemblance** *n* ▸**disˈsembler** *n*

disseminate ◑ (dɪˈsɛmɪˌneɪt) *vb* **disseminates, disseminating, disseminated.** (*tr*) to distribute or scatter about; diffuse. [C17: from L *dissēmināre,* from DIS-[1] + *sēmināre* to sow, from *sēmen* seed]
▸**disˌsemiˈnation** *n* ▸**disˈsemiˌnator** *n*

disseminated sclerosis *n* another name for **multiple sclerosis.**

dissension ◑ (dɪˈsɛnʃən) *n* disagreement, esp. when leading to a quarrel. [C13: from L *dissēnsiō,* from *dissentīre* to DISSENT]

dissent ◑ (dɪˈsɛnt) *vb* (*intr*) **1** to have a disagreement or withhold as-

THESAURUS

incommensurate, inordinate, out of proportion, too much, unbalanced, uneven, unreasonable

disprove *vb* = **prove false**, blow out of the water (*sl.*), confute, contradict, controvert, discredit, expose, give the lie to, invalidate, make a nonsense of, negate, rebut, refute
Antonyms *vb* ascertain, bear out, confirm, evince, prove, show, substantiate, verify

disputable *adj* = **debatable**, arguable, controversial, doubtful, dubious, iffy (*inf.*), moot, open to discussion, questionable, uncertain

disputant *n* **1** = **contestant**, adversary, antagonist, arguer, contender, debater, opponent

dispute *vb* **1** = **argue**, altercate, brawl, clash, contend, cross swords, debate, discuss, quarrel, row, spar, squabble, wrangle **2** = **doubt**, challenge, contest, contradict, controvert, deny, impugn, question, rebut ◆ *n* **5** = **disagreement**, altercation, argument, brawl, conflict, contention, controversy, debate, discord, discussion, dissension, disturbance, feud, friction, quarrel, shindig (*inf.*), shindy (*inf.*), strife, wrangle

disqualification *n* **1** = **unfitness**, disability, disablement, incapacitation, incapacity **2, 3** = **ban**, debarment, disenablement, disentitlement, elimination, exclusion, incompetence, ineligibility, rejection

disqualified *adj* **2, 3** = **ineligible**, debarred, eliminated, knocked out, out of the running

disqualify *vb* **1** = **invalidate**, disable, incapacitate, unfit (*rare*) **3** = **ban**, debar, declare ineligible, disentitle, preclude, prohibit, rule out

disquiet *n* **1** = **uneasiness**, alarm, angst, anxiety, concern, disquietude, distress, disturbance, fear, foreboding, fretfulness, nervousness, restlessness, trepidation, trouble, unrest, worry ◆ *vb* **2** = **make uneasy**, agitate, annoy, bother, concern, discompose, distress, disturb, fret, harass, hassle (*inf.*), incommode, perturb, pester, plague, trouble, unsettle, upset, vex, worry

disquieting *adj* **2** = **worrying**, annoying, bothersome, disconcerting, distressing, disturbing, harrowing, irritating, perturbing, troubling, unnerving, unsettling, upsetting, vexing

disregard *vb* **1, 2** = **ignore**, brush aside *or* away, discount, disobey, laugh off, leave out of account, make light of, neglect, overlook, pass over, pay no attention to, pay no heed to, take no notice of, turn a blind eye to ◆ *n* **3** = **inattention**, brushoff (*sl.*), contempt, disdain, disrespect, heedlessness, ignoring, indifference, neglect, negligence, oversight, slight, the cold shoulder
Antonyms *vb* ≠ **ignore:** attend, heed, listen to, mind, note, pay attention to, regard, respect, take into consideration, take notice of

disrepair *n* = **dilapidation**, collapse, decay, deterioration, ruination

disreputable *adj* **1** = **discreditable**, base, contemptible, derogatory, disgraceful, dishonourable, disorderly, ignominious, infamous, louche, low, mean, notorious, opprobrious, scandalous, shady (*inf.*), shameful, shocking, unprincipled, vicious, vile **2** = **scruffy**, bedraggled, dilapidated, dingy, dishevelled, down at heel, seedy, shabby, threadbare, worn
Antonyms *adj* ≠ **discreditable:** decent, reputable, respectable, respected, upright, worthy

disrepute *n* = **discredit**, disesteem, disfavour, disgrace, dishonour, ignominy, ill favour, ill repute, infamy, obloquy, shame, unpopularity

disrespect *n* = **contempt**, cheek, discourtesy, dishonour, disregard, impertinence, impoliteness, impudence, incivility, insolence, irreverence, lack of respect, lese-majesty, rudeness, sauce, unmannerliness
Antonyms *n* esteem, regard, respect

disrespectful *adj* = **contemptuous**, bad-mannered, cheeky, discourteous, ill-bred, impertinent, impolite, impudent, insolent, insulting, irreverent, misbehaved, rude, uncivil

disrobe *vb* **1** = **undress**, bare, denude, divest, doff, remove, shed, strip, take off, unclothe, uncover

disrupt *vb* **1** = **disturb**, agitate, confuse, convulse, disorder, disorganize, spoil, throw into disorder, upset **2** = **interrupt**, break up *or* into, interfere with, intrude, obstruct, unsettle, upset

disruption *n* **1, 2** = **disturbance**, confusion, disarray, disorder, disorderliness, interference, interruption, stoppage

disruptive *adj* = **disturbing**, confusing, disorderly, distracting, obstreperous, troublemaking, troublesome, unruly, unsettling, upsetting
Antonyms *adj* biddable, compliant, cooperative, docile, obedient, well-behaved

dissatisfaction *n* = **discontent**, annoyance, chagrin, disappointment, discomfort, dislike, dismay, displeasure, distress, exasperation, frustration, irritation, regret, resentment, unhappiness

dissatisfied *adj* = **discontented**, disappointed, disgruntled, displeased, fed up, frustrated, not satisfied, unfulfilled, ungratified, unhappy, unsatisfied
Antonyms *adj* content, contented, pleased, satisfied

dissatisfy *vb* = **discontent**, annoy, disappoint, disgruntle, displease, give cause for complaint, irritate, leave dissatisfied, not pass muster, not suffice, put out, vex

dissect *vb* **1** = **cut up** *or* **apart**, anatomize, dismember, lay open **2** = **analyse**, break down, explore, inspect, investigate, research, scrutinize, study

dissection *n* **1** = **cutting up**, anatomization, anatomy, autopsy, dismemberment, necropsy, postmortem (examination) **2** = **analysis**, breakdown, examination, inspection, investigation, research, scrutiny

dissemble *vb* **1** = **hide**, camouflage, cloak, conceal, cover up, disguise, dissimulate, mask **2** = **pretend**, affect, counterfeit, falsify, feign, sham, simulate

dissembler *n* **1, 2** = **fraud**, charlatan, con man (*inf.*), deceiver, dissimulator, feigner, hypocrite, impostor, pretender, trickster, whited sepulchre

disseminate *vb* = **spread**, broadcast, circulate, diffuse, disperse, dissipate, distribute, proclaim, promulgate, propagate, publicize, publish, scatter, sow

dissemination *n* = **spread**, broadcasting, circulation, diffusion, distribution, promulgation, propagation, publication, publishing

dissension *n* = **disagreement**, conflict, conflict of opinion, contention, difference, discord, discordance, dispute, dissent, friction, quarrel, row, strife, variance

dissent *vb* **1** = **disagree**, decline, differ, object,

sent. 2 *Christianity.* to reject the doctrines, beliefs, or practices of an established church, and to adhere to a different system of beliefs. ◆ *n* 3 a difference of opinion. 4 *Christianity.* separation from an established church; Nonconformism. 5 the voicing of a minority opinion in the decision on a case at law. [C16: from L *dissentīre* to disagree, from DIS-[1] + *sentīre* to feel]
▸**dis'senter** *n* ▸**dis'senting** *adj*

Dissenter (dɪ'sɛntə) *n Christianity, chiefly Brit.* a Nonconformist or a person who refuses to conform to the established church.

dissentient (dɪ'sɛnʃənt) *adj* 1 dissenting, esp. from the opinion of the majority. ◆ *n* 2 a dissenter.
▸**dis'sentience** *or* **dis'sentiency** *n*

dissertation ❶ (ˌdɪsə'teɪʃən) *n* 1 a written thesis, often based on original research, usually required for a higher degree. 2 a formal discourse. [C17: from L *dissertāre* to debate, from *disserere* to examine, from DIS-[1] + *serere* to arrange]
▸ˌ**disser'tational** *adj*

disserve (dɪs'sɜːv) *vb* **disserves, disserving, disserved.** (*tr*) *Arch.* to do a disservice to.

disservice ❶ (dɪs'sɜːvɪs) *n* an ill turn; wrong; injury, esp. when trying to help.

dissever (dɪ'sɛvə) *vb* 1 to break off or become broken off. 2 (*tr*) to divide up into parts. [C13: from OF *dessevrer*, from LL DIS-[1] + *sēparāre* to SEPARATE]
▸**dis'severance** *or* **dis'severment** *n*

dissident ❶ ('dɪsɪdənt) *adj* 1 disagreeing; dissenting. ◆ *n* 2 a person who disagrees, esp. one who disagrees with the government. [C16: from L *dissidēre* to be remote from, from DIS-[1] + *sedēre* to sit]
▸'**dissidence** *n* ▸'**dissidently** *adv*

dissimilar ❶ (dɪ'sɪmɪlə) *adj* not alike; not similar; different.
▸**dis'similarly** *adv* ▸ˌ**dissimi'larity** *n*

dissimilate (dɪ'sɪmɪˌleɪt) *vb* **dissimilates, dissimilating, dissimilated.** 1 to make or become dissimilar. 2 (usually foll. by *to*) *Phonetics.* to change or displace (a consonant) or (of a consonant) to be changed to or displaced by (another consonant) so that its manner of articulation becomes less similar to a speech sound in the same word. Thus (r) in the final syllable of French *marbre* is dissimilated to (l) in its English form *marble.* [C19: from DIS-[1] + ASSIMILATE]

dissimilation (ˌdɪsɪmɪ'leɪʃən) *n* 1 the act or an instance of making dissimilar. 2 *Phonetics.* the alteration or omission of a consonant as a result of being dissimilated.

dissimilitude ❶ (ˌdɪsɪ'mɪlɪˌtjuːd) *n* 1 dissimilarity; difference. 2 a point of difference.

dissimulate ❶ (dɪ'sɪmjʊˌleɪt) *vb* **dissimulates, dissimulating, dissimulated.** to conceal (one's real feelings) by pretence.
▸**disˌsimu'lation** *n* ▸**dis'simuˌlator** *n*

dissipate ❶ ('dɪsɪˌpeɪt) *vb* **dissipates, dissipating, dissipated.** 1 to exhaust or be exhausted by dispersion. 2 (*tr*) to scatter or break up. 3 (*intr*) to indulge in the pursuit of pleasure. [C15: from L *dissipāre* to disperse, from DIS-[1] + *supāre* to throw]
▸'**dissiˌpater** *or* '**dissiˌpator** *n* ▸'**dissiˌpative** *adj*

dissipated ❶ ('dɪsɪˌpeɪtɪd) *adj* 1 indulging without restraint in the pursuit of pleasure; debauched. 2 wasted, scattered, or exhausted.

dissipation ❶ (ˌdɪsɪ'peɪʃən) *n* 1 a dissipating or being dissipated. 2 unrestrained indulgence in physical pleasures. 3 excessive expenditure; wastefulness.

dissociate ❶ (dɪ'səʊʃɪˌeɪt, -sɪ-) *vb* **dissociates, dissociating, dissociated.** 1 to break or cause to break the association between (people, organizations, etc.). 2 (*tr*) to regard or treat as separate or unconnected. 3 to undergo or subject to dissociation.
▸**dis'sociative** *adj*

dissociation ❶ (dɪˌsəʊsɪ'eɪʃən, -ʃɪ-) *n* 1 a dissociating or being dissociated. 2 *Chem.* the decomposition of the molecules of a single compound into two or more other compounds, atoms, ions, or radicals. 3 *Psychiatry.* the separation of a group of mental processes or ideas from the rest of the personality, so that they lead an independent existence, as in cases of multiple personality.

dissoluble (dɪ'sɒljʊbᵊl) *adj* a less common word for **soluble.** [C16: from L *dissolūbilis*, from *dissolvere* to DISSOLVE]
▸**disˌsolu'bility** *n*

dissolute ❶ ('dɪsəˌluːt) *adj* given to dissipation; debauched. [C14: from L *dissolūtus* loose, from *dissolvere* to DISSOLVE]
▸'**dissoˌlutely** *adv* ▸'**dissoˌluteness** *n*

dissolution ❶ (ˌdɪsə'luːʃən) *n* 1 separation into component parts; disintegration. 2 destruction by breaking up and dispersing. 3 the termination of a meeting or assembly, such as Parliament. 4 the termination of a formal or legal relationship, such as a business, marriage, etc. 5 the act or process of dissolving.

dissolve ❶ (dɪ'zɒlv) *vb* **dissolves, dissolving, dissolved.** 1 to go or cause to go into solution. 2 to become or cause to become liquid; melt. 3 to disintegrate or disperse. 4 to come or bring to an end. 5 to dismiss (a meeting, Parliament, etc.) or (of a meeting, etc.) to be dismissed. 6 to collapse or cause to collapse emotionally: *to dissolve into tears.* 7 to lose or cause to lose distinctness. 8 (*tr*) to terminate legally, as a marriage, etc. 9 (*intr*) *Films, television.* to fade out one scene and replace with another to make two scenes merge imperceptibly or slowly overlap. ◆ *n* 10 *Films, television.* a scene filmed or televised by dissolving. [C14: from L *dissolvere* to make loose, from DIS-[1] + *solvere* to release]
▸**dis'solvable** *adj*

dissonance ❶ ('dɪsənəns) *or* **dissonancy** *n* 1 a discordant combination of sounds. 2 lack of agreement or consistency. 3 *Music.* 3a a sensation of harshness and incompleteness associated with certain intervals and chords. 3b an interval or chord of this kind.

dissonant ❶ ('dɪsənənt) *adj* 1 discordant. 2 incongruous or discrepant. 3 *Music.* characterized by dissonance. [C15: from L *dissonāre* to be discordant, from DIS-[1] + *sonāre* to sound]

dissuade ❶ (dɪ'sweɪd) *vb* **dissuades, dissuading, dissuaded.** (*tr*) 1 (often foll. by *from*) to deter (someone) by persuasion from a course of action, policy, etc. 2 to advise against (an action, etc.). [C15: from L *dissuādēre*, from DIS-[1] + *suādēre* to persuade]
▸**dis'suader** *n* ▸**dis'suasion** *n* ▸**dis'suasive** *adj*

THESAURUS

protest, refuse, withhold assent *or* approval ◆ *n* 3 = **disagreement**, difference, discord, dissension, dissidence, nonconformity, objection, opposition, refusal, resistance
Antonyms *vb* ≠ **disagree:** agree, assent, concur ◆ *n* ≠ **disagreement:** accord, agreement, assent, concurrence, consensus

dissenter *n* 1, 2 = **objector**, disputant, dissident, nonconformist, protestant

dissenting *adj* 1 = **disagreeing**, conflicting, differing, dissident, opposing, protesting

dissertation *n* = **thesis**, critique, discourse, disquisition, essay, exposition, treatise

disservice *n* = **bad turn**, disfavour, harm, ill turn, injury, injustice, unkindness, wrong
Antonyms *n* courtesy, good turn, indulgence, kindness, obligement (*Scot. or arch.*), service

dissidence *n* = **dissent**, difference of opinion, disagreement, discordance, dispute, feud, rupture, schism

dissident *adj* 1 = **dissenting**, differing, disagreeing, discordant, dissentient, heterodox, nonconformist, schismatic ◆ *n* 2 = **protester**, agitator, dissenter, rebel, recusant

dissimilar *adj* = **different**, disparate, divergent, diverse, heterogeneous, manifold, mismatched, not alike, not capable of comparison, not similar, unlike, unrelated, various
Antonyms *adj* alike, comparable, congruous, corresponding, in agreement, much the same, resembling, uniform

dissimilarity *n* = **difference**, discrepancy, disparity, dissimilitude, distinction, divergence, heterogeneity, incomparability, nonuniformity, unlikeness, unrelatedness

dissimilitude *n* 1 = **difference**, discrepancy, disparity, dissimilarity, diversity, heterogeneity, incomparability, nonuniformity, unlikeness, unrelatedness

dissimulate *vb* = **pretend**, camouflage, cloak, conceal, disguise, dissemble, feign, hide, mask

dissimulation *n* = **pretence**, concealment, deceit, deception, dissembling, double-dealing, duplicity, feigning, hypocrisy, play-acting, sham, wile

dissipate *vb* 2 = **disperse**, disappear, dispel, dissolve, drive away, evaporate, scatter, vanish 3 = **squander**, burn up, consume, deplete, expend, fritter away, indulge oneself, lavish, misspend, run through, spend, waste

dissipated *adj* 1 = **debauched**, abandoned, dissolute, intemperate, profligate, rakish, self-indulgent 2 = **squandered**, consumed, destroyed, exhausted, scattered, wasted

dissipation *n* 1 = **dispersal**, disappearance, disintegration, dissemination, dissolution, scattering, vanishing 2 = **debauchery**, abandonment, dissoluteness, drunkenness, excess, extravagance, indulgence, intemperance, lavishness, prodigality, profligacy, squandering, wantonness, waste

dissociate *vb* 1 = **break away**, break off, disband, disrupt, part company, quit 2 = **separate**, detach, disconnect, distance, divorce, isolate, segregate, set apart

dissociation *n* 1 = **separation**, break, detachment, disconnection, disengagement, distancing, disunion, division, divorce, isolation, segregation, severance

dissolute *adj* = **immoral**, abandoned, corrupt, debauched, degenerate, depraved, dissipated, lax, lewd, libertine, licentious, loose, profligate, rakish, unrestrained, vicious, wanton, wild
Antonyms *adj* chaste, clean-living, good, moral, squeaky-clean, upright, virtuous, worthy

dissolution *n* 1 = **breaking up**, disintegration, division, divorce, parting, resolution, separation 3 = **adjournment**, conclusion, disbandment, discontinuation, dismissal, end, ending, finish, suspension, termination
Antonyms *n* ≠ **breaking up:** alliance, amalgamation, coalition, combination, unification, union

dissolve *vb* 2 = **melt**, deliquesce, flux, fuse, liquefy, soften, thaw 3 = **disappear**, break down, crumble, decompose, diffuse, disintegrate, disperse, dissipate, dwindle, evanesce, evaporate, fade, melt away, perish, vanish, waste away 5 = **end**, break up, discontinue, dismiss, suspend, terminate, wind up 8 = **break up**, collapse, disorganize, disunite, divorce, loose, resolve into, separate, sever

dissonance *n* 1 = **discordance**, cacophony, discord, harshness, jangle, jarring, lack of harmony, unmelodiousness 2 = **disagreement**, difference, discord, discrepancy, disparity, dissension, incongruity, inconsistency, variance

dissonant *adj* 1 = **discordant**, cacophonous, grating, harsh, inharmonious, jangling, jarring, out of tune, raucous, strident, tuneless, unmelodious 2 = **disagreeing**, anomalous, at variance, different, differing, discrepant, dissentient, incompatible, incongruous, inconsistent, irreconcilable, irregular

dissuade *vb* 1, 2 = **deter**, advise against, discourage, disincline, divert, expostulate, persuade not to, put off, remonstrate, talk out of, urge not to, warn
Antonyms *vb* bring round (*inf.*), coax, convince, persuade, sway, talk into

dissuasion *n* 1, 2 = **deterrence**, caution, damper, determent, deterrent, discouragement, disincentive, expostulation, hindrance, remonstrance, setback

dissyllable (dɪˈsɪləbᵊl) *or* **disyllable** *n* a word of two syllables.
▸**dissyllabic** (ˌdɪsɪˈlæbɪk) *or* **disyllabic** (ˌdaɪsɪˈlæbɪk) *adj*

dissymmetry (dɪˈsɪmɪtrɪ, dɪsˈsɪm-) *n, pl* **dissymmetries.** **1** lack of symmetry. **2** the relationship between two objects when one is the mirror image of the other.
▸**dissymmetric** (ˌdɪsɪˈmɛtrɪk, ˌdɪssɪ-) *or* ˌ**dissymˈmetrical** *adj*

dist. *abbrev. for:* **1** distant. **2** distinguish(ed). **3** district.

distaff (ˈdɪstɑːf) *n* **1** the rod on which flax is wound preparatory to spinning. **2** *Figurative.* women's work. [OE *distæf,* from *dis-* bunch of flax + *stæf* STAFF[1]]

distaff side *n* the female side of a family.

distal (ˈdɪstᵊl) *adj Anat.* situated farthest from the centre or point of attachment or origin. [C19: from DISTANT + -AL[1]]
▸ˈ**distally** *adv*

distance ➊ (ˈdɪstəns) *n* **1** the space between two points. **2** the length of this gap. **3** the state of being apart in space; remoteness. **4** an interval between two points in time. **5** the extent of progress. **6** a distant place or time. **7** a separation or remoteness in relationship. **8** (preceded by *the*) the most distant or a faraway part of the visible scene. **9** *Horse racing.* **9a** *Brit.* a point on a racecourse 240 yards from the winning post. **9b** *US.* the part of a racecourse that a horse must reach before the winner passes the finishing line in order to qualify for later heats. **10 go the distance. 10a** *Boxing.* to complete a bout without being knocked out. **10b** to be able to complete an assigned task or responsibility. **11 keep one's distance.** to maintain a reserve in respect of another person. **12 middle distance.** halfway between the foreground or the observer and the horizon. ◆ *vb* **distances, distancing, distanced.** (*tr*) **13** to hold or place at a distance. **14** to separate (oneself) mentally from something. **15** to outdo; outstrip.

distance learning *n* a teaching system consisting of video, audio, and written material designed for a person to use in studying a subject at home.

distant ➊ (ˈdɪstənt) *adj* **1** far apart in space or time. **2** (*postpositive*) separated in space or time by a specified distance. **3** apart in relationship: *a distant cousin.* **4** coming from or going to a faraway place. **5** remote in manner; aloof. **6** abstracted; absent: *a distant look.* [C14: from L *distāre* to be distant, from DIS-[1] + *stāre* to stand]
▸ˈ**distantly** *adv* ▸ˈ**distantness** *n*

distaste ➊ (dɪsˈteɪst) *n* (often foll. by *for*) a dislike (of); aversion (to).

distasteful ➊ (dɪsˈteɪstfʊl) *adj* unpleasant or offensive.
▸**disˈtastefulness** *n*

distemper[1] (dɪsˈtɛmpə) *n* **1** any of various infectious diseases of animals, esp. **canine distemper,** a highly contagious viral disease of dogs. **2** *Arch.* **2a** a disorder. **2b** disturbance. **2c** discontent. [C14: from LL *distemperāre* to derange the health of, from L DIS-[1] + *temperāre* to mix in correct proportions]

distemper[2] (dɪsˈtɛmpə) *n* **1** a technique of painting in which the pigments are mixed with water, glue, size, etc.: used for poster, mural, and scene painting. **2** the paint used in this technique or any of various water-based paints. ◆ *vb* **3** to paint (something) with distemper. [C14: from Med. L *distemperāre* to soak, from L DIS-[1] + *temperāre* to mingle]

distend ➊ (dɪˈstɛnd) *vb* **1** to expand by or as if by pressure from within; swell; inflate. **2** (*tr*) to stretch out or extend. [C14: from L *distendere,* from DIS-[1] + *tendere* to stretch]
▸**disˈtensible** *adj* ▸**disˈtension** *or* **disˈtention** *n*

distich (ˈdɪstɪk) *n Prosody.* a unit of two verse lines, usually a couplet. [C16: from Gk *distikhos* having two lines, from DI-[1] + *stikhos* row, line]

distil ➊ *or US* **distill** (dɪsˈtɪl) *vb* **distils, distilling, distilled** *or US* **distills, distilling, distilled. 1** to subject to or undergo distillation. **2** (sometimes foll. by *out* or *off*) to purify, separate, or concentrate, or be purified, separated, or concentrated by distillation. **3** to obtain or be obtained by distillation. **4** to exude or give off (a substance) in drops. **5** (*tr*) to extract the essence of. [C14: from L *dēstillāre* to distil, from DE- + *stillāre* to drip]

distillate (ˈdɪstɪlɪt) *n* **1** the product of distillation. **2** a concentrated essence.

distillation ➊ (ˌdɪstɪˈleɪʃən) *n* **1** a distilling. **2** the process of evaporating or boiling a liquid and condensing its vapour. **3** purification or separation of mixtures by using different evaporation rates or boiling points of their components. **4** the process of obtaining the essence or an extract of a substance, usually by heating it in a solvent. **5** a distillate. **6** a concentrated essence.
▸**disˈtillatory** *adj*

distiller (dɪˈstɪlə) *n* a person or organization that distils, esp. a company that makes spirits.

distillery (dɪˈstɪlərɪ) *n, pl* **distilleries.** a place where alcoholic drinks, etc., are made by distillation.

distinct ➊ (dɪˈstɪŋkt) *adj* **1** easily sensed or understood; clear. **2** (when *postpositive,* foll. by *from*) not the same (as); separate (from). **3** not alike; different. **4** sharp; clear. **5** recognizable; definite. **6** explicit; unequivocal. **7** *Bot.* (of parts of a plant) not joined together; separate. [C14: from L *distinctus,* from *distinguere* to DISTINGUISH]
▸**disˈtinctly** *adv* ▸**disˈtinctness** *n*

distinction ➊ (dɪˈstɪŋkʃən) *n* **1** the act or an instance of distinguishing or differentiating. **2** a distinguishing feature. **3** the state of being different or distinguishable. **4** special honour, recognition, or fame. **5** excellence of character; distinctive qualities. **6** distinguished appearance. **7** a symbol of honour or rank.

distinctive ➊ (dɪˈstɪŋktɪv) *adj* serving or tending to distinguish; characteristic.
▸**disˈtinctively** *adv* ▸**disˈtinctiveness** *n*

distingué *French.* (distɛ̃ge) *adj* distinguished or noble.

distinguish ➊ (dɪˈstɪŋgwɪʃ) *vb* (*mainly tr*) **1** (when *intr,* foll. by *between* or *among*) to make, show, or recognize a difference (between or among); differentiate (between). **2** to be a distinctive feature of; characterize. **3** to make out; perceive. **4** to mark for a special honour. **5** to make (oneself) noteworthy. **6** to classify. [C16: from L *distinguere* to separate]
▸**disˈtinguishable** *adj* ▸**disˈtinguishing** *adj*

distinguished ➊ (dɪˈstɪŋgwɪʃt) *adj* **1** noble or dignified in appearance or behaviour. **2** eminent; famous; celebrated.

distort ➊ (dɪˈstɔːt) *vb* (*tr*) **1** (*often passive*) to twist or pull out of shape; contort; deform. **2** to alter or misrepresent (facts, etc.). **3** *Electronics.* to reproduce or amplify (a signal) inaccurately. [C16: from L

THESAURUS

dissuasive *adj* **1, 2** = **deterring,** admonitory, cautionary, discouraging, disincentive, dissuading, monitory, off-putting (*Brit. inf.*), remonstrative, warning

distance *n* **3** = **space,** absence, extent, gap, interval, lapse, length, range, reach, remoteness, remove, separation, span, stretch, width **7** = **reserve,** aloofness, coldness, coolness, frigidity, remoteness, restraint, stiffness **10 go the distance** = **finish,** bring to an end, complete, see through, stay the course **11 keep one's distance** = **be reserved,** avoid, be aloof, be indifferent, keep (someone) at arm's length, shun

distant *adj* **1** = **apart,** disparate, dispersed, distinct, scattered, separate **4** = **far-off,** abroad, afar, far, faraway, far-flung, outlying, out-of-the-way, remote, removed **5** = **reserved,** aloof, at arm's length, ceremonious, cold, cool, formal, haughty, restrained, reticent, standoffish, stiff, unapproachable, unfriendly, withdrawn
Antonyms *adj* ≠ **far-off:** adjacent, adjoining, at hand, close, handy, imminent, just round the corner, near, nearby, neighbouring, nigh, proximate, within sniffing distance (*inf.*) ≠ **reserved:** close, friendly, intimate, warm

distaste *n* = **dislike,** abhorrence, antipathy, aversion, detestation, disfavour, disgust, disinclination, displeasure, disrelish, dissatisfaction, horror, loathing, odium, repugnance, revulsion

distasteful *adj* = **unpleasant,** abhorrent, disagreeable, displeasing, loathsome, nauseous, objectionable, obnoxious, obscene, offensive, repugnant, repulsive, undesirable, uninviting, unpalatable, unsavoury
Antonyms *adj* agreeable, charming, enjoyable, pleasing, pleasurable

distend *vb* **1, 2** = **swell,** balloon, bloat, bulge, dilate, enlarge, expand, increase, inflate, puff, stretch, widen

distended *adj* **1** = **swollen,** bloated, dilated, enlarged, expanded, inflated, puffy, stretched, tumescent

distension *n* **1** = **swelling,** dilatation, dilation, enlargement, expansion, extension, inflation, intumescence, spread

distil *vb* **1-5** = **extract,** condense, draw out, evaporate, express, press out, purify, rectify, refine, sublimate, vaporize

distillation *n* **1, 6** = **essence,** elixir, extract, quintessence, spirit

distinct *adj* **3** = **different,** detached, discrete, dissimilar, individual, separate, unconnected **4** = **definite,** apparent, black-and-white, blatant, bold, clear, clear-cut, decided, evident, lucid, manifest, marked, noticeable, obvious, palpable, patent, plain, recognizable, sharp, unambiguous, unmistakable, well-defined
Antonyms *adj* ≠ **different:** common, connected, identical, indistinct, similar ≠ **definite:** fuzzy, indefinite, indistinct, obscure, unclear, vague

distinction *n* **1** = **differentiation,** discernment, discrimination, penetration, perception, separation **2** = **feature,** characteristic, distinctiveness, individuality, mark, particularity, peculiarity, quality **4** = **excellence,** account, celebrity, consequence, credit, eminence, fame, greatness, honour, importance, merit, name, note, prominence, quality, rank, renown, reputation, repute, superiority, worth

distinctive *adj* = **characteristic,** different, distinguishing, extraordinary, idiosyncratic, individual, original, peculiar, singular, special, typical, uncommon, unique
Antonyms *adj* common, ordinary, run-of-the-mill, typical

distinctly *adv* **4** = **definitely,** clearly, decidedly, evidently, manifestly, markedly, noticeably, obviously, palpably, patently, plainly, precisely, sharply, unmistakably

distinctness *n* **3** = **difference,** detachment, discreteness, disparateness, dissimilarity, dissociation, distinctiveness, individuality, separation **4** = **clearness,** clarity, lucidity, obviousness, plainness, sharpness, vividness

distinguish *vb* **1** = **differentiate,** ascertain, decide, determine, discriminate, judge, tell apart, tell between, tell the difference **3** = **make out,** discern, know, perceive, pick out, recognize, see, tell **4** = **make famous,** celebrate, dignify, honour, immortalize, signalize **6** = **characterize,** categorize, classify, individualize, make distinctive, mark, separate, set apart, single out

distinguishable *adj* **1** = **recognizable,** bold, clear, conspicuous, discernible, evident, manifest, noticeable, obvious, perceptible, plain, well-marked

distinguished *adj* **2** = **eminent,** acclaimed, celebrated, conspicuous, famed, famous, illustrious, notable, noted, renowned, well-known
Antonyms *adj* common, inferior, undistinguished, unknown

distinguishing *adj* **1** = **characteristic,** different, differentiating, distinctive, individualistic, marked, peculiar, typical

distort *vb* **1** = **deform,** bend, buckle, contort, disfigure, misshape, twist, warp, wrench, wrest

distortus, from *distorquēre* to turn different ways, from DIS-[1] + *torquēre* to twist]
▸**dis'torted** *adj*
distortion ⓘ (dɪ'stɔːʃən) *n* **1** a distorting or being distorted. **2** something that is distorted. **3** *Electronics.* an undesired change in the shape of an electrical wave or signal resulting in a loss of clarity in radio reception or sound reproduction.
▸**dis'tortional** *adj*
distract ⓘ (dɪ'strækt) *vb (tr)* **1** (*often passive*) to draw the attention of (a person) away from something. **2** to divide or confuse the attention of (a person). **3** to amuse or entertain. **4** to trouble greatly. **5** to make mad. [C14: from L *distractus* perplexed, from *distrahere* to pull in different directions, from DIS-[1] + *trahere* to drag]
distracted ⓘ (dɪ'stræktɪd) *adj* **1** bewildered; confused. **2** mad.
▸**dis'tractedly** *adv*
distraction ⓘ (dɪ'strækʃən) *n* **1** a distracting or being distracted. **2** something that serves as a diversion or entertainment. **3** an interruption; obstacle to concentration. **4** mental turmoil or madness.
distrain (dɪ'streɪn) *vb Law.* to seize (personal property) as security or indemnity for a debt. [C13: from OF *destreindre*, from L *distringere* to impede, from DIS-[1] + *stringere* to draw tight]
▸**dis'trainment** *n* ▸**dis'trainor** *or* **dis'trainer** *n*
distraint (dɪ'streɪnt) *n Law.* the act or process of distraining; distress.
distrait (dɪ'streɪ; *French* distrɛ) *adj* absent-minded; abstracted. [C18: from F, from *distraire* to DISTRACT]
distraught ⓘ (dɪ'strɔːt) *adj* **1** distracted or agitated. **2** *Rare.* mad. [C14: changed from obs. *distract* through influence of obs. *straught*, p.p. of STRETCH]
distress ⓘ (dɪ'strɛs) *vb (tr)* **1** to cause mental pain to; upset badly. **2** (*usually passive*) to subject to financial or other trouble. **3** to treat (something, esp. furniture or fabric) in order to make it appear older than it is. **4** *Law.* a less common word for **distrain.** ◆ *n* **5** mental pain; anguish. **6** a distressing or being distressed. **7** physical or financial trouble. **8 in distress.** (of a ship, etc.) in dire need of help. **9** *Law.* **9a** the seizure of property as security for or in satisfaction of a debt, claim, etc.; distraint. **9b** the property thus seized. **9c** *US* (*as modifier*): distress merchandise. [C13: from OF *destresse*, via Vulgar L, from L *districtus* divided in mind]
▸**dis'tressful** *adj* ▸**dis'tressing** *adj* ▸**dis'tressingly** *adv*
distressed ⓘ (dɪ'strɛst) *adj* **1** much troubled; upset; afflicted. **2** in financial straits; poor. **3** (of furniture, fabric, etc.) having signs of ageing artificially applied. **4** *Econ.* another word for **depressed.**
distress signal *n* a signal by radio, Very light, etc., from a ship in need of immediate assistance.
distribute ⓘ (dɪ'strɪbjuːt) *vb* **distributes, distributing, distributed.** *(tr)* **1** to give out in shares; dispense. **2** to hand out or deliver. **3** (*often passive*) to spread throughout an area. **4** (*often passive*) to divide into classes or categories. **5** *Printing.* to return (used type) to the correct positions in the typecase. **6** *Logic.* to incorporate in a distributed term of a categorical proposition. **7** *Maths.* to expand an expression containing two operators so as to change the order, as in expressing $a(b + c)$ as $ab + ac$. [C15: from L *distribuere*, from DIS-[1] + *tribuere* to give]
▸**dis'tributable** *adj*
distributed logic *n* a computer system in which remote terminals and electronic devices supplement the main computer by doing some of the computing or decision making.
distributed term *n Logic.* a term applying equally to every member of the class it designates, as *men* in *all men are mortal*.
distribution ⓘ (ˌdɪstrɪ'bjuːʃən) *n* **1** the act of distributing or the state or manner of being distributed. **2** a thing or portion distributed. **3** arrangement or location. **4** the process of physically satisfying the demand for goods and services. **5** *Econ.* the division of the total income of a community among its members. **6** *Statistics.* the set of possible values of a random variable, considered in terms of theoretical or observed frequency. **7** *Law.* the apportioning of the estate of a deceased intestate. **8** *Law.* the lawful division of the assets of a bankrupt among his creditors. **9** *Finance.* **9a** the division of part of a company's profit as a dividend to its shareholders. **9b** the amount paid by dividend in a particular distribution. **10** *Engineering.* the way in which the fuel-air mixture is supplied to each cylinder of a multicylinder internal-combustion engine.
▸ˌ**distri'butional** *adj*
distributive (dɪ'strɪbjʊtɪv) *adj* **1** characterized by or relating to distribution. **2** *Grammar.* referring separately to the individual people or items in a group, as the words *each* and *every*. ◆ *n* **3** *Grammar.* a distributive word.
▸**dis'tributively** *adv* ▸**dis'tributiveness** *n*
distributive law *n Maths, logic.* a theorem asserting that one operator can validly be distributed over another. See **distribute** (sense 7).
distributor (dɪ'strɪbjʊtə) *n* **1** a person or thing that distributes. **2** a wholesaler or middleman engaged in the distribution of a category of goods, esp. to retailers in a specific area. **3** the device in a petrol engine that distributes the high-tension voltage to the sparking plugs.
district ⓘ ('dɪstrɪkt) *n* **1a** an area of land marked off for administrative or other purposes. **1b** (*as modifier*): *district nurse*. **2** a locality separated by geographical attributes; region. **3** any subdivision of a territory, region, etc. **4** a political subdivision of a county, region, etc., that elects a council responsible for certain local services. ◆ *vb* **5** *(tr)* to divide into districts. [C17: from Med. L *districtus* area of jurisdiction, from L *distringere* to stretch out]
district attorney *n* (in the US) the state prosecuting officer in a specified judicial district.
District Court *n* **1** (in Scotland) a court of summary jurisdiction which deals with minor criminal offences. **2** (in the US) **2a** a Federal trial court in each US district. **2b** in some states, a court of general jurisdiction. **3** (in New Zealand) a court lower than a High Court. Formerly called: **magistrates' court.**
district high school *n* (in New Zealand) a school in a rural area providing both primary and secondary education.
district nurse *n* (in Britain) a nurse appointed to attend patients within a particular district, usually in the patients' homes.
distrust ⓘ (dɪs'trʌst) *vb* **1** to regard as untrustworthy or dishonest. ◆ *n* **2** suspicion; doubt.
▸**dis'truster** *n* ▸**dis'trustful** *adj*
disturb ⓘ (dɪ'stɜːb) *vb (tr)* **1** to intrude on; interrupt. **2** to destroy the quietness or peace of. **3** to disarrange; muddle. **4** (*often passive*) to

THESAURUS

2 = **misrepresent**, bias, colour, falsify, garble, pervert, slant, twist
distorted *adj* **1** = **deformed**, bent, buckled, contorted, crooked, disfigured, irregular, misshapen, twisted, warped **2** = **misrepresented**, biased, coloured, false, garbled, one-sided, partial, perverted, slanted, twisted
distortion *n* **1** = **misrepresentation**, bias, colouring, falsification, perversion, slant **2** = **deformity**, bend, buckle, contortion, crookedness, malformation, twist, twistedness, warp
distract *vb* **1** = **divert**, draw away, sidetrack, turn aside **3** = **amuse**, beguile, engross, entertain, occupy **4, 5** = **agitate**, bewilder, confound, confuse, derange, discompose, disconcert, disturb, harass, madden, perplex, puzzle, torment, trouble
distracted *adj* **1** = **agitated**, at sea, bemused, bewildered, confounded, confused, flustered, harassed, in a flap (*inf.*), perplexed, puzzled, troubled **2** = **frantic**, at the end of one's tether, crazy, deranged, desperate, distraught, frenzied, grief-stricken, insane, mad, overwrought, raving, wild
distracting *adj* **4** = **disturbing**, bewildering, bothering, confusing, disconcerting, dismaying, off-putting (*Brit. inf.*), perturbing
distraction *n* **2** = **entertainment**, amusement, beguilement, diversion, divertissement, pastime, recreation **3** = **diversion**, disturbance, interference, interruption **4** = **frenzy**, aberration, abstraction, agitation, alienation, bewilderment, commotion, confusion, delirium, derangement, desperation, discord, disorder, disturbance, hallucination, incoherence, insanity, mania
distraught *adj* **1, 2** = **frantic**, agitated, anxious, at the end of one's tether, beside oneself, crazed, desperate, distracted, distressed, hysterical, mad, out of one's mind, overwrought, raving, wild, worked-up, wrought-up
distress *vb* **1** = **upset**, afflict, agonize, bother, disturb, grieve, harass, harrow, pain, perplex, sadden, torment, trouble, worry, wound ◆ *n* **5** = **worry**, affliction, agony, anguish, anxiety, desolation, discomfort, grief, heartache, misery, pain, sadness, sorrow, suffering, torment, torture, woe, wretchedness **7** = **need**, adversity, calamity, destitution, difficulties, hardship, indigence, misfortune, poverty, privation, straits, trial, trouble
distressed *adj* **1** = **upset**, afflicted, agitated, anxious, distracted, distraught, saddened, tormented, troubled, worried, wretched **2** = **poverty-stricken**, destitute, down at heel, indigent, needy, poor, straitened
distressing *adj* **1** = **upsetting**, affecting, afflicting, distressful, disturbing, grievous, gut-wrenching, harrowing, heart-breaking, hurtful, lamentable, nerve-racking, painful, sad, worrying
distribute *vb* **1** = **share**, administer, allocate, allot, apportion, assign, deal, dispense, dispose, divide, dole out, give, measure out, mete **2** = **hand out**, circulate, convey, deliver, pass round **3** = **spread**, diffuse, disperse, disseminate, scatter, strew **4** = **classify**, arrange, assort, categorize, class, file, group
distribution *n* **1** = **spreading**, allocation, allotment, apportionment, circulation, diffusion, dispensation, dispersal, dispersion, dissemination, division, dole, partition, propagation, scattering, sharing **3** = **classification**, arrangement, assortment, disposition, grouping, location, organization, placement **4** = **delivery**, dealing, handling, mailing, marketing, trading, transport, transportation
district *n* **1-4** = **area**, community, locale, locality, neck of the woods (*inf.*), neighbourhood, parish, quarter, region, sector, vicinity, ward
distrust *vb* **1** = **suspect**, be sceptical of, be suspicious of, be wary of, disbelieve, discredit, doubt, misbelieve, mistrust, question, smell a rat (*inf.*), wonder about ◆ *n* **2** = **suspicion**, disbelief, doubt, dubiety, lack of faith, misgiving, mistrust, qualm, question, scepticism, wariness
Antonyms *vb* ≠ **suspect:** believe, depend, have confidence, have faith, trust ◆ *n* ≠ **suspicion:** confidence, faith, reliance, trust
distrustful *adj* **2** = **suspicious**, chary, cynical, disbelieving, distrusting, doubtful, doubting, dubious, leery (*sl.*), mistrustful, sceptical, uneasy, wary
disturb *vb* **1** = **interrupt**, bother, butt in on, disrupt, interfere with, intrude on, pester, rouse, startle **3** = **muddle**, confuse, derange, disarrange, disorder, disorganize, unsettle **4** = **upset**, agitate, alarm, annoy, confound, discompose, distract, distress, excite, fluster, harass, hassle (*inf.*), perturb, ruffle, shake, trouble, unnerve, unsettle, worry
Antonyms *vb* ≠ **upset:** calm, compose, lull, pacify, quiet, quieten, reassure, relax, relieve, settle, soothe

upset; trouble. **5** to inconvenience; put out. [C13: from L *disturbāre*, from DIS-[1] + *turbāre* to confuse]
▸**dis'turber** *n* ▸**dis'turbing** *adj* ▸**dis'turbingly** *adv*

disturbance ❶ (dɪ'stɜːbəns) *n* **1** a disturbing or being disturbed. **2** an interruption or intrusion. **3** an unruly outburst or tumult. **4** *Law.* an interference with another's rights. **5** *Geol.* a minor movement of the earth causing a small earthquake. **6** *Meteorol.* a small depression. **7** *Psychiatry.* a mental or emotional disorder.

disturbed ❶ (dɪ'stɜːbd) *adj Psychiatry.* emotionally upset, troubled, or maladjusted.

disulphide (daɪ'sʌlfaɪd) *n* any chemical compound containing two sulphur atoms per molecule.

disunite ❶ (ˌdɪsjʊ'naɪt) *vb* **disunites, disuniting, disunited. 1** to separate; disrupt. **2** (*tr*) to set at variance; estrange.
▸**dis'union** *n* ▸**dis'unity** *n*

disuse ❶ (dɪs'juːs) *n* the condition of being unused; neglect (often in **in** *or* **into disuse**).

disutility (ˌdɪsjuː'tɪlɪtɪ) *n, pl* **disutilities.** *Econ.* the shortcomings of a commodity or activity in satisfying human wants. Cf. **utility** (sense 4).

disyllable ('daɪˌsɪləbᵊl) *n* a variant of **dissyllable.**

ditch ❶ (dɪtʃ) *n* **1** a narrow channel dug in the earth, usually used for drainage, irrigation, or as a boundary marker. ◆ *vb* **2** to make a ditch in. **3** (*intr*) to edge with a ditch. **4** *Sl.* to crash, esp. deliberately, as to avoid more unpleasant circumstances: *he had to ditch the car.* **5** (*tr*) *Sl.* to abandon. **6** *Sl.* to land (an aircraft) on water in an emergency. **7** (*tr*) *US sl.* to evade. [OE *dīc*]
▸**'ditcher** *n*

ditchwater ('dɪtʃˌwɔːtə) *n* **1** stagnant water, esp. found in ditches. **2 as dull as ditchwater.** very dull; very uninteresting.

dither ❶ ('dɪðə) *vb* (*intr*) **1** *Chiefly Brit.* to be uncertain or indecisive. **2** *Chiefly US.* to be in an agitated state. **3** to tremble, as with cold. ◆ *n* **4** *Chiefly Brit.* a state of indecision. **5** a state of agitation. [C17: var. of C14 (N English dialect) *didder*, from ?]
▸**'ditherer** *n* ▸**'dithery** *adj*

dithyramb ('dɪθɪˌræm, -ˌræmb) *n* **1** (in ancient Greece) a passionate choral hymn in honour of Dionysus. **2** any utterance or a piece of writing that resembles this. [C17: from L *dīthyrambus*, from Gk *dithurambos*]
▸ˌ**dithy'rambic** *adj*

dittany ('dɪtənɪ) *n, pl* **dittanies. 1** an aromatic Cretan plant with pink flowers: formerly credited with medicinal properties. **2** a North American plant with purplish flowers. [C14: from OF *ditan*, from L *dictamnus*, from Gk *diktamnon*, ?from *Diktē*, mountain in Crete]

ditto ('dɪtəʊ) *n, pl* **dittos. 1** the aforementioned; the above; the same. Used in accounts, lists, etc., to avoid repetition, and symbolized by two small marks („) known as **ditto marks,** placed under the thing repeated. **2** *Inf.* a duplicate. ◆ *adv* **3** in the same way. ◆ *sentence substitute.* **4** *Inf.* used to avoid repeating or to confirm agreement with an immediately preceding sentence. ◆ *vb* **dittos, dittoing, dittoed. 5** (*tr*) to copy; repeat. [C17: from It. (dialect): var. of *detto* said, from *dicere* to say, from L]

ditty ('dɪtɪ) *n, pl* **ditties.** a short simple song or poem. [C13: from OF *ditie* poem, from *ditier* to compose, from L *dictāre* to DICTATE]

ditty bag *or* **box** *n* a sailor's bag or box for personal belongings or tools. [C19: ?from obs. *dutty* calico, from Hindi *dhōtī* loincloth]

ditzy *or* **ditsy** ('dɪtzɪ, 'dɪtsɪ) *adj* **ditzier, ditziest** *or* **ditsier, ditsiest.** *Sl.* silly and scatterbrained. [C20: perhaps from DOTTY + DIZZY]

diuretic (ˌdaɪjʊ'rɛtɪk) *adj* **1** acting to increase the flow of urine. ◆ *n* **2** a drug or agent that increases the flow of urine. [ME, from LL, from Gk, from *dia-* through + *ourein* to urinate]
▸**diuresis** (ˌdaɪjʊ'riːsɪs) *n*

diurnal ❶ (daɪ'ɜːnᵊl) *adj* **1** happening during the day or daily. **2** (of flowers) open during the day and closed at night. **3** (of animals) active during the day. ◆ Cf. **nocturnal.** [C15: from LL *diurnālis*, from L *diurnus*, from *diēs* day]
▸**di'urnally** *adv*

div (dɪv) *n Sl.* a shortened form of **divvy**[1].

div. *abbrev. for:* **1** divide(d). **2** dividend. **3** division. **4** divorce(d).

diva ❶ ('diːvə) *n, pl* **divas** *or* **dive** (-vɪ). a highly distinguished female singer; prima donna. [C19: via It. from L: a goddess, from *dīvus* DIVINE]

divagate ('daɪvəˌgeɪt) *vb* **divagates, divagating, divagated.** (*intr*) *Rare.* to digress or wander. [C16: from L DI-[2] + *vagārī* to wander]
▸ˌ**diva'gation** *n*

divalent (daɪ'veɪlənt, 'daɪˌveɪ-) *adj Chem.* **1** having a valency of two. **2** having two valencies. ◆ Also: **bivalent.**
▸**di'valency** *n*

divan (dɪ'væn) *n* **1a** a backless sofa or couch. **1b** a bed resembling such a couch. **2** (esp. formerly) a smoking room. **3a** a Muslim law court, council chamber, or counting house. **3b** a Muslim council of state. [C16: from Turkish *dīvān*, from Persian *dīwān*]

dive ❶ (daɪv) *vb* **dives, diving, dived** *or US* **dove** (dəʊv), **dived.** (*mainly intr*) **1** to plunge headfirst into water. **2** (of a submarine, etc.) to submerge under water. **3** (*also tr*) to fly in a steep nose-down descending path. **4** to rush, go, or reach quickly, as in a headlong plunge: *he dived for the ball.* **5** (*also tr;* foll. by *in* or *into*) to dip or put (one's hand) quickly or forcefully (into). **6** (usually foll. by *in* or *into*) to involve oneself (in something), as in eating food. ◆ *n* **7** a headlong plunge into water. **8** an act or instance of diving. **9** a steep nose-down descent of an aircraft. **10** *Sl.* a disreputable bar or club. **11** *Boxing sl.* the act of a boxer pretending to be knocked down or out. [OE *dȳfan*]

dive bomber *n* a military aircraft designed to release its bombs on a target during a steep dive.
▸**'dive-bomb** *vb* (*tr*)

diver ('daɪvə) *n* **1** a person or thing that dives. **2** a person who works or explores underwater. **3** any of various aquatic birds of northern oceans: noted for skill in diving. US and Canad. name: **loon. 4** any of various other diving birds.

diverge ❶ (daɪ'vɜːdʒ) *vb* **diverges, diverging, diverged. 1** to separate or cause to separate and go in different directions from a point. **2** (*intr*) to be at variance; differ. **3** (*intr*) to deviate from a prescribed course. **4** (*intr*) *Maths.* (of a series) to have no limit. [C17: from Med. L *dīvergere*, from L DI-[2] + *vergere* to turn]

divergence ❶ (daɪ'vɜːdʒəns) *or* **divergency** *n* **1** the act or result of diverging or the amount by which something diverges. **2** the condition of being divergent.

divergent ❶ (daɪ'vɜːdʒənt) *adj* **1** diverging or causing divergence. **2** *Maths.* (of a series) having no limit.
▸**di'vergently** *adv*

> **USAGE NOTE** The use of *divergent* to mean different as in *they hold widely divergent views* is considered by some people to be incorrect.

divergent thinking *n Psychol.* thinking in an unusual and unstereotyped way, for instance to generate several possible solutions to a problem.

divers ❶ ('daɪvəz) *determiner Arch. or literary.* various; sundry; some. [C13: from OF, from L *dīversus* turned in different directions]

diverse ❶ (daɪ'vɜːs, 'daɪvɜːs) *adj* **1** having variety; assorted. **2** distinct in kind. [C13: from L *dīversus;* see DIVERS]
▸**di'versely** *adv*

THESAURUS

disturbance *n* **1, 2 = interruption**, agitation, annoyance, bother, confusion, derangement, disorder, distraction, hindrance, intrusion, molestation, perturbation, upset **3 = disorder**, bother (*inf.*), brawl, commotion, fracas, fray, hubbub, riot, ruckus (*inf.*), ruction (*inf.*), rumpus, shindig (*inf.*), shindy (*inf.*), tumult, turmoil, upheaval, uproar

disturbed *adj Psychiatry* **= unbalanced**, disordered, maladjusted, neurotic, troubled, upset
Antonyms *adj* balanced, untroubled

disturbing *adj* **4 = worrying**, agitating, alarming, disconcerting, discouraging, dismaying, disquieting, distressing, frightening, harrowing, perturbing, startling, threatening, troubling, unsettling, upsetting

disunion *n* **1 = separation**, abstraction, detachment, disconnection, disjunction, division, partition, severance **2 = disagreement**, alienation, breach, discord, dissension, dissidence, estrangement, feud, rupture, schism, split

disunite *vb* **1 = separate**, detach, disband, disconnect, disengage, disjoin, disrupt, divide, part, segregate, sever, split, sunder **2 = set at odds**, alienate, embroil, estrange, set at variance

disunity *n* **2 = disagreement**, alienation, breach, discord, discordance, dissension, dissent, estrangement, rupture, schism, split, variance

disuse *n* **= neglect**, abandonment, decay, desuetude, discontinuance, idleness, nonemployment, nonuse
Antonyms *n* application, employment, practice, service, usage, use

ditch *n* **1 = channel**, drain, dyke, furrow, gully, moat, trench, watercourse ◆ *vb* **5** *Slang* **= get rid of**, abandon, axe (*inf.*), bin (*inf.*), chuck (*inf.*), discard, dispose of, drop, dump (*inf.*), jettison, junk (*inf.*), scrap, throw out *or* overboard

dither *Chiefly Brit.* ◆ *vb* **1 = vacillate**, faff about (*Brit. inf.*), falter, haver, hesitate, hum and haw, oscillate, shillyshally (*inf.*), swither (*Scot.*), teeter, waver ◆ *n* **4 = flutter**, bother, flap (*inf.*), fluster, pother, stew (*inf.*), tiz-woz (*inf.*), tizzy (*inf.*), twitter (*inf.*)
Antonyms *vb* ≠ **vacillate:** come to a conclusion, conclude, decide, make a decision, make up one's mind, reach *or* come to a decision, resolve, settle

dithery *adj* **1 = indecisive**, agitated, all of a dither *or* fluster, bothered, dithering, flustered, hesitant, in a flap *or* tizzy (*inf.*), irresolute, swithering (*Scot.*), tentative, uncertain, unsure, vacillating, wavering
Antonyms *adj* certain, decisive, firm, positive, resolute, sure, unhesitating

diurnal *adj* **1 = daily**, circadian, daytime, everyday, quotidian, regular

diva *n* **= prima donna**, opera singer, singer

dive *vb* **1-4 = plunge**, descend, dip, disappear, drop, duck, fall, go underwater, jump, leap, nose-dive, pitch, plummet, submerge, swoop ◆ *n* **7-9 = plunge**, dash, header (*inf.*), jump, leap, lunge, nose dive, spring **10** *Slang* **= sleazy bar**, honky-tonk (*US sl.*), joint (*sl.*)

diverge *vb* **1 = separate**, bifurcate, branch, divaricate, divide, fork, part, radiate, split, spread **2 = be at variance**, be at odds, conflict, differ, disagree, dissent **3 = deviate**, depart, digress, meander, stray, turn aside, wander

divergence *n* **1, 2 = separation**, branching out, deflection, departure, deviation, difference, digression, disparity, divagation, ramification, varying

divergent *adj* **1 = separate**, conflicting, deviating, different, differing, disagreeing, dissimilar, diverging, diverse, variant

divers *determiner Archaic or literary* **= various**, different, manifold, many, multifarious, numerous, several, some, sundry, varied

diverse *adj* **1 = various**, assorted, diversified, manifold, miscellaneous, of every description,

DICTIONARY

diversify Ⓣ (daɪˈvɜːsɪˌfaɪ) *vb* **diversifies, diversifying, diversified. 1** (*tr*) to create different forms of; variegate; vary. **2** (of an enterprise) to vary (products, operations, etc.) in order to spread risk, expand, etc. **3** to distribute (investments) among several securities in order to spread risk. [C15: from OF *diversifier,* from Med. L *dīversificāre,* from L *dīversus* DIVERSE + *facere* to make]
▸**diˌversifiˈcation** *n*

diversion Ⓣ (daɪˈvɜːʃən) *n* **1** the act of diverting from a specified course. **2** *Chiefly Brit.* an official detour used by traffic when a main route is closed. **3** something that distracts from business, etc.; amusement. **4** *Mil.* a feint attack designed to draw an enemy away from the main attack.
▸**diˈversional** *or* **diˈversionary** *adj*

diversity Ⓣ (daɪˈvɜːsɪtɪ) *n* **1** the state or quality of being different or varied. **2** a point of difference.

divert Ⓣ (daɪˈvɜːt) *vb* **1** to turn aside; deflect. **2** (*tr*) to entertain; amuse. **3** (*tr*) to distract the attention of. [C15: from F *divertir,* from L *dīvertere* to turn aside, from DI-[2] + *vertere* to turn]
▸**diˈverting** *adj* ▸**diˈvertingly** *adv*

diverticulitis (ˌdaɪvəˌtɪkjʊˈlaɪtɪs) *n* inflammation of one or more diverticula, esp. of the colon.

diverticulum (ˌdaɪvəˈtɪkjʊləm) *n, pl* **diverticula** (-lə). any sac or pouch formed by herniation of the wall of a tubular organ or part, esp. the intestines. [C16: from NL, from L *dēverticulum* by-path, from *dēvertere* to turn aside, from *vertere* to turn]

divertimento (dɪˌvɜːtɪˈmɛntəʊ) *n, pl* **divertimenti** (-tɪ). **1** a piece of entertaining music, often scored for a mixed ensemble and having no fixed form. **2** an episode in a fugue. [C18: from It.]

divertissement (dɪˈvɜːtɪsmənt) *n* a brief entertainment or diversion, usually between the acts of a play. [C18: from F: entertainment]

Dives (ˈdaɪviːz) *n* **1** a rich man in the parable in Luke 16:19–31. **2** a very rich man.

divest Ⓣ (daɪˈvɛst) *vb* (*tr;* usually foll. by *of*) **1** to strip (of clothes). **2** to deprive or dispossess. [C17: changed from earlier *devest*]
▸**divestiture** (daɪˈvɛstɪtʃə), **divesture** (daɪˈvɛstʃə), *or* **diˈvestment** *n*

divi (ˈdɪvɪ) *n* an alternative spelling of **divvy**[1].

divide Ⓣ (dɪˈvaɪd) *vb* **divides, dividing, divided. 1** to separate into parts; split up. **2** to share or be shared out in parts; distribute. **3** to diverge or cause to diverge in opinion or aim. **4** (*tr*) to keep apart or be a boundary between. **5** (*intr*) to vote by separating into two groups. **6** to categorize; classify. **7** to calculate the quotient of (one number or quantity) and (another number or quantity) by division. **8** (*intr*) to diverge: *the roads divide.* **9** (*tr*) to mark increments of (length, angle, etc.). ◆ *n* **10** *Chiefly US & Canad.* an area of relatively high ground separating drainage basins; watershed. **11** a division; split. [C14: from L *dīvidere* to force apart, from DIS-[1] + *vid-* separate, from the source of *viduus* bereaved]

divided (dɪˈvaɪdɪd) *adj* **1** *Bot.* another word for **dissected** (sense 1). **2** split; not united.

dividend Ⓣ (ˈdɪvɪˌdɛnd) *n* **1a** a distribution from the net profits of a company to its shareholders. **1b** a portion of this distribution received by a shareholder. **2** the share of a cooperative society's surplus allocated to members. **3** *Insurance.* a sum of money distributed from a company's net profits to the holders of certain policies. **4** something extra; a bonus. **5** a number or quantity to be divided by another number or quantity. **6** *Law.* the proportion of an insolvent estate payable to the creditors. [C15: from L *dīvidendum* what is to be divided]

divider (dɪˈvaɪdə) *n* **1** Also called: **room divider.** a screen or piece of furniture placed so as to divide a room into separate areas. **2** a person or thing that divides. **3** *Electronics.* an electrical circuit with an output that is a well-defined fraction of a given input: *a voltage divider.*

dividers (dɪˈvaɪdəz) *pl n* a type of compass with two pointed arms, used for measuring lines or dividing them.

divination Ⓣ (ˌdɪvɪˈneɪʃən) *n* **1** the art or practice of discovering future events or unknown things, as though by supernatural powers. **2** a prophecy. **3** a guess.
▸**divinatory** (dɪˈvɪnətərɪ, -trɪ) *adj*

divine Ⓣ (dɪˈvaɪn) *adj* **1** of God or a deity. **2** godlike. **3** of or associated with religion or worship. **4** of supreme excellence or worth. **5** *Inf.* splendid; perfect. ◆ *n* **6** (*often cap.;* preceded by *the*) another term for **God. 7** a priest, esp. one learned in theology. ◆ *vb* **divines, divining, divined. 8** to perceive (something) by intuition. **9** to conjecture (something); guess. **10** to discern (a hidden or future reality) as though by supernatural power. **11** (*tr*) to search for (water, metal, etc.) using a divining rod. [C14: from L *dīvīnus,* from *dīvus* a god]
▸**diˈvinely** *adv* ▸**diˈviner** *n*

divine office *n* (*sometimes cap.*) the canonical prayers recited daily by priests, etc. Also called: **Liturgy of the Hours.**

divine right of kings *n History.* the concept that the right to rule derives from God and that kings are answerable for their actions to God alone.

diving bell *n* an early diving submersible having an open bottom and being supplied with compressed air.

diving board *n* a platform or springboard from which swimmers may dive.

diving suit *or* **dress** *n* a waterproof suit used by divers, having a heavy detachable helmet and an air supply.

divining rod *n* a forked twig said to move when held over ground in which water, metal, etc., is to be found. Also called: **dowsing rod.**

divinity Ⓣ (dɪˈvɪnɪtɪ) *n, pl* **divinities. 1** the nature of a deity or the state of being divine. **2** a god. **3** (*often cap.;* preceded by *the*) another term for **God. 4** another word for **theology.**

divisible Ⓣ (dɪˈvɪzɪbᵊl) *adj* capable of being divided, usually with no remainder.
▸**diˌvisiˈbility** *or* **diˈvisibleness** *n* ▸**diˈvisibly** *adv*

division Ⓣ (dɪˈvɪʒən) *n* **1** a dividing or being divided. **2** the act of sharing out; distribution. **3** something that divides; boundary. **4** one of the parts, groups, etc., into which something is divided. **5** a part of a government, business, etc., that has been made into a unit for administrative or other reasons. **6** a formal vote in Parliament or a similar legislative body. **7** a difference of opinion. **8** (in sports) a section or class organized according to age, weight, skill, etc. **9** a mathematical operation in which the quotient of two numbers or quantities is calculated. Usually written: $a \div b$, a/b, $\frac{a}{b}$. **10** *Army.* a major formation, larger than a brigade but smaller than a corps, containing the necessary arms to sustain independent combat. **11** *Biol.* (in traditional classification systems) a major category of the plant kingdom that contains one or more related classes. Cf. **phylum** (sense 1). [C14: from L *dīvīsiō,* from *dīvidere* to DIVIDE]
▸**diˈvisional** *or* **diˈvisionary** *adj* ▸**diˈvisionally** *adv*

division sign *n* the symbol ÷, placed between the dividend and the divisor to indicate division, as in $12 \div 6 = 2$.

divisive Ⓣ (dɪˈvaɪsɪv) *adj* tending to cause disagreement or dissension.
▸**diˈvisively** *adv* ▸**diˈvisiveness** *n*

divisor (dɪˈvaɪzə) *n* **1** a number or quantity to be divided into another number or quantity (the dividend). **2** a number that is a factor of another number.

divorce Ⓣ (dɪˈvɔːs) *n* **1** the legal dissolution of a marriage. **2** a judicial

THESAURUS

several, sundry, varied **2** = **different,** differing, discrete, disparate, dissimilar, distinct, divergent, separate, unlike, varying

diversify *vb* **1** = **vary,** alter, assort, branch out, change, expand, have a finger in every pie, mix, modify, spread out, transform, variegate

diversion *n* **1** = **detour,** alteration, change, deflection, departure, deviation, digression, variation **3** = **pastime,** amusement, beguilement, delight, distraction, divertissement, enjoyment, entertainment, game, gratification, jollies (*sl.*), play, pleasure, recreation, relaxation, sport

diversity *n* **1** = **difference,** assortment, dissimilarity, distinctiveness, divergence, diverseness, diversification, heterogeneity, medley, multiplicity, range, unlikeness, variance, variegation, variety

divert *vb* **1** = **redirect,** avert, deflect, switch, turn aside **2** = **entertain,** amuse, beguile, delight, gratify, recreate, regale **3** = **distract,** detract, draw *or* lead away from, lead astray, sidetrack

diverted *adj* **1** = **redirected,** changed, deflected, made use of, rebudgeted, rechannelled, reclassified, taken over, turned aside **2** = **entertained,** amused, taken out of oneself, tickled

diverting *adj* **2** = **entertaining,** amusing, beguiling, enjoyable, fun, humorous, pleasant

divest *vb* **1** = **strip,** denude, disrobe, doff, remove, take off, unclothe, undress **2** = **deprive,** despoil, dispossess, strip

divide *vb* **1** = **separate,** bisect, cleave, cut (up), detach, disconnect, part, partition, segregate, sever, shear, split, subdivide, sunder **2** = **share,** allocate, allot, apportion, deal out, dispense, distribute, divvy (up) (*inf.*), dole out, measure out, portion **3** = **cause to disagree,** alienate, break up, come between, disunite, estrange, set at variance *or* odds, set *or* pit against one another, sow dissension, split **6** = **classify,** arrange, categorize, grade, group, put in order, separate, sort
Antonyms *vb* ≠ **separate:** combine, come together, connect, join, knit, marry, splice, unite

dividend *n* **4** = **bonus,** cut (*inf.*), divvy (*inf.*), extra, gain, plus, portion, share, surplus

divination *n* **1** = **prediction,** augury, clairvoyance, divining, foretelling, fortune-telling, presage, prognostication, prophecy, soothsaying, sortilege

divine *adj* **1, 2** = **heavenly,** angelic, celestial, godlike, holy, spiritual, superhuman, supernatural **3** = **sacred,** consecrated, holy, religious, sanctified, spiritual **5** *Informal* = **wonderful,** beautiful, excellent, glorious, marvellous, perfect, splendid, superlative ◆ *n* **7** = **priest,** churchman, clergyman, cleric, ecclesiastic, minister, pastor, reverend ◆ *vb* **8-10** = **infer,** apprehend, conjecture, deduce, discern, foretell, guess, intuit, perceive, prognosticate, suppose, surmise, suspect, understand **11** = **dowse**

diviner *n* **8-10** = **seer,** astrologer, augur, oracle, prophet, sibyl, soothsayer **11** = **dowser**

divinity *n* **1** = **godliness,** deity, divine nature, godhead, godhood, holiness, sanctity **2** = **god** *or* **goddess,** daemon, deity, genius, guardian spirit, spirit **4** = **theology,** religion, religious studies

divisible *adj* = **dividable,** fractional, separable, splittable

division *n* **1, 2** = **separation,** bisection, cutting up, detaching, dividing, partition, splitting up **3** = **dividing line,** border, boundary, demarcation, divide, divider, partition **4** = **sharing,** allotment, apportionment, distribution **5** = **part,** branch, category, class, compartment, department, group, head, portion, section, sector, segment **7** = **disagreement,** breach, difference of opinion, discord, disunion, estrangement, feud, rupture, split, variance
Antonyms *n* ≠ **disagreement:** accord, agreement, concord, harmony, peace, union, unity

divisive *adj* = **disruptive,** alienating, damaging, detrimental, discordant, estranging, inharmonious, pernicious, troublesome, unsettling

divorce *n* **1** = **separation,** annulment, breach, break, decree nisi, dissolution, disunion, rupture, severance, split-up ◆ *vb* **4, 5** = **separate,**

decree declaring a marriage to be dissolved. **3** a separation, esp. one that is total or complete. ◆ *vb* **divorces, divorcing, divorced. 4** to separate or be separated by divorce; give or obtain a divorce. **5** (*tr*) to remove or separate, esp. completely. [C14: from OF, from L *dīvortium,* from *dīvertere* to separate]
▸**di'vorceable** *adj*

divorcée (dɪvɔː'siː) *or* (*masc*) **divorcé** (dɪ'vɔːseɪ) *n* a person who has been divorced.

divot ('dɪvət) *n* a piece of turf dug out of a grass surface, esp. by a golf club or by horses' hooves. [C16: from Scot., from ?]

divulge ❶ (daɪ'vʌldʒ) *vb* **divulges, divulging, divulged.** (*tr; may take a clause as object*) to make known; disclose. [C15: from L *dīvulgāre,* from DI-[2] + *vulgāre* to spread among people, from *vulgus* the common people]
▸**di'vulgence** *or* **di'vulgement** *n* ▸**di'vulger** *n*

divvy[1] ❶ ('dɪvɪ) *Inf.* ◆ *n, pl* **divvies. 1** *Brit.* short for **dividend,** esp. (formerly) one paid by a cooperative society. **2** *US & Canad.* a share; portion. ◆ *vb* **divvies, divvying, divvied. 3** (*tr;* usually foll. by *up*) to divide and share.

divvy[2] ('dɪvɪ) *n, pl* **divvies.** *Sl.* a stupid or odd person; misfit. [C20: ? from DEVIANT]

Diwali (dɪ'wɑːlɪ) *n* a major Hindu religious festival, honouring Lakshmi, the goddess of wealth. Held over the New Year according to the Vikrama calendar, it is marked by feasting, gifts, and the lighting of lamps.

dixie ('dɪksɪ) *n* **1** *Chiefly mil.* a large metal pot for cooking, brewing tea, etc. **2** a mess tin. [C19: from Hindi *degcī,* dim. of *degcā* pot]

Dixie ('dɪksɪ) *n* **1** Also called: **Dixieland.** the southern states of the US. ◆ *adj* **2** of the southern states of the US. [C19: ?from the nickname of New Orleans, from *dixie* a ten-dollar bill printed there, from F *dix* ten]

Dixieland ('dɪksɪˌlænd) *n* **1** a form of jazz that originated in New Orleans in the 1920s. **2** a revival of this style in the 1950s. **3** See **Dixie** (sense 1).

DIY *or* **d.i.y.** *Brit., Austral., & NZ abbrev. for* do-it-yourself.

dizzy ❶ ('dɪzɪ) *adj* **dizzier, dizziest. 1** affected with a whirling or reeling sensation; giddy. **2** mentally confused or bewildered. **3** causing or tending to cause vertigo or bewilderment. **4** *Inf.* foolish or flighty. ◆ *vb* **dizzies, dizzying, dizzied. 5** (*tr*) to make dizzy. [OE *dysig* silly]
▸**'dizzily** *adv* ▸**'dizziness** *n*

DJ *or* **dj** ('diːˌdʒeɪ) *n* **1** a variant of **deejay. 2** an informal term for **dinner jacket.**

djellaba, djellabah *or* **jellaba, jellabah** ('dʒɛləbə) *n* a kind of loose cloak with a hood, worn by men esp. in N Africa and the Middle East. [from Ar. *jallabah*]

djinni *or* **djinny** (dʒɪ'niː, 'dʒɪnɪ) *n, pl* **djinn** (dʒɪn). variant spellings of **jinni.**

dl *symbol for* decilitre.

DLitt *or* **DLit** *abbrev. for:* **1** Doctor of Letters. **2** Doctor of Literature. [L *Doctor Litterarum*]

dm *symbol for* decimetre.

DM *abbrev. for* Deutschmark.

DMA *Computing. abbrev. for* direct memory access.

D-mark *or* **D-Mark** *n* short for **Deutschmark.**

DMF *abbrev. for* dimethylformamide.

DMs *Inf. abbrev. for* Doc Martens.

DMus *abbrev. for* Doctor of Music.

DNA *n* deoxyribonucleic acid, the main constituent of the chromosomes of all organisms (except some viruses) in the form of a double helix. DNA is self-replicating and is responsible for the transmission of hereditary characteristics.

DNAase (ˌdiːɛn'eɪeɪz) *or* **DNase** (ˌdiːɛn'eɪz) *n* deoxyribonuclease; any of a number of enzymes that hydrolyse DNA.

DNA fingerprinting *or* **profiling** *n* another name for **genetic fingerprinting.**

D-notice *n Brit.* an official notice sent to newspapers prohibiting the publication of certain security information. [C20: from their administrative classification letter]

do[1] ❶ (duː; *unstressed* dʊ, də) *vb* **does, doing, did, done. 1** to perform or complete (a deed or action): *to do a portrait.* **2** (often *intr;* foll. by *for*) to serve the needs of; be suitable for; suffice. **3** (*tr*) to arrange or fix. **4** (*tr*) to prepare or provide; serve: *this restaurant doesn't do lunch on Sundays.* **5** (*tr*) to make tidy, elegant, ready, etc.: *to do one's hair.* **6** (*tr*) to improve (esp. in **do something to** *or* **for**). **7** (*tr*) to find an answer to (a problem or puzzle). **8** (*tr*) to translate or adapt the form or language of: *the book was done into a play.* **9** (*intr*) to conduct oneself: *do as you please.* **10** (*intr*) to fare or manage. **11** (*tr*) to cause or produce: *complaints do nothing to help.* **12** (*tr*) to give or render: *do me a favour.* **13** (*tr*) to work at, esp. as a course of study or a profession. **14** (*tr*) to perform (a play, etc.); act. **15** (*tr*) to mimic or play the part of: *she does a wonderful elderly aunt.* **16** (*tr*) to travel at a specified speed, esp. as a maximum. **17** (*tr*) to travel or traverse (a distance). **18** (takes an infinitive without *to*) used as a way auxiliary **18a** before the subject of an interrogative sentence as a way of forming a question: *do you agree?* **18b** to intensify positive statements and commands: *I do like your new house; do hurry!* **18c** before a negative adverb to form negative statements or commands: *do not leave me here alone!* **18d** in inverted constructions: *little did he realize that.* **19** used as an auxiliary to replace an earlier verb or verb phrase: *he likes you as much as I do.* **20** (*tr*) *Inf.* to visit as a sightseer or tourist. **21** (*tr*) to wear out; exhaust. **22** (*intr*) to happen (esp. in **nothing doing**). **23** (*tr*) *Sl.* to serve (a period of time) as a prison sentence. **24** (*tr*) *Inf.* to cheat or swindle. **25** (*tr*) *Sl.* to rob. **26** (*tr*) *Sl.* **26a** to arrest. **26b** to convict of a crime. **27** (*tr*) *Austral. sl.* to spend (money). **28** (*tr*) *Sl., chiefly Brit.* to treat violently; assault. **29** *Sl.* to take or use (a drug). **30** (*tr*) *Taboo sl.* (of a male) to have sexual intercourse with. **31 do or die.** to make a final or supreme effort. **32 make do.** to manage with whatever is available. ◆ *n, pl* **dos** *or* **do's. 33** *Sl.* an act or instance of cheating or swindling. **34** *Inf., chiefly Brit. & NZ.* a formal or festive gathering; party. **35 do's and don'ts.** *Inf.* rules. ◆ See also **do away with, do by,** etc. [OE *dōn*]

do[2] (dəʊ) *n, pl* **dos.** a variant spelling of **doh.**

do. *abbrev. for* ditto.

DOA *abbrev. for* dead on arrival.

doable ('duːəb°l) *adj* capable of being done.

do away with ❶ *vb* (*intr, adv + prep*) **1** to kill or destroy. **2** to discard or abolish.

dobbin ('dɒbɪn) *n* a name for a horse, esp. a workhorse. [C16: from *Robin,* pet form of *Robert*]

Doberman pinscher ('dəʊbəmən 'pɪnʃə) *or* **Doberman** *n* a breed of large dog with a glossy black-and-tan coat. Also: **Dobermann.** [C19: after L. *Dobermann* (19th-cent. G dog breeder) who bred it + *Pinscher,* ? after *Pinzgau,* district in Austria]

dob in *vb* **dobs, dobbing, dobbed.** (*adv*) *Austral. & NZ sl.* **1** (*tr*) to inform against, esp. to the police. **2** to contribute to a fund.

dobra ('dəʊbrə) *n* the standard monetary unit of São Tomé e Principe.

do by *vb* (*intr, prep*) to treat in the manner specified.

doc (dɒk) *n Inf.* short for **doctor.**

DOC *abbrev. for* Denominazione di Origine Controllata: used of wines. [It., lit.: name of origin controlled]

docent ('dəʊs°nt) *n* a voluntary worker acting as a guide in a museum, art gallery, etc. [C19: from G *Dozent,* from L *docēns* from *docēre* to teach]

DOCG *abbrev. for* Denominazione di Origine Controllata Garantita: used of wines. [It., lit: name of origin guaranteed controlled]

docile ❶ ('dəʊsaɪl) *adj* **1** easy to manage or discipline; submissive. **2** *Rare.* easy to teach. [C15: from L *docilis* easily taught, from *docēre* to teach]
▸**'docilely** *adv* ▸**docility** (dəʊ'sɪlɪtɪ) *n*

dock[1] ❶ (dɒk) *n* **1** a wharf or pier. **2** a space between two wharves or piers for the mooring of ships. **3** an area of water that can accommodate a ship and can be closed off to allow regulation of the water level. **4** short for **dry dock. 5 in** *or* **into dock.** *Brit. inf.* **5a** (of people) in hospital. **5b** (of cars, etc.) in a repair shop. **6** *Chiefly US & Canad.* a platform from which lorries, goods trains, etc., are loaded and unloaded. ◆ *vb* **7** to moor or be moored at a dock. **8** to put (a vessel) into, or (of a

THESAURUS

annul, disconnect, dissociate, dissolve (*marriage*), disunite, divide, part, sever, split up, sunder

divulge *vb* = **make known,** betray, blow wide open (*sl.*), communicate, confess, cough (*sl.*), declare, disclose, exhibit, expose, get off one's chest (*inf.*), impart, leak, let slip, out (*inf.*), proclaim, promulgate, publish, reveal, spill (*inf.*), spill one's guts about (*sl.*), tell, uncover
Antonyms *vb* conceal, hide, keep secret

divvy[1] *Informal* ◆ *n* **1** = **share,** cut (*inf.*), dividend, percentage, portion, quota, whack (*inf.*) ◆ *vb* **3** *Informal* = **share (out),** apportion, cut, distribute, divide, parcel out, split

dizzy *adj* **1** = **giddy,** faint, light-headed, off balance, reeling, shaky, staggering, swimming, vertiginous, weak at the knees, wobbly, woozy (*inf.*) **2** = **confused,** at sea, befuddled, bemused, bewildered, dazed, dazzled, muddled **3** = **steep,** lofty, vertiginous **4** *Informal* = **scatterbrained,** capricious, ditzy *or* ditsy, fickle, flighty, foolish, frivolous, giddy, light-headed, silly

do[1] *vb* **1** = **perform,** accomplish, achieve, act, carry out, complete, conclude, discharge, end, execute, produce, transact, undertake, work **2** = **be adequate,** answer, be enough, be of use, be sufficient, cut the mustard, pass muster, satisfy, serve, suffice, suit **3** = **get ready,** arrange, be responsible for, fix, look after, make, make ready, organize, prepare, see to, take on **7** = **solve,** decipher, decode, figure out, puzzle out, resolve, work out **9** = **behave,** bear oneself, carry oneself, comport oneself, conduct oneself **10** = **get on,** fare, get along, make out, manage, proceed **11** = **cause,** bring about, create, effect, produce **14** = **perform,** act, give, present, produce, put on **20** *Informal* = **visit,** cover, explore, journey through *or* around, look at, stop in, tour, travel **24** *Informal* = **cheat,** con (*inf.*), cozen, deceive, defraud, diddle (*inf.*), dupe, fleece, hoax, pull a fast one on (*inf.*), skin (*sl.*), stiff (*sl.*), swindle, take (someone) for a ride (*inf.*), trick **32 make do** = **manage,** cope, get along *or* by, improvise, muddle through, scrape along *or* by ◆ *n* **34** *Informal, chiefly Brit. & NZ* = **event,** affair, function, gathering, occasion, party **35 do's and don'ts** *Informal* = **rules,** code, customs, etiquette, instructions, regulations, standards

do away with *vb* **1** = **kill,** blow away (*sl., chiefly US*), bump off (*sl.*), destroy, do in, exterminate, liquidate, murder, slay, take out (*sl.*) **2** = **get rid of,** abolish, axe (*inf.*), chuck (*inf.*), discard, discontinue, eliminate, junk (*inf.*), pull, put an end to, put paid to, remove

docile 1 *adj* = **submissive,** amenable, biddable, compliant, ductile, manageable, obedient, pliant, tractable
Antonyms *adj* difficult, intractable, obstreperous, troublesome, trying, uncooperative, unmanageable

docility *n* **1** = **submissiveness,** amenability, biddableness, compliance, ductility, manageability, meekness, obedience, pliancy, tractability

dock[1] *n* **1** = **wharf,** harbour, pier, quay, waterfront ◆ *vb* **7** = **moor,** anchor, berth, drop an-

vessel) to come into a dry dock. **9** (of two spacecraft) to link together in space or link together (two spacecraft) in space. [C14: from MDu. *docke;* ? rel. to L *ducere* to lead]

dock[2] ⓣ (dɒk) *n* **1** the bony part of the tail of an animal. **2** the part of an animal's tail left after the major part of it has been cut off. ♦ *vb (tr)* **3** to remove (the tail or part of the tail) of (an animal) by cutting through the bone. **4** to deduct (an amount) from (a person's wages, pension, etc.). [C14: *dok* from ?]

dock[3] (dɒk) *n* an enclosed space in a court of law where the accused sits or stands during his trial. [C16: from Flemish *dok* sty]

dock[4] (dɒk) *n* any of various weedy plants having greenish or reddish flowers and broad leaves. [OE *docce*]

dockage ('dɒkɪdʒ) *n* **1** a charge levied upon a vessel for using a dock. **2** facilities for docking vessels. **3** the practice of docking vessels.

docker ('dɒkə) *n Brit.* a man employed in the loading or unloading of ships. US and Canad. equivalent: **longshoreman.** Austral. and NZ equivalent: **watersider, wharfie.** See also **stevedore.**

docket ⓣ ('dɒkɪt) *n* **1** *Chiefly Brit.* a piece of paper accompanying or referring to a package or other delivery, stating contents, delivery instructions, etc., sometimes serving as a receipt. **2** *Law.* **2a** a summary of the proceedings in a court. **2b** a register containing this. **3** *Brit.* **3a** a customs certificate declaring that duty has been paid. **3b** a certificate giving particulars of a shipment. **4** a summary of contents, as in a document. **5** *US.* a list of things to be done. **6** *US law.* a list of cases awaiting trial. ♦ *vb* **dockets, docketing, docketed.** *(tr)* **7** to fix a docket to (a package, etc.). **8** *Law.* **8a** to make a summary of (a judgment, etc.). **8b** to abstract and enter in a register. **9** to endorse (a document, etc.) with a summary. [C15: from ?]

dockland ('dɒk,lænd) *n* the area around the docks.

dockside ('dɒk,saɪd) *n* an area beside a dock.

dockyard ('dɒk,jɑːd) *n* a naval establishment with docks, workshops, etc., for the building, fitting out, and repair of vessels.

Doc Martens (dɒk 'mɑːtənz) *pl n Trademark.* a brand of lace-up boots with thick lightweight resistant soles. In full: **Doctor Martens.** Abbrev.: **DMs.**

doctor ⓣ ('dɒktə) *n* **1** a person licensed to practise medicine. **2** a person who has been awarded a higher academic degree in any field of knowledge. **3** *Chiefly US & Canad.* a person licensed to practise dentistry or veterinary medicine. **4** *(often cap.)* Also called: **Doctor of the Church.** a title given to any of several of the early Fathers of the Christian Church. **5** *Angling.* any of various artificial flies. **6** *Inf.* a person who mends or repairs things. **7** *Sl.* a cook on a ship or at a camp. **8** *Arch.* a man, esp. a teacher, of learning. **9 go for the doctor.** *Austral. sl.* to make a great effort or move very fast. **10 what the doctor ordered.** something needed or desired. ♦ *vb* **11** *(tr)* to give medical treatment to. **12** *(intr) Inf.* to practise medicine. **13** *(tr)* to repair or mend. **14** *(tr)* to make different in order to deceive. **15** *(tr)* to adapt. **16** *(tr) Inf.* to castrate (a cat, dog, etc.). [C14: from L: teacher, from *docēre* to teach]
▸**'doctoral** *or* **doctorial** (dɒk'tɔːrɪəl) *adj*

doctorate ('dɒktərɪt, -trɪt) *n* the highest academic degree in any field of knowledge.

Doctor of Philosophy *n* a doctorate awarded for original research in any subject except law, medicine, or theology.

doctrinaire ⓣ (,dɒktrɪ'nɛə) *adj* **1** stubbornly insistent on the observation of the niceties of a theory, esp. without regard to practicality, suitability, etc. **2** theoretical; impractical. ♦ *n* **3** a person who stubbornly attempts to apply a theory without regard to practical difficulties.
▸**,doctri'nairism** *n* ▸**,doctri'narian** *n*

doctrine ⓣ ('dɒktrɪn) *n* **1** a creed or body of teachings of a religious, political, or philosophical group presented for acceptance or belief; dogma. **2** a principle or body of principles that is taught or advocated. [C14: from OF, from L *doctrīna* teaching, from *doctor;* see DOCTOR]
▸**doctrinal** (dɒk'traɪnᵊl) *adj* ▸**doc'trinally** *adv*

docudrama ('dɒkju,drɑːmə) *n* a film or television programme based on true events, presented in a dramatized form.

document ⓣ *n* ('dɒkjumənt). **1** a piece of paper, booklet, etc., providing information, esp. of an official nature. **2** a piece of text or graphics, such as a letter or article, stored in a computer as a file for manipulation by document processing software. **3** *Arch.* proof. ♦ *vb* ('dɒkju,mɛnt). *(tr)* **4** to record or report in detail, as in the press, on television, etc. **5** to support (statements in a book) with references, etc. **6** to support (a claim, etc.) with evidence. **7** to furnish (a vessel) with documents specifying its registration, dimensions, etc. [C15: from L *documentum* a lesson, from *docēre* to teach]

documentary (,dɒkju'mɛntərɪ) *adj* **1** Also: **documental.** consisting of or relating to documents. **2** presenting factual material with few or no fictional additions. ♦ *n, pl* **documentaries. 3** a factual film or television programme about an event, person, etc., presenting the facts with little or no fiction.
▸**,docu'mentarily** *adv*

documentation (,dɒkjumɛn'teɪʃən) *n* **1** the act of supplying with or using documents or references. **2** the documents or references supplied.

document reader *n Computing.* a device that reads and inputs into a computer marks and characters on a special form, as by optical or magnetic character recognition.

docu-soap *or* **docusoap** ('dɒkju,səup) *n* a television documentary series in which the lives of the people filmed are presented as entertainment or drama. [C20: from DOCU(MENTARY) + SOAP (OPERA)]

dodder[1] ⓣ ('dɒdə) *vb (intr)* **1** to move unsteadily; totter. **2** to shake or tremble, as from age. [C17: var. of earlier *dadder*]
▸**'dodderer** *n* ▸**'doddery** *adj*

dodder[2] ('dɒdə) *n* any of a genus of rootless parasitic plants lacking chlorophyll and having suckers for drawing nourishment from the host plant. [C13: of Gmc origin]

doddle ⓣ ('dɒdᵊl) *n Brit. inf.* something easily accomplished. [C20: ?from *doddle* (vb) to totter]

dodeca- *combining form.* indicating twelve: *dodecaphonic.* [from Gk *dōdeka* twelve]

dodecagon (dəu'dɛkə,gɒn) *n* a polygon having twelve sides.

dodecahedron (,dəudɛkə'hiːdrən) *n* a solid figure having twelve plane faces.
▸**,dodeca'hedral** *adj*

dodecaphonic (,dəudɛkə'fɒnɪk) *adj* of or relating to the twelve-tone system of serial music.

dodge ⓣ (dɒdʒ) *vb* **dodges, dodging, dodged. 1** to avoid or attempt to avoid (a blow, discovery, etc.), as by moving suddenly. **2** to evade by cleverness or trickery. **3** *(intr) Change-ringing.* to make a bell change places with its neighbour when sounding in successive changes. **4** *(tr) Photog.* to lighten or darken (selected areas on a print). ♦ *n* **5** a plan contrived to deceive. **6** a sudden evasive movement. **7** a clever contrivance. **8** *Change-ringing.* the act of dodging. [C16: from ?]

Dodgem ('dɒdʒəm) *n Trademark.* an electrically propelled vehicle driven and bumped against similar cars in a rink at a funfair.

dodger ('dɒdʒə) *n* **1** a person who evades or shirks. **2** a shifty dishonest person. **3** a canvas shelter on a ship's bridge, etc., to protect the helmsman from bad weather. **4** *Dialect & Austral.* food, esp. bread.

dodgy ⓣ ('dɒdʒɪ) *adj* **dodgier, dodgiest.** *Brit., Austral. & NZ inf.* **1** risky, difficult, or dangerous. **2** uncertain or unreliable; tricky.

dodo ('dəudəu) *n, pl* **dodos** *or* **dodoes. 1** any of a now extinct family of flightless birds formerly found on Mauritius. They had a hooked bill and short stout legs. **2** *Inf.* an intensely conservative person who is unaware of changing fashions, ideas, etc. **3 (as) dead as a dodo.** irretrievably defunct or out of date. [C17: from Port. *doudo,* from *duodo* stupid]

do down *vb (tr, adv)* **1** to belittle or humiliate. **2** to deceive or cheat.

doe (dəu) *n, pl* **does** *or* **doe.** the female of the deer, hare, rabbit, and certain other animals. [OE *dā*]

Doe (dəu) *n* **John.** *Law.* **1** (formerly) the plaintiff in a fictitious action, Doe versus Roe, to test a point of law. See also **Roe. 2** Also: **Jane Doe.** *US.* an unknown or unidentified person.

DOE (formerly, in Britain) *abbrev. for* Department of the Environment.

doek (dʊk) *n S. African inf.* a square of cloth worn mainly by African women to cover the head. [C18: from Afrik.: cloth]

doer ⓣ ('duːə) *n* **1** a person or thing that does something. **2** an active or energetic person. **3** a thriving animal, esp. a horse.

does (dʌz) *vb* (used with a singular noun or the pronouns *he, she,* or *it*) a form of the present tense (indicative mood) of **do**[1].

doeskin ('dəu,skɪn) *n* **1** the skin of a deer, lamb, or sheep. **2** a very supple leather made from this. **3** a heavy smooth cloth.

THESAURUS

chor, land, put in, tie up **9** = **link up**, couple, hook up, join, rendezvous, unite

dock[2] *vb* **3** = **cut off**, clip, crop, curtail, cut short, diminish, lessen, shorten **4** = **deduct**, decrease, diminish, lessen, reduce, subtract, withhold
Antonyms *vb* ≠ **deduct**: augment, boost, increase, raise

docket *n* **1** = **label**, bill, certificate, chit, chitty, counterfoil, receipt, tab, tag, tally, ticket, voucher ♦ *vb* **7** = **label**, catalogue, file, index, mark, register, tab, tag, ticket

doctor *n* **1** = **G.P.**, general practitioner, medic (*inf.*), medical practitioner, physician ♦ *vb* **14** = **change**, alter, disguise, falsify, fudge, misrepresent, pervert, tamper with

doctrinaire *adj* **1** = **dogmatic**, biased, fanatical, inflexible, insistent, opinionated, rigid **2** = **impractical**, hypothetical, ideological, speculative, theoretical, unpragmatic, unrealistic

doctrine *n* **1** = **teaching**, article, article of faith, belief, canon, concept, conviction, creed, dogma, opinion, precept, principle, tenet

document *n* **1** = **paper**, certificate, instrument, legal form, record, report ♦ *vb* **5, 6** = **support**, authenticate, back up, certify, cite, corroborate, detail, give weight to, instance, particularize, substantiate, validate, verify

dodder[1] *vb* **1, 2** = **totter**, quake, quaver, quiver, shake, shamble, shiver, shuffle, stagger, sway, teeter, tremble

doddering *adj* **1, 2** = **tottering**, aged, decrepit, doddery, faltering, feeble, floundering, infirm, senile, shaky, shambling, trembly, unsteady, weak

doddle *n Brit. informal* = **piece of cake** (*inf.*), cakewalk (*inf.*), child's play (*inf.*), cinch (*sl.*), easy-peasy (*sl.*), money for old rope, no sweat (*sl.*), picnic (*inf.*), pushover (*sl.*)

dodge *vb* **1** = **duck**, body-swerve (*Scot.*), dart, shift, sidestep, swerve, turn aside **2** = **evade**, avoid, body-swerve (*Scot.*), deceive, elude, equivocate, fend off, flannel (*Brit. inf.*), fudge, get out of, hedge, parry, shirk, shuffle, trick ♦ *n* **5** = **trick**, contrivance, device, feint, flannel (*Brit. inf.*), machination, ploy, ruse, scheme, stratagem, subterfuge, wheeze (*Brit. sl.*), wile

dodgy *adj* **1, 2** *Brit., Austral., & NZ* = **risky**, chancy (*inf.*), dangerous, delicate, dicey (*inf., chiefly Brit.*), dicky (*Brit. inf.*), difficult, problematic(al), ticklish, tricky, uncertain, unreliable

doer *n* **2** = **achiever**, active person, activist, bustler, dynamo, go-getter (*inf.*), live wire (*sl.*),

doff ❶ (dɒf) *vb (tr)* **1** to take off or lift (one's hat) in salutation. **2** to remove (clothing). [OE *dōn of*; see DO[1], OFF; cf. DON[1]] ▸**'doffer** *n*

do for ❶ *vb (prep) Inf.* **1** *(tr)* to convict of a crime or offence. **2** *(intr)* to cause the ruin, death, or defeat of. **3** *(intr)* to do housework for. **4 do well for oneself.** to thrive or succeed.

dog ❶ (dɒg) *n* **1** a domesticated canine mammal occurring in many breeds that show a great variety in size and form. **2** any other carnivore of the dog family, such as the dingo and coyote. **3** the male of animals of the dog family. **4** *(modifier)* spurious, inferior, or useless. **5** a mechanical device for gripping or holding. **6** *Inf.* a fellow; chap. **7** *Inf.* a man or boy regarded as unpleasant or wretched. **8** *Sl.* an unattractive girl or woman. **9** *US & Canad. inf.* something unsatisfactory or inferior. **10** short for **firedog. 11 a dog's chance.** no chance at all. **12 a dog's dinner** *or* **breakfast.** *Inf.* something messy or bungled. **13 a dog's life.** a wretched existence. **14 dog eat dog.** ruthless competition. **15 like a dog's dinner.** dressed smartly or ostentatiously. **16 put on the dog.** *US & Canad. inf.* to behave or dress in an ostentatious manner. ◆ *vb* **dogs, dogging, dogged.** *(tr)* **17** to pursue or follow after with determination. **18** to trouble; plague. **19** to chase with a dog. **20** to grip or secure by a mechanical device. ◆ *adv* **21** *(usually in combination)* thoroughly; utterly: *dog-tired.* ◆ See also **dogs.** [OE *docga*, from ?]

dog biscuit *n* a hard biscuit for dogs.

dog box *n NZ inf.* disgrace; disfavour: *in the dog box.*

dogcart ('dɒg,kɑːt) *n* a light horse-drawn two-wheeled vehicle.

dog-catcher *n Now chiefly US & Canad.* a local official whose job is to impound and dispose of stray dogs.

dog collar *n* **1** a collar for a dog. **2** *Inf.* a clerical collar. **3** *Inf.* a tight-fitting necklace.

dog days *pl n* the hot period of the summer reckoned in ancient times from the heliacal rising of Sirius (the Dog Star). [C16: translation of LL *diēs caniculārēs*, translation of Gk *hēmerai kunades*]

doge (dəʊdʒ) *n* (formerly) the chief magistrate in the republics of Venice and Genoa. [C16: via F from It. (Venetian dialect), from L *dux* leader]

dog-ear *vb* **1** *(tr)* to fold down the corner of (a page). ◆ *n also* **dog's-ear. 2** a folded-down corner of a page.

dog-eared *adj* **1** having dog-ears. **2** shabby or worn.

dog-end *n Inf.* a cigarette end.

dogfight ('dɒg,faɪt) *n* **1** close-quarters combat between fighter aircraft. **2** any rough fight.

dogfish ('dɒg,fɪʃ) *n, pl* **dogfish** *or* **dogfishes. 1** any of several small sharks. **2** a less common name for the **bowfin.**

dogged ❶ ('dɒgɪd) *adj* obstinately determined; wilful or tenacious. ▸**'doggedly** *adv* ▸**'doggedness** *n*

doggerel ('dɒgərəl) *or* **dogrel** ('dɒgrəl) *n* **1a** comic verse, usually irregular in measure. **1b** *(as modifier): a doggerel rhythm.* **2** nonsense. [C14 *dogerel* worthless, ?from *dogge* DOG]

doggish ('dɒgɪʃ) *adj* **1** of or like a dog. **2** surly; snappish.

doggo ('dɒgəʊ) *adv Brit. inf.* in hiding and keeping quiet (esp. in **lie doggo**). [C19: prob. from DOG]

doggone ('dɒgɒn) *US & Canad.* ◆ *interj* **1** an exclamation of annoyance, etc. ◆ *adj (prenominal), adv* **2** Also: **doggoned.** another word for **damn.** [C19: euphemism for *God damn*]

doggy *or* **doggie** ('dɒgɪ) *n, pl* **doggies. 1** a child's word for a **dog.** ◆ *adj* **doggier, doggiest. 2** of, like, or relating to a dog. **3** fond of dogs.

doggy bag *n* a bag in which leftovers from a meal may be taken away, supposedly for the diner's dog.

doggy paddle *or* **doggie paddle** *n, vb* another word for **dog paddle.**

doghouse ('dɒg,haʊs) *n* **1** the US and Canad. name for **kennel. 2** *Inf.* disfavour (in **in the doghouse**).

dogie, dogy, *or* **dogey** ('dəʊgɪ) *n, pl* **dogies** *or* **dogeys.** *US & Canad.* a motherless calf. [C19: from *dough-guts,* because they were fed on flour-and-water paste]

dog in the manger *n* a person who prevents others from using something he has no use for.

dog Latin *n* spurious or incorrect Latin.

dogleg ('dɒg,lɛg) *n* **1** a sharp bend or angle. ◆ *vb* **doglegs, doglegging, doglegged. 2** *(intr)* to go off at an angle. ◆ *adj* **3** of or with the shape of a dogleg. ▸**doglegged** (,dɒg'lɛgɪd, 'dɒg,lɛgd) *adj*

dogma ❶ ('dɒgmə) *n, pl* **dogmas** *or* **dogmata** (-mətə). **1** a religious doctrine or system of doctrines proclaimed by ecclesiastical authority as true. **2** a belief, principle, or doctrine or a code of beliefs, principles, or doctrines. [C17: via L from Gk: opinion, from *dokein* to seem good]

dogman ('dɒgmən) *n, pl* **dogmen.** *Austral.* a person who directs the operation of a crane whilst riding on an object being lifted by it.

dogmatic ❶ (dɒg'mætɪk) *or* **dogmatical** *adj* **1a** (of a statement, opinion, etc.) forcibly asserted as if authoritative and unchallengeable. **1b** (of a person) prone to making such statements. **2** of or constituting dogma. **3** based on assumption rather than observation. ▸**dog'matically** *adv*

dogmatics (dɒg'mætɪks) *n (functioning as sing)* the study of religious dogmas and doctrines. Also called: **dogmatic** (*or* **doctrinal**) **theology.**

dogmatize ❶ *or* **dogmatise** ('dɒgmə,taɪz) *vb* **dogmatizes, dogmatizing, dogmatized** *or* **dogmatises, dogmatising, dogmatised.** to say or state (something) in a dogmatic manner. ▸**'dogmatism** *n* ▸**'dogmatist** *n*

do-gooder *n Inf.* a well-intentioned person, esp. a naive or impractical one. ▸,**do-'gooding** *n, adj*

dog paddle *n* **1** a swimming stroke in which the swimmer paddles his hands in imitation of a swimming dog. ◆ *vb* **dog-paddle, dog-paddles, dog-paddling, dog-paddled. 2** *(intr)* to swim using the dog paddle. ◆ Also: **doggy paddle** *or* **doggie paddle.**

dog rose *n* a prickly wild European rose that has pink or white scentless flowers. [from belief that its root was effective against the bite of a mad dog]

dogs ❶ (dɒgz) *pl n* **1** *Sl.* the feet. **2** *Marketing inf.* goods with a low market share, which are unlikely to yield substantial profits. **3 go to the dogs.** *Inf.* to go to ruin physically or morally. **4 let sleeping dogs lie.** to leave things undisturbed. **5 the dogs.** *Brit. inf.* greyhound racing.

dogsbody ❶ ('dɒgz,bɒdɪ) *Inf.* ◆ *n, pl* **dogsbodies. 1** a person who carries out menial tasks for others. ◆ *vb* **dogsbodies, dogsbodying, dogsbodied.** *(intr)* **2** to act as a dogsbody.

dog's disease *n Austral. inf.* influenza.

dogsled ('dɒg,slɛd) *n Chiefly US & Canad.* a sleigh drawn by dogs. Also called (Brit.): **dog sledge.**

Dog Star *n* **the.** another name for **Sirius.**

dog-tired *adj (usually postpositive) Inf.* exhausted.

dogtooth ('dɒg,tuːθ) *n, pl* **dogteeth.** *Archit.* a carved ornament in the form of a series of four-cornered pyramids set diagonally and often decorated with leaf shapes along each edge, used in England in the 13th century.

dogtooth violet *n* any of a genus of plants, esp. a European plant with purple flowers.

dogtrot ('dɒg,trɒt) *n* a gently paced trot.

dog violet *n* any of three wild violets found in Britain and northern Europe.

dogwatch ('dɒg,wɒtʃ) *n* either of two two-hour watches aboard ship, from four to six p.m. or from six to eight p.m.

dogwood ('dɒg,wʊd) *n* any of various trees or shrubs, esp. a European shrub with small white flowers and black berries.

dogy ('dəʊgɪ) *n, pl* **dogies.** a variant of **dogie.**

doh (dəʊ) *n Music.* (in tonic sol-fa) the first degree of any major scale. [C18: from It., replacing *ut*; see GAMUT]

doily *or* **doyley** ('dɔɪlɪ) *n, pl* **doilies** *or* **doileys.** a decorative mat of lace or lacelike paper, etc., laid on plates. [C18: after *Doily,* a London draper]

do in ❶ *vb (tr, adv) Sl.* **1** to kill. **2** to exhaust.

doing ❶ ('duːɪŋ) *n* **1** an action or the performance of an action: *whose doing is this?* **2** *Inf.* a beating or castigation.

doings ❶ ('duːɪŋz) *n* **1** *(functioning as pl)* deeds, actions, or events. **2** *(functioning as sing) Inf.* anything of which the name is not known, or euphemistically left unsaid, etc.

do-it-yourself *n* **a** the hobby or process of constructing and repairing things oneself. **b** *(as modifier): a do-it-yourself kit.*

dol. *abbrev. for:* **1** *Music.* dolce. **2** *(pl* **dols.**) dollar.

Dolby ('dɒlbɪ) *n Trademark.* any of various specialized electronic circuits, esp. those used in tape recorders for noise reduction in high-frequency signals. [after R. *Dolby* (born 1933), US inventor]

THESAURUS

organizer, powerhouse (*sl.*), wheeler- dealer (*inf.*)

doff *vb* **1 = tip,** lift, raise, remove, take off, touch **2 = take off,** cast off, discard, remove, shed, slip off, slip out of, throw off, undress

do for *vb* **2** *Informal* **= destroy,** defeat, finish (off), kill, ruin, shatter, slay, undo

dog *n* **1 = hound,** bitch, canine, cur, kuri *or* goorie (*NZ*), man's best friend, mongrel, mutt (*sl.*), pooch (*sl.*), pup, puppy, tyke **7** *Informal* **= scoundrel,** beast, blackguard, cur, heel, knave (*arch.*), villain ◆ *vb* **17, 18 = trouble,** follow, haunt, hound, plague, pursue, shadow, tail (*inf.*), track, trail

dogged *adj* **= determined,** firm, immovable, indefatigable, obstinate, persevering, persistent, pertinacious, resolute, single-minded, staunch, steadfast, steady, stiff-necked, stubborn, tenacious, unflagging, unshakable, unyielding

Antonyms *adj* doubtful, half-hearted, hesitant, irresolute, undetermined, unsteady

doggedness *n* **= determination,** bulldog tenacity, endurance, obstinacy, perseverance, persistence, pertinacity, relentlessness, resolution, single-mindedness, steadfastness, steadiness, stubbornness, tenaciousness, tenacity

dogma *n* **1, 2 = doctrine,** article, article of faith, belief, credo, creed, opinion, precept, principle, teachings, tenet

dogmatic *adj* **1 = opinionated,** arbitrary, arrogant, assertive, categorical, dictatorial, doctrinaire, downright, emphatic, imperious, magisterial, obdurate, overbearing, peremptory **2 = doctrinal,** authoritative, canonical, categorical, ex cathedra, oracular, positive

dogmatism *n* **= opinionatedness,** arbitrariness, arrogance, dictatorialness, imperiousness, peremptoriness, positiveness, presumption

dogs *pl n* **3 go to the dogs** *Informal* **= go to ruin,** degenerate, deteriorate, go down the drain, go to pot

dogsbody *n* **1** *Informal* **= drudge,** general factotum, maid *or* man of all work, menial, skivvy (*chiefly Brit.*), slave

do in *vb Slang* **1 = kill,** blow away, butcher, dispatch, eliminate (*sl.*), execute, liquidate, murder, slaughter, slay, take out (*sl.*) **2 = exhaust,** fag (*inf.*), fatigue, knacker (*sl.*), shatter (*inf.*), tire, wear out, weary

doing *n* **1 = carrying out** *or* **through,** achievement, act, action, deed, execution, exploit, handiwork, implementation, performance

doings *pl n* **1 = deeds,** actions, affairs, concerns, dealings, events, exploits, goings-on (*inf.*), handiwork, happenings, proceedings, transactions

dolce ('dɒltʃɪ) *adj, adv Music.* (to be performed) gently and sweetly. [It.]
Dolcelatte (ˌdɒltʃiːˈlɑːtɪ) *n* a soft creamy blue-veined Italian cheese. [It., lit: sweet milk]
dolce vita ('dɒltʃɪ 'viːtə) *n* a life of luxury. [It., lit.: sweet life]
doldrums ➊ ('dɒldrəmz) *n* **the. 1** a depressed or bored state of mind. **2** a state of inactivity or stagnation. **3** a belt of light winds or calms along the equator. [C19: prob. from OE *dol* DULL, infl. by TANTRUM]
dole[1] ➊ (dəʊl) *n* **1** (usually preceded by *the*) *Brit. & Austral. inf.* money received from the state while out of work. **2 on the dole.** *Brit. & Austral. inf.* receiving such money. **3** a small portion of money or food given to a poor person. **4** the act of distributing such portions. **5** *Arch.* fate. ◆ *vb* **doles, doling, doled. 6** (*tr;* usually foll. by *out*) to distribute, esp. in small portions. [OE *dāl* share]
dole[2] (dəʊl) *n Arch.* grief or mourning. [C13: from OF, from LL *dolus*, from L *dolēre* to lament]
dole-bludger *n Austral. sl.* a person who draws unemployment benefit without making any attempt to get work.
doleful ➊ ('dəʊlfʊl) *adj* dreary; mournful.
▸**'dolefully** *adv* ▸**'dolefulness** *n*
dolerite ('dɒləˌraɪt) *n* **1** a dark basic igneous rock; a coarse-grained basalt. **2** any dark igneous rock whose composition cannot be determined with the naked eye. [C19: from F *dolérite*, from Gk *doleros* deceitful; from the difficulty in determining its composition]
dolichocephalic (ˌdɒlɪkəʊsɪˈfælɪk) *or* **dolichocephalous** (ˌdɒlɪkəʊˈsɛfələs) *adj* having a head much longer than it is broad. [C19: from Gk *dolichos* long + -CEPHALIC]
doll (dɒl) *n* **1** a small model or dummy of a human being, used as a toy. **2** *Sl.* a pretty girl or woman of little intelligence. [C16: prob. from *Doll*, pet name for *Dorothy*]
dollar ('dɒlə) *n* **1** the standard monetary unit of the US, divided into 100 cents. **2** the standard monetary unit, comprising 100 cents, of various other countries including: Australia, the Bahamas, Canada, Jamaica, Malaysia, New Zealand, Singapore, Taiwan, and Zimbabwe. [C16: from Low G *daler*, from G *Taler, Thaler*, short for *Joachimsthaler*, coin made from metal mined in *Joachimsthal* Jachymov, town in the Czech Republic]
dollarbird ('dɒləˌbɜːd) *n* a bird of S and SE Asia and Australia with a round white spot on each wing.
dollar diplomacy *n Chiefly US.* **1** a foreign policy that encourages and protects commercial and financial involvement abroad. **2** use of financial power as a diplomatic weapon.
dollop ➊ ('dɒləp) *Inf.* ◆ *n* **1** a semisolid lump. **2** a measure or serving. ◆ *vb* **3** (*tr;* foll. by *out*) to serve out (food). [C16: from ?]
doll up ➊ *vb* (*tr, adv*) *Sl.* to dress in a stylish or showy manner.
dolly ('dɒlɪ) *n, pl* **dollies. 1** a child's word for a **doll. 2** *Films, etc.* a wheeled support on which a camera may be mounted. **3** a cup-shaped anvil used to hold a rivet. **4** *Cricket.* **4a** a simple catch. **4b** a full toss bowled in a slow high arc. **5** Also called: **dolly bird.** *Sl., chiefly Brit.* an attractive and fashionable girl. ◆ *vb* **dollies, dollying, dollied. 6** *Films, etc.* to wheel (a camera) backwards or forwards on a dolly.
dolly mixture *n* **1** a mixture of tiny coloured sweets. **2** one such sweet.
dolma ('dɒlmə) *n, pl* **dolmas** *or* **dolmades** (dɒlˈmɑːdiːz). a vine leaf stuffed with a filling of meat and rice. [C19: Turkish *dolma* lit. something filled]
dolman sleeve ('dɒlmən) *n* a sleeve that is very wide at the armhole and tapers to a tight wrist. [C19: from *dolman*, a type of Turkish robe, ult. from Turkish *dolamak* to wind]
dolmen ('dɒlmɛn) *n* a Neolithic stone formation, consisting of a horizontal stone supported by several vertical stones, and thought to be a tomb. [C19: from F, prob. from OBreton *tol* table, from L *tabula* board + Breton *mēn* stone, of Celtic origin]
dolomite ('dɒləˌmaɪt) *n* **1** a mineral consisting of calcium magnesium carbonate. **2** a rock resembling limestone but consisting principally of the mineral dolomite. [C18: after Déodat de *Dolomieu* (1750–1801), F mineralogist]
▸**dolomitic** (ˌdɒləˈmɪtɪk) *adj*
doloroso (ˌdɒləˈrəʊsəʊ) *adj, adv Music.* (to be performed) in a sorrowful manner. [It.]
dolorous ➊ ('dɒlərəs) *adj* causing or involving pain or sorrow.
▸**'dolorously** *adv*
dolos ('dɒlɒs) *n, pl* **dolosse.** *S. African.* a knucklebone of a sheep, buck, etc., used esp. by diviners. [from ?]
dolour *or US* **dolor** ('dɒlə) *n Poetic.* grief or sorrow. [C14: from L, from *dolēre* to grieve]
dolphin ('dɒlfɪn) *n* **1** any of various marine mammals that are typically smaller than whales and larger than porpoises and have a beaklike snout. **2 river dolphin.** any of various freshwater mammals inhabiting rivers of North and South America and S Asia. **3** Also called: **dorado.** either of two large marine fishes that have an iridescent coloration. **4** *Naut.* a post or buoy for mooring a vessel. [C13: from OF *dauphin*, via L, from Gk *delphin-, delphis*]
dolphinarium (ˌdɒlfɪˈnɛərɪəm) *n, pl* **dolphinariums** *or* **dolphinaria** (-ɪə). a pool or aquarium for dolphins, esp. one in which they give public displays.
dolt ➊ (dəʊlt) *n* a slow-witted or stupid person. [C16: prob. rel. to OE *dol* stupid]
▸**'doltish** *adj* ▸**'doltishness** *n*
dom. *abbrev. for:* **1** domain. **2** domestic.
-dom *suffix forming nouns.* **1** state or condition: *freedom.* **2** rank, office, or domain of: *earldom.* **3** a collection of persons: *officialdom.* [OE *-dōm*]
domain ➊ (dəˈmeɪn) *n* **1** land governed by a ruler or government. **2** land owned by one person or family. **3** a field or scope of knowledge or activity. **4** a region having specific characteristics. **5** *Austral. & NZ.* a park or recreation reserve maintained by a public authority, often the government. **6** *Law.* the absolute ownership and right to dispose of land. **7** *Maths.* the set of values of the independent variable of a function for which the functional value exists. **8** *Logic.* another term for **universe of discourse. 9** *Philosophy.* range of significance. **10** *Physics.* one of the regions in a ferromagnetic solid in which all the atoms have their magnetic moments aligned in the same direction. **11** *Computing.* a group of computers that have the same suffix (**domain name**) in their names on the Internet, specifying the country, type of institution, etc. where they are located. [C17: from F *domaine*, from L *dominium* property, from *dominus* lord]
dome (dəʊm) *n* **1** a hemispherical roof or vault. **2** something shaped like this. **3** a slang word for the **head.** ◆ *vb* **domes, doming, domed.** (*tr*) **4** to cover with or as if with a dome. **5** to shape like a dome. [C16: from F, from It. *duomo* cathedral, from L *domus* house]
▸**'dome,like** *adj* ▸**domical** ('dəʊmɪk°l, 'dɒm-) *adj*
Domesday Book *or* **Doomsday Book** ('duːmzˌdeɪ) *n History.* the record of a survey of the land of England carried out by the commissioners of William I in 1086.
domestic ➊ (dəˈmɛstɪk) *adj* **1** of the home or family. **2** enjoying or accustomed to home or family life. **3** (of an animal) bred or kept by man as a pet or for purposes such as the supply of food. **4** of one's own country or a specific country: *domestic and foreign affairs.* ◆ *n* **5** a household servant. [C16: from OF *domestique*, from L *domesticus* belonging to the house, from *domus* house]
▸**do'mestically** *adv*
domesticate ➊ (dəˈmɛstɪˌkeɪt) *or US* (*sometimes*) **domesticize** (dəˈmɛstɪˌsaɪz) *vb* **domesticates, domesticating, domesticated** *or US* **domesticizes, domesticizing, domesticized.** (*tr*) **1** to bring or keep (wild animals or plants) under control or cultivation. **2** to accustom to home life. **3** to adapt to an environment.
▸**do'mesticable** *adj* ▸**do,mesti'cation** *n*
domesticity ➊ (ˌdəʊmɛˈstɪsɪtɪ) *n, pl* **domesticities. 1** home life. **2** devotion to or familiarity with home life. **3** (*usually pl*) a domestic duty or matter.
domestic science *n* the study of cooking, needlework, and other subjects concerned with household skills.

THESAURUS

doldrums *n* **1, 2 the doldrums** = **inactivity,** apathy, blues, boredom, depression, dullness, dumps (*inf.*), ennui, gloom, inertia, lassitude, listlessness, malaise, stagnation, tedium, the hump (*Brit. inf.*), torpor
dole[1] *n* **1** *Brit. & Austral. informal* = **benefit,** allowance, alms, donation, gift, grant, gratuity, handout, modicum, parcel, pittance, portion, quota, share ◆ *vb* **6 dole out** = **give out,** administer, allocate, allot, apportion, assign, deal, dispense, distribute, divide, hand out, mete, share
doleful *adj* = **mournful,** cheerless, depressing, dismal, distressing, dolorous, down in the mouth, dreary, forlorn, funereal, gloomy, low, lugubrious, melancholy, painful, pitiful, rueful, sad, sombre, sorrowful, woebegone, woeful, wretched
dollop *n* **1, 2** = **lump,** gob, helping, portion, scoop, serving
doll up *vb Slang* = **dress up,** deck out, get ready, preen, primp, prink, tart up (*sl.*), titivate, trick out
dolorous *adj* = **sorrowful,** anguished, dismal, distressing, doleful, grievous, harrowing, heart-rending, melancholy, miserable, mournful, painful, rueful, sad, woebegone, woeful, wretched
dolt *n* = **idiot,** ass, berk (*Brit. sl.*), blockhead, booby, charlie (*Brit. inf.*), chump (*inf.*), clot (*Brit. inf.*), coot, dimwit (*inf.*), dipstick (*Brit. sl.*), dope (*inf.*), dork (*sl.*), dullard, dumb-ass (*sl.*), dunce, fathead (*inf.*), fool, geek (*sl.*), gobshite (*Irish taboo sl.*), ignoramus, jerk (*sl., chiefly US & Canad.*), lamebrain (*inf.*), nerd *or* nurd (*sl.*), nitwit (*inf.*), numbskull *or* numskull, oaf, plank (*Brit. sl.*), plonker (*sl.*), prat (*sl.*), prick (*sl.*), schmuck (*US. sl.*), simpleton, thickhead, twit (*inf., chiefly Brit.*), wally (*sl.*)
doltish *adj* = **stupid,** asinine, boneheaded (*sl.*), brainless, clottish (*Brit. inf.*), dense, dim-witted (*inf.*), dopey (*inf.*), dumb (*inf.*), dumb-ass (*sl.*), foolish, goofy (*inf.*), halfwitted, idiotic, inane, mindless, silly
domain *n* **1** = **kingdom,** demesne, dominion, empire, estate, lands, policies (*Scot.*), province, realm, region, territory **3** = **area,** authority, bailiwick, concern, department, discipline, field, jurisdiction, orbit, power, realm, scope, speciality, sphere, sway
domestic *adj* **1** = **home,** domiciliary, family, household, private **2** = **home-loving,** domesticated, homely, housewifely, stay-at-home **3** = **domesticated,** house, house-trained, pet, tame, trained **4** = **native,** indigenous, internal, not foreign ◆ *n* **5** = **servant,** char (*inf.*), charwoman, daily, daily help, help, maid, woman (*inf.*)
domesticate *vb* **1** = **tame,** break, gentle, house-train, train **3** = **accustom,** acclimatize, familiarize, habituate, naturalize
domesticated *adj* **1** = **tame,** broken (in), naturalized, tamed **2** = **home-loving,** domestic, homely, house-trained (*jocular*), housewifely
Antonyms *adj* ≠ **tame:** feral, ferocious, savage, unbroken, undomesticated, untamed, wild
domesticity *n* **1, 2** = **home life,** domestication, home-lovingness, homemaking, housekeeping, housewifery

domicile Ⓣ ('dɒmɪˌsaɪl) *or* **domicil** ('dɒmɪsɪl) *Formal.* ◆ *n* **1** a dwelling place. **2** a permanent legal residence. **3** *Commerce, Brit.* the place where a bill of exchange is to be paid. ◆ *vb also* **domiciliate** (ˌdɒmɪ'sɪlɪˌeɪt), **domiciles, domiciling, domiciled** *or* **domiciliates, domiciliating, domiciliated. 4** to establish or be established in a dwelling place. [C15: from L *domicilium,* from *domus* house]
▸**domiciliary** (ˌdɒmɪ'sɪlɪərɪ) *adj*

dominance Ⓣ ('dɒmɪnəns) *n* control; ascendancy.

dominant Ⓣ ('dɒmɪnənt) *adj* **1** having primary authority or influence; governing; ruling. **2** predominant or primary: *the dominant topic of the day.* **3** occupying a commanding position. **4** *Genetics.* (of a gene) producing the same phenotype in the organism whether its allele is identical or dissimilar. Cf. **recessive. 5** *Music.* of or relating to the fifth degree of a scale. **6** *Ecology.* (of a plant or animal species) more prevalent than any other species and determining the appearance and composition of the community. ◆ *n* **7** *Genetics.* a dominant gene. **8** *Music.* **8a** the fifth degree of a scale. **8b** a key or chord based on this. **9** *Ecology.* a dominant plant or animal in a community.
▸'**dominantly** *adv*

dominant seventh chord *n Music.* a chord consisting of the dominant and the major third, perfect fifth, and minor seventh above it.

dominate Ⓣ ('dɒmɪˌneɪt) *vb* **dominates, dominating, dominated. 1** to control, rule, or govern. **2** to tower above (surroundings, etc.). **3** (*tr; usually passive*) to predominate in. [C17: from L *dominārī* to be lord over, from *dominus* lord]
▸'**domiˌnating** *adj* ▸ˌ**domi'nation** *n*

dominatrix (ˌdɒmɪ'neɪtrɪks) *n, pl* **dominatrices** (ˌdɒmɪnə'traɪsiːz). **1** a woman who is the dominant sexual partner in a sadomasochistic relationship. **2** a dominant woman. [C16: from L, fem of *dominātor,* from *dominārī* to be lord over]

dominee ('duːmɪnɪ, 'duə-) *n* (in South Africa) a minister in any of the Afrikaner Churches. [from Afrik., from Du.; cf. DOMINIE]

domineer Ⓣ (ˌdɒmɪ'nɪə) *vb* (*intr;* often foll. by *over*) to act with arrogance or tyranny; behave imperiously. [C16: from Du. *domineren,* from F *dominer* to DOMINATE]
▸ˌ**domi'neering** *adj*

dominical (də'mɪnɪkᵊl) *adj* **1** of Jesus Christ as Lord. **2** of Sunday as the Lord's Day. [C15: from LL *dominicālis,* from L *dominus* lord]

Dominican[1] (də'mɪnɪkən) *n* **1a** a member of an order of preaching friars founded by Saint Dominic in 1215; a Blackfriar. **1b** a nun of one of the orders founded under his patronage. ◆ *adj* **2** of Saint Dominic or the Dominican order.

Dominican[2] (də'mɪnɪkən) *adj* **1** of or relating to the Dominican Republic or Dominica. ◆ *n* **2** a native or inhabitant of the Dominican Republic or Dominica.

dominie ('dɒmɪnɪ) *n* **1** a Scots word for **schoolmaster. 2** a minister or clergyman. [C17: from L *domine,* vocative case of *dominus* lord]

dominion Ⓣ (də'mɪnjən) *n* **1** rule; authority. **2** the land governed by one ruler or government. **3** sphere of influence; area of control. **4** a name formerly applied to self-governing divisions of the British Empire. **5 the Dominion.** New Zealand. [C15: from OF, from L *dominium* ownership, from *dominus* master]

Dominion Day *n* the former name for **Canada Day.**

domino[1] ('dɒmɪˌnəʊ) *n, pl* **dominoes.** a small rectangular block marked with dots, used in dominoes. [C19: from F, from It., ?from *domino!* master!, said by the winner]

domino[2] ('dɒmɪˌnəʊ) *n, pl* **dominoes** *or* **dominos. 1** a large hooded cloak worn with an eye mask at a masquerade. **2** the eye mask worn with such a cloak. [C18: from F or It., prob. from L *dominus* lord, master]

domino effect *n* a series of similar or related events occurring as a direct and inevitable result of one initial event. [C20: alluding to a row of dominoes, each standing on end, all of which fall when one is pushed]

dominoes ('dɒmɪˌnəʊz) *n* (*functioning as sing*) any of several games in which dominoes with matching halves are laid together.

don[1] Ⓣ (dɒn) *vb* **dons, donning, donned.** (*tr*) to put on (clothing). [C14: from DO[1] + ON; cf. DOFF]

don[2] (dɒn) *n* **1** *Brit.* a member of the teaching staff at a university or college, esp. at Oxford or Cambridge. **2** the head of a student dormitory at certain Canadian universities and colleges. **3** a Spanish gentleman or nobleman. **4** (in the Mafia) the head of the family. **5** *Arch.* a person of rank. [C17: ult. from L *dominus* lord]

Don (dɒn) *n* a Spanish title equivalent to *Mr.* [C16: via Sp., from L *dominus* lord]

Doña ('dɒnjə) *n* a Spanish title of address equivalent to *Mrs* or *Madam.* [C17: via Sp., from L *domina*]

donate Ⓣ (dəʊ'neɪt) *vb* **donates, donating, donated.** to give (money, time, etc.), esp. to a charity.
▸**do'nator** *n*

donation Ⓣ (dəʊ'neɪʃən) *n* **1** the act of donating. **2** a contribution. [C15: from L *dōnātiō* a presenting, from *dōnāre* to give, from *dōnum* gift]

donative ('dəʊnətɪv) *n* **1** a gift or donation. **2** a benefice capable of being conferred as a gift. ◆ *adj* **3** of or like a donation. **4** being or relating to a benefice. [C15: from L *dōnātīvum* a donation made to soldiers by a Roman emperor, from *dōnāre* to present]

donder ('dɒndə) *S. African sl.* ◆ *vb* **1** (*tr*) to beat (someone) up. ◆ *n* **2** a wretch; swine. [from Afrik., from Du. *donderen* to swear, bully]

done Ⓣ (dʌn) *vb* **1** the past participle of **do**[1]. **2 be** *or* **have done with.** to end relations with. **3 have done.** to be completely finished: *have you done?* ◆ *interj* **4** an expression of agreement, as on the settlement of a bargain. ◆ *adj* **5** completed. **6** cooked enough. **7** used up. **8** socially acceptable. **9** *Inf.* cheated; tricked. **10 done for.** *Inf.* **10a** dead or almost dead. **10b** in serious difficulty. **11 done in** *or* **up.** *Inf.* exhausted.

donee (dəʊ'niː) *n* a person who receives a gift. [C16: from DON(OR) + -EE]

doner kebab ('dɒnə) *n* a fast-food dish comprising grilled meat and salad served in pitta bread with chilli sauce. [from Turkish *döner* rotating + KEBAB]

dong (dɒŋ) *n* **1** an imitation of the sound of a bell. **2** *Austral. & NZ inf.* a heavy blow. ◆ *vb* **3** (*intr*) to make such a sound. **4** *Austral. & NZ inf.* to strike or punch. [C19: imit.]

donga ('dɒŋgə) *n S. African, Austral., & NZ.* a steep-sided gully created by soil erosion. [C19: from Afrik., from Zulu]

donjon ('dʌndʒən, 'dɒn-) *n* the heavily fortified central tower or keep of a medieval castle. Also: **dungeon.** [C14: arch. var. of *dungeon*]

Don Juan ('dɒn 'dʒuːən) *n* **1** a legendary Spanish nobleman and philanderer: hero of many poems, plays, and operas. **2** a successful seducer of women.

donkey ('dɒŋkɪ) *n* **1** a long-eared member of the horse family. **2** a stupid or stubborn person. **3 talk the hind leg(s) off a donkey.** to talk endlessly. [C18: ?from *dun* dark + *-key,* as in *monkey*]

donkey jacket *n* a thick hip-length jacket, usually navy blue, with a waterproof panel across the shoulders.

donkey's years *pl n Inf.* a long time.

donkey vote *n Austral.* a vote in which the voter's order of preference follows the order in which the candidates are listed.

donkey-work *n* **1** groundwork. **2** drudgery.

Donna ('dɒnə) *n* an Italian title of address equivalent to *Madam.* [C17: from It., from L *domina* lady]

donnish Ⓣ ('dɒnɪʃ) *adj* of or resembling a university don, esp. denoting pedantry or fussiness.
▸'**donnishness** *n*

donnybrook ('dɒnɪˌbrʊk) *n* a rowdy brawl. [C19: after *Donnybrook Fair,* an annual event until 1855 near Dublin]

donor Ⓣ ('dəʊnə) *n* **1** a person who makes a donation. **2** *Med.* any per-

THESAURUS

domicile *n* **1, 2** = **dwelling,** abode, habitation, home, house, legal residence, mansion, pad (*sl.*), residence, residency, settlement

dominance *n* = **control,** ascendancy, authority, command, domination, government, mastery, paramountcy, power, rule, supremacy, sway

dominant *adj* **1** = **controlling,** ascendant, assertive, authoritative, commanding, governing, leading, presiding, ruling, superior, supreme **2** = **main,** chief, influential, outstanding, paramount, predominant, pre-eminent, prevailing, prevalent, primary, principal, prominent
Antonyms *adj* ≠ **controlling, main:** ancillary, auxiliary, inferior, junior, lesser, lower, minor, secondary, subservient, subsidiary

dominate *vb* **1** = **control,** direct, domineer, govern, have the upper hand over, have the whip hand over, keep under one's thumb, lead, lead by the nose (*inf.*), master, monopolize, overbear, rule, rule the roost, tyrannize **2** = **tower above,** bestride, loom over, overlook, stand head and shoulders above, stand over, survey **3** = **predominate,** detract from, eclipse, outshine, overrule, overshadow, prevail over

domination *n* **1** = **control,** ascendancy, authority, command, influence, mastery, power, rule, superiority, supremacy, sway

domineer *vb* = **boss around** *or* **about** (*inf.*), bluster, browbeat, bully, hector, intimidate, lord it over, menace, overbear, ride roughshod over, swagger, threaten, tyrannize

domineering *adj* = **overbearing,** arrogant, authoritarian, autocratic, bossy (*inf.*), coercive, despotic, dictatorial, high-handed, imperious, iron-handed, magisterial, masterful, oppressive, tyrannical
Antonyms *adj* meek, obsequious, servile, shy, submissive, subservient

dominion *n* **1** = **control,** ascendancy, authority, command, domination, government, jurisdiction, mastery, power, rule, sovereignty, supremacy, sway **2** = **kingdom,** country, domain, empire, patch, province, realm, region, territory, turf (*US. sl.*)

don[1] *vb* = **put on,** clothe oneself in, dress in, get into, pull on, slip on *or* into

donate *vb* = **give,** bequeath, bestow, chip in (*inf.*), contribute, gift, hand out, make a gift of, present, subscribe

donation *n* **2** = **contribution,** alms, benefaction, boon, gift, grant, gratuity, hand-out, largesse *or* largess, offering, present, stipend, subscription

done *interjection* **4** = **agreed,** it's a bargain, O.K. *or* okay (*inf.*), settled, you're on (*inf.*) ◆ *adj* **5** = **finished,** accomplished, completed, concluded, consummated, ended, executed, in the can (*inf.*), over, perfected, realized, terminated, through **6** = **cooked enough,** cooked, cooked sufficiently, cooked to a turn, ready **7** = **used up,** depleted, exhausted, finished, spent **8** = **acceptable,** conventional, *de rigueur,* proper **9** *Informal* = **cheated,** conned (*inf.*), duped, taken for a ride (*inf.*), tricked **10 done for** *Informal* = **finished,** beaten, broken, dashed, defeated, destroyed, doomed, foiled, lost, ruined, undone, wrecked **11 done in** *or* **up** *Informal* = **exhausted,** all in (*sl.*), bushed (*inf.*), clapped out (*Austral. & NZ inf.*), dead, dead beat (*inf.*), dog-tired (*inf.*), fagged out (*inf.*), knackered (*sl.*), on one's last legs, ready to drop, tired out, worn out, worn to a frazzle (*inf.*), zonked (*sl.*)

donnish *adj* = **scholarly,** bookish, erudite, formalistic, pedagogic, pedantic, precise, scholastic

donor *n* **1** = **giver,** almsgiver, benefactor, conson who gives blood, organs, etc., for use in the treatment of another person. **3** the atom supplying both electrons in a coordinate bond. [C15: from OF *doneur,* from L *dōnātor,* from *dōnāre* to give]

donor card *n* a card carried to show that the bodily organs specified on it may be used for transplants after the carrier's death.

Don Quixote ('dɒn kiː'həutiː, 'kwɪksət) *n* an impractical idealist. [after the hero of Cervantes' *Don Quixote de la Mancha* (1605)]

don't (dəunt) *contraction of* do not.

don't know *n* a person who has no definite opinion, esp. as a response to a questionnaire.

doodah ('duːdɑː) *or US & Canad.* **doodad** ('duːdæd) *n Inf.* an unnamed thing, esp. an object the name of which is unknown or forgotten. [C20: from ?]

doodle ('duːdᵊl) *Inf.* ◆ *vb* **doodles, doodling, doodled. 1** to scribble or draw aimlessly. **2** to play or improvise idly. **3** (*intr; often foll. by away*) *US.* to dawdle or waste time. ◆ *n* **4** a shape, picture, etc., drawn aimlessly. [C20: ?from C17: a foolish person, but infl. in meaning by DAWDLE]
▸ **'doodler** *n*

doodlebug ('duːdᵊlˌbʌg) *n* **1** another name for the **V-1. 2** a diviner's rod. **3** a US name for an **antlion** (the larva). [C20: prob. from DOODLE + BUG]

doo-doo ('duːˌduː) *n US & Canad. inf.* a child's word for **excrement.**

doohickey ('duːˌhɪkɪ) *n US & Canad. inf.* another name for **doodah.**

doom ❶ (duːm) *n* **1** death or a terrible fate. **2** a judgment. **3** (*sometimes cap.*) another term for the **Last Judgment.** ◆ *vb* **4** (*tr*) to destine or condemn to death or a terrible fate. [OE *dōm*]

doomsday *or* **domesday** ('duːmzˌdeɪ) *n* **1** (*sometimes cap.*) the day on which the Last Judgment will occur. **2** any day of reckoning. **3** (*modifier*) characterized by predictions of disaster: *doomsday scenario.* [OE *dōmes dæg* Judgment Day]

doona ('duːnə) *n* the Austral. name for **continental quilt.** [from a trademark]

door ❶ (dɔː) *n* **1** a hinged or sliding panel for closing the entrance to a room, cupboard, etc. **2** a doorway or entrance. **3** a means of access or escape: *a door to success.* **4 lay at someone's door.** to lay (the blame or responsibility) on someone. **5 out of doors.** in or into the open air. **6 show someone the door.** to order someone to leave. [OE *duru*]

do-or-die ❶ *adj* (*prenominal*) of a determined and sometimes reckless effort to succeed.

door furniture *n* locks, handles, etc., designed for use on doors.

doorjamb ('dɔːˌdʒæm) *n* one of the two vertical members forming the sides of a doorframe. Also called: **doorpost.**

doorkeeper ('dɔːˌkiːpə) *n* a person attending or guarding a door or gateway.

doorman ('dɔːˌmæn, -mən) *n, pl* **doormen.** a man employed to attend the doors of certain buildings.

doormat ('dɔːˌmæt) *n* **1** a mat, placed at an entrance, for wiping dirt from shoes. **2** *Inf.* a person who offers little resistance to ill-treatment.

doornail ('dɔːˌneɪl) *n* (**as**) **dead as a doornail.** dead beyond any doubt.

doorsill ('dɔːˌsɪl) *n* a horizontal member of wood, stone, etc., forming the bottom of a doorframe.

doorstep ('dɔːˌstɛp) *n* **1** a step in front of a door. **2** *Inf.* a thick slice of bread. ◆ *vb* **doorsteps, doorstepping, doorstepped.** (*tr*) **3** to canvass (a district or member of the public) by or in the course of door-to-door visiting. **4** (of journalists) to wait outside the house of (someone) in order to obtain an interview or photograph when he or she emerges.

doorstop ('dɔːˌstɒp) *n* **1** any device which prevents an open door from moving. **2** a piece of rubber, etc., fixed to the floor to stop a door striking a wall.

door to door *adj* (**door-to-door** *when prenominal*), *adv* **1** (of selling, etc.) from one house to the next. **2** (of journeys, etc.) direct.

doorway ('dɔːˌweɪ) *n* **1** an opening into a building, room, etc., esp. one that has a door. **2** a means of access or escape: *a doorway to freedom.*

do over *vb* (*tr, adv*) **1** *Inf.* to redecorate. **2** *Brit., Austral. & NZ sl.* to beat up; thrash.

doo-wop ('duːˌwɒp) *n* vocalizing based on rhythm-and-blues harmony. [C20: imit.]

dop (dɒp) *n S. African sl.* **1** Cape brandy. **2** a tot of this. [from Afrik., from ?]

dope ❶ (dəup) *n* **1** any of a number of preparations applied to fabric in order to improve strength, tautness, etc. **2** an additive, such as an antiknock compound added to petrol. **3** a thick liquid, such as a lubricant, applied to a surface. **4** a combustible absorbent material used to hold the nitroglycerine in dynamite. **5** *Sl.* an illegal drug, usually cannabis. **6** a drug administered to a racehorse or greyhound to affect its performance. **7** *Inf.* a stupid or slow-witted person. **8** *Inf.* news or facts, esp. confidential information. ◆ *vb* **dopes, doping, doped.** (*tr*) **9** *Electronics.* to add impurities to (a semiconductor) in order to produce or modify its properties. **10** to apply or add dope to. **11** to administer a drug to (oneself or another). [C19: from Du. *doop* sauce, from *doopen* to dip]

dopey ❶ *or* **dopy** ('dəupɪ) *adj* **dopier, dopiest. 1** *Sl.* silly. **2** *Inf.* half-asleep or semiconscious, as when under the influence of a drug.

doppelgänger ('dɒpᵊlˌgɛŋə) *n Legend.* a ghostly duplicate of a living person. [from G *Doppelgänger,* lit.: double-goer]

Doppler effect ('dɒplə) *n* a change in the apparent frequency of a sound or light wave, etc., as a result of relative motion between the observer and the source. Also called: **Doppler shift.** [C19: after C. J. *Doppler* (1803–53), Austrian physicist]

Doric ('dɒrɪk) *adj* **1** of the inhabitants of Doris in ancient Greece or their dialect. **2** of or denoting one of the five classical orders of architecture: characterized by a heavy fluted column and a simple capital. **3** (*sometimes not cap.*) rustic. ◆ *n* **4** one of four chief dialects of Ancient Greek. **5** any rural dialect of English, esp. a Scots one.

dorm (dɔːm) *n Inf.* short for **dormitory.**

dormant ❶ ('dɔːmənt) *adj* **1** quiet and inactive, as during sleep. **2** latent or inoperative. **3** (of a volcano) neither extinct nor erupting. **4** *Biol.* alive but in a resting condition with reduced metabolism. **5** (*usually postpositive*) *Heraldry.* (of a beast) in a sleeping position. [C14: from OF *dormant,* from *dormir* to sleep, from L *dormīre*]
▸ **'dormancy** *n*

dormer ('dɔːmə) *n* a construction with a gable roof and a window that projects from a sloping roof. Also called: **dormer window.** [C16: from OF *dormoir,* from L *dormītōrium* DORMITORY]

dormie *or* **dormy** ('dɔːmɪ) *adj Golf.* as many holes ahead of an opponent as there are still to play: *dormie three.* [C19: from ?]

dormitory ('dɔːmɪtərɪ, -trɪ) *n, pl* **dormitories. 1** a large room, esp. at a school, containing several beds. **2** *US.* a building, esp. at a college or camp, providing living and sleeping accommodation. **3** (*modifier*) *Brit.* denoting or relating to an area from which most of the residents commute to work (esp. in **dormitory suburb**). [C15: from L *dormītōrium,* from *dormīre* to sleep]

Dormobile ('dɔːməuˌbiːl) *n Trademark.* a vanlike vehicle specially equipped for living in while travelling.

dormouse ('dɔːˌmaus) *n, pl* **dormice.** a small Eurasian rodent resembling a mouse with a furry tail. [C15: *dor-,* ?from OF *dormir* to sleep, (from L *dormīre*) + MOUSE]

dorp (dɔːp) *n S. African.* a small town or village. [C16: from Du.]

dorsal ('dɔːsᵊl) *adj Anat., zool.* relating to the back or spinal part of the body. [C15: from Med. L *dorsālis,* from L *dorsum* back]
▸ **'dorsally** *adv*

dorsal fin *n* an unpaired fin on the back of a fish that maintains balance during locomotion.

dory[1] ('dɔːrɪ) *n, pl* **dories.** any of various spiny-finned food fishes, esp. the John Dory. [C14: from F *dorée* gilded, from LL *deaurāre* to gild, ult. from L *aurum* gold]

dory[2] ('dɔːrɪ) *n, pl* **dories.** *US & Canad.* a flat-bottomed rowing boat with a high bow, stern, and sides. [C18: from Amerind *dóri* dugout]

DOS (dɒs) *n Computers, trademark. acronym for* disk-operating system, often prefixed, as in MS-DOS and PC-DOS; a computer operating system.

dosage ('dəusɪdʒ) *n* **1** the administration of a drug or agent in prescribed amounts. **2** the optimum therapeutic dose and interval between doses. **3** another name for **dose** (senses 3, 4).

dose ❶ (dəus) *n* **1** *Med.* a specific quantity of a therapeutic drug or agent taken at any one time or at specified intervals. **2** *Inf.* something unpleasant to experience: *a dose of influenza.* **3** Also called: **dosage.** the total energy of ionizing radiation absorbed by unit mass of material, esp. of living tissue; usually measured in grays (SI unit) or rads. **4** Also called: **dosage.** a small amount of syrup added to wine during bottling. **5** *Sl.* a sexually transmitted infection. ◆ *vb* **doses, dosing, dosed.** (*tr*) **6** to administer a dose to (someone). **7** *Med.* to prescribe (a drug) in appropriate quantities. **8** to add syrup to (wine) during bottling. [C15: from F, from LL *dosis,* from Gk: a giving, from *didonai* to give]

THESAURUS

tributor, donator, grantor (*Law*), philanthropist
Antonyms *n* assignee, beneficiary, inheritor, legatee, payee, receiver, recipient

doom *n* **1 = destruction,** catastrophe, death, destiny, downfall, fate, fortune, lot, portion, ruin **2 = sentence,** condemnation, decision, decree, judgment, verdict ◆ *vb* **4 = condemn,** consign, damn, decree, destine, foreordain, judge, predestine, preordain, sentence, sound the death knell, threaten

doomed *adj* **4 = condemned,** bedevilled, bewitched, cursed, fated, hopeless, ill-fated, ill-omened, luckless, star-crossed

door *n* **1 = opening,** doorway, egress, entrance, entry, exit, ingress **4 lay at someone's door = blame,** censure, charge, hold responsible, impute to **5 out of doors = in the open air,** alfresco, out, outdoors, outside **6 show someone the door = throw out,** ask to leave, boot out, bounce (*sl.*), eject, oust, show out

do-or-die *adj* **= desperate,** death-or-glory, going for broke, hazardous, kill-or-cure, risky, win-or-bust

dope *n* **5** *Slang* **= drug,** narcotic, opiate **7** *Informal* **= idiot,** berk, blockhead, charlie (*Brit. inf.*), coot, dickhead (*sl.*), dimwit (*inf.*), dipstick (*Brit. sl.*), divvy (*Brit. sl.*), dolt, dork (*sl.*), dumb-ass (*sl.*), dunce, fathead (*inf.*), fool, geek (*sl.*), gobshite (*Irish taboo sl.*), jerk (*sl., chiefly US & Canad.*), lamebrain (*inf.*), nerd *or* nurd (*sl.*), nitwit (*inf.*), numbskull *or* numskull, oaf, pillock (*Brit. sl.*), plank (*Brit. sl.*), plonker (*sl.*), prat (*sl.*), prick (*sl.*), schmuck (*US sl.*), simpleton, twit (*inf., chiefly Brit.*), wally (*sl.*) **8 = information,** details, facts, gen (*Brit. inf.*), info (*inf.*), inside information, lowdown (*inf.*), news, tip ◆ *vb* **11 = drug,** anaesthetize, doctor, inject, knock out, narcotize, sedate, stupefy

dopey *adj* **1** *Informal* **= stupid,** asinine, dense, dozy, dumb (*inf.*), dumb-ass (*sl.*), foolish, goofy (*inf.*), idiotic, senseless, silly, simple, slow, thick **2 = drowsy,** dazed, drugged, groggy (*inf.*), half-asleep, muzzy, stupefied, woozy (*inf.*)

dormant *adj* **1-4 = inactive,** asleep, comatose, fallow, hibernating, inert, inoperative, latent, quiescent, sleeping, sluggish, slumbering, suspended, torpid
Antonyms *adj* active, alert, alive and kicking, aroused, awake, awakened, conscious, wakeful, wide-awake

dose *n* **1 = quantity,** dosage, draught, drench, measure, portion, potion, prescription

dosh (dɒʃ) *n Brit.* a slang word for **money.** [C20: of unknown origin]

dosimeter (dəʊˈsɪmɪtə) *n* an instrument for measuring the dose of radiation absorbed by matter or the intensity of a source of radiation.
▸**dosimetric** (ˌdəʊsɪˈmetrɪk) *adj*

dosing strip *n* (in New Zealand) an area set aside for treating dogs suspected of having hydatid disease.

doss (dɒs) *Brit. sl.* ◆ *vb* **1** (*intr;* often foll. by *down*) to sleep, esp. in a dosshouse. **2** (*intr;* often foll. by *around*) to pass time aimlessly. ◆ *n* **3** a bed, esp. in a dosshouse. **4** another word for **sleep. 5** short for **dosshouse. 6** a task or pastime requiring little effort: *making a film is a bit of a doss.* [C18: from ?]

dosser (ˈdɒsə) *n* **1** *Brit. sl.* a person who sleeps in dosshouses. **2** *Brit. sl.* another word for **dosshouse. 3** *Sl.* a lazy person.

dosshouse (ˈdɒsˌhaʊs) *n Brit. sl.* a cheap lodging house, esp. one used by tramps. US name: **flophouse.**

dossier (ˈdɒsɪˌeɪ) *n* a collection of papers about a subject or person. [C19: from F: a file with a label on the back, from *dos* back, from L *dorsum*]

dost (dʌst) *vb Arch. or dialect.* (used with *thou*) a singular form of the present tense (indicative mood) of **do**[1].

dot[1] ➊ (dɒt) *n* **1** a small round mark; spot; point. **2** anything resembling a dot; a small amount. **3** the mark (˙) above the letters *i, j.* **4** *Music.* **4a** the symbol (·) placed after a note or rest to increase its time value by half. **4b** this symbol written above or below a note indicating staccato. **5** *Maths, logic.* **5a** the symbol (.) indicating multiplication or logical conjunction. **5b** a decimal point. **6** the symbol (·) used, in combination with the symbol for *dash* (—), in Morse and other codes. **7 on the dot.** at exactly the arranged time. ◆ *vb* **dots, dotting, dotted. 8** (*tr*) to mark or form with a dot. **9** (*tr*) to scatter or intersperse (as with dots): *bushes dotting the plain.* **10** (*intr*) to make a dot or dots. **11 dot one's i's and cross one's t's.** *Inf.* to pay meticulous attention to detail. [OE *dott* head of a boil]
▸ˈ**dotter** *n*

dot[2] (dɒt) *n* a woman's dowry. [C19: from F from L *dōs;* rel. to *dōtāre* to endow, *dāre* to give]

dotage ➊ (ˈdəʊtɪdʒ) *n* **1** feebleness of mind, esp. as a result of old age. **2** foolish infatuation. [C14: from DOTE + -AGE]

dotard (ˈdəʊtəd) *n* a person who is weak-minded, esp. through senility. [C14: from DOTE + -ARD]
▸ˈ**dotardly** *adj*

dote ➊ (dəʊt) *vb* **dotes, doting, doted.** (*intr*) **1** (foll. by *on* or *upon*) to love to an excessive or foolish degree. **2** to be foolish or weak-minded, esp. as a result of old age. [C13: rel. to MDu. *doten* to be silly]
▸ˈ**doter** *n*

doth (dʌθ) *vb Arch. or dialect.* (used with *he, she,* or *it*) a singular form of the present tense of **do**[1].

dot-matrix printer *n Computing.* a printer in which each character is produced by a subset of an array of needles.

dotterel *or* **dottrel** (ˈdɒtrəl) *n* **1** a rare Eurasian plover with white bands around the head and neck. **2** *Dialect.* a person who is foolish or easily duped. [C15 *dotrelle;* see DOTE]

dottle (ˈdɒtᵊl) *n* the plug of tobacco left in a pipe after smoking. [C15: dim. of *dot* lump]

dotty ➊ (ˈdɒtɪ) *adj* **dottier, dottiest. 1** *Sl., chiefly Brit.* feeble-minded; slightly crazy. **2** *Brit. sl.* (foll. by *about*) extremely fond (of). **3** marked with dots. [C19: from DOT[1]]
▸ˈ**dottily** *adv* ▸ˈ**dottiness** *n*

Douay Bible *or* **Version** (ˈduːeɪ) *n* an English translation of the Bible from the Vulgate by Catholic scholars at Douai, a city in N France, in 1610.

double ➊ (ˈdʌbᵊl) *adj* (*usually prenominal*) **1** as much again in size, strength, number, etc.: *a double portion.* **2** composed of two equal or similar parts. **3** designed for two users: *a double room.* **4** folded in two; composed of two layers. **5** stooping; bent over. **6** having two aspects; ambiguous: *a double meaning.* **7** false, deceitful, or hypocritical: *a double life.* **8** (of flowers) having more than the normal number of petals. **9** *Music.* **9a** (of an instrument) sounding an octave lower: *a double bass.* **9b** (of time) duple. ◆ *adv* **10** twice over; twofold. **11** two together; two at a time (esp. in **see double**). ◆ *n* **12** twice the number, amount, size, etc. **13** a double measure of spirits. **14** a duplicate or counterpart, esp. a person who closely resembles another; understudy. **15** a ghostly apparition of a living person; doppelgänger. **16** a sharp turn, esp. a return on one's own tracks. **17** *Bridge.* a call that increases certain scoring points if the last preceding bid becomes the contract. **18** *Billiards, etc.* a strike in which the object ball is struck so as to make it rebound against the cushion to an opposite pocket. **19** a bet on two horses in different races in which any winnings from the first race are placed on the horse in the later race. **20a** the narrow outermost ring on a dartboard. **20b** a hit on this ring. **21 at** *or* **on the double. 21a** at twice normal marching speed. **21b** quickly or immediately. ◆ *vb* **doubles, doubling, doubled. 22** to make or become twice as much. **23** to bend or fold (material, etc.). **24** (*tr;* sometimes foll. by *up*) to clench (a fist). **25** (*tr;* often foll. by *together* or *up*) to join or couple. **26** (*tr*) to repeat exactly; copy. **27** (*intr*) to play two parts or serve two roles. **28** (*intr*) to turn sharply; follow a winding course. **29** *Naut.* to sail around (a headland or other point). **30** *Music.* **30a** to duplicate (a part) either in unison or at the octave above or below it. **30b** (*intr;* usually foll. by *on*) to be capable of performing (upon an additional instrument). **31** *Bridge.* to make a call that will double certain scoring points if the preceding bid becomes the contract. **32** *Billiards, etc.* to cause (a ball) to rebound or (of a ball) to rebound from a cushion. **33** (*intr;* foll. by *for*) to act as substitute. **34** (*intr*) to go or march at twice the normal speed. ◆ See also **double back, doubles, double up.** [C13: from OF, from L *duplus* twofold, from *duo* two + *-plus* -FOLD]
▸ˈ**doubler** *n*

double agent *n* a spy employed by two mutually antagonistic countries, companies, etc.

double back ➊ *vb* (*intr, adv*) to go back in the opposite direction (esp. in **double back on one's tracks**).

double-bank *vb Austral. & NZ inf.* to carry (a second person) on (a horse, bicycle, etc.). Also: **dub.**

double bar *n Music.* a symbol, consisting of two ordinary bar lines or a single heavy one, that marks the end of a composition or section.

double-barrelled *or US* **double-barreled** *adj* **1** (of a gun) having two barrels. **2** extremely forceful. **3** *Brit.* (of a surname) having hyphenated parts. **4** serving two purposes; ambiguous: *a double-barrelled remark.*

double bass (beɪs) *n* **1** Also called (US): **bass viol.** a stringed instrument, the largest and lowest member of the violin family with a range of almost three octaves. Inf. name: **bass fiddle.** ◆ *adj* **double-bass. 2** of an instrument whose pitch lies below the bass; contrabass.

double bassoon *n Music.* the lowest and largest instrument in the oboe class; contrabassoon.

double-blind *adj* of or denoting an experimental study of a new drug in which neither the experimenters nor the patients know which are the test subjects and which are the controls.

double boiler *n* the US and Canad. name for **double saucepan.**

double-breasted *adj* (of a garment) having overlapping fronts.

double-check *vb* **1** to check again; verify. ◆ *n* **double check. 2** a second examination or verification. **3** *Chess.* a simultaneous check from two pieces.

double chin *n* a fold of fat under the chin.
▸ˌ**double-**ˈ**chinned** *adj*

double concerto *n* a concerto for two solo instruments and orchestra.

double cream *n Brit.* thick cream with a high fat content.

double-cross ➊ *vb* **1** (*tr*) to cheat or betray. ◆ *n* **2** the act or an instance of double-crossing; betrayal.
▸ˌ**double-**ˈ**crosser** *n*

double dagger *n* a character (‡) used in printing to indicate a cross-reference. Also called: **diesis, double obelisk.**

double-dealing ➊ *n* **a** action characterized by treachery or deceit. **b** (*as modifier*): *double-dealing treachery.*
▸ˌ**double-**ˈ**dealer** *n*

double-decker *n* **1** *Chiefly Brit.* a bus with two passenger decks. **2** *Inf.* **2a** a thing or structure having two decks, layers, etc. **2b** (*as modifier*): *a double-decker sandwich.*

double-declutch *vb* (*intr*) *Brit., Austral, & NZ.* to change to a lower gear in a motor vehicle by first placing the gear lever into neutral before engaging the desired gear. US term: **double-clutch.**

double Dutch *n Brit. inf.* incomprehensible talk; gibberish.

double-edged *adj* **1** acting in two ways. **2** (of a remark, etc.) having two possible interpretations, esp. applicable both for and against, or

THESAURUS

dot[1] *n* **1** = **spot**, atom, circle, dab, fleck, full stop, iota, jot, mark, mite, mote, point, speck, speckle **7 on the dot** = **on time**, exactly, on the button (*inf.*), precisely, promptly, punctually, to the minute ◆ *vb* **8** = **spot**, dab, dabble, fleck, speckle, sprinkle, stipple, stud

dotage *n* **1** = **senility**, decrepitude, eld (*arch.*), feebleness, imbecility, old age, second childhood, weakness

dote on *vb* **1** = **adore**, admire, hold dear, idolize, lavish affection on, prize, treasure

doting *adj* **1** = **adoring**, devoted, fond, foolish, indulgent, lovesick

dotty *adj* **1** *Slang, chiefly Brit.* = **crazy**, batty, crackpot (*inf.*), doolally (*sl.*), eccentric, feeble-minded, loopy (*inf.*), oddball (*inf.*), off one's trolley (*sl.*), off-the-wall (*sl.*), outré, out to lunch (*inf.*), peculiar, potty (*Brit. inf.*), touched, up the pole (*inf.*) **2 dotty about** = **keen on**, crazy about (*inf.*), daft about (*inf.*), fond of, mad about (*inf.*)

double *adj* **1** = **twice**, binate (*Botany*), coupled, doubled, dual, duplicate, in pairs, paired, twin, twofold **7** = **deceitful**, dishonest, false, hypocritical, insincere, Janus-faced, knavish (*arch.*), perfidious, treacherous, two-faced, vacillating ◆ *n* **14** = **twin**, clone, copy, counterpart, dead ringer (*sl.*), Doppelgänger, duplicate, fellow, impersonator, lookalike, mate, replica, ringer (*sl.*), spitting image (*inf.*) **21 at** *or* **on the double** = **quickly**, at full speed, briskly, immediately, in double-quick time, posthaste, without delay ◆ *vb* **22** = **multiply**, duplicate, enlarge, fold, grow, increase, magnify, plait, repeat

double back *vb* = **backtrack**, circle, dodge, loop, retrace one's steps, return, reverse

double-cross *vb* **1** = **betray**, cheat, cozen, defraud, hoodwink, mislead, sell down the river (*inf.*), swindle, trick, two-time (*inf.*)

double-dealer *n* = **cheat**, betrayer, con man (*inf.*), cozener, deceiver, dissembler, double-crosser (*inf.*), fraud, fraudster, hypocrite, rogue, snake in the grass (*inf.*), swindler, traitor, two-timer (*inf.*)

double-dealing *n* **a** = **treachery**, bad faith, betrayal, cheating, deceit, deception, dishonesty, duplicity, foul play, hypocrisy, mendacity, perfidy, trickery, two-timing (*inf.*) ◆ *modifier* **b** = **treacherous**, cheating, crooked (*inf.*), deceitful, dishonest, duplicitous, fraudulent, hypocritical, lying, perfidious, sneaky, swindling, tricky, two-faced, two-timing (*inf.*), underhanded, untrustworthy, wily being malicious though apparently innocuous. **3** (of a knife, etc.) having a cutting edge on either side of the blade.

double entendre Ⓣ (ɑːnˈtɑːndrə) *n* **1** a word, phrase, etc., that can be interpreted in two ways, esp. one having one meaning that is indelicate. **2** the type of humour that depends upon this. [C17: from obs. F: double meaning]

double entry *n* **a** a book-keeping system in which any commercial transaction is entered as a debit in one account and as a credit in another. **b** (*as modifier*): *double-entry book-keeping.*

double exposure *n* **1** the act or process of recording two superimposed images on a photographic medium. **2** the photograph resulting from such an act.

double-faced *adj* **1** (of textiles) having a finished nap on each side; reversible. **2** insincere or deceitful.

double feature *n Films.* a programme showing two full-length films. Inf. name (US): **twin bill.**

double first *n Brit.* a first-class honours degree in two subjects.

double glazing *n* **1** two panes of glass in a window, fitted to reduce heat loss, etc. **2** the fitting of glass in such a manner.

double-header *n* **1** a train drawn by two locomotives coupled together. **2** Also called: **twin bill.** *Sport, US & Canad.* two games played consecutively. **3** *Austral. & NZ inf.* a coin with the impression of a head on each side. **4** *Austral. inf.* a double ice-cream cone.

double helix *n* the form of the molecular structure of DNA, consisting of two helical chains coiled around the same axis.

double-jointed *adj* having unusually flexible joints permitting an abnormal degree of motion.

double knitting *n* a widely used medium thickness of knitting wool.

double negative *n* a construction, often considered ungrammatical, in which two negatives are used where one is needed, as in *I wouldn't never have believed it.*

> **USAGE NOTE** There are two contexts where double negatives are found. An adjective with negative force is often used with a negative in order to express a nuance of meaning somewhere between the positive and the negative: *he was a not infrequent visitor; it is not an uncommon sight.* Two negatives are also found together where they reinforce each other rather than conflict: *he never went back, not even to collect his belongings.* These two uses of what is technically a double negative are acceptable. A third case, illustrated by *I shouldn't wonder if it didn't rain today,* has the force of a weak positive statement (*I expect it to rain today*) and is common in informal English.

double-park *vb* to park (a vehicle) alongside or opposite another already parked by the roadside, thereby causing an obstruction.

double pneumonia *n* pneumonia affecting both lungs.

double-quick *adj* **1** very quick; rapid. ◆ *adv* **2** in a very quick or rapid manner.

double-reed *adj* relating to or denoting a wind instrument having two reeds that vibrate against each other.

double refraction *n* the splitting of a ray of unpolarized light into two unequally refracted rays polarized in mutually perpendicular planes. Also called: **birefringence.**

doubles (ˈdʌbᵊlz) *n* (*functioning as sing or pl*) **a** a game between two pairs of players. **b** (*as modifier*): *a doubles match.*

double saucepan *n Brit.* a cooking utensil consisting of two saucepans: the lower pan is used to boil water to heat food in the upper pan. US and Canad. name: **double boiler.**

double-space *vb* **double-spaces, double-spacing, double-spaced.** to type (copy) with a full space between lines.

double spread *n Printing.* two facing pages of a publication treated as a single unit.

double standard *n* a set of principles that allows greater freedom to one person or group than to another.

double-stop *vb* **double-stops, double-stopping, double-stopped.** to play (two notes or parts) simultaneously on a violin or related instrument.

doublet Ⓣ (ˈdʌblɪt) *n* **1** (formerly) a man's close-fitting jacket, with or without sleeves (esp. in **doublet and hose**). **2a** a pair of similar things, esp. two words deriving ultimately from the same source. **2b** one of such a pair. **3** *Jewellery.* a false gem made by welding or fusing stones together. **4** *Physics.* a closely spaced pair of related spectral lines. **5** (*pl*) two dice each showing the same number of spots on one throw. [C14: from OF, from DOUBLE]

double take *n* (esp. in comedy) a delayed reaction by a person to a remark, situation, etc.

double talk *n* **1** rapid speech with a mixture of nonsense syllables and real words; gibberish. **2** empty, deceptive, or ambiguous talk.

doublethink (ˈdʌbᵊl,θɪŋk) *n* deliberate, perverse, or unconscious acceptance or promulgation of conflicting facts, principles, etc.

double time *n* **1** a doubled wage rate, paid for working on public holidays, etc. **2** *Music.* two beats per bar. **3** a slow running pace, keeping in step. **4** *US Army.* a fast march.

double up *vb* (*adv*) **1** to bend or cause to bend in two. **2** (*intr*) to share a room or bed designed for one person, family, etc. **3** (*intr*) *Brit.* to use the winnings from one bet as the stake for another. US and Canad. term: **parlay.**

double whammy *n Inf., chiefly US.* a devastating setback made up of two elements.

doubloon (dʌˈbluːn) *n* **1** a former Spanish gold coin. **2** (*pl*) *Sl.* money. [C17: from Sp. *doblón,* from *dobla,* from L *dupla,* fem. of *duplus* twofold]

doubly Ⓣ (ˈdʌblɪ) *adv* **1** to or in a double degree, quantity, or measure. **2** in two ways.

doubt Ⓣ (daʊt) *n* **1** uncertainty about the truth, fact, or existence of something (esp. in **in doubt, without doubt,** etc.). **2** (*often pl*) lack of belief in or conviction about something. **3** an unresolved difficulty, point, etc. **4** *Obs.* fear. **5 give (someone) the benefit of the doubt.** to presume (someone suspected of guilt) innocent. **6 no doubt.** almost certainly. ◆ *vb* **7** (*tr; may take a clause as object*) to be inclined to disbelieve. **8** (*tr*) to distrust or be suspicious of. **9** (*intr*) to feel uncertainty or be undecided. **10** (*tr*) *Arch.* to fear. [C13: from OF *douter,* from L *dubitāre*]
▶ˈ**doubtable** *adj* ▶ˈ**doubter** *n* ▶ˈ**doubtingly** *adv*

> **USAGE NOTE** Where a clause follows *doubt* in a positive sentence, it was formerly considered correct to use *whether:* (*I doubt whether he will come*), but now *if* and *that* are also acceptable. In negative statements, *doubt* is followed by *that: I do not doubt that he is telling the truth.* In such sentences, *but* (*I do not doubt but that he is telling the truth*) is redundant.

doubtful Ⓣ (ˈdaʊtful) *adj* **1** unlikely; improbable. **2** uncertain: *a doubtful answer.* **3** unsettled; unresolved. **4** of questionable reputation or morality. **5** having reservations or misgivings.
▶ˈ**doubtfully** *adv* ▶ˈ**doubtfulness** *n*

> **USAGE NOTE** It was formerly considered correct to use *whether* after *doubtful* (*it is doubtful whether he will come*), but now *if* and *that* are also acceptable.

doubting Thomas (ˈtɒməs) *n* a person who insists on proof before he will believe anything. [after *Thomas* (the apostle), who did not believe that Jesus had been resurrected until he had proof]

doubtless Ⓣ (ˈdaʊtlɪs) *adv also* **doubtlessly** (*sentence modifier*), *sentence substitute.* **1** certainly. **2** probably. ◆ *adj* **3** certain; assured.
▶ˈ**doubtlessness** *n*

douche (duːʃ) *n* **1** a stream of water directed onto or into the body for cleansing or medical purposes. **2** the application of such a stream of water. **3** an instrument for applying a douche. ◆ *vb* **douches, douching, douched. 4** to cleanse or treat or be cleansed or treated by means of a douche. [C18: from F, from It. *doccia* pipe]

dough (dəʊ) *n* **1** a thick mixture of flour or meal and water or milk, used for making bread, pastry, etc. **2** any similar pasty mass. **3** a slang word for **money.** [OE *dāg*]

doughboy (ˈdəʊ,bɔɪ) *n* **1** *US inf.* an infantryman, esp. in World War I. **2** dough that is boiled or steamed as a dumpling.

doughnut (ˈdəʊnʌt) *n* **1** a small cake of sweetened dough, often ring-shaped, cooked in hot fat. **2** anything shaped like a ring, such as the reaction vessel of a thermonuclear reactor. ◆ *vb* **doughnuts, doughnutting, doughnutted. 3** (*tr*) *Inf.* (of Members of Parliament) to surround (a speaker) during the televising of Parliament to give the impression that the chamber is crowded or the speaker is well supported.

doughty Ⓣ (ˈdaʊtɪ) *adj* **doughtier, doughtiest.** hardy; resolute. [OE *dohtig*]
▶ˈ**doughtily** *adv* ▶ˈ**doughtiness** *n*

THESAURUS

double entendre *n* **1** = **double meaning,** ambiguity, innuendo, play on words, pun

doublet *n* **1** *History* = **jacket,** jerkin, vest, waistcoat

doubly *adv* **1, 2** = **twice,** again, as much again, in double measure, in two ways, once more, over again, twofold

doubt *n* **1** = **suspicion,** apprehension, disquiet, distrust, fear, incredulity, lack of faith, misgiving, mistrust, qualm, scepticism **2** = **uncertainty,** dubiety, hesitancy, hesitation, indecision, irresolution, lack of conviction, suspense, vacillation **3** = **difficulty,** ambiguity, can of worms (*inf.*), confusion, dilemma, perplexity, problem, quandary **6 no doubt** = **certainly,** admittedly, assuredly, doubtless, doubtlessly, probably, surely ◆ *vb* **8** = **suspect,** discredit, distrust, fear, lack confidence in, misgive, mistrust, query, question **9** = **be uncertain,** be dubious, demur, fluctuate, hesitate, scruple, vacillate, waver
Antonyms *n* ≠ **suspicion:** confidence, trust ≠ **uncertainty:** belief, certainty, confidence, conviction ◆ *vb* ≠ **suspect:** accept, believe, buy (*sl.*), have faith in, swallow (*inf.*), take on board, trust

doubter *n* **7, 8** = **sceptic,** agnostic, disbeliever, doubting Thomas, questioner, unbeliever

doubtful *adj* **1** = **unlikely,** ambiguous, debatable, dodgy (*Brit., Austral., & NZ inf.*), dubious, equivocal, hazardous, iffy (*inf.*), improbable, inconclusive, indefinite, indeterminate, inexact, obscure, precarious, problematic(al), questionable, unclear, unconfirmed, unsettled, vague **2,** **3** = **unsure,** distrustful, hesitating, in two minds (*inf.*), irresolute, leery (*sl.*), perplexed, sceptical, suspicious, tentative, uncertain, unconvinced, undecided, unresolved, unsettled, vacillating, wavering **4** = **questionable,** disreputable, dodgy (*Brit., Austral., & NZ inf.*), dubious, shady (*inf.*), suspect, suspicious
Antonyms *adj* ≠ **unlikely:** certain, definite, indubitable ≠ **unsure:** certain, decided, positive, resolute

doubtless *adv* **1** = **certainly,** assuredly, clearly, indisputably, of course, precisely, surely, truly, undoubtedly, unquestionably, without doubt **2** = **probably,** apparently, most likely, ostensibly, presumably, seemingly, supposedly

doughty *adj Old-fashioned* = **intrepid,** bold,

doughy ('dəʊɪ) *adj* **doughier, doughiest.** resembling dough; soft, pallid, or flabby.

Douglas fir, spruce, *or* **hemlock** *n* a North American pyramidal coniferous tree, widely planted for ornament and for timber. [C19: after David *Douglas* (1798–1834), Scot. botanist]

Doukhobor *or* **Dukhobor** ('du:kəʊˌbɔ:) *n* a member of a Russian sect of Christians that originated in the 18th century. In the late 19th century a large number emigrated to W Canada, where most Doukhobors now live. [C19: from Russian *dukhoborets* spirit wrestlers]

do up *vb* (*adv; mainly tr*) **1** to wrap and make into a bundle: *to do up a parcel.* **2** to beautify or adorn. **3** (*also intr*) to fasten or be fastened. **4** *Inf.* to renovate or redecorate. **5** *Sl.* to assault. **6** *Inf.* to cause the downfall of (a person).

dour ❶ (dʊə, 'daʊə) *adj* **1** sullen. **2** hard or obstinate. [C14: prob. from L *dūrus* hard]
▸**'dourly** *adv* ▸**'dourness** *n*

douroucouli (ˌdu:ru:'ku:lɪ) *n* a nocturnal New World monkey of Central and South America with thick fur and large eyes. [from Amerind]

douse ❶ *or* **dowse** (daʊs) *vb* **douses, dousing, doused** *or* **dowses, dowsing, dowsed. 1** to plunge or be plunged into liquid; duck. **2** (*tr*) to drench with water. **3** (*tr*) to put out (a light, candle, etc.). ◆ *n* **4** an immersion. [C16: ? rel. to obs. *douse* to strike, from ?]

dove (dʌv) *n* **1** any of a family of birds having a heavy body, small head, short legs, and long pointed wings. **2** *Politics.* a person opposed to war. **3** a gentle or innocent person: used as a term of endearment. **4a** a greyish-brown colour. **4b** (*as adj*): *dove walls.* [OE *dūfe* (unattested except as a fem proper name)]
▸**'doveˌlike** *adj*

Dove (dʌv) *n* **the.** *Christianity.* a manifestation of the Holy Spirit (John 1:32).

dovecote ('dʌvˌkəʊt) *or* **dovecot** ('dʌvˌkɒt) *n* a structure for housing pigeons.

dovetail ❶ ('dʌvˌteɪl) *n* **1** a wedge-shaped tenon. **2** Also called: **dovetail joint.** a joint containing such tenons. ◆ *vb* **3** (*tr*) to join by means of dovetails. **4** to fit or cause to fit together closely or neatly.

dowager ('daʊədʒə) *n* **1a** a widow possessing property or a title obtained from her husband. **1b** (*as modifier*): *the dowager duchess.* **2** a wealthy or dignified elderly woman. [C16: from OF *douagiere*, from *douage* DOWER]

dowdy ❶ ('daʊdɪ) *adj* **dowdier, dowdiest. 1** (esp. of a woman or a woman's dress) shabby or old-fashioned. ◆ *n, pl* **dowdies. 2** a dowdy woman. [C14: *dowd* slut, from ?]
▸**'dowdily** *adv* ▸**'dowdiness** *n* ▸**'dowdyish** *adj*

dowel ('daʊəl) *n* a wooden or metal peg that fits into two corresponding holes to join two adjacent parts. [C14: from MLow G *dövel* plug, from OHG *tubili*]

dower ('daʊə) *n* **1** the life interest in a part of her husband's estate allotted to a widow by law. **2** an archaic word for **dowry** (sense 1). **3** a natural gift. ◆ *vb* **4** (*tr*) to endow. [C14: from OF *douaire*, from Med. L *dōtārium*, from L *dōs* gift]

dower house *n* a house for the use of a widow, often on her deceased husband's estate.

do with *vb* **1 could** *or* **can do with.** to find useful; benefit from. **2 have to do with.** to be involved in or connected with. **3 to do with.** concerning; related to. **4 what...do with. 4a** to put or place: *what did you do with my coat?* **4b** to handle or treat. **4c** to fill one's time usefully: *she didn't know what to do with herself when the project was finished.*

do without ❶ *vb* (*intr*) **1** to forgo; manage without. **2** (*prep*) not to require (uncalled-for comments): *we can do without your criticisms.*

Dow-Jones average ('daʊ'dʒəʊnz) *n US.* a daily index of average stock-exchange prices. [C20: after Charles H. *Dow* (died 1902) & Edward D. *Jones* (died 1920), American financial statisticians]

down[1] ❶ (daʊn) *prep* **1** used to indicate movement from a higher to a lower position. **2** at a lower or further level or position on, in, or along: *he ran down the street.* ◆ *adv* **3** downwards; at or to a lower level or position. **4** (*particle*) used with many verbs when the result of the verb's action is to lower or destroy its object: *knock down.* **5** (*particle*) used with several verbs to indicate intensity or completion: *calm down.* **6** immediately: *cash down.* **7** on paper: *write this down.* **8** arranged; scheduled. **9** in a helpless position. **10a** away from a more important place. **10b** away from a more northerly place. **10c** (of a member of some British universities) away from the university. **10d** in a particular part of a country: *down south.* **11** *Naut.* (of a helm) having the rudder to windward. **12** reduced to a state of lack or want: *down to the last pound.* **13** lacking a specified amount. **14** lower in price. **15** including all intermediate grades. **16** from an earlier to a later time. **17** to a finer or more concentrated state: *to grind down.* **18** *Sport.* being a specified number of points, goals, etc., behind another competitor, team, etc. **19** (of a person) being inactive, owing to illness: *down with flu.* **20** (*functioning as imperative*) (to dogs): *down, Rover!* **21** (*functioning as imperative*) **down with.** wanting the end of somebody or something: *down with the king!* **22 get down on something.** *Austral. & NZ.* to procure something, esp. in advance of needs or in anticipation of someone else. ◆ *adj* **23** (*postpositive*) depressed. **24** (*prenominal*) of or relating to a train or trains from a more important place or one regarded as higher: *the down line.* **25** (*postpositive*) (of a device, machine, etc., esp. a computer) temporarily out of action. **26** made in cash: *a down payment.* **27 down to.** the responsibility or fault of: *this defeat was down to me.* ◆ *vb* (*tr*) **28** to knock, push, or pull down. **29** to cause to go or come down. **30** *Inf.* to drink, esp. quickly. **31** to bring (someone) down, esp. by tackling. ◆ *n* **32** a descent; downward movement. **33** a lowering or a poor period (esp. in **ups and downs**). **34** (in American football) any of a series of four attempts to advance the ball ten yards. **35 have a down on.** *Inf.* to bear ill will towards. [OE *dūne*, short for *adūne*, var. of *of dūne*, lit.: from the hill]

down[2] (daʊn) *n* **1** soft fine feathers. **2** another name for **eiderdown** (sense 1). **3** *Bot.* a fine coating of soft hairs, as on certain leaves, fruits, and seeds. **4** any growth or coating of soft fine hair. [C14: from ON]

down[3] (daʊn) *n Arch.* a hill, esp. a sand dune. See also **downs.** [OE *dūn*]

down-and-out ❶ *adj* **1** without any means of livelihood; poor and, often, socially outcast. ◆ *n* **2** a person who is destitute and, often, homeless.

downbeat ❶ ('daʊnˌbi:t) *n* **1** *Music.* the first beat of a bar or the downward gesture of a conductor's baton indicating this. ◆ *adj Inf.* **2** depressed; gloomy. **3** relaxed.

downcast ❶ ('daʊnˌkɑ:st) *adj* **1** dejected. **2** (esp. of the eyes) directed downwards. ◆ *n* **3** *Mining.* a ventilation shaft.

downer ('daʊnə) *n Sl.* **1** a barbiturate, tranquillizer, or narcotic. **2** a depressing experience. **3** a state of depression.

downfall ❶ ('daʊnˌfɔ:l) *n* **1** a sudden loss of position, health, or reputation. **2** a fall of rain, snow, etc., esp. a sudden heavy one.

downgrade ❶ ('daʊnˌgreɪd) *vb* **downgrades, downgrading, downgraded.** (*tr*) **1** to reduce in importance or value, esp. to demote (a person) to a poorer job. **2** to speak of disparagingly. ◆ *n* **3** *Chiefly US & Canad.* a downward slope. **4 on the downgrade.** waning in importance, health, etc.

downhearted ❶ (ˌdaʊn'hɑ:tɪd) *adj* discouraged; dejected.
▸ˌ**down'heartedly** *adv*

downhill ('daʊn'hɪl) *adj* **1** going or sloping down. ◆ *adv* **2** towards the bottom of a hill; downwards. **3 go downhill.** *Inf.* to decline; deteriorate. ◆ *n* **4** the downward slope of a hill; a descent. **5** a skiing race downhill.

downhole ('daʊnˌhəʊl) *adj* (in the oil industry) denoting any piece of equipment used in the well itself.

downhome (ˌdaʊn'həʊm) *adj Sl., chiefly US.* of, relating to, or reminiscent of rural life, esp. in the southern US; unsophisticated; homely.

Downing Street ('daʊnɪŋ) *n* **1** a street in W central London: official

THESAURUS

brave, courageous, daring, dauntless, fearless, gallant, gritty, hardy, heroic, redoubtable, resolute, stouthearted, valiant, valorous

dour *adj* **1 = gloomy,** dismal, dreary, forbidding, grim, morose, sour, sullen, unfriendly
Antonyms *adj* carefree, cheerful, cheery, chirpy (*inf.*), genial, good-humoured, happy, jovial, pleasant, sunny

douse *vb* **1, 2 = drench,** duck, dunk, immerse, plunge into water, saturate, soak, souse, steep, submerge **3 = put out,** blow out, extinguish, smother, snuff (out)

dovetail *vb* **3 = fit together,** fit, interlock, join, link, mortise, tenon, unite **4 = correspond,** accord, agree, coincide, conform, harmonize, match, tally

dowdy *adj* **1 = frumpy,** dingy, drab, frowzy, frumpish, ill-dressed, old-fashioned, scrubby (*Brit. inf.*), shabby, slovenly, tacky (*US inf.*), unfashionable
Antonyms *adj* chic, dressy, fashionable, neat, smart, spruce, trim, well-dressed

do without *vb* **1 = manage without,** abstain from, dispense with, forgo, get along without, give up, kick (*inf.*)

down[1] *adj* **23 = depressed,** blue, dejected, disheartened, dismal, downcast, down in the dumps (*inf.*), low, miserable, sad, sick as a parrot (*inf.*), unhappy ◆ *vb* **28, 29 = bring down,** deck (*sl.*), fell, floor, knock down, overthrow, prostrate, subdue, tackle, throw, trip **30** *Informal* **= swallow,** drain, drink (down), gulp, put away, toss off ◆ *n* **32 = drop,** decline, descent, dropping, fall, falling, reverse **35 have a down on** *Informal* **= be antagonistic** *or* **hostile to,** be anti (*inf.*), bear a grudge towards, be contra (*inf.*), be prejudiced against, be set against, feel ill will towards, have it in for (*sl.*)

down-and-out *adj* **1 = destitute,** derelict, dirt-poor (*inf.*), flat broke (*inf.*), impoverished, on one's uppers (*inf.*), penniless, ruined, short, without two pennies to rub together (*inf.*) ◆ *n* **2 = tramp,** bag lady, beggar, bum (*inf.*), derelict, dosser (*Brit. sl.*), loser, outcast, pauper, vagabond, vagrant

downbeat *adj* **2** *Informal* **= gloomy,** depressed, discouraging, disheartening, flat, low-key, muted, negative, pessimistic, sober, sombre, subdued, unfavourable
Antonyms *adj* buoyant, cheerful, encouraging, favourable, heartening, optimistic, positive, upbeat

downcast *adj* **1 = dejected,** cheerless, choked, crestfallen, daunted, depressed, despondent, disappointed, disconsolate, discouraged, disheartened, dismal, dismayed, dispirited, down in the dumps (*inf.*), miserable, sad, sick as a parrot (*inf.*), unhappy
Antonyms *adj* cheerful, cheery, chirpy (*inf.*), contented, elated, genial, happy, joyful, lighthearted, optimistic

downfall *n* **1 = ruin,** breakdown, collapse, comedown, comeuppance (*sl.*), debacle, descent, destruction, disgrace, fall, overthrow, undoing **2 = rainstorm,** cloudburst, deluge, downpour

downgrade *vb* **1 = demote,** degrade, humble, lower *or* reduce in rank, take down a peg (*inf.*) **2 = run down,** decry, denigrate, detract from, disparage
Antonyms *vb* ≠ **demote:** advance, ameliorate, better, elevate, enhance, improve, promote, raise, upgrade

downhearted *adj* **= dejected,** blue, chapfallen, crestfallen, depressed, despondent, discouraged, disheartened, dismayed, dispirited, downcast, low-spirited, sad, sick as a parrot (*inf.*), sorrowful, unhappy residences of the prime minister of Great Britain and the Chancellor of the Exchequer. **2** the office of the prime minister. [after Sir George *Downing* (1623–84), E statesman]

download (ˈdaʊnˌləʊd) *vb* (*tr*) to copy or transfer (data or a program) from one computer's memory to that of another, esp. in a network of computing.

down-market Ⓣ *adj* relating to commercial products, services, etc., that are cheap, unfashionable, or poor quality.

down payment *n* the deposit paid on an item purchased on hire-purchase, mortgage, etc.

downpipe (ˈdaʊnˌpaɪp) *n Brit. and NZ.* a pipe for carrying rainwater from a roof gutter to ground level. Usual US & Canad. name: **downspout.**

downpour Ⓣ (ˈdaʊnˌpɔː) *n* a heavy continuous fall of rain.

downrange (ˈdaʊnˈreɪndʒ) *adj, adv* in the direction of the intended flight path of a rocket or missile.

downright Ⓣ (ˈdaʊnˌraɪt) *adj* **1** frank or straightforward; blunt. ◆ *adv, adj* (*prenominal*) **2** (intensifier): *downright rude.* ▸ **ˈdownˌrightly** *adv* ▸ **ˈdownˌrightness** *n*

downs (daʊnz) *pl n* **1** rolling upland, esp. in the chalk areas of S Britain, characterized by lack of trees and used mainly as pasture. **2** *Austral. & NZ.* a flat grassy area, not necessarily of uplands.

downshifting (ˈdaʊnˌʃɪftɪŋ) *n* the practice of simplifying one's lifestyle and becoming less materialistic.

downside Ⓣ (ˈdaʊnˌsaɪd) *n* the disadvantageous aspect of a situation: *the downside of twentieth-century living.*

downsize (ˈdaʊnˌsaɪz) *vb* **downsizes, downsizing, downsized.** (*tr*) **1** to reduce the number of people employed by (a company). **2** to upgrade (a computer system) by replacing a mainframe or minicomputer with a network of microcomputing. Cf. **rightsize.**

Down's syndrome (daʊnz) *n* **a** *Pathol.* a chromosomal abnormality resulting in a flat face and nose, a vertical fold of skin at the inner edge of the eye, and mental retardation. Former name: **mongolism. b** (*as modifier*): *a Down's syndrome baby.* [C19: after John *Langdon-Down* (1828–96), Brit. physician]

downstage (ˈdaʊnˈsteɪdʒ) *Theatre.* ◆ *adv* **1** at or towards the front of the stage. ◆ *adj* **2** of or relating to the front of the stage.

downstairs (ˈdaʊnˈsteəz) *adv* **1** down the stairs; to or on a lower floor. ◆ *n* **2a** a lower or ground floor. **2b** (*as modifier*): *a downstairs room.* **3** *Brit. inf., old-fashioned.* the servants of a household collectively.

downstream (ˈdaʊnˈstriːm) *adv, adj* in or towards the lower part of a stream; with the current. Cf. **upstream** (sense 1).

downswing (ˈdaʊnˌswɪŋ) *n* a statistical downward trend in business activity, the death rate, etc.

downtime (ˈdaʊnˌtaɪm) *n Commerce.* time during which a computer or machine is not working, as when under repair.

down-to-earth Ⓣ *adj* sensible; practical; realistic.

downtown (ˈdaʊnˈtaʊn) *Chiefly US, Canad., & NZ.* ◆ *n* **1** the central or lower part of a city, esp. the main commercial area. ◆ *adv* **2** towards, to, or into this area. ◆ *adj* **3** of, relating to, or situated in the downtown area: *a downtown cinema.*

downtrodden Ⓣ (ˈdaʊnˌtrɒdən) *adj* **1** subjugated; oppressed. **2** trodden down.

downturn (ˈdaʊnˌtɜːn) *n* a drop or reduction in the success of a business or economy.

down under *Inf.* ◆ *n* **1** Australia or New Zealand. ◆ *adv* **2** in or to Australia or New Zealand.

downward Ⓣ (ˈdaʊnwəd) *adj* **1** descending from a higher to a lower level, condition, position, etc. **2** descending from a beginning. ◆ *adv* **3** a variant of **downwards.** ▸ **ˈdownwardly** *adv*

downwards (ˈdaʊnwədz) *or* **downward** *adv* **1** from a higher to a lower place, level, etc. **2** from an earlier time or source to a later.

downwind (ˈdaʊnˈwɪnd) *adv, adj* in the same direction towards which the wind is blowing; with the wind from behind.

downy Ⓣ (ˈdaʊnɪ) *adj* **downier, downiest. 1** covered with soft fine hair or feathers. **2** light, soft, and fluffy. **3** made from or filled with down. **4** *Brit. sl.* sharp-witted. ▸ **ˈdowniness** *n*

dowry (ˈdaʊərɪ) *n, pl* **dowries. 1** the property brought by a woman to her husband at marriage. **2** a natural talent or gift. [C14: from Anglo-F *douarie,* from Med. L *dōtārium;* see DOWER]

dowse (daʊz) *vb* **dowses, dowsing, dowsed.** (*intr*) to search for underground water, minerals, etc., using a divining rod; divine. [C17: from ?] ▸ **ˈdowser** *n*

doxology (dɒkˈsɒlədʒɪ) *n, pl* **doxologies.** a hymn, verse, or form of words in Christian liturgy glorifying God. [C17: from Med. L *doxologia,* from Gk, from *doxologos* uttering praise, from *doxa* praise; see -LOGY] ▸ **doxological** (ˌdɒksəˈlɒdʒɪkəl) *adj*

doxy (ˈdɒksɪ) *n, pl* **doxies.** *Arch. sl.* a prostitute or mistress. [C16: prob. from MFlemish *docke* doll]

doyen (ˈdɔɪən) *n* the senior member of a group, profession, or society. [C17: from F, from LL *decānus* leader of a group of ten] ▸ **doyenne** (dɔɪˈɛn) *fem n*

doyley (ˈdɔɪlɪ) *n* a variant spelling of **doily.**

doz. *abbrev. for* dozen.

doze Ⓣ (dəʊz) *vb* **dozes, dozing, dozed.** (*intr*) **1** to sleep lightly or intermittently. **2** (often foll. by *off*) to fall into a light sleep. ◆ *n* **3** a short sleep. [C17: prob. from ON *dūs* lull] ▸ **ˈdozer** *n*

dozen (ˈdʌzən) *determiner* **1** (preceded by *a* or a numeral) twelve or a group of twelve. ◆ *n, pl* **dozens** *or* **dozen. 2 by the dozen.** in large quantities. **3 daily dozen.** *Brit.* regular physical exercises. **4 talk nineteen to the dozen.** to talk without stopping. [C13: from OF *douzaine,* from *douze* twelve, from L *duodecim,* from *duo* two + *decem* ten] ▸ **ˈdozenth** *adj*

dozy Ⓣ (ˈdəʊzɪ) *adj* **dozier, doziest. 1** drowsy. **2** *Brit. inf.* stupid. ▸ **ˈdozily** *adv* ▸ **ˈdoziness** *n*

DP *abbrev. for:* **1** data processing. **2** displaced person.

DPB (in New Zealand) *abbrev. for* domestic purposes benefit: an allowance paid to single parents.

DPhil *or* **DPh** *abbrev. for* Doctor of Philosophy. Also: **PhD.**

dpi *abbrev. for* dots per inch: a measure of the resolution of a typesetting machine, computer screen, etc.

DPP (in Britain) *abbrev. for* Director of Public Prosecutions.

dpt *abbrev. for:* **1** department. **2** depot.

dr *abbrev. for:* **1** Also: **dr.** dram. **2** debtor.

Dr *abbrev. for:* **1** Doctor. **2** Drive.

DR *abbrev. for* dry riser.

dr. *abbrev. for:* **1** debit. **2** drachma.

drab[1] Ⓣ (dræb) *adj* **drabber, drabbest. 1** dull; dingy. **2** cheerless; dreary. **3** of the colour drab. ◆ *n* **4** a light olive-brown colour. [C16: from OF *drap* cloth, from LL *drappus,* ? of Celtic origin] ▸ **ˈdrably** *adv* ▸ **ˈdrabness** *n*

drab[2] (dræb) *Arch.* ◆ *n* **1** a slatternly woman. **2** a whore. ◆ *vb* **drabs, drabbing, drabbed. 3** (*intr*) to consort with prostitutes. [C16: of Celtic origin]

drachm (dræm) *n* **1** Also called: **fluid dram.** *Brit.* one eighth of a fluid ounce. **2** *US.* another name for **dram** (sense 2). **3** another name for **drachma.** [C14: learned var. of DRAM]

drachma (ˈdrækmə) *n, pl* **drachmas** *or* **drachmae** (-miː). **1** the standard monetary unit of Greece. **2** *US.* another name for **dram** (sense 2). **3** a silver coin of ancient Greece. [C16: from L, from Gk *drakhmē* a handful, from *drassesthai* to seize]

drack *or* **drac** (dræk) *adj Austral. sl.* (of a woman) unattractive. [C20: ?from *Dracula's* daughter]

Draconian Ⓣ (dreɪˈkəʊnɪən) *or* **Draconic** (dreɪˈkɒnɪk) *adj* (*sometimes not cap.*) **1** of or relating to Draco (Athenian statesman, 7th century B.C.) or his code of laws. **2** harsh. ▸ **Draˈconianism** *n* ▸ **Draˈconically** *adv*

Dracula (ˈdrækjʊlə) *n* **1** a cruel or bloodthirsty person. **2** a person who preys ruthlessly on others. [C20: from the vampire in Bram Stoker's Gothic novel *Dracula* (1897)]

draff (dræf) *n* the residue of husks after fermentation of the grain in brewing, used as cattle fodder. [C13: from ON *draf*]

THESAURUS

down-market *adj* = **second-rate**, bush-league (*Austral. & NZ inf.*), cheap, cheap and nasty, inferior, lowbrow, low-grade, low-quality, shoddy, tacky (*inf.*), tawdry, two-bit (*US & Canad. sl.*)
Antonyms *adj* elite, exclusive, first-rate, high-brow, high-class, high-quality, posh (*inf., chiefly Brit.*), superior, top-quality, up-market

downpour *n* = **rainstorm**, cloudburst, deluge, flood, inundation, torrential rain

downright *adj* **1** = **blunt**, candid, forthright, frank, honest, open, outspoken, plain, sincere, straightforward, straight-from-the-shoulder, upfront (*inf.*) **2** = **complete**, absolute, arrant, blatant, categorical, clear, deep-dyed (*usually derogatory*), explicit, out-and-out, outright, plain, positive, simple, thoroughgoing, total, undisguised, unequivocal, unqualified, utter

downside *n* = **drawback**, bad *or* weak point, disadvantage, flip side, minus (*inf.*), other side of the coin (*inf.*), problem, snag, trouble
Antonyms *n* advantage, benefit, good *or* strong point, plus (*inf.*)

down-to-earth *adj* = **sensible**, common-sense, hard-headed, matter-of-fact, mundane, no-nonsense, plain-spoken, practical, realistic, sane, unsentimental

downtrodden *adj* **1** = **oppressed**, abused, afflicted, distressed, exploited, helpless, subjugated, subservient, tyrannized

downward *adj* **1** = **descending**, declining, earthward, heading down, sliding, slipping

downy *adj* **1** = **fluffy**, feathery, fleecy, plumate (*Zoology, Botany*), silky, soft, velvety, woolly

doze *vb* **1, 2** = **nap**, catnap, drop off (*inf.*), drowse, kip (*Brit. sl.*), nod, nod off (*inf.*), sleep, sleep lightly, slumber, snooze (*inf.*), zizz (*Brit. inf.*) ◆ *n* **3** = **nap**, catnap, forty winks (*inf.*), kip (*Brit. sl.*), little sleep, shuteye (*sl.*), siesta, snooze (*inf.*), zizz (*Brit. inf.*)

dozy *adj* **1** = **drowsy**, dozing, half asleep, nodding, sleepy **2** *Brit. informal* = **stupid**, daft (*inf.*), goofy (*inf.*), not all there, senseless, silly, simple, slow, slow-witted, witless

drab[1] *adj* **1, 2** = **dull**, cheerless, colourless, dingy, dismal, dreary, flat, gloomy, grey, lack-lustre, shabby, sombre, uninspired, vapid
Antonyms *adj* bright, cheerful, colourful, jazzy (*inf.*), vibrant, vivid

drabness *n* **1, 2** = **dullness**, banality, cheerlessness, colourlessness, dinginess, dreariness, flatness, gloom, gloominess, greyness, insipidity, monotony, sobriety, tediousness, vapidity
Antonyms *n* brightness, brilliance, character, cheerfulness, colour, colourfulness, gaiety, interest, liveliness, vividness

Draconian *adj* **2** *sometimes not cap.* = **severe**,

draft 🅣 (drɑːft) *n* **1** a plan, sketch, or drawing of something. **2** a preliminary outline of a book, speech, etc. **3** another word for **bill of exchange**. **4** a demand or drain on something. **5** *US & Austral.* selection for compulsory military service. **6** detachment of military personnel from one unit to another. **7** *Austral. & NZ.* a group of livestock separated from the rest of the herd or flock. ◆ *vb* (*tr*) **8** to draw up an outline or sketch for. **9** to prepare a plan or design of. **10** to detach (military personnel) from one unit to another. **11** *US & Austral.* to select for compulsory military service. **12** *Austral. & NZ.* **12a** to select (cattle or sheep) from a herd or flock. **12b** to select (farm stock) for sale. ◆ *n, vb* **13** the usual US spelling of **draught**. [C16: var. of DRAUGHT]
▸**'drafter** *n*

draftee (drɑːf'tiː) *n US.* a conscript.

drafty ('drɑːftɪ) *adj* **draftier, draftiest.** the usual US spelling of **draughty**.

drag 🅣 (dræg) *vb* **drags, dragging, dragged. 1** to pull or be pulled with force, esp. along the ground. **2** (*tr; often foll. by away or from*) to persuade to come away. **3** to trail or cause to trail on the ground. **4** (*tr*) to move with effort or difficulty. **5** to linger behind. **6** (often foll. by *on* or *out*) to prolong or be prolonged unnecessarily or tediously: *his talk dragged on for hours.* **7** (when *intr*, usually foll. by *for*) to search (the bed of a river, etc.) with a dragnet or hook. **8** (*tr;* foll. by *out* or *from*) to crush (clods) or level (a soil surface) by use of a drag. **9** (of hounds) to follow (a fox or its trail). **10** (*intr*) *Sl.* to draw (on a cigarette, etc.). **11** *Computing.* to move (a graphics image) from one place to another on the screen using a mouse. **12 drag anchor.** (of a vessel) to move away from its mooring because the anchor has failed to hold. **13 drag one's feet** *or* **heels.** *Inf.* to act with deliberate slowness. ◆ *n* **14** the act of dragging or the state of being dragged. **15** an implement, such as a dragnet, dredge, etc., used for dragging. **16** a type of harrow used to crush clods, level soil, etc. **17** a coach with seats inside and out, usually drawn by four horses. **18** a braking device. **19** a person or thing that slows up progress. **20** slow progress or movement. **21** *Aeronautics.* the resistance to the motion of a body passing through a fluid, esp. through air. **22** the trail of scent left by a fox, etc. **23** an artificial trail of scent drawn over the ground for hounds to follow. **24** See **drag hunt. 25** *Inf.* a person or thing that is very tedious. **26** *Sl.* a car. **27** short for **drag race. 28** *Sl.* **28a** women's clothes worn by a man (esp. in **in drag**). **28b** (*as modifier*): *a drag show.* **28c** clothes collectively. **29** *Inf.* a draw on a cigarette, etc. **30** *US sl.* influence. **31** *Chiefly US sl.* a street (esp. in **main drag**). ◆ See also **drag out of, drag up.** [OE *dragan* to DRAW]

dragée (dræ'ʒeɪ) *n* **1** a sweet coated with a hard sugar icing. **2** a tiny beadlike sweet used for decorating cakes, etc. **3** a medicinal pill coated with sugar. [C19: from F; see DREDGE[2]]

draggle ('dræg^{ə}l) *vb* **draggles, draggling, draggled. 1** to make or become wet or dirty by trailing on the ground; bedraggle. **2** (*intr*) to lag; dawdle. [ME, prob. frequentative of DRAG]

drag hunt *n* **1** a hunt in which hounds follow an artificial trail of scent. **2** a club that organizes such hunts.
▸**'drag-,hunt** *vb*

dragnet ('dræg,nɛt) *n* **1** a net used to scour the bottom of a pond, river, etc., as when searching for something. **2** any system of coordinated efforts to track down wanted persons.

dragoman ('drægəʊmən) *n, pl* **dragomans** *or* **dragomen.** (in some Middle Eastern countries, esp. formerly) a professional interpreter or guide. [C14: from F, from It., from Med. Gk *dragoumanos,* from Ar. *targumān,* ult. from Akkadian]

dragon ('drægən) *n* **1** a mythical monster usually represented as breathing fire and having a scaly reptilian body, wings, claws, and a long tail. **2** *Inf.* a fierce person, esp. a woman. **3** any of various very large lizards, esp. the Komodo dragon. **4** *Commerce.* a newly industrialized country, esp. one in SE Asia. **5 chase the dragon.** *Sl.* to smoke opium or heroin. [C13: from OF, from L *dracō,* from Gk *drakōn*]

dragonet ('drægənɪt) *n* a small fish with spiny fins, a flat head, and a tapering brighty coloured body. [C14 (meaning: small dragon): from F; applied to fish C18]

dragonfly ('drægən,flaɪ) *n, pl* **dragonflies.** a predatory insect having a long slender body and two pairs of iridescent wings that are outspread at rest.

dragon light *n* an extremely powerful light used by police to dazzle and immobilize criminal suspects.

dragonnade (,drægə'neɪd) *n* **1** *History.* the persecution of French Huguenots during the reign of Louis XIV by dragoons quartered in their villages and homes. **2** subjection by military force. ◆ *vb* **dragonnades, dragonnading, dragonnaded. 3** (*tr*) to subject to persecution by military troops. [C18: from F, from *dragon* DRAGOON]

dragoon 🅣 (drə'guːn) *n* **1** (originally) a mounted infantryman armed with a carbine. **2** (*sometimes cap.*) a domestic fancy pigeon. **3a** a type of cavalryman. **3b** (*pl; cap. when part of a name*): *the Royal Dragoons.* ◆ *vb* (*tr*) **4** to coerce; force. **5** to persecute by military force. [C17: from F *dragon* (special use of DRAGON), soldier armed with a carbine]

drag out of *vb* (*tr, adv + prep*) to obtain or extract (a confession, statement, etc.), esp. by force. Also: **drag from.**

drag race *n* a type of motor race in which specially built or modified cars or motorcycles are timed over a measured course.
▸**drag racing** *n*

dragster ('drægstə) *n* a car specially built or modified for drag racing.

drag up *vb* (*tr, adv*) *Inf.* **1** to rear (a child) poorly and in an undisciplined manner. **2** to introduce or revive (an unpleasant fact or story).

drain 🅣 (dreɪn) *n* **1** a pipe or channel that carries off water, sewage, etc. **2** an instance or cause of continuous diminution in resources or energy; depletion. **3** *Surgery.* a device, such as a tube, to drain off pus, etc. **4 down the drain.** wasted. ◆ *vb* **5** (*tr;* often foll. by *off*) to draw off or remove (liquid) from. **6** (*intr;* often foll. by *away*) to flow (away) or filter (off). **7** (*intr*) to dry or be emptied as a result of liquid running off or flowing away. **8** (*tr*) to drink the entire contents of (a glass, etc.). **9** (*tr*) to consume or make constant demands on (resources, energy, etc.); exhaust. **10** (*intr*) to disappear or leave, esp. gradually. **11** (of a river, etc.) to carry off the surface water from (an area). **12** (*intr*) (of an area) to discharge its surface water into rivers, streams, etc. [OE *drēahnian*]
▸**'drainer** *n*

drainage 🅣 ('dreɪnɪdʒ) *n* **1** the process or a method of draining. **2** a system of watercourses or drains. **3** liquid, sewage, etc., that is drained away.

drainage basin *or* **area** *n* another name for **catchment area.**

draining board *n* a sloping grooved surface at the side of a sink, used for draining washed dishes, etc. Also called: **drainer.**

drainpipe ('dreɪn,paɪp) *n* a pipe for carrying off rainwater, sewage, etc.; downpipe.

drainpipes ('dreɪn,paɪps) *pl n* trousers with very narrow legs, worn esp. by teddy boys in the 1950s.

drake (dreɪk) *n* the male of any duck. [C13: ?from Low G]

Dralon ('dreɪlɒn) *n Trademark.* an acrylic fibre fabric used esp. for upholstery.

dram 🅣 (dræm) *n* **1** one sixteenth of an ounce (avoirdupois). 1 dram is equivalent to 0.0018 kilogram. **2** *US.* one eighth of an apothecaries' ounce; 60 grains. 1 dram is equivalent to 0.0039 kilogram. **3** a small amount of an alcoholic drink, esp. a spirit; tot. **4** the standard monetary unit of Armenia. [C15: from OF *dragme,* from LL *dragma,* from Gk *drakhmē;* see DRACHMA]

DRAM *or* **D-RAM** ('diːræm) *n acronym for* dynamic random access memory: **a** a widely used type of random access memory. See **RAM**[1]. **b** a chip containing such a memory.

drama 🅣 ('drɑːmə) *n* **1** a work to be performed by actors; play. **2** the genre of literature represented by works intended for the stage. **3** the art of the writing and production of plays. **4** a situation that is highly emotional, tragic, or turbulent. [C17: from LL: a play, from Gk: something performed, from *drān* to do]

dramatic 🅣 (drə'mætɪk) *adj* **1** of drama. **2** like a drama in suddenness, emotional impact, etc. **3** striking; effective. **4** acting or performed in a flamboyant way.
▸**dra'matically** *adv*

dramatic irony *n Theatre.* the irony occurring when the implications of a situation, speech, etc., are understood by the audience but not by the characters in the play.

dramatics (drə'mætɪks) *n* **1** (*functioning as sing or pl*) **1a** the art of acting or producing plays. **1b** dramatic productions. **2** (*usually functioning as pl*) histrionic behaviour.

dramatis personae ('drɑːmətɪs pə'səʊnaɪ) *pl n* (*often functioning as sing*) the characters in a play. [C18: from NL]

dramatist 🅣 ('dræmətɪst) *n* a playwright.

THESAURUS

austere, drastic, hard, harsh, pitiless, punitive, stern, stringent

draft *n* **1, 2 = outline**, abstract, delineation, plan, preliminary form, rough, sketch, version **3 = order**, bill (*of exchange*), cheque, postal order ◆ *vb* **8, 9 = outline**, compose, delineate, design, draw, draw up, formulate, plan, sketch

drag *vb* **1 = pull**, draw, hale, haul, lug, tow, trail, tug, yank **4 = go slowly**, crawl, creep, inch, limp along, shamble, shuffle **5 = lag behind**, dawdle, draggle, linger, loiter, straggle, trail behind **6 drag on** *or* **out = last**, draw out, extend, keep going, lengthen, persist, prolong, protract, spin out, stretch out **13 drag one's feet** *or* **heels** *Informal* **= stall**, block, hold back, obstruct, procrastinate ◆ *n* **25** *Informal* **= nuisance**, annoyance, bore, bother, pain (*inf.*), pain in the arse (*taboo sl.*), pest

dragging *adj* **6 = tedious**, boring, dull, going slowly, humdrum, mind-numbing, monotonous, tiresome, wearisome

dragoon *vb* **4 = force**, browbeat, bully, coerce, compel, constrain, drive, impel, intimidate, railroad (*inf.*), strong-arm (*inf.*)

drain *n* **1 = pipe**, channel, conduit, culvert, ditch, duct, outlet, sewer, sink, trench, watercourse **2 = reduction**, depletion, drag, exhaustion, expenditure, sap, strain, withdrawal **4 down the drain = wasted**, gone, gone for good, lost, ruined ◆ *vb* **5 = remove**, bleed, draw off, dry, empty, evacuate, milk, pump off *or* out, tap, withdraw **6 = flow out**, discharge, effuse, exude, leak, ooze, seep, trickle, well out **8 = drink up**, finish, gulp down, quaff, swallow **9 = exhaust**, consume, deplete, dissipate, empty, sap, strain, tax, use up, weary

drainage *n* **3 = sewerage**, bilge (water), seepage, sewage, waste

dram *n* **3 = shot** (*inf.*), drop, glass, measure, slug, snifter (*inf.*), snort (*sl.*), tot

drama *n* **1 = play**, dramatization, show, stage play, stage show, theatrical piece **2 = theatre**, acting, dramatic art, dramaturgy, stagecraft, Thespian art **4 = excitement**, crisis, dramatics, histrionics, scene, spectacle, theatrics, turmoil

dramatic *adj* **1 = theatrical**, dramaturgic, dramaturgical, Thespian **2 = powerful**, affecting, effective, expressive, impressive, moving, striking, vivid **4 = exciting**, breathtaking, climactic, electrifying, emotional, high-octane (*inf.*), melodramatic, sensational, shock-horror (*facetious*), startling, sudden, suspenseful, tense, thrilling
Antonyms *adj* ≠ **powerful:** ordinary, run-of-the-mill, undramatic, unexceptional, unmemorable

dramatist *n* **= playwright**, dramaturge, screenwriter, scriptwriter

dramatize ❶ *or* **dramatise** (ˈdræməˌtaɪz) *vb* **dramatizes, dramatizing, dramatized** *or* **dramatises, dramatising, dramatised. 1** (*tr*) to put into dramatic form. **2** to express (something) in a dramatic or exaggerated way.
▸ **ˌdramatiˈzation** *or* **ˌdramatiˈsation** *n*

dramaturge (ˈdræməˌtɜːdʒ) *n* **1** Also called: **dramaturgist.** a dramatist. **2** Also called: **dramaturg.** a literary adviser on the staff of a theatre, film company, etc. [C19: prob. from F, from Gk *dramatourgos* playwright, from DRAMA + *ergon* work]

dramaturgy (ˈdræməˌtɜːdʒɪ) *n* the art and technique of the theatre; dramatics.
▸ **ˌdramaˈturgic** *or* **ˌdramaˈturgical** *adj*

drank (dræŋk) *vb* the past tense of **drink.**

drape ❶ (dreɪp) *vb* **drapes, draping, draped. 1** (*tr*) to hang or cover with material or fabric, usually in folds. **2** to hang or arrange or be hung or arranged, esp. in folds. **3** (*tr*) to place casually and loosely. ◆ *n* **4** (*often pl*) a cloth or hanging that covers something in folds. **5** the way in which fabric hangs. [C15: from OF *draper,* from *drap* piece of cloth; see DRAB[1]]

draper (ˈdreɪpə) *n* **1** *Brit.* a dealer in fabrics and sewing materials. **2** *Arch.* a maker of cloth.

drapery (ˈdreɪpərɪ) *n, pl* **draperies. 1** fabric or clothing arranged and draped. **2** (*often pl*) curtains or hangings that drape. **3** *Brit.* the occupation or shop of a draper. **4** fabrics and cloth collectively.
▸ **ˈdraperied** *adj*

drapes (dreɪps) *or* **draperies** (ˈdreɪpərɪz) *pl n Chiefly US & Canad.* curtains, esp. ones of heavy fabric.

drastic ❶ (ˈdræstɪk) *adj* extreme or forceful; severe. [C17: from Gk *drastikos,* from *drān* to do, act]
▸ **ˈdrastically** *adv*

drat (dræt) *interj Sl.* an exclamation of annoyance. [C19: prob. alteration of *God rot*]

draught ❶ *or US* **draft** (drɑːft) *n* **1** a current of air, esp. in an enclosed space. **2a** the act of pulling a load, as by a vehicle or animal. **2b** (*as modifier*): *a draught horse.* **3** the load or quantity drawn. **4** a portion of liquid to be drunk, esp. a dose of medicine. **5** the act or an instance of drinking; a gulp or swallow. **6** the act or process of drawing air, etc., into the lungs. **7** the amount of air, etc., inhaled. **8a** beer, wine, etc., stored in bulk, esp. in a cask. **8b** (*as modifier*): *draught beer.* **8c on draught.** drawn from a cask or keg. **9** any one of the flat discs used in the game of draughts. US and Canad. equivalent: **checker. 10** the depth of a loaded vessel in the water. **11 feel the draught.** to be short of money. [C14: prob. from ON *drahtr,* of Gmc origin]

draughtboard (ˈdrɑːftˌbɔːd) *n* a square board divided into 64 squares of alternating colours, used for playing draughts or chess.

draughts (drɑːfts) *n* (*functioning as sing*) a game for two players using a draughtboard and 12 draughtsmen each. US and Canad. name: **checkers.** [C14: pl of DRAUGHT (in obs. sense: a chess move)]

draughtsman *or US* **draftsman** (ˈdrɑːftsmən) *n, pl* **draughtsmen** *or US* **draftsmen. 1** a person employed to prepare detailed scale drawings of machinery, buildings, etc. **2** a person skilled in drawing. **3** *Brit.* any of the flat discs used in the game of draughts. US and Canad. equivalent: **checker.**
▸ **ˈdraughtsmanˌship** *or US* **ˈdraftsmanˌship** *n*

draughty *or US* **drafty** (ˈdrɑːftɪ) *adj* **draughtier, draughtiest** *or US* **draftier, draftiest.** characterized by or exposed to draughts of air.
▸ **ˈdraughtily** *or US* **ˈdraftily** *adv* ▸ **ˈdraughtiness** *or US* **ˈdraftiness** *n*

Dravidian (drəˈvɪdɪən) *n* **1** a family of languages spoken in S and central India and Sri Lanka, including Tamil, Malayalam, etc. **2** a member of one of the aboriginal races of India, pushed south by the Indo-Europeans and now mixed with them. ◆ *adj* **3** of or denoting this family of languages or these peoples.

draw ❶ (drɔː) *vb* **draws, drawing, drew, drawn. 1** to cause (a person or thing) to move towards or away by pulling. **2** to bring, take, or pull (something) out, as from a drawer, holster, etc. **3** (*tr*) to extract or pull or take out: *to draw teeth.* **4** (*tr;* often foll. by *off*) to take (liquid) out of a cask, etc., by means of a tap. **5** (*intr*) to move, esp. in a specified direction: *to draw alongside.* **6** (*tr*) to attract: *to draw attention.* **7** (*tr*) to cause to flow: *to draw blood.* **8** to depict or sketch (a figure, picture, etc.) in lines, as with a pencil or pen. **9** (*tr*) to make, formulate, or derive: *to draw conclusions.* **10** (*tr*) to write (a legal document) in proper form. **11** (*tr;* sometimes foll. by *in*) to suck or take in (air, etc.). **12** (*intr*) to induce or allow a draught to carry off air, smoke, etc. **13** (*tr*) to take or receive from a source: *to draw money from the bank.* **14** (*tr*) to earn: *draw interest.* **15** (*tr*) to write out (a bill of exchange, etc.). **16** (*tr*) to choose at random. **17** (*tr*) to reduce the diameter of (a wire) by pulling it through a die. **18** (*tr*) to shape (metal or glass) by rolling, by pulling through a die, or by stretching. **19** *Archery.* to bend (a bow) by pulling the string. **20** to steep (tea) or (of tea) to steep in boiling water. **21** (*tr*) to disembowel. **22** (*tr*) to cause (pus, etc.) to discharge from an abscess or wound. **23** (*intr*) (of two teams, etc.) to finish a game with an equal number of points, goals, etc.; tie. **24** (*tr*) *Bridge, whist.* to keep leading a suit in order to force out (all outstanding cards). **25 draw trumps.** *Bridge, whist.* to play the trump suit until the opponents have none left. **26** (*tr*) *Billiards.* to cause (the cue ball) to spin back after a direct impact with another ball. **27** (*tr*) to search (a place) in order to find wild animals, etc., for hunting. **28** *Golf.* to cause (a golf ball) to move with a controlled right-to-left trajectory or (of a golf ball) to veer gradually from right to left. **29** (*tr*) *Naut.* (of a vessel) to require (a certain depth) in which to float. **30 draw and quarter.** to disembowel and dismember (a person) after hanging. **31 draw stumps.** *Cricket.* to close play. **32 draw the shot.** *Bowls.* to deliver the bowl in such a way that it approaches the jack. ◆ *n* **33** the act of drawing. **34** *US.* a sum of money advanced to finance anticipated expenses. **35** *Inf.* an event, act, etc., that attracts a large audience. **36** a raffle or lottery. **37** something taken at random, as a ticket in a lottery. **38** a contest or game ending in a tie. **39** *US & Canad.* a small natural drainage way or gully. ◆ See also **drawback, draw in,** etc. [OE *dragan*]

drawback ❶ (ˈdrɔːˌbæk) *n* **1** a disadvantage or hindrance. **2** a refund of customs or excise paid on goods that are being exported or used in making goods for export. ◆ *vb* **draw back.** (*intr, adv;* often foll. by *from*) **3** to retreat; move backwards. **4** to turn aside from an undertaking.

drawbridge (ˈdrɔːˌbrɪdʒ) *n* a bridge that may be raised to prevent access or to enable vessels to pass.

drawee (drɔːˈiː) *n* the person or organization on which an order for payment is drawn.

drawer (ˈdrɔːə) *n* **1** a person or thing that draws, esp. a draughtsman. **2** a person who draws a cheque. See **draw** (sense 15). **3** a person who draws up a commercial paper. **4** *Arch.* a person who draws beer, etc., in a bar. **5** (drɔː). a boxlike container in a chest, table, etc., made for sliding in and out.

drawers (drɔːz) *pl n* a legged undergarment for either sex, worn below the waist.

draw in *vb* (*intr, adv*) **1** (of hours of daylight) to become shorter. **2** (of a train) to arrive at a station.

drawing ❶ (ˈdrɔːɪŋ) *n* **1** a picture or plan made by means of lines on a surface, esp. one made with a pencil or pen. **2** a sketch or outline. **3** the art of making drawings; draughtsmanship.

drawing pin *n Brit.* a short tack with a broad smooth head for fastening papers to a drawing board, etc. US and Canad. name: **thumbtack.**

drawing room *n* **1** a room where visitors are received and entertained; living room; sitting room. **2** *Arch.* a formal reception.

drawknife (ˈdrɔːˌnaɪf) *or* **drawshave** *n, pl* **drawknives** *or* **drawshaves.** a tool with two handles, used to shave wood. US name: **spokeshave.**

drawl ❶ (drɔːl) *vb* **1** to speak or utter (words) slowly, esp. prolonging the vowel sounds. ◆ *n* **2** the way of speech of someone who drawls. [C16: prob. frequentative of DRAW]
▸ **ˈdrawling** *adj*

drawn ❶ (drɔːn) *vb* **1** the past participle of **draw.** ◆ *adj* **2** haggard, tired, or tense in appearance.

drawn work *n* ornamental needlework done by drawing threads out of the fabric and using the remaining threads to form lacelike patterns. Also called: **drawn-thread work.**

draw off *vb* (*adv*) **1** (*tr*) to cause (a liquid) to flow from something. **2** to withdraw (troops).

draw on ❶ *vb* **1** (*intr, prep*) to use or exploit (a source, fund, etc.). **2** (*intr, adv*) to come near. **3** (*tr, prep*) to withdraw (money) from (an account). **4** (*tr, adv*) to put on (clothes). **5** (*tr, adv*) to lead further; entice.

draw out ❶ *vb* (*adv*) **1** to extend. **2** (*tr*) to cause (a person) to talk freely. **3** (*tr;* foll. by *of*) Also: **draw from.** to elicit (information) (from). **4** (*tr*) to withdraw (money) as from a bank account. **5** (*intr*) (of hours of daylight) to become longer. **6** (*intr*) (of a train) to leave a station. **7** (*tr*) to extend (troops) in line. **8** (*intr*) (of troops) to proceed from camp.

THESAURUS

dramatize *vb* **2** = **exaggerate,** act, lay it on (thick) (*sl.*), make a performance of, overdo, overstate, play-act, play to the gallery

drape *vb* **1** = **cover,** adorn, array, cloak, fold, swathe, wrap **2** = **hang,** dangle, droop, drop, lean over, let fall, suspend

drastic *adj* = **extreme,** desperate, dire, forceful, harsh, radical, severe, strong

draught *n* **1** = **breeze,** current, flow, influx, movement, puff **2a** = **pulling,** dragging, drawing, haulage, traction **4** = **drink,** cup, dose, drench, potion, quantity

draw *vb* **1** = **pull,** drag, haul, tow, tug **3** = **take out,** extort, extract, pull out **6** = **attract,** allure, bring forth, call forth, elicit, engage, entice, evoke, induce, influence, invite, persuade **8** = **sketch,** delineate, depict, design, map out, mark out, outline, paint, portray, trace **9** = **deduce,** derive, get, infer, make, take **11** = **inhale,** breathe in, drain, inspire, puff, pull, respire, suck **16** = **choose,** pick, select, single out, take **18** = **stretch,** attenuate, elongate, extend, lengthen ◆ *n* **35** *Informal* = **attraction,** enticement, lure, pull (*inf.*) **38** = **tie,** dead heat, deadlock, impasse, stalemate

drawback *n* **1** = **disadvantage,** defect, deficiency, detriment, difficulty, downside, fault, flaw, fly in the ointment (*inf.*), handicap, hazard, hindrance, hitch, impediment, imperfection, nuisance, obstacle, snag, stumbling block, trouble
Antonyms *n* advantage, asset, benefit, gain, help, service, use

draw back *vb* **3** = **recoil,** back off, retract, retreat, shrink, start back, withdraw

drawing *n* **1, 2** = **picture,** cartoon, delineation, depiction, illustration, outline, portrayal, representation, sketch, study

drawl *vb* **1** = **draw out,** drag out, extend, lengthen, prolong, protract

drawling *adj* **1** = **droning,** dragging, drawly, dull, twanging, twangy

drawn *adj* **2** = **tense,** fatigued, fraught, haggard, harassed, harrowed, pinched, sapped, strained, stressed, taut, tired, worn

draw on *vb* **1** = **make use of,** employ, exploit, extract, fall back on, have recourse to, rely on, take from, use

draw out *vb* **1** = **extend,** drag out, lengthen, make longer, prolong, protract, spin out, stretch, string out
Antonyms *vb* curtail, cut, cut short, dock, pare down, reduce, shorten, trim, truncate

drawstring ('drɔːˌstrɪŋ) *n* a cord, etc., run through a hem around an opening, so that when it is pulled tighter, the opening closes.

draw up ❶ *vb* (*adv*) **1** to come or cause to come to a halt. **2** (*tr*) **2a** to prepare a draft of (a document, etc.). **2b** to formulate and write out: *to draw up a contract.* **3** (*used reflexively*) to straighten oneself. **4** to form or arrange (a body of soldiers, etc.) in order or formation.

dray[1] (dreɪ) *n* **a** a low cart used for carrying heavy loads. **b** (*in combination*): *a drayman.* [OE *dræge* dragnet]

dray[2] (dreɪ) *n* a variant spelling of **drey.**

dread ❶ (drɛd) *vb* (*tr*) **1** to anticipate with apprehension or terror. **2** to fear greatly. **3** *Arch.* to be in awe of. ◆ *n* **4** great fear. **5** an object of terror. **6** *Sl.* a Rastafarian. **7** *Arch.* deep reverence. [OE *ondrǣdan*]

dreadful ❶ ('drɛdfʊl) *adj* **1** extremely disagreeable, shocking, or bad. **2** (intensifier): *a dreadful waste of time.* **3** causing dread; terrifying. **4** *Arch.* inspiring awe.

dreadfully ❶ ('drɛdfʊlɪ) *adv* **1** in a shocking or disagreeable manner. **2** (intensifier): *you're dreadfully kind.*

dreadlocks ('drɛdˌlɒks) *pl n Inf.* hair worn in the Rastafarian style of long tightly-curled strands.

dreadnought ('drɛdˌnɔːt) *n* **1** a battleship armed with heavy guns of uniform calibre. **2** an overcoat made of heavy cloth.

dream ❶ (driːm) *n* **1a** mental activity, usually an imagined series of events, occurring during sleep. **1b** (*as modifier*): *a dream sequence.* **1c** (*in combination*): *dreamland.* **2a** a sequence of imaginative thoughts indulged in while awake; daydream; fantasy. **2b** (*as modifier*): *a dream world.* **3** a person or thing seen or occurring in a dream. **4** a cherished hope; aspiration. **5** a vain hope. **6** a person or thing that is as pleasant or seemingly unreal as a dream. **7 go like a dream.** to move, develop, or work very well. ◆ *vb* **dreams, dreaming, dreamed** *or* **dreamt. 8** (*may take a clause as object*) to undergo or experience (a dream or dreams). **9** (*intr*) to indulge in daydreams. **10** (*intr*) to suffer delusions; be unrealistic. **11** (when *intr*, foll. by *of* or *about*) to have an image (of) or fantasy (about) in or as if in a dream. **12** (*intr;* foll. by *of*) to consider the possibility (of). ◆ *adj* **13** too good to be true; ideal: *dream kitchen.* [OE *drēam* song]
▸ **'dreamer** *n*

dreamboat ('driːmˌbəʊt) *n Sl.* an ideal or desirable person, esp. one of the opposite sex.

dreamt (drɛmt) *vb* a past tense and past participle of **dream.**

dream ticket *n* a combination of two people, usually candidates in an election, that is considered to be ideal.

Dreamtime ('driːmˌtaɪm) *n* **1** Also called: **alcheringa.** (in the mythology of Australian Aboriginal peoples) a mythical golden age of the past, when the first men were created. **2** *Austral. inf.* any remote period, out of touch with the realities of the present.

dream up ❶ *vb* (*tr, adv*) to invent by ingenuity and imagination: *to dream up an excuse.*

dreamy ❶ ('driːmɪ) *adj* **dreamier, dreamiest. 1** vague or impractical. **2** resembling a dream. **3** relaxing; gentle. **4** *Inf.* wonderful. **5** having dreams, esp. daydreams.
▸ **'dreamily** *adv* ▸ **'dreaminess** *n*

dreary ❶ ('drɪərɪ) *adj* **drearier, dreariest. 1** sad or dull. **2** wearying; boring. ◆ Also (literary): **drear.** [OE *drēorig* gory]
▸ **'drearily** *adv* ▸ **'dreariness** *n*

dredge[1] (drɛdʒ) *n* **1** a machine used to scoop or suck up material from a riverbed, channel, etc. **2** another name for **dredger.** ◆ *vb* **dredges, dredging, dredged. 3** to remove (material) from a riverbed, etc., by means of a dredge. **4** (*tr*) to search for (a submerged object) with or as if with a dredge; drag. [C16: ? ult. from OE *dragan* to DRAW]

dredge[2] (drɛdʒ) *vb* **dredges, dredging, dredged.** to sprinkle or coat (food) with flour, etc. [C16: from OF *dragie,* ?from L *tragēmata* spices, from Gk]
▸ **'dredger** *n*

dredger ('drɛdʒə) *n* **1** a vessel used for dredging. **2** another name for **dredge**[1] (sense 1).

dredge up ❶ *vb* (*tr, adv*) **1** *Inf.* to bring to notice, esp. with effort and from an obscure source. **2** to raise, as with a dredge.

dree (driː) *Scot., literary.* ◆ *vb* **drees, dreeing, dreed. 1** (*tr*) to endure. ◆ *adj* **2** dreary. [OE *drēogan*]

D region *or* **layer** *n* the lowest region of the ionosphere, extending from a height of about 60 km to about 90 km.

dregs ❶ (drɛgz) *pl n* **1** solid particles that settle at the bottom of some liquids. **2** residue or remains. **3 the dregs.** *Brit. sl.* a despicable person or people. [C14 *dreg,* from ON *dregg*]

dreich *or* **dreigh** (driːx) *adj Scot. dialect.* dreary. [ME *dreig, drih* enduring, from OE *drēog* (unattested)]

drench ❶ (drɛntʃ) *vb* (*tr*) **1** to make completely wet; soak. **2** to give liquid medicine to (an animal). ◆ *n* **3** a drenching. **4** a dose of liquid medicine given to an animal. [OE *drencan* to cause to drink]
▸ **'drenching** *n, adj*

Dresden china *n n* porcelain ware, esp. delicate and elegantly decorative objects and figures of high quality, made at Meissen, near Dresden, Germany, since 1710.

dress ❶ (drɛs) *vb* **1** to put clothes on; attire. **2** (*intr*) to put on more formal attire. **3** (*tr*) to provide (someone) with clothing; clothe. **4** (*tr*) to arrange merchandise in (a shop window). **5** (*tr*) to arrange (the hair). **6** (*tr*) to apply protective or therapeutic covering to (a wound, sore, etc.). **7** (*tr*) to prepare (food, esp. fowl and fish) by cleaning, gutting, etc. **8** (*tr*) to put a finish on (stone, metal, etc.). **9** (*tr*) to cultivate (land), esp. by applying fertilizer. **10** (*tr*) to trim (trees, etc.). **11** (*tr*) to groom (a horse). **12** (*tr*) to convert (tanned hides) into leather. **13** *Angling.* to tie (a fly). **14** *Mil.* to bring (troops) into line or (of troops) to come into line (esp. in **dress ranks**). **15 dress ship.** *Naut.* to decorate a vessel by displaying signal flags on lines. ◆ *n* **16** a one-piece garment for a woman, consisting of a skirt and bodice. **17** complete style of clothing; costume: *military dress.* **18** (*modifier*) suitable for a formal occasion: *a dress shirt.* **19** outer covering or appearance. ◆ See also **dress down, dress up.** [C14: from OF *drecier,* ult. from L *dīrigere* to DIRECT]

dressage ('drɛsɑːʒ) *n* **a** the training of a horse to perform manoeuvres in response to the rider's body signals. **b** the manoeuvres performed. [F: preparation, from OF *dresser* to prepare; see DRESS]

dress circle *n* a tier of seats in a theatre or other auditorium, usually the first gallery, in which evening dress formerly had to be worn.

dress code *n* a set of rules or guidelines regarding the manner of dress acceptable in an office, restaurant, etc.

dress down ❶ *vb* (*adv*) **1** (*tr*) *Inf.* to reprimand severely or scold (a person). **2** (*intr*) to dress in casual clothes.

dresser[1] ('drɛsə) *n* **1** a set of shelves, usually also with cupboards, for storing or displaying dishes, etc. **2** *US.* a chest of drawers for storing clothing, often having a mirror on top. [C14 *dressour,* from OF *dreceore,* from *drecier* to arrange; see DRESS]

dresser[2] ('drɛsə) *n* **1** a person who dresses in a specified way: *a fashionable dresser.* **2** *Theatre.* a person employed to assist actors with their costumes. **3** a tool used for dressing stone, etc. **4** *Brit.* a person who assists a surgeon during operations. **5** *Brit.* See **window-dresser.**

THESAURUS

draw up *vb* **1 = halt**, bring to a stop, pull up, run in, stop, stop short **2 = draft**, compose, formulate, frame, prepare, write out

dread *vb* **1 = fear**, anticipate with horror, cringe at, have cold feet (*inf.*), quail, shrink from, shudder, tremble ◆ *n* **4 = fear**, affright, alarm, apprehension, aversion, awe, dismay, fright, funk (*inf.*), heebie-jeebies (*sl.*), horror, terror, trepidation

dreadful *adj* **1 = terrible**, abysmal, alarming, appalling, atrocious, awful, dire, distressing, fearful, formidable, frightful, from hell (*inf.*), ghastly, grievous, hellacious (*US sl.*), hideous, horrendous, horrible, monstrous, shocking, tragic, tremendous

dreadfully *adv* **1 = terribly**, abysmally, alarmingly, appallingly, awfully, badly, disgracefully, disreputably, frightfully, horrendously, horribly, inadequately, monstrously, reprehensibly, shockingly, unforgivably, wickedly, woefully, wretchedly **2 = extremely**, awfully (*inf.*), badly, deeply, desperately, exceedingly, exceptionally, excessively, greatly, immensely, terribly, tremendously, very, very much

dream *n* **1a = vision**, delusion, hallucination, illusion, imagination, reverie, speculation, trance, vagary **2a = daydream**, fantasy, pipe dream **4 = ambition**, aim, aspiration, design, desire, goal, Holy Grail (*inf.*), hope, notion, thirst, wish **6 = delight**, beauty, gem, joy, marvel, pleasure, treasure ◆ *vb* **8 = have dreams**, conjure up, envisage, fancy, hallucinate, imagine, think, visualize **9 = daydream**, build castles in the air *or* in Spain, fantasize, stargaze

dreamer *n* **9 = idealist**, daydreamer, Don Quixote, escapist, fantasist, fantasizer, fantast, romancer, theorizer, utopian, visionary, Walter Mitty

dream up *vb* **= invent**, concoct, contrive, cook up (*inf.*), create, devise, hatch, imagine, spin, think up

dreamy *adj* **1 = impractical**, airy-fairy, dreamlike, fanciful, imaginary, quixotic, speculative, surreal, vague, visionary **3 = relaxing**, calming, gentle, lulling, romantic, soothing **5 = vague**, absent, abstracted, daydreaming, faraway, in a reverie, musing, pensive, preoccupied, with one's head in the clouds
Antonyms *adj* ≠ **impractical, vague:** *adj* commonsense, down-to-earth, feet-on-the-ground, practical, pragmatic, realistic, unromantic

dreary *adj* **1 = dismal**, bleak, cheerless, comfortless, depressing, doleful, downcast, forlorn, funereal, gloomy, glum, joyless, lonely, lonesome, melancholy, mournful, sad, solitary, sombre, sorrowful, wretched **2 = dull**, as dry as dust, boring, colourless, drab, ho-hum (*inf.*), humdrum, lifeless, mind-numbing, monotonous, routine, tedious, tiresome, uneventful, uninteresting, wearisome
Antonyms *adj* ≠ **dismal:** cheerful, happy, joyful ≠ **dull:** bright, interesting

dredge up *vb* **1** *Informal* **= dig up**, discover, drag up, draw up, fish up, raise, rake up, uncover, unearth

dregs *pl n* **1 = sediment**, deposit, draff, dross, grounds, lees, residue, residuum, scourings, scum, trash, waste **3 = scum**, *canaille*, down-and-outs, good-for-nothings, outcasts, rabble, ragtag and bobtail, riffraff

drench *vb* **1 = soak**, drown, duck, flood, imbrue, inundate, saturate, souse, steep, swamp, wet ◆ *n* **4** *Veterinary* **= dose**, physic, purge

dress *vb* **1 = put on**, attire, change, clothe, don, garb, robe, slip on *or* into **5 = arrange**, adjust, comb (out), do (up), groom, prepare, set, straighten **6 = bandage**, bind up, plaster, treat ◆ *n* **16 = frock**, costume, ensemble, garment, get-up (*inf.*), gown, outfit, rigout (*inf.*), robe, suit **17 = clothing**, apparel, attire, clothes, costume, garb, garments, gear (*inf.*), guise, habiliment, raiment (*arch. or poetic*), threads (*sl.*), togs, vestment
Antonyms *vb* ≠ **put on:** disrobe, divest oneself of, peel off (*sl.*), shed, strip, take off one's clothes

dress down *vb* **1** *Informal* **= reprimand**, bawl out (*inf.*), berate, carpet, castigate, chew out (*US & Canad. inf.*), give a rocket (*Brit. & NZ inf.*), haul over the coals, rap over the knuckles, read the riot act, rebuke, reprove, scold, slap on the wrist, tear into (*inf.*), tear (someone) off a strip (*Brit. inf.*), tell off (*inf.*), upbraid

dressing ('drɛsɪŋ) *n* **1** a sauce for food, esp. for salad. **2** the US and Canad. name for **stuffing** (sense 2). **3** a covering for a wound, etc. **4** fertilizer spread on land. **5** size used for stiffening textiles. **6** the processes in the conversion of hides into leather.
dressing-down *n Inf.* a severe scolding.
dressing gown *n* a full robe worn before dressing or for lounging.
dressing room *n* **1** *Theatre.* a room backstage for an actor to change clothing and to make up. **2** any room used for changing clothes.
dressing station *n Mil.* a first-aid post close to a combat area.
dressing table *n* a piece of bedroom furniture with a mirror and a set of drawers for clothes, cosmetics, etc.
dressmaker Ⓣ ('drɛsˌmeɪkə) *n* a person whose occupation is making clothes, esp. for women.
▸**'dressˌmaking** *n*
dress parade *n Mil.* a formal parade in dress uniform.
dress rehearsal *n* **1** the last rehearsal of a play, etc., using costumes, lighting, etc., as for the first night. **2** any full-scale practice.
dress shirt *n* a man's evening shirt, worn as part of formal evening dress.
dress suit *n* a man's evening suit, esp. tails.
dress uniform *n Mil.* formal ceremonial uniform.
dress up Ⓣ *vb (adv)* **1** to attire (oneself or another) very smartly or elaborately. **2** to put fancy dress, etc., on. **3** *(tr)* to improve the appearance or impression of: *to dress up the facts.*
dressy Ⓣ ('drɛsɪ) *adj* **dressier, dressiest. 1** (of clothes) elegant. **2** (of persons) dressing stylishly. **3** overelegant.
▸**'dressiness** *n*
drew (druː) *vb* the past tense of **draw.**
drey *or* **dray** (dreɪ) *n* a squirrel's nest. [C17: from ?]
dribble Ⓣ ('drɪbᵊl) *vb* **dribbles, dribbling, dribbled. 1** *(usually intr)* to flow or allow to flow in a thin stream or drops; trickle. **2** *(intr)* to allow saliva to trickle from the mouth. **3** (in soccer, basketball, hockey, etc.) to propel (the ball) by repeatedly tapping it with the hand, foot, or a stick. ◆ *n* **4** a small quantity of liquid falling in drops or flowing in a thin stream. **5** a small quantity or supply. **6** an act or instance of dribbling. [C16: frequentative of *drib*, var. of DRIP]
▸**'dribbler** *n* ▸**'dribbly** *adj*
driblet *or* **dribblet** ('drɪblɪt) *n* a small amount. [C17: from obs. *drib* to fall bit by bit + -LET]
dribs and drabs (drɪbz) *pl n Inf.* small sporadic amounts.
dried (draɪd) *vb* the past tense and past participle of **dry.**
drier[1] ('draɪə) *adj* a comparative of **dry.**
drier[2] ('draɪə) *n* a variant spelling of **dryer**[1].
driest ('draɪɪst) *adj* a superlative of **dry.**
drift Ⓣ (drɪft) *vb (mainly intr)* **1** *(also tr)* to be carried along as by currents of air or water or (of a current) to carry (a vessel, etc.) along. **2** to move aimlessly from one place or activity to another. **3** to wander away from a fixed course or point; stray. **4** *(also tr)* (of snow, etc.) to accumulate in heaps or to drive (snow, etc.) into heaps. ◆ *n* **5** something piled up by the wind or current, as a snowdrift. **6** tendency or meaning: *the drift of the argument.* **7** a state of indecision or inaction. **8** the extent to which a vessel, aircraft, etc., is driven off course by winds, etc. **9** a general tendency of surface ocean water to flow in the direction of the prevailing winds. **10** a driving movement, force, or influence; impulse. **11** a controlled four-wheel skid used to take bends at high speed. **12** a deposit of sand, gravel, etc., esp. one transported and deposited by a glacier. **13** a horizontal passage in a mine that follows the mineral vein. **14** something, esp. a group of animals, driven along. **15** a steel tool driven into holes to enlarge or align them. **16** an uncontrolled slow change in some operating characteristic of a piece of equipment. **17** *S. African.* a ford. [C13: from ON: snowdrift]
driftage ('drɪftɪdʒ) *n* **1** the act of drifting. **2** matter carried along by drifting. **3** the amount by which an aircraft or vessel has drifted.
drifter Ⓣ ('drɪftə) *n* **1** a person or thing that drifts. **2** a person who moves aimlessly from place to place. **3** a boat used for drift-net fishing.
drift ice *n* masses of ice floating in the sea.
drift net *n* a large fishing net that is allowed to drift with the tide or current.
driftwood ('drɪftˌwʊd) *n* wood floating on or washed ashore by the sea or other body of water.
drill[1] Ⓣ (drɪl) *n* **1** a machine or tool for boring holes. **2** *Mil.* **2a** training in procedures or movements, as for parades or the use of weapons. **2b** *(as modifier)*: *drill hall.* **3** strict and often repetitious training or exercises used in teaching. **4** *Inf.* correct procedure. **5** a marine mollusc that preys on oysters. ◆ *vb* **6** to pierce, bore, or cut (a hole) in (material) with or as if with a drill. **7** to instruct or be instructed in military procedures or movements. **8** *(tr)* to teach by rigorous exercises or training. **9** *(tr) Inf.* to riddle with bullets. [C17: from MDu. *drillen*]
▸**'driller** *n*
drill[2] (drɪl) *n* **1** a machine for planting seeds in rows. **2** a furrow in which seeds are sown. **3** a row of seeds planted by means of a drill. ◆ *vb* **4** to plant (seeds) by means of a drill. [C18: from ?; cf. G *Rille* furrow]
▸**'driller** *n*
drill[3] (drɪl) *n* a hard-wearing twill-weave cotton cloth, used for uniforms, etc. [C18: var. of G *Drillich*, from L *trilīx*, from TRI- + *līcium* thread]
drill[4] (drɪl) *n* an Old World monkey of W Africa, related to the mandrill. [C17: from a West African word]
drilling fluid *n* a fluid, usually consisting of a suspension of clay in water, pumped down when an oil well is being drilled. Also called: **mud.**
drilling platform *n* a structure, either fixed to the sea bed or mobile, which supports the drilling rig, stores, etc., required for drilling an offshore oil well.
drilling rig *n* **1** the complete machinery, equipment, and structures needed to drill an oil well. **2** a mobile drilling platform used for exploratory offshore drilling.
drillmaster ('drɪlˌmɑːstə) *n* **1** Also called: **drill sergeant.** a military drill instructor. **2** a person who instructs in a strict manner.
drill press *n* a machine tool for boring holes.
drily *or* **dryly** ('draɪlɪ) *adv* in a dry manner.
drink Ⓣ (drɪŋk) *vb* **drinks, drinking, drank, drunk. 1** to swallow (a liquid). **2** *(tr)* to soak up (liquid); absorb. **3** *(tr; usually foll. by in)* to pay close attention to. **4** *(tr)* to bring (oneself) into a certain condition by consuming alcohol. **5** *(tr; often foll. by away)* to dispose of or ruin by excessive expenditure on alcohol. **6** *(intr)* to consume alcohol, esp. to excess. **7** (when *intr*, foll. by *to*) to drink (a toast). **8 drink the health of.** to salute or celebrate with a toast. **9 drink with the flies.** *Austral. inf.* to drink alone. ◆ *n* **10** liquid suitable for drinking. **11** alcohol or its habitual or excessive consumption. **12** a portion of liquid for drinking; draught. **13 the drink.** *Inf.* the sea. [OE *drincan*]
▸**'drinkable** *adj* ▸**'drinker** *n*
drink-driving *n (modifier)* of or relating to driving a car after drinking alcohol: *drink-driving offences.*
drinking fountain *n* a device for providing a flow or jet of drinking water, esp. in public places.
drinking-up time *n* (in Britain) a short time for finishing drinks after last orders in a public house.
drinking water *n* water reserved or suitable for drinking.
drip Ⓣ (drɪp) *vb* **drips, dripping, dripped. 1** to fall or let fall in drops. ◆ *n* **2** the formation and falling of drops of liquid. **3** the sound made by falling drops. **4** a projection at the edge of a sill or cornice designed to throw water clear of the wall. **5** *Inf.* an inane, insipid person. **6** *Med.* **6a** the apparatus used for the intravenous drop-by-drop administration of a solution. **6b** the solution so administered. [OE *dryppan*, from *dropa* DROP]
drip-dry *adj* **1** designating clothing or a fabric that will dry relatively free of creases if hung up when wet. ◆ *vb* **drip-dries, drip-drying, drip-dried. 2** to dry or become dry thus.
drip-feed *vb* **drip-feeds, drip-feeding, drip-fed.** *(tr)* **1** to feed (someone) a liquid drop by drop, esp. intravenously. **2** *Inf.* to fund (a new company) in stages rather than by injecting a large sum at its inception. ◆ *n* **drip feed. 3** another term for **drip** (sense 6).

THESAURUS

dressmaker *n* = **seamstress,** couturier, modiste, sewing woman, tailor
dress up *vb* **1** = **dress formally,** doll up (*sl.*), dress for dinner, put on one's best bib and tucker (*inf.*), put on one's glad rags (*inf.*) **2** = **put on fancy dress,** disguise, play-act, wear a costume
dressy *adj* **1** = **elegant,** classy (*sl.*), elaborate, formal, ornate, ritzy (*sl.*), smart, stylish, swish (*inf., chiefly Brit.*)
dribble *vb* **1** = **run,** drip, drop, fall in drops, leak, ooze, seep, trickle **2** = **drool,** drip saliva, drivel, slaver, slobber
drift *vb* **1** = **float,** be carried along, coast, go (aimlessly), meander, stray, waft, wander **4** = **pile up,** accumulate, amass, bank up, drive, gather ◆ *n* **5** = **pile,** accumulation, bank, heap, mass, mound **6** = **meaning,** aim, design, direction, gist, implication, import, intention, object, purport, scope, significance, tendency, tenor, thrust **9** = **current,** course, direction, flow, impulse, movement, rush, sweep, trend
drifter *n* **2** = **wanderer,** bag lady (*chiefly US*), beachcomber, bum (*inf.*), hobo (*US*), itinerant, rolling stone, tramp, vagabond, vagrant
drill[1] *n* **1** = **boring tool,** bit, borer, gimlet, rotary tool **2a** = **training,** discipline, exercise, instruction, practice, preparation, repetition ◆ *vb* **6** = **bore,** penetrate, perforate, pierce, puncture, sink in **7, 8** = **train,** coach, discipline, exercise, instruct, practise, rehearse, teach
drink *vb* **1** = **swallow,** absorb, drain, gulp, guzzle, imbibe, partake of, quaff, sip, suck, sup, swig (*inf.*), swill, toss off, wash down, wet one's whistle (*inf.*) **3** *usually foll. by* **in** = **pay attention,** absorb, assimilate, be all ears (*inf.*), be fascinated by, be rapt, hang on (someone's) words, hang on the lips of **6** = **booze** (*inf.*), bend the elbow (*inf.*), bevvy (*dialect*), carouse, go on a binge *or* bender (*inf.*), hit the bottle (*inf.*), indulge, pub-crawl (*inf., chiefly Brit.*), revel, tipple, tope, wassail **7** *foll. by* **to** = **toast,** pledge, pledge the health of, salute ◆ *n* **10** = **beverage,** liquid, potion, refreshment, thirst quencher **11** = **alcohol,** booze (*inf.*), Dutch courage, hooch *or* hootch (*inf., chiefly US & Canad.*), liquor, spirits, the bottle (*inf.*) **12** = **glass,** cup, draught, gulp, noggin, sip, snifter (*inf.*), swallow, swig (*inf.*), taste, tipple **13 the drink** *Informal* = **the sea,** the briny (*inf.*), the deep, the main, the ocean
drinkable *adj* **1** = **fit to drink,** drinking, potable, quaffable
drinker *n* **4–6** = **alcoholic,** bibber, boozer (*inf.*), dipsomaniac, drunk, drunkard, guzzler, inebriate, lush (*sl.*), soak (*sl.*), sot, sponge (*inf.*), tippler, toper, wino (*inf.*)
drip *vb* **1** = **drop,** dribble, drizzle, exude, filter, plop, splash, sprinkle, trickle ◆ *n* **2** = **drop,** dribble, dripping, leak, trickle **5** *Informal* = **weakling,** milksop, mummy's boy (*inf.*),

dripping ('drɪpɪŋ) *n* **1** the fat exuded by roasting meat. **2** (*often pl*) liquid that falls in drops. ◆ *adv* **3** (intensifier): *dripping wet.*

drippy ('drɪpɪ) *adj* **drippier, drippiest. 1** *Inf.* mawkish, insipid, or inane. **2** tending to drip.

drive ❶ (draɪv) *vb* **drives, driving, drove, driven. 1** to push, propel, or be pushed or propelled. **2** to guide the movement of (a vehicle, animal, etc.). **3** (*tr*) to compel or urge to work or act, esp. excessively. **4** (*tr*) to goad into a specified attitude or state: *work drove him mad.* **5** (*tr*) to cause (an object) to make (a hole, crack, etc.). **6** to move rapidly by striking or throwing with force. **7** *Sport.* to hit (a ball) very hard and straight. **8** *Golf.* to strike (the ball) with a driver. **9** (*tr*) to chase (game) from cover. **10** to transport or be transported in a vehicle. **11** (*intr*) to rush or dash violently, esp. against an obstacle. **12** (*tr*) to transact with vigour (esp. in **drive a hard bargain**). **13** (*tr*) to force (a component) into or out of its location by means of blows or a press. **14** (*tr*) *Mining.* to excavate horizontally. **15 drive home. 15a** to cause to penetrate to the fullest extent. **15b** to make clear by special emphasis. ◆ *n* **16** the act of driving. **17** a journey in a driven vehicle. **18** a road for vehicles, esp. a private road leading to a house. **19** vigorous pressure, as in business. **20** a united effort, esp. towards a common goal. **21** *Brit.* a large gathering of persons to play cards, etc. **22** energy, ambition, or initiative. **23** *Psychol.* a motive or interest, such as sex or ambition. **24** a sustained and powerful military offensive. **25a** the means by which force, motion, etc., is transmitted in a mechanism. **25b** (*as modifier*): *a drive shaft.* **26** *Sport.* a hard straight shot or stroke. **27** a search for and chasing of game towards waiting guns. **28** *Electronics.* the signal applied to the input of an amplifier. [OE *drīfan*]
▸'**drivable** *or* '**driveable** *adj*

drive at ❶ *vb* (*intr, prep*) *Inf.* to intend or mean: *what are you driving at?*

drive-in *adj* **1** denoting a public facility or service designed to be used by patrons seated in their cars: *a drive-in bank.* ◆ *n* **2** *Chiefly US & Canad.* a cinema designed to be used in such a manner.

drivel ❶ ('drɪvᵊl) *vb* **drivels, drivelling, drivelled** *or US* **drivels, driveling, driveled. 1** to allow (saliva) to flow from the mouth; dribble. **2** (*intr*) to speak foolishly. ◆ *n* **3** foolish or senseless talk. **4** saliva flowing from the mouth; slaver. [OE *dreflian* to slaver]
▸'**driveller** *or US* '**driveler** *n*

driven ('drɪvᵊn) *vb* the past participle of **drive.**

driver ('draɪvə) *n* **1** a person who drives a vehicle. **2 in the driver's seat.** in a position of control. **3** a person who drives animals. **4** a mechanical component that exerts a force on another to produce motion. **5** *Golf.* a club, a No. 1 wood, used for tee shots. **6** *Electronics.* a circuit whose output provides the input of another circuit. **7** *Computing.* a computer program that controls a device.
▸'**driverless** *adj*

drive-thru *n* **a** a takeaway restaurant, bank, etc., designed so that customers can use it without leaving their cars. **b** (*as modifier*): *a drive-thru restaurant.*

drive-time *n* **a** the time of day when many people are driving to or from work, considered as a broadcasting slot. **b** (*as modifier*): *the daily drive-time show.*

driveway ('draɪv,weɪ) *n* a path for vehicles, often connecting a house with a public road.

driving chain *n Engineering.* a roller chain that transmits power from one toothed wheel to another. Also called: **drive chain.**

driving licence *n* an official document authorizing a person to drive a motor vehicle.

drizzle ❶ ('drɪzᵊl) *n* **1** very light rain. ◆ *vb* **drizzles, drizzling, drizzled. 2** (*intr*) to rain lightly. [OE *drēosan* to fall]
▸'**drizzly** *adj*

drogue (drəʊg) *n* **1** any funnel-like device used as a sea anchor. **2a** a small parachute released behind an aircraft to reduce its landing speed. **2b** a small parachute released during the landing of a spacecraft. **3** a device towed behind an aircraft as a target for firing practice. **4** a device on the end of the hose of a tanker aircraft, to assist location of the probe of the receiving aircraft. **5** a windsock. [C18: prob. based ult. on OE *dragan* to DRAW]

droll ❶ (drəʊl) *adj* amusing in a quaint or odd manner; comical. [C17: from F *drôle* scamp, from MDu.: imp]
▸'**drollness** *n* ▸'**drolly** *adv*

drollery ❶ ('drəʊlərɪ) *n, pl* **drolleries. 1** humour; comedy. **2** *Rare.* a droll act, story, or remark.

-drome *n combining form.* **1** a course or race-course: *hippodrome.* **2** a large place for a special purpose: *aerodrome.* [via L from Gk *dromos* race, course]

dromedary ('drʌmədərɪ) *n, pl* **dromedaries.** a type of Arabian camel bred for racing and riding, having a single hump. [C14: from LL *dromedārius* (*camēlus*), from Gk *dromas* running]

-dromous *adj combining form.* moving or running: *anadromous; catadromous.* [via NL from Gk *-dromos,* from *dromos* a running]

drone[1] ❶ (drəʊn) *n* **1** a male honeybee whose sole function is to mate with the queen. **2** a person who lives off the work of others. **3** a pilotless radio-controlled aircraft. [OE *drān;* see DRONE[2]]

drone[2] ❶ (drəʊn) *vb* **drones, droning, droned. 1** (*intr*) to make a monotonous low dull sound. **2** (when *intr,* often foll. by *on*) to utter (words) in a monotonous tone, esp. to talk without stopping. ◆ *n* **3** a monotonous low dull sound. **4** *Music.* a sustained bass note or chord. **5** one of the single-reed pipes in a set of bagpipes. **6** a person who speaks in a low monotonous tone. [C16: rel. to DRONE[1] & MDu. *drōnen,* G *dröhnen*]
▸'**droning** *adj*

drongo ('drɒŋgəʊ) *n, pl* **drongos. 1** any of various songbirds of the Old World tropics, having a glossy black plumage. **2** *Austral. & NZ sl.* a slow-witted person. [C19: from Malagasy]

drool ❶ (dru:l) *vb* **1** (*intr;* often foll. by *over*) to show excessive enthusiasm (for) or pleasure (in); gloat (over). ◆ *vb, n* **2** another word for **drivel** (senses 1, 2, 4). [C19: prob. alteration of DRIVEL]

droop ❶ (dru:p) *vb* **1** to sag or allow to sag, as from weakness. **2** (*intr*) to be overcome by weariness. **3** (*intr*) to lose courage. ◆ *n* **4** the act or state of drooping. [C13: from ON *drūpa*]
▸'**drooping** *adj* ▸'**droopy** *adj*

drop ❶ (drɒp) *n* **1** a small quantity of liquid that forms or falls in a spherical mass. **2** a very small quantity of liquid. **3** a very small quantity of anything. **4** something resembling a drop in shape or size. **5** the act or an instance of falling; descent. **6** a decrease in amount or value. **7** the vertical distance that anything may fall. **8** a steep incline or slope. **9** short for **fruit drop. 10** the act of unloading troops, etc., by parachute. **11** (in cable television) a short spur from a trunk cable that feeds signals to an individual house. **12** *Theatre.* See **drop curtain. 13** another word for **trap door** or **gallows. 14** *Chiefly US & Canad.* a slot through which an object can be dropped into a receptacle. **15** *Austral. cricket sl.* a fall of the wicket. **16** See **drop shot. 17 at the drop of a hat.** without hesitation or delay. **18 have the drop on (someone).** *US & NZ.* to have the advantage over (someone). ◆ *vb* **drops, dropping, dropped. 19** (of liquids) to fall or allow to fall in globules. **20** to fall or allow to fall vertically. **21** (*tr*) to allow to fall by letting go of. **22** to sink or fall or cause to sink to the ground, as from a blow, weariness, etc. **23** (*intr;* foll. by *back, behind,* etc.) to move in a specified manner, direction, etc. **24** (*intr;* foll. by *in, by,* etc.) *Inf.* to pay a casual visit (to). **25** to decrease in amount or value. **26** to sink or cause to sink to a lower position. **27** to make or become less in strength, volume, etc. **28** (*intr*) to decline in

THESAURUS

namby-pamby, ninny, softie (*inf.*), weed (*inf.*), wet (*Brit. inf.*)

drive *vb* **1** = **push**, herd, hurl, impel, propel, send, urge **2** = **operate**, direct, go, guide, handle, manage, motor, ride, steer, travel **4** = **goad**, actuate, coerce, compel, constrain, dragoon, force, harass, impel, motivate, oblige, overburden, overwork, press, prick, prod, prompt, railroad (*inf.*), rush, spur **5** = **thrust**, dig, hammer, plunge, push, ram, sink, stab ◆ *n* **17** = **run**, excursion, hurl (*Scot.*), jaunt, journey, outing, ride, spin (*inf.*), trip, turn **20** = **campaign**, action, advance, appeal, crusade, effort, push (*inf.*), surge **22** = **initiative**, ambition, effort, energy, enterprise, get-up-and-go (*inf.*), motivation, pep, pressure, push (*inf.*), vigour, zip (*inf.*)

drive at *vb Informal* = **mean**, aim, allude to, get at, have in mind, hint at, imply, indicate, insinuate, intend, intimate, refer to, signify, suggest

drivel *vb* **1** = **dribble**, drool, slaver, slobber **2** = **babble**, blether, gab (*inf.*), gas (*inf.*), maunder, prate, ramble, waffle (*inf., chiefly Brit.*) ◆ *n* **3** = **nonsense**, balderdash, balls (*taboo sl.*), bilge (*inf.*), blah (*sl.*), bosh (*inf.*), bull (*sl.*), bullshit (*taboo sl.*), bunk (*inf.*), bunkum *or* buncombe (*chiefly US*), cobblers (*Brit. taboo sl.*), crap (*sl.*), dross, eyewash (*inf.*), fatuity, garbage (*inf.*), gibberish, guff (*sl.*), hogwash, hokum (*sl., chiefly US & Canad.*), hot air (*inf.*), moonshine, pap, piffle (*inf.*), poppycock (*inf.*), prating, rot, rubbish, shit (*taboo sl.*), stuff, tommyrot, tosh (*sl., chiefly Brit.*), trash, tripe (*inf.*), twaddle, waffle (*inf., chiefly Brit.*) **4** = **saliva**, slaver, slobber

driving *adj* **22** = **forceful**, compelling, dynamic, energetic, galvanic, storming (*inf.*), sweeping, vigorous, violent

drizzle *n* **1** = **fine rain**, Scotch mist, smir (*Scot.*) ◆ *vb* **2** = **rain**, mizzle, shower, spot *or* spit with rain, spray, sprinkle

droll *adj* = **amusing**, clownish, comic, comical, diverting, eccentric, entertaining, farcical, funny, humorous, jocular, laughable, ludicrous, odd, oddball (*inf.*), off-the-wall (*sl.*), quaint, ridiculous, risible, waggish, whimsical

drollery *n* **1** = **humour**, absurdity, archness, buffoonery, farce, fun, jocularity, pleasantry, waggishness, whimsicality, wit

drone[1] *n* **2** = **parasite**, couch potato (*sl.*), idler, leech, loafer, lounger, scrounger (*inf.*), skiver (*Brit. sl.*), sluggard, sponger (*inf.*)

drone[2] *vb* **1** = **hum**, buzz, purr, thrum, vibrate, whirr **2 drone on** = **speak monotonously**, be boring, chant, drawl, intone, prose about, spout, talk interminably ◆ *n* **3** = **hum**, buzz, murmuring, purr, thrum, vibration, whirr, whirring

droning *adj* **1** = **humming**, buzzing, murmuring, purring, thrumming, vibrating, whirring **2** = **monotonous**, boring, drawling, soporific, tedious

drool *vb* **1 drool over** = **gloat over**, dote on, fondle, gush, make much of, pet, rave about (*inf.*), slobber over, spoil **2** = **dribble**, drivel, salivate, slaver, slobber, water at the mouth

droop *vb* **1** = **sag**, bend, dangle, drop, fall down, hang (down), sink **2** = **flag**, decline, diminish, fade, faint, languish, slump, wilt, wither

droopy *adj* **1** = **sagging**, drooping, flabby, floppy, languid, languorous, lassitudinous, limp, pendulous, stooped, wilting

drop *n* **1** = **droplet**, bead, bubble, driblet, drip, globule, pearl, tear **2, 3** = **dash**, dab, mouthful, nip, pinch, shot (*inf.*), sip, spot, taste, tot, trace, trickle **5, 6** = **decrease**, cut, decline, deterioration, downturn, fall-off, lowering, reduction, slump **7, 8** = **fall**, abyss, chasm, declivity, descent, plunge, precipice, slope ◆ *vb* **19** = **drip**, dribble, fall in drops, trickle **20** = **fall**, decline, depress, descend, diminish, dive, droop, lower, plummet, plunge, sink, tumble **24** *foll. by* **in** *Informal* = **visit**, blow in (*inf.*), call, call in, look in, look up, pop in, roll up (*inf.*), stop, turn up **33** = **set down**, deposit, leave, let off, unload **35** = **discontinue**, abandon, axe (*inf.*), cease, desert, forsake, give up, kick (*inf.*), leave, quit, relinquish, remit, terminate **36** *Informal* = **reject**, dis-

health or condition. **29** (*intr; sometimes foll. by into*) to pass easily into a condition: *to drop into a habit.* **30** (*intr*) to move gently as with a current of air. **31** (*tr*) to mention casually: *to drop a hint.* **32** (*tr*) to leave out (a word or letter). **33** (*tr*) to set down (passengers or goods). **34** (*tr*) to send or post: *drop me a line.* **35** (*tr*) to discontinue: *let's drop the matter.* **36** (*tr*) to cease to associate with. **37** (*tr*) *Sl., chiefly US.* to cease to employ. **38** (*tr; sometimes foll. by in, off, etc.*) *Inf.* to leave or deposit. **39** (of animals) to give birth to (offspring). **40** *Sl., chiefly US & Canad.* to lose (money). **41** (*tr*) to lengthen (a hem, etc.). **42** (*tr*) to unload (troops, etc.) by parachute. **43** (*tr*) *Naut.* to sail out of sight of. **44** (*tr*) *Sport.* to omit (a player) from a team. **45** (*tr*) to lose (a game, etc.). **46** (*tr*) *Golf, basketball, etc.* to hit or throw (a ball) into a goal. **47** (*tr*) to hit (a ball) with a drop shot. ◆ *n, vb* **48** *Rugby.* short for **drop kick** or **drop-kick.** ◆ See also **drop off, dropout, drops.** [OE *dropian*]

drop curtain *n Theatre.* a curtain that can be raised and lowered onto the stage.

drop-dead *adv Sl.* outstandingly or exceptionally: *drop-dead gorgeous.*

drop forge *n* a device for forging metal between two dies, one of which is fixed, the other acting by gravity or by pressure.
▸**'drop-ˌforge** *vb* (*tr*)

drop goal *n Rugby.* a goal scored with a drop kick during the run of play.

drop hammer *n* another name for **drop forge.**

drop-in centre *n* (in Britain) a daycentre run by the social services or a charity that clients may attend on an informal basis.

drop kick *n* **1** a kick in which the ball is dropped and kicked as it bounces from the ground. **2** a wrestling attack in which a wrestler leaps in the air and kicks his opponent. ◆ *vb* **drop-kick. 3** to kick (a ball, a wrestling opponent, etc.) by the use of a drop kick.

drop leaf *n* **a** a hinged flap on a table that can be raised to extend the surface. **b** (*as modifier*): *a drop-leaf table.*

droplet ('drɒplɪt) *n* a tiny drop.

drop lock *n Finance.* a variable-rate bank loan that is automatically replaced by a fixed-rate long-term bond if the long-term interest rates fall to a specified level.

drop off ❶ *vb* (*adv*) **1** (*intr*) to grow smaller or less. **2** (*tr*) to set down. **3** (*intr*) *Inf.* to fall asleep. ◆ *n* **drop-off. 4** a steep descent. **5** a sharp decrease.

dropout ❶ ('drɒpˌaʊt) *n* **1** a student who fails to complete a course. **2** a person who rejects conventional society. **3 drop-out.** *Rugby.* a drop kick taken to restart play. ◆ *vb* **drop out.** (*intr, adv; often foll. by of*) **4** to abandon or withdraw from (a school, job, etc.).

dropper ('drɒpə) *n* **1** a small tube having a rubber bulb at one end for dispensing drops of liquid. **2** a person or thing that drops.

droppings ❶ ('drɒpɪŋz) *pl n* the dung of certain animals, such as rabbits, sheep, and birds.

drops (drɒps) *pl n* any liquid medication applied by means of a dropper.

drop scone *n* a flat spongy cake made by dropping a spoonful of batter on a hot griddle.

drop shot *n* **a** *Tennis.* a softly played return that drops abruptly after clearing the net. **b** *Squash.* a shot that stops abruptly after hitting the front wall of the court.

dropsy ('drɒpsɪ) *n* **1** *Pathol.* a condition characterized by an accumulation of watery fluid in the tissues or in a body cavity. **2** *Sl.* a tip or bribe. [C13: from *ydropesie,* from L *hydrōpisis,* from Gk *hudrōps,* from *hudōr* water]
▸**dropsical** ('drɒpsɪk'l) *adj*

droshky ('drɒʃkɪ) *or* **drosky** ('drɒskɪ) *n, pl* **droshkies** *or* **droskies.** an open four-wheeled carriage, formerly used in Russia. [C19: from Russian, dim. of *drogi* wagon]

drosophila (drɒ'sɒfɪlə) *n, pl* **drosophilas** *or* **drosophilae** (-ˌliː). any of a genus of small flies that are widely used in laboratory genetics studies. Also called: **fruit fly.** [C19: NL, from Gk *drosos* dew + *-phila* -PHILE]

dross ❶ (drɒs) *n* **1** the scum formed on the surfaces of molten metals. **2** worthless matter; waste. [OE *drōs* dregs]
▸**'drossy** *adj* ▸**'drossiness** *n*

drought ❶ (draʊt) *n* **1** a prolonged period of scanty rainfall. **2** a prolonged shortage. [OE *drūgoth*]
▸**'droughty** *adj*

drove[1] (drəʊv) *vb* the past tense of **drive.**

drove[2] ❶ (drəʊv) *n* **1** a herd of livestock being driven together. **2** (*often pl*) a moving crowd of people. ◆ *vb* **droves, droving, droved.** (*tr*) **3** to drive (livestock), usually for a considerable distance. [OE *drāf* herd]

drover ('drəʊvə) *n* a person who drives sheep or cattle, esp. to and from market.

drown ❶ (draʊn) *vb* **1** to die or kill by immersion in liquid. **2** (*tr*) to get rid of: *he drowned his sorrows in drink.* **3** (*tr*) to drench thoroughly. **4** (*tr; sometimes foll. by out*) to render (a sound) inaudible by making a loud noise. [C13: prob. from OE *druncnian*]

drowse ❶ (draʊz) *vb* **drowses, drowsing, drowsed. 1** to be or cause to be sleepy, dull, or sluggish. ◆ *n* **2** the state of being drowsy. [C16: prob. from OE *drūsian* to sink]

drowsy ❶ ('draʊzɪ) *adj* **drowsier, drowsiest. 1** heavy with sleepiness; sleepy. **2** inducing sleep; soporific. **3** sluggish or lethargic; dull.
▸**'drowsily** *adv* ▸**'drowsiness** *n*

drub (drʌb) *vb* **drubs, drubbing, drubbed.** (*tr*) **1** to beat as with a stick. **2** to defeat utterly, as in a contest. **3** to drum or stamp (the feet). **4** to instil with force or repetition. ◆ *n* **5** a blow, as from a stick. [C17: prob. from Ar. *dáraba* to beat]

drubbing ❶ ('drʌbɪŋ) *n* **1** a beating. **2** a total defeat.

drudge ❶ (drʌdʒ) *n* **1** a person who works hard at wearisome menial tasks. ◆ *vb* **drudges, drudging, drudged. 2** (*intr*) to toil at such tasks. [C16: ?from *druggen* to toil]
▸**'drudger** *n* ▸**'drudgingly** *adv*

drudgery ❶ ('drʌdʒərɪ) *n, pl* **drudgeries.** hard, menial, and monotonous work.

drug ❶ (drʌg) *n* **1** any substance used in the treatment, prevention, or diagnosis of disease. Related adj: **pharmaceutical. 2** a chemical substance, esp. a narcotic, taken for the effects it produces. **3 drug on the market.** a commodity available in excess of demand. ◆ *vb* **drugs, drugging, drugged.** (*tr*) **4** to mix a drug with (food, etc.). **5** to administer a drug to. **6** to stupefy or poison with or as if with a drug. [C14: from OF *drogue,* prob. of Gmc origin]

drug addict ❶ *n* any person who is abnormally dependent on narcotic drugs.

drugget ('drʌgɪt) *n* a coarse fabric used as a protective floor covering, etc. [C16: from F *droguet* useless fabric, from *drogue* trash]

druggie ('drʌgɪ) *n Inf.* a drug addict.

druggist ('drʌgɪst) *n* a US and Canad. term for **pharmacist.**

drugstore ('drʌgˌstɔː) *n US & Canad.* a shop where medical prescriptions are made up and a wide variety of goods and sometimes light meals are sold.

druid ('druːɪd) *n* (*sometimes cap.*) **1** a member of an ancient order of priests in Gaul, Britain, and Ireland in the pre-Christian era. **2** a member of any of several modern movements attempting to revive druidism. [C16: from L *druides,* of Gaulish origin]
▸**'druidess** *fem n* ▸**dru'idic** *or* **dru'idical** *adj* ▸**'druidˌism** *n*

drum ❶ (drʌm) *n* **1** a percussion instrument sounded by striking a membrane stretched across the opening of a hollow cylinder or hemisphere. **2** the sound produced by a drum or any similar sound. **3**

THESAURUS

own, ignore, jilt, renounce, repudiate, throw over

drop off *vb* **1** = **decrease**, decline, diminish, dwindle, fall off, lessen, slacken **2** = **set down**, allow to alight, deliver, leave, let off **3** *Informal* = **fall asleep**, catnap, doze (off), drowse, have forty winks (*inf.*), nod (off), snooze (*inf.*)

drop out *vb* **4** = **leave**, abandon, back out, cop out (*sl.*), fall by the wayside, forsake, give up, quit, renege, stop, withdraw

droppings *pl n* = **excrement**, crap (*taboo sl.*), doo-doo (*inf.*), dung, excreta, faeces, guano, manure, ordure, shit (*taboo sl.*), stool, turd

dross *n* **1, 2** = **scum**, crust, debris, dregs, impurity, lees, recrement, refuse, remains, scoria, waste

drought *n* **1** = **dry spell**, aridity, dehydration, drouth (*Scot.*), dryness, dry weather, parchedness **2** = **shortage**, dearth, deficiency, insufficiency, lack, need, scarcity, want
Antonyms *n* ≠ **dry spell:** deluge, downpour, flood, flow, inundation, outpouring, rush, stream, torrent ≠ **shortage:** abundance, profusion

drove[2] *n* **1, 2** = **herd**, collection, company, crowd, flock, gathering, horde, mob, multitude, press, swarm, throng

drown *vb* **1** = **drench**, deluge, engulf, flood, go down, go under, immerse, inundate, sink, submerge, swamp **4** = **overpower**, deaden, engulf, muffle, obliterate, overcome, overwhelm, stifle, swallow up, wipe out

drowse *vb* **1** = **be sleepy**, be drowsy, be lethargic, doze, drop off (*inf.*), kip (*Brit. sl.*), nap, nod, sleep, slumber, snooze (*inf.*), zizz (*Brit. inf.*) ◆ *n* **2** = **sleep**, doze, forty winks (*inf.*), kip (*Brit. sl.*), nap, slumber, zizz (*Brit. inf.*)

drowsiness *n* **1** = **sleepiness**, doziness, heavy eyelids, languor, lethargy, oscitancy, sluggishness, somnolence, tiredness, torpidity, torpor
Antonyms *n* alertness, brightness, liveliness, perkiness, wakefulness

drowsy *adj* **1** = **sleepy**, comatose, dazed, dopey (*sl.*), dozy, drugged, half asleep, heavy, lethargic, nodding, somnolent, tired, torpid **2** = **peaceful**, dreamy, lulling, quiet, restful, sleepy, soothing, soporific
Antonyms *adj* ≠ **sleepy:** alert, awake, bright-eyed and bushy-tailed, full of beans (*inf.*), lively, perky

drubbing *n* **1** = **beating**, clobbering (*sl.*), flogging, hammering (*inf.*), licking (*inf.*), pasting (*sl.*), pounding, pummelling, thrashing, walloping (*inf.*), whipping **2** = **defeat**, clobbering, hammering (*inf.*), licking (*inf.*), pasting (*sl.*), thrashing, trouncing

drudge *n* **1** = **menial**, dogsbody (*inf.*), factotum, hack, maid *or* man of all work, plodder, scullion (*arch.*), servant, skivvy (*chiefly Brit.*), slave, toiler, worker ◆ *vb* **2** = **toil**, grind (*inf.*), keep one's nose to the grindstone, labour, moil (*arch. or dialect*), plod, plug away (*inf.*), slave, work

drudgery *n* = **menial labour**, chore, donkey-work, fag (*inf.*), grind (*inf.*), hack work, hard work, labour, skivvying (*Brit.*), slavery, slog, sweat (*inf.*), sweated labour, toil

drug *n* **1** = **medication**, medicament, medicine, physic, poison, remedy **2** = **dope** (*sl.*), narcotic, opiate, stimulant ◆ *vb* **5** = **dose**, administer a drug, dope (*sl.*), medicate, treat **6** = **knock out**, anaesthetize, deaden, numb, poison, stupefy

drug addict *n* = **junkie** (*inf.*), acid head (*inf.*), crack-head, dope-fiend (*sl.*), head (*inf.*), hophead (*inf.*), tripper (*inf.*)

drugged *adj* **2** = **stoned** (*sl.*), bombed (*sl.*), comatose, doped (*sl.*), dopey (*sl.*), flying (*sl.*), high (*inf.*), on a trip (*inf.*), out of it (*sl.*), out of one's mind (*sl.*), out to it (*Austral. & NZ sl.*), smashed (*sl.*), spaced out (*sl.*), stupefied, tripping (*inf.*), turned on (*sl.*), under the influence (*inf.*), wasted (*sl.*), wrecked (*sl.*), zonked (*sl.*)

drum *vb* **11** = **beat**, pulsate, rap, reverberate, tap, tattoo, throb **14** *foll. by* **into** = **drive home**, din into, hammer away, harp on, instil into, reiterate an object that resembles a drum in shape, such as a large spool or a cylindrical container. **4** *Archit.* a cylindrical block of stone used to construct the shaft of a column. **5** short for **eardrum.** **6** any of various North American fishes that utter a drumming sound. **7** a type of hollow rotor for steam turbines or axial compressors. **8** *Arch.* a drummer. **9 beat the drum for.** *Inf.* to attempt to arouse interest in. **10 the drum.** *Austral. inf.* the necessary information (esp. in **give (someone) the drum**). ◆ *vb* **drums, drumming, drummed. 11** to play (music) on or as if on a drum. **12** to tap rhythmically or regularly. **13** (*tr;* sometimes foll. by *up*) to summon or call by drumming. **14** (*tr*) to instil by constant repetition. ◆ See also **drum up.** [C16: prob. from MDu. *tromme,* imit.]

drumbeat ('drʌmˌbiːt) *n* the sound made by beating a drum.

drum brake *n* a type of brake used on the wheels of vehicles, consisting of two shoes that rub against the brake drum when the brake is applied.

drumhead ('drʌmˌhɛd) *n* **1** the part of a drum that is actually struck. **2** the head of a capstan. **3** another name for **eardrum.**

drumlin ('drʌmlɪn) *n* a streamlined mound of glacial drift. [C19: from Irish Gaelic *druim* ridge + *-lin* -LING[1]]

drum machine *n* a synthesizer specially programmed to reproduce the sound of drums and other percussion instruments in variable rhythms and combinations selected by the musician; the resulting beat is produced continually until stopped or changed.

drum major *n* the noncommissioned officer, usually of warrant officer's rank, who commands the corps of drums of a military band and who is in command of both the drums and the band when paraded together.

drum majorette *n* a girl who marches at the head of a procession, twirling a baton.

drummer ('drʌmə) *n* **1** a drum player. **2** *Chiefly US.* a travelling salesman.

drumstick ('drʌmˌstɪk) *n* **1** a stick used for playing a drum. **2** the lower joint of the leg of a cooked fowl.

drum up Ⓣ *vb* (*tr, adv*) to obtain (support, business, etc.) by solicitation or canvassing.

drunk Ⓣ (drʌŋk) *adj* **1** intoxicated with alcohol to the extent of losing control over normal functions. **2** overwhelmed by strong influence or emotion. ◆ *n* **3** a person who is drunk. **4** *Inf.* a drinking bout. [OE *druncen,* p.p. of *drincan* to drink]

drunkard Ⓣ ('drʌŋkəd) *n* a person who is frequently or habitually drunk.

drunken Ⓣ ('drʌŋkən) *adj* **1** intoxicated. **2** habitually drunk. **3** (*prenominal*) caused by or relating to alcoholic intoxication: *a drunken brawl.*
▸ **'drunkenly** *adv* ▸ **'drunkenness** *n*

drupe (druːp) *n* any fruit that has a fleshy or fibrous part around a stone that encloses a seed, as the peach, plum, and cherry. [C18: from L *druppa* wrinkled overripe olive, from Gk: olive]
▸ **drupaceous** (druːˈpeɪʃəs) *adj*

drupelet ('druːplɪt) *or* **drupel** ('druːpəl) *n* a small drupe, usually one of a number forming a compound fruit.

Druse *or* **Druze** (druːz) *n, pl* **Druse** *or* **Druze. a** a member of a religious sect, mainly living in Syria, Lebanon, and Israel, having certain characteristics in common with Muslims. **b** (*as modifier*): *Druse customs.* [C18: from Arabic *Durūz,* after Ismail al-*Darazi,* 11th-century founder of the sect]

dry Ⓣ (draɪ) *adj* **drier, driest** *or* **dryer, dryest. 1** lacking moisture; not damp or wet. **2** having little or no rainfall. **3** not in or under water. **4** having the water drained away or evaporated: *a dry river.* **5** not providing milk: *a dry cow.* **6** (of the eyes) free from tears. **7a** *Inf.* thirsty. **7b** causing thirst. **8** eaten without butter, jam, etc.: *dry toast.* **9** *Electronics* (of a soldered joint) imperfect because the solder has not adhered to the metal. **10** (of wine, etc.) not sweet. **11** not producing a mucous or watery discharge: *a dry cough.* **12** consisting of solid as opposed to liquid substances. **13** without adornment; plain: *dry facts.* **14** lacking interest: *a dry book.* **15** lacking warmth: *a dry greeting.* **16** (of humour) shrewd and keen in an impersonal, sarcastic, or laconic way. **17** *Inf.* opposed to or prohibiting the sale of alcoholic liquor: *a dry country.* ◆ *vb* **dries, drying, dried. 18** (when *intr,* often foll. by *off*) to make or become dry. **19** (*tr*) to preserve (fruit, etc.) by removing the moisture. ◆ *n, pl* **drys** *or* **dries. 20** *Brit. inf.* a Conservative politician who is a hardliner. **21 the dry.** (*sometimes cap.*) *Austral. inf.* the dry season. ◆ See also **dry out, dry up.** [OE *drȳge*]
▸ **'dryness** *n*

dryad ('draɪəd, -æd) *n, pl* **dryads** *or* **dryades** (-əˌdiːz). *Greek myth.* a nymph or divinity of the woods. [C14: from L *Dryas,* from Gk *Druas,* from *drus* tree]

dry battery *n* an electric battery consisting of two or more dry cells.

dry cell *n* a primary cell in which the electrolyte is in the form of a paste or is treated in some way to prevent it from spilling.

dry-clean *vb* (*tr*) to clean (fabrics, etc.) with a solvent other than water.
▸ **ˌdry-'cleaner** *n* ▸ **ˌdry-'cleaning** *n*

dry dock *n* a dock that can be pumped dry for work on a ship's bottom.

dryer[1] ('draɪə) *n* **1** a person or thing that dries. **2** an apparatus for removing moisture by forced draught, heating, or centrifuging. **3** any of certain chemicals added to oils to accelerate their drying when used in paints, etc.

dryer[2] ('draɪə) *adj* a variant spelling of **drier**[1].

dry fly *n Angling.* **a** an artificial fly designed to be floated on the surface of the water. **b** (*as modifier*): *dry-fly fishing.*

dry hole *n* (in the oil industry) a well which proves unsuccessful.

dry ice *n* solid carbon dioxide used as a refrigerant, and to create billows of smoke in stage shows. Also called: **carbon dioxide snow.**

drying ('draɪɪŋ) *n* the processing of timber until it has a moisture content suitable for the purposes for which it is to be used.

dryly ('draɪlɪ) *adv* a variant spelling of **drily.**

dry measure *n* a unit or system of units for measuring dry goods, such as fruit, grains, etc.

dry out *vb* (*adv*) **1** to make or become dry. **2** to undergo or cause to undergo treatment for alcoholism or drug addiction.

dry point *n* **1** a technique of intaglio engraving with a hard steel needle, without acid, on a copper plate. **2** the sharp steel needle used. **3** the engraving or print produced.

dry riser *n* a vertical pipe, not containing water, having connections on different floors of a building for a fireman's hose to be attached. A fire tender can be connected at the lowest level to make water rise under pressure within the pipe. Abbrev.: **DR.**

dry rot *n* **1** crumbling and drying of timber, bulbs, potatoes, or fruit, caused by certain fungi. **2** any fungus causing this decay. **3** moral degeneration or corruption.

dry run *n* **1** *Mil.* practice in firing without live ammunition. **2** *Inf.* a rehearsal.

drysalter ('draɪˌsɔːltə) *n Obs.* a dealer in dyestuffs and gums, and in dried, tinned, or salted foods and edible oils.

dry-stone *adj* (of a wall) made without mortar.

dry up Ⓣ *vb* (*adv*) **1** (*intr*) to become barren or unproductive; fail. **2** to dry (dishes, cutlery, etc.) with a tea towel after they have been washed. **3** (*intr*) *Inf.* to stop talking or speaking.

DS *or* **ds** *Music. abbrev. for* dal segno.

DSc *abbrev. for* Doctor of Science.

DSC *Mil. abbrev. for* Distinguished Service Cross.

DSM *Mil. abbrev. for* Distinguished Service Medal.

DSO *Brit. mil. abbrev. for* Distinguished Service Order.

DSS *Brit. abbrev. for:* **1** Department of Social Security. **2** Director of Social Services.

DST *abbrev. for* Daylight Saving Time.

DSW (in New Zealand) *abbrev. for* Department of Social Welfare.

DTI (in Britain) *abbrev. for* Department of Trade and Industry.

DTP *abbrev for* desktop publishing.

DT's *Inf. abbrev. for* delirium tremens.

Du. *abbrev. for* Dutch.

dual Ⓣ ('djuːəl) *adj* **1** relating to or denoting two. **2** twofold; double. **3** (in the grammar of some languages) denoting a form of a word indicating that exactly two referents are being referred to. **4** *Maths, logic.* (of a pair of operators) convertible into one another by the distribution of negation over either. ◆ *n* **5** *Grammar.* **5a** the dual number. **5b** a dual form of a word. [C17: from L *duālis* concerning two, from *duo* two]
▸ **'dually** *adv* ▸ **duality** (djuːˈælɪtɪ) *n*

THESAURUS

drum up *vb* = **canvass,** attract, bid for, obtain, petition, round up, solicit

drunk *adj* **1** = **intoxicated,** babalas (*S. Afr.*), bacchic, bevvied (*dialect*), blitzed (*sl.*), blotto (*sl.*), bombed (*sl.*), Brahms and Liszt (*sl.*), canned (*sl.*), drunken, flying (*sl.*), fu' (*Scot.*), fuddled, half seas over (*inf.*), inebriated, legless (*inf.*), lit up (*sl.*), loaded (*sl., chiefly US & Canad.*), maudlin, merry (*Brit. inf.*), muddled, out of it (*sl.*), out to it (*Austral. & NZ sl.*), paralytic (*inf.*), pickled (*inf.*), pie-eyed (*sl.*), pissed (*taboo sl.*), plastered (*sl.*), rat-arsed (*taboo sl.*), sloshed (*sl.*), smashed (*sl.*), soaked (*inf.*), steamboats (*Scot. sl.*), steaming (*sl.*), stewed (*sl.*), stoned (*sl.*), tanked up (*sl.*), tiddly (*sl., chiefly Brit.*), tight (*inf.*), tipsy, tired and emotional (*euphemistic*), under the influence (*inf.*), wasted (*sl.*), well-oiled (*sl.*), wrecked (*sl.*), zonked (*sl.*) ◆ *n* **3** = **drunkard,** alcoholic, boozer (*inf.*), inebriate, lush (*sl.*), soak (*sl.*), sot, toper, wino (*inf.*)

drunkard *n* = **drinker,** alcoholic, carouser, dipsomaniac, drunk, lush (*sl.*), soak (*sl.*), sot, tippler, toper, wino (*inf.*)

drunken *adj* **1** = **intoxicated,** bevvied (*dialect*), bibulous, blitzed, blotto (*sl.*), bombed (*sl.*), boozing (*inf.*), Brahms and Liszt (*sl.*), drunk, flying (*sl.*), (gin-)sodden, inebriate, legless (*inf.*), lit up (*sl.*), out of it (*sl.*), out to it (*Austral. & NZ sl.*), paralytic (*inf.*), pissed (*taboo sl.*), rat-arsed (*taboo sl.*), red-nosed, smashed (*sl.*), sottish, steamboats (*Scot. sl.*), steaming (*sl.*), tippling, toping, under the influence (*inf.*), wasted (*sl.*), wrecked (*sl.*), zonked (*sl.*) **3** = **debauched,** bacchanalian, bacchic, boozy (*inf.*), dionysian, dissipated, orgiastic, riotous, saturnalian

drunkenness *n* **1-3** = **intoxication,** alcoholism, bibulousness, dipsomania, inebriation, insobriety, intemperance, sottishness, tipsiness

dry *adj* **1, 2** = **dehydrated,** arid, barren, desiccated, dried up, juiceless, moistureless, parched, sapless, thirsty, torrid, waterless **14** = **dull,** boring, dreary, ho-hum (*inf.*), monotonous, plain, tedious, tiresome, uninteresting **16** = **sarcastic,** cutting, deadpan, droll, keen, low-key, quietly humorous, sharp, sly ◆ *vb* **18** = **dehydrate,** dehumidify, desiccate, drain, make dry, parch, sear

Antonyms *adj* ≠ **dehydrated:** damp, humid, moist, wet ≠ **dull:** entertaining, interesting, lively ◆ *vb* ≠ **dehydrate:** moisten, wet

dryness *n* **1, 2** = **aridity,** aridness, dehumidification, dehydration, drought, thirst, thirstiness

dry up *vb* **1** = **become dry,** become unproductive, harden, mummify, shrivel up, wilt, wither, wizen

dual *adj* **1, 2** = **twofold,** binary, coupled, double, duplex, duplicate, matched, paired, twin

duality *n* **1** = **dualism,** dichotomy, doubleness, duplexity, polarity

dual carriageway *n Brit.* a road on which traffic travelling in opposite directions is separated by a central strip of turf, etc. US and Canad. name: **divided highway.**

dualism ('dju:ə,lɪzəm) *n* **1** the state of being twofold or double. **2** *Philosophy.* the doctrine that reality consists of two basic types of substance, usually taken to be mind and matter or mental and physical entities. Cf. **monism** (sense 1). **3a** the theory that the universe has been ruled from its origins by two conflicting powers, one good and one evil. **3b** the theory that there are two personalities, one human and one divine, in Christ.
▸'**dualist** *n* ▸**dual'istic** *adj*

dub[1] ⓣ (dʌb) *vb* **dubs, dubbing, dubbed. 1** (*tr*) to invest (a person) with knighthood by tapping on the shoulder with a sword. **2** (*tr*) to invest with a title, name, or nickname. **3** (*tr*) to dress (leather) by rubbing. **4** *Angling.* to dress (a fly). [OE *dubbian*]

dub[2] (dʌb) *vb* **dubs, dubbing, dubbed. 1** to alter the soundtrack of (a film, etc.). **2** (*tr*) to provide (a film) with a new soundtrack, esp. in a different language. **3** (*tr*) to provide (a film or tape) with a soundtrack. ◆ *n* **4** the new sounds added. **5** *Music.* a style of record production associated with reggae, involving the use of echo, delay, etc. [C20: shortened from DOUBLE]

dub[3] (dʌb) *vb* **dubs, dubbing, dubbed.** *Austral. & NZ inf.* short for **double- bank.**

dubbin ('dʌbɪn) *n Brit.* a greasy preparation applied to leather to soften it and make it waterproof. [C18: from *dub* to dress leather]

dubbing[1] ('dʌbɪŋ) *n Films.* **1** the replacement of a soundtrack, esp. by one in another language. **2** the combination of several soundtracks. **3** the addition of a soundtrack to a film, etc.

dubbing[2] ('dʌbɪŋ) *n* **1** *Angling.* fibrous material used for the body of an artificial fly. **2** a variant of **dubbin.**

dubiety ⓣ (dju:'baɪɪtɪ) *n, pl* **dubieties. 1** the state of being doubtful. **2** a doubtful matter. [C18: from LL *dubietās,* from L *dubius* DUBIOUS]

dub in *or* **up** *vb* (*adv*) *Sl.* to contribute to the cost of something: *we'll all dub in a fiver for the trip.*

dubious ⓣ ('dju:bɪəs) *adj* **1** marked by or causing doubt. **2** uncertain; doubtful. **3** of doubtful quality; untrustworthy. **4** not certain in outcome. [C16: from L *dubius* wavering]
▸'**dubiously** *adv* ▸'**dubiousness** *n*

Dublin Bay prawn ('dʌblɪn) *n* a large prawn used in a dish of scampi.

dubnium ('dʌb,nɪəm) *n* a synthetic transactinide element produced in minute quantities by bombarding plutonium with high-energy neon ions. Symbol: Du; atomic no. 105. [C20: from *Dubna,* city in Russia where it was first reported]

ducal ('dju:kᵊl) *adj* of a duke or duchy. [C16: from F, from LL *ducālis* of a leader, from L *dux* leader]

ducat ('dʌkət) *n* **1** any of various former European gold or silver coins. **2** (*often pl*) money. [C14: from OF, from OIt. *ducato* coin stamped with the doge's image]

duce ('du:tʃɪ) *n* leader. [C20: from It., from L *dux*]

Duce (*Italian* 'du:tʃe) *n* **Il** (il). the title assumed by Mussolini as leader of Fascist Italy (1922–43).

Duchenne dystrophy (du'ʃɛn) *or* **Duchenne muscular dystrophy** *n* the most common form of muscular dystrophy, usually affecting only boys. [after Guillaume *Duchenne* (1806–75), F neurologist]

duchess ('dʌtʃɪs) *n* **1** the wife or widow of a duke. **2** a woman who holds the rank of duke in her own right. ◆ *vb* **3** (*tr*) *Austral. inf.* to overwhelm with flattering attention. [C14: from OF *duchesse*]

duchy ('dʌtʃɪ) *n, pl* **duchies.** the territory of a duke or duchess; dukedom. [C14: from OF *duche,* from *duc* DUKE]

duck[1] (dʌk) *n, pl* **ducks** *or* **duck. 1** any of a family of aquatic birds, esp. those having short legs, webbed feet, and a broad blunt bill. **2** the flesh of this bird, used as food. **3** the female of such a bird, as opposed to the male (drake). **4** Also: **ducks.** *Brit. inf.* dear or darling: used as a term of address. See also **ducky. 5** *Cricket.* a score of nothing by a batsman. **6 like water off a duck's back.** *Inf.* without effect. [OE *dūce* duck, diver; rel. to DUCK[2]]

duck[2] ⓣ (dʌk) *vb* **1** to move (the head or body) quickly downwards or away, esp. to escape observation or evade a blow. **2** to plunge suddenly under water. **3** (when *intr,* often foll. by *out*) *Inf.* to dodge or escape (a person, duty, etc.). **4** (*intr*) *Bridge.* to play a low card rather than try to win a trick. ◆ *n* **5** the act or an instance of ducking. [C14: rel. to OHG *tūhhan* to dive, MDu. *dūken*]
▸'**ducker** *n*

duck[3] (dʌk) *n* a heavy cotton fabric of plain weave, used for clothing, tents, etc. [C17: from MDu. *doek*]

duck[4] (dʌk) *n* an amphibious vehicle used in World War II. [C20: from code name DUKW]

duck-billed platypus *n* an amphibious egg-laying mammal of E Australia having dense fur, a broad bill and tail, and webbed feet.

duckboard ('dʌk,bɔ:d) *n* a board or boards laid so as to form a path over wet or muddy ground.

ducking stool *n History.* a chair used for punishing offenders by plunging them into water.

duckling ('dʌklɪŋ) *n* a young duck.

ducks and drakes *n* (*functioning as sing*) **1** a game in which a flat stone is bounced across the surface of water. **2 make ducks and drakes of** *or* **play (at) ducks and drakes with.** *Inf.* to use recklessly; squander.

duck's arse *n* a hairstyle in which the hair is swept back to a point at the nape of the neck, resembling a duck's tail. Abbrev.: **DA.**

duck soup *n US sl.* something that is easy to do.

duckweed ('dʌk,wi:d) *n* any of various small stemless aquatic plants that occur floating on still water in temperate regions.

ducky *or* **duckie** ('dʌkɪ) *Inf.* ◆ *n, pl* **duckies. 1** *Brit.* darling or dear: a term of endearment. ◆ *adj* **duckier, duckiest. 2** delightful; fine.

duct ⓣ (dʌkt) *n* **1** a tube, pipe, or canal by means of which a substance, esp. a fluid or gas, is conveyed. **2** any bodily passage, esp. one conveying secretions or excretions. **3** a narrow tubular cavity in plants. **4** a channel or pipe carrying electric wires. **5** a passage through which air can flow, as in air conditioning. [C17: from L *ductus* a leading (in Med. L: aqueduct), from *dūcere* to lead]
▸'**ductless** *adj*

ductile ⓣ ('dʌktaɪl) *adj* **1** (of a metal) able to sustain large deformations without fracture and able to be hammered into sheets or drawn out into wires. **2** able to be moulded. **3** easily led or influenced. [C14: from OF, from L *ductilis,* from *dūcere* to lead]
▸**ductility** (dʌk'tɪlɪtɪ) *n*

ductless gland *n Anat.* See **endocrine gland.**

dud ⓣ (dʌd) *Inf.* ◆ *n* **1** a person or thing that proves ineffectual. **2** a shell, etc., that fails to explode. **3** (*pl*) *Old-fashioned.* clothes or belongings. ◆ *adj* **4** failing in its purpose or function. [C15 (in the sense: an article of clothing, a thing, used disparagingly): from ?]

dude (du:d, dju:d) *n Inf.* **1** *Western US & Canad.* a city dweller, esp. one holidaying on a ranch. **2** *US & Canad.* a dandy. **3** *US & Canad.* any person: often used to any male in direct address. [C19: from ?]
▸'**dudish** *adj* ▸'**dudishly** *adv*

dude ranch *n US & Canad.* a ranch used as a holiday resort.

dudgeon ⓣ ('dʌdʒən) *n* anger or resentment (arch., except in **in high dudgeon**). [C16: from ?]

due ⓣ (dju:) *adj* **1** (*postpositive*) immediately payable. **2** (*postpositive*) owed as a debt. **3** fitting; proper. **4** (*prenominal*) adequate or sufficient. **5** (*postpositive*) expected or appointed to be present or arrive. **6 due to.** attributable to or caused by. ◆ *n* **7** something that is owed, required, or due. **8 give (a person) his due.** to give or allow what is deserved or right. ◆ *adv* **9** directly or exactly. [C13: from OF *deu,* from *devoir* to owe, from L *debēre*]

> **USAGE NOTE** The use of *due to* as a compound preposition (*the performance has been cancelled due to bad weather*) was formerly considered incorrect, but is now acceptable.

duel ⓣ ('dju:əl) *n* **1** a formal prearranged combat with deadly weapons between two people in the presence of seconds, usually to settle a quarrel. **2** a contest or conflict between two persons or parties. ◆ *vb* **duels, duelling, duelled** *or US* **duels, dueling, dueled.** (*intr*) **3** to fight in a duel. **4** to contest closely. [C15: from Med. L *duellum,* from L, poetical var. of *bellum* war; associated with L *duo* two]
▸'**dueller,** '**duellist** *or US* '**dueler,** '**duelist** *n*

duenna (dju:'ɛnə) *n* (in Spain and Portugal, etc.) an elderly woman retained by a family to act as governess and chaperon to girls. [C17: from Sp. *dueña,* from L *domina* lady]

due process of law *n* the administration of justice in accordance with established rules and principles.

dues ⓣ (dju:z) *pl n* (*sometimes sing*) charges, as for membership of a club or organization; fees.

THESAURUS

dub[1] *vb* **1** = **knight,** bestow, confer, confer knighthood upon, entitle **2** = **name,** call, christen, denominate, designate, label, nickname, style, term

dubiety *n* **1, 2** = **doubtfulness,** doubt, dubiosity, incertitude, indecision, misgiving, mistrust, qualm, scepticism, uncertainty

dubious *adj* **1** = **doubtful,** ambiguous, debatable, dodgy (*Brit., Austral., & NZ inf.*), equivocal **2** = **unsure,** doubtful, hesitant, iffy (*inf.*), leery, sceptical, uncertain, unconvinced, undecided, wavering **3** = **suspect,** dodgy (*Brit., Austral., & NZ inf.*), fishy (*inf.*), questionable, shady (*inf.*), suspicious, undependable, unreliable, untrustworthy
Antonyms *adj* ≠ **unsure:** certain, definite, positive, sure ≠ **suspect:** dependable, reliable, trustworthy

duck[2] *vb* **1** = **bob,** bend, bow, crouch, dodge, drop, lower, stoop **2** = **plunge,** dip, dive, douse, dunk, immerse, souse, submerge, wet **3** *Informal* = **dodge,** avoid, body-swerve (*Scot.*), escape, evade, shirk, shun, sidestep

duct *n* **1** = **pipe,** canal, channel, conduit, funnel, passage, tube

ductile *adj* **1, 2** = **pliable,** extensible, flexible, malleable, plastic, pliant, tensile **3** = **docile,** amenable, biddable, compliant, manageable, tractable, yielding

dud *Informal* ◆ *n* **1** = **failure,** clinker (*sl., chiefly US*), flop (*inf.*), washout (*inf.*) ◆ *adj* **4** = **useless,** broken, bust (*inf.*), duff (*Brit. inf.*), failed, inoperative, kaput (*inf.*), not functioning, valueless, worthless

dudgeon *n* **in high dudgeon** = **indignant,** angry, choked, fuming, offended, resentful, vexed

due *adj* **1, 2** = **payable,** in arrears, outstanding, owed, owing, unpaid **3** = **fitting,** appropriate, becoming, bounden, deserved, fit, just, justified, merited, obligatory, proper, requisite, right, rightful, suitable, well-earned **5** = **expected,** expected to arrive, scheduled ◆ *n* **7** = **right(s),** comeuppance, deserts, merits, prerogative, privilege ◆ *adv* **9** = **directly,** dead, direct, exactly, straight, undeviatingly

duel *n* **1** = **single combat,** affair of honour **2** = **contest,** clash, competition, encounter, engagement, fight, head-to-head, rivalry ◆ *vb* **3, 4** = **fight,** clash, compete, contend, contest, lock horns, rival, struggle, vie with

dues *pl n* = **membership fee,** charge, charges, contribution, fee, levy

duet (djuːˈɛt) *n* **1** a musical composition for two performers or voices. **2** a pair of closely connected individuals; duo. [C18: from It. *duetto* a little duet, from *duo* duet, from L: two]
▸**duˈettist** *n*

duff[1] (dʌf) *n* **1** a thick flour pudding boiled in a cloth bag. **2 up the duff.** *Sl.* pregnant. [C19: N English var. of DOUGH]

duff[2] Ⓣ (dʌf) *vb* (*tr*) **1** *Sl.* to give a false appearance to (old or stolen goods); fake. **2** (foll. by *up*) *Brit. sl.* to beat (a person) severely. **3** *Austral. sl.* to steal (cattle), altering the brand. **4** *Golf. inf.* to bungle a shot by hitting the ground behind the ball. ◆ *adj* **5** *Brit., Austral., & NZ inf.* bad or useless. [C19: prob. back formation from DUFFER]

duffel *or* **duffle** (ˈdʌfˀl) *n* **1** a heavy woollen cloth. **2** *Chiefly US & Canad.* equipment or supplies. [C17: after *Duffel*, Belgian town]

duffel bag *n* a cylindrical drawstring canvas bag, originally used esp. by sailors for carrying personal articles.

duffel coat *n* a usually knee-length wool coat, usually with a hood and fastened with toggles.

duffer Ⓣ (ˈdʌfə) *n* **1** *Inf.* a dull or incompetent person. **2** *Sl.* something worthless. **3** *Austral. sl.* **3a** an unproductive mine. **3b** a person who steals cattle. [C19: from ?]

dug[1] (dʌg) *vb* the past tense and past participle of **dig.**

dug[2] (dʌg) *n* a nipple, teat, udder, or breast. [C16: of Scand. origin]

dugong (ˈduːgɒŋ) *n* a whalelike mammal occurring in shallow tropical waters from E Africa to Australia. [C19: from Malay *duyong*]

dugout (ˈdʌgˌaʊt) *n* **1** a canoe made by hollowing out a log. **2** *Mil.* a covered excavation dug to provide shelter. **3** (at a sports ground) the covered bench where managers, substitutes, etc., sit. **4** (in the Canadian prairies) a reservoir dug on a farm in which water from rain and snow is collected for use in irrigation, watering livestock, etc.

duiker *or* **duyker** (ˈdaɪkə) *n, pl* **duikers, duiker** *or* **duykers, duyker. 1** Also: **duikerbok.** any of various small African antelopes. **2** *S. African.* any of several cormorants, esp. the long-tailed shag. [C18: via Afrik., from Du. *duiker* diver, from *duiken* to dive]

duke (djuːk) *n* **1** a nobleman of high rank: in the British Isles standing above the other grades of the nobility. **2** the prince or ruler of a small principality or duchy. [C12: from OF *duc*, from L *dux* leader]
▸ˈ**dukedom** *n*

dukes (djuːks) *pl n Sl.* the fists. [C19: from *Duke of Yorks* rhyming sl. for *forks* (fingers)]

dulcet Ⓣ (ˈdʌlsɪt) *adj* (of a sound) soothing or pleasant; sweet. [C14: from L *dulcis* sweet]

dulcimer (ˈdʌlsɪmə) *n* **1** a tuned percussion instrument consisting of a set of strings stretched over a sounding board and struck with hammers. **2** an instrument used in US folk music, with an elliptical body and usually three strings plucked with a goose quill. [C15: from OF *doulcemer*, from OIt. *dolcimelo*, from *dolce* (from L *dulcis* sweet) + *-melo*, ?from Gk *melos* song]

dull Ⓣ (dʌl) *adj* **1** slow to think or understand; stupid. **2** lacking in interest. **3** lacking in perception; insensitive. **4** lacking sharpness. **5** not acute, intense, or piercing. **6** (of weather) not bright or clear. **7** not active, busy, or brisk. **8** lacking in spirit; listless. **9** (of colour) lacking brilliance; sombre. **10** not loud or clear; muffled. ◆ *vb* **11** to make or become dull. [OE *dol*]
▸ˈ**dullish** *adj* ▸ˈ**dullness** *or* ˈ**dulness** *n* ▸ˈ**dully** *adv*

dullard Ⓣ (ˈdʌləd) *n* a dull or stupid person.

dulse (dʌls) *n* any of several seaweeds that occur on rocks and have large red edible fronds. [C17: from OIrish *duilesc* seaweed]

duly Ⓣ (ˈdjuːlɪ) *adv* **1** in a proper manner. **2** at the proper time. [C14: see DUE, -LY[2]]

duma *Russian.* (ˈduːmə) *n Russian history.* **1** (*usually cap.*) the elective legislative assembly established by Tsar Nicholas II in 1905: overthrown in 1917. **2** (before 1917) any official assembly or council. **3** short for **State Duma**, the lower chamber of the Russian parliament. [C20: from *duma* thought, of Gmc origin]

dumb Ⓣ (dʌm) *adj* **1** lacking the power to speak; mute. **2** lacking the power of human speech: *dumb animals.* **3** temporarily bereft of the power to speak: *struck dumb.* **4** refraining from speech; uncommunicative. **5** producing no sound: *a dumb piano.* **6** made, done, or performed without speech. **7** *Inf.* **7a** dim-witted. **7b** foolish. ◆ See also **dumb down.** [OE]
▸ˈ**dumbly** *adv* ▸ˈ**dumbness** *n*

dumbbell (ˈdʌmˌbel) *n* **1** an exercising weight consisting of a short bar with a heavy ball or disc at either end, used for single-arm movements. **2** a small wooden or rubber object of a similar shape used to train dogs in retrieval. **3** *Sl., chiefly US & Canad.* a fool.

dumb down *vb* (*tr*) to make less intellectually demanding or sophisticated: *the alleged dumbing down of BBC radio.*

dumbfound Ⓣ *or* **dumfound** (dʌmˈfaʊnd) *vb* (*tr*) to strike dumb with astonishment; amaze. [C17: from DUMB + (CON)FOUND]

dumb show *n* **1** formerly, a part of a play acted in pantomime. **2** meaningful gestures.

dumbstruck (ˈdʌmˌstrʌk) *adj* temporarily deprived of speech through shock or surprise.

dumbwaiter (ˈdʌmˌweɪtə) *n* **1** *Brit.* **1a** a stand placed near a dining table to hold food. **1b** a revolving circular tray placed on a table to hold food. US and Canad. name: **lazy Susan. 2** a lift for carrying food, rubbish, etc., between floors.

dumdum (ˈdʌmˌdʌm) *n* a soft-nosed bullet that expands on impact and inflicts extensive laceration. [C19: after *Dum-Dum*, town near Calcutta where orig. made]

dummy Ⓣ (ˈdʌmɪ) *n, pl* **dummies. 1** a figure representing the human form, used for displaying clothes, as a target, etc. **2a** a copy of an object, often lacking some essential feature of the original. **2b** (*as modifier*): *a dummy drawer.* **3** *Sl.* a stupid person. **4** *Derog., sl.* a person without the power of speech. **5** *Inf.* a person who says or does nothing. **6a** a person who appears to act for himself while acting on behalf of another. **6b** (*as modifier*): *a dummy buyer.* **7** *Mil.* a weighted round without explosives. **8** *Bridge.* **8a** the hand exposed on the table by the declarer's partner and played by the declarer. **8b** the declarer's partner. **9a** a prototype of a book, indicating the appearance of the finished product. **9b** a designer's layout of a page. **10** *Sport.* a feigned pass or move. **11** *Brit.* a rubber teat for babies to suck or bite on. US and Canad. equivalent: **pacifier. 12** (*modifier*) counterfeit; sham. **13** (*modifier*) (of a card game) played with one hand exposed or unplayed. **14 sell (someone) a dummy.** *Sport.* to trick (an opponent) with a dummy pass. [C16: see DUMB, -Y[3]]

dummy run Ⓣ *n* an experimental run; practice; rehearsal.

dump Ⓣ (dʌmp) *vb* **1** to drop, fall, or let fall heavily or in a mass. **2** (*tr*) to empty (objects or material) out of a container. **3** to unload or empty (a container), as by overturning. **4** (*tr*) **4a** *Inf.* to dispose of without subtlety or proper care. **4b** to dispose of (nuclear waste). **5** *Commerce.* to market (goods) in bulk and at low prices, esp. abroad, in

THESAURUS

duff[2] *adj* **5** *Brit., Austral., & NZ informal* = **useless**, bad, counterfeit, dud (*inf.*), fake, false, not working, worthless

duffer *n* **1** *Informal* = **clot** (*Brit. inf.*), blunderer, booby, bungler, clod, galoot (*sl., chiefly US*), lubber, lummox (*inf.*), oaf

dulcet *adj* = **sweet**, agreeable, charming, delightful, euphonious, harmonious, honeyed, mellifluent, mellifluous, melodious, musical, pleasant, pleasing, soothing

dull *adj* **1** = **stupid**, braindead (*inf.*), daft, dense, dim, dim-witted (*inf.*), doltish, dozy (*Brit. inf.*), obtuse, slow, stolid, thick, unintelligent **2** = **boring**, as dry as dust, commonplace, dozy, dreary, dry, flat, ho-hum (*inf.*), humdrum, mind-numbing, monotonous, plain, prosaic, run-of-the-mill, tedious, tiresome, unimaginative, uninteresting, vapid **4, 5** = **blunt**, blunted, dulled, edgeless, not keen, not sharp, unsharpened **6** = **cloudy**, dim, dismal, gloomy, leaden, opaque, overcast, turbid **8** = **lifeless**, apathetic, blank, callous, dead, empty, heavy, indifferent, insensible, insensitive, listless, passionless, slow, sluggish, unresponsive, unsympathetic, vacuous **9** = **drab**, faded, feeble, murky, muted, sombre, subdued, subfusc, toned-down ◆ *vb* **11** = **dampen**, deject, depress, discourage, dishearten, dispirit, sadden **11** = **relieve**, allay, alleviate, assuage, blunt, lessen, mitigate, moderate, palliate, paralyse, soften, stupefy, take the edge off **11** = **cloud**, darken, dim, fade, obscure, stain, sully, tarnish
Antonyms *adj* ≠ **stupid:** bright, clever, intelligent, sharp ≠ **boring:** exciting, interesting ≠ **blunt:** sharp ≠ **cloudy:** bright ≠ **lifeless:** active, full of beans (*inf.*), lively

dullard *n Old-fashioned* = **dolt**, blockhead, clod, dimwit (*inf.*), dope (*inf.*), dunce, fathead (*inf.*), gobshite (*Irish taboo sl.*), lamebrain (*inf.*), nitwit (*inf.*), numbskull *or* numskull, oaf

dullness *n* **1** = **stupidity**, dimness, dim-wittedness, dopiness (*sl.*), doziness, obtuseness, slowness, thickness **2** = **tediousness**, banality, dreariness, flatness, insipidity, monotony, vapidity **9** = **drabness**, colourlessness, dimness, dinginess, gloominess, greyness
Antonyms *n* ≠ **stupidity:** brightness, cleverness, intelligence, quickness, sharpness, smartness ≠ **tediousness:** colour, interest, liveliness ≠ **drabness:** brightness, brilliance, effulgence, incandescence, shine, sparkle

duly *adv* **1** = **properly**, accordingly, appropriately, befittingly, correctly, decorously, deservedly, fittingly, rightfully, suitably **2** = **on time**, at the proper time, punctually

dumb *adj* **1** = **mute**, at a loss for words, inarticulate, mum, silent, soundless, speechless, tongue-tied, voiceless, wordless **7** *Informal* = **stupid**, asinine, braindead (*inf.*), dense, dim-witted (*inf.*), dozy (*Brit. inf.*), dull, foolish, obtuse, thick, unintelligent
Antonyms *adj* ≠ **mute:** articulate ≠ **stupid:** bright, clever, intelligent, quick-witted, smart

dumbfound *vb* = **amaze**, astonish, astound, bewilder, bowl over (*inf.*), confound, confuse, flabbergast (*inf.*), flummox, nonplus, overwhelm, stagger, startle, stun, take aback

dumbfounded *adj* = **amazed**, astonished, astounded, at sea, bewildered, bowled over (*inf.*), breathless, confounded, confused, dumb, flabbergasted (*inf.*), flummoxed, gob- smacked (*Brit. sl.*), knocked for six (*inf.*), knocked sideways (*inf.*), lost for words, nonplussed, overcome, overwhelmed, speechless, staggered, startled, stunned, taken aback, thrown, thunderstruck

dummy *n* **1** = **model**, figure, form, lay figure, manikin, mannequin **2a** = **copy**, counterfeit, duplicate, imitation, sham, substitute **3** *Slang* = **fool**, berk, blockhead, charlie (*Brit. inf.*), coot, dickhead (*sl.*), dimwit (*inf.*), dipstick (*Brit. sl.*), divvy (*Brit. sl.*), dolt, dork (*sl.*), dullard, dumb-ass (*sl.*), dunce, fathead (*inf.*), geek (*sl.*), gobshite (*Irish taboo sl.*), idiot, jerk (*sl., chiefly US & Canad.*), lamebrain (*inf.*), nerd *or* nurd (*sl.*), nitwit (*inf.*), numbskull *or* numskull, oaf, pillock (*Brit. sl.*), plank (*Brit. sl.*), plonker (*sl.*), prat (*sl.*), prick (*sl.*), schmuck (*US sl.*), simpleton, wally (*sl.*), weenie (*US inf.*) ◆ *modifier* **12** = **imitation**, artificial, bogus, fake, false, mock, phoney *or* phony (*inf.*), sham, simulated

dummy run *n* = **practice**, mock, simulated, trial

dump *vb* **1** = **drop**, deposit, fling down, let fall, throw down **2–4** = **get rid of**, coup (*Scot.*), discharge, dispose of, ditch (*sl.*), empty out, jettison, scrap, throw away *or* out, tip, unload ◆ *n* **11** = **rubbish tip**, junkyard, refuse heap, rubbish order to maintain a high price in the home market and obtain a share of the foreign markets. **6** (*tr*) to store (supplies, etc.) temporarily. **7** (*intr*) *Sl., chiefly US.* to defecate. **8** (*tr*) *Surfing.* (of a wave) to hurl a swimmer or surfer down. **9** (*tr*) *Austral. & NZ.* to compact (bales of wool) by hydraulic pressure. **10** (*tr*) *Computing.* to record (the contents of the memory) on a storage device at a series of points during a computer run. ◆ *n* **11** a place or area where waste materials are dumped. **12** a pile or accumulation of rubbish. **13** the act of dumping. **14** *Inf.* a dirty or unkempt place. **15** *Mil.* a place where weapons, supplies, etc., are stored. **16** *Sl., chiefly US.* an act of defecation. [C14: prob. from ON]

dumper (ˈdʌmpə) *n* **1** a person or thing that dumps. **2** *Surfing.* a wave that hurls a swimmer or surfer down.

dumpling (ˈdʌmplɪŋ) *n* **1** a small ball of dough cooked and served with stew. **2** a pudding consisting of a round pastry case filled with fruit: *apple dumpling.* **3** *Inf.* a short plump person. [C16: *dump-,* ? var. of LUMP[1] + -LING[1]]

dumps Ⓣ (dʌmps) *pl n Inf.* a state of melancholy or depression (esp. in **down in the dumps**). [C16: prob. from MDu. *domp* haze]

dump truck *or* **dumper-truck** *n* a small truck used on building sites, having a load-bearing container at the front that can be tipped up to dump the contents.

dumpy Ⓣ (ˈdʌmpɪ) *adj* **dumpier, dumpiest.** short and plump; squat. [C18: ? rel. to DUMPLING]
▸ˈ**dumpily** *adv* ▸ˈ**dumpiness** *n*

dun[1] Ⓣ (dʌn) *vb* **duns, dunning, dunned. 1** (*tr*) to press (a debtor) for payment. ◆ *n* **2** a person, esp. a hired agent, who importunes another for the payment of a debt. **3** a demand for payment. [C17: from ?]

dun[2] (dʌn) *n* **1** a brownish-grey colour. **2** a horse of this colour. **3** *Angling.* **3a** an immature adult mayfly. **3b** an artificial fly resembling this. ◆ *adj* **dunner, dunnest. 4** of a dun colour. **5** gloomy. [OE *dunn*]

dunce Ⓣ (dʌns) *n* a person who is stupid or slow to learn. [C16: from *Dunses* or *Dunsmen,* term of ridicule applied to the followers of John *Duns Scotus* (?1265–1308), Scot. scholastic theologian, esp. by 16th-cent. humanists]

dunce cap *or* **dunce's cap** *n* a conical paper hat, formerly placed on the head of a dull child at school.

Dundee cake (dʌnˈdiː) *n Chiefly Brit.* a fairly rich fruit cake decorated with almonds. [after *Dundee,* a port in E Scotland]

dunderhead (ˈdʌndəˌhɛd) *n* a slow-witted person. [C17: prob. from Du. *donder* thunder + HEAD]
▸ˈ**dunderˌheaded** *adj*

dune (djuːn) *n* a mound or ridge of drifted sand. [C18: via OF from MDu. *dūne*]

dung (dʌŋ) *n* **1** excrement, esp. of animals; manure. **2** something filthy. ◆ *vb* **3** (*tr*) to cover with manure. [OE: prison; rel. to OHG *tunc* cellar roofed with dung, ON *dyngja* manure heap]

dungaree (ˌdʌŋgəˈriː) *n* **1** a coarse cotton fabric used chiefly for work clothes, etc. **2** (*pl*) **2a** a suit of workman's overalls made of this material, consisting of trousers with a bib attached. **2b** a casual garment resembling this, usually worn by women or children. **3** (*pl*) *US.* jeans. [C17: from Hindi, after *Dungrī,* district of Bombay, where this fabric originated]

dungeon Ⓣ (ˈdʌndʒən) *n* **1** a prison cell, often underground. **2** a variant spelling of **donjon.** [C14: from OF *donjon*]

dunghill (ˈdʌŋˌhɪl) *n* **1** a heap of dung. **2** a foul place, condition, or person.

dunk (dʌŋk) *vb* **1** to dip (bread, etc.) in tea, soup, etc., before eating. **2** to submerge or be submerged. [C20: from Pennsylvania Du., from MHG *dunken,* from OHG *dunkōn*]
▸ˈ**dunker** *n*

dunlin (ˈdʌnlɪn) *n* a small sandpiper of northern and arctic regions, having a brown back and black breast in summer. [C16: DUN[2] + -LING[1]]

dunnage (ˈdʌnɪdʒ) *n* loose material used for packing cargo. [C14: from ?]

dunno (dʌˈnəʊ, də-) *Sl. contraction of* (I) do not know.

dunnock (ˈdʌnək) *n* another name for a **hedge sparrow.** [C15: from DUN[2] + -OCK]

dunny (ˈdʌnɪ) *n, pl* **dunnies. 1** *Scot. dialect.* a cellar or basement. **2** *Austral. & NZ inf.* a lavatory, esp. one which is outside. [C20: from ?]

duo (ˈdjuːəʊ) *n, pl* **duos** *or* **dui** (ˈdjuːiː). **1** *Music.* **1a** a pair of performers. **1b** a duet. **2** a pair of actors, etc. **3** *Inf.* a pair of closely connected individuals. [C16: via It. from L: two]

duo- *combining form.* indicating two. [from L]

duodecimal (ˌdjuːəʊˈdɛsɪməl) *adj* **1** relating to twelve or twelfths. ◆ *n* **2** a twelfth. **3** one of the numbers in a duodecimal number system.
▸ˌ**duoˈdecimally** *adv*

duodecimo (ˌdjuːəʊˈdɛsɪˌməʊ) *n, pl* **duodecimos. 1** Also called: **twelvemo.** a book size resulting from folding a sheet of paper into twelve leaves. **2** a book of this size. [C17: from L *in duodecimō* in twelfth]

duodenum (ˌdjuːəʊˈdiːnəm) *n, pl* **duodena** (-nə) *or* **duodenums.** the first part of the small intestine, between the stomach and the jejunum. [C14: from Med. L, from *intestinum duodenum digitorum* intestine of twelve fingers' length]
▸ˌ**duoˈdenal** *adj*

duologue *or US* (*sometimes*) **duolog** (ˈdjuːəˌlɒg) *n* **1** a part or all of a play in which the speaking roles are limited to two actors. **2** a less common word for **dialogue.**

duopoly (djʊˈɒpəlɪ) *n, pl* **duopolies.** a situation in which control of a commodity or service in a particular market is vested in two producers or suppliers.
▸**duˌopoˈlistic** *adj*

dup. *abbrev. for* duplicate.

dupe Ⓣ (djuːp) *n* **1** a person who is easily deceived. ◆ *vb* **dupes, duping, duped. 2** (*tr*) to deceive; cheat; fool. [C17: from F, from OF *duppe,* contraction of *de huppe* of (a) hoopoe; from the bird's reputation for stupidity]
▸ˈ**dupable** *adj* ▸ˈ**duper** *n* ▸ˈ**dupery** *n*

duple (ˈdjuːpᵊl) *adj* **1** a less common word for **double. 2** *Music.* (of time or music) having two beats in a bar. [C16: from L *duplus* twofold]

duplex (ˈdjuːplɛks) *n* **1** *US & Canad.* a duplex apartment or house. **2** *Biochem.* a double-stranded region in a nucleic acid molecule. ◆ *adj* **3** having two parts. **4** having pairs of components of independent but identical function. **5** permitting the transmission of simultaneous signals in both directions. [C19: from L: twofold, from *duo* two + *-plex* -FOLD]
▸**duˈplexity** *n*

duplex apartment *n US & Canad.* an apartment on two floors.

duplex house *n US & Canad.* a house divided into two separate dwellings. Also called (US): **semidetached.**

duplicate Ⓣ *adj* (ˈdjuːplɪkɪt). **1** copied exactly from an original. **2** identical. **3** existing as a pair or in pairs. ◆ *n* (ˈdjuːplɪkɪt). **4** an exact copy. **5** something extra of the same kind. **6** two exact copies (esp. in **in duplicate**). ◆ *vb* (ˈdjuːplɪˌkeɪt), **duplicates, duplicating, duplicated.** (*tr*) **7** to make a replica of. **8** to do or make again. **9** to make in a pair; make double. [C15: from L *duplicāre* to double, from *duo* two + *plicāre* to fold]
▸ˈ**duplicable** *adj*

duplication (ˌdjuːplɪˈkeɪʃən) *n* **1** the act of duplicating or the state of being duplicated. **2** a copy; duplicate. **3** *Genetics.* a mutation in which there are two or more copies of a gene or of a segment of a chromosome.

duplicator (ˈdjuːplɪˌkeɪtə) *n* an apparatus for making replicas of an original, such as a machine using a stencil wrapped on an ink-loaded drum.

duplicity Ⓣ (djuːˈplɪsɪtɪ) *n, pl* **duplicities.** deception; double-dealing. [C15: from OF *duplicite,* from LL *duplicitās* a being double, from L DUPLEX]

durable Ⓣ (ˈdjʊərəbᵊl) *adj* long-lasting; enduring. [C14: from OF, from L *dūrābilis,* from *dūrāre* to last]
▸ˌ**duraˈbility** *n* ▸ˈ**durably** *adv*

durable goods *pl n* goods that require infrequent replacement. Also called: **durables.**

dural (ˈdjʊərəl) *adj* relating to or affecting the dura mater.

Duralumin (djʊˈræljʊmɪn) *n Trademark.* a light strong aluminium alloy containing copper, silicon, magnesium, and manganese.

dura mater (ˈdjʊərə ˈmeɪtə) *n* the outermost and toughest of the three membranes covering the brain and spinal cord. Often shortened to **dura.** [C15: from Med. L: hard mother]

duramen (djʊˈreɪmɛn) *n* another name for **heartwood.** [C19: from L: hardness, from *dūrāre* to harden]

THESAURUS

heap, tip **14** *Informal* = **pigsty**, hole (*inf.*), hovel, joint, mess, shack, shanty, slum

dumps *pl n As in* **down in the dumps** = **low spirits**, blues, dejection, depression, despondency, dolour, gloom, gloominess, melancholy, mopes, sadness, the hump (*Brit. inf.*), unhappiness, woe

dumpy *adj* = **podgy**, chubby, chunky, fubsy (*arch. or dialect*), homely, plump, pudgy, roly-poly, short, squab, squat, stout, tubby

dun[1] *vb* **1** = **pester**, beset, importune, plague, press, urge

dunce *n* = **simpleton**, ass, blockhead, bonehead, dimwit (*inf.*), dolt, donkey, duffer (*inf.*), dullard, dunderhead, fathead (*inf.*), goose (*inf.*), halfwit, ignoramus, lamebrain (*inf.*), loon (*inf.*), moron, nincompoop, nitwit (*inf.*), numbskull *or* numskull, oaf, thickhead

dungeon *n* **1** = **prison**, cage, calaboose (*US. inf.*), cell, donjon, lockup, oubliette, vault

dupe *n* **1** = **victim**, fall guy (*inf.*), gull, mug (*Brit. sl.*), pigeon (*sl.*), pushover, sap (*sl.*), simpleton, sucker (*sl.*) ◆ *vb* **2** = **deceive**, bamboozle (*inf.*), beguile, cheat, con (*inf.*), cozen, defraud, delude, gull (*arch.*), hoax, hoodwink, humbug, kid (*inf.*), outwit, overreach, pull a fast one on (*inf.*), rip off (*sl.*), swindle, take for a ride (*inf.*), trick

duplicate *adj* **1-3** = **identical**, corresponding, matched, matching, twin, twofold ◆ *n* **4, 5** = **copy**, carbon copy, clone, dead ringer (*sl.*), double, facsimile, fax, likeness, lookalike, match, mate, photocopy, Photostat (*Trademark*), replica, reproduction, ringer (*sl.*), twin, Xerox (*Trademark*) ◆ *vb* **7-9** = **copy**, clone, double, echo, fax, photocopy, Photostat (*Trademark*), reinvent the wheel, repeat, replicate, reproduce, Xerox (*Trademark*)

duplicity *n* = **deceit**, artifice, chicanery, deception, dishonesty, dissimulation, double-dealing, falsehood, fraud, guile, hypocrisy, perfidy
Antonyms *n* candour, honesty, straightforwardness

durability *n* = **durableness**, constancy, endurance, imperishability, lastingness, permanence, persistence

durable *adj* = **long-lasting**, abiding, constant, dependable, enduring, fast, firm, fixed, hard-wearing, lasting, permanent, persistent, reliable, resistant, sound, stable, strong, sturdy, substantial, tough
Antonyms *adj* breakable, brittle, delicate, fragile, impermanent, perishable, weak

durance ('djʊərəns) *n Arch. or literary.* **1** imprisonment. **2** duration. [C15: from OF, from *durer* to last, from L *dūrāre*]

duration ❶ (djʊ'reɪʃən) *n* the length of time that something lasts or continues. [C14: from Med. L *dūrātiō*, from L *dūrāre* to last]
▸**du'rational** *adj*

durative ('djʊərətɪv) *Grammar.* ◆ *adj* **1** denoting an aspect of verbs that includes the imperfective and the progressive. ◆ *n* **2a** the durative aspect of a verb. **2b** a verb in this aspect.

durbar ('dɜːbɑː, ˌdɜː'bɑː) *n* **a** (formerly) the court of a native ruler or a governor in India. **b** a levee at such a court. [C17: from Hindi *darbār*, from Persian, from *dar* door + *bār* entry, audience]

duress ❶ (djʊ'rɛs, djʊə-) *n* **1** compulsion by use of force or threat; coercion (often in **under duress**). **2** imprisonment. [C14: from OF *duresse*, from L *dūritia* hardness, from *dūrus* hard]

Durga Puja (ˌdʊəgə 'puːdʒə) *n* another name for **Navaratri.** [from Sanskr. *Durga* (Hindu goddess) and *puja* worship]

during ('djʊərɪŋ) *prep* **1** concurrently with (some other activity). **2** within the limit of (a period of time). [C14: from *duren* to last, ult. from L *dūrare* to last]

durmast *or* **durmast oak** ('dɜːˌmɑːst) *n* a large Eurasian oak tree with lobed leaves and sessile acorns. Also called: **sessile oak.** [C18: prob. from DUN[2] + MAST[2]]

durra ('dʌrə) *n* an Old World variety of sorghum, cultivated for grain and fodder. [C18: from Ar. *dhurah* grain]

durry ('dʌrɪ) *n, pl* **durries.** *Austral. sl.* a cigarette. [from *durrie* a type of Indian carpet]

durst (dɜːst) *vb* an archaic past tense of **dare.**

durum *or* **durum wheat** ('djʊərəm) *n* a variety of wheat with a high gluten content, used chiefly to make pastas. [C20: from NL *trīticum dūrum*, lit.: hard wheat]

dusk ❶ (dʌsk) *n* **1** the darker part of twilight. **2** *Poetic.* gloom; shade. ◆ *adj* **3** *Poetic.* shady. ◆ *vb* **4** *Poetic.* to make or become dark. [OE *dox*]

dusky ❶ ('dʌskɪ) *adj* **duskier, duskiest. 1** dark in colour; swarthy or dark-skinned. **2** dim.
▸**'duskily** *adv* ▸**'duskiness** *n*

dust ❶ (dʌst) *n* **1** dry fine powdery material, such as particles of dirt, earth, or pollen. **2** a cloud of such fine particles. **3a** the mortal body of man. **3b** the corpse of a dead person. **4** the earth; ground. **5** *Inf.* a disturbance; fuss (esp. in **kick up a dust, raise a dust**). **6** something of little worth. **7** short for **gold dust. 8** ashes or household refuse. **9 dust and ashes.** something that is very disappointing. **10 shake the dust off** (*or* **from**) **one's feet.** to depart angrily or contemptuously. **11 throw dust in the eyes of.** to confuse or mislead. ◆ *vb* **12** (*tr*) to sprinkle or cover (something) with (dust or some other powdery substance). **13** to remove dust (from) by wiping, sweeping, or brushing. **14** *Arch.* to make or become dirty with dust. ◆ See also **dust down, dust-up.** [OE *dūst*]
▸**'dustless** *adj*

dustbin ('dʌstˌbɪn) *n* a large container for rubbish, esp. one used by a household. US and Canad. names: **garbage can, trash can.**

dust bowl *n* a semiarid area in which the surface soil is exposed to wind erosion.

dustcart ('dʌstˌkɑːt) *n* a road vehicle for collecting refuse. US and Canad. name: **garbage truck.**

dust cover *n* **1** another name for **dustsheet. 2** another name for **dust jacket. 3** a Perspex cover for the turntable of a record player.

dust devil *n* a strong miniature whirlwind that whips up dust, litter, leaves, etc., into the air.

dust down *vb* (*tr, adv*). **1** to remove dust from by brushing or wiping. **2** to reprimand severely.
▸**dusting down** *n*

duster ('dʌstə) *n* **1** a cloth used for dusting. US name: **dust cloth. 2** a machine for blowing out dust. **3** a person or thing that dusts.

dusting-powder *n* fine powder (such as talcum powder) used to absorb moisture, etc.

dust jacket *or* **cover** *n* a removable paper cover used to protect a bound book.

dustman ('dʌstmən) *n, pl* **dustmen.** *Brit.* a man whose job is to collect domestic refuse.

dustpan ('dʌstˌpæn) *n* a short-handled hooded shovel into which dust is swept from floors, etc.

dustsheet ('dʌstˌʃiːt) *n Brit.* a large cloth to protect furniture from dust.

dust storm *n* a windstorm that whips up clouds of dust.

dust-up ❶ *Inf.* ◆ *n* **1** a fight or argument. ◆ *vb* **dust up. 2** (*tr, adv*) to attack (someone).

dusty ❶ ('dʌstɪ) *adj* **dustier, dustiest. 1** covered with or involving dust. **2** like dust. **3** (of a colour) tinged with grey; pale. **4 give** (*or* **get**) **a dusty answer.** to give (*or* get) an unhelpful or bad-tempered reply.
▸**'dustily** *adv* ▸**'dustiness** *n*

Dutch (dʌtʃ) *n* **1** the language of the Netherlands. **2 the Dutch.** (*functioning as pl*) the natives, citizens, or inhabitants of the Netherlands. **3** See **double Dutch. 4 in Dutch.** *Sl.* in trouble. ◆ *adj* **5** of the Netherlands, its inhabitants, or their language. ◆ *adv* **6 go Dutch.** *Inf.* to share expenses equally.

Dutch auction *n* an auction in which the price is lowered by stages until a buyer is found.

Dutch barn *n Brit.* a farm building consisting of a steel frame and a curved roof.

Dutch courage *n* **1** false courage gained from drinking alcohol. **2** alcoholic drink.

Dutch door *n* the US and Canad. name for **stable door.**

Dutch elm disease *n* a fungal disease of elm trees characterized by withering of the foliage and stems and eventual death of the tree.

Dutchman ('dʌtʃmən) *n, pl* **Dutchmen. 1** a native, citizen, or inhabitant of the Netherlands. **2** *S. African derog.* an Afrikaner.

Dutch medicine *n S. African.* patent medicine, esp. made of herbs.

Dutch oven *n* **1** an iron or earthenware container with a cover, used for stews, etc. **2** a metal box, open in front, for cooking in front of an open fire.

Dutch treat *n Inf.* an entertainment, meal, etc., where each person pays for himself.

Dutch uncle *n Inf.* a person who criticizes frankly and severely.

duteous ('djuːtɪəs) *adj Formal or arch.* dutiful; obedient.
▸**'duteously** *adv*

dutiable ('djuːtɪəbᵊl) *adj* (of goods) liable to duty.
▸ˌ**dutia'bility** *n*

dutiful ❶ ('djuːtɪfʊl) *adj* **1** exhibiting or having a sense of duty. **2** characterized by or resulting from a sense of duty: *a dutiful answer.*

duty ❶ ('djuːtɪ) *n, pl* **duties. 1** a task or action that a person is bound to perform for moral or legal reasons. **2** respect or obedience due to a superior, older persons, etc. **3** the force that binds one morally or legally to one's obligations. **4** a government tax, esp. on imports. **5** *Brit.* **5a** the quantity of work for which a machine is designed. **5b** a measure of the efficiency of a machine. **6a** a job or service allocated. **6b** (*as modifier*): *duty rota.* **7 do duty for.** to act as a substitute for. **8 on** (*or* **off**) **duty.** at (*or* not at) work. [C13: from Anglo-F *dueté*, from OF *deu* DUE]

duty-bound *adj* morally obliged.

duty-free *adj, adv* **1** with exemption from customs or excise duties. ◆ *n* **2** goods sold in a duty-free shop.

duty-free shop *n* a shop, esp. one at an airport or on board a ship, that sells perfume, tobacco, etc., at duty-free prices.

duumvir (djuː'ʌmvə) *n, pl* **duumvirs** *or* **duumviri** (-vɪˌriː). **1** *Roman history.* one of two coequal magistrates. **2** either of two men who exercise a joint authority. [C16: from L, from *duo* two + *vir* man]
▸**duumvirate** (djuː'ʌmvɪrɪt) *n*

duvet ('duːveɪ) *n* **1** another name for **continental quilt. 2** Also called: **duvet jacket.** a down-filled jacket. [C18: from F, from earlier *dumet*, from OF *dum* DOWN[2]]

dux (dʌks) *n* (esp. in Scottish schools) the top pupil in a class or school. [L: leader]

DV *abbrev. for:* **1** Deo volente. [L: God willing] **2** Douay Version (of the Bible).

DVD *abbrev. for* Digital Versatile Disk or (formerly) Digital Video Disk.

DVLA *abbrev. for* Driver and Vehicle Licensing Agency.

dwaal (dwɑːl) *n S. African.* a state of befuddlement; daze. [from Afrik. *dwaal* wander]

dwale (dweɪl) *n* another name for **deadly nightshade.** [C14: ?from ON]

dwarf ❶ (dwɔːf) *n, pl* **dwarfs** *or* **dwarves** (dwɔːvz). **1** an abnormally undersized person. **2a** an animal or plant much below the average height for the species. **2b** (*as modifier*): *a dwarf tree.* **3** (in folklore) a small ugly manlike creature, often possessing magical powers. **4** *Astron.* short for **dwarf star.** ◆ *vb* **5** to become or cause to become com-

THESAURUS

duration *n* = **length**, continuance, continuation, extent, period, perpetuation, prolongation, span, spell, stretch, term, time

duress *n* **1** = **pressure**, coercion, compulsion, constraint, threat **2** = **imprisonment**, captivity, confinement, constraint, hardship, incarceration, restraint

dusk *n* **1** = **twilight**, dark, evening, eventide, gloaming (*Scot. or poetic*), nightfall, sundown, sunset **2** *Poetic* = **shade**, darkness, gloom, murk, obscurity, shadowiness
Antonyms *n* ≠ **twilight:** aurora (*poetic*), cockcrow, dawn, dawning, daybreak, daylight, morning, sunlight, sunup

dusky *adj* **1** = **dark**, dark-complexioned, dark-hued, sable, swarthy **2** = **dim**, caliginous, cloudy, crepuscular, darkish, gloomy, murky, obscure, overcast, shadowy, shady, tenebrous, twilight, twilit, veiled

dust *n* **1, 2** = **grime**, dirt, earth, fine fragments, grit, ground, particles, powder, powdery dirt, soil **11 throw dust in the eyes of** = **mislead**, con (*sl.*), confuse, deceive, fool, have (someone) on, hoodwink, take in (*inf.*) ◆ *vb* **12** = **sprinkle**, cover, dredge, powder, scatter, sift, spray, spread

dust-up *n* **1** *Informal* = **fight**, argument, brush, conflict, encounter, fracas, punch-up (*Brit. inf.*), quarrel, scrap (*inf.*), set-to (*inf.*), shindig (*inf.*), skirmish, tussle

dusty *adj* **1** = **dirty**, grubby, sooty, unclean, undusted, unswept **2** = **powdery**, chalky, crumbly, friable, granular, sandy

dutiful *adj* **1** = **conscientious**, compliant, deferential, devoted, docile, duteous (*arch.*), filial, obedient, punctilious, respectful, reverential, submissive
Antonyms *adj* disobedient, disrespectful, insubordinate, remiss, uncaring

duty *n* **1** = **responsibility**, assignment, business, calling, charge, engagement, function, job, mission, obligation, office, onus, pigeon (*inf.*), province, role, service, task, work **2** = **loyalty**, allegiance, deference, obedience, respect, reverence **4** = **tax**, customs, due, excise, impost, levy, tariff, toll **8 off duty** = **off work**, at leisure, free, off, on holiday **8 on duty** = **at work**, busy, engaged, on active service

dwarf *n* **1** = **midget**, bantam, homunculus, hop-o'-my-thumb, Lilliputian, manikin, pygmy *or* pigmy, Tom Thumb **2b** *as modifier* = **miniature**, baby, bonsai, diminutive, dwarfed, Lilliputian, petite, pint-sized, pocket, small, teensy-

paratively small in size, importance, etc. **6** (*tr*) to stunt the growth of. [OE *dweorg*]
▸**'dwarfish** *adj*

dwarf star *n* any unevolved star, such as the sun, lying in the main sequence of the Hertzsprung-Russell diagram. Also called: **main sequence star.** See also **red dwarf, white dwarf.**

dwell Ⓣ (dwɛl) *vb* **dwells, dwelling, dwelt** *or* **dwelled.** (*intr*) **1** *Formal, literary.* to live as a permanent resident. **2** to live (in a specified state): *to dwell in poverty.* ◆ *n* **3** a regular pause in the operation of a machine. [OE *dwellan* to seduce, get lost]
▸**'dweller** *n*

dwelling Ⓣ ('dwɛlɪŋ) *n Formal, literary.* a place of residence.

dwell on Ⓣ *or* **upon** *vb* (*intr, prep*) to think, speak, or write at length about.

dwelt (dwelt) *vb* a past tense and past participle of **dwell.**

dwindle Ⓣ ('dwɪndᵊl) *vb* **dwindles, dwindling, dwindled.** to grow or cause to grow less in size, intensity, or number. [C16: from OE *dwīnan* to waste away]

Dy *the chemical symbol for* dysprosium.

dyad ('daɪæd) *n* **1** *Maths.* an operator that is the unspecified product of two vectors. **2** an atom or group that has a valency of two. **3** a group of two; couple. [C17: from LL *dyas,* from Gk *duas* two]
▸**dy'adic** *adj*

Dyak *or* **Dayak** ('daɪæk) *n, pl* **Dyaks, Dyak** *or* **Dayaks, Dayak.** a member of a Malaysian people of Borneo. [from Malay: upcountry, from *darat* land]

dybbuk ('dɪbək) *n, pl* **dybbuks** *or* **dybbukkim.** *Judaism.* (in folklore) the soul of a dead sinner that has transmigrated into the body of a living person. [from Yiddish: devil, from Heb.]

dye Ⓣ (daɪ) *n* **1** a staining or colouring substance. **2** a liquid that contains a colouring material and can be used to stain fabrics, skins, etc. **3** the colour produced by dyeing. ◆ *vb* **dyes, dyeing, dyed. 4** (*tr*) to impart a colour or stain to (fabric, hair, etc.) by or as if by the application of a dye. [OE *dēagian,* from *dēag* a dye]
▸**'dyable** *or* **'dyeable** *adj* ▸**'dyer** *n*

dyed-in-the-wool Ⓣ *adj* **1** uncompromising or unchanging in attitude, opinion, etc. **2** (of a fabric) made of dyed yarn.

dyeing ('daɪɪŋ) *n* the process or industry of colouring yarns, fabric, etc.

dyestuff ('daɪˌstʌf) *n* a substance that can be used as a dye or which yields a dye.

dying Ⓣ ('daɪɪŋ) *vb* **1** the present participle of **die**[1]. ◆ *adj* **2** relating to or occurring at the moment of death: *a dying wish.*

dyke[1] *or* **dike** (daɪk) *n* **1** an embankment constructed to prevent flooding, keep out the sea, or confine a river to a particular course. **2** a ditch or watercourse. **3** a bank made of earth alongside a ditch. **4** *Scot.* a wall, esp. a dry-stone wall. **5** a barrier or obstruction. **6** a wall-like mass of igneous rock in older sedimentary rock. **7** *Austral. & NZ inf.* a lavatory. ◆ *vb* **dykes, dyking, dyked. 8** (*tr*) to protect, enclose, or drain (land) with a dyke. [C13: from OE *dic* ditch]

dyke[2] *or* **dike** (daɪk) *n Sl.* a lesbian. [C20: from ?]

dynamic Ⓣ (daɪ'næmɪk) *adj* **1** of or concerned with energy or forces that produce motion, as opposed to *static.* **2** of or concerned with dynamics. **3** Also: **dynamical.** characterized by force of personality, ambition, energy, etc. **4** *Computing.* (of a memory) needing its contents refreshed periodically. [C19: from F *dynamique,* from Gk *dunamikos* powerful, from *dunamis* power, from *dunasthai* to be able]
▸**dy'namically** *adv*

dynamics (daɪ'næmɪks) *n* **1** (*functioning as sing*) the branch of mechanics concerned with the forces that change or produce the motions of bodies. **2** (*functioning as sing*) the branch of mechanics that includes statics and kinetics. **3** (*functioning as sing*) the branch of any science concerned with forces. **4** (*functioning as pl*) those forces that produce change in any field or system. **5** (*functioning as pl*) *Music.* **5a** the various degrees of loudness called for in performance. **5b** directions and symbols used to indicate degrees of loudness.

dynamism Ⓣ ('daɪnəˌmɪzəm) *n* **1** *Philosophy.* any of several theories that attempt to explain phenomena in terms of an immanent force or energy. **2** the forcefulness of an energetic personality.
▸**'dynamist** *n* ▸**ˌdyna'mistic** *adj*

dynamite ('daɪnəˌmaɪt) *n* **1** an explosive consisting of nitroglycerine mixed with an absorbent. **2** *Inf.* a spectacular or potentially dangerous person or thing. ◆ *vb* **dynamites, dynamiting, dynamited. 3** (*tr*) to blow up with dynamite. [C19 (coined by Alfred Nobel): from DYNAMO- + -ITE[1]]
▸**'dynaˌmiter** *n*

dynamo ('daɪnəˌməʊ) *n, pl* **dynamos. 1** a device for converting mechanical energy into electrical energy. **2** *Inf.* an energetic hard-working person. [C19: short for *dynamoelectric machine*]

dynamo- *or sometimes before a vowel* **dynam-** *combining form.* indicating power: *dynamite.* [from Gk, from *dunamis* power]

dynamoelectric (ˌdaɪnəməʊɪ'lɛktrɪk) *or* **dynamoelectrical** *adj* of or concerned with the interconversion of mechanical and electrical energy.

dynamometer (ˌdaɪnə'mɒmɪtə) *n* an instrument for measuring power or force.

dynamotor ('daɪnəˌməʊtə) *n* an electrical machine having two independent armature windings, one acting as a motor and the other a generator: used to convert direct current into alternating current.

dynast ('dɪnəst, -æst) *n* a ruler, esp. a hereditary one. [C17: from L *dynastēs,* from Gk, from *dunasthai* to be powerful]

dynasty Ⓣ ('dɪnəstɪ) *n, pl* **dynasties. 1** a sequence of hereditary rulers. **2** any sequence of powerful leaders of the same family. [C15: via LL from Gk, from *dunastēs* DYNAST]
▸**dynastic** (dɪ'næstɪk) *adj*

dyne (daɪn) *n* the cgs unit of force; the force that imparts an acceleration of 1 centimetre per second per second to a mass of 1 gram. 1 dyne is equivalent to 10^{-5} newton or 7.233×10^{-5} poundal. [C19: from F, from Gk *dunamis* power, force]

dys- *prefix* **1** diseased, abnormal, or faulty. **2** difficult or painful. **3** unfavourable or bad. [via L from Gk *dus-*]

dysentery ('dɪsᵊntrɪ) *n* infection of the intestine marked by severe diarrhoea with the passage of mucus and blood. [C14: via L from Gk, from *dusentera,* lit.: bad bowels, from DYS- + *enteron* intestine]
▸**dysenteric** (ˌdɪsᵊn'terɪk) *adj*

dysfunction (dɪs'fʌŋkʃən) *n* **1** *Med.* any disturbance or abnormality in the function of an organ or part. **2** (esp. of a family) failure to show the characteristics or fulfil the purposes held as normal or beneficial.

dysgraphia (dɪs'græfɪə) *n* inability to write correctly, caused by disease of part of the brain.

dyslexia (dɪs'lɛksɪə) *n* a developmental disorder which can cause learning difficulty in one or more of the areas of reading, writing, and numeracy. [C19: NL, from DYS- + *-lexia,* from Gk *lexis* word]
▸**dyslectic** (dɪs'lɛktɪk) *adj* ▸**dys'lexic** *adj, n*

dysmenorrhoea *or esp. US* **dysmenorrhea** (ˌdɪsmɛnə'rɪə) *n* abnormally difficult or painful menstruation. [C19: from DYS- + Gk *mēn* month + *rhoiā* a flowing]

dyspepsia (dɪs'pɛpsɪə) *n* indigestion or upset stomach. [C18: from L, from Gk *duspepsia,* from DYS- + *pepsis* digestion]

dyspeptic (dɪs'pɛptɪk) *adj* **1** relating to or suffering from dyspepsia. **2** irritable. ◆ *n* **3** a person suffering from dyspepsia.

dysphasia (dɪs'feɪzɪə) *n* a disorder of language caused by a brain lesion.
▸**dys'phasic** *adj, n*

dysphoria (dɪs'fɔːrɪə) *n* a feeling of being ill at ease. [C20: NL, from Gk DYS- + *-phoria,* from *pherein* to bear]

dyspnoea *or US* **dyspnea** (dɪsp'niːə) *n* difficulty in breathing or in catching the breath. [C17: via L from Gk *duspnoia,* from DYS- + *pnoē* breath, from *pnein* to breathe]
▸**dysp'noeal, dysp'noeic** *or US* **dysp'neal, dysp'neic** *adj*

dysprosium (dɪs'prəʊsɪəm) *n* a metallic element of the lanthanide series: used in laser materials and as a neutron absorber in nuclear control rods. Symbol: Dy; atomic no.: 66; atomic wt.: 162.50. [C20: NL, from Gk *dusprositos* difficult to get near + -IUM]

dysthymia (dɪs'θaɪmɪə) *n Psychiatry.* the characteristics of the neurotic and introverted, including anxiety, depression, and compulsive behaviour. [C19: NL, from Gk *dusthumia,* from DYS- + *thumos* mind]
▸**dys'thymic** *adj*

dysthymic disorder *n* a psychiatric disorder characterized by generalized depression that lasts for at least a year.

dystrophy ('dɪstrəfɪ) *n* any of various bodily disorders, characterized by wasting of tissues. See also **muscular dystrophy.** [C19: NL *dystrophia,* from DYS- + Gk *trophē* food]
▸**dystrophic** (dɪs'trɒfɪk) *adj*

dz. *abbrev. for* dozen.

dzo (zəʊ) *n, pl* **dzos** *or* **dzo.** a variant spelling of **zo.**

THESAURUS

weensy, teeny-weeny, tiny, undersized **3** = **gnome**, goblin ◆ *vb* **5** = **tower above** *or* **over**, dim, diminish, dominate, minimize, overshadow **6** = **stunt**, check, cultivate by bonsai, lower, retard

dwarfish *adj* **1, 2** = **undersized**, diminutive, dwarfed, knee high to a grasshopper (*inf.*), low, miniature, minute, pint-size (*inf.*), pygmaean, pygmy *or* pigmy, runtish, runty, short, small, stunted, teensy-weensy, teeny-weeny, tiny

dwell *vb* **1** *Formal, literary* = **live**, abide, establish oneself, hang out (*inf.*), inhabit, lodge, quarter, remain, reside, rest, settle, sojourn, stay, stop

dwelling *n Formal, literary* = **home**, abode, domicile, dwelling house, establishment, habitation, house, lodging, pad (*sl.*), quarters, residence

dwell on *vb* = **go on about** (*inf.*), be engrossed in, continue, elaborate, emphasize, expatiate, harp on, linger over, tarry over

dwindle *vb* = **lessen**, abate, contract, decay, decline, decrease, die away, die down, die out, diminish, ebb, fade, fall, grow less, peter out, pine, shrink, shrivel, sink, subside, taper off, wane, waste away, weaken, wither
Antonyms *vb* advance, amplify, develop, dilate, enlarge, escalate, expand, grow, heighten, increase, magnify, multiply, swell, wax

dye *n* **1, 2** = **colouring**, colorant, colour, pigment, stain, tinge, tint ◆ *vb* **4** = **colour**, pigment, stain, tincture, tinge, tint

dyed-in-the-wool *adj* **1** = **confirmed**, complete, deep-dyed (*usually derogatory*), deep-rooted, die-hard, entrenched, established, inveterate, through-and-through

dying *adj* **2** = **expiring**, at death's door, ebbing, fading, failing, final, going, *in extremis*, moribund, mortal, not long for this world, passing, perishing, sinking

dynamic *adj* **3** = **energetic**, active, alive and kicking, driving, electric, forceful, full of beans (*inf.*), go-ahead, go-getting (*inf.*), high-octane (*inf.*), high-powered, lively, magnetic, powerful, storming (*inf.*), vigorous, vital, zippy (*inf.*)
Antonyms *adj* apathetic, couldn't-care-less (*inf.*), impassive, inactive, listless, sluggish, torpid, undynamic, unenergetic

dynamism *n* **2** = **energy**, brio, drive, enterprise, forcefulness, get-up-and-go (*inf.*), go (*inf.*), initiative, liveliness, pep, push (*inf.*), vigour, zap (*sl.*), zip (*inf.*)

dynasty *n* **1, 2** = **lineage**, family, house, line

Ee

e *or* **E** (iː) *n, pl* **e's, E's,** *or* **Es. 1** the fifth letter and second vowel of the English alphabet. **2** any of several speech sounds represented by this letter, as in *he, bet,* or *below.*

e *symbol for:* **1** *Maths.* a transcendental number used as the base of natural logarithms. Approximate value: 2.718 282... **2** electron.

E *symbol for:* **1** *Music.* **1a** the third note of the scale of C major. **1b** the major or minor key having this note as its tonic. **2** earth. **3** East. **4** English. **5** Egypt(ian). **6** *Physics.* **6a** energy. **6b** electromotive force. **7** exa-. **8a** a person without a regular income, or who is dependent on the state on a long-term basis because of unemployment, sickness, old age, etc. **8b** (*as modifier*): *E worker.* ◆ See also **occupation groupings. 9** the drug ecstasy.

e. *abbrev. for* engineer(ing).

E. *abbrev. for* Earl.

e- *prefix* electronic: *e-mail; e-money.*

E- *prefix* used with numbers indicating a standardized system within the European Union, as of food additives. See also **E number.**

ea. *abbrev. for* each.

each Ⓣ (iːtʃ) *determiner* **1a** every (one) of two or more considered individually: *each day; each person.* **1b** (*as pron*): *each gave according to his ability.* ◆ *adv* **2** for, to, or from each one; apiece: *four apples each.* [OE *ǣlc*]

> **USAGE NOTE** *Each* is a singular pronoun and should be used with a singular form of a verb: *each of the candidates was* (not *were*) *interviewed separately.* See also at **either.**

eager Ⓣ ('iːɡə) *adj* **1** (*postpositive;* often foll. by *to* or *for*) impatiently desirous (of); anxious or avid (for). **2** characterized by or feeling expectancy or great desire: *an eager look.* **3** *Arch.* biting; sharp. [C13: from OF *egre,* from L *acer* sharp, keen]
▸'**eagerly** *adv* ▸'**eagerness** *n*

eager beaver *n Inf.* a person who displays conspicuous diligence.

eagle ('iːɡᵊl) *n* **1** any of various birds of prey having large broad wings and strong soaring flight. Related adj: **aquiline. 2** a representation of an eagle used as an emblem, etc., esp. representing power: *the Roman eagle.* **3** a standard, seal, etc., bearing the figure of an eagle. **4** *Golf.* a score of two strokes under par for a hole. **5** a former US gold coin worth ten dollars. ◆ *vb* **6** *Golf.* to score two strokes under par for a hole. [C14: from OF *aigle,* from OProvençal *aigla,* from L *aquila*]

eagle-eyed *adj* having keen or piercing eyesight.

eagle-hawk *n* a large brown Australian eagle. Also called: **wedge-tailed eagle.**

eagle owl *n* a large Eurasian owl with brownish speckled plumage and large ear tufts.

eaglet ('iːɡlɪt) *n* a young eagle.

ealdorman ('ɔːldəmən) *n, pl* **ealdormen.** an official of Anglo-Saxon England, appointed by the king, and responsible for law and order in his shire and for leading local militia. [OE *ealdor* lord + MAN]

-ean *suffix forming adjectives and nouns.* a variant of **-an:** *Caesarean.*

ear[1] Ⓣ (ɪə) *n* **1** the organ of hearing and balance in higher vertebrates (see **middle ear**). Related adj: **aural. 2** the outermost cartilaginous part of the ear in mammals, esp. man. **3** the sense of hearing. **4** sensitivity to musical sounds, poetic diction, etc.: *he has an ear for music.* **5** attention; consideration (esp. in **give ear to, lend an ear**). **6** an object resembling the external ear. **7 all ears.** very attentive; listening carefully. **8 a thick ear.** *Inf.* a blow on the ear. **9 fall on deaf ears.** to be ignored or pass unnoticed. **10 in one ear and out the other.** heard but unheeded. **11 keep** (*or* **have**) **one's ear to the ground.** to be or try to be well informed about current trends and opinions. **12 out on one's ear.** *Inf.* dismissed unceremoniously. **13 play by ear. 13a** *Inf.* to act according to the demands of a situation; improvise. **13b** to perform a musical piece on an instrument without written music. **14 turn a deaf ear.** to be deliberately unresponsive. **15 up to one's ears.** *Inf.* deeply involved, as in work or debt. [OE *ēare*]
▸**eared** *adj* ▸'**earless** *adj*

ear[2] (ɪə) *n* **1** the part of a cereal plant, such as wheat or barley, that contains the seeds, grains, or kernels. ◆ *vb* **2** (*intr*) (of cereal plants) to develop such parts. [OE *ēar*]

earache ('ɪərˌeɪk) *n* pain in the ear.

eardrum ('ɪəˌdrʌm) *n* the nontechnical name for **tympanic membrane.**

earful ('ɪəfʊl) *n Inf.* **1** something heard or overheard. **2** a rebuke or scolding.

earl (ɜːl) *n* (in Britain) a nobleman ranking below a marquess and above a viscount. Female equivalent: **countess.** [OE *eorl*]
▸'**earldom** *n*

Earl Grey *n* a variety of China tea flavoured with oil of bergamot.

Earl Marshal *n* an officer of the English peerage who presides over the College of Heralds and organizes royal processions and other important ceremonies.

early Ⓣ ('ɜːlɪ) *adj, adv* **earlier, earliest. 1** before the expected or usual time. **2** occurring in or characteristic of the first part of a period or sequence. **3** occurring in or characteristic of a period far back in time. **4** occurring in the near future. **5 in the early days.** during the first years of any enterprise, such as marriage. [OE *ǣrlīce,* from *ǣr* ERE + *-līce* -LY[2]]
▸'**earliness** *n*

early closing *n Brit.* the shutting of shops in a town one afternoon each week.

Early English *n* a style of architecture used in England in the 12th and 13th centuries, characterized by lancet arches and plate tracery.

early music *n* **1** music of the Middle Ages and Renaissance, sometimes also including music of the baroque and early classical periods. ◆ (*modifier*) **early-music. 2** of or denoting an approach to musical performance emphasizing the use of period instruments and historically researched scores and playing techniques: *the early-music movement.*

early warning *n* advance notice of some impending event.

earmark Ⓣ ('ɪəˌmɑːk) *vb* (*tr*) **1** to set aside or mark out for a specific purpose. **2** to make an identification mark on the ear of (a domestic animal). ◆ *n* **3** such a mark of identification. **4** any distinguishing mark or characteristic.

earmuff ('ɪəˌmʌf) *n* one of a joined pair of pads of fur or cloth for keeping the ears warm.

earn Ⓣ (ɜːn) *vb* **1** to gain or be paid (money or other payment) in return for work or service. **2** (*tr*) to acquire or deserve through behaviour or action. **3** (*tr*) (of securities, investments, etc.) to gain (interest, profit, etc.). [OE *earnian*]

earned income *n* income derived from paid employment.

earner ('ɜːnə) *n* **1** a person who earns money. **2** *Sl.* an activity or thing that produces income, esp. illicitly: *a nice little earner.*

earnest[1] Ⓣ ('ɜːnɪst) *adj* **1** serious in mind or intention. **2** characterized by sincerity of intention. **3** demanding or receiving serious attention. ◆ *n* **4 in earnest.** with serious or sincere intentions. [OE *eornost*]
▸'**earnestly** *adv* ▸'**earnestness** *n*

earnest[2] Ⓣ ('ɜːnɪst) *n* **1** a part of something given in advance as a guarantee of the remainder. **2** Also called: **earnest money.** *Contract law.* something given, usually a nominal sum of money, to confirm a contract. **3** any token of something to follow. [C13: from OF *erres* pledges, pl of *erre* earnest money, from L *arrha,* from *arrabō* pledge, from Gk *arrabon,* from Heb. *'ērābhōn* pledge]

THESAURUS

each *determiner* **1a** = **every** ◆ *pron* **1b** = **every one**, each and every one, each one, one and all ◆ *adv* **2** = **apiece**, for each, from each, individually, per capita, per head, per person, respectively, singly, to each

eager *adj* **1, 2** = **keen**, agog, anxious, ardent, athirst, avid, earnest, enthusiastic, fervent, fervid, greedy, hot, hungry, impatient, intent, longing, raring, vehement, yearning, zealous
Antonyms *adj* apathetic, blasé, impassive, indifferent, lazy, nonchalant, opposed, unambitious, unconcerned, unenthusiastic, unimpressed, uninterested

eagerness *n* = **keenness**, ardour, avidity, earnestness, enthusiasm, fervour, greediness, heartiness, hunger, impatience, impetuosity, intentness, longing, thirst, vehemence, yearning, zeal

ear[1] *n* **4** = **sensitivity**, appreciation, discrimination, musical perception, taste **5** = **attention**, consideration, hearing, heed, notice, regard **13a play by ear** *Informal* = **improvise**, ad lib, extemporize, rise to the occasion, take it as it comes

early *adj* **1** = **premature**, advanced, forward, untimely ◆ *adv* **1** = **too soon**, ahead of time, beforehand, betimes, in advance, in good time, prematurely ◆ *adj* **3** = **primitive**, primeval, primordial, undeveloped, young
Antonyms *adj* ≠ **premature:** developed, mature, ripe, seasoned ◆ *adv* ≠ **too soon:** behind, belated, late, overdue, tardy

earmark *vb* **1** = **set aside**, allocate, designate, flag, keep back, label, mark out, reserve, tag ◆ *n* **4** = **characteristic**, attribute, feature, hallmark, label, quality, signature, stamp, tag, token, trademark, trait

earn *vb* **1** = **make**, bring in, collect, draw, gain, get, gross, net, obtain, procure, realize, reap, receive **2** = **deserve**, acquire, attain, be entitled to, be worthy of, merit, rate, warrant, win

earnest[1] *adj* **1** = **serious**, close, constant, determined, firm, fixed, grave, intent, resolute, resolved, sincere, solemn, stable, staid, steady, thoughtful **2** = **heartfelt**, ablaze, ardent, devoted, eager, enthusiastic, fervent, fervid, impassioned, keen, keen as mustard, passionate, purposeful, urgent, vehement, warm, zealous ◆ *n* **4** *As in* **in earnest** = **seriousness**, determination, reality, resolution, sincerity, truth
Antonyms *adj* ≠ **serious:** flippant, frivolous, insincere, trifling ≠ **heartfelt:** apathetic, couldn't-care-less, half-hearted, indifferent, unconcerned, unenthusiastic, uninterested ◆ *n* ≠ **seriousness:** apathy, indifference, unconcern

earnest[2] *n* **1-3** = **down payment**, assurance, deposit, foretaste, guarantee, pledge, promise, security, token

earnestness *n* = **seriousness**, ardour, determination, devotion, eagerness, enthusiasm, fervour, gravity, intentness, keenness, passion, purposefulness, resolution, sincerity, urgency, vehemence, warmth, zeal

earnings ⓘ (ˈɜːnɪŋz) *pl n* **1** money or other payment earned. **2** the profits of an enterprise.

EAROM (ˈɪərɒm) *n Computing. acronym for* electrically alterable read only memory.

earphone (ˈɪəˌfəʊn) *n* a device for converting electric currents into sound waves, held close to or inserted into the ear.

ear piercing *n* **1** the making of a hole in the lobe of an ear, using a sterilized needle, so that earrings may be worn fastened in the hole. ◆ *adj* **ear-piercing. 2** so loud or shrill as to hurt the ears.

earplug (ˈɪəˌplʌg) *n* a piece of soft material placed in the ear to keep out noise or water.

earring (ˈɪəˌrɪŋ) *n* an ornament for the ear, usually clipped onto the lobe or fastened through a hole pierced in the lobe.

earshot (ˈɪəˌʃɒt) *n* the range or distance within which sound may be heard (esp. in **out of earshot,** etc.)

ear-splitting *adj* so loud or shrill as to hurt the ears.

earth ⓘ (ɜːθ) *n* **1** (*sometimes cap.*) the third planet from the sun, the only planet on which life is known to exist. Related adjs.: **terrestrial, telluric. 2** the inhabitants of this planet: *the whole earth rejoiced.* **3** the dry surface of this planet; land; ground. **4** the loose soft material on the surface of the ground that consists of disintegrated rock particles, mould, clay, etc.; soil. **5** worldly or temporal matters as opposed to the concerns of the spirit. **6** the hole in which a burrowing animal, esp. a fox, lives. **7** *Chem.* See **rare earth, alkaline earth. 8** Also (US and Canad.): **ground. 8a** a connection between an electric circuit or device and the earth, which is at zero potential. **8b** a terminal to which this connection is made. **9** (*modifier*) *Astrol.* of or relating to a group of three signs of the zodiac: Taurus, Virgo, and Capricorn. **10 come back** *or* **down to earth.** to return to reality from a fantasy or daydream. **11 on earth.** used as an intensifier in **what on earth, who on earth,** etc. **12 run to earth. 12a** to hunt (an animal, esp. a fox) to its earth and trap it there. **12b** to find (someone) after hunting. ◆ *vb* **13** Also (US and Canad.): **ground.** (*tr*) to connect (a circuit, device, etc.) to earth. ◆ See also **earth up.** [OE *eorthe*]

earthbound (ˈɜːθˌbaʊnd) *adj* **1** confined to the earth. **2** heading towards the earth.

earth closet *n* a type of lavatory in which earth is used to cover excreta.

earthen (ˈɜːθən) *adj* (*prenominal*) **1** made of baked clay: *an earthen pot.* **2** made of earth.

earthenware ⓘ (ˈɜːθənˌwɛə) *n* **a** vessels, etc., made of baked clay. **b** (*as adj*): *an earthenware pot.*

earth-grazer *n* an asteroid in an orbit that takes it close to the earth. Also called: **near-earth asteroid.**

earthly ⓘ (ˈɜːθlɪ) *adj* **earthlier, earthliest. 1** of or characteristic of the earth as opposed to heaven; materialistic; worldly. **2** (*usually with a negative*) *Inf.* conceivable or possible (in **not an earthly (chance),** etc.).
▸ˈ**earthliness** *n*

earthman (ˈɜːθˌmæn) *n, pl* **earthmen.** (esp. in science fiction) an inhabitant or native of the earth. Also called: **earthling.**

earthnut (ˈɜːθˌnʌt) *n* **1** a perennial umbelliferous plant of Europe and Asia, having edible dark brown tubers. **2** any of various plants having an edible root, tuber, or underground pod, such as the peanut or truffle.

earthquake (ˈɜːθˌkweɪk) *n* a series of vibrations at the earth's surface caused by movement along a fault plane, volcanic activity, etc. Related adj: **seismic.**

earth science *n* any of various sciences, such as geology and geography, that are concerned with the structure, age, etc., of the earth.

earth up *vb* (*tr, adv*) to cover (part of a plant) with soil to protect from frost, light, etc.

earthward (ˈɜːθwəd) *adj* **1** directed towards the earth. ◆ *adv* **2** a variant of **earthwards.**

earthwards (ˈɜːθwədz) *or* **earthward** *adv* towards the earth.

earthwork (ˈɜːθˌwɜːk) *n* **1** excavation of earth, as in engineering construction. **2** a fortification made of earth.

earthworm (ˈɜːθˌwɜːm) *n* any of numerous worms which burrow in the soil and help aerate and break up the ground.

earthy ⓘ (ˈɜːθɪ) *adj* **earthier, earthiest. 1** of, composed of, or characteristic of earth. **2** unrefined, coarse, or crude.
▸ˈ**earthily** *adv* ▸ˈ**earthiness** *n*

ear trumpet *n* a trumpet-shaped instrument held to the ear: an old form of hearing aid.

earwax (ˈɪəˌwæks) *n* the nontechnical name for **cerumen.**

earwig (ˈɪəˌwɪg) *n* **1** any of various insects that typically have an elongated body with small leathery forewings, semicircular membranous hindwings, and curved forceps at the tip of the abdomen. ◆ *vb* **earwigs, earwigging, earwigged. 2** (*intr*) *Inf.* to eavesdrop. **3** (*tr*) *Arch.* to attempt to influence (a person) by private insinuation. [OE *ēarwicga,* from *ēare* ear + *wicga* beetle, insect; prob. from superstition that the insect crept into human ears]

earwigging (ˈɪəˌwɪgɪŋ) *n Inf.* a scolding or harangue: *I'll give him an earwigging about that.*

ease ⓘ (iːz) *n* **1** freedom from discomfort, worry, or anxiety. **2** lack of difficulty, labour, or awkwardness. **3** rest, leisure, or relaxation. **4** freedom from poverty; affluence: *a life of ease.* **5** lack of restraint, embarrassment, or stiffness: *ease of manner.* **6 at ease. 6a** *Mil.* (of a standing soldier, etc.) in a relaxed position with the feet apart, rather than at attention. **6b** a command to adopt such a position. **6c** in a relaxed attitude or frame of mind. ◆ *vb* **eases, easing, eased. 7** to make or become less burdensome. **8** (*tr*) to relieve (a person) of worry or care; comfort. **9** (*tr*) to make comfortable or give rest to. **10** (*tr*) to make less difficult; facilitate. **11** to move or cause to move into, out of, etc., with careful manipulation. **12** (when *intr,* often foll. by *off* or *up*) to lessen or cause to lessen in severity, pressure, tension, or strain. **13 ease oneself** *or* **ease nature.** *Arch., euphemistic.* to urinate or defecate. [C13: from OF *aise* ease, opportunity, from L *adjacēns* neighbouring (area); see ADJACENT]
▸ˈ**easeful** *adj*

easel (ˈiːzᵊl) *n* a frame, usually an upright tripod, for supporting or displaying an artist's canvas, a blackboard, etc. [C17: from Du. *ezel*; ult. from L *asinus* ass]

easement (ˈiːzmənt) *n* **1** *Property law.* the right enjoyed by a landowner of making limited use of his neighbour's land, as by crossing it to reach his own property. **2** the act of easing or something that brings ease.

easily ⓘ (ˈiːzɪlɪ) *adv* **1** with ease; without difficulty or exertion. **2** by far; undoubtedly: *easily the best.* **3** probably; almost certainly.

> **USAGE NOTE** See at **easy.**

easiness (ˈiːzɪnɪs) *n* **1** the quality or condition of being easy to accomplish, do, obtain, etc. **2** ease or relaxation of manner; nonchalance.

east (iːst) *n* **1** the direction along a parallel towards the sunrise, at 90° to north; the direction of the earth's rotation. **2 the east.** (*often cap.*) any area lying in or towards the east. Related adj: **oriental. 3** (*usually cap.*) *Cards.* the player or position at the table corresponding to east on the compass. ◆ *adj* **4** situated in, moving towards, or facing the east. **5** (esp. of the wind) from the east. ◆ *adv* **6** in, to, or towards the east. **7 back East.** *Canad.* in or to E Canada, esp. east of Quebec. ◆ Symbol: E [OE *ēast*]

East (iːst) *n* **the. 1** the continent of Asia regarded as culturally distinct from Europe and the West; the Orient. **2** the countries under Communist rule and those under Communist rule until *c.* 1991, lying mainly in the E hemisphere. ◆ *adj* **3** of or denoting the eastern part of a specified country, area, etc.

eastbound (ˈiːstˌbaʊnd) *adj* going or leading towards the east.

east by north *n* one point on the compass north of east.

east by south *n* one point on the compass south of east.

Easter (ˈiːstə) *n* **1** a festival of the Christian Church commemorating the Resurrection of Christ: falls on the Sunday following the first full moon after the vernal equinox. **2** Also called: **Easter Sunday, Easter Day.** the day on which this festival is celebrated. **3** the period between Good Friday and Easter Monday. ◆ Related adj: **Paschal.** [OE *ēastre*]

Easter cactus *n* a Brazilian cactus, *Rhipsalidopsis gaertneri,* widely cultivated as an ornamental for its showy red flowers.

THESAURUS

earnings *pl n* **1, 2** = **income,** emolument, gain, pay, proceeds, profits, receipts, remuneration, return, reward, salary, stipend, takings, wages

earth *n* **1** = **world,** globe, orb, planet, sphere, terrestrial sphere **3, 4** = **soil,** clay, clod, dirt, ground, land, loam, mould, sod, topsoil, turf

earthenware *n* = **crockery,** ceramics, crocks, pots, pottery, terracotta

earthiness *n* **2** = **crudeness,** bawdiness, coarseness, crudity, lustiness, naturalness, ribaldry, robustness, uninhibitedness

earthly *adj* **1** = **worldly,** human, material, materialistic, mortal, non-spiritual, physical, profane, secular, temporal **2** *Informal* = **possible,** conceivable, feasible, imaginable, likely, practical
Antonyms *adj* ≠ **worldly:** ethereal, heavenly, immaterial, immortal, otherworldly, spiritual, supernatural, unearthly

earthy *adj* **2** = **crude,** bawdy, coarse, down-to-earth, homely, lusty, natural, raunchy (*sl.*), ribald, robust, rough, simple, uninhibited, unrefined, unsophisticated

ease *n* **1** = **peace of mind,** calmness, comfort, content, contentment, enjoyment, happiness, peace, quiet, quietude, serenity, tranquillity **2** = **effortlessness,** easiness, facility, readiness, simplicity **3** = **leisure,** relaxation, repose, rest, restfulness **5** = **freedom,** flexibility, informality, liberty, naturalness, unaffectedness, unconstraint, unreservedness ◆ *vb* **7, 8, 12** = **relieve,** abate, allay, alleviate, appease, assuage, calm, comfort, disburden, lessen, lighten, mitigate, moderate, mollify, pacify, palliate, quiet, relax, relent, slacken, soothe, still, tranquillize **10** = **make easier,** aid, assist, expedite, facilitate, forward, further, give a leg up (*inf.*), lessen the labour of, simplify, smooth, speed up **11** = **move carefully,** edge, guide, inch, manoeuvre, slide, slip, squeeze, steer
Antonyms *n* ≠ **peace of mind:** agitation, awkwardness, clumsiness, discomfort, disturbance, tension ≠ **effortlessness:** arduousness, awkwardness, clumsiness, difficulty, effort, exertion, toil ≠ **leisure:** difficulty, discomfort, hardship, irritation, pain, poverty, tribulation ≠ **freedom:** awkwardness, clumsiness, constraint, formality ◆ *vb* ≠ **relieve:** aggravate, discomfort, exacerbate, irritate, worsen ≠ **make easier:** hinder, retard

easily *adv* **1** = **without difficulty,** comfortably, effortlessly, facilely, like a knife through butter, readily, simply, smoothly, standing on one's head, with ease, with one hand tied behind one's back, with one's eyes closed *or* shut, without trouble **2** = **without a doubt,** absolutely, beyond question, by far, certainly, clearly, definitely, doubtlessly, far and away, indisputably, indubitably, plainly, surely, undeniably, undoubtedly, unequivocally, unquestionably

Easter egg *n* an egg given to children at Easter, usually a chocolate egg or a hen's egg with its shell painted.

easterly ('iːstəlɪ) *adj* **1** of or in the east. ◆ *adv, adj* **2** towards the east. **3** from the east: *an easterly wind.* ◆ *n, pl* **easterlies. 4** a wind from the east.

eastern ('iːstən) *adj* **1** situated in or towards the east. **2** facing or moving towards the east.

Eastern Church *n* **1** any of the Christian Churches of the former Byzantine Empire. **2** any Church owing allegiance to the Orthodox Church. **3** any Church having Eastern forms of liturgy and institutions.

Easterner ('iːstənə) *n* (*sometimes not cap.*) a native or inhabitant of the east of any specified region.

eastern hemisphere *n* (*often caps.*) **1** that half of the globe containing Europe, Asia, Africa, and Australia, lying east of the Greenwich meridian. **2** the lands in this, esp. Asia.

Eastern Orthodox Church *n* another name for the **Orthodox Church.**

Eastertide ('iːstəˌtaɪd) *n* the Easter season.

easting ('iːstɪŋ) *n* **1** *Naut.* the net distance eastwards made by a vessel moving towards the east. **2** *Cartography.* the distance eastwards of a point from a given meridian indicated by the first half of a map grid reference.

east-northeast *n* **1** the point on the compass or the direction midway between northeast and east. ◆ *adj, adv* **2** in, from, or towards this direction.

east-southeast *n* **1** the point on the compass or the direction midway between east and southeast. ◆ *adj, adv* **2** in, from, or towards this direction.

eastward ('iːstwəd) *adj* **1** situated or directed towards the east. ◆ *adv* **2** a variant of **eastwards.** ◆ *n* **3** the eastward part, direction, etc.
▸**'eastwardly** *adv, adj*

eastwards ('iːstwədz) *or* **eastward** *adv* towards the east.

easy Ⓣ ('iːzɪ) *adj* **easier, easiest. 1** not requiring much labour or effort; not difficult. **2** free from pain, care, or anxiety. **3** not restricting; lenient: *easy laws.* **4** tolerant and undemanding; easy-going: *an easy disposition.* **5** readily influenced; pliant: *an easy victim.* **6** not constricting; loose: *an easy fit.* **7** not strained or extreme; moderate: *an easy pace.* **8** *Inf.* ready to fall in with any suggestion made; not predisposed: *he is easy about what to do.* **9** *Sl.* sexually available. ◆ *adv* **10** *Inf.* in an easy or relaxed manner. **11 easy does it.** *Inf.* go slowly and carefully; be careful. **12 go easy.** (*usually imperative; often foll. by on*) to exercise moderation. **13 stand easy.** *Mil.* a command to soldiers standing at ease that they may relax further. **14 take it easy. 14a** to avoid stress or undue hurry. **14b** to remain calm. [C12: from OF *aisié,* p.p. of *aisier* to relieve, EASE]

> **USAGE NOTE** *Easy* is not used as an adverb by careful speakers and writers except in certain set phrases: *to take it easy; easy does it.* Where a fixed expression is not involved, the usual adverbial form of *easily* is preferred: *this polish goes on more easily* (not *easier*) *than the other.*

easy-care *adj* (esp. of a fabric or garment) hard-wearing and requiring no special treatment during washing, etc.

easy chair *n* a comfortable upholstered armchair.

easy-going Ⓣ ('iːzɪ'gəʊɪŋ) *adj* **1** relaxed in manner or attitude; excessively tolerant. **2** moving at a comfortable pace: *an easy-going horse.*

easy meat *n Inf.* **1** someone easily seduced or deceived. **2** something easy.

easy money *n* **1** money made with little effort, sometimes dishonestly. **2** *Commerce.* money that can be borrowed at a low interest rate.

Easy Street *n* (*sometimes not caps.*) *Inf.* a state of financial security.

eat Ⓣ (iːt) *vb* **eats, eating, ate, eaten. 1** to take into the mouth and swallow (food, etc.), esp. after biting and chewing. **2** (*tr;* often foll. by *away* or *up*) to destroy as if by eating: *the damp had eaten away the woodwork.* **3** (often foll. by *into*) to use up or waste: *taxes ate into his inheritance.* **4** (often foll. by *into* or *through*) to make (a hole, passage, etc.) by eating or gnawing: *rats ate through the floor.* **5** to take or have (a meal or meals): *we eat at six.* **6** (*tr*) to include as part of one's diet: *he doesn't eat fish.* **7** (*tr*) *Inf.* to cause to worry: *what's eating you?* ◆ See also **eat out, eats, eat up.** [OE *etan*]
▸**'eater** *n*

eatable Ⓣ ('iːtəb[ə]l) *adj* fit or suitable for eating; edible.

eatables ('iːtəb[ə]lz) *pl n* food.

eating ('iːtɪŋ) *n* **1** food, esp. in relation to quality or taste: *this fruit makes excellent eating.* ◆ *adj* **2** suitable for eating uncooked: *eating apples.* **3** relating to or for eating: *an eating house.*

eat out *vb* (*intr, adv*) to eat away from home, esp. in a restaurant.

eats (iːts) *pl n Inf.* articles of food; provisions.

eat up *vb* (*adv, mainly tr*) **1** (*also intr*) to eat or consume entirely. **2** *Inf.* to listen to with enthusiasm or appreciation: *the audience ate up his every word.* **3** (*often passive*) *Inf.* to affect grossly: *she was eaten up by jealousy.* **4** *Inf.* to travel (a distance) quickly: *we just ate up the miles.*

eau de Cologne (ˌəʊ də kə'ləʊn) *n* See **cologne.** [F, lit.: water of Cologne]

eau de nil (ˌəʊ də 'niːl) *n, adj* (of) a pale yellowish-green colour. [F, lit.: water of (the) Nile]

eau de vie (ˌəʊ də 'viː) *n* brandy or other spirits. [F, lit.: water of life]

eaves (iːvz) *pl n* the edge of a roof that projects beyond the wall. [OE *efes*]

eavesdrop Ⓣ ('iːvzˌdrɒp) *vb* **eavesdrops, eavesdropping, eavesdropped.** (*intr*) to listen secretly to the private conversation of others. [C17: back formation from *evesdropper,* from OE *yfesdrype* water dripping from the eaves]
▸**'eavesˌdropper** *n*

ebb Ⓣ (ɛb) *vb* (*intr*) **1** (of tide water) to flow back or recede. Cf. **flow** (sense 8). **2** to fall away or decline. ◆ *n* **3a** the flowing back of the tide from high to low water or the period in which this takes place. **3b** (*as modifier*): *the ebb tide.* Cf. **flood** (sense 3). **4 at a low ebb.** in a state of weakness or decline. [OE *ebba*]

EBCDIC ('ɛpsɪˌdɪk) *n acronym for* extended binary-coded decimal-interchange code: a computer code for representing alphanumeric characters.

ebon ('ɛb[ə]n) *adj, n* a poetic word for **ebony.** [C14: from L *hebenus;* see EBONY]

ebonite ('ɛbəˌnaɪt) *n* another name for **vulcanite.**

ebonize *or* **ebonise** ('ɛbəˌnaɪz) *vb* **ebonizes, ebonizing, ebonized** *or* **ebonises, ebonising, ebonised.** (*tr*) to stain or otherwise finish in imitation of ebony.

ebony ('ɛbənɪ) *n, pl* **ebonies. 1** any of various tropical and subtropical trees that have hard dark wood. **2** the wood of such a tree. **3a** a black colour. **3b** (*as adj*): *an ebony skin.* [C16 *hebeny,* from LL, from Gk, from *ebenos* ebony, from Egyptian]

Ebor. ('iːbɔː) *abbrev. for* Eboracensis. [L.: (Archbishop) of York]

EBRD *abbrev. for* European Bank for Reconstruction and Development.

ebullient Ⓣ (ɪ'bʌljənt, ɪ'bʊl-) *adj* **1** overflowing with enthusiasm or excitement. **2** boiling. [C16: from L *ēbullīre* to bubble forth, be boisterous, from *bullīre* to BOIL[1]]
▸**e'bullience** *or* **e'bulliency** *n*

ebulliometer (ɪˌbʌlɪ'ɒmɪtə) *n Physics.* a device used to determine the boiling point of a solution.

ebullition (ˌɛbə'lɪʃən) *n* **1** the process of boiling. **2** a sudden outburst, as of intense emotion. [C16: from LL *ēbullītiō;* see EBULLIENT]

EC *abbrev. for:* **1** European Community (now called European Union). **2** (in London postal codes) East Central.

ec- *combining form.* out from; away from: *eccentric; ecdysis.* [from Gk *ek* (before a vowel *ex*) out of, away from; see EX-[1]]

ECB *abbrev. for* European Central Bank.

eccentric Ⓣ (ɪk'sɛntrɪk) *adj* **1** deviating or departing from convention;

THESAURUS

easy *adj* **1 = not difficult,** a bed of roses, a piece of cake (*inf.*), child's play (*inf.*), clear, effortless, facile, light, no bother, no trouble, painless, plain sailing, simple, smooth, straightforward, uncomplicated, undemanding **2 = carefree,** calm, comfortable, contented, cushy (*inf.*), easeful, leisurely, peaceful, pleasant, quiet, relaxed, satisfied, serene, tranquil, undisturbed, untroubled, unworried, well-to-do **3 = tolerant,** easy-going, flexible, indulgent, lenient, liberal, light, mild, permissive, unburdensome, unoppressive **4 = relaxed,** affable, casual, easy-going, friendly, gentle, graceful, gracious, informal, laid-back, mild, natural, open, pleasant, smooth, tolerant, unaffected, unceremonious, unconstrained, undemanding, unforced, unpretentious **5 = accommodating,** amenable, biddable, compliant, docile, gullible, manageable, pliant, soft, submissive, suggestible, susceptible, tractable, trusting, yielding
Antonyms *adj* ≠ **not difficult:** arduous, complex, demanding, difficult, exacting, exhausting, formidable, hard, impossible, onerous, stiff ≠ **carefree:** difficult, insecure, stressful, uncomfortable, worried ≠ **tolerant:** demanding, dictatorial, difficult, exacting, hard, harsh, inflexible, intolerant, rigid, stern, strict, unyielding ≠ **relaxed:** affected, anxious, forced, formal, self-conscious, stiff, uncomfortable, unnatural, worried ≠ **accommodating:** difficult, impossible, unyielding

easy-going *adj* **1 = relaxed,** amenable, calm, carefree, casual, complacent, easy, easy-oasy (*sl.*), even-tempered, flexible, happy-go-lucky, indulgent, insouciant, laid-back (*inf.*), lenient, liberal, mild, moderate, nonchalant, permissive, placid, serene, tolerant, unconcerned, uncritical, undemanding, unhurried
Antonyms *adj* anxious, edgy, fussy, hung-up (*sl.*), intolerant, irritated, nervy (*Brit. inf.*), neurotic, on edge, strict, tense, uptight (*inf.*)

eat *vb* **1 = consume,** chew, devour, gobble, ingest, munch, scoff (*sl.*), swallow **2 = destroy,** corrode, crumble, decay, dissolve, erode, rot, waste away, wear away **5 = have a meal,** break bread, chow down (*sl.*), dine, feed, take food, take nourishment

eatable *adj* **= edible,** comestible (*rare*), digestible, esculent, fit to eat, good, harmless, palatable, wholesome

eavesdrop *vb* **= listen in,** bug (*inf.*), earwig (*inf.*), monitor, overhear, snoop (*inf.*), spy, tap

eavesdropper *n* **= listener,** monitor, snooper (*inf.*), spy

ebb *vb* **1 = flow back,** abate, fall away, fall back, go out, recede, retire, retreat, retrocede, sink, subside, wane, withdraw **2 = decline,** decay, decrease, degenerate, deteriorate, diminish, drop, dwindle, fade away, fall away, flag, lessen, peter out, shrink, sink, slacken, weaken ◆ *n* **3 = flowing back,** ebb tide, going out, low tide, low water, reflux, regression, retreat, retrocession, subsidence, wane, waning, withdrawal

ebullience *n* **1 = exuberance,** brio, buoyancy, effervescence, effusiveness, elation, enthusiasm, excitement, exhilaration, high spirits, vivacity, zest

ebullient *adj* **1 = exuberant,** buoyant, effervescent, effusive, elated, enthusiastic, excited, exhilarated, frothy, gushing, in high spirits, irrepressible, vivacious, zestful

eccentric *adj* **1 = odd,** aberrant, abnormal, anomalous, bizarre, capricious, erratic, freakish, idiosyncratic, irregular, oddball (*inf.*), out-

irregular or odd. **2** situated away from the centre or the axis. **3** not having a common centre: *eccentric circles.* **4** not precisely circular. ◆ *n* **5** a person who deviates from normal forms of behaviour. **6** a device for converting rotary motion to reciprocating motion. [C16: from Med. L *eccentricus,* from Gk *ekkentros,* from *ek-* EX-[1] + *kentron* centre]
▸**ec'centrically** *adv*

eccentricity Ⓣ (ˌɛksɛn'trɪsɪtɪ) *n, pl* **eccentricities. 1** unconventional or irregular behaviour. **2** the state of being eccentric. **3** deviation from a circular path or orbit. **4** *Geom.* a number that expresses the shape of a conic section. **5** the degree of displacement of the geometric centre of a part from the true centre, esp. of the axis of rotation of a wheel.

eccl. *or* **eccles.** *abbrev. for* ecclesiastic(al).

Eccles. *or* **Eccl.** *Bible. abbrev. for* Ecclesiastes.

ecclesiastic Ⓣ (ɪˌkliːzɪ'æstɪk) *n* **1** a clergyman or other person in holy orders. ◆ *adj* **2** of or associated with the Christian Church or clergy.

ecclesiastical (ɪˌkliːzɪ'æstɪkᵊl) *adj* of or relating to the Christian Church.
▸**ecˌclesi'astically** *adv*

ecclesiasticism (ɪˌkliːzɪ'æstɪˌsɪzəm) *n* exaggerated attachment to the practices or principles of the Christian Church.

ecclesiology (ɪˌkliːzɪ'ɒlədʒɪ) *n* **1** the study of the Christian Church. **2** the study of Church architecture and decoration.
▸**ecclesiological** (ɪˌkliːzɪə'lɒdʒɪkᵊl) *adj*

eccrine ('ɛkrɪn) *adj* of or denoting glands that secrete externally, esp. the sweat glands. Cf. **apocrine.** [from Gk *ekkrinein,* from *ek-* EC- + *krinein* to separate]
▸**eccrinology** (ˌɛkrɪ'nɒlədʒɪ) *n*

ecdemic (ɛk'dɛmɪk) *adj* not indigenous or endemic; foreign: *an ecdemic disease.*

ecdysis ('ɛkdɪsɪs) *n, pl* **ecdyses** (-ˌsiːz). the periodic shedding of the cuticle in insects and other arthropods or the outer epidermal layer in reptiles. [C19: NL, from Gk *ekdusis,* from *ekduein* to strip, from *ek-* EX-[1] + *duein* to put on]

ECG *abbrev. for:* **1** electrocardiogram. **2** electrocardiograph.

echelon Ⓣ ('ɛʃəˌlɒn) *n* **1** a level of command, responsibility, etc. (esp. in **the upper echelons**). **2** *Mil.* **2a** a formation in which units follow one another but are offset sufficiently to allow each unit a line of fire ahead. **2b** a group formed in this way. ◆ *vb* **3** to assemble in echelon. [C18: from F *échelon,* lit.: rung of a ladder, from OF *eschiele* ladder, from L *scāla*]

echidna (ɪ'kɪdnə) *n, pl* **echidnas** *or* **echidnae** (-niː). a spine-covered monotreme mammal of Australia and New Guinea, having a long snout and claws. Also called: **spiny anteater.** [C19: from NL, from L: viper, from Gk *ekhidna*]

echinoderm (ɪ'kaɪnəʊˌdɜːm) *n* any of various marine invertebrates characterized by tube feet, a calcite body-covering, and a five-part symmetrical body. The group includes the starfish, sea urchins, and sea cucumbers.

echinus (ɪ'kaɪnəs) *n, pl* **echini** (-naɪ). **1** *Archit.* a moulding between the shaft and the abacus of a Doric column. **2** any sea urchin of the genus *Echinus,* such as the Mediterranean edible sea urchin. [C14: from L, from Gk *ekhinos*]

echo Ⓣ ('ɛkəʊ) *n, pl* **echoes. 1a** the reflection of sound or other radiation by a reflecting medium, esp. a solid object. **1b** the sound so reflected. **2** a repetition or imitation, esp. an unoriginal reproduction of another's opinions. **3** something that evokes memories. **4** (*sometimes pl*) an effect that continues after the original cause has disappeared: *echoes of the French Revolution.* **5** a person who copies another, esp. one who obsequiously agrees with another's opinions. **6a** the signal reflected by a radar target. **6b** the trace produced by such a signal on a radar screen. ◆ *vb* **echoes, echoing, echoed. 7** to resound or cause to resound with an echo. **8** (*intr*) (of sounds) to repeat or resound by echoes; reverberate. **9** (*tr*) (of persons) to repeat (words, opinions, etc.) in imitation, agreement, or flattery. **10** (*tr*) (of things) to resemble or imitate (another style, an earlier model, etc.). [C14: via L from Gk *ēkhō;* rel. to Gk *ēkhē* sound]
▸**'echoing** *adj* ▸**'echoless** *adj* ▸**'echo-ˌlike** *adj*

echocardiography (ˌɛkəʊˌkɑːdɪ'ɒgrəfɪ) *n* examination of the heart using ultrasound techniques.

echo chamber *n* a room with walls that reflect sound. It is used to make acoustic measurements and as a recording studio when echo effects are required. Also called: **reverberation chamber.**

echography (ɛ'kɒgrəfɪ) *n* medical examination of the internal structures of the body by means of ultrasound.

echoic Ⓣ (ɛ'kəʊɪk) *adj* **1** characteristic of or resembling an echo. **2** onomatopoeic; imitative.

echolalia (ˌɛkəʊ'leɪlɪə) *n Psychiatry.* the tendency to repeat mechanically words just spoken by another person. [C19: from NL, from ECHO + Gk *lalia* talk, chatter]

echolocation (ˌɛkəʊləʊ'keɪʃən) *n* determination of the position of an object by measuring the time taken for an echo to return from it and its direction.

echo sounder *n* a navigation device that determines depth by measuring the time taken for a pulse of sound to reach the sea bed or a submerged object and for the echo to return.
▸**echo sounding** *n*

echovirus *or* **ECHO virus** ('ɛkəʊˌvaɪrəs) *n* any of a group of viruses that can cause symptoms of mild meningitis, the common cold, or infections of the intestinal and respiratory tracts. [C20: from initials of *Enteric Cytopathic Human Orphan* ("orphan" because orig. believed to be unrelated to any disease) + VIRUS]

éclair (eɪ'klɛə, ɪ'klɛə) *n* a finger-shaped cake of choux pastry, usually filled with cream and covered with chocolate. [C19: from F, lit.: lightning (prob. because it does not last long)]

eclampsia (ɪ'klæmpsɪə) *n Pathol.* a toxic condition that sometimes develops in the last three months of pregnancy, characterized by high blood pressure, weight gain, and convulsions. [C19: from NL, from Gk *eklampsis* a shining forth]

éclat Ⓣ (eɪ'klɑː) *n* **1** brilliant or conspicuous success, effect, etc. **2** showy display; ostentation. **3** social distinction. **4** approval; acclaim; applause. [C17: from F, from *éclater* to burst]

eclectic Ⓣ (ɪ'klɛktɪk, ɛ'klɛk-) *adj* **1** selecting from various styles, ideas, methods, etc. **2** composed of elements drawn from a variety of sources, styles, etc. ◆ *n* **3** a person who favours an eclectic approach. [C17: from Gk *eklektikos,* from *eklegein* to select, from *legein* to gather]
▸**e'clectically** *adv* ▸**e'clecticism** *n*

eclipse Ⓣ (ɪ'klɪps) *n* **1** the total or partial obscuring of one celestial body by another (**total eclipse** *or* **partial eclipse**). A **solar eclipse** occurs when the moon passes between the sun and the earth; a **lunar eclipse** when the earth passes between the sun and the moon. **2** the period of time during which such a phenomenon occurs. **3** any dimming or obstruction of light. **4** a loss of importance, power, fame, etc., esp. through overshadowing by another. ◆ *vb* **eclipses, eclipsing, eclipsed.** (*tr*) **5** to cause an eclipse of. **6** to cast a shadow upon; obscure. **7** to overshadow or surpass. [C13: back formation from OE *eclypsis,* from L, from Gk *ekleipsis* a forsaking, from *ekleipein* to abandon]
▸**e'clipser** *n*

eclipsing binary *n* a binary star whose orbital plane lies in or near the line of sight so that one component is regularly eclipsed by its companion.

ecliptic (ɪ'klɪptɪk) *n* **1** *Astron.* **1a** the great circle on the celestial sphere representing the apparent annual path of the sun relative to the stars. **1b** (*as modifier*): *the ecliptic plane.* **2** an equivalent great circle on the terrestrial globe. ◆ *adj* **3** of or relating to an eclipse.
▸**e'cliptically** *adv*

eclogue ('ɛklɒg) *n* a pastoral or idyllic poem, usually in the form of a conversation. [C15: from L *ecloga* short poem, collection of extracts, from Gk *eklogē* selection]

eclosion (ɪ'kləʊʒən) *n* the emergence of an insect larva from the egg or an adult from the pupal case. [C19: from F, from *éclore* to hatch, ult. from L *exclūdere* to shut out]

eco- *combining form.* denoting ecology or ecological: *ecocide; ecosphere.*

ecocentric (ˌiːkəʊ'sɛntrɪk) *adj* having a serious concern for environmental issues: *ecocentric management.*

ecofriendly ('iːkəʊˌfrɛndlɪ) *adj* having a beneficial effect on the environment or at least not causing environmental damage.

ecol. *abbrev. for:* **1** ecological. **2** ecology.

E. coli (iː'kəʊlaɪ) *n* short for *Escherichia coli,* see ***Escherichia.***

ecological (ˌiːkə'lɒdʒɪkᵊl) *adj* **1** of or relating to ecology. **2** (of a practice,

THESAURUS

landish, outré, peculiar, queer (*inf.*), quirky, rum (*Brit. sl.*), singular, strange, uncommon, unconventional, weird, whimsical ◆ *n* **5** = **crank** (*inf.*), card (*inf.*), case (*inf.*), character (*inf.*), freak (*inf.*), loose cannon, nonconformist, oddball (*inf.*), oddity, queer fish (*Brit. inf.*), weirdo (*inf.*)

Antonyms *adj* ≠ **odd:** average, conventional, normal, ordinary, regular, run-of-the-mill, straightforward, typical

eccentricity *n* **1, 2** = **oddity**, aberration, abnormality, anomaly, bizarreness, caprice, capriciousness, foible, freakishness, idiosyncrasy, irregularity, nonconformity, oddness, outlandishness, peculiarity, queerness (*inf.*), quirk, singularity, strangeness, unconventionality, waywardness, weirdness, whimsicality, whimsicalness

ecclesiastic *n* **1** = **clergyman**, churchman, cleric, divine, holy man, man of the cloth, minister, parson, pastor, priest ◆ *adj* **2** = **clerical**, church, churchly, divine, holy, pastoral, priestly, religious, spiritual

echelon *n* **1** = **level**, degree, grade, office, place, position, rank, tier

echo *n* **1** = **repetition**, answer, reverberation **2** = **copy**, imitation, mirror image, parallel, reflection, reiteration, reproduction **3** = **reminder**, allusion, evocation, hint, intimation, memory, suggestion, trace **4** *sometimes plural* = **repercussion**, aftereffect, aftermath, consequence ◆ *vb* **7, 8** = **repeat**, resound, reverberate **9, 10** = **copy**, ape, imitate, mirror, parallel, parrot, recall, reflect, reiterate, reproduce, resemble, ring, second

echoic *adj* **2** = **imitative**, onomatopoeic

éclat *n* **1** = **brilliance**, effect, success **2** = **showmanship**, display, lustre, ostentation, pomp, show, splendour **3** = **renown**, celebrity, distinction, fame, glory **4** = **acclaim**, acclamation, applause, approval, plaudits

eclectic *adj* **1, 2** = **comprehensive**, all-embracing, broad, catholic, dilettantish, diverse, diversified, general, heterogeneous, liberal, manifold, many-sided, multifarious, selective, varied, wide-ranging

eclipse *n* **1, 3** = **obscuring**, darkening, dimming, extinction, occultation, shading **4** = **decline**, diminution, failure, fall, loss ◆ *vb* **5, 6** = **obscure**, blot out, cloud, darken, dim, extinguish, overshadow, shroud, veil **7** = **surpass**, exceed, excel, outdo, outshine, put in the shade (*inf.*), transcend

policy, product, etc.) tending to benefit or cause minimal damage to the environment.
▸ˌ**ecoˈlogically** *adv*

ecology (ɪˈkɒlədʒɪ) *n* **1** the study of the relationships between living organisms and their environment. **2** the set of relationships of a particular organism with its environment. [C19: from G *Ökologie*, from Gk *oikos* house (hence, environment)]
▸**eˈcologist** *n*

econ. *abbrev. for:* **1** economical. **2** economics. **3** economy.

econometrics (ɪˌkɒnəˈmetrɪks) *n* (*functioning as sing*) the application of mathematical and statistical techniques to economic theories.
▸**eˌconoˈmetric** *or* **eˌconoˈmetrical** *adj* ▸**econometrician** (ɪˌkɒnəməˈtrɪʃən) *or* **econometrist** (ˌiːkəˈnɒmətrɪst, -ˌɛkə-) *n*

economic ➊ (ˌiːkəˈnɒmɪk, ˌɛkə-) *adj* **1** of or relating to an economy, economics, or finance. **2** *Brit.* capable of being produced, operated, etc., for profit; profitable. **3** concerning or affecting material resources or welfare: *economic pests.* **4** concerned with or relating to the necessities of life; utilitarian. **5** a variant of **economical**. **6** *Inf.* inexpensive; cheap.

economical ➊ (ˌiːkəˈnɒmɪkᵊl, ˌɛkə-) *adj* **1** using the minimum required; not wasteful. **2** frugal; thrifty. **3** a variant of **economic** (senses 1–4). **4** *Euphemistic.* deliberately withholding information (esp. in **economical with the truth**).
▸ˌ**ecoˈnomically** *adv*

economic indicator *n* a statistical measure representing an economic variable: *the retail price index is an economic indicator of the actual level of prices.*

economic migrant *or* **refugee** *n* a person who emigrates from a poor country to a developed one in the hope of improving his or her standard of living.

economics ➊ (ˌiːkəˈnɒmɪks, ˌɛkə-) *n* **1** (*functioning as sing*) the social science concerned with the production and consumption of goods and services and the analysis of the commercial activities of a society. **2** (*functioning as pl*) financial aspects.

economic sanctions *pl n* any actions taken by one nation or group of nations to harm the economy of another nation or group, often to force a political change.

economist (ɪˈkɒnəmɪst) *n* a specialist in economics.

economize ➊ *or* **economise** (ɪˈkɒnəˌmaɪz) *vb* **economizes, economizing, economized** *or* **economises, economising, economised.** (often foll. by *on*) to limit or reduce (expense, waste, etc.).
▸**eˌconomiˈzation** *or* **eˌconomiˈsation** *n*

economy ➊ (ɪˈkɒnəmɪ) *n, pl* **economies. 1** careful management of resources to avoid unnecessary expenditure or waste; thrift. **2** a means or instance of this; saving. **3** sparing, restrained, or efficient use. **4a** the complex of activities concerned with the production, distribution, and consumption of goods and services. **4b** a particular type or branch of this: *a socialist economy.* **5** the management of the resources, finances, income, and expenditure of a community, business enterprise, etc. **6a** a class of travel in aircraft, cheaper and less luxurious than first class. **6b** (*as modifier*): *economy class.* **7** (*modifier*) purporting to offer a larger quantity for a lower price: *economy pack.* **8** the orderly interplay between the parts of a system or structure. [C16: via L from Gk *oikonomia* domestic management, from *oikos* house + *-nomia*, from *nemein* to manage]

ecosphere (ˈiːkəʊˌsfɪə, ˈɛkəʊ-) *n* the parts of the universe, esp. on earth, where life can exist.

écossaise (ˌeɪkɒˈseɪz) *n* **1** a lively dance in two-four time. **2** the tune for such a dance. [C19: F, lit.: Scottish (dance)]

ecosystem (ˈiːkəʊˌsɪstəm, ˈɛkəʊ-) *n Ecology.* a system involving the interactions between a community and its nonliving environment. [C20: from ECO- + SYSTEM]

ecoterrorist (ˈiːkəʊˌterərɪst) *n* a person who uses violence in order to achieve environmentalist aims.

ecotourism (ˈiːkəʊˌtʊərɪzəm) *n* tourism which is designed to contribute to the protection of the environment or at least minimize damage to it, often involving travel to areas of natural interest in developing countries or participation in environmental projects.
▸**ˈecoˌtourist** *n*

ecru (ˈɛkruː, ˈeɪkruː) *n, adj* (of) a greyish-yellow to a light greyish colour. [C19: from F, from *é-* (intensive) + *cru* raw, from L *crūdus;* see CRUDE]

ecstasy ➊ (ˈɛkstəsɪ) *n, pl* **ecstasies. 1** (*often pl*) a state of exalted delight, joy, etc.; rapture. **2** intense emotion of any kind: *an ecstasy of rage.* **3** *Psychol.* overpowering emotion sometimes involving temporary loss of consciousness: often associated with mysticism. **4** *Sl.* 3,4-methylenedioxymethamphetamine: a powerful drug that acts as a stimulant and can produce hallucinations. [C14: from OF via Med. L from Gk *ekstasis* displacement, trance, from *ex-* out + *histanai* to cause to stand]

ecstatic ➊ (ɛkˈstætɪk) *adj* **1** in a trancelike state of rapture or delight. **2** showing or feeling great enthusiasm. ◆ *n* **3** a person who has periods of intense trancelike joy.
▸**ecˈstatically** *adv*

ECT *abbrev. for* electroconvulsive therapy.

ecto- *combining form.* indicating outer, outside. [from Gk *ektos* outside, from *ek, ex* out]

ectoblast (ˈɛktəʊˌblæst) *n* another name for **ectoderm.**
▸ˌ**ectoˈblastic** *adj*

ectoderm (ˈɛktəʊˌdɜːm) *or* **exoderm** *n* the outer germ layer of an animal embryo, which gives rise to epidermis and nervous tissue.
▸ˌ**ectoˈdermal** *or* ˌ**ectoˈdermic** *adj*

ectomorph (ˈɛktəʊˌmɔːf) *n* a type of person having a body build characterized by thinness, weakness, and a lack of weight.
▸ˌ**ectoˈmorphic** *adj* ▸**ˈectoˌmorphy** *n*

-ectomy *n combining form.* indicating surgical excision of a part: *appendectomy.* [from NL *-ectomia*, from Gk *ek-* out + -TOMY]

ectopic pregnancy (ɛkˈtɒpɪk) *n Pathol.* the abnormal development of a fertilized egg outside the uterus, usually within a Fallopian tube.

ectoplasm (ˈɛktəʊˌplæzəm) *n* **1** *Cytology.* the outer layer of cytoplasm. **2** *Spiritualism.* the substance supposedly emanating from the body of a medium during trances.
▸ˌ**ectoˈplasmic** *adj*

ECU (*also* ˈeɪkjuː, ˈekjuː) *abbrev. for* European Currency Unit.

ecumenical ➊, **oecumenical** (ˌiːkjʊˈmɛnɪkᵊl, ˌɛk-) *or* **ecumenic, oecumenic** *adj* **1** of or relating to the Christian Church throughout the world, esp. with regard to its unity. **2** tending to promote unity among Churches. [C16: via LL from Gk *oikoumenikos*, from *oikein* to inhabit, from *oikos* house]
▸ˌ**ecuˈmenically** *or* ˌ**oecuˈmenically** *adv*

ecumenism (ɪˈkjuːməˌnɪzəm, ˈɛkjʊm-), **ecumenicism** (ˌiːkjʊˈmɛnɪˌsɪzəm, ˌɛk-) *or* **ecumenicalism** (ˌiːkjʊˈmɛnɪkəˌlɪzəm, ˌɛk-) *n* the aim of unity among all Christian churches throughout the world.

eczema (ˈɛksɪmə) *n Pathol.* a skin inflammation with lesions that scale, crust, or ooze a serous fluid, often accompanied by intense itching. [C18: from NL, from Gk *ekzema*, from *ek-* out + *zein* to boil]
▸**eczematous** (ɛkˈsɛmətəs) *adj*

ed. *abbrev. for:* **1** edited. **2** (*pl* **eds.**) edition. **3** (*pl* **eds.**) editor. **4** education.

-ed[1] *suffix.* forming the past tense of most English verbs. [OE *-de, -ede, -ode, -ade*]

-ed[2] *suffix.* forming the past participle of most English verbs. [OE *-ed, -od, -ad*]

-ed[3] *suffix forming adjectives from nouns.* possessing or having the characteristics of: *salaried; red-blooded.* [OE *-ede*]

Edam (ˈiːdæm) *n* a round yellow cheese with a red outside covering. [after *Edam*, in Holland]

EDC *abbrev. for* European Defence Community.

Edda (ˈɛdə) *n* **1** Also called: **Elder Edda, Poetic Edda.** a 12th-century collection of mythological Old Norse poems. **2** Also called: **Younger Edda, Prose Edda.** a treatise on versification together with a collection of Scandinavian myths, legends, and poems (?1222). [C18: ON]
▸**Eddaic** (ɛˈdeɪɪk) *adj*

eddo (ˈɛdəʊ) *n, pl* **eddoes.** another name for **taro.**

eddy ➊ (ˈɛdɪ) *n, pl* **eddies. 1** a movement in air, water, or other fluid in which the current doubles back on itself causing a miniature whirlwind or whirlpool. **2** a deviation from or disturbance in the main trend of thought, life, etc. ◆ *vb* **eddies, eddying, eddied. 3** to move or cause to move against the main current. [C15: prob. from ON]

eddy current *n* an electric current induced in a massive conductor by an alternating magnetic field.

edelweiss (ˈeɪdᵊlˌvaɪs) *n* a small alpine flowering plant having white woolly oblong leaves and a tuft of floral leaves surrounding the flowers. [C19: G, lit.: noble white]

edema (ɪˈdiːmə) *n, pl* **edemata** (-mətə). the usual US spelling of **oedema.**

Eden (ˈiːdᵊn) *n* **1** Also called: **Garden of Eden.** *Bible.* the garden in which Adam and Eve were placed at the Creation. **2** a place or state of great

THESAURUS

economic *adj* **1** = **financial**, business, commercial, industrial, mercantile, trade **2** = **profitable**, money-making, productive, profit-making, remunerative, solvent, viable **3** = **monetary**, bread-and-butter (*inf.*), budgetary, financial, fiscal, material, pecuniary **6** *Informal* = **inexpensive**, cheap, fair, low, low-priced, modest, reasonable

economical *adj* **1** = **cost-effective**, efficient, money-saving, neat, sparing, time-saving, unwasteful, work-saving **2** = **thrifty**, careful, economizing, frugal, prudent, saving, scrimping, sparing
Antonyms *adj* ≠ **cost-effective:** loss-making, uneconomical, unprofitable, wasteful ≠ **thrifty:** extravagant, generous, imprudent, lavish, profligate, spendthrift, uneconomical, unthrifty, wasteful

economics *n* **1** = **finance**, commerce, the dismal science

economize *vb* = **cut back**, be economical, be frugal, be on a shoestring, be sparing, draw in one's horns, husband, pull in one's horns, retrench, save, scrimp, tighten one's belt
Antonyms *vb* be extravagant, push the boat out (*inf.*), spend, splurge, squander

economy *n* **1, 3** = **thrift**, frugality, husbandry, parsimony, providence, prudence, restraint, retrenchment, saving, sparingness, thriftiness

ecstasy *n* **1** = **rapture**, bliss, delight, elation, enthusiasm, euphoria, exaltation, fervour, frenzy, joy, ravishment, rhapsody, seventh heaven, trance, transport
Antonyms *n* affliction, agony, anguish, distress, hell, misery, pain, suffering, torment, torture

ecstatic *adj* **1, 2** = **rapturous**, blissful, cock-a-hoop, delirious, elated, enraptured, enthusiastic, entranced, euphoric, fervent, floating on air, frenzied, in seventh heaven, in transports of delight, joyful, joyous, on cloud nine (*inf.*), overjoyed, over the moon (*inf.*), rhapsodic, transported, walking on air

ecumenical *adj* **1, 2** = **unifying**, catholic, general, universal, worldwide

eddy *n* **1** = **swirl**, counter-current, counterflow, tideway, undertow, vortex, whirlpool ◆ *vb* **3** = **swirl**, whirl

delight or contentment. [C14: from LL, from Heb. *'ēdhen* place of pleasure]
▸**Edenic** (iː'dɛnɪk) *adj*

edentate (iː'dɛnteɪt) *n* **1** any mammal of the order *Edentata,* of tropical Central and South America, which have few or no teeth. The order includes anteaters, sloths, and armadillos. ◆ *adj* **2** of or relating to the order *Edentata.* [C19: from L *ēdentātus* lacking teeth, from *ēdentāre* to render toothless, from *e-* out + *dēns* tooth]

edge ❶ (ɛdʒ) *n* **1** a border, brim, or margin. **2** a brink or verge. **3** a line along which two faces or surfaces of a solid meet. **4** the sharp cutting side of a blade. **5** keenness, sharpness, or urgency. **6** force, effectiveness, or incisiveness: *the performance lacked edge.* **7** a ridge. **8 have the edge on** *or* **over.** to have a slight advantage or superiority over. **9 on edge. 9a** nervously irritable; tense. **9b** nervously excited or eager. **10 set (someone's) teeth on edge.** to make (someone) acutely irritated or uncomfortable. ◆ *vb* **edges, edging, edged. 11** (*tr*) to provide an edge or border for. **12** (*tr*) to shape or trim the edge or border of (something). **13** to push (one's way, someone, something, etc.) gradually, esp. edgeways. **14** (*tr*) *Cricket.* to hit (a bowled ball) with the edge of the bat. **15** (*tr*) to sharpen (a knife, etc.). [OE *ecg*]
▸**'edger** *n*

edgeways ('ɛdʒˌweɪz) *or esp. US & Canad.* **edgewise** ('ɛdʒˌwaɪz) *adv* **1** with the edge forwards or uppermost. **2** on, by, with, or towards the edge. **3 get a word in edgeways.** (*usually with a negative*) to interrupt a conversation in which someone else is talking incessantly.

edging ('ɛdʒɪŋ) *n* **1** anything placed along an edge to finish it, esp. as an ornament. **2** the act of making an edge. ◆ *adj* **3** used for making an edge: *edging shears.*

edgy ❶ ('ɛdʒɪ) *adj* **edgier, edgiest.** (*usually postpositive*) nervous, irritable, tense, or anxious.
▸**'edgily** *adv* ▸**'edginess** *n*

edh (ɛð) *or* **eth** (ɛθ, ɛð) *n* a character of the runic alphabet (ð) used to represent the voiced dental fricative as in *then, mother, bathe.*

edible ❶ ('ɛdɪbᵊl) *adj* fit to be eaten; eatable. [C17: from LL *edibilis,* from L *edere* to eat]
▸**ˌedi'bility** *n*

edibles ('ɛdɪbᵊlz) *pl n* articles fit to eat; food.

edict ❶ ('iːdɪkt) *n* **1** a decree or order issued by any authority. **2** any formal or authoritative command, proclamation, etc. [C15: from L *ēdictum,* from *ēdīcere* to declare]
▸**e'dictal** *adj*

edifice ❶ ('ɛdɪfɪs) *n* **1** a building, esp. a large or imposing one. **2** a complex or elaborate institution or organization. [C14: from OF, from L *aedificium,* from *aedificāre* to build; see EDIFY]

edify ❶ ('ɛdɪˌfaɪ) *vb* **edifies, edifying, edified.** (*tr*) to improve the morality, intellect, etc., of, esp. by instruction. [C14: from OF, from L *aedificāre* to construct, from *aedēs* a dwelling, temple + *facere* to make]
▸**ˌedifi'cation** *n* ▸**'ediˌfying** *adj*

edit ❶ ('ɛdɪt) *vb* **edits, editing, edited.** (*tr*) **1** to prepare (text) for publication by checking and improving its accuracy, clarity, etc. **2** to be in charge of (a publication, esp. a periodical). **3** to prepare (a film, tape, etc.) by rearrangement or selection of material. **4** (*tr*) to modify (a computer file). **5** (often foll. by *out*) to remove, as from a manuscript or film. [C18: back formation from EDITOR]

edit. *abbrev. for:* **1** edited. **2** edition. **3** editor.

edition ❶ (ɪ'dɪʃən) *n* **1** *Printing.* **1a** the entire number of copies of a book or other publication printed at one time. **1b** a copy from this number: *a first edition.* **2** one of a number of printings of a book or other publication, issued at separate times with alterations, amendments, etc. **3a** an issue of a work identified by its format: *a leather-bound edition.* **3b** an issue of a work identified by its editor or publisher: *the Oxford edition.* [C16: from L *ēditiō* a bringing forth, publishing, from *ēdere* to give out; see EDITOR]

editor ('ɛdɪtə) *n* **1** a person who edits written material for publication. **2** a person in overall charge of a newspaper or periodical. **3** a person in charge of one section of a newspaper or periodical: *the sports editor.* **4** *Films.* a person who makes a selection and arrangement of shots. **5** a person in overall control of a television or radio programme that consists of various items. [C17: from LL: producer, exhibitor, from *ēdere* to give out, publish, from *ē-* out + *dāre* to give]
▸**'editorˌship** *n*

editorial (ˌɛdɪ'tɔːrɪəl) *adj* **1** of or relating to editing or editors. **2** of, relating to, or expressed in an editorial. **3** of or relating to the content of a publication. ◆ *n* **4** an article in a newspaper, etc., expressing the opinion of the editor or the publishers.
▸**ˌedi'torially** *adv*

editorialize *or* **editorialise** (ˌɛdɪ'tɔːrɪəˌlaɪz) *vb* **editorializes, editorializing, editorialized** *or* **editorialises, editorialising, editorialised.** (*intr*) to express an opinion as in an editorial.
▸**ˌediˌtoriali'zation** *or* **ˌediˌtoriali'sation** *n*

EDT (in the US and Canada) *abbrev. for* Eastern Daylight Time.

educate ❶ ('ɛdjʊˌkeɪt) *vb* **educates, educating, educated.** (*mainly tr*) **1** (*also intr*) to impart knowledge by formal instruction to (a pupil); teach. **2** to provide schooling for. **3** to improve or develop (a person, taste, skills, etc.). **4** to train for some particular purpose or occupation. [C15: from L *ēducāre* to rear, educate, from *dūcere* to lead]
▸**'educable** *or* **'eduˌcatable** *adj* ▸**ˌeduca'bility** *or* **ˌeduˌcata'bility** *n* ▸**'educative** *adj*

educated ❶ ('ɛdjʊˌkeɪtɪd) *adj* **1** having an education, esp. a good one. **2** displaying culture, taste, and knowledge; cultivated. **3** (*prenominal*) based on experience or information (esp. in **an educated guess**).

education ❶ (ˌɛdjʊ'keɪʃən) *n* **1** the act or process of acquiring knowledge. **2** the knowledge or training acquired by this process. **3** the act or process of imparting knowledge, esp. at a school, college, or university. **4** the theory of teaching and learning. **5** a particular kind of instruction or training: *a university education.*
▸**ˌedu'cational** *adj* ▸**ˌedu'cationalist** *or* **ˌedu'cationist** *n*

educator ❶ ('ɛdjʊˌkeɪtə) *n* **1** a person who educates; teacher. **2** a specialist in education.

educe (ɪ'djuːs) *vb* **educes, educing, educed.** (*tr*) *Rare.* **1** to evolve or develop. **2** to draw out or elicit (information, solutions, etc.). [C15: from L *ēdūcere,* from *ē-* out + *dūcere* to lead]
▸**e'ducible** *adj* ▸**eductive** (ɪ'dʌktɪv) *adj*

Edwardian (ɛd'wɔːdɪən) *adj* of or characteristic of the reign of Edward VII, king of Great Britain and Ireland (1901–10).
▸**Ed'wardianˌism** *n*

-ee *suffix forming nouns.* **1** indicating a recipient of an action (as opposed, esp. in legal terminology, to the agent): *assignee; lessee.* **2** indicating a person in a specified state or condition: *absentee.* **3** indicating a diminutive form of something: *bootee.* [via OF *-é, -ée,* p.p. endings, from L *-ātus, -āta* -ATE[1]]

EEC *abbrev. for* (the former) European Economic Community.

EEG *abbrev. for:* **1** electroencephalogram. **2** electroencephalograph.

eel (iːl) *n* **1** any teleost fish such as the European freshwater eel, having a long snakelike body, a smooth slimy skin, and reduced fins. **2** any of various similar animals, such as the mud eel and the electric eel. **3** an evasive or untrustworthy person. [OE *ǣl*]
▸**'eel-ˌlike** *adj* ▸**'eely** *adj*

eelgrass ('iːlˌgrɑːs) *n* any of several perennial submerged marine plants having grasslike leaves.

THESAURUS

edge *n* **1, 2** = **border**, bound, boundary, brim, brink, contour, flange, fringe, limit, line, lip, margin, outline, perimeter, periphery, rim, side, threshold, verge **5, 6** = **sharpness**, acuteness, animation, bite, effectiveness, force, incisiveness, interest, keenness, point, pungency, sting, urgency, zest **8** *As in* **have the edge on** *or* **over** = **advantage**, ascendancy, dominance, lead, superiority, upper hand **9 on edge** = **nervous**, apprehensive, eager, edgy, excited, ill at ease, impatient, irritable, keyed up, on tenterhooks, tense, tetchy, twitchy (*inf.*), uptight (*inf.*), wired (*sl.*) ◆ *vb* **11, 12** = **border**, bind, fringe, hem, rim, shape, trim **13** = **inch**, creep, ease, sidle, steal, work, worm **15** = **sharpen**, hone, strop, whet

edginess *n* = **nervousness**, anxiety, irascibility, irritability, jitters (*inf.*), nerves, nervous tension, prickliness, restiveness, tenseness, tetchiness, touchiness, twitchiness

edgy *adj* = **nervous**, anxious, ill at ease, irascible, irritable, keyed up, nervy (*Brit. inf.*), neurotic, on edge, on pins and needles, on tenterhooks, restive, tense, tetchy, touchy, twitchy (*inf.*), uptight (*inf.*), wired (*sl.*)

edible *adj* = **eatable**, comestible (*rare*), digestible, esculent, fit to eat, good, harmless, palatable, wholesome
Antonyms *adj* baneful, harmful, indigestible, inedible, noxious, pernicious, poisonous, uneatable

edict *n* **1, 2** = **decree**, act, canon, command, demand, dictate, dictum, enactment, fiat, injunction, law, mandate, manifesto, order, ordinance, proclamation, pronouncement, pronunciamento, regulation, ruling, statute, ukase (*rare*)

edification *n* = **instruction**, education, elevation, enlightenment, guidance, improvement, information, nurture, schooling, teaching, tuition, uplifting

edifice *n* **1** = **building**, construction, erection, fabric (*rare*), habitation, house, pile, structure

edify *vb* = **instruct**, educate, elevate, enlighten, guide, improve, inform, nurture, school, teach, uplift

edifying *adj* = **instructional**, elevating, enlightening, improving, inspiring, uplifting

edit *vb* **1** = **revise**, adapt, annotate, censor, check, condense, correct, emend, polish, redact, rephrase, rewrite **2, 3** = **put together**, assemble, compose, rearrange, reorder, select

edition *n* **2, 3** = **version**, copy, impression, issue, number, printing, volume

educate *vb* **1-4** = **teach**, civilize, coach, cultivate, develop, discipline, drill, edify, enlighten, exercise, foster, improve, indoctrinate, inform, instruct, mature, rear, school, train, tutor

educated *adj* **1** = **taught**, coached, informed, instructed, nurtured, schooled, tutored **2** = **cultured**, civilized, cultivated, enlightened, experienced, informed, knowledgeable, learned, lettered, literary, polished, refined, sophisticated, tasteful
Antonyms *adj* ≠ **taught:** ignorant, illiterate, uneducated, unlettered, unread, unschooled, untaught ≠ **cultured:** benighted, lowbrow, philistine, uncultivated, uncultured, uneducated

education *n* **1-5** = **teaching**, breeding, civilization, coaching, cultivation, culture, development, discipline, drilling, edification, enlightenment, erudition, improvement, indoctrination, instruction, knowledge, nurture, scholarship, schooling, training, tuition, tutoring

educational *adj* **1-5** = **instructive**, cultural, didactic, edifying, educative, enlightening, heuristic, improving, informative

educative *adj* **1-4** = **instructive**, didactic, edifying, educational, enlightening, heuristic, improving, informative

educator *n* **1** = **teacher**, coach, edifier, educationalist *or* educationist, instructor, pedagogue, schoolmaster *or* schoolmistress, schoolteacher, trainer, tutor

eelpout (ˈiːlˌpaʊt) *n* **1** a marine eel-like fish. **2** another name for **burbot.** [OE *ǣlepūte*]

eelworm (ˈiːlˌwɜːm) *n* any of various nematode worms, esp. the wheatworm and the vinegar eel.

e'en (iːn) *adv, n Poetic or arch.* contraction of **even**[2] or **evening.**

e'er (ɛə) *adv Poetic or arch.* contraction of **ever.**

-eer *or* **-ier** *suffix.* **1** (*forming nouns*) indicating a person who is concerned with or who does something specified: *auctioneer; engineer; profiteer; mutineer.* **2** (*forming verbs*) to be concerned with something specified: *electioneer.* [from OF *-ier*, from L *-arius* -ARY]

eerie ❶ (ˈɪərɪ) *adj* **eerier, eeriest.** uncannily frightening or disturbing; weird. [C13: orig. Scot. & N English, prob. from OE *earg* cowardly]
▸ **ˈeerily** *adv* ▸ **ˈeeriness** *n*

EETPU (in Britain) *abbrev. for* Electrical, Electronic, Telecommunications, and Plumbing Union.

eff (ɛf) *vb* **1** euphemism for **fuck** (esp. in **eff off**). **2 eff and blind.** *Sl.* to use obscene language.
▸ **ˈeffing** *n, adj, adv*

efface ❶ (ɪˈfeɪs) *vb* **effaces, effacing, effaced.** (*tr*) **1** to obliterate or make dim. **2** to make (oneself) inconspicuous or humble. **3** to rub out; erase. [C15: from F *effacer*, lit.: to obliterate the face; see FACE]
▸ **efˈfaceable** *adj* ▸ **efˈfacement** *n* ▸ **efˈfacer** *n*

effect ❶ (ɪˈfɛkt) *n* **1** something produced by a cause or agent; result. **2** power to influence or produce a result. **3** the condition of being operative (esp. in **in** *or* **into effect**). **4 take effect.** to become operative or begin to produce results. **5** basic meaning or purpose (esp. in **to that effect**). **6** an impression, usually contrived (esp. in **for effect**). **7** a scientific phenomenon: *the Doppler effect.* **8 in effect. 8a** in fact; actually. **8b** for all practical purposes. **9** the overall impression or result. ◆ *vb* **10** (*tr*) to cause to occur; accomplish. [C14: from L *effectus* a performing, tendency, from *efficere* to accomplish, from *facere* to do]
▸ **efˈfecter** *n* ▸ **efˈfectible** *adj*

effective ❶ (ɪˈfɛktɪv) *adj* **1** productive of or capable of producing a result. **2** in effect; operative. **3** impressive: *an effective entrance.* **4** (*prenominal*) actual rather than theoretical. **5** (of a military force, etc.) equipped and prepared for action. ◆ *n* **6** a serviceman equipped and prepared for action.
▸ **efˈfectively** *adv* ▸ **efˈfectiveness** *n*

effects ❶ (ɪˈfɛkts) *pl n* **1** Also called: **personal effects.** personal belongings. **2** lighting, sounds, etc., to accompany a stage, film, or broadcast production.

effectual ❶ (ɪˈfɛktjʊəl) *adj* **1** capable of or successful in producing an intended result; effective. **2** (of documents, etc.) having legal force.
▸ **efˌfectuˈality** *or* **efˈfectualness** *n*

effectually (ɪˈfɛktjʊəlɪ) *adv* **1** with the intended effect. **2** in effect.

effectuate ❶ (ɪˈfɛktjʊˌeɪt) *vb* **effectuates, effectuating, effectuated.** (*tr*) to cause to happen; effect; accomplish.
▸ **efˌfectuˈation** *n*

effeminate ❶ (ɪˈfɛmɪnɪt) *adj* (of a man or boy) displaying characteristics regarded as typical of a woman; not manly. [C14: from L *effēmināre* to make into a woman, from *fēmina* woman]
▸ **efˈfeminacy** *or* **efˈfeminateness** *n*

effendi (ɛˈfɛndɪ) *n, pl* **effendis. 1** (in the Ottoman Empire) a title of respect. **2** (in Turkey since 1934) the oral title of address equivalent to *Mr.* [C17: from Turkish *efendi* master, from Mod. Gk *aphentēs*, from Gk *authentēs* lord, doer]

efferent (ˈɛfərənt) *adj Physiol.* carrying or conducting outwards, esp. from the brain or spinal cord. Cf. **afferent.** [C19: from L *efferre* to bear off, from *ferre* to bear]
▸ **ˈefference** *n*

effervesce ❶ (ˌɛfəˈvɛs) *vb* **effervesces, effervescing, effervesced.** (*intr*) **1** (of a liquid) to give off bubbles of gas. **2** (of a gas) to issue in bubbles from a liquid. **3** to exhibit great excitement, vivacity, etc. [C18: from L *effervescere* to foam up, ult. from *fervēre* to boil, ferment]
▸ **ˌefferˈvescingly** *adv*

effervescent ❶ (ˌɛfəˈvɛsᵊnt) *adj* **1** (of a liquid) giving off bubbles of gas. **2** high-spirited; vivacious.
▸ **ˌefferˈvescence** *n*

effete ❶ (ɪˈfiːt) *adj* **1** weak or decadent. **2** exhausted; spent. **3** (of animals or plants) no longer capable of reproduction. [C17: from L *effētus* exhausted by bearing, from *fētus* having brought forth; see FETUS]
▸ **efˈfeteness** *n*

efficacious ❶ (ˌɛfɪˈkeɪʃəs) *adj* capable of or successful in producing an intended result; effective. [C16: from L *efficāx* powerful, efficient, from *efficere* to achieve]
▸ **efficacy** (ˈɛfɪkəsɪ) *or* **ˌeffiˈcaciousness** *n*

efficiency ❶ (ɪˈfɪʃənsɪ) *n, pl* **efficiencies. 1** the quality or state of being efficient. **2** the ratio of the useful work done by a machine, etc., to the energy input, often expressed as a percentage.

efficient ❶ (ɪˈfɪʃənt) *adj* **1** functioning or producing effectively and with the least waste of effort; competent. **2** *Philosophy.* producing a direct effect. [C14: from L *efficiēns* effecting]

effigy ❶ (ˈɛfɪdʒɪ) *n, pl* **effigies. 1** a portrait, esp. as a monument. **2** a crude representation of someone, used as a focus for contempt or ridicule (often in **burn** *or* **hang in effigy**). [C18: from L *effigiēs*, from *effingere* to form, portray, from *fingere* to shape]

effleurage (ˌɛflɜːˈrɑːʒ) *n Med.* a light stroking movement used in massage. [C19: from F]

effloresce (ˌɛflɔːˈrɛs) *vb* **effloresces, efflorescing, effloresced.** (*intr*) **1** to burst forth as into flower; bloom. **2** to become powdery by loss of water or crystallization. **3** to become encrusted with powder or crystals as a result of chemical change or evaporation. [C18: from L *efflōrēscere* to blossom, from *flōrēscere*, from *flōs* flower]

efflorescence (ˌɛflɔːˈrɛsᵊns) *n* **1** a bursting forth or flowering. **2** *Chem.,*

THESAURUS

eerie *adj* = **frightening**, awesome, creepy (*inf.*), eldritch (*poetic*), fearful, ghostly, mysterious, scary (*inf.*), spectral, spooky (*inf.*), strange, uncanny, unearthly, uneasy, weird

efface *vb* **1, 3** = **obliterate**, annihilate, blot out, cancel, cross out, delete, destroy, dim, eradicate, erase, excise, expunge, extirpate, raze, rub out, wipe out **2 efface oneself** = **make oneself inconspicuous**, be bashful, be diffident, be modest, be retiring, be timid, be unassertive, humble oneself, lower oneself, withdraw

effect *n* **1** = **result**, aftermath, conclusion, consequence, end result, event, fruit, issue, outcome, upshot **2** = **power**, clout (*inf.*), effectiveness, efficacy, efficiency, fact, force, influence, reality, strength, use, validity, vigour, weight **3** = **operation**, action, enforcement, execution, force, implementation **4 take effect** = **produce results**, become operative, begin, come into force, work **5** = **impression**, drift, essence, impact, import, meaning, purport, purpose, sense, significance, tenor **8 in effect** = **in fact**, actually, effectively, essentially, for practical purposes, in actuality, in reality, in truth, really, to all intents and purposes, virtually ◆ *vb* **10** = **bring about**, accomplish, achieve, actuate, carry out, cause, complete, consummate, create, effectuate, execute, fulfil, give rise to, initiate, make, perform, produce

effective *adj* **1** = **efficient**, able, active, adequate, capable, competent, effectual, efficacious, energetic, operative, productive, serviceable, useful **2** = **in operation**, active, actual, current, in effect, in execution, in force, operative, real **3** = **powerful**, cogent, compelling, convincing, emphatic, forceful, forcible, impressive, moving, persuasive, potent, striking, telling
Antonyms *adj* ≠ **efficient:** futile, inadequate, incompetent, ineffective, inefficient, insufficient, otiose, unimpressive, unproductive, useless, vain, worthless ≠ **in operation:** inactive, inoperative ≠ **powerful:** feeble, ineffectual, pathetic, powerless, tame, weak

effectiveness *n* **1** = **power**, bottom, capability, clout (*inf.*), cogency, effect, efficacy, efficiency, force, influence, potency, strength, success, use, validity, vigour, weight

effects *pl n* **1** = **belongings**, chattels, furniture, gear, goods, movables, paraphernalia, possessions, property, things, trappings

effectual *adj* **1** = **effective**, capable, efficacious, efficient, forcible, influential, potent, powerful, productive, serviceable, successful, telling, useful **2** = **binding**, authoritative, in force, lawful, legal, licit (*rare*), sound, valid

effectuate *vb* = **bring about**, accomplish, achieve, carry out *or* through, cause, complete, create, do, effect, execute, fulfil, make, perform, procure, produce

effeminacy *n* = **womanliness**, delicacy, femininity, softness, tenderness, unmanliness, weakness, womanishness

effeminate *adj* = **womanly**, camp (*inf.*), delicate, feminine, poofy (*sl.*), sissy, soft, tender, unmanly, weak, wimpish *or* wimpy (*inf.*), womanish, womanlike
Antonyms *adj* butch (*sl.*), he-man (*inf.*), macho, manly, virile

effervesce *vb* **1** = **bubble**, ferment, fizz, foam, froth, sparkle

effervescence *n* **1** = **bubbling**, ferment, fermentation, fizz, foam, foaming, froth, frothing, sparkle **2** = **liveliness**, animation, brio, buoyancy, ebullience, enthusiasm, excitedness, excitement, exhilaration, exuberance, gaiety, high spirits, pizzazz *or* pizazz (*inf.*), vim (*sl.*), vitality, vivacity, zing (*inf.*)

effervescent *adj* **1** = **bubbling**, bubbly, carbonated, fermenting, fizzing, fizzy, foaming, foamy, frothing, frothy, sparkling **2** = **lively**, animated, bubbly, buoyant, ebullient, enthusiastic, excited, exhilarated, exuberant, gay, in high spirits, irrepressible, merry, vital, vivacious, zingy (*inf.*)
Antonyms *adj* ≠ **bubbling:** flat, flavourless, insipid, stale, watery, weak ≠ **lively:** boring, dull, flat, insipid, jejune, lacklustre, lifeless, spiritless, stale, unexciting, vapid

effete *adj* **1** = **decadent**, corrupt, debased, decayed, decrepit, degenerate, dissipated, enervated, enfeebled, feeble, ineffectual, overrefined, spoiled, weak **2** = **worn out**, burnt out, drained, enervated, exhausted, played out, spent, used up, wasted **3** = **sterile**, barren, fruitless, infecund, infertile, unfruitful, unproductive, unprolific

efficacious *adj* = **effective**, active, adequate, capable, competent, effectual, efficient, energetic, operative, potent, powerful, productive, serviceable, successful, useful
Antonyms *adj* abortive, futile, ineffective, ineffectual, inefficacious, unavailing, unproductive, unsuccessful, useless

efficacy *n* = **effectiveness**, ability, capability, competence, effect, efficaciousness, efficiency, energy, force, influence, potency, power, strength, success, use, vigour, virtue, weight

efficiency *n* **1** = **competence**, ability, adeptness, capability, economy, effectiveness, efficacy, power, productivity, proficiency, readiness, skilfulness, skill

efficient *adj* **1** = **competent**, able, adept, businesslike, capable, economic, effective, effectual, organized, powerful, productive, proficient, ready, skilful, well-organized, workmanlike
Antonyms *adj* cowboy (*inf.*), disorganized, incompetent, ineffectual, inefficient, inept, slipshod, sloppy, unbusinesslike, unproductive, wasteful

effigy *n* **1, 2** = **likeness**, dummy, figure, guy,

geol. **2a** the process of efflorescing. **2b** the powdery substance formed as a result of this process. **3** any skin rash or eruption.
▸ **ˌefflo'rescent** *adj*
effluence ❶ ('ɛfluəns) *or* **efflux** ('ɛflʌks) *n* **1** the act or process of flowing out. **2** something that flows out.
effluent ❶ ('ɛfluənt) *n* **1** liquid discharged as waste, as from an industrial plant or sewage works. **2** radioactive waste released from a nuclear power station. **3** a stream that flows out of another body of water. **4** something that flows out or forth. ◆ *adj* **5** flowing out or forth. [C18: from L *effluere* to run forth, from *fluere* to flow]
effluvium ❶ (ɛ'flu:vɪəm) *n, pl* **effluvia** (-vɪə) *or* **effluviums.** an unpleasant smell or exhalation, as of gaseous waste or decaying matter. [C17: from L: a flowing out; see EFFLUENT]
▸ **ef'fluvial** *adj*
effort ❶ ('ɛfət) *n* **1** physical or mental exertion. **2** a determined attempt. **3** achievement; creation. [C15: from OF *esfort,* from *esforcier* to force, ult. from L *fortis* strong]
▸ **'effortful** *adj* ▸ **'effortless** *adj*
effrontery ❶ (ɪ'frʌntərɪ) *n, pl* **effronteries.** shameless or insolent boldness. [C18: from F, from OF *esfront* barefaced, shameless, from LL *effrons,* lit.: putting forth one's forehead]
effulgent (ɪ'fʌldʒənt) *adj* radiant; brilliant. [C18: from L *effulgēre* to shine forth, from *fulgēre* to shine]
▸ **ef'fulgence** *n* ▸ **ef'fulgently** *adv*
effuse *vb* (ɪ'fju:z), **effuses, effusing, effused. 1** to pour or flow out. **2** to spread out; diffuse. ◆ *adj* (ɪ'fju:s). **3** *Bot.* (esp. of an inflorescence) spreading out loosely. [C16: from L *effūsus* poured out, from *effundere* to shed]
effusion ❶ (ɪ'fju:ʒən) *n* **1** an unrestrained outpouring in speech or words. **2** the act or process of being poured out. **3** something that is poured out. **4** *Med.* **4a** the escape of blood or other fluid into a body cavity or tissue. **4b** the fluid that has escaped.
effusive ❶ (ɪ'fju:sɪv) *adj* **1** extravagantly demonstrative of emotion; gushing. **2** (of rock) formed by the solidification of magma.
▸ **ef'fusively** *adv* ▸ **ef'fusiveness** *n*
EFL *abbrev. for* English as a Foreign Language.
eft (ɛft) *n* a dialect or archaic name for a **newt.** [OE *efeta*]
EFTA ('ɛftə) *n acronym for* European Free Trade Association; established in 1960 to eliminate trade tariffs on industrial products; the current members are Austria, Iceland, Norway, Sweden, and Switzerland.
EFTPOS ('ɛftpɒs) *n acronym for* electronic funds transfer at point of sale.
EFTS *abbrev. for* electronic funds transfer system.
Eg. *abbrev. for:* **1** Egypt(ian). **2** Egyptology.
e.g., eg, *or* **eg.** *abbrev. for* exempli gratia. [L: for example]
egad (ɪ'gæd, i:'gæd) *interj Arch.* a mild oath. [C17: prob. var. of *Ah God!*]
egalitarian (ɪˌgælɪ'tɛərɪən) *adj* **1** of or upholding the doctrine of the equality of mankind. ◆ *n* **2** an adherent of egalitarian principles. [C19: alteration of *equalitarian,* through infl. of F *égal* equal]
▸ **eˌgali'tarianˌism** *n*
egg[1] (ɛg) *n* **1** the oval or round reproductive body laid by the females of birds, reptiles, fishes, insects, and some other animals, consisting of a developing embryo, its food store, and sometimes jelly or albumen, all surrounded by an outer shell or membrane. **2** Also called: **egg cell.** any female gamete; ovum. **3** the egg of the domestic hen used as food. **4** something resembling an egg, esp. in shape. **5 good** (*or* **bad**) **egg.** *Old-fashioned inf.* a good (or bad) person. **6 put** *or* **have all one's eggs in one basket.** to stake everything on a single venture. **7 teach one's grandmother to suck eggs.** *Inf.* to presume to teach someone something that he knows already. **8 with egg on one's face.** *Inf.* made to look ridiculous. [C14: from ON *egg;* rel. to OE *ǣg*]
egg[2] ❶ (ɛg) *vb* (*tr;* usually foll. by *on*) to urge or incite, esp. to daring or foolish acts. [OE *eggian*]
egg-and-spoon race *n* a race in which runners carry an egg balanced in a spoon.
eggbeater ('ɛgˌbi:tə) *n* **1** Also called: **eggwhisk.** a utensil for beating eggs; whisk. **2** *Chiefly US & Canad.* an informal name for **helicopter.**
egger *or* **eggar** ('ɛgə) *n* any of various European moths having brown bodies and wings. [C18: from EGG[1], from the egg-shaped cocoon]
egghead ('ɛgˌhɛd) *n Inf.* an intellectual.
eggnog (ˌɛg'nɒg) *n* a drink made of eggs, milk, sugar, spice, and brandy, rum, or other spirit. Also called: **egg flip.** [C19: from EGG[1] + NOG]
eggplant ('ɛgˌplɑ:nt) *n* another name (esp. US, Canad., & Austral.) for **aubergine.**
eggshell ('ɛgˌʃɛl) *n* **1** the hard porous outer layer of a bird's egg. **2** (*modifier*) (of paint) having a very slight sheen.
eggshell porcelain *or* **china** *n* a very thin translucent porcelain originally from China.
egg tooth *n* (in embryo reptiles) a temporary tooth or (in birds) projection of the beak used for piercing the eggshell.
eglantine ('ɛglənˌtaɪn) *n* another name for **sweetbrier.** [C14: from OF *aiglent,* ult. from L *acus* needle, from *acer* sharp, keen]
EGM *abbrev. for* extraordinary general meeting.
ego ('i:gəʊ, 'ɛgəʊ) *n, pl* **egos. 1** the self of an individual person; the conscious subject. **2** *Psychoanalysis.* the conscious mind, based on perception of the environment: modifies the antisocial instincts of the id and is itself modified by the conscience (superego). **3** one's image of oneself; morale. **4** egotism; conceit. [C19: from L: I]
egocentric ❶ (ˌi:gəʊ'sɛntrɪk, ˌɛg-) *adj* **1** regarding everything only in relation to oneself; self-centred. ◆ *n* **2** a self-centred person; egotist.
▸ **ˌegocen'tricity** *n* ▸ **ˌego'centrism** *n*
egoism ('i:gəʊˌɪzəm, 'ɛg-) *n* **1** concern for one's own interests and welfare. **2** *Ethics.* the theory that the pursuit of one's own welfare is the highest good. **3** self-centredness; egotism.
▸ **'egoist** *n* ▸ **ˌego'istic** *or* **ˌego'istical** *adj*
egomania (ˌi:gəʊ'meɪnɪə, ˌɛg-) *n Psychiatry.* obsessive love for oneself.
▸ **ˌego'maniˌac** *n* ▸ **egomaniacal** (ˌi:gəʊmə'naɪɪk°l, ˌɛg-) *adj*
egotism ❶ ('i:gəˌtɪzəm, 'ɛgə-) *n* **1** an inflated sense of self-importance or superiority; self-centredness. **2** excessive reference to oneself. [C18: from L *ego* I + -ISM]
▸ **'egotist** *n* ▸ **ˌego'tistic** *or* **ˌego'tistical** *adj*
ego trip *n Inf.* something undertaken to boost or draw attention to a person's own image or appraisal of himself.
egregious (ɪ'gri:dʒəs, -dʒɪəs) *adj* **1** outstandingly bad; flagrant. **2** *Arch.* distinguished; eminent. [C16: from L *ēgregius* outstanding (lit.: standing out from the herd), from *ē-* out + *grex* flock, herd]
▸ **e'gregiousness** *n*
egress ❶ ('i:grɛs) *n* **1** Also: **egression.** the act of going or coming out; emergence. **2** a way out; exit. **3** the right to go out or depart. [C16: from L *ēgredī* to come forth, depart, from *gradī* to move, step]
egret ('i:grɪt) *n* any of various wading birds similar to herons but usually having white plumage and, in the breeding season, long feathery plumes. [C15: from OF *aigrette,* of Gmc origin]
Egyptian (ɪ'dʒɪpʃən) *adj* **1** of or relating to Egypt, a republic in NE Africa, its inhabitants, or their dialect of Arabic. **2** of or characteristic of the ancient Egyptians, their language, or culture. ◆ *n* **3** a native or inhabitant of Egypt. **4** a member of a people who established an advanced civilization in Egypt that flourished from the late fourth millennium B.C. **5** the extinct language of the ancient Egyptians.
Egyptology (ˌi:dʒɪp'tɒlədʒɪ) *n* the study of the archaeology and language of ancient Egypt.
▸ **ˌEgyp'tologist** *n*
eh (eɪ) *interj* an exclamation used to express questioning surprise or to seek the repetition or confirmation of a statement or question.
EHF *abbrev. for* extremely high frequency.
eider *or* **eider duck** ('aɪdə) *n* any of several sea ducks of the N hemisphere. See **eiderdown.** [C18: from ON *æthr*]
eiderdown ('aɪdəˌdaʊn) *n* **1** the breast down of the female eider duck, used for stuffing pillows, quilts, etc. **2** a thick, warm cover for a bed, enclosing a soft filling.
eidetic (aɪ'dɛtɪk) *adj Psychol.* **1** (of visual, or sometimes auditory, im-

THESAURUS

icon, idol, image, picture, portrait, representation, statue
effluence *n* **1, 2** = **outflow**, discharge, effluent, effluvium, efflux, emanation, emission, exhalation, flow, issue, outpouring, secretion
effluent *n* **1** = **waste**, effluvium, pollutant, sewage **4** = **outflow**, discharge, effluence, efflux, emanation, emission, exhalation, flow, issue, outpouring ◆ *adj* **5** = **outflowing**, discharged, emanating, emitted
effluvium *n* = **smell**, exhalation, exhaust, fumes, malodour, mephitis, miasma, niff (*Brit. sl.*), odour, pong (*Brit. inf.*), reek, stench, stink
effort *n* **1** = **exertion**, application, blood, sweat, and tears (*inf.*), elbow grease (*facetious*), endeavour, energy, force, labour, pains, power, strain, stress, stretch, striving, struggle, toil, travail (*literary*), trouble, work **2** = **attempt**, endeavour, essay, go (*inf.*), shot (*inf.*), stab (*inf.*), try **3** = **creation**, accomplishment, achievement, act, deed, feat, job, product, production
effortless *adj* **1** = **easy**, easy-peasy (*sl.*), facile, painless, plain sailing, simple, smooth, uncomplicated, undemanding, untroublesome
Antonyms *adj* demanding, difficult, formidable, hard, onerous, uphill
effrontery *n* = **insolence**, arrogance, assurance, audacity, boldness, brashness, brass neck (*Brit. inf.*), brazenness, cheek (*inf.*), cheekiness, chutzpah (*US & Canad. inf.*), disrespect, front, gall (*inf.*), impertinence, impudence, incivility, nerve, presumption, rudeness, shamelessness, temerity
effusion *n* **1** = **talk**, address, outpouring, speech, utterance, writing **2** = **outpouring**, discharge, effluence, efflux, emission, gush, issue, outflow, shedding, stream
effusive *adj* **1** = **demonstrative**, ebullient, enthusiastic, expansive, extravagant, exuberant, free-flowing, fulsome, gushing, lavish, overflowing, profuse, talkative, unreserved, unrestrained, wordy
egg[2] *usually with* **on** *vb* = **encourage**, exhort, goad, incite, prod, prompt, push, spur, urge
Antonyms *vb* deter, discourage, dissuade, hold back, put off, talk out of
egocentric *adj* **1** = **self-centred**, egoistic, egoistical, egotistic, egotistical, selfish
egotism *n* **1** = **self-centredness**, conceitedness, egocentricity, egomania, narcissism, self-absorption, self-admiration, self-conceit, self-esteem, self-importance, self-interest, selfishness, self-love, self-praise, self-regard, self-seeking, superiority, vainglory, vanity
egotist *n* **1** = **egomaniac**, bighead (*inf.*), blowhard (*inf.*), boaster, braggadocio, braggart, narcissist, self-admirer, self-seeker, swaggerer
egotistic *adj* **1** = **self-centred**, boasting, bragging, conceited, egocentric, egomaniacal, full of oneself, narcissistic, opinionated, self-absorbed, self-admiring, self-important, self-seeking, superior, vain, vainglorious
egress *n* **1, 2** = **exit**, departure, emergence,

ages) very vivid and allowing detailed recall of something previously perceived: thought to be common in children. **2** relating to or subject to such imagery. [C20: from Gk *eidētikos*, from *eidos* shape, form]
▸**ei'detically** *adv*

Eid-ul-Adha ('iːdʊl,ɑːdə) *n* an annual Muslim festival marking the end of the pilgrimage to Mecca. Animals are sacrificed and their meat shared among the poor. [from Ar. *id ul adha* festival of sacrifice]

Eid-ul-Fitr ('iːdʊl,fiːtə) *n* an annual Muslim festival marking the end of Ramadan, involving the exchange of gifts and a festive meal. [from Ar. *id ul fitr* festival of fast-breaking]

eight (eɪt) *n* **1** the cardinal number that is the sum of one and seven and the product of two and four. **2** a numeral, 8, VIII, etc., representing this number. **3** the amount or quantity that is one greater than seven. **4** something representing, represented by, or consisting of eight units. **5** *Rowing*. **5a** a racing shell propelled by eight oarsmen. **5b** the crew of such a shell. **6** Also called: **eight o'clock.** eight hours after noon or midnight. **7** **have one over the eight.** *Sl.* to be drunk. ◆ *determiner* **8a** amounting to eight. **8b** (*as pron*): *I could only find eight.* [OE *eahta*]

eighteen ('eɪ'tiːn) *n* **1** the cardinal number that is the sum of ten and eight and the product of two and nine. **2** a numeral, 18, XVIII, etc., representing this number. **3** the amount or quantity that is eight more than ten. **4** something represented by, representing, or consisting of 18 units. ◆ *determiner* **5a** amounting to eighteen: *eighteen weeks*. **5b** (*as pron*): *eighteen of them knew.* [OE *eahtatēne*]
▸**'eigh'teenth** *adj, n*

eightfold ('eɪt,fəʊld) *adj* **1** equal to or having eight times as many or as much. **2** composed of eight parts. ◆ *adv* **3** by eight times as much.

eighth (eɪtθ) *adj* **1** (*usually prenominal*) **1a** coming after the seventh and before the ninth in numbering, position, etc.; being the ordinal number of *eight:* often written 8th. **1b** (*as n*): *the eighth in line.* ◆ *n* **2a** one of eight equal parts of something. **2b** (*as modifier*): *an eighth part.* **3** the fraction one divided by eight (1/8). **4** another word for **octave.** ◆ *adv* **5** Also: **eighthly.** after the seventh person, position, event, etc.

eighth note *n Music.* the usual US and Canad. name for **quaver.**

eightsome reel ('eɪtsəm) *n* a Scottish dance for eight people.

eighty ('eɪtɪ) *n, pl* **eighties.** **1** the cardinal number that is the product of ten and eight. **2** a numeral, 80, LXXX, etc., representing this number. **3** (*pl*) the numbers 80-89, esp. the 80th to the 89th year of a person's life or of a century. **4** the amount or quantity that is eight times ten. **5** something represented by, representing, or consisting of 80 units. ◆ *determiner* **6a** amounting to eighty: *eighty pages of nonsense.* **6b** (*as pron*): *eighty are expected.* [OE *eahtatig*]
▸**'eightieth** *adj, n*

einsteinium (aɪn'staɪnɪəm) *n* a radioactive metallic transuranic element artificially produced from plutonium. Symbol: Es; atomic no.: 99; half-life of most stable isotope, ^{252}Es: 276 days. [C20: NL, after Albert *Einstein* (1879–1955), German-born US physicist and mathematician]

EIS *abbrev. for* Educational Institute of Scotland.

eisteddfod (aɪ'stɛdfəd) *n, pl* **eisteddfods** *or* **eisteddfodau** (*Welsh* aɪ,stɛð'vɒdaɪ). any of a number of annual festivals in Wales in which competitions are held in music, poetry, drama, and the fine arts. [C19: from Welsh, lit.: session, from *eistedd* to sit + *-fod*, from *bod* to be]

either ('aɪðə, 'iːðə) *determiner* **1a** one or the other (of two). **1b** (*as pron*): *either is acceptable.* **2** both one and the other: *at either end of the table.* ◆ *conj* **3** (*coordinating*) used preceding two or more possibilities joined by *"or"*. ◆ *adv* (*sentence modifier*) **4** (*with a negative*) used to indicate that the clause immediately preceding is a partial reiteration of a previous clause: *John isn't a liar, but he isn't exactly honest either.* [OE *ǣgther*, short for *ǣghwæther* each of two; see WHETHER]

> **USAGE NOTE** *Either* is followed by a singular verb in good usage: *either is good; either of these books is useful.* Care should be taken to avoid ambiguity when using *either* to mean *both* or *each*, as in the following sentence: *a ship could be moored on either side of the channel.* Agreement between verb and subject in *either...or...* constructions follows the pattern for *neither...nor...* See at **neither.**

ejaculate ❶ (ɪ'dʒækjʊ,leɪt) *vb* **ejaculates, ejaculating, ejaculated. 1** to eject or discharge (semen) in orgasm. **2** (*tr*) to utter abruptly; blurt out. ◆ *n* (ɪ'dʒækjʊlɪt). **3** another word for **semen.** [C16: from L *ējaculārī* to hurl out, from *jaculum* javelin, from *jacere* to throw]
▸**e,jacu'lation** *n* ▸**e'jaculatory** *or* **e'jaculative** *adj* ▸**e'jacu,lator** *n*

eject ❶ (ɪ'dʒɛkt) *vb* **1** (*tr*) to force out; expel or emit. **2** (*tr*) to compel (a person) to leave; evict. **3** (*tr*) to dismiss, as from office. **4** (*intr*) to leave an aircraft rapidly, using an ejection seat or capsule. [C15: from L *ejicere*, from *jacere* to throw]
▸**e'jection** *n* ▸**e'jective** *adj* ▸**e'jector** *n*

ejection seat *or* **ejector seat** *n* a seat, esp. in military aircraft, fired by a cartridge or rocket to eject the occupant in an emergency.

eke (iːk) *sentence connector. Arch.* also; moreover. [OE *eac*]

eke out ❶ (iːk) *vb* (*tr, adv*) **1** to make (a supply) last, esp. by frugal use. **2** to support (existence) with difficulty and effort. **3** to add to (something insufficient), esp. with effort. [from obs. *eke* to enlarge]

elaborate ❶ *adj* (ɪ'læbərɪt). **1** planned with care and exactness. **2** marked by complexity or detail. ◆ *vb* (ɪ'læbə,reɪt), **elaborates, elaborating, elaborated. 3** (*intr; usually foll. by on or upon*) to add detail (to an account); expand (upon). **4** (*tr*) to work out in detail; develop. **5** (*tr*) to produce by careful labour. **6** (*tr*) *Physiol.* to change (food or simple substances) into more complex substances for use in the body. [C16: from L *ēlabōrāre* to take pains, from *labōrāre* to toil]
▸**e'laborateness** *n* ▸**e,labo'ration** *n* ▸**elaborative** (ɪ'læbərətɪv) *adj* ▸**e'labo,rator** *n*

élan ❶ (eɪ'lɑːn) *n* a combination of style and vigour. [C19: from F, from *élancer* to throw forth, ult. from L *lancea* LANCE]

eland ('iːlənd) *n* **1** a large spiral-horned antelope inhabiting bushland in eastern and southern Africa. **2** **giant eland.** a similar but larger animal of central and W Africa. [C18: via Afrik., from Du. *eland* elk]

elapse ❶ (ɪ'læps) *vb* **elapses, elapsing, elapsed.** (*intr*) (of time) to pass by. [C17: from L *ēlābī* to slip away]

elasmobranch (ɪ'læsmə,bræŋk) *n* **1** any cartilaginous fish of the subclass *Elasmobranchii*, which includes sharks, rays, and skates. ◆ *adj* **2** of or relating to the *Elasmobranchii.* [C19: from NL *elasmobranchii*, from Gk *elasmos* metal plate + *brankhia* gills]

elastane (ɪ'læsteɪn) *n* a synthetic fibre characterized by its ability to revert to its original shape after being stretched.

elastic ❶ (ɪ'læstɪk) *adj* **1** (of a body or material) capable of returning to its original shape after compression, stretching, or other deformation. **2** capable of adapting to change. **3** quick to recover from fatigue, dejection, etc. **4** springy or resilient. **5** made of elastic. ◆ *n* **6** tape, cord, or fabric containing flexible rubber or similar substance allowing it to stretch and return to its original shape. [C17: from NL *elasticus* impulsive, from Gk *elastikos*, from *elaunein* to beat, drive]
▸**e'lastically** *adv* ▸**elas'ticity** *n*

elasticate (ɪ'læstɪ,keɪt) *vb* **elasticates, elasticating, elasticated.** (*tr*) to insert elastic into (a fabric or garment).
▸**e,lasti'cation** *n*

elastic band *n* another name for **rubber band.**

elasticize *or* **elasticise** (ɪ'læstɪ,saɪz) *vb* **elasticizes, elasticizing, elasticized** *or* **elasticises, elasticising, elasticised. 1** to make elastic. **2** another word for **elasticate.**

elastomer (ɪ'læstəmə) *n* any material, such as rubber, able to resume its original shape when a deforming force is removed. [C20: from ELASTIC + -MER]
▸**elastomeric** (ɪ,læstə'mɛrɪk) *adj*

Elastoplast (ɪ'læstə,plɑːst) *n Trademark.* a gauze surgical dressing backed by adhesive tape.

elate ❶ (ɪ'leɪt) *vb* **elates, elating, elated.** (*tr*) to fill with high spirits, exhila-

THESAURUS

escape, exodus, issue, outlet, passage out, vent, way out, withdrawal

ejaculate *vb* **1** = **discharge**, eject, emit, spurt **2** = **exclaim**, blurt out, burst out, cry out, shout

ejaculation *n* **1** = **discharge**, ejection, emission, spurt **2** = **exclamation**, cry, shout

eject *vb* **1** = **emit**, cast out, discharge, disgorge, expel, spew, spout, throw out, vomit **2** = **throw out**, banish, boot out (*inf.*), bounce, deport, dispossess, drive out, evacuate, evict, exile, expel, give the bum's rush (*sl.*), oust, relegate, remove, show one the door, throw out on one's ear (*inf.*), turn out **3** = **dismiss**, discharge, dislodge, fire (*inf.*), get rid of, kick out (*inf.*), oust, sack (*inf.*), throw out

ejection *n* **1** = **emission**, casting out, disgorgement, expulsion, spouting, throwing out **2** = **expulsion**, banishment, deportation, dispossession, evacuation, eviction, exile, ouster (*Law*), removal, the bum's rush (*sl.*) **3** = **dismissal**, discharge, dislodgement, firing (*inf.*), sacking (*inf.*), the boot (*sl.*), the sack (*inf.*)

eke out *vb* **1** = **be sparing with**, be economical with, be frugal with, economize on, husband, stretch out

elaborate *adj* **1** = **detailed**, careful, exact, intricate, laboured, minute, painstaking, perfected, precise, skilful, studied, thorough **2** = **complicated**, complex, decorated, detailed, extravagant, fancy, fussy, involved, ornamented, ornate, ostentatious, showy ◆ *vb* **3, 4** = **expand (upon)**, add detail, amplify, complicate, decorate, develop, devise, embellish, enhance, enlarge, flesh out, garnish, improve, ornament, polish, produce, refine, work out
Antonyms *adj* ≠ **complicated:** basic, minimal, modest, plain, severe, simple, unadorned, unembellished, unfussy ◆ *vb* ≠ **expand (upon):** abbreviate, condense, put in a nutshell, reduce to essentials, simplify, streamline, summarize, truncate

élan *n* = **style**, animation, brio, dash, esprit, flair, impetuosity, panache, spirit, verve, vigour, vivacity, zest

elapse *vb* = **pass**, glide by, go, go by, lapse, pass by, roll by, roll on, slip away, slip by

elastic *adj* **1, 4** = **flexible**, ductile, plastic, pliable, pliant, resilient, rubbery, springy, stretchable, stretchy, supple, tensile, yielding **2** = **adaptable**, accommodating, adjustable, complaisant, compliant, flexible, supple, tolerant, variable, yielding
Antonyms *adj* ≠ **flexible:** firm, immovable, inflexible, rigid, set, stiff, unyielding ≠ **adaptable:** firm, immovable, inflexible, intractable, obdurate, resolute, rigid, set, stiff, strict, stringent, unyielding

elasticity *n* **1, 4** = **flexibility**, ductileness, ductility, give (*inf.*), plasticity, pliability, pliancy, pliantness, resilience, rubberiness, springiness, stretch, stretchiness, suppleness **2** = **adaptability**, adjustability, complaisance, compliantness, flexibility, suppleness, tolerance, variability

elated *adj* = **joyful**, animated, cheered, cock-

ration, pride, or optimism. [C16: from p.p. of L *efferre* to bear away, from *ferre* to carry]
►e'lated *adj* ►e'latedly *adv* ►e'latedness *n*

elation ➊ (ɪ'leɪʃən) *n* joyfulness or exaltation of spirit, as from success, pleasure, or relief.

E layer *n* another name for **E region.**

elbow ➊ ('ɛlbəʊ) *n* **1** the joint between the upper arm and the forearm. **2** the corresponding joint of birds or mammals. **3** the part of a garment that covers the elbow. **4** something resembling an elbow, such as a sharp bend in a road. **5 at one's elbow.** within easy reach. **6 out at elbow(s).** ragged or impoverished. ◆ *vb* **7** to make (one's way) by shoving, jostling, etc. **8** (*tr*) to knock or shove as with the elbow. **9** (*tr*) to reject; dismiss (esp. in **give** or **get the elbow**). [OE *elnboga*]

elbow grease *n Facetious.* vigorous physical labour, esp. hard rubbing.

elbowroom ➊ ('ɛlbəʊ,ru:m, -,rʊm) *n* sufficient scope to move or function.

elder[1] ➊ ('ɛldə) *adj* **1** born earlier; senior. Cf. **older. 2** (in certain card games) denoting or relating to the nondealer (the **elder hand**), who has certain advantages in the play. **3** *Arch.* **3a** prior in rank or office. **3b** of a previous time. ◆ *n* **4** an older person; one's senior. **5** *Anthropol.* a senior member of a tribe who has authority. **6** (in certain Protestant Churches) a lay office. **7** another word for **presbyter.** [OE *eldra,* comp. of *eald* OLD]
►'elder,ship *n*

elder[2] ('ɛldə) *n* any of various shrubs or small trees having clusters of small white flowers and red, purple, or black berry-like fruits. Also called: **elderberry.** [OE *ellern*]

elderberry ('ɛldə,bɛrɪ) *n, pl* **elderberries. 1** the fruit of the elder. **2** another name for **elder**[2].

elder brother *n* one of the senior members of Trinity House.

elderly ('ɛldəlɪ) *adj* (of people) quite old; past middle age.
►'elderliness *n*

eldest ('ɛldɪst) *adj* being the oldest, esp. the oldest surviving child of the same parents. [OE *eldesta,* sup. of *eald* OLD]

El Dorado (ɛl dɒ'rɑ:dəʊ) *n* **1** a fabled city in South America, rich in treasure. **2** Also: **eldorado.** any place of great riches or fabulous opportunity. [C16: from Sp., lit.: the gilded (place)]

eldritch *or* **eldrich** ('ɛldrɪtʃ) *adj Poetic, Scot.* unearthly; weird. [C16: ?from OE *ælf* elf + *rīce* realm]

elect ➊ (ɪ'lɛkt) *vb* **1** (*tr*) to choose (someone) to be (a representative or official) by voting. **2** to select; choose. **3** (*tr*) (of God) to predestine for the grace of salvation. ◆ *adj* **4** (*immediately postpositive*) voted into office but not yet installed: *president elect.* **5a** chosen; elite. **5b** (*as collective n;* preceded by *the*): *the elect.* **6** *Christian theol.* **6a** predestined by God to receive salvation. **6b** (*as collective n;* preceded by *the*): *the elect.* [C15: from L *ēligere* to select, from *legere* to choose]
►e'lectable *adj*

elect. *or* **elec.** *abbrev. for:* **1** electric(al). **2** electricity.

election ➊ (ɪ'lɛkʃən) *n* **1** the selection by vote of a person or persons for a position, esp. a political office. **2** a public vote. **3** the act or an instance of choosing. **4** *Christian theol.* **4a** the doctrine that God chooses individuals for salvation without reference to faith or works. **4b** the doctrine that God chooses for salvation those who, by grace, persevere in faith and works.

electioneer (ɪ,lɛkʃə'nɪə) *vb* (*intr*) **1** to be active in a political election or campaign. ◆ *n* **2** a person who engages in this activity.
►e,lection'eering *n, adj*

elective (ɪ'lɛktɪv) *adj* **1** of or based on selection by vote. **2** selected by vote. **3** having the power to elect. **4** open to choice; optional. ◆ *n* **5** an optional course or hospital placement undertaken by a medical student.
►electivity (,i:lɛk'tɪvɪtɪ) *or* e'lectiveness *n*

elector ➊ (ɪ'lɛktə) *n* **1** someone who is eligible to vote in the election of a government. **2** (*often cap.*) a member of the US electoral college. **3** (*often cap.*) (in the Holy Roman Empire) any of the German princes entitled to take part in the election of a new emperor.
►e'lectoral *adj* ►e'lector,ship *n* ►e'lectress *fem n*

electoral college *n* (*often cap.*) **1** *US.* a body of electors chosen by the voters who formally elect the president and vice president. **2** any body of electors with similar functions.

electorate (ɪ'lɛktərɪt) *n* **1** the body of all qualified voters. **2** the rank, position, or territory of an elector of the Holy Roman Empire. **3** *Austral. & NZ.* the area represented by a Member of Parliament. **4** *Austral. & NZ.* the voters in a constituency.

electret (ɪ'lɛktrət) *n* a permanently polarized dielectric material; its field is similar to that of a permanent magnet. [C20: from *electr(icity + magn)et*]

electric ➊ (ɪ'lɛktrɪk) *adj* **1** of, derived from, produced by, producing, transmitting, or powered by electricity. **2** (of a musical instrument) amplified electronically. **3** very tense or exciting; emotionally charged. ◆ *n* **4** *Inf.* an electric train, car, etc. **5** (*pl*) an electric circuit or electric appliances. [C17: from NL *electricus* amber-like (because friction causes amber to become charged), from L *ēlectrum* amber, from Gk *ēlektron,* from ?]

USAGE NOTE See at **electronic.**

electrical (ɪ'lɛktrɪk°l) *adj* of, relating to, or concerned with electricity.
►e'lectrically *adv*

USAGE NOTE See at **electronic.**

electrical engineering *n* the branch of engineering concerned with practical applications of electricity.
►electrical engineer *n*

electric blanket *n* a blanket that contains an electric heating element, used to warm a bed.

electric chair *n* (in the US) **a** an electrified chair for executing criminals. **b** (usually preceded by *the*) execution by this method.

electric circuit *n Physics.* another name for **circuit** (sense 3a).

electric constant *n* the permittivity of free space, which has the value $8.854\ 185 \times 10^{-12}$ farad per metre.

electric discharge *n Physics.* another name for **discharge** (sense 17b).

electric displacement *n Physics.* the charge per unit area displaced across a layer of conductor in an electric field. Symbol: *D* Also called: **electric flux density.**

electric eel *n* an eel-like freshwater fish of N South America, having electric organs in the body.

electric eye *n* another name for **photocell.**

electric field *n* a field of force surrounding a charged particle within which another charged particle experiences a force.

electric flux *n* the amount of electricity displaced across a given area in a dielectric. Symbol: Ψ

electric flux density *n* another name for **electric displacement.**

electric guitar *n* an electrically amplified guitar, used mainly in pop music.

electrician (ɪlɛk'trɪʃən, ,i:lɛk-) *n* a person whose occupation is the installation, maintenance, and repair of electrical devices.

electricity (ɪlɛk'trɪsɪtɪ, ,i:lɛk-) *n* **1** any phenomenon associated with stationary or moving electrons, ions, or other charged particles. **2** the science of electricity. **3** an electric current or charge. **4** emotional tension or excitement.

electric motor *n* a device that converts electrical energy to mechanical torque.

electric organ *n* **1** *Music.* **1a** a pipe organ operated by electrical means. **1b** another name for **electronic organ. 2** a group of cells on certain fishes, such as the electric eel, that gives an electric shock to any animal touching them.

electric potential *n* **a** the work required to transfer a unit positive electric charge from an infinite distance to a given point. **b** the potential difference between the point and some other point. Sometimes shortened to **potential.**

electric ray *n* any ray of tropical and temperate seas, having a flat rounded body and an organ for producing electricity in each fin.

electric shock *n* the physiological reaction, characterized by pain and muscular spasm, to the passage of an electric current through the body. It can affect the respiratory system and heart rhythm. Sometimes shortened to **shock.**

electric susceptibility *n* another name for **susceptibility** (sense 4a).

electrify ➊ (ɪ'lɛktrɪ,faɪ) *vb* **electrifies, electrifying, electrified.** (*tr*) **1** to adapt or equip (a system, device, etc.) for operation by electrical power. **2** to charge with or subject to electricity. **3** to startle or excite intensely.
►e'lectri,fiable *adj* ►e,lectrifi'cation *n* ►e'lectri,fier *n*

electro (ɪ'lɛktrəʊ) *n, pl* **electros.** short for **electroplate** or **electrotype.**

electro- *or sometimes before a vowel* **electr-** *combining form.* **1** electric or

THESAURUS

a-hoop, delighted, ecstatic, euphoric, excited, exhilarated, exultant, floating *or* walking on air, gleeful, in high spirits, in seventh heaven, joyous, jubilant, overjoyed, over the moon (*inf.*), proud, puffed up, rapt, roused
Antonyms *adj* dejected, depressed, discouraged, dispirited, downcast, down in the dumps (*inf.*), miserable, sad, unhappy, woebegone

elation *n* = **joy,** bliss, delight, ecstasy, euphoria, exaltation, exhilaration, exultation, glee, high spirits, joyfulness, joyousness, jubilation, rapture

elbow *n* **4** = **joint,** angle, bend, corner, turn **5 at one's elbow** = **within reach,** at hand, close by, handy, near, to hand **6 out at elbow(s)** = **impoverished,** beggarly, down at heel, in rags, ragged, seedy, shabby, tattered ◆ *vb* **7, 8** = **push,** bump, crowd, hustle, jostle, knock, nudge, shoulder, shove

elbowroom *n* = **scope,** freedom, latitude, leeway, play, room, space

elder[1] *adj* **1** = **older,** ancient, earlier born, first-born, senior ◆ *n* **4** = **older person,** senior **6** = **church official,** office bearer, presbyter

elect *vb* **1, 2** = **choose,** appoint, decide upon, designate, determine, opt for, pick, pick out, prefer, select, settle on, vote ◆ *adj* **5** = **selected,** choice, chosen, elite, hand-picked, picked, preferred, select

election *n* **1-3** = **voting,** appointment, choice, choosing, decision, determination, judgment, preference, selection, vote

elector *n* **1-2** = **voter,** chooser, constituent, selector

electric *adj* **3** = **charged,** dynamic, exciting, high-octane (*inf.*), rousing, stimulating, stirring, tense, thrilling

electrify *vb* **3** = **startle,** amaze, animate, astonish, astound, excite, fire, galvanize, invigorate, jolt, rouse, shock, stimulate, stir, take one's breath away, thrill
Antonyms *vb* be tedious, bore, exhaust, fatigue, jade, send to sleep, tire, weary

electrically: *electrodynamic.* **2** electrolytic: *electrodialysis.* [from NL, from L *ēlectrum* amber, from Gk *ēlektron*]

electroacoustic (ɪˌlɛktrəʊəˈkuːstɪk) *adj* (of music) combining both computer-generated and acoustic sounds.

electrocardiograph (ɪˌlɛktrəʊˈkɑːdɪəʊˌgrɑːf) *n* an instrument for making tracings (**electrocardiograms**) recording the electrical activity of the heart.
▸**eˌlectroˌcardioˈgraphic** *or* **eˌlectroˌcardioˈgraphical** *adj* ▸**electrocardiography** (ɪˌlɛktrəʊˌkɑːdɪˈɒgrəfɪ) *n*

electrochemistry (ɪˌlɛktrəʊˈkɛmɪstrɪ) *n* the branch of chemistry concerned with electric cells and electrolysis.
▸**ˌelectroˈchemical** *adj* ▸**eˌlectroˈchemist** *n*

electroconvulsive therapy (ɪˌlɛktrəʊkənˈvʌlsɪv) *n Med.* the treatment of certain psychotic conditions by passing an electric current through the brain to induce coma or convulsions. See also **shock therapy.**

electrocute (ɪˈlɛktrəˌkjuːt) *vb* **electrocutes, electrocuting, electrocuted.** *(tr)* **1** to kill as a result of an electric shock. **2** *US.* to execute in the electric chair. [C19: from ELECTRO- + (EXE)CUTE]
▸**eˌlectroˈcution** *n*

electrode (ɪˈlɛktrəʊd) *n* **1** a conductor through which an electric current enters or leaves an electrolyte, an electric arc, or an electronic valve or tube. **2** an element in a semiconducting device that emits, collects, or controls the movement of electrons or holes.

electrodeposit (ɪˌlɛktrəʊdɪˈpɒzɪt) *vb* **1** *(tr)* to deposit (a metal) by electrolysis. ◆ *n* **2** the deposit so formed.
▸**electrodeposition** (ɪˌlɛktrəʊˌdɛpəˈzɪʃən) *n*

electrodynamics (ɪˌlɛktrəʊdaɪˈnæmɪks) *n (functioning as sing)* the branch of physics concerned with the interactions between electrical and mechanical forces.

electroencephalograph (ɪˌlɛktrəʊɛnˈsɛfələˌgrɑːf) *n* an instrument for making tracings (**electroencephalograms**) recording the electrical activity of the brain, usually by means of electrodes placed on the scalp. See also **brain wave.**
▸**eˌlectroenˌcephaloˈgraphic** *adj* ▸**electroencephalography** (ɪˌlɛktrəʊɛn-ˌsɛfəˈlɒgrəfɪ) *n*

electrolyse *or US* **electrolyze** (ɪˈlɛktrəʊˌlaɪz) *vb* **electrolyses, electrolysing, electrolysed** *or US* **electrolyzes, electrolyzing, electrolyzed.** *(tr)* **1** to decompose (a chemical compound) by electrolysis. **2** to destroy (living tissue, such as hair roots) by electrolysis.
▸**eˈlectroˌlyser** *or US* **eˈlectroˌlyzer** *n*

electrolysis (ɪlɛkˈtrɒlɪsɪs) *n* **1** the conduction of electricity by an electrolyte, esp. the use of this process to induce chemical changes. **2** the destruction of living tissue, such as hair roots, by an electric current, usually for cosmetic reasons.

electrolyte (ɪˈlɛktrəʊˌlaɪt) *n* **1** a solution or molten substance that conducts electricity. **2a** a chemical compound that dissociates in solution into ions. **2b** any of the ions themselves.

electrolytic (ɪˌlɛktrəʊˈlɪtɪk) *adj* **1** *Physics.* **1a** of, concerned with, or produced by electrolysis or electrodeposition. **1b** of, relating to, or containing an electrolyte. ◆ *n* **2** *Electronics.* Also called: **electrolytic capacitor.** a small capacitor consisting of two electrodes separated by an electrolyte.
▸**eˌlectroˈlytically** *adv*

electromagnet (ɪˌlɛktrəʊˈmægnɪt) *n* a magnet consisting of an iron or steel core wound with a coil of wire, through which a current is passed.

electromagnetic (ɪˌlɛktrəʊmægˈnɛtɪk) *adj* **1** of, containing, or operated by an electromagnet. **2** of, relating to, or consisting of electromagnetism. **3** of or relating to electromagnetic radiation.
▸**eˌlectromagˈnetically** *adv*

electromagnetic radiation *n* radiation consisting of an electric and magnetic field at right angles to each other and to the direction of propagation.

electromagnetics (ɪˌlɛktrəʊmægˈnɛtɪks) *n (functioning as sing) Physics.* another name for **electromagnetism** (sense 2).

electromagnetic spectrum *n* the complete range of electromagnetic radiation from the longest radio waves to the shortest gamma radiation.

electromagnetic unit *n* any unit of a system of electrical cgs units in which the magnetic constant is given the value of unity.

electromagnetic wave *n* a wave of energy propagated in an electromagnetic field.

electromagnetism (ɪˌlɛktrəʊˈmægnɪˌtɪzəm) *n* **1** magnetism produced by electric current. **2** Also called: **electromagnetics.** the branch of physics concerned with this magnetism and with the interaction of electric and magnetic fields.

electrometer (ɪlɛkˈtrɒmɪtə, ˌiːlɛk-) *n* an instrument for detecting or measuring a potential difference or charge by the electrostatic forces between charged bodies.
▸**electrometric** (ɪˌlɛktrəʊˈmɛtrɪk) *or* **eˌlectroˈmetrical** *adj* ▸**elecˈtrometry** *n*

electromotive (ɪˌlɛktrəʊˈməʊtɪv) *adj* of, concerned with, or producing an electric current.

electromotive force *n Physics.* **a** a source of energy that can cause current to flow in an electrical circuit. **b** the rate at which energy is drawn from this source when unit current flows through the circuit, measured in volts.

electromyography (ɪˌlɛktrəʊmaɪˈɒgrəfɪ) *n Med.* a technique for recording the electrical activity of muscles: used in the diagnosis of nerve and muscle disorders.

electron (ɪˈlɛktrɒn) *n* an elementary particle in all atoms, orbiting the nucleus in numbers equal to the atomic number of the element. [C19: from ELECTRO- + -ON]

electronegative (ɪˌlɛktrəʊˈnɛgətɪv) *adj* **1** having a negative electric charge. **2** (of an atom, molecule, etc.) tending to attract electrons and form negative ions or polarized bonds.

electron gun *n* a heated cathode for producing and focusing a beam of electrons, used esp. in cathode-ray tubes.

electronic (ɪlɛkˈtrɒnɪk, ˌiːlɛk-) *adj* **1** of, concerned with, using, or operated by devices, such as transistors, in which electrons are conducted through a semiconductor, free space, or gas. **2** of or concerned with electronics. **3** of or concerned with electrons. **4** involving or concerned with the representation, storage, or transmission of information by electronic systems: *electronic mail; electronic shopping.*
▸**elecˈtronically** *adv*

> **USAGE NOTE** *Electronic* is used to refer to equipment, such as television sets, computers, etc., in which current is controlled by transistors, valves, and similar components and also to the components themselves. *Electrical* is used in a more general sense, often to refer to the use of electricity as opposed to other forms of energy: *electrical engineering; an electrical appliance. Electric,* in many cases used interchangeably with *electrical,* is often restricted to the description of devices or to concepts relating to the flow of current: *electric fire; electric charge.*

electronic flash *n Photog.* an electronic device for producing a very bright flash of light by means of an electric discharge in a gas-filled tube.

electronic funds transfer at point of sale *n* a system for debiting a retail sale direct to the customer's bank, building-society, or credit-card account by means of a computer link using the telephone network. The customer inserts his debit card or credit card into the computer at the point of sale. Acronym: **EFTPOS.**

electronic ignition *n* any system that uses an electronic circuit to supply the voltage to the sparking plugs of an internal-combustion engine.

electronic keyboard *n* a typewriter keyboard used to operate an electronic device such as a computer.

electronic mail *n* the transmission of information, messages, facsimiles, etc., from one computer terminal to another. Often shortened to **E-mail, e-mail, email.**

electronic music *n* music consisting of sounds produced by electric currents either controlled from an instrument panel or keyboard or prerecorded on magnetic tape.

electronic organ *n Music.* an instrument played by means of a keyboard, in which sounds are produced by electronic or electrical means.

electronic organizer *n* a computerized personal organizer.

electronic point of sale *n* a computerized system for recording sales in retail shops, using a laser scanner at the cash till to read bar codes on the packages of the items sold. The retailer's stock record is automatically adjusted and the customer receives an itemized bill. Acronym: **EPOS.**

electronic publishing *n* the publication of information on magnetic tape, discs, etc., so that it can be accessed by a computer.

electronics (ɪlɛkˈtrɒnɪks, ˌiːlɛk-) *n* **1** *(functioning as sing)* the science and technology concerned with the development, behaviour, and applications of electronic devices and circuits. **2** *(functioning as pl)* the circuits and devices of a piece of electronic equipment.

electronic surveillance *n* **1** the use of such electronic devices as television monitors, video cameras, etc., to prevent burglary, shop lifting, break-ins, etc. **2** monitoring events, conversations, etc. at a distance by electronic means, esp. by such covert means as wire tapping or bugging.

electronic tag *n* another name for **tag**[1] (sense 2).

electronic transfer of funds *n* the transfer of money from one bank or building-society account to another by means of a computer link using the telephone network. Abbrev.: **ETF.**

electron lens *n* a system, such as an arrangement of electrodes or magnets, that produces a field for focusing a beam of electrons.

electron micrograph *n* a photograph of a specimen taken through an electron microscope.

electron microscope *n* a powerful microscope that uses electrons, rather than light, and electron lenses to produce a magnified image.

electron tube *n* an electrical device, such as a valve, in which a flow of electrons between electrodes takes place.

electronvolt (ɪˌlɛktrɒnˈvəʊlt) *n* a unit of energy equal to the work done on an electron accelerated through a potential difference of 1 volt.

electrophoresis (ɪˌlɛktrəʊfəˈriːsɪs) *n* the motion of charged particles in a colloid under the influence of an applied electric field.
▸**electrophoretic** (ɪˌlɛktrəʊfəˈrɛtɪk) *adj*

electrophorus (ɪlɛkˈtrɒfərəs, ˌiːlɛk-) *n* an apparatus for generating static electricity by induction. [C18: from ELECTRO- + *-phorus*, from Gk, from *pherein* to bear]

electroplate (ɪˈlɛktrəʊˌpleɪt) *vb* **electroplates, electroplating, electroplated.** **1** *(tr)* to plate (an object) by electrolysis. ◆ *n* **2** electroplated articles collectively, esp. when plated with silver.
▸**eˈlectroˌplater** *n*

electropositive (ɪˌlɛktrəʊˈpɒzɪtɪv) *adj* **1** having a positive electric charge. **2** (of an atom, molecule, etc.) tending to release electrons and form positive ions or polarized bonds.

electrorheology (ɪˌlɛktrəʊrɪˈɒlədʒɪ) *n* **1** the study of the flow of fluids under the influence of electric fields. **2** the way in which fluid flow is influenced by an electric field.
▸**eˌlectroˌrheoˈlogical** *adj*
electroscope (ɪˈlɛktrəʊˌskəʊp) *n* an apparatus for detecting an electric charge, typically consisting of a rod holding two gold foils that separate when a charge is applied.
▸**electroscopic** (ɪˌlɛktrəʊˈskɒpɪk) *adj*
electroshock therapy (ɪˈlɛktrəʊˌʃɒk) *n* another name for **electroconvulsive therapy.**
electrostatics (ɪˌlɛktrəʊˈstætɪks) *n* (*functioning as sing*) the branch of physics concerned with static electricity.
▸**eˌlectroˈstatic** *adj*
electrostatic unit *n* any unit of a system of electrical cgs units in which the electric constant is given the value of unity.
electrotherapeutics (ɪˌlɛktrəʊˌθɛrəˈpjuːtɪks) *n* (*functioning as sing*) the branch of medical science concerned with the use of electrotherapy.
▸**eˌlectroˌtheraˈpeutic** *or* **eˌlectroˌtheraˈpeutical** *adj*
electrotherapy (ɪˌlɛktrəʊˈθɛrəpɪ) *n* treatment in which electric currents are passed through the tissues to stimulate muscle function in paralysed patients.
▸**eˌlectroˈtherapist** *n*
electrotype (ɪˈlɛktrəʊˌtaɪp) *n* **1** a duplicate printing plate made by electrolytically depositing a layer of copper or nickel onto a mould of the original. ◆ *vb* **electrotypes, electrotyping, electrotyped. 2** (*tr*) to make an electrotype of (printed matter, etc.).
▸**eˈlectroˌtyper** *n*
electrovalent bond (ɪˌlɛktrəʊˈveɪlənt) *n* a type of chemical bond in which one atom loses an electron to form a positive ion and the other atom gains the electron to form a negative ion. The resulting ions are held together by electrostatic attraction.
▸**eˌlectroˈvalency** *n*
electroweak (ɪˌlɛktrəʊˈwiːk) *adj Physics.* involving both electromagnetic interaction and weak interaction.
electrum (ɪˈlɛktrəm) *n* an alloy of gold and silver. [C14: from L, from Gk *ēlektron* amber]
electuary (ɪˈlɛktjʊərɪ) *n, pl* **electuaries.** *Med.* a paste taken orally, containing a drug mixed with syrup or honey. [C14: from LL *ēlēctuārium*, prob. from Gk *ekleikton*, from *leikhein* to lick]
eleemosynary (ˌɛlɪiːˈmɒsɪnərɪ) *adj* **1** of or dependent on charity. **2** given as an act of charity. [C17: from Church L *eleēmosyna* ALMS]
elegance ❶ (ˈɛlɪgəns) *or* **elegancy** *n, pl* **elegances** *or* **elegancies. 1** dignified grace. **2** good taste in design, style, arrangement, etc. **3** something elegant; a refinement.
elegant ❶ (ˈɛlɪgənt) *adj* **1** tasteful in dress, style, or design. **2** dignified and graceful. **3** cleverly simple; ingenious: *an elegant solution.* [C16: from L *ēlegāns* tasteful; see ELECT]
elegiac ❶ (ˌɛlɪˈdʒaɪək) *adj* **1** resembling, characteristic of, relating to, or appropriate to an elegy. **2** lamenting; mournful. **3** denoting or written in elegiac couplets (which consist of a dactylic hexameter followed by a dactylic pentameter) or elegiac stanzas (which consist of a quatrain in iambic pentameters with alternate lines rhyming). ◆ *n* **4** (*often pl*) an elegiac couplet or stanza.
▸**ˌeleˈgiacally** *adv*
elegize *or* **elegise** (ˈɛlɪˌdʒaɪz) *vb* **elegizes, elegizing, elegized** *or* **elegises, elegising, elegised. 1** to compose an elegy (in memory of). **2** (*intr*) to write elegiacally.
▸**ˈelegist** *n*
elegy ❶ (ˈɛlɪdʒɪ) *n, pl* **elegies. 1** a mournful poem or song, esp. a lament for the dead. **2** poetry written in elegiac couplets or stanzas. [C16: via F & L from Gk, from *elegos* lament sung to flute accompaniment]

> **USAGE NOTE** Avoid confusion with **eulogy.**

elem. *abbrev. for:* **1** element(s). **2** elementary.
element ❶ (ˈɛlɪmənt) *n* **1** any of the 109 known substances that consist of atoms with the same number of protons in their nuclei. **2** one of the fundamental or irreducible components making up a whole. **3** a cause that contributes to a result; factor. **4** any group that is part of a larger unit, such as a military formation. **5** a small amount; hint. **6** a distinguishable section of a social group. **7** the most favourable environment for an animal or plant. **8** the situation in which a person is happiest or most effective (esp. in **in** *or* **out of one's element**). **9** the resistance wire that constitutes the electrical heater in a cooker, heater, etc. **10** one of the four substances thought in ancient and medieval cosmology to constitute the universe (earth, air, water, or fire). **11** (*pl*) atmospheric conditions, esp. wind, rain, and cold. **12** (*pl*) the basic principles. **13** *Christianity.* the bread or wine consecrated in the Eucharist. [C13: from L *elementum* a first principle, element]
elemental ❶ (ˌɛlɪˈmɛntᵊl) *adj* **1** fundamental; basic. **2** motivated by or symbolic of primitive powerful natural forces or passions. **3** of or relating to earth, air, water, and fire considered as elements. **4** of or relating to atmospheric forces, esp. wind, rain, and cold. **5** of or relating to a chemical element. ◆ *n* **6** *Rare.* a spirit or force that is said to appear in physical form.
▸**ˌeleˈmentalˌism** *n*
elementary ❶ (ˌɛlɪˈmɛntərɪ) *adj* **1** not difficult; rudimentary. **2** of or concerned with the first principles of a subject; introductory or fundamental. **3** *Chem.* another word for **elemental** (sense 5).
▸**ˌeleˈmentariness** *n*
elementary particle *n* any of several entities, such as electrons, neutrons, or protons, that are less complex than atoms.
elementary school *n* **1** *Brit.* a former name for **primary school. 2** *US & Canad.* a state school for the first six to eight years of a child's education.
elenchus (ɪˈlɛŋkəs) *n, pl* **elenchi** (-kaɪ). *Logic.* refutation of an argument by proving the contrary of its conclusion, esp. syllogistically. [C17: from L, from Gk, from *elenkhein* to refute]
▸**eˈlenctic** *adj*
elephant (ˈɛlɪfənt) *n, pl* **elephants** *or* **elephant.** either of two proboscidean mammals. The **African elephant** is the larger species, with large flapping ears and a less humped back than the **Indian elephant,** of S and SE Asia. [C13: from L, from Gk *elephas* elephant, ivory]
elephantiasis (ˌɛlɪfənˈtaɪəsɪs) *n Pathol.* a complication of chronic filariasis, in which nematode worms block the lymphatic vessels, usually in the legs or scrotum, causing extreme enlargement of the affected area. [C16: via L from Gk, from *elephas* ELEPHANT + -IASIS]
elephantine ❶ (ˌɛlɪˈfæntaɪn) *adj* **1** denoting, relating to, or characteristic of an elephant or elephants. **2** huge, clumsy, or ponderous.
elephant seal *n* either of two large earless seals, of southern oceans or of the N Atlantic, the males of which have a trunklike snout.
Eleusinian mysteries *pl n* a mystical religious festival, held at Eleusis in classical times, to celebrate the gods Persephone, Demeter, and Dionysus.
elev. *or* **el.** *abbrev. for* elevation.
elevate ❶ (ˈɛlɪˌveɪt) *vb* **elevates, elevating, elevated.** (*tr*) **1** to move to a higher place. **2** to raise in rank or status. **3** to put in a cheerful mood; elate. **4** to put on a higher cultural plane; uplift. **5** to raise the axis of a gun. **6** to raise the intensity or pitch of (the voice). [C15: from L *ēlevāre*, from *levāre* to raise, from *levis* (adj) light]
▸**ˈeleˌvatory** *adj*
elevated ❶ (ˈɛlɪˌveɪtɪd) *adj* **1** raised to or being at a higher level. **2** inflated or lofty; exalted. **3** in a cheerful mood. **4** *Inf.* slightly drunk.
elevation ❶ (ˌɛlɪˈveɪʃən) *n* **1** the act of elevating or the state of being elevated. **2** the height of something above a given place, esp. above sea level. **3** a raised area; height. **4** nobleness or grandeur. **5** a drawing to scale of the external face of a building or structure. **6** a ballet dancer's ability to leap high. **7** *Astron.* another name for **altitude** (sense 3). **8** the angle formed between the muzzle of a gun and the horizontal.
▸**ˌeleˈvational** *adj*
elevator (ˈɛlɪˌveɪtə) *n* **1** a person or thing that elevates. **2** a mechanical hoist, often consisting of a chain of scoops linked together on a conveyor belt. **3** the US and Canad. name for **lift** (sense 14a). **4** *Chiefly US & Canad.* a granary equipped with an elevator and, usually, facilities for cleaning and grading the grain. **5** a control surface on the tailplane of

THESAURUS

elegance *n* **1-2 = style,** beauty, courtliness, dignity, exquisiteness, gentility, grace, gracefulness, grandeur, luxury, polish, politeness, refinement, sumptuousness, taste
elegant *adj* **1-2 = stylish,** à la mode, artistic, beautiful, chic, choice, comely, courtly, cultivated, delicate, exquisite, fashionable, fine, genteel, graceful, handsome, luxurious, modish, nice, polished, refined, sumptuous, tasteful, urbane **3 = ingenious,** appropriate, apt, clever, effective, neat, simple
Antonyms *adj* ≠ **stylish:** awkward, clumsy, clunky (*inf.*), coarse, gauche, graceless, inelegant, misshapen, plain, tasteless, tawdry, ugly, uncouth, undignified, ungraceful, unrefined
elegiac *adj* **= lamenting,** dirgeful, funereal, keening, melancholy, mournful, nostalgic, plaintive, sad, threnodial, threnodic, valedictory
elegy *n* **1 = lament,** coronach (*Scot. & Irish*), dirge, keen, plaint (*arch.*), requiem, threnody
element *n* **2-4 = component,** basis, constituent, essential factor, factor, feature, ingredient, member, part, section, subdivision, unit **8** *As in* **in one's element = environment,** domain, field, habitat, medium, milieu, sphere **11** *plural* **= weather conditions,** atmospheric conditions, atmospheric forces, powers of nature **12** *plural* **= basics,** essentials, foundations, fundamentals, nuts and bolts (*inf.*), principles, rudiments
elemental *adj* **1 = basic,** elementary, essential, fundamental **2 = primal,** original, primitive, primordial **4 = atmospheric,** meteorological, natural
elementary *adj* **1 = simple,** clear, easy, facile, plain, rudimentary, straightforward, uncomplicated **2 = basic,** bog-standard (*inf.*), elemental, fundamental, initial, introductory, original, primary, rudimentary
Antonyms *adj* ≠ **simple:** complex, complicated, sophisticated ≠ **basic:** advanced, higher, highly-developed, progressive, secondary
elephantine *adj* **2 = massive,** bulky, clumsy, enormous, heavy, huge, hulking, humongous *or* humungous (*US sl.*), immense, laborious, lumbering, monstrous, ponderous, weighty
elevate *vb* **1 = raise,** heighten, hoist, lift, lift up, uplift, upraise **2 = promote,** advance, aggrandize, exalt, prefer, upgrade **3 = cheer,** animate, boost, brighten, buoy up, elate, excite, exhilarate, hearten, lift up, perk up, raise, rouse, uplift
elevated *adj* **2 = high-minded,** dignified, exalted, grand, high, high-flown, inflated, lofty, noble, sublime **3 = in high spirits,** animated, bright, cheerful, cheery, elated, excited, exhilarated, gleeful, overjoyed
Antonyms *adj* ≠ **high-minded:** humble, lowly, modest, simple
elevation *n* **1 = promotion,** advancement, aggrandizement, exaltation, preferment, upgrading **2 = altitude,** height **3 = rise,** acclivity, eminence, height, hill, hillock, mountain, rising ground

an aircraft, for making it climb or descend. **6** any muscle that raises a part of the body.

eleven (ɪˈlɛvᵊn) *n* **1** the cardinal number that is the sum of ten and one. **2** a numeral, 11, XI, etc., representing this number. **3** something representing, represented by, or consisting of 11 units. **4** (*functioning as sing or pl*) a team of 11 players in football, cricket, etc. **5** Also called: **eleven o'clock.** eleven hours after noon or midnight. ◆ *determiner* **6a** amounting to eleven. **6b** (*as pron*): *another eleven.* [OE *endleofan*]
▸**eˈleventh** *adj, n*

eleven-plus *n* (in Britain, esp. formerly) an examination taken by children aged 10 or 11 that determines the type of secondary education a child will be given.

elevenses (ɪˈlɛvᵊnzɪz) *pl n* (*sometimes functioning as sing*) *Brit. inf.* a light snack taken in mid-morning.

eleventh hour *n* the latest possible time; last minute.

elf (ɛlf) *n, pl* **elves. 1** (in folklore) one of a kind of legendary beings, usually characterized as small, manlike, and mischievous. **2** a mischievous or whimsical child. [OE *ælf*]
▸ **ˈelfish** *or* **ˈelvish** *adj*

elfin ➊ (ˈɛlfɪn) *adj* **1** of or like an elf or elves. **2** small, delicate, and charming.

elflock (ˈɛlfˌlɒk) *n* a lock of hair, fancifully regarded as having been tangled by the elves.

elicit ➊ (ɪˈlɪsɪt) *vb* (*tr*) **1** to give rise to; evoke. **2** to bring to light. [C17: from L *ēlicere*, from *licere* to entice]
▸**eˈlicitable** *adj* ▸**eˌliciˈtation** *n* ▸**eˈlicitor** *n*

elide (ɪˈlaɪd) *vb* **elides, eliding, elided.** to undergo or cause to undergo elision. [C16: from L *ēlīdere* to knock, from *laedere* to hit, wound]
▸**eˈlidible** *adj*

eligible ➊ (ˈɛlɪdʒəbᵊl) *adj* **1** fit, worthy, or qualified, as for office. **2** desirable, esp. as a spouse. [C15: from LL *ēligere* to ELECT]
▸ **ˌeligiˈbility** *n* ▸ **ˈeligibly** *adv*

eliminate ➊ (ɪˈlɪmɪˌneɪt) *vb* **eliminates, eliminating, eliminated.** (*tr*) **1** to remove or take out. **2** to reject; omit from consideration. **3** to remove (a competitor, team, etc.) from a contest, usually by defeat. **4** *Sl.* to murder in cold blood. **5** *Physiol.* to expel (waste) from the body. **6** *Maths.* to remove (an unknown variable) from simultaneous equations. [C16: from L *ēlīmināre* to turn out of the house, from *e-* out + *līmen* threshold]
▸**eˈliminable** *adj* ▸**eˌlimiˈnation** *n* ▸**eˈliminative** *adj* ▸**eˈlimiˌnator** *n*

> **USAGE NOTE** *Eliminate* is sometimes wrongly used to talk about avoiding the repetition of something undesirable: *we must prevent* (not *eliminate*) *further mistakes of this kind.*

ELISA (ɪˈlaɪzə) *n acronym for* enzyme-linked immunosorbent assay: an immunological technique for accurately measuring the amount of a substance, for example in a blood sample.

elision (ɪˈlɪʒən) *n* **1** omission of a syllable or vowel from a word. **2** omission of parts of a book, etc. [C16: from L *ēlīdere* to ELIDE]

elite ➊ *or* **élite** (ɪˈliːt, eɪ-) *n* **1** (*sometimes functioning as pl*) the most powerful, rich, or gifted members of a group, community, etc. **2** a typewriter type size having 12 characters to the inch. ◆ *adj* **3** of or suitable for an elite. [C18: from F, from OF *eslit* chosen, from L *ēligere* to ELECT]

elitism ➊ (ɪˈliːtɪzəm, eɪ-) *n* **1a** the belief that society should be governed by an elite. **1b** such government. **2** pride in or awareness of being one of an elite group.
▸**eˈlitist** *adj, n*

elixir ➊ (ɪˈlɪksə) *n* **1** an alchemical preparation supposed to be capable of prolonging life (**elixir of life**) or of transmuting base metals into gold. **2** anything that purports to be a sovereign remedy. **3** a quintessence. **4** a liquid containing a medicine with syrup, glycerine, or alcohol added to mask its unpleasant taste. [C14: from Med. L, from Ar., prob. from Gk *xērion* powder used for drying wounds]

Elizabethan (ɪˌlɪzəˈbiːθən) *adj* **1** of, characteristic of, or relating to the reigns of Elizabeth I (queen of England, 1558–1603) or Elizabeth II (queen of Great Britain and N Ireland since 1952). **2** of, relating to, or designating a style of architecture used in England during the reign of Elizabeth I. ◆ *n* **3** a person who lived in England during the reign of Elizabeth I.

Elizabethan sonnet *n* another term for **Shakespearean sonnet.**

elk (ɛlk) *n, pl* **elks** *or* **elk. 1** a large deer of N Europe and Asia: also occurs in N America, where it is called a moose. **2 American elk.** another name for **wapiti.** [OE *eolh*]

ell (ɛl) *n* an obsolete unit of length, approximately 45 inches. [OE *eln* forearm (the measure orig. being from elbow to fingertips)]

ellipse (ɪˈlɪps) *n* a closed conic section shaped like a flattened circle and formed by an inclined plane that does not cut the base of the cone. [C18: back formation from ELLIPSIS]

ellipsis (ɪˈlɪpsɪs) *n, pl* **ellipses** (-siːz). **1** omission of parts of a word or sentence. **2** *Printing.* a sequence of three dots (...) indicating an omission in text. [C16: from L, from Gk, from *en* in + *leipein* to leave]

ellipsoid (ɪˈlɪpsɔɪd) *n* **a** a geometric surface, symmetrical about the three coordinate axes, whose plane sections are ellipses or circles. **b** a solid having this shape.
▸**ellipsoidal** (ɪlɪpˈsɔɪdᵊl, ˌɛl-) *adj*

ellipsoid of revolution *n* a geometric surface produced by rotating an ellipse about one of its two axes and having circular plane sections perpendicular to the axis of revolution.

elliptical ➊ (ɪˈlɪptɪkᵊl) *adj* **1** relating to or having the shape of an ellipse. **2** relating to or resulting from ellipsis. **3** (of speech, literary style, etc.) **3a** very concise, often so as to be obscure or ambiguous. **3b** circumlocutory. ◆ Also (for senses 1 and 2): **elliptic.**
▸**elˈlipticalness** *n*

> **USAGE NOTE** The use of *elliptical* to mean *circumlocutory* should be avoided as it may be interpreted wrongly as meaning *condensed* or *concise.*

elm (ɛlm) *n* **1** any tree of the genus *Ulmus,* occurring in the N hemisphere, having serrated leaves and winged fruits (samaras). **2** the hard heavy wood of this tree. [OE *elm*]

El Niño (ɛl ˈniːnjəʊ) *n Meteorol.* a warming of the eastern tropical Pacific occurring every few years, which disrupts the weather pattern of the region. [from Sp.: The Child, i.e. Christ, referring to its original occurrence at Christmas time]

elocution ➊ (ˌɛləˈkjuːʃən) *n* the art of public speaking. [C15: from L *ēloquī*, from *loquī* to speak]
▸**ˌeloˈcutionary** *adj* ▸**ˌeloˈcutionist** *n* [C17: from Hebrew *'Elōhim*, plural (used to indicate uniqueness) of *'Elōah* God; probably related to *'El* God]

Elohist (ɛˈləʊhɪst) *n Bible.* the supposed author or authors of the Pentateuch, identified chiefly by the use of the word *Elohim* for God.

elongate ➊ (ˈiːlɒŋgeɪt) *vb* **elongates, elongating, elongated. 1** to make or become longer; stretch. ◆ *adj* **2** long and narrow. **3** lengthened or tapered. [C16: from LL *ēlongāre* to keep at a distance, from *ē-* away + L *longē* (adv) far]
▸**ˌelonˈgation** *n*

elope ➊ (ɪˈləʊp) *vb* **elopes, eloping, eloped.** (*intr*) to run away secretly with a lover, esp. in order to marry. [C16: from Anglo-F *aloper,* ?from MDu. *lōpen* to run; see LOPE]
▸**eˈlopement** *n* ▸**eˈloper** *n*

eloquence ➊ (ˈɛləkwəns) *n* **1** ease in using language. **2** powerful and effective language. **3** the quality of being persuasive or moving.

eloquent ➊ (ˈɛləkwənt) *adj* **1** (of speech, writing, etc.) fluent and persuasive. **2** visibly or vividly expressive: *an eloquent yawn.* [C14: from L *ēloquēns*, from *loquī* to speak]
▸ **ˈeloquentness** *n*

Elsan (ˈɛlsæn) *n Trademark.* a type of portable chemical lavatory. [C20: from initials of *E. L.* Jackson, manufacturer + SAN(ITATION)]

else (ɛls) *determiner* (*postpositive; used after an indefinite pronoun or an interrogative*) **1** in addition; more: *there is nobody else here.* **2** other; different: *where else could he be?* ◆ *adv* **3 or else. 3a** if not, then: *go away or else I won't finish my work today.* **3b** or something terrible will result: used as a threat: *sit down, or else!* [OE *elles*, genitive of *el-* strange, foreign]

THESAURUS

elfin *adj* **1 = rise**, elfish, elflike, elvish **2 = small**, arch, charming, frolicsome, impish, mischievous, playful, prankish, puckish, sprightly

elicit *vb* **1, 2 = bring about**, bring forth, bring out, bring to light, call forth, cause, derive, evolve, give rise to

eligible *adj* **1, 2 = qualified**, acceptable, appropriate, desirable, fit, preferable, proper, suitable, suited, worthy
Antonyms *adj* inappropriate, ineligible, unacceptable, unqualified, unsuitable, unsuited

eliminate *vb* **1 = get rid of**, cut out, dispose of, do away with, eradicate, exterminate, get shot of, remove, stamp out, take out, wipe from the face of the earth **2, 3 = drop**, axe (*inf.*), dispense with, disregard, eject, exclude, expel, ignore, knock out, leave out, omit, put out, reject, throw out **4** *Slang* **= murder**, annihilate, blow away (*sl., chiefly US*), bump off (*sl.*), kill, liquidate, rub out (*US sl.*), slay, take out (*sl.*), terminate, waste (*inf.*)

elite *n* **1 = best**, aristocracy, cream, *crème de la crème*, elect, flower, gentry, high society, nobility, pick, upper class ◆ *adj* **3 = best**, aristocratic, choice, crack (*sl.*), elect, exclusive, first-class, noble, pick, selected, upper-class
Antonyms *n* ≠ **best**: dregs, hoi polloi, rabble, riffraff

elitist *adj* **2 = snobbish**, exclusive, selective ◆ *n* **2 = snob**

elixir *n* **2 = panacea**, cure-all, nostrum, sovereign remedy **3 = essence**, concentrate, extract, pith, principle, quintessence **4 = syrup**, mixture, potion, solution, tincture

elliptical *adj* **1 = oval 3a = obscure**, abstruse, ambiguous, concentrated, concise, condensed, cryptic, laconic, recondite, terse

elocution *n* **= diction**, articulation, declamation, delivery, enunciation, oratory, pronunciation, public speaking, rhetoric, speech, speechmaking, utterance, voice production

elongate *vb* **1 = make longer**, draw out, extend, lengthen, prolong, protract, stretch

elongated *adj* **1 = drawn out**, extended, long, long-drawn-out, prolonged, protracted, stretched

elope *vb* **= run away**, abscond, bolt, decamp, disappear, escape, leave, run off, slip away, steal away

eloquence *n* **1-3 = expressiveness**, expression, fluency, forcefulness, oratory, persuasiveness, rhetoric, way with words

eloquent *adj* **1 = silver-tongued**, articulate, fluent, forceful, graceful, moving, persuasive, stirring, well-expressed **2 = expressive**, meaningful, pregnant, revealing, suggestive, telling, vivid
Antonyms *adj* ≠ **silver-tongued**: faltering, halting, hesitant, inarticulate, speechless, stumbling, tongue-tied, wordless

elsewhere ❶ (ˌɛlsˈwɛə) *adv* in or to another place; somewhere else. [OE *elles hwǣr;* see ELSE, WHERE]
ELT *abbrev. for* English Language Teaching.
eluate (ˈɛljuːˌeɪt) *n* a solution of adsorbed material in the eluant obtained during the process of elution.
elucidate ❶ (ɪˈluːsɪˌdeɪt) *vb* **elucidates, elucidating, elucidated.** to make clear (something obscure or difficult); clarify. [C16: from LL *ēlūcidāre* to enlighten; see LUCID]
▸**eˌluciˈdation** *n* ▸**eˈluciˌdative** *or* **eˈluciˌdatory** *adj* ▸**eˈluciˌdator** *n*
elude ❶ (ɪˈluːd) *vb* **eludes, eluding, eluded.** *(tr)* **1** to escape from or avoid, esp. by cunning. **2** to avoid fulfilment of (a responsibility, obligation, etc.); evade. **3** to escape discovery or understanding by; baffle. [C16: from L *ēlūdere* to deceive, from *lūdere* to play]
▸**eˈluder** *n* ▸**eˈlusion**

USAGE NOTE *Elude* is sometimes wrongly used where *allude* is meant: *he was alluding* (not *eluding*) *to his previous visit to the city.*

eluent *or* **eluant** (ˈɛljuənt) *n* a solvent used for eluting.
elusive ❶ (ɪˈluːsɪv) *adj* **1** difficult to catch. **2** preferring or living in solitude and anonymity. **3** difficult to remember.
▸**eˈlusiveness** *n*

USAGE NOTE See at **illusory.**

elute (iːˈluːt, ɪˈluːt) *vb* **elutes, eluting, eluted.** *(tr)* to wash out (a substance) by the action of a solvent, as in chromatography. [C18: from L *ēlūtus* rinsed out, from *luere* to wash, LAVE]
▸**eˈlution** *n*
elutriate (ɪˈluːtrɪˌeɪt) *vb* **elutriates, elutriating, elutriated.** *(tr)* to purify or separate (a substance or mixture) by washing and straining or decanting. [C18: from L *ēluere*, from *ē-* out + *lavere* to wash]
▸**eˌlutriˈation** *n*
elver (ˈɛlvə) *n* a young eel, esp. one migrating up a river. [C17: var. of *eelfare*, lit.: eel-journey; see EEL, FARE]
elves (ɛlvz) *n* the plural of **elf.**
elvish (ˈɛlvɪʃ) *adj* a variant of **elfish:** see **elf.**
Elysium (ɪˈlɪzɪəm) *n* **1** Also called: **Elysian fields.** *Greek myth.* the dwelling place of the blessed after death. **2** a state or place of perfect bliss. [C16: from L, from Gk *Ēlusion pedion* Elysian (that is, blessed) fields]
elytron (ˈɛlɪˌtrɒn) *or* **elytrum** (ˈɛlɪtrəm) *n, pl* **elytra** (-trə). either of the horny front wings of beetles and some other insects. [C18: from Gk *elutron* sheath]
em (ɛm) *n Printing.* **1** the square of a body of any size of type, used as a unit of measurement. **2** Also called: **pica em, pica.** a unit of measurement in printing, equal to twelve points or one sixth of an inch. [C19: from the name of the letter *M*]
em- *prefix* a variant of **en-**[1] and **en-**[2] before *b, m,* and *p.*
'em (əm) *pron* an informal variant of **them.**
emaciate ❶ (ɪˈmeɪsɪˌeɪt) *vb* **emaciates, emaciating, emaciated.** *(usually tr)* to become or cause to become abnormally thin. [C17: from L, from *macer* thin]
▸**eˈmaciˌated** *adj* ▸**eˌmaciˈation** *n*
E-mail, e-mail, *or* **email** (ˈiːmeɪl) *n* **1** short for **electronic mail.** ◆ *vb (tr)* **2** to contact (a person) by electronic mail. **3** to send (a message, document, etc.) by electronic mail.
emanate ❶ (ˈɛməˌneɪt) *vb* **emanates, emanating, emanated. 1** *(intr; often foll. by from)* to issue or proceed from or as from a source. **2** *(tr)* to send forth; emit. [C18: from L *ēmānāre* to flow out, from *mānāre* to flow]
▸**emanative** (ˈɛmənətɪv) *adj* ▸**ˈemaˌnator** *n* ▸**ˈemaˌnatory** *adj*
emanation ❶ (ˌɛməˈneɪʃən) *n* **1** an act or instance of emanating. **2** something that emanates or is produced. **3** a gaseous product of radioactive decay.
▸**ˌemaˈnational** *adj*
emancipate ❶ (ɪˈmænsɪˌpeɪt) *vb* **emancipates, emancipating, emancipated.** *(tr)* **1** to free from restriction or restraint, esp. social or legal restraint. **2** *(often passive)* to free from the inhibitions of conventional morality. **3** to liberate (a slave) from bondage. [C17: from L *ēmancipāre* to give independence (to a son), from *mancipāre* to transfer property; see MANCIPLE]
▸**eˈmanciˌpated** *adj* ▸**eˌmanciˈpation** *n* ▸**eˈmanciˌpator** *n* ▸**emancipatory** (ɪˈmænsɪpətərɪ, -trɪ) *adj*
emasculate ❶ *vb* (ɪˈmæskjʊˌleɪt), **emasculates, emasculating, emasculated.** *(tr)* **1** to remove the testicles of; castrate; geld. **2** to deprive of vigour, effectiveness, etc. **3** *Bot.* to remove the stamens from (a flower) to prevent self-pollination for the purposes of plant breeding. ◆ *adj* (ɪˈmæskjʊlɪt, -ˌleɪt). **4** castrated; gelded. **5** Also: **emasculated.** deprived of strength, effectiveness, etc. [C17: from L *ēmasculāre*, from *masculus* male; see MASCULINE]
▸**eˌmascuˈlation** *n* ▸**eˈmascuˌlator** *n* ▸**eˈmasculatory** *adj*
embalm ❶ (ɪmˈbɑːm) *vb (tr)* **1** to treat (a dead body) with preservatives to retard putrefaction. **2** to preserve or cherish the memory of. **3** *Poetic.* to give a sweet fragrance to. [C13: from OF *embaumer;* see BALM]
▸**emˈbalmer** *n* ▸**emˈbalmment** *n*
embank (ɪmˈbæŋk) *vb (tr)* to protect, enclose, or confine with an embankment.
embankment (ɪmˈbæŋkmənt) *n* a man-made ridge of earth or stone that carries a road or railway or confines a waterway.
embargo ❶ (ɛmˈbɑːgəʊ) *n, pl* **embargoes. 1** a government order prohibiting the departure or arrival of merchant ships in its ports. **2** any legal stoppage of commerce. **3** a restraint or prohibition. ◆ *vb* **embargoes, embargoing, embargoed.** *(tr)* **4** to lay an embargo upon. **5** to seize for use by the state. [C16: from Sp., from *embargar*, from L IM- + *barra* BAR[1]]
embark ❶ (ɛmˈbɑːk) *vb* **1** to board (a ship or aircraft). **2** *(intr; usually foll. by on or upon)* to commence or engage (in) a new project, venture, etc. [C16: via F from OF, from EM- + *barca* boat, BARQUE]
▸**ˌembarˈkation** *n*
embarrass ❶ (ɪmˈbærəs) *vb (mainly tr)* **1** to cause to feel confusion or self-consciousness; disconcert. **2** *(usually passive)* to involve in financial difficulties. **3** *Arch.* to complicate. **4** *Arch.* to impede or hamper. [C17 (in the sense: to impede): via F & Sp. from It., from *imbarrare* to confine within bars]
▸**emˈbarrassed** *adj* ▸**emˈbarrassing** *adj* ▸**emˈbarrassment** *n*
embassy (ˈɛmbəsɪ) *n, pl* **embassies. 1** the residence or place of business of an ambassador. **2** an ambassador and his entourage collectively. **3** the position, business, or mission of an ambassador. **4** any important or official mission. [C16: from OF *ambaisada;* see AMBASSADOR]
embattle (ɪmˈbætᵊl) *vb* **embattles, embattling, embattled.** *(tr)* **1** to deploy (troops) for battle. **2** to fortify (a position, town, etc.). **3** to provide with battlements. [C14: from OF *embataillier;* see EN-[1] BATTLE]
embay (ɪmˈbeɪ) *vb (tr) (usually passive)* **1** to form into a bay. **2** to enclose in or as if in a bay.
embed ❶ (ɪmˈbɛd) *vb* **embeds, embedding, embedded. 1** (usually foll. by *in*)

THESAURUS

elsewhere *adv* = **in** *or* **to another place**, abroad, away, hence (*arch.*), not here, somewhere else
elucidate *vb* = **clarify**, annotate, clear the air, clear up, explain, explicate, expound, gloss, illuminate, illustrate, interpret, make plain, shed *or* throw light upon, spell out, unfold
elucidation *n* = **clarification**, annotation, comment, commentary, explanation, explication, exposition, gloss, illumination, illustration, interpretation
elude *vb* **1, 2** = **escape**, avoid, body-swerve, circumvent, dodge, duck (*inf.*), evade, flee, get away from, outrun, shirk, shun, slip through one's fingers, slip through the net **3** = **baffle**, be beyond (someone), confound, escape, foil, frustrate, puzzle, stump, thwart
elusive *adj* **1** = **difficult to catch**, shifty, slippery, tricky **3** = **indefinable**, baffling, fleeting, intangible, puzzling, subtle, transient, transitory
emaciated *adj* = **skeletal**, atrophied, attenuate, attenuated, cadaverous, gaunt, haggard, lank, lean, meagre, pinched, scrawny, thin, undernourished, wasted
emaciation *n* = **thinness**, atrophy, attenuation, gauntness, haggardness, leanness, meagreness, scrawniness, wasting away
emanate *vb* **1** = **flow**, arise, come forth, derive, emerge, issue, originate, proceed, spring, stem **2** = **give out**, discharge, emit, exhale, give off, issue, radiate, send forth
emanation *n* **1** = **flow**, arising, derivation, emergence, origination, proceeding **2** = **emission**, discharge, effluent, efflux, effusion, exhalation **3** = **radiation**
emancipate *vb* **1-3** = **free**, deliver, discharge, disencumber, disenthral, enfranchise, liberate, manumit, release, set free, unbridle, unchain, unfetter, unshackle
Antonyms *vb* bind, capture, enchain, enslave, enthral, fetter, shackle, subjugate, yoke
emancipation *n* **1-3** = **freedom**, deliverance, discharge, enfranchisement, liberation, liberty, manumission, release
Antonyms *n* bondage, captivity, confinement, detention, enthralment, imprisonment, servitude, slavery, thraldom, vassalage
emasculate *vb* **1** = **castrate**, geld **2** = **weaken**, cripple, debilitate, deprive of force, enervate, impoverish, soften
embalm *vb* **1** = **preserve**, mummify **2** = **enshrine**, cherish, consecrate, conserve, immortalize, store, treasure
embargo *n* **1-3** = **ban**, bar, barrier, block, blockage, boycott, check, hindrance, impediment, interdict, interdiction, prohibition, proscription, restraint, restriction, stoppage ◆ *vb* **4** = **ban**, bar, block, boycott, check, impede, interdict, prohibit, proscribe, restrict, stop
embark *vb* **1** = **go aboard**, board ship, put on board, take on board, take ship **2** *usually with* **on** *or* **upon** = **begin**, broach, commence, engage, enter, get the show on the road (*inf.*), initiate, launch, plunge into, set about, set out, start, take up, undertake
Antonyms *vb* ≠ **go aboard:** alight, arrive, get off, go ashore, land, step out of
embarrass *vb* **1** = **shame**, abash, chagrin, confuse, discomfit, discompose, disconcert, discountenance, distress, faze, fluster, humiliate, mortify, put out of countenance, show up (*inf.*)
embarrassed *adj* **1** = **ashamed**, awkward, blushing, caught with egg on one's face, chagrined, confused, discomfited, disconcerted, discountenanced, flustered, humiliated, mortified, not knowing where to put oneself, put out of countenance, red-faced, self-conscious, sheepish, shown-up, thrown, upset, wishing the earth would swallow one up
embarrassing *adj* **1** = **humiliating**, awkward, blush-making, compromising, discomfiting, disconcerting, distressing, mortifying, sensitive, shameful, shaming, toe-curling (*sl.*), touchy, tricky, uncomfortable
embarrassment *n* **1** = **shame**, awkwardness, bashfulness, chagrin, confusion, discomfiture, discomposure, distress, humiliation, mortification, self-consciousness, showing up (*inf.*) **2** = **predicament**, bind (*inf.*), difficulty, mess, pickle (*inf.*), scrape (*inf.*)
embed *vb* **1** = **fix**, dig in, drive in, hammer in, implant, plant, ram in, root, set, sink

to fix or become fixed firmly and deeply in a surrounding solid mass. **2** (*tr*) to surround closely. **3** (*tr*) to fix or retain (a thought, idea, etc.) in the mind. ◆ Also: **imbed.**
▸**em'bedment** *n*

embellish ❶ (ɪm'bɛlɪʃ) *vb* (*tr*) **1** to beautify; adorn. **2** to make (a story, etc.) more interesting by adding detail. [C14: from OF *embelir*, from *bel* beautiful, from L *bellus*]
▸**em'bellisher** *n* ▸**em'bellishment** *n*

ember ❶ ('ɛmbə) *n* **1** a glowing or smouldering piece of coal or wood, as in a dying fire. **2** the remains of a past emotion. [OE *ǣmyrge*]

Ember days *pl n RC & Anglican Church.* any of four groups in the year of three days (always Wednesday, Friday, and Saturday) of prayer and fasting. [OE *ymbrendǣg*, from *ymb* around + *ryne* a course + *dǣg* day]

embezzle ❶ (ɪm'bɛzᵊl) *vb* **embezzles, embezzling, embezzled.** to convert (money or property entrusted to one) fraudulently to one's own use. [C15: from Anglo-F *embeseiller* to destroy, from OF *beseiller* to make away with, from ?]
▸**em'bezzlement** *n* ▸**em'bezzler** *n*

embitter ❶ (ɪm'bɪtə) *vb* (*tr*) **1** to make (a person) bitter. **2** to aggravate (a hostile feeling, difficult situation, etc.).
▸**em'bittered** *adj* ▸**em'bitterment** *n*

emblazon ❶ (ɪm'bleɪzᵊn) *vb* (*tr*) **1** to portray heraldic arms on (a shield, one's notepaper, etc.). **2** to make bright or splendid, as with colours, flowers, etc. **3** to glorify, praise, or extol.
▸**em'blazonment** *n*

emblem ❶ ('ɛmbləm) *n* a visible object or representation that symbolizes a quality, type, group, etc. [C15: from L *emblēma*, from Gk, from *emballein* to insert, from *en* in + *ballein* to throw]
▸ˌ**emblem'atic** *or* ˌ**emblem'atical** *adj* ▸ˌ**emblem'atically** *adv*

embody ❶ (ɪm'bɒdɪ) *vb* **embodies, embodying, embodied.** (*tr*) **1** to give a tangible, bodily, or concrete form to (an abstract concept). **2** to be an example of or express (an idea, principle, etc.). **3** (often foll. by *in*) to collect or unite in a comprehensive whole. **4** to invest (a spiritual entity) with bodily form.
▸**em'bodiment** *n*

embolden ❶ (ɪm'bəʊldᵊn) *vb* (*tr*) to encourage; make bold.

embolism ('ɛmbəˌlɪzəm) *n* the occlusion of a blood vessel by an embolus. [C14: from Med. L, from LGk *embolismos*; see EMBOLUS]
▸**embolic** (ɛm'bɒlɪk) *adj*

embolus ('ɛmbələs) *n, pl* **emboli** (-ˌlaɪ). material, such as part of a blood clot or an air bubble, that becomes lodged within a small blood vessel and impedes the circulation. [C17: via L from Gk *embolos* stopper; see EMBLEM]

embonpoint *French.* (ɑ̃bɔ̃pwɛ̃) *n* **1** plumpness or stoutness. ◆ *adj* **2** plump; stout. [C18: from *en bon point* in good condition]

embosom (ɪm'bʊzəm) *vb* (*tr*) *Arch.* **1** to enclose or envelop, esp. protectively. **2** to clasp to the bosom; hug. **3** to cherish.

emboss (ɪm'bɒs) *vb* **1** to mould or carve (a decoration) on (a surface) so that it is raised above the surface in low relief. **2** to cause to bulge; make protrude. [C14: from OF *embocer*, from EM- + *boce* BOSS[2]]
▸**em'bossed** *adj* ▸**em'bosser** *n* ▸**em'bossment** *n*

embouchure (ˌɒmbʊ'ʃʊə) *n* **1** the mouth of a river or valley. **2** *Music.* **2a** the correct application of the lips and tongue in playing a wind instrument. **2b** the mouthpiece of a wind instrument. [C18: from F, from OF, from *bouche* mouth, from L *bucca* cheek]

embower (ɪm'baʊə) *vb* (*tr*) *Arch.* to enclose in or as in a bower.

embrace ❶ (ɪm'breɪs) *vb* **embraces, embracing, embraced.** (*mainly tr*) **1** (*also intr*) (of a person) to take or clasp (another person) in the arms, or (of two people) to clasp each other, as in affection, greeting, etc.; hug. **2** to accept willingly or eagerly. **3** to take up (a new idea, faith, etc.); adopt. **4** to comprise or include as an integral part. **5** to encircle or enclose. **6** *Rare.* to perceive or understand. ◆ *n* **7** the act of embracing. [C14: from OF, from EM- + *brace* a pair of arms, from L *bracchia* arms]
▸**em'braceable** *adj* ▸**em'bracement** *n* ▸**em'bracer** *n*

embrasure (ɪm'breɪʒə) *n* **1** *Fortifications.* an opening or indentation, as in a battlement, for shooting through. **2** a door or window having splayed sides that increase the width of the opening in the interior. [C18: from F, from obs. *embraser* to widen]
▸**em'brasured** *adj*

embrocate ('ɛmbrəʊˌkeɪt) *vb* **embrocates, embrocating, embrocated.** (*tr*) to apply a liniment or lotion to (a part of the body). [C17: from Med. L *embrocha* poultice, from Gk, from *brokhē* a moistening]

embrocation (ˌɛmbrəʊ'keɪʃən) *n* a drug or agent for rubbing into the skin; liniment.

embroider (ɪm'brɔɪdə) *vb* **1** to do decorative needlework (upon). **2** to add fictitious or exaggerated detail to (a story, etc.). [C15: from OF *embroder*]
▸**em'broiderer** *n*

embroidery (ɪm'brɔɪdərɪ) *n, pl* **embroideries. 1** decorative needlework done usually on loosely woven cloth or canvas, often being a picture or pattern. **2** elaboration or exaggeration, esp. in writing or reporting; embellishment.

embroil ❶ (ɪm'brɔɪl) *vb* (*tr*) **1** to involve (a person, oneself, etc.) in trouble, conflict, or argument. **2** to throw (affairs, etc.) into a state of confusion or disorder; complicate; entangle. [C17: from F *embrouiller*, from *brouiller* to mingle, confuse]
▸**em'broiler** *n* ▸**em'broilment** *n*

embryo ❶ ('ɛmbrɪˌəʊ) *n, pl* **embryos. 1** an animal in the early stages of development up to birth or hatching. **2** the human product of conception up to approximately the end of the second month of pregnancy. Cf. **fetus. 3** a plant in the early stages of development. **4** an undeveloped or rudimentary state (esp. in **in embryo**). **5** something in an early stage of development. [C16: from LL, from Gk *embruon*, from *bruein* to swell]

embryology (ˌɛmbrɪ'ɒlədʒɪ) *n* **1** the scientific study of embryos. **2** the structure and development of the embryo of a particular organism.
▸**embryological** (ˌɛmbrɪə'lɒdʒɪkᵊl) *or* ˌ**embryo'logic** *adj* ▸ˌ**embry'ologist** *n*

embryonic ❶ (ˌɛmbrɪ'ɒnɪk) *or* **embryonal** ('ɛmbrɪənᵊl) *adj* **1** of or relating to an embryo. **2** in an early stage; rudimentary; undeveloped.
▸ˌ**embry'onically** *adv*

emcee (ˌɛm'siː) *Inf.* ◆ *n* **1** a master of ceremonies. ◆ *vb* **emcees, emceeing, emceed. 2** to act as master of ceremonies (for or at). [C20: from MC]

-eme *suffix forming nouns. Linguistics.* indicating a minimal distinctive unit of a specified type in a language: *morpheme; phoneme.* [C20: via F, abstracted from PHONEME]

emend ❶ (ɪ'mɛnd) *vb* (*tr*) to make corrections or improvements in (a text) by critical editing. [C15: from L, from *ē-* out + *mendum* a mistake]
▸**e'mendable** *adj*

emendation ❶ (ˌiːmɛn'deɪʃən) *n* **1** a correction or improvement in a text. **2** the act or process of emending.
▸**'emenˌdator** *n* ▸**emendatory** (ɪ'mɛndətərɪ, -trɪ) *adj*

emerald ('ɛmərəld, 'ɛmrəld) *n* **1** a green transparent variety of beryl: highly valued as a gem. **2a** its clear green colour. **2b** (*as adj*): *an emerald carpet.* [C13: from OF *esmeraude*, from L *smaragdus*, from Gk *smaragdos*]

Emerald Isle *n* a poetic name for Ireland.

emerge ❶ (ɪ'mɜːdʒ) *vb* **emerges, emerging, emerged.** (*intr*; often foll. by

THESAURUS

embellish *vb* **1, 2 = decorate**, adorn, beautify, bedeck, deck, dress up, elaborate, embroider, enhance, enrich, exaggerate, festoon, garnish, gild, gild the lily, grace, ornament, tart up (*sl.*), varnish

embellishment *n* **1, 2 = decoration**, adornment, elaboration, embroidery, enhancement, enrichment, exaggeration, gilding, ornament, ornamentation, trimming

ember *n* **1 = cinder**, ash, live coal

embezzle *vb* **= misappropriate**, abstract, appropriate, defalcate (*Law*), filch, have one's hand in the till (*inf.*), misapply, misuse, peculate, pilfer, purloin, rip off (*sl.*), steal

embezzlement *n* **= misappropriation**, abstraction, appropriation, defalcation (*Law*), filching, fraud, larceny, misapplication, misuse, peculation, pilferage, pilfering, purloining, stealing, theft, thieving

embitter *vb* **1 = make bitter** *or* **resentful**, alienate, anger, disaffect, disillusion, envenom, poison, sour **2 = aggravate**, exacerbate, exasperate, worsen

embittered *adj* **1 = resentful**, acid, angry, at daggers drawn (*inf.*), bitter, disaffected, disillusioned, nursing a grudge, rancorous, sour, soured, venomous, with a chip on one's shoulder (*inf.*)

emblazon *vb* **1, 2 = decorate**, adorn, blazon, colour, embellish, illuminate, ornament, paint **3 = publicize**, crack up (*inf.*), extol, glorify, laud (*literary*), praise, proclaim, publish, trumpet

emblem *n* **= symbol**, badge, crest, device, figure, image, insignia, mark, representation, sigil, sign, token, type

emblematic *adj* **= symbolic**, figurative, representative

embodiment *n* **1, 2 = personification**, epitome, example, exemplar, exemplification, expression, incarnation, incorporation, manifestation, realization, reification, representation, symbol, type **3 = incorporation**, bringing together, codification, collection, combination, comprehension, concentration, consolidation, inclusion, integration, organization, systematization

embody *vb* **1, 2 = personify**, concretize, exemplify, express, incarnate, incorporate, manifest, realize, reify, represent, stand for, symbolize, typify **3 = incorporate**, bring together, codify, collect, combine, comprehend, comprise, concentrate, consolidate, contain, include, integrate, organize, systematize

embolden *vb* **= encourage**, animate, cheer, fire, gee up, hearten, inflame, inspirit, invigorate, nerve, reassure, rouse, stimulate, stir, strengthen, vitalize

embrace *vb* **1 = hug**, clasp, cuddle, encircle, enfold, envelop, grasp, hold, neck (*inf.*), seize, squeeze, take *or* hold in one's arms **2, 3 = accept**, adopt, avail oneself of, espouse, grab, make use of, receive, seize, take on board, take up, welcome **4 = include**, comprehend, comprise, contain, cover, deal with, embody, encompass, involve, provide for, subsume, take in, take into account ◆ *n* **7 = hug**, canoodle (*sl.*), clasp, clinch (*sl.*), cuddle, squeeze

embroil *vb* **1, 2 = involve**, complicate, compromise, confound, confuse, disorder, disturb, encumber, enmesh, ensnare, entangle, implicate, incriminate, mire, mix up, muddle, perplex, stitch up (*sl.*), trouble

embryo *n* **5 = germ**, beginning, nucleus, root, rudiment

embryonic *adj* **2 = early**, beginning, germinal, immature, inchoate, incipient, primary, rudimentary, seminal, undeveloped
Antonyms *adj* advanced, developed, progressive

emend *vb* **= revise**, amend, correct, edit, improve, rectify, redact

emendation *n* **1, 2 = revision**, amendment, correction, editing, improvement, rectification, redaction

emerge *vb* **1, 2 = come into view**, appear, arise, become visible, come forth, come out, come up, emanate, issue, proceed, rise, spring up,

from) **1** to come up to the surface of or rise from water or other liquid. **2** to come into view, as from concealment or obscurity. **3** (foll. by *from*) to come out (of) or live (through (a difficult experience, etc.)). **4** to become apparent. [C17: from L *ēmergere* to rise up from, from *mergere* to dip]
▸**e'mergence** *n* ▸**e'merging** *adj*

emergency ❶ (ɪ'mɜːdʒənsɪ) *n, pl* **emergencies. 1a** an unforeseen or sudden occurrence, esp. of danger demanding immediate action. **1b** (*as modifier*): *an emergency exit.* **2a** a patient requiring urgent treatment. **2b** (*as modifier*): *an emergency ward.* **3** *NZ.* a player selected to stand by to replace an injured member of a team; reserve. **4 state of emergency.** a condition, declared by a government, in which martial law applies, usually because of civil unrest or natural disaster.

emergent ❶ (ɪ'mɜːdʒənt) *adj* **1** coming into being or notice. **2** (of a nation) recently independent.
▸**e'mergently** *adv*

emeritus (ɪ'merɪtəs) *adj* (*usually postpositive*) retired or honourably discharged from full-time work, but retaining one's title on an honorary basis: *a professor emeritus.* [C19: from L, from *merēre* to deserve; see MERIT]

emersion (ɪ'mɜːʃən) *n* **1** the act or an instance of emerging. **2** *Astron.* the reappearance of a celestial body after an eclipse or occultation. [C17: from L *ēmersus;* see EMERGE]

emery ('ɛmərɪ) *n* **a** a hard greyish-black mineral consisting of corundum with either magnetite or haematite: used as an abrasive and polishing agent. **b** (*as modifier*): *emery paper.* [C15: from OF *esmeril,* ult. from Gk *smuris* powder for rubbing]

emery board *n* a strip of cardboard or wood with a rough surface of crushed emery, for filing one's nails.

emetic ❶ (ɪ'metɪk) *adj* **1** causing vomiting. ◆ *n* **2** an emetic agent or drug. [C17: from LL, from Gk *emetikos,* from *emein* to vomit]

emf *or* **EMF** *abbrev. for* electromotive force.

-emia *n combining form.* a US variant of **-aemia.**

emigrant ('ɛmɪgrənt) *n* **a** a person who leaves one place, esp. his native country, to settle in another. **b** (*as modifier*): *an emigrant worker.*

emigrate ❶ ('ɛmɪˌgreɪt) *vb* **emigrates, emigrating, emigrated.** (*intr*) to leave one place, esp. one's native country, to settle in another. [C18: from L *ēmīgrāre,* from *mīgrāre* to depart, MIGRATE]
▸ˌ**emi'gration** *n* ▸'**emiˌgratory** *adj*

émigré ('ɛmɪˌgreɪ) *n* an emigrant, esp. one forced to leave his native country for political reasons. [C18: from F, from *émigrer* to EMIGRATE]

eminence ❶ ('ɛmɪnəns) *n* **1** a position of superiority or fame. **2** a high or raised piece of ground. ◆ Also: **eminency.** [C17: from F, from L *ēminentia* a standing out; see EMINENT]

Eminence ('ɛmɪnəns) *or* **Eminency** *n, pl* **Eminences** *or* **Eminencies.** (preceded by *Your* or *His*) a title used to address or refer to a cardinal.

éminence grise *French.* (eminɑ̃s griz) *n, pl* ***éminences grises*** (eminɑ̃s griz). a person who wields power and influence unofficially or behind the scenes. [lit.: grey eminence, orig. applied to Père Joseph, F monk, secretary of Cardinal Richelieu (1585–1642), F statesman]

eminent ❶ ('ɛmɪnənt) *adj* **1** above others in rank, merit, or reputation; distinguished. **2** (*prenominal*) noteworthy or outstanding. **3** projecting or protruding; prominent. [C15: from L *ēminēre* to project, stand out, from *minēre* to stand]

eminent domain *n Law.* the right of a state to confiscate private property for public use, payment usually being made in compensation.

emir (ɛ'mɪə) *n* (in the Islamic world) **1** an independent ruler or chieftain. **2** a military commander or governor. **3** a descendant of Mohammed. [C17: via F from Sp., from Ar. *'amīr* commander]
▸**e'mirate** *n*

emissary ❶ ('ɛmɪsərɪ, -ɪsrɪ) *n, pl* **emissaries. 1a** an agent sent on a mission, esp. one who represents a government or head of state. **1b** (*as modifier*): *an emissary delegation.* **2** an agent sent on a secret mission, as a spy. ◆ *adj* **3** (of veins) draining blood from sinuses in the dura mater to veins outside the skull. [C17: from L *ēmissārius,* from *ēmittere* to send out; see EMIT]

emission ❶ (ɪ'mɪʃən) *n* **1** the act of emitting or sending forth. **2** energy, in the form of heat, light, radio waves, etc., emitted from a source. **3** a substance, fluid, etc., that is emitted; discharge. **4** *Physiol.* any bodily discharge, esp. of semen. [C17: from L *ēmissiō,* from *ēmittere* to send forth, EMIT]
▸**e'missive** *adj*

emission spectrum *n* the spectrum or pattern of bright lines or bands seen when the electromagnetic radiation emitted by a substance is passed into a spectrometer.

emissivity (ˌiːmɪ'sɪvɪtɪ, ˌɛm-) *n* a measure of the ability of a surface to radiate energy; the ratio of the radiant flux emitted per unit area to that emitted by a black body at the same temperature.

emit ❶ (ɪ'mɪt) *vb* **emits, emitting, emitted.** (*tr*) **1** to give or send forth; discharge. **2** to give voice to; utter. **3** *Physics.* to give off (radiation or particles). [C17: from L *ēmittere* to send out, from *mittere* to send]

emitter (ɪ'mɪtə) *n* **1** a person or thing that emits. **2** a substance that emits radiation. **3** the region in a transistor in which the charge-carrying holes or electrons originate.

Emmenthal, Emmental ('ɛmənˌtɑːl), *or* **Emmenthaler** *n* a hard Swiss cheese with holes in it. [C20: after *Emmenthal,* valley in Switzerland]

Emmy ('ɛmɪ) *n, pl* **Emmys** *or* **Emmies.** (in the US) one of the statuettes awarded annually for outstanding television performances and productions. [C20: from *Immy,* short for *image orthicon tube*]

emollient (ɪ'mɒljənt) *adj* **1** softening or soothing, esp. to the skin. **2** helping to avoid confrontation; calming. ◆ *n* **3** any preparation or substance that has this effect. [C17: from L *ēmollīre* to soften, from *mollis* soft]
▸**e'mollience** *n*

emolument ❶ (ɪ'mɒljumənt) *n* the profit arising from an office or employment; fees or wages. [C15: from L *ēmolumentum* benefit; orig., fee paid to a miller, from *molere* to grind]

emote (ɪ'məut) *vb* **emotes, emoting, emoted.** (*intr*) to display exaggerated emotion, as in acting. [C20: back formation from EMOTION]
▸**e'moter** *n*

emotion ❶ (ɪ'məuʃən) *n* any strong feeling, as of joy, sorrow, or fear. [C16: from F, from OF, from L *ēmovēre* to disturb, from *movēre* to MOVE]

emotional ❶ (ɪ'məuʃənᵊl) *adj* **1** of, characteristic of, or expressive of emotion. **2** readily or excessively affected by emotion. **3** appealing to or arousing emotion. **4** caused or determined by emotion rather than reason: *an emotional argument.*
▸**eˌmotion'ality** *n*

emotionalism (ɪ'məuʃənəˌlɪzəm) *n* **1** emotional nature or quality. **2** a tendency to yield readily to the emotions. **3** an appeal to the emotions, esp. as to an audience.
▸**e'motionalist** *n* ▸**eˌmotional'istic** *adj*

emotionalize *or* **emotionalise** (ɪ'məuʃənəˌlaɪz) *vb* **emotionalizes, emotionalizing, emotionalized** *or* **emotionalises, emotionalising, emotionalised.** (*tr*) to make emotional; subject to emotional treatment.

emotive ❶ (ɪ'məutɪv) *adj* **1** tending or designed to arouse emotion. **2** of or characterized by emotion.
▸**e'motiveness** *or* ˌ**emo'tivity** *n*

> **USAGE NOTE** *Emotional* is preferred to *emotive* when describing a display of emotion: *he was given an emotional* (not *emotive*) *welcome.*

THESAURUS

surface **4** = **become apparent**, become known, come out, come out in the wash, come to light, crop up, develop, materialize, transpire, turn up
Antonyms *vb* ≠ **come into view**: depart, disappear, fade, fall, recede, retreat, sink, submerge, vanish from sight, wane, withdraw

emergence *n* **2, 4** = **coming**, advent, apparition, appearance, arrival, dawn, development, disclosure, emanation, issue, materialization, rise

emergency *n* **1** = **crisis**, danger, difficulty, exigency, extremity, necessity, panic stations (*inf.*), pass, pinch, plight, predicament, quandary, scrape (*inf.*), strait

emergent *adj* **1** = **developing**, appearing, budding, coming, rising

emetic *adj* **1** = **vomitory**, vomitive

emigrate *vb* = **move abroad**, migrate, move, remove

emigration *n* = **departure**, exodus, migration, removal

eminence *n* **1** = **prominence**, celebrity, dignity, distinction, esteem, fame, greatness, illustriousness, importance, notability, note, pre-eminence, prestige, rank, renown, reputation, repute, superiority **2** = **high ground**, elevation, height, hill, hillock, knoll, rise, summit

eminent *adj* **1, 2** = **prominent**, big-time (*inf.*), celebrated, conspicuous, distinguished, elevated, esteemed, exalted, famous, grand, great, high, high-ranking, illustrious, important, major league (*inf.*), notable, noted, noteworthy, outstanding, paramount, pre-eminent, prestigious, renowned, signal, superior, well-known
Antonyms *adj* anonymous, commonplace, infamous, lowly, ordinary, undistinguished, unheard-of, unimportant, unknown, unremarkable, unsung

emissary *n* **1** = **messenger**, agent, ambassador, courier, delegate, deputy, envoy, go-between, herald, legate, representative, scout **2** = **spy**, agent, secret agent

emission *n* **1** = **giving off** *or* **out**, diffusion, discharge, ejaculation, ejection, emanation, exhalation, exudation, issuance, issue, radiation, shedding, transmission, utterance, venting

emit *vb* **1-3** = **give off**, breathe forth, cast out, diffuse, discharge, eject, emanate, exhale, exude, give out, give vent to, issue, radiate, send forth, send out, shed, throw out, transmit, utter, vent
Antonyms *vb* absorb, assimilate, consume, devour, digest, drink in, incorporate, ingest, receive, soak up, suck up, take in

emolument *n* = **fee**, benefit, compensation, earnings, gain, hire, pay, payment, profits, recompense, remuneration, return, reward, salary, stipend, wages

emotion *n* = **feeling**, agitation, ardour, excitement, fervour, passion, perturbation, sensation, sentiment, vehemence, warmth

emotional *adj* **2** = **sensitive**, demonstrative, excitable, feeling, hot-blooded, passionate, responsive, sentimental, susceptible, temperamental, tender, touchy-feely (*inf.*), warm **3** = **moving**, affecting, emotive, exciting, heart-warming, pathetic, poignant, sentimental, stirring, tear-jerking (*inf.*), three-hankie (*inf.*), thrilling, touching
Antonyms *adj* ≠ **sensitive**: apathetic, cold, detached, insensitive, phlegmatic, undemonstrative, unemotional, unfeeling, unmoved, unsentimental ≠ **passionate**: dispassionate, unenthusiastic, unexcitable, unruffled

emotive *adj* **1** = **sensitive**, argumentative, controversial, delicate, touchy

Emp. *abbrev. for:* **1** Emperor. **2** Empire. **3** Empress.

empanel *or* **impanel** (ɪm'pænᵊl) *vb* **empanels, empanelling, empanelled** *or US* **empanels, empaneling, empaneled** *or* **impanels, impanelling, impanelled** *or US* **impanels, impaneling, impaneled.** (*tr*) *Law.* **1** to enter on a list (names of persons to be summoned for jury service). **2** to select (a jury) from such a list.
▸**em'panelment** *or* **im'panelment** *n*

empathize ➊ *or* **empathise** ('ɛmpəˌθaɪz) *vb* **empathizes, empathizing, empathized** *or* **empathises, empathising, empathised.** (*intr*) to engage in or feel empathy.

empathy ('ɛmpəθɪ) *n* **1** the power of understanding and imaginatively entering into another person's feelings. **2** the attribution to an object, such as a work of art, of one's own feelings about it. [C20: from Gk *empatheia* affection, passion]
▸**em'pathic** *or* ˌ**empa'thetic** *adj*

emperor ('ɛmpərə) *n* a monarch who rules or reigns over an empire. [C13: from OF, from L *imperāre* to command, from IM- + *parāre* to make ready]
▸**'emperorˌship** *n*

emperor penguin *n* an Antarctic penguin with orange-yellow patches on the neck: the largest penguin, reaching a height of 1.3 m (4 ft).

emphasis ➊ ('ɛmfəsɪs) *n, pl* **emphases** (-siːz). **1** special importance or significance. **2** an object, idea, etc., that is given special importance or significance. **3** stress on a particular syllable, word, or phrase in speaking. **4** force or intensity of expression. **5** sharpness or clarity of form or outline. [C16: via L from Gk: meaning, (in rhetoric) significant stress; see EMPHATIC]

emphasize ➊ *or* **emphasise** ('ɛmfəˌsaɪz) *vb* **emphasizes, emphasizing, emphasized** *or* **emphasises, emphasising, emphasised.** (*tr*) to give emphasis or prominence to; stress.

emphatic ➊ (ɪm'fætɪk) *adj* **1** expressed, spoken, or done with emphasis. **2** forceful and positive; definite; direct. **3** sharp or clear in form, contour, or outline. **4** important or significant; stressed. [C18: from Gk, from *emphainein* to display, from *phainein* to show]
▸**em'phatically** *adv*

emphysema (ˌɛmfɪ'siːmə) *n Pathol.* **1** a condition in which the air sacs of the lungs are grossly enlarged, causing breathlessness and wheezing. **2** the abnormal presence of air in a tissue or part. [C17: from NL, from Gk *emphusēma* a swelling up, from *phusan* to blow]

empire ➊ ('ɛmpaɪə) *n* **1** an aggregate of peoples and territories under the rule of a single person, oligarchy, or sovereign state. **2** any monarchy that has an emperor as head of state. **3** the period during which a particular empire exists. **4** supreme power; sovereignty. **5** a large industrial organization with many ramifications. [C13: from OF, from L, from *imperāre* to command, from *parāre* to prepare]

Empire ('ɛmpaɪə) *n* **the. 1.** the British Empire. **2** *French history.* **2a** the period of imperial rule in France from 1804 to 1815 under Napoleon Bonaparte. **2b** Also called: **Second Empire.** the period from 1852 to 1870 when Napoleon III ruled as emperor. ◆ *adj* **3** denoting, characteristic of, or relating to the British Empire. **4** denoting, characteristic of, or relating to either French Empire, esp. the first.

empire-builder *n Inf.* a person who seeks extra power, esp. by increasing the number of his staff.
▸**'empire-ˌbuilding** *n, adj*

Empire Day *n* the former name of **Commonwealth Day.**

empiric (ɛm'pɪrɪk) *n* **1** a person who relies on empirical methods. **2** a medical quack. ◆ *adj* **3** a variant of **empirical.** [C16: from L, from Gk *empeirikos* practised, from *peiran* to attempt]

empirical ➊ (ɛm'pɪrɪkᵊl) *adj* **1** derived from or relating to experiment and observation rather than theory. **2** (of medical treatment) based on practical experience rather than scientific proof. **3** *Philosophy.* (of knowledge) derived from experience rather than by logic from first principles. **4** of or relating to medical quackery.
▸**em'piricalness** *n*

empiricism (ɛm'pɪrɪˌsɪzəm) *n* **1** *Philosophy.* the doctrine that all knowledge derives from experience. **2** the use of empirical methods. **3** medical quackery.
▸**em'piricist** *n, adj*

emplace ➊ (ɪm'pleɪs) *vb* **emplaces, emplacing, emplaced.** (*tr*) to put in position.

emplacement ➊ (ɪm'pleɪsmənt) *n* **1** a prepared position for a gun or other weapon. **2** the act of putting or state of being put in place. [C19: from F, from obs. *emplacer* to put in position, from PLACE]

emplane (ɪm'pleɪn) *vb* **emplanes, emplaning, emplaned.** to board or put on board an aeroplane.

employ ➊ (ɪm'plɔɪ) *vb* (*tr*) **1** to engage or make use of the services of (a person) in return for money; hire. **2** to provide work or occupation for; keep busy. **3** to use as a means. ◆ *n* **4** the state of being employed (esp. in **in someone's employ**). [C15: from OF *emploier,* from L *implicāre* to entangle, engage, from *plicāre* to fold]
▸**em'ployable** *adj* ▸**emˌploya'bility** *n*

employee ➊ *or US* **employe** (ɛm'plɔɪiː, ˌɛmplɔɪ'iː) *n* a person who is hired to work for another or for a business, firm, etc., in return for payment.

employer ➊ (ɪm'plɔɪə) *n* **1** a person, firm, etc., that employs workers. **2** a person who employs.

employment ➊ (ɪm'plɔɪmənt) *n* **1** the act of employing or state of being employed. **2** a person's work or occupation.

employment exchange *n Brit.* a former name for **employment office.**

employment office *n Brit.* any government office established to collect and supply to the unemployed information about job vacancies and to employers information about availability of prospective workers. See also **Jobcentre.**

emporium ➊ (ɛm'pɔːrɪəm) *n, pl* **emporiums** *or* **emporia** (-rɪə). a large retail shop offering for sale a wide variety of merchandise. [C16: from L, from Gk, from *emporos* merchant, from *poros* a journey]

empower ➊ (ɪm'paʊə) *vb* (*tr*) **1** to give power or authority to; authorize. **2** to give ability to; enable or permit.
▸**em'powerment** *n*

empress ('ɛmprɪs) *n* **1** the wife or widow of an emperor. **2** a woman who holds the rank of emperor in her own right. [C12: from OF *empereriz,* from L *imperātrix;* see EMPEROR]

empty ➊ ('ɛmptɪ) *adj* **emptier, emptiest. 1** containing nothing. **2** without inhabitants; vacant or unoccupied. **3** carrying no load, passengers, etc. **4** without purpose, substance, or value: *an empty life.* **5** insincere or trivial: *empty words.* **6** not expressive or vital; vacant: *an empty look.* **7** *Inf.* hungry. **8** (*postpositive;* foll. by *of*) devoid; destitute. **9** *Inf.* drained of energy or emotion. **10** *Maths, logic.* (of a set or class) containing no members. ◆ *vb* **empties, emptying, emptied. 11** to make or become empty. **12** (when *intr,* foll. by *into*) to discharge (contents). **13** (*tr;* often foll. by *of*) to unburden or rid (oneself). ◆ *n, pl* **empties. 14** an empty container, esp. a bottle. [OE *æmtig*]
▸**'emptiable** *adj* ▸**'emptier** *n* ▸**'emptily** *adv* ▸**'emptiness** *n*

THESAURUS

empathize *vb* = **relate to,** feel for, identify with, put oneself in someone else's shoes (*inf.*)

emphasis *n* **1, 3, 4** = **stress,** accent, accentuation, attention, decidedness, force, importance, impressiveness, insistence, intensity, moment, positiveness, power, pre-eminence, priority, prominence, significance, strength, underscoring, weight

emphasize *vb* = **stress,** accent, accentuate, dwell on, foreground, give priority to, highlight, insist on, lay stress on, play up, press home, put the accent on, underline, underscore, weight
Antonyms *vb* gloss over, make light of, make little of, minimize, play down, soft-pedal (*inf.*), underplay

emphatic *adj* **2, 4** = **forceful,** absolute, categorical, certain, decided, definite, direct, distinct, earnest, energetic, forcible, important, impressive, insistent, in spades, marked, momentous, positive, powerful, pronounced, resounding, significant, striking, strong, telling, unequivocal, unmistakable, vigorous
Antonyms *adj* commonplace, equivocal, hesitant, insignificant, tame, tentative, uncertain, undecided, unremarkable, unsure, weak

empire *n* **1** = **kingdom,** commonwealth, domain, imperium (*rare*), realm **4** = **power,** authority, command, control, dominion, government, rule, sovereignty, supremacy, sway

empirical *adj* **1** = **first-hand,** experiential, experimental, observed, practical, pragmatic
Antonyms *adj* academic, assumed, conjectural, hypothetical, putative, speculative, theoretic(al)

emplace *vb* = **position,** insert, place, put, put in place, set up, station

emplacement *n* **1** = **position,** location, lodgment, platform, site, situation, station **2** = **positioning,** placement, placing, putting in place, setting up, stationing

employ *vb* **1** = **hire,** commission, engage, enlist, retain, take on **2** = **keep busy,** engage, fill, make use of, occupy, spend, take up, use up **3** = **use,** apply, bring to bear, exercise, exert, make use of, ply, put to use, utilize ◆ *n* **4** *As in* **in someone's employ** = **service,** employment, engagement, hire

employed *adj* **1** = **working,** active, busy, engaged, in a job, in employment, in work, occupied
Antonyms *adj* idle, jobless, laid off, on the dole (*Brit. inf.*), out of a job, out of work, redundant, unoccupied

employee *n* = **worker,** hand, job-holder, staff member, wage-earner, workman

employer *n* **1** = **boss** (*inf.*), business, company, establishment, firm, gaffer (*inf., chiefly Brit.*), organization, outfit (*inf.*), owner, patron, proprietor

employment *n* **1** = **use,** application, engagement, enlistment, exercise, hire, taking on, utilization **2** = **job,** avocation (*arch.*), business, calling, craft, employ, line, métier, occupation, profession, pursuit, service, trade, vocation, work

emporium *n* = **shop,** bazaar, market, mart, store, warehouse

empower *vb* **1, 2** = **enable,** allow, authorize, commission, delegate, entitle, license, permit, qualify, sanction, warrant

emptiness *n* **1, 2** = **bareness,** blankness, desertedness, desolation, destitution, vacancy, vacantness, vacuum, void, waste **4** = **purposelessness,** aimlessness, banality, barrenness, frivolity, futility, hollowness, inanity, ineffectiveness, meaninglessness, senselessness, silliness, unreality, unsatisfactoriness, unsubstantiality, vainness, valuelessness, vanity, worthlessness **5** = **insincerity,** cheapness, hollowness, idleness, triviality, trivialness **6** = **blankness,** absentness, expressionlessness, unintelligence, vacancy, vacantness, vacuity, vacuousness

empty *adj* **1, 2** = **bare,** blank, clear, deserted, desolate, destitute, hollow, unfurnished, uninhabited, unoccupied, untenanted, vacant, void, waste **4** = **purposeless,** aimless, banal, bootless, frivolous, fruitless, futile, hollow, inane, ineffective, meaningless, otiose, senseless, silly, unreal, unsatisfactory, unsubstantial, vain, valueless, worthless **5** = **insincere,** cheap, hollow, idle, trivial **6** = **blank,** absent, expres-

empty-handed *adj* **1** carrying nothing in the hands. **2** having gained nothing.

empty-headed ➊ *adj* lacking sense; frivolous.

empty-nester (-'nɛstə) *n Inf.* a married person whose children have grown up and left home.

empyema (ˌɛmpaɪ'iːmə) *n, pl* **empyemata** (-'iːmətə) *or* **empyemas.** a collection of pus in a body cavity, esp. in the chest. [C17: from Med. L, from Gk *empuēma* abscess, from *empuein* to suppurate, from *puon* pus]
▸ˌ**empy'emic** *adj*

empyrean (ˌɛmpaɪ'riːən) *n* **1** *Arch.* the highest part of the heavens, thought in ancient times to contain the pure element of fire and by early Christians to be the abode of God. **2** *Poetic.* the heavens or sky. ◆ *adj also* **empyreal. 3** of or relating to the sky. **4** heavenly or sublime. [C17: from LL, from Gk *empurios* fiery]

empyreuma (ˌɛmpɪ'ruːmə) *n, pl* **empyreumata** (-mətə). the smell and taste associated with burning vegetable and animal matter. [C17: from Gk, from *empureuein* to set on fire]

EMS *abbrev. for* European Monetary System.

emu ('iːmjuː) *n* a large Australian flightless bird, similar to the ostrich. [C17: changed from Port. *ema* ostrich, from Arab. *Na-'amah* ostrich]

EMU 1 *abbrev. for* European monetary union. **2** See **e.m.u.**

e.m.u. *or* **EMU** *abbrev. for* electromagnetic unit.

emu-bob *Austral. inf.* ◆ *vb* **emu-bobs, emu-bobbing, emu-bobbed. 1** (*intr*) to bend over to collect litter or small pieces of wood. ◆ *n* **2** Also called: **emu parade.** a parade of soldiers or schoolchildren for litter collection.
▸'**emu-**ˌ**bobbing** *n*

emulate ➊ ('ɛmjʊˌleɪt) *vb* **emulates, emulating, emulated.** (*tr*) **1** to attempt to equal or surpass, esp. by imitation. **2** to rival or compete with. [C16: from L *aemulus* competing with]
▸'**emulative** *adj* ▸ˌ**emu'lation** *n* ▸'**emu**ˌ**lator** *n*

emulous ('ɛmjʊləs) *adj* **1** desiring or aiming to equal or surpass another. **2** characterized by or arising from emulation. [C14: from L; see EMULATE]
▸'**emulousness** *n*

emulsifier (ɪ'mʌlsɪˌfaɪə) *n* an agent that forms an emulsion, esp. a food additive that prevents separation of processed foods.

emulsify (ɪ'mʌlsɪˌfaɪ) *vb* **emulsifies, emulsifying, emulsified.** to make or form into an emulsion.
▸**e**ˌ**mulsi'fiable** *or* **e'mulsible** *adj* ▸**e**ˌ**mulsifi'cation** *n*

emulsion (ɪ'mʌlʃən) *n* **1** *Photog.* a light-sensitive coating on a base, such as paper or film, consisting of silver bromide suspended in gelatine. **2** *Chem.* a colloid in which both phases are liquids. **3** a type of paint in which the pigment is suspended in a vehicle that is dispersed in water as an emulsion. **4** *Pharmacol.* a mixture in which an oily medicine is dispersed in another liquid. **5** any liquid resembling milk. [C17: from NL *ēmulsiō*, from L, from *ēmulgēre* to milk out, from *mulgēre* to milk]
▸**e'mulsive** *adj*

emu-wren *n* an Australian wren having long plumy tail feathers.

en (ɛn) *n Printing.* a unit of measurement, half the width of an em.

EN (in Britain) *abbrev. for:* **1** enrolled nurse. **2** English Nature.

en-[1] *or* **em-** *prefix forming verbs.* **1** (*from nouns*) **1a** put in or on: *entomb; enthrone.* **1b** go on or into: *enplane.* **1c** surround or cover with: *enmesh.* **1d** furnish with: *empower.* **2** (*from adjectives and nouns*) cause to be in a certain condition: *enable; enslave.* [via OF from L *in-* IN-[2]]

en-[2] *or* **em-** *prefix forming nouns and adjectives.* in; into; inside: *endemic.* [from Gk (often via L); cf. IN-[1], IN-[2]]

-en[1] *suffix forming verbs from adjectives and nouns.* cause to be; become; cause to have: *blacken; heighten.* [OE *-n-*, as in *fæst-n-ian* to fasten, of Gmc origin]

-en[2] *suffix forming adjectives from nouns.* of; made of; resembling: *ashen; wooden.* [OE *-en*]

enable ➊ (ɪn'eɪbᵊl) *vb* **enables, enabling, enabled.** (*tr*) **1** to provide (someone) with adequate power, means, opportunity, or authority (to do something). **2** to make possible.
▸**en'ablement** *n* ▸**en'abler** *n*

enabling act *n* a legislative act conferring certain specified powers on a person or organization.

enact ➊ (ɪn'ækt) *vb* (*tr*) **1** to make into an act or statute. **2** to establish by law; decree. **3** to represent or perform as in a play.
▸**en'actable** *adj* ▸**en'active** *or* **en'actory** *adj* ▸**en'actment** *or* **en'action** *n* ▸**en'actor** *n*

enamel (ɪ'næməl) *n* **1** a coloured glassy substance, translucent or opaque, fused to the surface of articles made of metal, glass, etc., for ornament or protection. **2** an article or articles ornamented with enamel. **3** an enamel-like paint or varnish. **4** any coating resembling enamel. **5** the hard white substance that covers the crown of each tooth. **6** (*modifier*) decorated or covered with enamel. ◆ *vb* **enamels, enamelling, enamelled** *or US* **enamels, enameling, enameled.** (*tr*) **7** to decorate with enamel. **8** to ornament with glossy variegated colours, as if with enamel. **9** to portray in enamel. [C15: from OF *esmail*, of Gmc origin]
▸**e'nameller, e'namellist** *or US* **e'nameler, e'namelist** *n* ▸**e'namel**ˌ**work** *n*

enamour ➊ *or US* **enamor** (ɪn'æmə) *vb* (*tr; usually passive* and foll. by *of*) to inspire with love; captivate. [C14: from OF, from *amour* love, from L *amor*]
▸**en'amoured** *or US* **en'amored** *adj*

en bloc *French.* (ɑ̃ blɔk) *adv* in a lump or block; as a body or whole; all together.

en brosse *French.* (ɑ̃ brɔs) *adj, adv* (of the hair) cut very short so that the hair stands up stiffly. [lit.: in the style of a brush]

enc. *abbrev. for:* **1** enclosed. **2** enclosure.

encamp (ɪn'kæmp) *vb* to lodge or cause to lodge in a camp.

encampment ➊ (ɪn'kæmpmənt) *n* **1** the act of setting up a camp. **2** the place where a camp, esp. a military camp, is set up.

encapsulate ➊ *or* **incapsulate** (ɪn'kæpsjʊˌleɪt) *vb* **encapsulates, encapsulating, encapsulated** *or* **incapsulates, incapsulating, incapsulated. 1** to enclose or be enclosed as in a capsule. **2** (*tr*) to sum up in a short or concise form.
▸**en**ˌ**capsu'lation** *or* **in**ˌ**capsu'lation** *n*

encase *or* **incase** (ɪn'keɪs) *vb* **encases, encasing, encased.** (*tr*) to place or enclose as in a case.
▸**en'casement** *or* **in'casement** *n*

encash (ɪn'kæʃ) *vb* (*tr*) *Brit., formal.* to exchange (a cheque) for cash.
▸**en'cashable** *adj* ▸**en'cashment** *n*

encaustic (ɪn'kɒstɪk) *Ceramics, etc.* ◆ *adj* **1** decorated by any process involving burning in colours, esp. by inlaying coloured clays and baking or by fusing wax colours to the surface. ◆ *n* **2** the process of burning in colours. **3** a product of such a process. [C17: from L *encausticus*, from Gk, from *enkaiein* to burn in, from *kaiein* to burn]
▸**en'caustically** *adv*

-ence *or* **-ency** *suffix forming nouns.* indicating an action, state, condition, or quality: *benevolence; residence; patience.* [via OF from L *-entia*, from *-ēns*, present participial ending]

enceinte (ɒn'sænt) *adj* another word for **pregnant.** [C17: from F, from L *inciēns* pregnant]

encephalic (ˌɛnsɪ'fælɪk) *adj* of or relating to the brain.

encephalin (ɛn'sɛfəlɪn) *n* a variant of **enkephalin.**

encephalitis (ˌɛnsɛfə'laɪtɪs) *n* inflammation of the brain.
▸**encephalitic** (ˌɛnsɛfə'lɪtɪk) *adj*

encephalitis lethargica (lɪ'θɑːdʒɪkə) *n* a technical name for **sleeping sickness** (sense 2).

encephalo- *or before a vowel* **encephal-** *combining form.* indicating the brain: *encephalogram; encephalitis.* [from NL, from Gk *enkephalos*, from *en-* in + *kephalē* head]

encephalogram (ɛn'sɛfələˌgræm) *n* **1** an X-ray photograph of the brain, esp. one (a **pneumoencephalogram**) taken after replacing some of the cerebrospinal fluid with air or oxygen. **2** short for **electroencephalogram;** see **electroencephalograph.**

encephalon (ɛn'sɛfəˌlɒn) *n, pl* **encephala** (-lə). a technical name for **brain.** [C18: from NL, from Gk *enkephalos* brain, from EN-[2] + *kephalē* head]
▸**en'cephalous** *adj*

encephalopathy (ˌɛnsɛfə'lɒpəθɪ) *n* any degenerative disease of the brain, often associated with toxic conditions. See also **BSE.**

enchain ➊ (ɪn'tʃeɪn) *vb* (*tr*) **1** to bind with chains. **2** to hold fast or captivate (the attention, etc.).
▸**en'chainment** *n*

enchant ➊ (ɪn'tʃɑːnt) *vb* (*tr*) **1** to cast a spell on; bewitch. **2** to delight or

THESAURUS

sionless, unintelligent, vacant, vacuous **7** *Informal* = **hungry**, esurient, famished, ravenous, starving (*inf.*), unfed, unfilled ◆ *vb* **11-13** = **evacuate**, clear, consume, deplete, discharge, drain, dump, exhaust, gut, pour out, unburden, unload, use up, vacate, void
Antonyms *adj* ≠ **bare:** full, inhabited, occupied, packed, stuffed ≠ **purposeless:** busy, fulfilled, full, interesting, meaningful, occupied, purposeful, satisfying, serious, significant, useful, valuable, worthwhile ◆ *vb* ≠ **evacuate:** cram, fill, pack, replenish, stock, stuff

empty-headed *adj* = **scatterbrained**, brainless, ditzy *or* ditsy (*sl.*), dizzy (*inf.*), featherbrained, flighty, frivolous, giddy, goofy (*inf.*), harebrained, inane, silly, skittish, vacuous

emulate *vb* **1** = **imitate**, copy, echo, follow, follow in the footsteps of, follow suit, follow the example of, mimic, take after, take a leaf out of someone's book **2** = **compete with**, challenge, contend with, rival, vie with

emulation *n* **1** = **imitation**, copying, following, mimicry **2** = **rivalry**, challenge, competition, contention, contest, envy, jealousy, strife

enable *vb* **1** = **allow**, authorize, capacitate, commission, empower, entitle, facilitate, fit, license, permit, prepare, qualify, sanction, warrant
Antonyms *vb* bar, block, hinder, impede, obstruct, prevent, stop, thwart

enact *vb* **2** = **establish**, authorize, command, decree, legislate, ordain, order, pass, proclaim, ratify, sanction **3** = **perform**, act, act out, appear as, depict, personate, play, play the part of, portray, represent

enactment *n* **2** = **decree**, authorization, canon, command, commandment, dictate, edict, law, legislation, order, ordinance, proclamation, ratification, regulation, statute **3** = **portrayal**, acting, depiction, performance, personation, play-acting, playing, representation

enamoured *adj* = **in love**, bewitched, captivated, charmed, crazy about (*inf.*), enchanted, enraptured, entranced, fascinated, fond, infatuated, smitten, swept off one's feet, taken, wild about (*inf.*)

encampment *n* **2** = **camp**, base, bivouac, camping ground, campsite, cantonment, quarters, tents

encapsulate *vb* **2** = **sum up**, abridge, compress, condense, digest, epitomize, précis, summarize

enchain *vb* **1** = **shackle**, bind, enslave, fetter, hold, hold fast, manacle, pinion, put in irons

enchant *vb* **1, 2** = **fascinate**, beguile, bewitch,

captivate utterly. [C14: from OF, from L *incantāre,* from *cantāre* to chant]
▸**en'chanted** *adj* ▸**en'chanter** *n* ▸**en'chantress** *fem n*

enchanting ❶ (ɪn'tʃɑːntɪŋ) *adj* pleasant; delightful.
▸**en'chantingly** *adv*

enchantment ❶ (ɪn'tʃɑːntmənt) *n* **1** the act of enchanting or state of being enchanted. **2** a magic spell. **3** great charm or fascination.

enchase (ɪn'tʃeɪs) *vb* **enchases, enchasing, enchased.** (*tr*) a less common word for **chase**[3]. [C15: from OF *enchasser* to enclose, set, from EN-[1] + *casse* CASE[2]]
▸**en'chaser** *n*

enchilada (ˌɛntʃɪ'lɑːdə) *n* a Mexican dish of a tortilla filled with meat, served with a chilli sauce. [American Sp., from *enchilado,* from *enchilar* to spice with chilli]

-enchyma *n combining form.* denoting cellular tissue. [C20: abstracted from PARENCHYMA]

encipher (ɪn'saɪfə) *vb* (*tr*) to convert (a message, etc.) into code or cipher.
▸**en'cipherer** *n* ▸**en'cipherment** *n*

encircle ❶ (ɪn'sɜːkᵊl) *vb* **encircles, encircling, encircled.** (*tr*) to form a circle around; enclose within a circle; surround.
▸**en'circlement** *n*

enclave ('ɛnkleɪv) *n* a part of a country entirely surrounded by foreign territory: viewed from the position of the surrounding territories. [C19: from F, from OF *enclaver* to enclose, from Vulgar L *inclāvāre* (unattested) to lock up, from L IN-[2] + *clavis* key]

enclitic (ɪn'klɪtɪk) *adj* **1** denoting or relating to a monosyllabic word or form that is treated as a suffix of the preceding word. ◆ *n* **2** an enclitic word or form. [C17: from LL, from Gk, from *enklinein* to cause to lean, from EN-[2] + *klinein* to lean]
▸**en'clitically** *adv*

enclose ❶ *or* **inclose** (ɪn'kləʊz) *vb* **encloses, enclosing, enclosed** *or* **incloses, inclosing, inclosed.** (*tr*) **1** to close; hem in; surround. **2** to surround (land) with or as if with a fence. **3** to put in an envelope or wrapper, esp. together with a letter. **4** to contain or hold.
▸**en'closable** *or* **in'closable** *adj* ▸**en'closer** *or* **in'closer** *n*

enclosed order *n* a Christian religious order that does not permit its members to go into the outside world.

enclosure *or* **inclosure** (ɪn'kləʊʒə) *n* **1** the act of enclosing or state of being enclosed. **2** an area enclosed as by a fence. **3** the act of appropriating land by setting up a fence, hedge, etc., around it. **4** a fence, wall, etc., that encloses. **5** something enclosed within an envelope or wrapper, esp. together with a letter. **6** *Brit.* a section of a sports ground, racecourse, etc., allotted to certain spectators.

encode (ɪn'kəʊd) *vb* **encodes, encoding, encoded.** (*tr*) to convert (a message) into code.
▸**en'codement** *n* ▸**en'coder** *n*

encomiast (ɛn'kəʊmɪˌæst) *n* a person who speaks or writes an encomium. [C17: from Gk, from *enkōmiazein* to utter an ENCOMIUM]
▸**enˌcomi'astic** *or* **enˌcomi'astical** *adj*

encomium (ɛn'kəʊmɪəm) *n, pl* **encomiums** *or* **encomia** (-mɪə). a formal expression of praise; eulogy. [C16: from L, from Gk, from EN-[2] + *kōmos* festivity]

encompass ❶ (ɪn'kʌmpəs) *vb* (*tr*) **1** to enclose within a circle; surround. **2** to bring about: *he encompassed the enemy's ruin.* **3** to include entirely or comprehensively.
▸**en'compassment** *n*

encore ('ɒŋkɔː) *sentence substitute.* **1** again: used by an audience to demand an extra or repeated performance. ◆ *n* **2** an extra or repeated performance given in response to enthusiastic demand. ◆ *vb* **encores, encoring, encored. 3** (*tr*) to demand an extra or repeated performance of (a work, piece of music, etc.) by (a performer). [C18: from F: still, again, ?from L *in hanc hōram* until this hour]

encounter ❶ (ɪn'kaʊntə) *vb* **1** to come upon or meet casually or unexpectedly. **2** to meet (an enemy, army, etc.) in battle or contest. **3** (*tr*) to be faced with; contend with. ◆ *n* **4** a casual or unexpected meeting. **5** a hostile meeting; contest. [C13: from OF, from Vulgar L *incontrāre* (unattested), from L IN-[2] + *contrā* against, opposite]

encounter group *n* a group of people who meet in order to develop self-awareness and mutual understanding by openly expressing their feelings, by confrontation, etc.

encourage ❶ (ɪn'kʌrɪdʒ) *vb* **encourages, encouraging, encouraged.** (*tr*) **1** to inspire (someone) with the courage or confidence (to do something). **2** to stimulate (something or someone) by approval or help.
▸**en'couragement** *n* ▸**en'courager** *n* ▸**en'couraging** *adj* ▸**en'couragingly** *adv*

encroach ❶ (ɪn'krəʊtʃ) *vb* (*intr*) **1** (often foll. by *on* or *upon*) to intrude gradually or stealthily upon the rights, property, etc., of another. **2** to advance beyond certain limits. [C14: from OF *encrochier* to seize, lit.: fasten upon with hooks, of Gmc origin]
▸**en'croacher** *n* ▸**en'croachment** *n*

encrust *or* **incrust** (ɪn'krʌst) *vb* **1** (*tr*) to cover or overlay with or as with a crust or hard coating. **2** to form or cause to form a crust or hard coating. **3** (*tr*) to decorate lavishly, as with jewels.
▸ˌ**encrus'tation** *or* ˌ**incrus'tation** *n*

encumber ❶ *or* **incumber** (ɪn'kʌmbə) *vb* (*tr*) **1** to hinder or impede; hamper. **2** to fill with superfluous or useless matter. **3** to burden with debts, obligations, etc. [C14: from OF, from EN-[1] + *combre* a barrier, from LL *combrus*]

encumbrance ❶ *or* **incumbrance** (ɪn'kʌmbrəns) *n* **1** a thing that impedes or is burdensome; hindrance. **2** *Law.* a burden or charge upon property, such as a mortgage or lien.

ency., encyc., *or* **encycl.** *abbrev. for* encyclopedia.

-ency *suffix forming nouns.* a variant of **-ence:** *fluency; permanency.*

encyclical (ɛn'sɪklɪkᵊl) *n* **1** a letter sent by the pope to all Roman Catholic bishops. ◆ *adj also* **encyclic. 2** (of letters) intended for general circulation. [C17: from LL, from Gk, from *kuklos* circle]

encyclopedia ❶ *or* **encyclopaedia** (ɛnˌsaɪkləʊ'piːdɪə) *n* a book, often in many volumes, containing articles, often arranged in alphabetical order, dealing either with the whole range of human knowledge or with one particular subject. [C16: from NL, erroneously for Gk *enkuklios paideia* general education]
▸**enˌcyclo'pedic** *or* **enˌcyclo'paedic** *adj*

encyclopedist *or* **encyclopaedist** (ɛnˌsaɪkləʊ'piːdɪst) *n* a person who compiles or contributes to an encyclopedia.
▸**enˌcyclo'pedism** *or* **enˌcyclo'paedism** *n*

encyst (ɛn'sɪst) *vb Biol.* to enclose or become enclosed by a cyst, thick membrane, or shell.
▸**en'cystment** *or* ˌ**encys'tation** *n*

end ❶ (ɛnd) *n* **1** the extremity of the length of something, such as a road, line, etc. **2** the surface at either extremity of an object. **3** the extreme extent, limit, or degree of something. **4** the most distant place or time that can be imagined: *the ends of the earth.* **5** the time at which

THESAURUS

captivate, cast a spell on, charm, delight, enamour, enrapture, enthral, hypnotize, mesmerize, ravish, spellbind

enchanter *n* **1** = **sorcerer**, conjuror, magician, magus, necromancer, spellbinder, warlock, witch, wizard

enchanting *adj* = **fascinating**, alluring, appealing, attractive, bewitching, captivating, charming, delightful, endearing, entrancing, lovely, Orphean, pleasant, ravishing, winsome

enchantment *n* **1, 3** = **fascination**, allure, allurement, beguilement, bliss, charm, delight, hypnotism, mesmerism, rapture, ravishment, transport **2** = **spell**, charm, conjuration, incantation, magic, necromancy, sorcery, witchcraft, wizardry

enchantress *n* **1** = **sorceress**, conjuror, lamia, magician, necromancer, spellbinder, witch **2** = **seductress**, charmer, *femme fatale,* siren, vamp (*inf.*)

encircle *vb* = **surround**, begird (*poetic*), circle, circumscribe, compass, enclose, encompass, enfold, envelop, environ, enwreath, gird in, girdle, hem in, ring

enclose *vb* **1, 2** = **surround**, bound, circumscribe, cover, encase, encircle, encompass, environ, fence, hedge, hem in, impound, pen, pound, shut in, wall in, wrap **3** = **send with**, include, insert, put in **4** = **include**, comprehend, contain, embrace, hold, incorporate

encompass *vb* **1** = **surround**, circle, circumscribe, encircle, enclose, envelop, environ, enwreath, girdle, hem in, ring **3** = **include**, admit, comprehend, comprise, contain, cover, embody, embrace, hold, incorporate, involve, subsume, take in

encounter *vb* **1** = **meet**, bump into (*inf.*), chance upon, come upon, confront, experience, face, happen on *or* upon, run across, run into (*inf.*) **2** = **battle with**, attack, clash with, combat, come into conflict with, contend, cross swords with, do battle with, engage, face off (*sl.*), fight, grapple with, join battle with, strive, struggle ◆ *n* **4** = **meeting**, brush, confrontation, rendezvous **5** = **battle**, action, clash, collision, combat, conflict, contest, dispute, engagement, face-off (*sl.*), fight, head-to-head, run-in (*inf.*), set to (*inf.*), skirmish

encourage *vb* **1** = **inspire**, animate, buoy up, cheer, comfort, console, embolden, gee up, hearten, incite, inspirit, rally, reassure, rouse, stimulate **2** = **spur**, abet, advance, advocate, aid, boost, commend, egg on, favour, forward, foster, further, help, promote, prompt, strengthen, succour, support, urge
Antonyms *vb* ≠ **inspire:** daunt, depress, deter, discourage, dishearten, dispirit, dissuade, hinder, inhibit, intimidate, prevent, retard, scare, throw cold water on (*inf.*)

encouragement *n* **1, 2** = **inspiration**, advocacy, aid, boost, cheer, clarion call, consolation, favour, gee-up, help, incitement, inspiritment, promotion, reassurance, security blanket (*inf.*), stimulation, stimulus, succour, support, urging

encouraging *adj* **1** = **promising**, bright, cheerful, cheering, comforting, good, heartening, hopeful, reassuring, rosy, satisfactory, stimulating
Antonyms *adj* daunting, depressing, disappointing, discouraging, disheartening, dispiriting, off-putting (*inf.*), unfavourable, unpropitious

encroach *vb* **1** = **intrude**, appropriate, arrogate, impinge, infringe, invade, make inroads, overstep, trench, trespass, usurp

encroachment *n* **1** = **intrusion**, appropriation, arrogation, impingement, incursion, infringement, inroad, invasion, trespass, usurpation, violation

encumber *vb* **1** = **burden**, clog, cramp, embarrass, hamper, handicap, hinder, impede, incommode, inconvenience, make difficult, obstruct, oppress, overload, retard, saddle, slow down, trammel, weigh down

encumbrance *n* **1** = **burden**, albatross, clog, difficulty, drag, embarrassment, handicap, hindrance, impediment, inconvenience, liability, load, millstone, obstacle, obstruction

encyclopedic *adj* = **comprehensive**, all-embracing, all-encompassing, all-inclusive, complete, exhaustive, thorough, universal, vast, wide-ranging

end *n* **1-4** = **extremity**, bound, boundary, edge, extent, extreme, limit, point, terminus, tip **5** = **finish**, cessation, close, closure, ending, expiration, expiry, stop, termination, wind-up **6** = **conclusion**, attainment, completion, consequence, consummation, culmination, denouement, ending, end result, finale, issue,

something is concluded. **6** the last section or part. **7** a share or part. **8** (*often pl*) a remnant or fragment (esp. in **odds and ends**). **9** a final state, esp. death; destruction. **10** the purpose of an action or existence. **11** *Sport.* either of the two defended areas of a playing field, rink, etc. **12** *Bowls, etc.* a section of play from one side of the rink to the other. **13 at an end.** exhausted or completed. **14 come to an end.** to become completed or exhausted. **15 have one's end away.** *sl.* to have sexual intercourse. **16 in the end.** finally. **17 keep one's end up. 17a** to sustain one's part in a joint undertaking. **17b** to hold one's own in an argument, contest, etc. **18 make (both) ends meet.** to spend no more than the money one has. **19 no end (of).** *Inf.* (intensifier): *I had no end of work.* **20 on end.** *Inf.* without pause or interruption. **21 the end.** *Sl.* the worst, esp. something that goes beyond the limits of endurance. ◆ *vb* **22** to bring or come to a finish; conclude. **23** to die or cause to die. **24** (*tr*) to surpass or outdo: *a novel to end all novels.* **25 end it all.** *Inf.* to commit suicide. ◆ See also **end up.** [OE *ende*]
▸**'ender** *n*

end- *combining form.* a variant of **endo-** before a vowel.

-end *suffix forming nouns.* See **-and.**

endamoeba *or US* **endameba** (ˌɛndəˈmiːbə) *n* variant spellings of **entamoeba.**

endanger ⓣ (ɪnˈdeɪndʒə) *vb* (*tr*) to put in danger or peril; imperil.
▸**en'dangerment** *n*

endangered (ɪnˈdeɪndʒəd) *adj* in danger, esp. of extinction: *an endangered species.*

endear ⓣ (ɪnˈdɪə) *vb* (*tr*) to cause to be beloved or esteemed.
▸**en'dearing** *adj*

endearment ⓣ (ɪnˈdɪəmənt) *n* something that endears, such as an affectionate utterance.

endeavour ⓣ *or US* **endeavor** (ɪnˈdɛvə) *vb* **1** to try (to do something). ◆ *n* **2** an effort to do or attain something. [C14 *endeveren,* from EN-[1] + *-deveren* from *dever* duty, from OF *deveir;* see DEVOIRS]
▸**en'deavourer** *or US* **en'deavorer** *n*

endemic (ɛnˈdɛmɪk) *adj also* **endemial** (ɛnˈdɛmɪəl) *or* **endemical. 1** present within a localized area or peculiar to persons in such an area. ◆ *n* **2** an endemic disease or plant. [C18: from NL *endēmicus,* from Gk *endēmos* native, from EN-[2] + *dēmos* the people]
▸**en'demically** *adv* ▸**'endemism** *or* **ˌende'micity** *n*

endermic (ɛnˈdɜːmɪk) *adj* (of a medicine, etc.) acting by absorption through the skin. [C19: from EN-[2] + Gk *derma* skin]

endgame (ˈɛndˌgeɪm) *n* the closing stage of any of certain games, esp. chess, when there are only a few pieces left in play.

ending ⓣ (ˈɛndɪŋ) *n* **1** the act of bringing to or reaching an end. **2** the last part of something. **3** the final part of a word, esp. a suffix.

endive (ˈɛndaɪv) *n* a plant cultivated for its crisp curly leaves, which are used in salads. Cf. **chicory.** [C15: from OF, from Med. L, from var. of L *intubus, entubus*]

endless ⓣ (ˈɛndlɪs) *adj* **1** having or seeming to have no end; eternal or infinite. **2** continuing too long or continually recurring. **3** formed with the ends joined.
▸**'endlessness** *n*

endmost (ˈɛndˌməʊst) *adj* nearest the end; most distant.

endo- *or before a vowel* **end-** *combining form.* inside; within: *endocrine.* [from Gk, from *endon* within]

endoblast (ˈɛndəʊˌblæst) *n* **1** *Embryol.* a less common name for **endoderm. 2** another name for **hypoblast.**
▸**ˌendo'blastic** *adj*

endocarditis (ˌɛndəʊkɑːˈdaɪtɪs) *n* inflammation of the lining of the heart. [C19: from NL, from ENDO- + Gk *kardia* heart + -ITIS]
▸**endocarditic** (ˌɛndəʊkɑːˈdɪtɪk) *adj*

endocarp (ˈɛndəˌkɑːp) *n* the inner layer of the pericarp of a fruit, such as the stone of a peach.
▸**ˌendo'carpal** *or* **ˌendo'carpic** *adj*

endocrine (ˈɛndəʊˌkraɪn) *adj also* **ˌendo'crinal, endocrinic** (ˌɛndəʊˈkrɪnɪk). **1** of or denoting endocrine glands or their secretions. ◆ *n* **2** an endocrine gland. [C20: from ENDO- + *-crine,* from Gk *krinein* to separate]

endocrine gland *n* any of the glands that secrete hormones directly into the bloodstream, e.g. the pituitary, pineal, and thyroid.

endocrinology (ˌɛndəʊkraɪˈnɒlədʒɪ, -krɪ-) *n* the branch of medical science concerned with the endocrine glands and their secretions.
▸**ˌendocri'nologist** *n*

endoderm (ˈɛndəʊˌdɜːm) *or* **entoderm** *n* the inner germ layer of an animal embryo, which gives rise to the lining of the digestive and respiratory tracts.
▸**ˌendo'dermal, ˌendo'dermic** *or* **ˌento'dermal, ˌento'dermic** *adj*

end of steel *n Canad.* **1** a point up to which railway tracks have been laid. **2** a town located at such a point.

endogamy (ɛnˈdɒgəmɪ) *n* **1** *Anthropol.* marriage within one's own tribe or similar unit. **2** pollination between two flowers on the same plant.
▸**en'dogamous** *or* **endogamic** (ˌɛndəʊˈgæmɪk) *adj*

endogenous (ɛnˈdɒdʒɪnəs) *adj* **1** *Biol.* developing or originating within an organism or part of an organism. **2** having no apparent external cause: *endogenous depression.*
▸**en'dogeny** *n*

endometritis (ˌɛndəʊmɪˈtraɪtɪs) *n* inflammation of the endometrium, which is caused by infection, as by bacteria, foreign bodies, etc.

endometrium (ˌɛndəʊˈmiːtrɪəm) *n, pl* **endometria** (-trɪə). the mucous membrane that lines the uterus. [C19: NL, from ENDO- + Greek *mētra* uterus]
▸**ˌendo'metrial** *adj*

endomorph (ˈɛndəʊˌmɔːf) *n* **1** a type of person having a body build characterized by fatness and heaviness. **2** a mineral that naturally occurs enclosed within another mineral.
▸**ˌendo'morphic** *adj* ▸**'endoˌmorphy** *n*

endomorphism (ˌɛndəʊˈmɔːˌfɪzəm) *n Geol.* metamorphism in which changes are induced in cooling molten rock by contact with older rocks.

endophyte (ˈɛndəʊˌfaɪt) *n* any plant, parasitic fungus, or alga that lives within a plant.
▸**endophytic** (ˌɛndəʊˈfɪtɪk) *adj*

endoplasm (ˈɛndəʊˌplæzəm) *n Cytology.* the inner cytoplasm of a cell.
▸**ˌendo'plasmic** *adj*

end organ *n Anat.* the expanded end of a peripheral motor or sensory nerve.

endorphin (ɛnˈdɔːfɪn) *n* any of a class of chemicals occurring in the brain, including enkephalin, which have a similar effect to morphine.

endorsation (ˌɛndɔːˈseɪʃən) *n Canad.* approval or support.

endorse ⓣ *or* **indorse** (ɪnˈdɔːs) *vb* **endorses, endorsing, endorsed** *or* **indorses, indorsing, indorsed.** (*tr*) **1** to give approval or sanction to. **2** to sign (one's name) on the back of (a cheque, etc.) to specify oneself as payee. **3** *Commerce.* **3a** to sign the back of (a document) to transfer ownership of the rights to a specified payee. **3b** to specify (a sum) as transferable to another as payee. **4** to write (a qualifying comment, etc.) on the back of a document. **5** to sign a document, as when confirming receipt of payment. **6** *Chiefly Brit.* to record a conviction on (a driving licence). [C16: from OF *endosser* to put on the back, from EN-[1] + *dos* back]
▸**en'dorsable** *or* **in'dorsable** *adj* ▸**en'dorser, en'dorsor** *or* **in'dorser, in'dorsor** *n* ▸**enˌdor'see** *or* **inˌdor'see** *n*

endorsement ⓣ *or* **indorsement** (ɪnˈdɔːsmənt) *n* **1** the act or an instance of endorsing. **2** something that endorses, such as a signature. **3** approval or support. **4** a record of a motoring offence on a driving licence.

endoscope (ˈɛndəʊˌskəʊp) *n* a medical instrument for examining the interior of hollow organs such as the stomach or bowel.
▸**endoscopic** (ˌɛndəʊˈskɒpɪk) *adj*

THESAURUS

outcome, resolution, result, sequel, upshot **8** = **remnant**, bit, butt, fragment, leftover, oddment, remainder, scrap, stub, tag end, tail end **9** = **destruction**, annihilation, death, demise, dissolution, doom, extermination, extinction, ruin, ruination **10** = **purpose**, aim, aspiration, design, drift, goal, intent, intention, object, objective, point, reason **21 the end** *Slang* = **the worst**, beyond endurance, insufferable, intolerable, the final blow, the last straw, the limit (*inf.*), too much (*inf.*), unbearable, unendurable ◆ *vb* **22** = **finish**, axe (*inf.*), belay (*Nautical*), bring to an end, cease, close, complete, conclude, culminate, dissolve, expire, nip in the bud, pull the plug on, put paid to, resolve, stop, terminate, wind up **23** = **destroy**, abolish, annihilate, exterminate, extinguish, kill, put to death, ruin
Antonyms *n* ≠ **finish:** beginning, birth, commencement, inception, launch, opening, origin, outset, prelude, source, start ◆ *vb* ≠ **finish:** begin, come into being, commence, initiate, launch, originate, start

endanger *vb* = **put at risk**, compromise, hazard, imperil, jeopardize, put in danger, risk, threaten
Antonyms *vb* defend, guard, preserve, protect, safeguard, save, secure

endear *vb* = **attract**, attach, bind, captivate, charm, engage, win

endearing *adj* = **attractive**, adorable, captivating, charming, cute, engaging, lovable, sweet, winning, winsome

endearment *n* = **loving word**, affectionate utterance, sweet nothing

endeavour *vb* **1** = **try**, aim, aspire, attempt, bend over backwards (*inf.*), do one's best, essay, give it one's best shot (*inf.*), have a go, knock oneself out (*inf.*), labour, make an effort, strive, struggle, take pains, undertake ◆ *n* **2** = **effort**, aim, attempt, crack (*inf.*), enterprise, essay, go (*inf.*), shot (*inf.*), stab (*inf.*), trial, try, undertaking, venture

ending *n* **1, 2** = **finish**, cessation, close, completion, conclusion, consummation, culmination, denouement, end, finale, resolution, termination, wind-up
Antonyms *n* birth, commencement, inauguration, inception, onset, opening, origin, preface, source, start, starting point

endless *adj* **1** = **eternal**, boundless, ceaseless, constant, continual, everlasting, immortal, incessant, infinite, interminable, limitless, measureless, perpetual, unbounded, unbroken, undying, unending, uninterrupted, unlimited **2** = **interminable**, monotonous, overlong **3** = **continuous**, unbroken, undivided, whole
Antonyms *adj* ≠ **eternal:** bounded, brief, circumscribed, finite, limited, passing, restricted, temporary, terminable, transient, transitory

endorse *vb* **1** = **approve**, advocate, affirm, authorize, back, champion, confirm, espouse, favour, prescribe, promote, ratify, recommend, sanction, subscribe to, support, sustain, vouch for, warrant **2-5** = **sign**, countersign, superscribe, undersign

endorsement *n* **1, 3** = **approval**, advocacy, affirmation, approbation, authorization, backing, championship, confirmation, espousal, favour, fiat, O.K. *or* okay (*inf.*), promotion, ratification, recommendation, sanction, seal of approval, subscription to, support, warrant **2** = **signature**,

endoskeleton (ˌɛndəʊˈskɛlɪtᵊn) *n* an internal skeleton, esp. the bony or cartilaginous skeleton of vertebrates.
▸ˌ**endoˈskeletal** *adj*

endosperm (ˈɛndəʊˌspɜːm) *n* the tissue within the seed of a flowering plant that surrounds and nourishes the embryo.
▸ˌ**endoˈspermic** *adj*

endothermic (ˌɛndəʊˈθɜːmɪk) *or* **endothermal** *adj* (of a chemical reaction or compound) occurring or formed with the absorption of heat.
▸ˌ**endoˈthermically** *adv* ▸ˌ**endoˈthermism** *n*

endow ❶ (ɪnˈdaʊ) *vb* (*tr*) **1** to provide with or bequeath a source of permanent income. **2** (usually foll. by *with*) to provide (with qualities, characteristics, etc.). [C14: from OF, from EN-[1] + *douer*, from L *dōtāre*, from *dōs* dowry]

endowment ❶ (ɪnˈdaʊmənt) *n* **1** the income with which an institution, etc., is endowed. **2** the act or process of endowing. **3** (*usually pl*) natural talents or qualities.

endowment assurance *or* **insurance** *n* a form of life insurance that provides for the payment of a specified sum directly to the policyholder at a designated date or to his beneficiary should he die before this date.

endpaper (ˈɛndˌpeɪpə) *n* either of two leaves at the front and back of a book pasted to the inside of the board covers and the first leaf of the book.

end point *n* **1** *Chem.* the point at which a titration is complete. **2** the point at which anything is complete.

end product *n* the final result of a process, series, etc., esp. in manufacturing.

endue ❶ *or* **indue** (ɪnˈdjuː) *vb* **endues, enduing, endued** *or* **indues, induing, indued.** (*tr*) (usually foll. by *with*) to invest or provide, as with some quality or trait. [C15: from OF, from L *indūcere*, from *dūcere* to lead]

end up ❶ *vb* (*adv*) **1** (*copula*) to become eventually; turn out to be. **2** (*intr*) to arrive, esp. by a circuitous or lengthy route or process.

endurance ❶ (ɪnˈdjʊərəns) *n* **1** the capacity, state, or an instance of enduring. **2** something endured; a hardship, strain, or privation.

endure ❶ (ɪnˈdjʊə) *vb* **endures, enduring, endured. 1** to undergo (hardship, strain, etc.) without yielding; bear. **2** (*tr*) to permit or tolerate. **3** (*intr*) to last or continue to exist. [C14: from OF, from L *indūrāre* to harden, from *dūrus* hard]
▸**enˈdurable** *adj*

enduring ❶ (ɪnˈdjʊərɪŋ) *adj* **1** permanent; lasting. **2** having forbearance; long-suffering.
▸**enˈduringly** *adv* ▸**enˈduringness** *n*

end user *n* **1** (in international trading) the person, organization, or nation that will be the ultimate user of goods such as arms. **2** *Computing.* the ultimate destination of information that is being transferred within a system.

endways (ˈɛndˌweɪz) *or esp. US & Canad.* **endwise** (ˈɛndˌwaɪz) *adv* **1** having the end forwards or upwards. ◆ *adj* **2** vertical or upright. **3** lengthways. **4** standing or lying end to end.

end zone *n American football.* the area behind the goals at each end of the field that the ball must cross for a touchdown to be awarded.

ENE *symbol for* east-northeast.

-ene *n combining form.* (in chemistry) indicating an unsaturated compound containing double bonds: *benzene; ethylene.* [from Gk *-ēnē*, fem. patronymic suffix]

enema (ˈɛnɪmə) *n, pl* **enemas** *or* **enemata** (-mətə). *Med.* **1** the introduction of liquid into the rectum to evacuate the bowels, medicate, or nourish. **2** the liquid so introduced. [C15: from NL, from Gk: injection, from *enienai* to send in]

enemy ❶ (ˈɛnəmɪ) *n, pl* **enemies. 1** a person hostile or opposed to a policy, cause, person, or group. **2a** an armed adversary; opposing military force. **2b** (*as modifier*): *enemy aircraft.* **3a** a hostile nation or people. **3b** (*as modifier*): *an enemy alien.* **4** something that harms or opposes. ◆ Related adj: **inimical.** [C13: from OF, from L *inimīcus* hostile, from IN-[1] + *amīcus* friend]

energetic ❶ (ˌɛnəˈdʒɛtɪk) *adj* having or showing energy; vigorous.
▸ˌ**enerˈgetically** *adv*

energize ❶ *or* **energise** (ˈɛnəˌdʒaɪz) *vb* **energizes, energizing, energized** *or* **energises, energising, energised. 1** to have or cause to have energy; invigorate. **2** (*tr*) to apply electric current or electromotive force to (a circuit, etc.).
▸ˈ**enerˌgizer** *or* ˈ**enerˌgiser** *n*

energy ❶ (ˈɛnədʒɪ) *n, pl* **energies. 1** intensity or vitality of action or expression; forcefulness. **2** capacity or tendency for intense activity; vigour. **3** *Physics.* **3a** the capacity of a body or system to do work. **3b** a measure of this capacity, measured in joules (SI units). [C16: from LL, from Gk *energeia* activity, from EN-[2] + *ergon* work]

energy band *n Physics.* a range of energies associated with the quantum states of electrons in a crystalline solid.

energy conversion *n* the process of changing one form of energy into another, such as nuclear energy into heat or solar energy into electrical energy.

enervate ❶ *vb* (ˈɛnəˌveɪt), **enervates, enervating, enervated. 1** (*tr*) to deprive of strength or vitality. ◆ *adj* (ɪˈnɜːvɪt). **2** deprived of strength or vitality. [C17: from L *ēnervāre* to remove the nerves from, from *nervus* nerve]
▸ˈ**enerˌvating** *adj* ▸ˌ**enerˈvation** *n*

en famille *French.* (ɑ̃ famij) *adv* **1** with one's family; at home. **2** in a casual way; informally.

enfant terrible *French.* (ɑ̃fɑ̃ tɛriblə) *n, pl* ***enfants terribles*** (ɑ̃fɑ̃ tɛriblə). a person given to unconventional conduct or indiscreet remarks. [C19: lit.: terrible child]

enfeeble ❶ (ɪnˈfiːbᵊl) *vb* **enfeebles, enfeebling, enfeebled.** (*tr*) to make weak.
▸**enˈfeeblement** *n* ▸**enˈfeebler** *n*

en fête *French.* (ɑ̃ fɛt) *adv* dressed for or engaged in a festivity. [C19: lit.: in festival]

enfilade (ˌɛnfɪˈleɪd) *Mil.* ◆ *n* **1** gunfire directed along the length of a position or formation. **2** a position or formation subject to such fire. ◆ *vb* **enfilades, enfilading, enfiladed.** (*tr*) **3** to attack (a position or formation) with enfilade. [C18: from F: suite, from *enfiler* to thread on string, from *fil* thread]

enfold ❶ *or* **infold** (ɪnˈfəʊld) *vb* (*tr*) **1** to cover by enclosing. **2** to embrace.
▸**enˈfolder** *or* **inˈfolder** *n* ▸**enˈfoldment** *or* **inˈfoldment** *n*

enforce ❶ (ɪnˈfɔːs) *vb* **enforces, enforcing, enforced.** (*tr*) **1** to ensure obedience to (a law, decision, etc.). **2** to impose (obedience, etc.) as by force. **3** to emphasize or reinforce (an argument, etc.).
▸**enˈforceable** *adj* ▸**enˌforceaˈbility** *n* ▸**enforcedly** (ɪnˈfɔːsɪdlɪ) *adv* ▸**enˈforcement** *n* ▸**enˈforcer** *n*

THESAURUS

comment, countersignature, qualification, superscription

endow *vb* **1, 2 = provide**, award, bequeath, bestow, confer, donate, endue, enrich, favour, finance, fund, furnish, give, grant, invest, leave, make over, purvey, settle on, supply, will

endowment *n* **1 = income**, award, bequest, boon, donation, fund, gift, grant, hand-out, largesse *or* largess, legacy, property, revenue, stipend **2 = provision**, award, benefaction, bestowal, donation, gift, presentation **3** *usually plural* **= talent**, ability, aptitude, attribute, capability, capacity, faculty, flair, genius, gift, power, qualification, quality

endue *vb* **= provide**, endow, fill, furnish, invest, supply

end up *vb* **1 = turn out to be**, become eventually, finish as, finish up, pan out (*inf.*) **2 = arrive**, come to a halt, fetch up (*inf.*), finish up, stop, wind up

endurable *adj* **1 = bearable**, acceptable, sufferable, supportable, sustainable, tolerable
Antonyms *adj* insufferable, insupportable, intolerable, too much (*inf.*), unbearable, unendurable

endurance *n* **1 = staying power**, bearing, fortitude, patience, perseverance, persistence, pertinacity, resignation, resolution, stamina, strength, submission, sufferance, tenacity, toleration

endure *vb* **1 = bear**, brave, cope with, experience, go through, stand, stick it out (*inf.*), suffer, support, sustain, take it (*inf.*), thole (*Scot.*), undergo, weather, withstand **2 = put up with**, abide, allow, bear, brook, countenance, hack (*sl.*), permit, stand, stick (*sl.*), stomach, submit to, suffer, swallow, take patiently, tolerate **3 = last**, abide, be durable, continue, have a good innings, hold, live, live on, persist, prevail, remain, stand, stay, survive, wear well

enduring *adj* **1 = long-lasting**, abiding, continuing, durable, eternal, firm, immortal, immovable, imperishable, lasting, living, perennial, permanent, persistent, persisting, prevailing, remaining, steadfast, steady, surviving, unfaltering, unwavering
Antonyms *adj* brief, ephemeral, fleeting, momentary, passing, short, short-lived, temporary, transient, transitory

enemy *n* **1-4 = foe**, adversary, antagonist, competitor, opponent, rival, the opposition, the other side
Antonyms *n* ally, confederate, friend, supporter

energetic *adj* **= vigorous**, active, alive and kicking, animated, brisk, dynamic, forceful, forcible, full of beans (*inf.*), high-powered, indefatigable, lively, potent, powerful, spirited, storming (*inf.*), strenuous, strong, tireless
Antonyms *adj* debilitated, dull, enervated, inactive, lazy, lethargic, lifeless, listless, slow, sluggish, torpid, weak

energize *vb* **1 = stimulate**, activate, animate, enliven, inspirit, invigorate, liven up, motivate, pep up, quicken, vitalize **2 = stimulate**, activate, electrify, kick-start, start up, switch on, turn on

energy *n* **1, 2 = vigour**, activity, animation, ardour, brio, drive, efficiency, élan, elbow grease (*facetious*), exertion, fire, force, forcefulness, get-up-and-go (*inf.*), go (*inf.*), intensity, life, liveliness, pep, pluck, power, spirit, stamina, strength, strenuousness, verve, vim (*sl.*), vitality, vivacity, zeal, zest, zip (*inf.*)

enervate *vb* **1 = weaken**, debilitate, devitalize, enfeeble, exhaust, fatigue, incapacitate, paralyse, prostrate, sap, tire, unnerve, wash out, wear out

enervation *n* **1 = weakness**, debilitation, debility, enfeeblement, exhaustedness, exhaustion, fatigue, feebleness, impotence, incapacity, infirmity, lassitude, paralysis, powerlessness, prostration, tiredness, weakening

enfeeble *vb* **= weaken**, debilitate, deplete, devitalize, diminish, exhaust, fatigue, render feeble, sap, undermine, unhinge, unnerve, wear out

enfold *vb* **1, 2 = wrap**, clasp, embrace, enclose, encompass, envelop, enwrap, fold, hold, hug, shroud, swathe, wrap up

enforce *vb* **1, 2 = impose**, administer, apply, carry out, coerce, compel, constrain, exact, execute, implement, insist on, oblige, prosecute, put in force, put into effect, reinforce, require, urge

enforced *adj* **1, 2 = imposed**, compelled, compulsory, constrained, dictated, involuntary, necessary, ordained, prescribed, required, unavoidable, unwilling

enforcement *n* **1, 2 = imposition**, administration, application, carrying out, exaction, execution, implementation, prosecution, reinforcement

enfranchise ⓣ (ɪn'fræntʃaɪz) *vb* **enfranchises, enfranchising, enfranchised.** (*tr*) **1** to grant the power of voting to. **2** to liberate, as from servitude. **3** (in England) to invest (a town, city, etc.) with the right to be represented in Parliament.
▸**en'franchisement** *n* ▸**en'franchiser** *n*
ENG *abbrev. for* electronic news gathering: TV news obtained at the point of action by means of modern video equipment.
Eng. *abbrev. for:* **1** England. **2** English.
engage ⓣ (ɪn'geɪdʒ) *vb* **engages, engaging, engaged.** (*mainly tr*) **1** to secure the services of. **2** to secure for use; reserve. **3** to involve (a person or his attention) intensely. **4** to attract (the affection) of (a person). **5** to draw (somebody) into conversation. **6** (*intr*) to take part; participate. **7** to promise (to do something). **8** (*also intr*) *Mil.* to begin an action with (an enemy). **9** to bring (a mechanism) into operation. **10** (*also intr*) to undergo or cause to undergo interlocking, as of the components of a driving mechanism. **11** *Machinery.* to locate (a locking device) in its operative position or to advance (a tool) into a workpiece to commence cutting. [C15: from OF, from EN-[1] + *gage* a pledge; see GAGE[1]]
▸**en'gager** *n*
engagé or (*fem*) ***engagée*** *French.* (ãgaʒe) *adj* (of an artist) committed to some ideology.
engaged ⓣ (ɪn'geɪdʒd) *adj* **1** pledged to be married; betrothed. **2** occupied or busy. **3** *Archit.* built against or attached to a wall or similar structure. **4** (of a telephone line) in use.
engaged tone *n Brit.* a repeated single note heard on a telephone when the number called is already in use.
engagement ⓣ (ɪn'geɪdʒmənt) *n* **1** a pledge of marriage; betrothal. **2** an appointment or arrangement, esp. for business or social purposes. **3** the act of engaging or condition of being engaged. **4** a promise, obligation, or other condition that binds. **5** a period of employment, esp. a limited period. **6** an action; battle.
engagement ring *n* a ring given by a man to a woman as a token of their betrothal.
engaging ⓣ (ɪn'geɪdʒɪŋ) *adj* pleasing, charming, or winning.
▸**en'gagingness** *n*
en garde *French.* (ã gard) *sentence substitute.* **1** on guard; a call to a fencer to adopt a defensive stance in readiness for an attack or bout. ◆ *adj* **2** (of a fencer) in such a stance.
engender ⓣ (ɪn'dʒendə) *vb* (*tr*) to bring about or give rise to; cause to be born. [C14: from OF, from L *ingenerāre,* from *generāre* to beget]
engin. *abbrev. for* engineering.
engine ⓣ ('ɛndʒɪn) *n* **1** any machine designed to convert energy into mechanical work. **2** a railway locomotive. **3** *Mil.* any piece of equipment formerly used in warfare, such as a battering ram. **4** *Obs.* any instrument or device. [C13: from OF, from L *ingenium* nature, talent, ingenious contrivance, from IN-[2] + *-genium,* rel. to *gignere* to beget, produce]
engine driver *n Chiefly Brit.* a man who drives a railway locomotive; train driver.
engineer ⓣ (,ɛndʒɪ'nɪə) *n* **1** a person trained in any branch of engineering. **2** the originator or manager of a situation, system, etc. **3** *US & Canad.* the driver of a railway locomotive. **4** an officer responsible for a ship's engines. **5** a member of the armed forces trained in engineering and construction work. ◆ *vb* (*tr*) **6** to originate, cause, or plan in a clever or devious manner. **7** to design, plan, or construct as a professional engineer. [C14 *enginer,* from OF, from *engignier* to contrive, ult. from L *ingenium* skill, talent; see ENGINE]
engineering (,ɛndʒɪ'nɪərɪŋ) *n* the profession of applying scientific principles to the design, construction, and maintenance of engines, cars, machines, etc. (**mechanical engineering**), buildings, bridges, roads, etc. (**civil engineering**), electrical machines and communication systems (**electrical engineering**), chemical plant and machinery (**chemical engineering**), or aircraft (**aeronautical engineering**).
English ('ɪŋglɪʃ) *n* **1** the official language of Britain, the US, most of the Commonwealth, and certain other countries. **2 the English.** (*functioning as pl*) the natives or inhabitants of England collectively. **3** (*often not cap.*) the usual US & Canad. term for **side** (in billiards). ◆ *adj* **4** of or relating to the English language. **5** relating to or characteristic of England or the English. ◆ *vb* (*tr*) **6** *Arch.* to translate or adapt into English.
▸**'Englishness** *n*
English horn *n Music.* another name for **cor anglais.**
Englishman ('ɪŋglɪʃmən) *or* (*fem*) **Englishwoman** *n, pl* **Englishmen** *or* **Englishwomen.** a native or inhabitant of England.
engorge ⓣ (ɪn'gɔːdʒ) *vb* **engorges, engorging, engorged.** (*tr*) **1** *Pathol.* to congest with blood. **2** to eat (food) greedily. **3** to gorge (oneself); glut.
▸**en'gorgement** *n*
engr *abbrev. for:* **1** engineer. **2** engraver.
engraft ⓣ *or* **ingraft** (ɪn'grɑːft) *vb* (*tr*) **1** to graft (a shoot, bud, etc.) onto a stock. **2** to incorporate in a firm or permanent way; implant.
▸**,engraf'tation, ,ingraf'tation** *or* **en'graftment, in'graftment** *n*
engrain ⓣ (ɪn'greɪn) *vb* a variant spelling of **ingrain.**
engrave ⓣ (ɪn'greɪv) *vb* **engraves, engraving, engraved.** (*tr*) **1** to inscribe (a design, writing, etc.) onto (a block, plate, or other printing surface) by carving, etching, or other process. **2** to print (designs or characters) from a plate so made. **3** to fix deeply or permanently in the mind. [C16: from EN-[1] + GRAVE[3], on the model of F *engraver*]
▸**en'graver** *n*
engraving ⓣ (ɪn'greɪvɪŋ) *n* **1** the art of a person who engraves. **2** a printing surface that has been engraved. **3** a print made from this.
engross ⓣ (ɪn'grəʊs) *vb* (*tr*) **1** to occupy one's attention completely; absorb. **2** to write or copy (manuscript) in large legible handwriting. **3** *Law.* to write or type out formally (a document) preparatory to execution. [C14 (in the sense: to buy up wholesale); C15 (in the sense: to write in large letters): from L *grossus* thick, GROSS]
▸**en'grossed** *adj* ▸**en'grossing** *adj* ▸**en'grossment** *n*
engulf ⓣ *or* **ingulf** (ɪn'gʌlf) *vb* (*tr*) **1** to immerse, plunge, bury, or swallow up. **2** (*often passive*) to overwhelm.
▸**en'gulfment** *n*
enhance ⓣ (ɪn'hɑːns) *vb* **enhances, enhancing, enhanced.** (*tr*) to intensify or increase in quality, value, power, etc.; improve; augment. [C14: from OF, from EN-[1] + *haucier* to raise, from Vulgar L *altiāre* (unattested), from L *altus* high]
▸**en'hancement** *n* ▸**en'hancer** *n*
enharmonic (,ɛnhɑː'mɒnɪk) *adj Music.* **1** denoting or relating to a small difference in pitch between two notes, such as A flat and G sharp: not present in instruments of equal temperament, but significant in the

THESAURUS

enfranchise *vb* **1** = **give the vote to**, grant suffrage to, grant the franchise to, grant voting rights to **2** = **free**, emancipate, liberate, manumit, release, set free
enfranchisement *n* **1** = **giving the vote**, granting suffrage *or* the franchise, granting voting rights **2** = **freeing**, emancipation, freedom, liberating, liberation, manumission, release, setting free
engage *vb* **1** = **employ**, appoint, commission, enlist, enrol, hire, retain, take on **2** = **book**, bespeak, charter, hire, lease, prearrange, rent, reserve, secure **3** = **occupy**, absorb, busy, engross, grip, involve, preoccupy, tie up **4** = **captivate**, allure, arrest, attach, attract, catch, charm, draw, enamour, enchant, fascinate, fix, gain, win **6** = **participate**, embark on, enter into, join, partake, practise, set about, take part, undertake **7** = **promise**, agree, bind, commit, contract, covenant, guarantee, obligate, oblige, pledge, undertake, vouch, vow **8** *Military* = **begin battle with**, assail, attack, combat, come to close quarters with, encounter, face off (*sl.*), fall on, fight with, give battle to, join battle with, meet, take on **9** = **set going**, activate, apply, bring into operation, energize, switch on **10** = **interlock**, dovetail, interact, interconnect, join, mesh
Antonyms *vb* ≠ **employ:** axe (*inf.*), discharge, dismiss, fire (*inf.*), give notice to, lay off, oust, remove, sack (*inf.*)
engaged *adj* **1** = **betrothed** (*arch.*), affianced, pledged, promised, spoken for **2** = **occupied**, absorbed, busy, committed, employed, engrossed, in use, involved, preoccupied, tied up, unavailable
Antonyms *adj* ≠ **betrothed:** available, fancy-free, free, unattached, uncommitted, unengaged ≠ **occupied:** available, free, uncommitted, unengaged
engagement *n* **1** = **betrothal**, troth (*arch.*) **2** = **appointment**, arrangement, commitment, date, meeting **4** = **promise**, assurance, bond, compact, contract, oath, obligation, pact, pledge, undertaking, vow, word **5** = **job**, commission, employment, gig (*inf.*), post, situation, stint, work **6** = **battle**, action, combat, conflict, confrontation, contest, encounter, face-off (*sl.*), fight
engaging *adj* = **charming**, agreeable, appealing, attractive, captivating, cute, enchanting, fascinating, fetching (*inf.*), likable *or* likeable, lovable, pleasant, pleasing, winning, winsome
Antonyms *adj* disagreeable, objectionable, obnoxious, offensive, repulsive, unattractive, unlikable *or* unlikeable, unlovely, unpleasant
engender *vb* = **produce**, beget, breed, bring about, cause, create, excite, foment, generate, give rise to, hatch, incite, induce, instigate, lead to, make, occasion, precipitate, provoke
engine *n* **1** = **machine**, mechanism, motor **4** *Obsolete* = **device**, agency, agent, apparatus, appliance, contrivance, implement, instrument, means, tool, weapon
engineer *vb* **6** = **bring about**, cause, concoct, contrive, control, create, devise, effect, encompass, finagle (*inf.*), manage, manoeuvre, mastermind, originate, plan, plot, scheme, wangle (*inf.*)
engorge *vb* **2, 3** = **gorge**, bolt, cram, devour, eat, fill, glut, gobble, gulp, guzzle, pig out (*sl.*), satiate, stuff, wolf
engraft *vb* **1, 2** = **incorporate**, graft, implant, inculcate, infix, infuse, ingrain, instil
engrain *see* **ingrain**
engrave *vb* **1** = **carve**, chase, chisel, cut, enchase (*rare*), etch, grave (*arch.*), inscribe **2** = **imprint**, impress, print **3** = **fix**, embed, impress, imprint, infix, ingrain, lodge
engraving *n* **1** = **cutting**, carving, chasing, chiselling, dry point, enchasing (*rare*), etching, inscribing, inscription **2** = **carving**, block, etching, inscription, plate, woodcut **3** = **print**, etching, impression
engross *vb* **1** = **absorb**, arrest, engage, engulf, hold, immerse, involve, occupy, preoccupy
engrossed *adj* **1** = **absorbed**, captivated, caught up, deep, enthralled, fascinated, gripped, immersed, intent, intrigued, lost, preoccupied, rapt, riveted
engrossing *adj* **1** = **absorbing**, captivating, compelling, enthralling, fascinating, gripping, interesting, intriguing, riveting
engulf *vb* **1, 2** = **immerse**, absorb, bury, consume, deluge, drown, encompass, engross, envelop, flood (out), inundate, overrun, overwhelm, plunge, submerge, swallow up, swamp
enhance *vb* = **improve**, add to, augment, boost, complement, elevate, embellish, exalt, heighten, increase, intensify, lift, magnify, raise, reinforce, strengthen, swell
Antonyms *vb* debase, decrease, depreciate, devalue, diminish, lower, minimize, reduce, spoil
enhancement *n* = **improvement**, addition, augmentation, boost, embellishment, enrichment, heightening, increase, increment, rise

intonation of stringed instruments. **2** denoting or relating to enharmonic modulation. [C17: from L, from Gk, from EN-[2] + *harmonia;* see HARMONY]
▸ˌenharˈmonically *adv*

enigma ❶ (ɪˈnɪgmə) *n* a person, thing, or situation that is mysterious, puzzling, or ambiguous. [C16: from L, from Gk, from *ainissesthai* to speak in riddles, from *ainos* fable, story]
▸**enigmatic** (ˌɛnɪgˈmætɪk) *or* ˌ**enigˈmatical** *adj* ▸ˌ**enigˈmatically** *adv*

enjambment *or* **enjambement** (ɪnˈdʒæmmənt) *n Prosody.* the running over of a sentence from one line of verse into the next. [C19: from F, lit.: a straddling, from EN-[1] + *jambe* leg; see JAMB]
▸**enˈjambed** *adj*

enjoin ❶ (ɪnˈdʒɔɪn) *vb (tr)* **1** to order (someone) to do something. **2** to impose or prescribe (a mode of behaviour, etc.). **3** *Law.* to require (a person) to do or refrain from some act, esp. by an injunction. [C13: from OF *enjoindre,* from L *injungere* to fasten to, from IN-[2] + *jungere* to JOIN]
▸**enˈjoiner** *n* ▸**enˈjoinment** *n*

enjoy ❶ (ɪnˈdʒɔɪ) *vb (tr)* **1** to receive pleasure from; take joy in. **2** to have the benefit of; use. **3** to have as a condition; experience. **4 enjoy oneself.** to have a good time. [C14: from OF, from EN-[1] + *joir* to find pleasure in, from L *gaudēre* to rejoice]
▸**enˈjoyable** *adj* ▸**enˈjoyableness** *n* ▸**enˈjoyably** *adv* ▸**enˈjoyer** *n*

enjoyment ❶ (ɪnˈdʒɔɪmənt) *n* **1** the act or condition of receiving pleasure from something. **2** the use or possession of something that is satisfying. **3** something that provides joy or satisfaction.

enkephalin (ɛnˈkɛfəlɪn) *or* **encephalin** (ɛnˈsɛfəlɪn) *n* a chemical occurring in the brain, having effects similar to those of morphine.

enkindle ❶ (ɪnˈkɪndᵊl) *vb* **enkindles, enkindling, enkindled.** *(tr)* **1** to set on fire; kindle. **2** to excite to activity or ardour; arouse.

enlace (ɪnˈleɪs) *vb* **enlaces, enlacing, enlaced.** *(tr)* **1** to bind or encircle with or as with laces. **2** to entangle; intertwine.
▸**enˈlacement** *n*

enlarge ❶ (ɪnˈlɑːdʒ) *vb* **enlarges, enlarging, enlarged. 1** to make or grow larger; increase or expand. **2** *(tr)* to make (a photographic print) of a larger size than the negative. **3** *(intr;* foll. by *on* or *upon)* to speak or write (about) in greater detail.
▸**enˈlargeable** *adj* ▸**enˈlargement** *n* ▸**enˈlarger** *n*

enlighten ❶ (ɪnˈlaɪtᵊn) *vb (tr)* **1** to give information or understanding to; instruct. **2** to free from prejudice, superstition, etc. **3** to give spiritual or religious revelation to. **4** *Poetic.* to shed light on.
▸**enˈlightening** *adj*

enlightened ❶ (ɪnˈlaɪtᵊnd) *adj* **1** well-informed, tolerant, and guided by rational thought: *an enlightened administration.* **2** claiming a spiritual revelation of truth.

enlightenment ❶ (ɪnˈlaɪtᵊnmənt) *n* the act or means of enlightening or the state of being enlightened.

Enlightenment (ɪnˈlaɪtᵊnmənt) *n* **the.** an 18th-century philosophical movement stressing the importance of reason.

enlist ❶ (ɪnˈlɪst) *vb* **1** to enter or persuade to enter the armed forces. **2** *(tr)* to engage or secure (a person or his support) for a venture, cause, etc. **3** *(intr;* foll. by *in)* to enter into or join an enterprise, cause, etc.
▸**enˈlister** *n* ▸**enˈlistment** *n*

enlisted man *n US.* a serviceman who holds neither a commission nor a warrant.

enliven ❶ (ɪnˈlaɪvᵊn) *vb (tr)* **1** to make active, vivacious, or spirited. **2** to make cheerful or bright; gladden.
▸**enˈlivening** *adj* ▸**enˈlivenment** *n*

en masse ❶ (*French* ɑ̃ mas) *adv* in a group or mass; as a whole; all together. [C19: from F]

enmesh ❶ (ɪnˈmɛʃ) *vb (tr)* to catch or involve in or as if in a net or snare; entangle.
▸**enˈmeshment** *n*

enmity ❶ (ˈɛnmɪtɪ) *n, pl* **enmities.** a feeling of hostility or ill will, as between enemies. [C13: from OF; see ENEMY]

ennoble ❶ (ɪˈnəubᵊl) *vb* **ennobles, ennobling, ennobled.** *(tr)* **1** to make noble, honourable, or excellent; dignify; exalt. **2** to raise to a noble rank.
▸**enˈnoblement** *n* ▸**enˈnobler** *n* ▸**enˈnobling** *adj*

ennui ❶ (ˈɒnwiː) *n* a feeling of listlessness and general dissatisfaction resulting from lack of activity or excitement. [C18: from F: apathy, from OF *enui* annoyance, vexation; see ANNOY]

enology (iːˈnɒlədʒɪ) *n* the usual US spelling of **oenology.**

enormity ❶ (ɪˈnɔːmɪtɪ) *n, pl* **enormities. 1** the quality or character of extreme wickedness. **2** an act of great wickedness; atrocity. **3** *Inf.* vastness of size or extent. [C15: from OF, from LL *ēnormitās* hugeness; see ENORMOUS]

> **USAGE NOTE** In modern English, it is common to talk about the *enormity* of something such as a task or a problem, but one should not talk about the *enormity* of an object or area: *distribution is a problem because of India's enormous size* (not *India's enormity*).

enormous ❶ (ɪˈnɔːməs) *adj* **1** unusually large in size, extent, or degree; immense; vast. **2** *Arch.* extremely wicked; heinous. [C16: from L, from *ē-* out of, away from + *norma* rule, pattern]
▸**eˈnormously** *adv* ▸**eˈnormousness** *n*

enosis (ˈɛnəusɪs) *n* the union of Greece and Cyprus: the aim of a group of Greek Cypriots. [C20: Mod. Gk: from Gk *henoun* to unite, from *heis* one]

enough ❶ (ɪˈnʌf) *determiner* **1a** sufficient to answer a need, demand or supposition. **1b** *(as pron): enough is now known.* **2 that's enough!** that will

THESAURUS

enigma *n* = **mystery**, conundrum, problem, puzzle, riddle, teaser

enigmatic *adj* = **mysterious**, ambiguous, cryptic, Delphic, doubtful, equivocal, incomprehensible, indecipherable, inexplicable, inscrutable, obscure, oracular, perplexing, puzzling, recondite, sphinxlike, uncertain, unfathomable, unintelligible
Antonyms *adj* clear, comprehensible, simple, straightforward, uncomplicated

enjoin *vb* **1, 2** = **order**, advise, bid, call upon, charge, command, counsel, demand, direct, instruct, prescribe, require, urge, warn **3** *Law* = **prohibit**, ban, bar, disallow, forbid, interdict, place an injunction on, preclude, proscribe, restrain

enjoy *vb* **1** = **take pleasure in** *or* **from**, appreciate, be entertained by, be pleased with, delight in, like, rejoice in, relish, revel in, take joy in **2, 3** = **have**, be blessed *or* favoured with, experience, have the benefit of, have the use of, own, possess, reap the benefits of, use **4 enjoy oneself** = **have a good time**, have a ball *(inf.)*, have a field day, have fun, let one's hair down, make merry
Antonyms *vb* ≠ **take pleasure in** *or* **from:** abhor, despise, detest, dislike, hate, have no taste *or* stomach for, loathe

enjoyable *adj* **1** = **pleasurable**, agreeable, amusing, delectable, delicious, delightful, entertaining, gratifying, pleasant, pleasing, satisfying, to one's liking
Antonyms *adj* despicable, disagreeable, displeasing, hateful, loathsome, obnoxious, offensive, repugnant, unenjoyable, unpleasant, unsatisfying, unsavoury

enjoyment *n* **1** = **pleasure**, amusement, beer and skittles *(inf.)*, delectation, delight, diversion, entertainment, fun, gladness, gratification, gusto, happiness, indulgence, joy, recreation, relish, satisfaction, zest

enkindle *vb* **1** = **set on fire**, fire, ignite, kindle, light, put a match to, put to the torch, set ablaze, set alight, set fire to, torch **2** = **arouse**, awake, excite, foment, incite, inflame, inspire, provoke, stir

enlarge *vb* **1, 2** = **increase**, add to, amplify, augment, blow up *(inf.)*, broaden, diffuse, dilate, distend, elongate, expand, extend, grow, heighten, inflate, lengthen, magnify, make *or* grow larger, multiply, stretch, swell, wax, widen **3** *with* **on** *or* **upon** = **expand on**, descant on, develop, elaborate on, expatiate on, give further details about
Antonyms *vb* ≠ **increase:** compress, condense, curtail, decrease, diminish, lessen, narrow, reduce, shorten, shrink, trim, truncate ≠ **expand on:** abbreviate, abridge, condense, shorten

enlighten *vb* **1** = **inform**, advise, apprise, cause to understand, civilize, counsel, edify, educate, instruct, make aware, teach

enlightened *adj* **1** = **informed**, aware, broad-minded, civilized, cultivated, educated, knowledgeable, liberal, literate, open-minded, reasonable, refined, sophisticated
Antonyms *adj* ignorant, narrow-minded, short-sighted, small-minded, unaware, uneducated, unenlightened

enlightenment *n* = **understanding**, awareness, broad-mindedness, civilization, comprehension, cultivation, edification, education, information, insight, instruction, knowledge, learning, literacy, open-mindedness, refinement, sophistication, teaching, wisdom

enlist *vb* **1, 3** = **join up**, enrol, enter (into), join, muster, register, sign up, volunteer **2** = **obtain**, engage, procure, recruit, secure

enliven *vb* **1, 2** = **cheer up**, animate, brighten, buoy up, cheer, excite, exhilarate, fire, gladden, hearten, inspire, inspirit, invigorate, pep up, perk up, quicken, rouse, spark, stimulate, vitalize, vivify, wake up
Antonyms *vb* chill, dampen, deaden, depress, put a damper on, repress, subdue

en masse *adv* = **all together**, all at once, as a group, as a whole, as one, ensemble, in a body, in a group, in a mass, together

enmesh *vb* = **entangle**, catch, embroil, ensnare, implicate, incriminate, involve, net, snare, snarl, tangle, trammel, trap

enmity *n* = **hostility**, acrimony, animosity, animus, antagonism, antipathy, aversion, bad blood, bitterness, hate, hatred, ill will, malevolence, malice, malignity, rancour, spite, venom
Antonyms *n* affection, amity, cordiality, friendliness, friendship, geniality, goodwill, harmony, love, warmth

ennoble *vb* **1** = **dignify**, aggrandize, elevate, enhance, exalt, glorify, honour, magnify, raise

ennui *n* = **boredom**, dissatisfaction, lassitude, listlessness, tedium, the doldrums

enormity *n* **1** = **wickedness**, atrociousness, atrocity, depravity, disgrace, evilness, heinousness, monstrousness, nefariousness, outrageousness, turpitude, viciousness, vileness, villainy **2** = **atrocity**, abomination, crime, disgrace, evil, horror, monstrosity, outrage, villainy **3** *Informal* = **hugeness**, enormousness, greatness, immensity, magnitude, massiveness, vastness

enormous *adj* **1** = **huge**, astronomic, Brobdingnagian, colossal, elephantine, excessive, gargantuan, gigantic, ginormous *(inf.)*, gross, humongous *or* humungous *(US sl.)*, immense, jumbo *(inf.)*, mammoth, massive, monstrous, mountainous, prodigious, stellar *(inf.)*, titanic, tremendous, vast **2** *Archaic* = **wicked**, abominable, atrocious, depraved, disgraceful, evil, heinous, monstrous, nefarious, odious, outrageous, vicious, vile, villainous
Antonyms *adj* ≠ **huge:** diminutive, dwarf, infinitesimal, insignificant, Lilliputian, little, meagre, microscopic, midget, minute, petite, pint-sized *(inf.)*, small, tiny, trivial, wee

enough *determiner* **1a** = **sufficient**, abundant, adequate, ample, plenty ◆ *pron* **1b** = **sufficiency**, abundance, adequacy, ample supply, do: used to put an end to an action, speech, performance, etc. ◆ *adv* **3** so as to be sufficient; as much as necessary. **4** (*not used with a negative*) very or quite; rather. **5** (intensifier): *oddly enough.* **6** just adequately; tolerably. [OE *genōh*]

en passant (ɒn pæ'sɑːnt) *adv* in passing: in chess, said of capturing a pawn that has made an initial move of two squares. The capture is made as if the captured pawn had moved one square instead of two. [C17: from F]

enprint ('ɛnprɪnt) *n* a standard photographic print (5 × 3·5 in.) produced from a negative.

enquire ❶ (ɪn'kwaɪə) *vb* **enquires, enquiring, enquired.** a variant of **inquire.**
▸**en'quirer** *n* ▸**en'quiry** *n*

enrage ❶ (ɪn'reɪdʒ) *vb* **enrages, enraging, enraged.** (*tr*) to provoke to fury; put into a rage.
▸**en'raged** *adj* ▸**en'ragement** *n*

en rapport *French.* (ɑ̃ rapɔr) *adj* (*postpositive*), *adv* in sympathy, harmony, or accord.

enrapture ❶ (ɪn'ræptʃə) *vb* **enraptures, enrapturing, enraptured.** (*tr*) to fill with delight; enchant.

enrich ❶ (ɪn'rɪtʃ) *vb* (*tr*) **1** to increase the wealth of. **2** to endow with fine or desirable qualities. **3** to make more beautiful; adorn; decorate. **4** to improve in quality, colour, flavour, etc. **5** to increase the food value of by adding nutrients. **6** to fertilize (soil). **7** *Physics.* to increase the concentration or abundance of one component or isotope in (a solution or mixture).
▸**en'riched** *adj* ▸**en'richment** *n*

enrol ❶ *or US* **enroll** (ɪn'rəʊl) *vb* **enrols** *or US* **enrolls, enrolling, enrolled.** (*mainly tr*) **1** to record or note in a roll or list. **2** (*also intr*) to become or cause to become a member; enlist; register. **3** to put on record.
▸**ˌenrol'lee** *n* ▸**en'roller** *n*

enrolment ❶ *or US* **enrollment** (ɪn'rəʊlmənt) *n* **1** the act of enrolling or state of being enrolled. **2** a list of people enrolled. **3** the total number of people enrolled.

en route ❶ (ɒn 'ruːt) *adv* on or along the way. [C18: from F]

Ens. *abbrev. for* Ensign.

ENSA ('ɛnsə) *n acronym for* Entertainments National Service Association.

ensconce ❶ (ɪn'skɒns) *vb* **ensconces, ensconcing, ensconced.** (*tr; often passive*) **1** to establish or settle firmly or comfortably. **2** to place in safety; hide. [C16: see EN-[1], SCONCE[2]]

ensemble ❶ (ɒn'sɒmbᵊl) *n* **1** all the parts of something considered together. **2** a person's complete costume; outfit. **3** the cast of a play other than the principals. **4** *Music.* a group of soloists singing or playing together. **5** *Music.* the degree of precision and unity exhibited by a group of instrumentalists or singers performing together. **6** the general effect of something made up of individual parts. ◆ *adv* **7** all together or at once. [C15: from F: together, from L, from IN-[2] + *simul* at the same time]

enshrine ❶ *or* **inshrine** (ɪn'ʃraɪn) *vb* **enshrines, enshrining, enshrined.** (*tr*) **1** to place or enclose as in a shrine. **2** to hold as sacred; cherish; treasure.
▸**en'shrinement** *n*

enshroud ❶ (ɪn'ʃraʊd) *vb* (*tr*) to cover or hide as with a shroud.

ensign ❶ ('ɛnsaɪn) *n* **1** (*also* 'ɛnsən). a flag flown by a ship, branch of the armed forces, etc., to indicate nationality, allegiance, etc. See also **Red Ensign, White Ensign.** **2** any flag, standard, or banner. **3** a standard-bearer. **4** a symbol or emblem; sign. **5** (in the US Navy) a commissioned officer of the lowest rank. **6** (in the British infantry) a colours bearer. **7** (formerly in the British infantry) a commissioned officer of the lowest rank. [C14: from OF *enseigne*, from L INSIGNIA]
▸**'ensignˌship** *or* **'ensigncy** *n*

ensilage ('ɛnsɪlɪdʒ) *n* **1** the process of ensiling green fodder. **2** a less common name for **silage.**

ensile (ɛn'saɪl, 'ɛnsaɪl) *vb* **ensiles, ensiling, ensiled.** (*tr*) **1** to store and preserve (green fodder) in a silo. **2** to turn (green fodder) into silage by causing it to ferment in a silo. [C19: from F, from Sp., from EN-[1] + *silo* SILO]

enslave ❶ (ɪn'sleɪv) *vb* **enslaves, enslaving, enslaved.** (*tr*) to make a slave of; subjugate.
▸**en'slavement** *n* ▸**en'slaver** *n*

ensnare ❶ *or* **insnare** (ɪn'snɛə) *vb* **ensnares, ensnaring, ensnared** *or* **insnares, insnaring, insnared.** (*tr*) **1** to catch or trap as in a snare. **2** to trap or gain power over (someone) by dishonest or underhand means.
▸**en'snarement** *n* ▸**en'snarer** *n*

ensue ❶ (ɪn'sjuː) *vb* **ensues, ensuing, ensued.** **1** (*intr*) to come next or afterwards. **2** (*intr*) to occur as a consequence; result. **3** (*tr*) *Obs.* to pursue. [C14: from Anglo-F, from OF, from EN-[1] + *suivre* to follow, from L *sequī*]
▸**en'suing** *adj*

en suite *French.* (ɑ̃ sɥit) *adv* forming a unit: *a room with bathroom en suite.* [lit.: in sequence]

ensure ❶ (ɛn'ʃʊə, -'ʃɔː) *or esp. US* **insure** *vb* **ensures, ensuring, ensured** *or US* **insures, insuring, insured.** (*tr*) **1** (*may take a clause as object*) to make certain or sure; guarantee. **2** to make safe or secure; protect.
▸**en'surer** *n*

ENT *Med. abbrev. for* ear, nose, and throat.

-ent *suffix forming adjectives and nouns.* causing or performing an action or existing in a certain condition; the agent that performs an action: *astringent; dependent.* [from L *-ent-, -ens,* present participial ending]

entablature (ɛn'tæblətʃə) *n Archit.* **1** the part of a classical temple above the columns, having an architrave, a frieze, and a cornice. **2** any similar construction. [C17: from F, from It. *intavolatura* something put on a table, hence, something laid flat, from *tavola* table]

entablement (ɪn'teɪbᵊlmənt) *n* the platform of a pedestal, above the dado, that supports a statue. [C17: from OF]

entail ❶ (ɪn'teɪl) *vb* (*tr*) **1** to bring about or impose inevitably: *this task entails careful thought.* **2** *Property law.* to restrict (the descent of an estate) to designated heirs. **3** *Logic.* to have as a necessary consequence. ◆ *n* **4** *Property law.* **4a** the restriction imposed by entailing an estate. **4b** an entailed estate. [C14 *entaillen*, from EN-[1] + *taille* limitation, TAIL[2]]
▸**en'tailer** *n* ▸**en'tailment** *n*

entamoeba (ˌɛntə'miːbə), **endamoeba** *or US* **entameba, endameba** *n, pl* **entamoebae** (-biː), **entamoebas, endamoebae, endamoebas** *or US* **entamebae, entamebas, endamebae, endamebas.** any parasitic amoeba of the genus *Entamoeba* (or *Endamoeba*) which lives in the intestines of man and causes amoebic dysentery.

entangle ❶ (ɪn'tæŋgᵊl) *vb* **entangles, entangling, entangled.** (*tr*) **1** to catch or involve in or as if in a tangle; ensnare or enmesh. **2** to make tangled or twisted; snarl. **3** to make complicated; confuse. **4** to involve in difficulties.
▸**en'tanglement** *n* ▸**en'tangler** *n*

entasis ('ɛntəsɪs) *n, pl* **entasises** (-siːz). a slightly convex curve given to the shaft of a column, or similar structure, to correct the illusion of concavity produced by a straight shaft. [C18: from Gk, from *enteinein* to stretch tight, from *teinein* to stretch]

entellus (ɛn'tɛləs) *n* an Old World monkey of S Asia. [C19: NL, apparently after a character in Virgil's *Aeneid*]

THESAURUS

plenty, right amount ◆ *adv* **3, 4** = **sufficiently,** abundantly, adequately, amply, fairly, moderately, passably, reasonably, satisfactorily, tolerably

enquire *see* **inquire**

enquiry *see* **inquiry**

enrage *vb* = **anger,** aggravate (*inf.*), exasperate, gall, get one's back up, incense, incite, inflame, infuriate, irritate, madden, make one's blood boil, make one see red (*inf.*), nark (*Brit., Austral., & NZ sl.*), provoke, put one's back up
Antonyms *vb* appease, assuage, calm, conciliate, mollify, pacify, placate, soothe

enraged *adj* = **furious,** aggravated (*inf.*), angered, angry, boiling mad, choked, cross, exasperated, fit to be tied (*sl.*), fuming, incandescent, incensed, inflamed, infuriated, irate, irritated, livid (*inf.*), mad (*inf.*), on the warpath, pissed (*taboo sl.*), pissed off (*taboo sl.*), raging, raging mad, wild

enrapture *vb* = **enchant,** absorb, beguile, bewitch, captivate, charm, delight, enamour, enthral, entrance, fascinate, ravish, spellbind, transport

enrich *vb* **1** = **make rich,** make wealthy **2, 4** = **enhance,** aggrandize, ameliorate, augment, cultivate, develop, endow, improve, refine, supplement

enrol *vb* **1, 3** = **record,** chronicle, inscribe, list, note **2** = **enlist,** accept, admit, engage, join up, matriculate, recruit, register, sign up *or* on, take on

enrolment *n* **1** = **enlistment,** acceptance, admission, engagement, matriculation, recruitment, registration

en route *adv* = **on** *or* **along the way,** in transit, on the road

ensconce *vb* **1** = **settle,** curl up, establish, install, nestle, snuggle up **2** = **hide,** conceal, cover, protect, screen, shelter, shield

ensemble *n* **1** = **whole,** aggregate, assemblage, collection, entirety, set, sum, total, totality, whole thing **2** = **outfit,** costume, get-up (*inf.*), suit **3** = **group,** band, cast, chorus, company, supporting cast, troupe ◆ *adv* **7** = **all together,** all at once, as a group, as a whole, at once, at the same time, en masse, in concert

enshrine *vb* **2** = **preserve,** apotheosize, cherish, consecrate, dedicate, embalm, exalt, hallow, revere, sanctify, treasure

enshroud *vb* = **cover,** cloak, cloud, conceal, enclose, enfold, envelop, enwrap, hide, obscure, pall, shroud, veil, wrap

ensign *n* **1, 2** = **flag,** badge, banner, colours, jack, pennant, pennon, standard, streamer

enslave *vb* = **subjugate,** bind, dominate, enchain, enthral, reduce to slavery, yoke

ensnare *vb* **1, 2** = **trap,** catch, embroil, enmesh, entangle, entrap, net, snare, snarl

ensue *vb* **1, 2** = **follow,** arise, attend, be consequent on, befall, come after, come next, come to pass (*arch.*), derive, flow, issue, proceed, result, stem, succeed, supervene, turn out *or* up
Antonyms *vb* antecede, come first, forerun, go ahead of, go before, introduce, lead, pave the way, precede, usher

ensure *vb* **1** = **make certain,** certify, confirm, effect, guarantee, make sure, secure, warrant **2** = **protect,** guard, make safe, safeguard, secure

entail *vb* **1** = **involve,** bring about, call for, cause, demand, encompass, give rise to, impose, lead to, necessitate, occasion, require, result in

entangle *vb* **1** = **tangle,** catch, compromise, embroil, enmesh, ensnare, entrap, foul, implicate, involve, knot, mat, mix up, ravel, snag, snare, trammel, trap **3** = **mix up,** bewilder, complicate, confuse, jumble, muddle, perplex, puzzle, snarl, twist
Antonyms *vb* ≠ **tangle:** detach, disconnect, disengage, disentangle, extricate, free, loose, separate, sever, unfold, unravel, unsnarl, untangle, untwist ≠ **mix up:** clarify, clear (up), resolve, simplify, work out

entanglement *n* **1-3** = **tangle,** complication, confusion, ensnarement, entrapment, imbroglio, involvement, jumble, knot, mesh, mess, mix-up, muddle, snare, snarl-up (*inf., chiefly Brit.*), toils, trap **4** = **difficulty,** embarrassment,

entente (*French* ãtãt) *n* **1** short for **entente cordiale. 2** the parties to an entente cordiale collectively. [C19: F: understanding]

entente cordiale 🅣 (*French* ãtãt kɔrdjal) *n* **1** a friendly understanding between political powers. **2** (*often caps.*) the understanding reached by France and Britain in 1904, over colonial disputes. [C19: F: cordial understanding]

enter 🅣 ('ɛntə) *vb* **1** to come or go into (a place, house, etc.). **2** to penetrate or pierce. **3** (*tr*) to introduce or insert. **4** to join (a party, organization, etc.). **5** (when *intr*, foll. by *into*) to become involved or take part (in). **6** (*tr*) to record (an item) in a journal, account, etc. **7** (*tr*) to record (a name, etc.) on a list. **8** (*tr*) to present or submit: *to enter a proposal.* **9** (*intr*) *Theatre.* to come on stage: used as a stage direction: *enter Juliet.* **10** (when *intr*, often foll. by *into*, *on*, or *upon*) to begin; start: *to enter upon a new career.* **11** (*intr;* often foll. by *upon*) to come into possession (of). **12** (*tr*) to place (evidence, etc.) before a court of law. [C13: from OF, from L *intrāre*, from *intrā* within]
▸**'enterable** *adj* ▸**'enterer** *n*

enteric (ɛn'tɛrɪk) *or* **enteral** ('ɛntərəl) *adj* intestinal. [C19: from Gk, from *enteron* intestine]

enter into *vb* (*intr, prep*) **1** to be considered as a necessary part of (one's plans, calculations, etc.). **2** to be in sympathy with.

enteritis (ˌɛntə'raɪtɪs) *n* inflammation of the intestine.

entero- *or before a vowel* **enter-** *combining form.* indicating an intestine: *enterovirus; enteritis.* [from NL, from Gk *enteron* intestine]

enterobiasis (ˌɛntərəʊ'baɪəsɪs) *n* a disease, common in children, caused by infestation of the large intestine with pinworms. [C20: NL, from *enterobius* (generic name of worm) + -IASIS]

enterprise 🅣 ('ɛntəˌpraɪz) *n* **1** a project or undertaking, esp. one that requires boldness or effort. **2** participation in such projects. **3** readiness to embark on new ventures; boldness and energy. **4a** initiative in business. **4b** (*as modifier*): *the enterprise culture.* **5** a company or firm. [C15: from OF *entreprise* (n), from *entreprendre* from *entre-* between (from L: INTER-) + *prendre* to take, from L *prehendere* to grasp]
▸**'enterˌpriser** *n*

Enterprise Allowance Scheme *n* (in Britain) a scheme to provide a weekly allowance to an unemployed person who wishes to set up a business and is willing to invest a specified amount in it during its first year.

enterprise zone *n* one of several areas in the UK in which industrial development is encouraged by tax and other concessions.

enterprising 🅣 ('ɛntəˌpraɪzɪŋ) *adj* ready to embark on new ventures; full of boldness and initiative.
▸**'enterˌprisingly** *adv*

entertain 🅣 (ˌɛntə'teɪn) *vb* **1** to provide amusement for (a person or audience). **2** to show hospitality to (guests). **3** (*tr*) to hold in the mind. [C15: from OF, from *entre-* mutually + *tenir* to hold]

entertainer (ˌɛntə'teɪnə) *n* **1** a professional performer in public entertainments. **2** any person who entertains.

entertaining 🅣 (ˌɛntə'teɪnɪŋ) *adj* serving to entertain or give pleasure; diverting; amusing.

entertainment 🅣 (ˌɛntə'teɪnmənt) *n* **1** the act or art of entertaining or state of being entertained. **2** an act, production, etc., that entertains; diversion; amusement.

enthral 🅣 *or US* **enthrall** (ɪn'θrɔːl) *vb* **enthrals** *or US* **enthralls, enthralling, enthralled.** (*tr*) **1** to hold spellbound; enchant; captivate. **2** *Obs.* to hold as thrall; enslave.
▸**en'thraller** *n* ▸**en'thralling** *adj* ▸**en'thralment** *or US* **en'thrallment** *n*

enthrone (ɛn'θrəʊn) *vb* **enthrones, enthroning, enthroned.** (*tr*) **1** to place on a throne. **2** to honour or exalt. **3** to assign authority to.
▸**en'thronement** *n*

enthuse (ɪn'θjuːz) *vb* **enthuses, enthusing, enthused.** to feel or show or cause to feel or show enthusiasm.

enthusiasm 🅣 (ɪn'θjuːzɪˌæzəm) *n* **1** ardent and lively interest or eagerness. **2** an object of keen interest. **3** *Arch.* extravagant religious fervour. [C17: from LL, from Gk, from *enthousiazein* to be possessed by a god, from EN-[2] + *theos* god]

enthusiast 🅣 (ɪn'θjuːzɪˌæst) *n* **1** a person motivated by enthusiasm; fanatic. **2** *Arch.* one whose zeal for religion is extravagant.
▸**enˌthusi'astic** *adj* ▸**enˌthusi'astically** *adv*

enthymeme ('ɛnθɪˌmiːm) *n Logic.* a syllogism in which one or more premises are unexpressed. [C16: via L from Gk *enthumeisthai* to infer, from EN-[2] + *thumos* mind]

entice 🅣 (ɪn'taɪs) *vb* **entices, enticing, enticed.** (*tr*) to attract by exciting hope or desire; tempt; allure. [C13: from OF, from Vulgar L *intitiāre* (unattested) to incite]
▸**en'ticement** *n* ▸**en'ticer** *n* ▸**en'ticing** *adj* ▸**en'ticingly** *adv*

entire 🅣 (ɪn'taɪə) *adj* **1** (*prenominal*) whole; complete. **2** (*prenominal*) without reservation or exception. **3** not broken or damaged. **4** undivided; continuous. **5** (of leaves, petals, etc.) having a smooth margin not broken up into teeth or lobes. **6** not castrated: *an entire horse.* **7** *Obs.* unmixed; pure. ◆ *n* **8** an uncastrated horse. [C14: from OF, from L *integer* whole, from IN-[1] + *tangere* to touch]
▸**en'tireness** *n*

entirely 🅣 (ɪn'taɪəlɪ) *adv* **1** wholly; completely. **2** solely or exclusively.

entirety 🅣 (ɪn'taɪərɪtɪ) *n, pl* **entireties. 1** the state of being entire or whole; completeness. **2** a thing, sum, amount, etc., that is entire; whole; total.

entitle 🅣 (ɪn'taɪtᵊl) *vb* **entitles, entitling, entitled.** (*tr*) **1** to give (a person) the right to do or have something; qualify; allow. **2** to give a name or title to. **3** to confer a title of rank or honour upon. [C14: from OF *entituler*, from LL, from L *titulus* TITLE]
▸**en'titlement** *n*

entity 🅣 ('ɛntɪtɪ) *n, pl* **entities. 1** something having real or distinct existence. **2** existence or being. [C16: from Med. L, from *ēns* being, from L *esse* to be]
▸**'entitative** *adj*

THESAURUS

imbroglio, involvement, liaison, predicament, tie

entente cordiale *n* **1 = agreement**, arrangement, compact, deal, friendship, pact, treaty, understanding

enter *vb* **1-3 = come** *or* **go in** *or* **into**, arrive, insert, introduce, make an entrance, pass into, penetrate, pierce **4, 5, 10 = join**, become a member of, begin, commence, commit oneself to, embark upon, enlist, enrol, participate in, set about, set out on, sign up, start, take part in, take up **6, 7 = record**, inscribe, list, log, note, register, set down, take down **8 = put forward**, offer, present, proffer, register, submit, tender
Antonyms *vb* ≠ **come** *or* **go in** *or* **into**: depart, exit, go, issue from, leave, take one's leave, withdraw ≠ **join**: drop out, go, leave, pull out, resign, retire, withdraw

enterprise *n* **1 = undertaking**, adventure, effort, endeavour, essay, operation, plan, programme, project, venture **3 = initiative**, activity, adventurousness, alertness, audacity, boldness, daring, dash, drive, eagerness, energy, enthusiasm, get-up-and-go (*inf.*), gumption (*inf.*), pep, push (*inf.*), readiness, resource, resourcefulness, spirit, vigour, zeal **5 = firm**, business, company, concern, establishment, operation

enterprising *adj* **= resourceful**, active, adventurous, alert, audacious, bold, daring, dashing, eager, energetic, enthusiastic, go-ahead, intrepid, keen, ready, spirited, stirring, up-and-coming, venturesome, vigorous, zealous

entertain *vb* **1 = amuse**, charm, cheer, delight, divert, occupy, please, recreate (*rare*), regale **2 = show hospitality to**, accommodate, be host to, harbour, have company, have guests *or* visitors, lodge, put up, treat **3 = consider**, cogitate on, conceive, contemplate, foster, harbour, hold, imagine, keep in mind, maintain, muse over, ponder, support, think about, think over

entertaining *adj* **= enjoyable**, amusing, charming, cheering, delightful, diverting, funny, humorous, interesting, pleasant, pleasing, pleasurable, recreative (*rare*), witty

entertainment *n* **1, 2 = enjoyment**, amusement, beer and skittles (*inf.*), cheer, distraction, diversion, fun, good time, leisure activity, pastime, play, pleasure, recreation, satisfaction, sport, treat

enthral *vb* **1 = fascinate**, absorb, beguile, captivate, charm, enchant, enrapture, entrance, grip, hold spellbound, hypnotize, intrigue, mesmerize, ravish, rivet, spellbind

enthralling *adj* **1 = fascinating**, beguiling, captivating, charming, compelling, compulsive, enchanting, entrancing, gripping, hypnotizing, intriguing, mesmerizing, riveting, spellbinding

enthusiasm *n* **1 = keenness**, ardour, avidity, devotion, eagerness, earnestness, excitement, fervour, frenzy, interest, passion, relish, vehemence, warmth, zeal, zest, zing (*inf.*) **2 = passion**, craze, fad (*inf.*), hobby, hobbyhorse, interest, mania, rage

enthusiast *n* **1 = lover**, admirer, aficionado, buff (*inf.*), devotee, fan, fanatic, fiend, follower, freak (*inf.*), supporter, zealot

enthusiastic *adj* **1 = keen**, ablaze, ardent, avid, bright-eyed and bushy-tailed (*inf.*), devoted, eager, earnest, ebullient, excited, exuberant, fervent, fervid, forceful, full of beans (*inf.*), hearty, keen as mustard, lively, passionate, spirited, unqualified, unstinting, vehement, vigorous, warm, wholehearted, zealous
Antonyms *adj* apathetic, blasé, bored, cool, dispassionate, half-hearted, indifferent, nonchalant, unconcerned, unenthusiastic, uninterested

entice *vb* **= attract**, allure, beguile, cajole, coax, dangle a carrot in front of (someone's) nose, decoy, draw, inveigle, lead on, lure, persuade, prevail on, seduce, tempt, wheedle

enticement *n* **= attraction**, allurement, bait, blandishments, cajolery, coaxing, come-on (*inf.*), decoy, incentive, inducement, inveiglement, lure, persuasion, seduction, temptation

enticing *adj* **= attractive**, alluring, beguiling, captivating, come-hither (*inf.*), intriguing, inviting, irresistible, persuasive, seductive, tempting, yummy (*inf.*)
Antonyms *adj* distasteful, off-putting (*Brit. inf.*), repellent, unappealing, unattractive

entire *adj* **1 = whole**, complete, full, gross, total **2 = total**, absolute, full, outright, thorough, undiminished, unmitigated, unreserved, unrestricted **3 = intact**, perfect, sound, unbroken, undamaged, unmarked, unmarred, whole, without a scratch **4 = continuous**, integrated, unbroken, undivided, unified

entirely *adv* **1 = completely**, absolutely, altogether, every inch, fully, in every respect, lock, stock and barrel, perfectly, thoroughly, totally, unreservedly, utterly, wholly, without exception, without reservation **2 = only**, exclusively, solely
Antonyms *adv* ≠ **completely**: incompletely, moderately, partially, partly, piecemeal, slightly, somewhat, to a certain extent *or* degree

entirety *n* **1 = wholeness**, absoluteness, completeness, fullness, totality, undividedness, unity **2 = whole**, aggregate, sum, total, unity

entitle *vb* **1 = give the right to**, accredit, allow, authorize, empower, enable, enfranchise, fit for, license, make eligible, permit, qualify for, warrant **2 = call**, characterize, christen, denominate, designate, dub, label, name, style, term, title

entity *n* **1 = thing**, being, body, creature, existence, individual, object, organism, presence, quantity, substance **2 = essential nature**, es-

ento- *combining form.* inside; within: *entoderm.* [NL, from Gk *entos* within]

entomb ❶ (ɪnˈtuːm) *vb (tr)* **1** to place in or as if in a tomb; bury; inter. **2** to serve as a tomb for.
▸**enˈtombment** *n*

entomo- *combining form.* indicating an insect: *entomology.* [from Gk *entomon* insect]

entomol. *or* **entom.** *abbrev. for* entomology.

entomology (ˌɛntəˈmɒlədʒɪ) *n* the branch of science concerned with the study of insects.
▸ˌ**entomoˈlogical** *adj* ▸ˌ**entoˈmologist** *n*

entophyte (ˈɛntəʊˌfaɪt) *n Bot.* a variant spelling of **endophyte.**
▸**entophytic** (ˌɛntəʊˈfɪtɪk) *adj*

entourage ❶ (ˌɒntʊˈrɑːʒ) *n* **1** a group of attendants or retainers; retinue. **2** surroundings. [C19: from F, from *entourer* to surround, from *tour* circuit; see TOUR, TURN]

entr'acte (ɒnˈtrækt) *n* **1** an interval between two acts of a play or opera. **2** (esp. formerly) an entertainment during such an interval. [C19: F, lit.: between-act]

entrails ❶ (ˈɛntreɪlz) *pl n* **1** the internal organs of a person or animal; intestines; guts. **2** the innermost parts of anything. [C13: from OF, from Med. L *intrālia,* changed from L *interānea* intestines]

entrain (ɪnˈtreɪn) *vb* to board or put aboard a train.
▸**enˈtrainment** *n*

entrance[1] ❶ (ˈɛntrəns) *n* **1** the act or an instance of entering; entry. **2** a place for entering, such as a door. **3a** the power, liberty, or right of entering. **3b** (*as modifier*): *an entrance fee.* **4** the coming of an actor or other performer onto a stage. [C16: from F, from *entrer* to ENTER]

entrance[2] ❶ (ɪnˈtrɑːns) *vb* **entrances, entrancing, entranced.** *(tr)* **1** to fill with wonder and delight; enchant. **2** to put into a trance; hypnotize.
▸**enˈtrancement** *n* ▸**enˈtrancing** *adj*

entrant ❶ (ˈɛntrənt) *n* a person who enters. [C17: from F, lit.: entering, from *entrer* to ENTER]

entrap ❶ (ɪnˈtræp) *vb* **entraps, entrapping, entrapped.** *(tr)* **1** to catch or snare as in a trap. **2** to trick into danger, difficulty, or embarrassment.
▸**enˈtrapment** *n* ▸**enˈtrapper** *n*

entreat ❶ *or* **intreat** (ɪnˈtriːt) *vb* **1** to ask (a person) earnestly; beg or plead with; implore. **2** to make an earnest request or petition for (something). **3** an archaic word for **treat** (sense 4). [C15: from OF, from EN-[1] + *traiter* to TREAT]
▸**enˈtreatment** *or* **inˈtreatment** *n*

entreaty ❶ (ɪnˈtriːtɪ) *n, pl* **entreaties.** an earnest request or petition; supplication; plea.

entrechat (*French* ɑ̃trəʃa) *n* a leap in ballet during which the dancer repeatedly crosses his feet or beats them together. [C18: from F *entrechase,* changed by folk etymology from It. (*capriola*) *intrecciata,* lit.: entwined (caper)]

entrecôte (*French* ɑ̃trəkot) *n* a beefsteak cut from between the ribs. [F, from *entre-* INTER- + *côte* rib]

entrée (ˈɒntreɪ) *n* **1** a dish served before a main course. **2** *Chiefly US.* the main course of a meal. **3** the power or right of entry. [C18: from F, from *entrer* to ENTER; in cookery, so called because formerly the course was served after an intermediate course called the *relevé* (remove)]

entremets (*French* ɑ̃trəmɛ) *n, pl* **entremets** (*French* -me). **1** a dessert. **2** a light dish formerly served between the main course and the dessert. [C18: from F, from OF, from *entre-* between + *mes* dish]

entrench ❶ *or* **intrench** (ɪnˈtrɛntʃ) *vb* **1** *(tr)* to construct a defensive position by digging trenches around it. **2** *(tr)* to fix or establish firmly. **3** *(intr;* foll. by *on* or *upon)* to trespass or encroach.
▸**enˈtrenched** *or* **inˈtrenched** *adj* ▸**enˈtrenchment** *or* **inˈtrenchment** *n*

entrepôt (*French* ɑ̃trəpo) *n* **1** a warehouse for commercial goods. **2a** a trading centre or port at which goods are imported and re-exported without incurring duty. **2b** (*as modifier*): *an entrepôt trade.* [C18: F, from *entreposer,* from *entre* between + *poser* to place; formed on the model of DEPOT]

entrepreneur ❶ (ˌɒntrəprəˈnɜː) *n* **1** the owner or manager of a business enterprise who, by risk and initiative, attempts to make profits. **2** a middleman or commercial intermediary. [C19: from F, from *entreprendre* to undertake; see ENTERPRISE]
▸ˌ**entrepreˈneurial** *adj* ▸ˌ**entrepreˈneurship** *n*

entropy (ˈɛntrəpɪ) *n, pl* **entropies. 1** a thermodynamic quantity that changes in a reversible process by an amount equal to the heat absorbed or emitted divided by the thermodynamic temperature. It is measured in joules per kelvin. **2** lack of pattern or organization; disorder. [C19: from EN-[2] + -TROPE]

entrust ❶ *or* **intrust** (ɪnˈtrʌst) *vb (tr)* **1** (usually foll. by *with*) to invest or charge (with a duty, responsibility, etc.). **2** (often foll. by *to*) to put into the care or protection of someone.
▸**enˈtrustment** *or* **inˈtrustment** *n*

> **USAGE NOTE** It is usually considered incorrect to talk about *entrusting* someone *to do* something: *the army cannot be trusted* (not *entrusted*) *to carry out orders.*

entry ❶ (ˈɛntrɪ) *n, pl* **entries. 1** the act or an instance of entering; entrance. **2** a point or place for entering, such as a door, etc. **3a** the right or liberty of entering. **3b** (*as modifier*): *an entry permit.* **4** the act of recording an item in a journal, account, etc. **5** an item recorded, as in a diary, dictionary, or account. **6** a person, horse, car, etc., entering a competition or contest. **7** the competitors entering a contest considered collectively. **8** the action of an actor in going on stage. **9** *Property law.* the act of going upon land with the intention of asserting the right to possession. **10** any point in a piece of music at which a performer commences or resumes singing or playing. **11** *Bridge, etc.* a card that enables one to transfer the lead from one's own hand to that of one's partner or to the dummy hand. **12** *Dialect.* a passage between the backs of two rows of houses. [C13: from OF *entree,* p.p. of *entrer* to ENTER]

entryism (ˈɛntrɪɪzəm) *n* the policy or practice of joining an existing political party with the intention of changing it instead of forming a new party.
▸ˈ**entryist** *n, adj*

entry-level *adj* **1** (of a job or worker) at the most elementary level in a career structure. **2** (of a product) characterized by being at the most appropriate level for use by a beginner: *an entry-level camera.*

entwine ❶ *or* **intwine** (ɪnˈtwaɪn) *vb* **entwines, entwining, entwined** *or* **intwines, intwining, intwined.** (of two or more things) to twine together or (of one or more things) to twine around (something else).
▸**enˈtwinement** *or* **inˈtwinement** *n*

E number *n* any of a series of numbers with the prefix E indicating a specific food additive recognized by the European Union.

enumerate ❶ (ɪˈnjuːməˌreɪt) *vb* **enumerates, enumerating, enumerated.** *(tr)* **1** to name one by one; list. **2** to determine the number of; count. [C17: from L, from *numerāre* to count, reckon; see NUMBER]
▸**eˈnumerable** *adj* ▸**eˌnumerˈation** *n* ▸**eˈnumerative** *adj*

enumerator (ɪˈnjuːməˌreɪtə) *n* **1** a person or thing that enumerates. **2** *Brit.* a person who issues and retrieves census forms.

enunciable (ɪˈnʌnsɪəbᵊl) *adj* capable of being enunciated.

enunciate ❶ (ɪˈnʌnsɪˌeɪt) *vb* **enunciates, enunciating, enunciated. 1** to articulate or pronounce (words), esp. clearly and distinctly. **2** *(tr)* to

THESAURUS

sence, quiddity (*Philosophy*), quintessence, real nature

entomb *vb* **1** = **bury,** inhume, inter, inurn, lay to rest, sepulchre

entombment *n* **1** = **burial,** inhumation, interment, inurnment, sepulture

entourage *n* **1** = **retinue,** associates, attendants, companions, company, cortege, court, escort, followers, following, retainers, staff, suite, train **2** = **surroundings,** ambience, environment, environs, milieu

entrails *pl n* **1** = **intestines,** bowels, guts, innards (*inf.*), insides, offal, viscera

entrance[1] *n* **1, 4** = **appearance,** arrival, coming in, entry, ingress, introduction **2** = **way in,** access, avenue, door, doorway, entry, gate, ingress, inlet, opening, passage, portal **3** = **admission,** access, admittance, entrée, entry, ingress, permission to enter
Antonyms *n* ≠ **appearance:** departure, egress, exit, exodus, leave-taking ≠ **way in:** exit, outlet, way out

entrance[2] *vb* **1** = **enchant,** absorb, bewitch, captivate, charm, delight, enrapture, enthral, fascinate, gladden, ravish, spellbind, transport **2** = **mesmerize,** hypnotize, put in a trance
Antonyms *vb* ≠ **enchant:** bore, disenchant, irritate, offend, put off, turn off (*inf.*)

entrant *n* = **competitor,** candidate, contestant, entry, participant, player

entrap *vb* **1** = **catch,** capture, ensnare, net, snare, trap **2** = **trick,** allure, beguile, decoy, embroil, enmesh, ensnare, entangle, entice, implicate, inveigle, involve, lead on, lure, seduce

entreat *vb* **1, 2** = **beg,** appeal to, ask, ask earnestly, beseech, conjure, crave, enjoin, exhort, implore, importune, petition, plead with, pray, request, supplicate

entreaty *n* = **plea,** appeal, earnest request, exhortation, importunity, petition, prayer, request, solicitation, suit, supplication

entrench *vb* **1** = **fortify,** construct defences, dig in, dig trenches **2** = **fix,** anchor, dig in, embed, ensconce, establish, implant, ingrain, install, lodge, plant, root, seat, set, settle **3** = **encroach,** impinge, infringe, interlope, intrude, make inroads, trespass

entrenched *adj* **2** = **fixed,** deep-rooted, deep-seated, firm, indelible, ineradicable, ingrained, rooted, set, unshakable, well-established

entrepreneur *n* **1** = **businessman** *or* **businesswoman,** contractor, director, financier, impresario, industrialist, magnate, tycoon

entrust *vb* **1, 2** = **give custody of,** assign, authorize, charge, commend, commit, confide, consign, delegate, deliver, hand over, invest, trust, turn over

entry *n* **1** = **coming in,** appearance, entering, entrance, initiation, introduction **2** = **way in,** access, avenue, door, doorway, entrance, gate, ingress, inlet, opening, passage, passageway, portal **3** = **admission,** access, entrance, entrée, free passage, permission to enter **5** = **record,** account, item, jotting, listing, memo, memorandum, minute, note, registration **6** = **competitor,** attempt, candidate, contestant, effort, entrant, participant, player, submission
Antonyms *n* ≠ **coming in:** departure, egress, exit, leave, leave-taking, withdrawal ≠ **way in:** exit, way out

entwine *vb* = **twist,** braid, embrace, encircle, entwist (*arch.*), interlace, intertwine, interweave, knit, plait, ravel, surround, twine, weave, wind
Antonyms *vb* disentangle, extricate, free, separate, straighten out, undo, unravel, untangle, unwind

enumerate *vb* **1** = **list,** cite, detail, itemize, mention, name, quote, recapitulate, recite, recount, rehearse, relate, specify, spell out, tell **2** = **count,** add up, calculate, compute, number, reckon, sum up, tally, total

enunciate *vb* **1** = **pronounce,** articulate, enounce, say, sound, speak, utter, vocalize,

state precisely or formally. [C17: from L *ēnuntiāre* to declare, from *nuntiāre* to announce]
▸**e,nunci'ation** *n* ▸**e'nunciative** *or* **e'nunciatory** *adj* ▸**e'nunci,ator** *n*

enuresis (,ɛnju'riːsɪs) *n* involuntary discharge of urine, esp. during sleep. [C19: from NL, from Gk EN-[2] + *ouron* urine]
▸**enuretic** (,ɛnju'rɛtɪk) *adj*

envelop ⓘ (ɪn'vɛləp) *vb* **envelops, enveloping, enveloped.** (*tr*) **1** to wrap or enclose as in a covering. **2** to conceal or obscure. **3** to surround (an enemy force). [C14: from OF *envoluper*, from EN-[1] + *voluper, voloper*, from ?]
▸**en'velopment** *n*

envelope ⓘ ('ɛnvə,ləʊp, 'ɒn-) *n* **1** a flat covering of paper, usually rectangular and with a flap that can be sealed, used to enclose a letter, etc. **2** any covering or wrapper. **3** *Biol.* any enclosing structure, such as a membrane, shell, or skin. **4** the bag enclosing gas in a balloon. **5** *Maths.* a curve or surface that is tangential to each one of a group of curves or surfaces. [C18: from F, from *envelopper* to wrap around; see ENVELOP]

envenom (ɪn'vɛnəm) *vb* (*tr*) **1** to fill or impregnate with venom; make poisonous. **2** to fill with bitterness or malice.

enviable ⓘ ('ɛnvɪəbᵊl) *adj* exciting envy; fortunate or privileged.
▸**'enviableness** *n*

envious ⓘ ('ɛnvɪəs) *adj* feeling, showing, or resulting from envy. [C13: from Anglo-Norman, ult. from L *invidiōsus* full of envy, INVIDIOUS; see ENVY]
▸**'enviously** *adv* ▸**'enviousness** *n*

environ ⓘ (ɪn'vaɪrən) *vb* (*tr*) to encircle or surround. [C14: from OF *environner* to surround, from EN-[1] + *viron* a circle, from *virer* to turn, VEER]

environment ⓘ (ɪn'vaɪrənmənt) *n* **1** external conditions or surroundings. **2** *Ecology.* the external surroundings in which a plant or animal lives, which influence its development and behaviour. **3** *Computing.* an operating system, program, or integrated suite of programs that provides all the facilities necessary for a particular application: *a word-processing environment.*
▸**en,viron'mental** *adj*

environmentalist ⓘ (ɪn,vaɪrən'mɛntəlɪst) *n* **1** a specialist in the maintenance of ecological balance and the conservation of the environment. **2** a person concerned with issues that affect the environment, such as pollution.

environs ⓘ (ɪn'vaɪrənz) *pl n* a surrounding area or region, esp. the suburbs or outskirts of a city.

envisage ⓘ (ɪn'vɪzɪdʒ) *vb* **envisages, envisaging, envisaged.** (*tr*) **1** to form a mental image of; visualize. **2** to conceive of as a possibility in the future. [C19: from F, from EN-[1] + *visage* face, VISAGE]
▸**en'visagement** *n*

> **USAGE NOTE** It was formerly considered incorrect to use a clause after *envisage* as in *it is envisaged that the new centre will cost £40 million*, but this use is now acceptable.

envision ⓘ (ɪn'vɪʒən) *vb* (*tr*) to conceive of as a possibility, esp. in the future; foresee.

envoy[1] ⓘ ('ɛnvɔɪ) *n* **1** Also called: **minister, minister plenipotentiary.** a diplomat ranking between an ambassador and a minister resident. **2** an accredited agent or representative. [C17: from F, from *envoyer* to send, from Vulgar L *inviāre* (unattested) to send on a journey, from IN-[2] + *via* road]
▸**'envoyship** *n*

envoy[2] *or* **envoi** ('ɛnvɔɪ) *n* **1** a brief concluding stanza, notably in ballades. **2** a postscript in other forms of verse or prose. [C14: from OF, from *envoyer* to send; see ENVOY[1]]

envy ⓘ ('ɛnvɪ) *n, pl* **envies. 1** a feeling of grudging or somewhat admiring discontent aroused by the possessions, achievements, or qualities of another. **2** the desire to have something possessed by another; covetousness. **3** an object of envy. ◆ *vb* **envies, envying, envied. 4** to be envious of (a person or thing). [C13: via OF from L *invidia*, from *invidēre* to eye maliciously, from IN-[2] + *vidēre* to see]
▸**'envier** *n* ▸**'envyingly** *adv*

enwrap *or* **inwrap** (ɪn'ræp) *vb* **enwraps, enwrapping, enwrapped.** (*tr*) **1** to wrap or cover up; envelop. **2** (*usually passive*) to engross or absorb.

enwreath (ɪn'riːð) *vb* (*tr*) to surround or encircle with or as with a wreath or wreaths.

enzootic (,ɛnzəʊ'ɒtɪk) *adj* **1** (of diseases) affecting animals within a limited region. ◆ *n* **2** an enzootic disease. [C19: from EN-[2] + Gk *zōion* animal + -OTIC]
▸**,enzo'otically** *adv*

enzyme ('ɛnzaɪm) *n* any of a group of complex proteins produced by living cells, that act as catalysts in specific biochemical reactions. [C19: from Med. Gk *enzumos* leavened, from Gk EN-[2] + *zumē* leaven]
▸**enzymatic** (,ɛnzaɪ'mætɪk, -zɪ-) *or* **enzymic** (ɛn'zaɪmɪk, -'zɪm-) *adj*

enzyme-linked immunosorbent assay (,ɪmjʊnəʊ'sɔːbənt) *n* the full name for **ELISA.**

eo- *combining form.* early or primeval: *Eocene; eohippus.* [from Gk, from *ēōs* dawn]

EOC *abbrev. for* Equal Opportunities Commission.

Eocene ('iːəʊ,siːn) *adj* **1** of or denoting the second epoch of the Tertiary period, during which hooved mammals appeared. ◆ *n* **2 the.** the Eocene epoch or rock series. [C19: from EO- + -CENE]

eohippus (,iːəʊ'hɪpəs) *n, pl* **eohippuses.** the earliest horse: an extinct Eocene dog-sized animal. [C19: NL, from EO- + Gk *hippos* horse]

Eolithic (,iːəʊ'lɪθɪk) *adj* denoting or relating to the early part of the Stone Age, characterized by the use of crude stone tools (**eoliths**).

eon ('iːən, 'iːɒn) *n* **1** the usual US spelling of **aeon. 2** *Geol.* the longest division of geological time, comprising two or more eras.

eosin ('iːəʊsɪn) *or* **eosine** ('iːəʊsɪn, -,siːn) *n* **1** a red fluorescent crystalline water-insoluble compound. Its soluble salts are used as dyes. **2** any of several similar dyes. [C19: from Gk *ēōs* dawn + -IN; referring to colour it gives to silk]

-eous *suffix forming adjectives.* relating to or having the nature of: *gaseous.* [from L *-eus*]

EP *n* an extended-play gramophone record, usually 7 inches (18 cm) in diameter: a longer recording than a single.

EPA *abbrev. for* eicosapentaenoic acid: a fatty acid, found in certain fish oils, that can reduce blood cholesterol.

epact ('iːpækt) *n* **1** the difference in time, about 11 days, between the solar year and the lunar year. **2** the number of days between the beginning of the calendar year and the new moon immediately preceding this. [C16: via LL from Gk *epaktē*, from *epagein* to bring in, intercalate]

eparch ('ɛpɑːk) *n* **1** a bishop or metropolitan in the Orthodox Church. **2** a governor of a subdivision of a province of modern Greece. [C17: from Gk *eparkhos*, from *epi-* over, on + -ARCH]
▸**'eparchy** *n*

epaulette *or US* **epaulet** ('ɛpə,lɛt, -lɪt) *n* a piece of ornamental material on the shoulder of a garment, esp. a military uniform. [C18: from F, from *épaule* shoulder, from L *spatula* shoulder blade]

épée ('ɛpeɪ) *n* a sword similar to the foil but with a heavier blade. [C19: from F: sword, from L *spatha*, from Gk *spathē* blade; see SPADE[1]]
▸**'épéeist** *n*

epeirogeny (,ɛpaɪ'rɒdʒɪnɪ) *or* **epeirogenesis** (ɪ,paɪrəʊ'dʒɛnɪsɪs) *n* the formation of continents by relatively slow displacements of the earth's crust. [C19: from Gk *ēpeiros* continent + -GENY]
▸**epeirogenic** (ɪ,paɪrəʊ'dʒɛnɪk) *or* **epeirogenetic** (ɪ,paɪrəʊdʒɪ'nɛtɪk) *adj*

epergne (ɪ'pɜːn) *n* an ornamental centrepiece for a table, holding fruit, flowers, etc. [C18: prob. from F *épargne* a saving, from *épargner* to economize, of Gmc origin]

epexegesis (ɛ,pɛksɪ'dʒiːsɪs) *n, pl* **epexegeses** (-,siːz). *Rhetoric.* **1** the addition of a phrase, clause, or sentence to a text to provide further explanation. **2** the phrase, clause, or sentence added for this purpose. [C17: from Gk; see EPI-, EXEGESIS]
▸**epexegetic** (ɛ,pɛksɪ'dʒɛtɪk) *or* **ep,exe'getical** *adj*

Eph. *or* **Ephes.** *Bible. abbrev. for* Ephesians.

ephah *or* **epha** ('iːfə) *n* a Hebrew unit of measure equal to approximately one bushel or about 33 litres. [C16: from Heb., from Egyptian]

ephedrine *or* **ephedrin** (ɪ'fɛdrɪn, 'ɛfɪ,driːn, -drɪn) *n* a white crystalline alkaloid used for the treatment of asthma and hay fever. [C19: from NL from L from Gk, from EPI- + *hedra* seat + -INE[2]]

ephemera (ɪ'fɛmərə) *n, pl* **ephemeras** *or* **ephemerae** (-ə,riː). **1** a mayfly, esp. one of the genus *Ephemera.* **2** something transitory or short-lived. **3** (*functioning as pl*) collectable items not originally intended to be

THESAURUS

voice **2** = **state**, declare, proclaim, promulgate, pronounce, propound, publish

envelop *vb* **1, 2** = **enclose**, blanket, cloak, conceal, cover, embrace, encase, encircle, encompass, enfold, engulf, enwrap, hide, obscure, sheathe, shroud, surround, swaddle, swathe, veil, wrap

envelope *n* **2** = **wrapping**, case, casing, coating, cover, covering, jacket, sheath, shell, skin, wrapper

enviable *adj* = **desirable**, advantageous, blessed, covetable, favoured, fortunate, lucky, much to be desired, privileged, to die for (*inf.*)
Antonyms *adj* disagreeable, painful, thankless, uncomfortable, undesirable, unenviable, unpleasant

envious *adj* = **covetous**, begrudging, green-eyed, green with envy, grudging, jaundiced, jealous, malicious, resentful, spiteful

environ *vb* = **surround**, beset, besiege, encircle, enclose, encompass, engird, envelop, gird, hem, invest (*rare*), ring

environment *n* **1** = **surroundings**, atmosphere, background, conditions, context, domain, element, habitat, locale, medium, milieu, scene, setting, situation, territory

environmental *adj* **2** = **ecological**, green

environmentalist *n* **1, 2** = **conservationist**, ecologist, friend of the earth, green

environs *pl n* = **surrounding area**, district, locality, neighbourhood, outskirts, precincts, purlieus, suburbs, vicinity

envisage *vb* **1** = **imagine**, conceive (of), conceptualize, contemplate, fancy, picture, think up, visualize **2** = **foresee**, anticipate, envision, predict, see

envision *vb* = **conceive of**, anticipate, contemplate, envisage, foresee, predict, see, visualize

envoy[1] *n* **2** = **messenger**, agent, ambassador, courier, delegate, deputy, diplomat, emissary, intermediary, legate, minister, plenipotentiary, representative

envy *n* **1, 2** = **covetousness**, enviousness, grudge, hatred, ill will, jealousy, malice, malignity, resentfulness, resentment, spite, the green-eyed monster (*inf.*) ◆ *vb* **4** = **covet**, be envious (of), begrudge, be jealous (of), grudge, resent long-lasting, such as tickets, posters, etc. **4** a plural of **ephemeron.** [C16: see EPHEMERAL]

ephemeral Ⓣ (ɪ'fɛmərəl) *adj* **1** transitory; short-lived: *ephemeral pleasure.* ◆ *n* **2** a short-lived organism, such as the mayfly. [C16: from Gk *ephēmeros* lasting only a day, from *hēmera* day]
▸**e͵phemer'ality** *or* **e'phemeralness** *n*

ephemerid (ɪ'fɛmərɪd) *n* any insect of the order *Ephemeroptera* (or *Ephemerida*), which comprises the mayflies. Also: **ephemeropteran.** [C19: from NL, from Gk *ephēmeros* short-lived + -ID[1]]

ephemeris (ɪ'fɛmərɪs) *n, pl* **ephemerides** (͵ɛfɪ'mɛrɪ͵diːz). a table giving the future positions of a planet, comet, or satellite during a specified period. [C16: from L, from Gk: diary, journal; see EPHEMERAL]

ephemeron (ɪ'fɛmə͵rɒn) *n, pl* **ephemera** (-ərə) *or* **ephemerons.** (*usually pl*). something transitory or short-lived. [C16: see EPHEMERAL]

ephod ('iːfɒd) *n Bible.* an embroidered vestment worn by priests in ancient Israel. [C14: from Heb.]

ephor ('ɛfɔː) *n, pl* **ephors** *or* **ephori** (-ə͵raɪ) (in ancient Greece) a senior magistrate, esp. one of the five Spartan ephors, who wielded effective power. [C16: from Gk, from *ephoran* to supervise, from EPI- + *horan* to look]
▸**'ephoral** *adj* ▸**'ephorate** *n*

epi-, eph-, *or before a vowel* **ep-** *prefix* **1** upon; above; over: *epidermis; epicentre.* **2** in addition to: *epiphenomenon.* **3** after: *epilogue.* **4** near; close to: *epicalyx.* [from Gk, from *epi* (prep)]

epic ('ɛpɪk) *n* **1** a long narrative poem recounting in elevated style the deeds of a legendary hero. **2** the genre of epic poetry. **3** any work of literature, film, etc., having qualities associated with the epic. **4** an episode in the lives of men in which heroic deeds are performed. ◆ *adj* **5** denoting, relating to, or characteristic of an epic or epics. **6** of heroic or impressive proportions. [C16: from L, from Gk *epikos*, from *epos* speech, word, song]

epicalyx (͵ɛpɪ'keɪlɪks, -'kæl-) *n, pl* **epicalyxes** *or* **epicalyces** (-lɪ͵siːz). *Bot.* a series of small sepal-like bracts forming an outer calyx beneath the true calyx in some flowers.

epicanthus (͵ɛpɪ'kænθəs) *n, pl* **epicanthi** (-θaɪ). a fold of skin extending vertically over the inner angle of the eye: characteristic of Mongolian peoples. [C19: NL, from EPI- + L *canthus* corner of the eye, from Gk *kanthos*]
▸͵**epi'canthic** *adj*

epicardium (͵ɛpɪ'kɑːdɪəm) *n, pl* **epicardia** (-dɪə). *Anat.* the innermost layer of the pericardium. [C19: NL, from EPI- + Gk *kardia* heart]
▸͵**epi'cardiac** *or* ͵**epi'cardial** *adj*

epicarp ('ɛpɪ͵kɑːp) *or* **exocarp** *n* the outermost layer of the pericarp of fruits. [C19: from F, from EPI- + Gk *karpos* fruit]

epicene ('ɛpɪ͵siːn) *adj* **1** having the characteristics of both sexes. **2** of neither sex; sexless. **3** effeminate. **4** *Grammar.* **4a** denoting a noun that may refer to a male or a female. **4b** (in Latin, Greek, etc.) denoting a noun that retains the same gender regardless of the sex of the referent. [C15: from L *epicoenus* of both genders, from Gk *epikoinos* common to many, from *koinos* common]
▸͵**epi'cenism** *n*

epicentre *or US* **epicenter** ('ɛpɪ͵sɛntə) *n* the point on the earth's surface immediately above the origin of an earthquake. [C19: from NL, from Gk *epikentros* over the centre, from EPI- + CENTRE]
▸͵**epi'central** *adj*

epicure Ⓣ ('ɛpɪ͵kjʊə) *n* **1** a person who cultivates a discriminating palate for good food and drink. **2** a person devoted to sensual pleasures. [C16: from Med. L *epicūrus*, after *Epicurus*; see EPICUREAN]
▸**'epicur͵ism** *n*

epicurean Ⓣ (͵ɛpɪkjʊ'riːən) *adj* **1** devoted to sensual pleasures, esp. food and drink. **2** suitable for an epicure. ◆ *n* **3** an epicure; gourmet.
▸͵**epicu'rean͵ism** *n*

Epicurean (͵ɛpɪkjʊ'riːən) *adj* **1** of or relating to the philosophy of Epicurus (341–270 B.C.), Greek philosopher, who held that the highest good is pleasure or freedom from pain. ◆ *n* **2** a follower of the philosophy of Epicurus.
▸͵**Epicu'rean͵ism** *n*

epicycle ('ɛpɪ͵saɪk[ə]l) *n* a circle that rolls around the inside or outside of another circle. [C14: from LL, from Gk; see EPI-, CYCLE]
▸**epicyclic** (͵ɛpɪ'saɪklɪk, -'sɪklɪk) *or* ͵**epi'cyclical** *adj*

epicyclic train *n* a cluster of gears consisting of a central gearwheel, a coaxial gearwheel of greater diameter, and one or more planetary gears engaging with both of them.

epicycloid (͵ɛpɪ'saɪklɔɪd) *n* the curve described by a point on the circumference of a circle as this circle rolls around the outside of another fixed circle.
▸͵**epicy'cloidal** *adj*

epideictic (͵ɛpɪ'daɪktɪk) *adj* designed to display something, esp. the skill of the speaker in rhetoric. Also: **epidictic** (͵ɛpɪ'dɪktɪk). [C18: from Gk, from *epideiknunai* to display, from *deiknunai* to show]

epidemic Ⓣ (͵ɛpɪ'dɛmɪk) *adj* **1** (esp. of a disease) attacking or affecting many persons simultaneously in a community or area. ◆ *n* **2** a widespread occurrence of a disease. **3** a rapid development, spread, or growth of something. [C17: from F, via LL from Gk *epidēmia*, lit.: among the people, from EPI- + *dēmos* people]
▸͵**epi'demically** *adv*

epidemiology (͵ɛpɪ͵diːmɪ'ɒlədʒɪ) *n* the branch of medical science concerned with the occurrence, distribution, and control of diseases in populations.
▸**epidemiological** (͵ɛpɪ͵diːmɪə'lɒdʒɪk[ə]l) *adj* ▸͵**epi͵demi'ologist** *n*

epidermis (͵ɛpɪ'dɜːmɪs) *n* **1** the thin protective outer layer of the skin. **2** the outer layer of cells of an invertebrate. **3** the outer protective layer of cells of a plant. [C17: via LL from Gk, from EPI- + *derma* skin]
▸͵**epi'dermal,** ͵**epi'dermic,** *or* ͵**epi'dermoid** *adj*

epidiascope (͵ɛpɪ'daɪə͵skəʊp) *n* an optical device for projecting a magnified image onto a screen.

epididymis (͵ɛpɪ'dɪdɪmɪs) *n, pl* **epididymides** (-dɪ'dɪmɪ͵diːz). *Anat.* a convoluted tube behind each testis, in which spermatozoa are stored and conveyed to the vas deferens. [C17: from Gk *epididumis*, from EPI- + *didumos* twin, testicle]

epidural (͵ɛpɪ'djʊərəl) *adj* **1** Also: **extradural.** upon or outside the dura mater. ◆ *n* **2** Also: **epidural anaesthesia, spinal anaesthesia. 2a** injection of anaesthetic into the space outside the dura mater enveloping the spinal cord. **2b** anaesthesia induced by this method. [C19: from EPI- + DUR(A MATER) + -AL[1]]

epigamic (͵ɛpɪ'gæmɪk) *adj Zool.* attractive to the opposite sex: *epigamic coloration.*

epigeal (͵ɛpɪ'dʒiːəl), **epigean,** *or* **epigeous** *adj* **1** of or relating to seed germination in which the cotyledons appear above the ground. **2** living or growing on or close to the surface of the ground. [C19: from Gk *epigeios* of the earth, from EPI- + *gē* earth]

epiglottis (͵ɛpɪ'glɒtɪs) *n, pl* **epiglottises** *or* **epiglottides** (-tɪ͵diːz). a thin cartilaginous flap that covers the entrance to the larynx during swallowing, preventing food from entering the trachea.
▸͵**epi'glottal** *or* ͵**epi'glottic** *adj*

epigram Ⓣ ('ɛpɪ͵græm) *n* **1** a witty, often paradoxical remark, concisely expressed. **2** a short poem, esp. one having a witty and ingenious ending. [C15: from L *epigramma*, from Gk: inscription, from *graphein* to write]
▸͵**epigram'matic** *adj* ▸͵**epigram'matically** *adv*

epigrammatize *or* **epigrammatise** (͵ɛpɪ'græmə͵taɪz) *vb* **epigrammatizes, epigrammatizing, epigrammatized** *or* **epigrammatises, epigrammatising, epigrammatised.** to make an epigram (about).
▸͵**epi'grammatism** *n* ▸͵**epi'grammatist** *n*

epigraph ('ɛpɪ͵grɑːf) *n* **1** a quotation at the beginning of a book, chapter, etc. **2** an inscription on a monument or building. [C17: from Gk; see EPIGRAM]
▸**epigraphic** (͵ɛpɪ'græfɪk) or ͵**epi'graphical** *adj*

epigraphy (ɪ'pɪgrəfɪ) *n* **1** the study of ancient inscriptions. **2** epigraphs collectively.
▸**e'pigraphist** *or* **e'pigrapher** *n*

epilator ('ɛpɪ͵leɪtə) *n* an electrical appliance consisting of a metal spiral head that rotates at high speed, plucking unwanted hair.

epilepsy ('ɛpɪ͵lɛpsɪ) *n* a disorder of the central nervous system characterized by periodic loss of consciousness with or without convulsions. [C16: from LL *epilēpsia*, from Gk, from *epilambanein* to attack, seize]

epileptic (͵ɛpɪ'lɛptɪk) *adj* **1** of, relating to, or having epilepsy. ◆ *n* **2** a person who has epilepsy.
▸͵**epi'leptically** *adv*

epilogue Ⓣ ('ɛpɪ͵lɒg) *n* **1a** a speech addressed to the audience by an actor at the end of a play. **1b** the actor speaking this. **2** a short postscript to any literary work. **3** *Brit.* the concluding programme of the day on a radio or television station. [C15: from L, from Gk *epilogos*, from *logos* word, speech]
▸**epilogist** (ɪ'pɪlədʒɪst) *n*

epinephrine (͵ɛpɪ'nɛfrɪn, -riːn) *or* **epinephrin** *n* a US name for **adrenaline.** [C19: from EPI- + *nephro-* + -INE[2]]

epiphany (ɪ'pɪfənɪ) *n, pl* **epiphanies. 1** the manifestation of a supernatural or divine reality. **2** any moment of great or sudden revelation.
▸**epiphanic** (͵ɛpɪ'fænɪk) *adj*

Epiphany (ɪ'pɪfənɪ) *n, pl* **Epiphanies.** a Christian festival held on Jan. 6, commemorating, in the Western Church, the manifestation of Christ to the Magi. [C17: via Church L from Gk *epiphaneia* an appearing, from EPI- + *phainein* to show]

epiphenomenon (͵ɛpɪfɪ'nɒmɪnən) *n, pl* **epiphenomena** (-nə). **1** a sec-

THESAURUS

ephemeral *adj* **1** = **brief,** evanescent, fleeting, flitting, fugacious, fugitive, impermanent, momentary, passing, short, short-lived, temporary, transient, transitory
Antonyms *adj* abiding, durable, enduring, eternal, immortal, lasting, long-lasting, persisting, steadfast

epicure *n* **1** = **gourmet,** *bon vivant,* epicurean, foodie, gastronome **2** = **hedonist,** glutton, gourmand, sensualist, sybarite, voluptuary

epicurean *adj* **1** = **hedonistic,** bacchanalian, gluttonous, libertine, luscious, lush, luxurious, pleasure-seeking, self-indulgent, sensual, sybaritic, voluptuous ◆ *n* **3** = **gourmet,** *bon vivant,* epicure, foodie, gastronome

epidemic *adj* **1** = **widespread,** general, pandemic, prevailing, prevalent, rampant, rife, sweeping, wide-ranging ◆ *n* **2** = **spread,** contagion, growth, outbreak, plague, rash, upsurge, wave

epigram *n* **1** = **witticism,** aphorism, bon mot, quip

epigrammatic *adj* **1** = **witty,** concise, laconic, piquant, pithy, pointed, pungent, sharp, short, succinct, terse

epilogue *n* **1, 2** = **conclusion,** afterword, coda, concluding speech, postscript
Antonyms *n* exordium, foreword, introduction, preamble, preface, prelude, prologue

ondary or additional phenomenon. **2** *Philosophy.* mind or consciousness regarded as a by-product of the biological activity of the human brain. **3** *Pathol.* an unexpected symptom or occurrence during the course of a disease.
▸ˌ**epipheˈnomenal** *adj*

epiphyte (ˈɛpɪˌfaɪt) *n* a plant that grows on another plant but is not parasitic on it. [C19: via NL from Gk, from EPI- + *phusis* growth]
▸**epiphytic** (ˌɛpɪˈfɪtɪk), ˌ**epiˈphytal,** *or* ˌ**epiˈphytical** *adj*

Epis. *abbrev. for:* **1** Also: **Episc.** Episcopal *or* Episcopalian. **2** *Bible.* Also: **Epist.** Epistle.

episcopacy (ɪˈpɪskəpəsɪ) *n, pl* **episcopacies. 1** government of a Church by bishops. **2** another word for **episcopate.**

episcopal (ɪˈpɪskəpᵊl) *adj* of, denoting, governed by, or relating to a bishop or bishops. [C15: from Church L, from *episcopus* BISHOP]

Episcopal (ɪˈpɪskəpᵊl) *adj* of or denoting the Episcopal Church, an autonomous church of Scotland and the US which is in full communion with the Church of England.

episcopalian (ɪˌpɪskəˈpeɪlɪən) *adj also* **episcopal. 1** practising or advocating the principle of Church government by bishops. ◆ *n* **2** an advocate of such Church government.
▸**eˌpiscoˈpalianism** *n*

Episcopalian (ɪˌpɪskəˈpeɪlɪən) *adj* **1** belonging to or denoting the Episcopal Church. ◆ *n* **2** a member or adherent of this Church.

episcopate (ɪˈpɪskəpɪt, -ˌpeɪt) *n* **1** the office, status, or term of office of a bishop. **2** bishops collectively.

episiotomy (ɪˌpiːzɪˈɒtəmɪ) *n, pl* **episiotomies.** surgical incision into the perineum during labour to prevent its laceration during childbirth. [C20: from Gk *epision* pubic region + -TOMY]

episode ➊ (ˈɛpɪˌsəʊd) *n* **1** an event or series of events. **2** any of the sections into which a serialized novel or radio or television programme is divided. **3** an incident or sequence that forms part of a narrative but may be a digression from the main story. **4** (in ancient Greek tragedy) a section between two choric songs. **5** *Music.* a contrasting section between statements of the subject, as in a fugue. [C17: from Gk *epeisodion* something added, from *epi-* (in addition) + *eisodios* coming in, from *eis-* in + *hodos* road]

episodic ➊ (ˌɛpɪˈsɒdɪk) *or* **episodical** *adj* **1** resembling or relating to an episode. **2** divided into episodes. **3** irregular or sporadic.
▸ˌ**epiˈsodically** *adv*

epistaxis (ˌɛpɪˈstæksɪs) *n* the technical name for **nosebleed.** [C18: from Gk: a dropping, from *epistazein* to drop on, from *stazein* to drip]

epistemology (ɪˌpɪstɪˈmɒlədʒɪ) *n* the theory of knowledge, esp. the critical study of its validity, methods, and scope. [C19: from Gk *epistēmē* knowledge]
▸**epistemological** (ɪˌpɪstɪməˈlɒdʒɪkᵊl) *adj* ▸**eˌpisteˈmologist** *n*

epistle ➊ (ɪˈpɪsᵊl) *n* **1** a letter, esp. one that is long, formal, or didactic. **2** a literary work in letter form, esp. a verse letter. [OE *epistol,* via L from Gk *epistolē*]

Epistle (ɪˈpɪsᵊl) *n* **1** *Bible.* any of the letters of the apostles. **2** a reading from one of the Epistles, part of the Eucharistic service in many Christian Churches.

epistolary (ɪˈpɪstələrɪ) *or* (*arch.*) **epistolatory** *adj* **1** relating to, denoting, conducted by, or contained in letters. **2** (of a novel, etc.) in the form of a series of letters.

epistyle (ˈɛpɪˌstaɪl) *n* another name for **architrave** (sense 1). [C17: via L from Gk, from EPI- + *stulos* column, STYLE]

epitaph ➊ (ˈɛpɪˌtɑːf) *n* **1** a commemorative inscription on a tombstone or monument. **2** a commemorative speech or written passage. **3** a final judgment on a person or thing. [C14: via L from Gk, from EPI- + *taphos* tomb]
▸**epitaphic** (ˌɛpɪˈtæfɪk) *adj* ▸ˈ**epiˌtaphist** *n*

epitaxy (ˈɛpɪˌtæksɪ) *n* the growth of a layer of one substance on the surface of a crystal so that the layer has the same structure as the underlying crystal.
▸**epitaxial** (ˌɛpɪˈtæksɪəl) *adj*

epithalamium (ˌɛpɪθəˈleɪmɪəm) *or* **epithalamion** *n, pl* **epithalamia** (-mɪə). a poem or song written to celebrate a marriage. [C17: from L, from Gk *epithalamion* marriage song, from *thalamos* bridal chamber]
▸**epithalamic** (ˌɛpɪθəˈlæmɪk) *adj*

epithelium (ˌɛpɪˈθiːlɪəm) *n, pl* **epitheliums** *or* **epithelia** (-lɪə). an animal cellular tissue covering the external and internal surfaces of the body. [C18: NL, from EPI- + Gk *thēlē* nipple]
▸ˌ**epiˈthelial** *adj*

epithet ➊ (ˈɛpɪˌθɛt) *n* a descriptive word or phrase added to or substituted for a person's name. [C16: from L, from Gk, from *epitithenai* to add, from *tithenai* to put]
▸ˌ**epiˈthetic** *or* ˌ**epiˈthetical** *adj*

epitome ➊ (ɪˈpɪtəmɪ) *n* **1** a typical example of a characteristic or class; embodiment; personification. **2** a summary of a written work; abstract. [C16: via L from Gk, from *epitemnein* to abridge, from EPI- + *temnein* to cut]
▸**epitomical** (ˌɛpɪˈtɒmɪkᵊl) *or* ˌ**epiˈtomic** *adj*

epitomize ➊ *or* **epitomise** (ɪˈpɪtəˌmaɪz) *vb* **epitomizes, epitomizing, epitomized** *or* **epitomises, epitomising, epitomised.** (*tr*) **1** to be a personification of; typify. **2** to make an epitome of.
▸**eˈpitomist** *n* ▸**eˌpitomiˈzation** *or* **eˌpitomiˈsation** *n*

epizootic (ˌɛpɪzəʊˈɒtɪk) *adj* **1** (of a disease) suddenly and temporarily affecting a large number of animals. ◆ *n* **2** an epizootic disease.

EPNS *abbrev. for* electroplated nickel silver.

epoch ➊ (ˈiːpɒk) *n* **1** a point in time beginning a new or distinctive period. **2** a long period of time marked by some predominant characteristic; era. **3** *Astron.* a precise date to which information relating to a celestial body is referred. **4** a unit of geological time within a period during which a series of rocks is formed. [C17: from NL, from Gk *epokhē* cessation]
▸**epochal** (ˈɛpˌɒkᵊl) *adj*

epode (ˈɛpəʊd) *n Greek prosody.* **1** the part of a lyric ode that follows the strophe and the antistrophe. **2** a type of lyric poem composed of couplets in which a long line is followed by a shorter one. [C16: via L from Gk, from *epaidein* to sing after, from *aidein* to sing]

eponym (ˈɛpənɪm) *n* **1** a name, esp. a place name, derived from the name of a real or mythical person. **2** the name of the person from which such a name is derived. [C19: from Gk *epōnumos* giving a significant name]
▸**eˈponymy** *n*

eponymous (ɪˈpɒnɪməs) *adj* **1** (of a person) being the person after whom a literary work, film, etc., is named: *the eponymous heroine in the film of Jane Eyre.* **2** (of a literary work, film, etc.) named after its central character or creator: *The Stooges' eponymous debut album.*
▸**eˈponymously** *adv*

EPOS (ˈiːpɒs) *n acronym for* electronic point of sale.

epoxidize *or* **epoxidise** *vb* **epoxidizes, epoxidizing, epoxidized** *or* **epoxidises, epoxidising, epoxidised.** (*tr*) to convert into or treat with an epoxy resin.

epoxy (ɪˈpɒksɪ) *adj Chem.* **1** of, consisting of, or containing an oxygen atom joined to two different groups that are themselves joined to other groups: *epoxy group.* **2** of, relating to, or consisting of an epoxy resin. ◆ *n, pl* **epoxies. 3** short for **epoxy resin.** [C20: from EPI- + OXY-²]

epoxy *or* **epoxide resin** (ɪˈpɒksaɪd) *n* any of various tough resistant thermosetting synthetic resins containing epoxy groups: used in surface coatings, laminates, and adhesives.

eps *abbrev. for* earnings per share.

epsilon (ˈɛpsɪˌlɒn) *n* the fifth letter of the Greek alphabet (Ε, ε). [Gk *e psilon,* lit.: simple *e*]

Epsom salts (ˈɛpsəm) *n* (*functioning as sing or pl*) a medicinal preparation of hydrated magnesium sulphate, used as a purgative, etc. [C18: after *Epsom,* a town in England, where they occur in the water]

equable ➊ (ˈɛkwəbᵊl) *adj* **1** even-tempered; placid. **2** unvarying; uniform: *an equable climate.* [C17: from L *aequābilis,* from *aequāre* to make equal]
▸ˌ**equaˈbility** *or* ˈ**equableness** *n*

equal ➊ (ˈiːkwəl) *adj* **1** (often foll. by *to* or *with*) identical in size, quantity, degree, intensity, etc. **2** having identical privileges, rights, status, etc. **3** having uniform effect or application: *equal opportunities.* **4** evenly balanced or proportioned. **5** (usually foll. by *to*) having the necessary or adequate strength, ability, means, etc. (for). ◆ *n* **6** a person or thing equal to another, esp. in merit, ability, etc. ◆ *vb* **equals, equalling, equalled** *or US* **equals, equaling, equaled. 7** (*tr*) to be equal to; match. **8** (*intr;* usually foll. by *out*) to become equal. **9** (*tr*) to make or do something equal to. [C14: from L *aequālis,* from *aequus* level]
▸ˈ**equally** *adv*

> **USAGE NOTE** The use of *more equal* as in *from now on their relationship will be a more equal one* is acceptable in modern English usage. *Equally* is preferred to *equally as* in sentences such as *reassuring the victims is equally important. Just as* is preferred to *equally as* in sentences such as *their surprise was just as great as his.*

THESAURUS

episode *n* **1 = event,** adventure, affair, business, circumstance, escapade, experience, happening, incident, matter, occurrence **2 = part,** chapter, instalment, passage, scene, section

episodic *adj* **3 = irregular,** anecdotal, digressive, disconnected, discursive, disjointed, intermittent, occasional, picaresque, rambling, sporadic, wandering

epistle *n* **1, 2 = letter,** communication, message, missive, note

epitaph *n* **1 = monument,** inscription

epithet *n* **= name,** appellation, description, designation, moniker *or* monicker (*sl.*), nickname, sobriquet, tag, title

epitome *n* **1 = personification,** archetype, embodiment, essence, exemplar, norm, quintessence, representation, type, typical example **2 = summary,** abbreviation, abridgment, abstract, compendium, condensation, conspectus, contraction, digest, précis, résumé, syllabus, synopsis

epitomize *vb* **1 = typify,** embody, exemplify, illustrate, incarnate, personify, represent, symbolize **2 = summarize,** abbreviate, abridge, abstract, condense, contract, curtail, cut, encapsulate, précis, reduce, shorten, synopsize

epoch *n* **2 = era,** age, date, period, time

equable *adj* **1 = even-tempered,** agreeable, calm, composed, easy-going, imperturbable, level-headed, placid, serene, temperate, unexcitable, unfazed (*inf.*), unflappable (*inf.*), unruffled **2 = constant,** consistent, even, on an even keel, regular, smooth, stable, steady, temperate, tranquil, unchanging, uniform, unvarying
Antonyms *adj* ≠ **even-tempered:** excitable, nervous, temperamental ≠ **constant:** changeable, fitful, inconsistent, irregular, temperamental, uneven, unstable, volatile

equal *adj* **1 = identical,** alike, commensurate, corresponding, equivalent, like, matched, one and the same, proportionate, tantamount, the same, uniform **4 = even,** balanced, evenly bal-

equalitarian (ɪˌkwɒlɪˈtɛərɪən) *adj, n* a less common word for **egalitarian.**
▸**eˌqualiˈtarianism** *n*

equality ❶ (ɪˈkwɒlɪtɪ) *n, pl* **equalities.** the state of being equal.

equalize ❶ *or* **equalise** (ˈiːkwəˌlaɪz) *vb* **equalizes, equalizing, equalized** *or* **equalises, equalising, equalised. 1** (*tr*) to make equal or uniform. **2** (*intr*) (in sports) to reach the same score as one's opponent or opponents.
▸**ˌequaliˈzation** *or* **ˌequaliˈsation** *n*

equal opportunity *n* **a** the offering of employment, pay, or promotion without discrimination as to sex, race, etc. **b** (*as modifier*): *an equal-opportunities employer.*

equal sign *or* **equals sign** *n* the symbol =, used to indicate a mathematical equality.

equanimity ❶ (ˌiːkwəˈnɪmɪtɪ, ˌɛkwə-) *n* calmness of mind or temper; composure. [C17: from L, from *aequus* even, EQUAL + *animus* mind, spirit]
▸**equanimous** (ɪˈkwænɪməs) *adj*

equate ❶ (ɪˈkweɪt) *vb* **equates, equating, equated.** (*mainly tr*) **1** to make or regard as equivalent or similar. **2** *Maths.* to indicate the equality of; form an equation from. **3** (*intr*) to be equal. [C15: from L *aequāre* to make EQUAL]
▸**eˈquatable** *adj* ▸**eˌquataˈbility** *n*

equation ❶ (ɪˈkweɪʒən, -ʃən) *n* **1** a mathematical statement that two expressions are equal. **2** the act of equating. **3** the state of being equal, equivalent, or equally balanced. **4** a representation of a chemical reaction using symbols of the elements. **5** a situation or problem in which a number of factors need to be considered.
▸**eˈquational** *adj* ▸**eˈquationally** *adv*

equator (ɪˈkweɪtə) *n* **1** the great circle of the earth, equidistant from the poles, dividing the N and S hemispheres. **2** a circle dividing a sphere into two equal parts. **3** *Astron.* See **celestial equator.** [C14: from Med. L (*circulus*) *aequātor* (*diei et noctis*) (circle) that equalizes (the day and night), from L *aequāre* to make EQUAL]

equatorial (ˌɛkwəˈtɔːrɪəl) *adj* **1** of, like, or existing at or near the equator. **2** *Astron.* of or referring to the celestial equator. **3** (of a telescope) mounted on perpendicular axes, one of which is parallel to the earth's axis. ◆ *n* **4** an equatorial mounting for a telescope.

equerry (ˈɛkwərɪ; *at the British court* ɪˈkwɛrɪ) *n, pl* **equerries. 1** an officer attendant upon the British sovereign. **2** (formerly) an officer in a royal household responsible for the horses. [C16: alteration (through infl. of L *equus* horse) of earlier *escuirie, from* OF: stable]

equestrian ❶ (ɪˈkwɛstrɪən) *adj* **1** of or relating to horses and riding. **2** on horseback; mounted. **3** of, relating to, or composed of knights. ◆ *n* **4** a person skilled in riding and horsemanship. [C17: from L *equestris,* from *equus* horse]
▸**eˈquestrianˌism** *n*

equi- *combining form.* equal or equally: *equidistant; equilateral.*

equiangular (ˌiːkwɪˈæŋgjʊlə) *adj* having all angles equal.

equidistant (ˌiːkwɪˈdɪstənt) *adj* equally distant.
▸**ˌequiˈdistance** *n* ▸**ˌequiˈdistantly** *adv*

equilateral (ˌiːkwɪˈlætərəl) *adj* **1** having all sides of equal length. ◆ *n* **2** a geometric figure having all sides of equal length. **3** a side that is equal in length to other sides.

equilibrant (ɪˈkwɪlɪbrənt) *n* a force capable of balancing another force.

equilibrate (ˌiːkwɪˈlaɪbreɪt, ɪˈkwɪlɪˌbreɪt) *vb* **equilibrates, equilibrating, equilibrated.** to bring to or be in equilibrium; balance. [C17: from LL, from *aequilībris* in balance; see EQUILIBRIUM]
▸**ˌequiliˈbration** *n*

equilibrist (ɪˈkwɪlɪbrɪst) *n* a person who performs balancing feats, esp. on a high wire.
▸**eˌquiliˈbristic** *adj*

equilibrium ❶ (ˌiːkwɪˈlɪbrɪəm) *n, pl* **equilibriums** *or* **equilibria** (-rɪə). **1** a stable condition in which forces cancel one another. **2** a state or feeling of mental balance; composure. **3** any unchanging state of a body, system, etc., resulting from the balance of the influences to which it is subjected. **4** *Physiol.* a state of bodily balance, maintained primarily by receptors in the inner ear. [C17: from L, from *aequi-* EQUI- + *lībra* pound, balance]

equine (ˈɛkwaɪn) *adj* of, relating to, or resembling a horse. [C18: from L, from *equus* horse]

equinoctial (ˌiːkwɪˈnɒkʃəl) *adj* **1** relating to or occurring at either or both equinoxes. **2** *Astron.* of or relating to the celestial equator. ◆ *n* **3** a storm or gale at or near an equinox. **4** another name for **celestial equator.** [C14: from L: see EQUINOX]

equinoctial circle *or* **line** *n* another name for **celestial equator.**

equinoctial point *n* either of two points at which the celestial equator intersects the ecliptic.

equinox (ˈiːkwɪˌnɒks) *n* **1** either of the two occasions, six months apart, when day and night are of equal length. In the N hemisphere the **vernal equinox** occurs around March 21 (Sept. 23 in the S hemisphere). The **autumnal equinox** occurs around Sept. 23 in the N hemisphere (March 21 in the S hemisphere). **2** another name for **equinoctial point.** [C14: from Med. L *equinoxium,* changed from L *aequinoctium,* from *aequi-* EQUI- + *nox* night]

equip ❶ (ɪˈkwɪp) *vb* **equips, equipping, equipped.** (*tr*) **1** to furnish (with necessary supplies, etc.). **2** (*usually passive*) to provide with abilities, understanding, etc. **3** to dress out; attire. [C16: from OF *eschiper* to embark, fit out (a ship), of Gmc origin]
▸**eˈquipper** *n*

equipage ❶ (ˈɛkwɪpɪdʒ) *n* **1** a horse-drawn carriage, esp. one attended by liveried footmen. **2** the stores and equipment of a military unit. **3** *Arch.* a set of useful articles.

equipment ❶ (ɪˈkwɪpmənt) *n* **1** an act or instance of equipping. **2** the items provided. **3** a set of tools, kit, etc., assembled for a specific purpose.

equipoise (ˈɛkwɪˌpɔɪz) *n* **1** even balance of weight; equilibrium. **2** a counterbalance; counterpoise. ◆ *vb* **equipoises, equipoising, equipoised. 3** (*tr*) to offset or balance.

equipollent (ˌiːkwɪˈpɒlənt) *adj* **1** equal or equivalent in significance, power, or effect. ◆ *n* **2** something that is equipollent. [C15: from L *aequipollēns* of equal importance, from EQUI- + *pollēre* to be able, be strong]
▸**ˌequiˈpollence** *or* **ˌequiˈpollency** *n*

equisetum (ˌɛkwɪˈsiːtəm) *n, pl* **equisetums** *or* **equiseta** (-tə). any plant of the horsetail genus. [C19: NL, from L, from *equus* horse + *saeta* bristle]

equitable ❶ (ˈɛkwɪtəbᵊl) *adj* **1** fair; just. **2** *Law.* relating to or valid in equity, as distinct from common law or statute law. [C17: from F, from *équité* EQUITY]
▸**ˈequitableness** *n*

equitation (ˌɛkwɪˈteɪʃən) *n* the study and practice of riding and horsemanship. [C16: from L *equitātiō,* from *equitāre* to ride, from *equus* horse]

equities (ˈɛkwɪtɪz) *pl n* another name for **ordinary shares.**

equity ❶ (ˈɛkwɪtɪ) *n, pl* **equities. 1** the quality of being impartial; fairness. **2** an impartial or fair act, decision, etc. **3** *Law.* a system of jurisprudence founded on principles of natural justice and fair conduct. It supplements common law, as by providing a remedy where none exists at law. **4** *Law.* an equitable right or claim. **5** the interest of ordinary shareholders in a company. **6** the value of a debtor's property in excess of debts to which it is liable. [C14: from OF, from L *aequitās,* from *aequus* level, EQUAL]

Equity (ˈɛkwɪtɪ) *n* the actors' trade union.

equity capital *n* the part of the share capital of a company owned by ordinary shareholders or in certain circumstances by other classes of shareholder.

equity-linked policy *n* an insurance or assurance policy in which premiums are invested partially or wholly in ordinary shares for the eventual benefit of the beneficiaries of the policy.

THESAURUS

anced, evenly matched, evenly proportioned, fifty-fifty (*inf.*), level pegging (*Brit. inf.*) **5** *usually with* **to** = **capable of**, able to, adequate for, competent to, fit for, good enough for, ready for, strong enough, suitable for, up to ◆ *n* **6** = **match**, brother, compeer, counterpart, equivalent, fellow, mate, parallel, peer, rival, twin ◆ *vb* **7** = **match**, agree with, amount to, balance, be equal to, be even with, be level with, be tantamount to, come up to, correspond to, equalize, equate, even, level, parallel, rival, square with, tally with, tie with

Antonyms *adj* ≠ **identical:** different, disproportionate, dissimilar, diverse, unequal, unlike ≠ **even:** unbalanced, unequal, uneven, unmatched ≠ **capable of:** inadequate, incapable, incompetent, not good enough, not up to, unequal, unfit ◆ *vb* ≠ **match:** be different, be unequal, disagree

equality *n* = **sameness**, balance, coequality, correspondence, equatability, equivalence, evenness, identity, likeness, similarity, uniformity

Antonyms *n* disparity, lack of balance, unevenness

equalize *vb* **1** = **make equal**, balance, equal, equate, even up, level, match, regularize, smooth, square, standardize

equanimity *n* = **composure**, aplomb, calm, calmness, coolness, imperturbability, levelheadedness, peace, phlegm, placidity, poise, presence of mind, sang-froid, self-possession, serenity, steadiness, tranquillity

equate *vb* **1, 3** = **make** *or* **be equal**, agree, balance, be commensurate, compare, correspond with *or* to, equalize, liken, match, mention in the same breath, offset, pair, parallel, square, tally, think of together

equation *n* **2, 3** = **equating**, agreement, balancing, comparison, correspondence, equality, equalization, equivalence, likeness, match, pairing, parallel

equestrian *adj* **2** = **on horseback**, in the saddle, mounted ◆ *n* **4** = **rider**, cavalier (*arch.*), horseman, knight

equilibrium *n* **1, 3** = **stability**, balance, counterpoise, equipoise, evenness, rest, steadiness, symmetry **2** = **composure**, calm, calmness, collectedness, coolness, equanimity, poise, self-possession, serenity, stability, steadiness

equip *vb* **1-3** = **supply**, accoutre, arm, array, attire, deck out, dress, endow, fit out, fit up, furnish, kit out, outfit, prepare, provide, rig, stock

equipage *n* **1** = **carriage**, coach **2** = **equipment**, accoutrements, apparatus, baggage, gear, materiel, munitions, stores

equipment *n* **2, 3** = **apparatus**, accoutrements, appurtenances, baggage, equipage, furnishings, furniture, gear, materiel, outfit, paraphernalia, rig, stuff, supplies, tackle, tools

equitable *adj* **1** = **fair**, candid, disinterested, dispassionate, due, even-handed, honest, impartial, just, nondiscriminatory, proper, proportionate, reasonable, right, rightful, unbiased, unprejudiced

equity *n* **1** = **fairness**, disinterestedness, equitableness, even-handedness, fair-mindedness, fair play, honesty, impartiality, integrity, justice, reasonableness, rectitude, righteousness, uprightness

Antonyms *n* bias, discrimination, injustice, partiality, preference, prejudice, unfairness

equivalence 🅣 (ɪˈkwɪvələns) *or* **equivalency** *n* **1** the state of being equivalent. **2** *Logic, maths.* another term for **biconditional.**

equivalent 🅣 (ɪˈkwɪvələnt) *adj* **1** equal in value, quantity, significance, etc. **2** having the same or a similar effect or meaning. **3** *Logic, maths.* (of two propositions) having a biconditional between them. ◆ *n* **4** something that is equivalent. **5** Also called: **equivalent weight.** the weight of a substance that will combine with or displace 8 grams of oxygen or 1.007 97 grams of hydrogen. [C15: from LL, from L *aequi-* EQUI- + *valēre* to be worth]
▸**eˈquivalently** *adv*

equivocal 🅣 (ɪˈkwɪvəkˡl) *adj* **1** capable of varying interpretations; ambiguous. **2** deliberately misleading or vague. **3** of doubtful character or sincerity. [C17: from LL, from L EQUI- + *vōx* voice]
▸**eˌquivoˈcality** *or* **eˈquivocalness** *n*

equivocate 🅣 (ɪˈkwɪvəˌkeɪt) *vb* **equivocates, equivocating, equivocated.** (*intr*) to use equivocal language, esp. to avoid speaking directly or honestly. [C15: from Med. L, from LL *aequivocus* ambiguous, EQUIVOCAL]
▸**eˈquivoˌcatingly** *adv* ▸**eˌquivoˈcation** *n* ▸**eˈquivoˌcator** *n* ▸**eˈquivocatory** *adj*

er (ə, ɜː) *interj* a sound made when hesitating in speech.

Er *the chemical symbol for* erbium.

ER *abbrev. for:* **1** Elizabeth Regina. [L: Queen Elizabeth] **2** Eduardus Rex. [L: King Edward]

-er[1] *suffix forming nouns.* **1** a person or thing that performs a specified action: *reader; lighter.* **2** a person engaged in a profession, occupation, etc.: *writer; baker.* **3** a native or inhabitant of: *Londoner; villager.* **4** a person or thing having a certain characteristic: *newcomer; fiver.* [OE *-ere*]

-er[2] *suffix.* forming the comparative degree of adjectives (*deeper, freer,* etc.) and adverbs (*faster, slower,* etc.). [OE *-rd, -re* (adj), *-or* (adv)]

era 🅣 (ˈɪərə) *n* **1** a period of time considered as being of a distinctive character; epoch. **2** an extended period of time the years of which are numbered from a fixed point: *the Christian era.* **3** a point in time beginning a new or distinctive period. **4** a major division of geological time, divided into periods. [C17: from L *aera* counters, pl of *aes* brass, pieces of brass money]

ERA (ˈɪərə) *n* (in Britain) *acronym for* Education Reform Act: the 1988 act which established the key elements of the National Curriculum and the Basic Curriculum.

eradicate 🅣 (ɪˈrædɪˌkeɪt) *vb* **eradicates, eradicating, eradicated.** (*tr*) **1** to obliterate. **2** to pull up by the roots. [C16: from L *ērādīcāre* to uproot, from EX-[1] + *rādīx* root]
▸**eˈradicable** *adj* ▸**eˌradiˈcation** *n* ▸**eˈradicative** *adj*

erase 🅣 (ɪˈreɪz) *vb* **erases, erasing, erased. 1** to obliterate or rub out (something written, typed, etc.). **2** (*tr*) to destroy all traces of. **3** to remove (a recording) from (magnetic tape). [C17: from L, from EX-[1] + *rādere* to scratch, scrape]
▸**eˈrasable** *adj*

eraser (ɪˈreɪzə) *n* an object, such as a piece of rubber, for erasing something written, typed, etc.

erasure (ɪˈreɪʒə) *n* **1** the act or an instance of erasing. **2** the place or mark, as on a piece of paper, where something has been erased.

Erato (ˈɛrəˌtəʊ) *n Greek myth.* the Muse of love poetry.

erbium (ˈɜːbɪəm) *n* a soft malleable silvery-white element of the lanthanide series of metals. Symbol: Er; atomic no.: 68; atomic wt.: 167.26. [C19: from NL, from (*Ytt*)*erb*(*y*), Sweden, where it was first found + -IUM]

ERDF *abbrev. for* European Regional Development Fund: a fund to provide money for specific projects for work on the infrastructure in countries of the European Union.

ere (ɛə) *conj, prep* a poetic word for **before.** [OE *ǣr*]

erect 🅣 (ɪˈrɛkt) *adj* **1** upright in posture or position. **2** *Physiol.* (of the penis, clitoris, or nipples) firm or rigid after swelling with blood, esp. as a result of sexual excitement. **3** (of plant parts) growing vertically or at right angles to the parts from which they arise. ◆ *vb* (*mainly tr*) **4** to put up; build. **5** to raise to an upright position. **6** to found or form; set up. **7** (*also intr*) *Physiol.* to become or cause to become firm or rigid by filling with blood. **8** to exalt. **9** to draw or construct (a line, figure, etc.) on a given line or figure. [C14: from L *ērigere* to set up, from *regere* to control, govern]
▸**eˈrectable** *adj* ▸**eˈrecter** *or* **eˈrector** *n* ▸**eˈrectness** *n*

erectile (ɪˈrɛktaɪl) *adj* **1** *Physiol.* (of tissues or organs, such as the penis or clitoris) capable of becoming erect. **2** capable of being erected.
▸**erectility** (ɪrɛkˈtɪlɪtɪ, ˌiːrɛk-) *n*

erection 🅣 (ɪˈrɛkʃən) *n* **1** the act of erecting or the state of being erected. **2** a building or construction. **3** *Physiol.* the enlarged state of erectile tissues or organs, esp. the penis, when filled with blood. **4** an erect penis.

E region *or* **layer** *n* a region of the ionosphere, extending from a height of 90 to about 150 kilometres. It reflects radio waves of medium wavelength.

eremite (ˈɛrɪˌmaɪt) *n* a Christian hermit or recluse. [C13: see HERMIT]
▸**eremitic** (ˌɛrɪˈmɪtɪk) or ˌ**ereˈmitical** *adj* ▸**ˈeremitˌism** *n*

erepsin (ɪˈrɛpsɪn) *n* a mixture of proteolytic enzymes secreted by the small intestine. [C20: *er-*, from L *ēripere* to snatch + (P)EPSIN]

erethism (ˈɛrɪˌθɪzəm) *n* **1** *Physiol.* an abnormal irritability or sensitivity in any part of the body. **2** *Psychiatry.* **2a** a personality disorder resulting from mercury poisoning. **2b** an abnormal tendency to become aroused quickly, esp. sexually, as the result of a verbal or psychic stimulus. [C18: from F, from Gk, from *erethizein* to excite, irritate]

erf (ɜːf) *n, pl* **erven** (ˈɜːvən). *S. African.* a plot of land, usually urban. [from Afrik., from Du.: inheritance]

Erf (ɜːf) *n acronym for* electrorheological fluid: a man-made liquid that thickens or solidifies when an electric current passes through it and returns to a liquid when the current ceases.

erg[1] (ɜːg) *n* the cgs unit of work or energy. [C19: from Gk *ergon* work]

erg[2] (ɜːg) *n, pl* **ergs** *or* **areg** (əˈrɛg). an area of shifting sand dunes, esp. in the Sahara Desert in N Africa. [C19: from Ar. *ˈirj*]

ergo 🅣 (ˈɜːgəʊ) *sentence connector.* therefore; hence. [C14: from L: therefore]

ergonomic (ˌɜːgəˈnɒmɪk) *adj* **1** of or relating to ergonomics. **2** designed to minimize physical effort and discomfort, and hence maximize efficiency.

ergonomics (ˌɜːgəˈnɒmɪks) *n* (*functioning as sing*) the study of the relationship between workers and their environment, esp. the equipment they use. [C20: from Gk *ergon* work + (ECO)NOMICS]
▸**ergonomist** (ɜːˈgɒnəmɪst) *n*

ergosterol (ɜːˈgɒstəˌrɒl) *n* a plant sterol that is converted into vitamin D by the action of ultraviolet radiation.

ergot (ˈɜːgət, -gɒt) *n* **1** a disease of cereals and other grasses caused by fungi of the genus *Claviceps.* **2** any fungus causing this disease. **3** the dried fungus, used as the source of certain alkaloids used in medicine. [C17: from F: spur (of a cock), from ?]

ergotism (ˈɜːgəˌtɪzəm) *n* ergot poisoning, producing either burning pains and eventually gangrene or itching skin and convulsions.

erica (ˈɛrɪkə) *n* any shrub of the ericaceous genus *Erica,* including the heaths and some heathers. [C19: via L from Gk *ereikē* heath]

ericaceous (ˌɛrɪˈkeɪʃəs) *adj* of or relating to the Ericaceae, a family of trees and shrubs with typically bell-shaped flowers: includes heather, rhododendron, azalea, and arbutus.

erigeron (ɪˈrɪdʒərən, -ˈrɪg-) *n* any plant of the genus *Erigeron,* whose flowers resemble asters. [C17: via L from Gk, from *ēri* early + *gerōn* old man; from the white down of some species]

Erin (ˈɪərɪn, ˈɛərɪn) *n* an archaic or poetic name for Ireland. [from Irish Gaelic *Éirinn,* dative of Ireland]

Erinyes (ɪˈrɪnɪˌiːz) *pl n, sing* **Erinys** (ɪˈrɪnɪs, ɪˈraɪ-). *Myth.* another name for the **Furies.** [Gk]

erk (ɜːk) *n Brit. sl.* an aircraftman or naval rating. [C20: ? a corruption of *AC* (aircraftman)]

ERM *abbrev. for* Exchange Rate Mechanism.

ermine (ˈɜːmɪn) *n, pl* **ermines** *or* **ermine. 1** the stoat in northern regions, where it has a white winter coat with a black-tipped tail. **2** the fur of this animal. **3** the dignity or office of a judge, noble, etc., whose state

THESAURUS

equivalence *n* **1 = equality,** agreement, alikeness, conformity, correspondence, evenness, identity, interchangeableness, likeness, match, parallel, parity, sameness, similarity, synonymy

equivalent *adj* **1, 2 = equal,** alike, commensurate, comparable, correspondent, corresponding, even, homologous, interchangeable, of a kind, of a piece, same, similar, synonymous, tantamount ◆ *n* **4 = equal,** correspondent, counterpart, match, opposite number, parallel, peer, twin
Antonyms *adj* ≠ **equal:** different, dissimilar, incomparable, unequal, unlike

equivocal *adj* **1-2 = ambiguous,** ambivalent, doubtful, dubious, evasive, indefinite, indeterminate, misleading, oblique, obscure, oracular, prevaricating, questionable, suspicious, uncertain, vague
Antonyms *adj* absolute, certain, clear, clear-cut, cut-and-dried (*inf.*), decisive, definite, evident, explicit, incontrovertible, indubitable, manifest, plain, positive, straight, unambiguous, unequivocal

equivocate *vb* **= be evasive,** avoid the issue, beat about the bush (*inf.*), dodge, evade, fence, flannel (*Brit. inf.*), fudge, hedge, parry, prevaricate, pussyfoot (*inf.*), quibble, shuffle, sidestep, tergiversate, waffle (*inf., chiefly Brit.*)

equivocation *n* **= ambiguity,** double talk, doubtfulness, evasion, hedging, prevarication, quibbling, shuffling, tergiversation, waffle (*inf., chiefly Brit.*), weasel words (*inf., chiefly US*)

era *n* **1 = age,** aeon, cycle, date, day *or* days, epoch, generation, period, stage, time

eradicate *vb* **1 = wipe out,** abolish, annihilate, deracinate, destroy, efface, eliminate, erase, excise, expunge, exterminate, extinguish, extirpate, get rid of, obliterate, put paid to, remove, root out, stamp out, uproot, weed out, wipe from the face of the earth

eradication *n* **1 = wiping out,** abolition, annihilation, deracination, destruction, effacement, elimination, erasure, expunction, extermination, extinction, extirpation, obliteration, removal

erase *vb* **1-3 = wipe out,** blot, cancel, delete, efface, excise, expunge, obliterate, remove, rub out, scratch out

erect *adj* **1 = upright,** elevated, firm, perpendicular, pricked-up, raised, rigid, standing, stiff, straight, vertical ◆ *vb* **4, 5 = build,** construct, elevate, lift, mount, pitch, put up, raise, rear, set up, stand up **6 = found,** create, establish, form, initiate, institute, organize, set up
Antonyms *adj* ≠ **upright:** bent, flaccid, horizontal, leaning, limp, prone, recumbent, relaxed, supine ◆ *vb* ≠ **build:** demolish, destroy, dismantle, raze, tear down

erection *n* **1 = building,** assembly, construction, creation, elevation, establishment, fabrication, manufacture **2 = structure,** building, construction, edifice, pile

ergo *sentence connector* **= therefore,** accordingly, consequently, for that reason, hence, in consequence, so, then, thus robes are trimmed with ermine. [C12: from OF, from Med. L *Armenius (mūs)* Armenian (mouse)]

erne *or* **ern** (ɜːn) *n* a fish-eating sea eagle. [OE *earn*]

Ernie (ˈɜːnɪ) *n* (in Britain) a machine that randomly selects winning numbers of Premium Bonds. [C20: acronym of *E*lectronic *R*andom *N*umber *I*ndicator *E*quipment]

erode ⓣ (ɪˈrəʊd) *vb* **erodes, eroding, eroded. 1** to grind or wear down or away or become ground or worn down or away. **2** to deteriorate or cause to deteriorate. [C17: from L, from EX-[1] + *rōdere* to gnaw] ▸**eˈrodible** *adj*

erogenous (ɪˈrɒdʒɪnəs) *or* **erogenic** (ˌɛrəˈdʒɛnɪk) *adj* **1** sensitive to sexual stimulation. **2** arousing sexual desire or giving sexual pleasure. [C19: from Gk *erōs* love, desire + -GENOUS] ▸**erogeneity** (ˌɛrədʒɪˈniːɪtɪ) *n*

erosion ⓣ (ɪˈrəʊʒən) *n* **1** the wearing away of rocks, soil, etc., by the action of water, ice, wind, etc. **2** the act or process of eroding or the state of being eroded. ▸**eˈrosive** *or* **eˈrosional** *adj*

erotic ⓣ (ɪˈrɒtɪk) *adj* **1** of, concerning, or arousing sexual desire or giving sexual pleasure. **2** marked by strong sexual desire or being especially sensitive to sexual stimulation. Also: **erotical.** [C17: from Gk *erōtikos*, from *erōs* love] ▸**eˈrotically** *adv*

erotica (ɪˈrɒtɪkə) *pl n* explicitly sexual literature or art. [C19: from Gk: see EROTIC]

eroticism (ɪˈrɒtɪˌsɪzəm) *or* **erotism** (ˈɛrəˌtɪzəm) *n* **1** erotic quality or nature. **2** the use of sexually arousing or pleasing symbolism in literature or art. **3** sexual excitement or desire.

erotogenic (ɪˌrɒtəˈdʒɛnɪk) *adj* originating from or causing sexual stimulation; erogenous.

err ⓣ (ɜː) *vb (intr)* **1** to make a mistake; be incorrect. **2** to deviate from a moral standard. **3** to act with bias, esp. favourable bias: *to err on the right side.* [C14 *erren* to wander, stray, from OF, from L *errāre*] ▸**ˈerrancy** *n*

errand ⓣ (ˈɛrənd) *n* **1** a short trip undertaken to perform a task or commission (esp. in **run errands**). **2** the purpose or object of such a trip. [OE *ǣrende*]

errant ⓣ (ˈɛrənt) *adj (often postpositive)* **1** *Arch. or literary.* wandering in search of adventure. **2** erring or straying from the right course or accepted standards. [C14: from OF: journeying, from Vulgar L *iterāre* (unattested), from L *iter* journey; infl. by L *errāre* to err] ▸**ˈerrantry** *n*

erratic ⓣ (ɪˈrætɪk) *adj* **1** irregular in performance, behaviour, or attitude; unpredictable. **2** having no fixed or regular course. ◆ *n* **3** a piece of rock that has been transported from its place of origin, esp. by glacial action. [C14: from L, from *errāre* to wander, err] ▸**erˈratically** *adv*

erratum ⓣ (ɪˈrɑːtəm) *n, pl* **errata** (-tə). **1** an error in writing or printing. **2** another name for **corrigendum.** [C16: from L: mistake, from *errāre* to err]

erroneous ⓣ (ɪˈrəʊnɪəs) *adj* based on or containing error; incorrect. [C14 (in the sense: deviating from what is right), from L, from *errāre* to wander] ▸**erˈroneousness** *n*

error ⓣ (ˈɛrə) *n* **1** a mistake or inaccuracy. **2** an incorrect belief or wrong judgment. **3** the condition of deviating from accuracy or correctness. **4** deviation from a moral standard; wrongdoing. **5** *Maths, statistics.* a measure of the difference between some quantity and an approximation of it, often expressed as a percentage. [C13: from L, from *errāre* to err] ▸**ˈerror-ˌfree** *adj*

ersatz ⓣ (ˈɛəzæts, ˈɜː-) *adj* **1** made in imitation; artificial. ◆ *n* **2** an ersatz substance or article. [C20: G, from *ersetzen* to substitute]

Erse (ɜːs) *n* **1** another name for Irish **Gaelic.** ◆ *adj* **2** of or relating to the Irish Gaelic language. [C14: from Lowland Scots *Erisch* Irish]

erst (ɜːst) *adv Arch.* **1** long ago; formerly. **2** at first. [OE *ǣrest* earliest, sup. of *ǣr* early]

erstwhile ⓣ (ˈɜːstˌwaɪl) *adj* **1** former; one-time. ◆ *adv* **2** *Arch.* long ago; formerly.

eruct (ɪˈrʌkt) *or* **eructate** *vb* **eructs, eructing, eructed** *or* **eructates, eructating, eructated. 1** to belch. **2** (of a volcano) to pour out (fumes or volcanic matter). [C17: from L, from *ructāre* to belch] ▸**eructation** (ɪˌrʌkˈteɪʃən, ˌiːrʌk-) *n*

erudite ⓣ (ˈɛrʊˌdaɪt) *adj* having or showing extensive scholarship; learned. [C15: from L, from *ērudīre* to polish] ▸**erudition** (ˌɛrʊˈdɪʃən) *or* **ˈeruˌditeness** *n*

erupt ⓣ (ɪˈrʌpt) *vb* **1** to eject (steam, water, and volcanic material) violently or (of volcanic material, etc.) to be so ejected. **2** *(intr)* (of a blemish) to appear on the skin. **3** *(intr)* (of a tooth) to emerge through the gum during normal tooth development. **4** *(intr)* to burst forth suddenly and violently. [C17: from L *ēruptus* having burst forth, from *ērumpere*, from *rumpere* to burst] ▸**eˈruptive** *adj* ▸**eˈruption** *n*

-ery *or* **-ry** *suffix forming nouns.* **1** indicating a place of business or activity: *bakery; refinery.* **2** indicating a class or collection of things: *cutlery.* **3** indicating qualities or actions: *snobbery; trickery.* **4** indicating a practice or occupation: *husbandry.* **5** indicating a state or condition: *slavery.* [from OF *-erie*; see -ER[1], -Y[3]]

erysipelas (ˌɛrɪˈsɪpɪləs) *n* an acute streptococcal infectious disease of the skin, characterized by fever and purplish lesions. [C16: from L, from Gk, from *erusi-* red + *-pelas* skin]

erythro- *or before a vowel* **erythr-** *combining form.* red: *erythrocyte.* [from Gk *eruthros* red]

erythrocyte (ɪˈrɪθrəʊˌsaɪt) *n* a blood cell of vertebrates that transports oxygen and carbon dioxide, combined with haemoglobin. ▸**erythrocytic** (ɪˌrɪθrəʊˈsɪtɪk) *adj*

erythromycin (ɪˌrɪθrəʊˈmaɪsɪn) *n* an antibiotic used in treating certain bacterial infections. [C20: from ERYTHRO- + Gk *mukēs* fungus + -IN]

erythropoiesis (ɪˌrɪθrəʊpɔɪˈiːsɪs) *n Physiol.* the formation of red blood cells. [C19: from ERYTHRO- + Gk *poiēs* a making, from *poiein* to make] ▸**erythropoietic** (ɪˌrɪθrəʊpɔɪˈɛtɪk) *adj*

Es *the chemical symbol for* einsteinium.

-es *suffix.* **1** a variant of -s[1] for nouns ending in *ch, s, sh, z,* postconsonantal *y*, for some nouns ending in a vowel, and nouns in *f* with *v* in the plural: *ashes; heroes; calves.* **2** a variant of -s[2] for verbs ending in *ch, s, sh, z,* postconsonantal *y*, or a vowel: *preaches; steadies; echoes.*

escadrille (ˌɛskəˈdrɪl) *n* a French squadron of aircraft, esp. in World War I. [from F: flotilla, from Sp., from *escuadra* SQUADRON]

escalade (ˌɛskəˈleɪd) *n* **1** an assault using ladders, esp. on a fortification. ◆ *vb* **escalades, escalading, escaladed. 2** to gain access to (a place) by ladders. [C16: from F, from It., from *scalare* to mount, SCALE[3]]

escalate ⓣ (ˈɛskəˌleɪt) *vb* **escalates, escalating, escalated.** to increase or be increased in extent, intensity, or magnitude. [C20: back formation from ESCALATOR] ▸**ˌescaˈlation** *n*

escalator (ˈɛskəˌleɪtə) *n* **1** a moving staircase consisting of stair treads fixed to a conveyor belt. **2** short for **escalator clause.** [C20: orig. a trademark]

escalator clause *n* a clause in a contract stipulating an adjustment in wages, prices, etc., in the event of specified changes in conditions, such as a large rise in the cost of living.

THESAURUS

erode *vb* **1, 2** = **wear down** *or* **away**, abrade, consume, corrode, destroy, deteriorate, disintegrate, eat away, grind down, spoil

erosion *n* **1, 2** = **deterioration**, abrasion, attrition, consumption, corrasion, corrosion, destruction, disintegration, eating away, grinding down, spoiling, wear, wearing down *or* away

erotic *adj* **1** = **sexual**, amatory, aphrodisiac, carnal, erogenous, lustful, rousing, seductive, sensual, sexy *(inf.)*, steamy *(inf.)*, stimulating, suggestive, titillating, voluptuous

err *vb* **1** = **make a mistake**, be inaccurate, be incorrect, be in error, blot one's copybook *(inf.)*, blunder, drop a brick *or* clanger *(inf.)*, go astray, go wrong, misapprehend, miscalculate, misjudge, mistake, put one's foot in it *(inf.)*, slip up *(inf.)* **2** = **sin**, be out of order, blot one's copybook *(inf.)*, deviate, do wrong, fall, go astray, lapse, misbehave, offend, transgress, trespass

errand *n* **1** = **job**, charge, commission, message, mission, task

errant *adj* **1** *Archaic or literary* = **wandering**, itinerant, journeying, nomadic, peripatetic, rambling, roaming, roving **2** = **sinning**, aberrant, deviant, erring, offending, straying, wayward, wrong

erratic *adj* **1** = **unpredictable**, aberrant, abnormal, capricious, changeable, desultory, eccentric, fitful, inconsistent, inconstant, irregular, shifting, uneven, unreliable, unstable, variable, wayward **2** = **wandering**, directionless, meandering, planetary
Antonyms *adj* ≠ **unpredictable:** certain, consistent, constant, dependable, invariable, natural, normal, predictable, regular, reliable, stable, steady, straight, unchanging, undeviating

erratum *n* **1, 2** = **misprint**, corrigendum, error, literal, omission, typo *(inf.)*

erroneous *adj* = **incorrect**, amiss, fallacious, false, faulty, flawed, inaccurate, inexact, invalid, mistaken, spurious, unfounded, unsound, untrue, wide of the mark, wrong
Antonyms *adj* accurate, correct, factual, faultless, flawless, precise, right, true, veracious

error *n* **1** = **mistake**, bloomer *(Brit. inf.)*, blunder, boner *(sl.)*, boob *(Brit. sl.)*, delusion, erratum, fallacy, fault, flaw, howler *(inf.)*, inaccuracy, misapprehension, miscalculation, misconception, oversight, slip, solecism **4** = **wrongdoing**, delinquency, deviation, fault, lapse, misdeed, offence, sin, transgression, trespass, wrong

ersatz *adj* **1** = **artificial**, bogus, counterfeit, fake, imitation, phoney *or* phony *(inf.)*, pretended, sham, simulated, spurious, substitute, synthetic

erstwhile *adj* **1** = **former**, bygone, ex *(inf.)*, late, old, once, one-time, past, previous, quondam, sometime

erudite *adj* = **learned**, cultivated, cultured, educated, knowledgeable, lettered, literate, scholarly, well-educated, well-read
Antonyms *adj* ignorant, illiterate, shallow, uneducated, uninformed, unlettered, unschooled, untaught, unthinking

erudition *n* = **learning**, education, knowledge, letters, lore, scholarship

erupt *vb* **1** = **explode**, be ejected, belch forth, blow up, break out, burst forth, burst into, burst out, discharge, flare up, gush, pour forth, spew forth *or* out, spit out, spout, throw off, vent, vomit **2** = **break out**, appear

eruption *n* **1** = **explosion**, discharge, ejection, flare-up, outbreak, outburst, sally, venting **2** = **inflammation**, outbreak, rash

escalate *vb* = **increase**, amplify, ascend, be increased, enlarge, expand, extend, grow, heighten, intensify, magnify, mount, raise, rise, step up
Antonyms *vb* abate, contract, decrease, descend, diminish, fall, lessen, limit, lower, shrink, wane, wind down

escalation *n* = **increase**, acceleration, amplifi-

DICTIONARY

escallop (ɛ'skɒləp, ɛ'skæl-) *n, vb* another word for **scallop.**

escalope ('ɛskə,lɒp) *n* a thin slice of meat, usually veal. [C19: from OF: shell]

escapade Ⓣ ('ɛskə,peɪd, ,ɛskə'peɪd) *n* **1** an adventure, esp. one that is mischievous or unlawful. **2** a prank; romp. [C17: from F, from OIt., from Vulgar L *excappāre* (unattested) to ESCAPE]

escape Ⓣ (ɪ'skeɪp) *vb* **escapes, escaping, escaped. 1** to get away or break free from (confinement, etc.). **2** to manage to avoid (danger, etc.). **3** (*intr; usually foll. by from*) (of gases, liquids, etc.) to issue gradually, as from a crack; seep; leak. **4** (*tr*) to elude; be forgotten by: *the figure escapes me.* **5** (*tr*) to be articulated inadvertently or involuntarily from: *a roar escaped his lips.* ◆ *n* **6** the act of escaping or state of having escaped. **7** avoidance of injury, harm, etc. **8a** a means or way of escape. **8b** (*as modifier*): *an escape route.* **9** a means of distraction or relief. **10** a gradual outflow; leakage; seepage. **11** Also called: **escape valve, escape cock.** a valve that releases air, steam, etc., above a certain pressure. **12** a plant originally cultivated but now growing wild. [C14: from OF, from Vulgar L *excappāre* (unattested) to escape (lit.: to slip out of one's cloak, hence free oneself), from EX-[1] + LL *cappa* cloak]
▸**es'capable** *adj* ▸**es'caper** *n*

escapee (ɪ,skeɪ'piː) *n* a person who has escaped, esp. an escaped prisoner.

escapement (ɪ'skeɪpmənt) *n* **1** a mechanism consisting of a toothed wheel (**escape wheel**) and anchor, used in timepieces to provide periodic impulses to the pendulum or balance. **2** any similar mechanism that regulates movement. **3** in pianos, the mechanism which allows the hammer to clear the string after striking, so the string can vibrate. **4** *Rare.* an act or means of escaping.

escape road *n* a road provided on a hill for a driver to drive into if his brakes fail or on a bend if he loses control of the turn.

escape velocity *n* the minimum velocity necessary for a body to escape from the gravitational field of the earth or other celestial body.

escapism (ɪ'skeɪpɪzəm) *n* an inclination to retreat from unpleasant reality, as through diversion or fantasy.
▸**es'capist** *n, adj*

escapologist (,ɛskə'pɒlədʒɪst) *n* an entertainer who specializes in freeing himself from confinement.
▸**,esca'pology** *n*

escargot *French.* (ɛskargo) *n* a variety of edible snail.

escarpment (ɪ'skɑːpmənt) *n* **1** the long continuous steep face of a ridge or plateau formed by erosion or faulting; scarp. **2** a steep artificial slope made immediately in front of a fortified place. [C19: from F *escarpe;* see SCARP]

-escent *suffix forming adjectives.* beginning to be, do, show, etc.: *convalescent; luminescent.* [via OF from L *-ēscent-,* stem of present participial suffix of *-ēscere,* ending of inceptive verbs]
▸**-escence** *suffix forming nouns.*

eschatology (,ɛskə'tɒlədʒɪ) *n* the branch of theology concerned with the end of the world. [C19: from Gk *eskhatos* last]
▸**eschatological** (,ɛskətə'lɒdʒɪk'l) *adj* ▸**,escha'tologist** *n*

escheat (ɪs'tʃiːt) *Law.* ◆ *n* **1** (in England before 1926) the reversion of property to the Crown in the absence of legal heirs. **2** *Feudalism.* the reversion of property to the feudal lord in the absence of legal heirs. **3** the property so reverting. ◆ *vb* **4** to take (land) by escheat or (of land) to revert by escheat. [C14: from OF, from *escheoir* to fall to the lot of, from LL *excadere* (unattested), from L *cadere* to fall]
▸**es'cheatable** *adj* ▸**es'cheatage** *n*

Escherichia (,ɛʃə'rɪkɪə) *n* a genus of bacteria that form acid and gas in the presence of carbohydrates and are found in the intestines of humans and many animals, esp. *E. coli,* which is sometimes pathogenic and is widely used in genetic research. [C19: after Theodor *Escherich* (1857–1911), G paediatrician]

eschew Ⓣ (ɪs'tʃuː) *vb* (*tr*) to keep clear of or abstain from (something disliked, injurious, etc.); shun; avoid. [C14: from OF *eschiver,* of Gmc origin; see SHY[1], SKEW]
▸**es'chewal** *n* ▸**es'chewer** *n*

eschscholzia *or* **eschscholtzia** (ɪs'kɒlʃə) *n* another name for **California poppy.** [C19: after J. F. von *Eschscholtz* (1793–1831), G botanist]

escort Ⓣ *n* ('ɛskɔːt). **1** one or more persons, soldiers, vehicles, etc., accompanying another or others for protection, as a mark of honour, etc. **2** a man or youth who accompanies a woman or girl on a social occasion. ◆ *vb* (ɪs'kɔːt). **3** (*tr*) to accompany or attend as an escort. [C16: from F, from It., from *scorgere* to guide, from L *corrigere* to straighten; see CORRECT]

escritoire (,ɛskrɪ'twɑː) *n* a writing desk with compartments and drawers. [C18: from F, from Med. L *scriptōrium* writing room in a monastery, from L *scrībere* to write]

escrow ('ɛskrəʊ, ɛ'skrəʊ) *Law.* ◆ *n* **1** money, goods, or a written document, held by a third party pending fulfilment of some condition. **2** the state or condition of being an escrow (esp. in **in escrow**). ◆ *vb* (*tr*) **3** to place (money, a document, etc.) in escrow. [C16: from OF *escroe,* of Gmc origin; see SCREED, SHRED, SCROLL]

escudo (ɛ'skuːdəʊ) *n, pl* **escudos. 1** the standard monetary unit of Cape Verde and Portugal. **2** a former standard monetary unit of Chile. **3** an old Spanish silver coin. [C19: Sp., lit.: shield, from L *scūtum*]

esculent ('ɛskjʊlənt) *n* **1** any edible substance. ◆ *adj* **2** edible. [C17: from L *ēsculentus* good to eat, from *ēsca* food, from *edere* to eat]

escutcheon (ɪ'skʌtʃən) *n* **1** a shield, esp. a heraldic one that displays a coat of arms. **2** a plate or shield around a keyhole, door handle, etc. **3** the place on the stern of a vessel where the name is shown. **4 blot on one's escutcheon.** a stain on one's honour. [C15: from OF *escuchon,* ult. from L *scūtum* shield]
▸**es'cutcheoned** *adj*

ESE *symbol for* east-southeast.

-ese *suffix forming adjectives and nouns.* indicating place of origin, language, or style: *Cantonese; Japanese; journalese.*

ESG (in Britain) *abbrev. for* Educational Support Grant: a government grant given to a Local Education Authority to fund educational schemes dealing with social issues, such as drug abuse.

esker ('ɛskə) *or* **eskar** ('ɛskɑː, -kə) *n* a long winding ridge of gravel, sand, etc., originally deposited by a meltwater stream running under a glacier. [C19: from OIrish *escir* ridge]

Eskimo ('ɛskɪ,məʊ) *n* **1** (*pl* **Eskimos** *or* **Eskimo**) a member of a group of peoples inhabiting N Canada, Greenland, Alaska, and E Siberia. The Eskimos are more properly referred to as the **Inuit. 2** the language of these peoples. ◆ *adj* **3** of or relating to the Eskimos. [C18 *Esquimawes:* rel. to *esquimantsic* (from a native language) eaters of raw flesh]

> **USAGE NOTE** *Eskimo* is considered by many people to be offensive, and in North America the term *Inuit* is often used.

Eskimo dog *n* a large powerful breed of dog with a long thick coat and curled tail, developed for hauling sledges.

Esky ('ɛskɪ) *n, pl* **Eskies.** (*sometimes not cap.*) *Austral. trademark.* a portable insulated container for keeping food and drink cool. [C20: from ESKIMO, alluding to the Eskimos' cold habitat]

ESN *abbrev. for* educationally subnormal; formerly used to designate a person of limited intelligence who needs special schooling.

esophagus (iː'sɒfəgəs) *n* the US spelling of **oesophagus.**

esoteric Ⓣ (,ɛsəʊ'tɛrɪk) *adj* **1** restricted to or intended for an enlightened or initiated minority. **2** difficult to understand; abstruse. **3** not openly admitted; private. [C17: from Gk, from *esōterō* inner]
▸**,eso'terically** *adv* ▸**,eso'teri,cism** *n*

ESP *abbrev. for* extrasensory perception.

esp. *abbrev. for* especially.

espadrille (,ɛspə'drɪl) *n* a light shoe with a canvas upper, esp. with a braided cord sole. [C19: from F, from Provençal *espardilho,* dim. of *espart* ESPARTO; from use of esparto for the soles]

espalier (ɪ'spæljə) *n* **1** an ornamental shrub or fruit tree trained to grow flat, as against a wall. **2** the trellis or framework on which such plants are trained. ◆ *vb* **3** (*tr*) to train (a plant) on an espalier. [C17: from F: trellis, from OIt.: shoulder supports, from *spalla* shoulder]

esparto *or* **esparto grass** (ɛ'spɑːtəʊ) *n, pl* **espartos.** any of various grasses of S Europe and N Africa, used to make ropes, mats, etc. [C18: from Sp., via L from Gk *spartos* a kind of rush]

especial Ⓣ (ɪ'spɛʃəl) *adj* (*prenominal*) **1** unusual; notable. **2** applying to one person or thing in particular; specific; peculiar: *he had an especial dislike of relatives.* [C14: from OF, from L *speciālis* individual; see SPECIAL]
▸**es'pecially** *adv*

> **USAGE NOTE** *Especial* and *especially* have a more limited use than *special* and *specially. Special* is always used in preference to

THESAURUS

cation, build-up, expansion, heightening, intensification, rise, upsurge

escapade *n* **1, 2** = **adventure,** antic, caper, fling, lark (*inf.*), mischief, prank, romp, scrape (*inf.*), spree, stunt, trick

escape *vb* **1** = **get away,** abscond, bolt, break free *or* out, decamp, do a bunk (*Brit. sl.*), do a runner (*sl.*), flee, fly, make one's getaway, make *or* effect one's escape, run away *or* off, skedaddle (*inf.*), skip, slip away, slip through one's fingers **2** = **avoid,** body-swerve (*Scot.*), circumvent, dodge, duck, elude, evade, pass, shun, slip **3** = **leak,** discharge, drain, emanate, exude, flow, gush, issue, pour forth, seep, spurt **4** = **be forgotten by,** baffle, be beyond (someone), elude, puzzle, stump ◆ *n* **6** = **getaway,** bolt, break, break-out, decampment, flight **7** = **avoidance,** circumvention, elusion, evasion **9** = **relaxation,** distraction, diversion, pastime, recreation, relief **10** = **leak,** discharge, drain, effluence, efflux, emanation, emission, gush, leakage, outflow, outpour, seepage, spurt

eschew *vb* = **avoid,** abandon, abjure, abstain from, elude, fight shy of, forgo, forswear, give a wide berth to, give up, have nothing to do with, keep *or* steer clear of, kick (*inf.*), refrain from, renounce, shun, swear off

escort *n* **1** = **guard,** bodyguard, company, convoy, cortege, entourage, protection, retinue, safeguard, train **2** = **companion,** attendant, beau, chaperon, guide, partner, protector, squire (*rare*) ◆ *vb* **3** = **accompany,** chaperon, conduct, convoy, guard, guide, hold (someone's) hand, lead, partner, protect, shepherd, squire, usher

esoteric *adj* **1-3** = **obscure,** abstruse, arcane, cabbalistic, cryptic, hidden, inner, inscrutable, mysterious, mystic, mystical, occult, private, recondite, secret

especial *adj* **1** = **exceptional,** chief, distinguished, extraordinary, marked, notable, noteworthy, outstanding, principal, signal, special, uncommon, unusual **2** = **particular,** exclusive, express, individual, peculiar, personal, private, singular, special, specific, unique

especially *adv* **1** = **exceptionally,** chiefly, conspicuously, extraordinarily, largely, mainly, markedly, notably, outstandingly, principally, *especial* when the sense is one of being out of the ordinary: *a special lesson; he has been specially trained. Special* is also used when something is referred to as being for a particular purpose: *the word was specially underlined for you.* Where an idea of pre-eminence or individuality is involved, either *especial* or *special* may be used: *he is my especial* (or *special*) *friend; he is especially* (or *specially*) *good at his job.* In informal English, however, *special* is usually preferred in all contexts.

Esperanto (ˌɛspəˈræntəʊ) *n* an international artificial language based on words common to the chief European languages. [C19: lit.: the one who hopes, pseudonym of Dr L. L. Zamenhof (1859–1917), its Polish inventor]
▸ˌ**Espeˈrantist** *n, adj*

espial (ɪˈspaɪəl) *n Arch.* **1** the act or fact of being seen or discovered. **2** the act of noticing. **3** the act of spying upon; secret observation.

espionage ❶ (ˈɛspɪəˌnɑːʒ) *n* **1** the use of spies to obtain secret information, esp. by governments. **2** the act of spying. [C18: from F, from *espion* spy]

esplanade (ˌɛspləˈneɪd) *n* **1** a long open level stretch of ground for walking along, esp. beside the seashore. Cf. **promenade** (sense 1). **2** an open area in front of a fortified place. [C17: from F, from OIt. *spianata,* from *spianare* to make level, from L *explānāre;* see EXPLAIN]

espousal ❶ (ɪˈspaʊzᵊl) *n* **1** adoption or support: *an espousal of new beliefs.* **2** (*sometimes pl*) *Arch.* a marriage or betrothal ceremony.

espouse ❶ (ɪˈspaʊz) *vb* **espouses, espousing, espoused.** (*tr*) **1** to adopt or give support to (a cause, ideal, etc.): *to espouse socialism.* **2** *Arch.* (esp. of a man) to take as spouse; marry. [C15: from OF *espouser,* from L *spōnsāre* to affiance, espouse]
▸**esˈpouser** *n*

espressivo (ˌɛsprɛˈsiːvəʊ) *adv Music.* in an expressive manner. [It.]

espresso (ɛˈsprɛsəʊ) *n, pl* **espressos. 1** coffee made by forcing steam or boiling water through ground coffee beans. **2** an apparatus for making coffee in this way. [C20: It., lit.: pressed]

esprit ❶ (ɛˈspriː) *n* spirit and liveliness, esp. in wit. [C16: from F, from L *spīritus* a breathing, SPIRIT[1]]

esprit de corps (ɛˈspriː də ˈkɔː) *n* consciousness of and pride in belonging to a particular group; the sense of shared purpose and fellowship.

espy ❶ (ɪˈspaɪ) *vb* **espies, espying, espied.** (*tr*) to catch sight of or perceive; detect. [C14: from OF *espier* to SPY, of Gmc origin]
▸**esˈpier** *n*

Esq. *abbrev. for* esquire.

-esque *suffix forming adjectives.* indicating a specified character, manner, style, or resemblance: *picturesque; Romanesque; statuesque.* [via F from It. *-esco*]

Esquimau (ˈɛskɪˌməʊ) *n, pl* **Esquimaus** *or* **Esquimau,** *adj* a former spelling of **Eskimo.**

esquire (ɪˈskwaɪə) *n* **1** *Chiefly Brit.* a title of respect, usually abbreviated *Esq.,* placed after a man's name. **2** (in medieval times) the attendant of a knight, subsequently often knighted himself. [C15: from OF *escuier,* from LL *scūtārius* shield bearer, from L *scūtum* shield]

ESRC (in Britain) *abbrev. for* Economic and Social Research Council.

ESRO (ˈɛzrəʊ) *n acronym for* European Space Research Organization.

-ess *suffix forming nouns.* indicating a female: *waitress; lioness.* [via OF from LL *-issa,* from Gk]

USAGE NOTE The suffix *-ess* in such words as *poetess, authoress* is now often regarded as disparaging; a sexually neutral term *poet, author* is preferred.

essay ❶ *n* (ˈɛseɪ; *senses 2, 3 also* ɛˈseɪ). **1** a short literary composition. **2** an attempt; effort. **3** a test or trial. ◆ *vb* (ɛˈseɪ). (*tr*) **4** to attempt or try. **5** to test or try out. [C15: from OF *essai* an attempt, from LL *exagium* a weighing, from L *agere* to do, infl. by *exigere* to investigate]

essayist (ˈɛseɪɪst) *n* a person who writes essays.

essence ❶ (ˈɛsᵊns) *n* **1** the characteristic or intrinsic feature of a thing, which determines its identity; fundamental nature. **2** a perfect or complete form of something. **3** *Philosophy.* the unchanging and unchangeable inward nature of something. **4a** the constituent of a plant, usually an oil, alkaloid, or glycoside, that determines its chemical properties. **4b** an alcoholic solution of such a substance. **5** a substance containing the properties of a plant or foodstuff in concentrated form: *vanilla essence.* **6** a rare word for **perfume. 7 in essence.** essentially; fundamentally. **8 of the essence.** indispensable; vitally important. [C14: from Med. L *essentia,* from L: the being (of something), from *esse* to be]

Essene (ˈɛsiːn, ɛˈsiːn) *n Judaism.* a member of an ascetic sect that flourished in Palestine from the second century B.C. to the second century A.D.
▸**Essenian** (ɛˈsiːnɪən) *or* **Essenic** (ɛˈsɛnɪk) *adj*

essential ❶ (ɪˈsɛnʃəl) *adj* **1** vitally important; absolutely necessary. **2** basic; fundamental. **3** absolute; perfect. **4** derived from or relating to an extract of a plant, drug, etc.: *an essential oil.* **5** *Biochem.* (of an amino acid or a fatty acid) necessary for the normal growth of an organism but not synthesized by the organism and therefore required in the diet. **6** *Pathol.* (of a disease) having no obvious external cause: *essential hypertension.* ◆ *n* **7** something fundamental or indispensable.
▸**essentiality** (ɪˌsɛnʃɪˈælɪtɪ) *or* **esˈsentialness** *n* ▸**esˈsentially** *adv*

essential element *n Biochem.* any chemical element required by an organism for healthy growth. It may be required in large amounts (**macronutrient**) or in very small amounts (**trace element**).

essentialism (ɪˈsɛnʃəˌlɪzəm) *n Philosophy.* any doctrine that material objects have an essence distinguishable from their attributes and existence.
▸**esˈsentialist** *n*

essential oil *n* any of various volatile oils in plants, having the odour or flavour of the plant from which they are extracted.

Essex Man (ˈɛsɪks) *n Inf., derog.* a self-made man, esp. of working-class origins, characterized by philistinism and bigoted right-wing views. [C20: from the supposed prevalence of such people in *Essex,* county of SE England]

EST *abbrev. for:* **1** (in the US and Canada) Eastern Standard Time. **2** electric-shock treatment.

est. *abbrev. for:* **1** established. **2** estimate(d).

-est[1] *suffix:* forming the superlative degree of adjectives and adverbs: *fastest.* [OE *-est, -ost*]

-est[2] *or* **-st** *suffix.* forming the archaic second person singular present and past indicative tense of verbs: *thou goest; thou hadst.* [OE *-est, -ast*]

establish ❶ (ɪˈstæblɪʃ) *vb* (*tr*) **1** to make secure or permanent in a certain place, condition, job, etc. **2** to create or set up (an organization, etc.) as on a permanent basis. **3** to prove correct; validate: *establish a fact.* **4** to cause (a principle, theory, etc.) to be accepted: *establish a precedent.* **5** to give (a Church) the status of a national institution. **6** to cause (a person) to become recognized and accepted. **7** (in works of imagination) to cause (a character, place, etc.) to be credible and recognized. [C14: from OF, from L *stabilis* STABLE[2]]
▸**esˈtablisher** *n*

Established Church *n* a Church that is officially recognized as a national institution, esp. the Church of England.

establishment ❶ (ɪˈstæblɪʃmənt) *n* **1** the act of establishing or state of being established. **2a** a business organization or other large institution. **2b** a place of business. **3** the staff and equipment of an organization. **4** any large organization or system. **5** a household; residence. **6** a

THESAURUS

remarkably, seriously (*inf.*), signally, specially, strikingly, supremely, uncommonly, unusually **2** = **particularly**, exclusively, expressly, peculiarly, singularly, specifically, uniquely

espionage *n* **1, 2** = **spying**, counter-intelligence, intelligence, surveillance, undercover work

espousal *n* **1** = **support**, adoption, advocacy, backing, championing, championship, defence, embracing, maintenance, promotion, taking up **2** *Archaic* = **engagement**, affiancing, betrothal, betrothing (*arch.*), espousing (*arch.*), marriage, nuptials, plighting, wedding

espouse *vb* **1** = **support**, adopt, advocate, back, champion, defend, embrace, maintain, promote, stand up for, take up, uphold **2** *Archaic* = **marry**, betroth (*arch.*), plight one's troth (*old-fashioned*), take as spouse, take to wife, wed

esprit *n* = **spirit**, animation, brio, élan, liveliness, quickness, sparkle, sprightliness, verve, vitality, vivacity, wit, zest

espy *vb* = **catch sight of**, behold, catch a glimpse of, descry, detect, discern, discover, glimpse, make out, notice, observe, perceive, sight, spot, spy

essay *n* **1** = **composition**, article, discourse, disquisition, dissertation, paper, piece, tract, treatise **2** = **attempt**, aim, bid, crack (*inf.*), effort, endeavour, go (*inf.*), shot (*inf.*), stab (*inf.*), try, undertaking, venture **3** = **test**, experiment, trial ◆ *vb* **4** = **attempt**, aim, endeavour, have a bash (*inf.*), have a crack (*inf.*), have a go, have a shot (*inf.*), strive, take on, try, undertake **5** = **test**, put to the test, try out

essence *n* **1** = **fundamental nature**, being, bottom line, core, crux, entity, heart, kernel, life, lifeblood, meaning, nature, pith, principle, quiddity, quintessence, significance, soul, spirit, substance **5** = **concentrate**, distillate, elixir, extract, spirits, tincture **7 in essence** = **essentially**, basically, fundamentally, in effect, in substance, in the main, materially, substantially, to all intents and purposes, virtually **8 of the essence** = **vitally important**, crucial, essential, indispensable, of the utmost importance, vital

essential *adj* **1** = **vital**, crucial, important, indispensable, necessary, needed, requisite **2** = **fundamental**, basic, cardinal, constitutional, elemental, elementary, immanent, inherent, innate, intrinsic, key, main, principal, radical **3** = **perfect**, absolute, complete, ideal, quintessential **4** = **concentrated**, distilled, extracted, rectified, refined, volatile ◆ *n* **7** = **prerequisite**, basic, fundamental, must, necessity, principle, requisite, rudiment, *sine qua non,* vital part
Antonyms *adj* ≠ **vital, fundamental:** accessory, dispensable, expendable, extra, extraneous, incidental, inessential, lesser, minor, nonessential, optional, secondary, superfluous, surplus, trivial, unimportant, unnecessary

establish *vb* **1, 2** = **create**, base, constitute, decree, enact, ensconce, entrench, fix, form, found, ground, implant, inaugurate, install, institute, organize, plant, put down roots, root, secure, settle, set up, sow the seeds, start **3** = **prove**, authenticate, certify, confirm, corroborate, demonstrate, ratify, show, substantiate, validate, verify

establishment *n* **1** = **creation**, enactment, formation, foundation, founding, inauguration, installation, institution, organization, setting up **2a** = **organization**, business, company, concern, corporation, enterprise, firm, house, institute, institution, outfit (*inf.*), setup (*inf.*), structure, system **2b** = **office**, building, factory, house, plant, quarters **5** = **house**, abode, domi-

body of employees or servants. **7** (*modifier*) belonging to or characteristic of the Establishment.

Establishment ➊ (ɪˈstæblɪʃmənt) *n* **the.** a group or class having institutional authority within a society: usually seen as conservative.

estate ➊ (ɪˈsteɪt) *n* **1** a large piece of landed property, esp. in the country. **2** *Chiefly Brit.* a large area of property development, esp. of new houses or (**trading estate**) of factories. **3** *Law.* **3a** property or possessions. **3b** the nature of interest that a person has in land or other property. **3c** the total extent of the property of a deceased person or bankrupt. **4** Also called: **estate of the realm.** an order or class in a political community, regarded as a part of the body politic: the lords spiritual (**first estate**), lords temporal or peers (**second estate**), and commons (**third estate**). See also **fourth estate. 5** state, period, or position in life: *youth's estate; a poor man's estate.* [C13: from OF *estat*, from L *status* condition, STATE]

estate agent *n* **1** *Brit.* an agent concerned with the valuation, management, lease, and sale of property. **2** the administrator of a large landed property; estate manager.

estate car *n Brit.* a car containing a large carrying space, reached through a rear door: usually the back seats fold forward to increase the carrying space.

estate duty *n* another name for **death duty.**

esteem ➊ (ɪˈsti:m) *vb* (*tr*) **1** to have great respect or high regard for. **2** *Formal.* to judge or consider; deem. ◆ *n* **3** high regard or respect; good opinion. **4** *Arch.* judgment; opinion. [C15: from OF *estimer*, from L *aestimāre* ESTIMATE]
▸**es'teemed** *adj*

ester (ˈɛstə) *n Chem.* any of a class of compounds produced by reaction between acids and alcohols with the elimination of water. [C19: from G, prob. a contraction of *Essigäther* acetic ether, from *Essig* vinegar (ult. from L *acētum*) + *Äther* ETHER]

Esth. *Bible. abbrev.for* Esther.

esthesia (i:sˈθi:zɪə) *n* a US spelling of **aesthesia.**

esthete (ˈi:sθi:t) *n* a US spelling of **aesthete.**

estimable ➊ (ˈɛstɪməbᵊl) *adj* worthy of respect; deserving of admiration.
▸**'estimableness** *n* ▸**'estimably** *adv*

estimate ➊ *vb* (ˈɛstɪˌmeɪt), **estimates, estimating, estimated. 1** to form an approximate idea of (size, cost, etc.); calculate roughly. **2** (*tr; may take a clause as object*) to form an opinion about; judge. **3** to submit (an approximate price) for (a job) to a prospective client. ◆ *n* (ˈɛstɪmɪt). **4** an approximate calculation. **5** a statement of the likely charge for certain work. **6** a judgment; appraisal. [C16: from L *aestimāre* to assess the worth of, from ?]
▸**'estiˌmator** *n* ▸**'estimative** *adj*

estimation ➊ (ˌɛstɪˈmeɪʃən) *n* **1** a considered opinion; judgment. **2** esteem; respect. **3** the act of estimating.

estival (i:ˈstaɪvᵊl, ˈɛstɪ-) *adj* the usual US spelling of **aestival.**

estivate (ˈi:stɪˌveɪt, ˈɛs-) *vb* **estivates, estivating, estivated.** (*intr*) the usual US spelling of **aestivate.**

Estonian *or* **Esthonian** (ɛˈstəʊnɪən, ɛˈsθəʊ-) *adj* **1** of, relating to, or characteristic of Estonia, a republic on the Gulf of Finland and the Baltic Sea. ◆ *n* **2** the official language of Estonia. **3** a native or inhabitant of Estonia.

estop (ɪˈstɒp) *vb* **estops, estopping, estopped.** (*tr*) **1** *Law.* to preclude by estoppel. **2** *Arch.* to stop. [C15: from OF *estoper* to plug, ult. from L *stuppa* tow; see STOP]
▸**es'toppage** *n*

estoppel (ɪˈstɒpᵊl) *n Law.* a rule of evidence whereby a person is precluded from denying the truth of a statement he has previously asserted. [C16: from OF *estoupail* plug; see ESTOP]

estovers (ɛˈstəʊvəz) *pl n Law.* necessaries allowed to tenants of land, esp. wood for fuel and repairs. [C15: from Anglo-F., pl of *estover*, from OF *estovoir* to be necessary, from L *est opus* there is need]

estradiol (ˌɛstrəˈdaɪɒl, ˌi:strə-) *n* the usual US spelling of **oestradiol.**

estrange ➊ (ɪˈstreɪndʒ) *vb* **estranges, estranging, estranged.** (*tr*) to antagonize or lose the affection of (someone previously friendly); alienate. [C15: from OF *estranger*, from LL *extrāneāre* to treat as a stranger, from L *extrāneus* foreign]
▸**es'tranged** *adj* ▸**es'trangement** *n*

estrogen (ˈɛstrədʒən, ˈi:strə-) *n* the usual US spelling of **oestrogen.**

estrus (ˈɛstrəs, ˈi:strəs) *n* the usual US spelling of **oestrus.**

estuary ➊ (ˈɛstjʊərɪ) *n, pl* **estuaries.** the widening channel of a river where it nears the sea. [C16: from L *aestuārium* marsh, channel, from *aestus* tide]
▸**estuarial** (ˌɛstjuˈɛərɪəl) *adj* ▸**'estuarine** *adj*

e.s.u. *or* **ESU** *abbrev. for* electrostatic unit.

ET (in Britain) *abbrev. for* Employment Training: a government scheme offering training in technology and business to unemployed people.

-et *suffix of nouns.* small or lesser: *islet; baronet.* [from OF *-et, -ete*]

eta (ˈi:tə) *n* the seventh letter in the Greek alphabet (Η, η). [Gk, from Phoenician]

ETA *abbrev. for* estimated time of arrival.

et al. *abbrev. for:* **1** et alibi. [L: and elsewhere] **2** et alii. [L: and others]

etalon (ˈɛtəˌlɒn) *n Physics.* a device used in spectroscopy to measure wavelengths by interference effects produced by multiple reflections between parallel half-silvered glass plates. [C20: F *étalon* a standard of weights & measures]

etc. *abbrev. for* et cetera.

et cetera ➊ *or* **etcetera** (ɪt ˈsɛtrə) *n and vb substitute.* **1** and the rest; and others; and so forth. **2** or the like; or something similar. [from L *et* and + *cetera* the other (things)]

> **USAGE NOTE** It is unnecessary to use *and* before *etc.* as *etc.* (*et cetera*) already means *and other things*. The repetition of *etc.*, as in *he brought paper, ink, notebooks, etc., etc.*, is avoided except in informal contexts.

etceteras (ɪtˈsɛtrəz) *pl n* miscellaneous extra things or persons.

etch ➊ (ɛtʃ) *vb* **1** (*tr*) to wear away the surface of (a metal, glass, etc.) by the action of an acid. **2** to cut or corrode (a design, etc.) on (a metal or other printing plate) by the action of acid on parts not covered by an acid-resistant coating. **3** (*tr*) to cut as with a sharp implement. **4** (*tr; usually passive*) to imprint vividly. [C17: from Du. *etsen*, from OHG *azzen* to feed, bite]
▸**'etcher** *n*

etching ➊ (ˈɛtʃɪŋ) *n* **1** the art, act, or process of preparing etched surfaces or of printing designs from them. **2** an etched plate. **3** an impression made from an etched plate.

ETD *abbrev. for* estimated time of departure.

eternal ➊ (ɪˈtɜ:nᵊl) *adj* **1a** without beginning or end; lasting forever. **1b** (*as n*): *the eternal.* **2** (*often cap.*) a name applied to God. **3** unchanged by time; immutable: *eternal truths.* **4** seemingly unceasing. [C14: from LL, from L *aeternus*; rel. to L *aevum* age]
▸**ˌeter'nality** *or* **e'ternalness** *n* ▸**e'ternally** *adv*

eternalize (ɪˈtɜ:nəˌlaɪz), **eternize** (ɪˈtɜ:naɪz), *or* **eternalise, eternise** *vb* **eternalizes, eternalizing, eternalized; eternizes, eternizing, eternized** *or* **eternalises, eternalising, eternalised; eternises, eternising, eternised.** (*tr*) **1** to make eternal. **2** to make famous forever; immortalize.
▸**eˌternali'zation, eˌterni'zation** *or* **eˌternali'sation, eternisation** *n*

eternal triangle *n* an emotional relationship usually involving three people, two of whom are rival lovers of the third person.

eternity ➊ (ɪˈtɜ:nɪtɪ) *n, pl* **eternities. 1** endless or infinite time. **2** the quality, state, or condition of being eternal. **3** (*usually pl*) any aspect of

THESAURUS

cile, dwelling, home, household, pad (*sl.*), residence

Establishment *n* = **the authorities**, established order, institutionalized authority, ruling class, the powers that be, the system

estate *n* **1** = **lands**, area, demesne, domain, holdings, manor, property **3** *Law* = **property**, assets, belongings, effects, fortune, goods, possessions, wealth **4** = **class**, caste, order, rank **5** = **status**, condition, lot, period, place, position, quality, rank, situation, standing, state, station

esteem *vb* **1** = **respect**, admire, be fond of, cherish, honour, like, love, prize, regard highly, revere, reverence, take off one's hat to, think highly of, treasure, value, venerate **2** *Formal* = **consider**, account, believe, calculate, deem, estimate, hold, judge, rate, reckon, regard, think, view ◆ *n* **3** = **respect**, admiration, Brownie points, consideration, credit, estimation, good opinion, honour, regard, reverence, veneration

estimable *adj* = **respectable**, admirable, esteemed, excellent, good, honourable, honoured, meritorious, reputable, respected, valuable, valued, worthy

estimate *vb* **1** = **calculate roughly**, appraise, assess, evaluate, gauge, guess, judge, number, reckon, value **2** = **form an opinion**, assess, believe, conjecture, consider, guess, judge, rank, rate, reckon, surmise, think ◆ *n* **4** = **approximate calculation**, appraisal, appraisement, assessment, ballpark estimate (*inf.*), ballpark figure (*inf.*), evaluation, guess, guesstimate (*inf.*), judgment, reckoning, valuation **6** = **opinion**, appraisal, appraisement, assessment, belief, conjecture, educated guess, estimation, judgment, surmise, thought(s)

estimation *n* **1** = **opinion**, appraisal, appreciation, assessment, belief, consideration, considered opinion, estimate, evaluation, judgment, view **2** = **respect**, admiration, Brownie points, credit, esteem, good opinion, honour, regard, reverence, veneration

estrange *vb* = **alienate**, antagonize, disaffect, disunite, divide, drive apart, lose *or* destroy the affection of, make hostile, part, separate, set at odds, withdraw, withhold
Antonyms *vb* ally, associate, coalesce, couple, fuse, join, link, marry, unite

estrangement *n* = **alienation**, antagonization, breach, break-up, disaffection, dissociation, disunity, division, hostility, parting, separation, split, withdrawal, withholding

estuary *n* = **inlet**, creek, firth, fjord, mouth

et cetera *n* **1** = **and the rest**, and others, and the like, et al.

etch *vb* **2** = **cut**, carve, corrode, eat into, engrave, furrow, impress, imprint, incise, ingrain, inscribe, stamp

etching *n* **1-3** = **print**, carving, engraving, impression, imprint, inscription

eternal *adj* **1** = **everlasting**, abiding, ceaseless, constant, deathless, endless, immortal, infinite, interminable, never-ending, perennial, perpetual, sempiternal (*literary*), timeless, unceasing, undying, unending, unremitting, without end **3** = **permanent**, deathless, enduring, everlasting, immortal, immutable, imperishable, indestructible, lasting, unchanging
Antonyms *adj* ≠ **everlasting:** finite, fleeting, infrequent, irregular, mortal, occasional, random, rare, temporal ≠ **permanent:** changing, ephemeral, evanescent, perishable, transient, transitory

eternity *n* **1, 2** = **infinity**, age, ages, endlessness, immortality, infinitude, perpetuity, timelessness, time without end **4** = **the afterlife**, heaven, paradise, the hereafter, the next world life and thought considered timeless. **4** the timeless existence, believed by some to characterize the afterlife. **5** a seemingly endless period of time.

eternity ring *n* a ring given as a token of lasting affection, esp. one set all around with stones to symbolize continuity.

etesian (ɪ'tiːʒɪən) *adj* (of NW winds) recurring annually in the summer in the E Mediterranean. [C17: from L *etēsius* yearly, from Gk *etos* year]

ETF *abbrev. for* electronic transfer of funds.

Eth. *abbrev. for:* **1** Ethiopia(n). **2** Ethiopic.

-eth[1] *suffix.* forming the archaic third person singular present indicative tense of verbs: *goeth; taketh.* [OE *-eth, -th*]

-eth[2] *suffix forming ordinal numbers.* a variant of **-th**[2]: *twentieth.*

ethanal ('ɛθəˌnæl) *n* the systematic name for **acetaldehyde.**

ethane ('iːθeɪn, 'ɛθ-) *n* a colourless odourless flammable gaseous alkane obtained from natural gas and petroleum: used as a fuel. Formula: C_2H_6. [C19: from ETH(YL)+ -ANE]

ethanediol ('iːθeɪnˌdaɪɒl, 'ɛθ-) *n* a colourless soluble liquid used as an antifreeze and solvent. Formula: $C_2H_4(OH)_2$. [C20: from ETHANE + DI-[1] + -OL[1]]

ethanoic acid (ˌɛθə'nəʊɪk, ˌiːθə-) *n* the systematic name for **acetic acid.**

ethanol ('ɛθəˌnɒl, 'iːθə-) *n* the systematic name for **alcohol** (sense 1).

ethene ('ɛθiːn) *n* the systematic name for **ethylene.**

ether ('iːθə) *n* **1** Also called: **diethyl ether, ethyl ether, ethoxyethane.** a colourless volatile highly flammable liquid: used as a solvent and anaesthetic. Formula: $C_2H_5OC_2H_5$. **2** any of a class of organic compounds with the general formula ROR′, as in methyl ethyl ether, $CH_3OC_2H_5$. **3** the medium formerly believed to fill all space and to support the propagation of electromagnetic waves. **4** *Greek myth.* the upper atmosphere; clear sky or heaven. ◆ Also (for senses 3 and 4): **aether.** [C17: from L, from Gk *aithein* to burn]
▸**e'theric** *adj*

ethereal ❶ (ɪ'θɪərɪəl) *adj* **1** extremely delicate or refined. **2** almost as light as air; airy. **3** celestial or spiritual. **4** of, containing, or dissolved in an ether, esp. diethyl ether. **5** of or relating to the ether. [C16: from L, from Gk *aithēr* ETHER]
▸**eˌthere'ality** *or* **e'therealness** *n*

etherealize *or* **etherealise** (ɪ'θɪərɪəˌlaɪz) *vb* **etherealizes, etherealizing, etherealized** *or* **etherealises, etherealising, etherealised.** (*tr*) **1** to make or regard as being ethereal. **2** to add ether to or make into ether.
▸**eˌthereali'zation** *or* **eˌthereali'sation** *n*

etherize *or* **etherise** ('iːθəˌraɪz) *vb* **etherizes, etherizing, etherized** *or* **etherises, etherising, etherised.** (*tr*) *Obs.* to subject (a person) to the anaesthetic influence of ether fumes; anaesthetize.
▸**ˌetheri'zation** *or* **ˌetheri'sation** *n* ▸**'etherˌizer** *or* **'etherˌiser** *n*

Ethernet ('iːθəˌnɛt) *n Trademark, computing.* a widely used type of local area network.

ethic ('ɛθɪk) *n* **1** a moral principle or set of moral values held by an individual or group. ◆ *adj* **2** another word for **ethical.** [C15: from L, from Gk *ēthos* custom]

ethical ❶ ('ɛθɪkᵊl) *adj* **1** in accordance with principles of conduct that are considered correct, esp. those of a given profession or group. **2** of or relating to ethics. **3** (of a medicinal agent) available legally only with a doctor's prescription.
▸**'ethically** *adv* ▸**'ethicalness** *or* **ˌethi'cality** *n*

ethical investment *n* an investment in a company whose activities or products are not considered by the investor to be unethical.

ethics ❶ ('ɛθɪks) *n* **1** (*functioning as sing*) the philosophical study of the moral value of human conduct and of the rules and principles that ought to govern it. **2** (*functioning as pl*) a code of behaviour considered correct, esp. that of a particular group, profession, or individual. **3** (*functioning as pl*) the moral fitness of a decision, course of action, etc.
▸**ethicist** ('ɛθɪsɪst) *n*

Ethiopian (ˌiːθɪ'əʊpɪən) *adj* **1** of or relating to Ethiopia (a state in NE Africa), its people, or any of their languages. ◆ *n* **2** a native or inhabitant of Ethiopia. **3** any of the languages of Ethiopia, esp. Amharic. ◆ *n, adj* **4** an archaic word for **Black.**

Ethiopic (ˌiːθɪ'ɒpɪk, -'əʊpɪk) *n* **1** the ancient Semitic language of Ethiopia: a Christian liturgical language. **2** the group of languages developed from this language, including Amharic. ◆ *adj* **3** denoting or relating to this language or group of languages. **4** a less common word for **Ethiopian.**

ethnic ❶ ('ɛθnɪk) *or* **ethnical** *adj* **1** of or relating to a human group having racial, religious, linguistic, and other traits in common. **2** relating to the classification of mankind into groups, esp. on the basis of racial characteristics. **3** denoting or deriving from the cultural traditions of a group of people. **4** characteristic of another culture, esp. a peasant one. ◆ *n* **5** *Chiefly US.* a member of an ethnic group, esp. a minority one. [C14 (in the senses: heathen, Gentile): from LL *ethnicus,* from Gk *ethnos* race]
▸**'ethnically** *adv* ▸**ethnicity** (ɛθ'nɪsɪtɪ) *n*

ethno- *combining form.* indicating race, people, or culture. [via F from Gk *ethnos* race]

ethnocentrism (ˌɛθnəʊ'sɛnˌtrɪzəm) *n* belief in the intrinsic superiority of the nation, culture, or group to which one belongs.
▸**ˌethno'centric** *adj* ▸**ˌethno'centrically** *adv* ▸**ˌethnocen'tricity** *n*

ethnography (ɛθ'nɒgrəfɪ) *n* the branch of anthropology that deals with the scientific description of individual human societies.
▸**ˌeth'nographer** *n* ▸**ethnographic** (ˌɛθnəʊ'græfɪk) *or* **ˌethno'graphical** *adj*

ethnology (ɛθ'nɒlədʒɪ) *n* the branch of anthropology that deals with races and peoples, their origins, characteristics, etc.
▸**ethnologic** (ˌɛθnə'lɒdʒɪk) *or* **ˌethno'logical** *adj* ▸**eth'nologist** *n*

ethnomusicology (ˌɛθnəʊˌmjuːzɪ'kɒlədʒɪ) *n* the study of the origins of music, esp. from non-European cultures.

ethology (ɪ'θɒlədʒɪ) *n* the study of the behaviour of animals in their normal environment. [C17 (in the obs. sense: mimicry): via L from Gk *ēthos* character; current sense, C19]
▸**ethological** (ˌɛθə'lɒdʒɪkᵊl) *adj* ▸**e'thologist** *n*

ethos ❶ ('iːθɒs) *n* the distinctive character, spirit, and attitudes of a people, culture, era, etc.: *the revolutionary ethos.* [C19: from LL: habit, from Gk]

ethyl ('iːθaɪl, 'ɛθɪl) *n* (*modifier*) of, consisting of, or containing the monovalent group C_2H_5–. [C19: from ETH(ER) + -YL]
▸**ethylic** (ɪ'θɪlɪk) *adj*

ethyl acetate *n* a colourless volatile flammable liquid ester: used in perfumes and flavourings and as a solvent. Formula: $CH_3COOC_2H_5$.

ethyl alcohol *n* another name for **alcohol** (sense 1).

ethylene ('ɛθɪˌliːn) *or* **ethene** ('ɛθiːn) *n* a colourless flammable gaseous alkene used in the manufacture of polythene and other chemicals. Formula: $CH_2{:}CH_2$.
▸**ethylenic** (ˌɛθɪ'liːnɪk) *adj*

ethylene glycol *n* another name for **ethanediol.**

ethylene group *or* **radical** *n Chem.* the divalent group, $–CH_2CH_2–$, derived from ethylene.

ethylene series *n Chem.* another name for **alkene series.**

ethyne ('ɛθaɪn) *n Chem.* the systematic name for **acetylene.**

ethyne series *n Chem.* another name for **acetylene series.**

etiolate ('iːtɪəʊˌleɪt) *vb* **etiolates, etiolating, etiolated. 1** *Bot.* to whiten (a green plant) through lack of sunlight. **2** to become or cause to become pale and weak. [C18: from F *étioler* to make pale, prob. from OF *estuble* straw, from L *stipula*]
▸**ˌetio'lation** *n*

etiology (ˌiːtɪ'ɒlədʒɪ) *n, pl* **etiologies.** a variant spelling of **aetiology.**

etiquette ❶ ('ɛtɪˌkɛt, ˌɛtɪ'kɛt) *n* **1** the customs or rules governing behaviour regarded as correct in social life. **2** a conventional code of practice followed in certain professions or groups. [C18: from F, from OF *estiquette* label, from *estiquier* to attach; see STICK[2]]

Eton collar ('iːtᵊn) *n* (formerly) a broad stiff white collar worn outside a boy's jacket.

Eton crop *n* a very short mannish hairstyle worn by women in the 1920s.

Eton jacket *n* a waist-length jacket with a V-shaped back, open in front, formerly worn by pupils of Eton College, a public school for boys in S England.

Etruscan (ɪ'trʌskən) *or* **Etrurian** (ɪ'trʊərɪən) *n* **1** a member of an ancient people of Etruria, in central Italy, whose civilization greatly influenced the Romans. **2** the language of the ancient Etruscans. ◆ *adj* **3** of or relating to Etruria, the Etruscans, their culture, or their language.

et seq. *abbrev. for:* **1** et sequens [L: and the following] **2** Also: **et seqq.** et sequentia [L: and those that follow]

-ette *suffix of nouns.* **1** small: *cigarette.* **2** female: *majorette.* **3** (esp. in trade names) imitation: *Leatherette.* [from F, fem of -ET]

étude ('eɪtjuːd) *n* a short musical composition for a solo instrument, esp. one designed as an exercise or exploiting virtuosity. [C19: from F: STUDY]

étui (ɛ'twiː) *n, pl* **étuis.** a small usually ornamented case for holding needles, cosmetics, or other small articles. [C17: F, from OF *estuier* to enclose; see TWEEZERS]

etymology (ˌɛtɪ'mɒlədʒɪ) *n, pl* **etymologies. 1** the study of the sources and development of words. **2** an account of the source and development of a word. [C14: via L from Gk; see ETYMON, -LOGY]
▸**etymological** (ˌɛtɪmə'lɒdʒɪkᵊl) *adj* ▸**ˌety'mologist** *n* ▸**ˌety'moloˌgize** *or* **ˌety'moloˌgise** *vb*

etymon ('ɛtɪˌmɒn) *n, pl* **etymons** *or* **etyma** (-mə). a form of a word, usually the earliest recorded form or a reconstructed form, from which an-

THESAURUS

ethereal *adj* **1** = **delicate**, dainty, exquisite, fine, light, rarefied, refined, subtle, tenuous **2** = **insubstantial**, aerial, airy, fairy, impalpable, intangible, light, rarefied **3** = **spiritual**, celestial, empyreal, heavenly, sublime, unearthly, unworldly

ethical *adj* **1** = **moral**, conscientious, correct, decent, fair, fitting, good, honest, honourable, just, principled, proper, right, righteous, upright, virtuous

Antonyms *adj* dishonourable, disreputable, immoral, improper, indecent, low-down (*inf.*), not cricket (*inf.*), underhand, unethical, unfair, unscrupulous, unseemly

ethics *n* **2** *plural* = **moral code**, conscience, morality, moral philosophy, moral values, principles, rules of conduct, standards

ethnic *adj* **3** = **cultural**, folk, indigenous, national, native, racial, traditional

ethos *n* = **spirit**, attitude, beliefs, character, disposition, ethic, tenor

etiquette *n* **1** = **good** *or* **proper behaviour**, civility, code, convention, courtesy, customs, decorum, formalities, manners, politeness, politesse, propriety, protocol, p's and q's, rules, usage other word is derived. [C16: via L from Gk *etumon* basic meaning, from *etumos* true, actual]

Eu *the chemical symbol for* europium.

EU *abbrev. for* European Union.

eu- *combining form.* well, pleasant, or good: *eupeptic; euphony.* [via L from Gk, from *eus* good]

eucalyptus (ˌjuːkəˈlɪptəs) *or* **eucalypt** (ˈjuːkəˌlɪpt) *n, pl* **eucalyptuses, eucalypti** (-ˈlɪptaɪ), *or* **eucalypts.** any tree of the mostly Australian genus *Eucalyptus,* widely cultivated for timber and gum, as ornament, and for the medicinal oil in their leaves (**eucalyptus oil**). [C19: NL, from EU- + Gk *kaluptos* covered, from *kaluptein* to cover, hide]

Eucharist (ˈjuːkərɪst) *n* **1** the Christian sacrament in which Christ's Last Supper is commemorated by the consecration of bread and wine. **2** the consecrated elements of bread and wine offered in the sacrament. [C14: via Church L from Gk *eukharistos* thankful, from EU- + *kharis* favour]
▸ **ˌEuchaˈristic** *or* **ˌEuchaˈristical** *adj*

euchre (ˈjuːkə) *n* **1** a US and Canad. card game for two, three, or four players, using a poker pack. **2** an instance of euchring another player. ◆ *vb* **euchres, euchring, euchred.** (*tr*) **3** to prevent (a player) from making his contracted tricks. **4** (usually foll. by *out*) *US, Canad., Austral., & NZ inf.* to outwit or cheat. [C19: from ?]

Euclidean *or* **Euclidian** (juːˈklɪdɪən) *adj* denoting a system of geometry based on the axioms of Euclid, 3rd-century B.C. Greek mathematician, esp. the axiom that parallel lines meet at infinity.

eucryphia (juːˈkrɪfɪə) *n* any of various mostly evergreen trees and shrubs of S America and Australia. [NL, from EU- + Gk *kryphios* covered]

eudiometer (ˌjuːdɪˈɒmɪtə) *n* a graduated glass tube used in the study and volumetric analysis of gas reactions. [C18: from Gk *eudios,* lit.: clear-skied + -METER]

eugenics (juːˈdʒɛnɪks) *n* (*functioning as sing*) the study of methods of improving the quality of the human race, esp. by selective breeding. [C19: from Gk *eugenēs* well-born, from EU- + *-genēs* born; see -GEN]
▸ **euˈgenic** *adj* ▸ **euˈgenically** *adv* ▸ **euˈgenicist** *n* ▸ **eugenist** (ˈjuːdʒənɪst) *n*

eukaryote *or* **eucaryote** (juˈkærɪəʊt) *n* an organism having cells each with a nucleus within which the genetic material is contained. Cf. **prokaryote.** [from EU- + KARYO- + *-ote* as in *zygote*]
▸ **eukaryotic** *or* **eucaryotic** (juˌkærɪˈɒtɪk) *adj*

eulogize ➊ *or* **eulogise** (ˈjuːləˌdʒaɪz) *vb* **eulogizes, eulogizing, eulogized** *or* **eulogises, eulogising, eulogised.** to praise (a person or thing) highly in speech or writing.
▸ **ˈeulogist, ˈeuloˌgizer,** *or* **ˈeuloˌgiser** *n* ▸ **ˌeuloˈgistic** *or* **ˌeuloˈgistical** *adj*

eulogy ➊ (ˈjuːlədʒɪ) *n, pl* **eulogies. 1** a speech or piece of writing praising a person or thing, esp. a person who has recently died. **2** high praise or commendation. ◆ Also called (archaic): **eulogium** (juːˈləʊdʒɪəm). [C16: from LL, from Gk: praise, from EU- + -LOGY]

USAGE NOTE Avoid confusion with **elegy.**

Eumenides (juːˈmɛnɪˌdiːz) *pl n* another name for the **Furies,** used by the Greeks as a euphemism. [from Gk, lit: the benevolent ones]

eunuch (ˈjuːnək) *n* **1** a man who has been castrated, esp. (formerly) for some office such as a guard in a harem. **2** *Inf.* an ineffective man. [C15: via L from Gk *eunoukhos* bedchamber attendant]

euonymus (juːˈɒnɪməs) *or* **evonymus** (ɛˈvɒnɪməs) *n* any tree or shrub of the N temperate genus *Euonymus,* such as the spindle tree. [C18: from L: spindle tree, from Gk *euōnumos* fortunately named, from EU- + *onoma* NAME]

eupepsia (juːˈpɛpsɪə) *or* **eupepsy** (juːˈpɛpsɪ) *n Physiol.* good digestion. [C18: from NL, from Gk, from EU- + *pepsis* digestion]
▸ **eupeptic** (juːˈpɛptɪk) *adj*

euphemism (ˈjuːfɪˌmɪzəm) *n* **1** an inoffensive word or phrase substituted for one considered offensive or hurtful. **2** the use of such inoffensive words or phrases. [C17: from Gk, from EU- + *phēmē* speech]
▸ **ˌeupheˈmistic** *adj* ▸ **ˌeupheˈmistically** *adv*

euphemize *or* **euphemise** (ˈjuːfɪˌmaɪz) *vb* **euphemizes, euphemizing, euphemized** *or* **euphemises, euphemising, euphemised.** to speak in euphemisms or refer to by means of a euphemism.
▸ **ˈeupheˌmizer** *or* **ˈeupheˌmiser** *n*

euphonic (juːˈfɒnɪk) *or* **euphonious** (juːˈfəʊnɪəs) *adj* **1** denoting or relating to euphony. **2** (of speech sounds) altered for ease of pronunciation.
▸ **euˈphonically** *or* **euˈphoniously** *adv* ▸ **euˈphoniousness** *n*

euphonium (juːˈfəʊnɪəm) *n* a brass musical instrument with four valves. [C19: NL, from EUPH(ONY + HARM)ONIUM]

euphonize *or* **euphonise** (ˈjuːfəˌnaɪz) *vb* **euphonizes, euphonizing, euphonized** *or* **euphonises, euphonising, euphonised. 1** to make pleasant to hear. **2** to change (speech sounds) so as to facilitate pronunciation.

euphony (ˈjuːfənɪ) *n, pl* **euphonies. 1** the alteration of speech sounds, esp. by assimilation, so as to make them easier to pronounce. **2** a pleasing sound, esp. in speech. [C17: from LL, from Gk, from EU- + *phōnē* voice]

euphorbia (juːˈfɔːbɪə) *n* any plant of the genus *Euphorbia,* such as the spurges. [C14 *euforbia,* from L *euphorbea* African plant, after *Euphorbus,* first-cent. A.D. Gk physician]

euphoria ➊ (juːˈfɔːrɪə) *n* a feeling of great elation, esp. when exaggerated. [C19: from Gk: good ability to endure, from EU- + *pherein* to bear]
▸ **euphoric** (juːˈfɒrɪk) *adj*

euphoriant (juːˈfɔːrɪənt) *adj* **1** able to produce euphoria. ◆ *n* **2** a euphoriant drug or agent.

euphotic (juːˈfəʊtɪk, -ˈfɒt-) *adj* denoting or relating to the uppermost part of a sea or lake, which receives enough light for photosynthesis to take place. [C20: from EU- + PHOTIC]

euphrasy (ˈjuːfrəsɪ) *n, pl* **euphrasies.** another name for **eyebright.** [C15: *eufrasie,* from Med. L, from Gk *euphrasia* gladness, from EU- + *phrēn* mind]

euphuism (ˈjuːfjuːˌɪzəm) *n* **1** an artificial prose style of the Elizabethan period, marked by extreme use of antithesis, alliteration, and extended similes and allusions. **2** any stylish affectation in speech or writing. [C16: after *Euphues,* prose romance by John Lyly]
▸ **ˈeuphuist** *n* ▸ **ˌeuphuˈistic** *or* **ˌeuphuˈistical** *adj*

eur. *or* **Eur.** *abbrev. for* Europe(an).

eur- *combining form.* (*sometimes cap.*) a variant of **euro-** before a vowel.

Eurasian (juəˈreɪʃən, -ʒən) *adj* **1** of or relating to Europe and Asia considered as a whole. **2** of mixed European and Asian descent. ◆ *n* **3** a person of mixed European and Asian descent.

Euratom (juəˈrætəm) *n* short for **European Atomic Energy Community;** an authority established by the EEC (now the EU) to develop peaceful uses of nuclear energy.

eureka (juˈriːkə) *interj* an exclamation of triumph on discovering or solving something. [C17: from Gk *heurēka* I have found (it), from *heuriskein* to find; traditionally the exclamation of Archimedes when he realized, during bathing, that the volume of an irregular solid could be calculated by measuring the water displaced when it was immersed]

eurhythmic (juːˈrɪðmɪk), **eurhythmical,** *or esp. US* **eurythmic, eurythmical** *adj* **1** having a pleasing and harmonious rhythm, order, or structure. **2** of or relating to eurhythmics. [C19: from L, from Gk, from EU- + *rhuthmos* proportion, RHYTHM]

eurhythmics *or esp. US* **eurythmics** (juːˈrɪðmɪks) *n* (*functioning as sing*) **1** a system of training through physical movement to music. **2** dancing of this style. [C20: from EURHYTHMIC]
▸ **euˈrhythmy** *or* **euˈrythmy** *n*

euro (ˈjuərəu) *n* the currency unit of the member countries of the European Union who have adopted European Monetary Union.

euro- (ˈjuərəu) *or before a vowel* **eur-** *combining form.* (*sometimes cap.*) Europe *or* European.

eurobond (ˈjuərəuˌbɒnd) *n* (*sometimes cap.*) a bond issued in a eurocurrency.

Eurocentric (ˌjuərəuˈsɛntrɪk) *adj* chiefly concerned with or concentrating on Europe and European culture: *the Eurocentric curriculum.*

eurocheque (ˈjuərəuˌtʃɛk) *n* (*sometimes cap.*) a cheque drawn on a European bank that can be cashed at any bank or bureau de change displaying the EU sign or that can be used to pay for goods or services at any outlet displaying this sign.

Eurocommunism (ˌjuərəuˈkɒmjuˌnɪzəm) *n* the policies, doctrines, and practices of Communist Parties in Western Europe in the 1970s and 1980s, esp. those rejecting democratic centralism and favouring nonalignment with the Soviet Union and China.
▸ **ˌEuroˈcommunist** *n, adj*

eurocrat (ˈjuərəˌkræt) *n* (*sometimes cap.*) a member of the administration of the European Union.

eurocurrency (ˈjuərəuˌkʌrənsɪ) *n* (*sometimes cap.*) the currency of any country held on deposit in Europe outside its home market: used as a source of short- or medium-term finance because of easy convertibility.

eurodollar (ˈjuərəuˌdɒlə) *n* (*sometimes cap.*) a US dollar as part of a European holding. See **eurocurrency.**

euromarket (ˈjuərəuˌmɑːkɪt) *n* **1** a market for financing international trade backed by the central banks and commercial banks of the European Union. **2** the European Union treated as one large market for the sale of goods and services.

Euro MP *n Inf.* a member of the European Parliament.

euronote (ˈjuərəuˌnəut) *n* a form of euro-commercial paper consisting of short-term negotiable bearer notes.

European (ˌjuərəˈpɪən) *adj* **1** of or relating to Europe or its inhabitants. **2** native to or derived from Europe. ◆ *n* **3** a native or inhabitant of Europe. **4** a person of European descent. **5** *S. African.* any White person.
▸ **ˌEuroˈpeanˌism** *n*

European Commission *n* the executive body of the European Union,

THESAURUS

eulogize *vb* = **praise,** acclaim, applaud, commend, compliment, crack up (*inf.*), cry up, exalt, extol, glorify, laud, magnify (*arch.*), panegyrize, pay tribute to, sing *or* sound the praises of

eulogy *n* **1** = **tribute,** accolade, encomium, paean, panegyric **2** = **praise,** acclaim, acclamation, applause, commendation, compliment, exaltation, glorification, laudation, plaudits

euphoria *n* = **elation,** bliss, ecstasy, exaltation, exhilaration, exultation, glee, high spirits, intoxication, joy, joyousness, jubilation, rapture, transport

Antonyms *n* depression, despair, despondency, dolefulness, downheartedness, dumps (*inf.*), gloominess, hopelessness, low spirits, melancholia, melancholy, sadness, the blues formed in 1967 to initiate action in the union and mediate between member governments.

European Community *or* **Communities** *n* the former name (until 1993) of the **European Union.**

European Council *n* an executive body of the European Union, made up of the President of the European Commission and representatives of the member states, including foreign and other ministers. The Council acts at the request of the Commission.

European Currency Unit *n* See **ECU.**

European Economic Community *n* the former W European economic association created by the Treaty of Rome (1957); in 1967 it merged with the European Coal and Steel Community and the European Atomic Energy Community to form the European Community, which was replaced in 1993 by the European Union. Informal name: **Common Market.** Abbrev.: **EEC.**

Europeanize *or* **Europeanise** (ˌjʊərəˈpɪəˌnaɪz) *vb* **Europeanizes, Europeanizing, Europeanized** *or* **Europeanises, Europeanising, Europeanised.** (*tr*) **1** to make European. **2** to integrate (a country, economy, etc.) into the European Union.
▸ **ˌEuroˌpeaniˈzation** *or* **ˌEuroˌpeaniˈsation** *n*

European Monetary System *n* the system used in the European Union for stabilizing exchange rates between the currencies of member states. It relies on the Exchange Rate Mechanism and the balance-of-payments support mechanism. Abbrev.: **EMS.**

European Parliament *n* the assembly of the European Union in Strasbourg.

European Union *n* the economic and political organization of European states created in 1967 (as the European Community) by the merger of the European Economic Community with the European Coal and Steel Community and the European Atomic Energy Community. The current members are Belgium, Denmark, France, Germany, Greece, Ireland, Italy, Luxembourg, the Netherlands, Portugal, Spain, and the UK; Austria, Finland, and Sweden joined in 1995. Abbrev.: **EU.**

Europhile (ˈjʊərəʊˌfaɪl) (*sometimes not cap.*) ◆ *n* **1** a person who admires Europe, Europeans, or the European Union. ◆ *adj* **2** marked by admiration for Europe, Europeans, or the European Union.

europium (jʊˈrəʊpɪəm) *n* a silvery-white element of the lanthanide series of metals. Symbol: Eu; atomic no.: 63; atomic wt.: 151.96. [C20: after *Europe* + -IUM]

Eurotunnel (ˈjʊərəʊˌtʌnᵊl) *n* another name for **Channel Tunnel.**

eurythmics (juːˈrɪðmɪks) *n* a variant spelling (esp. US) of **eurhythmics.**

Eustachian tube (juːˈsteɪʃən) *n* a tube that connects the middle ear with the pharynx and equalizes the pressure between the two sides of the eardrum. [C18: after Bartolomeo *Eustachio,* 16th-cent. It. anatomist]

eustatic (juːˈstætɪk) *adj* denoting or relating to worldwide changes in sea level, caused by the melting of ice sheets, sedimentation, etc. [C20: from Gk, from EU- + STATIC]

eutectic (juːˈtɛktɪk) *adj* **1** (of a mixture of substances) having the lowest freezing point of all possible mixtures of the substances. **2** concerned with or suitable for the formation of eutectic mixtures. ◆ *n* **3** a eutectic mixture. **4** the temperature at which a eutectic mixture forms. [C19: from Gk *eutēktos* melting readily, from EU- + *tēkein* to melt]

Euterpe (juːˈtɜːpɪ) *n Greek myth.* the Muse of lyric poetry and music.
▸ **Euˈterpean** *adj*

euthanasia (ˌjuːθəˈneɪzɪə) *n* the act of killing someone painlessly, esp. to relieve suffering from an incurable illness. [C17: via NL from Gk: easy death]

euthenics (juːˈθɛnɪks) *n* (*functioning as sing*) the study of the control of the environment, esp. with a view to improving the health and living standards of the human race. [C20: from Gk *euthēnein* to thrive]
▸ **euˈthenist** *n*

eutrophic (juːˈtrɒfɪk, -ˈtrəʊ-) *adj* (of lakes, etc.) rich in organic and mineral nutrients and supporting an abundant plant life. [C18: prob. from *eutrophy,* from Gk, from *eutrophos* well-fed]
▸ **ˈeutrophy** *n*

eV *abbrev. for* electronvolt.

EVA *Astronautics. abbrev. for* extravehicular activity.

evacuate ⓣ (ɪˈvækjʊˌeɪt) *vb* **evacuates, evacuating, evacuated.** (*mainly tr*) **1** (*also intr*) to withdraw or cause to withdraw (from a place of danger) to a place of safety. **2** to make empty. **3** (*also intr*) *Physiol.* **3a** to eliminate or excrete (faeces). **3b** to discharge (any waste) from (the body). **4** (*tr*) to create a vacuum in (a bulb, flask, etc.). [C16: from L *ēvacuāre* to void, from *vacuus* empty]
▸ **eˌvacuˈation** *n* ▸ **eˈvacuative** *adj* ▸ **eˈvacuˌator** *n* ▸ **eˌvacuˈee** *n*

evade ⓣ (ɪˈveɪd) *vb* **evades, evading, evaded.** (*mainly tr*) **1** to get away from or avoid (imprisonment, captors, etc.). **2** to get around, shirk, or dodge (the law, a duty, etc.). **3** (*also intr*) to avoid answering (a question). [C16: from F, from L *ēvādere* to go forth]
▸ **eˈvadable** *adj* ▸ **eˈvader** *n*

evaginate (ɪˈvædʒɪˌneɪt) *vb* **evaginates, evaginating, evaginated.** (*tr*) *Med.* to turn (an organ or part) inside out. [C17: from LL *ēvāgīnare* to unsheathe, from L *vāgīna* sheath]

evaluate ⓣ (ɪˈvæljʊˌeɪt) *vb* **evaluates, evaluating, evaluated.** (*tr*) **1** to ascertain or set the amount or value of. **2** to judge or assess the worth of. [C19: back formation from *evaluation,* from F, from *évaluer;* see VALUE]
▸ **eˌvaluˈation** *n* ▸ **eˈvaluative** *adj* ▸ **eˈvaluˌator** *n*

evanesce (ˌɛvəˈnɛs) *vb* **evanesces, evanescing, evanesced.** (*intr*) (of smoke, mist, etc.) to fade gradually from sight; vanish. [C19: from L *ēvānēscere* to disappear; see VANISH]

evanescent ⓣ (ˌɛvəˈnɛsᵊnt) *adj* **1** passing out of sight; fading away; vanishing. **2** ephemeral or transitory.
▸ **ˌevaˈnescence** *n*

evangel (ɪˈvændʒəl) *n* **1** *Arch.* the gospel of Christianity. **2** (*often cap.*) any of the four Gospels of the New Testament. **3** any body of teachings regarded as basic. **4** *US.* an evangelist. [C14: from Church L, from Gk *evangelion* good news, from EU- + *angelos* messenger; see ANGEL]

evangelical ⓣ (ˌiːvænˈdʒɛlɪkᵊl) *Christianity.* ◆ *adj* **1** of or following from the Gospels. **2** denoting or relating to any of certain Protestant sects, which emphasize personal conversion and faith in atonement through the death of Christ as a means of salvation. **3** denoting or relating to an evangelist. ◆ *n* **4** a member of an evangelical sect.
▸ **ˌevanˈgelicalism** *n* ▸ **ˌevanˈgelically** *adv*

evangelism (ɪˈvændʒɪˌlɪzəm) *n* **1** the practice of spreading the Christian gospel. **2** ardent or missionary zeal for a cause.

evangelist (ɪˈvændʒɪlɪst) *n* **1** an occasional preacher, sometimes itinerant. **2** a preacher of the Christian gospel.
▸ **eˌvangeˈlistic** *adj*

Evangelist (ɪˈvændʒɪlɪst) *n* any of the writers of the New Testament Gospels: Matthew, Mark, Luke, or John.

evangelize *or* **evangelise** (ɪˈvændʒɪˌlaɪz) *vb* **evangelizes, evangelizing, evangelized** *or* **evangelises, evangelising, evangelised.** **1** to preach the Christian gospel (to). **2** (*intr*) to advocate a cause with the object of making converts.
▸ **eˌvangeliˈzation** *or* **eˌvangeliˈsation** *n* ▸ **eˈvangeˌlizer** *or* **eˈvangeˌliser** *n*

evaporate ⓣ (ɪˈvæpəˌreɪt) *vb* **evaporates, evaporating, evaporated.** **1** to change or cause to change from a liquid or solid state to a vapour. **2** to lose or cause to lose liquid by vaporization leaving a more concentrated residue. **3** to disappear or cause to disappear. [C16: from LL, from L *vapor* steam; see VAPOUR]
▸ **eˈvaporable** *adj* ▸ **eˌvapoˈration** *n* ▸ **eˈvaporative** *adj* ▸ **eˈvapoˌrator** *n*

evaporated milk *n* thick unsweetened tinned milk from which some of the water has been evaporated.

evasion ⓣ (ɪˈveɪʒən) *n* **1** the act of evading, esp. a distasteful duty, responsibility, etc., by cunning or by illegal means: *tax evasion.* **2** cunning or deception used to dodge a question, duty, etc.; means of evading. [C15: from LL *ēvāsio;* see EVADE]

evasive ⓣ (ɪˈveɪsɪv) *adj* **1** tending or seeking to evade; not straightforward. **2** avoiding or seeking to avoid trouble or difficulties. **3** hard to catch or obtain; elusive.
▸ **eˈvasively** *adv* ▸ **eˈvasiveness** *n*

eve ⓣ (iːv) *n* **1** the evening or day before some special event. **2** the period immediately before an event: *the eve of war.* **3** an archaic word for **evening.** [C13: var. of EVEN[2]]

THESAURUS

evacuate *vb* **1** = **clear,** abandon, decamp, depart, desert, forsake, leave, move out, pull out, quit, relinquish, remove, vacate, withdraw **3** *Physiology* = **excrete,** crap (*taboo sl.*), defecate, discharge, eject, eliminate, empty, expel, shit (*taboo sl.*), void

evacuation *n* **1** = **clearance,** abandonment, departure, exodus, flight, leaving, moving out, pulling out, removal, vacation, withdrawal **3** *Physiology* = **excretion,** crap (*taboo sl.*), defecation, discharge, ejection, elimination, purging, shit (*taboo sl.*), voiding

evade *vb* **1, 2** = **avoid,** body-swerve (*Scot.*), circumvent, decline, dodge, duck, elude, escape, escape the clutches of, eschew, get away from, shirk, shun, sidestep, slip through one's fingers, slip through the net, steer clear of **3** = **avoid answering,** balk, beat about the bush, circumvent, cop out (*sl.*), equivocate, fence, fend off, flannel (*Brit. inf.*), fudge, hedge, parry, prevaricate, quibble, waffle (*inf., chiefly Brit.*)

Antonyms *vb* ≠ **avoid:** brave, confront, encounter, face, meet, meet face to face

evaluate *vb* **1, 2** = **assess,** appraise, assay, calculate, estimate, gauge, judge, rank, rate, reckon, size up (*inf.*), value, weigh

evaluation *n* **1, 2** = **assessment,** appraisal, calculation, estimate, estimation, judgment, opinion, rating, valuation

evanescent *adj* **1, 2** = **ephemeral,** brief, fading, fleeting, fugacious, fugitive, impermanent, momentary, passing, short-lived, transient, transitory, vanishing

evangelical *adj* **2** = **crusading,** missionary, propagandizing, proselytizing, zealous

evaporate *vb* **1** = **dry up,** dehydrate, desiccate, dry, vaporize **3** = **disappear,** dematerialize, dispel, disperse, dissipate, dissolve, evanesce, fade, fade away, melt, melt away, vanish

evaporation *n* **1** = **drying up,** dehydration, desiccation, drying, vaporization **3** = **disappearance,** dematerialization, dispelling, dispersal, dissipation, dissolution, evanescence, fading, fading away, melting, melting away, vanishing

evasion *n* **1** = **avoidance,** circumvention, dodging, elusion, escape **2** = **deception,** artifice, cop-out (*sl.*), cunning, equivocation, evasiveness, excuse, fudging, obliqueness, pretext, prevarication, ruse, shift, shirking, shuffling, sophism, sophistry, subterfuge, trickery, waffle (*inf., chiefly Brit.*)

evasive *adj* **1** = **deceptive,** cagey (*inf.*), casuistic, casuistical, cunning, deceitful, devious, dissembling, equivocating, indirect, misleading, oblique, prevaricating, shifty, shuffling, slippery, sophistical, tricky

Antonyms *adj* candid, direct, frank, guileless, honest, open, straight, straightforward, truthful, unequivocating

eve *n* **1** = **night before,** day before, vigil **2** = **brink,** edge, point, threshold, verge

even[1] Ⓣ ('iːvən) *adj* **1** level and regular; flat. **2** (*postpositive; foll. by with*) on the same level or in the same plane (as). **3** without variation or fluctuation; regular; constant. **4** not readily moved or excited; calm: *an even temper.* **5** equally balanced between two sides: *an even game.* **6** equal or identical in number, quantity, etc. **7a** (of a number) divisible by two. **7b** characterized or indicated by such a number: *the even pages.* Cf. **odd** (sense 4). **8** relating to or denoting two or either of two alternatives, events, etc., that have an equal probability: *an even chance of missing or catching a train.* **9** having no balance of debt; neither owing nor being owed. **10** just and impartial; fair. **11** exact in number, amount, or extent: *an even pound.* **12** equal, as in score; level. **13 even money. 13a** a bet in which the winnings are the same as the amount staked. **13b** (*as modifier*): *the even-money favourite.* **14 get even (with).** *Inf.* to exact revenge (on); settle accounts (with). ◆ *adv* **15** (intensifier; used to suggest that the content of a statement is unexpected or paradoxical): *even an idiot can do that.* **16** (intensifier; used with comparative forms): *even better.* **17** notwithstanding; in spite of. **18** used to introduce a more precise version of a word, phrase, or statement: *he is base, even depraved.* **19** used preceding a clause of supposition or hypothesis to emphasize that whether or not the condition in it is fulfilled, the statement in the main clause remains valid: *even if she died he wouldn't care.* **20** *Arch.* all the way; fully: *I love thee even unto death.* **21 even as.** (*conj*) at the very same moment or in the very same way that. **22 even so.** in spite of any assertion to the contrary: nevertheless. ◆ See also **even out, evens, even up.** [OE *efen*]
▸**'evener** *n* ▸**'evenly** *adv* ▸**'evenness** *n*

even[2] ('iːvən) *n* an archaic word for **eve** or **evening.** [OE *ǣfen*]

even-handed Ⓣ *adj* fair; impartial.
▸**ˌeven-'handedly** *adv* ▸**ˌeven-'handedness** *n*

evening Ⓣ ('iːvnɪŋ) *n* **1** the latter part of the day, esp. from late afternoon until nightfall. **2** the latter or concluding period: *the evening of one's life.* **3** the early part of the night spent in a specified way: *an evening at the theatre.* **4** (*modifier*) of, used in, or occurring in the evening: *the evening papers.* [OE *ǣfnung*]

evening dress *n* attire for a formal occasion during the evening.

evening primrose *n* any plant of the genus *Oenothera,* typically having yellow flowers that open in the evening.

evening primrose oil *n* an oil, obtained from the seeds of the evening primrose, that is claimed to stimulate the production of prostaglandins.

evenings ('iːvnɪŋz) *adv Inf.* in the evening, esp. regularly.

evening star *n* a planet, usually Venus, seen just after sunset during the time that the planet is east of the sun.

even out Ⓣ *vb* (*adv*) to make or become even, as by the removal of bumps, inequalities, etc.

evens ('iːvənz) *adj, adv* **1** (of a bet) winning the same as the amount staked if successful. **2** (of a runner) offered at such odds.

evensong ('iːvənˌsɒŋ) *n* **1** Also called: **Evening Prayer, vespers.** *Church of England.* the daily evening service. **2** *RC Church, arch.* another name for **vespers.**

event Ⓣ (ɪ'vɛnt) *n* **1** anything that takes place, esp. something important; an incident. **2** the actual or final outcome (esp. in **in the event, after the event**). **3** any one contest in a programme of sporting or other contests. **4 in any event** *or* **at all events.** regardless of circumstances; in any case. **5 in the event of.** in case of; if (such a thing) happens. **6 in the event that.** if it should happen that. [C16: from L *ēvenīre* to come forth, happen]

even-tempered Ⓣ *adj* not easily angered or excited; calm.

eventful Ⓣ (ɪ'vɛntfʊl) *adj* full of events.
▸**e'ventfully** *adv* ▸**e'ventfulness** *n*

event horizon *n Astron.* the spherical boundary of a black hole: objects passing through it would disappear completely and for ever, as no information can escape across the event horizon from the interior.

eventide ('iːvənˌtaɪd) *n Arch. or poetic.* another word for **evening.**

eventide home *n Euphemistic.* an old people's home.

eventing (ɪ'vɛntɪŋ) *n Chiefly Brit.* taking part in equestrian competitions (esp. **three-day events**), usually involving cross-country riding, jumping, and dressage.

eventual Ⓣ (ɪ'vɛntʃʊəl) *adj* **1** (*prenominal*) happening in due course of time; ultimate. **2** *Arch.* contingent or possible.

eventuality Ⓣ (ɪˌvɛntʃʊ'ælɪtɪ) *n, pl* **eventualities.** a possible event, occurrence, or result; contingency.

eventually Ⓣ (ɪ'vɛntʃʊəlɪ) *adv* **1** at the very end; finally. **2** (*sentence modifier*) after a long time or long delay: *eventually, he arrived.*

eventuate (ɪ'vɛntʃʊˌeɪt) *vb* **eventuates, eventuating, eventuated.** (*intr*) **1** (often foll. by *in*) to result ultimately (in). **2** to come about as a result.
▸**eˌventu'ation** *n*

even up Ⓣ *vb* (*adv*) to make or become equal, esp. in respect of claims or debts.

ever Ⓣ ('ɛvə) *adv* **1** at any time. **2** by any chance; in any case: *how did you ever find out?* **3** at all times; always. **4** in any possible way or manner: *come as fast as ever you can.* **5** *Inf., chiefly Brit.* (intensifier, in **ever so, ever such,** and **ever such a**). **6 is he** *or* **she ever!** *US & Canad. sl.* he *or* she displays the quality concerned in abundance. ◆ See also **forever.** [OE *ǣfre,* from ?]

evergreen ('ɛvəˌgriːn) *adj* **1** (of certain trees and shrubs) bearing foliage throughout the year. Cf. **deciduous. 2** remaining fresh and vital. ◆ *n* **3** an evergreen tree or shrub.

evergreen fund *n* a fund that provides capital for new companies and makes regular injections of capital to support their development.

everlasting Ⓣ (ˌɛvə'lɑːstɪŋ) *adj* **1** never coming to an end; eternal. **2** lasting for an indefinitely long period. **3** lasting so long or occurring so often as to become tedious. ◆ *n* **4** eternity. **5** Also called: **everlasting flower.** another name for **immortelle.**
▸**ˌever'lastingly** *adv*

evermore Ⓣ (ˌɛvə'mɔː) *adv* (often preceded by *for*) all time to come.

evert (ɪ'vɜːt) *vb* (*tr*) to turn (an eyelid or other bodily part) outwards or inside out. [C16: from L *ēvertere* to overthrow, from *vertere* to turn]
▸**e'versible** *adj* ▸**e'version** *n*

every Ⓣ ('ɛvrɪ) *determiner* **1** each one (of the class specified), without exception. **2** (*not used with a negative*) the greatest or best possible: *every hope.* **3** each: used before a noun phrase to indicate the recurrent, intermittent, or serial nature of a thing: *every third day.* **4 every bit.** (used in comparisons with *as*) quite; just; equally. **5 every other.** each alternate; every second. **6 every which way.** *US & Canad.* **6a** in all directions; everywhere. **6b** from all sides. [C15 *everich,* from OE *ǣfre ǣlc,* from *ǣfre* EVER + *ǣlc* EACH]

THESAURUS

even[1] *adj* **1** = **level,** flat, flush, horizontal, parallel, plane, plumb, smooth, steady, straight, true, uniform **3** = **regular,** constant, metrical, smooth, steady, unbroken, uniform, uninterrupted, unvarying, unwavering **4** = **calm,** composed, cool, equable, equanimous, even-tempered, imperturbable, peaceful, placid, serene, stable, steady, tranquil, undisturbed, unexcitable, unruffled, well-balanced **5, 6** = **equal,** coequal, commensurate, comparable, drawn, equalized, equally balanced, fifty-fifty (*inf.*), identical, level, level pegging (*Brit. inf.*), like, matching, neck and neck, on a par, parallel, similar, square, the same, tied, uniform **10** = **fair,** balanced, disinterested, dispassionate, equitable, fair and square, impartial, just, unbiased, unprejudiced **14 get even (with)** *Informal* = **pay back,** be revenged *or* revenge oneself, even the score, get one's own back, give tit for tat, pay (someone) back in his *or* her own coin, reciprocate, repay, requite, return like for like, settle the score, take an eye for an eye, take vengeance ◆ *adv* **17** = **despite,** disregarding, in spite of, notwithstanding **21 even as** = **while,** at the same time as, at the time that, during the time that, exactly as, just as, whilst **22 even so** = **nevertheless,** all the same, be that as it may, despite (that), however, in spite of (that), nonetheless, notwithstanding (that), still, yet
Antonyms *adj* ≠ **level:** asymmetrical, awry, bumpy, curving, rough, twisting, undulating, uneven, wavy ≠ **regular:** broken, changeable, changing, different, fluctuating, irregular, odd, uneven, variable ≠ **calm:** agitated, changeable, emotional, excitable, quick-tempered, unpredictable ≠ **equal:** disproportionate, ill-matched, imbalanced, irregular, unequal, uneven ≠ **fair:** biased, partial, prejudiced, unbalanced, unequal, unfair

even-handed *adj* = **fair,** balanced, disinterested, equitable, fair and square, impartial, just, unbiased, unprejudiced

evening *n* **1** = **dusk,** e'en (*arch. or poetic*), eve, even (*arch.*), eventide (*arch. or poetic*), gloaming (*Scot. or poetic*), twilight, vesper (*arch.*)

even out *vb* = **make** *or* **become level,** align, flatten, level, regularize, smooth, square, stabilize, steady

event *n* **1** = **incident,** adventure, affair, business, circumstance, episode, escapade, experience, fact, happening, matter, milestone, occasion, occurrence **2** *As in* **in the event** = **outcome,** conclusion, consequence, effect, end, issue, result, termination, upshot **3** = **competition,** bout, contest, game, tournament **4 in any event** *or* **at all events** = **whatever happens,** at any rate, come what may, in any case, regardless

even-tempered *adj* = **calm,** composed, cool, cool-headed, equable, imperturbable, level-headed, peaceful, placid, serene, steady, tranquil, unexcitable, unruffled
Antonyms *adj* emotional, excitable, hasty, highly-strung, hot-headed, hot-tempered, irascible, quick-tempered, temperamental, touchy, volatile

eventful *adj* = **exciting,** active, busy, consequential, critical, crucial, decisive, dramatic, fateful, full, historic, important, lively, memorable, momentous, notable, noteworthy, remarkable, significant
Antonyms *adj* commonplace, dull, humdrum, insignificant, ordinary, trivial, uneventful, unexceptional, unexciting, unimportant, uninteresting, unremarkable

eventual *adj* **1** = **final,** concluding, consequent, ensuing, future, later, overall, prospective, resulting, ultimate

eventuality *n* = **possibility,** case, chance, contingency, event, likelihood, probability

eventually *adv* **1** = **in the end,** after all, at the end of the day, finally, in the course of time, in the fullness of time, in the long run, one day, some day, some time, sooner or later, ultimately, when all is said and done

even up *vb* = **equalize,** balance, equal, match

ever *adv* **1, 2** = **at any time,** at all, at any period, at any point, by any chance, in any case, on any occasion **3** = **always,** at all times, aye (*Scot.*), constantly, continually, endlessly, eternally, everlastingly, evermore, for ever, incessantly, perpetually, relentlessly, to the end of time, unceasingly, unendingly

everlasting *adj* **1** = **eternal,** abiding, deathless, endless, immortal, imperishable, indestructible, infinite, interminable, never-ending, perpetual, timeless, undying **2** = **continual,** ceaseless, constant, continuous, endless, incessant, interminable, never-ending, unceasing, uninterrupted, unremitting
Antonyms *adj* ≠ **eternal:** brief, ephemeral, fleeting, impermanent, passing, short-lived, temporary, transient, transitory

evermore *adv* = **for ever,** always, eternally, ever, *in perpetuum,* to the end of time

every *determiner* **1** = **each,** all, each one, the whole number

everybody ❶ (ˈɛvrɪˌbɒdɪ) *pron* every person; everyone.

> **USAGE NOTE** See at **everyone.**

everyday ❶ (ˈɛvrɪˌdeɪ) *adj* **1** happening each day. **2** commonplace or usual. **3** suitable for or used on ordinary days.
Everyman (ˈɛvrɪˌmæn) *n* **1** a medieval English morality play in which the central figure represents mankind. **2** (*often not cap.*) the ordinary person; common man.
everyone ❶ (ˈɛvrɪˌwʌn, -wən) *pron* every person; everybody.

> **USAGE NOTE** *Everyone* and *everybody* are interchangeable, as are *no one* and *nobody*, and *someone* and *somebody*. Care should be taken to distinguish between *everyone* and *someone* as single words and *every one* and *some one* as two words, the latter form correctly being used to refer to each individual person or thing in a particular group: *every one of them is wrong.*

every one *pron* each person or thing in a group, without exception.
everything ❶ (ˈɛvrɪˌθɪŋ) *pron* **1** the entirety of a specified or implied class. **2** a great deal, esp. of something very important.
everywhere ❶ (ˈɛvrɪˌwɛə) *adv* to or in all parts or places.
evict ❶ (ɪˈvɪkt) *vb* (*tr*) **1** to expel (a tenant) from property by process of law; turn out. **2** to recover (property or the title to property) by judicial process or by virtue of a superior title. [C15: from LL *ēvincere*, from L: to vanquish utterly]
▸**eˈviction** *n* ▸**eˈvictor** *n*
evidence ❶ (ˈɛvɪdəns) *n* **1** ground for belief or disbelief; data on which to base proof or to establish truth or falsehood. **2** a mark or sign that makes evident. **3** *Law.* matter produced before a court of law in an attempt to prove or disprove a point in issue. **4 in evidence.** on display; apparent. ◆ *vb* **evidences, evidencing, evidenced.** (*tr*) **5** to make evident; show clearly. **6** to give proof of or evidence for.
evident ❶ (ˈɛvɪdənt) *adj* easy to see or understand; apparent. [C14: from L *ēvidēns*, from *vidēre* to see]
evidential (ˌɛvɪˈdɛnʃəl) *adj* relating to, serving as, or based on evidence.
▸ˌ**eviˈdentially** *adv*
evidently ❶ (ˈɛvɪdəntlɪ) *adv* **1** without question; clearly. **2** to all appearances; apparently.
evil ❶ (ˈiːvᵊl) *adj* **1** morally wrong or bad; wicked. **2** causing harm or injury. **3** marked or accompanied by misfortune: *an evil fate.* **4** (of temper, disposition, etc.) characterized by anger or spite. **5** infamous: *an evil reputation.* **6** offensive or unpleasant: *an evil smell.* **7** *Sl., chiefly US.* excellent or outstanding. ◆ *n* **8** the quality or an instance of being morally wrong; wickedness. **9** (*sometimes cap.*) a force or power that brings about wickedness or harm. ◆ *adv* **10** (*now usually in combination*) in an evil manner; badly: *evil-smelling.* [OE *yfel*]
▸ˈ**evilly** *adv* ▸ˈ**evilness** *n*
evildoer ❶ (ˈiːvᵊlˌduːə) *n* a person who does evil.
▸ˈ**evilˌdoing** *n*
evil eye *n* **the. 1** a look or glance superstitiously supposed to have the power of inflicting harm or injury. **2** the power to inflict harm, etc., by such a look.
▸ˌ**evil-ˈeyed** *adj*
evil-minded ❶ *adj* inclined to evil thoughts; malicious or spiteful.
▸ˌ**evil-ˈmindedly** *adv* ▸ˌ**evil-ˈmindedness** *n*
evince ❶ (ɪˈvɪns) *vb* **evinces, evincing, evinced.** (*tr*) to make evident; show (something) clearly. [C17: from L *ēvincere* to overcome; see EVICT]
▸**eˈvincible** *adj*

> **USAGE NOTE** *Evince* is sometimes wrongly used where *evoke* is meant: *the proposal evoked (not evinced) a storm of protest.*

eviscerate (ɪˈvɪsəˌreɪt) *vb* **eviscerates, eviscerating, eviscerated.** (*tr*) **1** to remove the internal organs of; disembowel. **2** to deprive of meaning or significance. [C17: from L *ēviscerāre*, from *viscera* entrails]
▸**eˌviscerˈation** *n* ▸**eˈviscerˌator** *n*
evocation (ˌɛvəˈkeɪʃən) *n* the act or an instance of evoking. [C17: from L: see EVOKE]
▸**evocative** (ɪˈvɒkətɪv) *adj*
evoke ❶ (ɪˈvəʊk) *vb* **evokes, evoking, evoked.** (*tr*) **1** to call or summon up (a memory, feeling, etc.), esp. from the past. **2** to provoke; elicit. **3** to cause (spirits) to appear; conjure up. [C17: from L *ēvocāre* to call forth, from *vocāre* to call]
▸**evocable** (ˈɛvəkəbᵊl) *adj* ▸**eˈvoker** *n*

> **USAGE NOTE** See at **evince** and **invoke.**

evolute (ˈɛvəˌluːt) *n* **1** a geometric curve that describes the locus of the centres of curvature of another curve (the **involute**). ◆ *adj* **2** *Biol.* having the margins rolled outwards. [C19: from L *ēvolūtus* unrolled, from *ēvolvere* to roll out, EVOLVE]
evolution ❶ (ˌiːvəˈluːʃən) *n* **1** *Biol.* a gradual change in the characteristics of a population of animals or plants over successive generations. **2** a gradual development, esp. to a more complex form: *the evolution of modern art.* **3** the act of throwing off, as heat, gas, vapour, etc. **4** a pattern formed by a series of movements or something similar. **5** an algebraic operation in which the root of a number, expression, etc., is extracted. **6** *Mil.* an exercise carried out in accordance with a set procedure or plan. [C17: from L *ēvolūtiō* an unrolling, from *ēvolvere* to EVOLVE]
▸ˌ**evoˈlutionary** *or* ˌ**evoˈlutional** *adj*
evolutionist (ˌiːvəˈluːʃənɪst) *n* **1** a person who believes in a theory of evolution. ◆ *adj* **2** of or relating to a theory of evolution.
▸ˌ**evoˈlutionism** *n* ▸ˌ**evolutionˈistic** *adj*
evolve ❶ (ɪˈvɒlv) *vb* **evolves, evolving, evolved. 1** to develop or cause to develop gradually. **2** (of animal or plant species) to undergo evolution of (organs or parts). **3** (*tr*) to yield, emit, or give off (heat, gas, vapour, etc.). [C17: from L *ēvolvere* to unfold, from *volvere* to roll]
▸**eˈvolvable** *adj* ▸**eˈvolvement** *n*
evzone (ˈɛvzəʊn) *n* a soldier in an elite Greek infantry regiment. [C19: from Mod. Gk, from Gk *euzōnos*, lit.: well-girt, from EU- + *zōne* girdle]

THESAURUS

everybody *pron* = **everyone**, all and sundry, each one, each person, every person, one and all, the whole world
everyday *adj* **1** = **daily**, quotidian **2** = **ordinary**, accustomed, banal, bog-standard (*Brit. & Irish sl.*), common, common or garden (*inf.*), commonplace, conventional, customary, dime-a-dozen (*inf.*), dull, familiar, frequent, habitual, informal, mundane, routine, run-of-the-mill, stock, unexceptional, unimaginative, usual, vanilla (*sl.*), wonted, workaday
Antonyms *adj* ≠ **daily:** infrequent, irregular, now and then, occasional, periodic ≠ **ordinary:** best, exceptional, exciting, extraordinary, incidental, individual, infrequent, interesting, irregular, now and then, occasional, original, outlandish, periodic, special, uncommon, unusual
everyone *pron* = **everybody**, all and sundry, each one, each person, every person, one and all, the whole world
everything *pron* **1** = **all**, each thing, the aggregate, the entirety, the lot, the sum, the total, the whole, the whole caboodle (*inf.*), the whole kit and caboodle (*inf.*), the whole lot
everywhere *adv* = **to** *or* **in every place**, all around, all over, far and wide *or* near, high and low, in each place, in every nook and cranny, omnipresent, the world over, ubiquitous, ubiquitously
evict *vb* **1** = **expel**, boot out (*inf.*), chuck out (*inf.*), dislodge, dispossess, eject, kick out (*inf.*), oust, put out, remove, show the door (to), throw on to the streets, throw out, turf out (*inf.*), turn out
eviction *n* **1** = **expulsion**, clearance, dislodgement, dispossession, ejection, ouster (*Law*), removal
evidence *n* **1, 2** = **proof**, affirmation, attestation, averment, confirmation, corroboration, data, declaration, demonstration, deposition, grounds, indication, manifestation, mark, sign, substantiation, testimony, token, witness ◆ *vb* **5, 6** = **show**, demonstrate, denote, display, evince, exhibit, indicate, manifest, prove, reveal, signify, testify to, witness
evident *adj* = **obvious**, apparent, blatant, bold, clear, conspicuous, incontestable, incontrovertible, indisputable, manifest, noticeable, palpable, patent, perceptible, plain, plain as the nose on your face, salient, tangible, unmistakable, visible
Antonyms *adj* ambiguous, concealed, doubtful, dubious, hidden, imperceptible, obscure, questionable, secret, uncertain, unclear, unknown, vague
evidently *adv* **1** = **obviously**, clearly, doubtless, doubtlessly, incontestably, incontrovertibly, indisputably, manifestly, patently, plainly, undoubtedly, unmistakably, without question **2** = **apparently**, it seems, it would seem, ostensibly, outwardly, seemingly, to all appearances
evil *adj* **1** = **wicked**, bad, base, corrupt, depraved, heinous, immoral, iniquitous, maleficent, malevolent, malicious, malignant, nefarious, reprobate, sinful, unholy, vicious, vile, villainous, wrong **2** = **harmful**, baneful (*arch.*), calamitous, catastrophic, deleterious, destructive, detrimental, dire, disastrous, hurtful, inauspicious, injurious, mischievous, painful, pernicious, ruinous, sorrowful, unfortunate, unlucky, woeful **6** = **offensive**, foul, mephitic, noxious, pestilential, putrid, unpleasant, vile ◆ *n* **8** = **wickedness**, badness, baseness, corruption, curse, depravity, heinousness, immorality, iniquity, maleficence, malignity, sin, sinfulness, turpitude, vice, viciousness, villainy, wrong, wrongdoing
evildoer *n* = **sinner**, bad hat (*inf., chiefly Brit*), blackguard, criminal, crook (*inf.*), culprit, delinquent, malefactor, mischief-maker, miscreant, offender, reprobate, rogue, villain, wrongdoer, wrong 'un (*inf.*)
evildoing *n* = **sin**, abomination, badness, crime, devilry, evil, fiendishness, harm, iniquity, injury, mischief-making, vice, viciousness, vileness, villainy, wickedness, wrongdoing
evil-minded *adj* = **nasty**, bitchy (*inf.*), depraved, dirty-minded, filthy, foul-mouthed, gossip-mongering, lewd, malicious, poisonous, salacious, snide, spiteful, venomous
evince *vb* = **show**, attest, bespeak, betoken, demonstrate, display, establish, evidence, exhibit, express, indicate, make clear, make evident, manifest, reveal, signify
evoke *vb* **1** = **arouse**, awaken, call, excite, give rise to, induce, recall, rekindle, stimulate, stir up, summon up **2** = **provoke**, call forth, educe (*rare*), elicit, produce **3** = **conjure up**, arouse, call, call forth, invoke, raise, summon
Antonyms *vb* ≠ **arouse:** contain, hold in check, inhibit, muffle, repress, restrain, smother, stifle, suppress
evolution *n* **2** = **development**, enlargement, evolvement, expansion, growth, increase, maturation, progress, progression, unfolding, unrolling, working out
evolve *vb* **1** = **develop**, disclose, educe, elabo-

ewe (juː) *n* **a** a female sheep. **b** (*as modifier*): *a ewe lamb.* [OE *ēowu*]

ewer ('juːə) *n* a large jug or pitcher with a wide mouth. [C14: from OF *evier*, from L *aquārius* water carrier, from *aqua* water]

ex[1] (ɛks) *prep* **1** *Finance.* excluding; without: *ex dividend.* **2** *Commerce.* without charge to the buyer until removed from: *ex warehouse.* [C19: from L: out of, from]

ex[2] (ɛks) *n Inf.* (a person's) former wife, husband, etc.

Ex. *Bible. abbrev. for* Exodus.

ex-[1] *prefix* **1** out of; outside of; from: *exclosure; exurbia.* **2** former: *ex-wife.* [from L, from *ex* (prep), identical with Gk *ex, ek;* see EC-]

ex-[2] *combining form.* a variant of **exo-** before a vowel: *exergonic.*

exa- *prefix* denoting 10^{18}: *exametres.* Symbol: E

exacerbate ❶ (ɪg'zæsəˌbeɪt, ɪk'sæs-) *vb* **exacerbates, exacerbating, exacerbated.** (*tr*) **1** to make (pain, disease, etc.) more intense; aggravate. **2** to irritate (a person). [C17: from L *exacerbāre* to irritate, from *acerbus* bitter]
▸**exˌacer'bation** *n*

exact ❶ (ɪg'zækt) *adj* **1** correct in every detail; strictly accurate. **2** precise, as opposed to approximate. **3** (*prenominal*) specific; particular. **4** operating with very great precision. **5** allowing no deviation from a standard; rigorous; strict. **6** based on measurement and the formulation of laws, as opposed to description and classification: *an exact science.* ◆ *vb* (*tr*) **7** to force or compel (payment, etc.); extort: *to exact tribute.* **8** to demand as a right; insist upon. **9** to call for or require. [C16: from L *exactus* driven out, from *exigere* to drive forth, from *agere* to drive]
▸**ex'actable** *adj* ▸**ex'actness** *n* ▸**ex'actor** *or* **ex'acter** *n*

exacting ❶ (ɪg'zæktɪŋ) *adj* making rigorous or excessive demands.
▸**ex'actingness** *n*

exaction ❶ (ɪg'zækʃən) *n* **1** the act or an instance of exacting. **2** an excessive or harsh demand, esp. for money. **3** a sum or payment exacted.

exactitude ❶ (ɪg'zæktɪˌtjuːd) *n* the quality of being exact; precision; accuracy.

exactly ❶ (ɪg'zæktlɪ) *adv* **1** in an exact manner; accurately or precisely. **2** in every respect; just. ◆ *sentence substitute.* **3** just so!, precisely! **4 not exactly.** *Ironical.* not at all; by no means.

exacum ('ɛksəkəm) *n* any of various Asian flowering herbs. [NL, from EX-[1] + Gk *ago* to arrive]

exaggerate ❶ (ɪg'zædʒəˌreɪt) *vb* **exaggerates, exaggerating, exaggerated. 1** to regard or represent as larger or greater, more important or more successful, etc., than is true. **2** (*tr*) to make greater, more noticeable, etc. [C16: from L *exaggerāre* to magnify, from *aggerāre* to heap, from *agger* heap]
▸**ex'aggerˌated** *adj* ▸**exˌagger'ation** *n* ▸**ex'aggerˌator** *n*

ex all *adv, adj Finance.* without the right to any benefits: *shares quoted ex all.*

exalt ❶ (ɪg'zɔːlt) *vb* (*tr*) **1** to elevate in rank, dignity, etc. **2** to praise highly; extol. **3** to stimulate; excite. **4** to fill with joy or delight; elate. [C15: from L *exaltāre* to raise, from *altus* high]
▸**ex'alted** *adj* ▸**ex'alter** *n*

> **USAGE NOTE** *Exalt* is sometimes wrongly used where *exult* is meant: *he was exulting* (not *exalting*) *in his win earlier that day.*

exaltation ❶ (ˌɛgzɔːl'teɪʃən) *n* **1** the act of exalting or state of being exalted. **2** exhilaration; elation; rapture.

exam (ɪg'zæm) *n* short for **examination.**

examination ❶ (ɪgˌzæmɪ'neɪʃən) *n* **1** the act of examining or state of being examined. **2** *Education.* **2a** written exercises, oral questions, etc., set to test a candidate's knowledge and skill. **2b** (*as modifier*): *an examination paper.* **3** *Med.* **3a** physical inspection of a patient. **3b** laboratory study of secretory or excretory products, tissue samples, etc. **4** *Law.* the formal interrogation of a person on oath.
▸**exˌami'national** *adj*

examine ❶ (ɪg'zæmɪn) *vb* **examines, examining, examined.** (*tr*) **1** to inspect or scrutinize carefully or in detail; investigate. **2** *Education.* to test the knowledge or skill of (a candidate) in (a subject or activity) by written or oral questions, etc. **3** *Law.* to interrogate (a person) formally on oath. **4** *Med.* to investigate the state of health of (a patient). [C14: from OF, from L *exāmināre* to weigh, from *exāmen* means of weighing]
▸**ex'aminable** *adj* ▸**exˌami'nee** *n* ▸**ex'aminer** *n* ▸**ex'amining** *adj*

example ❶ (ɪg'zɑːmpᵊl) *n* **1** a specimen or instance that is typical of its group or set; sample. **2** a person, action, thing, etc., that is worthy of imitation; pattern. **3** a precedent, illustration of a principle, or model. **4** a punishment or the recipient of a punishment intended to serve as a warning. **5 for example.** as an illustration; for instance. ◆ *vb* **examples, exampling, exampled. 6** (*tr; now usually passive*) to present an example of; exemplify. [C14: from OF, from L *exemplum* pattern, from *eximere* to take out]

exanthema (ˌɛksæn'θiːmə) *n, pl* **exanthemata** (-'θiːmətə) *or* **exanthemas.** a skin rash occurring in a disease such as measles. [C17: via LL from Gk, from *exanthein* to burst forth, from *anthein* to blossom]

exasperate ❶ (ɪg'zɑːspəˌreɪt) *vb* **exasperates, exasperating, exasperated.** (*tr*) **1** to cause great irritation or anger to. **2** to cause (something unpleasant) to worsen; aggravate. [C16: from L *exasperāre* to make rough, from *asper* rough]
▸**ex'asperˌatedly** *adv* ▸**ex'asperˌatingly** *adv* ▸**exˌasper'ation** *n*

THESAURUS

rate, enlarge, expand, grow, increase, mature, open, progress, unfold, unroll, work out

exacerbate *vb* **1 = make worse**, aggravate, inflame, intensify, worsen **2 = irritate**, aggravate (*inf.*), embitter, enrage, envenom, exasperate, infuriate, madden, provoke, vex

exact *adj* **1-3 = accurate**, careful, correct, definite, explicit, express, faithful, faultless, identical, literal, methodical, on the money (*US*), orderly, particular, precise, right, specific, true, unequivocal, unerring, veracious, very **5 = meticulous**, careful, exacting, painstaking, punctilious, rigorous, scrupulous, severe, strict ◆ *vb* **7-9 = demand**, call for, claim, command, compel, extort, extract, force, impose, insist upon, require, squeeze, wrest, wring
Antonyms *adj* ≠ **accurate:** approximate, careless, imprecise, inaccurate, incorrect, indefinite, inexact, loose, rough, slovenly

exacting *adj* **= demanding**, difficult, hard, harsh, imperious, oppressive, painstaking, rigid, rigorous, severe, stern, strict, stringent, taxing, tough, unsparing
Antonyms *adj* easy, easy-peasy (*sl.*), effortless, no bother, simple, undemanding

exaction *n* **1 = demand**, compulsion, contribution, extortion, imposition, oppression, rapacity, requirement, requisition, shakedown (*US sl.*), squeeze (*inf.*), tribute

exactitude *n* **= precision**, accuracy, carefulness, correctness, exactness, faithfulness, faultlessness, nicety, orderliness, painstakingness, preciseness, promptitude, regularity, rigorousness, rigour, scrupulousness, strictness, truth, unequivocalness, veracity

exactly *adv* **1 = precisely**, accurately, carefully, correctly, definitely, explicitly, faithfully, faultlessly, literally, methodically, rigorously, scrupulously, severely, strictly, truly, truthfully, unequivocally, unerringly, veraciously **2 = in every respect**, absolutely, bang, explicitly, expressly, indeed, just, on the button (*inf.*), particularly, precisely, prompt (*inf.*), quite, specifically, to the letter ◆ *sentence substitute* **3 = precisely**, absolutely, assuredly, as you say, certainly, indeed, just so, of course, quite, quite so, spot-on (*Brit. inf.*), truly **4 not exactly** *Ironical* **= not at all**, by no means, certainly not, hardly, in no manner, in no way, not by any means, not quite, not really

exactness *n* **1 = precision**, accuracy, carefulness, correctness, exactitude, faithfulness, faultlessness, nicety, orderliness, painstakingness, preciseness, promptitude, regularity, rigorousness, rigour, scrupulousness, strictness, truth, unequivocalness, veracity
Antonyms *n* imprecision, inaccuracy, incorrectness, inexactness, unfaithfulness

exaggerate *vb* **1 = overstate**, amplify, blow out of all proportion, embellish, embroider, emphasize, enlarge, exalt, hyperbolize, inflate, lay it on thick (*inf.*), magnify, make a federal case of (*US inf.*), make a mountain out of a molehill (*inf.*), make a production (out) of (*inf.*), overdo, overemphasize, overestimate

exaggerated *adj* **1 = overstated**, amplified, exalted, excessive, extravagant, fulsome, highly coloured, hyped, hyperbolic, inflated, overblown, overdone, overestimated, over the top (*inf.*), pretentious, tall (*inf.*)

exaggeration *n* **1 = overstatement**, amplification, embellishment, emphasis, enlargement, exaltation, excess, extravagance, hyperbole, inflation, magnification, overemphasis, overestimation, pretension, pretentiousness
Antonyms *n* litotes, meiosis, restraint, underplaying, understatement

exalt *vb* **1 = raise**, advance, aggrandize, dignify, elevate, ennoble, honour, promote, upgrade **2 = praise**, acclaim, apotheosize, applaud, bless, crack up (*inf.*), extol, glorify, idolize, laud, magnify (*arch.*), pay homage to, pay tribute to, reverence, set on a pedestal, worship **3 = stimulate**, animate, arouse, electrify, elevate, excite, fire the imagination (of), heighten, inspire, inspirit, uplift **4 = elate**, delight, exhilarate, fill with joy, thrill

exaltation *n* **1 = glorification**, acclamation, advancement, aggrandizement, apotheosis, elevation, ennoblement, lionization, magnification, praise, promotion, tribute, worship **2 = elation**, bliss, delight, ecstasy, exhilaration, exultation, joy, joyousness, jubilation, rapture, transport

exalted *adj* **1 = high-ranking**, august, dignified, elevated, eminent, grand, high, honoured, lofty, prestigious **4 = elated**, blissful, ecstatic, elevated, exhilarated, exultant, in seventh heaven, inspired, jubilant, rapturous, transported, uplifted

examination *n* **1 = inspection**, analysis, assay, checkup, exploration, interrogation, investigation, observation, once-over (*inf.*), perusal, recce (*sl.*), research, review, scrutiny, search, study, survey, test, trial **4 = questioning**, catechism, inquiry, inquisition, probe, quiz, test

examine *vb* **1 = inspect**, analyse, appraise, assay, check, check out, consider, explore, go over *or* through, investigate, look over, peruse, ponder, pore over, probe, recce (*sl.*), research, review, scan, scrutinize, sift, study, survey, take stock of, test, vet, weigh, work over **3 = question**, catechize, cross-examine, grill (*inf.*), inquire, interrogate, quiz, test

example *n* **1 = specimen**, case, case in point, exemplification, illustration, instance, sample **2, 3 = model**, archetype, exemplar, ideal, illustration, norm, paradigm, paragon, pattern, precedent, prototype, standard **4 = warning**, admonition, caution, lesson **5 for example = as an illustration**, by way of illustration, e.g., *exempli gratia,* for instance, to cite an instance, to illustrate

exasperate *vb* **1 = irritate**, aggravate, anger, annoy, bug (*inf.*), embitter, enrage, exacerbate, excite, gall, get on one's nerves (*inf.*), get on one's wick (*Brit. sl.*), hassle (*inf.*), incense, inflame, infuriate, irk, madden, nark (*Brit., Austral., & NZ sl.*), needle (*inf.*), nettle, peeve (*inf.*), pique, provoke, rankle, rile (*inf.*), rouse, try the patience of, vex
Antonyms *vb* appease, assuage, calm, conciliate, mollify, pacify, placate, soothe

exasperating *adj* **1 = irritating**, aggravating (*inf.*), annoying, enough to drive one up the

ex cathedra (ɛks kəˈθiːdrə) *adj, adv* **1** with authority. **2** *RC Church.* (of doctrines of faith or morals) defined by the pope as infallibly true, to be accepted by all Catholics. [L, lit.: from the chair]

excavate ➊ (ˈɛkskəˌveɪt) *vb* **excavates, excavating, excavated. 1** to remove (soil, earth, etc.) by digging; dig out. **2** to make (a hole or tunnel) in (solid matter) by hollowing. **3** to unearth (buried objects) methodically to discover information about the past. [C16: from L *cavāre* to make hollow, from *cavus* hollow]
▸**ˌexcaˈvation** *n* ▸**ˈexcaˌvator** *n*

exceed ➊ (ɪkˈsiːd) *vb* **1** to be superior (to); excel. **2** (*tr*) to go beyond the limit or bounds of. **3** (*tr*) to be greater in degree or quantity than. [C14: from L *excēdere* to go beyond]
▸**exˈceedable** *adj* ▸**exˈceeder** *n*

exceeding ➊ (ɪkˈsiːdɪŋ) *adj* **1** very great; exceptional or excessive. ◆ *adv* **2** *Arch.* to a great or unusual degree.
▸**exˈceedingly** *adv*

excel ➊ (ɪkˈsɛl) *vb* **excels, excelling, excelled. 1** to be superior to (another or others); surpass. **2** (*intr;* foll. by *in* or *at*) to be outstandingly good or proficient. [C15: from L *excellere* to rise up]

excellence ➊ (ˈɛksələns) *n* **1** the state or quality of excelling or being exceptionally good; extreme merit. **2** an action, feature, etc., in which a person excels.
▸**ˈexcellent** *adj* ▸**ˈexcellently** *adv*

Excellency (ˈɛksələnsɪ) *or* **Excellence** *n, pl* **Excellencies** *or* **Excellences. 1** (usually preceded by *Your, His,* or *Her*) a title used to address or refer to a high-ranking official, such as an ambassador. **2** *RC Church.* a title of bishops and archbishops in many non-English-speaking countries.

excelsior (ɪkˈsɛlsɪˌɔː) *interj, n* **1** excellent: used as a motto and as a trademark for various products. **2** upward. [C19: from L: higher]

except ➊ (ɪkˈsɛpt) *prep* **1** Also: **except for.** other than; apart from. **2 except that.** (*conj*) but for the fact that; were it not true that. ◆ *conj* **3** an archaic word for **unless. 4** *Inf. (not standard in the US)* except that; but for the fact that. ◆ *vb* **5** (*tr*) to leave out; omit; exclude. **6** (*intr;* often foll. by *to*) *Rare.* to take exception; object. [C14: from OF *excepter* to leave out, from L *excipere* to take out]

excepting (ɪkˈsɛptɪŋ) *prep* **1** except; except for (esp. in **not excepting**). ◆ *conj* **2** an archaic word for **unless.**

> **USAGE NOTE** The use of *excepting* is considered by many people to be acceptable only after *not, only, always,* or *without.* Elsewhere *except* is preferred: *every country agreed to the proposal except* (not *excepting*) *Spain; he was well again except for* (not *excepting*) *a slight pain in his chest.*

exception ➊ (ɪkˈsɛpʃən) *n* **1** the act of excepting or fact of being excepted; omission. **2** anything excluded from or not in conformance with a general rule, principle, class, etc. **3** criticism, esp. adverse; objection. **4** *Law.* (formerly) a formal objection in legal proceedings. **5 take exception. 5a** (usually foll. by *to*) to make objections (to); demur (at). **5b** (often foll. by *at*) to be offended (by); be resentful (at).

exceptionable ➊ (ɪkˈsɛpʃənəbᵊl) *adj* open to or subject to objection; objectionable.
▸**exˈceptionableness** *n* ▸**exˈceptionably** *adv*

exceptional ➊ (ɪkˈsɛpʃənᵊl) *adj* **1** forming an exception; not ordinary. **2** having much more than average intelligence, ability, or skill.

excerpt ➊ *n* (ˈɛksɜːpt). **1** a part or passage taken from a book, speech, etc.; extract. ◆ *vb* (ɛkˈsɜːpt). **2** (*tr*) to take (a part or passage) from a book, speech, etc. [C17: from L *excerptum,* lit.: (something) picked out, from *excerpere* to select, from *carpere* to pluck]
▸**exˈcerptible** *adj* ▸**exˈcerption** *n* ▸**exˈcerptor** *n*

excess ➊ *n* (ɪkˈsɛs, ˈɛksɛs). **1** the state or act of going beyond normal, sufficient, or permitted limits. **2** an immoderate or abnormal amount. **3** the amount, number, etc., by which one thing exceeds another. **4** overindulgence or intemperance. **5** *Insurance, chiefly Brit.* a specified contribution towards the cost of a claim, payable by the policyholder. US name: **deductible. 6 in excess of.** of more than; over. **7 to excess.** to an inordinate extent; immoderately. ◆ *adj* (ˈɛksɛs, ɪkˈsɛs). (*usually prenominal*) **8** more than normal, necessary, or permitted; surplus: *excess weight.* **9** payable as a result of previous underpayment: *excess postage.* [C14: from L *excēdere* to go beyond; see EXCEED]

excessive ➊ (ɪkˈsɛsɪv) *adj* exceeding the normal or permitted limits; immoderate; inordinate.
▸**exˈcessively** *adv* ▸**exˈcessiveness** *n*

excess luggage *or* **baggage** *n* luggage that is more in weight or number of pieces than an airline, etc., will carry free.

exchange ➊ (ɪksˈtʃeɪndʒ) *vb* **exchanges, exchanging, exchanged. 1** (*tr*) to give up or transfer (one thing) for an equivalent. **2** (*tr*) to give and receive (information, ideas, etc.); interchange. **3** (*tr*) to replace (one thing) with another, esp. to replace unsatisfactory goods. **4** to hand over (goods) in return for the equivalent value in kind; barter; trade. ◆ *n* **5** the act or process of exchanging. **6a** anything given or received as an equivalent or substitute for something else. **6b** (*as modifier*): *an exchange student.* **7** an argument or quarrel. **8** Also called: **telephone exchange.** a switching centre in which telephone lines are interconnected. **9** a place where securities or commodities are sold, bought, or traded, esp. by brokers or merchants. **10a** the system by which commercial debts are settled by commercial documents, esp. bills of exchange, instead of by direct payment of money. **10b** the percentage or fee charged for accepting payment in this manner. **11** a transfer or interchange of sums of money of equivalent value, as between different currencies. **12 win** (*or* **lose**) **the exchange.** *Chess.* to win (*or* lose) a rook in return for a bishop or knight. ◆ See also **bill of exchange, exchange rate, labour exchange.** [C14: from Anglo-French *eschaungier,* from Vulgar L *excambiāre* (unattested), from L *cambīre* to barter]
▸**exˈchangeable** *adj* ▸**exˌchangeaˈbility** *n* ▸**exˈchangeably** *adv* ▸**exˈchanger** *n*

exchange rate *n* the rate at which the currency unit of one country may be exchanged for that of another.

Exchange Rate Mechanism *n* the mechanism used in the European Monetary System in which participating governments commit themselves to maintain the values of their currencies in relation to the ECU. Abbrev.: **ERM.**

THESAURUS

wall (*inf.*), enough to try the patience of a saint, galling, infuriating, irksome, maddening, provoking, vexing

exasperation *n* **1 = irritation,** aggravation (*inf.*), anger, annoyance, exacerbation, fury, ire (*literary*), passion, pique, provocation, rage, vexation, wrath

excavate *vb* **1-3 = dig out,** burrow, cut, delve, dig, dig up, gouge, hollow, mine, quarry, scoop, trench, tunnel, uncover, unearth

excavation *n* **1-3 = hole,** burrow, cavity, cut, cutting, dig, diggings, ditch, dugout, hollow, mine, pit, quarry, shaft, trench, trough

exceed *vb* **1 = surpass,** beat, be superior to, better, cap (*inf.*), eclipse, excel, go beyond, knock spots off, outdistance, outdo, outreach, outrun, outshine, outstrip, overtake, pass, put in the shade (*inf.*), run rings around (*inf.*), surmount, top, transcend **2 = go over the limit of,** go beyond the bounds of, go over the top, overstep

exceeding *adj* **1 = extraordinary,** enormous, exceptional, excessive, great, huge, pre-eminent, streets ahead, superior, superlative, surpassing, vast

exceedingly *adv* **1 = extremely,** enormously, especially, exceptionally, excessively, extraordinarily, greatly, highly, hugely, inordinately, seriously (*inf.*), superlatively, surpassingly, to a fault, to the nth degree, unusually, vastly, very

excel *vb* **1 = be superior,** beat, better, cap (*inf.*), eclipse, exceed, go beyond, outdo, outrival, outshine, pass, put in the shade (*inf.*), run rings around (*inf.*), steal the show (*inf.*), surmount, surpass, top, transcend **2** *with* **in** *or* **at = be good at,** be master of, be proficient in, be skilful at, be talented at, have (something) down to a fine art, predominate in, shine at, show talent in

excellence *n* **1 = high quality,** distinction, eminence, fineness, goodness, greatness, merit, perfection, pre-eminence, purity, superiority, supremacy, transcendence, virtue, worth

excellent *adj* **1 = outstanding,** admirable, brilliant, capital, champion, choice, cracking, distinguished, estimable, exemplary, exquisite, fine, first-class, first-rate, good, great, meritorious, notable, noted, prime, select, sovereign, sterling, superb, superior, superlative, tiptop, top-notch (*inf.*), world-class, worthy
Antonyms *adj* abysmal, bad, dreadful, faulty, imperfect, incompetent, inexpert, inferior, lousy (*sl.*), mediocre, no great shakes (*inf.*), poor, rotten (*inf.*), second-class, second-rate, substandard, terrible, unskilled

except *prep* **1 = apart from,** bar, barring, besides, but, excepting, excluding, exclusive of, omitting, other than, save (*arch.*), saving, with the exception of ◆ *vb* **5 = exclude,** ban, bar, disallow, leave out, omit, pass over, reject, rule out

exception *n* **1 = exclusion,** debarment, disallowment, excepting, leaving out, omission, passing over, rejection **2 = special case,** anomaly, departure, deviation, freak, inconsistency, irregularity, oddity, peculiarity, quirk **5 take exception = object to,** be offended at, be resentful of, demur at, disagree with, quibble at, take offence at, take umbrage at

exceptionable *adj* **= objectionable,** disagreeable, inappropriate, unacceptable, unbearable, undesirable, unsatisfactory, unwelcome

exceptional *adj* **1 = unusual,** aberrant, abnormal, anomalous, atypical, deviant, extraordinary, inconsistent, irregular, odd, peculiar, rare, singular, special, strange, uncommon **2 = remarkable,** excellent, extraordinary, marvellous, notable, one in a million, outstanding, phenomenal, prodigious, special, superior
Antonyms *adj* ≠ **unusual:** average, common, customary, familiar, normal, ordinary, regular, straightforward, typical, unexceptional, unremarkable, usual ≠ **remarkable:** average, awful, bad, lousy (*sl.*), mediocre, no great shakes (*inf.*), second-rate

excerpt *n* **1 = extract,** citation, fragment, part, passage, pericope, piece, portion, quotation, quote (*inf.*), section, selection ◆ *vb* **2 = extract,** cite, cull, pick out, quote, select, take

excess *n* **2, 3 = surfeit,** glut, leftover, overabundance, overdose, overflow, overload, plethora, remainder, superabundance, superfluity, surplus, too much **4 = overindulgence,** debauchery, dissipation, dissoluteness, exorbitance, extravagance, immoderation, intemperance, prodigality, unrestraint ◆ *adj* **8 = spare,** extra, leftover, redundant, remaining, residual, superfluous, surplus
Antonyms *n* ≠ **surfeit:** dearth, deficiency, insufficiency, lack, shortage, want ≠ **overindulgence:** moderation, restraint, self-control, self-discipline, self-restraint, temperance

excessive *adj* **= immoderate,** disproportionate, enormous, exaggerated, exorbitant, extravagant, extreme, fulsome, inordinate, intemperate, needless, O.T.T. (*sl.*), overdone, overmuch, over the odds, over the top (*sl.*), prodigal, profligate, superfluous, too much, unconscionable, undue, unfair, unreasonable

exchange *vb* **1 = interchange,** bandy, barter, change, commute, convert into, reciprocate, swap, switch, trade, truck ◆ *n* **5 = interchange,** barter, dealing, quid pro quo, reciprocity, sub-

exchequer (ɪks'tʃɛkə) *n* **1** (*often cap.*) *Government.* (in Britain and certain other countries) the accounting department of the Treasury. **2** *Inf.* personal funds; finances. [C13 (in the sense: chessboard, counting table): from OF *eschequier,* from *eschec* CHECK]

excisable (ɪk'saɪzəbᵊl) *adj* **1** liable to an excise tax. **2** suitable for deletion.

excise[1] ❶ *n* ('ɛksaɪz, ɛk'saɪz). **1** Also called: **excise tax.** a tax on goods, such as spirits, produced for the home market. **2** a tax paid for a licence to carry out various trades, sports, etc. **3** *Brit.* that section of the government service responsible for the collection of excise, now the Board of Customs and Excise. ◆ *vb* (ɪk'saɪz), **excises, excising, excised. 4** (*tr*) *Rare.* to compel (a person) to pay excise. [C15: prob. from MDu. *excijs,* prob. from OF *assise* a sitting, assessment, from L *assidēre* to sit beside, assist in judging]
▸**ex'cisable** *adj*

excise[2] ❶ (ɪk'saɪz) *vb* **excises, excising, excised.** (*tr*) **1** to delete (a passage, sentence, etc.). **2** to remove (an organ or part) surgically. [C16: from L *excīdere* to cut down]
▸**excision** (ɪk'sɪʒən) *n*

exciseman ('ɛksaɪz,mæn) *n, pl* **excisemen.** *Brit.* (formerly) a government agent whose function was to collect excise and prevent smuggling.

excitable ❶ (ɪk'saɪtəbᵊl) *adj* **1** easily excited; volatile. **2** (esp. of a nerve) ready to respond to a stimulus.
▸**ex,cita'bility** *or* **ex'citableness** *n*

excitation (,ɛksɪ'teɪʃən) *n* **1** the act or process of exciting or state of being excited. **2** a means of exciting or cause of excitement. **3** the current in a field coil of a generator, motor, etc., or the magnetizing current in a transformer. **4** the action of a stimulus on an animal or plant organ, inducing it to respond.

excite ❶ (ɪk'saɪt) *vb* **excites, exciting, excited.** (*tr*) **1** to arouse (a person), esp. to pleasurable anticipation or nervous agitation. **2** to arouse or elicit (an emotion, response, etc.); evoke. **3** to cause or bring about; stir up. **4** to arouse sexually. **5** *Physiol.* to cause a response in or increase the activity of (an organ, tissue, or part); stimulate. **6** to raise (an atom, molecule, etc.) from the ground state to a higher energy level. **7** to supply electricity to (the coils of a generator or motor) in order to create a magnetic field. [C14: from L *exciēre* to stimulate, from *ciēre* to set in motion, rouse]
▸**ex'citant** *n* ▸**ex'citative** *or* **ex'citatory** *adj* ▸**ex'citer** *or* **ex'citor** *n*

excited ❶ (ɪk'saɪtɪd) *adj* **1** emotionally aroused, esp. to pleasure or agitation. **2** characterized by excitement. **3** sexually aroused. **4** (of an atom, molecule, etc.) having an energy level above the ground state.
▸**ex'citedness** *n*

excitement ❶ (ɪk'saɪtmənt) *n* **1** the state of being excited. **2** a person or thing that excites.

exciting ❶ (ɪk'saɪtɪŋ) *adj* causing excitement; stirring; stimulating.
▸**ex'citingly** *adv*

exclaim ❶ (ɪk'skleɪm) *vb* to cry out or speak suddenly or excitedly, as from surprise, delight, horror, etc. [C16: from L *exclāmāre,* from *clāmāre* to shout]
▸**ex'claimer** *n*

exclamation ❶ (,ɛksklə'meɪʃən) *n* **1** an abrupt or excited cry or utterance; ejaculation. **2** the act of exclaiming.
▸**,excla'mational** *adj* ▸**ex'clamatory** *adj*

exclamation mark *or US* **point** *n* **1** the punctuation mark ! used after exclamations and vehement commands. **2** this mark used for any other purpose, as to draw attention to an obvious mistake, in road warning signs, etc.

exclave ('ɛkskleɪv) *n* a part of a country entirely surrounded by foreign territory: viewed from the position of the home country. [C20: from EX-[1] + *-clave,* on the model of ENCLAVE]

exclosure (ɪk'skləʊʒə) *n* an area of land fenced round to keep out unwanted animals.

exclude ❶ (ɪk'sklu:d) *vb* **excludes, excluding, excluded.** (*tr*) **1** to keep out; prevent from entering. **2** to reject or not consider; leave out. **3** to expel forcibly; eject. [C14: from L *exclūdere,* from *claudere* to shut]
▸**ex'cludable** *or* **ex'cludible** *adj* ▸**ex'cluder** *n*

exclusion ❶ (ɪk'sklu:ʒən) *n* the act or an instance of excluding or the state of being excluded.
▸**ex'clusionary** *adj*

exclusion principle *n* See **Pauli exclusion principle.**

exclusive ❶ (ɪk'sklu:sɪv) *adj* **1** excluding all else; rejecting other considerations, events, etc. **2** belonging to a particular individual or group and to no other; not shared. **3** belonging to or catering for a privileged minority, esp. a fashionable clique. **4** (*postpositive;* foll. by *to*) limited (to); found only (in). **5** single; unique; only. **6** separate and incompatible. **7** (*immediately postpositive*) not including the numbers, dates, letters, etc., mentioned. **8** (*postpositive;* foll. by *of*) except (for); not taking account (of). **9** *Logic.* (of a disjunction) true if only one rather than both of its component propositions is true. ◆ *n* **10** an exclusive story; a story reported in only one newspaper.
▸**ex'clusively** *adv* ▸**exclusivity** (,ɛksklu:'sɪvɪtɪ) *or* **ex'clusiveness** *n*

exclusive OR circuit *or* **gate** *n Electronics.* a computer logic circuit having two or more input wires and one output wire and giving a high-voltage output signal if a low-voltage signal is fed to one or more, but not all, of the input wires. Cf. **OR circuit.**

excommunicate ❶ *RC Church.* ◆ *vb* (,ɛkskə'mju:nɪ,keɪt), **excommunicates, excommunicating, excommunicated. 1** (*tr*) to sentence (a member of the Church) to exclusion from the communion of believers and from the privileges and public prayers of the Church. ◆ *adj* (,ɛkskə'mju:nɪkɪt, -,keɪt). **2** having incurred such a sentence. ◆ *n* (,ɛkskə'mju:nɪkɪt, -,keɪt). **3** an excommunicated person. [C15: from LL *excommūnicāre,* lit.: to exclude from the community, from L *commūnis* COMMON]
▸**,excom,muni'cation** *n* ▸**,excom'muni,cator** *n*

excoriate (ɪk'skɔ:rɪ,eɪt) *vb* **excoriates, excoriating, excoriated.** (*tr*) **1** to strip the skin from (a person or animal). **2** to denounce vehemently. [C15: from LL *excoriāre* to strip, flay, from L *corium* skin, hide]
▸**ex,cori'ation** *n*

excrement ❶ ('ɛkskrɪmənt) *n* waste matter discharged from the body, esp. faeces; excreta. [C16: from L *excernere* to sift, EXCRETE]
▸**excremental** (,ɛkskrɪ'mentᵊl) *or* **excrementitious** (,ɛkskrɪmɛn'tɪʃəs) *adj*

excrescence ❶ (ɪk'skrɛsᵊns) *n* a projection or protuberance, esp. an outgrowth from an organ or part of the body.
▸**ex'crescent** *adj* ▸**excrescential** (,ɛkskrɪ'sɛnʃəl) *adj*

excreta (ɪk'skri:tə) *pl n* waste matter, such as urine, faeces, or sweat, discharged from the body. [C19: NL, from L: see EXCRETE]
▸**ex'cretal** *adj*

excrete ❶ (ɪk'skri:t) *vb* **excretes, excreting, excreted. 1** to discharge (waste matter, such as urine, sweat, or faeces) from the body. **2** (of plants) to eliminate (waste matter) through the leaves, roots, etc. [C17: from L *excernere* to separate, discharge, from *cernere* to sift]
▸**ex'creter** *n* ▸**ex'cretion** *n* ▸**ex'cretive** *or* **ex'cretory** *adj*

THESAURUS

stitution, swap, switch, tit for tat, trade, traffic, truck **9** = **market**, Bourse

excise[1] *n* **1** = **tax**, customs, duty, impost, levy, surcharge, tariff, toll

excise[2] *vb* **1** = **delete**, cross out, cut, destroy, eradicate, erase, expunge, exterminate, extirpate, strike out, wipe from the face of the earth **2** = **cut off** *or* **out**, extract, remove

excision *n* **1** = **deletion**, destruction, eradication, extermination, extirpation, removal

excitability *n* **1** = **nervousness**, high spirits, hot-headedness, restiveness, restlessness, volatility

excitable *adj* **1** = **nervous**, edgy, emotional, hasty, highly strung, hot-headed, hot-tempered, irascible, mercurial, passionate, quick-tempered, sensitive, susceptible, temperamental, testy, touchy, uptight (*inf.*), violent, volatile
Antonyms *adj* calm, cool, cool-headed, even-tempered, imperturbable, laid-back (*inf.*), placid, unexcitable, unruffled

excite *vb* **1-3** = **arouse**, agitate, animate, awaken, elicit, evoke, fire, foment, galvanize, incite, inflame, inspire, instigate, kindle, move, provoke, quicken, rouse, stimulate, stir up, waken, whet, work up

excited *adj* **1** = **worked up**, aflame, agitated, animated, aroused, awakened, discomposed, disturbed, enthusiastic, feverish, flurried, moved, nervous, overwrought, roused, stimulated, stirred, thrilled, tumultuous, wild

excitement *n* **1** = **agitation**, action, activity, ado, adventure, animation, commotion, discomposure, elation, enthusiasm, ferment, fever, flurry, furore, heat, kicks (*inf.*), passion, perturbation, thrill, tumult, warmth **2** = **stimulus**, impulse, incitement, instigation, motivation, motive, provocation, stimulation, urge

exciting *adj* = **stimulating**, dramatic, electrifying, exhilarating, inspiring, intoxicating, moving, provocative, rip-roaring, rousing, sensational, sexy (*inf.*), stirring, thrilling, titillating
Antonyms *adj* boring, dreary, dull, flat, humdrum, mind-numbing, monotonous, unexciting, uninspiring, uninteresting

exclaim *vb* = **cry out**, call, call out, cry, declare, ejaculate, proclaim, shout, utter, vociferate, yell

exclamation *n* **1** = **cry**, call, ejaculation, expletive, interjection, outcry, shout, utterance, vociferation, yell

exclude *vb* **1** = **keep out**, ban, bar, black, blackball, boycott, debar, disallow, embargo, forbid, interdict, ostracize, prohibit, proscribe, refuse, shut out, veto **2** = **leave out**, count out, eliminate, except, ignore, not count, omit, pass over, preclude, reject, repudiate, rule out, set aside **3** = **remove**, bounce (*sl.*), drive out, eject, evict, expel, force out, get rid of, oust, throw out
Antonyms *vb* ≠ **keep out, remove:** accept, admit, allow, let in, permit, receive, welcome ≠ **leave out:** accept, count, include

exclusion *n* = **ban**, bar, boycott, debarment, disqualification, embargo, forbiddance, interdict, nonadmission, preclusion, prohibition, proscription, refusal, rejection, removal, veto

exclusive *adj* **2** = **sole**, absolute, complete, entire, full, only, private, single, total, undivided, unique, unshared, whole **3** = **select**, aristocratic, chic, choice, cliquish, closed, elegant, fashionable, high-toned, limited, narrow, posh (*inf., chiefly Brit.*), private, restricted, restrictive, ritzy (*sl.*), snobbish, top-drawer, up-market **4** = **limited**, confined, peculiar, restricted, unique **8** *with* **of** = **except for**, debarring, excepting, excluding, leaving aside, not counting, omitting, restricting, ruling out
Antonyms *adj* ≠ **sole, limited:** inclusive, nonexclusive, partial, shared ≠ **select:** common, communal, open, popular, public, unrestricted

excommunicate *vb* **1** = **expel**, anathematize, ban, banish, cast out, denounce, eject, exclude, proscribe, remove, repudiate, unchurch

excrement *n* = **faeces**, crap (*taboo sl.*), droppings, dung, excreta, mess (*especially of a domestic animal*), motion, ordure, shit (*taboo sl.*), stool, turd (*taboo sl.*)

excrescence *n* = **protrusion**, knob, lump, outgrowth, process, projection, prominence, protuberance

excrete *vb* **1** = **defecate**, crap (*taboo sl.*), discharge, egest, eject, eliminate, evacuate, expel, exude, shit (*taboo sl.*), void

excruciate (ɪk'skruːʃɪˌeɪt) *vb* **excruciates, excruciating, excruciated.** *(tr)* to inflict mental suffering on; torment. [C16: from L *excruciāre*, from *cruciāre* to crucify, from *crux* cross]

excruciating ❶ (ɪk'skruːʃɪˌeɪtɪŋ) *adj* **1** unbearably painful; agonizing. **2** intense; extreme. **3** *Inf.* irritating; trying. **4** *Humorous.* very bad: *an excruciating pun.*

exculpate ❶ ('ɛkskʌlˌpeɪt, ɪk'skʌlpeɪt) *vb* **exculpates, exculpating, exculpated.** *(tr)* to free from blame or guilt; vindicate or exonerate. [C17: from Med. L, from L EX-[1] + *culpa* fault, blame]
▸ˌ**exculˈpation** *n* ▸**exˈculpatory** *adj*

excursion ❶ (ɪk'skɜːʃən, -ʒən) *n* **1** a short outward and return journey, esp. for sightseeing, etc.; outing. **2** a group going on such a journey. **3** *(modifier)* of or relating to reduced rates offered on certain journeys by rail: *an excursion ticket.* **4** a digression or deviation; diversion. **5** (formerly) a raid or attack. [C16: from L *excursiō* an attack, from *excurrere* to run out, from *currere* to run]
▸**exˈcursionist** *n*

excursive (ɪk'skɜːsɪv) *adj* **1** tending to digress. **2** involving detours; rambling. [C17: from L *excursus*, from *excurrere* to run forth]
▸**exˈcursively** *adv* ▸**exˈcursiveness** *n*

excuse ❶ *vb* (ɪk'skjuːz), **excuses, excusing, excused.** *(tr)* **1** to pardon or forgive. **2** to seek pardon or exemption for (a person, esp. oneself). **3** to make allowances for: *to excuse someone's ignorance.* **4** to serve as an apology or explanation for; justify: *her age excuses her.* **5** to exempt from a task, obligation, etc. **6** to dismiss or allow to leave. **7** to seek permission for (someone, esp. oneself) to leave. **8 be excused.** *Euphemistic.* to go to the lavatory. **9 excuse me!** an expression used to catch someone's attention or to apologize for an interruption, disagreement, etc. ◆ *n* (ɪk'skjuːs). **10** an explanation offered in defence of some fault or as a reason for not fulfilling an obligation, etc. **11** *Inf.* an inferior example of something; makeshift substitute: *she is a poor excuse for a hostess.* **12** the act of excusing. [C13: from L, from EX-[1] + *causa* cause, accusation]
▸**exˈcusable** *adj* ▸**exˈcusableness** *n* ▸**exˈcusably** *adv*

excuse-me *n* a dance in which a person may take another's partner.

ex-directory *adj Chiefly Brit.* not listed in a telephone directory, by request, and not disclosed to inquirers.

ex dividend *adj, adv* without the right to the current dividend: *to quote shares ex dividend.*

exeat ('ɛksɪət) *n Brit.* **1** leave of absence from school or some other institution. **2** a bishop's permission for a priest to leave his diocese in order to take up an appointment elsewhere. [C18: L, lit.: he may go out, from *exīre*]

exec. *abbrev. for:* **1** executive. **2** executor.

execrable ❶ ('ɛksɪkrəbᵊl) *adj* **1** deserving to be execrated; abhorrent. **2** of very poor quality. [C14: from L: see EXECRATE]
▸ˈ**execrableness** *n* ▸ˈ**execrably** *adv*

execrate ❶ ('ɛksɪˌkreɪt) *vb* **execrates, execrating, execrated.** **1** *(tr)* to loathe; detest; abhor. **2** *(tr)* to denounce; deplore. **3** to curse (a person or thing); damn. [C16: from L *exsecrārī* to curse, from EX-[1] + *-secrārī* from *sacer* SACRED]
▸ˌ**exeˈcration** *n* ▸ˈ**exeˌcrative** *or* ˈ**exeˌcratory** *adj*

execute ❶ ('ɛksɪˌkjuːt) *vb* **executes, executing, executed.** *(tr)* **1** to put (a condemned person) to death; inflict capital punishment upon. **2** to carry out; complete. **3** to perform; accomplish; effect. **4** to make or produce: *to execute a drawing.* **5** to carry into effect (a judicial sentence, the law, etc.). **6** *Law.* to render (a deed, etc.) effective, as by signing, sealing, and delivering. **7** to carry out the terms of (a contract, will, etc.). [C14: from OF *executer*, back formation from *executeur* EXECUTOR]
▸ˈ**exeˌcutable** *adj* ▸**executant** (ɪg'zɛkjʊtənt) *n* ▸ˈ**exeˌcuter** *n*

execution ❶ (ˌɛksɪ'kjuːʃən) *n* **1** the act or process of executing. **2** the carrying out or undergoing of a sentence of death. **3** the style or manner in which something is accomplished or performed; technique. **4a** the enforcement of the judgment of a court of law. **4b** the writ ordering such enforcement.

executioner ❶ (ˌɛksɪ'kjuːʃənə) *n* an official charged with carrying out the death sentence passed upon a condemned person.

executive ❶ (ɪg'zɛkjʊtɪv) *n* **1** a person or group responsible for the administration of a project, activity, or business. **2a** the branch of government responsible for carrying out laws, decrees, etc. **2b** any administration. ◆ *adj* **3** having the function of carrying plans, orders, laws, etc., into effect. **4** of or relating to an executive. **5** *Inf.* very expensive or exclusive: *executive housing.*
▸**exˈecutively** *adv*

Executive Council *n* (in Australia and New Zealand) a body of ministers of the Crown presided over by the governor or governor-general that formally approves cabinet decisions, etc.

executive director *n* a member of the board of directors of a company who is also an employee (usually full-time) and who often has a specified area of responsibility, such as finance or production. Cf. **nonexecutive director.**

executive officer *n* the second-in-command of any of certain military units.

executor (ɪg'zɛkjʊtə) *n* **1** *Law.* a person appointed by a testator to carry out his will. **2** a person who executes. [C14: from Anglo-F *executour*, from L *execūtor*]
▸**exˌecuˈtorial** *adj* ▸**exˈecutory** *adj* ▸**exˈecutorˌship** *n*

executrix (ɪg'zɛkjʊtrɪks) *n, pl* **executrices** (ɪgˌzɛkjʊ'traɪsiːz) *or* **executrixes.** *Law.* a female executor.

exegesis (ˌɛksɪ'dʒiːsɪs) *n, pl* **exegeses** (-siːz). explanation or critical interpretation of a text, esp. of the Bible. [C17: from Gk, from *exēgeisthai* to interpret, from EX-[1] + *hēgeisthai* to guide]
▸**exegetic** (ˌɛksɪ'dʒɛtɪk) *adj*

exegete ('ɛksɪˌdʒiːt) *or* **exegetist** (ˌɛksɪ'dʒiːtɪst, -'dʒɛt-) *n* a person who practises exegesis.

exemplar ❶ (ɪg'zɛmplə, -plɑː) *n* **1** a person or thing to be copied or imitated; model. **2** a typical specimen or instance; example. [C14: from L, from *exemplum* EXAMPLE]

exemplary ❶ (ɪg'zɛmplərɪ) *adj* **1** fit for imitation; model. **2** serving as a warning; admonitory. **3** representative; typical.
▸**exˈemplarily** *adv* ▸**exˈemplariness** *n*

exemplary damages *pl n Law.* damages awarded to a plaintiff above the value of actual loss sustained so that they serve also as a punishment to the defendant.

exemplify ❶ (ɪg'zɛmplɪˌfaɪ) *vb* **exemplifies, exemplifying, exemplified.** *(tr)* **1** to show by example. **2** to serve as an example of. **3** *Law.* to make an official copy of (a document) under seal. [C15: via OF from Med. L *exemplificāre*, from L *exemplum* EXAMPLE + *facere* to make]
▸**exˈempliˌfiable** *adj* ▸**exˌemplifiˈcation** *n* ▸**exˈempliˌcative** *adj* ▸**exˈempliˌfier** *n*

exempt ❶ (ɪg'zɛmpt) *vb* **1** *(tr)* to release from an obligation, tax, etc.; excuse. ◆ *adj* **2a** freed from or not subject to an obligation, tax, etc.; excused. **2b** *(in combination)*: *tax-exempt.* ◆ *n* **3** a person who is ex-

THESAURUS

excruciating *adj* **1 = agonizing**, acute, burning, exquisite, extreme, harrowing, insufferable, intense, piercing, racking, searing, severe, tormenting, torturous, unbearable, unendurable, violent

exculpate *vb* **= absolve**, acquit, clear, discharge, dismiss, excuse, exonerate, free, justify, pardon, release, vindicate

excursion *n* **1 = trip**, airing, day trip, expedition, jaunt, journey, outing, pleasure trip, ramble, tour **4 = digression**, detour, deviation, episode, excursus, wandering

excusable *adj* **1 = forgivable**, allowable, defensible, justifiable, minor, pardonable, permissible, slight, understandable, venial, warrantable

excuse *vb* **1, 3 = forgive**, absolve, acquit, bear with, exculpate, exonerate, extenuate, indulge, make allowances for, overlook, pardon, pass over, tolerate, turn a blind eye to, wink at **4 = justify**, apologize for, condone, defend, explain, mitigate, vindicate **5 = free**, absolve, discharge, exempt, let off, liberate, release, relieve, spare ◆ *n* **10 = justification**, apology, defence, explanation, grounds, mitigation, plea, pretext, reason, vindication **11** *Informal* **= poor substitute**, apology, makeshift, mockery, travesty
Antonyms *vb* ≠ **justify:** accuse, blame, censure, chasten, chastise, compel, condemn, correct, criticize, hold responsible, oblige, point a *or* the finger at, punish ≠ **free:** arraign, charge, convict, indict, sentence ◆ *n* ≠ **justification:** accusation, charge, imputation, indictment

execrable *adj* **1 = repulsive**, abhorrent, abominable, accursed, atrocious, damnable, deplorable, despicable, detestable, disgusting, foul, hateful, heinous, horrible, loathsome, nauseous, obnoxious, obscene, odious, offensive, revolting, sickening, vile

execrate *vb* **1, 2 = loathe**, abhor, abominate, condemn, denounce, deplore, despise, detest, excoriate, hate, revile, slam (*sl.*), vilify **3 = curse**, anathematize, damn, imprecate

execration *n* **1, 2 = loathing**, abhorrence, abomination, condemnation, contempt, detestation, excoriation, hate, hatred, odium, vilification **3 = curse**, anathema, damnation, imprecation, malediction

execute *vb* **1 = put to death**, behead, electrocute, guillotine, hang, kill, shoot **2-5 = carry out**, accomplish, achieve, administer, bring off, complete, consummate, discharge, do, effect, enact, enforce, finish, fulfil, implement, perform, prosecute, put into effect, realize, render **6** *Law* **= validate**, deliver, seal, serve, sign

execution *n* **1 = carrying out**, accomplishment, achievement, administration, completion, consummation, discharge, effect, enactment, enforcement, implementation, operation, performance, prosecution, realization, rendering **2 = killing**, capital punishment, hanging, necktie party (*inf.*) **3 = technique**, delivery, manner, mode, performance, rendition, style **4b = writ**, warrant

executioner *n* **= hangman**, headsman

executive *n* **1 = administrator**, director, manager, official **2 = administration**, directorate, directors, government, hierarchy, leadership, management ◆ *adj* **3 = administrative**, controlling, decision-making, directing, governing, managerial

exemplar *n* **1 = model**, criterion, epitome, example, ideal, paradigm, paragon, pattern, standard **2 = example**, exemplification, illustration, instance, prototype, specimen, type

exemplary *adj* **1 = ideal**, admirable, commendable, correct, estimable, excellent, fine, good, honourable, laudable, meritorious, model, praiseworthy, punctilious, sterling **2 = warning**, admonitory, cautionary, monitory **3 = typical**, characteristic, illustrative, representative

exemplification *n* **1, 2 = example**, embodiment, epitome, exemplar, illustration, manifestation, paradigm, personification, prototype, representation

exemplify *vb* **1, 2 = show**, demonstrate, depict, display, embody, evidence, exhibit, illustrate, instance, manifest, represent, serve as an example of

exempt *vb* **1 = grant immunity**, absolve, discharge, except, excuse, exonerate, free, let off, liberate, release, relieve, spare ◆ *adj* **2 = immune**, absolved, clear, discharged, excepted, excused, favoured, free, liberated, not liable, not subject, privileged, released, spared
Antonyms *adj* ≠ **immune:** accountable, answer-

empt. [C14: from L *exemptus* removed, from *eximere* to take out, from *emere* to buy, obtain]
▸**ex'emption** *n*

exequies ('ɛksɪkwɪz) *pl n, sing* **exequy.** the rites and ceremonies used at funerals. [C14: from L *exequiae* (pl) funeral procession, rites, from *exequī* to follow to the end]

exercise ('ɛksə,saɪz) *vb* **exercises, exercising, exercised.** (*mainly tr*) **1** to put into use; employ. **2** (*intr*) to take exercise or perform exercises. **3** to practise using in order to develop or train. **4** to perform or make use of: *to exercise one's rights.* **5** to bring to bear: *to exercise one's influence.* **6** (*often passive*) to occupy the attentions of, esp. so as to worry or vex: *to be exercised about a decision.* **7** *Mil.* to carry out or cause to carry out simulated combat, manoeuvres, etc. ◆ *n* **8** physical exertion, esp. for development, training, or keeping fit. **9** mental or other activity or practice, esp. to develop a skill. **10** a set of movements, tasks, etc., designed to train, improve, or test one's ability: *piano exercises.* **11** a performance or work of art done as practice or to demonstrate a technique. **12** the performance of a function: *the exercise of one's rights.* **13** (*usually pl*) *Mil.* a manoeuvre or simulated combat operation. **14** *Gymnastics.* a particular event, such as the horizontal bar. [C14: from OF, from L, from *exercēre* to drill, from EX-[1] + *arcēre* to ward off]
▸**'exer,cisable** *adj* ▸**'exer,ciser** *n*

exercise bike *or* **cycle** *n* a stationary exercise machine that is pedalled like a bicycle as a method of increasing cardiovascular fitness.

exercise book *n* a notebook used by pupils and students.

exercise price *n Stock Exchange.* the price at which the holder of a traded option may exercise his right to buy (or sell) a security.

exert (ɪg'zɜ:t) *vb* (*tr*) **1** to use (influence, authority, etc.) forcefully or effectively. **2** to apply (oneself) diligently; make a strenuous effort. [C17 (in the sense: push forth, emit): from L *exserere* to thrust out, from EX-[1] + *serere* to bind together, entwine]
▸**ex'ertion** *n* ▸**ex'ertive** *adj*

exeunt ('ɛksɪ,ʌnt) *Latin.* they go out: used as a stage direction.

exeunt omnes ('ɒmneɪz) *Latin.* they all go out: used as a stage direction.

exfoliate (ɛks'fəʊlɪ,eɪt) *vb* **exfoliates, exfoliating, exfoliated.** (of bark, skin, minerals, etc.) to peel off in layers, flakes, or scales. [C17: from LL *exfoliāre* to strip off leaves, from L *folium* leaf]
▸**ex,foli'ation** *n* ▸**ex'foliative** *adj*

ex gratia ('greɪʃə) *adj* given as a favour or gratuitously where no legal obligation exists: *an ex gratia payment.* [NL, lit.: out of kindness]

exhale (ɛks'heɪl, ɪg'zeɪl) *vb* **exhales, exhaling, exhaled. 1** to expel (breath, smoke, etc.) from the lungs; breathe out. **2** to give off (air, fumes, etc.) or (of air, etc.) to be given off. [C14: from L *exhālāre*, from *hālāre* to breathe]
▸**ex'halable** *adj* ▸**,exha'lation** *n*

exhaust (ɪg'zɔ:st) *vb* (*mainly tr*) **1** to drain the energy of; tire out. **2** to deprive of resources, etc. **3** to deplete totally; consume. **4** to empty (a container) by drawing off or pumping out (the contents). **5** to develop or discuss thoroughly so that no further interest remains. **6** to remove gas from (a vessel, etc.) in order to reduce pressure or create a vacuum. **7** (*intr*) (of steam or other gases) to be emitted or to escape from an engine after being expanded. ◆ *n* **8** gases ejected from an engine as waste products. **9** the expulsion of expanded gas or steam from an engine. **10a** the parts of an engine through which exhausted gases or steam pass. **10b** (*as modifier*): *exhaust pipe.* [C16: from L *exhaustus* made empty, from *exhaurīre* to draw out, from *haurīre* to draw, drain]
▸**ex'hausted** *adj* ▸**ex'haustible** *adj* ▸**ex'hausting** *adj*

exhaustion (ɪg'zɔ:stʃən) *n* **1** extreme tiredness. **2** the condition of being used up. **3** the act of exhausting or the state of being exhausted.

exhaustive (ɪg'zɔ:stɪv) *adj* **1** comprehensive; thorough. **2** tending to exhaust.
▸**ex'haustively** *adv* ▸**ex'haustiveness** *n*

exhibit (ɪg'zɪbɪt) *vb* (*mainly tr*) **1** (*also intr*) to display (something) to the public. **2** to manifest; display; show. **3** *Law.* to produce (a document or object) in court as evidence. ◆ *n* **4** an object or collection exhibited to the public. **5** *Law.* a document or object produced in court as evidence. [C15: from L *exhibēre* to hold forth, from *habēre* to have]
▸**ex'hibitor** *n* ▸**ex'hibitory** *adj*

exhibition (,ɛksɪ'bɪʃən) *n* **1** a public display of art, skills, etc. **2** the act of exhibiting or the state of being exhibited. **3 make an exhibition of oneself.** to behave so foolishly that one excites notice or ridicule. **4** *Brit.* an allowance or scholarship awarded to a student at a university or school.

exhibitioner (,ɛksɪ'bɪʃənə) *n Brit.* a student who has been awarded an exhibition.

exhibitionism (,ɛksɪ'bɪʃə,nɪzəm) *n* **1** a compulsive desire to attract attention to oneself, esp. by exaggerated behaviour. **2** a compulsive desire to expose one's genital organs publicly.
▸**,exhi'bitionist** *n* ▸**,exhi,bition'istic** *adj*

exhibitive (ɪg'zɪbɪtɪv) *adj* (*usually postpositive* and foll. by *of*) illustrative or demonstrative.

exhilarate (ɪg'zɪlə,reɪt) *vb* **exhilarates, exhilarating, exhilarated.** (*tr*) to make lively and cheerful; elate. [C16: from L *exhilarāre*, from *hilarāre* to cheer]
▸**ex'hila,rating** *adj* ▸**ex,hila'ration** *n* ▸**ex'hilarative** *adj*

exhort (ɪg'zɔ:t) *vb* to urge or persuade (someone) earnestly; advise strongly. [C14: from L *exhortārī*, from *hortārī* to urge]
▸**ex'hortative** *or* **ex'hortatory** *adj* ▸**,exhor'tation** *n* ▸**ex'horter** *n*

exhume (ɛks'hju:m) *vb* **exhumes, exhuming, exhumed.** (*tr*) **1** to dig up (something buried, esp. a corpse); disinter. **2** to reveal; disclose. [C18: from Med. L, from L EX-[1] + *humāre* to bury, from *humus* the ground]
▸**exhumation** (,ɛkshjʊ'meɪʃən) *n* ▸**ex'humer** *n*

ex hypothesi (ɛks haɪ'pɒθəsɪ) *adv* in accordance with the hypothesis stated. [C17: NL]

exigency ('ɛksɪdʒənsɪ, ɪg'zɪdʒənsɪ) *or* **exigence** ('ɛksɪdʒəns) *n, pl* **exi-**

THESAURUS

able, chargeable, liable, obligated, responsible, subject

exemption *n* **1 = immunity**, absolution, discharge, dispensation, exception, exoneration, freedom, privilege, release

exercise *vb* **1 = put to use**, apply, bring to bear, employ, enjoy, exert, practise, use, utilize, wield **3 = train**, discipline, drill, habituate, inure, practise, work out **6 = worry**, afflict, agitate, annoy, burden, distress, disturb, occupy, pain, perturb, preoccupy, trouble, try, vex ◆ *n* **8 = exertion**, action, activity, discipline, drill, drilling, effort, labour, toil, training, work, work-out **10 = task**, drill, lesson, practice, problem, schooling, schoolwork, work **12 = use**, accomplishment, application, discharge, employment, enjoyment, exertion, fulfilment, implementation, practice, utilization

exert *vb* **1 = use**, apply, bring into play, bring to bear, employ, exercise, expend, make use of, put forth, utilize, wield **2 exert oneself = make an effort**, apply oneself, bend over backwards (*inf.*), break one's neck (*inf.*), bust a gut (*inf.*), do one's best, endeavour, go for broke (*sl.*), knock oneself out (*inf.*), labour, pull one's finger out (*Brit. inf.*), strain, strive, struggle, toil, try hard, work

exertion *n* **1 = use**, application, employment, utilization **2 = effort**, action, attempt, elbow grease (*facetious*), endeavour, exercise, industry, labour, pains, strain, stretch, struggle, toil, travail (*literary*), trial

exhalation *n* **1 = breathing out**, breath, expiration **2 = giving off**, discharge, effluvium, emanation, emission, evaporation, exhaust, fog, fume, mist, smoke, steam, vapour

exhale *vb* **1 = breathe out**, breathe, expel, respire **2 = give off**, discharge, eject, emanate, emit, evaporate, issue, steam

exhaust *vb* **1 = tire out**, bankrupt, cripple, debilitate, disable, drain, enervate, enfeeble, fatigue, impoverish, prostrate, sap, tire, weaken, wear out **3 = use up**, consume, deplete, dissipate, expend, finish, run through, spend, squander, waste **4 = empty**, drain, dry, strain, void **7 = be emitted**, discharge, emanate, escape, issue

exhausted *adj* **1 = worn out**, all in, beat (*sl.*), dead beat (*inf.*), debilitated, dog-tired (*inf.*), done in (*inf.*), drained, enervated, enfeebled, fatigued, jaded, knackered (*sl.*), on one's last legs (*inf.*), out on one's feet (*inf.*), prostrated, ready to drop, sapped, spent, tired out, wasted, weak (*inf.*) **3 = used up**, at an end, consumed, depleted, dissipated, done, expended, finished, gone, spent, squandered, wasted **4 = empty**, bare, drained, dry, void
Antonyms *adj* ≠ **worn out**: active, alive and kicking, animated, enlivened, invigorated, refreshed, rejuvenated, restored, revived, stimulated ≠ **used up**: conserved, kept, preserved, replenished, restored

exhaustible *adj* **3 = limited**, delimited, finite

exhausting *adj* **1 = tiring**, arduous, backbreaking, crippling, debilitating, difficult, draining, enervating, fatiguing, gruelling, hard, laborious, punishing, sapping, strenuous, taxing, testing

exhaustion *n* **1 = tiredness**, debilitation, enervation, fatigue, feebleness, lassitude, prostration, weariness **3 = depletion**, consumption, emptying, using up

exhaustive *adj* **1 = thorough**, all-embracing, all-inclusive, all-out (*inf.*), complete, comprehensive, detailed, encyclopedic, extensive, far-reaching, full, full-scale, in-depth, intensive, sweeping, thoroughgoing, total
Antonyms *adj* casual, cursory, desultory, incomplete, perfunctory, sketchy, superficial

exhibit *vb* **1, 2 = display**, air, demonstrate, disclose, evidence, evince, expose, express, flaunt, indicate, make clear *or* plain, manifest, offer, parade, present, put on view, reveal, show ◆ *n* **4 = display**, exhibition, illustration, model, show

exhibition *n* **1, 2 = display**, airing, demonstration, exhibit, expo (*inf.*), exposition, fair, manifestation, performance, presentation, representation, show, showing, spectacle

exhilarate *vb* **= excite**, animate, cheer, delight, elate, enliven, exalt, gladden, inspirit, invigorate, lift, pep *or* perk up, rejoice, stimulate, thrill

exhilarating *adj* **= exciting**, breathtaking, cheering, enlivening, exalting, exhilarant, exhilarative, exhilaratory, gladdening, invigorating, stimulating, thrilling, vitalizing

exhilaration *n* **= excitement**, animation, cheerfulness, delight, elation, exaltation, gaiety, gladness, gleefulness, high spirits, hilarity, joy, joyfulness, liveliness, mirth, sprightliness, vivacity
Antonyms *n* dejection, depression, despondency, gloom, low spirits, melancholy, misery, sadness

exhort *vb* **= urge**, admonish, advise, beseech, bid, call upon, caution, counsel, encourage, enjoin, entreat, goad, incite, persuade, press, prompt, spur, warn

exhortation *n* **= urging**, admonition, advice, beseeching, bidding, caution, clarion call, counsel, encouragement, enjoinder (*rare*), entreaty, goading, incitement, lecture, persuasion, sermon, warning

exhume *vb* **1 = dig up**, disentomb, disinter, unbury, unearth
Antonyms *vb* bury, entomb, inearth, inhume, inter

exigency *n* **1 = urgency**, acuteness, constraint, criticalness, demandingness, difficulty, distress, emergency, imperativeness, necessity, needful-

DICTIONARY

gencies *or* **exigences. 1** urgency. **2** (*often pl*) an urgent demand; pressing requirement. **3** an emergency.

exigent ➊ ('ɛksɪdʒənt) *adj* **1** urgent; pressing. **2** exacting; demanding. [C15: from L *exigere* to drive out, weigh out, from *agere* to drive, compel]

exiguous (ɪg'zɪgjʊəs, ɪk'sɪg-) *adj* scanty or slender; meagre. [C17: from L *exiguus*, from *exigere* to weigh out; see EXIGENT]
▸**exiguity** (ˌɛksɪ'gjuːɪtɪ) *or* **ex'iguousness** *n*

exile ➊ ('ɛgzaɪl, 'ɛksaɪl) *n* **1** a prolonged, usually enforced absence from one's home or country. **2** the official expulsion of a person from his native land. **3** a person banished or living away from his home or country; expatriate. ◆ *vb* **exiles, exiling, exiled. 4** (*tr*) to expel from home or country, esp. by official decree; banish. [C13: from L *exsilium* banishment, from *exsul* banished person]
▸**exilic** (ɛg'zɪlɪk, ɛk'sɪlɪk) *adj*

exist ➊ (ɪg'zɪst) *vb* (*intr*) **1** to have being or reality; be. **2** to eke out a living; stay alive. **3** to be living; live. **4** to be present under specified conditions or in a specified place. [C17: from L *exsistere* to step forth, from EX-[1] + *sistere* to stand]
▸**ex'istent** *adj* ▸**ex'isting** *adj*

existence ➊ (ɪg'zɪstəns) *n* **1** the fact or state of existing; being. **2** the continuance or maintenance of life; living, esp. in adverse circumstances. **3** something that exists; a being or entity. **4** everything that exists.

existential (ˌɛgzɪ'stɛnʃəl) *adj* **1** of or relating to existence, esp. human existence. **2** *Philosophy.* known by experience rather than reason. **3** of a formula or proposition asserting the existence of at least one object fulfilling a given condition. **4** of or relating to existentialism.

existentialism (ˌɛgzɪ'stɛnʃəˌlɪzəm) *n* a modern philosophical movement stressing personal experience and responsibility and their demands on the individual, who is seen as a free agent in a deterministic and seemingly meaningless universe.
▸ˌ**exis'tentialist** *adj, n*

exit ➊ ('ɛgzɪt, 'ɛksɪt) *n* **1** a way out. **2** the act or an instance of going out. **3a** the act of leaving or right to leave a particular place. **3b** (*as modifier*): *an exit visa.* **4** departure from life; death. **5** *Theatre.* the act of going offstage. **6** *Brit.* a point at which vehicles may leave or join a motorway. ◆ *vb* **exits, exiting, exited. 7** (*intr*) to go away or out; depart. **8** (*intr*) *Theatre.* to go offstage: used as a stage direction: *exit Hamlet.* **9** *Computing.* to leave (a computer program or system). [C17: from L *exitus* a departure, from *exīre* to go out, from EX-[1] + *īre* to go]

exitance ('ɛksɪtəns) *n* a measure of the ability of a surface to emit radiation. [C20: from EXIT + -ANCE]

exit poll *n* a poll taken by asking people how they voted in an election as they leave a polling station.

ex libris (ɛks 'liːbrɪs) *prep* **1** from the collection or library of. ◆ *n* **ex-libris**, *pl* **ex-libris. 2** a bookplate bearing the owner's name, coat of arms, etc. [C19: from L, lit.: from the books (of)]

ex new *adv, adj* (of shares, etc.) without the right to take up any scrip issue or rights issue. Cf. **cum new.**

exo- *combining form.* external, outside, or beyond: *exothermal.* [from Gk *exō* outside]

exobiology (ˌɛksəʊbaɪ'ɒlədʒɪ) *n* another name for **astrobiology.**
▸ˌ**exobi'ologist** *n*

exocarp ('ɛksəʊˌkɑːp) *n* another name for **epicarp.**

exocrine ('ɛksəʊˌkraɪn, -krɪn) *adj* **1** of or relating to exocrine glands or their secretions. ◆ *n* **2** an exocrine gland. [C20: EXO- + *-crine* from Gk *krinein* to separate]

exocrine gland *n* any gland, such as a salivary or sweat gland, that secretes its products through a duct onto an epithelial surface.

Exod. *Bible. abbrev. for* Exodus.

exodus ➊ ('ɛksədəs) *n* the act or an instance of going out. [C17: via L from Gk *exodos*, from EX-[1] + *hodos* way]

Exodus ('ɛksədəs) *n* **1 the.** the departure of the Israelites from Egypt. **2** the second book of the Old Testament, recounting the events connected with this.

ex officio ('ɛks ə'fɪʃɪəʊ, ə'fɪsɪəʊ) *adv, adj* by right of position or office. [L]

exogamy (ɛk'sɒgəmɪ) *n Anthropol., sociol.* marriage outside one's own tribe or similar unit.
▸**ex'ogamous** *or* **exogamic** (ˌɛksəʊ'gæmɪk) *adj*

exogenous (ɛk'sɒdʒɪnəs) *adj* **1** having an external origin. **2** *Biol.* **2a** originating outside an organism. **2b** of or relating to external factors, such as light, that influence an organism. **3** *Psychiatry* (of a mental illness) caused by external factors.

exon ('ɛksɒn) *n Brit.* one of the four officers who command the Yeomen of the Guard. [C17: a pronunciation spelling of F *exempt* EXEMPT]

exonerate ➊ (ɪg'zɒnəˌreɪt) *vb* **exonerates, exonerating, exonerated.** (*tr*) **1** to absolve from blame or a criminal charge. **2** to relieve from an obligation. [C16: from L *exonerāre* to free from a burden, from *onus* a burden]
▸**exˌoner'ation** *n* ▸**ex'onerative** *adj* ▸**ex'onerˌator** *n*

exophthalmos (ˌɛksɒf'θælmɒs), **exophthalmus** (ˌɛksɒf'θælməs), *or* **exophthalmia** (ˌɛksɒf'θælmɪə) *n* abnormal protrusion of the eyeball, as caused by hyperthyroidism. [C19: via NL from Gk, from EX-[1] + *ophthalmos* eye]
▸ˌ**exoph'thalmic** *adj*

exorbitant ➊ (ɪg'zɔːbɪtᵊnt) *adj* (of prices, demands, etc.) excessive; extravagant; immoderate. [C15: from LL *exorbitāre* to deviate, from L *orbita* track]
▸**ex'orbitance** *n* ▸**ex'orbitantly** *adv*

exorcize ➊ *or* **exorcise** ('ɛksɔːˌsaɪz) *vb* **exorcizes, exorcizing, exorcized** *or* **exorcises, exorcising, exorcised.** (*tr*) to expel (evil spirits) from (a person or place), by adjurations and religious rites. [C15: from LL, from Gk, from EX-[1] + *horkizein* to adjure]
▸'**exorcism** *n* ▸'**exorcist** *n* ▸'**exorˌcizer** *or* '**exorˌciser** *n*

exordium (ɛk'sɔːdɪəm) *n, pl* **exordiums** *or* **exordia** (-dɪə). an introductory part or beginning, esp. of an oration or discourse. [C16: from L, from *exōrdīrī* to begin, from *ōrdīrī* to begin]
▸**ex'ordial** *adj*

exoskeleton (ˌɛksəʊ'skɛlɪtᵊn) *n* the protective or supporting structure covering the outside of the body of many animals, such as the thick cuticle of arthropods.
▸ˌ**exo'skeletal** *adj*

exosphere ('ɛksəʊˌsfɪə) *n* the outermost layer of the earth's atmosphere. It extends from about 400 kilometres above the earth's surface.

exothermic (ˌɛksəʊ'θɜːmɪk) *or* **exothermal** *adj* (of a chemical reaction or compound) occurring or formed with the evolution of heat.
▸ˌ**exo'thermically** *or* ˌ**exo'thermally** *adv*

exotic ➊ (ɪg'zɒtɪk) *adj* **1** originating in a foreign country, esp. one in the tropics; not native: *an exotic plant.* **2** having a strange or bizarre allure, beauty, or quality. ◆ *n* **3** an exotic person or thing. [C16: from L, from Gk *exōtikos* foreign, from *exō* outside]
▸**ex'otically** *adv* ▸**ex'otiˌcism** *n* ▸**ex'oticness** *n*

exotica (ɪg'zɒtɪkə) *pl n* exotic objects, esp. when forming a collection. [C19: L, neuter pl of *exōticus;* see EXOTIC]

exotic dancer *n* a striptease or belly dancer.

expand ➊ (ɪk'spænd) *vb* **1** to make or become greater in extent, volume, size, or scope. **2** to spread out; unfold; stretch out. **3** (*intr;* often

THESAURUS

ness, pressingness, pressure, stress **2** = **need**, constraint, demand, necessity, requirement, wont **3** = **emergency**, crisis, difficulty, extremity, fix (*inf.*), hardship, jam (*inf.*), juncture, panic stations (*inf.*), pass, pickle (*inf.*), pinch, plight, predicament, quandary, scrape (*inf.*), strait

exigent *adj* **1** = **urgent**, acute, constraining, critical, crucial, imperative, importunate, insistent, necessary, needful, pressing **2** = **demanding**, arduous, difficult, exacting, hard, harsh, rigorous, severe, stiff, strict, stringent, taxing, tough

exile *n* **2** = **banishment**, deportation, expatriation, expulsion, ostracism, proscription, separation **3** = **expatriate**, deportee, émigré, outcast, refugee ◆ *vb* **4** = **banish**, deport, drive out, eject, expatriate, expel, ostracize, oust, proscribe

exist *vb* **1, 3** = **be**, abide, be extant, be living, be present, breathe, continue, endure, happen, last, live, obtain, occur, prevail, remain, stand, survive **2** = **survive**, eke out a living, get along *or* by, keep one's head above water, stay alive, subsist

existence *n* **1** = **being**, actuality, animation, breath, continuance, continuation, duration, endurance, life, subsistence, survival **3** = **creature**, being, entity, thing **4** = **creation**, life, reality, the world

existent *adj* **1, 3** = **in existence**, abiding, alive, around, current, enduring, existing, extant, living, obtaining, present, prevailing, remaining, standing, surviving, to the fore (*Scot.*)

existing *adj* **3** = **in existence**, alive, alive and kicking, extant, living, remaining, surviving
Antonyms *adj* dead, defunct, died out, extinct, gone, lost, vanished

exit *n* **1** = **way out**, door, egress, gate, outlet, passage out, vent **2, 3** = **departure**, adieu, evacuation, exodus, farewell, going, goodbye, leave-taking, retirement, retreat, withdrawal **4** = **death**, decease, demise, expiry, passing away ◆ *vb* **7** = **depart**, bid farewell, go away, go offstage (*Theatre*), go out, issue, leave, make tracks, retire, retreat, say goodbye, take one's leave, withdraw
Antonyms *n* ≠ **way out:** entrance, entry, ingress, inlet, opening, way in ◆ *vb* ≠ **depart:** arrive, come *or* go in *or* into, enter, make an entrance

exodus *n* = **departure**, evacuation, exit, flight, going out, leaving, migration, retirement, retreat, withdrawal

exonerate *vb* **1** = **clear**, absolve, acquit, discharge, dismiss, exculpate, excuse, justify, pardon, vindicate **2** = **exempt**, discharge, dismiss, except, excuse, free, let off, liberate, release, relieve

exoneration *n* **1** = **acquittal**, absolution, amnesty, discharge, dismissal, exculpation, justification, pardon, vindication **2** = **exemption**, deliverance, discharge, dismissal, exception, freeing, liberation, release, relief

exorbitant *adj* = **excessive**, enormous, extortionate, extravagant, extreme, immoderate, inordinate, outrageous, preposterous, ridiculous, unconscionable, undue, unreasonable, unwarranted
Antonyms *adj* cheap, fair, moderate, reasonable

exorcism *n* = **driving out**, adjuration, casting out, deliverance, expulsion, purification

exorcize *vb* = **drive out**, adjure, cast out, deliver (from), expel, purify

exotic *adj* **1** = **foreign**, alien, external, extraneous, extrinsic, imported, introduced, naturalized, not native **2** = **unusual**, beyond one's ken, bizarre, colourful, curious, different, extraordinary, fascinating, glamorous, mysterious, outlandish, peculiar, strange, striking, unfamiliar
Antonyms *adj* ≠ **unusual:** conventional, familiar, ordinary, pedestrian, plain, run-of-the-mill, unmemorable, unremarkable

expand *vb* **1** = **increase**, amplify, augment, bloat, blow up, broaden, develop, dilate, distend, enlarge, extend, fatten, fill out, grow, heighten, inflate, lengthen, magnify, multiply,

foll. by *on*) to enlarge or expatiate (on a story, topic, etc.). **4** (*intr*) to become increasingly relaxed, friendly, or talkative. **5** *Maths.* to express (a function or expression) as the sum or product of terms. [C15: from L *expandere* to spread out]
▸**ex'pandable** *adj*

expanded (ɪk'spændɪd) *adj* (of a plastic) having been foamed during manufacture by a gas to make a light packaging material or heat insulator: *expanded polystyrene.*

expanded metal *n* an open mesh of metal used for reinforcing brittle or friable materials and in fencing.

expander (ɪk'spændə) *n* **1** a device for exercising and developing the muscles of the body. **2** an electronic device for increasing the variations in signal amplitude in a transmission system according to a specified law.

expanse Ⓣ (ɪk'spæns) *n* **1** an uninterrupted surface of something that extends, esp. over a wide area; stretch. **2** expansion or extension. [C17: from NL *expansum* the heavens, from L *expansus* spread out, from *expandere* to expand]

expansible (ɪk'spænsəb^əl) *adj* able to expand or be expanded.
▸**ex,pansi'bility** *n*

expansion Ⓣ (ɪk'spænʃən) *n* **1** the act of expanding or the state of being expanded. **2** something expanded. **3** the degree or amount by which something expands. **4** an increase or development, esp. in the activities of a company. **5** the increase in the dimensions of a body or substance when subjected to an increase in temperature, internal pressure, etc.
▸**ex'pansionary** *adj*

expansionism (ɪk'spænʃə,nɪzəm) *n* the doctrine or practice of expanding the economy or territory of a country.
▸**ex'pansionist** *n, adj* ▸**ex,pansion'istic** *adj*

expansive Ⓣ (ɪk'spænsɪv) *adj* **1** able or tending to expand or characterized by expansion. **2** wide; extensive. **3** friendly, open, or talkative. **4** grand or extravagant.
▸**ex'pansiveness** *n*

expansivity (,ɛkspæn'sɪvɪtɪ) *n* the fractional increase in length or volume of a substance or body on being heated through a one degree rise in temperature; coefficient of expansion.

ex parte (ɛks 'pɑːtɪ) *adj Law.* (of an application in a judicial proceeding) on behalf of one side or party only: *an ex parte injunction.*

expat (,ɛks'pæt) *n, adj Inf.* short for **expatriate.**

expatiate (ɪk'speɪʃɪ,eɪt) *vb* **expatiates, expatiating, expatiated.** (*intr*) **1** (foll. by *on* or *upon*) to enlarge (on a theme, topic, etc.); elaborate (on). **2** *Rare.* to wander about. [C16: from L *exspatiārī* to digress, from *spatiārī* to walk about]
▸**ex,pati'ation** *n* ▸**ex'pati,ator** *n*

expatriate Ⓣ *adj* (ɛks'pætrɪɪt, -,eɪt). **1** resident outside one's native country. **2** exiled or banished from one's native country. ◆ *n* (ɛks'pætrɪɪt, -,eɪt). **3** a person living outside his native country **4** an exile; expatriate person. ◆ *vb* (ɛks'pætrɪ,eɪt), **expatriates, expatriating, expatriated.** (*tr*) **5** to exile (oneself) from one's native country or cause (another) to go into exile. [C18: from Med. L, from L EX-[1] + *patria* native land]
▸**ex,patri'ation** *n*

expect Ⓣ (ɪk'spɛkt) *vb* (*tr; may take a clause as object or an infinitive*) **1** to regard as likely; anticipate. **2** to look forward to or be waiting for. **3** to decide that (something) is necessary; require: *the teacher expects us to work late.* ◆ See also **expecting.** [C16: from L *exspectāre* to watch for, from *spectāre* to look at]
▸**ex'pectable** *adj*

expectancy Ⓣ (ɪk'spɛktənsɪ) *or* **expectance** *n* **1** something expected, esp. on the basis of a norm or average: *his life expectancy was 30 years.* **2** anticipation; expectation. **3** the prospect of a future interest or possession.

expectant Ⓣ (ɪk'spɛktənt) *adj* **1** expecting, anticipating, or hopeful. **2** having expectations, esp. of possession of something. **3** pregnant. ◆ *n* **4** a person who expects something.
▸**ex'pectantly** *adv*

expectation Ⓣ (,ɛkspɛk'teɪʃən) *n* **1** the act or state of expecting or the state of being expected. **2** (*usually pl*) something looked forward to, whether feared or hoped for. **3** an attitude of expectancy or hope. **4** *Statistics.* **4a** the numerical probability that an event will occur. **4b** another term for **expected value.**

expected frequency *n Statistics.* the number of occasions on which an event may be presumed to occur on average in a given number of trials.

expected value *n Statistics.* the sum or integral of all possible values of a random variable, or any given function of it, multiplied by the respective probabilities of the values of the variable.

expecting Ⓣ (ɪk'spɛktɪŋ) *adj Inf.* pregnant.

expectorant (ɪk'spɛktərənt) *Med.* ◆ *adj* **1** promoting the secretion, liquefaction, or expulsion of sputum from the respiratory passages. ◆ *n* **2** an expectorant drug or agent.

expectorate (ɪk'spɛktə,reɪt) *vb* **expectorates, expectorating, expectorated.** to cough up and spit out (sputum from the respiratory passages). [C17: from L *expectorāre,* lit.: to drive from the breast, expel, from *pectus* breast]
▸**ex,pecto'ration** *n* ▸**ex'pecto,rator** *n*

expediency Ⓣ (ɪk'spiːdɪənsɪ) *or* **expedience** *n, pl* **expediencies** *or* **expediences. 1** appropriateness; suitability. **2** the use of or inclination towards methods that are advantageous rather than fair or just. **3** another word for **expedient** (sense 3).

expedient Ⓣ (ɪk'spiːdɪənt) *adj* **1** suitable to the circumstances; appropriate. **2** inclined towards methods that are advantageous rather than fair or just. ◆ *n also* **expediency. 3** something suitable or appropriate, esp. during an urgent situation. [C14: from L *expediēns* setting free; see EXPEDITE]

expedite Ⓣ ('ɛkspɪ,daɪt) *vb* **expedites, expediting, expedited.** (*tr*) **1** to hasten or assist the progress of. **2** to do or process with speed and efficiency. [C17: from L *expedīre,* lit.: to free the feet (as from a snare), hence, liberate, from EX-[1] + *pēs* foot]
▸**'expe,diter** *or* **'expe,ditor** *n*

expedition Ⓣ (,ɛkspɪ'dɪʃən) *n* **1** an organized journey or voyage, esp. for exploration or for a scientific or military purpose. **2** the people and equipment comprising an expedition. **3** promptness; dispatch. [C15: from L *expedīre* to prepare, EXPEDITE]
▸**,expe'ditionary** *adj*

expeditious Ⓣ (,ɛkspɪ'dɪʃəs) *adj* characterized by or done with speed and efficiency; prompt; quick.
▸**,expe'ditiously** *adv* ▸**,expe'ditiousness** *n*

expel Ⓣ (ɪk'spɛl) *vb* **expels, expelling, expelled.** (*tr*) **1** to eject or drive out

THESAURUS

prolong, protract, swell, thicken, wax, widen **2** = **spread (out)**, diffuse, open (out), outspread, stretch (out), unfold, unfurl, unravel, unroll **3** *with* **on** = **go into detail about**, amplify, develop, dilate, elaborate on, embellish, enlarge on, expatiate on, expound on, flesh out
Antonyms *vb* ≠ **increase:** condense, contract, decrease, reduce, shorten, shrink ≠ **go into detail about:** abbreviate, condense, shorten

expanse *n* **1** = **area**, breadth, extent, field, plain, range, space, stretch, sweep, tract

expansion *n* **1** = **increase**, amplification, augmentation, development, diffusion, dilatation, distension, enlargement, expanse, growth, inflation, magnification, multiplication, opening out, spread, swelling, unfolding, unfurling

expansive *adj* **1** = **expanding**, dilating, distending, elastic, enlargeable, extendable, inflatable, stretching, stretchy, swelling **2** = **wide**, all-embracing, broad, comprehensive, extensive, far-reaching, inclusive, thorough, voluminous, wide-ranging, widespread **3** = **talkative**, affable, communicative, easy, effusive, free, friendly, garrulous, genial, loquacious, open, outgoing, sociable, unreserved, warm

expatriate *adj* **1, 2** = **exiled**, banished, emigrant, émigré ◆ *n* **3, 4** = **exile**, emigrant, émigré, refugee ◆ *vb* **5** = **exile**, banish, expel, ostracize, proscribe

expect *vb* **1** = **think**, assume, believe, calculate, conjecture, forecast, foresee, imagine, presume, reckon, suppose, surmise, trust **2** = **look forward to**, anticipate, await, bargain for, contemplate, envisage, hope for, look ahead to, look for, predict, watch for **3** = **require**, call for, count on, demand, insist on, look for, rely upon, want, wish

expectancy *n* **1** = **likelihood**, outlook, prospect **2** = **expectation**, anticipation, assumption, belief, conjecture, hope, looking forward, prediction, presumption, probability, supposition, surmise, suspense, waiting

expectant *adj* **1** = **expecting**, anticipating, anxious, apprehensive, awaiting, eager, hopeful, in suspense, ready, watchful **3** = **pregnant**, enceinte, expecting (*inf.*), gravid

expectation *n* **1** = **anticipation**, apprehension, chance, expectancy, fear, hope, looking forward, outlook, possibility, prediction, promise, prospect, suspense

expected *adj* **1, 2** = **anticipated**, awaited, counted on, forecast, hoped-for, long-awaited, looked-for, predicted, promised, wanted

expecting *adj* = **pregnant**, enceinte, expectant, gravid, in the club (*Brit. sl.*), in the family way (*inf.*), with child

expediency *n* **1** = **suitability**, advantageousness, advisability, appropriateness, aptness, benefit, convenience, desirability, effectiveness, fitness, helpfulness, judiciousness, meetness, practicality, pragmatism, profitability, properness, propriety, prudence, usefulness, utilitarianism, utility **3** = **means**, contrivance, device, expedient, makeshift, manoeuvre, measure, method, resort, resource, scheme, shift, stopgap, stratagem, substitute

expedient *adj* **1** = **advantageous**, advisable, appropriate, beneficial, convenient, desirable, effective, fit, helpful, judicious, meet, opportune, politic, practical, pragmatic, profitable, proper, prudent, suitable, useful, utilitarian, worthwhile ◆ *n* **3** = **means**, contrivance, device, expediency, makeshift, manoeuvre, measure, method, resort, resource, scheme, shift, stopgap, stratagem, substitute
Antonyms *adj* ≠ **advantageous:** detrimental, disadvantageous, futile, harmful, ill-advised, impractical, imprudent, inadvisable, inappropriate, ineffective, inexpedient, unwise, wrong

expedite *vb* **1** = **speed (up)**, accelerate, advance, assist, dispatch, facilitate, forward, hasten, hurry, precipitate, press, promote, quicken, rush, urge
Antonyms *vb* block, curb, decelerate, delay, handicap, hold up, obstruct, restrict, slow up *or* down

expedition *n* **1** = **journey**, enterprise, excursion, exploration, mission, quest, safari, tour, trek, trip, undertaking, voyage **2** = **team**, company, crew, explorers, travellers, voyagers, wayfarers **3** = **speed**, alacrity, celerity, dispatch, expeditiousness, haste, hurry, promptness, quickness, rapidity, readiness, swiftness

expeditious *adj* = **quick**, active, alert, brisk, diligent, efficient, fast, hasty, immediate, instant, nimble, prompt, rapid, ready, speedy, swift

expel *vb* **1** = **drive out**, belch, cast out, discharge, dislodge, eject, remove, spew, throw out **2** = **dismiss**, ban, banish, bar, black, blackball, discharge, drum out, evict, exclude, exile,

with force. **2** to deprive of participation in or membership of a school, club, etc. [C14: from L *expellere* to drive out, from *pellere* to thrust, drive]
▸**ex'pellable** *adj* ▸**expellee** (ˌɛkspɛ'liː) *n* ▸**ex'peller** *n*

expellant *or* **expellent** (ɪk'spɛlənt) *adj* **1** forcing out or able to force out. ◆ *n* **2** a medicine used to expel undesirable substances or organisms from the body.

expend ❶ (ɪk'spɛnd) *vb* (*tr*) **1** to spend; disburse. **2** to consume or use up. [C15: from L *expendere*, from *pendere* to weigh]
▸**ex'pender** *n*

expendable ❶ (ɪk'spɛndəbᵊl) *adj* **1** that may be expended or used up. **2** able to be sacrificed to achieve an objective, esp. a military one. ◆ *n* **3** something expendable.
▸**exˌpenda'bility** *n*

expenditure ❶ (ɪk'spɛndɪtʃə) *n* **1** something expended, esp. money. **2** the act of expending.

expense ❶ (ɪk'spɛns) *n* **1** a particular payment of money; expenditure. **2** money needed for individual purchases; cost; charge. **3** (*pl*) money spent in the performance of a job, etc., usually reimbursed by an employer or allowable against tax. **4** something requiring money for its purchase or upkeep. **5 at the expense of.** to the detriment of. [C14: from LL, from L *expēnsus* weighed out; see EXPEND]

expense account *n* **1** an arrangement by which an employee's expenses are refunded by his employer or deducted from his income for tax purposes. **2** a record of such expenses.

expensive ❶ (ɪk'spɛnsɪv) *adj* high-priced; costly; dear.
▸**ex'pensiveness** *n*

experience ❶ (ɪk'spɪərɪəns) *n* **1** direct personal participation or observation. **2** a particular incident, feeling, etc., that a person has undergone. **3** accumulated knowledge, esp. of practical matters. ◆ *vb* **experiences, experiencing, experienced.** (*tr*) **4** to participate in or undergo. **5** to be moved by; feel. [C14: from L *experīrī* to prove; rel. to L *perīculum* PERIL]
▸**ex'perienceable** *adj*

experienced ❶ (ɪk'spɪərɪənst) *adj* having become skilful or knowledgeable from extensive participation or observation.

experiential (ɪkˌspɪərɪ'ɛnʃəl) *adj Philosophy.* relating to or derived from experience; empirical.

experiment ❶ *n* (ɪk'spɛrɪmənt). **1** a test or investigation, esp. one planned to provide evidence for or against a hypothesis. **2** the act of conducting such an investigation or test; research. **3** an attempt at something new or original. ◆ *vb* (ɪk'spɛrɪˌmɛnt). **4** (*intr*) to make an experiment or experiments. [C14: from L *experīmentum* proof, trial, from *experīrī* to test; see EXPERIENCE]
▸**ex'periˌmenter** *n*

experimental ❶ (ɪkˌspɛrɪ'mɛntᵊl) *adj* **1** relating to, based on, or having the nature of experiment. **2** based on or derived from experience; empirical. **3** tending to experiment. **4** tentative or provisional.
▸**exˌperi'mentalism** *n*

experimentation (ɪkˌspɛrɪmɛn'teɪʃən) *n* the act, process, or practice of experimenting.

expert ❶ ('ɛkspɜːt) *n* **1** a person who has extensive skill or knowledge in a particular field. ◆ *adj* **2** skilful or knowledgeable. **3** of, involving, or done by an expert: *an expert job.* [C14: from L *expertus* known by experience; see EXPERIENCE]
▸**'expertly** *adv* ▸**'expertness** *n*

expertise ❶ (ˌɛkspɜː'tiːz) *n* special skill, knowledge, or judgment; expertness. [C19: from F: expert skill, from EXPERT]

expiate ('ɛkspɪˌeɪt) *vb* **expiates, expiating, expiated.** (*tr*) to atone for (sin or wrongdoing); make amends for. [C16: from L *expiāre*, from *pius* dutiful; see PIOUS]
▸**'expiable** *adj* ▸ˌ**expi'ation** *n* ▸**'expiˌator** *n*

expiatory ('ɛkspɪətərɪ, -trɪ) *adj* **1** capable of making expiation. **2** offered in expiation.

expiration ❶ (ˌɛkspɪ'reɪʃən) *n* **1** the finish of something; expiry. **2** the act, process, or sound of breathing out.

expire ❶ (ɪk'spaɪə) *vb* **expires, expiring, expired.** **1** (*intr*) to finish or run out; come to an end. **2** to breathe out (air). **3** (*intr*) to die. [C15: from OF, from L *exspīrāre* to breathe out, from *spīrāre* to breathe]
▸**ex'pirer** *n*

expiry ❶ (ɪk'spaɪərɪ) *n, pl* **expiries. 1a** a coming to an end, esp. of a contract period; termination. **1b** (*as modifier*): *the expiry date.* **2** death.

explain ❶ (ɪk'spleɪn) *vb* **1** (when *tr, may take a clause as object*) to make (something) comprehensible, esp. by giving a clear and detailed account of it. **2** (*tr*) to justify or attempt to justify (oneself) by reasons for one's actions. [C15: from L *explānāre* to flatten, from *plānus* level]
▸**ex'plainable** *adj* ▸**ex'plainer** *n*

explain away *vb* (*tr, adv*) to offer excuses or reasons for (bad conduct, mistakes, etc.).

explanation ❶ (ˌɛksplə'neɪʃən) *n* **1** the act or process of explaining. **2** something that explains. **3** a clarification of disputed points.

explanatory ❶ (ɪk'splænətərɪ, -trɪ) *or* **explanative** *adj* serving or intended to serve as an explanation.
▸**ex'planatorily** *adv*

expletive (ɪk'spliːtɪv) *n* **1** an exclamation or swearword; an oath or sound expressing emotion rather than meaning. **2** any syllable, word, or phrase conveying no independent meaning, esp. one inserted in verse for the sake of metre. ◆ *adj also* **expletory** (ɪk'spliːtərɪ, -trɪ). **3** without particular meaning, esp. when filling out a line of verse. [C17: from LL *explētīvus* for filling out, from *explēre*, from *plēre* to fill]

explicable ❶ ('ɛksplɪkəbᵊl, ɪk'splɪk-) *adj* capable of being explained.

explicate ❶ ('ɛksplɪˌkeɪt) *vb* **explicates, explicating, explicated.** (*tr*) *Formal.* **1** to make clear or explicit; explain. **2** to formulate or develop (a theory, hypothesis, etc.). [C16: from L *explicāre* to unfold]
▸ˌ**expli'cation** *n*

explicit ❶ (ɪk'splɪsɪt) *adj* **1** precisely and clearly expressed, leaving nothing to implication; fully stated. **2** leaving little to the imagina-

THESAURUS

expatriate, oust, proscribe, relegate, send packing, show one the door, throw out, turf out (*inf.*)
Antonyms *vb* ≠ **dismiss:** admit, allow to enter, give access, let in, receive, take in, welcome

expend *vb* **1 = spend,** disburse, fork out (*sl.*), lay out (*inf.*), pay out, shell out **2 = use (up),** consume, dissipate, employ, exhaust, go through

expendable *adj* **2 = dispensable,** inessential, nonessential, replaceable, unimportant, unnecessary
Antonyms *adj* crucial, essential, indispensable, key, necessary, vital

expenditure *n* **2 = spending,** application, charge, consumption, cost, disbursement, expense, outgoings, outlay, output, payment, use

expense *n* **2 = cost,** charge, expenditure, outlay, payment

expensive *adj* **= dear,** costly, excessive, exorbitant, extravagant, high-priced, inordinate, lavish, overpriced, rich, steep (*inf.*), stiff
Antonyms *adj* bargain, budget, cheap, cut-price, economical, inexpensive, low-cost, low-priced, reasonable

experience *n* **1, 3 = knowledge,** contact, doing, evidence, exposure, familiarity, involvement, know-how (*inf.*), observation, participation, practice, proof, training, trial, understanding **2 = event,** adventure, affair, encounter, episode, happening, incident, occurrence, ordeal, test, trial ◆ *vb* **4, 5 = undergo,** apprehend, become familiar with, behold, encounter, endure, face, feel, go through, have, know, live through, meet, observe, participate in, perceive, sample, sense, suffer, sustain, taste, try

experienced *adj* **= knowledgeable,** accomplished, adept, capable, competent, expert, familiar, master, practised, professional, qualified, seasoned, skilful, tested, trained, tried, veteran, well-versed
Antonyms *adj* apprentice, green, incompetent, inexperienced, new, unqualified, unskilled, untrained, untried

experiment *n* **1, 2 = test,** assay, attempt, examination, experimentation, investigation, procedure, proof, research, trial, trial and error, trial run, venture ◆ *vb* **4 = test,** assay, examine, investigate, put to the test, research, sample, try, verify

experimental *adj* **1-4 = test,** empirical, exploratory, pilot, preliminary, probationary, provisional, speculative, tentative, trial, trial-and-error

expert *n* **1 = master,** ace (*inf.*), adept, authority, buff (*inf.*), connoisseur, dab hand (*Brit. inf.*), guru, maven (*US*), past master, pro (*inf.*), professional, specialist, virtuoso, whizz (*inf.*), wizard ◆ *adj* **2 = skilful,** able, adept, adroit, apt, clever, deft, dexterous, experienced, facile, handy, knowledgeable, master, masterly, practised, professional, proficient, qualified, skilled, trained, virtuoso
Antonyms *n* ≠ **master:** amateur, dabbler, ham, layman, nonprofessional, novice ◆ *adj* ≠ **skilful:** amateurish, cack-handed (*inf.*), clumsy, incompetent, inexperienced, unpractised, unqualified, unskilled, untrained

expertise *n* **= skill,** ableness, adroitness, aptness, cleverness, command, craft, deftness, dexterity, expertness, facility, grasp, grip, judgment, knack, know-how (*inf.*), knowing inside out, knowledge, masterliness, mastery, proficiency, skilfulness

expertness *n* **2 = skill,** ableness, adroitness, aptness, command, craft, deftness, dexterity, expertise, facility, grasp, grip, judgment, know-how (*inf.*), knowing inside out, knowledge, masterliness, mastery, proficiency, skilfulness

expiration *n* **1 = finish,** cessation, close, conclusion, end, expiry, finis, termination

expire *vb* **1 = finish,** cease, close, come to an end, conclude, end, lapse, run out, stop, terminate **2 = breathe out,** emit, exhale, expel **3 = die,** croak, decease, depart, kick the bucket (*inf.*), pass away or on, peg out (*inf.*), perish, pop one's clogs (*inf.*), snuff it (*inf.*)

expiry *n* **1 = ending,** cessation, close, conclusion, demise, end, expiration, lapsing, termination

explain *vb* **1 = make clear** *or* **plain,** clarify, clear up, define, demonstrate, describe, disclose, elucidate, explicate (*formal*), expound, illustrate, interpret, resolve, solve, teach, unfold **2 = account for,** excuse, give an explanation for, give a reason for, justify

explanation *n* **2 = reason,** account, answer, cause, excuse, justification, meaning, mitigation, motive, sense, significance, the why and wherefore, vindication **3 = description,** clarification, definition, demonstration, elucidation, explication, exposition, illustration, interpretation, resolution

explanatory *adj* **= descriptive,** demonstrative, elucidatory, explicative, expository, illuminative, illustrative, interpretive, justifying

explicable *adj* **= explainable,** accountable, definable, intelligible, interpretable, justifiable, resolvable, understandable

explicate *vb Formal* **1 = explain,** clarify, clear up, elucidate, expound, interpret, make clear or explicit, make plain, unfold, untangle **2 = develop,** construct, devise, evolve, formulate, work out

explicit *adj* **1, 3 = clear,** absolute, categorical, certain, definite, direct, distinct, exact, express, frank, open, outspoken, patent, plain, posi-

tion; graphically detailed. **3** openly expressed without reservations; unreserved. [C17: from L *explicitus* unfolded]
▸**ex'plicitly** *adv* ▸**ex'plicitness** *n*

explode ❶ (ɪk'spləud) *vb* **explodes, exploding, exploded.** **1** to burst or cause to burst with great violence, esp. through detonation of an explosive; blow up. **2** to destroy or be destroyed in this manner. **3** (of a gas) to undergo or cause (a gas) to undergo a sudden violent expansion, as a result of a fast exothermic chemical or nuclear reaction. **4** (*intr*) to react suddenly or violently with emotion, etc. **5** (*intr*) (esp. of a population) to increase rapidly. **6** (*tr*) to show (a theory, etc.) to be baseless. [C16: from L *explōdere* to drive off by clapping]
▸**ex'ploder** *n*

exploded view *n* a drawing or photograph of a mechanism that shows its parts separately, usually indicating their relative positions.

exploit ❶ *n* ('ɛksplɔɪt). **1** a notable deed or feat, esp. one that is heroic. ◆ *vb* (ɪk'splɔɪt). (*tr*) **2** to take advantage of (a person, situation, etc.) for one's own ends. **3** to make the best use of. [C14: from OF: accomplishment, from L *explicitum* (something) unfolded, from *explicāre* to EXPLICATE]
▸**ex'ploitable** *adj* ▸**ˌexploi'tation** *n* ▸**ex'ploitive** *or* **ex'ploitative** *adj*

exploration ❶ (ˌɛksplə'reɪʃən) *n* **1** the act or process of exploring. **2** an organized trip into unfamiliar regions, esp. for scientific purposes.
▸**exploratory** (ɪk'splɒrətərɪ, -trɪ) *or* **ex'plorative** *adj*

explore ❶ (ɪk'splɔː) *vb* **explores, exploring, explored.** **1** (*tr*) to examine or investigate, esp. systematically. **2** to travel into (unfamiliar regions), esp. for scientific purposes. **3** (*tr*) *Med.* to examine (an organ or part) for diagnostic purposes. [C16: from L, from EX-[1] + *plōrāre* to cry aloud; prob. from the shouts of hunters sighting prey]
▸**ex'plorer** *n*

explosion ❶ (ɪk'spləuʒən) *n* **1** the act or an instance of exploding. **2** a violent release of energy resulting from a rapid chemical or nuclear reaction. **3** a sudden or violent outburst of activity, noise, emotion, etc. **4** a rapid increase, esp. in a population. [C17: from L *explōsiō*, from *explōdere* to EXPLODE]

explosive ❶ (ɪk'spləusɪv) *adj* **1** of, involving, or characterized by explosion. **2** capable of exploding or tending to explode. **3** potentially violent or hazardous: *an explosive situation.* ◆ *n* **4** a substance capable of exploding or tending to explode.
▸**ex'plosiveness** *n*

expo ('ɛkspəu) *n, pl* **expos.** short for **exposition** (sense 3).

exponent ❶ (ɪk'spəunənt) *n* **1** (usually foll. by *of*) a person or thing that acts as an advocate (of an idea, cause, etc.). **2** a person or thing that explains or interprets. **3** a performer or artist. **4** Also called: **power, index.** *Maths.* a number or variable placed as a superscript to another number or quantity to indicate the number of times the designated number or quantity should appear in a repeated multiplication, as in $x^3 = x \times x \times x$, where 3 is the exponent. ◆ *adj* **5** offering a declaration, explanation, or interpretation. [C16: from L *expōnere* to set out, expound]

exponential (ˌɛkspəu'nɛnʃəl) *adj* **1** *Maths.* (of a function, curve, etc.) of or involving numbers or quantities raised to an exponent, esp. e^x. **2** *Maths.* raised to the power of e, the base of natural logarithms. **3** of or involving an exponent or exponents. **4** *Inf.* very rapid. ◆ *n* **5** *Maths.* an exponential function, etc.

exponential distribution *n Statistics.* a continuous single-parameter distribution used esp. when making statements about the length of life of materials or times between random events.

export *n* ('ɛkspɔːt). **1** (*often pl*) **1a** goods (**visible exports**) or services (**invisible exports**) sold to a foreign country or countries. **1b** (*as modifier*): *an export licence.* ◆ *vb* (ɪk'spɔːt, 'ɛkspɔːt). **2** to sell (goods or services) or ship (goods) to a foreign country. **3** (*tr*) to transmit or spread (an idea, institution, etc.) abroad. [C15: from L *exportāre* to carry away]
▸**ex'portable** *adj* ▸**exˌporta'bility** *n* ▸**ˌexpor'tation** *n* ▸**ex'porter** *n*

export reject *n* an article that fails to meet a standard of quality required for export and that is sold on the home market.

expose ❶ (ɪk'spəuz) *vb* **exposes, exposing, exposed.** (*tr*) **1** to display for viewing; exhibit. **2** to bring to public notice; disclose. **3** to divulge the identity of; unmask. **4** (foll. by *to*) to make subject or susceptible (to attack, criticism, etc.). **5** to abandon (a child, etc.) in the open to die. **6** (foll. by *to*) to introduce (to) or acquaint (with). **7** *Photog.* to subject (a film or plate) to light, X-rays, etc. **8 expose oneself.** to display one's sexual organs in public. [C15: from OF *exposer*, from L *expōnere* to set out]
▸**ex'posable** *adj* ▸**ex'posal** *n* ▸**ex'poser** *n*

exposé ❶ (ɛks'pəuzeɪ) *n* the act or an instance of bringing a scandal, crime, etc., to public notice.

exposed ❶ (ɪk'spəuzd) *adj* **1** not concealed; displayed for viewing. **2** without shelter from the elements. **3** susceptible to attack or criticism; vulnerable.

exposition ❶ (ˌɛkspə'zɪʃən) *n* **1** a systematic, usually written statement about or explanation of a subject. **2** the act of expounding or setting forth information or a viewpoint. **3** a large public exhibition, esp. of industrial products or arts and crafts. **4** the act of exposing or the state of being exposed. **5** *Music.* the first statement of the subjects or themes of a movement in sonata form or a fugue. **6** *RC Church.* the exhibiting of the consecrated Eucharistic Host or a relic for public veneration. [C14: from L *expositiō* a setting forth, from *expōnere* to display]
▸**ˌexpo'sitional** *adj*

expositor (ɪk'spɒzɪtə) *n* a person who expounds.

expository ❶ (ɪk'spɒzɪtərɪ, -trɪ) *or* **expositive** *adj* of or involving exposition; explanatory.

ex post facto (ɛks pəust 'fæktəu) *adj* having retrospective effect. [C17: from L *ex* from + *post* afterwards + *factus* done, from *facere* to do]

expostulate ❶ (ɪk'spɒstjuˌleɪt) *vb* **expostulates, expostulating, expostulated.** (*intr*; usually foll. by *with*) to argue or reason (with), esp. in order to dissuade. [C16: from L *expostulāre* to require, from *postulāre* to demand; see POSTULATE]
▸**exˌpostu'lation** *n* ▸**ex'postuˌlator** *n*

exposure ❶ (ɪk'spəuʒə) *n* **1** the act of exposing or the condition of being exposed. **2** the position or outlook of a house, building, etc.: *a southern exposure.* **3** lack of shelter from the weather, esp. the cold. **4** a surface that is exposed. **5** *Photog.* **5a** the act of exposing a film or plate to light, X-rays, etc. **5b** an area on a film or plate that has been exposed. **6** *Photog.* **6a** the intensity of light falling on a film or plate multiplied by the time for which it is exposed. **6b** a combination of lens aperture and shutter speed used in taking a photograph. **7** appearance before the public, as in a theatre, on television, etc.

exposure meter *n Photog.* an instrument for measuring the intensity of light so that suitable camera settings can be determined. Also called: **light meter.**

expound ❶ (ɪk'spaund) *vb* (when *intr*, foll. by *on* or *about*) to explain or set forth (an argument, theory, etc.) in detail. [C13: from OF, from L *expōnere* to set forth, from *pōnere* to put]
▸**ex'pounder** *n*

express ❶ (ɪk'sprɛs) *vb* (*tr*) **1** to transform (ideas) into words; utter; verbalize. **2** to show or reveal. **3** to communicate (emotion, etc.) without words, as through music, painting, etc. **4** to indicate through a sym-

THESAURUS

tive, precise, specific, stated, straightforward, unambiguous, unequivocal, unqualified, unreserved, upfront (*inf.*)
Antonyms *adj* ambiguous, cryptic, general, implicit, implied, indefinite, indirect, inexact, obscure, oracular, suggested, uncertain, vague

explode *vb* **1, 2** = **blow up**, burst, detonate, discharge, erupt, go off, set off, shatter, shiver **6** = **disprove**, belie, blow out of the water (*sl.*), debunk, discredit, give the lie to, invalidate, refute, repudiate

exploit *n* **1** = **feat**, accomplishment, achievement, adventure, attainment, deed, escapade, stunt ◆ *vb* **2** = **take advantage of**, abuse, dump on (*sl., chiefly US*), impose upon, manipulate, milk, misuse, play on *or* upon, shit on (*taboo sl.*) **3** = **make the best use of**, capitalize on, cash in on (*inf.*), live off the backs of, make capital out of, profit by *or* from, put to use, turn to account, use, use to advantage, utilize

exploitation *n* **2** = **misuse**, abuse, imposition, manipulation, trading upon, using **3** = **capitalization**, utilization

exploration *n* **1** = **investigation**, analysis, examination, inquiry, inspection, once-over (*inf.*), probe, research, scrutiny, search, study **2** = **expedition**, recce (*sl.*), reconnaissance, survey, tour, travel, trip

exploratory *adj* **1** = **investigative**, analytic, experimental, fact-finding, probing, searching, trial

explore *vb* **1** = **investigate**, analyse, examine, inquire into, inspect, look into, probe, prospect, research, scrutinize, search, work over **2** = **travel**, case (*sl.*), have *or* take a look around, range over, recce, reconnoitre, scout, survey, tour, traverse

explosion *n* **1** = **bang**, blast, burst, clap, crack, detonation, discharge, outburst, report **3** = **outburst**, eruption, fit, outbreak, paroxysm

explosive *adj* **2** = **unstable**, volatile **3** = **dangerous**, charged, hazardous, overwrought, perilous, tense, ugly

exponent *n* **1** = **advocate**, backer, champion, defender, promoter, propagandist, proponent, spokesman, spokeswoman, supporter, upholder **2** = **interpreter**, commentator, demonstrator, elucidator, expositor, expounder, illustrator **3** = **performer**, executant, interpreter, player, presenter

expose *vb* **1** = **uncover**, display, exhibit, manifest, present, put on view, reveal, show, take the wraps off, unveil **2, 3** = **reveal**, air, betray, blow wide open (*sl.*), bring to light, denounce, detect, disclose, divulge, lay bare, let out, make known, out (*inf.*), show up, smoke out, uncover, unearth, unmask **4** = **make vulnerable**, endanger, hazard, imperil, jeopardize, lay open, leave open, risk, subject **6** *with* **to** = **introduce to**, acquaint with, bring into contact with, familiarize with, make conversant with
Antonyms *vb* ≠ **uncover**: conceal, cover, hide, mask, protect, screen, shelter, shield ≠ **reveal**: conceal, cover, hide, keep secret

exposé *n* = **exposure**, disclosure, divulgence, revelation, uncovering

exposed *adj* **1** = **unconcealed**, bare, exhibited, laid bare, made manifest, made public, on display, on show, on view, revealed, shown, uncovered, unveiled **2** = **unsheltered**, open, open to the elements, unprotected **3** = **vulnerable**, in danger, in peril, laid bare, laid open, left open, liable, open, susceptible, wide open

exposition *n* **1** = **explanation**, account, commentary, critique, description, elucidation, exegesis, explication, illustration, interpretation, presentation **3** = **exhibition**, demonstration, display, expo (*inf.*), fair, presentation, show

expository *adj* = **explanatory**, descriptive, elucidative, exegetic, explicative, explicatory, hermeneutic, illustrative, interpretive

expostulate *vb* = **reason (with)**, argue (with), dissuade, protest, remonstrate (with)

exposure *n* **1** = **publicity**, baring, display, exhibition, manifestation, presentation, revelation, showing, uncovering, unveiling **2** = **position**, aspect, frontage, location, outlook, setting, view

expound *vb* = **explain**, describe, elucidate, explicate (*formal*), illustrate, interpret, set forth, spell out, unfold

express *vb* **1** = **state**, articulate, assert, asseverate, communicate, couch, declare, enunciate,

bol, formula, etc. **5** to squeeze out: *to express the juice from an orange.* **6 express oneself.** to communicate one's thoughts or ideas. ◆ *adj* (*prenominal*) **7** clearly indicated; explicitly stated. **8** done or planned for a definite reason; particular. **9** of or designed for rapid transportation of people, mail, etc.: *express delivery.* ◆ *n* **10a** a system for sending mail, money, etc., rapidly. **10b** mail, etc., conveyed by such a system. **10c** *Chiefly US & Canad.* an enterprise operating such a system. **11** Also: **express train.** a fast train stopping at no or only a few stations between its termini. ◆ *adv* **12** by means of express delivery. [C14: from L *expressus*, lit.: squeezed out, hence, prominent, from *exprimere* to force out, from EX-[1] + *premere* to press]
▸**ex'presser** *n* ▸**ex'pressible** *adj*

expression ❶ (ɪk'sprɛʃən) *n* **1** the act or an instance of transforming ideas into words. **2** a manifestation of an emotion, feeling, etc., without words. **3** communication of emotion through music, painting, etc. **4** a look on the face that indicates mood or emotion. **5** the choice of words, intonation, etc., in communicating. **6** a particular phrase used conventionally to express something. **7** the act or process of squeezing out a liquid. **8** *Maths.* a variable, function, or some combination of these.
▸**ex'pressional** *adj* ▸**ex'pressionless** *adj*

expressionism (ɪk'sprɛʃə,nɪzəm) *n* (*sometimes cap.*) an artistic and literary movement originating in the early 20th century, which sought to express emotions rather than to represent external reality: characterized by symbolism and distortion.
▸**ex'pressionist** *n, adj* ▸**ex,pression'istic** *adj*

expression mark *n* one of a set of musical directions, usually in Italian, indicating how a piece or passage is to be performed.

expressive ❶ (ɪk'sprɛsɪv) *adj* **1** of, involving, or full of expression. **2** (*postpositive; foll. by of*) indicative or suggestive (of). **3** having a particular meaning or force; significant.
▸**ex'pressiveness** *n*

expressly ❶ (ɪk'sprɛslɪ) *adv* **1** for an express purpose. **2** plainly, exactly, or unmistakably.

expresso (ɪk'sprɛsəʊ) *n, pl* **expressos.** a variant of **espresso.**

expressway (ɪk'spres,weɪ) *n* a motorway.

expropriate ❶ (ɛks'prəʊprɪ,eɪt) *vb* **expropriates, expropriating, expropriated.** (*tr*) to deprive (an owner) of (property), esp. by taking it for public use. [C17: from Med. L *expropriāre* to deprive of possessions, from *proprius* own]
▸**ex,propri'ation** *n* ▸**ex'propri,ator** *n*

expulsion ❶ (ɪk'spʌlʃən) *n* the act of expelling or the fact or condition of being expelled. [C14: from L *expulsiō* a driving out, from *expellere* to EXPEL]
▸**ex'pulsive** *adj*

expunge ❶ (ɪk'spʌndʒ) *vb* **expunges, expunging, expunged.** (*tr*) to delete or erase; blot out; obliterate. [C17: from L *expungere* to blot out, from *pungere* to prick]
▸**expunction** (ɪk'spʌŋkʃən) *n* ▸**ex'punger** *n*

expurgate ❶ ('ɛkspə,geɪt) *vb* **expurgates, expurgating, expurgated.** (*tr*) to amend (a book, text, etc.) by removing (offensive sections). [C17: from L *expurgāre* to clean out, from *purgāre* to purify; see PURGE]
▸**,expur'gation** *n* ▸**'expur,gator** *n*

exquisite ❶ (ɪk'skwɪzɪt, 'ɛkskwɪzɪt) *adj* **1** possessing qualities of unusual delicacy and craftsmanship. **2** extremely beautiful. **3** outstanding or excellent. **4** sensitive; discriminating. **5** fastidious and refined. **6** intense or sharp in feeling. ◆ *n* **7** *Obs.* a dandy. [C15: from L *exquīsītus* excellent, from *exquīrere* to search out, from *quaerere* to seek]
▸**ex'quisitely** *adv* ▸**ex'quisiteness** *n*

ex-serviceman *or* (*fem*) **ex-servicewoman** *n, pl* **ex-servicemen** *or* **ex-servicewomen.** a person who has served in the armed forces.

extant ❶ (ɛk'stænt, 'ɛkstənt) *adj* still in existence; surviving. [C16: from L *exstāns* standing out, from *exstāre*, from *stāre* to stand]

> **USAGE NOTE** *Extant* is sometimes wrongly used simply to say that something exists, without any connotation of survival: *plutonium is perhaps the deadliest element in existence* (not *the deadliest element extant*).

extemporaneous ❶ (ɪk,stɛmpə'reɪnɪəs) *or* **extemporary** (ɪk'stɛmpərərɪ) *adj* **1** spoken, performed, etc., without preparation; extempore. **2** done in a temporary manner; improvised.
▸**ex,tempo'raneously** *or* **ex'temporarily** *adv* ▸**ex,tempo'raneousness** *or* **ex'temporariness** *n*

extempore ❶ (ɪk'stɛmpərɪ) *adv, adj* without planning or preparation. [C16: from L *ex tempore* instantaneously, from EX-[1] out of + *tempus* time]

extemporize ❶ *or* **extemporise** (ɪk'stɛmpə,raɪz) *vb* **extemporizes, extemporizing, extemporized** *or* **extemporises, extemporising, extemporised. 1** to perform, speak, or compose (an act, speech, music, etc.) without preparation. **2** to use a temporary solution; improvise.
▸**ex,tempori'zation** *or* **ex,tempori'sation** *n* ▸**ex'tempo,rizer** *or* **ex'tempo,riser** *n*

extend ❶ (ɪk'stɛnd) *vb* **1** to draw out or be drawn out; stretch. **2** to last or cause to last for a certain time. **3** (*intr*) to reach a certain point in time or distance. **4** (*intr*) to exist or occur. **5** (*tr*) to increase (a building, etc.) in size; add to or enlarge. **6** (*tr*) to broaden the meaning or scope of: *the law was extended.* **7** (*tr*) to present or offer. **8** to stretch forth (an arm, etc.). **9** (*tr*) to lay out (a body) at full length. **10** (*tr*) to strain or exert (a person or animal) to the maximum. **11** (*tr*) to prolong (the time) for payment of (a debt or loan), completion of (a task), etc. [C14: from L *extendere* to stretch out, from *tendere* to stretch]
▸**ex'tendible** *or* **ex'tendable** *adj* ▸**ex,tendi'bility** *or* **ex,tenda'bility** *n*

extended family *n Sociol., anthropol.* the nuclear family together with relatives, often spanning three or more generations.

extended-play *adj* denoting an EP record.

extender (ɪk'stɛndə) *n* **1** a person or thing that extends. **2** a substance added to paints to give body and decrease their rate of settlement. **3** a substance added to glues and resins to dilute them or to modify their viscosity.

THESAURUS

phrase, pronounce, put, put across, put into words, say, speak, tell, utter, verbalize, voice, word **2** = **show**, bespeak, convey, denote, depict, designate, disclose, divulge, embody, evince, exhibit, indicate, intimate, make known, manifest, represent, reveal, signify, stand for, symbolize, testify **5** = **squeeze out**, extract, force out, press out ◆ *adj* **7** = **explicit**, accurate, categorical, certain, clear, definite, direct, distinct, exact, outright, plain, pointed, precise, unambiguous **8** = **specific**, clear-cut, deliberate, especial, particular, singular, special **9** = **fast**, direct, high-speed, nonstop, quick, quickie (*inf.*), rapid, speedy, swift

expression *n* **1** = **statement**, announcement, assertion, asseveration, communication, declaration, enunciation, mention, pronouncement, speaking, utterance, verbalization, voicing **2** = **indication**, demonstration, embodiment, exhibition, manifestation, representation, show, sign, symbol, token **4** = **look**, air, appearance, aspect, countenance, face, mien (*literary*) **5** = **choice of words**, delivery, diction, emphasis, execution, intonation, language, phraseology, phrasing, speech, style, wording **6** = **phrase**, idiom, locution, remark, set phrase, term, turn of phrase, word

expressionless *adj* **4** = **blank**, deadpan, dull, empty, inscrutable, poker-faced (*inf.*), straight-faced, vacuous, wooden

expressive *adj* **1** = **vivid**, eloquent, emphatic, energetic, forcible, lively, mobile, moving, poignant, striking, strong, sympathetic, telling **2** = **meaningful**, allusive, demonstrative, indicative, pointed, pregnant, revealing, significant, suggestive, thoughtful
Antonyms *adj* ≠ **vivid:** blank, dead-pan, dull, empty, impassive, inscrutable, poker-faced (*inf.*), straight-faced, vacuous, wooden

expressly *adv* **1** = **specifically**, deliberately, especially, exactly, intentionally, on purpose, particularly, precisely, purposely, specially **2** = **definitely**, absolutely, categorically, clearly, decidedly, distinctly, explicitly, in no uncertain terms, manifestly, outright, plainly, pointedly, positively, unambiguously, unequivocally, unmistakably

expropriate *vb* = **seize**, appropriate, arrogate, assume, commandeer, confiscate, impound, requisition, take, take over

expropriation *n* = **seizure**, commandeering, confiscation, disseisin (*Law*), impounding, requisitioning, sequestration, takeover

expulsion *n* = **ejection**, banishment, debarment, discharge, dislodgment, dismissal, eviction, exclusion, exile, expatriation, extrusion, proscription, removal

expunge *vb* = **erase**, abolish, annihilate, annul, blot out, cancel, delete, destroy, efface, eradicate, excise, exterminate, extinguish, extirpate, obliterate, raze, remove, strike out, wipe from the face of the earth, wipe out

expurgate *vb* = **censor**, blue-pencil, bowdlerize, clean up (*inf.*), cut, purge, purify, sanitize

exquisite *adj* **1** = **fine**, beautiful, dainty, delicate, elegant, lovely, precious **2** = **beautiful**, attractive, charming, comely, lovely, pleasing, striking **3** = **excellent**, admirable, choice, consummate, delicious, divine, fine, flawless, incomparable, matchless, outstanding, peerless, perfect, rare, select, splendid, superb, superlative **4, 5** = **refined**, appreciative, consummate, cultivated, discerning, discriminating, fastidious, impeccable, meticulous, polished, selective, sensitive **6** = **intense**, acute, excruciating, keen, piercing, poignant, sharp
Antonyms *adj* ≠ **beautiful:** ill-favoured, ugly, unattractive, unlovely, unsightly ≠ **excellent:** flawed, imperfect

extant *adj* = **in existence**, existent, existing, living, remaining, subsisting, surviving, undestroyed

extemporaneous *adj* **1** = **improvised**, ad-lib, extempore, free, impromptu, improvisatory, made-up, offhand, off-the-cuff (*inf.*), off the top of one's head, spontaneous, unplanned, unpremeditated, unprepared, unrehearsed **2** = **makeshift**, expedient, improvised, on-the-spot, temporary

extempore *adv, adj* = **impromptu**, ad lib, extemporaneous, extemporary, freely, improvised, offhand, off the cuff (*inf.*), off the top of one's head, on the spot, spontaneously, unplanned, unpremeditated, unprepared

extemporize *vb* **1** = **improvise**, ad-lib, busk, make up, play (it) by ear, vamp, wing it (*inf.*)

extend *vb* **1** = **make longer**, carry on, continue, drag out, draw out, elongate, lengthen, prolong, protract, spin out, spread out, stretch, unfurl, unroll **2** = **last**, carry on, continue, go on, take **3** = **reach**, amount to, attain, go as far as, spread **5, 6** = **widen**, add to, amplify, augment, broaden, develop, dilate, enhance, enlarge, expand, increase, spread, supplement **7** = **offer**, advance, bestow, confer, give, grant, hold out, impart, present, proffer, put forth, reach out, stretch out, yield
Antonyms *vb* ≠ **make longer:** condense, contract, curtail, cut, decrease, limit, reduce, restrict, shorten, take back ≠ **widen:** abbreviate, abridge, condense, contract, cut, decrease, reduce, restrict, shorten ≠ **offer:** take back, withdraw

extensible (ɪk'stɛnsɪbᵊl) *or* **extensile** (ɪk'stɛnsaɪl) *adj* capable of being extended.
▸**ex,tensi'bility** *or* **ex'tensibleness** *n*

extension Ⓣ (ɪk'stɛnʃən) *n* **1** the act of extending or the condition of being extended. **2** something that can be extended or that extends another object. **3** the length, range, etc., over which something is extended. **4** an additional telephone set connected to the same telephone line as another set. **5** a room or rooms added to an existing building. **6** a delay in the date originally set for payment of a debt or completion of a contract. **7** the property of matter by which it occupies space. **8a** the act of straightening or extending an arm or leg. **8b** its position after being straightened or extended. **9a** a service by which the facilities of an educational establishment, library, etc., are offered to outsiders. **9b** (*as modifier*): *a university extension course.* **10** *Logic.* the class of entities to which a given word correctly applies. [C14: from LL *extensiō* a stretching out; see EXTEND]
▸**ex'tensional** *adj* ▸**ex,tension'ality** *or* **ex'tensional,ism** *n*

extensive Ⓣ (ɪk'stɛnsɪv) *adj* **1** having a large extent, area, degree, etc. **2** widespread. **3** *Agriculture.* involving or farmed with minimum expenditure of capital or labour, esp. depending on a large extent of land. Cf. **intensive** (sense 3). **4** of or relating to logical extension.
▸**ex'tensiveness** *n*

extensor (ɪk'stɛnsə, -sɔː) *n* any muscle that stretches or extends an arm, leg, or other bodily part. Cf. **flexor.** [C18: from NL, from L *extensus* stretched out]

extent Ⓣ (ɪk'stɛnt) *n* **1** the range over which something extends; scope. **2** an area or volume. [C14: from OF, from L *extentus* extensive, from *extendere* to EXTEND]

extenuate Ⓣ (ɪk'stɛnjʊ,eɪt) *vb* **extenuates, extenuating, extenuated.** (*tr*) **1** to represent (an offence, fault, etc.) as being less serious than it appears, as by showing mitigating circumstances. **2** to cause to be or appear less serious; mitigate. **3** *Arch.* **3a** to emaciate or weaken. **3b** to dilute or thin out. [C16: from L *extenuāre* to make thin, from *tenuis* thin, frail]
▸**ex'tenu,ating** *adj* ▸**ex,tenu'ation** *n* ▸**ex'tenu,ator** *n*

exterior Ⓣ (ɪk'stɪərɪə) *n* **1** a part, surface, or region that is on the outside. **2** the outward behaviour or appearance of a person. **3** a film or scene shot outside a studio. ◆ *adj* **4** of, situated on, or suitable for the outside. **5** coming or acting from without. [C16: from L, comp. of *exterus* on the outside, from *ex* out of]
▸**ex'teriorly** *adv*

exterior angle *n* **1** an angle of a polygon contained between one side extended and the adjacent side. **2** any of the four angles made by a transversal that are outside the region between the two intersected lines.

exteriorize *or* **exteriorise** (ɪk'stɪərɪə,raɪz) *vb* **exteriorizes, exteriorizing, exteriorized** *or* **exteriorises, exteriorising, exteriorised.** (*tr*) **1** *Surgery.* to expose (an attached organ or part) outside the body. **2** another word for **externalize.**
▸**ex,teriori'zation** *or* **ex,teriori'sation** *n*

exterminate Ⓣ (ɪk'stɜːmɪ,neɪt) *vb* **exterminates, exterminating, exterminated.** (*tr*) to destroy (living things, esp. pests or vermin) completely; annihilate; eliminate. [C16: from L *extermināre* to drive away, from *terminus* boundary]
▸**ex'terminable** *adj* ▸**ex,termi'nation** *n* ▸**ex'termi,nator** *n*

external Ⓣ (ɪk'stɜːnᵊl) *adj* **1** of, situated on, or suitable for the outside; outer. **2** coming or acting from without. **3** of or involving foreign nations. **4** of, relating to, or designating a medicine that is applied to the outside of the body. **5** *Anat.* situated on or near the outside of the body. **6** (of a student) studying a university subject extramurally. **7** *Philosophy.* (of objects, etc.) taken to exist independently of a perceiving mind. ◆ *n* **8** (*often pl*) an external circumstance or aspect, esp. one that is superficial. **9** *Austral. & NZ.* an extramural student. [C15: from L *externus* outward, from *exterus* on the outside, from *ex* out of]
▸**ex'ternally** *adv* ▸**,exter'nality** *n*

externalize *or* **externalise** (ɪk'stɜːnə,laɪz) *vb* **externalizes, externalizing, externalized** *or* **externalises, externalising, externalised.** (*tr*) **1** to make external; give outward shape to. **2** *Psychol.* to attribute (one's feelings) to one's surroundings.
▸**ex,ternali'zation** *or* **ex,ternali'sation** *n*

extinct Ⓣ (ɪk'stɪŋkt) *adj* **1** (of an animal or plant species) having died out. **2** quenched or extinguished. **3** (of a volcano) no longer liable to erupt; inactive. [C15: from L *exstinctus* quenched, from *exstinguere* to EXTINGUISH]

extinction Ⓣ (ɪk'stɪŋkʃən) *n* **1** the act of making extinct or the state of being extinct. **2** the act of extinguishing or the state of being extinguished. **3** complete destruction; annihilation. **4** *Physics.* reduction of the intensity of radiation as a result of absorption or scattering by matter.

extinguish Ⓣ (ɪk'stɪŋgwɪʃ) *vb* (*tr*) **1** to put out or quench (a light, flames, etc.). **2** to remove or destroy entirely; annihilate. **3** *Arch.* to eclipse or obscure. [C16: from L *exstinguere*, from *stinguere* to quench]
▸**ex'tinguishable** *adj* ▸**ex'tinguisher** *n* ▸**ex'tinguishment** *n*

extirpate Ⓣ ('ɛkstə,peɪt) *vb* **extirpates, extirpating, extirpated.** (*tr*) **1** to remove or destroy completely. **2** to pull up or out; uproot. [C16: from L *exstirpāre* to root out, from *stirps* root, stock]
▸**,extir'pation** *n* ▸**'extir,pator** *n*

extol Ⓣ *or US* **extoll** (ɪk'stəʊl) *vb* **extols** *or US* **extolls, extolling, extolled.** (*tr*) to praise lavishly; exalt. [C15: from L *extollere* to elevate, from *tollere* to raise]
▸**ex'toller** *n* ▸**ex'tolment** *n*

extort Ⓣ (ɪk'stɔːt) *vb* (*tr*) **1** to secure (money, favours, etc.) by intimidation, violence, or the misuse of authority. **2** to obtain by importunate demands. [C16: from L *extortus* wrenched out, from *extorquēre* to wrest away, from *torquēre* to twist, wrench]
▸**ex'tortion** *n* ▸**ex'tortioner, ex'tortionist,** *or* **ex'torter** *n* ▸**ex'tortive** *adj*

extortionate Ⓣ (ɪk'stɔːʃənɪt) *adj* **1** (of prices, etc.) excessive; exorbitant. **2** (of persons) using extortion.
▸**ex'tortionately** *adv*

extra Ⓣ ('ɛkstrə) *adj* **1** being more than what is usual or expected; additional. ◆ *n* **2** a person or thing that is additional. **3** something for which an additional charge is made. **4** an additional edition of a newspaper, esp. to report a new development. **5** *Films.* a person temporarily engaged, usually for crowd scenes. **6** *Cricket.* a run not scored from the bat, such as a wide, no-ball, or bye. ◆ *adv* **7** unusually; exceptionally: *an extra fast car.* [C18: ? shortened from EXTRAORDINARY]

extra- *prefix* outside or beyond an area or scope: *extrasensory; extraterri-*

THESAURUS

extendible *adj* **1** = **flexible**, elastic, stretchy

extension *n* **1** = **lengthening**, amplification, augmentation, broadening, continuation, delay, development, dilatation, distension, elongation, enlargement, expansion, extent, increase, postponement, prolongation, protraction, spread, stretching, widening **2** = **annexe**, addendum, addition, add-on, adjunct, appendage, appendix, branch, ell, supplement, wing

extensive *adj* **1, 2** = **wide**, all-inclusive, broad, capacious, commodious, comprehensive, expanded, extended, far-flung, far-reaching, general, great, huge, humongous *or* humungous (*US sl.*), large, large-scale, lengthy, long, pervasive, prevalent, protracted, spacious, sweeping, thorough, universal, vast, voluminous, wholesale, widespread
Antonyms *adj* circumscribed, confined, constricted, limited, narrow, restricted, tight

extent *n* **1** = **range**, ambit, bounds, compass, play, reach, scope, sphere, sweep **2** = **size**, amount, amplitude, area, breadth, bulk, degree, duration, expanse, expansion, length, magnitude, measure, quantity, stretch, term, time, volume, width

extenuate *vb* **1** = **make light of**, discount, underestimate, underrate, undervalue **2** = **mitigate**, decrease, diminish, excuse, lessen, make allowances for, minimize, moderate, palliate, play down, qualify, reduce, soften, temper, weaken

extenuating *adj* **2** = **mitigating**, justifying, moderating, qualifying, serving as an excuse

exterior *n* **1** = **outside**, appearance, aspect, coating, covering, façade, face, finish, shell, skin, surface ◆ *adj* **4** = **outside**, external, outer, outermost, outward, superficial, surface **5** = **external**, alien, exotic, extraneous, extrinsic, foreign, outside
Antonyms *n* ≠ **outside**: inner, inside, interior ◆ *adj* ≠ **outside**: immanent, inherent, inside, interior, internal, intrinsic ≠ **external**: domestic, internal, intrinsic

exterminate *vb* = **destroy**, abolish, annihilate, eliminate, eradicate, extirpate

extermination *n* = **destruction**, annihilation, elimination, eradication, extirpation, genocide, massacre, mass murder, murder, slaughter, wiping out

external *adj* **1** = **outer**, apparent, exterior, outermost, outside, outward, superficial, surface, visible **2** = **outside**, alien, exotic, exterior, extramural, extraneous, extrinsic, foreign, independent
Antonyms *adj* ≠ **outer**: immanent, inherent, inner, inside, interior, internal, intrinsic ≠ **outside**: inside, interior, intrinsic

extinct *adj* **1** = **dead**, defunct, gone, lost, vanished **2** = **inactive**, doused, extinguished, out, quenched, snuffed out
Antonyms *adj* ≠ **dead**: active, alive, existing, extant, flourishing, living, surviving, thriving

extinction *n* **1, 3** = **dying out**, abolition, annihilation, death, destruction, eradication, excision, extermination, extirpation, obliteration, oblivion

extinguish *vb* **1** = **put out**, blow out, douse, quench, smother, snuff out, stifle **2** = **destroy**, abolish, annihilate, eliminate, end, eradicate, erase, expunge, exterminate, extirpate, kill, obscure, put paid to, remove, suppress, wipe out

extirpate *vb* **1** = **wipe out**, abolish, annihilate, deracinate, destroy, eliminate, eradicate, erase, excise, expunge, exterminate, extinguish, pull up by the roots, remove, root out, uproot, wipe from the face of the earth

extol *vb* = **praise**, acclaim, applaud, celebrate, commend, crack up (*inf.*), cry up, eulogize, exalt, glorify, laud, magnify (*arch.*), panegyrize, pay tribute to, sing the praises of

extort *vb* **1** = **force**, blackmail, bleed (*inf.*), bully, coerce, exact, extract, squeeze, wrest, wring

extortion *n* **1** = **force**, blackmail, coercion, compulsion, demand, exaction, oppression, rapacity, shakedown (*US sl.*)

extortionate *adj* **1** = **exorbitant**, excessive, extravagant, immoderate, inflated, inordinate, outrageous, preposterous, sky-high, unreasonable **2** = **grasping**, blood-sucking (*inf.*), exacting, hard, harsh, oppressive, rapacious, rigorous, severe, usurious
Antonyms *adj* ≠ **exorbitant**: fair, inexpensive, moderate, modest, reasonable

extra *adj* **1** = **additional**, added, auxiliary, further, more, spare, supererogatory, superfluous, supernumerary, supplemental, supplementary, surplus ◆ *n* **2** = **addition**, accessory, addendum, add-on, adjunct, affix, appendage, appurtenance, attachment, bonus, complement, extension, supernumerary, supplement ◆ *adv* **7** = **exceptionally**, especially, extraordinarily, extremely, particularly, remarkably, uncommonly, unusually
Antonyms *adj* ≠ **additional**: compulsory, essential, mandatory, necessary, needed, obligatory, required, requisite, vital ◆ *n* ≠ **addition**: essential,

torial. [from L *extrā* outside, beyond, from *extera,* from *exterus* outward]

extra cover *n Cricket.* a fielding position between cover and mid-off.

extract ❶ *vb* (ɪk'strækt). *(tr)* **1** to pull out or uproot by force. **2** to remove or separate. **3** to derive (pleasure, information, etc.) from some source. **4** to deduce or develop (a doctrine, policy, etc.). **5** *Inf.* to extort (money, etc.). **6** to obtain (a substance) from a mixture or material by a process, such as digestion, distillation, mechanical separation, etc. **7** to cut out or copy out (an article, passage, etc.) from a publication. **8** to determine the value of (the root of a number). ◆ *n* ('ɛkstrækt). **9** something extracted, such as a passage from a book, etc. **10** a preparation containing the active principle or concentrated essence of a material. [C15: from L *extractus* drawn forth, from *extrahere,* from *trahere* to drag]
▸**ex'tractable** *adj* ▸**ex,tracta'bility** *n* ▸**ex'tractive** *adj*

> **USAGE NOTE** *Extract* is sometimes wrongly used where *extricate* would be better: *he will find it difficult extricating* (not *extracting*) *himself from this situation.*

extraction ❶ (ɪk'strækʃən) *n* **1** the act of extracting or the condition of being extracted. **2** something extracted. **3** the act or an instance of extracting a tooth. **4** origin or ancestry.

extractor (ɪk'stræktə) *n* **1** a person or thing that extracts. **2** an instrument for pulling something out or removing tight-fitting components. **3** short for **extractor fan.**

extractor fan *or* **extraction fan** *n* a fan used in kitchens, bathrooms, workshops, etc., to remove stale air or fumes.

extracurricular (,ɛkstrəkə'rɪkjʊlə) *adj* **1** taking place outside the normal school timetable. **2** beyond the regular duties, schedule, etc.

extradite ('ɛkstrə,daɪt) *vb* **extradites, extraditing, extradited.** *(tr)* **1** to surrender (an alleged offender) for trial to a foreign state. **2** to procure the extradition of. [C19: back formation from EXTRADITION]
▸**'extra,ditable** *adj*

extradition (,ɛkstrə'dɪʃən) *n* the surrender of an alleged offender to the state where the alleged offence was committed. [C19: from F, from L *trāditiō* a handing over]

extrados (ɛk'streɪdɒs) *n, pl* **extrados** (-dəʊz) *or* **extradoses.** *Archit.* the outer curve of an arch or vault. [C18: from F, from EXTRA- + *dos* back]

extradural (,ɛkstrə'djʊərəl) *adj* another word for **epidural** (sense 1).

extragalactic (,ɛkstrəgə'læktɪk) *adj* occurring or existing beyond the Galaxy.

extramarital (,ɛkstrə'mærɪt'l) *adj* (esp. of sexual relations) occurring outside marriage.

extramural (,ɛkstrə'mjʊərəl) *adj* **1** connected with but outside the normal courses of a university, college, etc. **2** beyond the boundaries or walls of a city, castle, etc.

extraneous ❶ (ɪk'streɪnɪəs) *adj* **1** not essential. **2** not pertinent; irrelevant. **3** coming from without. **4** not belonging. [C17: from L *extrāneus* external, from *extrā* outside]
▸**ex'traneousness** *n*

extraordinary ❶ (ɪk'strɔːd'nrɪ) *adj* **1** very unusual or surprising. **2** not in an established manner or order. **3** employed for particular purposes. **4** *(usually postpositive)* (of an official, etc.) additional or subordinate. [C15: from L *extraordinārius* beyond what is usual; see ORDINARY]
▸**ex'traordinarily** *adv* ▸**ex'traordinariness** *n*

extraordinary general meeting *n* a meeting specially called to discuss an important item of a company's business. It may be called by a group of shareholders or by the directors. Abbrev.: **EGM.**

extrapolate (ɪk'stræpə,leɪt) *vb* **extrapolates, extrapolating, extrapolated. 1** *Maths.* to estimate (a value of a function etc.) beyond the known values, by the extension of a curve. Cf. **interpolate** (sense 4). **2** to infer (something) by using but not strictly deducing from known facts. [C19: EXTRA- + *-polate,* as in INTERPOLATE]
▸**ex,trapo'lation** *n* ▸**ex'trapolative** *or* **ex'trapolatory** *adj* ▸**ex'trapo,lator** *n*

extrasensory (,ɛkstrə'sɛnsərɪ) *adj* of or relating to extrasensory perception.

extrasensory perception *n* the supposed ability of certain individuals to obtain information about the environment without the use of normal sensory channels.

extraterritorial (,ɛkstrə,tɛrɪ'tɔːrɪəl) *or* **exterritorial** *adj* **1** beyond the limits of a country's territory. **2** of, relating to, or possessing extraterritoriality.

extraterritoriality (,ɛkstrə,tɛrɪ,tɔːrɪ'ælɪtɪ) *n* **1** the privilege granted to some aliens, esp. diplomats, of being exempt from the jurisdiction of the state in which they reside. **2** the right of a state to exercise authority in certain circumstances beyond the limits of its territory.

extra time *n Sport.* an additional period played at the end of a match, to compensate for time lost through injury or (in certain circumstances) to allow the teams to achieve a conclusive result.

extravagance ❶ (ɪk'strævɪgəns) *n* **1** excessive outlay of money; wasteful spending. **2** immoderate or absurd speech or behaviour.

extravagant ❶ (ɪk'strævɪgənt) *adj* **1** spending money excessively or immoderately. **2** going beyond usual bounds; unrestrained. **3** ostentatious; showy. **4** exorbitant in price; overpriced. [C14: from Med. L *extravagāns,* from L EXTRA- + *vagārī* to wander]

extravaganza ❶ (ɪk,strævə'gænzə) *n* **1** an elaborately staged light entertainment. **2** any lavish or fanciful display, literary composition, etc. [C18: from It.: extravagance]

extravasate (ɪk'strævə,seɪt) *vb* **extravasates, extravasating, extravasated.** *Pathol.* to cause (blood or lymph) to escape or (of blood or lymph) to escape into the surrounding tissues from their proper vessels. [C17: from L EXTRA- + *vās* vessel]
▸**ex,trava'sation** *n*

extravehicular (,ɛkstrəvɪ'hɪkjʊlə) *adj* occurring or used outside a spacecraft, either in space or on the surface of a planet.

extraversion (,ɛkstrə'vɜːʃən) *n* a variant spelling of **extroversion.**
▸**'extra,vert** *n, adj*

extra virgin *adj* (of olive oil) of the highest quality, extracted by cold pressing rather than chemical treatment.

extreme ❶ (ɪk'striːm) *adj* **1** being of a high or of the highest degree or intensity. **2** exceeding what is usual or reasonable; immoderate. **3** very strict or severe; drastic. **4** *(prenominal)* farthest or outermost. ◆ *n* **5** the highest or furthest degree (often in **in the extreme, go to extremes**). **6** *(often pl)* either of the two limits or ends of a scale or range. **7** *Maths.* the first or last term of a series or a proportion. [C15: from L *extrēmus* outermost, from *exterus* on the outside; see EXTERIOR]
▸**ex'tremely** *adv* ▸**ex'tremeness** *n*

> **USAGE NOTE** See at **very.**

extreme unction *n RC Church.* the former name for **anointing of the sick.**

THESAURUS

must, necessity, precondition, prerequisite, requirement, requisite

extract *vb* **1** = **pull out**, draw, extirpate, pluck out, pull, remove, take out, uproot, withdraw **3** = **derive**, bring out, draw, elicit, evoke, exact, gather, get, glean, obtain, reap, wrest, wring **4** = **develop**, deduce, derive, educe, elicit, evolve **6** = **obtain**, distil, draw out, express, press out, separate out, squeeze, take out **7** = **copy out**, abstract, choose, cite, cull, cut out, quote, select ◆ *n* **9** = **passage**, abstract, citation, clipping, cutting, excerpt, quotation, selection **10** = **essence**, concentrate, decoction, distillate, distillation, juice

extraction *n* **1** = **taking out**, drawing, extirpation, pulling, removal, uprooting, withdrawal **4** = **origin**, ancestry, birth, blood, derivation, descent, family, lineage, parentage, pedigree, race, stock

extraneous *adj* **1** = **nonessential**, accidental, additional, adventitious, extra, incidental, inessential, needless, peripheral, redundant, superfluous, supplementary, unessential, unnecessary, unneeded **2** = **irrelevant**, beside the point, immaterial, impertinent, inadmissible, inapplicable, inapposite, inappropriate, inapt, off the subject, unconnected, unrelated **3, 4** = **external**, adventitious, alien, exotic, extrinsic, foreign, out of place, strange

extraordinary *adj* **1** = **unusual**, amazing, beyond one's ken, bizarre, curious, exceptional, notable, odd, out of this world *(inf.)*, outstanding, particular, peculiar, phenomenal, rare, remarkable, singular, special, strange, surprising, uncommon, unfamiliar, unheard-of, unique, unprecedented, unwonted, weird, wonderful, wondrous *(arch. or literary)*
Antonyms *adj* banal, common, commonplace, customary, everyday, ordinary, unexceptional, unremarkable, usual

extravagance *n* **1** = **waste**, improvidence, lavishness, overspending, prodigality, profligacy, profusion, squandering, wastefulness **2** = **excess**, absurdity, dissipation, exaggeration, exorbitance, folly, immoderation, outrageousness, preposterousness, recklessness, unreasonableness, unrestraint, wildness

extravagant *adj* **1** = **wasteful**, excessive, having money to burn, improvident, imprudent, lavish, prodigal, profligate, spendthrift **2** = **excessive**, absurd, exaggerated, exorbitant, fanciful, fantastic, foolish, immoderate, inordinate, outrageous, outré, over the top *(sl.)*, preposterous, reckless, unreasonable, unrestrained, wild **3** = **showy**, fancy, flamboyant, flashy, garish, gaudy, grandiose, ornate, ostentatious, pretentious **4** = **overpriced**, costly, excessive, exorbitant, expensive, extortionate, inordinate, steep *(inf.)*, unreasonable
Antonyms *adj* ≠ **wasteful:** careful, close, economical, frugal, miserly, moderate, prudent, sensible, sparing, thrifty, tight-fisted *(inf.)* ≠ **excessive:** conservative, down-to-earth, moderate, prudent, realistic, reasonable, restrained, sensible, sober ≠ **showy:** conservative, moderate, restrained, sober ≠ **overpriced:** economical, moderate, reasonable

extravaganza *n* **1** = **show**, display, flight of fancy, pageant, spectacle, spectacular

extreme *adj* **1** = **maximum**, acute, great, greatest, high, highest, intense, severe, supreme, ultimate, utmost, uttermost, worst **2** = **excessive**, exaggerated, exceptional, extraordinary, extravagant, fanatical, immoderate, inordinate, intemperate, out-and-out, outrageous, over the top *(sl.)*, radical, remarkable, sheer, uncommon, unconventional, unreasonable, unusual **3** = **severe**, dire, drastic, harsh, radical, rigid, stern, strict, unbending, uncompromising **4** = **farthest**, faraway, far-off, final, last, most distant, outermost, remotest, terminal, ultimate, utmost, uttermost ◆ *n* **5** = **limit**, acme, apex, apogee, boundary, climax, consummation, depth, edge, end, excess, extremity, height, maximum, minimum, nadir, pinnacle, pole, termination, top, ultimate, zenith
Antonyms *adj* ≠ **maximum:** average, common, mild, moderate, modest, ordinary, reasonable, traditional, unremarkable ≠ **farthest:** nearest

extremely *adv* **1** = **very**, acutely, awfully *(inf.)*, exceedingly, exceptionally, excessively, extraordinarily, greatly, highly, inordinately, intensely, markedly, quite, severely, terribly, to a

extremist ⓘ (ɪk'striːmɪst) *n* **1** a person who favours immoderate or fanatical methods, esp. in being politically radical. ◆ *adj* **2** of or characterized by immoderate or excessive actions, opinions, etc.
▸**ex'tremism** *n*

extremity ⓘ (ɪk'stremɪtɪ) *n, pl* **extremities. 1** the farthest or outermost point or section. **2** the greatest degree. **3** an extreme condition or state, as of adversity. **4** a limb, such as a leg or wing, or the end of such a limb. **5** (*usually pl*) *Arch.* a drastic or severe measure.

extricate ⓘ ('ɛkstrɪˌkeɪt) *vb* **extricates, extricating, extricated.** (*tr*) to remove or free from complication, hindrance, or difficulty; disentangle. [C17: from L *extrīcāre* to disentangle]
▸**'extricable** *adj* ▸**ˌextri'cation** *n*

USAGE NOTE See at **extract.**

extrinsic ⓘ (ɛk'strɪnsɪk) *adj* **1** not contained or included within; extraneous. **2** originating or acting from outside. [C16: from LL *extrinsecus* (adj) outward, from L (adv), ult. from *exter* outward + *secus* alongside]
▸**ex'trinsically** *adv*

extroversion *or* **extraversion** (ˌɛkstrə'vɜːʃən) *n Psychol.* the directing of one's interest outwards, esp. towards social contacts. [C17: from *extro-* (var. of EXTRA-, contrasting with *intro-*) + *-version*, from L *vertere* to turn]
▸**ˌextro'versive** *or* **ˌextra'versive** *adj*

extrovert ⓘ *or* **extravert** ('ɛkstrəˌvɜːt) *Psychol.* ◆ *n* **1** a person concerned more with external reality than inner feelings. ◆ *adj* **2** of or characterized by extroversion. [C20: from *extro-* (var. of EXTRA-, contrasting with *intro-*) + *-vert*, from L *vertere* to turn]
▸**'extroˌverted** *or* **'extraˌverted** *adj*

extrude ⓘ (ɪk'struːd) *vb* **extrudes, extruding, extruded.** (*tr*) **1** to squeeze or force out. **2** to produce (moulded sections of plastic, metal, etc.) by ejection from a shaped nozzle or die. **3** to chop up or pulverize (an item of food) and re-form it to look like a whole. [C16: from L *extrūdere* to thrust out, from *trūdere* to push, thrust]
▸**ex'truded** *adj*

extrusion (ɪk'struːʒən) *n* **1** the act or process of extruding. **2a** the movement of magma through volcano craters and cracks in the earth's crust, forming igneous rock. **2b** any igneous rock formed in this way. **3** anything formed by the process of extruding.
▸**ex'trusive** *adj*

exuberant ⓘ (ɪg'zjuːbərənt) *adj* **1** abounding in vigour and high spirits. **2** lavish or effusive; excessively elaborate. **3** growing luxuriantly or in profusion. [C15: from L *exūberāns*, from *ūberāre* to be fruitful]
▸**ex'uberance** *n*

exuberate (ɪg'zjuːbəˌreɪt) *vb* **exuberates, exuberating, exuberated.** (*intr*) *Rare.* **1** to be exuberant. **2** to abound. [C15: from L *exūberāre* to be abundant; see EXUBERANT]

exude ⓘ (ɪg'zjuːd) *vb* **exudes, exuding, exuded. 1** to release or be released through pores, incisions, etc., as sweat or sap. **2** (*tr*) to make apparent by mood or behaviour. [C16: from L *exsūdāre*, from *sūdāre* to sweat]
▸**exudation** (ˌɛksju'deɪʃən) *n*

exult ⓘ (ɪg'zʌlt) *vb* (*intr*) **1** to be joyful or jubilant, esp. because of triumph or success. **2** (often foll. by *over*) to triumph (over). [C16: from L *exsultāre* to jump or leap for joy, from *saltāre* to leap]
▸**exultation** (ˌɛgzʌl'teɪʃən) *n* ▸**ex'ultingly** *adv*

USAGE NOTE See at **exalt.**

exultant ⓘ (ɪg'zʌltənt) *adj* elated or jubilant, esp. because of triumph or success.
▸**ex'ultantly** *adv*

exurbia (ɛks'ɜːbɪə) *n Chiefly US.* the region outside the suburbs of a city, consisting of residential areas (**exurbs**) occupied predominantly by rich commuters (**exurbanites**). [C20: from EX-[1] + L *urbs* city]
▸**ex'urban** *adj*

exuviate (ɪg'zjuːvɪˌeɪt) *vb* **exuviates, exuviating, exuviated.** to shed (a skin or similar outer covering). [C17: from L *exuere* to strip off]
▸**exˌuvi'ation** *n*

-ey *suffix.* a variant of **-y**[1] and **-y**[2].

eyas ('aɪəs) *n* a nestling hawk or falcon, esp. one reared for falconry. [C15: mistaken division of earlier *a nyas*, from OF *niais* nestling, from L *nīdus* nest]

eye[1] ⓘ (aɪ) *n* **1** the organ of sight of animals. Related adjs.: **ocular, ophthalmic. 2** (*often pl*) the ability to see; sense of vision. **3** the external part of an eye, often including the area around it. **4** a look, glance, expression, or gaze. **5** a sexually inviting or provocative look (esp. in **give (someone) the (glad) eye, make eyes at**). **6** attention or observation (often in **catch someone's eye, keep an eye on, cast an eye over**). **7** ability to recognize, judge, or appreciate. **8** (*often pl*) opinion, judgment, point of view, or authority: *in the eyes of the law*. **9** a structure or marking resembling an eye, such as the bud on a potato tuber or a spot on a butterfly wing. **10** a small loop or hole, as at one end of a needle. **11** a small area of low pressure and calm in the centre of a storm, hurricane, or tornado. **12 electric eye.** another name for **photocell. 13 all eyes.** *Inf.* acutely vigilant or observant. **14 (all) my eye.** *Inf.* rubbish; nonsense. **15 an eye for an eye.** retributive or vengeful justice; retaliation. **16 get one's eye in.** *Chiefly sport.* to become accustomed to the conditions, light, etc., with a consequent improvement in one's performance. **17 go eyes out.** *Austral.* & *NZ.* to make every possible effort. **18 half an eye.** a modicum of perceptiveness. **19 have eyes for.** to be interested in. **20 in one's mind's eye.** pictured within the mind; imagined or remembered vividly. **21 in the public eye.** exposed to public curiosity or publicity. **22 keep an eye open** *or* **out (for).** to watch with special attention (for). **23 keep one's eyes peeled** (*or* **skinned**). to watch vigilantly (for). **24 lay, clap,** *or* **set eyes on.** (*usually with a negative*) to see. **25 look (someone) in the eye.** to look openly and without shame or embarrassment at (someone). **26 make sheep's eyes (at).** *Old-fashioned.* to ogle amorously. **27 more than meets the eye.** hidden motives, meaning, or facts. **28 see eye to eye (with).** to agree (with). **29 turn a blind eye to** *or* **close one's eyes to.** to pretend not to notice or to ignore deliberately. **30 up to one's eyes (in).** extremely busy (with). **31 with** *or* **having an eye to.** (*prep*) **31a** regarding; with reference to. **31b** with the intention or purpose of. **32 with one's eyes open.** in the full knowledge of all relevant facts. **33 with one's eyes shut. 33a** with great ease, esp. as a result of thorough familiarity. **33b** without being aware of all the facts. ◆ *vb* **eyes, eyeing** *or* **eying, eyed.** (*tr*) **34** to look at carefully or warily. **35** Also: **eye up.** to look at in a manner indicating sexual interest; ogle. [OE *ēage*]
▸**'eyeless** *adj* ▸**'eyeˌlike** *adj*

eye[2] (aɪ) *n* another word for **nye.**

eyeball ('aɪˌbɔːl) *n* **1** the entire ball-shaped part of the eye. **2 eyeball to eyeball.** in close confrontation. ◆ *vb* **3** (*tr*) *Sl.* to stare at.

eyebank ('aɪˌbæŋk) *n* a place in which corneas are stored for use in corneal grafts.

eyebath ('aɪˌbɑːθ) *n* a small vessel for applying medicated or cleansing solutions to the eye. Also called (US and Canad.): **eyecup.**

eyeblack ('aɪˌblæk) *n* another name for **mascara.**

eyebright ('aɪˌbraɪt) *n* an annual plant having small white-and-purple flowers: formerly used in the treatment of eye disorders.

eyebrow ('aɪˌbraʊ) *n* **1** the transverse bony ridge over each eye. **2** the arch of hair that covers this ridge. **3 raise an eyebrow.** to give rise to doubt or disapproval.

eyebrow pencil *n* a cosmetic in pencil form for applying colour and shape to the eyebrows.

THESAURUS

fault, to *or* in the extreme, to the nth degree, ultra, uncommonly, unusually, utterly

extremist *n* **1** = **fanatic**, die-hard, radical, ultra, zealot

extremity *n* **1** = **limit**, acme, apex, apogee, border, bound, boundary, brim, brink, edge, end, extreme, farthest point, frontier, margin, maximum, minimum, nadir, pinnacle, pole, rim, terminal, termination, terminus, tip, top, ultimate, verge, zenith **3** = **crisis**, adversity, dire straits, disaster, emergency, exigency, hardship, pass, pinch, plight, setback, trouble

extricate *vb* = **free**, clear, deliver, disembarrass, disengage, disentangle, get out, get (someone) off the hook (*sl.*), liberate, release, relieve, remove, rescue, withdraw, wriggle out of

extrinsic *adj* **1, 2** = **external**, alien, exotic, exterior, extraneous, foreign, imported, outside, superficial

extrovert *adj* **2** = **outgoing**, amiable, exuberant, gregarious, hearty, sociable, social
Antonyms *adj* introspective, introverted, inward-looking, self-contained, withdrawn

extrude *vb* **1** = **force out**, eject, expel, press out, squeeze out, thrust out

exuberance *n* **1** = **high spirits**, animation, brio, buoyancy, cheerfulness, eagerness, ebullience, effervescence, energy, enthusiasm, excitement, exhilaration, life, liveliness, pep, spirit, sprightliness, vigour, vitality, vivacity, zest **2** = **fulsomeness**, effusiveness, exaggeration, excessiveness, lavishness, prodigality, superfluity **3** = **luxuriance**, abundance, copiousness, lavishness, lushness, plenitude, profusion, rankness, richness, superabundance

exuberant *adj* **1** = **high-spirited**, animated, buoyant, cheerful, chirpy (*inf.*), eager, ebullient, effervescent, elated, energetic, enthusiastic, excited, exhilarated, full of beans (*inf.*), full of life, in high spirits, lively, sparkling, spirited, sprightly, upbeat (*inf.*), vigorous, vivacious, zestful **2** = **fulsome**, effusive, exaggerated, excessive, lavish, overdone, prodigal, superfluous **3** = **luxuriant**, abundant, copious, lavish, lush, overflowing, plenteous, plentiful, profuse, rank, rich, superabundant, teeming
Antonyms *adj* ≠ **high-spirited:** apathetic, dull, lifeless, subdued, unenthusiastic

exude *vb* **1** = **seep**, bleed, discharge, emanate, emit, excrete, filter through, issue, leak, ooze, secrete, sweat, trickle, weep, well forth **2** = **radiate**, display, emanate, exhibit, manifest, show

exult *vb* **1** = **be joyful**, be delighted, be elated, be in high spirits, be jubilant, be overjoyed, celebrate, jubilate, jump for joy, make merry, rejoice **2** = **triumph**, boast, brag, crow, drool, gloat, glory (in), revel, take delight in, taunt, vaunt

exultant *adj* = **joyful**, cock-a-hoop, delighted, elated, exulting, flushed, gleeful, joyous, jubilant, overjoyed, over the moon (*inf.*), rapt, rejoicing, revelling, transported, triumphant

exultation *n* **1** = **joy**, celebration, delight, elation, glee, high spirits, joyousness, jubilation, merriness, rejoicing, transport **2** = **triumph**, boasting, bragging, crowing, gloating, glory, glorying, revelling

eye[1] *n* **1** = **eyeball**, optic (*inf.*), orb (*poetic*), peeper (*sl.*) **6 keep an eye on** = **watch**, guard, keep in view, keep tabs on (*inf.*), keep under surveillance, look after, look out for, monitor, observe, pay attention to, regard, scrutinize, supervise, survey, watch like a hawk, watch over **7** = **appreciation**, discernment, discrimination, judgment, perception, recognition, taste **8** *often plural* = **opinion**, belief, judgment, mind, point of view, viewpoint **15 an eye for an eye** = **retaliation**, justice, reprisal, requital, retribution, revenge, vengeance **24 lay, clap,** *or* **set eyes on** = **see**, behold, come across, encounter,

eye-catching ❶ *adj* tending to attract attention; striking.
eye contact *n* a direct look between two people; meeting of eyes.
eyed (aɪd) *adj* **a** having an eye or eyes (as specified). **b** (*in combination*): *brown-eyed*.
eye dog *n NZ*. a dog trained to control sheep by staring fixedly at them. Also called: **strong-eye dog**.
eyeful ❶ ('aɪfʊl) *n Inf.* **1** a view, glance, or gaze. **2** a beautiful or attractive sight, esp. a woman.
eyeglass ('aɪˌglɑːs) *n* **1** a lens for aiding or correcting defective vision, esp. a monocle. **2** another word for **eyepiece** or **eyebath**.
eyeglasses ('aɪˌglɑːsɪz) *pl n Now chiefly US*. another word for **spectacles**.
eyehole ('aɪˌhəʊl) *n* **1** a hole through which a rope, hook, etc., is passed. **2** the cavity that contains the eyeball. **3** another word for **peephole**.
eyelash ('aɪˌlæʃ) *n* **1** any one of the short curved hairs that grow from the edge of the eyelids. **2** a row or fringe of these hairs.
eyelet ('aɪlɪt) *n* **1** a small hole for a lace, cord, or hook to be passed through. **2** a small metal ring or tube reinforcing an eyehole in fabric. **3** a small opening, such as a peephole. **4** *Embroidery*. a small hole with finely stitched edges. **5** a small eye or eyelike marking. ◆ *vb* **6** (*tr*) to supply with an eyelet or eyelets. [C14: from OF *oillet*, lit.: a little eye, from *oill* eye, from L *oculus* eye]
eyelevel ('aɪˌlevᵊl) *adj* level with a person's eyes when looking straight ahead: *an eyelevel grill*.
eyelid ('aɪˌlɪd) *n* either of the two muscular folds of skin that can be moved to cover the exposed portion of the eyeball.
eyeliner ('aɪˌlaɪnə) *n* a cosmetic used to outline the eyes.
eye-opener *n Inf.* **1** something startling or revealing. **2** *US & Canad.* an alcoholic drink taken early in the morning.
eyepiece ('aɪˌpiːs) *n* the lens or lenses in an optical instrument nearest the eye of the observer.
eye rhyme *n* a rhyme involving words that are similar in spelling but not in sound, such as *stone* and *none*.
eye shadow *n* a coloured cosmetic put around the eyes.
eyeshot ('aɪˌʃɒt) *n* range of vision; view.
eyesight ❶ ('aɪˌsaɪt) *n* the ability to see; faculty of sight.
eyesore ❶ ('aɪˌsɔː) *n* something very ugly.
eyespot ('aɪˌspɒt) *n* **1** a small area of light-sensitive pigment in some simple organisms. **2** an eyelike marking, as on a butterfly wing.
eyestrain ('aɪˌstreɪn) *n* fatigue or irritation of the eyes, resulting from excessive use or uncorrected defects of vision.
Eyetie ('aɪtaɪ) *n, adj Brit. sl., offensive*. Italian. [C20: from jocular mispronunciation of *Italian*]
eyetooth (ˌaɪ'tuːθ) *n, pl* **eyeteeth**. **1** either of the two canine teeth in the upper jaw. **2 give one's eyeteeth for**. to go to any lengths to achieve or obtain (something).
eyewash ('aɪˌwɒʃ) *n* **1** a lotion for the eyes. **2** *Inf.* nonsense; rubbish.
eyewitness ❶ ('aɪˌwɪtnɪs) *n* a person present at an event who can describe what happened.
eyot (aɪt) *n Brit., obs. except in place names*. island. [var. of AIT]
eyrie ('ɪərɪ, 'eərɪ, 'aɪərɪ) *or* **aerie** *n* **1** the nest of an eagle or other bird of prey, built in a high inaccessible place. **2** any high isolated position or place. [C16: from Med. L *airea*, from L *ārea* open field, hence, nest]
eyrir ('eɪrɪə) *n, pl* **aurar** ('ɔɪrɑː). an Icelandic monetary unit worth one hundredth of a krona. [ON: ounce (of silver), money; rel. to L *aureus* golden]
Ez. *or* **Ezr.** *Bible. abbrev. for* Ezra.
Ezek. *Bible. abbrev. for* Ezekiel.

THESAURUS

meet, notice, observe, run into **28 see eye to eye = agree**, accord, back, be in unison, coincide, concur, fall in, get on, go along, harmonize, jibe (*inf.*), speak the same language, subscribe to **30 up to one's eyes = busy**, caught up, engaged, flooded out, fully occupied, inundated, overwhelmed, up to here, up to one's elbows, wrapped up in ◆ *vb* **34 = look at**, behold, check out (*inf.*), contemplate, eyeball (*sl.*), get a load of (*inf.*), glance at, have *or* take a look at, inspect, peruse, regard, scan, scrutinize, stare at, study, survey, view, watch **35 = ogle**, eye up (*inf.*), give (someone) the (glad) eye, leer at, make eyes at

eye-catching *adj* = **striking**, arresting, attractive, captivating, dramatic, showy, spectacular

eyeful *n* **1 = look**, butcher's (*Brit. sl.*), gander (*inf.*), gaze, glance, shufti (*Brit. sl.*), sight, view **2 = spectacle**, beauty, dazzler, humdinger (*sl.*), knockout (*inf.*), show, sight, sight for sore eyes (*inf.*), stunner (*inf.*), vision

eyesight *n* = **vision**, observation, perception, range of vision, sight

eyesore *n* = **mess**, atrocity, blemish, blight, blot, disfigurement, disgrace, horror, monstrosity, sight (*inf.*), ugliness

eyewitness *n* = **observer**, bystander, looker-on, onlooker, passer-by, spectator, viewer, watcher, witness

Ff

f *or* **F** (ɛf) *n, pl* **f's, F's,** *or* **Fs. 1** the sixth letter of the English alphabet. **2** a speech sound represented by this letter, as in *fat*.

f *symbol for:* **1** *Music.* forte: an instruction to play loudly. **2** *Physics.* frequency. **3** *Maths.* function (of). **4** *Physics.* femto-.

f, f/, *or* **f:** *symbol for* f-number.

F *symbol for:* **1** *Music.* **1a** the fourth note of the scale of C major. **1b** the major or minor key having this note as its tonic. **2** Fahrenheit. **3** farad(s). **4** *Chem.* fluorine. **5** *Physics.* force. **6** franc(s). **7** *Genetics.* a generation of filial offspring, F_1 being the first generation of offspring.

f. *or* **F.** *abbrev. for:* **1** fathom(s). **2** female. **3** *Grammar.* feminine. **4** (*pl* **ff.** *or* **FF.**) folio. **5** (*pl* **ff.**) following (page).

F- (of US military aircraft) *abbrev. for* fighter.

fa (fɑː) *n Music.* the syllable used in the fixed system of solmization for the note F. [C14: see GAMUT]

FA (in Britain) *abbrev. for* Football Association.

f.a. *or* **FA** *abbrev. for* fanny adams.

FAB *abbrev. for* fuel air bomb.

Fabian Ⓣ ('feɪbɪən) *adj* **1** of or resembling the delaying tactics of Q. Fabius Maximus, Roman general who wore out the strength of Hannibal while avoiding a pitched battle; cautious. ◆ *n* **2** a member of or sympathizer with the Fabian Society. [C19: from L *Fabiānus* of Fabius]
▸ **'Fabia,nism** *n*

Fabian Society *n* an association of British socialists advocating the establishment of socialism by gradual reforms.

fable Ⓣ ('feɪbᵊl) *n* **1** a short moral story, esp. one with animals as characters. **2** a false, fictitious, or improbable account. **3** a story or legend about supernatural or mythical characters or events. **4** legends or myths collectively. ◆ *vb* **fables, fabling, fabled. 5** to relate or tell (fables). **6** (*intr*) to tell lies. **7** (*tr*) to talk about or describe in the manner of a fable. [C13: from L *fābula* story, narrative, from *fārī* to speak, say]
▸ **'fabler** *n*

fabled Ⓣ ('feɪbᵊld) *adj* **1** made famous in fable. **2** fictitious.

fabliau ('fæblɪ,əʊ) *n, pl* **fabliaux** ('fæblɪ,əʊz). a comic usually ribald verse tale, popular in France in the 12th and 13th centuries. [C19: from F: a little tale, from *fable* tale]

Fablon ('fæblən, -lɒn) *n Trademark.* a brand of adhesive-backed plastic material used to cover and decorate shelves, worktops, etc.

fabric Ⓣ ('fæbrɪk) *n* **1** any cloth made from yarn or fibres by weaving, knitting, felting, etc. **2** the texture of a cloth. **3** a structure or framework: *the fabric of society.* **4** a style or method of construction. **5** *Rare.* a building. [C15: from L *fabrica* workshop, from *faber* craftsman]

fabricate Ⓣ ('fæbrɪ,keɪt) *vb* **fabricates, fabricating, fabricated.** (*tr*) **1** to make, build, or construct. **2** to devise or concoct (a story, etc.). **3** to fake or forge. [C15: from L, from *fabrica* workshop; see FABRIC]
▸ **,fabri'cation** *n* ▸ **'fabri,cator** *n*

fabulist ('fæbjʊlɪst) *n* **1** a person who invents or recounts fables. **2** a person who lies.

fabulous Ⓣ ('fæbjʊləs) *adj* **1** almost unbelievable; astounding; legendary: *fabulous wealth.* **2** *Inf.* extremely good: *a fabulous time at the party.* **3** of, relating to, or based upon fable: *a fabulous beast.* [C15: from L *fābulōsus* celebrated in fable, from *fābula* FABLE]
▸ **'fabulously** *adv* ▸ **'fabulousness** *n*

Fac. *abbrev. for* Faculty.

façade Ⓣ *or* **facade** (fə'sɑːd, fæ-) *n* **1** the face of a building, esp. the main front. **2** a front or outer appearance, esp. a deceptive one. [C17: from F, from It., from *faccia* FACE]

face Ⓣ (feɪs) *n* **1a** the front of the head from the forehead to the lower jaw. **1b** (*as modifier*): *face flannel.* **2a** the expression of the countenance: *a sad face.* **2b** a distorted expression, esp. to indicate disgust. **3** *Inf.* make-up (esp. in **put one's face on**). **4** outward appearance: *the face of the countryside is changing.* **5** appearance or pretence (esp. in **put a bold, good, bad,** etc., **face on**). **6** dignity (esp. in **lose** *or* **save face**). **7** *Inf.* impudence or effrontery. **8** the main side of an object, building, etc., or the front: *a cliff face.* **9** the marked surface of an instrument, esp. the dial of a timepiece. **10** the functional or working side of an object, as of a tool or playing card. **11a** the exposed area of a mine from which coal, ore, etc., may be mined. **11b** (*as modifier*): *face worker.* **12** the uppermost part or surface: *the face of the earth.* **13** Also called: **side.** any one of the plane surfaces of a crystal or other solid figure. **14** Also called: **typeface.** *Printing.* **14a** the printing surface of any type character. **14b** the style or design of the character on the type. **15** *NZ.* the exposed slope of a hill. **16** *Brit. sl.* a well-known or important person. **17 in (the) face of.** despite. **18 on the face of it.** to all appearances. **19 set one's face against.** to oppose with determination. **20 show one's face.** to make an appearance. **21 to someone's face.** in someone's presence: *I told him the truth to his face.* ◆ *vb* **faces, facing, faced. 22** (when *intr*, often foll. by *to, towards,* or *on*) to look or be situated or placed (in a specified direction): *the house faces onto the square.* **23** to be opposite: *facing page 9.* **24** (*tr*) to be confronted by: *he faces many problems.* **25** (*tr*) to provide with a surface of a different material. **26** to dress the surface of (stone or other material). **27** (*tr*) to expose (a card) with the face uppermost. **28** *Mil.* to order (a formation) to turn in a certain direction or (of a formation) to turn as required: *right face!* ◆ See also **face down, face up to.** [C13: from OF, from Vulgar L *facia* (unattested), from L *faciēs* form]

face card *n* the usual US and Canad. term for **court card.**

face cloth *or* **face flannel** *n Brit.* a small piece of cloth used to wash the face and hands. US equivalent: **washcloth.**

facedown ('feɪsdaʊn) *n Inf.* another word for **face-off** (sense 2).

face down *vb* (*tr, adv*) to confront and force (someone or something) to back down.

faceless Ⓣ ('feɪslɪs) *adj* **1** without a face. **2** without identity; anonymous.
▸ **'facelessness** *n*

face-lift Ⓣ *n* **1** a cosmetic surgical operation for tightening sagging skin and smoothing wrinkles on the face. **2** any improvement or renovation. ◆ *vb* (*tr*) **3** to improve the appearance of, as by a face-lift.

face-off *n* **1** *Ice hockey.* the method of starting a game, in which the referee drops the puck, etc. between two opposing players. **2** Also called **facedown.** a confrontation, esp. one in which each party attempts to make the other back down. ◆ *vb* **face off.** (*intr, adv*) **3** to start play by a face-off.

face powder *n* a cosmetic powder worn to make the face look less shiny, softer, etc.

facer Ⓣ ('feɪsə) *n* **1** a person or thing that faces. **2** *Brit. inf.* a difficulty or problem.

face-saving *adj* maintaining dignity or prestige.
▸ **'face-,saver** *n*

facet Ⓣ ('fæsɪt) *n* **1** any of the surfaces of a cut gemstone. **2** an aspect or phase, as of a subject or personality. ◆ *vb* **facets, faceting** *or* **facetting,**

THESAURUS

Fabian *adj* **1 = cautious,** attritional, circumspect, delaying, procrastinating

fable *n* **1, 3 = story,** allegory, apologue, legend, myth, parable, tale **2 = fiction,** fabrication, fairy story (*inf.*), falsehood, fantasy, fib, figment, invention, lie, romance, tall story (*inf.*), untruth, urban legend, urban myth, white lie, yarn (*inf.*)
Antonyms *n* actuality, certainty, fact, reality, truth, verity

fabled *adj* **1, 2 = legendary,** fabulous, famed, famous, fictional, mythical, storied

fabric *n* **1 = cloth,** material, stuff, textile, web **3, 4 = framework,** constitution, construction, foundations, infrastructure, make-up, organization, structure

fabricate *vb* **1 = build,** assemble, construct, erect, fashion, form, frame, make, manufacture, shape **2, 3 = make up,** coin, concoct, devise, fake, falsify, feign, forge, form, invent, trump up

fabrication *n* **1 = construction,** assemblage, assembly, building, erection, manufacture, production **2, 3 = forgery,** cock-and-bull story (*inf.*), concoction, fable, fairy story (*inf.*), fake, falsehood, fiction, figment, invention, lie, myth, pork pie (*Brit. sl.*), porky (*Brit. sl.*), untruth

fabulous *adj* **1 = astounding,** amazing, breathtaking, fictitious, immense, inconceivable, incredible, legendary, phenomenal, unbelievable **2** *Informal* **= wonderful,** brilliant, fantastic, magic (*inf.*), marvellous, out-of-this-world (*inf.*), sensational (*inf.*), spectacular, superb **3 = legendary,** apocryphal, fantastic, fictitious, imaginary, invented, made-up, mythical, unreal
Antonyms *adj* actual, common, commonplace, credible, genuine, natural, ordinary, real

façade *n* **1, 2 = appearance,** exterior, face, front, frontage, guise, mask, pretence, semblance, show, veneer

face *n* **1 = countenance,** clock, dial (*Brit. sl.*), features, kisser (*sl.*), lineaments, mug (*sl.*), phiz *or* phizog (*sl.*), physiognomy, visage **2 = scowl,** frown, grimace, *moue,* pout, smirk **4 = expression,** appearance, aspect, look **5** *As in* **put a good face on = façade,** air, appearance, disguise, display, exterior, front, mask, pretence, semblance, show **6** *As in* **save** or lose face **= self-respect,** authority, dignity, honour, image, prestige, reputation, standing, status **7** *Informal* **= impudence,** assurance, audacity, boldness, brass neck (*Brit. inf.*), cheek (*inf.*), chutzpah (*US & Canad. inf.*), confidence, effrontery, front, gall (*inf.*), neck (*inf.*), nerve, presumption, sauce (*inf.*) **12, 13 = side,** aspect, cover, exterior, facet, front, outside, right side, surface **18 on the face of it = to all appearances,** apparently, at first sight, seemingly, to the eye **20 = turn up,** appear **show one's face** approach, be seen, come, put in *or* make an appearance, show up (*inf.*) **21 to one's face = directly,** in one's presence, openly, straight ◆ *vb* **23 = look onto,** be opposite, front onto, give towards *or* onto, overlook **24 = confront,** be confronted by, brave, come up against, cope with, deal with, defy, encounter, experience, face off (*sl.*), meet, oppose, tackle **25, 26 = coat,** clad, cover, dress, finish, level, line, overlay, sheathe, surface, veneer

faceless *adj* **2 = impersonal,** anonymous, remote, unidentified, unknown

face-lift *n* **1 = cosmetic surgery,** plastic surgery **2 = renovation,** restoration

facer *n* **2** *Brit. informal* **= problem,** difficulty, dilemma, how-do-you-do (*inf.*), poser, puzzle, teaser

facet *n* **1 = aspect,** angle, face, part, phase, plane, side, slant, surface

facetious *adj* **1, 2 = funny,** amusing, comical,

faceted *or* **facetted. 3** (*tr*) to cut facets in (a gemstone). [C17: from F *facette* a little FACE]

facetiae (fəˈsiːʃɪˌiː) *pl n* **1** humorous or witty sayings. **2** obscene or coarsely witty books. [C17: from L: jests, pl of *facētia* witticism, from *facētus* elegant]

facetious ❶ (fəˈsiːʃəs) *adj* **1** characterized by love of joking. **2** jocular or amusing, esp. at inappropriate times: *facetious remarks.* [C16: from OF *facetieux,* from *facetie* witticism; see FACETIAE]
▸**faˈcetiously** *adv* ▸**faˈcetiousness** *n*

face to face ❶ *adv, adj* (**face-to-face** *as adj*) **1** opposite one another. **2** in confrontation.

face up to ❶ *vb* (*intr, adv + prep*) to accept (an unpleasant fact, reality, etc.).

face value *n* **1** the value written or stamped on the face of a commercial paper or coin. **2** apparent worth or value.

facia (ˈfeɪʃɪə) *n* a variant spelling of **fascia.**

facial (ˈfeɪʃəl) *adj* **1** of or relating to the face. ◆ *n* **2** a beauty treatment for the face involving massage and cosmetic packs.
▸**ˈfacially** *adv*

-facient *suffix forming adjectives and nouns.* indicating a state or quality: *absorbefacient.* [from L *facient-, faciēns,* present participle of *facere* to do]

facies (ˈfeɪʃɪˌiːz) *n, pl* **facies. 1** the general form and appearance of an individual or a group. **2** the characteristics of a rock or rocks reflecting their appearance and conditions of formation. **3** *Med.* the general facial expression of a patient. [C17: from L: appearance, FACE]

facile ❶ (ˈfæsaɪl) *adj* **1** easy to perform or achieve. **2** working or moving easily or smoothly. **3** superficial: *a facile solution.* [C15: from L *facilis* easy, from *facere* to do]
▸**ˈfacilely** *adv* ▸**ˈfacileness** *n*

facilitate ❶ (fəˈsɪlɪˌteɪt) *vb* **facilitates, facilitating, facilitated.** (*tr*) to assist the progress of.
▸**faˌciliˈtation** *n*

facility ❶ (fəˈsɪlɪtɪ) *n, pl* **facilities. 1** ease of action or performance. **2** ready skill or ease deriving from practice or familiarity. **3** (*often pl*) the means or equipment facilitating the performance of an action. **4** *Rare.* easy-going disposition. **5** (*usually pl*) a euphemistic word for **lavatory.** [C15: from L *facilitās,* from *facilis* easy; see FACILE]

facing ❶ (ˈfeɪsɪŋ) *n* **1** a piece of material used esp. to conceal the seam of a garment and prevent fraying. **2** (*usually pl*) the collar, cuffs, etc., of the jacket of a military uniform. **3** an outer layer or coat of material applied to the surface of a wall.

facsimile ❶ (fækˈsɪmɪlɪ) *n* **1** an exact copy or reproduction. **2** an image produced by facsimile transmission; fax. ◆ *vb* **facsimiles, facsimileing, facsimiled. 3** (*tr*) to make an exact copy of. [C17: from L *fac simile!* make something like it!, from *facere* to make + *similis* similar, like]

facsimile transmission *n* an international system of transmitting a written, printed, or pictorial document over the telephone system by scanning it photoelectrically and reproducing the image xerographically after transmission. Often shortened to **fax.**

fact ❶ (fækt) *n* **1** an event or thing known to have happened or existed. **2** a truth verifiable from experience or observation. **3** a piece of information: *get me all the facts of this case.* **4** (*often pl*) *Law.* an actual event, happening, etc., as distinguished from its legal consequences. **5 after** (*or* **before**) **the fact.** *Criminal law.* after (or before) the commission of the offence. **6 as a matter of fact, in fact, in point of fact.** in reality or actuality. **7 fact of life.** an inescapable truth, esp. an unpleasant one. See also **facts of life.** [C16: from L *factum* something done, from *factus* made, from *facere* to do, make]

faction[1] ❶ (ˈfækʃən) *n* **1** a group of people forming a minority within a larger body, esp. a dissentious group. **2** strife or dissension within a group. [C16: from L *factiō* a making, from *facere* to do, make]
▸**ˈfactional** *adj*

faction[2] (ˈfækʃən) *n* a television programme, film, or literary work comprising a dramatized presentation of actual events. [C20: a blend of FACT & FICTION]

faction fight *n* conflict between different groups within a larger body, esp. in S Africa a fight between Blacks of different tribes.

factious ❶ (ˈfækʃəs) *adj* given to, producing, or characterized by faction.
▸**ˈfactiously** *adv*

> **USAGE NOTE** See at **fractious.**

factitious ❶ (fækˈtɪʃəs) *adj* **1** artificial rather than natural. **2** not genuine; sham: *factitious enthusiasm.* [C17: from L *facticius,* from *facere* to do, make]
▸**facˈtitiously** *adv* ▸**facˈtitiousness** *n*

factitive (ˈfæktɪtɪv) *adj Grammar.* denoting a verb taking a direct object as well as a noun in apposition, as for example *elect* in *They elected John president,* where *John* is the direct object and *president* is the complement. [C19: from NL, from L *factitāre* to do frequently, from *facere* to do, make]

factoid (ˈfæktɔɪd) *n* a piece of unreliable information believed to be true because of the way it is presented or repeated in print. [C20: coined by Norman Mailer (born 1923), US author, from FACT + -OID]

factor ❶ (ˈfæktə) *n* **1** an element or cause that contributes to a result. **2** *Maths.* one of two or more integers or polynomials whose product is a given integer or polynomial: *2 and 3 are factors of 6.* **3** (foll. by identifying numeral) *Med.* any of several substances that participate in the clotting of blood: *factor VIII.* **4** a person who acts on another's behalf, esp. one who transacts business for another. **5** former name for a **gene. 6** *Commercial law.* a person to whom goods are consigned for sale and who is paid a commission. **7** (in Scotland) the manager of an estate. ◆ *vb* **8** (*intr*) to engage in the business of a factor. [C15: from L: one who acts, from *facere* to do, make]
▸**ˈfactorable** *adj* ▸**ˈfactorship** *n*

> **USAGE NOTE** *Factor* (sense 1) should only be used to refer to something which contributes to a result. It should not be used to refer to a part of something such as a plan or arrangement; instead a word such as *component* or *element* should be used.

factor VIII *n* a protein that participates in the clotting of blood. It is extracted from donated serum and used in the treatment of haemophilia.

factorial (fækˈtɔːrɪəl) *Maths.* ◆ *n* **1** the product of all the positive integers from one up to and including a given integer: *factorial four is* $1 \times 2 \times 3 \times 4$. ◆ *adj* **2** of or involving factorials or factors.
▸**facˈtorially** *adv*

factorize *or* **factorise** (ˈfæktəˌraɪz) *vb* **factorizes, factorizing, factorized** *or* **factorises, factorising, factorised.** (*tr*) *Maths.* to resolve (an integer or polynomial) into factors.
▸**ˌfactoriˈzation** *or* **ˌfactoriˈsation** *n*

factory ❶ (ˈfæktərɪ) *n, pl* **factories. a** a building or group of buildings containing a plant assembly for the manufacture of goods. **b** (*as modifier*): *a factory worker.* [C16: from LL *factorium;* see FACTOR]
▸**ˈfactory-ˌlike** *adj*

factory farm *n* a farm in which animals are intensively reared using modern industrial methods.
▸**factory farming** *n*

THESAURUS

droll, flippant, frivolous, humorous, jesting, jocose, jocular, merry, playful, pleasant, tongue in cheek, unserious, waggish, witty
Antonyms *adj* earnest, genuine, grave, lugubrious, pensive, sedate, serious, sincere, sober, thoughtful

face to face *adv, adj* **1, 2 = facing,** *à deux,* confronting, eyeball to eyeball, in confrontation, opposite, tête-à-tête, vis-à-vis

face up to *vb* **= accept,** acknowledge, come to terms with, confront, cope with, deal with, face the music, meet head-on, tackle

facile *adj* **1, 2 = easy,** adept, adroit, dexterous, effortless, fluent, light, proficient, quick, ready, simple, skilful, smooth, uncomplicated **3 = superficial,** cursory, glib, hasty, shallow, slick
Antonyms *adj* ≠ **easy:** awkward, careful, clumsy, difficult, intractable, maladroit, slow, thoughtful, unskilful

facilitate *vb* **= promote,** assist the progress of, ease, expedite, forward, further, help, make easy, oil the wheels, pave the way for, smooth the path of, speed up
Antonyms *vb* delay, encumber, frustrate, hamper, handicap, hinder, hold up *or* back, impede, obstruct, prevent, restrain, thwart

facility *n* **1, 2 = ease,** ability, adroitness, craft, dexterity, efficiency, effortlessness, expertness, fluency, gift, knack, proficiency, quickness, readiness, skilfulness, skill, smoothness, talent **3** *often plural* **= equipment,** advantage, aid, amenity, appliance, convenience, means, opportunity, resource
Antonyms *n* ≠ **ease:** awkwardness, clumsiness, difficulty, hardship, ineptness, maladroitness, pains

facing *n* **3 = overlay,** cladding, coating, façade, false front, front, plaster, reinforcement, revetment, stucco, surface, trimming, veneer

facsimile *n* **1, 2 = copy,** carbon, carbon copy, duplicate, fax, photocopy, Photostat (*Trademark*), print, replica, reproduction, transcript, Xerox (*Trademark*)

fact *n* **1 = event,** act, deed, *fait accompli,* happening, incident, occurrence, performance **2 = truth,** actuality, certainty, gospel (truth), naked truth, reality **3 = detail,** circumstance, feature, item, particular, point, specific **6 in fact = actually,** indeed, in point of fact, in reality, in truth, really, truly
Antonyms *n* ≠ **truth:** delusion, fable, fabrication, falsehood, fiction, invention, lie, tall story, untruth, yarn (*inf.*)

faction[1] *n* **1 = group,** bloc, cabal, camp, caucus, clique, coalition, combination, confederacy, contingent, coterie, division, gang, ginger group, junta, lobby, minority, party, pressure group, schism, section, sector, set, splinter group **2 = dissension,** conflict, disagreement, discord, disharmony, disunity, division, divisiveness, friction, infighting, rebellion, sedition, strife, tumult, turbulence
Antonyms *n* ≠ **dissension:** accord, agreement, amity, assent, concord, consensus, friendship, goodwill, harmony, peace, rapport, unanimity, unity

factious *adj* **= contentious,** conflicting, disputatious, dissident, divisive, insurrectionary, litigious, malcontent, mutinous, partisan, rebellious, refractory, rival, sectarian, seditious, troublemaking, tumultuous, turbulent, warring

factitious *adj* **1, 2 = artificial,** affected, assumed, counterfeited, engineered, fabricated, fake, false, imitation, insincere, made-up, manufactured, mock, phoney *or* phony (*inf.*), pinchbeck, pseudo (*inf.*), put-on, sham, simulated, spurious, synthetic, unnatural, unreal

factor *n* **1 = element,** aspect, cause, circumstance, component, consideration, determinant, influence, item, part, point, thing **7** *Scot.* **= agent,** deputy, estate manager, middleman, reeve, steward

factory *n* **= works,** manufactory, mill, plant

factory ship *n* a vessel that processes fish supplied by a fleet.

factotum ❶ (fæk'təutəm) *n* a person employed to do all kinds of work. [C16: from Med. L, from L *fac!* do! + *tōtum,* from *tōtus* (adj) all]

facts and figures ❶ *pl n* details.

factsheet ('fækt,ʃi:t) *n* a printed sheet containing information relating to items covered in a television or radio programme.

facts of life *pl n* **the.** the details of sexual behaviour and reproduction.

factual ❶ ('fæktʃuəl) *adj* **1** of, relating to, or characterized by facts. **2** real; actual.
▸ **'factually** *adv* ▸ **'factualness** *or* **,factu'ality** *n*

facula ('fækjulə) *n, pl* **faculae** (-,li:). any of the bright areas on the sun's surface, usually appearing just before a sunspot. [C18: from L: little torch, from *fax* torch]
▸ **'facular** *adj*

facultative ('fækəltətɪv) *adj* **1** empowering but not compelling the doing of an act. **2** that may or may not occur. **3** *Biol.* able to exist under more than one set of environmental conditions. **4** of or relating to a faculty.
▸ **'facultatively** *adv*

faculty ❶ ('fækəltɪ) *n, pl* **faculties. 1** one of the inherent powers of the mind or body, such as memory, sight, or hearing. **2** any ability or power, whether acquired or inherent. **3** a conferred power or right. **4a** a department within a university or college devoted to a particular branch of knowledge. **4b** the staff of such a department. **4c** *Chiefly US & Canad.* all the teaching staff at a university, school, etc. **5** all members of a learned profession. [C14 (in the sense: department of learning): from L *facultās* capability; rel. to L *facilis* easy]

FA Cup *n Soccer.* (in England and Wales) **1** an annual knockout competition among member teams of the Football Association. **2** the trophy itself.

fad ❶ (fæd) *n Inf.* **1** an intense but short-lived fashion. **2** a personal idiosyncrasy. [C19: from ?]
▸ **'faddish** *or* **'faddy** *adj*

fade ❶ (feɪd) *vb* **fades, fading, faded. 1** to lose or cause to lose brightness, colour, or clarity. **2** (*intr*) to lose vigour or youth. **3** (*intr;* usually foll. by *away* or *out*) to vanish slowly. **4a** to decrease the brightness or volume of (a television or radio programme) or (of a television programme, etc.) to decrease in this way. **4b** to decrease the volume of (a sound) in a recording system or (of a sound) to be so reduced in volume. **5** (*intr*) (of the brakes of a vehicle) to lose power. **6** to cause (a golf ball) to veer from a straight line or (of a golf ball) to veer from a straight flight. ◆ *n* **7** the act or an instance of fading. [C14: from *fade* (adj) dull, from OF, from Vulgar L *fatidus* (unattested), prob. blend of L *vapidus* VAPID + L *fatuus* FATUOUS]
▸ **'fadeless** *adj* ▸ **'fadedness** *n* ▸ **'fader** *n*

fade-in *n* **1** *Films.* an optical effect in which a shot appears gradually out of darkness. ◆ *vb* **fade in.** (*adv*) **2** to increase or cause to increase gradually, as vision or sound in a film or broadcast.

fade-out *n* **1** *Films.* an optical effect in which a shot slowly disappears into darkness. **2** a gradual and temporary loss of a radio or television signal. **3** a slow or gradual disappearance. ◆ *vb* **fade out.** (*adv*) **4** to decrease or cause to decrease gradually, as vision or sound in a film or broadcast.

faeces ❶ *or esp. US* **feces** ('fi:si:z) *pl n* bodily waste matter discharged through the anus. [C15: from L *faecēs,* pl. of *faex* sediment, dregs]
▸ **faecal** *or esp. US* **fecal** ('fi:kəl) *adj*

faerie *or* **faery** ('feɪərɪ, 'feərɪ) *n, pl* **faeries.** *Arch. or poetic.* **1** the land of fairies. ◆ *adj, n* **2** a variant spelling of **fairy.**

Faeroese *or* **Faroese** (,feərəu'i:z) *adj* **1** of or characteristic of the Faeroes, islands in the N Atlantic, their inhabitants, or their language. ◆ *n* **2** the language of the Faeroes, closely related to Icelandic. **3** (*pl* **Faeroese** *or* **Faroese**) a native or inhabitant of the Faeroes.

faff (fæf) *vb* (*intr;* often foll. by *about*) *Brit. inf.* to dither or fuss. [C19: from ?]

fag[1] ❶ (fæg) *n* **1** *Inf.* a boring or wearisome task. **2** *Brit.* (esp. formerly) a young public school boy who performs menial chores for an older boy or prefect. ◆ *vb* **fags, fagging, fagged. 3** (when *tr,* often foll. by *out*) *Inf.* to become or cause to become exhausted by hard work **4** (*usually intr*) *Brit.* to do or cause to do menial chores in a public school. [C18: from ?]

fag[2] (fæg) *n Brit. sl.* a cigarette. [C16 (in the sense: something hanging loose, flap): from ?]

fag[3] ❶ (fæg) *n Sl., chiefly US & Canad.* short for **faggot**[2].

fag end *n* **1** the last and worst part. **2** *Brit. inf.* the stub of a cigarette. [C17: see FAG[2]]

faggot[1] *or esp. US* **fagot** ('fægət) *n* **1** a bundle of sticks or twigs, esp. when used as fuel. **2** a bundle of iron bars, esp. to be forged into wrought iron. **3** a ball of chopped meat bound with herbs and bread and eaten fried. ◆ *vb* (*tr*) **4** to collect into a bundle or bundles. **5** *Needlework.* to do faggoting on (a garment, etc.). [C14: from OF, ?from Gk *phakelos* bundle]

faggot[2] ('fægət) *n Sl., chiefly US & Canad.* a male homosexual. [C20: special use of FAGGOT[1]]

faggoting *or esp. US* **fagoting** ('fægətɪŋ) *n* **1** decorative needlework done by tying vertical threads together in bundles. **2** a decorative way of joining two hems by crisscross stitches.

fag hag *n US sl., usually derog.* a heterosexual woman who prefers the company of homosexual men.

fah *n Music.* (in tonic sol-fa) the fourth degree of any major scale. [C14: later variant of *fa;* see GAMUT]

Fah. *or* **Fahr.** *abbrev. for* Fahrenheit.

Fahrenheit ('færən,haɪt) *adj* of or measured according to the Fahrenheit scale of temperature. Symbol: F [C18: after Gabriel *Fahrenheit* (1686–1736), G physicist]

Fahrenheit scale *n* a scale of temperatures in which 32° represents the melting point of ice and 212° represents the boiling point of pure water under standard atmospheric pressure. Cf. **Celsius scale.**

faïence (faɪ'ɑ:ns, feɪ-) *n* tin-glazed earthenware, usually that of French, German, Italian, or Scandinavian origin. [C18: from F, strictly: pottery from *Faenza,* N Italy]

fail ❶ (feɪl) *vb* **1** to be unsuccessful in an attempt (at something or to do something). **2** (*intr*) to stop operating or working properly: *the steering failed suddenly.* **3** to judge or be judged as being below the officially accepted standard required in (a course, examination, etc.). **4** (*tr*) to prove disappointing or useless to (someone). **5** (*tr*) to neglect or be unable (to do something). **6** (*intr*) to prove insufficient in quantity or extent. **7** (*intr*) to weaken. **8** (*intr*) to go bankrupt. ◆ *n* **9** a failure to attain the required standard. **10 without fail.** definitely. [C13: from OF *faillir,* ult. from L *fallere* to disappoint]

failing ❶ ('feɪlɪŋ) *n* **1** a weak point. ◆ *prep* **2** (*used to express a condition*) in default of: *failing a solution, the problem will have to wait until Monday.*

fail-safe *adj* **1** designed to return to a safe condition in the event of a failure or malfunction. **2** safe from failure; foolproof.

failure ❶ ('feɪljə) *n* **1** the act or an instance of failing. **2** a person or

THESAURUS

factotum *n* = **Man Friday** *or* **Girl Friday,** handyman, jack of all trades, man of all work, odd job man

facts and figures *pl n* = **information,** data, details, gen, info (*inf.*), ins and outs, the low-down (*inf.*), the score (*inf.*), the whole story

factual *adj* **1, 2** = **true,** accurate, authentic, circumstantial, close, correct, credible, exact, faithful, genuine, literal, matter-of-fact, objective, precise, real, sure, true-to-life, unadorned, unbiased, veritable
Antonyms *adj* embellished, fanciful, fictitious, fictive, figurative, imaginary, unreal

faculty *n* **1** *usually plural* = **powers,** capabilities, intelligence, reason, senses, wits **2** = **ability,** adroitness, aptitude, bent, capability, capacity, cleverness, dexterity, facility, gift, knack, power, propensity, readiness, skill, talent, turn **3** = **right,** authorization, licence, prerogative, privilege **4** = **department,** branch of learning, discipline, profession, school, teaching staff (*chiefly US*)
Antonyms *n* ≠ **ability:** failing, inability, shortcoming, unskilfulness, weakness, weak point

fad *n* **1, 2** = **craze,** affectation, fancy, fashion, mania, mode, rage, trend, vogue, whim

fade *vb* **1** = **pale,** blanch, bleach, blench, dim, discolour, dull, grow dim, lose colour, lose lustre, wash out **2, 2** *As in* **fade away** *or* **out** = **dwindle,** decline, die away, die out, dim, disappear, disperse, dissolve, droop, ebb, etiolate, evanesce, fail, fall, flag, languish, melt away, perish, shrivel, vanish, vanish into thin air, wane, waste away, wilt, wither

faded *adj* **1** = **discoloured,** bleached, dim, dull, etiolated, indistinct, lustreless, pale, washed out

fading *adj* **2, 3** = **declining,** decreasing, disappearing, dying, on the decline, vanishing

faeces *pl n* = **excrement,** bodily waste, droppings, dung, excreta, ordure, stools

fag[1] *n* **1** *Informal* = **chore,** bind (*inf.*), bore, bother, drag (*inf.*), inconvenience, irritation, nuisance

fag[3] *n Slang, chiefly U.S. & Canad.* = **homosexual,** bender (*sl.*), catamite, fairy (*sl.*), gay, homo (*inf.*), nancy boy (*sl.*), poof (*sl.*), poofter (*sl.*), queen (*sl.*), queer (*inf., derogatory*), woofter (*sl.*)

fail *vb* **1, 3** = **be unsuccessful,** be defeated, be found lacking *or* wanting, be in vain, bite the dust, break down, come a cropper (*inf.*), come to grief, come to naught, come to nothing, come unstuck, fall, fall by the wayside, fall flat, fall flat on one's face, fall short, fall short of, fall through, fizzle out (*inf.*), flop (*inf.*), founder, go astray, go belly-up (*sl.*), go by the board, go down, go up in smoke, meet with disaster, miscarry, misfire, miss, not make the grade (*inf.*), run aground, turn out badly **2** = **give out,** be on one's last legs (*inf.*), cease, conk out, cut out, decline, die, disappear, droop, dwindle, fade, fall apart at the seams, give up, go phut, gutter, languish, peter out, sicken, sink, stop working, wane, weaken **4** = **disappoint,** abandon, break one's word, desert, forget, forsake, let down, neglect, omit, turn one's back on **8** = **go bankrupt,** become insolvent, close down, crash, fold, go broke (*inf.*), go bust (*inf.*), go into receivership, go out of business, go to the wall, go under, smash ◆ *n* **10 without fail** = **regularly,** conscientiously, constantly, dependably, like clockwork, punctually, religiously, without exception
Antonyms *vb* ≠ **be unsuccessful:** bloom, flourish, grow, pass, prosper, strengthen, succeed, thrive, triumph

failing *n* **1** = **weakness,** blemish, blind spot, defect, deficiency, drawback, error, failure, fault, flaw, foible, frailty, imperfection, lapse, miscarriage, misfortune, shortcoming ◆ *prep* **2** = **in the absence of,** in default of, lacking
Antonyms *n* ≠ **weakness:** advantage, asset, forte, métier, speciality, strength, strong suit

failure *n* **1** = **lack of success,** abortion, breakdown, collapse, defeat, downfall, fiasco, frustration, miscarriage, overthrow, wreck **2** = **loser,** black sheep, clinker (*sl., chiefly US*), dead duck (*sl.*), disappointment, dud (*inf.*), flop (*inf.*), incompetent, ne'er-do-well, no-good, no-hoper (*chiefly Austral.*), nonstarter, washout (*inf.*) **3, 4** = **shortcoming,** default, deficiency, dereliction, neglect, negligence, nonobser-

thing that is unsuccessful or disappointing. **3** nonperformance of something required or expected: *failure to attend will be punished.* **4** cessation of normal operation: *a power failure.* **5** an insufficiency: *a crop failure.* **6** a decline or loss, as in health. **7** the fact of not reaching the required standard in an examination, test, etc. **8** bankruptcy.

fain ➊ (feɪn) *adv* **1** (usually with *would*) *Arch.* gladly: *she would fain be dead.* ◆ *adj* **2** *Obs.* **2a** willing. **2b** compelled. [OE *fægen;* see FAWN[2]]

faint ➊ (feɪnt) *adj* **1** lacking clarity, brightness, volume, etc. **2** lacking conviction or force: *faint praise.* **3** feeling dizzy or weak as if about to lose consciousness. **4** timid (esp. in **faint-hearted**). **5 not the faintest (idea** *or* **notion)**. no idea whatsoever: *I haven't the faintest.* ◆ *vb (intr)* **6** to lose consciousness, as through weakness. **7** *Arch. or poetic.* to become weak, esp. in courage. ◆ *n* **8** a sudden spontaneous loss of consciousness caused by an insufficient supply of blood to the brain. [C13: from OF, from *faindre* to be idle]
▸ **'faintish** *adj* ▸ **'faintly** *adv* ▸ **'faintness** *n*

fair[1] ➊ (feə) *adj* **1** free from discrimination, dishonesty, etc. **2** in conformity with rules or standards: *a fair fight.* **3** (of the hair or complexion) light in colour. **4** beautiful to look at. **5** quite good: *a fair piece of work.* **6** unblemished; untainted. **7** (of the tide or wind) favourable to the passage of a vessel. **8** fine or cloudless. **9** pleasant or courteous. **10** apparently good or valuable: *fair words.* **11 fair and square.** in a correct or just way. ◆ *adv* **12** in a fair way: *act fair, now!* **13** absolutely or squarely; quite. ◆ *vb* **14** *(intr) Dialect.* (of the weather) to become fine. ◆ *n* **15** *Arch.* a person or thing that is beautiful or valuable. [OE *fæger*]
▸ **'fairish** *adj* ▸ **'fairness** *n*

fair[2] ➊ (feə) *n* **1** a travelling entertainment with sideshows, rides, etc. **2** a gathering of producers of and dealers in a given class of products to facilitate business: *a world fair.* **3** a regular assembly at a specific place for the sale of goods, esp. livestock. [C13: from OF *feire,* from LL *fēria* holiday, from L *fēriae* days of rest]

fair game *n* a legitimate object for ridicule or attack.

fairground ('feə,graʊnd) *n* an open space used for a fair or exhibition.

fairing[1] ('feərɪŋ) *n* an external metal structure fitted around parts of an aircraft, car, etc., to reduce drag. [C20: from *fair* to streamline + -ING[1]]

fairing[2] ('feərɪŋ) *n Arch.* a present, esp. from a fair.

Fair Isle *n* an intricate multicoloured pattern knitted with Shetland wool into various garments, such as sweaters. [C19: after one of the Shetland Islands where this type of pattern originated]

fairly ➊ ('feəlɪ) *adv* **1** *(not used with a negative)* moderately. **2** as deserved; justly. **3** *(not used with a negative)* positively: *the hall fairly rang with applause.*

fair-minded ➊ *adj* just or impartial.
▸ **,fair-'mindedness** *n*

fair play *n* **1** an established standard of decency, etc. **2** abidance by this standard.

fair sex *n* **the.** women collectively.

fair-spoken *adj* civil, courteous, or elegant in speech.
▸ **,fair-'spokenness** *n*

fairway ('feə,weɪ) *n* **1** (on a golf course) the avenue approaching a green bordered by rough. **2** *Naut.* the navigable part of a river, harbour, etc.

fair-weather *adj* **1** suitable for use in fair weather only. **2** not reliable in situations of difficulty: *fair-weather friend.*

fairy ➊ ('feərɪ) *n, pl* **fairies. 1** an imaginary supernatural being, usually represented in diminutive human form and characterized as having magical powers. **2** *Sl.* a male homosexual. ◆ *adj (prenominal)* **3** of a fairy or fairies. **4** resembling a fairy or fairies. [C14: from OF *faerie* fairyland, from *feie* fairy, from L *Fāta* the Fates; see FATE, FAY]
▸ **'fairy-,like** *adj*

fairy cycle *n* a child's bicycle.

fairyfloss ('feərɪ,flɒs) *n* the Australian word for **candyfloss.**

fairy godmother *n* a benefactress, esp. an unknown one.

fairyland ('feərɪ,lænd) *n* **1** the imaginary domain of the fairies. **2** a fantasy world, esp. one resulting from a person's wild imaginings.

fairy lights *pl n* small coloured electric bulbs strung together and used as decoration, esp. on a Christmas tree.

fairy penguin *n* a small penguin with a bluish head and back, found on the Australian coast. Also called: **little** or **blue penguin.**

fairy ring *n* a ring of dark luxuriant vegetation in grassy ground corresponding to the outer edge of an underground fungal mycelium.

fairy tale ➊ *or* **story** *n* **1** a story about fairies or other mythical or magical beings. **2** a highly improbable account.

fairy-tale *adj* **1** of or relating to a fairy tale. **2** resembling a fairy tale, esp. in being extremely happy or fortunate: *a fairy-tale ending.* **3** highly improbable: *a fairy-tale account.*

fait accompli *French.* (fɛt akɔ̃pli) *n, pl* ***faits accomplis*** (fɛz akɔ̃pli). something already done and beyond alteration. [lit.: accomplished fact]

faith ➊ (feɪθ) *n* **1** strong or unshakeable belief in something, esp. without proof. **2** a specific system of religious beliefs: *the Jewish faith.* **3** *Christianity.* trust in God and in his actions and promises. **4** a conviction of the truth of certain doctrines of religion. **5** complete confidence or trust in a person, remedy, etc. **6** loyalty, as to a person or cause (esp. in **keep faith, break faith**). **7 bad faith.** dishonesty. **8 good faith.** honesty. **9** *(modifier)* using or relating to the supposed ability to cure bodily ailments by means of religious faith: *a faith healer.* ◆ *interj* **10** *Arch.* indeed. [C12: from Anglo-F *feid,* from L *fidēs* trust, confidence]

faithful ➊ ('feɪθfʊl) *adj* **1** remaining true or loyal. **2** maintaining sexual loyalty to one's lover or spouse. **3** consistently reliable: *a faithful worker.* **4** reliable or truthful. **5** accurate in detail: *a faithful translation.* ◆ *n* **6 the faithful. 6a** the believers in a religious faith, esp. Christianity. **6b** any group of loyal and steadfast followers.
▸ **'faithfully** *adv* ▸ **'faithfulness** *n*

faithless ➊ ('feɪθlɪs) *adj* **1** unreliable or treacherous. **2** dishonest or disloyal. **3** lacking religious faith.
▸ **'faithlessness** *n*

fajitas (fə'hiːtəz) *pl n* a Mexican dish of soft tortillas wrapped round fried strips of meat, vegetables, etc. [Mexican Sp.]

fake ➊ (feɪk) *vb* **fakes, faking, faked. 1** *(tr)* to cause (something inferior or not genuine) to appear more valuable or real by fraud or pretence. **2**

THESAURUS

vance, nonperformance, nonsuccess, omission, remissness, stoppage **4** = **breakdown**, decay, decline, deterioration, failing, loss **8** = **bankruptcy**, crash, downfall, folding (*inf.*), insolvency, liquidation, ruin
Antonyms *n* ≠ **lack of success:** adequacy, effectiveness, success, triumph ≠ **shortcoming:** care, observance ≠ **bankruptcy:** fortune, prosperity

fain *adv Archaic* **1** = **gladly**, as lief, as soon, cheerfully, eagerly, willingly ◆ *adj Obsolete* **2a** = **glad**, anxious, eager, well-pleased *Obsolete* **2b** = **compelled**, constrained, with no alternative but

faint *adj* **1** = **dim**, bleached, delicate, distant, dull, faded, faltering, feeble, hazy, hushed, ill-defined, indistinct, light, low, muffled, muted, soft, subdued, thin, vague, whispered **2** = **slight**, feeble, remote, unenthusiastic, weak **3** = **dizzy**, drooping, enervated, exhausted, faltering, fatigued, giddy, languid, lethargic, light-headed, muzzy, vertiginous, weak, woozy (*inf.*) **4** = **timid**, faint-hearted, lily-livered, spiritless, timorous ◆ *vb* **6** = **pass out**, black out, collapse, fade, fail, flake out (*inf.*), keel over (*inf.*), languish, lose consciousness, swoon (*literary*), weaken ◆ *n* **8** = **blackout**, collapse, swoon (*literary*), syncope (*Pathology*), unconsciousness
Antonyms *adj* ≠ **dim:** bright, clear, conspicuous, distinct, loud, powerful, strong ≠ **timid:** bold, brave, courageous ≠ **dizzy:** energetic, fresh, hearty, vigorous

faintly *adv* **1** = **softly**, feebly, in a whisper, indistinctly, weakly

faintness *n* **1-3** = **weakness**, dimness, dizziness, feebleness, giddiness, indistinctness, languor, loss of strength, shakiness

fair[1] *adj* **1, 2** = **unbiased**, above board, according to the rules, clean, disinterested, dispassionate, equal, equitable, even-handed, honest, honourable, impartial, just, lawful, legitimate, objective, on the level (*inf.*), proper, square, trustworthy, unprejudiced, upright **3** = **light**, blond, blonde, fair-haired, flaxen-haired, light-complexioned, tow-haired, towheaded **4** = **beautiful**, beauteous, bonny, comely, handsome, lovely, pretty, well-favoured **5** = **respectable**, adequate, all right, average, decent, mediocre, middling, moderate, not bad, O.K. or okay (*inf.*), passable, reasonable, satisfactory, so-so (*inf.*), tolerable **7, 8** = **fine**, bright, clear, clement, cloudless, dry, favourable, sunny, sunshiny, unclouded **11 fair and square** = **just**, above board, correct, honest, kosher (*inf.*), on the level (*inf.*), straight
Antonyms *adj* ≠ **unbiased:** bad, biased, bigoted, discriminatory, dishonest, inequitable, one-sided, partial, partisan, prejudiced, unfair, unjust ≠ **beautiful:** homely, plain, ugly

fair[2] *n* **1-3** = **carnival**, bazaar, expo (*inf.*), exposition, festival, fête, gala, market, show

fairly *adv* **1** = **moderately**, adequately, pretty well, quite, rather, reasonably, somewhat, tolerably **2** = **deservedly**, equitably, honestly, impartially, justly, objectively, properly, without fear or favour **3** = **positively**, absolutely, in a manner of speaking, really, veritably

fair-minded *adj* = **impartial**, disinterested, even-handed, just, open-minded, unbiased, unprejudiced

fairness *n* **1, 2** = **impartiality**, decency, disinterestedness, equitableness, equity, justice, legitimacy, rightfulness, uprightness

fairy *n* **1** = **sprite**, brownie, elf, hob, leprechaun, peri, pixie, Robin Goodfellow

fairy tale *n* **1** = **folk tale**, romance **2** = **lie**, cock-and-bull story, fabrication, fantasy, fiction, invention, pork pie (*Brit. sl.*), porky (*Brit. sl.*), tall story, untruth

faith *n* **1, 4, 5** = **confidence**, assurance, conviction, credence, credit, dependence, reliance, trust **2** = **religion**, belief, church, communion, creed, denomination, dogma, persuasion **6** = **allegiance**, constancy, faithfulness, fealty, fidelity, loyalty, troth (*arch.*), truth, truthfulness **8 good faith** = **honesty**, honour, pledge, promise, sincerity, vow, word, word of honour
Antonyms *n* ≠ **confidence:** apprehension, denial, disbelief, distrust, doubt, incredulity, misgiving, mistrust, rejection, scepticism, suspicion, uncertainty ≠ **religion:** agnosticism ≠ **allegiance:** infidelity

faithful *adj* **1, 3, 4** = **loyal**, attached, constant, dependable, devoted, immovable, reliable, staunch, steadfast, true, true-blue, trusty, truthful, unswerving, unwavering **5** = **accurate**, close, exact, just, precise, strict, true **6 the faithful** = **believers**, adherents, brethren, communicants, congregation, followers, the elect
Antonyms *adj* ≠ **loyal:** disloyal, doubting, faithless, false, false-hearted, fickle, inconstant, perfidious, recreant (*arch.*), traitorous, treacherous, unbelieving, unfaithful, unreliable, untrue, untrustworthy, untruthful

faithfulness *n* **1, 3, 4** = **loyalty**, adherence, constancy, dependability, devotion, fealty, fidelity, trustworthiness **5** = **accuracy**, closeness, exactness, justice, strictness, truth

faithless *adj* **1-3** = **disloyal**, doubting, false, false-hearted, fickle, inconstant, perfidious, recreant (*arch.*), traitorous, treacherous, unbelieving, unfaithful, unreliable, untrue, untrustworthy, untruthful

faithlessness *n* **1, 2** = **disloyalty**, betrayal, fickleness, inconstancy, infidelity, perfidy, treachery, unfaithfulness

fake *vb* **1, 2** = **sham**, affect, assume, copy, counterfeit, fabricate, feign, forge, pretend, put on, simulate ◆ *n* **3** = **impostor**, charlatan, copy,

to pretend to have (an illness, emotion, etc.). ◆ *n* **3** an object, person, or act that is not genuine; sham. ◆ *adj* **4** not genuine. [C18: prob. ult. from It. *facciare* to make or do]
▸**'faker** *n* ▸**'fakery** *n*

fakir ('feɪkɪə, fə'kɪə) *n* **1** a member of any religious order of Islam. **2** a Hindu ascetic mendicant. [C17: from Ar. *faqīr* poor]

falafel *or* **felafel** (fə'lɑːfəl) *n* a ball or cake of ground spiced chickpeas, deep-fried and often served with pitta bread. [C20: from Arabic *felāfil*]

Falange ('fælændʒ) *n* the Fascist movement founded in Spain in 1933. [Sp.: PHALANX]
▸**Fa'langist** *n, adj*

falcate ('fælkeɪt) *or* **falciform** ('fælsɪˌfɔːm) *adj Biol.* shaped like a sickle. [C19: from L *falcātus*, from *falx* sickle]

falchion ('fɔːltʃən, 'fɔːlʃən) *n* **1** a short and slightly curved medieval sword. **2** an archaic word for **sword.** [C14: from It., from *falce*, from L *falx* sickle]

falcon ('fɔːlkən, 'fɔːkən) *n* **1** a diurnal bird of prey such as the gyrfalcon, peregrine falcon, etc., having pointed wings and a long tail. **2a** any of these or related birds, trained to hunt small game. **2b** the female of such a bird (cf. **tercel**). [C13: from OF, from LL *falcō* hawk, prob. of Gmc origin; ? rel. to L *falx* sickle]

falconet ('fɔːlkəˌnɛt, 'fɔːkə-) *n* **1** any of various small falcons. **2** a small light cannon used from the 15th to 17th centuries.

falconry ('fɔːlkənrɪ, 'fɔːkən-) *n* the art of keeping falcons and training them to return from flight to a lure or to hunt quarry.
▸**'falconer** *n*

falderal ('fældəˌræl) *or* **folderol** ('fɒldəˌrɒl) *n* **1** a showy but worthless trifle. **2** foolish nonsense. **3** a nonsensical refrain in old songs.

faldstool ('fɔːldˌstuːl) *n* a backless seat, sometimes capable of being folded, used by bishops and certain other prelates. [C11 *fyldestol*, prob. a translation of Med. L *faldistolium* folding stool, of Gmc origin; cf. OHG *faldstuol*]

fall Ⓣ (fɔːl) *vb* **falls, falling, fell, fallen.** (*mainly intr*) **1** to descend by the force of gravity from a higher to a lower place. **2** to drop suddenly from an erect position. **3** to collapse to the ground, esp. in pieces. **4** to become less or lower in number, quality, etc.: *prices fell.* **5** to become lower in pitch. **6** to extend downwards: *her hair fell to her waist.* **7** to be badly wounded or killed. **8** to slope in a downward direction. **9** to yield to temptation or sin. **10** to diminish in status, estimation, etc. **11** to yield to attack: *the city fell under the assault.* **12** to lose power: *the government fell after the riots.* **13** to pass into or take on a specified condition: *to fall asleep.* **14** to adopt a despondent expression: *her face fell.* **15** to be averted: *her gaze fell.* **16** to come by chance or presumption: *suspicion fell on the butler.* **17** to occur; take place: *night fell.* **18** (foll. by *back, behind*, etc.) to move in a specified direction. **19** to occur at a specified place: *the accent falls on the last syllable.* **20** (foll. by *to*) to be inherited (by): *the estate falls to the eldest son.* **21** (often foll. by *into, under*, etc.) to be classified: *the subject falls into two main areas.* **22** to issue forth: *a curse fell from her lips.* **23** (*tr*) *Dialect, Austral. & NZ.* to fell (trees). **24** *Cricket.* (of a batsman's wicket) to be taken by the bowling side: *the sixth wicket fell for 96.* **25 fall short. 25a** to prove inadequate. **25b** (often foll. by *of*) to fail to reach or measure up to (a standard). ◆ *n* **26** an act or instance of falling. **27** something that falls: *a fall of snow.* **28** *Chiefly US.* autumn. **29** the distance that something falls: *a hundred-foot fall.* **30** a sudden drop from an upright position. **31** (*often pl*) **31a** a waterfall or cataract. **31b** (*cap. when part of a name*): *Niagara Falls.* **32** a downward slope or decline. **33** a decrease in value, number, etc. **34** a decline in status or importance. **35** a capture or overthrow: *the fall of the city.* **36** *Machinery, naut.* the end of a tackle to which power is applied to hoist it. **37** Also called: **pinfall.** *Wrestling.* a scoring move, pinning both shoulders of one's opponent to the floor for a specified period. **38a** the birth of an animal. **38b** the animals produced at a single birth. ◆ See also **fall about, fall away,** etc. [OE *feallan*: cf. FELL[2]]

Fall (fɔːl) *n* **the.** *Theol.* Adam's sin of disobedience and the state of innate sinfulness ensuing from this for himself and all mankind.

fall about *vb* (*intr, adv*) to laugh in an uncontrolled manner: *we fell about at the sight.*

fallacious Ⓣ (fə'leɪʃəs) *adj* **1** containing or involving a fallacy. **2** tending to mislead. **3** delusive or disappointing.
▸**fal'laciously** *adv*

fallacy Ⓣ ('fæləsɪ) *n, pl* **fallacies. 1** an incorrect or misleading notion or opinion based on inaccurate facts or invalid reasoning. **2** unsound reasoning. **3** the tendency to mislead. **4** *Logic.* an error in reasoning that renders an argument logically invalid. [C15: from L, from *fallax* deceitful, from *fallere* to deceive]

fall apart Ⓣ *vb* (*intr adv*) **1** to break owing to long use or poor construction: *the chassis is falling apart.* **2** to become disorganized and ineffective: *since you resigned, the office has fallen apart.*

fall away *vb* (*intr, adv*) **1** (of friendship, etc.) to be withdrawn. **2** to slope down.

fall back Ⓣ *vb* (*intr, adv*) **1** to recede or retreat. **2** (foll. by *on* or *upon*) to have recourse (to). ◆ *n* **fall-back. 3** a retreat. **4** a reserve, esp. money, that can be called upon in need. **5a** anything to which one can have recourse as a second choice. **5b** (*as modifier*): *a fall-back position.*

fall behind Ⓣ *vb* (*intr, adv*) **1** to drop back; fail to keep up. **2** to be in arrears, as with a payment.

fall down Ⓣ *vb* (*intr, adv*) **1** to drop suddenly or collapse. **2** (often foll. by *on*) *Inf.* to fail.

fallen Ⓣ ('fɔːlən) *vb* **1** the past participle of **fall.** ◆ *adj* **2** having sunk in reputation or honour: *a fallen woman.* **3** killed in battle with glory.

fallen arch *n* collapse of the arch formed by the instep of the foot, resulting in flat feet.

fall for Ⓣ *vb* (*intr, prep*) **1** to become infatuated with (a person). **2** to allow oneself to be deceived by (a lie, trick, etc.).

fall guy *n Inf.* **1** a person who is the victim of a confidence trick. **2** a scapegoat.

fallible Ⓣ ('fælɪbəl) *adj* **1** capable of being mistaken. **2** liable to mislead. [C15: from Med. L *fallibilis*, from L *fallere* to deceive]
▸**ˌfalli'bility** *n*

fall in Ⓣ *vb* (*intr, adv*) **1** to collapse. **2** to adopt a military formation, esp. as a soldier taking his place in a line. **3** (of a lease) to expire. **4** (often foll. by *with*) **4a** to meet and join. **4b** to agree with or support a person, suggestion, etc.

falling sickness *or* **evil** *n* a former name (nontechnical) for **epilepsy.**

falling star *n* an informal name for **meteor.**

fall off Ⓣ *vb* (*intr*) **1** to drop unintentionally to the ground from (a high object, bicycle, etc.), esp. after losing one's balance. **2** (*adv*) to diminish in size, intensity, etc. ◆ *n* **fall-off. 3** a decline or drop.

fall on Ⓣ *vb* (*intr, prep*) **1** Also: **fall upon.** to attack or snatch (an army,

THESAURUS

forgery, fraud, hoax, imitation, mountebank, phoney *or* phony (*inf.*), reproduction, sham ◆ *adj* **4 = artificial**, affected, assumed, counterfeit, false, forged, imitation, mock, phoney *or* phony (*inf.*), pinchbeck, pseudo (*inf.*), reproduction, sham
Antonyms *adj* ≠ **artificial:** actual, authentic, bona fide, faithful, genuine, honest, legitimate, real, true, veritable

faker *n* **1, 2 = fraud**, fake, humbug, impostor, phoney *or* phony (*inf.*), pretender, sham

fall *vb* **1-3 = descend**, be precipitated, cascade, collapse, come a cropper (*inf.*), crash, dive, drop, drop down, go head over heels, keel over, nose-dive, pitch, plummet, plunge, settle, sink, stumble, subside, topple, trip, trip over, tumble **4 = decrease**, abate, become lower, decline, depreciate, diminish, drop, dwindle, ebb, fall off, flag, go down, lessen, slump, subside **7 = die**, be a casualty, be killed, be lost, be slain, meet one's end, perish **8 = slope**, fall away, incline, incline downwards **9 = lapse**, backslide, err, go astray, offend, sin, transgress, trespass, yield to temptation **11 = be overthrown**, be taken, capitulate, give in *or* up, give way, go out of office, pass into enemy hands, resign, succumb, surrender, yield **17 = occur**, become, befall, chance, come about, come to pass, fall out, happen, take place **25 fall short = be lacking**, be deficient, be wanting, disappoint, fail, fall down on (*inf.*), miss, not come up to expectations *or* scratch (*inf.*), prove inadequate ◆ *n* **26, 30 = descent**, dive, drop, nose dive, plummet, plunge, slip, spill, tumble **31** *often plural* **= waterfall**, cascade, cataract, force (*N English dialect*), linn (*Scot.*), rapids **32 = slope**, declivity, descent, downgrade, incline, slant **33 = decrease**, cut, decline, diminution, dip, drop, dwindling, falling off, lessening, lowering, reduction, slump **35 = collapse**, capitulation, death, defeat, destruction, downfall, failure, overthrow, resignation, ruin, surrender
Antonyms *vb* ≠ **descend:** ascend, climb, go up, increase, mount, rise, scale, soar ≠ **decrease:** advance, appreciate, climb, escalate, extend, heighten, increase, wax ≠ **die:** endure, hold out, survive ≠ **be overthrown:** prevail, triumph

fallacious *adj* **1-3 = incorrect**, deceptive, delusive, delusory, erroneous, false, fictitious, illogical, illusory, misleading, mistaken, sophistic, sophistical, spurious, untrue, wrong

fallacy *n* **1, 2 = error**, casuistry, deceit, deception, delusion, falsehood, faultiness, flaw, illusion, inconsistency, misapprehension, misconception, mistake, sophism, sophistry, untruth

fall apart *vb* **1 = break up**, come apart at the seams, crumble, disband, disintegrate, disperse, dissolve, fall to bits, go *or* come to pieces, go to seed, lose cohesion, shatter

fall back *vb* **1 = retreat**, back off, draw back, recede, recoil, retire, withdraw **2** *foll. by* **on** *or* **upon = resort to**, call upon, employ, have recourse to, make use of, press into service

fall behind *vb* **1 = lag**, drop back, get left behind, lose one's place, trail **2 = be in arrears**

fall down *vb* **2 = fail**, disappoint, fail to make the grade, fall short, go wrong, prove unsuccessful

fallen *adj* **2 = dishonoured**, disgraced, immoral, loose, lost, ruined, shamed, sinful, unchaste **3 = killed**, dead, lost, perished, slain, slaughtered

fall for *vb* **1 = fall in love with**, become infatuated with, desire, lose one's head over, succumb to the charms of **2 = be fooled by**, accept, be deceived by, be duped by, be taken in by, buy (*sl.*), give credence to, swallow (*inf.*), take on board

fallible *adj* **1 = imperfect**, erring, frail, ignorant, mortal, prone to error, uncertain, weak
Antonyms *adj* divine, faultless, impeccable, infallible, omniscient, perfect, superhuman, unerring, unimpeachable

fall in *vb* **1 = collapse**, cave in, come down about one's ears, fall apart at the seams, sink **4b** *often foll. by* **with = go along with**, accept, agree with, assent, buy into (*inf.*), concur with, cooperate with, support, take on board

fall off *vb* **1 = tumble**, be unseated, come a cropper *or* purler (*inf.*), plummet, take a fall *or* tumble, topple **2 = decrease**, decline, diminish, drop, dwindle, ebb away, fade, fall away, go down *or* downhill, lessen, peter out, reduce, shrink, slacken, slump, subside, tail off (*inf.*), wane, weaken
Antonyms *vb* ≠ **decrease:** improve, increase, pick up, rally, recover, revive

fall on *vb* **1 = attack**, assail, assault, belabour,

booty, etc.). **2 fall on one's feet.** to emerge unexpectedly well from a difficult situation.

Fallopian tube (fəˈləupɪən) *n* either of a pair of slender tubes through which ova pass from the ovaries to the uterus in female mammals. [C18: after Gabriello *Fallopio* (1523–62), It. anatomist who first described the tubes]

fallout ➊ (ˈfɔːlˌaut) *n* **1** the descent of radioactive material following a nuclear explosion. **2** any particles that so descend. **3** secondary consequences. ◆ *vb* **fall out.** (*intr, adv*) **4** *Inf.* to disagree. **5** (*intr*) to occur. **6** *Mil.* to leave a disciplinary formation.

fallow[1] ➊ (ˈfæləu) *adj* **1** (of land) left unseeded after being ploughed to regain fertility for a crop. **2** (of an idea, etc.) undeveloped, but potentially useful. ◆ *n* **3** land treated in this way. ◆ *vb* **4** (*tr*) to leave (land) unseeded after ploughing it. [OE *fealga*]
▸ **ˈfallowness** *n*

fallow[2] (ˈfæləu) *n, adj* (of) a light yellowish-brown colour. [OE *fealu*]

fallow deer *n* either of two species of deer, one of which is native to the Mediterranean region and the other to Persia. The summer coat is reddish with white spots.

fall through ➊ *vb* (*intr, adv*) to fail.

fall to ➊ *vb* (*intr*) **1** (*adv*) to begin some activity, as eating, working, or fighting. **2** (*prep*) to devolve on (a person): *the task fell to me.*

false ➊ (fɔːls) *adj* **1** not in accordance with the truth or facts. **2** irregular or invalid: *a false start.* **3** untruthful or lying: *a false account.* **4** artificial; fake: *false teeth.* **5** being or intended to be misleading or deceptive: *a false rumour.* **6** treacherous: *a false friend.* **7** based on mistaken or irrelevant ideas or facts: *a false argument.* **8** (*prenominal*) (esp. of plants) superficially resembling the species specified: *false hellebore.* **9** serving to supplement or replace, often temporarily: *a false keel.* **10** *Music.* (of a note, interval, etc.) out of tune. ◆ *adv* **11** in a false or dishonest manner (esp. in **play (someone) false**). [OE *fals*]
▸ **ˈfalsely** *adv* ▸ **ˈfalseness** *n*

false colour *n* colour used in a computer or photographic display to help in interpreting the image, as in the use of red to show high temperatures and blue to show low temperatures in an infrared image converter.

false dawn *n* light appearing just before sunrise.

false diamond *n* any of a number of semiprecious stones that resemble diamond, such as zircon and white topaz.

falsehood ➊ (ˈfɔːlsˌhud) *n* **1** the quality of being untrue. **2** an untrue statement; lie. **3** the act of deceiving or lying.

false imprisonment *n Law.* the restraint of a person's liberty without lawful authority.

false pretences *pl n* a misrepresentation used to obtain anything, such as trust or affection (esp. in **under false pretences**).

false ribs *pl n* any of the lower five pairs of ribs in man, not attached directly to the breastbone.

false step *n* **1** an unwise action. **2** a stumble; slip.

falsetto (fɔːlˈsɛtəu) *n, pl* **falsettos.** a form of vocal production used by male singers to extend their range upwards by limiting the vibration of the vocal cords. [C18: from It., from *falso* false]

falsies (ˈfɔːlsɪz) *pl n Inf.* pads of soft material, such as foam rubber, worn to exaggerate the size of a woman's breasts.

falsify ➊ (ˈfɔːlsɪˌfaɪ) *vb* **falsifies, falsifying, falsified.** (*tr*) **1** to make (a report, evidence, etc.) false or inaccurate by alteration, esp. in order to deceive. **2** to prove false. [C15: from OF, from LL, from L *falsus* FALSE + *facere* to do, make]
▸ **ˈfalsiˌfiable** *adj* ▸ **falsification** (ˌfɔːlsɪfɪˈkeɪʃən) *n*

falsity ➊ (ˈfɔːlsɪtɪ) *n, pl* **falsities. 1** the state of being false or untrue. **2** a lie or deception.

Falstaffian (fɔːlˈstɑːfɪən) *adj* jovial, plump, and dissolute. [C19: after Sir John *Falstaff,* a character in Shakespeare's play *Henry IV*]

falter ➊ (ˈfɔːltə) *vb* **1** (*intr*) to be hesitant, weak, or unsure. **2** (*intr*) to move unsteadily or hesitantly. **3** to utter haltingly or hesitantly. ◆ *n* **4** hesitancy in speech or action. **5** a quavering sound. [C14: prob. from ON]
▸ **ˈfalterer** *n* ▸ **ˈfalteringly** *adv*

fame ➊ (feɪm) *n* **1** the state of being widely known or recognized. **2** *Arch.* rumour or public report. ◆ *vb* **fames, faming, famed. 3** (*tr; now usually passive*) to make famous: *he was famed for his ruthlessness.* [C13: from L *fāma* report; rel. to *fārī* to say]

familial (fəˈmɪlɪəl) *adj* **1** of or relating to the family. **2** occurring in the members of a family: *a familial disease.*

familiar ➊ (fəˈmɪlɪə) *adj* **1** well-known: *a familiar figure.* **2** frequent or customary: *a familiar excuse.* **3** (*postpositive;* foll. by *with*) acquainted. **4** friendly; informal. **5** close; intimate. **6** more intimate than is acceptable; presumptuous. ◆ *n* **7** Also called: **familiar spirit.** a supernatural spirit supposed to attend and aid a witch, wizard, etc. **8** a person attached to the household of the pope or a bishop, who renders service in return for support. **9** a friend. [C14: from L *familiāris* domestic, from *familia* FAMILY]
▸ **faˈmiliarly** *adv* ▸ **faˈmiliarness** *n*

familiarity ➊ (fəˌmɪlɪˈærɪtɪ) *n, pl* **familiarities. 1** knowledge, as of a subject or place. **2** close acquaintanceship. **3** undue intimacy. **4** (*sometimes pl*) an instance of unwarranted intimacy.

familiarize ➊ *or* **familiarise** (fəˈmɪljəˌraɪz) *vb* **familiarizes, familiarizing, familiarized** *or* **familiarises, familiarising, familiarised.** (*tr*) **1** to make (oneself or someone else) familiar, as with a particular subject. **2** to make (something) generally known.
▸ **faˌmiliariˈzation** *or* **faˌmiliariˈzatiˈsation** *n*

famille *French.* (famij) *n* a type of Chinese porcelain characterized either by a design on a background of yellow (***famille jaune***) or black (***famille noire***) or by a design in which the predominant colour is pink (***famille rose***) or green (***famille verte***). [C19: lit.: family]

family ➊ (ˈfæmɪlɪ, ˈfæmlɪ) *n, pl* **families. 1a** a primary social group consisting of parents and their offspring. **1b** (*as modifier*): *a family unit.* **2** one's wife or husband and one's children. **3** one's children, as distinguished from one's husband or wife. **4** a group descended from a common ancestor. **5** all the persons living together in one household.

THESAURUS

descend upon, lay into, pitch into (*inf.*), set upon *or* about, snatch, tear into (*inf.*)

fall out *vb* **4** *Informal* = **argue**, altercate, clash, come to blows, differ, disagree, fight, quarrel, squabble **5** = **happen**, chance, come to pass, occur, pan out (*inf.*), result, take place, turn out

fallow[1] *adj* **1** = **uncultivated**, dormant, idle, inactive, inert, resting, undeveloped, unplanted, untilled, unused

fall through *vb* = **fail**, come to nothing, fizzle out (*inf.*), go by the board, miscarry

fall to *vb* **1** = **begin**, apply oneself to, commence, set about, start **2** = **be the responsibility of**, be up to, come down to, devolve upon

false *adj* **1, 2** = **incorrect**, concocted, erroneous, faulty, fictitious, improper, inaccurate, inexact, invalid, mistaken, unfounded, unreal, wrong **3** = **untrue**, lying, mendacious, truthless, unreliable, unsound, untrustworthy, untruthful **4** = **artificial**, bogus, counterfeit, ersatz, fake, feigned, forged, imitation, mock, pretended, pseudo (*inf.*), sham, simulated, spurious, synthetic **5, 7** = **deceptive**, deceitful, deceiving, delusive, fallacious, fraudulent, hypocritical, misleading, trumped up **6** = **treacherous**, dishonest, dishonourable, disloyal, double-dealing, duplicitous, faithless, false-hearted, hypocritical, perfidious, treasonable, two-faced, unfaithful, untrustworthy ◆ *adv* **11 play (someone) false** = **deceive**, betray, cheat, double-cross, give the Judas kiss to, sell down the river (*inf.*), stab in the back

Antonyms *adj* ≠ **incorrect:** correct, exact, right, sound, valid ≠ **untrue:** reliable, true ≠ **artificial:** authentic, bona fide, genuine, honest, kosher (*inf.*), real, sincere ≠ **treacherous:** faithful, loyal, trustworthy

falsehood *n* **1, 3** = **untruthfulness**, deceit, deception, dishonesty, dissimulation, inveracity (*rare*), mendacity, perjury, prevarication **2** = **lie**, fabrication, fib, fiction, misstatement, pork pie (*Brit. sl.*), porky (*Brit. sl.*), story, untruth

falsification *n* **1** = **misrepresentation**, adulteration, deceit, dissimulation, distortion, forgery, perversion, tampering with

falsify *vb* **1** = **alter**, belie, cook (*sl.*), counterfeit, distort, doctor, fake, forge, garble, misrepresent, misstate, pervert, tamper with

falsity *n* **1** = **untruth**, deceit, deceptiveness, dishonesty, double-dealing, duplicity, fraudulence, hypocrisy, inaccuracy, mendacity, perfidy, treachery, unreality **2** = **lie**, cheating, deception, fraud, pork pie (*Brit. sl.*), porky (*Brit. sl.*)

falter *vb* **1-3** = **hesitate**, break, shake, speak haltingly, stammer, stumble, stutter, totter, tremble, vacillate, waver

Antonyms *vb* continue, endure, keep going, last, persevere, persist, proceed, stand firm, stick at, survive

faltering *adj* **1-3** = **hesitant**, broken, irresolute, stammering, tentative, timid, uncertain, weak

fame *n* **1** = **prominence**, celebrity, credit, eminence, glory, honour, illustriousness, name, public esteem, renown, reputation, repute, stardom

Antonyms *n* disgrace, dishonour, disrepute, ignominy, infamy, oblivion, obscurity, shame

famed *adj* **1** = **renowned**, acclaimed, celebrated, recognized, widely-known

familiar *adj* **1, 2** = **well-known**, accustomed, common, common or garden (*inf.*), conventional, customary, domestic, everyday, frequent, household, mundane, ordinary, recognizable, repeated, routine, stock **3** *foll. by* **with** = **acquainted with**, abreast of, at home with, *au courant with, au fait with,* aware of, conscious of, conversant with, introduced to, knowledgeable about, no stranger to, on speaking terms with, versed in, well up in **4, 5** = **friendly**, amicable, buddy-buddy, chummy (*inf.*), close, confidential, cordial, easy, free, free-and-easy, hail-fellow-well-met, informal, intimate, near, open, palsy-walsy (*inf.*), relaxed, unceremonious, unconstrained, unreserved **6** = **disrespectful**, bold, forward, impudent, intrusive, overfree, presuming, presumptuous

Antonyms *adj* ≠ **well-known:** infrequent, unaccustomed, uncommon, unfamiliar, unknown, unusual ≠ **acquainted with:** ignorant, unaccustomed, unacquainted, unfamiliar, uninformed, unskilled ≠ **friendly:** aloof, cold, detached, distant, formal, unfriendly

familiarity *n* **1** = **acquaintance**, acquaintanceship, awareness, experience, grasp, knowledge, understanding **2** = **friendliness**, absence of reserve, closeness, ease, fellowship, freedom, friendship, informality, intimacy, naturalness, openness, sociability, unceremoniousness **3, 4** = **disrespect**, boldness, forwardness, liberties, liberty, presumption

Antonyms *n* ≠ **acquaintance:** ignorance, inexperience, unfamiliarity ≠ **friendliness:** distance, formality, reserve ≠ **disrespect:** constraint, decorum, propriety, respect

familiarize *vb* **1** = **accustom**, bring into common use, coach, get to know (about), habituate, instruct, inure, make conversant, make used to, prime, school, season, train

family *n* **1-3, 5** = **relations**, brood, children, descendants, folk (*inf.*), household, issue, kin, kindred, kinsfolk, kinsmen, kith and kin, ménage, offspring, one's nearest and dearest, one's own flesh and blood, people, progeny, relatives **4** = **clan**, ancestors, ancestry, birth, blood, descent, dynasty, extraction, forebears, forefathers, ge-

6 any group of related things or beings, esp. when scientifically categorized. **7** *Biol.* any of the taxonomic groups into which an order is divided and which contains one or more genera. **8** a group of historically related languages assumed to derive from one original language. **9** *Maths.* a group of curves or surfaces whose equations differ from a given equation only in the values assigned to one or more constants. **10 in the family way.** *Inf.* pregnant. [C15: from L *familia* a household, servants of the house, from *famulus* servant]

family allowance *n* **1** (in Britain) a former name for **child benefit. 2** (*caps.*) the Canadian equivalent of **child benefit.**

family Bible *n* a large Bible in which births, marriages, and deaths of the members of a family are recorded.

Family Compact *n Canad.* **1 the.** the ruling oligarchy in Upper Canada in the early 19th century. **2** (*often not cap.*) any influential clique.

family credit *n* (in Britain) a means-tested allowance paid to families who have at least one dependent child and whose earnings from full-time work are low. It replaced **family income supplement.**

family man *n* a man who is married and has children, esp. one who is devoted to his family.

family name *n* a surname, esp. when regarded as representing the family honour.

family planning *n* the control of the number of children in a family and of the intervals between them, esp. by the use of contraceptives.

family support *n NZ.* a means-tested allowance for families in need.

family therapy *n* a form of psychotherapy in which the members of a family participate, with the aim of improving communications between them and the ways in which they relate to each other.

family tree ❶ *n* a chart showing the genealogical relationships and lines of descent of a family. Also called: **genealogical tree.**

famine ❶ ('fæmɪn) *n* **1** a severe shortage of food, as through crop failure or overpopulation. **2** acute shortage of anything. **3** violent hunger. [C14: from OF, via Vulgar L, from L *famēs* hunger]

famish ❶ ('fæmɪʃ) *vb* (*now usually passive*) to be or make very hungry or weak. [C14: from OF, from L *famēs* FAMINE]

famous ❶ ('feɪməs) *adj* **1** known to or recognized by many people. **2** *Inf.* excellent; splendid. [C14: from L *fāmōsus;* see FAME]
▸ **'famously** *adv* ▸ **'famousness** *n*

fan[1] ❶ (fæn) *n* **1** any device for creating a current of air by movement of a surface or number of surfaces, esp. a rotating device consisting of a number of blades attached to a central hub. **2** any of various hand-agitated devices for cooling oneself, esp. a collapsible semicircular series of flat segments of paper, ivory, etc. **3** something shaped like such a fan, such as the tail of certain birds. **4** *Agriculture.* a kind of basket formerly used for winnowing grain. ◆ *vb* **fans, fanning, fanned.** (*mainly tr*) **5** to cause a current of air to blow upon, as by means of a fan: *to fan one's face.* **6** to agitate or move (air, etc.) with or as if with a fan. **7** to make fiercer, more ardent, etc.: *fan one's passion.* **8** (*also intr;* often foll. by *out*) to spread out or cause to spread out in the shape of a fan. **9** to winnow (grain) by blowing the chaff away from it. [OE *fann,* from L *vannus*]
▸ **'fanlike** *adj* ▸ **'fanner** *n*

fan[2] ❶ (fæn) *n* **1** an ardent admirer of a pop star, football team, etc. **2** a devotee of a sport, hobby, etc. [C17, re-formed C19: from FAN(ATIC)]

Fanagalo ('fænəgələʊ) *or* **Fanakalo** *n* (in South Africa) a Zulu-based pidgin with English and Afrikaans components. [C20: from Fanagalo *fana ga lo,* lit.: to be like this]

fanatic ❶ (fə'nætɪk) *n* **1** a person whose enthusiasm or zeal for something is extreme or beyond normal limits. **2** *Inf.* a person devoted to a particular hobby or pastime. ◆ *adj* **3** a variant of **fanatical.** [C16: from L *fānāticus* belonging to a temple, hence, inspired by a god, frenzied, from *fānum* temple]

fanatical ❶ (fə'nætɪkᵊl) *adj* surpassing what is normal or accepted in enthusiasm for or belief in something.
▸ **fa'natically** *adv*

fanaticism ❶ (fə'nætɪˌsɪzəm) *n* wildly excessive or irrational devotion, dedication, or enthusiasm.

fan belt *n* the belt that drives a cooling fan in a car engine.

fancied ('fænsɪd) *adj* **1** imaginary; unreal. **2** thought likely to win or succeed: *a fancied runner.*

fancier ❶ ('fænsɪə) *n* **1** a person with a special interest in something. **2** a person who breeds special varieties of plants or animals: *a pigeon fancier.*

fanciful ❶ ('fænsɪful) *adj* **1** not based on fact: *fanciful notions.* **2** made or designed in a curious, intricate, or imaginative way. **3** indulging in or influenced by fancy.
▸ **'fancifully** *adv* ▸ **'fancifulness** *n*

fan club *n* **1** an organized group of admirers of a particular pop singer, film star, etc. **2 be a member of someone's fan club.** *Inf.* to approve of someone strongly.

fancy ❶ ('fænsɪ) *adj* **fancier, fanciest. 1** ornamented or decorative: *fancy clothes.* **2** requiring skill to perform: *a fancy dance routine.* **3** capricious or illusory. **4** (often used ironically) superior in quality. **5** higher than expected: *fancy prices.* **6** (of a domestic animal) bred for particular qualities. ◆ *n, pl* **fancies. 7** a sudden capricious idea. **8** a sudden or irrational liking for a person or thing. **9** the power to conceive and represent decorative and novel imagery, esp. in poetry. **10** an idea or thing produced by this. **11** a mental image. **12** *Music.* a composition for solo lute, keyboard, etc., current during the 16th and 17th centuries. **13 the fancy.** *Arch.* those who follow a particular sport, esp. prize fighting. ◆ *vb* **fancies, fancying, fancied.** (*tr*) **14** to picture in the imagination. **15** to imagine: *I fancy it will rain.* **16** (*often used with a negative*) to like: *I don't fancy your chances!* **17** (*reflexive*) to have a high or ill-founded opinion of oneself. **18** *Inf.* to have a wish for: *she fancied some chocolate.* **19** *Brit. inf.* to be physically attracted to (another person). **20** to breed (animals) for particular characteristics. ◆ *interj* **21** Also: **fancy that!** an exclamation of surprise. [C15 *fantsy,* shortened from *fantasie;* see FANTASY]
▸ **'fancily** *adv* ▸ **'fanciness** *n*

fancy dress *n* **a** costume worn at masquerades, etc., representing an historical figure, etc. **b** (*as modifier*): *a fancy-dress ball.*

fancy-free *adj* having no commitments.

fancy goods *pl n* small decorative gifts.

fancy man *n Sl.* **1** a woman's lover. **2** a pimp.

fancy woman *n Sl.* a mistress or prostitute.

fancywork ('fænsɪˌwɜːk) *n* any ornamental needlework, such as embroidery or crochet.

fan dance *n* a dance in which large fans are manipulated in front of the body, partially revealing or suggesting nakedness.

fandangle (fæn'dæŋgᵊl) *n Inf.* **1** elaborate ornament. **2** nonsense. [C19: ?from FANDANGO]

fandango (fæn'dæŋgəʊ) *n, pl* **fandangos. 1** an old Spanish courtship dance in triple time. **2** a piece of music composed for or in the rhythm of this dance. [C18: from Sp., from ?]

fane (feɪn) *n Arch. or poetic.* a temple or shrine. [C14: from L *fānum*]

fanfare ❶ ('fænfɛə) *n* **1** a flourish or short tune played on brass instruments. **2** an ostentatious flourish or display. [C17: from F, back formation from *fanfarer,* from Sp, from *fanfarron* boaster, from Ar. *farfār* garrulous]

fang ❶ (fæŋ) *n* **1** the long pointed hollow or grooved tooth of a venom-

THESAURUS

nealogy, house, line, lineage, parentage, pedigree, race, sept, stemma, stirps, strain, tribe **6** = **group**, class, classification, genre, kind, network, subdivision, system

family tree *n* = **lineage**, ancestry, extraction, genealogy, line, line of descent, pedigree, stemma, stirps

famine *n* **1, 2** = **hunger**, dearth, destitution, scarcity, starvation

famished *adj* = **starving**, ravening, ravenous, starved, voracious

famous *adj* **1** = **well-known**, acclaimed, celebrated, conspicuous, distinguished, eminent, excellent, far-famed, glorious, honoured, illustrious, legendary, lionized, much-publicized, notable, noted, prominent, remarkable, renowned, signal

Antonyms *adj* forgotten, mediocre, obscure, uncelebrated, undistinguished, unexceptional, unknown, unremarkable

fan[1] *n* **1, 2** = **blower**, air conditioner, blade, propeller, punkah (*in India*), vane, ventilator ◆ *vb* **5, 6** = **blow**, air-condition, air-cool, cool, refresh, ventilate, winnow (*rare*) **7** = **stimulate**, add fuel to the flames, agitate, arouse, enkindle, excite, impassion, increase, provoke, rouse, stir up, whip up, work up **8** *often foll. by* **out** = **spread out**, disperse, lay out, open out, space out, spread, unfurl

fan[2] *n* **1, 2** = **supporter**, addict, adherent, admirer, aficionado, buff (*inf.*), devotee, enthusiast, fiend (*inf.*), follower, freak (*inf.*), groupie (*sl.*), lover, rooter (*US*), zealot

fanatic *n* **1, 2** = **extremist**, activist, addict, bigot, buff (*inf.*), devotee, energumen, enthusiast, militant, visionary, zealot

fanatical *adj* = **obsessive**, bigoted, burning, enthusiastic, extreme, fervent, frenzied, immoderate, mad, overenthusiastic, passionate, rabid, visionary, wild, zealous

fanaticism *n* = **immoderation**, bigotry, dedication, devotion, enthusiasm, extremism, infatuation, madness, monomania, obsessiveness, overenthusiasm, single-mindedness, zeal, zealotry

fancier *n* **1, 2** = **expert**, aficionado, amateur, breeder, connoisseur

fanciful *adj* **1, 3** = **unreal**, capricious, chimerical, curious, extravagant, fabulous, fairy-tale, fantastic, ideal, imaginary, imaginative, mythical, poetic, romantic, visionary, whimsical, wild

Antonyms *adj* conventional, down-to-earth, dry, dull, literal, matter of fact, ordinary, pedestrian, predictable, routine, sensible, sober, unimaginative, uninspired

fancy *adj* **1** = **elaborate**, baroque, decorated, decorative, elegant, embellished, extravagant, fanciful, intricate, ornamental, ornamented, ornate **3** = **illusory**, capricious, chimerical, delusive, fanciful, fantastic, far-fetched, whimsical ◆ *n* **7** = **whim**, caprice, desire, humour, idea, impulse, inclination, notion, thought, urge **8** = **partiality**, fondness, hankering, inclination, liking, predilection, preference, relish, thirst **9** = **imagination**, conception, image, impression **11** = **delusion**, chimera, daydream, dream, fantasy, nightmare, phantasm, vision ◆ *vb* **15** = **suppose**, be inclined to think, believe, conceive, conjecture, guess (*inf., chiefly US & Canad.*), imagine, infer, reckon, surmise, think, think likely **18** = **wish for**, be attracted to, crave, desire, dream of, hanker after, have a yen for, hope for, long for, relish, thirst for, would like, yearn for **19** *Brit. informal* = **be attracted to**, be captivated by, desire, favour, go for, have an eye for, like, lust after, prefer, take a liking to, take to

Antonyms *adj* ≠ **elaborate:** basic, cheap, common, inferior, ordinary, plain, simple, unadorned, undecorated, unfussy ◆ *n* ≠ **partiality:** aversion, disinclination, dislike

fanfare *n* **1** = **trumpet call**, fanfaronade, flourish, trump (*arch.*), tucket (*arch.*)

fang *n* **1, 2, 4** = **tooth**, tusk

ous snake through which venom is injected. **2** any large pointed tooth, esp. the canine tooth of a carnivorous mammal. **3** the root of a tooth. **4** (*usually pl*) *Brit. inf.* a tooth. [OE *fang* what is caught, prey]
▸**fanged** *adj* ▸**'fangless** *adj*

fan heater *n* a space heater consisting of an electrically heated element with an electrically driven fan to disperse the heat.

fanjet ('fæn,dʒet) *n* another name for **turbofan.**

fanlight ('fæn,laɪt) *n* **1** a semicircular window over a door or window, often having sash bars like the ribs of a fan. **2** a small rectangular window over a door. US name: **transom.**

fan mail *n* mail sent to a famous person, such as a pop musician or film star, by admirers.

fanny ('fænɪ) *n, pl* **fannies.** *Sl.* **1** *Taboo, Brit.* the female genitals. **2** *Chiefly US & Canad.* the buttocks. [C20: ?from *Fanny*, pet name from *Frances*]

fanny adams *n Brit. sl.* **1** (usually preceded by *sweet*) absolutely nothing at all. **2** *Chiefly naut.* (formerly) tinned meat. [C19: from the name of a young murder victim whose body was cut up into small pieces. For sense 1: a euphemism for *fuck all*]

fantail ('fæn,teɪl) *n* **1** a breed of domestic pigeon having a large tail that can be opened like a fan. **2** an Old World flycatcher of Australia, New Zealand, and SE Asia, having a broad fan-shaped tail. **3** a tail shaped like an outspread fan. **4** an auxiliary sail on the upper portion of a windmill. **5** *US.* a part of the deck projecting aft of the sternpost of a ship.
▸**'fan-,tailed** *adj*

fan-tan *n* **1** a Chinese gambling game. **2** a card game played in sequence, the winner being the first to use up all his cards. [C19: from Chinese (Cantonese) *fan t'an* repeated divisions, from *fan* times + *t'an* division]

fantasia (fæn'teɪzɪə) *n* **1** any musical composition of a free or improvisatory nature. **2** a potpourri of popular tunes woven loosely together. [C18: from It.: fancy; see FANTASY]

fantasize **T** *or* **fantasise** ('fæntə,saɪz) *vb* **fantasizes, fantasizing, fantasized** *or* **fantasises, fantasising, fantasised. 1** (when *tr*, takes a clause as object) to conceive extravagant or whimsical ideas, images, etc. **2** (*intr*) to conceive pleasant mental images.

fantastic **T** (fæn'tæstɪk) *adj also* **fantastical. 1** strange or fanciful in appearance, conception, etc. **2** created in the mind; illusory. **3** unrealistic: *fantastic plans.* **4** incredible or preposterous: *a fantastic verdict.* **5** *Inf.* very large or extreme: *a fantastic fortune.* **6** *Inf.* very good; excellent. **7** of or characterized by fantasy. **8** capricious; fitful. [C14 *fantastik* imaginary, via LL from Gk *phantastikos* capable of imagining, from *phantazein* to make visible]
▸**fan,tasti'cality** *or* **fan'tasticalness** *n* ▸**fan'tastically** *adv*

fantasy **T** *or* **phantasy** ('fæntəsɪ) *n, pl* **fantasies** *or* **phantasies. 1a** imagination unrestricted by reality. **1b** (*as modifier*): *a fantasy world.* **2** a creation of the imagination, esp. a weird or bizarre one. **3** *Psychol.* a series of pleasing mental images, usually serving to fulfil a need not gratified in reality. **4** a whimsical or far-fetched notion. **5** an illusion or phantom. **6** a highly elaborate imaginative design or creation. **7** *Music.* another word for **fantasia. 8** literature, etc., having a large fantasy content. ◆ *vb* **fantasies, fantasying, fantasied** *or* **phantasies, phantasying, phantasied. 9** a less common word for **fantasize.** [C14 *fantasie*, from L, from Gk *phantazein* to make visible]

fan vaulting *n Archit.* vaulting having ribs that radiate like those of a fan and spring from the top of a capital. Also called: **palm vaulting.**

fanzine ('fæn,ziːn) *n* a magazine produced by amateurs for fans of a specific interest, pop group, etc. [C20: from FAN² + (MAGA)ZINE]

FAO *abbrev. for:* **1** Food and Agriculture Organization (of the United Nations). **2** for the attention of.

f.a.q. *abbrev. for:* **1** *Commerce.* fair average quality. **2** free alongside quay.

far **T** (fɑː) *adv* **farther** *or* **further, farthest** *or* **furthest. 1** at, to, or from a great distance. **2** at or to a remote time: *far in the future.* **3** to a considerable degree: *a far better plan.* **4 as far as. 4a** to the degree or extent that. **4b** to the distance or place of. **4c** *Inf.* with reference to; as for. **5 by far.** by a considerable margin. **6 far and away.** by a very great margin. **7 far and wide.** everywhere. **8 far be it from me.** on no account: *far be it from me to tell you what to do.* **9 go far. 9a** to be successful: *your son will go far.* **9b** to be sufficient or last long: *the wine didn't go far.* **10 go too far.** to exceed reasonable limits. **11 so far. 11a** up to the present moment. **11b** up to a certain point, extent, degree, etc. ◆ *adj* (*prenominal*) **12** remote in space or time: *in the far past.* **13** extending a great distance. **14** more distant: *the far end of the room.* **15 far from.** in a degree, state, etc. remote from: *he is far from happy.* [OE *feorr*]
▸**'farness** *n*

farad ('færəd) *n Physics.* the derived SI unit of electric capacitance; the capacitance of a capacitor between the plates of which a potential of 1 volt is created by a charge of 1 coulomb. Symbol: F [C19: see FARADAY]

faraday ('færə,deɪ) *n* a quantity of electricity, used in electrochemical calculations, equivalent to unit amount of substance of electrons. Symbol: *F* [C20: after Michael *Faraday*, (1791–1867), E physicist]

faradic (fə'rædɪk) *adj* of or concerned with an intermittent alternating current such as that induced in the secondary winding of an induction coil. [C19: from F *faradique*; see FARADAY]

farandole ('færən,dəʊl) *n* **1** a lively dance from Provence. **2** a piece of music composed for or in the rhythm of this dance. [C19: from F, from Provençal *farandoulo*, from ?]

faraway **T** ('fɑːrə,weɪ) *adj* (**far away** *when postpositive*). **1** very distant. **2** absent-minded.

farce **T** (fɑːs) *n* **1** a broadly humorous play based on the exploitation of improbable situations. **2** the genre of comedy represented by works of this kind. **3** a ludicrous situation or action. **4** another name for **forcemeat.** [C14 (in the sense: stuffing): from OF, from L *farcīre* to stuff, interpolate passages (in the mass, in religious plays, etc.)]

farcical **T** ('fɑːsɪkᵊl) *adj* **1** absurd. **2** of or relating to farce.
▸**,farci'cality** *n* ▸**'farcically** *adv*

fardel ('fɑːdᵊl) *n Arch.* a bundle or burden. [C13: from OF *farde*, ult. from Ar. *fardah*]

fare **T** (fɛə) *n* **1** the sum charged or paid for conveyance in a bus, train, etc. **2** a paying passenger, esp. when carried by taxi. **3** a range of food and drink. ◆ *vb* **fares, faring, fared.** (*intr*) **4** to get on (as specified): *he fared well.* **5** (with *it* as a subject) to happen as specified: *it fared badly with him.* **6** *Arch.* to eat: *we fared sumptuously.* **7** (often foll. by *forth*) *Arch.* to travel. [OE *faran*]
▸**'farer** *n*

Far East *n* **the.** the countries of E Asia, including China, Japan, North and South Korea, E Siberia, Indonesia, Malaysia, and the Philippines: sometimes extended to include all territories east of Afghanistan.
▸**Far Eastern** *adj*

fare stage *n* **1** a section of a bus journey for which a set charge is made. **2** the bus stop marking the end of such a section.

farewell **T** (,fɛə'wɛl) *sentence substitute.* **1** goodbye; adieu. ◆ *n* **2** a parting salutation. **3** an act of departure. **4** (*modifier*) expressing leave-taking: *a farewell speech.*

far-fetched **T** *adj* unlikely.

far-flung *adj* **1** widely distributed. **2** far distant; remote.

farina (fə'riːnə) *n* **1** flour or meal made from any kind of cereal grain. **2** *Chiefly Brit.* starch. [C18: from L *fār* spelt, coarse meal]

farinaceous (,færɪ'neɪʃəs) *adj* **1** consisting or made of starch. **2** having a mealy texture or appearance. **3** containing starch: *farinaceous seeds.*

THESAURUS

fantasize *vb* **1, 2** = **daydream**, build castles in the air, dream, envision, hallucinate, imagine, invent, live in a dream world, romance, see visions

fantastic *adj* **1** = **strange**, comical, eccentric, exotic, fanciful, freakish, grotesque, imaginative, odd, oddball (*inf.*), off-the-wall (*sl.*), outlandish, outré, peculiar, phantasmagorical, quaint, queer, rococo, unreal, weird, whimsical, zany **2, 3** = **unrealistic**, ambitious, chimerical, extravagant, far-fetched, grandiose, illusory, ludicrous, ridiculous, visionary, wild **4** = **implausible**, absurd, capricious, cock-and-bull (*inf.*), incredible, irrational, mad, preposterous, unlikely **5** *Informal* = **enormous**, extreme, great, overwhelming, severe, tremendous **6** *Informal* = **wonderful**, awesome, brill (*inf.*), cracking (*Brit. inf.*), crucial (*sl.*), def (*sl.*), dope (*sl.*), excellent, first-rate, jim-dandy (*sl.*), marvellous, mega (*sl.*), out of this world (*inf.*), sensational (*inf.*), sovereign, superb, topping (*Brit. sl.*), world-class
Antonyms ≠ **unrealistic, implausible:** credible, moderate, rational, realistic, sensible *adj* ≠ **wonderful:** common, everyday, normal, ordinary, poor, typical

fantasy *n* **1** = **imagination**, creativity, fancy, invention, originality **2** = **daydream**, apparition, delusion, dream, fancy, figment of the imagination, flight of fancy, hallucination, illusion, mirage, nightmare, pipe dream, reverie, vision

far *adv* **1** = **a long way**, afar, a good way, a great distance, deep, miles **3** = **much**, considerably, decidedly, extremely, greatly, incomparably, very much **5 by far** = **very much**, by a long chalk (*inf.*), by a long shot, by a long way, easily, far and away, immeasurably, incomparably, to a great degree **7 far and wide** = **extensively**, broadly, everywhere, far and near, here, there and everywhere, in every nook and cranny, widely, worldwide **11a so far** = **up to now**, thus far, to date, until now, up to the present ◆ *adj* **12** = **remote**, distant, faraway, far-flung, far-off, far-removed, long, outlying, out-of-the-way, removed
Antonyms *adj* ≠ **remote:** adjacent, adjoining, alongside, at close quarters, beside, bordering, close, contiguous, just round the corner, near, nearby, neighbouring, proximate, within sniffing distance (*inf.*)

faraway *adj* **1** = **distant**, beyond the horizon, far, far-flung, far-off, far-removed, outlying, remote **2** = **dreamy**, absent, abstracted, distant, lost, vague

farce *n* **1, 2** = **comedy**, broad comedy, buffoonery, burlesque, satire, slapstick **3** = **mockery**, absurdity, joke, nonsense, parody, ridiculousness, sham, travesty

farcical *adj* **1, 2** = **ludicrous**, absurd, amusing, comic, custard-pie, derisory, diverting, droll, funny, laughable, nonsensical, preposterous, ridiculous, risible, slapstick

fare *n* **1** = **charge**, passage money, price, ticket money, transport cost **2** = **passenger**, pick-up (*inf.*), traveller **3** = **food**, commons, diet, eatables, feed, meals, menu, nosebag (*sl.*), provisions, rations, sustenance, table, tack (*inf.*), victuals, vittles (*obs. or dialect*) ◆ *vb* **4** = **get on**, do, get along, make out, manage, prosper **5** *used impersonally* = **happen**, go, pan out (*inf.*), proceed, turn out

farewell *n* **2, 3** = **goodbye**, adieu, adieux *or* adieus, departure, leave-taking, parting, send-off (*inf.*), valediction

far-fetched *adj* = **unconvincing**, cock-and-bull (*inf.*), doubtful, dubious, fantastic, hard to swallow (*inf.*), implausible, improbable, incredible, preposterous, strained, unbelievable, unlikely, unnatural, unrealistic
Antonyms *adj* acceptable, authentic, believable, credible, feasible, imaginable, likely, plausible, possible, probable, realistic, reasonable

farm ❶ (fɑːm) *n* **1a** a tract of land, usually with house and buildings, cultivated as a unit or used to rear livestock. **1b** (*as modifier*): *farm produce*. **1c** (*in combination*): *farmland*. **2** a unit of land or water devoted to the growing or rearing of some particular type of vegetable, fruit, animal, or fish: *a fish farm*. **3** an installation for storage or disposal: *a sewage farm*. ◆ *vb* **4** (*tr*) **4a** to cultivate (land). **4b** to rear (stock, etc.) on a farm. **5** (*intr*) to engage in agricultural work, esp. as a way of life. **6** (*tr*) to look after a child for a fixed sum. **7** to collect the moneys due and retain the profits from (a tax district, business, etc.) for a specified period. ◆ See also **farm out**. [C13: from OF *ferme* rented land, ult. from L *firmāre* to settle]
▸**'farmable** *adj*

farmed (fɑːmd) *adj* (of fish and game) reared on a farm rather than caught in the wild.

farmer ❶ ('fɑːmə) *n* **1** a person who operates or manages a farm. **2** a person who obtains the right to collect and retain a tax, rent, etc., on payment of a fee. **3** a person who looks after a child for a fixed sum.

farmer's lung *n* inflammation of the alveoli of the lungs caused by an allergic response to fungal spores in hay.

farm hand *n* a person who is hired to work on a farm.

farmhouse ('fɑːmˌhaʊs) *n* a house attached to a farm, esp. the dwelling from which the farm is managed.

farming ❶ ('fɑːmɪŋ) *n* **a** the business or skill of agriculture. **b** (*as modifier*): *farming methods*.

farm out *vb* (*tr, adv*) **1** to send (work) to be done by another person, firm, etc. **2** to put (a child, etc.) into the care of a private individual. **3** to lease to another for a fee the right to collect (taxes).

farmstead ('fɑːmˌstɛd) *n* a farm or the part of a farm comprising its main buildings together with adjacent grounds.

farmyard ('fɑːmˌjɑːd) *n* an area surrounded by or adjacent to farm buildings.

Far North *n* **the**. the Arctic and sub-Arctic regions of the world.

faro ('fɛərəʊ) *n* a gambling game in which players bet against the dealer on what cards he will turn up. [C18: prob. spelling var. of *Pharoah*]

far-off *adj* (**far off** *when postpositive*). remote in space or time; distant.

farouche *French*. (faruʃ) *adj* sullen or shy. [C18: from F, from OF, from LL *forasticus* from without, from L *foras* out of doors]

far-out ❶ *Sl*. ◆ *adj* (**far out** *when postpositive*) **1** bizarre or avant-garde. **2** wonderful. ◆ *interj* **far out**. **3** an expression of amazement or delight.

farrago ❶ (fəˈrɑːgəʊ) *n, pl* **farragos** *or* **farragoes**. a hotchpotch. [C17: from L: mash for cattle (hence, a mixture), from *fār* spelt]
▸**farraginous** (fəˈrædʒɪnəs) *adj*

far-reaching ❶ *adj* extensive in influence, effect, or range.

farrier ('færɪə) *n Chiefly Brit*. **1** a person who shoes horses. **2** another name for **veterinary surgeon**. [C16: from OF, from L *ferrārius* smith, from *ferrum* iron]
▸**'farriery** *n*

farrow ('færəʊ) *n* **1** a litter of piglets. ◆ *vb* **2** (of a sow) to give birth to (a litter). [OE *fearh*]

far-seeing *adj* having shrewd judgment.

Farsi ('fɑːsɪ) *n* a language spoken in Iran.

far-sighted ❶ *adj* **1** possessing prudence and foresight. **2** another word for **long-sighted**.
▸ˌ**far-'sightedly** *adv* ▸ˌ**far-'sightedness** *n*

fart (fɑːt) *Taboo*. ◆ *n* **1** an emission of intestinal gas from the anus. **2** *Sl*. a contemptible person. ◆ *vb* (*intr*) **3** to break wind. **4** **fart about** *or* **around**. *Sl*. **4a** to behave foolishly. **4b** to waste time. [ME *farten*]

farther ('fɑːðə) *adv* **1** to or at a greater distance in space or time. **2** in addition. ◆ *adj* **3** more distant or remote in space or time. **4** additional. [C13: see FAR, FURTHER]

> **USAGE NOTE** *Farther, farthest, further,* and *furthest* can all be used to refer to literal distance, but *further* and *furthest* are regarded as more correct for figurative senses denoting greater or additional amount, time, etc.: *further to my letter*. *Further* and *furthest* are also preferred for figurative distance.

farthermost ('fɑːðəˌməʊst) *adj* most distant or remote.

farthest ('fɑːðɪst) *adv* **1** to or at the greatest distance in space or time. ◆ *adj* **2** most distant in space or time. **3** most extended. [C14 *ferthest*, from *ferther* FURTHER]

farthing ('fɑːðɪŋ) *n* **1** a former British bronze coin worth a quarter of an old penny: withdrawn in 1961. **2** something of negligible value; jot. [OE *fēorthing* from *fēortha* FOURTH + -ING[1]]

farthingale ('fɑːðɪŋˌgeɪl) *n* a hoop or framework worn under skirts, esp. in the Elizabethan period, to shape and spread them. [C16: from F *verdugale*, from OSp. *verdugado*, from *verdugo* rod]

fasces ('fæsiːz) *pl n, sing* **fascis** (-sɪs). **1** (in ancient Rome) one or more bundles of rods containing an axe with its blade protruding; a symbol of a magistrate's power. **2** (in modern Italy) such an object used as the symbol of Fascism. [C16: from L, pl of *fascis* bundle]

fascia *or* **facia** ('feɪʃɪə) *n, pl* **fasciae** *or* **faciae** (-ʃɪˌiː). **1** the flat surface above a shop window. **2** *Archit*. a flat band or surface, esp. a part of an architrave. **3** ('fæʃɪə). fibrous connective tissue occurring in sheets between muscles. **4** *Biol*. a distinctive band of colour, as on an insect or plant. **5** *Brit*. the outer panel which covers the dashboard of a motor vehicle. [C16: from L: band: rel. to *fascis* bundle]
▸**'fascial** *or* **'facial** *adj*

fasciate ('fæʃɪˌeɪt) *or* **fasciated** *adj* **1** *Bot*. (of stems and branches) abnormally flattened due to coalescence. **2** (of birds, insects, etc.) marked by bands of colour. [C17: prob. from NL *fasciātus* (unattested) having bands; see FASCIA]

fascicle ('fæsɪkᵊl) *n* **1** a bundle of branches, leaves, etc. **2** Also called: **fasciculus**. *Anat*. a small bundle of fibres, esp. nerve fibres. [C15: from L *fasciculus* a small bundle, from *fascis* a bundle]
▸**'fascicled** *adj* ▸**fascicular** (fəˈsɪkjʊlə) *or* **fasciculate** (fəˈsɪkjʊˌleɪt) *adj* ▸**fasˌcicu'lation** *n*

fascicule ('fæsɪˌkjuːl) *n* one part of a printed work that is published in instalments. Also called: **fascicle, fasciculus**.

fascinate ❶ ('fæsɪˌneɪt) *vb* **fascinates, fascinating, fascinated**. (*mainly tr*) **1** to attract and delight by arousing interest: *his stories fascinated me for hours*. **2** to render motionless, as by arousing terror or awe. **3** *Arch*. to put under a spell. [C16: from L, from *fascinum* a bewitching]
▸ˌ**fasci'nation** *n*

> **USAGE NOTE** A person can be fascinated *by* or *with* another person or thing. It is correct to speak of someone's fascination *with* a person or thing; one can also say a person or thing has a fascination *for* someone.

fascinating ❶ ('fæsɪˌneɪtɪŋ) *adj* **1** arousing great interest. **2** enchanting or alluring.

fascinator ('fæsɪˌneɪtə) *n Rare*. a lace or crocheted head covering for women.

Fascism ❶ ('fæʃɪzəm) *n* **1** the political movement, doctrine, system, or regime of Benito Mussolini in Italy (1922–43). Fascism encouraged militarism and nationalism, organizing the country along hierarchical authoritarian lines. **2** (*sometimes not cap*.) any ideology or movement modelled on or inspired by this. **3** *Inf*. (*often not cap*.) any doctrine, system, or practice, regarded as authoritarian, militaristic, or extremely right-wing. [C20: from It. *fascismo*, from *fascio* political group, from L *fascis* bundle; see FASCES]

Fascist ('fæʃɪst) *n* **1** a supporter or member of a Fascist movement. **2** (*sometimes not cap*.) any person regarded as having right-wing authoritarian views. ◆ *adj* **3** characteristic of or relating to Fascism.

fashion ❶ ('fæʃən) *n* **1a** style in clothes, behaviour, etc., esp. the latest style. **1b** (*as modifier*): *a fashion magazine*. **2** (*modifier*) designed to be in the current fashion. **3a** manner of performance: *in a striking fashion*. **3b** (*in combination*): *crab-fashion*. **4** a way of life that revolves around the activities, dress, interests, etc., that are most fashionable. **5** shape or form. **6** sort; kind. **7** **after** *or* **in a fashion**. in some manner, but not very well: *I mended it, after a fashion*. **8** **of fashion**. of high social standing. ◆ *vb* (*tr*) **9** to give a particular form to. **10** to make suitable or fitting. **11** *Obs*. to contrive. [C13 *facioun* form, manner, from OF *faceon*, from L, from *facere* to make]
▸**'fashioner** *n*

THESAURUS

farm *n* **1** = **smallholding**, acreage, acres, croft (*Scot*.), farmstead, grange, holding, homestead, land, plantation, ranch (*chiefly North American*), station (*Austral. & NZ*) ◆ *vb* **4** = **cultivate**, bring under cultivation, operate, plant, practise husbandry, till the soil, work

farmer *n* **1** = **agriculturist**, agronomist, husbandman, smallholder, yeoman

farming *n* = **agriculture**, agronomy, husbandry

far-out *adj* **1** = **strange**, advanced, avant-garde, bizarre, off-the-wall (*sl*.), outlandish, outré, unconventional, unusual, weird, wild

farrago *n* = **hotchpotch**, hash, hodgepodge, jumble, medley, *mélange*, miscellany, mishmash, mixed bag, mixture, potpourri

far-reaching *adj* = **extensive**, broad, important, momentous, pervasive, significant, sweeping, widespread

far-sighted *adj* **1** = **prudent**, acute, canny, cautious, discerning, far-seeing, judicious, politic, prescient, provident, sage, shrewd, wise

fascinate *vb* **1** = **entrance**, absorb, allure, beguile, bewitch, captivate, charm, delight, enamour, enchant, engross, enrapture, enthral, hold spellbound, hypnotize, infatuate, intrigue, mesmerize, ravish, rivet, spellbind, transfix
Antonyms *vb* alienate, bore, disenchant, disgust, irritate, jade, put one off, sicken, turn one off (*inf*.)

fascinated *adj* **1** = **entranced**, absorbed, beguiled, bewitched, captivated, charmed, engrossed, enthralled, hooked on, hypnotized, infatuated, smitten, spellbound, under a spell

fascinating *adj* **1** = **captivating**, alluring, bewitching, compelling, enchanting, engaging, engrossing, enticing, gripping, intriguing, irresistible, ravishing, riveting, seductive
Antonyms *adj* boring, dull, mind-numbing, unexciting, uninteresting

fascination *n* **1** = **attraction**, allure, charm, enchantment, glamour, lure, magic, magnetism, pull, sorcery, spell

Fascism *n* **2, 3** *sometimes not cap*. = **authoritarianism**, absolutism, autocracy, dictatorship, Hitlerism, totalitarianism

fashion *n* **1** = **style**, convention, craze, custom, fad, latest, latest style, look, mode, prevailing taste, rage, trend, usage, vogue **3** = **method**, attitude, demeanour, manner, mode, style, way **5** = **form**, appearance, configuration, cut, figure, guise (*arch*.), line, make, model, mould, pattern, shape, stamp **6** = **sort**, description, kind, stamp, type **7** **after a fashion** = **to some extent**, in a manner of speaking, in a way, moderately, somehow, somehow or other, to a degree ◆ *vb* **9** = **make**, construct, contrive, create, design,

fashionable ('fæʃənəbᵊl) *adj* **1** conforming to fashion; in vogue. **2** of or patronized by people of fashion: *a fashionable café.* **3** (usually foll. by *with*) patronized (by).
▸ **'fashionableness** *n* ▸ **'fashionably** *adv*

fashion plate *n* **1** an illustration of the latest fashion in dress. **2** a fashionably dressed person.

fashion victim *n Inf.* a person who slavishly follows fashion.

fast[1] (fɑːst) *adj* **1** acting or moving or capable of acting or moving quickly. **2** accomplished in or lasting a short time: *a fast visit.* **3** (*prenominal*) adapted to or facilitating rapid movement: *the fast lane of a motorway.* **4** (of a clock, etc.) indicating a time in advance of the correct time. **5** given to an active dissipated life. **6** of or characteristic of such activity: *a fast life.* **7** not easily moved; firmly fixed; secure. **8** firmly fastened or shut. **9** steadfast; constant (esp. in **fast friends**). **10** *Sport.* (of a playing surface, running track, etc.) conducive to rapid speed, as of a ball used on it or of competitors racing on it. **11** that will not fade or change colour readily. **12** proof against fading. **13** *Photog.* **13a** requiring a relatively short time of exposure to produce a given density: *a fast film.* **13b** permitting a short exposure time: *a fast shutter.* **14 a fast one.** *Inf.* a deceptive or unscrupulous trick (esp. in **pull a fast one**). **15 fast worker.** a person who achieves results quickly, esp. in seductions. ◆ *adv* **16** quickly; rapidly. **17** soundly; deeply: *fast asleep.* **18** firmly; tightly. **19** in quick succession. **20** in advance of the correct time: *my watch is running fast.* **21** in a reckless or dissipated way. **22 fast by** *or* **beside.** *Arch.* close by. **23 play fast and loose.** *Inf.* to behave in an insincere or unreliable manner. [OE *fæst* strong, tight]

fast[2] (fɑːst) *vb* **1** (*intr*) to abstain from eating all or certain foods or meals, esp. as a religious observance. ◆ *n* **2a** an act or period of fasting. **2b** (*as modifier*): *a fast day.* [OE *fæstan*]
▸ **'faster** *n*

fastback ('fɑːstˌbæk) *n* a car having a back that forms one continuous slope from roof to rear.

fast-breeder reactor *n* a nuclear reactor that uses little or no moderator and produces more fissionable material than it consumes.

fasten ('fɑːsᵊn) *vb* **1** to make or become fast or secure. **2** to make or become attached or joined. **3** to close or become closed by fixing firmly in place, locking, etc. **4** (*tr*; foll. by *in* or *up*) to enclose or imprison. **5** (*tr*; usually foll. by *on*) to cause (blame, a nickname, etc.) to be attached (to). **6** (usually foll. by *on* or *upon*) to direct or be directed in a concentrated way. **7** (*intr*; usually foll. by *on*) to take a firm hold (of). [OE *fæstnian; see* FAST[1]]
▸ **'fastener** *n*

fastening ('fɑːsᵊnɪŋ) *n* something that fastens, such as a clasp or lock.

fast food *n* **a** food, esp. hamburgers, fried chicken, etc., that is prepared and served very quickly. **b** (*as modifier*): *a fast-food restaurant.*

fast-forward *n* **1** (*sometimes not hyphenated*) the control on a tape deck or video recorder used to wind the tape or video forwards at speed. **2** *Inf.* a state of urgency or rapid progress: *put the deal into fast-forward.* ◆ *vb* (*tr*) **3** to wind (a tape, etc.) forward using the fast-forward control. **4** *Inf.* **4a** to deal with or dispatch (something) rapidly: *fast-forward this to the press.* **4b** to skip (something): *fast-forward the small talk and get down to business.*

fastidious (fæ'stɪdɪəs) *adj* **1** hard to please. **2** excessively particular about details. **3** exceedingly delicate. [C15: from L *fastīdiōsus* scornful, from *fastīdium* loathing, from *fastus* pride + *taedium* weariness]
▸ **fas'tidiously** *adv* ▸ **fas'tidiousness** *n*

fastigiate (fæ'stɪdʒɪɪt) *or* **fastigiated** *adj Biol.* (of parts or organs) united in a tapering group. [C17: from Med. L *fastīgiātus* lofty, from L *fastīgium* height]

fast lane *n* **1** the outside lane on a motorway for vehicles overtaking or travelling at high speed. **2** *Inf.* the quickest but most competitive route to success.

fastness ('fɑːstnɪs) *n* **1** a stronghold; fortress. **2** the state or quality of being firm or secure. [OE *fæstnes;* see FAST[1]]

fast-track *adj* taking the quickest but most competitive route to success or personal advancement: *fast-track executives.*
▸ **ˌfast-'tracker** *n*

fat (fæt) *n* **1** any of a class of naturally occurring soft greasy solids that are present in some plants and animals, and are used in making soap and paint and in the food industry. **2** vegetable or animal tissue containing fat. **3** corpulence, obesity, or plumpness. **4** the best or richest part of something. **5 the fat is in the fire.** an irrevocable action has been taken from which dire consequences are expected. **6 the fat of the land.** the best that is obtainable. ◆ *adj* **fatter, fattest. 7** having much or too much flesh or fat. **8** consisting of or containing fat; greasy. **9** profitable; lucrative. **10** affording great opportunities: *a fat part in the play.* **11** fertile or productive: *a fat land.* **12** thick, broad, or extended: *a fat log of wood.* **13** *Sl.* very little or none (in **a fat chance, a fat lot of good,** etc.). ◆ *vb* **fats, fatting, fatted. 14** to make or become fat; fatten. [OE *fǣtt,* p.p. of *fǣtan* to cram]
▸ **'fatless** *adj* ▸ **'fatly** *adv* ▸ **'fatness** *n* ▸ **'fattish** *adj*

fatal ('feɪtᵊl) *adj* **1** resulting in death: *a fatal accident.* **2** bringing ruin. **3** decisively important. **4** inevitable. [C14: from OF or L from L *fātum;* see FATE]
▸ **'fatally** *adv*

fatalism ('feɪtəˌlɪzəm) *n* **1** the philosophical doctrine that all events are predetermined so that man is powerless to alter his destiny. **2** the acceptance of and submission to this doctrine.
▸ **'fatalist** *n* ▸ **ˌfatal'istic** *adj*

fatality (fə'tælɪtɪ) *n, pl* **fatalities. 1** an accident or disaster resulting in death. **2** a person killed in an accident or disaster. **3** the power of causing death or disaster. **4** the quality or condition of being fated. **5** something caused by fate.

fate (feɪt) *n* **1** the ultimate agency that predetermines the course of events. **2** the inevitable fortune that befalls a person or thing. **3** the end or final result. **4** death, destruction, or downfall. ◆ *vb* **fates, fating, fated. 5** (*tr; usually passive*) to predetermine: *he was fated to lose.* [C14: from L *fātum* oracular utterance, from *fārī* to speak]

fated ('feɪtɪd) *adj* **1** destined. **2** doomed to death or destruction.

fateful ('feɪtfʊl) *adj* **1** having important consequences. **2** bringing death or disaster. **3** controlled by or as if by fate. **4** prophetic.
▸ **'fatefully** *adv* ▸ **'fatefulness** *n*

Fates (feɪts) *pl n Greek myth.* the three goddesses, Atropos, Clotho, and Lachesis, who control the destinies of the lives of man.

THESAURUS

forge, form, manufacture, mould, shape, work **10** = **fit**, accommodate, adapt, adjust, suit, tailor

fashionable *adj* **1** = **popular**, à la mode, all the go (*inf.*), all the rage, chic, cool (*sl.*), current, customary, genteel, happening (*inf.*), hip (*sl.*), in (*inf.*), in vogue, latest, modern, modish, prevailing, smart, stylish, trendsetting, trendy (*Brit. inf.*), up-to-date, up-to-the-minute, usual, voguish (*inf.*), with it (*inf.*)
Antonyms *adj* behind the times, dated, frumpy, obsolete, old-fashioned, old-hat, outmoded, out of date, out of the ark (*inf.*), uncool (*sl.*), unfashionable, unpopular, unstylish, untrendy (*Brit. inf.*)

fast[1] *adj* **1, 2** = **quick**, accelerated, brisk, fleet, flying, hasty, hurried, mercurial, nippy (*Brit. inf.*), quickie (*inf.*), rapid, speedy, swift, winged **5, 6** = **dissipated**, dissolute, extravagant, gadabout (*inf.*), giddy, immoral, intemperate, licentious, loose, profligate, promiscuous, rakish, reckless, self-indulgent, wanton, wild **7, 9** = **fixed**, close, constant, fastened, firm, fortified, immovable, impregnable, lasting, loyal, permanent, secure, sound, stalwart, staunch, steadfast, tight, unwavering **14 pull a fast one** *Informal* = **trick**, bamboozle (*inf.*), cheat, con (*inf.*), deceive, defraud, hoodwink, put one over on (*inf.*), swindle, take advantage of, take for a ride (*inf.*) ◆ *adv* **16** = **quickly**, apace, at a rate of knots, hastily, hell for leather (*inf.*), hotfoot, hurriedly, in haste, like a flash, like a shot (*inf.*), like lightning, posthaste, presto, rapidly, speedily, swiftly, with all haste **17, 18** = **soundly**, deeply, firmly, fixedly, securely, tightly **21** = **recklessly**, extravagantly, intemperately, loosely, promiscuously, rakishly, wildly
Antonyms *adj* ≠ **quick:** leisurely, plodding, slow, slow moving, unhurried ≠ **fixed:** inconstant, irresolute, unfaithful, unreliable, unstable, wavering, weak ◆ *adv* ≠ **quickly:** at a snail's pace, at one's leisure, gradually, leisurely, slowly, steadily, unhurriedly

fast[2] *vb* **1** = **go hungry**, abstain, deny oneself, go without food, practise abstention, refrain from food *or* eating ◆ *n* **2** = **fasting**, abstinence

fasten *vb* **1-3** = **fix**, affix, anchor, attach, bind, bolt, chain, connect, grip, join, lace, link, lock, make fast, make firm, seal, secure, tie, unite **6** = **direct**, aim, bend, concentrate, fix, focus, rivet

fastening *n* = **tie**, affixation, attachment, binding, bond, concatenation, connection, coupling, fusion, joint, junction, ligature, link, linking, union

fastidious *adj* **1-3** = **particular**, choosy, critical, dainty, difficult, discriminating, finicky, fussy, hard to please, hypercritical, meticulous, nice, overdelicate, overnice, pernickety, picky (*inf.*), punctilious, squeamish
Antonyms *adj* careless, casual, disorderly, easy-going, lenient, slack, slipshod, sloppy, slovenly, unsystematic

fat *n* **3** = **fatness**, adipose tissue, beef (*inf.*), blubber, bulk, cellulite, corpulence, flab, flesh, obesity, overweight, paunch, weight problem ◆ *adj* **7** = **overweight**, beefy (*inf.*), broad in the beam (*inf.*), corpulent, elephantine, fleshy, gross, heavy, obese, plump, podgy, portly, roly-poly, rotund, solid, stout, tubby **8** = **fatty**, adipose, greasy, lipid, oily, oleaginous, suety **9** = **profitable**, affluent, cushy, fertile, flourishing, fruitful, jammy (*Brit. sl.*), lucrative, lush, productive, prosperous, remunerative, rich, thriving
Antonyms *adj* ≠ **overweight:** angular, bony, empty, gaunt, lank, lean, scrawny, skinny, slender, slight, slim, spare, thin ≠ **fatty:** lean ≠ **profitable:** barren, poor, scanty, scarce, unproductive, unprofitable, unrewarding

fatal *adj* **1** = **lethal**, deadly, destructive, final, incurable, killing, malignant, mortal, pernicious, terminal **2** = **disastrous**, baleful, baneful, calamitous, catastrophic, lethal, ruinous **3** = **decisive**, critical, crucial, determining, fateful, final **4** = **inevitable**, destined, doomed, foreordained, predestined
Antonyms *adj* ≠ **lethal:** beneficial, benign, harmless, innocuous, inoffensive, non-lethal, non-toxic, salutary, vitalizing, wholesome ≠ **disastrous:** inconsequential, minor

fatalism *n* **1, 2** = **resignation**, acceptance, determinism, necessitarianism, passivity, predestinarianism, stoicism

fatality *n* **1, 3** = **death**, casualty, deadliness, disaster, fatal accident, lethalness, loss, mortality

fate *n* **1** = **destiny**, chance, divine will, fortune, kismet, nemesis, predestination, providence, weird (*arch.*) **2** = **fortune**, cup, horoscope, lot, portion, stars **3** = **outcome**, end, future, issue, upshot **4** = **downfall**, death, destruction, doom, end, ruin

fated *adj* **1** = **destined**, doomed, foreordained, ineluctable, inescapable, inevitable, marked down, predestined, pre-elected, preordained, sure, written

fateful *adj* **1** = **crucial**, critical, decisive, important, portentous, significant **2** = **disastrous**,

fat farm *n Sl.* a health farm or similar establishment to which people go to lose weight.

fathead ('fæt,hɛd) *n Inf.* a stupid person; fool.
▸'**fat,headed** *adj*

father ❶ ('fɑːðə) *n* **1** a male parent. **2** a person who founds a line or family; forefather. **3** any male acting in a paternal capacity. **4** (*often cap.*) a respectful term of address for an old man. **5** a male who originates something: *the father of modern psychology.* **6** a leader of an association, council, etc.: *a city father.* **7** *Brit.* the eldest or most senior member in a union, profession, etc. **8** (*often pl*) a senator in ancient Rome. ◆ *vb* (*tr*) **9** to procreate or generate (offspring). **10** to create, found, etc. **11** to act as a father to. **12** to acknowledge oneself as father or originator of. **13** (foll. by *on* or *upon*) to impose or foist upon. [OE *fæder*]
▸'**fatherhood** *n* ▸'**fatherless** *adj* ▸'**father-,like** *adj*

Father ('fɑːðə) *n* **1** God, esp. when considered as the first person of the Christian Trinity. **2** any of the early writers on Christian doctrine. **3** a title used for Christian priests.

father confessor *n* **1** *Christianity.* a priest who hears confessions. **2** any person to whom one tells private matters.

father-in-law *n, pl* **fathers-in-law.** the father of one's wife or husband.

fatherland ❶ ('fɑːðə,lænd) *n* **1** a person's native country. **2** the country of a person's ancestors.

fatherly ❶ ('fɑːðəlɪ) *adj* of, resembling, or suitable to a father, esp. in kindliness, encouragement, etc.
▸'**fatherliness** *n*

Father's Day *n* a day observed in honour of fathers; in Britain the third Sunday in June.

fathom ❶ ('fæðəm) *n* **1** a unit of length equal to six feet (1.829 metres), used to measure depths of water. ◆ *vb* (*tr*) **2** to measure the depth of, esp. with a sounding line. **3** to penetrate (a mystery, problem, etc.). [OE *fæthm*]
▸'**fathomable** *adj*

Fathometer (fə'ðɒmɪtə) *n Trademark.* a type of echo sounder used for measuring the depth of water.

fathomless ❶ ('fæðəmlɪs) *adj* another word for **unfathomable.**
▸'**fathomlessness** *n*

fatigue ❶ (fə'tiːg) *n* **1** physical or mental exhaustion due to exertion. **2** a tiring activity or effort. **3** *Physiol.* the temporary inability of an organ or part to respond to a stimulus because of overactivity. **4** the weakening of a material subjected to alternating stresses, esp. vibrations. **5** the temporary inability to respond to a situation resulting from overexposure to it: *compassion fatigue.* **6** any of the mainly domestic duties performed by military personnel, esp. as a punishment. **7** (*pl*) special clothing worn by military personnel to carry out such duties. ◆ *vb* **fatigues, fatiguing, fatigued. 8** to make or become weary or exhausted. [C17: from F, from *fatiguer* to tire, from L *fatīgāre*]
▸**fatigable** *or* **fatiguable** ('fætɪgəb'l) *adj*

fatshedera (fæts'hɛdərə) *n* a hybrid plant with five-lobed leaves. [from NL, from *Fatsia japonica* + *Hedera hibernica*]

fatsia ('fætsɪə) *n* an evergreen hardy shrub. Also known as the **false castor-oil plant.** [from NL]

fatso ('fætsəʊ) *n Sl.* a fat person.

fat-soluble *adj* soluble in substances, such as ether, chloroform, and oils. Fat-soluble compounds are often insoluble in water.

fat stock *n* livestock fattened and ready for market.

fatten ❶ ('fæt'n) *vb* **1** to grow or cause to grow fat or fatter. **2** (*tr*) to cause (an animal or fowl) to become fat by feeding it. **3** (*tr*) to make fuller or richer. **4** (*tr*) to enrich (soil).
▸'**fattening** *adj*

fatty ❶ ('fætɪ) *adj* **fattier, fattiest. 1** containing or derived from fat. **2** greasy; oily. **3** (esp. of tissues, organs, etc.) characterized by the excessive accumulation of fat. ◆ *n, pl* **fatties. 4** *Inf.* a fat person.
▸'**fattily** *adv* ▸'**fattiness** *n*

fatty acid *n* an aliphatic carboxylic acid, esp. one found in lipids, such as palmitic acid, stearic acid, and oleic acid.

fatty degeneration *n Pathol.* the abnormal formation of tiny globules of fat within the cytoplasm of a cell.

fatuity (fə'tjuːɪtɪ) *n, pl* **fatuities. 1** inanity. **2** a fatuous remark, act, sentiment, etc.
▸**fa'tuitous** *adj*

fatuous ❶ ('fætjʊəs) *adj* complacently or inanely foolish. [C17: from L *fatuus;* rel. to *fatiscere* to gape]
▸'**fatuously** *adv* ▸'**fatuousness** *n*

fatwa *or* **fatwah** ('fætwə) *n* a religious decree issued by a Muslim leader. [Ar.]

fauces ('fɔːsiːz) *n, pl* **fauces.** *Anat.* the area between the cavity of the mouth and the pharynx. [C16: from L: throat]
▸**faucal** ('fɔːk'l) *or* **faucial** ('fɔːʃəl) *adj*

faucet ('fɔːsɪt) *n* **1** a tap fitted to a barrel. **2** the US and Canad. name for **tap**[2] (sense 1). [C14: from OF from Provençal *falsar* to bore]

fault ❶ (fɔːlt) *n* **1** a failing or defect; flaw. **2** a mistake or error. **3** a misdeed. **4** responsibility for a mistake or misdeed. **5** *Electronics.* a defect in a circuit, component, or line, such as a short circuit. **6** *Geol.* a fracture in the earth's crust resulting in the relative displacement of the rocks on either side of it. **7** *Tennis, squash, etc.* an invalid serve. **8** (in showjumping) a penalty mark given for failing to clear, or refusing, a fence, etc. **9 at fault.** guilty of error; culpable. **10 find fault (with).** to seek out minor imperfections or errors (in). **11 to a fault.** excessively. ◆ *vb* **12** *Geol.* to undergo or cause to undergo a fault. **13** (*tr*) to criticize or blame. **14** (*intr*) to commit a fault. [C13: from OF *faute* ult. from L *fallere* to fail]

fault-finding ❶ *n* **1** continual criticism. ◆ *adj* **2** given to finding fault.
▸'**fault-,finder** *n*

faultless ❶ ('fɔːltlɪs) *adj* perfect or blameless.
▸'**faultlessly** *adv* ▸'**faultlessness** *n*

faulty ❶ ('fɔːltɪ) *adj* **faultier, faultiest.** defective or imperfect.
▸'**faultily** *adv* ▸'**faultiness** *n*

faun (fɔːn) *n* (in Roman legend) a rural deity represented as a man with a goat's ears, horns, tail, and hind legs. [C14: back formation from *Faunes* (pl), from L *Faunus* deity of forests]
▸'**faun,like** *adj*

fauna ('fɔːnə) *n, pl* **faunas** *or* **faunae** (-niː). **1** all the animal life of a given place or time. **2** a descriptive list of such animals. [C18: from NL, from LL *Fauna* a goddess of living things]
▸'**faunal** *adj*

Fauvism ('fəʊvɪzəm) *n* a form of expressionist painting characterized

THESAURUS

deadly, destructive, fatal, lethal, ominous, ruinous
Antonyms *adj* ≠ **crucial:** inconsequential, insignificant, nugatory, ordinary, unimportant

father *n* **1** = **daddy** (*inf.*), begetter, dad (*inf.*), governor (*inf.*), old boy (*inf.*), old man (*inf.*), pa (*inf.*), papa (*old-fashioned inf.*), pater, paterfamilias, patriarch, pop (*inf.*), sire **2** = **forefather,** ancestor, forebear, predecessor, progenitor **5** = **founder,** architect, author, creator, inventor, maker, originator, prime mover **6** = **leader,** city father, elder, patriarch, patron, senator ◆ *vb* **9** = **sire,** beget, get, procreate **10** = **originate,** create, engender, establish, found, institute, invent

fatherland *n* **1, 2** = **homeland,** land of one's birth, land of one's fathers, motherland, native land, old country

fatherly *adj* = **paternal,** affectionate, benevolent, benign, forbearing, indulgent, kind, kindly, patriarchal, protective, supportive, tender

fathom *vb* **2** = **measure,** divine, estimate, gauge, penetrate, plumb, probe, sound **3** = **understand,** comprehend, get to the bottom of, grasp, interpret

fathomless *adj* = **profound,** abysmal, bottomless, deep, immeasurable, impenetrable, incomprehensible, unfathomable, unplumbed

fatigue *n* **1** = **tiredness,** debility, ennui, heaviness, languor, lethargy, listlessness, over- tiredness ◆ *vb* **8** = **tire,** drain, drain of energy, exhaust, fag (out) (*inf.*), jade, knacker (*sl.*), overtire, poop (*inf.*), take it out of (*inf.*), weaken, wear out, weary, whack (*Brit. inf.*)
Antonyms *n* ≠ **tiredness:** alertness, animation, energy, freshness, get-up-and-go (*inf.*), go, indefatigability, life, vigour, zest ◆ *vb* ≠ **tire:** refresh, rejuvenate, relieve, rest, revive, stimulate

fatigued *adj* **8** = **tired,** all in (*sl.*), bushed (*inf.*), clapped out (*Austral. & NZ inf.*), dead beat (*inf.*), exhausted, fagged (out) (*inf.*), jaded, jiggered (*inf.*), knackered (*sl.*), overtired, tired out, wasted, weary, whacked (*Brit. inf.*), zonked (*sl.*)

fatness *n* **3** = **obesity,** beef (*inf.*), bulkiness, corpulence, *embonpoint,* flab, flesh, fleshiness, girth, grossness, heaviness, overweight, podginess, rotundity, size, stoutness, weight, weight problem

fatten *vb* **1** = **grow fat,** broaden, coarsen, expand, gain weight, put on weight, spread, swell, thicken, thrive **2** *often with* **up** = **feed up,** bloat, build up, cram, distend, feed, nourish, overfeed, stuff

fatty *adj* **1, 2** = **greasy,** adipose, fat, oily, oleaginous, rich

fatuous *adj* = **foolish,** absurd, asinine, brainless, dense, dull, idiotic, inane, ludicrous, lunatic, mindless, moronic, puerile, silly, stupid, vacuous, weak-minded, witless

fault *n* **1** = **flaw,** blemish, defect, deficiency, demerit, drawback, failing, imperfection, infirmity, lack, shortcoming, snag, weakness, weak point **2** = **mistake,** blunder, error, error of judgment, inaccuracy, indiscretion, lapse, negligence, offence, omission, oversight, slip, slip-up **3** = **misdeed,** delinquency, frailty, lapse, misconduct, misdemeanour, offence, peccadillo, sin, transgression, trespass, wrong **4** = **responsibility,** accountability, culpability, liability **9 at fault** = **guilty,** answerable, blamable, culpable, in the wrong, responsible, to blame **10 find fault (with)** = **criticize,** carp at, complain, pick holes in, pull to pieces, quibble, take to task **11 to a fault** = **excessively,** immoderately, in the extreme, needlessly, out of all proportion, overly (*US*), overmuch, preposterously, ridiculously, unduly ◆ *vb* **13** = **criticize,** blame, call to account, censure, find fault with, find lacking, hold (someone) accountable, hold (someone) responsible, hold (someone) to blame, impugn
Antonyms *n* ≠ **flaw:** asset, attribute, credit, goodness, merit, perfection, strength, virtue

fault-finding *n* **1** = **criticism,** carping, hairsplitting, nagging, niggling, nit-picking (*inf.*) ◆ *adj* **2** = **critical,** captious, carping, censorious, hypercritical, on (someone's) back (*inf.*), pettifogging
Antonyms *adj* ≠ **critical:** complimentary, easily pleased, indiscriminate, uncritical, undiscerning, unexacting, unfussy, unperceptive

faultless *adj* = **flawless,** accurate, classic, correct, exemplary, faithful, foolproof, impeccable, model, perfect, unblemished = **blameless,** above reproach, guiltless, immaculate, impeccable, innocent, irreproachable, pure, sinless, spotless, squeaky-clean, stainless, unblemished, unspotted, unsullied

faulty *adj* = **defective,** bad, blemished, broken, damaged, erroneous, fallacious, flawed, impaired, imperfect, imprecise, inaccurate, incorrect, invalid, malfunctioning, not working, out of order, unsound, weak, wrong

by the use of bright colours and simplified forms. [C20: from F, from *fauve* wild beast]
▸**Fauve** *n, adj* ▸ **'Fauvist** *n, adj*

faux pas ❶ (fəʊ pɑː) *n, pl* **faux pas** (fəʊ pɑːz). a social blunder. [C17: from F: false step]

favour ❶ *or US* **favor** ('feɪvə) *n* **1** an approving attitude; goodwill. **2** an act performed out of goodwill or mercy. **3** prejudice and partiality. **4** a condition of being regarded with approval (esp. in **in favour, out of favour**). **5** a token of love, goodwill, etc. **6** a small gift or toy given to a guest at a party. **7** *History.* a badge or ribbon worn or given to indicate loyalty. **8 find favour with.** to be approved of by someone. **9 in favour of. 9a** approving. **9b** to the benefit of. **9c** (of a cheque, etc.) made out to. **9d** in order to show preference for. ◆ *vb (tr)* **10** to regard with especial kindness. **11** to treat with partiality. **12** to support; advocate. **13** to oblige. **14** to help; facilitate. **15** *Inf.* to resemble: *he favours his father.* **16** to wear habitually: *she favours red.* **17** to treat gingerly: *a footballer favouring an injured leg.* [C14: from L, from *favēre* to protect]
▸ **'favourer** *or US* **'favorer** *n*

favourable ❶ *or US* **favorable** ('feɪvərəbᵊl) *adj* **1** advantageous, encouraging or promising. **2** giving consent.
▸ **'favourably** *or US* **'favorably** *adv*

-favoured *adj* (*in combination*) having an appearance (as specified): *ill-favoured.*

favourite ❶ *or US* **favorite** ('feɪvərɪt) *adj* **1** (*prenominal*) most liked. ◆ *n* **2** a person or thing regarded with especial preference or liking. **3** *Sport.* a competitor thought likely to win. [C16: from It., from *favorire* to favour, from L *favēre*]

favouritism ❶ *or US* **favoritism** ('feɪvərɪˌtɪzəm) *n* the practice of giving special treatment to a person or group.

fawn[1] ❶ (fɔːn) *n* **1** a young deer of either sex aged under one year. **2a** a light greyish-brown colour. **2b** (*as adj*): *a fawn raincoat.* ◆ *vb* **3** (of deer) to bear (young). [C14: from OF, from L *fētus* offspring; see FETUS]
▸ **'fawn,like** *adj*

fawn[2] ❶ (fɔːn) *vb* (*intr*; often foll. by *on* or *upon*) **1** to seek attention and admiration (from) by cringing and flattering. **2** (of animals, esp. dogs) to try to please by a show of extreme friendliness. [OE *fægnian* to be glad, from *fægen* glad; see FAIN]
▸ **'fawner** *n* ▸ **'fawning** *adj*

fax (fæks) *n* **1** short for **facsimile transmission. 2** a message or document sent by facsimile transmission. **3** Also called: **fax machine, facsimile machine.** a machine which transmits and receives exact copies of documents. ◆ *vb* **4** (*tr*) to send (a message or document) by facsimile transmission.

fay (feɪ) *n* a fairy or sprite. [C14: from OF *feie*, ult. from L *fātum* FATE]

faze (feɪz) *vb* **fazes, fazing, fazed.** (*tr*) *Inf.* to disconcert; worry; disturb. [C19: var. of arch. *feeze* to beat off]

FBA *abbrev. for* Fellow of the British Academy.

FBI (in the US) *abbrev. for* Federal Bureau of Investigation; an agency responsible for investigating violations of Federal laws.

FC (in Britain) *abbrev. for:* **1** Football Club. **2** Free Church.

fcap *abbrev. for* foolscap.

F clef *n* another name for **bass clef.**

FD *abbrev. for* Fidei Defensor. [L: Defender of the Faith]

Fe *the chemical symbol for* iron. [from NL *ferrum*]

fealty ❶ ('fiːəltɪ) *n, pl* **fealties.** (in feudal society) the loyalty sworn to one's lord on becoming his vassal. [C14: from OF, from L *fidēlitās* FIDELITY]

fear ❶ (fɪə) *n* **1** a feeling of distress, apprehension, or alarm caused by impending danger, pain, etc. **2** a cause of this feeling. **3** awe; reverence: *fear of God.* **4** concern; anxiety. **5** possibility; chance. **6 for fear of, that** *or* **lest.** to forestall or avoid. **7 no fear.** certainly not. ◆ *vb* **8** to be afraid (to do something) or of (a person or thing). **9** (*tr*) to revere; respect. **10** (*tr; takes a clause as object*) to be sorry: *I fear that you have not won.* **11** (*intr*; foll. by *for*) to feel anxiety about something. [OE *fǣr*]
▸ **'fearless** *adj* ▸ **'fearlessly** *adv* ▸ **'fearlessness** *n*

fearful ❶ ('fɪəfʊl) *adj* **1** afraid. **2** causing fear. **3** *Inf.* very unpleasant: *a fearful cold.*
▸ **'fearfully** *adv* ▸ **'fearfulness** *n*

fearsome ❶ ('fɪəsəm) *adj* **1** frightening. **2** timorous; afraid.
▸ **'fearsomely** *adv*

feasibility study *n* a study designed to determine the practicability of a system or plan.

feasible ❶ ('fiːzəbᵊl) *adj* **1** able to be done or put into effect; possible. **2** likely; probable. [C15: from Anglo-F *faisable*, from *faire* to do, from L *facere*]
▸ **,feasi'bility** *n* ▸ **'feasibly** *adv*

feast ❶ (fiːst) *n* **1** a large and sumptuous meal. **2** a periodic religious celebration. **3** something extremely pleasing: *a feast for the eyes.* **4 movable**

THESAURUS

faux pas *n* = **gaffe**, bloomer (*Brit. inf.*), blunder, breach of etiquette, clanger, gaucherie, impropriety, indiscretion, solecism

favour *n* **1** = **approval**, approbation, backing, bias, championship, espousal, esteem, favouritism, friendliness, good opinion, goodwill, grace, kindness, kind regard, partiality, patronage, promotion, support **2** = **good turn**, benefit, boon, courtesy, indulgence, kindness, obligement (*Scot. or arch.*), service **5, 6** = **memento**, gift, keepsake, love-token, present, souvenir, token **7** = **badge**, decoration, knot, ribbons, rosette **9a, 9b in favour of** = **for**, all for, backing, on the side of, pro, supporting, to the benefit of ◆ *vb* **10** = **prefer**, incline towards, single out **11** = **indulge**, be partial to, esteem, have in one's good books, pamper, pull strings for (*inf.*), reward, side with, smile upon, spoil, treat with partiality, value **12** = **support**, advocate, approve, back, be in favour of, champion, choose, commend, countenance, encourage, espouse, fancy, like, opt for, patronize **13, 14** = **help**, abet, accommodate, advance, aid, assist, befriend, do a kindness to, facilitate, oblige, promote, succour **15** *Informal* = **look like**, be the image *or* picture of, resemble, take after **17** = **ease**, extenuate, spare
Antonyms *n* ≠ **approval:** animosity, antipathy, disapproval, disfavour, ill will, malevolence ≠ **good turn:** disservice, harm, injury, wrong ◆ *vb* ≠ **prefer:** disapprove, disdain, dislike, object to ≠ **support:** oppose, thwart

favourable *adj* **1** = **advantageous**, appropriate, auspicious, beneficial, convenient, encouraging, fair, fit, good, helpful, hopeful, opportune, promising, propitious, suitable, timely **1** = **positive**, affirmative, agreeable, amicable, approving, benign, encouraging, enthusiastic, friendly, kind, reassuring, sympathetic, understanding, welcoming, well-disposed
Antonyms *adj* ≠ **advantageous:** disadvantageous, inauspicious, unfavourable, unhelpful, unpromising, useless ≠ **positive:** disapproving, ill-disposed, unfavourable, unfriendly, unsympathetic

favourably *adv* **1** = **advantageously**, auspiciously, conveniently, fortunately, opportunely, profitably, to one's advantage, well **1** = **positively**, agreeably, approvingly, enthusiastically, genially, graciously, helpfully, in a kindly manner, with approbation, with approval, with cordiality, without prejudice

favourite *adj* **1** = **preferred**, best-loved, choice, dearest, esteemed, fave (*inf.*), favoured ◆ *n* **2** = **darling**, beloved, blue-eyed boy (*inf.*), choice, dear, fave (*inf.*), idol, pet, pick, preference, teacher's pet, the apple of one's eye

favouritism *n* = **preferential treatment**, bias, cronyism, jobs for the boys (*inf.*), nepotism, one-sidedness, partiality, partisanship, preference
Antonyms *n* equality, equity, even-handedness, fairness, impartiality, neutrality, objectivity, open-mindedness

fawn[1] *adj* **2** = **beige**, buff, greyish-brown, neutral

fawn[2] *vb* **1** *often with* **on** *or* **upon** = **ingratiate oneself**, be obsequious, be servile, bow and scrape, brown-nose (*taboo sl.*), court, crawl, creep, cringe, curry favour, dance attendance, flatter, grovel, kneel, kowtow, lick (someone's) boots, pander to, pay court, toady, truckle

fawning[2] *adj* **1** = **obsequious**, abject, bootlicking (*inf.*), bowing and scraping, crawling, cringing, deferential, flattering, grovelling, prostrate, servile, slavish, sycophantic

fealty *n* = **loyalty**, allegiance, devotion, faith, faithfulness, fidelity, homage, obeisance, submission, troth (*arch.*)

fear *n* **1** = **dread**, alarm, apprehensiveness, awe, blue funk (*inf.*), consternation, cravenness, dismay, fright, horror, panic, qualms, terror, timidity, tremors, trepidation **2** = **bugbear**, bête noire, bogey, horror, nightmare, phobia, spectre **3** = **awe**, reverence, veneration, wonder **4** = **anxiety**, agitation, apprehension, concern, disquietude, distress, doubt, foreboding(s), misgiving(s), solicitude, suspicion, unease, uneasiness, worry ◆ *vb* **8** = **be afraid**, apprehend, be apprehensive, be frightened, be in a blue funk (*inf.*), be scared, dare not, dread, have a horror of, have a phobia about, have butterflies in one's stomach (*inf.*), have qualms, live in dread of, shake in one's shoes, shudder at, take fright, tremble at **9** = **revere**, respect, reverence, stand in awe of, venerate **11** *foll. by* **for** = **worry about**, be anxious about, be concerned about, be disquieted over, be distressed about, feel concern for, tremble for

fearful *adj* **1** = **scared**, afraid, alarmed, anxious, apprehensive, diffident, faint-hearted, frightened, hesitant, intimidated, jittery (*inf.*), jumpy, nervous, nervy (*Brit. inf.*), neurotic, panicky, pusillanimous, shrinking, tense, timid, timorous, uneasy, wired (*sl.*) **2** = **frightful**, appalling, atrocious, awful, dire, distressing, dreadful, ghastly, grievous, grim, gruesome, hair-raising, harrowing, hideous, horrendous, horrible, horrific, monstrous, shocking, terrible, unspeakable
Antonyms *adj* ≠ **scared:** bold, brave, confident, courageous, daring, dauntless, doughty, gallant, game (*inf.*), gutsy (*sl.*), heroic, indomitable, intrepid, lion-hearted, plucky, unabashed, unafraid, undaunted, unflinching, valiant, valorous

fearfully *adv* **1** = **nervously**, apprehensively, diffidently, in fear and trembling, timidly, timorously, uneasily, with bated breath, with many misgivings *or* forebodings, with one's heart in one's mouth

fearless *adj* **1** = **brave**, bold, confident, courageous, daring, dauntless, doughty, gallant, game (*inf.*), gutsy (*sl.*), heroic, indomitable, intrepid, lion-hearted, plucky, unabashed, unafraid, undaunted, unflinching, valiant, valorous

fearlessness *n* **1** = **bravery**, boldness, confidence, courage, dauntlessness, guts (*inf.*), indomitability, intrepidity, lion-heartedness, nerve, pluckiness

fearsome *adj* **1** = **terrifying**, alarming, appalling, awe-inspiring, awesome, awful, baleful, daunting, dismaying, formidable, frightening, hair-raising, horrendous, horrifying, menacing, unnerving

feasibility *n* **1, 2** = **possibility**, expediency, practicability, usefulness, viability, workability

feasible *adj* **1, 2** = **possible**, achievable, attainable, likely, practicable, realizable, reasonable, viable, workable
Antonyms *adj* impossible, impracticable, inconceivable, unreasonable, untenable, unviable, unworkable

feast *n* **1** = **banquet**, barbecue, beanfeast (*Brit. inf.*), beano (*Brit. sl.*), blowout (*sl.*), carousal, carouse, dinner, entertainment, festive board, jollification, junket, repast, revels, slap-up meal (*Brit. inf.*), spread (*inf.*), treat **2** = **festival**, cele-

feast. a festival of variable date. ◆ *vb* **5** (*intr*) **5a** to eat a feast. **5b** (usually foll. by *on*) to enjoy the eating (of): *to feast on cakes.* **6** (*tr*) to give a feast to. **7** (*intr;* foll. by *on*) to take great delight (in): *to feast on beautiful paintings.* **8** (*tr*) to regale or delight: *to feast one's eyes.* [C13: from OF, from L *festa,* neuter pl (later assumed to be fem sing) of *festus* joyful; rel. to L *fānum* temple, *fēriae* festivals]
▸ **'feaster** *n*

Feast of Dedication *n* a literal translation of **Chanukah.**

Feast of Lights *n* an English name for **Chanukah.**

Feast of Tabernacles *n* a literal translation of **Sukkoth.**

Feast of Weeks *n* a literal translation of **Shavuot.**

feat ⓘ (fi:t) *n* a remarkable, skilful, or daring action. [C14: from Anglo-F *fait,* from L *factum* deed; see FACT]

feather ⓘ ('fɛðə) *n* **1** any of the flat light waterproof structures forming the plumage of birds, each consisting of a hollow shaft having a vane of barbs on either side. **2** something resembling a feather, such as a tuft of hair or grass. **3** *Archery.* **3a** a bird's feather or artificial substitute fitted to an arrow to direct its flight. **3b** the feathered end of an arrow. **4** *Rowing.* the position of an oar turned parallel to the water between strokes. **5** condition of spirits; fettle: *in fine feather.* **6** something of negligible value: *I don't care a feather.* **7 feather in one's cap.** a cause for pleasure at one's achievements. ◆ *vb* **8** (*tr*) to fit, cover, or supply with feathers. **9** *Rowing.* to turn (an oar) parallel to the water during recovery between strokes, in order to lessen wind resistance. **10** to change the pitch of (an aircraft propeller) so that the chord lines of the blades are in line with the airflow. **11** (*intr*) (of a bird) to grow feathers. **12 feather one's nest.** to provide oneself with comforts. [OE *fether*]
▸ **'feathering** *n* ▸ **'feather-ˌlike** *adj* ▸ **'feathery** *adj*

feather bed *n* **1** a mattress filled with feathers or down. ◆ *vb* **feather-bed, featherbeds, featherbedding, featherbedded. 2** (*tr*) to pamper; spoil.

featherbedding ('fɛðəˌbɛdɪŋ) *n* the practice of limiting production or of overmanning in order to prevent redundancies or create jobs.

featherbrain ('fɛðəˌbreɪn) *or* **featherhead** *n* a frivolous or forgetful person.
▸ **'featherˌbrained** *or* **'featherˌheaded** *adj*

featheredge ('fɛðərˌɛdʒ) *n* a board or plank that tapers to a thin edge at one side.

featherstitch ('fɛðəˌstɪtʃ) *n* **1** a zigzag embroidery stitch. ◆ *vb* **2** to decorate (cloth) with featherstitch.

featherweight ('fɛðəˌweɪt) *n* **1a** something very light or of little importance. **1b** (*as modifier*): *featherweight considerations.* **2a** a professional boxer weighing 118–126 pounds (53.5–57 kg). **2b** an amateur boxer weighing 54–57 kg (119–126 pounds). **3** an amateur wrestler weighing usually 127–137 pounds (58–62 kg).

feature ⓘ ('fi:tʃə) *n* **1** any one of the parts of the face, such as the nose, chin, or mouth. **2** a prominent or distinctive part, as of a landscape, book, etc. **3** the principal film in a programme at a cinema. **4** an item or article appearing regularly in a newspaper, magazine, etc.: *a gardening feature.* **5** Also called: **feature story.** a prominent story in a newspaper, etc.: *a feature on prison reform.* **6** a programme given special prominence on radio or television. **7** *Arch.* general form. ◆ *vb* **features, featuring, featured. 8** (*tr*) to have as a feature or make a feature of. **9** to give prominence to (an actor, famous event, etc.) in a film or (of an actor, etc.) to have prominence in a film. **10** (*tr*) *Arch.* to draw the main features or parts of. [C14: from Anglo-F *feture,* from L *factūra* a making, from *facere* to make]
▸ **'featureless** *adj*

-featured *adj* (*in combination*) having features as specified: *heavy-featured.*

Feb. *abbrev. for* February.

febri- *combining form.* indicating fever: *febrifuge.* [from L *febris* fever]

febrifuge ('fɛbrɪˌfju:dʒ) *n* **1** any drug or agent for reducing fever. ◆ *adj* **2** serving to reduce fever. [C17: from Med. L *febrifugia* feverfew; see FEBRI-, -FUGE]
▸ **febrifugal** (fɪ'brɪfjugᵊl) *adj*

febrile ⓘ ('fi:braɪl) *adj* of or relating to fever; feverish. [C17: from Medical L *febrīlis,* from L *febris* fever]
▸ **febrility** (fɪ'brɪlɪtɪ) *n*

February ('fɛbrʊərɪ) *n, pl* **Februaries.** the second month of the year, consisting of 28 or (in a leap year) 29 days. [C13: from L *Februārius mēnsis* month of expiation, from *februa* Roman festival of purification held on February 15, from pl of *februum* a purgation]

feces ('fi:si:z) *pl n* the usual US spelling of **faeces.**
▸ **fecal** ('fi:kᵊl) *adj*

feckless ⓘ ('fɛklɪs) *adj* feeble; weak; ineffectual. [C16: from obs. *feck* value, effect + -LESS]
▸ **'fecklessly** *adv* ▸ **'fecklessness** *n*

feculent ('fɛkjʊlənt) *adj* **1** filthy or foul. **2** of or containing waste matter. [C15: from L *faeculentus;* see FAECES]
▸ **'feculence** *n*

fecund ⓘ ('fi:kənd, 'fɛk-) *adj* **1** fertile. **2** intellectually productive. [C14: from L *fēcundus*]
▸ **fecundity** (fɪ'kʌndɪtɪ) *n*

fecundate ('fi:kənˌdeɪt, 'fɛk-) *vb* **fecundates, fecundating, fecundated.** (*tr*) **1** to make fruitful. **2** to fertilize. [C17: from L *fēcundāre* to fertilize]
▸ **ˌfecun'dation** *n*

fed[1] (fɛd) *vb* **1** the past tense and past participle of **feed. 2 fed to death** *or* **fed (up) to the (back) teeth.** *Inf.* bored or annoyed.

fed[2] (fɛd) *n US sl.* an agent of the FBI.

Fed (fɛd) *n* short for **Federal Reserve System.**

Fed. *or* **fed.** *abbrev. for:* **1** Federal. **2** Federation. **3** Federated.

fedayee (fə'dɑ:ji:) *n, pl* **fedayeen** (-ji:n). **a** (*sometimes cap.*) (in Arab states) a commando, esp. one fighting against Israel. **b** (esp. in Iran and Afghanistan) a member of a guerrilla organization. [from Ar. *fidā'i* one who risks his life in a cause, from *fidā'* redemption]

federal ('fɛdərəl) *adj* **1** of or relating to a form of government or a country in which power is divided between one central and several regional governments. **2** of or relating to the central government of a federation. [C17: from L *foedus* league]
▸ **'federaˌlism** *n* ▸ **'federalist** *n, adj* ▸ **'federally** *adv*

Federal ('fɛdərəl) *adj* **1** characteristic of or supporting the Union government during the American Civil War. ◆ *n* **2** a supporter of the Union government during the American Civil War.

Federal Government *n* the national government of a federated state, such as the Canadian national government located in Ottawa.

federalize *or* **federalise** ('fɛdərəˌlaɪz) *vb* **federalizes, federalizing, federalized** *or* **federalises, federalising, federalised.** (*tr*) **1** to unite in a federal union. **2** to subject to federal control.
▸ **ˌfederali'zation** *or* **ˌfederali'sation** *n*

Federal Reserve System *n* (in the US) a banking system consisting of twelve **Federal Reserve Banks** and their member banks. It performs functions similar to those of the Bank of England.

federate ⓘ *vb* ('fɛdəˌreɪt), **federates, federating, federated. 1** to unite or cause to unite in a federal union. ◆ *adj* ('fɛdərɪt). **2** federal; federated.
▸ **'federative** *adj*

federation ⓘ (ˌfɛdə'reɪʃən) *n* **1** the act of federating. **2** the union of several provinces, states, etc., to form a federal union. **3** a political unit formed in such a way. **4** any league, alliance, or confederacy.

fedora (fɪ'dɔ:rə) *n* a soft felt brimmed hat, usually with a band. [C19: allegedly after *Fédora* (1882), play by Victorien Sardou (1831–1908)]

fed up ⓘ *adj* (*usually postpositive*) *Inf.* annoyed or bored: *I'm fed up with your conduct.*

fee ⓘ (fi:) *n* **1** a payment asked by professional people or public servants for their services: *school fees.* **2** a charge made for a privilege: *an entrance fee.* **3** *Property law.* an interest in land capable of being inherited. The interest can be with unrestricted rights of disposal (**fee simple**) or with restricted rights to one class of heirs (**fee tail**). **4** (in feudal Europe) the land granted by a lord to his vassal. **5 in fee.** *Law.* (of land) in absolute ownership. ◆ *vb* **fees, feeing, feed. 6** *Rare.* to give a fee to. **7** *Chiefly Scot.* to hire for a fee. [C14: from OF *fie,* of Gmc origin; see FIEF]

feeble ⓘ ('fi:bᵊl) *adj* **1** lacking in physical or mental strength. **2** uncon-

THESAURUS

bration, holiday, holy day, red-letter day, saint's day **3 = treat**, delight, enjoyment, gratification, pleasure ◆ *vb* **5 = eat one's fill**, eat to one's heart's content, fare sumptuously, gorge, gormandize, indulge, overindulge, pig out (*sl.*), stuff, stuff one's face (*sl.*), wine and dine **6 = treat**, entertain, hold a reception for, kill the fatted calf for, regale, wine and dine **7, 8 = delight**, gladden, gratify, rejoice, thrill

feat *n* **= accomplishment**, achievement, act, attainment, deed, exploit, feather in one's cap, performance

feather *n* **1** *plural* **= plumage**, down, plumes

feathery *adj* **1, 2 = downy**, feathered, fluffy, plumate *or* plumose (*Botany & Zoology*), plumed, plumy, wispy

feature 1 *plural* **= face**, countenance, lineaments, physiognomy *n* **2 = aspect**, attribute, characteristic, facet, factor, hallmark, mark, peculiarity, point, property, quality, trait **4 = article**, column, comment, item, piece, report, story ◆ *vb* **8, 9 = spotlight**, accentuate, call attention to, emphasize, foreground, give prominence to, give the full works (*sl.*), headline, play up, present, promote, set off, star

featured *adj* **8, 9 = highlighted**, given prominence, headlined, in the public eye, presented, promoted, recommended, specially presented, starred

featuring *adj* **8, 9 = highlighting**, calling attention to, displaying, drawing attention to, giving a star role, giving prominence to, giving the full works (*sl.*), making the main attraction, presenting, promoting, pushing, recommending, showing, showing off, starring, turning the spotlight on

febrile *adj* **= feverish**, delirious, fevered, fiery, flushed, hot, inflamed, pyretic (*Medical*)

feckless *adj* **= irresponsible**, aimless, feeble, futile, good-for-nothing, hopeless, incompetent, ineffectual, shiftless, useless, weak, worthless

fecund *adj* **1 = fertile**, fructiferous, fruitful, productive, prolific, teeming

fecundity *n* **1 = fertility**, fruitfulness, productiveness

federate *vb* **1 = unite**, amalgamate, associate, combine, confederate, integrate, syndicate, unify

federation *n* **2-4 = union**, alliance, amalgamation, association, *Bund*, coalition, combination, confederacy, copartnership, entente, federacy, league, syndicate

fed up *adj Informal* **= dissatisfied**, annoyed, blue, bored, brassed off (*Brit. sl.*), browned-off (*inf.*), depressed, discontented, dismal, down, down in the mouth, gloomy, glum, hacked (off) (*sl.*), pissed off (*taboo sl.*), sick and tired (*inf.*), tired, weary

fee *n* **1, 2 = charge**, account, bill, compensation, emolument, hire, honorarium, meed (*arch.*), pay, payment, recompense, remuneration, reward, toll

feeble *adj* **1 = weak**, debilitated, delicate, doddering, effete, enervated, enfeebled, etiolated, exhausted, failing, faint, frail, infirm, languid,

vincing: *feeble excuses.* **3** easily influenced. [C12: from OF *feble, fleible,* from L *flēbilis* to be lamented, from *flēre* to weep]
▸ **'feebleness** *n* ▸ **'feebly** *adv*

feeble-minded Ⓣ *adj* **1** lacking in intelligence. **2** mentally defective.

feed Ⓣ (fiːd) *vb* **feeds, feeding, fed.** (*mainly tr*) **1** to give food to: *to feed the cat.* **2** to give as food: *to feed meat to the cat.* **3** (*intr*) to eat food: *the horses feed at noon.* **4** to provide food for. **5** to gratify; satisfy. **6** (*also intr*) to supply (a machine, furnace, etc.) with (the necessary materials or fuel) for its operation, or (of such materials) to flow or move forwards into a machine, etc. **7** *Theatre, inf.* to cue (an actor, esp. a comedian) with lines. **8** *Sport.* to pass a ball to (a team-mate). **9** (*also intr; foll. by on or upon*) to eat or cause to eat. ◆ *n* **10** the act or an instance of feeding. **11** food, esp. that of animals or babies. **12** the process of supplying a machine or furnace with a material or fuel. **13** the quantity of material or fuel so supplied. **14** *Theatre, inf.* a performer, esp. a straight man, who provides cues. **15** *Inf.* a meal. [OE *fēdan*]
▸ **'feedable** *adj*

feedback ('fiːd,bæk) *n* **1** information or an opinion in response to an inquiry, proposal, etc. **2a** the return of part of the output of an electronic circuit, device, or mechanical system to its input. In **negative feedback** a rise in output energy reduces the input energy; in **positive feedback** an increase in output energy reinforces the input energy. **2b** that part of the output signal fed back into the input. **3** the return of part of the sound output of a loudspeaker to the microphone or pick-up, so that a high-pitched whistle is produced. **4** the whistling noise so produced. **5** the effect of a product or action in a cyclic biological reaction on another stage in the same reaction.

feeder ('fiːdə) *n* **1** a person or thing that feeds or is fed. **2** a child's feeding bottle or bib. **3** a person or device that feeds the working material into a system or machine. **4** a tributary channel. **5** a road, service, etc., that links secondary areas to the main traffic network. **6** a power line for transmitting electrical power from a generating station to a distribution network.

feeding bottle *n* a bottle fitted with a rubber teat from which infants suck liquids.

feel Ⓣ (fiːl) *vb* **feels, feeling, felt. 1** to perceive (something) by touching. **2** to have a physical or emotional sensation of (something): *to feel anger.* **3** (*tr*) to examine (something) by touch. **4** (*tr*) to find (one's way) by testing or cautious exploration. **5** (*copula*) to seem in respect of the sensation given: *it feels warm.* **6** to sense (esp. in **feel (it) in one's bones**). **7** to consider; believe; think. **8** (*intr; foll. by for*) to show sympathy or compassion (towards): *I feel for you in your sorrow.* **9** (*tr; often foll. by up*) *Sl.* to pass one's hands over the sexual organs of. **10 feel like.** to have an inclination (for something or doing something): *I don't feel like going to the pictures.* **11 feel up to.** (*usually used with a negative or in a question*) to be fit enough for (something or doing something): *I don't feel up to going out.* ◆ *n* **12** the act or an instance of feeling. **13** the quality of or an impression from something perceived through feeling: *a homely feel.* **14** the sense of touch. **15** an instinctive aptitude; knack: *she's got a feel for this sort of work.* [OE *fēlan*]

feeler Ⓣ ('fiːlə) *n* **1** a person or thing that feels. **2** an organ in certain animals, such as an antenna, that is sensitive to touch. **3** a remark designed to probe the reactions or intentions of others.

feeler gauge *n* a thin metal strip of known thickness used to measure a narrow gap or to set a gap between two parts.

feel-good *adj* causing or characterized by a feeling of self-satisfaction: *feel-good factor.*

feeling Ⓣ ('fiːlɪŋ) *n* **1** the sense of touch. **2a** the ability to experience physical sensations, such as heat, etc. **2b** the sensation so experienced. **3** a state of mind. **4** a physical or mental impression: *a feeling of warmth.* **5** fondness; sympathy: *to have a great deal of feeling for someone.* **6** a sentiment: *a feeling that the project is feasible.* **7** an emotional disturbance, esp. anger or dislike: *a lot of bad feeling.* **8** intuitive appreciation and understanding: *a feeling for words.* **9** sensibility in the performance of something. **10** (*pl*) emotional or moral sensitivity (esp. in **hurt** *or* **injure the feelings of**). ◆ *adj* **11** sentient; sensitive. **12** expressing or containing emotion.
▸ **'feelingly** *adv*

feet (fiːt) *n* **1** the plural of **foot. 2 at (someone's) feet.** as someone's disciple. **3 be run** *or* **rushed off one's feet.** to be very busy. **4 carry** *or* **sweep off one's feet.** to fill with enthusiasm. **5 feet of clay.** a weakness that is not widely known. **6 have** (*or* **keep**) **one's feet on the ground.** to be practical and reliable. **7 on one's** *or* **its feet. 7a** standing up. **7b** in good health. **8 stand on one's own feet.** to be independent.

feign Ⓣ (feɪn) *vb* **1** to pretend: *to feign innocence.* **2** (*tr*) to invent: *to feign an excuse.* **3** (*tr*) to copy; imitate. [C13: from OF, from L *fingere* to form, shape, invent]
▸ **'feigningly** *adv*

feijoa (fiː'dʒəʊə) *n* **1** an evergreen shrub of South America. **2** the fruit of this shrub. [C19: NL, after J. da Silva *Feijo*, 19th-cent. Sp. botanist]

feint[1] Ⓣ (feɪnt) *n* **1** a mock attack or movement designed to distract an adversary, as in boxing, fencing, etc. **2** a misleading action or appearance. ◆ *vb* **3** (*intr*) to make a feint. [C17: from F, from OF *feindre* to FEIGN]

feint[2] (feɪnt) *n Printing.* a narrow rule used in the production of ruled paper. [C19: var. of FAINT]

feisty ('faɪstɪ) *adj* **feistier, feistiest.** *Inf.* **1** lively, resilient, and self-reliant. **2** *US & Canad.* frisky. **3** *US & Canad.* irritable. [C19: dialect *feist, fist* small dog]

felafel (fə'lɑːfəl) *n* a variant spelling of **falafel.**

feldspar ('fɛld,spɑː, 'fɛl,spɑː) *or* **felspar** *n* any of a group of hard rock-forming minerals consisting of aluminium silicates of potassium, sodium, calcium, or barium: the principal constituents of igneous rocks. [C18: from G, from *Feld* field + *Spat(h)* SPAR[3]]
▸ **feldspathic** (fɛld'spæθɪk, fɛl'spæθ-) *or* **fel'spathic** *adj*

felicitate Ⓣ (fɪ'lɪsɪ,teɪt) *vb* **felicitates, felicitating, felicitated.** to congratulate.
▸ **fe,lici'tation** *n* ▸ **fe'lici,tator** *n*

felicitous Ⓣ (fɪ'lɪsɪtəs) *adj* **1** well-chosen; apt. **2** possessing an agreeable style. **3** marked by happiness.
▸ **fe'licitously** *adv*

felicity Ⓣ (fɪ'lɪsɪtɪ) *n, pl* **felicities. 1** happiness. **2** a cause of happiness. **3** an appropriate expression or style. **4** the display of such expressions or style. [C14: from L *fēlīcitās* happiness, from *fēlix* happy]

feline Ⓣ ('fiːlaɪn) *adj* **1** of, relating to, or belonging to a family of predatory mammals, including cats, lions, leopards, and cheetahs, having a round head and retractile claws. **2** resembling or suggestive of a cat, esp. in stealth or grace. ◆ *n* **3** any member of the cat family; a cat. [C17: from L, from *fēlēs* cat]
▸ **'felinely** *adv* ▸ **felinity** (fɪ'lɪnɪtɪ) *n*

fell[1] (fɛl) *vb* the past tense of **fall.**

fell[2] Ⓣ (fɛl) *vb* (*tr*) **1** to cut or knock down: *to fell a tree.* **2** *Needlework.* to fold under and sew flat (the edges of a seam). ◆ *n* **3** *US & Canad.* the timber felled in one season. **4** a seam finished by felling. [OE *fellan*; cf. FALL]
▸ **'feller** *n*

THESAURUS

powerless, puny, shilpit (*Scot.*), sickly, weakened, weedy (*inf.*) **2** = **flimsy**, flat, inadequate, incompetent, indecisive, ineffective, ineffectual, inefficient, insignificant, insufficient, lame, paltry, pathetic, poor, slight, tame, thin, unconvincing, weak
Antonyms *adj* ≠ **weak:** energetic, hale, healthy, hearty, lusty, robust, stalwart, strong, sturdy, vigorous ≠ **flimsy:** effective, forceful, successful

feeble-minded *adj* **1, 2** = **half-witted**, addle-pated, bone-headed, braindead (*inf.*), deficient, dim-witted (*inf.*), dozy (*Brit. inf.*), dull, dumb (*inf.*), idiotic, imbecilic, lacking, moronic, obtuse, retarded, simple, slow on the uptake, slow-witted, soft in the head (*inf.*), stupid, vacant, weak-minded
Antonyms *adj* astute, aware, bright, clear-headed, clever, intelligent, keen, quick-witted, smart

feebleness *n* **1** = **weakness**, debility, delicacy, effeteness, enervation, etiolation, exhaustion, frailness, frailty, incapacity, infirmity, lack of strength, languor, lassitude, sickliness **2** = **flimsiness**, inadequacy, incompetence, indecisiveness, ineffectualness, insignificance, insufficiency, lameness, weakness

feed *vb* **1, 4** = **cater for**, nourish, provide for, provision, supply, sustain, victual, wine and dine **9** *foll. by* **on** = **eat**, devour, exist on, fare, graze, live on, nurture, partake of, pasture, subsist, take nourishment ◆ *n* **11** = **food**, fodder, forage, pasturage, provender, silage **15** *Informal* = **meal**, feast, nosh (*sl.*), nosh-up (*Brit. sl.*), repast, spread (*inf.*), tuck-in (*inf.*)

feel *vb* **1** = **touch**, caress, finger, fondle, handle, manipulate, maul, paw, run one's hands over, stroke **2** = **experience**, be aware of, be sensible of, endure, enjoy, go through, have, have a sensation of, know, notice, observe, perceive, suffer, take to heart, undergo **3, 4** = **explore**, fumble, grope, sound, test, try **5** = **seem**, appear, resemble, strike one as **6** = **sense**, be convinced, feel in one's bones, have a hunch, have the impression, intuit **7** = **believe**, be of the opinion that, consider, deem, hold, judge, think **8** *foll. by* **for** = **feel compassion for**, be moved by, be sorry for, bleed for, commiserate, compassionate, condole with, empathize, pity, sympathize with **10 feel like** = **fancy**, could do with, desire, feel inclined, feel the need for, feel up to, have the inclination, want ◆ *n* **13** = **impression**, air, ambience, atmosphere, feeling, quality, sense, vibes (*sl.*)

feeler *n* **2** = **antenna**, tentacle, whisker **3** = **probe**, advance, approach

feeling *n* **1** = **sense of touch**, feel, perception, sensation, sense, touch **4** = **impression**, apprehension, consciousness, hunch, idea, inkling, notion, presentiment, sense, suspicion **5, 6** = **emotion**, affection, ardour, fervour, fondness, heat, intensity, passion, sentiment, sentimentality, warmth **5** = **sympathy**, appreciation, compassion, concern, empathy, pity, sensibility, sensitivity, understanding **7** = **hostility**, anger, dislike, distrust, enmity, upset **10** *plural* = **emotions**, ego, self-esteem, sensitivities, susceptibilities

feign *vb* **1, 3** = **pretend**, act, affect, assume, counterfeit, devise, dissemble, fabricate, fake, forge, give the appearance of, imitate, make a show of, put on, sham, simulate

feigned *adj* **1, 3** = **pretended**, affected, artificial, assumed, counterfeit, ersatz, fabricated, fake, false, imitation, insincere, pseudo (*inf.*), sham, simulated, spurious

feint[1] *n* **2** = **bluff**, artifice, blind, distraction, dodge, expedient, gambit, manoeuvre, mock attack, play, pretence, ruse, stratagem, subterfuge, wile

felicitate *vb* = **congratulate**, compliment, wish joy to

felicitous *adj* **1, 3** = **fitting**, apposite, appropriate, apropos, apt, happy, inspired, neat, opportune, pat, propitious, suitable, timely, well-chosen, well-timed

felicity *n* **1** = **happiness**, blessedness, bliss, blissfulness, delectation, ecstasy, joy **3** = **aptness**, applicability, appropriateness, becomingness, effectiveness, grace, propriety, suitability, suitableness

feline *adj* **1** = **catlike**, leonine **2** = **graceful**, flowing, sinuous, sleek, slinky, smooth, stealthy

fell[2] *vb* **1** = **cut down**, cut, deck (*sl.*), demolish,

fell[3] ❶ (fɛl) *adj* **1** *Arch.* cruel or fierce. **2** *Arch.* destructive or deadly. **3 one fell swoop.** a single hasty action or occurrence. [C13 *fel,* from OF: cruel, from Med. L *fellō* villain; see FELON[1]]

fell[4] (fɛl) *n* an animal skin or hide. [OE]

fell[5] (fɛl) *n* (*often pl*) *Scot. & N English.* **a** a mountain, hill, or moor. **b** (*in combination*): *fell-walking.* [C13: from ON *fjall;* rel. to OHG *felis* rock]

fellah ('fɛlə) *n, pl* **fellahs, fellahin,** *or* **fellaheen** (ˌfɛlə'hiːn). a peasant in Arab countries. [C18: from Ar., dialect var. of *fallāh,* from *falaha* to cultivate]

fellatio (fɪ'leɪʃɪəʊ) *n* a sexual activity in which the penis is stimulated by the mouth. [C19: NL, from L *fellāre* to suck]

felloe ('fɛləʊ) *or* **felly** ('fɛlɪ) *n, pl* **felloes** *or* **fellies.** a segment or the whole rim of a wooden wheel to which the spokes are attached. [OE *felge*]

fellow ❶ ('fɛləʊ) *n* **1** a man or boy. **2** an informal word for **boyfriend. 3** *Inf.* one or oneself: *a fellow has to eat.* **4** a person considered to be of little worth. **5a** (*often pl*) a companion; associate. **5b** (*as modifier*): *fellow travellers.* **6** a member of the governing body at any of various universities or colleges. **7** a postgraduate student employed, esp. for a fixed period, to undertake research. **8a** a person in the same group, class, or condition: *the surgeon asked his fellows.* **8b** (*as modifier*): *a fellow sufferer.* **9** one of a pair; counterpart; mate. [OE *fēolaga*]

Fellow ('fɛləʊ) *n* a member of any of various learned societies: *Fellow of the British Academy.*

fellow feeling ❶ *n* **1** mutual sympathy or friendship. **2** an opinion held in common.

fellowship ❶ ('fɛləʊˌʃɪp) *n* **1** the state of sharing mutual interests, activities, etc. **2** a society of people sharing mutual interests, activities, etc. **3** companionship; friendship. **4** the state or relationship of being a fellow. **5** *Education.* **5a** a financed research post providing study facilities, privileges, etc., often in return for teaching services. **5b** an honorary title carrying certain privileges awarded to a postgraduate student.

fellow traveller *n* **1** a companion on a journey. **2** a non-Communist who sympathizes with Communism.

felon[1] ('fɛlən) *n* **1** *Criminal law.* (formerly) a person who has committed a felony. ◆ *adj* **2** *Arch.* evil. [C13: from OF: villain, from Med. L *fellō,* from ?]

felon[2] ('fɛlən) *n* a purulent inflammation of the end joint of a finger. [C12: from Med. L *fellō,* ?from L *fel* poison]

felonious (fɪ'ləʊnɪəs) *adj* **1** *Criminal law.* of, involving, or constituting a felony. **2** *Obs.* wicked.
▸**fe'loniously** *adv* ▸**fe'loniousness** *n*

felony ('fɛlənɪ) *n, pl* **felonies.** *Criminal law.* (formerly) a serious crime, such as murder or arson.

felspar ('fɛlˌspɑː) *n* a variant spelling (esp. Brit.) of **feldspar.**
▸**felspathic** (fɛl'spæθɪk) *adj*

felt[1] (fɛlt) *vb* the past tense and past participle of **feel.**

felt[2] (fɛlt) *n* **1** a matted fabric of wool, hair, etc., made by working the fibres together under pressure or by heat or chemical action. **2** any material, such as asbestos, made by a similar process of matting. ◆ *vb* **3** (*tr*) to make into or cover with felt. **4** (*intr*) to become matted. [OE]

felt-tip pen *n* a pen whose writing point is made from pressed fibres. Also called: **fibre-tip pen.**

felucca (fɛ'lʌkə) *n* a narrow lateen-rigged vessel of the Mediterranean. [C17: from It., prob. from obs. Sp. *faluca,* prob. from Ar. *fulūk* ships, from Gk, from *ephelkein* to tow]

fem. *abbrev. for:* **1** female. **2** feminine.

female ('fiːmeɪl) *adj* **1** of, relating to, or designating the sex producing gametes (ova) that can be fertilized by male gametes (spermatozoa). **2** of or characteristic of a woman. **3** for or composed of women or girls: *a female choir.* **4** (of reproductive organs such as the ovary and carpel) capable of producing female gametes. **5** (of flowers) lacking, or having nonfunctional, stamens. **6** having an internal cavity into which a projecting male counterpart can be fitted: *a female thread.* ◆ *n* **7** a female animal or plant. [C14: from earlier *femelle* (infl. by *male*), from L *fēmella* a young woman, from *fēmina* a woman]
▸**'femaleness** *n*

female impersonator *n* a male theatrical performer who acts as a woman.

feminine ❶ ('fɛmɪnɪn) *adj* **1** suitable to or characteristic of a woman. **2** possessing qualities or characteristics considered typical of or appropriate to a woman. **3** effeminate; womanish. **4** *Grammar.* **4a** denoting or belonging to a gender of nouns that includes all kinds of referents as well as some female animate referents. **4b** (*as n*): *German* Zeit *"time" and* Ehe *"marriage" are feminines.* [C14: from L, from *fēmina* woman]
▸**'femininely** *adv* ▸**ˌfemi'ninity** *or* **'feminineness** *n*

feminism ('fɛmɪˌnɪzəm) *n* a doctrine or movement that advocates equal rights for women.
▸**'feminist** *n, adj*

feminize *or* **feminise** ('fɛmɪˌnaɪz) *vb* **feminizes, feminizing, feminized** *or* **feminises, feminising, feminised. 1** to make or become feminine. **2** to cause (a male animal) to develop female characteristics.
▸**ˌfemini'zation** *or* **ˌfemini'sation** *n*

femme fatale ❶ *French.* (fam fatal) *n, pl* ***femmes fatales*** (fam fatal). an alluring or seductive woman, esp. one who causes men to love her to their own distress. [fatal woman]

femto- *prefix* denoting 10^{-15}: *femtometer.* Symbol: f [from Danish or Norwegian *femten* fifteen]

femur ('fiːmə) *n, pl* **femurs** *or* **femora** ('fɛmərə). **1** the longest thickest bone of the human skeleton, with the pelvis above and the knee below. Nontechnical name: **thighbone. 2** the corresponding bone in other vertebrates or the corresponding segment of an insect's leg. [C18: from L: thigh]
▸**'femoral** *adj*

fen ❶ (fɛn) *n* low-lying flat land that is marshy or artificially drained. [OE *fenn*]
▸**'fenny** *adj*

fence ❶ (fɛns) *n* **1** a structure that serves to enclose an area such as a garden or field, usually made of posts of timber, concrete, or metal connected by wire netting, rails, or boards. **2** *Sl.* a dealer in stolen property. **3** an obstacle for a horse to jump in steeplechasing or showjumping. **4** *Machinery.* a guard or guide, esp. in a circular saw or plane. **5** (**sit**) **on the fence.** (to be) unable or unwilling to commit oneself. ◆ *vb* **fences, fencing, fenced. 6** (*tr*) to construct a fence on or around (a piece of land, etc.). **7** (*tr; foll. by in or off*) to close (in) or separate (off) with or as if with a fence: *he fenced in the livestock.* **8** (*intr*) to fight using swords or foils. **9** (*intr*) to evade a question or argument. **10** (*intr*) *Sl.* to receive stolen property. [C14 *fens,* shortened from *defens* DEFENCE]
▸**'fenceless** *adj* ▸**'fencer** *n*

fencible ('fɛnsəbᵊl) *n* (formerly) a person who undertook military service in immediate defence of his homeland only.

fencing ('fɛnsɪŋ) *n* **1** the practice, art, or sport of fighting with foils, épées, sabres, etc. **2a** wire, stakes, etc., used as fences. **2b** fences collectively.

fend ❶ (fɛnd) *vb* **1** (*intr;* foll. by *for*) to give support (to someone, esp. oneself). **2** (*tr;* usually foll. by *off*) to ward off or turn aside (blows, questions, etc.). ◆ *n* **3** *Scot. & N English dialect.* a shift or effort. [C13 *fenden,* shortened from *defenden* to DEFEND]

fender ('fɛndə) *n* **1** a low metal frame which confines falling coals to the hearth. **2** *Chiefly US.* a metal frame fitted to the front of locomotives to absorb shock, etc. **3** a cushion-like device, such as a car tyre hung over the side of a vessel to reduce damage resulting from collision. **4** the US and Canad. name for the wing of a car.

fenestra (fɪ'nɛstrə) *n, pl* **fenestrae** (-triː). **1** *Biol.* a small opening, esp. either of two openings between the middle and inner ears. **2** *Zool.* a transparent marking or spot, as on the wings of moths. **3** *Archit.* a window or window-like opening in the outside wall of a building. [C19: via NL from L: wall opening, window]

fenestrated (fɪ'nɛstreɪtɪd, 'fɛnɪˌstreɪtɪd) *or* **fenestrate** *adj* **1** *Archit.* having windows. **2** *Biol.* perforated or having fenestrae.

fenestration (ˌfɛnɪ'streɪʃən) *n* **1** the arrangement of windows in a building. **2** an operation to restore hearing by making an artificial opening into the labyrinth of the ear.

feng shui ('fʌŋ 'ʃweɪ) *n* the Chinese art of determining the most propitious design and placement of a grave, building, room, etc., so that the maximum harmony is achieved between the flow of chi of the

THESAURUS

flatten, floor, hew, knock down, level, prostrate, raze, strike down

fell[3] *adj* **1** *Archaic* = **cruel,** barbarous, bloody, ferocious, fierce, grim, implacable, inhuman, malicious, malignant, merciless, murderous, pitiless, relentless, ruthless, sanguinary, savage, vicious **2** *Archaic* = **deadly,** baneful, destructive, fatal, malign, mortal, noxious, pernicious, pestilential, ruinous

fellow *n* **1** = **man,** bloke (*Brit. inf.*), boy, chap (*inf.*), character, customer (*inf.*), guy (*inf.*), individual, person, punter (*inf.*) **5a** = **associate,** colleague, companion, compeer, comrade, co-worker, equal, friend, member, partner, peer ◆ *modifier* **5b, 8b** = **co-,** affiliated, akin, allied, associate, associated, like, related, similar ◆ *n* **9** = **counterpart,** brother, double, duplicate, match, mate, twin

fellow feeling *n* **1** = **sympathy,** compassion, empathy, friendship, pity, understanding

fellowship *n* **1, 3** = **camaraderie,** amity, brotherhood, communion, companionability, companionship, familiarity, fraternization, intercourse, intimacy, kindliness, sociability **2** = **society,** association, brotherhood, club, fraternity, guild, league, order, sisterhood, sodality

feminine *adj* **1, 2** = **womanly,** delicate, gentle, girlie, girlish, graceful, ladylike, modest, soft, tender **3** = **effeminate,** camp (*inf.*), effete, unmanly, unmasculine, weak, womanish
Antonyms *adj* Amazonian, butch, indelicate, manly, mannish, masculine, rough, unfeminine, unladylike, unwomanly, virile

femininity *n* **1, 2** = **womanliness,** delicacy, feminineness, gentleness, girlishness, muliebrity, softness, womanhood

femme fatale *n* = **seductress,** charmer, Circe, enchantress, siren, vamp (*inf.*)

fen *n* = **marsh,** bog, holm (*dialect*), morass, moss (*Scot.*), quagmire, slough, swamp

fence *n* **1** = **barrier,** barbed wire, barricade, defence, guard, hedge, paling, palisade, railings, rampart, shield, stockade, wall **5 on the fence** = **uncommitted,** between two stools, irresolute, uncertain, undecided, vacillating ◆ *vb* **6, 7** *often with* **in** *or* **off** = **enclose,** bound, circumscribe, confine, coop, defend, encircle, fortify, guard, hedge, impound, pen, pound, protect, restrict, secure, separate, surround **9** = **evade,** beat about the bush, cavil, dodge, equivocate, flannel (*Brit. inf.*), hedge, parry, prevaricate, quibble, shift, stonewall, tergiversate

fend *vb* **1** *foll. by* **for** = **look after,** make do, make provision for, provide for, shift for, support, sustain, take care of **2** *foll. by* **off** = **turn aside,** avert, beat off, deflect, drive back, hold *or* keep at bay, keep off, parry, repel, repulse, resist, stave off, ward off environment and that of the user, believed to bring good fortune. [C20: from Chinese *feng* wind + *shui* water]

Fenian (ˈfiːnɪən, ˈfiːnjən) *n* **1** (formerly) a member of an Irish revolutionary organization founded in the US in the 19th century to fight for an independent Ireland. ◆ *adj* **2** of or relating to the Fenians. [C19: from Irish Gaelic *fēinne,* after *Fiann* Irish folk hero]
▸ˈ**Fenianism** *n*

fennec (ˈfɛnɛk) *n* a very small nocturnal fox inhabiting deserts of N Africa and Arabia, having enormous ears. [C18: from Ar. *fenek* fox]

fennel (ˈfɛnᵊl) *n* a strong-smelling yellow-flowered umbelliferous plant whose seeds, feathery leaves, and bulbous aniseed-flavoured root are used in cookery. [OE *fenol*]

fenugreek (ˈfɛnjʊˌgriːk) *n* an annual heavily scented Mediterranean leguminous plant with hairy stems and white flowers. [OE *fēnogrēcum*]

feoff (fiːf) *History.* ◆ *n* **1** a variant spelling of **fief**. ◆ *vb* **2** (*tr*) to invest with a benefice or fief. [C13: from Anglo-F: a FIEF]
▸ˈ**feoffee** *n* ▸ˈ**feoffment** *n* ▸ˈ**feoffor** *or* ˈ**feoffer** *n*

-fer *n combining form.* indicating a person or thing that bears something specified: *crucifer; conifer.* [from L, from *ferre* to bear]

feral 🅣 (ˈfɪərəl) *adj* **1** (of animals and plants) existing in a wild or uncultivated state. **2** savage; brutal. [C17: from Med. L, from L, from *ferus* savage]

fer-de-lance (ˌfɛədəˈlɑːns) *n* a large highly venomous tropical American snake with a greyish-brown mottled coloration. [C19: from F, lit.: iron (head) of a lance]

feretory (ˈfɛrɪtərɪ, -trɪ) *n, pl* **feretories.** *Chiefly RC Church.* **1** a shrine, usually portable, for a saint's relics. **2** the chapel in which a shrine is kept. [C14: from MF *fiertre,* from L *feretrum* a bier, from Gk, from *pherein* to bear]

feria (ˈfɪərɪə) *n, pl* **ferias** *or* **feriae** (-rɪˌiː). *RC Church.* a weekday, other than Saturday, on which no feast occurs. [C19: from LL: day of the week (as in *prīma fēria* Sunday), sing of L *fēriae* festivals]
▸ˈ**ferial** *adj*

fermata (fəˈmɑːtə) *n, pl* **fermatas** *or* **fermate** (-tɪ). *Music.* another word for **pause** (sense 5). [from It., from *fermare* to stop, from L *firmāre* to establish]

ferment 🅣 *n* (ˈfɜːmɛnt). **1** any agent or substance, such as a bacterium, mould, yeast, or enzyme, that causes fermentation. **2** another word for **fermentation. 3** commotion; unrest. ◆ *vb* (fəˈmɛnt). **4** to undergo or cause to undergo fermentation. **5** to stir up or seethe with excitement. [C15: from L *fermentum* yeast, from *fervēre* to seethe]
▸**ferˈmentable** *adj*

> **USAGE NOTE** See at **foment.**

fermentation (ˌfɜːmɛnˈteɪʃən) *n* a chemical reaction in which an organic molecule splits into simpler substances, esp. the conversion of sugar to ethyl alcohol by yeast.
▸**ferˈmentative** *adj*

fermentation lock *n* a valve placed on the top of bottles of fermenting wine to allow bubbles to escape.

fermi (ˈfɜːmɪ) *n* a unit of length used in nuclear physics equal to 10^{-15} metre. [C20: see FERMION]

fermion (ˈfɜːmɪˌɒn) *n* any of a group of elementary particles, such as a nucleon, that has half-integral spin and obeys the Pauli exclusion principle. Cf. **boson.** [C20: after Enrico *Fermi* (1901–54), It. nuclear physicist; see -ON]

fermium (ˈfɜːmɪəm) *n* a transuranic element artificially produced by neutron bombardment of plutonium. Symbol: Fm; atomic no.: 100; half-life of most stable isotope, ^{257}Fm: 80 days (approx.). [C20: after Enrico *Fermi* (1901–54), It. nuclear physicist]

fern (fɜːn) *n* **1** a plant having roots, stems, and fronds and reproducing by spores formed in structures (sori) on the fronds. **2** any of certain similar but unrelated plants, such as the sweet fern. [OE *fearn*]
▸ˈ**ferny** *adj*

fernbird (ˈfɜːnˌbɜːd) *n* a New Zealand swamp bird with a fernlike tail.

ferocious 🅣 (fəˈrəʊʃəs) *adj* savagely fierce or cruel: *a ferocious tiger.* [C17: from L *ferox* fierce, warlike]
▸**ferocity** (fəˈrɒsɪtɪ) *n*

-ferous *adj combining form.* bearing or producing: *coniferous.* [from -FER + -OUS]

ferrate (ˈfɛreɪt) *n* a salt containing the divalent ion, FeO_4^{2-}. [C19: from L *ferrum* iron]

ferret 🅣 (ˈfɛrɪt) *n* **1** a domesticated albino variety of the polecat bred for hunting rats, rabbits, etc. **2** an assiduous searcher. ◆ *vb* **ferrets, ferreting, ferreted. 3** to hunt (rabbits, rats, etc.) with ferrets. **4** (*tr;* usually foll. by *out*) to drive from hiding: *to ferret out snipers.* **5** (*tr;* usually foll. by *out*) to find by persistent investigation. **6** (*intr*) to search around. [C14: from OF *furet,* from L *fur* thief]
▸ˈ**ferreter** *n* ▸ˈ**ferrety** *adj*

ferri- *combining form.* indicating the presence of iron, esp. in the trivalent state: *ferricyanide; ferriferous.* Cf. **ferro-.** [from L *ferrum* iron]

ferriage (ˈfɛrɪɪdʒ) *n* **1** transportation by ferry. **2** the fee charged for passage on a ferry.

ferric (ˈfɛrɪk) *adj* of or containing iron in the trivalent state; designating an iron(III) compound. [C18: from L *ferrum* iron]

ferric oxide *n* a red crystalline insoluble oxide of iron that occurs as haematite and rust, used as a pigment and metal polish (**jeweller's rouge**), and as a sensitive coating on magnetic tape. Formula: Fe_2O_3. Systematic name: **iron(III) oxide.**

ferrimagnetism (ˌfɛrɪˈmægnɪˌtɪzəm) *n* a phenomenon exhibited by certain substances, such as ferrites, in which the magnetic moments of neighbouring ions are nonparallel and unequal in magnitude.
▸**ferrimagnetic** (ˌfɛrɪmægˈnɛtɪk) *adj*

Ferris wheel (ˈfɛrɪs) *n* a fairground wheel having seats freely suspended from its rim. [C19: after G.W.G. *Ferris* (1859–96), American engineer]

ferrite (ˈfɛraɪt) *n* any of a class of nonconducting magnetic mixed-oxide ceramics.

ferrite-rod aerial *n* a type of aerial, normally used in radio reception, consisting of a small coil of wire mounted on a ferromagnetic ceramic core, the coil serving as a tuning inductance.

ferro- *combining form.* **1** indicating a property of iron or the presence of iron: *ferromagnetism.* **2** indicating the presence of iron in the divalent state: *ferrocyanide.* Cf. **ferri-.** [from L *ferrum* iron]

ferrocene (ˈfɛrəʊˌsiːn) *n* a reddish-orange compound in which the molecules have an iron atom sandwiched between two cyclopentadiene rings. Formula: $Fe(C_5H_5)_2$. [C20: from FERRO- + C(YCLOPENTADI)ENE]

ferroconcrete (ˌfɛrəʊˈkɒŋkriːt) *n* another name for **reinforced concrete.**

ferromagnetism (ˌfɛrəʊˈmægnɪˌtɪzəm) *n* the phenomenon exhibited by substances, such as iron, that have relative permeabilities much greater than unity and increasing magnetization with applied magnetizing field. Certain of these substances retain their magnetization in the absence of the applied field.
▸**ferromagnetic** (ˌfɛrəʊmægˈnɛtɪk) *adj*

ferromanganese (ˌfɛrəʊˈmæŋgəˌniːz) *n* an alloy of iron and manganese, used in making additions of manganese to cast iron and steel.

ferrous (ˈfɛrəs) *adj* of or containing iron in the divalent state; designating an iron(II) compound. [C19: from FERRI- + -OUS]

ferrous sulphate *n* an iron salt usually obtained as greenish crystals: used in inks, tanning, etc. Formula: $FeSO_4$. Systematic name: **iron(II) sulphate.** Also called: **copperas.**

ferruginous (fɛˈruːdʒɪnəs) *adj* **1** (of minerals, rocks, etc.) containing iron: *a ferruginous clay.* **2** rust-coloured. [C17: from L *ferrūgineus* of a rusty colour, from *ferrum* iron]

ferrule (ˈfɛruːl) *n* **1** a metal ring, tube, or cap placed over the end of a stick or post for added strength or to increase wear. **2** a small length of tube, etc., esp. one used for making a joint. [C17: from ME *virole,* from OF, from L, from *viria* bracelet; infl. by L *ferrum* iron]

ferry 🅣 (ˈfɛrɪ) *n, pl* **ferries. 1** Also called: **ferryboat.** a vessel for transporting passengers and usually vehicles across a body of water, esp. as a regular service. **2a** such a service. **2b** (*in combination*): *a ferryman.* **3** the delivering of aircraft by flying them to their destination. ◆ *vb* **ferries, ferrying, ferried. 4** to transport or go by ferry. **5** to deliver (an aircraft) by flying it to its destination. **6** (*tr*) to convey (passengers, goods, etc.). [OE *ferian* to carry, bring]

fertile 🅣 (ˈfɜːtaɪl) *adj* **1** capable of producing offspring. **2a** (of land) capable of sustaining an abundant growth of plants. **2b** (of farm animals) capable of breeding stock. **3** *Biol.* capable of undergoing growth and development: *fertile seeds; fertile eggs.* **4** producing many offspring; prolific. **5** highly productive: *a fertile brain.* **6** *Physics.* (of a substance) able to be transformed into fissile or fissionable material. [C15: from L *fertilis,* from *ferre* to bear]
▸ˈ**fertilely** *adv* ▸ˈ**fertileness** *n*

Fertile Crescent *n* an area of fertile land in the Middle East, extending

THESAURUS

feral *adj* **1** = **wild**, unbroken, uncultivated, undomesticated, untamed **2** = **savage**, bestial, brutal, fell, ferocious, fierce, vicious

ferment *n* **1** = **yeast**, bacteria, barm, fermentation agent, leaven, leavening, mother, mother-of-vinegar **3** = **commotion**, agitation, brouhaha, disruption, excitement, fever, frenzy, furore, glow, heat, hubbub, imbroglio, state of unrest, stew, stir, tumult, turbulence, turmoil, unrest, uproar ◆ *vb* **4** = **brew**, boil, bubble, concoct, effervesce, foam, froth, heat, leaven, rise, seethe, work **5** = **stir up**, agitate, boil, excite, fester, foment, heat, incite, inflame, provoke, rouse, seethe, smoulder

Antonyms *n* ≠ **commotion:** calmness, hush, peacefulness, quiet, restfulness, stillness, tranquillity

ferocious *adj* = **fierce**, feral, predatory, rapacious, ravening, savage, violent, wild = **cruel**, barbaric, barbarous, bloodthirsty, brutal, brutish, merciless, pitiless, relentless, ruthless, tigerish, vicious

Antonyms *adj* ≠ **fierce:** calm, docile, gentle, mild, subdued, submissive, tame

ferocity *n* = **savagery**, barbarity, bloodthirstiness, brutality, cruelty, ferociousness, fierceness, inhumanity, rapacity, ruthlessness, savageness, viciousness, wildness

ferret *vb* **5** *usually foll. by* **out** = **track down**, bring to light, dig up, disclose, discover, drive out, elicit, get at, nose out, root out, run to earth, search out, smell out, trace, unearth

ferry *n* **1** = **ferry boat**, packet, packet boat ◆ *vb* **6** = **carry**, chauffeur, convey, run, ship, shuttle, transport

fertile *adj* **1, 2, 4** = **productive**, abundant, fat, fecund, flowering, flowing with milk and honey, fruit-bearing, fruitful, generative, luxuriant, plenteous, plentiful, prolific, rich, teeming, yielding

Antonyms *adj* barren, dry, impotent, infecund, infertile, poor, sterile, unfruitful, unproductive around the Rivers Tigris and Euphrates in a semicircle from Israel to the Persian Gulf.

fertility ◐ (fɜːˈtɪlɪtɪ) *n* **1** the ability to produce offspring. **2** the state or quality of being fertile.

fertility drug *n* any of a group of preparations used to stimulate ovulation in women hitherto infertile.

fertilize ◐ *or* **fertilise** (ˈfɜːtɪˌlaɪz) *vb* **fertilizes, fertilizing, fertilized** *or* **fertilises, fertilising, fertilised.** (*tr*) **1** to provide (an animal, plant, etc.) with sperm or pollen to bring about fertilization. **2** to supply (soil or water) with nutrients to aid the growth of plants. **3** to make fertile.
▸ **ˌfertiliˈzation** *or* **ˌfertiliˈsation** *n*

fertilizer ◐ *or* **fertiliser** (ˈfɜːtɪˌlaɪzə) *n* **1** any substance, such as manure, added to soil or water to increase its productivity. **2** an object or organism that fertilizes an animal or plant.

ferula (ˈfɛrʊlə) *n, pl* **ferulas** *or* **ferulae** (-ˌliː). a large umbelliferous plant having thick stems and dissected leaves. [C14: from L: giant fennel]

ferule (ˈfɛruːl) *n* **1** a flat piece of wood, such as a ruler, used in some schools to cane children on the hand. ◆ *vb* **ferules, feruling, feruled. 2** (*tr*) *Rare.* to punish with a ferule. [C16: from L *ferula* giant fennel]

fervent ◐ (ˈfɜːvənt) *or* **fervid** (ˈfɜːvɪd) *adj* **1** intensely passionate; ardent. **2** *Arch. or poetic.* burning or glowing. [C14: from L *fervēre* to boil, glow]
▸ **ˈfervency** *n* ▸ **ˈfervently** *or* **ˈfervidly** *adv*

fervour ◐ *or US* **fervor** (ˈfɜːvə) *n* **1** great intensity of feeling or belief. **2** *Rare.* intense heat. [C14: from L *fervor* heat, from *fervēre* to glow, boil]

fescue (ˈfɛskjuː) *or* **fescue grass** *n* a widely cultivated pasture and lawn grass, having stiff narrow leaves. [C14: from OF *festu*, ult. from L *festūca* stem, straw]

fesse *or* **fess** (fɛs) *n Heraldry.* an ordinary consisting of a horizontal band across a shield. [C15: from Anglo-F, from L *fascia* band, fillet]

festal (ˈfɛstᵊl) *adj* another word for **festive.** [C15: from L *festum* holiday]
▸ **ˈfestally** *adv*

fester ◐ (ˈfɛstə) *vb* **1** to form or cause to form pus. **2** (*intr*) to become rotten; decay. **3** to become or cause to become bitter, irritated, etc., esp. over a long period of time. ◆ *n* **4** a small ulcer or sore containing pus. [C13: from OF *festre* suppurating sore, from L: FISTULA]

festival ◐ (ˈfɛstɪvᵊl) *n* **1** a day or period set aside for celebration or feasting, esp. one of religious significance. **2** any occasion for celebration. **3** an organized series of special events and performances: *a festival of drama.* **4** *Arch.* a time of revelry. **5** (*modifier*) relating to or characteristic of a festival. [C14: from Church L *fēstivālis* of a feast, from L *festīvus* FESTIVE]

festive ◐ (ˈfɛstɪv) *adj* appropriate to or characteristic of a holiday, etc. [C17: from L *festīvus* joyful, from *festus* of a FEAST]
▸ **ˈfestively** *adv*

festivity ◐ (fɛsˈtɪvɪtɪ) *n, pl* **festivities. 1** merriment characteristic of a festival, etc. **2** any festival or other celebration. **3** (*pl*) celebrations.

festoon ◐ (fɛˈstuːn) *n* **1** a decorative chain of flowers, ribbons, etc., suspended in loops. **2** a carved or painted representation of this, as in architecture, furniture, or pottery. ◆ *vb* (*tr*) **3** to decorate or join together with festoons. **4** to form into festoons. [C17: from F, from It. *festone* ornament for a feast, from *festa* FEAST]

festoon blind *n* a window blind consisting of vertical rows of horizontally gathered fabric that may be drawn up to form a series of ruches.

feta (ˈfɛtə) *n* a white sheep or goat cheese popular in Greece. [Mod. Gk, from the phrase *turi pheta*, from *turi* cheese + *pheta*, from It. *fetta* a slice]

fetal *or* **foetal** (ˈfiːtᵊl) *adj* of, relating to, or resembling a fetus.

fetal alcohol syndrome *n* a condition in newborn babies caused by excessive intake of alcohol by the mother during pregnancy: characterized by various defects including mental retardation.

fetch[1] ◐ (fɛtʃ) *vb* (*mainly tr*) **1** to go after and bring back: *to fetch help.* **2** to cause to come; bring or draw forth. **3** (*also intr*) to cost or sell for (a certain price): *the table fetched six hundred pounds.* **4** to utter (a sigh, groan, etc.). **5** *Inf.* to deal (a blow, slap, etc.). **6** (used esp. as a command to dogs) to retrieve (an object thrown, etc.). **7 fetch and carry.** to perform menial tasks or run errands. ◆ *n* **8** the reach, stretch, etc., of a mechanism. **9** a trick or stratagem. [OE *feccan*]
▸ **ˈfetcher** *n*

fetch[2] (fɛtʃ) *n* the ghost or apparition of a living person. [C18: from ?]

fetching ◐ (ˈfɛtʃɪŋ) *adj Inf.* **1** attractively befitting. **2** charming.

fetch up ◐ *vb* (*adv*) **1** (*intr;* usually foll. by *at* or *in*) *Inf.* to arrive (at) or end up (in): *to fetch up in New York.* **2** *Sl.* to vomit (food, etc.).

fête ◐ *or* **fete** (feɪt) *n* **1** a gala, bazaar, or similar entertainment, esp. one held outdoors in aid of charity. **2** a feast day or holiday, esp. one of religious significance. ◆ *vb* **fêtes, fêting, fêted** *or* **fetes, feting, feted. 3** (*tr*) to honour or entertain with or as if with a fête [C18: from F: FEAST]

fetid ◐ *or* **foetid** (ˈfɛtɪd, ˈfiː-) *adj* having a stale nauseating smell, as of decay. [C16: from L, from *fētēre* to stink; rel. to *fūmus* smoke]
▸ **ˈfetidly** *or* **ˈfoetidly** *adv* ▸ **ˈfetidness** *or* **ˈfoetidness** *n*

fetish ◐ (ˈfɛtɪʃ, ˈfiːtɪʃ) *n* **1** something, esp. an inanimate object, that is believed to have magical powers. **2a** a form of behaviour involving fetishism. **2b** any object that is involved in fetishism. **3** any object, activity, etc., to which one is excessively devoted. [C17: from F, from Port. *feitiço* (n) sorcery, from adj: artificial, from L *factīcius* made by art, FACTITIOUS]

fetishism (ˈfɛtɪˌʃɪzəm, ˈfiː-) *n* **1** a condition in which the handling of an inanimate object or a part of the body other than the sexual organs is a source of sexual satisfaction. **2** belief in or recourse to a fetish for magical purposes.
▸ **ˈfetishist** *n* ▸ **ˌfetishˈistic** *adj*

fetlock (ˈfɛtˌlɒk) *n* **1** a projection behind and above a horse's hoof. **2** Also called: **fetlock joint.** the joint at this part of the leg. **3** the tuft of hair growing from this part. [C14 *fetlak*]

fetor *or* **foetor** (ˈfiːtə) *n* an offensive stale or putrid odour. [C15: from L, from *fētēre* to stink]

fetter ◐ (ˈfɛtə) *n* **1** (*often pl*) a chain or bond fastened round the ankle. **2** (*usually pl*) a check or restraint. ◆ *vb* (*tr*) **3** to restrict or confine. **4** to bind in fetters. [OE *fetor*]

fettle (ˈfɛtᵊl) *vb* **fettles, fettling, fettled.** (*tr*) **1** to line or repair (the walls of a furnace). **2** *Brit. dialect.* **2a** to prepare or arrange (a thing, oneself, etc.). **2b** to repair or mend (something). ◆ *n* **3** state of health, spirits, etc. (esp. in **in fine fettle**). [C14 (in the sense: to put in order): back formation from *fetled* girded up, from OE *fetel* belt]

fettler (ˈfɛtlə) *n Austral.* a person employed to maintain railway tracks.

fetus *or* **foetus** (ˈfiːtəs) *n, pl* **fetuses** *or* **foetuses.** the embryo of a mammal in the later stages of development, esp. a human embryo from the end of the second month of pregnancy until birth. [C14: from L: offspring]

feu (fjuː) *n* **1** *Scot. legal history.* **1a** a feudal tenure of land for which rent was paid in money or grain instead of by the performance of military service. **1b** the land so held. **2** *Scots Law.* a right to the use of land in return for a fixed annual payment (**feu duty**). [C15: from OF; see FEE]

feud[1] ◐ (fjuːd) *n* **1** long and bitter hostility between two families, clans, or individuals. **2** a quarrel or dispute. ◆ *vb* **3** (*intr*) to carry on a feud. [C13 *fede*, from OF, from OHG *fēhida;* rel. to OE *fæhth* hostility; see FOE]
▸ **ˈfeudist** *n*

feud[2] *or* **feod** (fjuːd) *n Feudal law.* land held in return for service. [C17: from Med. L *feodum*, of Gmc origin; see FEE]

THESAURUS

fertility *n* **1, 2** = **fruitfulness**, abundance, fecundity, luxuriance, productiveness, richness

fertilization *n* **1** = **propagation**, implantation, impregnation, insemination, pollination, procreation **2** = **manuring**, dressing, mulching, top dressing

fertilize *vb* **1** = **make fruitful**, fecundate, fructify, impregnate, inseminate, make pregnant, pollinate **2** = **feed**, compost, dress, enrich, manure, mulch, top-dress

fertilizer *n* **1** = **compost**, dressing, dung, guano, manure, marl

fervent *adj* **1** = **intense**, animated, ardent, devout, eager, earnest, ecstatic, emotional, enthusiastic, excited, fiery, flaming, heartfelt, impassioned, passionate, perfervid (*literary*), vehement, warm, zealous
Antonyms *adj* apathetic, cold, cool, detached, dispassionate, frigid, impassive, unfeeling, unimpassioned

fervour *n* **1** = **intensity**, animation, ardour, eagerness, earnestness, enthusiasm, excitement, fervency, passion, vehemence, warmth, zeal

fester *vb* **1, 2** = **putrefy**, become inflamed, decay, gather, maturate, suppurate, ulcerate **3** = **intensify**, aggravate, chafe, gall, irk, rankle, smoulder

festering *adj* **1** = **septic**, gathering, inflamed, maturating, poisonous, purulent, pussy, suppurating, ulcerated

festival *n* **1** = **holy day**, anniversary, commemoration, feast, fête, fiesta, holiday, red-letter day, saint's day **1, 2** = **celebration**, carnival, entertainment, -fest, festivities, fête, field day, gala, jubilee, treat

festive *adj* = **celebratory**, back-slapping, carnival, cheery, Christmassy, convivial, festal, gala, gay, gleeful, happy, hearty, holiday, jolly, jovial, joyful, joyous, jubilant, light-hearted, merry, mirthful, sportive
Antonyms *adj* depressing, drab, dreary, funereal, gloomy, lugubrious, mournful, sad

festivity *n* **1** = **merrymaking**, amusement, conviviality, fun, gaiety, jollification, joviality, joyfulness, merriment, mirth, pleasure, revelry, sport **3** *often plural* = **celebration**, beano (*Brit. sl.*), carousal, entertainment, festival, festive event, festive proceedings, fun and games, hooley *or* hoolie (*chiefly Irish & NZ*), jollification, party, rave (*Brit. sl.*), rave-up (*Brit. sl.*)

festoon *n* **1** = **decoration**, chaplet, garland, lei, swag, swathe, wreath ◆ *vb* **3** = **decorate**, array, bedeck, beribbon, deck, drape, engarland, garland, hang, swathe, wreathe

fetch[1] *vb* **1** = **bring**, carry, conduct, convey, deliver, escort, get, go for, lead, obtain, retrieve, transport **2** = **produce**, draw forth, elicit, give rise to **3** = **sell for**, bring in, earn, go for, make, realize, yield

fetching *adj* **1, 2** = **attractive**, alluring, captivating, charming, cute, enchanting, enticing, fascinating, intriguing, sweet, taking, winsome

fetch up *vb* **1** *Informal* = **end up**, arrive, come, finish up, halt, land, reach, stop, turn up

fête *n* **1** = **fair**, bazaar, festival, gala, garden party, sale of work ◆ *vb* **3** = **entertain**, hold a reception for (someone), honour, kill the fatted calf for (someone), lionize, make much of, treat, wine and dine

fetid *adj* = **stinking**, corrupt, foul, malodorous, mephitic, noisome, noxious, offensive, olid, rancid, rank, reeking

fetish *n* **1** = **talisman**, amulet, cult object **2, 3** = **fixation**, *idée fixe*, mania, obsession, thing (*inf.*)

fetter *n* **1** *often plural* = **chains**, bilboes, bonds, gyves (*arch.*), irons, leg irons, manacles, shackles **2** *usually plural* = **restraint**, bondage, captivity, check, curb, hindrance, obstruction ◆ *vb* **3** = **restrict**, bind, clip someone's wings, confine, curb, encumber, hamper, hamstring, restrain, straiten, trammel **4** = **chain**, gyve (*arch.*), hobble, hold captive, manacle, put a straitjacket on, shackle, tie, tie up

feud[1] *n* **1, 2** = **hostility**, argument, bad blood, bickering, broil, conflict, contention, disagreement, discord, dissension, enmity, estrange-

feudal ('fjuːdᵊl) *adj* **1** of or characteristic of feudalism or its institutions. **2** of or relating to a fief. **3** *Disparaging.* old-fashioned. [C17: from Med. L, from *feudum* FEUD[2]]

feudalism ('fjuːdəˌlɪzəm) *n* the legal and social system that evolved in W Europe in the 8th and 9th centuries, in which vassals were protected and maintained by their lords, usually through the granting of fiefs, and were required to serve under them in war. Also called: **feudal system.**
▸**'feudalist** *n* ▸**ˌfeudal'istic** *adj*

feudality (fjuː'dælɪtɪ) *n, pl* **feudalities. 1** the state or quality of being feudal. **2** a fief or fee.

feudalize *or* **feudalise** ('fjuːdəˌlaɪz) *vb* **feudalizes, feudalizing, feudalized** *or* **feudalises, feudalising, feudalised.** (*tr*) to create feudal institutions in (a society, etc.).
▸**ˌfeudali'zation** *or* **ˌfeudali'sation** *n*

feudatory ('fjuːdətərɪ) (in feudal Europe) ◆ *n, pl* **feudatories. 1** a person holding a fief; vassal. ◆ *adj* **2** relating to or characteristic of the relationship between lord and vassal. [C16: from Med. L *feudātor*]

feuilleton (*French* fœjtɔ̃) *n* **1** the part of a European newspaper carrying reviews, serialized fiction, etc. **2** such a review or article. [C19: from F, from *feuillet* sheet of paper, dim. of *feuille* leaf, from L *folium*]

fever ⓣ ('fiːvə) *n* **1** an abnormally high body temperature, accompanied by a fast pulse rate, dry skin, etc. Related adj: **febrile. 2** any of various diseases, such as yellow fever or scarlet fever, characterized by a high temperature. **3** intense nervous excitement. ◆ *vb* **4** (*tr*) to affect with or as if with fever. [OE *fēfor,* from L *febris*]
▸**'fevered** *adj*

feverfew ('fiːvəˌfjuː) *n* a bushy European strong-scented perennial plant with white flower heads, formerly used medicinally. [OE *feferfuge,* from LL, from L *febris* fever + *fugāre* to put to flight]

feverish ⓣ ('fiːvərɪʃ) *or* **feverous** *adj* **1** suffering from fever. **2** in a state of restless excitement. **3** of, caused by, or causing fever.
▸**'feverishly** *or* **'feverously** *adv*

fever pitch *n* a state of intense excitement.

fever therapy *n* a former method of treating disease by raising the body temperature.

few ⓣ (fjuː) *determiner* **1a** hardly any: *few men are so cruel.* **1b** (*as pronoun; functioning as pl*): *many are called but few are chosen.* **2** (preceded by *a*) **2a** a small number of: *a few drinks.* **2b** (*as pronoun; functioning as pl*): *a few of you.* **3 a good few.** *Inf.* several. **4 few and far between. 4a** widely spaced. **4b** scarce. **5 not** *or* **quite a few.** *Inf.* several. ◆ *n* **6 the few.** a small number of people considered as a class: *the few who fell at Thermopylae.* [OE *fēawa*]
▸**'fewness** *n*

> **USAGE NOTE** See at **less.**

fey (feɪ) *adj* **1** interested in or believing in the supernatural. **2** clairvoyant; visionary. **3** *Chiefly Scot.* fated to die; doomed. **4** *Chiefly Scot.* in a state of high spirits. [OE *fæge* marked out for death]
▸**'feyness** *n*

fez (fez) *n, pl* **fezzes.** an originally Turkish brimless felt or wool cap, shaped like a truncated cone. [C19: via F from Turkish, from *Fès* city in Morocco]

ff *Music. symbol for* fortissimo.

ff. 1 *abbrev. for* folios. **2** *symbol for* and the following (pages, lines, etc.).

fiacre (fɪ'ɑːkrə) *n* a small four-wheeled horse-drawn carriage. [C17: after the Hotel de St *Fiacre,* Paris, where these vehicles were first hired out]

fiancé ⓣ *or* (*fem*) **fiancée** (fɪ'ɒnseɪ) *n* a person who is engaged to be married. [C19: from F, from OF *fiancier* to promise, betroth, from *fiance* a vow, from *fier* to trust, from L *fīdere*]

fiasco ⓣ (fɪ'æskəʊ) *n, pl* **fiascos** *or* **fiascoes.** a complete failure, esp. one that is ignominious or humiliating. [C19: from It., lit.: FLASK; sense development obscure]

fiat ('faɪət) *n* **1** official sanction. **2** an arbitrary order or decree. [C17: from L, lit.: let it be done]

fib ⓣ (fɪb) *n* **1** a trivial and harmless lie. ◆ *vb* **fibs, fibbing, fibbed. 2** (*intr*) to tell such a lie. [C17: ?from *fibble-fable* an unlikely story; see FABLE]
▸**'fibber** *n*

Fibonacci sequence *or* **series** (ˌfɪbə'nɑːtʃɪ) *n* the infinite sequence of numbers, 0, 1, 1, 2, 3, 5, 8, etc., in which each member (**Fibonacci number**) is the sum of the previous two. [after Leonardo *Fibonacci* (?1170–?1250), Florentine mathematician]

fibre ⓣ *or US* **fiber** ('faɪbə) *n* **1** a natural or synthetic filament that may be spun into yarn, such as cotton or nylon. **2** cloth or other material made from such yarn. **3** a long fine continuous thread or filament. **4** the texture of any material or substance. **5** essential substance or nature. **6** strength of character (esp. in **moral fibre**). **7** *Bot.* **7a** a narrow elongated thick-walled cell. **7b** a very small root or twig. **8** a fibrous substance, such as bran, as part of someone's diet: *dietary fibre.* [C14: from L *fibra* filament, entrails]
▸**'fibred** *or US* **'fibered** *adj*

fibreboard *or US* **fiberboard** ('faɪbəˌbɔːd) *n* a building material made of compressed wood or other plant fibres.

fibreglass *or US* **fiberglass** ('faɪbəˌglɑːs) *n* **1** material consisting of matted fine glass fibres, used as insulation in buildings, etc. **2** a light strong material made by bonding fibreglass with a synthetic resin; used for car bodies, etc.

fibre optics *or US* **fiber optics** *n* (*functioning as sing*) the transmission of information modulated on light down very thin flexible fibres of glass. See also **optical fibre.**
▸**ˌfibre-'optic** *or US* **ˌfiber-'optic** *adj*

fibrescope *or US* **fiberscope** ('faɪbəˌskəʊp) *n* a medical instrument using fibre optics used to examine internal organs, such as the stomach.

fibril ('faɪbrɪl) *or* **fibrilla** (faɪ'brɪlə) *n, pl* **fibrils** *or* **fibrillae** (-'brɪliː). **1** a small fibre or part of a fibre. **2** *Biol.* a root hair. [C17: from NL *fibrilla* a little FIBRE]
▸**fi'brillar** *or* **fi'brillose** *adj*

fibrillation (ˌfaɪbrɪ'leɪʃən, ˌfɪb-) *n* **1** a local and uncontrollable twitching of muscle fibres. **2** irregular twitchings of the muscular wall of the heart.

fibrin ('fɪbrɪn) *n* a white insoluble elastic protein formed from fibrinogen when blood clots: forms a network that traps red cells and platelets.

fibrinogen (fɪ'brɪnədʒən) *n* a soluble protein in blood plasma, converted to fibrin by the action of the enzyme thrombin when blood clots.

fibro ('faɪbrəʊ) *n Austral. inf.* **a** short for **fibrocement. b** (*as modifier*): *a fibro shack.*

fibro- *combining form.* **1** indicating fibrous tissue: *fibrosis.* **2** indicating fibre: *fibrocement.* [from L *fibra* FIBRE]

fibrocement (ˌfaɪbrəʊsɪ'ment) *n* cement combined with asbestos fibre, used esp. in sheets for building.

fibroid ('faɪbrɔɪd) *adj* **1** *Anat.* (of structures or tissues) containing or resembling fibres. ◆ *n* **2** a benign tumour, composed of fibrous and muscular tissue, occurring in the wall of the uterus and often causing heavy menstruation.

fibroin ('faɪbrəʊɪn) *n* a tough elastic protein that is the principal component of spiders' webs and raw silk.

fibroma (faɪ'brəʊmə) *n, pl* **fibromata** (-mətə) *or* **fibromas.** a benign tumour derived from fibrous connective tissue.

fibrosis (faɪ'brəʊsɪs) *n* the formation of an abnormal amount of fibrous tissue in an organ or part.

fibrositis (ˌfaɪbrə'saɪtɪs) *n* inflammation of white fibrous tissue, esp. that of muscle sheaths.

fibrous ('faɪbrəs) *adj* consisting of or resembling fibres: *fibrous tissue.*
▸**'fibrously** *adv*

fibula ('fɪbjʊlə) *n, pl* **fibulae** (-ˌliː) *or* **fibulas. 1** the outer and thinner of the two bones between the knee and ankle of the human leg. Cf. **tibia. 2** the corresponding bone in other vertebrates. **3** a metal brooch resembling a safety pin. [C17: from L: clasp, prob. from *figere* to fasten]
▸**'fibular** *adj*

-fic *suffix forming adjectives.* making or producing: *honorific.* [from L *-ficus,* from *facere* to do, make]

fiche (fiːʃ) *n* See **microfiche, ultrafiche.**

fichu ('fiːʃuː) *n* a woman's shawl worn esp. in the 18th century. [C19: from F: small shawl, from *ficher* to fix with a pin, from L *figere* to fasten, FIX]

fickle ⓣ ('fɪkᵊl) *adj* changeable in purpose, affections, etc. [OE *ficol* deceitful]
▸**'fickleness** *n*

THESAURUS

ment, faction, falling out, grudge, quarrel, rivalry, row, strife, vendetta ◆ *vb* **3 = quarrel**, be at daggers drawn, be at odds, bicker, brawl, clash, contend, dispute, duel, fall out, row, squabble, war

fever *n* **1 = ague**, pyrexia (*Medical*) **3 = excitement**, agitation, delirium, ecstasy, ferment, fervour, flush, frenzy, heat, intensity, passion, restlessness, turmoil, unrest

feverish *adj* **1 = hot**, burning, febrile, fevered, flaming, flushed, hectic, inflamed, pyretic (*Medical*) **2 = excited**, agitated, desperate, distracted, frantic, frenetic, frenzied, impatient, obsessive, overwrought, restless
Antonyms *adj* ≠ **excited:** calm, collected, composed, cool, dispassionate, nonchalant, offhand, serene, tranquil, unemotional, unexcitable, unfazed (*inf.*), unruffled

few *adj* **1a = not many**, hardly any, inconsiderable, infrequent, insufficient, meagre, negligible, rare, scant, scanty, scarce, scarcely any, scattered, sparse, sporadic, thin ◆ *pron* **1b = small number**, handful, scarcely any, scattering, some ◆ *adj* **4 few and far between = scarce**, at great intervals, hard to come by, infrequent, in short supply, irregular, rare, scattered, seldom met with, thin on the ground, uncommon, unusual, widely spaced
Antonyms *adj* ≠ **not many, scarce:** abundant, bounteous, divers (*arch.*), inexhaustible, manifold, many, multifarious, plentiful, sundry

fiancé *n* **= husband-to-be**, betrothed, intended, prospective spouse

fiancée *n* **= wife-to-be**, betrothed, intended, prospective spouse

fiasco *n* **= flop** (*inf.*), balls-up (*taboo sl.*), catastrophe, cock-up, debacle, disaster, failure, mess, rout, ruin, washout (*inf.*)

fib *n* **1 = lie**, fiction, pork pie (*Brit. sl.*), porky (*Brit. sl.*), prevarication, story, untruth, white lie, whopper (*inf.*)

fibre *n* **1, 3 = thread**, fibril, filament, pile, staple, strand, texture, wisp **5 = essence**, nature, quality, spirit, substance **6** *As in* **moral fibre = strength of character**, resolution, stamina, strength, toughness

fickle *adj* **= changeable**, blowing hot and cold,

fictile ('fɪktaɪl) *adj* **1** moulded or capable of being moulded from clay. **2** made of clay by a potter. [C17: from L *fictilis* that can be moulded, from *fingere* to shape]

fiction ➊ ('fɪkʃən) *n* **1** literary works invented by the imagination, such as novels or short stories. **2** an invented story or explanation. **3** the act of inventing a story. **4** *Law.* something assumed to be true for the sake of convenience, though probably false. [C14: from L *fictiō* a fashioning, hence something imaginary, from *fingere* to shape]
▸ **'fictional** *adj* ▸ **'fictionally** *adv* ▸ **'fictive** *adj*

fictionalize *or* **fictionalise** ('fɪkʃənəˌlaɪz) *vb* **fictionalizes, fictionalizing, fictionalized** *or* **fictionalises, fictionalising, fictionalised.** (*tr*) to make into fiction.
▸ **ˌfictionali'zation** *or* **ˌfictionali'sation** *n*

fictitious ➊ (fɪk'tɪʃəs) *adj* **1** not genuine or authentic: *to give a fictitious address.* **2** of, related to, or characteristic of fiction.
▸ **fic'titiously** *adv* ▸ **fic'titiousness** *n*

fid (fɪd) *n Naut.* **1** a spike for separating strands of rope in splicing. **2** a wooden or metal bar for supporting the topmast. [C17: from ?]

-fid *adj combining form.* divided into parts or lobes: *bifid.* [from L *-fidus*, from *findere* to split]

fiddle ➊ ('fɪdᵊl) *n* **1** *Inf. or disparaging.* the violin. **2** a violin played as a folk instrument. **3** *Naut.* a small railing around the top of a table to prevent objects from falling off it. **4** *Brit. inf.* an illegal transaction or arrangement. **5** *Brit. inf.* a manually delicate or tricky operation. **6 at** *or* **on the fiddle.** *Inf.* engaged in an illegal or fraudulent undertaking. **7 fit as a fiddle.** *Inf.* in very good health. **8 play second fiddle.** *Inf.* to play a minor part. ◆ *vb* **fiddles, fiddling, fiddled. 9** to play (a tune) on the fiddle. **10** (*intr;* often foll. by *with*) to make aimless movements with the hands. **11** (when *intr*, often foll. by *about* or *around*) *Inf.* to waste (time). **12** (often foll. by *with*) *Inf.* to interfere (with). **13** *Inf.* to contrive to do (something) by illicit means or deception. **14** (*tr*) *Inf.* to falsify (accounts, etc.). [OE *fithele;* see VIOLA[1]]

fiddle-faddle ('fɪdᵊlˌfædᵊl) *n, interj* **1** trivial matter; nonsense. ◆ *vb* **fiddle-faddles, fiddle-faddling, fiddle-faddled. 2** (*intr*) to fuss or waste time. [C16: reduplication of FIDDLE]
▸ **'fiddle-ˌfaddler** *n*

fiddler ('fɪdlə) *n* **1** a person who plays the fiddle. **2** See **fiddler crab. 3** *Inf.* a petty rogue.

fiddler crab *n* any of various burrowing crabs of American coastal regions, the males of which have one of their pincer-like claws enlarged. [C19: referring to the rapid fiddling movement of the enlarged anterior claw of the males, used to attract females]

fiddlestick ('fɪdᵊlˌstɪk) *n* **1** *Inf.* a violin bow. **2** any trifle. **3 fiddlesticks!** an expression of annoyance or disagreement.

fiddling ➊ ('fɪdlɪŋ) *adj* **1** trifling or insignificant. **2** another word for **fiddly.**

fiddly ('fɪdlɪ) *adj* **fiddlier, fiddliest.** small and awkward to do or handle.

Fidei Defensor *Latin.* ('faɪdɪˌaɪ dɪ'fɛnsɔː) *n* defender of the faith; a title given to Henry VIII by Pope Leo X, and appearing on British coins as FID DEF (before decimalization) or FD (after decimalization).

fidelity ➊ (fɪ'delɪtɪ) *n, pl* **fidelities. 1** devotion to duties, obligations, etc. **2** loyalty or devotion, as to a person or cause. **3** faithfulness to one's spouse, lover, etc. **4** accuracy in reporting detail. **5** *Electronics.* the degree to which an amplifier or radio accurately reproduces the characteristics of the input signal. [C15: from L, from *fidēs* faith, loyalty]

fidget ➊ ('fɪdʒɪt) *vb* **1** (*intr*) to move about restlessly. **2** (*intr;* often foll. by *with*) to make restless or uneasy movements (with something). **3** (*tr*) to cause to fidget. ◆ *n* **4** (*often pl*) a state of restlessness or unease: *he's got the fidgets.* **5** a person who fidgets. [C17: from earlier *fidge*, prob. from ON *fīkjast* to desire eagerly]
▸ **'fidgety** *adj*

fiducial (fɪ'djuːʃɪəl) *adj* **1** *Physics, etc.* used as a standard of reference or measurement: *a fiducial point.* **2** of or based on trust or faith. [C17: from LL *fīdūciālis*, from L *fīdūcia* confidence, from *fīdere* to trust]

fiduciary (fɪ'duːʃɪərɪ) *Law.* ◆ *n, pl* **fiduciaries. 1** a person bound to act for another's benefit, as a trustee. ◆ *adj* **2a** having the nature of a trust. **2b** of or relating to a trust or trustee. [C17: from L *fīdūciārius* relating to something held in trust, from *fīdūcia* trust]

fiduciary issue *n* an issue of banknotes not backed by gold.

fie (faɪ) *interj Obs. or facetious.* an exclamation of distaste or mock dismay. [C13: from OF *fi*, from L *fī*, exclamation of disgust]

fief *or* **feoff** (fiːf) *n* (in feudal Europe) the property or fee granted to a vassal for his maintenance by his lord in return for service. [C17: from OF *fie*, of Gmc origin; cf. OE *fēo* cattle, money, L *pecus* cattle, *pecūnia* money, Gk *pokos* fleece]

fiefdom ('fiːfdəm) *n* **1** (in feudal Europe) the property owned by a lord. **2** an area over which a person or organization exerts authority or influence.

field ➊ (fiːld) *n* **1** an open tract of uncultivated grassland; meadow. **2** a piece of land cleared of trees and undergrowth used for pasture or growing crops: *a field of barley.* **3** a limited or marked off area on which any of various sports, athletic competitions, etc., are held: *a soccer field.* **4** an area that is rich in minerals or other natural resources: *a coalfield.* **5** short for **battlefield** or **airfield. 6** the mounted followers that hunt with a pack of hounds. **7a** all the runners in a race or competitors in a competition. **7b** the runners in a race or competitors in a competition excluding the favourite. **8** *Cricket.* the fielders collectively, esp. with regard to their positions. **9** a wide or open expanse: *a field of snow.* **10a** an area of human activity: *the field of human knowledge.* **10b** a sphere or division of knowledge, etc.: *his field is physics.* **11** a place away from the laboratory, office, library, etc., where practical work is done. **12** the surface or background, as of a flag, coin, or heraldic shield, on which a design is displayed. **13** Also called: **field of view.** the area within which an object may be observed with a telescope, etc. **14** *Physics.* See **field of force. 15** *Maths.* a set of entities, such as numbers, subject to two binary operations, addition and multiplication, such that the set is a commutative group under addition and the set, minus the zero, is a commutative group under multiplication. **16** *Computing.* a set of one or more characters comprising a unit of information. **17 play the field.** *Inf.* to disperse one's interests or attentions among a number of activities, people, or objects. **18 take the field.** to begin or carry on activity, esp. in sport or military operations. **19** (*modifier*) *Mil.* of or relating to equipment, personnel, etc., specifically trained for operations in the field: *a field gun.* ◆ *vb* **20** (*tr*) *Sport.* to stop, catch, or return (the ball) as a fielder. **21** (*tr*) *Sport.* to send (a player or team) onto the field to play. **22** (*intr*) *Sport.* (of a player or team) to act or take turn as a fielder or fielders. **23** (*tr*) to enter (a person) in a competition: *each party fielded a candidate.* **24** (*tr*) *Inf.* to deal with or handle: *to field a question.* [OE *feld*]

field artillery *n* artillery capable of deployment in support of front-line troops, due mainly to its mobility.

field day *n* **1** a day spent in some special outdoor activity, such as nature study. **2** *Mil.* a day devoted to manoeuvres or exercises, esp. before an audience. **3** *Inf.* a day or time of exciting activity: *the children had a field day with their new toys.*

field effect transistor *n* a unipolar transistor in which the transverse application of an electric field produces amplification.

fielder ('fiːldə) *n Cricket, etc.* **a** a player in the field. **b** a member of the fielding side.

field event *n* a competition, such as the discus, etc., that takes place on a field or similar area as opposed to those on the running track.

fieldfare ('fiːldˌfɛə) *n* a large Old World thrush having a pale grey head, brown wings and back, and a blackish tail. [OE *feldefare;* see FIELD, FARE]

field glasses *pl n* another name for **binoculars.**

THESAURUS

capricious, faithless, fitful, flighty, inconstant, irresolute, mercurial, mutable, quicksilver, temperamental, unfaithful, unpredictable, unstable, unsteady, vacillating, variable, volatile
Antonyms *adj* changeless, constant, faithful, firm, invariable, loyal, reliable, resolute, settled, stable, staunch, steadfast, true, trustworthy

fickleness *n* = **inconstancy**, capriciousness, fitfulness, flightiness, mutability, unfaithfulness, unpredictability, unsteadiness, volatility

fiction *n* **1** = **tale**, fable, fantasy, legend, myth, novel, romance, story, storytelling, work of imagination, yarn (*inf.*) **2** = **lie**, cock and bull story (*inf.*), concoction, fabrication, falsehood, fancy, fantasy, figment of the imagination, imagination, improvisation, invention, pork pie (*Brit. sl.*), porky (*Brit. sl.*), tall story, untruth, urban legend, urban myth

fictional *adj* **1** = **imaginary**, invented, legendary, made-up, nonexistent, unreal

fictitious *adj* **1** = **false**, apocryphal, artificial, assumed, bogus, counterfeit, fabricated, fanciful, feigned, imaginary, imagined, improvised, invented, made-up, make-believe, mythical, spurious, unreal, untrue
Antonyms *adj* actual, authentic, genuine, legitimate, real, true, truthful, veracious, veritable

fiddle *n* **1** *Informal or disparaging* = **violin 4** *Brit. informal* = **fraud**, fix, graft (*inf.*), piece of sharp practice, racket, scam (*sl.*), sting (*inf.*), swindle, wangle (*inf.*) **7 fit as a fiddle** *Informal* = **healthy**, blooming, hale and hearty, in fine fettle, in good form, in good shape, in rude health, in the pink, sound, strong ◆ *vb* **10, 12** = **fidget**, finger, interfere with, mess about *or* around, play, tamper with, tinker, toy, trifle **14** *Informal* = **cheat**, cook the books (*inf.*), diddle (*inf.*), finagle (*inf.*), fix, gerrymander, graft (*inf.*), manoeuvre, racketeer, sting (*inf.*), swindle, wangle (*inf.*)

fiddling *adj* **1** = **trivial**, futile, insignificant, nickel-and-dime (*US sl.*), pettifogging, petty, trifling

fidelity *n* **1-3** = **loyalty**, allegiance, constancy, dependability, devotedness, devotion, faith, faithfulness, fealty, integrity, lealty (*arch. or Scot.*), staunchness, troth (*arch.*), true-heartedness, trustworthiness **4** = **accuracy**, adherence, closeness, correspondence, exactitude, exactness, faithfulness, preciseness, precision, scrupulousness
Antonyms *n* ≠ **loyalty**: disloyalty, faithlessness, falseness, infidelity, perfidiousness, treachery, unfaithfulness, untruthfulness ≠ **accuracy**: inaccuracy, inexactness

fidget *vb* **1-3** = **move restlessly**, be like a cat on hot bricks, bustle, chafe, fiddle (*inf.*), fret, jiggle, jitter (*inf.*), squirm, twitch, worry ◆ *n* **4** *often plural* = **restlessness**, fidgetiness, jitters (*inf.*), nervousness, unease, uneasiness

fidgety *adj* **1, 2** = **restless**, impatient, jerky, jittery (*inf.*), jumpy, nervous, on edge, restive, twitchy (*inf.*), uneasy

field *n* **1, 2** = **meadow**, grassland, green, greensward (*arch. or literary*), lea (*poetic*), mead (*arch.*), pasture **7** = **competitors**, applicants, candidates, competition, contestants, entrants, possibilities, runners **10** = **speciality**, area, bailiwick, bounds, confines, department, discipline, domain, environment, limits, line, metier, pale, province, purview, range, scope, specialty, sphere of activity, sphere of influence, sphere of interest, sphere of study, territory ◆ *vb* **20** *Sport* = **retrieve**, catch, pick up, return, stop **24** *Informal* = **deal with**, deflect, handle, turn aside

field goal *n* **1** *Basketball.* a goal scored while the ball is in normal play rather than from a free throw. **2** *American & Canadian football.* a score of three points made by kicking the ball through the opponent's goalposts above the crossbar.
field hockey *n US & Canad.* hockey played on a field, as distinguished from ice hockey.
field hospital *n* a temporary hospital set up near a battlefield for emergency treatment.
field magnet *n* a permanent magnet or an electromagnet that produces the magnetic field in a generator, electric motor, or similar device.
field marshal *n* an officer holding the highest rank in certain armies.
fieldmouse ('fiːld,maʊs) *n, pl* **fieldmice.** a nocturnal mouse inhabiting woods, fields, and gardens of the Old World that has yellowish-brown fur.
field officer *n* an officer holding the rank of major, lieutenant colonel, or colonel.
field of force *n* the region of space surrounding a body, such as a charged particle or a magnet, within which it can exert a force on another similar body not in contact with it.
fieldsman ('fiːldzmən) *n, pl* **fieldsmen.** *Cricket.* another name for **fielder.**
field sports *pl n* sports carried on in the countryside, such as hunting or fishing.
field tile *n Brit. & NZ.* an earthenware drain used in farm drainage.
field trial *n* (*often pl*) a test to display performance, efficiency, or durability, as of a vehicle or invention.
field trip *n* an expedition, as by a group of students, to study something at first hand.
field winding ('waɪndɪŋ) *n* the current-carrying coils on a field magnet that produce the magnetic field intensity required to set up the electrical excitation in a generator or motor.
fieldwork ('fiːld,wɜːk) *n Mil.* a temporary structure used in fortifying a place or position.
field work *n* an investigation or search for material, data, etc., made in the field as opposed to the classroom or laboratory.
▸**field worker** *n*
fiend ❶ (fiːnd) *n* **1** an evil spirit. **2** a cruel, brutal, or spiteful person. **3** *Inf.* **3a** a person who is intensely interested in or fond of something: *a fresh-air fiend.* **3b** an addict: *a drug fiend.* [OE *fēond*]
Fiend (fiːnd) *n* **the.** the devil; Satan.
fiendish ❶ ('fiːndɪʃ) *adj* **1** of or like a fiend. **2** diabolically wicked or cruel. **3** *Inf.* extremely difficult or unpleasant: *a fiendish problem.*
fierce ❶ (fɪəs) *adj* **1** having a violent and unrestrained nature: *a fierce dog.* **2** wild or turbulent in force, action, or intensity: *a fierce storm.* **3** intense or strong: *fierce competition.* **4** *Inf.* very unpleasant. [C13: from OF *fiers,* from L *ferus*]
▸'**fiercely** *adv* ▸'**fierceness** *n*
fiery ❶ ('faɪərɪ) *adj* **fierier, fieriest. 1** of, containing, or composed of fire. **2** resembling fire in heat, colour, ardour, etc.: *a fiery speaker.* **3** easily angered or aroused: *a fiery temper.* **4** (of food) producing a burning sensation: *a fiery curry.* **5** (of the skin or a sore) inflamed. **6** flammable.
▸'**fierily** *adv* ▸'**fieriness** *n*
fiesta ❶ (fɪ'ɛstə) *n* (esp. in Spain and Latin America) **1** a religious festival or celebration. **2** a holiday or carnival. [Sp., from L *festa;* see FEAST]
FIFA ('fiːfə) *n acronym for* Fédération Internationale de Football Association. [from F]
fife (faɪf) *n* **1** a small high-pitched flute similar to the piccolo, used esp. in military bands. ◆ *vb* **fifes, fifing, fifed. 2** to play (music) on a fife. [C16: from OHG *pfīfa;* see PIPE[1]]
▸'**fifer** *n*
FIFO ('faɪfəʊ) *n acronym for* first in, first out (as an accounting principle in costing stock). Cf. **LIFO.**
fifteen ('fɪf'tiːn) *n* **1** the cardinal number that is the sum of ten and five. **2** a numeral, 15, XV, etc., representing this number. **3** something represented by, representing, or consisting of 15 units. **4** a Rugby Union (football) team. ◆ *determiner* **5a** amounting to fifteen: *fifteen jokes.* **5b** (*as pronoun*): *fifteen of us danced.* [OE *fīftēne*]
▸'**fif'teenth** *adj, n*
fifth (fɪfθ) *adj* (*usually prenominal*) **1a** coming after the fourth in order, position, etc. Often written 5th. **1b** (*as n*): *he came on the fifth.* ◆ *n* **2a** one of five equal parts of an object, quantity, etc. **2b** (*as modifier*): *a fifth part.* **3** the fraction equal to one divided by five (1/5). **4** *Music.* **4a** the interval between one note and another five notes away from it in a diatonic scale. **4b** one of two notes constituting such an interval in relation to the other. ◆ *adv* **5** Also: **fifthly.** after the fourth person, position, event, etc. ◆ *sentence connector.* **6** Also: **fifthly.** as the fifth point. [OE *fifta*]
fifth column *n* **1** (originally) a group of Falangist sympathizers in Madrid during the Spanish Civil War who were prepared to join the insurgents marching on the city. **2** any group of hostile infiltrators.
▸**fifth columnist** *n*
fifth wheel *n* **1** a spare wheel for a four-wheeled vehicle. **2** a superfluous or unnecessary person or thing.
fifty ('fɪftɪ) *n, pl* **fifties. 1** the cardinal number that is the product of ten and five. **2** a numeral, 50, L, etc., representing this number. **3** something represented by, representing, or consisting of 50 units. ◆ *determiner* **4a** amounting to fifty: *fifty people.* **4b** (*as pronoun*): *fifty should be sufficient.* [OE *fīftig*]
▸'**fiftieth** *adj, n*
fifty-fifty *adj, adv Inf.* in equal parts.
fig (fɪg) *n* **1** a tree or shrub in which the flowers are borne inside a pear-shaped receptacle. **2** the fruit of any of these trees, which develops from the receptacle and has sweet flesh containing numerous seedlike structures. **3** (*used with a negative*) something of negligible value: *I don't care a fig for your opinion.* [C13: from OF, from *figa,* from L *ficus* fig tree]
fig. *abbrev. for:* **1** figurative(ly). **2** figure.
fight ❶ (faɪt) *vb* **fights, fighting, fought. 1** to oppose or struggle against (an enemy) in battle. **2** to oppose or struggle against (a person, cause, etc.) in any manner. **3** (*tr*) to engage in or carry on (a battle, contest, etc.). **4** (when *intr,* often foll. by *for*) to uphold or maintain (a cause, etc.) by fighting or struggling: *to fight for freedom.* **5** (*tr*) to make or achieve (a way) by fighting. **6** to engage (another or others) in combat. **7 fight it out.** to contend until a decisive result is obtained. **8 fight shy.** to keep aloof from. ◆ *n* **9** a battle, struggle, or physical combat. **10** a quarrel, dispute, or contest. **11** resistance (esp. in **to put up a fight**). **12** a boxing match. ◆ See also **fight off.** [OE *feohtan*]
fighter ❶ ('faɪtə) *n* **1** a person who fights, esp. a professional boxer. **2** a person who has determination. **3** *Mil.* an armed aircraft designed for destroying other aircraft.
fighter-bomber *n* an aircraft that combines the roles of fighter and bomber.
fighting chance *n* a slight chance of success dependent on a struggle.
fighting cock *n* **1** a gamecock. **2** a pugnacious person.
fighting fish *n* any of various tropical fishes of the genus *Betta,* esp. the Siamese fighting fish.
fight off ❶ *vb* (*tr, adv*) **1** to repulse; repel. **2** to struggle to avoid or repress: *to fight off a cold.*
fight-or-flight *n* (*modifier*) involving or relating to an involuntary response to stress in which the hormone adrenaline is secreted into the blood in readiness for physical action, such as fighting or running away.
fig leaf *n* **1** a leaf from a fig tree. **2** a representation of a fig leaf used in sculpture, etc. to cover the genitals of nude figures. **3** a device to conceal something regarded as shameful.
figment ❶ ('fɪgmənt) *n* a fantastic notion or fabrication: *a figment of the*

THESAURUS

fiend *n* **1** = **demon,** devil, evil spirit, hellhound **2** = **brute,** barbarian, beast, degenerate, ghoul, monster, ogre, savage **3** *Informal* = **enthusiast,** addict, energumen, fanatic, freak (*inf.*), maniac
fiendish *adj* **1, 2** = **wicked,** accursed, atrocious, black-hearted, cruel, demoniac, devilish, diabolical, hellish, implacable, infernal, inhuman, malevolent, malicious, malignant, monstrous, satanic, savage, ungodly, unspeakable
fierce *adj* **1** = **wild,** baleful, barbarous, brutal, cruel, dangerous, fell (*arch.*), feral, ferocious, fiery, menacing, murderous, passionate, savage, threatening, tigerish, truculent, uncontrollable, untamed, vicious **2** = **stormy,** blustery, boisterous, furious, howling, inclement, powerful, raging, strong, tempestuous, tumultuous, uncontrollable, violent **3** = **intense,** cut-throat, keen, relentless, strong
Antonyms *adj* ≠ **wild:** affectionate, calm, civilized, cool, docile, domesticated, gentle, harmless, kind, mild, peaceful, submissive, tame ≠ **stormy:** temperate, tranquil
fiercely *adv* **1** = **ferociously,** frenziedly, furiously, in a frenzy, like cat and dog, menacingly, passionately, savagely, tempestuously, tigerishly, tooth and nail, uncontrolledly, viciously, with bared teeth, with no holds barred
fierceness *n* **1** = **ferocity,** fieriness, mercilessness, ruthlessness, savageness, viciousness, wildness **2** = **storminess,** bluster, destructiveness, roughness, tempestuousness, turbulence, violence **3** = **intensity,** avidity, fervidness, fervour, passion, relentlessness, strength
fiery *adj* **1** = **burning,** ablaze, afire, aflame, blazing, flaming, glowing, in flames, on fire, red-hot **3** = **excitable,** choleric, fierce, hot-headed, impetuous, irascible, irritable, passionate, peppery, violent **5** = **feverish,** burning, febrile, fevered, flushed, heated, hot, inflamed
fiesta *n* **1, 2** = **carnival,** bacchanal *or* bacchanalia, carousal, celebration, fair, feast, festival, festivity, fête, gala, holiday, jamboree, jubilee, Mardi Gras, merrymaking, party, revel, revelry, saint's day, Saturnalia
fight *vb* **1, 3** = **battle,** assault, bear arms against, box, brawl, carry on war, clash, close, combat, come to blows, conflict, contend, cross swords, do battle, engage, exchange blows, feud, go to war, grapple, joust, lock horns, row, spar, struggle, take the field, take up arms against, tilt, tussle, wage war, war, wrestle **2** = **quarrel,** argue, bicker, dispute, fall out (*inf.*), squabble, wrangle **4** = **oppose,** contest, defy, dispute, make a stand against, resist, stand up to, strive, struggle, withstand **8 fight shy** = **avoid,** duck out (*inf.*), keep aloof, keep at arm's length, shun, steer clear ◆ *n* **9** = **battle,** action, affray (*Law*), altercation, bout, brawl, brush, clash, combat, conflict, contest, dispute, dissension, dogfight, duel, encounter, engagement, fracas, fray, hostilities, joust, melee *or* mêlée, passage of arms, riot, row, scrap (*inf.*), set-to (*inf.*), shindig (*inf.*), shindy (*inf.*), skirmish, sparring match, struggle, tussle, war **11** = **resistance,** belligerence, gameness, mettle, militancy, pluck, spirit, will to resist
fighter *n* **1** = **boxer,** bruiser (*inf.*), prize fighter, pugilist **1** = **soldier,** fighting man, man-at-arms, warrior **1** = **combatant,** antagonist, battler, belligerent, contender, contestant, disputant, militant
fighting *n* **1** = **battle,** bloodshed, blows struck, combat, conflict, hostilities, warfare
fight off *vb* **1** = **repel,** beat off, drive away, keep *or* hold at bay, repress, repulse, resist, stave off, ward off
figment *n As in* **figment of one's imagination** =

imagination. [C15: from LL *figmentum* a fiction, from L *fingere* to shape]

figurant ('fɪgjurənt) *n* a ballet dancer who does group work but no solo roles. [C18: from F, from *figurer* to represent, appear, FIGURE]
▸**figurante** (ˌfɪgju'rɒnt) *fem n*

figuration (ˌfɪgə'reɪʃən) *n* **1** *Music.* **1a** the employment of characteristic patterns of notes, esp. in variations on a theme. **1b** florid ornamentation. **2** the act or an instance of representing figuratively, as by means of allegory. **3** a figurative representation. **4** the act of decorating with a design.

figurative ➊ ('fɪgərətɪv) *adj* **1** involving a figure of speech; not literal; metaphorical. **2** using or filled with figures of speech. **3** representing by means of an emblem, likeness, etc.
▸'**figuratively** *adv* ▸'**figurativeness** *n*

figure ➊ ('fɪgə) *n* **1** any written symbol other than a letter, esp. a whole number. **2** another name for **digit** (sense 2). **3** an amount expressed numerically: *a figure of £1800 was suggested.* **4** (*pl*) calculations with numbers: *he's good at figures.* **5** visible shape or form; outline. **6** the human form: *a girl with a slender figure.* **7** a slim bodily shape (esp. in **keep** *or* **lose one's figure**). **8** a character or personage: *a figure in politics.* **9** the impression created by a person through behaviour (esp. in **to cut a fine, bold,** etc., **figure**). **10a** a person as impressed on the mind. **10b** (*in combination*): *father-figure.* **11** a representation in painting or sculpture, esp. of the human form. **12** an illustration or diagram in a text. **13** a representative object or symbol. **14** a pattern or design, as in wood. **15** a predetermined set of movements in dancing or skating. **16** *Geom.* any combination of points, lines, curves, or planes. **17** *Logic.* one of four possible arrangements of the terms in the major and minor premises of a syllogism that give the same conclusion. **18** *Music.* **18a** a numeral written above or below a note in a part. **18b** a characteristic short pattern of notes. ◆ *vb* **figures, figuring, figured. 19** (when *tr,* often foll. by *up*) to calculate or compute (sums, amounts, etc.). **20** (*tr; usually takes a clause as object*) *Inf., US, Canad., & NZ.* to consider. **21** (*tr*) to represent by a diagram or illustration. **22** (*tr*) to pattern or mark with a design. **23** (*tr*) to depict or portray in a painting, etc. **24** (*tr*) to imagine. **25** (*tr*) *Music.* to decorate (a melody line or part) with ornamentation. **26** (*intr;* usually foll. by *in*) to be included: *his name figures in the article.* **27** (*intr*) *Inf.* to accord with expectation: *it figures that he wouldn't come.* ◆ See also **figure out.** [C13: from L *figūra* a shape, from *fingere* to mould]
▸'**figurer** *n*

figured ➊ ('fɪgəd) *adj* **1** depicted as a figure in painting or sculpture. **2** decorated with a design. **3** having a form. **4** *Music.* **4a** ornamental. **4b** (of a bass part) provided with numerals indicating accompanying harmonies.

figured bass (beɪs) *n* a shorthand method of indicating a thorough-bass part in which each bass note is accompanied by figures indicating the intervals to be played in the chord above it.

figurehead ➊ ('fɪgəˌhɛd) *n* **1** a person nominally having a prominent position, but no real authority. **2** a carved bust on the bow of some sailing vessels.

figure of speech ➊ *n* an expression of language, such as metaphor, by which the literal meaning of a word is not employed.

figure out ➊ *vb* (*tr, adv; may take a clause as object*) *Inf.* **1** to calculate. **2** to understand.

figure skating *n* **1** ice skating in which the skater traces outlines of selected patterns. **2** the whole art of skating, as distinct from skating at speed.
▸**figure skater** *n*

figurine (ˌfɪgə'riːn) *n* a small carved or moulded figure; statuette. [C19: from F, from It. *figurina* a little FIGURE]

figwort ('fɪgˌwɜːt) *n* a plant related to the foxglove having square stems and small greenish flowers.

Fijian (fiː'dʒiːən) *n* **1** a member of the indigenous people inhabiting Fiji. **2** the language of this people, belonging to the Malayo-Polynesian family. ◆ *adj* **3** of or characteristic of Fiji or its inhabitants. ◆ Also: **Fiji.**

filagree ('fɪləˌgriː) *n, adj* a less common spelling of **filigree.**

filament ➊ ('fɪləmənt) *n* **1** the thin wire, usually tungsten, inside a light bulb that emits light when heated to incandescence by an electric current. **2** *Electronics.* a high-resistance wire forming the cathode in some valves. **3** a single strand of a natural or synthetic fibre. **4** *Bot.* the stalk of a stamen. **5** any slender structure or part. [C16: from NL, from Med. L *filāre* to spin, from L *filum* thread]
▸**filamentary** (ˌfɪlə'mɛntərɪ) *or* ˌ**fila'mentous** *adj*

filaria (fɪ'lɛərɪə) *n, pl* **filariae** (-ɪˌiː). a parasitic nematode worm that lives in the blood of vertebrates and is transmitted by insects: the cause of filariasis. [C19: NL (former name of genus), from L *filum* thread]
▸**fi'larial** *adj*

filariasis (ˌfɪlə'raɪəsɪs, fɪˌlɛərɪ'eɪsɪs) *n* a disease common in tropical and subtropical countries resulting from infestation of the lymphatic system with nematode worms transmitted by mosquitoes: characterized by inflammation. See also **elephantiasis.** [C19: from NL; see FILARIA]

filbert ('fɪlbət) *n* **1** any of several N temperate shrubs that have edible rounded brown nuts. **2** Also called: **hazelnut, cobnut.** the nut of any of these shrubs. [C14: after St *Philbert,* 7th-century Frankish abbot, because the nuts are ripe around his feast day, Aug. 22]

filch ➊ (fɪltʃ) *vb* (*tr*) to steal or take in small amounts. [C16 *filchen* to steal, attack, ?from OE *gefylce* band of men]
▸'**filcher** *n*

file[1] ➊ (faɪl) *n* **1** a folder, box, etc., used to keep documents or other items in order. **2** the documents, etc., kept in this way. **3** documents or information about a specific subject, person, etc. **4** a line of people in marching formation, one behind another. **5** any of the eight vertical rows of squares on a chessboard. **6** *Computing.* a named collection of information, in the form of text, programs, graphics, etc., held on a permanent storage device, such as a magnetic disk. **7 on file.** recorded or catalogued for reference, as in a file. ◆ *vb* **files, filing, filed. 8** to place (a document, etc.) in a file. **9** (*tr*) to place (a legal document) on public or official record. **10** (*tr*) to bring (a suit, esp. a divorce suit) in a court of law. **11** (*tr*) to submit (copy) to a newspaper. **12** (*intr*) to march or walk in a file or files: *the ants filed down the hill.* [C16 (in the sense: string on which documents are hung): from OF, from Med. L *filāre;* see FILAMENT]
▸'**filer** *n*

file[2] ➊ (faɪl) *n* **1** a hand tool consisting of a steel blade with small cutting teeth on some or all of its faces. It is used for shaping or smoothing. ◆ *vb* **files, filing, filed. 2** (*tr*) to shape or smooth (a surface) with a file. [OE *fīl*]
▸'**filer** *n*

filefish ('faɪlˌfɪʃ) *n, pl* **filefish** *or* **filefishes.** any tropical triggerfish having a narrow compressed body and a very long dorsal spine. [C18: referring to its file-like scales]

filename ('faɪlˌneɪm) *n* an arrangement of characters that enables a computer system to permit the user to have access to a particular file.

file server *n Computing.* the central unit of a local area network that controls its operation and provides access to separately stored data files.

filet ('fɪlɪt, 'fɪleɪ) *n* a variant spelling of **fillet** (senses 1–3). [C20: from F: net, from OF, from *fil* thread, from L *filum*]

filet mignon ('fɪleɪ 'miːnjɒn) *n* a small tender boneless cut of beef. [from F, lit.: dainty fillet]

filial ('fɪljəl) *adj* **1** of, resembling, or suitable to a son or daughter: *filial affection.* **2** *Genetics.* designating any of the generations following the parental generation. [C15: from LL *filiālis,* from L *filius* son]
▸'**filially** *adv*

filibeg *or* **philibeg** ('fɪlɪˌbɛg) *n* the kilt worn by Scottish Highlanders. [C18: from Scot. Gaelic *fēileadhbeag,* from *fēileadh* kilt + *beag* small]

filibuster ➊ ('fɪlɪˌbʌstə) *n* **1** the process of obstructing legislation by means of delaying tactics. **2** Also called: **filibusterer.** a legislator who engages in such obstruction. **3** a freebooter or military adventurer, esp. in a foreign country. ◆ *vb* **4** to obstruct (legislation) with delaying tactics. **5** (*intr*) to engage in unlawful military action. [C16: from Sp., from F *flibustier,* prob. from Du. *vrijbuiter* pirate, lit.: one plundering freely; see FREEBOOTER]
▸'**filiˌbusterer** *n*

filigree ➊ ('fɪlɪˌgriː) *or* **filagree** *n* **1** delicate ornamental work of twisted gold, silver, or other wire. **2** any fanciful delicate ornamentation.

THESAURUS

invention, creation, fable, fabrication, falsehood, fancy, fiction, improvisation, production

figurative *adj* **1 = symbolical,** allegorical, emblematical, metaphorical, representative, typical **2 = poetical,** descriptive, fanciful, florid, flowery, ornate, pictorial, tropical (*Rhetoric*)
Antonyms *adj* ≠ **symbolical:** accurate, exact, factual, faithful, literal ≠ **poetical:** prosaic, simple, true, unpoetical, unvarnished

figure *n* **1, 2 = number,** character, cipher, digit, numeral, symbol **3 = amount,** cost, price, sum, total, value **5 = outline,** form, shadow, shape, silhouette **6 = shape,** body, build, chassis (*sl.*), frame, physique, proportions, torso **8 = character,** big name, celebrity, dignitary, face (*inf.*), force, leader, notability, notable, personage, personality, presence, somebody, worthy **12 = diagram,** depiction, design, device, drawing, emblem, illustration, motif, pattern, representation, sketch ◆ *vb* **19 = calculate,** add, compute, count, reckon, sum, tally, tot up, work out **26** *usually foll. by* **in = feature,** act, appear, be conspicuous, be featured, be included, be mentioned, contribute to, have a place in, play a part

figured *adj* **2 = decorated,** adorned, embellished, marked, ornamented, patterned, variegated

figurehead *n* **1 = front man,** cipher, dummy, leader in name only, man of straw, mouthpiece, name, nonentity, puppet, straw man (*chiefly US*), titular *or* nominal head, token

figure of speech *n* **= expression,** conceit, image, trope, turn of phrase

figure out *vb* **1 = calculate,** compute, reckon, work out **2 = understand,** comprehend, decipher, fathom, make head or tail of (*inf.*), make out, resolve, see, suss (out) (*sl.*)

filament *n* **= strand,** cilium (*Biology & Zoology*), fibre, fibril, pile, staple, string, thread, wire, wisp

filch *vb* **= steal,** abstract, crib (*inf.*), embezzle, lift (*inf.*), misappropriate, nick (*sl., chiefly Brit.*), pilfer, pinch (*inf.*), purloin, rip off (*sl.*), swipe (*sl.*), take, thieve, walk off with

file[1] *n* **1, 2 = folder,** case, data, documents, dossier, information, portfolio **4 = line,** column, list, queue, row, string ◆ *vb* **8 = register,** document, enter, pigeonhole, put in place, record, slot in (*inf.*) **12 = march,** parade, troop

file[2] *vb* **2 = smooth,** abrade, burnish, furbish, polish, rasp, refine, rub, rub down, scrape, shape

filibuster *n* **1 = obstruction,** delay, hindrance, postponement, procrastination **3 = freebooter,** adventurer, buccaneer, corsair, pirate, sea robber, sea rover, soldier of fortune ◆ *vb* **4 = obstruct,** delay, hinder, play for time, prevent, procrastinate, put off

filigree *n* **1 = wirework,** lace, lacework, lattice, tracery

◆ *adj* **3** made of or as if with filigree. [C17: from earlier *filigreen,* from F *filigrane,* from L *filum* thread + *grānum* GRAIN]
▸ **'fili,greed** *adj*

filings ('faɪlɪŋz) *pl n* shavings or particles removed by a file: *iron filings.*

Filipino (ˌfɪlɪ'piːnəʊ) *n* **1** (*pl* **Filipinos**) Also (fem): **Filipina.** a native or inhabitant of the Philippines. **2** another name for **Tagalog.** ◆ *adj* **3** of or relating to the Philippines or their inhabitants.

fill ❶ (fɪl) *vb* (*mainly tr;* often foll. by *up*) **1** (*also intr*) to make or become full: *to fill up a bottle.* **2** to occupy the whole of: *the party filled the house.* **3** to plug (a gap, crevice, etc.). **4** to meet (a requirement or need) satisfactorily. **5** to cover (a page or blank space) with writing, drawing, etc. **6** to hold and perform the duties of (an office or position). **7** to appoint or elect an occupant to (an office or position). **8** (*also intr*) to swell or cause to swell with wind, as in manoeuvring the sails of a sailing vessel. **9** *Chiefly US & Canad.* to put together the necessary materials for (a prescription or order). **10 fill the bill.** *Inf.* to serve or perform adequately. ◆ *n* **11** material such as gravel, stones, etc., used to bring an area of ground up to a required level. **12 one's fill.** the quantity needed to satisfy one. ◆ See also **fill in, fill out,** etc. [OE *fyllan*]

filler ❶ ('fɪlə) *n* **1** a person or thing that fills. **2** an object or substance used to add weight or size to something or to fill in a gap. **3** a paste, used for filling in cracks, holes, etc., in a surface before painting. **4** the inner portion of a cigar. **5** *Journalism.* articles, photographs, etc., to fill space between more important articles in a newspaper or magazine.

fillet ('fɪlɪt) *n* **1a** Also called: **fillet steak.** a strip of boneless meat. **1b** the boned side of a fish. **2** a narrow strip of any material. **3** a thin strip of ribbon, lace, etc., worn in the hair or around the neck. **4** a narrow flat moulding, esp. one between other mouldings. **5** a narrow band between flutings on the shaft of a column. **6** *Heraldry.* a horizontal division of a shield. **7** a narrow decorative line, impressed on the cover of a book. ◆ *vb* **fillets, filleting, filleted.** (*tr*) **8** to cut or prepare (meat or fish) as a fillet. **9** to cut fillets from (meat or fish). **10** to bind or decorate with or as if with a fillet. ◆ Also (for senses 1–3): **filet.** [C14: from OF *filet,* from *fil* thread, from L *filum*]

fill in ❶ *vb* (*adv*) **1** (*tr*) to complete (a form, drawing, etc.). **2** (*intr*) to act as a substitute. **3** (*tr*) to put material into (a hole or cavity), esp. so as to make it level with a surface. **4** (*tr*) *Inf.* to inform with facts or news. ◆ *n* **fill-in. 5** a substitute.

filling ❶ ('fɪlɪŋ) *n* **1** the substance or thing used to fill a space or container: *pie filling.* **2** *Dentistry.* any of various substances (metal, plastic, etc.) for inserting into the prepared cavity of a tooth. **3** *Chiefly US.* the weft in weaving. ◆ *adj* **4** (of food or a meal) substantial and satisfying.

filling station *n* a place where petrol and other supplies for motorists are sold.

fillip ❶ ('fɪlɪp) *n* **1** something that adds stimulation or enjoyment. **2** the action of holding a finger towards the palm with the thumb and suddenly releasing it outwards to produce a snapping sound. **3** a quick blow or tap made by this. ◆ *vb* **4** (*tr*) to stimulate or excite. **5** (*tr*) to strike or project sharply with a fillip. **6** (*intr*) to make a fillip. [C15 *philippe,* imit.]

fill out *vb* (*adv*) **1** to make or become fuller, thicker, or rounder. **2** to make more substantial. **3** (*tr*) *Chiefly US & Canad.* to fill in (a form, etc.).

fill up *vb* (*adv*) **1** (*tr*) to complete (a form, application, etc.). **2** to make or become full. ◆ *n* **fill-up. 3** the act of filling something completely, esp. the petrol tank of a car.

filly ('fɪlɪ) *n, pl* **fillies.** a female horse or pony under the age of four. [C15: from ON *fylja;* see FOAL]

film ❶ (fɪlm) *n* **1a** a sequence of images of moving objects photographed by a camera and providing the optical illusion of continuous movement when projected onto a screen. **1b** a form of entertainment, etc., composed of such a sequence of images. **1c** (*as modifier*): *film techniques.* **2** a thin flexible strip of cellulose coated with a photographic emulsion, used to make negatives and transparencies. **3** a thin coating or layer. **4** a thin sheet of any material, as of plastic for packaging. **5** a fine haze, mist, or blur. **6** a gauzy web of filaments or fine threads. ◆ *vb* **7a** to photograph with a cine camera. **7b** to make a film of (a screenplay, event, etc.). **8** (often foll. by *over*) to cover or become covered or coated with a film. [OE *filmen* membrane]

filmic ('fɪlmɪk) *adj* **1** of or relating to films or the cinema. **2** suggestive of films or the cinema.
▸ **'filmically** *adv*

film noir (nwɑː) *n* a type of gangster thriller, made esp. in the 1940s in Hollywood, characterized by stark lighting, an involved plot, and an atmosphere of cynicism and corruption. [C20: F, lit.: black film]

filmography (fɪl'mɒgrəfɪ) *n* **1** a list of the films made by a particular director, actor, etc. **2** any writing that deals with films or the cinema.

filmset ('fɪlmˌset) *vb* **filmsets, filmsetting, filmset.** (*tr*) *Brit.* to set (type matter) by filmsetting.
▸ **'film,setter** *n*

filmsetting ('fɪlmˌsetɪŋ) *n Brit., printing.* typesetting by exposing type characters onto photographic film from which printing plates are made.

film speed *n* **1** the sensitivity to light of a photographic film, specified in terms of the film's ISO rating. **2** the rate at which the film passes through a motion picture camera or projector.

film strip *n* a strip of film composed of different images projected separately as slides.

filmy ❶ ('fɪlmɪ) *adj* **filmier, filmiest. 1** transparent or gauzy. **2** hazy; blurred.
▸ **'filmily** *adv* ▸ **'filminess** *n*

filo ('fiːləʊ) *n* a type of Greek flaky pastry in very thin sheets. [C20: Mod. Gk *phullon* leaf]

Filofax ('faɪləʊˌfæks) *n Trademark.* a type of loose-leaf ring binder with sets of different-coloured paper, used as a portable personal filing system, including appointments, addresses, etc.

filter ❶ ('fɪltə) *n* **1** a porous substance, such as paper or sand, that allows fluid to pass but retains suspended solid particles. **2** any device containing such a porous substance for separating suspensions from fluids. **3** any of various porous substances built into the mouth end of a cigarette or cigar for absorbing impurities such as tar. **4** any electronic, optical, or acoustic device that blocks signals or radiations of certain frequencies while allowing others to pass. **5** any transparent disc of gelatine or glass used to eliminate or reduce the intensity of given frequencies from the light leaving a lamp, entering a camera, etc. **6** *Brit.* a traffic signal at a road junction which permits vehicles to turn either left or right when the main signals are red. ◆ *vb* **7** (often foll. by *out*) to remove or separate (suspended particles, etc.) from (a liquid, gas, etc.) by the action of a filter. **8** (*tr*) to obtain by filtering. **9** (*intr;* foll. by *through*) to pass (through a filter or something like a filter). **10** (*intr*) to flow slowly; trickle. [C16 *filtre,* from Med. L *filtrum* piece of felt used as a filter, of Gmc origin]

filterable ('fɪltərəbᵊl) *or* **filtrable** ('fɪltrəbᵊl) *adj* **1** capable of being filtered. **2** (of most viruses and certain bacteria) capable of passing through the pores of a fine filter.

filter bed *n* a layer of sand or gravel in a tank or reservoir through which a liquid is passed so as to purify it.

filter feeding *n Zool.* a method of feeding in some aquatic animals, such as whalebone whales, in which minute food particles are filtered from the surrounding water.
▸ **filter feeder** *n*

filter out *or* **through** *vb* (*intr, adv*) to become known gradually; leak.

filter paper *n* a porous paper used for filtering liquids.

filter tip *n* **1** an attachment to the mouth end of a cigarette for trapping impurities such as tar during smoking. **2** a cigarette having such an attachment.
▸ **'filter-,tipped** *adj*

filth ❶ (fɪlθ) *n* **1** foul or disgusting dirt; refuse. **2** extreme physical or moral uncleanliness. **3** vulgarity or obscenity. **4 the filth.** *Sl.* the police. [OE *fylth*]

filthy ❶ ('fɪlθɪ) *adj* **filthier, filthiest. 1** very dirty or obscene. **2** offensive or vicious: *that was a filthy trick to play.* **3** *Inf., chiefly Brit.* extremely unpleasant: *filthy weather.* ◆ *adv* **4** extremely; disgustingly (esp. in **filthy rich**).
▸ **'filthily** *adv* ▸ **'filthiness** *n*

THESAURUS

fill *vb* **1** = **stuff,** brim over, cram, crowd, furnish, glut, gorge, inflate, pack, pervade, replenish, sate, satiate, satisfy, stock, store, supply, swell **2** = **saturate,** charge, imbue, impregnate, overspread, pervade, suffuse **3** = **plug,** block, bung, close, cork, seal, stop **6, 7** = **perform,** assign, carry out, discharge, engage, execute, fulfil, hold, occupy, officiate, take up ◆ *n* **12 one's fill** = **sufficient,** all one wants, ample, a sufficiency, enough, plenty
Antonyms *vb* ≠ **stuff:** diminish, drain, empty, exhaust, shrink, subside, vacate, void

filler *n* **2** = **padding,** makeweight, stopgap

fill in *vb* **1** = **complete,** answer, fill out (*US*), fill up **2** = **replace,** deputize, represent, stand in, sub, substitute, take the place of **4** *Informal* = **inform,** acquaint, apprise, bring up to date, give the facts *or* background, put wise (*sl.*)

filling *n* **1** = **stuffing,** contents, filler, innards (*inf.*), inside, insides, padding, wadding ◆ *adj* **4** = **satisfying,** ample, heavy, square, substantial

fillip *n* **1** = **stimulus,** goad, incentive, prod, push, spice, spur, zest

film *n* **1** = **movie,** flick (*sl.*), motion picture **3** = **layer,** coat, coating, covering, dusting, gauze, integument, membrane, pellicle, scum, skin, tissue **5** = **haze,** blur, cloud, haziness, mist, mistiness, opacity, veil ◆ *vb* **7** = **photograph,** shoot, take, video, videotape **8** *often foll. by* **over** = **cloud,** blear, blur, dull, haze, mist, veil

filmy *adj* **1** = **transparent,** chiffon, cobwebby, delicate, diaphanous, fine, finespun, flimsy, floaty, fragile, gauzy, gossamer, insubstantial, see-through, sheer **2** = **transparent,** bleared, bleary, blurred, blurry, cloudy, dim, hazy, membranous, milky, misty, opalescent, opaque, pearly

filter *n* **1** = **sieve,** gauze, membrane, mesh, riddle, strainer ◆ *vb* **7** = **purify,** clarify, filtrate, refine, screen, sieve, sift, strain, winnow **9, 10** = **trickle,** dribble, escape, exude, leach, leak, ooze, penetrate, percolate, seep, well

filth *n* **1** = **dirt,** carrion, contamination, crud (*sl.*), defilement, dung, excrement, excreta, faeces, filthiness, foul matter, foulness, garbage, grime, grot (*sl.*), muck, nastiness, ordure, pollution, putrefaction, putrescence, refuse, sewage, slime, sludge, squalor, uncleanness **2, 3** = **obscenity,** corruption, dirty- mindedness, impurity, indecency, pornography, smut, vileness, vulgarity

filthy *adj* **1** = **dirty,** faecal, feculent, foul, nasty, polluted, putrid, scummy, scuzzy (*sl., chiefly US*), slimy, squalid, unclean, vile **1** = **obscene,** bawdy, coarse, corrupt, depraved, dirty-minded, foul, foul-mouthed, impure, indecent, lewd, licentious, pornographic, smutty, suggestive, X-rated (*inf.*) **1** = **muddy,** begrimed, black, blackened, grimy, grubby, miry, mucky, mud-encrusted, scuzzy (*sl., chiefly US*), smoky, sooty, unwashed **2** = **despicable,** base, contemptible, low, mean, offensive, scurvy, vicious, vile

filtrate ('fɪltreɪt) *n* **1** a liquid or gas that has been filtered. ◆ *vb* **filtrates, filtrating, filtrated. 2** to filter. [C17: from Med. L *filtrāre* to FILTER]
▸**fil'tration** *n*

fin (fɪn) *n* **1** any of the firm appendages that are the organs of locomotion and balance in fishes and some other aquatic animals. **2** a part or appendage that resembles a fin. **3a** *Brit.* a vertical surface to which the rudder is attached at the rear of an aeroplane. **3b** a tail surface fixed to a rocket or missile to give stability. **4** *Naut.* a fixed or adjustable blade projecting under water from the hull of a vessel to give it stability or control. **5** a projecting rib to dissipate heat from the surface of an engine cylinder or radiator. ◆ *vb* **fins, finning, finned. 6** (*tr*) to provide with fins. [OE *finn*]
▸ **'finless** *adj* ▸**finned** *adj*

fin. *abbrev. for:* **1** finance. **2** financial.

Fin. *abbrev. for:* **1** Finland. **2** Finnish.

finable *or* **fineable** ('faɪnəbᵊl) *adj* liable to a fine.
▸ **'finableness** *or* **'fineableness** *n*

finagle (fɪ'neɪgᵊl) *vb* **finagles, finagling, finagled.** *Inf.* **1** (*tr*) to get or achieve by craftiness or persuasion. **2** to use trickery on (a person). [C20: ?from dialect *fainaigue* cheat]
▸**fi'nagler** *n*

final ➊ ('faɪnᵊl) *adj* **1** of or occurring at the end; last. **2** having no possibility of further discussion, action, or change: *a final decree of judgment.* **3** relating to or constituting an end or purpose: *a final clause may be introduced by "in order to".* **4** *Music.* another word for **perfect** (sense 9b.). ◆ *n* **5** a last thing; end. **6** a deciding contest between the winners of previous rounds in a competition. ◆ See also **finals.** [C14: from L *fīnālis*, from *finis* limit, boundary]

finale ➊ (fɪ'nɑːlɪ) *n* **1** the concluding part of any performance or presentation. **2** the closing section or movement of a musical composition. [C18: from It., n use of adj *finale*, from L *fīnālis* FINAL]

finalist ('faɪnəlɪst) *n* a contestant who has reached the last stage of a competition.

finality ➊ (faɪ'nælɪtɪ) *n, pl* **finalities. 1** the condition or quality of being final or settled: *the finality of death.* **2** a final or conclusive act.

finalize ➊ *or* **finalise** ('faɪnəˌlaɪz) *vb* **finalizes, finalizing, finalized** *or* **finalises, finalising, finalised. 1** (*tr*) to put into final form; settle: *to finalize plans for the merger.* **2** to reach agreement on a transaction.
▸ **ˌfinali'zation** *or* **ˌfinali'sation** *n*

> **USAGE NOTE** Although *finalize* has been in widespread use for some time, many speakers and writers still prefer to use *complete, conclude*, or *make final*, esp. in formal contexts.

finally ➊ ('faɪnəlɪ) *adv* **1** at last; eventually. **2** at the end or final point; lastly. **3** completely; conclusively. ◆ *sentence connector.* **4** in the end; lastly: *finally, he put his tie on.* **5** as the last or final point.

finals ('faɪnᵊlz) *pl n* **1** the deciding part of a competition. **2** *Education.* the last examinations in an academic or professional course.

finance ➊ (fɪ'næns, 'faɪnæns) *n* **1** the system of money, credit, etc., esp. with respect to government revenues and expenditures. **2** funds or the provision of funds. **3** (*pl*) financial condition. ◆ *vb* **finances, financing, financed. 4** (*tr*) to provide or obtain funds or credit for. [C14: from OF, from *finer* to end, settle by payment]

finance company *or* **house** *n* an enterprise engaged in the loan of money against collateral, esp. one specializing in the financing of hire-purchase contracts.

financial ➊ (fɪ'nænʃəl, faɪ-) *adj* **1** of or relating to finance or finances. **2** of or relating to persons who manage money, capital, or credit. **3** *Austral. & NZ inf.* having money; in funds. **4** *Austral. & NZ.* (of a club member) fully paid-up.
▸**fi'nancially** *adv*

financial futures *pl n* futures in a stock-exchange index, currency exchange rate, or interest rate enabling banks, building societies, brokers, and speculators to hedge their involvement in these markets.

Financial Ombudsman *n* any of five British ombudsmen: the **Banking Ombudsman**, set up in 1986 to investigate complaints from banking customers; the **Building Society Ombudsman**, set up in 1987 to investigate complaints from building society customers; the **Insurance Ombudsman**, set up in 1981 to investigate complaints by policyholders (since 1988 this ombudsman has also operated a **Unit Trust Ombudsman** scheme); the **Investment Ombudsman**, set up in 1989 to investigate complaints by investors (the **Personal Investment Authority Ombudsman** is responsible for investigating complaints by personal investors); and the **Pensions Ombudsman**, set up in 1993 to investigate complaints regarding pension schemes.

financial year *n Brit.* **1** any annual period at the end of which a firm's accounts are made up. **2** the annual period ending April 5, over which Budget estimates are made by the British Government. ◆ US and Canad. equivalent: **fiscal year.**

financier (fɪ'nænsɪə, faɪ-) *n* a person who is engaged in large-scale financial operations.

financing gap *n* the difference between a country's requirements for foreign exchange to finance its debts and imports and its income from overseas.

finback ('fɪnˌbæk) *n* another name for **rorqual.**

finch (fɪntʃ) *n* any of various songbirds having a short stout bill for feeding on seeds, such as the bullfinch, chaffinch, siskin, and canary. [OE *finc*]

find ➊ (faɪnd) *vb* **finds, finding, found.** (*mainly tr*) **1** to meet with or discover by chance. **2** to discover or obtain, esp. by search or effort: *to find happiness.* **3** (*may take a clause as object*) to realize: *he found that nobody knew.* **4** (*may take a clause as object*) to consider: *I find this wine a little sour.* **5** to look for and point out (something to be criticized). **6** (*also intr*) *Law.* to determine an issue and pronounce a verdict (upon): *the court found the accused guilty.* **7** to regain (something lost or not functioning): *to find one's tongue.* **8** to reach (a target): *the bullet found its mark.* **9** to provide, esp. with difficulty: *we'll find room for you too.* **10** to be able to pay: *I can't find that amount of money.* **11 find oneself.** to realize and accept one's true character; discover one's vocation. **12 find one's feet.** to become capable or confident. ◆ *n* **13** a person, thing, etc., that is found, esp. a valuable discovery. [OE *findan*]

finder ('faɪndə) *n* **1** a person or thing that finds. **2** *Physics.* a small telescope fitted to a more powerful larger telescope. **3** *Photog.* short for **viewfinder. 4 finders keepers.** *Inf.* whoever finds something has the right to keep it.

fin de siècle *French.* (fɛ̃ də sjɛklə) *n* **1** the end of the 19th century. ◆ *adj* ***fin-de-siècle.*** **2** of or relating to the close of the 19th century. **3** decadent, esp. in artistic tastes.

finding ➊ ('faɪndɪŋ) *n* **1** a thing that is found or discovered. **2** *Law.* the conclusion reached after a judicial inquiry; verdict.

find out ➊ *vb* (*adv*) **1** to gain knowledge of (something); learn. **2** to detect the crime, deception, etc., of (someone).

fine[1] ➊ (faɪn) *adj* **1** very good of its kind: *a fine speech.* **2** superior in skill or accomplishment: *a fine violinist.* **3** (of weather) clear and dry. **4** enjoyable or satisfying: *a fine time.* **5** (*postpositive*) *Inf.* quite well: *I feel fine.* **6** satisfactory; acceptable: *that's fine by me.* **7** of delicate composition or careful workmanship: *fine crystal.* **8** (of precious metals) pure or having a high degree of purity: *fine silver.* **9** discriminating: *a fine eye for antique brasses.* **10** abstruse or subtle: *a fine point.* **11** very thin or slender: *fine hair.* **12** very small: *fine print.* **13** (of edges, blades, etc.) sharp; keen. **14** ornate, showy, or smart. **15** good-looking: *a fine young woman.* **16** polished, elegant, or refined: *a fine gentleman.* **17** *Cricket.* (of a fielding position) oblique to and behind the wicket: *fine leg.* **18** (*prenominal*) *Inf.* disappointing or terrible: *a fine mess.* ◆ *adv* **19** *Inf.* all

THESAURUS

final *adj* **1 = last**, closing, concluding, end, eventual, last-minute, latest, terminal, terminating, ultimate **2 = conclusive**, absolute, decided, decisive, definite, definitive, determinate, finished, incontrovertible, irrevocable, settled
Antonyms *adj ≠ last*: earliest, first, initial, introductory, maiden, opening, original, precursory, prefatory, premier, preparatory

finale *n* **1 = ending**, climax, close, conclusion, crowning glory, culmination, denouement, epilogue, finis, last act
Antonyms *n* commencement, exordium, foreword, intro (*inf.*), lead-in, opening, overture, preamble, preface, preliminaries, prelude, proem, prolegomenon, prologue

finality *n* **1 = conclusiveness**, certitude, decidedness, decisiveness, definiteness, inevitableness, irrevocability, resolution, unavoidability

finalize *vb* **1, 2 = complete**, agree, clinch, conclude, decide, settle, sew up (*inf.*), shake hands, tie up, work out, wrap up (*inf.*)

finally *adv* **1 = eventually**, at last, at length, at long last, at the end of the day, at the last, at the last moment, in the end, in the fullness of time, in the long run, lastly, ultimately, when all is said and done **2 = in conclusion**, in summary, lastly, to conclude **3 = conclusively**, beyond the shadow of a doubt, completely, convincingly, decisively, for all time, for ever, for good, inescapably, inexorably, irrevocably, once and for all, permanently

finance *n* **1 = economics**, accounts, banking, business, commerce, financial affairs, investment, money, money management **3** *plural* = **resources**, affairs, assets, capital, cash, financial condition, funds, money, wherewithal ◆ *vb* **4 = fund**, back, bankroll (*US*), float, guarantee, pay for, provide security for, set up in business, subsidize, support, underwrite

financial *adj* **1 = economic**, budgeting, fiscal, monetary, money, pecuniary

financing *n* **4 = funding**, costs, expenditure, expense(s), operating expenses, outlay

find *vb* **1, 2 = discover**, catch sight of, chance upon, come across, come up with, descry, encounter, espy, expose, ferret out, hit upon, lay one's hand on, light upon, locate, meet, recognize, run to earth, run to ground, spot, stumble upon, track down, turn up, uncover, unearth **2 = get**, achieve, acquire, attain, earn, gain, obtain, procure, win **3 = realise**, arrive at, ascertain, become aware, detect, discover, experience, learn, note, notice, observe, perceive, remark **7 = regain**, get back, recover, repossess, retrieve **10 = provide**, be responsible for, bring, contribute, cough up (*inf.*), furnish, purvey, supply ◆ *n* **13 = discovery**, acquisition, asset, bargain, catch, good buy
Antonyms *vb ≠ discover*: lose, mislay, misplace, miss, overlook

finding *n* **2 = conclusion**, award, decision, decree, judgment, pronouncement, recommendation, verdict

find out *vb* **1 = learn**, detect, discover, note, observe, perceive, realize **2 = detect**, bring to light, catch, disclose, expose, reveal, rumble (*Brit. inf.*), uncover, unmask

fine[1] *adj* **1, 2 = excellent**, accomplished, admirable, beautiful, choice, divine, exceptional, exquisite, first-class, first-rate, great, magnificent, masterly, ornate, outstanding, rare, select, showy, skilful, splendid, sterling, superior, supreme, world-class **3 = sunny**, balmy, bright, clear, clement, cloudless, dry, fair, pleasant **6 = satisfactory**, acceptable, agreeable, all right, convenient, good, hunky-dory (*inf.*), O.K. *or* okay (*inf.*), suitable **7, 11 = delicate**, dainty, elegant, expensive, exquisite, fragile, quality **7, 11 = slender**, delicate, diaphanous, fine-grained,

right: *that suits me fine.* **20** finely. ◆ *vb* **fines, fining, fined. 21** to make or become finer; refine. **22** (often foll. by *down* or *away*) to make or become smaller. [C13: from OF *fin,* from L *finis* end, boundary, as in *finis honōrum* the highest degree of honour]
▸ **'finely** *adv* ▸ **'fineness** *n*

fine[2] ❶ (faɪn) *n* **1** a certain amount of money exacted as a penalty: *a parking fine.* **2** a payment made by a tenant at the start of his tenancy to reduce his subsequent rent; premium. **3 in fine. 3a** in short. **3b** in conclusion. ◆ *vb* **fines, fining, fined. 4** (*tr*) to impose a fine on. [C12 (in the sense: conclusion, settlement): from OF *fin;* see FINE[1]]

fine[3] ('fiːneɪ) *n Music.* the point at which a piece is to end. [It., from L *finis* end]

fine art *n* **1** art produced chiefly for its aesthetic value. **2** (*often pl*) any of the fields in which such art is produced, such as painting, sculpture, and engraving.

fine-draw *vb* **fine-draws, fine-drawing, fine-drew, fine-drawn.** (*tr*) to sew together so finely that the join is scarcely noticeable.

fine-drawn *adj* **1** (of arguments, distinctions, etc.) precise or subtle. **2** (of wire, etc.) drawn out until very fine.

fine-grained *adj* (of wood, leather, etc.) having a fine smooth even grain.

finery[1] ❶ ('faɪnərɪ) *n* elaborate or showy decoration, esp. clothing and jewellery.

finery[2] ('faɪnərɪ) *n, pl* **fineries.** a hearth for converting cast iron into wrought iron. [C17: from OF *finerie,* from *finer* to refine; see FINE[1]]

fines herbes (*French* finz ɛrb) *pl n* a mixture of finely chopped herbs, used to flavour omelettes, salads, etc.

finespun ('faɪn'spʌn) *adj* **1** spun or drawn out to a fine thread. **2** excessively subtle or refined.

finesse ❶ (fɪ'nɛs) *n* **1** elegant skill in style or performance. **2** subtlety and tact in handling difficult situations. **3** *Bridge, whist.* an attempt to win a trick when opponents hold a high card in the suit led by playing a lower card. **4** a trick, artifice, or strategy. ◆ *vb* **finesses, finessing, finessed. 5** to bring about with finesse. **6** to play (a card) as a finesse. [C15: from OF, from *fin* fine, delicate; see FINE[1]]

fine-tooth comb *or* **fine-toothed comb** *n* **1** a comb with fine teeth set closely together. **2 go over** (*or* **through**) **with a fine-tooth(ed) comb.** to examine very thoroughly.

fine-tune *vb* **fine-tunes, fine-tuning, fine-tuned.** (*tr*) to make fine adjustments to (something) in order to obtain optimum performance.

finger ❶ ('fɪŋgə) *n* **1a** any of the digits of the hand, often excluding the thumb. **1b** (*as modifier*): *a finger bowl.* **1c** (*in combination*): *a fingernail.* Related adj: **digital. 2** the part of a glove made to cover a finger. **3** something that resembles a finger in shape or function: *a finger of land.* **4** the length or width of a finger used as a unit of measurement. **5** a quantity of liquid in a glass, etc., as deep as a finger is wide. **6 get** *or* **pull one's finger out.** *Brit. inf.* to begin or speed up activity, esp. after initial delay. **7 have a** (*or* **one's**) **finger in the pie. 7a** to have an interest in or take part in some activity. **7b** to meddle or interfere. **8 lay** *or* **put one's finger on.** to indicate or locate accurately. **9 not lift** (*or* **raise**) **a finger.** (*foll. by an infinitive*) not to make any effort (to do something). **10 twist** *or* **wrap around one's little finger.** to have easy and complete control or influence over. **11 put the finger on.** *Inf.* to inform on or identify, esp. for the police. ◆ *vb* **12** (*tr*) to touch or manipulate with the fingers; handle. **13** (*tr*) *Inf., chiefly US.* to identify as a criminal or suspect. **14** to use one's fingers in playing (an instrument, such as a piano or clarinet). **15** to indicate on (a composition or part) the fingering required by a pianist, etc. [OE]
▸ **'fingerless** *adj*

fingerboard ('fɪŋgə,bɔːd) *n* the long strip of hard wood on a violin, guitar, etc. upon which the strings are stopped by the fingers.

finger bowl *n* a small bowl filled with water for rinsing the fingers at the table after a meal.

finger buffet ('bʊfeɪ) *n* a buffet meal at which food that may be picked up in the fingers (**finger food**), such as canapés or vol-au-vents, is served.

fingered ('fɪŋgəd) *adj* **1** marked or dirtied by handling. **2a** having a finger or fingers. **2b** (*in combination*): *red-fingered.* **3** (of a musical part) having numerals indicating the fingering.

fingering ('fɪŋgərɪŋ) *n* **1** the technique or art of using one's fingers in playing a musical instrument, esp. the piano. **2** the numerals in a musical part indicating this.

fingerling ('fɪŋgəlɪŋ) *n* a very young fish, esp. the parr of salmon or trout.

fingermark ('fɪŋgə,mɑːk) *n* a mark left by dirty or greasy fingers on paintwork, walls, etc.

fingernail ('fɪŋgə,neɪl) *n* a thin horny translucent plate covering part of the dorsal surface of the end joint of each finger.

finger painting *n* the process or art of painting with **finger paints** of starch, glycerine, and pigments, using the fingers, hand, or arm.

finger post *n* a signpost showing a pointing finger or hand.

fingerprint ('fɪŋgə,prɪnt) *n* **1** an impression of the pattern of ridges on the surface of the end joint of each finger and thumb. **2** any unique identifying characteristic. ◆ *vb* (*tr*) **3** to take an inked impression of the fingerprints of (a person). **4** to take a sample of (a person's) DNA.

fingerstall ('fɪŋgə,stɔːl) *n* a protective covering for a finger. Also called: **cot.**

fingertip ('fɪŋgə,tɪp) *n* **1** the end joint or tip of a finger. **2 at one's fingertips.** readily available.

finial ('faɪnɪəl) *n* **1** an ornament on top of a spire, etc., esp. in the form of a fleur-de-lys. **2** an ornament at the top of a piece of furniture, etc. [C14: from *finial* (adj), var. of FINAL]

finicky ❶ ('fɪnɪkɪ) *or* **finicking** *adj* **1** excessively particular; fussy. **2** overelaborate. [C19: from *finical,* from FINE[1]]

finis ('fɪnɪs) *n* the end; finish: used at the end of books, films, etc. [C15: from L]

finish ❶ ('fɪnɪʃ) *vb* (*mainly tr*) **1** to bring to an end; conclude or stop. **2** (*intr; sometimes foll. by up*) to be at or come to the end; use up. **3** to bring to a desired or complete condition. **4** to put a particular surface texture on (wood, cloth, etc.). **5** (often foll. by *off*) to destroy or defeat completely. **6** to train (a person) in social graces and talents. **7** (*intr;* foll. by *with*) to end a relationship or association. ◆ *n* **8** the final or last stage or part; end. **9** the death or absolute defeat of a person or one side in a conflict: *a fight to the finish.* **10** the surface texture or appearance of wood, cloth, etc.: *a rough finish.* **11** a thing, event, etc., that completes. **12** completeness and high quality of workmanship. **13** *Sport.* ability to sprint at the end of a race. [C14: from OF, from L *finīre;* see FINE[1]]
▸ **'finished** *adj* ▸ **'finisher** *n*

finishing school *n* a private school for girls that teaches social graces.

finite ❶ ('faɪnaɪt) *adj* **1** bounded in magnitude or spatial or temporal extent. **2** *Maths, logic.* having a countable number of elements. **3** limited or restricted in nature: *human existence is finite.* **4** denoting any form of a verb inflected for grammatical features such as person, number, and tense. [C15: from L *finītus* limited, from *finīre* to limit, end]
▸ **'finitely** *adv* ▸ **'finiteness** *or* **finitude** ('faɪnɪ,tjuːd) *n*

fink (fɪŋk) *n Sl., chiefly US & Canad.* **1** a strikebreaker. **2** an unpleasant or contemptible person. [C20: from ?]

THESAURUS

flimsy, gauzy, gossamer, light, lightweight, powdered, powdery, pulverized, sheer, small, thin **8** = **pure**, clear, refined, solid, sterling, unadulterated, unalloyed, unpolluted **10** = **subtle**, abstruse, acute, critical, discriminating, fastidious, hairsplitting, intelligent, keen, minute, nice, precise, quick, refined, sensitive, sharp, tasteful, tenuous **13** = **sharp**, brilliant, cutting, honed, keen, polished, razor-sharp **15** = **good-looking**, attractive, bonny, handsome, lovely, smart, striking, stylish, well-favoured
Antonyms *adj* ≠ **excellent:** indifferent, inferior, poor, second rate, substandard ≠ **sunny:** cloudy, dull, overcast, unpleasant ≠ **delicate:** blunt, coarse, crude, dull, heavy, rough

fine[2] *n* **1** = **penalty**, amercement (*obs.*), damages, forfeit, punishment ◆ *vb* **4** = **penalize**, amerce (*arch.*), mulct, punish

finery[1] *n* = **splendour**, best bib and tucker (*inf.*), decorations, frippery, gear (*inf.*), gewgaws, glad rags (*inf.*), ornaments, showiness, Sunday best, trappings, trinkets

finesse *n* **1, 2** = **skill**, adeptness, adroitness, artfulness, cleverness, craft, delicacy, diplomacy, discretion, know-how (*inf.*), polish, quickness, savoir-faire, sophistication, subtlety, tact **4** = **stratagem**, artifice, bluff, feint, manoeuvre, ruse, trick, wile

finger *n* **8 put one's finger on** = **identify**, bring to mind, discover, find out, hit the nail on the head, hit upon, indicate, locate, pin down, place, recall, remember ◆ *vb* **12** = **touch**, feel, fiddle with (*inf.*), handle, manipulate, maul, meddle with, paw (*inf.*), play about with, toy with

finicky *adj* **1** = **fussy**, choosy (*inf.*), critical, dainty, difficult, fastidious, finicking, hard to please, nit-picking (*inf.*), overnice, overparticular, particular, picky (*inf.*), scrupulous, squeamish

finish *vb* **1** = **stop**, accomplish, achieve, bring to a close *or* conclusion, carry through, cease, close, complete, conclude, culminate, deal with, discharge, do, end, execute, finalize, fulfil, get done, get out of the way, make short work of, put the finishing touch(es) to, put the tin lid on, round off, settle, terminate, wind up, wrap up (*inf.*) **2** = **consume**, deplete, devour, dispatch, dispose of, drain, drink, eat, empty, exhaust, expend, spend, use, use up **4** = **coat**, face, gild, lacquer, polish, smooth off, stain, texture, veneer, wax **5** = **destroy**, annihilate, best, bring down, defeat, dispose of, drive to the wall, exterminate, get rid of, kill, move in for the kill, overcome, overpower, put an end to, put paid to, rout, ruin, worst **6** = **perfect**, elaborate, polish, refine ◆ *n* **8** = **end**, cessation, close, closing, completion, conclusion, culmination, denouement, ending, finale, last stage(s), run-in, termination, winding up (*inf.*), wind-up **9** = **defeat**, annihilation, bankruptcy, curtains (*inf.*), death, end, end of the road, liquidation, ruin **10** = **surface**, appearance, grain, lustre, patina, polish, shine, smoothness, texture
Antonyms *vb* ≠ **stop:** begin, commence, create, embark on, instigate, start, undertake ◆ *n* ≠ **end:** beginning, birth, commencement, conception, genesis, inauguration, inception, instigation, preamble, preface, prologue

finished *adj* **1** = **over**, accomplished, achieved, closed, complete, completed, concluded, done, ended, entire, final, finalized, full, in the past, over and done with, sewed up (*inf.*), shut, terminated, through, tied up, wrapped up (*inf.*) **2** = **spent**, done, drained, empty, exhausted, gone, played out (*inf.*), used up **5** = **ruined**, bankrupt, defeated, devastated, done for (*inf.*), doomed, gone, liquidated, lost, through, undone, washed up (*inf., chiefly US*), wiped out, wound up, wrecked
Antonyms *adj* ≠ **over:** begun, incomplete

finite *adj* **1** = **limited**, bounded, circumscribed, conditioned, delimited, demarcated, restricted, subject to limitations, terminable
Antonyms *adj* boundless, endless, eternal, ever-

Finlandization *or* **Finlandisation** (ˌfɪnləndaɪˈzeɪʃən) *n* neutralization of a small country by a superpower, using conciliation rather than confrontation, as the former Soviet Union did in relation to Finland.

Finn (fɪn) *n* a native, inhabitant, or citizen of Finland. [OE *Finnas* (pl)]

finnan haddock (ˈfɪnən) *or* **haddie** (ˈhædɪ) *n* smoked haddock. [C18: *finnan* after *Findon,* a village in NE Scotland]

Finnic (ˈfɪnɪk) *n* **1** one of the two branches of the Finno-Ugric family of languages, including Finnish and several languages of NE Europe. ◆ *adj* **2** of or relating to this group of languages or to the Finns.

Finnish (ˈfɪnɪʃ) *adj* **1** of or characteristic of Finland, the Finns, or their language. ◆ *n* **2** the official language of Finland, belonging to the Finno-Ugric family.

Finno-Ugric (ˈfɪnəʊˈuːgrɪk, -ˈjuː-) *or* **Finno-Ugrian** *n* **1** a family of languages spoken in Scandinavia, E Europe, and W Asia, including Finnish, Estonian, and Hungarian. ◆ *adj* **2** of, relating to, speaking, or belonging to this family of languages.

finny (ˈfɪnɪ) *adj* **finnier, finniest. 1** *Poetic.* relating to or containing many fishes. **2** having or resembling a fin or fins.

fino (ˈfiːnəʊ) *n* a very dry sherry. [Sp.: FINE[1]]

fiord (fjɔːd) *n* a variant spelling of **fjord.**

fioriture (ˌfjɔːrɪˈtʊəreɪ) *pl n Music.* flourishes; embellishments. [C19: It, from *fiorire* to flower]

fipple (ˈfɪpᵊl) *n* a wooden plug forming a flue in the end of a pipe, as the mouthpiece of a recorder. [C17: from ?]

fipple flute *n* an end-blown flute provided with a fipple, such as the recorder or flageolet.

fir (fɜː) *n* **1** any of a genus of pyramidal coniferous trees having single needle-like leaves and erect cones. **2** any of various other related trees, such as the Douglas fir. **3** the wood of any of these trees. [OE *furh*]

fire ➊ (faɪə) *n* **1** the state of combustion in which inflammable material burns, producing heat, flames, and often smoke. **2a** a mass of burning coal, wood, etc., used esp. in a hearth to heat a room. **2b** (*in combination*): *firelighter.* **3** a destructive conflagration, as of a forest, building, etc. **4** a device for heating a room, etc. **5** something resembling a fire in light or brilliance: *a diamond's fire.* **6** the act of discharging weapons, artillery, etc. **7** a burst or rapid volley: *a fire of questions.* **8** intense passion; ardour. **9** liveliness, as of imagination, etc. **10** fever and inflammation. **11** a severe trial or torment (esp. in **go through fire and water**). **12 between two fires.** under attack from two sides. **13 catch fire.** to ignite. **14 on fire. 14a** in a state of ignition. **14b** ardent or eager. **15 open fire.** to start firing a gun, artillery, etc. **16 play with fire.** to be involved in something risky. **17 set fire to** *or* **set on fire. 17a** to ignite. **17b** to arouse or excite. **18 under fire.** being attacked, as by weapons or by harsh criticism. **19** (*modifier*) *Astrol.* of or relating to a group of three signs of the zodiac, Aries, Leo, and Sagittarius. ◆ *vb* **fires, firing, fired. 20** to discharge (a firearm or projectile), or (of a firearm, etc.) to be discharged. **21** to detonate (an explosive charge or device), or (of such a charge or device) to be detonated. **22** (*intr*) (of an engine) to start working; ignite. **23** (*tr*) *Inf.* to dismiss from employment. **24** (*tr*) *Ceramics.* to bake in a kiln to harden the clay, etc. **25** to kindle or be kindled. **26** (*tr*) to provide with fuel: *oil fires the heating system.* **27** (*tr*) to subject to heat. **28** (*tr*) to heat slowly so as to dry. **29** (*tr*) to arouse to strong emotion. **30** to glow or cause to glow. ◆ *sentence substitute.* **31** a cry to warn others of a fire. **32** the order to begin firing a gun, artillery, etc. [OE *fȳr*]
▸ˈ**firer** *n*

fire alarm *n* a device to give warning of fire, esp. a bell, siren, or hooter.

fire appliance *n* another name for fire engine.

firearm ➊ (ˈfaɪərˌɑːm) *n* a weapon from which a projectile can be discharged by an explosion caused by igniting gunpowder, etc.

fireback (ˈfaɪəˌbæk) *n* an ornamental iron slab against the back wall of a hearth.

fireball (ˈfaɪəˌbɔːl) *n* **1** a ball-shaped discharge of lightning. **2** the region of hot ionized gas at the centre of a nuclear explosion. **3** *Astron.* a large bright meteor. **4** *Sl.* an energetic person.

fire blight *n* a disease of apples, pears, and similar fruit trees, caused by a bacterium and characterized by blackening of the blossoms and leaves.

fireboat (ˈfaɪəˌbəʊt) *n* a motor vessel equipped with fire-fighting apparatus.

firebomb (ˈfaɪəˌbɒm) *n* another name for **incendiary** (sense 6).

firebox (ˈfaɪəˌbɒks) *n* the furnace chamber of a boiler in a steam locomotive.

firebrand ➊ (ˈfaɪəˌbrænd) *n* **1** a piece of burning wood. **2** a person who causes unrest.

firebreak (ˈfaɪəˌbreɪk) *n* a strip of open land in forest or prairie, serving to arrest the advance of a fire.

firebrick (ˈfaɪəˌbrɪk) *n* a refractory brick made of fire clay, used for lining furnaces, flues, etc.

fire brigade *n Chiefly Brit.* an organized body of firefighters.

firebug (ˈfaɪəˌbʌg) *n Inf.* a person who deliberately sets fire to property.

fire clay *n* a heat-resistant clay used in the making of firebricks, furnace linings, etc.

fire company *n* **1** an insurance company selling policies relating to fire risk. **2** *US.* an organized body of firemen.

fire control *n Mil.* the procedures by which weapons are brought to engage a target.

firecracker (ˈfaɪəˌkrækə) *n* a small cardboard container filled with explosive powder.

firecrest (ˈfaɪəˌkrest) *n* a small European warbler having a crown striped with yellow, black, and white.

firedamp (ˈfaɪəˌdæmp) *n* an explosive mixture of hydrocarbons, chiefly methane, formed in coal mines. See also **afterdamp.**

firedog (ˈfaɪəˌdɒg) *n* either of a pair of metal stands used to support logs in an open fire.

fire door *n* **1** a door made of noncombustible material that prevents a fire spreading within a building. **2** a similar door leading to the outside of a building that can be easily opened from inside; emergency exit.

fire-eater *n* **1** a performer who simulates the swallowing of fire. **2** a belligerent person.

fire engine *n* a vehicle that carries firemen and fire-fighting equipment to a fire.

fire escape *n* a means of evacuating persons from a building in the event of fire.

fire-extinguisher *n* a portable device for extinguishing fires, usually consisting of a canister with a directional nozzle used to direct a spray of water, etc., onto the fire.

firefighter (ˈfaɪəˌfaɪtə) *n* a person who assists in extinguishing fires and rescuing those endangered by them, usually a public employee or trained volunteer.
▸ˈ**fire-ˌfighting** *n, adj*

firefly (ˈfaɪəˌflaɪ) *n, pl* **fireflies.** a nocturnal beetle common in warm and tropical regions, having luminescent abdominal organs.

fireguard (ˈfaɪəˌgɑːd) *n* a meshed frame put before an open fire to protect against falling logs, sparks, etc.

fire hall *n Canad.* a fire station.

fire hydrant *n* a hydrant for use as an emergency supply for fighting fires.

fire insurance *n* insurance covering damage or loss caused by fire or lightning.

fire irons *pl n* metal fireside implements, such as poker, shovel, and tongs.

firelock (ˈfaɪəˌlɒk) *n* **1** an obsolete type of gunlock with a priming mechanism ignited by sparks. **2** a gun or musket having such a lock.

fireman (ˈfaɪəmən) *n, pl* **firemen. 1** a man who fights fires; firefighter. **2a** (on steam locomotives) the man who stokes the fire. **2b** (on diesel and electric locomotives) the driver's assistant. **3** a man who tends furnaces; stoker.

fire opal *n* an orange-red translucent variety of opal, valued as a gemstone.

fireplace (ˈfaɪəˌpleɪs) *n* **1** an open recess at the base of a chimney, etc., for a fire; hearth. **2** *Austral.* an authorized place or installation for outside cooking, esp. by a roadside.

fireplug (ˈfaɪəˌplʌg) *n* another name (esp. US and NZ) for **fire hydrant.**

fire power *n Mil.* **1** the amount of fire that can be delivered by a unit or weapon. **2** the capability of delivering fire.

fireproof (ˈfaɪəˌpruːf) *adj* **1** capable of resisting damage by fire. ◆ *vb* **2** (*tr*) to make resistant to fire.

fire raiser *n* a person who deliberately sets fire to property, etc.
▸**fire raising** *n*

fire screen *n* **1** a decorative screen placed in the hearth when there is no fire. **2** a screen placed before a fire to protect the face.

fire ship *n* a vessel loaded with explosives and used, esp. formerly, as a bomb by igniting it and directing it to drift among an enemy's warships.

fireside (ˈfaɪəˌsaɪd) *n* **1** the hearth. **2** family life; the home.

fire station *n* a building where fire-fighting vehicles and equipment are stationed and where firefighters on duty wait. Also called (US): **firehouse, station house.**

firestorm (ˈfaɪəˌstɔːm) *n* an uncontrollable blaze sustained by violent winds that are drawn into the column of rising hot air over the burning area: often the result of heavy bombing.

THESAURUS

lasting, immeasurable, infinite, interminable, limitless, perpetual, unbounded

fire *n* **1-3 = flames,** blaze, combustion, conflagration, inferno **6 = bombardment,** barrage, cannonade, flak, fusillade, hail, salvo, shelling, sniping, volley **8 = passion,** animation, ardour, brio, burning passion, dash, eagerness, élan, enthusiasm, excitement, fervency, fervour, force, heat, impetuosity, intensity, life, light, lustre, pizzazz *or* pizazz (*inf.*), radiance, scintillation, sparkle, spirit, splendour, verve, vigour, virtuosity, vivacity **14 on fire: a = ardent,** ablaze, aflame, alight, blazing, fiery, flaming, in flames **b = eager,** enthusiastic, excited, inspired, passionate ◆ *vb* **20, 21 = shoot,** detonate, discharge, eject, explode, hurl, launch, let loose (*inf.*), let off, loose, pull the trigger, set off, shell, touch off **23** *Informal* **= dismiss,** cashier, discharge, give marching orders, give the boot (*sl.*), give the bullet (*Brit. sl.*), give the push, make redundant, sack (*inf.*), show the door **25 = set fire to,** enkindle, ignite, kindle, light, put a match to, set ablaze, set aflame, set alight, set on fire, torch **29 = inspire,** animate, arouse, electrify, enliven, excite, galvanize, impassion, incite, inflame, inspirit, irritate, quicken, rouse, stir

firearm *n* **= weapon,** gun, handgun, heater (*US sl.*), piece (*sl.*), pistol, revolver, rod (*sl.*), shooter (*sl.*)

firebrand *n* **2 = rabble-rouser,** agitator, demagogue, fomenter, incendiary, instigator, soapbox orator, tub-thumper

fire trail *n Austral.* a permanent track cleared through the bush to provide access for fire-fighting.
firetrap ('faɪəˌtræp) *n* a building that would burn easily or one without fire escapes.
firewall ('faɪəˌwɔːl) *n* **1** a fireproof wall or partition used to impede the progress of a fire. **2** *Computing.* a computer system that isolates another computer from the Internet in order to prevent unauthorized access.
firewater ('faɪəˌwɔːtə) *n* any strong spirit, esp. whisky.
fireweed ('faɪəˌwiːd) *n* any of various plants that appear as first vegetation in burnt-over areas.
firework ('faɪəˌwɜːk) *n* a device, such as a Catherine wheel or rocket, in which combustible materials are ignited and produce coloured flames, sparks, and smoke.
fireworks 🅣 ('faɪəˌwɜːks) *pl n* **1** a show in which large numbers of fireworks are let off. **2** *Inf.* an exciting exhibition, as of musical virtuosity or wit. **3** *Inf.* a burst of temper.
firing ('faɪərɪŋ) *n* **1** the process of baking ceramics, etc., in a kiln. **2** the act of stoking a fire or furnace. **3** a discharge of a firearm. **4** something used as fuel, such as coal or wood.
firing line *n* **1** *Mil.* the positions from which fire is delivered. **2** the leading or most advanced position in an activity.
firkin ('fɜːkɪn) *n* **1** a small wooden barrel. **2** *Brit.* a unit of capacity equal to nine gallons. [C14 *fir*, from MDu. *vierde* FOURTH + -KIN]
firm[1] 🅣 (fɜːm) *adj* **1** not soft or yielding to a touch or pressure. **2** securely in position; stable or stationary. **3** decided; settled. **4** enduring or steady. **5** having determination or strength. **6** (of prices, markets, etc.) tending to rise. ◆ *adv* **7** in a secure or unyielding manner: *he stood firm.* ◆ *vb* **8** (sometimes foll. by *up*) to make or become firm. [C14: from L *firmus*]
▸ **'firmly** *adv* ▸ **'firmness** *n*
firm[2] 🅣 (fɜːm) *n* **1** a business partnership. **2** any commercial enterprise. **3** a team of doctors and their assistants. **4 the.** (*often cap.*) *Sl.* any organized group of people, such as intelligence agents, criminals, or football hooligans. [C16 (in the sense: signature): from Sp. *firma* signature, from *firmar* to sign, from L *firmāre* to confirm, from *firmus* firm]
firmament 🅣 ('fɜːməmənt) *n* the expanse of the sky; heavens. [C13: from LL *firmāmentum* sky (considered as fixed above the earth), from L: prop, support, from *firmāre* to make FIRM[1]]
firmware ('fɜːmˌwɛə) *n Computing.* a series of fixed instructions built into the hardware of a computer that can be changed only if the hardware itself is modified in some way.
first 🅣 (fɜːst) *adj* (*usually prenominal*) **1a** coming before all others. **1b** (*as n*): *I was the first to arrive.* **2** preceding all others in numbering or counting order; the ordinal number of *one.* Often written: 1st. **3** rated, graded, or ranked above all other levels. **4** denoting the lowest forward ratio of a gearbox in a motor vehicle. **5** *Music.* **5a** denoting the highest part assigned to one of the voice parts in a chorus or one of the sections of an orchestra: *the first violins.* **5b** denoting the principal player in a specific orchestral section: *he plays first horn.* **6 first thing.** as the first action of the day: *I'll see you first thing tomorrow.* ◆ *n* **7** the beginning; outset: *I couldn't see at first because of the mist.* **8** *Education, chiefly Brit.* an honours degree of the highest class. Full term: **first-class honours degree. 9** the lowest forward ratio of a gearbox in a motor vehicle. ◆ *adv* **10** Also: **firstly.** before anything else in order, time, importance, etc.: *do this first.* **11 first and last.** on the whole. **12 from first to last.** throughout. **13** for the first time: *I've loved you since I first saw you.* **14** (*sentence modifier*) in the first place or beginning of a series of actions. [OE *fyrest*]
first aid *n* **a** immediate medical assistance given in an emergency. **b** (*as modifier*): *first-aid box.*
first-born *adj* **1** eldest of the children in a family. ◆ *n* **2** the eldest child in a family.
first class 🅣 *n* **1** the class or grade of the best or highest value, quality, etc. ◆ *adj* (**first-class** *when prenominal*) **2** of the best or highest class or grade: *a first-class citizen.* **3** excellent. **4** of or denoting the most comfortable class of accommodation in a hotel, aircraft, train, etc. **5** (in Britain) of mail that is processed most quickly. ◆ *adv* **first-class. 6** by first-class mail, means of transportation, etc.
first-day cover *n Philately.* an envelope postmarked on the first day of the issue of its stamps.
first-degree burn *n Pathol.* the least severe type of burn, in which the skin surface is red and painful.
first-foot *Chiefly Scot.* ◆ *n also* **first-footer. 1** the first person to enter a household in the New Year. ◆ *vb* **2** to enter (a house) as first-foot.
▸ **'first-'footing** *n*
first fruits *pl n* **1** the first results or profits of an undertaking. **2** fruit that ripens first.
first-hand 🅣 *adj, adv* **1** from the original source: *he got the news first-hand.* **2 at first hand.** directly.
first lady *n* (*often caps.*) (in the US) the wife or official hostess of a state governor or a president.
firstling ('fɜːstlɪŋ) *n* the first, esp. the first offspring.
first-loss policy *n* an insurance policy for goods in which a total loss is extremely unlikely and the insurer agrees to provide cover for a sum less than the total value of the property.
firstly ('fɜːstlɪ) *adv* another word for **first.**
first mate *n* an officer second in command to the captain of a merchant ship.
First Minister *n* **1** the chief minister of the Northern Ireland Assembly. **2** the chief minister of the Scottish Parliament.
first mortgage *n* a mortgage that has priority over other mortgages on the same property.
first name *n* a name given to a person at birth, as opposed to a surname. Also called: **Christian name, forename, given name.**
First Nation *n Canad.* a formally recognized group of Indians on a reserve.
first night *n* **a** the first public performance of a play, etc. **b** (*as modifier*): *first-night nerves.*
first offender *n* a person convicted of a criminal offence for the first time.
first officer *n* **1** another name for **first mate. 2** the member of an aircraft crew who is second in command to the captain.
first-past-the-post *n* (*modifier*) of a voting system in which a candidate may be elected by a simple majority.
first person *n* a grammatical category of pronouns and verbs used by the speaker to refer to or talk about himself.
first-rate 🅣 *adj* **1** of the best or highest rated class or quality. **2** *Inf.* very good; excellent.
first reading *n* the introduction of a bill into a legislative assembly.
first refusal *n* the right to buy something before it is offered to others.
first-strike *adj* (of a nuclear missile) intended for use in an opening attack calculated to destroy the enemy's nuclear weapons.
first water *n* **1** the finest quality of diamond or other precious stone. **2** the highest grade or best quality.
firth (fɜːθ) *or* **frith** *n* a narrow inlet of the sea, esp. in Scotland. [C15: from ON *fjörthr* FJORD]
fiscal 🅣 ('fɪskᵊl) *adj* **1** of or relating to government finances, esp. tax revenues. **2** of or involving financial matters. ◆ *n* **3a** (in some countries) a public prosecutor. **3b** *Scot.* short for **procurator fiscal.** [C16: from L *fiscālis* concerning the state treasury, from *fiscus* public money]
▸ **'fiscally** *adv*
fiscal year *n* the US and Canad. term for **financial year.**

THESAURUS

fireworks *pl n* **1** = **pyrotechnics**, illuminations **3** *Informal* = **trouble**, fit of rage, hysterics, paroxysms, rage, row, storm, temper, uproar, wax (*inf., chiefly Brit.*)

firm[1] *adj* **1** = **hard**, close-grained, compact, compressed, concentrated, congealed, dense, inelastic, inflexible, jelled, jellified, rigid, set, solid, solidified, stiff, unyielding **2** = **secure**, anchored, braced, cemented, embedded, fast, fastened, fixed, immovable, motionless, riveted, robust, rooted, secured, stable, stationary, steady, strong, sturdy, taut, tight, unfluctuating, unmoving, unshakable **3-5** = **determined**, adamant, constant, definite, fixed, immovable, inflexible, obdurate, resolute, resolved, set on, settled, stalwart, staunch, steadfast, strict, true, unalterable, unbending, unfaltering, unflinching, unshakable, unshaken, unswerving, unwavering, unyielding
Antonyms *adj* ≠ **hard:** flabby, flaccid, limp, soft ≠ **secure:** flimsy, insecure, loose, shaky, unreliable, unstable, unsteady ≠ **determined:** inconstant, irresolute, wavering

firm[2] *n* **1, 2** = **company**, association, business, concern, conglomerate, corporation, enterprise, house, organization, outfit (*inf.*), partnership

firmament *n* = **sky**, empyrean (*poetic*), heaven, heavens, the blue, the skies, vault, vault of heaven, welkin (*arch.*)

firmly *adv* **4** = **securely**, enduringly, immovably, like a rock, motionlessly, steadily, tightly, unflinchingly, unshakably **4** = **resolutely**, determinedly, staunchly, steadfastly, strictly, through thick and thin, unchangeably, unwaveringly, with a rod of iron, with decision

firmness *n* **1** = **hardness**, compactness, density, fixedness, inelasticity, inflexibility, resistance, rigidity, solidity, stiffness **2** = **steadiness**, immovability, soundness, stability, strength, tautness, tensile strength, tension, tightness **3-5** = **resolve**, constancy, fixedness, fixity of purpose, inflexibility, obduracy, resolution, staunchness, steadfastness, strength of will, strictness

first *adj* **1** = **earliest**, initial, introductory, maiden, opening, original, premier, primeval, primitive, primordial, pristine **2** = **foremost**, chief, head, highest, leading, pre-eminent, prime, principal, ruling ◆ *n* **7** *As in* **from the first** = **start**, beginning, commencement, inception, introduction, outset, starting point, word go (*inf.*) ◆ *adv* **10** = **to begin with**, at the beginning, at the outset, before all else, beforehand, firstly, initially, in the first place, to start with

first class *adj* **first-class 2, 3** = **excellent**, A1 *or* A-one (*inf.*), ace (*inf.*), blue-chip, brilliant, capital, champion, choice, crack (*sl.*), elite, exceptional, exemplary, first-rate, five-star, great, marvellous, matchless, outstanding, premium, prime, second to none, sovereign, superb, superlative, tiptop, top, top-class, top-drawer, top-flight, top-notch (*inf.*), twenty-four carat, very good, world-class
Antonyms *adj* inferior, second-class, second-rate, shocking (*inf.*), terrible, third-rate

first-hand *adj, adv* **1** = **direct**, straight from the horse's mouth

first-rate *adj* **1, 2** = **excellent**, A1 *or* A-one, elite, exceptional, exclusive, first class, mean (*sl.*), mega (*sl.*), outstanding, prime, second to none, sovereign, superb, superlative, tiptop, top, top-notch (*inf.*), world-class

fiscal *adj* **2** = **financial**, budgetary, economic, monetary, money, pecuniary

fish ❶ (fɪʃ) *n, pl* **fish** *or* **fishes. 1a** any of a large group of cold-blooded aquatic vertebrates having jaws, gills, and usually fins and a skin covered in scales: includes the sharks, rays, teleosts, lungfish, etc. **1b** (*in combination*): *fishpond.* Related adj: **piscine. 2** any of various similar but jawless vertebrates, such as the hagfish and lamprey. **3** (*not in technical use*) any of various aquatic invertebrates, such as the cuttlefish and crayfish. **4** the flesh of fish used as food. **5** *Inf.* a person of little emotion or intelligence: *a poor fish.* **6 drink like a fish.** to drink (esp. alcohol) to excess. **7 have other fish to fry.** to have other activities to do, esp. more important ones. **8 like a fish out of water.** out of one's usual place. **9 make fish of one and flesh of another.** *Irish.* to discriminate unfairly between people. **10 neither fish, flesh, nor fowl.** neither this nor that. ◆ *vb* **11** (*intr*) to attempt to catch fish, as with a line and hook or with nets, traps, etc. **12** (*tr*) to fish in (a particular area of water). **13** to search (a body of water) for something or to search for something, esp. in a body of water. **14** (*intr; foll. by for*) to seek something indirectly: *to fish for compliments.* ◆ See also **fish out.** [OE *fisc*]
▸**'fish,like** *adj*

fish and chips *n* fish fillets coated with batter and deep-fried, eaten with potato chips.

fish cake *n* a fried flattened ball of flaked fish mixed with mashed potatoes.

fisher ('fɪʃə) *n* **1** a fisherman. **2** Also called: **pekan. 2a** a large North American marten having dark brown fur. **2b** the fur of this animal.

fisherman ('fɪʃəmən) *n, pl* **fishermen. 1** a person who fishes as a profession or for sport. **2** a vessel used for fishing.

fishery ('fɪʃərɪ) *n, pl* **fisheries. 1a** the industry of catching, processing, and selling fish. **1b** a place where this is carried on. **2** a place where fish are reared. **3** a fishing ground.

Fishes ('fɪʃɪz) *n* **the.** the constellation Pisces, the twelfth sign of the zodiac.

fisheye lens ('fɪʃ,aɪ) *n Photog.* a lens of small focal length, having a highly curved protruding front element that covers an angle of view of almost 180°.

fishfinger ('fɪʃ'fɪŋgə) *or US & Canad.* **fish stick** *n* an oblong piece of filleted or minced fish coated in breadcrumbs.

fish hawk *n* another name for the **osprey.**

fish-hook *n* a sharp hook used in angling, esp. one with a barb.

fishing ('fɪʃɪŋ) *n* **a** the occupation of catching fish. **b** (*as modifier*): *a fishing match.*

fishing ground *n* an area of water that is good for fishing.

fishing rod *n* a long tapered flexible pole for use with a fishing line and, usually, a reel.

fish joint *n* a connection formed by fishplates at the meeting point of two rails, beams, etc.

fishmeal ('fɪʃ,mi:l) *n* ground dried fish used as feed for farm animals, as a fertilizer, etc.

fishmonger ('fɪʃ,mʌŋgə) *n Chiefly Brit.* a retailer of fish.

fishnet ('fɪʃ,nɛt) *n* **a** an open mesh fabric resembling netting. **b** (*as modifier*): *fishnet tights.*

fish out ❶ *vb* (*tr, adv*) to find or extract (something): *to fish keys out of a pocket.*

fishplate ('fɪʃ,pleɪt) *n* a flat piece of metal joining one rail or beam to the next, esp. on railway tracks.

fishtail ('fɪʃ,teɪl) *n* **1** an aeroplane manoeuvre in which the tail is moved from side to side to reduce speed. **2** a nozzle having a long narrow slot at the top, placed over a Bunsen burner to produce a thin fanlike flame.

fishwife ('fɪʃ,waɪf) *n, pl* **fishwives. 1** a woman who sells fish. **2** a coarse scolding woman.

fishy ❶ ('fɪʃɪ) *adj* **fishier, fishiest. 1** of, involving, or suggestive of fish. **2** abounding in fish. **3** *Inf.* suspicious, doubtful, or questionable. **4** dull and lifeless: *a fishy look.*
▸**'fishily** *adv*

fissile ('fɪsaɪl) *adj* **1** *Brit.* capable of undergoing nuclear fission. **2** fissionable. **3** tending to split or capable of being split. [C17: from L, from *fissus* split]

fission ❶ ('fɪʃən) *n* **1** the act or process of splitting or breaking into parts. **2** *Biol.* a form of asexual reproduction involving a division into two or more equal parts. **3** short for **nuclear fission.** [C19: from L *fissiō* a cleaving]
▸**'fissionable** *adj*

fission-track dating *n* the dating of samples of minerals by comparing the tracks in them made by fission fragments of the uranium nuclei they contain, before and after irradiation by neutrons.

fissiparous (fɪ'sɪpərəs) *adj Biol.* reproducing by fission.
▸**fis'siparously** *adv*

fissure ❶ ('fɪʃə) *n* **1** any long narrow cleft or crack, esp. in a rock. **2** a weakness or flaw. **3** *Anat.* a narrow split or groove that divides an organ such as the brain, lung, or liver into lobes. ◆ *vb* **fissures, fissuring, fissured. 4** to crack or split apart. [C14: from Medical L *fissūra*, from L *fissus* split]

fist (fɪst) *n* **1** a hand with the fingers clenched into the palm, as for hitting. **2** Also called: **fistful.** the quantity that can be held in a fist or hand. **3** *Inf.* handwriting. **4** an informal word for **index** (sense 9). ◆ *vb* **5** (*tr*) to hit with the fist. [OE *fȳst*]

fisticuffs ('fɪstɪ,kʌfs) *pl n* combat with the fists. [C17: prob. from *fisty* with the fist + CUFF[2]]

fistula ('fɪstjʊlə) *n, pl* **fistulas** *or* **fistulae** (-,li:). *Pathol.* an abnormal opening between one hollow organ and another or between a hollow organ and the surface of the skin, caused by ulceration, malformation, etc. [C14: from L: pipe, tube, hollow reed, ulcer]
▸**'fistulous** *or* **'fistular** *adj*

fit[1] ❶ (fɪt) *vb* **fits, fitting, fitted** *or US* **fit. 1** to be appropriate or suitable for (a situation, etc.). **2** to be of the correct size or shape for (a container, etc.). **3** (*tr*) to adjust in order to render appropriate. **4** (*tr*) to supply with that which is needed. **5** (*tr*) to try clothes on (someone) in order to make adjustments if necessary. **6** (*tr*) to make competent or ready. **7** (*tr*) to locate with care. **8** (*intr*) to correspond with the facts or circumstances. ◆ *adj* **fitter, fittest. 9** appropriate. **10** having the right qualifications; qualifying. **11** in good health. **12** worthy or deserving. **13** (*foll. by an infinitive*) *Inf.* ready (to); strongly disposed (to): *she was fit to scream.* ◆ *n* **14** the manner in which something fits. **15** the act or process of fitting. **16** *Statistics.* the correspondence between observed and predicted characteristics of a distribution or model. ◆ See also **fit in, fit out.** [C14: prob. from MDu. *vitten;* rel. to ON *fitja* to knit]
▸**'fitly** *adv* ▸**'fittable** *adj*

fit[2] ❶ (fɪt) *n* **1** *Pathol.* a sudden attack or convulsion, such as an epileptic seizure. **2** a sudden spell of emotion: *a fit of anger.* **3** an impulsive period of activity or lack of activity. **4 have** *or* **throw a fit.** *Inf.* to become very angry. **5 in** *or* **by fits and starts.** in spasmodic spells. [OE *fitt* conflict]

fitch (fɪtʃ) *n* **1** a polecat. **2** the fur of the polecat. [C16: prob. from *ficheux,* from OF, from ?]

fitful ❶ ('fɪtfʊl) *adj* characterized by or occurring in irregular spells.
▸**'fitfully** *adv*

fit in *vb* **1** (*tr*) to give a place or time to. **2** (*intr, adv*) to belong or conform, esp. after adjustment: *he didn't fit in with their plans.*

fitment ('fɪtmənt) *n* **1** *Machinery.* an accessory attached to an assembly of parts. **2** *Chiefly Brit.* a detachable part of the furnishings of a room.

fitness ❶ ('fɪtnɪs) *n* **1** the state of being fit. **2** *Biol.* **2a** the degree of adaptation of an organism to its environment, determined by its genetic constitution. **2b** the ability of an organism to produce viable offspring capable of surviving to the next generation.

fit out *vb* (*tr, adv*) to equip.

fitted ❶ ('fɪtɪd) *adj* **1** designed for excellent fit: *a fitted suit.* **2** (of a carpet) cut or sewn to cover a floor completely. **3a** (of furniture) built to fit a particular space: *a fitted cupboard.* **3b** (of a room) equipped with fitted furniture: *a fitted kitchen.* **4** (of sheets) having ends that are elasticated and shaped to fit tightly over a mattress.

fitter ('fɪtə) *n* **1** a person who fits a garment, esp. when it is made for a

THESAURUS

fish *vb* **14** *foll. by* **for = seek**, angle for, elicit, hint at, hope for, hunt for, invite, look for, search for, solicit

fish out *vb* **= pull out**, extract, extricate, find, haul out, produce

fishy *adj* **1 = fishlike**, piscatorial, piscatory, piscine **3** *Informal* **= suspicious**, cock-and-bull, dodgy (*Brit., Austral., & NZ inf.*), doubtful, dubious, funny (*inf.*), implausible, improbable, odd, queer, questionable, rum (*Brit. sl.*), suspect, unlikely **4 = expressionless**, blank, deadpan, dull, glassy, glassy-eyed, inexpressive, lacklustre, lifeless, vacant, wooden

fission *n* **1 = splitting**, breaking, cleavage, division, parting, rending, rupture, schism, scission

fissure *n* **1 = crack**, breach, break, chink, cleavage, cleft, cranny, crevice, fault, fracture, gap, hole, interstice, opening, rent, rift, rupture, slit, split

fit[1] *vb* **2 = suit**, accord, agree, be consonant, belong, concur, conform, correspond, dovetail, go, interlock, join, match, meet, tally **3 = adapt**, adjust, alter, arrange, customize, dispose, fashion, modify, place, position, shape, tweak (*inf.*) **4 = equip**, accommodate, accoutre, arm, fit out, kit out, outfit, prepare, provide, rig out ◆ *adj* **9, 10, 12 = appropriate**, able, adapted, adequate, apposite, apt, becoming, capable, competent, convenient, correct, deserving, equipped, expedient, fitted, fitting, good enough, meet (*arch.*), prepared, proper, qualified, ready, right, seemly, suitable, trained, well-suited, worthy **11 = healthy**, able-bodied, as right as rain, hale, in good condition, in good shape, in good trim, robust, strapping, toned up, trim, well

Antonyms *adj* ≠ **appropriate:** amiss, ill-fitted, ill-suited, improper, inadequate, inappropriate, unfit, unprepared, unseemly, unsuitable, untimely ≠ **healthy:** flabby, in poor condition, out of shape, out of trim, unfit, unhealthy

fit[2] *n* **1 = seizure**, attack, bout, convulsion, paroxysm, spasm **2 = outbreak**, bout, burst, outburst, spell **5 in** *or* **by fits and starts = spasmodically**, erratically, fitfully, intermittently, irregularly, on and off, sporadically, unsystematically

fitful *adj* **= irregular**, broken, desultory, disturbed, erratic, flickering, fluctuating, haphazard, impulsive, inconstant, intermittent, spasmodic, sporadic, uneven, unstable, variable

Antonyms *adj* constant, equable, even, orderly, predictable, regular, steady, systematic, unchanging, uniform

fitfully *adv* **= irregularly**, by fits and starts, desultorily, erratically, in fits and starts, in snatches, intermittently, interruptedly, off and on, spasmodically, sporadically

fitness *n* **1 = appropriateness**, adaptation, applicability, aptness, competence, eligibility, pertinence, preparedness, propriety, qualifications, readiness, seemliness, suitability **1 = health**, good condition, good health, robustness, strength, vigour, wellness

fitted *adj* **3 = built-in**, permanent

particular person. **2** a person who is skilled in the assembly and adjustment of machinery, esp. of a specified sort.

fitting ('fɪtɪŋ) *adj* **1** appropriate or proper. ◆ *n* **2** an accessory or part: *an electrical fitting.* **3** (*pl*) furnishings or accessories in a building. **4** work carried out by a fitter. **5** the act of trying on clothes so that they can be adjusted to fit.
▸ **'fittingly** *adv*

Fitzgerald-Lorentz contraction *n Physics.* the contraction that a moving body exhibits when its velocity approaches that of light. [C19: after G. F. *Fitzgerald* (1851–1901), Irish physicist, and H. A. *Lorentz* (1853–1928), Du. physicist]

five (faɪv) *n* **1** the cardinal number that is the sum of four and one. **2** a numeral, 5, V, etc., representing this number. **3** the amount or quantity that is one greater than four. **4** something representing, represented by, or consisting of five units, such as a playing card with five symbols on it. **5 five o'clock.** five hours after noon or midnight. ◆ *determiner* **6a** amounting to five: *five nights.* **6b** (*as pronoun*): *choose any five you like.* ◆ See also **fives.** [OE *fīf*]

five-a-side *n* a version of soccer with five players on each side.

five-eighth *n Austral. & NZ.* a rugby player positioned between the halfbacks and three-quarters.

five-finger *n* any of various plants having five-petalled flowers or five lobed leaves, such as cinquefoil and Virginia creeper.

fivefold ('faɪv,fəʊld) *adj* **1** equal to or having five times as many or as much. **2** composed of five parts. ◆ *adv* **3** by or up to five times as many or as much.

five-o'clock shadow *n* beard growth visible late in the day on a man's shaven face.

fivepins ('faɪv,pɪnz) *n* (*functioning as sing*) a bowling game using five pins, played esp. in Canada.
▸ **'five,pin** *adj*

fiver ('faɪvə) *n Brit. inf.* a five-pound note.

fives (faɪvz) *n* (*functioning as sing*) a ball game similar to squash but played with bats or the hands.

Five-Year Plan *n* (in socialist economies) a government plan for economic development over a period of five years.

fix (fɪks) *vb* (*mainly tr*) **1** (*also intr*) to make or become firm, stable, or secure. **2** to attach or place permanently. **3** (often foll. by *up*) to settle definitely; decide. **4** to hold or direct (eyes, etc.) steadily: *he fixed his gaze on the woman.* **5** to call to attention or rivet. **6** to make rigid: *to fix one's jaw.* **7** to place or ascribe: *to fix the blame.* **8** to mend or repair. **9** *Inf.* to provide or be provided with: *how are you fixed for supplies?* **10** *Inf.* to influence (a person, etc.) unfairly, as by bribery. **11** *Sl.* to take revenge on. **12** *Inf.* to give (someone) his just deserts: *that'll fix him.* **13** *Inf., chiefly US & Canad.* to prepare: *to fix a meal.* **14** *Dialect or inf.* to spay or castrate (an animal). **15** *Photog.* to treat (a film, plate, or paper) with fixer to make permanent the image rendered visible by developer. **16** to convert (atmospheric nitrogen) into nitrogen compounds, as in the manufacture of fertilizers or the action of bacteria in the soil. **17** to reduce (a substance) to a solid state or a less volatile state. **18** (*intr*) *Sl.* to inject a narcotic drug. ◆ *n* **19** *Inf.* a predicament; dilemma. **20** the ascertaining of the navigational position, as of a ship, by radar, etc. **21** *Sl.* an intravenous injection of a narcotic such as heroin. ◆ See also **fix up.** [C15: from Med. L *fixāre,* from L *fixus* fixed, from L *figere*]
▸ **'fixable** *adj*

fixate (fɪk'seɪt) *vb* **fixates, fixating, fixated. 1** to become or cause to become fixed. **2** *Psychol.* to engage in fixation. **3** (*tr; usually passive*) *Inf.* to obsess. [C19: from L *fixus* fixed + -ATE[1]]

fixation (fɪk'seɪʃən) *n* **1** the act of fixing or the state of being fixed. **2** a preoccupation or obsession. **3** *Psychol.* **3a** the situation of being set in a certain way of thinking or acting. **3b** a strong attachment of a person to another person or an object in early life. **4** *Chem.* the conversion of nitrogen in the air into a compound, esp. a fertilizer. **5** the reduction of a substance to a nonvolatile or solid form.

fixative ('fɪksətɪv) *adj* **1** serving or tending to fix. ◆ *n* **2** a fluid sprayed over drawings to prevent smudging or one that fixes tissues and cells for microscopic study. **3** a substance added to a liquid, such as a perfume, to make it less volatile.

fixed (fɪkst) *adj* **1** attached or placed so as to be immovable. **2** stable: *fixed prices.* **3** steadily directed: *a fixed expression.* **4** established as to relative position: *a fixed point.* **5** always at the same time: *a fixed holiday.* **6** (of ideas, etc.) firmly maintained. **7** (of an element) held in chemical combination: *fixed nitrogen.* **8** (of a substance) nonvolatile. **9** arranged. **10** *Inf.* equipped or provided for, as with money, possessions, etc. **11** *Inf.* illegally arranged: *a fixed trial.*
▸ **fixedly** ('fɪksɪdlɪ) *adv* ▸ **'fixedness** *n*

fixed assets *pl n* nontrading business assets of a relatively permanent nature, such as plant, fixtures, or goodwill. Also called: **capital assets.**

fixed oil *n* a natural animal or vegetable oil that is not volatile: a mixture of esters of fatty acids.

fixed-point representation *n Computing.* the representation of numbers by a single set of digits such that the radix point has a predetermined location. Cf. **floating-point representation.**

fixed satellite *n* a satellite revolving in a stationary orbit so that it appears to remain over a fixed point on the earth's surface.

fixed star *n* an extremely distant star whose position appears to be almost stationary over a long period of time.

fixer ('fɪksə) *n* **1** a person or thing that fixes. **2** *Photog.* a solution used to dissolve unexposed silver halides after developing. **3** *Sl.* a person who makes arrangements, esp. by underhand or illegal means.

fixing ('fɪksɪŋ) *n* a means of attaching one thing to another, as a pipe to a wall, a slate to a roof, etc.

fixity ('fɪksɪtɪ) *n, pl* **fixities. 1** the state or quality of being fixed. **2** a fixture.

fixture ('fɪkstʃə) *n* **1** an object firmly fixed in place, esp. a household appliance. **2** a person or thing regarded as fixed in a particular place or position. **3** *Property law.* an article attached to land and regarded as part of it. **4** *Chiefly Brit.* **4a** a sports match or social occasion. **4b** the date of such an event. [C17: from LL *fixūra* a fastening (with *-t-* by analogy with *mixture*)]

fix up *vb* (*tr, adv*) **1** to arrange: *let's fix up a date.* **2** (often foll. by *with*) to provide: *I'm sure we can fix you up with a room.*

fizgig ('fɪz,gɪg) *n* **1** a frivolous or flirtatious girl. **2** a firework that fizzes as it moves. [C16: prob. from obs. *fise* a breaking of wind + *gig* girl]

fizz (fɪz) *vb* (*intr*) **1** to make a hissing or bubbling sound. **2** (of a drink) to produce bubbles of carbon dioxide. ◆ *n* **3** a hissing or bubbling sound. **4** the bubbly quality of a drink; effervescence. **5** any effervescent drink. [C17: imit.]
▸ **'fizzy** *adj* ▸ **'fizziness** *n*

fizzle ('fɪzᵊl) *vb* **fizzles, fizzling, fizzled.** (*intr*) **1** to make a hissing or bubbling sound. **2** (often foll. by *out*) *Inf.* to fail or die out, esp. after a promising start. ◆ *n* **3** a hissing or bubbling sound. **4** *Inf.* a failure. [C16: prob. from obs. *fist* to break wind]

fjord *or* **fiord** (fjɔːd) *n* a long narrow inlet of the sea between high steep cliffs, common in Norway. [C17: from Norwegian, from ON *fjörthr*; see FIRTH, FORD]

FL *abbrev. for:* **1** Flight Lieutenant. **2** Florida.

fl. *abbrev. for:* **1** floor. **2** floruit. **3** fluid.

Fl. *abbrev. for:* **1** Flanders. **2** Flemish.

flab (flæb) *n* unsightly or unwanted fat on the body. [C20: back formation from FLABBY]

flabbergast ('flæbə,gɑːst) *vb* (*tr; usually passive*) *Inf.* to amaze utterly; astound. [C18: from ?]

THESAURUS

fitting *adj* **1** = **appropriate**, apposite, becoming, *comme il faut*, correct, decent, decorous, desirable, meet (*arch.*), proper, right, seemly, suitable ◆ *n* **2** = **accessory**, attachment, component, connection, part, piece, unit **3** *plural* = **furnishings**, accessories, accoutrements, appointments, appurtenances, bells and whistles, conveniences, equipment, extras, furniture, trimmings
Antonyms *adj* ≠ **appropriate**: ill-suited, improper, unfitting, unseemly, unsuitable

fix *vb* **1** = **place**, anchor, embed, establish, implant, install, locate, plant, position, root, set, settle **2** = **fasten**, attach, bind, cement, connect, couple, glue, link, make fast, pin, secure, stick, tie **3** = **decide**, agree on, appoint, arrange, arrive at, conclude, define, determine, establish, limit, name, resolve, set, settle, specify **4, 5** = **focus**, direct, level at, rivet **8** = **repair**, adjust, correct, mend, patch up, put to rights, regulate, see to, sort **10** *Informal* = **rig**, bribe, fiddle (*inf.*), influence, manipulate, manoeuvre, pull strings **11** *Slang* = **sort (someone) out** (*inf.*), cook (someone's) goose (*inf.*), get even with (*inf.*), get revenge on, pay back, settle (someone's) hash (*inf.*), take retribution on, wreak vengeance on **17** = **set**, congeal, consolidate, harden, rigidify, solidify, stiffen, thicken ◆ *n* **19** *Informal* = **predicament**, difficult situation, difficulty, dilemma, embarrassment, hole, hot water (*inf.*), jam (*inf.*), mess, pickle (*inf.*), plight, quandary, spot (*inf.*), ticklish situation, tight spot

fixated *adj* **3** = **obsessed**, absorbed, attached, besotted, captivated, caught up in, devoted, engrossed, fascinated, hung up on (*sl.*), hypnotized, infatuated, mesmerized, monomaniacal, preoccupied, prepossessed, single-minded, smitten, spellbound, taken up with, wrapped up in
Antonyms *adj* detached, disinterested, dispassionate, indifferent, open-minded, uncommitted, unconcerned, uninvolved, unprepossessed

fixation *n* **2** = **obsession**, addiction, complex, hang-up (*inf.*), *idée fixe*, infatuation, mania, preoccupation, thing (*inf.*)

fixed *adj* **1** = **immovable**, anchored, attached, established, made fast, permanent, rigid, rooted, secure, set **3** = **steady**, intent, level, resolute, unbending, unblinking, undeviating, unflinching, unwavering **9** = **agreed**, arranged, decided, definite, established, planned, resolved, settled **11** *Informal* = **rigged**, framed, manipulated, packed, put-up
Antonyms *adj* ≠ **immovable**: bending, mobile, motile, moving, pliant, unfixed ≠ **steady**: inconstant, varying, wavering

fixity *n* **1** = **steadiness**, doggedness, intentness, perseverance, persistence, stability

fix up *vb* **1** = **arrange**, agree on, fix, organize, plan, settle, sort out **2** *often with* **with** = **provide**, accommodate, arrange for, bring about, furnish, lay on

fizz *vb* **1, 2** = **bubble**, effervesce, fizzle, froth, hiss, sparkle, sputter

fizzle *vb* **2** *often foll. by* **out** *Informal* = **die away**, abort, collapse, come to nothing, end in disappointment, fail, fall through, fold (*inf.*), miss the mark, peter out

fizzy *adj* **1, 2** = **bubbly**, bubbling, carbonated, effervescent, gassy, sparkling

flab *n* = **fat**, beef (*inf.*), flabbiness, flesh, fleshiness, heaviness, overweight, plumpness, slackness, weight

flabbergasted *adj* = **astonished**, abashed,

flabby ⓣ ('flæbɪ) *adj* **flabbier, flabbiest. 1** loose or yielding: *flabby muscles.* **2** having flabby flesh, esp. through being overweight. **3** lacking vitality; weak. [C17: alteration of *flappy* from FLAP + -Y[1]; cf. Du. *flabbe* drooping lip]
▸**'flabbiness** *n*

flaccid ⓣ ('flæksɪd) *adj* lacking firmness; soft and limp. [C17: from L *flaccidus*, from *flaccus*]
▸**flac'cidity** *n*

flacon (*French* flakõ) *n* a small stoppered bottle, esp. used for perfume. [C19: from F; see FLAGON]

flag[1] ⓣ (flæg) *n* **1** a piece of cloth, esp. bunting, often attached to a pole or staff, decorated with a design and used as an emblem, symbol, or standard or as a means of signalling. **2** a small piece of paper, etc., sold on flag days. **3** the conspicuously marked or shaped tail of a deer or of certain dogs. **4** anything used like a flag to attract attention, esp. a code inserted into a computer file to distinguish certain information. **5** *Brit., Austral., & NZ.* the part of a taximeter that is raised when a taxi is for hire. **6 show the flag. 6a** to assert a claim by military presence. **6b** *Inf.* to make an appearance. ◆ *vb* **flags, flagging, flagged.** (*tr*) **7** to decorate or mark with a flag or flags. **8** (often foll. by *down*) to warn or signal (a vehicle) to stop. **9** to send or communicate (messages, information, etc.) by flag. [C16: from ?]
▸**'flagger** *n*

flag[2] (flæg) *n* **1** any of various plants that have long swordlike leaves, esp. an iris (**yellow flag**). **2** the leaf of any such plant. [C14: prob. from ON]

flag[3] ⓣ (flæg) *vb* **flags, flagging, flagged.** (*intr*) **1** to hang down; droop. **2** to become weak or tired. [C16: from ?]

flag[4] (flæg) *n* **1** short for **flagstone.** ◆ *vb* **flags, flagging, flagged. 2** (*tr*) to furnish (a floor, etc.) with flagstones.

flag day *n Brit.* a day on which money is collected by a charity and small flags or emblems are given to contributors.

flagellant ('flædʒɪlənt, flə'dʒɛlənt) *or* **flagellator** ('flædʒɪˌleɪtə) *n* a person who whips himself or others either as part of a religious penance or for sexual gratification. [C16: from L *flagellāre* to whip, from FLAGELLUM]

flagellate ⓣ *vb* ('flædʒɪˌleɪt), **flagellates, flagellating, flagellated. 1** (*tr*) to whip; flog. ◆ *adj* ('flædʒɪlɪt), *also* **flagellated. 2** possessing one or more flagella. **3** whiplike. ◆ *n* ('flædʒɪlɪt). **4** a flagellate organism.
▸**ˌflagel'lation** *n*

flagellum (flə'dʒɛləm) *n, pl* **flagella** (-lə) *or* **flagellums. 1** *Biol.* a long whiplike outgrowth from a cell that acts as an organ of locomotion: occurs in some protozoans, gametes, etc. **2** *Bot.* a long thin shoot or runner. [C19: from L: a little whip, from *flagrum* a whip, lash]
▸**fla'gellar** *adj*

flageolet[1] (ˌflædʒə'lɛt) *n* a high-pitched musical instrument of the recorder family. [C17: from F, modification of OF *flajolet* a little flute, from Vulgar L *flabeolum* (unattested), from L *flāre* to blow]

flageolet[2] (ˌflædʒə'lɛt) *n* a type of kidney bean. [C19: from F, corruption of *fageolet*, dim. of *fageol*, from L *faseolus*]

flag fall *n Austral.* the minimum charge for hiring a taxi, to which the rate per kilometre is added.

flag of convenience *n* a national flag flown by a ship registered in that country to gain financial or legal advantage.

flag of truce *n* a white flag indicating an invitation to an enemy to negotiate.

flagon ('flægən) *n* **1** a large bottle of wine, cider, etc. **2** a vessel having a handle, spout, and narrow neck. [C15: from OF *flascon*, from LL *flascō*, prob. of Gmc origin; see FLASK]

flagpole ('flægˌpəʊl) *or* **flagstaff** ('flægˌstɑːf) *n, pl* **flagpoles, flagstaffs** *or* **flagstaves** (-ˌsteɪvz). a pole or staff on which a flag is hoisted and displayed.

flagrant ⓣ ('fleɪgrənt) *adj* openly outrageous. [C15: from L *flagrāre* to blaze, burn]
▸**'flagrancy** *n* ▸**'flagrantly** *adv*

flagrante delicto (flə'græntɪ dɪ'lɪktəʊ) *adv* See **in flagrante delicto.**

flagship ('flægˌʃɪp) *n* **1** a ship, esp. in a fleet, aboard which the commander of the fleet is quartered. **2** the most important ship belonging to a shipping company. **3** the item in a group considered most important esp. in establishing a public image: *costume drama is the flagship of the BBC.*

flagstone ⓣ ('flægˌstəʊn) *n* **1** a hard fine-textured rock that can be split up into slabs for paving. **2** a slab of such a rock. [C15 *flag* (in the sense: sod, turf), from ON *flaga* slab; cf. OE *flæcg* plaster, poultice]

flag-waving *n Inf.* an emotional appeal intended to arouse patriotic feeling.
▸**'flagˌwaver** *n*

flail ⓣ (fleɪl) *n* **1** an implement used for threshing grain, consisting of a wooden handle with a free-swinging metal or wooden bar attached to it. ◆ *vb* **2** (*tr*) to beat with or as if with a flail. **3** to thresh about: *with arms flailing.* [C12 *fleil*, ult. from LL *flagellum* flail, from L: whip]

flair ⓣ (flɛə) *n* **1** natural ability; talent. **2** perceptiveness. **3** *Inf.* stylishness or elegance: *to dress with flair.* [C19: from F, lit.: sense of smell, from OF: scent, ult. from L *frāgrāre* to smell sweet; see FRAGRANT]

flak ⓣ (flæk) *n* **1** anti-aircraft fire or artillery. **2** *Inf.* adverse criticism. [C20: from G *Fl(ieger)a(bwehr)k(anone)*, lit.: aircraft defence gun]

flake[1] ⓣ (fleɪk) *n* **1** a small thin piece or layer chipped off or detached from an object or substance. **2** a small piece or particle: *a flake of snow.* **3** *Archaeol.* a fragment removed by chipping from a larger stone used as a tool or weapon. **4** *Chiefly US sl.* an eccentric, crazy, or unreliable person. ◆ *vb* **flakes, flaking, flaked. 5** to peel or cause to peel off in flakes. **6** to cover or become covered with or as with flakes. **7** (*tr*) to form into flakes. [C14: from ON]

flake[2] (fleɪk) *n* a rack or platform for drying fish. [C14: from ON *flaki*; rel. to Du. *vlaak* hurdle]

flake out ⓣ *vb* (*intr, adv*) *Inf.* to collapse or fall asleep as through extreme exhaustion.

flake white *n* a pigment made from flakes of white lead.

flak jacket *n* a reinforced jacket for protection against gunfire or shrapnel worn by soldiers, policemen, etc.

flaky ('fleɪkɪ) *adj* **flakier, flakiest. 1** like or made of flakes. **2** tending to break easily into flakes. **3** Also spelt: **flakey.** *US sl.* eccentric; crazy.
▸**'flakily** *adv* ▸**'flakiness** *n*

flambé ('flɑːmbeɪ) **1** *adj* (of food, such as steak or pancakes) served in flaming brandy ◆ *vb* **flambés, flambéing, flambéed. 2** (*tr*) to serve (food) in such a manner. [F, p.p. of *flamber* to FLAME]

flambeau ('flæmbəʊ) *n, pl* **flambeaux** (-bəʊ, -bəʊz) *or* **flambeaus.** a burning torch, as used in night processions, etc. [C17: from OF: torch, lit.: a little flame, from *flambe* FLAME]

flamboyant ⓣ (flæm'bɔɪənt) *adj* **1** elaborate or extravagant; showy. **2** rich or brilliant in colour. **3** exuberant or ostentatious. **4** of the French Gothic style of architecture characterized by flamelike tracery and elaborate carving. [C19: from F: flaming, from *flamboyer* to FLAME]
▸**flam'boyance** *or* **flam'boyancy** *n* ▸**flam'boyantly** *adv*

flame ⓣ (fleɪm) *n* **1** a hot usually luminous body of burning gas emanating in flickering streams from burning material or produced by a jet of ignited gas. **2** (*often pl*) the state or condition of burning with flames: *to burst into flames.* **3** a brilliant light. **4a** a strong reddish-orange colour. **4b** (*as adj*): *a flame carpet.* **5** intense passion or ardour. **6** *Inf.* a lover or sweetheart (esp. in **an old flame**). **7** *Inf.* an abusive message sent by electronic mail. ◆ *vb* **flames, flaming, flamed. 8** to burn or cause to burn brightly. **9** (*intr*) to become red or fiery: *his face flamed with anger.* **10** (*intr*) to become angry or excited. **11** (*tr*) to apply a flame to (something). **12** *Inf.* to send an abusive message by elec-

THESAURUS

amazed, astounded, bowled over (*inf.*), confounded, dazed, disconcerted, dumbfounded, gobsmacked (*Brit. sl.*), lost for words, nonplussed, overcome, overwhelmed, speechless, staggered, struck dumb, stunned

flabbiness *n* **1, 2 = slackness**, bloatedness, flaccidity, limpness, looseness, pendulousness

flabby *adj* **1, 2 = limp**, baggy, drooping, flaccid, floppy, hanging, lax, loose, pendulous, sagging, slack, sloppy, toneless, unfit, yielding **3 = weak**, boneless, effete, enervated, feeble, impotent, ineffective, ineffectual, nerveless, spineless, wimpish *or* wimpy (*inf.*)
Antonyms *adj* ≠ **limp:** firm, hard, solid, strong, taut, tense, tight, tough

flaccid *adj* = **limp**, drooping, flabby, lax, loose, nerveless, slack, soft, weak

flaccidity *n* = **limpness**, flabbiness, looseness, nervelessness, slackness, softness

flag[1] *n* **1 = banner**, banderole, colours, ensign, gonfalon, jack, pennant, pennon, standard, streamer ◆ *vb* **7 = mark**, docket, indicate, label, note, tab **8** *often with* **down = hail**, salute, signal, warn, wave

flag[3] *vb* **1, 2 = weaken**, abate, decline, die, droop, ebb, fade, fail, faint, fall, fall off, feel the pace, languish, peter out, pine, sag, sink, slump, succumb, taper off, wane, weary, wilt

flagellate *vb* **1 = whip**, beat, castigate, chastise, flay, flog, lambast(e), lash, scourge, thrash

flagellation *n* **1 = whipping**, beating, flogging, lashing, thrashing

flagrancy *n* = **outrageousness**, blatancy, enormity, heinousness, infamy, insolence, ostentation, public display, shamelessness

flagrant *adj* = **outrageous**, arrant, atrocious, awful, barefaced, blatant, bold, brazen, crying, dreadful, egregious, enormous, flagitious, flaunting, glaring, heinous, immodest, infamous, notorious, open, ostentatious, out-and-out, scandalous, shameless, undisguised
Antonyms *adj* delicate, faint, implied, indirect, insinuated, slight, subtle, understated

flagstone *n* **2 = paving stone**, block, flag, slab

flail *vb* **2 = thrash**, beat, thresh, windmill

flair *n* **1 = ability**, accomplishment, aptitude, faculty, feel, genius, gift, knack, mastery, talent **3 = style**, chic, dash, discernment, elegance, panache, stylishness, taste

flak *n* **2** *Informal* = **criticism**, abuse, bad press, brickbats (*inf.*), censure, complaints, condemnation, denigration, disapprobation, disapproval, disparagement, fault-finding, hostility, opposition, stick (*sl.*)

flake[1] *n* **1 = chip**, disk, lamina, layer, peeling, scale, shaving, sliver, squama (*Biology*), wafer ◆ *vb* **5 = chip**, blister, desquamate, peel (off), scale (off)

flake out *vb* = **collapse**, faint, keel over, lose consciousness, pass out, swoon (*literary*)

flamboyance *n* **1, 3 = showiness**, bravura, brio, dash, élan, exhibitionism, extravagance, flair, flamboyancy, flashiness, floridity, glitz (*inf.*), ostentation, panache, pizzazz *or* pizazz (*inf.*), pomp, show, sparkle, style, stylishness, theatricality, verve
Antonyms *n* drabness, dullness, flatness, restraint, simplicity, unobtrusiveness

flamboyant *adj* **1, 3 = showy**, actorly, baroque, camp (*inf.*), dashing, elaborate, extravagant, florid, ornate, ostentatious, over the top (*inf.*), rich, rococo, swashbuckling, theatrical

flame *n* **1 = fire**, blaze, brightness, light **5 = passion**, affection, ardour, enthusiasm, fervency, fervour, fire, intensity, keenness, warmth **6** *Informal* = **sweetheart**, beau, beloved, boyfriend, girlfriend, heart-throb (*Brit.*), ladylove, lover ◆ *vb* **8 = burn**, blaze, flare, flash, glare, glow, shine

tronic mail. [C14: from Anglo-F, from OF *flambe*, from L *flammula* a little flame, from *flamma* flame]
▸ **'flame,like** *adj* ▸ **'flamy** *adj*

flame gun *n* a type of flame-thrower for destroying garden weeds, etc.

flamen ('fleɪmɛn) *n, pl* **flamens** *or* **flamines** ('flæmɪ,ni:z). (in ancient Rome) any of 15 priests who each served a particular deity. [C14: from L; prob. rel. to OE *blōtan* to sacrifice, Gothic *blotan* to worship]

flamenco (flə'mɛŋkəʊ) *n, pl* **flamencos.** **1** a type of dance music for vocal soloist and guitar, characterized by sad mood. **2** the dance performed to such music. [from Sp.: like a Gipsy, lit.: Fleming, from MDu. *Vlaminc* Fleming]

flameout ('fleɪm,aʊt) *n* the failure of an aircraft jet engine in flight due to extinction of the flame.

flame-thrower *n* a weapon that ejects a stream or spray of burning fluid.

flame tree *n* any of various tropical trees with red or orange flowers.

flaming ❶ ('fleɪmɪŋ) *adj* **1** burning with or emitting flames. **2** glowing brightly. **3** intense or ardent: *a flaming temper.* **4** *Inf.* (intensifier): *you flaming idiot.*

flamingo (flə'mɪŋgəʊ) *n, pl* **flamingos** *or* **flamingoes.** a large wading bird having a pink-and-red plumage and downward-bent bill and inhabiting brackish lakes. [C16: from Port., from Provençal, from L *flamma* flame + Gmc suffix *-ing* denoting descent from; cf. -ING[3]]

flammable ❶ ('flæməb^{ə}l) *adj* readily combustible; inflammable.
▸ **,flamma'bility** *n*

> **USAGE NOTE** *Flammable* and *inflammable* are interchangeable when used of the properties of materials. *Flammable* is, however, often preferred for warning labels as there is less likelihood of misunderstanding (*inflammable* being sometimes taken to mean *not flammable*). *Inflammable* is preferred in figurative contexts: *this could prove to be an inflammable situation.*

flan (flæn) *n* **1** an open pastry or sponge tart filled with fruit or a savoury mixture. **2** a piece of metal ready to receive the die or stamp in the production of coins. [C19: from F, from OF *flaon*, from LL *fladō* flat cake, of Gmc origin]

flange (flændʒ) *n* **1** a radially projecting collar or rim on an object for strengthening it or for attaching it to another object. **2** a flat outer face of a rolled-steel joist. ◆ *vb* **flanges, flanging, flanged. 3** (*tr*) to provide (a component) with a flange. [C17: prob. changed from earlier *flaunche* curved segment at side of a heraldic field, from F *flanc* FLANK]
▸ **flanged** *adj* ▸ **'flangeless** *adj*

flank ❶ (flæŋk) *n* **1** the side of a man or animal between the ribs and the hip. **2** a cut of beef from the flank. **3** the side of anything, such as a mountain or building. **4** the side of a naval or military formation. ◆ *vb* **5** (when *intr*, often foll. by *on* or *upon*) to be located at the side of (an object, etc.). **6** *Mil.* to position or guard on or beside the flank of (a formation, etc.). [C12: from OF *flanc*, of Gmc origin]

flanker ('flæŋkə) *n* **1** one of a detachment of soldiers detailed to guard the flanks. **2** a fortification used to protect a flank. **3** Also called: **flank forward.** *Rugby.* another name for **winger.**

flannel ❶ ('flæn^{ə}l) *n* **1** a soft light woollen fabric with a slight nap, used for clothing, etc. **2** (*pl*) trousers or other garments made of flannel. **3** *Brit.* a small piece of cloth used to wash the face and hands; face flannel. US and Canad. equivalent: **washcloth. 4** *Brit. inf.* indirect or evasive talk. ◆ *vb* **flannels, flannelling, flannelled** *or US* **flannels, flanneling, flanneled.** (*tr*) **5** to cover or wrap with flannel. **6** to rub or polish with flannel. **7** *Brit. inf.* to flatter. [C14: prob. var. of *flanen* sackcloth, from Welsh, from *gwlân* wool]
▸ **'flannelly** *adj*

flannelette (,flæn^{ə}'lɛt) *n* a cotton imitation of flannel.

flap ❶ (flæp) *vb* **flaps, flapping, flapped. 1** to move (wings or arms) up and down, esp. in or as if in flying, or (of wings or arms) to move in this way. **2** to move or cause to move noisily back and forth or up and down: *the curtains flapped in the breeze.* **3** (*intr*) *Inf.* to become agitated or flustered. **4** to deal (a person or thing) a blow with a broad flexible object. ◆ *n* **5** the action, motion, or noise made by flapping: *with one flap of its wings the bird was off.* **6** a piece of material, etc., attached at one edge and usually used to cover an opening, as on a tent, envelope, or pocket. **7** a blow dealt with a flat object. **8** a movable surface fixed to an aircraft wing that increases lift during takeoff and drag during landing. **9** *Inf.* a state of panic or agitation. [C14: prob. imit.]

flapdoodle ('flæp,du:d^{ə}l) *n Sl.* foolish talk; nonsense. [C19: from ?]

flapjack ('flæp,dʒæk) *n* **1** a chewy biscuit made with rolled oats. **2** *Chiefly US & Canad.* another word for **pancake.**

flapper ('flæpə) *n* (in the 1920s) a young woman, esp. one flaunting her unconventional behaviour.

flare ❶ (flɛə) *vb* **flares, flaring, flared. 1** to burn or cause to burn with an unsteady or sudden bright flame. **2** to burn off excess gas or oil. **3** to spread or cause to spread outwards from a narrow to a wider shape. ◆ *n* **4** an unsteady flame. **5** a sudden burst of flame. **6a** a blaze of light or fire used to illuminate, signal distress, alert, etc. **6b** the device producing such a blaze. **7** a spreading shape or anything with a spreading shape: *a skirt with a flare.* **8** an open flame used to burn off unwanted gas at an oil well. **9** *Astron.* short for **solar flare.** [C16 (to spread out): from ?]

flares (flɛəz) *pl n Inf.* trousers with legs that widen below the knee.

flare-up ❶ *n* **1** a sudden burst of fire or light. **2** *Inf.* a sudden burst of emotion or violence. ◆ *vb* **flare up.** (*intr, adv*). **3** to burst suddenly into fire or light. **4** *Inf.* to burst into anger.

flash ❶ (flæʃ) *n* **1** a sudden short blaze of intense light or flame: *a flash of sunlight.* **2** a sudden occurrence or display, esp. one suggestive of brilliance: *a flash of understanding.* **3** a very brief space of time: *over in a flash.* **4** Also called: **newsflash.** a short news announcement concerning a new event. **5** Also called: **patch.** *Chiefly Brit.* an insignia or emblem worn on a uniform, vehicle, etc., to identify its military formation. **6** a sudden rush of water down a river or watercourse. **7** *Photog., inf.* short for **flashlight** (sense 2). **8** (*modifier*) involving, using, or produced by a flash of heat, light, etc.: *flash distillation.* **9 flash in the pan.** a project, person, etc., that enjoys only short-lived success. ◆ *adj* **10** *Inf.* ostentatious or vulgar. **11** sham or counterfeit. **12** *Inf.* relating to or characteristic of the criminal underworld. **13** brief and rapid: *flash freezing.* ◆ *vb* **14** to burst or cause to burst suddenly or intermittently into flame. **15** to emit or reflect or cause to emit or reflect light suddenly or intermittently. **16** (*intr*) to move very fast: *he flashed by on his bicycle.* **17** (*intr*) to come rapidly (into the mind or vision). **18** (*intr*; foll. by *out* or *up*) to appear like a sudden light. **19a** to signal or communicate very fast: *to flash a message.* **19b** to signal by use of a light, such as car headlights. **20** (*tr*) *Inf.* to display ostentatiously: *to flash money around.* **21** (*tr*) *Inf.* to show suddenly and briefly. **22** (*intr*) *Brit. sl.* to expose oneself indecently. **23** to send a sudden rush of water down (a river, etc.), or to carry (a vessel) down by this method. [C14 (in the sense: to rush, as of water): from ?]
▸ **'flasher** *n*

flashback ('flæʃ,bæk) *n* a transition in a novel, film, etc., to an earlier scene or event.

flashboard ('flæʃ,bɔ:d) *n* a board or boarding that is placed along the top of a dam to increase its height and capacity.

flashbulb ('flæʃ,bʌlb) *n Photog.* a small expendable glass light bulb formerly used to produce a bright flash of light.

flashbulb memory *n Psychol.* the clear recollections that a person may have of the circumstances associated with a dramatic event.

flash burn *n Pathol.* a burn caused by momentary exposure to intense radiant heat.

flash card *n* a card on which are written or printed words for children to look at briefly, used as an aid to learning.

flashcube ('flæʃ,kju:b) *n* a boxlike camera attachment, holding four flashbulbs, that turns so that each flashbulb can be used.

flash flood *n* a sudden short-lived torrent, usually caused by a heavy storm, esp. in desert regions.

flashgun ('flæʃ,gʌn) *n* a type of electronic flash, attachable to or sometimes incorporated in a camera, that emits a very brief flash of light when the shutter is open.

flashing ('flæʃɪŋ) *n* a weatherproof material, esp. thin sheet metal, used to cover the valleys between the slopes of a roof, the junction between a chimney and a roof, etc.

flashlight ('flæʃ,laɪt) *n* **1** another word (esp. US and Canad.) for **torch. 2** *Photog.* the brief bright light emitted by an electronic flash unit. Often shortened to **flash.**

flash point *n* **1** the lowest temperature at which the vapour above a liquid can be ignited in air. **2** a critical time or place beyond which a situation will inevitably erupt into violence.

THESAURUS

flaming *adj* **1, 2** = **burning,** ablaze, afire, blazing, brilliant, fiery, glowing, ignited, in flames, raging, red, red-hot **3** = **intense,** angry, ardent, aroused, frenzied, hot, impassioned, raging, scintillating, vehement, vivid

flammable *adj* = **combustible,** ignitable, incendiary, inflammable

flank *n* **1, 2** = **side,** ham, haunch, hip, loin, quarter, thigh **3** = **wing,** side ◆ *vb* **5** = **border,** book-end, bound, edge, fringe, line, screen, skirt, wall

flannel *n* **4** *Brit. informal* = **prevarication,** baloney (*inf.*), blarney, equivocation, flattery, hedging, soft soap (*inf.*), sweet talk (*US inf.*), waffle (*inf., chiefly Brit.*) ◆ *vb* **7** *Brit. informal* = **prevaricate,** blarney, butter up, equivocate, flatter, hedge, pull the wool over (someone's) eyes, soft-soap (*inf.*), sweet-talk (*inf.*)

flap *vb* **2** = **flutter,** agitate, beat, flail, shake, swing, swish, thrash, thresh, vibrate, wag, wave **3** *Informal* = **panic,** dither (*chiefly Brit.*), fuss ◆ *n* **5** = **flutter,** bang, banging, beating, shaking, swinging, swish, waving **6** = **cover,** apron, fly, fold, lapel, lappet, overlap, skirt, tab, tail **9** *Informal* = **panic,** agitation, commotion, fluster, state (*inf.*), stew (*inf.*), sweat (*inf.*), tizzy (*inf.*), twitter (*inf.*)

flare *vb* **1** = **blaze,** burn up, dazzle, flicker, flutter, glare, waver **3** = **widen,** broaden, spread out ◆ *n* **4-6** = **flame,** blaze, burst, dazzle, flash, flicker, glare

flare up *vb* **4** = **lose one's temper,** blaze, blow one's top (*inf.*), boil over, break out, explode, fire up, fly off the handle (*inf.*), lose control, lose it (*inf.*), lose one's cool (*inf.*), lose the plot (*inf.*), throw a tantrum

flash *n* **1** = **blaze,** burst, coruscation, dazzle, flare, flicker, gleam, ray, scintillation, shaft, shimmer, spark, sparkle, streak, twinkle **2** = **burst,** demonstration, display, manifestation, outburst, show, sign, touch **3** = **moment,** bat of an eye, instant, jiffy (*inf.*), second, shake, split second, trice, twinkling, twinkling of an eye, two shakes of a lamb's tail (*inf.*) ◆ *adj* **10** *Informal* = **ostentatious,** cheap, glamorous, tacky (*inf.*), tasteless, vulgar ◆ *vb* **14, 15** = **blaze,** coruscate, flare, flicker, glare, gleam, glint, glisten, glitter, light, scintillate, shimmer, sparkle, twinkle **16** = **speed,** bolt, burn rubber (*inf.*), dart, dash, fly, race, shoot, sprint, streak, sweep,

flashy ➊ (ˈflæʃɪ) *adj* **flashier, flashiest. 1** brilliant and dazzling, esp. for a short time or in a superficial way. **2** cheap and ostentatious.
▸ˈ**flashily** *adv* ▸ˈ**flashiness** *n*

flask (flɑːsk) *n* **1** a bottle with a narrow neck, esp. used in a laboratory or for wine, oil, etc. **2** Also called: **hip flask.** a small flattened container of glass or metal designed to be carried in a pocket, esp. for liquor. **3** See **vacuum flask.** [C14: from OF, from Med. L *flasca, flasco*, ? of Gmc origin; cf. OE *flasce, flaxe*]

flat[1] ➊ (flæt) *adj* **flatter, flattest. 1** horizontal; level: *a flat roof*. **2** even or smooth, without projections or depressions: *a flat surface*. **3** lying stretched out at full length: *he lay flat on the ground*. **4** having little depth or thickness: *a flat dish*. **5** (*postpositive;* often foll. by *against*) having a surface or side in complete contact with another surface: *flat against the wall*. **6** (of a tyre) deflated. **7** (of shoes) having an unraised heel. **8** *Chiefly Brit.* **8a** (of races, racetracks, or racecourses) not having obstacles to be jumped. **8b** of, relating to, or connected with flat racing as opposed to steeplechasing and hurdling. **9** without qualification; total: *a flat denial*. **10** fixed: *a flat rate*. **11** (*prenominal or immediately postpositive*) neither more nor less; exact: *he did the journey in thirty minutes flat*. **12** unexciting: *a flat joke*. **13** without variation or resonance; monotonous: *a flat voice*. **14** (of beer, sparkling wines, etc.) having lost effervescence, as by exposure to air. **15** (of trade, business, etc.) commercially inactive. **16** (of a battery) fully discharged. **17** (of a print, photograph, or painting) lacking contrast. **18** (of paint) without gloss or lustre. **19** (of lighting) diffuse. **20** *Music.* **20a** (*immediately postpositive*) denoting a note of a given letter name (or the sound it represents) that has been lowered in pitch by one chromatic semitone: *B flat*. **20b** (of an instrument, voice, etc.) out of tune by being too low in pitch. Cf. **sharp** (sense 12). **21** *Phonetics.* **flat 21a** the vowel sound of *a* as in the usual US or S Brit. pronunciation of *hand, cat.* ◆ *adv* **22** in or into a prostrate, level, or flat state or position: *he held his hand out flat*. **23** completely or utterly; absolutely. **24** exactly; precisely: *in three minutes flat*. **25** *Music.* **25a** lower than a standard pitch. **25b** too low in pitch: *she sings flat*. Cf. **sharp** (sense 17). **26 fall flat (on one's face)**. to fail to achieve a desired effect. **27 flat out.** *Inf.* **27a** with the maximum speed or effort. **27b** totally exhausted. ◆ *n* **28** a flat object, surface, or part. **29** (*often pl*) a low-lying tract of land, esp. a marsh or swamp. **30** (*often pl*) a mud bank exposed at low tide. **31** *Music.* **31a** an accidental that lowers the pitch of a note by one chromatic semitone. Usual symbol: ♭ **31b** a note affected by this accidental. Cf. **sharp** (sense 18). **32** *Theatre.* a wooden frame covered with painted canvas, etc., used to form part of a stage setting. **33** a punctured car tyre. **34** (*often cap.; preceded by the*) *Chiefly Brit.* **34a** flat racing, esp. as opposed to steeplechasing and hurdling. **34b** the season of flat racing. **35** *US & Canad.* a shallow box used for holding plants, etc. ◆ *vb* **flats, flatting, flatted. 36** to make or become flat. [C14: from ON *flatr*]
▸ˈ**flatly** *adv* ▸ˈ**flatness** *n* ▸ˈ**flattish** *adj*

flat[2] ➊ (flæt) *n* a set of rooms comprising a residence entirely on one floor of a building. Usual US and Canad. name: **apartment.** [OE *flett* floor, hall, house]

flatbed lorry (ˈflæt,bɛd) *n* a lorry with a flat platform for its body.

flatbed scanner *n Computing.* a computer-controlled device that electronically scans images placed on its flat glass, to produce digitized images for use in desktop publishing, etc.

flatboat (ˈflæt,bəʊt) *n* any boat with a flat bottom, usually for transporting goods on a canal.

flatette (,flætˈɛt) *n Austral.* a very small flat.

flatfish (ˈflæt,fɪʃ) *n, pl* **flatfish** *or* **flatfishes.** any of an order of marine spiny-finned fish including the halibut, plaice, turbot, and sole, all of which have a flat body which has both eyes on the uppermost side.

flatfoot (ˈflæt,fʊt) *n* **1** Also called: **splayfoot.** a condition in which the instep arch of the foot is flattened. **2** (*pl* **flatfoots** *or* **flatfeet**) a slang word (usually derogatory) for a **policeman.**

flat-footed (,flætˈfʊtɪd) *adj* **1** having flatfoot. **2** *Inf.* **2a** awkward. **2b** downright. **3** *Inf.* off guard (often in **catch flat-footed**).
▸,**flat-ˈfootedly** *adv* ▸,**flat-ˈfootedness** *n*

flathead (ˈflæt,hɛd) *n, pl* **flathead** *or* **flatheads.** a Pacific food fish which resembles the gurnard.

flatiron (ˈflæt,aɪən) *n* (formerly) an iron for pressing clothes that was heated by being placed on a stove, etc.

flatlet (ˈflætlɪt) *n* a flat having only a few rooms.

flatmate (ˈflæt,meɪt) *n* a person with whom one shares a flat.

flat racing *n* **a** the racing of horses on racecourses without jumps. **b** (*as modifier*): *the flat-racing season.*

flat spin *n* **1** an aircraft spin in which the longitudinal axis is more nearly horizontal than vertical. **2** *Inf.* a state of confusion; dither.

flat spot *n* **1** *Engineering.* a region of poor acceleration over a narrow range of throttle openings, caused by a weak mixture in the carburettor. **2** any narrow region of poor performance in a mechanical device.

flatten ➊ (ˈflætᵊn) *vb* **1** (sometimes foll. by *out*) to make or become flat or flatter. **2** (*tr*) *Inf.* **2a** to knock down or injure. **2b** to crush or subdue. **3** (*tr*) *Music.* to lower the pitch of (a note) by one chromatic semitone.
▸ˈ**flattener** *n*

flatter ➊ (ˈflætə) *vb* **1** to praise insincerely, esp. in order to win favour or reward. **2** to show to advantage: *that dress flatters her*. **3** (*tr*) to make to appear more attractive, etc., than in reality. **4** to gratify the vanity of (a person). **5** (*tr*) to encourage, esp. falsely. **6** (*tr*) to deceive (oneself): *I flatter myself that I am the best*. [C13: prob. from OF *flater* to lick, fawn upon, of Frankish origin]
▸ˈ**flatterable** *adj* ▸ˈ**flatterer** *n*

flattery ➊ (ˈflætərɪ) *n, pl* **flatteries. 1** the act of flattering. **2** excessive or insincere praise.

flattie (ˈflætɪ) *n NZ inf.* a flounder or other flatfish.

flatties (ˈflætɪz) *pl n* shoes with flat heels.

flat top *n* a style of haircut in which the hair is cut shortest on the top of the head so that it stands up from the scalp and appears flat from the crown to the forehead.

flatulent ➊ (ˈflætjʊlənt) *adj* **1** suffering from or caused by an excessive amount of gas in the alimentary canal. **2** generating excessive gas in the alimentary canal. **3** pretentious. [C16: from NL *flātulentus*, from L *flatus*, from *flāre* to breathe, blow]
▸ˈ**flatulence** *or* ˈ**flatulency** *n* ▸ˈ**flatulently** *adv*

flatus (ˈfleɪtəs) *n, pl* **flatuses.** gas generated in the alimentary canal. [C17: from L: a blowing, from *flāre* to breathe, blow]

flatworm (ˈflæt,wɜːm) *n* any parasitic or free-living invertebrate of the phylum *Platyhelminthes*, including flukes and tapeworms, having a flattened body.

flaunt ➊ (flɔːnt) *vb* **1** to display (possessions, oneself, etc.) ostentatiously. **2** to wave or cause to wave freely. ◆ *n* **3** the act of flaunting. [C16: ? of Scand. origin]

> **USAGE NOTE** *Flaunt* is sometimes wrongly used where *flout* is meant: *they must be prevented from flouting* (not *flaunting*) *the law.*

flautist (ˈflɔːtɪst) *or US & Canad.* **flutist** (ˈfluːtɪst) *n* a player of the flute. [C19: from It. *flautista*, from *flauto* FLUTE]

flavescent (fləˈvɛsᵊnt) *adj* turning yellow; yellowish. [C19: from L *flāvēscere* to become yellow]

flavin *or* **flavine** (ˈfleɪvɪn) *n* **1** a heterocyclic ketone that forms the nucleus of certain natural yellow pigments, such as riboflavin. **2** any yellow pigment based on flavin. [C19: from L *flāvus* yellow]

THESAURUS

whistle, zoom **20** *Informal* = **show**, display, exhibit, expose, flaunt, flourish

flashy *adj* **2** = **showy**, brash, cheap, cheap and nasty, flamboyant, flaunting, garish, gaudy, glittery, glitzy (*sl.*), in poor taste, jazzy (*inf.*), loud, meretricious, ostentatious, over the top (*inf.*), snazzy (*inf.*), tacky (*inf.*), tasteless, tawdry, tinselly
Antonyms *adj* downbeat, low-key, modest, natural, plain, unaffected, understated

flat[1] *adj* **1, 2** = **even**, horizontal, level, levelled, low, planar, plane, smooth, unbroken **3** = **horizontal**, laid low, lying full length, outstretched, prone, prostrate, reclining, recumbent, supine **6** = **punctured**, blown out, burst, collapsed, deflated, empty **9** = **absolute**, categorical, direct, downright, explicit, final, fixed, out-and-out, peremptory, plain, positive, straight, unconditional, unequivocal, unmistakable, unqualified **12, 13** = **dull**, boring, dead, flavourless, ho-hum (*inf.*), insipid, jejune, lacklustre, lifeless, monotonous, pointless, prosaic, spiritless, stale, tedious, tiresome, uninteresting, vapid, watery, weak ◆ *adv* **23, 24** = **completely**, absolutely, categorically, exactly, point blank, precisely, utterly **27a flat out** *Informal* = **at full speed**, all out, at full gallop, at full tilt, for all one is worth, hell for leather (*inf.*), posthaste, under full steam ◆ *n* **29, 30** *often plural* = **plain**, lowland, marsh, mud flat, shallow, shoal, strand, swamp
Antonyms *adj* ≠ **even**: broken, hilly, irregular, rolling, rough, rugged, slanting, sloping, uneven, up and down ≠ **horizontal**: on end, perpendicular, straight, upright, vertical ≠ **dull**: bubbly, effervescent, exciting, fizzy, palatable, sparkling, tasty, zestful

flat[2] *n* = **apartment**, rooms

flatly *adv* **23** = **absolutely**, categorically, completely, positively, unhesitatingly

flatness *n* **1, 2** = **evenness**, horizontality, levelness, smoothness, uniformity **12, 13** = **dullness**, emptiness, insipidity, monotony, staleness, tedium, vapidity

flatten *vb* **1** = **level**, compress, even out, iron out, plaster, raze, roll, smooth off, squash, trample **2a** *Informal* = **knock down**, bowl over, deck (*sl.*), fell, floor, knock off one's feet, prostrate **2b** *Informal* = **crush**, subdue

flatter *vb* **1** = **praise**, blandish, butter up, cajole, compliment, court, fawn, flannel (*Brit. inf.*), humour, inveigle, lay it on (thick) (*sl.*), pander to, puff, soft-soap (*inf.*), sweet-talk (*inf.*), wheedle **2, 3** = **suit**, become, do something for, enhance, set off, show to advantage

flattering *adj* **1** = **ingratiating**, adulatory, complimentary, fawning, fulsome, gratifying, honeyed, honey-tongued, laudatory, sugary **2, 3** = **becoming**, effective, enhancing, kind, well-chosen
Antonyms *adj* ≠ **ingratiating**: blunt, candid, honest, straight, uncomplimentary ≠ **becoming**: not shown in the best light, not shown to advantage, plain, unattractive, unbecoming, unflattering, warts and all

flattery *n* **1, 2** = **obsequiousness**, adulation, blandishment, blarney, cajolery, false praise, fawning, flannel (*Brit. inf.*), fulsomeness, honeyed words, servility, soft-soap (*inf.*), sweet-talk (*inf.*), sycophancy, toadyism

flatulence *n* **1** = **wind**, borborygmus (*Medical*), eructation **3** = **pretentiousness**, boasting, bombast, claptrap, empty words, fustian, hot air (*inf.*), pomposity, prolixity, rodomontade, twaddle

flatulent *adj* **3** = **pretentious**, bombastic, inflated, long-winded, pompous, prolix, swollen, tedious, tiresome, turgid, wordy

flaunt *vb* **1** = **show off**, boast, brandish, display, disport, exhibit, flash about, flourish, make a (great) show of, make an exhibition of, parade, sport (*inf.*), vaunt

flavine ('fleɪvɪn) *n* another name for **acriflavine hydrochloride.**
flavone ('fleɪvəʊn) *n* **1** a crystalline compound occurring in plants. **2** any of a class of yellow plant pigments derived from flavone. [C19: from G, from L *flāvus* yellow + -ONE]
flavoprotein (ˌfleɪvəʊ'prəʊtiːn) *n* any of a group of enzymes that contain a derivative of riboflavin linked to a protein and catalyse oxidation in cells.
flavour ➊ *or US* **flavor** ('fleɪvə) *n* **1** taste perceived in food or liquid in the mouth. **2** a substance added to food, etc., to impart a specific taste. **3** a distinctive quality or atmosphere. **4** *Physics.* a property of quarks that distinguishes different types. ◆ *vb* **5** (*tr*) to impart a flavour or quality to. [C14: from OF *flaour,* from LL *flātor* (unattested) bad smell, breath, from L *flāre* to blow]
▸ **'flavourless** *or US* **'flavorless** *adj* ▸ **'flavourful** *or US* **'flavorful** *adj*
flavour enhancer *n* another term for **monosodium glutamate.**
flavouring *or US* **flavoring** ('fleɪvərɪŋ) *n* a substance used to impart a particular flavour to food.
flaw[1] ➊ (flɔː) *n* **1** an imperfection or blemish. **2** a crack or rift. **3** *Law.* an invalidating defect in a document or proceeding. ◆ *vb* **4** to make or become blemished or imperfect. [C14: prob. from ON *flaga* stone slab]
▸ **'flawless** *adj*
flaw[2] (flɔː) *n* a sudden short gust of wind; squall. [C16: of Scand. origin]
flax (flæks) *n* **1** a herbaceous plant or shrub that has blue flowers and is cultivated for its seeds (flaxseed) and for the fibres of its stems. **2** the fibre of this plant, made into thread and woven into linen fabrics. **3** any of various similar plants. **4** *NZ.* a swamp plant producing a fibre that is used by Maoris for clothing, baskets, etc. [OE *fleax*]
flaxen ('flæksən) *adj* **1** of or resembling flax. **2** of a soft yellow colour: *flaxen hair.*
flaxseed ('flæksˌsiːd) *n* the seed of the flax plant, which yields linseed oil. Also called: **linseed.**
flay ➊ (fleɪ) *vb* (*tr*) **1** to strip off the skin or covering of, esp. by whipping. **2** to attack with savage criticism. [OE *flēan*]
▸ **'flayer** *n*
flea (fliː) *n* **1** a small wingless parasitic blood-sucking jumping insect living on the skin of mammals and birds. **2 flea in one's ear.** *Inf.* a sharp rebuke. [OE *flēah*]
fleabane ('fliːˌbeɪn) *n* any of several plants, including one having purplish tubular flower heads with orange centres and one having yellow daisy-like flower heads, that are reputed to ward off fleas.
fleabite ('fliːˌbaɪt) *n* **1** the bite of a flea. **2** a slight or trifling annoyance or discomfort.
flea-bitten ➊ *adj* **1** bitten by or infested with fleas. **2** *Inf.* shabby or decrepit.
flea market *n* an open-air market selling cheap and often second-hand goods.
fleapit ('fliːˌpɪt) *n Inf.* a shabby cinema or theatre.
fleawort ('fliːˌwɜːt) *n* **1** any of various plants with yellow daisy-like flowers and rosettes of downy leaves. **2** a Eurasian plantain whose seeds were formerly used as a flea repellent.
flèche (fleɪʃ, flɛʃ) *n* a slender spire, esp. over the intersection of the nave and transept ridges of a church roof. Also called: **spirelet.** [C18: from F: spire (lit.: arrow), prob. of Gmc origin]
fleck ➊ (flɛk) *n* **1** a small marking or streak. **2** a speck: *a fleck of dust.* ◆ *vb* **3** (*tr*) Also: **flecker.** to speckle. [C16: prob. from ON *flekkr* stain, spot]
fled (flɛd) *vb* the past tense and past participle of **flee.**
fledge (flɛdʒ) *vb* **fledges, fledging, fledged.** (*tr*) **1** to feed and care for (a young bird) until it is able to fly. **2** Also called: **fletch.** to fit (something, esp. an arrow) with a feather or feathers. **3** to cover or adorn with or as if with feathers. [OE *-flycge,* as in *unflycge* unfledged; see FLY[1]]
fledgling ➊ *or* **fledgeling** ('flɛdʒlɪŋ) *n* **1** a young bird that has grown feathers. **2** a young and inexperienced person.
flee ➊ (fliː) *vb* **flees, fleeing, fled. 1** to run away from (a place, danger, etc.). **2** (*intr*) to run or move quickly. [OE *flēon*]
▸ **'fleer** *n*
fleece ➊ (fliːs) *n* **1** the coat of wool that covers the body of a sheep or similar animal. **2** the wool removed from a single sheep. **3** something resembling a fleece. **4** sheepskin or a fabric with soft pile, used as a lining for coats, etc. ◆ *vb* **fleeces, fleecing, fleeced.** (*tr*) **5** to defraud or charge exorbitantly. **6** another term for **shear** (sense 1). [OE *flēos*]
fleecie ('fliːsɪ) *n NZ.* a person who collects fleeces after shearing and prepares them for baling. Also called: **fleece-oh.**
fleecy ➊ ('fliːsɪ) *adj* **fleecier, fleeciest.** of or resembling fleece.
▸ **'fleecily** *adv*
fleer (flɪə) *Arch.* ◆ *vb* **1** to scoff; sneer. ◆ *n* **2** a derisory glance. [C14: from ON; cf. Norwegian *flire* to snigger]
fleet[1] ➊ (fliːt) *n* **1** a number of warships organized as a tactical unit. **2** all the warships of a nation. **3** a number of aircraft, ships, buses, etc., operating together or under the same ownership. [OE *flēot*]
fleet[2] (fliːt) *adj* **1** rapid in movement; swift. **2** *Poetic.* fleeting. ◆ *vb* **3** (*intr*) to move rapidly. **4** (*tr*) *Obs.* to cause (time) to pass rapidly. [prob. OE *flēotan* to float, glide rapidly]
▸ **'fleetly** *adv* ▸ **'fleetness** *n*
Fleet Air Arm *n* the aviation branch of the Royal Navy.
fleet chief petty officer *n* a noncommissioned officer in the Royal Navy comparable in rank to a warrant officer in the army or the Royal Air Force.
fleeting ➊ ('fliːtɪŋ) *adj* rapid and transient: *a fleeting glimpse of the sea.*
▸ **'fleetingly** *adv*
fleet rate *or* **rating** *n* a reduced rate quoted by an insurance company to underwrite the risks to a fleet of vehicles, aircraft, etc.
Fleet Street *n* **1** a street in central London in which many newspaper offices were formerly situated. **2** British journalism or journalists collectively.
Fleming ('flɛmɪŋ) *n* a native or inhabitant of Flanders, a medieval principality in the Low Countries, or of Flemish-speaking Belgium.
Flemish ('flɛmɪʃ) *n* **1** one of the two official languages of Belgium. **2 the Flemish.** (*functioning as pl*) the Flemings collectively. ◆ *adj* **3** of or characteristic of Flanders, the Flemings, or their language.
flense (flɛns), **flench** (flɛntʃ), *or* **flinch** (flɪntʃ) *vb* **flenses, flensing, flensed** *or* **flenches, flenching, flenched** *or* **flinches, flinching, flinched.** (*tr*) to strip (a whale, seal, etc.) of (its blubber or skin). [C19: from Danish *flense;* rel. to Du. *flensen*]
flesh ➊ (flɛʃ) *n* **1** the soft part of the body of an animal or human, esp. muscular tissue, as distinct from bone and viscera. **2** *Inf.* excess weight; fat. **3** *Arch.* the edible tissue of animals as opposed to that of fish or, sometimes, fowl. **4** the thick soft part of a fruit or vegetable. **5** the human body and its physical or sensual nature as opposed to the soul or spirit. Related adj: **carnal. 6** mankind in general. **7** animate creatures in general. **8** one's own family; kin (esp. in **one's own flesh and blood**). **9a** a yellowish-pink colour. **9b** (*as adj*): *flesh tights.* **10 in the flesh.** in person; actually present. **11 press the flesh.** *Inf.* to shake hands, usually with large numbers of people, esp. as a political campaigning ploy. ◆ *vb* **12** (*tr*) *Hunting.* to stimulate the hunting instinct of (hounds or falcons) by giving them small quantities of raw flesh. **13** *Arch. or poetic.* to accustom or incite to bloodshed or battle by initial experience. **14** to fatten; fill out. [OE *flǣsc*]
fleshings ('flɛʃɪŋz) *pl n* flesh-coloured tights.
fleshly ➊ ('flɛʃlɪ) *adj* **fleshlier, fleshliest. 1** relating to the body; carnal: *fleshly desire.* **2** worldly as opposed to spiritual. **3** fat.

THESAURUS

flavour *n* **1 = taste,** aroma, essence, extract, flavouring, odour, piquancy, relish, savour, seasoning, smack, tang, zest, zing (*inf.*) **2 = quality,** aspect, character, essence, feel, feeling, property, *soupçon,* stamp, style, suggestion, tinge, tone, touch ◆ *vb* **5 = season,** ginger up, imbue, infuse, lace, leaven, spice
Antonyms *n* ≠ **taste:** blandness, flatness, insipidity, odourlessness, tastelessness, vapidity
flaw[1] *n* **1 = weakness,** blemish, chink in one's armour, defect, disfigurement, failing, fault, imperfection, scar, speck, spot, weak spot **2 = crack,** breach, break, cleft, crevice, fissure, fracture, rent, rift, scission, split, tear
flawed *adj* **1, 2 = damaged,** blemished, broken, chipped, cracked, defective, erroneous, faulty, imperfect, unsound
flawless *adj* **1 = perfect,** faultless, impeccable, spotless, unblemished, unsullied **2 = intact,** sound, unbroken, undamaged, whole
flay *vb* **1 = skin,** excoriate **2 = upbraid,** castigate, excoriate, execrate, pull to pieces (*inf.*), revile, slam (*sl.*), tear a strip off, tear into (*inf.*)
flea-bitten *adj* **1, 2 = shabby,** crawling, decrepit, fetid, flea-ridden, frowsty, grotty (*sl.*), grubby, infested, insalubrious, lousy, mean, mucky, pediculous (*Medical*), run-down, scabby, scruffy, scurfy, sleazy, slummy, sordid, squalid, tatty, unhygienic
fleck *n* **1, 2 = mark,** dot, pinpoint, speck, speckle, spot, streak ◆ *vb* **3 = speckle,** bespeckle, besprinkle, dapple, dot, dust, mark, mottle, spot, stipple, streak, variegate
fledgling *n* **1 = chick,** nestling **2 = novice,** apprentice, beginner, learner, neophyte, newcomer, rookie (*inf.*), trainee, tyro
flee *vb* **1, 2 = run away,** abscond, avoid, bolt, cut and run (*inf.*), decamp, depart, do a runner (*sl.*), escape, fly, get away, hook it (*sl.*), leave, make a quick exit, make off, make oneself scarce (*inf.*), make one's escape, make one's getaway, scarper (*Brit. sl.*), skedaddle (*inf.*), slope off, split (*sl.*), take flight, take off (*inf.*), turn tail, vanish
fleece *n* **1, 2 = wool** ◆ *vb* **5 = cheat,** bleed, con (*inf.*), cozen, defraud, despoil, diddle (*inf.*), overcharge, plunder, rifle, rip off (*sl.*), rob, rook (*sl.*), skin (*sl.*), steal, stiff (*sl.*), swindle, take for a ride (*inf.*), take to the cleaners (*sl.*) **6 = shear,** clip
fleecy *adj* **= woolly,** downy, fluffy, shaggy, soft
fleet[1] *n* **1, 2 = navy,** argosy, armada, flotilla, naval force, sea power, squadron, task force, vessels, warships
fleet[2] *adj* **1 = swift,** fast, flying, mercurial, meteoric, nimble, nimble-footed, quick, rapid, speedy, winged
fleeting *adj* **= momentary,** brief, ephemeral, evanescent, flitting, flying, fugacious, fugitive, passing, short, short-lived, temporary, transient, transitory
Antonyms *adj* abiding, continuing, durable, enduring, eternal, imperishable, lasting, long-lasting, long-lived, permanent
fleetness *n* **1 = swiftness,** celerity, lightning speed, nimble-footedness, nimbleness, quickness, rapidity, speed, speediness, velocity
flesh *n* **1 = meat,** beef (*inf.*), body, brawn, fat, fatness, food, tissue, weight **5 = physical nature,** animality, body, carnality, flesh and blood, human nature, physicality, sensuality **6 = mankind,** homo sapiens, humankind, human race, living creatures, man, mortality, people, race, stock, world **8 one's own flesh and blood = family,** blood, kin, kindred, kinsfolk, kith and kin, relations, relatives
fleshiness *n* **1 = plumpness,** chubbiness, corpulence, flabbiness, heaviness, obesity, stoutness
fleshly *adj* **1 = carnal,** animal, bodily, erotic, lascivious, lecherous, lustful, sensual **2 =**

▸ 'fleshliness *n*

flesh out *vb* (*adv*) **1** (*tr*) to give substance to (an argument, description, etc.). **2** (*intr*) to expand or become more substantial.

fleshpots ('flɛʃ,pɒts) *pl n Often facetious.* **1** luxurious living. **2** places where bodily desires are gratified. [C16: from the Biblical use as applied to Egypt (Exodus 16:3)]

flesh wound (wu:nd) *n* a wound affecting superficial tissues.

fleshy ❶ ('flɛʃɪ) *adj* **fleshier, fleshiest. 1** plump. **2** related to or resembling flesh. **3** *Bot.* (of some fruits, etc.) thick and pulpy.
▸ **'fleshiness** *n*

fletcher ('flɛtʃə) *n* a person who makes arrows. [C14: from OF *flechier*, from *fleche* arrow; see FLÈCHE]

fleur-de-lys *or* **fleur-de-lis** (,flɜ:də'li:) *n, pl* **fleurs-de-lys** *or* **fleurs-de-lis** (,flɜ:də'li:z). **1** *Heraldry.* a charge representing a lily with three distinct petals. **2** another name for **iris** (sense 2). [C19: from OF *flor de lis*, lit.: lily flower]

fleurette *or* **fleuret** (flʊə'rɛt) *n* an ornament or motif resembling a flower. [C19: F, lit.: a small flower, from *fleur* flower]

flew (flu:) *vb* the past tense of **fly**[1].

flews (flu:z) *pl n* the fleshy hanging upper lip of a bloodhound or similar dog. [C16: from ?]

flex ❶ (flɛks) *n* **1** *Brit.* a flexible insulated electric cable, used esp. to connect appliances to mains. US and Canad. name: **cord.** ◆ *vb* **2** to bend or be bent: *he flexed his arm.* **3** to contract (a muscle) or (of a muscle) to contract. **4** (*intr*) to work flexitime. [C16: from L *flexus* bent, winding, from *flectere* to bend, bow]

flexible ❶ ('flɛksɪbᵊl) *adj* **1** Also **flexile** ('flɛksaɪl). able to be bent easily without breaking. **2** adaptable or variable: *flexible working hours.* **3** able to be persuaded easily.
▸ ,**flexi'bility** *n* ▸ **'flexibly** *adv*

flexion ('flɛkʃən) *or* **flection** *n* **1** the act of bending a joint or limb. **2** the condition of the joint or limb so bent.
▸ **'flexional** *adj*

flexitime ('flɛksɪ,taɪm) *n* a system permitting flexibility of working hours at the beginning or end of the day, provided an agreed period (**core time**) is spent at work. Also called: **flextime.**

flexor ('flɛksə) *n* any muscle whose contraction serves to bend a joint or limb. Cf. **extensor.** [C17: NL; see FLEX]

flexuous ('flɛksjuəs) *adj* full of bends or curves; winding. [C17: from L *flexuōsus* full of bends, tortuous, from *flexus* a bending; see FLEX]
▸ **'flexuously** *adv*

flexure ('flɛkʃə) *n* **1** the act of flexing or the state of being flexed. **2** a bend, turn, or fold.

flex-wing *n Aeronautics.* a collapsible fabric delta wing, as used with hang-gliders.

flibbertigibbet ('flɪbətɪ,dʒɪbɪt) *n* an irresponsible, silly, or gossipy person. [C15: from ?]

flick[1] ❶ (flɪk) *vb* **1** (*tr*) to touch with or as if with the finger or hand in a quick jerky movement. **2** (*tr*) to propel or remove by a quick jerky movement, usually of the fingers or hand. **3** to move or cause to move quickly or jerkily. **4** (*intr; foll. by through*) to read or look at (a book, etc.) quickly or idly. ◆ *n* **5** a tap or quick stroke with the fingers, a whip, etc. **6** the sound made by such a stroke. **7** a fleck or particle. **8 give (someone) the flick.** to dismiss (someone) from consideration. [C15: imit.; cf. F *flicflac*]

flick[2] (flɪk) *n Sl.* **1** a cinema film. **2 the flicks.** the cinema: *what's on at the flicks tonight?*

flicker[1] ❶ ('flɪkə) *vb* **1** (*intr*) to shine with an unsteady or intermittent light. **2** (*intr*) to move quickly to and fro. **3** (*tr*) to cause to flicker. ◆ *n* **4** an unsteady or brief light or flame. **5** a swift quivering or fluttering movement. [OE *flicorian*]

flicker[2] ('flɪkə) *n* a North American woodpecker which has a yellow undersurface to the wings and tail. [C19: ? imit. of the bird's call]

flick knife *n* a knife with a retractable blade that springs out when a button is pressed.

flier ❶ ('flaɪə) *n* a variant spelling of **flyer.**

flight[1] ❶ (flaɪt) *n* **1** the act, skill, or manner of flying. **2** a journey made by a flying animal or object. **3** a group of flying birds or aircraft: *a flight of swallows.* **4** the basic tactical unit of a military air force. **5** a journey through space, esp. of a spacecraft. **6** an aircraft flying on a scheduled journey. **7** a soaring mental journey above or beyond the normal everyday world: *a flight of fancy.* **8** a single line of hurdles across a track in a race. **9** a feather or plastic attachment fitted to an arrow or dart to give it stability in flight. **10** a set of steps or stairs between one landing or floor and the next. ◆ *vb* (*tr*) **11** *Sport.* to cause (a ball, dart, etc.) to float slowly towards its target. **12** to shoot (a bird) in flight. **13** to fledge (an arrow or dart). [OE *flyht*]

flight[2] ❶ (flaɪt) *n* **1** the act of fleeing or running away, as from danger. **2 put to flight.** to cause to run away. **3 take (to) flight.** to run away; flee. [OE *flyht* (unattested)]

flight attendant *n* a person who attends to the needs of passengers on a commercial flight.

flight deck *n* **1** the crew compartment in an airliner. **2** the upper deck of an aircraft carrier from which aircraft take off.

flightless ('flaɪtlɪs) *adj* (of certain birds and insects) unable to fly. See also **ratite.**

flight lieutenant *n* an officer holding a commissioned rank senior to a flying officer and junior to a squadron leader in the Royal Air Force.

flight path *n* the course through the air of an aircraft, rocket, or projectile.

flight recorder *n* an electronic device fitted to an aircraft for collecting and storing information concerning its performance in flight. It is often used to determine the cause of a crash. Also called: **black box.**

flight sergeant *n* a noncommissioned officer in the Royal Air Force, junior in rank to that of master aircrew.

flight simulator *n* a ground-training device that reproduces exactly the conditions experienced on the flight deck of an aircraft.

flighty ❶ ('flaɪtɪ) *adj* **flightier, flightiest. 1** frivolous and irresponsible. **2** mentally erratic or wandering.
▸ **'flightiness** *n*

flimflam ('flɪm,flæm) *Inf.* ◆ *n* **1a** nonsense; rubbish; foolishness. **1b** (*as modifier*): *flimflam arguments.* **2** a deception; trick; swindle. ◆ *vb* **flimflams, flimflamming, flimflammed. 3** (*tr*) to deceive; trick; swindle; cheat. [C16: prob. of Scand. origin]
▸ **'flim,flammer** *n*

flimsy ❶ ('flɪmzɪ) *adj* **flimsier, flimsiest. 1** not strong or substantial: *a flimsy building.* **2** light and thin: *a flimsy dress.* **3** unconvincing; weak: *a flimsy excuse.* ◆ *n* **4** thin paper used for making carbon copies of a letter, etc. **5** a copy made on such paper. [C17: from ?]
▸ **'flimsiness** *n*

flinch ❶ (flɪntʃ) *vb* (*intr*) **1** to draw back suddenly, as from pain, shock, etc.; wince. **2** (often foll. by *from*) to avoid contact (with): *he never flinched from his duty.* [C16: from OF *flenchir*; rel. to MHG *lenken* to bend, direct]
▸ **'flinchingly** *adv*

flinders ('flɪndəz) *pl n Rare.* small fragments or splinters (esp. in **fly into flinders**). [C15: prob. from ON; cf. Norwegian *flindra* thin piece of stone]

fling ❶ (flɪŋ) *vb* **flings, flinging, flung.** (*mainly tr*) **1** to throw, esp. with force or abandon. **2** to put or send without warning or preparation: *to fling someone into jail.* **3** (*also intr*) to move (oneself or a part of the body) with abandon or speed. **4** (usually foll. by *into*) to apply (oneself) diligently and with vigour (to). **5** to cast aside: *she flung away her scruples.* ◆ *n* **6** the act or an instance of flinging. **7** a period or occasion of unrestrained or extravagant behaviour. **8** any of various vigorous Scottish

THESAURUS

worldly, corporal, corporeal, earthly, human, material, mundane, of this world, physical, secular, terrestrial

fleshy *adj* **1** = **plump**, ample, beefy (*inf.*), brawny, chubby, chunky, corpulent, fat, hefty, meaty, obese, overweight, podgy, stout, tubby, well-padded

flex *vb* **2, 3** = **bend**, angle, contract, crook, curve, tighten

flexibility *n* **1** = **pliancy**, elasticity, give, pliability, resilience, springiness, tensility **2** = **adaptability**, adjustability, complaisance

flexible *adj* **1** = **pliable**, bendable, ductile, elastic, limber, lissom(e), lithe, mouldable, plastic, pliant, springy, stretchy, supple, tensile, willowy, yielding **2** = **adaptable**, adjustable, discretionary, open, variable **3** = **compliant**, amenable, biddable, complaisant, docile, gentle, manageable, responsive, tractable
Antonyms *adj* ≠ **pliable**: fixed, immovable, inflexible, rigid, stiff, tough, unyielding ≠ **adaptable**: absolute, inflexible ≠ **compliant**: determined, inexorable, inflexible, intractable, obdurate, staunch, unyielding

flick[1] *vb* **1** = **strike**, dab, fillip, flip, hit, jab, peck, rap, tap, touch **4** *foll. by* **through** = **browse**, flip through, glance at, skim, skip, thumb ◆ *n* **5** = **tap**, fillip, flip, jab, peck, rap, touch

flicker[1] *vb* **1** = **twinkle**, flare, flash, glimmer, gutter, shimmer, sparkle **2** = **flutter**, quiver, vibrate, waver ◆ *n* **4** = **glimmer**, flare, flash, gleam, spark

flickering *adj* **1** = **wavering**, fitful, guttering, twinkling, unsteady

flier *see* **flyer**

flight[1] *n* **1** = **flying**, mounting, soaring, winging **2** = **journey**, trip, voyage **4** = **flock**, cloud, formation, squadron, swarm, unit, wing

flight[2] *n* **1** = **escape**, departure, exit, exodus, fleeing, getaway, retreat, running away **2 put to flight** = **drive off**, chase off, disperse, rout, scare off, scatter, send packing, stampede **3 take (to) flight** = **run away** *or* **off**, abscond, beat a retreat, bolt, decamp, do a bunk (*Brit. sl.*), do a runner (*sl.*), fleet, skedaddle (*inf.*), turn tail, withdraw hastily

flightiness *n* **1, 2** = **frivolity**, capriciousness, fickleness, flippancy, giddiness, irresponsibility, levity, lightness, mercurialness, volatility

flighty *adj* **1, 2** = **frivolous**, capricious, changeable, ditzy *or* ditsy (*sl.*), dizzy, fickle, giddy, harebrained, impetuous, impulsive, irresponsible, light-headed, mercurial, scatterbrained, skittish, thoughtless, unbalanced, unstable, unsteady, volatile, wild

flimsy *adj* **1** = **fragile**, delicate, frail, gimcrack, insubstantial, makeshift, rickety, shaky, shallow, slight, superficial, unsubstantial **2** = **thin**, chiffon, gauzy, gossamer, light, sheer, transparent **3** = **unconvincing**, feeble, frivolous, implausible, inadequate, pathetic, poor, tenuous, thin, transparent, trivial, unsatisfactory, weak
Antonyms *adj* ≠ **fragile**: durable, heavy, robust, solid, sound, stout, strong, sturdy, substantial

flinch *vb* **1** = **recoil**, back off, baulk, blench, cower, cringe, draw back, duck, flee, quail, retreat, shirk, shrink, shy away, start, swerve, wince, withdraw

fling *vb* **1** = **throw**, cast, catapult, chuck (*inf.*), heave, hurl, jerk, let fly, lob (*inf.*), pitch, precipitate, propel, send, shy, sling, toss ◆ *n* **6** = **throw**, cast, lob, pitch, shot, toss **7** = **binge** (*inf.*), bash, beano (*Brit. sl.*), bit of fun, good time, hooley *or* hoolie (*chiefly Irish & NZ*), indulgence, party, rave (*Brit. sl.*), rave-up (*Brit. sl.*), spree **9** = **try**, attempt, bash (*inf.*), crack, gamble, go (*inf.*), shot (*inf.*), stab (*inf.*), trial, venture, whirl (*inf.*)

reels full of leaps and turns, such as the Highland fling. **9** a trial; try: *to have a fling at something different.* [C13: from ON]
▸ **'flinger** *n*

flint (flɪnt) *n* **1** an impure greyish-black form of quartz that occurs in chalk. It produces sparks when struck with steel and is used in the manufacture of pottery and road-construction materials. Formula: SiO_2. **2** any piece of flint, esp. one used as a primitive tool or for striking fire. **3** a small cylindrical piece of an iron alloy, used in cigarette lighters. **4** Also called: **flint glass.** colourless glass other than plate glass. [OE]

flintlock ('flɪnt,lɒk) *n* **1** an obsolete gunlock in which the charge is ignited by a spark produced by a flint in the hammer. **2** a firearm having such a lock.

flinty ❶ ('flɪntɪ) *adj* **flintier, flintiest. 1** of or resembling flint. **2** hard or cruel; unyielding.
▸ **'flintily** *adv* ▸ **'flintiness** *n*

flip ❶ (flɪp) *vb* **flips, flipping, flipped. 1** to throw (something light or small) carelessly or briskly. **2** to throw or flick (an object such as a coin) so that it turns or spins in the air. **3** to flick: *to flip a crumb across the room.* **4** (foll. by *through*) to read or look at (a book, etc.) quickly, idly, or incompletely. **5** (*intr*) to make a snapping movement or noise with the finger and thumb. **6** (*intr*) *Sl.* to fly into a rage or an emotional outburst (also in **flip one's lid, flip one's top, flip out**). ◆ *n* **7** a snap or tap, usually with the fingers. **8** a rapid jerk. **9** any alcoholic drink containing beaten egg. ◆ *adj* **10** *Inf.* flippant or pert. [C16: prob. imit.; see FILLIP]

flip chart *n* a pad, containing large sheets of paper that can be easily turned over, mounted on a stand and used to present reports, data, etc.

flip-flop *n* **1** a backward handspring. **2** Also called: **bistable.** an electronic device or circuit that can assume either of two states by the application of a suitable pulse. **3** a complete change of opinion, policy, etc. **4** a repeated flapping noise. **5** Also called (esp. US, Austral., NZ, and Canad.): **thong** or (S. Afr.) **slip-slop.** a rubber-soled sandal attached to the foot by a thong between the big toe and the next toe. ◆ *vb* **flip-flops, flip-flopping, flip-flopped. 6** (*intr*) to move with repeated flaps. [C16: reduplication of FLIP]

flippant ❶ ('flɪpənt) *adj* **1** marked by inappropriate levity; frivolous. **2** impertinent; saucy. [C17: ?from FLIP]
▸ **'flippancy** *n* ▸ **'flippantly** *adv*

flipper ('flɪpə) *n* **1** the flat broad limb of seals, whales, etc., specialized for swimming. **2** (*often pl*) either of a pair of rubber paddle-like devices worn on the feet as an aid in swimming.

flip side *n* **1** another term for **B-side. 2** another, less familiar, aspect of a person or thing.

flirt ❶ (flɜːt) *vb* **1** (*intr*) to behave or act amorously without emotional commitment. **2** (*intr;* usually foll. by *with*) to deal playfully or carelessly (with something dangerous or serious): *the motorcyclist flirted with death.* **3** (*intr;* usually foll. by *with*) to toy (with): *to flirt with the idea of leaving.* **4** (*intr*) to dart; flit. **5** (*tr*) to flick or toss. ◆ *n* **6** a person who acts flirtatiously. [C16: from ?]
▸ **'flirter** *n* ▸ **'flirty** *adj*

flirtation ❶ (flɜː'teɪʃən) *n* **1** behaviour intended to arouse sexual feelings or advances without emotional commitment. **2** any casual involvement.

flirtatious ❶ (flɜː'teɪʃəs) *adj* **1** given to flirtation. **2** expressive of playful sexual invitation: *a flirtatious glance.*
▸ **flir'tatiously** *adv*

flit ❶ (flɪt) *vb* **flits, flitting, flitted.** (*intr*) **1** to move along rapidly and lightly. **2** to fly rapidly and lightly. **3** to pass quickly: *a memory flitted into his mind.* **4** *Scot. & N English dialect.* to move house. **5** *Brit. inf.* to depart hurriedly and stealthily in order to avoid obligations. ◆ *n* **6** the act or an instance of flitting. **7** *Brit. inf.* a hurried and stealthy departure in order to avoid obligations. [C12: from ON *flytja* to carry]
▸ **'flitter** *n*

flitch (flɪtʃ) *n* **1** a side of pork salted and cured. **2** a piece of timber cut lengthways from a tree trunk. [OE *flicce;* cf. FLESH]

flitter ('flɪtə) *vb* a less common word for **flutter.**

flittermouse ('flɪtə,maʊs) *n, pl* **flittermice.** a dialect name for **bat**[2] (sense 1). [C16: translation of G *Fledermaus*]

float ❶ (fləʊt) *vb* **1** to rest or cause to rest on the surface of a fluid or in a fluid or space without sinking: *oil floats on water.* **2** to move or cause to move buoyantly, lightly, or freely across a surface or through air, water, etc. **3** to move about aimlessly, esp. in the mind: *thoughts floated before him.* **4** (*tr*) **4a** to launch or establish (a commercial enterprise, etc.). **4b** to offer for sale (stock or bond issues, etc.) on the stock market. **5** (*tr*) *Finance.* to allow (a currency) to fluctuate against other currencies in accordance with market forces. **6** (*tr*) to flood, inundate, or irrigate (land). ◆ *n* **7** something that floats. **8** *Angling.* an indicator attached to a baited line that sits on the water and moves when a fish bites. **9** a small hand tool with a rectangular blade used for smoothing plaster, etc. **10** Also called: **paddle.** a blade of a paddle wheel. **11** *Brit.* a buoyant garment or device to aid a person in staying afloat. **12** a structure fitted to the underside of an aircraft to allow it to land on water. **13** a motor vehicle used to carry a tableau or exhibit in a parade, esp. a civic parade. **14** a small delivery vehicle, esp. one powered by batteries: *a milk float.* **15** *Austral. & NZ.* a vehicle for transporting horses. **16** a sum of money used by shopkeepers to provide change at the start of the day's business. **17** the hollow floating ball of a ballcock. [OE *flotian;* see FLEET[2]]
▸ **'floatable** *adj* ▸ **,floata'bility** *n* ▸ **'floaty** *adj*

floatage ('fləʊtɪdʒ) *n* a variant spelling of **flotage.**

floatation (fləʊ'teɪʃən) *n* a variant spelling of **flotation.**

floatel (fləʊ'tɛl) *n* a variant spelling of **flotel.**

floater ('fləʊtə) *n* **1** a person or thing that floats. **2** a dark spot that appears in one's vision as a result of dead cells or cell fragments in the eye. **3** *US & Canad.* a person of no fixed political opinion. **4** *US inf.* a person who often changes employment, residence, etc.

float glass *n* polished glass made by floating molten glass on liquid metal in a reservoir.

floating ❶ ('fləʊtɪŋ) *adj* **1** having little or no attachment. **2** (of an organ or part) displaced from the normal position or abnormally movable: *a floating kidney.* **3** uncommitted or unfixed: *floating voters.* **4** *Finance.* **4a** (of capital) available for current use. **4b** (of debt) short-term and unfunded, usually raised to meet current expenses. **4c** (of a currency) free to fluctuate against other currencies in accordance with market forces.
▸ **'floatingly** *adv*

floating-point representation *n Computing.* the representation of numbers by two sets of digits (*a, b*), the set *a* indicating the significant digits, the set *b* giving the position of the radix point. Also called: **floating decimal point representation.** Cf. **fixed-point representation.**

floating rib *n* any rib of the lower two pairs of ribs in man, which are not attached to the breastbone.

floats (fləʊts) *pl n Theatre.* another word for **footlights.**

flob (flɒb) *vb* **flobs, flobbing, flobbed.** (*intr*) *Brit. sl.* to spit. [C20: from?]

flocculate ('flɒkjʊ,leɪt) *vb* **flocculates, flocculating, flocculated.** to form or be formed into an aggregated flocculent mass.
▸ **,floccu'lation** *n*

flocculent ('flɒkjʊlənt) *adj* **1** like wool; fleecy. **2** *Chem.* aggregated in woolly cloudlike masses: *a flocculent precipitate.* **3** *Biol.* covered with tufts or flakes. [C19: from L *floccus* FLOCK[2] + -ULENT]
▸ **'flocculence** *n*

flocculus ('flɒkjʊləs) *n, pl* **flocculi** (-,laɪ). **1** Also called: **plage.** a cloudy marking on the sun's surface. It consists of calcium when lighter than the surroundings and of hydrogen when darker. **2** *Anat.* a tiny prominence on each side of the cerebellum.

flock[1] ❶ (flɒk) *n* (*sometimes functioning as pl*) **1** a group of animals of one kind, esp. sheep or birds. **2** a large number of people. **3** a body of Christians regarded as the pastoral charge of a priest, bishop, etc. ◆ *vb* (*intr*) **4** to gather together or move in a flock. **5** to go in large numbers: *people flocked to the church.* [OE *flocc*]

flock[2] (flɒk) *n* **1** a tuft, as of wool, hair, cotton, etc. **2** waste from fabrics such as cotton or wool used for stuffing mattresses, etc. **3** Also called: **flocking.** very small tufts of wool applied to fabrics, wallpaper, etc., to give a raised pattern. [C13: from OF *floc,* from L *floccus*]
▸ **'flocky** *adj*

floe (fləʊ) *n* See **ice floe.** [C19: prob. from Norwegian *flo* slab, layer, from ON; see FLAW[1]]

flog ❶ (flɒg) *vb* **flogs, flogging, flogged. 1** (*tr*) to beat harshly, esp. with a whip, strap, etc. **2** *Brit. sl.* to sell. **3** (*intr*) to make progress by painful work. **4 flog a dead horse.** *Chiefly Brit.* **4a** to harp on some long discarded subject. **4b** to pursue the solution of a problem long realized to be insoluble. [C17: prob. from L *flagellāre;* see FLAGELLANT]
▸ **'flogger** *n*

THESAURUS

flinty *adj* **2** = **hard,** adamant, cruel, hard-hearted, harsh, heartless, inflexible, obdurate, pitiless, steely, stern, stony, unfeeling, unmerciful, unyielding

flip *vb, n* **1-3, 8** = **toss,** cast, flick, jerk, pitch, snap, spin, throw, twist

flippancy *n* **1, 2** = **frivolity,** cheek (*inf.*), cheekiness, disrespectfulness, impertinence, irreverence, levity, pertness, sauciness

flippant *adj* **1, 2** = **frivolous,** cheeky, disrespectful, flip (*inf.*), glib, impertinent, impudent, irreverent, offhand, pert, rude, saucy, superficial

Antonyms *adj* gracious, mannerly, polite, respectful, serious, sincere, solicitous, well-mannered

flirt *vb* **1** = **chat up** (*inf.*), coquet, dally, lead on, make advances, make eyes at, make sheep's eyes at, philander **2, 3** *usually foll. by* **with** = **toy with,** consider, dabble in, entertain, expose oneself to, give a thought to, play with, trifle with ◆ *n* **6** = **tease,** coquette, heart-breaker, philanderer, trifler, wanton

flirtation *n* **1** = **teasing,** coquetry, dalliance, intrigue, philandering, toying, trifling

flirtatious *adj* **1, 2** = **teasing,** amorous, arch, come-hither, come-on (*inf.*), coquettish, coy, enticing, flirty, provocative, sportive

flit *vb* **1-3** = **fly,** dart, flash, fleet, flutter, pass, skim, speed, whisk, wing

float *vb* **1, 2** = **be buoyant,** be *or* lie on the surface, displace water, hang, hover, poise, rest on water, stay afloat **2** = **glide,** bob, drift, move gently, sail, slide, slip along **4** = **launch,** get going, promote, push off, set up

Antonyms *vb* ≠ **be buoyant:** dip, drown, founder, go down, settle, sink, submerge ≠ **launch:** abolish, annul, cancel, dissolve, terminate

floating *adj* **3** = **free,** fluctuating, migratory, movable, unattached, uncommitted, unfixed, variable, wandering

flock[1] *n* **1** = **herd,** colony, drove, flight, gaggle, skein **2** = **crowd,** assembly, bevy, collection, company, congregation, convoy, gathering, group, herd, host, mass, multitude, throng ◆ *vb* **4** = **gather,** collect, congregate, converge, crowd, group, herd, huddle, mass, throng, troop

flog *vb* **1** = **beat,** castigate, chastise, flagellate, flay, lambast(e), lash, scourge, thrash, trounce, whack, whip **3** = **strain,** drive, oppress, overexert, overtax, overwork, punish, push, tax

flogging *n* **1** = **beating,** caning, flagellation,

flong (flɒŋ) *n Printing.* a material used for making moulds in stereotyping. [C20: var. of FLAN]

flood ➊ (flʌd) *n* **1a** the inundation of land that is normally dry through the overflowing of a body of water, esp. a river. **1b** the state of a river that is at an abnormally high level. Related adj: **diluvial. 2** a great outpouring or flow: *a flood of words.* **3a** the rising of the tide from low to high water. **3b** (*as modifier*): *the flood tide.* Cf. **ebb** (sense 3). **4** *Theatre.* short for **floodlight.** ◆ *vb* **5** (of water) to inundate or submerge (land) or (of land) to be inundated or submerged. **6** to fill or be filled to overflowing, as with a flood. **7** (*intr*) to flow; surge: *relief flooded through him.* **8** to supply an excessive quantity of petrol to (a carburettor or petrol engine) or (of a carburettor, etc.) to be supplied with such an excess. **9** (*intr*) to overflow. **10** (*intr*) to bleed profusely from the uterus, as following childbirth. [OE *flōd*; see FLOW, FLOAT]

Flood (flʌd) *n Old Testament.* **the.** the flood from which Noah and his family and livestock were saved in the ark (Genesis 7–8).

floodgate ('flʌd,geɪt) *n* **1** Also called: **head gate, water gate.** a gate in a sluice that is used to control the flow of water. **2** (*often pl*) a control or barrier against an outpouring or flow.

flooding ('flʌdɪŋ) *n* **1** *Psychol.* a method of eliminating anxiety in a given situation, by exposing a person to the situation until the anxiety subsides. **2** *Pathol.* excessive bleeding from the uterus.

floodlight ('flʌd,laɪt) *n* **1** a broad intense beam of artificial light, esp. as used in the theatre or to illuminate the exterior of buildings. **2** the lamp producing such light. ◆ *vb* **floodlights, floodlighting, floodlit. 3** (*tr*) to illuminate as by floodlight.

flood plain *n* the flat area bordering a river, composed of sediment deposited during flooding.

floor ➊ (flɔː) *n* **1** Also called: **flooring.** the inner lower surface of a room. **2** a storey of a building: *the second floor.* **3** a flat bottom surface in or on any structure: *a dance floor.* **4** the bottom surface of a tunnel, cave, sea, etc. **5** that part of a legislative hall in which debate and other business is conducted. **6** the right to speak in a legislative body (esp. in **get, have,** *or* **be given the floor**). **7** the room in a stock exchange where trading takes place. **8** the earth; ground. **9** a minimum price charged or paid. **10 take the floor.** to begin dancing on a dance floor. ◆ *vb* **11** to cover with or construct a floor. **12** (*tr*) to knock to the floor or ground. **13** (*tr*) *Inf.* to disconcert, confound, or defeat. [OE *flōr*]

floorboard ('flɔː,bɔːd) *n* one of the boards forming a floor.

flooring ('flɔːrɪŋ) *n* **1** the material used in making a floor. **2** another word for **floor** (sense 1).

floor manager *n* **1** the stage manager of a television programme. **2** a person in overall charge of one floor of a large shop.

floor plan *n* a drawing to scale of the arrangement of rooms on one floor of a building.

floor show *n* a series of entertainments, such as singing and dancing, performed in a nightclub.

floozy, floozie, *or* **floosie** ('fluːzɪ) *n, pl* **floozies** *or* **floosies.** *Sl.* a disreputable woman. [C20: from ?]

flop ➊ (flɒp) *vb* **flops, flopping, flopped. 1** (*intr*) to bend, fall, or collapse loosely or carelessly: *his head flopped backwards.* **2** (when *intr*, often foll. by *into, onto,* etc.) to fall, cause to fall, or move with a sudden noise. **3** (*intr*) *Inf.* to fail: *the scheme flopped.* **4** (*intr*) to fall flat onto the surface of water. **5** (*intr;* often foll. by *out*) *Sl.* to go to sleep. ◆ *n* **6** the act of flopping. **7** *Inf.* a complete failure. [C17: var. of FLAP]

floppy ➊ ('flɒpɪ) *adj* **floppier, floppiest. 1** limp or hanging loosely. ◆ *n, pl* **floppies. 2** short for **floppy disk.**
▸**'floppily** *adv* ▸**'floppiness** *n*

floppy disk *n* a flexible magnetic disk that stores information and can be used to store data in the memory of a digital computer.

flops *abbrev.* (*sometimes caps.*) *for* floating-point operations per second: a measure of computer processing power.

flora ('flɔːrə) *n, pl* **floras** *or* **florae** (-riː). **1** all the plant life of a given place or time. **2** a descriptive list of such plants, often including a key for identification. [C18: from NL, from *Flōra* goddess of flowers, from *flōs* FLOWER]

floral ➊ ('flɔːrəl) *adj* **1** decorated with or consisting of flowers or patterns of flowers. **2** of or associated with flowers.
▸**'florally** *adv*

Florentine ('flɒrən,taɪn) *adj* **1** of or relating to Florence, in Italy. ◆ *n* **2** a native or inhabitant of Florence.

florescence ➊ (flɔː'rɛsəns) *n* the process, state, or period of flowering. [C18: from NL, from L *flōrēscere* to come into flower]

floret ('flɔːrɪt) *n* a small flower, esp. one of many making up the head of a composite flower. [C17: from OF, from *flor* FLOWER]

floriated *or* **floreated** ('flɔːrɪ,eɪtɪd) *adj Archit.* having ornamentation based on flowers and leaves. [C19: from L *flōs* FLOWER]

floribunda (,flɔːrɪ'bʌndə) *n* any of several varieties of cultivated hybrid roses whose flowers grow in large sprays. [C19: from NL, fem of *flōribundus* flowering freely]

floriculture ('flɔːrɪ,kʌltʃə) *n* the cultivation of flowering plants.
▸**,flori'cultural** *adj* ▸**,flori'culturist** *n*

florid ➊ ('flɒrɪd) *adj* **1** having a red or flushed complexion. **2** excessively ornate; flowery: *florid architecture.* [C17: from L *flōridus* blooming]
▸**flo'ridity** *n* ▸**'floridly** *adv*

floriferous (flɔː'rɪfərəs) *adj* bearing or capable of bearing many flowers.

florin ('flɒrɪn) *n* **1** a former British coin, originally silver, equivalent to ten (new) pence. **2** (formerly) another name for **guilder** (sense 1). [C14: from F, from OIt. *fiorino* Florentine coin, from *fiore* flower, from L *flōs*]

florist ('flɒrɪst) *n* a person who grows or deals in flowers.

floristic (flɒ'rɪstɪk) *adj* of or relating to flowers or a flora.
▸**flo'ristically** *adv*

-florous *adj combining form.* indicating number or type of flowers: *tubuliflorous.*

floruit *Latin.* ('flɒruːɪt) *vb* (he or she) flourished: used to indicate the period when a figure, whose birth and death dates are unknown, was most active.

floss (flɒs) *n* **1** the mass of fine silky fibres obtained from cotton and similar plants. **2** any similar fine silky material. **3** untwisted silk thread used in embroidery, etc. **4** See **dental floss.** ◆ *vb* **5** (*tr*) to clean (between one's teeth) with dental floss. [C18: ?from OF *flosche* down]

flossy ➊ ('flɒsɪ) *adj* **flossier, flossiest.** consisting of or resembling floss.

flotage *or* **floatage** ('fləʊtɪdʒ) *n* **1** the act or state of floating. **2** power or ability to float. **3** flotsam.

flotation *or* **floatation** (fləʊ'teɪʃən) *n* **1a** the launching or financing of a commercial enterprise by bond or share issues. **1b** the raising of a loan or new capital by bond or share issues. **2** power or ability to float. **3** Also called: **froth flotation.** a process to concentrate the valuable ore in low-grade ores by using induced differences in surface tension to carry the valuable fraction to the surface.

flotel *or* **floatel** (fləʊ'tel) *n* a rig used for accommodation of workers in off-shore oil fields. [C20: FLO(ATING) + (HO)TEL]

flotilla (flə'tɪlə) *n* a small fleet or a fleet of small vessels. [C18: from Sp., from F *flotte,* ult. from ON *floti*]

flotsam ➊ ('flɒtsəm) *n* **1** wreckage from a ship found floating. Cf. **jetsam. 2** odds and ends (esp. in **flotsam and jetsam**). **3** vagrants. [C16: from Anglo-F *floteson,* from *floter* to FLOAT]

flounce[1] ➊ (flaʊns) *vb* **flounces, flouncing, flounced. 1** (*intr;* often foll. by *about, away, out,* etc.) to move or go with emphatic movements. ◆ *n* **2** the act of flouncing. [C16: of Scand. origin]

flounce[2] (flaʊns) *n* an ornamental gathered ruffle sewn to a garment by its top edge. [C18: from OF, from *froncir* to wrinkle, of Gmc origin]

flounder[1] ➊ ('flaʊndə) *vb* (*intr*) **1** to move with difficulty, as in mud. **2** to make mistakes. ◆ *n* **3** the act of floundering. [C16: prob. a blend of FOUNDER[2] + BLUNDER; ? infl. by FLOUNDER[2]]

> **USAGE NOTE** *Flounder* is sometimes wrongly used where *founder* is meant: *the project foundered* (not *floundered*) *because of lack of funds.*

flounder[2] ('flaʊndə) *n, pl* **flounder** *or* **flounders.** a European flatfish having a greyish-brown body covered with prickly scales: an important food fish. [C14: from ON]

flour ('flaʊə) *n* **1** a powder, which may be either fine or coarse, prepared by grinding the meal of a grass, esp. wheat. **2** any finely powdered substance. ◆ *vb* (*tr*) **3** to make (grain, etc.) into flour. **4** to dredge or

THESAURUS

hiding (*inf.*), horsewhipping, lashing, scourging, thrashing, trouncing, whipping

flood *n* **1, 3 = deluge,** downpour, flash flood, freshet, inundation, overflow, spate, tide, torrent **2 = torrent,** abundance, flow, glut, multitude, outpouring, profusion, rush, stream ◆ *vb* **5, 6 = immerse,** brim over, deluge, drown, inundate, overflow, pour over, submerge, swamp, teem **7, 9 = engulf,** flow, gush, overwhelm, rush, surge, swarm, sweep **8 = oversupply,** choke, fill, glut, saturate

floor *n* **2 = tier,** level, stage, storey ◆ *vb* **12 = knock down,** deck (*sl.*), prostrate **13** *Informal* **= disconcert,** baffle, beat, bewilder, bowl over (*inf.*), confound, conquer, defeat, discomfit, dumbfound, faze, nonplus, overthrow, perplex, puzzle, stump, throw (*inf.*)

flop *vb* **1, 2 = fall,** collapse, dangle, droop, drop, hang limply, sag, slump, topple, tumble **3** *Informal* **= fail,** bomb (*US & Canad. sl.*), close, come to nothing, come unstuck, fall flat, fall short, fold (*inf.*), founder, go belly-up (*sl.*), misfire ◆ *n* **7** *Informal* **= failure,** debacle, disaster, fiasco, loser, nonstarter, washout (*inf.*)
Antonyms *vb* **≠ fail:** flourish, make a hit, make it (*inf.*), prosper, succeed, triumph, work ◆ *n* **≠ failure:** hit, success, triumph

floppy *adj* **1 = droopy,** baggy, flaccid, flapping, flip-flop, hanging, limp, loose, pendulous, sagging, soft

floral *adj* **1 = flowery,** flower-patterned

florescence *n* **= flowering,** blooming, blossoming, development, flourishing, fruition, maturity

florid *adj* **1 = flushed,** blowsy, high-coloured, high-complexioned, rubicund, ruddy **2 = ornate,** baroque, busy, embellished, euphuistic, figurative, flamboyant, flowery, fussy, grandiloquent, high-flown, overelaborate
Antonyms *adj* **≠ flushed:** anaemic, bloodless, pale, pallid, pasty, wan, washed out **≠ ornate:** bare, dull, plain, unadorned

flossy *adj* **= fluffy,** downy, feathery, satiny, silky, soft

flotsam *n* **1, 2 = debris,** detritus, jetsam, junk, odds and ends, sweepings, wreckage

flounce[1] *vb* **1 = bounce,** fling, jerk, spring, stamp, storm, throw, toss

flounder[1] *vb* **1 = struggle,** blunder, fumble, grope, muddle, plunge, stumble, thrash, toss, tumble, wallow

sprinkle (food or utensils) with flour. [C13 *flur* finer portion of meal, FLOWER]
▸ '**floury** *adj*

flourish ● ('flʌrɪʃ) *vb* **1** (*intr*) to thrive; prosper. **2** (*intr*) to be at the peak of condition. **3** (*intr*) to be healthy: *plants flourish in the light.* **4** to wave or cause to wave in the air with sweeping strokes. **5** to display or make a display. **6** to play (a fanfare, etc.) on a musical intrument. ◆ *n* **7** the act of waving or brandishing. **8** a showy gesture: *he entered with a flourish.* **9** an ornamental embellishment in writing. **10** a display of ornamental language or speech. **11** a grandiose passage of music. [C13: from OF, ult. from L *flōrēre* to flower, from *flōs* a flower]
▸ '**flourisher** *n*

flout ● (flaʊt) *vb* (when *intr*, usually foll. by *at*) to show contempt (for). [C16: ?from ME *flouten* to play the flute, from OF *flauter*]
▸ '**floutingly** *adv*

USAGE NOTE See at **flaunt.**

flow ● (fləʊ) *vb* (*mainly intr*) **1** (of liquids) to move or be conveyed as in a stream. **2** (of blood) to circulate around the body. **3** to move or progress freely as if in a stream: *the crowd flowed into the building.* **4** to be produced continuously and effortlessly: *ideas flowed from her pen.* **5** to be marked by smooth or easy movement. **6** to hang freely or loosely: *her hair flowed down her back.* **7** to be present in abundance: *wine flows at their parties.* **8** (of tide water) to advance or rise. Cf. **ebb** (sense 1). **9** (of rocks such as slate) to yield to pressure so that the structure and arrangement of the constituent minerals are altered. ◆ *n* **10** the act, rate, or manner of flowing: *a fast flow.* **11** a continuous stream or discharge. **12** continuous progression. **13** the advancing of the tide. **14** *Scot.* **14a** a marsh or swamp. **14b** an inlet or basin of the sea. **14c** (*cap. when part of a name*): *Scapa Flow.* [OE *flōwan*]

flow chart *or* **sheet** *n* a diagrammatic representation of the sequence of operations in an industrial process, computer program, etc.

flower ● ('flaʊə) *n* **1a** a bloom or blossom on a plant. **1b** a plant that bears blooms or blossoms. **2** the reproductive structure of angiosperm plants, consisting of stamens and carpels surrounded by petals and sepals. In some plants it is brightly coloured and attracts insects for pollination. Related adj: **floral. 3** any similar reproductive structure in other plants. **4** the prime; peak: *in the flower of his youth.* **5** the choice or finest product, part, or representative. **6** a decoration or embellishment. **7** (*pl*) fine powder, usually produced by sublimation: *flowers of sulphur.* ◆ *vb* **8** (*intr*) to produce flowers; bloom. **9** (*intr*) to reach full growth or maturity. **10** (*tr*) to deck or decorate with flowers or floral designs. [C13: from OF *flor*, from L *flōs*]
▸ '**flowerless** *adj* ▸ '**flower-,like** *adj*

flowered ('flaʊəd) *adj* **1** having flowers. **2** decorated with flowers or a floral design.

floweret ('flaʊərɪt) *n* another name for **floret.**

flower girl *n* a girl or woman who sells flowers in the street.

flowering ● ('flaʊərɪŋ) *adj* (of certain species of plants) capable of producing conspicuous flowers.

flowerpot ('flaʊə,pɒt) *n* a pot in which plants are grown.

flower power *n Inf.* a youth cult of the late 1960s advocating peace and love; associated with drug-taking. Its adherents were known as **flower children** or **flower people.**

flowery ● ('flaʊərɪ) *adj* **1** abounding in flowers. **2** decorated with flowers or floral patterns. **3** like or suggestive of flowers. **4** (of language or style) elaborate.
▸ '**floweriness** *n*

flown (fləʊn) *vb* the past participle of **fly**[1].

flow-on *n Austral. & NZ.* **a** a wage or salary increase granted to one group of workers as a consequence of a similar increase granted to another group. **b** (*as modifier*): *a flow-on effect.*

fl. oz. *abbrev. for* fluid ounce.

flu (fluː) *n Inf.* **1** (often preceded by *the*) short for **influenza. 2** any of various viral infections, esp. a respiratory or intestinal infection.

fluctuate ● ('flʌktjʊ,eɪt) *vb* **fluctuates, fluctuating, fluctuated. 1** to change or cause to change position constantly. **2** (*intr*) to rise and fall like a wave. [C17: from L, from *fluctus* a wave, from *fluere* to flow]
▸ '**fluctuant** *adj* ▸ ,**fluctu'ation** *n*

flue (fluː) *n* a shaft, tube, or pipe, esp. as used in a chimney, to carry off smoke, gas, etc. [C16: from ?]

fluent ● ('fluːənt) *adj* **1** able to speak or write a specified foreign language with facility. **2** spoken or written with facility. **3** graceful in motion or shape. **4** flowing or able to flow freely. [C16: from L: flowing, from *fluere* to flow]
▸ '**fluency** *n* ▸ '**fluently** *adv*

flue pipe *or* **flue** *n* an organ pipe whose sound is produced by the passage of air across a fissure in the side, as distinguished from a **reed pipe.**

fluff ● (flʌf) *n* **1** soft light particles, such as the down or nap of cotton or wool. **2** any light downy substance. **3** *Inf.* a mistake, esp. in speaking or reading lines or performing music. **4** *Inf.* a young woman (esp. in **a bit of fluff**). ◆ *vb* **5** to make or become soft and puffy. **6** *Inf.* to make a mistake in performing (an action, music, etc.). [C18: ?from *flue* downy matter]

fluffy ● ('flʌfɪ) *adj* **fluffier, fluffiest. 1** of, resembling, or covered with fluff. **2** soft and light.
▸ '**fluffily** *adv* ▸ '**fluffiness** *n*

flugelhorn ('fluːgᵊl,hɔːn) *n* a type of valved brass instrument consisting of a tube of conical bore with a cup-shaped mouthpiece, used esp. in brass bands. [G, from *Flügel* wing + *Horn* HORN]

fluid ● ('fluːɪd) *n* **1** a substance, such as a liquid or gas, that can flow, has no fixed shape, and offers little resistance to an external stress. ◆ *adj* **2** capable of flowing and easily changing shape. **3** of or using a fluid or fluids. **4** constantly changing or apt to change. **5** flowing. [C15: from L, from *fluere* to flow]
▸ '**fluidal** *adj* ▸ **flu'idity** *or* '**fluidness** *n*

fluidics (fluː'ɪdɪks) *n* (*functioning as sing*) the study and use of systems in which the flow of fluids in tubes simulates the flow of electricity in conductors.
▸ **flu'idic** *adj*

fluidize *or* **fluidise** ('fluːɪ,daɪz) *vb* **fluidizes, fluidizing, fluidized** *or* **fluidises, fluidising, fluidised.** (*tr*) to make fluid, esp. to make (solids) fluid by pulverizing them so that they can be transported in gas as if they were liquids.
▸ ,**fluidi'zation** *or* ,**fluidi'sation** *n*

fluid mechanics *n* (*functioning as sing*) the study of the mechanical and flow properties of fluids, esp. as they apply to practical engineering. Also called: **hydraulics.**

fluid ounce *n* **1** *Brit.* a unit of capacity equal to one twentieth of an Imperial pint. **2** *US.* a unit of capacity equal to one sixteenth of a US pint.

fluke[1] (fluːk) *n* **1** a flat bladelike projection at the end of the arm of an anchor. **2** either of the two lobes of the tail of a whale. **3** the barb of a harpoon, arrow, etc. [C16: ? a special use of FLUKE[3] (in the sense: a flounder)]

fluke[2] ● (fluːk) *n* **1** an accidental stroke of luck. **2** any chance happening. ◆ *vb* **flukes, fluking, fluked. 3** (*tr*) to gain, make, or hit by a fluke. [C19: from ?]

THESAURUS

flourish *vb* **1** = **thrive**, bear fruit, be in one's prime, be successful, be vigorous, bloom, blossom, boom, burgeon, develop, do well, flower, get ahead, get on, go great guns (*sl.*), go up in the world, grow, grow fat, increase, prosper, succeed **4, 5** = **wave**, brandish, display, flaunt, flutter, shake, sweep, swing, swish, twirl, vaunt, wag, wield ◆ *n* **7, 8** = **wave**, brandishing, dash, display, fanfare, parade, shaking, show, showy gesture, twirling **9** = **ornamentation**, curlicue, decoration, embellishment, plume, sweep
Antonyms *vb* ≠ **thrive:** decline, diminish, dwindle, fade, fail, grow less, pine, shrink, wane

flourishing *adj* **1** = **successful**, blooming, burgeoning, doing well, going places, going strong, in the pink, in top form, lush, luxuriant, mushrooming, on a roll, on the up and up (*inf.*), prospering, rampant, thriving

flout *vb* = **defy**, deride, gibe at, insult, jeer at, laugh in the face of, mock, outrage, ridicule, scoff at, scorn, show contempt for, sneer at, spurn, taunt, treat with disdain
Antonyms *vb* attend, esteem, heed, honour, mind, note, pay attention to, regard, respect, revere, value

flow *vb* **1, 5** = **run**, circulate, course, glide, move, purl, ripple, roll, slide **3, 7** = **pour**, cascade, deluge, flood, gush, inundate, issue, overflow, run, run out, rush, spew, spill, spurt, squirt, stream, surge, sweep, swirl, teem, well forth, whirl **4** = **issue**, arise, emanate, emerge, pour, proceed, result, spring ◆ *n* **10** = **stream**, course, current, drift, flood, flux, gush, issue, outflow, outpouring, spate, tide, tideway, undertow **11** = **outpouring**, abundance, deluge, effusion, emanation, outflow, plenty, plethora, succession, train

flower *n* **1** = **bloom**, blossom, efflorescence **4, 5** = **elite**, best, choicest part, cream, *crème de la crème,* freshness, greatest *or* finest point, height, pick, vigour ◆ *vb* **8, 9** = **bloom**, blossom, blow, burgeon, effloresce, flourish, mature, open, unfold

flowering *adj* = **blooming**, abloom, blossoming, in bloom, in blossom, in flower, open, out, ready

flowery *adj* **4** = **ornate**, baroque, embellished, euphuistic, fancy, figurative, florid, high-flown, overwrought, rhetorical
Antonyms *adj* austere, bare, basic, modest, muted, plain, restrained, simple, spartan, unadorned, unembellished

fluctuate *vb* **1, 2** = **change**, alter, alternate, ebb and flow, go up and down, hesitate, oscillate, rise and fall, seesaw, shift, swing, undulate, vacillate, vary, veer, waver

fluctuation *n* **1, 2** = **change**, alternation, fickleness, inconstancy, instability, oscillation, shift, swing, unsteadiness, vacillation, variation, wavering

fluency *n* **1, 2** = **ease**, articulateness, assurance, command, control, facility, glibness, readiness, slickness, smoothness, volubility

fluent *adj* **1, 2** = **effortless**, articulate, easy, facile, flowing, glib, natural, ready, smooth, smooth-spoken, voluble, well-versed
Antonyms *adj* faltering, halting, hesitant, hesitating, inarticulate, stammering, stumbling, tongue-tied

fluff *n* **1, 2** = **fuzz**, down, dust, dustball, lint, nap, oose (*Scot.*), pile ◆ *vb* **6** *Informal* = **mess up** (*inf.*), bungle, foul up (*inf.*), make a mess off, make a nonsense of, muddle, screw up (*inf.*), spoil

fluffy *adj* **1** = **soft**, downy, feathery, fleecy, flossy, fuzzy, gossamer, silky

fluid *n* **1** = **liquid**, liquor, solution ◆ *adj* **2, 5** = **liquid**, aqueous, flowing, in solution, liquefied, melted, molten, running, runny, watery **4** = **changeable**, adaptable, adjustable, flexible, floating, fluctuating, indefinite, mercurial, mobile, mutable, protean, shifting
Antonyms *adj* ≠ **liquid:** firm, hard, rigid, set, solid ≠ **changeable:** definite, firm, fixed, immobile, immutable

fluke[2] *n* **1, 2** = **stroke of luck**, accident, blessing, break, chance, chance occurrence, coinci-

fluke[3] (flu:k) *n* any parasitic flatworm, such as the blood fluke and liver fluke. [OE *flōc;* rel. to ON *flōki* flounder]

fluky ⓘ *or* **flukey** ('flu:kɪ) *adj* **flukier, flukiest.** *Inf.* **1** done or gained by an accident, esp. a lucky one. **2** variable; uncertain.
▸ **'flukiness** *n*

flume (flu:m) *n* **1** a ravine through which a stream flows. **2** a narrow artificial channel made for providing water for power, floating logs, etc. **3** a slide in the form of a long and winding tube with a stream of water running through it that descends into a purpose-built pool. ◆ *vb* **flumes, fluming, flumed. 4** (*tr*) to transport (logs) in a flume. [C12: from OF, ult. from L *flūmen* stream, from *fluere* to flow]

flummery ('flʌmərɪ) *n, pl* **flummeries. 1** *Inf.* meaningless flattery. **2** *Chiefly Brit.* a cold pudding of oatmeal, etc. [C17: from Welsh *llymru*]

flummox ⓘ ('flʌməks) *vb* (*tr*) to perplex or bewilder. [C19: from ?]

flung (flʌŋ) *vb* the past tense and past participle of **fling.**

flunk ⓘ (flʌŋk) *vb Inf., US, Canad., & NZ.* **1** to fail or cause to fail to reach the required standard in (an examination, course, etc.). **2** (*intr;* foll. by *out*) to be dismissed from a school. [C19: ?from FLINCH + FUNK[1]]

flunky ⓘ *or* **flunkey** ('flʌŋkɪ) *n, pl* **flunkies** *or* **flunkeys. 1** a servile person. **2** a person who performs menial tasks. **3** *Usually derog.* a manservant in livery. [C18: from ?]

fluor ('flu:ɔ:) *n* another name for **fluorspar.** [C17: from L: a flowing; so called from its use as a metallurgical flux]

fluor- *combining form.* a variant of **fluoro-** before a vowel: *fluorine.*

fluoresce (ˌfluə'rɛs) *vb* **fluoresces, fluorescing, fluoresced.** (*intr*) to exhibit fluorescence. [C19: back formation from FLUORESCENCE]

fluorescence (ˌfluə'rɛsəns) *n* **1** *Physics.* **1a** the emission of light or other radiation from atoms or molecules that are bombarded by particles, such as electrons, or by radiation from a separate source. **1b** such an emission of photons that ceases as soon as the bombarding radiation is discontinued. **2** the radiation emitted as a result of fluorescence. Cf. **phosphorescence.** [C19: FLUOR + *-escence* (as in *opalescence*)]
▸ **ˌfluo'rescent** *adj*

fluorescent lamp *n* a type of lamp in which ultraviolet radiation from an electrical gas discharge causes a thin layer of phosphor on a tube's inside surface to fluoresce.

fluoridate ('fluərɪˌdeɪt) *vb* **fluoridates, fluoridating, fluoridated.** to subject (water) to fluoridation.

fluoridation (ˌfluərɪ'deɪʃən) *n* the addition of fluorides to the public water supply as a protection against tooth decay.

fluoride ('fluəˌraɪd) *n* **1** any salt of hydrofluoric acid, containing the fluoride ion, F^-. **2** any compound containing fluorine, such as methyl fluoride.

fluorinate ('fluərɪˌneɪt) *vb* **fluorinates, fluorinating, fluorinated.** to treat or combine with fluorine.
▸ **ˌfluori'nation** *n*

fluorine ('fluəri:n) *n* a toxic pungent pale yellow gas of the halogen group that is the most electronegative and reactive of all the elements: used in the production of uranium, fluorocarbons, and other chemicals. Symbol: F; atomic no.: 9; atomic wt.: 18.998.

fluorite ('fluəraɪt) *n* the US and Canad. name for **fluorspar.**

fluoro- *or before a vowel* **fluor-** *combining form.* **1** indicating the presence of fluorine: *fluorocarbon.* **2** indicating fluorescence: *fluoroscope.*

fluorocarbon (ˌfluərəu'kɑ:bᵊn) *n* any compound derived by replacing all or some of the hydrogen atoms in hydrocarbons by fluorine atoms. Many of them are used as lubricants, solvents, coatings, and aerosol propellants. See also **Freon, CFC.**

fluorometer (ˌfluə'rɒmɪtə) *or* **fluorimeter** (ˌfluə'rɪmɪtə) *n* a device for detecting and measuring ultraviolet radiation by determining the amount of fluorescence that it produces from a phosphor.

fluoroscope ('fluərəˌskəup) *n* a device consisting of a fluorescent screen and an X-ray source that enables an X-ray image of an object, person, or part to be observed directly.

fluoroscopy (fluə'rɒskəpɪ) *n* examination of a person or object by means of a fluoroscope.

fluorosis (fluə'rəusɪs) *n* fluoride poisoning, due to ingestion of too much fluoride.

fluorspar ('fluəˌspɑ:), **fluor,** *or US & Canad.* **fluorite** *n* a white or colourless soft mineral, sometimes fluorescent or tinted by impurities, consisting of calcium fluoride (CaF) in crystalline form: the chief ore of fluorine.

flurry ⓘ ('flʌrɪ) *n, pl* **flurries. 1** a sudden commotion. **2** a light gust of wind or rain or fall of snow. ◆ *vb* **flurries, flurrying, flurried. 3** to confuse or bewilder or be confused or bewildered. [C17: from obs. *flurr* to scatter, ? formed on analogy with HURRY]

flush[1] ⓘ (flʌʃ) *vb* **1** to blush or cause to blush. **2** to flow or flood or cause to flow or flood with or as if with water. **3** to glow or shine or cause to glow or shine with a rosy colour. **4** to send a volume of water quickly through (a pipe, etc.) or into (a toilet) for the purpose of cleansing, etc. **5** (*tr; usually passive*) to excite or elate. ◆ *n* **6** a rosy colour, esp. in the cheeks. **7** a sudden flow or gush, as of water. **8** a feeling of excitement or elation: *the flush of success.* **9** freshness: *the flush of youth.* **10** redness of the skin, as from the effects of a fever, alcohol, etc. [C16: (in the sense: to gush forth): ?from FLUSH[3]]
▸ **'flusher** *n*

flush[2] ⓘ (flʌʃ) *adj* (*usually postpositive*) **1** level or even with another surface. **2** directly adjacent; continuous. **3** *Inf.* having plenty of money. **4** *Inf.* abundant or plentiful, as money. **5** full to the brim. ◆ *adv* **6** so as to be level or even. **7** directly or squarely. ◆ *vb* (*tr*) **8** to cause (surfaces) to be on the same level or in the same plane. ◆ *n* **9** a period of fresh growth of leaves, shoots, etc. [C18: prob. from FLUSH[1] (in the sense: spring out)]
▸ **'flushness** *n*

flush[3] ⓘ (flʌʃ) *vb* (*tr*) to rouse (game, etc.) and put to flight. [C13 *flusshen,* ? imit.]

flush[4] (flʌʃ) *n* (in poker and similar games) a hand containing only one suit. [C16: from OF, from L *fluxus* FLUX]

fluster ⓘ ('flʌstə) *vb* **1** to make or become nervous or upset. ◆ *n* **2** a state of confusion or agitation. [C15: from ON]

flute (flu:t) *n* **1** a wind instrument consisting of an open cylindrical tube of wood or metal having holes in the side stopped either by the fingers or by pads controlled by keys. The breath is directed across a mouth hole cut in the side. **2** *Archit.* a rounded shallow concave groove on the shaft of a column, pilaster, etc. **3** a tall narrow wineglass. ◆ *vb* **flutes, fluting, fluted. 4** to produce or utter (sounds) in the manner or tone of a flute. **5** (*tr*) to make grooves or furrows in. [C14: from OF *flahute,* from Vulgar L *flabeolum* (unattested); ? also infl. by OF *laut* lute]
▸ **'fluteˌlike** *adj* ▸ **'fluty** *adj*

fluting ('flu:tɪŋ) *n* a design or decoration of flutes on a column, pilaster, etc.

flutist ('flu:tɪst) *n Now chiefly US & Canad.* a variant spelling of **flautist.**

flutter ⓘ ('flʌtə) *vb* **1** to wave or cause to wave rapidly. **2** (*intr*) (of birds, butterflies, etc.) to flap the wings. **3** (*intr*) to move, esp. downwards, with an irregular motion. **4** (*intr*) *Pathol.* (of the heart) to beat abnormally rapidly, esp. in a regular rhythm. **5** to be or make nervous or restless. **6** (*intr*) to move about restlessly. ◆ *n* **7** a quick flapping or vibrating motion. **8** a state of nervous excitement or confusion. **9** excited interest; stir. **10** *Brit. inf.* a modest bet or wager. **11** *Pathol.* an abnormally rapid beating of the heart, esp. in a regular rhythm. **12** *Electronics.* a slow variation in pitch in a sound-reproducing system, similar to wow but occurring at higher frequencies. **13** a potentially dangerous oscillation of an aircraft, or part of an aircraft. **14** Also called: **flutter tonguing.** *Music.* a method of sounding a wind instrument, esp. the flute, with a rolling movement of the tongue. [OE *floterian* to float to and fro]
▸ **'flutterer** *n* ▸ **'fluttery** *adj*

THESAURUS

dence, fortuity, freak, lucky break, quirk, quirk of fate, serendipity, stroke, windfall

fluky *adj Informal* **1** = **lucky,** accidental, coincidental, fortuitous **2** = **uncertain,** at the mercy of events, chancy, incalculable, variable

flummox *vb* = **baffle,** bamboozle (*inf.*), bewilder, defeat, fox, mystify, nonplus, perplex, puzzle, stump, stymie

flummoxed *adj* = **baffled,** at a loss, at sea, bewildered, foxed, mystified, nonplussed, puzzled, stumped, stymied

flunk *Informal, U.S., Canad., & N.Z. vb* **1** = **fail,** be found lacking, be unsuccessful, bust, fall short, flop (*inf.*), founder, miss, not come up to scratch, not come up to the mark (*inf.*), not make the grade (*inf.*), underachieve, underperform, wash out **2** = **be expelled,** be dismissed, drop out (*inf.*), go down
Antonyms *vb* ≠ **fail:** be successful, come up to scratch (*inf.*), excel, get by *or* through, get pass marks, make it, make the grade, meet *or* satisfy requirements, pass, pass with flying colours, stand the test ≠ **be expelled:** graduate

flunky *n* **1, 2** = **minion,** assistant, cohort, drudge, hanger-on, menial, slave, toady, tool, underling, yes man **3** = **manservant,** footman, lackey, valet

flurry *n* **1** = **commotion,** ado, agitation, bustle, disturbance, excitement, ferment, flap, fluster, flutter, furore, fuss, hurry, stir, to-do, tumult, whirl **2** = **gust,** flaw, squall ◆ *vb* **3** = **confuse,** agitate, bewilder, bother, disconcert, disturb, faze, fluster, flutter, fuss, hassle (*inf.*), hurry, hustle, rattle (*inf.*), ruffle, unnerve, unsettle, upset

flush[1] *vb* **1** = **blush,** burn, colour, colour up, crimson, flame, glow, go as red as a beetroot, go red, redden, suffuse **2, 4** = **rinse out,** cleanse, douche, drench, eject, expel, flood, hose down, swab, syringe, wash out ◆ *n* **6, 10** = **blush,** bloom, colour, freshness, glow, redness, rosiness

flush[2] *adj* **1** = **level,** even, flat, plane, square, true **3** *Informal* = **wealthy,** in funds, in the money (*inf.*), moneyed, rich, rolling (*sl.*), well-heeled (*inf.*), well-off, well-supplied **4** *Informal* = **abundant,** affluent, full, generous, lavish, liberal, overflowing, prodigal ◆ *adv* **6, 7** = **level with,** even with, hard against, in contact with, squarely, touching

flush[3] *vb* = **drive out,** discover, disturb, put to flight, rouse, start, uncover

flushed *adj* **1** = **blushing,** burning, crimson, embarrassed, feverish, glowing, hot, red, rosy, rubicund, ruddy **5** *often foll. by* **with** = **exhilarated,** animated, aroused, elated, enthused, excited, high (*inf.*), inspired, intoxicated, thrilled

fluster *vb* **1** = **upset,** agitate, bother, bustle, confound, confuse, disturb, excite, flurry, hassle (*inf.*), heat, hurry, make nervous, perturb, rattle (*inf.*), ruffle, throw off balance, unnerve ◆ *n* **2** = **turmoil,** agitation, bustle, commotion, disturbance, dither (*chiefly Brit.*), flap (*inf.*), flurry, flutter, furore, perturbation, ruffle, state (*inf.*)

fluted *adj* **5** = **grooved,** channelled, corrugated, furrowed

flutter *vb* **1, 2, 4** = **beat,** agitate, bat, flap, flicker, flit, flitter, fluctuate, hover, palpitate, quiver, ripple, ruffle, shiver, tremble, vibrate, waver ◆ *n* **7, 11** = **vibration,** palpitation, quiver, quivering, shiver, shudder, tremble, tremor, twitching **8** = **agitation,** commotion, confusion, dither (*chiefly Brit.*), excitement, flurry, fluster, perturbation, state (*inf.*), state of nervous excitement, tremble, tumult

fluvial ('flu:vɪəl) *adj* of or occurring in a river: *fluvial deposits.* [C14: from L, from *fluvius* river, from *fluere* to flow]

flux ❶ (flʌks) *n* **1** a flow or discharge. **2** continuous change; instability. **3** a substance, such as borax or salt, that gives a low melting-point mixture with a metal oxide to assist in fusion. **4** *Metallurgy.* a chemical used to increase the fluidity of refining slags. **5** *Physics.* **5a** the rate of flow of particles, energy, or a fluid, such as that of neutrons (**neutron flux**) or of light energy (**luminous flux**). **5b** the strength of a field in a given area: *magnetic flux.* **6** *Pathol.* an excessive discharge of fluid from the body, such as watery faeces in diarrhoea. ◆ *vb* **7** to make or become fluid. **8** (*tr*) to apply flux to (a metal, soldered joint, etc.). [C14: from L *fluxus* a flow, from *fluere* to flow]

flux density *n Physics.* the amount of flux per unit of cross-sectional area.

fluxion ('flʌkʃən) *n Maths., obs.* the rate of change of a function, especially the instantaneous velocity of a moving body; derivative. [C16: from LL *fluxiō* a flowing]

fly[1] ❶ (flaɪ) *vb* **flies, flying, flew, flown. 1** (*intr*) (of birds, aircraft, etc.) to move through the air in a controlled manner using aerodynamic forces. **2** to travel over (an area of land or sea) in an aircraft. **3** to operate (an aircraft or spacecraft). **4** to float, flutter, or be displayed in the air or cause to float, etc., in this way: *they flew the flag.* **5** to transport or be transported by or through the air by aircraft, wind, etc. **6** (*intr*) to move or be moved very quickly, or suddenly: *the door flew open.* **7** (*intr*) to pass swiftly: *time flies.* **8** to escape from (an enemy, place, etc.); flee. **9** (*intr;* may be foll. by *at* or *upon*) to attack a person. **10 fly a kite. 10a** to procure money by an accommodation bill. **10b** to release information or take a step in order to test public opinion. **11 fly high.** *Inf.* **11a** to have a high aim. **11b** to prosper or flourish. **12 let fly.** *Inf.* **12a** to lose one's temper (with a person): *she really let fly at him.* **12b** to shoot or throw (an object). ◆ *n, pl* **flies. 13** (*often pl*) Also called: **fly front.** a closure that conceals a zip, buttons, or other fastening, by having one side overlapping, as on trousers. **14** Also called: **fly sheet. 14a** a flap forming the entrance to a tent. **14b** a piece of canvas drawn over the ridgepole of a tent to form an outer roof. **15** short for **flywheel. 16a** the outer edge of a flag. **16b** the distance from the outer edge of a flag to the staff. **17** *Brit.* a light one-horse covered carriage formerly let out on hire. **18** (*pl*) *Theatre.* the space above the stage out of view of the audience, used for storing scenery, etc. **19** *Rare.* the act of flying. [OE *flēogan*]

▸ **'flyable** *adj*

fly[2] ❶ (flaɪ) *n, pl* **flies. 1** any dipterous insect, esp. the housefly, characterized by active flight. **2** any of various similar but unrelated insects, such as the caddis fly, firefly, and dragonfly. **3** *Angling.* a lure made from a fish-hook dressed with feathers, tinsel, etc., to resemble any of various flies or nymphs: used in fly-fishing. **4 fly in the ointment.** *Inf.* a slight flaw that detracts from value or enjoyment. **5 fly on the wall. 5a** a person who watches others, while not being noticed himself. **5b** (*as modifier*): *a fly-on-the-wall documentary.* **6 there are no flies on him, her,** etc. *Inf.* he, she, etc., is no fool. [OE *flēoge*]

▸ **'flyless** *adj*

fly[3] ❶ (flaɪ) *adj Sl., chiefly Brit.* knowing and sharp; smart. [C19: from ?]

fly agaric *n* a woodland fungus having a scarlet cap with white warts and white gills: poisonous but rarely fatal. [so named from its use as a poison on flypaper]

fly ash *n* fine solid particles of ash carried into the air during combustion.

flyaway ('flaɪəˌweɪ) *adj* **1** (of hair or clothing) loose and fluttering. **2** frivolous or flighty; giddy.

flyblow ('flaɪˌbləʊ) *vb* **flyblows, flyblowing, flyblew, flyblown. 1** (*tr*) to contaminate, esp. with the eggs or larvae of the blowfly; taint. ◆ *n* **2** (*usually pl*) the eggs or young larva of a blowfly.

flyblown ('flaɪˌbləʊn) *adj* **1** covered with flyblows. **2** contaminated; tainted.

flybook ('flaɪˌbʊk) *n* a small case or wallet used by anglers for storing artificial flies.

flyby ('flaɪˌbaɪ) *n, pl* **flybys.** a flight past a particular position or target, esp. the close approach of a spacecraft to a planet or satellite.

fly-by-night ❶ *Inf.* ◆ *adj* **1** unreliable or untrustworthy, esp. in finance. ◆ *n* **2** an untrustworthy person, esp. one who departs secretly or by night to avoid paying debts.

flycatcher ('flaɪˌkætʃə) *n* **1** a small insectivorous songbird of the Old World having a small slender bill fringed with bristles. **2** an American passerine bird.

fly-drive *adj, adv* describing a type of package-deal holiday in which the price includes outward and return flights and car hire while away.

flyer ❶ *or* **flier** ('flaɪə) *n* **1** a person or thing that flies or moves very fast. **2** an aviator or pilot. **3** *Inf.* a large flying leap. **4** a rectangular step in a straight flight of stairs. Cf. **winder** (sense 5). **5** *Athletics inf.* a flying start. **6** *Chiefly US.* a speculative business transaction. **7** a small handbill.

fly-fish *vb* (*intr*) *Angling.* to fish using artificial flies as lures.

▸ **'fly-ˌfishing** *n*

fly half *n Rugby.* another name for **stand-off half.**

flying ❶ ('flaɪɪŋ) *adj* **1** (*prenominal*) hurried; fleeting: *a flying visit.* **2** (*prenominal*) designed for fast action. **3** (*prenominal*) moving or passing quickly on or as if on wings: *flying hours.* **4** hanging, waving, or floating freely: *flying hair.* ◆ *n* **5** the act of piloting, navigating, or travelling in an aircraft. **6** (*modifier*) relating to, accustomed to, or adapted for flight: *a flying machine.*

flying boat *n* a seaplane in which the fuselage consists of a hull that provides buoyancy.

flying bridge *n* an auxiliary bridge of a vessel.

flying buttress *n* a buttress supporting a wall or other structure by an arch that transmits the thrust outwards and downwards.

flying colours *pl n* conspicuous success; triumph: *he passed his test with flying colours.*

flying doctor *n* (in areas of sparse or scattered population) a doctor who visits patients by aircraft.

flying fish *n* a fish common in warm and tropical seas, having enlarged winglike pectoral fins used for gliding above the surface of the water.

flying fox *n* **1** any large fruit bat of tropical Africa and Asia. **2** *Austral. & NZ.* a cable mechanism used for transportation across a river, gorge, etc.

flying gurnard *n* a marine spiny-finned gurnard-like fish having enlarged fan-shaped pectoral fins used to glide above the surface of the sea.

flying jib *n* the jib set furthest forward or outboard on a vessel with two or more jibs.

flying lemur *n* either of the two arboreal mammals of S and SE Asia that resemble lemurs but have a fold of skin between the limbs enabling movement by gliding leaps.

flying officer *n* an officer holding commissioned rank senior to a pilot officer but junior to a flight lieutenant in the British and certain other air forces.

flying phalanger *n* a nocturnal arboreal phalanger of E Australia and New Guinea, moving with gliding leaps using folds of skin between the hind limbs and forelimbs.

flying picket *n* (in industrial disputes) a member of a group of pickets organized to be able to move quickly from place to place.

flying saucer *n* any unidentified disc-shaped flying object alleged to come from outer space.

flying squad *n* a small group of police, soldiers, etc., ready to move into action quickly.

flying squirrel *n* a nocturnal rodent of Asia and North America, related to the squirrel. Furry folds of skin between the forelegs and hind legs enable these animals to move by gliding leaps.

flying start *n* **1** (in sprinting) a start by a competitor anticipating the starting signal. **2** a start to a race in which the competitor is already travelling at speed as he passes the starting line. **3** any promising beginning. **4** an initial advantage.

flying wing *n* **1** an aircraft consisting mainly of one large wing or tailplane and no fuselage. **2** (in Canadian football) the twelfth player, who has a variable position behind the scrimmage line.

flyleaf ('flaɪˌli:f) *n, pl* **flyleaves.** the inner leaf of the endpaper of a book, pasted to the first leaf.

flyover ('flaɪˌəʊvə) *n* **1** *Brit.* an intersection of two roads at which one is carried over the other by a bridge. **2** the US name for **fly-past.**

flypaper ('flaɪˌpeɪpə) *n* paper with a sticky and poisonous coating, usually hung from the ceiling to trap flies.

fly-past *n* a ceremonial flight of aircraft over a given area.

THESAURUS

flux *n* **1** = **flow,** fluidity, motion **2** = **change,** alteration, fluctuation, instability, modification, mutability, mutation, transition, unrest

fly[1] *vb* **1** = **take wing,** flit, flutter, hover, mount, sail, soar, take to the air, wing **3** = **pilot,** aviate, be at the controls, control, manoeuvre, operate **4** = **display,** flap, float, flutter, show, wave **6** = **rush,** barrel (along), be off like a shot (*inf.*), bolt, burn rubber (*inf.*), career, dart, dash, hare (*Brit. inf.*), hasten, hurry, race, scamper, scoot, shoot, speed, sprint, tear, whizz (*inf.*), zoom **7** = **pass,** elapse, flit, glide, pass swiftly, roll on, run its course, slip away **8** = **flee,** abscond, avoid, beat a retreat, clear out, cut and run (*inf.*), decamp, disappear, do a runner (*sl.*), escape, get away, hasten away, make a getaway, make a quick exit, make one's escape, run, run for it, run from, shun, skedaddle (*inf.*), take flight, take off **9** = **attack,** assail, assault, belabour, fall upon, get stuck into (*inf.*), go for, go for the jugular, have a go at (*inf.*), lay about, pitch into (*inf.*), rush at **12 let fly** *Informal* **a** = **throw,** burst forth, give free reign, keep nothing back, lash out, let (someone) have it, tear into (*inf.*), vent **b** cast, chuck (*inf.*), fire, fling, heave, hurl, hurtle, launch, let off, lob (*inf.*), shoot, sling

fly[2] *n* **4** *Informal* **fly in the ointment** = **snag,** difficulty, drawback, flaw, hitch, problem, rub, small problem

fly[3] *adj Slang, chiefly Brit.* = **cunning,** astute, canny, careful, knowing, nobody's fool, not born yesterday, on the ball (*inf.*), sharp, shrewd, smart, wide-awake

fly-by-night *adj* **1** *Informal* = **unreliable,** cowboy (*inf.*), dubious, questionable, shady, undependable, untrustworthy

flyer *n* **1** = **goer,** racer, runner, scorcher (*inf.*), speed merchant (*inf.*), sprinter **2** = **pilot,** aeronaut, airman *or* airwoman, aviator *or* aviatrix **3** *Informal* = **jump,** bound, flying *or* running jump, hurdle, jeté, leap, spring, vault **7** = **leaflet,** advert, bill, booklet, circular, handbill, handout, leaf, literature (*inf.*), notice, pamphlet, promotional material, publicity material, release, throwaway (*US*)

flying *adj* **1** = **hurried,** brief, fleeting, fugacious, hasty, rushed, short-lived, transitory **2, 3** = **fast,** express, fleet, mercurial, mobile, rapid, speedy, winged **4** = **airborne,** flapping, floating, fluttering, gliding, hovering, in the air, soaring, streaming, volitant, waving, wind-borne, winging

flyposting ('flaɪˌpəʊstɪŋ) *n* the posting of advertising or political posters, etc., in unauthorized places.
flyscreen ('flaɪˌskriːn) *n* a wire-mesh screen over a window to prevent flies entering a room.
fly sheet *n* **1** another term for **fly**[1] (sense 14). **2** a short handbill.
flyspeck ('flaɪˌspɛk) *n* **1** the small speck of the excrement of a fly. **2** a small spot or speck. ◆ *vb* **3** (*tr*) to mark with flyspecks.
fly spray *n* a liquid used to destroy flies and other insects, sprayed from an aerosol.
fly-tipping *n* the deliberate dumping of rubbish in an unauthorized place.
flytrap ('flaɪˌtræp) *n* **1** any of various insectivorous plants. **2** a device for catching flies.
fly way *n* the usual route used by birds when migrating.
flyweight ('flaɪˌweɪt) *n* **1a** a professional boxer weighing not more than 112 pounds (51 kg). **1b** an amateur boxer weighing 48–51 kg (106–112 pounds). **2** an amateur wrestler weighing 107–115 pounds (49–52 kg).
flywheel ('flaɪˌwiːl) *n* a heavy wheel that stores kinetic energy and smooths the operation of a reciprocating engine by maintaining a constant speed of rotation over the whole cycle.
fm *abbrev. for:* **1** fathom. **2** from.
Fm *the chemical symbol for* fermium.
FM *abbrev. for:* **1** frequency modulation. **2** Field Marshal.
f-number, f number, f-stop, *or* **f stop** *n Photog.* the numerical value of the relative aperture. If the relative aperture is f8, 8 is the f-number.
FO *abbrev. for:* **1** *Army.* Field Officer. **2** *Air Force.* Flying Officer. **3** Foreign Office.
fo. *abbrev. for* folio.
foal (fəʊl) *n* **1** the young of a horse or related animal. ◆ *vb* **2** to give birth to (a foal). [OE *fola*]
foam ➊ (fəʊm) *n* **1** a mass of small bubbles of gas formed on the surface of a liquid, such as the froth produced by a solution of soap or detergent in water. **2** frothy saliva sometimes formed in and expelled from the mouth, as in rabies. **3** the frothy sweat of a horse or similar animal. **4a** any of a number of light cellular solids made by creating bubbles of gas in the liquid material: used as insulation and packaging. **4b** (*as modifier*): *foam rubber; foam plastic.* ◆ *vb* **5** to produce or cause to produce foam; froth. **6** (*intr*) to be very angry (esp. in **foam at the mouth**). [OE *fām*]
▸ **'foamless** *adj*
foamy ➊ ('fəʊmɪ) *adj* **foamier, foamiest.** of, resembling, consisting of, or covered with foam.
fob[1] (fɒb) *n* **1** a chain or ribbon by which a pocket watch is attached to a waistcoat. **2** any ornament hung on such a chain. **3** a small pocket in a man's waistcoat, etc., for holding a watch. [C17: prob. of Gmc origin]
fob[2] (fɒb) *vb* **fobs, fobbing, fobbed.** (*tr*) *Arch.* to cheat. [C15: prob. from G *foppen* to trick]
f.o.b. *or* **FOB** *Commerce. abbrev. for* free on board.
fob off ➊ *vb* (*tr, adv*) **1** to trick (a person) with lies or excuses. **2** to dispose of (goods) by trickery.
focal ('fəʊkᵊl) *adj* **1** of or relating to a focus. **2** situated at or measured from the focus.
focalize *or* **focalise** ('fəʊkəˌlaɪz) *vb* **focalizes, focalizing, focalized** *or* **focalises, focalising, focalised.** a less common word for **focus.**
▸ **ˌfocali'zation** *or* **ˌfocali'sation** *n*
focal length *or* **distance** *n* the distance from the focal point of a lens or mirror to the reflecting surface of the mirror or the centre point of the lens.
focal plane *n* the plane that is perpendicular to the axis of a lens or mirror and passes through the focal point.
focal point *n* the point on the axis of a lens or mirror to which parallel rays of light converge or from which they appear to diverge after refraction or reflection. Also called: **focus.**
fo'c's'le *or* **fo'c'sle** ('fəʊksᵊl) *n* a variant spelling of **forecastle.**
focus ➊ ('fəʊkəs) *n, pl* **focuses** *or* **foci** (-saɪ). **1** a point of convergence of light or sound waves, etc., or a point from which they appear to diverge. **2** another name for **focal point** or **focal length. 3** *Optics.* the state of an optical image when it is distinct and clearly defined or the state of an instrument producing this image: *the telescope is out of focus.* **4** a point upon which attention, activity, etc., is concentrated. **5** *Geom.* a fixed reference point on the concave side of a conic section, used when defining its eccentricity. **6** the point beneath the earth's surface at which an earthquake originates. **7** *Pathol.* the main site of an infection. ◆ *vb* **focuses, focusing, focused** *or* **focusses, focussing, focussed. 8** to bring or come to a focus or into focus. **9** (*tr;* often foll. by *on*) to concentrate. [C17: via NL from L: hearth, fireplace]
▸ **'focuser** *n*
focus group *n* a group of people gathered by a market research company to discuss and assess a product or service.
focus puller *n Films.* the member of a camera crew who adjusts the focus of the lens as the camera is tracked in or out.
fodder ➊ ('fɒdə) *n* **1** bulk feed for livestock, esp. hay, straw, etc. ◆ *vb* **2** (*tr*) to supply (livestock) with fodder. [OE *fōdor*]
foe ➊ (fəʊ) *n Formal or literary.* another word for **enemy.** [OE *fāh* hostile]
FoE *or* **FOE** *abbrev. for* Friends of the Earth.
foehn (fɜːn; *German* føːn) *n Meteorol.* a variant spelling of **föhn.**
foeman ('fəʊmən) *n, pl* **foemen.** *Arch. & poetic.* an enemy in war; foe.
foetal ('fiːtᵊl) *adj* a variant spelling of **fetal.**
foetid ('fɛtɪd, 'fiː-) *adj* a variant spelling of **fetid.**
▸ **'foetidly** *adv* ▸ **'foetidness** *n*
foetus ('fiːtəs) *n, pl* **foetuses.** a variant spelling of **fetus.**
fog[1] ➊ (fɒg) *n* **1** a mass of droplets of condensed water vapour suspended in the air, often greatly reducing visibility. **2** a cloud of any substance in the atmosphere reducing visibility. **3** a state of mental uncertainty. **4** *Photog.* a blurred area on a developed negative, print, or transparency. ◆ *vb* **fogs, fogging, fogged. 5** to envelop or become enveloped with or as if with fog. **6** to confuse or become confused. **7** *Photog.* to produce fog on (a negative, print, or transparency) or (of a negative, print, or transparency) to be affected by fog. [C16: ? back formation from *foggy* damp, boggy, from FOG[2]]
fog[2] (fɒg) *n* a second growth of grass after the first mowing. [C14: prob. from ON]
fog bank *n* a distinct mass of fog, esp. at sea.
fogbound ('fɒgˌbaʊnd) *adj* prevented from operation by fog: *the airport was fogbound.*
fogbow ('fɒgˌbəʊ) *n* a faint arc of light sometimes seen in a fog bank.
fogey ➊ *or* **fogy** ('fəʊgɪ) *n, pl* **fogeys** *or* **fogies.** an extremely fussy or conservative person (esp. in **old fogey**). [C18: from ?]
▸ **'fogeyish** *or* **'fogyish** *adj*
foggy ➊ ('fɒgɪ) *adj* **foggier, foggiest. 1** thick with fog. **2** obscure or confused. **3 not the foggiest** (**idea** *or* **notion**). no idea whatsoever: *I haven't the foggiest.*
▸ **'fogginess** *n*
foghorn ('fɒgˌhɔːn) *n* **1** a mechanical instrument sounded at intervals to serve as a warning to vessels in fog. **2** *Inf.* a loud deep resounding voice.
fog signal *n* a signal used to warn railway engine drivers in fog, consisting of a detonator placed on the line.
föhn *or* **foehn** (fɜːn; *German* føːn) *n* a warm dry wind blowing down the northern slopes of the Alps. [G, from OHG, from L *favōnius;* rel. to *fovēre* to warm]
foible ➊ ('fɔɪbᵊl) *n* **1** a slight peculiarity or minor weakness; idiosyncrasy. **2** the most vulnerable part of a sword's blade, from the middle to the tip. [C17: from obs. F, from obs. adj: FEEBLE]
foie gras (*French* fwa grɑ) *n* See **pâté de foie gras.**
foil[1] ➊ (fɔɪl) *vb* (*tr*) **1** to baffle or frustrate (a person, attempt, etc.). **2** *Hunting.* (of hounds, hunters, etc.) to obliterate the scent left by a hunted animal or (of a hunted animal) to run back over its own trail. ◆ *n* **3** *Arch.* a setback or defeat. [C13 *foilen* to trample, from OF, *fuler* tread down]
▸ **'foilable** *adj*
foil[2] ➊ (fɔɪl) *n* **1** metal in the form of very thin sheets: *tin foil.* **2** the thin metallic sheet forming the backing of a mirror. **3** a thin leaf of shiny metal set under a gemstone to add brightness or colour. **4** a person or thing that gives contrast to another. **5** *Archit.* a small arc between cusps. **6** short for **hydrofoil.** ◆ *vb* (*tr*) **7** Also: **foliate.** *Archit.* to ornament (windows, etc.) with foils. [C14: from OF, from L *folia* leaves]
foil[3] (fɔɪl) *n* a light slender flexible sword tipped by a button. [C16: from ?]
foist ➊ (fɔɪst) *vb* (*tr*) **1** (often foll. by *off* or *on*) to sell or pass off (some-

THESAURUS

foam *n* **1** = **froth,** bubbles, head, lather, spray, spume, suds ◆ *vb* **5** = **bubble,** boil, effervesce, fizz, froth, lather
foamy *adj* = **bubbly,** foaming, frothy, lathery, spumescent, sudsy
fob off *vb* **1** = **put off,** appease, deceive, equivocate with, flannel (*Brit. inf.*), give (someone) the run-around (*inf.*), stall **2** = **pass off,** dump, foist, get rid of, inflict, palm off, unload
focus *n* **4** = **centre,** bull's eye, centre of activity, centre of attraction, core, cynosure, focal point, headquarters, heart, hub, meeting place, target ◆ *vb* **9** = **concentrate,** aim, bring to bear, centre, converge, direct, fix, join, meet, pinpoint, rivet, spotlight, zero in (*inf.*), zoom in
fodder *n* **1** = **feed,** food, foodstuff, forage, provender, rations, tack (*inf.*), victuals, vittles (*obs. or dialect*)
foe *n* = **enemy,** adversary, antagonist, foeman (*arch.*), opponent, rival
Antonyms *n* ally, companion, comrade, confederate, friend, partner
fog[1] *n* **1** = **mist,** gloom, miasma, murk, murkiness, peasouper (*inf.*), smog **3** = **obscurity,** blindness, confusion, daze, haze, mist, perplexity, stupor, trance ◆ *vb* **5** = **mist over** *or* **up,** cloud, steam up **6** = **obscure,** becloud, bedim, befuddle, bewilder, blear, blind, cloud, confuse, darken, daze, dim, muddle, muddy the waters, obfuscate, perplex, stupefy
fogey *n* = **fuddy-duddy** (*inf.*), anachronism, antique (*inf.*), back number (*inf.*), dinosaur, dodo (*inf.*), fossil (*inf.*), relic, square (*inf.*), stick-in-the-mud (*inf.*)
foggy *adj* **1** = **misty,** blurred, brumous (*rare*), cloudy, dim, grey, hazy, indistinct, murky, nebulous, obscure, smoggy, soupy, vaporous **2** = **unclear,** befuddled, bewildered, clouded, cloudy, confused, dark, dazed, dim, indistinct, muddled, obscure, stupefied, stupid, vague
Antonyms *adj* ≠ **misty:** bright, clear ≠ **unclear:** accurate, alert, awake, clear, decisive, distinct, lucid, palpable, sharp, shrewd, undimmed
foible *n* **1** = **idiosyncrasy,** defect, failing, fault, imperfection, infirmity, peculiarity, quirk, weakness, weak point
foil[1] *vb* **1** = **thwart,** baffle, balk, check, checkmate, circumvent, cook (someone's) goose (*inf.*), counter, defeat, disappoint, elude, frustrate, nip in the bud, nullify, outwit, stop
foil[2] *n* **4** = **contrast,** antithesis, background, complement, setting
foist *vb* **1, 2** = **impose,** fob off, get rid of, insert,

thing, esp. an inferior article) as genuine, valuable, etc. **2** (usually foll. by *in* or *into*) to insert surreptitiously or wrongfully. [C16: prob. from obs. Du. *vuisten* to enclose in one's hand, from MDu. *vuist* fist]

FOL (in New Zealand) *abbrev. for* Federation of Labour.

fol. *abbrev. for:* **1** folio. **2** following.

fold[1] ➊ (fəʊld) *vb* **1** to bend or be bent double so that one part covers another. **2** (*tr*) to bring together and intertwine (the arms, legs, etc.). **3** (*tr*) (of birds, insects, etc.) to close (the wings) together from an extended position. **4** (*tr;* often foll. by *up* or *in*) to enclose in or as if in a surrounding material. **5** (*tr;* foll. by *in*) to clasp (a person) in the arms. **6** (*tr;* usually foll. by *round, about,* etc.) to wind (around); entwine. **7** Also: **fold in.** (*tr*) to mix (a whisked mixture) with other ingredients by gently turning one part over the other with a spoon. **8** (*intr;* often foll. by *up*) *Inf.* to collapse; fail: *the business folded.* ◆ *n* **9** a piece or section that has been folded: *a fold of cloth.* **10** a mark, crease, or hollow made by folding. **11** a hollow in undulating terrain. **12** a bend in stratified rocks that results from movements within the earth's crust. **13** a coil, as in a rope, etc. [OE *fealdan*]
▸**'foldable** *adj*

fold[2] (fəʊld) *n* **1a** a small enclosure or pen for sheep or other livestock, where they can be gathered. **1b** a flock of sheep. **2** a church or the members of it. ◆ *vb* **3** (*tr*) to gather or confine (sheep, etc.) in a fold. [OE *falod*]

-fold *suffix forming adjectives and adverbs.* having so many parts or being so many times as much or as many: *three-hundredfold.* [OE *-fald, -feald*]

foldaway ('fəʊldə,weɪ) *adj* (*prenominal*) (of a bed, etc.) able to be folded away when not in use.

folded dipole *n* a type of aerial consisting of two parallel dipoles connected together at their outer ends and fed at the centre of one of them. The length is usually half the operating wavelength.

folder ➊ ('fəʊldə) *n* **1** a binder or file for holding loose papers, etc. **2** a folded circular. **3** a person or thing that folds.

folderol ('fɒldə,rɒl) *n* a variant spelling of **falderal.**

folding door *n* a door in the form of two or more vertical hinged leaves that can be folded one against another.

folding money *n Inf.* paper money.

foley *or* **foley artist** ('fəʊlɪ) *n Films.* the US name for **footsteps editor.** [C20: after the inventor of the technique]

foliaceous (,fəʊlɪ'eɪʃəs) *adj* **1** having the appearance of the leaf of a plant. **2** bearing leaves or leaflike structures. **3** *Geol.* consisting of thin layers. [C17: from L *foliāceus*]

foliage ('fəʊlɪɪdʒ) *n* **1** the green leaves of a plant. **2** sprays of leaves used for decoration. **3** an ornamental leaflike design. [C15: from OF *fuellage,* from *fuelle* leaf; infl. in form by L *folium*]

foliar ('fəʊlɪə) *adj* of or relating to a leaf or leaves. [C19: from F, from L *folium* leaf]

foliate *adj* ('fəʊlɪɪt, -,eɪt). **1a** relating to, possessing, or resembling leaves. **1b** (*in combination*): *trifoliate.* ◆ *vb* ('fəʊlɪ,eɪt), **foliates, foliating, foliated. 2** (*tr*) to ornament with foliage or with leaf forms such as foils. **3** to hammer or cut (metal) into thin plates or foil. **4** (*tr*) to number the leaves of (a book, etc.). Cf. **paginate. 5** (*intr*) (of plants) to grow leaves. [C17: from L *foliātus* leaved, leafy]

foliation (,fəʊlɪ'eɪʃən) *n* **1** *Bot.* **1a** the process of producing leaves. **1b** the state of being in leaf. **1c** the arrangement of leaves in a leaf bud. **2** *Archit.* ornamentation consisting of cusps and foils. **3** the consecutive numbering of the leaves of a book. **4** *Geol.* the arrangement of the constituents of a rock in leaflike layers, as in schists.

folic acid ('fəʊlɪk) *n* any of a group of vitamins of the B complex, used in the treatment of anaemia. Also called: **folacin.** [C20: from L *folium* leaf; so called because it may be obtained from green leaves]

folio ('fəʊlɪəʊ) *n, pl* **folios. 1** a sheet of paper folded in half to make two leaves for a book. **2** a book of the largest common size made up of such sheets. **3a** a leaf of paper numbered on the front side only. **3b** the page number of a book. **4** *Law.* a unit of measurement of the length of legal documents, determined by the number of words, generally 72 or 90 in Britain and 100 in the US. ◆ *adj* **5** relating to or having the format of a folio: *a folio edition.* [C16: from L phrase *in foliō* in a leaf, from *folium* leaf]

folk ➊ (fəʊk) *n, pl* **folk** *or* **folks. 1** (*functioning as pl; often pl in form*) people in general, esp. those of a particular group or class: *country folk.* **2** (*functioning as pl; usually pl in form*) *Inf.* members of a family. **3** (*functioning as sing*) *Inf.* short for **folk music. 4** a people or tribe. **5** (*modifier*) originating from or traditional to the common people of a country: *a folk song.* [OE *folc*]
▸**'folkish** *adj*

folk dance *n* **1** any of various traditional rustic dances. **2** a piece of music composed for or in the rhythm of such a dance.
▸**folk dancing** *n*

folk etymology *n* the gradual change in the form of a word through the influence of a more familiar word or phrase with which it becomes associated, as for example *sparrow-grass* for *asparagus.*

folkie *or* **folky** ('fəʊkɪ) *n, pl* **folkies.** *Inf.* a devotee of folk music.

folklore ('fəʊk,lɔː) *n* **1** the unwritten literature of a people as expressed in folk tales, songs, etc. **2** the body of stories and legends attached to a particular place, group, etc.: *rugby folklore.* **3** study of folkloric materials.
▸**'folk,loric** *adj* ▸**'folk,lorist** *n, adj*

folk medicine *n* medicine as practised among rustic communities and primitive peoples, consisting typically of the use of herbal remedies.

folk music *n* **1** music that is passed on from generation to generation. **2** any music composed in this idiom.

folk-rock *n* a style of rock music influenced by folk.

folk song *n* **1** a song which has been handed down among the common people. **2** a modern song which reflects the folk idiom.

folksy ('fəʊksɪ) *adj* **folksier, folksiest. 1** of or like ordinary people; sometimes used derogatorily to describe affected simplicity. **2** *Inf., chiefly US.* friendly; affable.

folk tale *or* **story** *n* a tale or legend originating among a people and becoming part of an oral tradition.

folk weave *n* a type of fabric with a loose weave.

follicle ('fɒlɪkᵊl) *n* **1** any small sac or cavity in the body having an excretory, secretory, or protective function: *a hair follicle.* **2** *Bot.* a dry fruit that splits along one side only to release its seeds. [C17: from L *folliculus* small bag, from *follis* pair of bellows, leather money-bag]
▸**follicular** (fɒ'lɪkjʊlə), **folliculate** (fɒ'lɪkjʊ,leɪt), *or* **fol'licu,lated** *adj*

follow ➊ ('fɒləʊ) *vb* **1** to go or come after in the same direction. **2** (*tr*) to accompany: *she followed her sister everywhere.* **3** to come after as a logical or natural consequence. **4** (*tr*) to keep to the course or track of: *she followed the towpath.* **5** (*tr*) to act in accordance with: *to follow instructions.* **6** (*tr*) to accept the ideas or beliefs of (a previous authority, etc.): *he followed Donne in most of his teachings.* **7** to understand (an explanation, etc.): *the lesson was difficult to follow.* **8** to watch closely or continuously: *she followed his progress.* **9** (*tr*) to have a keen interest in: *to follow athletics.* **10** (*tr*) to help in the cause of: *the men who followed Napoleon.* [OE *folgian*]

follower ➊ ('fɒləʊə) *n* **1** a person who accepts the teachings of another: *a follower of Marx.* **2** an attendant. **3** a supporter, as of a sport or team. **4** (esp. formerly) a male admirer.

following ➊ ('fɒləʊɪŋ) *adj* **1a** (*prenominal*) about to be mentioned, specified, etc.: *the following items.* **1b** (*as n*): *will the following please raise their hands?* **2** (of winds, currents, etc.) moving in the same direction as a vessel. ◆ *n* **3** a group of supporters or enthusiasts: *he attracted a large following.* ◆ *prep* **4** as a result of: *he was arrested following a tip-off.*

> **USAGE NOTE** The use of *following* to mean *as a result of* is very common in journalism, but should be avoided in other kinds of writing.

follow-on *Cricket.* ◆ *n* **1** an immediate second innings forced on a team scoring a prescribed number of runs fewer than its opponents in the first innings. ◆ *vb* **follow on. 2** (*intr, adv*) (of a team) to play a follow-on.

follow out *vb* (*tr, adv*) to implement (an idea or action) to a conclusion.

follow through ➊ *vb* (*adv*) **1** *Sport.* to complete (a stroke or shot) by continuing the movement to the end of its arc. **2** (*tr*) to pursue (an aim) to a conclusion. ◆ *n* **follow-through. 3** the act of following through.

follow up ➊ *vb* (*tr, adv*) **1** to pursue or investigate (a person, etc.)

THESAURUS

insinuate, interpolate, introduce, palm off, pass off, put over, sneak in, unload

fold[1] *vb* **1, 2** = **bend**, crease, crumple, dog-ear, double, double over, gather, intertwine, overlap, pleat, tuck, turn under **4** = **wrap**, do up, enclose, enfold, entwine, envelop, wrap up **8** *Informal* = **go bankrupt**, be ruined, close, collapse, crash, fail, go belly-up (*sl.*), go bust (*inf.*), go by the board, go to the wall, go under, shut down ◆ *n* **9, 10** = **crease**, bend, double thickness, folded portion, furrow, knife-edge, layer, overlap, pleat, turn, wrinkle

folder *n* **1** = **file**, binder, envelope, portfolio

folk *n* **1, 2, 4** = **people**, clan, ethnic group, family, kin, kindred, race, tribe

follow *vb* **1** = **come after**, come next, step into the shoes of, succeed, supersede, supplant, take the place of **1** = **pursue**, chase, dog, hound, hunt, run after, shadow, stalk, tail (*inf.*), track, trail **2** = **accompany**, attend, bring up the rear, come after, come *or* go with, escort, tag along, tread on the heels of **3** = **result**, arise, be consequent, develop, emanate, ensue, flow, issue, proceed, spring, supervene **5** = **obey**, act in accordance with, be guided by, comply, conform, give allegiance to, heed, mind, note, observe, regard, toe the line, watch **7** = **understand**, appreciate, catch, catch on (*inf.*), comprehend, fathom, get, get the hang of (*inf.*), get the picture, grasp, keep up with, realize, see, take in **9** = **be interested in**, be a devotee *or* supporter of, be devoted to, cultivate, keep abreast of, support
Antonyms *vb* ≠ **come after:** guide, lead, precede ≠ **pursue:** avoid, elude, escape ≠ **obey:** abandon, desert, disobey, flout, forsake, give up, ignore, reject, renounce, shun

follower *n* **1, 3** = **supporter**, adherent, admirer, apostle, backer, believer, cohort (*chiefly US*), convert, devotee, disciple, fan, fancier, habitué, henchman, partisan, protagonist, pupil, representative, votary, worshipper **2** = **attendant**, companion, hanger-on, helper, henchman, lackey, minion, retainer (*History*), sidekick (*sl.*)
Antonyms *n* ≠ **supporter:** guru, leader, mentor, svengali, swami, teacher, tutor ≠ **attendant:** antagonist, contender, enemy, foe, opponent, rival

following *adj* **1** = **next**, coming, consequent, consequential, ensuing, later, specified, subsequent, succeeding, successive ◆ *n* **3** = **supporters**, audience, circle, clientele, coterie, entourage, fans, patronage, public, retinue, suite, support, train

follow through *vb* **2** = **complete**, bring to a conclusion, conclude, consummate, pursue, see through

follow up *vb* **1** = **investigate**, check out, find

closely. **2** to continue (action) after a beginning, esp. to increase its effect. ◆ *n* **follow-up. 3a** something done to reinforce an initial action. **3b** (*as modifier*): *a follow-up letter.* **4** *Med.* an examination of a patient at intervals after treatment.

folly ⓘ ('fɒlɪ) *n, pl* **follies. 1** the state or quality of being foolish. **2** a foolish action, idea, etc. **3** a building in the form of a castle, temple, etc., built to satisfy a fancy or conceit. **4** (*pl*) *Theatre.* an elaborately costumed revue. [C13: from OF *folie* madness, from *fou* mad; see FOOL[1]]

foment ⓘ (fə'mɛnt) *vb* (*tr*) **1** to encourage or instigate (trouble, discord, etc.). **2** *Med.* to apply heat and moisture to (a part of the body) to relieve pain. [C15: from LL, from L *fōmentum* a poultice, ult. from *fovēre* to foster]
▸**fomentation** (ˌfəʊmɛn'teɪʃən) *n* ▸**fo'menter** *n*

> **USAGE NOTE** Both *foment* and *ferment* can be used to talk about stirring up trouble: *he was accused of fomenting/fermenting unrest.* Only *ferment* can be used intransitively or as a noun: *his anger continued to ferment* (not *foment*); *rural areas were unaffected by the ferment in the cities.*

fond ⓘ (fɒnd) *adj* **1** (*postpositive;* foll. by *of*) having a liking (for). **2** loving; tender. **3** indulgent: *a fond mother.* **4** (of hopes, wishes, etc.) cherished but unlikely to be realized: *he had fond hopes of starting his own firm.* **5** *Arch. or dialect.* **5a** foolish. **5b** credulous. [C14 *fonned,* from *fonne* a fool]
▸**'fondly** *adv* ▸**'fondness** *n*

fondant ('fɒndənt) *n* **1** a thick flavoured paste of sugar and water, used in sweets and icings. **2** a sweet made of this mixture. ◆ *adj* **3** (of a colour) soft, pastel. [C19: from F, lit.: melting, from *fondre* to melt, from L *fundere;* see FOUND[3]]

fondle ⓘ ('fɒnd°l) *vb* **fondles, fondling, fondled.** (*tr*) to touch or stroke tenderly. [C17: from (obs.) vb *fond* to fondle; see FOND]
▸**'fondler** *n*

fondue ('fɒndjuː; *French* fɔ̃dy) *n* a Swiss dish, consisting of melted cheese into which small pieces of bread are dipped. [C19: from F, fem of *fondu* melted; see FONDANT]

font[1] (fɒnt) *n* **1a** a large bowl for baptismal water. **1b** a receptacle for holy water. **2** the reservoir for oil in an oil lamp. **3** *Arch. or poetic.* a fountain or well. [OE, from Church L *fons,* from L: fountain]

font[2] (fɒnt) *n Printing.* another name (esp. US and Canad.) for **fount**[2].

fontanelle *or chiefly US* **fontanel** (ˌfɒntə'nɛl) *n Anat.* any of the soft membranous gaps between the bones of the skull in a fetus or infant. [C16 (in the sense: hollow between muscles): from OF *fontanele,* lit.: a little spring, from *fontaine* FOUNTAIN]

food ⓘ (fuːd) *n* **1** any substance that can be ingested by a living organism and metabolized into energy and body tissue. Related adj: **alimentary. 2** nourishment in more or less solid form: *food and drink.* **3** anything that provides mental nourishment or stimulus. [OE *fōda*]

food additive *n* any of various natural or synthetic substances, such as salt or citric acid, used in the commercial processing of food as preservatives, antioxidants, emulsifiers, etc.

food chain *n Ecology.* a series of organisms in a community, each member of which feeds on another in the chain and is in turn eaten.

foodie ⓘ *or* **foody** ('fuːdɪ) *n, pl* **foodies.** a person having an enthusiastic interest in the preparation and consumption of good food.

food poisoning *n* an acute illness caused by food that is either naturally poisonous or contaminated by bacteria.

food processor *n Cookery.* an electric domestic appliance for automatic chopping, grating, blending, etc.

foodstuff ('fuːdˌstʌf) *n* any material, substance, etc., that can be used as food.

food value *n* the relative degree of nourishment obtained from different foods.

fool[1] ⓘ (fuːl) *n* **1** a person who lacks sense or judgement. **2** a person who is made to appear ridiculous. **3** (formerly) a professional jester living in a royal or noble household. **4** *Obs.* an idiot or imbecile: *the village fool.* **5 play** *or* **act the fool.** to deliberately act foolishly. ◆ *vb* **6** (*tr*) to deceive (someone), esp. in order to make him look ridiculous. **7** (*intr;* foll. by *with, around with,* or *about with*) *Inf.* to act or play (with) irresponsibly or aimlessly. **8** (*intr*) to speak or act in a playful or jesting manner. **9** (*tr;* foll. by *away*) to squander; fritter. ◆ *adj* **10** *US inf.* short for **foolish.** [C13: from OF *fol* mad person, from LL *follis* empty-headed fellow, from L: bellows]

fool[2] (fuːl) *n Chiefly Brit.* a dessert made from a purée of fruit with cream. [C16: ?from FOOL[1]]

foolery ⓘ ('fuːlərɪ) *n, pl* **fooleries. 1** foolish behaviour. **2** an instance of this.

foolhardy ⓘ ('fuːlˌhɑːdɪ) *adj* **foolhardier, foolhardiest.** heedlessly rash or adventurous. [C13: from OF, from *fol* foolish + *hardi* bold]
▸**'foolˌhardily** *adv* ▸**'foolˌhardiness** *n*

foolish ⓘ ('fuːlɪʃ) *adj* **1** unwise; silly. **2** resulting from folly or stupidity. **3** ridiculous or absurd. **4** weak-minded; simple.
▸**'foolishly** *adv* ▸**'foolishness** *n*

foolproof ⓘ ('fuːlˌpruːf) *adj Inf.* **1** proof against failure. **2** (esp. of machines, etc.) proof against human misuse, error, etc.

foolscap ('fuːlzˌkæp) *n Chiefly Brit.* a size of writing or printing paper, 13½ by 17 inches. [C17: see FOOL[1], CAP; so called from the watermark formerly used on this kind of paper]

fool's cap *n* **1** a hood or cap with bells or tassels, worn by court jesters. **2** a dunce's cap.

fool's errand *n* a fruitless undertaking.

THESAURUS

out about, look into, make inquiries, pursue, research **2** = **continue**, consolidate, make sure, reinforce

folly *n* **1** = **foolishness**, absurdity, daftness, fatuity, idiocy, imbecility, imprudence, indiscretion, irrationality, lunacy, madness, nonsense, preposterousness, rashness, recklessness, silliness, stupidity
Antonyms *n* judgment, level-headedness, moderation, prudence, rationality, reason, sanity, sense, wisdom

foment *vb* **1** = **stir up**, abet, agitate, arouse, brew, encourage, excite, fan the flames, foster, goad, incite, instigate, promote, provoke, quicken, raise, rouse, sow the seeds of, spur, stimulate, whip up

fomenter *n* **1** = **instigator**, agitator, demagogue, firebrand, incendiary, inciter, rabble-rouser, stirrer (*inf.*), troublemaker

fond *adj* **1** *foll. by* **of** = **keen on**, addicted to, attached to, enamoured of, having a fancy for, having a liking for, having a soft spot for, having a taste for, hooked on, into (*inf.*), partial to, predisposed towards **2, 3** = **loving**, adoring, affectionate, amorous, caring, devoted, doting, indulgent, tender, warm **4** = **foolish**, absurd, credulous, deluded, delusive, delusory, empty, indiscreet, naive, overoptimistic, vain
Antonyms *adj* ≠ **loving:** aloof, austere, averse, disinterested, indifferent, unaffectionate, unconcerned, undemonstrative ≠ **foolish:** rational, sensible

fondle *vb* = **caress**, cuddle, dandle, pat, pet, stroke

fondly *adv* **2, 3** = **lovingly**, affectionately, dearly, indulgently, possessively, tenderly, with affection **4** = **foolishly**, credulously, naively, stupidly, vainly

fondness *n* **1** = **liking**, attachment, fancy, love, partiality, penchant, predilection, preference, soft spot, susceptibility, taste, weakness **2** = **devotion**, affection, attachment, kindness, love, tenderness

Antonyms *n* abhorrence, animosity, animus, antagonism, antipathy, aversion, bad blood, coldness, contempt, detestation, dislike, enmity, harshness, hatred, hostility, ill will, loathing, malevolence, malice, opposition, repugnance, repulsion, resentment, unfriendliness

food *n* **1** = **nourishment**, aliment, board, bread, chow (*inf.*), comestibles, commons, cooking, cuisine, diet, eatables (*sl.*), edibles, fare, feed, foodstuffs, grub (*sl.*), meat, nosh (*sl.*), nutriment, nutrition, provender, provisions, rations, refreshment, scoff (*sl.*), stores, subsistence, survival rations, sustenance, table, tuck (*inf.*), tucker (*Austral. & NZ inf.*), viands, victuals, vittles (*obs. or dialect*)

foodie *n* = **gourmet**, *bon vivant, bon viveur,* connoisseur, epicure, gastronome, gourmand

fool[1] *n* **1** = **simpleton**, ass, blockhead, bonehead (*sl.*), charlie (*Brit. inf.*), chump, coot, dimwit (*inf.*), dolt, dope (*inf.*), dork (*sl.*), dunce, fathead (*inf.*), goose (*inf.*), halfwit, idiot, ignoramus, illiterate, imbecile (*inf.*), jackass, jerk (*sl., chiefly US & Canad.*), loon, mooncalf, moron, nerd *or* nurd (*sl.*), nincompoop, ninny, nit (*inf.*), nitwit (*inf.*), numbskull *or* numskull, oaf, sap (*sl.*), schmuck (*US sl.*), silly, twerp *or* twirp (*inf.*), twit (*inf., chiefly Brit.*), wally (*sl.*) **2** = **dupe**, butt, chump (*inf.*), easy mark (*inf.*), fall guy (*inf.*), greenhorn (*inf.*), gull (*arch.*), laughing stock, mug (*Brit. sl.*), stooge (*sl.*), sucker (*sl.*) **3** = **clown**, buffoon, comic, harlequin, jester, merry-andrew, motley, pierrot, punchinello **5** **play** *or* act the fool = **clown**, act the goat, act up, be silly, cavort, cut capers, frolic, lark about (*inf.*), mess about, play (silly) games, show off (*inf.*) ◆ *vb* **6** = **deceive**, bamboozle, beguile, bluff, cheat, con, delude, dupe, gull (*arch.*), have (someone) on, hoax, hoodwink, kid (*inf.*), make a fool of, mislead, play a trick on, pull a fast one on (*inf.*), put one over on (*inf.*), stiff (*sl.*), take in, trick **7** *with* **with, around with,** *or* **about with** *Informal* = **play**, fiddle (*inf.*), meddle, mess, monkey, tamper, toy, trifle

Antonyms *n* ≠ **simpleton:** expert, genius, master, sage, savant, scholar, wise man

foolery *n* **1, 2** = **nonsense**, antics, capers, carry-on (*inf., chiefly Brit.*), childishness, clowning, folly, fooling, horseplay, larks, mischief, monkey tricks (*inf.*), practical jokes, pranks, shenanigans (*inf.*), silliness, tomfoolery

foolhardy *adj* = **rash**, adventurous, bold, hot-headed, impetuous, imprudent, incautious, irresponsible, madcap, precipitate, reckless, temerarious, venturesome, venturous
Antonyms *adj* alert, careful, cautious, chary, circumspect, heedful, judicious, prudent, shrewd, solicitous, thoughtful, wary, watchful

foolish *adj* **1** = **unwise**, absurd, asinine, ill-advised, ill-considered, ill-judged, imprudent, inane, incautious, indiscreet, injudicious, nonsensical, senseless, short-sighted, silly, unintelligent, unreasonable **3, 4** = **silly**, as daft as a brush (*inf., chiefly Brit.*), brainless, crackpot (*inf.*), crazy, daft (*inf.*), doltish, fatuous, goofy (*inf.*), half-baked (*inf.*), half-witted, hare-brained, idiotic, imbecilic, inane, loopy (*inf.*), ludicrous, mad, moronic, off one's head (*inf.*), potty (*Brit. inf.*), ridiculous, senseless, simple, stupid, weak, witless
Antonyms *adj* bright, cautious, clever, commonsensical, intelligent, judicious, prudent, rational, sagacious, sane, sensible, sharp, smart, sound, thoughtful, wise

foolishly *adv* **1** = **unwisely**, absurdly, idiotically, ill-advisedly, imprudently, incautiously, indiscreetly, injudiciously, like a fool, mistakenly, short-sightedly, stupidly, without due consideration

foolishness *n* **1, 2** = **stupidity**, absurdity, folly, idiocy, imprudence, inanity, indiscretion, irresponsibility, silliness, weakness **3** = **nonsense**, bunk (*inf.*), bunkum *or* buncombe (*chiefly US*), claptrap (*inf.*), foolery, rigmarole, rubbish, trash

foolproof *adj* **1** = **infallible**, certain, guaran-

fool's gold *n* any of various yellow minerals, esp. pyrite, that can be mistaken for gold.
fool's paradise *n* illusory happiness.
fool's-parsley *n* an evil-smelling Eurasian umbelliferous plant with small white flowers.
foot (fʊt) *n, pl* **feet.** **1** the part of the vertebrate leg below the ankle joint that is in contact with the ground during standing and walking. Related adj: **pedal. 2** the part of a garment covering a foot. **3** any of various organs of locomotion or attachment in invertebrates, including molluscs. **4** *Bot.* the lower part of some plants or plant structures. **5** a unit of length equal to one third of a yard or 12 inches. 1 foot is equivalent to 0.3048 metre. **6** any part resembling a foot in form or function: *the foot of a chair.* **7** the lower part of something; bottom: *the foot of a hill.* **8** the end of a series or group: *the foot of the list.* **9** manner of walking or moving: *a heavy foot.* **10a** infantry, esp. in the British army. **10b** (*as modifier*): *a foot soldier.* **11** any of various attachments on a sewing machine that hold the fabric in position. **12** *Prosody.* a group of two or more syllables in which one syllable has the major stress, forming the basic unit of poetic rhythm. **13 my foot!** an expression of disbelief, often of the speaker's own preceding statement. **14 of foot.** *Arch.* in manner of movement: *fleet of foot.* **15 one foot in the grave.** *Inf.* near to death. **16 on foot. 16a** walking or running. **16b** astir; afoot. **17 put a foot wrong.** to make a mistake. **18 put one's best foot forward. 18a** to try to do one's best. **18b** to hurry. **19 put one's foot down.** *Inf.* to act firmly. **20 put one's foot in it.** *Inf.* to blunder. **21 under foot.** on the ground; beneath one's feet. ◆ *vb* **22** to dance to music (esp. in **foot it**). **23** (*tr*) to walk over or set foot on (esp. in **foot it**). **24** (*tr*) to pay the entire cost of (esp. in **foot the bill**). [OE *fōt*] ◆ See also **feet.**
▸ **'footless** *adj*

> **USAGE NOTE** In front of another noun, the plural for the unit of length is *foot: a 20-foot putt; his 70-foot ketch. Foot* can also be used instead of *feet* when mentioning a quantity and in front of words like *tall: four foot of snow; he is at least six foot tall.*

footage ('fʊtɪdʒ) *n* **1** a length or distance measured in feet. **2** the extent of film material shot and exposed.
foot-and-mouth disease *n* an acute highly infectious viral disease of cattle, pigs, sheep, and goats, characterized by the formation of vesicular eruptions in the mouth and on the feet.
football ('fʊt,bɔːl) *n* **1a** any of various games played with a round or oval ball and usually based on two teams competing to kick, head, carry, or otherwise propel the ball into each other's goal, territory, etc. **1b** (*as modifier*): *a football supporter.* **2** the ball used in any of these games or their variants. **3** a problem, issue, etc., that is continually passed from one group or person to another as a pretext for argument.
▸ **'foot,baller** *n*
footboard ('fʊt,bɔːd) *n* **1** a board for a person to stand or rest his feet on. **2** a treadle or foot-operated lever on a machine. **3** a vertical board at the foot of a bed.
footbridge ('fʊt,brɪdʒ) *n* a narrow bridge for the use of pedestrians.
-footed *adj* **1** having a foot or feet as specified: *four-footed.* **2** having a tread as specified: *heavy-footed.*
footer[1] ('fʊtə) *n* (*in combination*) a person or thing of a specified length or height in feet: *a six-footer.*
footer[2] ('fʊtə) *n Brit. inf.* short for **football** (the game).
footfall ('fʊt,fɔːl) *n* the sound of a footstep.
foot fault *n Tennis.* a fault that occurs when the server fails to keep both feet behind the baseline until he has served.
foothill ('fʊt,hɪl) *n* (*often pl*) a relatively low hill at the foot of a mountain.
foothold ('fʊt,həʊld) *n* **1** a ledge or other place affording a secure grip, as during climbing. **2** a secure position from which further progress may be made.
footing 🅣 ('fʊtɪŋ) *n* **1** the basis or foundation on which something is established: *the business was on a secure footing.* **2** the relationship or status existing between two persons, groups, etc. **3** a secure grip by or for the feet. **4** the lower part of a foundation of a column, wall, building, etc.
footle ('fuːtᵊl) *vb* **footles, footling, footled.** (*intr*; often foll. by *around* or *about*) *Inf.* to loiter aimlessly. [C19: prob. from F *foutre* to copulate with, from L *futuere*]
▸ **'footling** *adj*
footlights ('fʊt,laɪts) *pl n Theatre.* lights set in a row along the front of the stage floor.
footloose ('fʊt,luːs) *adj* **1** free to go or do as one wishes. **2** restless: *to feel footloose.*
footman ('fʊtmən) *n, pl* **footmen. 1** a male servant, esp. one in livery. **2** (formerly) a foot soldier.
footnote ('fʊt,nəʊt) *n* **1** a note printed at the bottom of a page, to which attention is drawn by means of a mark in the text. ◆ *vb* **footnotes, footnoting, footnoted. 2** (*tr*) to supply (a page, etc.) with footnotes.
footpad ('fʊt,pæd) *n Arch.* a robber or highwayman, on foot rather than horseback.
footpath ('fʊt,pɑːθ) *n* **1** a narrow path for walkers only. **2** *Chiefly Austral. & NZ.* another word for **pavement.**
footplate ('fʊt,pleɪt) *n Chiefly Brit.* a platform in the cab of a locomotive on which the crew stand to operate the controls.
foot-pound-second *n* See **fps units.**
footprint ('fʊt,prɪnt) *n* an indentation or outline of the foot of a person or animal on a surface.
footrest ('fʊt,rest) *n* something that provides a support for the feet, such as a low stool, rail, etc.
foot rot *n Vet. science.* See **rot** (sense 10).
footsie ('fʊtsɪ) *n Inf.* flirtation involving the touching together of feet, etc.
Footsie ('fʊtsɪ) *n Brit. inf.* the Financial Times Stock Exchange 100 index. See **FT Index** (sense 2).
foot soldier *n* an infantryman.
footsore ('fʊt,sɔː) *adj* having sore or tired feet, esp. from much walking.
▸ **'foot,soreness** *n*
footstep 🅣 ('fʊt,step) *n* **1** the action of taking a step in walking. **2** the sound made by walking. **3** the distance covered with a step. **4** a footmark. **5** a single stair. **6 follow in someone's footsteps.** to continue the example of another.
footsteps editor *n Brit. films.* the technician who adds sound effects, such as doors closing, rain falling, etc., during the postproduction sound-dubbing process. US name: **foley** *or* **foley artist.**
footstool ('fʊt,stuːl) *n* a low stool used for supporting or resting the feet of a seated person.
footwear 🅣 ('fʊt,weə) *n* anything worn to cover the feet.
footwork ('fʊt,wɜːk) *n* the use of the feet, esp. in sports, dancing, etc.
footy *or* **footie** ('fʊtɪ) *n Inf.* **a** football. **b** (*as modifier*): *footy boots.*
fop 🅣 (fɒp) *n* a man who is excessively concerned with fashion and elegance. [C15: rel. to G *foppen* to trick]
▸ **'foppery** *n* ▸ **'foppish** *adj*
for (fɔː; *unstressed* fə) *prep* **1** directed or belonging to: *there's a phone call for you.* **2** to the advantage of: *I only did it for you.* **3** in the direction of: *heading for the border.* **4** over a span of (time or distance): *working for six days.* **5** in favour of: *vote for me.* **6** in order to get or achieve: *I do it for money.* **7** designed to meet the needs of: *these kennels are for puppies.* **8** at a cost of: *I got it for hardly any money.* **9** such as explains or results in: *his reason for changing his job was not given.* **10** in place of: *a substitute for the injured player.* **11** because of: *she wept for pure relief.* **12** with regard or consideration to the usual characteristics of: *it's cool for this time of year.* **13** concerning: *desire for money.* **14** as being: *I know that for a fact.* **15** at a specified time: *a date for the next evening.* **16** to do or partake of: *an appointment for supper.* **17** in the duty or task of: *that's for him to say.* **18** to allow of: *too big a job for us to handle.* **19** despite: *she's a good wife, for all her nagging.* **20** in order to preserve, retain, etc.: *to fight for survival.* **21** as a direct equivalent to: *word for word.* **22** in order to become or enter: *to train for the priesthood.* **23** in recompense for: *I paid for it last week.* **24 for it.** *Brit. inf.* liable for punishment or blame: *you'll be for it if she catches you.* ◆ *conj* **25** (*coordinating*) because; seeing that: *I couldn't stay, for the area was violent.* [OE]
for- *prefix* **1** indicating rejection or prohibition: *forbid.* **2** indicating falsity: *forswear.* **3** used to give intensive force: *forlorn.* [OE *for-*]
forage 🅣 ('fɒrɪdʒ) *n* **1** food for horses or cattle, esp. hay or straw. **2** the act of searching for food or provisions. ◆ *vb* **forages, foraging, foraged. 3** to search (the countryside or a town) for food, etc. **4** (*intr*) *Mil.* to carry out a raid. **5** (*tr*) to obtain by searching about. **6** (*tr*) to give food or other provisions to. **7** (*tr*) to feed (cattle or horses) with such food. [C14: from OF *fourrage*, prob. of Gmc origin]
▸ **'forager** *n*
forage cap *n* a soldier's undress cap.
foramen (fɒ'reɪmen) *n, pl* **foramina** (-'ræmɪnə) *or* **foramens.** a natural hole, esp. one in a bone. [C17: from L, from *forāre* to bore, pierce]
foraminifer (,fɒrə'mɪnɪfə) *n* a protozoan of the phylum *Foraminifera*, having a shell with numerous openings through which the cytoplasmic processes protrude. [C19: from NL, from FORAMEN + -FER]
forasmuch as (fərəz'mʌtʃ) *conj* (*subordinating*) *Arch. or legal.* seeing that.
foray 🅣 ('fɒreɪ) *n* **1** a short raid or incursion. ◆ *vb* **2** to raid or ravage (a town, district, etc.). [C14: from *forrayen* to pillage, from OF, from *fuerre* fodder]

THESAURUS

teed, never-failing, safe, sure-fire (*inf.*), unassailable, unbreakable
footing *n* **1** = **basis**, establishment, foot-hold, foundation, ground, groundwork, installation, settlement **2** = **relationship**, condition, grade, position, rank, relations, standing, state, status, terms
footling *adj* = **trivial**, fiddling, fussy, hairsplitting, immaterial, insignificant, irrelevant, minor, nickel-and-dime (*US sl.*), niggly, petty, pointless, silly, time-wasting, trifling, unimportant
footstep *n* **2** = **step**, footfall, tread **4** = **footprint**, footmark, trace, track
footwear *n* = **footgear**
fop *n* = **dandy**, beau, Beau Brummel, clotheshorse, coxcomb (*arch.*), fashion plate, peacock, popinjay, smoothie *or* smoothy (*sl.*), swell
foppish *adj* = **dandyish**, dandified, dapper, dressy (*inf.*), finical, natty (*inf.*), preening, prinking, spruce, vain
forage *n* **1** = **fodder**, feed, food, foodstuffs, provender ◆ *vb* **3-5** = **search**, cast about, explore, hunt, look round, plunder, raid, ransack, rummage, scavenge, scour, scrounge (*inf.*), seek
foray *n* **1** = **raid**, depredation, descent, incursion, inroad, invasion, irruption, reconnaissance, sally, sortie, swoop

forbade (fə'bæd, -'beɪd) *or* **forbad** (fə'bæd) *vb* the past tense of **forbid.**

forbear[1] ❶ (fɔː'bɛə) *vb* **forbears, forbearing, forbore, forborne. 1** (when *intr*, often foll. by *from* or an infinitive) to cease or refrain (from doing something). **2** *Arch.* to tolerate (misbehaviour, etc.). [OE *forberan*]

forbear[2] ('fɔːˌbɛə) *n* a variant spelling of **forebear.**

forbearance ❶ (fɔː'bɛərəns) *n* **1** the act of forbearing. **2** self-control; patience.

forbid ❶ (fə'bɪd) *vb* **forbids, forbidding, forbade** *or* **forbad, forbidden** *or* **forbid.** (*tr*) **1** to prohibit (a person) in a forceful or authoritative manner (from doing or having something). **2** to make impossible. **3** to shut out or exclude. [OE *forbēodan*; see FOR-, BID]
▸**for'bidder** *n*

> **USAGE NOTE** It was formerly considered incorrect to talk of *forbidding* someone *from* doing something, but in modern usage either *from* or *to* can be used: *he was forbidden from entering/to enter the building.*

forbidden ❶ (fə'bɪdᵊn) *adj* **1** not permitted by order or law. **2** *Physics.* involving a change in quantum numbers that is not permitted by certain rules derived from quantum mechanics.

forbidden fruit *n* any pleasure or enjoyment regarded as illicit, esp. sexual indulgence.

forbidding ❶ (fə'bɪdɪŋ) *adj* **1** hostile or unfriendly. **2** dangerous or ominous.

forbore (fɔː'bɔː) *vb* the past tense of **forbear**[1].

forborne (fɔː'bɔːn) *vb* the past participle of **forbear**[1].

force[1] ❶ (fɔːs) *n* **1** strength or energy; power: *the force of the blow.* **2** exertion or the use of exertion against a person or thing that resists. **3** *Physics.* **3a** a dynamic influence that changes a body from a state of rest to one of motion or changes its rate of motion. **3b** a static influence that produces a strain in a body or system. Symbol: *F* **4a** intellectual, political, or moral influence or strength: *the force of his argument.* **4b** a person or thing with such influence: *he was a force in the land.* **5** vehemence or intensity: *she spoke with great force.* **6** a group of persons organized for military or police functions: *armed forces.* **7** (*sometimes cap.*; preceded by *the*) *Inf.* the police force. **8** a group of persons organized for particular duties or tasks: *a workforce.* **9** *Criminal law.* violence unlawfully committed or threatened. **10 in force. 10a** (of a law) having legal validity. **10b** in great strength or numbers. ◆ *vb* **forces, forcing, forced.** (*tr*) **11** to compel or cause (a person, group, etc.) to do something through effort, superior strength, etc. **12** to acquire or produce through effort, superior strength, etc.: *to force a confession.* **13** to propel or drive despite resistance. **14** to break down or open (a lock, door, etc.). **15** to impose or inflict: *he forced his views on them.* **16** to cause (plants or farm animals) to grow or fatten artificially at an increased rate. **17** to strain to the utmost: *to force the voice.* **18** to rape. **19** *Cards.* **19a** to compel a player by the lead of a particular suit to play (a certain card). **19b** (in bridge) to induce (a bid) from one's partner. [C13: from OF, from Vulgar L *fortia* (unattested), from L *fortis* strong]
▸**'forceable** *adj* ▸**'forceless** *adj* ▸**'forcer** *n*

force[2] (fɔːs) *n* (in N England) a waterfall. [C17: from ON *fors*]

forced ❶ (fɔːst) *adj* **1** done because of force: *forced labour.* **2** false or unnatural: *a forced smile.* **3** due to an emergency or necessity: *a forced landing.*

force de frappe (*French* fɔrs də frap) *n* a military strike force, esp. the independent nuclear strike force of France. [C20: F, lit.: striking force]

force-feed *vb* **force-feeds, force-feeding, force-fed.** (*tr*) to force (a person or animal) to eat or swallow food.

forceful ❶ ('fɔːsfʊl) *adj* **1** powerful. **2** persuasive or effective.
▸**'forcefully** *adv* ▸**'forcefulness** *n*

forcemeat ('fɔːsˌmiːt) *n* a mixture of chopped ingredients used for stuffing. Also called: **farce.** [C17: from *force* (see FARCE) + MEAT]

forceps ('fɔːsɪps) *n, pl* **forceps. 1a** a surgical instrument in the form of a pair of pincers, used esp. in the delivery of babies. **1b** (*as modifier*): *a forceps baby.* **2** any part of an organism shaped like a forceps. [C17: from L, from *formus* hot + *capere* to seize]

force pump *n* a pump that ejects fluid under pressure. Cf. **lift pump.**

Forces ('fɔːsɪz) *pl n* (usually preceded by *the*) the armed services of a nation.

forcible ❶ ('fɔːsəbᵊl) *adj* **1** done by, involving, or having force. **2** convincing or effective: *a forcible argument.*
▸**'forcibly** *adv*

ford (fɔːd) *n* **1** a shallow area in a river that can be crossed by car, on horseback, etc. ◆ *vb* **2** (*tr*) to cross (a river, brook, etc.) over a shallow area. [OE]
▸**'fordable** *adj*

fore[1] (fɔː) *adj* **1** (*usually in combination*) located at, in, or towards the front: *the forelegs of a horse.* ◆ *n* **2** the front part. **3** something located at, or towards the front. **4 fore and aft.** located at both ends of a vessel: *a fore-and-aft rig.* **5 to the fore.** to the front or conspicuous position. ◆ *adv* **6** at or towards a ship's bow. **7** *Obs.* before. ◆ *prep, conj* **8** a less common word for **before.** [OE]

fore[2] (fɔː) *sentence substitute.* (in golf) a warning shout made by a player about to make a shot. [C19: prob. short for BEFORE]

fore- *prefix* **1** before in time or rank: *forefather.* **2** at or near the front: *forecourt.* [OE, from *fore* (adv)]

fore-and-after *n Naut.* **1** any vessel with a fore-and-aft rig. **2** a double-ended vessel.

forearm[1] ('fɔːrˌɑːm) *n* the part of the arm from the elbow to the wrist. [C18: from FORE- + ARM[1]]

forearm[2] (fɔːr'ɑːm) *vb* (*tr*) to prepare or arm (someone) in advance. [C16: from FORE- + ARM[2]]

forebear ❶ *or* **forbear** ('fɔːˌbɛə) *n* an ancestor.

forebode ❶ (fɔː'bəʊd) *vb* **forebodes, foreboding, foreboded. 1** to warn of or indicate (an event, result, etc.) in advance. **2** to have a premonition of (an event).

foreboding ❶ (fɔː'bəʊdɪŋ) *n* **1** a feeling of impending evil, disaster, etc. **2** an omen or portent. ◆ *adj* **3** presaging something.

forebrain ('fɔːˌbreɪn) *n* the nontechnical name for **prosencephalon.**

forecast ❶ ('fɔːˌkɑːst) *vb* **forecasts, forecasting, forecast** *or* **forecasted. 1** to predict or calculate (weather, events, etc.), in advance. **2** (*tr*) to serve as an early indication of. ◆ *n* **3** a statement of probable future weather calculated from meteorological data. **4** a prediction. **5** the practice or power of forecasting.
▸**'foreˌcaster** *n*

forecastle, fo'c's'le, *or* **fo'c'sle** ('fəʊksᵊl) *n* the part of a vessel at the bow where the crew is quartered.

foreclose (fɔː'kləʊz) *vb* **forecloses, foreclosing, foreclosed. 1** *Law.* to deprive (a mortgagor, etc.) of the right to redeem (a mortgage or

THESAURUS

forbear[1] *vb* **1 = refrain,** abstain, avoid, cease, decline, desist, eschew, hold back, keep from, omit, pause, resist the temptation to, restrain oneself, stop, withhold

forbearance *n* **1 = abstinence,** avoidance, refraining **2 = patience,** indulgence, leniency, lenity, longanimity (*rare*), long-suffering, mildness, moderation, resignation, restraint, self-control, temperance, tolerance
Antonyms *n* ≠ **patience:** anger, impatience, impetuosity, intolerance, irritability, shortness

forbearing *adj* **2 = patient,** clement, easy, forgiving, indulgent, lenient, long-suffering, merciful, mild, moderate, tolerant

forbid *vb* **1 = prohibit,** ban, debar, disallow, exclude, hinder, inhibit, interdict, outlaw, preclude, proscribe, rule out, veto
Antonyms *vb* allow, approve, authorize, bid, enable, endorse, grant, let, license, O.K. *or* okay (*inf.*), order, permit, sanction

forbidden *adj* **1 = prohibited,** banned, outlawed, out of bounds, proscribed, taboo, *verboten*, vetoed

forbidding *adj* **1, 2 = threatening,** baleful, daunting, foreboding, frightening, grim, hostile, menacing, ominous, sinister, unfriendly
Antonyms *adj* alluring, attractive, beguiling, enticing, inviting, magnetic, tempting, welcoming, winning

force[1] *n* **1 = power,** dynamism, energy, impact, impulse, life, might, momentum, muscle, potency, pressure, stimulus, strength, stress, vigour **2 = compulsion,** arm-twisting (*inf.*), coercion, constraint, duress, enforcement, pressure, violence **4 = influence,** bite, cogency, effect, effectiveness, efficacy, persuasiveness, power, punch (*inf.*), strength, validity, weight **5 = intensity,** drive, emphasis, fierceness, persistence, vehemence, vigour **6 = army,** battalion, body, corps, detachment, division, host, legion, patrol, regiment, squad, squadron, troop, unit **10 in force: a = valid,** binding, current, effective, in operation, on the statute book, operative, working **b = in great numbers,** all together, in full strength ◆ *vb* **11 = compel,** bring pressure to bear upon, coerce, constrain, dragoon, drive, impel, impose, make, necessitate, obligate, oblige, overcome, press, press-gang, pressure, pressurize, put the screws on (*inf.*), put the squeeze on (*inf.*), railroad (*inf.*), strong-arm (*inf.*), twist (someone's) arm, urge **12 = extort,** drag, exact, wring **13 = push,** propel, thrust **14 = break open,** blast, prise, use violence on, wrench, wrest
Antonyms *n* ≠ **power:** debility, enervation, feebleness, fragility, frailty, impotence, ineffectiveness, irresolution, powerlessness, weakness ◆ *vb* ≠ **extort:** coax, convince, induce, persuade, prevail, talk into

forced *adj* **1 = compulsory,** conscripted, enforced, involuntary, mandatory, obligatory, slave, unwilling **2 = false,** affected, artificial, contrived, insincere, laboured, stiff, strained, unnatural, wooden
Antonyms *adj* ≠ **compulsory:** spontaneous, voluntary ≠ **false:** easy, natural, simple, sincere, spontaneous, unforced, unpretending

forceful *adj* **1, 2 = powerful,** cogent, compelling, convincing, dynamic, effective, persuasive, pithy, potent, telling, vigorous, weighty
Antonyms *adj* enervated, exhausted, faint, feeble, frail, powerless, spent, weak

forcible *adj* **1 = violent,** aggressive, armed, coercive, compulsory, drastic **2 = compelling,** active, cogent, effective, efficient, energetic, forceful, impressive, mighty, potent, powerful, strong, telling, valid, weighty

forcibly *adv* **1 = by force,** against one's will, by main force, compulsorily, under compulsion, under protest, willy-nilly

forebear *n* **= ancestor,** father, forefather, forerunner, predecessor, progenitor

forebode *vb* **1 = portend,** augur, betoken, foreshadow, foreshow, foretell, foretoken, forewarn, indicate, predict, presage, prognosticate, promise, vaticinate (*rare*), warn of

foreboding *n* **1 = dread,** anxiety, apprehension, apprehensiveness, chill, fear, misgiving, premonition, presentiment **2 = omen,** augury, foreshadowing, foretoken, portent, prediction, presage, prognostication, sign, token, warning

forecast *vb* **1 = predict,** anticipate, augur, calculate, call, divine, estimate, foresee, foretell, plan, prognosticate, prophesy, vaticinate (*rare*) ◆ *n* **4 = prediction,** anticipation, conjecture, foresight, forethought, guess, outlook, planning, prognosis, projection, prophecy

pledge). **2** (*tr*) to shut out; bar. **3** (*tr*) to prevent or hinder. [C15: from OF, from *for-* out + *clore* to close, from L *claudere*]
▸**fore'closable** *adj* ▸**foreclosure** (fɔː'kləʊʒə) *n*

forecourt ('fɔːˌkɔːt) *n* **1** a courtyard in front of a building, as one in a filling station. **2** the section of the court in tennis, badminton, etc., between the service line and the net.

foredoom (fɔː'duːm) *vb* (*tr*) to doom or condemn beforehand.

forefather Ⓣ ('fɔːˌfɑːðə) *n* an ancestor, esp. a male.
▸**'foreˌfatherly** *adj*

forefinger ('fɔːˌfɪŋgə) *n* the finger next to the thumb. Also called: **index finger.**

forefoot ('fɔːˌfʊt) *n, pl* **forefeet.** either of the front feet of a quadruped.

forefront Ⓣ ('fɔːˌfrʌnt) *n* **1** the extreme front. **2** the position of most prominence or action.

foregather *or* **forgather** (fɔː'gæðə) *vb* (*intr*) **1** to gather together. **2** (foll. by *with*) to socialize.

forego[1] Ⓣ (fɔː'gəʊ) *vb* **foregoes, foregoing, forewent, foregone.** to precede in time, place, etc. [OE *foregān*]

forego[2] (fɔː'gəʊ) *vb* **foregoes, foregoing, forewent, foregone.** (*tr*) a variant spelling of **forgo.**

foregoing Ⓣ (fɔː'gəʊɪŋ) *adj* (*prenominal*) (esp. of writing or speech) going before; preceding.

foregone (fɔː'gɒn, 'fɔːˌgɒn) *adj* gone or completed; past.
▸**fore'goneness** *n*

foregone conclusion *n* an inevitable result or conclusion.

foreground Ⓣ ('fɔːˌgraʊnd) *n* **1** the part of a scene situated towards the front or nearest to the viewer. **2** a conspicuous position.

forehand ('fɔːˌhænd) *adj* (*prenominal*) **1** *Tennis, squash, etc.* (of a stroke) made with the palm of the hand facing the direction of the stroke. ◆ *n* **2** *Tennis, squash, etc.* **2a** a forehand stroke. **2b** the side on which such strokes are made. **3** the part of a horse in front of the saddle.

forehead ('fɒrɪd, 'fɔːˌhɛd) *n* the part of the face between the natural hairline and the eyes. Related adj: **frontal.** [OE *forhēafod*]

foreign Ⓣ ('fɒrɪn) *adj* **1** of, located in, or coming from another country, area, people, etc.: *a foreign resident.* **2** dealing or concerned with another country, area, people, etc.: *a foreign office.* **3** not pertinent or related: *a matter foreign to the discussion.* **4** not familiar; strange. **5** in an abnormal place or position: *foreign matter.* [C13: from OF, from Vulgar L *forānus* (unattested) on the outside, from L *foris* outside]
▸**'foreignness** *n*

foreign affairs *pl n* matters abroad that involve the homeland, such as relations with another country.

foreigner Ⓣ ('fɒrɪnə) *n* **1** a person from a foreign country. **2** an outsider. **3** something from a foreign country, such as a ship or product.

foreign minister *or* **secretary** *n* (*often caps.*) a cabinet minister who is responsible for a country's dealings with other countries. US equivalent: **secretary of state.**

foreign office *n* the ministry of a country or state that is concerned with dealings with other states. US equivalent: **State Department.**

foreknowledge Ⓣ (fɔː'nɒlɪdʒ) *n* knowledge of a thing before it exists or occurs; prescience.
▸**fore'know** *vb* ▸**fore'knowable** *adj*

foreland ('fɔːlənd) *n* **1** a headland, cape, or promontory. **2** land lying in front of something, such as water.

foreleg ('fɔːˌlɛg) *n* either of the front legs of a horse, sheep, or other quadruped.

forelimb ('fɔːˌlɪm) *n* either of the front or anterior limbs of a four-limbed vertebrate.

forelock ('fɔːˌlɒk) *n* a lock of hair growing or falling over the forehead.

foreman ('fɔːmən) *n, pl* **foremen. 1** a person, often experienced, who supervises other workmen. **2** *Law.* the principal juror, who presides at the deliberations of a jury.

foremast ('fɔːˌmɑːst; *Naut.* 'fɔːməst) *n* the mast nearest the bow on vessels with two or more masts.

foremost Ⓣ ('fɔːˌməʊst) *adj, adv* first in time, place, rank, etc. [OE, from *forma* first]

forename Ⓣ ('fɔːˌneɪm) *n* another term for **first name.**

forenamed ('fɔːˌneɪmd) *adj* (*prenominal*) named or mentioned previously; aforesaid.

forenoon ('fɔːˌnuːn) *n* the daylight hours before or just before noon.

forensic (fə'rɛnsɪk) *adj* used in, or connected with a court of law: *forensic science.* [C17: from L *forēnsis* public, from FORUM]
▸**fo'rensically** *adv*

forensic medicine *n* the use of medical knowledge, esp. pathology, for the purposes of the law, as in determining the cause of death. Also called: **medical jurisprudence.**

foreordain Ⓣ (ˌfɔːrɔː'deɪn) *vb* (*tr; may take a clause as object*) to determine (events, etc.) in the future.
▸**foreordination** (ˌfɔːrɔːdɪ'neɪʃən) *n*

forepaw ('fɔːˌpɔː) *n* either of the front feet of most land mammals that do not have hoofs.

foreplay ('fɔːˌpleɪ) *n* mutual sexual stimulation preceding sexual intercourse.

forequarter ('fɔːˌkwɔːtə) *n* the front portion, including the leg, of half of a carcass, as of beef.

forequarters ('fɔːˌkwɔːtəz) *pl n* the part of the body of a horse, etc. that consists of the forelegs, shoulders, and adjoining parts.

forerun (fɔː'rʌn) *vb* **foreruns, forerunning, foreran, forerun.** (*tr*) **1** to serve as a herald for. **2** to precede. **3** to forestall.

forerunner Ⓣ ('fɔːˌrʌnə) *n* **1** a person or thing that precedes another. **2** a person or thing coming in advance to herald the arrival of someone or something. **3** an omen; portent.

foresail ('fɔːˌseɪl; *Naut.* 'fɔːsᵊl) *n Naut.* **1** the aftermost headsail of a fore-and-aft rigged vessel. **2** the lowest sail set on the foremast of a square-rigged vessel.

foresee Ⓣ (fɔː'siː) *vb* **foresees, foreseeing, foresaw, foreseen.** (*tr; may take a clause as object*) to see or know beforehand: *he did not foresee that.*
▸**fore'seeable** *adj* ▸**fore'seer** *n*

foreshadow Ⓣ (fɔː'ʃædəʊ) *vb* (*tr*) to show, indicate, or suggest in advance; presage.

foreshank ('fɔːˌʃæŋk) *n* **1** the top of the front leg of an animal. **2** a cut of meat from this part.

foresheet ('fɔːˌʃiːt) *n* **1** the sheet of a foresail. **2** (*pl*) the part forward of the foremost thwart of a boat.

foreshock ('fɔːˌʃɒk) *n Chiefly US.* a relatively small earthquake heralding the arrival of a much larger one.

foreshore ('fɔːˌʃɔː) *n* **1** the part of the shore that lies between the limits for high and low tides. **2** the part of the shore that lies just above the high water mark.

foreshorten (fɔː'ʃɔːtᵊn) *vb* (*tr*) to represent (a line, form, object, etc.) as shorter than actual length in order to give an illusion of recession or projection.

foreshow (fɔː'ʃəʊ) *vb* **foreshows, foreshowing, foreshowed; foreshown** *or* **foreshowed.** (*tr*) *Arch.* to indicate in advance.

foresight Ⓣ ('fɔːˌsaɪt) *n* **1** provision for or insight into future problems, needs, etc. **2** the act or ability of foreseeing. **3** the act of looking forward. **4** *Surveying.* a reading taken looking forwards. **5** the front sight on a firearm.
▸**ˌfore'sighted** *adj* ▸**ˌfore'sightedly** *adv* ▸**ˌfore'sightedness** *n*

foreskin ('fɔːˌskɪn) *n Anat.* the nontechnical name for **prepuce.**

forest ('fɒrɪst) *n* **1** a large wooded area having a thick growth of trees and plants. **2** the trees of such an area. **3** *NZ.* an area planted with pines or similar trees, not native trees. Cf. **bush**[1] (sense 4). **4** something resembling a large wooded area, esp. in density: *a forest of telegraph poles.* **5** *Law.* (formerly) an area of woodland, esp. one owned by the sovereign and set apart as a hunting ground. **6** (*modifier*) of, involving, or living in a forest or forests: *a forest glade.* ◆ *vb* **7** (*tr*) to create a forest. [C13: from OF, from Med. L *forestis* unfenced woodland, from L *foris* outside]
▸**'forested** *adj*

forestall Ⓣ (fɔː'stɔːl) *vb* (*tr*) **1** to delay, stop, or guard against beforehand. **2** to anticipate. **3** to buy up merchandise for profitable resale. [C14 *forestallen* to waylay, from OE, from *fore-* in front of + *steall* place]
▸**fore'staller** *n* ▸**fore'stalment** *n*

forestation (ˌfɒrɪ'steɪʃən) *n* the planting of trees over a wide area.

forestay ('fɔːˌsteɪ) *n Naut.* an adjustable stay leading from the truck of the foremast to the deck, for controlling the bending of the mast.

forester ('fɒrɪstə) *n* **1** a person skilled in forestry or in charge of a forest.

THESAURUS

forefather *n* = **ancestor**, father, forebear, forerunner, predecessor, primogenitor, procreator, progenitor

forefront *n* **1, 2** = **lead**, centre, fore, foreground, front, prominence, spearhead, van, vanguard

forego[2] *see* **forgo**

foregoing *adj* = **preceding**, above, antecedent, anterior, former, previous, prior

foreground *n* **2** = **front**, centre, forefront, limelight, prominence

foreign *adj* **1, 4** = **alien**, beyond one's ken, borrowed, distant, exotic, external, imported, outlandish, outside, overseas, remote, strange, unfamiliar, unknown **3** = **extraneous**, extrinsic, incongruous, irrelevant, unassimilable, uncharacteristic, unrelated
Antonyms *adj* ≠ **alien:** customary, domestic, familiar, native, well-known ≠ **extraneous:** applicable, characteristic, intrinsic, pertinent, relevant, suited

foreigner *n* **1** = **alien**, immigrant, incomer, newcomer, outlander, stranger

foreknowledge *n* = **prior knowledge**, clairvoyance, foresight, forewarning, precognition, prescience, prevision

foremost *adj* = **leading**, chief, first, front, headmost, highest, inaugural, initial, paramount, pre-eminent, primary, prime, principal, supreme

forename *n* = **first name**, Christian name, given name

foreordain *vb* = **predestine**, doom, fate, foredoom, prearrange, predetermine, preordain, reserve

forerunner *n* **1, 2** = **precursor**, ancestor, announcer, envoy, forebear, foregoer, harbinger, herald, predecessor, progenitor, prototype **3** = **omen**, augury, foretoken, indication, portent, premonition, prognostic, sign, token

foresee *vb* = **predict**, anticipate, divine, envisage, forebode, forecast, foretell, prophesy, vaticinate (*rare*)

foreshadow *vb* = **predict**, adumbrate, augur, betoken, bode, forebode, imply, indicate, portend, prefigure, presage, promise, prophesy, signal

foresight *n* **1, 2** = **forethought**, anticipation, care, caution, circumspection, far-sightedness, precaution, premeditation, preparedness, prescience, prevision (*rare*), provision, prudence
Antonyms *n* carelessness, hindsight, imprudence, inconsideration, lack of foresight, neglect, retrospection, thoughtlessness, unpreparedness

forestall *vb* **1, 2** = **prevent**, anticipate, balk, circumvent, frustrate, head off, hinder, intercept, nip in the bud, obviate, parry, preclude, provide against, thwart

2 a person or animal that lives in a forest. 3 (*cap.*) a member of the Ancient Order of Foresters, a friendly society.

forest park *n NZ.* a recreational reserve which may include bush and exotic trees.

forestry ➊ ('fɒrɪstrɪ) *n* **1** the science of planting and caring for trees. **2** the planting and management of forests. **3** *Rare.* forest land.

foretaste ➊ ('fɔːˌteɪst) *n* an early but limited experience of something to come.

foretell ➊ (fɔː'tɛl) *vb* **foretells, foretelling, foretold.** (*tr; may take a clause as object*) to tell or indicate (an event, a result, etc.) beforehand.

forethought ➊ ('fɔːˌθɔːt) *n* **1** advance consideration or deliberation. **2** thoughtful anticipation of future events.

foretoken ➊ *n* ('fɔːˌtəʊkən). **1** a sign of a future event. ◆ *vb* (fɔː'təʊkən). **2** (*tr*) to foreshadow.

foretop ('fɔːˌtɒp; *Naut.* 'fɔːtəp) *n Naut.* a platform at the top of the foremast.

fore-topgallant (ˌfɔːtɒp'gælənt; *Naut.* ˌfɔːtə'gælənt) *adj Naut.* of, relating to, or being the topmost portion of a foremast.

fore-topmast (fɔː'tɒpˌmɑːst; *Naut.* fɔː'tɒpməst) *n Naut.* a mast stepped above a foremast.

fore-topsail (fɔː'tɒpˌseɪl; *Naut.* fɔː'tɒpsᵊl) *n Naut.* a sail set on a fore-topmast.

forever ➊ (fɔː'rɛvə, fə-) *adv* **1** Also: **for ever.** without end; everlastingly. **2** at all times. **3** *Inf.* for a very long time: *he went on speaking forever.* ◆ *n* **forever. 4** (*as object*) *Inf.* a very long time: *it took him forever to reply.*

USAGE NOTE *Forever* and *for ever* can both be used to say that something is without end. For all other meanings, *forever* is the preferred form.

for evermore *or* **forevermore** (fɔːˌrɛvə'mɔː, fə-) *adv* a more emphatic or emotive term for **forever.**

forewarn ➊ (fɔː'wɔːn) *vb* (*tr*) to warn beforehand.
▸**fore'warner** *n*

forewent (fɔː'wɛnt) *vb* the past tense of **forego.**

forewing ('fɔːˌwɪŋ) *n* either wing of the anterior pair of an insect's two pairs of wings.

foreword ➊ ('fɔːˌwɜːd) *n* an introductory statement to a book. [C19: literal translation of G *Vorwort*]

forfaiting ('fɔːˌfeɪtɪŋ) *n* the financial service of discounting, without recourse, a promissory note, bill of exchange, letter of credit, etc., received from an overseas buyer by an exporter; a form of debt discounting. [C20: from F *forfaire* to forfeit or surrender]

forfeit ➊ ('fɔːfɪt) *n* **1** something lost or given up as a penalty for a fault, mistake, etc. **2** the act of losing or surrendering something in this manner. **3** *Law.* something confiscated as a penalty for an offence, etc. **4** (*sometimes pl*) **4a** a game in which a player has to give up an object, perform a specified action, etc., if he commits a fault. **4b** an object so given up. ◆ *vb* (*tr*) **5** to lose or be liable to lose in consequence of a mistake, fault, etc. **6** *Law.* to confiscate as punishment. ◆ *adj* **7** surrendered or liable to be surrendered as a penalty. [C13: from OF *forfet* offence, from *forfaire* to commit a crime, from Med. L, from L *foris* outside + *facere* to do]
▸**'forfeiter** *n*

forfeiture ➊ ('fɔːfɪtʃə) *n* **1** something forfeited. **2** the act of forfeiting or paying a penalty.

forfend *or* **forefend** (fɔː'fɛnd) *vb* (*tr*) **1** *US.* to protect or secure. **2** *Obs.* to prevent.

forgather (fɔː'gæðə) *vb* a variant spelling of **foregather.**

forgave (fə'geɪv) *vb* the past tense of **forgive.**

forge[1] ➊ (fɔːdʒ) *n* **1** a place in which metal is worked by heating and hammering; smithy. **2** a hearth or furnace used for heating metal. ◆ *vb* **forges, forging, forged. 3** (*tr*) to shape (metal) by heating and hammering. **4** (*tr*) to form, make, or fashion (objects, etc.). **5** (*tr*) to invent or devise (an agreement, etc.). **6** to make a fraudulent imitation of (a signature, etc.) or to commit forgery. [C14: from OF *forgier* to construct, from L *fabricāre*, from *faber* craftsman]
▸**'forger** *n*

forge[2] (fɔːdʒ) *vb* **forges, forging, forged.** (*intr*) **1** to move at a steady pace. **2** **forge ahead.** to increase speed. [C17: from ?]

forgery ➊ ('fɔːdʒərɪ) *n, pl* **forgeries. 1** the act of reproducing something for a fraudulent purpose. **2** something forged, such as an antique. **3** *Criminal law.* **3a** the false making or altering of a document, such as a cheque, etc., or any tape or disc storing information, with intent to defraud. **3b** something forged.

forget ➊ (fə'gɛt) *vb* **forgets, forgetting, forgot, forgotten** *or* (*Arch. or dialect*) **forgot. 1** (when *tr, may take a clause as object or an infinitive*) to fail to recall (someone or something once known). **2** (*tr; may take a clause as object or an infinitive*) to neglect, either as the result of an unintentional error or intentionally. **3** (*tr*) to leave behind by mistake. **4 forget oneself. 4a** to act in an improper manner. **4b** to be unselfish. **4c** to be deep in thought. [OE *forgietan*]
▸**for'gettable** *adj* ▸**for'getter** *n*

forgetful ➊ (fə'gɛtfʊl) *adj* **1** tending to forget. **2** (*often postpositive;* foll. by *of*) inattentive (to) or neglectful (of).
▸**for'getfully** *adv* ▸**for'getfulness** *n*

forget-me-not *n* a temperate low-growing plant having clusters of small blue flowers.

forgive ➊ (fə'gɪv) *vb* **forgives, forgiving, forgave, forgiven. 1** to cease to blame (someone or something). **2** to grant pardon for (a mistake, etc.). **3** (*tr*) to free (someone) from penalty. **4** (*tr*) to free from the obligation of (a debt, etc.). [OE *forgiefan*]
▸**for'givable** *adj* ▸**for'giver** *n*

forgiveness ➊ (fə'gɪvnɪs) *n* **1** the act of forgiving or the state of being forgiven. **2** willingness to forgive.

forgiving ➊ (fə'gɪvɪŋ) *adj* willing to forgive.

forgo ➊ *or* **forego** (fɔː'gəʊ) *vb* **forgoes, forgoing, forwent, forgone.** (*tr*) to give up or do without. [OE *forgān*]

forgot (fə'gɒt) *vb* **1** the past tense of **forget. 2** *Arch. or dialect.* a past participle of **forget.**

forgotten ➊ (fə'gɒtᵊn) *vb* a past participle of **forget.**

forint (*Hungarian* 'forint) *n* the standard monetary unit of Hungary. [from Hungarian, from It. *fiorino* FLORIN]

fork ➊ (fɔːk) *n* **1** a small usually metal implement consisting of two, three, or four long thin prongs on the end of a handle, used for lifting food to the mouth, etc. **2** a similar-shaped agricultural tool, used for lifting, digging, etc. **3** a pronged part of any machine, device, etc. **4** (of a road, river, etc.) **4a** a division into two or more branches. **4b** the point where the division begins. **4c** such a branch. ◆ *vb* **5** (*tr*) to pick up, dig, etc., with a fork. **6** (*tr*) *Chess.* to place (two enemy pieces) under attack with one of one's own pieces. **7** (*intr*) to be divided into two or more branches. **8** to take one or other branch at a fork in a road, etc. [OE *forca*, from L *furca*]

THESAURUS

forestry *n* **1 = woodcraft**, arboriculture, dendrology (*Botany*), silviculture, woodmanship

foretaste *n* **= sample**, example, foretoken, indication, prelude, preview, trailer, warning, whiff

foretell *vb* **= predict**, adumbrate, augur, bode, call, forebode, forecast, foreshadow, foreshow, forewarn, portend, presage, prognosticate, prophesy, signify, soothsay, vaticinate (*rare*)

forethought *n* **2 = anticipation**, far-sightedness, foresight, precaution, providence, provision, prudence
Antonyms *n* carelessness, imprudence, impulsiveness, inconsideration, neglect, unpreparedness

foretoken *vb* **2 = portend**, augur, forebode, foreshadow, foreshow, give notice of, give warning of, presage, signify, warn of

forever *adv* **1 = evermore**, always, for all time, for good and all (*inf.*), for keeps, in perpetuity, till Doomsday, till the cows come home (*inf.*), till the end of time, world without end **2 = constantly**, all the time, continually, endlessly, eternally, everlastingly, incessantly, interminably, perpetually, unremittingly

forewarn *vb* **= caution**, admonish, advise, alert, apprise, dissuade, give fair warning, put on guard, put on the qui vive, tip off

foreword *n* **= introduction**, preamble, preface, preliminary, prolegomenon, prologue

forfeit *n* **1 = penalty**, amercement, damages, fine, forfeiture, loss, mulct ◆ *vb* **5 = lose**, be deprived of, be stripped of, give up, relinquish, renounce, say goodbye to, surrender

forfeiture *n* **2 = loss**, confiscation, giving up, relinquishment, sequestration (*Law*), surrender

forge[1] *vb* **3, 4 = create**, construct, contrive, devise, fabricate, fashion, form, frame, hammer out, invent, make, mould, shape, work **6 = fake**, coin, copy, counterfeit, falsify, feign, imitate

forged *adj* **3, 4 = formed**, beat out, cast, crafted, fashioned, founded, framed, hammered out, minted, modelled, moulded, shaped, stamped, worked **6 = fake**, artificial, bogus, copy, copycat (*inf.*), counterfeit, duplicate, ersatz, fabricated, false, falsified, fraudulent, imitation, mock, phony *or* phoney (*inf.*), pretend, pseudo, quasi, reproduction, sham, simulated, synthetic, ungenuine, unoriginal
Antonyms *adj* ≠ **fake:** actual, authentic, bona fide, *echt*, genuine, honest, kosher (*inf.*), legitimate, original, real, true

forger *n* **6 = counterfeiter**, coiner, falsifier

forgery *n* **1 = falsification**, coining, counterfeiting, fraudulence, fraudulent imitation **2 = fake**, counterfeit, falsification, imitation, phoney *or* phony (*inf.*), sham

forget *vb* **1 = dismiss from one's mind**, consign to oblivion, let bygones be bygones, let slip from the memory **3 = neglect**, leave behind, lose sight of, omit, overlook
Antonyms *vb* bring to mind, mind, recall, recollect, remember, retain

forgetful *adj* **1, 2 = absent-minded**, apt to forget, careless, dreamy, having a memory like a sieve, heedless, inattentive, lax, neglectful, negligent, oblivious, slapdash, slipshod, unmindful, vague
Antonyms *adj* attentive, careful, mindful, retentive, unforgetful, unforgetting

forgetfulness *n* **1, 2 = absent-mindedness**, abstraction, carelessness, dreaminess, heedlessness, inattention, lapse of memory, laxity, laxness, oblivion, obliviousness, woolgathering

forgive *vb* **1, 2 = excuse**, absolve, accept (someone's) apology, acquit, bear no malice, condone, exonerate, let bygones be bygones, let off (*inf.*), pardon, remit
Antonyms *vb* blame, censure, charge, condemn, find fault with, reproach, reprove

forgiveness *n* **1 = pardon**, absolution, acquittal, amnesty, condonation, exoneration, mercy, overlooking, remission

forgiving *adj* **= lenient**, clement, compassionate, forbearing, humane, magnanimous, merciful, mild, soft-hearted, tolerant

forgo *vb* **= give up**, abandon, abjure, cede, do without, kick (*inf.*), leave alone *or* out, relinquish, renounce, resign, sacrifice, say goodbye to, surrender, waive, yield

forgotten *adj* **1, 3 = unremembered**, blotted out, buried, bygone, consigned to oblivion, gone (clean) out of one's mind, left behind, lost, obliterated, omitted, past, past recall

fork *vb* **7 = branch**, bifurcate, branch off, diverge, divide, go separate ways, part, split

forked ❶ (fɔːkt) *adj* **1a** having a fork or forklike parts. **1b** (*in combination*): *two-forked.* **2** zigzag: *forked lightning.*
▸**forkedly** ('fɔːkɪdlɪ) *adv*

fork-lift truck *n* a vehicle having two power-operated horizontal prongs that can be raised and lowered for transporting and unloading goods. Sometimes shortened to **fork-lift.**

fork out, over, *or* **up** *vb* (*adv*) *Sl.* to pay (money, goods, etc.), esp. with reluctance.

forlorn ❶ (fə'lɔːn) *adj* **1** miserable or cheerless. **2** forsaken. **3** (*postpositive;* foll. by *of*) bereft: *forlorn of hope.* **4** desperate: *the last forlorn attempt.* [OE *forloren* lost, from *forlēosan* to lose]
▸**for'lornness** *n*

forlorn hope *n* **1** a hopeless enterprise. **2** a faint hope. **3** *Obs.* a group of soldiers assigned to an extremely dangerous duty. [C16 (in the obs. sense): changed (by folk etymology) from Du. *verloren hoop* lost troop, from *verloren,* p.p. of *verliezen* to lose + *hoop* troop (lit.: heap)]

form ❶ (fɔːm) *n* **1** the shape or configuration of something as distinct from its colour, texture, etc. **2** the particular mode, appearance, etc., in which a thing or person manifests itself: *water in the form of ice.* **3** a type or kind: *imprisonment is a form of punishment.* **4** a printed document, esp. one with spaces in which to insert facts or answers: *an application form.* **5** physical or mental condition, esp. good condition, with reference to ability to perform: *off form.* **6** the previous record of a horse, athlete, etc., esp. with regard to fitness. **7** *Brit. sl.* a criminal record. **8** a fixed mode of artistic expression or representation in literary, musical, or other artistic works: *sonata form.* **9** a mould, frame, etc., that gives shape to something. **10** *Education, chiefly Brit.* a group of children who are taught together. **11** behaviour or procedure, esp. as governed by custom or etiquette: *good form.* **12** formality or ceremony. **13** a prescribed set or order of words, terms, etc., as in a religious ceremony or legal document. **14** *Philosophy.* **14a** the structure of anything as opposed to its content. **14b** essence as opposed to matter. **15** See **logical form. 16** *Brit., Austral., & NZ.* a bench, esp. one that is long, low, and backless. **17** a hare's nest. **18** any of the various ways in which a word may be spelt or inflected. ◆ *vb* **19** to give shape or form to or to take shape or form, esp. a particular shape. **20** to come or bring into existence: *a scum formed.* **21** to make or construct or be made or constructed. **22** to construct or develop in the mind: *to form an opinion.* **23** (*tr*) to train or mould by instruction or example. **24** (*tr*) to acquire or develop: *to form a habit.* **25** (*tr*) to be an element of or constitute: *this plank will form a bridge.* **26** (*tr*) to organize: *to form a club.* [C13: from OF, from L *forma* shape, model]

-form *adj combining form.* having the shape or form of or resembling: *cruciform; vermiform.* [from NL *-formis,* from L, from *fōrma* FORM]

formal ❶ ('fɔːməl) *adj* **1** of or following established forms, conventions, etc.: *a formal document.* **2** characterized by observation of conventional forms of ceremony, behaviour, etc.: *a formal dinner.* **3** methodical or stiff. **4** suitable for occasions organized according to conventional ceremony: *formal dress.* **5** denoting idiom, vocabulary, etc., used by educated speakers and writers of a language. **6** acquired by study in academic institutions. **7** symmetrical in form: *a formal garden.* **8** of or relating to the appearance, form, etc., of something as distinguished from its substance. **9** logically deductive: *formal proof.* **10** denoting a second-person pronoun in some languages: *in French the pronoun "vous" is formal, while "tu" is informal.* [C14: from L *formālis*]
▸**'formally** *adv* ▸**'formalness** *n*

formaldehyde (fɔː'mældɪˌhaɪd) *n* a colourless poisonous irritating gas with a pungent characteristic odour, used as formalin and in the manufacture of synthetic resins. Formula: HCHO. Systematic name: **methanal.** [C19: FORM(IC) + ALDEHYDE; on the model of G *Formaldehyd*]

formalin ('fɔːməlɪn) *n* a solution of formaldehyde in water, used as a disinfectant, preservative for biological specimens, etc.

formalism ('fɔːməˌlɪzəm) *n* **1** scrupulous or excessive adherence to outward form at the expense of content. **2** the mathematical or logical structure of a scientific argument as distinguished from its subject matter. **3** *Theatre.* a stylized mode of production. **4** (in Marxist criticism, etc.) excessive concern with artistic technique at the expense of social values, etc.
▸**'formalist** *n* ▸**ˌformal'istic** *adj*

formality ❶ (fɔː'mælɪtɪ) *n, pl* **formalities. 1** a requirement of custom, etiquette, etc. **2** the quality of being formal or conventional. **3** strict or excessive observance of ceremony, etc.

formalize *or* **formalise** ('fɔːməˌlaɪz) *vb* **formalizes, formalizing, formalized** *or* **formalises, formalising, formalised. 1** to be or make formal. **2** (*tr*) to make official or valid. **3** (*tr*) to give a definite shape or form to.
▸**ˌformali'zation** *or* **ˌformali'sation** *n*

formal language *n* any of various languages designed for use in fields such as mathematics, logic, or computer programming, the symbols and formulas of which stand in precisely specified syntactic and semantic relations to one another.

formal logic *n* the study of systems of deductive argument in which symbols are used to represent precisely defined categories of expressions.

formant ('fɔːmənt) *n Acoustics, phonetics.* any of the constituents of a sound, esp. a vowel sound, that impart to the sound its own special quality, tone colour, or timbre.

format ❶ ('fɔːmæt) *n* **1** the general appearance of a publication, including type style, paper, binding, etc. **2** style, plan, or arrangement, as of a television programme. **3** *Computing.* **3a** the defined arrangement of data encoded in a file or, for example, on magnetic disk or CD-ROM, that is essential for the correct recording and recovery of data on different devices. **3b** the arrangement of text on printed output or on a display screen. ◆ *vb* **formats, formatting, formatted.** (*tr*) **4** to arrange (a book, page, etc.) into a specified format. [C19: via F from G, from L *liber formātus* volume formed]

formation ❶ (fɔː'meɪʃən) *n* **1** the act of giving or taking form or existence. **2** something that is formed. **3** the manner in which something is arranged. **4a** a formal arrangement of a number of persons or things acting as a unit, such as a troop of soldiers or a football team. **4b** (*as modifier*): *formation dancing.* **5** a series of rocks with certain characteristics in common.

formative ❶ ('fɔːmətɪv) *adj* **1** of or relating to formation, development, or growth: *formative years.* **2** shaping; moulding: *a formative experience.* **3** functioning in the formation of derived, inflected, or compound words. ◆ *n* **4** an inflectional or derivational affix.
▸**'formatively** *adv* ▸**'formativeness** *n*

form class *n* **1** another term for **part of speech. 2** a group of words distinguished by common inflections, such as the weak verbs of English.

form criticism *n* literary criticism concerned esp. with analysing the Bible in terms of the literary forms used, such as proverbs, songs, or stories, and relating them to their historical forms and background.
▸**form critic** *n* ▸**form critical** *adj*

forme *or US* **form** (fɔːm) *n Printing.* type matter, blocks, etc., assembled in a chase and ready for printing. [C15: from F: FORM]

former[1] ❶ ('fɔːmə) *adj* (*prenominal*) **1** belonging to or occurring in an earlier time: *former glory.* **2** having been at a previous time: *a former colleague.* **3** denoting the first or first mentioned of two. ◆ *n* **4 the former.** the first or first mentioned of two: distinguished from *latter.*

former[2] ('fɔːmə) *n* **1** a person or thing that forms or shapes. **2** *Electrical engineering.* a tool for giving a coil or winding the required shape.

formerly ❶ ('fɔːməlɪ) *adv* at or in a former time; in the past.

formic ('fɔːmɪk) *adj* **1** of, relating to, or derived from ants. **2** of, containing, or derived from formic acid. [C18: from L *formīca* ant; the acid occurs naturally in ants]

Formica (fɔː'maɪkə) *n Trademark.* any of various laminated plastic sheets used esp. for heat-resistant surfaces.

THESAURUS

forked *adj* **1, 2** = **branching**, angled, bifurcate(d), branched, divided, pronged, split, tined, zigzag

forlorn *adj* **1, 2** = **miserable**, abandoned, bereft, cheerless, comfortless, deserted, desolate, destitute, disconsolate, down in the dumps (*inf.*), forgotten, forsaken, friendless, helpless, homeless, hopeless, lonely, lost, pathetic, pitiable, pitiful, unhappy, woebegone, wretched
Antonyms *adj* busy, cheerful, happy, hopeful, optimistic, thriving

form *n* **1** = **shape**, appearance, cast, configuration, construction, cut, fashion, formation, model, mould, pattern, stamp, structure **2** = **mode**, arrangement, character, design, guise, manifestation, semblance **3** = **type**, description, kind, manner, method, order, practice, sort, species, stamp, style, system, variety, way **4** = **document**, application, paper, sheet **5** = **condition**, fettle, fitness, good condition, good spirits, health, shape, trim **10** = **class**, grade, rank **11, 12** = **procedure**, behaviour, ceremony, conduct, convention, custom, done thing, etiquette, formality, manners, protocol, ritual, rule ◆ *vb* **20** = **take shape**, accumulate, appear, become visible, come into being, crystallize, grow, materialize, rise, settle, show up **21** = **make**, assemble, bring about, build, concoct, construct, contrive, create, devise, establish, fabricate, fashion, forge, found, invent, manufacture, model, mould, produce, put together, set up, shape, stamp **23** = **train**, bring up, discipline, educate, instruct, rear, school, teach **24** = **develop**, acquire, contract, cultivate, get into (*inf.*), pick up **25** = **constitute**, compose, comprise, make, make up, serve as **26** = **arrange**, combine, design, dispose, draw up, frame, organize, pattern, plan, think up

formal *adj* **1, 3** = **official**, approved, ceremonial, explicit, express, fixed, lawful, legal, methodical, prescribed, *pro forma*, regular, rigid, ritualistic, set, solemn, strict **3** = **conventional**, affected, aloof, ceremonious, correct, exact, precise, prim, punctilious, reserved, starched, stiff, unbending
Antonyms *adj* casual, easy-going, informal, laid-back (*inf.*), relaxed, unceremonious, unofficial

formality *n* **2** = **convention**, ceremony, conventionality, custom, form, gesture, matter of form, procedure, red tape, rite, ritual **3** = **correctness**, ceremoniousness, decorum, etiquette, politesse, protocol, p's and q's, punctilio

format *n* **1, 2** = **arrangement**, appearance, construction, form, layout, look, make-up, plan, style, type

formation *n* **1** = **development**, accumulation, compilation, composition, constitution, crystallization, establishment, evolution, forming, generation, genesis, manufacture, organization, production **3** = **arrangement**, configuration, design, disposition, figure, grouping, pattern, rank, structure

formative *adj* **1** = **impressionable**, malleable, mouldable, pliant, sensitive, susceptible **2** = **developmental**, determinative, influential, moulding, shaping

former[1] *adj* **1** = **past**, ancient, bygone, departed, long ago, long gone, of yore, old, old-time **2** = **previous**, antecedent, anterior, earlier, erstwhile, ex-, late, one-time, prior, quondam **3** = **aforementioned**, above, aforesaid, first mentioned, foregoing, preceding
Antonyms ≠ **past:** current, future, modern, present, present-day *adj* ≠ **previous:** coming, current, ensuing, following, future, latter, subsequent, succeeding

formerly *adv* = **previously**, aforetime (*arch.*),

formic acid *n* a colourless corrosive liquid carboxylic acid found in some insects, esp. ants, and many plants: used in the manufacture of insecticides. Formula: HCOOH. Systematic name: **methanoic acid.**

formidable ◉ ('fɔːmɪdəbᵊl) *adj* **1** arousing or likely to inspire fear or dread. **2** extremely difficult to defeat, overcome, manage, etc. **3** tending to inspire awe or admiration because of great size, excellence, etc. [C15: from L, from *formīdāre* to dread, from *formīdō* fear]
▸ **'formidably** *adv*

formless ◉ ('fɔːmlɪs) *adj* without a definite shape or form; amorphous.
▸ **'formlessly** *adv*

form letter *n* a single copy of a letter that has been mechanically reproduced in large numbers for circulation.

formula ◉ ('fɔːmjʊlə) *n, pl* **formulas** *or* **formulae** (-ˌliː). **1** an established form or set of words, as used in religious ceremonies, legal proceedings, etc. **2** *Maths., physics.* a general relationship, principle, or rule stated, often as an equation, in the form of symbols. **3** *Chem.* a representation of molecules, radicals, ions, etc., expressed in the symbols of the atoms of their constituent elements. **4a** a method, pattern, or rule for doing or producing something, often one proved to be successful. **4b** (*as modifier*): *formula fiction.* **5** *US & Canad.* a prescription for making up a medicine, baby's food, etc. **6** *Motor racing.* the category in which a type of car competes, judged according to engine size, weight, and fuel capacity. [C17: from L: dim. of *forma* FORM]
▸ **formulaic** (ˌfɔːmjʊ'leɪɪk) *adj*

Formula One *n* **1** the top class of professional motor racing. **2** the most important world championship in motor racing.

formularize *or* **formularise** ('fɔːmjʊləˌraɪz) *vb* **formularizes, formularizing, formularized** *or* **formularises, formularising, formularised.** a less common word for **formulate** (sense 1).

formulary ('fɔːmjʊlərɪ) *n, pl* **formularies. 1** a book of prescribed formulas, esp. relating to religious procedure or doctrine. **2** a formula. **3** *Pharmacol.* a book containing a list of pharmaceutical products with their formulas. ◆ *adj* **4** of or relating to a formula.

formulate ◉ ('fɔːmjʊˌleɪt) *vb* **formulates, formulating, formulated.** (*tr*) **1** to put into or express in systematic terms; express in or as if in a formula. **2** to devise.
▸ **ˌformu'lation** *n*

formwork ('fɔːmˌwɜːk) *n* an arrangement of wooden boards, etc., used to shape concrete while it is setting.

fornicate ('fɔːnɪˌkeɪt) *vb* **fornicates, fornicating, fornicated.** (*intr*) to commit fornication. [C16: from LL *fornicārī*, from L *fornix* vault, brothel situated therein]
▸ **'forniˌcator** *n*

fornication ◉ (ˌfɔːnɪ'keɪʃən) *n* **1** voluntary sexual intercourse outside marriage. **2** *Bible.* sexual immorality in general, esp. adultery.

forsake ◉ (fə'seɪk) *vb* **forsakes, forsaking, forsook, forsaken.** (*tr*) **1** to abandon. **2** to give up (something valued or enjoyed). [OE *forsacan*]
▸ **for'saker** *n*

forsaken ◉ (fə'seɪkən) *vb* **1** the past participle of **forsake.** ◆ *adj* **2** completely deserted or helpless.
▸ **for'sakenly** *adv* ▸ **for'sakenness** *n*

forsook (fə'sʊk) *vb* the past tense of **forsake.**

forsooth (fə'suːθ) *adv Arch.* in truth; indeed. [OE *forsōth*]

forswear ◉ (fɔː'swɛə) *vb* **forswears, forswearing, forswore, forsworn. 1** (*tr*) to reject or renounce with determination or as upon oath. **2** (*tr*) to deny or disavow absolutely or upon oath. **3** to perjure (oneself). [OE *forswearian*]
▸ **for'swearer** *n*

forsworn (fɔː'swɔːn) *vb* the past participle of **forswear.**
▸ **for'swornness** *n*

forsythia (fɔː'saɪθɪə) *n* a shrub native to China, Japan, and SE Europe but widely cultivated for its showy yellow bell-shaped flowers, which appear in spring before the foliage. [C19: NL, after William *Forsyth* (1737–1804), E botanist]

fort ◉ (fɔːt) *n* **1** a fortified enclosure, building, or position able to be defended against an enemy. **2 hold the fort.** *Inf.* to guard something temporarily. [C15: from OF, from *fort* (adj) strong, from L *fortis*]

fort. *abbrev. for:* **1** fortification. **2** fortified.

forte[1] ◉ (fɔːt, 'fɔːteɪ) *n* **1** something at which a person excels: *cooking is my forte.* **2** *Fencing.* the stronger section of a sword, between the hilt and the middle. [C17: from F, from *fort* (adj) strong, from L *fortis*]

forte[2] ('fɔːtɪ) *Music.* ◆ *adj, adv* **1** loud or loudly. Symbol: f ◆ *n* **2** a loud passage in music. [C18: from It., from L *fortis* strong]

forte-piano (ˌfɔːtɪ'pjɑːnəʊ) *Music.* ◆ *adj, adv* **1** loud and then immediately soft. Symbol: fp ◆ *n* **2** a note played in this way.

forth ◉ (fɔːθ) *adv* **1** forward in place, time, order, or degree. **2** out, as from concealment or inaction. **3** away, as from a place or country. **4 and so forth.** and so on. ◆ *prep* **5** *Arch.* out of. [OE]

forthcoming ◉ (ˌfɔːθ'kʌmɪŋ) *adj* **1** approaching in time: *the forthcoming debate.* **2** about to appear: *his forthcoming book.* **3** available or ready. **4** open or sociable.

forthright ◉ *adj* ('fɔːθˌraɪt). **1** direct and outspoken. ◆ *adv* (ˌfɔːθ'raɪt, 'fɔːθˌraɪt), *also* **forthrightly. 2** in a direct manner; frankly. **3** at once.
▸ **'forthˌrightness** *n*

forthwith ◉ (ˌfɔːθ'wɪθ) *adv* at once.

fortification ◉ (ˌfɔːtɪfɪ'keɪʃən) *n* **1** the act, art, or science of fortifying or strengthening. **2a** a wall, mound, etc., used to fortify a place. **2b** such works collectively.

fortify ◉ ('fɔːtɪˌfaɪ) *vb* **fortifies, fortifying, fortified.** (*mainly tr*) **1** (*also intr*) to make (a place) defensible, as by building walls, etc. **2** to strengthen physically, mentally, or morally. **3** to add alcohol to (wine), in order to produce sherry, port, etc. **4** to increase the nutritious value of (a food), as by adding vitamins. **5** to confirm: *to fortify an argument.* [C15: from OF, from LL, from L *fortis* strong + *facere* to make]
▸ **'fortiˌfiable** *adj* ▸ **'fortiˌfier** *n*

fortissimo (fɔː'tɪsɪˌməʊ) *Music.* ◆ *adj, adv* **1** very loud. Symbol: ff ◆ *n* **2** a very loud passage in music. [C18: from It., from L, from *fortis* strong]

fortitude ◉ ('fɔːtɪˌtjuːd) *n* strength and firmness of mind. [C15: from L *fortitūdō* courage]

fortnight ('fɔːtˌnaɪt) *n* a period of 14 consecutive days; two weeks. [OE *fēowertīene niht* fourteen nights]

fortnightly ('fɔːtˌnaɪtlɪ) *Chiefly Brit.* ◆ *adj* **1** occurring or appearing once each fortnight. ◆ *adv* **2** once a fortnight. ◆ *n, pl* **fortnightlies. 3** a publication issued at intervals of two weeks.

Fortran ('fɔːtræn) *n* a high-level computer programming language for mathematical and scientific purposes. [C20: from *for(mula) tran(slation)*]

fortress ◉ ('fɔːtrɪs) *n* **1** a large fort or fortified town. **2** a place or source

THESAURUS

already, at one time, before, heretofore, lately, once

formidable *adj* **1** = **intimidating**, appalling, baleful, dangerous, daunting, dismaying, dreadful, fearful, frightful, horrible, menacing, shocking, terrifying, threatening **2** = **difficult**, arduous, challenging, colossal, mammoth, onerous, overwhelming, staggering, toilsome **3** = **impressive**, awesome, great, indomitable, mighty, powerful, puissant, redoubtable, terrific, tremendous
Antonyms *adj* ≠ **intimidating:** cheering, comforting, encouraging, genial, heartening, pleasant, reassuring ≠ **difficult:** easy

formless *adj* = **shapeless**, amorphous, disorganized, inchoate, incoherent, indefinite, nebulous, unformed, vague

formula *n* **1** = **form of words**, formulary, rite, ritual, rubric **4** = **method**, blueprint, modus operandi, precept, prescription, principle, procedure, recipe, rule, way

formulate *vb* **1** = **define**, codify, detail, express, frame, give form to, particularize, set down, specify, systematize **2** = **devise**, coin, develop, evolve, forge, invent, map out, originate, plan, work out

fornication *n* **1** = **adultery**, extra-curricular sex (*inf.*), extra-marital congress *or* relations *or* sex, infidelity, living in sin, pre-marital congress *or* relations *or* sex, unfaithfulness **2** = **immorality**, debauchery, dissipation, dissoluteness, easy virtue, immodesty, impurity, incontinence, indecency, indelicacy, lasciviousness, lechery, libertinism, loose morals, looseness, promiscuity, salaciousness, shamelessness, sin, sleeping around, unchastity, uncleanness

forsake *vb* **1** = **desert**, abandon, cast off, disown, jettison, jilt, leave, leave in the lurch, quit, repudiate, strand, throw over **2** = **give up**, abdicate, forgo, forswear, have done with, kick (*inf.*), relinquish, renounce, set aside, surrender, turn one's back on, yield

forsaken *adj* **2** = **deserted**, abandoned, cast off, destitute, disowned, ditched, forlorn, friendless, ignored, isolated, jilted, left behind, left in the lurch, lonely, marooned, outcast, solitary, stranded

forswear *vb* **1** = **renounce**, abandon, abjure, drop, forgo, forsake, give up, swear off **2** = **reject**, deny, disavow, disclaim, disown, recant, repudiate, retract **3** = **lie**, perjure oneself, renege, swear falsely

fort *n* **1** = **fortress**, blockhouse, camp, castle, citadel, fastness, fortification, garrison, redoubt, station, stronghold **2 hold the fort** *Informal* = **carry on**, keep things moving, keep things on an even keel, maintain the status quo, stand in, take over the reins

forte[1] *n* **1** = **speciality**, gift, long suit (*inf.*), métier, strength, strong point, talent
Antonyms *n* Achilles heel, chink in one's armour, defect, failing, imperfection, shortcoming, weak point

forth *adv* **1-3** = **forward**, ahead, away, into the open, onward, out, out of concealment, outward

forthcoming *adj* **1, 2** = **approaching**, coming, expected, future, imminent, impending, prospective, upcoming **3** = **available**, accessible, at hand, in evidence, obtainable, on tap (*inf.*), ready **4** = **communicative**, chatty, expansive, free, informative, open, sociable, talkative, unreserved

forthright *adj* **1** = **outspoken**, above-board, blunt, candid, direct, downright, frank, open, plain-spoken, straightforward, straight from the shoulder (*inf.*), upfront (*inf.*)
Antonyms *adj* dishonest, furtive, secret, secretive, sneaky, underhand, untruthful

forthwith *adv* = **at once**, directly, immediately, instantly, quickly, right away, straightaway, *tout de suite*, without delay

fortification *n* **1** = **strengthening**, embattlement, reinforcement **2** = **defence**, bastion, bulwark, castle, citadel, fastness, fort, fortress, keep, protection, stronghold

fortify *vb* **1** = **protect**, augment, brace, buttress, embattle, garrison, reinforce, secure, shore up, strengthen, support **2, 5** = **strengthen**, brace, cheer, confirm, embolden, encourage, hearten, invigorate, reassure, stiffen, sustain
Antonyms *vb* ≠ **strengthen:** debilitate, demoralize, dilute, dishearten, impair, reduce, sap the strength of, weaken

fortitude *n* = **courage**, backbone, bravery, dauntlessness, determination, endurance, fearlessness, firmness, grit, guts (*inf.*), hardihood, intrepidity, patience, perseverance, pluck, resolution, staying power, stoutheartedness, strength, strength of mind, valour

fortress *n* **1** = **castle**, citadel, fastness, fort, redoubt, stronghold of refuge or support. ◆ *vb* **3** (*tr*) to protect. [C13: from OF, from Med. L *fortalitia*, from L *fortis* strong]

Fort Sumter ('sʌmtə) *n* a fort in SE South Carolina, guarding Charleston Harbour. Its capture by Confederate forces (1861) was the first action of the Civil War.

fortuitous ➊ (fɔː'tjuːɪtəs) *adj* happening by chance, esp. by a lucky chance. [C17: from L *fortuitus* happening by chance, from *fors* chance, luck]
▸ **for'tuitously** *adv*

fortuity (fɔː'tjuːɪtɪ) *n, pl* **fortuities. 1** a chance or accidental occurrence. **2** chance or accident.

fortunate ➊ ('fɔːtʃənɪt) *adj* **1** having good luck. **2** occurring by or bringing good fortune or luck.
▸ **'fortunately** *adv*

fortune ➊ ('fɔːtʃən) *n* **1** an amount of wealth or material prosperity, esp. a great amount. **2 small fortune.** a large sum of money. **3** a power or force, often personalized, regarded as being responsible for human affairs. **4** luck, esp. when favourable. **5** (*often pl*) a person's destiny. ◆ *vb* **fortunes, fortuning, fortuned. 6** (*intr*) *Arch.* to happen by chance. [C13: from OF, from L, from *fors* chance]

fortune-hunter *n* a person who seeks to secure a fortune, esp. through marriage.

fortune-teller *n* a person who makes predictions about the future as by looking into a crystal ball, etc.
▸ **'fortune-ˌtelling** *adj, n*

forty ('fɔːtɪ) *n, pl* **forties. 1** the cardinal number that is the product of ten and four. **2** a numeral, 40, XL, etc., representing this number. **3** something representing, represented by, or consisting of 40 units. ◆ *determiner* **4a** amounting to forty: *forty thieves*. **4b** (*as pronoun*): *there were forty in the herd*. [OE *fēowertig*]
▸ **'fortieth** *adj, n*

forty-five *n* a gramophone record played at 45 revolutions per minute.

Forty-Five *n* **the.** *British history.* another name for the **Jacobite Rebellion** of 1745–46. See **Young Pretender.**

forty-niner *n* (*sometimes cap.*) *US history.* a prospector who took part in the California gold rush of 1849.

forty winks *n* (*functioning as sing or pl*) *Inf.* a short light sleep; nap.

forum ➊ ('fɔːrəm) *n, pl* **forums** *or* **fora** (-rə). **1** a meeting for the open discussion of subjects of public interest. **2** a medium for open discussion, such as a magazine. **3** a public meeting place for open discussion. **4** a court; tribunal. **5** (in ancient Italy) an open space serving as a city's marketplace and centre of public business. [C15: from L: public place]

Forum *or* **Forum Romanum** (rəʊ'mɑːnəm) *n* **the.** the main forum of ancient Rome.

forward ➊ ('fɔːwəd) *adj* **1** directed or moving ahead. **2** lying or situated in or near the front part of something. **3** presumptuous, pert, or impudent. **4** well developed or advanced, esp. in physical or intellectual development. **5a** of or relating to the future or favouring change. **5b** (*in combination*): *forward-looking*. **6** (*often postpositive*) *Arch.* ready, eager, or willing. **7** *Commerce.* relating to fulfilment at a future date. ◆ *n* **8** an attacking player in any of various sports, such as soccer. ◆ *adv* **9** a variant of **forwards. 10** ('fɔːwəd; *Naut.* 'fɒrəd). towards the front or bow of an aircraft or ship. **11** into a position of being subject to public scrutiny: *the witness came forward*. ◆ *vb* (*tr*) **12** to send forward or pass on to an ultimate destination: *the letter was forwarded*. **13** to advance or promote: *to forward one's career*. [OE *foreweard*]
▸ **'forwarder** *n* ▸ **'forwardly** *adv* ▸ **'forwardness** *n*

forwards ('fɔːwədz) *or* **forward** *adv* **1** towards or at a place ahead or in advance, esp. in space but also in time. **2** towards the front.

forwent (fɔː'wɛnt) *vb* the past tense of **forgo.**

forza ('fɔːtsə) *n Music.* force. [C19: It., lit.: force]

fossa ('fɒsə) *n, pl* **fossae** (-siː). an anatomical depression or hollow area. [C19: from L: ditch, from *fossus* dug up, from *fodere* to dig up]

fosse *or* **foss** (fɒs) *n* a ditch or moat, esp. one dug as a fortification. [C14: from OF, from L *fossa*; see FOSSA]

fossick ('fɒsɪk) *vb Austral. & NZ.* **1** (*intr*) to search for gold or precious stones in abandoned workings, rivers, etc. **2** to rummage or search for (something): *to fossick around for*. [C19: Austral., prob. from E dialect *fussock* to bustle about, from FUSS]
▸ **'fossicker** *n*

fossil ('fɒsᵊl) *n* **1a** a relic or representation of a plant or animal that existed in a past geological age, occurring in the form of mineralized bones, shells, etc. **1b** (*as modifier*): *fossil insects*. **2** *Inf., derog.* a person, idea, thing, etc., that is outdated or incapable of change. **3** *Linguistics.* a form once current but now appearing only in one or two special contexts. [C17: from L *fossilis* dug up, from *fodere* to dig]

fossil fuel *n* any naturally occurring fuel, such as coal, and natural gas, formed by the decomposition of prehistoric organisms.

fossiliferous (ˌfɒsɪ'lɪfərəs) *adj* (of sedimentary rocks) containing fossils.

fossilize *or* **fossilise** ('fɒsɪˌlaɪz) *vb* **fossilizes, fossilizing, fossilized** *or* **fossilises, fossilising, fossilised. 1** to convert or be converted into a fossil. **2** to become or cause to become antiquated or inflexible.
▸ **ˌfossili'zation** *or* **ˌfossili'sation** *n*

fossorial (fɒ'sɔːrɪəl) *adj* (of the forelimbs and skeleton of burrowing animals) adapted for digging. [C19: from Med. L, from L *fossor* digger, from *fodere* to dig]

foster ➊ ('fɒstə) *vb* (*tr*) **1** to promote the growth or development of. **2** to bring up (a child, etc.). **3** to cherish (a plan, hope, etc.) in one's mind. **4** *Chiefly Brit.* **4a** to place (a child) in the care of foster parents. **4b** to bring up under fosterage. ◆ *adj* **5** indicating relationship through fostering and not through birth: *foster child, foster mother*. **6** of or involved in the rearing of a child by persons other than his natural parents: *foster home*. [OE *fōstrian* to feed, from *fōstor* FOOD]
▸ **'fosterer** *n* ▸ **'fostering** *n*

fosterage ('fɒstərɪdʒ) *n* **1** the act of caring for a foster child. **2** the state of being a foster child. **3** the act of encouraging.

fought (fɔːt) *vb* the past tense and past participle of **fight.**

foul ➊ (faʊl) *adj* **1** offensive to the senses; revolting. **2** stinking. **3** charged with or full of dirt or offensive matter. **4** (of food) putrid; rotten. **5** morally or spiritually offensive. **6** obscene; vulgar: *foul language*. **7** unfair: *to resort to foul means*. **8** (esp. of weather) unpleasant or adverse. **9** blocked or obstructed with dirt or foreign matter: *a foul drain*. **10** (of the bottom of a vessel) covered with barnacles that slow forward motion. **11** *Inf.* unsatisfactory; bad: *a foul book*. ◆ *n* **12** *Sport.* **12a** a violation of the rules. **12b** (*as modifier*): *a foul blow*. **13** an entanglement or collision, esp. in sailing or fishing. ◆ *vb* **14** to make or become polluted. **15** to become or cause to become entangled. **16** (*tr*) to disgrace. **17** to become or cause to become clogged. **18** (*tr*) *Naut.* (of underwater growth) to cling to (the bottom of a vessel) so as to slow its motion. **19** (*tr*) *Sport.* to commit a foul against (an opponent). **20** (*intr*) *Sport.* to infringe the rules. **21** to collide (with a boat, etc.). ◆ *adv* **22** in a foul manner. **23 fall foul of. 23a** come into conflict with. **23b** *Naut.* to come into collision with. [OE *fūl*]
▸ **'foully** *adv* ▸ **'foulness** *n*

THESAURUS

fortuitous *adj* = **chance**, accidental, arbitrary, casual, contingent, incidental, random, unforeseen, unplanned = **lucky**, fluky (*inf.*), fortunate, happy, providential, serendipitous

fortunate *adj* **1** = **lucky**, bright, favoured, golden, happy, having a charmed life, in luck, jammy (*Brit. sl.*), on a roll, prosperous, rosy, sitting pretty (*inf.*), successful, well-off **2** = **providential**, advantageous, auspicious, convenient, encouraging, expedient, favourable, felicitous, fortuitous, helpful, opportune, profitable, promising, propitious, timely
Antonyms *adj* hapless, ill-fated, ill-starred, miserable, poor, unfortunate, unhappy, unlucky, unsuccessful, wretched

fortunately *adv* **2** = **luckily**, by a happy chance, by good luck, happily, providentially

fortune *n* **1** = **wealth**, affluence, an arm and a leg (*inf.*), big money, bomb (*Brit. sl.*), bundle (*sl.*), gold mine, king's ransom, megabucks (*US & Canad. sl.*), mint, opulence, packet (*sl.*), pile (*inf.*), possessions, pretty penny (*inf.*), property, prosperity, riches, tidy sum (*inf.*), treasure, wad (*US & Canad. sl.*) **3** = **luck**, accident, chance, contingency, destiny, fate, fortuity, hap (*arch.*), hazard, kismet, providence **5** *often plural* = **destiny**, adventures, circumstances, doom, expectation, experiences, history, life, lot, portion, star, success
Antonyms *n* ≠ **wealth:** destitution, hardship, indigence, penury, poverty, privation

forum *n* **1** = **meeting**, assemblage, assembly, body, caucus (*chiefly US & Canad.*), colloquium, conclave, conference, congregation, congress, convention, convergence, convocation, council, court, diet, gathering, get- together (*inf.*), moot, parliament, rally, seminar, senate, symposium, synod, tribunal (*arch. or literary*) **3** = **meeting**, amphitheatre, arena, chamber, court, meeting place, platform, pulpit, rostrum, stage

forward *adj* **2** = **leading**, advance, first, fore, foremost, front, head **3** = **presumptuous**, assuming, bare-faced, bold, brash, brass-necked (*Brit. inf.*), brazen, brazen-faced, cheeky, confident, familiar, fresh (*inf.*), impertinent, impudent, overassertive, overweening, pert, presuming, pushy (*inf.*), sassy (*US inf.*) **4** = **well-developed**, advanced, advancing, early, forward-looking, onward, precocious, premature, progressive ◆ *adv* **9** = **forth**, ahead, on, onward **11** = **to the front**, into consideration, into prominence, into the open, into view, out, to light, to the surface ◆ *vb* **12** = **send**, dispatch, freight, post, route, send on, ship, transmit **13** = **promote**, advance, aid, assist, back, encourage, expedite, favour, foster, further, hasten, help, hurry, speed, support
Antonyms *adj* ≠ **presumptuous:** backward, diffident, modest, regressive, retiring, shy ◆ *adv* ≠ **forth:** backward(s) ◆ *vb* ≠ **promote:** bar, block, hinder, hold up, impede, obstruct, retard, thwart

forwardness *n* **3** = **impertinence**, boldness, brashness, brazenness, cheek (*inf.*), cheekiness, chutzpah (*US & Canad. inf.*), impudence, overconfidence, pertness, presumption

foster *vb* **1** = **promote**, cultivate, encourage, feed, foment, nurture, stimulate, support, uphold **2** = **bring up**, mother, nurse, raise, rear, take care of **3** = **cherish**, accommodate, entertain, harbour, nourish, sustain
Antonyms *vb* ≠ **promote:** combat, curb, curtail, hold out against, inhibit, oppose, resist, restrain, subdue, suppress, withstand

foul *adj* **1, 2, 4** = **dirty**, contaminated, disgusting, fetid, filthy, grotty (*sl.*), impure, loathsome, malodorous, mephitic, nasty, nauseating, noisome, offensive, olid, polluted, putrid, rank, repulsive, revolting, rotten, squalid, stinking, sullied, tainted, unclean **5** = **offensive**, abhorrent, abominable, base, despicable, detestable, disgraceful, dishonourable, egregious, hateful, heinous, infamous, iniquitous, nefarious, notorious, scandalous, shameful, shitty (*taboo sl.*), vicious, vile, wicked **6** = **obscene**, abusive, blasphemous, blue, coarse, dirty, filthy, foul-mouthed, gross, indecent, lewd, low, profane, scatological, scurrilous, smutty, vulgar **7** = **unfair**, crooked, dirty, dishonest, fraudulent, inequitable, shady (*inf.*), underhand, unjust, unscrupulous, unsportsmanlike **8** = **stormy**, bad, blustery, disagreeable, foggy, murky, rainy, rough, wet, wild ◆ *vb* **14** =

foulard (fuːˈlɑːd) *n* a soft light fabric of plain-weave or twill-weave silk or rayon, usually with a printed design. [C19: from F, from ?]

foul play ❶ *n* **1** violent or treacherous conduct, esp. murder. **2** a violation of the rules in a game or sport.

foul up ❶ *vb (adv)* **1** *(tr)* to bungle. **2** *(tr)* to contaminate. **3** to be or cause to be blocked, choked, or entangled. ◆ *n* **foul-up. 4** a state of confusion or muddle caused by bungling.

found[1] (faʊnd) *vb* **1** the past tense and past participle of **find.** ◆ *adj* **2** furnished or fitted out. **3** *Brit.* with meals, heating, etc., provided without extra charge.

found[2] ❶ (faʊnd) *vb* **1** *(tr)* to bring into being or establish (something, such as an institution, etc.). **2** *(tr)* to build or establish the foundation of. **3** *(also intr;* foll. by *on* or *upon)* to have a basis (in). [C13: from OF, from L, from *fundus* bottom]

found[3] (faʊnd) *vb (tr)* **1** to cast (a material, such as metal or glass) by melting and pouring into a mould. **2** to make (articles) in this way. [C14: from OF, from L *fundere* to melt]

foundation ❶ (faʊnˈdeɪʃən) *n* **1** that on which something is founded. **2** *(often pl)* a construction below the ground that distributes the load of a building, wall, etc. **3** the base on which something stands. **4** the act of founding or establishing or the state of being founded or established. **5** an endowment for the support of an institution such as a school. **6** an institution supported by an endowment, often one that provides funds for charities, research, etc. **7** a cosmetic used as a base for make-up.
▸**founˈdational** *adj*

foundation garment *n* a woman's undergarment worn to shape and support the figure. Also called: **foundation.**

foundation stone *n* a stone laid at a ceremony to mark the foundation of a new building.

foundation subjects *pl n Brit. education.* the subjects studied as part of the National Curriculum, including the compulsory core subjects.

founder[1] ❶ (ˈfaʊndə) *n* a person who establishes an institution, society, etc. [C14: see FOUND[2]]

founder[2] ❶ (ˈfaʊndə) *vb (intr)* **1** (of a ship, etc.) to sink. **2** to break down or fail: *the project foundered.* **3** to sink into or become stuck in soft ground. **4** to collapse. **5** (of a horse) to stumble or go lame. [C13: from OF *fondrer* to submerge, from L *fundus* bottom]

> **USAGE NOTE** *Founder* is sometimes wrongly used where *flounder* is meant: *this unexpected turn of events left him floundering* (not *foundering*).

founder[3] (ˈfaʊndə) *n* **a** a person who makes metal castings. **b** *(in combination): an iron founder.* [C15: see FOUND[3]]

foundling ❶ (ˈfaʊndlɪŋ) *n* an abandoned infant whose parents are not known. [C13 *foundeling;* see FIND]

foundry (ˈfaʊndrɪ) *n, pl* **foundries.** a place in which metal castings are produced. [C17: from OF, from *fondre;* see FOUND[3]]

fount[1] (faʊnt) *n* **1** *Poetic.* a spring or fountain. **2** source. [C16: back formation from FOUNTAIN]

fount[2] (faʊnt, fɒnt) *n Printing.* a complete set of type of one style and size. Also called (esp. US and Canad.): **font.** [C16: from OF *fonte* a founding, casting, from Vulgar L *funditus* (unattested) a casting, from L *fundere* to melt]

fountain ❶ (ˈfaʊntɪn) *n* **1** a jet or spray of water or some other liquid. **2** a structure from which such a jet or a number of such jets spurt. **3** a natural spring of water, esp. the source of a stream. **4** a stream, jet, or cascade of sparks, lava, etc. **5** a principal source. **6** a reservoir, as for oil in a lamp. [C15: from OF, from LL, from L *fons* spring, source]
▸**ˈfountained** *adj*

fountainhead ❶ (ˈfaʊntɪnˌhɛd) *n* **1** a spring that is the source of a stream. **2** a principal or original source.

fountain pen *n* a pen the nib of which is supplied with ink from a cartridge or a reservoir in its barrel.

four (fɔː) *n* **1** the cardinal number that is the sum of three and one. **2** a numeral, 4, IV, etc., representing this number. **3** something representing, represented by, or consisting of four units, such as a playing card with four symbols on it. **4** Also called: **four o'clock.** four hours after noon or midnight. **5** *Cricket.* **5a** a shot that crosses the boundary after hitting the ground. **5b** the four runs scored for such a shot. **6** *Rowing.* **6a** a racing shell propelled by four oarsmen. **6b** the crew of such a shell. ◆ *determiner* **7a** amounting to four: *four times.* **7b** *(as pronoun): four are ready.* [OE *fēower*]

four-by-four *n* a vehicle equipped with four-wheel drive.

four flush *n* a useless poker hand, containing four of a suit and one odd card.

fourfold (ˈfɔːˌfəʊld) *adj* **1** equal to or having four times as many or as much. **2** composed of four parts. ◆ *adv* **3** by or up to four times as many or as much.

four-in-hand *n* **1** a road vehicle drawn by four horses and driven by one driver. **2** a four-horse team. **3** *US.* a long narrow tie tied in a flat slipknot with the ends dangling.

four-leaf clover *or* **four-leaved clover** *n* a clover with four leaves rather than three, supposed to bring good luck.

four-letter word *n* any of several short English words referring to sex or excrement: regarded generally as offensive or obscene.

four-o'clock *n* a tropical American plant, cultivated for its tubular yellow, red, or white flowers that open in late afternoon. Also called: **marvel-of-Peru.**

four-poster *n* a bed with posts at each corner supporting a canopy and curtains.

fourscore (ˌfɔːˈskɔː) *determiner* an archaic word for **eighty.**

foursome (ˈfɔːsəm) *n* **1** a set or company of four. **2** Also called: **four-ball.** *Golf.* a game between two pairs of players.

foursquare (ˌfɔːˈskwɛə) *adv* **1** squarely; firmly. ◆ *adj* **2** solid and strong. **3** forthright. **4** a rare word for **square.**

four-stroke *adj* designating an internal-combustion engine in which the piston makes four strokes for every explosion.

fourteen (ˈfɔːˈtiːn) *n* **1** the cardinal number that is the sum of ten and four. **2** a numeral, 14, XIV, etc., representing this number. **3** something represented by or consisting of 14 units. ◆ *determiner* **4a** amounting to fourteen: *fourteen cats.* **4b** *(as pronoun): the fourteen who remained.* [OE *fēowertiene*]
▸**ˈfourˈteenth** *adj, n*

fourth (fɔːθ) *adj (usually prenominal)* **1a** coming after the third in order, position, time, etc. Often written: 4th. **1b** *(as n): the fourth in succession.* **2** denoting the highest forward ratio of a gearbox in most motor vehicles. ◆ *n* **3** *Music.* **3a** the interval between one note and another four notes away from it in a diatonic scale. **3b** one of two notes constituting such an interval in relation to the other. **4** the fourth forward ratio of a gearbox in a motor vehicle, usually the highest gear in cars. **5** a less common word for **quarter** (sense 2). ◆ *adv also:* **fourthly. 6** after the third person, position, event, etc. ◆ *sentence connector. also:* **fourthly. 7** as the fourth point.

fourth dimension *n* **1** the dimension of time, which in addition to three spatial dimensions specifies the position of a point or particle. **2** the concept in science fiction of a dimension in addition to three spatial dimensions.
▸**ˌfourth-diˈmensional** *adj*

fourth estate *n (sometimes caps.)* journalists or their profession; the press.

four-wheel drive *n* a system used in motor vehicles in which all four wheels are connected to the source of power.

fovea (ˈfəʊvɪə) *n, pl* **foveae** (-vɪˌiː). *Anat.* any small pit or depression in the surface of a bodily organ or part. [C19: from L: a small pit]

fowl (faʊl) *n* **1** Also called: **domestic fowl.** a domesticated gallinaceous bird occurring in many varieties. **2** any other bird that is used as food or hunted as game. **3** the flesh or meat of fowl, esp. of chicken. **4** an archaic word for any **bird.** ◆ *vb* **5** *(intr)* to hunt or snare wildfowl. [OE *fugol*]
▸**ˈfowler** *n* ▸**ˈfowling** *n, adj*

fowl pest *n* an acute and usually fatal viral disease of domestic fowl, characterized by discoloration of the comb and wattles.

fox (fɒks) *n, pl* **foxes** *or* **fox. 1** any canine mammal of the genus *Vulpes* and related genera. They are mostly predators and have a pointed muzzle and a bushy tail. **2** the fur of any of these animals, usually reddish-brown or grey in colour. **3** a person who is cunning and sly. ◆ *vb* **4** *(tr) Inf.* to perplex: *to fox a person with a problem.* **5** to cause (paper, wood, etc.) to become discoloured with spots, or (of paper, etc.) to be-

THESAURUS

dirty, begrime, besmear, besmirch, contaminate, defile, pollute, smear, smirch, soil, stain, sully, taint **15, 17 = clog,** block, catch, choke, ensnare, entangle, jam, snarl, twist ◆ *adv* **23a fall foul of = come into conflict with,** brush with, cross swords with, have trouble with, make an enemy of

Antonyms *adj* ≠ **offensive:** admirable, attractive, decent, pleasant, respectable ≠ **dirty:** clean, clear, fair, fragrant, fresh, pure, spotless, undefiled ◆ *vb* ≠ **dirty:** clean, cleanse, clear, purge, purify, sanitize

foul play *n* **1 = crime,** chicanery, corruption, deception, dirty work, double-dealing, duplicity, fraud, perfidy, roguery, sharp practice, skulduggery, treachery, villainy

foul up *vb* **1 = bungle,** bodge *(inf.)*, botch, cock up *(Brit. sl.)*, make a mess of, make a nonsense of, make a pig's ear of *(inf.)*, mismanage, muck up *(sl.)*, put a spanner in the works *(Brit. inf.)*, spoil

found[2] *vb* **1, 2 = establish,** bring into being, constitute, construct, create, endow, erect, fix, inaugurate, institute, organize, originate, plant, raise, settle, set up, start **3 = base,** bottom, build, ground, rest, root, sustain

foundation *n* **1, 3 = basis,** base, bedrock, bottom, footing, groundwork, substructure, underpinning **4 = setting up,** endowment, establishment, inauguration, institution, organization, settlement

founder[1] *n* **= initiator,** architect, author, beginner, benefactor, builder, constructor, designer, establisher, father, framer, generator, institutor, inventor, maker, organizer, originator, patriarch

founder[2] *vb* **1 = sink,** be lost, go down, go to the bottom, submerge **2 = fail,** abort, bite the dust, break down, collapse, come to grief, come to nothing, come unstuck, fall by the wayside, fall through, go belly-up *(sl.)*, go down like a lead balloon *(inf.)*, miscarry, misfire **4, 5 = stumble,** collapse, fall, go lame, lurch, sprawl, stagger, trip

foundling *n* **= orphan,** outcast, stray, waif

fountain *n* **1, 3 = jet,** font, fount, reservoir, spout, spray, spring, well **5 = source,** beginning, cause, commencement, derivation, fount, fountainhead, genesis, origin, rise, wellhead, wellspring

fountainhead *n* **2 = source,** *fons et origo,* fount, inspiration, mainspring, origin, spring, well, wellspring

come discoloured. **6** (*tr*) to trick; deceive. **7** (*intr*) to act deceitfully or craftily. [OE]
▸ **'fox,like** *adj*

foxfire ('fɒks,faɪə) *n* a luminescent glow emitted by certain fungi on rotting wood.

foxglove ('fɒks,glʌv) *n* a plant having spikes of purple or white thimble-like flowers. The soft wrinkled leaves are a source of digitalis. [OE]

foxhole ('fɒks,həʊl) *n Mil.* a small pit dug to provide shelter against hostile fire.

foxhound ('fɒks,haʊnd) *n* a breed of short-haired hound, usually kept for hunting foxes.

fox hunt *n* **1a** the hunting of foxes with hounds. **1b** an instance of this. **2** an organization for fox hunting within a particular area.
▸ **'fox-,hunter** *n* ▸ **'fox-,hunting** *n*

foxtail ('fɒks,teɪl) *n* any grass of Europe, Asia, and South America, having soft cylindrical spikes of flowers: cultivated as a pasture grass.

fox terrier *n* either of two breeds of small tan-black-and-white terrier, the wire-haired and the smooth.

foxtrot ('fɒks,trɒt) *n* **1** a ballroom dance in quadruple time, combining short and long steps in various sequences. ◆ *vb* **foxtrots, foxtrotting, foxtrotted. 2** (*intr*) to perform this dance.

foxy ❶ ('fɒksɪ) *adj* **foxier, foxiest. 1** of or resembling a fox, esp. in craftiness. **2** of a reddish-brown colour. **3** (of paper, etc.) spotted, esp. by mildew. **4** *Sl.* sexy; sexually attractive.
▸ **'foxily** *adv* ▸ **'foxiness** *n*

foyer ❶ ('fɔɪeɪ, 'fɔɪə) *n* a hall, lobby, or anteroom, as in a hotel, theatre, cinema, etc. [C19: from F: fireplace, from Med. L, from L *focus* fire]

fp *Music. abbrev. for* forte-piano.

FP *abbrev. for:* **1** fire plug. **2** former pupil. **3** Also: **fp.** freezing point.

FPA *abbrev. for* Family Planning Association.

fps *abbrev. for:* **1** feet per second. **2** foot-pound-second. **3** *Photog.* frames per second.

fps units *pl, n* an Imperial system of units based on the foot, pound, and second as the units of length, mass, and time.

Fr *abbrev. for:* **1** *Christianity:* **1a** Father. **1b** Frater. [L: brother] **2** *the chemical symbol for* francium.

fr. *abbrev. for:* **1** fragment. **2** franc. **3** from.

Fr. *abbrev. for:* **1** France. **2** French.

Fra (frɑː) *n* brother: a title given to an Italian monk or friar. [It., short for *frate* brother, from L *frāter* BROTHER]

fracas ❶ ('frækɑː) *n* a noisy quarrel; brawl. [C18: from F, from *fracasser* to shatter, from L *frangere* to break, infl. by *quassāre* to shatter]

fractal ('fræktəl) *n* any of various irregular and fragmented shapes or surfaces that are generated by a series of successive subdivisions. [C20: from L *frāctus*, p.p. of *frangere* to break]

fraction ❶ ('frækʃən) *n* **1** *Maths.* a ratio of two expressions or numbers other than zero. **2** any part or subdivision. **3** a small piece; fragment. **4** *Chem.* a component of a mixture separated by fractional distillation. **5** *Christianity.* the formal breaking of the bread in Communion. [C14: from LL, from L *fractus* broken, from *frangere* to break]
▸ **'fractional** *adj* ▸ **'fraction,ize** *or* **'fraction,ise** *vb*

fractional crystallization *n Chem.* the process of separating the components of a solution on the basis of their different solubilities, by means of evaporating the solution until the least soluble component crystallizes out.

fractional distillation *n* the process of separating the constituents of a liquid mixture by heating it and condensing separately the components according to their different boiling points. Sometimes shortened to **distillation.**

fractionate ('frækʃə,neɪt) *vb* **fractionates, fractionating, fractionated. 1** to separate or cause to separate into constituents. **2** (*tr*) *Chem.* to obtain (a constituent of a mixture) by a fractional process.
▸ **,fraction'ation** *n*

fractious ❶ ('frækʃəs) *adj* **1** irritable. **2** unruly. [C18: from (obs.) *fraction* discord + -OUS]
▸ **'fractiously** *adv* ▸ **'fractiousness** *n*

> **USAGE NOTE** *Fractious* is sometimes wrongly used where *factious* is meant: *this factious* (not *fractious*) *dispute has split the party still further.*

fracture ❶ ('fræktʃə) *n* **1** the act of breaking or the state of being broken. **2a** the breaking or cracking of a bone or the tearing of a cartilage. **2b** the resulting condition. **3** a division, split, or breach. **4** *Mineralogy.* **4a** the characteristic appearance of the surface of a freshly broken mineral or rock. **4b** the way in which a mineral or rock naturally breaks. ◆ *vb* **fractures, fracturing, fractured. 5** to break or cause to break. **6** to break or crack (a bone) or (of a bone) to become broken or cracked. [C15: from OF, from L, from *frangere* to break]
▸ **'fractural** *adj*

fraenum *or* **frenum** ('friːnəm) *n, pl* **fraena** *or* **frena** (-nə). a fold of membrane or skin, such as the fold beneath the tongue. [C18: from L: bridle]

fragile ❶ ('frædʒaɪl) *adj* **1** able to be broken easily. **2** in a weakened physical state. **3** delicate; light: *a fragile touch.* **4** slight; tenuous. [C17: from L *fragilis*, from *frangere* to break]
▸ **'fragilely** *adv* ▸ **fragility** (frə'dʒɪlɪtɪ) *n*

fragment ❶ *n* ('frægmənt). **1** a piece broken off or detached. **2** an incomplete piece: *fragments of a novel.* **3** a scrap; bit. ◆ *vb* (fræg'ment). **4** to break or cause to break into fragments. [C15: from L *fragmentum*, from *frangere* to break]
▸ **,fragmen'tation** *n*

fragmentary ❶ ('frægməntərɪ) *adj* made up of fragments; disconnected. Also: **fragmental.**

fragrance ❶ ('freɪgrəns) *or* **fragrancy** *n, pl* **fragrances** *or* **fragrancies. 1** a pleasant or sweet odour. **2** the state of being fragrant.

fragrant ❶ ('freɪgrənt) *adj* having a pleasant or sweet smell. [C15: from L, from *frāgrāre* to emit a smell]
▸ **'fragrantly** *adv*

frail[1] ❶ (freɪl) *adj* **1** physically weak and delicate. **2** fragile: *a frail craft.* **3** easily corrupted or tempted. [C13: from OF *frele*, from L *fragilis*, FRAGILE]

frail[2] (freɪl) *n* **1** a rush basket for figs or raisins. **2** a quantity of raisins or figs equal to between 50 and 75 pounds. [C13: from OF *fraiel*, from ?]

frailty ❶ ('freɪltɪ) *n, pl* **frailties. 1** physical or moral weakness. **2** (*often pl*) a fault symptomatic of moral weakness.

framboesia *or US* **frambesia** (fræm'biːzɪə) *n Pathol.* another name for **yaws.** [C19: from NL, from F *framboise* raspberry; from its raspberry-like excrescences]

frame ❶ (freɪm) *n* **1** an open structure that gives shape and support to something, such as the ribs of a ship's hull or an aircraft's fuselage or the beams of a building. **2** an enclosing case or border into which something is fitted: *the frame of a picture.* **3** the system around which something is built up: *the frame of government.* **4** the structure of the human body. **5** a condition; state (esp. in **frame of mind**). **6a** one of a series of exposures on film used in making motion pictures. **6b** an exposure on a film used in still photography. **7** a television picture scanned by one or more electron beams at a particular frequency. **8** *Snooker, etc.* **8a** the wooden triangle used to set up the balls. **8b** the balls when set up. **8c** a single game finished when all the balls have been potted. **9** short for **cold frame. 10** one of the sections of which a beehive is composed, esp. one designed to hold a honeycomb. **11** *Sta-*

THESAURUS

foxy *adj* **1** = **crafty**, artful, astute, canny, cunning, devious, guileful, knowing, sharp, shrewd, sly, tricky, wily

foyer *n* = **entrance hall**, antechamber, anteroom, lobby, reception area, vestibule

fracas *n* = **brawl**, affray (*Law*), aggro, disturbance, donnybrook, fight, free-for-all (*inf.*), melee *or* mêlée, quarrel, riot, row, rumpus, scrimmage, scuffle, shindig (*inf.*), shindy (*inf.*), skirmish, trouble, uproar

fraction *n* **1, 2** = **piece**, cut, division, moiety, part, percentage, portion, proportion, quota, ratio, section, sector, segment, share, slice, subdivision **3** = **fragment**, atom, bit, bite, chip, crumb, drop, flake, grain, granule, iota, jot, morsel, mote, particle, scrap, shard, shred, sliver, smithereen (*inf.*), splinter, whit

fractious *adj* **1, 2** = **irritable**, awkward, captious, crabby, cross, fretful, froward (*arch.*), grouchy, peevish, pettish, petulant, querulous, ratty (*Brit. & NZ inf.*), recalcitrant, refractory, testy, tetchy, touchy, unruly
Antonyms *adj* affable, agreeable, amiable, biddable, complaisant, genial, good-natured, good-tempered, tractable

fracture *n* **3** = **break**, breach, cleft, crack, fissure, gap, opening, rent, rift, rupture, schism, split ◆ *vb* **5, 6** = **break**, crack, rupture, splinter, split

fragile *adj* **1** = **delicate**, breakable, brittle, dainty, feeble, fine, flimsy, frail, frangible, infirm, slight, weak
Antonyms *adj* durable, elastic, flexible, hardy, lasting, reliable, resilient, robust, strong, sturdy, tough

fragility *n* **1** = **delicacy**, brittleness, feebleness, frailty, frangibility, infirmity, weakness

fragment *n* **1-3** = **piece**, bit, chip, fraction, morsel, oddment, part, particle, portion, remnant, scrap, shiver, shred, sliver ◆ *vb* **4** = **break**, break up, come apart, come to pieces, crumble, disintegrate, disunite, divide, shatter, shiver, splinter, split, split up
Antonyms *vb* ≠ **break:** bond, combine, compound, fuse, join together, link, marry, merge, synthesize, unify

fragmentary *adj* = **incomplete**, bitty, broken, disconnected, discrete, disjointed, incoherent, partial, piecemeal, scattered, scrappy, sketchy, unsystematic

fragrance *n* **1** = **scent**, aroma, balm, bouquet, fragrancy, perfume, redolence, smell, sweet odour
Antonyms *n* effluvium, miasma, offensive smell, pong (*Brit. inf.*), reek, smell, stink, whiff (*Brit. sl.*)

fragrant *adj* = **aromatic**, ambrosial, balmy, odoriferous, odorous, perfumed, redolent, sweet-scented, sweet-smelling
Antonyms *adj* fetid, foul-smelling, malodorous, noisome, olid, pongy (*Brit. inf.*), reeking, smelling, smelly, stinking

frail[1] **1, 2** *adj* = **weak**, breakable, brittle, decrepit, delicate, feeble, flimsy, fragile, frangible, infirm, insubstantial, puny, slight, tender, unsound, vulnerable, wispy
Antonyms *adj* hale, healthy, robust, sound, stalwart, strong, sturdy, substantial, tough, vigorous

frailty *n* **1** = **weakness**, fallibility, feebleness, frailness, infirmity, peccability, puniness, susceptibility **2** = **fault**, blemish, chink in one's armour, defect, deficiency, failing, flaw, foible, imperfection, peccadillo, shortcoming, vice, weak point
Antonyms *n* ≠ **weakness:** fortitude, might, robustness, strength ≠ **fault:** asset, strong point, virtue

frame *n* **1** = **casing**, construction, fabric, form, framework, scheme, shell, structure, system **2** = **mounting**, mount, setting **4** = **physique**, anatomy, body, build, carcass, morphology, skeleton **5** = **mood**, attitude, disposition, fettle,

tistics. an enumeration of a population for the purposes of sampling. **12** *Sl.* another word for **frame-up. 13** *Obs.* shape; form. ◆ *vb* **frames, framing, framed.** (*mainly tr*) **14** to construct by fitting parts together. **15** to draw up the plans or basic details for: *to frame a policy.* **16** to compose or conceive: *to frame a reply.* **17** to provide, support, or enclose with a frame: *to frame a picture.* **18** to form (words) with the lips, esp. silently. **19** *Sl.* to conspire to incriminate (someone) on a false charge. [OE *framiae* to avail]
▸**'frameless** *adj* ▸**'framer** *n*

frame house *n* a house that has a timber framework and cladding.

frame of reference *n* **1** *Sociol.* a set of standards that determines and sanctions behaviour. **2** any set of planes or curves, such as the three coordinate axes, used to locate a point in space.

frame-up ❶ *n Sl.* **1** a conspiracy to incriminate someone on a false charge. **2** a plot to bring about a dishonest result, as in a contest.

framework ❶ ('freɪm,wɜːk) *n* **1** a structural plan or basis of a project. **2** a structure or frame supporting or containing something.

franc (fræŋk; *French* frɑ̃) *n* **1** the standard monetary unit of France, French dependencies, and Monaco, divided into 100 centimes. Also called: **French franc. 2** the standard monetary and currency unit, comprising 100 centimes, of various countries including Belgium, the Central African Republic, Gabon, Guinea, Liechtenstein, Luxembourg, Mauritania, Niger, the Republic of Congo, Senegal, Switzerland, Togo, etc. **3** a Moroccan monetary unit worth one hundredth of a dirham. [C14: from OF; from L *Rex Francōrum* King of the Franks, inscribed on 14th-century francs]

franchise ❶ ('fræntʃaɪz) *n* **1** (usually preceded by *the*) the right to vote, esp. for representatives in a legislative body. **2** any exemption, privilege, or right granted to an individual or group by a public authority. **3** *Commerce.* authorization granted by a manufacturing enterprise to a distributor to market the manufacturer's products. **4** the full rights of citizenship. ◆ *vb* **franchises, franchising, franchised. 5** (*tr*) *Commerce, chiefly US & Canad.* to grant (a person, firm, etc.) a franchise. [C13: from OF, from *franchir* to set free, from *franc* free]
▸**,franchi'see** *n* ▸**franchisement** ('fræntʃɪzmənt) *n* ▸**'franchiser** *n*

Franciscan (fræn'sɪskən) *n* **a** a member of a Christian religious order of friars or nuns tracing their origins back to Saint Francis of Assisi. **b** (*as modifier*): *a Franciscan friary.*

francium ('frænsɪəm) *n* an unstable radioactive element of the alkali-metal group, occurring in minute amounts in uranium ores. Symbol: Fr; atomic no.: 87; half-life of most stable isotope, ^{223}Fr: 22 minutes. [C20: from NL, from *France* + -IUM; because first found in France]

Franco- ('fræŋkəʊ-) *combining form.* indicating France or French: *Franco-Prussian.* [from Med. L *Francus,* from LL: FRANK]

francolin ('fræŋkəʊlɪn) *n* an African or Asian partridge. [C17: from F, from OIt. *francolino,* from ?]

Francophobe ('fræŋkəʊ,fəʊb) *n* **1** a person who hates or fears France or its people. **2** *Canad.* a person who hates or fears Canadian Francophones.

Francophone ('fræŋkəʊ,fəʊn) (*often not cap.*) ◆ *n* **1** a person who speaks French, esp. a native speaker. ◆ *adj* **2** speaking French as a native language. **3** using French as a lingua franca.

frangible ('frændʒɪbᵊl) *adj* breakable or fragile. [C15: from OF, ult. from L *frangere* to break]
▸**,frangi'bility** *or* **'frangibleness** *n*

frangipane ('frændʒɪ,peɪn) *n* **1** a pastry filled with cream and flavoured with almonds. **2** a variant of **frangipani** (the perfume).

frangipani (,frændʒɪ'pɑːnɪ) *n, pl* **frangipanis** *or* **frangipani. 1** a tropical American shrub cultivated for its waxy white or pink flowers, which have a sweet overpowering scent. **2** a perfume prepared from this plant or resembling the odour of its flowers. **3 native frangipani.** *Austral.* an Australian evergreen tree with large fragrant yellow flowers. [C17: via F from It.: perfume for scenting gloves, after the Marquis Muzio *Frangipani,* 16th-century Roman nobleman who invented it]

Franglais (*French* frɑ̃glɛ) *n* informal French containing a high proportion of English. [C20: from F *français* French + *anglais* English]

frank ❶ (fræŋk) *adj* **1** honest and straightforward in speech or attitude: *a frank person.* **2** outspoken or blunt. **3** open and avowed: *frank interest.* ◆ *vb* (*tr*) **4** *Chiefly Brit.* to put a mark on (a letter, etc.), either cancelling the postage stamp or in place of a stamp, ensuring free carriage. **5** to mark (a letter, etc.) with an official mark or signature, indicating the right of free delivery. **6** to facilitate or assist (a person) to enter easily. **7** to obtain immunity for (a person). ◆ *n* **8** an official mark or signature affixed to a letter, etc., ensuring free delivery or delivery without stamps. [C13: from OF, from Med. L *francus* free; identical with FRANK (in Frankish Gaul only members of this people enjoyed full freedom)]
▸**'frankable** *adj* ▸**'franker** *n* ▸**'frankness** *n*

Frank (fræŋk) *n* a member of a group of West Germanic peoples who spread from the east in the late 4th century A.D., gradually conquering most of Gaul and Germany. [OE *Franca;* ?from the name of a Frankish weapon (cf. OE *franca* javelin)]

franked investment income *n* dividends from one UK company received by another on which the paying company has paid corporation tax.

Frankenstein ('fræŋkɪn,staɪn) *n* **1** a person who creates something that brings about his ruin. **2** Also called: **Frankenstein's monster.** a thing that destroys its creator. [C19: after Baron *Frankenstein,* who created a destructive monster from parts of corpses in the novel by Mary Shelley (1818)]
▸**,Franken'steinian** *adj*

frankfurter ('fræŋk,fɜːtə) *n* a smoked sausage, made of finely minced pork or beef. [C20: short for G *Frankfurter Wurst* sausage from *Frankfurt am Main* in Germany]

frankincense ('fræŋkɪn,sens) *n* an aromatic gum resin obtained from trees of the genus *Boswellia,* which occur in Asia and Africa. [C14: from OF *franc* free, pure + *encens* INCENSE[1]; see FRANK]

Frankish ('fræŋkɪʃ) *n* **1** the ancient West Germanic language of the Franks. ◆ *adj* **2** of or relating to the Franks or their language.

franklin ('fræŋklɪn) *n* (in 14th- and 15th-century England) a substantial landholder of free but not noble birth. [C13: from Anglo-F, from OF *franc* free, on the model of CHAMBERLAIN]

frankly ❶ ('fræŋklɪ) *adv* **1** (*sentence modifier*) to be honest. **2** in a frank manner.

frantic ❶ ('fræntɪk) *adj* **1** distracted with fear, pain, joy, etc. **2** marked by or showing frenzy: *frantic efforts.* [C14: from OF, from L *phrenēticus* mad]
▸**'frantically** *or* **'franticly** *adv*

frappé ('fræpeɪ) *n* **1** a drink consisting of a liqueur, etc., poured over crushed ice. ◆ *adj* **2** (*postpositive*) (esp. of drinks) chilled. [C19: from F, from *frapper* to strike, hence, chill]

frater ('freɪtə) *n Arch.* a refectory. [C13: from OF *fraiteur,* from *refreitor,* from LL *rēfectōrium* REFECTORY]

fraternal (frə'tɜːnᵊl) *adj* **1** of or suitable to a brother; brotherly. **2** of a fraternity. **3** designating twins of the same or opposite sex that developed from two separate fertilized ova. Cf. **identical** (sense 3). [C15: from L, from *frāter* brother]
▸**fra'ternalism** *n*

fraternity ❶ (frə'tɜːnɪtɪ) *n, pl* **fraternities. 1** a body of people united in interests, aims, etc.: *the teaching fraternity.* **2** brotherhood. **3** *US & Canad.* a secret society joined by male students, functioning as a social club.

fraternize ❶ *or* **fraternise** ('frætə,naɪz) *vb* **fraternizes, fraternizing, fraternized** *or* **fraternises, fraternising, fraternised.** (*intr;* often foll. by *with*) to associate on friendly terms.
▸**,fraterni'zation** *or* **,fraterni'sation** *n* ▸**'frater,nizer** *or* **'frater,niser** *n*

fratricide ('frætrɪ,saɪd, 'freɪ-) *n* **1** the act of killing one's brother. **2** a person who kills his brother. [C15: from L, from *frater* brother + -CIDE]
▸**,fratri'cidal** *adj*

Frau (fraʊ) *n, pl* **Frauen** ('fraʊən) *or* **Fraus.** a married German woman: usually used as a title equivalent to *Mrs.* [from OHG *frouwa*]

fraud ❶ (frɔːd) *n* **1** deliberate deception, trickery, or cheating intended to gain an advantage. **2** an act or instance of such deception. **3** *Inf.* a person who acts in a false or deceitful way. [C14: from OF, from L *fraus* deception]

THESAURUS

humour, outlook, spirit, state, temper ◆ *vb* **14** = **construct**, assemble, build, constitute, fabricate, fashion, forge, form, institute, invent, make, manufacture, model, mould, put together, set up **15, 16** = **devise**, block out, compose, conceive, concoct, contrive, cook up, draft, draw up, form, formulate, hatch, map out, plan, shape, sketch **17** = **mount**, case, enclose, surround

frame-up *n* **1** *Slang* = **false charge**, fabrication, fit-up (*sl.*), put-up job, trumped-up charge

framework *n* **1, 2** = **structure**, core, fabric, foundation, frame, frame of reference, groundwork, plan, schema, shell, skeleton, the bare bones

franchise *n* **1** = **vote**, suffrage **2** = **right**, authorization, charter, exemption, freedom, immunity, prerogative, privilege

frank *adj* **1, 2** = **honest**, artless, blunt, candid, direct, downright, forthright, free, ingenuous, open, outright, outspoken, plain, plain-spoken, round, sincere, straightforward, straight from the shoulder (*inf.*), transparent, truthful, unconcealed, undisguised, unreserved, unrestricted, upfront (*inf.*)
Antonyms *adj* artful, crafty, cunning, evasive, indirect, inscrutable, reserved, reticent, secretive, shifty, shy, underhand

frankly *adv* **1** = **honestly**, candidly, in truth, to be honest **2** = **openly**, bluntly, directly, freely, overtly, plainly, straight, straight from the shoulder, without reserve

frankness *n* **1, 2** = **outspokenness**, absence of reserve, bluntness, candour, forthrightness, ingenuousness, laying it on the line, openness, plain speaking, truthfulness

frantic *adj* **1** = **distraught**, at one's wits' end, at the end of one's tether, berserk, beside oneself, distracted, furious, mad, overwrought, raging, raving, uptight (*inf.*), wild **2** = **hectic**, desperate, fraught (*inf.*), frenetic, frenzied
Antonyms *adj* calm, collected, composed, cool, laid-back, poised, self-possessed, together (*sl.*), unfazed (*inf.*), unruffled

fraternity *n* **1** = **association**, brotherhood, circle, clan, club, company, guild, league, order, set, sodality, union **2** = **companionship**, brotherhood, camaraderie, comradeship, fellowship, kinship

fraternize *vb* = **associate**, concur, consort, cooperate, go around with, hang out (*inf.*), hobnob, keep company, mingle, mix, socialize, sympathize, unite
Antonyms *vb* avoid, eschew, keep away from, shun, steer clear of

fraud *n* **1, 2** = **deception**, artifice, canard, cheat, chicane, chicanery, craft, deceit, double-dealing, duplicity, guile, hoax, humbug, imposture, scam (*sl.*), sharp practice, spuriousness, sting (*inf.*), stratagems, swindling, treachery, trickery **3** *Informal* = **impostor**, bluffer, charlatan, cheat, counterfeit, double-dealer, fake, forgery, fraudster, hoax, hoaxer, mountebank, phoney *or* phony (*inf.*), pretender, quack, sham, swindler
Antonyms *n* ≠ **deception:** fairness, good faith, hon-

DICTIONARY

fraudster ('frɔːdstə) *n* a swindler.

fraudulent ❶ ('frɔːdjʊlənt) *adj* **1** acting with or having the intent to deceive. **2** relating to or proceeding from fraud. [C15: from L *fraudulentus* deceitful]
▸ **'fraudulence** *n* ▸ **'fraudulently** *adv*

fraught ❶ (frɔːt) *adj* **1** (*usually postpositive* and foll. by *with*) filled or charged: *a venture fraught with peril.* **2** *Inf.* showing or producing tension or anxiety. [C14: from MDu. *vrachten,* from *vracht* FREIGHT]

Fräulein (*German* 'frɔylaɪn) *n, pl* **Fräulein** *or English* **Fräuleins.** an unmarried German woman: often used as a title equivalent to *Miss.* [from MHG *vrouwelīn,* dim. of *vrouwe* lady]

Fraunhofer lines ('fraunhəufə) *pl n* a set of dark lines appearing in the continuous emission spectrum of the sun. [C19: after Joseph von *Fraunhofer* (1787–1826), G physicist]

fraxinella (ˌfræksɪ'nɛlə) *n* another name for **gas plant.** [C17: from NL: a little ash tree, from L *frāxinus* ash]

fray[1] ❶ (freɪ) *n* **1** a noisy quarrel. **2** a fight or brawl. [C14: short for AFFRAY]

fray[2] ❶ (freɪ) *vb* **1** to wear or cause to wear away into loose threads, esp. at an edge or end. **2** to make or become strained or irritated. **3** to rub or chafe (another object). [C14: from F *frayer* to rub, from L *fricāre* to rub]

frazil ('freɪzɪl) *n* small pieces of ice that form in water moving turbulently enough to prevent the formation of a sheet of ice. [C19: from Canad. F, from F *fraisil* cinders, ult. from L *fax* torch]

frazzle ('fræzəl) *Inf.* ◆ *vb* **frazzles, frazzling, frazzled. 1** to make or become exhausted or weary. ◆ *n* **2** the state of being frazzled or exhausted. **3** **to a frazzle.** completely (esp. in **burnt to a frazzle**). [C19: prob. from ME *faselen* to fray, from *fasel* fringe; infl. by FRAY[2]]

freak ❶ (friːk) *n* **1** a person, animal, or plant that is abnormal or deformed. **2a** an object, event, etc., that is abnormal. **2b** (*as modifier*): *a freak storm.* **3** a personal whim or caprice. **4** *Inf.* a person who acts or dresses in a markedly unconventional way. **5** *Inf.* a person who is ardently fond of something specified: *a jazz freak.* ◆ *vb* **6** See **freak out.** [C16: from ?]
▸ **'freakish** *adj* ▸ **'freaky** *adj*

freak out *vb* (*adv*) *Inf.* to be or cause to be in a heightened emotional state.

freckle ('frɛkəl) *n* **1** a small brownish spot on the skin developed by exposure to sunlight. Technical name: **lentigo. 2** any small area of discoloration. ◆ *vb* **freckles, freckling, freckled. 3** to mark or become marked with freckles or spots. [C14: from ON *freknur*]
▸ **'freckled** *or* **'freckly** *adj*

free ❶ (friː) *adj* **freer, freest. 1** able to act at will; not under compulsion or restraint. **2a** not enslaved or confined. **2b** (*as n*): *land of the free.* **3** (*often postpositive* and foll. by *from*) not subject (to) or restricted (by some regulation, constraint, etc.): *free from pain.* **4** (of a country, etc.) autonomous or independent. **5** exempt from external direction: *free will.* **6** not subject to conventional constraints: *free verse.* **7** not exact or literal: *a free translation.* **8** provided without charge: *free entertainment.* **9** *Law.* (of property) **9a** not subject to payment of rent or performance of services; freehold. **9b** not subject to any burden or charge; unencumbered. **10** (*postpositive;* often foll. by *of* or *with*) ready or generous in using or giving: *free with advice.* **11** not occupied or in use; available: *a free cubicle.* **12** (of a person) not busy. **13** open or available to all. **14** without charge to the subscriber or user: *freepost; freephone.* **15** not fixed or joined; loose: *the free end of a chain.* **16** without obstruction or impediment: *free passage.* **17** *Chem.* chemically uncombined: *free nitrogen.* **18** *Logic.* denoting an occurrence of a variable not bound by a quantifier. Cf. **bound**[1] (sense 8). **19** (of routines in figure skating competitions) chosen by the competitor. **20** (of jazz) totally improvised. **21 for free.** *Nonstandard.* without charge or cost. **22 free and easy.** casual or tolerant; easy-going. **23 make free with.** to behave too familiarly towards. ◆ *adv* **24** in a free manner; freely. **25** without charge or cost. **26** *Naut.* with the wind blowing from the quarter. ◆ *vb* **frees, freeing, freed.** (*tr*) **27** to set at liberty; release. **28** to remove obstructions or impediments from. **29** (often foll. by *of* or *from*) to relieve or rid (of obstacles, pain, etc.). [OE *frēo*]
▸ **'freely** *adv* ▸ **'freeness** *n*

-free *adj combining form.* free from: *trouble-free; lead-free petrol.*

free alongside ship *adj* (of a shipment of goods) delivered to the dock without charge to the buyer, but excluding the cost of loading onto the vessel. Cf. **free on board.**

free association *n Psychoanal.* a method of exploring a person's unconscious by eliciting words and thoughts that are associated with key words provided by a psychoanalyst.

freebase ('friːˌbeɪs) *Sl.* ◆ *n* **1** cocaine that has been refined by heating it in ether or some other solvent. ◆ *vb* **freebases, freebasing, freebased. 2** to refine (cocaine) in this way. **3** to smoke or inhale the fumes from (refined cocaine).

freebie ('friːbɪ) *n Sl.* something provided without charge.

freeboard ('friːˌbɔːd) *n* the space or distance between the deck of a vessel and the waterline.

freebooter ❶ ('friːˌbuːtə) *n* a person, such as a pirate, living from plunder. [C16: from Du., from *vrijbuit* booty; see FILIBUSTER]
▸ **'freeboot** *vb* (*intr*)

freeborn ('friːˌbɔːn) *adj* **1** not born in slavery. **2** of or suitable for people not born in slavery.

Free Church *n Chiefly Brit.* any Protestant Church, esp. the Presbyterian, other than the Established Church.

free city *n* a sovereign or autonomous city.

freedman ('friːdˌmæn) *n, pl* **freedmen.** a man who has been freed from slavery.

freedom ❶ ('friːdəm) *n* **1** personal liberty, as from slavery, serfdom, etc. **2** liberation, as from confinement or bondage. **3** the quality or state of being free, esp. to enjoy political and civil liberties. **4** (usually foll. by *from*) exemption or immunity: *freedom from taxation.* **5** the right or privilege of unrestricted use or access: *the freedom of a city.* **6** autonomy, self-government, or independence. **7** the power or liberty to order one's own actions. **8** *Philosophy.* the quality, esp. of the will or the individual, of not being totally constrained. **9** ease or frankness of manner: *she talked with complete freedom.* **10** excessive familiarity of manner. **11** ease and grace, as of movement. [OE *frēodōm*]

freedom fighter *n* a militant revolutionary.

free energy *n* a thermodynamic property that expresses the capacity of a system to perform work under certain conditions.

free enterprise *n* an economic system in which commercial organizations compete for profit with little state control.

THESAURUS

esty, integrity, probity, rectitude, trustworthiness, virtue

fraudulent *adj* **1** = **deceitful**, counterfeit, crafty, criminal, crooked (*inf.*), deceptive, dishonest, double-dealing, duplicitous, false, knavish, phoney *or* phony (*inf.*), sham, spurious, swindling, treacherous
Antonyms *adj* above board, genuine, honest, honourable, lawful, principled, reputable, true, trustworthy, upright

fraught *adj* **1** *with* **with** = **filled**, abounding, accompanied, attended, bristling, charged, full, heavy, laden, replete, stuffed **2** *Informal* = **tense**, agitated, anxious, difficult, distracted, distressed, distressing, emotionally charged, emotive, hag-ridden, on tenterhooks, strung-up, tricky, trying, uptight (*inf.*), wired (*sl.*)

fray[1] *n* **1, 2** = **fight**, affray (*Law*), battle, battle royal, brawl, broil, clash, combat, conflict, disturbance, donnybrook, melee *or* mêlée, quarrel, riot, row, ruckus (*inf.*), rumble (*US & NZ sl.*), rumpus, scrimmage, scuffle, set-to (*inf.*), shindig (*inf.*), shindy (*inf.*), skirmish

fray[2] *vb* **1, 3** = **wear thin**, become threadbare, chafe, fret, rub, wear, wear away

frayed *adj* **1** = **worn**, frazzled, out at elbows, ragged, tattered, threadbare

freak *n* **1, 2a** = **oddity**, aberration, abnormality, abortion, anomaly, grotesque, malformation, monster, monstrosity, mutant, queer fish (*Brit. inf.*), *rara avis*, sport (*Biology*), teratism, weirdo *or* weirdie (*inf.*) ◆ *modifier* **2b** = **abnormal**, aberrant, atypical, bizarre, erratic, exceptional, fluky (*inf.*), fortuitous, odd, queer, unaccountable, unexpected, unforeseen, unparalleled, unpredictable, unusual ◆ *n* **3** = **whim**, caprice, crotchet, fad, fancy, folly, humour, irregularity, quirk, turn, twist, vagary, whimsy **5** *Informal* = **enthusiast**, addict, aficionado, buff (*inf.*), devotee, fan, fanatic, fiend (*inf.*), nut (*sl.*)

freakish *adj* **1, 2** = **odd**, aberrant, abnormal, fantastic, freaky (*sl.*), grotesque, malformed, monstrous, outlandish, outré, preternatural, strange, teratoid (*Biology*), unconventional, weird **3** = **whimsical**, arbitrary, capricious, changeable, erratic, fanciful, fitful, humorous, odd, unpredictable, vagarious (*rare*), wayward

freaky *adj* **1** = **weird**, abnormal, bizarre, crazy, far-out (*sl.*), freakish, odd, queer, rum (*Brit. sl.*), strange, unconventional, wild

free *adj* **1** = **allowed**, able, clear, disengaged, loose, open, permitted, unattached, unengaged, unhampered, unimpeded, unobstructed, unregulated, unrestricted, untrammelled **2** = **at liberty**, at large, footloose, independent, liberated, loose, off the hook (*sl.*), on the loose, uncommitted, unconstrained, unengaged, unfettered, unrestrained **4** = **independent**, autarchic, autonomous, democratic, emancipated, self-governing, self- ruling, sovereign **8** = **complimentary**, buckshee (*Brit. sl.*), for free (*inf.*), for nothing, free of charge, gratis, gratuitous, on the house, unpaid, without charge **11, 12** = **available**, at leisure, empty, extra, idle, not tied down, spare, unemployed, uninhabited, unoccupied, unused, vacant **22** **free and easy** = **relaxed**, casual, easy-going, informal, laid-back (*inf.*), lax, lenient, liberal, tolerant, unceremonious ◆ *adv* **24** = **freely**, abundantly, copiously, idly, loosely **25** = **without charge**, at no cost, for love, gratis ◆ *vb* **27** = **release**, deliver, discharge, disenthrall, emancipate, let go, let out, liberate, loose, manumit, set at liberty, set free, turn loose, unbridle, uncage, unchain, unfetter, unleash, untie **28, 29** = **clear**, cut loose, deliver, disengage, disentangle, exempt, extricate, ransom, redeem, relieve, rescue, rid, unburden, undo, unshackle
Antonyms *adj* ≠ **at liberty**: bound, captive, confined, dependent, fettered, immured, incarcerated, restrained, restricted, secured ◆ *vb* ≠ **release**: confine, imprison, incarcerate, inhibit, limit, restrain, restrict, straiten

freebooter *n* = **pirate**, bandit, brigand, buccaneer, cateran (*Scot.*), highwayman, looter, marauder, pillager, plunderer, raider, reiver (*dialect*), robber, rover

freedom *n* **4** = **exemption**, immunity, impunity, privilege **6** = **liberty**, autonomy, deliverance, emancipation, home rule, independence, manumission, release, self-government **7** = **licence**, ability, a free hand, blank cheque, carte blanche, discretion, elbowroom, facility, flexibility, free rein, latitude, leeway, opportunity, play, power, range, scope **9** = **openness**, abandon, candour, directness, ease, familiarity, frankness, informality, ingenuousness, lack of restraint *or* reserve, unconstraint **10** = **overfamiliarity**, boldness, brazenness, disrespect, forwardness, impertinence, laxity, licence, presumption
Antonyms *n* ≠ **liberty**: bondage, captivity, dependence, imprisonment, servitude, slavery, thraldom ≠ **licence**: limitation, restriction ≠ **open-**

free fall *n* **1** free descent of a body in which the gravitational force is the only force acting on it. **2** the part of a parachute descent before the parachute opens.
free flight *n* the flight of a rocket, missile, etc., when its engine has ceased to produce thrust.
free-for-all ❶ *n Inf.* **1** a disorganized brawl or argument, usually involving all those present. **2a** a contest, discussion, etc., that is open to everyone. **2b** (*as modifier*): *a free-for-all contest.*
free-form *adj Arts.* freely flowing, spontaneous.
free hand ❶ *n* **1** unrestricted freedom to act (esp. in **give (someone) a free hand**). ◆ *adj, adv* **freehand. 2** (done) by hand without the use of guiding instruments: *a freehand drawing.*
free-handed *adj* generous or liberal; unstinting.
▸ **ˌfree-ˈhandedly** *adv*
freehold (ˈfriːˌhəʊld) *Property law.* ◆ *n* **1a** tenure by which land is held in fee simple, fee tail, or for life. **1b** an estate held by such tenure. ◆ *adj* **2** relating to or having the nature of freehold.
▸ **ˈfreeholder** *n*
free house *n Brit.* a public house not bound to sell only one brewer's products.
free kick *n Soccer.* a place kick awarded for a foul or infringement.
freelance (ˈfriːˌlɑːns) *n* **1a** Also called: **freelancer.** a self-employed person, esp. a writer or artist, who is hired to do specific assignments. **1b** (*as modifier*): *a freelance journalist.* **2** (in medieval Europe) a mercenary soldier or adventurer. ◆ *vb* **freelances, freelancing, freelanced. 3** to work as a freelance on (an assignment, etc.). ◆ *adv* **4** as a freelance. [C19 (in sense 2): later applied to politicians, writers, etc.]
free-living *adj* **1** given to ready indulgence of the appetites. **2** (of animals and plants) not parasitic.
▸ **ˌfree-ˈliver** *n*
freeloader (ˈfriːˌləʊdə) *n Sl.* a person who habitually depends on others for food, shelter, etc.
free love *n* the practice of sexual relationships without fidelity to a single partner.
freeman (ˈfriːmən) *n, pl* **freemen. 1** a person who is not a slave. **2** a person who enjoys political and civil liberties. **3** a person who enjoys a privilege, such as the freedom of a city.
free market *n* **a** an economic system that allows supply and demand to regulate prices, wages, etc., rather than government policy. **b** (*as modifier*): *a free-market economy.*
freemartin (ˈfriːˌmɑːtɪn) *n* the female of a pair of twin calves of unlike sex that is imperfectly developed and sterile. [C17: from ?]
Freemason (ˈfriːˌmeɪsᵊn) *n* a member of the widespread secret order, constituted in London in 1717, of **Free and Accepted Masons,** pledged to brotherly love, faith, and charity. Sometimes shortened to **Mason.**
freemasonry (ˈfriːˌmeɪsᵊnrɪ) *n* natural or tacit sympathy and understanding.
Freemasonry (ˈfriːˌmeɪsᵊnrɪ) *n* **1** the institutions, rites, practices, etc., of Freemasons. **2** Freemasons collectively.
free on board *adj* (of a shipment of goods) delivered on board ship or other carrier without charge to the buyer. Cf. **free alongside ship.**
free port *n* **1** a port open to all commercial vessels on equal terms. **2** a port that permits the duty-free entry of foreign goods intended for re-export.
free radical *n* an atom or group of atoms containing at least one unpaired electron and existing for a brief period of time before reacting to produce a stable molecule.
free-range *adj Chiefly Brit.* kept or produced in natural conditions: *free-range eggs.*
free-select *vb* (*tr*) *Austral. history.* to select (areas of crown land) and acquire the freehold by a series of annual payments.
▸ **ˈfree-seˈlection** *n* ▸ **ˈfree-seˈlector** *n*
freesia (ˈfriːzɪə) *n* a plant of Southern Africa, cultivated for its white, yellow, or pink tubular fragrant flowers. [C19: NL, after F. H. T. *Freese* (died 1876), G physician]
free skating *n* either of two parts in a figure-skating competition in which the skater chooses the sequence of figures and the music and which are judged on technique and artistic presentation. The short programme consists of specified movements and the long programme is entirely the skater's own choice.
free space *n* a region that has no gravitational and electromagnetic fields. It is used as an absolute standard and was formerly referred to as a vacuum.
free-spoken *adj* speaking frankly or without restraint.
▸ **ˌfree-ˈspokenly** *adv*
freestanding (ˌfriːˈstændɪŋ) *adj* not attached to or supported by another object.
freestone (ˈfriːˌstəʊn) *n* **1** any fine-grained stone, esp. sandstone or limestone, that can be worked in any direction without breaking. **2** *Bot.* a fruit, such as a peach, in which the flesh separates readily from the stone.
freestyle (ˈfriːˌstaɪl) *n* **1** a competition or race, as in swimming, in which each participant may use a style of his or her choice instead of a specified style. **2a International freestyle.** an amateur style of wrestling with an agreed set of rules. **2b** Also called: **all-in wrestling.** a style of professional wrestling with no internationally agreed set of rules.
freethinker ❶ (ˌfriːˈθɪŋkə) *n* a person who forms his ideas and opinions independently of authority or accepted views, esp. in matters of religion.
▸ **free thought** *n*
free trade *n* **1** international trade that is free of such government interference as protective tariffs. **2** *Arch.* smuggling.
free verse *n* unrhymed verse without a metrical pattern.
freeware (ˈfriːˌwɛə) *n* computer software that may be distributed and used without payment.
freeway (ˈfriːˌweɪ) *n US.* **1** an expressway. **2** a major road that can be used without paying a toll.
freewheel ❶ (ˌfriːˈwiːl) *n* **1** a ratchet device in the rear hub of a bicycle wheel that permits the wheel to rotate freely while the pedals are stationary. ◆ *vb* **2** (*intr*) to coast on a bicycle using the freewheel.
free will *n* **1a** the apparent human ability to make choices that are not externally determined. **1b** the doctrine that such human freedom of choice is not illusory. Cf. **determinism. 2** the ability to make a choice without outside coercion: *he left of his own free will.*
Free World *n* **the.** the non-Communist countries collectively.
freeze ❶ (friːz) *vb* **freezes, freezing, froze, frozen. 1** to change (a liquid) into a solid as a result of a reduction in temperature, or (of a liquid) to solidify in this way. **2** (when *intr*, sometimes foll. by *over* or *up*) to cover, clog, or harden with ice, or become so covered, clogged, or hardened. **3** to fix fast or become fixed (to something) because of the action of frost. **4** (*tr*) to preserve (food) by subjection to extreme cold, as in a freezer. **5** to feel or cause to feel the sensation or effects of extreme cold. **6** to die or cause to die of extreme cold. **7** to become or cause to become paralysed, fixed, or motionless, esp. through fear, shock, etc. **8** (*tr*) to cause (moving film) to stop at a particular frame. **9** to make or become formal, haughty, etc., in manner. **10** (*tr*) to fix (prices, incomes, etc.) at a particular level. **11** (*tr*) to forbid by law the exchange, liquidation, or collection of (loans, assets, etc.). **12** (*tr*) to stop (a process) at a particular stage of development. **13** (*intr;* foll. by *onto*) *Inf., chiefly US.* to cling. ◆ *n* **14** the act of freezing or state of being frozen. **15** *Meteorol.* a spell of temperatures below freezing point, usually over a wide area. **16** the fixing of incomes, prices, etc., by legislation. ◆ *sentence substitute.* **17** *Chiefly US.* a command to stop instantly or risk being shot. [OE *frēosan*]
▸ **ˈfreezable** *adj*
freeze-dry *vb* **freeze-dries, freeze-drying, freeze-dried.** (*tr*) to preserve (a substance) by rapid freezing and subsequently drying in a vacuum.
freeze-frame *n* **1** *Films, television.* a single frame of a film repeated to give an effect like a still photograph. **2** *Video.* a single frame of a video recording viewed as a still by stopping the tape.
freeze out *vb* (*tr, adv*) *Inf.* to exclude, as by unfriendly behaviour, etc.
freezer (ˈfriːzə) *n* an insulated cold-storage cabinet for long-term storage of perishable foodstuffs. Also called: **deepfreeze.**
freezing ❶ (ˈfriːzɪŋ) *adj Inf.* extremely cold.
freezing point *n* the temperature below which a liquid turns into a solid.
freezing works *n Austral. & NZ.* a slaughterhouse at which animal carcasses are frozen for export.
freight ❶ (freɪt) *n* **1a** commercial transport that is slower and cheaper than express. **1b** the price charged for such transport. **1c** goods transported by this means. **1d** (*as modifier*): *freight transport.* **2** *Chiefly Brit.* a ship's cargo or part of it. ◆ *vb* (*tr*) **3** to load with goods for transport. [C16: from MDu *vrecht*, var. of *vracht*]
freightage (ˈfreɪtɪdʒ) *n* **1** the commercial conveyance of goods. **2** the goods so transported. **3** the price charged for such conveyance.
freighter (ˈfreɪtə) *n* **1** a ship or aircraft designed for transporting cargo. **2** a person concerned with the loading of a ship.
freightliner (ˈfreɪtˌlaɪnə) *n Trademark.* a type of goods train carrying containers that can be transferred onto lorries or ships.
French (frentʃ) *n* **1** the official language of France: also an official language of Switzerland, Belgium, Canada, and certain other countries. Historically, French is an Indo-European language belonging to the Romance group. **2 the French.** (*functioning as pl*) the natives, citizens, or inhabitants of France collectively. ◆ *adj* **3** relating to, denoting, or characteristic of France, the French, or their language. **4** (in Canada) of French Canadians. [OE *Frencisc* French, Frankish]
▸ **ˈFrenchness** *n*
French bread *n* white bread in a long slender loaf that has a crisp brown crust.

THESAURUS

ness: caution, restraint ≠ **overfamiliarity:** respectfulness
free-for-all *n* **1** *Informal* = **fight**, affray (*Law*), brawl, donnybrook, dust-up (*inf.*), fracas, melee *or* mêlée, riot, row, scrimmage, shindig (*inf.*), shindy (*inf.*)
free hand *n* **1** = **freedom**, authority, blank cheque, carte blanche, discretion, latitude, liberty, scope
freethinker *n* = **unbeliever**, agnostic, deist, doubter, infidel, sceptic
freewheel *vb* **2** = **coast**, drift, float, glide
freeze *vb* **1, 5** = **chill**, benumb, congeal, glaciate, harden, ice over *or* up, stiffen **12** = **suspend**, fix, hold up, inhibit, peg, stop
freezing *adj Informal* = **icy**, arctic, biting, bitter, chill, chilled, cold as ice, cutting, frostbound, frosty, glacial, numbing, parky (*Brit. inf.*), penetrating, polar, raw, Siberian, wintry
freight *n* **1a** = **transportation**, carriage, conveyance, shipment **1c, 2** = **cargo**, bales, bulk, burden, consignment, contents, goods, haul, lading, load, merchandise, payload, tonnage
French *adj* **3** = **Gallic**

DICTIONARY

French Canadian *n* **1** a Canadian citizen whose native language is French. ◆ *adj* **French-Canadian. 2** of or relating to French Canadians or their language.

French chalk *n* a variety of talc used to mark cloth, remove grease stains, or as a dry lubricant.

French doors *pl n* the US and Canad. name for **French windows.**

French dressing *n* a salad dressing made from oil and vinegar with seasonings; vinaigrette.

French fried potatoes *pl n* a more formal name for chips. Often shortened to **French fries, fries.**

French horn *n Music.* a valved brass instrument with a funnel-shaped mouthpiece and a tube of conical bore coiled into a spiral.

Frenchify ('frɛntʃɪˌfaɪ) *vb* **Frenchifies, Frenchifying, Frenchified.** *Inf.* to make or become French in appearance, etc.

French kiss *n* a kiss involving insertion of the tongue into the partner's mouth.

French knickers *pl n* women's wide-legged underpants.

French leave *n* an unauthorized or unannounced absence or departure. [C18: alluding to a custom in France of leaving without saying goodbye to one's host or hostess]

French letter *n Brit.* a slang term for **condom.**

Frenchman ('frɛntʃmən) *n, pl* **Frenchmen.** a native, citizen, or inhabitant of France.
▸ **'French,woman** *fem n*

French mustard *n* a mild mustard paste made with vinegar rather than water.

French polish *n* **1** a varnish for wood consisting of shellac dissolved in alcohol. **2** the gloss finish produced by this polish.

French-polish *vb* to treat with French polish or give a French polish (to).

French seam *n* a seam in which the edges are not visible.

French toast *n* **1** *Brit.* toast cooked on one side only. **2** bread dipped in beaten egg and lightly fried.

French windows *pl n (sometimes sing) Brit.* a pair of casement windows extending to floor level and opening onto a balcony, garden, etc.

frenetic ❶ (frɪ'nɛtɪk) *adj* distracted or frantic. [C14: via OF, from L, from Gk, from *phrenitis* insanity, from *phrēn* mind]
▸ **fre'netically** *adv*

frenum ('friːnəm) *n, pl* **frena** (-nə). a variant spelling (esp. US) of **fraenum.**

frenzy ❶ ('frɛnzɪ) *n, pl* **frenzies. 1** violent mental derangement. **2** wild excitement or agitation. **3** a bout of wild or agitated activity: *a frenzy of preparations.* ◆ *vb* **frenzies, frenzying, frenzied. 4** *(tr)* to drive into a frenzy. [C14: from OF, from LL *phrēnēsis* madness, from LGk, ult. from Gk *phrēn* mind]
▸ **'frenzied** *adj*

Freon ('friːˌɒn) *n Trademark.* any of a group of chemically unreactive gaseous or liquid derivatives of methane in which hydrogen atoms have been replaced by chlorine and fluorine atoms: used as aerosol propellants, refrigerants, and solvents.

freq. *abbrev. for:* **1** frequent(ly). **2** frequentative.

frequency ❶ ('friːkwənsɪ) *n, pl* **frequencies. 1** the state of being frequent. **2** the number of times that an event occurs within a given period. **3** *Physics.* the number of times that a periodic function or vibration repeats itself in a specified time, often 1 second. It is usually measured in hertz. **4** *Statistics.* **4a** the number of individuals in a class (**absolute frequency**). **4b** the ratio of this number to the total number of individuals under survey (**relative frequency**). **5** *Ecology.* the number of individuals of a species within a given area. [C16: from L, from *frequēns* crowded]

frequency distribution *n Statistics.* the function of the distribution of a sample corresponding to the probability density function of the underlying population and tending to it as the sample size increases.

frequency modulation *n* a method of transmitting information using a radio-frequency carrier wave. The frequency of the carrier wave is varied in accordance with the amplitude of the input signal, the amplitude of the carrier remaining unchanged. Cf. **amplitude modulation.**

frequent ❶ *adj* ('friːkwənt). **1** recurring at short intervals. **2** habitual. ◆ *vb* (frɪ'kwɛnt). **3** *(tr)* to visit repeatedly or habitually. [C16: from L *frequēns* numerous]
▸ **ˌfrequen'tation** *n* ▸ **fre'quenter** *n* ▸ **'frequently** *adv*

frequentative (frɪ'kwɛntətɪv) *Grammar.* ◆ *adj* **1** denoting an aspect of verbs in some languages used to express repeated or habitual action. **2** (in English) denoting a verb or an affix meaning repeated action, such as the verb *wrestle,* from *wrest.* ◆ *n* **3** a frequentative verb or affix.

fresco ('frɛskəʊ) *n, pl* **frescoes** *or* **frescos. 1** a very durable method of wall-painting using watercolours on wet plaster. **2** a painting done in this way. [C16: from It.: fresh plaster, from *fresco* (adj) fresh, cool, of Gmc origin]

fresh ❶ (frɛʃ) *adj* **1** newly made, harvested, etc.: *fresh bread; fresh strawberries.* **2** newly acquired, found, etc.: *fresh publications.* **3** novel; original: *a fresh outlook.* **4** most recent: *fresh developments.* **5** further; additional: *fresh supplies.* **6** not canned, frozen, or otherwise preserved: *fresh fruit.* **7** (of water) not salt. **8** bright or clear: *a fresh morning.* **9** chilly or invigorating: *a fresh breeze.* **10** not tired; alert. **11** not worn or faded: *fresh colours.* **12** having a healthy or ruddy appearance. **13** newly or just arrived: *fresh from the presses.* **14** youthful or inexperienced. **15** *Inf.* presumptuous or disrespectful; forward. ◆ *n* **16** the fresh part or time of something. **17** another name for **freshet.** ◆ *adv* **18** in a fresh manner. [OE *fersc* fresh, unsalted]
▸ **'freshly** *adv* ▸ **'freshness** *n*

fresh breeze *n* a wind of force 5 on the Beaufort scale, blowing at speeds between 19 and 24 mph.

freshen ❶ ('frɛʃən) *vb* **1** to make or become fresh or fresher. **2** (often foll. by *up*) to refresh (oneself), esp. by washing. **3** *(intr)* (of the wind) to increase.

fresher ('frɛʃə) *or* **freshman** ('frɛʃmən) *n, pl* **freshers** *or* **freshmen.** a first-year student at college or university.

freshet ('frɛʃɪt) *n* **1** the sudden overflowing of a river caused by heavy rain or melting snow. **2** a stream of fresh water emptying into the sea.

freshwater ('frɛʃˌwɔːtə) *n (modifier)* **1** of or living in fresh water. **2** (esp. of a sailor who has not sailed on the sea) inexperienced. **3** *US.* little known: *a freshwater school.*

fresnel ('freɪnɛl) *n* a unit of frequency equivalent to 10^{12} hertz. [C20: after A. J. *Fresnel* (1788–1827), F physicist]

fret[1] ❶ (frɛt) *vb* **frets, fretting, fretted. 1** to distress or be distressed. **2** to rub or wear away. **3** to feel or give annoyance or vexation. **4** to eat away or be eaten away, as by chemical action. **5** *(tr)* to make by wearing away; erode. ◆ *n* **6** a state of irritation or anxiety. [OE *fretan* to eat]

fret[2] (frɛt) *n* **1** a repetitive geometrical figure, esp. one used as an ornamental border. **2** such a pattern made in relief; fretwork. ◆ *vb* **frets, fretting, fretted. 3** *(tr)* to ornament with fret or fretwork. [C14: from OF *frete* interlaced design used on a shield, prob. of Gmc origin]
▸ **'fretless** *adj*

fret[3] (frɛt) *n* any of several small metal bars set across the fingerboard of a musical instrument of the lute, guitar, or viol family at various points along its length so as to produce the desired notes. [C16: from ?]
▸ **'fretless** *adj*

fretboard ('frɛtbɔːd) *n* a fingerboard with frets on a stringed instrument.

THESAURUS

frenetic *adj* = **wild,** demented, distraught, excited, fanatical, frantic, frenzied, hyped up (*sl.*), insane, mad, maniacal, obsessive, overwrought, unbalanced

frenzied *adj* **4** = **uncontrolled,** agitated, all het up (*inf.*), berserk, convulsive, distracted, distraught, excited, feverish, frantic, frenetic, furious, hysterical, mad, maniacal, rabid, wild

frenzy *n* **1, 2** = **fury,** aberration, agitation, delirium, derangement, distraction, hysteria, insanity, lunacy, madness, mania, paroxysm, passion, rage, seizure, transport, turmoil **3** = **fit,** bout, burst, convulsion, outburst, paroxysm, spasm
Antonyms *n* ≠ **fury:** calm, collectedness, composure, coolness, sanity

frequency *n* **1** = **recurrence,** constancy, frequentness, periodicity, prevalence, repetition

frequent *adj* **1, 2** = **common,** constant, continual, customary, everyday, familiar, habitual, incessant, numerous, persistent, recurrent, recurring, reiterated, repeated, usual ◆ *vb* **3** = **visit,** attend, be a regular customer of, be found at, hang out at (*inf.*), haunt, patronize, resort
Antonyms *adj* ≠ **common:** few, few and far between, infrequent, occasional, rare, scanty, sporadic ◆ *vb* ≠ **visit:** avoid, keep away, shun, spurn

frequenter *n* **3** = **regular visitor,** client, fan, habitué, haunter, patron, regular, regular customer

frequently *adv* **1, 2** = **often,** commonly, customarily, habitually, many a time, many times, much, not infrequently, oft, oftentimes (*arch.*), over and over again, repeatedly, thick and fast, very often
Antonyms *adv* hardly ever, infrequently, occasionally, once in a blue moon (*inf.*), rarely, seldom

fresh *adj* **3, 4** = **new,** different, groundbreakkng, latest, left-field (*inf.*), modern, modernistic, new-fangled, novel, original, recent, this season's, unconventional, unusual, up-to-date **5** = **additional,** added, auxiliary, extra, further, more, other, renewed, supplementary **6** = **natural,** crude, green, raw, uncured, undried, unprocessed, unsalted **8, 9** = **invigorating,** bracing, bright, brisk, clean, clear, cool, crisp, pure, refreshing, spanking, sparkling, stiff, sweet, unpolluted **10** = **lively,** alert, bouncing, bright, bright-eyed and bushy-tailed (*inf.*), chipper (*inf.*), energetic, full of beans (*inf.*), full of vim and vigour (*inf.*), invigorated, keen, like a new man, refreshed, rested, restored, revived, sprightly, spry, vigorous, vital **11** = **vivid,** dewy, undimmed, unfaded, unwearied, unwithered, verdant, young **12** = **rosy,** blooming, clear, fair, florid, glowing, good, hardy, healthy, ruddy, wholesome **14** = **inexperienced,** artless, callow, green, natural, new, raw, uncultivated, untrained, untried, youthful **15** *Informal* = **cheeky,** bold, brazen, disrespectful, familiar, flip (*inf.*), forward, impudent, insolent, pert, presumptuous, sassy (*US inf.*), saucy, smart-alecky (*inf.*)
Antonyms *adj* ≠ **new:** dull, old, ordinary, stereotyped, trite ≠ **natural:** frozen, pickled, preserved, salted, tinned ≠ **invigorating:** impure, musty, stale, warm ≠ **lively:** exhausted, weary ≠ **vivid:** old, weary ≠ **rosy:** pallid, sickly ≠ **inexperienced:** experienced, old ≠ **cheeky:** well-mannered

freshen *vb* **1, 2** = **refresh,** enliven, freshen up, liven up, restore, revitalize, rouse, spruce up, titivate

freshness *n* **3, 4** = **novelty,** innovativeness, inventiveness, newness, originality **11** = **cleanness,** bloom, brightness, clearness, dewiness, glow, shine, sparkle, vigour, wholesomeness

fret[1] *vb* **1** = **worry,** agonize, anguish, brood, lose sleep over, obsess about, upset *or* distress oneself **2** = **rub,** abrade, chafe, erode, fray, gall, wear, wear away **3** = **annoy,** agitate, bother, chagrin, distress, disturb, gall, goad, grieve, harass, irk, irritate, nag, nettle, peeve (*inf.*), pique, provoke, rankle with, rile, ruffle, torment, trouble, vex

fretful ⓣ ('frɛtful) *adj* peevish, irritable, or upset.
▸'**fretfully** *adv* ▸'**fretfulness** *n*

fret saw *n* a fine-toothed saw with a long thin narrow blade, used for cutting designs in thin wood or metal.

fretwork ('frɛt,wɜːk) *n* decorative geometrical carving or openwork.

Freudian ('frɔɪdɪən) *adj* **1** of or relating to Sigmund Freud (1856–1939), Austrian psychiatrist, or his ideas. ◆ *n* **2** a person who follows or believes in the basic ideas of Sigmund Freud.
▸'**Freudian,ism** *n*

Freudian slip *n* any action, such as a slip of the tongue, that may reveal an unconscious thought.

Fri. *abbrev. for* Friday.

friable ⓣ ('fraɪəbᵊl) *adj* easily broken up; crumbly. [C16: from L, from *friāre* to crumble]
▸,**fria'bility** *or* '**friableness** *n*

friar ('fraɪə) *n* a member of any of various chiefly mendicant religious orders of the Roman Catholic Church. [C13 *frere*, from OF: brother, from L *frāter* BROTHER]

friar's balsam *n* a compound containing benzoin, mixed with hot water and used as an inhalant to relieve colds and sore throats.

friary ('fraɪərɪ) *n, pl* **friaries**. *Christianity*. a convent or house of friars.

fricandeau ('frɪkən,dəʊ) *n, pl* **fricandeaus** *or* **fricandeaux** (-,dəʊz). a larded and braised veal fillet. [C18: from OF, prob. based on FRICASSEE]

fricassee (,frɪkə'siː, 'frɪkəsɪ) *n* **1** stewed meat, esp. chicken or veal, served in a thick white sauce. ◆ *vb* **fricassees, fricasseeing, fricasseed. 2** (*tr*) to prepare (meat, etc.) as a fricassee. [C16: from OF, from *fricasser* to fricassee]

fricative ('frɪkətɪv) *n* **1** a consonant produced by partial occlusion of the airstream, such as (f) or (z). ◆ *adj* **2** relating to or denoting a fricative. [C19: from NL, from L *fricāre* to rub]

friction ⓣ ('frɪkʃən) *n* **1** a resistance encountered when one body moves relative to another body with which it is in contact. **2** the act, effect, or an instance of rubbing one object against another. **3** disagreement or conflict. [C16: from F, from L *frictiō* a rubbing, from *fricāre* to rub]
▸'**frictional** *adj* ▸'**frictionless** *adj*

Friday ('fraɪdɪ) *n* **1** the sixth day of the week; fifth day of the working week. **2** See **man Friday**. [OE *Frīgedæg*]

fridge (frɪdʒ) *n* short for **refrigerator**.

fried (fraɪd) *vb* the past tense and past participle of **fry**[1].

friend ⓣ (frɛnd) *n* **1** a person known well to another and regarded with liking, affection, and loyalty. **2** an acquaintance or associate. **3** an ally in a fight or cause. **4** a fellow member of a party, society, etc. **5** a patron or supporter. **6 be friends (with)**. to be friendly (with). **7 make friends (with)**. to become friendly (with). ◆ *vb* **8** (*tr*) an archaic word for **befriend**. [OE *frēond*]
▸'**friendless** *adj* ▸'**friendship** *n*

Friend (frɛnd) *n* a member of the Religious Society of Friends; Quaker.

friend at court *n* an influential acquaintance who can promote one's interests.

friendly ⓣ ('frɛndlɪ) *adj* **friendlier, friendliest. 1** showing or expressing liking, goodwill, or trust. **2** on the same side; not hostile. **3** tending or disposed to help or support: *a friendly breeze helped them escape.* ◆ *n, pl* **friendlies. 4** Also: **friendly match**. *Sport*. a match played for its own sake.
▸'**friendlily** *adv* ▸'**friendliness** *n*

-friendly *adj combining form*. helpful, easy, or good for the person or thing specified: *ozone-friendly*.

friendly fire *n Mil*. firing by one's own side, esp. when it harms one's own personnel.

friendly society *n Brit*. an association of people who pay regular dues or other sums in return for old-age pensions, sickness benefits, etc.

Friends of the Earth *n* an organization of environmentalists and conservationists.

frier ('fraɪə) *n* a variant spelling of **fryer**. See **fry**[1].

fries (fraɪz) *pl n* short for **French fried potatoes**; chips.

Friesian ('friːʒən) *n* **1** *Brit*. any of several breeds of black-and-white dairy cattle having a high milk yield. **2** see **Frisian**.

frieze[1] (friːz) *n* **1** *Archit*. **1a** the horizontal band between the architrave and cornice of a classical entablature. **1b** the upper part of the wall of a room, below the cornice. **2** any ornamental band on a wall. [C16: from F *frise*, ?from Med. L *frisium*, changed from L *Phrygium* Phrygian (work), from Phrygia, famous for embroidery in gold]

frieze[2] (friːz) *n* a heavy woollen fabric used for coats, etc. [C15: from OF, from MDu. ?from *Vriese* Frisian]

frigate ('frɪgɪt) *n* **1** a medium-sized square-rigged warship of the 18th and 19th centuries. **2a** *Brit*. a warship smaller than a destroyer. **2b** *US*. (formerly) a warship larger than a destroyer. **2c** *US*. a small escort vessel. [C16: from F *frégate*, from It. *fregata*, from ?]

frigate bird *n* a bird of tropical and subtropical seas, having a long bill, a wide wingspan, and a forked tail.

fright ⓣ (fraɪt) *n* **1** sudden fear or alarm. **2** a sudden alarming shock. **3** *Inf*. a horrifying or ludicrous person or thing: *she looks a fright*. **4 take fright**. to become frightened. ◆ *vb* **5** a poetic word for **frighten**. [OE *fryhto*]

frighten ⓣ ('fraɪtᵊn) *vb* (*tr*) **1** to terrify; scare. **2** to drive or force to go (away, off, out, in, etc.) by making afraid.
▸'**frightener** *n* ▸'**frighteningly** *adv*

frightful ⓣ ('fraɪtful) *adj* **1** very alarming or horrifying. **2** unpleasant, annoying, or extreme: *a frightful hurry*.
▸'**frightfully** *adv* ▸'**frightfulness** *n*

frigid ⓣ ('frɪdʒɪd) *adj* **1** formal or stiff in behaviour or temperament. **2** (esp. of women) lacking sexual responsiveness. **3** characterized by physical coldness: *a frigid zone*. [C15: from L *frigidus* cold, from *frīgēre* to be cold]
▸**fri'gidity** *or* '**frigidness** *n* ▸'**frigidly** *adv*

Frigid Zone *n* the cold region inside the Arctic or Antarctic Circle where the sun's rays are very oblique.

frijol (*Spanish* fri'xol) *n, pl* **frijoles** (*Spanish* -'xoles). a variety of bean extensively cultivated for food in Mexico. [C16: from Sp., ult. from L *phaseolus*, from Gk *phasēlos* bean with edible pod]

frill ⓣ (frɪl) *n* **1** a gathered, ruched, or pleated strip of cloth sewn on at one edge only, as on garments, as ornament, or to give extra body. **2** a

THESAURUS

fretful *adj* = **irritable**, captious, complaining, cross, crotchety (*inf.*), edgy, fractious, out of sorts, peevish, petulant, querulous, short-tempered, splenetic, testy, tetchy, touchy, uneasy

friable *adj* = **crumbly**, brittle, crisp, powdery, pulverizable

friction *n* **1, 2** = **rubbing**, abrasion, attrition, chafing, erosion, fretting, grating, irritation, rasping, resistance, scraping, wearing away **3** = **hostility**, animosity, antagonism, bad blood, bad feeling, bickering, conflict, disagreement, discontent, discord, disharmony, dispute, dissension, incompatibility, opposition, resentment, rivalry, wrangling

friend *n* **1** = **companion**, Achates, alter ego, boon companion, bosom friend, buddy (*inf.*), china (*Brit. sl.*), chum (*inf.*), cock (*Brit. inf.*), comrade, confidant, crony, familiar, homeboy (*sl., chiefly US*), intimate, mate (*inf.*), pal, partner, playmate, soul mate **2, 3, 5** = **supporter**, adherent, advocate, ally, associate, backer, benefactor, partisan, patron, protagonist, well-wisher
Antonyms *n* adversary, antagonist, competitor, enemy, foe, opponent, rival

friendless *adj* **1** = **alone**, abandoned, alienated, all alone, cut off, deserted, estranged, forlorn, forsaken, isolated, lonely, lonesome, ostracized, shunned, solitary, unattached, with no one to turn to, without a friend in the world, without ties

friendliness *n* **1-3** = **amiability**, affability, companionability, congeniality, conviviality, geniality, kindliness, mateyness *or* matiness (*Brit. inf.*), neighbourliness, open arms, sociability, warmth

friendly *adj* **1-3** = **amiable**, affable, affectionate, amicable, attached, attentive, auspicious, beneficial, benevolent, benign, chummy (*inf.*), close, clubby, companionable, comradely, conciliatory, confiding, convivial, cordial, familiar, favourable, fond, fraternal, genial, good, helpful, intimate, kind, kindly, neighbourly, on good terms, on visiting terms, outgoing, pally (*inf.*), peaceable, propitious, receptive, sociable, sympathetic, thick (*inf.*), welcoming, well-disposed
Antonyms *adj* antagonistic, belligerent, cold, contentious, distant, inauspicious, sinister, uncongenial, unfriendly

friendship *n* **1** = **friendliness**, affection, affinity, alliance, amity, attachment, benevolence, closeness, concord, familiarity, fondness, good-fellowship, goodwill, harmony, intimacy, love, rapport, regard
Antonyms *n* animosity, antagonism, antipathy, aversion, bad blood, conflict, enmity, hatred, hostility, resentment, strife, unfriendliness

fright *n* **1, 2** = **fear**, alarm, apprehension, (blue) funk (*inf.*), cold sweat, consternation, dismay, dread, fear and trembling, horror, panic, quaking, scare, shock, terror, the shivers, trepidation **3** *Informal* = **sight** (*inf.*), eyesore, frump, mess (*inf.*), scarecrow
Antonyms *n* ≠ **fear**: boldness, bravery, courage, pluck, valor

frighten *vb* **1** = **scare**, affright (*arch.*), alarm, appal, cow, daunt, dismay, freeze one's blood, get the wind up, intimidate, petrify, put the wind up (someone) (*inf.*), scare (someone) stiff, shock, startle, terrify, terrorize, throw into a fright, throw into a panic, unman, unnerve
Antonyms *vb* allay, assuage, calm, comfort, encourage, hearten, reassure, soothe

frightened *adj* **1** = **afraid**, abashed, affrighted (*arch.*), alarmed, cowed, dismayed, frozen, in a cold sweat, in a panic, in fear and trepidation, numb with fear, panicky, petrified, scared, scared shitless (*taboo sl.*), scared stiff, startled, terrified, terrorized, terror-stricken, unnerved

frightening *adj* **1** = **terrifying**, alarming, appalling, baleful, bloodcurdling, daunting, dismaying, dreadful, fearful, fearsome, hair-raising, horrifying, intimidating, menacing, scary (*inf.*), shocking, spooky (*inf.*), unnerving

frightful *adj* **1** = **terrifying**, alarming, appalling, awful, dire, dread, dreadful, fearful, from hell (*inf.*), ghastly, grim, grisly, gruesome, harrowing, hideous, horrendous, horrible, horrid, lurid, macabre, petrifying, shocking, terrible, traumatic, unnerving, unspeakable **2** = **dreadful**, annoying, awful, disagreeable, extreme, great, insufferable, terrible, terrific, unpleasant
Antonyms *adj* ≠ **terrifying**: attractive, beautiful, calming, lovely, nice, pleasant, soothing ≠ **dreadful**: moderate, pleasant, slight

frigid *adj* **1** = **unresponsive**, aloof, austere, cold as ice, cold-hearted, forbidding, formal, icy, lifeless, passionless, passive, repellent, rigid, stiff, unapproachable, unbending, unfeeling, unloving **3** = **cold**, arctic, chill, cool, frost-bound, frosty, frozen, gelid, glacial, icy, Siberian, wintry
Antonyms *adj* ≠ **unresponsive**: ardent, cordial, friendly, hospitable, hot, impassioned, passionate, responsive, sensual, warm ≠ **cold**: hot, stifling, sweltering, warm

frigidity *n* **1** = **unresponsiveness**, aloofness, austerity, chill, cold-heartedness, coldness, frostiness, iciness, impassivity, lack of response, lifelessness, passivity, touch-me-not attitude, unapproachability, wintriness

frill *n* **1, 2** = **ruffle**, flounce, furbelow, gathering,

ruff of hair or feathers around the neck of a dog or bird or a fold of skin around the neck of a reptile or amphibian. **3** (*often pl*) *Inf.* a superfluous or pretentious thing or manner; affectation: *he made a plain speech with no frills.* ◆ *vb* **4** (*tr*) to adorn or fit with a frill or frills. **5** to form into a frill or frills. [C14: ? of Flemish origin]
▸ **'frilliness** *n* ▸ **'frilly** *adj*

frilled lizard *n* a large arboreal insectivorous Australian lizard having an erectile fold of skin around the neck.

fringe ❶ (frɪndʒ) *n* **1** an edging consisting of hanging threads, tassels, etc. **2a** an outer edge; periphery. **2b** (*as modifier*): *a fringe area.* **3** (*modifier*) unofficial; not conventional in form: *fringe theatre.* **4** *Chiefly Brit.* a section of the front hair cut short over the forehead. **5** an ornamental border. **6** *Physics.* any of the light and dark bands produced by diffraction or interference of light. ◆ *vb* **fringes, fringing, fringed.** (*tr*) **7** to adorn with a fringe or fringes. **8** to be a fringe for. [C14: from OF *frenge,* ult. from L *fimbria* fringe, border]
▸ **'fringeless** *adj*

fringe benefit *n* an additional advantage, esp. a benefit provided by an employer to supplement an employee's regular pay.

fringing reef *n* a coral reef close to the shore to which it is attached, having a steep seaward edge.

frippery ❶ ('frɪpərɪ) *n, pl* **fripperies. 1** ornate or showy clothing or adornment. **2** ostentation. **3** trifles; trivia. [C16: from OF, from *frepe* frill, rag, from Med. L *faluppa* a straw, splinter, from ?]

Frisbee ('frɪzbɪ) *n Trademark.* a light plastic disc thrown with a spinning motion for recreation or in competition.

Frisian ('frɪʒən) *or* **Friesian** *n* **1** a language spoken in the NW Netherlands, parts of N Germany, and some of the adjacent islands. **2** a speaker of this language or a native or inhabitant of Friesland. ◆ *adj* **3** of or relating to this language, its speakers, or the peoples and culture of Friesland. [C16: from L *Frīsiī* people of northern Germany]

frisk ❶ (frɪsk) *vb* **1** (*intr*) to leap, move about, or act in a playful manner. **2** (*tr*) (esp. of animals) to whisk or wave briskly: *the dog frisked its tail.* **3** (*tr*) *Inf.* to search (someone) by feeling for concealed weapons, etc. ◆ *n* **4** a playful antic or movement. **5** *Inf.* an instance of frisking a person. [C16: from OF *frisque,* of Gmc origin]
▸ **'frisker** *n*

frisky ❶ ('frɪskɪ) *adj* **friskier, friskiest.** lively, high-spirited, or playful.
▸ **'friskily** *adv*

frisson *French.* (frisɔ̃) *n* a shiver; thrill. [C18 (but in common use only from C20): lit.: shiver]

frit (frɪt) *n* **1a** the basic materials, partially or wholly fused, for making glass, glazes for pottery, enamel, etc. **1b** a glassy substance used in some soft-paste porcelain. ◆ *vb* **frits, fritting, fritted. 2** (*tr*) to fuse (materials) in making frit. [C17: from It. *fritta,* lit.: fried, from *friggere* to fry, from L *frīgere*]

fritillary (frɪ'tɪlərɪ) *n, pl* **fritillaries. 1** a liliaceous plant having purple or white drooping bell-shaped flowers, typically marked in a chequered pattern. **2** any of various butterflies having brownish wings chequered with black and silver. [C17: from NL *fritillāria,* from L *fritillus* dice box; prob. with reference to the markings]

fritter[1] ❶ ('frɪtə) *vb* (*tr*) **1** (usually foll. by *away*) to waste: *to fritter away time.* **2** to break into small pieces. [C18: prob. from obs. *fitter* to break into small pieces, ult. from OE *fitt* a piece]

fritter[2] ('frɪtə) *n* a piece of food, such as apple, that is dipped in batter and fried in deep fat. [C14: from OF, from L *frictus* fried, from *frīgere* to fry]

frivolous ❶ ('frɪvələs) *adj* **1** not serious or sensible in content, attitude, or behaviour. **2** unworthy of serious or sensible treatment: *frivolous details.* [C15: from L *frīvolus*]
▸ **'frivolously** *adv* ▸ **'frivolousness** *or* **frivolity** (frɪ'vɒlɪtɪ) *n*

frizz (frɪz) *vb* **1** (of the hair, nap, etc.) to form or cause (the hair, etc.) to form tight curls or crisp tufts. ◆ *n* **2** hair that has been frizzed. **3** the state of being frizzed. [C19: from F *friser* to curl]

frizzle[1] ('frɪzᵊl) *vb* **frizzles, frizzling, frizzled. 1** to form (the hair) into tight crisp curls. ◆ *n* **2** a tight curl. [C16: prob. rel. to OE *frīs* curly]

frizzle[2] ❶ ('frɪzᵊl) *vb* **frizzles, frizzling, frizzled. 1** to scorch or be scorched, esp. with a sizzling noise. **2** (*tr*) to fry (bacon, etc.) until crisp. [C16: prob. blend of FRY[1] + SIZZLE]

frizzy ❶ ('frɪzɪ) *or* **frizzly** ('frɪzlɪ) *adj* **frizzier, frizziest** *or* **frizzlier, frizzliest.** (of the hair) in tight crisp wiry curls.
▸ **'frizziness** *or* **'frizzliness** *n*

fro (frəʊ) *adv* back or from. [C12: from ON *frā*]

frock (frɒk) *n* **1** a girl's or woman's dress. **2** a loose garment of several types, such as a peasant's smock. **3** a wide-sleeved outer garment worn by members of some religious orders. ◆ *vb* **4** (*tr*) to invest (a person) with the office of a cleric. [C14: from OF *froc*]

frock coat *n* a man's single- or double-breasted skirted coat, as worn in the 19th century.

Froebel ('frəʊbᵊl) *adj* of, denoting, or relating to a system of kindergarten education developed by Friedrich Froebel (1782–1852), German educator, or to the training and qualification of teachers to use this system.

frog[1] (frɒg) *n* **1** an insectivorous amphibian, having a short squat tailless body with a moist smooth skin and very long hind legs specialized for hopping. **2** any of various similar amphibians, such as the tree frog. **3** any spiked object that is used to support plant stems in a flower arrangement. **4 a frog in one's throat.** phlegm on the vocal cords that affects one's speech. [OE *frogga*]
▸ **'froggy** *adj*

frog[2] (frɒg) *n* **1** (*often pl*) a decorative fastening of looped braid or cord, as on a military uniform. **2** an attachment on a belt to hold the scabbard of a sword, etc. [C18: ? ult. from L *floccus* tuft of hair]
▸ **frogged** *adj* ▸ **'frogging** *n*

frog[3] (frɒg) *n* a tough elastic horny material in the centre of the sole of a horse's foot. [C17: from ?]

frog[4] (frɒg) *n* a plate of iron or steel to guide train wheels over an intersection of railway lines. [C19: from ?; ? a special use of FROG[1]]

Frog (frɒg) *or* **Froggy** ('frɒgɪ) *n, pl* **Frogs** *or* **Froggies.** *Brit. sl.* a derogatory word for a French person.

froghopper ('frɒg,hɒpə) *n* any small leaping insect whose larvae secrete a protective spittle-like substance around themselves.

frogman ('frɒgmən) *n, pl* **frogmen.** a swimmer equipped with a rubber suit, flippers, and breathing equipment for working underwater.

frogmarch ('frɒg,mɑːtʃ) *Chiefly Brit.* ◆ *n* **1** a method of carrying a resisting person in which each limb is held and the victim is carried horizontally and face downwards. **2** any method of making a person move against his will. ◆ *vb* **3** (*tr*) to carry in a frogmarch or cause to move forward unwillingly.

frogmouth ('frɒg,maʊθ) *n* a nocturnal insectivorous bird of SE Asia and Australia, similar to the nightjars.

frogspawn ('frɒg,spɔːn) *n* a mass of fertilized frogs' eggs surrounded by a protective nutrient jelly.

frog spit *or* **spittle** *n* **1** another name for **cuckoo spit. 2** a foamy mass of threadlike green algae floating on ponds.

frolic ❶ ('frɒlɪk) *n* **1** a light-hearted entertainment or occasion. **2** light-hearted activity; gaiety. ◆ *vb* **frolics, frolicking, frolicked. 3** (*intr*) to caper about. ◆ *adj* **4** *Arch.* full of fun; gay. [C16: from Du. *vrolijk,* from MDu. *vro* happy]
▸ **'frolicker** *n*

frolicsome ❶ ('frɒlɪksəm) *adj* merry and playful.
▸ **'frolicsomely** *adv*

from (frɒm; *unstressed* frəm) *prep* **1** used to indicate the original location, situation, etc.: *from behind the bushes.* **2** in a period of time starting at: *he lived from 1910 to 1970.* **3** used to indicate the distance between two things or places: *a hundred miles from here.* **4** used to indicate a lower amount: *from five to fifty pounds.* **5** showing the model of: *painted from life.* **6** used with the gerund to mark prohibition, etc.:

THESAURUS

purfle, ruche, ruching, ruff, tuck **3** *often plural* = **trimmings**, additions, affectation(s), bells and whistles, bits and pieces, decoration(s), dressing up, embellishments, extras, fanciness, fandangles, finery, frilliness, frippery, fuss, gewgaws, icing on the cake, jazz (*sl.*), mannerisms, nonsense, ornamentation, ostentation, superfluities, tomfoolery

frilly *adj* **1** = **ruffled**, fancy, flouncy, frothy, lacy, ruched

fringe *n* **1** = **border**, binding, edging, hem, tassel, trimming **2** = **edge**, borderline, limits, march, marches, margin, outskirts, perimeter, periphery ◆ *modifier* **3** = **unofficial**, unconventional, unorthodox ◆ *vb* **7, 8** = **border**, edge, enclose, skirt, surround, trim

fringed *adj* **8** = **edged**, befringed, bordered, margined, outlined, overhung

frippery *n* **1** = **decoration**, adornment, bauble, fandangle, gewgaw, icing on the cake, knickknack, ornament, toy, trinket **1, 2** = **frills**, fanciness, finery, flashiness, foppery, frilliness, fussiness, gaudiness, glad rags (*inf.*), meretriciousness, nonsense, ostentation, pretentiousness, showiness, tawdriness

frisk *vb* **1** = **frolic**, bounce, caper, cavort, curvet, dance, gambol, hop, jump, play, prance, rollick, romp, skip, sport, trip **3** *Informal* = **search**, check, inspect, run over, shake down (*US sl.*)

frisky *adj* = **lively**, bouncy, coltish, frolicsome, full of beans, full of joie de vivre, high-spirited, in high spirits, kittenish, playful, rollicking, romping, spirited, sportive
Antonyms *adj* demure, dull, lacklustre, pensive, sedate, stodgy, stolid, wooden

fritter[1] *vb* **1** *usually foll. by* **away** = **waste**, dally away, dissipate, fool away, idle away, misspend, run through, spend like water, squander

frivolity *n* **1, 2** = **flippancy**, childishness, desipience, flightiness, flummery, folly, frivolousness, fun, gaiety, giddiness, jest, levity, light-heartedness, lightness, nonsense, puerility, shallowness, silliness, superficiality, trifling, triviality
Antonyms *n* earnestness, gravity, humourlessness, importance, sedateness, seriousness, significance, soberness, sobriety

frivolous *adj* **1** = **flippant**, childish, ditzy *or* ditsy (*sl.*), dizzy, empty-headed, flighty, flip (*inf.*), foolish, giddy, idle, ill-considered, juvenile, light-minded, nonserious, puerile, silly, superficial **2** = **trivial**, extravagant, footling (*inf.*), impractical, light, minor, nickel-and-dime (*US sl.*), niggling, paltry, peripheral, petty, pointless, shallow, trifling, unimportant
Antonyms *adj* ≠ **flippant**: earnest, mature, practical, responsible, sensible, serious, solemn ≠ **trivial**: important, serious, vital

frizzle[2] *vb* **1, 2** = **crisp**, fry, hiss, roast, scorch, sizzle, sputter

frizzy *adj* = **tight-curled**, corrugated, crimped, crisp, frizzed, wiry

frolic *n* **1** = **revel**, antic, blast (*US sl.*), escapade, gambado, gambol, game, lark, prank, romp, spree **2** = **merriment**, amusement, drollery, fun, fun and games, gaiety, high jinks, skylarking (*inf.*), sport ◆ *vb* **3** = **play**, caper, cavort, cut capers, frisk, gambol, lark, make merry, rollick, romp, sport

frolicsome *adj* = **playful**, coltish, frisky, full of *nothing prevents him from leaving.* **7** because of: *exhausted from his walk.* [OE *fram*]

fromage frais ('frɒmɑːʒ 'freɪ; *French* frɔmaʒ fre) *n* a low-fat soft cheese with a smooth light texture. [F, lit.: fresh cheese]

frond (frɒnd) *n* **1** the compound leaf of a fern. **2** the leaf of a palm. [C18: from L *frōns*]

front ➊ (frʌnt) *n* **1** that part or side that is forward, or most often seen or used. **2** a position or place directly before or ahead: *a fountain stood at the front of the building.* **3** the beginning, opening, or first part. **4** the position of leadership: *in the front of scientific knowledge.* **5** land bordering a lake, street, etc. **6** land along a seashore or large lake, esp. a promenade. **7** *Mil.* **7a** the total area in which opposing armies face each other. **7b** the space in which a military unit is operating: *to advance on a broad front.* **8** *Meteorol.* the dividing line or plane between two air masses of different origins. **9** outward aspect or bearing, as when dealing with a situation: *a bold front.* **10** *Inf.* a business or other activity serving as a respectable cover for another, usually criminal, organization. **11** Also called: **front man.** a nominal leader of an organization etc.; figurehead. **12** *Inf.* outward appearance of rank or wealth. **13** a particular field of activity: *on the wages front.* **14** a group of people with a common goal: *a national liberation front.* **15** a false shirt front; a dicky. **16** *Arch.* the forehead or the face. ◆ *adj* (*prenominal*) **17** of, at, or in the front: *a front seat.* **18** *Phonetics.* of or denoting a vowel articulated with the tongue brought forward, as for the sound of *ee* in English *see* or *a* in English *hat.* ◆ *vb* **19** (when *intr,* foll. by *on* or *onto*) to face (onto): *this house fronts the river.* **20** (*tr*) to be a front of or for. **21** (*tr*) to appear as a presenter in a television show. **22** (*tr*) to be the lead singer or player in (a band). **23** (*tr*) to confront. **24** to supply a front for. **25** (*intr;* often foll. by *up*) *Austral. inf.* to appear (at): *to front up at the police station.* [C13 (in the sense: forehead, face): from L *frōns* forehead, foremost part]
▸ **'frontless** *adj*

frontage ('frʌntɪdʒ) *n* **1** the façade of a building or the front of a plot of ground. **2** the extent of the front of a shop, plot of land, etc. **3** the direction in which a building faces.

frontal ('frʌntᵊl) *adj* **1** of, at, or in the front. **2** of or relating to the forehead: *frontal artery.* ◆ *n* **3** a decorative hanging for the front of an altar. [C14 (in the sense: adornment for forehead, altarcloth): via OF *frontel,* from L *frōns* forehead]
▸ **'frontally** *adv*

frontal lobe *n Anat.* the anterior portion of each cerebral hemisphere.

front bench *n* **1** *Brit.* **1a** the foremost bench of either the Government or Opposition in the House of Commons. **1b** the leadership (**frontbenchers**) of either group, who occupy this bench. **2** the leadership of the government or opposition in various legislative assemblies.

front-end *adj* (of money, costs, etc.) required or incurred in advance of a project in order to get it under way.

frontier ➊ ('frʌntɪə, frʌn'tɪə) *n* **1a** the region of a country bordering on another or a line, barrier, etc., marking such a boundary. **1b** (*as modifier*): *a frontier post.* **2** *US.* the edge of the settled area of a country. **3** (*often pl*) the limit of knowledge in a particular field: *the frontiers of physics have been pushed back.* [C14: from OF, from *front* (in the sense: part which is opposite)]

frontiersman ('frʌntɪəzmən, frʌn'tɪəz-) *or* (*fem*) **frontierswoman** (-,wʊmən) *n, pl* **frontiersmen** *or* **frontierswomen.** (formerly) a person living on a frontier, esp. in a newly pioneered territory of the US.

frontispiece ('frʌntɪs,piːs) *n* **1** an illustration facing the title page of a book. **2** the principal façade of a building. **3** a pediment over a door, window, etc. [C16 *frontispice,* from F, from LL *frontispicium* façade, from L *frōns* forehead + *specere* to look at; infl. by PIECE]

frontlet ('frʌntlɪt) *n Judaism.* a phylactery attached to the forehead. [C15: from OF *frontelet* a little FRONTAL]

front line *n* **1** *Military.* **1a** the most advanced military units in a battle. **1b** (*modifier*): of, relating to, or suitable for the military front line: *frontline troops.* **2** (*modifier*) close to a hostile country or scene of armed conflict: *the frontline states.*

front loader *n* a washing machine with a door at the front which opens one side of the drum into which washing is placed.

front-page *n* (*modifier*) important enough to be put on the front page of a newspaper.

frontrunner ('frʌnt,rʌnə) *n Inf.* the leader or a favoured contestant in a race, election, etc.

frontrunning ('frʌnt,rʌnɪŋ) *n Stock Exchange.* the practice by market makers of using advance information provided by their own investment analysts before it has been given to clients.

frost ➊ (frɒst) *n* **1** a white deposit of ice particles, esp. one formed on objects out of doors at night. **2** an atmospheric temperature of below freezing point, characterized by the production of this deposit. **3 degrees of frost.** degrees below freezing point. **4** *Inf.* something given a cold reception; failure. **5** *Inf.* coolness of manner. **6** the act of freezing. ◆ *vb* **7** to cover or be covered with frost. **8** (*tr*) to give a frostlike appearance to (glass, etc.), as by means of a fine-grained surface. **9** (*tr*) *Chiefly US & Canad.* to decorate (cakes, etc.) with icing or frosting. **10** (*tr*) to kill or damage (crops, etc.) with frost. [OE *frost*]

frostbite ('frɒst,baɪt) *n* destruction of tissues, esp. those of the fingers, ears, toes, and nose, by freezing.
▸ **'frost,bitten** *adj*

frosted ('frɒstɪd) *adj* **1** covered or injured by frost. **2** covered with icing, as a cake. **3** (of glass, etc.) having a surface roughened to prevent clear vision through it.

frost hollow *n* a depression in a hilly area in which cold air collects, becoming very cold at night.

frosting ('frɒstɪŋ) *n* **1** another word (esp. US and Canad.) for **icing. 2** a rough or matt finish on glass, silver, etc.

frosty ➊ ('frɒstɪ) *adj* **frostier, frostiest. 1** characterized by frost: *a frosty night.* **2** covered by or decorated with frost. **3** lacking warmth or enthusiasm: *the new plan had a frosty reception.*
▸ **'frostily** *adv* ▸ **'frostiness** *n*

froth ➊ (frɒθ) *n* **1** a mass of small bubbles of air or a gas in a liquid, produced by fermentation, etc. **2** a mixture of saliva and air bubbles formed at the lips in certain diseases, such as rabies. **3** trivial ideas or entertainment. ◆ *vb* **4** to produce or cause to produce froth. **5** (*tr*) to give out in the form of froth. [C14: from ON *frotha* or *frauth*]
▸ **'frothy** *adj* ▸ **'frothily** *adv*

froufrou ('fruː,fruː) *n* a swishing sound, as made by a long silk dress. [C19: from F, imit.]

froward ('frəʊəd) *adj Arch.* obstinate; contrary. [C14: see FRO, -WARD]
▸ **'frowardly** *adv* ▸ **'frowardness** *n*

frown ➊ (fraʊn) *vb* **1** (*intr*) to draw the brows together and wrinkle the forehead, esp. in worry, anger, or concentration. **2** (*intr;* foll. by *on* or *upon*) to look disapprovingly (upon). **3** (*tr*) to express (worry, etc.) by frowning. ◆ *n* **4** the act of frowning. **5** a show of dislike or displeasure. [C14: from OF *froigner,* of Celtic origin]
▸ **'frowner** *n* ▸ **'frowningly** *adv*

frowst (fraʊst) *n Brit. inf.* a hot and stale atmosphere; fug. [C19: back formation from *frowsty* musty, stuffy, var. of FROWZY]

frowsty ➊ ('fraʊstɪ) *adj* **frowstier, frowstiest.** ill-smelling; stale; musty.
▸ **'frowstiness** *n*

frowzy ➊ *or* **frowsy** ('fraʊzɪ) *adj* **frowzier, frowziest,** *or* **frowsier, frowsiest. 1** untidy or unkempt in appearance. **2** ill-smelling; frowsty. [C17: from ?]
▸ **'frowziness** *or* **'frowsiness** *n*

froze (frəʊz) *vb* the past tense of **freeze.**

frozen ➊ ('frəʊzᵊn) *vb* **1** the past participle of **freeze.** ◆ *adj* **2** turned into or covered with ice. **3** killed or stiffened by extreme cold. **4** (of a region or climate) icy or snowy. **5** (of food) preserved by a freezing process. **6a** (of prices, wages, etc.) arbitrarily pegged at a certain level. **6b** (of business assets) not convertible into cash. **7** frigid or disdainful in manner. **8** motionless or unyielding: *he was frozen with horror.*
▸ **'frozenly** *adv*

frozen shoulder *n Pathol.* painful stiffness in a shoulder joint.

FRS (in Britain) *abbrev. for* Fellow of the Royal Society.

FRSNZ *abbrev. for* Fellow of the Royal Society of New Zealand.

fructify ('frʌktɪ,faɪ) *vb* **fructifies, fructifying, fructified. 1** to bear or cause to bear fruit. **2** to make or become fruitful. [C14: from OF, from LL *frūctificāre,* from L *frūctus* fruit + *facere* to produce]
▸ **,fructifi'cation** *n* ▸ **fruc'tiferous** *adj* ▸ **'fructi,fier** *n*

fructose ('frʌktəʊs) *n* a white crystalline sugar occurring in many fruits. Formula: $C_6H_{12}O_6$. [C19: from L *frūctus* fruit + -OSE²]

frugal ➊ ('fruːgᵊl) *adj* **1** practising economy; thrifty. **2** not costly; meagre. [C16: from L, from *frūgī* useful, temperate, from *frux* fruit]
▸ **fru'gality** *n* ▸ **'frugally** *adv*

THESAURUS

beans (*inf.*), gay, kittenish, lively, merry, rollicking, sportive, sprightly, wanton (*arch.*)

front *n* **1** = **exterior**, anterior, façade, face, facing, foreground, forepart, frontage, obverse **2** = **forefront**, beginning, fore, front line, head, lead, top, van, vanguard **9** = **appearance**, air, aspect, bearing, countenance, demeanour, expression, exterior, face, manner, mien, show **10** *Informal* = **disguise**, blind, cover, cover-up, façade, mask, pretext, show ◆ *adj* **17** = **foremost**, first, head, headmost, lead, leading, topmost ◆ *vb* **19** = **face onto**, look over *or* onto, overlook
Antonyms *adj* ≠ **foremost**: aft, back, back end, behind, hindmost, nethermost, rear

frontier *n* **1, 3** = **boundary**, borderland, borderline, bound, confines, edge, limit, marches, perimeter, verge

frost *n* **1** = **hoarfrost**, freeze, freeze-up, Jack Frost, rime

frosty *adj* **1, 2** = **cold**, chilly, frozen, hoar (*rare*), ice-capped, icicled, icy, parky (*Brit. inf.*), rimy, wintry **3** = **unfriendly**, cold as ice, discouraging, frigid, off-putting (*Brit. inf.*), standoffish, unenthusiastic, unwelcoming

froth *n* **1** = **foam**, bubbles, effervescence, head, lather, scum, spume, suds ◆ *vb* **4** = **fizz**, bubble over, come to a head, effervesce, foam, lather

frothy *adj* **1** = **foamy**, foaming, spumescent, spumous, spumy, sudsy **3** = **trivial**, empty, frilly, frivolous, light, petty, slight, trifling, unnecessary, unsubstantial, vain

frown *vb* **1** = **scowl**, give a dirty look, glare, glower, knit one's brows, look daggers, lour *or* lower **2** *foll. by* **on** *or* **upon** = **disapprove of**, discountenance, discourage, dislike, look askance at, not take kindly to, show disapproval *or* displeasure, take a dim view of, view with disfavour

frowsty *adj* = **stale**, close, fuggy, fusty, ill-smelling, musty, stuffy

frowzy *adj* **1** = **slovenly**, blowsy, dirty, draggletailed (*arch.*), frumpy, messy, slatternly, sloppy, sluttish, ungroomed, unkempt, untidy, unwashed

frozen *adj* **2, 4** = **icy**, arctic, chilled, chilled to the marrow, frigid, frosted, icebound, ice-cold, ice-covered, numb **6** = **fixed**, pegged (*of prices*), stopped, suspended **8** = **motionless**, petrified, rooted, stock-still, turned to stone

frugal *adj* **1, 2** = **thrifty**, abstemious, careful, cheeseparing, economical, meagre, niggardly,

frugivorous (fruː'dʒɪvərəs) *adj* fruit-eating. [C18: from *frugi-* (as in FRUGAL) + -VOROUS]

fruit ❶ (fruːt) *n* **1** *Bot.* the ripened ovary of a flowering plant, containing one or more seeds. It may be dry, as in the poppy, or fleshy, as in the peach. **2** any fleshy part of a plant that supports the seeds and is edible, such as the strawberry. **3** any plant product useful to man, including grain, vegetables, etc. **4** (*often pl*) the result or consequence of an action or effort. **5** *Arch.* offspring of man or animals. **6** *Inf., chiefly US & Canad.* a male homosexual. ◆ *vb* **7** to bear or cause to bear fruit. [C12: from OF, from L *frūctus* enjoyment, fruit, from *frūī* to enjoy]
▸ **'fruit,like** *adj*

fruit bat *n* a large Old World bat occurring in tropical and subtropical regions and feeding on fruit.

fruitcake ('fruːt,keɪk) *n* a rich cake containing mixed dried fruit, lemon peel, etc.

fruit drop *n* **1** the premature shedding of fruit from a tree before fully ripe. **2** a boiled sweet with a fruity flavour.

fruiterer ('fruːtərə) *n Chiefly Brit.* a fruit dealer or seller.

fruit fly *n* **1** a small dipterous fly which feeds on and lays its eggs in plant tissues. **2** any dipterous fly of the genus *Drosophila.* See **drosophila.**

fruitful ❶ ('fruːtfʊl) *adj* **1** bearing fruit in abundance. **2** productive or prolific. **3** producing results or profits: *a fruitful discussion.*
▸ **'fruitfully** *adv* ▸ **'fruitfulness** *n*

fruition ❶ (fruː'ɪʃən) *n* **1** the attainment of something worked for or desired. **2** enjoyment of this. **3** the act or condition of bearing fruit. [C15: from LL, from L *fruī* to enjoy]

fruitless ❶ ('fruːtlɪs) *adj* **1** yielding nothing or nothing of value; unproductive. **2** without fruit.
▸ **'fruitlessly** *adv* ▸ **'fruitlessness** *n*

fruit machine *n Brit.* a gambling machine that pays out when certain combinations of diagrams, usually of fruit, appear on a dial.

fruit salad *n* a dessert consisting of sweet fruits cut up and served in a syrup.

fruit sugar *n* another name for **fructose.**

fruit tree *n* any tree that bears edible fruit.

fruity ❶ ('fruːtɪ) *adj* **fruitier, fruitiest. 1** of or resembling fruit. **2** (of a voice) mellow or rich. **3** *Inf., chiefly Brit.* erotically stimulating; salacious. **4** *Inf., chiefly US & Canad.* homosexual.
▸ **'fruitily** *adv* ▸ **'fruitiness** *n*

frumenty ('fruːməntɪ) *or* **furmenty** *n Brit.* a kind of porridge made from hulled wheat boiled with milk, sweetened, and spiced. [C14: from OF, from *frument* grain, from L *frūmentum*]

frump (frʌmp) *n* a woman who is dowdy, drab, or unattractive. [C16 (in the sense: to be sullen; C19: dowdy woman): from MDu. *verrompelen* to wrinkle]
▸ **'frumpy** *or* **'frumpish** *adj*

frustrate ❶ (frʌ'streɪt) *vb* **frustrates, frustrating, frustrated.** (*tr*) **1** to hinder or prevent (the efforts, plans, or desires) of. **2** to upset, agitate, or tire. ◆ *adj* **3** *Arch.* frustrated or thwarted. [C15: from L *frustrāre* to cheat, from *frustrā* in error]
▸ **frus'tration** *n*

frustrated ❶ (frʌ'streɪtɪd) *adj* having feelings of dissatisfaction or lack of fulfilment.

frustum ('frʌstəm) *n, pl* **frustums** *or* **frusta** (-tə). *Geom.* **a** the part of a solid, such as a cone or pyramid, contained between the base and a plane parallel to the base that intersects the solid. **b** the part of such a solid contained between two parallel planes intersecting the solid. [C17: from L: piece]

fry[1] (fraɪ) *vb* **fries, frying, fried. 1** (when *tr*, sometimes foll. by *up*) to cook or be cooked in fat, oil, etc., usually over direct heat. **2** *Sl., chiefly US.* to kill or be killed by electrocution. ◆ *n, pl* **fries. 3** a dish of something fried, esp. the offal of a specified animal: *pig's fry.* **4 fry-up.** *Brit. inf.* the act of preparing a mixed fried dish or the dish itself. [C13: from OF *frire*, from L *frīgere* to fry]
▸ **'fryer** *or* **'frier** *n*

fry[2] (fraɪ) *pl n* **1** the young of various species of fish. **2** the young of certain other animals, such as frogs. [C14 (in the sense: young, offspring): from OF *freier* to spawn, from L *fricāre* to rub]

frying pan *n* **1** a long-handled shallow pan used for frying. **2 out of the frying pan into the fire.** from a bad situation to a worse one.

f-stop ('ɛf,stɒp) *n* any of the settings for the f-number of a camera.

ft. *abbrev. for* foot *or* feet.

fth. *or* **fthm.** *abbrev. for* fathom.

FT Index *abbrev. for:* **1** Financial Times Industrial Ordinary Share Index: an index designed to show the general trend in share prices, produced daily by the *Financial Times* newspaper. **2** Financial Times Stock Exchange 100 Index: an index produced by the *Financial Times* based on an average of 100 securities and giving the best indication of daily movements. Also: **FTSE Index.** Informal name: **Footsie.**

FTP *abbrev.* (*sometimes not caps.*) *for* file transfer protocol: the standard mechanism used to transfer files between computer systems or across the Internet.

fuchsia ('fjuːʃə) *n* **1** a shrub widely cultivated for its showy drooping purple, red, or white flowers. **2a** a reddish-purple to purplish-pink colour. **2b** (*as adj*): *a fuchsia dress.* [C18: from NL, after Leonhard *Fuchs* (1501–66), G botanist]

fuchsin ('fuːksɪn) *or* **fuchsine** ('fuːksiːn, -sɪn) *n* an aniline dye forming a red solution in water: used as a textile dye and a biological stain. [C19: from FUCHS(IA) + -IN; from its similarity in colour to the flower]

fuck (fʌk) *Taboo.* ◆ *vb* **1** to have sexual intercourse with (someone). ◆ *n* **2** an act of sexual intercourse. **3** *Sl.* a partner in sexual intercourse. **4 not care** *or* **give a fuck.** not to care at all. ◆ *interj* **5** *Offens.* an expression of strong disgust or anger. [C16: of Gmc origin]

fucus ('fjuːkəs) *n, pl* **fuci** (-saɪ) *or* **fucuses.** a seaweed of the genus *Fucus*, having greenish-brown slimy fronds. [C16: from L: rock lichen, from Gk *phukos* seaweed, of Semitic origin]

fuddle ('fʌdᵊl) *vb* **fuddles, fuddling, fuddled. 1** (*tr; often passive*) to cause to be confused or intoxicated. ◆ *n* **2** a muddled or confused state. [C16: from ?]

fuddy-duddy ❶ ('fʌdɪ,dʌdɪ) *n, pl* **fuddy-duddies.** *Inf.* a person, esp. an elderly one, who is extremely conservative or dull. [C20: from ?]

fudge[1] (fʌdʒ) *n* a soft variously flavoured sweet made from sugar, butter, etc. [C19: from ?]

fudge[2] (fʌdʒ) *n* **1** foolishness; nonsense. ◆ *interj* **2** a mild exclamation of annoyance. [C18: from ?]

fudge[3] ❶ (fʌdʒ) *n* **1** a small section of type matter in a box in a newspaper allowing late news to be included without the whole page having to be remade. **2** the late news so inserted. **3** an unsatisfactory compromise reached to evade a difficult problem or controversial issue. ◆ *vb* **fudges, fudging, fudged. 4** (*tr*) to make or adjust in a false or clumsy way. **5** (*tr*) to misrepresent; falsify. **6** to evade (a problem, issue, etc.). [C19: ? rel. to arch. *fadge* to agree, succeed]

fuel ❶ (fjʊəl) *n* **1** any substance burned as a source of heat or power, such as coal or petrol. **2** the material, containing a fissile substance such as uranium-235, that produces energy in a nuclear reactor. **3** something that nourishes or builds up emotion, action, etc. ◆ *vb* **fuels, fuelling, fuelled** *or US* **fuels, fueling, fueled. 4** to supply with or receive fuel. [C14: from OF, from *feu* fire, ult. from L *focus* hearth]

fuel air bomb *n* a type of bomb that spreads a cloud of gas, which is then detonated, over the target area, causing extensive destruction.

fuel cell *n* a cell in which chemical energy is converted directly into electrical energy.

fuel injection *n* a system for introducing fuel directly into the combustion chambers of an internal-combustion engine without the use of a carburettor.

THESAURUS

parsimonious, penny-wise, provident, prudent, saving, sparing
Antonyms *adj* excessive, extravagant, imprudent, lavish, luxurious, prodigal, profligate, spendthrift, wasteful

frugality *n* **1, 2** = **thrift**, carefulness, conservation, economizing, economy, good management, husbandry, moderation, providence, thriftiness

fruit *n* **1** = **produce**, crop, harvest, product, yield **4** *often plural* = **result**, advantage, benefit, consequence, effect, end result, outcome, profit, return, reward

fruitful *adj* **1** = **fertile**, fecund, fructiferous **2** = **plentiful**, abundant, copious, flush, plenteous, productive, profuse, prolific, rich, spawning **3** = **useful**, advantageous, beneficial, effective, gainful, productive, profitable, rewarding, successful, well-spent, worthwhile
Antonyms ≠ fertile: barren, fruitless, infertile, sterile, unfruitful, unproductive **≠ plentiful:** scarce *adj* **≠ useful:** fruitless, futile, ineffectual, pointless, unfruitful, unproductive, useless, vain

fruition *n* **1, 2** = **fulfilment**, actualization, attainment, completion, consummation, enjoyment, materialization, maturation, maturity, perfection, realization, ripeness

fruitless *adj* **1** = **useless**, abortive, bootless, futile, idle, ineffectual, in vain, pointless, profitless, to no avail, to no effect, unavailing, unfruitful, unproductive, unprofitable, unsuccessful, vain **2** = **barren**, unfruitful, unproductive, unprolific
Antonyms *adj* **≠ useless:** effective, fruitful, productive, profitable, useful **≠ barren:** abundant, fecund, fertile, fruitful, productive, prolific

fruity *adj* **2** = **rich**, full, mellow, resonant **3** *Informal, chiefly Brit.* = **risqué**, bawdy, blue, hot, indecent, indelicate, juicy, near the knuckle (*inf.*), racy, ripe, salacious, sexy, smutty, spicy (*inf.*), suggestive, titillating, vulgar

frumpy *adj* = **dowdy**, badly-dressed, dated, dingy, drab, dreary, mumsy, out of date

frustrate *vb* **1** = **thwart**, baffle, balk, block, check, circumvent, confront, counter, defeat, disappoint, foil, forestall, hobble, inhibit, neutralize, nullify, render null and void, stymie
Antonyms *vb* advance, encourage, endorse, forward, further, promote, satisfy, stimulate

frustrated *adj* = **disappointed**, choked, discontented, discouraged, disheartened, embittered, foiled, irked, resentful, sick as a parrot (*inf.*)

frustration *n* **1** = **annoyance**, disappointment, dissatisfaction, grievance, irritation, resentment, vexation

fuddled *adj* **1** = **confused**, muddled, muzzy **1** = **drunk**, babalas, bevvied (*dialect*), inebriated, intoxicated, legless (*inf.*), paralytic (*inf.*), smashed (*sl.*), sozzled (*inf.*), steamboats (*Scot. sl.*), steaming (*sl.*), stupefied, tipsy, wasted (*sl.*), woozy (*inf.*), wrecked (*sl.*)

fuddy-duddy *n Informal* = **conservative**, dinosaur, dodo (*inf.*), fossil, museum piece, (old) fogey, square (*inf.*), stick-in-the-mud (*inf.*), stuffed shirt (*inf.*)

fudge[3] *vb* **5, 6** = **misrepresent**, avoid, cook (*sl.*), dodge, equivocate, evade, fake, falsify, flannel (*Brit. inf.*), hedge, patch up, shuffle, slant, stall

fuel *n* **1, 3** = **incitement**, ammunition, encouragement, fodder, food, material, means, nourishment, provocation ◆ *vb* **4** = **inflame**, charge, fan, feed, fire, incite, nourish, stoke up, sustain

fuel oil *n* a liquid petroleum product used as a substitute for coal in industrial furnaces, ships, and locomotives.

fug Ⓣ (fʌg) *n Chiefly Brit.* a hot, stale, or suffocating atmosphere. [C19: ? var. of FOG[1]]
▸**'fuggy** *adj*

fugacity (fjuː'gæsɪtɪ) *n Thermodynamics.* a property of a gas that expresses its tendency to escape or expand.

-fuge *n combining form.* indicating an agent or substance that expels or drives away: *vermifuge.* [from L *fugāre* to expel]

fugitive Ⓣ ('fjuːdʒɪtɪv) *n* **1** a person who flees. **2** a thing that is elusive or fleeting. ◆ *adj* **3** fleeing, esp. from arrest or pursuit. **4** not permanent; fleeting. [C14: from L, from *fugere* to take flight]
▸**'fugitively** *adv*

fugleman ('fjuːgᵊlmən) *n, pl* **fuglemen. 1** (formerly) a soldier used as an example for those learning drill. **2** a leader or example. [C19: from G *Flügelmann,* from *Flügel* wing + *Mann* MAN]

fugue (fjuːg) *n* **1** a musical form consisting of a theme repeated a fifth above or a fourth below the continuing first statement. **2** *Psychiatry.* a dreamlike altered state of consciousness, during which a person may lose his memory and wander away. [C16: from F, from It. *fuga,* from L: a running away]
▸**'fugal** *adj*

Führer *or* ***Fuehrer*** *German.* ('fyːrər) *n* a leader: applied esp. to Adolf Hitler while he was Chancellor. [G, from *führen* to lead]

-ful *suffix.* **1** (*forming adjectives*) full of or characterized by: *painful; restful.* **2** (*forming adjectives*) able or tending to: *useful.* **3** (*forming nouns*) indicating as much as will fill the thing specified: *mouthful.* [OE *-ful, -full,* from FULL[1]]

> **USAGE NOTE** Where the amount held by a spoon, etc., is used as a rough unit of measurement, the correct form is *spoonful,* etc.: *take a spoonful of this medicine every day. Spoon full* is used in a sentence such as *he held out a spoon full of dark liquid,* where *full of* describes the spoon. A plural form such as *spoonfuls* is preferred by many speakers and writers to *spoonsful.*

fulcrum ('fʊlkrəm, 'fʌl-) *n, pl* **fulcrums** *or* **fulcra** (-krə). **1** the pivot about which a lever turns. **2** something that supports or sustains; prop. [C17: from L: foot of a couch, from *fulcire* to prop up]

fulfil Ⓣ *or US* **fulfill** (fʊl'fɪl) *vb* **fulfils, fulfilling, fulfilled** *or US* **fulfills, fulfilling, fulfilled.** (*tr*) **1** to bring about the completion or achievement of (a desire, promise, etc.). **2** to carry out or execute (a request, etc.). **3** to conform with or satisfy (regulations, etc.). **4** to finish or reach the end of. **5 fulfil oneself.** to achieve one's potential or desires. [OE *fulfyllan*]
▸**ful'filment** *or US* **ful'fillment** *n*

fulgent ('fʌldʒənt) *adj Poetic.* shining brilliantly; gleaming. [C15: from L *fulgēre* to shine]

fulgurate ('fʌlgjʊˌreɪt) *vb* **fulgurates, fulgurating, fulgurated.** (*intr*) *Rare.* to flash like lightning. [C17: from L, from *fulgur* lightning]

fulgurite ('fʌlgjʊˌraɪt) *n* glassy mineral matter found in sand and rock, formed by the action of lightning. [C19: from L *fulgur* lightning]

fuliginous (fjuː'lɪdʒɪnəs) *adj* **1** sooty or smoky. **2** of the colour of soot. [C16: from LL *fūlīginōsus* full of soot, from L *fūlīgō* soot]

full[1] Ⓣ (fʊl) *adj* **1** holding or containing as much as possible. **2** abundant in supply, quantity, number, etc.: *full of energy.* **3** having consumed enough food or drink. **4** (esp. of the face or figure) rounded or plump. **5** (*prenominal*) complete: *a full dozen.* **6** (*prenominal*) with all privileges, rights, etc.: *a full member.* **7** (*prenominal*) having the same parents: *a full brother.* **8** filled with emotion or sentiment: *a full heart.* **9** (*postpositive;* foll. by *of*) occupied or engrossed (with): *full of his own projects.* **10** *Music.* **10a** powerful or rich in volume and sound. **10b** completing a piece or section; concluding: *a full close.* **11** (of a garment, esp. a skirt) containing a large amount of fabric. **12** (of sails, etc.) distended by wind. **13** (of wine, such as a burgundy) having a heavy body. **14** (of a colour) rich; saturated. **15** *Inf.* drunk. **16 full of oneself.** full of pride or conceit. **17 full up.** filled to capacity. **18 in full swing.** at the height of activity: *the party was in full swing.* ◆ *adv* **19a** completely; entirely. **19b** (*in combination*): *full-fledged.* **20** directly; right: *he hit him full in the stomach.* **21** very; extremely (esp. in **full well**). ◆ *n* **22** the greatest degree, extent, etc. **23 in full.** without omitting or shortening: *we paid in full for our mistake.* **24 to the full.** thoroughly; fully. ◆ *vb* **25** (*tr*) *Needlework.* to gather or tuck. **26** (*intr*) (of the moon) to be fully illuminated. [OE]
▸**'fullness** *or esp. US* **'fulness** *n*

full[2] (fʊl) *vb* (of cloth, yarn, etc.) to become or to make (cloth, yarn, etc.) more compact during manufacture through shrinking and pressing. [C14: from OF *fouler,* ult. from L *fullō* a FULLER]

fullback ('fʊlˌbæk) *n Soccer, hockey, rugby.* **a** a defensive player. **b** the position held by this player.

full-blooded Ⓣ *adj* **1** (esp. of horses) of unmixed ancestry. **2** having great vigour or health; hearty.
▸**ˌfull-'bloodedness** *n*

full-blown Ⓣ *adj* **1** characterized by the fullest, strongest, or best development. **2** in full bloom.

full board *n* accommodation at a hotel, etc., that includes all meals.

full-bodied Ⓣ *adj* having a full rich flavour or quality.

full-court press *n Basketball.* the tactic of harrying the opposing team in all areas of the court, as opposed to the more usual practice of trying to defend one's own basket.

full dress *n* **a** a formal style of dress, such as white tie and tails for a man. **b** (*as modifier*): *full-dress uniform.*

full employment *n* a state in which the labour force and other economic resources of a country are utilized to their maximum extent.

fuller ('fʊlə) *n* a person who fulls cloth for his living. [OE *fullere*]

fuller's earth *n* a natural absorbent clay used, after heating, for clarifying oils and fats, fulling cloth, etc.

full face *adj* facing towards the viewer, with the entire face visible.

full-fledged *adj* See **fully fledged.**

full-frontal *Inf.* ◆ *adj* **1** (of a nude person or a photograph of a nude person) exposing the genitals to full view. **2** all-out; unrestrained. ◆ *n* **full frontal. 3** a full-frontal photograph.

full house *n* **1** *Poker.* a hand with three cards of the same value and another pair. **2** a theatre, etc., filled to capacity. **3** (in bingo, etc.) the set of numbers needed to win.

full-length *n* (*modifier*) **1** showing the complete length. **2** not abridged.

full moon *n* one of the four phases of the moon when the moon is visible as a fully illuminated disc.

full monty ('mɒntɪ) *n* **the.** *Inf.* something in its entirety. [from ?]

full nelson *n* a wrestling hold in which a wrestler places both arms under his opponent's arms from behind and exerts pressure on the back of the neck.

full-on *adj Inf.* complete; unrestrained: *full-on military intervention; full-on hard rock.*

full sail *adv* **1** at top speed. ◆ *adj* (*postpositive*), *adv* **2** with all sails set.

full-scale Ⓣ *n* (*modifier*) **1** (of a plan, etc.) of actual size. **2** using all resources; all-out.

full stop *or* **full point** *n* the punctuation mark (.) used at the end of a sentence that is not a question or exclamation, after abbreviations, etc. Also called (esp. US and Canad.): **period.**

full time *n* the end of a football or other match.

full-time *adj* **1** for the entire time appropriate to an activity: *a full-time job.* ◆ *adv* **full time. 2** on a full-time basis: *he works full time.* ◆ Cf. **part-time.**
▸**ˌfull-'timer** *n*

full toss *or* **full pitch** *n Cricket.* a bowled ball that reaches the batsman without bouncing.

fully Ⓣ ('fʊlɪ) *adv* **1** to the greatest degree or extent. **2** amply; adequately: *they were fully fed.* **3** at least: *it was fully an hour before she came.*

fully fashioned *adj* (of stockings, knitwear, etc.) shaped and seamed so as to fit closely.

THESAURUS

fug *n* = **stale air,** fetidity, fetor, frowst, frowstiness, fustiness, reek, staleness, stink

fuggy *adj* = **stuffy,** airless, fetid, foul, frowsty, noisome, noxious, stale, suffocating, unventilated

fugitive *n* **1** = **runaway,** deserter, escapee, refugee, runagate (*arch.*) ◆ *adj* **3, 4** = **momentary,** brief, ephemeral, evanescent, fleeing, fleeting, flitting, flying, fugacious, passing, short, short-lived, temporary, transient, transitory, unstable

fulfil *vb* **1, 2, 4** = **achieve,** accomplish, bring to completion, carry out, complete, conclude, discharge, effect, execute, finish, keep, perfect, perform, realise, satisfy **3** = **comply with,** answer, conform to, fill, meet, obey, observe
Antonyms *vb* disappoint, dissatisfy, fail in, fail to meet, fall short of, neglect

fulfilment *n* **1, 2, 4** = **achievement,** accomplishment, attainment, carrying out *or* through, completion, consummation, crowning, discharge, discharging, effecting, end, implementation, observance, perfection, realization

full[1] *adj* **1** = **crammed,** chock-a-block, chock-full, crowded, in use, jammed, occupied, packed, taken **2** = **extensive,** abundant, adequate, all-inclusive, ample, broad, comprehensive, copious, detailed, exhaustive, generous, maximum, plenary, plenteous, plentiful, thorough, unabridged **3** = **filled,** brimful, brimming, bursting at the seams, complete, entire, gorged, intact, loaded, replete, sated, satiated, satisfied, saturated, stocked, sufficient **4** = **plump,** buxom, curvaceous, rounded, voluptuous **10a** = **rich,** clear, deep, distinct, loud, resonant, rounded **11** = **voluminous,** baggy, balloon-like, capacious, large, loose, puffy ◆ *n* **23 in full** = **completely,** in its entirety, in total, *in toto,* without exception **24 to the full** = **thoroughly,** completely, entirely, fully, to the utmost, without reservation
Antonyms *adj* ≠ **extensive:** abridged, incomplete, limited, partial ≠ **filled, crammed:** blank, devoid, empty, vacant, void ≠ **rich:** faint, thin ≠ **voluminous:** restricted, tight

full-blooded *adj* **2** = **vigorous,** gutsy (*sl.*), hearty, lusty, mettlesome, red-blooded, virile

full-blown *adj* **1** = **fully developed,** advanced, complete, developed, entire, full, full-scale, full-sized, fully fledged, fully formed, fully grown, progressed, total, whole **2** = **in full bloom,** blossoming, flowering, full, opened out, unfolded
Antonyms *adj* ≠ **fully developed:** dormant, latent, potential, undeveloped

full-bodied *adj* = **rich,** fruity, full-flavoured, heady, heavy, mellow, redolent, strong, well-matured

fullness *n* **2** = **plenty,** abundance, adequateness, ampleness, copiousness, fill, glut, profusion, repletion, satiety, saturation, sufficiency **4** = **roundness,** curvaceousness, dilation, distension, enlargement, swelling, tumescence, voluptuousness **10a** = **richness,** clearness, loudness, resonance, strength

full-scale *adj* **2** = **major,** all-encompassing, all-out, comprehensive, exhaustive, extensive, full-dress, in-depth, proper, sweeping, thorough, thoroughgoing, wide-ranging

fully *adv* **1** = **totally,** absolutely, altogether, completely, entirely, every inch, from first to

fully fledged ⓣ *or* **full-fledged** *adj* **1** (of a young bird) having acquired adult feathers, enabling it to fly. **2** developed to the fullest degree. **3** of full rank or status.

fulmar ('fʊlmə) *n* a heavily built short-tailed oceanic bird of polar regions. [C17: of Scand. origin]

fulminate ⓣ ('fʌlmɪˌneɪt) *vb* **fulminates, fulminating, fulminated. 1** (*intr;* often foll. by *against*) to make severe criticisms or denunciations; rail. **2** to explode with noise and violence. ◆ *n* **3** any salt or ester of **fulminic acid,** an isomer of cyanic acid, which is used as a detonator. [C15: from Med. L, from L, from *fulmen* lightning that strikes]
▸**'fulminant** *adj* ▸**ˌfulmi'nation** *n* ▸**'fulmiˌnatory** *adj*

fulsome ⓣ ('fʊlsəm) *adj* **1** excessive or insincere, esp. in an offensive or distasteful way: *fulsome compliments.* **2** *Not standard.* extremely complimentary.
▸**'fulsomely** *adv* ▸**'fulsomeness** *n*

fulvous ('fʌlvəs) *adj* of a dull brownish-yellow colour. [C17: from L *fulvus* reddish yellow]

fumarole ('fjuːməˌrəʊl) *n* a vent in or near a volcano from which hot gases, esp. steam, are emitted. [C19: from F, from LL *fūmāriolum* smoke hole, from L *fūmus* smoke]

fumble ⓣ ('fʌmbᵊl) *vb* **fumbles, fumbling, fumbled. 1** (*intr;* often foll. by *for* or *with*) to grope about clumsily or blindly, esp. in searching. **2** (*intr;* foll. by *at* or *with*) to finger or play with, esp. in an absent-minded way. **3** to say or do awkwardly: *he fumbled the introduction badly.* **4** to fail to catch or grasp (a ball, etc.) cleanly. ◆ *n* **5** the act of fumbling. [C16: prob. of Scand. origin]
▸**'fumbler** *n* ▸**'fumblingly** *adv*

fume ⓣ (fjuːm) *vb* **fumes, fuming, fumed. 1** (*intr*) to be overcome with anger or fury. **2** to give off (fumes) or (of fumes) to be given off, esp. during a chemical reaction. **3** (*tr*) to fumigate. ◆ *n* **4** (*often pl*) a pungent or toxic vapour, gas, or smoke. **5** a sharp or pungent odour. [C14: from OF *fum,* from L *fūmus* smoke, vapour]
▸**'fumeless** *adj* ▸**'fumingly** *adv* ▸**'fumy** *adj*

fumed (fjuːmd) *adj* (of wood, esp. oak) having a dark colour and distinctive grain from exposure to ammonia fumes.

fumigant ('fjuːmɪgənt) *n* a substance used for fumigating.

fumigate ⓣ ('fjuːmɪˌgeɪt) *vb* **fumigates, fumigating, fumigated.** to treat (something contaminated or infected) with fumes or smoke. [C16: from L, from *fūmus* smoke + *agere* to drive]
▸**ˌfumi'gation** *n* ▸**'fumiˌgator** *n*

fuming sulphuric acid *n* a mixture of acids, made by dissolving sulphur trioxide in concentrated sulphuric acid. Also called: **oleum.**

fumitory ('fjuːmɪtərɪ) *n, pl* **fumitories.** any plant of the genus *Fumaria* having spurred flowers and formerly used medicinally. [C14: from OF, from Med. L *fūmus terrae,* lit.: smoke of the earth]

fun ⓣ (fʌn) *n* **1** a source of enjoyment, amusement, diversion, etc. **2** pleasure, gaiety, or merriment. **3** jest or sport (esp. in **in** *or* **for fun**). **4 fun and games.** *Ironic or facetious.* frivolous or hetic activity. **5 make fun of** *or* **poke fun at.** to ridicule or deride. **6** (*modifier*) full of amusement, diversion, gaiety, etc.: *a fun sport.* [C17: ?from obs. *fon* to make a fool of; see FOND]

funambulist (fjuː'næmbjʊlɪst) *n* a tightrope walker. [C18: from L, from *fūnis* rope + *ambulāre* to walk]
▸**fu'nambulism** *n*

function ⓣ ('fʌŋkʃən) *n* **1** the natural action of a person or thing: *the function of the kidneys is to filter waste products from the blood.* **2** the intended purpose of a person or thing in a specific role: *the function of a hammer is to hit nails into wood.* **3** an official or formal social gathering or ceremony. **4** a factor dependent upon another or other factors. **5** Also called: **map, mapping.** *Maths, logic.* a relation between two sets that associates a unique element (the value) of the second (the range) with each element (the argument) of the first (the domain). Symbol: $f(x)$. The value of $f(x)$ for $x=2$ is $f(2)$. ◆ *vb* (*intr*) **6** to operate or perform as specified. **7** (foll. by *as*) to perform the action or role (of something or someone else): *a coin may function as a screwdriver.* [C16: from L *functiō,* from *fungī* to perform]

functional ⓣ ('fʌŋkʃənᵊl) *adj* **1** of, involving, or containing a function or functions. **2** practical rather than decorative; utilitarian. **3** capable of functioning; working. **4** *Med.* affecting a function of an organ without structural change.
▸**'functionally** *adv*

functionalism ('fʌŋkʃənəˌlɪzəm) *n* **1** the theory of design that the form of a thing should be determined by its use. **2** any doctrine that stresses purpose.
▸**'functionalist** *n, adj*

functionary ⓣ ('fʌŋkʃənərɪ) *n, pl* **functionaries.** a person acting in an official capacity, as for a government; an official.

fund ⓣ (fʌnd) *n* **1** a reserve of money, etc., set aside for a certain purpose. **2** a supply or store of something; stock: *it exhausted his fund of wisdom.* ◆ *vb* (*tr*) **3** to furnish money to in the form of a fund. **4** to place or store up in a fund. **5** to convert (short-term floating debt) into long-term debt bearing fixed interest and represented by bonds. **6** to accumulate a fund for the discharge of (a recurrent liability): *to fund a pension plan.* ◆ See also **funds.** [C17: from L *fundus* the bottom, piece of land]
▸**'funder** *n*

fundament ('fʌndəmənt) *n Euphemistic or facetious.* the buttocks. [C13: from L, from *fundāre* to FOUND[2]]

fundamental ⓣ (ˌfʌndə'mɛntᵊl) *adj* **1** of, involving, or comprising a foundation; basic. **2** of, involving, or comprising a source; primary. **3** *Music.* denoting or relating to the principal or lowest note of a harmonic series. ◆ *n* **4** a principle, law, etc., that serves as the basis of an idea or system. **5a** the principal or lowest note of a harmonic series. **5b** the bass note of a chord in root position.
▸**ˌfundamen'tality** *n* ▸**ˌfunda'mentally** *adv*

fundamental interaction *n* any of the four basic interactions that occur in nature: the gravitational, electromagnetic, strong, and weak interactions.

fundamentalism (ˌfʌndə'mɛntəˌlɪzəm) *n* **1** *Christianity.* the view that the Bible is divinely inspired and is therefore literally true. **2** *Islam.* a movement favouring strict observance of the teachings of the Koran and Islamic law.
▸**ˌfunda'mentalist** *n, adj*

fundamental particle *n* another name for **elementary particle.**

fundamental unit *n* one of a set of unrelated units that form the basis of a system of units. For example, the metre, kilogram, and second are fundamental SI units.

funded debt *n* that part of the British national debt that the government is not obliged to repay by a fixed date.

fundraiser ('fʌndˌreɪzə) *n* **1** a person engaged in fundraising. **2** an event held to raise money for a cause.

fundraising ('fʌndˌreɪzɪŋ) *n* **1** the activity involved in raising money for a cause. ◆ *adj* **2** of, for, or related to fundraising.

THESAURUS

last, heart and soul, in all respects, intimately, lock, stock and barrel, one hundred per cent, perfectly, positively, thoroughly, to the hilt, utterly, wholly **2** = **adequately,** abundantly, amply, comprehensively, enough, plentifully, satisfactorily, sufficiently **3** = **at least,** quite, without (any) exaggeration, without a word of a lie (*inf.*)

fully fledged *adj* **3** = **experienced,** mature, professional, proficient, qualified, senior, time-served, trained

fulminate *vb* **1** = **criticize,** animadvert upon, berate, blast, castigate, censure, curse, denounce, denunciate, excoriate, execrate, fume, inveigh against, lambast(e), protest against, put down, rage, rail against, reprobate, tear into (*inf.*), thunder, upbraid, vilify, vituperate

fulmination *n* **1** = **condemnation,** denunciation, diatribe, excoriation, invective, obloquy, philippic, reprobation, tirade

fulsome *adj* **1** = **extravagant,** adulatory, cloying, excessive, fawning, gross, immoderate, ingratiating, inordinate, insincere, nauseating, overdone, over the top, saccharine, sickening, smarmy (*Brit. inf.*), sycophantic, unctuous

fumble *vb* **1** = **grope,** bumble, feel around, flounder, paw (*inf.*), scrabble

fume *vb* **1** = **rage,** blow a fuse (*sl., chiefly US*), boil, chafe, crack up (*inf.*), fly off the handle (*inf.*), go ballistic (*sl.*), go off the deep end (*inf.*), go up the wall (*sl.*), rant, rave, see red (*inf.*), seethe, smoulder, storm ◆ *n* **4** *often plural* = **smoke,** effluvium, exhalation, exhaust, gas, haze, miasma, pollution, reek, smog, vapour

fumigate *vb* = **disinfect,** clean out *or* up, cleanse, purify, sanitize, sterilize

fuming *adj* **1** = **furious,** angry, at boiling point (*inf.*), choked, enraged, fit to be tied (*sl.*), foaming at the mouth, in a rage, incandescent, incensed, on the warpath (*inf.*), raging, roused, seething, up in arms

fun *n* **1** = **joking,** buffoonery, clowning, foolery, game, horseplay, jesting, jocularity, nonsense, play, playfulness, skylarking (*inf.*), sport, teasing, tomfoolery **2** = **enjoyment,** amusement, beer and skittles (*inf.*), cheer, distraction, diversion, entertainment, frolic, gaiety, good time, high jinks, jollification, jollity, joy, junketing, living it up, merriment, merrymaking, mirth, pleasure, recreation, romp, sport, treat, whoopee (*inf.*) **3 in** *or* **for fun** = **for a joke,** facetiously, for a laugh, in jest, jokingly, lightheartedly, mischievously, playfully, roguishly, teasingly, tongue in cheek, with a gleam *or* twinkle in one's eye, with a straight face **5 make fun of** = **mock,** deride, hold up to ridicule, lampoon, laugh at, make a fool of, parody, poke fun at, rag, rib (*inf.*), ridicule, satirize, scoff at, send up (*Brit. inf.*), sneer at, take off, taunt ◆ *modifier* **6** = **enjoyable,** amusing, convivial, diverting, entertaining, lively, witty
Antonyms *n* ≠ **enjoyment:** depression, desolation, despair, distress, gloom, grief, melancholy, misery, sadness, sorrow, unhappiness, woe

function *n* **2** = **purpose,** activity, business, capacity, charge, concern, duty, employment, exercise, job, mission, occupation, office, operation, part, post, province, *raison d'être,* responsibility, role, situation, task **3** = **reception,** affair, do (*inf.*), gathering, lig (*Brit. sl.*), social occasion ◆ *vb* **6** = **work,** act, act the part of, behave, be in business, be in commission, be in operation *or* action, be in running order, do duty, go, officiate, operate, perform, run, serve, serve one's turn

functional *adj* **2** = **practical,** hard-wearing, serviceable, useful, utilitarian, utility **3** = **working,** operative

functionary *n* = **officer,** dignitary, employee, office bearer, office holder, official

fund *n* **1** = **reserve,** capital, endowment, fall-back, foundation, kitty, pool, stock, store, supply, tontine **2** = **store,** hoard, mine, repository, reserve, reservoir, source, treasury, vein ◆ *vb* **3** = **finance,** capitalize, endow, float, pay for, promote, stake, subsidize, support

fundamental *adj* **1, 2** = **essential,** basic, cardinal, central, constitutional, crucial, elementary, first, important, indispensable, integral, intrinsic, key, necessary, organic, primary, prime, principal, radical, rudimentary, underlying, vital ◆ *n* **4** = **principle,** axiom, basic, cornerstone, essential, first principle, law, rudiment, rule, *sine qua non*
Antonyms *adj* ≠ **essential:** advanced, back-up, extra, incidental, lesser, secondary, subsidiary, superfluous

fundamentally *adv* **2** = **essentially,** at bot-

funds ❶ (fʌndz) *pl n* **1** money that is readily available. **2** British government securities representing national debt.
fundus ('fʌndəs) *n, pl* **fundi** (-daɪ). *Anat.* the base of an organ or the part farthest away from its opening. [C18: from L, lit.: the bottom]
funeral ❶ ('fju:nərəl) *n* **1a** a ceremony at which a dead person is buried or cremated. **1b** (*as modifier*): *funeral service.* **2** a procession of people escorting a corpse to burial. **3** *Inf.* concern; affair: *it's your funeral.* [C14: from Med. L, from LL, from L *fūnus* funeral]
▸**'funerary** *adj*
funeral director *n* an undertaker.
funeral parlour *n* a place where the dead are prepared for burial or cremation. Usual US name: **funeral home.**
funereal ❶ (fju:'nɪərɪəl) *adj* suggestive of a funeral; gloomy or mournful. Also: **funebrial.** [C18: from L *fūnereus*]
▸**fu'nereally** *adv*
funfair ('fʌnˌfeə) *n Brit.* an amusement park or fairground.
fungible ('fʌndʒɪbᵊl) *n Law.* (*often pl*) moveable perishable goods of a sort that may be estimated by number or weight, such as grain, wine, etc. [C18: from Med. L *fungibilis,* from L *fungī* to perform]
▸**ˌfungi'bility** *n*
fungicide ('fʌndʒɪˌsaɪd) *n* a substance or agent that destroys or is capable of destroying fungi.
▸**ˌfungi'cidal** *adj*
fungoid ('fʌŋgɔɪd) *adj* resembling a fungus or fungi.
fungous ('fʌŋgəs) *adj* appearing suddenly and spreading quickly like a fungus.
fungus ('fʌŋgəs) *n, pl* **fungi** ('fʌŋgaɪ, 'fʌndʒaɪ, 'fʌndʒɪ) *or* **funguses. 1** any member of a kingdom of organisms, formerly classified as plants, that lack chlorophyll, leaves, true stems, and roots, reproduce by spores, and live as saprotrophs or parasites. **2** something resembling a fungus, esp. in suddenly growing. **3** *Pathol.* any soft tumorous growth. [C16: from L: mushroom, fungus]
▸**'fungal** *adj*
funicular (fju:'nɪkjʊlə) *n* **1** Also called: **funicular railway.** a railway up the side of a mountain, consisting of two cars at either end of a cable passing round a driving wheel at the summit. ◆ *adj* **2** relating to or operated by a rope, etc. [C17: from L, from *fūnis* rope]
funk[1] ❶ (fʌŋk) *Inf., chiefly Brit.* ◆ *n* **1** Also called: **blue funk.** a state of nervousness, fear, or depression. **2** a coward. ◆ *vb* **3** to flinch from (responsibility, etc.) through fear. **4** (*tr; usually passive*) to make afraid. [C18: university sl., ? rel. to *funk* to smoke]
funk[2] (fʌŋk) *n* a type of polyrhythmic Black dance music with heavy syncopation. [C20: back formation from FUNKY]
funky ('fʌŋkɪ) *adj* **funkier, funkiest.** *Inf.* (of jazz, pop, etc.) passionate; soulful. [C20: from *funk* to smoke (tobacco), ? alluding to music that was smelly, that is, earthy]
funnel ❶ ('fʌnᵊl) *n* **1** a hollow utensil with a wide mouth tapering to a small hole, used for pouring liquids, etc., into a narrow-necked vessel. **2** something resembling this in shape or function. **3** a smokestack for smoke and exhaust gases, as on a steam locomotive. ◆ *vb* **funnels, funnelling, funnelled** *or US* **funnels, funneling, funneled. 4** to move or cause to move or pour through or as if through a funnel. [C15: from OProvençal *fonilh,* ult. from L *infundibulum,* from *infundere* to pour in]
▸**'funnel-ˌlike** *adj*
funnel-web *n Austral.* a large poisonous black spider that constructs funnel-shaped webs.
funny ❶ ('fʌnɪ) *adj* **funnier, funniest. 1** causing amusement or laughter; humorous. **2** peculiar; odd. **3** suspicious or dubious (esp. in **funny business**). **4** *Inf.* faint or ill. ◆ *n, pl* **funnies. 5** *Inf.* a joke or witticism.
▸**'funnily** *adv* ▸**'funniness** *n*
funny bone *n* the area near the elbow where the ulnar nerve is close to the surface of the skin: when it is struck, a sharp tingling sensation is experienced.
fun run *n* a long run or part-marathon run for exercise and pleasure, often by large numbers of people.
fuoco (fu:'əʊkəʊ) *Music.* ◆ *n* **1** fire. ◆ *adv, adj* **2 con fuoco.** in a fiery manner. [C19: It., lit.: fire]
fur (fɜ:) *n* **1** the dense coat of fine silky hairs on such mammals as the cat and mink. **2a** the dressed skin of certain fur-bearing animals, with the hair left on. **2b** (*as modifier*): *a fur coat.* **3** a garment made of fur, such as a stole. **4** a pile fabric made in imitation of animal fur. **5** *Heraldry.* any of various stylized representations of animal pelts used in coats of arms. **6 make the fur fly.** to cause a scene or disturbance. **7** *Inf.* a whitish coating on the tongue, caused by excessive smoking, illness, etc. **8** *Brit.* a whitish-grey deposit precipitated from hard water onto the insides of pipes, kettles, etc. ◆ *vb* **furs, furring, furred. 9** (*tr*) to line or trim a garment, etc., with fur. **10** (often foll. by *up*) to cover or become covered with a furlike lining or deposit. [C14: from OF *forrer* to line a garment, from *fuerre* sheath, of Gmc origin]
▸**'furless** *adj*
fur. *abbrev. for* furlong.
furbelow ('fɜ:bɪˌləʊ) *n* **1** a flounce, ruffle, or other ornamental trim. **2** (*often pl*) showy ornamentation. ◆ *vb* **3** (*tr*) to put a furbelow on (a garment, etc.). [C18: by folk etymology from F dialect *farbella* a frill]
furbish ❶ ('fɜ:bɪʃ) *vb* (*tr*) **1** to make bright by polishing. **2** (often foll. by *up*) to renovate; restore. [C14: from OF *fourbir* to polish, of Gmc origin]
▸**'furbisher** *n*
furcate ('fɜ:keɪt) *vb* **furcates, furcating, furcated. 1** to divide into two parts. ◆ *adj* **2** forked: *furcate branches.* [C19: from LL, from L *furca* a fork]
▸**fur'cation** *n*
furfuraceous (ˌfɜ:fjʊ'reɪʃəs) *adj* **1** relating to or resembling bran. **2** *Med.* resembling dandruff. [C17: from L *furfur* bran, scurf + -ACEOUS]
Furies ('fjʊərɪz) *pl n, sing* **Fury.** *Classical myth.* the snake-haired goddesses of vengeance, usually three in number, who pursued unpunished criminals. Also called: **Erinyes, Eumenides.**
furioso (ˌfjʊərɪ'əʊsəʊ) *Music.* ◆ *adj, adv* **1** in a frantically rushing manner. ◆ *n* **2** a passage or piece to be performed in this way. [C19: It., lit.: furious]
furious ❶ ('fjʊərɪəs) *adj* **1** extremely angry or annoyed. **2** violent or unrestrained, as in speed, energy, etc.
▸**'furiously** *adv* ▸**'furiousness** *n*
furl (fɜ:l) *vb* **1** to roll up (an umbrella, flag, etc.) neatly and securely or (of an umbrella, flag, etc.) to be rolled up in this way. ◆ *n* **2** the act or an instance of furling. **3** a single rolled-up section. [C16: from OF, from *ferm* tight (from L *firmus* FIRM[1]) + *lier* to bind, from L *ligāre*]
▸**'furlable** *adj*
furlong ('fɜ:ˌlɒŋ) *n* a unit of length equal to 220 yards (201.168 metres). [OE *furlang,* from *furh* furrow + *lang* long]
furlough ('fɜ:ləʊ) *n* **1** leave of absence from military duty. ◆ *vb* (*tr*) **2** to grant a furlough to. [C17: from Du. *verlof,* from *ver-* FOR- + *lof* leave, permission]
furnace ('fɜ:nɪs) *n* **1** an enclosed chamber in which heat is produced to destroy refuse, smelt or refine ores, etc. **2** a very hot place. [C13: from OF, from L *fornax* oven, furnace]
furnish ❶ ('fɜ:nɪʃ) *vb* (*tr*) **1** to provide (a house, room, etc.) with furniture, etc. **2** to equip with what is necessary. **3** to supply: *the records furnished the information.* [C15: from OF *fournir,* of Gmc origin]
▸**'furnisher** *n*
furnishings ('fɜ:nɪʃɪŋz) *pl n* furniture, carpets, etc., with which a room or house is furnished.
furniture ❶ ('fɜ:nɪtʃə) *n* **1** the movable articles that equip a room, house, etc. **2** the equipment necessary for a ship, factory, etc. **3** *Printing.* lengths of wood, plastic, or metal, used in assembling formes to surround the type. ◆ See also **door furniture, street furniture.** [C16: from F, from *fournir* to equip]
furore ❶ (fjʊ'rɔ:rɪ) *or esp. US* **furor** ('fjʊərɔ:) *n* **1** a public outburst; uproar. **2** a sudden widespread enthusiasm; craze. **3** frenzy; rage. [C15: from L: frenzy, from *furere* to rave]
furphy ('fɜ:fɪ) *n, pl* **furphies.** *Austral. sl.* a rumour or fictitious story. [C20: from *Furphy* carts (used for water or sewage in World War I), made at a foundry established by the Furphy family]
furred (fɜ:d) *adj* **1** made of, lined with, or covered in fur. **2** wearing fur. **3** (of animals) having fur. **4** another word for **furry** (sense 3). **5** provided with furring strips. **6** (of a pipe, kettle, etc.) lined with hard lime.
furrier ('fʌrɪə) *n* a person whose occupation is selling, making, or repairing fur garments. [C14: *furour,* from OF *fourrer* to trim with FUR]

THESAURUS

tom, at heart, basically, intrinsically, primarily, radically
funds *pl n* **1** = **money**, brass (*N English dialect*), bread (*sl.*), capital, cash, dosh (*Brit. & Austral. sl.*), dough (*sl.*), finance, hard cash, necessary (*inf.*), ready money, resources, savings, shekels (*inf.*), silver, spondulicks (*sl.*), the wherewithal, tin (*sl.*)
funeral *n* **1** = **burial**, cremation, inhumation, interment, obsequies
funereal *adj* = **gloomy**, dark, deathlike, depressing, dirge-like, dismal, dreary, grave, lamenting, lugubrious, mournful, sad, sepulchral, solemn, sombre, woeful
funk[1] *vb* **3** = **chicken out of** (*inf.*), dodge, duck out of (*inf.*), flinch from, recoil from, take fright, turn tail
funnel *vb* **4** = **channel**, conduct, convey, direct, filter, move, pass, pour
funny *adj* **1** = **humorous**, amusing, comic, comical, diverting, droll, entertaining, facetious, farcical, hilarious, jocose, jocular, jolly, killing (*inf.*), laughable, ludicrous, rich, ridiculous, riotous, risible, side-splitting, silly, slapstick, waggish, witty **2** = **peculiar**, curious, dubious, mysterious, odd, perplexing, puzzling, queer, remarkable, rum (*Brit. sl.*), strange, suspicious, unusual, weird ◆ *n* **5** *Informal* = **joke**, crack (*sl.*), jest, play on words, pun, quip, wisecrack, witticism
Antonyms *adj* ≠ **humorous:** grave, humourless, melancholy, serious, sober, solemn, stern, unfunny
furbish *vb* **1, 2** = **renovate**, brighten, burnish, polish, restore, rub, shine, smarten up, spruce up
furious *adj* **1** = **angry**, beside oneself, boiling, choked, cross, enraged, frantic, frenzied, fuming, incandescent, incensed, infuriated, in high dudgeon, livid (*inf.*), mad, maddened, on the warpath (*inf.*), raging, up in arms, wrathful, wroth (*arch.*) **2** = **violent**, boisterous, fierce, impetuous, intense, savage, stormy, tempestuous, tumultuous, turbulent, ungovernable, unrestrained, vehement, wild
Antonyms *adj* ≠ **angry:** calm, dispassionate, impassive, imperturbable, mild, placated, pleased, serene, tranquil
furnish *vb* **1, 2** = **decorate**, appoint, equip, fit, fit out, fit up, outfit, provide, provision, purvey, rig, stock, store, supply **3** = **supply**, afford, bestow, endow, give, grant, hand out, offer, present, provide, reveal
furniture *n* **1** = **household goods**, appliances, appointments, chattels, effects, equipment, fittings, furnishings, goods, movable property, movables, possessions, things (*inf.*)
furore *n* **1** = **commotion**, brouhaha, disturbance, excitement, flap (*inf.*), hullabaloo, out-

▸'furriery *n*

furring ('fɜːrɪŋ) *n* **1** short for **furring strip. 2** the formation of fur on the tongue. **3** trimming of animal fur, as on a coat.

furring strip *n* a strip of wood or metal fixed to a wall, floor, or ceiling to provide a surface for the fixing of plasterboard, floorboards, etc.

furrow Ⓣ ('fʌrəʊ) *n* **1** a long narrow trench made in the ground by a plough. **2** any long deep groove, esp. a deep wrinkle on the forehead. ◆ *vb* **3** to develop or cause to develop furrows or wrinkles. **4** to make a furrow or furrows in (land). [OE *furh*]
▸'**furrower** *n* ▸'**furrowless** *adj* ▸'**furrowy** *adj*

furry ('fɜːrɪ) *adj* **furrier, furriest. 1** covered with fur or something furlike. **2** of, relating to, or resembling fur. **3** Also: **furred.** (of the tongue) coated with whitish cellular debris.
▸'**furrily** *adv* ▸'**furriness** *n*

further Ⓣ ('fɜːðə) *adv* **1** in addition; furthermore. **2** to a greater degree or extent. **3** to or at a more advanced point. **4** to or at a greater distance in time or space. ◆ *adj* **5** additional; more. **6** more distant or remote in time or space. ◆ *vb* **7** (*tr*) to assist the progress of. ◆ See also **far, furthest.** [OE *furthor*]

USAGE NOTE See at **farther.**

furtherance Ⓣ ('fɜːðərəns) *n* **1** the act of furthering. **2** something that furthers.

further education *n* (in Britain) formal education beyond school other than at a university or polytechnic.

furthermore Ⓣ ('fɜːðəˌmɔː) *adv* in addition; moreover.

furthermost ('fɜːðəˌməʊst) *adj* most distant; furthest.

furthest Ⓣ ('fɜːðɪst) *adv* **1** to the greatest degree or extent. **2** to or at the greatest distance in time or space; farthest. ◆ *adj* **3** most distant or remote in time or space; farthest.

furtive Ⓣ ('fɜːtɪv) *adj* characterized by stealth; sly and secretive. [C15: from L *furtīvus* stolen, from *furtum* a theft, from *fūr* a thief]
▸'**furtively** *adv* ▸'**furtiveness** *n*

furuncle ('fjʊərʌŋkᵊl) *n Pathol.* the technical name for **boil**[2]. [C17: from L *fūrunculus* pilferer, sore, from *fūr* thief]
▸**furuncular** (fjʊ'rʌŋkjʊlə) *or* **fu'runculous** *adj*

furunculosis (fjʊˌrʌŋkjʊ'ləʊsɪs) *n* **1** a skin condition characterized by the presence of multiple boils. **2** a disease of salmon and trout caused by a bacterium.

fury Ⓣ ('fjʊərɪ) *n, pl* **furies. 1** violent or uncontrolled anger. **2** an outburst of such anger. **3** uncontrolled violence: *the fury of the storm.* **4** a person, esp. a woman, with a violent temper. **5** See **Furies. 6 like fury.** *Inf.* violently; furiously. [C14: from L, from *furere* to be furious]

furze (fɜːz) *n* another name for **gorse.** [OE *fyrs*]
▸'**furzy** *adj*

fuscous ('fʌskəs) *adj* of a brownish-grey colour. [C17: from L *fuscus* dark, swarthy, tawny]

fuse[1] *or chiefly US* **fuze** (fjuːz) *n* **1** a lead of combustible black powder (**safety fuse**), or a lead containing an explosive (**detonating fuse**), used to fire an explosive charge. **2** any device by which an explosive charge is ignited. ◆ *vb* **fuses, fusing, fused** *or chiefly US* **fuzes, fuzing, fuzed. 3** (*tr*) to equip with such a fuse. [C17: from It. *fuso* spindle, from L *fūsus*]
▸'**fuseless** *adj*

fuse[2] Ⓣ (fjuːz) *vb* **fuses, fusing, fused. 1** to unite or become united by melting, esp. by the action of heat. **2** to become or cause to become liquid, esp. by the action of heat. **3** to join or become combined. **4** (*tr*) to equip (a plug, etc.) with a fuse. **5** *Brit.* to fail or cause to fail as a result of the blowing of a fuse: *the lights fused.* ◆ *n* **6** a protective device for safeguarding electric circuits, etc., containing a wire that melts and breaks the circuit when the current exceeds a certain value. [C17: from L *fūsus* melted, cast, from *fundere* to pour out; sense 5 infl. by FUSE[1]]

fusee *or* **fuzee** (fjuː'ziː) *n* **1** (in early clocks and watches) a spirally grooved spindle, functioning as an equalizing force on the unwinding of the mainspring. **2** a friction match with a large head. [C16: from F *fusée* spindleful of thread, from OF *fus* spindle, from L *fūsus*]

fuselage ('fjuːzɪˌlɑːʒ) *n* the main body of an aircraft. [C20: from F, from *fuseler* to shape like a spindle, from OF *fusel* spindle]

fusel oil *or* **fusel** ('fjuːzᵊl) *n* a poisonous by-product formed in the distillation of fermented liquors and used as a source of amyl alcohols. [C19: from G *Fusel* bad spirits]

fusible ('fjuːzəbᵊl) *adj* capable of being fused or melted.
▸ˌ**fusi'bility** *n* ▸'**fusibly** *adv*

fusiform ('fjuːzɪˌfɔːm) *adj* elongated and tapering at both ends. [C18: from L *fūsus* spindle]

fusil ('fjuːzɪl) *n* a light flintlock musket. [C16 (in the sense: steel for a tinderbox): from OF, from Vulgar L *focīlis* (unattested), from L *focus* fire]

fusilier (ˌfjuːzɪ'lɪə) *n* **1** (formerly) an infantryman armed with a light musket. **2** Also: **fusileer. 2a** a soldier, esp. a private, serving in any of certain British or other infantry regiments. **2b** (*pl; cap. when part of a name*): *the Royal Welch Fusiliers.* [C17: from F; see FUSIL]

fusillade Ⓣ (ˌfjuːzɪ'leɪd) *n* **1** a rapid continual discharge of firearms. **2** a sudden outburst, as of criticism. ◆ *vb* **fusillades, fusillading, fusilladed. 3** (*tr*) to attack with a fusillade. [C19: from F, from *fusiller* to shoot; see FUSIL]

fusion Ⓣ ('fjuːʒən) *n* **1** the act or process of fusing or melting together. **2** the state of being fused. **3** something produced by fusing. **4** a kind of popular music that is a blend of two or more styles, such as jazz and funk. **5** See **nuclear fusion. 6** a coalition of political parties. [C16: from L *fūsiō* a pouring out, melting, from *fundere* to pour out, FOUND[3]]

fusion bomb *n* a type of bomb in which most of the energy is provided by nuclear fusion. Also called: **thermonuclear bomb, fission-fusion bomb.**

fuss Ⓣ (fʌs) *n* **1** nervous activity or agitation, esp. when unnecessary. **2** complaint or objection: *he made a fuss over the bill.* **3** an exhibition of affection or admiration: *they made a great fuss over the new baby.* **4** a quarrel. ◆ *vb* **5** (*intr*) to worry unnecessarily. **6** (*intr*) to be excessively concerned over trifles. **7** (when *intr*, usually foll. by *over*) to show great or excessive concern, affection, etc. (for). **8** (*tr*) to bother (a person). [C18: from ?]
▸'**fusser** *n*

fusspot Ⓣ ('fʌsˌpɒt) *n Brit. inf.* a person who fusses unnecessarily.

fussy Ⓣ ('fʌsɪ) *adj* **fussier, fussiest. 1** inclined to fuss over minor points. **2** very particular about detail. **3** characterized by overelaborate detail.
▸'**fussily** *adv* ▸'**fussiness** *n*

fustanella (ˌfʌstə'nelə) *n* a white knee-length pleated skirt worn by men in Greece and Albania. [C19: from It., from Mod. Gk *phoustani*, prob. from It. *fustagno* FUSTIAN]

fustian ('fʌstɪən) *n* **1a** a hard-wearing fabric of cotton mixed with flax or wool. **1b** (*as modifier*): *a fustian jacket.* **2** pompous talk or writing. ◆ *adj* **3** cheap; worthless. **4** bombastic. [C12: from OF, from Med. L *fustāneum*, from L *fustis* cudgel]

fustic ('fʌstɪk) *n* **1** Also called: **old fustic.** a large tropical American tree. **2** the yellow dye obtained from the wood of this tree. **3** any of various trees or shrubs that yield a similar dye, esp. a European sumach (**young fustic**). [C15: from F *fustoc*, from Sp., from Ar. *fustuq*, from Gk *pistakē* pistachio tree]

fusty Ⓣ ('fʌstɪ) *adj* **fustier, fustiest. 1** smelling of damp or mould. **2**

THESAURUS

burst, outcry, stir, to-do, uproar **2** = **craze**, enthusiasm, mania, rage

furrow *n* **1, 2** = **groove**, channel, corrugation, crease, crow's-foot, fluting, hollow, line, rut, seam, trench, wrinkle ◆ *vb* **3** = **wrinkle**, corrugate, crease, draw together, flute, knit, seam

further *adv* **1** = **in addition**, additionally, also, as well as, besides, furthermore, into the bargain, moreover, on top of, over and above, to boot, what's more, yet ◆ *adj* **5** = **additional**, extra, fresh, more, new, other, supplementary ◆ *vb* **7** = **promote**, advance, aid, assist, champion, contribute to, encourage, expedite, facilitate, forward, foster, hasten, help, lend support to, patronize, pave the way for, plug (*inf.*), push, speed, succour, work for
Antonyms *vb* ≠ **promote:** foil, frustrate, hinder, hobble, impede, obstruct, oppose, prevent, retard, stop, thwart

furtherance *n* **1** = **promotion**, advancement, advocacy, backing, boosting, carrying-out, championship, prosecution, pursuit

furthermore *adv* = **besides**, additionally, as well, further, in addition, into the bargain, moreover, not to mention, to boot, too, what's more

furthest *adj* **3** = **most distant**, extreme, farthest, furthermost, outermost, outmost, remotest, ultimate, uttermost

furtive *adj* = **sly**, behind someone's back, clandestine, cloaked, conspiratorial, covert, hidden, secret, secretive, skulking, slinking, sneaking, sneaky, stealthy, surreptitious, underhand, under-the-table
Antonyms *adj* above-board, candid, forthright, frank, open, public, straightforward, undisguised, unreserved

fury *n* **1** = **anger**, frenzy, impetuosity, ire, madness, passion, rage, red mist (*inf.*), wrath **3** = **violence**, ferocity, fierceness, force, intensity, power, savagery, severity, tempestuousness, turbulence, vehemence **4** = **spitfire**, bacchante, hag, hellcat, shrew, termagant, virago, vixen
Antonyms *n* ≠ **anger:** calm, calmness, composure, equanimity ≠ **violence:** hush, peace, peacefulness, serenity, stillness, tranquillity

fuse[2] *vb* **1-3** = **join**, agglutinate, amalgamate, blend, coalesce, combine, commingle, dissolve, federate, integrate, intermingle, intermix, meld, melt, merge, run together, smelt, solder, unite, weld
Antonyms *vb* diffuse, dispense, disseminate, dissipate, disunite, scatter, separate, spread, strew

fusillade *n* **1, 2** = **barrage**, broadside, burst, fire, hail, outburst, salvo, volley

fusion *n* **1-3** = **merging**, alloy, amalgam, amalgamation, blend, blending, coalescence, commingling, commixture, federation, integration, liquefaction, meld, merger, mixture, smelting, synthesis, union, uniting, welding

fuss *n* **1** = **bother**, ado, agitation, bustle, commotion, confusion, excitement, fidget, flap (*inf.*), flurry, fluster, flutter, hue and cry, hurry, palaver, pother, stir, storm in a teacup (*Brit.*), to-do, upset, worry **2** = **argument**, altercation, bother, complaint, difficulty, display, furore, hassle (*inf.*), objection, row, squabble, trouble, unrest, upset ◆ *vb* **5** = **worry**, bustle, chafe, fidget, flap (*inf.*), fret, fume, get in a stew (*inf.*), get worked up, labour over, make a meal of (*inf.*), make a thing of (*inf.*), niggle, take pains

fusspot *n Brit. informal* = **perfectionist**, fidget, old woman, worrier

fussy *adj* **1, 2** = **particular**, choosy (*inf.*), dainty, difficult, discriminating, exacting, faddish, faddy, fastidious, finicky, hard to please, nit-picking (*inf.*), old-maidish, old womanish, overparticular, pernickety, picky (*inf.*), squeamish **3** = **overelaborate**, busy, cluttered, overdecorated, overembellished, overworked, rococo

fustiness *n* **1** = **staleness**, airlessness, damp-

old-fashioned in attitude. [C14: from *fust* wine cask, from OF: cask, from L *fūstis* cudgel]
▸ **'fustily** *adv* ▸ **'fustiness** *n*

fut. *abbrev. for* future.

futhark ('fu:θɑ:k) *or* **futhorc, futhork** ('fu:θɔ:k) *n* a phonetic alphabet consisting of runes. [C19: from the first six letters: *f, u, th, a, r, k*]

futile ❶ ('fju:taɪl) *adj* **1** having no effective result; unsuccessful. **2** pointless; trifling. **3** inane or foolish. [C16: from L *futtilis* pouring out easily, from *fundere* to pour out]
▸ **'futilely** *adv* ▸ **futility** (fju:'tɪlɪtɪ) *n*

futon ('fu:ˌtɒn) *n* a Japanese padded quilt, laid on the floor as a bed. [C19: from Japanese]

futtock ('fʌtək) *n Naut.* one of the ribs in the frame of a wooden vessel. [C13: ? var. of *foothook*]

future ❶ ('fju:tʃə) *n* **1** the time yet to come. **2** undetermined events that will occur in that time. **3** the condition of a person or thing at a later date: *the future of the school is undecided.* **4** likelihood of later improvement: *he has a future as a singer.* **5** *Grammar.* **5a** a tense of verbs used when the action or event described is to occur after the time of utterance. **5b** a verb in this tense. **6 in future.** from now on. ◆ *adj* **7** that is yet to come or be. **8** of or expressing time yet to come. **9** (*prenominal*) destined to become. **10** *Grammar.* in or denoting the future as a tense of verbs. ◆ See also **futures.** [C14: from L *fūtūrus* about to be, from *esse* to be]
▸ **'futureless** *adj*

future perfect *Grammar.* ◆ *adj* **1** denoting a tense of verbs describing an action that will have been performed by a certain time. ◆ *n* **2a** the future perfect tense. **2b** a verb in this tense.

futures ('fju:tʃəz) *pl n* **a** commodities or other financial products bought or sold at an agreed price for delivery at a specified future date. See also **financial futures. b** (*as modifier*): *futures contract; futures market.*

future value *n* the value that a sum of money invested at compound interest will have after a specified period.

futurism ('fju:tʃəˌrɪzəm) *n* an artistic movement that arose in Italy in 1909 to replace traditional aesthetic values with the characteristics of the machine age.
▸ **'futurist** *n, adj*

futuristic (ˌfju:tʃə'rɪstɪk) *adj* **1** denoting or relating to design, etc., that is thought likely to be fashionable at some future time. **2** of or relating to futurism.
▸ **ˌfutur'istically** *adv*

futurity (fju:'tjʊərɪtɪ) *n, pl* **futurities. 1** a less common word for **future. 2** the quality of being in the future. **3** a future event.

futurology (ˌfju:tʃə'rɒlədʒɪ) *n* the study or prediction of the future of mankind.
▸ **ˌfutur'ologist** *n*

fuze (fju:z) *n, vb* **fuzes, fuzing, fuzed.** *Chiefly US.* a variant spelling of **fuse**[1].

fuzee (fju:'zi:) *n* a variant spelling of **fusee.**

fuzz[1] ❶ (fʌz) *n* **1** a mass or covering of fine or curly hairs, fibres, etc. **2** a blur. ◆ *vb* **3** to make or become fuzzy. **4** to make or become indistinct. [C17: ?from Low G *fussig* loose]

fuzz[2] (fʌz) *n* a slang word for **police** or **policeman.** [C20: from ?]

fuzzy ❶ ('fʌzɪ) *adj* **fuzzier, fuzziest. 1** of, resembling, or covered with fuzz. **2** unclear or distorted. **3** (of the hair) tightly curled or very wavy.
▸ **'fuzzily** *adv* ▸ **'fuzziness** *n*

fuzzy logic *n* a branch of logic that allows degrees of imprecision in reasoning and knowledge to be represented in such a way that the information can be processed by computer.

fuzzy-wuzzy ('fʌzɪˌwʌzɪ) *n, pl* **fuzzy-wuzzies.** *Offens. arch. sl.* a Black fuzzy-haired native of any of various countries.

fwd *abbrev. for* forward.

f-word *n* **the.** (*sometimes cap.*) a euphemistic way of referring to the word **fuck.** [from F(UCK) + WORD]

FX *n Films, inf.* short for **special effects.** [C20: a phonetic respelling of EFFECTS]

-fy *suffix forming verbs.* to make or become: *beautify.* [from OF *-fier*, from L *-ficāre*, from *-ficus* -FIC]

fylfot ('faɪlfɒt) *n* a rare word for **swastika.** [C16 (apparently meaning: a sign or device for the lower part or foot of a painted window): from *fillen* to fill + *fot* foot]

THESAURUS

ness, frowstiness, fug, mouldiness, mustiness, smell of decay, stuffiness

fusty *adj* **1 = stale**, airless, damp, frowsty, ill-smelling, malodorous, mildewed, mildewy, mouldering, mouldy, musty, rank, stuffy **2 = old-fashioned**, antediluvian, antiquated, archaic, old-fogeyish, outdated, out-of-date, out of the ark (*inf.*), passé

futile *adj* **1 = useless**, abortive, barren, bootless, empty, forlorn, fruitless, hollow, ineffectual, in vain, nugatory, otiose, profitless, sterile, to no avail, unavailing, unproductive, unprofitable, unsuccessful, vain, valueless, without rhyme or reason, worthless **2 = trivial**, idle, pointless, trifling, unimportant
Antonyms *adj* ≠ **useless:** constructive, effective, fruitful, profitable, purposeful, successful, useful, valuable, worthwhile ≠ **trivial:** important, significant

futility *n* **1 = uselessness**, bootlessness, emptiness, fruitlessness, hollowness, ineffectiveness, spitting in the wind **2 = triviality**, pointlessness, unimportance, vanity

future *n* **1 = time to come**, hereafter **3 = prospect**, expectation, outlook ◆ *adj* **7, 9 = forthcoming**, approaching, coming, destined, eventual, expected, fated, impending, in the offing, later, prospective, subsequent, to be, to come, ultimate, unborn
Antonyms *adj* ≠ **forthcoming:** bygone, erstwhile, ex-, former, late, past, preceding, previous, quondam

fuzz[1] *n* **1 = fluff**, down, fibre, floss, hair, lint, nap, pile

fuzzy *adj* **1 = fluffy**, down-covered, downy, flossy, frizzy, linty, napped, woolly **2 = indistinct**, bleary, blurred, distorted, faint, ill-defined, muffled, out of focus, shadowy, unclear, unfocused, vague
Antonyms *adj* ≠ **indistinct:** clear, defined, detailed, distinct, in focus, precise

Gg

g *or* **G** (dʒiː) *n, pl* **g's, G's,** *or* **Gs. 1** the seventh letter of the English alphabet. **2** a speech sound represented by this letter, usually either as in *grass,* or as in *page.*

g *symbol for:* **1** gallon(s). **2** gram(s). **3** grav. **4** acceleration of free fall (due to gravity).

G *symbol for:* **1** *Music.* **1a** the fifth note of the scale of C major. **1b** the major or minor key having this note as its tonic. **2** gauss. **3** gravitational constant. **4** *Physics.* conductance. **5** *Biochem.* guanine. **6** German. **7** giga. **8** good. **9** *Sl., chiefly US.* grand (a thousand dollars or pounds). **10** (in Australia) **10a** general exhibition (used to describe a category of film certified as suitable for viewing by anyone). **10b** (*as modifier*): *a G film.*

G. *or* **g.** *abbrev. for:* **1** gauges. **2** gelding. **3** guilder(s). **4** guinea(s). **5** Gulf.

G3 *abbrev. for* Group of Three.

G5 *abbrev. for* Group of Five.

G7 *abbrev. for* Group of Seven.

G10 *abbrev. for* Group of Ten.

G24 *abbrev. for* Group of Twenty-Four.

G77 *abbrev. for* Group of Seventy-Seven.

Ga *the chemical symbol for* gallium.

GA *abbrev. for:* **1** General Assembly (of the United Nations). **2** general average. **3** Georgia.

gab ❶ (gæb) *Inf.* ◆ *vb* **gabs, gabbing, gabbed. 1** (*intr*) to talk excessively or idly; gossip. ◆ *n* **2** idle or trivial talk. **3 gift of the gab.** ability to speak glibly or persuasively. [C18: prob. from Irish Gaelic *gob* mouth]
▸ **'gabber** *n*

gabardine *or* **gaberdine** ('gæbəˌdiːn, ˌgæbə'diːn) *n* **1** a twill-weave worsted, cotton, or spun-rayon fabric. **2** an ankle-length loose coat or frock worn by men, esp. by Jews, in the Middle Ages. **3** any of various other garments made of gabardine, esp. a child's raincoat. [C16: from OF *gauvardine* pilgrim's garment, from MHG *wallewart* pilgrimage]

gabble ❶ ('gæbᵊl) *vb* **gabbles, gabbling, gabbled. 1** to utter (words, etc.) rapidly and indistinctly; jabber. **2** (*intr*) (of geese, etc.) to utter rapid cackling noises. ◆ *n* **3** rapid and indistinct speech or noises. [C17: from MDu. *gabbelen,* imit.]
▸ **'gabbler** *n*

gabbro ('gæbrəʊ) *n, pl* **gabbros.** a dark coarse-grained igneous rock consisting of feldspar, pyroxene, and often olivine. [C19: from It., prob. from L *glaber* smooth, bald]

gabby ❶ ('gæbɪ) *adj* **gabbier, gabbiest.** *Inf.* inclined to chatter; talkative.

gabfest ('gæbˌfest) *n Inf., chiefly US & Canad.* **1** prolonged gossiping or conversation. **2** an informal gathering for conversation. [C19: from GAB + FEST]

gabion ('geɪbɪən) *n* **1** a cylindrical metal container filled with stones, used in the construction of underwater foundations. **2** a wickerwork basket filled with stones or earth, used (esp. formerly) as part of a fortification. [C16: from F: basket, from It., from *gabbia* cage, from L *cavea;* see CAGE]

gable ('geɪbᵊl) *n* **1** the triangular upper part of a wall between the sloping ends of a pitched roof (**gable roof**). **2** a triangular ornamental feature, esp. as used over a door or window. [C14: OF, prob. from ON *gafl*]
▸ **'gabled** *adj*

gable end *n* the end wall of a building on the side which is topped by a gable.

gaboon (gə'buːn) *n* a dark mahogany-like wood from an African tree, used in plywood, for furniture, and as a veneer. [C20: altered from *Gabon*]

gaboon viper *n* a large venomous viper of African rainforests. It has brown and purple markings and hornlike projections on its snout.

gaby ('geɪbɪ) *n, pl* **gabies.** *Arch. or dialect.* a simpleton. [C18: from ?]

gad ❶ (gæd) *vb* **gads, gadding, gadded. 1** (*intr;* often foll. by *about* or *around*) to go out in search of pleasure; gallivant. ◆ *n* **2** carefree adventure (esp. in **on the gad**). [C15: back formation from obs. *gadling* companion, from OE, from *gæd* fellowship]
▸ **'gadder** *n*

gadabout ❶ ('gædəˌbaʊt) *n Inf.* a person who restlessly seeks amusement, etc.

Gadarene ('gædəˌriːn) *adj* relating to or engaged in a headlong rush. [C19: via LL from Gk *Gadarēnos,* of Gadara (Palestine), alluding to the Gadarene swine (Matthew 8:28ff.)]

gadfly ('gædˌflaɪ) *n, pl* **gadflies. 1** any of various large dipterous flies, esp. the horsefly, that annoy livestock by sucking their blood. **2** a constantly irritating person. [C16: from *gad* sting + FLY²]

gadget ❶ ('gædʒɪt) *n* **1** a small mechanical device or appliance. **2** any object that is interesting for its ingenuity. [C19: ?from F *gâchette* lock catch, dim. of *gâche* staple]

gadgetry ('gædʒɪtrɪ) *n* **1** gadgets collectively. **2** use of or preoccupation with gadgets.

gadoid ('geɪdɔɪd) *adj* **1** of or belonging to an order of marine soft-finned fishes typically having the pectoral and pelvic fins close together and small cycloid scales. The group includes cod and hake. ◆ *n* **2** any gadoid fish. [C19: from NL *Gadidae,* from *gadus* cod; see -OID]

gadolinium (ˌgædə'lɪnɪəm) *n* a ductile malleable silvery-white ferromagnetic element of the lanthanide series of metals. Symbol: Gd; atomic no.: 64; atomic wt.: 157.25. [C19: NL, after Johan *Gadolin* (1760–1852), Finnish mineralogist]

gadroon *or* **godroon** (gə'druːn) *n* a decorative moulding composed of a series of convex flutes and curves, used esp. as an edge to silver articles. [C18: from F *godron,* ?from OF *godet* cup, goblet]

gadwall ('gædˌwɔːl) *n, pl* **gadwalls** *or* **gadwall.** a duck related to the mallard. The male has a grey body and black tail. [C17: from ?]

gadzooks (gæd'zuːks) *interj Arch.* a mild oath. [C17: ?from *God's hooks* (the nails of the cross) from *Gad* arch. euphemism for God]

Gael (geɪl) *n* a person who speaks a Gaelic language, esp. a Highland Scot or an Irishman. [C19: from Gaelic *Gaidheal*]
▸ **'Gaeldom** *n*

Gaelic ('geɪlɪk, 'gæ-) *n* **1** any of the closely related languages of the Celts in Ireland, Scotland, or the Isle of Man. ◆ *adj* **2** of, denoting, or relating to the Celtic people of Ireland, Scotland, or the Isle of Man or their language or customs.

Gaelic coffee *n* another name for **Irish coffee.**

Gaeltacht ('geːltəxt) *n* any of the regions in Ireland in which Irish Gaelic is the vernacular speech. [C20: from Irish Gaelic]

gaff¹ (gæf) *n* **1** *Angling.* a stiff pole with a stout prong or hook attached for landing large fish. **2** *Naut.* a boom hoisted aft of a mast to support a fore-and-aft sail. **3** a metal spur fixed to the leg of a gamecock. ◆ *vb* **4** (*tr*) *Angling.* to hook or land (a fish) with a gaff. [C13: from F *gaffe,* from Provençal *gaf* boat hook]

gaff² (gæf) *n* **1** *Sl.* nonsense. **2 blow the gaff.** *Brit. sl.* to divulge a secret. [C19: from ?]

gaffe ❶ (gæf) *n* a social blunder, esp. a tactless remark. [C19: from F]

gaffer ❶ ('gæfə) *n* **1** an old man: often used affectionately or patronizingly. **2** *Inf., chiefly Brit.* a boss, foreman, or owner of a factory, etc. **3** *Inf.* the senior electrician on a television or film set. [C16: from GODFATHER]

gag¹ ❶ (gæg) *vb* **gags, gagging, gagged. 1** (*tr*) to stop up (a person's mouth), esp. with a piece of cloth, etc., to prevent him from speaking or crying out. **2** (*tr*) to suppress or censor (free expression, information, etc.). **3** to retch or cause to retch. **4** (*intr*) to struggle for breath; choke. ◆ *n* **5** a piece of cloth, rope, etc., stuffed into or tied across the mouth. **6** any restraint on or suppression of information, free speech, etc. **7** *Parliamentary procedure.* another word for **closure** (sense 4). [C15 *gaggen;* ? imit. of a gasping sound]

gag² ❶ (gæg) *Inf.* ◆ *n* **1** a joke or humorous story, esp. one told by a professional comedian. **2** a hoax, practical joke, etc. ◆ *vb* **gags, gagging, gagged. 3** (*intr*) to tell jokes or funny stories, as comedians in nightclubs, etc. [C19: ? special use of GAG¹]

gaga ('gɑːgɑː) *adj Inf.* **1** senile; doting. **2** slightly crazy. [C20: from F, imit.]

gage¹ (geɪdʒ) *n* **1** something deposited as security against the fulfilment of an obligation; pledge. **2** (formerly) a glove or other object thrown down to indicate a challenge to combat. ◆ *vb* **gages, gaging,**

THESAURUS

gab *vb* **1** = **chatter**, babble, blabber, blather, buzz, chew the fat *or* rag (*sl.*), gossip, jabber, jaw (*sl.*), prattle, rabbit (*Brit. inf.*), spout, talk, waffle (*inf., chiefly Brit.*), yak (*sl.*) ◆ *n* **2** = **chatter**, blab, blarney, blather, chat, chitchat, conversation, gossip, loquacity, palaver, small talk, talk, tête-à-tête, tittle-tattle, tongue-wagging, waffle (*inf., chiefly Brit.*)

gabble *vb* **1** = **prattle**, babble, blab, blabber, cackle, chatter, gaggle, gibber, gush, jabber, rabbit (*Brit. inf.*), rattle, splutter, spout, sputter, waffle (*inf., chiefly Brit.*) ◆ *n* **3** = **gibberish**, babble, blabber, cackling, chatter, drivel, jargon, pap, prattle, twaddle, waffle (*inf., chiefly Brit.*)

gabby *adj* = **talkative**, chatty, effusive, garrulous, glib, gossiping, gushing, long-winded, loquacious, mouthy, prattling, prolix, verbose, voluble, windy, wordy

gad *vb* **1** *with* **about** *or* **around** = **gallivant**, ramble, range, roam, rove, run around, stravaig (*Scot. & N English dialect*), stray, traipse (*inf.*), wander

gadabout *n* = **pleasure-seeker**, gallivanter, rambler, rover, wanderer

gadget *n* **1** = **device**, appliance, contraption, contrivance, gimmick, gizmo (*sl., chiefly US*), instrument, invention, novelty, thing, tool, waldo

gaffe *n* = **blunder**, bloomer (*inf.*), boob (*Brit. sl.*), boo-boo (*inf.*), clanger (*inf.*), faux pas, gaucherie, howler, indiscretion, lapse, mistake, slip, solecism

gaffer *n* **1** = **old man**, granddad, greybeard, old boy, old fellow, old-timer (*US*) **2** *Informal* = **manager**, boss (*inf.*), foreman, ganger, overseer, superintendent, supervisor

gag¹ *vb* **1, 2** = **suppress**, curb, muffle, muzzle, quiet, silence, stifle, still, stop up, throttle **3** = **retch**, barf (*sl.*), disgorge, heave, puke (*sl.*), spew, throw up (*inf.*), vomit **4** = **choke**, gasp, pant, struggle for breath

gag² *n* **1, 2** = **joke**, crack, funny (*inf.*), hoax, jest, wisecrack (*inf.*), witticism

gaged. 3 (*tr*) *Arch.* to stake, pledge, or wager. [C14: from OF, of Gmc origin]

gage[2] (geɪdʒ) *n* short for **greengage.**

gage[3] (geɪdʒ) *n, vb* **gages, gaging, gaged.** *US.* a variant spelling (esp. in technical senses) of **gauge.**

gaggle ('gægᵊl) *vb* **gaggles, gaggling, gaggled.** 1 (*intr*) (of geese) to cackle. ◆ *n* 2 a flock of geese. 3 *Inf.* a disorderly group of people. [C14: of Gmc origin; imit.]

Gaia hypothesis *or* **theory** ('gaɪə) *n* the theory that the earth and everything on it constitutes a single self-regulating living entity. [C20: *Gaia,* variant of *Gaea,* Gk goddess of the earth]

gaiety Ⓣ ('geɪətɪ) *n, pl* **gaieties.** 1 the state or condition of being merry, bright, or lively. 2 festivity; merrymaking. 3 bright appearance.

> **USAGE NOTE** See at **gay.**

gaillardia (geɪ'lɑːdɪə) *n* a plant of the composite family having ornamental flower heads with yellow or red rays and purple discs. [C19: from NL, after *Gaillard* de Marentonneau, 18th-cent. F amateur botanist]

gaily Ⓣ ('geɪlɪ) *adv* 1 in a gay manner; merrily. 2 with bright colours; showily.

gain Ⓣ (geɪn) *vb* 1 (*tr*) to acquire (something desirable); obtain. 2 (*tr*) to win in competition: *to gain the victory.* 3 to increase, improve, or advance: *the car gained speed.* 4 (*tr*) to earn (a wage, living, etc.). 5 (*intr;* usually foll. by *on* or *upon*) 5a to get nearer (to) or catch up (on). 5b to get farther away (from). 6 (*tr*) (esp. of ships) to get to; reach: *the steamer gained port.* 7 (of a timepiece) to operate too fast, so as to indicate a time ahead of the true time. ◆ *n* 8 something won, acquired, earned, etc.; profit; advantage. 9 an increase in size, amount, etc. 10 the act of gaining; attainment; acquisition. 11 Also called: **amplification.** *Electronics.* the ratio of the output signal of an amplifier to the input signal, usually measured in decibels. [C15: from OF *gaaignier,* of Gmc origin]

gainer ('geɪnə) *n* 1 a person or thing that gains. 2 a type of dive in which the diver leaves the board facing forward and completes a full backward somersault to enter the water feet first with his back to the diving board.

gainful Ⓣ ('geɪnfʊl) *adj* profitable; lucrative.
▸ **'gainfully** *adv* ▸ **'gainfulness** *n*

gainsay Ⓣ (geɪn'seɪ) *vb* **gainsays, gainsaying, gainsaid.** (*tr*) *Arch. or literary.* to deny (an allegation, statement, etc.); contradict. [C13 *gainsaien,* from *gain-* AGAINST + *saien* to SAY]
▸ **gain'sayer** *n*

'gainst *or* **gainst** (genst, geɪnst) *prep Poetic.* short for **against.**

gait Ⓣ (geɪt) *n* 1 manner of walking or running. 2 (used esp. of horses and dogs) the pattern of footsteps at a particular speed, as the walk, canter, etc. ◆ *vb* 3 (*tr*) to teach (a horse) a particular gait. [C16: var. of GATE]

gaiter ('geɪtə) *n* (*often pl*) 1 a cloth or leather covering for the leg or ankle. 2 Also called: **spat.** a similar covering extending from the ankle to the instep. [C18: from F *guêtre,* prob. of Gmc origin]

gal (gæl) *n Sl.* a girl.

gal. *or* **gall.** *abbrev. for* gallon.

Gal. *Bible. abbrev. for* Galatians.

gala Ⓣ ('gɑːlə, 'geɪlə) *n* 1a a celebration; festive occasion. 1b (*as modifier*): *a gala occasion.* 2 *Chiefly Brit.* a sporting occasion involving competitions in several events: *a swimming gala.* [C17: from F or It., from OF *gale,* from *galer* to make merry, prob. of Gmc origin]

galactic (gə'læktɪk) *adj* 1 *Astron.* of or relating to a galaxy, esp. the Galaxy. 2 **galactic plane.** the plane passing through the spiral arms of the Galaxy, contained by the great circle of the celestial sphere (**galactic equator**) and perpendicular to an imaginary line joining opposite points (**galactic poles**) on the celestial sphere. 3 *Med.* of or relating to milk. [C19: from Gk *galaktikos;* see GALAXY]

galactic halo *n Astron.* a spheroidal aggregation of globular clusters, individual stars, dust, and gas that surrounds the Galaxy.

galago (gə'lɑːgəʊ) *n, pl* **galagos.** another name for **bushbaby.** [C19: from NL, ?from Wolof *golokh* monkey]

galah (gə'lɑː) *n* 1 an Australian cockatoo, having grey wings, back, and crest, and a pink body. 2 *Austral. sl.* a fool or simpleton. [C19: from Abor.]

Galahad ('gælə,hæd) *n* 1 **Sir.** (in Arthurian legend) the most virtuous knight of the Round Table. 2 a pure or noble man.

galantine ('gælən,tiːn) *n* a cold dish of meat or poultry, which is boned, cooked, then pressed and glazed. [C14: from OF, from Med. L *galatina,* prob. from L *gelātus* frozen, set]

galaxy ('gæləksɪ) *n, pl* **galaxies.** 1 any of a vast number of star systems held together by gravitational attraction. 2 a splendid gathering, esp. one of famous or distinguished people. [C14 (in the sense: the Milky Way): from Med. L *galaxia,* from L, from Gk, from *gala* milk]

Galaxy ('gæləksɪ) *n* **the.** the spiral galaxy that contains the solar system about three fifths of the distance from its centre. Also called: the **Milky Way System.**

galbanum ('gælbənəm) *n* a bitter aromatic gum resin extracted from any of several Asian umbelliferous plants. [C14: from L, from Gk, from Heb. *helbenāh*]

gale Ⓣ (geɪl) *n* 1 a strong wind, specifically one of force 8 on the Beaufort scale or from 39-46 mph. 2 (*often pl*) a loud outburst, esp. of laughter. 3 *Arch. & poetic.* a gentle breeze. [C16: from ?]

galea ('geɪlɪə) *n, pl* **galeae** (-lɪ,iː). a part shaped like a helmet, such as the petals of certain flowers. [C18: from L: helmet]
▸ **'gale,ate** *or* **'gale,ated** *adj*

galena (gə'liːnə) *or* **galenite** (gə'liːnaɪt) *n* a soft heavy bluish-grey or black mineral consisting of lead sulphide: the chief source of lead. Formula: PbS. [C17: from L: lead ore]

Galenic (geɪ'lenɪk, gə-) *adj* of or relating to Galen, 2nd-century Greek physician, or his teachings or methods.

Galilean[1] (,gælɪ'liːən) *n* 1 a native or inhabitant of Galilee. 2 **the.** an epithet of Jesus Christ. ◆ *adj* 3 of Galilee.

Galilean[2] (,gælɪ'leɪən) *adj* of or relating to Galileo (1564–1642), It. astronomer and physicist.

galingale ('gælɪŋ,geɪl) *or* **galangal** (gə'læŋgᵊl) *n* a European plant with rough-edged leaves, reddish spikelets of flowers, and aromatic roots. [C13: from OF, from Ar., from Chinese]

galiot *or* **galliot** ('gælɪət) *n* 1 a small swift galley formerly sailed on the Mediterranean. 2 a ketch formerly used along the coasts of Germany and the Netherlands. [C14: from OF, from It., from Med. L *galea* GALLEY]

galipot ('gælɪ,pɒt) *n* a resin obtained from several species of pine. [C18: from F, from ?]

gall[1] Ⓣ (gɔːl) *n* 1 *Inf.* impudence. 2 bitterness; rancour. 3 something bitter or disagreeable. 4 *Physiol.* an obsolete term for **bile.** See also **gall bladder.** [from ON, replacing OE *gealla*]

gall[2] Ⓣ (gɔːl) *n* 1 a sore on the skin caused by chafing. 2 something that causes vexation or annoyance. 3 irritation; exasperation. ◆ *vb* 4 to abrade (the skin, etc.) as by rubbing. 5 (*tr*) to irritate or annoy; vex. [C14: of Gmc origin; rel. to OE *gealla* sore on a horse, & ? to GALL[1]]

gall[3] (gɔːl) *n* an abnormal outgrowth in plant tissue caused by certain parasitic insects, fungi, or bacteria. [C14: from OF, from L *galla*]

gall. *or* **gal.** *abbrev. for* gallon.

gallant Ⓣ *adj* ('gælənt). 1 brave and high-spirited; courageous and honourable: *a gallant warrior.* 2 (gə'lænt, 'gælənt). (of a man) attentive to women; chivalrous. 3 imposing; dignified; stately: *a gallant ship.* 4

THESAURUS

gaiety *n* 1 = **cheerfulness**, animation, blitheness, blithesomeness (*literary*), effervescence, elation, exhilaration, glee, good humour, high spirits, hilarity, *joie de vivre*, jollity, joviality, joyousness, light-heartedness, liveliness, merriment, mirth, sprightliness, vivacity 2 = **merrymaking**, celebration, conviviality, festivity, fun, jollification, revelry, revels 3 = **colour**, brightness, brilliance, colourfulness, gaudiness, glitter, show, showiness, sparkle
Antonyms *n* ≠ **cheerfulness:** despondency, gloom, melancholy, misery, sadness

gaily *adv* 1 = **cheerfully**, blithely, gleefully, happily, joyfully, light-heartedly, merrily 2 = **colourfully**, brightly, brilliantly, flamboyantly, flashily, gaudily, showily

gain *vb* 1, 2 = **acquire**, achieve, attain, bag, bring in, capture, clear, collect, earn, gather, get, glean, harvest, land, make, net, obtain, procure, realize, reap, score (*sl.*), secure, win 3 = **improve**, advance, build up, increase, pick up, profit 5a *with* **on** *or* **upon** = **get nearer**, approach, catch up with, close, narrow the gap, overtake 6 = **reach**, arrive at, attain, come to, get to ◆ *n* 8 = **profit**, accretion, achievement, acquisition, advantage, attainment, benefit, dividend, earnings, emolument, headway, income, lucre, proceeds, produce, return, winnings, yield 9 = **increase**, advance, advancement, growth, improvement, increment, progress, rise
Antonyms *vb* ≠ **acquire:** forfeit, lose ≠ **improve:** fail, worsen ◆ *n* ≠ **profit:** forfeiture, loss ≠ **increase:** damage, injury

gainful *adj* = **profitable**, advantageous, beneficial, expedient, fruitful, lucrative, moneymaking, paying, productive, remunerative, rewarding, useful, worthwhile

gainsay *vb* = **contradict**, contravene, controvert, deny, disaffirm, disagree with, dispute, rebut, retract
Antonyms *vb* agree with, back, confirm, support

gait *n* 1 = **walk**, bearing, carriage, pace, step, stride, tread

gala *n* 1a = **festival**, beano (*Brit. sl.*), carnival, celebration, festivity, fête, hooley *or* hoolie (*chiefly Irish & NZ*), jamboree, pageant, party, rave (*Brit. sl.*), rave-up (*Brit. sl.*) ◆ *modifier* 1b = **festive**, celebratory, convivial, festal, gay, jovial, joyful, merry

gale *n* 1 = **storm**, blast, cyclone, hurricane, squall, tempest, tornado, typhoon 2 = **outburst**, burst, eruption, explosion, fit, howl, outbreak, paroxysm, peal, shout, shriek, storm

gall[1] *n* 1 *Informal* = **impudence**, brass neck (*Brit. inf.*), brazenness, cheek (*inf.*), chutzpah (*US & Canad. inf.*), effrontery, face (*inf.*), impertinence, insolence, neck (*inf.*), nerve (*inf.*) 2 = **bitterness**, acrimony, animosity, animus, antipathy, bad blood, bile, enmity, hostility, malevolence, malice, malignity, rancour, sourness, spite, spleen, venom

gall[2] *n* 1 = **sore**, abrasion, chafe, excoriation, raw spot, scrape, sore spot, wound 2, 3 = **irritation**, aggravation (*inf.*), annoyance, bother, botheration (*inf.*), exasperation, harassment, irritant, nuisance, pest, provocation, vexation ◆ *vb* 4 = **scrape**, abrade, bark, chafe, excoriate, fret, graze, irritate, rub raw, skin 5 = **annoy**, aggravate (*inf.*), be on one's back (*sl.*), bother, exasperate, fret, get on one's nerves (*inf.*), harass, hassle (*inf.*), irk, irritate, nag, nark (*Brit., Austral., & NZ sl.*), nettle, peeve (*inf.*), pester, plague, provoke, rankle, rile (*inf.*), rub up the wrong way, ruffle, vex

gallant *adj* 1 = **brave**, bold, courageous, daring, dashing, dauntless, doughty, fearless, game (*inf.*), heroic, high-spirited, honourable, intrepid, lion-hearted, manful, manly, mettlesome, noble, plucky, valiant, valorous 2 = **courteous**, attentive, chivalrous, courtly, gentlemanly, gracious, magnanimous, noble,

Arch. showy in dress. ◆ *n* (ˈgælənt, gəˈlænt). *Arch.* **5** a woman's lover or suitor. **6** a dashing or fashionable young man, esp. one who pursues women. **7** a brave, high-spirited, or adventurous man. ◆ *vb* (gəˈlænt, ˈgælənt). *Rare.* **8** (when *intr,* usually foll. by *with*) to court or flirt (with). [C15: from OF, from *galer* to make merry, from *gale* enjoyment, of Gmc origin]
▸**ˈgallantly** *adv*

gallantry Ⓣ (ˈgæləntrɪ) *n, pl* **gallantries. 1** conspicuous courage, esp. in war. **2** polite attentiveness to women. **3** a gallant action, speech, etc.

gall bladder *n* a muscular sac, attached to the right lobe of the liver, that stores bile.

galleass (ˈgælɪˌæs) *n* a three-masted galley used as a warship in the Mediterranean from the 15th to the 18th centuries. [C16: from F, from It., from Med. L *galea* GALLEY]

galleon (ˈgælɪən) *n* a large sailing ship having three or more masts, used as a warship or trader from the 15th to the 18th centuries. [C16: from Sp. *galeón,* from F, from OF *galie* GALLEY]

gallery (ˈgælərɪ) *n, pl* **galleries. 1** a room or building for exhibiting works of art. **2** a covered passageway open on one side or on both sides. **3** a balcony running along or around the inside wall of a church, hall, etc. **4** *Theatre.* **4a** an upper floor that projects from the rear and contains the cheapest seats. **4b** the seats there. **4c** the audience seated there. **5** a long narrow room, esp. one used for a specific purpose: *a shooting gallery.* **6** an underground passage, as in a mine, etc. **7** a small ornamental railing, esp. one surrounding the top of a desk, table, etc. **8** any group of spectators, as at a golf match. **9** a glass-fronted soundproof room overlooking a television studio, used for lighting, etc. **10 play to the gallery.** to try to gain popular favour, esp. by crude appeals. [C15: from OF, from Med. L, prob. from *galilea* galilee, porch or chapel at entrance to medieval church]
▸**ˈgalleried** *adj*

galley (ˈgælɪ) *n* **1** any of various kinds of ship propelled by oars or sails used in ancient or medieval times. **2** the kitchen of a ship, boat, or aircraft. **3** any of various long rowing boats. **4** *Printing.* **4a** a tray for holding composed type. **4b** short for **galley proof.** [C13: from OF *galie,* from Med. L *galea,* from Gk *galaia,* from ?]

galley proof *n* a printer's proof, esp. one taken from type in a galley, used to make corrections before the matter has been split into pages. Often shortened to **galley.**

galley slave *n* **1** a criminal or slave condemned to row in a galley. **2** *Inf.* a drudge.

gallfly (ˈgɔːlˌflaɪ) *n, pl* **gallflies.** any of several small insects that produce galls in plant tissues.

galliard (ˈgæljəd) *n* **1** a spirited dance in triple time for two persons, popular in the 16th and 17th centuries. **2** a piece of music composed for or in the rhythm of this dance. [C14: from OF *gaillard* valiant, ? of Celtic origin]

Gallic (ˈgælɪk) *adj* **1** of or relating to France. **2** of or relating to ancient Gaul or the Gauls.

gallic acid *n* a colourless crystalline compound obtained from tannin: used as a tanning agent and in making inks and paper. [C18: from F *gallique;* see GALL[3]]

Gallicism (ˈgælɪˌsɪzəm) *n* a word or idiom borrowed from French.

Gallicize *or* **Gallicise** (ˈgælɪˌsaɪz) *vb* **Gallicizes, Gallicizing, Gallicized** *or* **Gallicises, Gallicising, Gallicised.** to make or become French in attitude, language, etc.

galligaskins (ˌgælɪˈgæskɪnz) *pl n* **1** loose wide breeches or hose, esp. as worn by men in the 17th century. **2** leather leggings, as worn in the 19th century. [C16: from obs. F, from It. *grechesco* Greek, from L *Graecus*]

gallimaufry (ˌgælɪˈmɔːfrɪ) *n, pl* **gallimaufries.** a jumble; hotchpotch. [C16: from F *galimafrée* ragout, hash, from ?]

gallinacean (ˌgælɪˈneɪʃən) *n* any gallinaceous bird.

gallinaceous (ˌgælɪˈneɪʃəs) *adj* of, relating to, or belonging to an order of birds, including domestic fowl, pheasants, grouse, etc., having a heavy rounded body, short bill, and strong legs. [C18: from L, from *gallīna* hen]

galling Ⓣ (ˈgɔːlɪŋ) *adj* irritating, exasperating, or bitterly humiliating.
▸**ˈgallingly** *adv*

gallinule (ˈgælɪˌnjuːl) *n* any of various aquatic birds, typically having a dark plumage, red bill, and a red shield above the bill. [C18: from NL *Gallīnula,* from L *gallīna* hen]

galliot (ˈgælɪət) *n* a variant spelling of **galiot.**

gallipot (ˈgælɪˌpɒt) *n* a small earthenware pot used by pharmacists as a container for ointments, etc. [C16: prob. from GALLEY + POT[1]; because imported in galleys]

gallium (ˈgælɪəm) *n* a silvery metallic element that is liquid for a wide temperature range. It is used in high-temperature thermometers and low-melting alloys. **Gallium arsenide** is a semiconductor. Symbol: Ga; atomic no.: 31; atomic wt.: 69.72. [C19: from NL, from L *gallus* cock, translation of F *coq* in the name of its discoverer, *Lecoq* de Boisbaudran, 19th-cent. F chemist]

gallivant Ⓣ (ˈgælɪˌvænt) *vb* (*intr*) to go about in search of pleasure, etc.; gad about. [C19: ? whimsical from GALLANT]

galliwasp (ˈgælɪˌwɒsp) *n* a lizard of the Caribbean. [C18: from ?]

gallnut (ˈgɔːlˌnʌt) *or* **gall-apple** *n* a type of plant gall that resembles a nut.

Gallo- (ˈgæləʊ) *combining form.* denoting Gaul or France: *Gallo-Roman.* [from L *Gallus* a Gaul]

gallon (ˈgælən) *n* **1** Also called: **imperial gallon.** *Brit.* a unit of capacity equal to 277.42 cubic inches. 1 Brit. gallon is equivalent to 1.20 US gallons or 4.55 litres. **2** *US.* a unit of capacity equal to 231 cubic inches. 1 US gallon is equivalent to 0.83 imperial gallon or 3.79 litres. **3** (*pl*) *Inf.* great quantities. [C13: from ONorthern F *galon* (OF *jalon*), ? of Celtic origin]

gallonage (ˈgælənɪdʒ) *n* a capacity measured in gallons.

galloon (gəˈluːn) *n* a narrow band of cord, embroidery, silver or gold braid, etc., used on clothes and furniture. [C17: from F, from OF *galonner* to trim with braid, from ?]

gallop Ⓣ (ˈgæləp) *vb* **gallops, galloping, galloped. 1** (*intr*) (of a horse or other quadruped) to run fast with a two-beat stride in which all four legs are off the ground at once. **2** to ride (a horse, etc.) at a gallop. **3** (*intr*) to move, read, progress, etc., rapidly. ◆ *n* **4** the fast two-beat gait of horses. **5** an instance of galloping. [C16: from OF *galoper,* from ?]
▸**ˈgalloper** *n*

gallows (ˈgæləʊz) *n, pl* **gallowses** *or* **gallows. 1** a wooden structure usually consisting of two upright posts with a crossbeam, used for hanging criminals. **2** any timber structure resembling this. **3 the gallows.** execution by hanging. [C13: from ON *galgi,* replacing OE *gealga*]

gallows bird *n Inf.* a person considered deserving of hanging.

gallows humour *n* sinister and ironic humour.

gallows tree *or* **gallow tree** *n* another name for **gallows** (sense 1).

gallsickness (ˈgɔːlˌsɪknɪs) *n* a disease of cattle and sheep, caused by infection with rickettsiae, resulting in anaemia and jaundice. Also called: **anaplasmosis.**

gallstone (ˈgɔːlˌstəʊn) *n* a small hard concretion formed in the gall bladder or its ducts.

Gallup Poll (ˈgæləp) *n* a sampling of the views of a representative cross section of the population, used esp. as a means of forecasting voting. [C20: after G. H. *Gallup* (1901–84), US statistician]

galluses (ˈgæləsɪz) *pl n Dialect.* braces for trousers. [C18: var. of *gallowses,* from GALLOWS (in the obs. sense: braces)]

gall wasp *n* any small solitary wasp that produces galls in plant tissue.

galoot *or* **galloot** (gəˈluːt) *n Sl., chiefly US.* a clumsy or uncouth person. [C19: from ?]

galop (ˈgæləp) *n* **1** a 19th-century dance in quick duple time. **2** a piece of music for this dance. [C19: from F; see GALLOP]

galore Ⓣ (gəˈlɔː) *determiner* (*immediately postpositive*) in great numbers or quantity: *there were daffodils galore in the park.* [C17: from Irish Gaelic *go leór* to sufficiency]

galoshes *or* **goloshes** (gəˈlɒʃɪz) *pl n* (*sometimes sing*) a pair of waterproof overshoes. [C14 (in the sense: wooden shoe): from OF, from LL *gallicula* Gallic shoe]

galumph (gəˈlʌmpf, -ˈlʌmf) *vb* (*intr*) *Inf.* to leap or move about clumsily or joyfully. [C19 (coined by Lewis Carroll): prob. a blend of GALLOP + TRIUMPH]

galvanic (gælˈvænɪk) *adj* **1** of, producing, or concerned with an electric current, esp. a direct current produced chemically. **2** *Inf.* resembling the effect of an electric shock; convulsive, startling, or energetic.
▸**galˈvanically** *adv*

galvanism (ˈgælvəˌnɪzəm) *n* **1** *Obs.* electricity, esp. when produced by chemical means as in a cell or battery. **2** *Med.* treatment involving the application of electric currents to tissues. [C18: via F from It. *galvanismo,* after Luigi *Galvani* (1737–98), It. physiologist]

galvanize Ⓣ *or* **galvanise** (ˈgælvəˌnaɪz) *vb* **galvanizes, galvanizing, galvanized** *or* **galvanises, galvanising, galvanised.** (*tr*) **1** to stimulate to action; excite; startle. **2** to cover (iron, steel, etc.) with a protective zinc coating. **3** to stimulate by application of an electric current.
▸**ˌgalvaniˈzation** *or* **ˌgalvaniˈsation** *n*

galvanized iron *or* **galvanised iron** *n Building trades.* iron, esp. a sheet of corrugated iron, covered with a protective coating of zinc.

THESAURUS

polite **3** = **elegant,** august, dignified, glorious, grand, imposing, lofty, magnificent, noble, splendid, stately ◆ *n* **6** = **ladies' man,** beau, blade (*arch.*), buck (*inf.*), dandy, fop, lady-killer (*inf.*), man about town, man of fashion
Antonyms *adj* ≠ **brave:** cowardly, fearful, ignoble ≠ **courteous:** churlish, discourteous, ill-mannered, impolite, rude

gallantry *n* **1** = **bravery,** audacity, boldness, courage, courageousness, daring, dauntlessness, derring-do (*arch.*), fearlessness, heroism, intrepidity, manliness, mettle, nerve, pluck, prowess, spirit, valiance, valour **2** = **courtesy,** attentiveness, chivalry, courteousness, courtliness, elegance, gentlemanliness, graciousness, nobility, politeness
Antonyms *n* ≠ **bravery:** cowardice, irresolution ≠ **courtesy:** churlishness, discourtesy, rudeness, ungraciousness

galling *adj* = **annoying,** aggravating (*inf.*), bitter, bothersome, exasperating, harassing, humiliating, irksome, irritating, nettlesome, plaguing, provoking, rankling, vexatious, vexing

gallivant *vb* = **wander,** gad about, ramble, range, roam, rove, run around, stravaig (*Scot. & N English dialect*), stray, traipse (*inf.*)

gallop *vb* **3** = **run,** barrel (along) (*inf., chiefly US & Canad.*), bolt, career, dart, dash, fly, hasten, hie (*arch.*), hurry, race, rush, scud, shoot, speed, sprint, tear along, zoom

galore *determiner* = **in abundance,** à gogo (*inf.*), all over the place, aplenty, everywhere, in great quantity, in numbers, in profusion, to spare

galvanize *vb* **1** = **stimulate,** arouse, awaken, electrify, excite, fire, inspire, invigorate, jolt,

galvano- *combining form.* indicating a galvanic current: *galvanometer.*
galvanometer (ˌgælvəˈnɒmɪtə) *n* any sensitive instrument for detecting or measuring small electric currents.
▸**galvanometric** (ˌgælvənəʊˈmɛtrɪk, gælˌvænəʊ-) *adj* ▸ˌ**galvaˈnometry** *n*
gam (gæm) *n Sl.* a leg. [C18: from F *jambe* leg]
gambier *or* **gambir** (ˈgæmbɪə) *n* an astringent resinous substance obtained from a tropical Asian plant: used as an astringent and tonic and in tanning. [C19: from Malay]
gambit (ˈgæmbɪt) *n* **1** *Chess.* an opening move in which a chessman, usually a pawn, is sacrificed to secure an advantageous position. **2** an opening comment, manoeuvre, etc., intended to secure an advantage. [C17: from F, from It. *gambetto* a tripping up, from *gamba* leg]
gamble ❶ (ˈgæmbᵊl) *vb* **gambles, gambling, gambled. 1** (*intr*) to play games of chance to win money, etc. **2** to risk or bet (money, etc.) on the outcome of an event, sport, etc. **3** (*intr; often foll. by on*) to act with the expectation of: *to gamble on its being a sunny day.* **4** (often foll. by *away*) to lose by or as if by betting; squander. ◆ *n* **5** a risky act or venture. **6** a bet or wager. [C18: prob. var. of GAME[1]]
▸ˈ**gambler** *n* ▸ˈ**gambling** *n*
gamboge (gæmˈbəʊdʒ, -ˈbuːʒ) *n* **1a** a gum resin used as the source of a yellow pigment and as a purgative. **1b** the pigment made from this resin. **2 gamboge tree.** any of several tropical Asian trees that yield this resin. [C18: from NL *gambaugium, from Cambodia,* where first found]
gambol ❶ (ˈgæmbᵊl) *vb* **gambols, gambolling, gambolled** *or US* **gambols, gamboling, gamboled. 1** (*intr*) to skip or jump about in a playful manner; frolic. ◆ *n* **2** a playful antic; frolic. [C16: from F *gambade;* see JAMB]
gambrel (ˈgæmbrəl) *n* **1** the hock of a horse or similar animal. **2** short for **gambrel roof.** [C16: from OF, from *gambe* leg]
gambrel roof *n* **1** *Chiefly Brit.* a hipped roof having a small gable at both ends. **2** *Chiefly US & Canad.* a roof having two slopes on both sides, the lower slopes being steeper than the upper.
game[1] ❶ (geɪm) *n* **1** an amusement or pastime; diversion. **2** a contest with rules, the result being determined by skill, strength, or chance. **3** a single period of play in such a contest, sport, etc. **4** the score needed to win a contest. **5** a single contest in a series; match. **6** (*pl; often cap.*) an event consisting of various sporting contests, esp. in athletics: *Olympic Games.* **7** equipment needed for playing certain games. **8** short for **computer game. 9** style or ability in playing a game. **10** a scheme, proceeding, etc., practised like a game: *the game of politics.* **11** an activity undertaken in a spirit of levity; joke: *marriage is just a game to him.* **12a** wild animals, including birds and fish, hunted for sport, food, or profit. **12b** (*as modifier*): *game laws.* **13** the flesh of such animals, used as food. **14** an object of pursuit; quarry; prey (esp. in **fair game**). **15** *Inf.* work or occupation. **16** *Inf.* a trick, strategy, or device: *I can see through your little game.* **17** *Sl., chiefly Brit.* prostitution (esp. in **on the game**). **18 give the game away.** to reveal one's intentions or a secret. **19 make (a) game of.** to make fun of; ridicule; mock. **20 play the game.** to behave fairly or in accordance with the rules. **21 the game is up.** there is no longer a chance of success. ◆ *adj* **22** *Inf.* full of fighting spirit; plucky; brave. **23** (usually foll. by *for*) *Inf.* prepared or ready; willing: *I'm game for a try.* ◆ *vb* **games, gaming, gamed. 24** (*intr*) to play games of chance for money, stakes, etc.; gamble. [OE *gamen*]
▸ˈ**gamely** *adv* ▸ˈ**gameness** *n*
game[2] ❶ (geɪm) *adj* a less common word for **lame** (esp. in **game leg**). [C18: prob. from Irish *cam* crooked]
gamecock (ˈgeɪmˌkɒk) *n* a cock bred and trained for fighting. Also called: **fighting cock.**
game fish *n* any fish providing sport for the angler.
gamekeeper (ˈgeɪmˌkiːpə) *n* a person employed to take care of game, as on an estate.
gamelan (ˈgæmɪˌlæn) *n* a type of percussion orchestra common in the East Indies. [from Javanese]
game laws *pl n* laws governing the hunting and preservation of game.
game plan *n* **1** a strategy. **2** a plan of campaign, esp. in politics.
game point *n Tennis, etc.* a stage at which winning one further point would enable one player or side to win a game.
gamesmanship (ˈgeɪmzmənˌʃɪp) *n Inf.* the art of winning games or defeating opponents by cunning practices without actually cheating.
gamesome (ˈgeɪmsəm) *adj* full of merriment; sportive.
▸ˈ**gamesomeness** *n*
gamester (ˈgeɪmstə) *n* a person who habitually plays games for money; gambler.
gametangium (ˌgæmɪˈtændʒɪəm) *n, pl* **gametangia** (-dʒɪə). *Biol.* an organ or cell in which gametes are produced, esp. in algae and fungi. [C19: NL, from GAMETO- + Gk *angeion* vessel]
gamete (ˈgæmiːt, gəˈmiːt) *n* a haploid germ cell that fuses with another during fertilization. [C19: from NL, from Gk *gametē* wife, from *gamos* marriage]
▸**gametic** (gəˈmɛtɪk) *adj*
gamete intrafallopian transfer (ˌɪntrəfəˈləʊpɪən) *n* See **GIFT.**
game theory *n* mathematical theory concerned with the optimum choice of strategy in situations involving a conflict of interest.
gameto- *or sometimes before a vowel* **gamet-** *combining form.* gamete: *gametophyte.*
gametophyte (gəˈmiːtəʊˌfaɪt) *n* the plant body, in species showing alternation of generations, that produces the gametes.
▸**gametophytic** (ˌgæmɪtəʊˈfɪtɪk) *adj*
gamey *or* **gamy** (ˈgeɪmɪ) *adj* **gamier, gamiest. 1** having the smell or flavour of game, esp. high game. **2** *Inf.* spirited; plucky; brave.
▸ˈ**gamily** *adv* ▸ˈ**gaminess** *n*
gamin ❶ (ˈgæmɪn) *n* a street urchin. [from F]
gamine (ˈgæmiːn) *n* a slim and boyish girl or young woman; an elfish tomboy. [from F]
gaming (ˈgeɪmɪŋ) *n* **a** gambling on games of chance. **b** (*as modifier*): *gaming house.*
gamma (ˈgæmə) *n* **1** the third letter in the Greek alphabet (Γ, γ). **2** the third in a group or series. [C14: from Gk]
gamma distribution *n Statistics.* a continuous two-parameter distribution from which the chi-square and exponential distributions are derived.
gamma globulin *n* any of a group of proteins in blood plasma that includes most known antibodies.
gamma radiation *n* electromagnetic radiation of shorter wavelength and higher energy than X-rays.
gamma-ray astronomy *n* the investigation of cosmic gamma rays, such as those from quasars.
gamma rays *pl n* streams of gamma radiation.
gamma stock *n* any of the third rank of active securities on the London stock exchange. Prices displayed by market makers are given as an indication rather than an offer to buy or sell.
gammer (ˈgæmə) *n Rare, chiefly Brit.* a dialect word for an old woman: now chiefly humorous or contemptuous. [C16: prob. from GODMOTHER or GRANDMOTHER]
gammon[1] (ˈgæmən) *n* **1** a cured or smoked ham. **2** the hindquarter of a side of bacon, cooked either whole or in rashers. [C15: from OF *gambon,* from *gambe* leg]
gammon[2] (ˈgæmən) *n* **1** a double victory in backgammon in which one player throws off all his pieces before his opponent throws any. ◆ *vb* **2** (*tr*) to score such a victory over. [C18: prob. special use of ME *gamen* GAME[1]]
gammon[3] (ˈgæmən) *Brit. inf.* ◆ *n* **1** deceitful nonsense; humbug. ◆ *vb* **2** to deceive (a person). [C18: ? special use of GAMMON[1]]
gammy (ˈgæmɪ) *adj* **gammier, gammiest.** *Brit. sl.* (esp. of the leg) malfunctioning, injured, or lame; game. [C19: dialect var. of GAME[2]]
gamo- *or before a vowel* **gam-** *combining form.* **1** indicating sexual union or reproduction: *gamogenesis.* **2** united or fused: *gamopetalous.* [from Gk *gamos* marriage]
gamopetalous (ˌgæməʊˈpɛtələs) *adj* (of flowers) having petals that are united or partly united, as the primrose.
gamp (gæmp) *n Brit. inf.* an umbrella. [C19: after Mrs Sarah *Gamp,* a nurse in Dickens' *Martin Chuzzlewit,* who carried a faded cotton umbrella]
gamut ❶ (ˈgæmət) *n* **1** entire range or scale, as of emotions. **2** *Music.* **2a** a scale, esp. (in medieval theory) one starting on the G on the bottom line of the bass staff. **2b** the whole range of notes. **3** *Physics.* the range of chromaticities that can be obtained by mixing three colours. [C14: from Med. L, from *gamma,* the lowest note of the hexachord as established by Guido d'Arezzo + *ut* (now, *doh*), the first of the notes of the scale *ut, re, mi, fa, sol, la, si*]
-gamy *n combining form.* denoting marriage or sexual union: *bigamy.* [from Gk, from *gamos* marriage]
▸**-gamous** *adj combining form.*
gander (ˈgændə) *n* **1** a male goose. **2** *Inf.* a quick look (esp. in **take** (*or* **have**) **a gander**). **3** *Inf.* a simpleton. [OE *gandra, ganra*]
Gandhian (ˈgændɪən) *adj* **1.** of or relating to the Indian political and

THESAURUS

kick-start, move, prod, provoke, quicken, shock, spur, startle, stir, thrill, vitalize, wake

gamble *vb* **1, 2 = bet,** back, game, have a flutter (*inf.*), lay *or* make a bet, play, punt, put one's shirt on, stake, try one's luck, wager **3 = risk,** back, chance, hazard, put one's faith *or* trust in, skate on thin ice, speculate, stake, stick one's neck out (*inf.*), take a chance, take the plunge, venture ◆ *n* **5 = risk,** chance, leap in the dark, lottery, speculation, uncertainty, venture **6 = bet,** flutter (*inf.*), punt, wager
Antonyms *n* ≠ **risk:** banker, certainty, foregone conclusion, safe bet, sure thing

gambol *vb* **1 = frolic,** caper, cavort, curvet, cut a caper, frisk, hop, jump, prance, rollick, skip ◆ *n* **2 = frolic,** antic, caper, gambado, hop, jump, prance, skip, spring

game[1] *n* **1 = pastime,** amusement, distraction, diversion, entertainment, frolic, fun, jest, joke, lark, merriment, play, recreation, romp, sport **2 = match,** competition, contest, event, head-to-head, meeting, round, tournament **10 = undertaking,** adventure, business, enterprise, line, occupation, plan, proceeding, scheme **12 = wild animals,** chase, prey, quarry **16 = scheme,** design, device, plan, plot, ploy, stratagem, strategy, tactic, trick **20 play the game = play fair,** conform, follow the rules, go along with, keep in step, play by the rules, toe the line ◆ *adj* **22 = brave,** bold, courageous, dauntless, dogged, fearless, feisty (*inf., chiefly US & Canad.*), gallant, gritty, have-a-go (*inf.*), heroic, intrepid, persevering, persistent, plucky, resolute, spirited, unflinching, valiant, valorous **23 = willing,** desirous, disposed, eager, inclined, interested, keen, prepared, ready, up for it (*inf.*)
Antonyms *n* ≠ **pastime:** business, chore, duty, job, labour, toil, work ◆ *adj* ≠ **brave:** cowardly, fearful, irresolute

game[2] *adj* **= lame,** bad, crippled, deformed, disabled, gammy (*Brit. sl.*), incapacitated, injured, maimed

gamin *n* **= (street) urchin,** guttersnipe, mudlark (*sl.*), ragamuffin, street Arab (*offens.*), waif

gamut *n* **1 = range,** area, catalogue, compass, field, scale, scope, series, sweep spiritual leader Mahatma Gandhi (1869–1948) or his ideas. ◆ *n* **2** a follower of Gandhi or his ideas.

gang[1] ➊ (gæŋ) *n* **1** a group of people who associate together or act as an organized body, esp. for criminal or illegal purposes. **2** an organized group of workmen. **3** a series of similar tools arranged to work simultaneously in parallel. ◆ *vb* **4** to form into, become part of, or act as a gang. ◆ See also **gang up.** [OE: journey]

gang[2] (gæŋ) *n* a variant spelling of **gangue.**

gang[3] (gæŋ) *vb* (*intr*) *Scot.* to go or walk. [OE *gangan*]

gangbang ('gæŋ,bæŋ) *n Sl.* an instance of sexual intercourse between one woman and several men one after the other, esp. against her will.

gang-banger *n US sl.* a member of a street gang.
▸**'gang-,banging** *n*

ganger ('gæŋə) *n Chiefly Brit.* the foreman of a gang of labourers.

gangland ('gæŋ,lænd, -lənd) *n* the criminal underworld.

gangling ➊ ('gæŋglɪŋ) *or* **gangly** *adj* tall, lanky, and awkward in movement. [see GANG[3]]

ganglion ('gæŋglɪən) *n, pl* **ganglia** (-glɪə) *or* **ganglions. 1** an encapsulated collection of nerve-cell bodies, usually located outside the brain and spinal cord. **2** any concentration or centre of energy, activity, or strength. **3** a cystic tumour on a tendon sheath. [C17: from LL: swelling, from Gk: cystic tumour]
▸**'gangliar** *adj* ▸**,gangli'onic** *or* **'gangli,ated** *adj*

gangplank ('gæŋ,plæŋk) *or* **gangway** *n Naut.* a portable bridge for boarding and leaving a vessel at dockside.

gangrene ('gæŋgriːn) *n* **1** death and decay of tissue due to an interrupted blood supply, disease, or injury. ◆ *vb* **gangrenes, gangrening, gangrened. 2** to become or cause to become affected with gangrene. [C16: from L, from Gk *gangraina* an eating sore]
▸**gangrenous** ('gæŋgrɪnəs) *adj*

gang-saw *n* a multiple saw used in a timber mill to cut planks from logs.

gangster ➊ ('gæŋstə) *n* a member of an organized gang of criminals.

gangue *or* **gang** (gæŋ) *n* valueless and undesirable material in an ore. [C19: from F, from G *Gang* vein of metal, course]

gang up *vb* (*intr, adv;* often foll. by *on* or *against*) *Inf.* to combine in a group (against).

gangway ('gæŋ,weɪ) *n* **1** another word for **gangplank. 2** an opening in a ship's side to take a gangplank. **3** *Brit.* an aisle between rows of seats. **4** temporary planks over mud, as on a building site. ◆ *sentence substitute.* **5** clear a path!

ganister *or* **gannister** ('gænɪstə) *n* a refractory siliceous sedimentary rock occurring beneath coal seams: used for lining furnaces. [C20: from ?]

gannet ('gænɪt) *n* **1** any of several heavily built marine birds having a long stout bill and typically white plumage with dark markings. **2** *Sl.* a greedy person. [OE *ganot*]

ganoid ('gænɔɪd) *adj* **1** (of the scales of certain fishes) consisting of an inner bony layer and an outer layer of an enamel-like substance (**ganoin**). **2** denoting fishes, including the sturgeon, having such scales. ◆ *n* **3** a ganoid fish. [C19: from F, from Gk *ganos* brightness + -OID]

gantry ('gæntrɪ) *n, pl* **gantries. 1** a bridgelike framework used to support a travelling crane, signals over a railway track, etc. **2** Also called: **gantry scaffold.** the framework tower used to attend to a large rocket on its launch pad. **3** a supporting framework for a barrel. **4a** the area behind a bar where bottles, esp. spirit bottles mounted in optics, are kept. **4b** the range or quality of the spirits on display there. [C16 (in the sense: wooden platform for barrels): from OF *chantier,* from Med. L, from L *canthērius* supporting frame, pack ass]

Gantt chart (gænt) *n* a chart showing, in horizontal lines, activity planned to take place during specified periods, which are indicated in vertical bands. [C20: named after Henry L. *Gantt* (1861–1919), US management consultant]

gaol ➊ (dʒeɪl) *n, vb* (*tr*) *Brit.* a variant spelling of **jail.**
▸**'gaoler** *n*

gap ➊ (gæp) *n* **1** a break or opening in a wall, fence, etc. **2** a break in continuity; interruption; hiatus. **3** a break in a line of hills or mountains affording a route through. **4** *Chiefly US.* a gorge or ravine. **5** a divergence or difference; disparity: *the generation gap.* **6** *Electronics.* **6a** a break in a magnetic circuit that increases the inductance and saturation point of the circuit. **6b** See **spark gap. 7 bridge, close, fill,** *or* **stop a gap.** to remedy a deficiency. ◆ *vb* **gaps, gapping, gapped. 8** (*tr*) to make a breach or opening in. [C14: from ON *gap* chasm]
▸**'gappy** *adj*

gape ➊ (geɪp) *vb* **gapes, gaping, gaped.** (*intr*) **1** to stare in wonder, esp. with the mouth open. **2** to open the mouth wide, esp. involuntarily, as in yawning. **3** to be or become wide open: *the crater gaped under his feet.* ◆ *n* **4** the act of gaping. **5** a wide opening. **6** the width of the widely opened mouth of a vertebrate. **7** a stare of astonishment. [C13: from ON *gapa*]
▸**'gaper** *n* ▸**'gaping** *adj*

gapes (geɪps) *n* (*functioning as sing*) **1** a disease of young domestic fowl, characterized by gaping and caused by parasitic worms (**gapeworms**). **2** *Inf.* a fit of yawning.

gap year *n* a year's break taken by a student between leaving school and starting further education.

gar (gɑː) *n, pl* **gar** *or* **gars.** short for **garpike.**

garage ('gærɑːʒ, -rɪdʒ) *n* **1** a building used to house a motor vehicle. **2** a commercial establishment in which motor vehicles are repaired, serviced, bought, and sold, and which usually also sells motor fuels. ◆ *vb* **garages, garaging, garaged. 3** (*tr*) to put into or keep in a garage. [C20: from F, from OF: to protect, from OHG *warōn*]

garage band *n* a rough-and-ready amateurish rock group. [?from the practice of such bands rehearsing in a garage]

garage sale *n* a sale of personal belongings or household effects held at a person's home, usually in the garage.

garb ➊ (gɑːb) *n* **1** clothes, esp. the distinctive attire of an occupation: *clerical garb.* **2** style of dress; fashion. **3** external appearance, covering, or attire. ◆ *vb* **4** (*tr*) to clothe; attire. [C16: from OF: graceful contour, from OIt. *garbo* grace, prob. of Gmc origin]

garbage ➊ ('gɑːbɪdʒ) *n* **1** worthless, useless, or unwanted matter. **2** another word (esp. US and Canad.) for **rubbish. 3** *Computing.* invalid data. **4** *Inf.* nonsense. [C15: prob. from Anglo-F *garbelage* removal of discarded matter, from ?]

garble ➊ ('gɑːb[ə]l) *vb* **garbles, garbling, garbled.** (*tr*) **1** to jumble (a story, quotation, etc.), esp. unintentionally. **2** to distort the meaning of (an account, text, etc.), as by making misleading omissions; corrupt. ◆ *n* **3a** the act of garbling. **3b** garbled matter. [C15: from OIt. *garbellare* to strain, sift, from Ar., from LL *crībellum* small sieve]
▸**'garbler** *n*

garboard ('gɑː,bɔːd) *n Naut.* the bottommost plank of a vessel's hull. Also called: **garboard strake.** [C17: from Du. *gaarboord,* prob. from MDu. *gaderen* to GATHER + *boord* BOARD]

garbology (gɑː'bɒlədʒɪ) *n Chiefly US.* **1** analysis of refuse as a means of investigating the lifestyle of the person or people who produced it. **2** the study of waste disposal. [C20: from GARBAGE + -OLOGY]
▸**gar'bologist** *n*

garçon (*French* garsɔ̃) *n* a waiter or male servant, esp. if French. [C19: from OF *gars* lad, prob. of Gmc origin]

garda ('gɑːrdə) *n, pl* **gardaí** ('gɑːrdɪ). a member of the **Garda Síochána,** the police force of the Republic of Ireland.

garden ('gɑːd[ə]n) *n* **1** *Brit.* **1a** an area of land, usually planted with grass, trees, flowerbeds, etc., adjoining a house. US and Canad. word: **yard. 1b** (*as modifier*): *a garden chair.* **2a** an area of land used for the cultivation of ornamental plants, herbs, fruit, vegetables, trees, etc. **2b** (*as modifier*): *garden tools.* Related adj: **horticultural. 3** (*often pl*) such an area of land that is open to the public, sometimes part of a park: *botanical gardens.* **4** a fertile and beautiful region. **5 lead (a person) up the garden path.** *Inf.* to mislead or deceive. ◆ *vb* **6** to work in, cultivate, or take care of (a garden, plot of land, etc.). [C14: from OF *gardin,* of Gmc origin]
▸**'gardener** *n* ▸**'gardening** *n*

garden centre *n* a place where gardening tools and equipment, plants, seeds, etc., are sold.

garden city *n Brit.* a planned town of limited size surrounded by a rural belt.

gardenia (gɑː'diːnɪə) *n* **1** any evergreen shrub or tree of the Old World tropical genus *Gardenia,* cultivated for their large fragrant waxlike typically white flowers. **2** the flower of any of these shrubs. [C18: NL, after Dr Alexander *Garden* (1730–91), American botanist]

garderobe ('gɑːd,rəʊb) *n Arch.* **1** a wardrobe or its contents. **2** a private room. **3** a privy. [C14: from F, from *garder* to keep + *robe* dress, clothing; see WARDROBE]

THESAURUS

gang[1] *n* **2** = **group,** band, bevy, camp, circle, clique, club, company, coterie, crew (*inf.*), crowd, herd, horde, lot, mob, pack, party, posse (*sl.*), ring, set, shift, squad, team, troupe

gangling *adj* = **tall,** angular, awkward, lanky, loose-jointed, rangy, rawboned, skinny, spindly

gangster *n* = **racketeer,** bandit, brigand, crook (*inf.*), desperado, gang member, heavy (*sl.*), hood, hoodlum (*chiefly US*), mobster (*US sl.*), robber, ruffian, thug, tough, tsotsi (*S. Afr.*)

gaol *see* **jail**

gap *n* **1** = **opening,** blank, breach, break, chink, cleft, crack, cranny, crevice, discontinuity, divide, hole, interstice, rent, rift, space, vacuity, void **2** = **interval,** breathing space, entr'acte, hiatus, interlude, intermission, interruption, lacuna, lull, pause, recess, respite **5** = **difference,** disagreement, disparity, divergence, inconsistency

gape *vb* **1** = **stare,** gawk, gawp (*Brit. sl.*), goggle, wonder **3** = **open,** crack, split, yawn

gaping *adj* **3** = **wide,** broad, cavernous, great, open, vast, wide open, yawning

garb *n* **1** = **clothes,** apparel, array, attire, clothing, costume, dress, garment, gear (*sl.*), habiliment, habit, outfit, raiment (*arch.*), robes, uniform, vestments, wear **2** = **fashion,** cut, look, mode, style **3** = **appearance,** aspect, attire, covering, guise, outward form ◆ *vb* **4** = **clothe,** apparel, attire, cover, dress, rig out, robe

garbage *n* **1** = **junk,** bits and pieces, debris, detritus, litter, odds and ends, rubbish, scraps **2** = **waste,** dreck (*sl., chiefly US*), dross, filth, muck, offal, refuse, rubbish, scourings, slops, sweepings, swill, trash (*chiefly US*), wack (*US sl.*) **4** = **nonsense,** bunkum *or* buncombe (*chiefly US*), claptrap (*inf.*), codswallop (*Brit. sl.*), drivel, gibberish, guff (*sl.*), hogwash, hokum (*sl., chiefly US & Canad.*), hot air (*inf.*), moonshine, piffle (*inf.*), poppycock (*inf.*), rot, stuff and nonsense, tommyrot, tosh (*inf.*), trash, tripe (*inf.*), twaddle

garble *vb* **1** = **jumble,** confuse, mix up **2** = **distort,** corrupt, doctor, falsify, misinterpret, misquote, misreport, misrepresent, misstate, mistranslate, mutilate, pervert, slant, tamper with, twist

Antonyms *vb* clarify, decipher, make intelligible

garbled *adj* **1** = **jumbled,** confused, distorted, double-Dutch, incomprehensible, mixed up, unintelligible

garfish ('gɑːˌfɪʃ) *n, pl* **garfish** *or* **garfishes. 1** another name for **garpike** (sense 1). **2** an elongated marine teleost fish with long toothed jaws: related to the flying fishes. [OE *gār* spear + FISH]

garganey ('gɑːgənɪ) *n* a small Eurasian duck closely related to the mallard. The male has a white stripe over each eye. [C17: from It. dialect *garganei*, imit.]

gargantuan ❶ (gɑː'gæntjʊən) *adj* (*sometimes cap.*) huge; enormous. [after *Gargantua*, a giant in Rabelais' satire *Gargantua and Pantagruel* (1534)]

> **USAGE NOTE** Some people think that *gargantuan* should only be used to describe things connected with food: *a gargantuan meal; his gargantuan appetite.*

gargle ('gɑːgᵊl) *vb* **gargles, gargling, gargled. 1** to rinse the mouth and throat with (a liquid, esp. a medicinal fluid) by slowly breathing out through the liquid. ◆ *n* **2** the liquid used for gargling. **3** the sound produced by gargling. [C16: from OF, from *gargouille* throat, ? imit.]

gargoyle ('gɑːgɔɪl) *n* **1** a waterspout carved in the form of a grotesque face or creature and projecting from a roof gutter. **2** a person with a grotesque appearance. [C15: from OF *gargouille* gargoyle, throat; see GARGLE]

garibaldi (ˌgærɪ'bɔːldɪ) *n Brit.* a type of biscuit having a layer of currants in the centre.

garish ❶ ('gɛərɪʃ) *adj* gay or colourful in a crude manner; gaudy. [C16: from earlier *gaure* to stare + -ISH]
▸ **'garishly** *adv* ▸ **'garishness** *n*

garland ❶ ('gɑːlənd) *n* **1** a wreath of flowers, leaves, etc., worn round the head or neck or hung up. **2** a collection of short literary pieces, such as poems; anthology. ◆ *vb* **3** (*tr*) to adorn with a garland or garlands. [C14: from OF *garlande*, ? of Gmc origin]

garlic ('gɑːlɪk) *n* **1** a hardy widely cultivated Asian alliaceous plant having whitish flowers. **2** the bulb of this plant, made up of small segments (cloves) that have a strong odour and pungent taste and are used in cooking. [OE *gārlēac*, from *gār* spear + *lēac* LEEK]
▸ **'garlicky** *adj*

garment ❶ ('gɑːmənt) *n* **1** (*often pl*) an article of clothing. **2** outer covering. ◆ *vb* **3** (*tr; usually passive*) to cover or clothe. [C14: from OF *garniment*, from *garnir* to equip; see GARNISH]

garner ❶ ('gɑːnə) *vb* (*tr*) **1** to gather or store as in a granary. ◆ *n* **2** an archaic word for **granary. 3** *Arch.* a place for storage. [C12: from OF: granary, from L *grānārium*, from *grānum* grain]

garnet ('gɑːnɪt) *n* any of a group of hard glassy red, yellow, or green minerals consisting of silicates in cubic crystalline form: used as a gemstone and abrasive. [C13: from OF, from *grenat* (adj) red, from *pome grenate* POMEGRANATE]

garnish ❶ ('gɑːnɪʃ) *vb* (*tr*) **1** to decorate; trim. **2** to add something to (food) in order to improve its appearance or flavour. **3** *Law.* **3a** to serve with notice of proceedings; warn. **3b** to attach (a debt). ◆ *n* **4** a decoration; trimming. **5** something, such as parsley, added to a dish for its flavour or decorative effect. [C14: from OF *garnir* to adorn, equip, of Gmc origin]
▸ **'garnisher** *n*

garnishee (ˌgɑːnɪ'ʃiː) *Law.* ◆ *n* **1** a person upon whom a garnishment has been served. ◆ *vb* **garnishees, garnisheeing, garnisheed.** (*tr*) **2** to attach (a debt or other property) by garnishment. **3** to serve (a person) with a garnishment.

garnishment ('gɑːnɪʃmənt) *n* **1** decoration or embellishment. **2** *Law.* **2a** a notice or warning. **2b** *Obs.* a summons to court proceedings already in progress. **2c** a notice warning a person holding money or property belonging to a debtor whose debt has been attached to hold such property until directed by the court to apply it.

garniture ('gɑːnɪtʃə) *n* decoration or embellishment. [C16: from F, from *garnir* to GARNISH]

garpike ('gɑːˌpaɪk) *n* **1** Also called: **garfish, gar.** any primitive freshwater elongated bony fish of North and Central America, having very long toothed jaws and a body covering of thick scales. **2** another name for **garfish** (sense 2).

garret ('gærɪt) *n* another word for **attic** (sense 1). [C14: from OF: watchtower, from *garir* to protect, of Gmc origin]

garret window *n* a skylight that lies along the slope of the roof.

garrison ❶ ('gærɪsᵊn) *n* **1** the troops who maintain and guard a base or fortified place. **2** the place itself. ◆ *vb* **3** (*tr*) to station (troops) in (a fort, etc.). [C13: from OF, from *garir* to defend, of Gmc origin]

garron ('gærən) *n* a small sturdy pony bred and used chiefly in Scotland and Ireland. [C16: from Gaelic *gearran*]

garrotte *or* **garotte** (gə'rɒt) *n* **1** a Spanish method of execution by strangulation. **2** the device, usually an iron collar, used in such executions. **3** *Obs.* strangulation of one's victim while committing robbery. ◆ *vb* **garrottes, garrotting, garrotted** *or* **garottes, garotting, garotted.** (*tr*) **4** to execute by means of the garrotte. **5** to strangle, esp. in order to commit robbery. [C17: from Sp. *garrote*, ?from OF *garrot* cudgel; from ?]
▸ **gar'rotter** *or* **ga'rotter** *n*

garrulous ❶ ('gærʊləs) *adj* **1** given to constant chatter; talkative. **2** wordy or diffuse. [C17: from L, from *garrīre* to chatter]
▸ **'garrulously** *adv* ▸ **'garrulousness** *or* **garrulity** (gæ'ruːlɪtɪ) *n*

garryowen (ˌgærɪ'əʊɪn) *n* (in rugby union) another term for **up-and-under.** [from *Garryowen* RFC, Ireland]

garter ('gɑːtə) *n* **1** a band, usually of elastic, worn round the leg to hold up a sock or stocking. **2** the US and Canad. word for **suspender.** ◆ *vb* **3** (*tr*) to fasten or secure as with a garter. [C14: from OF *gartier*, from *garet* bend of the knee, prob. of Celtic origin]

Garter ('gɑːtə) *n* **the. 1 Order of the Garter.** the highest order of British knighthood, open to women since 1987. **2** (*sometimes not cap.*) **2a** the badge of this Order. **2b** membership of this Order.

garter snake *n* a nonvenomous North American snake, typically marked with longitudinal stripes.

garter stitch *n* knitting in which all the rows are knitted in plain stitch.

garth (gɑːθ) *n* **1** a courtyard surrounded by a cloister. **2** *Arch.* a yard or garden. [C14: from ON *garthr*]

gas (gæs) *n, pl* **gases** *or* **gasses. 1** a substance in a physical state in which it does not resist change of shape and will expand indefinitely to fill any container. Cf. **liquid** (sense 1), **solid** (sense 1). **2** any substance that is gaseous at room temperature and atmospheric pressure. **3** any gaseous substance that is above its critical temperature and therefore not liquefiable by pressure alone. Cf. **vapour** (sense 2). **4a** a fossil fuel in the form of a gas, used as a source of domestic and industrial heat. **4b** (*as modifier*): *a gas cooker; gas fire.* **5** a gaseous anaesthetic, such as nitrous oxide. **6** *Mining.* firedamp or the explosive mixture of firedamp and air. **7** the usual US, Canad., Austral., and NZ word for **petrol,** a shortened form of **gasoline. 8 step on the gas.** *Inf.* **8a** to accelerate a motor vehicle. **8b** to hurry. **9** a toxic, etc., substance in suspension in air used against an enemy, etc. **10** *Inf.* idle talk or boasting. **11** *Sl.* a delightful or successful person or thing: *his latest record is a gas.* **12** *US.* an informal name for **flatus.** ◆ *vb* **gases** *or* **gasses, gassing, gassed. 13** (*tr*) to provide or fill with gas. **14** (*tr*) to subject to gas fumes, esp. so as to asphyxiate or render unconscious. **15** (*intr; foll. by to*) *Inf.* to talk in an idle or boastful way (to a person). [C17 (coined by J. B. van Helmont (1577–1644), Flemish chemist): from Gk *khaos* atmosphere]

gasbag ('gæsˌbæg) *n Inf.* a person who talks in a voluble way, esp. about unimportant matters.

gas chamber *or* **oven** *n* an airtight room into which poison gas is introduced to kill people or animals.

gas chromatography *n* a technique for analysing a mixture of volatile substances in which the mixture is carried by an inert gas through a column packed with a selective adsorbent or absorbent and a detector records on a moving strip the conductivity of the gas leaving the tube.

Gascon ('gæskən) *n* **1** a native or inhabitant of Gascony. **2** the dialect of French spoken in Gascony. ◆ *adj* **3** of or relating to Gascony, its inhabitants, or their dialect of French.

gasconade (ˌgæskə'neɪd) *Rare.* ◆ *n* **1** boastful talk or bluster. ◆ *vb* **gasconades, gasconading, gasconaded. 2** (*intr*) to boast, brag, or bluster. [C18: from F, from *gasconner* to chatter, boast like a GASCON]

gas constant *n* the constant in the gas equation, having the value 8.3143 joules per kelvin per mole. Symbol *R* Also called: **universal gas constant.**

gas-cooled reactor *n* a nuclear reactor using a gas as the coolant.

gas-discharge tube *n Electronics.* any tube in which an electric discharge takes place through a gas.

THESAURUS

gargantuan *adj* = **huge**, big, colossal, elephantine, enormous, giant, gigantic, ginormous (*inf.*), humongous *or* humungous (*US sl.*), immense, mammoth, massive, monstrous, monumental, mountainous, prodigious, titanic, towering, tremendous, vast
Antonyms *adj* little, meagre, miniature, minute, paltry, petite, puny, pygmy *or* pigmy, small, tiny

garish *adj* = **gaudy**, brash, brassy, brummagem, cheap, flash (*inf.*), flashy, flaunting, glaring, glittering, loud, meretricious, naff (*Brit. sl.*), raffish, showy, tacky (*inf.*), tasteless, tawdry, vulgar
Antonyms *adj* conservative, elegant, modest, plain, refined, sedate, sombre, unobtrusive

garland *n* **1** = **wreath**, bays, chaplet, coronal, crown, festoon, honours, laurels ◆ *vb* **3** = **adorn**, crown, deck, festoon, wreathe

garment *n* **1** *plural* = **clothes**, apparel, array, articles of clothing, attire, clothing, costume, dress, duds (*inf.*), garb, gear (*sl.*), habiliment, habit, outfit, raiment (*arch.*), robes, threads (*sl.*), togs, uniform, vestments, wear

garner *vb* **1** = **collect**, accumulate, amass, assemble, deposit, gather, hoard, husband, lay in *or* up, put by, reserve, save, stockpile, store, stow away, treasure ◆ *n* **2, 3** *Archaic* = **storehouse**, depository, granary, store, vault

garnish *vb* **1** = **decorate**, adorn, beautify, bedeck, deck, embellish, enhance, festoon, grace, ornament, set off, trim ◆ *n* **4** = **decoration**, adornment, embellishment, enhancement, festoon, garniture, ornament, ornamentation, trim, trimming
Antonyms *vb* ≠ **decorate**: denude, spoil, strip

garrison *n* **1** = **troops**, armed force, command, detachment, unit **2** = **fort**, base, camp, encampment, fortification, fortress, post, station, stronghold ◆ *vb* **3** = **station**, assign, mount, position, post, put on duty

garrulous *adj* **1** = **talkative**, babbling, chattering, chatty, effusive, gabby (*inf.*), glib, gossiping, gushing, loquacious, mouthy, prating, prattling, verbose, voluble **2** = **long-winded**, diffuse, gassy (*sl.*), prolix, prosy, verbose, windy, wordy
Antonyms *adj* ≠ **talkative**: reserved, reticent, taciturn, tight-lipped, uncommunicative ≠ **long-winded**: concise, succinct, terse

garrulousness *n* **1** = **talkativeness**, babble, babbling, chatter, chattering, chattiness, effusiveness, gabbiness (*inf.*), garrulity, gift of the gab (*inf.*), glibness, loquacity, mouthiness, prating, prattle, verbosity, volubility **2** =

gaseous ('gæsɪəs, -ʃəs, -ʃɪəs, 'geɪ-) *adj* of, concerned with, or having the characteristics of a gas.
▸ **'gaseousness** *n*

gas equation *n* an equation relating the product of the pressure and the volume of an ideal gas to the product of its thermodynamic temperature and the gas constant.

gas gangrene *n* gangrene resulting from infection of a wound by anaerobic bacteria that cause gas bubbles in the surrounding tissues.

gas guzzler *n Sl., chiefly US.* a car that consumes large quantities of petrol.

gash ❶ (gæʃ) *vb* **1** (*tr*) to make a long deep cut in; slash. ◆ *n* **2** a long deep cut. [C16: from OF *garser* to scratch, from Vulgar L, from Gk *kharassein*]

gasholder ('gæs,həʊldə) *n* **1** Also called: **gasometer.** a large tank for storing coal gas or natural gas prior to distribution to users. **2** any vessel for storing or measuring a gas.

gasify ('gæsɪ,faɪ) *vb* **gasifies, gasifying, gasified.** to make into or become a gas.
▸ **,gasifi'cation** *n*

gasket ('gæskɪt) *n* **1** a compressible packing piece of paper, rubber, asbestos, etc., sandwiched between the faces of a metal joint to provide a seal. **2** *Naut.* a piece of line used as a sail stop. [C17 (in the sense: rope lashing a furled sail): prob. from F *garcette* rope's end, lit.: little girl, from OF]

gaslight ('gæs,laɪt) *n* **1** a type of lamp in which the illumination is produced by an incandescent mantle heated by a jet of gas. **2** the light produced by such a lamp.

gasman ('gæs,mæn) *n, pl* **gasmen.** a man employed to read household gas meters, supervise gas fittings, etc.

gas mantle *n* a mantle for use in a gaslight. See **mantle** (sense 4).

gas mask *n* a mask fitted with a chemical filter to enable the wearer to breathe air free of poisonous or corrosive gases.

gas meter *n* an apparatus for measuring and recording the amount of gas passed through it.

gasoline *or* **gasolene** ('gæsə,liːn) *n* a US and Canad. name for **petrol.**

gasometer (gæs'ɒmɪtə) *n* a nontechnical name for **gasholder.**

gasp ❶ (gɑːsp) *vb* **1** (*intr*) to draw in the breath sharply or with effort, esp. in expressing awe, horror, etc. **2** (*intr;* foll. by *after* or *for*) to crave. **3** (*tr;* often foll. by *out*) to utter breathlessly. ◆ *n* **4** a short convulsive intake of breath. **5 at the last gasp. 5a** at the point of death. **5b** at the last moment. [C14: from ON *geispa* to yawn]

gasper ('gɑːspə) *n* **1** a person who gasps. **2** *Brit. dated sl.* a cheap cigarette.

gas plant *n* an aromatic white-flowered Eurasian plant that emits vapour capable of being ignited. Also called: **burning bush, dittany, fraxinella.**

gas ring *n* a circular assembly of gas jets, used esp. for cooking.

gassy ('gæsɪ) *adj* **gassier, gassiest. 1** filled with, containing, or resembling gas. **2** *Inf.* full of idle or vapid talk.
▸ **'gassiness** *n*

gasteropod ('gæstərə,pɒd) *n, adj* a variant spelling of **gastropod.**

gas thermometer *n* a device for measuring temperature by observing the pressure of gas at a constant volume or the volume of a gas kept at a constant pressure.

gastric ('gæstrɪk) *adj* of, relating to, near, or involving the stomach.

gastric juice *n* a digestive fluid secreted by the stomach, containing hydrochloric acid, pepsin, rennin, etc.

gastric ulcer *n* an ulcer of the mucous membrane lining the stomach.

gastritis (gæs'traɪtɪs) *n* inflammation of the stomach.

gastro- *or often before a vowel* **gastr-** *combining form.* stomach: *gastroenteritis; gastritis.* [from Gk *gastēr*]

gastrocolic (,gæstrəʊ'kɒlɪk) *adj* of or relating to the stomach and colon: *gastrocolic reflex.*

gastroenteritis (,gæstrəʊ,entə'raɪtɪs) *n* inflammation of the stomach and intestines.

gastrointestinal (,gæstrəʊɪn'testɪn°l) *adj* of or relating to the stomach and intestinal tract.

gastronome ('gæstrə,nəʊm), **gastronomer** (gæs'trɒnəmə), *or* **gastronomist** *n* less common words for **gourmet.**

gastronomy (gæs'trɒnəmɪ) *n* the art of good eating. [C19: from F, from Gk, from *gastēr* stomach; see -NOMY]
▸ **gastronomic** (,gæstrə'nɒmɪk) *or* **,gastro'nomical** *adj* ▸ **,gastro'nomically** *adv*

gastropod ('gæstrə,pɒd) *or* **gasteropod** *n* any of a class of molluscs typically having a flattened muscular foot for locomotion and a head that bears stalked eyes. The class includes the snails, whelks, and slugs.
▸ **gastropodan** (gæs'trɒpəd°n) *adj, n*

gastroscope ('gæstrə,skəʊp) *n* a medical instrument for examining the interior of the stomach.

gastrula ('gæstrʊlə) *n, pl* **gastrulas** *or* **gastrulae** (-,liː). a saclike animal embryo consisting of three layers of cells surrounding a central cavity with a small opening to the exterior. [C19: NL: little stomach, from Gk *gastēr* belly]

gas turbine *n* an internal-combustion engine in which the expanding gases emerging from one or more combustion chambers drive a turbine.

gasworks ('gæs,wɜːks) *n* (*functioning as sing*) a plant in which gas, esp. coal gas, is made.

gat (gæt) *vb Arch.* a past tense of **get.**

gate ❶ (geɪt) *n* **1** a movable barrier, usually hinged, for closing an opening in a wall, fence, etc. **2** an opening to allow passage into or out of an enclosed place. **3** any means of entrance or access. **4** a mountain pass or gap, esp. one providing entry into another country or region. **5a** the number of people admitted to a sporting event or entertainment. **5b** the total entrance money received from them. **6** *Electronics.* a logic circuit having one or more input terminals and one output terminal, the output being switched between two voltage levels determined by the combination of input signals. **7** a component in a motion-picture camera or projector that holds each frame flat and momentarily stationary behind the lens. **8** a slotted metal frame that controls the positions of the gear lever in a motor vehicle. ◆ *vb* **gates, gating, gated. 9** (*tr*) *Brit.* to restrict (a student) to the school or college grounds as a punishment. [OE *geat*]

gâteau ('gætəʊ) *n, pl* **gâteaux** (-təʊz). a rich cake usually layered with cream and elaborately decorated. [F: cake]

gate-crash *vb Inf.* to gain entry to (a party, concert, etc.) without invitation or payment.
▸ **'gate-,crasher** *n*

gatefold ('geɪt,fəʊld) *n* an oversize page in a book or magazine that is folded in. Also called: **foldout.**

gatehouse ('geɪt,haʊs) *n* **1** a building at or above a gateway, used by a porter or guard, or, formerly, as a fortification. **2** a small house at the entrance to the grounds of a country mansion.

gatekeeper ('geɪt,kiːpə) *n* **1** a person who has charge of a gate and controls who may pass through it. **2** a manager in a large organization who controls the flow of information, esp. to parent and subsidiary companies. **3** any of several Eurasian butterflies having brown-bordered orange wings.

gate-leg table *or* **gate-legged table** *n* a table with one or two leaves supported by a hinged leg swung out from the frame.

gatepost ('geɪt,pəʊst) *n* **1a** the post on which a gate is hung. **1b** the post to which a gate is fastened when closed. **2 between you, me, and the gatepost.** confidentially.

gateway ('geɪt,weɪ) *n* **1** an entrance that may be closed by or as by a gate. **2** a means of entry or access: *Bombay, gateway to India.* **3** *Computing.* hardware and software that connect incompatible computer networks.

gather ❶ ('gæðə) *vb* **1** to assemble or cause to assemble. **2** to collect or be collected gradually; muster. **3** (*tr*) to learn from information given; conclude or assume. **4** (*tr*) to pick or harvest (flowers, fruit, etc.). **5** (*tr*) to bring close (to). **6** to increase or cause to increase gradually, as in force, speed, intensity, etc. **7** to contract (the brow) or (of the brow) to become contracted into wrinkles; knit. **8** (*tr*) to assemble (sections of a book) in the correct sequence for binding. **9** (*tr*) to prepare or make ready: *to gather one's wits.* **10** to draw (material) into a series of small tucks or folds. **11** (*intr*) (of a boil or other sore) to come to a head; form pus. ◆ *n* **12a** the act of gathering. **12b** the amount gathered. **13** a small fold in material, as made by a tightly pulled stitch; tuck. [OE *gadrian*]
▸ **'gatherer** *n*

gathering ❶ ('gæðərɪŋ) *n* **1** a group of people, things, etc., that are gathered together; assembly. **2** *Sewing.* a series of gathers in material. **3** *Inf.* **3a** the formation of pus in a boil. **3b** the pus so formed. **4** *Printing.* an informal name for **section** (sense 16).

Gatling gun ('gætlɪŋ) *n* a machine gun equipped with a rotating cluster of barrels that are fired in succession. [C19: after R. J. *Gatling* (1818–1903), its US inventor]

GATT (gæt) *n acronym for* General Agreement on Tariffs and Trade: a multilateral international treaty signed in 1947 to promote trade; replaced in 1995 by the World Trade Organization.

gauche ❶ (gəʊʃ) *adj* lacking ease of manner; tactless. [C18: F: awkward, left, from OF *gauchir* to swerve, ult. of Gmc origin]
▸ **'gauchely** *adv* ▸ **'gaucheness** *n*

THESAURUS

long-windedness, diffuseness, prolixity, prosiness, verbosity, windiness, wordiness

gash *vb* **1** = **cut**, cleave, gouge, incise, lacerate, rend, slash, slit, split, tear, wound ◆ *n* **2** = **cut**, cleft, gouge, incision, laceration, rent, slash, slit, split, tear, wound

gasp *vb* **1** = **gulp**, blow, catch one's breath, choke, fight for breath, pant, puff ◆ *n* **4** = **gulp**, blow, ejaculation, exclamation, intake of breath, pant, puff, sharp intake of breath

gate *n* **1-3** = **barrier**, access, door, doorway, egress, entrance, exit, gateway, opening, passage, port (*Scot.*), portal

gather *vb* **1, 2** = **assemble**, accumulate, amass, bring *or* get together, collect, congregate, convene, flock, foregather, garner, group, heap, hoard, marshal, mass, muster, pile up, round up, stack up, stockpile **3** = **learn**, assume, be led to believe, conclude, deduce, draw, hear, infer, make, surmise, understand **4** = **pick**, crop, cull, garner, glean, harvest, pluck, reap, select **5** = **enfold**, clasp, draw, embrace, hold, hug **6** = **intensify**, build, deepen, enlarge, expand, grow, heighten, increase, rise, swell, thicken, wax **10** = **fold**, pleat, pucker, ruffle, shirr, tuck
Antonyms *vb* ≠ **assemble:** diffuse, disperse, dissipate, scatter, separate

gathering *n* **1** = **assembly**, assemblage, collection, company, conclave, concourse, congregation, congress, convention, convocation, crowd, flock, get-together (*inf.*), group, knot, mass, meeting, muster, party, rally, throng, turnout **3** *Informal* = **pimple**, abscess, boil, carbuncle, pustule, sore, spot, tumour, ulcer

gauche *adj* = **awkward**, clumsy, graceless, ig-

gaucherie ➊ (ˌɡəʊʃəˈriː, ˈɡəʊʃərɪ) *n* **1** the quality of being gauche. **2** a gauche act.

gaucho (ˈɡaʊtʃəʊ) *n, pl* **gauchos.** a cowboy of the South American pampas, usually one of mixed Spanish and Indian descent. [C19: from American Sp., prob. from Quechuan *wáhcha* orphan, vagabond]

gaud (ɡɔːd) *n* an article of cheap finery. [C14: prob. from OF *gaudir* to be joyful, from L *gaudēre*]

gaudy[1] ➊ (ˈɡɔːdɪ) *adj* **gaudier, gaudiest.** bright or colourful in a crude or vulgar manner. [C16: from GAUD]
▸ **ˈgaudily** *adv* ▸ **ˈgaudiness** *n*

gaudy[2] (ˈɡɔːdɪ) *n, pl* **gaudies.** *Brit.* a celebratory feast held at some schools and colleges. [C16: from L *gaudium* joy, from *gaudēre* to rejoice]

gauge ➊ *or* **gage** (ɡeɪdʒ) *vb* **gauges, gauging, gauged** *or* **gages, gaging, gaged.** (*tr*) **1** to measure or determine the amount, quantity, size, condition, etc., of. **2** to estimate or appraise; judge. **3** to check for conformity or bring into conformity with a standard measurement, etc. ◆ *n* **4** a standard measurement, dimension, capacity, or quantity. **5** any of various instruments for measuring a quantity: *a pressure gauge.* **6** any of various devices used to check for conformity with a standard measurement. **7** a standard or means for assessing; test; criterion. **8** scope, capacity, or extent. **9** the diameter of the barrel of a gun, esp. a shotgun. **10** the thickness of sheet metal or the diameter of wire. **11** the distance between the rails of a railway track. **12** the distance between two wheels on the same axle of a vehicle, truck, etc. **13** *Naut.* the position of a vessel in relation to the wind and another vessel. **14** a measure of the fineness of woven or knitted fabric. **15** the width of motion-picture film or magnetic tape. ◆ *adj* **16** (of a pressure measurement) measured on a pressure gauge that registers zero at atmospheric pressure. [C15: from OF, prob. of Gmc origin]
▸ **ˈgaugeable** *or* **ˈgageable** *adj*

gauge boson *n Physics.* a boson that mediates the interaction between elementary particles. There are four types: photons for electromagnetic interactions, gluons for strong interactions, intermediate vector bosons for weak interactions, and gravitons for gravitational interactions.

gauge theory *n Physics.* a type of theory of elementary particles designed to explain the strong, weak, and electromagnetic interactions in terms of exchange of virtual particles.

Gaul (ɡɔːl) *n* **1** a native of ancient Gaul, a region in Roman times stretching from what is now N Italy to the S Netherlands. **2** a Frenchman.

Gauleiter (ˈɡaʊˌlaɪtə) *n* **1** a provincial governor in Germany under Hitler. **2** (*sometimes not cap.*) a person in a position of petty authority who behaves in an overbearing manner. [G, from *Gau* district + *Leiter* leader]

Gaulish (ˈɡɔːlɪʃ) *n* **1** the extinct Celtic language of the pre-Roman Gauls. ◆ *adj* **2** of ancient Gaul, the Gauls, or their language.

gaunt ➊ (ɡɔːnt) *adj* **1** bony and emaciated in appearance. **2** (of places) bleak or desolate. [C15: ?from ON]
▸ **ˈgauntly** *adv* ▸ **ˈgauntness** *n*

gauntlet[1] (ˈɡɔːntlɪt) *n* **1** a medieval armoured leather glove. **2** a heavy glove with a long cuff. **3 take up** (*or* **throw down**) **the gauntlet.** to accept (*or* offer) a challenge. [C15: from OF *gantelet*, dim. of *gant* glove, of Gmc origin]

gauntlet[2] (ˈɡɔːntlɪt) *n* **1** a punishment in which the victim is forced to run between two rows of men who strike at him as he passes: formerly a military punishment. **2 run the gauntlet. 2a** to suffer this punishment. **2b** to endure an onslaught, as of criticism. **3** a testing ordeal. [C15: changed (through infl. of GAUNTLET[1]) from earlier *gantlope*, from Swedish *gatlopp* passageway]

gaur (ˈɡaʊə) *n* a large wild ox of mountainous regions of S Asia. [C19: from Hindi, from Sansk. *gāura*]

gauss (ɡaʊs) *n, pl* **gauss.** the cgs unit of magnetic flux density. 1 gauss is equivalent to 10^{-4} tesla. [after K. F. *Gauss* (1777–1855), G mathematician]

Gaussian distribution (ˈɡaʊsɪən) *n* another name for **normal distribution.**

gauze (ɡɔːz) *n* **1** a transparent cloth of loose weave. **2** a surgical dressing of muslin or similar material. **3** any thin openwork material, such as wire. **4** a fine mist or haze. [C16: from F *gaze*, ?from *Gaza*, Israel, where it was believed to originate]

gauzy ➊ (ˈɡɔːzɪ) *adj* **gauzier, gauziest.** resembling gauze; thin and transparent.
▸ **ˈgauzily** *adv* ▸ **ˈgauziness** *n*

gave (ɡeɪv) *vb* the past tense of **give.**

gavel (ˈɡævᵊl) *n* a small hammer used by a chairman, auctioneer, etc., to call for order or attention. [C19: from ?]

gavial (ˈɡeɪvɪəl), **gharial,** *or* **garial** (ˈɡærɪəl) *n* a large fish-eating Indian crocodile with a very long slender snout. [C19: from F, from Hindi]

gavotte *or* **gavot** (ɡəˈvɒt) *n* **1** an old formal dance in quadruple time. **2** a piece of music composed for or in the rhythm of this dance. [C17: from F, from Provençal, from *gavot* mountaineer, dweller in the Alps (where the dance originated)]

gawk ➊ (ɡɔːk) *n* **1** a clumsy stupid person; lout. ◆ *vb* **2** (*intr*) to stare in a stupid way; gape. [C18: from ODanish *gaukr*; prob. rel. to GAPE]

gawky ➊ (ˈɡɔːkɪ) *adj* **gawkier, gawkiest.** clumsy or ungainly; awkward. Also: **gawkish.**
▸ **ˈgawkily** *adv* ▸ **ˈgawkiness** *n*

gawp *or* **gaup** (ɡɔːp) *vb* (*intr*; often foll. by *at*) *Brit. sl.* to stare stupidly; gape. [C14 *galpen*; prob. rel. to OE *gielpan* to boast, YELP]
▸ **ˈgawper** *n*

gay ➊ (ɡeɪ) *adj* **1a** homosexual. **1b** of or for homosexuals: *a gay club.* **2** carefree and merry: *a gay temperament.* **3** brightly coloured; brilliant: *a gay hat.* **4** given to pleasure, esp. in social entertainment: *a gay life.* ◆ *n* **5** a homosexual. [C13: from OF *gai*, from OProvençal, of Gmc origin]
▸ **ˈgayness** *n*

> **USAGE NOTE** *Gayness* is the state of being homosexual. The noun which refers to the state of being carefree and merry is *gaiety.*

gazania (ɡæˈzeɪnɪə) *n* any of a genus of S. African plants of the composite family having large showy flowers. [? after Theodore of *Gaza* (1398–1478), who translated the botanical works of Theophrastus into Latin]

gaze ➊ (ɡeɪz) *vb* **gazes, gazing, gazed. 1** (*intr*) to look long and fixedly, esp. in wonder. ◆ *n* **2** a fixed look. [C14: from Swedish dialect *gasa* to gape at]
▸ **ˈgazer** *n*

gazebo (ɡəˈziːbəʊ) *n, pl* **gazebos** *or* **gazeboes.** a summerhouse, garden pavilion, or belvedere, sited to command a view. [C18: ? a pseudo-Latin coinage based on GAZE]

gazelle (ɡəˈzɛl) *n, pl* **gazelles** *or* **gazelle.** any small graceful usually fawn-coloured antelope of Africa and Asia. [C17: from OF, from Ar. *ghazāl*]

gazette ➊ (ɡəˈzɛt) *n* **1** a newspaper or official journal. **2** *Brit.* an official

THESAURUS

norant, ill-bred, ill-mannered, inelegant, inept, insensitive, lacking in social graces, maladroit, tactless, uncultured, unpolished, unsophisticated
Antonyms *adj* elegant, gracious, polished, polite, refined, sophisticated, tasteful, urbane, well-mannered

gaucherie *n* **1** = **awkwardness**, bad taste, clumsiness, gaucheness, gracelessness, ignorance, ill-breeding, inelegance, ineptness, insensitivity, lack of polish, maladroitness, tactlessness, unsophisticatedness **2** = **blunder**, bloomer, boob (*sl.*), breach of etiquette, clanger (*inf.*), faux pas, gaffe, indiscretion, lapse, mistake, slip, solecism

gaudiness *n* = **garishness**, brashness, flashiness, loudness, naffness, ostentation, poor taste, tastelessness, tawdriness, vulgarity

gaudy[1] *adj* = **garish**, brash, bright, brilliant, brummagem, flash (*inf.*), flashy, florid, gay, gimcrack, glaring, jazzy (*inf.*), loud, meretricious, naff (*Brit. sl.*), ostentatious, raffish, showy, tacky (*inf.*), tasteless, tawdry, vulgar
Antonyms *adj* colourless, conservative, dull, elegant, modest, quiet, refined, sedate, subtle, tasteful

gauge *vb* **1** = **measure**, ascertain, calculate, check, compute, count, determine, weigh **2** = **judge**, adjudge, appraise, assess, estimate, evaluate, guess, rate, reckon, value ◆ *n* **4, 7** = **indicator**, basis, criterion, example, exemplar, guide, guideline, measure, meter, model, par, pattern, rule, sample, standard, test, touchstone, yardstick **9-12** = **size**, bore, capacity, degree, depth, extent, height, magnitude, measure, scope, span, thickness, width

gaunt *adj* **1** = **thin**, angular, attenuated, bony, cadaverous, emaciated, haggard, lank, lean, meagre, pinched, rawboned, scraggy, scrawny, skeletal, skin and bone, skinny, spare, wasted **2** = **bleak**, bare, desolate, dismal, dreary, forbidding, forlorn, grim, harsh, stark
Antonyms *adj* ≠ **thin:** chubby, corpulent, fat, lush, obese, plump, stout, well-fed ≠ **bleak:** inviting, lush, luxurious

gauntness *n* **1** = **thinness**, angularity, boniness, cadaverousness, emaciation, leanness, scragginess, scrawniness, wasted frame **2** = **bleakness**, desolation, forlornness, grimness, harshness, starkness

gauzy *adj* = **delicate**, diaphanous, filmy, flimsy, gossamer, insubstantial, light, see-through, sheer, thin, translucent, transparent

gawk *n* **1** = **oaf**, boor, churl, clod, clodhopper (*inf.*), dolt, dunderhead, galoot (*sl.*), ignoramus, lout, lubber, lummox (*inf.*) ◆ *vb* **2** = **stare**, gape, gawp (*sl.*), gaze open-mouthed, goggle

gawky *adj* = **awkward**, clownish, clumsy, gauche, loutish, lumbering, lumpish, maladroit, oafish, uncouth, ungainly
Antonyms *adj* elegant, graceful, self-assured, well-coordinated

gay *adj* **1** = **homosexual**, bent, dykey (*sl.*), lesbian, pink (*inf.*), queer (*inf., derogatory*) **2** = **cheerful**, animated, blithe, carefree, debonair, full of beans (*inf.*), glad, gleeful, happy, hilarious, insouciant, jolly, jovial, joyful, joyous, light-hearted, lively, merry, sparkling, sunny, vivacious **3** = **colourful**, bright, brilliant, flamboyant, flashy, fresh, garish, gaudy, rich, showy, vivid **4** = **merry**, convivial, festive, frivolous, frolicsome, fun-loving, gamesome, playful, pleasure-seeking, rakish, rollicking, sportive, waggish ◆ *n* **5** = **homosexual**, bull dyke (*offens. sl.*), dyke (*offens. sl.*), faggot (*US offens. sl.*), fairy, invert, lesbian, poof (*offens. sl.*), queer (*offens. sl.*)
Antonyms *adj, n* ≠ **homosexual:** heterosexual, straight ◆ *adj* ≠ **cheerful:** cheerless, down in the dumps (*inf.*), grave, grim, melancholy, miserable, sad, sedate, serious, sober, solemn, sombre, unhappy ≠ **colourful:** colourless, conservative, drab, dull, sombre

gaze *vb* **1** = **stare**, contemplate, eyeball (*sl.*), gape, look, look fixedly, regard, view, watch, wonder ◆ *n* **2** = **stare**, fixed look, look

gazette *n* **1** = **newspaper**, journal, news-sheet, organ, paper, periodical document containing public notices, appointments, etc. ◆ *vb* **gazettes, gazetting, gazetted. 3** (*tr*) *Brit.* to announce or report (facts or an event) in a gazette. [C17: from F, from It., from Venetian dialect *gazeta* news-sheet costing one *gazet*, small copper coin]

gazetteer (ˌgæzɪˈtɪə) *n* **1** a book or section of a book that lists and describes places. **2** *Arch.* a writer for a gazette.

gazpacho (gəzˈpɑːtʃəʊ, gæs-) *n* a Spanish soup made from tomatoes, peppers, etc., and served cold. [from Sp.]

gazump (gəˈzʌmp) *Brit.* ◆ *vb* **1** to raise the price of something, esp. a house, after agreeing a price verbally with (an intending buyer). **2** (*tr*) to swindle or overcharge. ◆ *n* **3** an instance of gazumping. [C20: from ?]
▸**gaˈzumper** *n*

gazunder (gəˈzʌndə) *Brit.* ◆ *vb* **1** to reduce an offer on a property immediately before exchanging contracts, having previously agreed to a higher price with (the seller). ◆ *n* **2** an act or instance of gazundering. [C20: modelled on GAZUMP]
▸**gaˈzunderer** *n*

GB *abbrev. for* Great Britain.

GBE *abbrev. for* (Knight or Dame) Grand Cross of the British Empire (a Brit. title).

GBH *abbrev. for* grievous bodily harm.

GC *abbrev. for* George Cross (a Brit. award for bravery).

GCB *abbrev. for* (Knight) Grand Cross of the Bath (a Brit. title).

gcd *or* **GCD** *abbrev. for* greatest common divisor.

GCE (in Britain) *abbrev. for* General Certificate of Education: a public examination in specified subjects taken as qualifying examinations for entry into a university, college, etc. The GCSE has replaced it at O level. See also **A level, S level.**

GCHQ (in Britain) *abbrev. for* Government Communications Headquarters.

G clef *n* another name for **treble clef.**

GCMG *abbrev. for* (Knight or Dame) Grand Cross of the Order of St Michael and St George (a Brit. title).

GCSE (in Britain) *abbrev. for* General Certificate of Secondary Education: a public examination in specified subjects for 16-year-old schoolchildren. It replaced GCE O level and CSE.

GCVO *abbrev. for* (Knight or Dame) Grand Cross of the Royal Victorian Order (a Brit. title).

Gd *the chemical symbol for* gadolinium.

g'day *or* **gidday** (gəˈdaɪ) *sentence substitute.* an Australian and NZ informal variant of **good day.**

Gdns *abbrev. for* Gardens.

Ge *the chemical symbol for* germanium.

gean (giːn) *n* a white-flowered tree of the rose family of Europe, W Asia, and N Africa; the ancestor of the cultivated sweet cherries.

gear **T** (gɪə) *n* **1** a toothed wheel that engages with another toothed wheel or with a rack in order to change the speed or direction of transmitted motion. **2** a mechanism for transmitting motion by gears. **3** the engagement or specific ratio of a system of gears: *in gear; high gear.* **4** personal belongings. **5** equipment and supplies for a particular operation, sport, etc. **6** *Naut.* all equipment or appurtenances belonging to a certain vessel, sailor, etc. **7** short for **landing gear. 8** *Inf.* up-to-date clothes and accessories. **9** *Sl.* drugs of any type. **10** a less common word for **harness** (sense 1). **11 out of gear.** out of order; not functioning properly. ◆ *vb* **12** (*tr*) to adjust or adapt (one thing) so as to fit in or work with another: *to gear our output to current demand.* **13** (*tr*) to equip with or connect by gears. **14** (*intr*) to be in or come into gear. **15** (*tr*) to equip with a harness. [C13: from ON *gervi*]

gearbox (ˈgɪəˌbɒks) *n* **1** the metal casing within which a train of gears is sealed. **2** this metal casing and its contents, esp. in a motor vehicle.

gearing (ˈgɪərɪŋ) *n* **1** an assembly of gears designed to transmit motion. **2** the act or technique of providing gears to transmit motion. **3** Also called: **capital gearing.** *Accounting, Brit.* the ratio of a company's debt capital to its equity capital. US word: **leverage.**

gear lever *or US & Canad.* **gearshift** (ˈgɪəˌʃɪft) *n* a lever used to move gearwheels relative to each other, esp. in a motor vehicle.

gear train *n Engineering.* a system of gears that transmits power from one shaft to another.

gearwheel (ˈgɪəˌwiːl) *n* another name for **gear** (sense 1).

gecko (ˈgɛkəʊ) *n, pl* **geckos** *or* **geckoes.** a small insectivorous terrestrial lizard of warm regions. [C18: from Malay *geˈkok*, imit.]

gee[1] (dʒiː) *interj* **1** Also: **gee up!** an exclamation, as to a horse or draught animal, to encourage it to turn to the right, go on, or go faster. ◆ *vb* **gees, geeing, geed. 2** (usually foll. by *up*) to move (an animal, esp. a horse) ahead; urge on. [C17: from ?]

gee[2] (dʒiː) *interj US & Canad. inf.* a mild exclamation of surprise, admiration, etc. Also: **gee whizz.** [C20: euphemism for JESUS]

geebung (ˈdʒiːbʌŋ) *n* **1** any of several Australian trees or shrubs with edible but tasteless fruit. **2** the fruit of these trees. [from Abor.]

geek (giːk) *n Sl.* **1** a boring or unattractive social misfit. **2** a degenerate. [C19: prob. from Scot. *geck* fool]
▸**ˈgeeky** *adj*

geelbek (ˈxiːlˌbɛk) *n S. African.* an edible marine fish with yellow jaws. Also called: **Cape salmon.** [from Afrik. *geel* yellow + *bek* mouth]

geese (giːs) *n* the plural of **goose**[1].

geezer (ˈgiːzə) *n Inf.* a man. [C19: prob. from dialect pronunciation of GUISER]

Gehenna (gɪˈhɛnə) *n* **1** *Old Testament.* the valley below Jerusalem, where children were sacrificed and, later, unclean things were burnt. **2** *New Testament, Judaism.* a place where the wicked are punished after death. **3** a place or state of pain and torment. [C16: from LL, from Gk, from Heb. *Gê' Hinnōm*, lit.: valley of Hinnom, symbolic of hell]

Geiger counter (ˈgaɪgə) *or* **Geiger-Müller counter** (ˈmʊlə) *n* an instrument for detecting and measuring the intensity of ionizing radiation. [C20: after Hans *Geiger* and W. *Müller*, 20th-cent. G physicists]

geisha (ˈgeɪʃə) *n, pl* **geisha** *or* **geishas.** a professional female companion for men in Japan, trained in music, dancing, and the art of conversation. [C19: from Japanese, from Ancient Chinese]

Geissler tube (ˈgaɪslə) *n* a glass or quartz vessel for maintaining an electric discharge in a low-pressure gas as a source of visible or ultraviolet light for spectroscopy, etc. [C19: after Heinrich *Geissler* (1814–79), G mechanic]

gel (dʒɛl) *n* **1** a semirigid jelly-like colloid in which a liquid is dispersed in a solid: *nondrip paint is a gel.* **2** a jelly-like substance applied to the hair before styling in order to retain the style. ◆ *vb* **gels, gelling, gelled. 3** to become or cause to become a gel. **4** a variant spelling of **jell.** [C19: from GELATINE]

gelatine (ˈdʒɛləˌtiːn) *or* **gelatin** (ˈdʒɛlətɪn) *n* **1** a colourless or yellowish water-soluble protein prepared by boiling animal hides and bones: used in foods, glue, photographic emulsions, etc. **2** an edible jelly made of this substance. [C19: from F *gélatine*, from Med. L, from L *gelāre* to freeze]

gelatinize *or* **gelatinise** (dʒɪˈlætɪˌnaɪz) *vb* **gelatinizes, gelatinizing, gelatinized** *or* **gelatinises, gelatinising, gelatinised. 1** to make or become gelatinous. **2** (*tr*) *Photog.* to coat (glass, paper, etc.) with gelatine.
▸**geˌlatiniˈzation** *or* ▸**geˌlatiniˈsation** *n*

gelatinous **T** (dʒɪˈlætɪnəs) *adj* **1** consisting of or resembling jelly; viscous. **2** of, containing, or resembling gelatine.
▸**geˈlatinously** *adv* ▸**geˈlatinousness** *n*

gelation[1] (dʒɪˈleɪʃən) *n* the act or process of freezing a liquid. [C19: from L *gelātiō* a freezing; see GELATINE]

gelation[2] (dʒɪˈleɪʃən) *n* the act or process of forming into a gel. [C20: from GEL]

geld (gɛld) *vb* **gelds, gelding, gelded** *or* **gelt** (gɛlt). (*tr*) **1** to castrate (a horse or other animal). **2** to deprive of virility or vitality; emasculate; weaken. [C13: from ON, from *geldr* barren]

gelding (ˈgɛldɪŋ) *n* a castrated male horse. [C14: from ON *geldingr*; see GELD, -ING[1]]

gelid (ˈdʒɛlɪd) *adj* very cold, icy, or frosty. [C17: from L *gelidus*, from *gelu* frost]
▸**geˈlidity** *n*

gelignite (ˈdʒɛlɪgˌnaɪt) *n* a type of dynamite in which the nitrogelatine is absorbed in a base of wood pulp and potassium or sodium nitrate. Also called (informal): **gelly.** [C19: from GEL(ATINE) + L *ignis* fire + -ITE[1]]

gem **T** (dʒɛm) *n* **1** a precious or semiprecious stone used in jewellery as a decoration; jewel. **2** a person or thing held to be a perfect example; treasure. ◆ *vb* **gems, gemming, gemmed. 3** (*tr*) to set or ornament with gems. [C14: from OF, from L *gemma* bud, precious stone]
▸**ˈgemˌlike** *adj* ▸**ˈgemmy** *adj*

Gemara (gɛˈmɑːrə; *Hebrew* gemaˈra) *n Judaism.* the later main part of the Talmud, being a commentary on the Mishnah: the primary source of Jewish religious law. [C17: from Aramaic *gemārā* completion]

geminate *adj* (ˈdʒɛmɪnɪt, -ˌneɪt) *also* **geminated. 1** combined in pairs; doubled: *a geminate leaf.* ◆ *vb* (ˈdʒɛmɪˌneɪt), **geminates, geminating, geminated. 2** to arrange or be arranged in pairs: *the "t"s in "fitted" are geminated.* [C17: from L *gemināre* to double, from *geminus* twin]
▸**ˈgeminately** *adv* ▸**ˌgemiˈnation** *n*

Gemini (ˈdʒɛmɪˌnaɪ, -ˌniː) *n* **1** *Astron.* a zodiacal constellation in the N hemisphere containing the stars Castor and Pollux. **2** *Astrol.* Also called: the **Twins.** the third sign of the zodiac. The sun is in this sign between about May 21 and June 20.

gemma (ˈdʒɛmə) *n, pl* **gemmae** (-miː). **1** a small asexual reproductive structure in mosses, etc., that becomes detached from the parent and develops into a new individual. **2** *Zool.* another name for **gemmule.** [C18: from L: bud, GEM]

gemmate (ˈdʒɛmeɪt) *adj* **1** (of some plants and animals) having or reproducing by gemmae. ◆ *vb* **gemmates, gemmating, gemmated. 2** (*intr*) to produce or reproduce by gemmae.
▸**gemˈmation** *n*

gemmiparous (dʒɛˈmɪpərəs) *adj* (of plants and animals) reproducing by gemmae or buds. Also: **gemmiferous.**

gemmule (ˈdʒɛmjuːl) *n* **1** *Zool.* a cell or mass of cells produced asexually by sponges and developing into a new individual; bud. **2** *Bot.* a small gemma. [C19: from F, from L *gemmula* a little bud; see GEM]

THESAURUS

gear *n* **1 = cog**, cogwheel, gearwheel, toothed wheel **2 = mechanism**, cogs, gearing, machinery, works **4 = belongings**, baggage, effects, kit, luggage, stuff, things **5 = equipment**, accessories, accoutrements, apparatus, harness, instruments, outfit, paraphernalia, supplies, tackle, tools, trappings **8 = clothing**, apparel, array, attire, clothes, costume, dress, garb, garments, habit, outfit, rigout (*inf.*), threads (*sl.*), togs, wear ◆ *vb* **12 = equip**, adapt, adjust, fit, rig, suit, tailor

gelatinous *adj* **1 = jelly-like**, gluey, glutinous, gummy, mucilaginous, sticky, viscid, viscous

gem *n* **1 = precious stone**, jewel, semiprecious stone, stone **2 = prize**, flower, jewel, masterpiece, pearl, pick, treasure

gemology *or* **gemmology** (dʒɛˈmɒlədʒɪ) *n* the branch of mineralogy concerned with gems and gemstones.
▸**gemological** *or* **gemmological** (ˌdʒɛməˈlɒdʒɪkᵊl) *adj* ▸**gemˈologist** *or* **gemˈmologist** *n*

gemsbok *or* **gemsbuck** (ˈgɛmzˌbʌk) *n, pl* **gemsbok, gemsboks** *or* **gemsbuck, gemsbucks.** an oryx of southern Africa, marked with a broad black band along its flanks. [C18: from Afrik., from G *Gemsbock,* from *Gemse* chamois + *Bock* BUCK[1]]

gemstone (ˈdʒɛmˌstəʊn) *n* a precious or semiprecious stone, esp. one cut and polished.

gen (dʒɛn) *n Brit., Austral., & NZ inf.* information: *give me the gen on your latest project.* See also **gen up.** [C20: from *gen(eral information)*]

gen. *abbrev. for:* **1** gender. **2** general(ly). **3** generic. **4** genitive. **5** genus.

Gen. *abbrev. for:* **1** General. **2** *Bible.* Genesis.

-gen *suffix forming nouns.* **1** producing or that which produces: *hydrogen.* **2** something produced: *carcinogen.* [via F *-gène,* from Gk *-genēs* born]

gendarme (ˈʒɒndɑːm) *n* **1** a member of the police force in France or in countries influenced or controlled by France. **2** a sharp pinnacle of rock on a mountain ridge. [C16: from F, from *gens d'armes* people of arms]

gendarmerie *or* **gendarmery** (ʒɒnˈdɑːmərɪ) *n* **1** the whole corps of gendarmes. **2** the headquarters of a body of gendarmes.

gender (ˈdʒɛndə) *n* **1** a set of two or more grammatical categories into which the nouns of certain languages are divided. **2** any of the categories, such as masculine, feminine, neuter, or common, within such a set. **3** *Inf.* the state of being male, female, or neuter. **4** *Inf.* all the members of one sex: *the female gender.* [C14: from OF, from L *genus* kind]

gender-bender *n Inf.* a person who adopts an androgynous style of dress, hair, etc.

gene (dʒiːn) *n* a unit of heredity composed of DNA occupying a fixed position on a chromosome and transmitted from parent to offspring during reproduction. [C20: from G *Gen,* shortened from *Pangen;* see PAN-, -GEN]

-gene *suffix forming nouns.* a variant of **-gen.**

genealogy 🅣 (ˌdʒiːnɪˈælədʒɪ) *n, pl* **genealogies. 1** the direct descent of an individual or group from an ancestor. **2** the study of the evolutionary development of animals and plants from earlier forms. **3** a chart showing the relationships and descent of an individual, group, etc. [C13: from OF, from LL, from Gk, from *genea* race]
▸**genealogical** (ˌdʒiːnɪəˈlɒdʒɪkᵊl) *adj* ▸ˌ**geneaˈlogically** *adv* ▸ˌ**geneˈalogist** *n*

gene bank *n Bot.* a collection of seeds, plants, tissue cultures, etc., of potentially useful species, esp. species containing genes of significance to the breeding of crops.

gene clone *n* See **clone** (sense 2).

genecology (ˌdʒɛnɪˈkɒlədʒɪ) *n* the study of the gene frequency of a species in relation to its population distribution within a particular environment.

gene library *n* a collection of gene clones that represents the genetic material of an organism: used in genetic engineering.

gene pool *n* the total of all the genes and their alleles in a population of a plant or animal species.

genera (ˈdʒɛnərə) *n* a plural of **genus.**

general 🅣 (ˈdʒɛnərəl, ˈdʒɛnrəl) *adj* **1** common; widespread. **2** of, applying to, or participated in by all or most of the members of a group, category, or community. **3** relating to various branches of an activity, profession, etc.; not specialized: *general office work.* **4** including various or miscellaneous items: *general knowledge; a general store.* **5** not specific as to detail; overall: *a general description.* **6** not definite; vague: *the general idea.* **7** applicable or true in most cases; usual. **8** *(prenominal or immediately postpositive)* having superior or extended authority or rank: *general manager; consul general.* ◆ *n* **9** an officer of a rank senior to lieutenant general, esp. one who commands a large military formation. **10** any person acting as a leader and applying strategy or tactics. **11** a general condition or principle: opposed to *particular.* **12** a title for the head of a religious order, congregation, etc. **13** *Arch.* the people; public. **14 in general.** generally; mostly or usually. [C13: from L *generālis* of a particular kind, from *genus* kind]

general anaesthetic *n* See **anaesthesia.**

General Assembly *n* **1** the deliberative assembly of the United Nations. Abbrev.: **GA. 2** *NZ.* an older name for **parliament. 3** the supreme governing body of certain religious denominations, esp. of the Presbyterian Church.

general average *n Insurance.* loss or damage to a ship or its cargo that is shared among the shipowners and all the cargo owners. Abbrev.: **GA.** Cf. **particular average.**

General Certificate of Education *n* See **GCE.**

General Certificate of Secondary Education *n* See **GCSE.**

general election *n* **1** an election in which representatives are chosen in all constituencies of a state. **2** *US.* a final election from which successful candidates are sent to a legislative body. **3** *US & Canad.* a national, state, or provincial election.

generalissimo (ˌdʒɛnərəˈlɪsɪˌməʊ, ˌdʒɛnrə-) *n, pl* **generalissimos.** a supreme commander of combined military, naval, and air forces. [C17: from It., sup. of *generale* GENERAL]

generality 🅣 (ˌdʒɛnəˈrælɪtɪ) *n, pl* **generalities. 1** a principle or observation having general application. **2** the state or quality of being general. **3** *Arch.* the majority.

generalization *or* **generalisation** (ˌdʒɛnrəlaɪˈzeɪʃən) *n* **1** a principle, theory, etc., with general application. **2** the act or an instance of generalizing. **3** *Logic.* the derivation of a general statement from a particular one, formally by prefixing a quantifier and replacing a subject term by a bound variable. If the quantifier is universal (**universal generalization**) the argument is not in general valid; if it is existential (**existential generalization**) it is valid.

generalize *or* **generalise** (ˈdʒɛnrəˌlaɪz) *vb* **generalizes, generalizing, generalized** *or* **generalises, generalising, generalised. 1** to form (general principles or conclusions) from (detailed facts, experience, etc.); infer. **2** *(intr)* to think or speak in generalities, esp. in a prejudiced way. **3** *(tr; usually passive)* to cause to become widely used or known.

generally 🅣 (ˈdʒɛnrəlɪ) *adv* **1** usually; as a rule. **2** commonly or widely. **3** without reference to specific details or facts; broadly.

general practitioner *n* a physician who does not specialize but has a medical practice (**general practice**) in which he treats all illnesses. Informal name: **family doctor.** Abbrev.: **GP.**

general-purpose *adj* having a range of uses; not restricted to one function.

generalship (ˈdʒɛnrəlˌʃɪp) *n* **1** the art or duties of exercising command of a major military formation or formations. **2** tactical or administrative skill.

general staff *n* officers assigned to advise commanders in the planning and execution of military operations.

general strike *n* a strike by all or most of the workers of a country, province, city, etc.

General Synod *n* the governing body, under Parliament, of the Church of England, made up of the bishops and elected clerical and lay representatives.

generate 🅣 (ˈdʒɛnəˌreɪt) *vb* **generates, generating, generated.** *(mainly tr)* **1** to produce or bring into being; create. **2** *(also intr)* to produce (electricity). **3** to produce (a substance) by a chemical process. **4** *Maths, linguistics.* to provide a precise criterion for membership in (a set). **5** *Geom.* to trace or form by moving a point, line, or plane in a specific way: *circular motion of a line generates a cylinder.* [C16: from L *generāre* to beget, from *genus* kind]
▸ˈ**generable** *adj*

generation 🅣 (ˌdʒɛnəˈreɪʃən) *n* **1** the act or process of bringing into being; production or reproduction, esp. of offspring. **2** a successive stage in natural descent of people or animals or the individuals produced at each stage. **3** the average time between two such generations of a species: about 35 years for humans. **4** all the people of approximately the same age, esp. when considered as sharing certain attitudes, etc. **5** production of electricity, heat, etc. **6** *(modifier, in combination)* **6a** belonging to a generation specified as having been born in or as having parents, grandparents, etc., born in a given country: *a third-generation American.* **6b** belonging to a specified stage of development in manufacture: *a second-generation computer.*

generation gap *n* the years separating one generation from the next, esp. when regarded as representing the difference in outlook and the lack of understanding between them.

generative (ˈdʒɛnərətɪv) *adj* **1** of or relating to the production of offspring, parts, etc. **2** capable of producing or originating.

generative grammar *n* a description of a language in terms of ex-

THESAURUS

genealogy *n* **1 = ancestry**, blood line, derivation, descent, extraction, family tree, line, lineage, pedigree, stemma, stirps, stock, strain

general *adj* **1 = common**, accepted, broad, extensive, popular, prevailing, prevalent, public, universal, widespread **5 = universal**, across-the-board, all-inclusive, blanket, broad, catholic, collective, comprehensive, encyclopedic, generic, indiscriminate, miscellaneous, overall, overarching, panoramic, sweeping, total **6 = imprecise**, approximate, ill-defined, inaccurate, indefinite, inexact, loose, undetailed, unspecific, vague **7 = ordinary**, accustomed, conventional, customary, everyday, habitual, normal, regular, typical, usual
Antonyms *adj* ≠ **common, universal:** distinctive, exceptional, extraordinary, individual, peculiar, special, unusual ≠ **imprecise:** definite, exact, particular, precise, specific ≠ **ordinary:** infrequent, rare

generality *n* **1 = generalization**, abstract principle, loose statement, sweeping statement, vague notion **2 = commonness**, acceptedness, breadth, comprehensiveness, extensiveness, popularity, prevalence, ubiquity, universality

generally *adv* **1 = usually**, almost always, as a rule, by and large, conventionally, customarily, for the most part, habitually, in most cases, largely, mainly, normally, on average, on the whole, ordinarily, regularly, typically **2 = commonly**, extensively, popularly, publicly, universally, widely **3 = broadly**, approximately, chiefly, for the most part, in the main, largely, mainly, mostly, on the whole, predominantly, principally
Antonyms *adv* ≠ **usually:** especially, occasionally, rarely, unusually ≠ **commonly:** individually, particularly

generate *vb* **1 = produce**, beget, breed, bring about, cause, create, engender, form, give rise to, initiate, make, originate, procreate, propagate, spawn, whip up
Antonyms *vb* annihilate, crush, destroy, end, extinguish, kill, terminate

generation *n* **1 = production**, begetting, breeding, creation, engenderment, formation, genesis, origination, procreation, propagation, reproduction **2 = age group**, breed, crop **3 = age**, day, days, epoch, era, period, time, times plicit rules that ideally generate all and only the grammatical sentences of the language.

generator ('dʒɛnəˌreɪtə) *n* **1** *Physics.* **1a** any device for converting mechanical energy into electrical energy. **1b** a device for producing a voltage electrostatically. **2** an apparatus for producing a gas. **3** a person or thing that generates.

generatrix ('dʒɛnəˌreɪtrɪks) *n, pl* **generatrices** ('dʒɛnəˌreɪtrɪˌsi:z). a point, line, or plane moved in a specific way to produce a geometric figure.

generic ❶ (dʒɪ'nɛrɪk) *adj* **1** applicable or referring to a whole class or group; general. **2** *Biol.* of, relating to, or belonging to a genus: *the generic name.* **3** (of a drug, food product, etc.) not having a trademark. [C17: from F; see GENUS]
▸**ge'nerically** *adv*

generic advertising *n* advertising designed to promote a class of product rather than a particular brand.

generosity ❶ (ˌdʒɛnə'rɒsɪtɪ) *n, pl* **generosities.** **1** willingness and liberality in giving away one's money, time, etc.; magnanimity. **2** freedom from pettiness in character and mind. **3** a generous act. **4** abundance; plenty.

generous ❶ ('dʒɛnərəs, 'dʒɛnrəs) *adj* **1** willing and liberal in giving away one's money, time, etc.; munificent. **2** free from pettiness in character and mind. **3** full or plentiful: *a generous portion.* **4** (of wine) rich in alcohol. [C16: via OF from L *generōsus* nobly born, from *genus* race]
▸**'generously** *adv* ▸**'generousness** *n*

genesis ❶ ('dʒɛnɪsɪs) *n, pl* **geneses** (-ˌsi:z). a beginning or origin of anything. [OE: via L from Gk; rel. to Gk *gignesthai* to be born]

Genesis ('dʒɛnɪsɪs) *n* the first book of the Old Testament recounting the Creation of the world.

-genesis *n combining form.* indicating genesis, development, or generation: *parthenogenesis.* [NL, from L: GENESIS]
▸**-genetic** *or* **-genic** *adj combining form.*

genet[1] ('dʒɛnɪt) *or* **genette** (dʒɪ'nɛt) *n* **1** an agile catlike mammal of Africa and S Europe, having thick spotted fur and a very long tail. **2** the fur of such an animal. [C15: from OF, from Ar. *jarnayt*]

genet[2] ('dʒɛnɪt) *n* an obsolete spelling of **jennet.**

gene therapy *n* the replacement or alteration of defective genes in order to prevent the occurrence of such inherited diseases as haemophilia. Effected by genetic engineering techniques, it is still at an early stage of development.

genetic (dʒɪ'nɛtɪk) *or* **genetical** *adj* of or relating to genetics, genes, or the origin of something. [C19: from GENESIS]
▸**ge'netically** *adv*

genetic code *n Biochem.* the order in which the four nitrogenous bases of DNA are arranged in the molecule, which determines the type and amount of protein synthesized in the cell.

genetic counselling *n* the provision of advice for couples with a history of inherited disorders who wish to have children, including the likelihood of having affected children, the course and management of the disorder, etc.

genetic engineering *n* alteration of the DNA of a cell as a means of manufacturing animal proteins, making improvements to plants and animals bred by man, etc.

genetic fingerprint *n* the pattern of DNA unique to each individual, that can be analysed in a sample of blood, saliva, or tissue: used as a means of identification.
▸**genetic fingerprinting** *n*

genetic map *n* a graphic representation of the order of genes within chromosomes by means of detailed analysis of the DNA. See also **chromosome map.**
▸**genetic mapping** *n*

genetics (dʒɪ'nɛtɪks) *n* **1** (*functioning as sing*) the study of heredity and variation in organisms. **2** (*functioning as pl*) the genetic features and constitution of a single organism, species, or group.
▸**ge'neticist** *n*

Geneva bands (dʒɪ'ni:və) *pl n* a pair of white linen strips hanging from the front of the collar of some ecclesiastical robes. [C19: after *Geneva*, Switzerland, where orig. worn by Swiss Calvinist clergy]

Geneva Convention *n* the international agreement, first formulated in 1864 at Geneva, establishing a code for wartime treatment of the sick or wounded: revised and extended to cover maritime warfare and prisoners of war.

Geneva gown *n* a black gown with wide sleeves worn by Protestant clerics. [C19: after *Geneva*; see GENEVA BANDS]

Geneva protocol *n* the agreement in 1925 to ban the use of asphyxiating, poisonous, or other gases in war. It does not ban the development or manufacture of such gases.

genial[1] ❶ ('dʒi:njəl, -nɪəl) *adj* **1** cheerful, easy-going, and warm in manner. **2** pleasantly warm, so as to give life, growth, or health. [C16: from L *geniālis* relating to birth or marriage, from *genius* tutelary deity; see GENIUS]
▸**geniality** (ˌdʒi:nɪ'ælɪtɪ) *n* ▸**'genially** *adv*

genial[2] (dʒɪ'ni:əl) *adj Anat.* of or relating to the chin. [C19: from Gk, from *genus* jaw]

genic ('dʒɛnɪk) *adj* of or relating to a gene or genes.

-genic *adj combining form.* **1** relating to production or generation: *carcinogenic.* **2** suited to or suitable for: *photogenic.* [from -GEN + -IC]

genie ('dʒi:nɪ) *n* **1** (in fairy tales and stories) a servant who appears by magic and fulfils a person's wishes. **2** another word for **jinni.** [C18: from F, from Ar. *jinni* demon, infl. by L *genius* attendant spirit; see GENIUS]

genista (dʒɪ'nɪstə) *n* any of a genus of leguminous deciduous shrubs, usually having yellow, often fragrant, flowers; broom. [C17: from L]

genital ('dʒɛnɪtᵊl) *adj* **1** of or relating to the sexual organs or to reproduction. **2** *Psychoanal.* relating to the mature stage of psychosexual development. [C14: from L *genitālis* concerning birth, from *gignere* to beget]

genital herpes *n* a sexually transmitted disease caused by the herpes simplex virus, in which painful blisters occur in the genital region.

genitals ❶ ('dʒɛnɪtᵊlz) *or* **genitalia** (ˌdʒɛnɪ'teɪlɪə, -'teɪljə) *pl n* the external sexual organs.

genitive ('dʒɛnɪtɪv) *Grammar.* ◆ *adj* **1** denoting a case of nouns, pronouns, and adjectives in inflected languages used to indicate a relation of ownership or association. ◆ *n* **2a** the genitive case. **2b** a word or speech element in this case. [C14: from L *genetīvus* relating to birth, from *gignere* to produce]
▸**genitival** (ˌdʒɛnɪ'taɪvᵊl) *adj*

genitourinary (ˌdʒɛnɪtəʊ'jʊərɪnərɪ) *adj* of or relating to both the reproductive and excretory organs; urogenital: *genitourinary medicine.*

genius ❶ ('dʒi:nɪəs, -njəs) *n, pl* **geniuses** *or* (*for senses 5, 6*) **genii** ('dʒi:nɪˌaɪ). **1** a person with exceptional ability, esp. of a highly original kind. **2** such ability. **3** the distinctive spirit of a nation, era, language, etc. **4** a person considered as exerting influence of a certain sort: *an evil genius.* **5** *Roman myth.* **5a** the guiding spirit who attends a person from birth to death. **5b** the guardian spirit of a place. **6** (*usually pl*) *Arabic myth.* a demon; jinn. [C16: from L, from *gignere* to beget]

genizah (ge'ni:zə) *n, pl* **genizahs** *or* **genizoth** (ge'ni:zəθ). *Judaism.* a repository for sacred objects which can no longer be used but which may not be destroyed. [C19: from Heb., lit.: a hiding place]

genoa ('dʒɛnəʊə) *n Yachting.* a large jib sail.

genocide ('dʒɛnəʊˌsaɪd) *n* the policy of deliberately killing a nationality or ethnic group. [C20: from Gk *genos* race + -CIDE]
▸**ˌgeno'cidal** *adj*

Genoese (ˌdʒɛnəʊ'i:z) *or* **Genovese** (ˌdʒɛnə'vi:z) *n, pl* **Genoese** *or* **Genovese.** **1** a native or inhabitant of Genoa. ◆ *adj* **2** of or relating to Genoa or its inhabitants.

genome ('dʒi:ˌnəʊm) *n* the complete set of haploid chromosomes that an organism passes on to its offspring in its reproductive cells. [C20: from GEN(E) + (CHROMOS)OME]

genotype ('dʒɛnəʊˌtaɪp) *n* **1** the genetic constitution of an organism. **2** a group of organisms with the same genetic constitution.
▸**genotypic** (ˌdʒɛnəʊ'tɪpɪk) *adj*

-genous *adj combining form.* **1** yielding or generating: *erogenous.* **2** generated by or issuing from: *endogenous.* [from -GEN + -OUS]

genre ❶ ('ʒɑ:nrə) *n* **1a** kind, category, or sort, esp. of literary or artistic work. **1b** (*as modifier*): *genre fiction.* **2** a category of painting in which incidents from everyday life are depicted. [C19: from F, from OF *gendre;* see GENDER]

THESAURUS

generic *adj* **1** = **collective**, all-encompassing, blanket, common, comprehensive, general, inclusive, sweeping, universal, wide
Antonyms *adj* individual, particular, precise, specific

generosity *n* **1** = **liberality**, beneficence, benevolence, bounteousness, bounty, charity, kindness, largesse *or* largess, munificence, open-handedness **2** = **unselfishness**, disinterestedness, goodness, high-mindedness, magnanimity, nobleness

generous *adj* **1** = **liberal**, beneficent, benevolent, bounteous, bountiful, charitable, free, hospitable, kind, lavish, munificent, open-handed, princely, prodigal, ungrudging, unstinting **2** = **unselfish**, big-hearted, disinterested, good, high-minded, lofty, magnanimous, noble **3** = **plentiful**, abundant, ample, copious, full, fulsome, lavish, liberal, overflowing, rich, unstinting
Antonyms *adj* ≠ **liberal:** avaricious, close-fisted, greedy, mean, miserly, parsimonious, selfish, stingy, tight ≠ **plentiful:** cheap, minimal, scanty, small, tiny

genesis *n* = **beginning**, birth, commencement, creation, dawn, engendering, formation, generation, inception, origin, outset, propagation, root, source, start
Antonyms *n* completion, conclusion, end, finish, termination

genial[1] *adj* **1** = **cheerful**, affable, agreeable, amiable, cheery, congenial, convivial, cordial, easy-going, enlivening, friendly, glad, good-natured, happy, hearty, jolly, jovial, joyous, kind, kindly, merry, pleasant, sunny, warm, warm-hearted
Antonyms *adj* cheerless, cool, discourteous, frigid, morose, rude, sardonic, sullen, unfriendly, ungracious, unpleasant

geniality *n* **1** = **cheerfulness**, affability, agreeableness, amiability, cheeriness, congenialness, conviviality, cordiality, friendliness, gladness, good cheer, good nature, happiness, heartiness, jollity, joviality, joy, joyousness, kindliness, kindness, mirth, pleasantness, sunniness, warm-heartedness, warmth

genitals *pl n* = **sex organs**, genitalia, loins, private parts, pudenda, reproductive organs

genius *n* **1** = **master**, adept, brainbox, buff (*inf.*), expert, hotshot, intellect (*inf.*), maestro, master-hand, mastermind, maven (*US*), virtuoso, whiz (*inf.*) **2** = **brilliance**, ability, aptitude, bent, capacity, creative power, endowment, faculty, flair, gift, inclination, knack, propensity, talent, turn
Antonyms *n* ≠ **master:** dolt, dunce, fool, half-wit, idiot, imbecile, nincompoop, simpleton

genre *n* **1** = **type**, brand, category, character, class, fashion, genus, group, kind, school, sort, species, stamp, style

gens (dʒɛnz) *n, pl* **gentes** ('dʒɛnti:z). **1** (in ancient Rome) any of a group of families, having a common name and claiming descent from a common ancestor in the male line. **2** *Anthropol.* a group based on descent in the male line. [C19: from L: race]

gent (dʒɛnt) *n Inf.* short for **gentleman.**

genteel ❶ (dʒɛn'ti:l) *adj* **1** affectedly proper or refined; excessively polite. **2** respectable, polite, and well-bred. **3** appropriate to polite or fashionable society. [C16: from F *gentil* well-born; see GENTLE]
▸**gen'teelly** *adv* ▸**gen'teelness** *n*

gentian ('dʒɛnʃən) *n* **1** any plant of the genus *Gentiana,* having blue, yellow, white, or red showy flowers. **2** the bitter-tasting roots of the yellow gentian, which can be used as a tonic. [C14: from L *gentiāna*; ? after *Gentius,* a second-century B.C. Illyrian king, reputedly the first to use it medicinally]

gentian violet *n* a greenish crystalline substance that forms a violet solution in water, used as an indicator, antiseptic, and in the treatment of burns.

Gentile ('dʒɛntaɪl) *n* **1** a person, esp. a Christian, who is not a Jew. **2** a Christian, as contrasted with a Jew. **3** a person who is not a member of one's own church: used esp. by Mormons. **4** a heathen or pagan. ◆ *adj* **5** of or relating to a race or religion that is not Jewish. **6** Christian, as contrasted with Jewish. **7** not being a member of one's own church: used esp. by Mormons. **8** pagan or heathen. [C15 *gentil,* from LL *gentīlis,* from L: one belonging to the same tribe]

gentility ❶ (dʒɛn'tɪlɪtɪ) *n, pl* **gentilities. 1** respectability and polite good breeding. **2** affected politeness. **3** noble birth or ancestry. **4** people of noble birth. [C14: from OF, from L *gentīlitās* relationship of those belonging to the same tribe or family; see GENS]

gentle ❶ ('dʒɛnt^əl) *adj* **1** having a mild or kindly nature or character. **2** soft or temperate; mild; moderate. **3** gradual: *a gentle slope.* **4** easily controlled; tame. **5** *Arch.* of good breeding; noble: *gentle blood.* **6** *Arch.* gallant; chivalrous. ◆ *vb* **gentles, gentling, gentled.** (*tr*) **7** to tame or subdue (a horse, etc.). **8** to appease or mollify. ◆ *n* **9** a maggot, esp. when used as bait in fishing. [C13: from OF *gentil* noble, from L *gentīlis* belonging to the same family; see GENS]
▸**'gentleness** *n* ▸**'gently** *adv*

gentle breeze *n* a wind of force 3 on the Beaufort scale, blowing at 8-12 mph.

gentlefolk ('dʒɛnt^əl,fəʊk) *or* **gentlefolks** *pl n* persons regarded as being of good breeding.

gentleman ❶ ('dʒɛnt^əlmən) *n, pl* **gentlemen. 1** a man regarded as having qualities of refinement associated with a good family. **2** a man who is cultured, courteous, and well-educated. **3** a polite name for a man. **4** the personal servant of a gentleman (esp. in **gentleman's gentleman**).
▸**'gentlemanly** *adj* ▸**'gentlemanliness** *n*

gentleman-farmer *n, pl* **gentlemen-farmers. 1** a person who engages in farming but does not depend on it for his living. **2** a person who owns farmland but does not farm it personally.

gentlemen's agreement *or* **gentleman's agreement** *n* an understanding or arrangement based on honour and not legally binding.

gentlewoman ('dʒɛnt^əl,wʊmən) *n, pl* **gentlewomen. 1** *Arch.* a woman regarded as being of good family or breeding; lady. **2** (formerly) a woman in personal attendance on a high-ranking lady.

gentrification (,dʒɛntrɪfɪ'keɪʃən) *n Brit.* a process by which middle-class people take up residence in a traditionally working-class area, changing its character. [C20: from *gentrify* (to become GENTRY)]
▸**'gentri,fier** *n*

gentry ❶ ('dʒɛntrɪ) *n* **1** *Brit.* persons just below the nobility in social rank. **2** people of a particular class, esp. one considered to be inferior. [C14: from OF *genterie,* from *gentil* GENTLE]

gents (dʒɛnts) *n* (*functioning as sing*) *Brit. inf.* a men's public lavatory.

genuflect ('dʒɛnjʊ,flɛkt) *vb* (*intr*) **1** to act in a servile or deferential manner. **2** *RC Church.* to bend one or both knees as a sign of reverence. [C17: from Med. L, from L *genu* knee + *flectere* to bend]
▸**,genu'flection** *or* (*esp. Brit.*) **,genu'flexion** *n* ▸**'genu,flector** *n*

genuine ❶ ('dʒɛnjʊɪn) *adj* **1** not fake or counterfeit; original; real; authentic. **2** not pretending; frank; sincere. **3** being of authentic or original stock. [C16: from L *genuīnus* inborn, hence (in LL) authentic]
▸**'genuinely** *adv* ▸**'genuineness** *n*

gen up *vb* **gens, genning, genned.** (*adv; often passive;* when *intr,* usually foll. by *on*) *Brit. inf.* to make or become fully conversant (with).

genus ❶ ('dʒi:nəs) *n, pl* **genera** *or* **genuses. 1** *Biol.* any of the taxonomic groups into which a family is divided and which contains one or more species. **2** *Logic.* a class of objects or individuals that can be divided into two or more groups or species. **3** a class, group, etc., with common characteristics. [C16: from L: race]

-geny *n combining form.* origin or manner of development: *phylogeny.* [from Gk, from *-genēs* born]
▸**-genic** *adj combining form.*

geo- *combining form.* indicating earth: *geomorphology.* [from Gk, from *gē* earth]

geocentric (,dʒi:əʊ'sɛntrɪk) *adj* **1** having the earth at its centre. **2** measured as from the centre of the earth.
▸**,geo'centrically** *adv*

geochronology (,dʒi:əʊkrə'nɒlədʒɪ) *n* the branch of geology concerned with ordering and dating events in the earth's history.
▸**geochronological** (,dʒi:əʊ,krɒnə'lɒdʒɪk^əl) *adj*

geode ('dʒi:əʊd) *n* a cavity, usually lined with crystals, within a rock mass or nodule. [C17: from L *geōdēs* a precious stone, from Gk: earthlike; see GEO-, -ODE[1]]
▸**geodic** (dʒɪ'ɒdɪk) *adj*

geodesic (,dʒi:əʊ'dɛsɪk, -'di:-) *adj* **1** Also: **geodetic.** relating to the geometry of curved surfaces. ◆ *n* **2** Also called: **geodesic line.** the shortest line between two points on a curved surface.

geodesic dome *n* a light structural framework arranged as a set of polygons in the form of a shell.

geodesy (dʒɪ'ɒdɪsɪ) *n* the branch of science concerned with determining the exact position of geographical points and the shape and size of the earth. [C16: from F, from Gk *geōdaisia,* from GEO- + *daiein* to divide]
▸**ge'odesist** *n*

geodetic (,dʒi:əʊ'dɛtɪk) *adj* **1** of or relating to geodesy. **2** another word for **geodesic.**
▸**,geo'detically** *adv*

geog. *abbrev. for:* **1** geographer. **2** geographic(al). **3** geography.

geographical mile *n* a former name for **nautical mile.**

geography (dʒɪ'ɒgrəfɪ) *n, pl* **geographies. 1** the study of the natural features of the earth's surface, including topography, climate, soil, vegetation, etc., and man's response to them. **2** the natural features of a region.
▸**ge'ographer** *n* ▸**geographical** (,dʒɪə'græfɪk^əl) *or* **,geo'graphic** *adj*
▸**,geo'graphically** *adv*

geoid ('dʒi:ɔɪd) *n* **1** a hypothetical surface that corresponds to mean sea level and extends under the continents. **2** the shape of the earth.

geol. *abbrev. for:* **1** geologic(al). **2** geologist. **3** geology.

geology (dʒɪ'ɒlədʒɪ) *n* **1** the scientific study of the origin, structure, and composition of the earth. **2** the geological features of a district or country.
▸**geological** (,dʒɪə'lɒdʒɪk^əl) *or* **,geo'logic** *adj* ▸**,geo'logically** *adv* ▸**ge'ologist** *n*

geom. *abbrev. for:* **1** geometric(al). **2** geometry.

geomagnetism (,dʒi:əʊ'mægnɪ,tɪzəm) *n* **1** the magnetic field of the earth. **2** the branch of physics concerned with this.
▸**geomagnetic** (,dʒi:əʊmæg'nɛtɪk) *adj*

geometric (,dʒɪə'mɛtrɪk) *or* **geometrical** *adj* **1** of, relating to, or following the methods and principles of geometry. **2** consisting of, formed by, or characterized by points, lines, curves, or surfaces. **3** (of design or ornamentation) composed predominantly of simple geometric forms, such as circles, triangles, etc.
▸**,geo'metrically** *adv*

geometric mean *n* the average value of a set of *n* integers, terms, or quantities, expressed as the *n*th root of their product.

THESAURUS

genteel *adj* **2** = **refined,** aristocratic, civil, courteous, courtly, cultivated, cultured, elegant, fashionable, formal, gentlemanly, ladylike, mannerly, polished, polite, respectable, sophisticated, stylish, urbane, well-bred, well-mannered
Antonyms *adj* discourteous, ill-bred, impolite, inelegant, low-bred, natural, plebeian, rude, unaffected, uncultured, unmannerly, unpolished, unrefined

gentility *n* **1** = **nobility,** blue blood, gentle birth, good family, high birth, rank **2** = **refinement,** breeding, civility, courtesy, courtliness, cultivation, culture, decorum, elegance, etiquette, formality, good breeding, good manners, mannerliness, polish, politeness, propriety, respectability, sophistication, urbanity **4** = **aristocracy,** elite, gentlefolk, gentry, nobility, nobles, ruling class, upper class

gentle *adj* **1** = **mild,** amiable, benign, bland, compassionate, dove-like, humane, kind, kindly, lenient, meek, merciful, pacific, peaceful, placid, quiet, soft, sweet-tempered, tender **2** = **moderate,** balmy, calm, clement, easy, light, low, mild, muted, placid, quiet, serene, slight, smooth, soft, soothing, temperate, tranquil, untroubled **3** = **gradual,** easy, imperceptible, light, mild, moderate, slight, slow **4** = **tame,** biddable, broken, docile, manageable, placid, tractable **5** *Archaic* = **well-bred,** aristocratic, civil, courteous, cultured, elegant, genteel, gentlemanlike, gentlemanly, high-born, ladylike, noble, polished, polite, refined, upper-class, well-born
Antonyms *adj* ≠ **mild:** aggressive, cruel, fierce, hard, harsh, heartless, impolite, rough, savage, sharp, unkind ≠ **moderate:** powerful, strong, violent, wild ≠ **gradual:** sudden ≠ **tame:** fierce, savage, unmanageable, wild

gentlemanly *adj* **2** = **polite,** civil, civilized, courteous, cultivated, debonair, gallant, genteel, gentlemanlike, honourable, mannerly, noble, obliging, polished, refined, reputable, suave, urbane, well-bred, well-mannered

gentleness *n* **1** = **tenderness,** compassion, kindliness, kindness, lightness of touch, mansuetude (*arch.*), mildness, softness, sweetness

gentry *n* **1** = **nobility,** aristocracy, elite, gentility, gentlefolk, nobles, ruling class, upper class, upper crust (*inf.*)

genuine *adj* **1** = **authentic,** actual, bona fide, honest, legitimate, natural, on the level, original, pure, real, sound, sterling, the real McCoy, true, unadulterated, unalloyed, veritable **2** = **sincere,** artless, candid, earnest, frank, heartfelt, honest, unaffected, unfeigned
Antonyms *adj* ≠ **authentic:** artificial, bogus, counterfeit, fake, false, fraudulent, imitation, phoney, pseudo (*inf.*), sham, simulated, spurious ≠ **sincere:** affected, false, feigned, hypocritical, insincere, phoney

genus *n* **3** = **type,** breed, category, class, genre, group, kind, order, race, set, sort

geometric progression *n* **1** a sequence of numbers, each of which differs from the succeeding one by a constant ratio, as 1, 2, 4, 8, ... Cf. **arithmetic progression. 2 geometric series.** such numbers written as a sum.

geometrid (dʒɪ'ɒmɪtrɪd) *n* any of a family of moths, the larvae of which are called measuring worms, inchworms, or loopers. [C19: from NL, from L, from Gk *geometrēs* land measurer, from the looping gait of the larvae]

geometry (dʒɪ'ɒmɪtrɪ) *n* **1** the branch of mathematics concerned with the properties, relationships, and measurement of points, lines, curves, and surfaces. **2** a shape, configuration, or arrangement. [C14: from L, from Gk, from *geōmetrein* to measure the land]
▸**ge,ome'trician** *n*

geomorphology (ˌdʒiːəʊmɔː'fɒlədʒɪ) *n* the branch of geology that is concerned with the structure, origin, and development of the topographical features of the earth's crust.
▸**geomorphological** (ˌdʒiːəʊˌmɔːfə'lɒdʒɪkᵊl) *or* **ˌgeoˌmorpho'logic** *adj*

geophysics (ˌdʒiːəʊ'fɪzɪks) *n* (*functioning as sing*) the study of the earth's physical properties and of the physical processes acting upon, above, and within the earth. It includes seismology, meteorology, and oceanography.
▸**ˌgeo'physical** *adj* ▸**ˌgeo'physicist** *n*

geopolitics (ˌdʒiːəʊ'pɒlɪtɪks) *n* **1** (*functioning as sing*) the study of the effect of geographical factors on politics. **2** (*functioning as pl*) the combination of geographical and political factors affecting a country or area. **3** (*functioning as pl*) politics as they affect the whole world; global politics.
▸**geopolitical** (ˌdʒiːəʊpə'lɪtɪkᵊl) *adj*

Geordie ('dʒɔːdɪ) *Brit.* ◆ *n* **1** a person who comes from or lives in Tyneside. **2** the dialect spoken by these people. ◆ *adj* **3** of or relating to these people or their dialect. [C19: a dim. of *George*]

George Cross (dʒɔːdʒ) *n* a British award for bravery, esp. of civilians. Abbrev.: **GC.**

georgette *or* **georgette crepe** (dʒɔː'dʒɛt) *n* a thin silk or cotton crepe fabric. [C20: from Mme *Georgette*, a F modiste]

Georgian ('dʒɔːdʒjən) *adj* **1** of or relating to any or all of the four kings who ruled Great Britain from 1714 to 1830, or to their reigns. **2** of or relating to George V of Great Britain or his reign (1910–36): *the Georgian poets.* **3** of or relating to Georgia, its people, or their language. **4** of or relating to the American State of Georgia or its inhabitants. **5** (of furniture, architecture, etc.) in or imitative of the style prevalent in Britain during the 18th century. ◆ *n* **6** the official language of Georgia, belonging to the South Caucasian family. **7** a native or inhabitant of Georgia. **8** a native or inhabitant of the American State of Georgia.

geostatics (ˌdʒiːəʊ'stætɪks) *n* (*functioning as sing*) the branch of physics concerned with the statics of rigid bodies, esp. the balance of forces within the earth.

geostationary (ˌdʒiːəʊ'steɪʃənərɪ) *adj* (of a satellite, etc.) in a circular equatorial orbit in which it circles the earth once in 24 hours so that it appears stationary in relation to the earth's surface.

geostrophic (ˌdʒiːəʊ'strɒfɪk) *adj* of, relating to, or caused by the force produced by the rotation of the earth: *geostrophic wind.*

geosynchronous (ˌdʒiːəʊ'sɪŋkrənəs) *n* (of a satellite) in an orbit in which it circles the earth once in 24 hours.

geosyncline (ˌdʒiːəʊ'sɪŋklaɪn) *n* a broad elongated depression in the earth's crust.

geotextile (ˌdʒiːəʊ'tɛkstaɪl) *n* any strong synthetic fabric used in civil engineering, as to retain an embankment.

geothermal (ˌdʒiːəʊ'θɜːməl) *or* **geothermic** *adj* of or relating to the heat in the interior of the earth.

geotropism (dʒɪ'ɒtrəˌpɪzəm) *n* the response of a plant part to the stimulus of gravity. Plant stems, which grow upwards irrespective of the position in which they are placed, show **negative geotropism.**
▸**geotropic** (ˌdʒiːəʊ'trɒpɪk) *adj*

Ger. *abbrev. for:* **1** German. **2** Germany.

geranium (dʒɪ'reɪnɪəm) *n* **1** a cultivated plant of the genus *Pelargonium* having scarlet, pink, or white showy flowers. See also **pelargonium. 2** any plant such as cranesbill and herb Robert, having divided leaves and pink or purplish flowers. [C16: from L: cranesbill, from Gk, from *geranos* CRANE]

gerbera ('dʒɜːbərə) *n* a genus of African or Asian plants belonging to the composite family, esp. the Transvaal daisy. [C19: from NL, after T. *Gerber* (died 1743), G naturalist]

gerbil *or* **gerbille** ('dʒɜːbɪl) *n* a burrowing rodent inhabiting hot dry regions of Asia and Africa. [C19: from F, from NL *gerbillus* a little JERBOA]

gerfalcon ('dʒɜːˌfɔːlkən, -ˌfɔːkən) *n* a variant spelling of **gyrfalcon.**

geriatric (ˌdʒɛrɪ'ætrɪk) *adj* **1** of or relating to geriatrics or to elderly people. **2** *Inf.* old, decrepit, or useless. ◆ *n* **3** an elderly person. [C20: from Gk *gēras* old age + IATRIC]

geriatrics (ˌdʒɛrɪ'ætrɪks) *n* (*functioning as sing*) the branch of medical science concerned with the diagnosis and treatment of diseases affecting elderly people.
▸**ˌgeria'trician** *n*

germ ❶ (dʒɜːm) *n* **1** a microorganism, esp. one that produces disease. **2** (*often pl*) the rudimentary or initial form of something: *the germs of revolution.* **3** a simple structure that is capable of developing into a complete organism. [C17: from F, from L *germen* sprout, seed]

german ('dʒɜːmən) *adj* **1** (used in combination) **1a** having the same parents as oneself: *a brother-german.* **1b** having a parent that is a brother or sister of either of one's own parents: *cousin-german.* **2** a less common word for **germane.** [C14: via OF, from L *germānus* of the same race, from *germen* sprout, offshoot]

German ('dʒɜːmən) *n* **1** the official language of Germany and Austria and one of the official languages of Switzerland. **2** a native, inhabitant, or citizen of Germany. **3** a person whose native language is German. ◆ *adj* **4** denoting, relating to, or using the German language. **5** relating to, denoting, or characteristic of any German state or its people.

germander (dʒɜː'mændə) *n* any of several plants of Europe, having two-lipped flowers with a very small upper lip. [C15: from Med. L, ult. from Gk *khamai* on the ground + *drus* oak tree]

germane ❶ (dʒɜː'meɪn) *adj* (*postpositive;* usually foll. by *to*) related (to the topic being considered); akin; relevant. [var. of GERMAN]
▸**ger'manely** *adv* ▸**ger'maneness** *n*

Germanic (dʒɜː'mænɪk) *n* **1** a branch of the Indo-European family of languages that includes English, Dutch, German, the Scandinavian languages, and Gothic. Abbrev.: **Gmc. 2** Also called: **Proto-Germanic.** the unrecorded language from which all of these languages developed. ◆ *adj* **3** of, denoting, or relating to this group of languages. **4** of, relating to, or characteristic of the German language or any people that speaks a Germanic language. **5** (formerly) of the German people.

germanium (dʒɜː'meɪnɪəm) *n* a brittle crystalline grey element that is a semiconducting metalloid: used in transistors, and to strengthen alloys. Symbol: Ge; atomic no.: 32; atomic wt.: 72.59. [C19: NL, after *Germany*]

German measles *n* (*functioning as sing*) a nontechnical name for **rubella.**

German shepherd dog *n* another name for **Alsatian.**

German silver *n* another name for **nickel silver.**

germ cell *n* a sexual reproductive cell.

germicide ('dʒɜːmɪˌsaɪd) *n* any substance that kills germs.
▸**ˌgermi'cidal** *adj*

germinal ('dʒɜːmɪnᵊl) *adj* **1** of, relating to, or like germs or a germ cell. **2** of or in the earliest stage of development. [C19: from NL, from L *germen* bud; see GERM]
▸**'germinally** *adv*

germinate ❶ ('dʒɜːmɪˌneɪt) *vb* **germinates, germinating, germinated. 1** to cause (seeds or spores) to sprout or (of seeds or spores) to sprout. **2** to grow or cause to grow; develop. **3** to come or bring into existence; originate: *the idea germinated with me.* [C17: from L *germināre* to sprout; see GERM]
▸**'germinative** *adj* ▸**ˌgermi'nation** *n* ▸**'germiˌnator** *n*

germ plasm *n* **a** the part of a germ cell that contains hereditary material. **b** the germ cells collectively.

germ warfare *n* the military use of disease-spreading bacteria against an enemy.

gerontology (ˌdʒɛrɒn'tɒlədʒɪ) *n* the scientific study of ageing and the problems associated with elderly people.
▸**gerontological** (ˌdʒɛrɒntə'lɒdʒɪkᵊl) *adj* ▸**ˌgeron'tologist** *n*

-gerous *adj combining form.* bearing or producing: *armigerous.* [from L *-ger* bearing + -OUS]

gerrymander ('dʒɛrɪˌmændə) *vb* **1** to divide the constituencies of (a voting area) so as to give one party an unfair advantage. **2** to manipulate or adapt to one's advantage. ◆ *n* **3** an act or result of gerrymandering. [C19: from Elbridge *Gerry*, US politician + (SALA)MANDER; from the salamander-like outline of an electoral district reshaped (1812) for political purposes while Gerry was governor of Massachusetts]

gerund ('dʒɛrənd) *n* a noun formed from a verb, ending in *-ing*, denoting an action or state: *the living is easy.* [C16: from LL, from L *gerundum* something to be carried on, from *gerere* to wage]
▸**gerundial** (dʒɪ'rʌndɪəl) *adj*

gerundive (dʒɪ'rʌndɪv) *n* **1** (in Latin grammar) an adjective formed from a verb, expressing the desirability, etc., of the activity denoted by the verb. ◆ *adj* **2** of or relating to the gerund or gerundive. [C17: from LL, from *gerundium* GERUND]
▸**gerundival** (ˌdʒɛrən'daɪvᵊl) *adj*

gesso ('dʒɛsəʊ) *n* **1** a white ground of plaster and size, used to prepare panels or canvas for painting or gilding. **2** any white substance, esp. plaster of Paris, that forms a ground when mixed with water. [C16: from It.: chalk, GYPSUM]

gest *or* **geste** (dʒɛst) *n Arch.* **1** a notable deed or exploit. **2** a tale of adventure or romance, esp. in verse. [C14: from OF, from L *gesta* deeds, from *gerere* to carry out]

Gestalt psychology (gə'ʃtælt) *n* a system of thought that regards all mental phenomena as being arranged in patterns or structures (**gestalts**) perceived as a whole and not merely as the sum of their parts. [C20: from G *Gestalt* form]

THESAURUS

germ *n* **1** = **microbe**, bacterium, bug (*inf.*), microorganism, virus **2** = **beginning**, bud, cause, embryo, origin, root, rudiment, seed, source, spark **3** = **embryo**, bud, egg, nucleus, ovule, ovum, seed, spore, sprout

germane *adj* = **relevant**, akin, allied, apposite, appropriate, apropos, apt, cognate, connected, fitting, kindred, material, pertinent, proper, related, suitable, to the point *or* purpose

Antonyms *adj* extraneous, foreign, immaterial, inappropriate, irrelevant, unrelated

germinate *vb* **1** = **sprout**, bud, develop, generate, grow, originate, pullulate, shoot, swell, vegetate

Gestapo (gɛ'stɑːpəʊ) *n* the secret state police in Nazi Germany. [from G *Ge(heime) Sta(ats)po(lizei)*, lit.: secret state police]

gestate ➊ ('dʒɛsteɪt) *vb* **gestates, gestating, gestated. 1** (*tr*) to carry (developing young) in the uterus during pregnancy. **2** (*tr*) to develop (a plan or idea) in the mind. **3** (*intr*) to be in the process of gestating. [C19: from L p.p. of *gestare*, from *gerere* to bear]
▸**ges'tation** *n*

gesticulate ➊ (dʒɛ'stɪkjʊˌleɪt) *vb* **gesticulates, gesticulating, gesticulated.** to express by or make gestures. [C17: from L, from *gesticulus* (unattested except in LL) gesture, from *gerere* to bear, conduct]
▸**geˌsticu'lation** *n* ▸**ge'sticulative** *adj* ▸**ges'ticuˌlator** *n* ▸**ges'ticulatory** *adj*

gesture ➊ ('dʒɛstʃə) *n* **1** a motion of the hands, head, or body to express or emphasize an idea or emotion. **2** something said or done as a formality or as an indication of intention. ◆ *vb* **gestures, gesturing, gestured. 3** to express by or make gestures; gesticulate. [C15: from Med. L *gestūra* bearing, from L *gestus*, p.p. of *gerere* to bear]
▸**'gestural** *adj*

get ➊ (gɛt) *vb* **gets, getting, got;** **got** *or esp. US* **gotten.** (*mainly tr*) **1** to come into possession of; receive or earn. **2** to bring or fetch. **3** to contract or be affected by: *he got a chill.* **4** to capture or seize: *the police got him.* **5** (*also intr*) to become or cause to become or act as specified: *to get one's hair cut; get wet.* **6** (*intr;* foll. by a preposition or adverbial particle) to succeed in going, coming, leaving, etc.: *get off the bus.* **7** (*takes an infinitive*) to manage or contrive: *how did you get to be captain?* **8** to make ready or prepare: *to get a meal.* **9** to hear, notice, or understand: *I didn't get your meaning.* **10** to learn or master by study. **11** (*intr;* often foll. by *to*) to come (to) or arrive (at): *we got home safely; to get to London.* **12** to catch or enter: *to get a train.* **13** to induce or persuade: *get him to leave.* **14** to reach by calculation: *add 2 and 2 and you will get 4.* **15** to receive (a broadcast signal). **16** to communicate with (a person or place), as by telephone. **17** (*also intr;* foll. by *to*) *Inf.* to have an emotional effect (on): *that music really gets me.* **18** *Inf.* to annoy or irritate: *her voice gets me.* **19** *Inf.* to bring a person into a difficult position from which he cannot escape. **20** *Inf.* to puzzle; baffle. **21** *Inf.* to hit: *the blow got him in the back.* **22** *Inf.* to be revenged on, esp. by killing. **23** *Inf.* to have the better of: *your extravagant habits will get you in the end.* **24** (*intr;* foll. by present participle) *Inf.* to begin: *get moving.* **25** (used as a command) *Inf.* go! leave now! **26** *Arch.* to beget or conceive. **27 get with child.** *Arch.* to make pregnant. ◆ *n* **28** *Rare.* the act of begetting. **29** *Rare.* something begotten; offspring. **30** *Brit. sl.* a variant of **git**. ◆ See also **get about, get across,** etc. [OE *gietan*]
▸**'getable** *or* **'gettable** *adj* ▸**'getter** *n*

> **USAGE NOTE** The use of *off* after *get* as in *I got this chair off an antique dealer* is acceptable in conversation, but should not be used in formal writing.

get about *or* **around** *vb* (*intr, adv*) **1** to move around, as when recovering from an illness. **2** to be socially active. **3** (of news, rumour, etc.) to become known; spread.

get across ➊ *vb* **1** to cross or cause to cross. **2** (*adv*) to be or cause to be understood.

get at ➊ *vb* (*intr, prep*) **1** to gain access to. **2** to mean or intend: *what are you getting at?* **3** to irritate or annoy persistently; criticize: *she is always getting at him.* **4** to influence or seek to influence, esp. illegally by bribery, intimidation, etc.: *someone had got at the witness before the trial.*

get away ➊ *vb* (*adv, mainly intr*) **1** to make an escape; leave. **2** to make a start. **3 get away with. 3a** to steal and escape with (money, goods, etc.). **3b** to do (something wrong, illegal, etc.) without being discovered or punished. ◆ *interj* **4** an exclamation indicating mild disbelief. ◆ *n* **getaway. 5** the act of escaping, esp. by criminals. **6** a start or acceleration. **7** a short holiday away from home. **8** (*modifier*) used for escaping: *a getaway car.*

get back ➊ *vb* (*adv*) **1** (*tr*) to recover or retrieve. **2** (*intr;* often foll. by *to*) to return, esp. to a former position or activity. **3** (*intr;* foll. by *at*) to retaliate (against); wreak vengeance (on). **4 get one's own back.** *Inf.* to obtain one's revenge.

get by ➊ *vb* **1** to pass; go past or overtake. **2** (*intr, adv*) *Inf.* to manage, esp. in spite of difficulties. **3** (*intr*) to be accepted or permitted: *that book will never get by the authorities.*

get in ➊ *vb* (*mainly adv*) **1** (*intr*) to enter a car, train, etc. **2** (*intr*) to arrive, esp. at one's home or place of work. **3** (*tr*) to bring in or inside: *get the milk in.* **4** (*tr*) to insert or slip in: *he got his suggestion in before anyone else.* **5** (*tr*) to gather or collect (crops, debts, etc.). **6** to be elected or cause to be elected. **7** (*intr*) to obtain a place at university, college, etc. **8** (foll. by *on*) to join or cause to join (an activity or organization).

get off ➊ *vb* **1** (*intr, adv*) to escape the consequences of an action: *he got off very lightly.* **2** (*adv*) to be or cause to be acquitted: *a good lawyer got him off.* **3** (*adv*) to depart or cause to depart: *to get the children off to school.* **4** (*intr*) to descend (from a bus, train, etc.); dismount: *she got off at the terminus.* **5** to move or cause to move to a distance (from): *get off the field.* **6** (*tr, adv*) to remove; take off: *get your coat off.* **7** (*adv*) to go or send to sleep. **8** (*adv*) to send (letters) or (of letters) to be sent. **9 get off with.** *Brit. inf.* to establish an amorous or sexual relationship (with).

get on ➊ *vb* (*mainly adv*) **1** Also (*when prep*): **get onto.** to board or cause or help to board (a bus, train, etc.). **2** (*tr*) to dress in (clothes as specified). **3** (*intr*) to grow late or (of time) to elapse: *it's getting on and I must go.* **4** (*intr*) (of a person) to grow old. **5** (*intr;* foll. by *for*) to approach (a time, age, amount, etc.): *she is getting on for seventy.* **6** (*intr*) to make progress, manage, or fare: *how did you get on in your exam?* **7** (*intr;* often foll. by *with*) to establish a friendly relationship: *he gets on well with other people.* **8** (*intr;* foll. by *with*) to continue to do: *get on with your homework!*

get out ➊ *vb* (*adv*) **1** to leave or escape or cause to leave or escape: used in the imperative when dismissing a person. **2** to make or become known; publish or be published. **3** (*tr*) to express with difficulty. **4** (*tr;* often foll. by *of*) to extract (information or money) (from a person): *to get a confession out of a criminal.* **5** (*tr*) to gain or receive something, esp. something of significance or value. **6** (foll. by *of*) to avoid or cause to avoid: *she always gets out of swimming.* **7** *Cricket.* to dismiss or be dismissed.

get over ➊ *vb* **1** to cross or surmount (something). **2** (*intr, prep*) to recover from (an illness, shock, etc.). **3** (*intr, prep*) to overcome or master (a problem). **4** (*intr, prep*) to appreciate fully: *I just can't get over seeing you again.* **5** (*tr, adv*) to communicate effectively. **6** (*tr, adv;* sometimes foll. by *with*) to bring (something necessary but unpleasant) to an end: *let's get this job over with quickly.*

get round ➊ *or* **around** *vb* (*intr*) **1** (*prep*) to circumvent or overcome. **2** (*prep*) *Inf.* to have one's way with; cajole: *that girl can get round anyone.* **3** (*prep*) to evade (a law or rules). **4** (*adv;* foll. by *to*) to reach or come to at length: *I'll get round to that job in an hour.*

get through *vb* **1** to succeed or cause or help to succeed in an examination, test, etc. **2** to bring or come to a destination, esp. after overcoming problems: *we got through the blizzards to the survivors.* **3** (*intr, adv*) to contact, as by telephone. **4** (*intr, prep*) to use, spend, or consume (money, supplies, etc.). **5** to complete or cause to complete (a task, process, etc.): *to get a bill through Parliament.* **6** (*adv;* foll. by *to*) to reach the awareness and understanding (of a person): *I just can't get the message through to him.*

THESAURUS

gestation *n* **1, 2** = **development**, evolution, incubation, maturation, pregnancy, ripening

gesticulate *vb* = **signal**, gesture, indicate, make a sign, motion, sign, wave

gesticulation *n* = **signalling**, arm-waving, gestures, waving

gesture *n* **1** = **signal**, action, gesticulation, indication, motion, sign ◆ *vb* **3** = **signal**, gesticulate, indicate, motion, sign, wave

get *vb* **1** = **obtain**, achieve, acquire, attain, bag, bring, come by, come into possession of, earn, fall heir to, fetch, gain, glean, inherit, land, make, net, pick up, procure, realize, reap, receive, score (*sl.*), secure, succeed to, win **3** = **contract**, be afflicted with, become infected with, be smitten by, catch, come down with, fall victim to, take **4** = **capture**, arrest, collar (*inf.*), grab, lay hold of, nab (*inf.*), nail (*inf.*), seize, take, trap **5** = **become**, come to be, grow, turn, wax **7** = **arrange**, contrive, fix, manage, succeed, wangle (*inf.*) **9** = **understand**, catch, comprehend, fathom, follow, get the picture, hear, notice, perceive, see, suss (out) (*sl.*), take in, work out **11** = **arrive**, come, make it (*inf.*), reach **13** = **persuade**, coax, convince, induce, influence, prevail upon, sway, talk into, wheedle, win over **16** = **contact**, communicate with, get in touch with, reach **17** *Informal* = **impress**, affect, arouse, excite, have an effect on, impact on, move, stimulate, stir, touch, tug at (someone's) heartstrings (*often facetious*) **18** *Informal* = **annoy**, bother, bug (*inf.*), gall, get (someone's) goat (*sl.*), irk, irritate, nark (*Brit., Austral., & NZ sl.*), pique, rub (someone) up the wrong way, upset, vex **20** = **puzzle**, baffle, confound, mystify, nonplus, perplex, stump

get across *vb* **1** = **cross**, ford, negotiate, pass over, traverse **2** = **communicate**, bring home to, convey, get (something) through to, impart, make clear *or* understood, put over, transmit

get at *vb* **1** = **gain access to**, acquire, attain, come to grips with, get, get hold of, reach **2** = **imply**, hint, intend, lead up to, mean, suggest **3** = **criticize**, annoy, attack, be on one's back (*sl.*), blame, carp, find fault with, hassle (*inf.*), irritate, nag, nark (*Brit., Austral., & NZ sl.*), pick on, put the boot into (*sl.*), taunt **4** = **corrupt**, bribe, buy off, influence, suborn, tamper with

get away *vb* **1** = **escape**, abscond, break free, break out, decamp, depart, disappear, flee, leave, make good one's escape, slope off ◆ *n* **getaway 5** = **escape**, break, break-out, decampment, flight

get back *vb* **1** = **regain**, recoup, recover, repossess, retrieve **2** = **return**, arrive home, come back *or* home, revert, revisit **3** *with* **at** = **retaliate**, be avenged, get even with, get one's own back, give tit for tat, hit back, settle the score with, take vengeance on

get by *vb* **1** = **pass**, circumvent, get ahead of, go around, go past, overtake, round **2** = **manage**, contrive, cope, exist, fare, get along, keep one's head above water, make both ends meet, subsist, survive

get in *vb* **1** = **enter**, embark, mount, penetrate **2** = **arrive**, alight, appear, come, land

get off *vb* **3, 4** = **leave**, alight, depart, descend, disembark, dismount, escape, exit **6** = **remove**, detach, shed, take off

get on *vb* **1** = **board**, ascend, climb, embark, mount **6** = **progress**, advance, cope, cut it (*inf.*), fare, get along, make out (*inf.*), manage, prosper, succeed **7** = **be friendly**, agree, be compatible, concur, get along, harmonize, hit it off (*inf.*)

get out *vb* **1** = **leave**, alight, break out, clear out, decamp, escape, evacuate, extricate oneself, free oneself, vacate, withdraw **6** *with* **of** = **avoid**, body-swerve (*Scot.*), dodge, escape, evade, shirk

get over *vb* **1** = **cross**, ford, get across, pass, pass over, surmount, traverse **2** = **recover from**, come round, get better, mend, pull through, rally, revive, survive **3** = **overcome**, defeat, get the better of, master, shake off **5** = **communicate**, convey, get *or* put across, impart, make clear *or* understood

get round *vb* **1** = **bypass**, circumvent, edge, evade, outmanoeuvre, skirt **2** *Informal* = **win over**, cajole, coax, convert, persuade, prevail upon, talk round, wheedle

get-together ⓣ *n* 1 *Inf.* a small informal meeting or social gathering. ◆ *vb* **get together.** (*adv*) 2 (*tr*) to gather or collect. 3 (*intr*) (of people) to meet socially. 4 (*intr*) to discuss, esp. in order to reach an agreement.

get up ⓣ *vb* (*mainly adv*) 1 to wake and rise from one's bed or cause to wake and rise from bed. 2 (*intr*) to rise to one's feet; stand up. 3 (*also prep*) to ascend or cause to ascend. 4 to increase or cause to increase in strength: *the wind got up at noon.* 5 (*tr*) *Inf.* to dress (oneself) in a particular way, esp. elaborately. 6 (*tr*) *Inf.* to devise or create: *to get up an entertainment for Christmas.* 7 (*tr*) *Inf.* to study or improve one's knowledge of: *I must get up my history.* 8 (*intr; foll. by to*) *Inf.* to be involved in: *he's always getting up to mischief.* ◆ *n* **get-up.** *Inf.* 9 a costume or outfit. 10 the arrangement or production of a book, etc.

get-up-and-go *n Inf.* energy or drive.

geum ('dʒiːəm) *n* any herbaceous plant of the rose type, having compound leaves and red, orange, yellow, or white flowers. [C19: NL, from L: herb bennet, avens]

gewgaw ('gjuːgɔː, 'guː-) *n* a showy but valueless trinket. [C15: from ?]

geyser ('giːzə; *US* 'gaɪzər) *n* 1 a spring that discharges steam and hot water. 2 *Brit.* a domestic gas water heater. [C18: from Icelandic *Geysir,* from ON *geysa* to gush]

G-force *n* the force of gravity.

gharry *or* **gharri** ('gærɪ) *n, pl* **gharries.** a horse-drawn vehicle used in India. [C19: from Hindi *gārī*]

ghastly ⓣ ('gɑːstlɪ) *adj* **ghastlier, ghastliest.** 1 *Inf.* very bad or unpleasant. 2 deathly pale; wan. 3 *Inf.* extremely unwell; ill. 4 terrifying; horrible. ◆ *adv* 5 unhealthily; sickly: *ghastly pale.* [OE *gāstlīc* spiritual]
▸'**ghastliness** *n*

ghat (gɔːt) *n* (in India) 1 stairs or a passage leading down to a river. 2 a mountain pass. 3 a place of cremation. [C17: from Hindi, from Sansk.]

ghazi ('gɑːzɪ) *n, pl* **ghazis.** 1 a Muslim fighter against infidels. 2 (*often cap.*) a Turkish warrior of high rank. [C18: from Ar., from *ghazā* he made war]

ghee (giː) *n* a clarified butter used in Indian cookery. [C17: from Hindi *ghī,* from Sansk. *ghri* sprinkle]

gherkin ('gɜːkɪn) *n* 1 the small immature fruit of any of various cucumbers, used for pickling. 2a a tropical American climbing plant. 2b its small spiny edible fruit. [C17: from Du., dim. of *gurk,* ult. from Gk *angourion*]

ghetto ('getəʊ) *n, pl* **ghettos** *or* **ghettoes.** 1 a densely populated slum area of a city inhabited by a socially and economically deprived minority. 2 an area or community that is segregated or isolated. 3 an area in a European city in which Jews were formerly required to live. [C17: from It., ?from *borghetto,* dim. of *borgo* settlement outside a walled city, or from *ghetto* foundry, because one occupied the site of the later Venetian ghetto]

ghettoblaster ('getəʊˌblɑːstə) *n Inf.* a large portable cassette recorder with built-in speakers.

ghettoize *or* **ghettoise** ('getəʊˌaɪz) *vb* **ghettoizes, ghettoizing, ghettoized** *or* **ghettoises, ghettoising, ghettoised.** (*tr*) to confine or restrict to a particular area, activity, or category: *to ghettoize women as housewives.*
▸ˌ**ghettoi'zation** *or* ˌ**ghettoi'sation** *n*

ghillie ('gɪlɪ) *n* a variant spelling of **gillie.**

ghost ⓣ (gəʊst) *n* 1 the disembodied spirit of a dead person, supposed to haunt the living as a pale or shadowy vision; phantom. Related adj: **spectral.** 2 a haunting memory: *the ghost of his former life rose up before him.* 3 a faint trace or possibility of something; glimmer: *a ghost of a smile.* 4 the spirit; soul (archaic, except in **the Holy Ghost**). 5 *Physics.* 5a a faint secondary image produced by an optical system. 5b a similar image on a television screen. 6 (*modifier*) falsely recorded as doing a particular job or fulfilling a particular function in order that some benefit, esp. money, may be obtained: *a ghost worker.* 7 **give up the ghost.** to die. ◆ *vb* 8 See **ghostwrite.** 9 (*tr*) to haunt. [OE *gāst*]
▸'**ghostˌlike** *adj* ▸'**ghostly** *adj*

ghost town *n* a deserted town, esp. one in the western US that was formerly a boom town.

ghost word *n* a word that has entered the language through the perpetuation, in dictionaries, etc., of an error.

ghostwrite ('gəʊstˌraɪt) *vb* **ghostwrites, ghostwriting, ghostwrote, ghostwritten.** to write (an article, etc.) on behalf of a person who is then credited as the author. Often shortened to **ghost.**
▸'**ghostˌwriter** *n*

ghoul ⓣ (guːl) *n* 1 a malevolent spirit or ghost. 2 a person interested in morbid or disgusting things. 3 a person who robs graves. 4 (in Muslim legend) an evil demon thought to eat corpses. [C18: from Ar. *ghūl,* from *ghāla* he seized]
▸'**ghoulish** *adj* ▸'**ghoulishly** *adv* ▸'**ghoulishness** *n*

GHQ *Mil. abbrev. for* General Headquarters.

ghyll (gɪl) *n* a variant spelling of **gill**[3].

GI *US inf.* ◆ *n* 1 (*pl* **GIs** *or* **GI's**) a soldier in the US Army, esp. an enlisted man. ◆ *adj* 2 conforming to US Army regulations. [C20: abbrev. of *government issue*]

gi. *abbrev. for* gill (unit of measure).

giant ⓣ ('dʒaɪənt) *n* 1 Also (fem): **giantess** ('dʒaɪəntɪs). a mythical figure of superhuman size and strength, esp. in folklore or fairy tales. 2 a person or thing of exceptional size, reputation, etc. ◆ *adj* 3 remarkably or supernaturally large. [C13: from OF *geant,* from L *gigant-, gigās,* from Gk]

giant hogweed *n* a species of cow parsley that grows up to 3½ metres (10 ft) and whose irritant hairs and sap can cause a severe reaction.

giantism ('dʒaɪənˌtɪzəm) *n* another term for **gigantism** (sense 1).

giant panda *n* See **panda** (sense 1).

giant slalom *n Skiing.* a type of slalom in which the course is longer and the obstacles are further apart than in a standard slalom.

giant star *n* any of a class of stars that have swelled and brightened as they approach the end of their life, their energy supply having changed.

giaour ('dʒaʊə) *n* a derogatory term for a non-Muslim, esp. a Christian. [C16: from Turkish: unbeliever, from Persian *gaur*]

gib (gɪb) *n* 1 a metal wedge, pad, or thrust bearing, esp. a brass plate let into a steam engine crosshead. ◆ *vb* **gibs, gibbing, gibbed.** 2 (*tr*) to fasten or supply with a gib. [C18: from ?]

gibber[1] ⓣ ('dʒɪbə) *vb* 1 to utter rapidly and unintelligibly; prattle. 2 (*intr*) (of monkeys and related animals) to make characteristic chattering sounds. [C17: imit.]

gibber[2] ('gɪbə) *n Austral.* 1 a stone or boulder. 2 (*modifier*) of or relating to a dry flat area of land covered with wind-polished stones: *gibber plains.* [C19: from Abor.]

gibberellin (ˌdʒɪbə'relɪn) *n* any of several plant hormones whose main action is to cause elongation of the stem. [C20: from NL *Gibberella,* lit.: a little hump, from L *gibber* hump + -IN]

gibberish ⓣ ('dʒɪbərɪʃ) *n* 1 rapid chatter. 2 incomprehensible talk; nonsense.

gibbet ('dʒɪbɪt) *n* 1a a wooden structure resembling a gallows, from which the bodies of executed criminals were formerly hung to public view. 1b a gallows. ◆ *vb* (*tr*) 2 to put to death by hanging on a gibbet. 3 to hang (a corpse) on a gibbet. 4 to expose to public ridicule. [C13: from OF: gallows, lit.: little cudgel, from *gibe* cudgel; from ?]

gibbon ('gɪbᵊn) *n* a small agile arboreal anthropoid ape inhabiting forests in S Asia. [C18: from F, prob. from an Indian dialect word]

gibbous ⓣ ('gɪbəs) *or* **gibbose** ('gɪbəʊs) *adj* 1 (of the moon or a planet) more than half but less than fully illuminated. 2 hunchbacked. 3 bulging. [C17: from LL *gibbōsus* humpbacked, from L *gibba* hump]
▸'**gibbously** *adv* ▸'**gibbousness** *or* **gibbosity** (gɪ'bɒsɪtɪ) *n*

gibe[1] ⓣ *or* **jibe** (dʒaɪb) *vb* **gibes, gibing, gibed** *or* **jibes, jibing, jibed.** 1 to make jeering or scoffing remarks (at); taunt. ◆ *n* 2 a derisive or provoking remark. [C16: ?from OF *giber* to treat roughly, from ?]
▸'**giber** *or* '**jiber** *n*

gibe[2] (dʒaɪb) *vb* **gibes, gibing, gibed,** *n Naut.* a variant spelling of **gybe.**

giblets ('dʒɪblɪts) *pl n* (*sometimes sing*) the gizzard, liver, heart, and neck of a fowl. [C14: from OF *gibelet* stew of game birds, prob. from *gibier* game, of Gmc origin]

gidday (gə'daɪ) *sentence substitute.* a variant spelling of **g'day.**

giddy ⓣ ('gɪdɪ) *adj* **giddier, giddiest.** 1 affected with a reeling sensation and feeling as if about to fall; dizzy. 2 causing or tending to cause vertigo. 3 impulsive; scatterbrained. ◆ *vb* **giddies, giddying, giddied.** 4 to

THESAURUS

get-together *n* 1 = **gathering**, celebration, conference, do (*inf.*), function, knees-up (*Brit. inf.*), meeting, party, reception, social ◆ *vb* **get together** 2 = **collect**, accumulate, assemble, gather 3 = **meet**, congregate, convene, converge, gather, join, muster, rally

get up *vb* 2-4 = **arise**, ascend, climb, increase, mount, rise, scale, stand

ghastly *adj* 2 = **pale**, ashen, cadaverous, deathlike, deathly pale, like death warmed up (*inf.*), livid, pallid, spectral, wan 4 = **horrible**, dreadful, frightful, from hell (*inf.*), grim, grisly, gruesome, hideous, horrendous, horrid, loathsome, repellent, shocking, terrible, terrifying
Antonyms *adj* ≠ **pale**: appealing, attractive, beautiful, blooming, charming, healthy, lovely, pleasing

ghost *n* 1 = **spirit**, apparition, eidolon, manes, phantasm, phantom, revenant, shade (*literary*), soul, spectre, spook (*inf.*), wraith 3 = **trace**, glimmer, hint, possibility, semblance, shadow, suggestion

ghostly *adj* 1 = **supernatural**, eerie, ghostlike, illusory, insubstantial, phantasmal, phantom, spectral, spooky (*inf.*), uncanny, unearthly, weird, wraithlike

ghoulish *adj* 2 = **macabre**, disgusting, grisly, gruesome, morbid, sick (*inf.*), unwholesome

giant *n* 1 = **ogre**, behemoth, colossus, Hercules, leviathan, monster, titan ◆ *adj* 3 = **huge**, colossal, elephantine, enormous, gargantuan, gigantic, ginormous, immense, jumbo (*inf.*), large, mammoth, monstrous, prodigious, stellar (*inf.*), titanic, vast
Antonyms *adj* ≠ **huge**: dwarf, Lilliputian, miniature, pygmy *or* pigmy, tiny

gibber[1] *vb* 1 = **gabble**, babble, blab, blabber, blather, cackle, chatter, jabber, prattle, rabbit (*Brit. inf.*), waffle (*inf., chiefly Brit.*)

gibberish *n* 2 = **nonsense**, all Greek (*inf.*), babble, balderdash, blather, bunkum *or* buncombe (*chiefly US*), double talk, drivel, gabble, garbage (*inf.*), gobbledegook (*inf.*), guff (*sl.*), hogwash, hokum (*sl., chiefly US & Canad.*), jabber, moonshine, mumbo jumbo, poppycock (*inf.*), prattle, tommyrot, tosh (*sl., chiefly Brit.*), tripe (*inf.*), twaddle

gibbous *adj* 1, 3 = **bulging**, convex, protuberant, rounded 2 = **hunchbacked**, crookbacked, humpbacked, humped, hunched

gibe[1] *vb* 1 = **taunt**, deride, flout, jeer, make fun of, mock, poke fun at, ridicule, scoff, scorn, sneer, take the piss out of (*sl.*), twit ◆ *n* 2 = **taunt**, barb, crack (*sl.*), cutting remark, derision, dig, jeer, mockery, ridicule, sarcasm, scoffing, sneer

giddiness *n* 1 = **dizziness**, faintness, lightheadedness, vertigo

giddy *adj* 1 = **dizzy**, faint, light-headed, reeling, unsteady, vertiginous 3 = **scatterbrained**, capri-

make or become giddy. [OE *gydig* mad, frenzied, possessed by God; rel. to GOD]
▸'**giddily** *adv* ▸'**giddiness** *n*

gidgee *or* **gidjee** ('gɪdʒiː) *n Austral.* **1** a small acacia tree yielding useful timber. **2** a spear made of this. [C19: from Abor.]

gie (giː) *vb* **gies, gi'ing, gi'ed.** a Scot. word for **give.**

gift ❶ (gɪft) *n* **1** something given; a present. **2** a special aptitude, ability, or power; talent. **3** the power or right to give or bestow (esp. in **in the gift of, in (someone's) gift**). **4** the act or process of giving. **5 look a gift-horse in the mouth.** (*usually negative*) to find fault with a free gift or chance benefit. ◆ *vb* (*tr*) **6** to present (something) as a gift to (a person). [OE *gift* payment for a wife, dowry; see GIVE]

GIFT (gɪft) *n acronym for* gamete intrafallopian transfer: a technique, similar to IVF, that enables some women who cannot conceive to bear children.

gifted ❶ ('gɪftɪd) *adj* having or showing natural talent or aptitude: *a gifted musician.*
▸'**giftedly** *adv* ▸'**giftedness** *n*

gift of tongues *n* an utterance, partly or wholly unintelligible, produced under the influence of ecstatic religious emotion. Also called: **glossolalia.**

giftwrap ('gɪft,ræp) *vb* **giftwraps, giftwrapping, giftwrapped.** to wrap (a gift) attractively.

gig[1] (gɪg) *n* **1** a light two-wheeled one-horse carriage without a hood. **2** *Naut.* a light tender for a vessel. **3** a long light rowing boat, used esp. for racing. ◆ *vb* **gigs, gigging, gigged. 4** (*intr*) to travel in a gig. [C13 (in the sense: flighty girl, spinning top): ?from ON]

gig[2] (gɪg) *n* **1** a cluster of barbless hooks drawn through a shoal of fish to try to impale them. ◆ *vb* **gigs, gigging, gigged. 2** to catch (fish) with a gig. [C18: ? shortened from obs. *fishgig* or *fizgig* kind of harpoon]

gig[3] (gɪg) *n* **1** a job, esp. a single booking for jazz or pop musicians. **2** the performance itself. ◆ *vb* **gigs, gigging, gigged. 3** (*intr*) to perform at a gig or gigs. [C20: from ?]

giga- ('gɪgə, 'gaɪgə) *combining form.* **1** denoting 10^9: *gigahertz.* **2** *Computing.* denoting 2^{30}: *gigabyte.* Symbol: G [from Gk *gigas* GIANT]

gigaflop ('gaɪgə,flɒp) *n Computing.* a measure of processing speed, consisting of a thousand million floating-point operations a second. [C20: from GIGA- + *flo(ating) p(oint)*]

gigantic ❶ (dʒaɪ'gæntɪk) *adj* **1** very large; enormous. **2** Also: **gigantesque** (,dʒaɪgæn'tɛsk). of or suitable for giants. [C17: from Gk *gigantikos,* from *gigas* GIANT]
▸**gi'gantically** *adv*

gigantism ('dʒaɪgæn,tɪzəm, dʒaɪ'gæntɪzəm) *n* **1** Also called: **giantism.** excessive growth of the entire body, caused by overproduction of growth hormone by the pituitary gland. **2** the state or quality of being gigantic.

giggle ❶ ('gɪgᵊl) *vb* **giggles, giggling, giggled. 1** (*intr*) to laugh nervously or foolishly. ◆ *n* **2** such a laugh. **3** *Inf.* something or someone that causes amusement. [C16: imit.]
▸'**giggler** *n* ▸'**giggling** *adj, n* ▸'**giggly** *adj*

gigolo ('ʒɪgə,ləʊ) *n, pl* **gigolos. 1** a man who is kept by a woman, esp. an older woman. **2** a man who is paid to dance with or escort women. [C20: from F, back formation from *gigolette* girl for hire as a dancing partner, prostitute, ult. from *gigue* a fiddle]

gigot ('dʒɪgət) *n* **1** a leg of lamb or mutton. **2** a leg-of-mutton sleeve. [C16: from OF: leg, a small fiddle, from *gigue* a fiddle, of Gmc origin]

gigue (ʒiːg) *n* a piece of music, usually in six-eight time, incorporated into the classical suite. [C17: from F, from It. *giga,* lit.: a fiddle; see GIGOT]

Gila monster ('hiːlə) *n* a large venomous brightly coloured lizard inhabiting deserts of the southwestern US and Mexico. [C19: after the *Gila,* a river in New Mexico and Arizona]

gilbert ('gɪlbət) *n* the cgs unit of magnetomotive force. Symbol: Gb, Gi [C19: after William *Gilbert* (1540–1603), E scientist]

gild[1] ❶ (gɪld) *vb* **gilds, gilding, gilded** *or* **gilt.** (*tr*) **1** to cover with or as if with gold. **2 gild the lily. 2a** to adorn unnecessarily something already beautiful. **2b** to praise someone inordinately. **3** to give a falsely attractive or valuable appearance to. [OE *gyldan,* from *gold* GOLD]
▸'**gilder** *n*

gild[2] (gɪld) *n* a variant spelling of **guild.**

gilding ('gɪldɪŋ) *n* **1** the act or art of applying gilt to a surface. **2** the surface so produced. **3** another word for **gilt**[1] (sense 2).

gilet (dʒɪ'leɪ) *n* a garment resembling a waistcoat. [C20: F, lit.: waistcoat]

gill[1] (gɪl) *n* **1** the respiratory organ in many aquatic animals. **2** any of the radiating leaflike spore-producing structures on the undersurface of the cap of a mushroom. [C14: from ON]
▸**gilled** *adj*

gill[2] (dʒɪl) *n* a unit of liquid measure equal to one quarter of a pint. [C14: from OF *gille* vat, tub, from LL *gillō,* from ?]

gill[3] *or* **ghyll** (gɪl) *n Dialect.* **1** a narrow stream; rivulet. **2** a wooded ravine. [C11: from ON *gil* steep-sided valley]

gillie, ghillie, *or* **gilly** ('gɪlɪ) *n, pl* **gillies** *or* **ghillies.** *Scot.* **1** an attendant or guide for hunting or fishing. **2** (formerly) a Highland chieftain's male attendant. [C17: from Scot. Gaelic *gille* boy, servant]

gills (gɪlz) *pl n* **1** (*sometimes sing*) the wattle of birds such as domestic fowl. **2** the cheeks and jowls of a person. **3 green about the gills.** *Inf.* looking or feeling nauseated.

gillyflower *or* **gilliflower** ('dʒɪlɪ,flaʊə) *n* **1** any of several plants having fragrant flowers, such as the stock and wallflower. **2** an archaic name for **carnation.** [C14: from *gilofre,* from OF *girofle,* from Med. L, from Gk: clove tree, from *karuon* nut + *phullon* leaf]

gilt[1] (gɪlt) *vb* **1** a past tense and past participle of **gild**[1]. ◆ *n* **2** gold or a substance simulating it, applied in gilding. **3** another word for **gilding** (senses 1, 2). **4** superficial or false appearance of excellence. **5** a gilt-edged security. **6 take the gilt off the gingerbread.** to destroy the part of something that gives it its appeal. ◆ *adj* **7** covered with or as if with gold or gilt; gilded.

gilt[2] (gɪlt) *n* a young female pig, esp. one that has not had a litter. [C15: from ON *gyltr*]

gilt-edged *adj* **1** denoting government securities on which interest payments will certainly be met and that will certainly be repaid at par on the due date. **2** of the highest quality: *the last track on the album is a gilt-edged classic.* **3** (of books, papers, etc.) having gilded edges.

gimbals ('dʒɪmbᵊlz, 'gɪm-) *pl n* a device, consisting of two or three pivoted rings at right angles to each other, that provides free suspension in all planes for a compass, chronometer, etc. Also called: **gimbal ring.** [C16: var. of earlier *gimmal,* from OF *gemel* double finger ring, from L *gemellus,* dim. of *geminus* twin]

gimcrack ('dʒɪm,kræk) *adj* **1** cheap; shoddy. ◆ *n* **2** a cheap showy trifle or gadget. [C18: from C14 *gibecrake* little ornament, from ?]
▸'**gim,crackery** *n*

gimlet ('gɪmlɪt) *n* **1** a small hand tool consisting of a pointed spiral tip attached at right angles to a handle, used for boring small holes in wood. **2** *US.* a cocktail consisting of half gin or vodka and half lime juice. ◆ *vb* **3** (*tr*) to make holes in (wood) using a gimlet. ◆ *adj* **4** penetrating; piercing (esp. in **gimlet-eyed**). [C15: from OF *guimbelet,* of Gmc origin, see WIMBLE]

gimmick ❶ ('gɪmɪk) *n Inf.* **1** something designed to attract extra attention, interest, or publicity. **2** any clever device, gadget, or stratagem, esp. one used to deceive. [C20: orig. US sl., from ?]
▸'**gimmickry** *n* ▸'**gimmicky** *adj*

gimp *or* **guimpe** (gɪmp) *n* a tapelike trimming. [C17: prob. from Du. *gimp,* from ?]

gin[1] (dʒɪn) *n* an alcoholic drink obtained by distillation of the grain of malted barley, rye, or maize, flavoured with juniper berries. [C18: from Du. *genever,* via OF from L *jūniperus* JUNIPER]

gin[2] (dʒɪn) *n* **1** a primitive engine in which a vertical shaft is turned by horses driving a horizontal beam in a circle. **2** Also called: **cotton gin.** a machine of this type used for separating seeds from raw cotton. **3** a trap for catching small mammals, consisting of a noose of thin strong wire. ◆ *vb* **gins, ginning, ginned.** (*tr*) **4** to free (cotton) of seeds with a gin. **5** to trap or snare (game) with a gin. [C13 *gyn,* from ENGINE]

gin[3] (gɪn) *vb* **gins, ginning, gan** (gæn), **gun** (gʌn). an archaic word for **begin.**

gin[4] (dʒɪn) *n Austral. offens. sl.* an Aboriginal woman. [C19: from Abor.]

ginger ('dʒɪndʒə) *n* **1** any of several plants of the East Indies, cultivated throughout the tropics for their spicy hot-tasting underground stems. **2** the underground stem of this plant, which is used fresh or powdered as a flavouring or crystallized as a sweetmeat. **3a** a reddish-brown or yellowish-brown colour. **3b** (*as adj*): *ginger hair.* **4** *Inf.* liveliness; vigour. [C13: from OF *gingivre,* ult. from Sansk. *śṛṅgaveram,* from *śṛṅga-* horn + *vera-* body, referring to its shape]
▸'**gingery** *adj*

ginger ale *n* a sweetened effervescent nonalcoholic drink flavoured with ginger extract.

ginger beer *n* a slightly alcoholic drink made by fermenting a mixture of syrup and root ginger.

gingerbread ('dʒɪndʒə,brɛd) *n* **1** a moist brown cake, flavoured with ginger and treacle. **2a** a biscuit, similarly flavoured, cut into various shapes. **2b** (*as modifier*): *gingerbread man.* **3** an elaborate but unsubstantial ornamentation.

THESAURUS

cious, careless, changeable, changeful, ditzy *or* ditsy (*sl.*), dizzy, erratic, fickle, flighty, frivolous, heedless, impulsive, inconstant, irresolute, irresponsible, reckless, silly, thoughtless, unbalanced, unstable, unsteady, vacillating, volatile, wild

Antonyms *adj* ≠ **scatterbrained:** calm, constant, determined, earnest, resolute, serious, steady

gift *n* **1** = **donation,** benefaction, bequest, bonus, boon, bounty, contribution, grant, gratuity, hand-out, largesse *or* largess, legacy, offering, present **2** = **talent,** ability, aptitude, attribute, bent, capability, capacity, endowment, faculty, flair, genius, knack, power, turn

gifted *adj* = **talented,** able, accomplished, adroit, brilliant, capable, clever, expert, ingenious, intelligent, masterly, skilled

Antonyms *adj* amateur, backward, dull, incapable, inept, retarded, slow, talentless, unskilled

gigantic *adj* **1** = **enormous,** Brobdingnagian, colossal, Cyclopean, elephantine, gargantuan, giant, herculean, huge, immense, mammoth, monstrous, prodigious, stellar (*inf.*), stupendous, titanic, tremendous, vast

Antonyms *adj* diminutive, insignificant, little, miniature, puny, small, tiny, weak

giggle *vb* **1** = **laugh,** cackle, chortle, chuckle, snigger, tee-hee, titter, twitter ◆ *n* **2** = **laugh,** cackle, chortle, chuckle, snigger, tee-hee, titter, twitter

gild[1] *vb* **3** = **embellish,** adorn, beautify, bedeck, brighten, coat, deck, dress up, embroider, enhance, enrich, garnish, grace, ornament

gimmick *n* **1, 2** = **stunt,** contrivance, device, dodge, gadget, gambit, gizmo (*sl., chiefly US*), ploy, scheme, stratagem, trick

ginger group *n Chiefly Brit.* a group within a party, association, etc., that enlivens or radicalizes its parent body.

gingerly Ⓣ (ˈdʒɪndʒəlɪ) *adv* **1** in a cautious, reluctant, or timid manner. ◆ *adj* **2** cautious, reluctant, or timid. [C16: ?from OF *gensor* dainty, from *gent* of noble birth; see GENTLE]

ginger nut *or* **snap** *n* a crisp biscuit flavoured with ginger.

gingham (ˈgɪŋəm) *n* a cotton fabric, usually woven of two coloured yarns in a checked or striped design. [C17: from F, from Malay *ginggang* striped cloth]

gingili (ˈdʒɪndʒɪlɪ) *n* **1** the oil obtained from sesame seeds. **2** another name for **sesame**. [C18: from Hindi *jingalī*]

gingiva (ˈdʒɪndʒɪvə, dʒɪnˈdʒaɪvə) *n, pl* **gingivae** (-dʒɪˌviː, -ˈdʒaɪviː). *Anat.* the technical name for the **gum**[2]. [from L]
▸ ˈ**gingival** *adj*

gingivitis (ˌdʒɪndʒɪˈvaɪtɪs) *n* inflammation of the gums.

ginglymus (ˈdʒɪŋglɪməs, ˈgɪŋ-) *n, pl* **ginglymi** (-ˌmaɪ). *Anat.* a hinge joint. [C17: NL, from Gk *ginglumos* hinge]

gink (gɪŋk) *n Sl.* a man or boy, esp. one considered to be odd. [C20: from ?]

ginkgo (ˈgɪŋkgəʊ) *or* **gingko** (ˈgɪŋkəʊ) *n, pl* **ginkgoes** *or* **gingkoes.** a widely planted ornamental Chinese tree with fan-shaped deciduous leaves and fleshy yellow fruit. Also called: **maidenhair tree.** [C18: from Japanese, from Ancient Chinese: silver + apricot]

ginormous (dʒaɪˈnɔːməs) *adj Inf.* very large. [C20: blend of *giant* or *gigantic* & *enormous*]

gin palace (dʒɪn) *n* (formerly) a gaudy drinking house.

gin rummy (dʒɪn) *n* a version of rummy in which a player may go out if the odd cards outside his sequences total less than ten points. [C20: from GIN[1] + RUMMY]

ginseng (ˈdʒɪnsɛŋ) *n* **1** either of two plants of China or of North America, whose forked aromatic roots are used medicinally. **2** the root of either of these plants or a substance obtained from the roots, believed to possess tonic and energy-giving properties. [C17: from Mandarin Chinese *jen shen*]

Gioconda (*Italian* dʒoˈkonda) *n* **1 La.** Also called: **Mona Lisa.** the portrait by Leonardo da Vinci of a young woman with an enigmatic smile. ◆ *adj* **2** mysterious or enigmatic. [It.: the smiling (lady)]

giocoso (dʒəˈkəʊzəʊ) *adj Music.* jocose. [It.]

gip (dʒɪp) *vb* **gips, gipping, gipped. 1** a variant spelling of **gyp**[1]. ◆ *n* **2** a variant spelling of **gyp**[2].

Gipsy (ˈdʒɪpsɪ) *n, pl* **Gipsies.** (*sometimes not cap.*) a variant spelling of **Gypsy.**

gipsy moth *n* a variant spelling of **gypsy moth.**

giraffe (dʒɪˈrɑːf, -ˈræf) *n, pl* **giraffes** *or* **giraffe.** a large ruminant mammal inhabiting savannas of tropical Africa: the tallest mammal, with very long legs and neck. [C17: from It. *giraffa*, from Ar. *zarāfah*, prob. of African origin]

girandole (ˈdʒɪrənˌdəʊl) *n* **1** a branched wall candleholder. **2** an earring or pendant having a central gem surrounded by smaller ones. **3** a revolving firework. **4** *Artillery.* a group of connected mines. [C17: from F, from It. *girandola*, from L *gȳrāre* to GYRATE]

girasol *or* **girasole** (ˈdʒɪrəˌsɒl, -ˌsəʊl) *n* a type of opal that has a red or pink glow; fire opal. [C16: from It., from *girare* to revolve (see GYRATE) + *sole* the sun]

gird[1] Ⓣ (gɜːd) *vb* **girds, girding, girded** *or* **girt.** (*tr*) **1** to put a belt, girdle, etc., around (the waist or hips). **2** to bind or secure with or as if with a belt: *to gird on one's armour.* **3** to surround; encircle. **4** to prepare (oneself) for action (esp. in **gird (up) one's loins**). [OE *gyrdan*, of Gmc origin]

gird[2] (gɜːd) *N English dialect.* ◆ *vb* **1** (when *intr*, foll. by *at*) to jeer (at someone); mock. ◆ *n* **2** a taunt; gibe. [C13 *girden* to strike, cut, from ?]

girder (ˈgɜːdə) *n* a large beam, esp. one made of steel, used in the construction of bridges, buildings, etc.

girdle[1] Ⓣ (ˈgɜːdᵊl) *n* **1** a woman's elastic corset covering the waist to the thigh. **2** anything that surrounds or encircles. **3** a belt or sash. **4** *Jewellery.* the outer edge of a gem. **5** *Anat.* any encircling structure or part. **6** the mark left on a tree trunk after the removal of a ring of bark. ◆ *vb* **girdles, girdling, girdled.** (*tr*) **7** to put a girdle on or around. **8** to surround or encircle. **9** to remove a ring of bark from (a tree). [OE *gyrdel*, of Gmc origin; see GIRD[1]]

girdle[2] (ˈgɜːdᵊl) *n Scot. & N English dialect.* another word for **griddle.**

girl Ⓣ (gɜːl) *n* **1** a female child from birth to young womanhood. **2** a young unmarried woman; lass; maid. **3** *Inf.* a sweetheart or girlfriend. **4** *Inf.* a woman of any age. **5** a female employee, esp. a female servant. **6** *S. African derog.* a Black female servant. [C13: from ?; ? rel. to Low G *Göre* boy, girl]
▸ ˈ**girlish** *adj*

girlfriend (ˈgɜːlˌfrɛnd) *n* **1** a female friend with whom a person is romantically or sexually involved. **2** any female friend.

Girl Guide *n* See **Guide.**

girlhood (ˈgɜːlˌhʊd) *n* the state or time of being a girl.

girlie (ˈgɜːlɪ) *adj* **1** *Inf.* featuring nude or scantily dressed women: *a girlie magazine.* **2** suited to or designed to appeal to young women: *a real girlie night out.*

giro (ˈdʒaɪrəʊ) *n, pl* **giros. 1** a system of transferring money within a financial organization, such as a bank or post office, directly from the account of one person into that of another. **2** *Brit. inf.* a jobseeker's allowance or income support payment by giro cheque. [C20: ult. from Gk *guros* circuit]

girt[1] (gɜːt) *vb* a past tense and past participle of **gird**[1].

girt[2] (gɜːt) *vb* **1** (*tr*) to bind or encircle; gird. **2** to measure the girth of (something).

girth Ⓣ (gɜːθ) *n* **1** the distance around something; circumference. **2** a band around a horse's belly to keep the saddle in position. ◆ *vb* **3** (usually foll. by *up*) to fasten a girth on (a horse). **4** (*tr*) to encircle or surround. [C14: from ON *gjörth* belt; see GIRD[1]]

gist Ⓣ (dʒɪst) *n* the point or substance of an argument, speech, etc. [C18: from Anglo-F, as in *cest action gist en* this action consists in, lit.: lies in, from OF *gésir*, from L *jacēre*]

git (gɪt) *n Brit. sl.* **1** a contemptible person, often a fool. **2** a bastard. [C20: from GET (in the sense: *to beget*, hence a bastard, fool)]

gîte (ʒiːt) *n* a self-catering holiday cottage for let in France. [C20: F]

gittern (ˈgɪtɜːn) *n* an obsolete medieval stringed instrument resembling the guitar. [C14: from OF, ult. from OSp. *guitarra* GUITAR; see CITTERN]

giusto (ˈdʒuːstəʊ) *adj Music.* (of tempo) exact; strict. [It.]

give Ⓣ (gɪv) *vb* **gives, giving, gave, given.** (*mainly tr*) **1** (*also intr*) to present or deliver voluntarily (something that is one's own) to another. **2** (often foll. by *for*) to transfer (something that is one's own, esp. money) to the possession of another as part of an exchange: *to give fifty pounds for a painting.* **3** to place in the temporary possession of another: *I gave him my watch while I went swimming.* **4** (when *intr*, foll. by *of*) to grant, provide, or bestow: *give me some advice.* **5** to administer: *to give a reprimand.* **6** to award or attribute: *to give blame, praise*, etc. **7** to be a source of: *he gives no trouble.* **8** to impart or communicate: *to give news.* **9** to utter or emit: *to give a shout.* **10** to perform, make, or do: *the car gave a jolt.* **11** to sacrifice or devote: *he gave his life for his country.* **12** to surrender: *to give place to others.* **13** to concede or yield: *I will give you this game.* **14** (*intr*) *Inf.* to happen: *what gives?* **15** (often foll. by *to*) to cause; lead: *she gave me to believe that she would come.* **16** to perform or present as an entertainment: *to give a play.* **17** to act as a host of (a party, etc.). **18** (*intr*) to yield or break under force or pressure: *this surface will give if you sit on it.* **19 give as good as one gets.** to respond to verbal or bodily blows to at least an equal extent as those received. **20 give or take.** plus or minus: *three thousand people came, give or take a few hundred.* ◆ *n* **21** tendency to yield under pressure; resilience. ◆ See also **give away, give in**, etc. [OE *giefan*]
▸ ˈ**givable** *or* ˈ**giveable** *adj* ▸ ˈ**giver** *n*

give-and-take *n* **1** mutual concessions, shared benefits, and cooperation. **2** a smoothly flowing exchange of ideas and talk. ◆ *vb* **give and take.** (*intr*) **3** to make mutual concessions.

give away Ⓣ *vb* (*tr, adv*) **1** to donate or bestow as a gift, prize, etc. **2** to sell very cheaply. **3** to reveal or betray. **4** to fail to use (an opportunity) through folly or neglect. **5** to present (a bride) formally to her husband in a marriage ceremony. ◆ *n* **giveaway. 6** a betrayal or disclosure esp. when unintentional. **7** (*modifier*) **7a** very cheap (esp. in **giveaway prices**). **7b** free of charge: *a giveaway property magazine.*

give in Ⓣ *vb* (*adv*) **1** (*intr*) to yield; admit defeat. **2** (*tr*) to submit or deliver (a document).

given Ⓣ (ˈgɪvᵊn) *vb* **1** the past participle of **give.** ◆ *adj* **2** (*postpositive*; foll. by *to*) tending (to); inclined or addicted (to). **3** specific or previously stated. **4** assumed as a premise. **5** *Maths.* known or determined independently: *a given volume.* **6** (on official documents) issued or executed, as on a stated date.

THESAURUS

gingerly *adv* **1** = **cautiously**, carefully, charily, circumspectly, daintily, delicately, fastidiously, hesitantly, reluctantly, squeamishly, suspiciously, timidly, warily ◆ *adj* **2** = **cautious**, careful, chary, circumspect, dainty, delicate, fastidious, hesitant, reluctant, squeamish, suspicious, timid, wary
Antonyms *adv* ≠ **cautiously:** boldly, carelessly, confidently, rashly

gird[1] *vb* **1, 2** = **girdle**, belt, bind **3** = **surround**, blockade, encircle, enclose, encompass, enfold, environ, hem in, pen, ring **4** *As in* **gird (up) one's loins** = **prepare**, brace, fortify, make ready, ready, steel

girdle[1] *n* **3** = **belt**, band, cincture, cummerbund, fillet, sash, waistband ◆ *vb* **8** = **surround**, bind, bound, encircle, enclose, encompass, environ, enwreath, gird, hem, ring

girl *n* **1, 2** = **female child**, bird (*sl.*), chick (*sl.*), colleen (*Irish*), damsel (*arch.*), daughter, lass, lassie (*inf.*), maid (*arch.*), maiden (*arch.*), miss, wench

girth *n* **1** = **circumference**, bulk, measure, size

gist *n* = **point**, core, drift, essence, force, idea, import, marrow, meaning, nub, pith, quintessence, sense, significance, substance

give *vb* **1** = **present**, accord, administer, allow, award, bestow, commit, confer, consign, contribute, deliver, donate, entrust, furnish, grant, hand over *or* out, make over, permit, provide, purvey, supply, vouchsafe **7** = **produce**, cause, do, engender, lead, make, occasion, perform **8** = **announce**, be a source of, communicate, emit, impart, issue, notify, pronounce, publish, render, transmit, utter **12** = **surrender**, cede, devote, hand over, lend, relinquish, yield **13** = **concede**, allow, grant **18** = **break**, bend, collapse, fall, recede, retire, sink
Antonyms *vb* ≠ **present:** accept, get, hold, keep, receive, take, withdraw

give away *vb* **3** = **reveal**, betray, disclose, divulge, expose, grass (*Brit. sl.*), grass up (*sl.*), inform on, leak, let out, let slip, let the cat out of the bag (*inf.*), put the finger on (*inf.*), shop (*sl., chiefly Brit.*), uncover

give in *vb* **1** = **admit defeat**, capitulate, cave in (*inf.*), collapse, comply, concede, quit, submit, succumb, surrender, yield

given *adj* **2** = **inclined**, addicted, apt, disposed, liable, likely, prone

given name *n* another term (esp. US) for **first name.**

give off Ⓣ *vb (tr, adv)* to emit or discharge: *the mothballs gave off an acrid odour.*

give out Ⓣ *vb (adv)* **1** *(tr)* to emit or discharge. **2** *(tr)* to publish or make known: *the chairman gave out that he would resign.* **3** *(tr)* to hand out or distribute: *they gave out free chewing gum.* **4** *(intr)* to become exhausted; fail: *the supply of candles gave out.*

give over *vb (adv)* **1** *(tr)* to transfer, esp. to the care or custody of another. **2** *(tr)* to assign or resign to a specific purpose or function: *the day was given over to pleasure.* **3** *Inf.* to cease (an activity): *give over fighting, will you!*

give up Ⓣ *vb (adv)* **1** to abandon hope (for). **2** *(tr)* to renounce (an activity, belief, etc.): *I have given up smoking.* **3** *(tr)* to relinquish or resign from: *he gave up the presidency.* **4** *(tr; usually reflexive)* to surrender: *the escaped convict gave himself up.* **5** *(intr)* to admit one's defeat or inability to do something. **6** *(tr; often passive or reflexive)* to devote completely (to): *she gave herself up to caring for the sick.*

gizmo *or* **gismo** (ˈgɪzməʊ) *n, pl* **gizmos, gismos.** *Sl.* a device; gadget. [C20: from ?]

gizzard (ˈgɪzəd) *n* **1** the thick-walled part of a bird's stomach, in which hard food is broken up. **2** *Inf.* the stomach and entrails generally. [C14: from OF *guisier* fowl's liver, from L *gigēria* entrails of poultry when cooked, from ?]

Gk *abbrev. for* Greek.

glabella (gləˈbɛlə) *n, pl* **glabellae** (-liː). *Anat.* a smooth elevation of the frontal bone just above the bridge of the nose. [C19: NL, from L, from *glaber* bald, smooth]
▸**glaˈbellar** *adj*

glabrous (ˈgleɪbrəs) *adj Biol.* without hair or a similar growth; smooth. [C17 *glabrous*, from L *glaber*]

glacé (ˈglæsɪ) *adj* **1** crystallized or candied: *glacé cherries.* **2** covered in icing. **3** (of leather, silk, etc.) having a glossy finish. ◆ *vb* **glacés, glacéing, glacéed. 4** *(tr)* to ice or candy (cakes, fruits, etc.). [C19: from F *glacé*, lit.: iced, from *glacer* to freeze, from L *glaciēs* ice]

glacial Ⓣ (ˈgleɪsɪəl, -ʃəl) *adj* **1** characterized by the presence of masses of ice. **2** relating to, caused by, or deposited by a glacier. **3** extremely cold; icy. **4** cold or hostile in manner. **5** (of a chemical compound) of or tending to form crystals that resemble ice.
▸ˈ**glacially** *adv*

glacial acetic acid *n* pure acetic acid.

glacial period *n* **1** any period of time during which a large part of the earth's surface was covered with ice, due to the advance of glaciers. **2** *(often caps.)* the Pleistocene epoch. ◆ Also called: **glacial epoch, ice age.**

glaciate (ˈgleɪsɪˌeɪt) *vb* **glaciates, glaciating, glaciated. 1** to cover or become covered with glaciers or masses of ice. **2** *(tr)* to subject to the effects of glaciers, such as denudation and erosion.
▸ˌ**glaciˈation** *n*

glacier (ˈglæsɪə, ˈgleɪs-) *n* a slowly moving mass of ice originating from an accumulation of snow. [C18: from F (dialect), from OF *glace* ice, from LL, from L *glaciēs* ice]

glaciology (ˌglæsɪˈɒlədʒɪ, ˌgleɪ-) *n* the study of the distribution, character, and effects of glaciers.
▸**glaciological** (ˌglæsɪəˈlɒdʒɪkᵊl, ˌgleɪ-) *adj* ▸ˌ**glaciˈologist** *n*

glacis (ˈglæsɪs, ˈglæsɪ, ˈgleɪ-) *n, pl* **glacises** *or* **glacis** (-iːz, -ɪz). **1** a slight incline; slope. **2** an open slope in front of a fortified place. [C17: from F, from OF *glacier* to freeze, slip, from L, from *glaciēs* ice]

glad[1] Ⓣ (glæd) *adj* **gladder, gladdest. 1** happy and pleased; contented. **2** causing happiness or contentment. **3** *(postpositive; foll. by to)* very willing: *he was glad to help.* **4** *(postpositive; foll. by of)* happy or pleased to have: *glad of her help.* ◆ *vb* **glads, gladding, gladded. 5** *(tr)* an archaic word for **gladden.** [OE *glæd*]
▸ˈ**gladly** *adv* ▸ˈ**gladness** *n*

glad[2] (glæd) *n Inf.* short for **gladiolus.**

gladden Ⓣ (ˈglædᵊn) *vb* to make or become glad and joyful.
▸ˈ**gladdener** *n*

glade (gleɪd) *n* an open place in a forest; clearing. [C16: from ?; ? rel. to GLAD[1] (in obs. sense: bright); see GLEAM]

glad eye *n Inf.* an inviting or seductive glance (esp. in **give (someone) the glad eye**).

gladiator (ˈglædɪˌeɪtə) *n* **1** (in ancient Rome) a man trained to fight in arenas to provide entertainment. **2** a person who supports and fights publicly for a cause. [C16: from L: swordsman, from *gladius* sword]
▸**gladiatorial** (ˌglædɪəˈtɔːrɪəl) *adj*

gladiolus (ˌglædɪˈəʊləs) *n, pl* **gladiolus, gladioli** (-laɪ), *or* **gladioluses.** any plant of a widely cultivated genus having sword-shaped leaves and spikes of funnel-shaped brightly coloured flowers. Also called: **gladiola.** [C16: from L: a small sword, sword lily, from *gladius* a sword]

glad rags *pl n Inf.* best clothes or clothes used on special occasions.

gladsome (ˈglædsəm) *adj* an archaic word for **glad**[1].
▸ˈ**gladsomely** *adv* ▸ˈ**gladsomeness** *n*

Gladstone bag (ˈglædstən) *n* a piece of hand luggage consisting of two equal-sized hinged compartments. [C19: after W. E. *Gladstone* (1809–98), Brit. statesman]

Glagolitic (ˌglægəˈlɪtɪk) *adj* of, relating to, or denoting a Slavic alphabet whose invention is attributed to Saint Cyril. [C19: from NL, from Serbo-Croat *glagolica* the Glagolitic alphabet]

glair (glɛə) *n* **1** white of egg, esp. when used as a size or adhesive. **2** any substance resembling this. ◆ *vb* **3** *(tr)* to apply glair to (something). [C14: from OF *glaire*, from Vulgar L *clāria* (unattested) CLEAR, from L *clārus*]
▸ˈ**glairy** *or* ˈ**glaireous** *adj*

glam (glæm) *adj Inf.* short for **glamorous.**

glamorize, glamorise, *or US (sometimes)* **glamourize** (ˈglæməˌraɪz) *vb* **glamorizes, glamorizing, glamorized; glamorises, glamorising, glamorised** *or US (sometimes)* **glamourizes, glamourizing, glamourized.** *(tr)* to cause to be or seem glamorous; romanticize or beautify.
▸ˌ**glamoriˈzation** *or* ˌ**glamoriˈsation** *n*

glamorous Ⓣ (ˈglæmərəs) *adj* **1** possessing glamour; alluring and fascinating. **2** beautiful and smart, esp. in a showy way: *a glamorous woman.*
▸ˈ**glamorously** *adv*

glamour Ⓣ *or US (sometimes)* **glamor** (ˈglæmə) *n* **1** charm and allure; fascination. **2a** fascinating or voluptuous beauty. **2b** *(as modifier): a glamour girl.* **3** *Arch.* a magic spell; charm. [C18: Scot. var. of GRAMMAR (hence a magic spell, because occult practices were popularly associated with learning)]

glance[1] Ⓣ (glɑːns) *vb* **glances, glancing, glanced. 1** *(intr)* to look hastily or briefly. **2** *(intr; foll. by over, through, etc.)* to look over briefly: *to glance through a report.* **3** *(intr)* to reflect, glint, or gleam: *the sun glanced on the water.* **4** *(intr; usually foll. by off)* to depart (from an object struck) at an oblique angle: *the arrow glanced off the tree.* ◆ *n* **5** a hasty or brief look; peep. **6** a flash or glint of light; gleam. **7** the act or an instance of an object glancing off another. **8** a brief allusion. [C15: from *glacen* to strike obliquely, from OF *glacier* to slide (see GLACIS)]
▸ˈ**glancing** *adj* ▸ˈ**glancingly** *ad*

> **USAGE NOTE** *Glance* is sometimes wrongly used where *glimpse* is meant: *he caught a glimpse* (not *glance*) *of her making her way through the crowd.*

glance[2] (glɑːns) *n* any mineral having a metallic lustre. [C19: from G *Glanz* brightness, lustre]

gland[1] (glænd) *n* **1** a cell or organ in man and other animals that synthesizes chemical substances and secretes them for the body to use or eliminate, either through a duct (exocrine gland) or directly into the bloodstream (endocrine gland). **2** a structure, such as a lymph node, that resembles a gland in form. **3** a cell or organ in plants that synthesizes and secretes a particular substance. [C17: from L *glāns* acorn]

gland[2] (glænd) *n* a device that prevents leakage of fluid along a rotating shaft or reciprocating rod passing between areas of high and low

THESAURUS

give off *vb* = **emit,** discharge, exhale, exude, produce, release, send out, throw out, vent

give out *vb* **1** = **emit,** discharge, exhale, exude, produce, release, send out, throw out, vent **2** = **make known,** announce, broadcast, communicate, disseminate, impart, notify, publish, shout from the rooftops (*inf.*), transmit, utter

give up *vb* **2-5** = **abandon,** call it a day *or* night, capitulate, cave in (*inf.*), cease, cede, cut out, desist, despair, fall by the wayside, forswear, hand over, kick (*inf.*), kiss (something) goodbye, leave off, quit, relinquish, renounce, resign, say goodbye to, step down (*inf.*), stop, surrender, throw in the sponge, throw in the towel, waive

glacial *adj* **3** = **icy,** arctic, biting, bitter, chill, chilly, cold, freezing, frigid, frosty, frozen, gelid, piercing, polar, raw, wintry **4** = **unfriendly,** antagonistic, cold, frigid, hostile, icy, inimical

glad[1] *adj* **1** = **happy,** cheerful, chuffed (*sl.*), contented, delighted, gay, gleeful, gratified, jocund, jovial, joyful, overjoyed, pleased **2** = **pleasing,** animated, cheerful, cheering, cheery, delightful, felicitous, gratifying, joyous, merry, pleasant

Antonyms *adj* ≠ **happy:** depressed, discontented, displeased, melancholy, miserable, sad, sorrowful, unhappy

gladden *vb* = **please,** cheer, delight, elate, enliven, exhilarate, gratify, hearten, rejoice

gladly *adv* **3** = **happily,** cheerfully, freely, gaily, gleefully, jovially, joyfully, joyously, lief (*rare*), merrily, readily, willingly, with (a) good grace, with pleasure

Antonyms *adv* dolefully, grudgingly, reluctantly, sadly, unenthusiastically, unwillingly

gladness *n* **1** = **happiness,** animation, blitheness, cheerfulness, delight, felicity, gaiety, glee, high spirits, hilarity, jollity, joy, joyousness, mirth, pleasure

glamorous *adj* **1, 2** = **elegant,** alluring, attractive, beautiful, bewitching, captivating, charming, dazzling, enchanting, entrancing, exciting, fascinating, glittering, glitzy (*sl.*), glossy, lovely, prestigious, smart

Antonyms *adj* colourless, dull, plain, unattractive, unexciting, unglamorous

glamour *n* **1** = **charm,** allure, appeal, attraction, beauty, bewitchment, enchantment, fascination, magnetism, prestige, ravishment, witchery

glance[1] *vb* **1** = **peek,** check, check out (*inf.*), clock (*Brit. inf.*), gaze, glimpse, look, peep, scan, take a dekko at (*Brit. sl.*), view **2** *with* **over, through,** *etc.* = **scan,** browse, dip into, flip through, leaf through, riffle through, run over *or* through, skim through, thumb through **3** = **gleam,** flash, glimmer, glint, glisten, glitter, reflect, shimmer, shine, twinkle **4** = **graze,** bounce, brush, rebound, ricochet, skim ◆ *n* **5** = **peek,** brief look, butcher's (*Brit. sl.*), dekko (*sl.*), gander (*inf.*), glimpse, look, peep, quick look, shufti (*Brit. sl.*), squint, view **6** = **gleam,** flash, glimmer, glint, reflection, sparkle, twinkle **8** = **allusion,** passing mention, reference

Antonyms *vb* ≠ **peek:** peruse, scrutinize, study ◆ *n* ≠ **peek:** examination, good look, inspection, perusal pressure. It often consists of a flanged metal sleeve bedding into a stuffing box. [C19: from ?]

glanders (ˈglændəz) *n* (*functioning as sing*) a highly infectious bacterial disease of horses, sometimes communicated to man, characterized by inflammation and ulceration of the mucous membranes of the air passages, skin and lymph glands. [C16: from OF *glandres*, from L *glandulae*, lit.: little acorns, from *glāns* acorn; see GLAND[1]]

glandular (ˈglændjʊlə) *or* **glandulous** (ˈglændjʊləs) *adj* of, relating to, containing, functioning as, or affecting a gland. [C18: from L *glandula*, lit.: a little acorn; see GLANDERS]
▸ **ˈglandularly** *or* **ˈglandulously** *adv*

glandular fever *n* another name for **infectious mononucleosis.**

glandule (ˈglændjuːl) *n* a small gland.

glans (glænz) *n, pl* **glandes** (ˈglændiːz). *Anat.* any small rounded body or glandlike mass, such as the head of the penis (**glans penis**). [C17: from L: acorn; see GLAND[1]]

glare ➊ (glɛə) *vb* **glares, glaring, glared. 1** (*intr*) to stare angrily; glower. **2** (*tr*) to express by glowering. **3** (*intr*) (of light, colour, etc.) to be very bright and intense. **4** (*intr*) to be dazzlingly ornamented or garish. ◆ *n* **5** an angry stare. **6** a dazzling light or brilliance. **7** garish ornamentation or appearance. [C13: prob. from MLow G, MDu. *glaren* to gleam]

glaring ➊ (ˈglɛərɪŋ) *adj* **1** conspicuous: *a glaring omission.* **2** dazzling or garish.
▸ **ˈglaringly** *adv* ▸ **ˈglaringness** *n*

glasnost (ˈglæsˌnɒst) *n* the policy of public frankness and accountability developed in the former Soviet Union under the leadership of Mikhail Gorbachov. [C20: Russian, lit.: publicity, openness]

glass (glɑːs) *n* **1a** a hard brittle transparent or translucent noncrystalline solid, consisting of metal silicates or similar compounds. It is made from a fused mixture of oxides, such as lime, silicon dioxide, phosphorus pentoxide, etc. **1b** (*as modifier*): *a glass bottle.* Related adj: **vitreous. 2** something made of glass, esp. a drinking vessel, a barometer, or a mirror. **3** Also called: **glassful.** the amount or volume contained in a drinking glass: *he drank a glass of wine.* **4** glassware collectively. **5** See **fibreglass.** ◆ *vb* **6** (*tr*) to cover with, enclose in, or fit with glass. [OE *glæs*]
▸ **ˈglassless** *adj* ▸ **ˈglassˌlike** *adj*

glass-blowing *n* the process of shaping a mass of molten glass by blowing air into it through a tube.
▸ **ˈglass-ˌblower** *n*

glass ceiling *n* a situation in which progress, esp. promotion, appears to be possible but restrictions or discrimination create a barrier that prevents it.

glasses (ˈglɑːsɪz) *pl n* a pair of lenses for correcting faulty vision, in a frame that rests on the bridge of the nose and hooks behind the ears. Also called: **spectacles, eyeglasses.**

glass fibre *n* another name for **fibreglass.**

glass harmonica *n* a musical instrument of the 18th century consisting of a set of glass bowls of graduated pitches, played by rubbing the fingers over the moistened rims or by a keyboard mechanism. Sometimes shortened to **harmonica.** Also called: **musical glasses.**

glasshouse (ˈglɑːsˌhaʊs) *n* **1** *Brit.* a glass building, esp. a greenhouse, used for growing plants in protected or controlled conditions. **2** *Inf., chiefly Brit.* a military detention centre.

glassine (glæˈsiːn) *n* a glazed translucent paper.

glass snake *n* any snakelike lizard of Europe, Asia, or North America, with vestigial hind limbs and a tail that breaks off easily.

glassware (ˈglɑːsˌwɛə) *n* articles made of glass, esp. drinking glasses.

glass wool *n* fine spun glass massed into a wool-like bulk, used in insulation, filtering, etc.

glasswort (ˈglɑːsˌwɜːt) *n* **1** any plant of salt marshes having fleshy stems and scalelike leaves: formerly used as a source of soda for glass-making. **2** another name for **saltwort.**

glassy ➊ (ˈglɑːsɪ) *adj* **glassier, glassiest. 1** resembling glass, esp. in smoothness or transparency. **2** void of expression, life, or warmth: *a glassy stare.*
▸ **ˈglassily** *adv* ▸ **ˈglassiness** *n*

Glaswegian (glæzˈwiːdʒən) *adj* **1.** of or relating to Glasgow, a city in Scotland, or its inhabitants. ◆ *n* **2** a native or inhabitant of Glasgow. [C19: infl. by NORWEGIAN]

Glauber's salt (ˈglaʊbəz) *or* **Glauber salt** *n* the crystalline decahydrate of sodium sulphate: used in making glass, detergents, and pulp. [C18: after J. R. *Glauber* (1604–68), G chemist]

glaucoma (glɔːˈkəʊmə) *n* a disease of the eye in which increased pressure within the eyeball causes impaired vision, sometimes progressing to blindness. [C17: from L, from Gk, from *glaukos;* see GLAUCOUS]
▸ **glauˈcomatous** *adj*

glaucous (ˈglɔːkəs) *adj* **1** *Bot.* covered with a waxy or powdery bloom. **2** bluish-green. [C17: from L *glaucus* silvery, bluish-green, from Gk *glaukos*]

glaze ➊ (gleɪz) *vb* **glazes, glazing, glazed. 1** (*tr*) to fit or cover with glass. **2** (*tr*) *Ceramics.* to cover with a vitreous solution, rendering impervious to liquid. **3** (*tr*) to cover (foods) with a shiny coating by applying beaten egg, sugar, etc. **4** (*tr*) to make glossy or shiny. **5** (when *intr*, often foll. by *over*) to become or cause to become glassy: *his eyes were glazing over.* ◆ *n* **6** *Ceramics.* **6a** a vitreous coating. **6b** the substance used to produce such a coating. **7** a smooth lustrous finish on a fabric produced by applying various chemicals. **8** something used to give a glossy surface to foods: *a syrup glaze.* [C14 *glasen*, from *glas* GLASS]
▸ **glazed** *adj* ▸ **ˈglazer** *n*

glaze ice *n Brit.* a thin clear layer of ice caused by the freezing of rain in the air or by refreezing after a thaw.

glazier (ˈgleɪzɪə) *n* a person who fits windows, doors, etc., with glass.
▸ **ˈglaziery** *n*

glazing (ˈgleɪzɪŋ) *n* **1** the surface of a glazed object. **2** glass fitted, or to be fitted, in a door, frame, etc.

GLC *abbrev. for* Greater London Council; abolished 1986.

gleam ➊ (gliːm) *n* **1** a small beam or glow of light, esp. reflected light. **2** a brief or dim indication: *a gleam of hope.* ◆ *vb* (*intr*) **3** to send forth or reflect a beam of light. **4** to appear, esp. briefly. [OE *glǣm*]
▸ **ˈgleaming** *adj* ▸ **ˈgleamingly** *adv* ▸ **ˈgleamy** *adj*

glean ➊ (gliːn) *vb* **1** to gather (something) slowly and carefully in small pieces: *to glean information.* **2** to gather (the useful remnants of a crop) from the field after harvesting. [C14: from OF *glener*, from LL *glennāre*, prob. of Celtic origin]
▸ **ˈgleaner** *n*

gleanings (ˈgliːnɪŋz) *pl n* the useful remnants of a crop that can be gathered from the field after harvesting.

glebe (gliːb) *n* **1** *Brit.* land granted to a clergyman as part of his benefice. **2** *Poetic.* land, esp. for growing things. [C14: from L *glaeba*]

glee ➊ (gliː) *n* **1** great merriment or delight, often caused by someone else's misfortune. **2** a type of song originating in 18th-century England, sung by three or more unaccompanied voices. [OE *gléo*]

glee club *n Now chiefly US & Canad.* a society organized for the singing of choral music.

gleeful ➊ (ˈgliːfʊl) *adj* full of glee; merry.
▸ **ˈgleefully** *adv* ▸ **ˈgleefulness** *n*

gleeman (ˈgliːmən) *n, pl* **gleemen.** *Obs.* a minstrel.

glen (glɛn) *n* a narrow and deep mountain valley, esp. in Scotland or Ireland. [C15: from Scot. Gaelic *gleann*, from OIrish *glend*]

glengarry (glɛnˈgærɪ) *n, pl* **glengarries.** a brimless Scottish cap with a crease down the crown, often with ribbons at the back. Also called: **glengarry bonnet.** [C19: after *Glengarry*, Scotland]

glia (ˈgliːə) *n* the delicate web of connective tissue that surrounds and supports nerve cells. Also called: **neuroglia.**
▸ **ˈglial** *adj*

glib ➊ (glɪb) *adj* **glibber, glibbest.** fluent and easy, often in an insincere or deceptive way. [C16: prob. from MLow G *glibberich* slippery]
▸ **ˈglibly** *adv* ▸ **ˈglibness** *n*

glide ➊ (glaɪd) *vb* **glides, gliding, glided. 1** to move or cause to move easily without jerks or hesitations. **2** (*intr*) to pass slowly or without perceptible change: *to glide into sleep.* **3** to cause (an aircraft) to come into land without engine power, or (of an aircraft) to land in this way. **4** (*intr*) to fly a glider. **5** (*intr*) *Music.* to execute a portamento from one note to another. **6** (*intr*) *Phonetics.* to produce a glide. ◆ *n* **7** a smooth easy movement. **8a** any of various dances featuring gliding steps. **8b** a step in such a dance. **9** a manoeuvre in which an aircraft makes a gen-

THESAURUS

glare *vb* **1** = **scowl**, frown, give a dirty look, glower, look daggers, lour *or* lower, stare angrily **3** = **dazzle**, blaze, flame, flare ◆ *n* **5** = **scowl**, angry stare, black look, dirty look, frown, glower, lour *or* lower **6** = **dazzle**, blaze, brilliance, flame, flare, glow

glaring *adj* **1** = **conspicuous**, audacious, blatant, egregious, flagrant, gross, manifest, obvious, open, outrageous, outstanding, overt, patent, rank, unconcealed, visible **2** = **dazzling**, blazing, bright, flashy, florid, garish, glowing, loud
Antonyms *adj* ≠ **conspicuous:** concealed, hidden, inconspicuous, obscure ≠ **dazzling:** soft, subdued, subtle

glassy *adj* **1** = **transparent**, clear, glossy, icy, shiny, slick, slippery, smooth **2** = **expressionless**, blank, cold, dazed, dull, empty, fixed, glazed, lifeless, vacant

glaze *vb* **2** = **coat**, burnish, enamel, furbish, gloss, lacquer, polish, varnish ◆ *n* **6a** = **coat**, enamel, finish, gloss, lacquer, lustre, patina, polish, shine, varnish

gleam *n* **1** = **glow**, beam, flash, glimmer, ray, sparkle **2** = **trace**, flicker, glimmer, hint, inkling, ray, suggestion ◆ *vb* **3** = **shine**, coruscate, flare, flash, glance, glimmer, glint, glisten, glitter, glow, scintillate, shimmer, sparkle

gleaming *adj* **3** = **bright**, bright as a button, brilliant, burnished, catching the light, glimmering, glistening, glowing, lustrous, scintillating, shining, sparkling
Antonyms *adj* dull, lustreless, unpolished

glean *vb* **1, 2** = **gather**, accumulate, amass, collect, cull, garner, harvest, learn, pick, pick up, reap, select

glee *n* **1** = **delight**, cheerfulness, elation, exhilaration, exuberance, exultation, fun, gaiety, gladness, hilarity, jocularity, jollity, joviality, joy, joyfulness, joyousness, liveliness, merriment, mirth, sprightliness, triumph, verve
Antonyms *n* depression, gloom, melancholy, misery, sadness

gleeful *adj* = **delighted**, cheerful, chirpy, cock-a-hoop, elated, exuberant, exultant, gay, gratified, happy, jocund, jovial, joyful, joyous, jubilant, merry, mirthful, overjoyed, over the moon (*inf.*), pleased, rapt, triumphant

glib *adj* = **smooth**, artful, easy, fast-talking, fluent, garrulous, insincere, plausible, quick, ready, slick, slippery, smooth-tongued, suave, talkative, voluble
Antonyms *adj* halting, hesitant, implausible, sincere, tongue-tied

glibness *n* = **smoothness**, fluency, gift of the gab, patter, plausibility, readiness, slickness

glide *vb* **1** = **slide**, coast, drift, float, flow, fly, roll, run, sail, skate, skim, slip, soar

tle descent without engine power. **10** the act or process of gliding. **11** *Music.* a portamento or slur. **12** *Phonetics.* a transitional sound as the speech organs pass from the articulatory position of one speech sound to that of the next. [OE *glīdan*]
▸ **'glidingly** *adv*

glide path *n* the path of an aircraft as it descends to land.

glider ('glaɪdə) *n* **1** an aircraft capable of gliding and soaring in air currents without the use of an engine. **2** a person or thing that glides.

glide time *n* the NZ term for **flexitime.**

glimmer ❶ ('glɪmə) *vb* (*intr*) **1** (of a light) to glow faintly or flickeringly. **2** to be indicated faintly: *hope glimmered in his face.* ◆ *n* **3** a glow or twinkle of light. **4** a faint indication. [C14: cf. MHG *glimmern*]
▸ **'glimmeringly** *adv*

glimpse ❶ (glɪmps) *n* **1** a brief or incomplete view: *to catch a glimpse of the sea.* **2** a vague indication. **3** *Arch.* a glimmer of light. ◆ *vb* **glimpses, glimpsing, glimpsed. 4** (*tr*) to catch sight of momentarily. [C14: of Gmc origin; cf. MHG *glimsen* to glimmer]
▸ **'glimpser** *n*

USAGE NOTE *Glimpse* is sometimes wrongly used where *glance* is meant: *he gave a quick glance* (not *glimpse*) *at his watch.*

glint ❶ (glɪnt) *vb* **1** to gleam or cause to gleam brightly. ◆ *n* **2** a bright gleam or flash. **3** brightness or gloss. **4** a brief indication. [C15: prob. from ON]

glioma (glaɪ'əʊmə) *n, pl* **gliomata** (-mətə) *or* **gliomas.** a tumour of the brain and spinal cord, composed of glia cells and fibres. [C19: from NL, from Gk *glia* glue + -OMA]

glissade (glɪ'sɑːd, -'seɪd) *n* **1** a gliding step in ballet. **2** a controlled slide down a snow slope. ◆ *vb* **glissades, glissading, glissaded. 3** (*intr*) to perform a glissade. [C19: from F, from *glisser* to slip, from OF *glicier,* of Frankish origin]

glissando (glɪ'sændəʊ) *n, pl* **glissandi** (-diː) *or* **glissandos.** a rapidly executed series of notes, each of which is discretely audible. [C19: prob. It. var. of GLISSADE]

glisten ❶ ('glɪsᵊn) *vb* (*intr*) **1** (of a wet or glossy surface) to gleam by reflecting light. **2** (of light) to reflect with brightness: *the sunlight glistens on wet leaves.* ◆ *n* **3** *Rare.* a gleam or gloss. [OE *glisnian*]

glister ('glɪstə) *vb, n* an archaic word for **glitter.** [C14: prob. from MDu. *glisteren*]

glitch ❶ (glɪtʃ) *n* **1** a sudden instance of malfunctioning in an electronic system. **2** a change in the rotation rate of a pulsar. [C20: from ?]

glitter ❶ ('glɪtə) *vb* (*intr*) **1** (of a hard, wet, or polished surface) to reflect light in bright flashes. **2** (of light) to be reflected in bright flashes. **3** (usually foll. by *with*) to be decorated or enhanced by the glamour (of): *the show glitters with famous actors.* ◆ *n* **4** sparkle or brilliance. **5** show and glamour. **6** tiny pieces of shiny decorative material. **7** *Canad.* Also called: **silver thaw.** ice formed from freezing rain. [C14: from ON *glitra*]
▸ **'glitteringly** *adv* ▸ **'glittery** *adj*

glitterati (ˌglɪtə'rɑːtiː) *pl n Inf.* the leaders of society, esp. the rich and beautiful. [C20: from GLITTER + *-ati* as in LITERATI]

glitzy ('glɪtsɪ) *adj* **glitzier, glitziest.** *Sl.* showily attractive; flashy or glittery. [C20: prob. via Yiddish from G *glitzern* to glitter]

gloaming ❶ ('gləʊmɪŋ) *n Scot. or poetic.* twilight or dusk. [OE *glōmung,* from *glōm*]

gloat ❶ (gləʊt) *vb* **1** (*intr;* often foll. by *over*) to dwell (on) with malevolent smugness or exultation. ◆ *n* **2** the act of gloating. [C16: prob. of Scand. origin; cf. ON *glotta* to grin, MHG *glotzen* to stare]
▸ **'gloater** *n*

glob (glɒb) *n Inf.* a rounded mass of some thick fluid substance. [C20: prob. from GLOBE, infl. by BLOB]

global ❶ ('gləʊbᵊl) *adj* **1** covering or relating to the whole world. **2** comprehensive; total.
▸ **'globally** *adv*

globalization *or* **globalisation** (ˌgləʊbᵊlaɪ'zeɪʃən) *n* **1** the process enabling financial and investment markets to operate internationally, largely as a result of deregulation and improved communications. **2** the process by which a company, etc., expands to operate internationally.

globalize *or* **globalise** ('gləʊbᵊˌlaɪz) *vb* **globalizes, globalizing, globalized** *or* **globalises, globalising, globalised.** (*tr*) to put into effect or spread worldwide.

global product *n* a commercial product, such as Coca Cola, that is marketed throughout the world under the same brand name.

global warming *n* an increase in the average temperature worldwide believed to be caused by the greenhouse effect.

globe ❶ (gləʊb) *n* **1** a sphere on which a map of the world is drawn. **2** **the globe.** the world; the earth. **3** a planet or some other astronomical body. **4** an object shaped like a sphere, such as a glass lampshade or fishbowl. **5** an orb, usually of gold, symbolic of sovereignty. ◆ *vb* **globes, globing, globed. 6** to form or cause to form into a globe. [C16: from OF, from L *globus*]
▸ **'globeˌlike** *adj*

globefish ('gləʊbˌfɪʃ) *n, pl* **globefish** *or* **globefishes.** another name for **puffer.**

globeflower ('gləʊbˌflaʊə) *n* a plant having pale yellow, white, or orange globe-shaped flowers.

globetrotter ('gləʊbˌtrɒtə) *n* a habitual worldwide traveller, esp. a tourist.
▸ **'globeˌtrotting** *n, adj*

globigerina (gləʊˌbɪdʒə'raɪnə) *n, pl* **globigerinas** *or* **globigerinae** (-niː). **1** a marine protozoan having a rounded shell with spiny processes. **2** **globigerina ooze.** a deposit on the ocean floor consisting of the shells of these protozoans. [C19: from NL, from L *globus* GLOBE + *gerere* to bear]

globoid ('gləʊbɔɪd) *adj* **1** shaped like a globe. ◆ *n* **2** a globoid body.

globose ('gləʊbəʊs, gləʊ'bəʊs) *or* **globous** ('gləʊbəs) *adj* spherical or approximately spherical. [C15: from L *globōsus;* see GLOBE]
▸ **'globosely** *adv*

globular ❶ ('glɒbjʊlə) *or* **globulous** *adj* **1** shaped like a globe or globule. **2** having or consisting of globules.

globule ❶ ('glɒbjuːl) *n* a small globe, esp. a drop of liquid. [C17: from L *globulus,* dim. of *globus* GLOBE]

globulin ('glɒbjʊlɪn) *n* any of a group of simple proteins that are generally insoluble in water but soluble in salt solutions.

glockenspiel ('glɒkənˌspiːl, -ˌʃpiːl) *n* a percussion instrument consisting of a set of tuned metal plates played with a pair of small hammers. [C19: G, from *Glocken* bells + *Spiel* play]

glomerate ('glɒmərɪt) *adj* **1** gathered into a compact rounded mass. **2** *Anat.* (esp. of glands) conglomerate in structure. [C18: from L *glomerāre,* from *glomus* ball]
▸ **ˌglome'ration** *n*

glomerule ('glɒməˌruːl) *n Bot.* an inflorescence in the form of a ball-like cluster of flowers. [C18: from NL *glomerulus*]

gloom ❶ (gluːm) *n* **1** partial or total darkness. **2** a state of depression or melancholy. **3** an appearance or expression of despondency or melancholy. **4** *Poetic.* a dim or dark place. ◆ *vb* **5** (*intr*) to look sullen or depressed. **6** to make or become dark or gloomy. [C14 *gloumben* to look sullen]

gloomy ❶ ('gluːmɪ) *adj* **gloomier, gloomiest. 1** dark or dismal. **2** causing depression or gloom: *gloomy news.* **3** despairing; sad.
▸ **'gloomily** *adv* ▸ **'gloominess** *n*

gloop (gluːp) *or esp. US* **glop** (glɒp) *n Inf.* any messy sticky fluid or substance. [C20: from ?]
▸ **'gloopy** *or esp. US* **'gloppy** *adj*

THESAURUS

glimmer *vb* **1** = **flicker,** blink, gleam, glisten, glitter, glow, shimmer, shine, sparkle, twinkle ◆ *n* **3** = **gleam,** blink, flicker, glow, ray, shimmer, sparkle, twinkle **4** = **trace,** flicker, gleam, grain, hint, inkling, ray, suggestion

glimpse *n* **1** = **look,** brief view, butcher's (*Brit. sl.*), gander (*inf.*), glance, peek, peep, quick look, shufti (*Brit. sl.*), sight, sighting, squint ◆ *vb* **4** = **catch sight of,** clock (*Brit. inf.*), descry, espy, sight, spot, spy, view

glint *vb* **1** = **gleam,** flash, glimmer, glitter, shine, sparkle, twinkle ◆ *n* **2** = **gleam,** flash, glimmer, glitter, shine, sparkle, twinkle, twinkling

glisten *vb* **1, 2** = **gleam,** coruscate, flash, glance, glare, glimmer, glint, glitter, scintillate, shimmer, shine, sparkle, twinkle

glitch *n* **1** = **problem,** blip, bug (*inf.*), difficulty, fault, flaw, fly in the ointment, gremlin, hitch, interruption, kink, malfunction, snag

glitter *vb* **1, 2** = **shine,** coruscate, flare, flash, glare, gleam, glimmer, glint, glisten, scintillate, shimmer, sparkle, twinkle ◆ *n* **4** = **shine,** beam, brightness, brilliance, flash, glare, gleam, lustre, radiance, scintillation, sheen, shimmer, sparkle **5** = **glamour,** display, gaudiness, gilt, pageantry, show, showiness, splendour, tinsel

gloaming *n* = **twilight,** dusk, eventide (*arch.*), half-light, nightfall

gloat *vb* **1** = **relish,** crow, drool, exult, glory, revel in, rub it in (*inf.*), rub one's hands, rub someone's nose in it, triumph, vaunt

global *adj* **1** = **worldwide,** international, pandemic, planetary, universal, world **2** = **comprehensive,** all-encompassing, all-inclusive, all-out, encyclopedic, exhaustive, general, thorough, total, unbounded, unlimited
Antonyms *adj* ≠ **comprehensive:** limited, narrow, parochial, restricted, sectional

globe *n* **2** = **earth,** planet, world **4** = **sphere,** ball, orb, round

globular *adj* **1** = **spherical,** globate, globelike, globoid, globose, globous, globulous, orbicular, round, spheroid

globule *n* = **droplet,** bead, bubble, drop, particle, pearl, pellet

gloom *n* **1** = **darkness,** blackness, cloud, cloudiness, dark, dimness, dullness, dusk, duskiness, gloominess, murk, murkiness, obscurity, shade, shadow, twilight **2** = **depression,** blues, dejection, desolation, despair, despondency, downheartedness, low spirits, melancholy, misery, sadness, sorrow, the hump (*Brit. inf.*), unhappiness, woe
Antonyms *n* ≠ **darkness:** daylight, light, radiance ≠ **depression:** brightness, cheerfulness, delight, happiness, high spirits, jollity, joy, mirth

gloomy *adj* **1** = **dark,** black, crepuscular, dim, dismal, dreary, dull, dusky, grey, murky, obscure, overcast, shadowy, sombre, Stygian, tenebrous **2** = **depressing,** bad, black, cheerless, comfortless, disheartening, dismal, dispiriting, dreary, funereal, joyless, sad, saddening, sombre **3** = **miserable,** blue, chapfallen, cheerless, crestfallen, dejected, despondent, dismal, dispirited, down, downcast, downhearted, down in the dumps (*inf.*), down in the mouth, glum, in low spirits, low, melancholy, moody, morose, pessimistic, sad, saturnine, sullen
Antonyms *adj* ≠ **dark:** brilliant, light, radiant, sunny ≠ **miserable:** blithe, bright, cheerful, chirpy (*inf.*), happy, high-spirited, jolly, jovial, light, merry, upbeat (*inf.*)

gloria ('glɔːrɪə) *n* a halo or nimbus, esp. as represented in art. [C16: from L: GLORY]

Gloria ('glɔːrɪə, -ˌɑː) *n* **1** any of several doxologies beginning with the word *Gloria*. **2** a musical setting of one of these.

glorify ➊ ('glɔːrɪˌfaɪ) *vb* **glorifies, glorifying, glorified.** (*tr*) **1** to make glorious. **2** to make more splendid; adorn. **3** to worship, exalt, or adore. **4** to extol. **5** to cause to seem more splendid or imposing than reality.
▸**ˌglorifi'cation** *n*

gloriole ('glɔːrɪˌəʊl) *n* another name for a **halo.** [C19: from L *glōriola*, lit.: a small GLORY]

glorious ➊ ('glɔːrɪəs) *adj* **1** having or full of glory; illustrious. **2** conferring glory or renown: *a glorious victory.* **3** brilliantly beautiful. **4** delightful or enjoyable.
▸**'gloriously** *adv* ▸**'gloriousness** *n*

glory ➊ ('glɔːrɪ) *n, pl* **glories. 1** exaltation, praise, or honour. **2** something that brings or is worthy of praise (esp. in **crowning glory**). **3** thanksgiving, adoration, or worship: *glory be to God.* **4** pomp; splendour: *the glory of the king's reign.* **5** radiant beauty; resplendence: *the glory of the sunset.* **6** the beauty and bliss of heaven. **7** a state of extreme happiness or prosperity. **8** another word for **halo** or **nimbus.** ◆ *vb* **glories, glorying, gloried. 9** (*intr;* often foll. by *in*) to triumph or exalt. ◆ *interj* **10** *Inf.* a mild interjection to express pleasure or surprise (often **glory be!**). [C13: from OF *glorie*, from L *glōria*, from ?]

glory box *n Austral. & NZ.* (esp. formerly) a box in which a young woman stores clothes, etc., in preparation for marriage.

glory hole *n* **1** a cupboard or storeroom, esp. one which is very untidy. **2** *Naut.* another term for **lazaretto** (sense 1).

Glos *abbrev. for* Gloucestershire.

gloss[1] ➊ (glɒs) *n* **1a** lustre or sheen, as of a smooth surface. **1b** (*as modifier*): *gloss paint.* **2** a superficially attractive appearance. **3** a cosmetic used to give a sheen. ◆ *vb* **4** to give a gloss to or obtain a gloss. **5** (*tr;* often foll. by *over*) to hide under a deceptively attractive surface or appearance. [C16: prob. of Scand. origin]
▸**'glosser** *n*

gloss[2] ➊ (glɒs) *n* **1** a short or expanded explanation or interpretation of a word, expression, or foreign phrase in the margin or text of a manuscript, etc. **2** an intentionally misleading explanation. **3** short for **glossary.** ◆ *vb* (*tr*) **4** to add glosses to. **5** (often foll. by *over*) to give a false or misleading interpretation of. [C16: from L *glōssa* unusual word requiring explanatory note, from Ionic Gk]

glossary ('glɒsərɪ) *n, pl* **glossaries.** an alphabetical list of terms peculiar to a field of knowledge with explanations. [C14: from LL *glossārium;* see GLOSS[2]]
▸**glossarial** (glɒ'sɛərɪəl) *adj* ▸**'glossarist** *n*

glosseme ('glɒsiːm) *n* the smallest meaningful unit of a language, such as stress, form, etc. [C20: from Gk; see GLOSS[2], -EME]

glossitis (glɒ'saɪtɪs) *n* inflammation of the tongue.
▸**glossitic** (glɒ'sɪtɪk) *adj*

glosso- *or before a vowel* **gloss-** *combining form.* indicating a tongue or language: *glossolaryngeal.* [from Gk *glossa* tongue]

glossolalia (ˌglɒsə'leɪlɪə) *n* another term for **gift of tongues.** [C19: NL, from GLOSSO- + Gk *lalein* to babble]

glossy ➊ ('glɒsɪ) *adj* **glossier, glossiest. 1** smooth and shiny; lustrous. **2** superficially attractive; plausible. **3** (of a magazine) lavishly produced on shiny paper. ◆ *n, pl* **glossies. 4** Also called (US): **slick.** an expensively produced magazine, printed on shiny paper and containing high-quality colour photography. **5** a photograph printed on paper that has a smooth shiny surface.
▸**'glossily** *adv* ▸**'glossiness** *n*

glottal ('glɒtᵊl) *adj* **1** of or relating to the glottis. **2** *Phonetics.* articulated or pronounced at or with the glottis.

glottal stop *n* a plosive speech sound produced by tightly closing the glottis and allowing the air pressure to build up before opening the glottis, causing the air to escape with force.

glottis ('glɒtɪs) *n, pl* **glottises** *or* **glottides** (-tɪˌdiːz). the vocal apparatus of the larynx, consisting of the two true vocal cords and the opening between them. [C16: from NL, from Gk, from Attic form of Ionic *glōssa* tongue; see GLOSS[2]]

glove (glʌv) *n* **1** (*often pl*) a shaped covering for the hand with individual sheaths for the fingers and thumb, made of leather, fabric, etc. **2** any of various large protective hand covers worn in sports, such as a boxing glove. ◆ *vb* **gloves, gloving, gloved. 3** (*tr*) to cover or provide with or as if with gloves. [OE *glōfe*]

glove box *n* a closed box in which toxic or radioactive substances can be handled by an operator who places his hands through protective gloves sealed to the box.

glove compartment *n* a small compartment in a car dashboard for the storage of miscellaneous articles.

glover ('glʌvə) *n* a person who makes or sells gloves.

glow ➊ (gləʊ) *n* **1** light emitted by a substance or object at a high temperature. **2** a steady even light without flames. **3** brilliance of colour. **4** brightness of complexion. **5** a feeling of wellbeing or satisfaction. **6** intensity of emotion. ◆ *vb* (*intr*) **7** to emit a steady even light without flames. **8** to shine intensely, as if from great heat. **9** to be exuberant, as from excellent health or intense emotion. **10** to experience a feeling of wellbeing or satisfaction: *to glow with pride.* **11** (esp. of the complexion) to show a strong bright colour, esp. red. **12** to be very hot. [OE *glōwan*]

glow discharge *n* a silent luminous discharge of electricity through a low-pressure gas.

glower ➊ ('glaʊə) *vb* **1** (*intr*) to stare hard and angrily. ◆ *n* **2** a sullen or angry stare. [C16: prob. of Scand. origin]
▸**'gloweringly** *adv*

glowing ➊ ('gləʊɪŋ) *adj* **1** emitting light without flames: *glowing embers.* **2** warm and rich in colour: *glowing shades of gold and orange.* **3** flushed and rosy: *glowing cheeks.* **4** displaying or indicative of extreme pride or emotion: *a glowing account of his son's achievements.*

glow-worm *n* a European beetle, the females and larvae of which bear luminescent organs producing a soft greenish light.

gloxinia (glɒk'sɪnɪə) *n* any of several tropical plants cultivated for their large white, red, or purple bell-shaped flowers. [C19: after Benjamin P. *Gloxin*, 18th-cent. G physician & botanist]

gloze (gləʊz) *vb* **glozes, glozing, glozed.** *Arch.* **1** (*tr;* often foll. by *over*) to explain away; minimize the effect or importance of. **2** to make explanatory notes or glosses on (a text). **3** to use flattery (on). [C13: from OF *glosser* to comment; see GLOSS[2]]

glucose ('gluːkəʊz, -kəʊs) *n* **1** a white crystalline sugar, the most abundant form being dextrose. Formula: $C_6H_{12}O_6$. **2** a yellowish syrup obtained by incomplete hydrolysis of starch: used in confectionery, fermentation, etc. [C19: from F, from Gk *gleukos* sweet wine; rel. to Gk *glukus* sweet]

glucoside ('gluːkəʊˌsaɪd) *n Biochem.* any of a large group of glycosides that yield glucose on hydrolysis.
▸**glucosidic** (ˌgluːkəʊ'sɪdɪk) *adj*

glue ➊ (gluː) *n* **1** any natural or synthetic adhesive, esp. a sticky gelatinous substance prepared by boiling animal products such as bones, skin, and horns. **2** any other sticky or adhesive substance. ◆ *vb* **glues,**

THESAURUS

glorify *vb* **2** = **enhance**, add lustre to, adorn, aggrandize, augment, dignify, elevate, ennoble, illuminate, immortalize, lift up, magnify, raise **3** = **worship**, adore, apotheosize, beatify, bless, canonize, deify, enshrine, exalt, honour, idolize, pay homage to, revere, sanctify, venerate **4** = **praise**, celebrate, crack up (*inf.*), cry up (*inf.*), eulogize, extol, hymn, laud, lionize, magnify, panegyrize, sing *or* sound the praises of
Antonyms *vb* ≠ **enhance:** debase, defile, degrade ≠ **worship:** desecrate, dishonour ≠ **praise:** condemn, humiliate, mock

glorious *adj* **1** = **famous**, celebrated, distinguished, elevated, eminent, excellent, famed, grand, honoured, illustrious, magnificent, majestic, noble, noted, renowned, sublime, triumphant **3** = **splendid**, beautiful, bright, brilliant, dazzling, divine, effulgent, gorgeous, radiant, resplendent, shining, splendiferous (*facetious*), superb **4** = **delightful**, enjoyable, excellent, fine, gorgeous, great, heavenly (*inf.*), marvellous, pleasurable, splendid, splendiferous (*facetious*), wonderful
Antonyms *adj* ≠ **famous:** minor, ordinary, trivial, unimportant, unknown ≠ **splendid, delightful:** awful, dreary, dull, gloomy, horrible, unimpressive, unpleasant

glory *n* **1** = **honour**, celebrity, dignity, distinction, eminence, exaltation, fame, illustriousness, immortality, kudos, praise, prestige, renown **3** = **worship**, adoration, benediction, blessing, gratitude, homage, laudation, praise, thanksgiving, veneration **4** = **splendour**, éclat, grandeur, greatness, magnificence, majesty, nobility, pageantry, pomp, sublimity, triumph **5** = **beauty**, brilliance, effulgence, gorgeousness, lustre, radiance, resplendence ◆ *vb* **9** = **triumph**, boast, crow, drool, exult, gloat, pride oneself, relish, revel, take delight
Antonyms *n* ≠ **honour:** condemnation, disgrace, dishonour, disrepute, infamy, shame ≠ **worship:** blasphemy ≠ **splendour:** triviality ≠ **beauty:** ugliness

gloss[1] *n* **1** = **shine**, brightness, brilliance, burnish, gleam, lustre, patina, polish, sheen, varnish, veneer **2** = **façade**, appearance, front, mask, semblance, show, surface ◆ *vb* **4** = **glaze**, burnish, finish, furbish, lacquer, polish, shine, varnish, veneer **5** *with* **over** = **conceal**, camouflage, cover up, disguise, hide, mask, smooth over, sweep under the carpet (*inf.*), veil, whitewash (*inf.*)

gloss[2] *n* **1** = **comment**, annotation, commentary, elucidation, explanation, footnote, interpretation, note, scholium, translation ◆ *vb* **4** = **interpret**, annotate, comment, construe, elucidate, explain, translate

glossy *adj* **1** = **shiny**, bright, brilliant, burnished, glassy, glazed, lustrous, polished, sheeny, shining, silken, silky, sleek, smooth
Antonyms *adj* drab, dull, mat *or* matt, subfusc

glow *n* **1** = **light**, burning, gleam, glimmer, incandescence, lambency, luminosity, phosphorescence **3** = **radiance**, brightness, brilliance, effulgence, splendour, vividness **4** = **blush**, bloom, flush, reddening, rosiness **6** = **passion**, ardour, earnestness, enthusiasm, excitement, fervour, gusto, impetuosity, intensity, vehemence, warmth ◆ *vb* **7** = **shine**, brighten, burn, gleam, glimmer, redden, smoulder **10, 11** = **blush**, be suffused, colour, fill, flush, radiate, thrill, tingle
Antonyms *n* ≠ **radiance:** dullness, greyness ≠ **blush:** paleness, pallor, wanness ≠ **passion:** chill, coolness, half-heartedness, iciness, indifference

glower *vb* **1** = **scowl**, frown, give a dirty look, glare, look daggers, lour *or* lower ◆ *n* **2** = **scowl**, angry stare, black look, dirty look, frown, glare, lour *or* lower

glowing *adj* **1** = **bright**, aglow, beaming, flaming, florid, flushed, lambent, luminous, radiant, red, rich, ruddy, suffused, vibrant, vivid, warm **4** = **complimentary**, adulatory, ecstatic, enthusiastic, eulogistic, laudatory, panegyrical, rave (*inf.*), rhapsodic
Antonyms *adj* ≠ **bright:** colourless, cool, dull, grey, pale, pallid, wan ≠ **complimentary:** cruel, dispassionate, scathing, unenthusiastic

glue *n* **1, 2** = **adhesive**, cement, gum, mucilage, paste ◆ *vb* **3** = **stick**, affix, agglutinate, cement, fix, gum, paste, seal

gluing *or* **glueing, glued. 3** (*tr*) to join or stick together as with glue. [C14: from OF *glu,* from LL *glūs*]
▸'**glue,like** *adj* ▸'**gluer** *n* ▸'**gluey** *adj*

glue ear *n* accumulation of fluid in the middle ear in children, caused by infection and resulting in deafness.

glue-sniffing *n* the practice of inhaling the fumes of certain types of glue to produce intoxicating or hallucinatory effects.
▸'**glue-,sniffer** *n*

gluhwein ('gluː,vaɪn) *n* mulled wine. [G]

glum Ⓣ (glʌm) *adj* **glummer, glummest.** silent or sullen, as from gloom. [C16: var. of GLOOM]
▸'**glumly** *adv* ▸'**glumness** *n*

glume (gluːm) *n Bot.* one of a pair of dry membranous bracts at the base of the spikelet of grasses. [C18: from L *glūma* husk of corn]
▸**glu'maceous** *adj*

gluon ('gluːɒn) *n* a hypothetical particle believed to be exchanged between quarks in order to bind them together to form particles. [C20: coined from GLUE + -ON]

glut Ⓣ (glʌt) *n* **1** an excessive amount, as in the production of a crop. **2** the act of glutting or state of being glutted. ◆ *vb* **gluts, glutting, glutted.** (*tr*) **3** to feed or supply beyond capacity. **4** to supply (a market, etc.) with a commodity in excess of the demand for it. [C14: prob. from OF *gloutir,* from L *gluttīre;* see GLUTTON[1]]

glutamic acid (gluː'tæmɪk) *n* an amino acid, occurring in proteins.

gluten ('gluːtᵊn) *n* a protein present in cereal grains, esp. wheat. [C16: from L: GLUE]
▸'**glutenous** *adj*

gluteus (glʊ'tiːəs) *n, pl* **glutei** (-'tiːaɪ). any one of the three large muscles that form the human buttock. [C17: from NL, from Gk *gloutos* buttock, rump]
▸**glu'teal** *adj*

glutinous Ⓣ ('gluːtɪnəs) *adj* resembling glue in texture; sticky.
▸'**glutinously** *adv*

glutton[1] Ⓣ ('glʌtᵊn) *n* **1** a person devoted to eating and drinking to excess; greedy person. **2** a person who has or appears to have a voracious appetite for something: *a glutton for punishment.* [C13: from OF *glouton,* from L from *gluttīre* to swallow]
▸'**gluttonous** *adj* ▸'**gluttonously** *adv*

glutton[2] ('glʌtᵊn) *n* another name for **wolverine.** [C17: from GLUTTON[1], apparently translating G *Vielfrass* great eater]

gluttony Ⓣ ('glʌtənɪ) *n* the act or practice of eating to excess.

glyceride ('glɪsə,raɪd) *n* any fatty-acid ester of glycerol.

glycerine ('glɪsəriːn, ,glɪsə'riːn) *or* **glycerin** ('glɪsərɪn) *n* another name (not in technical usage) for **glycerol.** [C19: from F, from Gk *glukeros* sweet + *-ine* -IN; rel. to Gk *glukus* sweet]

glycerol ('glɪsə,rɒl) *n* a colourless odourless syrupy liquid: a by-product of soap manufacture, used as a solvent, antifreeze, plasticizer, and sweetener (**E422**). Formula: $CH_2OHCHOHCH_2OH$. [C19: from GLYCER(IN) + -OL[1]]

glycine ('glaɪsiːn, glaɪ'siːn) *n* a white sweet crystalline amino acid occurring in most proteins. [C19: GLYCO- + -INE[2]]

glyco- *or before a vowel* **glyc-** *combining form.* sugar: *glycogen.* [from Gk *glukus* sweet]

glycogen ('glaɪkəʊdʒən) *n* a polysaccharide consisting of glucose units: the form in which carbohydrate is stored in animals.
▸**glycogenic** (,glaɪkəʊ'dʒenɪk) *adj* ▸**,glyco'genesis** *n*

glycol ('glaɪkɒl) *n* another name (not in technical usage) for **ethanediol.**

glycolic acid (glaɪ'kɒlɪk) *n* a colourless crystalline compound found in sugar cane and sugar beet: used in the manufacture of pharmaceuticals, pesticides, and plasticizers.

glycolysis (glaɪ'kɒlɪsɪs) *n Biochem.* the breakdown of glucose by enzymes with the liberation of energy.

glycoside ('glaɪkəʊ,saɪd) *n* any of a group of substances derived from simple sugars by replacing the hydroxyl group by another group.
▸**glycosidic** (,glaɪkəʊ'sɪdɪk) *adj*

glycosuria (,glaɪkəʊ'sjʊərɪə) *n* the presence of excess sugar in the urine, as in diabetes. [C19: from NL, from F *glycose* GLUCOSE + -URIA]

glyph (glɪf) *n* **1** a carved channel or groove, esp. a vertical one. **2** *Now rare.* another word for **hieroglyphic.** [C18: from F, from Gk, from *gluphein* to carve]
▸'**glyphic** *adj*

glyptic ('glɪptɪk) *adj* of or relating to engraving or carving, esp. on precious stones. [C19: from F, from Gk, from *gluphein* to carve]

glyptodont ('glɪptə,dɒnt) *n* an extinct mammal of South America which resembled the giant armadillo. [C19: from Gk *gluptos* carved + -ODONT]

GM *abbrev. for:* **1** general manager. **2** genetically modified. **3** (in Britain) George Medal. **4** Grand Master. **5** grant-maintained.

G-man *n, pl* **G-men. 1** *US sl.* an FBI agent. **2** *Irish.* a political detective.

Gmc *abbrev. for* Germanic.

GMT *abbrev. for* Greenwich Mean Time.

GMWU (in Britain) *abbrev. for* National Union of General and Municipal Workers.

gnarl (nɑːl) *n* **1** any knotty swelling on a tree. ◆ *vb* **2** (*tr*) to knot or cause to knot. [C19: back formation from *gnarled*]

gnarled Ⓣ (nɑːld) *or* **gnarly** *adj* **1** having gnarls: *the gnarled trunk of the old tree.* **2** (esp. of hands) rough, twisted, and weather-beaten.

gnash (næʃ) *vb* **1** to grind (the teeth) together, as in pain or anger. **2** (*tr*) to bite or chew as by grinding the teeth. ◆ *n* **3** the act of gnashing the teeth. [C15: prob. from ON; cf. *gnastan* gnashing of teeth]

gnat (næt) *n* any of various small fragile biting two-winged insects. [OE *gnætt*]

gnathic ('næθɪk) *adj Anat.* of or relating to the jaw. [C19: from Gk *gnathos* jaw]

-gnathous *adj combining form.* indicating or having a jaw of a specified kind: *prognathous.* [from NL, from Gk *gnathos* jaw]

gnaw Ⓣ (nɔː) *vb* **gnaws, gnawing, gnawed; gnawed** *or* **gnawn. 1** (when *intr,* often foll. by *at* or *upon*) to bite (at) or chew (upon) constantly so as to wear away little by little. **2** (*tr*) to form by gnawing: *to gnaw a hole.* **3** to cause erosion of (something). **4** (when *intr,* often foll. by *at*) to cause constant distress or anxiety (to). ◆ *n* **5** the act or an instance of gnawing. [OE *gnagan*]

gnawing ('nɔːɪŋ) *n* a dull persistent pang or pain, esp. of hunger.

gneiss (naɪs) *n* any coarse-grained metamorphic rock that is banded or foliated. [C18: from G *Gneis,* prob. from MHG *ganeist* spark]
▸'**gneissic,** '**gneissoid,** *or* '**gneissose** *adj*

gnocchi ('nɒkɪ) *pl n* dumplings made of pieces of semolina pasta, or sometimes potato, served with sauce. [It., pl of *gnocco* lump, prob. of Gmc origin]

gnome (nəʊm) *n* **1** one of a species of legendary creatures, usually resembling small misshapen old men, said to live in the depths of the earth and guard buried treasure. **2** the statue of a gnome, esp. in a garden. **3** a very small or ugly person. **4** *Facetious or derog.* an international banker or financier (esp. in **gnomes of Zürich**). [C18: from F, from NL *gnomus,* coined by Paracelsus (1493-1541), Swiss alchemist, from ?]
▸'**gnomish** *adj*

gnomic ('nəʊmɪk, 'nɒm-) *adj* of or relating to aphorisms; pithy.
▸'**gnomically** *adv*

gnomon ('nəʊmɒn) *n* **1** the stationary arm that projects the shadow on a sundial. **2** a geometric figure remaining after a parallelogram has been removed from one corner of a larger parallelogram. [C16: from L, from Gk: interpreter, from *gignōskein* to know]
▸**gno'monic** *adj*

-gnosis *n combining form.* (esp. in medicine) recognition or knowledge: *diagnosis.* [via L from Gk: knowledge]
▸**-gnostic** *adj combining form.*

gnostic ('nɒstɪk) *adj* of, relating to, or possessing knowledge, esp. spiritual knowledge.

Gnostic ('nɒstɪk) *n* **1** an adherent of Gnosticism. ◆ *adj* **2** of or relating to Gnostics or to Gnosticism. [C16: from LL, from Gk *gnōstikos* relating to knowledge]

Gnosticism ('nɒstɪ,sɪzəm) *n* a religious movement characterized by a belief in intuitive spiritual knowledge: regarded as a heresy by the Christian Church.

gnotobiotic (,nəʊtəʊbaɪ'ɒtɪk) *adj* of or pertaining to germ-free conditions, esp. in a laboratory in which animals are injected with known strains of organisms. [C20: from Gk *gnōtos,* from *gignōskein* to know + BIOTIC]

GNP *abbrev. for* gross national product.

gnu (nuː) *n, pl* **gnus** *or* **gnu.** either of two sturdy antelopes inhabiting the savannas of Africa, having an oxlike head and a long tufted tail. Also called: **wildebeest.** [C18: from Xhosa *nqu*]

GNVQ (in Britain) *abbrev. for* general national vocational qualification: a qualification which rewards the development of skills likely to be of use to employers.

go Ⓣ (gəʊ) *vb* **goes, going, went, gone.** (*mainly intr*) **1** to move or proceed, esp. to or from a point or in a certain direction: *go home.* **2** (*tr; takes an infinitive,* often with *to* omitted or replaced by *and*) to proceed towards a particular person or place with some specified purpose: *I must go and*

THESAURUS

glum *adj* = **gloomy,** chapfallen, churlish, crabbed, crestfallen, crusty, dejected, doleful, down, gruff, grumpy, huffy, ill-humoured, low, moody, morose, pessimistic, saturnine, sour, sulky, sullen, surly
Antonyms *adj* cheerful, cheery, chirpy (*inf.*), jolly, joyful, merry, upbeat (*inf.*)

glut *n* **1** = **surfeit,** excess, overabundance, oversupply, plethora, saturation, superabundance, superfluity, surplus ◆ *vb* **3** = **overfeed,** cram, fill, gorge, satiate, stuff **4** = **saturate,** choke, clog, deluge, flood, inundate, overload, oversupply
Antonyms *n* ≠ **surfeit:** dearth, lack, paucity, scarcity, shortage, want

glutinous *adj* = **sticky,** adhesive, cohesive, gluey, gooey, gummy, mucilaginous, viscid, viscous

glutton[1] *n* **1** = **gourmand,** gannet (*sl.*), gobbler, gorger, gormandizer, pig (*inf.*)

gluttonous[1] *adj* **1** = **greedy,** edacious, gormandizing, hoggish, insatiable, piggish, rapacious, ravenous, voracious

gluttony *n* = **greed,** edacity, gormandizing, gourmandism, greediness, piggishness, rapacity, voraciousness, voracity

gnarled *adj* **1, 2** = **twisted,** contorted, knotted, knotty, knurled, leathery, rough, rugged, weather-beaten, wrinkled

gnaw *vb* **1** = **bite,** chew, munch, nibble **3** = **erode,** consume, devour, eat away *or* into, fret, wear away *or* down **4** = **distress,** fret, harry, haunt, nag, plague, prey on one's mind, trouble, worry

go *vb* **1** = **move,** advance, fare (*arch.*), journey, make for, pass, proceed, repair, set off, travel **3** = **leave,** decamp, depart, make tracks, move out, slope off, withdraw **6** = **function,** move, operate, perform, run, work **11** = **lead,** connect, extend, fit, give access, reach, run, span, spread, stretch **13** = **contribute,** avail, concur, conduce, incline, lead to, serve, tend, work towards **14** = **fare,** develop, eventuate, fall out, *get that book.* **3** to depart: *we'll have to go at eleven.* **4** to start, as in a race: often used in commands. **5** to make regular journeys: *this train service goes to the east coast.* **6** to operate or function effectively: *the radio won't go.* **7** (*copula*) to become: *his face went red.* **8** to make a noise as specified: *the gun went bang.* **9** to enter into a specified state or condition: *to go into hysterics.* **10** to be or continue to be in a specified state or condition: *to go in rags; to go in poverty.* **11** to lead, extend, or afford access: *this route goes to the north.* **12** to proceed towards an activity: *to go to sleep.* **13** (*tr; takes an infinitive*) to serve or contribute: *this letter goes to prove my point.* **14** to follow a course as specified; fare: *the lecture went badly.* **15** to be applied or allotted to a particular purpose or recipient: *his money went on drink.* **16** to be sold: *the necklace went for three thousand pounds.* **17** to be ranked; compare: *this meal is good as my meals go.* **18** to blend or harmonize: *these chairs won't go with the rest of your furniture.* **19** (foll. by *by* or *under*) to be known (by a name or disguise). **20** to have a usual or proper place: *those books go on this shelf.* **21** (of music, poetry, etc.) to be sounded; expressed, etc.: *how does that song go?* **22** to fail or give way: *my eyesight is going.* **23** to break down or collapse abruptly: *the ladder went at the critical moment.* **24** to die: *the old man went at 2 a.m.* **25** (often foll. by *by*) **25a** (of time, etc.) to elapse: *the hours go by so slowly.* **25b** to travel past: *the train goes by her house.* **25c** to be guided (by). **26** to occur: *happiness does not always go with riches.* **27** to be eliminated, abolished, or given up: *this entry must go to save space.* **28** to be spent or finished: *all his money has gone.* **29** to attend: *go to school.* **30** to join a stated profession: *go on the stage.* **31** (foll. by *to*) to have recourse (to); turn: *to go to arbitration.* **32** (foll. by *to*) to subject or put oneself (to): *she goes to great pains to please him.* **33** to proceed, esp. up to or beyond certain limits: *you will go too far one day and then you will be punished.* **34** to be acceptable or tolerated: *anything goes.* **35** to carry the weight of final authority: *what the boss says goes.* **36** (*tr*) *Nonstandard.* to say: *Then she goes, "Give it to me!" and she just snatched it.* **37** (foll. by *into*) to be contained in: *four goes into twelve three times.* **38** (often foll. by *for*) to endure or last out: *we can't go for much longer without water.* **39** (*tr*) *Cards.* to bet or bid: *I go two hearts.* **40 be going.** to intend or be about to start (to do or be doing something): often used as an alternative future construction: *what's going to happen to us?* **41 go and.** *Inf.* to be so foolish or unlucky as to: *then she had to go and lose her hat.* **42 go it.** *Sl.* to do something or move energetically. **43 go it alone.** *Inf.* to act or proceed without allies or help. **44 go one better.** *Inf.* to surpass or outdo (someone). **45 let go. 45a** to relax one's hold (on); release. **45b** to discuss or consider no further. **46 let oneself go. 46a** to act in an uninhibited manner. **46b** to lose interest in one's appearance, manners, etc. **47 to go. 47a** remaining. **47b** *US & Canad. inf.* (of food served by a restaurant) for taking away. ◆ *n, pl* **goes. 48** the act of going. **49a** an attempt or try: *he had a go at the stamp business.* **49b** an attempt at stopping a person suspected of a crime: *the police are not always in favour of the public having a go.* **49c** an attack, esp. verbal: *she had a real go at them.* **50** a turn: *it's my go next.* **51** *Inf.* the quality of being active and energetic: *she has much more go than I have.* **52** *Inf.* hard or energetic work: *it's all go.* **53** *Inf.* a successful venture or achievement: *he made a go of it.* **54** *Inf.* a bargain or agreement. **55 from the word go.** *Inf.* from the very beginning. **56 no go.** *Inf.* impossible; abortive or futile: *it's no go, I'm afraid.* **57 on the go.** *Inf.* active and energetic. ◆ *adj* **58** (*postpositive*) *Inf.* functioning properly and ready for action: esp. used in astronautics: *all systems are go.* ◆ See also **go about, go against,** etc. [OE *gān*]

go about ❶ *vb* (*intr*) **1** (*prep*) to busy oneself with: *to go about one's duties.* **2** (*prep*) to tackle (a problem or task). **3** to circulate (in): *there's a lot of flu going about.* **4** (*adv*) (of a sailing ship) to change from one tack to another.

goad ❶ (gəʊd) *n* **1** a sharp pointed stick for urging on cattle, etc. **2** anything that acts as a spur or incitement. ◆ *vb* **3** (*tr*) to drive as if with a goad; spur; incite. [OE *gād*, of Gmc origin]

go against *vb* (*intr, prep*) **1** to be contrary to (principles or beliefs). **2** to be unfavourable to (a person): *the case went against him.*

go-ahead ❶ *n* **1** (usually preceded by *the*) *Inf.* permission to proceed. ◆ *adj* **2** enterprising or ambitious.

goal ❶ (gəʊl) *n* **1** the aim or object towards which an endeavour is directed. **2** the terminal point of a journey or race. **3** (in various sports) the net, basket, etc., into or over which players try to propel the ball, puck, etc., to score. **4** *Sport.* **4a** a successful attempt at scoring. **4b** the score so made. **5** (in soccer, hockey, etc.) the position of goalkeeper. [C16: ? rel. to ME *gol* boundary, OE *gǣlan* to hinder]
▸ **'goalless** *adj*

goalball ('gəʊl,bɔ:l) *n* **1** a game played by two teams who compete to score goals by throwing a ball that emits sound when in motion. Players are blindfolded during play. **2** the ball used in this game.

goalie ('gəʊlɪ) *n Inf.* short for **goalkeeper.**

goalkeeper ('gəʊl,ki:pə) *n Sport.* a player in the goal whose duty is to prevent the ball, puck, etc., from entering or crossing it.

goal kick *n Soccer.* a kick taken from the six-yard line by the defending team after the ball has been put out of play by an opposing player.

goal line *n Sport.* the line marking each end of the pitch, on which the goals stand.

go along ❶ *vb* (*intr, adv;* often foll. by *with*) to refrain from disagreement; assent.

goalpost ('gəʊl,pəʊst) *n* **1** either of two upright posts supporting the crossbar of a goal. **2 move the goalposts.** to change the target required during negotiations, etc.

goanna (gəʊ'ænə) *n* any of various Australian monitor lizards. [C19: from IGUANA]

goat (gəʊt) *n* **1** any sure-footed agile ruminant mammal with hollow horns, naturally inhabiting rough stony ground in Europe, Asia, and N Africa. **2** *Inf.* a lecherous man. **3** a foolish person. **4 get (someone's) goat.** *Sl.* to cause annoyance to (someone). [OE *gāt*]
▸ **'goatish** *adj*

Goat (gəʊt) *n* **the.** the constellation Capricorn, the tenth sign of the zodiac.

go at ❶ *vb* (*intr, prep*) **1** to make an energetic attempt at (something). **2** to attack vehemently.

goatee (gəʊ'ti:) *n* a pointed tuftlike beard on the chin. [C19: from GOAT + *-ee* (see -Y[2])]

goatherd ('gəʊt,hɜ:d) *n* a person employed to tend or herd goats.

goatsbeard *or* **goat's-beard** ('gəʊts,bɪəd) *n* **1** Also called: **Jack-go-to-bed-at-noon.** a Eurasian plant of the composite family, with woolly stems and large heads of yellow rayed flowers. **2** an American plant with long spikes of small white flowers.

goatskin ('gəʊt,skɪn) *n* **1** the hide of a goat. **2** something made from the hide of a goat, such as leather or a container for wine.

goatsucker ('gəʊt,sʌkə) *n* the US and Canad. name for **nightjar.**

gob[1] ❶ (gɒb) *n* **1** a lump or chunk, esp. of a soft substance. **2** (*often pl*) *Inf.* a great quantity or amount. **3** *Inf.* a globule of spittle or saliva. **4** a lump of molten glass used to make a piece of glassware. ◆ *vb* **gobs, gobbing, gobbed. 5** (*intr*) *Brit. inf.* to spit. [C14: from OF *gobe* lump, from *gober;* see GOBBET]

gob[2] (gɒb) *n* a slang word (esp. Brit.) for the **mouth.** [C16: ?from Gaelic *gob*]

go back ❶ *vb* (*intr, adv*) **1** to return. **2** (often foll. by *to*) to originate (in): *the links with France go back to the Norman Conquest.* **3** (foll. by *on*) to change one's mind about; repudiate (esp. in **go back on one's word**).

gobbet ('gɒbɪt) *n* a chunk, lump, or fragment, esp. of raw meat. [C14: from OF *gobet*, from *gober* to gulp down]

gobble[1] ❶ ('gɒb°l) *vb* **gobbles, gobbling, gobbled. 1** (when *tr*, often foll. by *up*) to eat or swallow (food) hastily and in large mouthfuls. **2** (*tr;* often foll. by *up*) *Inf.* to snatch. [C17: prob. from GOB[1]]

gobble[2] ('gɒb°l) *n* **1** the loud rapid gurgling sound made by male turkeys. ◆ *vb* **gobbles, gobbling, gobbled. 2** (*intr*) (of a turkey) to make this sound. [C17: prob. imit.]

gobbledegook ❶ *or* **gobbledygook** ('gɒb°l dɪ,gu:k) *n* pretentious or unintelligible jargon, such as that used by officials. [C20: whimsical formation from GOBBLE[2]]

gobbler ('gɒblə) *n Inf.* a male turkey.

Gobelin ('gəʊbəlɪn; *French* gɔblɛ̃) *adj* **1** of or resembling tapestry made at the Gobelins' factory in Paris, having vivid pictorial scenes. ◆ *n* **2** a tapestry of this kind. [C19: from the *Gobelin* family, who founded the factory]

go-between ❶ *n* a person who acts as agent or intermediary for two people or groups in a transaction or dealing.

goblet ('gɒblɪt) *n* **1** a vessel for drinking, with a base and stem but with-

THESAURUS

happen, pan out (*inf.*), proceed, result, turn out, work out **18** = **harmonize**, accord, agree, blend, chime, complement, correspond, fit, match, suit **24** = **die**, croak (*sl.*), expire, give up the ghost, kick the bucket (*sl.*), pass away, peg out (*inf.*), perish, pop one's clogs (*inf.*), snuff it (*inf.*) **25a** = **elapse**, expire, flow, lapse, pass, slip away ◆ *n* **49a** = **attempt**, bid, crack (*inf.*), effort, essay, shot (*inf.*), stab (*inf.*), try, turn, whack (*inf.*), whirl (*inf.*) **51** *Informal* = **energy**, activity, animation, brio, drive, force, get-up-and-go (*inf.*), life, oomph (*inf.*), pep, spirit, verve, vigour, vitality, vivacity **56 no go** *Informal* = **impossible**, futile, hopeless, not on (*inf.*), vain

Antonyms *vb* ≠ **move:** arrive, halt, reach, remain, stay, stop ≠ **function:** break (down), fail, malfunction, stop

go about *vb* **1** = **busy** *or* **occupy oneself with**, devote oneself to **2** = **tackle**, approach, begin, get the show on the road, set about, take the bit between one's teeth, undertake **3** = **move around**, circulate, pass around, wander

goad *n* **2** = **provocation**, impetus, incentive, incitement, irritation, motivation, pressure, spur, stimulation, stimulus, urge ◆ *vb* **3** = **provoke**, annoy, arouse, drive, egg on, exhort, harass, hound, impel, incite, instigate, irritate, lash, prick, prod, prompt, propel, spur, stimulate, sting, urge, worry

go-ahead *n* **1** *Informal* = **permission**, assent, authorization, consent, green light, leave, O.K. *or* okay (*inf.*) ◆ *adj* **2** = **enterprising**, ambitious, go-getting (*inf.*), pioneering, progressive, up-and-coming

goal *n* **1, 2** = **aim**, ambition, design, destination, end, Holy Grail (*inf.*), intention, limit, mark, object, objective, purpose, target

go along *vb* = **agree**, acquiesce, assent, concur, cooperate, follow

go at *vb* **2** = **attack**, argue, blame, blast, criticize, go for the jugular, impugn, lambast(e), put down, set about, tear into (*inf.*)

gob[1] *n* **1** = **piece**, blob, chunk, clod, gobbet, hunk, lump, nugget, wad, wodge (*Brit. inf.*)

go back *vb* **1** = **return**, retrocede, revert **3** *with* **on** = **repudiate**, change one's mind about, desert, forsake, renege on, retract

gobble[1] *vb* **1** = **devour**, bolt, cram, gorge, gulp, guzzle, pig out on (*US & Canad. sl.*), stuff, swallow, wolf

gobbledegook *n* = **nonsense**, babble, cant, double talk, gabble, gibberish, Greek (*inf.*), hocus-pocus, jabber, jargon, mumbo jumbo, officialese, rigmarole, twaddle

go-between *n* = **intermediary**, agent, broker,

out handles. **2** *Arch.* a large drinking cup. [C14: from OF *gobelet* a little cup, ult. of Celtic origin]

goblin ('gɒblɪn) *n* (in folklore) a small grotesque supernatural creature, regarded as malevolent towards human beings. [C14: from OF, from MHG *kobolt;* cf. COBALT]

gobo ('gəʊbəʊ) *n, pl* **gobos** *or* **goboes.** a shield placed round a microphone to exclude unwanted sounds, or round a camera lens, etc., to reduce the incident light. [C20: from ?]

gobshite ('gɒb,ʃaɪt) *n Irish taboo sl.* a stupid person. [C20: from GOB² + *shite* excrement; see SHIT]

gobsmacked ('gɒb,smækt) *adj Brit. sl.* astounded; astonished. [C20: from GOB² + SMACK]

goby ('gəʊbɪ) *n, pl* **goby** *or* **gobies.** a small spiny-finned fish of coastal or brackish waters, having a large head, an elongated tapering body, and the ventral fins modified as a sucker. [C18: from L *gōbius* gudgeon from Gk *kōbios*]

go-by *n Sl.* a deliberate snub or slight (esp. in **give (a person) the go-by**).

go by ❶ *vb (intr)* **1** to pass: *as the years go by.* **2** *(prep)* to be guided by: *in the darkness we could only go by the stars.* **3** *(prep)* to use as a basis for forming an opinion or judgment: *it's wise not to go only by appearances.*

go-cart *n* See **kart.**

god (gɒd) *n* **1** a supernatural being, who is worshipped as the controller of some part of the universe or some aspect of life in the world or is the personification of some force. **2** an image, idol, or symbolic representation of such a deity. **3** any person or thing to which excessive attention is given: *money was his god.* **4** a man who has qualities regarded as making him superior to other men. **5** *(pl)* the gallery of a theatre. [OE *god*]

God (gɒd) *n* **1** the sole Supreme Being, eternal, spiritual, and transcendent, who is the Creator and ruler of all and is infinite in all attributes; the object of worship in monotheistic religions. ◆ *interj* **2** an oath or exclamation used to indicate surprise, annoyance, etc. (and in such expressions as **My God!** or **God Almighty!**).

godchild ('gɒd,tʃaɪld) *n, pl* **godchildren.** a person who is sponsored by adults at baptism.

goddaughter ('gɒd,dɔːtə) *n* a female godchild.

goddess ('gɒdɪs) *n* **1** a female divinity. **2** a woman who is adored or idealized, esp. by a man.

godetia (gəˈdiːʃə) *n* any plant of the American genus *Godetia,* esp. one grown as a showy-flowered annual garden plant. [C19: after C. H. *Godet* (died 1879), Swiss botanist]

godfather ('gɒd,fɑːðə) *n* **1** a male godparent. **2** the head of a Mafia family or other criminal ring. **3** an originator or leading exponent: *the godfather of South African pop.*

godfather offer *n Inf.* a takeover bid pitched so high that the management of the target company is unable to dissuade shareholders from accepting it. [from the 1972 film *The Godfather,* in which a character was made an offer he could not refuse]

God-fearing *adj* pious; devout.

godforsaken ❶ ('gɒdfə,seɪkən) *adj* *(sometimes cap.)* **1** *(usually prenominal)* desolate; dreary; forlorn. **2** wicked.

Godhead ('gɒd,hɛd) *n* *(sometimes not cap.)* **1** the essential nature and condition of being God. **2 the Godhead.** God.

godhood ('gɒd,hʊd) *n* the state of being divine.

godless ❶ ('gɒdlɪs) *adj* **1** wicked or unprincipled. **2** lacking a god. **3** refusing to acknowledge God.
▸**'godlessly** *adv* ▸**'godlessness** *n*

godlike ❶ ('gɒd,laɪk) *adj* resembling or befitting a god or God; divine.

godly ❶ ('gɒdlɪ) *adj* **godlier, godliest.** having a religious character; pious; devout.
▸**'godliness** *n*

godmother ('gɒd,mʌðə) *n* a female godparent.

godown ('gəʊ,daʊn) *n* (in the East, esp. in India) a warehouse. [C16: from Malay *godong*]

go down ❶ *vb (intr, mainly adv)* **1** *(also prep)* to move or lead to or as if to a lower place or level; sink, decline, decrease, etc. **2** to be defeated; lose. **3** to be remembered or recorded (esp. in **go down in history**). **4** to be received: *his speech went down well.* **5** (of food) to be swallowed. **6** *Brit.* to leave a college or university at the end of a term. **7** (usually foll. by *with*) to fall ill; be infected. **8** (of a celestial body) to sink or set. **9 go down on.** *Taboo sl.* to perform cunnilingus or fellatio on.

godparent ('gɒd,pɛərənt) *n* a person who stands sponsor to another at baptism.

God's acre *n Literary.* a churchyard or burial ground. [C17: translation of G *Gottesacker*]

godsend ❶ ('gɒd,send) *n* a person or thing that comes unexpectedly but is particularly welcome. [C19: from C17 *God's send,* alteration of *goddes sand* God's message, from OE *sand;* see SEND]

godslot ('gɒd,slɒt) *n Inf.* a time in a television or radio schedule traditionally reserved for religious broadcasts.

godson ('gɒd,sʌn) *n* a male godchild.

Godspeed ('gɒd'spiːd) *sentence substitute, n* an expression of good wishes for a person's success and safety. [C15: from *God spede* may God prosper (you)]

godsquad ('gɒd,skwɒd) *n Inf., derog.* any group of evangelical Christians, members of which are regarded as intrusive and exuberantly pious.

godwit ('gɒdwɪt) *n* a large shore bird of the sandpiper family having long legs and a long upturned bill. [C16: from ?]

goer ('gəʊə) *n* **1a** a person who attends something regularly. **1b** *(in combination): filmgoer.* **2** a person or thing that goes, esp. one that goes very fast. **3** an energetic person. **4** *Austral. inf.* an acceptable or feasible idea, proposal, etc.

go-faster stripe *n Inf.* a decorative line, often suggestive of high speed, on the bodywork of a car.

gofer ('gəʊfə) *n Sl.* a person who runs errands. [C20: from GO + FOR]

goffer ('gəʊfə) *vb (tr)* **1** to press pleats into (a frill). **2** to decorate (the edges of a book). ◆ *n* **3** an ornamental frill made by pressing pleats. **4** the decoration formed by goffering books. **5** the iron or tool used in making goffers. [C18: from F *gaufrer* to impress a pattern, from *gaufre,* from MLow G *wāfel;* see WAFFLE¹, WAFER]

go for ❶ *vb (intr, prep)* **1** to go somewhere in order to have or fetch: *he went for a drink.* **2** to seek to obtain: *I'd go for that job if I were you.* **3** to prefer or choose; like: *I really go for that new idea of yours.* **4** to make a physical or verbal attack on. **5** to be considered to be of a stated importance or value: *his twenty years went for nothing when he was made redundant.* **6 go for it.** *Inf.* to make the maximum effort to achieve a particular goal.

go-getter *n Inf.* an ambitious enterprising person.
▸**,go-'getting** *adj*

gogga ('xɒxə) *n S. African inf.* any small animal that crawls or flies, esp. an insect. [C20: from Khoikhoi *xoxon* insects collectively]

goggle ❶ ('gɒgᵊl) *vb* **goggles, goggling, goggled. 1** *(intr)* to stare fixedly, as in astonishment. **2** to cause (the eyes) to roll or bulge or (of the eyes) to roll or bulge. ◆ *n* **3** a bulging stare. **4** *(pl)* spectacles, often of coloured glass or covered with gauze: used to protect the eyes. [C14: from *gogelen* to look aside, from ?; see AGOG]
▸**'goggle-,eyed** *adj*

gogglebox ('gɒgᵊl,bɒks) *n Brit. sl.* a television set.

Go-Go *n* a form of soul music originating in Washington, DC, characterized by the use of funk rhythms and a brass section.

go-go dancer *n* a dancer, usually scantily dressed, who performs rhythmic and often erotic modern dance routines, esp. in a nightclub.

Goidelic (gɔɪ'dɛlɪk) *n* **1** the N group of Celtic languages, consisting of Irish Gaelic, Scottish Gaelic, and Manx. ◆ *adj* **2** of, relating to, or characteristic of this group of languages. [C19: from OIrish *Goídel* a Celt, from OWelsh, from *gwydd* savage]

go in ❶ *vb (intr, adv)* **1** to enter. **2** *(prep)* See **go into. 3** (of the sun) to become hidden behind a cloud. **4 go in for. 4a** to enter as a competitor or contestant. **4b** to adopt as an activity, interest, or guiding principle: *she went in for nursing.*

going ('gəʊɪŋ) *n* **1** a departure or farewell. **2** the condition of a surface such as a road or field with regard to walking, riding, etc.: *muddy going.* **3** *Inf.* speed, progress, etc.: *we made good going on the trip.* ◆ *adj* **4** thriving (esp. in **a going concern**). **5** current or accepted: *the going rate.* **6** *(postpositive)* available: *the best going.*

going-over ❶ *n, pl* **goings-over.** *Inf.* **1** a check, examination, or investigation. **2** a castigation or thrashing.

goings-on *pl n Inf.* **1** actions or conduct, esp. when regarded with disapproval. **2** happenings or events, esp. when mysterious or suspicious.

go into ❶ *vb (intr, prep)* **1** to enter. **2** to start a career in: *to go into publishing.* **3** to investigate or examine. **4** to discuss: *we won't go into that now.* **5** to be admitted to, esp. temporarily: *she went into hospital.* **6** to enter a specified state: *she went into fits of laughter.*

goitre *or US* **goiter** ('gɔɪtə) *n Pathol.* a swelling of the thyroid gland, in

THESAURUS

dealer, factor, liaison, mediator, medium, middleman

go by *vb* **1** = **pass**, elapse, exceed, flow on, move onward, proceed **2, 3** = **follow**, adopt, be guided by, heed, judge from, observe, take as guide

godforsaken *adj* **1** = **desolate**, abandoned, backward, bleak, deserted, dismal, dreary, forlorn, gloomy, lonely, neglected, remote, wretched

godless *adj* **1** = **wicked**, depraved, evil, impious, unprincipled, unrighteous **3** = **profane**, atheistic, irreligious, ungodly

godlike *adj* = **divine**, celestial, deific, deiform, heavenly, superhuman, transcendent

godly *adj* = **devout**, god-fearing, good, holy, pious, religious, righteous, saintly

go down *vb* **2** = **fall**, be beaten, collapse, decline, decrease, drop, founder, go under, lose, set, sink, submerge, submit, suffer defeat **3** = **be recorded**, be commemorated, be recalled, be remembered

godsend *n* = **blessing**, boon, manna, stroke of luck, windfall

go for *vb* **2** = **seek**, clutch at, fetch, obtain, reach, stretch for **3** = **favour**, admire, be attracted to, be fond of, choose, hold with, like, prefer **4** = **attack**, assail, assault, launch oneself at, rush upon, set about *or* upon, spring upon

goggle *vb* **1** = **stare**, gape, gawk, gawp, peer, rubberneck *(sl.)*

go in *vb* **4 go in for** = **enter**, adopt, embrace, engage in, espouse, practise, pursue, take up, undertake

going-over *n* **1** = **examination**, analysis, check, inspection, investigation, perusal, recce *(sl.)*, review, scrutiny, study, survey **2** = **beating**, buffeting, castigation, chastisement, doing *(inf.)*, drubbing, pasting *(sl.)*, rebuke, thrashing, thumping, whipping

go into *vb* **1, 2** = **enter**, begin, develop, participate in, undertake **3** = **investigate**, analyse, consider, delve into, discuss, examine, inquire into,

some cases nearly doubling the size of the neck. [C17: from F, from OF *goitron* ult. from L *guttur* throat]
▸'**goitred** *or US* '**goitered** *adj* ▸'**goitrous** *adj*

go-kart *or* **go-cart** *n* See **kart**.

Golconda (gɒl'kɒndə) *n* (*sometimes not cap.*) a source of wealth or riches, esp. a mine. [C18: from former city in India, renowned for its diamond mines]

gold (gəʊld) *n* **1a** a dense inert bright yellow element that is the most malleable and ductile metal, occurring in rocks and alluvial deposits: used as a monetary standard and in jewellery, dentistry, and plating. Symbol: Au; atomic no.: 79; atomic wt.: 196.97. Related adj: **auric. 1b** (*as modifier*): *a gold mine.* **2** a coin or coins made of this metal. **3** money; wealth. **4** something precious, beautiful, etc., such as a noble nature (esp. in **heart of gold**). **5a** a deep yellow colour, sometimes with a brownish tinge. **5b** (*as adj*): *a gold carpet.* **6** short for **gold medal.** [OE *gold*]

gold card *n* a credit card issued by credit-card companies to favoured clients, entitling them to high unsecured overdrafts, some insurance cover, etc.

goldcrest ('gəʊld,krest) *n* a small Old World warbler having a greenish plumage and a bright yellow-and-black crown.

gold-digger *n* **1** a person who prospects or digs for gold. **2** *Inf.* a woman who uses her sexual attractions to accumulate gifts and wealth.

gold disc *n* **1** (in Britain) an LP record certified to have sold 100 000 copies or a single certified to have sold 400 000 copies. **2** (in the US) an LP record or single certified to have sold 500 000 copies.

gold dust *n* gold in the form of small particles or powder.

golden ❶ ('gəʊldən) *adj* **1** of the yellowish colour of gold: *golden hair.* **2** made from or largely consisting of gold: *a golden statue.* **3** happy or prosperous: *golden days.* **4** (*sometimes cap.*) (of anniversaries) the 50th in a series: *Golden Jubilee; golden wedding.* **5** *Inf.* very successful or destined for success: *the golden girl of tennis.* **6** extremely valuable or advantageous: *a golden opportunity.*
▸'**goldenly** *adv* ▸'**goldenness** *n*

golden age *n* **1** *Classical myth.* the first and best age of mankind, when existence was happy, prosperous, and innocent. **2** the most flourishing and outstanding period, esp. in the history of an art or nation: *the golden age of poetry.*

golden eagle *n* a large eagle of mountainous regions of the N hemisphere, having a plumage that is golden brown on the back.

goldeneye ('gəʊldən,aɪ) *n, pl* **goldeneyes** *or* **goldeneye.** either of two black-and-white diving ducks of northern regions.

Golden Fleece *n Greek myth.* the fleece of a winged ram stolen by Jason and the Argonauts.

golden goose *n* a goose in folklore that laid a golden egg every day until its greedy owner killed it in an attempt to get all the gold at once.

golden handcuffs *pl n* payments deferred over a number of years that induce a person to stay with a particular company or in a particular job.

golden handshake *n Inf.* a sum of money given to an employee, either on retirement or as compensation for loss of employment.

golden hello *n* a payment made to a sought-after recruit on signing a contract of employment with a company.

golden hour *n* the first hour after a serious accident, when it is crucial that the victim receives medical treatment in order to have a chance of surviving.

golden mean *n* **1** the middle course between extremes. **2** another term for **golden section.**

golden number *n* a number between 1 and 19, used to indicate the position of any year in the Metonic cycle: so called from its importance in fixing the date of Easter.

golden parachute *n Inf.* a clause in the employment contract of a senior executive providing for special benefits if the executive's employment is terminated as a result of a takeover.

golden retriever *n* a breed of retriever with a silky wavy coat of a golden colour.

goldenrod (,gəʊldən'rɒd) *n* a plant of the composite family of North America, Europe, and Asia, having spikes of small yellow flowers.

golden rule *n* **1** any of a number of rules of fair conduct, such as *Whatsoever ye would that men should do to you, do ye even so to them* (Matthew 7:12). **2** any important principle: *a golden rule of sailing is to wear a life jacket.* **3** another name for **rule of three.**

golden section *or* **mean** *n* the proportion of the two divisions of a straight line such that the smaller is to the larger as the larger is to the sum of the two.

golden share *n* a share in a company that controls at least 51% of the voting rights, esp. one retained by the UK government in some privatization issues.

Golden Starfish *n* an award given to a bathing beach that meets EU standards of cleanliness but that does not provide facilities.

golden syrup *n Brit.* a light golden-coloured treacle produced by the evaporation of cane sugar juice, used to flavour cakes, puddings, etc.

Golden Triangle *n* **the.** an opium-producing area of SE Asia, comprising parts of Myanmar, Laos, and Thailand.

golden wattle *n* **1** an Australian yellow-flowered plant that yields a useful gum and bark. **2** any of several similar and related Australian plants.

goldfinch ('gəʊld,fɪntʃ) *n* a common European finch, the adult of which has a red-and-white face and yellow-and-black wings.

goldfish ('gəʊld,fɪʃ) *n, pl* **goldfish** *or* **goldfishes.** a freshwater fish of E Europe and Asia, esp. China, widely introduced as a pond or aquarium fish. It resembles the carp and has a typically golden or orange-red coloration.

gold foil *n* thin gold sheet that is thicker than gold leaf.

gold leaf *n* very thin gold sheet produced by rolling or hammering gold and used for gilding woodwork, etc.

gold medal *n* a medal of gold, awarded to the winner of a competition or race.

gold plate *n* **1** a thin coating of gold, usually produced by electroplating. **2** vessels or utensils made of gold.
▸,**gold-'plate** *vb* (*tr*)

gold reserve *n* the gold reserved by a central bank to support domestic credit expansion, to cover balance of payments deficits, and to protect currency.

gold rush *n* a large-scale migration of people to a territory where gold has been found.

goldsmith ('gəʊld,smɪθ) *n* **1** a dealer in articles made of gold. **2** an artisan who makes such articles.

gold standard *n* a monetary system in which the unit of currency is defined with reference to gold.

golf (gɒlf) *n* **1** a game played on a large open course, the object of which is to hit a ball using clubs, with as few strokes as possible, into each of usually 18 holes. ◆ *vb* **2** (*intr*) to play golf. [C15: ?from MDu. *colf* CLUB]
▸'**golfer** *n*

golf ball *n* **1** a small resilient, usually white, ball of either two-piece or three-piece construction, the former consisting of a solid inner core with a thick covering of toughened material, the latter consisting of a liquid centre, rubber-wound core, and a thin layer of balata. **2** (in some electric typewriters) a small detachable metal sphere, around the surface of which type characters are arranged.

golf club *n* **1** any of various long-shafted clubs with wood or metal heads used to strike a golf ball. **2a** an association of golf players, usually having its own course and facilities. **2b** the premises of such an association.

golf course *or* **links** *n* an area of ground laid out for the playing of golf.

Goliath (gə'laɪəθ) *n Bible.* a Philistine giant who was killed by David with a stone from his sling (I Samuel 17).

golliwog ('gɒlɪ,wɒg) *n* a soft doll with a black face, usually made of cloth or rags. [C19: from a doll in a series of American children's books]

gollop ('gɒləp) *vb* **gollops, golloping, golloped.** to eat or drink (something) quickly or greedily. [dialect var. of GULP]

golly ('gɒlɪ) *interj* an exclamation of mild surprise. [C19: orig. a euphemism for GOD]

goloshes (gə'lɒʃɪz) *pl n* a less common spelling of **galoshes.**

-gon *n combining form.* indicating a figure having a specified number of angles: *pentagon.* [from Gk *-gōnon,* from *gōnia* angle]

gonad ('gɒnæd) *n* an animal organ in which gametes are produced, such as a testis or an ovary. [C19: from NL *gonas,* from Gk *gonos* seed]
▸'**gonadal** *or* **gonadial** (gɒ'neɪdɪəl) *adj*

gonadotrophin (,gɒnədəʊ'trəʊfɪn) *or* **gonadotropin** (-'trəʊpɪn) *n* any of several hormones that stimulate the gonads. See also **HCG.**
▸**gonadotrophic** (,gɒnədəʊ'trɒfɪk) *or* ,**gonado'tropic** *adj*

gondola ('gɒndələ) *n* **1** a long narrow flat-bottomed boat with a high ornamented stem: traditionally used on the canals of Venice. **2a** a car or cabin suspended from an airship or balloon. **2b** a moving cabin suspended from a cable across a valley, etc. **3** a flat-bottomed barge used on canals and rivers of the US. **4** *US & Canad.* a low open flat-bottomed railway goods wagon. **5** a set of island shelves in a self-service shop: used for displaying goods. **6** *Canad.* a broadcasting booth built close to the roof of an ice-hockey stadium. [C16: from It. (dialect), from Med. L, ? ult. from Gk *kondu* drinking vessel]

gondolier (,gɒndə'lɪə) *n* a man who propels a gondola.

Gondwanaland (gɒnd'wɑːnə,lænd) *n* one of the two ancient supercontinents comprising chiefly what are now Africa, South America, Australia, Antarctica, and the Indian subcontinent. [C19: from *Gondwana,* region in central north India, where the rock series was orig. found]

gone ❶ (gɒn) *vb* **1** the past participle of **go.** ◆ *adj* (*usually postpositive*) **2** ended; past. **3** lost; ruined. **4** dead. **5** spent; consumed; used up. **6** *Inf.*

THESAURUS

look into, probe, pursue, research, review, scrutinize, study, work over

golden *adj* **1** = **yellow**, blond, blonde, bright, brilliant, flaxen, resplendent, shining **3** = **successful**, best, blissful, delightful, flourishing, glorious, halcyon, happy, joyful, joyous, precious, prosperous, rich **6** = **promising**, advantageous, auspicious, excellent, favourable, opportune, propitious, rosy, valuable
Antonyms *adj* ≠ **yellow:** black, brunette, dark, dull ≠ **successful:** poorest, sad, unfavourable, worst ≠ **promising:** black, dark, sad, unfavourable, untimely, wretched

gone *adj* **2** = **past**, elapsed, ended, finished, over **3** = **missing**, absent, astray, away, lacking, lost, vanished **4** = **dead**, deceased, defunct, departed, extinct, no more **5** = **used up**, consumed, done, finished, spent faint or weak. **7** *Inf.* having been pregnant (for a specified time): *six months gone.* **8** (usually foll. by *on*) *Sl.* in love (with).

goner ('gɒnə) *n Sl.* a person or thing beyond help or recovery, esp. a person who is about to die.

gonfalon ('gɒnfələn) *n* **1** a banner hanging from a crossbar, used esp. by certain medieval Italian republics. **2** a battle flag suspended crosswise on a staff, usually having a serrated edge. [C16: from OIt., from OF, of Gmc origin]

gong (gɒŋ) *n* **1** a percussion instrument consisting of a metal platelike disc struck with a soft-headed drumstick. **2** a rimmed metal disc, hollow metal hemisphere, or metal strip, tube, or wire that produces a note when struck. **3** a fixed saucer-shaped bell, as on an alarm clock, struck by a mechanically operated hammer. **4** *Brit. sl.* a medal, esp. a military one. ◆ *vb* **5** (*intr*) to sound a gong. **6** (*tr*) (of traffic police) to summon (a driver) to stop by sounding a gong. [C17: from Malay, imit.]

goniometer (ˌgəʊnɪ'ɒmɪtə) *n* **1** an instrument for measuring the angles between the faces of a crystal. **2** an instrument used to determine the bearing of a distant radio station. [C18: via F from Gk *gōnia* angle]
▸**goniometric** (ˌgəʊnɪə'mɛtrɪk) *adj* ▸ˌ**goni'ometry** *n*

-gonium *n combining form.* indicating a seed or reproductive cell: *archegonium.* [from NL, from Gk *gonos* seed]

gonococcus (ˌgɒnəʊ'kɒkəs) *n, pl* **gonococci** (-'kɒksaɪ). a spherical bacterium that causes gonorrhoea.

gonorrhoea *or esp. US* **gonorrhea** (ˌgɒnə'rɪə) *n* an infectious venereal disease characterized by a discharge of mucus and pus from the urethra or vagina. [C16: from L, from Gk *gonos* semen + *rhoia* flux]
▸ˌ**gonor'rhoeal** *or esp. US* ˌ**gonor'rheal** *adj*

-gony *n combining form.* genesis, origin, or production: *cosmogony.* [from L, from Gk, from *gonos* seed, procreation]

gonzo ('gɒnzəʊ) *Sl.* ◆ *adj* **1** wild or crazy. **2** (of journalism) focusing on the eccentric personality or lifestyle of the reporter as much as on the events reported. ◆ *n, pl* **gonzos. 3** a wild or crazy person. [C20: coined by Hunter S. Thompson, US journalist, ? from It., lit.: fool, or Sp. *ganso* idiot (lit.: goose)]

goo (guː) *n Inf.* **1** a sticky substance. **2** coy or sentimental language or ideas. [C20: from ?]

good ➊ (gʊd) *adj* **better, best. 1** having admirable, pleasing, superior, or positive qualities; not negative, bad, or mediocre: *a good teacher.* **2a** morally excellent or admirable; virtuous; righteous: *a good man.* **2b** (*as collective n;* preceded by *the*): *the good.* **3** suitable or efficient for a purpose: *a good winter coat.* **4** beneficial or advantageous: *vegetables are good for you.* **5** not ruined or decayed: *the meat is still good.* **6** kindly or generous: *you are good to him.* **7** valid or genuine: *I would not do this without good reason.* **8** honourable or held in high esteem: *a good family.* **9** financially secure, sound, or safe: *a good investment.* **10** (of a draft, etc.) drawn for a stated sum. **11** (of debts) expected to be fully paid. **12** clever, competent, or talented: *he's good at science.* **13** obedient or well-behaved: *a good dog.* **14** reliable, safe, or recommended: *a good make of clothes.* **15** affording material pleasure: *the good life.* **16** having a well-proportioned or generally fine appearance: *a good figure.* **17** complete; full: *I took a good look round the house.* **18** propitious; opportune: *a good time to ask for a rise.* **19** satisfying or gratifying: *a good rest.* **20** comfortable: *did you have a good night?* **21** newest or of the best quality: *keep the good plates for guests.* **22** fairly large, extensive, or long: *a good distance away.* **23** sufficient; ample: *we have a good supply of food.* **24 a good one. 24a** an unbelievable assertion. **24b** a very funny joke. **25 as good as.** virtually; practically: *it's as good as finished.* **26 good and.** *Inf.* (intensifier): *good and mad.* ◆ *interj* **27** an exclamation of approval, agreement, pleasure, etc. ◆ *n* **28** moral or material advantage or use; benefit or profit: *for the good of our workers; what is the good of worrying?* **29** positive moral qualities; goodness; virtue; righteousness; piety. **30** (*sometimes cap.*) moral qualities seen as an abstract entity: *we must pursue the Good.* **31** a good thing. **32 for good (and all).** forever; permanently: *I have left them for good.* **33 good for** *or* **on you.** well done, well said, etc.: a term of congratulation. **34 make good. 34a** to recompense or repair damage or injury. **34b** to be successful. **34c** to prove the truth of (a statement or accusation). **34d** to secure and retain (a position). **34e** to effect or fulfil (something intended or promised). ◆ See also **goods.** [OE *gōd*]
▸'**goodish** *adj*

Good Book *n* a name for the **Bible.**

goodbye ➊ (ˌgʊd'baɪ) *sentence substitute.* **1** farewell: a conventional expression used at leave-taking or parting with people. ◆ *n* **2** a leave-taking; parting: *they prolonged their goodbyes.* **3** a farewell: *they said goodbyes to each other.* [C16: from *God be with ye*]

good day *sentence substitute.* a conventional expression of greeting or farewell used during the day.

good-for-nothing ➊ *n* **1** an irresponsible or worthless person. ◆ *adj* **2** irresponsible; worthless.

Good Friday *n* the Friday before Easter, observed as a commemoration of the Crucifixion of Jesus.

good-humoured ➊ *adj* being in or expressing a pleasant, tolerant, and kindly state of mind.
▸ˌ**good-'humouredly** *adv*

goodies ('gʊdɪz) *pl n* any objects, rewards, etc., considered particularly desirable.

good-looking ➊ *adj* handsome or pretty.

goodly ➊ ('gʊdlɪ) *adj* **goodlier, goodliest. 1** considerable: *a goodly amount of money.* **2** *Obs.* attractive, pleasing, or fine.
▸'**goodliness** *n*

goodman ('gʊdmən) *n, pl* **goodmen.** *Arch.* **1** a husband. **2** a man not of gentle birth: used as a title. **3** a master of a household.

good morning *sentence substitute.* a conventional expression of greeting or farewell used in the morning.

good-natured ➊ *adj* of a tolerant and kindly disposition.
▸ˌ**good-'naturedly** *adv*

goodness ➊ ('gʊdnɪs) *n* **1** the state or quality of being good. **2** generosity; kindness. **3** moral excellence; piety; virtue. **4** what is good in something; essence. ◆ *interj* **5** a euphemism for **God:** used as an exclamation of surprise.

goodness of fit *n Statistics.* the extent to which observed sample values of a variable approximate to values derived from a theoretical density.

good night *sentence substitute.* a conventional expression of farewell, used in the evening or at night, esp. when departing to bed.

good-oh *or* **good-o** ('gʊd'əʊ) *interj Brit. & Austral. inf.* an exclamation of pleasure, agreement, etc.

good oil *n* (usually preceded by *the*) *Austral. sl.* true or reliable facts, information, etc.

goods ➊ (gʊdz) *pl n* **1** possessions and personal property. **2** (*sometimes sing*) *Econ.* commodities that are tangible, usually movable, and generally not consumed at the same time as they are produced. **3** articles of commerce; merchandise. **4** *Chiefly Brit.* **4a** merchandise when

THESAURUS

good *adj* **1 = excellent**, admirable, agreeable, capital, choice, commendable, divine, fine, first-class, first-rate, great, pleasant, pleasing, positive, precious, satisfactory, splendid, super (*inf.*), superior, tiptop, valuable, world-class, worthy **2 = honourable**, admirable, estimable, ethical, exemplary, honest, moral, praiseworthy, right, righteous, trustworthy, upright, virtuous, worthy **4 = favourable**, adequate, advantageous, auspicious, beneficial, convenient, fit, fitting, healthy, helpful, opportune, profitable, propitious, salubrious, salutary, suitable, useful, wholesome **5 = eatable**, fit to eat, sound, uncorrupted, untainted, whole **6 = kind**, altruistic, approving, beneficent, benevolent, charitable, friendly, gracious, humane, kind-hearted, kindly, merciful, obliging, well-disposed **7 = valid**, authentic, bona fide, dependable, genuine, honest, legitimate, proper, real, reliable, sound, true, trustworthy **12 = expert**, able, accomplished, adept, adroit, capable, clever, competent, dexterous, efficient, first-rate, proficient, reliable, satisfactory, serviceable, skilled, sound, suitable, talented, thorough, useful **13 = well-behaved**, decorous, dutiful, mannerly, obedient, orderly, polite, proper, seemly, well-mannered **15 = enjoyable**, agreeable, cheerful, congenial, convivial, gratifying, happy, pleasant, pleasing, pleasurable, satisfying **17, 23 = full**, adequate, ample, complete, considerable, entire, extensive, large, long, sizable *or* sizeable, solid, substantial, sufficient, whole **21 = best**, fancy, finest, newest, nicest, precious, smartest, special, valuable ◆ *n* **28 = benefit**, advantage, avail, behalf, gain, interest, mileage (*inf.*), profit, service, use, usefulness, welfare, wellbeing, worth **29 = virtue**, excellence, goodness, merit, morality, probity, rectitude, right, righteousness, uprightness, worth **32 for good = permanently**, finally, for ever, irrevocably, never to return, once and for all, *sine die*

Antonyms *adj* ≠ **excellent:** awful, bad, boring, disagreeable, dull, inadequate, rotten, tedious, unpleasant ≠ **honourable:** bad, base, corrupt, dishonest, dishonourable, evil, immoral, improper, sinful ≠ **favourable:** inappropriate, pathetic, unbecoming, unbefitting, unfavourable, unfitting, unsuitable, useless ≠ **eatable:** bad, decayed, mouldy, off, rotten, unsound ≠ **kind:** cruel, evil, mean (*inf.*), selfish, unkind, vicious, wicked ≠ **valid:** counterfeit, false, fraudulent, invalid, phoney ≠ **expert:** bad, incompetent, inefficient, unsatisfactory, unskilled ≠ **well-behaved:** ill-mannered, mischievous, naughty, rude ≠ **full:** scant, short ◆ *n* ≠ **benefit:** detriment, disadvantage, failure, ill-fortune, loss ≠ **virtue:** badness, baseness, corruption, cruelty, dishonesty, evil, immorality, meanness, wickedness

goodbye *n* **2 = farewell**, adieu, leave-taking, parting

good-for-nothing *n* **1 = layabout**, black sheep, idler, ne'er-do-well, numb-nut (*US sl.*), profligate, rapscallion, scapegrace, skiver (*Brit. sl.*), slacker (*inf.*), waster, wastrel ◆ *adj* **2 = worthless**, feckless, idle, irresponsible, useless

good-humoured *adj* **= cheerful**, affable, amiable, congenial, genial, good-tempered, happy, pleasant

good-looking *adj* **= attractive**, comely, fair, handsome, personable, pretty, well-favoured

goodly *adj* **1 = considerable**, ample, large, significant, sizable *or* sizeable, substantial, tidy (*inf.*) **2 = attractive**, agreeable, comely, desirable, elegant, fine, good-looking, graceful, handsome, personable, pleasant, pleasing, well-favoured

good-natured *adj* **= kindly**, agreeable, amiable, benevolent, friendly, good-hearted, helpful, kind, tolerant, warm-hearted, well-disposed, willing to please

goodness *n* **1 = excellence**, merit, quality, superiority, value, worth **2 = kindness**, beneficence, benevolence, friendliness, generosity, goodwill, graciousness, humaneness, kind-heartedness, kindliness, mercy, obligingness **3 = virtue**, honesty, honour, integrity, merit, morality, probity, rectitude, righteousness, uprightness **4 = benefit**, advantage, nourishment, nutrition, salubriousness, wholesomeness

Antonyms *n* ≠ **virtue:** badness, corruption, dishonesty, evil, immorality, wickedness, worthlessness ≠ **benefit:** detriment, disadvantage

goods *pl n* **1 = property**, appurtenances, belongings, chattels, effects, furnishings, furniture, gear, movables, paraphernalia, posses-

transported, esp. by rail; freight. **4b** (*as modifier*): *a goods train.* **5 the goods. 5a** *Inf.* that which is expected or promised: *to deliver the goods.* **5b** *Sl.* the real thing. **5c** *US & Canad. sl.* incriminating evidence (esp. in **have the goods on someone**).

Good Samaritan *n* **1** *New Testament.* a figure in one of Christ's parables (Luke 10:30–37) who is an example of compassion towards those in distress. **2** a kindly person who helps another in difficulty or distress.

Good Shepherd *n New Testament.* a title given to Jesus Christ in John 10:11–12.

good-sized *adj* quite large.

good-tempered *adj* of a kindly and generous disposition.

good turn *n* a helpful and friendly act; favour.

goodwife (ˈgʊd,waɪf) *n, pl* **goodwives.** *Arch.* **1** the mistress of a household. **2** a woman not of gentle birth: used as a title.

goodwill Ⓣ (,gʊdˈwɪl) *n* **1** benevolence, approval, and kindly interest. **2** willingness or acquiescence. **3** an intangible asset of an enterprise reflecting its commercial reputation, customer connections, etc.

goody[1] (ˈgʊdɪ) *interj* **1** a child's exclamation of pleasure. ◆ *n, pl* **goodies. 2** short for **goody-goody. 3** *Inf.* the hero in a film, book, etc. **4** See **goodies.**

goody[2] (ˈgʊdɪ) *n, pl* **goodies.** *Arch. or literary.* a married woman of low rank: used as a title: *Goody Two-Shoes.* [C16: from GOODWIFE]

goody-goody *n, pl* **goody-goodies. 1** *Inf.* a smugly virtuous or sanctimonious person. ◆ *adj* **2** smug and sanctimonious.

gooey Ⓣ (ˈguːɪ) *adj* **gooier, gooiest.** *Inf.* **1** sticky, soft, and often sweet. **2** oversweet and sentimental.
▸ **ˈgooily** *adv*

goof (guːf) *Inf.* ◆ *n* **1** a foolish error. **2** a stupid person. ◆ *vb* **3** to bungle (something); botch. **4** (*intr; often foll. by about or around*) to fool (around); mess (about). [C20: prob. from (dialect) *goff* simpleton, from OF *goffe* clumsy, from It. *goffo,* from ?]

go off Ⓣ *vb* (*intr*) **1** (*adv*) (of power, a water supply, etc.) to cease to be available or functioning: *the lights suddenly went off.* **2** (*adv*) to explode. **3** (*adv*) to occur as specified: *the meeting went off well.* **4** to leave (a place): *the actors went off stage.* **5** (*adv*) (of a sensation) to gradually cease to be felt. **6** (*adv*) to fall asleep. **7** (*adv*) (of concrete, mortar, etc.) to harden. **8** (*adv*) *Brit. inf.* (of food, etc.) to become stale or rotten. **9** (*prep*) *Brit. inf.* to cease to like.

goofy (ˈguːfɪ) *adj* **goofier, goofiest.** *Inf.* foolish; silly.
▸ **ˈgoofily** *adv* ▸ **ˈgoofiness** *n*

goog (gʊg) *n Austral. sl.* an egg. [?from Du. *oog*]

googly (ˈguːglɪ) *n, pl* **googlies.** *Cricket.* an off break bowled with a leg break action. [C20: Austral. from ?]

goolie *or* **gooly** (ˈguːlɪ) *n, pl* **goolies. 1** (*usually pl*) *Taboo sl.* a testicle. **2** *Austral. sl.* a stone or pebble. [from Hindi *goli* ball]

goon (guːn) *n* **1** a stupid or deliberately foolish person. **2** *US inf.* a thug hired to commit acts of violence or intimidation, esp. in an industrial dispute. [C20: partly from dialect *gooney* fool, partly after the character Alice the *Goon,* created by E. C. Segar (1894–1938), American cartoonist]

go on Ⓣ *vb* (*intr, mostly adv*) **1** to continue or proceed. **2** to happen: *there's something peculiar going on here.* **3** (*prep*) to ride on, esp. as a treat: *children love to go on donkeys at the seaside.* **4** *Theatre.* to make an entrance on stage. **5** to talk excessively; chatter. **6** to continue talking, esp. after a short pause. **7** to criticize or nag: *stop going on at me all the time!* ◆ *sentence substitute.* **8** I don't believe what you're saying.

gooney bird (ˈguːnɪ) *n* an informal name for **albatross,** esp. the black-footed albatross. [C19 *gony* (orig. sailors' sl.), prob. from dialect *gooney* fool, from ?]

goop (guːp) *n US & Canad. sl.* **1** a rude or ill-mannered person. **2** any sticky or semiliquid substance. [C20: coined by G. Burgess (1866–1951), American humorist]
▸ **ˈgoopy** *adj*

goorie *or* **goory** (ˈguːrɪ) *n, pl* **goories.** *NZ inf.* a mongrel dog. [from Maori *kuri*]

goosander (guːˈsændə) *n* a common merganser (a duck) of Europe and North America, having a dark head and white body in the male. [C17: prob. from GOOSE[1] + ON *önd* (genitive *andar*) duck]

goose[1] (guːs) *n, pl* **geese. 1** any of various web-footed long-necked birds typically larger and less aquatic than ducks. They are gregarious and migratory. **2** the female of such a bird, as opposed to the male (gander). **3** *Inf.* a silly person. **4** (*pl* **gooses**) a pressing iron with a long curving handle, used esp. by tailors. **5** the flesh of the goose, used as food. **6 cook someone's goose.** *Inf.* **6a** to spoil someone's chances or plans completely. **6b** to bring about someone's downfall. **7 kill the goose that lays the golden eggs.** See **golden goose.** [OE *gōs*]

goose[2] (guːs) *Sl.* ◆ *vb* **gooses, goosing, goosed. 1** (*tr*) to prod (a person) playfully in the bottom. ◆ *n, pl* **gooses. 2** such a prod. [C19: from GOOSE[1], prob. from a comparison with the jabbing of a goose's bill]

gooseberry (ˈgʊzbərɪ, -brɪ) *n, pl* **gooseberries. 1** a Eurasian shrub having ovoid yellow-green or red-purple berries. **2a** the berry of this plant. **2b** (*as modifier*): *gooseberry jam.* **3** *Brit. inf.* an unwanted single person, esp. a third person with a couple (often in **play gooseberry**).

goose flesh *n* the bumpy condition of the skin induced by cold, fear, etc., caused by contraction of the muscles at the base of the hair follicles with consequent erection of papillae. Also called: **goose bumps, goose pimples, goose skin.**

goosefoot (ˈguːs,fʊt) *n, pl* **goosefoots.** any typically weedy plant having small greenish flowers and leaves shaped like a goose's foot.

goosegog (ˈgʊzgɒg) *n Brit.* a dialect or informal word for **gooseberry.** [from *goose* in GOOSEBERRY + *gog,* var. of GOB[1]]

goosegrass (ˈguːs,grɑːs) *n* another name for **cleavers.**

gooseneck (ˈguːs,nɛk) *n* something, such as a jointed pipe, in the form of the neck of a goose.

goose step *n* **1** a military march step in which the leg is swung rigidly to an exaggerated height. ◆ *vb* **goose-step, goose-steps, goose-stepping, goose-stepped. 2** (*intr*) to march in goose step.

go out Ⓣ *vb* (*intr, adv*) **1** to depart from a room, house, country, etc. **2** to cease to illuminate, burn, or function: *the fire has gone out.* **3** to cease to be fashionable or popular: *that style went out ages ago!* **4** (of a broadcast) to be transmitted. **5** to go to entertainments, social functions, etc. **6** (usually foll. by *with* or *together*) to associate (with a person of the opposite sex) regularly. **7** (of workers) to begin to strike. **8** *Card games, etc.* to get rid of the last card, token, etc., in one's hand.

go over Ⓣ *vb* (*intr*) **1** to be received in a specified manner: *the concert went over very well.* **2** (*prep*) Also: **go through.** to examine and revise as necessary: *he went over the accounts.* **3** (*prep*) to check and repair: *can you go over my car, please?* **4** (*prep*) Also: **go through.** to rehearse: *I'll go over my lines before the play.*

gopak (ˈgəʊ,pæk) *n* a spectacular high-leaping Russian peasant dance for men. [from Russian]

gopher (ˈgəʊfə) *n* **1** Also called: **pocket gopher.** a burrowing rodent of North and Central America, having a thickset body, short legs, and cheek pouches. **2** another name for **ground squirrel. 3** a burrowing tortoise of SE North America. [C19: from earlier *megopher* or *magopher,* from ?]

goral (ˈgɔːrəl) *n* a small goat antelope inhabiting mountainous regions of S Asia. [C19: from Hindi, prob. from Sansk.]

Gordian knot (ˈgɔːdɪən) *n* **1** (in Greek legend) a complicated knot, tied by King Gordius of Phrygia, that Alexander the Great cut with a sword. **2** a complicated and intricate problem (esp. in **cut the Gordian knot**).

gore[1] Ⓣ (gɔː) *n* **1** blood shed from a wound, esp. when coagulated. **2** *Inf.* killing, fighting, etc. [OE *gor* dirt]

gore[2] Ⓣ (gɔː) *vb* **gores, goring, gored.** (*tr*) (of an animal, such as a bull) to pierce or stab (a person or another animal) with a horn or tusk. [C16: prob. from OE *gār* spear]

gore[3] (gɔː) *n* **1** a tapering or triangular piece of material used in making a shaped skirt, umbrella, etc. ◆ *vb* **gores, goring, gored. 2** (*tr*) to make into or with a gore or gores. [OE *gāra*]
▸ **gored** *adj*

gorge Ⓣ (gɔːdʒ) *n* **1** a deep ravine, esp. one through which a river runs. **2** the contents of the stomach. **3** feelings of disgust or resentment (esp. in **one's gorge rises**). **4** an obstructing mass: *an ice gorge.* **5** *Fortifications.* a narrow rear entrance to a work. **6** *Arch.* the throat or gullet. ◆ *vb* **gorges, gorging, gorged. 7** to swallow (food) ravenously. **8** (*tr*) to stuff (oneself) with food. [C14: from OF *gorger* to stuff, from *gorge* throat, from LL *gurga,* from L *gurges* whirlpool]

gorgeous Ⓣ (ˈgɔːdʒəs) *adj* **1** strikingly beautiful or magnificent: *a gorgeous array; a gorgeous girl.* **2** *Inf.* extremely pleasing, fine, or good: *gorgeous weather.* [C15: from OF *gorgias* elegant, from *gorge;* see GORGE]
▸ **ˈgorgeously** *adv* ▸ **ˈgorgeousness** *n*

gorget (ˈgɔːdʒɪt) *n* **1** a collar-like piece of armour worn to protect the throat. **2** a part of a wimple worn by women to cover the throat and chest, esp. in the 14th century. **3** a band of distinctive colour on the throat of an animal, esp. a bird. [C15: from OF, from *gorge;* see GORGE]

Gorgio (ˈgɔːdʒɪəʊ) *n, pl* **Gorgios.** the Gypsy name for a non-Gypsy. [C19: from Romany]

THESAURUS

sions, things, trappings **3** = **merchandise,** commodities, stock, stuff, wares

goodwill *n* **1** = **friendliness,** amity, benevolence, favour, friendship, heartiness, kindliness, zeal

gooey *adj* **1** = **sticky,** gluey, glutinous, mucilaginous, soft, tacky, viscous **2** = **sentimental,** maudlin, mawkish, slushy (*inf.*), syrupy (*inf.*), tear-jerking (*inf.*)

go off *vb* **2** = **explode,** blow up, detonate, fire **3** = **happen,** occur, take place **4** = **leave,** decamp, depart, go away, hook it (*sl.*), move out, pack one's bags (*inf.*), part, quit, slope off **8** *Informal* = **rot,** go bad, go stale

go on *vb* **1** = **continue,** endure, happen, last, occur, persist, proceed, stay **5** = **chatter,** blether, carry on, prattle, rabbit (*Brit. inf.*), ramble on, waffle (*inf., chiefly Brit.*), witter (on) (*inf.*)

go out *vb* **1** = **leave,** depart, exit **2** = **be extinguished,** die out, expire, fade out

go over *vb* **2** = **examine,** inspect, rehearse, reiterate, review, revise, study, work over

gore[1] *n* **2** = **blood,** bloodshed, butchery, carnage, slaughter

gore[2] *vb* = **pierce,** impale, spit, stab, transfix, wound

gorge *n* **1** = **ravine,** canyon, chasm, cleft, clough (*dialect*), defile, fissure, pass ◆ *vb* **7, 8** = **overeat,** bolt, cram, devour, feed, fill, glut, gobble, gormandize, gulp, guzzle, pig out (*US & Canad. sl.*), raven, sate, satiate, stuff, surfeit, swallow, wolf

gorgeous *adj* **1** = **beautiful,** brilliant, dazzling, drop-dead (*sl.*), elegant, glittering, grand, luxuriant, magnificent, opulent, ravishing, resplendent, showy, splendid, splendiferous (*facetious*), stunning (*inf.*), sumptuous, superb **2** *Informal* = **pleasing,** attractive, bright, delightful, enjoyable, exquisite, fine, glorious, good, good-looking, lovely
Antonyms *adj* cheap, dismal, dreary, dull, gloomy, homely, plain, repulsive, shabby, shoddy, sombre, ugly, unattractive, unsightly

Gorgon ('gɔːgən) *n* **1** *Greek myth.* any of three winged monstrous sisters who had live snakes for hair, huge teeth, and brazen claws. **2** (*often not cap.*) *Inf.* a fierce or unpleasant woman. [via L *Gorgō* from Gk, from *gorgos* terrible]

gorgonian (gɔː'gəʊnɪən) *n* any of various corals having a horny or calcareous branching skeleton, such as the sea fans and red corals.

Gorgonzola (ˌgɔːgən'zəʊlə) *n* a semihard blue-veined cheese of sharp flavour, made from pressed milk. [C19: after *Gorgonzola*, It. town where it originated]

gorilla (gə'rɪlə) *n* **1** the largest anthropoid ape, inhabiting the forests of central W Africa. It is stocky with a short muzzle and coarse dark hair. **2** *Inf.* a large, strong, and brutal-looking man. [C19: NL, from Gk *Gorillai*, an African tribe renowned for their hirsute appearance]

gormand ('gɔːmənd) *n* a less common spelling of **gourmand.**

gormandize *or* **gormandise** ('gɔːmənˌdaɪz) *vb* **gormandizes, gormandizing, gormandized** *or* **gormandises, gormandising, gormandised.** to eat (food) greedily and voraciously.
▸ **'gormandˌizer** *or* **'gormandˌiser** *n*

gormless ('gɔːmlɪs) *adj Brit. inf.* stupid; dull. [C19: var. of C18 *gaumless*, from dialect *gome*, from OE *gom, gome*, from ON *gaumr* heed]

go round *vb* (*intr*) **1** (*adv*) to be sufficient: *are there enough sweets to go round?* **2** to circulate (in): *measles is going round the school.* **3** to be long enough to encircle: *will that belt go round you?*

gorse (gɔːs) *n* an evergreen shrub which has yellow flowers and thick green spines instead of leaves. Also called: **furze, whin.** [OE *gors*]
▸ **'gorsy** *adj*

gory ❶ ('gɔːrɪ) *adj* **gorier, goriest. 1** horrific or bloodthirsty: *a gory story.* **2** involving bloodshed and killing: *a gory battle.* **3** covered in gore.
▸ **'gorily** *adv* ▸ **'goriness** *n*

gosh (gɒʃ) *interj* an exclamation of mild surprise or wonder. [C18: euphemistic for GOD]

goshawk ('gɒsˌhɔːk) *n* a large hawk of Europe, Asia, and North America, having a bluish-grey back and wings and paler underparts: used in falconry. [OE *gōshafoc*; see GOOSE[1], HAWK[1]]

gosling ('gɒzlɪŋ) *n* **1** a young goose. **2** an inexperienced or youthful person. [C15: from ON *gæslingr*; rel. to Danish *gäsling*; see GOOSE[1], -LING[1]]

go-slow *n* **1** *Brit.* a deliberate slackening of the rate of production by organized labour as a tactic in industrial conflict. US and Canad. equivalent: **slowdown.** ◆ *vb* **go slow. 2** (*intr*) to work deliberately slowly as a tactic in industrial conflict.

gospel ❶ ('gɒspᵊl) *n* **1** Also called: **gospel truth.** an unquestionable truth: *to take someone's word as gospel.* **2** a doctrine maintained to be of great importance. **3** Black religious music originating in the churches of the Southern states of the United States. **4** the message or doctrine of a religious teacher. **5a** the story of Christ's life and teachings as narrated in the Gospels. **5b** the good news of salvation in Jesus Christ. **5c** (*as modifier*): *the gospel story.* [OE *gōdspell*, from *gōd* GOOD + *spell* message; see SPELL[2]]

Gospel ('gɒspᵊl) *n* **1** any of the first four books of the New Testament, namely Matthew, Mark, Luke, and John. **2** a reading from one of these in a religious service.

gossamer ('gɒsəmə) *n* **1** a gauze or silk fabric of the very finest texture. **2** a filmy cobweb often seen on foliage or floating in the air. **3** anything resembling gossamer in fineness or filminess. [C14 (in sense 2): prob. from *gos* GOOSE[1] + *somer* SUMMER; the phrase refers to *St Martin's summer*, a period in November when goose was traditionally eaten; from the prevalence of the cobweb in the autumn]
▸ **'gossamery** *adj*

gossip ❶ ('gɒsɪp) *n* **1** casual and idle chat. **2** a conversation involving malicious chatter or rumours about other people. **3** Also called: **gossipmonger.** a person who habitually talks about others, esp. maliciously. **4** light easy communication: *to write a letter full of gossip.* **5** *Arch.* a close woman friend. ◆ *vb* **gossips, gossiping, gossiped. 6** (*intr*; often foll. by *about*) to talk casually or maliciously (about other people). [OE *godsibb* godparent, from GOD + SIB; came to be applied esp. to a woman's female friends at the birth of a child, hence a woman fond of light talk]
▸ **'gossiper** *n* ▸ **'gossipy** *adj*

gossypol ('gɒsɪˌpɒl) *n* a toxic crystalline pigment that is a constituent of cottonseed oil. [C19: from Mod. L *gossypium* cotton plant + -OL[1]]

got (gɒt) *vb* **1** the past tense and past participle of **get. 2 have got. 2a** to possess. **2b** (*takes an infinitive*) used as an auxiliary to express compulsion: *I've got to get a new coat.*

Goth (gɒθ) *n* **1** a member of an East Germanic people from Scandinavia who settled south of the Baltic early in the first millennium A.D. They moved on to the Ukrainian steppes and raided and later invaded many parts of the Roman Empire from the 3rd to the 5th century. **2** a rude or barbaric person. [C14: from LL (pl) *Gothī* from Gk *Gothoi*]

Gothic ('gɒθɪk) *adj* **1** denoting, relating to, or resembling the style of architecture that was used in W Europe from the 12th to the 16th centuries, characterized by the lancet arch, the ribbed vault, and the flying buttress. See also **Gothic Revival. 2** of or relating to the style of sculpture, painting, or other arts as practised in W Europe from the 12th to the 16th centuries. **3** (*sometimes not cap.*) of or relating to a literary style characterized by gloom, the grotesque, and the supernatural, popular esp. in the late 18th century: when used of modern literature, films, etc., sometimes spelt: **Gothick. 4** of, relating to, or characteristic of the Goths or their language. **5** (*sometimes not cap.*) primitive and barbarous in style, behaviour, etc. **6** of or relating to the Middle Ages. ◆ *n* **7** Gothic architecture or art. **8** the extinct language of the ancient Goths, known mainly from fragments of a translation of the Bible made in the 4th century by Bishop Wulfila. **9** Also called (esp. Brit): **black letter.** a family of heavy script typefaces.
▸ **'Gothically** *adv*

Gothic Revival *n* a Gothic style of architecture popular between the late 18th and late 19th centuries, exemplified by the Houses of Parliament in London (1840). Also called: **neogothic.**

go through ❶ *vb* (*intr*) **1** (*adv*) to be approved or accepted: *the amendment went through.* **2** (*prep*) to consume; exhaust: *we went through our supplies in a day.* **3** (*prep*) Also: **go over.** to examine: *he went through the figures.* **4** (*prep*) to suffer: *she went through tremendous pain.* **5** (*prep*) Also: **go over.** to rehearse: *let's just go through the details again.* **6** (*prep*) to search: *she went through the cupboards.* **7** (*adv*; foll. by *with*) to come or bring to a successful conclusion, often by persistence.

go together ❶ *vb* (*intr, adv*) **1** to be mutually suited; harmonize: *the colours go well together.* **2** *Inf.* (of two people) to have a romantic or sexual relationship: *they had been going together for two years.*

gotten ('gɒtᵊn) *vb Chiefly US.* a past participle of **get.**

Götterdämmerung (ˌgɒtə'dɛməˌrʊŋ) *n German myth.* the twilight of the gods; their ultimate destruction in a battle with the forces of evil.

gouache (gʊ'ɑːʃ) *n* **1** Also called: **body colour.** a painting technique using opaque watercolour in which the pigments are bound with glue and lighter tones contain white. **2** the paint used in this technique. **3** a painting done by this method. [C19: from F, from It. *guazzo* puddle, from L, from *aqua* water]

Gouda ('gaʊdə) *n* a large round mild Dutch cheese, orig. made in the town of Gouda.

gouge ❶ (gaʊdʒ) *vb* **gouges, gouging, gouged.** (*mainly tr*) **1** (usually foll. by *out*) to scoop or force (something) out of its position. **2** (sometimes foll. by *out*) to cut (a hole or groove) in (something) with a sharp instrument or tool. **3** *US & Canad. inf.* to extort from. **4** (*also intr*) *Austral.* to dig for (opal). ◆ *n* **5** a type of chisel with a blade that has a concavo-convex section. **6** a mark or groove made as with a gouge. **7** *US & Canad. inf.* extortion; swindling. [C15: from F, from LL *gulbia* a chisel, of Celtic origin]
▸ **'gouger** *n*

goujon ('guːʒɒn) *n* a small strip of fish or chicken, coated in breadcrumbs and deep-fried. [F, lit.: gudgeon]

goulash ('guːlæʃ) *n* **1** Also called: **Hungarian goulash.** a rich stew, originating in Hungary, made of beef, lamb, or veal highly seasoned with paprika. **2** *Bridge.* a method of dealing in threes and fours without first shuffling the cards, to produce freak hands. [C19: from Hungarian *gulyás hus* herdsman's meat]

go under ❶ *vb* (*intr, mainly adv*) **1** (*also prep*) to sink below (a surface). **2** to be overwhelmed: *the firm went under in the economic crisis.*

go up *vb* (*intr, mainly adv*) **1** (*also prep*) to move or lead as to a higher place or level; rise; increase: *prices are always going up.* **2** to be destroyed: *the house went up in flames.* **3** *Brit.* to go or return (to college or university) at the beginning of a term or academic year.

gourami ('gʊərəmɪ) *n, pl* **gourami** *or* **gouramis. 1** a large SE Asian labyrinth fish used for food. **2** any of various other labyrinth fishes, many of which are brightly coloured and popular aquarium fishes. [from Malay *gurami*]

gourd (gʊəd) *n* **1** the fruit of any of various plants of the cucumber family, esp. the bottle gourd and some squashes, whose dried shells are used for ornament, drinking cups, etc. **2** any plant that bears this fruit. **3** a bottle or flask made from the dried shell of the bottle gourd. [C14: from OF *gourde*, ult. from L *cucurbita*]

gourmand ('gʊəmənd) *or* **gormand** *n* a person devoted to eating and drinking, esp. to excess. [C15: from OF *gourmant*, from ?]
▸ **'gourmandˌism** *n*

THESAURUS

gory *adj* **1-3** = **bloodthirsty**, blood-soaked, bloodstained, bloody, ensanguined (*literary*), murderous, sanguinary

gospel *n* **1** = **truth**, certainty, fact, the last word, verity **2** = **doctrine**, credo, creed, message, news, revelation, tidings

gossip *n* **1** = **idle talk**, blether, bush telegraph, buzz, chinwag (*Brit. inf.*), chitchat, clishmaclaver (*Scot.*), dirt (*US sl.*), gen (*Brit. inf.*), hearsay, jaw (*sl.*), latest (*inf.*), newsmongering (*old-fashioned*), prattle, scandal, scuttlebutt (*US sl.*), small talk, tittle-tattle **3** = **busybody**, babbler, blatherskite, blether, chatterbox (*inf.*), chatterer, flibbertigibbet, gossip-monger, newsmonger (*old-fashioned*), prattler, quidnunc, scandalmonger, tattler, telltale ◆ *vb* **6** = **chat**, blather, blether, chew the fat *or* rag (*sl.*), dish the dirt (*inf.*), gabble, jaw (*sl.*), prate, prattle, schmooze (*sl.*), shoot the breeze (*sl., chiefly US*), tattle

go through *vb* **2** = **use up**, consume, exhaust, squander **3** = **examine**, check, explore, forage, hunt, look, search, work over **4** = **suffer**, bear, brave, endure, experience, tolerate, undergo, withstand

go together *vb* **1** = **harmonize**, accord, agree, fit, make a pair, match **2** *Informal* = **go out**, court, date (*inf., chiefly US*), escort, go steady (*inf.*)

gouge *vb* **1, 2** = **scoop**, chisel, claw, cut, dig (out), gash, hollow (out), incise, score, scratch ◆ *n* **6** = **gash**, cut, furrow, groove, hollow, incision, notch, scoop, score, scratch, trench

go under *vb* **2** = **sink**, default, die, drown, fail, fold (*inf.*), founder, go down, submerge, succumb

DICTIONARY

gourmet ➊ (ˈɡʊəmeɪ) *n* a person who cultivates a discriminating palate for the enjoyment of good food and drink. [C19: from F, from OF *gromet* serving boy]

gout (ɡaʊt) *n* **1** a metabolic disease characterized by painful inflammation of certain joints, esp. of the big toe, caused by deposits of sodium urate. **2** *Arch.* a drop or splash, esp. of blood. [C13: from OF, from L *gutta* a drop]
▸ **ˈgouty** *adj* ▸ **ˈgoutily** *adv* ▸ **ˈgoutiness** *n*

Gov. *or* **gov.** *abbrev. for:* **1** government. **2** governor.

govern ➊ (ˈɡʌvᵊn) *vb* (*mainly tr*) **1** (*also intr*) to direct and control the actions, affairs, policies, functions, etc., of (an organization, nation, etc.); rule. **2** to exercise restraint over; regulate or direct: *to govern one's temper.* **3** to decide or determine (something): *his injury governed his decision to avoid sports.* **4** to control the speed of (an engine, machine, etc.) using a governor. **5** (of a word) to determine the inflection of (another word): *Latin nouns govern adjectives that modify them.* [C13: from OF, from L *gubernāre* to steer, from Gk *kubernan*]
▸ **ˈgovernable** *adj*

governance (ˈɡʌvənəns) *n* **1** government, control, or authority. **2** the action, manner, or system of governing.

governess (ˈɡʌvənɪs) *n* a woman teacher employed in a private household to teach and train the children.

government ➊ (ˈɡʌvənmənt, ˈɡʌvəmənt) *n* **1** the exercise of political authority over the actions, affairs, etc., of a political unit, people, etc.; the action of governing; political rule and administration. **2** the system or form by which a community, etc., is ruled: *tyrannical government.* **3a** the executive policy-making body of a political unit, community, etc.; ministry or administration. **3b** (*cap. when of a specific country*): *the British Government.* **4a** the state and its administration: *blame it on the government.* **4b** (*as modifier*): *a government agency.* **5** regulation; direction. **6** *Grammar.* the determination of the form of one word by another word.
▸**governmental** (ˌɡʌvənˈmɛntᵊl, ˌɡʌvəˈmɛntᵊl) *adj* ▸**ˌgovernˈmentally** *adv*

governor ➊ (ˈɡʌvənə) *n* **1** a person who governs. **2** the ruler or chief magistrate of a colony, province, etc. **3** the representative of the Crown in a British colony. **4** *Brit.* the senior administrator of a society, prison, etc. **5** the chief executive of any state in the US. **6** a device that controls the speed of an engine, esp. by regulating the supply of fuel. **7** *Brit. inf.* a name or title of respect for a father, employer, etc.
▸ **ˈgovernorˌship** *n*

governor general *n, pl* **governors general** *or* **governor generals. 1** the representative of the Crown in a dominion of the Commonwealth or a British colony; vicegerent. **2** *Brit.* a governor with jurisdiction or precedence over other governors.
▸ **ˌgovernor-ˈgeneralˌship** *n*

Govt *or* **govt** *abbrev. for* government.

go with ➊ *vb* (*intr, prep*) **1** to accompany. **2** to blend or harmonize: *that new wallpaper goes well with the furniture.* **3** to be a normal part of: *three acres of land go with the house.* **4** (of two people of the opposite sex) to associate frequently with each other.

go without ➊ *vb* (*intr*) *Chiefly Brit.* to be denied or deprived of (something, esp. food): *if you don't like your tea you can go without.*

gowk (ɡaʊk) *n Scot. & N English dialect.* **1** a fool. **2** a cuckoo. [from ON *gaukr* cuckoo]

gown ➊ (ɡaʊn) *n* **1** any of various outer garments, such as a woman's elegant or formal dress, a dressing robe, or a protective garment, esp. one worn by surgeons during operations. **2** a loose wide garment indicating status, such as worn by academics. **3** the members of a university as opposed to the other residents of the university town. ◆ *vb* **4** (*tr*) to supply with or dress in a gown. [C14: from OF, from LL *gunna* garment made of leather or fur, of Celtic origin]

goy (ɡɔɪ) *n, pl* **goyim** (ˈɡɔɪɪm) *or* **goys.** a Jewish word for a **Gentile.** [from Yiddish, from Heb. *goi* people]
▸ **ˈgoyish** *adj*

GP *abbrev. for:* **1** Gallup Poll. **2** *Music.* general pause. **3** general practitioner. **4** (in Britain) graduated pension. **5** Grand Prix.

GPMU (in Britain) *abbrev. for* Graphical, Paper and Media Union.

GPO *abbrev. for* general post office.

Gr. *abbrev. for:* **1** Grecian. **2** Greece. **3** Greek.

Graafian follicle (ˈɡrɑːfɪən) *n* a fluid-filled vesicle in the mammalian ovary containing a developing egg cell. [C17: after R. de *Graaf* (1641–73), Du. anatomist]

grab ➊ (ɡræb) *vb* **grabs, grabbing, grabbed. 1** to seize hold of (something). **2** (*tr*) to seize illegally or unscrupulously. **3** (*tr*) to arrest; catch. **4** (*tr*) *Inf.* to catch the attention or interest of; impress. ◆ *n* **5** the act or an instance of grabbing. **6** a mechanical device for gripping objects, esp. the hinged jaws of a mechanical excavator. **7** something that is grabbed. [C16: prob. from MLow G or MDu. *grabben*]
▸ **ˈgrabber** *n*

grab bag *n* **1** a collection of miscellaneous things. **2** *US, Canad., & Austral.* a bag or other container from which gifts are drawn at random.

grabby (ˈɡræbɪ) *adj* **grabbier, grabbiest. 1** grasping or avaricious. **2** seizing the attention: *a grabby headline; a grabby performance.*

grace ➊ (ɡreɪs) *n* **1** elegance and beauty of movement, form, expression, or proportion. **2** a pleasing or charming quality. **3** goodwill or favour. **4** a delay granted for the completion of a task or payment of a debt. **5** a sense of propriety and consideration for others. **6** (*pl*) **6a** affectation of manner (esp. in **airs and graces**). **6b in (someone's) good graces.** regarded favourably and with kindness by (someone). **7** mercy; clemency. **8** *Christian theol.* **8a** the free and unmerited favour of God shown towards man. **8b** the divine assistance given to man in spiritual rebirth. **8c** the condition of being favoured or sanctified by God. **8d** an unmerited gift, favour, etc., granted by God. **9** a short prayer recited before or after a meal to give thanks for it. **10** *Music.* a melodic ornament or decoration. **11 with (a) bad grace.** unwillingly or grudgingly. **12 with (a) good grace.** willingly or cheerfully. ◆ *vb* **graces, gracing, graced. 13** (*tr*) to add elegance and beauty to: *flowers graced the room.* **14** (*tr*) to honour or favour: *to grace a party with one's presence.* **15** to ornament or decorate (a melody, part, etc.) with nonessential notes. [C12: from OF, from L *grātia,* from *grātus* pleasing]

Grace (ɡreɪs) *n* (preceded by *your, his,* or *her*) a title used to address or refer to a duke, duchess, or archbishop.

grace-and-favour *n* (*modifier*) *Brit.* (of a house, flat, etc.) owned by the sovereign and granted free of rent to a person to whom the sovereign wishes to express gratitude.

graceful ➊ (ˈɡreɪsfʊl) *adj* characterized by beauty of movement, style, form, etc.
▸ **ˈgracefully** *adv* ▸ **ˈgracefulness** *n*

graceless ➊ (ˈɡreɪslɪs) *adj* **1** lacking manners. **2** lacking elegance.
▸ **ˈgracelessly** *adv* ▸ **ˈgracelessness** *n*

grace note *n Music.* a note printed in small type to indicate that it is melodically and harmonically nonessential.

Graces (ˈɡreɪsɪz) *pl n Greek myth.* three sister goddesses, givers of charm and beauty.

gracious ➊ (ˈɡreɪʃəs) *adj* **1** characterized by or showing kindness and courtesy. **2** condescendingly courteous, benevolent, or indulgent. **3** characterized by or suitable for a life of elegance, ease, and indulgence: *gracious living.* **4** merciful or compassionate. ◆ *interj* **5** an expression of mild surprise or wonder.
▸ **ˈgraciously** *adv* ▸ **ˈgraciousness** *n*

grackle (ˈɡrækᵊl) *n* **1** an American songbird of the oriole family, having a dark iridescent plumage. **2** any of various starlings, such as the Indian grackle or hill myna. [C18: from NL, from L *grāculus* jackdaw]

THESAURUS

gourmet *n* = **connoisseur,** *bon vivant,* epicure, foodie (*inf.*), gastronome

govern *vb* **1** = **rule,** administer, be in power, call the shots, call the tune, command, conduct, control, direct, guide, handle, hold sway, lead, manage, order, oversee, pilot, reign, steer, superintend, supervise **3** = **determine,** decide, guide, influence, rule, sway, underlie **4** = **restrain,** bridle, check, contain, control, curb, direct, discipline, get the better of, hold in check, inhibit, keep a tight rein on, master, regulate, subdue, tame

government *n* **1** = **rule,** administration, authority, dominion, execution, governance, law, polity, sovereignty, state, statecraft **3** = **executive,** administration, ministry, powers-that-be, regime **5** = **guidance,** authority, command, control, direction, domination, management, regulation, restraint, superintendence, supervision, sway

governmental *adj* **1** = **administrative,** bureaucratic, executive, ministerial, official, political, sovereign, state

governor *n* **1** = **leader,** administrator, boss (*inf.*), chief, commander, comptroller, controller, director, executive, head, manager, overseer, ruler, superintendent, supervisor

go with *vb* **2** = **match,** agree, blend, complement, concur, correspond, fit, harmonize, suit

go without *vb* = **be deprived of,** abstain, be denied, deny oneself, do without, go short, lack, want

gown *n* **1** = **dress,** costume, frock, garb, garment, habit, robe

grab *vb* **1** = **snatch,** bag, capture, catch, catch *or* take hold of, clutch, grasp, grip, latch on to, nab (*inf.*), nail (*inf.*), pluck, seize, snap up

grace *n* **1, 2** = **elegance,** attractiveness, beauty, charm, comeliness, ease, finesse, gracefulness, loveliness, pleasantness, poise, polish, refinement, shapeliness, tastefulness **3** = **goodwill,** benefaction, beneficence, benevolence, favour, generosity, goodness, kindliness, kindness **5** = **manners,** breeding, consideration, cultivation, decency, decorum, etiquette, mannerliness, propriety, tact **7** = **indulgence,** charity, clemency, compassion, forgiveness, leniency, lenity, mercy, pardon, quarter, reprieve **9** = **prayer,** benediction, blessing, thanks, thanksgiving ◆ *vb* **13, 14** = **honour,** adorn, beautify, bedeck, deck, decorate, dignify, distinguish, elevate, embellish, enhance, enrich, favour, garnish, glorify, ornament, set off
Antonyms *n* ≠ **elegance:** awkwardness, clumsiness, inelegance, stiffness, tastelessness, ugliness, ungainliness ≠ **goodwill:** disfavour, ill will ≠ **manners:** bad manners, tactlessness ◆ *vb* ≠ **honour:** desecrate, dishonour, insult, ruin, spoil

graceful *adj* = **elegant,** agile, beautiful, becoming, charming, comely, easy, fine, flowing, gracile (*rare*), natural, pleasing, smooth, symmetrical, tasteful
Antonyms *adj* awkward, clumsy, gawky, inelegant, plain, ponderous, stiff, ugly, ungainly, ungraceful

graceless *adj* **1** = **ill-mannered,** barbarous, boorish, coarse, crude, improper, indecorous, loutish, rude, shameless, unmannerly, unsophisticated, vulgar **2** = **inelegant,** awkward, clumsy, forced, gauche, gawky, rough, uncouth, ungainly, untutored

gracious *adj* **1, 2, 4** = **kind,** accommodating, affable, amiable, beneficent, benevolent, benign, benignant, charitable, chivalrous, civil, compassionate, considerate, cordial, courteous, courtly, friendly, hospitable, indulgent, kindly, lenient, loving, merciful, mild, obliging, pleasing, polite, well-mannered
Antonyms *adj* brusque, cold, discourteous, gruff, haughty, impolite, mean, remote, rude, surly, unfriendly, ungracious, unpleasant

grad. *abbrev. for:* **1** *Maths.* gradient. **2** *Education.* graduate(d).

gradate (grəˈdeɪt) *vb* **gradates, gradating, gradated. 1** to change or cause to change imperceptibly, as from one colour, tone, or degree to another. **2** *(tr)* to arrange in grades or ranks.

gradation Ⓣ (grəˈdeɪʃən) *n* **1** a series of systematic stages; gradual progression. **2** *(often pl)* a stage or degree in such a series or progression. **3** the act or process of arranging or forming in stages, grades, etc., or of progressing evenly. **4** (in painting, drawing, or sculpture) transition from one colour, tone, or surface to another through a series of very slight changes. **5** *Linguistics.* any change in the quality or length of a vowel within a word indicating certain distinctions, such as inflectional or tense differentiations. See **ablaut.**
► **graˈdational** *adj*

grade Ⓣ (greɪd) *n* **1** a position or degree in a scale, as of quality, rank, size, or progression: *high-grade timber.* **2** a group of people or things of the same category. **3** *Chiefly US.* a military or other rank. **4** a stage in a course of progression. **5** a mark or rating indicating achievement or the worth of work done, as at school. **6** *US & Canad.* a unit of pupils of similar age or ability taught together at school. **7 make the grade.** *Inf.* **7a** to reach the required standard. **7b** to succeed. ◆ *vb* **grades, grading, graded. 8** *(tr)* to arrange according to quality, rank, etc. **9** *(tr)* to determine the grade of or assign a grade to. **10** *(intr)* to achieve or deserve a grade or rank. **11** to change or blend (something) gradually; merge. **12** *(tr)* to level (ground, a road, etc.) to a suitable gradient. [C16: from F, from L *gradus* step, from *gradī* to step]

-grade *adj combining form.* indicating a kind or manner of movement or progression: *plantigrade; retrograde.* [via F from L *-gradus,* from *gradus* a step, from *gradī* to walk]

gradely (ˈgreɪdlɪ) *adj* **gradelier, gradeliest.** *Midland English dialect.* fine; excellent. [C13: from ON *greidhligr,* from *greidhr* ready]

grader (ˈgreɪdə) *n* **1** a person or thing that grades. **2** a machine that levels earth, rubble, etc., as in road construction.

gradient Ⓣ (ˈgreɪdɪənt) *n* **1** Also called (esp. US): **grade.** a part of a railway, road, etc., that slopes upwards or downwards; inclination. **2** Also called (esp. US and Canad.): **grade.** a measure of such a slope, esp. the ratio of the vertical distance between two points on the slope to the horizontal distance between them. **3** *Physics.* a measure of the change of some physical quantity, such as temperature or electric potential, over a specified distance. **4** *Maths.* (of a curve) the slope of the tangent at any point on a curve with respect to the horizontal axis. ◆ *adj* **5** sloping uniformly. [C19: from L *gradiēns* stepping, from *gradī* to go]

gradin (ˈgreɪdɪn) *or* **gradine** (grəˈdiːn) *n* **1** a ledge above or behind an altar for candles, etc., to stand on. **2** one of a set of steps or seats arranged on a slope, as in an amphitheatre. [C19: from F, from It. *gradino,* dim. of *grado* a step]

gradual Ⓣ (ˈgrædjʊəl) *adj* **1** occurring, developing, moving, etc., in small stages: *a gradual improvement in health.* **2** not steep or abrupt: *a gradual slope.* ◆ *n* **3** *(often cap.) Christianity.* **3a** an antiphon usually from the Psalms, sung or recited immediately after the epistle at Mass. **3b** a book of plainsong containing the words and music of the parts of the Mass that are sung by the cantors and choir. [C16: from Med. L: relating to steps, from L *gradus* a step]
► **ˈgradually** *adv* ► **ˈgradualness** *n*

gradualism (ˈgrædjʊəˌlɪzəm) *n* **1** the policy of seeking to change something gradually, esp. in politics. **2** the theory that explains major changes in fossils, rock strata, etc., in terms of gradual evolutionary processes rather than sudden violent catastrophes.
► **ˈgradualist** *n, adj* ► **ˌgradualˈistic** *adj*

graduand (ˈgrædjʊˌænd) *n Chiefly Brit.* a person who is about to graduate. [C19: from Med. L gerundive of *graduārī* to GRADUATE]

graduate Ⓣ *n* (ˈgrædjʊɪt). **1** a person who has been awarded a first degree from a university or college. **2** *US & Canad.* a student who has completed a course of studies at a high school and received a diploma. ◆ *vb* (ˈgrædjʊˌeɪt), **graduates, graduating, graduated. 3** to receive or cause to receive a degree or diploma. **4** *Chiefly US & Canad.* to confer a degree, diploma, etc., upon. **5** *(tr)* to mark (a thermometer, flask, etc.) with units of measurement; calibrate. **6** *(tr)* to arrange or sort into groups according to type, quality, etc. **7** *(intr; often foll. by to)* to change by degrees (from something to something else). [C15: from Med. L *graduārī* to take a degree, from L *gradus* a step]
► **ˈgraduˌator** *n*

graduated pension *n* (in Britain) a national pension scheme in which employees' contributions are scaled in accordance with their wage rate.

graduation (ˌgrædjʊˈeɪʃən) *n* **1** the act of graduating or the state of being graduated. **2** the ceremony at which school or college degrees and diplomas are conferred. **3** a mark or division or all the marks or divisions that indicate measure on an instrument or vessel.

Graecism *or esp. US* **Grecism** (ˈgriːsɪzəm) *n* **1** Greek characteristics or style. **2** admiration for or imitation of these, as in sculpture or architecture. **3** a form of words characteristic of the idiom of the Greek language.

Graeco- *or esp. US* **Greco-** (ˈgriːkəʊ, ˈgrɛkəʊ) *combining form.* Greek: *Graeco-Roman.*

Graeco-Roman *or esp. US* **Greco-Roman** *adj* of, characteristic of, or relating to Greek and Roman influences.

graffiti (græˈfiːtɪ) *pl n (sometimes functioning as sing)* drawings, messages, etc., often obscene, scribbled on the walls of public lavatories, advertising posters, etc. [C19: see GRAFFITO]

graffito (græˈfiːtəʊ) *n, pl* **graffiti** (-tɪ). **1** *Archaeol.* any inscription or drawing scratched onto a surface, esp. rock or pottery. **2** See **graffiti.** [C19: from It.: a little scratch, from L *graphium* stylus, from Gk *grapheion;* see GRAFT[1]]

graft[1] Ⓣ (grɑːft) *n* **1** *Horticulture.* **1a** a small piece of plant tissue (the scion) that is made to unite with an established plant (the stock), which supports and nourishes it. **1b** the plant resulting from the union of scion and stock. **1c** the point of union between the scion and the stock. **2** *Surgery.* a piece of tissue transplanted from a donor or from the patient's own body to an area of the body in need of the tissue. **3** the act of joining one thing to another as by grafting. ◆ *vb* **4** *Horticulture.* **4a** to induce (a plant or part of a plant) to unite with another part or (of a plant or part of a plant) to unite in this way. **4b** to produce (fruit, flowers, etc.) by this means or (of fruit, etc.) to grow by this means. **5** to transplant (tissue) or (of tissue) to be transplanted. **6** to attach or incorporate or become attached or incorporated: *to graft a happy ending onto a sad tale.* [C15: from OF *graffe,* from Med. L *graphium,* from L: stylus, from Gk *grapheion,* from *graphein* to write]
► **ˈgrafting** *n*

graft[2] (grɑːft) *n* **1** *Inf.* work (esp. in **hard graft**). **2a** the acquisition of money, power, etc., by dishonest or unfair means, esp. by taking advantage of a position of trust. **2b** something gained in this way. **2c** a payment made to a person profiting by such a practice. ◆ *vb* **3** *(intr) Inf.* to work, esp. hard. **4** to acquire by or practise graft. [C19: from ?]
► **ˈgrafter** *n*

Grail (greɪl) *n* See **Holy Grail.**

grain Ⓣ (greɪn) *n* **1** the small hard seedlike fruit of a grass, esp. a cereal plant. **2** a mass of such fruits, esp. when gathered for food. **3** the plants, collectively, from which such fruits are harvested. **4** a small hard particle: *a grain of sand.* **5a** the general direction or arrangement of the fibres, layers, or particles in wood, leather, stone, etc. **5b** the pattern or texture resulting from such an arrangement. **6** the relative size of the particles of a substance: *sugar of fine grain.* **7** the granular texture of a rock, mineral, etc. **8** the outer layer of a hide or skin from which the hair or wool has been removed. **9** the smallest unit of weight in the avoirdupois, Troy, and apothecaries' systems: equal to 0.0648 gram. **10** the threads or direction of threads in a woven fabric. **11** *Photog.* any of a large number of particles in a photographic emulsion. **12** cleavage lines in crystalline material. **13** *Chem.* any of a large number of small crystals forming a solid. **14** a very small amount: *a grain of truth.* **15** natural disposition, inclination, or character (esp. in **go against the grain**). **16** *Astronautics.* a homogenous mass of solid propellant in a form designed to give the required combustion characteristics for a particular rocket. **17** (not in technical usage) kermes or a red dye made from this insect. ◆ *vb (mainly tr)* **18** *(also intr)* to form grains or cause to form into grains; granulate; crystallize. **19** to give a granular or roughened appearance or texture to. **20** to paint, stain, etc., in imitation of the grain of wood or leather. **21a** to remove the hair or wool from (a hide or skin) before tanning. **21b** to raise the grain pattern on (leather). [C13: from OF, from L *grānum*]

grain alcohol *n* ethanol containing about 10 per cent of water, made by the fermentation of grain.

grain elevator *n* a machine for raising grain to a higher level, esp. one having an endless belt fitted with scoops.

graining (ˈgreɪnɪŋ) *n* **1** the pattern or texture of the grain of wood, leather, etc. **2** the process of painting, printing, staining, etc., a surface in imitation of a grain. **3** a surface produced by such a process.

grainy (ˈgreɪnɪ) *adj* **grainier, grainiest. 1** resembling, full of, or composed of grain; granular. **2** resembling the grain of wood, leather, etc. **3** *Photog.* having poor definition because of large grain size.
► **ˈgraininess** *n*

THESAURUS

gradation *n* **1** = **progression**, array, sequence, series, succession **2** = **stage**, degree, grade, level, mark, measurement, notch, place, point, position, rank, step **3** = **classification**, arrangement, grouping, ordering, sorting

grade *n* **1, 4** = **level**, brand, category, class, condition, degree, echelon, group, mark, notch, order, place, position, quality, rank, rung, size, stage, station, step **7 make the grade** *Informal* = **succeed**, come through with flying colours, come up to scratch (*inf.*), measure up, measure up to expectations, pass muster, prove acceptable, win through ◆ *vb* **8** = **classify**, arrange, brand, class, evaluate, group, order, range, rank, rate, sequence, sort, value

gradient *n* **1** = **slope**, acclivity, bank, declivity, grade, hill, incline, rise

gradual *adj* **1** = **steady**, continuous, even, gentle, graduated, moderate, piecemeal, progressive, regular, slow, successive, unhurried
Antonyms *adj* abrupt, broken, instantaneous, overnight, sudden

gradually *adv* **1** = **steadily**, bit by bit, by degrees, drop by drop, evenly, gently, little by little, moderately, piece by piece, piecemeal, progressively, slowly, step by step, unhurriedly

graduate *vb* **5** = **mark off**, calibrate, grade, measure out, proportion, regulate **6** = **classify**, arrange, grade, group, order, range, rank, sequence, sort

graft[1] *n* **1a** = **shoot**, bud, implant, scion, splice, sprout ◆ *vb* **4a** = **transplant**, affix, implant, ingraft, insert, join, splice

grain *n* **1** = **seed**, grist, kernel **3** = **cereals**, corn **10** = **texture**, fibre, nap, pattern, surface, weave **14** = **bit**, atom, crumb, fragment, granule, iota, jot, mite, modicum, molecule, morsel, mote, ounce, particle, piece, scrap, scruple, spark, speck, suspicion, trace, whit **15** *As in* **go against the grain** = **inclination**, character, disposition, humour, make-up, temper

grallatorial (ˌgrælə'tɔːrɪəl) *adj* of or relating to long-legged wading birds. [C19: from NL, from L *grallātor* one who walks on stilts, from *grallae* stilts]

gram[1] (græm) *n* a metric unit of mass equal to one thousandth of a kilogram. Symbol: g [C18: from F *gramme*, from LL *gramma*, from Gk: small weight, from *graphein* to write]

gram[2] (græm) *n* **1** any of several leguminous plants whose seeds are used as food in India. **2** the seed of any of these plants. [C18: from Port. *gram* (modern spelling: *grão*), from L *grānum* GRAIN]

gram. *abbrev. for:* **1** grammar. **2** grammatical.

-gram *n combining form.* indicating a drawing or something written or recorded: *hexagram; telegram.* [from L *-gramma*, from Gk, from *gramma* letter & *grammē* line]

gram atom *or* **gram-atomic weight** *n* an amount of an element equal to its atomic weight expressed in grams: now replaced by the mole.

gramineous (grə'mɪnɪəs) *adj* **1** of, relating to, or belonging to the grass family. **2** resembling a grass; grasslike. ◆ Also: **graminaceous** (ˌgræmɪ'neɪʃəs). [C17: from L, from *grāmen* grass]

graminivorous (ˌgræmɪ'nɪvərəs) *adj* (of animals) feeding on grass. [C18: from L *grāmen* grass + -VOROUS]

grammar ➊ ('græmə) *n* **1** the branch of linguistics that deals with syntax and morphology, sometimes also phonology and semantics. **2** the abstract system of rules in terms of which a person's mastery of his native language can be explained. **3** a systematic description of the grammatical facts of a language. **4** a book containing an account of the grammatical facts of a language or recommendations as to rules for the proper use of a language. **5** the use of language with regard to its correctness or social propriety, esp. in syntax: *the teacher told him to watch his grammar.* [C14: from OF, from L, from Gk *grammatikē* (*tekhnē*) the grammatical (art), from *grammatikos* concerning letters, from *gramma* letter]

grammarian (grə'meərɪən) *n* **1** a person whose occupation is the study of grammar. **2** the author of a grammar.

grammar school *n* **1** *Brit.* (esp. formerly) a state-maintained secondary school providing an education with an academic bias. **2** *US.* another term for **elementary school. 3** *Austral.* a private school, esp. one controlled by a church. **4** *NZ.* a secondary school forming part of the public education system.

grammatical (grə'mætɪkᵊl) *adj* **1** of or relating to grammar. **2** (of a sentence) well formed; regarded as correct.
▸**gram'matically** *adv* ▸**gram'maticalness** *n*

gram molecule *or* **gram-molecular weight** *n* an amount of a compound equal to its molecular weight expressed in grams: now replaced by the mole. See **mole**[3].

Grammy ('græmɪ) *n, pl* **Grammys** *or* **Grammies.** (in the US) one of the gold-plated discs awarded annually for outstanding achievement in the record industry. [C20: from GRAM(OPHONE) + *-my* as in EMMY]

gramophone ('græməˌfəʊn) *n* **1a** Also called: **record player.** a device for reproducing the sounds stored on a record: now usually applied to the early type that uses an acoustic horn. US and Canad. word: **phonograph. 1b** (*as modifier*): *a gramophone record.* **2** the technique of recording sound on disc: *the gramophone has made music widely available.* [C19: orig. a trademark, ? based on an inversion of *phonogram;* see PHONO-, -GRAM]

grampus ('græmpəs) *n, pl* **grampuses. 1** a widely distributed slaty-grey dolphin with a blunt snout. **2** another name for **killer whale.** [C16: from OF *graspois*, from *gras* fat (from L *crassus*) + *pois* fish (from L *piscis*)]

Gram's method (græmz) *n Bacteriol.* **1** a technique used to classify bacteria by staining them with a violet iodine solution. **2 Gram-positive** (*or* **Gram-negative**). *adj* denoting bacteria that do (*or* do not) retain this stain. [C19: after H. C. J. *Gram* (1853–1938), Danish physician]

gran (græn) *n* an informal word for **grandmother.**

granadilla (ˌgrænə'dɪlə) *n* **1** any of various passionflowers that have edible egg-shaped fleshy fruit. **2** Also called: **passion fruit.** the fruit of such a plant. [C18: from Sp., dim. of *granada* pomegranate, from LL *grānātum*]

granary ('grænərɪ; *US* 'greɪnərɪ) *n, pl* **granaries. 1** a building for storing threshed grain. **2** a region that produces a large amount of grain. ◆ *adj* **3** (*cap.*) *Trademark.* (of bread, flour, etc.) containing malted wheat grain. [C16: from L *grānārium*, from *grānum* GRAIN]

grand ➊ (grænd) *adj* **1** large or impressive in size, extent, or consequence: *grand mountain scenery.* **2** characterized by or attended with magnificence or display; sumptuous: *a grand feast.* **3** of great distinction or pretension; dignified or haughty. **4** designed to impress: *grand gestures.* **5** very good; wonderful. **6** comprehensive; complete: *a grand total.* **7** worthy of respect; fine: *a grand old man.* **8** large or impressive in conception or execution: *grand ideas.* **9** most important; chief: *the grand arena.* ◆ *n* **10** See **grand piano. 11** (*pl* **grand**) *Sl.* a thousand pounds or dollars. [C16: from OF, from L *grandis*]
▸**'grandly** *adv* ▸**'grandness** *n*

grand- *prefix* (in designations of kinship) one generation removed in ascent or descent: *grandson; grandfather.* [from F *grand-*, on the model of L *magnus* in such phrases as *avunculus magnus* great-uncle]

grandad, granddad ('grænˌdæd) *or* **grandaddy, granddaddy** ('grænˌdædɪ) *n, pl* **grandads, granddads** *or* **grandaddies, granddaddies.** informal words for **grandfather.**

grandam ('grændəm, -dæm) *or* **grandame** ('grændeɪm, -dəm) *n* an archaic word for **grandmother.** [C13: from Anglo-F *grandame*, from OF GRAND- + *dame* lady, mother]

grandaunt ('grændˌɑːnt) *n* another name for **great-aunt.**

grandchild ('grænˌtʃaɪld) *n, pl* **grandchildren.** the son or daughter of one's child.

granddaughter ('grænˌdɔːtə) *n* a daughter of one's son or daughter.

grand duchess *n* **1** the wife or widow of a grand duke. **2** a woman who holds the rank of grand duke in her own right.

grand duchy *n* the territory, state, or principality of a grand duke or grand duchess.

grand duke *n* **1** a prince or nobleman who rules a territory, state, or principality. **2** a son or a male descendant in the male line of a Russian tsar. **3** a medieval Russian prince who ruled over other princes.

grande dame *French.* (grɑ̃d dam) *n* a woman regarded as the most experienced, prominent, or venerable member of her profession, etc.

grandee (græn'diː) *n* **1** a Spanish or Portuguese prince or nobleman of the highest rank. **2** a person of high station. [C16: from Sp. *grande*]

grandeur ➊ ('grændʒə) *n* **1** personal greatness, esp. when based on dignity, character, or accomplishments. **2** magnificence; splendour. **3** pretentious or bombastic behaviour.

grandfather ('grænˌfɑːðə, 'grænd-) *n* **1** the father of one's father or mother. **2** (*often pl*) a male ancestor. **3** (*often cap.*) a familiar term of address for an old man.
▸**'grandˌfatherly** *adj*

grandfather clock *n* a long-pendulum clock in a tall standing wooden case.

Grand Guignol *French.* (grɑ̃ giɲɔl) *n* **a** a brief sensational play intended to horrify. **b** (*modifier*) of or like plays of this kind. [C20: after *Le Grand Guignol*, a small theatre in Montmartre, Paris]

grandiloquent (græn'dɪləkwənt) *adj* inflated, pompous, or bombastic in style or expression. [C16: from L *grandiloquus*, from *grandis* great + *loquī* to speak]
▸**gran'diloquence** *n* ▸**gran'diloquently** *adv*

grandiose ➊ ('grændɪˌəʊs) *adj* **1** pretentiously grand or stately. **2** imposing in conception or execution. [C19: from F, from It., from *grande* great; see GRAND]
▸**'grandiˌosely** *adv* ▸**grandiosity** (ˌgrændɪ'ɒsɪtɪ) *n*

grand jury *n Law.* (esp. in the US and, now rarely, in Canada) a jury summoned to inquire into accusations of crime and ascertain whether the evidence is adequate to found an indictment. Abolished in Britain in 1948.

grand larceny *n* **1** (formerly, in England) the theft of property valued at over 12 pence. Abolished in 1827. **2** (in some states of the US) the theft of property of which the value is above a specified figure.

grandma ('grænˌmɑː), **grandmama,** *or* **grandmamma** ('grænməˌmɑː) *n* informal words for **grandmother.**

grand mal (grɒn mæl) *n* a form of epilepsy characterized by loss of consciousness for up to five minutes and violent convulsions. Cf. **petit mal.** [F: great illness]

grandmaster ('grændˌmɑːstə) *n* **1** *Chess.* one of the top chess players of a particular country. **2** a leading exponent of any of various arts.

Grand Master *n* the title borne by the head of any of various societies, orders, and other organizations, such as the Templars, Freemasons, or the various martial arts.

grandmother ('grænˌmʌðə, 'grænd-) *n* **1** the mother of one's father or mother. **2** (*often pl*) a female ancestor.
▸**'grandˌmotherly** *adj*

Grand National *n* **the.** an annual steeplechase run at Aintree, Liverpool, since 1839.

grandnephew ('grænˌnevjuː, -ˌnefjuː, 'grænd-) *n* another name for **great-nephew.**

grandniece ('grænˌniːs, 'grænd-) *n* another name for **great-niece.**

THESAURUS

grammar *n* **2** = **syntax**, rules of language

grand *adj* **1-3** = **impressive**, ambitious, august, dignified, elevated, eminent, exalted, fine, glorious, gorgeous, grandiose, great, haughty, illustrious, imposing, large, lofty, lordly, luxurious, magnificent, majestic, monumental, noble, opulent, ostentatious, palatial, pompous, pretentious, princely, regal, splendid, stately, striking, sublime, sumptuous, superb **5** = **excellent**, admirable, divine, fine, first-class, first-rate, great (*inf.*), marvellous (*inf.*), outstanding, smashing (*inf.*), splendid, super (*inf.*), superb, terrific (*inf.*), very good, wonderful, world-class **9** = **chief**, big-time (*inf.*), head, highest, lead, leading, main, major league (*inf.*), pre-eminent, principal, supreme
Antonyms *adj* ≠ **impressive:** undignified, unimposing ≠ **excellent:** awful, bad, common, contemptible, mean, petty, poor, terrible, worthless ≠ **chief:** inferior, insignificant, little, secondary, small, trivial, unimportant

grandeur *n* **1, 2** = **splendour**, augustness, dignity, greatness, importance, loftiness, magnificence, majesty, nobility, pomp, state, stateliness, sublimity
Antonyms *n* commonness, inferiority, insignificance, lowliness, pettiness, smallness, triviality, unimportance

grandiose *adj* **1** = **pretentious**, affected, ambitious, bombastic, extravagant, flamboyant, high-flown, ostentatious, pompous, showy **2** = **imposing**, ambitious, grand, impressive, lofty, magnificent, majestic, monumental, stately
Antonyms *adj* ≠ **pretentious:** down-to-earth, unpretentious ≠ **imposing:** humble, modest, small-scale

grand opera *n* an opera that has a serious plot and is entirely in musical form, with no spoken dialogue.

grandpa ('græn,pɑː) *or* **grandpapa** ('grænpə,pɑː) *n* informal words for **grandfather.**

grandparent ('græn,pɛərənt, 'grænd-) *n* the father or mother of either of one's parents.

grand piano *n* a form of piano in which the strings are arranged horizontally.

Grand Prix (*French* grɑ̃ pri) *n* **1** any of a series of formula motor races to determine the annual Driver's World Championship. **2** a very important competitive event in various other sports, such as athletics, snooker, or powerboating. [F: great prize]

grandsire ('græn,saɪə, 'grænd-) *n* an archaic word for **grandfather.**

grand slam *n* **1** *Bridge, etc.* the winning of 13 tricks by one player or side or the contract to do so. Cf. **little slam. 2** the winning of all major competitions in a season, esp. in tennis and golf. **3** (*often caps.*) *Rugby union.* the winning of all five games in the annual Six Nations Championship involving Scotland, England, Wales, Ireland, Italy, and France.

grandson ('grænsʌn, 'grænd-) *n* a son of one's son or daughter.

grandstand ('græn,stænd, 'grænd-) *n* **1** a terraced block of seats commanding the best view at racecourses, football pitches, etc. **2** the spectators in a grandstand.

grand tour *n* **1** (formerly) an extended tour through the major cities of Europe, esp. one undertaken by a rich or aristocratic Englishman to complete his education. **2** *Inf.* an extended sightseeing trip, tour of inspection, etc.

granduncle ('grænd,ʌŋkᵊl) *n* another name for **great-uncle.**

grand unified theory *n Physics.* any of a number of theories of elementary particles and fundamental interactions designed to explain the electromagnetic, strong, and weak interactions in terms of a single mathematical formalism. Abbrev.: **GUT.**

grange (greɪndʒ) *n* **1** *Chiefly Brit.* a farm, esp. a farmhouse or country house with its various outbuildings. **2** *Arch.* a granary or barn. [C13: from Anglo-F *graunge,* from Med. L *grānica,* from L *grānum* GRAIN]

granite ('grænɪt) *n* **1** a light-coloured coarse-grained acid plutonic igneous rock consisting of quartz and feldspars: widely used for building. **2** great hardness, endurance, or resolution. [C17: from It. *granito* grained, from *grano* grain, from L *grānum*]
▸**granitic** (grə'nɪtɪk) *adj*

graniteware ('grænɪt,wɛə) *n* **1** iron vessels coated with enamel of a granite-like appearance. **2** a type of pottery with a speckled glaze.

granivorous (græ'nɪvərəs) *adj* (of animals) feeding on seeds and grain.
▸**granivore** ('grænɪ,vɔː) *n*

granny *or* **grannie** ('grænɪ) *n, pl* **grannies. 1** informal words for **grandmother. 2** *Inf.* an irritatingly fussy person. **3** See **granny knot.**

granny bond *n Brit. inf.* a savings scheme available originally only to people over retirement age.

granny farm *n Derog. sl.* an old people's home, esp. one that charges high fees and offers poor care.

granny flat *n* self-contained accommodation within or built onto a house, suitable for an elderly parent.

granny knot *or* **granny's knot** *n* a reef knot with the ends crossed the wrong way, making it liable to slip or jam.

grant ❶ (grɑːnt) *vb* (*tr*) **1** to consent to perform or fulfil: *to grant a wish.* **2** (*may take a clause as object*) to permit as a favour, indulgence, etc.: *to grant an interview.* **3** (*may take a clause as object*) to acknowledge the validity of; concede: *I grant what you say is true.* **4** to bestow, esp. in a formal manner. **5** to transfer (property) to another, esp. by deed; convey. **6 take for granted. 6a** to accept or assume without question: *one takes certain amenities for granted.* **6b** to fail to appreciate the value, merit, etc., of (a person). ◆ *n* **7** a sum of money provided by a government, local authority, or public fund to finance educational study, building repairs, overseas aid, etc. **8** a privilege, right, etc., that has been granted. **9** the act of granting. **10** a transfer of property by deed; conveyance. [C13: from OF *graunter,* from Vulgar L *credentāre* (unattested), from L *crēdere* to believe]
▸'**grantable** *adj* ▸'**granter** *or* (*Law*) '**grantor** *n*

grantee (grɑːn'tiː) *n Law.* a person to whom a grant is made.

Granth (grʌnt) *n* the sacred scripture of the Sikhs. [from Hindi, from Sansk. *grantha* a book]

grant-in-aid *n, pl* **grants-in-aid.** a sum of money granted by one government to a lower level of government for a programme, etc.

grant-maintained *adj* (**grant maintained** *when postpositive*) (of schools or educational institutions) funded directly by central government.

gran turismo ('græn tʊə'rɪzməʊ) *n, pl* **gran turismos.** See **GT.** [C20: from It.]

granular ❶ ('grænjʊlə) *adj* **1** of, like, or containing granules. **2** having a grainy surface.
▸**granularity** (,grænjʊ'lærɪtɪ) *n* ▸'**granularly** *adv*

granulate ❶ ('grænjʊ,leɪt) *vb* **granulates, granulating, granulated. 1** (*tr*) to make into grains: *granulated sugar.* **2** to make or become roughened in surface texture.
▸,**granu'lation** *n* ▸'**granulative** *adj* ▸'**granu,lator** *or* '**granu,later** *n*

granule ❶ ('grænjuːl) *n* a small grain. [C17: from LL *grānulum* a small GRAIN]

granulocyte ('grænjʊlə,saɪt) *n* any of a group of unpigmented blood cells having cytoplasmic granules that take up various dyes.

grape (greɪp) *n* **1** the fruit of the grapevine, which has a purple or green skin and sweet flesh: eaten raw, dried to make raisins, currants, or sultanas, or used for making wine. **2** See **grapevine** (sense 1). **3 the grape.** *Inf.* wine. **4** See **grapeshot.** [C13: from OF *grape* bunch of grapes, of Gmc origin; rel. to CRAMP², GRAPPLE]
▸'**grapey** *or* '**grapy** *adj*

grapefruit ('greɪp,fruːt) *n, pl* **grapefruit** *or* **grapefruits. 1** a tropical or subtropical evergreen tree. **2** the large round edible fruit of this tree, which has yellow rind and juicy slightly bitter pulp.

grape hyacinth *n* any of various Eurasian bulbous plants of the lily family with clusters of rounded blue flowers resembling tiny grapes.

grapeshot ('greɪp,ʃɒt) *n* ammunition for cannons consisting of a cluster of iron balls that scatter after firing.

grape sugar *n* another name for **dextrose.**

grapevine ('greɪp,vaɪn) *n* **1** any of several vines of E Asia, widely cultivated for its fruit (grapes). **2** *Inf.* an unofficial means of relaying information, esp. from person to person.

graph (grɑːf) *n* **1** Also called: **chart.** a drawing depicting the relation between certain sets of numbers or quantities by means of a series of dots, lines, etc., plotted with reference to a set of axes. **2** *Maths.* a drawing depicting a functional relation between two or three variables by means of a curve or surface containing only those points whose coordinates satisfy the relation. **3** *Linguistics.* a symbol in a writing system not further subdivisible into other such symbols. ◆ *vb* **4** (*tr*) to draw or represent in a graph. [C19: short for *graphic formula*]

-graph *n combining form.* **1** an instrument that writes or records: *telegraph.* **2** a writing, record, or drawing: *autograph; lithograph.* [via L from Gk, from *graphein* to write]
▸**-graphic** *or* **-graphical** *adj combining form.* ▸**-graphically** *adv combining form.*

grapheme ('græfiːm) *n Linguistics.* the complete class of letters or combinations of letters that represent one speech sound: for instance, the *f* in *full,* the *gh* in *cough,* and the *ph* in *photo* are members of the same grapheme. [C20: from Gk *graphēma* a letter]
▸**gra'phemically** *adv*

-grapher *n combining form.* **1** indicating a person skilled in a subject: *geographer; photographer.* **2** indicating a person who writes or draws in a specified way: *stenographer; lithographer.*

graphic ❶ ('græfɪk) *or* **graphical** *adj* **1** vividly or clearly described: *a graphic account of the disaster.* **2** of or relating to writing: *graphic symbols.* **3** *Maths.* using, relating to, or determined by a graph: *a graphic representation of the figures.* **4** of or relating to the graphic arts. **5** *Geol.* having or denoting a texture resembling writing: *graphic granite.* [C17: from L *graphicus,* from Gk *graphikos,* from *graphein* to write]
▸'**graphically** *adv* ▸'**graphicness** *n*

graphicacy ('græfɪkəsɪ) *n* the ability to understand and use maps, symbols, etc. [C20: formed on the model of *literacy*]

graphical user interface *n* an interface between a user and a computer system that allows the user to operate the system by means of pictorial devices, such as menus and icons.

graphic arts *pl n* any of the fine or applied visual arts based on drawing or the use of line, esp. illustration and printmaking of all kinds.

graphic equalizer *n* a tone control that enables the output signal of an audio amplifier to be adjusted in each of a series of frequency bands by means of sliding contacts.

graphic novel *n* a novel in the form of a comic strip.

graphics ('græfɪks) *n* **1** (*functioning as sing*) the process or art of drawing in accordance with mathematical principles. **2** (*functioning as sing*) the study of writing systems. **3** (*functioning as pl*) the drawings, photographs, etc., in a magazine or book, or in a television or film production. **4** (*functioning as pl*) *Computing.* information displayed in the form of diagrams, graphs, etc.

graphite ('græfaɪt) *n* a blackish soft form of carbon used in pencils, electrodes, as a lubricant, as a moderator in nuclear reactors, and, in carbon fibre form, for tough lightweight sports equipment. [C18: from G *Graphit,* from Gk *graphein* to write + -ITE¹]
▸**graphitic** (grə'fɪtɪk) *adj*

graphology (græ'fɒlədʒɪ) *n* **1** the study of handwriting, esp. to analyse the writer's character. **2** *Linguistics.* the study of writing systems.
▸,**grapho'logical** *adj* ▸**gra'phologist** *n*

THESAURUS

grant *vb* **1, 2 = consent to,** accede to, accord, agree to, allow, permit **3 = admit,** acknowledge, cede, concede **4 = give,** allocate, allot, assign, award, bestow, confer, donate, hand out, impart, present, vouchsafe **5 = transfer,** assign, convey, transmit ◆ *n* **7 = award,** bequest, boon, bounty, donation, endowment, gift, hand-out, present, stipend, subsidy **9 = allowance,** admission, allocation, allotment, concession, endowment

granular *adj* **1 = grainy,** crumbly, granulated, gravelly, gritty, rough, sandy

granulate *vb* **1 = crystallize,** crumble, crush, grind, levigate (*Chemistry*), pound, powder, pulverize, triturate

granule *n* **= grain,** atom, crumb, fragment, iota, jot, molecule, particle, scrap, speck

graphic *adj* **1 = vivid,** clear, descriptive, detailed, explicit, expressive, forcible, illustrative, lively, lucid, picturesque, striking, telling, well-drawn **4 = pictorial,** delineated, diagrammatic, drawn, illustrative, representational, seen, visible, visual

Antonyms *adj* ≠ **vivid:** generalized, imprecise, unspecific, vague, woolly ≠ **pictorial:** impressionistic

graph paper *n* paper printed with intersecting lines for drawing graphs, diagrams, etc.

-graphy *n combining form.* **1** indicating a form of writing, representing, etc.: *calligraphy; photography.* **2** indicating an art or descriptive science: *choreography; oceanography.* [via L from Gk, from *graphein* to write]

grapnel ('græpnᵊl) *n* **1** a device with a multiple hook at one end and attached to a rope, which is thrown or hooked over a firm mooring to secure an object attached to the other end of the rope. **2** a light anchor for small boats. [C14: from OF *grapin,* from *grape* a hook; see GRAPE]

grappa ('græpə) *n* a spirit distilled from the fermented remains of grapes after pressing. [It.: grape stalk, of Gmc origin; see GRAPE]

grapple ❶ ('græpᵊl) *vb* **grapples, grappling, grappled. 1** to come to grips with (one or more persons), esp. to struggle in hand-to-hand combat. **2** (*intr;* foll. by *with*) to cope or contend: *to grapple with a financial problem.* **3** (*tr*) to secure with a grapple. ◆ *n* **4** any form of hook or metal instrument by which something is secured, such as a grapnel. **5a** the act of gripping or seizing, as in wrestling. **5b** a grip or hold. [C16: from OF *grappelle* a little hook, from *grape* hook; see GRAPNEL]
▸ **'grappler** *n*

grappling iron *or* **hook** *n* a grapnel, esp. one used for securing ships.

graptolite ('græptəˌlaɪt) *n* an extinct Palaeozoic colonial animal: a common fossil. [C19: from Gk *graptos* written, from *graphein* to write + -LITE]

grasp ❶ (grɑːsp) *vb* **1** to grip (something) firmly as with the hands. **2** (when *intr,* often foll. by *at*) to struggle, snatch, or grope (for). **3** (*tr*) to understand, esp. with effort. ◆ *n* **4** the act of grasping. **5** a grip or clasp, as of a hand. **6** total rule or possession. **7** understanding; comprehension. [C14: from Low G *grapsen;* rel. to OE *græppian* to seize]
▸ **'graspable** *adj* ▸ **'grasper** *n*

grasping ❶ ('grɑːspɪŋ) *adj* greedy; avaricious.
▸ **'graspingly** *adv* ▸ **'graspingness** *n*

grass (grɑːs) *n* **1** any of a family of plants having jointed stems sheathed by long narrow leaves, flowers in spikes, and seedlike fruits. The family includes cereals, bamboo, etc. **2** such plants collectively, in a lawn, meadow, etc. Related adj: **verdant. 3** ground on which such plants grow; a lawn, field, etc. **4** ground on which animals are grazed; pasture. **5** a slang word for **marijuana. 6** *Brit. sl.* a person who informs, esp. on criminals. **7 let the grass grow under one's feet.** to squander time or opportunity. ◆ *vb* **8** to cover or become covered with grass. **9** to feed or be fed with grass. **10** (*tr*) to spread (cloth, etc.) out on grass for drying or bleaching in the sun. **11** (*intr;* usually foll. by *on*) *Brit. sl.* to inform, esp. to the police. ◆ See also **grass up.** [OE *græs*]
▸ **'grassˌlike** *adj*

grass hockey *n* in W Canada, field hockey, as contrasted with ice hockey.

grasshopper ('grɑːsˌhɒpə) *n* an insect having hind legs adapted for leaping: typically terrestrial, feeding on plants, and producing a ticking sound by rubbing the hind legs against the leathery forewings.

grassland ('grɑːsˌlænd) *n* **1** land, such as a prairie, on which grass predominates. **2** land reserved for natural grass pasture.

grass roots *pl n* **1** ordinary people as distinct from the active leadership of a group or organization, esp. a political party. **2** the essentials.

grass snake *n* **1** a harmless nonvenomous European snake having a brownish-green body with variable markings. **2** any of several similar related European snakes.

grass tree *n* **1** Also called: **blackboy.** an Australian plant of the lily family, having a woody stem, stiff grasslike leaves, and a spike of small white flowers. **2** any of several similar Australasian plants.

grass up *vb* (*tr, adv*) *Sl.* to inform on (someone), esp. to the police.

grass widow *or* (*masc*) **grass widower** *n* a person whose spouse is regularly away for a short period. [C16: ? an allusion to a grass bed as representing an illicit relationship]

grassy ('grɑːsɪ) *adj* **grassier, grassiest.** covered with, containing, or resembling grass.
▸ **'grassiness** *n*

grate[1] ❶ (greɪt) *vb* **grates, grating, grated. 1** (*tr*) to reduce to small shreds by rubbing against a rough or sharp perforated surface: *to grate carrots.* **2** to scrape (an object) against something or (objects) together, producing a harsh rasping sound, or (of objects) to scrape with such a sound. **3** (*intr;* foll. by *on* or *upon*) to annoy. [C15: from OF *grater* to scrape, of Gmc origin]
▸ **'grater** *n*

grate[2] (greɪt) *n* **1** a framework of metal bars for holding fuel in a fireplace, stove, or furnace. **2** a less common word for **fireplace. 3** another name for **grating**[1]. ◆ *vb* **4** (*tr*) to provide with a grate or grates. [C14: from OF, from L *crātis* hurdle]

grateful ❶ ('greɪtfʊl) *adj* **1** thankful for gifts, favours, etc.; appreciative. **2** showing gratitude: *a grateful letter.* **3** favourable or pleasant: *a grateful rest.* [C16: from obs. *grate,* from L *grātus* + -FUL]
▸ **'gratefully** *adv* ▸ **'gratefulness** *n*

graticule ('grætɪˌkjuːl) *n* **1** the grid of intersecting lines of latitude and longitude on which a map is drawn. **2** another name for **reticle.** [C19: from F, from L *crāticula,* from *crātis* wickerwork]

gratify ❶ ('grætɪˌfaɪ) *vb* **gratifies, gratifying, gratified.** (*tr*) **1** to satisfy or please. **2** to yield to or indulge (a desire, whim, etc.). [C16: from L *grātificārī,* from *grātus* grateful + *facere* to make]
▸ **ˌgratifi'cation** *n* ▸ **'gratiˌfier** *n* ▸ **'gratiˌfying** *adj* ▸ **'gratiˌfyingly** *adv*

gratin (*French* gratɛ̃) See **au gratin.**

grating[1] ❶ ('greɪtɪŋ) *n* a framework of metal bars in the form of a grille set into a wall, pavement, etc., serving as a cover or guard but admitting air and sometimes light. Also called: **grate.**

grating[2] ❶ ('greɪtɪŋ) *adj* **1** (of sounds) harsh and rasping. **2** annoying; irritating. ◆ *n* **3** (*often pl*) something produced by grating.
▸ **'gratingly** *adv*

gratis ❶ ('greɪtɪs, 'grætɪs, 'grɑːtɪs) *adv, adj* (*postpositive*) without payment; free of charge. [C15: from L: out of kindness, from *grātiīs,* ablative pl of *grātia* favour]

gratitude ❶ ('grætɪˌtjuːd) *n* a feeling of thankfulness, as for gifts or favours. [C16: from Med. L *grātitūdō,* from L *grātus* GRATEFUL]

gratuitous ❶ (grə'tjuːɪtəs) *adj* **1** given or received without payment or obligation. **2** without cause; unjustified. [C17: from L *grātuītus* from *grātia* favour]
▸ **gra'tuitously** *adv* ▸ **gra'tuitousness** *n*

gratuity ❶ (grə'tjuːɪtɪ) *n, pl* **gratuities. 1** a gift or reward, usually of money, for services rendered; tip. **2** *Mil.* a financial award granted for long or meritorious service.

gratulatory ('grætjʊlətərɪ) *adj* expressing congratulation. [C16: from L *grātulārī* to congratulate]

grav (græv) *n* a unit of acceleration equal to the standard acceleration of free fall. 1 grav is equivalent to 9.806 65 metres per second per second. Symbol: g

gravadlax ('grævədˌlæks) *n* another name for **gravlax.**

gravamen (grə'veɪmen) *n, pl* **gravamina** (-'væmɪnə). **1** *Law.* that part of an accusation weighing most heavily against an accused. **2** *Law.* the substance or material grounds of a complaint. **3** a rare word for **grievance.** [C17: from LL: trouble, from L *gravis* heavy]

grave[1] ❶ (greɪv) *n* **1** a place for the burial of a corpse, esp. beneath the ground and usually marked by a tombstone. Related adj: **sepulchral. 2** something resembling a grave or resting place: *the ship went to its grave.* **3** (often preceded by *the*) a poetic term for **death. 4 make (someone) turn in his grave.** to do something that would have shocked or distressed a person now dead. [OE *græf*]

grave[2] ❶ (greɪv) *adj* **1** serious and solemn: *a grave look.* **2** full of or sug-

THESAURUS

grapple *vb* **1 = grip,** catch, clasp, clutch, come to grips, fasten, grab, grasp, hold, hug, lay *or* take hold, make fast, seize, wrestle **2 = deal with,** address oneself to, attack, battle, clash, combat, confront, contend, cope, do battle, encounter, engage, face, fight, get to grips with, struggle, tackle, take on, tussle, wrestle

grasp *vb* **1 = grip,** catch, clasp, clinch, clutch, grab, grapple, hold, lay *or* take hold of, seize, snatch **3 = understand,** catch on, catch *or* get the drift of, comprehend, follow, get, get the hang of (*inf.*), get the message, get the picture, realize, see, take in ◆ *n* **5 = grip,** clasp, clutches, embrace, hold, possession, tenure **6 = control,** capacity, compass, extent, mastery, power, range, reach, scope, sway, sweep **7 = understanding,** awareness, comprehension, grip, ken, knowledge, mastery, perception, realization

grasping *adj* **= greedy,** acquisitive, avaricious, close-fisted, covetous, mean, miserly, niggardly, penny-pinching (*inf.*), rapacious, selfish, stingy, tightfisted, usurious, venal
Antonyms *adj* altruistic, generous, unselfish

grate[1] *vb* **1 = shred,** mince, pulverize, triturate **2 = scrape,** creak, grind, rasp, rub, scratch **3 = annoy,** chafe, exasperate, fret, gall, get one down, get on one's nerves (*inf.*), irk, irritate, jar, nark (*Brit., Austral., & NZ sl.*), nettle, peeve, rankle, rub one up the wrong way, set one's teeth on edge, vex

grateful *adj* **1 = thankful,** appreciative, beholden, indebted, obliged

gratification *n* **1 = satisfaction,** delight, enjoyment, fruition, fulfilment, glee, indulgence, joy, kick *or* kicks (*inf.*), pleasure, recompense, relish, reward, thrill
Antonyms *n* control, denial, disappointment, discipline, dissatisfaction, frustration, pain, restraint, sorrow

gratify *vb* **1, 2 = please,** cater to, delight, favour, fawn on, feed, fulfil, give pleasure, gladden, humour, indulge, pander to, recompense, requite, satisfy, thrill

grating[1] *n* **= grille,** grate, grid, gridiron, lattice, trellis

grating[2] *adj* **1, 2 = irritating,** annoying, disagreeable, discordant, displeasing, grinding, harsh, irksome, jarring, offensive, rasping, raucous, scraping, squeaky, strident, unpleasant, vexatious
Antonyms *adj* agreeable, calming, mellifluous, musical, pleasing, soft, soothing

gratis *adj* **= free,** buckshee (*Brit. sl.*), for nothing, freely, free of charge, gratuitously, on the house, unpaid

gratitude *n* **= thankfulness,** appreciation, gratefulness, indebtedness, obligation, recognition, sense of obligation, thanks
Antonyms *n* ingratitude, ungratefulness, unthankfulness

gratuitous *adj* **1 = voluntary,** buckshee (*Brit. sl.*), complimentary, free, gratis, spontaneous, unasked-for, unpaid, unrewarded **2 = unjustified,** assumed, baseless, causeless, groundless, irrelevant, needless, superfluous, uncalled-for, unfounded, unmerited, unnecessary, unprovoked, unwarranted, wanton
Antonyms *adj* ≠ **voluntary:** compulsory, involuntary, paid ≠ **unjustified:** justifiable, provoked, relevant, well-founded

gratuity *n* **1 = tip,** baksheesh, benefaction, bonus, boon, bounty, donation, gift, largesse *or* largess, perquisite, *pourboire,* present, recompense, reward

grave[1] *n* **1 = tomb,** burying place, crypt, last resting place, mausoleum, pit, sepulchre, vault

grave[2] *adj* **1 = solemn,** dignified, dour, dull, earnest, gloomy, grim-faced, heavy, leaden, long-

gesting danger: *a grave situation.* **3** important; crucial: *grave matters of state.* **4** (of colours) sober or dull. **5** (grɑːv). *Phonetics.* of or relating to an accent (`) over vowels, denoting a pronunciation with lower or falling musical pitch (as in ancient Greek), with certain special quality (as in French), or in a manner that gives the vowel status as a syllable (as in English *agèd*). ◆ *n* **6** (*also* grɑːv). a grave accent. [C16: from OF, from L *gravis*]
▸**'gravely** *adv* ▸**'graveness** *n*

grave[3] (greɪv) *vb* **graves, graving, graved; graved** *or* **graven.** (*tr*) *Arch.* **1** to carve or engrave. **2** to fix firmly in the mind. [OE *grafan*]

grave[4] ('grɑːveɪ) *adj Music.* solemn. [It.]

grave clothes (greɪv) *pl n* the wrappings in which a dead body is interred.

gravel ('grævᵊl) *n* **1** a mixture of rock fragments and pebbles that is coarser than sand. **2** *Pathol.* small rough calculi in the kidneys or bladder. ◆ *vb* **gravels, gravelling, gravelled** *or US* **gravels, graveling, graveled.** (*tr*) **3** to cover with gravel. **4** to confound or confuse. **5** *US inf.* to annoy or disturb. [C13: from OF *gravele*, dim. of *grave*, ? of Celtic origin]

gravel-blind *adj Literary.* almost completely blind. [C16: from GRAVEL + BLIND]

gravelly ('grævəlɪ) *adj* **1** consisting of or abounding in gravel. **2** of or like gravel. **3** (esp. of a voice) harsh and grating.

graven ('greɪvᵊn) *vb* **1** a past participle of **grave**[3]. ◆ *adj* **2** strongly fixed.

graven image *n Chiefly Bible.* a carved image used as an idol.

graver ('greɪvə) *n* any of various engraving or sculpting tools, such as a burin.

Graves (grɑːv) *n* (*sometimes not cap.*) a white or red wine from the district around Bordeaux, France.

gravestone ('greɪv,stəʊn) *n* a stone marking a grave.

graveyard ➊ ('greɪv,jɑːd) *n* a place for graves; a burial ground, esp. a small one or one in a churchyard.

graveyard shift *n US.* the working shift between midnight and morning.

graveyard slot *n Television.* the hours from late night until early morning when the number of people watching television is at its lowest.

gravid ('grævɪd) *adj* the technical word for **pregnant.** [C16: from L *gravidus*, from *gravis* heavy]

gravimeter (grə'vɪmɪtə) *n* **1** an instrument for measuring the earth's gravitational field at points on its surface. **2** an instrument for measuring relative density. [C18: from F *gravimètre*, from L *gravis* heavy]
▸**gra'vimetry** *n*

gravimetric (,grævɪ'mɛtrɪk) *adj* **1** of, concerned with, or using measurement by weight. **2** *Chem.* of analysis of quantities by weight.

graving dock *n* another term for **dry dock.**

gravitas ➊ ('grævɪ,tæs) *n* seriousness or solemnity, esp. of conduct or demeanour; weight or authority. [C20: from L *gravitās* weight, from *gravis* heavy]

gravitate ➊ ('grævɪ,teɪt) *vb* **gravitates, gravitating, gravitated.** (*intr*) **1** *Physics.* to move under the influence of gravity. **2** (usually foll. by *to* or *towards*) to be influenced or drawn, as by strong impulses. **3** to sink or settle.
▸**'gravi,tater** *n* ▸**'gravi,tative** *adj*

gravitation (,grævɪ'teɪʃən) *n* **1** the force of attraction that bodies exert on one another as a result of their mass. **2** any process or result caused by this interaction. ◆ Also called: **gravity.**
▸**,gravi'tational** *adj* ▸**,gravi'tationally** *adv*

gravitational constant *n* the factor relating force to mass and distance in Newton's law of gravitation. Symbol: *G*

gravitational field *n* the field of force surrounding a body of finite mass in which another body would experience an attractive force that is proportional to the product of the masses and inversely proportional to the square of the distance between them.

gravitational mass *n* the mass of a body expressed in terms of the gravitational force between it and the earth. Cf. **inertial mass.**

graviton ('grævɪ,tɒn) *n* a postulated quantum of gravitational energy, usually considered to be a particle with zero charge and rest mass and a spin of 2.

gravity ➊ ('grævɪtɪ) *n, pl* **gravities. 1** the force of attraction that moves or tends to move bodies towards the centre of a celestial body, such as the earth or moon. **2** the property of being heavy or having weight. **3** another name for **gravitation. 4** seriousness or importance, esp. as a consequence of an action or opinion. **5** manner or conduct that is solemn or dignified. **6** lowness in pitch. **7** (*modifier*) of or relating to gravity or gravitation or their effects: *gravity feed.* [C16: from L *gravitās* weight, from *gravis* heavy]

gravity wave *n Physics.* **1** a wave propagated in a gravitational field, predicted to occur as a result of an accelerating mass. **2** a surface wave on water or other liquid propagated because of the weight of liquid in the crests. ◆ Also called: **gravitational wave.**

gravlax ('græv,læks) *or* **gravadlax** *n* dry-cured salmon, marinated in salt, sugar, and spices, as served in Scandinavia. [C20: from Norwegian, from *grav* grave (because the salmon is left to ferment) + *laks* or Swedish *lax* salmon]

gravure (grə'vjʊə) *n* **1** a method of intaglio printing using a plate with many small etched recesses. See also **rotogravure. 2** See **photogravure. 3** matter printed by this process. [C19: from F, from *graver* to engrave]

gravy ('greɪvɪ) *n, pl* **gravies. 1a** the juices that exude from meat during cooking. **1b** the sauce made by thickening and flavouring such juices. **2** *Sl.* money or gain acquired with little effort, esp. above that needed for ordinary living. [C14: from OF *gravé*, from ?]

gravy boat *n* a small often boat-shaped vessel for serving gravy or other sauces.

gray[1] (greɪ) *adj, n, vb* a variant spelling (now esp. US) of **grey.**

gray[2] (greɪ) *n* the derived SI unit of the absorbed dose of ionizing radiation: equal to 1 joule per kilogram. Symbol: Gy [C20: after L. H. Gray, Brit. radiobiologist]

grayling ('greɪlɪŋ) *n, pl* **grayling** *or* **graylings. 1** a freshwater food fish of the salmon family of the N hemisphere, having a long spiny dorsal fin, a silvery back, and greyish-green sides. **2** any of various European butterflies having grey or greyish-brown wings.

graze[1] ➊ (greɪz) *vb* **grazes, grazing, grazed. 1** to allow (animals) to consume the vegetation on (an area of land), or (of animals) to feed thus. **2** (*tr*) to tend (livestock) while at pasture. **3** (*intr*) *Inf.* to eat snacks throughout the day rather than formal meals. **4** (*intr*) *US.* to pilfer and eat sweets, vegetables, etc., from supermarket shelves while shopping. [OE *grasian*, from *græs* GRASS]

graze[2] ➊ (greɪz) *vb* **grazes, grazing, grazed. 1** (when *intr*, often foll. by *against* or *along*) to brush or scrape (against) gently, esp. in passing. **2** (*tr*) to break the skin of (a part of the body) by scraping. ◆ *n* **3** the act of grazing. **4** a scrape or abrasion made by grazing. [C17: prob. special use of GRAZE[1]]

grazier ('greɪzɪə) *n* a rancher or farmer who rears or fattens cattle or sheep on grazing land.

grazing ('greɪzɪŋ) *n* **1** the vegetation on pastures that is available for livestock to feed upon. **2** the land on which this is growing.

grazioso (,grɑːtsɪ'əʊsəʊ) *adj Music.* graceful. [It.]

grease ➊ (griːs, griːz) *n* **1** animal fat in a soft or melted condition. **2** any thick fatty oil, esp. one used as a lubricant for machinery, etc. ◆ *vb* **greases, greasing, greased.** (*tr*) **3** to soil, coat, or lubricate with grease. **4 grease the palm** (*or* **hand**) **of.** *Sl.* to bribe; influence by giving money to. [C13: from OF *craisse*, from L *crassus* thick]
▸**'greaser** *n*

grease gun *n* a device for forcing grease through nipples into bearings.

grease monkey *n Inf.* a mechanic, esp. one who works on cars or aircraft.

grease nipple *n* a metal nipple designed to engage with a grease gun for injecting grease into a bearing, etc.

greasepaint ('griːs,peɪnt) *n* **1** a waxy or greasy substance used as make-up by actors. **2** theatrical make-up.

greaseproof paper ('griːs,pruːf) *n* any paper that is resistant to penetration by greases and oils.

greasy ➊ ('griːsɪ, -zɪ) *adj* **greasier, greasiest. 1** coated or soiled with or as if with grease. **2** composed of or full of grease. **3** resembling grease. **4** unctuous or oily in manner.
▸**'greasily** *adv* ▸**'greasiness** *n*

greasy wool *n* untreated wool still retaining the lanolin; used for waterproof clothing.

great ➊ (greɪt) *adj* **1** relatively large in size or extent; big. **2** relatively large in number; having many parts or members: *a great assembly.* **3** of relatively long duration: *a great wait.* **4** of larger size or more importance than others of its kind: *the great auk.* **5** extreme or more than usual: *great worry.* **6** of significant importance or consequence: *a great*

THESAURUS

faced, muted, quiet, sage (*obs.*), sedate, serious, sober, sombre, staid, subdued, thoughtful, unsmiling **2, 3** = **important**, acute, critical, crucial, dangerous, exigent, hazardous, life-and-death, momentous, of great consequence, perilous, pressing, serious, severe, significant, threatening, urgent, vital, weighty
Antonyms *adj* ≠ **solemn:** carefree, exciting, flippant, happy, joyous, merry, undignified ≠ **important:** frivolous, insignificant, mild, trifling, unimportant

graveyard *n* = **cemetery**, boneyard (*inf.*), burial ground, charnel house, churchyard, God's acre (*literary*), necropolis

gravitas *n* = **seriousness**, gravity, solemnity

gravitate *vb* **2** *with* **to** *or* **towards** = **be drawn**, be attracted, be influenced, be pulled, incline, lean, move, tend **3** = **fall**, be precipitated, descend, drop, precipitate, settle, sink

gravity *n* **4** = **importance**, acuteness, consequence, exigency, hazardousness, moment, momentousness, perilousness, pressingness, seriousness, severity, significance, urgency, weightiness **5** = **solemnity**, demureness, dignity, earnestness, gloom, gravitas, grimness, reserve, sedateness, seriousness, sobriety, thoughtfulness
Antonyms *n* ≠ **importance:** inconsequentiality, insignificance, triviality, unimportance ≠ **solemnity:** flippancy, frivolity, gaiety, happiness, joy, levity, merriment, thoughtlessness

graze[1] *vb* **1** = **feed**, browse, crop, pasture

graze[2] *vb* **1** = **touch**, brush, glance off, kiss, rub, scrape, shave, skim **2** = **scratch**, abrade, bark, chafe, scrape, skin ◆ *n* **4** = **scratch**, abrasion, scrape

grease *vb* **4 grease someone's palm** *Slang* = **bribe**, buy, corrupt, fix (*inf.*), give a backhander (*sl.*), induce, influence, pay off (*inf.*), square, suborn

greasy *adj* **1-3** = **fatty**, oily, oleaginous, slick, slimy, slippery **4** = **sycophantic**, fawning, glib, grovelling, ingratiating, oily, slick, smarmy (*Brit. inf.*), smooth, toadying, unctuous

great *adj* **1** = **large**, big, bulky, colossal, elephantine, enormous, extensive, gigantic, huge, immense, mammoth, prodigious, stellar (*inf.*), stupendous, tremendous, vast, voluminous **3** = **long**, extended, lengthy, prolonged, protracted **4** = **major**, big-time (*inf.*), capital, chief, grand, head, lead, leading, main, major league (*inf.*),

decision. **7a** of exceptional talents or achievements; remarkable: *a great writer.* **7b** (*as n*): *the great; one of the greats.* **8** doing or exemplifying (something) on a large scale: *she's a great reader.* **9** arising from or possessing idealism in thought, action, etc.; heroic: *great deeds.* **10** illustrious or eminent: *a great history.* **11** impressive or striking: *a great show of wealth.* **12** active or enthusiastic: *a great walker.* **13** (often foll. by *at*) skilful or adroit: *a great carpenter; you are great at singing.* **14** *Inf.* excellent; fantastic. ◆ *n* **15** Also called: **great organ.** the principal manual on an organ. [OE *grēat*]
▸'**greatly** *adv* ▸'**greatness** *n*

great- *prefix* **1** being the parent of a person's grandparent (in the combinations **great-grandfather, great-grandmother, great-grandparent**). **2** being the child of a person's grandchild (in the combinations **great-grandson, great-granddaughter, great-grandchild**).

great auk *n* a large flightless auk, extinct since the middle of the 19th century.

great-aunt *or* **grandaunt** *n* an aunt of one's father or mother; sister of one's grandfather or grandmother.

Great Bear *n* **the.** the English name for **Ursa Major.**

great circle *n* a circular section of a sphere that has a radius equal to that of the sphere.

greatcoat ('greɪtˌkəʊt) *n* a heavy overcoat.

Great Dane *n* one of a very large breed of dog with a short smooth coat.

great gross *n* a unit of quantity equal to one dozen gross (or 1728).

great-hearted *adj* benevolent or noble; magnanimous.
▸ˌ**great-'heartedness** *n*

great-nephew *or* **grandnephew** *n* a son of one's nephew or niece; grandson of one's brother or sister.

great-niece *or* **grandniece** *n* a daughter of one's nephew or niece; grand-daughter of one's brother or sister.

Great Red Spot *n* a large long-lived oval feature, south of Jupiter's equator, that is an anticyclonic disturbance in the atmosphere.

Great Russian *n* **1** *Linguistics.* the technical name for **Russian. 2** a member of the chief East Slavonic people of Russia. ◆ *adj* **3** of or relating to this people or their language.

Greats (greɪts) *pl n* (at Oxford University) **1** the Honour School of Literae Humaniores, involving the study of Greek and Roman history and literature and philosophy. **2** the final examinations at the end of this course.

great seal *n* (*often caps.*) the principal seal of a nation, sovereign, etc., used to authenticate documents of the highest importance.

great tit *n* a Eurasian tit with yellow-and-black underparts and a black-and-white head.

great-uncle *or* **granduncle** *n* an uncle of one's father or mother; brother of one's grandfather or grandmother.

Great War *n* another name for **World War I.**

greave (griːv) *n* (*often pl*) a piece of armour worn to protect the shin. [C14: from OF *greve,* ?from *graver* to part the hair, of Gmc origin]

grebe (griːb) *n* an aquatic bird, such as the great crested grebe and little grebe, similar to the divers but with lobate rather than webbed toes and a vestigial tail. [C18: from F *grèbe,* from ?]

Grecian ('griːʃən) *adj* **1** (esp. of beauty or architecture) conforming to Greek ideals. ◆ *n* **2** a scholar of Greek. ◆ *adj, n* **3** another word for **Greek.**

Grecism ('griːˌsɪzəm) *n* a variant spelling (esp. US) of **Graecism.**

Greco- ('griːkəʊ, 'grɛkəʊ) *combining form.* a variant (esp. US) of **Graeco-.**

greed ❶ (griːd) *n* **1** excessive consumption of or desire for food. **2** excessive desire, as for wealth or power. [C17: back formation from GREEDY]

greedy ❶ ('griːdɪ) *adj* **greedier, greediest. 1** excessively desirous of food or wealth, esp. in large amounts; voracious. **2** (*postpositive;* foll. by *for*) eager (for): *a man greedy for success.* [OE *grǣdig*]
▸'**greedily** *adv* ▸'**greediness** *n*

greegree ('griːgriː) *n* a variant spelling of **grigri.**

Greek ❶ (griːk) *n* **1** the official language of Greece, constituting the Hellenic branch of the Indo-European family of languages. **2** a native or inhabitant of Greece or a descendant of such a native. **3** a member of the Greek Orthodox Church. **4** *Inf.* anything incomprehensible (esp. in **it's (all) Greek to me**). ◆ *adj* **5** denoting, relating to, or characteristic of Greece, the Greeks, or the Greek language; Hellenic. **6** of, relating to, or designating the Greek Orthodox Church.
▸'**Greekness** *n*

Greek cross *n* a cross with each of the four arms of the same length.

Greek fire *n* a Byzantine weapon consisting of an unknown mixture that caught fire when wetted.

Greek gift *n* a gift given with the intention of tricking and causing harm to the recipient. [C19: in allusion to Virgil's *Aeneid* ii 49; see also TROJAN HORSE]

Greek Orthodox Church *n* **1** Also called: **Greek Church.** the established Church of Greece, governed by the holy synod of Greece, in which the Metropolitan of Athens has primacy of honour. **2** another name for **Orthodox Church.**

green ❶ (griːn) *n* **1** any of a group of colours, such as that of fresh grass, that lie between yellow and blue in the visible spectrum. Related adj: **verdant. 2** a dye or pigment of or producing these colours. **3** something of the colour green. **4** a small area of grassland, esp. in the centre of a village. **5** an area of smooth turf kept for a special purpose: *a putting green.* **6** (*pl*) **6a** the edible leaves and stems of certain plants, eaten as a vegetable. **6b** freshly cut branches of ornamental trees, shrubs, etc., used as a decoration. **7** (*sometimes cap.*) a person, esp. a politician, who supports environmentalist issues. ◆ *adj* **8** of the colour green. **9** greenish in colour or having parts or marks that are greenish. **10** (*sometimes cap.*) of or concerned with conservation of natural resources and improvement of the environment: used esp. in a political context. **11** vigorous; not faded: *a green old age.* **12** envious or jealous. **13** immature, unsophisticated, or gullible. **14** characterized by foliage or green plants: *a green wood; a green salad.* **15** denoting a unit of account that is adjusted in accordance with fluctuations between the currencies of the EU nations and is used to make payments to agricultural producers within the EU: *green pound.* **16** fresh, raw, or unripe: *green bananas.* **17** unhealthily pale in appearance: *he was green after his boat trip.* **18** (of meat) not smoked or cured: *green bacon.* **19** (of timber) freshly felled; not dried or seasoned. ◆ *vb* **20** to make or become green. [OE *grēne*]
▸'**greenish** *or* '**greeny** *adj* ▸'**greenly** *adv* ▸'**greenness** *n*

greenback ('griːnˌbæk) *n US.* **1** *Inf.* a legal-tender US currency note. **2** *Sl.* a dollar bill.

green ban *n Austral.* a trade-union ban on any development that might be considered harmful to the environment.

green bean *n* any bean plant, such as the French bean, having narrow green edible pods.

green belt *n* a zone of farmland, parks, and open country surrounding a town or city.

Green Cross Code *n Brit.* a code for children giving rules for road safety.

greenery ('griːnərɪ) *n, pl* **greeneries.** green foliage, esp. when used for decoration.

green-eyed *adj* **1** jealous or envious. **2 the green-eyed monster.** jealousy or envy.

greenfield ('griːnˌfiːld) *n* (*modifier*). denoting or located in a rural area which has not previously been built on.

greenfinch ('griːnˌfɪntʃ) *n* a European finch the male of which has a dull green plumage with yellow patches on the wings and tail.

THESAURUS

paramount, primary, principal, prominent, superior **5** = **extreme,** considerable, decided, excessive, extravagant, grievous, high, inordinate, prodigious, pronounced, serious (*inf.*), strong **6** = **important,** consequential, critical, crucial, grave, heavy, momentous, serious, significant, weighty **7** = **famous,** celebrated, distinguished, eminent, exalted, excellent, famed, glorious, illustrious, notable, noteworthy, outstanding, prominent, remarkable, renowned, superb, superlative, talented, world-class **9** = **noble,** august, chivalrous, dignified, distinguished, exalted, fine, glorious, grand, heroic, high-minded, idealistic, impressive, lofty, magnanimous, princely, sublime **12** = **enthusiastic,** active, devoted, keen, zealous **13** = **skilful,** able, adept, adroit, crack (*sl.*), expert, good, masterly, proficient, skilled **14** *Informal* = **excellent,** admirable, cracking (*Brit. inf.*), fantastic (*inf.*), fine, first-rate, good, hunky-dory (*inf.*), jim-dandy (*sl.*), marvellous (*inf.*), sovereign, superb, terrific (*inf.*), tremendous (*inf.*), wonderful
Antonyms *adj* ≠ **large:** diminutive, little, small ≠ **important:** inconsequential, inconsiderable, insignificant, petty, trivial, unimportant ≠ **noble:** base, hateful, ignoble, inhumane, mean, unkind ≠ **skilful:** inexperienced, unskilled, untrained ≠ **excellent:** average, inferior, poor, secondary, second-rate, undistinguished, unnotable

greatly *adv* **5** = **very much,** abundantly, by leaps and bounds, by much, considerably, enormously, exceedingly, extremely, highly, hugely, immensely, markedly, mightily, much, notably, powerfully, remarkably, seriously (*inf.*), to the nth degree, tremendously, vastly

greatness *n* **1** = **immensity,** bulk, enormity, hugeness, largeness, length, magnitude, mass, prodigiousness, size, vastness **6** = **importance,** gravity, heaviness, import, moment, momentousness, seriousness, significance, urgency, weight **7** = **fame,** celebrity, distinction, eminence, glory, grandeur, illustriousness, lustre, note, renown **9** = **grandeur,** chivalry, dignity, disinterestedness, generosity, heroism, high-mindedness, idealism, loftiness, majesty, nobility, nobleness, stateliness, sublimity

greed *n* **1** = **gluttony,** edacity, esurience, gormandizing, hunger, insatiableness, ravenousness, voracity **2** = **avarice,** acquisitiveness, avidity, covetousness, craving, cupidity, desire, eagerness, graspingness, longing, rapacity, selfishness
Antonyms *n* ≠ **avarice:** altruism, benevolence, generosity, largesse *or* largess, munificence, self-restraint, unselfishness

greedy *adj* **1** = **grasping,** acquisitive, avaricious, covetous, edacious, esurient, gluttonous, gormandizing, hoggish, hungry, insatiable, piggish, rapacious, ravenous, selfish, voracious **2** = **eager,** avid, craving, desirous, hungry, impatient
Antonyms *adj* ≠ **grasping:** altruistic, benevolent, generous, munificent, self-restrained, unselfish

Greek *n* **2** = **Hellene** ◆ *adj* **5** = **Hellenic**

green *n* **4** = **lawn,** common, sward, turf ◆ *adj* **10** = **ecological,** conservationist, ecologically sound, environment-friendly, non-polluting, ozone-friendly **12** = **jealous,** covetous, envious, grudging, resentful **13** = **inexperienced,** callow, credulous, gullible, ignorant, immature, inexpert, ingenuous, innocent, naive, new, raw, unpolished, unpractised, unskilful, unsophisticated, untrained, unversed, wet behind the ears (*inf.*) **14** = **leafy,** blooming, budding, flourishing, fresh, grassy, new, undecayed, verdant, verdurous **16** = **new,** fresh, immature, raw, recent, unripe **17** = **nauseous,** ill, pale, sick, under the weather, unhealthy, wan

green fingers *pl n* considerable talent or ability to grow plants.

greenfly ('griːnˌflaɪ) *n, pl* **greenflies.** a greenish aphid commonly occurring as a pest on garden and crop plants.

greengage ('griːnˌgeɪdʒ) *n* **1** a cultivated variety of plum tree with edible green plumlike fruits. **2** the fruit of this tree. [C18: GREEN + *-gage,* after Sir W. *Gage* (1777–1864), E botanist who brought it from France]

greengrocer ('griːnˌgrəʊsə) *n Chiefly Brit.* a retail trader in fruit and vegetables.
▸**'green,grocery** *n*

greenheart ('griːnˌhɑːt) *n* **1** Also called: **bebeeru.** a tropical American tree that has dark green durable wood. **2** any of various similar trees. **3** the wood of any of these trees.

greenhorn 🅣 ('griːnˌhɔːn) *n* **1** an inexperienced person, esp. one who is extremely gullible. **2** *Chiefly US.* a newcomer. [C17: orig. an animal with *green* (that is, young) horns]

greenhouse ('griːnˌhaʊs) *n* **1** a building with glass walls and roof for the cultivation of plants under controlled conditions. ◆ *adj* **2** relating to or contributing to the greenhouse effect: *greenhouse gases, such as carbon dioxide.*

greenhouse effect *n* **1** an effect occurring in greenhouses, etc., in which ultraviolet radiation from the sun passes through the glass warming the contents, the infrared radiation from inside being trapped by the glass. **2** the application of this effect to a planet's atmosphere, esp. the warming up of the earth as man-made carbon dioxide in the atmosphere traps the infrared radiation emitted by the earth's surface. The greenhouse effect is made more serious by damage to the ozone layer, which permits more ultraviolet radiation to reach the earth.

greenie ('griːnɪ) *n Austral. inf.* a conservationist.

greenkeeper ('griːnˌkiːpə) *n* a person responsible for maintaining a golf course or bowling green.

Greenland whale *n* another name for **bowhead.**

green leek *n* any of several Australian parrots with a green or mostly green plumage.

green light 🅣 *n* **1** a signal to go, esp. a green traffic light. **2** permission to proceed with a project, etc. ◆ *vb* **greenlight, greenlights, greenlighting, greenlighted.** (*tr*) **3** to permit (a project, etc.) to proceed.

greenmail ('griːnˌmeɪl) *n* (esp. in the US) the practice of a company buying sufficient shares in another company to threaten takeover and making a quick profit as a result of the threatened company buying back its shares at a higher price.

green monkey disease *n* another name for **Marburg disease.**

green paper *n* (*often caps.*) (in Britain) a government document containing policy proposals to be discussed, esp. by Parliament.

Green Party *n* a political party whose policies are based on concern for the environment.

Greenpeace ('griːnˌpiːs) *n* a conservationist organization founded in 1971: members take active but nonviolent measures against what are regarded as threats to environmental safety, such as the dumping of nuclear waste at sea.

green pepper *n* the green unripe fruit of the sweet pepper, eaten raw or cooked.

green pound *n* a unit of account used in calculating Britain's contributions to and payments from the Community Agricultural Fund of the EU. See also **green** (sense 15).

greenroom ('griːnˌruːm, -ˌrʊm) *n* (esp. formerly) a backstage room in a theatre where performers may rest or receive visitors. [C18: prob. from its original colour]

greensand ('griːnˌsænd) *n* an olive-green sandstone consisting mainly of quartz and glauconite.

greenshank ('griːnˌʃæŋk) *n* a large European sandpiper with greenish legs and a slightly upturned bill.

greensickness ('griːnˌsɪknɪs) *n* an informal name for **chlorosis.**

greenstick fracture ('griːnˌstɪk) *n* a fracture in children in which the bone is partly bent and splinters only on the convex side of the bend. [C20: alluding to the similar way in which a green stick splinters]

greenstone ('griːnˌstəʊn) *n* **1** any basic dark green igneous rock. **2** a variety of jade formerly used in New Zealand by Maoris for ornaments and tools, now used for jewellery.

greensward ('griːnˌswɔːd) *n Arch. or literary.* fresh green turf or an area of such turf.

green tea *n* a sharp tea made from tea leaves that have been dried quickly without fermenting.

green turtle *n* a mainly tropical edible turtle, with greenish flesh.

green-wellie *n* (*modifier*) characterizing or belonging to the upper-class set devoted to hunting, shooting, and fishing: *the green-wellie brigade.*

Greenwich Mean Time *or* **Greenwich Time** ('grɪnɪdʒ, -ɪtʃ, 'grɛn-) *n* mean solar time on the 0° meridian passing through Greenwich, England, measured from midnight: formerly a standard time in Britain and a basis for calculating times throughout most of the world, it has been replaced by an atomic timescale. See **universal time.** Abbrev.: **GMT.**

> **USAGE NOTE** The name **Greenwich mean time** is ambiguous, having been measured from mean midday in astronomy up to 1925, and is not used for scientific purposes. It is generally and incorrectly used in the sense of **universal coordinated time,** an atomic timescale available since 1972 from broadcast signals, in addition to the earliest sense of **universal time,** adopted internationally in 1928 as the name for GMT measured from midnight.

greenwood ('griːnˌwʊd) *n* a forest or wood when the leaves are green.

greet[1] 🅣 (griːt) *vb* (*tr*) **1** to meet or receive with expressions of gladness or welcome. **2** to send a message of friendship to. **3** to receive in a specified manner: *her remarks were greeted by silence.* **4** to become apparent to: *the smell of bread greeted him.* [OE *grētan*]
▸**'greeter** *n*

greet[2] (griːt) *Scot. or dialect.* ◆ *vb* **1** (*intr*) to weep; lament. ◆ *n* **2** weeping; lamentation. [from OE *grētan,* N dialect var. of *grætan*]

greeting 🅣 ('griːtɪŋ) *n* **1** the act or an instance of welcoming or saluting on meeting. **2** (*often pl*) **2a** an expression of friendly salutation. **2b** (*as modifier*): *a greetings card.*

gregarious 🅣 (grɪ'gɛərɪəs) *adj* **1** enjoying the company of others. **2** (of animals) living together in herds or flocks. **3** (of plants) growing close together. **4** of or characteristic of crowds or communities. [C17: from L, from *grex* flock]
▸**gre'gariously** *adv* ▸**gre'gariousness** *n*

Gregorian calendar (grɪ'gɔːrɪən) *n* the revision of the Julian calendar introduced in 1582 by Pope Gregory XIII and still in force, whereby the ordinary year is made to consist of 365 days.

Gregorian chant *n* another name for **plainsong.**

Gregorian telescope *n* a type of reflecting astronomical telescope with a concave secondary mirror and the eyepiece set in the centre of the parabolic primary mirror. [C18: after J. *Gregory* (died 1675), Scot. mathematician]

gremial ('griːmɪəl) *n RC Church.* a cloth spread upon the lap of a bishop when seated during Mass. [C17: from L *gremium* lap]

gremlin ('grɛmlɪn) *n* **1** an imaginary imp jokingly said to be responsible for mechanical troubles in aircraft, esp. in World War II. **2** any mischievous troublemaker. [C20: from ?]

grenade (grɪ'neɪd) *n* **1** a small container filled with explosive thrown by hand or fired from a rifle. **2** a sealed glass vessel that is thrown and shatters to release chemicals, such as tear gas. [C16: from F, from Sp.: pomegranate, from LL, from L *grānātus* seedy; see GRAIN]

grenadier (ˌgrɛnə'dɪə) *n* **1** *Mil.* **1a** (in the British Army) a member of the senior regiment of infantry in the Household Brigade. **1b** (formerly) a member of a special formation, usually selected for strength and height. **1c** (formerly) a soldier trained to throw grenades. **2** any of various deep-sea fish, typically having a large head and a long tapering tail. [C17: from F; see GRENADE]

grenadine[1] (ˌgrɛnə'diːn) *n* a light thin fabric of silk, wool, rayon, or nylon, used for dresses, etc. [C19: from F]

grenadine[2] (ˌgrɛnə'diːn, 'grɛnəˌdiːn) *n* a syrup made from pomegranate juice, used as a sweetening and colouring agent in various drinks. [C19: from F: a little pomegranate; see GRENADE]

Gresham's law *or* **theorem** ('grɛʃəmz) *n* the economic hypothesis that bad money drives good money out of circulation; the superior currency will tend to be hoarded and the inferior will thus dominate the circulation. [C16: after Sir T. *Gresham* (?1519–79), E financier]

gressorial (grɛ'sɔːrɪəl) *or* **gressorious** *adj* **1** (of the feet of certain birds) specialized for walking. **2** (of birds, such as the ostrich) having such feet. [C19: from NL, from *gressus* having walked, from *gradī* to step]

grew (gruː) *vb* the past tense of **grow.**

grey 🅣 *or US* **gray** (greɪ) *adj* **1** of a neutral tone, intermediate between black and white, that has no hue and reflects and transmits only a little light. **2** greyish in colour or having greyish marks. **3** dismal or dark, esp. from lack of light; gloomy. **4** conventional or dull, esp. in character or opinion. **5** having grey hair. **6** of or relating to people of middle age or above: *grey power.* **7** ancient; venerable. ◆ *n* **8** any of a group of grey tones. **9** grey cloth or clothing. **10** an animal, esp. a horse, that is grey or whitish. ◆ *vb* **11** to become or make grey. [OE *grǣg*]
▸**'greyish** *or US* **'grayish** *adj* ▸**'greyly** *or US* **'grayly** *adv* ▸**'greyness** *or US* **'grayness** *n*

grey area *n* **1** an area or part of something existing between two extremes and having mixed characteristics of both. **2** an area, situation, etc., lacking clearly defined characteristics.

THESAURUS

greenhorn *n* **1** = **novice,** apprentice, beginner, ignoramus, ingénue, learner, naïf, neophyte, newcomer, raw recruit, simpleton, tyro

green light *n* **2** = **permission,** approval, authorization, blessing, clearance, confirmation, go-ahead (*inf.*), imprimatur, O.K. *or* okay, sanction

greet[1] *vb* **1** = **welcome,** accost, address, compliment, hail, meet, nod to, receive, salute, tip one's hat to

greeting *n* **1** = **welcome,** address, hail, reception, salutation, salute **2** *plural* = **best wishes,** compliments, devoirs, good wishes, regards, respects, salutations

gregarious *adj* **1** = **outgoing,** affable, companionable, convivial, cordial, friendly, sociable, social
Antonyms *adj* antisocial, reserved, solitary, standoffish, unsociable, withdrawn

grey *adj* **3** = **dismal,** cheerless, cloudy, dark, depressing, dim, drab, dreary, dull, foggy, gloomy, misty, murky, overcast, sunless **4** = **characterless,** anonymous, colourless, dull, indistinct, neutral, unclear, unidentifiable **7** = **old,** aged, ancient, elderly, experienced, hoary, mature, venerable

greybeard *or US* **graybeard** ('greɪˌbɪəd) *n* **1** an old man, esp. a sage. **2** a large stoneware or earthenware jar or jug for spirits.
grey eminence *n* the English equivalent of ***éminence grise.***
Grey Friar *n* a Franciscan friar.
greyhen ('greɪˌhɛn) *n* the female of the black grouse.
greyhound ('greɪˌhaʊnd) *n* a tall slender fast-moving breed of dog.
grey knight *n Inf.* an ambiguous intervener in a takeover battle, who makes a counterbid for the shares of the target company without having made his intentions clear. Cf. **black knight, white knight.**
greylag *or* **greylag goose** ('greɪˌlæg) *n* a large grey Eurasian goose: the ancestor of many domestic breeds of goose. US spelling: **graylag.** [C18: from GREY + LAG[1], from its migrating later than other species]
grey market *n* **1** trade in newly-issued shares before they have been formally listed and traded on the Stock Exchange. **2** a practice in which supermarkets buy excess stock of branded goods from other retailers at a low margin and then sell them at discounted prices.
grey matter *n* **1** the greyish tissue of the brain and spinal cord, containing nerve cell bodies and fibres. **2** *Inf.* brains or intellect.
grey squirrel *n* a grey-furred squirrel, native to E North America but now widely established.
greywacke ('greɪˌwækə) *n* any dark sandstone or grit having a matrix of clay minerals. [C19: partial translation of G *Grauwacke;* see WACKE]
grey water *n* water that has been used for one purpose but can be used again for another without repurification (e.g. bathwater, which can be used to water plants).
grey wolf *n* another name for **timber wolf.**
grid (grɪd) *n* **1** See **gridiron. 2** a network of horizontal and vertical lines superimposed over a map, building plan, etc., for locating points. **3** a grating consisting of parallel bars. **4 the grid.** the national network of transmission lines, pipes, etc., by which electricity, gas, or water is distributed. **5** Also called: **control grid.** *Electronics.* an electrode usually consisting of a cylindrical mesh of wires, that controls the flow of electrons between the cathode and anode of a valve. **6** See **starting grid. 7** a plate in an accumulator that carries the active substance. **8** any interconnecting system of links: *the bus service formed a grid across the country.* [C19: back formation from GRIDIRON]
grid bias *n* the fixed voltage applied between the control grid and cathode of a valve.
griddle ('grɪdᵊl) *n* **1** Also called: **girdle.** *Brit.* a thick round iron plate with a half hoop handle over the top, for making scones, etc. **2** any flat heated surface, esp. on the top of a stove, for cooking food. ◆ *vb* **griddles, griddling, griddled. 3** (*tr*) to cook (food) on a griddle. [C13: from OF *gridil,* from LL *crāticulum* (unattested) fine wickerwork; see GRILL]
griddlecake ('grɪdᵊlˌkeɪk) *n* another name for **drop scone.**
gridiron ('grɪdˌaɪən) *n* **1** a utensil of parallel metal bars, used to grill meat, fish, etc. **2** any framework resembling this utensil. **3** a framework above the stage in a theatre from which suspended scenery, lights, etc., are manipulated. **4a** the field of play in American football. **4b** an informal name for **American football.** ◆ Often shortened to **grid.** [C13 *gredire,* ? a var. (through influence of *ire* IRON) of *gredile* GRIDDLE]
gridlock ❶ ('grɪdˌlɒk) *Chiefly US.* ◆ *n* **1** obstruction of urban traffic caused by queues of vehicles forming across junctions and causing further queues to form in the intersecting streets. **2** a point in a dispute at which no agreement can be reached: *political gridlock.* ◆ *vb* **3** (*tr*) (of traffic) to block or obstruct (an area).
grief ❶ (griːf) *n* **1** deep or intense sorrow, esp. at the death of someone. **2** something that causes keen distress. **3 come to grief.** *Inf.* to end unsuccessfully or disastrously. [C13: from Anglo-F *gref,* from *grever* to GRIEVE]
grievance ❶ ('griːvᵊns) *n* **1** a real or imaginary wrong causing resentment and regarded as grounds for complaint. **2** a feeling of resentment or injustice at having been unfairly treated. [C15 *grevance,* from OF, from *grever* to GRIEVE]
grieve ❶ (griːv) *vb* **grieves, grieving, grieved.** to feel or cause to feel great sorrow or distress, esp. at the death of someone. [C13: from OF *grever,* from L *gravāre* to burden, from *gravis* heavy]
▸**'griever** *n* ▸**'grieving** *n, adj*
grievous ❶ ('griːvəs) *adj* **1** very severe or painful: *a grievous injury.* **2** very serious; heinous: *a grievous sin.* **3** showing or marked by grief. **4** causing great pain or suffering.
▸**'grievously** *adv* ▸**'grievousness** *n*
grievous bodily harm *n Criminal law.* serious injury caused by one person to another.
griffin ('grɪfɪn), **griffon,** *or* **gryphon** *n* a winged monster with an eagle-like head and the body of a lion. [C14: from OF *grifon,* from L *grȳphus,* from Gk *grups,* from *grupos* hooked]
griffon ('grɪfᵊn) *n* **1** any of various small wire-haired breeds of dog, originally from Belgium. **2** a large vulture of Africa, S Europe, and SW Asia, having a pale plumage with black wings. [C19: from F: GRIFFIN] a variant of **griffin**[1]. a variant of **griffin.**
grifter ('grɪftə) *n Sl., chiefly US.* a petty criminal or gambler. [C20: a blend of GR(AFT)[2] (sense 2) + DRIFTER (sense 2)]
grigri, gris-gris, *or* **greegree** ('griːgriː) *n, pl* **grigris, gris-gris** (-griːz) *or* **greegrees.** an African talisman, amulet, or charm. [of African origin]
grill (grɪl) *vb* **1** to cook (meat, etc.) by direct heat, as under a grill or over a hot fire, or (of meat, etc.) to be cooked in this way. Usual US and Canad. word: **broil. 2** (*tr; usually passive*) to torment with or as if with extreme heat: *the travellers were grilled by the scorching sun.* **3** (*tr*) *Inf.* to subject to insistent or prolonged questioning. ◆ *n* **4** a device with parallel bars of thin metal on which meat, etc., may be cooked by a fire; gridiron. **5** a device on a cooker that radiates heat downwards for grilling meat, etc. **6** food cooked by grilling. **7** See **grillroom.** [C17: from F *gril* gridiron, from L *crātīcula* fine wickerwork; see GRILLE]
▸**grilled** *adj* ▸**'griller** *n*
grillage ('grɪlɪdʒ) *n* an arrangement of beams and crossbeams used as a foundation on soft ground. [C18: from F, from *griller* to furnish with a grille]
grille *or* **grill** (grɪl) *n* **1** a framework, esp. of metal bars arranged to form an ornamental pattern, used as a screen or partition. **2** Also called: **radiator grille.** a grating that admits cooling air to the radiator of a motor vehicle. **3** a metal or wooden openwork grating used as a screen or divider. **4** a protective screen, usually plastic or metal, in front of the loudspeaker in a radio, record player, etc. [C17: from OF, from L *crātīcula* fine hurdlework, from *crātis* a hurdle]
grillroom ('grɪlˌruːm, -ˌrʊm) *n* a restaurant where grilled steaks and other meat are served.
grilse (grɪls) *n, pl* **grilses** *or* **grilse.** a young salmon that returns to fresh water after one winter in the sea. [C15 *grilles* (pl), from ?]
grim ❶ (grɪm) *adj* **grimmer, grimmest. 1** stern; resolute: *grim determination.* **2** harsh or formidable in manner or appearance. **3** harshly ironic or sinister: *grim laughter.* **4** cruel, severe, or ghastly: *a grim accident.* **5** *Arch. or poetic.* fierce: *a grim warrior.* **6** *Inf.* unpleasant; disagreeable. [OE *grimm*]
▸**'grimly** *adv* ▸**'grimness** *n*
grimace ❶ (grɪ'meɪs) *n* **1** an ugly or distorted facial expression, as of wry humour, disgust, etc. ◆ *vb* **grimaces, grimacing, grimaced. 2** (*intr*) to contort the face. [C17: from F, of Gmc origin; rel. to Sp. *grimazo* caricature]
▸**gri'macer** *n*
grimalkin (grɪ'mælkɪn, -'mɔːl-) *n* **1** an old cat, esp. an old female cat. **2** a crotchety or shrewish old woman. [C17: from GREY + *malkin,* dim. of female name *Maud*]
grime ❶ (graɪm) *n* **1** dirt, soot, or filth, esp. when ingrained. ◆ *vb* **grimes, griming, grimed. 2** (*tr*) to make dirty or coat with filth. [C15: from MDu. *grime*]
▸**'grimy** *adj* ▸**'griminess** *n*
grin (grɪn) *vb* **grins, grinning, grinned. 1** to smile with the lips drawn back revealing the teeth or express (something) by such a smile: *to grin a welcome.* **2** (*intr*) to draw back the lips revealing the teeth, as in a snarl or grimace. **3 grin and bear it.** *Inf.* to suffer trouble or hardship without complaint. ◆ *n* **4** a broad smile. **5** a snarl or grimace. [OE *grennian*]
▸**'grinning** *adj, n*
grind ❶ (graɪnd) *vb* **grinds, grinding, ground. 1** to reduce or be reduced to small particles by pounding or abrading: *to grind corn.* **2** (*tr*) to smooth, sharpen, or polish by friction or abrasion: *to grind a knife.* **3** to scrape or grate together (two things, esp. the teeth) with a harsh rasping sound or (of such objects) to be scraped together. **4** (*tr; foll. by out*) to speak or say something in a rough voice. **5** (*tr; often foll. by down*) to hold

THESAURUS

gridlock *n* **2** = **standstill**, deadlock, full stop, halt, impasse, stalemate
grief *n* **1** = **sadness**, affliction, agony, anguish, bereavement, dejection, distress, grievance, hardship, heartache, heartbreak, misery, mournfulness, mourning, pain, regret, remorse, sorrow, suffering, trial, tribulation, trouble, woe **3 come to grief** *Informal* = **fail**, come unstuck, fall flat on one's face, meet with disaster, miscarry
Antonyms *n* ≠ **sadness:** cheer, comfort, consolation, delight, gladness, happiness, joy, rejoicing, solace
grievance *n* **1** = **complaint**, affliction, beef, gripe (*inf.*), hardship, injury, injustice, protest, wrong **2** = **unhappiness**, axe to grind, chip on one's shoulder (*inf.*), distress, grief, resentment, sorrow, tribulation, trouble
grieve *vb* = **mourn**, ache, bemoan, bewail, complain, deplore, lament, regret, rue, sorrow, suffer, wail, weep = **sadden**, afflict, agonize, break the heart of, crush, distress, hurt, injure, make one's heart bleed, pain, wound
Antonyms *vb* ≠ **sadden:** cheer, comfort, console, ease, gladden, please, rejoice, solace
grievous *adj* **1** = **severe**, afflicting, calamitous, damaging, distressing, dreadful, grave, harmful, heavy, hurtful, injurious, lamentable, oppressive, painful, wounding **2** = **deplorable**, appalling, atrocious, dreadful, egregious, flagrant, glaring, heinous, intolerable, lamentable, monstrous, offensive, outrageous, shameful, shocking, unbearable
Antonyms *adj* ≠ **severe:** insignificant, mild, trivial, unimportant ≠ **deplorable:** delightful, glad, happy, joyous, pleasant
grim *adj* **1** = **stern**, hard, implacable, relentless, resolute, unrelenting, unyielding **2-4** = **forbidding**, cruel, ferocious, fierce, formidable, frightful, ghastly, grisly, gruesome, harsh, hideous, horrible, horrid, merciless, morose, ruthless, severe, shocking, sinister, terrible
Antonyms *adj* ≠ **forbidding:** amiable, attractive, benign, cheerful, easy, genial, gentle, happy, kind, pleasant, soft, sympathetic
grimace *n* **1** = **scowl**, face, frown, mouth, sneer, wry face ◆ *vb* **2** = **scowl**, frown, lour *or* lower, make a face *or* faces, mouth, sneer
grime *n* **1** = **dirt**, filth, grot (*sl.*), smut, soot
grimy *adj* **1** = **dirty**, begrimed, besmeared, besmirched, filthy, foul, grubby, scuzzy (*sl.*), smutty, soiled, sooty, unclean
grind *vb* **1** = **crush**, abrade, comminute, granulate, grate, kibble, mill, pound, powder, pulverize, triturate **2** = **smooth**, file, polish, sand, sharpen, whet **3** = **scrape**, gnash, grate, grit **5** *with* **down** = **oppress**, afflict, harass, hold down, hound, persecute, plague, trouble, tyrannize (over) ◆ *n* **9** *Informal* = **hard work**, chore, drudgery, labour, sweat (*inf.*), task, toil

down; oppress; tyrannize. **6** (*tr*) to operate (a machine) by turning a handle. **7** (*tr; foll. by out*) to produce in a routine or uninspired manner: *he ground out his weekly article for the paper.* **8** (*intr*) *Inf.* to study or work laboriously. ◆ *n* **9** *Inf.* laborious or routine work or study. **10** a specific grade of pulverization, as of coffee beans: *coarse grind.* **11** the act or sound of grinding. [OE *grindan*]
▸'**grindingly** *adv*

grinder ('graɪndə) *n* **1** a person who grinds, esp. one who grinds cutting tools. **2** a machine for grinding. **3** a molar tooth.

grindstone ('graɪnd,stəʊn) *n* **1a** a machine having a circular block of stone rotated for sharpening tools or grinding metal. **1b** the stone used in this machine. **1c** any stone used for sharpening; whetstone. **2 keep** *or* **have one's nose to the grindstone.** to work hard and perseveringly.

gringo ('grɪŋgəʊ) *n, pl* **gringos.** a person from an English-speaking country: used as a derogatory term by Latin Americans. [C19: from Sp.: foreigner, prob. from *griego* Greek, hence an alien]

grip Ⓣ (grɪp) *n* **1** the act or an instance of grasping and holding firmly: *he lost his grip on the slope.* **2** Also called: **handgrip.** the strength or pressure of such a grasp, as in a handshake. **3** the style or manner of grasping an object, such as a tennis racket. **4** understanding, control, or mastery of a subject, problem, etc. **5** a person who manoeuvres the cameras in a film or television studio. **6 get** *or* **come to grips.** (often foll. by *with*) **6a** to deal with (a problem or subject). **6b** to tackle (an assailant). **7** Also called: **handgrip.** a part by which an object is grasped; handle. **8** Also called: **handgrip.** a travelling bag or holdall. **9** See **hairgrip. 10** any device that holds by friction, such as certain types of brake. ◆ *vb* **grips, gripping, gripped. 11** to take hold of firmly or tightly, as by a clutch. **12** to hold the interest or attention of: *the thrilling performance gripped the audience.* [OE *gripe* grasp]
▸'**gripper** *n* ▸'**gripping** *adj*

gripe Ⓣ (graɪp) *vb* **gripes, griping, griped. 1** (*intr*) *Inf.* to complain, esp. in a persistent nagging manner. **2** to cause sudden intense pain in the intestines of (a person) or (of a person) to experience this pain. **3** *Arch.* to clutch; grasp. **4** (*tr*) *Arch.* to afflict. ◆ *n* **5** (*usually pl*) a sudden intense pain in the intestines; colic. **6** *Inf.* a complaint or grievance. **7** *Now rare.* **7a** the act of gripping. **7b** a firm grip. **7c** a device that grips. [OE *grīpan*]
▸'**griper** *n*

Gripe Water *n Brit., trademark.* a solution given to infants to relieve colic.

grippe *or* **grip** (grɪp) *n* a former name for **influenza.** [C18: from F *grippe*, from *gripper* to seize, of Gmc origin; see GRIP]

grisaille (grɪ'zeɪl) *n* **1** a technique of monochrome painting in shades of grey, imitating the effect of relief. **2** a painting, stained-glass window, etc., in this manner. [C19: from F, from *gris* grey]

griseofulvin (,grɪzɪəʊ'fʊlvɪn) *n* an antibiotic used to treat fungal infections of the skin and hair. [C20: from NL, ult. from Med. L *griseus* grey + L *fulvus* reddish-yellow]

grisette (grɪ'zɛt) *n* (esp. formerly) a French working girl. [C18: from F, from grey fabric used for dresses, from *gris* grey]

gris-gris ('gri:gri:) *n, pl* **gris-gris** (-gri:z). a variant spelling of **grigri.**

grisly Ⓣ ('grɪzlɪ) *adj* **grislier, grisliest.** causing horror or dread; gruesome. [OE *grislic*]
▸'**grisliness** *n*

> **USAGE NOTE** See at **grizzly.**

grist (grɪst) *n* **1a** grain intended to be or that has been ground. **1b** the quantity of such grain processed in one grinding. **2** *Brewing.* malt grains that have been cleaned and cracked. **3 grist to** (*or* **for**) **the** (*or* **one's**) **mill.** anything that can be turned to profit or advantage. [OE *grīst*]

gristle ('grɪs^{ə}l) *n* cartilage, esp. when in meat. [OE *gristle*]
▸'**gristly** *adj* ▸'**gristliness** *n*

grit Ⓣ (grɪt) *n* **1** small hard particles of sand, earth, stone, etc. **2** Also called: **gritstone.** any coarse sandstone that can be used as a grindstone or millstone. **3** indomitable courage, toughness, or resolution. ◆ *vb* **grits, gritting, gritted. 4** to clench or grind together (two objects, esp. the teeth). **5** to cover (a surface, such as icy roads) with grit. [OE *grēot*]
▸'**gritter** *n*

Grit (grɪt) *n, adj Canad.* an informal word for **Liberal.**

grits (grɪts) *pl n* **1** hulled or coarsely ground grain. **2** *US.* See **hominy grits.** [OE *grytt*]

gritty Ⓣ ('grɪtɪ) *adj* **grittier, grittiest. 1** courageous; hardy; resolute. **2** of, like, or containing grit.
▸'**grittily** *adv* ▸'**grittiness** *n*

grizzle[1] ('grɪz^{ə}l) *vb* **grizzles, grizzling, grizzled. 1** to make or become grey. ◆ *n* **2** a grey colour. **3** grey hair. [C15: from OF *grisel*, from *gris*, of Gmc origin]

grizzle[2] Ⓣ ('grɪz^{ə}l) *vb* **grizzles, grizzling, grizzled.** (*intr*) *Inf., chiefly Brit.* (esp. of a child) to fret; whine. [C18: of Gmc origin]
▸'**grizzler** *n*

grizzled Ⓣ ('grɪz^{ə}ld) *adj* **1** streaked or mixed with grey; grizzly. **2** having grey hair.

grizzly ('grɪzlɪ) *adj* **grizzlier, grizzliest. 1** somewhat grey; grizzled. ◆ *n, pl* **grizzlies. 2** See **grizzly bear.**

> **USAGE NOTE** *Grizzly* is sometimes wrongly used where *grisly* is meant: *a grisly* (not *grizzly*) *murder.*

grizzly bear *n* a variety of the brown bear, formerly widespread in W North America; its brown fur has cream or white tips on the back, giving a grizzled appearance. Often shortened to **grizzly.**

groan Ⓣ (grəʊn) *n* **1** a prolonged stressed dull cry expressive of agony, pain, or disapproval. **2** a loud harsh creaking sound, as of a tree bending in the wind. **3** *Inf.* a grumble or complaint, esp. a persistent one. ◆ *vb* **4** to utter (low inarticulate sounds) expressive of pain, grief, disapproval, etc. **5** (*intr*) to make a sound like a groan. **6** (*intr; usually foll. by beneath* or *under*) to be weighed down (by) or suffer greatly (under). **7** (*intr*) *Inf.* to complain or grumble. [OE *grānian*]
▸'**groaner** *n* ▸'**groaning** *adj, n* ▸'**groaningly** *adv*

groat (grəʊt) *n* an obsolete English silver coin worth four pennies. [C14: from MDu. *groot*, from MLow G *gros*, from Med. L (*denarius*) *grossus* thick (coin); see GROSCHEN]

groats (grəʊts) *pl n* the hulled and crushed grain of oats, wheat, or certain other cereals. [OE *grot* particle]

grocer ('grəʊsə) *n* a dealer in foodstuffs and other household supplies. [C15: from OF *grossier*, from *gros* large; see GROSS]

groceries ('grəʊsərɪz) *pl n* merchandise, esp. foodstuffs, sold by a grocer.

grocery ('grəʊsərɪ) *n, pl* **groceries.** the business or premises of a grocer.

grog (grɒg) *n* **1** diluted spirit, usually rum, as an alcoholic drink. **2** *Austral. & NZ inf.* alcoholic drink in general, esp. spirits. [C18: from Old *Grog*, nickname of Edward Vernon (1684–1757), Brit. admiral, who in 1740 issued naval rum diluted with water; his nickname arose from his grogram cloak]

groggy Ⓣ ('grɒgɪ) *adj* **groggier, groggiest.** *Inf.* **1** dazed or staggering, as from exhaustion, blows, or drunkenness. **2** faint or weak.
▸'**groggily** *adv* ▸'**grogginess** *n*

grogram ('grɒgrəm) *n* a coarse fabric of silk, wool, or silk mixed with wool or mohair, often stiffened with gum, formerly used for clothing. [C16: from F *gros grain* coarse grain; see GROSGRAIN]

groin (grɔɪn) *n* **1** the depression or fold where the legs join the abdomen. **2** *Euphemistic.* the genitals, esp. the testicles. **3** a variant spelling (esp. US) of **groyne. 4** *Archit.* a curved arris formed where two intersecting vaults meet. ◆ *vb* **5** (*tr*) *Archit.* to provide or construct with groins. [C15: ?from E *grynde* abyss]

grommet ('grɒmɪt) *or* **grummet** *n* **1** a ring of rubber or plastic or a metal eyelet designed to line a hole to prevent a cable or pipe passed through it from chafing. **2** *Med.* a small tube inserted into the eardrum in order to drain fluid from the middle ear, as in glue ear. [C15: from obs. F *gourmette* chain linking the ends of a bit, from *gourmer* bridle, from ?]

groom Ⓣ (gru:m, grʊm) *n* **1** a person employed to clean and look after horses. **2** See **bridegroom. 3** any of various officers of a royal or noble

THESAURUS

grip *n* **1** = **clasp**, handclasp (*US*), hold, purchase **4** = **control**, command, comprehension, domination, grasp, mastery, tenure, understanding **6 get** *or* **come to grips** *often foll. by* **with** = **tackle**, close with, confront, contend with, cope with, deal with, encounter, face up to, grapple with, grasp, handle, meet, take on, take the bit between one's teeth, undertake ◆ *vb* **11** = **grasp**, clasp, clutch, hold, latch on to, seize, take hold of **12** = **engross**, absorb, catch up, compel, enthral, entrance, fascinate, hold, involve, mesmerize, rivet, spellbind

gripe *vb* **1** *Informal* = **complain**, beef (*sl.*), bellyache (*sl.*), bitch (*sl.*), bleat, carp, groan, grouch (*inf.*), grouse, grumble, kvetch (*US sl.*), moan, nag, whine **2** = **ache**, compress, cramp, hurt, pain, pinch, press, squeeze ◆ *n* **5** *usually plural* = **pain**, ache, aching, affliction, colic, cramps, distress, griping, pang, pinching, stomachache, twinge **6** *Informal* = **complaint**, beef (*sl.*), grievance, groan, grouch (*inf.*), grouse, grumble, moan, objection, protest

gripping *adj* **12** = **fascinating**, compelling, compulsive, engrossing, enthralling, entrancing, exciting, riveting, spellbinding, thrilling, unputdownable (*inf.*)

grisly *adj* = **gruesome**, abominable, appalling, awful, dreadful, frightful, ghastly, grim, hellacious (*US sl.*), hideous, horrible, horrid, macabre, shocking, sickening, terrible, terrifying
Antonyms *adj* agreeable, attractive, charming, innocuous, nice, pleasant

grit *n* **1** = **gravel**, dust, pebbles, sand **3** = **courage**, backbone, balls, determination, doggedness, fortitude, gameness, guts (*inf.*), hardihood, mettle, nerve, perseverance, pluck, resolution, spirit, tenacity, toughness ◆ *vb* **4** = **grind**, clench, gnash, grate

gritty *adj* **1** = **courageous**, ballsy (*taboo sl.*), brave, determined, dogged, feisty (*inf., chiefly US & Canad.*), game, hardy, mettlesome, plucky, resolute, spirited, steadfast, tenacious, tough **2** = **rough**, abrasive, dusty, grainy, granular, gravelly, rasping, sandy

grizzle[2] *vb* = **whine**, fret, girn (*Scot.*), pule, snivel, whimper, whinge (*inf.*)

grizzled *adj* **1, 2** = **grey**, canescent, grey-haired, grey-headed, greying, griseous, grizzly, hoary

groan *n* **1** = **moan**, cry, sigh, whine **3** *Informal* = **complaint**, beef (*sl.*), gripe (*inf.*), grouse, grumble, objection, protest ◆ *vb* **4** = **moan**, cry, sigh, whine **7** *Informal* = **complain**, beef (*sl.*), bemoan, bitch (*sl.*), gripe (*inf.*), grouse, grumble, lament, object

groggy *adj* **1, 2** = **dizzy**, befuddled, confused, dazed, faint, muzzy, punch-drunk, reeling, shaky, staggering, stunned, stupefied, unsteady, weak, wobbly, woozy (*inf.*)

groom *n* **1** = **stableman**, currier (*rare*), hostler *or* household. **4** *Arch.* a male servant. ◆ *vb* (*tr*) **5** to make or keep (clothes, appearance, etc.) clean and tidy. **6** to rub down, clean, and smarten (a horse, dog, etc.). **7** to train or prepare for a particular task, occupation, etc.: *to groom someone for the Presidency.* [C13 *grom* manservant; ? rel. to OE *grōwan* to GROW]

groomsman (ˈgruːmzmən, ˈgrʊmz-) *n, pl* **groomsmen.** a man who attends the bridegroom at a wedding, usually the best man.

groove Ⓣ (gruːv) *n* **1** a long narrow channel or furrow, esp. one cut into wood by a tool. **2** the spiral channel in a gramophone record. **3** a settled existence, routine, etc., to which one is suited or accustomed. **4** *Dated sl.* an experience, event, etc., that is groovy. **5 in the groove. 5a** *Jazz.* playing well and apparently effortlessly, with a good beat, etc. **5b** *US.* fashionable. ◆ *vb* **grooves, grooving, grooved. 6** (*tr*) to form or cut a groove in. **7** (*intr*) *Dated sl.* to enjoy oneself or feel in rapport with one's surroundings. **8** (*intr*) *Jazz.* to play well, with a good beat, etc. [C15: from obs. Du. *groeve,* of Gmc origin]

groovy (ˈgruːvɪ) *adj* **groovier, grooviest.** *Sl., often jocular.* attractive, fashionable, or exciting.

grope Ⓣ (grəʊp) *vb* **gropes, groping, groped. 1** (*intr;* usually foll. by *for*) to feel or search about uncertainly (for something) with the hands. **2** (*intr;* usually foll. by *for* or *after*) to search uncertainly or with difficulty (for a solution, answer, etc.). **3** (*tr*) to find (one's way) by groping. **4** (*tr*) *Sl.* to fondle the body of (someone) for sexual gratification. ◆ *n* **5** the act of groping. [OE *grāpian*]
▸**ˈgropingly** *adv*

groper (ˈgrəʊpə) *or* **grouper** *n, pl* **groper, gropers** *or* **grouper, groupers.** a large marine fish of warm and tropical seas. [C17: from Port. *garupa,* prob. from a South American Indian word]

grosbeak (ˈgrəʊs,biːk, ˈgrɒs-) *n* any of various finches that have a massive powerful bill. [C17: from F *grosbec,* from OF *gros* large, thick + *bec* BEAK[1]]

groschen (ˈgrəʊʃən) *n, pl* **groschen. 1** an Austrian monetary unit worth one hundredth of a schilling. **2** a German coin worth ten pfennigs. **3** a former German silver coin. [C17: from G: alteration of MHG *grosse,* from Med. L (*denarius*) *grossus* thick (penny); see GROSS, GROAT]

grosgrain (ˈgrəʊ,greɪn) *n* a heavy ribbed silk or rayon fabric or tape for trimming clothes, etc. [C19: from F *gros grain* coarse grain; see GROSS, GRAIN]

gros point (ˈgrəʊ ˈpɔɪnt; *French* gro pwɛ̃) *n* **1** a needlepoint stitch covering two horizontal and two vertical threads. **2** work done in this stitch. [OF: large point]

gross Ⓣ (grəʊs) *adj* **1** repellently or excessively fat or bulky. **2** with no deductions for expenses, tax, etc.; total: *gross sales.* Cf. **net**[2]. **3** (of personal qualities, tastes, etc.) conspicuously coarse or vulgar. **4** obviously or exceptionally culpable or wrong; flagrant: *gross inefficiency.* **5** lacking in perception, sensitivity, or discrimination: *gross judgments.* **6** (esp. of vegetation) dense; thick; luxuriant. ◆ *n* **7** (*pl* **gross**). a unit of quantity equal to 12 dozen. **8** (*pl* **grosses**). **8a** the entire amount. **8b** the great majority. ◆ *interj* **9** *Sl.* an exclamation indicating disgust. ◆ *vb* (*tr*) **10** to earn as total revenue, before deductions for expenses, tax, etc. [C14: from OF *gros* large, from LL *grossus* thick]
▸**ˈgrossly** *adv* ▸**ˈgrossness** *n*

gross domestic product *n* the total value of all goods and services produced domestically by a nation during a year. It is equivalent to gross national product minus net investment incomes from foreign nations. Abbrev.: **GDP.**

gross national product *n* the total value of all final goods and services produced annually by a nation. Abbrev.: **GNP.**

gross profit *n Accounting.* the difference between total revenue from sales and the total cost of purchases or materials, with an adjustment for stock.

gross weight *n* total weight of an article inclusive of the weight of the container and packaging.

grot (grɒt) *n Sl.* rubbish; dirt. [C20: from GROTTY]

grotesque Ⓣ (grəʊˈtɛsk) *adj* **1** strangely or fantastically distorted; bizarre. **2** of or characteristic of the grotesque in art. **3** absurdly incongruous; in a ludicrous context. ◆ *n* **4** a 16th-century decorative style in which parts of human, animal, and plant forms are distorted and mixed. **5** a decorative device, as in painting or sculpture, in this style. **6** *Printing.* the family of 19th-century sans serif display types. **7** any grotesque person or thing. [C16: from F, from OIt. (*pittura*) *grottesca* cave painting, from *grotta* cave; see GROTTO]
▸**groˈtesquely** *adv* ▸**groˈtesqueness** *n* ▸**groˈtesquery** *or* **groˈtesquerie** *n*

grotto (ˈgrɒtəʊ) *n, pl* **grottoes** *or* **grottos. 1** a small cave, esp. one with attractive features. **2** a construction in the form of a cave, esp. as in landscaped gardens during the 18th century. [C17: from OIt. *grotta,* from LL *crypta* vault; see CRYPT]

grotty (ˈgrɒtɪ) *adj* **grottier, grottiest.** *Brit. sl.* **1** nasty or unattractive. **2** of poor quality or in bad condition. [C20: from GROTESQUE]

grouch Ⓣ (graʊtʃ) *Inf.* ◆ *vb* (*intr*) **1** to complain; grumble. ◆ *n* **2** a complaint, esp. a persistent one. **3** a person who is always grumbling. [C20: from obs. *grutch,* from OF *grouchier* to complain; see GRUDGE]
▸**ˈgrouchy** *adj* ▸**ˈgrouchily** *adv* ▸**ˈgrouchiness** *n*

ground[1] Ⓣ (graʊnd) *n* **1** the land surface. **2** earth or soil. **3** (*pl*) the land around a dwelling house or other building. **4** (*sometimes pl*) an area of land given over to a purpose: *football ground.* **5** land having a particular characteristic: *high ground.* **6** matter for consideration or debate; field of research or inquiry: *the report covered a lot of ground.* **7** a position or viewpoint, as in an argument or controversy (esp. in **give ground, hold, stand,** *or* **shift one's ground**). **8** position or advantage, as in a subject or competition (esp. in **gain ground, lose ground,** etc.). **9** (*often pl*) reason; justification: *grounds for complaint.* **10** *Arts.* **10a** the prepared surface applied to a wall, canvas, etc., to prevent it reacting with or absorbing the paint. **10b** the background of a painting against which the other parts of a work of art appear superimposed. **11a** the first coat of paint applied to a surface. **11b** (*as modifier*): *ground colour.* **12** the bottom of a river or the sea. **13** (*pl*) sediment or dregs, esp. from coffee. **14** *Chiefly Brit.* the floor of a room. **15** *Cricket.* the area from the popping crease back past the stumps, in which a batsman may legally stand. **16** *Electrical.* the usual US and Canad. word for **earth** (sense 8). **17 break new ground.** to do something that has not been done before. **18 common ground.** an agreed basis for identifying issues in an argument. **19 cut the ground from under someone's feet.** to anticipate someone's action or argument and thus make it irrelevant or meaningless. **20 (down) to the ground.** *Brit. inf.* completely; absolutely: *it suited him down to the ground.* **21 home ground.** a familiar area or topic. **22 into the ground.** beyond what is requisite or can be endured; to exhaustion. **23** (*modifier*) on or concerned with the ground: *ground frost; ground forces.* ◆ *vb* **24** (*tr*) to put or place on the ground. **25** (*tr*) to instruct in fundamentals. **26** (*tr*) to provide a basis or foundation for; establish. **27** (*tr*) to confine (an aircraft, pilot, etc.) to the ground. **28** (*tr*) to confine (a teenager) to the house as a punishment. **29** the usual US and Canad. word for **earth** (sense 13). **30** (*tr*) *Naut.* to run (a vessel) aground. **31** (*intr*) to hit or reach the ground. [OE *grund*]

ground[2] (graʊnd) *vb* **1** the past tense and past participle of **grind.** ◆ *adj* **2** having the surface finished, thickness reduced, or an edge sharpened by grinding. **3** reduced to fine particles by grinding.

groundage (ˈgraʊndɪdʒ) *n Brit.* a fee levied on a vessel entering a port or anchored off a shore.

groundbait (ˈgraʊnd,beɪt) *n Angling.* bait, such as bread or maggots, thrown into an area of water to attract fish.

ground bass (beɪs) *n Music.* a short melodic bass line that is repeated over and over again.

ground-breaking *adj* innovative: *a ground-breaking novel.*

ground control *n* **1** the personnel, radar, computers, etc., on the ground that monitor the progress of aircraft or spacecraft. **2** a system

THESAURUS

ostler (*arch.*), stableboy ◆ *vb* **5** = **smarten up,** clean, dress, get up (*inf.*), preen, primp, spruce up, tidy, turn out **6** = **rub down,** brush, clean, curry, tend **7** = **train,** coach, drill, educate, make ready, nurture, prepare, prime, ready

groove *n* **1** = **indentation,** channel, cut, cutting, flute, furrow, gutter, hollow, rebate, rut, score, trench, trough

grope *vb* **1, 2** = **feel,** cast about, fish, flounder, forage, fumble, grabble, scrabble, search

gross *adj* **1** = **fat,** big, bulky, corpulent, dense, great, heavy, hulking, large, lumpish, massive, obese, overweight, thick **2** = **total,** aggregate, before deductions, before tax, entire, whole **3** = **vulgar,** coarse, crude, improper, impure, indecent, indelicate, lewd, low, obscene, offensive, ribald, rude, sensual, smutty, unseemly, X-rated (*inf.*) **4** = **blatant,** apparent, arrant, downright, egregious, flagrant, glaring, grievous, heinous, manifest, obvious, outrageous, plain, rank, serious, shameful, sheer, shocking, unmitigated, unqualified, utter **5** = **coarse,** boorish, callous, crass, dull, ignorant, imperceptive, insensitive, tasteless, uncultured, undiscriminating, unfeeling, unrefined, unsophisticated ◆ *vb* **10** = **earn,** bring in, make, rake in (*inf.*), take

Antonyms *adj* ≠ **fat:** delicate, little, petite, slim, small, svelte, thin ≠ **total:** net ≠ **vulgar:** decent, delicate, proper, pure ≠ **blatant:** partial, qualified ≠ **coarse:** cultivated, elegant

grossness *n* **1** = **obesity,** bigness, bulkiness, corpulence, fatness, greatness, heaviness, lumpishness, thickness **3** = **coarseness,** bestiality, crudity, impurity, indecency, indelicacy, licentiousness, obscenity, offensiveness, ribaldry, rudeness, sensuality, smut, smuttiness, unseemliness, vulgarity **4** = **blatancy,** egregiousness, flagrancy, grievousness, obviousness, rankness, seriousness, shamefulness **5** = **insensitivity,** coarseness, crassness, ignorance, lack of taste, pig-ignorance (*sl.*), tastelessness

grotesque *adj* **1, 3** = **unnatural,** absurd, bizarre, deformed, distorted, extravagant, fanciful, fantastic, freakish, incongruous, ludicrous, malformed, misshapen, odd, outlandish, preposterous, ridiculous, strange, weird, whimsical

Antonyms *adj* average, classic, graceful, natural, normal, realistic

grouch *vb* **1** = **complain,** beef (*sl.*), bellyache (*sl.*), bitch (*sl.*), bleat, carp, find fault, gripe (*inf.*), grouse, grumble, kvetch (*US sl.*), moan, whine, whinge (*inf.*) ◆ *n* **2** = **complaint,** beef (*sl.*), grievance, gripe (*inf.*), grouse, grumble, moan, objection, protest **3** = **moaner,** complainer, crab (*inf.*), crosspatch (*inf.*), curmudgeon, faultfinder, grouser, grumbler, malcontent, whiner

grouchy *adj* **3** = **bad-tempered,** cantankerous, cross, discontented, grumbling, grumpy, huffy, ill-tempered, irascible, irritable, liverish, peevish, petulant, querulous, ratty (*Brit. & NZ inf.*), sulky, surly, testy, tetchy

ground[1] *n* **1, 2** = **earth,** clod, dirt, dry land, dust, field, land, loam, mould, sod, soil, terra firma, terrain, turf **3** *plural* = **land,** area, country, district, domain, estate, fields, gardens, habitat, holding, property, realm, terrain, territory, tract **4** = **stadium,** arena, field, park (*inf.*), pitch **9** *often plural* = **reason,** account, argument, base, basis, call, cause, excuse, factor, foundation, inducement, justification, motive, occasion, premise, pretext, rationale **13** *plural* = **dregs,** deposit, grouts, lees, sediment, settlings ◆ *vb* **25** = **instruct,** acquaint with, coach, familiarize with, inform, initiate, prepare, teach, train, tutor **26** = **base,** establish, fix, found, set, settle for feeding radio messages to an aircraft pilot to enable him to make a blind landing.

ground cover *n* dense low herbaceous plants and shrubs that grow over the surface of the ground.

ground elder *n* a widely naturalized Eurasian umbelliferous plant with white flowers and creeping underground stems. Also called: **bishop's weed, goutweed.**

ground floor *n* **1** the floor of a building level or almost level with the ground. **2 get in on the ground floor.** *Inf.* to be in a project, undertaking, etc., from its inception.

ground frost *n* the condition resulting from a temperature reading of 0°C or below on a thermometer in contact with a grass surface.

ground glass *n* **1** glass that has a rough surface produced by grinding, used for diffusing light. **2** glass in the form of fine particles produced by grinding, used as an abrasive.

groundhog ('graʊnd,hɒg) *n* another name for **woodchuck.**

grounding ('graʊndɪŋ) *n* a foundation, esp. the basic general knowledge of a subject.

ground ivy *n* a creeping or trailing Eurasian aromatic herbaceous plant with scalloped leaves and purplish-blue flowers.

groundless ❶ ('graʊndlɪs) *adj* without reason or justification: *his suspicions were groundless.*
▸'**groundlessly** *adv* ▸'**groundlessness** *n*

groundling ('graʊndlɪŋ) *n* **1** any animal or plant that lives close to the ground or at the bottom of a lake, river, etc. **2** (in Elizabethan theatre) a spectator standing in the yard in front of the stage and paying least. **3** a person on the ground as distinguished from one in an aircraft.

groundnut ('graʊnd,nʌt) *n* **1** a North American climbing leguminous plant with small edible underground tubers. **2** the tuber of this plant. **3** *Brit.* another name for **peanut.**

ground plan *n* **1** a drawing of the ground floor of a building, esp. one to scale. **2** a preliminary or basic outline.

ground rule *n* a procedural or fundamental principle.

groundsel ('graʊnsəl) *n* any of certain plants of the composite family, esp. a Eurasian weed with heads of small yellow flowers. [OE, from *gundeswilge,* from *gund* pus + *swelgan* to swallow; after its use in poultices]

groundsheet ('graʊnd,ʃi:t) *n* a waterproof rubber, plastic, or polythene sheet placed on the ground in a tent, etc., to keep out damp.

groundsill ('graʊnd,sɪl) *n* a joist forming the lowest member of a timber frame. Also called: **ground plate.**

groundsman ('graʊndzmən) *n, pl* **groundsmen.** a person employed to maintain a sports ground, park, etc.

groundspeed ('graʊnd,spi:d) *n* the speed of an aircraft relative to the ground.

ground squirrel *n* a burrowing rodent resembling a chipmunk and occurring in North America, E Europe, and Asia. Also called: **gopher.**

groundswell ('graʊnd,swɛl) *n* **1** a considerable swell of the sea, often caused by a distant storm or earthquake. **2** a rapidly developing general feeling or opinion.

ground water *n* underground water that is held in the soil and in pervious rocks.

groundwork ❶ ('graʊnd,wɜ:k) *n* **1** preliminary work as a foundation or basis. **2** the ground or background of a painting, etc.

ground zero *n* a point on the ground directly below the centre of a nuclear explosion.

group ❶ (gru:p) *n* **1** a number of persons or things considered as a collective unit. **2a** a number of persons bound together by common social standards, interests, etc. **2b** (*as modifier*): *group behaviour.* **3** a small band of players or singers, esp. of pop music. **4** a number of animals or plants considered as a unit because of common characteristics, habits, etc. **5** an association of companies under a single ownership and control. **6** two or more figures or objects forming a design in a painting or sculpture. **7** a military formation comprising complementary arms and services: *a brigade group.* **8** an air force organization of higher level than a squadron. **9** Also called: **radical.** *Chem.* two or more atoms that are bound together in a molecule and behave as a single unit: *a methyl group* $-CH_3$. **10** a vertical column of elements in the periodic table that all have similar electronic structures, properties, and valencies: *the halogen group.* **11** *Maths.* a set under an operation involving any two members of the set such that the set is closed, associative, and contains both an identity and the inverse of each member. **12** See **blood group.** ◆ *vb* **13** to arrange or place (things, people, etc.) in or into a group, or (of things, etc.) to form into a group. [C17: from F *groupe,* of Gmc origin; cf. It. *gruppo;* see CROP]

group captain *n* an officer holding commissioned rank senior to a wing commander but junior to an air commodore in the RAF and certain other air forces.

group dynamics *n* (*functioning as sing*) *Psychol.* a field of social psychology concerned with the nature of human groups, their development, and their interactions.

grouper ('gru:pə) *n* a variant spelling of **groper.**

groupie ('gru:pɪ) *n Sl.* **1** an ardent fan of a celebrity, esp. a girl who follows the members of a pop group on tour in order to have sexual relations with them. **2** an enthusiastic follower of some activity: *a political groupie.*

Group of Five *n* France, Japan, the UK, the US, and Germany acting as a group to stabilize their currency exchange rates. Abbrev.: **G5.**

Group of Seven *n* the seven leading industrial nations excepting Russia, i.e. Canada, France, Germany, Italy, Japan, the UK, and the US, whose heads of state and finance ministers meet regularly to coordinate economic policy. Abbrev.: **G7.**

Group of Seventy-Seven *n* the developing countries of the world. Abbrev.: **G77.**

Group of Ten *n* the ten nations who met in Paris in 1961 to arrange the special drawing rights of the IMF; Belgium, Canada, France, Italy, Japan, the Netherlands, Sweden, the UK, the US, and West Germany. Also called: **Paris Club.** Abbrev.: **G10.**

Group of Three *n* Japan, the US, and Germany, regarded as the largest industrialized nations. Abbrev.: **G3.**

group practice *n* a group of doctors who together run a general practice.

group therapy *n Psychol.* the simultaneous treatment of a number of individuals who are brought together to share their problems in group discussion.

groupuscule ('gru:pə,skju:l) *n Usually derog.* a small group within a political party or movement. [C20: a blend of GROUP + *corpuscule;* see CORPUSCLE]

groupware ('gru:p,wɛə) *n* software that enables a group of computers to work together, so that users may access shared files, exchange messages, etc.

grouse[1] (graʊs) *n, pl* **grouse** *or* **grouses.** a game bird occurring mainly in the N hemisphere, having a stocky body and feathered legs and feet. [C16: from ?]

grouse[2] ❶ (graʊs) *vb* **grouses, grousing, groused. 1** (*intr*) to grumble; complain. ◆ *n* **2** a persistent complaint. [C19: from ?]
▸'**grouser** *n*

grouse[3] (graʊs) *adj Austral. & NZ sl.* fine; excellent. [from ?]

grout (graʊt) *n* **1** a thin mortar for filling joints between tiles, masonry, etc. **2** a fine plaster used as a finishing coat. **3** (*pl*) sediment or dregs. ◆ *vb* **4** (*tr*) to fill (joints) or finish (walls, etc.) with grout. [OE *grūt*]
▸'**grouter** *n*

grove ❶ (grəʊv) *n* **1** a small wooded area. **2** a road lined with houses and trees, esp. in a suburban area. [OE *grāf*]

grovel ❶ ('grɒvᵊl) *vb* **grovels, grovelling, grovelled** *or US* **grovels, groveling, groveled.** (*intr*) **1** to humble or abase oneself, as in making apologies or showing respect. **2** to lie or crawl face downwards, as in fear or humility. **3** (often foll. by *in*) to indulge or take pleasure (in sensuality or vice). [C16: back formation from obs. *groveling* (adv), from ME *on grufe* on the face, of Scand. origin; see -LING[2]]
▸'**groveller** *or US* ,**groveler** *n*

grow ❶ (grəʊ) *vb* **grows, growing, grew, grown. 1** (of an organism or part of an organism) to increase in size or develop (hair, leaves, or other structures). **2** (*intr; usually foll. by* *out of* or *from*) to originate, as from an initial cause or source: *the federation grew out of the Empire.* **3** (*intr*) to increase in size, number, degree, etc.: *the population is growing rapidly.* **4** (*intr*) to change in length or amount in a specified direction: *some plants grow downwards.* **5** (*copula; may take an infinitive*) (esp. of emotions, physical states, etc.) to develop or come into existence or being gradually: *to grow cold.* **6** (*intr;* foll. by *together*) to be joined gradually by or as by growth. **7** (when *intr,* foll. by *with*) to become covered with a growth: *the path grew with weeds.* **8** to produce (plants) by controlling or encouraging their growth, esp. for home consump-

THESAURUS

groundless *adj* = **unjustified,** baseless, chimerical, empty, false, idle, illusory, imaginary, unauthorized, uncalled-for, unfounded, unprovoked, unsupported, unwarranted
Antonyms *adj* justified, logical, proven, real, reasonable, substantial, supported, true, well-founded

groundwork *n* **1** = **preliminaries,** base, basis, cornerstone, footing, foundation, fundamentals, preparation, spadework, underpinnings

group *n* **1** = **set,** aggregation, assemblage, association, band, batch, bevy, bunch, camp, category, circle, class, clique, clump, cluster, collection, company, congregation, coterie, crowd, faction, formation, gang, gathering, organization, pack, party, posse (*sl.*), troop ◆ *vb* **13** = **arrange,** assemble, associate, assort, bracket, class, classify, congregate, dispose, gather, marshal, order, organize, put together, range, sort

grouse[2] *vb* **1** = **complain,** beef, bellyache (*sl.*), bitch (*sl.*), bleat, carp, find fault, gripe (*inf.*), grouch (*inf.*), grumble, kvetch (*US sl.*), moan, whine, whinge (*inf.*) ◆ *n* **2** = **complaint,** beef (*sl.*), grievance, gripe (*inf.*), grouch (*inf.*), grumble, moan, objection, protest

grove *n* **1** = **wood,** brake, coppice, copse, covert, hurst (*arch.*), plantation, spinney, thicket, woodland

grovel *vb* **1** = **humble oneself,** abase oneself, bootlick (*inf.*), bow and scrape, brown-nose (*taboo sl.*), cower, crawl, creep, cringe, crouch, demean oneself, fawn, flatter, kiss ass (*taboo sl.*), kowtow, lick someone's arse (*taboo sl.*), lick someone's boots, pander to, sneak, toady
Antonyms *vb* be proud, domineer, face, hold one's head high, intimidate

grow *vb* **1** = **spring up,** develop, flourish, germinate, shoot, sprout, vegetate **2** = **originate,** arise, issue, spring, stem **3** = **increase,** develop, enlarge, expand, extend, fill out, get bigger, get taller, heighten, multiply, spread, stretch, swell, thicken, widen **5** = **become,** come to be, develop (into), get, turn, wax **8** = **improve,** advance, expand, flourish, progress, prosper, succeed, thrive
Antonyms *vb* ≠ **increase:** decline, decrease, die, diminish, dwindle, fail, lessen, shrink, subside, wane

tion or on a commercial basis. ◆ See also **grow into, grow on,** etc. [OE *grōwan*]
▸ **'growable** *adj* ▸ **'grower** *n*

grow bag *n* a plastic bag containing a sterile growing medium that enables a plant to be grown to full size in it, usually for one season only. [C20: from *Gro-bag,* trademark for the first ones marketed]

growing pains *pl n* **1** pains in muscles or joints sometimes experienced by growing children. **2** difficulties besetting a new enterprise in its early stages.

grow into *vb (intr, prep)* to become big or mature enough for: *clothes big enough for him to grow into.*

growl (graʊl) *vb* **1** (of animals, esp. when hostile) to utter (sounds) in a low inarticulate manner: *the dog growled.* **2** to utter (words) in a gruff or angry manner. **3** *(intr)* to make sounds suggestive of an animal growling: *the thunder growled.* ◆ *n* **4** the act or sound of growling. [C18: from earlier *grolle,* from OF *grouller* to grumble]
▸ **'growler** *n*

grown (grəʊn) *adj* **a** developed or advanced: *fully grown.* **b** *(in combination): half-grown.*

grown-up ❶ *adj* **1** having reached maturity; adult. **2** suitable for or characteristic of an adult. ◆ *n* **3** an adult.

grow on *vb (intr, prep)* to become progressively more acceptable or pleasant to.

grow out of *vb (intr, adv + prep)* to become too big or mature for: *she soon grew out of her girlish ways.*

growth ❶ (grəʊθ) *n* **1** the process or act of growing. **2** an increase in size, number, significance, etc. **3** something grown or growing: *a new growth of hair.* **4** a stage of development: *a full growth.* **5** any abnormal tissue, such as a tumour. **6** *(modifier)* of, relating to, causing, or characterized by growth: *a growth industry; growth hormone.*

growth curve *n* a curve on a graph in which a variable is plotted against time to illustrate the growth of the variable.

grow up *vb (intr, adv)* **1** to reach maturity; become adult. **2** to come into existence; develop.

groyne *or esp. US* **groin** (grɔɪn) *n* a wall or jetty built out from a riverbank or seashore to control erosion. Also called: **spur, breakwater.** [C16: ?from OF *groign* snout, promontory]

grub ❶ (grʌb) *vb* **grubs, grubbing, grubbed. 1** (when *tr,* often foll. by *up* or *out*) to search for and pull up (roots, stumps, etc.) by digging in the ground. **2** to dig up the surface of (ground, soil, etc.), esp. to clear away roots, stumps, etc. **3** *(intr;* often foll. by *in* or *among)* to search carefully. **4** *(intr)* to work unceasingly, esp. at a dull task. ◆ *n* **5** the short legless larva of certain insects, esp. beetles. **6** *Sl.* food; victuals. **7** a person who works hard, esp. in a dull plodding way. [C13: of Gmc origin; cf. OHG *grubilōn* to dig]
▸ **'grubber** *n*

grubby ❶ ('grʌbɪ) *adj* **grubbier, grubbiest. 1** dirty; slovenly. **2** mean; beggarly. **3** infested with grubs.
▸ **'grubbily** *adv* ▸ **'grubbiness** *n*

grub screw *n* a small headless screw used to secure a sliding component in position.

grubstake ('grʌbˌsteɪk) *US & Canad. inf.* ◆ *n* **1** supplies provided for a prospector on the condition that the donor has a stake in any finds. ◆ *vb* **grubstakes, grubstaking, grubstaked.** *(tr)* **2** to furnish with such supplies. **3** to supply (a person) with a stake in a gambling game.
▸ **'grubˌstaker** *n*

Grub Street *n* **1** a former street in London frequented by literary hacks and needy authors. **2** the world or class of literary hacks, etc. ◆ *adj also* **Grubstreet. 3** *(sometimes not cap.)* relating to or characteristic of hack literature.

grudge ❶ (grʌdʒ) *n* **1** a persistent feeling of resentment, esp. one due to an insult or injury. **2** *(modifier)* planned or carried out in order to settle a grudge: *a grudge fight.* ◆ *vb* **grudges, grudging, grudged. 3** *(tr)* to give unwillingly. **4** to feel resentful or envious about (someone else's success, etc.). [C15: from OF *grouchier* to grumble, prob. of Gmc origin]
▸ **'grudging** *adj* ▸ **'grudgingly** *adv*

gruel ('gruːəl) *n* a drink or thin porridge made by boiling meal, esp. oatmeal, in water or milk. [C14: from OF, of Gmc origin]

gruelling ❶ *or US* **grueling** ('gruːəlɪŋ) *adj* **1** extremely severe or tiring. ◆ *n* **2** *Inf.* a severe or tiring experience, esp. punishment. [C19: from obs. *gruel* (vb) to punish]

gruesome ❶ ('gruːsəm) *adj* inspiring repugnance and horror; ghastly. [C16: orig. Northern E and Scot., of Scand. origin]
▸ **'gruesomely** *adv* ▸ **'gruesomeness** *n*

gruff ❶ (grʌf) *adj* **1** rough or surly in manner, speech, etc. **2** (of a voice, bark, etc.) low and throaty. [C16: orig. Scot., from Du. *grof,* of Gmc origin; rel. to OE *hrēof*]
▸ **'gruffly** *adv* ▸ **'gruffness** *n*

grumble ❶ ('grʌmbᵊl) *vb* **grumbles, grumbling, grumbled. 1** to utter (complaints) in a nagging way. **2** *(intr)* to make low rumbling sounds. ◆ *n* **3** a complaint. **4** a low rumbling sound. [C16: from MLow G *grommelen,* of Gmc origin]
▸ **'grumbler** *n* ▸ **'grumblingly** *adv* ▸ **'grumbly** *adj*

grumbling appendix *n Inf.* a condition in which the appendix causes intermittent pain or discomfort but appendicitis has not developed.

grummet ('grʌmɪt) *n* a variant of **grommet.**

grump (grʌmp) *Inf.* ◆ *n* **1** a surly or bad-tempered person. **2** *(pl)* a sulky or morose mood (esp. in **have the grumps**). ◆ *vb* **3** *(intr)* to complain or grumble. [C18: dialect: surly remark, prob. imit.]

grumpy ❶ ('grʌmpɪ) *or* **grumpish** *adj* **grumpier, grumpiest.** peevish; sulky. [C18: from GRUMP + -Y[1]]
▸ **'grumpily** *or* **'grumpishly** *adv* ▸ **'grumpiness** *or* **'grumpishness** *n*

Grundy ('grʌndɪ) *n* a narrow-minded person who keeps critical watch on the propriety of others. [C18: after Mrs *Grundy,* the character in T. Morton's play *Speed the Plough* (1798)]
▸ **'Grundyˌism** *n* ▸ **'Grundyist** *or* **'Grundyite** *n*

grungy ('grʌndʒɪ) *adj* **grungier, grungiest. 1** *Sl., chiefly US & Canad.* squalid, seedy, grotty. **2** (of pop music) characterized by a loud fuzzy guitar sound. [from ?]

grunion ('grʌnjən) *n* a Californian marine fish that spawns on beaches. [C20: prob. from Sp. *gruñón* a grunter]

grunt (grʌnt) *vb* **1** *(intr)* (esp. of pigs and some other animals) to emit a low short gruff noise. **2** (when *tr, may take a clause as object*) to express something gruffly: *he grunted his answer.* ◆ *n* **3** the characteristic low short gruff noise of pigs, etc., or a similar sound, as of disgust. **4** any of various mainly tropical marine fishes that utter a grunting sound when caught. [OE *grunnettan,* prob. imit.; cf. OHG *grunnizōn, grunni* moaning]
▸ **'grunter** *n*

Gruyère *or* **Gruyère cheese** ('gruːjɛə) *n* a hard flat whole-milk cheese, pale yellow in colour and with holes. [C19: after *Gruyère,* Switzerland, where it originated]

gr. wt. *abbrev. for* gross weight. a variant of **griffin**[1]. a variant of **griffin.**

grysbok ('graɪsˌbɒk) *n* either of two small antelopes of central and southern Africa, having small straight horns. [C18: Afrik., from Du. *grijs* grey + *bok* BUCK[1]]

GS *abbrev. for:* **1** General Secretary. **2** General Staff.

GST (in New Zealand) *abbrev. for* goods and services tax.

G-string *n* **1** a piece of cloth worn by striptease artistes covering the pubic area and attached to a narrow waistband. **2** a strip of cloth attached to the front and back of a waistband and covering the loins. **3** *Music.* a string tuned to G.

G-suit *n* a close-fitting garment that is worn by the crew of high-speed aircraft and can be pressurized to prevent blackout during manoeuvres. [C20: from *g(ravity) suit*]

GSVQ (in Britain) *abbrev. for* General Scottish Vocational Qualification: the Scottish equivalent of GNVQ.

THESAURUS

grown-up *adj* **1** = **mature**, adult, fully-grown, of age ◆ *n* **3** = **adult**, man, woman

growth *n* **1** = **cultivation**, crop, development, germination, produce, production, shooting, sprouting, vegetation **2** = **increase**, advance, advancement, enlargement, expansion, extension, improvement, proliferation, rise **5** = **tumour**, excrescence, lump
Antonyms *n* ≠ **increase:** decline, decrease, drop, dwindling, failure, fall, lessening, shrinkage, slackening, subsiding

grub *vb* **1** = **search**, ferret, forage, hunt, rummage, scour, uncover, unearth **2** = **dig up**, burrow, probe, pull up, root *(inf.)*, rootle *(Brit.)*, search for, uproot ◆ *n* **5** = **larva**, caterpillar, maggot **6** *Slang* = **food**, eats *(sl.)*, feed, nosebag *(sl.)*, nosh *(sl.)*, rations, sustenance, tack *(inf.)*, victuals, vittles *(obs. or dialect)*

grubby *adj* **1** = **dirty**, besmeared, filthy, frowzy, grimy, grungy *(sl., chiefly US & Canad.)*, manky *(Scot. dialect)*, mean, messy, mucky, scruffy, scuzzy *(sl.)*, seedy, shabby, slovenly, smutty, soiled, sordid, squalid, unkempt, untidy, unwashed

grudge *n* **1** = **resentment**, animosity, animus, antipathy, aversion, bitterness, chip on one's shoulder *(inf.)*, dislike, enmity, grievance, hard feelings, hate, ill will, malevolence, malice, pique, rancour, spite, venom ◆ *vb* **4** = **resent**, begrudge, be reluctant, complain, covet, envy, hold back, mind, stint
Antonyms *n* ≠ **resentment:** appreciation, goodwill, liking, thankfulness ◆ *vb* ≠ **resent:** be glad for, celebrate, welcome

gruelling *adj* **1** = **exhausting**, arduous, backbreaking, brutal, crushing, demanding, difficult, fatiguing, fierce, grinding, hard, harsh, laborious, punishing, severe, stiff, strenuous, taxing, tiring, trying
Antonyms *adj* cushy *(inf.)*, easy, enjoyable, light, pleasant, undemanding

gruesome *adj* = **horrific**, abominable, awful, fearful, from hell *(inf.)*, ghastly, grim, grisly, hellacious *(US sl.)*, hideous, horrendous, horrible, horrid, horrifying, loathsome, macabre, obscene, repugnant, repulsive, shocking, spine-chilling, terrible
Antonyms *adj* appealing, benign, cheerful, pleasant, sweet

gruff *adj* **1** = **surly**, bad-tempered, bearish, blunt, brusque, churlish, crabbed, crusty, curt, discourteous, grouchy *(inf.)*, grumpy, ill-humoured, ill-natured, impolite, rough, rude, sour, sullen, uncivil, ungracious, unmannerly **2** = **hoarse**, croaking, guttural, harsh, husky, low, rasping, rough, throaty
Antonyms *adj* ≠ **surly:** courteous, good-tempered, gracious, kind, pleasant, polite ≠ **hoarse:** mellifluous, smooth, sweet

grumble *vb* **1** = **complain**, beef *(sl.)*, bellyache *(sl.)*, bitch *(sl.)*, bleat, carp, find fault, gripe *(inf.)*, grouch *(inf.)*, grouse, kvetch *(US sl.)*, moan, repine, whine, whinge *(inf.)* **2** = **rumble**, growl, gurgle, murmur, mutter, roar ◆ *n* **3** = **complaint**, beef *(sl.)*, grievance, gripe *(inf.)*, grouch *(inf.)*, grouse, moan, objection, protest **4** = **rumble**, growl, gurgle, murmur, muttering, roar

grumpy *adj* = **irritable**, bad-tempered, cantankerous, crabbed, cross, crotchety *(inf.)*, edgy, grouchy *(inf.)*, grumbling, huffy, ill-tempered, liverish, peevish, petulant, querulous, sulky, sullen, surly, testy, tetchy

GT *abbrev. for* gran turismo: a touring car; usually a fast sports car with a hard fixed roof.

gtd *abbrev. for* guaranteed.

guaiacum ('gwaɪəkəm) *n* **1** any of a family of tropical American evergreen trees such as the lignum vitae. **2** the hard heavy wood of any of these trees. **3** a brownish resin obtained from the lignum vitae, used medicinally and in making varnishes. [C16: NL, from Sp. *guayaco,* of Amerind origin]

guanaco (gwɑːˈnɑːkəʊ) *n, pl* **guanacos.** a cud-chewing South American mammal closely related to the domesticated llama. [C17: from Sp., from Quechuan *huanacu*]

guanine ('gwɑːniːn, 'guːəˌniːn) *n* a white almost insoluble compound: one of the purine bases in nucleic acids. [C19: from GUANO + -INE^2]

guano ('gwɑːnəʊ) *n, pl* **guanos. 1** the dried excrement of fish-eating sea birds, deposited in rocky coastal regions of South America: used as a fertilizer. **2** any similar but artificially produced fertilizer. [C17: from Sp., from Quechuan *huano* dung]

Guarani (ˌgwɑːrəˈniː) *n* **1** (*pl* **Guarani** *or* **Guaranis**) a member of a South American Indian people of Paraguay, S Brazil, and Bolivia. **2** the language of this people.

guarantee Ⓣ (ˌgærənˈtiː) *n* **1** a formal assurance, esp. in writing, that a product, service, etc., will meet certain standards or specifications. **2** *Law.* a promise, esp. a collateral agreement, to answer for the debt, default, or miscarriage of another. **3a** a person, company, etc., to whom a guarantee is made. **3b** a person, company, etc., who gives a guarantee. **4** a person who acts as a guarantor. **5** something that makes a specified condition or outcome certain. **6** a variant spelling of **guaranty.** ◆ *vb* **guarantees, guaranteeing, guaranteed.** (*mainly tr*) **7** (*also intr*) to take responsibility for (someone else's debts, obligations, etc.). **8** to serve as a guarantee for. **9** to secure or furnish security for: *a small deposit will guarantee any dress.* **10** (usually foll. by *from* or *against*) to undertake to protect or keep secure, as against injury, loss, etc. **11** to ensure: *good planning will guarantee success.* **12** (*may take a clause as object or an infinitive*) to promise or make certain. [C17: ?from Sp. *garante* or F *garant,* of Gmc origin; cf. WARRANT]

guarantor Ⓣ (ˌgærənˈtɔː) *n* a person who gives or is bound by a guarantee or guaranty; surety.

guaranty ('gærəntɪ) *n, pl* **guaranties. 1** a pledge of responsibility for fulfilling another person's obligations in case of that person's default. **2** a thing given or taken as security for a guaranty. **3** the act of providing security. **4** a person who acts as a guarantor. ◆ *vb* **guaranties, guarantying, guarantied. 5** a variant spelling of **guarantee.** [C16: from OF *garantie,* var. of *warantie,* of Gmc origin; see WARRANTY]

guard Ⓣ (gɑːd) *vb* **1** to watch over or shield (a person or thing) from danger or harm; protect. **2** to keep watch over (a prisoner or other potentially dangerous person or thing), as to prevent escape. **3** (*tr*) to control: *to guard one's tongue.* **4** (*intr;* usually foll. by *against*) to take precautions. **5** to control entrance and exit through (a gate, door, etc.). **6** (*tr*) to provide (machinery, etc.) with a device to protect the operator. **7** (*tr*) **7a** *Chess, cards.* to protect or cover (a chessman or card) with another. **7b** *Curling, bowling.* to protect or cover (a stone or bowl) by placing one's own stone or bowl between it and another player. ◆ *n* **8** a person or group who keeps a protecting, supervising, or restraining watch or control over people, such as prisoners, things, etc. Related adj: **custodial. 9** a person or group of people, such as soldiers, who form a ceremonial escort. **10** *Brit.* the official in charge of a train. **11a** the act or duty of protecting, restraining, or supervising. **11b** (*as modifier*): *guard duty.* **12** a device, part, or attachment on an object, such as a weapon or machine tool, designed to protect the user against injury. **13** anything that provides or is intended to provide protection: *a guard against infection.* **14** *Sport.* an article of light tough material worn to protect any of various parts of the body. **15** the posture of defence or readiness in fencing, boxing, cricket, etc. **16 mount guard. 16a** (of a sentry, etc.) to begin to keep watch. **16b** (with *over*) to take a protective or defensive stance (towards something). **17 off (one's) guard.** having one's defences down; unprepared. **18 on (one's) guard.** prepared to face danger, difficulties, etc. **19 stand guard.** (of a sentry, etc.) to keep watch. [C15: from OF, from *garder* to protect, of Gmc origin; see WARD]
▸'**guarder** *n*

guarded Ⓣ ('gɑːdɪd) *adj* **1** protected or kept under surveillance. **2** prudent, restrained, or noncommittal: *a guarded reply.*
▸'**guardedly** *adv* ▸'**guardedness** *n*

guard hair *n* any of the coarse hairs that form the outer fur in certain mammals.

guardhouse ('gɑːdˌhaʊs) *or* **guardroom** ('gɑːdˌruːm, -rʊm) *n Mil.* a building serving as headquarters for military police and in which military prisoners are detained.

guardian Ⓣ ('gɑːdɪən) *n* **1** one who looks after, protects, or defends: *the guardian of public morals.* **2** *Law.* someone legally appointed to manage the affairs of a person incapable of acting for himself, as a minor or person of unsound mind. ◆ *adj* **3** protecting or safeguarding.
▸'**guardian,ship** *n*

Guardian Angels *pl n* vigilante volunteers who patrol the New York Underground and elsewhere, wearing red berets, to deter violent crime.

guard ring *n* **1** Also called: **keeper ring.** a ring worn to prevent another from slipping off the finger. **2** an electrode used to counteract distortion of the electric fields at the edges of other electrodes.

Guards (gɑːdz) *pl n* (esp. in European armies) any of various regiments responsible for ceremonial duties and, formerly, the protection of the head of state: *the Life Guards.*

guardsman ('gɑːdzmən) *n, pl* **guardsmen. 1** (in Britain) a member of a Guards battalion or regiment. **2** (in the US) a member of the National Guard. **3** a guard.

guard's van *n Railways, Brit. & NZ.* the van in which the guard travels, usually attached to the rear of a train. US and Canad. equivalent: **caboose.**

guava ('gwɑːvə) *n* **1** any of various tropical American trees, grown esp. for their edible fruit. **2** the fruit of such a tree, having yellow skin and pink pulp. [C16: from Sp. *guayaba,* from a South American Indian word]

guayule (gwəˈjuːlɪ) *n* **1** a bushy shrub of the southwestern US. **2** rubber derived from the sap of this plant. [from American Sp., from Nahuatl *cuauhuli,* from *cuahuitl* tree + *uli* gum]

gubbins ('gʌbɪnz) *n* **1** (*functioning as sing*) an object of little value. **2** (*functioning as sing*) a small gadget. **3** (*functioning as pl*) odds and ends; rubbish. **4** (*functioning as sing*) a silly person. [C16 (meaning: fragments): from obs. *gobbon*]

gubernatorial (ˌgjuːbənəˈtɔːrɪəl, ˌguː-) *adj Chiefly US.* of or relating to a governor. [C18: from L *gubernātor* governor]

guddle ('gʌd^{ə}l) *Scot.* ◆ *vb* **guddles, guddling, guddled. 1** to catch (fish) by groping with the hands under the banks or stones of a stream. ◆ *n* **2** a muddle; confusion. [C19: from ?]

gudgeon[1] ('gʌdʒən) *n* **1** a small slender European freshwater fish with a barbel on each side of the mouth: used as bait by anglers. **2** any of various other fishes, such as the goby. **3** *Sl.* a person who is easy to trick or cheat. ◆ *vb* **4** (*tr*) *Sl.* to trick or cheat. [C15: from OF *gougon,* prob. from L *gōbius;* see GOBY]

gudgeon[2] ('gʌdʒən) *n* **1** the female or socket portion of a pinned hinge. **2** *Naut.* one of two or more looplike sockets, fixed to the transom of a boat, into which the pintles of a rudder are fitted. [C14: from OF *goujon,* ?from LL *gulbia* chisel]

gudgeon pin *n Brit.* the pin through the skirt of a piston in an internal-combustion engine, to which the little end of the connecting rod is attached. US and Canad. name: **wrist pin.**

guelder-rose ('gɛldəˌrəʊz) *n* a Eurasian shrub with clusters of white flowers and small red fruits. [C16: from Du. *geldersche roos,* from *Gelderland* or *Gelders,* province of Holland]

guenon (gəˈnɒn) *n* a slender agile Old World monkey inhabiting wooded regions of Africa and having long hind limbs and tail and long hair surrounding the face. [C19: from F, from ?]

guerdon ('gɜːd^{ə}n) *Poetic.* ◆ *n* **1** a reward or payment. ◆ *vb* **2** (*tr*) to give a guerdon to. [C14: from OF *gueredon,* of Gmc origin; final element infl. by L *dōnum* gift]

Guernsey ('gɜːnzɪ) *n* **1** a breed of dairy cattle producing rich creamy milk, originating from the island of Guernsey, one of the Channel Islands. **2** (*sometimes not cap.*) a seaman's knitted woollen sweater. **3** (*not cap.*) *Austral.* a sleeveless woollen shirt or jumper worn by a football player. **4 get a guernsey.** *Austral.* to be selected or gain recognition for something.

guerrilla Ⓣ *or* **guerilla** (gəˈrɪlə) *n* **a** a member of an irregular usually politically motivated armed force that combats stronger regular forces. **b** (*as modifier*): *guerrilla warfare.* [C19: from Sp., dim. of *guerra* WAR]

guess Ⓣ (gɛs) *vb* (when *tr, may take a clause as object*) **1** (when *intr,* often foll. by *at* or *about*) to form or express an uncertain estimate or conclusion (about something), based on insufficient information: *guess what we're having for dinner.* **2** to arrive at a correct estimate of (something) by guessing: *he guessed my age.* **3** *Inf., chiefly US & Canad.* to be-

THESAURUS

guarantee *n* **1** = **assurance,** bond, certainty, collateral, covenant, earnest, guaranty, pledge, promise, security, surety, undertaking, warranty, word, word of honour ◆ *vb* **7, 11** = **ensure,** answer for, assure, certify, insure, maintain, make certain, pledge, promise, protect, secure, stand behind, swear, vouch for, warrant

guarantor *n* = **underwriter,** backer, bailsman (*rare*), bondsman, guarantee, sponsor, supporter, surety, voucher, warrantor

guard *vb* **1** = **watch over,** cover, defend, escort, keep, mind, oversee, patrol, police, preserve, protect, safeguard, save, screen, secure, shelter, shield, supervise, tend, watch ◆ *n* **8** = **protector,** custodian, defender, lookout, picket, sentinel, sentry, warder, watch, watchman **9** = **escort,** convoy, patrol **11** = **watchfulness,** attention, care, caution, heed, vigilance, wariness **12, 13** = **protection,** buffer, bulwark, bumper, defence, pad, rampart, safeguard, screen, security, shield **17 off guard** = **unprepared,** napping, unready, unwary, with one's defences down **18 on guard** = **prepared,** alert, cautious, circumspect, on the alert, on the lookout, on the qui vive, ready, vigilant, wary, watchful

guarded *adj* **2** = **cautious,** cagey (*inf.*), careful, circumspect, discreet, leery (*sl.*), noncommittal, prudent, reserved, restrained, reticent, suspicious, wary

guardian *n* **1** = **keeper,** attendant, champion, curator, custodian, defender, escort, guard, preserver, protector, trustee, warden, warder

guerrilla *n* = **freedom fighter,** irregular, member of the underground *or* resistance, partisan, underground fighter

guess *vb* **1** = **estimate,** conjecture, fathom, hypothesize, penetrate, predict, solve, speculate, work out **3** = **suppose,** believe, conjecture, dare say, deem, divine, fancy, hazard, imagine, judge, reckon, surmise, suspect, think ◆ *n* **4** = **supposition,** ballpark figure (*inf.*), conjecture,

lieve, think, or suppose (something): *I guess I'll go now.* ◆ *n* **4** an estimate or conclusion arrived at by guessing: *a bad guess.* **5** the act of guessing. [C13: prob. from ON]
▸'**guesser** *n*

guesstimate *or* **guestimate** *Inf.* ◆ *n* ('gestɪmɪt). **1** an estimate calculated mainly or only by guesswork. ◆ *vb* ('gestɪ,meɪt), **guesstimates, guesstimating, guesstimated.** (*tr*) **2** to form a guesstimate of.

guesswork ❶ ('gɛs,wɜːk) *n* **1** a set of conclusions, estimates, etc., arrived at by guessing. **2** the process of making guesses.

guest ❶ (gest) *n* **1** a person who is entertained, taken out to eat, etc., and paid for by another. **2a** a person who receives hospitality at the home of another. **2b** (*as modifier*): *the guest room.* **3a** a person who receives the hospitality of a government, establishment, or organization. **3b** (*as modifier*): *a guest speaker.* **4a** an actor, contestant, entertainer, etc., taking part as a visitor in a programme in which there are also regular participants. **4b** (*as modifier*): *a guest appearance.* **5** a patron of a hotel, boarding house, restaurant, etc. ◆ *vb* **6** (*intr*) (in theatre and broadcasting) to be a guest: *to guest on a show.* [OE *giest* guest, stranger, enemy]

guest beer *n* a draught beer stocked by a bar, often for a limited period, in addition to its usual range.

guesthouse ('gest,haʊs) *n* a private home or boarding house offering accommodation.

guest rope *n Naut.* any line trailed over the side of a vessel as a convenience for boats drawing alongside, as an aid in towing, etc.

guff ❶ (gʌf) *n Sl.* ridiculous or insolent talk. [C19: imit. of empty talk]

guffaw (gʌ'fɔː) *n* **1** a crude and boisterous laugh. ◆ *vb* **2** to laugh or express (something) in this way. [C18: imit.]

guidance ❶ ('gaɪdᵊns) *n* **1** leadership, instruction, or direction. **2a** counselling or advice on educational, vocational, or psychological matters. **2b** (*as modifier*): *the marriage-guidance counsellor.* **3** something that guides. **4** any process by which the flight path of a missile is controlled in flight.

guide ❶ (gaɪd) *vb* **guides, guiding, guided. 1** to lead the way for (a person). **2** to control the movement or course of (an animal, vehicle, etc.) by physical action; steer. **3** to supervise or instruct (a person). **4** (*tr*) to direct the affairs of (a person, company, nation, etc.). **5** (*tr*) to advise or influence (a person) in his standards or opinions: *let truth guide you.* ◆ *n* **6a** a person, animal, or thing that guides. **6b** (*as modifier*): *a guide dog.* **7** a person, usually paid, who conducts tour expeditions, etc. **8** a model or criterion, as in moral standards or accuracy. **9** Also called: **guidebook.** a handbook with information for visitors to a place. **10** a book that instructs or explains the fundamentals of a subject or skill. **11** any device that directs the motion of a tool or machine part. **12** a mark, sign, etc., that points the way. **13a** *Naval.* a ship in a formation used as a reference for manoeuvres. **13b** *Mil.* a soldier stationed to one side of a column or line to regulate alignment, show the way, etc. [C14: from (O)F *guider,* of Gmc origin]
▸'**guidable** *adj* ▸'**guider** *n*

Guide (gaɪd) *n* (*sometimes not cap.*) a member of an organization for girls equivalent to the Scouts. US equivalent: **Girl Scout.**

guided missile *n* a missile, esp. one that is rocket-propelled, having a flight path controlled either by radio signals or by internal preset or self-actuating homing devices.

guide dog *n* a dog that has been specially trained to accompany someone who is blind, enabling the blind person to move about safely.

guideline ('gaɪd,laɪn) *n* a principle put forward to set standards or determine a course of action.

guidepost ('gaɪd,pəʊst) *n* **1** a sign on a post by a road indicating directions. **2** a principle or guideline.

Guider ('gaɪdə) *n* (*sometimes not cap.*) a woman leader of a company of Guides or of a pack of Brownie Guides.

guidon ('gaɪdᵊn) *n* **1** a small pennant, used as a marker or standard, esp. by cavalry regiments. **2** the man or vehicle that carries this. [C16: from F, from OProvençal *guidoo,* from *guida* GUIDE]

guild ❶ *or* **gild** (gɪld) *n* **1** an organization, club, or fellowship. **2** (esp. in medieval Europe) an association of men sharing the same interests, such as merchants or artisans: formed for mutual aid and protection and to maintain craft standards. [C14: from ON; cf. *gjald* payment, *gildi* guild; rel. to OE *gield* offering, OHG *gelt* money]
▸'**guildsman,** '**gildsman** *or* (*fem*) '**guildswoman,** '**gildswoman** *n*

guilder ('gɪldə) *or* **gulden** *n, pl* **guilders, guilder** *or* **guldens, gulden. 1** Also: **gilder, florin.** the standard monetary unit of the Netherlands, divided into 100 cents. **2** any of various former gold or silver coins of Germany, Austria, or the Netherlands. [C15: from MDu. *gulden,* lit.: GOLDEN]

guildhall ('gɪld,hɔːl) *n Brit.* **a** the hall of a guild or corporation. **b** a town hall.

guile ❶ (gaɪl) *n* clever or crafty character or behaviour. [C18: from OF *guile,* of Gmc origin; see WILE]
▸'**guileful** *adj* ▸'**guilefully** *adv* ▸'**guilefulness** *n* ▸'**guileless** *adj* ▸'**guilelessly** *adv* ▸'**guilelessness** *n*

guillemot ('gɪlɪ,mɒt) *n* a northern oceanic diving bird having a black-and-white plumage and long narrow bill. [C17: from F, dim. of *Guillaume* William]

guilloche (gɪ'lɒʃ) *n* an ornamental border with a repeating pattern of two or more interwoven wavy lines, as in architecture. [C19: from F: tool used in ornamental work, ?from *Guillaume* William]

guillotine *n* ('gɪlə,tiːn). **1a** a device for beheading persons, consisting of a weighted blade set between two upright posts. **1b the guillotine.** execution by this instrument. **2** a device for cutting or trimming sheet material, such as paper or sheet metal, consisting of a slightly inclined blade that descends onto the sheet. **3** a surgical instrument for removing tonsils, growths in the throat, etc. **4** (in Parliament, etc.) a form of closure under which a bill is divided into compartments, groups of which must be completely dealt with each day. ◆ *vb* (,gɪlə'tiːn), **guillotines, guillotining, guillotined.** (*tr*) **5** to behead (a person) by guillotine. **6** (in Parliament, etc.) to limit debate on (a bill, motion, etc.) by the guillotine. [C18: from F, after Joseph Ignace *Guillotin* (1738–1814), F physician, who advocated its use in 1789]
▸,**guillo'tiner** *n*

guilt ❶ (gɪlt) *n* **1** the fact or state of having done wrong or committed an offence. **2** responsibility for a criminal or moral offence deserving punishment or a penalty. **3** remorse or self-reproach caused by feeling that one is responsible for a wrong or offence. **4** *Arch.* sin or crime. [OE *gylt,* from ?]

guiltless ❶ ('gɪltlɪs) *adj* free of all responsibility for wrongdoing or crime; innocent.
▸'**guiltlessly** *adv* ▸'**guiltlessness** *n*

guilty ❶ ('gɪltɪ) *adj* **guiltier, guiltiest. 1** responsible for an offence or misdeed. **2** *Law.* having committed an offence or adjudged to have done so: *the accused was found guilty.* **3** of, showing, or characterized by guilt.
▸'**guiltily** *adv* ▸'**guiltiness** *n*

guimpe (gɪmp) *n* a variant spelling of **gimp.**

guinea ('gɪnɪ) *n* **1a** a British gold coin taken out of circulation in 1813, worth 21 shillings. **1b** the sum of 21 shillings (1.05), still used in quoting professional fees. **2** See **guinea fowl.** [C16: the coin was orig. made of gold from Guinea]

guinea fowl *or* **guinea** *n* a domestic fowl of Africa and SW Asia, having a dark plumage mottled with white, a naked head and neck, and a heavy rounded body.

THESAURUS

feeling, hypothesis, judgment, notion, prediction, reckoning, shot in the dark, speculation, surmise, suspicion, theory
Antonyms *vb* ≠ **estimate, suppose:** be certain, be sure, know, prove, show ◆ *n* ≠ **supposition:** certainty, fact

guesswork *n* **1** = **speculation,** conjecture, estimation, presumption, supposition, surmise, suspicion, theory

guest *n* **2** = **visitor,** boarder, caller, company, lodger, visitant

guff *n* = **nonsense,** balderdash, bull (*sl.*), bunkum *or* buncombe (*chiefly US*), drivel, empty talk, eyewash (*inf.*), garbage (*inf.*), hogwash, hokum (*sl., chiefly US & Canad.*), hot air (*inf.*), humbug, moonshine, pap, piffle (*inf.*), poppycock (*inf.*), rot, rubbish, tommyrot, tosh (*sl., chiefly Brit.*), trash, tripe (*inf.*)

guidance *n* **1** = **advice,** auspices, conduct, control, counsel, counselling, direction, government, help, instruction, intelligence, leadership, management, teaching

guide *vb* **1** = **lead,** accompany, attend, conduct, convoy, direct, escort, pilot, shepherd, show the way, steer, usher **2** = **steer,** command, control, direct, handle, manage, manoeuvre **3, 5** = **supervise,** advise, counsel, educate, govern, influence, instruct, oversee, regulate, rule, superintend, sway, teach, train ◆ *n* **6** = **escort,** adviser, attendant, chaperon, cicerone, conductor, controller, counsellor, director, dragoman, guru, leader, mentor, monitor, pilot, steersman, teacher, torchbearer, usher **8** = **model,** criterion, example, exemplar, ideal, imago (*Psychoanalysis*), inspiration, lodestar, master, par, paradigm, standard **9, 10** = **guidebook,** Baedeker, catalogue, directory, handbook, instructions, key, manual, vade mecum **12** = **pointer,** beacon, clue, guiding light, key, landmark, lodestar, mark, marker, sign, signal, signpost

guild *n* **1** = **society,** association, brotherhood, club, company, corporation, fellowship, fraternity, league, lodge, order, organization, union

guile *n* = **cunning,** art, artfulness, artifice, cleverness, craft, craftiness, deceit, deception, duplicity, gamesmanship (*inf.*), knavery, ruse, sharp practice, slyness, treachery, trickery, trickiness, wiliness
Antonyms *n* candour, frankness, honesty, sincerity, truthfulness

guileful *adj* = **cunning,** artful, clever, crafty, deceitful, duplicitous, foxy, sly, sneaky, treacherous, tricky, underhand, wily

guileless *adj* = **artless,** above-board, candid, frank, genuine, honest, ingenuous, innocent, naive, natural, open, simple, simple-minded, sincere, straightforward, truthful, undesigning, unsophisticated, upfront (*inf.*)

guilt *n* **1, 2** = **culpability,** blame, blameworthiness, criminality, delinquency, guiltiness, iniquity, misconduct, responsibility, sinfulness, wickedness, wrong, wrongdoing **3** = **remorse,** bad conscience, contrition, disgrace, dishonour, guiltiness, guilty conscience, infamy, regret, self-condemnation, self-reproach, shame, stigma
Antonyms *n* ≠ **culpability:** blamelessness, innocence, righteousness, sinlessness, virtue ≠ **remorse:** honour, pride, self-respect

guiltless *adj* = **innocent,** blameless, clean (*sl.*), clear, immaculate, impeccable, irreproachable, pure, sinless, spotless, squeaky-clean, unimpeachable, unsullied, untainted, untarnished

guilty *adj* **1, 2** = **culpable,** at fault, blameworthy, convicted, criminal, delinquent, erring, evil, felonious, iniquitous, offending, reprehensible, responsible, sinful, to blame, wicked, wrong **3** = **remorseful,** ashamed, conscience-stricken, contrite, hangdog, regretful, rueful, shamefaced, sheepish, sorry
Antonyms *adj* ≠ **culpable:** blameless, innocent, moral, righteous, virtuous ≠ **remorseful:** proud

guinea hen *n* a guinea fowl, esp. a female.

guinea pig *n* **1** a domesticated cavy, commonly kept as a pet and used in scientific experiments. **2** a person or thing used for experimentation. [C17: from ?]

guipure (gɪˈpjʊə) *n* **1** Also called: **guipure lace.** any of many types of heavy lace that have their pattern connected by threads, rather than supported on a net mesh. **2** a heavy corded trimming; gimp. [C19: from OF, from *guiper* to cover with cloth, of Gmc origin]

guise 🅣 (gaɪz) *n* **1** semblance or pretence: *under the guise of friendship.* **2** external appearance in general. **3** *Arch.* manner or style of dress. [C13: from OF *guise*, of Gmc origin]

guising (ˈgaɪzɪŋ) *n* (in Scotland and N England) the practice or custom of disguising oneself in fancy dress, often with mask, and visiting people's houses, esp. at Halloween.
▸**ˈguiser** *n*

guitar (gɪˈtɑː) *n* a plucked stringed instrument originating in Spain, usually having six strings, a flat sounding board with a circular sound hole in the centre, a flat back, and a fretted fingerboard. [C17: from Sp. *guitarra*, from Ar. *qītār*, from Gk: CITHARA]
▸**guiˈtarist** *n*

Gulag (ˈguːlæg) *n* **1** (formerly) the central administrative department of the Soviet security service, responsible for maintaining prisons and labour camps. **2** (*not cap.*) any system used to silence dissidents. [C20: from Russian *G(lavnoye) U(pravleniye Ispravitelno-Trudovykh) Lag(erei)* Main Administration for Corrective Labour Camps]

gulch (gʌltʃ) *n US & Canad.* a narrow ravine cut by a fast stream. [C19: from ?]

gulden (ˈgʊldᵊn) *n, pl* **guldens** *or* **gulden.** a variant of **guilder.**

gules (gjuːlz) *adj* (*usually postpositive*), *n Heraldry.* red. [C14: from OF *gueules* red fur worn around the neck, from *gole* throat, from L *gula* GULLET]

gulf 🅣 (gʌlf) *n* **1** a large deep bay. **2** a deep chasm. **3** something that divides or separates, such as a lack of understanding. **4** something that engulfs, such as a whirlpool. ◆ *vb* **5** (*tr*) to swallow up; engulf. [C14: from OF *golfe*, from It. *golfo*, from Gk *kolpos*]

Gulf States *pl n* **the. 1** the oil-producing states around the Persian Gulf: Iran, Iraq, Kuwait, Saudi Arabia, Bahrain, Qatar, the United Arab Emirates, and Oman. **2** the states of the US that border on the Gulf of Mexico: Alabama, Florida, Louisiana, Mississippi, and Texas.

Gulf Stream *n* a relatively warm ocean current flowing northeastwards from the Gulf of Mexico towards NW Europe. Also called: **North Atlantic Drift.**

Gulf War *n* **1** the war (1991) between US-led UN forces and Iraq, following Iraq's invasion of Kuwait. **2** See **Iran-Iraq War.**

Gulf War syndrome *n* a group of various debilitating symptoms experienced by many soldiers who served in the Gulf War of 1991. It is claimed to be associated with damage to the central nervous system, caused by exposure to pesticides containing organophosphates.

gulfweed (ˈgʌlf,wiːd) *n* a brown seaweed having air bladders and forming dense floating masses in tropical Atlantic waters, esp. the Gulf Stream. Also called: **sargasso, sargasso weed.**

gull[1] (gʌl) *n* an aquatic bird such as the common gull or mew having long pointed wings, short legs, and a mostly white plumage. [C15: of Celtic origin]

gull[2] 🅣 (gʌl) *Arch.* ◆ *n* **1** a person who is easily fooled or cheated. ◆ *vb* **2** (*tr*) to fool, cheat, or hoax. [C16: ?from dialect *gull* unfledged bird, prob. from *gul*, from ON *gulr* yellow]

gullet 🅣 (ˈgʌlɪt) *n* **1** a less formal name for the **oesophagus. 2** the throat or pharynx. [C14: from OF *goulet*, dim. of *goule*, from L *gula* throat]

gullible 🅣 (ˈgʌlɪbᵊl) *adj* easily taken in or tricked.
▸**,gulliˈbility** *n* ▸**ˈgullibly** *adv*

gully 🅣 *or* **gulley** (ˈgʌlɪ) *n, pl* **gullies** *or* **gulleys. 1** a channel or small valley, esp. one cut by heavy rainwater. **2** *NZ.* a bush-clad small valley. **3** *Cricket.* **3a** a fielding position between the slips and point. **3b** a fielder in this position. ◆ *vb* **gullies, gullying, gullied** *or* **gulleys, gulleying, gulleyed. 4** (*tr*) to make channels in (the ground, sand, etc.). [C16: from F *goulet* neck of a bottle; see GULLET]

gulp 🅣 (gʌlp) *vb* **1** (*tr*; often foll. by *down*) to swallow rapidly, esp. in large mouthfuls. **2** (*tr*; often foll. by *back*) to stifle or choke: *to gulp back sobs.* **3** (*intr*) to swallow air convulsively because of nervousness, surprise, etc. **4** (*intr*) to make a noise, as when swallowing too quickly. ◆ *n* **5** the act of gulping. **6** the quantity taken in a gulp. [C15: from MDu. *gulpen*, imit.]
▸**ˈgulper** *n* ▸**ˈgulpingly** *adv* ▸**ˈgulpy** *adj*

gum[1] 🅣 (gʌm) *n* **1** any of various sticky substances that exude from certain plants, hardening on exposure to air and dissolving or forming viscous masses in water. **2** any of various products, such as adhesives, that are made from such substances. **3** any sticky substance used as an adhesive; mucilage; glue. **4** See **chewing gum, bubble gum,** and **gumtree. 5** *NZ.* See **kauri gum. 6** *Chiefly Brit.* a gumdrop. ◆ *vb* **gums, gumming, gummed. 7** to cover or become covered, clogged, or stiffened as with gum. **8** (*tr*) to stick together or in place with gum. **9** (*intr*) to emit or form gum. ◆ See also **gum up.** [C14: from OF *gomme*, from L *gummi*, from Gk *kommi*, from Egyptian *kemai*]

gum[2] (gʌm) *n* the fleshy tissue that covers the jawbones around the bases of the teeth. Technical name: **gingiva.** Related adj: **gingival.** [OE *gōma* jaw]

gum ammoniac *n* another name for **ammoniac.**

gum arabic *n* a gum exuded by certain acacia trees, used in the manufacture of ink, food thickeners, pills, emulsifiers, etc. Also called: **gum acacia.**

gumbo (ˈgʌmbəʊ) *n, pl* **gumbos.** *US.* **1** the mucilaginous pods of okra. **2** another name for **okra. 3** a soup or stew thickened with okra pods. **4** a fine soil in the W prairies that becomes muddy when wet. [C19: from Louisiana F *gombo*, of Bantu origin]

gumboil (ˈgʌm,bɔɪl) *n* an abscess on the gums.

gumboots (ˈgʌm,buːts) *pl n* another name for **Wellington boots** (sense 1).

gum-digger *n NZ.* a person who digs for fossilized kauri gum in a **gum-field,** an area where it is found buried.

gumdrop (ˈgʌm,drɒp) *n* a small jelly-like sweet containing gum arabic and various colourings and flavourings. Also called (esp. Brit.): **gum.**

gummy[1] 🅣 (ˈgʌmɪ) *adj* **gummier, gummiest. 1** sticky or tacky. **2** consisting of, coated with, or clogged by gum or a similar substance. **3** producing gum. [C14: from GUM[1] + -Y[1]]
▸**ˈgumminess** *n*

gummy[2] (ˈgʌmɪ) *adj* **gummier, gummiest. 1** toothless. ◆ *n, pl* **gummies. 2** Also called: **gummy shark.** *Austral.* a small crustacean-eating shark with flat crushing teeth. [C20: from GUM[2] + -Y[1]]

gum nut *n Austral.* the hardened seed container of the gumtree *Eucalyptus gummifera.*

gumption 🅣 (ˈgʌmpʃən) *n Inf.* **1** *Brit.* common sense or resourcefulness. **2** initiative or courage. [C18: orig. Scot., from ?]

gum resin *n* a mixture of resin and gum obtained from various plants and trees.

gumtree (ˈgʌm,triː) *n* **1** any of various trees that yield gum, such as the eucalyptus, sweet gum, and sour gum. Sometimes shortened to **gum. 2 up a gumtree.** *Inf.* in a very awkward position; in difficulties.

gum up *vb* (*tr, adv*) **1** to cover, dab, or stiffen with gum. **2** *Inf.* to make a mess of; bungle (often in **gum up the works**).

gun 🅣 (gʌn) *n* **1a** a weapon with a metallic tube or barrel from which a missile is discharged, usually by force of an explosion. It may be portable or mounted. **1b** (*as modifier*): *a gun barrel.* **2** the firing of a gun as a salute or signal, as in military ceremonial. **3** a member of or a place in a shooting party or syndicate. **4** any device used to project something under pressure: *a spray gun.* **5** *US sl.* an armed criminal; gunman. **6** *Austral. & NZ sl.* **6a** an expert. **6b** (*as modifier*): *a gun shearer.* **7 give it the gun.** *Sl.* to increase speed, effort, etc., to a considerable or maximum degree. **8 go great guns.** *Sl.* to act or function with great speed, intensity, etc. **9 jump** *or* **beat the gun. 9a** (of a runner, etc.) to set off before the starting signal is given. **9b** *Inf.* to act prematurely. **10 stick to one's guns.** *Inf.* to maintain one's opinions or intentions in spite of opposition. ◆ *vb* **guns, gunning, gunned. 11** (when *tr*, often foll. by *down*) to shoot (someone) with a gun. **12** (*tr*) to press hard on the accelerator of (an engine): *to gun the engine.* **13** (*intr*) to hunt with a gun. ◆ See also **gun for.** [C14: prob. from a female pet name, from the Scand. name *Gunnhildr* (from ON *gunnr* war + *hildr* war)]

gunboat (ˈgʌn,bəʊt) *n* a small shallow-draft vessel carrying mounted guns and used by coastal patrols, etc.

gunboat diplomacy *n* diplomacy conducted by threats of military intervention.

guncotton (ˈgʌn,kɒtᵊn) *n* cellulose nitrate containing a relatively large amount of nitrogen: used as an explosive.

gun dog *n* **1** a dog trained to work with a hunter or gamekeeper, esp. in retrieving, pointing at, or flushing game. **2** a dog belonging to any breed adapted to these activities.

gunfight (ˈgʌn,faɪt) *n Chiefly US.* a fight between persons using firearms.
▸**ˈgun,fighter** *n*

THESAURUS

guise *n* **1, 2 = form,** air, appearance, aspect, behaviour, demeanour, disguise, dress, façade, face, fashion, front, mask, mode, pretence, semblance, shape, show

gulf *n* **1 = bay,** bight, sea inlet **2 = chasm,** abyss, breach, cleft, gap, opening, rent, rift, separation, split, void, whirlpool

gull[2] *n* **1 = dupe,** babe in arms (*inf.*), chump, easy mark (*sl.*), fool, mug (*sl.*), sap (*sl.*), simpleton, sucker (*sl.*) ◆ *vb* **2 = deceive,** beguile, cheat, con (*sl.*), cozen, defraud, dupe, hoax, pull a fast one on (*inf.*), put one over on (*inf.*), rook (*sl.*), sell a pup to, skin (*sl.*), stiff (*sl.*), swindle, take for a ride (*inf.*), take in (*inf.*), trick

gullet *n* **1 = oesophagus 2 = throat,** craw, crop, maw

gullibility *n* **= credulity,** innocence, naïveté, simplicity, trustingness

gullible *adj* **= naive,** as green as grass, born yesterday, credulous, easily taken in, foolish, green, innocent, silly, simple, trusting, unsceptical, unsophisticated, unsuspecting, wet behind the ears (*inf.*)
Antonyms *adj* cynical, sophisticated, suspicious, untrusting, worldly

gully *n* **1 = channel,** ditch, gutter, watercourse

gulp *vb* **1 = swallow,** bolt, devour, gobble, guzzle, knock back (*inf.*), quaff, swig (*inf.*), swill, toss off, wolf **2 = gasp,** choke, stifle, swallow ◆ *n* **6 = swallow,** draught, mouthful, swig (*inf.*)

gum[1] *n* **3 = glue,** adhesive, cement, exudate, mucilage, paste, resin ◆ *vb* **6 = clog,** stiffen **7 = stick,** affix, cement, glue, paste

gummy[1] *adj* **1 = sticky,** adhesive, gluey, tacky, viscid

gumption *n* **1, 2 = resourcefulness,** ability, acumen, astuteness, cleverness, common sense, discernment, enterprise, get-up-and-go (*inf.*), horse sense, initiative, mother wit, nous (*Brit. sl.*), sagacity, savvy (*sl.*), shrewdness, spirit, wit(s)

gun *n* **1 = firearm,** handgun, heater (*US sl.*), piece (*sl.*), rod (*sl.*), shooter (*sl.*)

gunfire ('gʌnˌfaɪə) *n* **1** the firing of one or more guns, esp. when done repeatedly. **2** the use of firearms, as contrasted with other military tactics.

gun for *vb* (*intr, prep*) **1** to search for in order to reprimand, punish, or kill. **2** to try earnestly for: *he was gunning for promotion.*

gunge (gʌndʒ) *Inf.* ◆ *n* **1** sticky, rubbery, or congealed matter. ◆ *vb* **gunges, gunging, gunged. 2** (*tr; usually passive;* foll. by *up*) to block or encrust with gunge; clog. [C20: imit., ? infl. by GOO & SPONGE]
▸ **'gungy** *adj*

gunk (gʌŋk) *n Inf.* slimy, oily, or filthy matter. [C20: ? imit.]

gunlock ('gʌnˌlɒk) *n* the mechanism in some firearms that causes the charge to be exploded.

gunman ➊ ('gʌnmən) *n, pl* **gunmen. 1** a man armed with a gun, esp. unlawfully. **2** a man skilled with a gun.

gunmetal ('gʌnˌmetᵊl) *n* **1** a type of bronze containing copper, tin, and zinc. **2a** a dark grey colour. **2b** (*as adj*): *gunmetal chiffon.*

gunnel[1] ('gʌnᵊl) *n* any eel-like fish occurring in coastal regions of northern seas. [C17: from ?]

gunnel[2] ('gʌnᵊl) *n* a variant spelling of **gunwale.**

gunner ('gʌnə) *n* **1** a serviceman who works with, uses, or specializes in guns. **2** *Naval.* (formerly) a warrant officer responsible for the training of gun crews, their performance in action, and accounting for ammunition. **3** (in the British Army) an artilleryman, esp. a private. **4** a person who hunts with a rifle or shotgun.

gunnery ('gʌnərɪ) *n* **1** the art and science of the efficient design and use of ordnance, esp. artillery. **2** guns collectively. **3** the use and firing of guns.

gunny ('gʌnɪ) *n, pl* **gunnies.** *Chiefly US.* **1** a coarse hard-wearing fabric usually made from jute and used for sacks, etc. **2** Also called: **gunny sack.** a sack made from this fabric. [C18: from Hindi, from Sansk. *gōnī* sack, prob. of Dravidian origin]

gunplay ('gʌnˌpleɪ) *n Chiefly US.* the use of firearms, as by criminals, etc.

gunpoint ('gʌnˌpɔɪnt) *n* **1** the muzzle of a gun. **2 at gunpoint.** being under or using the threat of being shot.

gunpowder ('gʌnˌpaʊdə) *n* an explosive mixture of potassium nitrate, charcoal, and sulphur: used in time fuses and in fireworks.

gun room *n* **1** (esp. in the Royal Navy) the mess allocated to junior officers. **2** a room where guns are stored.

gunrunning ('gʌnˌrʌnɪŋ) *n* the smuggling of guns and ammunition or other weapons of war into a country.
▸ **'gunˌrunner** *n*

gunshot ('gʌnˌʃɒt) *n* **1a** shot fired from a gun. **1b** (*as modifier*): *gunshot wounds.* **2** the range of a gun. **3** the shooting of a gun.

gunslinger ('gʌnˌslɪŋə) *n Sl.* a gunfighter or gunman, esp. in the Old West.

gunsmith ('gʌnˌsmɪθ) *n* a person who makes or repairs firearms, esp. portable guns.

gunstock ('gʌnˌstɒk) *n* the wooden handle or support to which is attached the barrel of a rifle.

Gunter's chain ('gʌntəz) *n Surveying.* a measuring chain 22 yards in length, or this length as a unit. [C17: after E. *Gunter* (1581–1626), E mathematician]

gunwale *or* **gunnel** ('gʌnᵊl) *n Naut.* the top of the side of a boat or ship. [C15: from GUN + WALE from its use to support guns]

gunyah ('gʌnjə) *n Austral.* a bush hut or shelter. [C19: from Abor.]

guppy ('gʌpɪ) *n, pl* **guppies.** a small brightly coloured freshwater fish of N South America and the Caribbean: a popular aquarium fish. [C20: after R. J. L. *Guppy,* 19th-cent. clergyman of Trinidad who first presented specimens to the British Museum]

gurdwara ('gɜːdwɑːrə) *n* a Sikh place of worship. [C20: from Punjabi *gurduārā,* from Sansk. *guru* teacher + *dvārā* door]

gurgle ➊ ('gɜːgᵊl) *vb* **gurgles, gurgling, gurgled.** (*intr*) **1** (of liquids, esp. of streams, etc.) to make low bubbling noises when flowing. **2** to utter low throaty bubbling noises, esp. as a sign of contentment: *the baby gurgled with delight.* ◆ *n* **3** the act or sound of gurgling. [C16: ?from Vulgar L *gurgulāre,* from L *gurguliō* gullet]

Gurkha ('gɜːkə) *n* **1** a member of a Hindu people, descended from Brahmins and Rajputs, living chiefly in Nepal. **2** a member of a Gurkha regiment in the Indian or British army.

gurnard ('gɜːnəd) *or* **gurnet** ('gɜːnɪt) *n, pl* **gurnard, gurnards** *or* **gurnet, gurnets.** a European marine fish having a heavily armoured head and finger-like pectoral fins. [C14: from OF *gornard,* from *grognier* to grunt, from L *grunnīre*]

guru ➊ ('gʊruː, 'guːruː) *n* **1** a Hindu or Sikh religious teacher or leader, giving personal spiritual guidance to his disciples. **2** *Often derog.* a leader or chief theoretician of a movement, esp. a spiritual or religious cult. **3** *Often facetious.* a leading authority in a particular field: *a cricketing guru.* [C17: from Hindi *gurū,* from Sansk. *guruḥ* weighty]

gush ➊ (gʌʃ) *vb* **1** to pour out or cause to pour out suddenly and profusely, usually with a rushing sound. **2** to act or utter in an overeffusive, affected, or sentimental manner. ◆ *n* **3** a sudden copious flow or emission, esp. of liquid. **4** something that flows out or is emitted. **5** an extravagant and insincere expression of admiration, sentiment, etc. [C14: prob. imit.; cf. ON *gjósa*]
▸ **'gushing** *adj* ▸ **'gushingly** *adv*

gusher ('gʌʃə) *n* **1** a person who gushes, as in being effusive or sentimental. **2** something, such as a spurting oil well, that gushes.

gushy ➊ ('gʌʃɪ) *adj* **gushier, gushiest.** *Inf.* displaying excessive admiration or sentimentality.
▸ **'gushily** *adv* ▸ **'gushiness** *n*

gusset ('gʌsɪt) *n* **1** an inset piece of material used esp. to strengthen or enlarge a garment. **2** a triangular metal plate for strengthening a corner joist. ◆ *vb* **3** (*tr*) to put a gusset in (a garment). [C15: from OF *gousset* a piece of mail, dim. of *gousse* pod, from ?]
▸ **'gusseted** *adj*

gust ➊ (gʌst) *n* **1** a sudden blast of wind. **2** a sudden rush of smoke, sound, etc. **3** an outburst of emotion. ◆ *vb* **4** (*intr*) to blow in gusts. [C16: from ON *gustr;* rel. to *gjōsa* to GUSH; see GEYSER]

gustation (gʌ'steɪʃən) *n* the act of tasting or the faculty of taste. [C16: from L *gustātiō,* from *gustāre* to taste]
▸ **gustatory** ('gʌstətərɪ) *adj*

gusto ➊ ('gʌstəʊ) *n* vigorous enjoyment, zest, or relish: *the aria was sung with great gusto.* [C17: from Sp.: taste, from L *gustus* a tasting]

gusty ➊ ('gʌstɪ) *adj* **gustier, gustiest. 1** blowing in gusts or characterized by blustery weather: *a gusty wind.* **2** given to sudden outbursts, as of emotion.
▸ **'gustily** *adv* ▸ **'gustiness** *n*

gut ➊ (gʌt) *n* **1a** the lower part of the alimentary canal; intestine. **1b** the entire alimentary canal. Related adj: **visceral. 2** (*often pl*) the bowels or entrails, esp. of an animal. **3** *Sl.* the belly; paunch. **4** See **catgut. 5** a silky fibrous substance extracted from silkworms, used in the manufacture of fishing tackle. **6** a narrow channel or passage. **7** (*pl*) *Inf.* courage, willpower, or daring; forcefulness. **8** (*pl*) *Inf.* the essential part: *the guts of a problem.* ◆ *vb* **guts, gutting, gutted.** (*tr*) **9** to remove the entrails from (fish, etc.). **10** (esp. of fire) to destroy the inside of (a building). **11** to take out the central points of (an article, etc.), esp. in summary form. ◆ *adj* **12** *Inf.* instinctive, basic, or fundamental: *a gut feeling; capital punishment is a gut issue.* [OE *gutt;* rel. to *gēotan* to flow]

GUT (gʌt) *n acronym for* grand unified theory.

gutless ➊ ('gʌtlɪs) *adj Inf.* lacking courage or determination.

gut reaction *n* the first, instinctive, reaction to a situation.

gutsy ➊ ('gʌtsɪ) *adj* **gutsier, gutsiest.** *Sl.* **1** gluttonous; greedy. **2** full of courage or boldness. **3** passionate; lusty.

gutta-percha ('gʌtə'pɜːtʃə) *n* **1** any of several tropical trees with leathery leaves. **2** a whitish rubber substance derived from the coagulated milky latex of any of these trees: used in electrical insulation and dentistry. [C19: from Malay *getah* gum + *percha* tree that produces it]

guttate ('gʌteɪt) *adj Biol.* (esp. of plants) covered with small drops or droplike markings. [C19: from L *guttātus* dappled, from *gutta* a drop]

gutted ('gʌtɪd) *adj Inf.* disappointed and upset.

gutter ➊ ('gʌtə) *n* **1** a channel along the eaves or on the roof of a building, used to collect and carry away rainwater. **2** a channel running along the kerb or the centre of a road to collect and carry away rainwater. **3** either of the two channels running parallel to a tenpin bowling lane. **4** *Printing.* the white space between the facing pages of an open book. **5** *Surfing.* a dangerous deep channel formed by currents

THESAURUS

gunman *n* **1** = **terrorist**, assassin, bandit, bravo, desperado, gangster, gunslinger (*US sl.*), heavy (*sl.*), hit man (*sl.*), killer, mobster (*US sl.*), murderer, thug

gurgle *vb* **1** = **murmur**, babble, bubble, burble, crow, lap, plash, purl, ripple, splash ◆ *n* **3** = **murmur**, babble, purl, ripple

guru *n* **2** = **teacher**, authority, guiding light, leader, maharishi, mahatma, master, mentor, sage, Svengali, swami, torchbearer, tutor

gush *vb* **1** = **flow**, burst, cascade, flood, issue, jet, pour, run, rush, spout, spurt, stream **2** = **enthuse**, babble, blather, chatter, effervesce, effuse, jabber, overstate, spout ◆ *n* **3** = **stream**, burst, cascade, flood, flow, issue, jet, outburst, outflow, rush, spout, spurt, torrent **5** = **babble**, blather, chatter, effusion, exuberance

gushy *adj* = **effusive**, cloying, emotional, excessive, fulsome, gushing, mawkish, overdone, overenthusiastic, over the top, sentimental

gust *n* **1** = **blast**, blow, breeze, flurry, gale, puff, rush, squall **3** = **surge**, burst, eruption, explosion, fit, gale, outburst, paroxysm, passion, storm ◆ *vb* **4** = **blow**, blast, puff, squall

gusto *n* = **relish**, appetite, appreciation, brio, delight, enjoyment, enthusiasm, exhilaration, fervour, liking, pleasure, savour, verve, zeal, zest
Antonyms *n* apathy, coolness, disinterest, distaste, inertia

gusty *adj* **1** = **windy**, blowy, blustering, blustery, breezy, inclement, squally, stormy, tempestuous

gut *n* **2** *plural* = **intestines**, belly, bowels, entrails, innards (*inf.*), insides (*inf.*), inwards, stomach, viscera **3** *Slang* = **paunch**, belly, potbelly, spare tyre (*Brit. sl.*) **7** *plural Informal* = **courage**, audacity, backbone, boldness, bottle (*sl.*), daring, forcefulness, grit, hardihood, mettle, nerve, pluck, spirit, spunk (*inf.*), willpower ◆ *vb* **9** = **disembowel**, clean, draw, dress, eviscerate ◆ *adj* **12** = **instinctive**, basic, deep-seated, emotional, heartfelt, innate, intuitive, involuntary, natural, spontaneous, unthinking, visceral

gutless *adj* = **faint-hearted**, abject, boneless, chicken (*sl.*), cowardly, craven, feeble, irresolute, lily-livered, spineless, submissive, timid, weak
Antonyms *adj* bold, brave, courageous, determined, resolute

gutsy *adj* **2** = **brave**, bold, courageous, determined, feisty (*inf., chiefly US & Canad.*), gallant, game (*inf.*), gritty, have-a-go (*inf.*), indomitable, mettlesome, plucky, resolute, spirited, staunch

gutter *n* **1** = **drain**, channel, conduit, ditch, duct, pipe, sluice, trench, trough, tube

and waves. **6 the gutter.** a poverty-stricken, degraded, or criminal environment. ◆ *vb* **7** (*tr*) to make gutters in. **8** (*intr*) to flow in a stream. **9** (*intr*) (of a candle) to melt away as the wax forms channels and runs down in drops. **10** (*intr*) (of a flame) to flicker and be about to go out. [C13: from Anglo-F *goutiere,* from OF *goute* a drop, from L *gutta*]
▸ **'guttering** *n*

gutter press *n* the section of the popular press that seeks sensationalism in its coverage.

guttersnipe Ⓣ ('gʌtə,snaɪp) *n* a child who spends most of his time in the streets, esp. in a slum area.

guttural Ⓣ ('gʌtərəl) *adj* **1** *Anat.* of or relating to the throat. **2** *Phonetics.* pronounced in the throat or the back of the mouth. **3** raucous. ◆ *n* **4** *Phonetics.* a guttural consonant. [C16: from NL *gutturālis,* from L *guttur* gullet]
▸ **'gutturally** *adv*

guy[1] Ⓣ (gaɪ) *n* **1** *Inf.* a man or youth. **2** *Brit.* a crude effigy of Guy Fawkes, usually made of old clothes stuffed with straw or rags, that is burnt on top of a bonfire on Guy Fawkes Day. **3** *Brit.* a person in shabby or ludicrously odd clothes. **4** (*pl*) *Inf.* persons of either sex. ◆ *vb* **5** (*tr*) to make fun of; ridicule. [C19: short for *Guy* Fawkes, who plotted to blow up King James I and the Houses of Parliament (1605)]

guy[2] (gaɪ) *n* **1** a rope, chain, wire, etc., for anchoring an object in position or for steadying or guiding it. ◆ *vb* **2** (*tr*) to anchor, steady, or guide with a guy or guys. [C14: prob. from Low G; cf. OF *guie* guide, from *guier* to GUIDE]

guzzle Ⓣ ('gʌzᵊl) *vb* **guzzles, guzzling, guzzled.** to consume (food or drink) excessively or greedily. [C16: from ?]
▸ **'guzzler** *n*

gybe, gibe, *or* **jibe** (dʒaɪb) *Naut.* ◆ *vb* **gybes, gybing, gybed, gibes, gibing, gibed** *or* **jibes, jibing, jibed. 1** (*intr*) (of a fore-and-aft sail) to shift suddenly from one side of the vessel to the other when running before the wind. **2** to cause (a sailing vessel) to gybe or (of a sailing vessel) to undergo gybing. ◆ *n* **3** an instance of gybing. [C17: from obs. Du. *gijben* (now *gijpen*), from ?]

gym (dʒɪm) *n, adj* short for **gymnasium, gymnastics, gymnastic.**

gymkhana (dʒɪm'kɑːnə) *n* **1** *Chiefly Brit.* an event in which horses and riders display skill and aptitude in various races and contests. **2** (in Anglo-India) a place providing sporting and athletic facilities. [C19: from Hindi *gend-khānā,* lit.: ball house]

gymnasium (dʒɪm'neɪzɪəm) *n, pl* **gymnasiums** *or* **gymnasia** (-zɪə). **1** a large room or hall equipped with bars, weights, ropes, etc., for physical training. **2** (in various European countries) a secondary school that prepares pupils for university. [C16: from L: school for gymnastics, from Gk *gumnasion,* from *gumnazein* to exercise naked]

gymnast ('dʒɪmnæst) *n* a person who is skilled or trained in gymnastics.

gymnastic (dʒɪm'næstɪk) *adj* of, like, or involving gymnastics.
▸ **gym'nastically** *adv*

gymnastics (dʒɪm'næstɪks) *n* **1** (*functioning as sing*) practice or training in exercises that develop physical strength and agility or mental capacity. **2** (*functioning as pl*) gymnastic exercises.

gymno- *combining form.* naked, bare, or exposed: *gymnosperm.* [from Gk *gumnos* naked]

gymnosperm ('dʒɪmnəʊ,spɜːm, 'gɪm-) *n* any seed-bearing plant in which the ovules are borne naked on open scales, which are often arranged in cones; any conifer or related plant. Cf. **angiosperm.**
▸ **,gymno'spermous** *adj*

gympie ('gɪmpɪ) *n* a tall Australian tree with stinging hairs on its leaves. Also: **nettle tree.**

gym shoe *n* another name for **plimsoll.**

gymslip ('dʒɪm,slɪp) *n* a tunic or pinafore dress worn by schoolgirls, often part of a school uniform.

gyn- *combining form.* a variant of **gyno-** before a vowel.

gynaeco- *or US* **gyneco-** *combining form.* relating to women; female: *gynaecology.* [from Gk, from *gunē, gunaik-* woman, female]

gynaecology *or US* **gynecology** (,gaɪnɪ'kɒlədʒɪ) *n* the branch of medicine concerned with diseases and conditions specific to women.
▸ **gynaecological** (,gaɪnɪkə'lɒdʒɪkᵊl), **,gynaeco'logic** *or US* **,gyneco'logical, ,gyneco'logic** *adj* ▸ **,gynae'cologist** *or US* **,gyne'cologist** *n*

gynandromorph (dʒɪ'nændrəʊ,mɔːf, gaɪ-) *n* an abnormal organism, esp. an insect, that has both male and female physical characteristics.

gynandrous (dʒaɪ'nændrəs, gaɪ-) *adj* (of flowers such as the orchid) having the stamens and styles united in a column. [C19: from Gk *gunandros* of uncertain sex, from *gunē* woman + *anēr* man]

gyno- *or before a vowel* **gyn-** *combining form.* **1** relating to women; female: *gynarchy.* **2** denoting a female reproductive organ: *gynophore.* [from Gk, from *gunē* woman]

gynoecium, gynaeceum, *or esp. US* **gynecium** (dʒaɪ'niːsɪəm, gaɪ-) *n, pl* **gynoecia, gynaecea** *or esp. US* **gynecia** (-sɪə). the carpels of a flowering plant collectively. [C18: NL, from Gk *gunaikeion* women's quarters, from *gunaik-, gunē* woman + *-eion,* suffix indicating place]

gynophore ('dʒaɪnəʊ,fɔː, 'gaɪ-) *n* a stalk in some plants that bears the gynoecium above the level of the other flower parts.

-gynous *adj combining form.* **1** of or relating to women or females: *androgynous; misogynous.* **2** relating to female organs: *epigynous.* [from NL, from Gk, from *gunē* woman]
▸ **-gyny** *n combining form.*

gyp[1] *or* **gip** (dʒɪp) *Sl.* ◆ *vb* **gyps, gypping, gypped** *or* **gips, gipping, gipped. 1** (*tr*) to swindle, cheat, or defraud. ◆ *n* **2** an act of cheating. **3** a person who gyps. [C18: back formation from GYPSY]

gyp[2] *or* **gip** (dʒɪp) *n Brit. & NZ sl.* severe pain; torture: *his arthritis gave him gyp.* [C19: prob. a contraction of *gee up!;* see GEE[1]]

gyp[3] (dʒɪp) *n* a college servant at the universities of Cambridge or Durham. [C18: ?from obs. *gippo* scullion]

gypsophila (dʒɪp'sɒfɪlə) *n* any of a Mediterranean genus of plants, having small white or pink fragrant flowers. [C18: NL, from Gk *gupsos* chalk + *philos* loving]

gypsum ('dʒɪpsəm) *n* a mineral consisting of hydrated calcium sulphate that occurs in sedimentary rocks and clay and is used principally in making plasters and cements, esp. plaster of Paris. Formula: $CaSO_4.2H_2O$. [C17: from L, from Gk *gupsos* chalk, plaster, cement, of Semitic origin]
▸ **gypseous** ('dʒɪpsɪəs) *adj*

Gypsy Ⓣ *or* **Gipsy** ('dʒɪpsɪ) *n, pl* **Gypsies** *or* **Gipsies.** (*sometimes not cap.*) **1a** a member of a people scattered throughout Europe and North America, who maintain a nomadic way of life in industrialized societies. They migrated from NW India about the 9th century onwards. **1b** (*as modifier*): *a Gypsy fortune-teller.* **2** the language of the Gypsies; Romany. **3** a person who looks or behaves like a Gypsy. [C16: from EGYPTIAN, since they were thought to have come orig. from Egypt]
▸ **'Gypsyish** *or* **'Gipsyish** *adj*

gypsy moth *or* **gipsy moth** *n* a European moth whose caterpillars are pests on deciduous trees.

gyrate Ⓣ *vb* (dʒaɪ'reɪt), **gyrates, gyrating, gyrated. 1** (*intr*) to rotate or spiral, esp. about a fixed point or axis. ◆ *adj* ('dʒaɪrɪt). **2** *Biol.* curved or coiled into a circle. [C19: from LL *gȳrāre,* from L *gȳrus* circle, from Gk *guros*]
▸ **gy'ration** *n* ▸ **gy'rator** *n* ▸ **gyratory** ('dʒaɪrətərɪ) *adj*

gyre ('dʒaɪə) *Chiefly literary.* ◆ *n* **1** a circular or spiral movement or path. **2** a ring, circle, or spiral. ◆ *vb* **gyres, gyring, gyred. 3** (*intr*) to whirl. [C16: from L *gȳrus* circle, from Gk *guros*]

gyrfalcon *or* **gerfalcon** ('dʒɜː,fɔːlkən, -,fɔːkən) *n* a very large rare falcon of northern and arctic regions. [C14: from OF *gerfaucon,* ?from ON *geirfalki,* from *geirr* spear + *falki* falcon]

gyro ('dʒaɪrəʊ) *n, pl* **gyros. 1** See **gyrocompass. 2** See **gyroscope.**

gyro- *or before a vowel* **gyr-** *combining form.* **1** indicating rotating or gyrating motion: *gyroscope.* **2** indicating a gyroscope: *gyrocompass.* [via L from Gk, from *guros* circle]

gyrocompass ('dʒaɪrəʊ,kʌmpəs) *n* a nonmagnetic compass that uses a motor-driven gyroscope to indicate true north.

gyrodyne ('dʒaɪrəʊ,daɪn) *n* an aircraft that uses a powered rotor to take off and manoeuvre, but uses autorotation when cruising.

gyromagnetic (,dʒaɪrəʊmæg'nɛtɪk) *adj* of or caused by magnetic properties resulting from the spin of a charged particle, such as an electron.

gyroscope ('dʒaɪrə,skəʊp) *n* a device containing a disc rotating on an axis that can turn freely in any direction so that the disc maintains the same orientation irrespective of the movement of the surrounding structure.
▸ **gyroscopic** (,dʒaɪrə'skɒpɪk) *adj* ▸ **,gyro'scopically** *adv*

gyrostabilizer *or* **gyrostabiliser** (,dʒaɪrəʊ'steɪbɪ,laɪzə) *n* a gyroscopic device used to stabilize the rolling motion of a ship.

gyve (dʒaɪv) *Arch.* ◆ *vb* **gyves, gyving, gyved. 1** (*tr*) to shackle or fetter. ◆ *n* **2** (*usually pl*) fetter. [C13: from ?]

THESAURUS

guttersnipe *n* = **street urchin**, gamin, mudlark (*sl.*), ragamuffin, street Arab (*offens.*), waif

guttural *adj* **3** = **throaty**, deep, gravelly, gruff, hoarse, husky, low, rasping, rough, thick

guy[1] *n* **1** *Informal* = **man**, bloke (*Brit. inf.*), cat (*sl.*), chap, fellow, lad, person, youth ◆ *vb* **5** = **mock**, caricature, make fun of, poke fun at, rib (*inf.*), ridicule, send up (*Brit. inf.*), take off (*inf.*)

guzzle *vb* = **devour**, bolt, carouse, cram, drink, gobble, gorge, gormandize, knock back (*inf.*), pig out (*US & Canad. sl.*), quaff, stuff (oneself), swill, tope, wolf

Gypsy *n* **1** = **Romany 3** = **traveller**, Bohemian, nomad, rambler, roamer, rover, vagabond, vagrant, wanderer

gyrate *vb* **1** = **rotate**, circle, pirouette, revolve, spin, spiral, twirl, whirl

gyration *n* **1** = **rotation**, convolution, pirouette, revolution, spin, spinning, spiral, whirl, whirling

Hh

h *or* **H** (eɪtʃ) *n, pl* **h's, H's,** *or* **Hs. 1** the eighth letter of the English alphabet. **2** a speech sound represented by this letter. **3a** something shaped like an H. **3b** (*in combination*): *an H-beam.*

h *symbol for:* **1** *Physics.* Planck constant. **2** hecto-. **3** hour.

H *symbol for:* **1** *Chem.* hydrogen. **2** *Physics.* magnetic field strength. **3** *Electronics.* henry. **4** (on Brit. pencils, signifying degree of hardness of lead) hard.

h. *or* **H.** *abbrev. for:* **1** harbour. **2** height. **3** high. **4** hour. **5** hundred. **6** husband.

ha[1] *or* **hah** (hɑː) *interj* **1** an exclamation expressing derision, triumph, surprise, etc. **2** (*reiterated*) a representation of the sound of laughter.

ha[2] *symbol for* hectare.

haar (hɑː) *n Eastern Brit.* a cold sea mist or fog off the North Sea. [C17: rel. to Du. dialect *harig* damp]

Hab. *Bible. abbrev. for* Habakkuk.

habanera (ˌhæbəˈnɛərə) *n* **1** a slow Cuban dance in duple time. **2** a piece of music for this dance. [from Sp. *danza habanera* dance from Havana]

habeas corpus (ˈheɪbɪəs ˈkɔːpəs) *n Law.* a writ ordering a person to be brought before a court or judge, esp. so that the court may ascertain whether his detention is lawful. [C15: from the opening of the L writ, lit.: you may have the body]

haberdasher (ˈhæbəˌdæʃə) *n* **1** *Brit.* a dealer in small articles for sewing, such as buttons and ribbons. **2** *US.* a men's outfitter. [C14: from Anglo-F *hapertas* small items of merchandise, from ?]

haberdashery (ˈhæbəˌdæʃərɪ) *n, pl* **haberdasheries.** the goods or business kept by a haberdasher.

habergeon (ˈhæbədʒən) *n* a light sleeveless coat of mail worn in the 14th century under the plated hauberk. [C14: from OF *haubergeon* a little HAUBERK]

Haber process (ˈhɑːbə) *n* an industrial process for producing ammonia by reacting atmospheric nitrogen with hydrogen at high pressure and temperature in the presence of a catalyst. [after Fritz *Haber* (1868–1934), G chemist]

habiliment (həˈbɪlɪmənt) *n* (*often pl*) dress or attire. [C15: from OF *habillement,* from *habiller* to dress]

habilitate (həˈbɪlɪˌteɪt) *vb* **habilitates, habilitating, habilitated. 1** (*tr*) *US.* to equip and finance (a mine). **2** (*intr*) to qualify for office. [C17: from Med. L *habilitāre* to make fit, from L *habilitās* aptness]
▸**haˌbiliˈtation** *n*

habit ➊ (ˈhæbɪt) *n* **1** a tendency or disposition to act in a particular way. **2** established custom, usual practice, etc. **3** *Psychol.* a learned behavioural response to a particular situation. **4** mental disposition or attitude: *a good working habit of mind.* **5a** a practice or substance to which a person is addicted: *drink has become a habit with him.* **5b** the state of being dependent on something, esp. a drug. **6** *Bot., zool.* method of growth, type of existence, or general appearance: *a burrowing habit.* **7** the customary apparel of a particular occupation, rank, etc., now esp. the costume of a nun or monk. **8** Also called: **riding habit.** a woman's riding dress. ◆ *vb* **habits, habiting, habited.** (*tr*) **9** to clothe. **10** an archaic word for **inhabit.** [C13: from L *habitus* custom, from *habēre* to have]

habitable (ˈhæbɪtəbᵊl) *adj* able to be lived in.
▸ˌ**habitaˈbility** *or* ˈ**habitableness** *n* ▸ˈ**habitably** *adv*

habitant (ˈhæbɪtᵊnt) *n* **1** a less common word for **inhabitant. 2a** an early French settler in Canada or Louisiana. **2b** a descendant of these settlers, esp. a farmer.

habitat ➊ (ˈhæbɪˌtæt) *n* **1** the natural home of an animal or plant. **2** the place in which a person, group, class, etc., is normally found. [C18: from L: it inhabits, from *habitāre* to dwell, from *habēre* to have]

habitation ➊ (ˌhæbɪˈteɪʃən) *n* **1** a dwelling place. **2** occupation of a dwelling place.

habit-forming ➊ *adj* tending to become a habit or addiction.

habitual ➊ (həˈbɪtjuəl) *adj* **1** (*usually prenominal*) done or experienced regularly and repeatedly: *the habitual Sunday walk.* **2** (*usually prenominal*) by habit: *a habitual drinker.* **3** customary; usual.
▸**haˈbitually** *adv* ▸**haˈbitualness** *n*

habituate ➊ (həˈbɪtjuˌeɪt) *vb* **habituates, habituating, habituated. 1** to accustom; make used to. **2** *US & Canad. arch.* to frequent.
▸**haˌbituˈation** *n*

habitude (ˈhæbɪˌtjuːd) *n Rare.* habit; tendency.

habitué ➊ (həˈbɪtjuˌeɪ) *n* a frequent visitor to a place. [C19: from F, from *habituer* to frequent]

HAC *abbrev. for* Honourable Artillery Company.

hachure (hæˈʃjuə) *n* shading of short lines drawn on a relief map to indicate gradients. [C19: from F, from *hacher* to chop up]

hacienda (ˌhæsɪˈɛndə) *n* (in Spain or Spanish-speaking countries) **1a** a ranch or large estate. **1b** any substantial manufacturing establishment in the country. **2** the main house on such a ranch or establishment. [C18: from Sp., from L *facienda* things to be done, from *facere* to do]

hack[1] ➊ (hæk) *vb* **1** (when *intr*, usually foll. by *at* or *away*) to chop (at) roughly or violently. **2** to cut and clear (a way), as through undergrowth. **3** (in sport, esp. rugby) to foul (an opposing player) by kicking his shins. **4** (*intr*) to cough in short dry bursts. **5** (*tr*) to cut (a story, article, etc.) in a damaging way. **6** (*intr;* usually foll. by *into*) to manipulate a computer program skilfully, esp. to gain unauthorized access to another computer system. ◆ *n* **7** a cut or gash. **8** any tool used for shallow digging, such as a mattock or pick. **9** a chopping blow. **10** a dry spasmodic cough. **11** a kick on the shins, as in rugby. [OE *haccian*]

hack[2] ➊ (hæk) *n* **1** a horse kept for riding. **2** an old or overworked horse. **3** a horse kept for hire. **4** *Brit.* a country ride on horseback. **5** a drudge. **6** a person who produces mediocre literary work. **7** *US inf.* **7a** a cab driver. **7b** a taxi. ◆ *vb* **8** *Brit.* to ride (a horse) cross-country for pleasure. **9** (*tr*) *Inf.* to write (an article, etc.) in the manner of a hack. ◆ *adj* **10** (*prenominal*) banal, mediocre, or unoriginal: *hack writing.* [C17: short for HACKNEY]

hack[3] (hæk) *n* **1** a rack used for fodder for livestock. **2** a board on which meat is placed for a hawk. **3** a pile or row of unfired bricks stacked to dry. [C16: var. of HATCH[2]]

hackamore (ˈhækəˌmɔː) *n US & NZ.* a rope or rawhide halter used for unbroken foals. [C19: from Sp. *jáquima* headstall, ult. from Ar. *shaqīmah*]

hackberry (ˈhækˌbɛrɪ) *n, pl* **hackberries. 1** an American tree having edible cherry-like fruits. **2** the fruit. [C18: var. of C16 *hagberry*, of Scand. origin]

hacker (ˈhækə) *n* **1** a person that hacks. **2** *Sl.* a computer fanatic, esp. one who through a personal computer breaks into the computer system of a company, government, etc.

hackery (ˈhækərɪ) *n* **1** *Ironic.* journalism; hackwork. **2** *Inf.* a variant of **hacking**[2].

hacking[1] (ˈhækɪŋ) *adj* (of a cough) harsh, dry, and spasmodic.

hacking[2] (ˈhækɪŋ) *n* the practice of gaining illegal access to a computer system.

hackle (ˈhækᵊl) *n* **1** any of the long slender feathers on the neck of poultry and other birds. **2** *Angling.* parts of an artificial fly made from hackle feathers, representing the legs and sometimes the wings of a real fly. **3** a feathered ornament worn in the headdress of some British regiments. **4** a steel flax comb. ◆ *vb* **hackles, hackling, hackled.** (*tr*) **5** to comb (flax) using a hackle. [C15: *hakell* prob. from OE]

hackles (ˈhækᵊlz) *pl n* **1** the hairs on the back of the neck and the back of a dog, cat, etc., which rise when the animal is angry or afraid. **2** anger or resentment: *to make one's hackles rise.*

hackney (ˈhæknɪ) *n* **1** a compact breed of harness horse with a high-stepping trot. **2** a coach or carriage that is for hire. **3** a popular term for **hack**[2] (sense 1). ◆ *vb* **4** (*tr; usually passive*) to make com-

THESAURUS

habit *n* **1** = **mannerism**, bent, custom, disposition, manner, practice, proclivity, propensity, quirk, tendency, way **2** = **custom**, convention, mode, practice, routine, rule, tradition, usage, wont **5** = **addiction**, dependence, fixation, obsession, weakness **7** = **dress**, apparel, garb, garment, habiliment, riding dress ◆ *vb* **9** = **clothe**, array, attire, dress, equip

habitat *n* **1, 2** = **home**, abode, element, environment, home ground, locality, natural home, surroundings, terrain, territory

habitation *n* **1** = **dwelling**, abode, domicile, dwelling house, home, house, living quarters, lodging, pad (*sl.*), quarters, residence **2** = **occupation**, inhabitance, inhabitancy, occupancy, tenancy

habit-forming *adj* = **addictive**, compulsive, moreish (*inf.*)

habitual *adj* **1** = **customary**, accustomed, common, familiar, fixed, natural, normal, ordinary, regular, routine, standard, traditional, usual, wonted **2** = **persistent**, chronic, confirmed, constant, established, frequent, hardened, ingrained, inveterate, recurrent
Antonyms *adj* ≠ **customary**: abnormal, exceptional, extraordinary, irregular, rare, strange, uncommon, unusual ≠ **persistent**: infrequent, irregular, occasional

habituate *vb* **1** = **accustom**, acclimatize, acquaint, break in, condition, discipline, familiarize, harden, inure, make used to, school, season, train

habituated *adj* **1** = **accustomed**, acclimatized, adapted, broken in, conditioned, disciplined, familiarized, hardened, inured, schooled, seasoned, trained, used (to)
Antonyms *adj* unaccustomed, unfamiliar, unused (to)

habitué *n* = **frequent visitor**, constant customer, frequenter, regular (*inf.*), regular patron

hack[1] *vb* **1** = **cut**, chop, gash, hew, kick, lacerate, mangle, mutilate, notch, slash ◆ *n* **4** = **cough**, bark, rasp **7** = **cut**, chop, gash, notch, slash

hack[2] *n* **2** = **horse**, crock, jade, nag **5** = **drudge**, plodder, slave **6** = **scribbler**, literary hack ◆ *adj* **10** = **unoriginal**, banal, mediocre, pedestrian, poor, stereotyped, tired, undistinguished, uninspired monplace and banal by too frequent use. [C14: prob. after *Hackney,* London, where horses were formerly raised]

hackneyed ('hæknɪd) *adj* used so often as to be trite, dull, and stereotyped.

hacksaw ('hæk,sɔː) *n* a handsaw for cutting metal, with a blade in a frame under tension.

hackwork ('hæk,wɜːk) *n* undistinguished literary work produced to order.

had (hæd) *vb* the past tense and past participle of **have.**

haddock ('hædək) *n, pl* **haddocks** *or* **haddock.** a North Atlantic gadoid food fish similar to but smaller than the cod. [C14: from ?]

hade (heɪd) *Geol.* ◆ *n* **1** the angle made to the vertical by the plane of a fault or vein. ◆ *vb* **hades, hading, haded. 2** *(intr)* to incline from the vertical. [C18: from ?]

hadedah ('hɑːdɪ,dɑː) *n* a large grey-green S. African ibis. [imit.]

Hades ('heɪdiːz) *n* **1** *Greek myth.* **1a** the underworld abode of the souls of the dead. **1b** Pluto, the god of the underworld. **2** *(often not cap.)* hell.

Hadith ('hædɪθ, hɑː'diːθ) *n* the body of tradition about Mohammed and his followers. [Ar.]

hadj (hædʒ) *n* a variant spelling of **hajj.**

hadji ('hædʒɪ) *n, pl* **hadjis.** a variant spelling of **hajji.**

hadn't ('hædənt) *contraction of* had not.

hadron ('hædrɒn) *n* an elementary particle capable of taking part in a strong nuclear interaction. [C20: from Gk *hadros* heavy, from *hadēn* enough + -ON]
▸**had'ronic** *adj*

hadst (hædst) *vb Arch. or dialect.* (used with the pronoun *thou*) a singular form of the past tense (indicative mood) of **have.**

haecceity (hɛk'siːɪtɪ, hiːk-) *n, pl* **haecceities.** *Philosophy.* the property that uniquely identifies an object. [C17: from Med. L *haecceitas,* lit.: thisness, from *haec,* fem. of *hic* this]

haem *or US* **heme** (hiːm) *n Biochem.* a complex red organic pigment containing ferrous iron, present in haemoglobin. [C20: from HAEMATIN]

haem- *combining form.* a variant of **haemo-** before a vowel. Also (US): **hem-.**

haemal *or US* **hemal** ('hiːməl) *adj* **1** of the blood. **2** denoting or relating to the region of the body containing the heart.

haematemesis *or US* **hematemesis** (,hiːmə'temɪsɪs) *n* vomiting of blood, esp. as the result of a bleeding ulcer. [C19: from HAEMATO- + Gk *emesis* vomiting]

haematic *or US* **hematic** (hiː'mætɪk) *adj* relating to, acting on, having the colour of, or containing blood. Also: **haemic** *or US* **hemic.**

haematin *or US* **hematin** ('hɛmətɪn, 'hiː-) *n Biochem.* a dark bluish or brownish pigment obtained by the oxidation of haem.

haematite ('hiːmə,taɪt, 'hɛm-) *n* a variant spelling of **hematite.**

haemato- *or before a vowel* **haemat-** *combining form.* indicating blood: *haematology.* Also: **haemo-** or (US) **hemato-, hemat-, hemo-.** [from Gk *haima, haimat-* blood]

haematocrit *or US* **hematocrit** ('hɛmətəʊkrɪt, 'hiː-) *n* **1** a centrifuge for separating blood cells from plasma. **2** the ratio of the volume occupied by these cells, esp. the red cells, to the total volume of blood, expressed as a percentage. [C20: from HAEMATO- + *-crit,* from Gk *kritēs* judge, from *krinein* to separate]

haematology *or US* **hematology** (,hiːmə'tɒlədʒɪ) *n* the branch of medical science concerned with diseases of the blood.
▸**haematologic** (,hiːmətə'lɒdʒɪk), **,haemato'logical** *or US* **,hemato'logic, ,hemato'logical** *adj*

haematoma *or US* **hematoma** (,hiːmə'təʊmə) *n, pl* **haematomas, haematomata** *or US* **hematomas, hematomata** (-mətə). *Pathol.* a tumour of clotted blood.

haematuria *or US* **hematuria** (,hiːmə'tjʊərɪə) *n Pathol.* the presence of blood or red blood cells in the urine.

-haemia *or esp. US* **-hemia** *n combining form.* variants of **-aemia.**

haemo-, haema-, *or before a vowel* **haem-** *combining form.* denoting blood. Also: (US) **hemo-, hema-,** or **hem-.** [from Gk *haima* blood]

haemocyanin *or US* **hemocyanin** (,hiːməʊ'saɪənɪn) *n* a blue copper-containing respiratory pigment in crustaceans and molluscs that functions as haemoglobin.

haemocytometer *or US* **hemocytometer** (,hiːməʊsaɪ'tɒmɪtə) *n Med.* an apparatus for counting the number of cells in a quantity of blood.

haemodialysis *or US* **hemodialysis** (,hiːməʊdaɪ'ælɪsɪs) *n, pl* **haemodialyses** *or US* **hemodialyses** (-,siːz). *Med.* the filtering of circulating blood through a membrane in an apparatus (**haemodialyser** *or* **artificial kidney**) to remove waste products: performed in cases of kidney failure. [C20: from HAEMO- + DIALYSIS]

haemoglobin *or US* **hemoglobin** (,hiːməʊ'gləʊbɪn) *n* a protein that gives red blood cells their characteristic colour. It combines reversibly with oxygen and is thus very important in the transportation of oxygen to tissues. [C19: shortened from *haematoglobulin:* see HAEMATIN + GLOBULIN]

haemolysis (hɪ'mɒlɪsɪs), **haematolysis** (,hiːmətɒlɪsɪs) *or US* **hemolysis, hematolysis** *n, pl* **haemolyses, haematolyses** *or US* **hemolyses, hematolyses** (-,siːz). the disintegration of red blood cells, with the release of haemoglobin.
▸**haemolytic** *or US* **hemolytic** (,hiːməʊ'lɪtɪk) *adj*

haemophilia *or US* **hemophilia** (,hiːməʊ'fɪlɪə) *n* an inheritable disease, usually affecting only males, characterized by loss or impairment of the normal clotting ability of blood.
▸**,haemo'philiac** *or US* **,hemo'philiac** *n* ▸**,haemo'philic** *or US* **,hemo'philic** *adj*

haemoptysis *or US* **hemoptysis** (hɪ'mɒptɪsɪs) *n, pl* **haemoptyses** *or US* **hemoptyses** (-,siːz). spitting or coughing up of blood, as in tuberculosis. [C17: from HAEMO- + *-ptysis,* from Gk *ptyein* to spit]

haemorrhage *or US* **hemorrhage** ('hɛmərɪdʒ) *n* **1** profuse bleeding from ruptured blood vessels. **2** a steady or severe loss or depletion of resources, staff, etc. ◆ *vb* **haemorrhages, haemorrhaging, haemorrhaged** *or US* **hemorrhages, hemorrhaging, hemorrhaged. 3** *(intr)* to bleed profusely. [C17: from L *haemorrhagia;* see HAEMO-, -RRHAGIA]

haemorrhoids *or US* **hemorrhoids** ('hɛmə,rɔɪdz) *pl n Pathol.* swollen and twisted veins in the region of the anus. Nontechnical name: **piles.** [C14: from L *haemorrhoidae* (pl), from Gk, from *haimorrhoos* discharging blood, from *haimo-* HAEMO- + *rhein* to flow]
▸**,haemor'rhoidal** *or US* **,hemor'rhoidal** *adj*

haemostasis *or US* **hemostasis** (,hiːməʊ'steɪsɪs) *n* the stopping of bleeding or of blood circulation, as during a surgical operation. [C18: from NL, from HAEMO- + Gk *stasis* a standing still]
▸**,haemo'static** *or US* **,hemo'static** *adj*

haemostat *or US* **hemostat** ('hiːməʊ,stæt) *n* a surgical instrument or chemical agent that retards or stops bleeding.

haeremai ('haɪrə,maɪ) *NZ.* ◆ *sentence substitute.* **1** an expression of greeting or welcome. ◆ *n* **2** the act of saying "haeremai". [C18: Maori, lit.: come hither]

hafiz ('hɑːfɪz) *n Islam.* **1** a title for a person who knows the Koran by heart. **2** the guardian of a mosque. [from Persian, from Ar., from *hafiza* to guard]

hafnium ('hæfnɪəm) *n* a bright metallic element found in zirconium ores. Symbol: Hf; atomic no.: 72; atomic wt.: 178.49. [C20: NL, after *Hafnia,* L name of Copenhagen + -IUM]

haft (hɑːft) *n* **1** the handle of an axe, knife, etc. ◆ *vb* **2** *(tr)* to provide with a haft. [OE *hæft*]

hag[1] (hæg) *n* **1** an unpleasant or ugly old woman. **2** a witch. **3** short for **hagfish.** [OE *hægtesse* witch]
▸**'haggish** *adj*

hag[2] (hæg) *n Scot. & N English dialect.* **1** a firm spot in a bog. **2** a soft place in a moor. [C13: from ON]

Hag. *Bible. abbrev. for* Haggai.

hagfish ('hæg,fɪʃ) *n, pl* **hagfish** *or* **hagfishes.** an eel-like marine vertebrate having a round sucking mouth and feeding on the tissues of other animals and on dead organic material.

Haggadah *or* **Haggodoh** (hə'gɑːdə) *n, pl* **Haggadahs, Haggadas** *or* **Haggadoth** (hægə'dəʊt). *Judaism.* **a** a book containing the order of service of the traditional Passover meal. **b** the narrative of the Exodus from Egypt that constitutes the main part of that service. ◆ See also **Seder.** [C19: from Heb.: story, from *hagged* to tell]
▸**haggadic** (hə'gædɪk, -'gɑː-) *adj*

haggard ('hægəd) *adj* **1** careworn or gaunt, as from anxiety or starvation. **2** wild or unruly. **3** (of a hawk) having reached maturity in the wild before being caught. ◆ *n* **4** *Falconry.* a haggard hawk. [C16: from OF *hagard,* ? rel. to HEDGE]
▸**'haggardly** *adv* ▸**'haggardness** *n*

haggis ('hægɪs) *n* a Scottish dish made from sheep's or calf's offal, oatmeal, suet, and seasonings boiled in a skin made from the animal's stomach. [C15: ?from *haggen* to HACK[1]]

haggle ('hægəl) *vb* **haggles, haggling, haggled.** *(intr; often foll. by over)* to bargain or wrangle (over a price, terms of an agreement, etc.); barter. [C16: of Scand. origin]
▸**'haggler** *n*

hagio- *or before a vowel* **hagi-** *combining form.* indicating a saint, saints, or holiness: *hagiography.* [via LL from Gk, from *hagios* holy]

Hagiographa (,hægɪ'ɒgrəfə) *n* the third of the three main parts into which the books of the Old Testament are divided in Jewish tradition (the other two parts being the Law and the Prophets).

hagiographer (,hægɪ'ɒgrəfə) *or* **hagiographist** *n* **1** a person who writes about the lives of the saints. **2** one of the writers of the Hagiographa.

hagiography (,hægɪ'ɒgrəfɪ) *n, pl* **hagiographies. 1** the writing of the lives of the saints. **2** a biography that idealizes or idolizes its subject.
▸**hagiographic** (,hægɪə'græfɪk) *or* **,hagio'graphical** *adj*

hagiolatry (,hægɪ'ɒlətrɪ) *n* worship or veneration of saints.

hagiology (,hægɪ'ɒlədʒɪ) *n, pl* **hagiologies.** literature concerned with the lives and legends of saints.
▸**hagiological** (,hægɪə'lɒdʒɪkəl) *adj* ▸**,hagi'ologist** *n*

hag-ridden *adj* tormented or worried, as if by a witch.

THESAURUS

hackneyed *adj* **1 = unoriginal,** banal, clichéd, common, commonplace, overworked, pedestrian, played out *(inf.),* run-of-the-mill, stale, stereotyped, stock, threadbare, timeworn, tired, trite, worn-out
Antonyms *adj* fresh, imaginative, new, novel, original, striking, unusual

Hades *n* **1 = underworld,** hell, infernal regions, lower world, nether regions, realm of Pluto, (the) inferno

haft *n* **1 = handle,** helve, shaft

hag[1] *n* **1 = crone,** fury, harridan, shrew, termagant, virago, vixen **2 = witch**

haggard *adj* **1 = gaunt,** careworn, drawn, emaciated, ghastly, hollow-eyed, pinched, shrunken, thin, wan, wasted, wrinkled
Antonyms *adj* bright-eyed, brisk, energetic, fresh, hale, robust, sleek, vigorous

haggle *vb* **= bargain,** barter, beat down, dicker *(chiefly US),* drive a hard bargain, wrangle

hah (hɑː) *interj* a variant spelling of **ha**[1].

ha-ha[1] ('hɑː'hɑː) *or* **haw-haw** ('hɔː'hɔː) *interj* **1** a representation of the sound of laughter. **2** an exclamation expressing derision, mockery, etc.

ha-ha[2] ('hɑːhɑː) *or* **haw-haw** ('hɔːhɔː) *n* a wall or other boundary marker that is set in a ditch so as not to interrupt the landscape. [C18: from F *haha,* prob. based on *ha!* ejaculation denoting surprise]

hahnium ('hɑːnɪəm) *n* the former name for **hassium.** [C20: after Otto *Hahn* (1879–1968), G physicist]

haik *or* **haick** (haɪk, heɪk) *n* a traditional Arabian outer garment for the head and body. [C18: from Ar.]

haiku ('haɪkuː) *or* **hokku** ('hɒkuː) *n, pl* **haiku** *or* **hokku.** an epigrammatic Japanese verse form in 17 syllables. [from Japanese, from *hai* amusement + *ku* verse]

hail[1] ❶ (heɪl) *n* **1** small pellets of ice falling from cumulonimbus clouds when there are strong rising air currents. **2** a storm of such pellets. **3** words, ideas, missiles, etc., directed with force and in great quantity: *a hail of abuse.* ◆ *vb* **4** (*intr;* with *it* as subject) to be the case that hail is falling. **5** (often with *it* as subject) to fall or cause to fall as or like hail. [OE *hægl*]

hail[2] ❶ (heɪl) *vb* (*mainly tr*) **1** to greet, esp. enthusiastically: *the crowd hailed the actress with joy.* **2** to acclaim or acknowledge: *they hailed him as their hero.* **3** to attract the attention of by shouting or gesturing: *to hail a taxi.* **4** (*intr;* foll. by *from*) to be a native of: *she hails from India.* ◆ *n* **5** the act or an instance of hailing. **6** a distance across which one can attract attention (esp. in **within hail**). ◆ *sentence substitute.* **7** *Poetic.* an exclamation of greeting. [C12: from ON *heill* healthy]

hail-fellow-well-met ❶ *adj* genial and familiar, esp. in an offensive or ingratiating way.

Hail Mary *n* **1** Also called: **Ave Maria.** *RC Church.* a prayer to the Virgin Mary, based on the salutations of the angel Gabriel (Luke 1:28) and Elizabeth (Luke 1:42) to her. **2** *American football sl.* a very long high pass into the end zone, made in the final seconds of a half or of a game.

hailstone ('heɪl,stəʊn) *n* a pellet of hail.

hailstorm ('heɪl,stɔːm) *n* a storm during which hail falls.

hair ❶ (hɛə) *n* **1** any of the threadlike structures that grow from follicles beneath the skin of mammals. **2** a growth of such structures, as on an animal's body, which helps prevent heat loss. **3** *Bot.* any threadlike outgrowth, such as a root hair. **4** a fabric made from the hair of some animals. **5** another word for **hair's-breadth:** *to lose by a hair.* **6 get in someone's hair.** *Inf.* to annoy someone persistently. **7 hair of the dog (that bit one).** an alcoholic drink taken as an antidote to a hangover. **8 keep your hair on!** *Brit. inf.* keep calm. **9 let one's hair down.** to behave without reserve. **10 not turn a hair.** to show no surprise, anger, fear, etc. **11 split hairs.** to make petty and unnecessary distinctions. [OE *hær*]
▸ **'hairless** *adj* ▸ **'hair,like** *adj*

haircloth ('hɛə,klɒθ) *n* a cloth woven from horsehair, used (esp. formerly) in upholstery, etc.

haircut ('hɛə,kʌt) *n* **1** the act of cutting the hair. **2** the style in which hair has been cut.

hairdo ('hɛə,duː) *n, pl* **hairdos.** the arrangement of a person's hair, esp. after styling and setting.

hairdresser ❶ ('hɛə,drɛsə) *n* **1** a person whose business is cutting, dyeing, and arranging hair. **2** a hairdresser's establishment. ◆ Related adj: **tonsorial.**
▸ **'hair,dressing** *n*

-haired *adj* having hair as specified: *long-haired.*

hair gel *n* a preparation used in hair styling.

hairgrip ('hɛə,grɪp) *n Chiefly Brit.* a small tightly bent metal hair clip. Also called (US, Canad., and NZ): **bobby pin.**

hairline ('hɛə,laɪn) *n* **1** the natural margin formed by hair on the head. **2a** a very narrow line. **2b** (*as modifier*): *a hairline crack.*

hairline fracture *n* a very fine crack in a bone.

hairnet ('hɛə,nɛt) *n* any of several kinds of light netting worn over the hair to keep it in place.

hairpiece ❶ ('hɛə,piːs) *n* **1** a wig or toupee. **2** a section of extra hair attached to a woman's real hair to give it greater bulk or length.

hairpin ('hɛə,pɪn) *n* **1** a thin double-pronged pin used to fasten the hair. **2** (*modifier*) (esp. of a bend in a road) curving very sharply.

hair-raising ❶ *adj* inspiring horror; terrifying.

hair's-breadth ❶ *n* **a** a very short or imperceptible margin or distance. **b** (*as modifier*): *a hair's-breadth escape.*

hair shirt *n* **1** a shirt made of haircloth worn next to the skin as a penance. **2** a secret trouble or affliction.

hair slide *n* a hinged clip with a tortoiseshell, bone, or similar back, used to fasten a girl's hair.

hairsplitting ❶ ('hɛə,splɪtɪŋ) *n* **1** the making of petty distinctions. ◆ *adj* **2** occupied with or based on petty distinctions.
▸ **'hair,splitter** *n*

hairspring ('hɛə,sprɪŋ) *n* a fine spiral spring in some timepieces which, in combination with the balance wheel, controls the timekeeping.

hairstreak ('hɛə,striːk) *n* a small butterfly having fringed wings with narrow white streaks.

hairstyle ❶ ('hɛə,staɪl) *n* a particular mode of arranging the hair.
▸ **'hair,stylist** *n*

hair trigger *n* **1** a trigger of a firearm that responds to very slight pressure. **2** *Inf.* any mechanism, reaction, etc., set in operation by slight provocation.

hairy ❶ ('hɛərɪ) *adj* **hairier, hairiest. 1** covered with hair. **2** *Sl.* **2a** difficult or problematic. **2b** dangerous or exciting.
▸ **'hairiness** *n*

hajj *or* **hadj** (hædʒ) *n* the pilgrimage to Mecca that every Muslim is required to make at least once. [from Ar.]

hajji, hadji, *or* **haji** ('hædʒɪ) *n, pl* **hajjis, hadjis,** *or* **hajis. 1** a Muslim who has made a pilgrimage to Mecca: also used as a title. **2** a Christian who has visited Jerusalem.

haka ('hɑːkə) *n NZ.* **1** a Maori war chant accompanied by gestures. **2** a similar performance by, for instance, a rugby team.

hake (heɪk) *n, pl* **hake** *or* **hakes. 1** a gadoid food fish of the N hemisphere, having an elongated body with a large head and two dorsal fins. **2** a similar North American fish. [C15: ?from ON *haki* hook]

hakea ('hɑːkɪə, 'heɪkɪə) *n* any shrub or tree of the Australian genus *Hakea,* having a hard woody fruit and often yielding a useful wood. [C19: NL, after C. L. von *Hake* (died 1818), G botanist]

hakim *or* **hakeem** (hɑː'kiːm) *n* **1** a Muslim judge, ruler, or administrator. **2** a Muslim physician. [C17: from Ar., from *hakama* to rule]

Halakah *or* **Halacha** (,hɑːlə'kɑː, hə'lɑːkə) *n* that part of traditional Jewish literature concerned with the law, as contrasted with Haggadah. [C19: from Heb.: way, from *hālakh* to go]
▸ **Halakic** *or* **Halachic** (hə'lækɪk) *adj*

halal *or* **hallal** (hɑː'lɑːl) *n* **1** meat from animals that have been killed according to Muslim law. ◆ *adj* **2** of or relating to such meat: *a halal butcher.* ◆ *vb* **halals, halalling, halalled** *or* **hallals, hallalling, hallalled.** (*tr*) **3** to kill (animals) according to Muslim law. [from Ar.: lawful]

halation (hə'leɪʃən) *n Photog.* fogging usually seen as a bright ring surrounding a source of light. [C19: from HALO + -ATION]

halberd ('hælbəd) *or* **halbert** ('hælbət) *n* a weapon consisting of a long shaft with an axe blade and a pick, topped by a spearhead: used in 15th- and 16th-century warfare. [C15: from OF *hallebarde,* from MHG *helm* handle + *barde* axe]
▸ **,halber'dier** *n*

halcyon ❶ ('hælsɪən) *adj* **1** peaceful, gentle, and calm. **2 halcyon days. 2a** a fortnight of calm weather during the winter solstice. **2b** a period of peace and happiness. ◆ *n* **3** *Greek myth.* a fabulous bird associated with the winter solstice. **4** a poetic name for the **kingfisher.** [C14: from L *alcyon,* from Gk *alkuōn* kingfisher, from ?]

hale[1] ❶ (heɪl) *adj* healthy and robust (esp. in **hale and hearty**). [OE *hæl* WHOLE]
▸ **'haleness** *n*

hale[2] (heɪl) *vb* **hales, haling, haled.** (*tr*) to pull or drag. [C13: from OF *haler,* of Gmc origin]
▸ **'haler** *n*

half ❶ (hɑːf) *n, pl* **halves** (hɑːvz). **1a** either of two equal or corresponding parts that together comprise a whole. **1b** a quantity equalling such a

THESAURUS

hail[1] *n* **3** = **shower,** barrage, bombardment, downpour, pelting, rain, storm, volley ◆ *vb* **5** = **shower,** barrage, batter, beat down upon, bombard, pelt, rain, rain down on, storm, volley

hail[2] *vb* **1** = **salute,** greet, welcome **2** = **acclaim,** acknowledge, applaud, cheer, exalt, glorify, honour **3** = **flag down,** accost, address, call, halloo, shout to, signal to, sing out, speak to, wave down **4** *foll. by* **from** = **come from,** be a native of, be born in, originate in
Antonyms *vb* ≠ **salute:** avoid, cut (*inf.*), ignore, snub ≠ **acclaim:** boo, condemn, criticize, hiss, insult, jeer

hail-fellow-well-met *adj* = **overfriendly,** back-slapping, familiar, free-and-easy, genial, hearty, unceremonious

hair *n* **2** = **locks,** head of hair, mane, mop, shock, tresses **5** = **narrow margin,** fraction of an inch, hair's-breadth, split second, the skin of one's teeth, whisker **6 get in one's hair** *Informal* = **annoy,** aggravate (*inf.*), be on one's back (*sl.*), exasperate, get on one's nerves (*inf.*), harass, hassle (*inf.*), irritate, nark (*Brit., Austral., & NZ sl.*), pester, piss one off (*taboo sl.*), plague **9 let one's hair down** = **let oneself go,** chill out (*sl., chiefly US*), let it all hang out, let off steam (*inf.*), mellow out (*inf.*), relax, veg out (*sl., chiefly US*) **10 not turn a hair** = **remain calm,** keep one's cool (*sl.*), keep one's hair on (*Brit. inf.*), not bat an eyelid **11 split hairs** = **quibble,** cavil, find fault, overrefine, pettifog

hairdresser *n* **1** = **stylist,** barber, coiffeur *or* coiffeuse

hairless *adj* **2** = **bare,** bald, baldheaded, beardless, clean-shaven, depilated, shorn

hairpiece *n* **1** = **wig,** toupee

hair-raising *adj* = **frightening,** alarming, bloodcurdling, breathtaking, creepy, exciting, horrifying, petrifying, scary, shocking, spine-chilling, startling, terrifying, thrilling

hair's-breadth *n* **a** = **fraction,** hair, jot, narrow margin, whisker ◆ *modifier* **b** = **narrow,** close, hazardous

hairsplitting *adj* **2** = **fault-finding,** captious, carping, cavilling, fine, finicky, nice, niggling, nit-picking (*inf.*), overrefined, pettifogging, quibbling, subtle

hairstyle *n* = **haircut,** coiffure, cut, hairdo, style

hairy *adj* **1** = **shaggy,** bearded, bewhiskered, bushy, fleecy, furry, hirsute, pileous (*Biology*), pilose (*Biology*), stubbly, unshaven, woolly **2b** *Slang* = **dangerous,** hazardous, perilous, risky

halcyon *adj* **1** = **peaceful,** calm, gentle, mild, pacific, placid, quiet, serene, still, tranquil, undisturbed, unruffled **2b halcyon days** = **happy,** carefree, flourishing, golden, palmy, prosperous

hale[1] *adj* = **healthy,** able-bodied, blooming, fit, flourishing, hearty, in fine fettle, in the pink, right as rain (*Brit. inf.*), robust, sound, strong, vigorous, well

half *n* **1** = **equal part,** bisection, division, fifty per cent, fraction, hemisphere, portion, section **11 by halves** = **incompletely,** imperfectly, scrappily, skimpily ◆ *adj* **14** = **partial,** incomplete, limited, part: *half a dozen.* **2** half a pint, esp. of beer. **3** *Scot.* a small drink of spirits, esp. whisky. **4** *Football, hockey, etc.* the half of the pitch regarded as belonging to one team. **5** *Golf.* an equal score with an opponent. **6** (in various games) either of two periods of play separated by an interval. **7** a half-price ticket on a bus, etc. **8** short for **half-hour. 9** *Sport.* short for **halfback. 10** *Obs.* a half-year period. **11 by halves.** (*used with a negative*) without being thorough: *we don't do things by halves.* **12 go halves.** (often foll. by *on, in,* etc.) **12a** to share expenses. **12b** to share the whole amount (of something): *to go halves on an orange.* ◆ *determiner* **13a** being a half or approximately a half: *half the kingdom.* **13b** (*as pron; functioning as sing or pl*): *half of them came.* ◆ *adj* **14** not perfect or complete: *he only did a half job on it.* ◆ *adv* **15** to the amount or extent of a half. **16** to a great amount or extent. **17** partially; to an extent. **18 by half.** to an excessive degree: *he's too arrogant by half.* **19 half two,** etc. *Inf.* 30 minutes after two o'clock, etc. **20 have half a mind to.** to have a vague intention to. **21 not half.** *Inf.* **21a** not in any way: *he's not half clever enough.* **21b** *Brit.* very: *he isn't half stupid.* **21c** yes, indeed. [OE *healf*]

half- *prefix* **1** one of two equal parts: *half-moon.* **2** related through one parent only: *half-brother.* **3** not completely; partly: *half-hardy.*

half-and-half *n* **1** a mixture of half one thing and half another thing. **2** a drink consisting of equal parts of beer and stout, or equal parts of bitter and mild.

halfback ('hɑːf,bæk) *n* **1** *Soccer.* any of three players positioned behind the line of forwards and in front of the fullbacks. **2** *Rugby.* either the scrum half or the stand-off half. **3** any of certain similar players in other team sports.

half-baked Ⓣ *adj* **1** insufficiently baked. **2** *Inf.* foolish; stupid. **3** *Inf.* poorly planned.

halfbeak ('hɑːf,biːk) *n* a marine and freshwater teleost fish having an elongated body with a short upper jaw and a long protruding lower jaw.

half-binding *n* a type of bookbinding in which the backs are bound in one material and the sides in another.

half-blood *n* **1a** the relationship between individuals having only one parent in common. **1b** an individual having such a relationship. **2** a less common name for a **half-breed.**
▸,**half-'blooded** *adj*

half board *n* accommodation at a hotel, etc., that includes breakfast and one main meal. Also called: **demi-pension.**

half-boot *n* a boot reaching to the midcalf.

half-bottle *n* a bottle of spirits or wine that contains half the quantity of a standard bottle.

half-breed *n* **1** *Often offens.* a person whose parents are of different races, esp. the offspring of a White person and an American Indian. ◆ *adj also* **half-bred. 2** of, relating to, or designating offspring of people or animals of different races or breeds.

half-brother *n* the son of either of one's parents by another partner.

half-butt *n* a snooker cue that is longer than an ordinary cue.

half-caste ◆ *Offens. n* **1** a person having parents of different races, esp. the offspring of a European and an Indian. ◆ *adj* **2** of, relating to, or designating such a person.

half-century *n* **1** a period of 50 years. **2** a score or grouping of 50: *he scored his first half-century for England.*

half-cock *n* **1** the halfway position of a firearm's hammer when the trigger is cocked by the hammer and the hammer cannot reach the primer to fire the weapon. **2 go off at half-cock** *or* **half-cocked.** to fail as a result of inadequate preparation or premature starting.

half-crown *n* a former British coin worth two shillings and sixpence (12½p). Also called: **half-a-crown.**

half-cut *adj Brit. sl.* rather drunk.

half-dozen *n* six.

half gainer *n* a type of dive in which the diver completes a half backward somersault to enter the water headfirst facing the diving board.

half-hardy *adj* (of a cultivated plant) able to survive out of doors except during severe frost.

half-hearted Ⓣ *adj* without enthusiasm or determination.
▸,**half-'heartedly** *adv*

half-hitch *n* a knot made by passing the end of a piece of rope around itself and through the loop thus made.

half-hour *n* **1** a period of 30 minutes. **2** the point of time 30 minutes after the beginning of an hour.
▸,**half-'hourly** *adv, adj*

half-hunter *n* a watch with a hinged lid in which a small circular opening or crystal allows the approximate time to be read.

half landing *n* a landing halfway up a flight of stairs.

half-life *n* the time taken for half of the atoms in a radioactive material to undergo decay.

half-light *n* a dim light, as at dawn or dusk.

half-mast *n* the lower than normal position to which a flag is lowered on a mast as a sign of mourning.

half measure *n* (*often pl*) an inadequate measure or action; compromise.

half-moon *n* **1** the moon at first or last quarter when half its face is illuminated. **2** the time at which a half-moon occurs. **3** something shaped like a half-moon.

half-nelson *n* a wrestling hold in which a wrestler places an arm under one of his opponent's arms from behind and exerts pressure with his palm on the back of his opponent's neck.

half-note *n* the usual US name for **minim** (sense 2).

halfpenny *or* **ha'penny** ('heɪpnɪ, *for sense 1* 'hɑːf,penɪ) *n* **1** (*pl* **halfpennies** *or* **ha'pennies**) a small British coin worth half a new penny (withdrawn 1985). **2** (*pl* **halfpennies** *or* **ha'pennies**) an old British coin worth half an old penny. **3** (*pl* **halfpence**) something of negligible value.
▸**halfpennyworth** *or* **ha'p'orth** ('heɪpəθ) *n*

half-pie *adj NZ inf.* ill planned; not properly thought out: *a half-pie scheme.* [from Maori *pai* good]

half-pint *n Sl.* a small or insignificant person.

half-plate *or* **half-print** *n Photog.* a size of plate measuring 6½ × 4½ inches.

half-rotten *adj* partially rotted or decomposed.

half seas over *adj Brit. inf.* drunk.

half-section *n Engineering.* a scale drawing of a section through a symmetrical object that shows only half the object.

half-sister *n* the daughter of either of one's parents by another partner.

half-size *n* any size, esp. in clothing, that is halfway between two sizes.

half-sole *n* a sole from the shank of a shoe to the toe.

half term *n Brit. education.* a short holiday midway through an academic term.

half-timbered *or* **half-timber** *adj* (of a building) having an exposed timber framework filled with brick, stone, or plastered laths, as in Tudor architecture.
▸,**half-'timbering** *n*

half-time *n Sport.* **a** a rest period between the two halves of a game. **b** (*as modifier*): *the half-time score.*

half-title *n* **1** the short title of a book as printed on the right-hand page preceding the title page. **2** a title on a separate page preceding a section of a book.

halftone ('hɑːf,təʊn) *n* **1** a process used to reproduce an illustration by photographing it through a fine screen to break it up into dots. **2** the print obtained. **3** *Music.* the usual US and Canad. name for **semitone.**

half-track *n* a vehicle with caterpillar tracks on the wheels that supply motive power only.

half-truth *n* a partially true statement intended to mislead.
▸,**half-'true** *adj*

half volley *n Sport.* a stroke or shot in which the ball is hit immediately after it bounces.

halfway Ⓣ (,hɑːf'weɪ) *adv, adj* **1** at or to half the distance. **2** in or of an incomplete manner. **3 meet halfway.** to compromise with.

halfway house *n* **1** a place to rest midway on a journey. **2** the halfway point in any progression. **3** a centre or hostel designed to facilitate the readjustment to private life of released prisoners, mental patients, etc.

halfwit Ⓣ ('hɑːf,wɪt) *n* **1** a feeble-minded person. **2** a foolish or inane person.
▸,**half'witted** *adj*

half-year *n* a period of six months.

halibut ('hælɪbət) *n, pl* **halibuts** *or* **halibut.** the largest flatfish: a dark green North Atlantic species that is a very important food fish. [C15: from *hali* HOLY (because it was eaten on holy days) + *butte* flat-fish, from MDu.]

halide ('hælaɪd) *or* **halid** ('hælɪd) *n* a binary compound containing a halogen atom or ion in combination with a more electropositive element.

halite ('hælaɪt) *n* a mineral consisting of sodium chloride in cubic crystalline form, occurring in sedimentary beds and dried salt lakes: an important source of table salt. Also called: **rock salt.** [C19: from NL *halītes,* from Gk *hals* salt + -ITE[2]]

halitosis (,hælɪ'təʊsɪs) *n* the state or condition of having bad breath. [C19: NL, from L *hālitus* breath, from *hālāre* to breathe]

hall Ⓣ (hɔːl) *n* **1** a room serving as an entry area. **2** (*sometimes cap.*) a

THESAURUS

moderate ◆ *adv* **17** = **partially**, after a fashion, all but, barely, inadequately, incompletely, in part, partly, pretty nearly, slightly **18 by half** = **excessively**, considerably, very much

half-baked *adj Informal* **2** = **stupid**, brainless, crackpot, crazy, dumb-ass (*sl.*), foolish, harebrained, inane, loopy (*inf.*), senseless, silly *Informal* **3** = **poorly planned**, ill-conceived, ill-judged, impractical, short-sighted, unformed, unthought out *or* through

half-hearted *adj* = **unenthusiastic**, apathetic, cool, indifferent, lacklustre, listless, lukewarm, neutral, passive, perfunctory, spiritless, tame, uninterested
Antonyms *adj* ambitious, animated, avid, concerned, determined, eager, emotional, energetic, enthusiastic, excited, spirited, warm, wholehearted, zealous

halfway *adv* **1** = **midway**, to *or* in the middle, to the midpoint **2** = **partially**, incompletely, moderately, nearly, partly, rather **3 meet halfway** = **compromise**, accommodate, come to terms, concede, give and take, strike a balance, trade off

halfwit *n* **1** = **mental defective**, imbecile, moron, simpleton **2** = **fool**, berk (*Brit. sl.*), dimwit (*inf.*), divvy (*Brit. sl.*), dolt, dork (*sl.*), dullard, dunce, dunderhead, fathead (*inf.*), idiot, imbecile (*inf.*), jerk (*sl., chiefly US & Canad.*), nitwit (*inf.*), numbskull *or* numskull, pillock (*Brit. sl.*), twit (*inf., chiefly Brit.*), wally (*sl.*)

halfwitted *adj* **1** = **feeble-minded**, dull, dull-witted, simple, simple-minded **2** = **foolish**, barmy (*sl.*), batty, crazy, doltish, doolally (*sl.*), dumb (*inf.*), idiotic, moronic, obtuse, silly, stupid

hall *n* **1** = **entrance hall**, corridor, entry, foyer, hallway, lobby, passage, passageway, vestibule building for public meetings. **3** (*often cap.*) the great house of an estate; manor. **4** a large building or room used for assemblies, dances, etc. **5** a residential building, esp. in a university; hall of residence. **6a** a large room, esp. for dining, in a college or university. **6b** a meal eaten in this room. **7** the large room of a house, castle, etc. **8** *US & Canad.* a corridor into which rooms open. **9** (*often pl*) *Inf.* short for **music hall.** [OE *heall*]

hallelujah, halleluiah (ˌhælɪ'luːjə), *or* **alleluia** (ˌælɪ'luːjə) *interj* **1** an exclamation of praise to God. ◆ *n* **2** an exclamation of "Hallelujah". **3** a musical composition that uses the word *Hallelujah* as its text. [C16: from Heb. *hallēl* to praise + *yāh* the Lord]

halliard ('hæljəd) *n* a variant spelling of **halyard.**

hallmark ❶ ('hɔːlˌmɑːk) *n* **1** *Brit.* an official series of marks stamped by the London Guild of Goldsmiths on gold, silver, or platinum articles to guarantee purity, date of manufacture, etc. **2** a mark of authenticity or excellence. **3** an outstanding feature. ◆ *vb* **4** (*tr*) to stamp with or as if with a hallmark. [C18: after Goldsmiths' *Hall* in London, where items were graded and stamped]

hallo (hə'ləʊ) *sentence substitute, n* **1** a variant spelling of **hello.** ◆ *sentence substitute, n, vb* **2** a variant spelling of **halloo.**

halloo ❶ (hə'luː), **hallo,** *or* **halloa** (hə'ləʊ) *sentence substitute.* **1** a shout to attract attention, esp. to call hounds at a hunt. ◆ *n, pl* **halloos, hallos,** *or* **halloas. 2** a shout of "halloo". ◆ *vb* **halloos, hallooing, hallooed; hallos, halloing, halloed;** *or* **halloas, halloaing, halloaed. 3** to shout. **4** (*tr*) to urge on (dogs) with shouts. [C16: ? var. of *hallow* to encourage hounds by shouting]

hallow ('hæləʊ) *vb* (*tr*) **1** to consecrate or set apart as being holy. **2** to venerate as being holy. [OE *hālgian,* from *hālig* HOLY]
▸**'hallower** *n*

hallowed ❶ ('hæləʊd; *liturgical* 'hæləʊɪd) *adj* **1** set apart as sacred. **2** consecrated or holy.

Halloween *or* **Hallowe'en** (ˌhæləʊ'iːn) *n* the eve of All Saints' Day celebrated on Oct. 31; Allhallows Eve. [C18: see ALLHALLOWS, EVEN[2]]

hall stand *or esp. US* **hall tree** *n* a piece of furniture for hanging coats, hats, etc., on.

Hallstatt ('hælstæt) *adj* of a late Bronze Age culture extending from central Europe to Britain and lasting from the 9th to the 5th century B.C. [C19: after *Hallstatt,* Austrian village where remains were found]

hallucinate ❶ (hə'luːsɪˌneɪt) *vb* **hallucinates, hallucinating, hallucinated.** (*intr*) to experience hallucinations. [C17: from L *ālūcinārī* to wander in mind]
▸**hal'luciˌnator** *n*

hallucination ❶ (həˌluːsɪ'neɪʃən) *n* the alleged perception of an object when no object is present, occurring under hypnosis, in some mental disorders, etc.
▸**hal'lucinatory** *adj*

hallucinogen (hə'luːsɪnəˌdʒɛn) *n* any drug that induces hallucinations.
▸**hallucinogenic** (həˌluːsɪnə'dʒɛnɪk) *adj*

hallux ('hæləks) *n* the first digit on the hind foot of a mammal, bird, reptile, or amphibian; the big toe of man. [C19: NL, from LL *allex* big toe]

hallway ('hɔːlˌweɪ) *n* a hall or corridor.

halm (hɔːm) *n* a variant spelling of **haulm.**

halma ('hælmə) *n* a board game in which players attempt to transfer their pieces from their own to their opponents' bases. [C19: from Gk *halma* leap]

halo ❶ ('heɪləʊ) *n, pl* **haloes** *or* **halos. 1** a disc or ring of light around the head of an angel, saint, etc., as in painting. **2** the aura surrounding a famous or admired person, thing, or event. **3** a circle of light around the sun or moon, caused by the refraction of light by particles of ice. ◆ *vb* **haloes** *or* **halos, haloing, haloed. 4** to surround with or form a halo. [C16: from Med. L, from L *halōs* circular threshing floor, from Gk]

halogen ('hæləˌdʒɛn) *n* any of the chemical elements fluorine, chlorine, bromine, iodine, and astatine. They are all monovalent and readily form negative ions. [C19: from Swedish, from Gk *hals* salt + -GEN]
▸**halogenous** (hə'lɒdʒɪnəs) *adj*

halogenate ('hælədʒəˌneɪt) *vb* **halogenates, halogenating, halogenated.** *Chem.* to treat or combine with a halogen.
▸ˌ**halogen'ation** *n*

haloid ('hælɔɪd) *Chem.* ◆ *adj* **1** derived from a halogen: *a haloid salt.* ◆ *n* **2** a compound containing halogen atoms in its molecules.

halon ('hælɒn) *n* any of a class of chemical compounds derived from hydrocarbons by replacing one or more hydrogen atoms by bromine atoms and other hydrogen atoms by other halogen atoms (chlorine, fluorine, or iodine).

halt[1] ❶ (hɔːlt) *n* **1** an interruption or end to movement or progress. **2** *Chiefly Brit.* a minor railway station, without permanent buildings. **3 call a halt (to).** to put an end (to); stop. ◆ *n, sentence substitute.* **4** a command to halt, esp. as an order when marching. ◆ *vb* **5** to come or bring to a halt. [C17: from *to make halt,* translation of G *halt machen,* from *halten* to stop]

halt[2] ❶ (hɔːlt) *vb* (*intr*) **1** (esp. of verse) to falter or be defective. **2** to be unsure. **3** *Arch.* to be lame. ◆ *adj* **4** *Arch.* **4a** lame. **4b** (*as collective n; preceded by the*): *the halt.* [OE *healt* lame]

halter ('hɔːltə) *n* **1** headgear for a horse, usually with a rope for leading. **2** Also: **halterneck.** a style of woman's top fastened behind the neck and waist, leaving the back and arms bare. **3** a rope having a noose for hanging a person. **4** death by hanging. ◆ *vb* (*tr*) **5** to put on a halter. **6** to hang (someone). [OE *hælfter*]

haltere ('hæltɪə) *n, pl* **halteres** (hæl'tɪəriːz). one of a pair of short projections in dipterous insects that are modified hind wings, used for maintaining equilibrium during flight. [C18: from Gk *haltēres* (pl) hand-held weights used as balancers or to give impetus in leaping, from *hallesthai* to leap]

halting ❶ ('hɔːltɪŋ) *adj* **1** hesitant: *halting speech.* **2** lame.
▸**'haltingly** *adv*

halvah, halva ('hælvɑː), *or* **halavah** ('hæləvɑː) *n* an Eastern sweetmeat made of honey and containing sesame seeds, nuts, etc. [from Yiddish *halva,* ult. from Ar. *halwā*]

halve ❶ (hɑːv) *vb* **halves, halving, halved.** (*mainly tr*) **1** to divide into two approximately equal parts. **2** to share equally. **3** (*also intr*) to reduce by half, as by cutting. **4** *Golf.* to take the same number of strokes on (a hole or round) as one's opponent. [OE *hielfan*]

halyard *or* **halliard** ('hæljəd) *n Naut.* a line for hoisting or lowering a sail, flag, or spar. [C14 *halier,* infl. by YARD[1]; see HALE[2]]

ham[1] (hæm) *n* **1** the part of the hindquarters of a pig between the hock and the hip. **2** the meat of this part. **3** *Inf.* the back of the leg above the knee. [OE *hamm*]

ham[2] (hæm) *n* **1** *Theatre, inf.* **1a** an actor who overacts or relies on stock gestures. **1b** overacting or clumsy acting. **1c** (*as modifier*): *a ham actor.* **2** *Inf.* a licensed amateur radio operator. ◆ *vb* **hams, hamming, hammed. 3** *Inf.* to overact. [C19: special use of HAM[1]; in some senses prob. infl. by AMATEUR]

hamadryad (ˌhæmə'draɪəd) *n* **1** *Classical myth.* a nymph who inhabits a tree and dies with it. **2** another name for **king cobra.** [C14: from L *Hamādryas,* from Gk *Hamadruas,* from *hama* together with + *drus* tree]

hamadryas (ˌhæmə'draɪəs) *n* a baboon of Arabia and NE Africa, having long silvery hair on the head, neck, and chest. [C19: via NL from L; see HAMADRYAD]

hamba ('hæmbə) *sentence substitute. S. African, usually offens.* go away; be off. [from a Bantu language, from *ukuttamba* to go]

hamburger ('hæmˌbɜːgə) *n* a cake of minced beef, often served in a bread roll. Also called: **beefburger.** [C20: from *Hamburger steak* (steak in the fashion of *Hamburg,* Germany)]

hame (heɪm) *n* either of the two curved bars holding the traces of the harness, attached to the collar of a draught animal. [C14: from MDu. *hame*]

ham-fisted ❶ *or* **ham-handed** *adj Inf.* lacking dexterity or elegance; clumsy.

Hamitic (hæ'mɪtɪk, hə-) *n* **1** a group of N African languages related to Semitic. ◆ *adj* **2** denoting or belonging to this group of languages. **3** denoting or characteristic of the Hamites, a group of peoples of N Africa, including the ancient Egyptians, supposedly descended from Noah's son Ham.

hamlet ('hæmlɪt) *n* a small village, esp. (in Britain) one without its own church. [C14: from OF *hamelet,* dim. of *hamel,* from *ham,* of Gmc origin]

hammer ❶ ('hæmə) *n* **1** a hand tool consisting of a heavy usually steel head held transversely on the end of a handle, used for driving in nails, etc. **2** any tool or device with a similar function, such as the

THESAURUS

2, 4 = meeting place, assembly room, auditorium, chamber, concert hall

hallmark *n* **2 = seal**, authentication, device, endorsement, mark, sign, signet, stamp, symbol **3 = indication**, badge, emblem, sure sign, telltale sign

halloo *vb* **3 = call**, cry, hail, shout

hallowed *adj* **1, 2 = sanctified**, beatified, blessed, consecrated, dedicated, holy, honoured, inviolable, revered, sacred, sacrosanct

hallucinate *vb* **= imagine**, daydream, envision, fantasize, freak out (*inf.*), have hallucinations, trip (*inf.*)

hallucination *n* **= illusion**, apparition, delusion, dream, fantasy, figment of the imagination, mirage, phantasmagoria, vision

hallucinogenic *adj* **= psychedelic**, hallucinatory, mind-blowing (*inf.*), mind-expanding, psychoactive, psychotropic

halo *n* **3 = ring of light**, aura, aureole *or* aureola, corona, nimbus, radiance

halt[1] *n* **1 = stop**, arrest, break, close, end, impasse, interruption, pause, stand, standstill, stoppage, termination ◆ *vb* **5 = stop**, arrest, belay (*Nautical*), block, break off, bring to an end, call it a day, cease, check, close down, come to an end, curb, cut short, desist, draw up, end, pull up, rest, stand still, wait

Antonyms *n* ≠ **stop:** beginning, commencement, continuation, resumption, start ◆ *vb* ≠ **stop:** begin, commence, continue, go ahead, maintain, proceed, resume, start

halt[2] *vb* **1 = falter**, be defective, hobble, limp, stumble **2 = be unsure**, boggle, dither (*chiefly Brit.*), haver, hesitate, pause, stammer, swither (*Scot.*), think twice, waver ◆ *adj* **3** *Archaic* **= lame**, crippled, limping

halting *adj* **1 = faltering**, awkward, hesitant, imperfect, laboured, stammering, stumbling, stuttering

halve *vb* **1 = bisect**, cut in half, divide equally, split in two **3 = reduce by fifty per cent**

ham-fisted *adj Informal* **= clumsy**, all fingers and thumbs, awkward, bungling, butterfingered (*inf.*), cack-handed (*inf.*), ham-handed (*inf.*), inept, maladroit, unhandy

hammer *vb* **12 = hit**, bang, beat, drive, knock, strike, tap **13 = fashion**, beat out, forge, form, make, shape **15** *often with* **into = impress upon**, din into, drive home, drub into, drum into, grind into, instruct, repeat **16** *often with* **away = work**, beaver away (*Brit. inf.*), drudge, grind, keep on, peg away, persevere, persist, plug

striking head on a bell. **3** a power-driven striking tool, esp. one used in forging. **4** a part of a gunlock that strikes the primer or percussion cap when the trigger is pulled. **5** *Athletics.* **5a** a heavy metal ball attached to a flexible wire: thrown in competitions. **5b** the sport of throwing the hammer. **6** an auctioneer's gavel. **7** a device on a piano that is made to strike a string or group of strings causing them to vibrate. **8** *Anat.* the nontechnical name for **malleus. 9 go under the hammer.** to be offered for sale by an auctioneer. **10 hammer and tongs.** with great effort or energy. **11 on someone's hammer.** *Austral. & NZ sl.* persistently demanding and critical of someone. ◆ *vb* **12** to strike or beat with or as if with a hammer. **13** (*tr*) to shape with or as if with a hammer. **14** (*tr; foll. by in or into*) to force (facts, ideas, etc.) into (someone) through constant repetition. **15** (*intr*) to feel or sound like hammering. **16** (*intr; often foll. by away*) to work at constantly. **17** (*tr*) *Brit.* to criticize severely. **18** (*tr*) *Inf.* to defeat. **19** (*tr*) *Stock Exchange.* **19a** to announce the default of (a member). **19b** to cause prices of (securities, the market, etc.) to fall by bearish selling. [OE *hamor*]
▸ **'hammer-,like** *adj*

hammer and sickle *n* the emblem on the flag of the former Soviet Union, representing the industrial workers and the peasants respectively.

hammer beam *n* either of a pair of short horizontal beams that project from opposite walls to support arched braces and struts.

hammerhead ('hæmə,hɛd) *n* **1** a shark having a flattened hammer-shaped head. **2** a tropical African wading bird having a dark plumage and a long backward-pointing crest. **3** a large African fruit bat with a hammer-shaped muzzle.
▸ **'hammer,headed** *adj*

hammerlock ('hæmə,lɒk) *n* a wrestling hold in which a wrestler twists his opponent's arm upwards behind his back.

hammer out Ⓣ *vb* (*tr, adv*) **1** to shape or remove with or as if with a hammer. **2** to settle or reconcile (differences, problems, etc.).

hammertoe ('hæmə,təʊ) *n* a deformity causing the toe to be bent in a clawlike arch.

hammock ('hæmək) *n* a length of canvas, net, etc., suspended at the ends and used as a bed. [C16: from Sp. *hamaca*, from Amerind]

hammy ('hæmɪ) *adj* **hammier, hammiest.** *Inf.* **1** (of an actor) tending to overact. **2** (of a play, performance, etc.) overacted or exaggerated.

hamper[1] Ⓣ ('hæmpə) *vb* **1** (*tr*) to prevent the progress or free movement of. ◆ *n* **2** *Naut.* gear aboard a vessel that, though essential, is often in the way. [C14: from ?; ? rel. to OE *hamm* enclosure, *hemm* HEM[1]]

hamper[2] ('hæmpə) *n* **1** a large basket, usually with a cover. **2** *Brit.* a selection of food and drink packed in a hamper or other container. [C14: var. of earlier *hanaper* a small basket, from OF, of Gmc origin]

hamster ('hæmstə) *n* a Eurasian burrowing rodent having a stocky body, short tail, and cheek pouches: a popular pet. [C17: from G, from OHG *hamustro*, of Slavic origin]

hamstring Ⓣ ('hæm,strɪŋ) *n* **1** one of the tendons at the back of the knee. **2** the large tendon at the back of the hind leg of a horse, etc. ◆ *vb* **hamstrings, hamstringing, hamstrung.** (*tr*) **3** to cripple by cutting the hamstring of. **4** to thwart. [C16: HAM[1] + STRING]

hamulus ('hæmjʊləs) *n, pl* **hamuli** (-,laɪ). *Biol.* a hook or hooklike process, between the fore and hind wings of a bee. [C18: from L: a little hook, from *hāmus* hook]

hand Ⓣ (hænd) *n* **1** the prehensile part of the body at the end of the arm, consisting of a thumb, four fingers, and a palm. Related adj: **manual. 2** the corresponding part in animals. **3** something resembling this in shape or function. **4a** the cards dealt in one round of a card game. **4b** a player holding such cards. **4c** one round of a card game. **5** agency or influence: *the hand of God.* **6** a part in something done: *he had a hand in the victory.* **7** assistance: *to give someone a hand.* **8** a pointer on a dial, indicator, or gauge, esp. on a clock. **9** acceptance or pledge of partnership, as in marriage. **10** a position indicated by its location to the side of an object or the observer: *on the right hand.* **11** a contrastive aspect, condition, etc.: *on the other hand.* **12** source or origin: *a story heard at third hand.* **13** a person, esp. one who creates something: *a good hand at painting.* **14** a manual worker. **15** a member of a ship's crew: *all hands on deck.* **16** a person's handwriting: *the letter was in his own hand.* **17** a round of applause: *give him a hand.* **18** a characteristic way of doing something: *the hand of a master.* **19** a unit of length equalling four inches, used for measuring the height of horses. **20** a cluster of bananas. **21** (*modifier*) **21a** of or involving the hand: *a hand grenade.* **21b** carried in or worn on the hand: *hand luggage.* **21c** operated by hand: *a hand drill.* **22** (*in combination*) made by hand rather than machine: *hand-sewn.* **23 a free hand.** freedom to do as desired. **24 a hand's turn.** (*usually used with a negative*) a small amount of work: *he hasn't done a hand's turn.* **25 a heavy hand.** tyranny or oppression: *he ruled with a heavy hand.* **26 a high hand.** a dictatorial manner. **27 by hand. 27a** by manual rather than mechanical means. **27b** by messenger or personally: *the letter was delivered by hand.* **28 force someone's hand.** to force someone to act. **29 from hand to mouth. 29a** in poverty: *living from hand to mouth.* **29b** without preparation or planning. **30 hand and foot.** in all ways possible; completely: *they waited on him hand and foot.* **31 hand in glove.** in close association. **32 hand over fist.** steadily and quickly: *he makes money hand over fist.* **33 hold one's hand.** to stop or postpone a planned action or punishment. **34 hold someone's hand.** to support, help, or guide someone, esp. by giving sympathy. **35 in hand. 35a** under control. **35b** receiving attention. **35c** available in reserve. **35d** with deferred payment: *he works a week in hand.* **36 keep one's hand in.** to maintain a limited involvement in an activity so as to preserve one's proficiency at it. **37 (near) at hand.** very close, esp. in time. **38 on hand.** close by; present. **39 out of hand. 39a** beyond control. **39b** without reservation or deeper examination: *he condemned him out of hand.* **40 show one's hand.** to reveal one's stand, opinion, or plans. **41 take in hand.** to discipline; control. **42 throw one's hand in.** to give up a venture, game, etc. **43 to hand.** accessible. **44 try one's hand.** to attempt to do something. ◆ *vb* (*tr*) **45** to transmit or offer by the hand or hands. **46** to help or lead with the hand. **47** *Naut.* to furl (a sail). **48 hand it to someone.** to give credit to someone. ◆ See also **hand down, hand in,** etc., **hands.** [OE *hand*]
▸ **'handless** *adj*

handbag ('hænd,bæg) *n* **1** Also called: **bag, purse** (US and Canad.), **pocketbook** (chiefly US). a woman's small bag carried to contain personal articles. **2** a small suitcase that can be carried by hand.

handball ('hænd,bɔːl) *n* **1** a game in which two teams of seven players try to throw a ball into their opponent's goal. **2** a game in which two or four people strike a ball against a wall with the hand. **3** *Soccer.* the offence committed when a player other than a goalkeeper in his own penalty area touches the ball with a hand. ◆ *vb* **4** *Australian Rules football.* to pass (the ball) with a blow of the fist.

handbarrow ('hænd,bærəʊ) *n* a flat tray for transporting loads, usually carried by two men.

handbill ('hænd,bɪl) *n* a small printed notice for distribution by hand.

handbook Ⓣ ('hænd,bʊk) *n* a reference book listing brief facts on a subject or place or directions for maintenance or repair, as of a car.

handbrake ('hænd,breɪk) *n* **1** a brake operated by a hand lever. **2** the lever that operates the handbrake.

handbrake turn *n* a turn sharply reversing the direction of a vehicle by speedily applying the handbrake while turning the steering wheel.

handbreadth ('hænd,brɛtθ, -,brɛdθ) *or* **hand's-breadth** *n* the width of a hand used as an indication of length.

h and c *abbrev. for* hot and cold (water).

handcart ('hænd,kɑːt) *n* a simple cart, usually with one or two wheels, pushed or drawn by hand.

handcraft ('hænd,krɑːft) *n* **1** another word for **handicraft.** ◆ *vb* **2** (*tr*) to make by handicraft.
▸ **'hand,crafted** *adj*

handcuff Ⓣ ('hænd,kʌf) *vb* **1** (*tr*) to put handcuffs on (a person); manacle. ◆ *n* **2** (*pl*) a pair of locking metal rings joined by a short bar or chain for securing prisoners, etc.

hand down Ⓣ *vb* (*tr, adv*) **1** to bequeath. **2** to pass (an outgrown garment) on from one member of a family to a younger one. **3** *US & Canad. law.* to announce (a verdict).

-handed *adj* of, for, or using a hand or hands as specified: *left-handed; a four-handed game of cards.*

handful Ⓣ ('hændfʊl) *n, pl* **handfuls. 1** the amount or number that can be held in the hand. **2** a small number or quantity. **3** *Inf.* a person or thing difficult to manage or control.

handgun Ⓣ ('hænd,gʌn) *n US & Canad.* a firearm that can be fired with one hand, such as a pistol.

THESAURUS

away (*inf.*), pound away, stick at **18** *Informal* = **defeat**, beat, blow out of the water (*sl.*), clobber (*sl.*), drub, lick (*inf.*), master, run rings around (*inf.*), tank (*sl.*), thrash, trounce, undo, wipe the floor with (*inf.*), worst

hammer out *vb* **2** = **work out**, accomplish, bring about, come to a conclusion, complete, finish, form a resolution, make a decision, negotiate, produce, settle, sort out, thrash out

hamper[1] *vb* **1** = **hinder**, bind, cramp, curb, embarrass, encumber, entangle, fetter, frustrate, hamstring, handicap, hobble, hold up, impede, interfere with, obstruct, prevent, restrain, restrict, slow down, thwart, trammel
Antonyms *vb* aid, assist, boost, encourage, expedite, forward, further, help, promote, speed

hamstring *vb* **3** = **lame**, cripple, disable, hock, injure **4** = **thwart**, balk, foil, frustrate, prevent, ruin, stop

hamstrung *adj* **3** = **incapacitated**, crippled, disabled, helpless, *hors de combat*, paralysed

hand *n* **1** = **palm**, fist, hook, mitt (*sl.*), paw (*inf.*) **5** = **influence**, agency, direction, part, participation, share **7** = **assistance**, aid, help, support **14** = **worker**, artificer, artisan, craftsman, employee, hired man, labourer, operative, workman **16** = **penmanship**, calligraphy, chirography, handwriting, longhand, script **17** = **round of applause**, clap, ovation **29a from hand to mouth** = **in poverty**, by necessity, improvidently, insecurely, on the breadline (*inf.*), precariously, uncertainly **31 hand in glove** = **in league**, allied, in cahoots (*inf.*), in partnership **32 hand over fist** = **steadily**, by leaps and bounds, easily, swiftly **35 in hand: a** = **in reserve**, in order, receiving attention **c** available for use, put by, ready **37 (near) at hand** = **imminent**, approaching, close, just round the corner, near **38 on hand** = **nearby**, at one's fingertips, available, close, handy, near, on tap (*inf.*), ready, within reach ◆ *vb* **45** = **give**, deliver, hand over, pass **46** = **help**, aid, assist, conduct, convey, guide, lead

handbook *n* = **guidebook**, guide, instruction book, manual

handcuff *vb* **1** = **shackle**, fetter, manacle ◆ *pl n* **2** = **shackles**, bracelets (*sl.*), cuffs, fetters, manacles

hand down *vb* **1** = **pass on** *or* **down**, bequeath, give, grant, transfer, will

handful *n* **2** = **few**, small number, small quantity, smattering, sprinkling
Antonyms *n* a lot, crowd, heaps, horde, large number, large quantity, loads (*inf.*), masses (*inf.*), mob, plenty, scores, stacks

handgun *n* = **pistol**, automatic, derringer, piece (*US sl.*), revolver, rod (*US sl.*), shooter (*inf.*)

handicap ❶ ('hændɪ,kæp) *n* **1** something that hampers or hinders. **2a** a contest, esp. a race, in which competitors are given advantages or disadvantages of weight, distance, etc., in an attempt to equalize their chances. **2b** the advantage or disadvantage prescribed. **3** *Golf.* the number of strokes by which a player's averaged score exceeds par for the course. **4** any disability or disadvantage resulting from physical, mental, or social impairment or abnormality. ◆ *vb* **handicaps, handicapping, handicapped.** (*tr*) **5** to be a hindrance or disadvantage to. **6** to assign a handicap to. **7** to organize (a contest) by handicapping. [C17: prob. from *hand in cap*, a lottery game in which players drew forfeits from a cap or deposited money in it]
▸**'handi,capper** *n*

handicapped ('hændɪ,kæpt) *adj* **1a** physically or mentally disabled. **1b** (*as collective n; preceded by the*): *the handicapped.* **2** (of a competitor) assigned a handicap.

handicraft ❶ ('hændɪ,krɑːft) *n* **1** skill in working with the hands. **2** a particular skill performed with the hands, such as weaving. **3** the work so produced. ◆ Also called: **handcraft.** [C15: changed from HANDCRAFT through infl. of HANDIWORK]

hand in *vb* (*tr, adv*) to return or submit (something, such as an examination paper).

handiwork ❶ ('hændɪ,wɜːk) *n* **1** work produced by hand. **2** the result of the action or endeavours of a person or thing. [OE *handgeweorc*, from HAND + *ge-* (collective prefix) + *weorc* WORK]

handkerchief ❶ ('hæŋkətʃɪf, -tʃiːf) *n* a small square of soft absorbent material carried and used to wipe the nose, etc.

handle ❶ ('hænd°l) *n* **1** the part of a utensil, drawer, etc., designed to be held in order to move, use, or pick up the object. **2** *Sl.* a person's name or title. **3** *CB radio.* a slang name for **call sign. 4** an excuse for doing something: *his background served as a handle for their mockery.* **5** the quality, as of textiles, perceived by feeling. **6** *NZ.* a glass beer mug with a handle. **7 fly off the handle.** *Inf.* to become suddenly extremely angry. ◆ *vb* **handles, handling, handled.** (*mainly tr*) **8** to hold, move, or touch with the hands. **9** to operate using the hands: *the boy handled the reins well.* **10** to control: *my wife handles my investments.* **11** to manage successfully: *a secretary must be able to handle clients.* **12** to discuss (a theme, subject, etc.). **13** to deal with in a specified way: *I was handled with great tact.* **14** to trade or deal in (specified merchandise). **15** (*intr*) to react in a specified way to operation: *the car handles well on bends.* [OE]
▸**'handled** *adj* ▸**'handling** *n*

handlebar moustache ('hænd°l,bɑː) *n* a bushy extended moustache with curled ends.

handlebars ('hænd°l,bɑːz) *pl n* (*sometimes sing*) a metal tube having its ends curved to form handles, used for steering a bicycle, etc.

handler ('hændlə) *n* **1** a person who trains and controls an animal, esp. a police dog. **2** the trainer or second of a boxer.

handmade (,hænd'meɪd) *adj* made by hand, not by machine, esp. with care or craftsmanship.

handmaiden ('hænd,meɪd°n) *or* **handmaid** *n* **1** a person or thing that serves a useful but subordinate purpose. **2** *Arch.* a female servant.

hand-me-down *n Inf.* **1** something, esp. an outgrown garment, passed down from one person to another. **2** anything that has already been used by another.

hand-off *Rugby.* ◆ *n* **1** the act of warding off an opposing player with the open hand. ◆ *vb* **hand off. 2** (*tr, adv*) to ward off thus.

hand on *vb* (*tr, adv*) to pass to the next in a succession.

hand organ *n* another name for **barrel organ.**

hand-out ❶ *n* **1** clothing, food, or money given to a needy person. **2** a leaflet, free sample, etc., given out to publicize something. **3** a statement distributed to the press or an audience to confirm or replace an oral presentation. ◆ *vb* **hand out. 4** (*tr, adv*) to distribute.

hand over ❶ *vb* **1** (*tr, adv*) to surrender possession of; transfer. ◆ *n* **handover. 2** a transfer; surrender.

hand-pick ❶ *vb* (*tr*) to select with great care, as for a special job.
▸**,hand-'picked** *adj*

handrail ('hænd,reɪl) *n* a rail alongside a stairway, etc., to provide support.

hands ❶ (hændz) *pl n* **1** power or keeping: *your welfare is in his hands.* **2** Also called: **handling.** *Soccer.* the infringement of touching the ball with the hand or arm. **3 change hands.** to pass from the possession of one person to another. **4 hands down.** without effort; easily. **5 have one's hands full. 5a** to be completely occupied. **5b** to be beset with problems. **6 have one's hands tied.** to be unable to act. **7 lay hands on** *or* **upon. 7a** to get possession of. **7b** to beat up; assault. **7c** to find. **7d** *Christianity.* to place hands on (someone) in order to confirm or ordain. **8 off one's hands.** for which one is no longer responsible. **9 on one's hands. 9a** for which one is responsible: *I've got too much on my hands to help.* **9b** to spare: *time on my hands.* **10 wash one's hands of.** to have nothing more to do with; refuse to accept responsibility for.

handsaw ('hænd,sɔː) *n* any saw for use in one hand only.

hand's-breadth *n* another name for **handbreadth.**

handsel *or* **hansel** ('hæns°l) *Arch. or dialect.* ◆ *n* **1** a gift for good luck at the beginning of a new year, new venture, etc. ◆ *vb* **handsels, handselling, handselled** *or* **hansels, hanselling, hanselled;** *or US* **handsels, handseling, handseled** *or* **hansels, hanseling, hanseled.** (*tr*) **2** to give a handsel to (a person). **3** to inaugurate. [OE *handselen* delivery into the hand]

handset ('hænd,sɛt) *n* a telephone mouthpiece and earpiece mounted as a single unit.

handshake ('hænd,ʃeɪk) *n* the act of grasping and shaking a person's hand, as when being introduced or agreeing on a deal.

hands-off *adj* **1** (of a machine, device, etc.) without need of manual operation. **2** denoting a policy, etc., of deliberate noninvolvement: *a hands-off strategy towards industry.*

handsome ❶ ('hænsəm) *adj* **1** (of a man) good-looking. **2** (of a woman) fine-looking in a dignified way. **3** well-proportioned; stately: *a handsome room.* **4** liberal: *a handsome allowance.* **5** gracious or generous: *a handsome action.* [C15 *handsom* easily handled]
▸**'handsomely** *adv* ▸**'handsomeness** *n*

hands-on *adj* involving practical experience of equipment, etc.: *hands-on training in computing.*

handspring ('hænd,sprɪŋ) *n* a gymnastic feat in which a person starts from a standing position and leaps forwards or backwards into a handstand and then onto his feet.

handstand ('hænd,stænd) *n* the act of supporting the body on the hands in an upside-down position.

hand-to-hand *adj, adv* at close quarters.

hand-to-mouth *adj, adv* with barely enough money or food to satisfy immediate needs.

handwork ('hænd,wɜːk) *n* work done by hand rather than by machine.
▸**'hand,worked** *adj*

handwriting ❶ ('hænd,raɪtɪŋ) *n* **1** writing by hand rather than by typing or printing. **2** a person's characteristic writing style: *that is in my handwriting.*
▸**'hand,written** *adj*

handy ❶ ('hændɪ) *adj* **handier, handiest. 1** conveniently within reach. **2** easy to handle or use. **3** skilful with one's hands.
▸**'handily** *adv* ▸**'handiness** *n*

THESAURUS

handicap *n* **1 = disadvantage,** albatross, barrier, block, drawback, encumbrance, hazard, hindrance, impediment, limitation, millstone, obstacle, restriction, shortcoming, stumbling block **2b = advantage,** edge, head start, odds, penalty, upper hand **4 = disability,** impairment ◆ *vb* **5 = hinder,** burden, encumber, hamper, hamstring, hobble, hold back, impede, limit, place at a disadvantage, restrict, retard
Antonyms *n* ≠ **disadvantage:** advantage, asset, benefit, boost, edge ◆ *vb* ≠ **hinder:** aid, assist, benefit, boost, forward, further, help, promote

handicraft *n* **1 = craftsmanship,** art, artisanship, craft, handiwork, skill, workmanship

handily *adv* **1 = conveniently,** accessibly, advantageously, helpfully, readily, suitably **3 = skilfully,** adroitly, capably, cleverly, deftly, dexterously, expertly, proficiently

handiness *n* **1 = convenience,** accessibility, availability, closeness, practicality, proximity, usefulness **3 = skill,** adroitness, aptitude, cleverness, deftness, dexterity, efficiency, expertise, knack, proficiency

handiwork *n* **1 = handicraft,** craft, handwork **2 = creation,** achievement, artefact, design, invention, product, production, result

handkerchief *n* **= hanky** (*inf.*), tissue

handle *n* **1 = grip,** haft, handgrip, helve, hilt, knob, stock **7 fly off the handle** *Informal* **= lose one's temper,** blow one's top, explode, flip one's lid (*sl.*), fly into a rage, go ballistic (*sl., chiefly US*), have a tantrum, hit *or* go through the roof (*inf.*), let fly (*inf.*), lose it (*inf.*), lose one's cool (*sl.*), lose the plot (*inf.*) ◆ *vb* **8 = hold,** feel, finger, fondle, grasp, maul, paw (*inf.*), pick up, poke, touch **9 = control,** direct, guide, manage, manipulate, manoeuvre, operate, steer, use, wield **11 = manage,** cope with, deal with, take care of **12 = discuss,** discourse, treat **13 = deal with,** treat **14 = deal in,** carry, market, sell, stock, trade, traffic in

handling *n* **11, 13 = management,** administration, approach, conduct, direction, running, treatment

hand-out *n* **1 = charity,** alms, dole **2 = leaflet,** bulletin, circular, free sample, literature (*inf.*), mailshot ◆ *vb* **hand out 4 = distribute,** deal out, disburse, dish out (*inf.*), dispense, disseminate, give out, mete

hand over *vb* **1 = give,** deliver, donate, fork out *or* up (*sl.*), present, release, surrender, transfer, turn over, yield

hand-picked *adj* **= selected,** choice, chosen, elect, elite, recherché, select
Antonyms *adj* haphazard, indiscriminate, random, run-of-the-mill, wholesale

hands *pl n* **1 = control,** authority, care, charge, command, custody, disposal, guardianship, keeping, possession, power, supervision **4 hands down = easily,** effortlessly, with no contest, with no trouble **7 lay hands on: a = bless,** acquire, get, grab, grasp, seize **b** assault, beat up, lay into (*inf.*), set on, work over (*sl.*) **c** find, unearth **d** *Christianity* confirm, consecrate, ordain **10 wash one's hands of = have nothing to do with,** abandon, accept no responsibility for, give up on, leave to one's own devices

handsome *adj* **1 = good-looking,** attractive, dishy (*inf., chiefly Brit.*), gorgeous **2 = majestic,** comely, elegant, graceful, personable **4 = generous,** abundant, ample, bountiful, considerable, large, liberal, plentiful, sizable *or* sizeable **5 = gracious,** generous, magnanimous
Antonyms *adj* ≠ **good-looking:** ugly, unattractive, unprepossessing, unsightly ≠ **generous:** base, cheap, meagre, mean, miserly, selfish, small, stingy, ungenerous

handsomely *adv* **4 = generously,** abundantly, amply, bountifully, liberally, munificently, plentifully, richly

handwriting *n* **2 = penmanship,** calligraphy, chirography, fist, hand, scrawl, script

handy *adj* **1 = convenient,** accessible, at hand, at one's fingertips, available, close, just round

handyman ❶ ('hændɪˌmæn) *n, pl* **handymen.** a man employed to do or skilled in odd jobs, etc.

hanepoot ('hɑːnəˌpɔːt) *n S. African.* a kind of grape for eating or wine making. [from Du.]

hang ❶ (hæŋ) *vb* **hangs, hanging, hung. 1** to fasten or be fastened from above, esp. by a cord, chain, etc. **2** to place or be placed in position as by a hinge so as to allow free movement: *to hang a door.* **3** (*intr;* sometimes foll. by *over*) to be suspended; hover: *a pall of smoke hung over the city.* **4** (*intr;* sometimes foll. by *over*) to threaten. **5** (*intr*) to be or remain doubtful (esp. in **hang in the balance**). **6** (*p.t. & p.p.* **hanged**) to suspend or be suspended by the neck until dead. **7** (*tr*) to decorate, furnish, or cover with something suspended. **8** (*tr*) to fasten to a wall: *to hang wallpaper.* **9** to exhibit or be exhibited in an art gallery, etc. **10** to droop or allow to droop: *to hang one's head.* **11** (of cloth, clothing, etc.) to drape, fall, or flow: *her skirt hangs well.* **12** (*tr*) to suspend (game such as pheasant) so that it becomes slightly decomposed and therefore more tasty. **13** (of a jury) to prevent or be prevented from reaching a verdict. **14** (*p.t. & p.p.* **hanged**) *Sl.* to damn or be damned: used in mild curses or interjections. **15** (*intr*) to pass slowly (esp. in **time hangs heavily**). **16 hang fire.** to be delayed or to procrastinate. ◆ *n* **17** the way in which something hangs. **18** (*usually used with a negative*) *Sl.* a damn: *I don't care a hang.* **19 get the hang of.** *Inf.* **19a** to understand the technique of doing something. **19b** to perceive the meaning of. ◆ See also **hang about, hang back,** etc. [OE *hangian*]

hang about ❶ *or* **around** *vb* (*intr*) **1** to waste time; loiter. **2** (*adv;* foll. by *with*) to frequent the company (of someone).

hangar ('hæŋə) *n* a large building for storing and maintaining aircraft. [C19: from F: shed, ?from Med. L *angārium* shed used as a smithy, from ?]

hang back ❶ *vb* (*intr, adv;* often foll. by *from*) to be reluctant to go forward or carry on.

hangdog ❶ ('hæŋˌdɒg) *adj* downcast, furtive, or guilty in appearance or manner.

hanger ('hæŋə) *n* **1a** any support, such as a peg or loop, on or by which something may be hung. **1b** See **coat hanger. 2a** a person who hangs something. **2b** (*in combination*): *paperhanger.* **3** a type of dagger worn on a sword belt. **4** *Brit.* a wood on a steep hillside.

hanger-on ❶ *n, pl* **hangers-on.** a sycophantic follower or dependant.

hang-glider *n* an unpowered aircraft consisting of a large wing made of cloth or plastic stretched over a light framework from which the pilot hangs in a harness.
▸**'hang-ˌgliding** *n*

hangi ('hʌŋiː) *n NZ.* **1** an open-air cooking pit. **2** the food cooked in it. **3** the social gathering at the resultant meal. [from Maori]

hang in *vb* (*intr, prep*) *Inf., chiefly US & Canad.* to persist: *just hang in there for a bit longer.*

hanging ❶ ('hæŋɪŋ) *n* **1a** the putting of a person to death by suspending the body by the neck. **1b** (*as modifier*): *a hanging offence.* **2** (*often pl*) a decorative drapery hung on a wall or over a window. ◆ *adj* **3** not supported from below; suspended. **4** undecided; still under discussion. **5** projecting downwards; overhanging. **6** situated on a steep slope. **7** (*prenominal*) given to issuing death sentences: *a hanging judge.*

hanging valley *n Geog.* a tributary valley entering a main valley at a much higher level because of overdeepening of the main valley, esp. by glacial erosion.

hangman ('hæŋmən) *n, pl* **hangmen.** an official who carries out a sentence of hanging.

hangnail ('hæŋˌneɪl) *n* a piece of skin torn away from, but still attached to, the base or side of a fingernail. [C17: from OE *angnægl,* from *enge* tight + *nægl* nail; infl. by HANG]

hang on ❶ *vb* (*intr*) **1** (*adv*) to continue or persist, esp. with effort or difficulty. **2** (*adv*) to grasp or hold. **3** (*prep*) to depend on: *everything hangs on this deal.* **4** (*prep*) Also: **hang onto, hang upon.** to listen attentively to. **5** (*adv*) *Inf.* to wait: *hang on for a few minutes.*

hang out ❶ *vb* (*adv*) **1** to suspend, be suspended, or lean. **2** (*intr*) *Inf.* to frequent a place. **3 let it all hang out.** *Inf., chiefly US.* **3a** to relax completely in an unassuming way. **3b** to act or speak freely. ◆ *n* **hang-out. 4** *Inf.* a place that one frequents.

hangover ❶ ('hæŋˌəʊvə) *n* **1** the delayed aftereffects of drinking too much alcohol. **2** a person or thing left over from or influenced by a past age.

Hang Seng Index (hæŋ sɛŋ) *n* an index of share prices based on an average of 33 stocks quoted on the Hong Kong Stock Exchange. [name of a Hong Kong bank]

hang together *vb* (*intr, adv*) **1** to be cohesive or united. **2** to be consistent: *your statements don't quite hang together.*

hang up ❶ *vb* (*adv*) **1** (*tr*) to put on a hook, hanger, etc. **2** to replace (a telephone receiver) on its cradle at the end of a conversation. **3** (*tr; usually passive;* usually foll. by *on*) *Inf.* to cause to have an emotional or psychological preoccupation or problem: *he's really hung up on his mother.* ◆ *n* **hang-up.** *Inf.* **4** an emotional or psychological preoccupation or problem. **5** a persistent cause of annoyance.

hank ❶ (hæŋk) *n* **1** a loop, coil, or skein, as of rope. **2** *Naut.* a ringlike fitting that can be opened to admit a stay for attaching the luff of a sail. **3** a unit of measurement of cloth, such as a length of 840 yards (767 m) of cotton or 560 yards (512 m) of worsted yarn. [C13: from ON]

hanker ❶ ('hæŋkə) *vb* (foll. by *for, after,* or an infinitive) to have a yearning. [C17: prob. from Du. dialect *hankeren*]
▸**'hankering** *n*

hanky *or* **hankie** ('hæŋkɪ) *n, pl* **hankies.** *Inf.* short for **handkerchief.**

hanky-panky ❶ ('hæŋkɪ'pæŋkɪ) *n Inf.* **1** dubious or foolish behaviour. **2** illicit sexual relations. [C19: var. of HOCUS-POCUS]

Hanoverian (ˌhænə'vɪərɪən) *adj* of or relating to the British royal house ruling from 1714 to 1901. [from the princely House of *Hanover,* former province of Germany]

Hansard ('hænsɑːd) *n* **1** the official verbatim report of the proceedings of the British Parliament. **2** a similar report kept by the Canadian House of Commons and other legislative bodies. [C19: after L. *Hansard* (1752–1828) and his descendants, who compiled the reports until 1889]

Hanse (hæns) *n* **1** a medieval guild of merchants. **2** a fee paid by the new members of a medieval trading guild. **3** another name for the **Hanseatic League.** [C12: of Gmc origin]
▸**Hanseatic** (ˌhænsɪ'ætɪk) *adj*

Hanseatic League *n* a commercial organization of towns in N Germany formed in the mid-14th century to protect and control trade.

hansel ('hænsᵊl) *n, vb* a variant spelling of **handsel.**

hansom ('hænsəm) *n* (*sometimes cap.*) a two-wheeled one-horse carriage with a fixed hood. The driver sits on a high outside seat at the rear. Also called: **hansom cab.** [C19: after its designer J. A. *Hansom* (1803–82)]

Hants (hænts) *abbrev. for* Hampshire.

Hanukkah ('hɑːnəkə, -nʊˌkɑː) *n* a variant of **Chanukah.**

Hanuman (ˌhʌnʊ'mɑːn) *n* **1** (*pl* **Hanumans**) another word for **entellus** (the monkey). **2** the monkey chief of Hindu mythology. [from Hindi, from Sansk. *hanumant* having (conspicuous) jaws, from *hanu* jaw]

hap (hæp) *Arch.* ◆ *n* **1** luck; chance. **2** an occurrence. ◆ *vb* **haps, happing, happed. 3** (*intr*) to happen. [C13: from ON *happ* good luck]

ha'penny ('heɪpnɪ) *n, pl* **ha'pennies.** *Brit.* a variant spelling of **halfpenny.**

haphazard ❶ (hæp'hæzəd) *adv, adj* **1** at random. ◆ *adj* **2** careless.
▸**hap'hazardly** *adv* ▸**hap'hazardness** *n*

hapless ❶ ('hæplɪs) *adj* unfortunate; wretched.

THESAURUS

the corner, near, nearby, on hand, within reach **2** = **useful,** convenient, easy to use, helpful, manageable, neat, practical, serviceable, user-friendly **3** = **skilful,** adept, adroit, clever, deft, dexterous, expert, nimble, proficient, ready, skilled

Antonyms *adj* ≠ **convenient:** awkward, inaccessible, inconvenient, out of the way, unavailable ≠ **useful:** awkward, inconvenient, unwieldy, useless ≠ **skilful:** clumsy, ham-fisted, incompetent, inept, inexpert, maladroit, unaccomplished, unskilful, unskilled, useless

handyman *n* = **odd-jobman,** DIY expert, handy Andy (*inf.*), jack-of-all-trades

hang *vb* **1** = **suspend,** be pendent, dangle, depend, droop, incline **3** = **hover,** be poised, drift, float, remain, swing **4** *sometimes with* **over** = **threaten,** be imminent, impend, loom, menace **6** = **execute,** gibbet, lynch, send to the gallows, string up (*inf.*) **7** = **fasten,** attach, cover, deck, decorate, drape, fix, furnish **10** = **droop,** bend downward, bend forward, bow, dangle, incline, lean over, let droop, loll, lower, sag, trail **16 hang fire** = **put off,** be slow, be suspended, delay, hang back, procrastinate, stall, stick, vacillate ◆ *n* **19 get the hang of** = **grasp,** comprehend, get the knack *or* technique, understand

hang about *vb* **1** = **loiter,** dally, linger, roam, tarry, waste time **2** = **associate with,** frequent, hang out (*inf.*), hang with (*inf., chiefly US*), haunt, resort

hang back *vb* = **be reluctant,** be backward, demur, hesitate, hold back, recoil

hangdog *adj* = **guilty,** abject, browbeaten, cowed, cringing, defeated, downcast, furtive, shamefaced, wretched

hanger-on *n* = **parasite,** cohort (*chiefly US*), dependant, follower, freeloader (*sl.*), lackey, leech, ligger (*sl.*), minion, sponger (*inf.*), sycophant

hanging *adj* **3** = **suspended,** dangling, drooping, flapping, flopping, floppy, loose, pendent, swinging, unattached, unsupported **4** = **undecided,** unresolved, unsettled, up in the air (*inf.*) **5** = **projecting,** beetle, beetling, jutting, overhanging, prominent

hang on *vb* **1** = **continue,** carry on, endure, go on, hold on, hold out, persevere, persist, remain, stay the course **2** = **grasp,** cling, clutch, grip, hold fast **3** = **depend on,** be conditional upon, be contingent on, be dependent on, be determined by, hinge, rest, turn on **4** = **listen attentively,** be rapt, give ear **5** *Informal* = **wait,** hold on, hold the line, remain, stop

hang out *n* **hang-out 4** *Informal* = **haunt,** den, dive (*sl.*), home, joint (*sl.*), resort

hangover *n* **1** = **aftereffects,** crapulence, head (*inf.*), morning after (*inf.*)

hang up *n* **hang-up** *Informal* **4** = **preoccupation,** block, difficulty, inhibition, obsession, problem, thing (*inf.*)

hank *n* **1** = **coil,** length, loop, piece, roll, skein

hanker *vb, with* **for** *or* **after** = **desire,** ache, covet, crave, eat one's heart out over, hope, hunger, itch, long, lust, pine, set one's heart on, thirst, want, wish, yearn

hankering *n* = **desire,** ache, craving, hope, hunger, itch, longing, pining, thirst, urge, wish, yearning, yen (*inf.*)

hanky-panky *n Informal* **1** = **mischief,** chicanery, deception, devilry, funny business (*inf.*), jiggery-pokery (*inf., chiefly Brit.*), knavery, machinations, monkey business (*inf.*), shenanigans (*inf.*), subterfuge, trickery

haphazard *adj* **1** = **random,** accidental, arbitrary, chance, fluky (*inf.*) **2** = **unsystematic,** aimless, careless, casual, disorderly, disorganized, hit or miss, indiscriminate, slapdash, slipshod, unmethodical

Antonyms *adj* ≠ **random:** arranged, deliberate, planned ≠ **unsystematic:** careful, considered, methodical, orderly, organized, systematic, thoughtful

hapless *adj* = **unlucky,** cursed, ill-fated, ill-

▸ 'haplessly *adv* ▸ 'haplessness *n*

haplography (hæp'lɒgrəfɪ) *n, pl* **haplographies.** the accidental omission of a letter or syllable which recurs, as in spelling *endodontics* as *endontics.* [C19: from Gk, from *haplous* single + -GRAPHY]

haploid ('hæplɔɪd) *Biol.* ◆ *adj* **1** (esp. of gametes) having a single set of unpaired chromosomes. ◆ *n* **2** a haploid cell or organism. [C20: from Gk *haploeidēs,* from *haplous* single]
▸ 'haploidy *n*

haplology (hæp'lɒlədʒɪ) *n* omission of a repeated occurrence of a sound or syllable in fluent speech, as for example in the pronunciation of *library* as ('laɪbrɪ).

haply ('hæplɪ) *adv* (*sentence modifier*) an archaic word for **perhaps.**

happen Ⓣ ('hæpᵊn) *vb* **1** (*intr*) to take place; occur. **2** (*intr;* foll. by *to*) (of some unforeseen event, esp. death) to fall to the lot (of): *if anything happens to me it'll be your fault.* **3** (*tr*) to chance (to be or do something): *I happen to know him.* **4** (*tr; takes a clause as object*) to be the case, esp. by chance: *it happens that I know him.* ◆ *adv, sentence substitute.* **5** *N English dialect.* another word for **perhaps.** [C14: see HAP, -EN[1]]

USAGE NOTE See at **occur.**

happening Ⓣ ('hæpənɪŋ, 'hæpnɪŋ) *n* **1** an event. **2** an improvised or spontaneous performance consisting of bizarre events. ◆ *adj* **3** *Inf.* fashionable and up-to-the-minute.

happen on Ⓣ *or* **upon** *vb* (*intr; prep*) to find by chance.

happy Ⓣ ('hæpɪ) *adj* **happier, happiest. 1** feeling or expressing joy; pleased. **2** willing: *I'd be happy to show you around.* **3** causing joy or gladness. **4** fortunate: *the happy position of not having to work.* **5** aptly expressed; appropriate: *a happy turn of phrase.* **6** (*postpositive*) *Inf.* slightly intoxicated. [C14: see HAP, -Y[1]]
▸ 'happily *adv* ▸ 'happiness *n*

happy event *n Inf.* the birth of a child.

happy-go-lucky Ⓣ *adj* carefree or easy-going.

happy hour *n* a period during which some public houses, bars, restaurants, etc., charge reduced prices.

happy hunting ground *n* **1** (in Amerind legend) the paradise to which a person passes after death. **2** a productive or profitable area to explore.

happy medium *n* a course or state that avoids extremes.

haptic ('hæptɪk) *adj* relating to or based on the sense of touch. [C19: from Gk, from *haptein* to touch]

hapuka *or* **hapuku** (hə'pu:kə, 'hɑ:pʊkə) *n NZ.* another name for **groper.** [from Maori]

hara-kiri Ⓣ (ˌhærə'kɪrɪ) *or* **hari-kari** (ˌhærɪ'kɑ:rɪ) *n* (formerly, in Japan) ritual suicide by disembowelment when disgraced or under sentence of death. Also called: **seppuku.** [C19: from Japanese, from *hara* belly + *kiri* cutting]

harangue Ⓣ (hə'ræŋ) *vb* **harangues, haranguing, harangued. 1** to address (a person or crowd) in an angry, vehement, or forcefully persuasive way. ◆ *n* **2** a loud, forceful, or angry speech. [C15: from OF, from OIt. *aringa* public speech, prob. of Gmc origin]
▸ ha'ranguer *n*

harass Ⓣ ('hærəs, hə'ræs) *vb* (*tr*) to trouble, torment, or confuse by continual persistent attacks, questions, etc. [C17: from F *harasser,* var. of OF *harer* to set a dog on, of Gmc origin]
▸ 'harassed *adj* ▸ 'harassment *n*

harbinger Ⓣ ('hɑ:bɪndʒə) *n* **1** a person or thing that announces or indicates the approach of something; forerunner. ◆ *vb* **2** (*tr*) to announce the approach or arrival of. [C12: from OF *herbergere,* from *herberge* lodging, from OSaxon]

harbour Ⓣ *or US* **harbor** ('hɑ:bə) *n* **1** a sheltered port. **2** a place of refuge or safety. ◆ *vb* **3** (*tr*) to give shelter to: *to harbour a criminal.* **4** (*tr*) to maintain secretly: *to harbour a grudge.* **5** to shelter (a vessel) in a harbour or (of a vessel) to seek shelter. [OE *herebeorg,* from *here* army + *beorg* shelter]

harbourage *or US* **harborage** ('hɑ:bərɪdʒ) *n* shelter or refuge, as for a ship.

harbour master *n* an official in charge of a harbour.

hard Ⓣ (hɑ:d) *adj* **1** firm or rigid. **2** toughened; not soft or smooth: *hard skin.* **3** difficult to do or accomplish: *a hard task.* **4** difficult to understand: *a hard question.* **5** showing or requiring considerable effort or application: *hard work.* **6** demanding: *a hard master.* **7** harsh; cruel: *a hard fate.* **8** inflicting pain, sorrow, or hardship: *hard times.* **9** tough or violent: *a hard man.* **10** forceful: *a hard knock.* **11** cool or uncompromising: *we took a long hard look at our profit factor.* **12** indisputable; real: *hard facts.* **13** *Chem.* (of water) impairing the formation of a lather by soap. **14** practical, shrewd, or calculating: *he is a hard man in business.* **15** harsh: *hard light.* **16a** (of currency) in strong demand, esp. as a result of a good balance of payments situation. **16b** (of credit) difficult to obtain; tight. **17** (of alcoholic drink) being a spirit rather than a wine, beer, etc. **18** (of a drug) highly addictive. **19** *Physics.* (of radiation) having high energy and the ability to penetrate solids. **20** *Chiefly US.* (of goods) durable. **21** short for **hard-core. 22** *Phonetics.* (not in technical usage) denoting the consonants *c* and *g* when they are pronounced as in *cat* and *got.* **23a** heavily fortified. **23b** (of nuclear missiles) located underground. **24** politically extreme: *the hard left.* **25** *Brit. & NZ inf.* incorrigible or disreputable (esp. in **a hard case**). **26 a hard nut to crack. 26a** a person not easily won over. **26b** a thing not easily done or understood. **27 hard by.** close by. **28 hard of hearing.** slightly deaf. **29 hard up.** *Inf.* **29a** in need of money. **29b** (foll. by *for*) in great need (of): *hard up for suggestions.* ◆ *adv* **30** with great energy, force, or vigour: *the team always played hard.* **31** as far as possible: *hard left.* **32** earnestly or intently: *she thought hard about the formula.* **33** with great intensity: *his son's death hit him hard.* **34** (foll. by *on, upon, by,* or *after*) close; near: *hard on his heels.* **35** (foll. by *at*) assiduously; devotedly. **36a** with effort or difficulty: *their victory was hard won.* **36b** (*in combination*): *hard-earned.* **37** slowly: *prejudice dies hard.* **38 go hard with.** to cause pain or difficulty to (someone). **39 hard put (to it).** scarcely having the capacity (to do something). ◆ *n* **40** *Brit.* a roadway across a foreshore. **41** *Sl.* hard labour. **42**

THESAURUS

starred, jinxed, luckless, miserable, unfortunate, unhappy, wretched

happen *vb* **1 = occur,** appear, arise, come about, come off (*inf.*), come to pass, crop up (*inf.*), develop, ensue, eventuate, follow, materialize, present itself, result, see the light of day, take place, transpire (*inf.*) **2 = befall,** become of, betide **4 = chance,** fall out, have the fortune to be, pan out (*inf.*), supervene, turn out

happening *n* **1 = event,** accident, adventure, affair, case, chance, episode, escapade, experience, incident, occasion, occurrence, phenomenon, proceeding, scene

happen on *vb* **= find,** chance upon, come upon, discover unexpectedly, hit upon, light upon, stumble on, turn up

happily *adv* **1 = joyfully,** blithely, cheerfully, gaily, gleefully, joyously, merrily **2 = willingly,** agreeably, contentedly, delightedly, enthusiastically, freely, gladly, heartily, lief (*rare*), with pleasure **4 = luckily,** auspiciously, favourably, fortunately, opportunely, propitiously, providentially, seasonably **5 = aptly,** appropriately, felicitously, successfully

happiness *n* **1 = joy,** beatitude, blessedness, bliss, cheer, cheerfulness, cheeriness, contentment, delight, ecstasy, elation, enjoyment, exuberance, felicity, gaiety, gladness, high spirits, jubilation, light-heartedness, merriment, pleasure, prosperity, satisfaction, wellbeing
Antonyms *n* annoyance, bane, depression, despondency, distress, grief, low spirits, misery, misfortune, sadness, sorrow, unhappiness

happy *adj* **1 = joyful,** blessed, blest, blissful, blithe, cheerful, cock-a-hoop, content, contented, delighted, ecstatic, elated, floating on air, glad, gratified, jolly, joyous, jubilant, merry, on cloud nine (*inf.*), overjoyed, over the moon (*inf.*), pleased, rapt, sunny, thrilled, walking on air (*inf.*) **4 = fortunate,** advantageous, auspicious, convenient, enviable, favourable, felicitous, lucky, promising, propitious, satisfactory, successful **5 = apt,** appropriate, befitting, opportune, seasonable, timely, well-timed
Antonyms *adj* ≠ **joyful:** depressed, despondent, discontented, displeased, down in the dumps (*inf.*), forlorn, gloomy, joyless, low, melancholy, miserable, mournful, sad, sombre, sorrowful, sorry, unhappy ≠ **fortunate:** unfortunate, unhappy, unlucky

happy-go-lucky *adj* **= carefree,** blithe, casual, devil-may-care, easy-going, heedless, improvident, insouciant, irresponsible, lighthearted, nonchalant, unconcerned, untroubled
Antonyms *adj* careworn, cheerless, gloomy, melancholy, morose, sad, serious, unhappy

hara-kiri *n* **= ritual suicide,** seppuku

harangue *vb* **1 = rant,** address, declaim, exhort, hold forth, lecture, spout (*inf.*) ◆ *n* **2 = speech,** address, declamation, diatribe, exhortation, lecture, oration, spiel (*inf.*), tirade

harass *vb* **= annoy,** badger, bait, beleaguer, be on one's back (*sl.*), bother, breathe down someone's neck, chivvy (*Brit.*), devil (*inf.*), disturb, exasperate, exhaust, fatigue, harry, hassle (*inf.*), hound, perplex, persecute, pester, plague, tease, tire, torment, trouble, vex, weary, worry

harassed *adj* **= hassled** (*inf.*), careworn, distraught, harried, plagued, strained, tormented, troubled, under pressure, under stress, vexed, worried

harassment *n* **= hassle** (*inf.*), aggravation (*inf.*), annoyance, badgering, bedevilment, bother, grief (*inf.*), irritation, molestation, nuisance, persecution, pestering, torment, trouble, vexation

harbinger *n* **1 = herald,** forerunner, foretoken, indication, messenger, omen, portent, precursor, sign

harbour *n* **1 = port,** anchorage, destination, haven **2 = sanctuary,** asylum, covert, haven, refuge, retreat, sanctum, security, shelter ◆ *vb* **3 = shelter,** conceal, hide, lodge, protect, provide refuge, secrete, shield **4 = maintain,** brood over, cherish, cling to, entertain, foster, hold, nurse, nurture, retain

hard *adj* **1, 2 = tough,** compact, dense, firm, impenetrable, inflexible, rigid, rocklike, solid, stiff, stony, strong, unyielding **3, 5 = strenuous,** arduous, backbreaking, burdensome, exacting, exhausting, fatiguing, formidable, Herculean, laborious, rigorous, toilsome, tough, uphill, wearying **4 = difficult,** baffling, complex, complicated, intricate, involved, knotty, perplexing, puzzling, tangled, thorny, unfathomable **7 = harsh,** callous, cold, cruel, exacting, grim, hardhearted, implacable, obdurate, pitiless, ruthless, severe, stern, strict, stubborn, unfeeling, unjust, unkind, unrelenting, unsparing, unsympathetic **8 = grim,** calamitous, dark, disagreeable, disastrous, distressing, grievous, intolerable, painful, unpleasant **10 = forceful,** driving, fierce, heavy, powerful, strong, violent **12 = indisputable,** actual, bare, cold, definite, plain, undeniable, unvarnished, verified **29a hard up** *Informal* **= poor,** bankrupt, broke (*inf.*), bust (*inf.*), cleaned out (*sl.*), dirt-poor (*inf.*), down and out, flat broke (*inf.*), impecunious, impoverished, in queer street, in the red (*inf.*), on one's uppers (*inf.*), on the breadline, out of pocket, penniless, short, short of cash *or* funds, skint (*Brit. sl.*), strapped for cash (*inf.*), without two pennies to rub together (*inf.*) ◆ *adv* **30 = energetically,** fiercely, forcefully, forcibly, heavily, intensely, powerfully, severely, sharply, strongly, vigorously, violently, with all one's

Taboo sl. an erection of the penis (esp. in **get** or **have a hard on**). [OE *heard*]
▸ **'hardness** *n*

hard and fast ⓣ *adj* (**hard-and-fast** *when prenominal*). (of rules, etc.) invariable or strict.

hardback ('hɑːdˌbæk) *n* **1** a book with covers of cloth, cardboard, or leather. ◆ *adj* **2** Also: **casebound, hardbound, hardcover.** of or denoting a hardback or the publication of hardbacks.

hard-bitten ⓣ *adj Inf.* tough and realistic.

hardboard ('hɑːdˌbɔːd) *n* a thin stiff sheet made of compressed sawdust and wood pulp bound together under heat and pressure.

hard-boiled *adj* **1** (of an egg) boiled until solid. **2** *Inf.* **2a** tough, realistic. **2b** cynical.

hard card *n* a hard disk, mounted on a card, that can be added to a personal computer.

hard cash *n* money or payment in money, as opposed to payment by cheque, credit, etc.

hard coal *n* another name for **anthracite.**

hard copy *n* computer output printed on paper, as contrasted with machine-readable output such as magnetic tape.

hardcore ('hɑːdˌkɔː) *n* **1** a style of rock music characterized by short fast songs with minimal melody and aggressive delivery. **2** a type of dance music with a very fast beat.

hard core ⓣ *n* **1** the members of a group who form an intransigent nucleus resisting change. **2** material, such as broken stones, used to form a foundation for a road, etc. ◆ *adj* **hard-core. 3** (of pornography) describing or depicting sexual acts in explicit detail. **4** extremely committed or fanatical: *a hard-core Communist.*

hard disk *n Computing.* a disk of rigid magnetizable material that is used to store data for computers: it is permanently mounted in its disk drive and usually has a storage capacity of a few gigabytes.

harden ⓣ ('hɑːdᵊn) *vb* **1** to make or become hard or harder; freeze, stiffen, or set. **2** to make or become tough or unfeeling. **3** to make or become stronger or firmer. **4** (*intr*) *Commerce.* **4a** (of prices, a market, etc.) to cease to fluctuate. **4b** (of price) to rise higher.
▸ **'hardener** *n*

hardened ⓣ ('hɑːdᵊnd) *adj* **1** rigidly set, as in a mode of behaviour. **2** toughened; seasoned.

harden off *vb* (*tr, adv*) to cause (plants) to become resistant to cold, frost, etc., by gradually exposing them to such conditions.

hard feeling *n* (*often pl; often used with a negative*) resentment; ill will: *no hard feelings?*

hard hat *n* **1** a hat made of a hard material for protection, worn esp. by construction workers, equestrians, etc. **2** *Inf., chiefly US.* a construction worker.

hard-headed ⓣ *adj* tough, realistic, or shrewd; not moved by sentiment.

hardhearted ⓣ (ˌhɑːd'hɑːtɪd) *adj* unkind or intolerant.
▸ **ˌhard'heartedness** *n*

hardihood ⓣ ('hɑːdɪˌhʊd) *n* courage or daring.

hard labour *n Criminal law.* (formerly) the penalty of compulsory physical labour imposed in addition to a sentence of imprisonment.

hard landing *n* **1** a landing by a rocket or spacecraft in which the vehicle is destroyed on impact. **2** a solution to a problem, esp. an economic problem, that involves hardship.

hard line *n* an uncompromising course or policy.
▸ **ˌhard'liner** *n*

hardly ⓣ ('hɑːdlɪ) *adv* **1** scarcely; barely: *we hardly knew the family.* **2** only just: *he could hardly hold the cup.* **3** *Often used ironically.* not at all: *he will hardly incriminate himself.* **4** with difficulty. **5** *Rare.* harshly or cruelly.

> **USAGE NOTE** Since *hardly, scarcely,* and *barely* already have negative force, it is redundant to use another negative in the same clause: *he had hardly had* (not *he hadn't hardly had*) *time to think; there was scarcely any* (not *scarcely no*) *bread left.*

hard-nosed ⓣ *adj Inf.* tough, shrewd, and practical.

hard pad *n* (in dogs) an abnormal increase in the thickness of the foot pads: one of the clinical signs of canine distemper. See **distemper**[1].

hard palate *n* the anterior bony portion of the roof of the mouth.

hardpan ('hɑːdˌpæn) *n* a hard impervious layer of clay below the soil.

hard paste *n* **a** porcelain made with kaolin and petuntse, of Chinese origin and made in Europe from the early 18th century. **b** (*as modifier*): *hard-paste porcelain.*

hard-pressed ⓣ *adj* **1** in difficulties. **2** subject to severe competition or attack. **3** closely pursued.

hard rock *n* rhythmically simple rock music that is very loud.

hard sauce *n* another name for **brandy butter.**

hard science *n* one of the natural or physical sciences, such as physics, chemistry, biology, geology, or astronomy.
▸ **hard scientist** *n*

hard sell *n* an aggressive insistent technique of selling or advertising.

hard-shell *adj also* **hard-shelled. 1** *Zool.* having a shell or carapace that is thick, heavy, or hard. **2** *US.* strictly orthodox.

hardship ⓣ ('hɑːdʃɪp) *n* **1** conditions of life difficult to endure. **2** something that causes suffering or privation.

hard shoulder *n Brit.* a surfaced verge running along the edge of a motorway for emergency stops.

hardtack ('hɑːdˌtæk) *n* a kind of hard saltless biscuit, formerly eaten esp. by sailors as a staple aboard ship. Also called: **ship's biscuit, sea biscuit.**

hardtop ('hɑːdˌtɒp) *n* a car with a metal or plastic roof that is sometimes detachable.

hardware ('hɑːdˌwɛə) *n* **1** metal tools, implements, etc., esp. cutlery or cooking utensils. **2** *Computing.* the physical equipment used in a computer system, such as the central processing unit, peripheral devices, and memory. Cf. **software. 3** mechanical equipment, components, etc. **4** heavy military equipment, such as tanks and missiles. **5** *Inf.* a gun.

hard-wired *adj* (of a circuit or instruction) permanently wired into a computer, replacing separate software.

hardwood ('hɑːdˌwʊd) *n* **1** the wood of any of numerous broad-leaved trees, such as oak, beech, ash, etc., as distinguished from the wood of a conifer. **2** any tree from which this wood is obtained.

hardy ⓣ ('hɑːdɪ) *adj* **hardier, hardiest. 1** having or demanding a tough constitution; robust. **2** bold; courageous. **3** foolhardy; rash. **4** (of plants) able to live out of doors throughout the winter. [C13: from OF *hardi,* p.p. of *hardir* to become bold, of Gmc origin; cf. OE *hierdan* to HARDEN, ON *hertha,* OHG *herten*]
▸ **'hardily** *adv* ▸ **'hardiness** *n*

THESAURUS

might, with might and main **32 = intently,** assiduously, determinedly, diligently, doggedly, earnestly, industriously, persistently, steadily, strenuously, untiringly **36 = with difficulty,** agonizingly, badly, distressingly, harshly, laboriously, painfully, roughly, severely
Antonyms *adj* ≠ **tough:** flexible, malleable, pliable, soft, weak ≠ **strenuous:** easy, easy-peasy (*sl.*), lazy, light, soft ≠ **difficult:** clear, direct, easy, easy-peasy (*sl.*), simple, straightforward, uncomplicated ≠ **harsh:** agreeable, amiable, careless, flexible, friendly, gentle, good, humane, kind, lenient, merciful, mild, permissive, pleasant ≠ **poor:** affluent, comfortable (*inf.*), fortunate, loaded (*sl.*), rich, wealthy, well-heeled (*inf.*), well-off ◆ *adv* ≠ **energetically:** lazily, lightly, loosely, softly, weakly ≠ **intently:** easily, gently, softly

hard and fast *adj* = **fixed,** binding, immutable, incontrovertible, inflexible, invariable, rigid, set, strict, stringent, unalterable

hard-bitten *adj Informal* = **tough,** case-hardened, cynical, down-to-earth, hard-headed, hard-nosed (*inf.*), matter-of-fact, practical, realistic, shrewd, unsentimental
Antonyms *adj* benign, compassionate, gentle, humane, idealistic, merciful, mild, romantic, sympathetic

hard core *adj* **hard-core 3 = explicit,** obscene, X-rated (*inf.*) **4 = dyed-in-the-wool,** dedicated, die-hard, extreme, intransigent, obstinate, rigid, staunch, steadfast

harden *vb* **1 = solidify,** anneal, bake, cake, freeze, set, stiffen **2 = accustom,** brutalize, case-harden, habituate, inure, season, train **3 = reinforce,** brace, buttress, fortify, gird, indurate, nerve, steel, strengthen, toughen

hardened *adj* **1 = habitual,** chronic, fixed, incorrigible, inveterate, irredeemable, reprobate, set, shameless **2 = seasoned,** accustomed, habituated, inured, toughened
Antonyms *adj* infrequent, irregular, occasional, rare, unaccustomed

hard-headed *adj* = **shrewd,** astute, cool, hard-boiled (*inf.*), level-headed, practical, pragmatic, realistic, sensible, tough, unsentimental
Antonyms *adj* idealistic, impractical, sentimental, unrealistic

hardhearted *adj* = **unsympathetic,** callous, cold, cruel, hard, hard as nails, heartless, indifferent, inhuman, insensitive, intolerant, merciless, pitiless, stony, uncaring, unfeeling, unkind
Antonyms *adj* compassionate, forgiving, gentle, humane, kind, loving, merciful, sensitive, soft-hearted, sympathetic, understanding, warm, warm-hearted

hardihood *n* = **courage,** backbone, boldness, bottle (*Brit. sl.*), bravery, daring, determination, firmness, grit, guts (*inf.*), intrepidity, mettle, nerve, pluck, resolution, spirit, spunk (*inf.*), strength

hardiness *n* **1 = resilience,** robustness, ruggedness, sturdiness, toughness **2 = boldness,** courage, fortitude, intrepidity, resolution, valour

hardly *adv* **1, 2 = barely,** almost not, faintly, infrequently, just, not quite, only, only just, scarcely **3 = not at all,** by no means, no way **4 = with difficulty,** at a push
Antonyms *adv* ≠ **barely:** abundantly, amply, by all means, certainly, completely, fully, indubitably, more than, really, truly, undoubtedly, well over

hard-nosed *adj Informal* = **tough,** businesslike, down-to-earth, hard-headed, hardline, practical, pragmatic, realistic, shrewd, uncompromising, unsentimental

hard-pressed *adj* **1, 2 = under pressure,** harried, in difficulties, pushed (*inf.*), under attack, up against it (*inf.*), with one's back to the wall

hardship *n* **1, 2 = suffering,** adversity, affliction, austerity, burden, calamity, destitution, difficulty, fatigue, grievance, labour, misery, misfortune, need, oppression, persecution, privation, toil, torment, trial, tribulation, trouble, want
Antonyms *n* aid, blessing, boon, comfort, ease, good fortune, happiness, help, prosperity, relief

hardy *adj* **1 = strong,** firm, fit, hale, healthy, hearty, in fine fettle, lusty, robust, rugged, sound, stalwart, stout, sturdy, tough, vigorous **2 = courageous,** bold, brave, daring, feisty (*inf., chiefly US & Canad.*), gritty, heroic, intrepid, manly, plucky, resolute, stouthearted, valiant, valorous **3 = rash,** audacious, brazen, foolhardy, headstrong, impudent, reckless
Antonyms *adj* ≠ **strong:** delicate, feeble, fragile, frail, sickly, soft, weak, weedy ≠ **courageous:** faint-hearted, feeble, soft, weak, weedy (*inf.*), wimpish *or* wimpy (*inf.*)

hare (hɛə) *n, pl* **hares** *or* **hare. 1** a solitary mammal which is larger than a rabbit, has longer ears and legs, and lives in a shallow nest (form). **2 run with the hare and hunt with the hounds.** to be on good terms with both sides. **3 start a hare.** to raise a topic for conversation. ◆ *vb* **hares, haring, hared. 4** (*intr; often foll. by off, after*, etc.) *Brit. inf.* to run fast or wildly. [OE *hara*]
▸ **'hare,like** *adj*

hare and hounds *n* (*functioning as sing*) a game in which certain players (**hares**) run across country scattering pieces of paper that the other players (**hounds**) follow in an attempt to catch the hares.

harebell ('hɛə,bel) *n* a N temperate plant having slender stems and leaves, and bell-shaped blue flowers.

harebrained Ⓣ *or* **hairbrained** ('hɛə,breɪnd) *adj* rash, foolish, or badly thought out.

Hare Krishna ('hɑːrɪ 'krɪʃnə) *n* **1** a Hindu sect devoted to a form of Hinduism (**Krishna Consciousness**) based on the worship of the god Krishna. **2** (*pl* **Hare Krishnas**) a member or follower of this sect. [C20: from Hindi, literally: Lord Krishna (vocative): the opening words of a sacred verse often chanted in public by adherents of the movement]

harelip ('hɛə,lɪp) *n* a congenital cleft or fissure in the midline of the upper lip, resembling the cleft upper lip of a hare, often occurring with cleft palate.
▸ **'hare,lipped** *adj*

harem Ⓣ ('hɛərəm, hɑː'riːm) *or* **hareem** (hɑː'riːm) *n* **1** the part of an Oriental house reserved strictly for wives, concubines, etc. **2** a Muslim's wives and concubines collectively. **3** a group of female animals that are the mates of a single male. [C17: from Ar. *harīm* forbidden (place)]

hare's-foot *n* a plant that grows on sandy soils in Europe and NW Asia and has downy heads of white or pink flowers.

haricot ('hærɪkəʊ) *n* a variety of French bean with light-coloured edible seeds, which can be dried and stored. [C17: from F, ?from Amerind]

Harijan ('hʌrɪdʒən) *n* a member of certain classes in India, formerly considered inferior and untouchable. [Hindi, lit.: man of God (so called by Mahatma Gandhi)]

hari-kari (,hærɪ'kɑːrɪ) *n* a non-Japanese variant spelling of **hara-kiri**.

hark Ⓣ (hɑːk) *vb* (*intr; usually imperative*) to listen; pay attention. [OE *heorcnian* to HEARKEN]

hark back Ⓣ *vb* (*intr, adv*) to return to an earlier subject in speech or thought.

harken ('hɑːkən) *vb* a variant spelling (esp. US) of **hearken**.
▸ **'harkener** *n*

harl (hɑːl) *n Angling.* a variant of **herl**.

harlequin ('hɑːlɪkwɪn) *n* **1** (*sometimes cap.*) *Theatre.* a stock comic character originating in the commedia dell'arte; the foppish lover of Columbine in the English harlequinade. He is usually represented in diamond-patterned multicoloured tights, wearing a black mask. **2** a clown or buffoon. ◆ *adj* **3** varied in colour or decoration. [C16: from OF *Herlequin, Hellequin* leader of band of demon horsemen]

harlequinade (,hɑːlɪkwɪ'neɪd) *n* **1** (*sometimes cap.*) *Theatre.* a play in which harlequin has a leading role. **2** buffoonery.

Harley Street ('hɑːlɪ) *n* a street in central London famous for its large number of medical specialists' consulting rooms.

harlot Ⓣ ('hɑːlət) *n* a prostitute. [C13: from OF *herlot* rascal, from ?]
▸ **'harlotry** *n*

harm Ⓣ (hɑːm) *n* **1** physical or mental injury. **2** moral wrongdoing. ◆ *vb* **3** (*tr*) to injure physically, morally, or mentally. [OE *hearm*]

harmattan (hɑː'mætᵊn) *n* a dry dusty wind from the Sahara blowing towards the W African coast. [C17: from native African language *haramata*, ?from Ar. *harām* forbidden thing; see HAREM]

harmful Ⓣ ('hɑːmful) *adj* causing or tending to cause harm; injurious.
▸ **'harmfully** *adv*

harmless Ⓣ ('hɑːmlɪs) *adj* **1** not causing or tending to cause harm. **2** unlikely to annoy or worry people: *a harmless sort of man.*
▸ **'harmlessly** *adv*

harmonic (hɑː'mɒnɪk) *adj* **1** of, producing, or characterized by harmony; harmonious. **2** *Music.* of or belonging to harmony. **3** *Maths.* **3a** capable of expression in the form of sine and cosine functions. **3b** of or relating to numbers whose reciprocals form an arithmetic progression. **4** *Physics.* of or concerned with a harmonic or harmonics. ◆ *n* **5** *Physics, music.* a component of a periodic quantity, such as a musical tone, with a frequency that is an integral multiple of the fundamental frequency. **6** *Music.* (not in technical use) overtone. ◆ See also **harmonics**. [C16: from L *harmonicus* relating to HARMONY]
▸ **har'monically** *adv*

harmonica (hɑː'mɒnɪkə) *n* **1** Also called: **mouth organ.** a small wind instrument in which reeds of graduated lengths set into a metal plate enclosed in a narrow oblong box are made to vibrate by blowing and sucking. **2** See **glass harmonica.** [C18: from L *harmonicus* relating to HARMONY]

harmonic analysis *n* the representation of a periodic function by means of the summation and integration of simple trigonometric functions.

harmonic mean *n* the reciprocal of the arithmetic mean of the reciprocals of a set of specified numbers: the harmonic mean of 2, 3, and 4 is $3/(\frac{1}{2} + \frac{1}{3} + \frac{1}{4}) = 36/13$.

harmonic minor scale *n Music.* a minor scale modified from the natural by the sharpening of the seventh degree.

harmonic motion *n* a periodic motion in which the displacement is symmetrical about a point or a periodic motion that is composed of such motions.

harmonic progression *n* a sequence of numbers whose reciprocals form an arithmetic progression, as $1, \frac{1}{2}, \frac{1}{3}, \ldots$

harmonics (hɑː'mɒnɪks) *n* **1** (*functioning as sing*) the science of musical sounds and their acoustic properties. **2** (*functioning as pl*) the overtones of a fundamental note, as produced by lightly touching the string of a stringed instrument at one of its node points while playing.

harmonic series *n* **1** *Maths.* a series whose terms are in harmonic progression, as in $1 + \frac{1}{2} + \frac{1}{3} + \ldots$ **2** *Acoustics.* the series of tones with frequencies strictly related to one another and to the fundamental tone, as obtained by touching lightly the node points of a string while playing it.

harmonious Ⓣ (hɑː'məʊnɪəs) *adj* **1** (esp. of colours or sounds) fitting together well. **2** having agreement. **3** tuneful or melodious.

harmonist ('hɑːmənɪst) *n* **1** a person skilled in the art and techniques of harmony. **2** a person who combines and collates parallel narratives.

harmonium (hɑː'məʊnɪəm) *n* a musical keyboard instrument in which air from pedal-operated bellows causes the reeds to vibrate. [C19: from F, from *harmonie* HARMONY]

harmonize Ⓣ *or* **harmonise** ('hɑːmə,naɪz) *vb* **harmonizes, harmonizing, harmonized** *or* **harmonises, harmonising, harmonised. 1** to make or become harmonious. **2** (*tr*) *Music.* to provide a harmony for (a tune, etc.). **3** (*intr*) to sing in harmony, as with other singers. **4** to collate parallel narratives.
▸ **,harmoni'zation** *or* **,harmoni'sation** *n*

harmony Ⓣ ('hɑːmənɪ) *n, pl* **harmonies. 1** agreement in action, opinion, feeling, etc. **2** order or congruity of parts to their whole or to one another. **3** agreeable sounds. **4** *Music.* **4a** any combination of notes sounded simultaneously. **4b** the vertically represented structure of a piece of music. Cf. **melody** (sense 1b). **4c** the art or science concerned with combinations of chords. **5** a collation of parallel narratives, esp. of the four Gospels. [C14: from L *harmonia* concord of sounds, from Gk: harmony, from *harmos* a joint]

harness Ⓣ ('hɑːnɪs) *n* **1** an arrangement of straps fitted to a draught animal in order that the animal can be attached to and pull a cart. **2**

THESAURUS

harebrained *adj* = **foolish**, asinine, careless, empty-headed, flighty, giddy, half-baked (*inf.*), harum-scarum, heedless, inane, mindless, rash, reckless, scatterbrained, unstable, unsteady, wild

harem *n* **1** = **women's quarters**, seraglio

hark *vb* = **listen**, attend, give ear, give heed, hear, hearken (*arch.*), mark, notice, pay attention

hark back *vb* = **return**, look back, recall, recollect, regress, remember, revert, think back

harlot *n* = **prostitute**, call girl, fallen woman, hussy, loose woman, pro (*sl.*), scrubber (*Brit. & Austral. sl.*), slag (*Brit. sl.*), slapper (*Brit. sl.*), streetwalker, strumpet, tart (*inf.*), tramp (*sl.*), whore, working girl (*facetious sl.*)

harm *n* **1** = **injury**, abuse, damage, detriment, disservice, hurt, ill, impairment, loss, mischief, misfortune **2** = **sin**, evil, immorality, iniquity, sinfulness, vice, wickedness, wrong ◆ *vb* **3** = **injure**, abuse, blemish, damage, hurt, ill-treat, ill-use, impair, lay a finger on, maltreat, mar, molest, ruin, spoil, wound
Antonyms *n* ≠ **injury:** aid, assistance, benefit, blessing, boon, gain, good, help, improvement, reparation ≠ **sin:** good, goodness, righteousness ◆ *vb* ≠ **injure:** aid, alleviate, ameliorate, assist, benefit, better, cure, heal, help, improve, repair

harmful *adj* = **injurious**, baleful, baneful, damaging, deleterious, destructive, detrimental, disadvantageous, evil, hurtful, maleficent, noxious, pernicious
Antonyms *adj* beneficial, good, harmless, healthy, helpful, innocuous, safe, wholesome

harmless *adj* **1** = **safe**, innocent, nontoxic, not dangerous **2** = **inoffensive**, gentle, innocuous, unobjectionable
Antonyms *adj* ≠ **safe:** dangerous, destructive, harmful, unhealthy, unsafe, unwholesome

harmonious *adj* **1** = **compatible**, agreeable, congruous, consonant, coordinated, correspondent, matching **2** = **friendly**, agreeable, amicable, compatible, concordant, congenial, cordial, *en rapport*, fraternal, in accord, in harmony, in unison, of one mind, sympathetic **3** = **melodious**, concordant, dulcet, euphonic, euphonious, harmonic, harmonizing, mellifluous, musical, sweet-sounding, symphonious (*literary*), tuneful
Antonyms *adj* ≠ **compatible:** contrasting, discordant, incompatible, inconsistent, unlike ≠ **friendly:** discordant, unfriendly ≠ **melodious:** cacophonous, discordant, grating, harsh, unmelodious

harmonize *vb* **1** = **go together**, accord, adapt, agree, arrange, attune, be in unison, be of one mind, blend, chime with, cohere, coordinate, correspond, match, reconcile, suit, tally, tone in with

harmony *n* **1** = **agreement**, accord, amicability, amity, assent, compatibility, concord, conformity, consensus, cooperation, friendship, goodwill, like-mindedness, order, peace, rapport, sympathy, unanimity, understanding, unity **2** = **compatibility**, balance, concord, congruity, consistency, consonance, coordination, correspondence, fitness, suitability, symmetry **4a** = **tunefulness**, euphony, melodiousness, melody, tune, unison
Antonyms *n* ≠ **agreement:** antagonism, conflict, contention, disagreement, dissension, hostility, opposition ≠ **compatibility:** conflict, disagreement, incongruity, inconsistency, unsuitability ≠ **tunefulness:** cacophony

harness *n* **1, 2** = **equipment**, gear, tack, tackle,

something resembling this, esp. for attaching something to the body: *a parachute harness.* **3** *Weaving.* the part of a loom that raises and lowers the warp threads. **4** *Arch.* armour. **5 in harness.** at one's routine work. ◆ *vb (tr)* **6** to put a harness on (a horse). **7** (usually foll. by *to*) to attach (a draught animal) to (a cart, etc.). **8** to control so as to employ the energy or potential power of: *to harness the atom.* **9** to equip with armour. [C13: from OF *harneis* baggage, prob. from ON *hernest* (unattested), from *herr* army + *nest* provisions]
▸**'harnesser** *n*

harness race *n Horse racing.* a trotting or pacing race for horses pulling sulkies.

harp ➊ (hɑːp) *n* **1** a large triangular plucked stringed instrument consisting of a soundboard connected to an upright pillar by means of a curved crossbar from which the strings extend downwards. ◆ *vb (intr)* **2** to play the harp. **3** (foll. by *on* or *upon*) to speak or write in a persistent and tedious manner. [OE *hearpe*]
▸**'harper** *or* **'harpist** *n*

harpoon (hɑː'puːn) *n* **1a** a barbed missile attached to a long cord and hurled or fired from a gun when hunting whales, etc. **1b** *(as modifier): a harpoon gun.* ◆ *vb* **2** *(tr)* to spear with or as if with a harpoon. [C17: prob. from Du. *harpoen,* from OF *harpon* clasp, ? of Scand. origin]
▸**har'pooner** *or* **,harpoon'eer** *n*

harp seal *n* a brownish-grey North Atlantic and Arctic seal, having a dark mark on its back.

harpsichord ('hɑːpsɪ,kɔːd) *n* a horizontally strung stringed keyboard instrument, triangular in shape, with strings plucked by pivoted plectra mounted on jacks. [C17: from NL *harpichordium,* from LL *harpa* HARP + L *chorda* CHORD[1]]
▸**'harpsi,chordist** *n*

harpy ('hɑːpɪ) *n, pl* **harpies.** a cruel grasping woman. [C16: from L *Harpyia,* from Gk *Harpuiai* the Harpies, lit.: snatchers, from *harpazein* to seize]

Harpy ('hɑːpɪ) *n, pl* **Harpies.** *Greek myth.* a ravenous creature with a woman's head and trunk and a bird's wings and claws.

harquebus ('hɑːkwɪbəs) *n, pl* **harquebuses.** a variant spelling of **arquebus.**

harridan ➊ ('hærɪdᵊn) *n* a scolding old woman; nag. [C17: from ?; ? rel. to F *haridelle,* lit.: broken-down horse]

harrier[1] ('hærɪə) *n* **1** a person or thing that harries. **2** a diurnal bird of prey having broad wings and long legs and tail.

harrier[2] ('hærɪə) *n* **1** a smallish breed of hound used originally for hare-hunting. **2** a cross-country runner. [C16: from HARE + -ER[1]; infl. by HARRIER[1]]

Harris Tweed ('hærɪs) *n Trademark.* a loose-woven tweed made in the Outer Hebrides.

harrow ➊ ('hærəʊ) *n* **1** any of various implements used to level the ground, stir the soil, break up clods, destroy weeds, etc., in soil. ◆ *vb (tr)* **2** to draw a harrow over (land). **3** to distress; vex. [C13: from ON]
▸**'harrower** *n* ▸**'harrowing** *adj*

harrumph (hə'rʌmf) *vb (intr) Chiefly US & Canad.* to clear or make the noise of clearing the throat.

harry ➊ ('hærɪ) *vb* **harries, harrying, harried. 1** *(tr)* to harass; worry. **2** to ravage (a town, etc.), esp. in war. [OE *hergian;* rel. to *here* army, ON *herja* to lay waste]

harsh ➊ (hɑːʃ) *adj* **1** rough or grating to the senses. **2** stern, severe, or cruel. [C16: prob. of Scand. origin]
▸**'harshly** *adv* ▸**'harshness** *n*

hart (hɑːt) *n, pl* **harts** *or* **hart.** the male of the deer, esp. the red deer aged five years or more. [OE *heorot*]

hartal (hɑː'tɑːl) *n* (in India) the act of closing shops or suspending work, esp. in political protest. [C20: from Hindi *hartāl,* from *hāt* shop + *tālā* bolt for a door, from Sansk.]

hartebeest ('hɑːtɪ,biːst) *or* **hartbeest** ('hɑːt,biːst) *n* either of two large African antelopes having an elongated muzzle, lyre-shaped horns, and a fawn-coloured coat. [C18: via Afrik. from Du.; see HART, BEAST]

hartshorn ('hɑːts,hɔːn) *n* an obsolete name for **sal volatile.** [OE *heortes horn* hart's horn (formerly a chief source of ammonia)]

hart's-tongue *n* an evergreen Eurasian fern with narrow undivided fronds.

harum-scarum ➊ ('hɛərəm'skɛərəm) *adj, adv* **1** in a reckless way or of a reckless nature. ◆ *n* **2** a person who is impetuous or rash. [C17: ?from *hare* (in obs. sense: harass) + *scare,* var. of STARE]

haruspex (hə'rʌspɛks) *n, pl* **haruspices** (hə'rʌspɪ,siːz). (in ancient Rome) a priest who practised divination, esp. by examining the entrails of animals. [C16: from L, prob. from *hīra* gut + *specere* to look]
▸**haruspicy** (hə'rʌspɪsɪ) *n*

harvest ➊ ('hɑːvɪst) *n* **1** the gathering of a ripened crop. **2** the crop itself. **3** the season for gathering crops. **4** the product of an effort, action, etc.: *a harvest of love.* ◆ *vb* **5** to gather (a ripened crop) from (the place where it has been growing). **6** *(tr)* to receive (consequences). [OE *hærfest*]
▸**'harvesting** *n*

harvester ('hɑːvɪstə) *n* **1** a person who harvests. **2** a harvesting machine, esp. a combine harvester.

harvest home *n* **1** the bringing in of the harvest. **2** *Chiefly Brit.* a harvest supper.

harvestman ('hɑːvɪstmən) *n, pl* **harvestmen. 1** a person engaged in harvesting. **2** Also called (US and Canad.): **daddy-longlegs.** an arachnid having a small rounded body and very long thin legs.

harvest moon *n* the full moon occurring nearest to the autumnal equinox.

harvest mouse *n* a very small reddish-brown Eurasian mouse inhabiting cornfields, hedgerows, etc.

has (hæz) *vb* (used with *he, she, it,* or a singular noun) a form of the present tense (indicative mood) of **have.**

has-been *n Inf.* a person or thing that is no longer popular, successful, effective, etc.

hash[1] ➊ (hæʃ) *n* **1** a dish of diced cooked meat, vegetables, etc., reheated in a sauce. **2** a reuse or rework of old material. **3 make a hash of.** *Inf.* to mess up or destroy. **4 settle someone's hash.** *Inf.* to subdue or silence someone. ◆ *vb (tr)* **5** to chop into small pieces. **6** to mess up. [C17: from OF *hacher* to chop up, from *hache* HATCHET]

hash[2] (hæʃ) *n Sl.* short for **hashish.**

hashish ('hæʃiːʃ, -ɪʃ) *or* **hasheesh** *n* a resinous extract of the dried flower tops of the female hemp plant, used as a hallucinogenic. See also **cannabis.** [C16: from Ar. *hashīsh* hemp]

haslet ('hæzlɪt) *or* **harslet** *n* a loaf of cooked minced pig's offal, eaten cold. [C14: from OF *hastelet* piece of spit-roasted meat, from *haste* spit, of Gmc origin]

hasn't ('hæzᵊnt) *contraction of* has not.

hasp (hɑːsp) *n* **1** a metal fastening consisting of a hinged strap with a slot that fits over a staple and is secured by a pin, bolt, or padlock. ◆ *vb* **2** *(tr)* to secure (a door, window, etc.) with a hasp. [OE *hæpse*]

Hassid ('hæsɪd) *n* a variant spelling of **Chassid.**

hassium ('hæsɪəm) *n* a synthetic element produced in small quantities by high-energy ion bombardment. Symbol: Hs; atomic no. 108. Former name: **hahnium.** [C20: from L, from *Hesse,* German state where it was discovered]

hassle ➊ ('hæsᵊl) *Inf.* ◆ *n* **1** a great deal of trouble. **2** a prolonged argument. ◆ *vb* **hassles, hassling, hassled. 3** *(tr)* to cause annoyance or trouble to (someone); harass. **4** *(intr)* to quarrel or wrangle. [C20: from ?]

hassock ('hæsək) *n* **1** a firm upholstered cushion used for kneeling on, esp. in church. **2** a thick clump of grass. [OE *hassuc* matted grass]

hast (hæst) *vb Arch. or dialect.* (used with the pronoun *thou*) a singular form of the present tense (indicative mood) of **have.**

hastate ('hæsteɪt) *adj* (of a leaf) having a pointed tip and two outward-pointing lobes at the base. [C18: from L *hastātus,* from *hasta* spear]

haste ➊ (heɪst) *n* **1** speed, esp. in an action. **2** the act of hurrying in a

THESAURUS

trappings **5 in harness = working,** active, at work, busy, in action ◆ *vb* **6 = put in harness,** saddle **7 = yoke,** couple, hitch up **8 = exploit,** apply, channel, control, employ, make productive, mobilize, render useful, turn to account, utilize

harp *vb* **3** *with* **on** *or* **upon = go on,** dwell on, labour, press, reiterate, renew, repeat, rub it in

harridan *n* **= shrew,** ballbreaker (*sl.*), battleaxe (*inf.*), nag, scold, tartar, termagant, virago, witch

harried *adj* **1 = harassed,** agitated, anxious, beset, bothered, distressed, hard-pressed, hassled (*inf.*), plagued, tormented, troubled, worried

harrow *vb* **3 = distress,** agonize, harass, perturb, rack, tear, torment, torture, vex, wound

harrowing *adj* **3 = distressing,** agonizing, alarming, chilling, disturbing, excruciating, frightening, gut-wrenching, heartbreaking, heart-rending, nerve-racking, painful, racking, scaring, terrifying, tormenting, traumatic

harry *vb* **1 = pester,** annoy, badger, bedevil, be on one's back, bother, breathe down someone's neck, disturb, get in one's hair (*inf.*), harass, hassle (*inf.*), molest, persecute, plague, tease, torment, trouble, vex, worry **2 = ravage,** despoil, devastate, pillage, plunder, raid, rob, sack

harsh *adj* **1 = rough,** coarse, croaking, discordant, dissonant, grating, guttural, jarring, rasping, raucous, strident, unmelodious **2 = severe,** abusive, austere, bitter, bleak, brutal, comfortless, cruel, Draconian, drastic, grim, hard, pitiless, punitive, relentless, ruthless, sharp, Spartan, stern, stringent, tough, unfeeling, unkind, unpleasant, unrelenting

Antonyms *adj* ≠ **raucous:** harmonious, mellifluous, smooth, soft, soothing, sweet ≠ **severe:** agreeable, gentle, kind, loving, merciful, mild, pleasant, sweet

harshly *adv* **2 = severely,** brutally, cruelly, grimly, roughly, sharply, sternly, strictly

harshness *n* **2 = severity,** acerbity, acrimony, asperity, austerity, bitterness, brutality, coarseness, hardness, ill-temper, rigour, roughness, sourness, sternness

harum-scarum *adj* **1 = reckless,** careless, erratic, giddy, haphazard, harebrained, hasty, ill-considered, impetuous, imprudent, irresponsible, precipitate, rash, scatterbrained, scatty (*Brit. inf.*), wild

harvest *n* **1, 3 = gathering,** harvesting, harvest-time, reaping **2 = crop,** produce, yield **4 = product,** consequence, effect, fruition, result, return ◆ *vb* **5 = gather,** mow, pick, pluck, reap

hash[1] *n* **3 make a hash of** *Informal* **= mess up,** bodge, botch, bungle, cock up (*Brit. sl.*), jumble, make a nonsense of (*inf.*), make a pig's ear of (*inf.*), mishandle, mismanage, mix, muddle

hassle *Informal n* **1 = trouble,** bother, difficulty, grief (*inf.*), inconvenience, problem, struggle, trial, upset **2 = argument,** altercation, bickering, disagreement, dispute, fight, quarrel, row, squabble, tussle, wrangle ◆ *vb* **3 = bother,** annoy, badger, be on one's back (*sl.*), breath down someone's neck, bug (*inf.*), get in one's hair (*inf.*), get on one's nerves (*inf.*), harass, harry, hound, pester

hassled *adj* **3 = bothered,** browbeaten, hot and bothered, hounded, hunted, pressured, stressed, under pressure, uptight, worried

haste *n* **1 = speed,** alacrity, briskness, celerity,

careless manner. **3** a necessity for hurrying; urgency. **4 make haste.** to hurry. ◆ *vb* **hastes, hasting, hasted. 5** a poetic word for **hasten.** [C14: from OF *haste,* of Gmc origin]

hasten ⓣ ('heɪsᵊn) *vb* **1** (*may take an infinitive*) to hurry or cause to hurry; rush. **2** (*tr*) to be anxious (to say something).
▸**'hastener** *n*

hasty ⓣ ('heɪstɪ) *adj* **hastier, hastiest. 1** rapid; swift; quick. **2** excessively or rashly quick. **3** short-tempered. **4** showing irritation or anger: *hasty words.*
▸**'hastily** *adv* ▸**'hastiness** *n*

hat (hæt) *n* **1** a head covering, esp. one with a brim and a shaped crown. **2** *Inf.* a role or capacity. **3 I'll eat my hat.** *Inf.* I will be greatly surprised if (something that proves me wrong) happens. **4 keep (something) under one's hat.** to keep (something) secret. **5 pass** (*or* **send**) **the hat round.** to collect money, as for a cause. **6 take off one's hat to.** to admire or congratulate. **7 talk through one's hat. 7a** to talk foolishly. **7b** to deceive or bluff. ◆ *vb* **hats, hatting, hatted. 8** (*tr*) to supply (a person, etc.) with a hat or put a hat on (someone). [OE *hætt*]
▸**'hatless** *adj*

hatband ('hætˌbænd) *n* a band or ribbon around the base of the crown of a hat.

hatbox ('hætˌbɒks) *n* a box or case for a hat.

hatch[1] ⓣ (hætʃ) *vb* **1** to cause (the young of various animals, esp. birds) to emerge from the egg or (of young birds, etc.) to emerge from the egg. **2** to cause (eggs) to break and release the fully developed young or (of eggs) to break and release the young animal within. **3** (*tr*) to contrive or devise (a scheme, plot, etc.). ◆ *n* **4** the act or process of hatching. **5** a group of newly hatched animals. [C13: of Gmc origin]

hatch[2] (hætʃ) *n* **1** a covering for a hatchway. **2a** short for **hatchway. 2b** a door in an aircraft or spacecraft. **3** Also called: **serving hatch.** an opening in a wall separating a kitchen from a dining area. **4** the lower half of a divided door. **5** a sluice in a dam, dyke, or weir. **6 down the hatch.** *Sl.* (used as a toast) drink up! **7 under hatches. 7a** below decks. **7b** out of sight. **7c** dead. [OE *hæcc*]

hatch[3] (hætʃ) *vb Drawing, engraving, etc.* to mark (a figure, etc.) with fine parallel or crossed lines to indicate shading. [C15: from OF *hacher* to chop, from *hache* HATCHET]
▸**'hatching** *n*

hatch[4] (hætʃ) *n Inf.* short for **hatchback.**

hatchback ('hætʃˌbæk) *n* **1** a sloping rear end of a car having a single door that is lifted to open. **2** a car having such a rear end.

hatchery ('hætʃərɪ) *n, pl* **hatcheries.** a place where eggs are hatched under artificial conditions.

hatchet ⓣ ('hætʃɪt) *n* **1** a short axe used for chopping wood, etc. **2** a tomahawk. **3** (*modifier*) of narrow dimensions and sharp features: *a hatchet face.* **4 bury the hatchet.** to cease hostilities and become reconciled. [C14: from OF *hachette,* from *hache* axe, of Gmc origin]

hatchet job *n Inf.* a malicious or devastating verbal or written attack.

hatchet man ⓣ *n Inf.* **1** a person carrying out unpleasant assignments for an employer or superior. **2** a severe or malicious critic.

hatchling ('hætʃlɪŋ) *n* a young animal that has newly emerged from the egg. [C19: from HATCH[1] + -LING[1]]

hatchment ('hætʃmənt) *n Heraldry.* a diamond-shaped tablet displaying the coat of arms of a dead person. [C16: changed from earlier use of *achievement* in this sense]

hatchway ('hætʃˌweɪ) *n* **1** an opening in the deck of a vessel to provide access below. **2** a similar opening in a wall, floor, ceiling, or roof.

hate ⓣ (heɪt) *vb* **hates, hating, hated. 1** to dislike (something) intensely; detest. **2** (*intr*) to be unwilling (to be or do something). ◆ *n* **3** intense dislike. **4** *Inf.* a person or thing that is hated (esp. in **pet hate**). **5** (*modifier*) expressing or arousing feelings of hatred: *hate mail.* [OE *hatian*]
▸**'hateable** *or* **'hatable** *adj* ▸**'hater** *n*

hateful ⓣ ('heɪtfʊl) *adj* **1** causing or deserving hate; loathsome; detestable. **2** *Arch.* full of hate.
▸**'hatefully** *adv* ▸**'hatefulness** *n*

hath (hæθ) *vb Arch. or dialect.* (used with the pronouns *he, she,* or *it* or a singular noun) a form of the present tense (indicative mood) of **have.**

hatred ⓣ ('heɪtrɪd) *n* intense dislike; enmity.

hat stand *or esp. US* **hat tree** *n* a pole equipped with hooks for hanging up hats, etc.

hatter ('hætə) *n* **1** a person who makes and sells hats. **2 mad as a hatter.** eccentric.

hat trick *n* **1** *Cricket.* the achievement of a bowler in taking three wickets with three successive balls. **2** any achievement of three successive points, victories, etc.

hauberk ('hɔːbɜːk) *n* a long coat of mail, often sleeveless. [C13: from OF *hauberc,* of Gmc origin; cf. OHG *halsberc,* OE *healsbeorg,* from *heals* neck + *beorg* protection]

haughty ⓣ ('hɔːtɪ) *adj* **haughtier, haughtiest.** having or showing arrogance. [C16: from OF *haut* lofty, from L *altus* high]
▸**'haughtily** *adv* ▸**'haughtiness** *n*

haul ⓣ (hɔːl) *vb* **1** to drag (something) with effort. **2** (*tr*) to transport, as in a lorry. **3** *Naut.* to alter the course of (a vessel), esp. so as to sail closer to the wind. **4** (*intr*) *Naut.* (of the wind) to blow from a direction nearer the bow. ◆ *n* **5** the act of dragging with effort. **6** (esp. of fish) the amount caught at a single time. **7** something that is hauled. **8** the goods obtained from a robbery. **9** a distance of hauling or travelling. **10** the amount of a contraband seizure: *arms haul, drugs haul.* [C16: from OF *haler,* of Gmc origin]
▸**'hauler** *n*

haulage ('hɔːlɪdʒ) *n* **1** the act or labour of hauling. **2** a rate or charge levied for the transportation of goods, esp. by rail.

haulier ('hɔːljə) *n* **1** *Brit.* a person or firm that transports goods by road. **2** a mine worker who conveys coal from the workings to the foot of the shaft.

haulm *or* **halm** (hɔːm) *n* **1** the stalks of beans, peas, potatoes, grasses, etc., collectively. **2** a single stem of such a plant. [OE *healm*]

haul up *vb* (*adv*) **1** (*tr*) *Inf.* to call to account or criticize. **2** *Naut.* to sail (a vessel) closer to the wind.

haunch (hɔːntʃ) *n* **1** the human hip or fleshy hindquarter of an animal. **2** the leg and loin of an animal, used for food. **3** *Archit.* the part of an arch between the impost and apex. [C13: from OF *hanche;* rel. to Sp., It. *anca,* of Gmc origin]

haunt ⓣ (hɔːnt) *vb* **1** to visit (a person or place) in the form of a ghost. **2** (*tr*) to recur to (the memory, thoughts, etc.): *he was haunted by the fear of insanity.* **3** to visit (a place) frequently. **4** to associate with (someone) frequently. ◆ *n* **5** (*often pl*) a place visited frequently. **6** a place to which animals habitually resort for food, drink, shelter, etc. [C13: from OF *hanter,* of Gmc origin]

haunted ⓣ ('hɔːntɪd) *adj* **1** frequented or visited by ghosts. **2** (*postpositive*) obsessed or worried.

THESAURUS

dispatch, expedition, fleetness, nimbleness, promptitude, quickness, rapidity, rapidness, swiftness, urgency, velocity **2** = **rush**, bustle, hastiness, helter-skelter, hurry, hustle, impetuosity, precipitateness, rashness, recklessness
Antonyms *n* ≠ **speed:** slowness, sluggishness ≠ **rush:** calmness, care, delay, deliberation, leisureliness, sureness

hasten *vb* **1** = **hurry (up)**, accelerate, advance, barrel (along) (*inf., chiefly US & Canad.*), beetle, bolt, burn rubber (*inf.*), dash, dispatch, expedite, fly, get one's skates on (*inf.*), haste, make haste, precipitate, press, push forward, quicken, race, run, rush, scurry, scuttle, speed (up), sprint, step on it (*inf.*), step up (*inf.*), tear (along), urge
Antonyms *vb* ≠ **hurry (up):** crawl, creep, dawdle, decelerate, delay, hinder, impede, move slowly, retard, slow, slow down

hastily *adv* **1** = **quickly**, apace, double-quick, fast, hotfoot, posthaste, promptly, pronto (*inf.*), rapidly, speedily, straightaway **2** = **hurriedly**, heedlessly, impetuously, impulsively, on the spur of the moment, precipitately, rashly, recklessly, too quickly

hasty *adj* **1** = **speedy**, brief, brisk, cursory, eager, expeditious, fast, fleeting, hurried, passing, perfunctory, prompt, rapid, rushed, short, superficial, swift, urgent **2** = **rash**, foolhardy, headlong, heedless, impetuous, impulsive, indiscreet, precipitate, reckless, thoughtless, unduly quick **3** = **impatient**, brusque, excited, fiery, hot-headed, hot-tempered, irascible, irritable, passionate, quick-tempered, snappy
Antonyms *adj* ≠ **speedy:** leisurely, long, protracted ≠ **rash:** careful, cautious, detailed, thorough, thoughtful ≠ **impatient:** dispassionate

hatch[1] *vb* **1, 2** = **incubate**, breed, bring forth, brood **3** = **devise**, conceive, concoct, contrive, cook up, design, dream up (*inf.*), manufacture, plan, plot, project, scheme, think up, trump up

hatchet *n* **1** = **axe**, cleaver, machete **2** = **tomahawk**

hatchet man *n Informal* **2** = **detractor**, defamer, smear campaigner, traducer

hate *vb* **1** = **detest**, abhor, abominate, be hostile to, be repelled by, be sick of, despise, dislike, execrate, have an aversion to, loathe, recoil from **2** = **be unwilling**, be loath, be reluctant, be sorry, dislike, feel disinclined, have no stomach for, shrink from ◆ *n* **3** = **dislike**, abhorrence, abomination, animosity, animus, antagonism, antipathy, aversion, detestation, enmity, execration, hatred, hostility, loathing, odium
Antonyms *vb* ≠ **detest:** be fond of, cherish, dote on, enjoy, esteem, fancy, like, love, relish, treasure, wish ◆ *n* ≠ **dislike:** affection, amity, devotion, fondness, goodwill, liking, love

hateful *adj* **1** = **despicable**, abhorrent, abominable, detestable, disgusting, execrable, forbidding, foul, heinous, horrible, loathsome, obnoxious, obscene, odious, offensive, repellent, repugnant, repulsive, revolting, vile
Antonyms *adj* attractive, beautiful, charming, desirable, good, likable *or* likeable, lovable, pleasant, wonderful

hatred *n* = **dislike**, abomination, animosity, animus, antagonism, antipathy, aversion, detestation, enmity, execration, hate, ill will, odium, repugnance, revulsion
Antonyms *n* affection, amity, attachment, devotion, fondness, friendliness, goodwill, liking, love

haughtiness *n* = **pride**, airs, aloofness, arrogance, conceit, contempt, contemptuousness, disdain, hauteur, insolence, loftiness, pomposity, snobbishness, superciliousness

haughty *adj* = **proud**, arrogant, assuming, conceited, contemptuous, disdainful, high, high and mighty (*inf.*), hoity-toity (*inf.*), imperious, lofty, on one's high horse (*inf.*), overweening, scornful, snobbish, snooty (*inf.*), stuck-up (*inf.*), supercilious, uppish (*Brit. inf.*)
Antonyms *adj* humble, meek, mild, modest, self-effacing, subservient, wimpish *or* wimpy (*inf.*)

haul *vb* **1** = **drag**, draw, hale, heave, lug, pull, tow, trail, tug **2** = **transport**, carry, cart, convey, hump (*Brit. sl.*), move ◆ *n* **5** = **drag**, heave, pull, tug **10** = **yield**, booty, catch, find, gain, harvest, loot, spoils, takings

haunt *vb* **1** = **visit**, walk **2** = **plague**, beset, come back, obsess, possess, prey on, recur, stay with, torment, trouble, weigh on **3** = **frequent**, hang around *or* about, repair, resort, visit ◆ *n* **5** = **meeting place**, den, gathering place, hangout (*inf.*), rendezvous, resort, stamping ground

haunted *adj* **1** = **possessed**, cursed, eerie, ghostly, jinxed, spooky (*inf.*) **2** = **preoccupied**,

DICTIONARY

haunting Ⓣ (ˈhɔːntɪŋ) *adj* **1** (of memories) poignant or persistent. **2** poignantly sentimental; eerily evocative. ▸ˈ**hauntingly** *adv*

Hausa (ˈhaʊsə) *n* **1** (*pl* **Hausas** *or* **Hausa**) a member of a Negroid people of W Africa, living chiefly in N Nigeria. **2** the language of this people, widely used as a trading language throughout W Africa.

hausfrau (ˈhaʊsˌfraʊ) *n* a German housewife. [G, from *Haus* house + *Frau* woman, wife]

hautboy (ˈəʊbɔɪ) *n* **1** a strawberry with large fruit. **2** an archaic word for **oboe.** [C16: from F *hautbois,* from *haut* high + *bois* wood, of Gmc origin]

haute couture *French.* (ot kutyr) *n* high fashion. [lit.: high dressmaking]

haute cuisine *French.* (ot kwizin) *n* high-class cooking. [lit.: high cookery]

haute école *French.* (ot ekɔl) *n* the classical art of riding. [lit.: high school]

hauteur Ⓣ (əʊˈtɜː) *n* pride; haughtiness. [C17: from F, from *haut* high; see HAUGHTY]

haut monde *French.* (o mɔ̃d) *n* high society. [lit.: high world]

Havana cigar (həˈvænə) *n* any of various cigars manufactured in Cuba, known esp. for their high quality. Also: **Havana.**

have Ⓣ (hæv) *vb* **has, having, had.** (*mainly tr*) **1** to be in possession of; own: *he has two cars.* **2** to possess as a quality or attribute: *he has dark hair.* **3** to receive, take, or obtain: *she had a present; have a look.* **4** to hold in the mind: *to have an idea.* **5** to possess a knowledge of: *I have no German.* **6** to experience: *to have a shock.* **7** to suffer from: *to have a cold.* **8** to gain control of or advantage over: *you have me on that point.* **9** (*usually passive*) *Sl.* to cheat or outwit: *he was had by that dishonest salesman.* **10** (foll. by *on*) to exhibit (mercy, etc., towards). **11** to take part in: *to have a conversation.* **12** to arrange or hold: *to have a party.* **13** to cause, compel, or require to (be, do, or be done): *have my shoes mended.* **14** (takes an infinitive with *to*) used as an auxiliary to express compulsion or necessity: *I had to run quickly to escape him.* **15** to eat, drink, or partake of. **16** *Taboo sl.* to have sexual intercourse with. **17** (*used with a negative*) to tolerate or allow: *I won't have all this noise.* **18** to state or assert: *rumour has it that they will marry.* **19** to place: *I'll have the sofa in this room.* **20** to receive as a guest: *to have people to stay.* **21** to be pregnant with or bear (offspring). **22** (*takes a past participle*) used as an auxiliary to form compound tenses expressing completed action: *I have gone; I had gone.* **23 had rather** *or* **sooner.** to consider preferable that: *I had rather you left at once.* **24 have had it.** *Inf.* **24a** to be exhausted, defeated, or killed. **24b** to have lost one's last chance. **24c** to become unfashionable. **25 have it away** (*or* **off**). *Taboo, Brit. sl.* to have sexual intercourse. **26 have it so good.** to have so many material benefits. **27 have to do with.** **27a** to have dealings with. **27b** to be of relevance to. **28 let (someone) have it.** *Sl.* to launch an attack on (someone). ◆ *n* **29** (*usually pl*) *Inf.* a person or group in possession of wealth, security, etc.: *the haves and the have-nots.* ◆ See also **have at, have on,** etc. [OE *habban*]

have-a-go *adj Inf.* (of members of the public at the scene of a crime) intervening physically in an attempt to catch or thwart a criminal, esp. one who is armed: *a have-a-go pensioner.*

have at *vb* (*intr, prep*) *Arch.* to make an opening attack on, esp. in fencing.

havelock (ˈhævlɒk) *n* a light-coloured cover for a service cap with a flap extending over the back of the neck to protect the head and neck from the sun. [C19: after Sir H. *Havelock* (1795–1857), E general in India]

haven Ⓣ (ˈheɪvᵊn) *n* **1** a harbour or other sheltered place for shipping. **2** a place of safety; shelter. ◆ *vb* **3** (*tr*) to shelter as in a haven. [OE *hæfen,* from ON *höfn*]

have-not *n* (*usually pl*) a person or group in possession of relatively little material wealth.

haven't (ˈhævᵊnt) *contraction of* have not.

have on Ⓣ *vb* (*tr*) **1** (*usually adv*) to wear. **2** (*usually adv*) to have a commitment: *what does your boss have on this afternoon?* **3** (*adv*) *Inf.* to trick or tease (a person). **4** (*prep*) to have available (information, esp. when incriminating) about (a person).

have out *vb* (*tr, adv*) **1** to settle (a matter) or come to (a final decision), esp. by fighting or by frank discussion (often in **have it out**). **2** to have extracted or removed.

haver (ˈheɪvə) *vb* (*intr*) **1** *Scot. & N English dialect.* to babble; talk nonsense. **2** to dither. ◆ *n* **3** (*usually pl*) *Scot.* nonsense. [C18: from ?]

haversack (ˈhævəˌsæk) *n* a canvas bag for provisions or equipment, carried on the back or shoulder. [C18: from F *havresac,* from G *Habersack* oat bag, from OHG *habaro* oats + *Sack* SACK[1]]

haversine (ˈhævəˌsaɪn) *n* half the value of the versed sine. [C19: combination of *half + versed + sine*[1]]

have up *vb* (*tr, adv; usually passive*) to cause to appear for trial: *he was had up for breaking and entering.*

havildar (ˈhævɪlˌdɑː) *n* a noncommissioned officer in the Indian army, equivalent in rank to sergeant. [C17: from Hindi, from Persian *hawāldār* one in charge]

havoc Ⓣ (ˈhævək) *n* **1** destruction; devastation; ruin. **2** *Inf.* confusion; chaos. **3 cry havoc.** *Arch.* to give the signal for pillage and destruction. **4 play havoc.** (often foll. by *with*) to cause a great deal of damage, distress, or confusion (to). [C15: from OF *havot* pillage, prob. of Gmc origin]

haw[1] (hɔː) *n* **1** the fruit of the hawthorn. **2** another name for **hawthorn.** [OE *haga,* identical with *haga* hedge]

haw[2] (hɔː) *n, interj* **1** an inarticulate utterance, as of hesitation, embarrassment, etc.; hem. ◆ *vb* **2** (*intr*) to make this sound. [C17: imit.]

haw[3] (hɔː) *n* the nictitating membrane of a horse or other domestic animal. [C15: from ?]

Hawaiian (həˈwaɪən) *adj* **1** of or relating to Hawaii, a state of the US consisting of over 20 islands and atolls in the central Pacific, its people, or their language. ◆ *n* **2** a native or inhabitant of Hawaii. **3** a language of Hawaii belonging to the Malayo-Polynesian family.

hawfinch (ˈhɔːˌfɪntʃ) *n* an uncommon European finch having a very stout bill.

hawk[1] (hɔːk) *n* **1** any of various diurnal birds of prey of the family Accipitridae, typically having short rounded wings and a long tail. **2** a person who advocates or supports war or warlike policies. Cf. **dove** (sense 2). **3** a ruthless or rapacious person. ◆ *vb* **4** (*intr*) to hunt with falcons, hawks, etc. **5** (*intr*) (of falcons or hawks) to fly in quest of prey. **6** to pursue or attack on the wing, as a hawk. [OE *hafoc*] ▸ˈ**hawking** *n* ▸ˈ**hawkish** *adj* ▸ˈ**hawkˌlike** *adj*

hawk[2] Ⓣ (hɔːk) *vb* **1** to offer (goods) for sale, as in the street. **2** (*tr;* often foll. by *about*) to spread (news, gossip, etc.). [C16: back formation from HAWKER[1]]

hawk[3] (hɔːk) *vb* **1** (*intr*) to clear the throat noisily. **2** (*tr*) to force (phlegm, etc.) up from the throat. [C16: imit.]

hawk[4] (hɔːk) *n* a small square board with a handle underneath, for carrying wet mortar. Also called: **mortarboard.** [from ?]

hawker[1] Ⓣ (ˈhɔːkə) *n* a person who travels from place to place selling goods. [C16: prob. from MLow G *hōker,* from *hōken* to peddle; see HUCKSTER]

hawker[2] (ˈhɔːkə) *n* a person who hunts with hawks, falcons, etc. [OE *hafecere*]

hawk-eyed Ⓣ *adj* **1** having extremely keen sight. **2** vigilant, watchful, or observant.

hawk moth *n* any of various moths having long narrow wings and powerful flight, with the ability to hover over flowers when feeding from the nectar.

hawksbill turtle *or* **hawksbill** (ˈhɔːksˌbɪl) *n* a small tropical turtle with a hooked beaklike mouth: a source of tortoiseshell.

hawkweed (ˈhɔːkˌwiːd) *n* a hairy plant with clusters of dandelion-like flowers.

hawse (hɔːz) *n Naut.* **1** the part of the bows of a vessel where the hawseholes are. **2** short for **hawsehole** or **hawsepipe.** **3** the distance from the bow of an anchored vessel to the anchor. **4** the arrangement of port and starboard anchor ropes when a vessel is riding on both anchors. [C14: from earlier *halse,* prob. from ON *háls* neck, ship's bow]

hawsehole (ˈhɔːzˌhəʊl) *n Naut.* one of the holes in the upper part of the bows of a vessel through which the anchor ropes pass.

hawsepipe (ˈhɔːzˌpaɪp) *n Naut.* a strong metal pipe through which an anchor rope passes.

hawser (ˈhɔːzə) *n Naut.* a large heavy rope. [C14: from Anglo-F *hauceour,* from OF *haucier* to hoist, ult. from L *altus* high]

hawthorn (ˈhɔːˌθɔːn) *n* any of various thorny trees or shrubs of a N temperate genus, having white or pink flowers and reddish fruits (haws). Also called (in Britain): **may, may tree, mayflower.** [OE *haguthorn,* from *haga* hedge + *thorn* thorn]

hay (heɪ) *n* **1a** grass, clover, etc., cut and dried as fodder. **1b** (*in combina-*

THESAURUS

obsessed, plagued, tormented, troubled, worried

haunting *adj* **1, 2 = evocative,** disturbing, eerie, indelible, nostalgic, persistent, poignant, recurrent, recurring, unforgettable

hauteur *n* **= haughtiness,** affectedness, airs, arrogance, contempt, dignity, disdain, loftiness, pride, snobbishness, stateliness, superciliousness

have *vb* **1, 2 = possess,** hold, keep, obtain, occupy, own, retain **3 = receive,** accept, acquire, gain, get, obtain, procure, secure, take **6 = experience,** endure, enjoy, feel, meet with, suffer, sustain, undergo **9** *Slang* **= cheat,** deceive, dupe, fool, outwit, stiff (*sl.*), swindle, take in (*inf.*), trick **14 = be obliged,** be bound, be compelled, be forced, have got to, must, ought, should **17 = put up with** (*inf.*), allow, consider, entertain, permit, think about, tolerate **21 = give birth to,** bear, beget, bring forth, bring into the world, deliver **24 have had it** *Informal* **a = be exhausted,** be defeated, be finished, be pooped (*US sl.*)

haven *n* **1 = harbour,** anchorage, port, roads (*Nautical*) **2 = sanctuary,** asylum, refuge, retreat, sanctum, shelter

have on *vb* **1 = wear,** be clothed in, be dressed in **2 = have planned,** be committed to, be engaged to, have on the agenda **3** *Informal* **= tease,** deceive, kid (*inf.*), play a joke on, pull someone's leg, take the mickey, trick, wind up (*Brit. sl.*)

havoc *n* **1 = devastation,** carnage, damage, desolation, despoliation, destruction, rack and ruin, ravages, ruin, slaughter, waste, wreck **2** *Informal* **= disorder,** chaos, confusion, disruption, mayhem, shambles **4 play havoc (with) = wreck,** bring into chaos, confuse, convulse, demolish, destroy, devastate, disorganize, disrupt

hawk[2] *vb* **1 = peddle,** bark (*inf.*), cry, market, sell, tout (*inf.*), vend **2** *often with* **about = spread,** bandy about (*inf.*), bruit about, buzz, noise abroad, put about, rumour

hawker *n*[1] **= pedlar,** barrow boy (*Brit.*), cheap-jack (*inf.*), crier, huckster, vendor

hawk-eyed *adj* **1 = sharp-eyed,** gimlet-eyed, keen-sighted, lynx-eyed **2 = vigilant,** Argus-eyed, having eyes in the back of one's head (*inf.*), observant, perceptive *tion): a hayfield.* **2 hit the hay.** *Sl.* to go to bed. **3 make hay of.** to throw into confusion. **4 make hay while the sun shines.** to take full advantage of an opportunity. **5 roll in the hay.** *Inf.* sexual intercourse or heavy petting. ◆ *vb* **6** to cut, dry, and store (grass, etc.) as fodder. [OE *hieg*]

haybox ('heɪˌbɒks) *n* an airtight box full of hay used for cooking preheated food by retained heat.

haycock ('heɪˌkɒk) *n* a small cone-shaped pile of hay left in the field until dry.

hay fever *n* an allergic reaction to pollen, dust, etc., characterized by sneezing, runny nose, and watery eyes due to inflammation of the mucous membranes of the eyes and nose.

haymaker ('heɪˌmeɪkə) *n* **1** a person who helps to cut, turn, or carry hay. **2** either of two machines, one designed to crush stems of hay, the other to break and bend them, in order to cause more rapid and even drying. **3** *Boxing sl.* a wild swinging punch.
▸ **'hayˌmaking** *adj, n*

haymow ('heɪˌmaʊ) *n* **1** a part of a barn where hay is stored. **2** a quantity of hay stored.

hayseed ('heɪˌsiːd) *n* **1** seeds or fragments of grass or straw. **2** *US & Canad. inf., derog.* a yokel.

haystack ('heɪˌstæk) *or* **hayrick** *n* a large pile of hay, esp. one built in the open air and covered with thatch.

haywire ❶ ('heɪˌwaɪə) *adj (postpositive) Inf.* **1** (of things) not functioning properly. **2** (of people) erratic or crazy. [C20: from the disorderly tangle of wire removed from bales of hay]

hazard ❶ ('hæzəd) *n* **1** exposure or vulnerability to injury, loss, etc. **2 at hazard.** at risk; in danger. **3** a thing likely to cause injury, etc. **4** *Golf.* an obstacle such as a bunker, a road, rough, water, etc. **5** chance; accident. **6** a gambling game played with two dice. **7** *Real Tennis.* **7a** the receiver's side of the court. **7b** one of the winning openings. **8** *Billiards.* a scoring stroke made either when a ball other than the striker's is pocketed (**winning hazard**) or the striker's cue ball itself (**losing hazard**). ◆ *vb (tr)* **9** to risk. **10** to venture (an opinion, guess, etc.). **11** to expose to danger. [C13: from OF *hasard,* from Ar. *az-zahr* the die]

hazard lights *pl n* the indicator lights of a motor vehicle when flashing simultaneously to indicate that the vehicle is stationary and temporarily obstructing the traffic. Also called: **hazard warning lights, hazards.**

hazardous ❶ ('hæzədəs) *adj* **1** involving great risk. **2** depending on chance.
▸ **'hazardously** *adv* ▸ **'hazardousness** *n*

hazard warning device *n* an appliance fitted to a motor vehicle that operates the hazard lights.

haze[1] ❶ (heɪz) *n* **1** *Meteorol.* reduced visibility in the air as a result of condensed water vapour, dust, etc., in the atmosphere. **2** obscurity of perception, feeling, etc. ◆ *vb* **hazes, hazing, hazed. 3** (when *intr,* often foll. by *over*) to make or become hazy. [C18: back formation from HAZY]

haze[2] (heɪz) *vb* **hazes, hazing, hazed.** *(tr)* **1** *Chiefly US & Canad.* to subject (fellow students) to ridicule or abuse. **2** *Naut.* to harass with humiliating tasks. [C17: from ?]

hazel ('heɪzᵊl) *n* **1** Also called: **cob.** any of several shrubs of a N temperate genus, having edible rounded nuts. **2** the wood of any of these trees. **3** short for **hazelnut. 4a** a light yellowish-brown colour. **4b** *(as adj): hazel eyes.* [OE *hæsel*]

hazelhen ('heɪzᵊlˌhɛn) *n* a European woodland gallinaceous bird with a speckled brown plumage and slightly crested crown.

hazelnut ('heɪzᵊlˌnʌt) *n* the nut of a hazel shrub, having a smooth shiny hard shell. Also called: **filbert,** (Brit.) **cobnut, cob.**

hazy ❶ ('heɪzɪ) *adj* **hazier, haziest.** misty; indistinct; vague. [C17: from ?]
▸ **'hazily** *adv* ▸ **'haziness** *n*

Hb *symbol for* haemoglobin.

HB (on Brit. pencils) *symbol for* hard-black: denoting a medium-hard lead.

HBC *abbrev. for* Hudson's Bay Company.

HBM (in Britain) *abbrev. for* His (*or* Her) Britannic Majesty.

H-bomb *n* short for **hydrogen bomb.**

HC *abbrev. for:* **1** Holy Communion. **2** (in Britain) House of Commons.

HCF *or* **hcf** *abbrev. for* highest common factor.

HCG *abbrev. for* human chorionic gonadotrophin; a hormone produced by the placenta during pregnancy: its presence in the urine is used as the basis of most pregnancy tests.

hcp *abbrev. for* handicap.

HD *abbrev. for* heavy duty.

hdqrs *abbrev. for* headquarters.

HDTV *abbrev. for* high definition television.

he (hiː; *unstressed* iː) *pron (subjective)* **1** refers to a male person or animal. **2** refers to an indefinite antecedent such as *whoever* or *anybody: everybody can do as he likes.* **3** refers to a person or animal of unknown or unspecified sex: *a member may vote as he sees fit.* ◆ *n* **4a** a male person or animal. **4b** *(in combination): he-goat.* **5** (in children's play) another name for **tag**[2] (sense 1), **it** (sense 7). [OE *hē*]

He *the chemical symbol for* helium.

HE *abbrev. for:* **1** high explosive. **2** His Eminence. **3** His (*or* Her) Excellency.

head ❶ (hɛd) *n* **1** the upper or front part of the body in vertebrates, including man, that contains and protects the brain, eyes, mouth, nose, and ears. Related adj: **cephalic. 2** the corresponding part of an invertebrate animal. **3** something resembling a head in form or function, such as the top of a tool. **4a** the person commanding most authority within a group, organization, etc. **4b** *(as modifier): head buyer.* **4c** *(in combination): headmaster.* **5** the position of leadership or command. **6** the most forward part of a thing; front: *the head of a queue.* **7** the highest part of a thing; upper end: *the head of the pass.* **8** the froth on the top of a glass of beer. **9** aptitude, intelligence, and emotions (esp. in **over one's head, lose one's head,** etc.): *she has a good head for figures.* **10** *(pl* **head)** a person or animal considered as a unit: *the show was two pounds per head; six hundred head of cattle.* **11** the head considered as a measure: *he's a head taller than his mother.* **12** *Bot.* **12a** a dense inflorescence such as that of the daisy. **12b** any other compact terminal part of a plant, such as the leaves of a cabbage. **13** a culmination or crisis (esp. in **bring** or **come to a head). 14** the pus-filled tip or central part of a pimple, boil, etc. **15** the source of a river or stream. **16** *(cap. when part of a name)* a headland or promontory. **17** the obverse of a coin, usually bearing a portrait of the head of a monarch, etc. **18** a main point of an argument, discourse, etc. **19** *(often pl)* a headline or heading. **20** *(often pl) Naut.* a lavatory. **21** the taut membrane of a drum, tambourine, etc. **22a** the height of the surface of liquid above a specific point, esp. as a measure of the pressure at that point: *a head of four feet.* **22b** pressure of water, caused by height or velocity, measured in terms of a vertical column of water. **22c** any pressure: *a head of steam in the boiler.* **23** *Sl.* **23a** a person who regularly takes drugs, esp. LSD or cannabis. **23b** *(in combination): an acidhead.* **24** *Mining.* a road driven into the coalface. **25a** the terminal point of a route. **25b** *(in combination): railhead.* **26** a device on a turning or boring machine equipped with one or more cutting tools held to the work by this device. **27 cylinder head.** See **cylinder** (sense 4). **28** an electromagnet that can read, write, or erase information on a magnetic medium, used in computers, tape recorders, etc. **29** *Inf.* short for **headmaster** *or* **headmistress. 30** a narrow margin of victory (esp. in **(win) by a head). 31** *Inf.* short for **headache. 32 bite** *or* **snap someone's head off.** to speak sharply to someone. **33 give someone** (*or* **something) his** (*or* **its) head. 33a** to allow a person greater freedom or responsibility. **33b** to allow a horse to gallop by lengthening the reins. **34 go to one's head. 34a** to make one dizzy or confused, as might an alcoholic drink. **34b** to make one conceited: *his success has gone to his head.* **35 head and shoulders above.** greatly superior to. **36 head over heels. 36a** turning a complete somersault. **36b** completely; utterly (esp. in **head over heels in love). 37 hold up one's head.** to be unashamed. **38 keep one's head.** to remain calm. **39 keep one's head above water.** to manage to survive difficulties, esp. financial ones. **40 make head or tail of.** *(used with a negative)* to attempt to understand (a problem, etc.). **41 off** (*or* **out of) one's head.** *Sl.* insane or delirious. **42 on one's (own) head.** at a one's (own) risk or responsibility. **43 over someone's head. 43a** without a person in the obvious position being considered: *the graduate was promoted over the heads of several of his seniors.* **43b** without consulting a person in the obvious position but referring to a higher authority: *he went straight to the director, over the head of his imme-*

THESAURUS

haywire *adj* **1** = **chaotic,** confused, disarranged, disordered, disorganized, mixed up, on the blink (*sl.*), out of commission, out of order, shambolic (*inf.*), tangled, topsy-turvy **2** = **crazy,** erratic, mad, wild

hazard *n* **1, 3** = **danger,** endangerment, imperilment, jeopardy, peril, pitfall, risk, threat **5** = **chance,** accident, coincidence, fluke, luck, misfortune, mishap, stroke of luck ◆ *vb* **9** = **gamble,** chance, dare, risk, stake **10** = **conjecture,** advance, offer, presume, proffer, speculate, submit, suppose, throw out, venture, volunteer **11** = **jeopardize,** endanger, expose, imperil, risk, threaten

hazardous *adj* **1** = **dangerous,** dicey (*inf., chiefly Brit.*), difficult, fraught with danger, hairy (*sl.*), insecure, perilous, precarious, risky, unsafe **2** = **unpredictable,** chancy, haphazard, precarious, uncertain

Antonyms *adj* reliable, safe, secure, sound, stable, sure

haze[1] *n* **1** = **mist,** cloud, dimness, film, fog, obscurity, smog, smokiness, steam, vapour

hazy *adj* = **unclear,** blurry, cloudy, dim, dull, faint, foggy, fuzzy, ill-defined, indefinite, indistinct, misty, muddled, muzzy, nebulous, obscure, overcast, smoky, uncertain, vague, veiled

Antonyms *adj* ≠ **unclear:** bright, certain, clear, detailed, well-defined

head *n* **1, 2** = **skull,** bean (*US & Canad. sl.*), conk (*sl.*), cranium, loaf (*sl.*), noddle (*inf., chiefly Brit.*), noggin, nut (*sl.*), pate **4a** = **leader,** boss (*inf.*), captain, chief, chieftain, commander, director, headmaster *or* headmistress, head teacher, manager, master, principal, superintendent, supervisor ◆ *modifier* **4b** = **chief,** arch, first, foremost, front, highest, leading, main, pre-eminent, premier, prime, principal, supreme, topmost ◆ *n* **6** = **front,** cutting edge, first place, fore, forefront, van, vanguard **7** = **top,** apex, crest, crown, height, peak, pinnacle, pitch, summit, tip, vertex **9** = **mind,** ability, aptitude, brain, brains (*inf.*), capacity, faculty, flair, intellect, intelligence, mentality, talent, thought, understanding **13** = **culmination,** climax, conclusion, crisis, end, turning point **15** = **source,** beginning, commencement, origin, rise, start **16** = **headland,** cape, foreland, point, promontory **go to one's head 34a** = **intoxicate,** dizzy **34b** = **excite,** make conceited, puff up **36b head over heels** = **completely,** intensely, thoroughly, uncontrollably, utterly, wholeheartedly **44 put (our, their,** *etc.***) heads together** *Informal* = **consult,** confab, confabulate, confer, deliberate, discuss, palaver, powwow, talk over ◆ *vb* **47** = **lead,** be *or* go first, cap, crown, lead the way, precede, top **48** = **be in charge of,** command, control, direct, govern, guide, lead, manage,

diate boss. **43c** beyond a person's comprehension. **44 put (our, their, etc.) heads together.** *Inf.* to consult together. **45 take it into one's head.** to conceive a notion (to do something). **46 turn someone's head.** to make someone vain, conceited, etc. ◆ *vb* **47** (*tr*) to be at the front or top of: *to head the field.* **48** (*tr;* often foll. by *up*) to be in the commanding or most important position. **49** (often foll. by *for*) to go or cause to go (towards): *where are you heading?* **50** to turn or steer (a vessel) as specified: *to head into the wind.* **51** *Soccer.* to propel (the ball) by striking it with the head. **52** (*tr*) to provide with or be a head or heading for. **53** (*tr*) to cut the top branches or shoots off a tree or plant. **54** (*intr*) to form a head, as a plant. **55** (*intr;* often foll. by *in*) (of streams, rivers, etc.) to originate or rise. ◆ See also **head off, heads.** [OE *hēafod*]
▸ **'headless** *adj* ▸ **'head,like** *adj*

-head *n combining form.* indicating a person having a preoccupation as specified: *breadhead.*

headache Ⓣ ('hɛd,eɪk) *n* **1** a continuous pain in the head. **2** *Inf.* any cause of worry, difficulty, or annoyance.
▸ **'head,achy** *adj*

headband ('hɛd,bænd) *n* **1** a ribbon or band worn around the head. **2** a narrow cloth band attached to the top of the spine of a book for protection or decoration.

headbang ('hɛd,bæŋ) *vb* (*intr*) *Sl.* to nod one's head violently to the beat of heavy-metal rock music.

head-banger *n Sl.* **1** a heavy-metal rock fan. **2** a crazy or stupid person.

headboard ('hɛd,bɔːd) *n* a vertical board or terminal at the head of a bed.

head-butt *vb* (*tr*) **1** to strike (someone) deliberately with the head. ◆ *n* **head butt. 2** an act or an instance of deliberately striking someone with the head.

headdress ('hɛd,drɛs) *n* any head covering, esp. an ornate one or one denoting a rank.

headed ('hɛdɪd) *adj* **1a** having a head or heads. **1b** (*in combination*): *two-headed; bullet-headed.* **2** having a heading: *headed notepaper.*

header ('hɛdə) *n* **1** a machine that trims the heads from castings, forgings, etc., or one that forms heads, as in wire, to make nails. **2** a person who operates such a machine. **3** Also called: **header tank.** a reservoir that maintains a gravity feed or a static fluid pressure in an apparatus. **4** a brick or stone laid across a wall so that its end is flush with the outer surface. **5** the action of striking a ball with the head. **6** *Inf.* a headlong fall or dive.

headfirst Ⓣ ('hɛd'fɜːst) *adj, adv* **1** with the head foremost; headlong. ◆ *adv* **2** rashly.

headgear ('hɛd,gɪə) *n* **1** a hat. **2** any part of a horse's harness that is worn on the head. **3** the hoisting mechanism at the pithead of a mine.

headguard ('hɛd,gɑːd) *n* a lightweight helmet-like piece of equipment worn to protect the head in various sports.

head-hunting *n* **1** the practice among certain peoples of removing the heads of slain enemies and preserving them as trophies. **2** *US sl.* the destruction or neutralization of political opponents. **3** (of a company or corporation) the recruitment of, or a drive to recruit, new high-level personnel, esp. in management or in specialist fields.
▸ **'head-,hunter** *n*

heading Ⓣ ('hɛdɪŋ) *n* **1** a title for a page, chapter, etc. **2** a main division, as of a speech. **3** *Mining.* **3a** a horizontal tunnel. **3b** the end of such a tunnel. **4** the angle between the direction of an aircraft and a specified meridian, often due north. **5** the compass direction parallel to the keel of a vessel. **6** the act of heading.

headland Ⓣ *n* **1** ('hɛdlənd). a narrow area of land jutting out into a sea, lake, etc. **2** ('hɛd,lænd). a strip of land along the edge of an arable field left unploughed to allow space for machines.

headlight ('hɛd,laɪt) *or* **headlamp** *n* a powerful light, equipped with a reflector and attached to the front of a motor vehicle, etc.

headline ('hɛd,laɪn) *n* **1a** a phrase at the top of a newspaper or magazine article indicating the subject of the article, usually in larger and heavier type. **1b** a line at the top of a page indicating the title, page number, etc. **2 hit the headlines.** to become prominent in the news. **3** (*usually pl*) the main points of a television or radio news broadcast, read out before the full broadcast. ◆ *vb* **headlines, headlining, headlined. 4** (*tr*) to furnish (a story or page) with a headline. **5** to have top billing (in).

headlong Ⓣ ('hɛd,lɒŋ) *adv, adj* **1** with the head foremost; headfirst. **2** with great haste. ◆ *adj* **3** *Arch.* (of slopes, etc.) very steep; precipitous.

headman ('hɛdmən) *n, pl* **headmen. 1** *Anthropol.* a chief or leader. **2** a foreman or overseer.

headmaster Ⓣ (,hɛd'mɑːstə) *or* (*fem*) **headmistress** *n* the principal of a school.

headmost ('hɛd,məʊst) *adj* foremost.

head off Ⓣ *vb* (*tr, adv*) **1** to intercept and force to change direction. **2** to prevent or forestall.

head-on *adv, adj* **1** front foremost: *a head-on collision.* **2** with directness or without compromise: *in his usual head-on fashion.*

headphones ('hɛd,fəʊnz) *pl n* an electrical device consisting of two earphones held in position by a flexible metallic strap passing over the head. Informal name: **cans.**

headpiece ('hɛd,piːs) *n* **1** *Printing.* a decorative band at the top of a page, etc. **2** a helmet. **3** *Arch.* the intellect.

headpin ('hɛd,pɪn) *n Tenpin bowling.* another word for **kingpin** (sense 2).

headquarters (,hɛd'kwɔːtəz) *pl n* (*sometimes functioning as sing*) **1** any centre from which operations are directed, as in the police. **2** a military formation comprising the commander and his staff. ◆ Abbrev.: **HQ, h.q.**

headrace ('hɛd,reɪs) *n* a channel that carries water to a water wheel, turbine, etc.

headrest ('hɛd,rɛst) *n* a support for the head, as on a dentist's chair or car seat.

head restraint *n* an adjustable support for the head, attached to a car seat, to prevent the neck from being jolted backwards sharply in the event of a crash or sudden stop.

headroom ('hɛd,rʊm, -,ruːm) *or* **headway** *n* the height of a bridge, room, etc.; clearance.

heads (hɛdz) *interj, adv* with the obverse side of a coin uppermost, esp. if it has a head on it: used as a call before tossing a coin.

headscarf ('hɛd,skɑːf) *n, pl* **headscarves.** a scarf for the head, often worn tied under the chin.

headset ('hɛd,sɛt) *n* a pair of headphones, esp. with a microphone attached.

headship ('hɛdʃɪp) *n* **1** the position or state of being a leader; command. **2** *Brit.* the position of headmaster or headmistress of a school.

headshrinker ('hɛd,ʃrɪŋkə) *n* **1** a slang name for **psychiatrist.** Often shortened to **shrink. 2** a head-hunter who shrinks the heads of his victims.

headsman ('hɛdzmən) *n, pl* **headsmen.** (formerly) an executioner who beheaded condemned persons.

headstall ('hɛd,stɔːl) *n* the part of a bridle that fits round a horse's head.

head start *n* an initial advantage in a competitive situation.

headstock ('hɛd,stɒk) *n* the part of a machine that supports and transmits the drive.

headstone ('hɛd,stəʊn) *n* **1** a memorial stone at the head of a grave. **2** *Archit.* another name for **keystone.**

headstream ('hɛd,striːm) *n* a stream that is the source or a source of a river.

headstrong Ⓣ ('hɛd,strɒŋ) *adj* **1** self-willed; obstinate. **2** (of an action) heedless; rash.

head-to-head *Inf.* ◆ *adj* **1** in direct competition. ◆ *n* **2** a competition involving two people, teams, etc.

head-up display *n* a projection of readings from instruments onto a windscreen, enabling a pilot or driver to see them without moving his eyes.

head voice *or* **register** *n* the high register of the human voice, in which the vibrations of sung notes are felt in the head.

headwaters ('hɛd,wɔːtəz) *pl n* the tributary streams of a river in the area in which it rises.

headway Ⓣ ('hɛd,weɪ) *n* **1** motion forward: *the vessel made no headway.* **2** progress: *he made no headway with the problem.* **3** another name for **headroom. 4** the interval between consecutive trains, buses, etc., on the same route.

headwind ('hɛd,wɪnd) *n* a wind blowing directly against the course of an aircraft or ship.

headword ('hɛd,wɜːd) *n* a key word placed at the beginning of a line, paragraph, etc., as in a dictionary entry.

headwork ('hɛd,wɜːk) *n* **1** mental work. **2** the ornamentation of the keystone of an arch.

heady Ⓣ ('hɛdɪ) *adj* **headier, headiest. 1** (of alcoholic drink) intoxicating. **2** strongly affecting the senses; extremely exciting. **3** rash; impetuous.
▸ **'headily** *adv* ▸ **'headiness** *n*

heal Ⓣ (hiːl) *vb* **1** to restore or be restored to health. **2** (*intr;* often foll. by *over* or *up*) (of a wound) to repair by natural processes, as by scar for-

THESAURUS

rule, run, supervise **49** = **make for,** aim, go to, make a beeline for, point, set off for, set out, start towards, steer, turn

headache *n* **1** = **migraine,** head (*inf.*), neuralgia **2** *Informal* = **problem,** bane, bother, inconvenience, nuisance, trouble, vexation, worry

headfirst *adj, adv* **1** = **headlong,** diving, head-on **2** = **recklessly,** carelessly, hastily, head over heels, precipitately, rashly

heading *n* **1** = **title,** caption, headline, name, rubric **2** = **division,** category, class, section

headland *n* **1** = **promontory,** bill, bluff, cape, cliff, foreland, head, mull (*Scot.*), point

headlong *adv, adj* **1** = **headfirst,** headforemost, head-on ◆ *adv* **2** = **hastily,** heedlessly, helter-skelter, hurriedly, pell-mell, precipitately, rashly, thoughtlessly, wildly ◆ *adj* **3** *Archaic* = **steep,** breakneck, dangerous, precipitate

headmaster *or* **headmistress** *n* = **principal,** head, head teacher, rector

head off *vb* **1** = **intercept,** block off, cut off, deflect, divert, interpose, intervene **2** = **prevent,** avert, fend off, forestall, parry, stop, ward off

headstrong *adj* **1** = **self-willed,** contrary, intractable, mulish, obstinate, perverse, pig-headed, stiff-necked, stubborn, ungovernable, unruly, wilful **2** = **rash,** foolhardy, heedless, imprudent, impulsive, reckless

Antonyms *adj* ≠ **self-willed:** impressionable, manageable, pliant, subservient, tractable ≠ **rash:** cautious

headway *n* **1, 2** = **advance,** improvement, progress, progression, way

heady *adj* **1** = **intoxicating,** inebriating, potent, spirituous, strong **2** = **exciting,** exhilarating, intoxicating, overwhelming, stimulating, thrilling **3** = **rash,** hasty, impetuous, impulsive, inconsiderate, precipitate, reckless, thoughtless

heal *vb* **1, 3** = **cure,** make well, mend, remedy,

mation. **3** (*tr*) to cure (a disease or disorder). **4** to restore or be restored to friendly relations, harmony, etc. [OE *hælan*; see HALE[1], WHOLE]
▸ **'healer** *n* ▸ **'healing** *n, adj*

health ❶ (hɛlθ) *n* **1** the state of being bodily and mentally vigorous and free from disease. **2** the general condition of body and mind: *in poor health.* **3** the condition of any unit, society, etc.: *the economic health of a nation.* **4** a toast to a person. **5** (*modifier*) of or relating to food or other goods reputed to be beneficial to the health: *health food.* **6** (*modifier*) of or relating to health: *health care; health service.* [OE *hælth*; rel. to *hāl* HALE[1]]

health centre *n* (in Britain) premises providing health care for a local community and usually housing a group practice, nursing staff, a child-health clinic, etc.

health farm *n* a residential establishment, often in the country, visited by those who wish to improve their health by losing weight, eating health foods, taking exercise, etc.

health food *n* **a** food eaten for its alleged benefits to health, esp. fruit, vegetables, etc., that are organically grown, high in dietary fibre, and without additives. **b** (*as modifier*): *a health-food shop.*

healthful ❶ ('hɛlθfʊl) *adj* a less common word for **healthy** (senses 1–3).

health salts *pl n* magnesium sulphate or similar salts taken as a mild laxative.

health visitor *n* (in Britain) a nurse employed by a district health authority to visit people in their homes and give help and advice on health and social welfare, esp. to mothers of preschool children, and to handicapped and elderly people.

healthy ❶ ('hɛlθɪ) *adj* **healthier, healthiest. 1** enjoying good health. **2** sound: *the company's finances are not very healthy.* **3** conducive to health. **4** indicating soundness of body or mind: *a healthy appetite.* **5** *Inf.* considerable: *a healthy sum.*
▸ **'healthily** *adv* ▸ **'healthiness** *n*

heap ❶ (hiːp) *n* **1** a collection of articles or mass of material gathered in a pile. **2** (*often pl; usually foll. by of*) *Inf.* a large number or quantity. **3** *Inf.* a thing that is very old, unreliable, etc.: *the car was a heap.* ◆ *adv* **4 heaps.** (intensifier): *he was heaps better.* ◆ *vb* **5** (often foll. by *up* or *together*) to collect or be collected into or as if into a pile. **6** (*tr; often foll. by with, on,* or *upon*) to load (with) abundantly: *to heap with riches.* [OE *héap*]

hear ❶ (hɪə) *vb* **hears, hearing, heard** (hɜːd). **1** (*tr*) to perceive (a sound) with the sense of hearing. **2** (*tr; may take a clause as object*) to listen to: *did you hear what I said?* **3** (when *intr,* sometimes foll. by *of* or *about;* when *tr, may take a clause as object*) to be informed (of); receive information (about). **4** *Law.* to give a hearing to (a case). **5** (when *intr,* usually foll. by *of* and used with a negative) to listen (to) with favour, assent, etc.: *she wouldn't hear of it.* **6** (*intr;* foll. by *from*) to receive a letter (from). **7 hear! hear!** an exclamation of approval. **8 hear tell (of).** *Dialect.* to be told (about). [OE *hieran*]
▸ **'hearer** *n*

hearing ❶ ('hɪərɪŋ) *n* **1** the sense by which sound is perceived. **2** an opportunity to be listened to. **3** the range within which sound can be heard; earshot. **4** the investigation of a matter by a court of law, esp. the preliminary inquiry into an indictable crime by magistrates.

hearing aid *n* a device for assisting the hearing of partially deaf people, typically a small battery-powered amplifier worn in or behind the ear. Also called: **deaf aid.**

hearing dog *n* a dog that has been specially trained to help deaf or partially deaf people by alerting them to such sounds as a ringing doorbell, an alarm, etc.

hearken *or US (sometimes)* **harken** ('hɑːkən) *vb Arch.* to listen to (something). [OE *heorcnian*]

hear out *vb* (*tr, adv*) to listen in regard to every detail and give a proper or full hearing to.

hearsay ❶ ('hɪə,seɪ) *n* gossip; rumour.

hearsay evidence *n Law.* evidence based on what has been reported to a witness by others rather than what he has himself observed.

hearse (hɜːs) *n* a vehicle, such as a car or carriage, used to carry a coffin to the grave. [C14: from OF *herce,* from L *hirpex* harrow]

heart ❶ (hɑːt) *n* **1** the hollow muscular organ in vertebrates whose contractions propel the blood through the circulatory system. Related adj: **cardiac. 2** the corresponding organ in invertebrates. **3** this organ considered as the seat of emotions, esp. love. **4** emotional mood: *a change of heart.* **5** tenderness or pity: *you have no heart.* **6** courage or spirit. **7** the most central part: *the heart of the city.* **8** the most important part: *the heart of the matter.* **9** (of vegetables, such as cabbage) the inner compact part. **10** the breast: *she held him to her heart.* **11** a dearly loved person: *dearest heart.* **12** a conventionalized representation of the heart, having two rounded lobes at the top meeting in a point at the bottom. **13a** a red heart-shaped symbol on a playing card. **13b** a card with one or more of these symbols or (*when pl*) the suit of cards so marked. **14** a fertile condition in land (esp. in **in good heart**). **15 after one's own heart.** appealing to one's own disposition or taste. **16 break one's** (*or* **someone's**) **heart.** to grieve (or cause to grieve) very deeply, esp. through love. **17 by heart.** by committing to memory. **18 eat one's heart out.** to brood or pine with grief or longing. **19 from (the bottom of) one's heart.** very sincerely or deeply. **20 have a change of heart.** to experience a profound change of outlook, attitude, etc. **21 have one's heart in one's mouth** (*or* **throat**). to be full of apprehension, excitement, or fear. **22 have one's heart in the right place.** to be kind, thoughtful, or generous. **23 have the heart.** (*usually used with a negative*) to have the necessary will, callousness, etc. (to do something): *I didn't have the heart to tell him.* **24 heart of hearts.** the depths of one's conscience or emotions. **25 heart of oak.** a brave person. **26 lose heart.** to become despondent or disillusioned (over something). **27 lose one's heart to.** to fall in love with. **28 set one's heart on.** to have as one's ambition to obtain; covet. **29 take heart.** to become encouraged. **30 take to heart.** to take seriously or be upset about. **31 wear one's heart on one's sleeve.** to show one's feelings openly. **32 with all one's heart.** very willingly. ◆ *vb* (*intr*) **33** (of vegetables) to form a heart. ◆ See also **hearts.** [OE *heorte*]

heartache ❶ ('hɑːt,eɪk) *n* intense anguish or mental suffering.

heart attack *n* any sudden severe instance of abnormal heart functioning, esp. coronary thrombosis.

heartbeat ('hɑːt,biːt) *n* one complete pulsation of the heart.

heart block *n* impaired conduction of the impulse that regulates the heartbeat, resulting in a lack of coordination between the beating of the atria and the ventricles.

heartbreak ❶ ('hɑːt,breɪk) *n* intense and overwhelming grief, esp. through disappointment in love.
▸ **'heart,breaker** *n* ▸ **'heart,breaking** *adj*

heartburn ('hɑːt,bɜːn) *n* a burning sensation beneath the breastbone caused by irritation of the oesophagus. Technical names: **cardialgia, pyrosis.**

-hearted *adj* having a heart or disposition as specified: *cold-hearted; heavy-hearted.*

THESAURUS

restore, treat **4** = **reconcile,** alleviate, ameliorate, compose, conciliate, harmonize, patch up, settle, soothe
Antonyms *vb* aggravate, exacerbate, harm, hurt, make worse, reopen

healing *adj* **1, 3** = **medicinal,** analeptic, curative, remedial, restorative, restoring, sanative, therapeutic **4** = **soothing,** assuaging, comforting, emollient, gentle, lenitive, mild, mitigative, palliative

health *n* **1** = **wellbeing,** fitness, good condition, haleness, healthiness, robustness, salubrity, soundness, strength, vigour, wellness **2, 3** = **condition,** constitution, fettle, form, shape, state, tone
Antonyms *n* ≠ **wellbeing:** debility, disease, frailty, illness, sickness, weakness

healthful *adj* = **healthy,** beneficial, bracing, good for one, health-giving, invigorating, nourishing, nutritious, salubrious, salutary, wholesome

healthy *adj* **1** = **well,** active, alive and kicking, blooming, fighting fit, fit, fit as a fiddle (*inf.*), flourishing, hale, hale and hearty, hardy, hearty, in fine feather, in fine fettle, in fine form, in good condition, in good shape (*inf.*), in the pink, physically fit, right as rain (*Brit. inf.*), robust, sound, strong, sturdy, vigorous **3** = **wholesome,** beneficial, bracing, good for one, healthful, health-giving, hygienic, invigorating, nourishing, nutritious, salubrious, salutary
Antonyms *adj* ≠ **well:** ailing, at death's door, debilitated, delicate, diseased, feeble, fragile, frail, ill, infirm, poorly (*inf.*), sick, sickly, unfit, unhealthy, unsound, unwell, weak, weedy (*inf.*) ≠ **wholesome:** unhealthy, unwholesome

heap *n* **1** = **pile,** accumulation, aggregation, collection, hoard, lot, mass, mound, mountain, rick, stack, stockpile, store **2** *often plural Informal* = **a lot,** abundance, great deal, lashings (*Brit. inf.*), load(s) (*inf.*), lots (*inf.*), mass, mint, ocean(s), oodles (*inf.*), plenty, pot(s) (*inf.*), quantities, stack(s), tons ◆ *vb* **5** = **pile,** accumulate, amass, augment, bank, collect, gather, hoard, increase, mound, stack, stockpile, store **6** = **load,** assign, bestow, burden, confer, shower upon

hear *vb* **2** = **listen to,** attend, be all ears (*inf.*), catch, eavesdrop, give attention, hark, hearken (*arch.*), heed, listen in, overhear **3** = **learn,** ascertain, be informed, be told of, discover, find out, gather, get wind of (*inf.*), hear tell (*dialect*), pick up, understand **4** *Law* = **try,** examine, investigate, judge

hearing *n* **1** = **perception,** audition, ear **2** = **chance to speak,** audience, audition, interview **3** = **earshot,** auditory range, hearing distance, range, reach, sound **4** = **inquiry,** industrial tribunal, investigation, review, trial

hearsay *n* = **rumour,** buzz, dirt, gossip, grapevine (*inf.*), idle talk, report, talk, talk of the town, tittle-tattle, word of mouth

heart *n* **3, 4** = **nature,** character, disposition, emotion, feeling, inclination, sentiment, soul, sympathy, temperament **5** = **tenderness,** affection, benevolence, compassion, concern, humanity, love, pity, understanding **6** = **courage,** balls (*taboo sl.*), boldness, bravery, fortitude, guts (*inf.*), mettle, mind, nerve, pluck, purpose, resolution, spirit, spunk (*inf.*), will **7** = **centre,** central part, core, crux, essence, hub, kernel, marrow, middle, nucleus, pith, quintessence, root **17 by heart** = **by memory,** by rote, off pat, parrot-fashion (*inf.*), pat, word for word **18 eat one's heart out** = **grieve,** agonize, brood, mope, mourn, obsess, pine, regret, repine, sorrow **19 from (the bottom of) one's heart** = **sincerely,** deeply, devoutly, fervently, heart and soul, heartily, with all one's heart **29 take heart** = **be encouraged,** be comforted, be heartened, brighten up, buck up (*inf.*), cheer up, perk up, revive

heartache *n* = **sorrow,** affliction, agony, anguish, bitterness, despair, distress, grief, heartbreak, heartsickness, pain, remorse, suffering, torment, torture

heartbreak *n* = **grief,** anguish, desolation, despair, misery, pain, sorrow, suffering

heartbreaking *adj* = **sad,** agonizing, bitter, desolating, disappointing, distressing, grievous, gut-wrenching, harrowing, heart-rending, pitiful, poignant, tragic
Antonyms *adj* cheerful, cheery, comic, glorious, happy, jolly, joyful, joyous, light-hearted

hearten 🅣 (ˈhɑːtᵊn) *vb* to make or become cheerful.
▸ **ˈheartening** *adj*

heart failure *n* **1** a condition in which the heart is unable to pump an adequate amount of blood to the tissues. **2** sudden cessation of the heartbeat, resulting in death.

heartfelt 🅣 (ˈhɑːtˌfelt) *adj* sincerely and strongly felt.

hearth (hɑːθ) *n* **1a** the floor of a fireplace, esp. one that extends outwards into the room. **1b** (*as modifier*): *hearth rug.* **2** this as a symbol of the home, etc. **3** the bottom part of a metallurgical furnace in which the molten metal is produced or contained. [OE *heorth*]

hearthstone (ˈhɑːθˌstəʊn) *n* **1** a stone that forms a hearth. **2** soft stone used (esp. formerly) to clean and whiten floors, steps, etc.

heartily 🅣 (ˈhɑːtɪlɪ) *adv* **1** thoroughly or vigorously. **2** in a sincere manner.

heartland (ˈhɑːtˌlænd) *n* the central or most important region of a country or continent.

heartless 🅣 (ˈhɑːtlɪs) *adj* unkind or cruel.
▸ **ˈheartlessly** *adv* ▸ **ˈheartlessness** *n*

heart-lung machine *n* a machine used to maintain the circulation and oxygenation of the blood during heart surgery.

heart-rending 🅣 *adj* causing great mental pain and sorrow.
▸ **ˈheart-ˌrendingly** *adv*

hearts (hɑːts) *n* (*functioning as sing*) a card game in which players must avoid winning tricks containing hearts or the queen of spades. Also called: **Black Maria.**

heart-searching *n* examination of one's feelings or conscience.

heartsease *or* **heart's-ease** (ˈhɑːtsˌiːz) *n* **1** another name for the **wild pansy. 2** peace of mind.

heartsick 🅣 (ˈhɑːtˌsɪk) *adj* deeply despondent.
▸ **ˈheartˌsickness** *n*

heartstrings (ˈhɑːtˌstrɪŋz) *pl n Often facetious.* deep emotions. [C15: orig. referring to the tendons supposed to support the heart]

heart-throb *n* **1** an object of infatuation. **2** a heartbeat.

heart-to-heart 🅣 *adj* **1** (esp. of a conversation) concerned with personal problems or intimate feelings. ◆ *n* **2** an intimate conversation.

heart-warming 🅣 *adj* **1** pleasing; gratifying. **2** emotionally moving.

heartwood (ˈhɑːtˌwʊd) *n* the central core of dark hard wood in tree trunks, consisting of nonfunctioning xylem tissue that has become blocked with resins, tannins, and oils.

hearty 🅣 (ˈhɑːtɪ) *adj* **heartier, heartiest. 1** warm and unreserved in manner. **2** vigorous and heartfelt: *hearty dislike.* **3** healthy and strong (esp. in **hale and hearty**). **4** substantial and nourishing. ◆ *n, pl* **hearties.** *Inf.* **5** a comrade, esp. a sailor. **6** a vigorous sporting man: *a rugby hearty.*
▸ **ˈheartiness** *n*

heat 🅣 (hiːt) *n* **1** the energy transferred as a result of a difference in temperature. Related adjs.: **thermal, calorific. 2** the sensation caused by heat energy; warmth. **3** the state of being hot. **4** hot weather: *the heat of summer.* **5** intensity of feeling: *the heat of rage.* **6** pressure: *the political heat on the government over the economy.* **7** the most intense part: *the heat of the battle.* **8** a period of sexual excitement in female mammals that occurs at oestrus. **9** *Sport.* **9a** a preliminary eliminating contest in a competition. **9b** a single section of a contest. **10** *Sl.* police activity after a crime: *the heat is off.* **11** *Sl., chiefly US.* criticism or abuse: *he took a lot of heat for that mistake.* **12 in the heat of the moment.** without pausing to think. **13 on** *or* **in heat. 13a** Also: **in season.** (of some female mammals) sexually receptive. **13b** in a state of sexual excitement. ◆ *vb* **14** to make or become hot or warm. **15** to make or become excited or intense. [OE *hǣtu*]

heat barrier *n* another name for **thermal barrier.**

heat capacity *n* the heat required to raise the temperature of a substance by unit temperature interval under specified conditions.

heat death *n Thermodynamics.* the condition of any closed system when its total entropy is a maximum and it has no available energy. If the universe is a closed system it should eventually reach this state.

heated 🅣 (ˈhiːtɪd) *adj* **1** made hot. **2** impassioned or highly emotional.
▸ **ˈheatedly** *adv*

heat engine *n* an engine that converts heat energy into mechanical energy.

heater (ˈhiːtə) *n* **1** any device for supplying heat, such as a convector. **2** *US sl.* a pistol. **3** *Electronics.* a conductor carrying a current that indirectly heats the cathode in some types of valve.

heat exchanger *n* a device for transferring heat from one fluid to another without allowing them to mix.

heat exhaustion *n* a condition resulting from exposure to intense heat, characterized by dizziness, abdominal cramp, and prostration.

heath (hiːθ) *n* **1** *Brit.* a large open area, usually with sandy soil and scrubby vegetation, esp. heather. **2** Also called: **heather.** a low-growing evergreen shrub having small bell-shaped typically pink or purple flowers. **3** any of several heathlike plants, such as sea heath. [OE *hǣth*]
▸ **ˈheathˌlike** *adj* ▸ **ˈheathy** *adj*

heathen 🅣 (ˈhiːðən) *n, pl* **heathens** *or* **heathen. 1** a person who does not acknowledge the God of Christianity, Judaism, or Islam; pagan. **2** an uncivilized or barbaric person. ◆ *adj* **3** irreligious; pagan. **4** uncivilized; barbaric. **5** of or relating to heathen peoples or their customs and beliefs. [OE *hǣthen*]
▸ **ˈheathendom** *n* ▸ **ˈheathenism** *or* **ˈheathenry** *n*

heathenize *or* **heathenise** (ˈhiːðəˌnaɪz) *vb* **heathenizes, heathenizing, heathenized** *or* **heathenises, heathenising, heathenised.** to render or become heathen.

heather (ˈheðə) *n* **1** Also called: **ling, heath.** a low-growing evergreen Eurasian shrub that grows in dense masses on open ground and has clusters of small bell-shaped typically pinkish-purple flowers. **2** a purplish-red to pinkish-purple colour. ◆ *adj* **3** of a heather colour. **4** of or relating to interwoven yarns of mixed colours: *heather mixture.* [C14: orig. Scot. & N English, prob. from HEATH]
▸ **ˈheathery** *adj*

Heath Robinson *adj* (of a mechanical device) absurdly complicated in design and having a simple function. [C20: after William *Heath Robinson* (1872–1944), E cartoonist who drew such contrivances]

heating (ˈhiːtɪŋ) *n* **1** a device or system for supplying heat, esp. central heating, to a building. **2** the heat supplied.

heat pump *n* a device for extracting heat from a source and delivering it elsewhere at a higher temperature.

heat rash *n* a nontechnical name for **miliaria.**

heat-seeking *adj* (of a missile, detecting device, etc.) able to detect a source of heat, as from an aircraft engine: *a heat-seeking missile.*
▸ **heat seeker** *n*

heat shield *n* a coating or barrier for shielding from excessive heat, such as that experienced by a spacecraft on re-entry into the earth's atmosphere.

heat sink *n* **1** a metal plate designed to conduct and radiate heat from an electrical component. **2** a layer within the outer skin of high-speed aircraft to absorb heat.

heatstroke (ˈhiːtˌstrəʊk) *n* a condition resulting from prolonged exposure to intense heat, characterized by high fever.

heat-treat *vb* (*tr*) to apply heat to (a metal or alloy) in one or more temperature cycles to give it desirable properties.
▸ **heat treatment** *n*

heat wave *n* **1** a continuous spell of abnormally hot weather. **2** an extensive slow-moving air mass at a relatively high temperature.

heave 🅣 (hiːv) *vb* **heaves, heaving, heaved** *or* **hove. 1** (*tr*) to lift or move with a great effort. **2** (*tr*) to throw (something heavy) with effort. **3** to utter (sounds) noisily or unhappily: *to heave a sigh.* **4** to rise and fall or

THESAURUS

hearten *vb* = **encourage**, animate, assure, buck up (*inf.*), buoy up, cheer, comfort, console, embolden, gee up, incite, inspire, inspirit, raise someone's spirits, reassure, revivify, rouse, stimulate

heartfelt *adj* = **sincere**, ardent, cordial, deep, devout, earnest, fervent, genuine, hearty, honest, profound, unfeigned, warm, wholehearted
Antonyms *adj* false, feigned, flippant, fraudulent, frivolous, half-hearted, hypocritical, insincere, phoney *or* phony (*inf.*), pretended, put on, reserved, unenthusiastic, unimpassioned

heartily *adv* **1** = **thoroughly**, absolutely, completely, eagerly, earnestly, enthusiastically, resolutely, totally, very, vigorously, zealously **2** = **sincerely**, cordially, deeply, feelingly, genuinely, profoundly, unfeignedly, warmly

heartless *adj* = **cruel**, affectless, brutal, callous, cold, cold-blooded, cold-hearted, hard, hardhearted, harsh, inhuman, merciless, pitiless, uncaring, unfeeling, unkind
Antonyms *adj* compassionate, generous, humane, kind, merciful, sensitive, sympathetic, warm-hearted

heart-rending *adj* = **moving**, affecting, distressing, gut-wrenching, harrowing, heartbreaking, pathetic, piteous, pitiful, poignant, sad, tragic

heartsick *adj* = **despondent**, dejected, dispirited, downcast, heartsore, heavy-hearted, sick at heart

heart-to-heart *adj* **1** = **intimate**, candid, open, personal, sincere, unreserved ◆ *n* **2** = **cosy chat**, tête-à-tête

heart-warming *adj* **1** = **gratifying**, pleasing, rewarding, satisfying **2** = **moving**, affecting, cheering, encouraging, heartening, touching, warming

hearty *adj* **1** = **friendly**, affable, ardent, back-slapping, cordial, eager, ebullient, effusive, enthusiastic, generous, genial, jovial, unreserved, warm **2** = **wholehearted**, earnest, genuine, heartfelt, honest, real, sincere, true, unfeigned **3** = **healthy**, active, alive and kicking, energetic, hale, hardy, right as rain (*Brit. inf.*), robust, sound, strong, vigorous, well **4** = **substantial**, ample, filling, nourishing, sizable *or* sizeable, solid, square
Antonyms *adj* ≠ **friendly:** cold, cool, unfriendly ≠ **wholehearted:** half-hearted, insincere, mild ≠ **healthy:** delicate, feeble, frail, sickly, unhealthy, weak

heat *n* **2, 3** = **hotness**, calefaction, fever, fieriness, high temperature, warmness, warmth **4** = **hot weather**, high temperature, sultriness, swelter, torridity **5** = **passion**, agitation, ardour, earnestness, excitement, fervour, fever, fury, impetuosity, intensity, vehemence, violence, warmth, zeal ◆ *vb* **14** = **warm up**, become warm, chafe, flush, glow, grow hot, make hot, reheat **15** = **stimulate**, animate, excite, impassion, inflame, inspirit, rouse, stir, warm
Antonyms *n* ≠ **hotness:** cold, coldness, coolness ≠ **passion:** calmness, coldness, composure, coolness ◆ *vb* ≠ **warm up:** chill, cool, cool off, freeze

heated *adj* **2** = **impassioned**, angry, bitter, excited, fierce, fiery, frenzied, furious, intense, passionate, raging, stormy, tempestuous, vehement, violent
Antonyms *adj* calm, civilized, dispassionate, friendly, half-hearted, mellow, mild, peaceful, quiet, rational, reasoned, serene, subdued, unemotional, unfazed (*inf.*), unruffled

heathen *n* **1** = **pagan**, idolater, idolatress, infidel, unbeliever **2** = **barbarian**, philistine, savage ◆ *adj* **3** = **pagan**, godless, heathenish, idolatrous, infidel, irreligious **4** = **uncivilized**, barbaric, philistine, savage, unenlightened

heave *vb* **1** = **lift**, drag (up), elevate, haul (up), heft, hoist, lever, pull (up), raise, tug **2** = **throw**,

cause to rise and fall heavily. **5** (*p.t. & p.p.* **hove**) *Naut.* **5a** to move or cause to move in a specified direction: *to heave in sight.* **5b** (*intr*) (of a vessel) to pitch or roll. **6** (*tr*) to displace (rock strata, etc.) in a horizontal direction. **7** (*intr*) to retch. ◆ *n* **8** the act of heaving. **9** a horizontal displacement of rock strata at a fault. ◆ See also **heave to, heaves.** [OE *hebban*]
▸ **'heaver** *n*

heave-ho *interj* a sailors' cry, as when hoisting anchor.

heaven ⓣ ('hɛvᵊn) *n* **1** (*sometimes cap.*) *Christianity.* **1a** the abode of God and the angels. **1b** a state of communion with God after death. **2** (*usually pl*) the firmament surrounding the earth. **3** (in various mythologies) a place, such as Elysium or Valhalla, to which those who have died in the gods' favour are brought to dwell in happiness. **4** a place or state of happiness. **5** (*sing* or *pl; sometimes cap.*) God or the gods, used in exclamatory phrases: *for heaven's sake.* **6 move heaven and earth.** to do everything possible (to achieve something). [OE *heofon*]

heavenly ⓣ ('hɛvᵊnlı) *adj* **1** *Inf.* wonderful. **2** of or occurring in space: *a heavenly body.* **3** holy.
▸ **'heavenliness** *n*

heavenward ('hɛvᵊnwəd) *adj* **1** directed towards heaven or the sky. ◆ *adv* **2** Also **heavenwards.** towards heaven or the sky.

heaves (hiːvz) *n* (*functioning as sing or pl*) a chronic respiratory disorder of animals of the horse family, of unknown cause. Also called: **broken wind.**

heave to *vb* (*adv*) to stop (a vessel) or (of a vessel) to stop, as by trimming the sails, etc.

Heaviside layer ('hɛvı,saıd) *n* another name for **E region** (of the ionosphere). [C20: after O. *Heaviside* (1850–1925), E physicist who predicted its existence (1902)]

heavy ⓣ ('hɛvı) *adj* **heavier, heaviest. 1** of comparatively great weight. **2** having a relatively high density: *lead is a heavy metal.* **3** great in yield, quality, or quantity: *heavy traffic.* **4** considerable: *heavy emphasis.* **5** hard to bear or fulfil: *heavy demands.* **6** sad or dejected: *heavy at heart.* **7** coarse or broad: *heavy features.* **8** (of soil) having a high clay content; cloggy. **9** solid or fat: *heavy legs.* **10** (of an industry) engaged in the large-scale complex manufacture of capital goods or extraction of raw materials. **11** serious; grave. **12** *Mil.* **12a** equipped with large weapons, armour, etc. **12b** (of guns, etc.) of a large and powerful type. **13** (of a syllable) having stress or accentuation. **14** dull and uninteresting: *a heavy style.* **15** prodigious: *a heavy drinker.* **16** (of cakes, etc.) insufficiently leavened. **17** deep and loud: *a heavy thud.* **18** (of music, literature, etc.) **18a** dramatic and powerful. **18b** not immediately comprehensible or appealing. **19** *Sl.* (of rock music) having a powerful beat; hard. **20** burdened: *heavy with child.* **21 heavy on.** *Inf.* using large quantities of: *this car is very heavy on petrol.* **22** clumsy and slow: *heavy going.* **23** cloudy or overcast: *heavy skies.* **24** not easily digestible: *a heavy meal.* **25** (of an element or compound) being or containing an isotope with greater atomic weight than that of the naturally occurring element: *heavy water.* **26** (of the going on a racecourse) soft and muddy. **27** *Sl.* using, or prepared to use, violence or brutality. ◆ *n, pl* **heavies. 28a** a villainous role. **28b** an actor who plays such a part. **29** *Mil.* **29a** a large fleet unit, esp. an aircraft carrier or battleship. **29b** a large piece of artillery. **30** (*usually pl; often preceded by the*) *Inf.* a serious newspaper: *the Sunday heavies.* **31** *Inf.* a heavyweight boxer, wrestler, etc. **32** *Sl.* a man hired to threaten violence or deter others by his presence. ◆ *adv* **33a** in a heavy manner; heavily: *time hangs heavy.* **33b** (*in combination*): *heavy-laden.* [OE *hefig*]
▸ **'heavily** *adv* ▸ **'heaviness** *n*

heavy-duty *n* (*modifier*) made to withstand hard wear, bad weather, etc.

heavy-handed ⓣ *adj* **1** clumsy. **2** harsh and oppressive.
▸ **,heavy-'handedly** *adv*

heavy-hearted ⓣ *adj* sad; melancholy.

heavy hydrogen *n* another name for **deuterium.**

heavy metal *n* a type of rock music characterized by high volume, a driving beat, and extended guitar solos, often with violent, nihilistic, and misogynistic lyrics.

heavy middleweight *n* a professional wrestler weighing 177–187 pounds (81–85 kg).

heavy spar *n* another name for **barytes.**

heavy water *n* water that has been electrolytically decomposed to reduce the amount of normal hydrogen present and enrich it in deuterium in the form D_2O or HDO. See also **deuterium oxide.**

heavyweight ('hɛvı,weıt) *n* **1** a person or thing that is heavier than average. **2a** a professional boxer weighing more than 175 pounds (79 kg). **2b** an amateur boxer weighing more than 81 kg (179 pounds). **3a** a professional wrestler weighing over 209 pounds (95 kg). **3b** an amateur wrestler weighing over 220 pounds (100kg). **4** *Inf.* an important or highly influential person.

Heb. *or* **Hebr.** *abbrev. for:* **1** Hebrew (language). **2** *Bible.* Hebrews.

hebdomadal (hɛb'dɒmədᵊl) *adj* weekly. [C18: from L, from Gk *hebdomas* seven (days), from *hepta* seven]

hebetate ('hɛbı,teıt) *adj* **1** (of plant parts) having a blunt or soft point. ◆ *vb* **hebetates, hebetating, hebetated. 2** *Rare.* to make or become blunted. [C16: from L *hebetāre* to make blunt, from *hebes* blunt]
▸ **,hebe'tation** *n*

Hebraic (hı'breıık) *or* **Hebraical** *adj* of, relating to, or characteristic of the Hebrews or their language or culture.
▸ **He'braically** *adv*

Hebraism ('hiːbreı,ızəm) *n* a linguistic usage, custom, or other feature borrowed from or particular to the Hebrew language, or to the Jewish people or their culture.
▸ **'Hebraist** *n* ▸ **'Hebra,ize** *or* **'Hebra,ise** *vb*

Hebrew ('hiːbruː) *n* **1** the ancient language of the Hebrews, revived as the official language of Israel. **2** a member of an ancient Semitic people claiming descent from Abraham; an Israelite. **3** *Arch. or offens.* a Jew. ◆ *adj* **4** of or relating to the Hebrews or their language. **5** *Arch. or offens.* Jewish. [C13: from OF *Ebreu*, ult. from Heb. *'ibhrī* one from beyond (the river)]

hecatomb ('hɛkə,təʊm, -,tuːm) *n* **1** (in ancient Greece or Rome) any great public sacrifice and feast, originally one in which 100 oxen were sacrificed. **2** a great sacrifice. [C16: from L *hecatombē*, from Gk, from *hekaton* hundred + *bous* ox]

heck (hɛk) *interj* a mild exclamation of surprise, irritation, etc. [C19: euphemistic for *hell*]

heckelphone ('hɛkəl,fəʊn) *n Music.* a type of bass oboe. [C20: after W. *Heckel* (1856-1909), G inventor]

heckle ⓣ ('hɛkᵊl) *vb* **heckles, heckling, heckled. 1** to interrupt (a public speaker, etc.) by comments, questions, or taunts. **2** (*tr*) Also: **hackle, hatchel.** to comb (hemp or flax). ◆ *n* **3** an instrument for combing flax or hemp. [C15: N English & East Anglian form of HACKLE]
▸ **'heckler** *n*

hectare ('hɛktɑː) *n* one hundred ares (10 000 square metres or 2.471 acres). Symbol: ha [C19: from F; see HECTO-, ARE[2]]

hectic ⓣ ('hɛktık) *adj* **1** characterized by extreme activity or excitement. **2** associated with or symptomatic of tuberculosis (esp. in **hectic fever, hectic flush**). ◆ *n* **3** a hectic fever or flush. **4** *Rare.* a person who is consumptive. [C14: from LL *hecticus*, from Gk *hektikos* habitual, from *hexis* state, from *ekhein* to have]
▸ **'hectically** *adv*

THESAURUS

cast, fling, hurl, pitch, send, sling, toss **3 = sigh,** breathe heavily, groan, puff, sob, utter wearily **4 = surge,** billow, breathe, dilate, exhale, expand, palpitate, pant, rise, swell, throb **7 = vomit,** barf (*US sl.*), be sick, chuck (up) (*sl., chiefly US*), chunder (*sl., chiefly Austral.*), do a technicolour yawn (*sl.*), gag, retch, spew, throw up (*inf.*), toss one's cookies (*US sl.*)

heaven *n* **1, 3 = paradise,** abode of God, bliss, Elysium *or* Elysian fields (*Greek myth*), happy hunting ground (*Native American legend*), Happy Valley, hereafter, life everlasting, life to come, next world, nirvana (*Buddhism, Hinduism*), Valhalla (*Norse myth*), Zion (*Christianity*) **2** *usually plural* **= sky,** empyrean (*poetic*), ether, firmament, welkin (*arch.*) **4 = happiness,** bliss, dreamland, ecstasy, enchantment, felicity, paradise, rapture, seventh heaven, sheer bliss, transport, utopia

heavenly *adj* **1** *Informal* **= wonderful,** alluring, beautiful, blissful, delightful, divine (*inf.*), entrancing, exquisite, glorious, lovely, rapturous, ravishing, sublime **2 = celestial,** empyrean (*poetic*), extraterrestrial **3 = holy,** angelic, beatific, blessed, blest, cherubic, divine, godlike, immortal, paradisaical, seraphic, superhuman, supernal (*literary*), supernatural
Antonyms *adj* ≠ **wonderful:** abominable, abysmal, appalling, awful, bad, depressing, dire, disagreeable, dreadful, dreary, dull, frightful, gloomy, grim, hellacious (*US sl.*), horrible, horrid, lousy (*sl.*), miserable, rotten (*inf.*), terrible, unpleasant, vile ≠ **holy:** earthly, human, secular, worldly

heavily *adv* **3 = densely,** closely, compactly, fast, hard, thick, thickly **5 = laboriously,** painfully, with difficulty **15 = excessively,** a great deal, considerably, copiously, frequently, to excess, very much **22 = ponderously,** awkwardly, clumsily, weightily

heaviness *n* **1 = weight,** gravity, heftiness, ponderousness **5 = onerousness,** arduousness, grievousness, oppressiveness, severity, weightiness **6 = sadness,** dejection, depression, despondency, gloom, gloominess, glumness, melancholy, seriousness

heavy *adj* **1 = weighty,** bulky, hefty, massive, ponderous, portly **4 = considerable,** abundant, copious, large, profuse **5 = onerous,** burdensome, difficult, grievous, hard, harsh, intolerable, laborious, oppressive, severe, tedious, vexatious, wearisome **6 = sad,** crestfallen, dejected, depressed, despondent, disconsolate, downcast, gloomy, grieving, melancholy, sorrowful **18b = serious,** complex, deep, difficult, grave, profound, solemn, weighty **20 = burdened,** encumbered, laden, loaded, oppressed, weighted **23 = overcast,** cloudy, dull, gloomy, leaden, louring *or* lowering
Antonyms *adj* ≠ **weighty:** agile, compact, handy, light, slight, small ≠ **considerable:** light, moderate, slight, sparse ≠ **onerous:** bearable, easy, gentle, light, mild, moderate, soft ≠ **sad:** calm, cheerful, happy, joyful ≠ **serious:** exciting, inconsequential, trivial, unimportant

heavy-handed *adj* **1 = clumsy,** awkward, bungling, graceless, ham-fisted (*inf.*), ham-handed (*inf.*), inept, inexpert, like a bull in a china shop (*inf.*), maladroit, unhandy **2 = oppressive,** autocratic, domineering, harsh, overbearing
Antonyms *adj* ≠ **clumsy:** adept, adroit, competent, dexterous, effectual, efficient, gentle, graceful, skilful, smooth ≠ **oppressive:** considerate, submissive, subservient

heavy-hearted *adj* **= sad,** crushed, depressed, despondent, discouraged, disheartened, dismal, downcast, downhearted, down in the dumps (*inf.*), forlorn, heartsick, melancholy, miserable, morose, mournful, sick as a parrot (*inf.*), sorrowful

heckle *vb* **1 = jeer,** bait, barrack (*inf.*), boo, disrupt, interrupt, pester, shout down, taunt

hectic *adj* **1 = frantic,** animated, boisterous, chaotic, excited, fevered, feverish, flurrying, flustering, frenetic, frenzied, furious, heated, riotous, rumbustious, tumultuous, turbulent, wild

hecto- *or before a vowel* **hect-** *prefix* denoting 100: *hectogram.* Symbol: h [via F from Gk *hekaton* hundred]

hectog *abbrev. for* hectogram.

hectogram *or* **hectogramme** ('hɛktəʊ,græm) *n* one hundred grams (3.527 ounces). Symbol: hg

hectograph ('hɛktəʊ,grɑːf) *n* **1** a process for copying type or manuscript from a glycerine-coated gelatine master to which the original has been transferred. **2** a machine using this process.

hector ❶ ('hɛktə) *vb* **1** to bully or torment by teasing. ◆ *n* **2** a blustering bully. [C17: after *Hector* (son of Priam), in the sense: a bully]

he'd (hiːd; *unstressed* iːd, hɪd, ɪd) *contraction of* he had *or* he would.

heddle ('hɛdᵊl) *n* one of a set of frames of vertical wires on a loom, each wire having an eye through which a warp thread can be passed. [OE *hefeld* chain]

hedera ('hɛdərə) *n* the genus name of **ivy** (sense 1). [L]

hedge ❶ (hɛdʒ) *n* **1** a row of shrubs or bushes forming a boundary. **2** a barrier or protection against something. **3** the act or a method of reducing the risk of loss on an investment, etc. **4** a cautious or evasive statement. **5** (*as modifier*) low, inferior, or illiterate: *hedge priest.* ◆ *vb* **hedges, hedging, hedged. 6** (*tr*) to enclose or separate with or as if with a hedge. **7** (*intr*) to make or maintain a hedge. **8** (*tr;* often foll. by *in, about,* or *around*) to hinder or restrict. **9** (*intr*) to evade decision, esp. by making noncommittal statements. **10** (*tr*) to guard against the risk of loss in (a bet, etc.), esp. by laying bets with other bookmakers. **11** (*intr*) to protect against loss through future price fluctuations, as by investing in futures. [OE *hecg*]
▸**'hedger** *n* ▸**'hedging** *n*

hedge fund *n* a largely unregulated speculative fund which offers substantial returns for high-risk investments.

hedgehog ('hɛdʒ,hɒg) *n* a small nocturnal Old World mammal having a protective covering of spines on the back.

hedgehop ('hɛdʒ,hɒp) *vb* **hedgehops, hedgehopping, hedgehopped.** (*intr*) (of an aircraft) to fly close to the ground, as in crop spraying.
▸**'hedge,hopping** *n, adj*

hedgerow ('hɛdʒ,rəʊ) *n* a hedge of shrubs or low trees, esp. one bordering a field.

hedge sparrow *n* a small brownish European songbird. Also called: **dunnock.**

hedonics (hiː'dɒnɪks) *n* (*functioning as sing*) **1** the branch of psychology concerned with the study of pleasant and unpleasant sensations. **2** (in philosophy) the study of pleasure.

hedonism ❶ ('hiːdᵊ,nɪzəm, 'hɛd-) *n* **1** *Ethics.* **1a** the doctrine that moral value can be defined in terms of pleasure. **1b** the doctrine that the pursuit of pleasure is the highest good. **2** indulgence in sensual pleasures. [C19: from Gk *hēdonē* pleasure]
▸**,hedon'istic** *adj* ▸**'hedonist** *n*

-hedron *n combining form.* indicating a solid having a specified number of surfaces: *tetrahedron.* [from Gk *-edron* -sided, from *hedra* seat, base]
▸**-hedral** *adj combining form.*

heebie-jeebies ('hiːbɪ'dʒiːbɪz) *pl n* **the.** *Sl.* apprehension and nervousness. [C20: coined by W. De Beck (1890–1942), American cartoonist]

heed ❶ (hiːd) *n* **1** careful attention; notice: *to take heed.* ◆ *vb* **2** to pay close attention to (someone or something). [OE *hēdan*]
▸**'heedful** *adj* ▸**'heedfully** *adv* ▸**'heedfulness** *n*

heedless ❶ ('hiːdlɪs) *adj* taking no notice; careless or thoughtless.
▸**'heedlessly** *adv* ▸**'heedlessness** *n*

heehaw (,hiː'hɔː) *interj* an imitation or representation of the braying sound of a donkey.

heel[1] ❶ (hiːl) *n* **1** the back part of the human foot. **2** the corresponding part in other vertebrates. **3** the part of a stocking, etc., designed to fit the heel. **4** the outer part of a shoe underneath the heel. **5** the end or back section of something: *the heel of a loaf.* **6** *Horticulture.* the small part of the parent plant that remains attached to a young shoot cut for propagation. **7** the back part of a golf club head where it bends to join the shaft. **8** *Sl.* a contemptible person. **9 at** (*or* **on**) **one's heels.** following closely. **10 down at heel. 10a** shabby or worn. **10b** slovenly. **11 kick** (*or* **cool**) **one's heels.** to wait or be kept waiting. **12 take to one's heels.** to run off. **13 to heel.** under control, as a dog walking by a person's heel. ◆ *vb* **14** (*tr*) to repair or replace the heel of (a shoe, etc.). **15** (*tr*) *Golf.* to strike (the ball) with the heel of the club. **16** to follow at the heels of (a person). [OE *hēla*]
▸**'heelless** *adj*

heel[2] ❶ (hiːl) *vb* **1** (of a vessel) to lean over; list. ◆ *n* **2** inclined position from the vertical. [OE *hieldan*]

heelball ('hiːl,bɔːl) *n* **a** a mixture of beeswax and lampblack used by shoemakers to blacken the edges of heels and soles. **b** a similar substance used to take rubbings, esp. brass rubbings.

heeler ('hiːlə) *n* **1** *US.* See **ward heeler. 2** a person or thing that heels. **3** *Austral. & NZ.* a dog that herds cattle, etc., by biting at their heels.

heel in *vb* (*tr, adv*) to insert (cuttings, shoots, etc.) into the soil before planting to keep them moist.

heeltap ('hiːl,tæp) *n* **1** a layer of leather, etc., in the heel of a shoe. **2** a small amount of alcoholic drink left at the bottom of a glass.

heft (hɛft) *vb* (*tr*) *Brit. dialect. & US inf.* **1** to assess the weight of (something) by lifting. **2** to lift. ◆ *n* **3** weight. **4** *US.* the main part. [C19: prob. from HEAVE, by analogy with *thieve, theft, cleave, cleft*]

hefty ❶ ('hɛftɪ) *adj* **heftier, heftiest.** *Inf.* **1** big and strong. **2** characterized by vigour or force: *a hefty blow.* **3** bulky or heavy. **4** sizable; involving a large amount of money: *a hefty bill.*
▸**'heftily** *adv*

Hegelian (hɪ'geɪlɪən, heɪ'giː-) *adj* relating to G. W. F. Hegel (1770–1831), German philosopher, or his system of thought, esp. his concept of dialectic, in which the contradiction between a proposition (thesis) and its antithesis is resolved at a higher level of truth (synthesis).

hegemony (hɪ'gemənɪ) *n, pl* **hegemonies.** ascendancy or domination of one power or state within a league, confederation, etc. [C16: from Gk *hēgemonia,* from *hēgemōn* leader, from *hēgeisthai* to lead]
▸**hegemonic** (,hɛgə'mɒnɪk) *adj*

Hegira *or* **Hejira** ('hɛdʒɪrə) *n* **1** the flight of Mohammed from Mecca to Medina in 622 A.D.; the starting point of the Muslim era. **2** the Muslim era itself. **3** (*often not cap.*) an emigration, escape, or flight. [C16: from Med. L, from Ar. *hijrah* emigration or flight]

heifer ('hɛfə) *n* a young cow. [OE *heahfore*]

heigh-ho ('heɪ'həʊ) *interj* an exclamation of weariness, surprise, or happiness.

height ❶ (haɪt) *n* **1** the vertical distance from the bottom of something to the top. **2** the vertical distance of a place above sea level. **3** relatively great altitude. **4** the topmost point; summit. **5** *Astron.* the angular distance of a celestial body above the horizon. **6** the period of greatest intensity: *the height of the battle.* **7** an extreme example: *the height of rudeness.* **8** (*often pl*) an area of high ground. [OE *hīehthu;* see HIGH]

heighten ❶ ('haɪtᵊn) *vb* to make or become higher or more intense.
▸**'heightened** *adj*

height of land *n US & Canad.* a watershed.

heinous ❶ ('heɪnəs, 'hiː-) *adj* evil; atrocious. [C14: from OF *haineus,* from *haine* hatred, of Gmc origin]
▸**'heinously** *adv*

THESAURUS

Antonyms *adj* calm, peaceful, relaxing, tranquil

hector *vb* **1 = bully,** bluster, boast, browbeat, bullyrag, harass, huff and puff, intimidate, menace, provoke, ride roughshod over, roister, threaten, worry

hedge *n* **1 = hedgerow,** quickset **2 = barrier,** boundary, screen, windbreak **3 = insurance cover,** compensation, counterbalance, guard, protection ◆ *vb* **6 = enclose,** border, edge, fence, surround **8 = restrict,** block, confine, hem about, hem around, hem in, hinder, obstruct **9 = dodge,** beg the question, be noncommittal, duck, equivocate, evade, flannel (*Brit. inf.*), prevaricate, pussyfoot (*inf.*), quibble, sidestep, temporize, waffle (*inf., chiefly Brit.*) **10, 11 = insure,** cover, fortify, guard, protect, safeguard, shield

hedonism *n* **1 = pursuit of pleasure,** dolce vita, gratification, luxuriousness, pleasure-seeking, self-indulgence, sensualism, sensuality **2 = sybaritism,** epicureanism, epicurism

hedonist *n* **2 = pleasure seeker,** *bon vivant,* epicure, epicurean, sensualist, sybarite, voluptuary

hedonistic *adj* **2 = pleasure-seeking,** bacchanalian, epicurean, luxurious, self-indulgent, sybaritic, voluptuous

heed *n* **1 = care,** attention, caution, consideration, ear, heedfulness, mind, note, notice, regard, respect, thought, watchfulness ◆ *vb* **2 = pay attention to,** attend, bear in mind, be guided by, consider, follow, give ear to, listen to, mark, mind, note, obey, observe, regard, take notice of, take to heart

Antonyms *n* ≠ **care:** carelessness, disregard, inattention, laxity, laxness, neglect, thoughtlessness ◆ *vb* ≠ **pay attention to:** be inattentive to, discount, disobey, disregard, flout, ignore, neglect, overlook, reject, shun, turn a deaf ear to

heedful *adj* **1 = careful,** attentive, cautious, chary, circumspect, mindful, observant, prudent, vigilant, wary, watchful

heedless *adj* **= careless,** foolhardy, imprudent, inattentive, incautious, neglectful, negligent, oblivious, precipitate, rash, reckless, thoughtless, unmindful, unobservant, unthinking

Antonyms *adj* attentive, aware, careful, cautious, concerned, heedful, mindful, observant, thoughtful, vigilant, wary, watchful

heel[1] *n* **5 = end,** crust, remainder, rump, stub, stump **8** *Slang* **= swine,** blackguard, bounder, cad (*Brit. inf.*), rotter (*sl., chiefly Brit.*), scally (*Northwest English dialect*), scoundrel, scumbag (*sl.*) **10 down at heel = shabby,** dowdy, impoverished, out at elbows, run-down, seedy, slipshod, slovenly, worn **12 take to one's heels = flee,** escape, hook it (*sl.*), run away *or* off, show a clean pair of heels, skedaddle (*inf.*), take flight, turn tail, vamoose (*sl., chiefly US*)

heel[2] *vb* **1 = lean over,** cant, careen, incline, keel over, list, tilt

hefty *adj Informal* **1 = big,** beefy (*inf.*), brawny, burly, hulking, husky (*inf.*), massive, muscular, robust, strapping, strong **2 = forceful,** heavy, powerful, thumping (*sl.*), vigorous **3 = heavy,** ample, awkward, bulky, colossal, cumbersome, large, massive, ponderous, substantial, tremendous, unwieldy, weighty

Antonyms *adj* ≠ **big:** diminutive, inconsequential, ineffectual, infinitesimal, insignificant, little, minute, narrow, pocket-sized, scanty, short, slight, slim, small, thin, tiny ≠ **forceful:** feeble, frail, mild, soft, weak, weedy (*inf.*), wimpish *or* wimpy (*inf.*) ≠ **heavy:** agile, light

height *n* **1 = tallness,** highness, loftiness, stature **2, 3 = altitude,** elevation **4 = peak,** apex, apogee, crest, crown, elevation, hill, mountain, pinnacle, summit, top, vertex, zenith **6, 7 = culmination,** climax, extremity, limit, maximum, *ne plus ultra,* ultimate, utmost degree, uttermost

Antonyms *n* ≠ **tallness:** depth, lowness, shortness, smallness ≠ **peak:** abyss, base, bottom, canyon, chasm, depth, lowland, nadir, ravine, valley ≠ **culmination:** low point, minimum, nadir

heighten *vb* **= intensify,** add to, aggravate, amplify, augment, enhance, improve, increase, magnify, sharpen, strengthen

heinous *adj* **= shocking,** abhorrent, abomina-

heir Ⓣ (ɛə) *n* **1** the person legally succeeding to all property of a deceased person. **2** any person or thing that carries on some tradition, circumstance, etc., from a forerunner. [C13: from OF, from L *hērēs*]
▸ **'heirdom** *or* **'heirship** *n*

heir apparent *n, pl* **heirs apparent.** a person whose right to succeed to certain property cannot be defeated, provided such person survives his ancestor.

heiress ('ɛərɪs) *n* **1** a woman who inherits or expects to inherit great wealth. **2** a female heir.

heirloom ('ɛəˌluːm) *n* **1** an object that has been in a family for generations. **2** an item of personal property inherited in accordance with the terms of a will. [C15: from HEIR + *lome* tool; see LOOM[1]]

heir presumptive *n Property law.* a person who expects to succeed to an estate but whose right may be defeated by the birth of one nearer in blood to the ancestor.

heist (haɪst) *Sl., chiefly US & Canad.* ◆ *n* **1** a robbery. ◆ *vb* **2** (*tr*) to steal. [var. of HOIST]

Hejira ('hɛdʒɪrə) *n* a variant spelling of **Hegira.**

held (hɛld) *vb* the past tense and past participle of **hold**[1].

helenium (hɛ'liːnɪəm) *n* a perennial garden plant with yellow, bronze, or crimson flowers. [from Gk *helenion* name of a plant]

heliacal rising (hɪ'laɪək[ə]l) *n* **1** the rising of a celestial object at the same time as the sun. **2** the date at which such a celestial object first becomes visible. [C17: from LL *hēliacus* relating to the sun, from Gk, from *hēlios* sun]

helianthemum (hiːlɪ'ænθəməm) *n* any of a genus of dwarf shrubs with brightly coloured flowers: often grown in rockeries. [from Gk *helios* sun + *anthemon* flower]

helianthus (ˌhiːlɪ'ænθəs) *n, pl* **helianthuses.** a plant of the composite family having large yellow daisy-like flowers with yellow, brown, or purple centres. [C18: NL, from Gk *hēlios* sun + *anthos* flower]

helical ('hɛlɪk[ə]l) *adj* of or like a helix; spiral.

helical gear *n* a gearwheel having the tooth form generated on a helical path about the axis of the wheel.

helices ('hɛlɪˌsiːz) *n* a plural of **helix.**

helichrysum (ˌhɛlɪ'kraɪzəm) *n* any plant of the genus *Helichrysum,* whose flowers retain their shape and colour when dried. [C16: from L, from Gk, from *helix* spiral + *khrusos* gold]

helicoid ('hɛlɪˌkɔɪd) *adj* **1** *Biol.* shaped like a spiral: *a helicoid shell.* ◆ *n* **2** *Geom.* any surface resembling that of a screw thread.

helicon ('hɛlɪkən) *n* a bass tuba made to coil over the shoulder of a band musician. [C19: prob. from *Helicon,* Gk mountain, believed to be source of poetic inspiration; associated with Gk *helix* spiral]

helicopter ('hɛlɪˌkɒptə) *n* an aircraft capable of hover, vertical flight, and horizontal flight in any direction. Most get their lift and propulsion from overhead rotating blades. [C19: from F, from Gk *helix* spiral + *pteron* wing]

helicopter gunship *n* a large heavily armed helicopter used for ground attack.

helio- *or before a vowel* **heli-** *combining form.* indicating the sun: *heliocentric.* [from Gk, from *hēlios* sun]

heliocentric (ˌhiːlɪəʊ'sɛntrɪk) *adj* **1** having the sun at its centre. **2** measured from or in relation to the sun.
▸ **ˌhelio'centrically** *adv*

heliograph ('hiːlɪəʊˌgrɑːf) *n* **1** an instrument with mirrors and a shutter used for sending messages in Morse code by reflecting the sun's rays. **2** a device used to photograph the sun.
▸ **ˌheli'ography** *n*

heliometer (ˌhiːlɪ'ɒmɪtə) *n* a refracting telescope used to determine angular distances between celestial bodies.
▸ **ˌheli'ometry** *n*

heliopsis (ˌhɛlɪ'ɒpsɪs) *n* a perennial plant with yellow daisy-like flowers.

heliostat ('hiːlɪəʊˌstæt) *n* an astronomical instrument used to reflect the light of the sun in a constant direction.
▸ **ˌhelio'static** *adj*

heliotrope ('hiːlɪəˌtrəʊp, 'hɛljə-) *n* **1** any plant of the genus *Heliotropium,* esp. the South American variety, cultivated for its small fragrant purple flowers. **2a** a bluish-violet to purple colour. **2b** (*as adj*): *a heliotrope dress.* **3** another name for **bloodstone.** [C17: from L *hēliotropium,* from Gk, from *hēlios* sun + *trepein* to turn]

heliotropism (ˌhiːlɪ'ɒtrəˌpɪzəm) *n* the growth of a plant in response to the stimulus of sunlight.
▸**heliotropic** (ˌhiːlɪəʊ'trɒpɪk) *adj*

heliport ('hɛlɪˌpɔːt) *n* an airport for helicopters. [C20: from HELI(COPTER) + PORT[1]]

helium ('hiːlɪəm) *n* a very light nonflammable colourless odourless element that is an inert gas, occurring in certain natural gases. Symbol: He; atomic no.: 2; atomic wt.: 4.0026. [C19: NL, from HELIO- + -IUM; because first detected in the solar spectrum]

helix ('hiːlɪks) *n, pl* **helices** *or* **helixes. 1** a spiral. **2** the incurving fold that forms the margin of the external ear. **3** another name for **volute** (sense 2). **4** any terrestrial mollusc of the genus *Helix,* including the garden snail. [C16: from L, from Gk: spiral; prob. rel. to Gk *helissein* to twist]

hell Ⓣ (hɛl) *n* **1** (*sometimes cap.*) *Christianity.* **1a** the place or state of eternal punishment of the wicked after death. **1b** forces of evil regarded as residing there. **2** (*sometimes cap.*) (in various religions and cultures) the abode of the spirits of the dead. **3** pain, extreme difficulty, etc. **4** *Inf.* a cause of such suffering: *war is hell.* **5** *US & Canad.* high spirits or mischievousness. **6** *Now rare.* a gambling house. **7** (**come**) **hell or high water.** *Inf.* whatever difficulties may arise. **8 for the hell of it.** *Inf.* for the fun of it. **9 from hell.** *Inf.* denoting a person or thing that is particularly bad or alarming: *job from hell.* **10 give someone hell.** *Inf.* **10a** to give someone a severe reprimand or punishment. **10b** to be a source of torment to someone. **11 hell for leather.** at great speed. **12 hell to pay.** *Inf.* serious consequences, as of a foolish action. **13 the hell.** *Inf.* **13a** (intensifier): used in such phrases as **what the hell. 13b** an expression of strong disagreement: *the hell I will.* ◆ *interj* **14** *Inf.* an exclamation of anger, surprise, etc. [OE *hell*]

he'll (hiːl; *unstressed* iːl, hɪl, ɪl) *contraction of* he will *or* he shall.

hellacious (hɛ'leɪʃəs) *adj US sl.* **1** remarkable; horrifying. **2** wonderful; excellent. [C20: from HELL + *-acious* as in AUDACIOUS]

Helladic (hɛ'lædɪk) *adj* of or relating to the Bronze Age civilization that flourished about 2900 to 1100 B.C. on the Greek mainland and islands.

Hellas ('hɛləs) *n* transliteration of the Ancient Greek name for Greece.

hellbent Ⓣ (ˌhɛl'bɛnt) *adj* (*postpositive;* foll. by *on*) *Inf.* strongly or rashly intent.

hellcat ('hɛlˌkæt) *n* a spiteful fierce-tempered woman.

hellebore ('hɛlɪˌbɔː) *n* **1** any plant of the Eurasian genus *Helleborus,* typically having showy flowers and poisonous parts. See also **Christmas rose. 2** any of various plants that yield alkaloids used in the treatment of heart disease. [C14: from Gk *helleboros,* from ?]

Hellene ('hɛliːn) *or* **Hellenian** (hɛ'liːnɪən) *n* another name for a **Greek.**

Hellenic (hɛ'lɛnɪk, -'liː-) *adj* **1** of or relating to the ancient or modern Greeks or their language. **2** of or relating to ancient Greece or the Greeks of the classical period (776–323 B.C.). Cf. **Hellenistic.** ◆ *n* **3** the Greek language in its various ancient and modern dialects.

Hellenism ('hɛlɪˌnɪzəm) *n* **1** the principles, ideals, and pursuits associated with classical Greek civilization. **2** the spirit or national character of the Greeks. **3** imitation of or devotion to the culture of ancient Greece.
▸ **'Hellenist** *n*

Hellenistic (ˌhɛlɪ'nɪstɪk) *or* **Hellenistical** *adj* **1** characteristic of or relating to Greek civilization in the Mediterranean world, esp. from the death of Alexander the Great (323 B.C.) to the defeat of Antony and Cleopatra (30 B.C.). **2** of or relating to the Greeks or to Hellenism.
▸ **ˌHellen'istically** *adv*

Hellenize *or* **Hellenise** ('hɛlɪˌnaɪz) *vb* **Hellenizes, Hellenizing, Hellenized** *or* **Hellenises, Hellenising, Hellenised.** to make or become like the ancient Greeks.
▸ **ˌHelleni'zation** *or* **ˌHelleni'sation** *n*

hellfire ('hɛlˌfaɪə) *n* **1** the torment of hell, envisaged as eternal fire. **2** (*modifier*) characterizing sermons that emphasize this.

hellion ('hɛljən) *n Chiefly US inf.* a rowdy person, esp. a child; troublemaker. [C19: prob. from dialect *hallion* rogue, from ?]

hellish Ⓣ ('hɛlɪʃ) *adj* **1** of or resembling hell. **2** wicked; cruel. **3** *Inf.* very unpleasant. ◆ *adv* **4** *Brit. inf.* (intensifier): *a hellish good idea.*

hello Ⓣ**, hallo,** *or* **hullo** (hɛ'ləʊ, hə-; 'hɛləʊ) *sentence substitute.* **1** an expression of greeting. **2** a call used to attract attention. **3** an expression of surprise. ◆ *n, pl* **hellos, hallos** *or* **hullos. 4** the act of saying or calling "hello". [C19: see HOLLO]

Hell's Angel *n* a member of a motorcycle gang who typically dress in Nazi-style paraphernalia and are noted for their lawless behaviour.

helm[1] Ⓣ (hɛlm) *n* **1** *Naut.* **1a** the wheel or entire apparatus by which a vessel is steered. **1b** the position of the helm: that is, on the side of the keel opposite from that of the rudder. **2** a position of leadership or control (esp. in **at the helm**). ◆ *vb* **3** (*tr*) to steer. [OE *helma*]
▸ **'helmsman** *n*

helm[2] (hɛlm) *n* an archaic or poetic word for **helmet.** [OE *helm*]

helmet ('hɛlmɪt) *n* **1** a piece of protective or defensive armour for the head worn by soldiers, policemen, firemen, divers, etc. See also **crash**

THESAURUS

ble, atrocious, awful, evil, execrable, flagrant, grave, hateful, hideous, infamous, iniquitous, monstrous, nefarious, odious, outrageous, revolting, unspeakable, vicious, villainous

heir *n* **1** = **successor**, beneficiary, heiress (*fem.*), inheritor, inheritress *or* inheritrix, next in line, scion

hell *n* **1, 2** = **underworld**, Abaddon, abode of the damned, abyss, Acheron (*Greek myth*), bottomless pit, fire and brimstone, Gehenna, Hades (*Greek myth*), hellfire, infernal regions, inferno, lower world, nether world, Tartarus (*Greek myth*) **3** *Informal* = **torment**, affliction, agony, anguish, martyrdom, misery, nightmare, ordeal, suffering, trial, wretchedness **11 hell for leather** = **speedily**, at a rate of knots, at the double, full-tilt, headlong, hotfoot, hurriedly, like a bat out of hell (*sl.*), pell-mell, posthaste, quickly, swiftly

hellbent *adj Informal* = **intent**, bent, determined, fixed, resolved, set, settled

hellish *adj* **1** = **devilish**, damnable, damned, demoniacal, diabolical, fiendish, infernal **2** = **atrocious**, abominable, accursed, barbarous, cruel, detestable, execrable, inhuman, monstrous, nefarious, vicious, wicked

Antonyms *adj* ≠ **atrocious:** admirable, agreeable, benevolent, delightful, fine, gentle, good, harmless, honourable, humane, innocuous, kind, merciful, noble, pleasant, virtuous, wonderful

hello *sentence substitute* **1** = **hi** (*Informal*), good afternoon, good evening, good morning, greetings, how do you do?, welcome

helm[1] *n* **1a** *Nautical* = **tiller**, rudder, steering gear, wheel **2** = **control**, command, driving seat, saddle

helmet, pith helmet. 2 *Biol.* a part or structure resembling a helmet, esp. the upper part of the calyx of certain flowers. [C15: from OF, dim. of *helme,* of Gmc origin]
▸**'helmeted** *adj*

helminth ('hɛlmɪnθ) *n* any parasitic worm, esp. a nematode or fluke. [C19: from Gk *helmins* parasitic worm]
▸**hel'minthic** *or* **helminthoid** ('hɛlmɪnˌθɔɪd, hɛl'mɪnθɔɪd) *adj*

helminthiasis (ˌhɛlmɪn'θaɪəsɪs) *n* infestation of the body with parasitic worms. [C19: from NL, from Gk *helminthian* to be infested with worms]

helot ('hɛlət, 'hiː-) *n* **1** (*cap.*) (in ancient Sparta) a member of the class of serfs owned by the state. **2** a serf or slave. [C16: from L *Hēlotēs,* from Gk *Heilōtes,* alleged to have meant orig.: inhabitants of Helos, who, after its conquest, were serfs of the Spartans]
▸**'helotism** *n* ▸**'helotry** *n*

help Ⓣ (hɛlp) *vb* **1** to assist (someone to do something), esp. by sharing the work, cost, or burden of something. **2** to alleviate the burden of (someone else) by giving assistance. **3** (*tr*) to assist (a person) to go in a specified direction: *help the old lady up.* **4** to contribute to: *to help the relief operations.* **5** to improve (a situation, etc.): *crying won't help.* **6** (*tr; preceded by can, could,* etc.; *usually used with a negative*) **6a** to refrain from: *we can't help wondering who he is.* **6b** (usually foll. by *it*) to be responsible for: *I can't help it if it rains.* **7** to alleviate (an illness, etc.). **8** (*tr*) to serve (a customer). **9** (*tr;* foll. by *to*) **9a** to serve (someone with food, etc.) (usually in **help oneself**). **9b** to provide (oneself with) without permission. **10 cannot help but.** to be unable to do anything else except: *I cannot help but laugh.* **11 so help me. 11a** on my honour. **11b** no matter what: *so help me, I'll get revenge.* ◆ *n* **12** the act of helping or being helped, or a person or thing that helps. **13a** a person hired for a job, esp. a farm worker or domestic servant. **13b** (*functioning as sing*) several employees collectively. **14** a remedy: *there's no help for it.* ◆ *sentence substitute.* **15** used to ask for assistance. ◆ See also **help out.** [OE *helpan*]
▸**'helper** *n*

helpful Ⓣ ('hɛlpfʊl) *adj* giving help.
▸**'helpfully** *adv* ▸**'helpfulness** *n*

helping Ⓣ ('hɛlpɪŋ) *n* a single portion of food.

helping hand *n* assistance: *many people lent a helping hand in making arrangements.*

helpless Ⓣ ('hɛlplɪs) *adj* **1** unable to manage independently. **2** made weak: *they were helpless from giggling.*
▸**'helplessly** *adv* ▸**'helplessness** *n*

helpline ('hɛlpˌlaɪn) *n* a telephone line operated by a charitable organization for people in distress or by a commercial organization to provide information.

helpmate Ⓣ ('hɛlpˌmeɪt) *n* a companion and helper, esp. a wife.

helpmeet ('hɛlpˌmiːt) *n* a less common word for **helpmate.** [C17: from *an helpe meet* (suitable) *for him* Genesis 2:18]

help out *vb* (*adv*) to assist, esp. by sharing the burden or cost of something with (another person).

helter-skelter Ⓣ ('hɛltə'skɛltə) *adj* **1** haphazard or careless. ◆ *adv* **2** in a helter-skelter manner. ◆ *n* **3** *Brit.* a high spiral slide, as at a fairground. **4** disorder. [C16: prob. imit.]

helve (hɛlv) *n* the handle of a hand tool such as an axe or pick. [OE *hielfe*]

Helvetian (hɛl'viːʃən) *adj* **1** Swiss. ◆ *n* **2** a native or citizen of Switzerland. [from L *Helvetia* Switzerland]

hem[1] Ⓣ (hɛm) *n* **1** an edge to a piece of cloth, made by folding the raw edge under and stitching it down. **2** short for **hemline.** ◆ *vb* **hems, hemming, hemmed.** (*tr*) **3** to provide with a hem. **4** (usually foll. by *in, around,* or *about*) to enclose or confine. [OE *hemm*]
▸**'hemmer** *n*

hem[2] Ⓣ (hɛm) *n, interj* **1** a representation of the sound of clearing the throat, used to gain attention, etc. ◆ *vb* **hems, hemming, hemmed. 2** (*intr*) to utter this sound. **3 hem** (*or* **hum**) **and haw.** to hesitate in speaking.

he-man Ⓣ *n, pl* **he-men.** *Inf.* a strongly built muscular man.

hematite *or* **haematite** ('hɛməˌtaɪt, 'hiːm-) *n* a red, grey, or black mineral, found as massive beds and in veins and igneous rocks. It is the chief source of iron. Composition: iron (ferric) oxide. Crystal structure: hexagonal (rhombohedral). [C16: via L from Gk *haimatitēs* resembling blood, from *haima* blood]
▸**hematitic** *or* **haematitic** (ˌhɛmə'tɪtɪk, ˌhiː-) *adj*

hemato- *or before a vowel* **hemat-** *combining form.* US variants of **haemato-.**

hemeralopia (ˌhɛmərə'ləʊpɪə) *n* inability to see clearly in bright light. Nontechnical name: **day blindness.** [C18: NL, from Gk, from *hēmera* day + *alaos* blind + *ōps* eye]

hemerocallis (hɛmər'ɒkælɪs) *n* a N temperate plant with large funnel-shaped orange flowers: each single flower lasts for only one day. Also called: **day lily.** [C17: from Gk *hēmera* day + *kallos* beauty]

hemi- *prefix* half: *hemicycle; hemisphere.* [from L, from Gk *hēmi-*]

-hemia *n combining form.* a US variant of **-aemia.**

hemidemisemiquaver (ˌhɛmɪˌdɛmɪ'sɛmɪˌkweɪvə) *n Music.* a note having the time value of one sixty-fourth of a semibreve. Usual US & Canad. name: **sixty-fourth note.**

hemiplegia (ˌhɛmɪ'pliːdʒɪə) *n* paralysis of one side of the body.
▸**ˌhemi'plegic** *adj*

hemipode ('hɛmɪˌpəʊd) *n* a small quail-like bird occurring in tropical and subtropical regions of the Old World. Also called: **button quail.**

hemipteran (hɪ'mɪptərən) *n* any hemipterous insect. [C19: from HEMI- + Gk *pteron* wing]

hemipterous (hɪ'mɪptərəs) *adj* of or belonging to a large order of insects having sucking or piercing mouthparts.

hemisphere ('hɛmɪˌsfɪə) *n* **1** one half of a sphere. **2a** half of the terrestrial globe, divided into **northern** and **southern hemispheres** by the equator or into **eastern** and **western hemispheres** by some meridians, usually 0° and 180°. **2b** a map or projection of one of the hemispheres. **3** *Anat.* short for **cerebral hemisphere,** a half of the cerebrum.
▸**hemispheric** (ˌhɛmɪ'sfɛrɪk) *or* **ˌhemi'spherical** *adj*

hemistich ('hɛmɪˌstɪk) *n Prosody.* a half line of verse.

hemline ('hɛmˌlaɪn) *n* the level to which the hem of a skirt or dress hangs.

hemlock ('hɛmˌlɒk) *n* **1** an umbelliferous poisonous Eurasian plant having finely divided leaves, spotted stems, and small white flowers. **2** a poisonous drug derived from this plant. **3** Also called: **hemlock spruce.** a coniferous tree of North America and Asia. [OE *hymlic*]

hemo- *combining form.* a US variant of **haemo-.**

hemp (hɛmp) *n* **1** Also called: **cannabis, marijuana.** an Asian plant having tough fibres, deeply lobed leaves, and small greenish flowers. See also **Indian hemp. 2** the fibre of this plant, used to make canvas, rope, etc. **3** any of several narcotic drugs obtained from some varieties of this plant, esp. from Indian hemp. [OE *hænep*]
▸**'hempen** *or* **'hempˌlike** *adj*

hemstitch ('hɛmˌstɪtʃ) *n* **1** a decorative edging stitch, usually for a hem, in which the cross threads are stitched in groups. ◆ *vb* **2** to decorate (a hem, etc.) with hemstitches.

hen (hɛn) *n* **1** the female of any bird, esp. of the domestic fowl. **2** the female of certain other animals, such as the lobster. **3** *Scot. dialect.* a term of address used to women. [OE *henn*]

henbane ('hɛnˌbeɪn) *n* a poisonous Mediterranean plant with sticky hairy leaves: yields the drug hyoscyamine.

hence Ⓣ (hɛns) *sentence connector.* **1** for this reason; therefore. ◆ *adv* **2** from this time: *a year hence.* **3** *Arch.* from here; away. ◆ *sentence substitute.* **4** *Arch.* begone! away! [OE *hionane*]

henceforth Ⓣ ('hɛns'fɔːθ), **henceforwards,** *or* **henceforward** *adv* from now on.

THESAURUS

help *vb* **1 = aid,** abet, assist, back, befriend, cooperate, encourage, give a leg up (*inf.*), lend a hand, lend a helping hand, promote, relieve, save, second, serve, stand by, succour, support **5 = improve,** mitigate, relieve **6a = refrain from,** abstain, avoid, control, eschew, forbear, hinder, keep from, prevent, resist, shun, withstand **7 = alleviate,** ameliorate, cure, heal, remedy, restore ◆ *n* **12 = assistance,** advice, aid, avail, benefit, cooperation, guidance, helping hand, promotion, service, support, use, utility **13a = assistant,** employee, hand, helper, worker **14 = remedy,** balm, corrective, cure, relief, restorative, salve, succour
Antonyms *vb* ≠ **aid:** bar, block, discourage, fight, foil, frustrate, hinder, hobble, impede, obstruct, oppose ≠ **improve:** aggravate, irritate, make worse ◆ *n* ≠ **assistance:** aggravation, bane, block, discouragement, hindrance, irritant, obstruction, opposition

helper *n* **1 = assistant,** abettor, adjutant, aide, aider, ally, attendant, auxiliary, coadjutor, collaborator, colleague, deputy, helpmate, henchman, mate, partner, protagonist, right-hand man, second, subsidiary, supporter

helpful *adj* **= useful,** accommodating, advantageous, beneficent, beneficial, benevolent, caring, considerate, constructive, cooperative, favourable, fortunate, practical, productive, profitable, serviceable, supportive, timely

helpfulness *n* **= usefulness,** advantage, assistance, benefit, cooperation, friendliness, kindness, neighbourliness, rallying round, support, sympathy

helping *n* **= portion,** dollop (*inf.*), piece, plateful, ration, serving

helpless *adj* **1 = vulnerable,** abandoned, defenceless, dependent, destitute, exposed, forlorn, stranded, unprotected, wide open **2 = powerless,** debilitated, disabled, feeble, impotent, incapable, incompetent, infirm, paralysed, unfit, weak
Antonyms *adj* ≠ **vulnerable:** invulnerable, safe, secure, well-protected ≠ **powerless:** able, capable, competent, equipped, fit, hardy, healthy, hearty, mighty, powerful, robust, solid, strong, sturdy, thriving, tough

helplessness *n* **1 = vulnerability,** defencelessness, exposed position, forlornness **2 = weakness,** disability, feebleness, impotence, infirmity, powerlessness

helpmate *n* **= partner,** assistant, associate, companion, consort, helper, helpmeet, husband, significant other (*US inf.*), spouse, support, wife

helter-skelter *adj* **1 = haphazard,** confused, disordered, higgledy-piggledy (*inf.*), hit-or-miss, jumbled, muddled, random, topsy-turvy ◆ *adv* **2 = carelessly,** anyhow, hastily, headlong, hurriedly, pell-mell, rashly, recklessly, wildly

hem[1] *n* **1 = edge,** border, fringe, margin, trimming ◆ *vb* **4** *usually with* **in = surround,** beset, border, circumscribe, confine, edge, enclose, environ, hedge in, restrict, shut in, skirt

hem[2] *vb* **3 hem and haw** *or* **hum and haw = hesitate,** falter, fumble, pause, stammer, stutter

he-man *n Informal* **= muscle man,** Atlas, beefcake, Hercules, hunk (*sl.*), Tarzan (*inf.*)

hence *sentence connector* **1 = therefore,** ergo, for this reason, on that account, thus

henceforth *adv* **= from now on,** from this day forward, hence, hereafter, hereinafter, in the future

henchman ➊ ('hɛntʃmən) *n, pl* **henchmen. 1** a faithful attendant or supporter. **2** *Arch.* a squire; page. [C14 *hengestman,* from OE *hengest* stallion + MAN]

hendeca- *combining form.* eleven: *hendecagon; hendecasyllable.* [from Gk *hendeka,* from *hen,* neuter of *heis* one + *deka* ten]

hendecagon (hɛn'dɛkəgən) *n* a polygon having 11 sides.
▸**hendecagonal** (ˌhɛndɪ'kægənᵊl) *adj*

hendecasyllable ('hɛndɛkəˌsɪləbᵊl) *n Prosody.* a verse line of 11 syllables. [C18: from Gk]

hendiadys (hɛn'daɪədɪs) *n* a rhetorical device by which two nouns joined by a conjunction are used instead of a noun and a modifier, as in *to run with fear and haste* instead of *to run with fearful haste.* [C16: from Med. L, from Gk *hen dia duoin,* lit.: one through two]

henequen, henequin, *or* **heniquen** ('hɛnɪkɪn) *n* **1** an agave plant that is native to Mexico. **2** the fibre of this plant, used in making rope, twine, and coarse fabrics. [C19: from American Sp. *henequén,* prob. of Amerind origin]

henge (hɛndʒ) *n* a circular monument, often containing a circle of stones, dating from the Neolithic and Bronze Ages. [back formation from *Stonehenge,* site of important megalithic ruins on Salisbury Plain, S England]

hen harrier *n* a common harrier that nests in marshes and open land.

henhouse ('hɛnˌhaʊs) *n* a coop for hens.

henna ('hɛnə) *n* **1** a shrub or tree of Asia and N Africa. **2** a reddish dye obtained from the powdered leaves of this plant, used as a cosmetic and industrial dye. **3a** a reddish-brown colour. **3b** (*as adj*): *henna tresses.* ◆ *vb* **hennas, hennaing, hennaed. 4** (*tr*) to dye with henna. [C16: from Ar. *hinnā'*; see ALKANET]

hen night *n Inf.* a party for women only, esp. held for a woman shortly before she is married. Cf. **hen party, stag night.**

henotheism ('hɛnəʊθiːˌɪzəm) *n* the worship of one deity (of several) as the special god of one's family, clan, or tribe. [C19: from Gk *heis* one + *theos* god]
▸ˌ**henothe'istic** *adj*

hen party *n Inf.* a party at which only women are present. Cf. **hen night, stag night.**

henpeck ➊ ('hɛnˌpɛk) *vb* (*tr*) (of a woman) to harass or torment (a man, esp. her husband) by persistent nagging.
▸'**hen,pecked** *adj*

henry ('hɛnrɪ) *n, pl* **henry, henries,** *or* **henrys.** the derived SI unit of electric inductance; the inductance of a closed circuit in which an emf of 1 volt is produced when the current varies uniformly at the rate of 1 ampere per second. Symbol: H [C19: after Joseph *Henry* (1797–1878), US physicist]

hep (hɛp) *adj* **hepper, heppest.** *Sl.* an earlier word for **hip**[4].

heparin ('hɛpərɪn) *n* a polysaccharide, containing sulphate groups, present in most body tissues: an anticoagulant used in the treatment of thrombosis. [C20: from Gk *hēpar* the liver + -IN]

hepatic (hɪ'pætɪk) *adj* **1** of the liver. **2** having the colour of liver. ◆ *n* **3** any of various drugs for use in treating diseases of the liver. [C15: from L *hēpaticus,* from Gk *hēpar* liver]

hepatica (hɪ'pætɪkə) *n* a woodland plant of a N temperate genus, having three-lobed leaves and white, mauve, or pink flowers. [C16: from Med. L: liverwort, from L *hēpaticus* of the liver]

hepatitis (ˌhɛpə'taɪtɪs) *n* inflammation of the liver.

hepatitis A *n* a form of hepatitis caused by a virus transmitted in contaminated food or drink.

hepatitis B *n* a form of hepatitis caused by a virus transmitted by infected blood (as in transfusions), contaminated hypodermic needles, sexual contact, or by contact with any other body fluid. Former name: **serum hepatitis.**

Hepplewhite ('hɛpᵊlˌwaɪt) *adj* of or in a style of ornamental and carved 18th-century English furniture. [C18: after George *Hepplewhite* (1727–86), E cabinetmaker]

hepta- *or before a vowel* **hept-** *combining form.* seven: *heptameter.* [from Gk]

heptad ('hɛptæd) *n* a group or series of seven. [C17: from Gk *heptas* seven]

heptagon ('hɛptəgən) *n* a polygon having seven sides.
▸**heptagonal** (hɛp'tægənᵊl) *adj*

heptahedron (ˌhɛptə'hiːdrən) *n* a solid figure having seven plane faces.
▸ˌ**hepta'hedral** *adj*

heptameter (hɛp'tæmɪtə) *n Prosody.* a verse line of seven metrical feet.
▸**heptametrical** (ˌhɛptə'mɛtrɪkᵊl) *adj*

heptane ('hɛpteɪn) *n* an alkane which is found in petroleum and used as an anaesthetic. [C19: from HEPTA- + -ANE, because it has seven carbon atoms]

heptarchy ('hɛptɑːkɪ) *n, pl* **heptarchies. 1** government by seven rulers. **2** the seven kingdoms into which Anglo-Saxon England is thought to have been divided from about the 7th to the 9th centuries A.D.
▸'**heptarch** *n* ▸**hep'tarchic** *or* **hep'tarchal** *adj*

heptathlon (hɛp'tæθlɒn) *n* an athletic contest for women in which each athlete competes in seven different events. [C20: from HEPTA- + Gk *athlon* contest]
▸**hep'tathlete** *n*

heptavalent (hɛp'tævələnt, ˌhɛptə'veɪlənt) *adj Chem.* having a valency of seven.

her (hɜː; *unstressed* hə, ə) *pron* (*objective*) **1** refers to a female person or animal: *he loves her.* **2** refers to things personified as feminine or traditionally to ships and nations. ◆ *determiner* **3** of, belonging to, or associated with her: *her hair.* [OE *hire,* genitive & dative of *hēo* SHE, fem. of *hē* HE]

USAGE NOTE See at **me**[1].

herald ➊ ('hɛrəld) *n* **1** a person who announces important news. **2** *Often literary.* a forerunner; harbinger. **3** the intermediate rank of heraldic officer, between king-of-arms and pursuivant. **4** (in the Middle Ages) an official at a tournament. ◆ *vb* (*tr*) **5** to announce publicly. **6** to precede or usher in. [C14: from OF *herault,* of Gmc origin]

heraldic (hɛ'rældɪk) *adj* of or relating to heraldry or heralds.
▸**he'raldically** *adv*

heraldry ('hɛrəldrɪ) *n, pl* **heraldries. 1** the study concerned with the classification of armorial bearings, the tracing of genealogies, etc. **2** armorial bearings, insignia, etc. **3** the show and ceremony of heraldry.
▸'**heraldist** *n*

herb (hɜːb; *US* ɜːrb) *n* **1** a plant whose aerial parts do not persist above ground at the end of the growing season; herbaceous plant. **2** any of various usually aromatic plants, such as parsley and rosemary, that are used in cookery and medicine. [C13: from OF *herbe,* from L *herba* grass, green plants]
▸'**herb,like** *adj* ▸'**herby** *adj*

herbaceous (hɜː'beɪʃəs) *adj* **1** designating or relating to plants that are fleshy as opposed to woody: *a herbaceous plant.* **2** (of petals and sepals) green and leaflike.

herbaceous border *n* a flower bed that contains perennials rather than annuals.

herbage ('hɜːbɪdʒ) *n* **1** herbaceous plants collectively, esp. the edible parts on which cattle, sheep, etc., graze. **2** the vegetation of pasture land; pasturage.

herbal ('hɜːbᵊl) *adj* **1** of herbs. ◆ *n* **2** a book describing the properties of plants.

herbalist ('hɜːbᵊlɪst) *n* **1** a person who grows or specializes in the use of herbs, esp. medicinal herbs. **2** (formerly) a descriptive botanist.

herbarium (hɜː'bɛərɪəm) *n, pl* **herbariums** *or* **herbaria** (-rɪə). **1** a collection of dried plants that are mounted and classified systematically. **2** a room, etc., in which such a collection is kept.

herb bennet ('bɛnɪt) *n* a Eurasian and N African plant with yellow flowers. Also called: **wood avens, bennet.** [from OF *herbe benoite,* lit.: blessed herb, from Med. L *herba benedicta*]

herbicide ('hɜːbɪˌsaɪd) *n* a chemical that destroys plants, esp. one used to control weeds.

herbivore ('hɜːbɪˌvɔː) *n* **1** an animal that feeds on grass and other plants. **2** *Inf.* a liberal, idealistic, or nonmaterialistic person. [C19: from NL *herbivora* grass-eaters]
▸**her'bivorous** *adj*

herb Paris ('pærɪs) *n, pl* **herbs Paris.** a Eurasian woodland plant with a whorl of four leaves and a solitary yellow flower. [C16: from Med. L *herba paris,* lit.: herb of a pair: because the four leaves on the stalk look like a true lovers' knot]

herb Robert ('rɒbət) *n, pl* **herbs Robert.** a low-growing N temperate plant with strongly scented divided leaves and small purplish flowers. [C13: from Med. L *herba Roberti* herb of Robert, prob. after St *Robert,* 11th-cent. F ecclesiastic]

herculean ➊ (ˌhɜːkjʊ'liːən) *adj* **1** requiring tremendous effort, strength, etc. **2** (*sometimes cap.*) resembling Hercules, hero of classical myth, in strength, courage, etc.

herd[1] ➊ (hɜːd) *n* **1** a large group of mammals living and feeding together, esp. cattle. **2** *Often disparaging.* a large group of people. ◆ *vb* **3** to collect or be collected into or as if into a herd. [OE *heord*]

herd[2] (hɜːd) *n* **1a** *Arch. or dialect.* a man who tends livestock; herdsman.

THESAURUS

henchman *n* **1** = **attendant**, aide, associate, bodyguard, cohort (*chiefly US*), crony, follower, heavy (*sl.*), minder (*sl.*), minion, right-hand man, satellite, sidekick (*sl.*), subordinate, supporter

henpeck *vb* = **nag**, browbeat, bully, carp, chide, criticize, find fault, harass, hector, intimidate, niggle, pester, pick at, scold, torment

henpecked *adj* = **dominated**, browbeaten, bullied, cringing, led by the nose, meek, subject, subjugated, tied to someone's apron strings, timid, treated like dirt

Antonyms *adj* aggressive, assertive, bossy (*inf.*), dominating, domineering, forceful, macho, overbearing, self-assertive, spirited, wilful

herald *n* **1** = **messenger**, bearer of tidings, crier **2** *Often literary* = **forerunner**, harbinger, indication, omen, precursor, sign, signal, token ◆ *vb* **5** = **announce**, advertise, broadcast, proclaim, publicize, publish, trumpet **6** = **precede**, foretoken, harbinger, indicate, pave the way, portend, presage, promise, show, usher in

herculean *adj* **1** = **arduous**, demanding, difficult, exhausting, formidable, gruelling, hard, heavy, laborious, onerous, prodigious, strenuous, toilsome, tough **2** = **strong**, athletic, brawny, husky (*inf.*), mighty, muscular, powerful, rugged, sinewy, stalwart, strapping, sturdy

herd[1] *n* **1** = **flock**, assemblage, collection, crowd, crush, drove, horde, mass, mob, multitude, press, swarm, throng **2** *Often disparaging* = **mob**, populace, rabble, riffraff, the hoi polloi, the masses, the plebs ◆ *vb* **3** = **collect**, assemble, associate, congregate, flock, force, gather, guide, huddle, lead, muster, rally, shepherd

1b (*in combination*): *goatherd.* ◆ *vb* (*tr*) **2** to drive forwards in a large group. **3** to look after (livestock). [OE *hirde:* see HERD[1]]

herd instinct *n Psychol.* the inborn tendency to associate with others and follow the group's behaviour.

herdsman 🅣 ('hɜːdzmən) *n, pl* **herdsmen.** *Chiefly Brit.* a person who breeds or cares for cattle or (rarely) other livestock. US equivalent: **herder.**

here (hɪə) *adv* **1** in, at, or to this place, point, case, or respect: *we come here every summer; here comes Roy.* **2 here and there.** at several places in or throughout an area. **3 here's to.** a formula used in proposing a toast to someone or something. **4 neither here nor there.** of no relevance or importance. ◆ *n* **5** this place or point: *they leave here tonight.* [OE *hēr*]

hereabouts ('hɪərə,bauts) *or* **hereabout** *adv* in this region or neighbourhood.

hereafter 🅣 (,hɪər'ɑːftə) *adv* **1** *Formal or law.* in a subsequent part of this document, matter, case, etc. **2** a less common word for **henceforth. 3** at some time in the future. **4** in a future life after death. ◆ *n* (usually preceded by *the*) **5** life after death. **6** the future.

hereat (,hɪər'æt) *adv Arch.* because of this.

hereby (,hɪə'baɪ) *adv* (used in official statements, etc.) by means of or as a result of this.

hereditable (hɪ'redɪtəbᵊl) *adj* a less common word for **heritable.**
▸**he,redita'bility** *n*

hereditament (,herɪ'dɪtəmənt) *n Property law.* any kind of property capable of being inherited.

hereditary 🅣 (hɪ'redɪtərɪ, -trɪ) *adj* **1** of or denoting factors that can be transmitted genetically from one generation to another. **2** *Law.* **2a** descending to succeeding generations by inheritance. **2b** transmitted according to established rules of descent. **3** derived from one's ancestors; traditional: *hereditary feuds.*
▸**he'reditarily** *adv* ▸**he'reditariness** *n*

heredity 🅣 (hɪ'redɪtɪ) *n, pl* **heredities. 1** the transmission from one generation to another of genetic factors that determine individual characteristics. **2** the sum total of the inherited factors in an organism. [C16: from OF *heredite,* from L *hērēditās* inheritance; see HEIR]

herein (,hɪər'ɪn) *adv* **1** *Formal or law.* in or into this place, thing, document, etc. **2** *Rare.* in this respect, circumstance, etc.

hereinafter (,hɪərɪn'ɑːftə) *adv Formal or law.* from this point on in this document, etc.

hereinto (,hɪər'ɪntuː) *adv Formal or law.* into this place, circumstance, etc.

hereof (,hɪər'ɒv) *adv Formal or law.* of or concerning this.

hereon (,hɪər'ɒn) *adv* an archaic word for **hereupon.**

heresiarch (hɪ'riːzɪ,ɑːk) *n* the leader or originator of a heretical movement or sect.

heresy 🅣 ('herəsɪ) *n, pl* **heresies. 1a** an opinion contrary to the orthodox tenets of a religious body. **1b** the act of maintaining such an opinion. **2** any belief that is or is thought to be contrary to official or established theory. **3** adherence to unorthodox opinion. [C13: from OF *eresie,* from LL, from L: sect, from Gk, from *hairein* to choose]

heretic 🅣 ('herətɪk) *n* **1** *Now chiefly RC Church.* a person who maintains beliefs contrary to the established teachings of his Church. **2** a person who holds unorthodox opinions in any field.
▸**heretical** (hɪ'retɪkᵊl) *adj* ▸**he'retically** *adv*

hereto (,hɪə'tuː) *adv Formal or law.* to this place, thing, matter, document, etc.

heretofore (,hɪətu'fɔː) *adv Formal or law.* until now; before this time.

hereunder (,hɪər'ʌndə) *adv Formal or law.* **1** (in documents, etc.) below this; subsequently; hereafter. **2** under the terms or authority of this.

hereupon (,hɪərə'pɒn) *adv* **1** following immediately after this; at this stage. **2** *Formal or law.* upon this thing, point, subject, etc.

herewith (,hɪə'wɪð, -'wɪθ) *adv Formal.* together with this: *we send you herewith your statement of account.*

heriot ('herɪət) *n* (in medieval England) a death duty paid by villeins and free tenants to their lord, often consisting of the dead man's best beast or chattel. [OE *heregeatwa,* from *here* army + *geatwa* equipment]

heritable ('herɪtəbᵊl) *adj* **1** capable of being inherited; inheritable. **2** *Chiefly law.* capable of inheriting. [C14: from OF, from *heriter* to INHERIT]
▸**,herita'bility** *n* ▸**'heritably** *adv*

heritage 🅣 ('herɪtɪdʒ) *n* **1** something inherited at birth. **2** anything that has been transmitted from the past or handed down by tradition. **3** the evidence of the past, such as historical sites, and the unspoilt natural environment, considered as the inheritance of present-day society. **4** *Law.* any property, esp. land, that by law has descended or may descend to an heir. [C13: from OF; see HEIR]

herl (hɜːl) *or* **harl** *n Angling.* **1** the barb or barbs of a feather, used to dress fishing flies. **2** an artificial fly dressed with such barbs. [C15: from MLow G *herle,* from ?]

hermaphrodite 🅣 (hɜː'mæfrə,daɪt) *n* **1** *Biol.* an animal or flower that has both male and female reproductive organs. **2** a person having both male and female sexual characteristics. **3** a person or thing in which two opposite qualities are combined. ◆ *adj* **4** having the characteristics of a hermaphrodite. [C15: from L *hermaphrodītus,* from Gk, after *Hermaphroditus,* a son of Hermes and Aphrodite, who merged with the nymph Salmacis to form one body]
▸**her,maphro'ditic** *or* **her,maphro'ditical** *adj* ▸**her'maphrodit,ism** *n*

hermaphrodite brig *n* a sailing vessel with two masts, rigged square on the foremast and fore-and-aft on the aftermast.

hermeneutic (,hɜːmɪ'njuːtɪk) *or* **hermeneutical** *adj* **1** of or relating to the interpretation of Scripture. **2** interpretive.
▸**,herme'neutically** *adv*

hermeneutics (,hɜːmɪ'njuːtɪks) *n* (*functioning as sing*) **1** the science of interpretation, esp. of Scripture. **2** *Philosophy.* **2a** the study and interpretation of human behaviour and social institutions. **2b** (in existentialist thought) discussion of the purpose of life. [C18: from Gk *hermēneutikos* expert in interpretation, from *hermēneuein* to interpret, from ?]

hermetic (hɜː'metɪk) *or* **hermetical** *adj* **1a** (of a seal) airtight. **1b** (of a vessel, etc.) sealed so as to be airtight. **2** of or relating to alchemy or other forms of ancient science: *the hermetic arts.* **3** esoteric or recondite. **4** hidden or protected from the outside world: *the hermetic world of Vatican politics.* [C17: from Med. L *hermēticus* belonging to *Hermes Trismegistus* (Gk, lit.: Hermes thrice-greatest), traditionally the inventor of a magic seal]
▸**her'metically** *adv*

hermit 🅣 ('hɜːmɪt) *n* **1** one of the early Christian recluses. **2** any person living in solitude. [C13: from OF *hermite,* from LL, from Gk *erēmitēs* living in the desert, from *erēmos* lonely]
▸**her'mitic** *or* **her'mitical** *adj*

hermitage ('hɜːmɪtɪdʒ) *n* **1** the abode of a hermit. **2** any retreat.

hermit crab *n* a small soft-bodied crustacean living in and carrying about the empty shells of whelks or similar molluscs.

hernia ('hɜːnɪə) *n, pl* **hernias** *or* **herniae** (-nɪ,iː). the projection of an organ or part through the lining of the cavity in which it is normally situated, esp. the intestine through the front wall of the abdominal cavity. Also called: **rupture.** [C14: from L]
▸**'hernial** *adj* ▸**'herni,ated** *adj*

hero 🅣 ('hɪərəʊ) *n, pl* **heroes. 1** a man distinguished by exceptional courage, nobility, etc. **2** a man who is idealized for possessing superior qualities in any field. **3** *Classical myth.* a being of extraordinary strength and courage, often the offspring of a mortal and a god. **4** the principal male character in a novel, play, etc. [C14: from L *hērōs,* from Gk]

heroic 🅣 (hɪ'rəʊɪk) *or* **heroical** *adj* **1** of, like, or befitting a hero. **2** courageous but desperate. **3** treating of heroes and their deeds. **4** of or resembling the heroes of classical mythology. **5** (of language, manner, etc.) extravagant. **6** *Prosody.* of or resembling heroic verse. **7** (of the arts, esp. sculpture) larger than life-size; smaller than colossal.
▸**he'roically** *adv*

heroic age *n* the period in an ancient culture, when legendary heroes are said to have lived.

heroic couplet *n Prosody.* a verse form consisting of two rhyming lines in iambic pentameter.

heroics (hɪ'rəʊɪks) *pl n* **1** *Prosody.* short for **heroic verse. 2** extravagant or melodramatic language, behaviour, etc.

heroic verse *n Prosody.* a type of verse suitable for epic or heroic subjects, such as the classical hexameter or the French Alexandrine.

heroin ('herəʊɪn) *n* a white bitter-tasting crystalline powder derived from morphine: a highly addictive narcotic. [C19: coined in G as a trademark, prob. from HERO, referring to its aggrandizing effect on the personality]

heroine 🅣 ('herəʊɪn) *n* **1** a woman possessing heroic qualities. **2** a

THESAURUS

herdsman *n Chiefly Brit.* = **stockman**, cowherd, cowman, drover, grazier

hereafter *adv* **2** = **in future**, after this, from now on, hence, henceforth, henceforward ◆ *n* **5** = **afterlife**, future life, life after death, next world, the beyond

hereditary *adj* **1** = **genetic**, family, inborn, inbred, inheritable, transmissible **2** *Law* = **inherited**, bequeathed, handed down, patrimonial, transmitted, willed **3** = **traditional**, ancestral

heredity *n* **1, 2** = **genetics**, congenital traits, constitution, genetic make-up, inheritance

heresy *n* **1-3** = **unorthodoxy**, apostasy, dissidence, heterodoxy, iconoclasm, impiety, revisionism, schism

heretic *n* **1, 2** = **nonconformist**, apostate, dissenter, dissident, renegade, revisionist, schismatic, sectarian, separatist

heretical *adj* **1, 2** = **unorthodox**, freethinking, heterodox, iconoclastic, idolatrous, impious, revisionist, schismatic

heritage *n* **1, 2, 4** = **inheritance**, bequest, birthright, endowment, estate, legacy, lot, patrimony, portion, share, tradition

hermaphrodite *n* **2** = **androgyne**, bisexual, epicene

hermaphroditic *adj* **2** = **androgynous**, AC/DC, bisexual, epicene, gynandrous

hermit *n* **1** = **recluse**, anchorite, eremite, monk, stylite **2** = **recluse**, loner (*inf.*), recluse, solitary

hero *n* **2** = **idol**, celeb (*inf.*), celebrity, champion, conqueror, exemplar, great man, heart-throb (*Brit.*), man of the hour, megastar (*inf.*), popular figure, star, superstar, victor **4** = **leading man**, lead actor, male lead, principal male character, protagonist

heroic *adj* **1, 2** = **courageous**, bold, brave, daring, dauntless, doughty, fearless, gallant, intrepid, lion-hearted, stouthearted, undaunted, valiant, valorous **3, 4** = **classical**, Homeric, legendary, mythological **5** = **extravagant**, classic, elevated, epic, exaggerated, grand, grandiose, high-flown, inflated

Antonyms *adj* ≠ **courageous:** base, chicken (*sl.*), cowardly, craven, faint-hearted, ignoble, irresolute, mean, timid ≠ **extravagant:** lowbrow, simple, unadorned

heroine *n* **2** = **idol**, celeb (*inf.*), celebrity, goddess, megastar (*inf.*), woman of the hour **3** = **leading lady**, diva, female lead, lead actress, woman idealized for possessing superior qualities. **3** the main female character in a novel, play, film, etc.

heroism ❶ ('hɛrəʊˌɪzəm) *n* the state or quality of being a hero.

heron ('hɛrən) *n* any of various wading birds having a long neck, slim body, and a plumage that is commonly grey or white. [C14: from OF *hairon,* of Gmc origin]

heronry ('hɛrənrɪ) *n, pl* **heronries.** a colony of breeding herons.

hero worship ❶ *n* **1** admiration for heroes or idealized persons. **2** worship by the ancient Greeks and Romans of heroes. ◆ *vb* **hero-worship, hero-worships, hero-worshipping, hero-worshipped** *or US* **hero-worships, hero-worshiping, hero-worshiped. 3** (*tr*) to feel admiration or adulation for.
▸**'hero-ˌworshipper** *or US* **'hero-ˌworshiper** *n*

herpes ('hɜːpiːz) *n* any of several inflammatory diseases of the skin, esp. herpes simplex. [C17: via L from Gk, from *herpein* to creep]
▸**herpetic** (hɜː'pɛtɪk) *adj, n*

herpes simplex ('sɪmplɛks) *n* an acute viral disease characterized by formation of clusters of watery blisters, esp. on the lips or the genitals. See **cold sore, genital herpes.** [NL: simple herpes]

herpes zoster ('zɒstə) *n* a technical name for **shingles.** [NL: girdle herpes, from HERPES + Gk *zōstēr* girdle]

herpetology (ˌhɜːpɪ'tɒlədʒɪ) *n* the study of reptiles and amphibians. [C19: from Gk *herpeton* creeping animal]
▸**herpetologic** (ˌhɜːpɪtə'lɒdʒɪk) *or* **ˌherpeto'logical** *adj*

Herr (*German* hɛr) *n, pl* **Herren** ('hɛrən). a German man: used before a name as a title equivalent to *Mr.* [G, from OHG *herro* lord]

Herrenvolk *German.* ('hɛrənfɔlk) *n* a race, nation, or group, such as the Germans or Nazis as viewed by Hitler, believed by themselves to be superior to other races. Also called: **master race.** [lit.: master race, from *Herren,* pl. of HERR + *Volk* folk]

herring ('hɛrɪŋ) *n, pl* **herrings** *or* **herring.** an important food fish of northern seas, having an elongated body covered with large silvery scales. [OE *hǣring*]

herringbone ('hɛrɪŋˌbəʊn) *n* **1a** a pattern consisting of two or more rows of short parallel strokes slanting in alternate directions to form a series of zigzags. **1b** (*as modifier*): *a herringbone pattern.* **2** *Skiing.* a method of ascending a slope by walking with the skis pointing outwards and one's weight on the inside edges. ◆ *vb* **herringbones, herringboning, herringboned. 3** to decorate (textiles, brickwork, etc.) with herringbone. **4** (*intr*) *Skiing.* to ascend a slope in herringbone fashion.

herring gull *n* a common gull that has a white plumage with black-tipped wings.

hers (hɜːz) *pron* **1** something or someone belonging to her: *hers is the nicest dress; that cat is hers.* **2 of hers.** belonging to her. [C14 *hires;* see HER]

herself (hə'sɛlf) *pron* **1a** the reflexive form of *she* or *her.* **1b** (intensifier): *the queen herself signed.* **2** (*preceded by a copula*) her normal self: *she looks herself again.*

hertz (hɜːts) *n, pl* **hertz.** the derived SI unit of frequency; the frequency of a periodic phenomenon that has a periodic time of 1 second; 1 cycle per second. Symbol: Hz [C20: after H. R. *Hertz* (1857–94), G physicist]

Hertzian wave ('hɜːtsɪən) *n* an electromagnetic wave with a frequency in the range from about 3×10^{10} hertz to about 1.5×10^5 hertz. [C19: after H. R. *Hertz*]

Hertzsprung-Russell diagram ('hɜːtssprʌŋ'rʌsᵊl) *n* a graph in which the spectral types of stars are plotted against their absolute magnitudes. Stars fall into different groupings in different parts of the graph. [C20: after E. *Hertzsprung* (1873–1967), Danish astronomer, and H. N. *Russell* (1877–1957), US astronomer]

he's (hiːz) *contraction of* he is *or* he has.

hesitant ❶ ('hɛzɪtᵊnt) *adj* wavering, hesitating, or irresolute.
▸**'hesitantly** *adv*

hesitate ❶ ('hɛzɪˌteɪt) *vb* **hesitates, hesitating, hesitated.** (*intr*) **1** to be slow in acting; be uncertain. **2** to be reluctant (to do something). **3** to stammer or pause in speaking. [C17: from L *haesitāre,* from *haerēre* to cling to]
▸**hesitancy** ('hɛzɪtᵊnsɪ) *or* **ˌhesi'tation** *n* ▸**'hesiˌtatingly** *adv*

Hesperian (hɛ'spɪərɪən) *adj* **1** *Poetic.* western. **2** of or relating to the Hesperides or Islands of the Blessed where, in Greek mythology, the souls of the good went after death.

hesperidium (ˌhɛspə'rɪdɪəm) *n Bot.* the fruit of citrus plants, in which the flesh consists of fluid-filled hairs and is protected by a tough rind. [C19: NL; alluding to the fruit in the garden of the *Hesperides,* nymphs in Gk myth (daughters of Hesperus)]

Hesperus ('hɛspərəs) *n* an evening star, esp. Venus. [from L, from Gk, from *hesperos* western]

hessian ('hɛsɪən) *n* a coarse jute fabric similar to sacking. [C18: from HESSIAN]

Hessian ('hɛsɪən) *n* **1** a native or inhabitant of Hesse, a state of Germany. **2** a Hessian soldier in any of the mercenary units of the British Army in the War of American Independence or the Napoleonic Wars. ◆ *adj* **3** of Hesse or its inhabitants.

Hessian fly *n* a small dipterous fly whose larvae damage wheat, barley, and rye. [C18: thought to have been introduced into America by Hessian soldiers]

hest (hest) *n* an archaic word for **behest.** [OE *hǣs*]

hetaera (hɪ'tɪərə) *or* **hetaira** (hɪ'taɪrə) *n, pl* **hetaerae** (-'tɪəriː) *or* **hetairai** (-'taɪraɪ). (esp. in ancient Greece) a prostitute, esp. an educated courtesan. [C19: from Gk *hetaira* concubine]

hetaerism (hɪ'tɪərɪzəm) *or* **hetairism** (hɪ'taɪrɪzəm) *n* **1** the state of being a concubine. **2** *Sociol., anthropol.* a social system attributed to some primitive societies, in which women are communally shared.

hetero- *combining form.* other, another, or different: *heterosexual.* [from Gk *heteros* other]

heteroclite ('hɛtərəˌklaɪt) *adj also* **heteroclitic** (ˌhɛtərə'klɪtɪk). **1** (esp. of the form of a word) irregular or unusual. ◆ *n* **2** an irregularly formed word. [C16: from LL *heteroclitus* declining irregularly, from Gk, from HETERO- + *klinein* to inflect]

heterocyclic (ˌhɛtərəʊ'saɪklɪk, -'sɪk-) *adj* (of an organic compound) containing a closed ring of atoms, at least one of which is not a carbon atom.

heterodox ❶ ('hɛtərəʊˌdɒks) *adj* **1** at variance with established or accepted doctrines or beliefs. **2** holding unorthodox opinions. [C17: from Gk *heterodoxos,* from HETERO- + *doxa* opinion]
▸**'heteroˌdoxy** *n*

heterodyne ('hɛtərəʊˌdaɪn) *vb* **heterodynes, heterodyning, heterodyned. 1** *Electronics.* to combine by modulation (two alternating signals) to produce two signals having frequencies corresponding to the sum and the difference of the original frequencies. ◆ *adj* **2** produced by, operating by, or involved in heterodyning two signals.

heteroecious (ˌhɛtə'riːʃəs) *adj* (of parasites) undergoing different stages of the life cycle on different host species. [from HETERO- + *-oecious,* from Gk *oikia* house]
▸**heteroecism** (ˌhɛtə'riːˌsɪzəm) *n*

heterogamete (ˌhɛtərəʊgæ'miːt) *n* a gamete that differs in size and form from the one with which it unites in fertilization.

heterogamy (ˌhɛtə'rɒgəmɪ) *n* **1** a type of sexual reproduction in which the gametes differ in both size and form. **2** a condition in which different types of reproduction occur in successive generations of an organism. **3** the presence of both male and female flowers in one inflorescence.
▸**ˌheter'ogamous** *adj*

heterogeneous ❶ (ˌhɛtərəʊ'dʒiːnɪəs) *adj* **1** composed of unrelated parts. **2** not of the same type. [C17: from Med. L *heterogeneus,* from Gk, from HETERO- + *genos* sort]
▸**heterogeneity** (ˌhɛtərəʊdʒɪ'niːɪtɪ) *or* **ˌhetero'geneousness** *n*

heterogony (ˌhɛtə'rɒgənɪ) *n* **1** *Biol.* the alternation of parthenogenetic and sexual generations in rotifers and similar animals. **2** the condition in plants, such as the primrose, of having flowers that differ from each other in the length of their stamens and styles.
▸**ˌheter'ogonous** *adj*

heterologous (ˌhɛtə'rɒləgəs) *adj* **1** *Pathol.* designating cells or tissues not normally present in a particular part of the body. **2** differing in structure or origin.
▸**ˌheter'ology** *n*

heteromerous (ˌhɛtə'rɒmərəs) *adj Biol.* having parts that differ, esp. in number.

heteromorphic (ˌhɛtərəʊ'mɔːfɪk) *or* **heteromorphous** *adj Biol.* **1** differing from the normal form. **2** (esp. of insects) having different forms at different stages of the life cycle.
▸**ˌhetero'morphism** *n*

heteronomous (ˌhɛtə'rɒnɪməs) *adj* **1** subject to an external law. **2** (of parts of an organism) differing in the manner of growth, development, or specialization.
▸**ˌheter'onomy** *n*

heteronym ('hɛtərəʊˌnɪm) *n* one of two or more words pronounced differently but spelt alike: *the two English words spelt "bow" are heteronyms.* Cf. **homograph.** [C17: from LGk *heteronumos,* from Gk HETERO- + *onoma* name]

THESAURUS

prima donna, principal female character, protagonist

heroism *n* = **bravery**, boldness, courage, courageousness, daring, fearlessness, fortitude, gallantry, intrepidity, prowess, spirit, valour

hero worship *n* **1** = **idolization**, admiration, adoration, adulation, idealization, putting on a pedestal, veneration

hesitant *adj* = **uncertain**, diffident, doubtful, half-hearted, halting, hanging back, hesitating, irresolute, lacking confidence, reluctant, sceptical, shy, timid, unsure, vacillating, wavering
Antonyms *adj* arrogant, avid, can-do (*inf.*), clear, confident, definite, determined, dogmatic, eager, enthusiastic, firm, forceful, keen, positive, resolute, self-assured, spirited, sure, unhesitating, unwavering

hesitate *vb* **1** = **waver**, be uncertain, delay, dither (*chiefly Brit.*), doubt, haver (*Brit.*), hum and haw, pause, shillyshally (*inf.*), swither (*Scot.*), vacillate, wait **2** = **be reluctant**, balk, be unwilling, boggle, demur, hang back, scruple, shrink from, think twice **3** = **falter**, fumble, hem and haw *or* hum and haw, stammer, stumble, stutter
Antonyms *vb* ≠ **waver:** be confident, be decisive, be firm, continue, decide ≠ **be reluctant:** be determined, resolve, welcome

hesitation *n* **1** = **indecision**, delay, doubt, dubiety, hesitancy, irresolution, uncertainty, vacillation **2** = **reluctance**, demurral, misgiving(s), qualm(s), scruple(s), unwillingness **3** = **faltering**, fumbling, hemming and hawing, stammering, stumbling, stuttering

heterodox *adj* **1, 2** = **unorthodox**, dissident, heretical, iconoclastic, revisionist, schismatic, unsound

heterogeneous *adj* **1, 2** = **diverse**, assorted, contrary, contrasted, different, discrepant, disparate, dissimilar, divergent, diversified, incongruous, manifold, miscellaneous, mixed, motley, opposed, unlike, unrelated, varied

heterophyllous (ˌhɛtərəʊˈfɪləs, ˌhɛtəˈrɒfɪləs) *adj* having more than one type of leaf on the same plant.
▸ˈ**hetero,phylly** *n*

heteropterous (ˌhɛtəˈrɒptərəs) *or* **heteropteran** *adj* of or belonging to a suborder of hemipterous insects, including bedbugs, water bugs, etc., in which the forewings are membranous but have leathery tips. [C19: from NL *Heteroptera,* from HETERO- + Gk *pteron* wing]

heterosexism (ˌhɛtərəʊˈsɛkˌsɪzəm) *n* discrimination on the basis of sexual orientation, practised by heterosexuals against homosexuals.
▸**hetero'sexist** *adj, n*

heterosexual (ˌhɛtərəʊˈsɛksjʊəl) *n* **1** a person who is sexually attracted to the opposite sex. ◆ *adj* **2** of or relating to heterosexuality.
▸ˌ**hetero,sexu'ality** *n*

heterotaxis (ˌhɛtərəʊˈtæksɪs) *or* **heterotaxy** *n* an abnormal or asymmetrical arrangement of parts, as of the organs of the body.

heterotrophic (ˌhɛtərəʊˈtrɒfɪk) *adj* (of animals and some plants) using complex organic compounds to manufacture their own organic constituents. [C20: from HETERO- + Gk *trophikos* concerning food, from *trophē* nourishment]
▸ˈ**hetero,troph** *n*

heterozygote (ˌhɛtərəʊˈzaɪgəʊt) *n* an animal or plant that is heterozygous; a hybrid.

heterozygous (ˌhɛtərəʊˈzaɪgəs) *adj Genetics.* (of an organism) having dissimilar alleles for any one gene: *heterozygous for eye colour.*

hetman (ˈhɛtmən) *n, pl* **hetmans.** an elected leader of the Cossacks. Also called: **ataman.** [C18: from Polish, from G *Hauptmann* headman]

het up *adj Inf.* angry; excited: *don't get het up.* [C19: from dialect p.p. of HEAT]

heuchera (ˈhɔɪkərə) *n* a North American shrub with red or pink flowers and ornamental foliage. [after J. H. *Heucher* (1677–1747), G botanist]

heuristic (hjʊəˈrɪstɪk) *adj* **1** helping to learn; guiding in investigation. **2** (of a method of teaching) allowing pupils to learn things for themselves. **3a** *Maths, science, philosophy.* using or obtained by exploration of possibilities rather than by following set rules. **3b** *Computing.* denoting a rule of thumb for solving a problem without the exhaustive application of an algorithm: *a heuristic solution.* ◆ *n* **4** (*pl*) the science of heuristic procedure. [C19: from NL *heuristicus,* from Gk *heuriskein* to discover]
▸**heu'ristically** *adv*

hew ❶ (hjuː) *vb* **hews, hewing, hewed, hewed** *or* **hewn. 1** to strike (something, esp. wood) with cutting blows, as with an axe. **2** (*tr; often foll. by out*) to carve from a substance. **3** (*tr; often foll. by away, off,* etc.) to sever from a larger portion. **4** (*intr; often foll. by to*) *US & Canad.* to conform. [OE *hēawan*]
▸ˈ**hewer** *n*

hex[1] (hɛks) *n* **a** short for **hexadecimal (notation). b** (*as modifier*): *hex code.*

hex[2] (hɛks) *US & Canad. inf.* ◆ *vb* **1** (*tr*) to bewitch. ◆ *n* **2** an evil spell. **3** a witch. [C19: via Pennsylvania Du. from G *Hexe* witch, from MHG *hecse,* ?from OHG *hagzissa*]

hex. *abbrev. for:* **1** hexachord. **2** hexagon(al).

hexa- *or before a vowel* **hex-** *combining form.* six: *hexachord; hexameter.* [from Gk, from *hex* SIX]

hexachlorophene (ˌhɛksəˈklɔːrəfiːn) *n* an insoluble white bactericidal substance used in antiseptic soaps, deodorants, etc. Formula: $(C_6HCl_3OH)_2CH_2$.

hexachord (ˈhɛksəˌkɔːd) *n* (in medieval musical theory) any of three diatonic scales based upon C, F, and G, each consisting of six notes, from which solmization was developed.

hexad (ˈhɛksæd) *n* a group or series of six. [C17: from Gk *hexas,* from *hex* six]

hexadecane (ˈhɛksədɛˌkeɪn, ˌhɛksəˈdɛkeɪn) *n* the systematic name for **cetane.**

hexadecanoic acid (ˌhɛksəˌdɛkəˈnəʊɪk) *n* the systematic name for **palmitic acid.**

hexadecimal notation *or* **hexadecimal** (ˌhɛksəˈdɛsɪməl) *n* a number system having a base 16; the symbols for the numbers 0 – 9 are the same as those used in the decimal system, and the numbers 10 – 15 are usually represented by the letters A – F. The system is used as a convenient way of representing the internal binary code of a computer.

hexagon (ˈhɛksəgən) *n* a polygon having six sides.
▸**hex'agonal** *adj*

hexagram (ˈhɛksəˌgræm) *n* a star-shaped figure formed by extending the sides of a regular hexagon to meet at six points.

hexahedron (ˌhɛksəˈhiːdrən) *n* a solid figure having six plane faces.
▸ˌ**hexa'hedral** *adj*

hexameter (hɛkˈsæmɪtə) *n Prosody.* **1** a verse line consisting of six metrical feet. **2** (in Greek and Latin epic poetry) a verse line of six metrical feet, of which the first four are usually dactyls or spondees, the fifth almost always a dactyl, and the sixth a spondee or trochee.
▸**hexametric** (ˌhɛksəˈmɛtrɪk) *or* ˌ**hexa'metrical** *adj*

hexane (ˈhɛkseɪn) *n* a liquid alkane found in petroleum and used as a solvent. Formula: C_6H_{14}. [C19: from HEXA- + -ANE]

hexapla (ˈhɛksəplə) *n* an edition of the Old Testament compiled by Origen (?185–?254 A.D.), Christian theologian, containing six versions of the text. [C17: from Gk *hexaploos* sixfold]
▸ˈ**hexaplar** *adj*

hexapod (ˈhɛksəˌpɒd) *n* an insect.

hexavalent (ˌhɛksəˈveɪlənt) *adj Chem.* having a valency of six. Also: **sexivalent.**

hexose (ˈhɛksəʊs, -əʊz) *n* a monosaccharide, such as glucose, that contains six carbon atoms per molecule.

hey (heɪ) *interj* **1** an expression indicating surprise, dismay, discovery, etc. **2 hey presto!** an exclamation used by conjurors to herald the climax of a trick. [C13: imit.]

heyday ❶ (ˈheɪˌdeɪ) *n* the time of most power, popularity, vigour, etc. [C16: prob. based on HEY]

hf *abbrev. for* half.

Hf *the chemical symbol for* hafnium.

HF *or* **h.f.** *abbrev. for* high frequency.

hg *abbrev. for* hectogram.

Hg *the chemical symbol for* mercury. [from NL *hydrargyrum*]

HG *abbrev. for* His (*or* Her) Grace.

hgt *abbrev. for* height.

HGV (formerly, in Britain) *abbrev. for* heavy goods vehicle.

HH *abbrev. for:* **1** His (*or* Her) Highness. **2** His Holiness (title of the Pope). ◆ **3** (on Brit. pencils) *symbol for* double hard.

hi (haɪ) *sentence substitute.* an informal word for **hello.** [C20: prob. from *how are you?*]

hiatus ❶ (haɪˈeɪtəs) *n, pl* **hiatuses** *or* **hiatus. 1** (esp. in manuscripts) a break or interruption in continuity. **2** a break between adjacent vowels in the pronunciation of a word. [C16: from L: gap, cleft, from *hiāre* to gape]

hiatus hernia *n* protrusion of part of the stomach through the diaphragm at the oesophageal opening.

Hib (hɪb) *n acronym for* Haemophilus influenzae type b: a vaccine against a type of bacterial meningitis, administered to children.

hibachi (hɪˈbɑːtʃɪ) *n* a portable brazier for heating and cooking food. [from Japanese, from *hi* fire + *bachi* bowl]

hibakusha (hɪˈbɑːkuʃə) *n, pl* **hibakusha** *or* **hibakushas.** a survivor of either of the atomic-bomb attacks on Hiroshima and Nagasaki in 1945. [C20: from Japanese, from *hibaku* bombed + *-sha* -person]

hibernal (haɪˈbɜːnᵊl) *adj* of or occurring in winter. [C17: from L *hībernālis,* from *hiems* winter]

hibernate ❶ (ˈhaɪbəˌneɪt) *vb* **hibernates, hibernating, hibernated.** (*intr*) **1** (of some animals) to pass the winter in a dormant condition with metabolism greatly slowed down. **2** to cease from activity. [C19: from L *hībernāre* to spend the winter, from *hībernus* of winter]
▸ˌ**hiber'nation** *n* ▸ˈ**hiber,nator** *n*

Hibernia (haɪˈbɜːnɪə) *n* the Roman name for Ireland: used poetically in later times.
▸**Hi'bernian** *adj, n*

Hibernicism (haɪˈbɜːnɪˌsɪzəm) *n* an Irish expression, idiom, trait, custom, etc.

Hiberno- (haɪˈbɜːnəʊ) *combining form.* denoting Irish or Ireland: *Hiberno-English.*

hibiscus (hɪˈbɪskəs) *n, pl* **hibiscuses.** any plant of the chiefly tropical and subtropical genus *Hibiscus,* cultivated for its large brightly coloured flowers. [C18: from L, from Gk *hibiskos* marsh mallow]

hiccup (ˈhɪkʌp) *n* **1** a spasm of the diaphragm producing a sudden breathing in of air resulting in a characteristic sharp sound. **2** (*pl*) the state of having such spasms. **3** *Inf.* a minor difficulty. ◆ *vb* **hiccups, hiccuping, hiccuped** *or* **hiccups, hiccupping, hiccupped. 4** (*intr*) to make a hiccup or hiccups. **5** (*tr*) to utter with a hiccup. ◆ Also: **hiccough** (ˈhɪkʌp). [C16: imit.]

hic jacet *Latin.* (hɪk ˈjækɛt) (on gravestones, etc.) here lies.

hick (hɪk) *n Inf., chiefly US & Canad.* a country bumpkin. [C16: after *Hick,* familiar form of *Richard*]

hickory (ˈhɪkərɪ) *n, pl* **hickories. 1** a tree of a chiefly North American genus having nuts with edible kernels and hard smooth shells. **2** the hard tough wood of this tree. [C17: ult. from Algonquian *pawcohiccora* food made from ground hickory nuts]

hid (hɪd) *vb* the past tense and a past participle of **hide**[1].

hidalgo (hɪˈdælgəʊ) *n, pl* **hidalgos.** a member of the lower nobility in Spain. [C16: from Sp., from OSp. *fijo dalgo* nobleman, from L *filius* son + *dē* of + *aliquid* something]

hidden ❶ (ˈhɪdᵊn) *vb* **1** a past participle of **hide**[1]. ◆ *adj* **2** concealed or obscured: *a hidden cave; a hidden meaning.*

hidden agenda *n* a hidden motive or intention behind an overt action, policy, etc.

hide[1] ❶ (haɪd) *vb* **hides, hiding, hid, hidden** *or* **hid. 1** to conceal (oneself or an object) from view or discovery: *to hide a pencil; to hide from the police.* **2** (*tr*) to obscure: *clouds hid the sun.* **3** (*tr*) to keep secret. **4** (*tr*) to turn

THESAURUS

hew *vb* **1 = cut,** axe, chop, hack, lop, split **2 = carve,** fashion, form, make, model, sculpt, sculpture, shape, smooth

heyday *n* **= prime,** bloom, flowering, pink, prime of life, salad days

hiatus *n* **1 = interruption,** break, discontinuity, gap, interval, lacuna, pause

hibernate *vb* **1 = lie dormant,** hole up, overwinter, remain torpid, sleep snug, vegetate, winter

hidden *adj* **2 = concealed,** abstruse, clandestine, close, covered, covert, cryptic, dark, hermetic, hermetical, latent, masked, mysterious, mystic, mystical, obscure, occult, recondite, secret, shrouded, ulterior, under wraps, unrevealed, unseen, veiled

hide[1] *vb* **1 = conceal,** cache, go into hiding, go to ground, go underground, hole up, lie low, secrete, stash (*inf.*), take cover **2 = disguise,** blot out, bury, camouflage, cloak, conceal, cover, eclipse, mask, obscure, screen, shelter, shroud,

(one's eyes, etc.) away. ◆ *n* **5** *Brit.* a place of concealment, usually disguised to appear as part of the natural environment, used by hunters, birdwatchers, etc. US and Canad. equivalent: **blind.** [OE *hȳdan*]
▸ **'hider** *n*

hide[2] Ⓣ (haɪd) *n* **1** the skin of an animal, either tanned or raw. **2** *Inf.* the human skin. ◆ *vb* **hides, hiding, hided. 3** (*tr*) *Inf.* to flog. [OE *hȳd*]

hide[3] (haɪd) *n* an obsolete Brit. land measure, varying from about 60 to 120 acres. [OE *hīgid*]

hide-and-seek *or US, Canad., & Scot.* **hide-and-go-seek** *n* a game in which one player covers his eyes while the others hide, and he then tries to find them.

hideaway Ⓣ ('haɪdəˌweɪ) *n* a hiding place or secluded spot.

hidebound Ⓣ ('haɪdˌbaʊnd) *adj* **1** restricted by petty rules, a conservative attitude, etc. **2** (of cattle, etc.) having the skin closely attached to the flesh as a result of poor feeding.

hideous Ⓣ ('hɪdɪəs) *adj* **1** extremely ugly; repulsive. **2** terrifying and horrific. [C13: from OF *hisdos*, from *hisde* fear; from ?]
▸ **'hideously** *adv* ▸ **'hideousness** *n*

hide-out Ⓣ *n* a hiding place, esp. a remote place used by outlaws, etc.; hideaway.

hiding[1] ('haɪdɪŋ) *n* **1** the state of concealment: *in hiding.* **2 hiding place.** a place of concealment.

hiding[2] Ⓣ ('haɪdɪŋ) *n Inf.* a flogging; beating.

hidrosis (hɪ'drəʊsɪs) *n* a technical word for **perspiration** or **sweat.** [C18: via NL from Gk, from *hidrōs* sweat]
▸**hidrotic** (hɪ'drɒtɪk) *adj*

hidy-hole *or* **hidey-hole** *n Inf.* a hiding place.

hie (haɪ) *vb* **hies, hieing** *or* **hying, hied.** *Arch. or poetic.* to hurry; speed. [OE *hīgian* to strive]

hierarch ('haɪəˌrɑːk) *n* **1** a high priest. **2** a person at a high level in a hierarchy.
▸ **ˌhier'archal** *adj*

hierarchy Ⓣ ('haɪəˌrɑːkɪ) *n, pl* **hierarchies. 1** a system of persons or things arranged in a graded order. **2** a body of persons in holy orders organized into graded ranks. **3** the collective body of those so organized. **4** a series of ordered groupings within a system, such as the arrangement of plants into classes, orders, etc. **5** government by a priesthood. [C14: from Med. L *hierarchia*, from LGk, from *hierarkhēs* high priest; see HIERO-, -ARCHY]
▸ **ˌhier'archical** *or* **ˌhier'archic** *adj* ▸ **'hierˌarchism** *n*

hieratic (ˌhaɪə'rætɪk) *adj* **1** of priests. **2** of a cursive form of hieroglyphics used by priests in ancient Egypt. **3** of styles in art that adhere to certain fixed types, as in ancient Egypt. ◆ *n* **4** the hieratic script of ancient Egypt. [C17: from L *hierāticus*, from Gk, from *hiereus* priest]
▸ **ˌhier'atically** *adv*

hiero- *or before a vowel* **hier-** *combining form.* holy or divine: *hierarchy.* [from Gk, from *hieros* holy]

hieroglyphic Ⓣ (ˌhaɪərə'glɪfɪk) *adj also* **hieroglyphical. 1** of or relating to a form of writing using picture symbols, esp. as used in ancient Egypt. **2** difficult to decipher. ◆ *n also* **hieroglyph. 3** a picture or symbol representing an object, concept, or sound. **4** a symbol that is difficult to decipher. [C16: from LL *hieroglyphicus*, from Gk, from HIERO- + *gluphē*, from *gluphein* to carve]
▸ **ˌhiero'glyphically** *adv*

hieroglyphics (ˌhaɪərə'glɪfɪks) *n* (*functioning as sing or pl*) **1** a form of writing, esp. as used in ancient Egypt, in which pictures or symbols are used to represent objects, concepts, or sounds. **2** difficult or undecipherable writing.

hierophant ('haɪərəˌfænt) *n* **1** (in ancient Greece) a high priest of religious mysteries. **2** a person who interprets esoteric mysteries. [C17: from LL *hierophanta*, from Gk, from HIERO- + *phainein* to reveal]
▸ **ˌhiero'phantic** *adj*

hi-fi ('haɪˌfaɪ) *n Inf.* **1a** short for **high fidelity. 1b** (*as modifier*): *hi-fi equipment.* **2** a set of high-quality sound-reproducing equipment.

higgledy-piggledy Ⓣ ('hɪgᵊldɪ'pɪgᵊldɪ) *Inf.* ◆ *adj, adv* **1** in a jumble. ◆ *n* **2** a muddle.

high Ⓣ (haɪ) *adj* **1** being a relatively great distance from top to bottom; tall: *a high building.* **2** situated at a relatively great distance above sea level: *a high plateau.* **3** (*postpositive*) being a specified distance from top to bottom: *three feet high.* **4** extending from or performed at an elevation: *a high dive.* **5** (*in combination*) coming up to a specified level: *knee-high.* **6** being at its peak: *high noon.* **7** of greater than average height: *a high collar.* **8** greater than normal in intensity or amount: *a high wind; high mileage.* **9** (of sound) acute in pitch. **10** (of latitudes) relatively far north or south from the equator. **11** (of meat) slightly decomposed, regarded as enhancing the flavour of game. **12** very important: *the high priestess.* **13** exalted in style or character: *high drama.* **14** expressing contempt or arrogance: *high words.* **15** elated; cheerful: *high spirits.* **16** *Inf.* being in a state of altered consciousness induced by alcohol, narcotics, etc. **17** *Inf.* overexcited: *by Christmas the children are high.* **18** luxurious or extravagant: *high life.* **19** advanced in complexity: *high finance.* **20** (of a gear) providing a relatively great forward speed for a given engine speed. **21** *Phonetics.* denoting a vowel whose articulation is produced by raising the tongue, such as for the *ee* in *see* or *oo* in *moon.* **22** (*cap. when part of a name*) formal and elaborate: *High Mass.* **23** (*usually cap.*) relating to the High Church. **24** *Cards.* having a relatively great value in a suit. **25 high and dry.** stranded; destitute. **26 high and mighty.** *Inf.* arrogant. **27 high opinion.** a favourable opinion. ◆ *adv* **28** at or to a height: *he jumped high.* **29** in a high manner. **30** *Naut.* close to the wind with sails full. ◆ *n* **31** a high place or level. **32** *Inf.* a state of altered consciousness induced by alcohol, narcotics, etc. **33** another word for **anticyclone. 34 on high. 34a** at a height. **34b** in heaven. [OE *hēah*]

High Arctic *n* the regions of Canada, esp. the northern islands, within the Arctic Circle.

highball ('haɪˌbɔːl) *n Chiefly US.* a long iced drink consisting of spirits with soda water, etc.

highborn Ⓣ ('haɪˌbɔːn) *adj* of noble birth.

highboy ('haɪˌbɔɪ) *n US & Canad.* a tallboy.

highbrow Ⓣ ('haɪˌbraʊ) *Often disparaging.* ◆ *n* **1** a person of scholarly and erudite tastes. ◆ *adj also* **highbrowed. 2** appealing to highbrows.

highchair ('haɪˌtʃɛə) *n* a long-legged chair for a child, esp. one with a table-like tray.

High Church *n* **1** the party or movement within the Church of England stressing continuity with Catholic Christendom, the authority of bishops, and the importance of sacraments. ◆ *adj* **High-Church. 2** of or relating to this party or movement.
▸ **'High-'Churchman** *n*

high-class Ⓣ *adj* **1** of very good quality: *a high-class grocer.* **2** belonging to or exhibiting the characteristics of an upper social class.

high-coloured *adj* (of the complexion) deep red or purplish; florid.

THESAURUS

veil **3** = **suppress**, draw a veil over, hush up, keep dark, keep secret, keep under one's hat, withhold
Antonyms *vb* admit, bare, confess, disclose, display, divulge, exhibit, expose, find, flaunt, reveal, show, uncover, unveil

hide[2] *n* **1** = **skin**, fell, pelt

hideaway *n* = **hiding place**, haven, hide-out, nest, refuge, retreat, sanctuary

hidebound *adj* **1** = **conventional**, brassbound, narrow, narrow-minded, puritan, rigid, set, set in one's ways, strait-laced, ultraconservative
Antonyms *adj* broad-minded, flexible, liberal, open, receptive, tolerant, unconventional, unorthodox

hideous *adj* **1** = **ugly**, ghastly, grim, grisly, grotesque, gruesome, monstrous, repulsive, revolting, unsightly **2** = **terrifying**, abominable, appalling, awful, detestable, disgusting, dreadful, horrendous, horrible, horrid, horrific, loathsome, macabre, obscene, odious, shocking, sickening, terrible
Antonyms *adj* ≠ **ugly:** appealing, beautiful, captivating, charming, entrancing, lovely, pleasant, pleasing

hide-out *n* = **hiding place**, den, hideaway, lair, secret place, shelter

hiding[2] *n* = **beating**, caning, drubbing, flogging, larruping (*Brit. dialect*), lathering (*inf.*), licking (*inf.*), spanking, tanning (*sl.*), thrashing, walloping (*inf.*), whaling, whipping

hierarchy *n* **1** = **grading**, pecking order, ranking

hieroglyphic *adj* **2** = **indecipherable**, enigmatical, figurative, obscure, runic, symbolical

higgledy-piggledy *Informal adj* **1** = **haphazard**, helter-skelter, indiscriminate, jumbled, muddled, pell-mell, topsy-turvy ◆ *adv* **2** = **haphazardly**, all over the place, all over the shop (*inf.*), anyhow, any old how, confusedly, helter-skelter, pell-mell, topsy-turvy

high *adj* **1** = **tall**, elevated, lofty, soaring, steep, towering **8** = **extreme**, excessive, extraordinary, great, intensified, sharp, strong **9** = **high-pitched**, acute, penetrating, piercing, piping, sharp, shrill, soprano, strident, treble **11** = **gamey**, niffy (*Brit. sl.*), pongy (*Brit. inf.*), strong-flavoured, tainted, whiffy (*Brit. sl.*) **12** = **important**, arch, big-time (*inf.*), chief, consequential, distinguished, eminent, exalted, influential, leading, major league (*inf.*), notable, powerful, prominent, ruling, significant, superior **14** = **haughty**, arrogant, boastful, bragging, despotic, domineering, lofty, lordly, ostentatious, overbearing, proud, tyrannical, vainglorious **15** = **cheerful**, boisterous, bouncy (*inf.*), elated, excited, exhilarated, exuberant, joyful, light-hearted, merry **16** *Informal* = **intoxicated**, freaked out (*inf.*), inebriated, on a trip (*inf.*), spaced out (*sl.*), stoned (*sl.*), tripping (*inf.*), turned on (*sl.*), zonked (*sl.*) **17** *Informal* = **euphoric**, delirious, hyped up (*sl.*) **18** = **luxurious**, extravagant, grand, lavish, rich **25 high and dry** = **abandoned**, bereft, destitute, helpless, stranded **26 high and mighty** *Informal* = **self-important**, arrogant, cavalier, conceited, disdainful, haughty, imperious, overbearing, snobbish, stuck-up (*inf.*), superior ◆ *adv* **28** = **aloft**, at great height, far up, way up ◆ *n* **31** = **peak**, apex, crest, height, record level, summit, top **32** *Informal* = **intoxication**, delirium, ecstasy, euphoria, trip (*inf.*)
Antonyms *adj* ≠ **tall:** dwarfed, low, short, stunted ≠ **extreme:** average, low, mild, moderate, reduced, restrained, routine, suppressed ≠ **high-pitched:** alto, bass, deep, gruff, low, low-pitched ≠ **important:** average, common, degraded, ignoble, inconsequential, insignificant, low, lowly, low-ranking, menial, routine, secondary, undistinguished, unimportant ≠ **cheerful:** angry, dejected, depressed, gloomy, low, melancholy, sad

highborn *adj* = **noble**, aristocratic, blue-blooded, gentle (*arch.*), patrician, pedigreed, thoroughbred, well-born

highbrow *Often disparaging n* **1** = **intellectual**, aesthete, Brahmin (*US*), brain (*inf.*), brainbox (*sl.*), egghead (*inf.*), mastermind, savant, scholar ◆ *adj* **2** = **intellectual**, bookish, brainy (*inf.*), cultivated, cultured, deep, highbrowed, sophisticated
Antonyms *n* ≠ **intellectual:** idiot, ignoramus, illiterate, imbecile (*inf.*), lowbrow, moron, philistine ◆ *adj* ≠ **intellectual:** ignorant, lowbrow, philistine, shallow, uncultivated, uninformed, unintellectual, unlearned, unsophisticated

high-class *adj* **1** = **high-quality**, A1 *or* A-one (*inf.*), choice, classy (*sl.*), elite, exclusive, first-rate, high-toned, posh (*inf., chiefly Brit.*),

high comedy *n* comedy set largely among cultured and articulate people and featuring witty dialogue.
high commissioner *n* the senior diplomatic representative sent by one Commonwealth country to another instead of an ambassador.
high country *n* (often preceded by *the*) *NZ.* sheep pastures in the foothills of the Southern Alps, New Zealand.
High Court *n* **1** Also called: **High Court of Justice.** (in England) the supreme court dealing with civil law cases. **2** (in Australia) the highest court of appeal, deciding esp. constitutional issues. **3** (in New Zealand) a court of law that is superior to a District Court. Former name: **Supreme Court.**
high definition television *n* a television system using 1000 or more scanning lines and a higher field repetition rate. Abbrev.: **HDTV.**
high-energy physics *n* (*functioning as sing*) another name for **particle physics.**
higher ('haɪə) *adj* **1** the comparative of **high.** ◆ *n* (*usually cap.*) (in Scotland) **2a** the advanced level of the Scottish Certificate of Education. **2b** (*as modifier*): *Higher Latin.* **3** a pass in a subject at Higher level: *she has four Highers.*
higher education *n* education and training at colleges, universities, etc.
higher mathematics *n* (*functioning as sing*) mathematics that is more abstract than normal arithmetic, algebra, geometry, and trigonometry.
higher-rate tax *n* (in Britain) a rate of income tax that is higher than the basic rate and becomes payable on taxable income in excess of a specified limit.
higher-up ❶ *n Inf.* a person of higher rank or in a superior position.
highest common factor *n* the largest number or quantity that is a factor of each member of a group of numbers or quantities.
high explosive *n* an extremely powerful chemical explosive, such as TNT or gelignite.
highfalutin ❶ (ˌhaɪfə'luːtɪn) *or* **highfaluting** *adj Inf.* pompous or pretentious. [C19: from HIGH + *-falutin*, ? var. of *fluting*, from FLUTE]
high fidelity *n* **a** the reproduction of sound using electronic equipment that gives faithful reproduction with little or no distortion. **b** (*as modifier*): *a high-fidelity amplifier.* ◆ Often shortened to **hi-fi.**
high-five *n Sl.* a gesture of greeting or congratulation in which two people slap raised right palms together.
high-flown ❶ *adj* extravagant or pretentious in conception or intention: *high-flown ideas.*
high-flyer *or* **high-flier** *n* **1** a person who is extreme in aims, ambition, etc. **2** a person of great ability, esp. in a career.
▸ˌ**high-'flying** *adj, n*
high frequency *n* a radio frequency lying between 30 and 3 megahertz. Abbrev.: **HF.**
High German *n* the standard German language, historically developed from the form of West Germanic spoken in S Germany.
high-handed ❶ *adj* tactlessly overbearing and inconsiderate.
▸ˌ**high-'handedness** *n*
high-hat *Inf.* ◆ *adj* **1** snobbish and arrogant. ◆ *vb* **high-hats, high-hatting, high-hatted.** (*tr*) **2** *Chiefly US & Canad.* to treat in a snobbish or offhand way. ◆ *n* **3** a snobbish person.
high hurdles *n* (*functioning as sing*) a race in which competitors leap over hurdles 42 inches (107 cm) high.
highjack ('haɪˌdʒæk) *vb, n* a less common spelling of **hijack.**
▸'**highˌjacker** *n*
high jump *n* **1** (usually preceded by *the*) an athletic event in which a competitor has to jump over a high bar. **2 be for the high jump.** *Brit. inf.* to be liable to receive a severe reprimand or punishment.
▸**high jumper** *n* ▸**high jumping** *n*
high-key *adj* (of a painting, etc.) having a predominance of light tones or colours. Cf. **low-key** (sense 3).
highland ('haɪlənd) *n* **1** relatively high ground. **2** (*modifier*) of or relating to a highland.
▸'**highlander** *n*
Highland ('haɪlənd) *n* **1** a council area in N Scotland, formed in 1975 as Highland Region and reorganized in 1996. Administrative centre: Inverness. Pop.: 206 900 (1996 est.). Area: 25 149 sq. km (9710 sq. miles). **2** (*modifier*) of or denoting the Highlands of Scotland.
▸'**Highlander** *n*
Highland cattle *n* a breed of cattle with shaggy reddish-brown hair and long horns.
Highland dress *n* **1** the historical costume including the plaid and kilt, of Highland clansmen and soldiers. **2** a modern version of this worn for formal occasions.
Highland fling *n* a vigorous Scottish solo dance.
Highland Games *n* (*functioning as sing or pl*) a meeting in which competitions in sport, piping, and dancing are held: originating in the Highlands of Scotland.
Highlands ❶ ('haɪləndz) *n* **the. 1a** the part of Scotland that lies to the northwest of the great fault that runs from Dumbarton to Stonehaven. **1b** a mountainous region of NW Scotland: distinguished by Gaelic culture. **2** (*often not cap.*) the highland region of any country.
high-level *adj* (of conferences, talks, etc.) involving very important people.
high-level language *n Computing.* a programming language that resembles natural language or mathematical notation and is designed to reflect the requirements of a problem.
high-level waste *n* high-activity radioactive waste, such as spent nuclear fuel, needing cooling for several decades before disposal. Cf. **intermediate-level waste, low-level waste.**
highlight ❶ ('haɪˌlaɪt) *n* **1** an area of the lightest tone in a painting, photograph, etc. **2** Also called: **high spot.** the most exciting or memorable part or time. **3** (*pl*) a lightened or brightened effect produced in the hair by bleaching selected strands. ◆ *vb* (*tr*) **4** *Painting, photog., etc.* to mark with light tone. **5** to bring emphasis to. **6** to produce highlights in (the hair).
highlighter ('haɪˌlaɪtə) *n* **1** a cosmetic cream or powder applied to the face to highlight the cheekbones, eyes, etc. **2** a fluorescent felt-tip pen used as a marker to emphasize a section of text without obscuring it.
highly ❶ ('haɪlɪ) *adv* **1** (intensifier): *highly disappointed.* **2** with great approbation: *we spoke highly of it.* **3** in a high position: *placed highly in class.* **4** at or for a high cost.
highly strung ❶ *or US & Canad.* **high-strung** *adj* tense and easily upset; excitable; nervous.
High Mass *n* a solemn and elaborate sung Mass.
high-minded ❶ *adj* **1** having or characterized by high moral principles. **2** *Arch.* arrogant; haughty.
▸ˌ**high-'mindedness** *n*
highness ('haɪnɪs) *n* the condition of being high.
Highness ('haɪnɪs) *n* (preceded by *Your, His,* or *Her*) a title used to address or refer to a royal person.
high-octane *adj* **1** (of petrol) having a high octane number. **2** *Inf.* dynamic, forceful, or intense: *high-octane drive and efficiency.*
high-pass filter *n Electronics.* a filter that transmits all frequencies above a specified value, attenuating frequencies below this value.
high-pitched *adj* **1** pitched high in tone. **2** (of a roof) having steeply sloping sides. **3** (of an argument, style, etc.) lofty or intense.
high-powered ❶ *adj* **1** (of an optical instrument or lens) having a high magnification. **2** dynamic and energetic; highly capable.
high-pressure ❶ *adj* **1** having, using, or designed to withstand pressure above normal. **2** *Inf.* (of selling) persuasive in an aggressive and persistent manner.
high priest *n* **1** *Bible.* the priest of highest rank who alone was permitted to enter the holy of holies of the Temple. **2** Also (fem): **high priestess.** the head of a cult.
▸**high priesthood** *n*
high profile *n* a position or attitude characterized by a deliberate seeking of prominence or publicity.
high-rise *adj* **1** (*prenominal*) of or relating to a building that has many

THESAURUS

ritzy (*sl.*), select, superior, swish (*inf., chiefly Brit.*), tip-top, tops (*sl.*), up-market
Antonyms *adj* cheap, cheapo (*inf.*), common, inferior, mediocre, ordinary, run-of-the-mill
higher-up *n Informal* = **superior**, boss, director, executive, gaffer (*inf., chiefly Brit.*), manager, senior
highfalutin *adj Informal* = **pompous**, arty-farty (*inf.*), big, bombastic, florid, grandiose, high-flown, high-sounding, lofty, magniloquent, pretentious, supercilious, swanky (*inf.*)
high-flown *adj* = **extravagant**, arty-farty (*inf.*), elaborate, exaggerated, florid, grandiose, highfalutin (*inf.*), inflated, lofty, magniloquent, overblown, pretentious
Antonyms *adj* down-to-earth, moderate, modest, practical, pragmatic, realistic, reasonable, restrained, sensible, simple, straightforward, unpretentious
high-handed *adj* = **dictatorial**, arbitrary, autocratic, bossy (*inf.*), despotic, domineering, imperious, inconsiderate, oppressive, overbearing, peremptory, self-willed, tyrannical, wilful
Highlands *pl n* **2** *often not cap.* = **uplands**, heights, hill country, hills, mesa, mountainous region, plateau, tableland
highlight *n* **2** = **high point**, best part, climax, feature, focal point, focus, high spot, main feature, memorable part, peak ◆ *vb* **5** = **emphasize**, accent, accentuate, bring to the fore, feature, focus attention on, foreground, give prominence to, play up, set off, show up, spotlight, stress, underline
Antonyms *n* ≠ **high point:** disappointment, lowlight, low point ◆ *vb* ≠ **emphasize:** de-emphasize, gloss over, neglect, overlook, play down
highly *adv* **1** = **extremely**, decidedly, eminently, exceptionally, extraordinarily, greatly, immensely, seriously (*inf.*), supremely, tremendously, vastly, very, very much **2** = **favourably**, appreciatively, approvingly, enthusiastically, warmly, well
highly strung *adj* = **nervous**, easily upset, edgy, excitable, irascible, irritable, nervy (*Brit. inf.*), neurotic, on pins and needles, on tenterhooks, restless, sensitive, stressed, taut, temperamental, tense, tetchy, twitchy (*inf.*), wired (*sl.*)
Antonyms *adj* calm, collected, easy-going, even-tempered, laid-back (*inf.*), placid, relaxed, serene, unfazed (*inf.*)
high-minded *adj* **1** = **principled**, elevated, ethical, fair, good, honourable, idealistic, magnanimous, moral, noble, pure, righteous, upright, virtuous, worthy
Antonyms *adj* dishonest, dishonourable, unethical, unfair
high-mindedness *n* **1** = **integrity**, probity, rectitude, scrupulousness, uprightness
high-powered *adj* **2** = **dynamic**, aggressive, driving, effective, energetic, enterprising, fast-track, forceful, go-ahead, go-getting (*inf.*), highly capable, high-octane (*inf.*), vigorous
high-pressure *Informal* **2** *adj* = **forceful**, aggressive, bludgeoning, coercive, compelling, high-powered, importunate, insistent, intensive, in-your-face (*sl.*), persistent, persuasive, pushy (*inf.*)

storeys, esp. one used for flats or offices: *a high-rise block.* ◆ *n* **2** a high-rise building.
high-risk *adj* (*prenominal*) denoting a group, part, etc., that is particularly subject to a danger.
highroad ('haɪˌrəʊd) *n* **1** a main road; highway. **2** (usually preceded by *the*) the sure way: *the highroad to fame.*
high school *n* **1** *Brit.* another term for **grammar school. 2** *US, Canad., NZ, & Scot.* a secondary school.
high seas *pl n* (*sometimes sing*) the open seas, outside the jurisdiction of any one nation.
high season *n* the most popular time of year at a holiday resort, etc.
high-sounding ⓘ *adj* another term for **high-flown.**
high-spirited ⓘ *adj* vivacious, bold, or lively.
▸ˌ**high-'spiritedness** *n*
High Street *n* (*often not cap.*; usually preceded by *the*) *Brit.* the main street of a town, usually where the principal shops are situated.
high table *n* (*sometimes cap.*) the table in the dining hall of a school, college, etc., at which the principal teachers, fellows, etc., sit.
hightail ('haɪˌteɪl) *vb* (*intr*) *Inf., chiefly US & Canad.* to go or move in a great hurry.
high tea *n Brit.* See **tea** (sense 4b).
high tech (tɛk) *n* a variant spelling of **hi tech.**
high technology *n* any type of sophisticated industrial process, esp. electronic.
high-tension *n* (*modifier*) carrying or operating at a relatively high voltage.
high tide *n* **1** the tide at its highest level. **2** a culminating point.
high time *Inf.* ◆ *adv* **1** the latest possible time: *it's high time you left.* ◆ *n* **2** Also: **high old time.** an enjoyable and exciting time.
high-toned *adj* **1** having a superior social, moral, or intellectual quality. **2** affectedly superior. **3** high in tone.
high tops *pl n* training shoes that reach to above the ankles.
high treason *n* an act of treason directly affecting a sovereign or state.
high-up *n Inf.* a person who holds an important or influential position.
highveld ('haɪˌfɛlt) *n* **the.** the high grassland region of NE South Africa.
high water *n* **1** another name for **high tide. 2** the state of any stretch of water at its highest level, as during a flood. ◆ Abbrev.: **HW.**
high-water mark *n* **1** the level reached by sea water at high tide or by other stretches of water in flood. **2** the highest point.
highway ('haɪˌweɪ) *n* **1** a public road that all may use. **2** *Now chiefly US & Canad. except in legal contexts.* a main road, esp. one that connects towns. **3** a direct path or course.
Highway Code *n* (in Britain) a booklet compiled by the Department of Transport for the guidance of users of public roads.
highwayman ('haɪweɪmən) *n, pl* **highwaymen.** (formerly) a robber, usually on horseback, who held up travellers on public roads.
high wire *n* a tightrope stretched high in the air for balancing acts.
HIH *abbrev. for* His (*or* Her) Imperial Highness.
hijack ⓘ *or* **highjack** ('haɪˌdʒæk) *vb* **1** (*tr*) to seize or divert (a vehicle or the goods it carries) while in transit: *to hijack an aircraft.* ◆ *n* **2** the act or an instance of hijacking. [C20: from ?]
▸'**hiˌjacker** *or* '**highˌjacker** *n*
hike ⓘ (haɪk) *vb* **hikes, hiking, hiked. 1** (*intr*) to walk a long way, usually for pleasure, esp. in the country. **2** (usually foll. by *up*) to pull or be pulled; hitch. **3** (*tr;* usually foll. by *up*) to raise (prices). ◆ *n* **4** a long walk. **5** a rise in price. [C18: from ?]
▸'**hiker** *n*
hilarious ⓘ (hɪ'lɛərɪəs) *adj* very funny. [C19: from L *hilaris* glad, from Gk *hilaros*]
▸**hi'lariously** *adv* ▸**hi'lariousness** *n*
hilarity ⓘ (hɪ'lærɪtɪ) *n* mirth and merriment.
Hilary term *n* the spring term at Oxford University, the Inns of Court, and some other educational establishments. [C16: after Saint *Hilary* of Poitiers (?315–?367), F bishop]
hill ⓘ (hɪl) *n* **1a** a natural elevation of the earth's surface, less high or craggy than a mountain. **1b** (*in combination*): *a hillside.* **2a** a heap or mound. **2b** (*in combination*): *a dunghill.* **3** an incline; slope. **4 over the hill. 4a** *Inf.* beyond one's prime. **4b** *Mil. sl.* absent without leave or deserting. ◆ *vb* (*tr*) **5** to form into a hill. **6** to cover or surround with a heap of earth. [OE *hyll*]
▸'**hilly** *adj*
hillbilly ('hɪlˌbɪlɪ) *n, pl* **hillbillies. 1** *Usually disparaging.* an unsophisticated person, esp. from the mountainous areas in the southeastern US. **2** another name for **country and western.** [C20: from HILL + *Billy* (the nickname)]
hillock ⓘ ('hɪlək) *n* a small hill or mound. [C14 *hilloc*]
▸'**hillocked** *or* '**hillocky** *adj*
hills (hɪlz) *pl n* **1 as old as the hills.** very old. **2 the.** a hilly and often remote region.
hill station *n* (in northern India, etc.) a settlement or resort at a high altitude.
hilt ⓘ (hɪlt) *n* **1** the handle or shaft of a sword, dagger, etc. **2 to the hilt.** to the full. [OE]
hilum ('haɪləm) *n, pl* **hila** (-lə). *Bot.* a scar on a seed marking its point of attachment to the seed stalk. [C17: from L: trifle]
him (hɪm; *unstressed* ɪm) *pron* (*objective*) refers to a male person or animal: *they needed him; she baked him a cake; not him again!* [OE *him,* dative of *hē* HE]

USAGE NOTE See at **me**[1].

HIM *abbrev. for* His (*or* Her) Imperial Majesty.
himation (hɪ'mætɪˌɒn) *n, pl* **himatia** (-ɪə). (in ancient Greece) a cloak draped around the body. [C19: from Gk, from *heima* dress, from *hennunai* to clothe]
himself (hɪm'sɛlf; *medially often* ɪm'sɛlf) *pron* **1a** the reflexive form of *he* or *him.* **1b** (intensifier): *the king himself waved to me.* **2** (*preceded by a copula*) his normal self: *he seems himself once more.* [OE *him selfum,* dative sing of *hē self;* see HE, SELF]
Hinayana (ˌhiːnə'jɑːnə) *n* any of various early forms of Buddhism. [from Sansk., from *hīna* lesser + *yāna* vehicle]
hind[1] ⓘ (haɪnd) *adj* **hinder, hindmost** *or* **hindermost.** (*prenominal*) (esp. of parts of the body) situated at the back: *a hind leg.* [OE *hindan* at the back, rel. to G *hinten*]
hind[2] (haɪnd) *n, pl* **hinds** *or* **hind. 1** the female of the deer, esp. the red deer when aged three years or more. **2** any of several marine fishes related to the groper. [OE *hind*]
hind[3] (haɪnd) *n* (formerly) **1** a simple peasant. **2** (in Scotland and N England) a skilled farm worker. **3** a steward. [OE *hīne,* from *hīgna,* genitive pl of *hīgan* servants]
hinder[1] ⓘ ('hɪndə) *vb* **1** to be or get in the way of (someone or something); hamper. **2** (*tr*) to prevent. [OE *hindrian*]
hinder[2] ('haɪndə) *adj* (*prenominal*) situated at or further towards the back; posterior. [OE]
Hindi ('hɪndɪ) *n* **1** a language or group of dialects of N central India. See also **Hindustani. 2** a formal literary dialect of this language, the official language of India. **3** a person whose native language is Hindi. [C18: from Hindi, from *Hind* India, from OPersian *Hindu* the river Indus]
hindmost ⓘ ('haɪndˌməʊst) *or* **hindermost** ('hɪndəˌməʊst) *adj* furthest back; last.
Hindoo ('hɪnduː, hɪn'duː) *n, pl* **Hindoos,** *adj* an older spelling of **Hindu.**
▸'**HindooˌIsm** *n*
hindquarter ('haɪndˌkwɔːtə) *n* **1** one of the two back quarters of a carcass of beef, lamb, etc. **2** (*pl*) the rear, esp. of a four-legged animal.
hindrance ⓘ ('hɪndrəns) *n* **1** an obstruction or snag; impediment. **2** the act of hindering.
hindsight ('haɪndˌsaɪt) *n* **1** the ability to understand, after something has happened, what should have been done. **2** a firearm's rear sight.
Hindu ('hɪnduː, hɪn'duː) *n, pl* **Hindus. 1** a person who adheres to Hinduism. **2** an inhabitant or native of Hindustan or India. ◆ *adj* **3** relating to Hinduism, Hindus, or India. [C17: from Persian *Hindū,* from *Hind* India; see HINDI]
Hinduism ('hɪndʊˌɪzəm) *n* the complex of beliefs and customs comprising the dominant religion of India, characterized by the worship of many gods, a caste system, belief in reincarnation, etc.
Hindustani (ˌhɪndʊ'stɑːnɪ) *n* **1** the dialect of Hindi spoken in Delhi:

THESAURUS

high-sounding *adj* = **extravagant,** affected, artificial, bombastic, flamboyant, florid, grandiloquent, grandiose, high-flown, imposing, magniloquent, ostentatious, overblown, pompous, pretentious, stilted, strained
high-spirited *adj* = **lively,** alive and kicking, animated, boisterous, bold, bouncy, daring, dashing, ebullient, effervescent, energetic, exuberant, frolicsome, full of beans (*inf.*), full of life, fun-loving, gallant, mettlesome, sparky, spirited, spunky (*inf.*), vibrant, vital, vivacious
hijack *vb* **1** = **seize,** commandeer, expropriate, skyjack, take over
hike *vb* **1** = **walk,** back-pack, hoof it (*sl.*), leg it (*inf.*), ramble, tramp **2** *usually with* **up** = **raise,** hitch up, jack up, lift, pull up ◆ *n* **4** = **walk,** journey on foot, march, ramble, tramp, trek
hiker *n* **1** = **walker,** backpacker, rambler
hilarious *adj* = **funny,** amusing, comical, entertaining, humorous, mirthful, side-splitting, uproarious
Antonyms *adj* dull, gloomy, sad, serious
hilarity *n* = **merriment,** amusement, glee, laughter, levity, mirth
hill *n* **1** = **mount,** brae (*Scot.*), down (*arch.*), elevation, eminence, fell, height, hillock, hilltop, knoll, mound, prominence, tor **2** = **heap,** drift, hummock, mound, pile, rick, stack **3** = **slope,** acclivity, brae, climb, gradient, incline, rise
hillock *n* = **mound,** barrow, hummock, knap (*dialect*), knoll
hilly *adj* **1** = **mountainous,** rolling, steep, undulating
hilt *n* **1** = **handle,** grip, haft, handgrip, helve **2 to the hilt** = **fully,** completely, entirely, totally, wholly
hind[1] *adj* = **back,** after, hinder, posterior, rear
hinder[1] *vb* **1** = **obstruct,** arrest, block, check, debar, delay, deter, encumber, frustrate, hamper, hamstring, handicap, hobble, hold up *or* back, impede, interrupt, oppose, retard, slow down, stymie, throw a spanner in the works, thwart, trammel **2** = **stop,** prevent
Antonyms *vb* accelerate, advance, aid, benefit, encourage, expedite, facilitate, further, help, hurry, promote, quicken, speed, support
hindmost *adj* = **last,** concluding, final, furthest, furthest behind, most remote, rearmost, terminal, trailing, ultimate
hindrance *n* **1** = **obstacle,** bar, barrier, block, check, deterrent, difficulty, drag, drawback, encumbrance, handicap, hazard, hitch, impediment, interruption, limitation, obstruction, restraint, restriction, snag, stoppage, stumbling block, trammel
Antonyms *n* advantage, aid, asset, assistance, benefit, boon, boost, encouragement, furtherance, help, support

used as a lingua franca throughout India. **2** all the spoken forms of Hindi and Urdu considered together. ◆ *adj* **3** of or relating to these languages or Hindustan.

hinge ❶ (hɪndʒ) *n* **1** a device for holding together two parts such that one can swing relative to the other. **2** a natural joint, such as the knee joint, that functions in only one plane. **3** a similar structure in invertebrate animals, such as the joint between the two halves of a bivalve shell. **4** something on which events, opinions, etc., turn. **5** Also called: **mount.** *Philately.* a small transparent strip of gummed paper for affixing a stamp to a page. ◆ *vb* **hinges, hinging, hinged. 6** *(tr)* to fit a hinge to (something). **7** *(intr;* usually foll. by *on* or *upon)* to depend (on). **8** *(intr)* to hang or turn on or as if on a hinge. [C13: prob. of Gmc origin]
▸**hinged** *adj*

hinny[1] ('hɪnɪ) *n, pl* **hinnies.** the sterile hybrid offspring of a male horse and a female donkey. [C19: from L *hinnus,* from Gk *hinnos*]

hinny[2] ('hɪnɪ) *n Scot. & N English dialect.* a term of endearment, esp. for a woman. [var. of HONEY]

Hi-NRG (,haɪ'enədʒɪ) *n* a type of dance music, originating in the late 1980s, that has a very fast tempo and a strong beat. [C20: from HIGH + ENERGY]

hint ❶ (hɪnt) *n* **1** a suggestion given in an indirect or subtle manner. **2** a helpful piece of advice. **3** a small amount; trace. ◆ *vb* **4** (when *intr,* often foll. by *at;* when *tr, takes a clause as object)* to suggest indirectly. [C17: from ?]

hinterland ('hɪntə,lænd) *n* **1** land lying behind something, esp. a coast or the shore of a river. **2** remote or undeveloped areas. **3** an area near and dependent on a large city, esp. a port. [C19: from G, from *hinter* behind + *land* LAND]

hip[1] (hɪp) *n* **1** *(often pl)* either side of the body below the waist and above the thigh. **2** another name for **pelvis** (sense 1). **3** short for **hip joint. 4** the angle formed where two sloping sides of a roof meet. [OE *hype*]
▸'**hipless** *adj*

hip[2] (hɪp) *n* the berry-like brightly coloured fruit of a rose plant. Also called: **rosehip.** [OE *héopa*]

hip[3] (hɪp) *interj* an exclamation used to introduce cheers (in **hip, hip, hurrah**). [C18: from ?]

hip[4] ❶ (hɪp) *adj* **hipper, hippest.** *Sl.* **1** aware of or following the latest trends. **2** *(often postpositive;* foll. by *to)* informed (about). [var. of earlier *hep*]

hip bath *n* a portable bath in which the bather sits.

hipbone ('hɪp,bəʊn) *n* the nontechnical name for **innominate bone.**

hip flask *n* a small metal flask for spirits, etc.

hip-hop ('hɪp,hɒp) *n* a US pop culture movement of the 1980s comprising rap music, graffiti, and break dancing.

hip joint *n* the ball-and-socket joint that connects each leg to the trunk of the body.

hippeastrum (,hɪpɪ'æstrəm) *n* any plant of a South American genus cultivated for their large funnel-shaped typically red flowers. [C19: NL, from Gk *hippeus* knight + *astron* star]

hipped[1] (hɪpt) *adj* **1a** having a hip or hips. **1b** *(in combination): broad-hipped.* **2** (esp. of cows, sheep, etc.) having an injury to the hip, such as a dislocation. **3** *Archit.* having a hip or hips: *hipped roof.*

hipped[2] (hɪpt) *adj (often postpositive;* foll. by *on) US & Canad. dated sl.* very enthusiastic. [C20: from HIP[4]]

hippie *n, pl* **hippies.** a variant of **hippy**[1].

hippo ('hɪpəʊ) *n, pl* **hippos.** *Inf.* short for **hippopotamus.**

hippocampus (,hɪpəʊ'kæmpəs) *n, pl* **hippocampi** (-paɪ). **1** a mythological sea creature with the forelegs of a horse and the tail of a fish. **2** any of various small sea fishes with a horselike head; sea horse. **3** an area of cerebral cortex that forms a ridge in the floor of the brain, which in cross section has the shape of a sea horse. It functions as part of the limbic system. [C16: from L, from Gk *hippos* horse + *kampos* a sea monster]

hippocras ('hɪpəʊ,kræs) *n* an old English drink of wine flavoured with spices. [C14 *ypocras,* from OF: *Hippocrates,* prob. referring to a filter called *Hippocrates' sleeve,* Hippocrates being regarded as the father of medicine]

Hippocratic oath (,hɪpəʊ'krætɪk) *n* an oath taken by a doctor to observe a code of medical ethics derived from that of Hippocrates (?460–?377 B.C.), Greek physician.

hippodrome ('hɪpə,drəʊm) *n* **1** a music hall, variety theatre, or circus. **2** (in ancient Greece or Rome) an open-air course for horse and chariot races. [C16: from L *hippodromos,* from Gk *hippos* horse + *dromos* race]

hippogriff *or* **hippogryph** ('hɪpəʊ,grɪf) *n* a monster with a griffin's head, wings, and claws and a horse's body. [C17: from It. *ippogrifo,* from *ippo-* horse (from Gk) + *grifo* GRIFFIN]

hippopotamus (,hɪpə'pɒtəməs) *n, pl* **hippopotamuses** *or* **hippopotami** (-,maɪ). a very large gregarious mammal living in or around the rivers of tropical Africa. [C16: from L, from Gk: river horse, from *hippos* horse + *potamos* river]

hippy[1] ❶ *or* **hippie** ('hɪpɪ) *n, pl* **hippies.** (esp. during the 1960s) a person whose behaviour, dress, use of drugs, etc., implies a rejection of conventional values. [C20: see HIP[4]]

hippy[2] ('hɪpɪ) *adj* **hippier, hippiest.** *Inf.* (esp. of a woman) having large hips.

hip roof *n* a roof having sloping ends and sides.

hipster ('hɪpstə) *n* **1** *Sl., now rare.* **1a** an enthusiast of modern jazz. **1b** an outmoded word for **hippy**[1]. **2** *(modifier)* (of trousers) cut so that the top encircles the hips.

hipsters ('hɪpstəz) *pl n Brit.* trousers cut so that the top encircles the hips. Usual US word: **hip-huggers.**

hircine ('hɜːsaɪn, -sɪn) *adj* **1** *Arch.* of or like a goat. **2** *Literary.* lascivious. [C17: from L *hircīnus,* from *hircus* goat]

hire ❶ ('haɪə) *vb* **hires, hiring, hired.** *(tr)* **1** to acquire the temporary use of (a thing) or the services of (a person) in exchange for payment. **2** to employ (a person) for wages. **3** (often foll. by *out)* to provide (something) or the services of (oneself or others) for payment, usually for an agreed period. **4** (foll. by *out) Chiefly Brit.* to pay independent contractors for (work to be done). ◆ *n* **5a** the act of hiring or the state of being hired. **5b** *(as modifier): a hire car.* **6** the price for a person's services or the temporary use of something. **7 for** *or* **on hire.** available for hire. [OE *hȳrian*]
▸'**hirable** *or* '**hireable** *adj* ▸'**hirer** *n*

hireling ('haɪəlɪŋ) *n Derog.* a person who works only for money. [OE *hȳrling*]

hire-purchase *n Brit.* a system in which a buyer takes possession of merchandise on payment of a deposit and completes the purchase by paying a series of instalments while the seller retains ownership until the final instalment is paid. Abbrev.: **HP, h.p.** US and Canad. equivalents: **installment plan, instalment plan.**

hirsute ❶ ('hɜːsjuːt) *adj* **1** covered with hair. **2** (of plants) covered with long but not stiff hairs. **3** (of a person) having long, thick, or untrimmed hair. [C17: from L *hirsūtus* shaggy]
▸'**hirsuteness** *n*

his (hɪz; *unstressed* ɪz) *determiner* **1a** of, belonging to, or associated with him: *his knee; I don't like his being out so late.* **1b** *(as pron): his is on the left; that book is his.* **2 his and hers.** for a man and woman respectively. ◆ *pron* **3 of his.** belonging to him. [OE *his,* genitive of *hē* HE & of *hit* IT]

Hispanic (hɪ'spænɪk) *adj* **1** of or derived from Spain or the Spanish. ◆ *n* **2** *US.* a US citizen of Latin-American descent.
▸**His'panicism** *n*

hispid ('hɪspɪd) *adj Biol.* covered with stiff hairs or bristles. [C17: from L *hispidus* bristly]

hiss ❶ (hɪs) *n* **1** a sound like that of a prolonged *s.* **2** such a sound as an exclamation of derision, contempt, etc. ◆ *vb* **3** *(intr)* to produce or utter a hiss. **4** *(tr)* to express with a hiss. **5** *(tr)* to show derision or anger towards (a speaker, performer, etc.) by hissing. [C14: imit.]

hist (hɪst) *interj* an exclamation used to attract attention or as a warning to be silent.

histamine ('hɪstə,miːn) *n* an amine released by the body tissues in allergic reactions, causing irritation. [C20: from HIST- + AMINE]
▸**histaminic** (,hɪstə'mɪnɪk) *adj*

histo- *or before a vowel* **hist-** *combining form.* indicating animal or plant tissue: *histology; histochemistry.* [from Gk, from *histos* web]

histogenesis (,hɪstəʊ'dʒenɪsɪs) *n* the formation of tissues and organs from undifferentiated cells.
▸**histogenetic** (,hɪstəʊdʒə'netɪk) *or* ,**histo'genic** *adj*

histogram ('hɪstə,græm) *n* a statistical graph that represents the frequency of values of a quantity by vertical rectangles of varying heights and widths. [C20: ?from HISTO(RY) + -GRAM]

histology (hɪ'stɒlədʒɪ) *n* the study of the tissues of an animal or plant.
▸**histological** (,hɪstə'lɒdʒɪk'l) *or* ,**histo'logic** *adj*

histolysis (hɪ'stɒlɪsɪs) *n* the disintegration of organic tissues.
▸**histolytic** (,hɪstə'lɪtɪk) *adj*

historian ❶ (hɪ'stɔːrɪən) *n* a person who writes or studies history, esp. one who is an authority on it.

historic ❶ (hɪ'stɒrɪk) *adj* **1** famous in history; significant. **2** *Linguistics.* (of Latin, Greek, or Sanskrit verb tenses) referring to past time.

USAGE NOTE A distinction is usually made between *historic* (important, significant) and *historical* (pertaining to history): *a historic decision; a historical perspective.*

THESAURUS

hinge *vb* **7** *usually with* **on** *or* **upon** = **depend on,** be contingent on, be subject to, hang on, pivot on, rest on, revolve around, turn on

hint *n* **1** = **indication,** allusion, clue, implication, inkling, innuendo, insinuation, intimation, mention, reminder, suggestion, tip-off, word to the wise **2** = **advice,** help, pointer, suggestion, tip, wrinkle *(inf.)* **3** = **trace,** breath, dash, *soupçon,* speck, suggestion, suspicion, taste, tinge, touch, undertone, whiff, whisper ◆ *vb* **4** = **suggest,** allude, cue, imply, indicate, insinuate, intimate, let it be known, mention, prompt, tip off, tip the wink *(inf.)*

hip[4] *adj Slang* **1** = **fashionable,** in, trendy *(Brit. inf.),* with it *(inf.)* **2** = **informed,** aware, clued-up *(inf.),* in on, knowledgeable, onto, wise *(sl.)*

hippy[1] *n* = **bohemian,** beatnik, dropout, flower child

hire *vb* **1** = **rent,** charter, engage, lease, let **2** = **employ,** appoint, commission, engage, sign up, take on ◆ *n* **6** = **rental,** charge, cost, fee, price, rent

hirsute *adj* **1, 3** = **hairy,** bearded, bewhiskered, bristly, shaggy, unshaven

hiss *n* **1** = **sibilation,** buzz, hissing, sibilance **2** = **catcall,** boo, contempt, derision, jeer, raspberry ◆ *vb* **3** = **whistle,** rasp, shrill, sibilate, wheeze, whirr, whiz **5** = **jeer,** blow a raspberry, boo, catcall, condemn, damn, decry, deride, hoot, mock, revile, ridicule

historian *n* = **chronicler,** annalist, biographer, historiographer, recorder

historic *adj* **1** = **significant,** celebrated, conse-

historical ⓣ (hɪˈstɒrɪkəl) *adj* **1** belonging to or typical of the study of history: *historical methods.* **2** concerned with events of the past: *historical accounts.* **3** based on or constituting factual material as distinct from legend or supposition. **4** based on history: *a historical novel.* **5** occurring in history.
▸**hisˈtorically** *adv*

USAGE NOTE See at **historic.**

historical-cost accounting *n* a method of accounting that values assets at the original cost. In times of high inflation profits can be overstated. Cf. **current-cost accounting.**
historical linguistics *n* (*functioning as sing*) the study of language as it changes in the course of time.
historical present *n* the present tense used to narrate past events, employed for effect or in informal use, as in *a week ago I see this accident.*
historicism (hɪˈstɒrɪˌsɪzəm) *n* **1** the belief that natural laws govern historical events. **2** the doctrine that each period of history has its own beliefs and values inapplicable to any other. **3** excessive emphasis on history, past styles, etc.
▸**hisˈtoricist** *n, adj*
historicity (ˌhɪstəˈrɪsɪtɪ) *n* historical authenticity.
historiographer (hɪˌstɔːrɪˈɒgrəfə) *n* **1** a historian, esp. one concerned with historical method. **2** a historian employed to write the history of a group or public institution.
▸**hiˌstoriˈography** *n*
history ⓣ (ˈhɪstərɪ) *n, pl* **histories. 1** a record or account of past events, developments, etc. **2** all that is preserved of the past, esp. in written form. **3** the discipline of recording and interpreting past events. **4** past events, esp. when considered as an aggregate. **5** an event in the past, esp. one that has been reduced in importance: *their quarrel was just history.* **6** the past, previous experiences, etc., of a thing or person: *the house had a strange history.* **7** a play that depicts historical events. **8** a narrative relating the events of a character's life: *the history of Joseph Andrews.* [C15: from L *historia*, from Gk: inquiry, from *historein* to narrate, from *histōr* judge]
histrionic ⓣ (ˌhɪstrɪˈɒnɪk) *adj* **1** excessively dramatic or artificial: *histrionic gestures.* **2** *Now rare.* dramatic. ◆ *n* **3** (*pl*) melodramatic displays of temperament. **4** *Rare.* (*pl; functioning as sing*) dramatics. [C17: from LL *histriōnicus*, from L *histriō* actor]
▸ˌ**histriˈonically** *adv*
hit ⓣ (hɪt) *vb* **hits, hitting, hit.** (*mainly tr*) **1** (*also intr*) to deal (a blow) to (a person or thing); strike. **2** to come into violent contact with: *the car hit the tree.* **3** to strike with a missile: *to hit a target.* **4** to knock or bump: *I hit my arm on the table.* **5** to propel by striking: *to hit a ball.* **6** *Cricket.* to score (runs). **7** to affect (a person, place, or thing), esp. suddenly or adversely: *his illness hit his wife very hard.* **8** to reach: *unemployment hit a new high.* **9** to experience: *I've hit a slight snag here.* **10** *Sl.* to murder (a rival criminal) in fulfilment of an underworld vendetta. **11** *Inf.* to set out on: *let's hit the road.* **12** *Inf.* to arrive: *he will hit town tomorrow.* **13** *Inf., chiefly US & Canad.* to demand or request from: *he hit me for a pound.* **14 hit the bottle.** *Sl.* to drink an excessive amount of alcohol. ◆ *n* **15** an impact or collision. **16** a shot, blow, etc., that reaches its object. **17** an apt, witty, or telling remark. **18** *Inf.* **18a** a person or thing that gains wide appeal: *she's a hit with everyone.* **18b** (*as modifier*): *a hit record.* **19** *Inf.* a stroke of luck. **20** *Sl.* **20a** a murder carried out as the result of an underworld vendetta. **20b** (*as modifier*): *a hit squad.* **21** *Computing sl.* a single visit to a website. **22 make a hit with.** *Inf.* to make a favourable impression on. ◆ See also **hit off, hit on, hit out.** [OE *hittan*, from ON *hitta*]
▸ˈ**hitter** *n*
hit-and-miss ⓣ *adj Inf.* random; haphazard: *a hit-and-miss affair; the technique is very hit and miss.* Also: **hit or miss.**
hit-and-run *adj* (*prenominal*) **1** denoting a motor-vehicle accident in which the driver leaves the scene without stopping to give assistance, inform the police, etc. **2** (of an attack, raid, etc.) relying on surprise allied to a rapid departure from the scene of operations: *hit-and-run tactics.*
hitch ⓣ (hɪtʃ) *vb* **1** to fasten or become fastened with a knot or tie. **2** (*tr;* often foll. by *up*) to pull up (the trousers, etc.) with a quick jerk. **3** (*intr*) *Chiefly US.* to move in a halting manner. **4** (*tr; passive*) *Sl.* to marry (esp. in **get hitched**). **5** *Inf.* to obtain (a ride) by hitchhiking. ◆ *n* **6** an impediment or obstacle, esp. one that is temporary or minor. **7** a knot that can be undone by pulling against the direction of the strain that holds it. **8** a sudden jerk: *he gave it a hitch and it came loose.* **9** *Inf.* a ride obtained by hitchhiking. [C15: from ?]
▸ˈ**hitcher** *n*
hitchhike (ˈhɪtʃˌhaɪk) *vb* **hitchhikes, hitchhiking, hitchhiked.** (*intr*) to travel by obtaining free lifts in motor vehicles.
▸ˈ**hitchˌhiker** *n*
hi tech *or* **high tech** (tɛk) *n* **1** short for **high technology. 2** a style of interior design using features of industrial equipment. ◆ *adj* **hi-tech** *or* **high-tech. 3** designed for or using high technology. **4** of or in the interior design style. ◆ Cf. **low tech.**
hither ⓣ (ˈhɪðə) *adv* **1** to or towards this place (esp. in **come hither**). **2 hither and thither.** this way and that, as in confusion. ◆ *adj* **3** *Arch. or dialect.* (of a side or part) nearer; closer. [OE *hider*]
hithermost (ˈhɪðəˌməust) *adj Now rare.* nearest to this place or in this direction.
hitherto ⓣ (ˌhɪðəˈtuː) *adv, adj* until this time: *hitherto, there have been no problems; hitherto private aristocratic homes.*
Hitlerism (ˈhɪtləˌrɪzəm) *n* the policies, principles, and methods of the Nazi party as developed by Adolf Hitler.
hit list *n Inf.* **1** a list of people to be murdered: *a terrorist hit list.* **2** a list of targets to be eliminated in some way: *a hit list of pits to be closed.*
hit man *n* a hired assassin.
hit off ⓣ *vb* **1** (*tr, adv*) to represent or mimic accurately. **2 hit it off with.** *Inf.* to have a good relationship with.
hit on ⓣ *vb* (*prep*) **1** (*tr*) to discover unexpectedly or guess correctly. Also: **hit upon. 2** (*tr*) *US & Canad.* to make sexual advances to.
hit out ⓣ *vb* (*intr, adv;* often foll. by *at*) **1** to direct blows forcefully and vigorously. **2** to make a verbal attack (upon someone).
Hittite (ˈhɪtaɪt) *n* **1** a member of an ancient people of Anatolia, who built a great empire in N Syria and Asia Minor in the second millennium B.C. **2** the extinct language of this people. ◆ *adj* **3** of or relating to this people, their civilization, or their language.
hit wicket *n Cricket.* an instance of a batsman breaking the wicket with the bat or a part of the body while playing a stroke and so being out.
HIV *abbrev. for* human immunodeficiency virus; the cause of AIDS.
hive ⓣ (haɪv) *n* **1** a structure in which social bees live. **2** a colony of social bees. **3** a place showing signs of great industry (esp. in **a hive of activity**). **4** a teeming multitude. ◆ *vb* **hives, hiving, hived. 5** to cause (bees) to collect or (of bees) to collect inside a hive. **6** to live or cause to live in or as if in a hive. **7** (*tr;* often foll. by *up* or *away*) to store, esp. for future use. [OE *hȳf*]
hive off *vb* (*adv*) **1** to transfer or be transferred from a larger group or unit. **2** (*usually tr*) to transfer (profitable activities of a nationalized industry) back to private ownership.
hives (haɪvz) *n* (*functioning as sing or pl*) *Pathol.* a nontechnical name for **urticaria.** [C16: from ?]
hiya (ˈhaɪjə, ˌharˈjɑː) *sentence substitute.* an informal term of greeting. [C20: shortened from *how are you?*]
hl *abbrev. for* hectolitre.
HL (in Britain) *abbrev. for* House of Lords.
hm *symbol for* hectometre.
h'm (*spelling pron* hmmm) *interj* used to indicate hesitation, doubt, assent, pleasure, etc.
HM *abbrev. for:* **1** His (*or* Her) Majesty. **2** headmaster; headmistress.
HMAS *abbrev. for* His (*or* Her) Majesty's Australian Ship.
HMCS *abbrev. for* His (*or* Her) Majesty's Canadian Ship.
HMI (in Britain) *abbrev. for* His (*or* Her) Majesty's Inspector; a government official who examines and supervises schools.

THESAURUS

quential, epoch-making, extraordinary, famous, ground-breaking, momentous, notable, outstanding, red-letter, remarkable
Antonyms *adj* ordinary, uncelebrated, unimportant, unknown
historical *adj* **3** = **factual**, actual, archival, attested, authentic, chronicled, documented, real, verifiable
Antonyms *adj* contemporary, current, fabulous, fictional, legendary, mythical, present-day
history *n* **1** = **chronicle**, account, annals, autobiography, biography, memoirs, narration, narrative, recapitulation, recital, record, relation, saga, story **4** = **the past**, ancient history, antiquity, bygone times, days of old, days of yore, olden days, the good old days, the old days, yesterday, yesteryear
histrionic *adj* **1** = **theatrical**, actorly, actressy, affected, artificial, bogus, camp (*inf.*), dramatic, forced, insincere, melodramatic, sensational, unnatural ◆ *n* **3** *plural* = **temperament**, dramatics, performance, scene, staginess, tantrums, theatricality
hit *vb* **1, 4** = **strike**, bang, bash (*inf.*), batter, beat, belt, clip (*inf.*), clobber (*sl.*), clout (*inf.*), cuff, deck (*sl.*), flog, knock, lay one on (*sl.*), lob, punch, slap, smack, smite (*arch.*), sock (*sl.*), swat, thump, tonk (*sl.*), wallop (*inf.*), whack **2** = **collide with**, bang into, bump, clash with, crash against, meet head-on, run into, smash into **7** = **affect**, damage, devastate, impact on, impinge on, influence, leave a mark on, make an impact or impression on, move, overwhelm, touch **8** = **reach**, accomplish, achieve, arrive at, attain, gain, secure, strike, touch ◆ *n* **15** = **stroke**, belt (*inf.*), blow, bump, clash, clout, collision, cuff, impact, knock, rap, shot, slap, smack, swipe (*inf.*), wallop (*inf.*) **18** = **success**, sellout, sensation, smash (*inf.*), triumph, winner
hit-and-miss *adj Informal* = **haphazard**, aimless, casual, cursory, disorganized, indiscriminate, perfunctory, random, undirected, uneven
Antonyms *adj* arranged, deliberate, organized, planned, systematic
hitch *vb* **1** = **fasten**, attach, connect, couple, harness, join, make fast, tether, tie, unite, yoke **2** *often foll. by* **up** = **pull up**, hoick, jerk, tug, yank **5** *Informal* = **hitchhike**, thumb a lift ◆ *n* **6** = **problem**, catch, check, delay, difficulty, drawback, hassle (*inf.*), hazard, hindrance, hold-up, impediment, mishap, obstacle, snag, stoppage, trouble
hither *adv* **1** = **here**, close, closer, near, nearer, nigh (*arch.*), over here, to this place
hitherto *adv* = **previously**, heretofore, so far, thus far, till now, until now, up to now
hit off *vb* **1** = **mimic**, capture, catch, impersonate, represent, take off (*inf.*) **2 hit it off with** *Informal* = **get on (well) with**, be on good terms with, click with (*sl.*), get on with like a house on fire (*inf.*), take to, warm to
hit on *vb* **1** = **think up**, arrive at, chance upon, come upon, discover, guess, invent, light upon, realize, strike upon, stumble on
hit out *vb* **2** = **attack**, assail, castigate, condemn, denounce, inveigh against, lash out, rail against, strike out at
hive *n* **2** = **colony**, cluster, swarm **3** *As in* **hive of activity** = **centre**, heart, hub, powerhouse (*sl.*)

H.M.S. *or* **HMS** *abbrev. for:* **1** His (*or* Her) Majesty's Service. **2** His (*or* Her) Majesty's Ship.

HMSO (in Britain) *abbrev. for* His (*or* Her) Majesty's Stationery Office.

HNC (in Britain) *abbrev. for* Higher National Certificate; a qualification recognized by many national technical and professional institutions.

HND (in Britain) *abbrev. for* Higher National Diploma; a qualification in technical subjects equivalent to a degree.

ho (həʊ) *interj* **1** Also: **ho-ho.** an imitation or representation of a deep laugh. **2** an exclamation used to attract attention, etc. [C13: imit.]

Ho *the chemical symbol for* holmium.

hoar (hɔː) *n* **1** short for **hoarfrost.** ◆ *adj* **2** *Rare.* covered with hoarfrost. **3** *Arch.* a poetic variant of **hoary.** [OE *hār*]

hoard 🅣 (hɔːd) *n* **1** an accumulated store hidden away for future use. **2** a cache of ancient coins, etc. ◆ *vb* **3** to accumulate (a hoard). [OE *hord*]
▸'**hoarder** *n*

> **USAGE NOTE** *Hoard* is sometimes wrongly written where *horde* is meant: *hordes* (not *hoards*) *of tourists.*

hoarding ('hɔːdɪŋ) *n* **1** Also called (esp. US and Canad.): **billboard.** a large board used for displaying advertising posters, as by a road. **2** a temporary wooden fence erected round a building or demolition site. [C19: from C15 *hoard* fence, from OF *hourd* palisade, of Gmc origin]

hoarfrost ('hɔːˌfrɒst) *n* a deposit of needle-like ice crystals formed on the ground by direct condensation at temperatures below freezing point. Also called: **white frost.**

hoarhound ('hɔːˌhaʊnd) *n* a variant spelling of **horehound.**

hoarse 🅣 (hɔːs) *adj* **1** gratingly harsh in tone. **2** having a husky voice, as through illness, shouting, etc. [C14: from ON]
▸'**hoarsely** *adv* ▸'**hoarseness** *n*

hoarsen ('hɔːsən) *vb* to make or become hoarse.

hoary 🅣 ('hɔːrɪ) *adj* **hoarier, hoariest. 1** having grey or white hair. **2** white or whitish-grey in colour. **3** ancient or venerable.
▸'**hoariness** *n*

hoatzin (həʊ'ætsɪn) *n* a unique South American bird with clawed wing digits in the young. [C17: from American Sp., from Nahuatl *uatzin* pheasant]

hoax 🅣 (həʊks) *n* **1** a deception, esp. a practical joke. ◆ *vb* **2** (*tr*) to deceive or play a joke on (someone). [C18: prob. from HOCUS]
▸'**hoaxer** *n*

hob[1] (hɒb) *n* **1** the flat top part of a cooking stove, or a separate flat surface, containing hotplates or burners. **2** a shelf beside an open fire, for keeping kettles, etc., hot. **3** a steel pattern used in forming a mould or die in cold metal. [C16: var. of obs. *hubbe;* ? rel. to HUB]

hob[2] (hɒb) *n* **1** a hobgoblin or elf. **2 raise** *or* **play hob.** *US inf.* to cause mischief. **3** a male ferret. [C14: var. of *Rob,* short for *Robin* or *Robert*]

hobble 🅣 ('hɒbəl) *vb* **hobbles, hobbling, hobbled. 1** (*intr*) to walk with a lame awkward movement. **2** (*tr*) to fetter the legs of (a horse) in order to restrict movement. **3** (*intr*) to progress with difficulty. ◆ *n* **4** a strap, rope, etc., used to hobble a horse. **5** a limping gait. ◆ Also (for senses 2, 4): **hopple.** [C14: prob. from Low G]
▸'**hobbler** *n*

hobbledehoy (ˌhɒbəldɪ'hɔɪ) *n* a clumsy or bad-mannered youth. [C16: from earlier *hobbard de hoy,* from ?]

hobby[1] 🅣 ('hɒbɪ) *n, pl* **hobbies. 1** an activity pursued in spare time for pleasure or relaxation. **2** *Arch.* a small horse. **3** short for **hobbyhorse** (sense 1). **4** an early form of bicycle, without pedals. [C14 *hobyn,* prob. var. of name *Robin*]
▸'**hobbyist** *n*

hobby[2] ('hɒbɪ) *n, pl* **hobbies.** any of several small Old World falcons. [C15: from OF *hobet,* from *hobe* falcon]

hobbyhorse ('hɒbɪˌhɔːs) *n* **1** a toy consisting of a stick with a figure of a horse's head at one end. **2** a rocking horse. **3** a figure of a horse attached to a performer's waist in a morris dance, etc. **4** a favourite topic (esp. in **on one's hobbyhorse**). [C16: from HOBBY[1], orig. a small horse; then generalized to apply to any pastime]

hobgoblin 🅣 (ˌhɒb'gɒblɪn) *n* **1** a mischievous goblin. **2** a bogey; bugbear. [C16: from HOB[2] + GOBLIN]

hobnail ('hɒbˌneɪl) *n* **a** a short nail with a large head for protecting the soles of heavy footwear. **b** (*as modifier*): *hobnail boots.* [C16: from HOB[1] (in archaic sense: peg) + NAIL]
▸'**hobˌnailed** *adj*

hobnob 🅣 ('hɒbˌnɒb) *vb* **hobnobs, hobnobbing, hobnobbed.** (*intr;* often foll. by *with*) **1** to socialize or talk informally. **2** *Obs.* to drink (with). [C18: from *hob or nob* to drink to one another in turns, ult. from OE *habban* to HAVE + *nabban* not to have]

hobo ('həʊbəʊ) *n, pl* **hobos** *or* **hoboes.** *Chiefly US & Canad.* **1** a tramp; vagrant. **2** a migratory worker. [C19 (US): from ?]
▸'**hoboism** *n*

Hobson's choice ('hɒbsənz) *n* the choice of taking what is offered or nothing at all. [C16: after Thomas *Hobson* (1544–1631), E liveryman who gave his customers no choice but had them take the nearest horse]

hock[1] (hɒk) *n* **1** the joint at the tarsus of a horse or similar animal, corresponding to the human ankle. ◆ *vb* **2** another word for **hamstring.** [C16: short for *hockshin,* from OE *hōhsinu* heel sinew]

hock[2] (hɒk) *n* any of several white wines from the German Rhine. [C17: short for obs. *hockamore* from G *Hochheimer*]

hock[3] (hɒk) *Inf., chiefly US & Canad.* ◆ *vb* **1** (*tr*) to pawn or pledge. ◆ *n* **2** the state of being in pawn. **3 in hock. 3a** in prison. **3b** in debt. **3c** in pawn. [C19: from Du. *hok* prison, debt]

hockey ('hɒkɪ) *n* **1** Also called (esp. US and Canad.): **field hockey.** a game played on a field by two opposing teams of 11 players each, who try to hit a ball into their opponents' goal using long sticks curved at the end. **2** See **ice hockey.** [C19: from earlier *hawkey,* from ?]

hocus ('həʊkəs) *vb* **hocuses, hocusing, hocused** *or* **hocusses, hocussing, hocussed.** (*tr*) *Now rare.* **1** to trick. **2** to stupefy, esp. with a drug. **3** to drug (a drink).

hocus-pocus 🅣 ('həʊkəs'pəʊkəs) *n* **1** trickery or chicanery. **2** an incantation used by conjurors or magicians. **3** conjuring skill. ◆ *vb* **hocus-pocuses, hocus-pocusing, hocus-pocused** *or* **hocus-pocusses, hocus-pocussing, hocus-pocussed. 4** to deceive or trick (someone). [C17: ? dog Latin invented by jugglers]

hod (hɒd) *n* **1** an open wooden box attached to a pole, for carrying bricks, mortar, etc. **2** a tall narrow coal scuttle. [C14: ?from C13 dialect *hot,* from OF *hotte* pannier, prob. of Gmc origin]

hodgepodge ('hɒdʒˌpɒdʒ) *n* a variant spelling (esp. US and Canad.) of **hotchpotch.**

Hodgkin's disease ('hɒdʒkɪnz) *n* a malignant disease, a form of lymphoma, characterized by enlargement of the lymph nodes, spleen, and liver. [C19: after Thomas *Hodgkin* (1798–1866), London physician, who first described it]

hodograph ('hɒdəˌgrɑːf) *n* a curve of which the radius vector represents the velocity of a moving particle. [C19: from Gk *hodos* way + -GRAPH]

hodometer (hɒ'dɒmɪtə) *n* another name for **odometer.**
▸**ho'dometry** *n*

hoe (həʊ) *n* **1** any of several kinds of long-handled hand implement used to till the soil, weed, etc. ◆ *vb* **hoes, hoeing, hoed. 2** to dig, scrape, weed, or till (surface soil) with or as if with a hoe. [C14: via OF *houe,* of Gmc origin]
▸'**hoer** *n*

hoedown ('həʊˌdaʊn) *n US & Canad.* **1** a boisterous square dance. **2** a party at which hoedowns are danced.

hog 🅣 (hɒg) *n* **1** a domesticated pig, esp. a castrated male. **2** *US & Canad.* any mammal of the family Suidae; pig. **3** Also: **hogg.** *Dialect, Austral. & NZ.* another name for **hogget. 4** *Inf.* a greedy person. **5 go the whole hog.** *Sl.* to do something thoroughly or unreservedly. ◆ *vb* **hogs, hogging, hogged.** (*tr*) **6** *Sl.* to take more than one's share of. **7** to arch (the back) like a hog. **8** to cut (the mane) of (a horse) very short. [OE *hogg,* of Celtic origin]
▸'**hogger** *n* ▸'**hogˌlike** *adj*

hogan ('həʊgən) *n* a wooden dwelling covered with earth, typical of the Navaho Indians of North America. [of Amerind origin]

hogback ('hɒgˌbæk) *n* **1** Also called: **hog's back.** a narrow ridge with steep sides. **2** *Archaeol.* a tomb with sloping sides.

hogfish ('hɒgˌfɪʃ) *n, pl* **hogfish** *or* **hogfishes.** a wrasse that occurs in the Atlantic. The head of the male resembles a pig's snout.

THESAURUS

hoard *n* **1** = **store,** accumulation, cache, fall-back, fund, heap, mass, pile, reserve, stash, stockpile, supply ◆ *vb* **3** = **save,** accumulate, amass, buy up, cache, collect, deposit, garner, gather, hive, lay up, put away, put by, stash away (*inf.*), stockpile, store, treasure

hoarder *n* **3** = **saver,** collector, magpie (*Brit.*), miser, niggard

hoarse *adj* **1** = **rough,** discordant, grating, gravelly, growling, harsh, rasping, raucous **2** = **husky,** croaky, gruff, guttural, throaty
Antonyms *adj* harmonious, mellifluous, mellow, melodious, smooth

hoarseness *n* **2** = **croakiness,** a frog in one's throat, gruffness, huskiness, rasping, sore throat, throatiness, wheeziness

hoary *adj* **1** = **white-haired,** grey, grey-haired, grizzled **2** = **white,** frosty, grey, hoar, silvery **3** = **old,** aged, ancient, antiquated, antique, venerable

hoax *n* **1** = **trick,** canard, cheat, con (*inf.*), deception, fast one (*inf.*), fraud, imposture, joke, practical joke, prank, ruse, spoof (*inf.*), swindle ◆ *vb* **2** = **deceive,** bamboozle (*inf.*), befool, bluff, con (*sl.*), delude, dupe, fool, gull (*arch.*), hoodwink, hornswoggle (*sl.*), kid (*inf.*), swindle, take in (*inf.*), take (someone) for a ride (*inf.*), trick, wind up (*Brit. sl.*)

hoaxer *adj* **2** = **trickster,** bamboozler (*inf.*), hoodwinker, humbug, joker, practical joker, prankster, spoofer (*inf.*)

hobble *vb* **1, 3** = **limp,** dodder, falter, halt, shamble, shuffle, stagger, stumble, totter **2** = **tie,** clog, fasten, fetter, hamstring, restrict, shackle

hobby[1] *n* **1** = **pastime,** diversion, favourite occupation, (leisure) activity, leisure pursuit, relaxation, sideline

hobgoblin *n* **1** = **imp,** apparition, goblin, hob, spectre, spirit, sprite

hobnob *vb* **1** = **socialize,** associate, consort, fraternize, hang about, hang out (*inf.*), keep company, mingle, mix

hocus-pocus *n* **1** *Informal* = **trickery,** artifice, cheat, chicanery, deceit, deception, delusion, hoax, humbug, imposture, swindle **2** = **mumbo jumbo,** abracadabra, cant, gibberish, gobbledegook (*inf.*), Greek (*inf.*), hokum (*sl., chiefly US & Canad.*), jargon, nonsense, rigmarole **3** = **conjuring,** jugglery, legerdemain, prestidigitation, sleight of hand

hog *vb* **6** *Slang* = **monopolize,** be a dog in the manger, corner, corner the market in, dominate, tie up

hogget ('hɒgɪt) *n Dialect, Austral. & NZ.* a young sheep that has yet to be sheared. Also: **hog, hogg.**

hoggish Ⓣ ('hɒgɪʃ) *adj* selfish, gluttonous, or dirty.

Hogmanay (ˌhɒgmə'neɪ) *n* (*sometimes not cap.*) New Year's Eve in Scotland. [C17: ?from Norman F *hoguinane,* from OF *aguillanneuf* a New Year's Eve gift]

hognose snake ('hɒgˌnəʊz) *n* a North American nonvenomous snake that has a trowel-shaped snout and inflates its body when alarmed. Also called: **puff adder.**

hogshead ('hɒgzˌhed) *n* **1** a unit of capacity, used esp. for alcoholic beverages. It has several values. **2** a large cask. [C14: from ?]

hogtie ('hɒgˌtaɪ) *vb* **hogties, hogtying, hogtied.** (*tr*) *Chiefly US.* **1** to tie together the legs or the arms and legs of. **2** to impede, hamper, or thwart.

hogwash Ⓣ ('hɒgˌwɒʃ) *n* **1** *Inf.* nonsense. **2** pigswill.

hogweed ('hɒgˌwiːd) *n* any of several coarse weedy plants.

ho-hum ('həʊˌhʌm) *adj Inf.* lacking interest or inspiration; dull; mediocre: *a ho-hum collection of new releases.*

hoick (hɔɪk) *vb* to rise or raise abruptly and sharply. [C20: from ?]

hoi polloi Ⓣ (ˈhɔɪ pəˈlɔɪ) *n* **the.** *Often derog.* the masses; common people. [Gk, lit.: the many]

hoist Ⓣ (hɔɪst) *vb* **1** (*tr*) to raise or lift up, esp. by mechanical means. ◆ *n* **2** any apparatus or device for hoisting. **3** the act of hoisting. **4** *Naut.* a group of signal flags. **5** the inner edge of a flag next to the staff. [C16: var. of *hoise,* prob. from Low G]

▸ **'hoister** *n*

hoity-toity Ⓣ (ˌhɔɪtɪ'tɔɪtɪ) *adj Inf.* arrogant or haughty. [C17: rhyming compound based on C16 *hoit* to romp, from ?]

hokey cokey ('həʊkɪ 'kəʊkɪ) *n* a dance routine performed to a cockney song of the same name.

hokonui (ˌhəʊkə'nuːiː) *n NZ.* illicit whisky. [from *Hokonui,* district of Southland region, NZ]

hokum ('həʊkəm) *n Sl., chiefly US & Canad.* **1** claptrap; bunk. **2** obvious or hackneyed material of a sentimental nature in a play, film, etc. [C20: prob. a blend of HOCUS-POCUS & BUNKUM]

Holarctic (hɒ'lɑːktɪk) *adj* of or denoting a zoogeographical region consisting of the entire arctic regions. [C19: from HOLO- + ARCTIC]

hold[1] Ⓣ (həʊld) *vb* **holds, holding, held. 1** to have or keep (an object) with or within the hands, arms, etc.; clasp. **2** (*tr*) to support: *to hold a drowning man's head above water.* **3** to maintain or be maintained in a specified state: *to hold firm.* **4** (*tr*) to set aside or reserve: *they will hold our tickets until tomorrow.* **5** (when *intr, usually used in commands*) to restrain or be restrained from motion, action, departure, etc.: *hold that man until the police come.* **6** (*intr*) to remain fast or unbroken: *that cable won't hold much longer.* **7** (*intr*) (of the weather) to remain dry and bright. **8** (*tr*) to keep the attention of. **9** (*tr*) to engage in or carry on: *to hold a meeting.* **10** (*tr*) to have the ownership, possession, etc., of: *he holds a law degree; who's holding the ace?* **11** (*tr*) to have the use of or responsibility for: *to hold office.* **12** (*tr*) to have the capacity for: *the carton will hold eight books.* **13** (*tr*) to be able to control the outward effects of drinking beer, spirits, etc. **14** (often foll. by *to* or *by*) to remain or cause to remain committed (to): *hold him to his promise.* **15** (*tr; takes a clause as object*) to claim: *he holds that the theory is incorrect.* **16** (*intr*) to remain relevant, valid, or true: *the old philosophies don't hold nowadays.* **17** (*tr*) to consider in a specified manner: *I hold him very dear.* **18** (*tr*) to defend successfully: *hold the fort against the attack.* **19** (sometimes foll. by *on*) *Music.* to sustain the sound of (a note) throughout its specified duration. **20** (*tr*) *Computing.* to retain (data) in a storage device after copying onto another storage device or location. **21 hold (good) for.** to apply or be relevant to: *the same rules hold for everyone.* **22 there is no holding him.** he is so spirited that he cannot be restrained. ◆ *n* **23** the act or method of holding fast or grasping. **24** something to hold onto, as for support or control. **25** an object or device that holds fast or grips something else. **26** controlling influence: *she has a hold on him.* **27** a short pause. **28** a prison or a cell in a prison. **29** *Wrestling.* a way of seizing one's opponent. **30** *Music.* a pause or fermata. **31a** a tenure, esp. of land. **31b** (*in combination*): *freehold.* **32** *Arch.* a fortified place. **33 no holds barred.** all limitations removed. ◆ See also **hold back, hold down,** etc. [OE *healdan*]

▸ **'holdable** *adj*

hold[2] (həʊld) *n* the space in a ship or aircraft for storing cargo. [C16: var. of HOLE]

holdall ('həʊldˌɔːl) *n Brit.* a large strong bag or basket. Usual US and Canad. name: **carryall.**

hold back Ⓣ *vb* (*adv*) **1** to restrain or be restrained. **2** (*tr*) to withhold: *he held back part of the payment.*

hold down *vb* (*tr, adv*) **1** to restrain or control. **2** *Inf.* to manage to retain or keep possession of: *to hold down two jobs at once.*

holder Ⓣ ('həʊldə) *n* **1** a person or thing that holds. **2a** a person who has possession or control of something. **2b** (*in combination*): *householder.* **3** *Law.* a person who has possession of a bill of exchange, cheque, or promissory note that he is legally entitled to enforce.

holdfast ('həʊldˌfɑːst) *n* **1** the act of gripping strongly. **2** any device used to secure an object, such as a hook, clamp, etc. **3** the organ of attachment of a seaweed or related plant.

hold forth Ⓣ *vb* (*adv*) **1** (*intr*) to speak for a long time or in public. **2** (*tr*) to offer (an attraction or enticement).

hold in *vb* (*tr, adv*) **1** to curb, control, or keep in check. **2** to conceal (feelings).

holding Ⓣ ('həʊldɪŋ) *n* **1** land held under a lease. **2** (*often pl*) property to which the holder has legal title, such as land, stocks, shares, and other investments. **3** *Sport.* the obstruction of an opponent with the hands or arms, esp. in boxing. ◆ *adj* **4** *Austral. inf.* in funds; having money.

holding company *n* a company with controlling shareholdings in one or more other companies.

holding operation *n* a plan or procedure devised to prolong the existing situation.

holding paddock *n Austral. & NZ.* a paddock in which cattle or sheep are kept temporarily, as before shearing, etc.

holding pattern *n* the oval or circular path of an aircraft flying around an airport awaiting permission to land.

hold off Ⓣ *vb* (*adv*) **1** (*tr*) to keep apart or at a distance. **2** (*intr;* often foll. by *from*) to refrain (from doing something).

hold on *vb* (*intr, adv*) **1** to maintain a firm grasp. **2** to continue or persist. **3** (foll. by *to*) to keep or retain: *hold on to those stamps as they'll soon be valuable.* **4** *Inf.* to keep a telephone line open. ◆ *sentence substitute.* **5** *Inf.* stop! wait!

hold out Ⓣ *vb* (*adv*) **1** (*tr*) to offer. **2** (*intr*) to last or endure. **3** (*intr*) to continue to stand firm, as a person refusing to succumb to persuasion. **4** *Chiefly US.* to withhold (something due). **5 hold out for.** to wait patiently for (the fulfilment of one's demands). **6 hold out on.** *Inf.* to keep from telling (a person) some important information.

hold over Ⓣ *vb* (*tr, mainly adv*) **1** to defer or postpone. **2** (*prep*) to intimidate (a person) with (a threat).

hold-up Ⓣ *n* **1** a robbery, esp. an armed one. **2** a delay; stoppage. ◆ *vb* **hold up.** (*tr, adv*) **3.** to delay; hinder. **4** to support. **5** to waylay in order to rob, esp. using a weapon. **6** to exhibit or present.

THESAURUS

hoggish *adj* = **greedy,** brutish, dirty, edacious, filthy, gluttonous, gross, mean, piggish, rapacious, ravenous, selfish, sordid, squalid, swinish, unclean

hogwash *n* **1** *Informal* = **nonsense,** balderdash, bilge (*inf.*), bosh (*inf.*), bunk, bunkum *or* buncombe (*chiefly US*), cobblers (*Brit. taboo sl.*), crap (*sl.*), drivel, garbage (*inf.*), hokum (*sl., chiefly US & Canad.*), hooey (*sl.*), hot air (*inf.*), piffle (*inf.*), poppycock (*inf.*), rot, rubbish, shit (*taboo sl.*), tommyrot, tosh (*sl., chiefly Brit.*), trash, tripe (*inf.*), twaddle

hoi polloi *n Often derog.* = **the common people,** *canaille,* commonalty, riffraff, the (common) herd, the great unwashed (*inf. & derogatory*), the lower orders, the masses, the plebs, the populace, the proles (*derogatory sl., chiefly Brit.*), the proletariat, the rabble, the third estate, the underclass

hoist *vb* **1** = **raise,** elevate, erect, heave, lift, rear, upraise ◆ *n* **2** = **lift,** crane, elevator, tackle, winch

hoity-toity *adj Informal* = **haughty,** arrogant, conceited, disdainful, high and mighty (*inf.*), lofty, overweening, proud, scornful, snobbish, snooty (*inf.*), stuck-up (*inf.*), supercilious, toffee-nosed (*sl., chiefly Brit.*), uppish (*Brit. inf.*)

hold[1] *vb* **1** = **grasp,** clasp, cleave, clinch, cling, clutch, cradle, embrace, enfold, grip **2** = **support,** bear, brace, carry, prop, shoulder, sustain, take **3** = **continue,** endure, last, persevere, persist, remain, resist, stay, wear **5** = **restrain,** arrest, bind, check, confine, curb, detain, impound, imprison, pound, stay, stop, suspend **9** = **convene,** assemble, call, carry on, celebrate, conduct, have, officiate at, preside over, run, solemnize **10** = **own,** have, keep, maintain, occupy, possess, retain **12** = **accommodate,** comprise, contain, have a capacity for, seat, take **15** = **consider,** assume, believe, deem, judge, maintain, presume, reckon, regard, think, view **16** = **apply,** be in force, be the case, exist, hold good, operate, remain true, remain valid, stand up ◆ *n* **23** = **grip,** clasp, clutch, grasp **24** = **foothold,** anchorage, footing, leverage, prop, purchase, stay, support, vantage **26** = **control,** ascendancy, authority, clout (*inf.*), dominance, dominion, influence, mastery, pull (*inf.*), sway

Antonyms *vb* ≠ **support:** break, come undone, give way, loosen ≠ **restrain:** free, let go, let loose, release ≠ **convene:** call off, cancel, postpone ≠ **own:** bestow, give, give away, give up, hand over, offer, turn over ≠ **consider:** deny, disavow, disclaim, put down, refute, reject

hold back *vb* **1** = **restrain,** check, control, curb, inhibit, rein, repress, stem the flow, suppress **2** = **withhold,** desist, forbear, keep back, refuse

holder *n* **1** = **case,** container, cover, housing, receptacle, sheath **2** = **owner,** bearer, custodian, incumbent, keeper, occupant, possessor, proprietor, purchaser

hold forth *vb* **1** = **speak,** declaim, descant, discourse, go on, harangue, lecture, orate, preach, speechify, spiel (*inf.*), spout (*inf.*)

holding *n* **2** *often plural* = **property,** assets, estate, investments, land interests, possessions, resources, securities, stocks and shares

hold off *vb* **1** = **fend off,** keep off, rebuff, repel, repulse, stave off **2** = **put off,** avoid, defer, delay, keep from, postpone, refrain

hold out *vb* **1** = **offer,** extend, give, present, proffer **2** = **last,** carry on, continue, endure, hang on, persevere, persist, stand fast, stay the course, withstand

hold over *vb* **1** = **postpone,** adjourn, defer, delay, put off, suspend, take a rain check on (*US & Canad. inf.*), waive

hold-up *n* **1** = **robbery,** burglary, mugging (*inf.*), steaming (*inf.*), stick-up (*sl., chiefly US*), theft **2** = **delay,** bottleneck, difficulty, hitch, obstruction, setback, snag, stoppage, traffic jam, trouble, wait ◆ *vb* **hold up 3** = **delay,** detain, hinder, impede, retard, set back, slow down, stop **4** = **support,** bolster, brace, buttress, jack up, prop, shore up, sustain **5** = **rob,** mug (*inf.*), stick up (*sl., chiefly US*), waylay **6** = **exhibit,** display, flaunt, present, show

hold with ❶ *vb (intr, prep)* to support; approve of.

hole ❶ (həʊl) *n* **1** an area hollowed out in a solid. **2** an opening in or through something. **3** an animal's burrow. **4** *Inf.* an unattractive place, such as a town. **5** a fault (esp. in **pick holes in**). **6** *Sl.* a difficult and embarrassing situation. **7** the cavity in various games into which the ball must be thrust. **8** (on a golf course) **8a** each of the divisions of a course (usually 18) represented by the distance between the tee and a green. **8b** the score made in striking the ball from the tee into the hole. **9** *Physics.* a vacancy in a nearly full band of quantum states of electrons in a semiconductor or an insulator. Under the action of an electric field holes behave as carriers of positive charge. **10 hole in the wall.** *Inf.* a small dingy place, esp. one difficult to find. **11 in holes.** so worn as to be full of holes. **12 make a hole in.** to consume or use a great amount of (food, drink, money, etc.). ◆ *vb* **holes, holing, holed. 13** to make a hole or holes in (something). **14** (when *intr*, often foll. by *out*) *Golf.* to hit (the ball) into the hole. [OE *hol*]
▸**'holey** *adj*

hole-and-corner ❶ *adj (usually prenominal) Inf.* furtive or secretive.

hole in one *n Golf.* a shot from the tee that finishes in the hole. Also (esp. US): **ace.**

hole in the heart *n* a defect of the heart in which there is an abnormal opening in any of the walls dividing the four heart chambers.

hole up ❶ *vb (intr, adv)* **1** (of an animal) to hibernate. **2** *Inf.* to hide or remain secluded.

Holi ('həʊlɪ) *n* a Hindu spring festival, celebrated for two to five days, commemorating Krishna's dalliance with the cowgirls. Bonfires are lit and coloured powder and water thrown over celebrants. [after *Holika*, legendary female demon]

-holic *suffix forming noun* indicating desire for or dependence on; *workaholic; chocoholic.* [C20: abstracted from *(alco)holic*]

holiday ❶ ('hɒlɪˌdeɪ) *n* **1** *(often pl) Chiefly Brit.* a period in which a break is taken from work or studies for rest, travel, or recreation. US and Canad. word: **vacation. 2** a day on which work is suspended by law or custom, such as a religious festival, bank holiday, etc. Related adj: **ferial.** ◆ *vb* **3** *(intr) Chiefly Brit.* to spend a holiday. [OE *hāligdæg*, lit.: holy day]

holiday camp *n Brit.* a place, esp. one at the seaside, providing accommodation, recreational facilities, etc., for holiday-makers.

holiday-maker *n Brit.* a person who goes on holiday. US and Canad. equivalents: **vacationer, vacationist.**

holily ('həʊlɪlɪ) *adv* in a holy, devout, or sacred manner.

holiness ❶ ('həʊlɪnɪs) *n* the state or quality of being holy.

Holiness ('həʊlɪnɪs) *n* (preceded by *His* or *Your*) a title reserved for the pope.

holism ('həʊlɪzəm) *n* **1** any doctrine that a system may have properties over and above those of its parts and their organization. **2** (in medicine) the consideration of the complete person in the treatment of disease. [C20: from HOLO- + -ISM]
▸**ho'listic** *adj*

holland ('hɒlənd) *n* a coarse linen cloth. [C15: after *Holland*, where it was made]

hollandaise sauce (ˌhɒlən'deɪz, 'hɒlənˌdeɪz) *n* a rich sauce of egg yolks, butter, vinegar, etc. [C19: from F *sauce hollandaise* Dutch sauce]

Hollands ('hɒləndz) *n (functioning as sing)* Dutch gin, often sold in stone bottles. [C18: from Du. *hollandsch genever*]

holler ❶ ('hɒlə) *Inf.* ◆ *vb* **1** to shout or yell (something). ◆ *n* **2** a shout; call. [var. of C16 *hollow*, from *holla*, from F *holà* stop! (lit.: ho there!)]

hollo ('hɒləʊ) *or* **holla** ('hɒlə) *n, pl* **hollos** *or* **hollas,** *interj* **1** a cry for attention, or of encouragement. ◆ *vb* **2** *(intr)* to shout. [C16: from F *holà* ho there!]

hollow ❶ ('hɒləʊ) *adj* **1** having a hole or space within; not solid. **2** having a sunken area; concave. **3** deeply set: *hollow cheeks.* **4** (of sounds) as if resounding in a hollow place. **5** without substance or validity. **6** hungry or empty. **7** insincere; cynical. ◆ *adv* **8 beat (someone) hollow.** *Brit. inf.* to defeat thoroughly. ◆ *n* **9** a cavity, opening, or space in or within something. **10** a depression in the land. ◆ *vb* (often foll. by *out*, usually when *tr*) **11** to make or become hollow. **12** to form (a hole, cavity, etc.) or (of a hole, etc.) to be formed. [C12: from *holu*, inflected form of OE *holh* cave]
▸**'hollowly** *adv* ▸**'hollowness** *n*

hollow-eyed *adj* with the eyes appearing to be sunk into the face, as from excessive fatigue.

holly ('hɒlɪ) *n, pl* **hollies. 1** a tree or shrub having bright red berries and shiny evergreen leaves with prickly edges. **2** its branches, used for Christmas decorations. **3 holly oak.** another name for **holm oak.** [OE *holegn*]

hollyhock ('hɒlɪˌhɒk) *n* a tall plant with stout hairy stems and spikes of white, yellow, red, or purple flowers. Also called (US): **rose mallow.** [C16: from HOLY + *hock*, from OE *hoc* mallow]

Hollywood ('hɒlɪˌwʊd) *n* **1** a NW suburb of Los Angeles, California: centre of the US film industry. **2a** the US film industry. **2b** *(as modifier): a Hollywood star.*

holm[1] (həʊm) *n Dialect, chiefly northwestern English.* **1** an island in a river or lake. **2** low flat land near a river. [OE *holm* sea, island]

holm[2] (həʊm) *n* **1** short for **holm oak. 2** *Chiefly Brit.* a dialect word for **holly.** [C14: var. of obs. *holin*, from OE *holegn* holly]

holmium ('hɒlmɪəm) *n* a malleable silver-white metallic element of the lanthanide series. Symbol: Ho; atomic no.: 67; atomic wt.: 164.93. [C19: from NL *Holmia* Stockholm]

holm oak *n* an evergreen Mediterranean oak tree with prickly leaves resembling holly. Also called: **holm, holly oak, ilex.**

holo- *or before a vowel* **hol-** *combining form.* whole or wholly: *holograph.* [from Gk *holos*]

holocaust ❶ ('hɒləˌkɔːst) *n* **1** great destruction or loss of life or the source of such destruction, esp. fire. **2** *(usually cap.)* **the.** the mass murder of some six million European Jews by the Germans during World War II. **3** a rare word for **burnt offering.** [C13: from LL *holocaustum* whole burnt offering, from Gk, from HOLO- + *kaiein* to burn]

Holocene ('hɒləˌsiːn) *adj* **1** of, denoting, or formed in the second and most recent epoch of the Quaternary period, which began 10 000 years ago. ◆ *n* **2 the.** the Holocene epoch or rock series. ◆ Also: **Recent.**

hologram ('hɒləˌgræm) *n* a photographic record produced by illuminating the object with coherent light (as from a laser) and, without using lenses, exposing a film to light reflected from this object and to a direct beam of coherent light. When interference patterns on the film are illuminated by the coherent light a three-dimensional image is produced.

holograph ('hɒləˌgrɑːf) *n* a book or document handwritten by its author; original manuscript; autograph.

holography (hɒ'lɒgrəfɪ) *n* the science or practice of producing holograms.
▸**holographic** (ˌhɒlə'græfɪk) *adj* ▸ˌ**holo'graphically** *adv*

holohedral (ˌhɒlə'hiːdrəl) *adj* (of a crystal) exhibiting all the planes required for the symmetry of the crystal system.

holophytic (ˌhɒlə'fɪtɪk) *adj* (of plants) capable of synthesizing their food from inorganic molecules, esp. by photosynthesis.

holothurian (ˌhɒlə'θjʊərɪən) *n* **1** an echinoderm of the class *Holothuroidea*, having a leathery elongated body with a ring of tentacles around the mouth. ◆ *adj* **2** of the *Holothuroidea.* [C19: from NL *Holothūria*, name of type genus, from L: water polyp, from Gk, from ?]

hols (hɒlz) *pl n Brit. school sl.* holidays.

holster ('həʊlstə) *n* a sheathlike leather case for a pistol, attached to a belt or saddle. [C17: via Du., of Gmc origin]

holt[1] (həʊlt) *n Arch. or poetic.* a wood or wooded hill. [OE *holt*]

holt[2] (həʊlt) *n* the lair of an animal, esp. an otter. [C16: from HOLD[1]]

holy ❶ ('həʊlɪ) *adj* **holier, holiest. 1** of or associated with God or a deity; sacred. **2** endowed or invested with extreme purity. **3** devout or virtuous. **4 holier-than-thou.** offensively sanctimonious or self-righteous. ◆ *n, pl* **holies. 5** a sacred place. [OE *hālig, hǣlig*]

THESAURUS

hold with *vb* = **approve of**, agree to *or* with, be in favour of, countenance, subscribe to, support, take kindly to
Antonyms *vb* be against, disagree with, disapprove of, hold out against, oppose

hole *n* **1** = **cavity**, cave, cavern, chamber, depression, excavation, hollow, pit, pocket, scoop, shaft **2** = **opening**, aperture, breach, break, crack, fissure, gap, orifice, outlet, perforation, puncture, rent, split, tear, vent **3** = **burrow**, covert, den, earth, lair, nest, retreat, shelter **4** *Informal* = **hovel**, dive, dump (*inf.*), joint (*sl.*), slum **5** = **fault**, defect, discrepancy, error, fallacy, flaw, inconsistency, loophole **6** *Slang* = **predicament**, dilemma, fix (*inf.*), hot water (*inf.*), imbroglio, jam (*inf.*), mess, quandary, scrape (*inf.*), spot (*inf.*), tangle, tight spot

hole-and-corner *adj Informal* = **furtive**, backstairs, clandestine, secret, secretive, sneaky (*inf.*), stealthy, surreptitious, underhand, under the counter (*inf.*)
Antonyms *adj* above-board, candid, frank, open, public

hole up *vb* **1** = **hibernate 2** *Informal* = **hide**, go into hiding, go to earth, shelter, take cover, take refuge

holiday *n* **1** = **vacation**, away day, break, leave, recess, time off **2** = **festival**, anniversary, bank holiday, celebration, feast, festivity, fête, gala, public holiday, red-letter day, saint's day

holiness *n* = **sanctity**, blessedness, devoutness, divinity, godliness, piety, purity, religiousness, righteousness, sacredness, saintliness, spirituality, virtuousness

holler *Informal* ◆ *vb, n* **1, 2** = **yell**, bawl, bellow, call, cheer, clamour, cry, hail, halloo, hollo, hurrah, huzzah, roar, shout, whoop

hollow *adj* **1** = **empty**, not solid, unfilled, vacant, void **2, 3** = **sunken**, cavernous, concave, deep-set, depressed, indented **4** = **toneless**, deep, dull, expressionless, flat, low, muffled, muted, reverberant, rumbling, sepulchral **5** = **toneless**, empty, fruitless, futile, meaningless, pointless, Pyrrhic, specious, unavailing, useless, vain, worthless **6** = **hungry**, empty, esurient, famished, ravenous, starved **7** = **insincere**, artificial, cynical, deceitful, faithless, false, flimsy, hollow-hearted, hypocritical, treacherous, unsound, weak ◆ *adv* **8 beat (someone) hollow** *Brit. informal* = **defeat**, hammer (*inf.*), outdo, overcome, rout, thrash, trounce, worst ◆ *n* **9** = **cavity**, basin, bowl, cave, cavern, concavity, crater, cup, den, dent, depression, dimple, excavation, hole, indentation, pit, trough **10** = **valley**, bottom, dale, dell, dingle, glen ◆ *vb* **11** = **scoop**, channel, dig, dish, excavate, furrow, gouge, groove, pit
Antonyms *adj* ≠ **empty**: full, occupied, solid ≠ **sunken**: convex, rounded ≠ **toneless**: expressive, vibrant ≠ **worthless**: gratifying, meaningful, pleasing, satisfying, valuable, worthwhile ≠ **insincere**: genuine ◆ *n* ≠ **cavity**: bump, mound, projection ≠ **valley**: bluff, height, hill, knoll, mountain, rise

holocaust *n* **1** = **genocide**, annihilation, carnage, conflagration, destruction, devastation, fire, inferno, massacre, mass murder, pogrom

holy *adj* **1** = **sacred**, blessed, consecrated, dedicated, hallowed, sacrosanct, sanctified, vener-

Holy Communion *n* **1** the celebration of the Eucharist. **2** the consecrated elements.
holy day *n* a day on which a religious festival is observed.
Holy Father *n RC Church.* the pope.
Holy Ghost *n* another name for the **Holy Spirit.**
Holy Grail *n* **1** Also called: **Grail, Sangraal.** (in medieval legend) the bowl used by Jesus at the Last Supper. It was brought to Britain by Joseph of Arimathea, where it became the quest of many knights. **2** *Inf.* any desired ambition or goal: *the Holy Grail of infrared astronomy.* [C14: *grail* from OF *graal,* from Med. L *gradālis* bowl, from ?]
Holy Land *n* **the.** another name for Palestine.
holy of holies *n* **1** any place of special sanctity. **2** (*cap.*) the innermost compartment of the Jewish tabernacle, where the Ark was enshrined.
holy orders *pl n* **1** the sacrament whereby a person is admitted to the Christian ministry. **2** the grades of the Christian ministry. **3** the status of an ordained Christian minister.
Holy Roman Empire *n* the complex of European territories under the rule of the Frankish or German king who bore the title of Roman emperor, beginning with the coronation of Charlemagne in 800 A.D.
Holy Scripture *n* another term for **Scripture.**
Holy See *n RC Church.* **1** the see of the pope as bishop of Rome. **2** the Roman curia.
Holy Spirit *n Christianity.* the third person of the Trinity. Also called: **Holy Ghost.**
holystone ('həʊlɪˌstəʊn) *n* **1** a soft sandstone used for scrubbing the decks of a vessel. ◆ *vb* **holystones, holystoning, holystoned. 2** (*tr*) to scrub (a vessel's decks) with a holystone. [C19: ?from its being used in a kneeling position]
holy synod *n* the governing body of any of the Orthodox Churches.
holy water *n* water that has been blessed by a priest for use in symbolic rituals of purification.
Holy Week *n* the week preceding Easter Sunday.
Holy Willie ('wɪlɪ) *n* a person who is hypocritically pious. [C18: from Burns' *Holy Willie's Prayer*]
Holy Writ *n* another term for **Scripture.**
homage ➊ ('hɒmɪdʒ) *n* **1** a public show of respect or honour towards someone or something (esp. in **pay** *or* **do homage to**). **2** (in feudal society) the act of respect and allegiance made by a vassal to his lord. [C13: from OF, from *home* man, from L *homo*]
homburg ('hɒmbɜːg) *n* a man's hat of soft felt with a dented crown and a stiff upturned brim. [C20: after *Homburg,* in Germany, where orig. made]
home ➊ (həʊm) *n* **1** the place where one lives. **2** a house or other dwelling. **3** a family or other group living in a house. **4** a person's country, city, etc., esp. viewed as a birthplace or a place dear to one. **5** the habitat of an animal. **6** the place where something is invented, founded, or developed. **7** a building or organization set up to care for people in a certain category, such as orphans, the aged, etc. **8** *Sport.* one's own ground: *the match is at home.* **9a** the objective towards which a player strives in certain sports. **9b** an area where a player is safe from attack. **10 a home from home.** a place other than one's own home where one can be at ease. **11 at home. 11a** in one's own home or country. **11b** at ease. **11c** giving an informal party at one's own home. **12 at home in, on,** *or* **with.** familiar with. **13 home and dry.** *Brit. sl.* definitely safe or successful. Austral. and NZ equivalent: **home and hosed. 14 near home.** concerning one deeply. ◆ *adj* (*usually prenominal*) **15** of one's home, country, etc.; domestic. **16** (of an activity) done in one's house: *home taping.* **17** *Sport.* relating to one's own ground: *a home game.* **18** *US.* central; principal: *the company's home office.* ◆ *adv* **19** to or at home: *I'll be home tomorrow.* **20** to or on the point. **21** to the fullest extent: *hammer the nail home.* **22 bring home to. 22a** to make clear to. **22b** to place the blame on. **23 nothing to write home about.** *Inf.* of no particular interest: *the film was nothing to write home about.* ◆ *vb* **homes, homing, homed. 24** (*intr*) (of birds and other animals) to return home accurately from a distance. **25** (often foll. by *in on* or *onto*) to direct or be directed onto a point or target, esp. by automatic navigational aids. **26** to send or go home. **27** (*tr*) to furnish with a home. **28** (*intr;* often foll. by *in* or *in on*) to be directed towards a goal, target, etc. [OE *hām*]
home banking *n* a system whereby a person at home or in an office can use a computer with a modem to call up information from a bank or to transfer funds electronically.
homeboy ('həʊmˌbɔɪ) *n Sl., chiefly US.* **1** a close friend. **2** a person from one's home town or neighbourhood. **3** a member of a neighbourhood gang. [C20: US rap-music usage]
► **'homeˌgirl** *fem n*
home-brew *n* **1** a beer or other alcoholic drink brewed at home rather than commercially. **2** *Canad. inf.* a professional football player who was born in Canada and is not an import.
► **ˌhome-'brewed** *adj*
homecoming ('həʊmˌkʌmɪŋ) *n* **1** the act of coming home. **2** *US.* an annual celebration held by a university, college, or school for former students.
Home Counties *pl n* the counties surrounding London.
home economics *n* (*functioning as sing or pl*) the study of diet, budgeting, child care, and other subjects concerned with running a home.
home farm *n Brit.* (esp. formerly) a farm attached to and providing food for a large country house.
Home Guard *n* a volunteer part-time military force recruited to defend the United Kingdom in World War II.
home help *n Brit.* a woman employed, esp. by a local authority, to do housework in a person's home. NZ equivalent: **home aid.**
homeland ➊ ('həʊmˌlænd) *n* **1** the country in which one lives or was born. **2** the official name for a **Bantustan.**
homeless ➊ ('həʊmlɪs) *adj* **a** having nowhere to live. **b** (*as collective n;* preceded by *the*): *the homeless.*
► **'homelessness** *n*
homely ➊ ('həʊmlɪ) *adj* **homelier, homeliest. 1** characteristic of or suited to the ordinary home; unpretentious. **2** (of a person) **2a** *Brit.* warm and domesticated. **2b** *Chiefly US & Canad.* plain.
► **'homeliness** *n*
home-made *adj* **1** (esp. of foods) made at home or on the premises, esp. of high quality ingredients. **2** crudely fashioned.
homeo-, homoeo-, *or* **homoio-** *combining form.* like or similar: *homeomorphism.* [from L *homoeo-,* from Gk *homoio-,* from *homos* same]
Home Office *n Brit. government.* the department responsible for the maintenance of law and order, and all other domestic affairs not assigned to another department.
homeopathy *or* **homoeopathy** (ˌhəʊmɪ'ɒpəθɪ) *n* a method of treating disease by the use of small amounts of a drug that, in healthy persons, produces symptoms similar to those of the disease being treated.
► **homeopathic** *or* **homoeopathic** (ˌhəʊmɪə'pæθɪk) *adj* ► **homeopathist, homoeopathist** (ˌhəʊmɪ'ɒpəθɪst) *or* **homeopath, homoeopath** ('həʊmɪəˌpæθ) *n*
homeostasis *or* **homoeostasis** (ˌhəʊmɪəʊ'steɪsɪs) *n* **1** the maintenance of metabolic equilibrium within an animal by a tendency to compensate for disrupting changes. **2** the maintenance of equilibrium within a social group, person, etc.
homeowner ('həʊmˌəʊnə) *n* a person who owns the house in which he or she lives.
► **ˌhome'ownership** *n*
home page *n Computing.* (on a website) the main document relating to an individual or an institution that provides introductory information about a website with links to the actual details of services or information provided.
homer ('həʊmə) *n* a homing pigeon.
Homeric (həʊ'merɪk) *adj* **1** of, relating to, or resembling Homer, Greek poet (circa 800 B.C.), to whom are attributed the *Iliad* and the *Odyssey,* or his poems. **2** imposing or heroic.
home rule *n* **1** self-government, esp. in domestic affairs. **2** the partial autonomy sometimes granted to a national minority or a colony.
Home Secretary *n Brit. government.* the head of the Home Office.
homesick ('həʊmˌsɪk) *adj* depressed or melancholy at being away from home and family.
► **'homeˌsickness** *n*
homespun ➊ ('həʊmˌspʌn) *adj* **1** having plain or unsophisticated character. **2** woven or spun at home. ◆ *n* **3** cloth made at home or made of yarn spun at home.
homestead ('həʊmˌsted, -stɪd) *n* **1** a house or estate and the adjoining land, buildings, etc., esp. a farm. **2** (in the US) a house and adjoining land designated by the owner as his fixed residence and exempt

THESAURUS

able, venerated **2** = **devout**, divine, faithful, god-fearing, godly, hallowed, pious, pure, religious, righteous, saintly, sublime, virtuous **4** **holier-than-thou** = **self-righteous**, goody-goody, pietistic, pietistical, priggish, religiose, sanctimonious, self-satisfied, smug, squeaky-clean, unctuous
Antonyms *adj* ≠ **sacred**: desecrated, unconsecrated, unhallowed, unholy, unsanctified ≠ **devout**: blasphemous, corrupt, earthly, evil, human, immoral, impious, irreligious, sacrilegious, secular, sinful, unholy, wicked, worldly

homage *n* **1** = **respect**, admiration, adoration, adulation, awe, deference, devotion, duty, esteem, honour, reverence, worship **2** = **allegiance**, devotion, faithfulness, fealty, fidelity, loyalty, obeisance, service, tribute, troth (*arch.*)
Antonyms *n* ≠ **respect**: condemnation, contempt, disdain, disregard, disrespect, irreverence, scorn

home *n* **1, 2** = **dwelling**, abode, domicile, dwelling place, habitation, house, pad (*sl.*), residence **4** = **birthplace**, family, fireside, hearth, homestead, home town, household **5** = **territory**, abode, element, environment, habitat, habitation, haunt, home ground, range, stamping ground **11 at home: a** = **having guests**, available, present **b** comfortable, familiar, relaxed **c** entertaining, giving a party, receiving **12 at home in, on,** *or* **with** = **familiar with**, conversant with, knowledgeable, proficient, skilled, well-versed ◆ *adj* **15** = **domestic**, central, familiar, family, household, inland, internal, local, national, native ◆ *n* **22a bring home to** = **make clear**, drive home, emphasize, impress upon, press home

homeland *n* **1** = **native land**, country of origin, fatherland, mother country, motherland

homeless *adj* **a** = **destitute**, abandoned, displaced, dispossessed, down-and-out, exiled, forlorn, forsaken, outcast, unsettled ◆ *n* **b the homeless** = **vagrants**, dossers (*Brit. sl.*), squatters

homely *adj* **1** = **comfortable**, comfy (*inf.*), cosy, domestic, downhome (*sl., chiefly US*), down-to-earth, everyday, familiar, friendly, homelike, homespun, homy, informal, modest, natural, ordinary, plain, simple, unaffected, unassuming, unfussy, unpretentious, welcoming
Antonyms *adj* affected, elaborate, elegant, grand, ostentatious, pretentious, refined, regal, sophisticated, splendid

homespun *adj* **1** = **unsophisticated**, artless,

under the homestead laws from seizure and forced sale for debts. **3** (in western Canada) a piece of land granted to a settler by the federal government. **4** *Austral. & NZ.* (on a sheep or cattle station) the owner's or manager's residence; in New Zealand, the term includes all outbuildings.

Homestead Act *n* **1** an act passed by the US Congress in 1862 making available to settlers 160-acre tracts of public land for cultivation. **2** (in Canada) a similar act passed by the Canadian Parliament in 1872.

homesteader ('həʊmˌstedə) *n US and Canad.* a person who possesses land under a homestead law.

homestead law *n* (in the US and Canada) any of various laws conferring privileges on owners of homesteads.

home straight *n* **1** *Horse racing.* the section of a racecourse forming the approach to the finish. **2** the final stage of an undertaking. ◆ Also (chiefly US): **home stretch.**

home truth *n* (*often pl*) an unpleasant fact told to a person about himself.

home unit *n Austral. & NZ.* a self-contained residence which is part of a series of similar residences. Often shortened to **unit.**

homeward ('həʊmwəd) *adj* **1** going home. **2** (of a voyage, etc.) returning to the home port. ◆ *adv also* **homewards. 3** towards home.

homework ('həʊmˌwɜːk) *n* **1** school work done at home. **2** any preparatory study. **3** work done at home for pay.

homey ('həʊmɪ) *adj* **homier, homiest.** a variant spelling (esp. US) of **homy.**
▸**'homeyness** *n*

homicide ➊ ('hɒmɪˌsaɪd) *n* **1** the killing of a human being by another person. **2** a person who kills another. [C14: from OF, from L *homo* man + *caedere* to slay]
▸ˌ**homi'cidal** *adj*

homiletics (ˌhɒmɪ'letɪks) *n* (*functioning as sing*) the art of preaching or writing sermons. [C17: from Gk *homilētikos* cordial, from *homilein*; see HOMILY]

homily ➊ ('hɒmɪlɪ) *n, pl* **homilies. 1** a sermon. **2** moralizing talk or writing. [C14: from Church L *homīlia*, from Gk: discourse, from *homilein* to converse with, from *homilos* crowd, from *homou* together + *ilē* crowd]
▸ˌ**homi'letic** *adj* ▸**'homilist** *n*

homing ('həʊmɪŋ) *n* (*modifier*) **1** *Zool.* relating to the ability to return home after travelling great distances. **2** (of an aircraft, missile, etc.) capable of guiding itself onto a target.

homing pigeon *n* any breed of pigeon developed for its homing instinct, used for racing. Also called: **homer.**

hominid ('hɒmɪnɪd) *n* **1** any primate of the family Hominidae, which includes modern man (*Homo sapiens*) and the extinct precursors of man. ◆ *adj* **2** of or belonging to the Hominidae. [C19: via NL from L *homo* man + -ID[1]]

hominoid ('hɒmɪˌnɔɪd) *adj* **1** of or like man; manlike. **2** of or belonging to the primate family, which includes the anthropoid apes and man. ◆ *n* **3** a hominoid animal. [C20: from L *homin-*, *homo* man + -OID]

hominy ('hɒmɪnɪ) *n Chiefly US.* coarsely ground maize prepared as a food by boiling in milk or water. [C17: prob. of Algonquian origin]

hominy grits *pl n US.* finely ground hominy.

homo ('həʊməʊ) *n, pl* **homos.** *Inf., derog.* short for **homosexual.**

Homo ('həʊməʊ) *n* a genus of hominids including modern man (see ***Homo sapiens***) and several extinct species of primitive man. [L: man]

homo- *combining form.* same or like: *homologous; homosexual.* [via L from Gk *homos* same]

homocyclic (ˌhəʊməʊ'saɪklɪk) *adj* (of a chemical compound) containing a closed ring of atoms of the same kind, esp. carbon atoms.

homoeo- *combining form.* a variant of **homeo-.**

homogamy (hɒ'mɒgəmɪ) *n* **1** a condition in which all the flowers of an inflorescence are either of the same sex or hermaphrodite. **2** the maturation of the anthers and stigmas at the same time, ensuring self-pollination.
▸**ho'mogamous** *adj*

homogeneous ➊ (ˌhəʊmə'dʒiːnɪəs, ˌhɒm-) *adj* **1** composed of similar or identical parts or elements. **2** of uniform nature. **3** similar in kind or nature. **4** *Maths.* containing terms of the same degree with respect to all the variables, as in $x^2 + 2xy + y^2$.
▸**homogeneity** (ˌhəʊməʊdʒɪ'niːɪtɪ, ˌhɒm-) *n* ▸ˌ**homo'geneousness** *n*

homogenize *or* **homogenise** (hɒ'mɒdʒɪˌnaɪz) *vb* **homogenizes, homogenizing, homogenized** *or* **homogenises, homogenising, homogenised. 1** (*tr*) to break up the fat globules in (milk or cream) so that they are evenly distributed. **2** to make or become homogeneous.
▸**hoˌmogeni'zation** *or* **hoˌmogeni'sation** *n* ▸**ho'mogeˌnizer** *or* **ho'mogeˌniser** *n*

homogenous (hə'mɒdʒɪnəs) *adj* of, relating to, or exhibiting homogeny.

homogeny (hɒ'mɒdʒɪnɪ) *n Biol.* similarity in structure because of common ancestry. [C19: from Gk *homogeneia* community of origin, from *homogenēs* of the same kind]

homograph ('hɒməˌgrɑːf) *n* one of a group of words spelt in the same way but having different meanings.
▸ˌ**homo'graphic** *adj*

homoiothermic (həʊˌmɔɪə'θɜːmɪk) *or* **homothermal** (ˌhəʊməʊ'θɜːməl, ˌhɒm-) *adj* having a constant body temperature, usually higher than the temperature of the surroundings; warm-blooded.
▸**ho'moioˌthermy** *or* **'homoˌthermy** *n*

homologize *or* **homologise** (hɒ'mɒləˌdʒaɪz) *vb* **homologizes, homologizing, homologized** *or* **homologises, homologising, homologised.** to be, show to be, or make homologous.

homologous ➊ (həʊ'mɒləgəs, hɒ-), **homological** (ˌhəʊ-mə'lɒdʒɪkᵊl, ˌhɒm-), *or* **homologic** *adj* **1** having a related or similar position, structure, etc. **2** *Biol.* (of organs and parts) having the same evolutionary origin but different functions: *the wing of a bat and the paddle of a whale are homologous.*
▸ˌ**homo'logically** *adv* ▸**'homoˌlogue** *or US* (*sometimes*) **'homolog** *n*

homology (həʊ'mɒlədʒɪ) *n, pl* **homologies.** the condition of being homologous. [C17: from Gk *homologia* agreement, from *homologos* agreeing, from HOMO- + *legein* to speak]

homolosine projection (hɒ'mɒləˌsaɪn) *n* a map projection of the world on which the oceans are distorted to allow for greater accuracy in representing the continents. [C20: from Gk *homologos* agreeing + SINE[1]]

homomorphism (ˌhəʊməʊ'mɔːfɪzəm, ˌhɒm-) *or* **homomorphy** *n Biol.* similarity in form.
▸ˌ**homo'morphic** *or* ˌ**homo'morphous** *adj*

homonym ('hɒmənɪm) *n* **1** one of a group of words spelt in the same way but having different meanings. Cf. **homograph, homophone. 2** *Biol.* a specific or generic name that has been used for two or more different organisms. [C17: from L *homōnymum*, from Gk, from *homōnumos* of the same name; see HOMO-, -ONYM]
▸ˌ**homo'nymic** *or* **ho'monymous** *adj*

homophobia (ˌhəʊməʊ'fəʊbɪə) *n* intense hatred or fear of homosexuals or homosexuality. [C20: from HOMO(SEXUAL) + -PHOBIA]
▸**'homoˌphobe** *n* ▸ˌ**homo'phobic** *adj*

homophone ('hɒməˌfəʊn) *n* **1** one of a group of words pronounced in the same way but differing in meaning or spelling or both, as *bear* and *bare*. **2** a written letter or combination of letters that represents the same speech sound as another: *"ph" is a homophone of "f".*

homophonic (ˌhɒmə'fɒnɪk) *adj* of or relating to music in which the parts move together rather than exhibit individual rhythmic independence.

homopterous (həʊ'mɒptərəs) *or* **homopteran** *adj* of or belonging to a suborder of hemipterous insects having wings of a uniform texture held over the back at rest. [C19: from Gk *homopteros*, from HOMO- + *pteron* wing]

Homo sapiens ('sæpɪˌenz) *n* the specific name of modern man; the only extant species of the genus *Homo*. This species also includes some extinct types of primitive man, such as Cro-Magnon man. [NL, from L *homo* man + *sapiens* wise]

homosexual ➊ (ˌhəʊməʊ'seksjʊəl, ˌhɒm-) *n* **1** a person who is sexually attracted to members of the same sex. ◆ *adj* **2** of or relating to homosexuals or homosexuality. **3** of or relating to the same sex.

homosexuality (ˌhəʊməʊˌseksjʊ'ælɪtɪ, ˌhɒm-) *n* sexual attraction to or sexual relations with members of the same sex.

homozygote (ˌhəʊməʊ'zaɪgəʊt) *n* an animal or plant that is homozygous and breeds true to type.
▸**homozygotic** (ˌhəʊməʊzaɪ'gɒtɪk) *adj*

homozygous (ˌhəʊməʊ'zaɪgəs) *adj Genetics.* (of an organism) having identical alleles for any one gene: *these two fruit flies are homozygous for red eye colour.*

homunculus (hɒ'mʌŋkjʊləs) *n, pl* **homunculi** (-ˌlaɪ). a miniature man; midget. Also called: **homuncule** (həʊ'mʌŋkjuːl). [C17: from L, dim. of *homo* man]
▸**ho'muncular** *adj*

homy ➊ *or esp. US* **homey** ('həʊmɪ) *adj* **homier, homiest.** like a home; cosy.
▸**'hominess** *or esp. US* **'homeyness** *n*

hon. *abbrev. for:* **1** honorary. **2** honourable.

Hon. *abbrev. for* Honourable (title).

honcho ('hɒntʃəʊ) *n, pl* **honchos.** *Inf., chiefly US.* the person in charge; the boss. [C20: from Japanese *han'chō* group leader]

THESAURUS

homely, home-made, inelegant, plain, rough, rude, rustic, unpolished

homicidal *adj* **1, 2** = **murderous,** deadly, death-dealing, lethal, maniacal, mortal

homicide *n* **1** = **murder,** bloodshed, killing, manslaughter, slaying **2** = **murderer,** killer, slayer

homily *n* **1** = **sermon,** address, discourse, lecture, preaching, preachment

homogeneity *n* **1-3** = **uniformity,** analogousness, comparability, consistency, correspondence, identicalness, oneness, sameness, similarity

homogeneous *adj* **1-3** = **uniform,** akin, alike, analogous, cognate, comparable, consistent, identical, kindred, similar, unvarying
Antonyms *adj* different, disparate, dissimilar, divergent, diverse, heterogeneous, manifold, mixed, unlike, unrelated, varied, various, varying

homologous *adj* **1** = **similar,** analogous, comparable, correspondent, corresponding, like, parallel, related

homosexual *adj* **2** = **gay,** bent (*sl.*), camp (*inf.*), dykey (*sl.*), homoerotic, lesbian, pink (*inf.*), queer (*inf., derogatory*), sapphic

homy *adj* = **cosy,** comfortable, comfy (*inf.*), congenial, domestic, familiar, friendly, informal, intimate, pleasant, warm

hone ⓣ (həʊn) *n* **1** a fine whetstone for sharpening. ◆ *vb* **hones, honing, honed. 2** (*tr*) to sharpen or polish with or as if with a hone. [OE *hān* stone]

> **USAGE NOTE** *Hone* is sometimes wrongly used where *home* is meant: *this device makes it easier to home in on* (not *hone in on*) *the target.*

honest ⓣ (ˈɒnɪst) *adj* **1** not given to lying, cheating, stealing, etc.; trustworthy. **2** not false or misleading; genuine. **3** just or fair: *honest wages.* **4** characterized by sincerity: *an honest appraisal.* **5** without pretensions: *honest farmers.* **6** *Arch.* (of a woman) respectable. **7 honest broker.** a mediator in disputes, esp. international ones. **8 make an honest woman of.** to marry (a woman, esp. one who is pregnant) to prevent scandal. [C13: from OF *honeste,* from L *honestus* distinguished, from *honōs* HONOUR]

honestly ⓣ (ˈɒnɪstlɪ) *adv* **1** in an honest manner. **2** (intensifier): *I honestly don't believe it.*

honesty ⓣ (ˈɒnɪstɪ) *n, pl* **honesties. 1** the condition of being honest. **2** *Arch.* virtue or respect. **3** Also called: **moonwort, satinpod.** a purple-flowered European plant cultivated for its flattened silvery pods, which are used for indoor decoration.

honey (ˈhʌnɪ) *n* **1** a sweet viscid substance made by bees from nectar and stored in their nests or hives as food. **2** anything that is sweet or delightful. **3** (*often cap.*) *Chiefly US & Canad.* a term of endearment. **4** *Inf., chiefly US & Canad.* something very good of its kind. ◆ *vb* **honeys, honeying, honeyed. 5** (*tr*) to sweeten with or as if with honey. **6** (often foll. by *up*) to talk to (someone) in a flattering way. [OE *huneg*]
▸ **ˈhoney-ˌlike** *adj*

honey badger *n* another name for **ratel.**

honeybee (ˈhʌnɪˌbiː) *n* any of various social bees widely domesticated as a source of honey and beeswax. Also called: **hive bee.**

honey buzzard *n* a common European bird of prey having broad wings and a typically dull brown plumage with white-streaked underparts.

honeycomb (ˈhʌnɪˌkəʊm) *n* **1** a waxy structure, constructed by bees in a hive, that consists of adjacent hexagonal cells in which honey is stored, eggs are laid, and larvae develop. **2** something resembling this in structure. **3** *Zool.* another name for **reticulum** (sense 2). ◆ *vb* (*tr*) **4** to pierce with holes, cavities, etc. **5** to permeate: *honeycombed with spies.*

honey creeper *n* a small tropical American songbird having a slender downward-curving bill and feeding on nectar.

honeydew (ˈhʌnɪˌdjuː) *n* **1** a sugary substance excreted by aphids and similar insects. **2** a similar substance exuded by certain plants.

honeydew melon *n* a variety of muskmelon with a smooth greenish-white rind and sweet greenish flesh.

honey-eater (ˈhʌnɪˌiːtə) *n* a small Australasian songbird having a downward-curving bill and a brushlike tongue specialized for extracting nectar from flowers.

honeyed ⓣ *or* **honied** (ˈhʌnɪd) *adj Poetic.* **1** flattering or soothing. **2** made sweet or agreeable: *honeyed words.* **3** full of honey.

honey guide *n* a small bird inhabiting tropical forests of Africa and Asia and feeding on beeswax, honey, and insects.

honeymoon (ˈhʌnɪˌmuːn) *n* **1** a holiday taken by a newly married couple. **2** a holiday considered to resemble a honeymoon: *a second honeymoon.* **3** the early, usually calm period of a relationship or enterprise. ◆ *vb* **4** (*intr*) to take a honeymoon. [C16: traditionally explained as an allusion to the feelings of married couples as changing with the phases of the moon]
▸ **ˈhoneyˌmooner** *n*

honeysuckle (ˈhʌnɪˌsʌkᵊl) *n* **1** a temperate climbing shrub with fragrant white, yellow, or pink tubular flowers. **2** any of various Australian trees or shrubs of the genus *Banksia,* having flowers in dense spikes. [OE *hunigsūce,* from HONEY + SUCK]

honeytrap (ˈhʌnɪˌtræp) *n Inf.* a scheme in which a victim is lured into a compromising sexual situation that provides the opportunity for blackmail.

honk (hɒŋk) *n* **1** a representation of the sound made by a goose. **2** any sound resembling this, esp. a motor horn. **3** *Brit. & Austral. sl.* a bad smell. ◆ *vb* **4** to make or cause (something) to make such a sound. **5** (*intr*) *Brit. sl.* to vomit. **6** (*intr*) *Brit. & Austral. sl.* to have a bad smell.

honky (ˈhɒnkɪ) *n, pl* **honkies.** *Derog. sl., chiefly US.* a White man or White men collectively. [C20: from ?]

honky-tonk (ˈhɒŋkɪˌtɒŋk) *n* **1** *US & Canad. sl.* a cheap disreputable nightclub, bar, etc. **2a** a style of ragtime piano-playing, esp. on a tinny-sounding piano. **2b** (*as modifier*): *honky-tonk music.* [C19: rhyming compound based on HONK]

honorarium (ˌɒnəˈrɛərɪəm) *n, pl* **honorariums** *or* **honoraria** (-rɪə). a fee paid for a nominally free service. [C17: from L: something presented on being admitted to a post of HONOUR]

honorary ⓣ (ˈɒnərərɪ) *adj* (*usually prenominal*) **1a** held or given only as an honour, without the normal privileges or duties: *an honorary degree.* **1b** (of a secretary, treasurer, etc.) unpaid. **2** having such a position or title. **3** depending on honour rather than legal agreement.

honorific (ˌɒnəˈrɪfɪk) *adj* **1** showing respect. **2a** (of a pronoun, verb inflection, etc.) indicating the speaker's respect for the addressee. **2b** (*as n*): *a Japanese honorific.*
▸ **ˌhonorˈifically** *adv*

honour ⓣ *or US* **honor** (ˈɒnə) *n* **1** personal integrity; allegiance to moral principles. **2a** fame or glory. **2b** a person who wins this for his country, school, etc. **3** (*often pl*) great respect, esteem, etc., or an outward sign of this. **4** (*often pl*) high or noble rank. **5** a privilege or pleasure: *it is an honour to serve you.* **6** a woman's chastity. **7a** *Bridge, etc.* any of the top five cards in a suit or any of the four aces at no trumps. **7b** *Whist.* any of the top four cards. **8** *Golf.* the right to tee off first. **9 in honour bound.** under a moral obligation. **10 in honour of.** out of respect for. **11 on one's honour.** on the pledge of one's word or good name. ◆ *vb* (*tr*) **12** to hold in respect. **13** to show courteous behaviour towards. **14** to worship. **15** to confer a distinction upon. **16** to accept and then pay when due (a cheque, draft, etc.). **17** to keep (one's promise); fulfil (a previous agreement). **18** to bow or curtsy to (one's dancing partner). [C12: from OF *onor,* from L *honor* esteem]

Honour (ˈɒnə) *n* (preceded by *Your, His,* or *Her*) a title used to or of certain judges.

honourable ⓣ *or US* **honorable** (ˈɒnərəbᵊl) *adj* **1** possessing or characterized by high principles. **2** worthy of honour or esteem. **3** consistent with or bestowing honour.
▸ **ˈhonourably** *or US* **ˈhonorably** *adv*

Honourable *or US* **Honorable** (ˈɒnərəbᵊl) *adj* (*prenominal*) **the.** a title of respect placed before a name: used of various officials in the English-speaking world, as a courtesy title in Britain for the children of certain peers, and in Parliament by one member speaking of another. Abbrev.: **Hon.**

honours ⓣ *or US* **honors** (ˈɒnəz) *pl n* **1** observances of respect. **2** (*often cap.*) **2a** (in a university degree course) a rank of the highest academic standard. **2b** (*as modifier*): *an honours degree.* Abbrev.: **Hons. 3** a high mark awarded for an examination; distinction. **4 do the honours.** to serve as host or hostess. **5 last** (*or* **funeral**) **honours.** observances of respect at a funeral. **6 military honours.** ceremonies performed by troops in honour of royalty, at the burial of an officer, etc.

honours of war *pl n Mil.* the honours granted by the victorious to the defeated, esp. as of marching out with all arms and flags flying.

hooch *or* **hootch** (huːtʃ) *n Inf., chiefly US & Canad.* alcoholic drink, esp. illicitly distilled spirits. [C20: of Amerind origin, *Hootchinoo,* name of a tribe that distilled a type of liquor]

THESAURUS

hone *vb* **2** = **sharpen**, edge, file, grind, point, polish, strop, whet

honest *adj* **1** = **trustworthy**, conscientious, decent, ethical, high-minded, honourable, law-abiding, reliable, reputable, scrupulous, trusty, truthful, upright, veracious, virtuous **2** = **genuine**, above board, authentic, bona fide, honest to goodness, on the level (*inf.*), on the up and up, proper, real, straight, true **3** = **fair**, equitable, fair and square, impartial, just **4** = **open**, candid, direct, forthright, frank, ingenuous, outright, plain, round, sincere, straightforward, undisguised, unfeigned, upfront (*inf.*)
Antonyms *adj* ≠ **trustworthy:** bad, corrupt, crooked, deceitful, dishonest, guilty, immoral, treacherous, unethical, unfair, unfaithful, unlawful, unprincipled, unreliable, unrighteous, unscrupulous, untrustworthy, untruthful ≠ **genuine:** counterfeit, false, fraudulent, illegitimate ≠ **open:** disguised, false, insincere, secretive

honestly *adv* **1** = **ethically**, by fair means, cleanly, honourably, in good faith, lawfully, legally, legitimately, on the level (*inf.*), with clean hands ◆ *intensifier* **2** = **frankly**, candidly, in all sincerity, truthfully

honesty *n* **1** = **integrity**, bluntness, candour, equity, even-handedness, fairness, faithfulness, fidelity, frankness, genuineness, honour, incorruptibility, morality, openness, outspokenness, plainness, probity, rectitude, reputability, scrupulousness, sincerity, straightforwardness, straightness, trustworthiness, truthfulness, uprightness, veracity, virtue

honeyed *adj Poetic* **1, 2** = **flattering**, agreeable, alluring, cajoling, dulcet, enticing, mellow, melodious, seductive, soothing, sweet, sweetened, unctuous

honorary *adj* **1a** = **nominal**, complimentary, ex officio, formal, *honoris causa,* in name or title only, titular, unofficial **1b** = **unpaid**

honour *n* **1** = **integrity**, decency, fairness, goodness, honesty, morality, principles, probity, rectitude, righteousness, trustworthiness, uprightness **2a, 4** = **prestige**, credit, dignity, distinction, elevation, eminence, esteem, fame, glory, high standing, rank, renown, reputation, repute **3** = **tribute**, acclaim, accolade, adoration, Brownie points, commendation, deference, homage, kudos, praise, recognition, regard, respect, reverence, veneration **5** = **privilege**, compliment, credit, favour, pleasure, source of pride *or* satisfaction **6** = **virginity**, chastity, innocence, modesty, purity, virtue ◆ *vb* **12–14** = **respect**, admire, adore, appreciate, esteem, exalt, glorify, hallow, prize, revere, reverence, value, venerate, worship **15** = **acclaim**, celebrate, commemorate, commend, compliment, crack up (*inf.*), decorate, dignify, exalt, glorify, laud, lionize, praise **16** = **pay**, accept, acknowledge, cash, clear, credit, pass, take **17** = **fulfil**, be as good as (*inf.*), be faithful to, be true to, carry out, discharge, keep, live up to, observe
Antonyms *n* ≠ **integrity:** degradation, dishonesty, dishonour, insincerity, lowness, meanness, unscrupulousness ≠ **prestige:** disgrace, dishonour, disrepute, disrespect, infamy, shame ≠ **tribute:** condemnation, contempt, disfavour, insult, scorn, slight ◆ *vb* ≠ **respect, acclaim:** condemn, defame, degrade, dishonour, insult, offend, scorn, slight ≠ **pay:** refuse

honourable *adj* **1** = **principled**, ethical, fair, high-minded, honest, just, moral, true, trustworthy, trusty, upright, upstanding, virtuous **2** = **respected**, creditable, estimable, proper, reputable, respectable, right, righteous, virtuous **3** = **prestigious**, distinguished, eminent, great, illustrious, noble, notable, noted, renowned, venerable

honours *pl n* **1** = **titles**, adornments, awards, decorations, dignities, distinctions, laurels

hood[1] (hʊd) *n* **1** a loose head covering either attached to a cloak or coat or made as a separate garment. **2** something resembling this in shape or use. **3** the US and Canad. name for **bonnet** (of a car). **4** the folding roof of a convertible car. **5** a hoodlike garment worn over an academic gown, indicating its wearer's degree and university. **6** *Biol.* a hoodlike structure, such as the fold of skin on the head of a cobra. ◆ *vb* **7** (*tr*) to cover with or as if with a hood. [OE *hōd*]
▸ **'hood,like** *adj*

hood[2] (hʊd) *n Sl.* short for **hoodlum.**

-hood *suffix forming nouns.* **1** indicating state or condition: *manhood.* **2** indicating a body of persons: *knighthood; priesthood.* [OE *-hād*]

hooded ('hʊdɪd) *adj* **1** covered with, having, or shaped like a hood. **2** (of eyes) having heavy eyelids that appear to be half closed.

hooded crow *n* a crow that has a grey body and black head, wings, and tail. Also called (Scot.): **hoodie** ('hʊdɪ), **hoodie crow.**

hoodlum ('huːdləm) *n* **1** a petty gangster. **2** a lawless youth. [C19: ?from Southern G *Haderlump* ragged good-for-nothing]

hoodman-blind (,hʊdmən'blaɪnd) *n Brit., arch.* blind man's buff.

hoodoo ⓣ ('huːduː) *n, pl* **hoodoos. 1** a variant of **voodoo. 2** *Inf.* a person or thing that brings bad luck. **3** *Inf.* bad luck. ◆ *vb* **hoodoos, hoodooing, hoodooed. 4** (*tr*) *Inf.* to bring bad luck to.

hoodwink ⓣ ('hʊd,wɪŋk) *vb* (*tr*) **1** to dupe; trick. **2** *Obs.* to cover or hide. [C16: orig., to cover the eyes with a hood, blindfold]

hooey ('huːɪ) *n, interj Sl.* nonsense. [C20: from ?]

hoof (huːf) *n, pl* **hooves** *or* **hoofs. 1a** the horny covering of the end of the foot in the horse, deer, and all other ungulate mammals. **1b** (*in combination*): *a hoofbeat.* Related adj: **ungular. 2** the foot of an ungulate mammal. **3** a hoofed animal. **4** *Facetious.* a person's foot. **5 on the hoof. 5a** (of livestock) alive. **5b** in an impromptu manner: *he did his thinking on the hoof.* ◆ *vb* **6 hoof it.** *Sl.* **6a** to walk. **6b** to dance. [OE *hōf*]
▸ **hoofed** *adj*

hoofer ('huːfə) *n Sl.* a professional dancer.

hoo-ha ('huː,hɑː) *n* a noisy commotion or fuss. [C20: from ?]

hook ⓣ (hʊk) *n* **1** a curved piece of material, usually metal, used to suspend, hold, or pull something. **2** short for **fish-hook. 3** a trap or snare. **4** something resembling a hook in design or use. **5a** a sharp bend, esp. in a river. **5b** a sharply curved spit of land. **6** *Boxing.* a short swinging blow delivered with the elbow bent. **7** *Cricket.* a shot in which the ball is hit square on the leg side with the bat held horizontally. **8** *Golf.* a shot that causes the ball to go to the player's left. **9** a hook-shaped stroke used in writing, such as a part of a letter extending above or below the line. **10** *Music.* a stroke added to the stem of a note to indicate time values shorter than a crotchet. **11** a sickle. **12** *Naut.* an anchor. **13 by hook or (by) crook.** by any means. **14 hook, line, and sinker.** *Inf.* completely: *he fell for it hook, line, and sinker.* **15 off the hook.** *Sl.* free from obligation or guilt. **16 sling one's hook.** *Brit. sl.* to leave. ◆ *vb* **17** (often foll. by *up*) to fasten or be fastened with or as if with a hook or hooks. **18** (*tr*) to catch (something, such as a fish) on a hook. **19** to curve like or into the shape of a hook. **20** (*tr*) to make (a rug) by hooking yarn through a stiff fabric backing with a special instrument. **21** *Boxing.* to hit (an opponent) with a hook. **22** *Cricket, etc.* to play (a ball) with a hook. **23** *Rugby.* to obtain and pass (the ball) backwards from a scrum, using the feet. **24** (*tr*) *Sl.* to steal. [OE *hōc*]
▸ **'hook,like** *adj*

hookah *or* **hooka** ('hʊkə) *n* an oriental pipe for smoking marijuana, tobacco, etc., consisting of one or more long flexible stems connected to a container of water or other liquid through which smoke is drawn and cooled. Also called: **hubble-bubble, water pipe.** [C18: from Ar. *huqqah*]

hooked ⓣ (hʊkt) *adj* **1** bent like a hook. **2** having a hook or hooks. **3** caught or trapped. **4** a slang word for **married. 5** *Sl.* addicted to a drug. **6** (often foll. by *on*) obsessed (with).

hooker ('hʊkə) *n* **1** a person or thing that hooks. **2** *Sl.* a prostitute. **3** *Rugby.* the central forward in the front row of a scrum.

Hooke's law (hʊks) *n* the principle that the stress imposed on a solid is directly proportional to the strain produced, within the elastic limit. [C18: after R. *Hooke* (1635–1703), E scientist]

hook-up *n* **1** the contact of an aircraft in flight with the refuelling hose of a tanker aircraft. **2** an alliance or relationship. **3** the linking of broadcasting equipment or stations to transmit a special programme. ◆ *vb* **hook up** (*adv*). **4** to connect (two or more people or things).

hookworm ('hʊk,wɜːm) *n* any of various parasitic bloodsucking worms which cause disease. They have hooked mouthparts and enter their hosts by boring through the skin. Cf. **ancylostomiasis.**

hooky *or* **hookey** ('hʊkɪ) *n Inf., chiefly US, Canad., & NZ.* truancy, usually from school (esp. in **play hooky**). [C20: ?from *hook it* to escape]

hooligan ⓣ ('huːlɪgən) *n Sl.* a rough lawless young person. [C19: ? var. of *Houlihan,* Irish surname]
▸ **'hooliganism** *n*

hoop[1] ⓣ (huːp) *n* **1** a rigid circular band of metal or wood. **2** something resembling this. **3** a band of iron that holds the staves of a barrel together. **4** a child's toy shaped like a hoop and rolled on the ground or whirled around the body. **5** *Croquet.* any of the iron arches through which the ball is driven. **6a** a light curved frame to spread out a skirt. **6b** (*as modifier*): *a hoop skirt.* **7** *Basketball.* the round metal frame to which the net is attached to form the basket. **8** a large ring through which performers or animals jump. **9 go** *or* **be put through the hoop.** to be subjected to an ordeal. ◆ *vb* **10** (*tr*) to surround with or as if with a hoop. [OE *hōp*]
▸ **hooped** *adj*

hoop[2] (huːp) *n, vb* a variant spelling of **whoop.**

hoopla ('huːplɑː) *n* **1** *Brit.* a fairground game in which a player tries to throw a hoop over an object and so win it. **2** *US & Canad. sl.* **2a** noise; bustle. **2b** nonsense; ballyhoo. [C20: see WHOOP, LA[2]]

hoopoe ('huːpuː) *n* an Old World bird having a pinkish-brown plumage with black-and-white wings and an erectile crest. [C17: from earlier *hoopoop,* imit.]

hoop pine *n* a fast-growing timber tree of Australia having rough bark with hooplike cracks around the trunk and branches.

hooray (huː'reɪ) *interj, n, vb* **1** a variant spelling of **hurrah.** ◆ *sentence substitute.* **2** Also: **hooroo** (huː'ruː). *Austral. & NZ.* cheerio.

Hooray Henry ('huː,reɪ 'henrɪ) *n, pl* **Hooray Henries** *or* **Hooray Henrys.** a young upper-class man, often with affectedly hearty voice and manners. Sometimes shortened to **Hooray.**

hoosegow *or* **hoosgow** ('huːsgaʊ) *n US.* a slang word for **jail.** [C20: from Mexican Sp. *jusgado* prison, from Sp.: court of justice, ult. from L *judex* a JUDGE]

hoot[1] ⓣ (huːt) *n* **1** the mournful wavering cry of some owls. **2** a similar sound, such as that of a train whistle. **3** a jeer of derision. **4** *Inf.* an amusing person or thing. ◆ *vb* **5** (often foll. by *at*) to jeer or yell (something) contemptuously (at someone). **6** (*tr*) to drive (speakers, actors on stage, etc.) off by hooting. **7** (*intr*) to make a hoot. **8** (*intr*) *Brit.* to blow a horn. [C13 *hoten,* imit.]

hoot[2] (huːt) *n Austral. & NZ.* a slang word for **money.** [from Maori *utu* price]

hootenanny ('huːtᵊ,nænɪ) *or* **hootnanny** ('huːt,nænɪ) *n, pl* **hootenannies** *or* **hootnannies.** *US & Canad.* an informal performance by folk singers. [C20: from ?]

hooter ('huːtə) *n Chiefly Brit.* **1** a person or thing that hoots, esp. a car horn. **2** *Sl.* a nose.

Hoover ('huːvə) *n* **1** *Trademark.* a type of vacuum cleaner. ◆ *vb* (*usually not cap.*) **2** to vacuum-clean (a carpet, etc.). **3** (*tr*; often foll. by *up*) to consume or dispose of (something) quickly and completely: *he hoovered up his grilled fish.*

hooves (huːvz) *n* a plural of **hoof.**

hop[1] ⓣ (hɒp) *vb* **hops, hopping, hopped. 1** (*intr*) to jump forwards or upwards on one foot. **2** (*intr*) (esp. of frogs, birds, etc.) to move forwards in short jumps. **3** (*tr*) to jump over. **4** (*intr*) *Inf.* to move quickly (in, on, out of, etc.): *hop on a bus.* **5** (*tr*) *Inf.* to cross (an ocean) in an aircraft. **6** (*tr*) *US & Canad. inf.* to travel by means of: *he hopped a train to Chicago.* **7** (*intr*) another word for **limp**[1] (senses 1 and 2). **8 hop it** (*or* **off**). *Brit. sl.* to go away. ◆ *n* **9** the act or an instance of hopping. **10** *Inf.* an informal dance. **11** *Inf.* a trip, esp. in an aircraft. **12 on the hop.** *Inf.* **12a** active or busy. **12b** *Brit.* unawares or unprepared. [OE *hoppian*]

hop[2] (hɒp) *n* **1** a climbing plant which has green conelike female flowers and clusters of small male flowers. **2 hop garden.** a field of hops. **3** *Obs. sl.* opium or any other narcotic drug. ◆ See also **hops.** [C15: from MDu. *hoppe*]

hope ⓣ (həʊp) *n* **1** (*sometimes pl*) a feeling of desire for something and confidence in the possibility of its fulfilment: *his hope for peace was justified.* **2** a reasonable ground for this feeling: *there is still hope.* **3** a person or thing that gives cause for hope. **4** a thing, situation, or event that is desired: *my hope is that prices will fall.* **5 not a hope** *or* **some hope.** used ironically to express little confidence that expectations will be

THESAURUS

hoodoo *n* **1** = **voodoo 2, 3** *Informal* = **jinx**, bad luck, curse, evil eye, evil star, hex (*US & Canad. inf.*)

hoodwink *vb* **1** = **deceive**, bamboozle (*inf.*), befool, cheat, con (*inf.*), cozen, delude, dupe, fool, gull (*arch.*), hoax, impose, kid (*inf.*), lead up the garden path (*inf.*), mislead, pull a fast one on (*inf.*), rook (*sl.*), sell a pup, swindle, take (someone) for a ride (*inf.*), trick

hook *n* **1** = **fastener**, catch, clasp, hasp, holder, link, lock, peg **3** = **trap**, noose, snare, springe **13 by hook or by crook** = **by any means**, by fair means or foul, somehow, somehow or other, someway **14 hook, line, and sinker** *Informal* = **completely**, entirely, lock, stock and barrel, thoroughly, through and through, totally, utterly, wholly **15 off the hook** *Slang* = **let off**, acquitted, cleared, exonerated, in the clear, under no obligation, vindicated ◆ *vb* **17** = **fasten**, catch, clasp, fix, hasp, secure **18** = **catch**, enmesh, ensnare, entrap, snare, trap

hooked *adj* **1** = **bent**, aquiline, beaked, beaky, curved, hooklike, hook-shaped, uncinate (*Biology*) **5** *Slang* = **addicted 6** *often foll. by* **on** = **obsessed**, devoted, enamoured, taken

hooligan *n Slang* = **delinquent**, casual, hoodlum (*chiefly US*), lager lout, rowdy, ruffian, tough, vandal, yob *or* yobbo (*Brit. sl.*)

hooliganism *n* = **delinquency**, disorder, loutishness, rowdiness, vandalism, violence, yobbishness

hoop[1] *n* **1, 2** = **ring**, band, circlet, girdle, loop, round, wheel

hoot[1] *n* **1** = **cry**, call **2** = **toot 3** = **catcall**, boo, hiss, jeer, yell **4** *Informal* = **laugh**, card (*inf.*), caution (*inf.*), scream (*inf.*) ◆ *vb* **5, 6** = **jeer**, boo, catcall, condemn, decry, denounce, hiss, howl down, yell at **7** = **cry**, scream, shout, shriek, whoop, yell **8** *Brit.* = **toot**

hop[1] *vb* **2, 3** = **jump**, bound, caper, dance, leap, skip, spring, trip, vault ◆ *n* **9** = **jump**, bounce, bound, leap, skip, spring, step, vault

hope *n* **1** = **belief**, ambition, anticipation, assumption, confidence, desire, dream, expectancy, expectation, faith, longing ◆ *vb* **6** = **desire**, anticipate, aspire, await, believe, contemplate, count on, cross one's fingers, expect, foresee, keep one's fingers crossed, long, look forward to, rely, set one's heart on, trust
Antonyms *n* ≠ **belief**: despair, distrust, doubt, dread, hopelessness

fulfilled. ◆ *vb* **hopes, hoping, hoped. 6** (*tr; takes a clause as object or an infinitive*) to desire (something) with some possibility of fulfilment: *I hope to tell you.* **7** (*intr;* often foll. by *for*) to have a wish. **8** (*tr; takes a clause as object*) to trust or believe: *we hope that this is satisfactory.* [OE *hopa*]

hope chest *n* the US, Canad., and NZ name for **bottom drawer.**

hopeful ◑ ('həʊpfʊl) *adj* **1** having or expressing hope. **2** inspiring hope; promising. ◆ *n* **3** a person considered to be on the brink of success (esp. in **a young hopeful**).
▸ **'hopefulness** *n*

hopefully ◑ ('həʊpfʊlɪ) *adv* **1** in a hopeful manner. **2** *Inf.* it is hoped: *hopefully they will be married soon.*

> **USAGE NOTE** The use of *hopefully* to mean *it is hoped* used to be considered incorrect by some people but has now become acceptable in informal contexts.

hopeless ◑ ('həʊplɪs) *adj* **1** having or offering no hope. **2** impossible to solve. **3** unable to learn, function, etc. **4** *Inf.* without skill or ability.
▸ **'hopelessly** *adv* ▸ **'hopelessness** *n*

Hopi ('həʊpɪ) *n* **1** (*pl* **Hopis** *or* **Hopi**) a member of a North American Indian people of NE Arizona. **2** the language of this people. [from Hopi *Hópi* peaceful]

hoplite ('hɒplaɪt) *n* (in ancient Greece) a heavily armed infantryman. [C18: from Gk *hoplitēs*, from *hoplon* weapon, from *hepein* to prepare]

hopper ('hɒpə) *n* **1** a person or thing that hops. **2** a funnel-shaped reservoir from which solid materials can be discharged into a receptacle below, esp. for feeding fuel to a furnace, loading a truck, etc. **3** a machine used for picking hops. **4** any of various long-legged hopping insects. **5** an open-topped railway truck for loose minerals, etc., unloaded through doors on the underside. **6** *S. African.* another name for **cocopan. 7** *Computing.* a device for holding punched cards and feeding them to a card reader.

hopping ('hɒpɪŋ) *adv* **hopping mad.** in a terrible rage.

hops (hɒps) *pl n* the dried flowers of the hop plant, used to give a bitter taste to beer.

hopsack ('hɒp,sæk) *n* **1** a roughly woven fabric of wool, cotton, etc., used for clothing. **2** Also called: **hopsacking.** a coarse fabric used for bags, etc., made generally of hemp or jute.

hopscotch ('hɒp,skɒtʃ) *n* a children's game in which a player throws a small stone or other object to land in one of a pattern of squares marked on the ground and then hops over to it to pick it up. [C19: HOP[1] + SCOTCH[1]]

horary ('hɔːrərɪ) *adj Arch.* **1** relating to the hours. **2** hourly. [C17: from Med. L *hōrārius*, from L *hora*]

horde ◑ (hɔːd) *n* **1** a vast crowd; throng; mob. **2** a nomadic group of people, esp. an Asiatic group. **3** a large moving mass of animals, esp. insects. [C16: from Polish *horda*, from Turkish *ordū* camp]

> **USAGE NOTE** *Horde* is sometimes wrongly written where *hoard* is meant: *a hoard* (not *horde*) *of gold coins.*

horehound *or* **hoarhound** ('hɔː,haʊnd) *n* a downy herbaceous Old World plant with small white flowers that contain a bitter juice formerly used as a cough medicine and flavouring. [OE *hārhūne*, from *hār* grey + *hūne* horehound, from ?]

horizon ◑ (hə'raɪzᵊn) *n* **1** Also called: **visible horizon, apparent horizon.** the apparent line that divides the earth and the sky. **2** *Astron.* **2a** Also called: **sensible horizon.** the circular intersection with the celestial sphere of the plane tangential to the earth at the position of the observer. **2b** Also called: **celestial horizon.** the great circle on the celestial sphere, the plane of which passes through the centre of the earth and is parallel to the sensible horizon. **3** the range or limit of scope, interest, knowledge, etc. **4** a layer of rock within a stratum that has a particular composition by which the stratum may be dated. [C14: from L, from Gk *horizōn kuklos* limiting circle, from *horizein* to limit]

horizontal ◑ (,hɒrɪ'zɒntᵊl) *adj* **1** parallel to the plane of the horizon; level; flat. **2** of or relating to the horizon. **3** in a plane parallel to that of the horizon. **4** applied uniformly to all members of a group. **5** *Econ.* relating to identical stages of commercial activity: *horizontal integration.* ◆ *n* **6** a horizontal plane, position, line, etc.
▸ **,horizon'tality** *n* ▸ **,hori'zontally** *adv*

horizontal bar *n Gymnastics.* a raised bar on which swinging and vaulting exercises are performed.

hormone ('hɔːməʊn) *n* **1** a chemical substance produced in an endocrine gland and transported in the blood to a certain tissue, on which it exerts a specific effect. **2** an organic compound produced by a plant that is essential for growth. **3** any synthetic substance having the same effects. [C20: from Gk *hormōn*, from *horman* to stir up, from *hormē* impulse]
▸ **hor'monal** *adj*

hormone replacement therapy *n* a form of oestrogen treatment used to control menopausal symptoms and in the prevention of osteoporosis. Abbrev.: **HRT.**

horn (hɔːn) *n* **1** either of a pair of permanent bony outgrowths on the heads of cattle, antelopes, etc. **2** the outgrowth from the nasal bone of a rhinoceros, consisting of a mass of fused hairs. **3** any hornlike projection, such as the eyestalk of a snail. **4** the antler of a deer. **5a** the constituent substance, mainly keratin, of horns, hooves, etc. **5b** (*in combination*): *horn-rimmed spectacles.* **6** a container or device made from this substance or an artificial substitute: *a drinking horn.* **7** an object resembling a horn in shape, such as a cornucopia. **8** a primitive musical wind instrument made from horn. **9** any musical instrument consisting of a pipe or tube of brass fitted with a mouthpiece. See **French horn, cor anglais. 10** *Jazz sl.* any wind instrument. **11a** a device for producing a warning or signalling noise. **11b** (*in combination*): *a foghorn.* **12** (*usually pl*) the imaginary hornlike parts formerly supposed to appear on the forehead of a cuckold. **13a** a hollow conical device coupled to a gramophone to control the direction and quality of the sound. **13b** a similar device attached to an electrical loudspeaker, esp. in a public-address system. **14** a stretch of land or water shaped like a horn. **15** *Brit. taboo sl.* an erection of the penis. ◆ *vb* (*tr*) **16** to provide with a horn or horns. **17** to gore or butt with a horn. **18** to remove or shorten the horns of (cattle, etc.). ◆ See also **horn in.** [OE]
▸ **horned** *adj* ▸ **'hornless** *adj*

hornbeam ('hɔːn,biːm) *n* **1** a tree of Europe and Asia having smooth grey bark and hard white wood. **2** its wood. ◆ Also called: **ironwood.** [C14: from HORN + BEAM, referring to its tough wood]

hornbill ('hɔːn,bɪl) *n* a bird of tropical Africa and Asia, having a very large bill with a basal bony protuberance.

hornblende ('hɔːn,blend) *n* a mineral of the amphibole group consisting of the aluminium silicates of calcium, sodium, magnesium, and iron: varies in colour from green to black. [C18: from G *Horn* horn + BLENDE]

hornbook ('hɔːn,bʊk) *n* a page bearing a religious text or the alphabet, held in a frame with a thin window of horn over it.

horned toad *or* **lizard** *n* a small insectivorous burrowing lizard inhabiting desert regions of America, having a flattened toadlike body covered with spines.

horned viper *n* a venomous snake that occurs in desert regions of N Africa and SW Asia and has a small horny spine above each eye.

hornet ('hɔːnɪt) *n* **1** any of various large social wasps that can inflict a severe sting. **2 hornet's nest.** a strongly unfavourable reaction (often in **stir up a hornet's nest**). [OE *hyrnetu*]

horn in *vb* (*intr, adv;* often foll. by *on*) *Sl.* to interrupt or intrude.

horn of plenty *n* another term for **cornucopia.**

hornpipe ('hɔːn,paɪp) *n* **1** an obsolete reed instrument with a mouthpiece made of horn. **2** an old British solo dance to a hornpipe accompaniment, traditionally performed by sailors. **3** a piece of music for such a dance.

hornswoggle ('hɔːn,swɒgᵊl) *vb* **hornswoggles, hornswoggling, hornswoggled.** (*tr*) *Sl.* to cheat or trick; bamboozle. [C19: from ?]

horny ◑ ('hɔːnɪ) *adj* **hornier, horniest. 1** of, like, or hard as horn. **2** having a horn or horns. **3** *Sl.* **3a** sexually aroused. **3b** provoking or intended to provoke sexual arousal. **3c** sexually eager or lustful.
▸ **'horniness** *n*

horologe ('hɒrə,lɒdʒ) *n* a rare word for **timepiece.** [C14: from L *hōrologium*, from Gk *hōrologion*, from *hōra* HOUR + *-logos* from *legein* to tell]

horologist (hɒ'rɒlədʒɪst) *or* **horologer** *n* a person skilled in horology.

horology (hɒ'rɒlədʒɪ) *n* the art or science of making timepieces or of measuring time.
▸ **horologic** (,hɒrə'lɒdʒɪk) *or* **,horo'logical** *adj*

horoscope ('hɒrə,skəʊp) *n* **1** the prediction of a person's future based on zodiacal data for the time of birth. **2** the configuration of the planets, sun, and moon in the sky at a particular moment. **3** a diagram showing the positions of the planets, sun, moon, etc., at a particular time and place. [OE *horoscopus*, from L, from Gk *hōroskopos*, from *hōra* HOUR + -SCOPE]
▸ **horoscopic** (,hɒrə'skɒpɪk) *adj* ▸ **horoscopy** (hɒ'rɒskəpɪ) *n*

THESAURUS

hopeful *adj* **1** = **optimistic**, anticipating, assured, buoyant, confident, expectant, looking forward to, sanguine **2** = **promising**, auspicious, bright, cheerful, encouraging, heartening, propitious, reassuring, rosy
Antonyms *adj* ≠ **optimistic:** cheerless, dejected, despairing, hopeless, pessimistic ≠ **promising:** depressing, discouraging, disheartening, unpromising

hopefully *adv* **1** = **optimistically**, confidently, expectantly, sanguinely **2** *Informal* = **it is hoped**, all being well, conceivably, expectedly, feasibly, probably

hopeless *adj* **1** = **pessimistic**, abject, defeatist, dejected, demoralized, despairing, desperate, despondent, disconsolate, downhearted, forlorn, in despair, woebegone **2** = **impossible**, forlorn, futile, impracticable, not having a prayer, no-win, pointless, unachievable, unattainable, useless, vain **4** *Informal* = **no good**, inadequate, incompetent, ineffectual, inferior, pathetic, poor, useless (*inf.*)
Antonyms *adj* ≠ **pessimistic:** assured, cheerful, confident, expectant, happy, heartened, hopeful, optimistic, uplifted

hopelessly *adv* **1** = **without hope**, beyond all hope, despairingly, in despair, irredeemably, irremediably

horde *n* **1** = **crowd**, band, crew, drove, gang, host, mob, multitude, pack, press, swarm, throng, troop

horizon *n* **1** = **skyline**, field of vision, vista **3** = **scope**, ambit, compass, ken, perspective, prospect, purview, range, realm, sphere, stretch

horizontal *adj* **1** = **level**, flat, parallel, plane, supine

horny *adj* **3a, 3c** = **aroused**, amorous, excited, lustful, randy (*inf., chiefly Brit.*), raunchy (*sl.*), turned on (*sl.*)

horrendous (hɒˈrɛndəs) *adj* another word for **horrific**. [C17: from L *horrendus* fearful, from *horrēre* to bristle, shudder, tremble; see HORROR]
▸**horˈrendously** *adv*

horrible ❶ (ˈhɒrɪbᵊl) *adj* **1** causing horror; dreadful. **2** disagreeable. **3** *Inf.* cruel or unkind. [C14: via OF from L *horribilis*, from *horrēre* to tremble]
▸**ˈhorribleness** *n* ▸**ˈhorribly** *adv*

horrid ❶ (ˈhɒrɪd) *adj* **1** disagreeable; unpleasant: *a horrid meal.* **2** repulsive or frightening. **3** *Inf.* unkind. [C16 (in the sense: bristling, shaggy): from L *horridus* prickly, from *horrēre* to bristle]
▸**ˈhorridly** *adv* ▸**ˈhorridness** *n*

horrific ❶ (hɒˈrɪfɪk, hə-) *adj* provoking horror; horrible.
▸**horˈrifically** *adv*

horrify ❶ (ˈhɒrɪˌfaɪ) *vb* **horrifies, horrifying, horrified.** (*tr*) **1** to cause feelings of horror in; terrify. **2** to shock greatly.
▸**ˌhorrifiˈcation** *n* ▸**ˈhorriˌfied** *adj* ▸**ˈhorriˌfying** *adj* ▸**ˈhorriˌfyingly** *adv*

horripilation (hɒˌrɪpɪˈleɪʃən) *n Physiol.* a technical name for **goose flesh.** [C17: from LL *horripilātiō* a bristling, from L *horrēre* to stand on end + *pilus* hair]

horror ❶ (ˈhɒrə) *n* **1** extreme fear; terror; dread. **2** intense hatred. **3** (*often pl*) a thing or person causing fear, loathing, etc. **4** (*modifier*) having a frightening subject: *a horror film.* [C14: from L: a trembling with fear]

horrors (ˈhɒrəz) *pl n* **1** *Sl.* a fit of depression or anxiety. **2** *Inf.* See **delirium tremens.** ◆ *interj* **3** an expression of dismay, sometimes facetious.

hors de combat *French.* (ɔr də kɔ̃ba) *adj* (*postpositive*), *adv* disabled or injured. [lit.: out of (the) fight]

hors d'oeuvre (ɔː ˈdɜːvr) *n, pl* **hors d'oeuvre** *or* **hors d'oeuvres** (ˈdɜːvr). an appetizer, usually served before the main meal. [C18: from F, lit.: outside the work]

horse ❶ (hɔːs) *n* **1** a solid-hoofed, herbivorous, domesticated mammal used for draught work and riding. Related adj: **equine. 2** the adult male of this species; stallion. **3 wild horse.** another name for **Przewalski's horse. 4** (*functioning as pl*) horsemen, esp. cavalry: *a regiment of horse.* **5** Also called: **buck.** *Gymnastics.* a padded apparatus on legs, used for vaulting, etc. **6** a narrow board supported by a pair of legs at each end, used as a frame for sawing or as a trestle, barrier, etc. **7** a contrivance on which a person may ride and exercise. **8** a slang word for **heroin. 9** *Mining.* a mass of rock within a vein of ore. **10** *Naut.* a rod, rope, or cable, fixed at the ends, along which something may slide; traveller. **11** *Inf.* short for **horsepower. 12** (*modifier*) drawn by a horse or horses: *a horse cart.* **13 a horse of another** *or* **a different colour.** a completely different topic, argument, etc. **14 be** (*or* **get**) **on one's high horse.** *Inf.* to act disdainfully aloof. **15 hold one's horses.** to restrain oneself. **16 horses for courses.** a policy, course of action, etc. modified slightly to take account of special circumstances without departing in essentials from the original. **17 the horse's mouth.** the most reliable source. ◆ *vb* **horses, horsing, horsed. 18** (*tr*) to provide with a horse or horses. **19** to put or be put on horseback. [OE *hors*]
▸**ˈhorseˌlike** *adj*

horse around ❶ *or* **about** *vb* (*intr, adv*) *Inf.* to indulge in horseplay.

horseback (ˈhɔːsˌbæk) *n* **a** a horse's back (esp. in **on horseback**). **b** *Chiefly US.* (*as modifier*): *horseback riding.*

horsebox (ˈhɔːsˌbɒks) *n Brit.* a van or trailer used for carrying horses.

horse brass *n* a decorative brass ornament, originally attached to a horse's harness.

horse chestnut *n* **1** a tree having palmate leaves, erect clusters of white, pink, or red flowers, and brown shiny inedible nuts enclosed in a spiky bur. **2** Also called: **conker.** the nut of this tree. [C16: from its having been used in the treatment of respiratory disease in horses]

horseflesh (ˈhɔːsˌflɛʃ) *n* **1** horses collectively. **2** the flesh of a horse, esp. edible horse meat.

horsefly (ˈhɔːsˌflaɪ) *n, pl* **horseflies.** a large stout-bodied dipterous fly, the female of which sucks the blood of mammals, esp. horses, cattle, and man. Also called: **gadfly, cleg.**

horsehair (ˈhɔːsˌhɛə) *n* hair taken chiefly from the tail or mane of a horse, used in upholstery and for fabric, etc.

horsehide (ˈhɔːsˌhaɪd) *n* **1** the hide of a horse. **2** leather made from this hide.

horse latitudes *pl n Naut.* the latitudes near 30°N or 30°S at sea, characterized by baffling winds, calms, and high barometric pressure. [C18: referring either to the high mortality of horses on board ship in these latitudes or to *dead horse* (nautical slang: advance pay), which sailors expected to work off by this stage of a voyage]

horse laugh *n* a coarse or raucous laugh.

horseleech (ˈhɔːsˌliːtʃ) *n* **1** any of several large carnivorous freshwater leeches. **2** an archaic name for a **veterinary surgeon.**

horse mackerel *n* **1** Also called: **scad.** a mackerel-like fish of European Atlantic waters, with a row of bony scales along the lateral line. Sometimes called (US): **saurel. 2** any of various large tunnies or related fishes.

horseman (ˈhɔːsmən) *n, pl* **horsemen. 1** a person skilled in riding. **2** a person who rides a horse.
▸**ˈhorsemanˌship** *n* ▸**ˈhorseˌwoman** *fem n*

horse mushroom *n* a large edible mushroom, with a white cap and greyish gills.

horse pistol *n* a large holstered pistol formerly carried by horsemen.

horseplay ❶ (ˈhɔːsˌpleɪ) *n* rough or rowdy play.

horsepower (ˈhɔːsˌpaʊə) *n* an fps unit of power, equal to 550 foot-pounds per second (equivalent to 745.7 watts). Abbrev.: **HP, h.p.**

horseradish (ˈhɔːsˌrædɪʃ) *n* a coarse Eurasian plant cultivated for its thick white pungent root, which is ground and combined with vinegar, etc., to make a sauce.

horse sense *n* another term for **common sense.**

horseshoe (ˈhɔːsˌʃuː) *n* **1** a piece of iron shaped like a U nailed to the underside of the hoof of a horse to protect the soft part of the foot: commonly thought to be a token of good luck. **2** an object of similar shape.

horseshoe bat *n* any of numerous large-eared Old World bats with a fleshy growth around the nostrils, used in echolocation.

horseshoe crab *n* a marine arthropod of North America and Asia, having a rounded heavily armoured body with a long pointed tail. Also called: **king crab.**

horsetail (ˈhɔːsˌteɪl) *n* **1** a plant having jointed stems with whorls of small dark toothlike leaves and producing spores within conelike structures at the tips of the stems. **2** a stylized horse's tail formerly used as the emblem of a pasha.

horse trading *n* shrewd bargaining.

horsewhip (ˈhɔːsˌwɪp) *n* **1** a whip, usually with a long thong, used for managing horses. ◆ *vb* **horsewhips, horsewhipping, horsewhipped. 2** (*tr*) to flog with such a whip.
▸**ˈhorseˌwhipper** *n*

horsey *or* **horsy** (ˈhɔːsɪ) *adj* **horsier, horsiest. 1** of or relating to horses: *a horsey smell.* **2** dealing with or devoted to horses. **3** like a horse: *a horsey face.*
▸**ˈhorsily** *adv* ▸**ˈhorsiness** *n*

horst (hɔːst) *n* a ridge of land that has been forced upwards between two parallel faults. [C20: from G *Horst* thicket]

hortatory (ˈhɔːtətərɪ) *or* **hortative** (ˈhɔːtətɪv) *adj* tending to exhort; encouraging. [C16: from LL *hortātōrius*, from L *hortārī* to EXHORT]
▸**horˈtation** *n* ▸**ˈhortatorily** *or* **ˈhortatively** *adv*

horticulture (ˈhɔːtɪˌkʌltʃə) *n* the art or science of cultivating gardens. [C17: from L *hortus* garden + CULTURE; cf. AGRICULTURE]
▸**ˌhortiˈcultural** *adj* ▸**ˌhortiˈculturalist** *or* **ˌhortiˈculturist** *n*

Hos. *Bible. abbrev. for* Hosea.

hosanna (həʊˈzænə) *interj* an exclamation of praise, esp. one to God. [OE *osanna*, via LL from Gk, from Heb. *hōshiʿāh nnā* save now, we pray]

hose[1] (həʊz) *n* **1** a flexible pipe, for conveying a liquid or gas. ◆ *vb* **hoses, hosing, hosed. 2** (sometimes foll. by *down*) to wash, water, or sprinkle (a person or thing) with or as if with a hose. [C15: later use of HOSE[2]]

hose[2] (həʊz) *n, pl* **hose** *or* **hosen** (ˈhəʊzᵊn). **1** stockings, socks, and tights collectively. **2** *History.* a man's garment covering the legs and reaching up to the waist. **3 half-hose.** socks. [OE *hosa*]

hosier (ˈhəʊzɪə) *n* a person who sells stockings, etc.

hosiery (ˈhəʊzɪərɪ) *n* stockings, socks, and knitted underclothing collectively.

hospice (ˈhɒspɪs) *n* **1** a nursing home that specializes in caring for the terminally ill. **2** *Arch.* a place of shelter for travellers, esp. one kept by a monastic order. [C19: from F, from L *hospitium* hospitality, from *hospes* guest]

hospitable ❶ (ˈhɒspɪtəbᵊl, hɒˈspɪt-) *adj* **1** welcoming to guests or

THESAURUS

horrible *adj* **1 = terrifying,** abhorrent, abominable, appalling, awful, dreadful, fearful, frightful, from hell (*inf.*), ghastly, grim, grisly, gruesome, heinous, hellacious (*US sl.*), hideous, horrid, loathsome, obscene, repulsive, revolting, shameful, shocking, terrible **2, 3 = dreadful,** awful, beastly (*inf.*), cruel, disagreeable, ghastly (*inf.*), horrid, mean, nasty, terrible, unkind, unpleasant
Antonyms *adj* agreeable, appealing, attractive, charming, cute, delightful, enchanting, fetching, lovely, pleasant, wonderful

horrid *adj* **1 = unpleasant,** awful, disagreeable, disgusting, dreadful, horrible, nasty, obscene, offensive, terrible, yucky *or* yukky (*sl.*) **2 = repulsive,** abominable, alarming, appalling, formidable, frightening, from hell (*inf.*), hair-raising, harrowing, hideous, horrific, odious, revolting, shocking, terrifying, terrorizing **3** *Informal* **= unkind,** beastly (*inf.*), cruel, mean, nasty

horrific *adj* **= horrifying,** appalling, awful, dreadful, frightening, frightful, from hell, ghastly, grim, grisly, hellacious (*US sl.*), horrendous, shocking, terrifying

horrify *vb* **1 = terrify,** affright, alarm, frighten, gross out (*US sl.*), intimidate, make one's hair stand on end, petrify, put the wind up (*inf.*), scare, terrorize **2 = shock,** appal, disgust, dismay, outrage, sicken
Antonyms *vb* comfort, delight, enchant, encourage, gladden, hearten, please, reassure, soothe

horror *n* **1 = terror,** alarm, apprehension, awe, consternation, dismay, dread, fear, fright, panic **2 = hatred,** abhorrence, abomination, antipathy, aversion, detestation, disgust, loathing, odium, repugnance, revulsion
Antonyms *n* ≠ **hatred:** affinity, approval, attraction, delight, liking, love

horse *n* **1 = nag,** colt, cuddy *or* cuddie (*dialect, chiefly Scot.*), filly, gee-gee (*sl.*), gelding, jade, mare, moke (*Austral. sl.*), mount, stallion, steed (*arch. or literary*), studhorse *or* stud, yarraman (*Austral.*), yearling

horse around *vb Informal* **= play around,** clown, fool about *or* around, misbehave, play the fool, play the goat, roughhouse (*sl.*)

horseplay *n* **= rough-and-tumble,** buffoonery, clowning, fooling around, high jinks, pranks, romping, roughhousing (*sl.*), skylarking (*inf.*)

hospitable *adj* **1, 2 = welcoming,** amicable, bountiful, cordial, friendly, generous, genial, gracious, kind, liberal, sociable
Antonyms *adj* ≠ **welcoming:** inhospitable, parsimonious

strangers. **2** fond of entertaining. [C16: from Med. L *hospitāre* to receive as a guest, from L *hospes* guest]
▸ **'hospitableness** *n* ▸ **'hospitably** *adv*

hospital ('hɒspɪt°l) *n* **1** an institution for the medical or psychiatric care and treatment of patients. **2** (*modifier*) having the function of a hospital: *a hospital ship.* **3** a repair shop for something specified: *a dolls' hospital.* **4** *Arch.* a charitable home, hospice, or school. [C13: from Med. L *hospitāle* hospice, from L, from *hospes* guest]

hospitality ➊ (ˌhɒspɪ'tælɪtɪ) *n, pl* **hospitalities.** kindness in welcoming strangers or guests.

hospitality suite *n* a room or suite, as at a conference, where free drinks are offered.

hospitalize *or* **hospitalise** ('hɒspɪtəˌlaɪz) *vb* **hospitalizes, hospitalizing, hospitalized** *or* **hospitalises, hospitalising, hospitalised.** (*tr*) to admit or send (a person) into a hospital.
▸ **ˌhospitali'zation** *or* **ˌhospitali'sation** *n*

hospitaller *or US* **hospitaler** ('hɒspɪtələ) *n* a person, esp. a member of certain religious orders, dedicated to hospital work, ambulance services, etc. [C14: from OF *hospitalier,* from Med. L, from *hospitāle* hospice; see HOSPITAL]

Hospitaller *or US* **Hospitaler** ('hɒspɪtələ) *n* a member of the order of the Knights Hospitallers.

host[1] ➊ (həʊst) *n* **1** a person who receives or entertains guests, esp. in his own home. **2a** a country or organization which provides facilities for and receives visitors to an event. **2b** (*as modifier*): *the host nation.* **3** the compere of a show or television programme. **4** *Biol.* **4a** an animal or plant that supports a parasite. **4b** an animal into which tissue is experimentally grafted. **5** *Computing.* a computer that is connected to others on a network. **6** the owner or manager of an inn. ◆ *vb* **7** to be the host of (a party, programme, etc.): *to host one's own show.* [C13: from F *hoste,* from L *hospes* guest]

host[2] ➊ (həʊst) *n* **1** a great number; multitude. **2** an archaic word for **army.** [C13: from OF *hoste,* from L *hostis* stranger]

Host (həʊst) *n Christianity.* the wafer of unleavened bread consecrated in the Eucharist. [C14: from OF *oiste,* from L *hostia* victim]

hosta ('hɒstə) *n* a plant cultivated esp. for its ornamental foliage. [C19: NL, after N. T. *Host* (1761–1834), Austrian physician]

hostage ➊ ('hɒstɪdʒ) *n* **1** a person held as a security or pledge or to be ransomed, exchanged for prisoners, etc. **2** the state of being held as a hostage. **3** any security or pledge. **4 give hostages to fortune.** to place oneself in a position in which misfortune may strike through the loss of what one values most. [C13: from OF, from *hoste* guest]

hostel ('hɒst°l) *n* **1** a building providing overnight accommodation, as for homeless people. **2** See **youth hostel. 3** *Brit.* a supervised lodging house for nurses, workers, etc. **4** *Arch.* another word for **hostelry.** [C13: from OF, from Med. L *hospitāle* hospice; see HOSPITAL]

hosteller *or US* **hosteler** ('hɒstələ) *n* **1** a person who stays at youth hostels. **2** an archaic word for **innkeeper.**

hostelling *or US* **hosteling** ('hɒstəlɪŋ) *n* the practice of staying at youth hostels when travelling.

hostelry ('hɒstəlrɪ) *n, pl* **hostelries.** *Arch. or facetious.* an inn.

hostess ('həʊstɪs) *n* **1** a woman acting as host. **2** a woman who receives and entertains patrons of a club, restaurant, etc. **3** See **air hostess.**

hostile ➊ ('hɒstaɪl) *adj* **1** antagonistic; opposed. **2** of or relating to an enemy. **3** unfriendly. [C16: from L *hostīlis,* from *hostis* enemy]
▸ **'hostilely** *adv*

hostility ➊ (hɒ'stɪlɪtɪ) *n, pl* **hostilities. 1** enmity. **2** an act expressing enmity. **3** (*pl*) fighting; warfare.

hostler ('ɒslə) *n* a variant (esp. Brit.) of **ostler.**

hot ➊ (hɒt) *adj* **hotter, hottest. 1** having a relatively high temperature. **2** having a temperature higher than desirable. **3** causing a sensation of bodily heat. **4** causing a burning sensation on the tongue: *a hot curry.* **5** expressing or feeling intense emotion, such as anger or lust. **6** intense or vehement. **7** recent; new: *hot from the press.* **8** *Ball games.* (of a ball) thrown or struck hard, and so difficult to respond to. **9** much favoured: *a hot favourite.* **10** *Inf.* having a dangerously high level of radioactivity. **11** *Sl.* stolen or otherwise illegally obtained. **12** *Sl.* (of people) being sought by the police. **13** (of a colour) intense; striking: *hot pink.* **14** following closely: *hot on the scent.* **15** *Inf.* at a dangerously high electric potential. **16** *Sl.* good (esp. in **not so hot**). **17** *Jazz sl.* arousing great excitement by inspired improvisation, strong rhythms, etc. **18** *Inf.* dangerous or unpleasant (esp. in **make it hot for someone**). **19** (in various games) very near the answer. **20** *Metallurgy.* (of a process) at a sufficiently high temperature for metal to be in a soft workable state. **21** *Austral. & NZ inf.* (of a price, etc.) excessive. **22 hot on.** *Inf.* **22a** very severe: *the police are hot on drunk drivers.* **22b** particularly knowledgeable about. **23 hot under the collar.** *Inf.* aroused with anger, annoyance, etc. **24 in hot water.** *Inf.* in trouble. ◆ *adv* **25** in a hot manner; hotly. ◆ See also **hots, hot up.** [OE *hāt*]
▸ **'hotly** *adv* ▸ **'hotness** *n* ▸ **'hottish** *adj*

hot air ➊ *n Inf.* empty and usually boastful talk.

hotbed ➊ ('hɒtˌbɛd) *n* **1** a glass-covered bed of soil, usually heated, for propagating plants, forcing early vegetables, etc. **2** a place offering ideal conditions for the growth of an idea, activity, etc., esp. one considered bad.

hot-blooded ➊ *adj* **1** passionate or excitable. **2** (of a horse) being of thoroughbred stock.

hotchpotch ➊ ('hɒtʃˌpɒtʃ) *or esp. US & Canad.* **hodgepodge** *n* **1** a jumbled mixture. **2** a thick soup or stew. [C15: var. of *hotchpot* from OF, from *hocher* to shake + POT[1]]

hot cross bun *n* a yeast bun marked with a cross and traditionally eaten on Good Friday.

hot desking ('dɛskɪŋ) *n* the practice of not assigning permanent desks in a workplace, so that employees may work at any available desk.

hot dog[1] *n* a sausage, esp. a frankfurter, usually served hot in a long roll split lengthways. [C20: from the supposed resemblance of the sausage to a dachshund]

hot dog[2] *n* **1** *Chiefly US.* a person who performs showy acrobatic manoeuvres when skiing or surfing. ◆ *vb* **hot-dog, hot-dogs, hot-dogging, hot-dogged. 2** (*intr*) to perform a series of manoeuvres in skiing, surfing, etc.

hotel (həʊ'tɛl) *n* a commercially run establishment providing lodging and usually meals for guests and often containing a public bar. [C17: from F *hôtel,* from OF *hostel;* see HOSTEL]

hotelier (hɒ'tɛljɪɪ) *n* an owner or manager of one or more hotels.

hotel ship *n* an accommodation barge anchored near an oil production rig.

hot flush *or US* **hot flash** *n* a sudden unpleasant hot feeling experienced by menopausal women.

hotfoot ➊ ('hɒtˌfʊt) *adv* with all possible speed.

hothead ➊ ('hɒtˌhɛd) *n* an excitable person.

hot-headed ➊ *adj* impetuous, rash, or hot-tempered.
▸ **ˌhot-'headedness** *n*

hothouse ➊ ('hɒtˌhaʊs) *n* **1a** a greenhouse in which the temperature is maintained at a fixed level. **1b** (*as modifier*): *a hothouse plant.* **2a** an environment that encourages rapid development. **2b** (*as modifier*): *a hothouse atmosphere.* **3** (*modifier*) *Inf., often disparaging.* sensitive or delicate: *a hothouse temperament.*

hot key *n Computing.* a single key on the keyboard of a computer which carries out a series of commands.

hotline ('hɒtˌlaɪn) *n* **1** a direct telephone, teletype, or other communications link between heads of government, etc., for emergency use. **2** any such direct line kept for urgent use.

hot link *n Computing.* a word or phrase in a hypertext document that can be selected to access additional information.

THESAURUS

hospitality *n* = **welcome,** cheer, conviviality, cordiality, friendliness, geniality, heartiness, hospitableness, neighbourliness, sociability, warmth

host[1] *n* **1** = **master of ceremonies,** entertainer, innkeeper, landlord *or* landlady, proprietor **3** = **presenter,** anchorman *or* anchorwoman, compere (*Brit.*) ◆ *vb* **7** = **present,** compere (*Brit.*), front (*inf.*), introduce

host[2] *n* **1** = **multitude,** array, drove, horde, legion, myriad, swarm, throng **2** = **army**

hostage *n* = **prisoner,** captive, gage, pawn, pledge, security, surety

hostile *adj* **1, 3** = **unfriendly,** antagonistic, anti (*inf.*), bellicose, belligerent, contrary, ill-disposed, inimical, malevolent, opposed, opposite, rancorous, unkind, warlike
Antonyms *adj* affable, agreeable, amiable, approving, cordial, friendly, kind, peaceful, sympathetic, warm

hostility *n* **1** = **unfriendliness,** abhorrence, animosity, animus, antagonism, antipathy, aversion, bad blood, detestation, enmity, hatred, ill will, malevolence, malice, opposition, resentment **3** *plural* = **warfare,** conflict, fighting, state of war, war
Antonyms *n* ≠ **unfriendliness:** agreement, amity, approval, congeniality, cordiality, friendliness, goodwill, sympathy ≠ **warfare:** alliance, ceasefire, peace, treaty, truce

hot *adj* **1-3** = **burning,** blistering, boiling, fiery, flaming, heated, piping hot, roasting, scalding, scorching, searing, steaming, sultry, sweltering, torrid, warm **4** = **spicy,** acrid, biting, peppery, piquant, pungent, sharp **5, 6** = **passionate,** ablaze, animated, ardent, excited, fervent, fervid, fierce, fiery, flaming, impetuous, inflamed, intense, irascible, lustful, raging, stormy, touchy, vehement, violent **7** = **new,** fresh, just out, latest, recent, up to the minute **9** = **popular,** approved, favoured, in demand, in vogue, sought-after **14** = **following closely,** close, in hot pursuit, near
Antonyms *adj* ≠ **heated:** chilly, cold, cool, freezing, frigid, frosty, icy, parky (*Brit. inf.*) ≠ **spicy:** mild ≠ **passionate:** apathetic, calm, dispassionate, half-hearted, indifferent, mild, moderate ≠ **new:** old, stale, trite ≠ **popular:** out of favour, unpopular ≠ **following closely:** cold

hot air *n Informal* = **empty talk,** blether, bombast, bosh (*inf.*), bunkum *or* buncombe (*chiefly US*), claptrap (*inf.*), rant, verbiage, wind

hotbed *n* **1** = **nursery,** forcing house, seedbed **2** = **breeding ground,** den, nest

hot-blooded *adj* **1** = **passionate,** ardent, excitable, fervent, fiery, heated, impulsive, rash, spirited, temperamental, wild
Antonyms *adj* apathetic, calm, cold, cool, frigid, impassive, restrained, unenthusiastic

hotchpotch *n* **1** = **mixture,** conglomeration, farrago, gallimaufry, hash, hodgepodge (*US*), jumble, medley, *mélange,* mess, miscellany, mishmash, olio, olla podrida, potpourri

hotfoot *adv* = **speedily,** hastily, helter-skelter, hurriedly, pell-mell, posthaste, quickly

hothead *n* = **tearaway,** adrenalin junky (*sl.*), daredevil, desperado, hotspur, madcap

hot-headed *adj* = **rash,** fiery, foolhardy, hasty, hot-tempered, impetuous, precipitate, quick-tempered, reckless, unruly, volatile

hothouse *n* **1** = **greenhouse,** conservatory, glasshouse ◆ *modifier* **3** = **delicate,** coddled, dainty, exotic, fragile, frail, overprotected, pampered, sensitive

hotly *adv* **5, 6** = **passionately,** angrily, fiercely, heatedly, impetuously, indignantly, vehemently, with indignation **14** = **enthusiastically,** closely, eagerly, hotfoot, with enthusiasm

hot money *n* capital that is transferred from one financial centre to another seeking the best opportunity for short-term gain.

hotplate ('hɒt,pleɪt) *n* **1** an electrically heated plate on a cooker or one set into a working surface. **2** a portable device on which food can be kept warm.

hotpot ('hɒt,pɒt) *n* **1** *Brit.* a casserole covered with a layer of potatoes. **2** *Austral. sl.* a heavily backed horse.

hot potato *n Sl.* a delicate or awkward matter.

hot-press *n* **1** a machine for applying a combination of heat and pressure to give a smooth surface to paper, to express oil from it, etc. ◆ *vb* **2** (*tr*) to subject (paper, cloth, etc.) to such a process.

hot rod *n* a car with an engine that has been radically modified to produce increased power.

hots (hɒts) *pl n* **the.** *Sl.* intense sexual desire; lust (esp. in the phrase **have the hots for (someone)**).

hot seat *n* **1** *Inf.* a difficult or dangerous position. **2** *US.* a slang term for **electric chair.**

hot spot *n* **1** an area of potential violence. **2** a lively nightclub. **3** any local area of high temperature in a part of an engine, etc. **4** *Med.* **4a** a small area on the surface or within a body with an exceptionally high level of radioactivity or of some chemical or mineral considered harmful. **4b** a similar area that generates an abnormal amount of heat, as revealed by thermography.

hot spring *n* a natural spring of mineral water at 21°C (70°F) or above, found in areas of volcanic activity. Also called: **thermal spring.**

hotspur ('hɒt,spɜː) *n* an impetuous or fiery person. [C15: from *Hotspur*, nickname of Sir Henry Percy (1364–1403)]

hot stuff *n Inf.* **1** a person, object, etc., considered important, attractive, etc. **2** a pornographic or erotic book, play, film, etc.

Hottentot ('hɒtᵊn,tɒt) *n* another name for **Khoikhoi.**

hotting ('hɒtɪŋ) *n Inf.* the practice of stealing from cars and putting on a show of skilful but dangerous driving.
▸**'hotter** *n*

hot up *vb* **hots, hotting, hotted.** (*adv*) *Inf.* **1** to make or become more exciting, active, or intense. **2** (*tr*) another term for **soup up.**

hot-water bottle *n* a receptacle now usually made of rubber, designed to be filled with hot water and used for warming a bed.

hot-wire *vb* **hot-wires, hot-wiring, hot-wired.** (*tr*) *Sl.* to start the engine of (a motor vehicle) by bypassing the ignition switch.

hough (hɒk) *Brit.* ◆ *n* **1** a variant of **hock**[1]. ◆ *vb* (*tr*) **2** to hamstring (cattle, horses, etc.). [C14: from OE *hōh* heel]

hound ❶ (haʊnd) *n* **1a** any of several breeds of dog used for hunting. **1b** (*in combination*): *a deerhound.* **2** a dog, esp. one regarded as annoying. **3** a despicable person. **4** (in hare and hounds) a runner who pursues a hare. **5** *Sl., chiefly US & Canad.* an enthusiast. **6 ride to hounds** *or* **follow the hounds.** to take part in a fox hunt. **7 the hounds.** a pack of foxhounds, etc. ◆ *vb* (*tr*) **8** to pursue relentlessly. **9** to urge on. [OE *hund*]
▸**'hounder** *n*

hound's-tongue *n* a plant which has small reddish-purple flowers and spiny fruits. Also called: **dog's-tongue.** [OE *hundestunge*, translation of L *cynoglōssos*, from Gk, from *kuōn* dog + *glōssa* tongue; referring to the shape of its leaves]

hound's-tooth check *n* a pattern of broken or jagged checks, esp. on cloth. Also called: **dog's-tooth check, dogtooth check.**

hour ('aʊə) *n* **1** a period of time equal to 3600 seconds; 1/24th of a calendar day. Related adj: **horary. 2** any of the points on the face of a timepiece that indicate intervals of 60 minutes. **3** the time. **4** the time allowed for or used for something: *lunch hour.* **5** a special moment: *our finest hour.* **6** the distance covered in an hour: *we live an hour away.* **7** *Astron.* an angular measurement of right ascension equal to 15° or a 24th part of the celestial equator. **8 one's last hour.** the time of one's death. **9 the hour.** an exact number of complete hours: *the bus leaves on the hour.* ◆ See also **hours.** [C13: from OF *hore*, from L *hōra*, from Gk: season]

hour circle *n* a great circle on the celestial sphere passing through the celestial poles and a specified point, such as a star.

hourglass ('aʊə,glɑːs) *n* **1** a device consisting of two transparent chambers linked by a narrow channel, containing a quantity of sand that takes a specified time to trickle from one chamber to the other. **2** (*modifier*) well-proportioned with a small waist: *an hourglass figure.*

hour hand *n* the pointer on a timepiece that indicates the hour.

houri ('hʊərɪ) *n, pl* **houris. 1** (in Muslim belief) any of the nymphs of Paradise. **2** any alluring woman. [C18: from F, from Persian, from Ar. *hūr*, pl. of *haurā'* woman with dark eyes]

hourly ('aʊəlɪ) *adj* **1** of, occurring, or done every hour. **2** done in or measured by the hour: *an hourly rate.* **3** continual or frequent. ◆ *adv* **4** every hour. **5** at any moment.

hours ('aʊəz) *pl n* **1** a period regularly appointed for work, etc. **2** one's times of rising and going to bed: *he keeps late hours.* **3 till all hours.** until very late. **4** an indefinite time. **5** *RC Church.* Also called: **canonical hours. 5a** the seven times of the day laid down for the recitation of the prayers of the divine office. **5b** the prayers recited at these times.

house ❶ *n* (haʊs), *pl* **houses** ('haʊzɪz). **1a** a building used as a home; dwelling. **1b** (*as modifier*): *house dog.* **2** the people present in a house. **3a** a building for some specific purpose. **3b** (*in combination*): *a schoolhouse.* **4** (*often cap.*) a family or dynasty: *the House of York.* **5a** a commercial company: *a publishing house.* **5b** (*as modifier*): *a house journal.* **6** a legislative body. **7** a quorum in such a body (esp. in **make a house**). **8** a dwelling for a religious community. **9** *Astrol.* any of the 12 divisions of the zodiac. **10** any of several divisions of a large school. **11** a hotel, restaurant, club, etc., or the management of such an establishment. **12** (*modifier*) (of wine) sold unnamed by a restaurant, at a lower price than wines specified on the wine list: *the house red.* **13** the audience in a theatre or cinema. **14** an informal word for **brothel. 15** a hall in which a legislative body meets. **16** See **full house. 17** *Naut.* any structure or shelter on the weather deck of a vessel. **18 bring the house down.** *Theatre.* to win great applause. **19 like a house on fire.** *Inf.* very well. **20 on the house.** (usually of drinks) paid for by the management of the hotel, bar, etc. **21 put one's house in order.** to settle or organize one's affairs. **22 safe as houses.** *Brit.* very secure. ◆ *vb* (haʊz), **houses, housing, housed. 23** (*tr*) to provide with or serve as accommodation. **24** to give or receive lodging. **25** (*tr*) to contain or cover; protect. **26** (*tr*) to fit (a piece of wood) into a mortise, etc. [OE *hūs*]
▸**'houseless** *adj*

house agent *n Brit.* another name for **estate agent.**

house arrest *n* confinement to one's own home rather than in prison.

houseboat ('haʊs,bəʊt) *n* a stationary boat or barge used as a home.

housebound ('haʊs,baʊnd) *adj* unable to leave one's house because of illness, injury, etc.

housebreaking ('haʊs,breɪkɪŋ) *n Criminal law.* the act of entering a building as a trespasser for an unlawful purpose. Assimilated with burglary (1968).
▸**'house,breaker** *n*

housecoat ('haʊs,kəʊt) *n* a woman's loose robelike informal garment.

house-craft *n* skill in domestic management.

housefly ('haʊs,flaɪ) *n, pl* **houseflies.** a common dipterous fly that frequents human habitations, spreads disease, and lays its eggs in carrion, decaying vegetables, etc.

household ❶ ('haʊs,həʊld) *n* **1** the people living together in one house. **2** (*modifier*) relating to the running of a household: *household management.*

householder ❶ ('haʊs,həʊldə) *n* a person who owns or rents a house.
▸**'house,holder,ship** *n*

household name *or* **word** *n* a person or thing that is very well known.

housekeeper ('haʊs,kiːpə) *n* a person, esp. a woman, employed to run a household.

housekeeping ❶ ('haʊs,kiːpɪŋ) *n* **1** the running of a household. **2** money allotted for this. **3** general maintenance as of records, data, etc., in an organization.

houseleek ('haʊs,liːk) *n* an Old World plant which has a rosette of succulent leaves and pinkish flowers: grows on walls.

house lights *pl n* the lights in the auditorium of a theatre, cinema, etc.

housemaid ('haʊs,meɪd) *n* a girl or woman employed to do housework, esp. one who is resident in the household.

housemaid's knee *n* inflammation and swelling of the bursa in front of the kneecap, caused esp. by constant kneeling on a hard surface. Technical name: **prepatellar bursitis.**

houseman ('haʊsmən) *n, pl* **housemen.** *Med.* a junior doctor who is a member of the medical staff of a hospital. US and Canad. equivalent: **intern.**

house martin *n* a Eurasian swallow with a forked tail.

house mouse *n* any of various greyish mice, a common household pest in most parts of the world.

House music *or* **House** *n* a type of disco music of the late 1980s, based on funk, with fragments of other recordings edited in electronically.

House of Assembly *n* a legislative assembly or the lower chamber of such an assembly.

house of cards *n* **1** a tiered structure created by balancing playing cards on their edges. **2** an unstable situation, etc.

House of Commons *n* (in Britain, Canada, etc.) the lower chamber of Parliament.

house of correction *n* (formerly) a place of confinement for persons convicted of minor offences.

house of ill repute *or* **ill fame** *n* a euphemistic name for **brothel.**

House of Keys *n* the lower chamber of the legislature of the Isle of Man.

House of Lords *n* (in Britain) the upper chamber of Parliament, composed of the peers of the realm.

THESAURUS

hound *vb* **8** = **pursue**, chase, drive, give chase, hunt, hunt down **9** = **harass**, badger, goad, harry, impel, persecute, pester, prod, provoke

house *n* **1a** = **home**, abode, building, domicile, dwelling, edifice, habitation, homestead, pad (*sl.*), residence **2** = **household**, family, ménage **4** = **dynasty**, ancestry, clan, family tree, kindred, line, lineage, race, tribe **5a** = **firm**, business, company, concern, establishment, organization, outfit (*inf.*), partnership **6** = **assembly**, Commons, legislative body, parliament **11** = **inn**, hotel, public house, tavern **20 on the house** = **free**, for nothing, gratis, without expense ◆ *vb* **23, 24** = **accommodate**, billet, board, domicile, harbour, lodge, put up, quarter, take in **25** = **contain**, cover, keep, protect, sheathe, shelter, store

household *n* **1** = **family**, home, house, ménage ◆ *modifier* **2** = **domestic**, domiciliary, family

householder *n* = **occupant**, homeowner, resident, tenant

housekeeping *n* **1** = **household management**, home economy, homemaking, housecraft, housewifery

House of Representatives *n* **1** (in the US) the lower chamber of Congress, or of many state legislatures. **2** (in Australia) the lower chamber of Parliament. **3** the sole chamber of New Zealand's Parliament.

houseparent ('haʊsˌpɛərənt) *n* a person in charge of the welfare of a group of children in an institution.

house party *n* **1** a party, usually in a country house, at which guests are invited to stay for several days. **2** the guests who are invited.

house plant *n* a plant that can be grown indoors.

house-proud *adj* proud of the appearance, cleanliness, etc., of one's house, sometimes excessively so.

houseroom ('haʊsˌrʊm, -ˌruːm) *n* **1** room for storage or lodging. **2 give (something) houseroom.** (*used with a negative*) to have or keep (something) in one's house.

Houses of Parliament *n* (in Britain) **1** the building in which the House of Commons and the House of Lords assemble. **2** these two chambers considered together.

house sparrow *n* a small Eurasian bird, now established in North America and Australia. It has a brown plumage with grey underparts. Also called (US): **English sparrow.**

housetop ('haʊsˌtɒp) *n* **1** the roof of a house. **2 proclaim from the housetops.** to announce (something) publicly.

house-train *vb* (*tr*) *Brit.* to train (pets) to urinate and defecate outside the house.
▸**'house-ˌtrained** *adj*

house-warming *n* a party given after moving into a new home.

housewife *n, pl* **housewives. 1** ('haʊsˌwaɪf). a woman who keeps house. **2** ('hʌzɪf). Also called: **hussy, huswife.** *Chiefly Brit.* a small sewing kit.
▸**housewifery** ('haʊsˌwɪfərɪ) *n* ▸**'housewifely** *adj*

housework ('haʊsˌwɜːk) *n* the work of running a home, such as cleaning, cooking, etc.

housey-housey ('haʊsɪ'haʊsɪ) *n* another name for **bingo** or **lotto.** [C20: from the cry of "house!" shouted by the winner, prob. from FULL HOUSE]

housing[1] **T** ('haʊzɪŋ) *n* **1a** houses collectively. **1b** (*as modifier*): *a housing problem.* **2** the act of providing with accommodation. **3** a hole or slot made in one wooden member to receive another. **4** a part designed to contain or support a component or mechanism: *a wheel housing.*

housing[2] ('haʊzɪŋ) *n* (*often pl*) *Arch.* another word for **trappings** (sense 2). [C14: from OF *houce* covering, of Gmc origin]

housing estate *n* a planned area of housing, often with its own shops and other amenities.

housing scheme *n* a local-authority housing estate. Often shortened to **scheme.**

hove (həʊv) *vb Chiefly naut.* a past tense and past participle of **heave.**

hovel T ('hɒvᵊl) *n* **1** a ramshackle dwelling place. **2** an open shed for livestock, carts, etc. **3** the conical building enclosing a kiln. [C15: from ?]

hover T ('hɒvə) *vb* (*intr*) **1** to remain suspended in one place. **2** (of certain birds, esp. hawks) to remain in one place in the air by rapidly beating the wings. **3** to linger uncertainly. **4** to be in a state of indecision. ◆ *n* **5** the act of hovering. [C14: *hoveren*, var. of *hoven*, from ?]
▸**'hoverer** *n*

hovercraft ('hɒvəˌkrɑːft) *n* a vehicle that is able to travel across both land and water on a cushion of air.

hover fly *n* a dipterous fly with a hovering flight.

hoverport ('hɒvəˌpɔːt) *n* a port for hovercraft.

hovertrain ('hɒvəˌtreɪn) *n* a train that moves over a concrete track and is supported by a cushion of air supplied by powerful fans.

how (haʊ) *adv* **1** in what way? by what means?: *how did it happen?* Also used in indirect questions: *tell me how he did it.* **2** to what extent?: *how tall is he?* **3** how good? how well? what...like?: *how did she sing?* **4 and how!** (intensifier) very much so! **5 how about?** used to suggest something: *how about a cup of tea?* **6 how are you?** what is your state of health? **7 how come?** *Inf.* what is the reason (that)?: *how come you told him?* **8 how's that? 8a** what is your opinion? **8b** *Cricket.* Also written: **howzat** (haʊ'zæt). (an appeal to the umpire) is the batsman out? **9 how now?** *or* **how so?** *Arch.* what is the meaning of this? **10** in whatever way: *do it how you wish.* ◆ *n* **11** the way a thing is done: *the how of it.* [OE *hu*]

howbeit (haʊ'biːɪt) *Arch.* ◆ *sentence connector.* **1** however. ◆ *conj* **2** (*subordinating*) though; although.

howdah ('haʊdə) *n* a seat for riding on an elephant's back, esp. one with a canopy. [C18: from Hindi *haudah*, from Ar. *haudaj* load carried by elephant or camel]

how do you do *sentence substitute.* **1** a formal greeting said by people who are being introduced to each other. ◆ *n* **how-do-you-do. 2** *Inf.* a difficult situation.

howdy ('haʊdɪ) *sentence substitute. Chiefly US.* an informal word for **hello.** [C16: from *how d'ye do*]

however T (haʊ'ɛvə) *sentence connector.* **1** still; nevertheless. **2** on the other hand; yet. ◆ *adv* **3** by whatever means. **4** (*used with adjectives of quantity or degree*) no matter how: *however long it takes, finish it.* **5** an emphatic form of **how** (sense 1).

howitzer ('haʊɪtsə) *n* a cannon having a short barrel with a low muzzle velocity and a steep angle of fire. [C16: from Du. *houwitser*, from G, from Czech *houfnice* stone-sling]

howl T (haʊl) *n* **1** a long plaintive cry characteristic of a wolf or hound. **2** a similar cry of pain or sorrow. **3** a prolonged outburst of laughter. **4** *Electronics.* an unwanted high-pitched sound produced by a sound-producing system as a result of feedback. ◆ *vb* **5** to express in a howl or utter such cries. **6** (*intr*) (of the wind, etc.) to make a wailing noise. **7** (*intr*) *Inf.* to shout or laugh. [C14: *houlen*]

howl down *vb* (*tr, adv*) to prevent (a speaker) from being heard by shouting disapprovingly.

howler T ('haʊlə) *n* **1** Also called: **howler monkey.** a large New World monkey inhabiting tropical forests in South America and having a loud howling cry. **2** *Inf.* a glaring mistake. **3** a person or thing that howls.

howling ('haʊlɪŋ) *adj* (*prenominal*) *Inf.* (intensifier): *a howling success; a howling error.*

howsoever (ˌhaʊsəʊ'ɛvə) *sentence connector, adv* a less common word for **however.**

how-to *adj* (of a book or guide) giving basic instructions to the lay person on how to do or make something: *a how-to book on carpentry.*

hoy[1] (hɔɪ) *n Naut.* **1** a freight barge. **2** a coastal fishing and trading vessel used during the 17th and 18th centuries. [C15: from MDu. *hoei*]

hoy[2] (hɔɪ) *interj* a cry used to attract attention or drive animals. [C14: var. of HEY]

hoya ('hɔɪə) *n* any plant of the genus *Hoya*, of E Asia and Australia, esp. the waxplant. [C19: after Thomas *Hoy* (died 1821), E gardener]

hoyden *or* **hoiden** ('hɔɪdᵊn) *n* a wild boisterous girl; tomboy. [C16: ?from MDu. *heidijn* heathen]
▸**'hoydenish** *or* **'hoidenish** *adj*

Hoyle (hɔɪl) *n* an authoritative book of rules for card games. [after Sir Edmund *Hoyle*, 18th-cent. E authority on games, its compiler]

HP *abbrev. for:* **1** *Brit.* hire-purchase. **2** horsepower. **3** high pressure. **4** (in Britain) Houses of Parliament. ◆ Also (for senses 1–3): **h.p.**

HPV *abbrev. for* human papilloma virus.

HQ *or* **h.q.** *abbrev. for* headquarters.

hr *abbrev. for* hour.

HRH *abbrev. for* His (*or* Her) Royal Highness.

HRT *abbrev. for* hormone replacement therapy.

HS (in Britain) *abbrev. for* Home Secretary.

HSH *abbrev. for* His (*or* Her) Serene Highness.

ht *abbrev. for* height.

HT *Physics. abbrev. for* high tension.

HTLV *abbrev. for* human T-cell lymphotropic virus: any one of a family of viruses that cause certain rare human diseases in the T-cells. HTLV-III was an early name for the AIDS virus.

HTML *abbrev. for* hypertext markup language: a text description language that is used for electronic publishing, esp. on the World Wide Web.

HTTP *abbrev. for* hypertext transfer protocol, used esp. on the World Wide Web. See also **hypertext.**

hub T (hʌb) *n* **1** the central portion of a wheel, propeller, fan, etc., through which the axle passes. **2** the focal point. [C17: prob. var. of HOB[1]]

hubble-bubble ('hʌbᵊl'bʌbᵊl) *n* **1** another name for **hookah. 2** turmoil. **3** a gargling sound. [C17: rhyming jingle based on BUBBLE]

Hubble's law *n Astron.* a law stating that the velocity of recession of a galaxy is proportional to its distance from the observer. [C20: after E. P. *Hubble* (1889–1953), US astronomer]

Hubble telescope *n* a telescope launched into orbit around the earth in 1990 to provide information about the universe.

hubbub T ('hʌbʌb) *n* **1** a confused noise of many voices. **2** tumult; uproar. [C16: prob. from Irish *hooboobbes*]

hubby ('hʌbɪ) *n, pl* **hubbies.** an informal word for **husband.** [C17: by shortening and altering]

hubcap ('hʌbˌkæp) *n* a cap fitting over the hub of a wheel.

hubris T ('hjuːbrɪs) *n* **1** pride or arrogance. **2** (in Greek tragedy) ambition, arrogance, etc., ultimately causing the transgressor's ruin. [C19: from Gk]
▸**hu'bristic** *adj*

THESAURUS

housing[1] *n* **1a = accommodation**, dwellings, homes, houses **4 = case**, casing, container, cover, covering, enclosure, sheath

hovel *n* **1 = hut**, cabin, den, hole, shack, shanty, shed

hover *vb* **1, 2 = float**, be suspended, drift, flutter, fly, hang, poise **3 = linger**, hang about, wait nearby **4 = waver**, alternate, dither, falter, fluctuate, haver (*Brit.*), oscillate, pause, seesaw, swither (*Scot. dialect*), vacillate

however *sentence connector* **1 = nevertheless**, after all, anyhow, be that as it may, but, even though, nonetheless, notwithstanding, still, though **2 = on the other hand**, yet

howl *n* **1, 2 = cry**, bawl, bay, bell, bellow, clamour, groan, hoot, outcry, roar, scream, shriek, ululation, wail, yelp, yowl ◆ *vb* **5 = cry**, bawl, bell, bellow, cry out, lament, quest (*used of hounds*), roar, scream, shout, shriek, ululate, wail, weep, yell, yelp

howler *n* **2** *Informal* **= mistake**, bloomer (*Brit. inf.*), blunder, boner, boob (*Brit. sl.*), bull (*sl.*), clanger (*inf.*), error, malapropism, schoolboy howler

hub *n* **2 = centre**, core, focal point, focus, heart, middle, nerve centre, pivot

hubbub *n* **1, 2 = noise**, babel, bedlam, brouhaha, clamour, confusion, din, disorder, disturbance, hue and cry, hullabaloo, hurly-burly, pandemonium, racket, riot, ruckus (*inf.*), ruction (*inf.*), rumpus, tumult, uproar

hubris *n* **1 = pride**, arrogance **2 = nemesis**

huckaback ('hʌkəˌbæk) *n* a coarse absorbent linen or cotton fabric used for towels, etc. Also: **huck** (hʌk). [C17: from ?]

huckleberry ('hʌkᵊlˌbərɪ) *n, pl* **huckleberries. 1** an American shrub having edible dark blue berries. **2** the fruit of this shrub. **3** a Brit. name for **whortleberry** (sense 1,2). [C17: prob. var. of *hurtleberry,* from ?]

huckster ❶ ('hʌkstə) *n* **1** a person who uses aggressive or questionable methods of selling. **2** *Now rare.* a person who sells small articles or fruit in the street. **3** *US.* a person who writes for radio or television advertisements. ◆ *vb* **4** (*tr*) to peddle. **5** (*tr*) to sell or advertise aggressively or questionably. **6** to haggle (over). [C12: ?from MDu. *hoekster,* from *hoeken* to carry on the back]

huddle ❶ ('hʌdᵊl) *n* **1** a heaped or crowded mass of people or things. **2** *Inf.* a private or impromptu conference (esp. in **go into a huddle**). ◆ *vb* **huddles, huddling, huddled. 3** to crowd or nestle closely together. **4** (often foll. by *up*) to hunch (oneself), as through cold. **5** (*intr*) *Inf.* to confer privately. **6** (*tr*) *Chiefly Brit.* to do (something) in a careless way. **7** (*tr*) *Rare.* to put on (clothes) hurriedly. [C16: from ?; cf. ME *hoderen* to wrap up]
▸ **'huddler** *n*

hue ❶ (hjuː) *n* **1** the attribute of colour that enables an observer to classify it as red, blue, etc., and excludes white, black, and grey. **2** a shade of a colour. **3** aspect: *a different hue on matters.* [OE *hīw* beauty]
▸ **hued** *adj*

hue and cry ❶ *n* **1** (formerly) the pursuit of a suspected criminal with loud cries in order to raise the alarm. **2** any loud public outcry. [C16: from Anglo-F *hu et cri,* from OF *hue* outcry, from *hu!* shout of warning + *cri* CRY]

huff ❶ (hʌf) *n* **1** a passing mood of anger or pique (esp. in **in a huff**). ◆ *vb* **2** to make or become angry or resentful. **3** (*intr*) to blow or puff heavily. **4** Also: **blow.** *Draughts.* to remove (an opponent's draught) from the board for failure to make a capture. **5** (*tr*) *Obs.* to bully. **6 huffing and puffing.** empty threats or objections: bluster. [C16: imit.; cf. PUFF]
▸ **'huffish** *or* **'huffy** *adj* ▸ **'huffily** *or* **'huffishly** *adv*

hug ❶ (hʌg) *vb* **hugs, hugging, hugged.** (*mainly tr*) **1** (*also intr*) to clasp tightly, usually with affection; embrace. **2** to keep close to a shore, kerb, etc. **3** to cling to (beliefs, etc.); cherish. **4** to congratulate (oneself). ◆ *n* **5** a tight or fond embrace. [C16: prob. of Scand. origin]
▸ **'huggable** *adj*

huge ❶ (hjuːdʒ) *adj* extremely large. [C13: from OF *ahuge,* from ?]
▸ **'hugely** *adv* ▸ **'hugeness** *n*

hugger-mugger ('hʌgəˌmʌgə) *n* **1** confusion. **2** *Rare.* secrecy. ◆ *adj, adv Arch.* **3** with secrecy. **4** in confusion. ◆ *vb Obs.* **5** (*tr*) to keep secret. **6** (*intr*) to act secretly. [C16: from ?]

Huguenot ('hjuːgəˌnəʊ, -ˌnɒt) *n* **1** a French Calvinist, esp. of the 16th or 17th centuries. ◆ *adj* **2** designating the French Protestant Church. [C16: from F, from Genevan dialect *eyguenot* one who opposed annexation by Savoy, ult. from Swiss G *Eidgenoss* confederate]

huh (*spelling pron* hʌ) *interj* an exclamation of derision, bewilderment, inquiry, etc.

huhu ('huːhuː) *n* a New Zealand beetle with a hairy body. [from Maori]

hui ('huːɪ) *n NZ.* **1** a Maori social gathering. **2** *Inf.* any party. [from Maori]

huia ('hʊɪjə) *n* an extinct New Zealand bird, prized by early Maoris for its distinctive tail feathers. [from Maori]

hula ('huːlə) *or* **hula-hula** *n* a Hawaiian dance performed by a woman. [from Hawaiian]

Hula Hoop *n Trademark.* a light hoop that is whirled around the body by movements of the waist and hips.

hulk ❶ (hʌlk) *n* **1** the body of an abandoned vessel. **2** *Disparaging.* a large or unwieldy vessel. **3** *Disparaging.* a large ungainly person or thing. **4** (*often pl*) the hull of a ship, used as a storehouse, etc., or (esp. in 19th-century Britain) as a prison. [OE *hulc,* from Med. L *hulca,* from Gk *holkas* barge, from *helkein* to tow]

hulking ❶ ('hʌlkɪŋ) *adj* big and ungainly.

hull ❶ (hʌl) *n* **1** the main body of a vessel, tank, etc. **2** the outer covering of a fruit or seed. **3** the calyx at the base of a strawberry, raspberry, or similar fruit. **4** the outer casing of a missile, rocket, etc. ◆ *vb* **5** to remove the hulls from (fruit or seeds). **6** (*tr*) to pierce the hull of (a vessel, tank, etc.). [OE *hulu*]

hullabaloo ❶ *or* **hullaballoo** (ˌhʌləbə'luː) *n, pl* **hullabaloos** *or* **hullaballoos.** loud confused noise; commotion. [C18: ?from HALLO + Scot. *baloo* lullaby]

hullo (hʌ'ləʊ) *sentence substitute, n* a variant spelling of **hello.**

hum ❶ (hʌm) *vb* **hums, humming, hummed.** (*intr*) **1** to make a low continuous vibrating sound. **2** (of a person) to sing with the lips closed. **3** to utter an indistinct sound, as in hesitation; hem. **4** *Inf.* to be in a state of feverish activity. **5** *Brit. & Irish sl.* to smell unpleasant. **6 hum and haw.** See **hem**[2] (sense 3). ◆ *n* **7** a low continuous murmuring sound. **8** *Electronics.* an undesired low-frequency noise in the output of an amplifier or receiver. ◆ *interj, n* **9** an indistinct sound of hesitation, embarrassment, etc.; hem. [C14: imit.]

human ❶ ('hjuːmən) *adj* **1** of or relating to mankind: *human nature.* **2** consisting of people: *a human chain.* **3** having the attributes of man as opposed to animals, divine beings, or machines: *human failings.* **4a** kind or considerate. **4b** natural. ◆ *n* **5** a human being; person. [C14: from L *hūmānus;* rel. to L *homō* man]
▸ **'humanness** *n*

human being *n* a member of any of the races of *Homo sapiens;* person; man, woman, or child.

humane ❶ (hjuː'meɪn) *adj* **1** characterized by kindness, sympathy, etc. **2** inflicting as little pain as possible: *a humane killing.* **3** civilizing or liberal: *humane studies.* [C16: var. of HUMAN]
▸ **hu'manely** *adv* ▸ **hu'maneness** *n*

human interest *n* (in a newspaper story, etc.) reference to individuals and their emotions, sometimes from exploitative motives.

humanism ('hjuːməˌnɪzəm) *n* **1** the rejection of religion in favour of a belief in the advancement of humanity by its own efforts. **2** (*often cap.*) a cultural movement of the Renaissance, based on classical studies. **3** interest in the welfare of people.
▸ **'humanist** *n* ▸ **ˌhuman'istic** *adj*

humanitarian ❶ (hjuːˌmænɪ'tɛərɪən) *adj* **1** having the interests of mankind at heart. ◆ *n* **2** a philanthropist.
▸ **huˌmani'tarianism** *n*

humanity ❶ (hjuː'mænɪtɪ) *n, pl* **humanities. 1** the human race. **2** the quality of being human. **3** kindness or mercy. **4** (*pl; usually preceded by the*) the study of literature, philosophy, and the arts, esp. study of Ancient Greece and Rome.

humanize ❶ *or* **humanise** ('hjuːməˌnaɪz) *vb* **humanizes, humanizing, hu-**

THESAURUS

huckster *n* **1, 2** = **pedlar**, barker, hawker, pitchman (*US*), salesman, vendor

huddle *n* **1** = **crowd**, confusion, disorder, heap, jumble, mass, mess, muddle **2** *Informal* = **conference**, confab (*inf.*), discussion, meeting, powwow ◆ *vb* **3** = **crowd**, cluster, converge, flock, gather, press, throng **4** = **curl up**, crouch, cuddle, hunch up, make oneself small, nestle, snuggle

hue *n* **1, 2** = **colour**, dye, shade, tincture, tinge, tint, tone **3** = **aspect**, cast, complexion, light

hue and cry *n* **2** = **outcry**, brouhaha, clamour, furore, hullabaloo, much ado, ruction (*inf.*), rumpus, uproar

huff *n* **1** = **sulk**, anger, bad mood, bate (*Brit. sl.*), passion, pet, pique, rage, temper, wax (*inf., chiefly Brit.*) ◆ *vb* **3** = **puff**, blow, exhale

huffy *adj* **1** = **resentful**, angry, cross, crotchety, curt, disgruntled, edgy, grumpy, irritable, moody, moping, offended, peevish, pettish, petulant, querulous, ratty (*Brit. & NZ inf.*), shirty (*sl., chiefly Brit.*), snappy, sulky, sullen, surly, testy, tetchy
Antonyms *adj* amiable, calm, cheerful, friendly, gay, good-humoured, happy, pleasant, sunny

hug *vb* **1** = **clasp**, cuddle, embrace, enfold, hold close, squeeze, take in one's arms **2** = **follow closely**, cling to, keep close, stay near **3** = **cherish**, cling, hold onto, nurse, retain ◆ *n* **5** = **embrace**, bear hug, clasp, clinch (*sl.*), squeeze

huge *adj* = **enormous**, Brobdingnagian, bulky, colossal, elephantine, extensive, gargantuan, giant, gigantic, ginormous (*inf.*), great, humongous *or* humungous (*US sl.*), immense, jumbo (*inf.*), large, mammoth, massive, mega (*sl.*), monumental, mountainous, prodigious, stupendous, titanic, tremendous, vast
Antonyms *adj* insignificant, little, microscopic, minute, petty, puny, small, tiny

hugely *adv* = **immensely**, by leaps and bounds, enormously, massively, monumentally, on a grand scale, prodigiously, stupendously

hulk *n* **1** = **wreck**, derelict, frame, hull, shell, shipwreck **3** *Disparaging* = **oaf**, lout, lubber, lump (*inf.*)

hulking *adj* = **ungainly**, awkward, bulky, clumsy, clunky (*inf.*), cumbersome, gross, lubberly, lumbering, lumpish, massive, oafish, overgrown, ponderous, unwieldy

hull *n* **1** = **frame**, body, casing, covering, framework, skeleton **2** = **husk**, peel, pod, rind, shell, shuck, skin ◆ *vb* **5** = **peel**, husk, shell, shuck, skin, trim

hullabaloo *n* = **commotion**, babel, bedlam, brouhaha, clamour, confusion, din, disturbance, furore, hubbub, hue and cry, hurly-burly, noise, outcry, pandemonium, racket, ruckus (*inf.*), ruction (*inf.*), rumpus, to-do, tumult, turmoil, upheaval, uproar

hum *vb* **1** = **drone**, bombinate *or* bombilate (*literary*), buzz, croon, mumble, murmur, purr, sing, throb, thrum, vibrate, whir **4** *Informal* = **be busy**, be active, bustle, buzz, move, pulsate, pulse, stir, vibrate

human *adj* **1, 3** = **mortal**, anthropoid, fleshly, manlike **4a** = **kind**, approachable, compassionate, considerate, humane, kindly, understanding ◆ *n* **5** = **human being**, body, child, creature, individual, man *or* woman, mortal, person, soul, wight (*arch.*)
Antonyms *adj* ≠ **mortal:** animal, nonhuman ≠ **kind:** beastly, brutish, cruel, inhuman, unsympathetic ◆ *n* ≠ **human being:** animal, god, nonhuman

humane *adj* **1** = **kind**, benevolent, benign, charitable, clement, compassionate, forbearing, forgiving, gentle, good, good-natured, kind-hearted, kindly, lenient, merciful, mild, sympathetic, tender, understanding
Antonyms *adj* barbarous, brutal, cruel, inhuman, inhumane, ruthless, uncivilized, unkind, unmerciful, unsympathetic

humanitarian *adj* **1** = **philanthropic**, altruistic, beneficent, benevolent, charitable, compassionate, humane, public-spirited ◆ *n* **2** = **philanthropist**, altruist, benefactor, Good Samaritan

humanitarianism *n* **1** = **philanthropy**, beneficence, benevolence, charity, generosity, goodwill, humanism

humanity *n* **1** = **human race**, flesh, Homo sapiens, humankind, man, mankind, men, mortality, people **2** = **human nature**, humanness, mortality **3** = **kindness**, benevolence, benignity, brotherly love, charity, compassion, fellow feeling, kind-heartedness, mercy, philanthropy, sympathy, tenderness, tolerance, understanding **4** *plural* = **classical studies**, classics, liberal arts, literae humaniores

humanize *vb* **2** = **civilize**, cultivate, educate, enlighten, improve, mellow, polish, reclaim, refine, soften, tame

manized *or* **humanises, humanising, humanised. 1** to make or become human. **2** to make or become humane.
▸**,humani'zation** *or* **,humani'sation** *n*

humankind (,hjuːmən'kaɪnd) *n* the human race; humanity.

> **USAGE NOTE** See at **mankind.**

humanly ('hjuːmənlɪ) *adv* **1** by human powers or means. **2** in a human or humane manner.

human nature *n* the qualities common to humanity, esp. with reference to human weakness.

humanoid ('hjuːmə,nɔɪd) *adj* **1** like a human being in appearance. ◆ *n* **2** a being with human rather than anthropoid characteristics. **3** (in science fiction) a robot or creature resembling a human being.

human papilloma virus *n* any of a class of viruses that cause tumours, including warts, in humans. Certain strains have been implicated as a cause of cervical cancer. Abbrev.: **HPV.**

human rights *pl n* the rights of individuals to liberty, justice, etc.

humble ❶ ('hʌmbᵊl) *adj* **1** conscious of one's failings. **2** unpretentious; lowly: *a humble cottage; my humble opinion.* **3** deferential or servile. ◆ *vb* **humbles, humbling, humbled.** (*tr*) **4** to cause to become humble; humiliate. **5** to lower in status. [C13: from OF, from L *humilis* low, from *humus* the ground]
▸**'humbleness** *n* ▸**'humbly** *adv*

humblebee ('hʌmbᵊl,biː) *n* another name for the **bumblebee.** [C15: rel. to MDu. *hommel* bumblebee, OHG *humbal*]

humble pie *n* **1** (formerly) a pie made from the heart, entrails, etc., of a deer. **2 eat humble pie.** to be forced to behave humbly; be humiliated. [C17: earlier *an umble pie,* by mistaken word division from *a numble pie,* from *numbles* offal of a deer, ult. from L *lumbulus* a little loin]

humbug ❶ ('hʌm,bʌg) *n* **1** a person or thing that deceives. **2** nonsense. **3** *Brit.* a hard boiled sweet, usually having a striped pattern. ◆ *vb* **humbugs, humbugging, humbugged. 4** to cheat or deceive (someone). [C18: from ?]
▸**'hum,bugger** *n* ▸**'hum,buggery** *n*

humdinger ('hʌm,dɪŋə) *n Sl.* an excellent person or thing. [C20: from ?]

humdrum ❶ ('hʌm,drʌm) *adj* **1** ordinary; dull. ◆ *n* **2** a monotonous routine, task, or person. [C16: rhyming compound, prob. based on HUM]

humectant (hjuː'mektənt) *adj* **1** producing moisture. ◆ *n* **2** a substance added to another to keep it moist. [C17: from L *ūmectāre* to wet, from *ūmēre* to be moist]

humerus ('hjuːmərəs) *n, pl* **humeri** (-mə,raɪ). **1** the bone that extends from the shoulder to the elbow in man. **2** the corresponding bone in other vertebrates. [C17: from L *umerus;* rel. to Gothic *ams* shoulder, Gk *ōmos*]
▸**'humeral** *adj*

humid ❶ ('hjuːmɪd) *adj* moist; damp. [C16: from L *ūmidus,* from *ūmēre* to be wet]
▸**'humidly** *adv* ▸**'humidness** *n*

humidex ('hjuːmɪ,deks) *n Canad.* an index of discomfort showing the combined effect of humidity and temperature.

humidify (hjuː'mɪdɪ,faɪ) *vb* **humidifies, humidifying, humidified.** (*tr*) to make (air, etc.) humid or damp.
▸**hu,midifi'cation** *n* ▸**hu'midi,fier** *n*

humidity ❶ (hjuː'mɪdɪtɪ) *n* **1** dampness. **2** a measure of the amount of moisture in the air.

humidor ('hjuːmɪ,dɔː) *n* a humid place or container for storing cigars, tobacco, etc.

humify ('hjuːmɪ,faɪ) *vb* **humifies, humifying, humified.** to convert or be converted into humus.
▸**,humifi'cation** *n*

humiliate ❶ (hjuː'mɪlɪ,eɪt) *vb* **humiliates, humiliating, humiliated.** (*tr*) to lower or hurt the dignity or pride of. [C16: from LL *humiliāre,* from L *humilis* HUMBLE]
▸**hu'mili,atingly** *adv* ▸**hu,mili'ation** *n* ▸**hu'mili,ator** *n*

humility ❶ (hjuː'mɪlɪtɪ) *n, pl* **humilities.** the state or quality of being humble.

hummingbird ('hʌmɪŋ,bɜːd) *n* a very small American bird having a brilliant iridescent plumage, long slender bill, and wings specialized for very powerful vibrating flight.

hummock ('hʌmək) *n* **1** a hillock; knoll. **2** a ridge or mound of ice in an ice field. **3** *Chiefly southern US.* a wooded area lying above the level of an adjacent marsh. [C16: from ?; cf. HUMP]
▸**'hummocky** *adj*

hummus *or* **houmous** ('huməs) *n* a creamy dip originating in the Middle East, made from puréed chickpeas. [from Turkish *humus*]

> **USAGE NOTE** Avoid confusion with **humus.**

humoral ('hjuːmərəl) *adj* **1** *Immunol.* denoting or relating to a type of immunity caused by free antibodies circulating in the blood. **2** *Obs.* of or relating to the four bodily fluids (humours).

humoresque (,hjuːmə'resk) *n* a short lively piece of music. [C19: from G *Humoreske,* ult. from E HUMOUR]

humorist ❶ ('hjuːmərɪst) *n* a person who acts, speaks, or writes in a humorous way.

humorous ❶ ('hjuːmərəs) *adj* **1** funny; comical; amusing. **2** displaying or creating humour.
▸**'humorously** *adv* ▸**'humorousness** *n*

humour ❶ *or US* **humor** ('hjuːmə) *n* **1** the quality of being funny. **2** Also called: **sense of humour.** the ability to appreciate or express that which is humorous. **3** situations, speech, or writings that are humorous. **4a** a state of mind; mood. **4b** (*in combination*): *good humour.* **5** temperament or disposition. **6** a caprice or whim. **7** any of various fluids in the body: *aqueous humour.* **8** Also called: **cardinal humour.** *Arch.* any of the four bodily fluids (blood, phlegm, choler or yellow bile, melancholy or black bile) formerly thought to determine emotional and physical disposition. **9 out of humour.** in a bad mood. ◆ *vb* (*tr*) **10** to gratify; indulge: *he humoured the boy's whims.* **11** to adapt oneself to: *to humour someone's fantasies.* [C14: from L *humor* liquid; rel. to L *ūmēre* to be wet]
▸**'humourless** *or US* **'humorless** *adj*

hump ❶ (hʌmp) *n* **1** a rounded protuberance or projection. **2** a

THESAURUS

humble *adj* **1** = **modest**, meek, self-effacing, submissive, unassuming, unostentatious, unpretentious **2** = **lowly**, common, commonplace, insignificant, low, low-born, mean, modest, obscure, ordinary, plebeian, poor, simple, undistinguished, unimportant, unpretentious **3** = **servile**, courteous, deferential, obliging, obsequious, polite, respectful, subservient ◆ *vb* **4, 5** = **humiliate**, abase, abash, break, bring down, chagrin, chasten, crush, debase, degrade, demean, disgrace, lower, mortify, put down (*sl.*), put (someone) in their place, reduce, shame, sink, subdue, take down a peg (*inf.*)
Antonyms *adj* ≠ **modest:** arrogant, assuming, conceited, haughty, immodest, lordly, ostentatious, overbearing, pompous, presumptuous, pretentious, proud, snobbish, superior, vain ≠ **lowly:** aristocratic, distinguished, elegant, famous, glorious, high, important, rich, significant, superior, wealthy ◆ *vb* ≠ **humiliate:** elevate, exalt, magnify, raise

humbly *adv* **1, 3** = **meekly**, cap in hand, deferentially, diffidently, modestly, obsequiously, on bended knee, respectfully, servilely, submissively, subserviently, unassumingly

humbug *n* **1** = **fraud**, charlatan, cheat, con man (*inf.*), faker, fraudster, impostor, phoney *or* phony (*inf.*), quack, swindler, trickster **1** = **deception**, bluff, canard, cheat, deceit, dodge, feint, fraud, hoax, imposition, imposture, ruse, sham, swindle, trick, trickery, wile **2** = **nonsense**, baloney (*inf.*), cant, charlatanry, claptrap, eyewash (*inf.*), gammon (*Brit. inf.*), hypocrisy, rubbish, trash ◆ *vb* **4** = **deceive**, bamboozle (*inf.*), befool, beguile, cheat, con (*inf.*), cozen, delude, dupe, fool, gull (*arch.*), hoax, hoodwink, impose, mislead, swindle, take in (*inf.*), trick

humdrum *adj* **1** = **dull**, banal, boring, commonplace, dreary, ho-hum (*inf.*), mind-numbing, monotonous, mundane, ordinary, repetitious, routine, tedious, tiresome, uneventful, uninteresting, unvaried, wearisome
Antonyms *adj* dramatic, entertaining, exciting, extraordinary, interesting, lively, sexy (*inf.*), stimulating

humid *adj* = **damp**, clammy, dank, moist, muggy, steamy, sticky, sultry, watery, wet
Antonyms *adj* arid, dry, sunny, torrid

humidity *n* **1** = **damp**, clamminess, dampness, dankness, dew, humidness, moistness, moisture, mugginess, sogginess, wetness

humiliate *vb* = **embarrass**, abase, abash, bring low, chagrin, chasten, crush, debase, degrade, discomfit, disgrace, humble, make (someone) eat humble pie, mortify, put down, put (someone) in their place, shame, subdue, take down a peg (*inf.*), take the wind out of someone's sails
Antonyms *vb* elevate, honour, magnify, make proud

humiliating *adj* = **embarrassing**, cringe-making (*Brit. inf.*), cringeworthy (*Brit. inf.*), crushing, degrading, disgracing, humbling, ignominious, mortifying, shaming

humiliation *n* = **embarrassment**, abasement, affront, chagrin, condescension, degradation, disgrace, dishonour, humbling, ignominy, indignity, loss of face, mortification, put-down, resignation, self-abasement, shame, submission, submissiveness

humility *n* = **modesty**, diffidence, humbleness, lack of pride, lowliness, meekness, self-abasement, servility, submissiveness, unpretentiousness
Antonyms *n* arrogance, conceit, disdain, haughtiness, pomposity, presumption, pretentiousness, pride, snobbishness, superciliousness, superiority, vanity

humorist *n* = **comedian**, card (*inf.*), comic, eccentric, funny man, jester, joker, wag, wit

humorous *adj* **1, 2** = **funny**, amusing, comic, comical, droll, entertaining, facetious, farcical, hilarious, jocose, jocular, laughable, ludicrous, merry, playful, pleasant, side-splitting, waggish, whimsical, witty
Antonyms *adj* earnest, grave, sad, serious, sober, solemn

humour *n* **1** = **funniness**, amusement, comedy, drollery, facetiousness, fun, jocularity, ludicrousness **3** = **joking**, comedy, farce, gags (*inf.*), jesting, jests, jokes, pleasantry, wisecracks (*inf.*), wit, witticisms, wittiness **4** = **mood**, disposition, frame of mind, spirits, temper **5** = **whim**, bent, bias, fancy, freak, mood, propensity, quirk, vagary ◆ *vb* **10** = **indulge**, accommodate, cosset, favour, fawn on, feed, flatter, go along with, gratify, mollify, pamper, pander to, spoil
Antonyms *n* ≠ **funniness:** gravity, grief, melancholy, sadness, seriousness, sobriety, solemnity, sorrow ◆ *vb* ≠ **indulge:** aggravate, excite, oppose, rouse, stand up to

humourless *adj* **1, 2** = **serious**, dour, dry, heavy-going, intense, po-faced, solemn, straight, unamused, unamusing, unfunny, unsmiling

hump *n* **1** = **lump**, bulge, bump, hunch, knob, mound, projection, protrusion, protuberance, swelling **4 the hump** *Brit. informal* = **sulks**, blues,

rounded deformity of the back, consisting of a spinal curvature. **3** a rounded protuberance on the back of a camel or related animal. **4 the hump.** *Brit. inf.* a fit of sulking. ◆ *vb* **5** to form or become a hump; hunch; arch. **6** (*tr*) *Sl.* to carry or heave. **7** *Taboo sl.* to have sexual intercourse with (someone). [C18: prob. from earlier *humpbacked*]
▸ **'humpy** *adj*

humpback ('hʌmpˌbæk) *n* **1** another word for **hunchback. 2** Also called: **humpback whale.** a large whalebone whale with a humped back and long flippers. **3** a Pacific salmon, the male of which has a humped back. **4** Also: **humpback bridge.** *Brit.* a road bridge having a sharp incline and decline and usually a narrow roadway. [C17: alteration of earlier *crumpbacked,* ? infl. by HUNCHBACK]
▸ **'humpˌbacked** *adj*

humph (*spelling pron* hʌmf) *interj* an exclamation of annoyance, indecision, etc.

humpty dumpty ('hʌmptɪ 'dʌmptɪ) *n, pl* **humpty dumpties.** *Chiefly Brit.* **1** a short fat person. **2** a person or thing that once broken cannot be mended. [C18: from the nursery rhyme *Humpty Dumpty*]

humpy ('hʌmpɪ) *n, pl* **humpies.** *Austral.* a primitive hut. [C19: from Abor.]

humus ('hju:məs) *n* a dark brown or black colloidal mass of partially decomposed organic matter in the soil. It improves the fertility and water retention of the soil. [C18: from L: soil]

USAGE NOTE Avoid confusion with **hummus.**

Hun (hʌn) *n, pl* **Huns** *or* **Hun. 1** a member of any of several Asiatic nomadic peoples who dominated much of Asia and E Europe from before 300 B.C., invading the Roman Empire in the 4th and 5th centuries A.D. **2** *Inf.* (esp. in World War I) a derogatory name for a **German. 3** *Inf.* a vandal. [OE *Hūnas,* from LL *Hūnī,* from Turkish *Hun-yū*]
▸ **'Hunnish** *adj* ▸ **'HunˌIike** *adj*

hunch ➊ (hʌntʃ) *n* **1** an intuitive guess or feeling. **2** another word for **hump. 3** a lump or large piece. ◆ *vb* **4** to draw (oneself or a part of the body) up or together. **5** (*intr;* usually foll. by *up*) to sit in a hunched position. [C16: from ?]

hunchback ➊ ('hʌntʃˌbæk) *n* **1** a person having an abnormal curvature of the spine. **2** such a curvature. ◆ Also called: **humpback.** [C18: from earlier *hunchbacked*]
▸ **'hunchˌbacked** *adj*

hundred ('hʌndrəd) *n, pl* **hundreds** *or* **hundred. 1** the cardinal number that is the product of ten and ten; five score. **2** a numeral, 100, C, etc., representing this number. **3** (*often pl*) a large but unspecified number, amount, or quantity. **4** (*pl*) the 100 years of a specified century: *in the sixteen hundreds.* **5** something representing, represented by, or consisting of 100 units. **6** *Maths.* the position containing a digit representing that number followed by two zeros: *in 4376, 3 is in the hundred's place.* **7** an ancient division of a county. ◆ *determiner* **8** amounting to or approximately a hundred: *a hundred reasons for that.* [OE]
▸ **'hundredth** *adj, n*

hundreds and thousands *pl n* tiny beads of coloured sugar, used in decorating cakes, etc.

hundredweight ('hʌndrədˌweɪt) *n, pl* **hundredweights** *or* **hundredweight. 1** Also called: **long hundredweight.** *Brit.* a unit of weight equal to 112 pounds (50.802 kg). **2** Also called: **short hundredweight.** *US & Canad.* a unit of weight equal to 100 pounds (45.359 kg). **3** Also called: **metric hundredweight.** a metric unit of weight equal to 50 kilograms. ◆ Abbrev. (for senses 1, 2): **cwt.**

hung (hʌŋ) *vb* **1** the past tense and past participle of **hang** (except in the sense of *to execute*). ◆ *adj* **2** (of a political party, jury, etc.) not having a majority: *a hung parliament.* **3 hung over.** *Inf.* suffering from the effects of a hangover. **4 hung up.** *Sl.* **4a** impeded by some difficulty or delay. **4b** emotionally disturbed. **5 hung up on.** *Sl.* obsessively interested in.

Hungarian (hʌŋ'geərɪən) *n* **1** the official language of Hungary, also spoken in Romania and elsewhere, belonging to the Finno-Ugric family. **2** a native, inhabitant, or citizen of Hungary. ◆ *adj* **3** of or relating to Hungary, its people, or their language. ◆ Cf. **Magyar.**

hunger ➊ ('hʌŋgə) *n* **1** a feeling of emptiness or weakness induced by lack of food. **2** desire or craving: *hunger for a woman.* ◆ *vb* **3** (*intr;* usually foll. by *for* or *after*) to have a great appetite or desire (for). [OE]

hunger march *n* a procession of protest or demonstration, esp. by the unemployed.

hunger strike *n* a voluntary fast undertaken, usually by a prisoner, as a means of protest.
▸ **hunger striker** *n*

hungry ➊ ('hʌŋgrɪ) *adj* **hungrier, hungriest. 1** desiring food. **2** (*postpositive;* foll. by *for*) having a craving, desire, or need (for). **3** expressing or appearing to express greed, craving, or desire. **4** lacking fertility; poor. **5** *Austral. & NZ.* greedy; mean. **6** *NZ.* (of timber) dry and bare.
▸ **'hungrily** *adv* ▸ **'hungriness** *n*

hunk ➊ (hʌŋk) *n* **1** a large piece. **2** *Sl.* a sexually attractive man. [C19: prob. rel. to Flemish *hunke*]

hunkers ('hʌŋkəz) *pl n* haunches. [C18: from ?]

hunky-dory (ˌhʌŋkɪ'dɔ:rɪ) *adj Inf.* very satisfactory; fine. [C20: from ?]

hunt ➊ (hʌnt) *vb* **1** to seek out and kill (animals) for food or sport. **2** (*intr;* often foll. by *for*) to search (for): *to hunt for a book.* **3** (*tr*) to use (hounds, horses, etc.) in the pursuit of wild animals, game, etc.: *to hunt a pack of hounds.* **4** (*tr*) to search (country) to hunt game, etc.: *to hunt the parkland.* **5** (*tr;* often foll. by *down*) to track diligently so as to capture: *to hunt down a criminal.* **6** (*tr; usually passive*) to persecute; hound. **7** (*intr*) (of a gauge indicator, etc.) to oscillate about a mean value or position. **8** (*intr*) (of an aircraft, rocket, etc.) to oscillate about a flight path or its course axis. ◆ *n* **9** the act or an instance of hunting. **10** chase or search, esp. of animals. **11** the area of a hunt. **12** a party or institution organized for the pursuit of wild animals, esp. for sport. **13** the members of such a party or institution. [OE *huntian*]

huntaway ('hʌntəˌweɪ) *n NZ.* a dog trained to drive sheep at a long distance from the shepherd.

hunted ➊ ('hʌntɪd) *adj* harassed: *a hunted look.*

hunter ➊ ('hʌntə) *n* **1** a person or animal that seeks out and kills or captures game. Fem.: **huntress** ('hʌntrɪs). **2a** a person who looks diligently for something. **2b** (*in combination*): *a fortune-hunter.* **3** a specially bred horse used in hunting, characterized by strength and stamina. **4** a watch with a hinged metal lid or case (**hunting case**) to protect the crystal.

hunter-killer *adj* denoting a type of submarine designed and equipped to pursue and destroy enemy craft.

hunter's moon *n* the full moon following the harvest moon.

hunting ('hʌntɪŋ) *n* **a** the pursuit and killing or capture of wild animals, regarded as a sport. **b** (*as modifier*): *hunting lodge.*

hunting horn *n* a long straight metal tube with a flared end, used in giving signals in hunting.

Huntington's disease ('hʌntɪŋtənz) *n* a hereditary form of chorea associated with progressive dementia. Former name: **Huntington's chorea.** [after G. *Huntington* (1850–1916), US physician]

huntsman ('hʌntsmən) *n, pl* **huntsmen. 1** a person who hunts. **2** a person who trains hounds, beagles, etc., and manages them during a hunt.

Huon pine ('hju:ɒn) *n* a tree of Australasia, SE Asia, and Chile, with scalelike leaves and cup-shaped berry-like fruits. [after the *Huon* River, Tasmania]

hurdle ➊ ('hɜ:dᵊl) *n* **1a** *Athletics.* one of a number of light barriers over which runners leap in certain events. **1b** a low barrier used in certain horse races. **2** an obstacle: *the next hurdle in his career.* **3** a light framework of interlaced osiers, etc., used as a temporary fence. **4** a sledge on which criminals were dragged to their executions. ◆ *vb* **hurdles, hurdling, hurdled. 5** to jump (a hurdle). **6** (*tr*) to surround with hurdles. **7** (*tr*) to overcome. [OE *hyrdel*]
▸ **'hurdler** *n*

hurdy-gurdy ('hɜ:dɪ'gɜ:dɪ) *n, pl* **hurdy-gurdies.** any mechanical musical instrument, such as a barrel organ. [C18: rhyming compound, prob. imit.]

hurl ➊ (hɜ:l) *vb* (*tr*) **1** to throw with great force. **2** to utter with force; yell: *to hurl insults.* ◆ *n* **3** the act of hurling. [C13: prob. imit.]

hurling ('hɜ:lɪŋ) *or* **hurley** *n* a traditional Irish game resembling hockey, played with sticks and a ball between two teams of 15 players.

hurly-burly ➊ ('hɜ:lɪ'bɜ:lɪ) *n, pl* **hurly-burlies.** confusion or commotion. [C16: from earlier *hurling and burling,* rhyming phrase based on *hurling* in obs. sense of uproar]

Huron ('hjʊərən) *n* **1** (*pl* **Hurons** *or* **Huron**) a member of a North American Indian people formerly living in the region east of Lake Huron. **2** the Iroquoian language of this people.

hurrah (hʊ'rɑ:), **hooray** (hu:'reɪ), *or* **hurray** (hʊ'reɪ) *interj, n* **1** a cheer of

THESAURUS

doldrums, dumps (*inf.*), grumps, megrims (*rare*), mopes ◆ *vb* **5** = **hunch**, arch, curve, form a hump, lift, tense **6** *Slang* = **carry**, heave, hoist, lug, shoulder

hunch *n* **1** = **feeling**, idea, impression, inkling, intuition, premonition, presentiment, suspicion ◆ *vb* **4, 5** = **draw in**, arch, bend, crouch, curve, huddle, hump, squat, stoop, tense

hunchback *n* **1** = **Quasimodo**, humpback **2** = **humpback**, crookback (*rare*), crouch-back (*arch.*), kyphosis (*Pathology*)

hunchbacked *adj* **2** = **humpbacked**, deformed, humped, malformed, misshapen, stooped

hunger *n* **1** = **appetite**, emptiness, esurience, hungriness, ravenousness, voracity **2** = **desire**, ache, appetence, appetite, craving, greediness, itch, lust, thirst, yearning, yen (*inf.*) ◆ *vb* **3** = **want**, ache, crave, desire, hanker, hope, itch, long, pine, starve, thirst, wish, yearn

hungry *adj* **1** = **empty**, esurient, famished, famishing, hollow, peckish (*inf., chiefly Brit.*), ravenous, sharp-set, starved, starving, voracious **2** = **eager**, athirst, avid, covetous, craving, desirous, greedy, keen, yearning

hunk *n* **1** = **lump**, block, chunk, gobbet, mass, nugget, piece, slab, wedge, wodge (*Brit. inf.*)

hunt *vb* **1** = **stalk**, chase, gun for, hound, pursue, track, trail **2** = **search**, ferret about, forage, go in quest of, look, look high and low, rummage through, scour, seek, try to find ◆ *n* **9** = **search**, chase, hunting, investigation, pursuit, quest

hunted *adj* = **harassed**, careworn, desperate, distraught, gaunt, haggard, harried, persecuted, stricken, terror-stricken, tormented, worn

hunter *n* **1** = **huntsman** *or* **huntress**, sportsman *or* sportswoman

hurdle *n* **1b** = **fence**, barricade, barrier, block, hedge, wall **2** = **obstacle**, barrier, block, complication, difficulty, handicap, hazard, hindrance, impediment, obstruction, snag, stumbling block

hurl *vb* **1** = **throw**, cast, chuck (*inf.*), fire, fling, heave, launch, let fly, pitch, project, propel, send, shy, sling, toss

hurly-burly *n* = **commotion**, bedlam, brouhaha, chaos, confusion, disorder, furore, hubbub, pandemonium, tumult, turbulence, turmoil, upheaval, uproar

Antonyms *n* composure, order, organization, tidiness

joy, victory, etc. ◆ *vb* **2** to shout "hurrah". [C17: prob. from G *hurra;* cf. HUZZAH]

hurricane Ⓣ ('hʌrɪk^{ə}n) *n* **1** a severe, often destructive storm, esp. a tropical cyclone. **2** a wind of force 12 on the Beaufort scale, with speeds over 72 mph. [C16: from Sp. *huracán,* of Amerind origin, from *hura* wind]

hurricane deck *n* a ship's deck that is covered by a light deck as a sunshade.

hurricane lamp *n* a paraffin lamp with a glass covering. Also called: **storm lantern.**

hurried Ⓣ ('hʌrɪd) *adj* performed with great or excessive haste.
▸ **'hurriedly** *adv* ▸ **'hurriedness** *n*

hurry Ⓣ ('hʌrɪ) *vb* **hurries, hurrying, hurried. 1** (*intr;* often foll. by *up*) to hasten; rush. **2** (*tr;* often foll. by *along*) to speed up the completion, progress, etc., of. ◆ *n* **3** haste. **4** urgency or eagerness. **5 in a hurry.** *Inf.* **5a** easily: *you won't beat him in a hurry.* **5b** willingly: *we won't go there again in a hurry.* [C16 *horyen,* prob. imit.]

hurst (hɜːst) *n Arch.* **1** a wood. **2** a sandbank. [OE *hyrst*]

hurt Ⓣ (hɜːt) *vb* **hurts, hurting, hurt. 1** (*tr*) to cause physical pain to (someone or something). **2** (*tr*) to cause emotional pain or distress to (someone). **3** to produce a painful sensation in (someone): *the bruise hurts.* **4** (*intr*) *Inf.* to feel pain. ◆ *n* **5** physical or mental pain or suffering. **6** a wound, cut, or sore. **7** damage or injury; harm. ◆ *adj* **8** injured or pained: *a hurt knee; a hurt look.* [C12 *hurten* to hit, from OF *hurter* to knock against, prob. of Gmc origin]

hurtful Ⓣ ('hɜːtfʊl) *adj* causing distress or injury: *to say hurtful things.*
▸ **'hurtfully** *adv*

hurtle Ⓣ ('hɜːt^{ə}l) *vb* **hurtles, hurtling, hurtled.** to project or be projected very quickly, noisily, or violently. [C13 *hurtlen,* from *hurten* to strike; see HURT]

husband Ⓣ ('hʌzbənd) *n* **1** a woman's partner in marriage. **2** *Arch.* a manager of an estate. ◆ *vb* **3** to manage or use (resources, finances, etc.) thriftily. **4** (*tr*) *Arch.* to find a husband for. **5** (*tr*) *Obs.* to till (the soil). [OE *hūsbonda,* from ON *hūsbōndi,* from *hūs* house + *bōndi* one who has a household]
▸ **'husbander** *n*

husbandman ('hʌzbəndmən) *n, pl* **husbandmen.** *Arch.* a farmer.

husbandry Ⓣ ('hʌzbəndrɪ) *n* **1** farming, esp. when regarded as a science, skill, or art. **2** management of affairs and resources.

hush Ⓣ (hʌʃ) *vb* **1** to make or become silent; quieten; soothe. ◆ *n* **2** stillness; silence. ◆ *interj* **3** a plea or demand for silence. [C16: prob. from earlier *husht* quiet!, the *-t* being thought to indicate a past participle]
▸**hushed** *adj*

hushaby ('hʌʃə,baɪ) *interj* **1** used in quietening a baby or child to sleep. ◆ *n, pl* **hushabies. 2** a lullaby. [C18: from HUSH + *by,* as in BYE-BYES]

hush-hush Ⓣ *adj Inf.* (esp. of official work, documents, etc.) secret; confidential.

hush money *n Sl.* money given to a person to ensure that something is kept secret.

hush up Ⓣ *vb* (*tr, adv*) to suppress information or rumours about.

husk Ⓣ (hʌsk) *n* **1** the external green or membranous covering of certain fruits and seeds. **2** any worthless outer covering. ◆ *vb* **3** (*tr*) to remove the husk from. [C14: prob. based on MDu. *huusken* little house, from *hūs* house]

husky^{1} Ⓣ ('hʌskɪ) *adj* **huskier, huskiest. 1** (of a voice, utterance, etc.) slightly hoarse or rasping. **2** of or containing husks. **3** *Inf.* big and strong. [C19: prob. from HUSK, from the toughness of a corn husk]
▸ **'huskily** *adv* ▸ **'huskiness** *n*

husky^{2} ('hʌskɪ) *n, pl* **huskies. 1** a breed of Arctic sled dog with a thick dense coat, pricked ears, and a curled tail. **2** *Canad. sl.* **2a** a member of the Inuit people. **2b** their language. [C19: prob. based on ESKIMO]

hussar (hʊ'zɑː) *n* **1** a member of any of various light cavalry regiments, renowned for their elegant dress. **2** a Hungarian horseman of the 15th century. [C15: from Hungarian *huszár* hussar, formerly freebooter, ult. from OIt. *corsaro* CORSAIR]

Hussite ('hʌsaɪt) *n* **1** an adherent of the ideas of John Huss, 14th-century Bohemian religious reformer, or a member of the movement initiated by him. ◆ *adj* **2** of or relating to John Huss, his teachings, followers, etc.
▸ **'Hussitism** *n*

hussy Ⓣ ('hʌsɪ, -zɪ) *n, pl* **hussies.** *Contemptuous.* a shameless or promiscuous woman. [C16 (in the sense: housewife): from *hussif* HOUSEWIFE]

hustings ('hʌstɪŋz) *n* (*functioning as pl or sing*) **1** *Brit.* (before 1872) the platform on which candidates were nominated for Parliament and from which they addressed the electors. **2** the proceedings at a parliamentary election. [C11: from ON *hūsthing,* from *hūs* HOUSE + *thing* assembly]

hustle Ⓣ ('hʌs^{ə}l) *vb* **hustles, hustling, hustled. 1** to shove or crowd (someone) roughly. **2** to move hurriedly or furtively: *he hustled her out of sight.* **3** (*tr*) to deal with hurriedly: *to hustle legislation through.* **4** *Sl.* to obtain (something) forcefully. **5** *US & Canad. sl.* (of procurers and prostitutes) to solicit. ◆ *n* **6** an instance of hustling. [C17: from Du. *husselen* to shake, from MDu. *hutsen*]
▸ **'hustler** *n*

hut Ⓣ (hʌt) *n* **1** a small house or shelter. ◆ *vb* **huts, hutting, hutted. 2** to furnish with or live in a hut. [C17: from F *hutte,* of Gmc origin]
▸ **'hut,like** *adj*

hutch (hʌtʃ) *n* **1** a cage, usually of wood and wire mesh, for small animals. **2** *Inf., derog.* a small house. **3** a cart for carrying ore. [C14 *hucche,* from OF *huche,* from Med. L *hutica,* from ?]

hutment ('hʌtmənt) *n Chiefly mil.* a number or group of huts.

huzzah (hə'zɑː) *interj, n, vb* an archaic word for **hurrah.** [C16: from ?]

HV *or* **h.v.** *abbrev. for* high voltage.

HWM *abbrev. for* high-water mark.

hwyl ('huːɪl) *n* emotional fervour, as in the recitation of poetry. [C19: Welsh]

hyacinth ('haɪəsɪnθ) *n* **1** any plant of the Mediterranean genus *Hyacinthus,* esp. a cultivated variety having a thick flower stalk bearing bell-shaped fragrant flowers. **2** the flower or bulb of such a plant. **3** any similar plant, such as the grape hyacinth. **4** Also called: **jacinth.** a reddish transparent variety of the mineral zircon, used as a gemstone. **5a** any of the varying colours of the hyancinth flower or stone. **5b** (*as adj*): *hyacinth eyes.* [C16: from L *hyacinthus,* from Gk *huakinthos*]
▸ **,hya'cinthine** *adj*

Hyades^{1} ('haɪə,diːz) *pl n* an open cluster of stars in the constellation Taurus, formerly believed to bring rain when they rose with the sun. [C16: via L from Gk *huades,* ?from *huein* to rain]

hyaena (haɪ'iːnə) *n* a variant spelling of **hyena.**

hyaline ('haɪəlɪn) *adj Biol.* clear and translucent, as a common type of cartilage. [C17: from LL *hyalinus,* from Gk, from *hualos* glass]

hyalite ('haɪə,laɪt) *n* a clear and colourless variety of opal in globular form.

hyaloid ('haɪə,lɔɪd) *adj Anat., zool.* clear and transparent; hyaline. [C19: from Gk *hualoeidēs*]

THESAURUS

hurricane *n* **1, 2 = storm,** cyclone, gale, tempest, tornado, twister (*US inf.*), typhoon, willy-willy (*Austral.*), windstorm

hurried *adj* **= hasty,** breakneck, brief, cursory, hectic, perfunctory, precipitate, quick, quickie (*inf.*), rushed, short, slapdash, speedy, superficial, swift

hurriedly *adv* **= hastily,** hurry-scurry, in a rush, perfunctorily, quickly

hurry *vb* **1 = rush,** barrel (along), burn rubber (*inf.*), dash, fly, get a move on (*inf.*), get one's skates on (*inf.*), lose no time, make haste, scoot, scurry, step on it (*inf.*) **2 = speed (up),** accelerate, expedite, goad, hasten, hustle, push on, quicken, urge ◆ *n* **3 = haste,** bustle, celerity, commotion, dispatch, expedition, flurry, precipitation, promptitude, quickness, rush, speed, urgency
Antonyms *vb* ≠ **rush:** crawl, creep, dawdle, drag one's feet, move slowly ≠ **speed (up):** delay, retard, slow, slow down ◆ *n* ≠ **haste:** calmness, slowness

hurt *vb* **1 = harm,** bruise, damage, disable, impair, injure, lay a finger on, mar, spoil, wound **2 = upset,** afflict, aggrieve, annoy, cut to the quick, distress, grieve, pain, sadden, sting, wound **3 = ache,** be sore, be tender, burn, smart, sting, throb ◆ *n* **5 = distress,** discomfort, pain, pang, soreness, suffering **6 = wound,** bruise, sore **7 = harm,** damage, detriment, disadvantage, injury, loss, mischief, wrong ◆ *adj* **8 = injured,** bruised, cut, damaged, grazed, harmed, scarred, scraped, scratched, wounded **8 = upset,** aggrieved, crushed, injured, miffed (*inf.*), offended, pained, piqued, rueful, sad, wounded
Antonyms *vb* ≠ **harm:** alleviate, cure, heal, relieve, repair, restore, soothe ◆ *n* ≠ **distress:** delight, happiness, joy, pleasure, pride, satisfaction ◆ *adj* ≠ **injured:** alleviated, assuaged, healed, relieved, repaired, restored, soothed ≠ **upset:** calmed, consoled, placated

hurtful *adj* **= unkind,** cruel, cutting, damaging, destructive, detrimental, disadvantageous, distressing, harmful, injurious, maleficent, malicious, mean, mischievous, nasty, pernicious, prejudicial, spiteful, upsetting, wounding

hurtle *vb* **= rush,** barrel (along) (*inf., chiefly US & Canad.*), burn rubber (*inf.*), charge, crash, fly, go hell for leather (*inf.*), plunge, race, rush headlong, scoot, scramble, shoot, speed, spurt, stampede, tear

husband *n* **1 = partner,** better half (*humorous*), bridegroom, man (*inf.*), mate, old man (*inf.*), significant other (*US inf.*), spouse ◆ *vb* **3 = economize,** budget, conserve, hoard, manage thriftily, save, store, use sparingly
Antonyms *vb* ≠ **economize:** be extravagant, fritter away, spend, splash out (*inf., chiefly Brit.*), squander

husbandry *n* **1 = farming,** agriculture, agronomy, cultivation, land management, tillage **2 = thrift,** careful management, economy, frugality, good housekeeping

hush *vb* **1 = quieten,** allay, appease, calm, compose, mollify, mute, muzzle, shush, silence, soothe, still, suppress ◆ *n* **2 = quiet,** calm, peace, peacefulness, silence, still (*poetic*), stillness, tranquillity

hush-hush *adj Informal* **= secret,** classified, confidential, restricted, top-secret, under wraps

hush up *vb* **= cover up,** conceal, draw a veil over, keep dark, keep secret, sit on (*inf.*), smother, squash, suppress, sweep under the carpet (*inf.*)

husk *n* **1 = rind,** bark, chaff, covering, hull, shuck

huskiness *n* **1 = hoarseness,** dryness, harshness, raspingness, roughness

husky^{1} *adj* **1 = hoarse,** croaking, croaky, gruff, guttural, harsh, rasping, raucous, rough, throaty **3** *Informal* **= muscular,** beefy (*inf.*), brawny, burly, hefty, powerful, rugged, stocky, strapping, thickset

hussy *n Contemptuous* **= slut,** baggage (*inf., old-fashioned*), floozy (*sl.*), jade, scrubber, slapper (*Brit. sl.*), strumpet, tart (*inf.*), tramp (*sl.*), trollop, wanton

hustle *vb* **1, 2 = jostle,** bustle, crowd, elbow, force, haste, hasten, hurry, impel, jog, push, rush, shove, thrust

hut *n* **1 = shed,** cabin, den, hovel, lean-to, refuge, shanty, shelter

hyaloid membrane *n* the delicate transparent membrane enclosing the vitreous humour of the eye.

hybrid ⓣ ('haɪbrɪd) *n* **1** an animal or plant resulting from a cross between genetically unlike individuals; usually sterile. **2** anything of mixed ancestry. **3** a word, part of which is derived from one language and part from another, such as *monolingual*. ◆ *adj* **4** denoting or being a hybrid; of mixed origin. [C17: from L *hibrida* offspring of a mixed union (human or animal)]
▸**'hybridism** *n* ▸**hy'bridity** *n*

hybrid computer *n* a computer that uses both analogue and digital techniques.

hybridize *or* **hybridise** ('haɪbrɪˌdaɪz) *vb* **hybridizes, hybridizing, hybridized** *or* **hybridises, hybridising, hybridised.** to produce or cause to produce hybrids; crossbreed.
▸**ˌhybridi'zation** *or* **ˌhybridi'sation** *n*

hybridoma (ˌhaɪbrɪ'dəʊmə) *n* a hybrid cell formed by the fusion of two different types of cell, esp. one capable of producing antibodies fused with an immortal tumour cell. [C20: from HYBRID + -OMA]

hybrid vigour *n Biol.* the increased size, strength, etc., of a hybrid as compared to either of its parents. Also called: **heterosis.**

hydatid ('haɪdətɪd) *n* **1** a large bladder containing encysted larvae of the tapeworm *Echinococcus:* causes serious disease in man. **2** Also called: **hydatid cyst.** a sterile fluid-filled cyst produced in man and animals during infestation by *Echinococcus* larval forms. [C17: from Gk *hudatis* watery vesicle, from *hudōr, hudat-* water]

hydr- *combining form.* a variant of **hydro-** before a vowel.

hydra ('haɪdrə) *n, pl* **hydras** *or* **hydrae** (-driː). **1** a freshwater coelenterate in which the body is a slender polyp with tentacles around the mouth. **2** a persistent trouble or evil. [C16: from L, from Gk *hudra* water serpent]

hydracid (haɪ'dræsɪd) *n* an acid, such as hydrochloric acid, that does not contain oxygen.

hydrangea (haɪ'dreɪndʒə) *n* a shrub or tree of an Asian and American genus cultivated for their large clusters of white, pink, or blue flowers. [C18: from NL, from Gk *hudōr* water + *angeion* vessel: prob. from the cup-shaped fruit]

hydrant ('haɪdrənt) *n* an outlet from a water main, usually an upright pipe with a valve attached, from which water can be tapped for fighting fires, etc. [C19: from HYDRO- + -ANT]

hydrate ('haɪdreɪt) *n* **1** a chemical compound containing water that is chemically combined with a substance. **2** a crystalline chemical compound containing weakly bound water molecules. ◆ *vb* **hydrates, hydrating, hydrated. 3** to undergo or cause to undergo treatment or impregnation with water.
▸**hy'dration** *n* ▸**'hydrator** *n*

hydrated ('haɪdreɪtɪd) *adj* (of a compound) chemically bonded to water molecules.

hydraulic (haɪ'drɒlɪk) *adj* **1** operated by pressure transmitted through a pipe by a liquid, such as water or oil. **2** of or employing liquids in motion. **3** of hydraulics. **4** hardening under water: *hydraulic cement.* [C17: from L *hydraulicus,* from Gk *hudraulikos,* from *hudraulos* water organ, from HYDRO- + *aulos* pipe]
▸**hy'draulically** *adv*

hydraulic brake *n* a type of brake, used in motor vehicles, in which the braking force is transmitted from the brake pedal to the brakes by a liquid under pressure.

hydraulic coupling *n* another name for **torque converter.**

hydraulic press *n* a press that utilizes liquid pressure to enable a small force applied to a small piston to produce a large force on a larger piston.

hydraulic ram *n* **1** the larger or working piston of a hydraulic press. **2** a form of water pump utilizing the kinetic energy of running water to provide static pressure to raise water to a reservoir higher than the source.

hydraulics (haɪ'drɒlɪks) *n* (*functioning as sing*) another name for **fluid mechanics.**

hydraulic suspension *n* a system of motor-vehicle suspension using hydraulic members, often with hydraulic compensation between front and rear systems (**hydroelastic suspension**).

hydrazine ('haɪdrəˌziːn, -zɪn) *n* a colourless liquid made from sodium hypochlorite and ammonia: used as a rocket fuel. Formula: N_2H_4. [C19: from HYDRO- + AZO + -INE[2]]

hydric ('haɪdrɪk) *adj* **1** of or containing hydrogen. **2** containing or using moisture.

hydride ('haɪdraɪd) *n* any compound of hydrogen with another element.

hydrilla (haɪ'drɪlə) *n* a type of underwater aquatic weed that was introduced from Asia into the south US, where it has become a serious problem, choking fish and hindering navigation. [C20: NL, prob. from L *hydra:* see HYDRA]

hydriodic acid (ˌhaɪdrɪ'ɒdɪk) *n* a solution of hydrogen iodide in water: a strong acid. [C19: from HYDRO- + IODIC]

hydro[1] ('haɪdrəʊ) *n, pl* **hydros.** *Brit.* (esp. formerly) a hotel or resort, often near a spa, offering facilities for hydropathic treatment.

hydro[2] ('haɪdrəʊ) *adj* **1** short for **hydroelectric.** ◆ *n* **2** a Canadian name for **electricity.**

Hydro ('haɪdrəʊ) *n* (esp. in Canada) a hydroelectric power company or board.

hydro- *or sometimes before a vowel* **hydr-** *combining form.* **1** indicating water or fluid: *hydrodynamics.* **2** indicating hydrogen in a chemical compound: *hydrochloric acid.* **3** indicating a hydroid: *hydrozoan.* [from Gk *hudōr* water]

hydrobromic acid (ˌhaɪdrəʊ'brəʊmɪk) *n* a solution of hydrogen bromide in water: a strong acid.

hydrocarbon (ˌhaɪdrəʊ'kɑːbᵊn) *n* any organic compound containing only carbon and hydrogen.

hydrocele ('haɪdrəʊˌsiːl) *n* an abnormal collection of fluid in any saclike space.

hydrocephalus (ˌhaɪdrəʊ'sɛfələs) *or* **hydrocephaly** (ˌhaɪdrəʊ'sɛfəlɪ) *n* accumulation of cerebrospinal fluid within the ventricles of the brain because its normal outlet has been blocked by congenital malformation or disease. Nontechnical name: **water on the brain.**
▸**hydrocephalic** (ˌhaɪdrəʊsɪ'fælɪk) *or* **ˌhydro'cephalous** *adj*

hydrochloric acid (ˌhaɪdrə'klɒrɪk) *n* a solution of hydrogen chloride in water: a strong acid used in many industrial and laboratory processes.

hydrochloride (ˌhaɪdrə'klɔːraɪd) *n* a quaternary salt formed by the addition of hydrochloric acid to an organic base.

hydrocyanic acid (ˌhaɪdrəʊsaɪ'ænɪk) *n* another name for **hydrogen cyanide.**

hydrodynamics (ˌhaɪdrəʊdaɪ'næmɪks, -dɪ-) *n* (*functioning as sing*) the branch of science concerned with the mechanical properties of fluids, esp. liquids. Also called: **hydromechanics.**

hydroelastic suspension (ˌhaɪdrəʊɪ'læstɪk) *n* See **hydraulic suspension.**

hydroelectric (ˌhaɪdrəʊɪ'lɛktrɪk) *adj* **1** generated by the pressure of falling water: *hydroelectric power.* **2** of the generation of electricity by water pressure: *a hydroelectric scheme.*
▸**hydroelectricity** (ˌhaɪdrəʊɪlɛk'trɪsɪtɪ) *n*

hydrofluoric acid (ˌhaɪdrəʊfluː'ɒrɪk) *n* a solution of hydrogen fluoride in water: a strong acid that attacks glass.

hydrofoil ('haɪdrəˌfɔɪl) *n* **1** a fast light vessel the hull of which is raised out of the water on one or more pairs of fixed vanes. **2** any of these vanes.

hydroforming ('haɪdrəʊˌfɔːmɪŋ) *n* **1** *Chem.* the catalytic reforming of petroleum to increase the proportion of aromatic and branched-chain hydrocarbons. **2** *Engineering.* a forming process in which a metal is shaped by a punch forced against a die, consisting of a flexible bag containing a fluid.

hydrogen ('haɪdrɪdʒən) *n* **a** a flammable colourless gas that is the lightest and most abundant element in the universe. It occurs in water and in most organic compounds. Symbol: H; atomic no.: 1; atomic wt.: 1.007 94. **b** (*as modifier*): *hydrogen bomb.* [C18: from F *hydrogène,* from HYDRO- + -GEN; because its combustion produces water]
▸**hydrogenous** (haɪ'drɒdʒɪnəs) *adj*

hydrogenate ('haɪdrədʒɪˌneɪt, haɪ'drɒdʒɪˌneɪt) *vb* **hydrogenates, hydrogenating, hydrogenated.** to undergo or cause to undergo a reaction with hydrogen: *to hydrogenate ethylene.*
▸**ˌhydrogen'ation** *n*

hydrogen bomb *n* a type of bomb in which energy is released by fusion of hydrogen nuclei to give helium nuclei. The energy required to initiate the fusion is provided by the detonation of an atomic bomb, which is surrounded by a hydrogen-containing substance. Also called: **H-bomb.**

hydrogen bond *n* a weak chemical bond between an electronegative atom, such as fluorine, oxygen, or nitrogen, and a hydrogen atom bound to another electronegative atom.

hydrogen bromide *n* **1** a colourless pungent gas used in organic synthesis. Formula: HBr. **2** an aqueous solution of hydrogen bromide; hydrobromic acid.

hydrogen carbonate *n* another name for **bicarbonate.**

hydrogen chloride *n* **1** a colourless pungent corrosive gas obtained by the action of sulphuric acid on sodium chloride: used in making vinyl chloride and other organic chemicals. Formula: HCl. **2** an aqueous solution of hydrogen chloride; hydrochloric acid.

hydrogen cyanide *n* a colourless poisonous liquid with a faint odour of bitter almonds. It forms prussic acid in aqueous solution and is used for making plastics and as a war gas. Formula: HCN. Also called: **hydrocyanic acid.**

hydrogen fluoride *n* **1** a colourless poisonous corrosive gas or liquid made by reaction between calcium fluoride and sulphuric acid: used as a fluorinating agent and catalyst. Formula: HF. **2** an aqueous solution of hydrogen fluoride; hydrofluoric acid.

hydrogen iodide *n* **1** a colourless poisonous corrosive gas obtained by a catalysed reaction between hydrogen and iodine vapour: used in making iodides. Formula HI. **2** an aqueous solution of this gas; hydriodic acid.

THESAURUS

hybrid *n* **1, 2** = **crossbreed,** amalgam, composite, compound, cross, half-blood, half-breed, mixture, mongrel, mule

hydrogen ion *n* an ionized hydrogen atom, occurring in aqueous solutions of acids; proton. Formula: H^+.
hydrogenize *or* **hydrogenise** ('haɪdrədʒɪ,naɪz, haɪ'drɒdʒɪ,naɪz) *vb* **hydrogenizes, hydrogenizing, hydrogenized** *or* **hydrogenises, hydrogenising, hydrogenised.** a variant of **hydrogenate.**
hydrogen peroxide *n* a colourless oily unstable liquid used as a bleach and as an oxidizer in rocket fuels. Formula: H_2O_2.
hydrogen sulphide *n* a colourless poisonous gas with an odour of rotten eggs. Formula: H_2S. Also called: **sulphuretted hydrogen.**
hydrography (haɪ'drɒgrəfɪ) *n* the study, surveying, and mapping of the oceans, seas, and rivers.
▸**hy'drographer** *n* ▸**hydrographic** (,haɪdrə'græfɪk) *adj*
hydroid ('haɪdrɔɪd) *adj* **1** of or relating to the *Hydroida,* an order of hydrozoan coelenterates that have the polyp phase dominant. **2** having or consisting of hydra-like polyps. ◆ *n* **3** a hydroid colony or individual.
hydrokinetics (,haɪdrəʊkɪ'nɛtɪks, -kaɪ-) *n* (*functioning as sing*) the branch of science concerned with the behaviour and properties of fluids in motion. Also called: **hydrodynamics.**
hydrolase ('haɪdrə,leɪz) *n* an enzyme that controls hydrolysis.
hydrology (haɪ'drɒlədʒɪ) *n* the study of the distribution, conservation, use, etc., of the water of the earth and its atmosphere.
▸**hydrological** (,haɪdrə'lɒdʒɪkᵊl) *adj* ▸**hy'drologist** *n*
hydrolyse *or US* **hydrolyze** ('haɪdrə,laɪz) *vb* **hydrolyses, hydrolysing, hydrolysed** *or US* **hydrolyzes, hydrolyzing, hydrolyzed.** to subject to or undergo hydrolysis.
hydrolysis (haɪ'drɒlɪsɪs) *n* a chemical reaction in which a compound reacts with water to produce other compounds.
▸**hydrolytic** (,haɪdrə'lɪtɪk) *adj*
hydrolyte ('haɪdrə,laɪt) *n* a substance subjected to hydrolysis.
hydromel ('haɪdrəʊ,mɛl) *n Arch.* another word for **mead** (the drink). [C15: from L, from Gk *hudromeli,* from HYDRO- + *meli* honey]
hydrometer (haɪ'drɒmɪtə) *n* an instrument for measuring the relative density of a liquid.
▸**hydrometric** (,haɪdrəʊ'mɛtrɪk) *or* ,**hydro'metrical** *adj*
hydronaut ('haɪdrəʊ,nɔːt) *n US Navy.* a person trained to operate deep submergence vessels. [C20: from Gk, from HYDRO- + *-naut,* as in *astronaut*]
hydropathy (haɪ'drɒpəθɪ) *n* a pseudoscientific method of treating disease by the use of large quantities of water both internally and externally.
▸**hydropathic** (,haɪdrəʊ'pæθɪk) *adj*
hydrophilic (,haɪdrəʊ'fɪlɪk) *adj Chem.* tending to dissolve in, mix with, or be wetted by water: *a hydrophilic colloid.*
▸**hydrophile** ('haɪdrəʊ,faɪl) *n*
hydrophobia (,haɪdrə'fəʊbɪə) *n* **1** another name for **rabies. 2** a fear of drinking fluids, esp. that of a person with rabies, because of painful spasms when trying to swallow.
▸,**hydro'phobic** *adj*
hydrophone ('haɪdrə,fəʊn) *n* an electroacoustic transducer that converts sound travelling through water into electrical oscillations.
hydrophyte ('haɪdrəʊ,faɪt) *n* a plant that grows only in water or very moist soil.
hydroplane ('haɪdrəʊ,pleɪn) *n* **1** a motorboat equipped with hydrofoils or with a shaped bottom that raises its hull out of the water at high speeds. **2** an attachment to an aircraft to enable it to glide along the surface of the water. **3** another name for a **seaplane. 4** a horizontal vane on the hull of a submarine for controlling its vertical motion. ◆ *vb* **hydroplanes, hydroplaning, hydroplaned. 5** (*intr*) (of a boat) to rise out of the water in the manner of a hydroplane.
hydroponics (,haɪdrəʊ'pɒnɪks) *n* (*functioning as sing*) a method of cultivating plants by growing them in gravel, etc., through which water containing dissolved inorganic nutrient salts is pumped. [C20: from HYDRO- + (*geo*)*ponics* science of agriculture]
▸,**hydro'ponic** *adj* ▸,**hydro'ponically** *adv*
hydropower ('haɪdrəʊ,paʊə) *n* hydroelectric power.
hydroquinone (,haɪdrəʊkwɪ'nəʊn) *or* **hydroquinol** (,haɪdrəʊ'kwɪnɒl) *n* a white crystalline soluble phenol used as a photographic developer.
hydrosphere ('haɪdrə,sfɪə) *n* the watery part of the earth's surface, including oceans, lakes, water vapour in the atmosphere, etc.
hydrostatics (,haɪdrəʊ'stætɪks) *n* (*functioning as sing*) the branch of science concerned with the mechanical properties and behaviour of fluids that are not in motion.
▸,**hydro'static** *adj*
hydrotherapeutics (,haɪdrəʊ,θɛrə'pjuːtɪks) *n* (*functioning as sing*) the branch of medical science concerned with hydrotherapy.
hydrotherapy (,haɪdrəʊ'θɛrəpɪ) *n Med.* the treatment of certain diseases by the application of water, esp. by exercising in water to mobilize stiff joints or strengthen weak muscles.
hydrothermal (,haɪdrəʊ'θɜːməl) *adj* of or relating to the action of water under conditions of high temperature, esp. in forming rocks.
hydrotropism (haɪ'drɒtrə,pɪzəm) *n* the directional growth of plants in response to the stimulus of water.
hydrous ('haɪdrəs) *adj* containing water.
hydrovane ('haɪdrəʊ,veɪn) *n* a vane on a seaplane conferring stability on water (a sponson) or facilitating takeoff (a hydrofoil).
hydroxide (haɪ'drɒksaɪd) *n* **1** a base or alkali containing the ion OH^-. **2** any compound containing an -OH group.
hydroxy (haɪ'drɒksɪ) *adj* (of a chemical compound) containing one or more hydroxyl groups. [C19: HYDRO- + OXY(GEN)]
hydroxyl (haɪ'drɒksɪl) *n* (*modifier*) of, consisting of, or containing the monovalent group -OH or the ion OH^-: *a hydroxyl group or radical.*
hydroxytryptamine (haɪ,drɒksɪ'trɪptə,miːn) *n* 5-hydroxytryptamine: another name for **serotonin.** Abbrev.: **5HT.**
hydrozoan (,haɪdrəʊ'zəʊən) *n* **1** any coelenterate of the class *Hydrozoa,* which includes the hydra and the Portuguese man-of-war. ◆ *adj* **2** of the *Hydrozoa.*
hyena *or* **hyaena** (haɪ'iːnə) *n* any of several long-legged carnivorous doglike mammals such as the spotted or laughing hyena, of Africa and S Asia. [C16: from Med. L, from L *hyaena,* from Gk, from *hus* hog]
▸**hy'enic** *or* **hy'aenic** *adj*
hygiene ➊ ('haɪdʒiːn) *n* **1** Also called: **hygienics.** the science concerned with the maintenance of health. **2** clean or healthy practices or thinking: *personal hygiene.* [C18: from NL *hygiēna,* from Gk *hugieinē,* from *hugiēs* healthy]
hygienic ➊ (haɪ'dʒiːnɪk) *adj* promoting health or cleanliness; sanitary.
▸**hy'gienically** *adv*
hygienics (haɪ'dʒiːnɪks) *n* (*functioning as sing*) another word for **hygiene** (sense 1).
hygienist ('haɪdʒiːnɪst) *n* a person skilled in the practice of hygiene.
hygro- *or before a vowel* **hygr-** *combining form.* indicating moisture: *hygrometer.* [from Gk *hugros* wet]
hygrometer (haɪ'grɒmɪtə) *n* any of various instruments for measuring humidity.
▸**hygrometric** (,haɪgrə'mɛtrɪk) *adj*
hygrophyte ('haɪgrə,faɪt) *n* any plant that grows in wet or waterlogged soil.
▸**hygrophytic** (,haɪgrə'fɪtɪk) *adj*
hygroscope ('haɪgrə,skəʊp) *n* any device that indicates the humidity of the air without necessarily measuring it.
hygroscopic (,haɪgrə'skɒpɪk) *adj* (of a substance) tending to absorb water from the air.
▸,**hygro'scopically** *adv*
hying ('haɪɪŋ) *vb* a present participle of **hie.**
hyla ('haɪlə) *n* a tree frog of tropical America. [C19: from NL, from Gk *hulē* forest]
hylomorphism (,haɪlə'mɔːfɪzəm) *n* the philosophical doctrine that identifies matter with the first cause of the universe.
hylozoism (,haɪlə'zəʊɪzəm) *n* the philosophical doctrine that life is one of the properties of matter. [C17: from Gk *hulē* wood, matter + *zōē* life]
hymen ('haɪmɛn) *n Anat.* a fold of mucous membrane that partly covers the entrance to the vagina and is usually ruptured when sexual intercourse takes place for the first time. [C17: from Gk: membrane]
▸'**hymenal** *adj*
hymeneal (,haɪmɛ'niːəl) *adj* **1** *Chiefly poetic.* of or relating to marriage. ◆ *n* **2** a wedding song or poem.
hymenopteran (,haɪmɪ'nɒptərən) *or* **hymenopteron** *n, pl* **hymenopterans, hymenoptera** (-tərə), *or* **hymenopterons.** any hymenopterous insect.
hymenopterous (,haɪmɪ'nɒptərəs) *adj* of or belonging to an order of insects, including bees, wasps, and ants, having two pairs of membranous wings. [C19: from Gk *humenopteros* membrane wing; see HYMEN, -PTEROUS]
hymn ➊ (hɪm) *n* **1** a Christian song of praise sung to God or a saint. **2** a similar song praising other gods, a nation, etc. ◆ *vb* **3** to express (praises, thanks, etc.) by singing hymns. [C13: from L *hymnus,* from Gk *humnos*]
▸**hymnic** ('hɪmnɪk) *adj*
hymnal ('hɪmnᵊl) *n* **1** Also: **hymn book.** a book of hymns. ◆ *adj* **2** of, relating to, or characteristic of hymns.
hymnody ('hɪmnədɪ) *n* **1** the composition or singing of hymns. **2** hymns collectively. ◆ Also called: **hymnology.** [C18: from Med. L *hymnōdia,* from Gk, from *humnōidein,* from HYMN + *aeidein* to sing]
hymnology (hɪm'nɒlədʒɪ) *n* **1** the study of hymn composition. **2** another word for **hymnody.**
▸**hym'nologist** *n*
hyoid ('haɪɔɪd) *adj* of or relating to the **hyoid bone,** the horseshoe-shaped bone that lies at the base of the tongue. [C19: from NL *hyoïdes,* from Gk *huoeidēs* having the shape of the letter UPSILON, from *hu* upsilon + -OID]
hyoscine ('haɪə,siːn) *n* another name for **scopolamine.** [C19: from *huosc*(*yamus*) a medicinal plant + -INE[2]; see HYOSCYAMINE]
hyoscyamine (,haɪə'saɪə,miːn) *n* a poisonous alkaloid occurring in henbane and related plants: used in medicine. [C19: from NL, from Gk *huoskuamos* (from *hus* pig + *kuamos* bean) + AMINE]
hyp. *abbrev. for:* **1** hypotenuse. **2** hypothesis. **3** hypothetical.

THESAURUS

hygiene *n* **1, 2** = **cleanliness,** hygienics, sanitary measures, sanitation
hygienic *adj* = **clean,** aseptic, disinfected, germ-free, healthy, pure, salutary, sanitary, sterile
Antonyms *adj* dirty, filthy, germ-ridden, harmful, insanitary, polluted, unhealthy, unhygienic, unwholesome
hymn *n* **1, 2** = **song of praise,** anthem, canticle, carol, chant, doxology, paean, psalm

hypaethral *or US* **hypethral** (hɪ'pi:θrəl, haɪ-) *adj* (esp. of a classical temple) having no roof. [C18: from L *hypaethrus* uncovered, from Gk, from HYPO- + *aithros* clear sky]

hypallage (haɪ'pælə,dʒi:) *n Rhetoric.* a figure of speech in which the natural relations of two words in a statement are interchanged, as in *the fire spread the wind.* [C16: via LL from Gk *hupallagē,* from HYPO- + *allassein* to exchange]

hype[1] ❶ (haɪp) *Sl.* ◆ *n* **1** an intensive or exaggerated publicity or sales promotion. **2** a deception or racket. ◆ *vb* **hypes, hyping, hyped. 3** (*tr*) to market or promote (a product) using intensive or exaggerated publicity. [C20: from ?]

hype[2] (haɪp) *Sl.* ◆ *n* **1** a hypodermic needle or injection. ◆ *vb* **hypes, hyping, hyped. 2** (*intr;* usually foll. by *up*) to inject oneself with a drug. **3** (*tr*) to stimulate artificially or excite. [C20: shortened from HYPODERMIC]

hyped up *adj Sl.* stimulated or excited by or as if by the effect of a stimulating drug.

hyper ('haɪpə) *adj Inf.* overactive; overexcited. [C20: prob. independent use of HYPER-]

hyper- *prefix* **1** above, over, or in excess: *hypercritical.* **2** denoting an abnormal excess: *hyperacidity.* **3** indicating that a chemical compound contains a greater than usual amount of an element: *hyperoxide.* [from Gk *huper* over]

hyperacidity (,haɪpərə'sɪdɪtɪ) *n* excess acidity of the gastrointestinal tract, esp. the stomach, producing a burning sensation.

hyperactive (,haɪpər'æktɪv) *adj* abnormally active.
▸**,hyperac'tivity** *n*

hyperaemia *or US* **hyperemia** (,haɪpər'i:mɪə) *n Pathol.* an excessive amount of blood in an organ or part.

hyperaesthesia *or US* **hyperesthesia** (,haɪpəri:s'θi:zɪə) *n Pathol.* increased sensitivity of any of the sense organs.
▸**hyperaesthetic** *or US* **hyperesthetic** (,haɪpəri:s'θetɪk) *adj*

hyperbaton (haɪ'pɜ:bə,tɒn) *n Rhetoric.* a figure of speech in which the normal order of words is reversed, as in *cheese I love.* [C16: via L from Gk, lit.: an overstepping, from HYPER- + *bainein* to step]

hyperbola (haɪ'pɜ:bələ) *n, pl* **hyperbolas** *or* **hyperbole** (-,li:). a conic section formed by a plane that cuts both bases of a cone: it consists of two branches asymptotic to two intersecting fixed lines. [C17: from Gk *huperbolē,* lit.: excess, extravagance, from HYPER- + *ballein* to throw]

hyperbole ❶ (haɪ'pɜ:bəlɪ) *n* a deliberate exaggeration used for effect: *he embraced her a thousand times.* [C16: from Gk, from HYPER- + *bolē,* from *ballein* to throw]
▸**hy'perbolism** *n*

hyperbolic (,haɪpə'bɒlɪk) *or* **hyperbolical** *adj* **1** of a hyperbola. **2** *Rhetoric.* of a hyperbole.
▸**,hyper'bolically** *adv*

hyperbolic function *n* any of a group of functions of an angle expressed as a relationship between the distances of a point on a hyperbola to the origin and to the coordinate axes.

hyperbolize *or* **hyperbolise** (haɪ'pɜ:bə,laɪz) *vb* **hyperbolizes, hyperbolizing, hyperbolized** *or* **hyperbolises, hyperbolising, hyperbolised.** to express (something) by means of hyperbole.

hyperboloid (haɪ'pɜ:bə,lɔɪd) *n* a geometric surface consisting of one sheet, or of two sheets separated by a finite distance, whose sections parallel to the three coordinate planes are hyperbolas or ellipses.

Hyperborean (,haɪpə'bɔ:rɪən) *n* **1** *Greek myth.* one of a people believed to have lived beyond the North Wind in a sunny land. **2** an inhabitant of the extreme north. ◆ *adj* **3** (*sometimes not cap.*) of or relating to the extreme north. [C16: from L *hyperboreus,* from Gk, from HYPER- + *Boreas* the north wind]

hypercharge ('haɪpə,tʃɑ:dʒ) *n* a property of baryons that is used to account for the absence of certain strong interaction decays.

hypercholesterolaemia *or US* **hypercholesterolemia** (,haɪpəkə,lestərɒl'i:mɪə) *n* the condition of having high levels of cholesterol in the blood, predisposing to atherosclerosis of the coronary arteries.

hypercorrect (,haɪpəkə'rekt) *adj* **1** excessively correct or fastidious. **2** resulting from or characterized by hypercorrection.

hypercorrection (,haɪpəkə'rekʃən) *n* a mistaken correction to text or speech made through a desire to avoid nonstandard pronunciation or grammar: *"between you and I" is a hypercorrection of "between you and me."*

hypercritical ❶ (,haɪpə'krɪtɪk°l) *adj* excessively or severely critical.
▸**,hyper'critically** *adv*

hyperfocal distance (,haɪpə'fəʊk°l) *n* the distance from a camera lens to the point beyond which all objects appear sharp and clearly defined.

hyperglycaemia *or US* **hyperglycemia** (,haɪpəglaɪ'si:mɪə) *n Pathol.* an abnormally large amount of sugar in the blood. [C20: from HYPER- + GLYCO- + -AEMIA]
▸**,hypergly'caemic** *or US* **,hypergly'cemic** *adj*

hypergolic (,haɪpə'gɒlɪk) *adj* (of a rocket fuel) able to ignite spontaneously on contact with an oxidizer. [C20: from G *Hypergol* (?from HYP(ER-) + ERG[1] + -OL[2]) + -IC]

hypericum (haɪ'perɪkəm) *n* any herbaceous plant or shrub of the temperate genus *Hypericum.* See **rose of Sharon, Saint John's wort.** [C16: via L from Gk *hupereikon,* from HYPER- + *ereikē* heath]

hyperinflation (,haɪpəɪn'fleɪʃən) *n* an extremely high level of inflation (with price rises of 50 percent per month), often involving social disorder.

hypermarket ('haɪpə,mɑ:kɪt) *n Brit.* a huge self-service store, usually built on the outskirts of a town. [C20: translation of F *hypermarché*]

hypermedia ('haɪpə,mi:dɪə) *n* computer software and hardware that allows users to interact with text, graphics, sound, and video, each of which can be accessed from within any of the others. Cf. **hypertext.**

hypermetropia (,haɪpəmɪ'trəʊpɪə) *or* **hypermetropy** (,haɪpə'metrəpɪ) *n Pathol.* a variant of **hyperopia.** [C19: from Gk *hupermetros* beyond measure (from HYPER- + *metron* measure) + -OPIA]

hyperon ('haɪpə,rɒn) *n Physics.* any baryon that is not a nucleon. [C20: from HYPER- + -ON]

hyperopia (,haɪpə'rəʊpɪə) *n* inability to see near objects clearly because the images received by the eye are focused behind the retina; long-sightedness.
▸**hyperopic** (,haɪpə'rɒpɪk) *adj*

hyperphysical (,haɪpə'fɪzɪk°l) *adj* beyond the physical; supernatural or immaterial.

hyperpyrexia (,haɪpəpaɪ'reksɪə) *n Pathol.* an extremely high fever, with a temperature of 41°C (106°F) or above.

hypersensitive (,haɪpə'sensɪtɪv) *adj* **1** having unduly vulnerable feelings. **2** abnormally sensitive to an allergen, a drug, or other agent.
▸**,hyper'sensitiveness** *or* **,hyper,sensi'tivity** *n*

hypersonic (,haɪpə'sɒnɪk) *adj* concerned with or having a velocity of at least five times that of sound in the same medium under the same conditions.
▸**,hyper'sonics** *n*

hyperspace (,haɪpə'speɪs) *n* **1** *Maths.* space having more than three dimensions. **2** (in science fiction) a theoretical dimension within which conventional space-time relationship does not apply.

hypersthene ('haɪpə,sθi:n) *n* a green, brown, or black pyroxene mineral. [C19: from HYPER- + Gk *sthenos* strength]

hypertension (,haɪpə'tenʃən) *n Pathol.* abnormally high blood pressure.
▸**hypertensive** (,haɪpə'tensɪv) *adj, n*

hypertext ('haɪpə,tekst) *n* computer software and hardware that allows users to create, store, and view text and move between related items easily and in a nonsequential way.

hyperthermia (,haɪpə'θɜ:mɪə) *or* **hyperthermy** (,haɪpə'θɜ:mɪ) *n Pathol.* a variant of **hyperpyrexia.**
▸**,hyper'thermal** *adj*

hyperthyroidism (,haɪpə'θaɪrɔɪ,dɪzəm) *n* overproduction of thyroid hormone by the thyroid gland, causing nervousness, insomnia, and sensitivity to heat.
▸**,hyper'thyroid** *adj, n*

hypertonic (,haɪpə'tɒnɪk) *adj* **1** (esp. of muscles) being in a state of abnormally high tension. **2** (of a solution) having a higher osmotic pressure than that of a specified solution.

hypertrophy (haɪ'pɜ:trəfɪ) *n, pl* **hypertrophies. 1** enlargement of an organ or part resulting from an increase in the size of the cells. ◆ *vb* **hypertrophies, hypertrophying, hypertrophied. 2** to undergo or cause to undergo this condition.

hyperventilation (,haɪpə,ventɪ'leɪʃən) *n* an increase in the rate of breathing, sometimes resulting in cramp and dizziness.
▸**,hyper'venti,late** *vb*

hypha ('haɪfə) *n, pl* **hyphae** (-fi:). any of the filaments that constitute the body (mycelium) of a fungus. [C19: from NL, from Gk *huphē* web]
▸**'hyphal** *adj*

hyphen ('haɪf°n) *n* **1** the punctuation mark **hyphen,** used to separate parts of compound words, to link the words of a phrase, and between syllables of a word split between two consecutive lines. ◆ *vb* **2** (*tr*) another word for **hyphenate.** [C17: from LL (meaning: the combining of two words), from Gk *huphen* (adv) together, from HYPO- + *heis* one]

hyphenate ('haɪf°,neɪt) *vb* **hyphenates, hyphenating, hyphenated.** (*tr*) to separate (words, etc.) with a hyphen.
▸**,hyphen'ation** *n*

hyphenated ('haɪf°,neɪtɪd) *adj* **1** containing or linked with a hyphen. **2** *Chiefly US.* having a nationality denoted by a hyphenated word: *Irish-American.*

hypno- *or before a vowel* **hypn-** *combining form.* **1** indicating sleep: *hypnopaedia.* **2** relating to hypnosis: *hypnotherapy.* [from Gk *hupnos* sleep]

hypnoid ('hɪp,nɔɪd) *or* **hypnoidal** (hɪp'nɔɪd°l) *adj Psychol.* of or relating to a state resembling sleep or hypnosis.

hypnology (hɪp'nɒlədʒɪ) *n Psychol.* the study of sleep and hypnosis.
▸**hyp'nologist** *n*

hypnopaedia (,hɪpnəʊ'pi:dɪə) *n* the learning of lessons heard during sleep. [C20: from HYPNO- + Gk *paideia* education]

hypnopompic (,hɪpnəʊ'pɒmpɪk) *adj Psychol.* relating to the state existing between sleep and full waking, characterized by the persistence of

THESAURUS

hype[1] *Slang n* **1 = publicity,** ballyhoo (*inf.*), brouhaha, build-up, plugging (*inf.*), promotion, puffing, racket, razzmatazz (*sl.*)

hyperbole *n* **= exaggeration,** amplification, enlargement, magnification, overstatement

hypercritical *adj* **= fault-finding,** captious, carping, cavilling, censorious, finicky, fussy, hairsplitting, niggling, overcritical, over- exacting, overscrupulous, pernickety (*inf.*), strict dreamlike imagery. [C20: from HYPNO- + Gk *pompē* a sending forth, escort + -IC]

hypnosis (hɪpˈnəʊsɪs) *n, pl* **hypnoses** (-siːz). an artificially induced state of relaxation and concentration in which deeper parts of the mind become more accessible.

hypnotherapy (ˌhɪpnəʊˈθɛrəpɪ) *n* the use of hypnosis in the treatment of emotional and psychogenic problems.
▸ˌ**hypnoˈtherapist** *n*

hypnotic ❶ (hɪpˈnɒtɪk) *adj* **1** of or producing hypnosis or sleep. **2** (of a person) susceptible to hypnotism. ◆ *n* **3** a drug that induces sleep. **4** a person susceptible to hypnosis. [C17: from LL *hypnōticus*, from Gk, from *hupnoun* to put to sleep, from *hupnos* sleep]
▸**hypˈnotically** *adv*

hypnotism (ˈhɪpnəˌtɪzəm) *n* **1** the scientific study and practice of hypnosis. **2** the process of inducing hypnosis.
▸ˈ**hypnotist** *n*

hypnotize ❶ *or* **hypnotise** (ˈhɪpnəˌtaɪz) *vb* **hypnotizes, hypnotizing, hypnotized** *or* **hypnotises, hypnotising, hypnotised.** (*tr*) **1** to induce hypnosis in (a person). **2** to charm or beguile; fascinate.
▸ˌ**hypnotiˈzation** *or* ˌ**hypnotiˈsation** *n* ▸ˈ**hypnoˌtizer** *or* ˈ**hypnoˌtiser** *n*

hypo[1] (ˈhaɪpəʊ) *n* short for **hyposulphite.** [C19]

hypo[2] (ˈhaɪpəʊ) *n, pl* **hypos.** *Inf.* short for **hypodermic syringe.**

hypo- *or before a vowel* **hyp-** *prefix* **1** beneath or below: *hypodermic.* **2** lower: *hypogastrium.* **3** less than; denoting a deficiency: *hypothyroid.* **4** indicating that a chemical compound contains an element in a lower oxidation state than usual: *hypochlorous acid.* [from Gk, from *hupo* under]

hypoallergenic (ˌhaɪpəʊˌæləˈdʒɛnɪk) *adj* (of cosmetics, earrings, etc.) not likely to cause an allergic reaction.

hypoblast (ˈhaɪpəˌblæst) *n Embryol.* the inner layer of an embryo at an early stage of development that becomes the endoderm.

hypocaust (ˈhaɪpəˌkɔːst) *n* an ancient Roman heating system in which hot air circulated under the floor and between double walls. [C17: from L *hypocaustum*, from Gk, from *hupokaiein* to light a fire beneath, from HYPO- + *kaiein* to burn]

hypocentre (ˈhaɪpəʊˌsɛntə) *n* the point immediately below the centre of explosion of a nuclear bomb. Also called: **ground zero.**

hypochlorite (ˌhaɪpəˈklɔːraɪt) *n* any salt or ester of hypochlorous acid.

hypochlorous acid (ˌhaɪpəˈklɔːrəs) *n* an unstable acid known only in solution and in the form of its salts: a strong oxidizing and bleaching agent. Formula: HOCl.

hypochondria (ˌhaɪpəˈkɒndrɪə) *n* chronic abnormal anxiety concerning the state of one's health. Also called: **hypochondriasis** (ˌhaɪpəkɒnˈdraɪəsɪs). [C18: from LL: abdomen, supposedly the seat of melancholy, from Gk, from *hupokhondrios*, from HYPO- + *khondros* cartilage]

hypochondriac (ˌhaɪpəˈkɒndrɪˌæk) *n* **1** a person suffering from hypochondria. ◆ *adj also* **hypochondriacal** (ˌhaɪpəkɒnˈdraɪəkᵊl). **2** relating to or suffering from hypochondria.

hypocorism (haɪˈpɒkəˌrɪzəm) *n* a pet name, esp. one using a diminutive affix: *"Sally" is a hypocorism for "Sarah".* [C19: from Gk *hupo-korisma*, from *hupokorizesthai* to use pet names, from *hypo-* beneath + *korizesthai*, from *korē* girl, *koros* boy]
▸**hypocoristic** (ˌhaɪpəkɔːˈrɪstɪk) *adj*

hypocotyl (ˌhaɪpəˈkɒtɪl) *n* the part of an embryo plant between the cotyledons and the radicle. [C19: from HYPO- + COTYL(EDON)]

hypocrisy ❶ (hɪˈpɒkrəsɪ) *n, pl* **hypocrisies. 1** the practice of professing standards, beliefs, etc., contrary to one's real character or actual behaviour. **2** an act or instance of this.

hypocrite ❶ (ˈhɪpəkrɪt) *n* a person who pretends to be what he is not. [C13: from OF *ipocrite*, via LL from Gk *hupokritēs* one who plays a part, from *hupokrinein* to feign, from *krinein* to judge]
▸ˌ**hypoˈcritical** *adj* ▸ˌ**hypoˈcritically** *adv*

hypocycloid (ˌhaɪpəˈsaɪklɔɪd) *n* a curve described by a point on the circumference of a circle as the circle rolls around the inside of a fixed coplanar circle.
▸ˌ**hypocyˈcloidal** *adj*

hypodermic ❶ (ˌhaɪpəˈdɜːmɪk) *adj* **1** of or relating to the region of the skin beneath the epidermis. **2** injected beneath the skin. ◆ *n* **3** a hypodermic syringe or needle. **4** a hypodermic injection.
▸ˌ**hypoˈdermically** *adv*

hypodermic syringe *n Med.* a type of syringe consisting of a hollow cylinder, usually of glass or plastic, a tightly fitting piston, and a hollow needle (**hypodermic needle**), used for withdrawing blood samples, etc.

hypodermis (ˌhaɪpəˈdɜːmɪs) *or* **hypoderm** *n* **1** *Bot.* a layer of thick-walled supportive or water-storing cells beneath the epidermis in some plants. **2** *Zool.* the epidermis of arthropods, annelids, etc. [C19: from HYPO- + EPIDERMIS]

hypogastrium (ˌhaɪpəˈgæstrɪəm) *n, pl* **hypogastria** (-trɪə). *Anat.* the lower front central region of the abdomen. [C17: from NL, from Gk *hupogastrion*, from HYPO- + *gastrion*, dim. of *gastēr* stomach]

hypogeal (ˌhaɪpəˈdʒiːəl) *or* **hypogeous** *adj* occurring or living below the surface of the ground. [C19: from L *hypogēus*, from Gk, from HYPO- + *gē* earth]

hypogene (ˈhaɪpəˌdʒiːn) *adj* formed or originating beneath the surface of the earth.

hypogeum (ˌhaɪpəˈdʒiːəm) *n, pl* **hypogea** (-ˈdʒiːə). an underground vault, esp. one used for burials. [C18: from L, from Gk *hupogeion*; see HYPOGEAL]

hypoid gear (ˈhaɪpɔɪd) *n* a gear having a tooth form generated by a hypocycloidal curve. [C20: *hypoid*, shortened from HYPOCYCLOID]

hyponasty (ˈhaɪpəˌnæstɪ) *n* increased growth of the lower surface of a plant part, resulting in an upward bending of the part.
▸ˌ**hypoˈnastic** *adj*

hypophosphate (ˌhaɪpəˈfɒsfeɪt) *n* any salt or ester of hypophosphoric acid.

hypophosphite (ˌhaɪpəˈfɒsfaɪt) *n* any salt of hypophosphorous acid.

hypophosphoric acid (ˌhaɪpəfɒsˈfɒrɪk) *n* a tetrabasic acid produced by the slow oxidation of phosphorus in moist air. Formula: $H_4P_2O_6$.

hypophosphorous acid (ˌhaɪpəˈfɒsfərəs) *n* a monobasic acid and a reducing agent. Formula: H_3PO_2.

hypophysis (haɪˈpɒfɪsɪs) *n, pl* **hypophyses** (-ˌsiːz). the technical name for **pituitary gland.** [C18: from Gk: outgrowth, from HYPO- + *phuein* to grow]
▸**hypophyseal** *or* **hypophysial** (ˌhaɪpəˈfɪzɪəl, haɪˌpɒfɪˈsiːəl) *adj*

hypostasis (haɪˈpɒstəsɪs) *n, pl* **hypostases** (-ˌsiːz). **1** *Metaphysics.* the essential nature of a substance. **2** *Christianity.* **2a** any of the three persons of the Godhead. **2b** the one person of Christ in which the divine and human natures are united. **3** the accumulation of blood in an organ or part as the result of poor circulation. [C16: from LL: substance, from Gk *hupostasis* foundation, from *huphistasthai*, from HYPO- + *histanai* to cause to stand]
▸**hypostatic** (ˌhaɪpəˈstætɪk) *or* ˌ**hypoˈstatical** *adj*

hypostyle (ˈhaɪpəʊˌstaɪl) *adj* **1** having a roof supported by columns. ◆ *n* **2** a building constructed in this way.

hyposulphite (ˌhaɪpəˈsʌlfaɪt) *n* another name for **sodium thiosulphate,** esp. when used as a photographic fixer. Often shortened to **hypo.**

hyposulphurous acid (ˌhaɪpəˈsʌlfərəs) *n* an unstable acid known only in solution: a powerful reducing agent. Formula $H_2S_2O_4$.

hypotension (ˌhaɪpəʊˈtɛnʃən) *n Pathol.* abnormally low blood pressure.
▸**hypotensive** (ˌhaɪpəʊˈtɛnsɪv) *adj*

hypotenuse (haɪˈpɒtɪˌnjuːz) *n* the side in a right-angled triangle that is opposite the right angle. Abbrev.: **hyp.** [C16: from L *hypotēnūsa*, from Gk *hupoteinousa grammē* subtending line, from HYPO- + *teinein* to stretch]

hypothalamus (ˌhaɪpəˈθæləməs) *n, pl* **hypothalami** (-ˌmaɪ). a neural control centre at the base of the brain, concerned with hunger, thirst, satiety, and other autonomic functions.
▸**hypothalamic** (ˌhaɪpəθəˈlæmɪk) *adj*

hypothec (haɪˈpɒθɪk) *n Roman & Scots Law.* a charge on property in favour of a creditor. [C16: from LL *hypotheca*, from Gk *hupothēkē* pledge, from *hupotithenai* to deposit as a security, from HYPO- + *tithenai* to place]

hypothecate (haɪˈpɒθɪˌkeɪt) *vb* **hypothecates, hypothecating, hypothecated.** (*tr*) *Law.* to pledge (personal property or a ship) as security for a debt without transferring possession or title.
▸**hyˌpotheˈcation** *n* ▸**hyˈpotheˌcator** *n*

hypothermia (ˌhaɪpəʊˈθɜːmɪə) *n* **1** *Pathol.* an abnormally low body temperature, as induced in the elderly by exposure to cold weather. **2** *Med.* the intentional reduction of normal body temperature to reduce the patient's metabolic rate.

hypothesis ❶ (haɪˈpɒθɪsɪs) *n, pl* **hypotheses** (-ˌsiːz). **1** a suggested explanation for a group of facts or phenomena, either accepted as a basis for further verification (**working hypothesis**) or accepted as likely to be true. **2** an assumption used in an argument; supposition. [C16: from Gk, from *hupotithenai* to propose, lit.: put under; see HYPO-, THESIS]
▸**hyˈpothesist** *n*

hypothesize *or* **hypothesise** (haɪˈpɒθɪˌsaɪz) *vb* **hypothesizes, hypothesizing, hypothesized** *or* **hypothesises, hypothesising, hypothesised.** to form or assume as a hypothesis.
▸**hyˈpotheˌsizer** *or* **hyˈpotheˌsiser** *n*

hypothetical ❶ (ˌhaɪpəˈθɛtɪkᵊl) *or* **hypothetic** *adj* **1** having the nature

THESAURUS

hypnotic *adj* **1** = **mesmerizing,** mesmeric, narcotic, opiate, sleep-inducing, somniferous, soothing, soporific, spellbinding

hypnotize *vb* **1** = **mesmerize,** put in a trance, put to sleep **2** = **fascinate,** absorb, entrance, magnetize, spellbind

hypocrisy *n* **1, 2** = **insincerity,** cant, deceit, deceitfulness, deception, dissembling, duplicity, falsity, imposture, pharisaism, phariseeism, phoneyness *or* phoniness (*inf.*), pretence, sanctimoniousness, speciousness, two-facedness
Antonyms *n* honesty, sincerity, truthfulness

hypocrite *n* = **fraud,** charlatan, deceiver, dissembler, impostor, pharisee, phoney *or* phony (*inf.*), pretender, whited sepulchre

hypocritical *adj* = **insincere,** canting, deceitful, deceptive, dissembling, duplicitous, false, fraudulent, hollow, pharisaical, phoney *or* phony (*inf.*), sanctimonious, specious, spurious, two-faced

hypodermic *n* **3** = **syringe,** needle

hypothesis *n* **1, 2** = **assumption,** postulate, premise *or* premiss, proposition, supposition, theory, thesis

hypothetical *adj* **1, 2** = **theoretical,** academic, assumed, conjectural, imaginary, putative, speculative, supposed
Antonyms *adj* actual, confirmed, established, known, proven, real, true

of a hypothesis. **2** assumed or thought to exist. **3** *Logic.* another word for **conditional** (sense 3).
▸ ˌ**hypoˈthetically** *adv*

hypothyroidism (ˌhaɪpəʊˈθaɪrɔɪˌdɪzəm) *n Pathol.* **1** insufficient production of thyroid hormones by the thyroid gland. **2** any disorder, such as cretinism or myxoedema, resulting from this.
▸ ˌ**hypoˈthyroid** *n, adj*

hypotonic (ˌhaɪpəˈtɒnɪk) *adj* **1** *Pathol.* (of muscles) lacking normal tone or tension. **2** (of a solution) having a lower osmotic pressure than that of a specified solution.

hypoxia (haɪˈpɒksɪə) *n* deficiency in the amount of oxygen delivered to the body tissues. [C20: from HYPO- + OXY-[2] + -IA]
▸ **hypoxic** (haɪˈpɒksɪk) *adj*

hypso- *or before a vowel* **hyps-** *combining form.* indicating height: *hypsometry.* [from Gk *hupsos*]

hypsography (hɪpˈsɒgrəfɪ) *n* the scientific study and mapping of the earth's topography above sea level.

hypsometer (hɪpˈsɒmɪtə) *n* **1** an instrument for measuring altitudes by determining the boiling point of water at a given altitude. **2** any instrument used to calculate the heights of trees by triangulation.

hypsometry (hɪpˈsɒmɪtrɪ) *n* (in mapping) the establishment of height above sea level.

hyrax (ˈhaɪræks) *n, pl* **hyraxes** *or* **hyraces** (ˈhaɪrəˌsiːz). any of various agile herbivorous mammals of Africa and SW Asia. They resemble rodents but have feet with hooflike toes. Also called: **dassie.** [C19: from NL, from Gk *hurax* shrewmouse]

hyssop (ˈhɪsəp) *n* **1** a widely cultivated Asian plant with spikes of small blue flowers and aromatic leaves, used as a condiment and in perfumery and folk medicine. **2** a Biblical plant, used for sprinkling in the ritual practices of the Hebrews. [OE *ysope,* from L *hyssōpus,* from Gk *hussōpos,* of Semitic origin]

hysterectomy (ˌhɪstəˈrɛktəmɪ) *n, pl* **hysterectomies.** surgical removal of the uterus.

hysteresis (ˌhɪstəˈriːsɪs) *n Physics.* the lag in a variable property of a system with respect to the effect producing it as this effect varies, esp. the phenomenon in which the magnetic induction of a ferromagnetic material lags behind the changing external field. [from Gk *husterēsis,* from *husteros* coming after]
▸ **hysteretic** (ˌhɪstəˈrɛtɪk) *adj*

hysteresis loop *n* a closed curve showing the variation of the magnetic induction of a ferromagnetic material with the external magnetic field producing it, when this field is changed through a complete cycle.

hysteria ❶ (hɪˈstɪərɪə) *n* **1** a mental disorder characterized by emotional outbursts and, often, symptoms such as paralysis. **2** any frenzied emotional state, esp. of laughter or crying. [C19: from NL, from L *hystericus* HYSTERIC]

hysteric (hɪˈstɛrɪk) *n* **1** a hysterical person. ◆ *adj* **2** hysterical. [C17: from L *hystericus,* lit.: of the womb, from Gk, from *hustera* womb; from the belief that hysteria in women originated in disorders of the womb]

hysterical ❶ (hɪˈstɛrɪkᵊl) *adj* **1** suggesting hysteria: *hysterical cries.* **2** suffering from hysteria. **3** *Inf.* wildly funny.
▸ **hysˈterically** *adv*

hysterics (hɪˈstɛrɪks) *n* (*functioning as pl or sing*) **1** an attack of hysteria. **2** *Inf.* wild uncontrollable bursts of laughter.

hystero- *or before a vowel* **hyster-** *combining form.* the uterus: *hysterectomy.* [from Gk *hustera* womb]

hysteron proteron (ˈhɪstəˌrɒn ˈprɒtəˌrɒn) *n* **1** *Logic.* a fallacious argument in which the proposition to be proved is assumed as a premise. **2** *Rhetoric.* a figure of speech in which the normal order of two sentences, clauses, etc., is reversed: *bred and born* (for *born and bred*). [C16: from LL, from Gk *husteron proteron* the latter (placed as) former]

hystricomorph (hɪˈstraɪkəʊˌmɔːf) *n* **1** any rodent of the suborder *Hystricomorpha,* which includes porcupines, cavies, agoutis, and chinchillas. ◆ *adj* also: **hystricomorphic** (hɪˌstraɪkəʊˈmɔːfɪk). **2** of the *Hystricomorpha.* [C19: from L *hystrix* porcupine, from Gk *hustrix*]

Hz *symbol for* hertz.

THESAURUS

hysteria *n* **2** = **frenzy,** agitation, delirium, hysterics, madness, panic, unreason

hysterical *adj* **1, 2** = **frenzied,** berserk, beside oneself, convulsive, crazed, distracted, distraught, frantic, mad, overwrought, raving, uncontrollable **3** *Informal* = **hilarious,** comical, farcical, screaming, side-splitting, uproarious, wildly funny

Antonyms *adj* ≠ **frenzied:** calm, composed, poised, self-possessed, unfazed (*inf.*) ≠ **hilarious:** grave, melancholy, sad, serious

i *or* **I** (aɪ) *n, pl* **i's, I's,** *or* **Is. 1** the ninth letter and third vowel of the English alphabet. **2** any of several speech sounds represented by this letter. **3a** something shaped like an I. **3b** (*in combination*): *an I-beam.*

i *symbol for* the imaginary number √–1.

I[1] (aɪ) *pron* (*subjective*) refers to the speaker or writer. [C12: from OE *ic;* cf. OSaxon *ik,* OHG *ih,* Sansk. *ahām*]

I[2] *symbol for:* **1** *Chem.* iodine. **2** *Physics.* current. **3** *Physics.* isospin. ◆ **4** *the Roman numeral for* one. See **Roman numerals.**

I. *abbrev. for:* **1** Independence. **2** Independent. **3** Institute. **4** International. **5** Island; Isle.

-ia *suffix forming nouns.* **1** in place names: *Columbia.* **2** in names of diseases: *pneumonia.* **3** in words denoting condition or quality: *utopia.* **4** in names of botanical genera and zoological classes: *Reptilia.* **5** in collective nouns borrowed from Latin: *regalia.* [(for senses 1–4) NL, from L & Gk, suffix of fem nouns; (for sense 5) from L, neuter pl suffix]

IAA *abbrev. for* indoleacetic acid.

IAEA *abbrev. for* International Atomic Energy Agency.

-ial *suffix forming adjectives.* of or relating to: *managerial.* [from L *-iālis,* adj. suffix; cf. -AL[1]]

iamb (ˈaɪæm, ˈaɪæmb) *or* **iambus** (aɪˈæmbəs) *n, pl* **iambs, iambi** (aɪˈæmbaɪ), *or* **iambuses.** *Prosody.* **1** a metrical foot of two syllables, a short one followed by a long one. **2** a line of verse of such feet. [C19 *iamb,* from C16 *iambus,* from L, from Gk *iambos*]

iambic (aɪˈæmbɪk) *Prosody.* ◆ *adj* **1** of, relating to, or using an iamb. **2** (in Greek literature) denoting a satirical verse written in iambs. ◆ *n* **3** a metrical foot, line, or stanza consisting of iambs. **4** an ancient Greek satirical verse written in iambs.

-ian *suffix.* a variant of **-an:** *Etonian.* [from L *-iānus*]

-iana *suffix forming nouns.* a variant of **-ana.**

IAP *abbrev. for* Internet access provider.

-iasis *or* **-asis** *n combining form.* (in medicine) indicating a diseased condition: *psoriasis.* Cf. **-osis** (sense 2). [from NL, from Gk, suffix of action]

IATA (aɪˈɑːtə, iːˈɑːtə) *n acronym for* International Air Transport Association.

-iatrics *n combining form.* indicating medical care or treatment: *paediatrics.* [C19: from Gk, from *iasthai* to heal]

iatrogenic (aɪˌætrəʊˈdʒenɪk) *adj Med.* (of an illness) induced in a patient as the result of a physician's action.
▸**iatrogenicity** (aɪˌætrəʊdʒɪˈnɪsɪtɪ) *n*

-iatry *n combining form.* indicating healing or medical treatment: *psychiatry.* Cf. **-iatrics.** [from NL *-iatria,* from Gk *iatreia* the healing art, from *iatros* healer, physician]
▸**-iatric** *adj combining form.*

IBA (in Britain) *abbrev. for* Independent Broadcasting Authority.

I-beam *n* a rolled steel joist or a girder with a cross section in the form of a capital *I.*

Iberian (aɪˈbɪərɪən) *n* **1** a member of a group of ancient Caucasoid peoples who inhabited the Iberian Peninsula, in classical times. **2** a native or inhabitant of the Iberian Peninsula; a Spaniard or Portuguese. **3** a native or inhabitant of ancient Iberia. ◆ *adj* **4** relating to the pre-Roman peoples of the Iberian Peninsula or of Caucasian Iberia. **5** of or relating to the Iberian Peninsula, its inhabitants, or any of their languages.

iberis (aɪˈbɪərɪs) *n* any of various Mediterranean plants with white, lilac, or purple flowers. Also called: **candytuft.** [from Gk *ibēris* pepperwort]

ibex (ˈaɪbeks) *n, pl* **ibexes, ibices** (ˈɪbɪˌsiːz, ˈaɪ-), *or* **ibex.** any of three species of wild goat of mountainous regions of Europe, Asia, and North Africa, having large backward-curving horns. [C17: from L: chamois]

ibid. *or* **ib.** (referring to a book, etc., previously cited) *abbrev. for* ibidem. [L: in the same place]

ibis (ˈaɪbɪs) *n, pl* **ibises** *or* **ibis.** any of various wading birds such as the sacred ibis, that occur in warm regions and have a long thin down-curved bill. [C14: via L from Gk, from Egyptian *hby*]

-ible *suffix forming adjectives.* a variant of **-able.**
▸**-ibly** *suffix forming adverbs.* ▸**-ibility** *suffix forming nouns.*

Ibo *or* **Igbo** (ˈiːbəʊ) *n* **1** (*pl* **Ibos** *or* **Ibo**) a member of a Negroid people of W Africa, living in S Nigeria. **2** their language, belonging to the Niger-Congo family.

IBRD *abbrev. for* International Bank for Reconstruction and Development (the World Bank).

ibuprofen (aɪˈbjuːˌprəʊfən) *n* a drug that relieves pain and reduces inflammation: used to treat arthritis and muscular strains.

i/c *abbrev. for:* **1** in charge (of). **2** internal combustion.

-ic *suffix forming adjectives.* **1** of, relating to, or resembling: *periodic.* See also **-ical. 2** (in chemistry) indicating that an element is chemically combined in the higher of two possible valence states: *ferric.* Cf. **-ous** (sense 2). [from L *-icus* or Gk *-ikos; -ic* also occurs in nouns that represent a substantive use of adjectives (*magic*) and in nouns borrowed directly from L or Gk (*critic, music*)]

ICA *abbrev. for:* **1** (in Britain) Institute of Contemporary Arts. **2** Institute of Chartered Accountants.

-ical *suffix forming adjectives.* a variant of **-ic,** but having a less literal application than corresponding adjectives ending in *-ic: economical.* [from L *-icālis*]
▸**-ically** *suffix forming adverbs.*

ICAO *abbrev. for* International Civil Aviation Organization.

ICBM *abbrev. for* intercontinental ballistic missile: a missile with a range greater than 5550 km.

ice ❶ (aɪs) *n* **1** water in the solid state, formed by freezing liquid water. Related adj: **glacial. 2** a portion of ice cream. **3** *Sl.* a diamond or diamonds. **4** *Sl.* a concentrated and highly potent form of methamphetamine with dangerous side effects. **5 break the ice. 5a** to relieve shyness, etc., esp. between strangers. **5b** to be the first of a group to do something. **6 on ice.** in abeyance; pending. **7 on thin ice.** unsafe; vulnerable. ◆ *vb* **ices, icing, iced. 8** (often foll. by *up, over,* etc.) to form ice; freeze. **9** (*tr*) to mix with ice or chill (a drink, etc.). **10** (*tr*) to cover (a cake, etc.) with icing. [OE *īs*]
▸**iced** *adj*

ICE (in Britain) *abbrev. for* Institution of Civil Engineers.

ice age *n* another name for **glacial period.**

ice axe *n* a light axe used by mountaineers for cutting footholds in ice.

ice bag *n* a waterproof bag used as an ice pack.

iceberg (ˈaɪsbɜːg) *n* **1** a large mass of ice floating in the sea. **2 tip of the iceberg.** the small visible part of something, esp. a problem, that is much larger. **3** *Sl., chiefly US.* a person considered to have a cold or reserved manner. [C18: prob. part translation of MDu. *ijsberg* ice mountain; cf. Norwegian *isberg*]

iceberg lettuce *n* a type of lettuce with very crisp pale leaves tightly enfolded.

iceblink (ˈaɪsˌblɪŋk) *n* a reflected glare in the sky over an ice field. Also called: **blink.**

icebound (ˈaɪsˌbaʊnd) *adj* covered or made immobile by ice; frozen in: *an icebound ship.*

icebox (ˈaɪsˌbɒks) *n* **1** a compartment in a refrigerator for storing or making ice. **2** an insulated cabinet packed with ice for storing food. **3** a US and Canad. name for **refrigerator.**

icebreaker (ˈaɪsˌbreɪkə) *n* **1** Also called: **iceboat.** a vessel with a reinforced bow for breaking up the ice in bodies of water. **2** a device for breaking ice into smaller pieces. **3** something intended to relieve shyness between strangers.

icecap (ˈaɪsˌkæp) *n* a thick mass of glacial ice that permanently covers an area, such as the polar regions or the peak of a mountain.

ice cream *n* a sweetened frozen liquid, made from cream, milk, or a custard base, flavoured in various ways.

ice dance *n* any of a number of dances, mostly based on ballroom dancing, performed by a couple skating on ice.
▸**ice dancer** *n* ▸**ice dancing** *n*

icefall (ˈaɪsˌfɔːl) *n* a steep part of a glacier that resembles a frozen waterfall.

ice field *n* **1** a large ice floe. **2** a large mass of ice permanently covering an extensive area of land.

ice floe *n* a sheet of ice, of variable size, floating in the sea. See also **ice field** (sense 1).

ice hockey *n* a game played on ice by two teams wearing skates, who try to propel a flat puck into their opponents' goal with long sticks.

ice house *n* a building for storing ice.

Icelander (ˈaɪslændə, ˈaɪsləndə) *n* a native or inhabitant of Iceland.

Icelandic (aɪsˈlændɪk) *adj* **1** of or relating to Iceland, its people, or their language. ◆ *n* **2** the official language of Iceland.

Iceland poppy (ˌaɪslənd) *n* any of various arctic poppies with white or yellow nodding flowers.

Iceland spar *n* a pure transparent variety of calcite with double-refracting crystals.

ice lolly *n Brit. inf.* a water ice or an ice cream on a stick. Also called: **lolly.**

ice pack *n* **1** a bag or folded cloth containing ice, applied to a part of the body to reduce swelling, etc. **2** another name for **pack ice. 3** a sachet containing a gel that retains its temperature for an extended period of time, used esp. in cool bags.

ice pick *n* a pointed tool used for breaking ice.

ice plant *n* a low-growing plant of southern Africa, with fleshy leaves covered with icelike hairs and pink or white rayed flowers.

ice point *n* the temperature at which a mixture of ice and water are in

THESAURUS

ice *n* **5 break the ice = begin,** initiate the proceedings, kick off (*inf.*), lead the way, make a start, start *or* set the ball rolling (*inf.*), take the plunge (*inf.*) **7 on thin ice = unsafe,** at risk, in jeopardy, open to attack, out on a limb, sticking one's neck out (*inf.*), vulnerable equilibrium at a pressure of one atmosphere. It is 0° on the Celsius scale and 32° on the Fahrenheit scale. Cf. **steam point.**

ice sheet *n* a thick layer of ice covering a large area of land for a long time, esp. the layer that covered much of the N hemisphere during the last glacial period.

ice shelf *n* a thick mass of ice that is permanently attached to the land but projects into and floats on the sea.

ice skate *n* **1** a boot having a steel blade fitted to the sole to enable the wearer to glide over ice. **2** the steel blade on such a boot. ◆ *vb* **ice-skate, ice-skates, ice-skating, ice-skated. 3** (*intr*) to glide over ice on ice skates.
▸**'ice-ˌskater** *n*

ice station *n* a scientific research station in polar regions, where ice movement, weather, and environmental conditions are monitored.

IChemE *abbrev. for* Institution of Chemical Engineers.

I Ching ('iː 'tʃɪŋ) *n* an ancient Chinese book of divination and a source of Confucian and Taoist philosophy.

ichneumon (ɪk'njuːmən) *n* a mongoose of Africa and S Europe, having greyish-brown speckled fur. [C16: via L from Gk, lit.: tracker, hunter, from *ikhneuein* to track, from *ikhnos* a footprint; so named from the animal's alleged ability to locate the eggs of crocodiles]

ichneumon fly *or* **wasp** *n* any hymenopterous insect whose larvae are parasitic in caterpillars and other insect larvae.

ichnography (ɪk'nɒgrəfɪ) *n* **1** the art of drawing ground plans. **2** the ground plan of a building. [C16: from L, from Gk, from *ikhnos* trace, track]
▸**ichnographic** (ˌɪknə'græfɪk) *or* **ˌichno'graphical** *adj*

ichor ('aɪkɔː) *n* **1** *Greek myth.* the fluid said to flow in the veins of the gods. **2** *Pathol.* a foul-smelling watery discharge from a wound or ulcer. [C17: from Gk *ikhōr,* from ?]
▸**'ichorous** *adj*

ichthyo- *or before a vowel* **ichthy-** *combining form.* indicating or relating to fishes: *ichthyology.* [from L, from Gk *ikhthus* fish]

ichthyoid ('ɪkθɪˌɔɪd) *adj also* **ichthyoidal. 1** resembling a fish. ◆ *n* **2** a fishlike vertebrate.

ichthyology (ˌɪkθɪ'ɒlədʒɪ) *n* the study of fishes.
▸**ichthyologic** (ˌɪkθɪə'lɒdʒɪk) *or* **ˌichthyo'logical** *adj* ▸**ˌichthy'ologist** *n*

ichthyosaur ('ɪkθɪəˌsɔː) *or* **ichthyosaurus** (ˌɪkθɪə'sɔːrəs) *n, pl* **ichthyosaurs, ichthyosauruses,** *or* **ichthyosauri** (-'sɔːraɪ). an extinct marine Mesozoic reptile which had a porpoise-like body with dorsal and tail fins and paddle-like limbs. See also **plesiosaur.**

ichthyosis (ˌɪkθɪ'əʊsɪs) *n* a congenital disease in which the skin is coarse, dry, and scaly.
▸**ichthyotic** (ˌɪkθɪ'ɒtɪk) *adj*

ICI *abbrev. for* Imperial Chemical Industries.

-ician *suffix forming nouns.* indicating a person skilled or involved in a subject or activity: *physician; beautician.* [from F *-icien;* see -IC, -IAN]

icicle ('aɪsɪkᵊl) *n* a hanging spike of ice formed by the freezing of dripping water. [C14: from ICE + *ickel,* from OE *gicel* icicle, rel. to ON *jökull* glacier]

icing ('aɪsɪŋ) *n* **1** Also (esp. US and Canad.): **frosting.** a sugar preparation, variously flavoured and coloured, for coating and decorating cakes, etc. **2 icing on the cake** any unexpected extra or bonus. **3** the formation of ice, as on a ship, due to the freezing of moisture in the atmosphere.

icing sugar *n Brit.* a very finely ground sugar used for icings, confections, etc. US term: **confectioners' sugar.**

icon *or* **ikon** ('aɪkɒn) *n* **1** a representation of Christ or a saint, esp. one painted in oil on a wooden panel in a traditional Byzantine style and venerated in the Eastern Church. **2** an image, picture, etc. **3** a symbol resembling or analogous to the thing it represents. **4** a person regarded as a sex symbol or as a symbol of a belief or cultural movement. **5** a pictorial representation of a facility available on a computer that can be implemented by a cursor rather than by a textual instruction. [C16: from L, from Gk *eikōn* image, from *eikenai* to be like]

icono- *or before a vowel* **icon-** *combining form.* indicating an image or likeness: *iconology.*

iconoclast (aɪ'kɒnəˌklæst) *n* **1** a person who attacks established or traditional concepts, principles, etc. **2a** a destroyer of religious images or objects. **2b** an adherent of a heretical iconoclastic movement within the Greek Orthodox Church from 725 to 842 A.D. [C16: from LL, from LGk *eikonoklastes,* from *eikōn* icon + *klastes* breaker]
▸**iˌcono'clastic** *adj* ▸**i'conoˌclasm** *n*

iconography (ˌaɪkɒ'nɒgrəfɪ) *n, pl* **iconographies. 1a** the symbols used in a work of art. **1b** the conventional significance attached to such symbols. **2** a collection of pictures of a particular subject. **3** the representation of the subjects of icons or portraits, esp. on coins.
▸**ˌico'nographer** *n* ▸**iconographic** (aɪˌkɒnə'græfɪk) *or* **iˌcono'graphical** *adj*

iconolatry (ˌaɪkɒ'nɒlətrɪ) *n* the worship of icons as idols.
▸**ˌico'nolater** *n* ▸**ˌico'nolatrous** *adj*

iconology (ˌaɪkɒ'nɒlədʒɪ) *n* **1** the study of icons. **2** icons collectively. **3** the symbolic representation of icons.
▸**iconological** (aɪˌkɒnə'lɒdʒɪkᵊl) *adj* ▸**ˌico'nologist** *n*

iconoscope (aɪ'kɒnəˌskəʊp) *n* a television camera tube in which an electron beam scans a surface, converting an optical image into electrical pulses.

iconostasis (ˌaɪkəʊ'nɒstəsɪs) *or* **iconostas** (aɪ'kɒnəˌstæs) *n, pl* **iconostases** (ˌaɪkəʊ'nɒstəˌsiːz *or* aɪ'kɒnəˌstæsɪz). *Eastern Church.* a screen with doors and with icons set in tiers, which separates the sanctuary from the nave. [C19: Church L, from LGk *eikonostasion* shrine, lit.: area where images are placed, from *icono-* + *histanai* to stand]

icosahedron (ˌaɪkəsə'hiːdrən) *n, pl* **icosahedrons** *or* **icosahedra** (-drə). a solid figure having 20 faces. [C16: from Gk, from *eikosi* twenty + *-edron* -HEDRON]
▸**ˌicosa'hedral** *adj*

-ics *suffix forming nouns; functioning as sing* **1** indicating a science, art, or matters relating to a particular subject: *politics.* **2** indicating certain activities: *acrobatics.* [pl. of *-ic,* representing L *-ica,* from Gk *-ika*]

ictus ('ɪktəs) *n, pl* **ictuses** *or* **ictus. 1** *Prosody.* metrical or rhythmic stress in verse feet, as contrasted with the stress accent on words. **2** *Med.* a sudden attack or stroke. [C18: from L *icere* to strike]
▸**'ictal** *adj*

ICU *abbrev. for* intensive care unit.

icy ❶ ('aɪsɪ) *adj* **icier, iciest. 1** made of, covered with, or containing ice. **2** resembling ice. **3** freezing or very cold. **4** cold or reserved in manner; aloof.
▸**'icily** *adv* ▸**'iciness** *n*

id (ɪd) *n Psychoanal.* the primitive instincts and energies in the unconscious mind that, modified by the ego and the superego, underlie all psychic activity. [C20: NL, from L: it; used to render G *Es*]

ID *abbrev. for:* **1.** identification. **2** Also **i.d.** intradermal(ly).

id. *abbrev. for* idem.

I'd (aɪd) *contraction of* I had *or* I would.

-id[1] *suffix forming nouns and adjectives.* indicating members of a zoological family: *cyprinid.* [from NL *-idae* or *-ida,* from Gk *-idēs* suffix indicating offspring]

-id[2] *suffix forming nouns.* a variant of **-ide.**

IDA *abbrev. for* International Development Association.

-idae *suffix forming plural proper nouns.* indicating names of zoological families: *Felidae.* [NL, from L, from Gk *-idai,* suffix indicating offspring]

-ide *or* **-id** *suffix forming nouns.* **1** (*added to the combining form of the nonmetallic or electronegative elements*) indicating a binary compound: *sodium chloride.* **2** indicating an organic compound derived from another: *acetanilide.* **3** indicating one of a class of compounds or elements: *peptide.* [from G *-id,* from F *oxide* OXIDE, based on the suffix of *acide* ACID]

idea ❶ (aɪ'dɪə) *n* **1** any product of mental activity; thought. **2** the thought of something: *the idea appals me.* **3** a belief; opinion. **4** a scheme, intention, plan, etc. **5** a vague notion; inkling: *he had no idea of the truth.* **6** a person's conception of something: *her idea of honesty is not the same as mine.* **7** significance or purpose: *the idea of the game is to discover the murderer.* **8** *Philosophy.* **8a** an immediate object of thought or perception. **8b** (*sometimes cap.*) (in Plato) the universal essence or archetype of any class of things or concepts. **9 get ideas.** to become ambitious, restless, etc. **10 not one's idea of.** not what one regards as (hard work, a holiday, etc.). **11 that's an idea.** that is worth considering. **12 the very idea!** that is preposterous, unreasonable, etc. [C16: via LL from Gk: model, notion, from *idein* to see]

> **USAGE NOTE** It is usually considered correct to say that someone has the *idea of doing* something, rather than *the idea to do it: he had the idea of taking* (not *the idea to take*) *a short holiday.*

ideal ❶ (aɪ'dɪəl) *n* **1** a conception of something that is perfect. **2** a person or thing considered to represent perfection. **3** something existing only as an idea. **4** a pattern or model, esp. of ethical behaviour. ◆ *adj* **5** conforming to an ideal. **6** of, involving, or existing in the form of an idea. **7** *Philosophy.* **7a** of or relating to a highly desirable and possible state of affairs. **7b** of or relating to idealism.
▸**i'deally** *adv* ▸**i'dealness** *n*

ideal element *n* any element added to a mathematical theory in order

THESAURUS

icy *adj* **2 = slippery,** glacial, glassy, like a sheet of glass, rimy, slippy (*inf. or dialect*) **3 = cold,** arctic, biting, bitter, chill, chilling, chilly, freezing, frost-bound, frosty, frozen over, ice-cold, parky (*Brit. inf.*), raw **4 = unfriendly,** aloof, cold, distant, forbidding, frigid, frosty, glacial, hostile, indifferent, steely, stony, unwelcoming
Antonyms *adj* ≠ **cold:** blistering, boiling, hot, sizzling, warm ≠ **unfriendly:** cordial, friendly, gracious, warm

idea *n* **1 = thought,** abstraction, concept, conception, conclusion, fancy, impression, judgment, perception, understanding **3 = belief,** conviction, doctrine, interpretation, notion, opinion, teaching, view, viewpoint **4 = plan,** design, hypothesis, recommendation, scheme, solution, suggestion, theory **5 = impression,** approximation, ballpark figure, clue, estimate, guess, hint, inkling, intimation, notion, suspicion **7 = intention,** aim, end, import, meaning, object, objective, plan, purpose, *raison d'être,* reason, sense, significance **8b** *Philosophy* **= pattern,** archetype, essence, form

ideal *n* **1, 2 = model,** archetype, criterion, epitome, example, exemplar, last word, nonpareil, paradigm, paragon, pattern, perfection, prototype, standard, standard of perfection **4 = principle,** moral value, standard ◆ *adj* **5 = perfect,** archetypal, classic, complete, consummate, model, optimal, quintessential, supreme **6 = hypothetical,** abstract, conceptual, intellectual, mental, notional, theoretical, transcendental
Antonyms *adj* ≠ **perfect:** deficient, flawed, impaired, imperfect, unsuitable ≠ **hypothetical:** actual, factual, literal, mundane, ordinary, real

to eliminate special cases. The ideal element i = √–1 allows all algebraic equations to be solved.

ideal gas *n* a hypothetical gas which obeys Boyle's law exactly at all temperatures and pressures, and which has internal energy that depends only upon the temperature.

idealism ❶ (aɪˈdɪəˌlɪzəm) *n* **1** belief in or pursuance of ideals. **2** the tendency to represent things in their ideal forms, rather than as they are. **3** *Philosophy.* the doctrine that material objects and the external world do not exist in reality, but are creations of the mind. Cf. **materialism.** ▸**iˈdealist** *n* ▸**iˌdealˈistic** *adj* ▸**iˌdealˈistically** *adv*

idealize ❶ *or* **idealise** (aɪˈdɪəˌlaɪz) *vb* **idealizes, idealizing, idealized** *or* **idealises, idealising, idealised. 1** to consider or represent (something) as ideal. **2** (*tr*) to portray as ideal; glorify. **3** (*intr*) to form an ideal or ideals. ▸**iˌdealiˈzation** *or* **iˌdealiˈsation** *n* ▸**iˈdealˌizer** *or* **iˈdealˌiser** *n*

idée fixe ❶ *French.* (ide fiks) *n, pl* ***idées fixes*** (ide fiks). a fixed idea; obsession.

idem *Latin.* (ˈaɪdɛm, ˈɪdɛm) *pron, adj* the same: used to refer to an article, chapter, etc., previously cited.

identic (aɪˈdɛntɪk) *adj Diplomacy.* (esp. of opinions expressed by two or more governments) having the same wording or intention regarding another power.

identical ❶ (aɪˈdɛntɪkᵊl) *adj* **1** being the same: *we got the identical hotel room as last year.* **2** exactly alike or equal. **3** designating either or both of a pair of twins of the same sex who developed from a single fertilized ovum that split into two. Cf. **fraternal** (sense 3). [C17: from Med. L *identicus,* from L *idem* the same] ▸**iˈdentically** *adv*

identification ❶ (aɪˌdɛntɪfɪˈkeɪʃən) *n* **1** the act of identifying or the state of being identified. **2a** something that identifies a person or thing. **2b** (*as modifier*): *an identification card.* **3** *Psychol.* **3a** the process of recognizing specific objects as the result of remembering. **3b** the process by which one incorporates aspects of another person's personality. **3c** the transferring of a response from one situation to another because the two bear similar features.

identification parade *n* a group of persons, including one suspected of a crime, assembled for the purpose of discovering whether a witness can identify the suspect.

identify ❶ (aɪˈdɛntɪˌfaɪ) *vb* **identifies, identifying, identified.** (*mainly tr*) **1** to prove or recognize as being a certain person or thing; determine the identity of. **2** to consider as the same or equivalent. **3** (*also intr; often* foll. by *with*) to consider (oneself) as similar to another. **4** to determine the taxonomic classification of (a plant or animal). **5** (*intr;* usually foll. by *with*) *Psychol.* to engage in identification. ▸**iˈdentiˌfiable** *adj* ▸**iˈdentiˌfiableness** *n* ▸**iˈdentiˌfier** *n*

Identikit (aɪˈdɛntɪˌkɪt) *n Trademark.* **1a** a set of transparencies of typical facial characteristics that can be superimposed on one another to build up a picture of a person sought by the police. **1b** (*as modifier*): *an Identikit picture.* **2** (*modifier*) artificially created by copying different elements in an attempt to form a whole: *an Identikit pop group.*

identity ❶ (aɪˈdɛntɪtɪ) *n, pl* **identities. 1** the state of having unique identifying characteristics. **2** the individual characteristics by which a person or thing is recognized. **3** the state of being the same in nature, quality, etc.: *linked by the identity of their tastes.* **4** the state of being the same as a person or thing described or known: *the identity of the stolen goods was soon established.* **5** *Maths.* **5a** an equation that is valid for all values of its variables, as in $(x-y)(x+y) = x^2 - y^2$. Often denoted by the symbol ≡. **5b** Also called: **identity element.** a member of a set that when operating on another member, *x,* produces that member *x:* the identity for multiplication of numbers is 1 since $x.1 = 1.x = x$. **6** *Logic.* the relationship between an object and itself. **7** *Austral. inf.* a well-known local person; figure: *a Barwidgee identity.* **8** *Austral. & NZ inf.* an eccentric; character: *an old identity in the town.* [C16: from LL *identitās,* from L *idem* the same]

identity card *n* a card that establishes a person's identity, esp. one issued to all members of the population in wartime, to the staff of an organization, etc.

ideo- *combining form.* of or indicating idea or ideas: *ideology.* [from F *idéo-,* from Gk *idea* IDEA]

ideogram (ˈɪdɪəʊˌgræm) *or* **ideograph** (ˈɪdɪəʊˌgrɑːf) *n* **1** a sign or symbol, used in a writing system such as that of China, that directly represents a concept or thing, rather than a word for it. **2** any graphic sign or symbol, such as % or &.

ideography (ˌɪdɪˈɒgrəfɪ) *n* the use of ideograms to communicate ideas.

ideology ❶ (ˌaɪdɪˈɒlədʒɪ) *n, pl* **ideologies. 1** a body of ideas that reflects the beliefs of a nation, political system, class, etc. **2** speculation that is imaginary or visionary. **3** the study of the nature and origin of ideas. ▸**ideological** (ˌaɪdɪəˈlɒdʒɪkᵊl) *or* ˌ**ideoˈlogic** *adj* ▸ˌ**ideoˈlogically** *adv* ▸ˌ**ideˈologist** *or* ˈ**ideoˌlogue** *n*

ides (aɪdz) *n* (*functioning as sing*) (in the Roman calendar) the 15th day in March, May, July, and October and the 13th day of each other month. [C15: from OF, from L *īdūs* (pl), from ?]

id est *Latin.* (ˈɪd ˈɛst) the full form of **i.e.**

idiocy ❶ (ˈɪdɪəsɪ) *n, pl* **idiocies. 1** (*not in technical usage*) severe mental retardation. **2** foolishness; stupidity. **3** a foolish act or remark.

idiom ❶ (ˈɪdɪəm) *n* **1** a group of words whose meaning cannot be predicted from the constituent words: (*It was raining*) *cats and dogs.* **2** linguistic usage that is grammatical and natural to native speakers. **3** the characteristic vocabulary or usage of a specific human group or subject. **4** the characteristic artistic style of an individual, school, etc. [C16: from L *idiōma* peculiarity of language, from Gk *idios* private, separate] ▸**idiomatic** (ˌɪdɪəˈmætɪk) *adj* ▸ˌ**idioˈmatically** *adv*

idiosyncrasy ❶ (ˌɪdɪəʊˈsɪŋkrəsɪ) *n, pl* **idiosyncrasies. 1** a tendency, type of behaviour, etc., of a person; quirk. **2** the composite physical or psychological make-up of a person. **3** an abnormal reaction of an individual to specific foods, drugs, etc. [C17: from Gk, from *idios* private, separate + *sunkrasis* mixture, temperament] ▸**idiosyncratic** (ˌɪdɪəʊsɪŋˈkrætɪk) *adj* ▸ˌ**idiosynˈcratically** *adv*

idiot ❶ (ˈɪdɪət) *n* **1** a person with severe mental retardation. **2** a foolish or senseless person. [C13: from L *idiōta* ignorant person, from Gk *idiōtēs* private person, ignoramus]

idiot board *n* a slang name for **Autocue.**

idiot box *n Sl.* a television set.

idiotic ❶ (ˌɪdɪˈɒtɪk) *adj* of or resembling an idiot; foolish; senseless. ▸ˌ**idiˈotically** *adv*

idiot savant (ˈiːdjəʊ sæˈvɑ̃, ˈɪdɪət ˈsævənt) *n, pl* **idiots savants** (ˈiːdjəʊ sæˈvɑ̃) *or* **idiot savants.** a person of subnormal intelligence who performs brilliantly at some specialized intellectual task.

idiot tape *n Computing.* a tape that prints out information in a continuous stream, with no line breaks.

idle ❶ (ˈaɪdᵊl) *adj* **1** unemployed or unoccupied; inactive. **2** not operating or being used. **3** (of money) not used to earn interest, etc. **4** not wanting to work; lazy. **5** (*usually prenominal*) frivolous or trivial: *idle pleasures.* **6** ineffective or powerless; vain. **7** without basis; unfounded. ◆ *vb* **idles, idling, idled. 8** (when *tr,* often foll. by *away*) to waste or pass

THESAURUS

idealist *n* **1** = **romantic,** dreamer, Utopian, visionary

idealistic *adj* **1** = **perfectionist,** impracticable, optimistic, quixotic, romantic, starry-eyed, Utopian, visionary
Antonyms *adj* down-to-earth, practical, pragmatic, realistic, sensible

idealization *n* **2** = **glorification,** ennoblement, exaltation, magnification, worship

idealize *vb* **2** = **romanticize,** apotheosize, deify, ennoble, exalt, glorify, magnify, put on a pedestal, worship

ideally *adv* **5** = **in a perfect world,** all things being equal, if one had one's way, under the best of circumstances

idée fixe *n* = **obsession,** bee in one's bonnet, fixation, fixed idea, hobbyhorse, monomania, one-track mind (*inf.*), preoccupation, thing (*inf.*)

identical *adj* **1, 2** = **alike,** a dead ringer (*sl.*), corresponding, duplicate, equal, equivalent, indistinguishable, interchangeable, like, like two peas in a pod, matching, selfsame, the same, twin
Antonyms *adj* different, disparate, distinct, diverse, separate, unlike

identifiable *adj* **1** = **noticeable,** ascertainable, detectable, discernible, distinguishable, known, recognizable, unmistakable

identification *n* **1** = **recognition,** cataloguing, classifying, establishment of identity, labelling, naming, pinpointing **2** = **identity card,** credentials, ID, letters of introduction, papers **3** = **sympathy,** association, connection, empathy, fellow feeling, involvement, rapport, relationship

identify *vb* **1** = **recognize,** catalogue, classify, diagnose, flag, label, make out, name, pick out, pinpoint, place, put one's finger on (*inf.*), single out, spot, tag **3** *with* **with** = **relate to,** ally with, associate with, empathize with, feel for, put in the same category as, put oneself in the place *or* shoes of, respond to, see through another's eyes, think of in connection with

identity *n* **2** = **existence,** distinctiveness, individuality, oneness, particularity, personality, self, selfhood, singularity, uniqueness **3** = **sameness,** accord, correspondence, empathy, rapport, unanimity, unity

ideology *n* **1** = **philosophy,** articles of faith, belief(s), creed, dogma, ideas, principles, tenets, *Weltanschauung,* world view

idiocy *n* **2** = **foolishness,** abject stupidity, asininity, cretinism, fatuity, fatuousness, imbecility, inanity, insanity, lunacy, senselessness, tomfoolery
Antonyms *n* acumen, sagacity, sanity, sense, soundness, wisdom

idiom *n* **1** = **phrase,** expression, locution, set phrase, turn of phrase **2, 3** = **language,** jargon, mode of expression, parlance, style, talk, usage, vernacular

idiomatic *adj* **2** = **vernacular,** dialectal, native

idiosyncrasy *n* **1** = **peculiarity,** affectation, characteristic, eccentricity, habit, mannerism, oddity, personal trait, quirk, singularity, trick

idiosyncratic *adj* **1** = **distinctive,** individual, individualistic, peculiar

idiot *n* **2** = **fool,** ass, berk (*Brit. sl.*), blockhead, booby, charlie (*Brit. inf.*), chump, coot, cretin, dimwit (*inf.*), dork (*sl.*), dunderhead, geek (*sl.*), halfwit, imbecile, jerk (*sl., chiefly US & Canad.*), lamebrain (*inf.*), mooncalf, moron, nerd *or* nurd (*sl.*), nincompoop, nitwit (*inf.*), numbskull *or* numskull, oaf, prat (*sl.*), schmuck (*US sl.*), simpleton, twit (*inf., chiefly Brit.*)

idiotic *adj* = **foolish,** asinine, braindead (*inf.*), crackpot (*inf.*), crazy, daft (*inf.*), dumb (*inf.*), dumb-ass (*sl.*), fatuous, foolhardy, halfwitted, harebrained, imbecile, imbecilic, inane, insane, loopy (*inf.*), lunatic, moronic, senseless, stupid, unintelligent
Antonyms *adj* brilliant, commonsensical, intelligent, sensible, thoughtful, wise

idle *adj* **1** = **inactive,** dead, empty, gathering dust, jobless, mothballed, out of action *or* operation, out of work, redundant, stationary, ticking over, unemployed, unoccupied, unused, vacant **4** = **lazy,** good-for-nothing, indolent, lackadaisical, shiftless, slothful, sluggish **5** = **trivial,** frivolous, insignificant, irrelevant, nugatory, superficial, unhelpful, unnecessary **6** = **useless,** abortive, bootless, fruitless, futile, groundless,

(time) fruitlessly or inactively. **9** (*intr*) (of a shaft, etc.) to turn without doing useful work. **10** (*intr*) (of an engine) to run at low speed with the transmission disengaged. [OE *īdel*]
▸**'idleness** *n* ▸**'idly** *adv*

idle pulley *or* **idler pulley** *n* a freely rotating pulley used to control the tension or direction of a belt. Also called: **idler.**

idler ❶ ('aɪdlə) *n* **1** a person who idles. **2** another name for **idle pulley** or **idle wheel.**

idle wheel *n* a gearwheel interposed between two others to transmit torque without changing the direction of rotation or the velocity ratio. Also called: **idler.**

idol ❶ ('aɪdᵊl) *n* **1** a material object that is worshipped as a god. **2** *Christianity, Judaism.* any being (other than the one God) to which divine honour is paid. **3** a person who is revered, admired, or highly loved. [C13: from LL, from L: image, from Gk, from *eidos* shape, form]

idolatry ❶ (aɪ'dɒlətrɪ) *n* **1** the worship of idols. **2** great devotion or reverence.
▸**i'dolater** *n or* **i'dolatress** *fem n* ▸**i'dolatrous** *adj*

idolize ❶ *or* **idolise** ('aɪdəˌlaɪz) *vb* **idolizes, idolizing, idolized** *or* **idolises, idolising, idolised. 1** (*tr*) to admire or revere greatly. **2** (*tr*) to worship as an idol. **3** (*intr*) to worship idols.
▸**ˌidoli'zation** *or* **ˌidoli'sation** *n* ▸**'idolˌizer** *or* **'idolˌiser** *n*

idolum (ɪ'dəʊlʊm) *n* **1** a mental picture; idea. **2** a false idea; fallacy. [C17: from L: IDOL]

IDP *abbrev. for* integrated data processing.

idyll ❶ *or US* (*sometimes*) **idyl** ('ɪdɪl) *n* **1** a poem or prose work describing an idealized rural life, pastoral scenes, etc. **2** a charming or picturesque scene or event. **3** a piece of music with a pastoral character. [C17: from L, from Gk *eidullion,* from *eidos* shape, (literary) form]
▸**i'dyllic** *adj* ▸**i'dyllically** *adv*

IE *abbrev. for* Indo-European (languages).

i.e. *abbrev. for* id est. [L: that is (to say); in other words]

-ie *suffix forming nouns.* a variant of **-y**²: *groupie.*

IEE *abbrev. for* Institution of Electrical Engineers.

-ier *suffix forming nouns.* a variant of **-eer:** *brigadier.* [from OE *-ere* -ER¹ or (in some words) from OF *-ier,* from L *-ārius* -ARY]

if ❶ (ɪf) *conj* (*subordinating*) **1** in case that, or on condition that: *if you try hard it might work.* **2** used to introduce an indirect question. In this sense, *if* approaches the meaning of *whether.* **3** even though: *an attractive if awkward girl.* **4a** used to introduce expressions of desire, with *only: if I had only known.* **4b** used to introduce exclamations of surprise, dismay, etc.: *if this doesn't top everything!* ◆ *n* **5** an uncertainty or doubt: *the big if is whether our plan will work.* **6** a condition or stipulation: *I won't have any ifs or buts.* [OE *gif*]

IF *or* **i.f.** *Electronics. abbrev. for* intermediate frequency.

IFA *abbrev. for* independent financial adviser.

IFC *abbrev. for* International Finance Corporation.

-iferous *suffix forming adjectives.* containing or yielding: *carboniferous.*

iffy ❶ ('ɪfɪ) *adj* **iffier, iffiest.** *Inf.* uncertain or subject to contingency. [C20: from IF + -Y¹]

-ify *suffix forming verbs.* a variant of **-fy:** *intensify.*
▸**-ification** *suffix forming nouns.*

Igbo ('iːbəʊ) *n, pl* **Igbo** *or* **Igbos.** a variant spelling of **Ibo.**

igloo *or* **iglu** ('ɪgluː) *n, pl* **igloos** *or* **iglus. 1** a dome-shaped Eskimo house, built of blocks of solid snow. **2** a hollow made by a seal in the snow over its breathing hole in the ice. [C19: from Eskimo *igdlu* house]

igneous ('ɪgnɪəs) *adj* **1** (of rocks) derived from magma or lava that has solidified on or below the earth's surface. **2** of or relating to fire. [C17: from L *igneus* fiery, from *ignis* fire]

ignis fatuus ('ɪgnɪs 'fætjʊəs) *n, pl* **ignes fatui** ('ɪgniːz 'fætjʊˌaɪ). another name for **will-o'-the-wisp.** [C16: from Med. L, lit.: foolish fire]

ignite ❶ (ɪg'naɪt) *vb* **ignites, igniting, ignited. 1** to catch fire or set fire to; burn or cause to burn. **2** (*tr*) *Chem.* to heat strongly. [C17: from L, from *ignis* fire]
▸**ig'nitable** *or* **ig'nitible** *adj* ▸**igˌnita'bility** *or* **igˌniti'bility** *n* ▸**ig'niter** *n*

ignition (ɪg'nɪʃən) *n* **1** the act or process of initiating combustion. **2** the process of igniting the fuel in an internal-combustion engine. **3** (preceded by *the*) the devices used to ignite the fuel in an internal-combustion engine.

ignition coil *n* an induction coil that supplies the high voltage to the sparking plugs on an internal-combustion engine.

ignition key *n* the key used in a motor vehicle to turn the switch that connects the battery to the ignition system.

ignitron (ɪg'naɪtrɒn, 'ɪgnɪˌtrɒn) *n* a rectifier controlled by a subsidiary electrode, the igniter, partially immersed in a mercury cathode. A current passed between igniter and cathode forms a hot spot sufficient to strike an arc between cathode and anode. [C20: from *igniter* + ELECTRON]

ignoble ❶ (ɪg'nəʊbᵊl) *adj* **1** dishonourable; base; despicable. **2** of low birth or origins; humble; common. **3** of low quality; inferior. [C16: from L, from IN-¹ + OL *gnōbilis* NOBLE]
▸**ˌigno'bility** *or* **ig'nobleness** *n* ▸**ig'nobly** *adv*

ignominy ❶ ('ɪgnəˌmɪnɪ) *n, pl* **ignominies. 1** disgrace or public shame; dishonour. **2** a cause of disgrace; a shameful act. [C16: from L *ignōminia* disgrace, from *ig-* (see IN-²) + *nōmen* name, reputation]
▸**ˌigno'minious** *adj* ▸**ˌigno'miniously** *adv* ▸**ˌigno'miniousness** *n*

ignoramus ❶ (ˌɪgnə'reɪməs) *n, pl* **ignoramuses.** an ignorant person; fool. [C16: from legal L, lit.: we have no knowledge of, from L *ignōrāre* to be ignorant of; see IGNORE; modern usage originated from use of *Ignoramus* as the name of an unlettered lawyer in a play by G. Ruggle, 17th-century E dramatist]

ignorance ❶ ('ɪgnərəns) *n* lack of knowledge, information, or education; the state of being ignorant.

ignorant ❶ ('ɪgnərənt) *adj* **1** lacking in knowledge or education; unenlightened. **2** (*postpositive;* often foll. by *of*) lacking in awareness or knowledge (of): *ignorant of the law.* **3** resulting from or showing lack of knowledge or awareness: *an ignorant remark.*
▸**'ignorantly** *adv*

ignore ❶ (ɪg'nɔː) *vb* **ignores, ignoring, ignored.** (*tr*) to fail or refuse to notice; disregard. [C17: from L *ignōrāre* not to know, from *ignārus* ignorant of]
▸**ig'norer** *n*

THESAURUS

ineffective, of no avail, otiose, pointless, unavailing, unproductive, unsuccessful, vain, worthless ◆ *vb* **8** *often with* **away = laze,** dally, dawdle, fool, fritter, hang out (*inf.*), kill time, loaf, loiter, lounge, potter, take it easy, vegetate, waste, while

Antonyms *adj* ≠ **inactive, lazy:** active, busy, employed, energetic, functional, industrious, occupied, operative, working ≠ **trivial:** important, meaningful ≠ **useless:** advantageous, effective, fruitful, profitable, useful, worthwhile

idleness *n* **1 = inactivity,** inaction, leisure, time on one's hands, unemployment **4 = laziness,** hibernation, inertia, shiftlessness, sloth, sluggishness, torpor, vegetating **8 = loafing,** dilly-dallying (*inf.*), lazing, pottering, skiving (*Brit. sl.*), time-wasting, trifling

idler *n* **1 = loafer,** clock-watcher, couch potato (*sl.*), dawdler, deadbeat (*inf., chiefly US & Canad.*), dodger, drone, laggard, layabout, lazybones, lounger, malingerer, shirker, skiver (*Brit. sl.*), slacker, sloth, slouch (*inf.*), sluggard, time-waster

idly *adv* **4 = lazily,** apathetically, casually, inactively, indolently, inertly, lackadaisically, languidly, languorously, lethargically, passively, shiftlessly, slothfully, sluggishly, unthinkingly

Antonyms *adv* actively, animatedly, busily, dynamically, energetically, industriously

idol *n* **1, 2 = graven image,** deity, god, image, pagan symbol **3 = hero,** beloved, darling, fave (*inf.*), favourite, pet, pin-up (*sl.*), superstar

idolater *n* **1 = heathen,** idol-worshipper, pagan **2 = admirer,** adorer, devotee, idolizer, votary, worshipper

idolatrous *adj* **2 = adoring,** adulatory, reverential, uncritical, worshipful

idolatry *n* **2 = adoration,** adulation, apotheosis, deification, exaltation, glorification, hero worship, idolizing

idolize *vb* **1 = worship,** admire, adore, apotheosize, bow down before, deify, dote upon, exalt, glorify, hero-worship, look up to, love, revere, reverence, venerate, worship to excess

idyllic *adj* **2 = idealized,** arcadian, charming, halcyon, heavenly, ideal, out of this world, pastoral, peaceful, picturesque, rustic, unspoiled

if *conj* **1 = provided,** admitting, allowing, assuming, granting, in case, on condition that, on the assumption that, providing, supposing, though, whenever, wherever **2 = whether** ◆ *n* **5 = doubt,** condition, hesitation, stipulation, uncertainty

iffy *adj* **= uncertain,** chancy (*inf.*), conditional, doubtful, in the lap of the gods, problematical, undecided, unpredictable, up in the air

ignite *vb* **1 = set fire to,** burn, burst into flames, fire, flare up, inflame, kindle, light, put a match to (*inf.*), set alight, take fire, torch, touch off

ignoble *adj* **1 = dishonourable,** abject, base, contemptible, craven, dastardly, degenerate, degraded, despicable, disgraceful, heinous, infamous, low, mean, petty, shabby, shameless, unworthy, vile, wretched **2 = lowly,** baseborn (*arch.*), common, humble, lowborn (*rare*), mean, of humble birth, peasant, plebeian, vulgar

ignominious *adj* **1 = humiliating,** abject, despicable, discreditable, disgraceful, dishonourable, disreputable, indecorous, inglorious, mortifying, scandalous, shameful, sorry, undignified

Antonyms *adj* creditable, honourable, reputable, worthy

ignominy *n* **1 = disgrace,** bad odour, contempt, discredit, dishonour, disrepute, humiliation, infamy, mortification, obloquy, odium, opprobrium, reproach, shame, stigma

Antonyms *n* credit, honour, repute

ignoramus *n* **= dunce,** ass, blockhead, bonehead (*sl.*), dolt, donkey, duffer (*inf.*), dullard, fathead (*inf.*), fool, illiterate, lowbrow, numbskull *or* numskull, simpleton

ignorance *n* **= lack of education,** benightedness, greenness, inexperience, innocence, nescience (*literary*), oblivion, unawareness, unconsciousness, unfamiliarity

Antonyms *n* comprehension, enlightenment, insight, intelligence, knowledge, understanding, wisdom

ignorant *adj* **1 = uneducated,** as green as grass, green, illiterate, naive, unaware, uncultivated, unknowledgeable, unlearned, unlettered, unread, untaught, untrained, untutored, wet behind the ears (*inf.*) **2 = uninformed,** benighted, blind to, inexperienced, innocent, in the dark about, oblivious, out of the loop, unaware, unconscious, unenlightened, uninitiated, unknowing, unschooled, unwitting **3 = insensitive,** crass, crude, gross, half-baked (*inf.*), rude, shallow, superficial, uncomprehending, unscholarly

Antonyms *adj* ≠ **uneducated:** astute, brilliant, cultured, educated, knowledgeable, learned, literate, sagacious, sophisticated, wise ≠ **uninformed:** aware, conscious, informed, in the loop

ignore *vb* **= overlook,** be oblivious to, blank (*sl.*), bury one's head in the sand, cold-shoulder, cut, discount, disregard, give the cold shoulder to, neglect, pass over, pay no attention to, reject, send (someone) to Coventry, shut one's eyes to, take no notice of, turn a

iguana (ɪ'gwɑːnə) *n* either of two large tropical American arboreal herbivorous lizards, esp. the common iguana, having a greyish-green body with a row of spines along the back. [C16: from Sp., from S Amerind *iwana*]
▸**i'guanian** *n, adj*

iguanodon (ɪ'gwɑːnəˌdɒn) *n* a massive herbivorous long-tailed bipedal dinosaur common in Europe and N Africa in Jurassic and Cretaceous times. [C19: NL, from IGUANA + Gk *odōn* tooth]

IHC (in New Zealand) *abbrev. for* intellectually handicapped child.

IHS the first three letters of the name Jesus in Greek (ΙΗΣΟΥΣ), often used as a Christian emblem.

ikat ('iːkæt) *n* a method of creating patterns in fabric by tie-dyeing the yarn before weaving. [C20: from Malay, lit.: to tie, bind]

ikebana (ˌiːkə'bɑːnə) *n* the Japanese decorative art of flower arrangement.

ikon ('aɪkɒn) *n* a variant spelling of **icon.**

il- *prefix* a variant of **in-**[1] and **in-**[2] before *l*.

-ile *or* **-il** *suffix forming adjectives and nouns.* indicating capability, liability, or a relationship with something: *agile; juvenile.* [via F from L or directly from L *-ilis*]
▸**-ility** *suffix forming nouns.*

ileitis (ˌɪlɪ'aɪtɪs) *n* inflammation of the ileum.

ileostomy (ˌɪlɪ'ɒstəmɪ) *n, pl* **ileostomies.** the surgical formation of a permanent opening through the abdominal wall into the ileum.

ileum ('ɪlɪəm) *n* the part of the small intestine between the jejunum and the caecum. [C17: NL, from L *īlium, īleum* flank, groin, from ?]
▸**'ileˌac** *adj*

ilex ('aɪleks) *n* **1** any of a genus of trees or shrubs such as the holly and inkberry. **2** another name for the **holm oak.** [C16: from L]

ilium ('ɪlɪəm) *n, pl* **ilia** (-ɪə). the uppermost and widest of the three sections of the hipbone.

ilk ❶ (ɪlk) *n* **1** a type; class; sort (esp. in **of that, his,** etc., **ilk**): *people of that ilk should not be allowed here.* **2 of that ilk.** *Scot.* of the place of the same name: to indicate that the person is laird of the place named: *Moncrieff of that ilk.* [OE *ilca* the same family, same kind]

> **USAGE NOTE** Although the use of *ilk* in sense 1 is sometimes condemned as being the result of a misunderstanding of the original Scottish expression *of that ilk*, it is nevertheless well established and generally acceptable.

ill ❶ (ɪl) *adj* **worse, worst. 1** (*usually postpositive*) not in good health; sick. **2** characterized by or intending harm, etc.; hostile: *ill deeds.* **3** causing pain, harm, adversity, etc. **4** ascribing or imputing evil to something referred to: *ill repute.* **5** promising an unfavourable outcome; unpropitious: *an ill omen.* **6** harsh; lacking kindness: *ill will.* **7** not up to an acceptable standard; faulty: *ill manners.* **8 ill at ease.** unable to relax; uncomfortable. ◆ *n* **9** evil or harm; misfortune; trouble. **10** a mild disease. ◆ *adv* **11** badly: *the title ill befits him.* **12** with difficulty; hardly: *he can ill afford the money.* **13** not rightly: *he ill deserves such good fortune.* [C11 (in the sense: evil): from ON *illr* bad]

ill. *abbrev. for:* **1** illustrated. **2** illustration.

I'll (aɪl) *contraction of* I will *or* I shall.

ill-advised ❶ *adj* **1** acting without reasonable care or thought: *you would be ill-advised to sell your house now.* **2** badly thought out; not or insufficiently considered: *an ill-advised plan of action.*
▸**ill-advisedly** (ˌɪləd'vaɪzɪdlɪ) *adv*

ill-affected *adj* (often foll. by *towards*) not well disposed; disaffected.

ill-assorted ❶ *adj* badly matched; incompatible.

illative (ɪ'leɪtɪv) *adj* **1** relating to inference; inferential. **2** *Grammar.* denoting a word or morpheme used to signal inference, for example *so* or *therefore.* **3** (esp. in Finnish grammar) denoting a case of nouns expressing a relation of motion or direction, usually translated by *into* or *towards.* ◆ *n* **4** *Grammar.* **4a** the illative case. **4b** an illative word or speech element. [C16: from LL *illātīvus* inferring, concluding]
▸**il'latively** *adv*

ill-bred ❶ *adj* badly brought up; lacking good manners.
▸ˌ**ill-'breeding** *n*

ill-considered ❶ *adj* done without due consideration; not thought out: *an ill-considered decision.*

ill-defined ❶ *adj* imperfectly defined; having no clear outline.

ill-disposed ❶ *adj* (often foll. by *towards*) not kindly disposed.

illegal ❶ (ɪ'liːgᵊl) *adj* **1** forbidden by law; unlawful; illicit. **2** unauthorized or prohibited by a code of official or accepted rules. ◆ *n* **3** a person who has entered or attempted to enter a country illegally.
▸**il'legally** *adv* ▸ˌ**ille'gality** *n*

illegible ❶ (ɪ'ledʒɪbᵊl) *adj* unable to be read or deciphered.
▸**ilˌlegi'bility** *or* **il'legibleness** *n* ▸**il'legibly** *adv*

illegitimate ❶ (ˌɪlɪ'dʒɪtɪmɪt) *adj* **1a** born of parents who were not married to each other at the time of birth; bastard. **1b** occurring outside marriage: *of illegitimate birth.* **2** illegal; unlawful. **3** contrary to logic; incorrectly reasoned. ◆ *n* **4** an illegitimate person; bastard.
▸ˌ**ille'gitimacy** *or* ˌ**ille'gitimateness** *n* ▸ˌ**ille'gitimately** *adv*

ill-fated ❶ *adj* doomed or unlucky.

ill-favoured ❶ *adj* **1** unattractive or repulsive in appearance; ugly. **2** disagreeable or objectionable.
▸ˌ**ill-'favouredly** *adv* ▸ˌ**ill-'favouredness** *n*

ill feeling ❶ *n* hostile feeling; animosity.

ill-founded ❶ *adj* not founded on true or reliable premises; unsubstantiated.

ill-gotten *adj* obtained dishonestly or illegally (esp. in **ill-gotten gains**).

ill humour ❶ *n* a disagreeable or sullen mood; bad temper.
▸ˌ**ill-'humoured** *adj* ▸ˌ**ill-'humouredly** *adv*

THESAURUS

blind eye to, turn a deaf ear to, turn one's back on

Antonyms *vb* acknowledge, heed, note, pay attention to, recognize, regard

ilk *n* **1** = **type**, brand, breed, character, class, description, disposition, kidney, kind, sort, stamp, style, variety

ill *adj* **1** = **unwell**, ailing, at death's door, dicky (*Brit. inf.*), diseased, funny (*inf.*), green about the gills, indisposed, infirm, laid up (*inf.*), off-colour, out of sorts (*inf.*), poorly (*inf.*), queasy, queer, seedy (*inf.*), sick, under the weather (*inf.*), unhealthy, valetudinarian **2** = **harmful**, bad, damaging, deleterious, detrimental, evil, foul, iniquitous, injurious, ruinous, unfortunate, unlucky, vile, wicked, wrong **5** = **ominous**, disturbing, foreboding, inauspicious, sinister, threatening, unfavourable, unhealthy, unlucky, unpromising, unpropitious, unwholesome **6** = **hostile**, acrimonious, adverse, antagonistic, cantankerous, cross, harsh, hateful, hurtful, inimical, malevolent, malicious, sullen, surly, unfriendly, unkind **8 ill at ease** = **uncomfortable**, anxious, awkward, disquieted, disturbed, edgy, faltering, fidgety, hesitant, like a fish out of water, nervous, neurotic, on edge, on pins and needles (*inf.*), on tenterhooks, out of place, restless, self-conscious, strange, tense, twitchy (*inf.*), uneasy, unquiet, unrelaxed, unsettled, unsure ◆ *n* **9** = **harm**, affliction, evil, hardship, hurt, injury, misery, misfortune, pain, trial, tribulation, trouble, unpleasantness, wickedness, woe ◆ *adv* **11** = **badly**, hard, inauspiciously, poorly, unfavourably, unfortunately, unluckily **12** = **hardly**, barely, by no means, insufficiently, scantily

Antonyms *adj* ≠ **unwell:** hale, healthy, strong, well ≠ **harmful:** favourable, good ≠ **hostile:** generous, kind ◆ *n* ≠ **harm:** good, kindness ◆ *adv* ≠ **hardly:** easily, well

ill-advised *adj* **1, 2** = **misguided**, foolhardy, foolish, ill-considered, ill-judged, impolitic, imprudent, inappropriate, incautious, indiscreet, injudicious, overhasty, rash, reckless, short-sighted, thoughtless, unseemly, unwise, wrong-headed

Antonyms *adj* appropriate, cautious, discreet, judicious, politic, prudent, seemly, sensible, wise

ill-assorted *adj* = **incompatible**, incongruous, inharmonious, mismatched, uncongenial, unsuited

ill-bred *adj* = **bad-mannered**, boorish, churlish, coarse, crass, discourteous, ill-mannered, impolite, indelicate, rude, uncivil, uncivilized, uncouth, ungallant, ungentlemanly, unladylike, unmannerly, unrefined, vulgar

Antonyms *adj* civil, courteous, delicate, mannerly, refined, urbane, well-bred

ill-considered *adj* = **unwise**, careless, hasty, heedless, improvident, imprudent, injudicious, overhasty, precipitate, rash

ill-defined *adj* = **unclear**, blurred, dim, fuzzy, indistinct, nebulous, shadowy, vague, woolly

Antonyms *adj* apparent, bold, clear, conspicuous, cut-and-dried, distinct, evident, manifest, obvious, plain

ill-disposed *adj* = **unfriendly**, against, antagonistic, anti (*inf.*), antipathetic, averse, disobliging, down on (*inf.*), hostile, inimical, opposed, uncooperative, unwelcoming

Antonyms *adj* amicable, cooperative, friendly, obliging, welcoming, well-disposed

illegal *adj* **1** = **unlawful**, actionable (*Law*), banned, black-market, bootleg, criminal, felonious, forbidden, illicit, lawless, off limits, outlawed, prohibited, proscribed, unauthorized, unconstitutional, under-the-counter, under-the-table, unlicensed, unofficial, wrongful

Antonyms *adj* lawful, legal, licit, permissible

illegality *n* **1** = **crime**, criminality, felony, illegitimacy, illicitness, lawlessness, unlawfulness, wrong, wrongness

illegible *adj* = **indecipherable**, crabbed, faint, hard to make out, hieroglyphic, obscure, scrawled, undecipherable, unreadable

Antonyms *adj* clear, decipherable, legible, plain, readable

illegitimacy *n* **1** = **bastardy**, bastardism **2** = **illegality**, illicitness, irregularity, unconstitutionality, unlawfulness

illegitimate *adj* **1** = **born out of wedlock**, baseborn, bastard, born on the wrong side of the blanket, fatherless, misbegotten (*literary*), natural, spurious (*rare*) **2** = **unlawful**, illegal, illicit, improper, unauthorized, unconstitutional, under-the-table, unsanctioned **3** = **invalid**, illogical, incorrect, spurious, unsound

Antonyms *adj* ≠ **unlawful:** authorized, constitutional, lawful, legal, legitimate, proper, sanctioned

ill-fated *adj* = **doomed**, blighted, hapless, ill-omened, ill-starred, luckless, star-crossed, unfortunate, unhappy, unlucky

ill-favoured *adj* **1** = **ugly**, hideous, no oil painting, plain, repulsive, unattractive, unlovely, unprepossessing, unsightly

ill feeling *n* = **hostility**, animosity, animus, antagonism, bad blood, bitterness, chip on one's shoulder, disgruntlement, dissatisfaction, dudgeon (*arch.*), enmity, frustration, hard feelings, ill will, indignation, offence, rancour, resentment

Antonyms *n* amity, benevolence, favour, friendship, goodwill, satisfaction

ill-founded *adj* = **groundless**, baseless, empty, idle, unjustified, unproven, unreliable, unsubstantiated, unsupported

ill humour *n* = **irascibility**, (bad) mood, (bad) temper, bate, crabbiness, crossness, disagreeableness, grumpiness, irritability, moodiness, moroseness, petulance, pique, sharpness, spleen, sulkiness, sulks, tartness, testiness

ill-humoured *adj* = **bad-tempered**, acrimonious, crabbed, crabby, cross, disagreeable, grumpy, impatient, irascible, irritable, liverish,

illiberal Ⓣ (ɪˈlɪbərəl) *adj* **1** narrow-minded; prejudiced; bigoted; intolerant. **2** not generous; mean. **3** lacking in culture or refinement.
▸**il͵liberˈality** *n* ▸**ilˈliberally** *adv*

illicit Ⓣ (ɪˈlɪsɪt) *adj* **1** another word for **illegal. 2** not allowed or approved by common custom, rule, or standard: *illicit sexual relations.*
▸**ilˈlicitly** *adv* ▸**ilˈlicitness** *n*

illimitable Ⓣ (ɪˈlɪmɪtəbᵊl) *adj* limitless; boundless.
▸**il͵limitaˈbility** *or* **ilˈlimitableness** *n*

illiterate Ⓣ (ɪˈlɪtərɪt) *adj* **1** unable to read and write. **2** violating accepted standards in reading and writing: *an illiterate scrawl.* **3** uneducated, ignorant, or uncultured: *scientifically illiterate.* ◆ *n* **4** an illiterate person.
▸**ilˈliteracy** *or* **ilˈliterateness** *n* ▸**ilˈliterately** *adv*

ill-judged Ⓣ *adj* rash; ill-advised.

ill-mannered Ⓣ *adj* having bad manners; rude; impolite.
▸͵**ill-ˈmanneredly** *adv*

ill-natured Ⓣ *adj* naturally unpleasant and mean.
▸͵**ill-ˈnaturedly** *adv* ▸͵**ill-ˈnaturedness** *n*

illness Ⓣ (ˈɪlnɪs) *n* **1** a disease or indisposition; sickness. **2** a state of ill health.

illogical Ⓣ (ɪˈlɒdʒɪkᵊl) *adj* **1** characterized by lack of logic; senseless or unreasonable. **2** disregarding logical principles.
▸**illogicality** (ɪ͵lɒdʒɪˈkælɪtɪ) *or* **ilˈlogicalness** *n* ▸**ilˈlogically** *adv*

ill-starred Ⓣ *adj* unlucky; unfortunate; ill-fated.

ill temper Ⓣ *n* bad temper; irritability.
▸͵**ill-ˈtempered** *adj* ▸͵**ill-ˈtemperedly** *adv*

ill-timed Ⓣ *adj* occurring at or planned for an unsuitable time.

ill-treat Ⓣ *vb* (*tr*) to behave cruelly or harshly towards; misuse; maltreat.
▸͵**ill-ˈtreatment** *n*

illuminance (ɪˈluːmɪnəns) *n* the luminous flux incident on unit area of a surface. Sometimes called: **illumination.** Cf. **irradiance.**

illuminant (ɪˈluːmɪnənt) *n* **1** something that provides or gives off light. ◆ *adj* **2** giving off light; illuminating.

illuminate Ⓣ *vb* (ɪˈluːmɪ͵neɪt), **illuminates, illuminating, illuminated. 1** (*tr*) to throw light in or into; light up. **2** (*tr*) to make easily understood; clarify. **3** to adorn, decorate, or be decorated with lights. **4** (*tr*) to decorate (a letter, etc.) by the application of colours, gold, or silver. **5** (*intr*) to become lighted up. ◆ *adj* (ɪˈluːmɪnɪt, -͵neɪt). **6** *Arch.* made clear or bright with light. ◆ *n* (ɪˈluːmɪnɪt, -͵neɪt). **7** a person who claims to have special enlightenment. [C16: from L *illūmināre* to light up, from *lūmen* light]
▸**ilˈlumi͵nating** *adj* ▸**ilˈluminative** *adj* ▸**ilˈlumi͵nator** *n*

illuminati (ɪ͵luːmɪˈnɑːtiː) *pl n, sing* **illuminato** (-təʊ). **1** a group of persons claiming exceptional enlightenment on some subject, esp. religion. **2** (*cap.*) any of several groups of illuminati, esp. in 18th-century France and Bavaria or 16th-century Spain. [C16: from L, lit.: the enlightened ones, from *illūmināre* to ILLUMINATE]

illumination Ⓣ (ɪ͵luːmɪˈneɪʃən) *n* **1** the act of illuminating or the state of being illuminated. **2** a source of light. **3** (*often pl*) *Chiefly Brit.* a light or lights used as decoration in streets, parks, etc. **4** spiritual or intellectual enlightenment; insight or understanding. **5** the act of making understood; clarification. **6** decoration in colours, gold, or silver used on some manuscripts. **7** *Physics.* another name (not in technical usage) for **illuminance.**

illumine (ɪˈluːmɪn) *vb* **illumines, illumining, illumined.** a literary word for **illuminate.** [C14: from L *illūmināre* to make light]
▸**ilˈluminable** *adj*

ill-use *vb* (ˈɪlˈjuːz), **ill-uses, ill-using, ill-used. 1** to use badly or cruelly; abuse; maltreat. ◆ *n* (ˈɪlˈjuːs), *also* **ill-usage. 2** harsh or cruel treatment; abuse.

illusion Ⓣ (ɪˈluːʒən) *n* **1** a false appearance or deceptive impression of reality: *the mirror gives an illusion of depth.* **2** a false or misleading perception or belief; delusion. **3** *Psychol.* a perception that is not true to reality, having been altered subjectively in the mind of the perceiver. See also **hallucination.** [C14: from L *illūsiō* deceit, from *illūdere* to sport with, from *ludus* game]
▸**ilˈlusionary** *or* **ilˈlusional** *adj* ▸**ilˈlusioned** *adj*

illusionism (ɪˈluːʒə͵nɪzəm) *n* **1** *Philosophy.* the doctrine that the external world exists only in illusory sense perceptions. **2** the use of highly illusory effects in art.

illusionist (ɪˈluːʒənɪst) *n* **1** a person given to illusions; visionary; dreamer. **2** *Philosophy.* a person who believes in illusionism. **3** an artist who practises illusionism. **4** a conjuror; magician.
▸**il͵lusionˈistic** *adj*

illusory Ⓣ (ɪˈluːsərɪ) *or* **illusive** (ɪˈluːsɪv) *adj* producing or based on illusion; deceptive or unreal.
▸**ilˈlusorily** *adv* ▸**ilˈlusoriness** *n*

> **USAGE NOTE** *Illusive* is sometimes wrongly used where *elusive* is meant: *they fought hard, but victory remained elusive* (not *illusive*).

illust. *or* **illus.** *abbrev. for:* **1** illustrated. **2** illustration.

illustrate Ⓣ (ˈɪlə͵streɪt) *vb* **illustrates, illustrating, illustrated. 1** to clarify or explain by use of examples, analogy, etc. **2** (*tr*) to be an example of. **3** (*tr*) to explain or decorate (a book, text, etc.) with pictures. [C16: from L, from *lustrāre* to purify, brighten; see LUSTRUM]
▸ˈ**illus͵trative** *adj* ▸ˈ**illus͵trator** *n*

THESAURUS

moody, morose, out of sorts, out of temper, petulant, sharp, snappish, snappy, sulky, sullen, tart, testy, tetchy, thin-skinned, touchy, unpleasant, waspish
Antonyms *adj* affable, agreeable, amiable, charming, congenial, delightful, genial, good-humoured, good-natured, pleasant

illiberal *adj* **1** = **intolerant**, bigoted, hidebound, narrow-minded, prejudiced, reactionary, small-minded, uncharitable, ungenerous **2** = **mean**, close-fisted, miserly, niggardly, parsimonious, selfish, sordid, stingy, tight, tight-arsed (*taboo sl.*), tight as a duck's arse (*taboo sl.*), tight-assed (*US taboo sl.*), tightfisted, ungenerous
Antonyms *adj* ≠ **intolerant:** broad-minded, charitable, generous, liberal, open-minded, politically correct *or* PC, right-on (*inf.*), tolerant

illicit *adj* **1** = **illegal**, black-market, bootleg, contraband, criminal, felonious, illegitimate, off limits, prohibited, unauthorized, unlawful, unlicensed **2** = **forbidden**, clandestine, furtive, guilty, immoral, improper, wrong
Antonyms *adj* ≠ **illegal:** above-board, lawful, legal, legitimate, licit, permissible

illimitable *adj* **1** = **unlimited**, boundless, eternal, immeasurable, immense, infinite, limitless, unbounded, unending, vast, without end

illiteracy *n* **1** = **lack of education**, benightedness, ignorance, illiterateness

illiterate *adj* **1** = **uneducated**, benighted, ignorant, uncultured, unlettered, untaught, untutored
Antonyms *adj* cultured, educated, lettered, literate, taught, tutored

ill-judged *adj* = **misguided**, foolish, ill-advised, ill-considered, injudicious, overhasty, rash, short-sighted, unwise, wrong-headed

ill-mannered *adj* = **rude**, badly behaved, boorish, churlish, coarse, discourteous, ill-behaved, ill-bred, impolite, insolent, loutish, uncivil, uncouth, unmannerly
Antonyms *adj* civil, courteous, cultivated, mannerly, polished, polite, refined, well-mannered

ill-natured *adj* = **unkind**, bad-tempered, catty (*inf.*), churlish, crabbed, cross, cross-grained, disagreeable, disobliging, malevolent, malicious, mean, nasty, perverse, petulant, shrewish, spiteful, sulky, sullen, surly, unfriendly, unpleasant
Antonyms *adj* agreeable, amiable, cheerful, congenial, friendly, good-natured, kind, obliging, pleasant

illness *n* **1, 2** = **sickness**, affliction, ailment, attack, complaint, disability, disease, disorder, ill health, indisposition, infirmity, lurgy (*inf.*), malady, malaise, poor health

illogical *adj* **1** = **irrational**, absurd, fallacious, faulty, inconclusive, inconsistent, incorrect, invalid, meaningless, senseless, sophistical, specious, spurious, unreasonable, unscientific, unsound
Antonyms *adj* coherent, consistent, correct, logical, rational, reasonable, scientific, sound, valid

ill-starred *adj* = **doomed**, hapless, ill-fated, ill-omened, inauspicious, star-crossed, unfortunate, unhappy, unlucky

ill temper *n* = **irascibility**, annoyance, bad temper, crossness, curtness, impatience, irritability, petulance, sharpness, spitefulness, tetchiness

ill-tempered *adj* = **irascible**, annoyed, bad-tempered, choleric, cross, curt, grumpy, ill-humoured, impatient, irritable, liverish, ratty (*Brit. & NZ inf.*), sharp, spiteful, testy, tetchy, touchy
Antonyms *adj* benign, cheerful, good-natured, mild-mannered, patient, pleasant, sweet-tempered

ill-timed *adj* = **inopportune**, awkward, inappropriate, inconvenient, inept, unseasonable, untimely, unwelcome
Antonyms *adj* appropriate, convenient, opportune, seasonable, timely, well-timed

ill-treat *vb* = **abuse**, damage, dump on (*sl., chiefly US*), handle roughly, harass, harm, harry, ill-use, injure, knock about *or* around, maltreat, mishandle, misuse, oppress, shit on (*taboo sl.*), wrong

ill-treatment *n* = **abuse**, damage, harm, ill-use, injury, mistreatment, misuse, rough handling

illuminate *vb* **1** = **light up**, brighten, illumine (*literary*), irradiate, light **2** = **clarify**, clear up, elucidate, enlighten, explain, explicate, give insight into, instruct, interpret, make clear, shed light on **3** = **decorate**, adorn, illustrate, ornament
Antonyms *vb* ≠ **light up:** black out, darken, dim, obscure, overshadow ≠ **clarify:** befog, cloud, dull, obfuscate, overcast, shade, veil

illuminating *adj* **2** = **informative**, enlightening, explanatory, helpful, instructive, revealing
Antonyms *adj* confusing, obscuring, puzzling, unhelpful

illumination *n* **1, 2** = **light**, beam, brightening, brightness, lighting, lighting up, lights, radiance, ray **3** *plural* = **lights**, decorations, fairy lights **4** = **enlightenment**, awareness, clarification, edification, insight, inspiration, instruction, perception, revelation, understanding

illusion *n* **1** = **fantasy**, chimera, daydream, figment of the imagination, hallucination, ignis fatuus, mirage, mockery, phantasm, semblance, will-o'-the-wisp **2** = **misconception**, deception, delusion, error, fallacy, false impression, fancy, misapprehension
Antonyms *n* actuality, fact, reality, truth

illusory *adj* = **unreal**, apparent, Barmecide, beguiling, chimerical, deceitful, deceptive, delusive, fallacious, false, hallucinatory, misleading, mistaken, seeming, sham, untrue
Antonyms *adj* authentic, down-to-earth, factual, genuine, real, reliable, solid, true

illustrate *vb* **1** = **demonstrate**, bring home, clarify, elucidate, emphasize, exemplify, exhibit, explain, explicate, instance, interpret, make clear, make plain, point up, show **3** = **draw**, adorn, decorate, depict, ornament, picture, sketch

illustrated *adj* **3** = **pictorial**, decorated, em-

illustration ❶ (ˌɪləˈstreɪʃən) *n* **1** pictorial matter used to explain or decorate a text. **2** an example: *an illustration of his ability.* **3** the act of illustrating or the state of being illustrated.
▸ˌ**illusˈtrational** *adj*

illustrious ❶ (ɪˈlʌstrɪəs) *adj* **1** of great renown; famous and distinguished. **2** glorious or great: *illustrious deeds.* [C16: from L *illustris* bright, famous, from *illūstrāre* to make light; see ILLUSTRATE]
▸**ilˈlustriously** *adv* ▸**ilˈlustriousness** *n*

ill will ❶ *n* hostile feeling; enmity; antagonism.

ILO *abbrev. for* International Labour Organisation.

IM *or* **i.m.** *abbrev. for* intramuscular(ly).

I'm (aɪm) *contraction of* I am.

im- *prefix* a variant of **in-**[1] and **in-**[2] before *b, m,* and *p.*

image ❶ (ˈɪmɪdʒ) *n* **1** a representation or likeness of a person or thing, esp. in sculpture. **2** an optically formed reproduction of an object, such as one formed by a lens or mirror. **3** a person or thing that resembles another closely; double or copy. **4** a mental picture; idea produced by the imagination. **5** the personality presented to the public by a person, organization, etc.: *a politician's image.* **6** the pattern of light that is focused onto the retina. **7** *Psychol.* the mental experience of something that is not immediately present to the senses, often involving memory. See also **imagery**. **8** a personification of a specified quality; epitome: *the image of good breeding.* **9** a mental picture or association of ideas evoked in a literary work. **10** a figure of speech such as a simile or metaphor. ◆ *vb* **images, imaging, imaged.** (*tr*) **11** to picture in the mind; imagine. **12** to make or reflect an image of. **13** to project or display on a screen, etc. **14** to portray or describe. **15** to be an example or epitome of; typify. [C13: from OF *imagene,* from L *imāgō* copy, representation; rel. to L *imitārī* to IMITATE]
▸**ˈimageable** *adj* ▸**ˈimageless** *adj*

image converter *or* **tube** *n* an electronic device that converts an invisible image, esp. one formed by X-rays, into an image that is visible on a fluorescent screen.

image enhancement *n* a method of improving the definition of a video picture by a computer program which reduces the lowest grey values to black and the highest to white: used for pictures from microscopes, surveillance cameras, and scanners.

image intensifier *or* **tube** *n* any of various devices for amplifying the intensity of an optical image, sometimes used in conjunction with an image converter.

image orthicon *n* a television camera tube in which electrons, emitted from a surface in proportion to the intensity of the incident light, are focused onto the target causing secondary emission of electrons.

imagery (ˈɪmɪdʒrɪ, -dʒərɪ) *n, pl* **imageries. 1** figurative or descriptive language in a literary work. **2** images collectively. **3** *Psychol.* **3a** the materials or general processes of the imagination. **3b** the characteristic kind of mental images formed by a particular individual. See also **image** (sense 7), **imagination** (sense 1).

image tube *n* another name for **image converter** or **image intensifier.**

imaginary ❶ (ɪˈmædʒɪnərɪ, -dʒɪnrɪ) *adj* **1** existing in the imagination; unreal; illusory. **2** *Maths.* involving or containing imaginary numbers.
▸**imˈaginarily** *adv*

imaginary number *n* any complex number of the form $a + ib$, where b is not zero and $i = \sqrt{-1}$.

imagination ❶ (ɪˌmædʒɪˈneɪʃən) *n* **1** the faculty or action of producing ideas, esp. mental images of what is not present or has not been experienced. **2** mental creative ability. **3** the ability to deal resourcefully with unexpected or unusual problems, circumstances, etc.

imaginative ❶ (ɪˈmædʒɪnətɪv) *adj* **1** produced by or indicative of a creative imagination. **2** having a vivid imagination.
▸**imˈaginatively** *adv* ▸**imˈaginativeness** *n*

imagine ❶ (ɪˈmædʒɪn) *vb* **imagines, imagining, imagined. 1** (when *tr, may take a clause as object*) to form a mental image of. **2** (when *tr, may take a clause as object*) to think, believe, or guess. **3** (*tr; takes a clause as object*) to suppose; assume: *I imagine he'll come.* **4** (*tr; takes a clause as object*) to believe without foundation: *he imagines he knows the whole story.* [C14: from L *imāginārī* to fancy, picture mentally, from *imāgō* likeness; see IMAGE]
▸**imˈaginable** *adj* ▸**imˈaginably** *adv* ▸**imˈaginer** *n*

imagism (ˈɪmɪˌdʒɪzəm) *n* an early 20th-century poetic movement, advocating the use of ordinary speech and the precise presentation of images.
▸**ˈimagist** *n, adj* ▸ˌ**imagˈistic** *adj*

imago (ɪˈmeɪgəʊ) *n, pl* **imagoes** *or* **imagines** (ɪˈmædʒəˌniːz). **1** an adult sexually mature insect. **2** *Psychoanal.* an idealized image of another person, usually a parent, carried in the unconscious. [C18: NL, from L: likeness]

imam (ɪˈmɑːm) *or* **imaum** (ɪˈmɑːm, ɪˈmɔːm) *n Islam.* **1** a leader of congregational prayer in a mosque. **2** a caliph, as leader of a Muslim community. **3** any of a succession of Muslim religious leaders regarded by their followers as divinely inspired. [C17: from Ar.: leader]

imamate (ɪˈmɑːmeɪt) *n Islam.* **1** the region or territory governed by an imam. **2** the office, rank, or period of office of an imam.

imbalance ❶ (ɪmˈbæləns) *n* a lack of balance, as in emphasis, proportion, etc.: *the political imbalance of the programme.*

imbecile ❶ (ˈɪmbɪˌsiːl, -ˌsaɪl) *n* **1** *Psychol.* a person of very low intelligence (IQ of 25 to 50). **2** *Inf.* an extremely stupid person; dolt. ◆ *adj also* **imbecilic** (ˌɪmbɪˈsɪlɪk). **3** of or like an imbecile; mentally deficient; feeble-minded. **4** stupid or senseless: *an imbecile thing to do.* [C16: from L *imbēcillus* feeble (physically or mentally)]
▸**ˈimbeˌcilely** *or* ˌ**imbeˈcilically** *adv* ▸ˌ**imbeˈcility** *n*

imbed (ɪmˈbɛd) *vb* **imbeds, imbedding, imbedded.** a less common spelling of **embed.**

imbibe ❶ (ɪmˈbaɪb) *vb* **imbibes, imbibing, imbibed. 1** to drink (esp. alcoholic drinks). **2** *Literary.* to take in or assimilate (ideas, etc.): *to imbibe the spirit of the Renaissance.* **3** (*tr*) to take in as if by drinking: *to imbibe fresh air.* **4** to absorb or cause to absorb liquid or moisture; assimilate or saturate. [C14: from L *imbibere,* from *bibere* to drink]
▸**imˈbiber** *n*

imbricate *adj* (ˈɪmbrɪkɪt, -ˌkeɪt), *also* **imbricated. 1** *Archit.* relating to or having tiles, shingles, or slates that overlap. **2** (of leaves, scales, etc.) overlapping each other. ◆ *vb* (ˈɪmbrɪˌkeɪt), **imbricates, imbricating, imbricated. 3** (*tr*) to decorate with a repeating pattern resembling scales or overlapping tiles. [C17: from L *imbricāre* to cover with overlapping tiles, from *imbrex* pantile]
▸**ˈimbricately** *adv* ▸ˌ**imbriˈcation** *n*

imbroglio ❶ (ɪmˈbrəʊlɪˌəʊ) *n, pl* **imbroglios. 1** a confused or perplexing political or interpersonal situation. **2** *Obs.* a confused heap; jumble. [C18: from It., from *imbrogliare* to confuse, EMBROIL]

imbrue (ɪmˈbruː) *vb* **imbrues, imbruing, imbrued.** (*tr*) *Rare.* **1** to stain, esp.

THESAURUS

bellished, graphic, illuminated, picture, pictured, with illustrations

illustration *n* **1** = **picture**, adornment, decoration, figure, plate, sketch **2** = **example**, analogy, case, case in point, clarification, demonstration, elucidation, exemplification, explanation, instance, interpretation, specimen

illustrative *adj* **1** = **explanatory**, descriptive, explicatory, expository, illustrational, interpretive, representative, sample, typical **3** = **pictorial**, delineative, diagrammatic, graphic

illustrious *adj* **1** = **famous**, brilliant, celebrated, distinguished, eminent, exalted, famed, glorious, great, noble, notable, noted, prominent, remarkable, renowned, resplendent, signal, splendid
Antonyms *adj* humble, ignoble, infamous, lowly, meek, notorious, obscure, unassuming

ill will *n* = **hostility**, acrimony, animosity, animus, antagonism, antipathy, aversion, bad blood, dislike, enmity, envy, grudge, hard feelings, hatred, malevolence, malice, no love lost, rancour, resentment, spite, unfriendliness, venom
Antonyms *n* amiability, amity, charity, congeniality, cordiality, friendship, goodwill

image *n* **1** = **representation**, appearance, effigy, figure, icon, idol, likeness, picture, portrait, reflection, statue **3** = **replica**, chip off the old block (*inf.*), counterpart, (dead) ringer (*sl.*), Doppelgänger, double, facsimile, similitude, spit (*inf., chiefly Brit.*), spitting image (*inf.*) **4** = **concept**, conception, idea, impression, mental picture, perception **10** = **figure**, conceit, trope

imaginable *adj* **2** = **possible**, believable, comprehensible, conceivable, credible, likely, plausible, supposable, thinkable, under the sun, within the bounds of possibility
Antonyms *adj* impossible, incomprehensible, inconceivable, incredible, unbelievable, unimaginable, unlikely, unthinkable

imaginary *adj* **1** = **fictional**, assumed, chimerical, dreamlike, fancied, fanciful, fictitious, hallucinatory, hypothetical, ideal, illusive, illusory, imagined, invented, legendary, made-up, mythological, nonexistent, phantasmal, shadowy, supposed, unreal, unsubstantial, visionary
Antonyms *adj* actual, factual, genuine, known, proven, real, substantial, tangible, true

imagination *n* **1** = **unreality**, chimera, conception, idea, ideality, illusion, image, invention, notion, supposition **2, 3** = **creativity**, enterprise, fancy, ingenuity, insight, inspiration, invention, inventiveness, originality, resourcefulness, vision, wit, wittiness

imaginative *adj* **1** = **creative**, clever, dreamy, enterprising, fanciful, fantastic, ingenious, inspired, inventive, original, poetical, visionary, vivid, whimsical
Antonyms *adj* literal, mundane, ordinary, uncreative, unimaginative, uninspired, unoriginal, unpoetical, unromantic

imagine *vb* **1** = **envisage**, conceive, conceptualize, conjure up, create, devise, dream up (*inf.*), fantasize, form a mental picture of, frame, invent, picture, plan, project, scheme, see in the mind's eye, think of, think up, visualize **2, 3** = **believe**, apprehend, assume, conjecture, deduce, deem, fancy, gather, guess (*inf., chiefly US & Canad.*), infer, realize, suppose, surmise, suspect, take for granted, take it, think

imbalance *n* = **unevenness**, bias, disproportion, inequality, lack of proportion, lopsidedness, partiality, top-heaviness, unfairness

imbecile *n* **2** = **idiot**, berk (*Brit. sl.*), chump, coot, cretin, dolt, dork (*sl.*), fool, halfwit, jerk (*sl., chiefly US & Canad.*), moron, nerd *or* nurd (*sl.*), numbskull *or* numskull, pillock (*Brit. sl.*), prat (*sl.*), schmuck (*US sl.*), thickhead, twit (*inf., chiefly Brit.*) ◆ *adj* **4** = **stupid**, asinine, braindead (*inf.*), dead from the neck up, dumb-ass (*sl.*), fatuous, feeble-minded, foolish, idiotic, imbecilic, inane, ludicrous, moronic, simple, simple-minded, thick, witless

imbecility *n* **2** = **stupidity**, asininity, childishness, cretinism, fatuity, foolishness, idiocy, inanity, incompetency
Antonyms *n* comprehension, intelligence, perspicacity, reasonableness, sagacity, sense, soundness, wisdom

imbibe *vb* **1** = **drink**, consume, knock back (*inf.*), quaff, sink (*inf.*), suck, swallow, swig (*inf.*) **2** = **absorb**, acquire, assimilate, gain, gather, ingest, receive, take in

imbroglio *n* **1** = **complication**, complexity, embarrassment, entanglement, involvement, misunderstanding, quandary

with blood. **2** to permeate or impregnate. [C15: from OF *embreuver*, from L *imbibere* to IMBIBE]
▸**im'bruement** *n*

imbue ❶ (ɪm'bjuː) *vb* **imbues, imbuing, imbued.** (*tr*; usually foll. by *with*) **1** to instil or inspire (with ideals, principles, etc.). **2** *Rare.* to soak, esp. with dye, etc. [C16: from L *imbuere* to stain, accustom]
▸**im'buement** *n*

IMechE *abbrev. for* Institution of Mechanical Engineers.

IMF *abbrev. for* International Monetary Fund.

imit. *abbrev. for:* **1** imitation. **2** imitative.

imitate ❶ ('ɪmɪˌteɪt) *vb* **imitates, imitating, imitated.** (*tr*) **1** to try to follow the manner, style, etc., of or take as a model: *many writers imitated the language of Shakespeare.* **2** to pretend to be or to impersonate, esp. for humour; mimic. **3** to make a copy or reproduction of; duplicate. [C16: from L *imitārī*; see IMAGE]
▸**imitable** ('ɪmɪtəbᵊl) *adj* ▸ˌ**imita'bility** *n* ▸'**imiˌtator** *n*

imitation ❶ (ˌɪmɪ'teɪʃən) *n* **1** the act or practice of imitating; mimicry. **2** an instance or product of imitating, such as a copy of the manner of a person; impression. **3a** a copy of a genuine article; counterfeit. **3b** (*as modifier*): *imitation jewellery.* **4** *Music.* the repetition of a phrase or figure in one part after its appearance in another, as in a fugue.
▸ˌ**imi'tational** *adj*

imitative ❶ ('ɪmɪtətɪv) *adj* **1** imitating or tending to copy. **2** characterized by imitation. **3** copying or reproducing an original, esp. in an inferior manner: *imitative painting.* **4** another word for **onomatopoeic.**
▸'**imitatively** *adv* ▸'**imitativeness** *n*

immaculate ❶ (ɪ'mækjʊlɪt) *adj* **1** completely clean; extremely tidy: *his clothes were immaculate.* **2** completely flawless, etc.: *an immaculate rendering of the symphony.* **3** morally pure; free from sin or corruption. **4** *Biol.* with no spots or markings. [C15: from L, from IM- (not) + *macula* blemish]
▸**im'maculacy** *or* **im'maculateness** *n* ▸**im'maculately** *adv*

Immaculate Conception *n Christian theol., RC Church.* the doctrine that the Virgin Mary was conceived without any stain of original sin.

immanent ('ɪmənənt) *adj* **1** existing, operating, or remaining within; inherent. **2** (of God) present throughout the universe. [C16: from L *immanēre* to remain in]
▸'**immanence** *or* '**immanency** *n* ▸'**immanently** *adv* ▸'**immanenˌtism** *n*

immaterial ❶ (ˌɪmə'tɪərɪəl) *adj* **1** of no real importance; inconsequential. **2** not formed of matter; incorporeal; spiritual.
▸ˌ**immaˌteri'ality** *n* ▸ˌ**imma'terially** *adv*

immaterialism (ˌɪmə'tɪərɪəˌlɪzəm) *n Philosophy.* the doctrine that the material world exists only in the mind.
▸ˌ**imma'terialist** *n*

immature ❶ (ˌɪmə'tjʊə, -'tʃʊə) *adj* **1** not fully grown or developed. **2** deficient in maturity; lacking wisdom, insight, emotional stability, etc.
▸ˌ**imma'turely** *adv* ▸ˌ**imma'turity** *or* ˌ**imma'tureness** *n*

immeasurable ❶ (ɪ'mɛʒərəbᵊl) *adj* incapable of being measured, esp. by virtue of great size; limitless.
▸**imˌmeasura'bility** *or* **im'measurableness** *n* ▸**im'measurably** *adv*

immediate ❶ (ɪ'miːdɪət) *adj* (*usually prenominal*) **1** taking place or accomplished without delay: *an immediate reaction.* **2** closest or most direct in effect or relationship: *the immediate cause of his downfall.* **3** having no intervening medium; direct in effect: *an immediate influence.* **4** contiguous in space, time, or relationship: *our immediate neighbour.* **5** present; current: *the immediate problem is food.* **6** *Philosophy.* of or relating to a concept that is directly known or intuited. [C16: from Med. L, from L IM- (not) + *mediāre* to be in the middle; see MEDIATE]
▸**im'mediacy** *or* **im'mediateness** *n*

immediately ❶ (ɪ'miːdɪətlɪ) *adv* **1** without delay or intervention; at once; instantly. **2** very closely or directly: *this immediately concerns you.* **3** near or close by: *somewhere immediately in this area.* ◆ *conj* **4** (*subordinating*) *Chiefly Brit.* as; as soon as: *immediately he opened the door, there was a gust of wind.*

immemorial ❶ (ˌɪmɪ'mɔːrɪəl) *adj* originating in the distant past; ancient (postpositive in **time immemorial**). [C17: from Med. L, from L IM- (not) + *memoria* MEMORY]
▸ˌ**imme'morially** *adv*

immense ❶ (ɪ'mɛns) *adj* **1** unusually large; huge; vast. **2** without limits; immeasurable. **3** *Inf.* very good; excellent. [C15: from L *immensus*, lit.: unmeasured, from IM- (not) + *mētīrī* to measure]
▸**im'mensely** *adv* ▸**im'menseness** *n*

immensity ❶ (ɪ'mɛnsɪtɪ) *n, pl* **immensities. 1** the state of being immense; vastness; enormity. **2** enormous expanse, distance, or volume. **3** *Inf.* a huge amount: *an immensity of wealth.*

immerse ❶ (ɪ'mɜːs) *vb* **immerses, immersing, immersed.** (*tr*) **1** (often foll. by *in*) to plunge or dip into liquid. **2** (*often passive;* often foll. by *in*) to involve deeply; engross: *to immerse oneself in a problem.* **3** to baptize by dipping the whole body into water. [C17: from L *immergere*, from IM- (in) + *mergere* to dip]
▸**im'mersible** *adj* ▸**im'mersion** *n*

immerser (ɪ'mɜːsə) *n* an informal term for **immersion heater.**

immersion heater *n* an electrical device, usually thermostatically controlled, for heating the liquid in which it is immersed, esp. as a fixture in a domestic hot-water tank.

immigrant ❶ ('ɪmɪgrənt) *n* **1a** a person who immigrates. **1b** (*as modifier*): *an immigrant community.* **2** *Brit.* a person who has been settled in a country of which he is not a native for less than ten years.

immigrate ('ɪmɪˌgreɪt) *vb* **immigrates, immigrating, immigrated. 1** (*intr*) to come to a place or country of which one is not a native in order to settle there. **2** (*tr*) to introduce or bring in as an immigrant. [C17: from L *immigrāre* to go into]
▸ˌ**immi'gration** *n* ▸'**immiˌgrator** *n* ▸'**immiˌgratory** *adj*

imminent ❶ ('ɪmɪnənt) *adj* **1** liable to happen soon; impending. **2** *Obs.*

THESAURUS

imbue *vb* **1** = **instil**, bathe, impregnate, inculcate, infuse, permeate, pervade, saturate, steep

imitate *vb* **1-3** = **copy**, affect, ape, burlesque, caricature, counterfeit, do (*inf.*), do an impression of, duplicate, echo, emulate, follow, follow in the footsteps of, follow suit, impersonate, mimic, mirror, mock, parody, personate, repeat, send up (*Brit. inf.*), simulate, spoof (*inf.*), take a leaf out of (someone's) book, take off (*inf.*), travesty

imitation *n* **1** = **mimicry**, aping, copy, counterfeit, counterfeiting, duplication, echoing, likeness, resemblance, simulation **2, 3a** = **replica**, carbon copy (*inf.*), fake, forgery, impersonation, impression, mockery, parody, reflection, reproduction, sham, substitution, takeoff (*inf.*), travesty ◆ *modifier* **3b** = **artificial**, dummy, ersatz, man-made, mock, phoney *or* phony (*inf.*), pseudo (*inf.*), repro, reproduction, sham, simulated, synthetic
Antonyms *modifier* ≠ **artificial:** authentic, genuine, original, real, true, valid

imitative *adj* **1-4** = **derivative**, copied, copycat (*inf.*), copying, echoic, mimetic, mimicking, mock, onomatopoeic, parrot-like, plagiarized, pseudo (*inf.*), put-on, second-hand, simulated, unoriginal

imitator *n* **1** = **copier**, carbon copy (*inf.*), copycat (*inf.*), echo, epigone (*rare*), follower, parrot, shadow **2** = **impersonator**, impressionist, mimic

immaculate *adj* **1** = **clean**, impeccable, neat, neat as a new pin, spick-and-span, spotless, spruce, squeaky-clean, trim **3** = **pure**, above reproach, faultless, flawless, guiltless, impeccable, incorrupt, innocent, perfect, sinless, squeaky-clean, stainless, unblemished, uncontaminated, undefiled, unexceptionable, unpolluted, unsullied, untarnished, virtuous
Antonyms *adj* ≠ **clean:** dirty, filthy, unclean ≠ **pure:** contaminated, corrupt, impeachable, impure, polluted, stained, tainted

immaterial *adj* **1** = **irrelevant**, a matter of indifference, extraneous, impertinent, inapposite, inconsequential, inconsiderable, inessential, insignificant, of little account, of no consequence, of no importance, trifling, trivial, unimportant, unnecessary **2** = **spiritual**, airy, disembodied, ethereal, ghostly, incorporeal, metaphysical, unembodied, unsubstantial
Antonyms *adj* ≠ **irrelevant:** crucial, essential, germane, important, material, relevant, significant, substantial ≠ **spiritual:** earthly, physical, real, tangible

immature *adj* **1** = **young**, adolescent, crude, green, imperfect, premature, raw, undeveloped, unfinished, unfledged, unformed, unripe, unseasonable, untimely **2** = **childish**, babyish, callow, inexperienced, infantile, jejune, juvenile, puerile, wet behind the ears (*inf.*)
Antonyms *adj* adult, developed, fully-fledged, mature, mellow, ripe

immaturity *n* **1** = **unripeness**, crudeness, crudity, greenness, imperfection, rawness, unpreparedness **2** = **childishness**, babyishness, callowness, inexperience, juvenility, puerility

immeasurable *adj* = **incalculable**, bottomless, boundless, endless, illimitable, immense, inestimable, inexhaustible, infinite, limitless, measureless, unbounded, unfathomable, unlimited, vast
Antonyms *adj* bounded, calculable, estimable, exhaustible, fathomable, finite, limited, measurable

immediate *adj* **1** = **instant**, instantaneous **4** = **nearest**, adjacent, close, contiguous, direct, near, next, primary, proximate, recent **5** = **current**, actual, existing, extant, on hand, present, pressing, up to date, urgent
Antonyms *adj* ≠ **instant:** delayed, late, later, leisurely, postponed, slow, tardy ≠ **nearest:** distant, far, remote

immediately *adv* **1** = **at once**, before you could say Jack Robinson (*inf.*), directly, forthwith, instantly, now, on the nail, posthaste, promptly, pronto (*inf.*), right away, right now, straight away, this instant, this very minute, *tout de suite,* unhesitatingly, without delay, without hesitation **2** = **closely**, at first hand, directly, nearly

immemorial *adj* = **age-old**, ancient, archaic, fixed, long-standing, of yore, olden (*arch.*), rooted, time-honoured, traditional

immense *adj* **1** = **huge**, colossal, elephantine, enormous, extensive, giant, gigantic, ginormous (*inf.*), great, humongous *or* humungous (*US sl.*), jumbo (*inf.*), large, mammoth, massive, mega (*sl.*), monstrous, monumental, prodigious, stellar (*inf.*), stupendous, titanic, tremendous, vast **2** = **immeasurable**, illimitable, infinite, interminable
Antonyms *adj* ≠ **huge:** infinitesimal, little, microscopic, minuscule, minute, puny, small, tiny

immensity *n* **1-3** = **size**, bulk, enormity, expanse, extent, greatness, hugeness, infinity, magnitude, massiveness, scope, sweep, vastness

immerse *vb* **1** = **plunge**, bathe, dip, douse, duck, dunk, sink, submerge, submerse **2** = **engross**, absorb, busy, engage, involve, occupy, take up

immersed *adj* **2** = **engrossed**, absorbed, bound up, buried, busy, consumed, deep, in a brown study, involved, mesmerized, occupied, rapt, spellbound, taken up, wrapped up

immersion *n* **1, 3** = **dipping**, baptism, bathe, dip, dousing, ducking, dunking, plunging, submerging **2** = **involvement**, absorption, concentration, preoccupation

immigrant *n* **1** = **settler**, incomer, newcomer

imminent *adj* **1** = **near**, at hand, brewing, close, coming, fast-approaching, forthcoming, gathering, impending, in the air, in the offing, in the pipeline, just round the corner, looming,

overhanging. [C16: from L *imminēre* to project over; rel. to *mons* mountain]
▸'**imminence** *n* ▸'**imminently** *adv*

immiscible (ɪ'mɪsɪbᵊl) *adj* (of liquids) incapable of being mixed: *oil and water are immiscible.*
▸**im,misci'bility** *n* ▸**im'miscibly** *adv*

immitigable (ɪ'mɪtɪgəbᵊl) *adj Rare.* unable to be mitigated.
▸**im,mitiga'bility** *n* ▸**im'mitigably** *adv*

immobile ❶ (ɪ'məubaɪl) *adj* **1** not moving; motionless. **2** not able to move or be moved; fixed.
▸**immobility** (,ɪməu'bɪlɪtɪ) *n*

immobilize ❶ *or* **immobilise** (ɪ'məubɪ,laɪz) *vb* **immobilizes, immobilizing, immobilized** *or* **immobilises, immobilising, immobilised.** (*tr*) **1** to make immobile: *to immobilize a car.* **2** *Finance.* to convert (circulating capital) into fixed capital.
▸**im,mobili'zation** *or* **im,mobili'sation** *n* ▸**im'mobi,lizer** *or* **im'mobi,liser** *n*

immoderate ❶ (ɪ'mɒdərɪt, ɪ'mɒdrɪt) *adj* lacking in moderation; excessive: *immoderate demands.*
▸**im'moderately** *adv* ▸**im,moder'ation** *or* **im'moderateness** *n*

immodest ❶ (ɪ'mɒdɪst) *adj* **1** indecent, esp. with regard to sexual propriety; improper. **2** bold, impudent, or shameless.
▸**im'modestly** *adv* ▸**im'modesty** *n*

immolate ('ɪməu,leɪt) *vb* **immolates, immolating, immolated.** (*tr*) **1** to kill or offer as a sacrifice, esp. by fire. **2** *Literary.* to sacrifice (something highly valued). [C16: from L *immolāre* to sprinkle an offering with sacrificial meal, sacrifice; see MILL]
▸,**immo'lation** *n* ▸'**immo,lator** *n*

immoral ❶ (ɪ'mɒrəl) *adj* **1** transgressing accepted moral rules; corrupt. **2** sexually dissolute; profligate or promiscuous. **3** unscrupulous or unethical: *immoral trading.* **4** tending to corrupt or resulting from corruption: *immoral earnings.*
▸**im'morally** *adv*

immorality ❶ (,ɪmə'rælɪtɪ) *n, pl* **immoralities. 1** the quality or state of being immoral. **2** immoral behaviour, esp. in sexual matters; licentiousness; promiscuity. **3** an immoral act.

immortal ❶ (ɪ'mɔːtᵊl) *adj* **1** not subject to death or decay; having perpetual life. **2** having everlasting fame; remembered throughout time. **3** everlasting; perpetual; constant. **4** of or relating to immortal beings or concepts. ◆ *n* **5** an immortal being. **6** (*often pl*) a person who is remembered enduringly, esp. an author.
▸,**immor'tality** *n* ▸**im'mortally** *adv*

immortalize ❶ *or* **immortalise** (ɪ'mɔːtə,laɪz) *vb* **immortalizes, immortalizing, immortalized** *or* **immortalises, immortalising, immortalised.** (*tr*) **1** to give everlasting fame to, as by treating in a literary work: *Macbeth was immortalized by Shakespeare.* **2** to give immortality to.
▸**im,mortali'zation** *or* **im,mortali'sation** *n* ▸**im'mortal,izer** *or* **im'mortal,iser** *n*

immortelle (,ɪmɔː'tel) *n* any of various composite plants that retain their colour when dried. Also called: **everlasting.** [C19: from F (*fleur*) *immortelle* everlasting (flower)]

immovable ❶ *or* **immoveable** (ɪ'muːvəbᵊl) *adj* **1** unable to move or be moved; immobile. **2** unable to be diverted from one's intentions; steadfast. **3** unaffected by feeling; impassive. **4** unchanging; unalterable. **5** (of feasts, etc.) on the same date every year. **6** *Law.* **6a** (of property) not liable to be removed; fixed. **6b** of or relating to immovable property.
▸**im,mova'bility, im,movea'bility** *or* **im'movableness, im'moveableness** *n*
▸**im'movably** *or* **im'moveably** *adv*

immune ❶ (ɪ'mjuːn) *adj* **1** protected against a specific disease by inoculation or as the result of innate or acquired resistance. **2** relating to or conferring immunity: *an immune body* (see **antibody**). **3** (*usually postpositive*; foll. by *to*) unsusceptible (to) or secure (against): *immune to inflation.* **4** exempt from obligation, penalty, etc. ◆ *n* **5** an immune person or animal. [C15: from L *immūnis* exempt from a public service]

immune response *n* the reaction of an organism's body to foreign materials (antigens), including the production of antibodies.

immunity ❶ (ɪ'mjuːnɪtɪ) *n, pl* **immunities. 1** the ability of an organism to resist disease, either through the activities of specialized blood cells or antibodies produced by them in response to natural exposure or inoculation (**active immunity**) or by the injection of antiserum or the transfer of antibodies from a mother to her baby via the placenta or breast milk (**passive immunity**). See also **acquired immunity, natural immunity. 2** freedom from obligation or duty, esp. exemption from tax, legal liability, etc.

immunize ❶ *or* **immunise** ('ɪmjʊ,naɪz) *vb* **immunizes, immunizing, immunized** *or* **immunises, immunising, immunised.** (*tr*) to make immune, esp. by inoculation.
▸,**immuni'zation** *or* ,**immuni'sation** *n* ▸'**immu,nizer** *or* '**immu,niser** *n*

immuno- *or before a vowel* **immun-** *combining form.* indicating immunity or immune: *immunology.*

immunoassay (,ɪmjunəu'æseɪ) *n Immunol.* a technique of identifying a substance, esp. a protein, through its action as an antigen.

immunocompromised (,ɪmjunəu'kɒmprəmaɪzd) *adj* having an impaired immune system and therefore incapable of an effective immune response, usually as a result of disease, such as AIDS, that damages the immune system.

immunodeficiency (,ɪmjunəudɪ'fɪʃənsɪ) *n* a deficiency in or breakdown of a person's immune system.

immunogenic (,ɪmjunəu'dʒenɪk) *adj* causing or producing immunity or an immune response.
▸,**immuno'genically** *adv*

immunoglobulin (,ɪmjunəu'glɒbjulɪn) *n* any of five classes of proteins, all of which show antibody activity.

immunology (,ɪmju'nɒlədʒɪ) *n* the branch of biological science concerned with the study of immunity.
▸**immunologic** (,ɪmjunə'lɒdʒɪk) *or* ,**immuno'logical** *adj* ▸,**immuno'logically** *adv* ▸,**immu'nologist** *n*

immunoreaction (ɪ,mjuːnəurɪ'ækʃən) *n* the reaction between an antigen and its antibody.

immunosuppression (,ɪmjunəusə'preʃən) *n* medical suppression of the body's immune system, esp. in order to reduce the likelihood of rejection of a transplanted organ.
▸,**immunosup'pressant** *n, adj*

immunosuppressive (,ɪmjunəusə'presɪv) *n* **1** any drug that lessens the body's rejection, esp. of a transplanted organ. ◆ *adj* **2** of or relating to such a drug.

THESAURUS

menacing, nigh (*arch.*), on the cards, on the horizon, on the way, threatening, upcoming
Antonyms *adj* delayed, distant, far-off, remote

immobile *adj* **1, 2** = **stationary**, at a standstill, at rest, fixed, frozen, immobilized, immotile, immovable, like a statue, motionless, rigid, riveted, rooted, stable, static, stiff, still, stock-still, stolid, unmoving
Antonyms *adj* active, mobile, movable, on the move, pliant, portable, vigorous

immobility *n* **1, 2** = **stillness**, absence of movement, firmness, fixity, immovability, inertness, motionlessness, stability, steadiness

immobilize *vb* **1** = **paralyse**, bring to a standstill, cripple, disable, freeze, halt, lay up (*inf.*), put out of action, render inoperative, stop, transfix

immoderate *adj* = **excessive**, egregious, enormous, exaggerated, exorbitant, extravagant, extreme, inordinate, intemperate, over the odds (*inf.*), over the top (*sl.*), profligate, steep (*inf.*), uncalled-for, unconscionable, uncontrolled, undue, unjustified, unreasonable, unrestrained, unwarranted, wanton
Antonyms *adj* controlled, judicious, mild, moderate, reasonable, restrained, temperate

immoderation *n* = **excess**, exorbitance, extravagance, intemperance, lack of restraint *or* balance, overindulgence, prodigality, unrestraint

immodest *adj* **1** = **indecent**, bawdy, coarse, depraved, flirtatious, gross, immoral, improper, impure, indecorous, indelicate, lewd, obscene, revealing, titillating, unchaste **2** = **shameless**, bold, bold as brass, brass-necked (*Brit. inf.*), brazen, forward, fresh (*inf.*), impudent, pushy (*inf.*), unblushing

immodesty *n* **1** = **lewdness**, bawdiness, coarseness, impurity, indecorousness, indelicacy, obscenity **2** = **shamelessness**, audacity, boldness, brass neck (*Brit. inf.*), forwardness, gall, impudence, temerity
Antonyms *n* ≠ **lewdness:** decency, decorousness, delicacy, modesty, restraint, sobriety

immoral *adj* **1** = **wicked**, abandoned, bad, corrupt, debauched, degenerate, depraved, dishonest, dissolute, evil, impure, indecent, iniquitous, lewd, licentious, nefarious, obscene, profligate, reprobate, sinful, sink, unchaste, unethical, unprincipled, vicious, vile, wrong
Antonyms *adj* conscientious, good, honourable, inoffensive, law-abiding, moral, pure, upright, virtuous

immorality *n* **1, 2** = **wickedness**, badness, corruption, debauchery, depravity, dissoluteness, evil, iniquity, licentiousness, profligacy, sin, turpitude, vice, wrong
Antonyms *n* goodness, honesty, lawfulness, morality, purity

immorally *adv* **1** = **wickedly**, corruptly, degenerately, dishonestly, dissolutely, evilly, sinfully, unethically, unrighteously

immortal *adj* **1, 3** = **eternal**, abiding, constant, death-defying, deathless, endless, enduring, everlasting, imperishable, incorruptible, indestructible, lasting, perennial, perpetual, sempiternal (*literary*), timeless, undying, unfading ◆ *n* **5** = **god**, goddess, Olympian **6** = **great**, genius, hero, paragon
Antonyms *adj* ≠ **eternal:** ephemeral, fading, fleeting, mortal, passing, perishable, temporary, transitory

immortality *n* **1** = **eternity**, deathlessness, endlessness, everlasting life, incorruptibility, indestructibility, perpetuity, timelessness **2** = **fame**, celebrity, glorification, gloriousness, glory, greatness, renown

immortalize *vb* **1** = **commemorate**, apotheosize, celebrate, enshrine, eternalize, eternize, exalt, glorify, memorialize, perpetuate, solemnize

immovable *adj* **1** = **fixed**, fast, firm, immutable, jammed, rooted, secure, set, stable, stationary, stuck, unbudgeable **2** = **inflexible**, adamant, constant, impassive, obdurate, resolute, steadfast, stony-hearted, unchangeable, unimpressionable, unshakable, unshaken, unwavering, unyielding
Antonyms *adj* ≠ **inflexible:** changeable, flexible, impressionable, movable, shakable, wavering, yielding

immune *adj* **1, 3, 4** = **exempt**, clear, free, insusceptible, invulnerable, let off (*inf.*), not affected, not liable, not subject, proof (against), protected, resistant, safe, unaffected
Antonyms *adj* exposed, liable, prone, susceptible, unprotected, vulnerable

immunity *n* **1** = **resistance**, immunization, protection **2** = **exemption**, amnesty, charter, exoneration, franchise, freedom, indemnity, invulnerability, liberty, licence, prerogative, privilege, release, right
Antonyms *n* ≠ **resistance:** exposure, liability, openness, proneness, susceptibility, vulnerability

immunize *vb* = **vaccinate**, inoculate, protect, safeguard

DICTIONARY

immunotherapy (ˌɪmjʊnəʊˈθɛrəpɪ) *n* the treatment of disease by stimulating or modifying the immune response.
▸**immunotherapeutic** (ˌɪmjʊnəʊˌθɛrəˈpjuːtɪk) *adj*

immure (ɪˈmjʊə) *vb* **immures, immuring, immured.** (*tr*) **1** *Arch. or literary.* to enclose within or as if within walls; imprison. **2** to shut (oneself) away from society. [C16: from Med. L, from L IM- (in) + *mūrus* wall]
▸**imˈmurement** *n*

immutable ❶ (ɪˈmjuːtəbᵊl) *adj* unchanging through time; unalterable; ageless: *immutable laws.*
▸**imˌmutaˈbility** *or* **imˈmutableness** *n*

imp ❶ (ɪmp) *n* **1** a small demon or devil; mischievous sprite. **2** a mischievous child. ◆ *vb* **3** (*tr*) *Falconry.* to insert new feathers in order to repair (the wing of a falcon). [OE *impa* bud, graft, hence offspring, child, from *impian* to graft]

imp. *abbrev. for:* **1** imperative. **2** imperfect. **3** imperial. **4** impersonal. **5** import. **6** importer.

impact ❶ *n* (ˈɪmpækt). **1** the act of one body, etc., striking another; collision. **2** the force with which one thing hits another. **3** the impression made by an idea, social group, etc. ◆ *vb* (ɪmˈpækt). **4** to drive or press (an object) firmly into (another object, thing, etc.) or (of two objects) to be driven or pressed firmly together. **5** to have an impact or strong effect (on). [C18: from L *impactus* pushed against, fastened on, from *impingere* to thrust at, from *pangere* to drive in]
▸**imˈpaction** *n*

impacted (ɪmˈpæktɪd) *adj* **1** (of a tooth) unable to erupt, esp. because of being wedged against another tooth below the gum. **2** (of a fracture) having the jagged broken ends wedged into each other.

impair ❶ (ɪmˈpɛə) *vb* (*tr*) to reduce or weaken in strength, quality, etc.: *his hearing was impaired by an accident.* [C14: from OF *empeirer* to make worse, from LL, from L *pēior* worse; see PEJORATIVE]
▸**imˈpairable** *adj* ▸**imˈpairer** *n* ▸**imˈpairment** *n*

impala (ɪmˈpɑːlə) *n, pl* **impalas** *or* **impala.** an antelope of southern and eastern Africa, having lyre-shaped horns and able to move with enormous leaps. [from Zulu]

impale ❶ *or* **empale** (ɪmˈpeɪl) *vb* **impales, impaling, impaled** *or* **empales, empaling, empaled.** (*tr*) **1** (often foll. by *on, upon,* or *with*) to pierce with a sharp instrument: *they impaled his severed head on a spear.* **2** *Heraldry.* to charge (a shield) with two coats of arms placed side by side. [C16: from Med. L, from L IM- (in) + *pālus* PALE[2]]
▸**imˈpalement** *or* **emˈpalement** *n*

impalpable ❶ (ɪmˈpælpəbᵊl) *adj* **1** imperceptible, esp. to the touch: *impalpable shadows.* **2** difficult to understand; abstruse.
▸**imˌpalpaˈbility** *n* ▸**imˈpalpably** *adv*

impanel (ɪmˈpænᵊl) *vb* **impanels, impanelling, impanelled** *or US* **impanels, impaneling, impaneled.** a variant spelling (esp. US) of **empanel.**
▸**imˈpanelment** *n*

impart ❶ (ɪmˈpɑːt) *vb* (*tr*) **1** to communicate (information, etc.); relate. **2** to give or bestow (an abstract quality): *to impart wisdom.* [C15: from OF, from L, from IM- (in) + *partīre* to share, from *pars* part]
▸**imˈpartable** *adj* ▸ˌ**imparˈtation** *or* **imˈpartment** *n*

impartial ❶ (ɪmˈpɑːʃəl) *adj* not prejudiced towards or against any particular side; fair; unbiased.
▸**imˌpartiˈality** *or* **imˈpartialness** *n* ▸**imˈpartially** *adv*

impartible (ɪmˈpɑːtəbᵊl) *adj Law.* (of land, an estate, etc.) incapable of partition; indivisible.
▸**imˌpartiˈbility** *n* ▸**imˈpartibly** *adv*

impassable ❶ (ɪmˈpɑːsəbᵊl) *adj* (of terrain, roads, etc.) not able to be travelled through or over.
▸**imˌpassaˈbility** *or* **imˈpassableness** *n* ▸**imˈpassably** *adv*

impasse ❶ (æmˈpɑːs, ˈæmpɑːs) *n* a situation in which progress is blocked; an insurmountable difficulty; stalemate. [C19: from F; see IM-, PASS]

impassible (ɪmˈpæsəbᵊl) *adj Rare.* **1** not susceptible to pain or injury. **2** impassive or unmoved.
▸**imˌpassiˈbility** *or* **imˈpassibleness** *n* ▸**imˈpassibly** *adv*

impassion (ɪmˈpæʃən) *vb* (*tr*) to arouse the passions of; inflame.

impassioned ❶ (ɪmˈpæʃənd) *adj* filled with passion; fiery; inflamed: *an impassioned appeal.*
▸**imˈpassionedly** *adv* ▸**imˈpassionedness** *n*

impassive ❶ (ɪmˈpæsɪv) *adj* **1** not revealing or affected by emotion; reserved. **2** calm; serene; imperturbable.
▸**imˈpassively** *adv* ▸**imˈpassiveness** *or* **impassivity** (ˌɪmpæˈsɪvɪtɪ) *n*

impasto (ɪmˈpæstəʊ) *n* **1** paint applied thickly, so that brush marks are evident. **2** the technique of painting in this way. [C18: from It., from *impastare,* from *pasta* PASTE]

impatience ❶ (ɪmˈpeɪʃəns) *n* **1** lack of patience; intolerance of or irritability with anything that impedes or delays. **2** restless desire for change and excitement.

impatiens (ɪmˈpeɪʃɪˌɛnz) *n, pl* **impatiens.** a plant with explosive pods, such as balsam, touch-me-not, and busy Lizzie. [C18: NL from L: impatient; from the fact that the ripe pods burst open when touched]

impatient ❶ (ɪmˈpeɪʃənt) *adj* **1** lacking patience; easily irritated at delay, etc. **2** exhibiting lack of patience. **3** (*postpositive;* foll. by *of*) intolerant (of) or indignant (at): *impatient of indecision.* **4** (*postpositive;* often foll. by *for*) restlessly eager (for *or* to do something).
▸**imˈpatiently** *adv*

impeach ❶ (ɪmˈpiːtʃ) *vb* (*tr*) **1** *Criminal law.* to bring a charge or accusation against. **2** *Brit. criminal law.* to accuse of a crime against the state. **3** *Chiefly US.* to charge (a public official) with an offence committed in office. **4** to challenge or question (a person's honesty, etc.). [C14: from OF, from LL *impedicāre* to entangle, catch, from L IM- (in) + *pedica* a fetter, from *pēs* foot]
▸**imˈpeachable** *adj* ▸**imˈpeachment** *n*

impeccable ❶ (ɪmˈpɛkəbᵊl) *adj* **1** without flaw or error; faultless: *an impeccable record.* **2** *Rare.* incapable of sinning. [C16: from LL *impeccābilis* sinless, from L IM- (not) + *peccāre* to sin]
▸**imˌpeccaˈbility** *n* ▸**imˈpeccably** *adv*

impecunious ❶ (ˌɪmpɪˈkjuːnɪəs) *adj* without money; penniless. [C16: from IM- (not) + from L *pecūniōsus* wealthy, from *pecūnia* money]
▸ˌ**impeˈcuniously** *adv* ▸ˌ**impeˈcuniousness** *or* **impecuniosity** (ˌɪmpɪkjuːnɪˈɒsɪtɪ) *n*

THESAURUS

immutability *n* = **permanence**, agelessness, changelessness, constancy, durability, invariability, stability, unalterableness, unchangeableness

immutable *adj* = **unchanging**, abiding, ageless, changeless, constant, enduring, fixed, immovable, inflexible, invariable, permanent, perpetual, sacrosanct, stable, steadfast, unalterable, unchangeable

imp *n* **1** = **demon**, devil, sprite **2** = **rascal**, brat, gamin, minx, pickle (*Brit. inf.*), rogue, scamp, urchin

impact *n* **1** = **collision**, bang, blow, bump, concussion, contact, crash, force, jolt, knock, shock, smash, stroke, thump **3** = **effect**, brunt, burden, consequences, full force, impression, influence, meaning, power, repercussions, significance, thrust, weight ◆ *vb* **4** = **hit**, clash, collide, crash, crush, strike

impair *vb* = **worsen**, blunt, damage, debilitate, decrease, deteriorate, diminish, enervate, enfeeble, harm, hinder, injure, lessen, mar, reduce, spoil, undermine, vitiate, weaken
Antonyms *vb* ameliorate, amend, better, enhance, facilitate, improve, strengthen

impaired *adj* = **damaged**, defective, faulty, flawed, imperfect, unsound

impale *vb* **1** = **pierce**, lance, run through, skewer, spear, spike, spit, stick, transfix

impalpable *adj* **1** = **intangible**, airy, delicate, disembodied, fine, imperceptible, incorporeal, indistinct, insubstantial, shadowy, tenuous, thin, unsubstantial

impart *vb* **1** = **communicate**, convey, disclose, discover, divulge, make known, pass on, relate, reveal, tell **2** = **give**, accord, afford, bestow, confer, contribute, grant, lend, offer, yield

impartial *adj* = **neutral**, detached, disinterested, equal, equitable, even-handed, fair, just, nondiscriminating, nonpartisan, objective, open-minded, unbiased, unprejudiced, without fear or favour
Antonyms *adj* biased, bigoted, influenced, partial, prejudiced, swayed, unfair, unjust

impartiality *n* = **neutrality**, detachment, disinterest, disinterestedness, dispassion, equality, equity, even-handedness, fairness, lack of bias, nonpartisanship, objectivity, open-mindedness
Antonyms *n* bias, favouritism, partiality, partisanship, subjectivity, unfairness

impassable *adj* = **blocked**, closed, impenetrable, obstructed, pathless, trackless, unnavigable

impasse *n* = **deadlock**, blind alley, dead end, stalemate, standoff, standstill

impassioned *adj* = **intense**, ablaze, animated, ardent, blazing, excited, fervent, fervid, fiery, flaming, furious, glowing, heated, inflamed, inspired, passionate, rousing, stirring, vehement, violent, vivid, warm, worked up
Antonyms *adj* apathetic, cool, impassive, indifferent, objective, reasoned

impassive *adj* **1, 2** = **unemotional**, aloof, apathetic, callous, calm, composed, cool, dispassionate, emotionless, impassible (*rare*), imperturbable, indifferent, inscrutable, insensible, insusceptible, phlegmatic, poker-faced (*inf.*), reserved, self-contained, serene, stoical, stolid, unconcerned, unexcitable, unfazed (*inf.*), unfeeling, unimpressible, unmoved, unruffled

impassiveness *n* **1, 2** = **inscrutability**, aloofness, calmness, composure, dispassion, imperturbability, indifference, insensibility, nonchalance, phlegm, stoicism, stolidity

impatience *n* **1** = **irritability**, intolerance, irritableness, quick temper, shortness, snappiness **2** = **restlessness**, agitation, anxiety, avidity, disquietude, eagerness, edginess, fretfulness, nervousness, restiveness, uneasiness
Antonyms *n* ≠ **irritability:** control, forbearance, patience, restraint, tolerance ≠ **restlessness:** calm, composure, serenity

impatient *adj* **1** = **irritable**, demanding, hot-tempered, intolerant, quick-tempered, snappy, testy **2** = **hasty**, abrupt, brusque, curt, headlong, impetuous, indignant, sudden, vehement, violent **4** = **restless**, agog, athirst, chafing, eager, edgy, fretful, like a cat on hot bricks (*inf.*), straining at the leash
Antonyms *adj* ≠ **irritable:** easy-going, tolerant ≠ **restless:** calm, composed, cool, imperturbable, patient, quiet, serene

impeach *vb* **1** = **charge**, accuse, arraign, blame, censure, criminate (*rare*), denounce, indict, tax **4** = **challenge**, call into question, cast aspersions on, cast doubt on, disparage, impugn, question

impeachment *n* **1** = **accusation**, arraignment, indictment

impeccable *adj* **1** = **faultless**, above suspicion, blameless, exact, exquisite, flawless, immaculate, incorrupt, innocent, irreproachable, perfect, precise, pure, sinless, squeaky-clean, stainless, unblemished, unerring, unimpeachable
Antonyms *adj* blameworthy, corrupt, defective, deficient, faulty, flawed, shallow, sinful

impecunious *adj* = **poor**, broke (*inf.*), cleaned out (*sl.*), destitute, dirt-poor (*inf.*), down and out, flat broke (*inf.*), indigent, in queer street, insolvent, penniless, poverty-stricken, short, skint (*Brit. sl.*), stony (*Brit. sl.*), strapped (*sl.*), without two pennies to rub together (*inf.*)

DICTIONARY

impedance (ɪmˈpiːdᵊns) *n* **1** a measure of the opposition to the flow of an alternating current equal to the square root of the sum of the squares of the resistance and the reactance, expressed in ohms. **2** the ratio of the sound pressure in a medium to the rate of alternating flow through a specified surface due to the sound wave. **3** the ratio of the mechanical force to the velocity of the resulting vibration.

impede Ⓣ (ɪmˈpiːd) *vb* **impedes, impeding, impeded.** (*tr*) to restrict or retard in action, progress, etc.; obstruct. [C17: from L *impedīre* to hinder, lit.: shackle the feet, from *pēs* foot]
▸**imˈpeder** *n* ▸**imˈpedingly** *adv*

impediment Ⓣ (ɪmˈpɛdɪmənt) *n* **1** a hindrance or obstruction. **2** a physical defect, esp. one of speech, such as a stammer. **3** (*pl* **impediments** *or* **impedimenta** (-ˈmɛntə)) *Law.* an obstruction to the making of a contract, esp. one of marriage.
▸**imˌpediˈmental** *or* **imˌpediˈmentary** *adj*

impedimenta Ⓣ (ɪmˌpɛdɪˈmɛntə) *pl n* **1** any objects that impede progress, esp. the baggage and equipment carried by an army. **2** a plural of **impediment** (sense 3). [C16: from L, pl of *impedīmentum* hindrance; see IMPEDE]

impel Ⓣ (ɪmˈpɛl) *vb* **impels, impelling, impelled.** (*tr*) **1** to urge or force (a person) to an action; constrain or motivate. **2** to push, drive, or force into motion. [C15: from L *impellere* to push against, drive forward]
▸**imˈpellent** *n, adj*

impeller (ɪmˈpɛlə) *n* the vaned rotating disc of a centrifugal pump, compressor, etc.

impend Ⓣ (ɪmˈpɛnd) *vb* (*intr*) **1** (esp. of something threatening) to be imminent. **2** (foll. by *over*) *Rare.* to be suspended; hang. [C16: from L *impendēre* to overhang, from *pendēre* to hang]
▸**imˈpendence** *or* **imˈpendency** *n* ▸**imˈpending** *adj*

impenetrable Ⓣ (ɪmˈpɛnɪtrəbᵊl) *adj* **1** incapable of being pierced through or penetrated: *an impenetrable forest.* **2** incapable of being understood; incomprehensible. **3** incapable of being seen through: *impenetrable gloom.* **4** not susceptible to ideas, influence, etc.: *impenetrable ignorance.* **5** *Physics.* (of a body) incapable of occupying the same space as another body.
▸**imˌpenetraˈbility** *n* ▸**imˈpenetrableness** *n* ▸**imˈpenetrably** *adv*

impenitent Ⓣ (ɪmˈpɛnɪtənt) *adj* not sorry or penitent; unrepentant.
▸**imˈpenitence, imˈpenitency,** *or* **imˈpenitentness** *n* ▸**imˈpenitently** *adv*

imper. *abbrev. for* imperative.

imperative Ⓣ (ɪmˈpɛrətɪv) *adj* **1** extremely urgent or important; essential. **2** peremptory or authoritative: *an imperative tone of voice.* **3** Also: **imperatival** (ɪmˌpɛrəˈtaɪvᵊl). *Grammar.* denoting a mood of verbs used in giving orders, making requests, etc. ◆ *n* **4** something that is urgent or essential. **5** an order or command. **6** *Grammar.* **6a** the imperative mood. **6b** a verb in this mood. [C16: from LL, from L *imperāre* to command]
▸**imˈperatively** *adv* ▸**imˈperativeness** *n*

imperator (ˌɪmpəˈrɑːtɔː) *n* (in ancient Rome) a title bestowed upon generals and, later, emperors. [C16: from L: commander, from *imperāre* to command]
▸**imperatorial** (ɪmˌpɛrəˈtɔːrɪəl) *adj* ▸**ˌimpeˈratorˌship** *n*

imperceptible Ⓣ (ˌɪmpəˈsɛptɪbᵊl) *adj* too slight, subtle, gradual, etc., to be perceived.
▸**ˌimperˌceptiˈbility** *or* **ˌimperˈceptibleness** *n* ▸**ˌimperˈceptibly** *adv*

imperceptive Ⓣ (ˌɪmpəˈsɛptɪv) *adj, also* **impercipient** (ˌɪmpəˈsɪpɪənt). lacking in perception; obtuse.
▸**ˌimperˈception** *n* ▸**ˌimperˈceptively** *adv* ▸**ˌimperˈceptiveness** *or* **ˌimperˈcipience** *n*

imperf. *abbrev. for:* **1** Also: **impf.** imperfect. **2** (of stamps) imperforate.

imperfect Ⓣ (ɪmˈpɜːfɪkt) *adj* **1** exhibiting or characterized by faults, mistakes, etc.; defective. **2** not complete or finished; deficient. **3** *Grammar.* denoting a tense of verbs used most commonly in describing continuous or repeated past actions or events. **4** *Law.* legally unenforceable. **5** *Music.* **5a** proceeding to the dominant from the tonic, subdominant, or any chord other than the dominant. **5b** of or relating to all intervals other than the fourth, fifth, and octave. Cf. **perfect** (sense 9). ◆ *n* **6** *Grammar.* **6a** the imperfect tense. **6b** a verb in this tense.
▸**imˈperfectly** *adv* ▸**imˈperfectness** *n*

imperfection Ⓣ (ˌɪmpəˈfɛkʃən) *n* **1** the condition or quality of being imperfect. **2** a fault or defect.

imperfective (ˌɪmpəˈfɛktɪv) *Grammar.* ◆ *adj* **1** denoting an aspect of the verb to indicate that the action is in progress without regard to its completion. Cf. **perfective.** ◆ *n* **2a** the imperfective aspect of a verb. **2b** a verb in this aspect.
▸**ˌimperˈfectively** *adv*

imperforate (ɪmˈpɜːfərɪt, -ˌreɪt) *adj* **1** not perforated. **2** (of a postage stamp) not provided with perforation or any other means of separation. **3** *Anat.* without the normal opening.
▸**imˌperfoˈration** *n*

imperial Ⓣ (ɪmˈpɪərɪəl) *adj* **1** of or relating to an empire, emperor, or empress. **2** characteristic of an emperor; majestic; commanding. **3** exercising supreme authority; imperious. **4** (esp. of products) of a superior size or quality. **5** (*usually prenominal*) (of weights, measures, etc.) conforming to standards legally established in Great Britain. ◆ *n* **6** a book size, esp. 7½ by 11 inches or 11 by 15 inches. **7** a size of writing paper, 23 by 31 inches (US and Canad.) or 22 by 30 inches (Brit.). **8** *US.* **8a** the top of a carriage. **8b** a luggage case carried there. **9** a small tufted beard popularized by the French emperor Napoleon III. **10** a wine bottle holding the equivalent of eight normal bottles. [C14: from LL, from L *imperium* command, authority, empire]
▸**imˈperially** *adv* ▸**imˈperialness** *n*

imperialism (ɪmˈpɪərɪəˌlɪzəm) *n* **1** the policy or practice of extending a state's rule over other territories. **2** the extension or attempted extension of authority, influence, power, etc., by any person, country, institution, etc.: *cultural imperialism.* **3** a system of imperial government or rule by an emperor. **4** the spirit, character, authority, etc., of an empire.
▸**imˈperialist** *adj, n* ▸**imˌperialˈistic** *adj* ▸**imˌperialˈistically** *adv*

imperil Ⓣ (ɪmˈpɛrɪl) *vb* **imperils, imperilling, imperilled** *or US* **imperils, imperiling, imperiled.** (*tr*) to place in danger or jeopardy; endanger.
▸**imˈperilment** *n*

imperious Ⓣ (ɪmˈpɪərɪəs) *adj* **1** domineering; overbearing. **2** *Rare.* urgent. [C16: from L, from *imperium* command, power]
▸**imˈperiously** *adv* ▸**imˈperiousness** *n*

imperishable Ⓣ (ɪmˈpɛrɪʃəbᵊl) *adj* **1** not subject to decay or deterioration. **2** not likely to be forgotten: *imperishable truths.*
▸**imˌperishaˈbility** *or* **imˈperishableness** *n* ▸**imˈperishably** *adv*

THESAURUS

Antonyms *adj* affluent, prosperous, rich, wealthy, well-off, well-to-do

impede *vb* = **hinder**, bar, block, brake, check, clog, cumber, curb, delay, disrupt, encumber, hamper, hold up, obstruct, restrain, retard, slow (down), stop, throw a spanner in the works (*Brit. inf.*), thwart
Antonyms *vb* advance, aid, assist, further, help, promote

impediment *n* **1** = **obstacle**, bar, barrier, block, check, clog, curb, defect, difficulty, encumbrance, fly in the ointment, hazard, hindrance, millstone around one's neck, obstruction, snag, stumbling block
Antonyms *n* advantage, aid, assistance, benefit, encouragement, relief, support

impedimenta *pl n* **1** = **baggage**, accoutrements, belongings, effects, equipment, gear, junk (*inf.*), luggage, movables, odds and ends, paraphernalia, possessions, stuff, things, trappings, traps

impel *vb* **1** = **force**, actuate, chivy, compel, constrain, drive, goad, incite, induce, influence, inspire, instigate, motivate, move, oblige, power, prod, prompt, propel, push, require, spur, stimulate, urge
Antonyms *vb* check, discourage, dissuade, rebuff, repulse, restrain

impending *adj* **1** = **looming**, approaching, brewing, coming, forthcoming, gathering, hovering, imminent, in the offing, in the pipeline, menacing, near, nearing, on the horizon, threatening, upcoming

impenetrable *adj* **1** = **impassable**, dense, hermetic, impermeable, impervious, inviolable, solid, thick, unpierceable **2** = **incomprehensible**, arcane, baffling, cabbalistic, dark, enigmatic, enigmatical, hidden, indiscernible, inexplicable, inscrutable, mysterious, obscure, unfathomable, unintelligible
Antonyms *adj* ≠ **impassable:** accessible, enterable, passable, penetrable, pierceable, vulnerable ≠ **incomprehensible:** clear, explicable, obvious, soluble, understandable

impenitence *n* = **hardheartedness**, impenitency, incorrigibility, obduracy, stubbornness

impenitent *adj* = **unrepentant**, defiant, hardened, hardhearted, incorrigible, obdurate, recidivistic, relentless, remorseless, unabashed, unashamed, uncontrite, unreformed

imperative *adj* **1** = **urgent**, compulsory, crucial, essential, exigent, indispensable, insistent, obligatory, pressing, vital **2** = **commanding**, authoritative, autocratic, dictatorial, domineering, high-handed, imperious, lordly, magisterial, peremptory
Antonyms *adj* ≠ **urgent:** avoidable, discretional, nonessential, optional, unimportant, unnecessary

imperceptible *adj* = **undetectable**, faint, fine, gradual, impalpable, inappreciable, inaudible, indiscernible, indistinguishable, infinitesimal, insensible, invisible, microscopic, minute, shadowy, slight, small, subtle, teensy-weensy, teeny-weeny, tiny, unnoticeable
Antonyms *adj* audible, detectable, discernible, distinguishable, noticeable, perceptible, visible

imperceptibly *adv* = **invisibly**, by a hair's-breadth, inappreciably, indiscernibly, little by little, slowly, subtly, unnoticeably, unobtrusively, unseen

imperceptive *adj* = **unobservant**, impercipient, insensitive, obtuse, superficial, unappreciative, unaware, undiscerning, unseeing

imperfect *adj* **1, 2** = **flawed**, broken, damaged, defective, deficient, faulty, immature, impaired, incomplete, inexact, limited, partial, patchy, rudimentary, sketchy, undeveloped, unfinished
Antonyms *adj* complete, developed, exact, finished, flawless, perfect

imperfection *n* **1, 2** = **fault**, blemish, defect, deficiency, failing, fallibility, flaw, foible, frailty, inadequacy, incompleteness, infirmity, insufficiency, peccadillo, scar, shortcoming, stain, taint, weakness, weak point
Antonyms *n* adequacy, completeness, consummation, excellence, faultlessness, flawlessness, perfection, sufficiency

imperial *adj* **1** = **royal**, kingly, majestic, princely, queenly, regal, sovereign **3** = **supreme**, august, exalted, grand, great, high, imperious, lofty, magnificent, noble, superior

imperil *vb* = **endanger**, expose, hazard, jeopardize, risk
Antonyms *vb* care for, guard, protect, safeguard, secure

imperious *adj* **1** = **domineering**, arrogant, authoritative, autocratic, bossy (*inf.*), commanding, despotic, dictatorial, exacting, haughty, high-handed, imperative, lordly, magisterial, overbearing, overweening, tyrannical, tyrannous

imperishable *adj* **1** = **indestructible**, abiding,

impermanent ⓣ (ɪmˈpɜːmənənt) *adj* not permanent; fleeting. ▸**imˈpermanence** *or* **imˈpermanency** *n* ▸**imˈpermanently** *adv*

impermeable ⓣ (ɪmˈpɜːmɪəbᵊl) *adj* (of a substance) not allowing the passage of a fluid through interstices; not permeable. ▸**im͵permeaˈbility** *or* **imˈpermeableness** *n* ▸**imˈpermeably** *adv*

impermissible (͵ɪmpəˈmɪsɪbᵊl) *adj* not permissible; not allowed. ▸**͵imper͵missiˈbility** *n*

impersonal ⓣ (ɪmˈpɜːsənᵊl) *adj* **1** without reference to any individual person; objective: *an impersonal assessment.* **2** devoid of human warmth or sympathy; cold: *an impersonal manner.* **3** not having human characteristics: *an impersonal God.* **4** *Grammar.* (of a verb) having no logical subject: *it is raining.* **5** *Grammar.* (of a pronoun) not denoting a person. ▸**im͵personˈality** *n* ▸**imˈpersonally** *adv*

impersonalize *or* **impersonalise** (ɪmˈpɜːsənə͵laɪz) *vb* **impersonalizes, impersonalizing, impersonalized** *or* **impersonalises, impersonalising, impersonalised.** (*tr*) to make impersonal, esp. to rid of such human characteristics as sympathy, etc.; dehumanize. ▸**im͵personaliˈzation** *or* **im͵personaliˈsation** *n*

impersonate ⓣ (ɪmˈpɜːsə͵neɪt) *vb* **impersonates, impersonating, impersonated.** (*tr*) **1** to pretend to be (another person). **2** to imitate the character, mannerisms, etc., of (another person). **3** *Rare.* to play the part or character of. **4** an archaic word for **personify.** ▸**im͵personˈation** *n* ▸**imˈperson͵ator** *n*

impertinence ⓣ (ɪmˈpɜːtɪnəns) *or* **impertinency** *n* **1** disrespectful behaviour or language; rudeness; insolence. **2** an impertinent act, gesture, etc. **3** *Rare.* lack of pertinence; irrelevance; inappropriateness.

impertinent ⓣ (ɪmˈpɜːtɪnənt) *adj* **1** rude; insolent; impudent. **2** irrelevant or inappropriate. [C14: from L *impertinēns* not belonging, from L IM- (not) + *pertinēre* to be relevant; see PERTAIN] ▸**imˈpertinently** *adv*

imperturbable ⓣ (͵ɪmpɜːˈtɜːbəbᵊl) *adj* not easily perturbed; calm; unruffled. ▸**͵imper͵turbaˈbility** *or* **͵imperˈturbableness** *n* ▸**͵imperˈturbably** *adv*

impervious ⓣ (ɪmˈpɜːvɪəs) *or* **imperviable** *adj* **1** not able to be penetrated, as by water, light, etc.; impermeable. **2** (*often postpositive;* foll. by *to*) not able to be influenced (by) or not receptive (to): *impervious to argument.* ▸**imˈperviously** *adv* ▸**imˈperviousness** *n*

impetigo (͵ɪmpɪˈtaɪgəʊ) *n* a contagious pustular skin disease. [C16: from L: scabby eruption, from *impetere* to assail; see IMPETUS; for form, cf. VERTIGO] ▸**impetiginous** (͵ɪmpɪˈtɪdʒɪnəs) *adj*

impetuous ⓣ (ɪmˈpetjʊəs) *adj* **1** liable to act without consideration; rash; impulsive. **2** resulting from or characterized by rashness or haste. **3** *Poetic.* moving with great force or violence; rushing: *the impetuous stream hurtled down the valley.* [C14: from LL *impetuōsus* violent; see IMPETUS] ▸**imˈpetuously** *adv* ▸**imˈpetuousness** *or* **impetuosity** (ɪm͵petjuˈɒsɪtɪ) *n*

impetus ⓣ (ˈɪmpɪtəs) *n, pl* **impetuses. 1** an impelling movement or force; incentive or impulse; stimulus. **2** *Physics.* the force that sets a body in motion or that tends to resist changes in a body's motion. [C17: from L: attack, from *impetere* to assail, from IM- (in) + *petere* to make for, seek out]

impf. *or* **imperf.** *abbrev. for* imperfect.

impi (ˈɪmpɪ) *n, pl* **impi** *or* **impies.** a group of Bantu warriors. [C19: from Zulu]

impiety ⓣ (ɪmˈpaɪɪtɪ) *n, pl* **impieties. 1** lack of reverence or proper respect for a god. **2** any lack of proper respect. **3** an impious act.

impinge ⓣ (ɪmˈpɪndʒ) *vb* **impinges, impinging, impinged. 1** (*intr;* usually foll. by *on* or *upon*) to encroach or infringe; trespass: *to impinge on someone's time.* **2** (*intr;* usually foll. by *on, against,* or *upon*) to collide (with); strike. [C16: from L *impingere* to drive at, dash against, from *pangere* to fasten, drive in] ▸**imˈpingement** *n* ▸**imˈpinger** *n*

impious ⓣ (ˈɪmpɪəs) *adj* **1** lacking piety or reverence for a god. **2** lacking respect; undutiful. ▸**ˈimpiously** *adv* ▸**ˈimpiousness** *n*

impish ⓣ (ˈɪmpɪʃ) *adj* of or like an imp; mischievous. ▸**ˈimpishly** *adv* ▸**ˈimpishness** *n*

implacable ⓣ (ɪmˈplækəbᵊl) *adj* **1** incapable of being placated or pacified; unappeasable. **2** inflexible; intractable. ▸**im͵placaˈbility** *n* ▸**imˈplacably** *adv*

implant ⓣ *vb* (ɪmˈplɑːnt). (*tr*) **1** to inculcate; instil: *to implant sound moral principles.* **2** to plant or embed; infix; entrench. **3** *Surgery.* to graft or insert (a tissue, hormone, etc.) into the body. ◆ *n* (ˈɪmplɑːnt). **4** anything implanted, esp. surgically, such as a tissue graft or hormone. ▸**͵implanˈtation** *n*

implausible ⓣ (ɪmˈplɔːzəbᵊl) *adj* not plausible; provoking disbelief; unlikely. ▸**im͵plausiˈbility** *or* **imˈplausibleness** *n* ▸**imˈplausibly** *adv*

implement ⓣ *n* (ˈɪmplɪmənt). **1** a piece of equipment; tool or utensil: *gardening implements.* **2** a means to achieve a purpose; agent. ◆ *vb* (ˈɪmplɪ͵ment). (*tr*) **3** to carry out; put into action: *to implement a plan.* **4** *Rare.* to supply with tools. [C17: from LL *implēmentum,* lit.: a filling up, from L *implēre* to fill up, satisfy, fulfil] ▸**͵impleˈmental** *adj* ▸**͵implemenˈtation** *n*

implicate ⓣ (ˈɪmplɪ͵keɪt) *vb* **implicates, implicating, implicated.** (*tr*) **1** to show to be involved, esp. in a crime. **2** to imply: *his protest implicated censure by the authorities.* **3** *Rare.* to entangle. [C16: from L *implicāre* to involve, from *plicāre* to fold] ▸**implicative** (ɪmˈplɪkətɪv) *adj* ▸**imˈplicatively** *adv*

THESAURUS

enduring, eternal, everlasting, immortal, perennial, permanent, perpetual, undying, unfading, unforgettable
Antonyms *adj* destructible, dying, fading, forgettable, mortal, perishable

impermanent *adj* = **temporary,** brief, elusive, ephemeral, evanescent, fleeting, fly-by-night, flying, fugacious, fugitive, here today, gone tomorrow (*inf.*), inconstant, momentary, mortal, passing, perishable, short-lived, transient, transitory

impermeable *adj* = **impenetrable,** hermetic, impassable, impervious, nonporous, proof, resistant

impersonal *adj* **2** = **detached,** aloof, bureaucratic, businesslike, cold, dispassionate, formal, inhuman, neutral, remote
Antonyms *adj* friendly, intimate, outgoing, personal, warm

impersonate *vb* **1** = **pass oneself off as,** masquerade as, personate, pose as (*inf.*) **2** = **imitate,** act, ape, caricature, do (*inf.*), do an impression of, enact, mimic, parody, take off (*inf.*)

impersonation *n* **2** = **imitation,** caricature, impression, mimicry, parody, takeoff (*inf.*)

impertinence *n* **1** = **rudeness,** assurance, audacity, backchat (*inf.*), boldness, brass neck (*Brit. inf.*), brazenness, cheek (*inf.*), chutzpah (*US & Canad. inf.*), disrespect, effrontery, face (*inf.*), forwardness, front, impudence, incivility, insolence, neck (*inf.*), nerve (*inf.*), pertness, presumption, sauce (*inf.*)

impertinent *adj* **1** = **rude,** bold, brazen, cheeky (*inf.*), discourteous, disrespectful, flip (*inf.*), forward, fresh (*inf.*), impolite, impudent, insolent, interfering, lippy (*US & Canad. sl.*), pert, presumptuous, sassy (*US inf.*), saucy (*inf.*), uncivil, unmannerly **2** = **inappropriate,** inapplicable, incongruous, irrelevant
Antonyms *adj* ≠ **rude:** mannerly, polite, respectful ≠ **inappropriate:** appropriate, germane, important, pertinent, relevant, vital

imperturbable *adj* = **calm,** collected, complacent, composed, cool, equanimous, nerveless, sedate, self-possessed, serene, stoic, stoical, tranquil, undisturbed, unexcitable, unfazed (*inf.*), unflappable (*inf.*), unmoved, unruffled
Antonyms *adj* agitated, excitable, frantic, jittery (*inf.*), nervous, panicky, ruffled, touchy, upset

impervious *adj* **1** = **sealed,** hermetic, impassable, impenetrable, impermeable, imperviable, invulnerable, resistant **2** = **unaffected,** closed, immune, invulnerable, proof against, unmoved, unreceptive, unswayable, untouched

impetuous *adj* **1** = **rash,** ardent, eager, fierce, furious, hasty, headlong, impassioned, impulsive, passionate, precipitate, spontaneous, spur-of-the-moment, unbridled, unplanned, unpremeditated, unreflecting, unrestrained, unthinking, vehement, violent
Antonyms *adj* cautious, leisurely, mild, slow, wary

impetuously *adv* **1** = **rashly,** helter-skelter, impulsively, in the heat of the moment, on the spur of the moment, passionately, recklessly, spontaneously, unthinkingly, vehemently, without thinking

impetuousness *n* **1** = **haste,** hastiness, impulsiveness, precipitancy, precipitateness, rashness, vehemence, violence

impetus *n* **1** = **incentive,** catalyst, goad, impulse, impulsion, motivation, push, spur, stimulus **2** = **force,** energy, momentum, power

impiety *n* **1** = **sacrilege,** godlessness, iniquity, irreligion, irreverence, profaneness, profanity, sinfulness, ungodliness, unholiness, unrighteousness, wickedness
Antonyms *n* devoutness, godliness, holiness, piety, respect, reverence, righteousness

impinge *vb* **1** = **encroach,** infringe, invade, make inroads, obtrude, trespass, violate

impious *adj* **1** = **sacrilegious,** blasphemous, godless, iniquitous, irreligious, irreverent, profane, sinful, ungodly, unholy, unrighteous, wicked
Antonyms *adj* devout, godly, holy, pious, religious, reverent, righteous

impish *adj* = **mischievous,** devilish, elfin, prankish, puckish, rascally, roguish, sportive, waggish

implacability *n* **1, 2** = **pitilessness,** implacableness, inexorability, inflexibility, intractability, mercilessness, relentlessness, ruthlessness, unforgivingness, vengefulness

implacable *adj* **1, 2** = **unyielding,** cruel, inexorable, inflexible, intractable, merciless, pitiless, rancorous, relentless, remorseless, ruthless, unappeasable, unbending, uncompromising, unforgiving, unrelenting
Antonyms *adj* appeasable, flexible, lenient, merciful, relenting, tolerant, yielding

implant *vb* **1** = **instil,** inculcate, infix, infuse, inseminate, sow **2** = **insert,** embed, fix, graft, ingraft, place, plant, root, sow

implausible *adj* = **improbable,** cock-and-bull (*inf.*), dubious, far-fetched, flimsy, incredible, suspect, unbelievable, unconvincing, unlikely, unreasonable, weak

implement *n* **1** = **tool,** apparatus, appliance, device, gadget, instrument, utensil ◆ *vb* **3** = **carry out,** bring about, complete, effect, enforce, execute, fulfil, perform, put into action *or* effect, realize
Antonyms *vb* ≠ **carry out:** delay, hamper, hinder, impede, weaken

implementation *n* **3** = **carrying out,** accomplishment, discharge, effecting, enforcement, execution, fulfilment, performance, performing, realization

implicate *vb* **1** = **incriminate,** associate, compromise, concern, embroil, entangle, include, inculpate, involve, mire, stitch up (*sl.*), tie up with
Antonyms *vb* acquit, disentangle, dissociate, eliminate, exclude, exculpate, rule out

implicated *adj* **1** = **involved,** incriminated, suspected, under suspicion

implication Ⓣ (ˌɪmplɪˈkeɪʃən) *n* **1** the act of implicating. **2** something that is implied. **3** *Logic.* a relation between two propositions, such that the second can be logically deduced from the first.

implicit Ⓣ (ɪmˈplɪsɪt) *adj* **1** not explicit; implied; indirect. **2** absolute and unreserved; unquestioning: *implicit trust.* **3** (when *postpositive,* foll. by *in*) contained or inherent: *to bring out the anger implicit in the argument.* [C16: from L *implicitus,* var. of *implicātus* interwoven; see IMPLICATE]
▸**imˈplicitly** *adv* ▸**imˈplicitness** *n*

implied Ⓣ (ɪmˈplaɪd) *adj* hinted at or suggested; not directly expressed: *an implied criticism.*

implode (ɪmˈpləʊd) *vb* **implodes, imploding, imploded.** to collapse inwards. Cf. **explode.** [C19: from IM- + (EX)PLODE]

implore Ⓣ (ɪmˈplɔː) *vb* **implores, imploring, implored.** (*tr*) to beg or ask (someone) earnestly (to do something); plead with; beseech; supplicate. [C16: from L *implōrāre,* from IM- + *plōrāre* to bewail]
▸ˌ**imploˈration** *n* ▸**imˈploratory** *adj* ▸**imˈploringly** *adv*

imply Ⓣ (ɪmˈplaɪ) *vb* **implies, implying, implied.** (*tr; may take a clause as object*) **1** to express or indicate by a hint; suggest. **2** to suggest or involve as a necessary consequence. [C14: from OF *emplier,* from L; see IMPLICATE]

> **USAGE NOTE** See at **infer.**

impolder (ɪmˈpəʊldə) *or* **empolder** *vb* to make into a polder; reclaim (land) from the sea. [C19: from Du. *inpolderen,* see IN-[2], POLDER]

impolite Ⓣ (ˌɪmpəˈlaɪt) *adj* discourteous; rude.
▸ˌ**impoˈlitely** *adv* ▸ˌ**impoˈliteness** *n*

impolitic Ⓣ (ɪmˈpɒlɪtɪk) *adj* not politic or expedient; unwise.
▸**imˈpoliticly** *adv*

imponderable (ɪmˈpɒndərəbᵊl, -drəbᵊl) *adj* **1** unable to be weighed or assessed. ◆ *n* **2** something difficult or impossible to assess.
▸**imˌponderaˈbility** *or* **imˈponderableness** *n* ▸**imˈponderably** *adv*

import Ⓣ *vb* (ɪmˈpɔːt, ˈɪmpɔːt). **1** to buy or bring in (goods or services) from a foreign country. **2** (*tr*) to bring in from an outside source: *to import foreign words into the language.* **3** *Rare.* to signify; mean: *to import doom.* ◆ *n* (ˈɪmpɔːt). **4** (*often pl*) **4a** goods or services that are bought from foreign countries. **4b** (*as modifier*): *an import licence.* **5** importance: *a man of great import.* **6** meaning. **7** *Inf.* a sportsman or -woman who is not native to the country in which he or she plays. [C15: from L *importāre* to carry in]
▸**imˈportable** *adj* ▸**imˈporter** *n*

importance Ⓣ (ɪmˈpɔːtᵊns) *n* **1** the state of being important; significance. **2** social status; standing; esteem: *a man of importance.* **3** *Obs.* **3a** meaning or signification. **3b** an important matter. **3c** importunity.

important Ⓣ (ɪmˈpɔːtᵊnt) *adj* **1** of great significance or value; outstanding. **2** of social significance; notable; eminent; esteemed: *an important man in the town.* **3** (when postpositive, usually foll. by *to*) of great concern (to); valued highly (by): *your wishes are important to me.* [C16: from OIt., from Med. L *importāre* to signify, be of consequence, from L: to carry in]
▸**imˈportantly** *adv*

> **USAGE NOTE** The use of *more importantly* as in *more importantly, the local council is opposed to this proposal* has become very common, but many people still prefer to use *more important.*

importation (ˌɪmpɔːˈteɪʃən) *n* **1** the act, business, or process of importing goods or services. **2** an imported product or service.

importunate Ⓣ (ɪmˈpɔːtjʊnɪt) *adj* **1** persistent or demanding; insistent. **2** *Rare.* troublesome; annoying.
▸**imˈportunately** *adv* ▸**imˈportunateness** *n*

importune Ⓣ (ɪmˈpɔːtjuːn, ˌɪmpɔːˈtjuːn) *vb* **importunes, importuning, importuned.** (*tr*) **1** to harass with persistent requests; demand of (someone) insistently. **2** to beg for persistently; request with insistence. [C16: from L *importūnus* tiresome, from *im-* IN-[1] + *-portūnus* as in *opportūnus* OPPORTUNE]
▸**imˈportunely** *adv* ▸**imˈportuner** *n* ▸ˌ**imporˈtunity** *or* **imˈportunacy** *n*

impose Ⓣ (ɪmˈpəʊz) *vb* **imposes, imposing, imposed.** (usually foll. by *on* or *upon*) **1** (*tr*) to establish something to be obeyed or complied with; enforce. **2** to force (oneself, one's presence, etc.) on others; obtrude. **3** (*intr*) to take advantage, as of a person or quality: *to impose on someone's kindness.* **4** (*tr*) *Printing.* to arrange (pages, type, etc.) in a chase so that the pages will be in the correct order. **5** (*tr*) to pass off deceptively; foist. [C15: from OF, from L *impōnere* to place upon, from *pōnere* to place, set]
▸**imˈposable** *adj* ▸**imˈposer** *n*

imposing Ⓣ (ɪmˈpəʊzɪŋ) *adj* grand or impressive: *an imposing building.*
▸**imˈposingly** *adv* ▸**imˈposingness** *n*

imposition Ⓣ (ˌɪmpəˈzɪʃən) *n* **1** the act of imposing. **2** something imposed unfairly on someone. **3** a task set as a school punishment. **4** the arrangement of pages for printing.

impossibility Ⓣ (ɪmˌpɒsəˈbɪlɪtɪ, ˌɪmpɒs-) *n, pl* **impossibilities. 1** the state or quality of being impossible. **2** something that is impossible.

impossible Ⓣ (ɪmˈpɒsəbᵊl) *adj* **1** incapable of being done, undertaken, or experienced. **2** incapable of occurring or happening. **3** absurd or inconceivable; unreasonable. **4** *Inf.* intolerable; outrageous: *those children are impossible.*
▸**imˈpossibleness** *n* ▸**imˈpossibly** *adv*

impossible figure *n* a picture of an object that at first sight looks three-dimensional but cannot be a two-dimensional projection of a real three-dimensional object, for example a picture of a staircase that re-enters itself while appearing to ascend continuously.

impost[1] (ˈɪmpəʊst) *n* **1** a tax, esp. a customs duty. **2** the weight that a horse must carry in a handicap race. ◆ *vb* **3** (*tr*) *US.* to classify (imported goods) according to the duty payable on them. [C16: from Med. L *impostus* tax, from L *impositus* imposed; see IMPOSE]
▸ˈ**imposter** *n*

impost[2] (ˈɪmpəʊst) *n Archit.* a member at the top of a column that sup-

THESAURUS

implication *n* **1** = **involvement**, association, connection, entanglement, incrimination **2** = **suggestion**, conclusion, inference, innuendo, meaning, overtone, presumption, ramification, significance, signification

implicit *adj* **1, 3** = **implied**, contained, inferred, inherent, latent, tacit, taken for granted, undeclared, understood, unspoken **2** = **absolute**, constant, entire, firm, fixed, full, steadfast, total, unhesitating, unqualified, unreserved, unshakable, unshaken, wholehearted
Antonyms *adj* ≠ **implied:** declared, explicit, expressed, obvious, patent, spoken, stated

implicitly *adv* **2** = **absolutely**, completely, firmly, unconditionally, unhesitatingly, unreservedly, utterly, without reservation

implied *adj* = **unspoken**, hinted at, implicit, indirect, inherent, insinuated, suggested, tacit, undeclared, unexpressed, unstated

implore *vb* = **beg**, beseech, conjure, crave, entreat, go on bended knee to, importune, plead with, pray, solicit, supplicate

imply *vb* **1** = **hint**, connote, give (someone) to understand, insinuate, intimate, signify, suggest **2** = **entail**, betoken, denote, evidence, import, include, indicate, involve, mean, point to, presuppose

impolite *adj* = **bad-mannered**, boorish, churlish, discourteous, disrespectful, ill-bred, ill-mannered, indecorous, indelicate, insolent, loutish, rough, rude, uncivil, uncouth, ungallant, ungentlemanly, ungracious, unladylike, unmannerly, unrefined
Antonyms *adj* courteous, decorous, gallant, gracious, mannerly, polite, refined, respectful, well-bred

impoliteness *n* = **bad manners**, boorishness, churlishness, discourtesy, disrespect, incivility, indelicacy, insolence, rudeness, unmannerliness
Antonyms *n* civility, courtesy, delicacy, mannerliness, politeness, respect

impolitic *adj* = **unwise**, ill-advised, ill-judged, imprudent, indiscreet, inexpedient, injudicious, maladroit, misguided, undiplomatic, untimely
Antonyms *adj* diplomatic, discreet, expedient, judicious, politic, prudent, timely, wise

import *vb* **1** = **bring in**, introduce, land ◆ *n* **5** = **importance**, bottom, consequence, magnitude, moment, significance, substance, weight **6** = **meaning**, bearing, drift, gist, implication, intention, message, purport, sense, significance, thrust

importance *n* **1** = **significance**, concern, consequence, import, interest, moment, momentousness, substance, usefulness, value, weight, worth **2** = **prestige**, bottom, distinction, eminence, esteem, influence, mark, pre-eminence, prominence, standing, status

important *adj* **1** = **significant**, far-reaching, grave, large, material, meaningful, momentous, of substance, primary, salient, seminal, serious, signal, substantial, urgent, weighty **2** = **powerful**, big-time (*inf.*), eminent, foremost, high-level, high-ranking, influential, leading, major league (*inf.*), notable, noteworthy, of note, outstanding, pre-eminent, prominent **3** *usually with* **to** = **of concern**, basic, essential, of interest, relevant, valuable, valued
Antonyms *adj* ≠ **significant:** inconsequential, insignificant, minor, needless, negligible, secondary, trivial, undistinctive, unimportant, unnecessary

importunate *adj* **1** = **persistent**, burning, clamant, clamorous, demanding, dogged, earnest, exigent, insistent, pertinacious, pressing, solicitous, troublesome, urgent

importune *vb* **1** = **pester**, badger, beset, besiege, dun, entreat, harass, hound, lay siege to, plague, press, solicit

importunity *n* **1** = **persistence**, cajolery, dunning, entreaties, insistence, pressing, solicitations, urging

impose *vb* **1** = **establish**, decree, enforce, exact, fix, institute, introduce, lay, levy, ordain, place, prescribe, promulgate, put, set **2** = **intrude**, butt in, encroach, foist, force oneself, gate-crash (*inf.*), inflict, obtrude, presume, take liberties, trespass **3** = **take advantage of**, abuse, exploit, play on, use

imposing *adj* = **impressive**, august, commanding, dignified, effective, grand, majestic, stately, striking
Antonyms *adj* insignificant, mean, modest, ordinary, petty, poor, unimposing

imposition *n* **1** = **application**, decree, introduction, laying on, levying, promulgation **2** = **intrusion**, cheek, encroachment, liberty, presumption

impossibility *n* **1** = **hopelessness**, impracticability, inability, inconceivability

impossible *adj* **2** = **inconceivable**, beyond one, beyond the bounds of possibility, hopeless, impracticable, not to be thought of, out of the question, unachievable, unattainable, unobtainable, unthinkable **3** = **absurd**, inadmissible, insoluble, intolerable, ludicrous, outrageous, preposterous, unacceptable, unanswerable, ungovernable, unreasonable, unsuitable, unworkable
Antonyms *adj* ≠ **inconceivable:** conceivable, imaginable, likely, plausible, possible, reasonable

ports an arch. [C17: from F *imposte,* from L *impositus* placed upon; see IMPOSE]

impostor Ⓣ *or* **imposter** (ɪmˈpɒstə) *n* a person who deceives others, esp. by assuming a false identity; charlatan. [C16: from LL: deceiver; see IMPOSE]

imposture Ⓣ (ɪmˈpɒstʃə) *n* the act or an instance of deceiving others, esp. by assuming a false identity. [C16: from F, from LL, from L *impōnere;* see IMPOSE]
▸**impostrous** (ɪmˈpɒstrəs) *or* **impostorous** (ɪmˈpɒstərəs) *adj*

impotent Ⓣ (ˈɪmpətənt) *adj* **1** (when *postpositive,* often takes an infinitive) lacking sufficient strength; powerless. **2** (esp. of males) unable to perform sexual intercourse.
▸**ˈimpotence** *or* **ˈimpotency** *n* ▸**ˈimpotently** *adv*

impound (ɪmˈpaʊnd) *vb (tr)* **1** to confine (animals, etc.) in a pound. **2** to take legal possession of (a document, evidence, etc.). **3** to collect (water) in a reservoir or dam.
▸**imˈpoundable** *adj* ▸**imˈpoundage** *or* **imˈpoundment** *n* ▸**imˈpounder** *n*

impoverish Ⓣ (ɪmˈpɒvərɪʃ) *vb (tr)* **1** to make poor or diminish the quality of: *to impoverish society by cutting the grant to the arts.* **2** to deprive (soil, etc.) of fertility. [C15: from OF *empovrir,* from *povre* POOR]
▸**imˈpoverishment** *n*

impracticable Ⓣ (ɪmˈpræktɪkəbᵊl) *adj* **1** incapable of being put into practice or accomplished; not feasible. **2** unsuitable for a desired use; unfit.
▸**imˌpracticaˈbility** *or* **imˈpracticableness** *n* ▸**imˈpracticably** *adv*

impractical Ⓣ (ɪmˈpræktɪkᵊl) *adj* **1** not practical or workable: *an impractical solution.* **2** not given to practical matters or gifted with practical skills.
▸**imˌpractiˈcality** *or* **imˈpracticalness** *n* ▸**imˈpractically** *adv*

imprecate Ⓣ (ˈɪmprɪˌkeɪt) *vb* **imprecates, imprecating, imprecated. 1** *(intr)* to swear or curse. **2** *(tr)* to invoke or bring down (evil, a curse, etc.). [C17: from L *imprecārī* to invoke, from *im-* IN-[2] + *precārī* to PRAY]
▸**ˌimpreˈcation** *n* ▸**ˈimpreˌcatory** *adj*

imprecise Ⓣ (ˌɪmprɪˈsaɪs) *adj* not precise; inexact or inaccurate.
▸**ˌimpreˈcisely** *adv* ▸**imprecision** (ˌɪmprɪˈsɪʒən) *or* **ˌimpreˈciseness** *n*

impregnable[1] Ⓣ (ɪmˈprɛgnəbᵊl) *adj* **1** unable to be broken into or taken by force: *an impregnable castle.* **2** unshakable: *impregnable self-confidence.* **3** incapable of being refuted: *an impregnable argument.* [C15 *imprenable,* from OF, from IM- (not) + *prenable* able to be taken, from *prendre* to take]
▸**imˌpregnaˈbility** *n* ▸**imˈpregnably** *adv*

impregnable[2] (ɪmˈprɛgnəbᵊl) *or* **impregnatable** (ˌɪmprɛgˈneɪtəbᵊl) *adj* able to be impregnated; fertile.

impregnate Ⓣ *vb* (ˈɪmprɛgˌneɪt), **impregnates, impregnating, impregnated.** *(tr)* **1** to saturate, soak, or infuse. **2** to imbue or permeate; pervade. **3** to cause to conceive; make pregnant; fertilize. **4** to make (land, soil, etc.) fruitful. ◆ *adj* (ɪmˈprɛgnɪt, -ˌneɪt). **5** pregnant or fertilized. [C17: from LL, from L *im-* IN-[2] + *praegnans* PREGNANT]
▸**ˌimpregˈnation** *n* ▸**imˈpregnator** *n*

impresario (ˌɪmprəˈsɑːrɪˌəʊ) *n, pl* **impresarios.** the director or manager of an opera, ballet, etc. [C18: from It., lit.: one who undertakes]

imprescriptible (ˌɪmprɪˈskrɪptəbᵊl) *adj Law.* immune or exempt from prescription.
▸**ˌimpreˌscriptiˈbility** *n* ▸**ˌimpreˈscriptibly** *adv*

impress[1] Ⓣ *vb* (ɪmˈprɛs). *(tr)* **1** to make an impression on; have a strong, lasting, or favourable effect on: *I am impressed by your work.* **2** to produce (an imprint, etc.) by pressure in or on (something): *to impress a seal in wax.* **3** (often foll. by *on*) to stress (something to a person); urge; emphasize. **4** to exert pressure on; press. ◆ *n* (ˈɪmprɛs). **5** the act or an instance of impressing. **6** a mark, imprint, or effect produced by impressing. [C14: from L *imprimere* to press into, imprint]
▸**imˈpresser** *n* ▸**imˈpressible** *adj*

impress[2] *vb* (ɪmˈprɛs). **1** to commandeer or coerce (men or things) into government service; press-gang. ◆ *n* (ˈɪmprɛs). **2** the act of commandeering or coercing into government service. [C16: see *im-* IN-[2], PRESS[2]]

impression Ⓣ (ɪmˈprɛʃən) *n* **1** an effect produced in the mind by a stimulus; sensation: *he gave the impression of wanting to help.* **2** an imprint or mark produced by pressing. **3** a vague idea, consciousness, or belief: *I had the impression we had met before.* **4** a strong, favourable, or remarkable effect. **5** the act of impressing or the state of being impressed. **6** *Printing.* **6a** the act, process, or result of printing from type, plates, etc. **6b** the total number of copies of a publication printed at one time. **7** an imprint of the teeth and gums for preparing crowns, dentures, etc. **8** an imitation or impersonation.
▸**imˈpressional** *adj* ▸**imˈpressionally** *adv*

impressionable Ⓣ (ɪmˈprɛʃənəbᵊl, -ˈprɛʃnə-) *adj* easily influenced or characterized by susceptibility to influence: *an impressionable age.*
▸**imˌpressionaˈbility** *or* **imˈpressionableness** *n*

impressionism (ɪmˈprɛʃəˌnɪzəm) *n (often cap.)* a 19th-century movement in French painting, having the aim of objectively recording experience by a system of fleeting impressions, esp. of natural light.
▸**imˈpressionist** *n*

impressive Ⓣ (ɪmˈprɛsɪv) *adj* capable of impressing, esp. by size, magnificence, etc.; awe-inspiring; commanding.
▸**imˈpressively** *adv* ▸**imˈpressiveness** *n*

imprest (ɪmˈprɛst) *n* **1** a fund of cash from which a department, etc., pays incidental expenses, topped up periodically from central funds. **2** *Chiefly Brit.* an advance from government funds for some public business or service. [C16: prob. from It. *imprestare* to lend, from L *in-* towards + *praestāre* to pay, from *praestō* at hand; see PRESTO]

imprimatur (ˌɪmprɪˈmeɪtə, -ˈmɑː-) *n* **1** sanction or approval for something to be printed. **2** *RC Church.* a licence certifying the Church's approval. [C17: NL, lit.: let it be printed]

imprint Ⓣ *n* (ˈɪmprɪnt). **1** a mark or impression produced by pressure, printing, or stamping. **2** a characteristic mark or indication; stamp: *the imprint of great sadness on his face.* **3a** the publisher's name and address, often with the date of publication, printed in a book, usually on the title page or the verso title page. **3b** the printer's name and address on any printed matter. ◆ *vb* (ɪmˈprɪnt). *(tr)* **4** to produce (a mark, impression, etc.) on (a surface) by pressure, printing, or stamping: *to imprint a seal on wax.* **5** to establish firmly; impress: *to imprint the details on one's mind.* **6** to cause (a young animal) to undergo the process of imprinting: *chicks can be imprinted on human beings.*

THESAURUS

impostor *n* = **impersonator,** charlatan, cheat, deceiver, fake, fraud, hypocrite, knave *(arch.),* phoney *or* phony *(inf.),* pretender, quack, rogue, sham, trickster

imposture *n* = **deception,** artifice, canard, cheat, con trick *(inf.),* counterfeit, fraud, hoax, impersonation, imposition, quackery, swindle, trick

impotence *n* **1** = **powerlessness,** disability, enervation, feebleness, frailty, helplessness, inability, inadequacy, incapacity, incompetence, ineffectiveness, inefficacy, inefficiency, infirmity, paralysis, uselessness, weakness
Antonyms *n* ability, adequacy, competence, effectiveness, efficacy, efficiency, powerfulness, strength, usefulness

impotent *adj* **1** = **powerless,** disabled, emasculate, enervated, feeble, frail, helpless, incapable, incapacitated, incompetent, ineffective, infirm, nerveless, paralysed, unable, unmanned, weak
Antonyms *adj* able, capable, competent, effective, manned, potent, powerful, strong

impoverish *vb* **1** = **bankrupt,** beggar, break, pauperize, ruin **2** = **diminish,** deplete, drain, exhaust, reduce, sap, use up, wear out

impoverished *adj* **1** = **poor,** bankrupt, destitute, distressed, impecunious, indigent, in reduced *or* straitened circumstances, necessitous, needy, on one's uppers, penurious, poverty-stricken, ruined, straitened **2** = **depleted,** barren, denuded, drained, empty, exhausted, played out, reduced, spent, sterile, worn out
Antonyms *adj* ≠ **poor:** affluent, rich, wealthy, well-off ≠ **depleted:** fecund, fertile, productive

impracticability *n* **1, 2** = **impracticality,** futility, hopelessness, impossibility, unsuitableness, unworkability, uselessness

impracticable *adj* **1** = **unfeasible,** impossible, out of the question, unachievable, unattainable, unworkable **2** = **unsuitable,** awkward, impractical, inapplicable, inconvenient, unserviceable, useless
Antonyms *adj* ≠ **unfeasible:** feasible, possible, practicable ≠ **unsuitable:** practical, serviceable, suitable

impractical *adj* **1** = **unworkable,** impossible, impracticable, inoperable, nonviable, unrealistic, unserviceable, visionary, wild **2** = **idealistic,** romantic, starry-eyed, unbusinesslike, unrealistic, visionary
Antonyms *adj* ≠ **unworkable:** possible, practical, serviceable, viable, workable ≠ **idealistic:** down-to-earth, realistic, sensible

impracticality *n* **1** = **unworkability,** hopelessness, impossibility, inapplicability

imprecation *n* **2** = **curse,** anathema, blasphemy, denunciation, execration, malediction, profanity, vilification

imprecise *adj* = **indefinite,** ambiguous, blurred round the edges, careless, equivocal, estimated, fluctuating, hazy, ill-defined, inaccurate, indeterminate, inexact, inexplicit, loose, rough, sloppy *(inf.),* vague, wide of the mark, woolly
Antonyms *adj* accurate, careful, definite, determinate, exact, explicit, precise

impregnable[1] *adj* **1-3** = **invulnerable,** immovable, impenetrable, indestructible, invincible, secure, strong, unassailable, unbeatable, unconquerable, unshakable
Antonyms *adj* destructible, exposed, insecure, open, pregnable, shakable, vulnerable

impregnate *vb* **1, 2** = **saturate,** fill, imbrue *(rare),* imbue, infuse, percolate, permeate, pervade, seep, soak, steep, suffuse **3** = **fertilize,** get with child, inseminate, make pregnant **4** = **fecundate,** fructify

impress[1] *vb* **1** = **excite,** affect, grab *(inf.),* influence, inspire, make an impression, move, stir, strike, sway, touch **2** = **imprint,** emboss, engrave, indent, mark, print, stamp **3** = **stress,** bring home to, emphasize, fix, inculcate, instil into

impression *n* **2** = **mark,** brand, dent, hollow, impress, imprint, indentation, outline, stamp, stamping **3** = **idea,** belief, concept, conviction, fancy, feeling, funny feeling *(inf.),* hunch, memory, notion, opinion, recollection, sense, suspicion **4** = **effect,** feeling, impact, influence, reaction, sway **6** = **edition,** imprinting, issue, printing **8** = **imitation,** impersonation, parody, send-up *(Brit. inf.),* takeoff *(inf.)*

impressionability *n* = **suggestibility,** ingenuousness, receptiveness, receptivity, sensitivity, susceptibility, vulnerability

impressionable *adj* = **suggestible,** feeling, gullible, ingenuous, open, receptive, responsive, sensitive, susceptible, vulnerable
Antonyms *adj* blasé, hardened, insensitive, jaded, unresponsive

impressive *adj* = **grand,** affecting, awesome, dramatic, exciting, forcible, moving, powerful, stirring, striking, touching
Antonyms *adj* ordinary, unimposing, unimpressive, uninspiring, unmemorable, weak

imprint *n* **1** = **mark,** impression, indentation, print, sign, stamp ◆ *vb* **4, 5** = **fix,** engrave, establish, etch, impress, print, stamp

DICTIONARY

imprinting (ɪmˈprɪntɪŋ) *n* the development in young animals of recognition of and attraction to members of their own species or surrogates.

imprison Ⓣ (ɪmˈprɪzən) *vb* (*tr*) to confine in or as if in prison.
▸**imˈprisonment** *n*

improbable Ⓣ (ɪmˈprɒbəᵊl) *adj* not likely or probable; doubtful; unlikely.
▸**imˌprobaˈbility** *or* **imˈprobableness** *n* ▸**imˈprobably** *adv*

improbity Ⓣ (ɪmˈprəʊbɪtɪ) *n, pl* **improbities.** dishonesty, wickedness, or unscrupulousness.

impromptu Ⓣ (ɪmˈprɒmptju:) *adj* **1** unrehearsed; spontaneous. **2** produced or done without care or planning; improvised. ◆ *adv* **3** in a spontaneous or improvised way: *he spoke impromptu.* ◆ *n* **4** something that is impromptu. **5** a short piece of instrumental music, sometimes improvisatory in character. [C17: from F, from L *in promptū* in readiness, from *promptus* (adj) ready, PROMPT]

improper Ⓣ (ɪmˈprɒpə) *adj* **1** lacking propriety; not seemly. **2** unsuitable for a certain use or occasion; inappropriate. **3** irregular or abnormal.
▸**imˈproperly** *adv* ▸**imˈproperness** *n*

improper fraction *n* a fraction in which the numerator is greater than the denominator, as 7/6.

impropriate *vb* (ɪmˈprəʊprɪˌeɪt), **impropriates, impropriating, impropriated. 1** (*tr*) to transfer (property, rights, etc.) from the Church into lay hands. ◆ *adj* (ɪmˈprəʊprɪɪt, -ˌeɪt). **2** transferred in this way. [C16: from Med. L *impropriāre* to make one's own, from L *im-* IN-[2] + *propriāre* to APPROPRIATE]
▸**imˌpropriˈation** *n* ▸**imˈpropriˌator** *n*

impropriety Ⓣ (ˌɪmprəˈpraɪɪtɪ) *n, pl* **improprieties. 1** lack of propriety; indecency; indecorum. **2** an improper act or use. **3** the state of being improper.

improve Ⓣ (ɪmˈpru:v) *vb* **improves, improving, improved. 1** to make or become better in quality; ameliorate. **2** (*tr*) to make (buildings, land, etc.) more valuable by additions or betterment. **3** (*intr*; usually foll. by *on* or *upon*) to achieve a better standard or quality in comparison (with): *to improve on last year's crop.* [C16: from Anglo-F *emprouer* to turn to profit, from LL *prōde* beneficial, from L *prōdesse* to be advantageous]
▸**imˈprovable** *adj* ▸**imˌprovaˈbility** *or* **imˈprovableness** *n* ▸**imˈprover** *n*

improvement Ⓣ (ɪmˈpru:vmənt) *n* **1** the act of improving or the state of being improved. **2** something that improves, esp. an addition or alteration. **3** (*usually pl*) *Austral. & NZ.* a building, etc., on a piece of land, adding to its value.

improvident Ⓣ (ɪmˈprɒvɪdənt) *adj* **1** not provident; thriftless, imprudent, or prodigal. **2** heedless or incautious; rash.
▸**imˈprovidence** *n* ▸**imˈprovidently** *adv*

improvise Ⓣ (ˈɪmprəˌvaɪz) *vb* **improvises, improvising, improvised. 1** to perform or make quickly from materials and sources available, without previous planning. **2** to perform (a poem, play, piece of music, etc.), composing as one goes along. [C19: from F, from It., from L *imprōvīsus* unforeseen, from *prōvidēre* to foresee; see PROVIDE]
▸**ˈimproˌviser** *n* ▸**ˌimproviˈsation** *n* ▸**improvisatory** (ˌɪmprəˈvaɪzətərɪ, -ˈvɪz-, ˌɪmprəvaɪzˈeɪtərɪ) *adj*

imprudent Ⓣ (ɪmˈpru:dᵊnt) *adj* not prudent; rash, heedless, or indiscreet.
▸**imˈprudence** *n* ▸**imˈprudently** *adv*

impudence Ⓣ (ˈɪmpjʊdəns) *or* **impudency** *n* **1** the quality of being impudent. **2** an impudent act or statement. [C14: from L *impudēns* shameless]

impudent Ⓣ (ˈɪmpjʊdənt) *adj* **1** mischievous, impertinent, or disrespectful. **2** *Obs.* immodest.
▸**ˈimpudently** *adv* ▸**ˈimpudentness** *n*

impugn Ⓣ (ɪmˈpju:n) *vb* (*tr*) to challenge or attack as false; criticize. [C14: from OF, from L *impugnāre* to fight against, attack]
▸**imˈpugnable** *adj* ▸**imˈpugnment** *n* ▸**imˈpugner** *n*

impulse Ⓣ (ˈɪmpʌls) *n* **1** an impelling force or motion; thrust; impetus. **2** a sudden desire, whim, or inclination. **3** an instinctive drive; urge. **4** tendency; current; trend. **5** *Physics.* **5a** the product of the average magnitude of a force acting on a body and the time for which it acts. **5b** the change in the momentum of a body as a result of a force acting upon it. **6** *Physiol.* See **nerve impulse. 7 on impulse.** spontaneously or impulsively. [C17: from L *impulsus* a pushing against, incitement, from *impellere* to strike against; see IMPEL]

impulse buying *n* the buying of merchandise prompted by a whim.
▸**impulse buyer** *n*

impulsion (ɪmˈpʌlʃən) *n* **1** the act of impelling or the state of being impelled. **2** motion produced by an impulse; propulsion. **3** a driving force; compulsion.

impulsive Ⓣ (ɪmˈpʌlsɪv) *adj* **1** characterized by actions based on sudden desires, whims, or inclinations: *an impulsive man.* **2** based on emotional impulses or whims; spontaneous. **3** forceful, inciting, or impelling. **4** (of physical forces) acting for a short time; not continuous. **5** (of a sound) brief, loud, and having a wide frequency range.
▸**imˈpulsively** *adv* ▸**imˈpulsiveness** *n*

impundulu (ˈɪmpʊnˌdʊlʊ) *n S. African.* a mythical bird often associated with witchcraft. [from Bantu]

impunity Ⓣ (ɪmˈpju:nɪtɪ) *n, pl* **impunities. 1** exemption or immunity from punishment, recrimination, or other unpleasant consequences. **2 with impunity.** with no care or heed for such consequences. [C16:

THESAURUS

imprison *vb* = **jail**, confine, constrain, detain, immure, incarcerate, intern, lock up, put away, put under lock and key, send down (*inf.*), send to prison
Antonyms *vb* discharge, emancipate, free, liberate, release

imprisoned *adj* = **jailed**, behind bars, captive, confined, immured, incarcerated, in irons, in jail, inside (*sl.*), interned, locked up, put away, under lock and key

imprisonment *n* = **custody**, confinement, detention, durance (*arch.*), duress, incarceration, internment, porridge (*sl.*)

improbability *n* = **doubt**, doubtfulness, dubiety, uncertainty, unlikelihood

improbable *adj* = **doubtful**, cock-and-bull, dubious, fanciful, far-fetched, implausible, questionable, unbelievable, uncertain, unconvincing, unlikely, weak
Antonyms *adj* certain, convincing, doubtless, likely, plausible, probable, reasonable

improbity *n* = **dishonesty**, chicanery, crookedness (*inf.*), faithlessness, fraud, knavery, unfairness, unscrupulousness, villainy

impromptu *adj* **1, 2** = **unprepared**, ad-lib, extemporaneous, extempore, extemporized, improvised, offhand, off the cuff (*inf.*), spontaneous, unpremeditated, unrehearsed, unscripted, unstudied ◆ *adv* **3** = **spontaneously**, ad lib, off the cuff (*inf.*), off the top of one's head (*inf.*), on the spur of the moment, without preparation
Antonyms *adj* ≠ **unprepared:** considered, planned, premeditated, prepared, rehearsed

improper *adj* **1** = **indecent**, impolite, indecorous, indelicate, off-colour, risqué, smutty, suggestive, unbecoming, unfitting, unseemly, untoward, vulgar **2** = **inappropriate**, ill-timed, inapplicable, inapposite, inapt, incongruous, infelicitous, inopportune, malapropos, out of place, uncalled-for, unfit, unseasonable, unsuitable, unsuited, unwarranted **3** = **incorrect**, abnormal, erroneous, false, inaccurate, irregular, wrong
Antonyms *adj* ≠ **indecent:** becoming, decent, decorous, delicate, fitting, proper, seemly ≠ **inappropriate:** apposite, appropriate, apt, felicitous, opportune, seasoned, suitable

impropriety *n* **1** = **indecency**, bad taste, immodesty, incongruity, indecorum, unsuitability, vulgarity **2** = **lapse**, bloomer (*Brit. inf.*), blunder, faux pas, gaffe, gaucherie, mistake, slip, solecism
Antonyms *n* ≠ **indecency:** decency, decorum, delicacy, modesty, propriety, suitability

improve *vb* **1** = **enhance**, ameliorate, amend, augment, better, correct, help, increase, mend, polish, rectify, touch up, upgrade
Antonyms *vb* damage, harm, impair, injure, mar, worsen

improvement *n* **1** = **enhancement**, advancement, amelioration, amendment, augmentation, betterment, correction, development, face-lift, furtherance, gain, increase, progress, rectification, rise, upswing

improvidence *n* **1** = **imprudence**, carelessness, extravagance, heedlessness, lavishness, negligence, prodigality, profligacy, shortsightedness, thriftlessness, wastefulness

improvident *adj* **1** = **imprudent**, careless, heedless, inconsiderate, negligent, prodigal, profligate, reckless, shiftless, short-sighted, spendthrift, thoughtless, thriftless, uneconomical, unthrifty, wasteful
Antonyms *adj* careful, considerate, economical, heedful, provident, prudent, thrifty

improvisation *n* **2** = **spontaneity**, ad-libbing, extemporizing, invention

improvise *vb* **1** = **concoct**, contrive, devise, make do, throw together **2** = **extemporize**, ad-lib, busk, coin, invent, play it by ear (*inf.*), speak off the cuff (*inf.*), vamp, wing it (*inf.*)

improvised *adj* **2** = **unprepared**, ad-lib, extemporaneous, extempore, extemporized, makeshift, off the cuff (*inf.*), spontaneous, spur-of-the-moment, unrehearsed

imprudence *n* = **rashness**, carelessness, folly, foolhardiness, foolishness, heedlessness, improvidence, inadvisability, incaution, incautiousness, inconsideration, indiscretion, irresponsibility, recklessness, temerity

imprudent *adj* = **unwise**, careless, foolhardy, foolish, heedless, ill-advised, ill-considered, ill-judged, impolitic, improvident, incautious, inconsiderate, indiscreet, injudicious, irresponsible, overhasty, rash, reckless, temerarious, unthinking
Antonyms *adj* careful, cautious, considerate, discreet, judicious, politic, provident, prudent, responsible, wise

impudence *n* **1** = **boldness**, assurance, audacity, backchat (*inf.*), brazenness, bumptiousness, cheek (*inf.*), chutzpah (*US & Canad. inf.*), effrontery, face (*inf.*), front, impertinence, insolence, lip (*sl.*), nerve (*inf.*), pertness, presumption, rudeness, shamelessness

impudent *adj* **1** = **bold**, audacious, bold-faced, brazen, bumptious, cheeky (*inf.*), cocky (*inf.*), forward, fresh (*inf.*), immodest, impertinent, insolent, lippy (*US & Canad. sl.*), pert, presumptuous, rude, sassy (*US inf.*), saucy (*inf.*), shameless
Antonyms *adj* courteous, modest, polite, respectful, retiring, self-effacing, timid, well-behaved

impugn *vb* = **challenge**, assail, attack, call into question, cast aspersions upon, cast doubt upon, criticize, dispute, gainsay (*arch. or literary*), oppose, question, resist, traduce

impulse *n* **1** = **force**, catalyst, impetus, momentum, movement, pressure, push, stimulus, surge, thrust **2, 3** = **urge**, caprice, drive, feeling, incitement, inclination, influence, instinct, motive, notion, passion, resolve, whim, wish

impulsive *adj* **1, 2** = **instinctive**, devil-may-care, emotional, hasty, headlong, impetuous, intuitive, passionate, precipitate, quick, rash, spontaneous, unconsidered, unpredictable, unpremeditated
Antonyms *adj* calculating, cautious, considered, cool, deliberate, halting, planned, premeditated, rehearsed, restrained

impunity *n* **1** = **security**, dispensation, exemp-

from L, from *impūnis* unpunished, from IM- (not) + *poena* punishment]

impure ❶ (ɪmˈpjʊə) *adj* **1** not pure; combined with something else; tainted or sullied. **2** (in certain religions) ritually unclean. **3** (of a colour) mixed with another colour. **4** of more than one origin or style, as of architecture.
▸**imˈpurely** *adv* ▸**imˈpureness** *n*

impurity ❶ (ɪmˈpjʊərɪtɪ) *n, pl* **impurities. 1** the quality of being impure. **2** an impure thing, constituent, or element: *impurities in the water.* **3** *Electronics.* a small quantity of an element added to a pure semiconductor crystal to control its electrical conductivity.

impute ❶ (ɪmˈpjuːt) *vb* **imputes, imputing, imputed.** (*tr*) **1** to attribute or ascribe (something dishonest or dishonourable) to a person. **2** to attribute to a source or cause: *I impute your success to nepotism.* **3** *Commerce.* to give (a notional value) to goods, etc., when the real value is unknown. [C14: from L, from IM- + *putāre* to think, calculate]
▸ˌ**impuˈtation** *n* ▸**imˈputative** *adj* ▸**imˈputer** *n* ▸**imˈputable** *adj*

IMunE *abbrev. for* Institution of Municipal Engineers.

in (ɪn) *prep* **1** inside; within: *no smoking in the auditorium.* **2** at a place where there is: *in the shade.* **3** indicating a state, situation, or condition: *in silence.* **4** when (a period of time) has elapsed: *return in one year.* **5** using: *written in code.* **6** concerned with, esp. as an occupation: *in journalism.* **7** while or by performing the action of: *in crossing the street he was run over.* **8** used to indicate purpose: *in honour of the king.* **9** (of certain animals) pregnant with: *in calf.* **10** a variant of **into**: *she fell in the water.* **11 have it in one.** (often foll. by an infinitive) to have the ability (to do something). **12 in that** *or* **in so far as.** (*conj*) because or to the extent that: *I regret my remark in that it upset you.* **13 nothing in it.** no difference or interval between two things. ◆ *adv* (*particle*) **14** in or into a particular place; inward or indoors: *come in.* **15** so as to achieve office or power: *Labour got in at the last election.* **16** so as to enclose: *block in.* **17** (in certain games) so as to take one's turn of the play: *you have to get the other side out before you go in.* **18** *NZ.* competing: *you've got to be in to win.* **19** *Brit.* (of a fire) alight. **20** (*in combination*) indicating an activity or gathering: *teach-in; work-in.* **21 in at.** present at (the beginning, end, etc.). **22 in for.** about to be affected by (something, esp. something unpleasant): *you're in for a shock.* **23 in on.** acquainted with or sharing in: *I was in on all his plans.* **24 in with.** associated with; friendly with; regarded highly by. **25 have (got) it in for.** to wish or intend harm towards. ◆ *adj* **26** (*stressed*) fashionable; modish: *the in thing to do.* ◆ *n* **27 ins and outs.** intricacies or complications; details. [OE]

In *the chemical symbol for* indium.

in. *abbrev. for* inch(es).

in-[1], **il-, im-,** *or* **ir-** *prefix* **a** not; non-: *incredible; illegal; imperfect; irregular.* **b** lack of: *inexperience.* Cf. **un-**. [from L *in-*; rel. to *ne-, nōn* not]

in-[2], **il-, im-,** *or* **ir-** *prefix* **1** in; into; towards; within; on: *infiltrate; immigrate.* **2** having an intensive or causative function: *inflame; imperil.* [from IN (prep, adv)]

-in *suffix forming nouns.* **1** indicating a neutral organic compound, including proteins, glucosides, and glycerides: *insulin; tripalmitin.* **2** indicating an enzyme in certain nonsystematic names: *pepsin.* **3** indicating a pharmaceutical substance: *penicillin; aspirin.* **4** indicating a chemical substance in certain nonsystematic names: *coumarin.* [from NL *-ina;* cf. -INE[2]]

in absentia *Latin.* (ɪn æbˈsɛntɪə) *adv* in the absence of (someone indicated).

inaccessible ❶ (ˌɪnækˈsɛsəbᵊl) *adj* not accessible; unapproachable.
▸ˌ**inacˌcessiˈbility** *or* ˌ**inacˈcessibleness** *n* ▸ˌ**inacˈcessibly** *adv*

inaccuracy ❶ (ɪnˈækjʊrəsɪ) *n, pl* **inaccuracies. 1** lack of accuracy; imprecision. **2** an error, mistake, or slip.
▸**inˈaccurate** *adj*

inaction ❶ (ɪnˈækʃən) *n* lack of action; idleness; inertia.

inactivate (ɪnˈæktɪˌveɪt) *vb* **inactivates, inactivating, inactivated.** (*tr*) to render inactive.
▸**inˌactiˈvation** *n*

inactive ❶ (ɪnˈæktɪv) *adj* **1** idle or inert; not active. **2** sluggish or indolent. **3** *Mil.* of or relating to persons or equipment not in active service. **4** *Chem.* (of a substance) having little or no reactivity.
▸**inˈactively** *adv* ▸ˌ**inacˈtivity** *n*

inadequate ❶ (ɪnˈædɪkwɪt) *adj* **1** not adequate; insufficient. **2** not capable; lacking.
▸**inˈadequacy** *n* ▸**inˈadequately** *adv*

inadvertence (ˌɪnədˈvɜːtᵊns) *or* **inadvertency** *n* **1** lack of attention; heedlessness. **2** an oversight; slip.

inadvertent ❶ (ˌɪnədˈvɜːtᵊnt) *adj* **1** failing to act carefully or considerately; inattentive. **2** resulting from heedless action; unintentional.
▸ˌ**inadˈvertently** *adv*

-inae *suffix forming plural proper nouns.* occurring in names of zoological subfamilies: *Felinae.* [NL, from L, fem pl of *-īnus* -INE[1]]

inalienable ❶ (ɪnˈeɪljənəbᵊl) *adj* not able to be transferred to another; not alienable: *the inalienable rights of the citizen.*
▸**inˌalienaˈbility** *or* **inˈalienableness** *n* ▸**inˈalienably** *adv*

inalterable (ɪnˈɔːltərəbᵊl) *adj* not alterable; unalterable.
▸**inˌalteraˈbility** *or* **inˈalterableness** *n* ▸**inˈalterably** *adv*

inamorata (ɪnˌæməˈrɑːtə, ˌɪnæmə-) *or* (*masc*) **inamorato** (ɪnˌæməˈrɑːtəʊ, ˌɪnæmə-) *n, pl* **inamoratas** *or* (*masc*) **inamoratos.** a person with whom one is in love; lover. [C17: from It., from *innamorare* to cause to fall in love, from *amore* love, from L *amor*]

inane ❶ (ɪˈneɪn) *adj* **1** senseless, unimaginative, or empty; unintelligent: *inane remarks.* ◆ *n* **2** *Arch.* something empty or vacant, esp. the void of space. [C17: from L *inānis* empty]
▸**inˈanely** *adv*

inanimate ❶ (ɪnˈænɪmɪt) *adj* **1** lacking the qualities of living beings; not animate: *inanimate objects.* **2** lacking any sign of life or consciousness; appearing dead. **3** lacking vitality; dull.
▸**inˈanimately** *adv* ▸**inˈanimateness** *or* **inanimation** (ɪnˌænɪˈmeɪʃən) *n*

inanition (ˌɪnəˈnɪʃən) *n* **1** exhaustion resulting from lack of food. **2** mental, social, or spiritual weakness or lassitude. [C14: from LL *inānītio* emptiness, from L *inānis* empty; see INANE]

inanity ❶ (ɪˈnænɪtɪ) *n, pl* **inanities. 1** lack of intelligence or imagination; senselessness; silliness. **2** a senseless action, remark, etc. **3** an archaic word for **emptiness.**

THESAURUS

tion, freedom, immunity, liberty, licence, nonliability, permission

impure *adj* **1 = unrefined**, admixed, adulterated, alloyed, debased, mixed **2 = unclean**, contaminated, defiled, dirty, filthy, foul, infected, polluted, sullied, tainted, unwholesome, vitiated
Antonyms *adj* ≠ **unclean:** clean, immaculate, spotless, squeaky-clean, undefiled, unsullied

impurity *n* **1 = contamination**, befoulment, defilement, dirtiness, filth, foulness, infection, pollution, taint, uncleanness **2 = dirt**, bits, contaminant, dross, foreign body, foreign matter, grime, marks, pollutant, scum, spots, stains

imputable *adj* **2 = attributable**, accreditable, ascribable, chargeable, referable, traceable

imputation *n* **1 = blame**, accusation, ascription, aspersion, attribution, censure, charge, insinuation, reproach, slander, slur

impute *vb* **2 = attribute**, accredit, ascribe, assign, credit, lay at the door of, refer, set down to

inaccessible *adj* **= out of reach**, impassable, out of the way, remote, unapproachable, unattainable, un-get-at-able (*inf.*), unreachable
Antonyms *adj* accessible, approachable, attainable, reachable

inaccuracy *n* **1 = imprecision**, erroneousness, incorrectness, inexactness, unfaithfulness, unreliability **2 = error**, blunder, boob, corrigendum, defect, erratum, fault, howler (*inf.*), lapse, miscalculation, mistake, slip

inaccurate *adj* **1 = incorrect**, careless, defective, discrepant, erroneous, faulty, imprecise, in error, inexact, mistaken, off base (*US & Canad. inf.*), off beam (*inf.*), out, unfaithful, unreliable, unsound, way off beam (*inf.*), wide of the mark, wild, wrong
Antonyms *adj* accurate, correct, exact, precise, reliable, sound

inaction *n* **= inactivity**, dormancy, idleness, immobility, inertia, rest, torpidity, torpor

inactive *adj* **1 = unused**, abeyant, dormant, idle, immobile, inert, inoperative, jobless, kicking one's heels, latent, mothballed, out of service, out of work, unemployed, unoccupied **2 = slothful**, dull, indolent, lazy, lethargic, low-key (*inf.*), passive, quiet, sedentary, slow, sluggish, somnolent, torpid
Antonyms *adj* ≠ **unused:** employed, mobile, occupied, operative, running, used, working ≠ **slothful:** active, busy, diligent, energetic, industrious, vibrant

inactivity *n* **1 = immobility**, dormancy, hibernation, inaction, passivity, unemployment **2 = sloth**, dilatoriness, *dolce far niente*, dullness, heaviness, indolence, inertia, inertness, lassitude, laziness, lethargy, quiescence, sluggishness, stagnation, torpor, vegetation
Antonyms *n* action, activeness, bustle, employment, exertion, mobility, movement

inadequacy *n* **1 = shortage**, dearth, inadequateness, incompleteness, insufficiency, meagreness, paucity, poverty, scantiness, skimpiness **2 = incompetence**, defectiveness, deficiency, faultiness, inability, inaptness, incapacity, incompetency, ineffectiveness, inefficacy, unfitness, unsuitableness

inadequate *adj* **1 = insufficient**, incommensurate, incomplete, insubstantial, meagre, niggardly, scant, scanty, short, sketchy, skimpy, sparse **2 = incapable**, defective, deficient, faulty, found wanting, imperfect, inapt, incompetent, not up to scratch (*inf.*), pathetic, unequal, unfitted, unqualified
Antonyms *adj* ≠ **insufficient:** adequate, ample, complete, perfect, satisfactory, substantial, sufficient ≠ **incapable:** apt, capable, competent, equal, fit, qualified

inadequately *adv* **1 = insufficiently**, imperfectly, meagrely, poorly, scantily, sketchily, skimpily, sparsely, thinly

inadvertent *adj* **2 = unintentional**, accidental, careless, chance, heedless, negligent, thoughtless, unheeding, unintended, unplanned, unpremeditated, unthinking, unwitting

inadvertently *adv* **1 = carelessly**, heedlessly, in an unguarded moment, negligently, thoughtlessly, unguardedly, unthinkingly **2 = unintentionally**, accidentally, by accident, by mistake, involuntarily, mistakenly, unwittingly
Antonyms *adv* carefully, consciously, deliberately, heedfully, intentionally

inalienable *adj* **= sacrosanct**, absolute, entailed (*Law*), inherent, inviolable, non-negotiable, nontransferable, unassailable, untransferable

inane *adj* **1 = senseless**, asinine, daft (*inf.*), devoid of intelligence, empty, fatuous, frivolous, futile, idiotic, imbecilic, mindless, puerile, silly, stupid, trifling, unintelligent, vacuous, vain, vapid, worthless
Antonyms *adj* meaningful, profound, sensible, serious, significant, weighty, worthwhile

inanimate *adj* **1, 2 = lifeless**, cold, dead, defunct, extinct, inactive, inert, insensate, insentient, quiescent, soulless, spiritless
Antonyms *adj* active, alive, alive and kicking, animate, full of beans (*inf.*), lively, living, moving

inanity *n* **1 = senselessness**, asininity, daftness (*inf.*), fatuity, folly, frivolity, imbecility, puerility, silliness, vacuity, vapidity, worthlessness

inapposite Ⓣ (ɪnˈæpəzɪt) *adj* not appropriate or pertinent; unsuitable. ▸**inˈappositely** *adv* ▸**inˈappositeness** *n*

inapt Ⓣ (ɪnˈæpt) *adj* **1** not apt or fitting; inappropriate. **2** lacking skill; inept. ▸**inˈaptiˌtude** *or* **inˈaptness** *n* ▸**inˈaptly** *adv*

inarch (ɪnˈɑːtʃ) *vb* (*tr*) to graft (a plant) by uniting stock and scion while both are still growing independently.

inasmuch as (ˌɪnəzˈmʌtʃ) *conj* (*subordinating*) **1** in view of the fact that; seeing that; since. **2** to the extent or degree that; in so far as.

inaugural Ⓣ (ɪnˈɔːgjʊrəl) *adj* **1** characterizing or relating to an inauguration. ◆ *n* **2** a speech made at an inauguration, esp. by a president of the US.

inaugurate Ⓣ (ɪnˈɔːgjʊˌreɪt) *vb* **inaugurates, inaugurating, inaugurated.** (*tr*) **1** to commence officially or formally; initiate. **2** to place in office formally and ceremonially; induct. **3** to open ceremonially; dedicate formally: *to inaugurate a factory.* [C17: from L *inaugurāre*, lit.: to take omens, practise augury, hence to install in office after taking auguries; see IN-[2], AUGUR] ▸**inˌauguˈration** *n* ▸**inˈauguˌrator** *n* ▸**inauguratory** (ɪnˈɔːgjʊrətərɪ, -trɪ) *adj*

in-between *adj* intermediate: *he's at the in-between stage, neither a child nor an adult.*

inboard (ˈɪnˌbɔːd) *adj* **1** (esp. of a boat's motor or engine) situated within the hull. **2** situated between the wing tip of an aircraft and its fuselage: *an inboard engine.* ◆ *adv* **3** towards the centre line of or within a vessel, aircraft, etc.

inborn Ⓣ (ˈɪnˈbɔːn) *adj* existing from birth; congenital; innate.

inbred Ⓣ (ˈɪnˈbrɛd) *adj* **1** produced as a result of inbreeding. **2** deeply ingrained; innate: *inbred good manners.*

inbreed (ˈɪnˈbriːd) *vb* **inbreeds, inbreeding, inbred. 1** to breed from unions between closely related individuals, esp. over several generations. **2** (*tr*) to develop within; engender. ▸**ˈinˈbreeding** *n, adj*

in-built Ⓣ *adj* built-in, integral.

inc. *abbrev. for:* **1** including. **2** inclusive. **3** income. **4** increase.

Inc. (esp. US) *abbrev. for* incorporated.

incalculable Ⓣ (ɪnˈkælkjʊləbᵊl) *adj* beyond calculation; unable to be predicted or determined. ▸**inˌcalculaˈbility** *n* ▸**inˈcalculably** *adv*

incandesce (ˌɪnkænˈdɛs) *vb* **incandesces, incandescing, incandesced.** (*intr*) to make or become incandescent.

incandescent Ⓣ (ˌɪnkænˈdɛsᵊnt) *adj* **1** emitting light as a result of being heated; red-hot or white-hot. **2** *Inf.* extremely angry. [C18: from L *incandescere* to become hot, glow, from *candēre* to be white; see CANDID] ▸ˌ**incanˈdescently** *adv* ▸ˌ**incanˈdescence** *n*

incandescent lamp *n* a source of light that contains a heated solid, such as an electrically heated filament.

incantation Ⓣ (ˌɪnkænˈteɪʃən) *n* **1** ritual recitation of magic words or sounds. **2** the formulaic words or sounds used; a magic spell. [C14: from LL *incantātiō* an enchanting, from *incantāre* to repeat magic formulas, from L, from IN-[2] + *cantāre* to sing; see ENCHANT] ▸ˌ**incanˈtational** *or* **inˈcantatory** *adj*

incapacitate Ⓣ (ˌɪnkəˈpæsɪˌteɪt) *vb* **incapacitates, incapacitating, incapacitated.** (*tr*) **1** to deprive of power, strength, or capacity; disable. **2** to deprive of legal capacity or eligibility. ▸ˌ**incaˌpaciˈtation** *n*

incapacity Ⓣ (ˌɪnkəˈpæsɪtɪ) *n, pl* **incapacities. 1** lack of power, strength, or capacity; inability. **2** *Law.* legal disqualification or ineligibility.

in-car *adj* (of hi-fi equipment, etc.) installed inside a car.

incarcerate Ⓣ (ɪnˈkɑːsəˌreɪt) *vb* **incarcerates, incarcerating, incarcerated.** (*tr*) to confine or imprison. [C16: from Med. L, from L IN-[2] + *carcer* prison] ▸**inˌcarcerˈation** *n* ▸**inˈcarcerˌator** *n*

incarnadine (ɪnˈkɑːnəˌdaɪn) *Arch. or literary.* ◆ *vb* **incarnadines, incarnadining, incarnadined. 1** (*tr*) to tinge or stain with red. ◆ *adj* **2** of a pinkish or reddish colour similar to that of flesh or blood. [C16: from F *incarnadin* flesh-coloured, from It., from LL *incarnātus* made flesh, INCARNATE]

incarnate Ⓣ *adj* (ɪnˈkɑːnɪt, -neɪt). (*usually immediately postpositive*) **1** possessing bodily form, esp. the human form: *a devil incarnate.* **2** personified or typified: *stupidity incarnate.* ◆ *vb* (ɪnˈkɑːneɪt), **incarnates, incarnating, incarnated.** (*tr*) **3** to give a bodily or concrete form to. **4** to be representative or typical of. [C14: from LL *incarnāre* to make flesh, from L IN-[2] + *carō* flesh]

incarnation Ⓣ (ˌɪnkɑːˈneɪʃən) *n* **1** the act of manifesting or state of being manifested in bodily form, esp. human form. **2** a bodily form assumed by a god, etc. **3** a person or thing that typifies or represents some quality, idea, etc.

Incarnation (ˌɪnkɑːˈneɪʃən) *n Christian theol.* the assuming of a human body by the Son of God.

incarvillea (ˌɪnkɑːˈvɪlɪə) *n* any of various perennials with pink flowers and pinnate leaves. Also called: **Chinese trumpet flower.** [C18: after Pierre d'*Incarville*, F missionary in China]

incase (ɪnˈkeɪs) *vb* **incases, incasing, incased.** a variant spelling of **encase.** ▸**inˈcasement** *n*

incautious Ⓣ (ɪnˈkɔːʃəs) *adj* not careful or cautious. ▸**inˈcautiously** *adv* ▸**inˈcautiousness** *or* **inˈcaution** *n*

incendiary Ⓣ (ɪnˈsɛndɪərɪ) *adj* **1** of or relating to the illegal burning of property, goods, etc. **2** tending to create strife, violence, etc. **3** (of a substance) capable of catching fire or burning readily. ◆ *n, pl* **incendiaries. 4** a person who illegally sets fire to property, goods, etc.; arsonist. **5** (esp. formerly) a person who stirs up civil strife, violence, etc.; agitator. **6** Also called: **incendiary bomb.** a bomb that is designed to start fires. **7** an incendiary substance, such as phosphorus. [C17: from L, from *incendium* fire, from *incendere* to kindle] ▸**inˈcendiaˌrism** *n*

incense[1] Ⓣ (ˈɪnsɛns) *n* **1** any of various aromatic substances burnt for their fragrant odour, esp. in religious ceremonies. **2** the odour or smoke so produced. **3** any pleasant fragrant odour; aroma. ◆ *vb* **incenses, incensing, incensed. 4** to burn incense in honour of (a deity). **5** (*tr*) to perfume or fumigate with incense. [C13: from OF *encens*, from Church L *incensum*, from L *incendere* to kindle]

incense[2] Ⓣ (ɪnˈsɛns) *vb* **incenses, incensing, incensed.** (*tr*) to enrage greatly. [C15: from L *incensus* set on fire, from *incendere* to kindle] ▸**inˈcensement** *n*

incensory (ˈɪnsɛnsərɪ) *n, pl* **incensories.** a less common name for **censer.** [C17: from Med. L *incensorium*]

incentive Ⓣ (ɪnˈsɛntɪv) *n* **1** a motivating influence; stimulus. **2a** an additional payment made to employees to increase production. **2b** (*as modifier*): *an incentive scheme.* ◆ *adj* **3** serving to incite to action. [C15: from LL, from L: striking up, setting the tune, from *incinere* to sing]

incept (ɪnˈsɛpt) *vb* (*tr*) **1** (of organisms) to ingest (food). **2** *Brit.* (formerly) to take a master's or doctor's degree at a university. [C19:

THESAURUS

inapposite *adj* = **inappropriate**, impertinent, inapplicable, infelicitous, irrelevant, out of place, unfit, unsuitable

inapt *adj* **1** = **inappropriate**, ill-fitted, ill-suited, inapposite, infelicitous, unsuitable, unsuited **2** = **incompetent**, awkward, clumsy, dull, gauche, inept, inexpert, maladroit, slow, stupid
Antonyms *adj* ≠ **inappropriate:** apposite, appropriate, apt, felicitous, fitting, suitable, suited

inaptitude *n* **2** = **incompetence**, awkwardness, clumsiness, maladroitness, unfitness, unreadiness, unsuitableness

inaugural *adj* **1** = **first**, dedicatory, initial, introductory, maiden, opening

inaugurate *vb* **1** = **launch**, begin, commence, get under way, initiate, institute, introduce, kick off (*inf.*), originate, set in motion, set up, usher in **2** = **invest**, induct, install, instate **3** = **open**, commission, dedicate, ordain

inauguration *n* **1** = **launch**, initiation, institution, launching, opening, setting up **2** = **investiture**, induction, installation

inborn *adj* = **natural**, congenital, connate, hereditary, immanent, inbred, ingrained, inherent, inherited, innate, in one's blood, instinctive, intuitive, native

inbred *adj* **2** = **innate**, constitutional, deep-seated, immanent, ingrained, inherent, native, natural

in-built *adj* = **integral**, built-in, component, incorporated

incalculable *adj* = **countless**, boundless, enormous, immense, incomputable, inestimable, infinite, innumerable, limitless, measureless, numberless, uncountable, untold, vast, without number

incandescent *adj* **1** = **glowing**, brilliant, Day-Glo, luminous, phosphorescent, radiant, red-hot, shining, white-hot

incantation *n* **2** = **chant**, abracadabra, charm, conjuration, formula, hex (*US & Canad. inf.*), invocation, spell

incapacitate *vb* **1** = **disable**, cripple, disqualify, immobilize, lay up (*inf.*), paralyse, prostrate, put out of action (*inf.*), scupper (*Brit. sl.*), unfit (*rare*)

incapacitated *adj* **1** = **indisposed**, disqualified, *hors de combat*, immobilized, laid up (*inf.*), out of action (*inf.*), unfit

incapacity *n* **1** = **inability**, disqualification, feebleness, impotence, inadequacy, incapability, incompetency, ineffectiveness, powerlessness, unfitness, weakness

incarcerate *vb* = **imprison**, commit, confine, coop up, detain, immure, impound, intern, jail *or* gaol, lock up, put under lock and key, restrain, restrict, send down (*Brit.*), throw in jail

incarceration *n* = **imprisonment**, bondage, captivity, confinement, detention, internment, porridge (*sl.*), restraint

incarnate *adj* **1** = **made flesh**, in bodily form, in human form, in the flesh **2** = **personified**, embodied, typified

incarnation *n* **2, 3** = **embodiment**, avatar, bodily form, epitome, exemplification, impersonation, manifestation, personification, type

incautious *adj* = **careless**, hasty, heedless, ill-advised, ill-judged, improvident, imprudent, impulsive, inconsiderate, indiscreet, injudicious, negligent, precipitate, rash, reckless, thoughtless, unguarded, unthinking, unwary
Antonyms *adj* careful, cautious, considerate, discreet, guarded, heedful, judicious, prudent, thoughtful, wary

incautiously *adv* = **rashly**, imprudently, impulsively, indiscreetly, precipitately, recklessly, thoughtlessly, unthinkingly

incendiary *adj* **2** = **inflammatory**, dissentious, provocative, rabble-rousing, seditious, subversive ◆ *n* **4** = **arsonist**, firebug (*inf.*), fire raiser, pyromaniac **5** = **agitator**, demagogue, firebrand, insurgent, rabble-rouser, revolutionary

incense[1] *n* **2, 3** = **perfume**, aroma, balm, bouquet, fragrance, redolence, scent

incense[2] *vb* = **anger**, enrage, exasperate, excite, gall, inflame, infuriate, irritate, madden, make one's blood boil (*inf.*), make one see red (*inf.*), make one's hackles rise, nark (*Brit., Austral., & NZ sl.*), provoke, rile (*inf.*), rub one up the wrong way

incentive *n* **1** = **encouragement**, bait, carrot (*inf.*), carrot and stick, enticement, goad, impetus, impulse, inducement, lure, motivation, motive, spur, stimulant, stimulus
Antonyms *n* deterrent, discouragement, disincentive, dissuasion, warning

DICTIONARY

from L *inceptus* begun, attempted, from *incipere* to begin, take in hand]
▸**inˈceptor** *n*

inception Ⓣ (ɪnˈsɛpʃən) *n* the beginning, as of a project or undertaking.

inceptive (ɪnˈsɛptɪv) *adj* **1** beginning; incipient; initial. **2** Also called: **inchoative.** *Grammar.* denoting a verb used to indicate the beginning of an action. ◆ *n* **3** *Grammar.* an inceptive verb.
▸**inˈceptively** *adv*

incertitude (ɪnˈsɜːtɪˌtjuːd) *n* **1** uncertainty; doubt. **2** a state of mental or emotional insecurity.

incessant Ⓣ (ɪnˈsɛsᵊnt) *adj* not ceasing; continual. [C16: from LL, from L IN-[1] + *cessāre* to CEASE]
▸**inˈcessancy** *n* ▸**inˈcessantly** *adv*

incest (ˈɪnsɛst) *n* sexual intercourse between two persons who are too closely related to marry. [C13: from L, from IN-[1] + *castus* CHASTE]

incestuous (ɪnˈsɛstjʊəs) *adj* **1** relating to or involving incest: *an incestuous union.* **2** guilty of incest. **3** resembling incest in excessive or claustrophobic intimacy.
▸**inˈcestuously** *adv* ▸**inˈcestuousness** *n*

inch[1] (ɪntʃ) *n* **1** a unit of length equal to one twelfth of a foot or 0.0254 metre. **2** *Meteorol.* **2a** an amount of precipitation that would cover a surface with water one inch deep. **2b** a unit of pressure equal to a mercury column one inch high in a barometer. **3** a very small distance, degree, or amount. **4 every inch.** in every way; completely: *every inch an aristocrat.* **5 inch by inch.** gradually; little by little. **6 within an inch of one's life.** almost to death. ◆ *vb* **7** to move or be moved very slowly or in very small steps: *the car inched forward.* **8** (*tr*; foll. by *out*) to defeat (someone) by a very small margin. [OE *ynce;* see OUNCE[1]]

inch[2] (ɪntʃ) *n Scot. & Irish.* a small island. [C15: from Gaelic *innis* island; cf. Welsh *ynys*]

inchoate *adj* (ɪnˈkəʊeɪt, -ˈkəʊɪt). **1** just beginning; incipient. **2** undeveloped; immature; rudimentary. ◆ *vb* (ɪnˈkəʊeɪt), **inchoates, inchoating, inchoated.** (*tr*) **3** to begin. [C16: from L *incohāre* to make a beginning, lit.: to hitch up, from IN-[2] + *cohum* yokestrap]
▸**inˈchoately** *adv* ▸**inˈchoateness** *n* ▸**ˌinchoˈation** *n* ▸**inchoative** (ɪnˈkəʊətɪv) *adj*

inchworm (ˈɪntʃˌwɜːm) *n* another name for **measuring worm.**

incidence Ⓣ (ˈɪnsɪdəns) *n* **1** degree, extent, or frequency of occurrence; amount: *a high incidence of death from pneumonia.* **2** the act or manner of impinging on or affecting by proximity or influence. **3** *Physics.* the arrival of a beam of light or particles at a surface. See also **angle of incidence. 4** *Geom.* the partial coincidence of two configurations, such as a point on a circle.

incident Ⓣ (ˈɪnsɪdənt) *n* **1** a definite occurrence; event. **2** a minor, subsidiary, or related event. **3** a relatively insignificant event that might have serious consequences. **4** a public disturbance. ◆ *adj* **5** (*postpositive;* foll. by *to*) related (to) or dependent (on). **6** (when *postpositive,* often foll. by *to*) having a subsidiary or minor relationship (with). **7** (esp. of a beam of light or particles) arriving at or striking a surface. [C15: from Med. L, from L *incidere,* lit.: to fall into, hence befall, happen]

incidental Ⓣ (ˌɪnsɪˈdɛntᵊl) *adj* **1** happening in connection with or resulting from something more important; casual or fortuitous. **2** (*postpositive;* foll. by *to*) found in connection (with); related (to). **3** (*postpositive;* foll. by *upon*) caused (by). **4** occasional or minor: *incidental expenses.* ◆ *n* **5** (*often pl*) a minor expense, event, or action.
▸**ˌinciˈdentalness** *n*

incidentally Ⓣ (ˌɪnsɪˈdɛntəlɪ) *adv* **1** as a subordinate or chance occurrence. **2** (*sentence modifier*) by the way.

incidental music *n* background music for a film, etc.

incinerate Ⓣ (ɪnˈsɪnəˌreɪt) *vb* **incinerates, incinerating, incinerated.** to burn up completely; reduce to ashes. [C16: from Med. L, from L IN-[2] + *cinis* ashes]
▸**inˌcinerˈation** *n*

incinerator (ɪnˈsɪnəˌreɪtə) *n* a furnace or apparatus for incinerating something, esp. refuse.

incipient Ⓣ (ɪnˈsɪpɪənt) *adj* just starting to be or happen; beginning. [C17: from L, from *incipere* to begin, take in hand]
▸**inˈcipience** *or* **inˈcipiency** *n* ▸**inˈcipiently** *adv*

incise Ⓣ (ɪnˈsaɪz) *vb* **incises, incising, incised.** (*tr*) to produce (lines, a design, etc.) by cutting into the surface of (something) with a sharp tool. [C16: from L *incīdere* to cut into]

incision Ⓣ (ɪnˈsɪʒən) *n* **1** the act of incising. **2** a cut, gash, or notch. **3** a cut made with a knife during a surgical operation.

incisive Ⓣ (ɪnˈsaɪsɪv) *adj* **1** keen, penetrating, or acute. **2** biting or sarcastic; mordant: *an incisive remark.* **3** having a sharp cutting edge: *incisive teeth.*
▸**inˈcisively** *adv* ▸**inˈcisiveness** *n*

incisor (ɪnˈsaɪzə) *n* a chisel-edged tooth at the front of the mouth.

incite Ⓣ (ɪnˈsaɪt) *vb* **incites, inciting, incited.** (*tr*) to stir up or provoke to action. [C15: from L, from IN-[2] + *citāre* to excite]
▸**ˌinciˈtation** *n* ▸**inˈcitement** *n* ▸**inˈciter** *n* ▸**inˈcitingly** *adv*

incivility Ⓣ (ˌɪnsɪˈvɪlɪtɪ) *n, pl* **incivilities. 1** lack of civility or courtesy; rudeness. **2** an impolite or uncivil act or remark.

incl. *abbrev. for:* **1** including. **2** inclusive.

inclement Ⓣ (ɪnˈklɛmənt) *adj* **1** (of weather) stormy, severe, or tempestuous. **2** severe or merciless.
▸**inˈclemency** *n* ▸**inˈclemently** *adv*

inclination Ⓣ (ˌɪnklɪˈneɪʃən) *n* **1** (often foll. by *for, to, towards,* or an infinitive) a particular disposition, esp. a liking; tendency: *I've no inclination for such dull work.* **2** the degree of deviation from a particular plane, esp. a horizontal or vertical plane. **3** a sloping or slanting surface; incline. **4** the act of inclining or the state of being inclined. **5** the act of bowing or nodding the head. **6** another name for **dip** (sense 24).
▸**ˌincliˈnational** *adj*

incline Ⓣ *vb* (ɪnˈklaɪn), **inclines, inclining, inclined. 1** to deviate from a particular plane, esp. a vertical or horizontal plane; slope or slant. **2** (when *tr,* may take an infinitive) to be disposed or cause to be disposed (towards some attitude or to do something). **3** to bend or lower (part of the body, esp. the head), as in a bow or in order to listen. **4 incline one's ear.** to listen favourably (to). ◆ *n* (ˈɪnklaɪn, ɪnˈklaɪn). **5** an inclined surface or slope; gradient. [C13: from L *inclīnāre* to cause to lean, from *clīnāre* to bend; see LEAN[1]]
▸**inˈclined** *adj* ▸**inˈcliner** *n*

inclined plane *n* a plane whose angle to the horizontal is less than a right angle.

inclinometer (ˌɪnklɪˈnɒmɪtə) *n* an aircraft instrument that indicates the angle an aircraft makes with the horizontal.

THESAURUS

inception *n* = **beginning**, birth, commencement, dawn, inauguration, initiation, kickoff (*inf.*), origin, outset, rise, start
Antonyms *n* completion, conclusion, end, ending, finish, termination

incessant *adj* = **endless**, ceaseless, constant, continual, continuous, eternal, everlasting, interminable, never-ending, nonstop, perpetual, persistent, relentless, unbroken, unceasing, unending, unrelenting, unremitting
Antonyms *adj* infrequent, intermittent, occasional, periodic, rare, sporadic

incessantly *adv* = **endlessly**, all the time, ceaselessly, constantly, continually, eternally, everlastingly, interminably, nonstop, perpetually, persistently, without a break

incidence *n* **1** = **prevalence**, amount, degree, extent, frequency, occurrence, rate

incident *n* **1** = **happening**, adventure, circumstance, episode, event, fact, matter, occasion, occurrence **4** = **disturbance**, brush, clash, commotion, confrontation, contretemps, mishap, scene, skirmish

incidental *adj* **1** = **accidental**, casual, chance, fortuitous, odd, random **2** = **accompanying**, attendant, by-the-way, concomitant, contingent, contributory, related **4** = **secondary**, ancillary, minor, nonessential, occasional, subordinate, subsidiary ◆ *n* **5** *plural* = **odds and ends**, contingencies, extras, minutiae
Antonyms *adj* ≠ **secondary:** crucial, essential, important, necessary, vital

incidentally *adv* **1** = **accidentally**, by chance, casually, fortuitously **2** = **parenthetically**, by the bye, by the way, in passing

incinerate *vb* = **burn up**, carbonize, char, consume by fire, cremate, reduce to ashes

incipient *adj* = **beginning**, commencing, developing, embryonic, inceptive, inchoate, nascent, originating, starting

incise *vb* = **cut into**, carve, chisel, engrave, etch, inscribe

incision *n* **2** = **cut**, gash, notch, opening, slash, slit

incisive *adj* **1** = **penetrating**, acute, keen, perspicacious, piercing, sharp, trenchant
Antonyms *adj* dense, dull, superficial, vague, woolly

incisiveness *n* **1** = **perspicacity**, keenness, penetration, sharpness, trenchancy

incite *vb* = **provoke**, agitate for *or* against, animate, drive, egg on, encourage, excite, foment, goad, impel, inflame, instigate, prod, prompt, put up to, rouse, set on, spur, stimulate, stir up, urge, whip up
Antonyms *vb* dampen, deter, discourage, dishearten, dissuade, restrain

incitement *n* = **provocation**, agitation, clarion call, encouragement, goad, impetus, impulse, inducement, instigation, motivation, motive, prompting, spur, stimulus

incivility *n* **1** = **rudeness**, bad manners, boorishness, discourteousness, discourtesy, disrespect, ill-breeding, impoliteness, unmannerliness
Antonyms *n* civility, courteousness, courtesy, good manners, mannerliness, politeness, respect

inclemency *n* **1** = **storminess**, bitterness, boisterousness, rawness, rigour, roughness, severity **2** = **harshness**, callousness, cruelty, mercilessness, severity, tyranny, unfeelingness

inclement *adj* **1** = **stormy**, bitter, boisterous, foul, harsh, intemperate, rigorous, rough, severe, tempestuous **2** = **cruel**, callous, draconian, harsh, intemperate, merciless, pitiless, rigorous, severe, tyrannical, unfeeling, unmerciful
Antonyms *adj* ≠ **stormy:** balmy, calm, clement, fine, mild, pleasant, temperate ≠ **cruel:** compassionate, gentle, humane, kind, merciful, tender

inclination *n* **1** = **tendency**, affection, aptitude, bent, bias, desire, disposition, fancy, fondness, leaning, liking, partiality, penchant, predilection, predisposition, prejudice, proclivity, proneness, propensity, stomach, taste, thirst, turn, turn of mind, wish **2, 3** = **slope**, angle, bend, bending, deviation, gradient, incline, leaning, pitch, slant, tilt **5** = **bow**, bending, bowing, nod
Antonyms *n* ≠ **tendency:** antipathy, aversion, disinclination, dislike, revulsion

incline *vb* **1** = **slope**, bend, bevel, cant, deviate, diverge, heel, lean, slant, tend, tilt, tip, veer **2** = **predispose**, be disposed *or* predisposed, bias, influence, persuade, prejudice, sway, tend, turn **3** = **bend**, bow, lower, nod, stoop ◆ *n* **5** = **slope**, acclivity, ascent, declivity, descent, dip, grade, gradient, ramp, rise

inclined *adj* **2** = **disposed**, apt, given, liable, likely, minded, of a mind (*inf.*), predisposed, prone, willing

inclose ❶ (ɪn'kləʊz) *vb* **incloses, inclosing, inclosed.** a less common spelling of **enclose.**
▸**in'closure** *n*

include ❶ (ɪn'klu:d) *vb* **includes, including, included.** (*tr*) **1** to have as contents or part of the contents; be made up of or contain. **2** to add as part of something else; put in as part of a set, group, or category. **3** to contain as a secondary or minor ingredient or element. [C15 (in the sense: to enclose): from L, from IN-[2] + *claudere* to close]
▸**in'cludable** *or* **in'cludible** *adj*

include out *vb* (*tr, adv*) *Inf.* to exclude: *you can include me out of that deal.*

inclusion ❶ (ɪn'klu:ʒən) *n* **1** the act of including or the state of being included. **2** something included.

inclusion body *n Pathol.* any of the small particles found in cells infected with certain viruses.

inclusive ❶ (ɪn'klu:sɪv) *adj* **1** (*postpositive;* foll. by *of*) considered together (with): *capital inclusive of profit.* **2** (*postpositive*) including the limits specified: *Monday to Friday inclusive.* **3** comprehensive. **4** *Logic.* (of a disjunction) true if at least one of its component propositions is true.
▸**in'clusively** *adv* ▸**in'clusiveness** *n*

incognito ❶ (ˌɪnkɒg'ni:təʊ, ɪn'kɒgnɪtəʊ) *or* (*fem*) **incognita** *adv, adj* (*postpositive*) **1** under an assumed name or appearance; in disguise. ◆ *n, pl* **incognitos** *or* (*fem*) **incognitas. 2** a person who is incognito. **3** the assumed name or disguise of such a person. [C17: from It., from L *incognitus* unknown]

incognizant (ɪn'kɒgnɪzənt) *adj* (when *postpositive,* often foll. by *of*) unaware (of).
▸**in'cognizance** *n*

incoherent ❶ (ˌɪnkəʊ'hɪərənt) *adj* **1** lacking in clarity or organization; disordered. **2** unable to express oneself clearly; inarticulate. **3** *Physics.* (of two or more waves) having the same frequency but not the same phase: *incoherent light.*
▸ˌ**inco'herently** *adv* ▸ˌ**inco'herence** *or* ˌ**inco'herency** *n*

income ❶ ('ɪnkʌm, 'ɪnkəm) *n* **1** the amount of monetary or other returns, either earned or unearned, accruing over a given period of time. **2** receipts; revenue. [C13 (in the sense: arrival, entrance): from OE *incumen* a coming in]

incomer ❶ ('ɪnkʌmə) *n* a person who comes to live in a place in which he was not born.

incomes policy *n* an economic policy that attempts to reduce or control inflation by limiting incomes.

income support *n* (in Britain, formerly) a social security payment for people on very low incomes.

income tax *n* a personal tax levied on annual income subject to certain deductions.

incoming ❶ ('ɪnˌkʌmɪŋ) *adj* **1** coming in; entering. **2** about to come into office; succeeding. **3** (of interest, dividends, etc.) being received; accruing. ◆ *n* **4** the act of coming in; entrance. **5** (*usually pl*) income or revenue.

incommensurable (ˌɪnkə'mɛnʃərəb[ə]l) *adj* **1** incapable of being judged, measured, or considered comparatively. **2** (*postpositive;* foll. by *with*) not in accordance; incommensurate. **3** *Maths.* not having a common factor other than 1, such as 2 and √–5. ◆ *n* **4** something incommensurable.
▸ˌ**incomˌmensura'bility** *n* ▸ˌ**incom'mensurably** *adv*

incommensurate ❶ (ˌɪnkə'mɛnʃərɪt) *adj* **1** (when *postpositive,* often foll. by *with*) not commensurate; disproportionate. **2** incommensurable.
▸ˌ**incom'mensurately** *adv* ▸ˌ**incom'mensurateness** *n*

incommode ❶ (ˌɪnkə'məʊd) *vb* **incommodes, incommoding, incommoded.** (*tr*) to bother, disturb, or inconvenience. [C16: from L *incommodāre* to be troublesome, from *incommodus* inconvenient; see COMMODE]

incommodious (ˌɪnkə'məʊdɪəs) *adj* **1** insufficiently spacious; cramped. **2** troublesome or inconvenient.
▸ˌ**incom'modiously** *adv*

incommodity (ˌɪnkə'mɒdɪtɪ) *n, pl* **incommodities.** anything that causes inconvenience.

incommunicado ❶ (ˌɪnkəˌmju:nɪ'kɑ:dəʊ) *adv, adj* (*postpositive*) deprived of communication with other people, as while in solitary confinement. [C19: from Sp., from *incomunicar* to deprive of communication; see IN-[1], COMMUNICATE]

incomparable ❶ (ɪn'kɒmpərəb[ə]l, -prəb[ə]l) *adj* **1** beyond or above comparison; matchless; unequalled. **2** lacking a basis for comparison; not having qualities or features that can be compared.
▸**inˌcompara'bility** *or* **in'comparableness** *n* ▸**in'comparably** *adv*

incompatible ❶ (ˌɪnkəm'pætəb[ə]l) *adj* **1** incapable of living or existing together in harmony; conflicting. **2** opposed in nature or quality; inconsistent. **3** *Med.* (esp. of two drugs or two types of blood) incapable of being combined or used together; antagonistic. **4** *Logic.* (of two propositions) unable to be both true at the same time. **5** (of plants) incapable of self-fertilization. ◆ *n* **6** (*often pl*) a person or thing that is incompatible with another.
▸ˌ**incomˌpati'bility** *or* ˌ**incom'patibleness** *n* ▸ˌ**incom'patibly** *adv*

incompetent ❶ (ɪn'kɒmpɪtənt) *adj* **1** not possessing the necessary ability, skill, etc., to do or carry out a task; incapable. **2** marked by lack of ability, skill, etc. **3** *Law.* not legally qualified: *an incompetent witness.* ◆ *n* **4** an incompetent person.
▸**in'competence** *or* **in'competency** *n* ▸**in'competently** *adv*

incomplete ❶ (ˌɪnkəm'pli:t) *adj* **1** not complete or finished. **2** not completely developed; imperfect.
▸ˌ**incom'pletely** *adv* ▸ˌ**incom'pleteness** *or* ˌ**incom'pletion** *n*

incomprehensible ❶ (ˌɪnkɒmprɪ'hɛnsəb[ə]l, ɪn'kɒm-) *adj* **1** incapable of being understood; unintelligible. **2** *Archaic.* limitless; boundless.
▸ˌ**incompreˌhensi'bility** *or* ˌ**incompre'hensibleness** *n* ▸ˌ**incompre'hensibly** *adv*

inconceivable ❶ (ˌɪnkən'si:vəb[ə]l) *adj* incapable of being conceived, imagined, or considered.
▸ˌ**inconˌceiva'bility** *or* ˌ**incon'ceivableness** *n* ▸ˌ**incon'ceivably** *adv*

inconclusive ❶ (ˌɪnkən'klu:sɪv) *adj* not conclusive or decisive; not finally settled; indeterminate.
▸ˌ**incon'clusively** *adv* ▸ˌ**incon'clusiveness** *n*

incongruous ❶ (ɪn'kɒŋgrʊəs) *or* **incongruent** *adj* **1** (when *postpositive,*

THESAURUS

inclose *see* **enclose**

include *vb* **1 = contain**, comprehend, comprise, cover, embody, embrace, encompass, incorporate, involve, subsume, take in, take into account **2 = introduce**, add, allow for, build in, count, enter, insert, number among
Antonyms *vb* eliminate, exclude, leave out, omit, rule out

inclusion *n* **1 = addition**, incorporation, insertion
Antonyms *n* exception, exclusion, omission, rejection

inclusive *adj* **3 = comprehensive**, across-the-board, all-embracing, all in, all together, blanket, catch-all (*chiefly US*), full, general, global, *in toto*, overall, overarching, sweeping, umbrella, without exception
Antonyms *adj* confined, exclusive, limited, narrow, restricted, unique

incognito *adj* **1 = in disguise**, disguised, under an assumed name, unknown, unrecognized

incoherence *n* **1 = disjointedness**, disconnectedness **2 = unintelligibility**, inarticulateness

incoherent *adj* **1 = disordered**, confused, disconnected, disjointed, inconsistent, jumbled, loose, muddled, unconnected, uncoordinated, wild **2 = unintelligible**, inarticulate, rambling, stammering, stuttering, wandering
Antonyms *adj* coherent, connected, intelligible, logical, rational

income *n* **1, 2 = revenue**, earnings, gains, interest, means, pay, proceeds, profits, receipts, salary, takings, wages

incomer *n* **= immigrant**

incoming *adj* **1 = arriving**, approaching, entering, homeward, landing, returning **2 = succeeding**, new
Antonyms *adj* ≠ **arriving:** departing, exiting, leaving, outgoing

incommensurate *adj* **1 = disproportionate**, inadequate, inequitable, insufficient, unequal

incommode *vb* **= inconvenience**, annoy, be a trouble to, bother, disturb, embarrass, get in one's hair (*inf.*), give (someone) bother *or* trouble, hassle (*inf.*), hinder, impede, irk, put out, put (someone) to trouble, trouble, upset, vex

incommunicado *adv* **= in purdah**, under house arrest

incomparable *adj* **1 = unequalled**, beyond compare, inimitable, matchless, paramount, peerless, superlative, supreme, transcendent, unmatched, unparalleled, unrivalled

incomparably *adv* **1 = immeasurably**, beyond compare, by far, easily, eminently, far and away

incompatibility *n* **1, 2 = inconsistency**, antagonism, conflict, discrepancy, disparateness, incongruity, irreconcilability, uncongeniality

incompatible *adj* **1, 2 = inconsistent**, antagonistic, antipathetic, conflicting, contradictory, discordant, discrepant, disparate, ill-assorted, incongruous, inconsonant, irreconcilable, mismatched, uncongenial, unsuitable, unsuited
Antonyms *adj* alike, appropriate, compatible, congenial, consistent, harmonious, reconcilable, suitable, suited

incompetence *n* **2 = ineptitude**, inability, inadequacy, incapability, incapacity, incompetency, ineffectiveness, ineptness, insufficiency, unfitness, uselessness

incompetent *adj* **2 = inept**, bungling, cowboy (*inf.*), floundering, incapable, incapacitated, ineffectual, inexpert, insufficient, unable, unfit, unfitted, unskilful, useless
Antonyms *adj* able, capable, competent, expert, fit, proficient, skilful

incomplete *adj* **1 = unfinished**, broken, defective, deficient, fragmentary, imperfect, insufficient, lacking, partial, short, unaccomplished, undeveloped, undone, unexecuted, wanting
Antonyms *adj* accomplished, complete, developed, finished, perfect, unified, whole

incomprehensible *adj* **1 = unintelligible**, above one's head, all Greek to one (*inf.*), baffling, beyond comprehension, beyond one's grasp, enigmatic, impenetrable, inconceivable, inscrutable, mysterious, obscure, opaque, perplexing, puzzling, unfathomable, unimaginable, unthinkable
Antonyms *adj* apparent, clear, comprehensible, conceivable, evident, intelligible, manifest, obvious, understandable

inconceivable *adj* **= unimaginable**, beyond belief, impossible, incomprehensible, incredible, mind-boggling (*inf.*), not to be thought of, out of the question, staggering (*inf.*), unbelievable, unheard-of, unknowable, unthinkable
Antonyms *adj* believable, comprehensible, conceivable, credible, imaginable, likely, plausible, possible, reasonable

inconclusive *adj* **= indecisive**, ambiguous, indeterminate, open, uncertain, unconvincing, undecided, unsettled, up in the air (*inf.*), vague

incongruous *adj* **1 = inappropriate**, absurd, conflicting, contradictory, contrary, disconsonant, discordant, extraneous, improper, inapt, incoherent, incompatible, inconsistent, out of keeping, out of place, unbecoming, unsuitable, unsuited
Antonyms *adj* appropriate, becoming, compatible, consistent, harmonious, suitable, suited

incongruousness *n* **1 = inappropriateness**, conflict, discrepancy, disparity, inaptness, in-

foll. by *with* or *to*) incompatible with (what is suitable); inappropriate. **2** containing disparate or discordant elements or parts.
▸**in'congruously** *adv* ▸**in'congruousness** *or* **incongruity** (ˌɪnkɒŋ'gruːɪtɪ) *n*

inconnu ('ɪnkənjuː, 'ɪnkənuː) *n Canad.* a whitefish of Far Northern waters. [C19: from F, lit.: unknown]

inconsequential ➊ (ˌɪnkɒnsɪ'kwenʃəl, ɪnˌkɒn-) *or* **inconsequent** (ɪn'kɒnsɪkwənt) *adj* **1** not following logically as a consequence. **2** trivial or insignificant. **3** not in a logical sequence; haphazard.
▸ˌ**inconseˌquenti'ality**, ˌ**inconse'quentialness**, *or* **in'consequence** *n*
▸ˌ**inconse'quentially** *or* **in'consequently** *adv*

inconsiderable ➊ (ˌɪnkən'sɪdərəbᵊl) *adj* **1** relatively small. **2** not worthy of consideration; insignificant.
▸ˌ**incon'siderableness** *n* ▸ˌ**incon'siderably** *adv*

inconsiderate ➊ (ˌɪnkən'sɪdərɪt) *adj* lacking in care or thought for others; thoughtless.
▸ˌ**incon'siderately** *adv* ▸ˌ**incon'siderateness** *or* ˌ**inconˌsider'ation** *n*

inconsistency ➊ (ˌɪnkən'sɪstənsɪ) *n, pl* **inconsistencies. 1** lack of consistency or agreement; incompatibility. **2** an inconsistent feature or quality.

inconsistent ➊ (ˌɪnkən'sɪstənt) *adj* **1** lacking in consistency, agreement, or compatibility; at variance. **2** containing contradictory elements. **3** irregular or fickle in behaviour or mood. **4** *Logic.* (of a set of propositions) enabling an explicit contradiction to be validly derived.
▸ˌ**incon'sistently** *adv*

inconsolable ➊ (ˌɪnkən'səʊləbᵊl) *adj* incapable of being consoled or comforted; disconsolate.
▸ˌ**inconˌsola'bility** *or* ˌ**incon'solableness** *n* ▸ˌ**incon'solably** *adv*

inconsonant (ɪn'kɒnsənənt) *adj* lacking in harmony or compatibility; discordant.
▸**in'consonance** *n* ▸**in'consonantly** *adv*

inconspicuous ➊ (ˌɪnkən'spɪkjʊəs) *adj* not easily noticed or seen; not prominent or striking.
▸ˌ**incon'spicuously** *adv* ▸ˌ**incon'spicuousness** *n*

incontinent[1] ➊ (ɪn'kɒntɪnənt) *adj* **1** relating to or exhibiting involuntary urination or defecation. **2** lacking in restraint or control, esp. sexually. **3** (foll. by *of*) having little or no control (over). **4** unrestrained; uncontrolled. [C14: from OF, from L, from IN-[1] + *continere* to hold, restrain]
▸**in'continence** *n* ▸**in'continently** *adv*

incontinent[2] (ɪn'kɒntɪnənt) *or* **incontinently** *adv* obsolete words for **immediately.** [C15: from LL *in continentī tempore,* lit.: in continuous time, that is, with no interval]

incontrovertible ➊ (ˌɪnkɒntrə'vɜːtəbᵊl, ɪnˌkɒn-) *adj* incapable of being contradicted or disputed; undeniable.
▸ˌ**incontroˌverti'bility** *n* ▸ˌ**incontro'vertibly** *adv*

inconvenience ➊ (ˌɪnkən'viːnjəns, -'viːnɪəns) *n* **1** the state or quality of being inconvenient. **2** something inconvenient; a hindrance, trouble, or difficulty. ◆ *vb* **3** (*tr*) to cause inconvenience to; trouble or harass.

inconvenient ➊ (ˌɪnkən'viːnjənt, -'viːnɪənt) *adj* not convenient; troublesome, awkward, or difficult.
▸ˌ**incon'veniently** *adv*

incorporate ➊ *vb* (ɪn'kɔːpəˌreɪt), **incorporates, incorporating, incorporated. 1** to include or be included as a part or member of a united whole. **2** to form a united whole or mass; merge or blend. **3** to form into a corporation or other organization with a separate legal identity. ◆ *adj* (ɪn'kɔːpərɪt, -prɪt). **4** combined into a whole; incorporated. **5** formed into or constituted as a corporation. [C14 (in the sense: put into the body of something else): from LL *incorporāre* to embody, from L IN-[2] + *corpus* body]
▸**in'corpoˌrated** *adj* ▸**inˌcorpo'ration** *n* ▸**in'corporative** *adj*

incorporeal (ˌɪnkɔː'pɔːrɪəl) *adj* **1** without material form, body, or substance. **2** spiritual or metaphysical. **3** *Law.* having no material existence but existing by reason of its annexation of something material: *an incorporeal hereditament.*
▸ˌ**incor'poreally** *adv* ▸**incorporeity** (ɪnˌkɔːpə'riːɪtɪ) *or* ˌ**incorpore'ality** *n*

incorrect ➊ (ˌɪnkə'rekt) *adj* **1** false; wrong: *an incorrect calculation.* **2** not fitting or proper: *incorrect behaviour.*
▸ˌ**incor'rectly** *adv* ▸ˌ**incor'rectness** *n*

incorrigible ➊ (ɪn'kɒrɪdʒəbᵊl) *adj* **1** beyond correction, reform, or alteration. **2** firmly rooted; ineradicable. ◆ *n* **3** a person or animal that is incorrigible.
▸**inˌcorrigi'bility** *or* **in'corrigibleness** *n* ▸**in'corrigibly** *adv*

incorruptible ➊ (ˌɪnkə'rʌptəbᵊl) *adj* **1** incapable of being corrupted; honest; just. **2** not subject to decay or decomposition.
▸ˌ**incorˌrupti'bility** *n* ▸ˌ**incor'ruptibly** *adv*

incr. *abbrev. for:* **1** increase. **2** increased. **3** increasing.

incrassate *adj* (ɪn'kræsɪt, -eɪt), *also* **incrassated. 1** *Biol.* thickened or swollen. ◆ *vb* (ɪn'kræseɪt), **incrassates, incrassating, incrassated. 2** *Obs.* to make or become thicker. [C17: from LL, from L *crassus* thick, dense]
▸ˌ**incras'sation** *n*

increase ➊ *vb* (ɪn'kriːs), **increases, increasing, increased. 1** to make or become greater in size, degree, frequency, etc.; grow or expand. ◆ *n* ('ɪnkriːs). **2** the act of increasing; augmentation. **3** the amount by which something increases. **4 on the increase.** increasing, esp. becoming more frequent. [C14: from OF *encreistre,* from L, from IN-[2] + *crēscere* to grow]
▸**in'creasable** *adj* ▸**increasedly** (ɪn'kriːsɪdlɪ) *or* **in'creasingly** *adv* ▸**in'creaser** *n*

incredible ➊ (ɪn'kredəbᵊl) *adj* **1** beyond belief or understanding; unbelievable. **2** *Inf.* marvellous; amazing.
▸**inˌcredi'bility** *or* **in'credibleness** *n* ▸**in'credibly** *adv*

THESAURUS

compatibility, inconsistency, inharmoniousness, unsuitability

inconsequential *adj* **2** = **unimportant**, immaterial, inconsiderable, insignificant, measly, minor, negligible, nickel-and-dime (*US sl.*), of no significance, paltry, petty, trifling, trivial

inconsiderable *adj* **2** = **insignificant**, exiguous, inconsequential, light, minor, negligible, petty, slight, small, small-time (*inf.*), trifling, trivial, unimportant

inconsiderate *adj* = **selfish**, careless, indelicate, insensitive, intolerant, rude, self-centred, tactless, thoughtless, uncharitable, ungracious, unkind, unthinking
Antonyms *adj* attentive, careful, considerate, gracious, kind, sensitive, tactful, thoughtful, tolerant

inconsistency *n* **1** = **incompatibility**, contrariety, disagreement, discrepancy, disparity, divergence, incongruity, inconsonance, paradox, variance

inconsistent *adj* **1** = **incompatible**, at odds, at variance, conflicting, contradictory, contrary, discordant, discrepant, incoherent, in conflict, incongruous, inconstant, irreconcilable, out of step **3** = **changeable**, capricious, erratic, fickle, inconstant, irregular, uneven, unpredictable, unstable, unsteady, vagarious (*rare*), variable
Antonyms *adj* ≠ **incompatible:** coherent, compatible, homogeneous, orderly, reconcilable, uniform ≠ **changeable:** consistent, constant, predictable, reliable, stable, steady, unchanging

inconsistently *adv* **1** = **unpredictably**, contradictorily, differently, eccentrically, erratically, inequably, randomly, unequally, unfairly, variably

inconsolable *adj* = **heartbroken**, brokenhearted, desolate, despairing, heartsick, prostrate with grief, sick at heart

inconspicuous *adj* = **unobtrusive**, camouflaged, hidden, insignificant, modest, muted, ordinary, plain, quiet, retiring, unassuming, unnoticeable, unostentatious
Antonyms *adj* bold, conspicuous, noticeable, obtrusive, obvious, salient, significant, visible

incontinent[1] *adj* **2** = **promiscuous**, debauched, lascivious, lecherous, lewd, loose, lustful, profligate, unchaste, wanton **4** = **unrestrained**, unbridled, unchecked, uncontrollable, uncontrolled, ungovernable, ungoverned

incontrovertible *adj* = **indisputable**, beyond dispute, certain, established, incontestable, indubitable, irrefutable, positive, sure, undeniable, unquestionable, unshakable

inconvenience *n* **1** = **awkwardness**, cumbersomeness, unfitness, unhandiness, unsuitableness, untimeliness, unwieldiness **2** = **trouble**, annoyance, awkwardness, bother, difficulty, disadvantage, disruption, disturbance, downside, drawback, fuss, hassle (*inf.*), hindrance, nuisance, uneasiness, upset, vexation ◆ *vb* **3** = **trouble**, bother, discommode, disrupt, disturb, give (someone) bother *or* trouble, hassle (*inf.*), irk, make (someone) go out of his way, put out, put to trouble, upset

inconvenient *adj* = **troublesome**, annoying, awkward, bothersome, cumbersome, difficult, disadvantageous, disturbing, embarrassing, inopportune, tiresome, unhandy, unmanageable, unseasonable, unsuitable, untimely, unwieldy, vexatious
Antonyms *adj* convenient, handy, opportune, seasonable, suitable, timely

incorporate *vb* **1, 2** = **include**, absorb, amalgamate, assimilate, blend, coalesce, combine, consolidate, embody, fuse, integrate, meld, merge, mix, subsume, unite

incorporation *n* **1, 2** = **inclusion**, absorption, amalgamation, assimilation, blend, coalescence, federation, fusion, integration, merger, unifying

incorrect *adj* **1** = **false**, erroneous, faulty, flawed, inaccurate, inexact, mistaken, off base (*US & Canad. inf.*), off beam (*inf.*), out, specious, untrue, wide of the mark (*inf.*), wrong **2** = **inappropriate**, improper, unfitting, unsuitable, wrong
Antonyms *adj* ≠ **false:** accurate, correct, exact, faultless, right, true ≠ **inappropriate:** fitting, flawless, suitable

incorrectness *n* **1** = **inaccuracy**, erroneousness, error, fallacy, faultiness, impreciseness, imprecision, inexactness, speciousness, unsoundness **2** = **impropriety**, unsuitability, wrongness

incorrigible *adj* **1** = **incurable**, hardened, hopeless, intractable, inveterate, irredeemable, unreformed

incorruptibility *n* **1** = **integrity**, honesty, honour, justness, uprightness

incorruptible *adj* **1** = **honest**, above suspicion, honourable, just, straight, trustworthy, unbribable, upright **2** = **imperishable**, everlasting, undecaying

increase *vb* **1** = **grow**, add to, advance, aggrandize, amplify, augment, boost, build up, develop, dilate, enhance, enlarge, escalate, expand, extend, heighten, inflate, intensify, magnify, mount, multiply, proliferate, prolong, raise, snowball, spread, step up (*inf.*), strengthen, swell, wax ◆ *n* **2** = **growth**, addition, augmentation, boost, development, enlargement, escalation, expansion, extension, gain, increment, intensification, rise, upsurge, upturn **4 on the increase** = **growing**, developing, escalating, expanding, increasing, multiplying, on the rise, proliferating, spreading
Antonyms *vb* ≠ **grow:** abate, abbreviate, abridge, condense, curtail, decline, decrease, deflate, diminish, dwindle, lessen, reduce, shorten, shrink

increasingly *adv* **1** = **progressively**, more and more, to an increasing extent

incredible *adj* **1** = **implausible**, absurd, beyond belief, cock-and-bull (*inf.*), far-fetched, impossible, improbable, inconceivable, not able to hold water, preposterous, unbelievable, unimaginable, unthinkable **2** *Informal* = **amaz-**

incredulity Ⓣ (ˌɪnkrɪˈdjuːlɪtɪ) *n* lack of belief; scepticism.

incredulous Ⓣ (ɪnˈkrɛdjʊləs) *adj* (often foll. by *of*) not prepared or willing to believe (something); unbelieving.
▸**inˈcredulously** *adv* ▸**inˈcredulousness** *n*

increment Ⓣ (ˈɪnkrɪmənt) *n* **1** an increase or addition, esp. one of a series. **2** the act of increasing; augmentation. **3** *Maths.* a small positive or negative change in a variable or function. [C15: from L *incrēmentum* growth, INCREASE]
▸**incremental** (ˌɪnkrɪˈmɛntᵊl) *adj*

incremental plotter *n* a device that plots graphs on paper from computer-generated instructions.

incriminate Ⓣ (ɪnˈkrɪmɪˌneɪt) *vb* **incriminates, incriminating, incriminated.** (*tr*) **1** to imply or suggest the guilt or error of (someone). **2** to charge with a crime or fault. [C18: from LL *incrīmināre* to accuse, from L *crīmen* accusation; see CRIME]
▸**inˌcrimiˈnation** *n* ▸**inˈcrimiˌnator** *n* ▸**inˈcriminatory** *adj*

incrust (ɪnˈkrʌst) *vb* a variant spelling of **encrust.**
▸**inˈcrustant** *n, adj* ▸**ˌincrusˈtation** *n*

incubate (ˈɪnkjʊˌbeɪt) *vb* **incubates, incubating, incubated. 1** (of birds) to supply (eggs) with heat for their development, esp. by sitting on them. **2** to cause (bacteria, etc.) to develop, esp. in an incubator or culture medium. **3** (*intr*) (of embryos, etc.) to develop in favourable conditions, esp. in an incubator. **4** (*intr*) (of disease germs) to remain inactive in an animal or human before causing disease. **5** to develop gradually; foment or be fomented. [C18: from L *incubāre* to lie upon, hatch, from IN-[2] + *cubāre* to lie down]
▸**ˌincuˈbation** *n* ▸**ˌincuˈbational** *adj* ▸**ˈincuˌbative** *or* **ˈincuˌbatory** *adj*

incubation period *n Med.* the time between exposure to an infectious disease and the appearance of the first signs or symptoms.

incubator (ˈɪnkjʊˌbeɪtə) *n* **1** *Med.* an apparatus for housing prematurely born babies until they are strong enough to survive. **2** a container in which birds' eggs can be artificially hatched or bacterial cultures grown. **3** a person, animal, or thing that incubates.

incubus (ˈɪnkjʊbəs) *n, pl* **incubi** (-ˌbaɪ) *or* **incubuses. 1** a demon believed in folklore to have sexual intercourse with sleeping women. Cf. **succubus. 2** something that oppresses or disturbs greatly, esp. a nightmare or obsession. [C14: from LL, from L *incubāre* to lie upon; see INCUBATE]

inculcate (ˈɪnkʌlˌkeɪt, ɪnˈkʌlkeɪt) *vb* **inculcates, inculcating, inculcated.** (*tr*) to instil by insistent repetition. [C16: from L *inculcāre* to tread upon, ram down, from IN-[2] + *calcāre* to trample, from *calx* heel]
▸**ˌinculˈcation** *n* ▸**ˈinculˌcator** *n*

inculpate (ˈɪnkʌlˌpeɪt, ɪnˈkʌlpeɪt) *vb* **inculpates, inculpating, inculpated.** (*tr*) to incriminate; cause blame to be imputed to. [C18: from LL, from L *culpāre* to blame, from *culpa* fault, blame]
▸**ˌinculˈpation** *n* ▸**inculpative** (ɪnˈkʌlpətɪv) *or* **inculpatory** (ɪnˈkʌlpətərɪ, -trɪ) *adj*

incumbency (ɪnˈkʌmbənsɪ) *n, pl* **incumbencies. 1** the state or quality of being incumbent. **2** the office, duty, or tenure of an incumbent.

incumbent Ⓣ (ɪnˈkʌmbənt) *adj* **1** *Formal.* (often *postpositive* and foll. by *on* or *upon* and an infinitive) morally binding; obligatory: *it is incumbent on me to attend.* **2** (usually *postpositive* and foll. by *on*) resting or lying (on). **3** (usually *prenominal*) occupying or holding an office. ◆ *n* **4** a person who holds an office, esp. a clergyman holding a benefice. [C16: from L *incumbere* to lie upon, devote one's attention to]

incunabula (ˌɪnkjʊˈnæbjʊlə) *pl n, sing* **incunabulum** (-ləm). **1** any book printed before 1500. **2** the earliest stages of something; beginnings. [C19: from L, orig.: swaddling clothes, hence beginnings, from IN-[2] + *cūnābula* cradle]
▸**ˌincuˈnabular** *adj*

incur Ⓣ (ɪnˈkɜː) *vb* **incurs, incurring, incurred.** (*tr*) **1** to make oneself subject to (something undesirable); bring upon oneself. **2** to run into or encounter. [C16: from L *incurrere* to run into, from *currere* to run]
▸**inˈcurrable** *adj*

incurable Ⓣ (ɪnˈkjʊərəbᵊl) *adj* **1** (esp. of a disease) not curable; unresponsive to treatment. ◆ *n* **2** a person having an incurable disease.
▸**inˌcuraˈbility** *or* **inˈcurableness** *n* ▸**inˈcurably** *adv*

incurious Ⓣ (ɪnˈkjʊərɪəs) *adj* not curious; indifferent or uninterested.
▸**incuriosity** (ɪnˌkjʊərɪˈɒsɪtɪ) *or* **inˈcuriousness** *n* ▸**inˈcuriously** *adv*

incursion Ⓣ (ɪnˈkɜːʃən) *n* **1** a sudden invasion, attack, or raid. **2** the act of running or leaking into; penetration. [C15: from L *incursiō* onset, attack, from *incurrere* to run into; see INCUR]
▸**incursive** (ɪnˈkɜːsɪv) *adj*

incus (ˈɪŋkəs) *n, pl* **incudes** (ɪnˈkjuːdiːz). the central of the three small bones in the middle ear of mammals. Cf. **malleus, stapes.** [C17: from L: anvil, from *incūdere* to forge]

incuse (ɪnˈkjuːz) *n* **1** a design stamped or hammered onto a coin. ◆ *vb* **incuses, incusing, incused. 2** to impress (a coin) with a design by hammering or stamping. ◆ *adj* **3** stamped or hammered onto a coin. [C19: from L *incūsus* hammered; see INCUS]

ind. *abbrev. for:* **1** independence. **2** independent. **3** index. **4** indicative. **5** indirect. **6** industrial. **7** industry.

Ind. *abbrev. for:* **1** Independent. **2** India. **3** Indian. **4** Indies.

indaba (ɪnˈdɑːbə) *n* **1** (among Bantu peoples of southern Africa) a meeting to discuss a serious topic. **2** *S. African inf.* a matter of concern or for discussion. [C19: from Zulu: topic]

indebted Ⓣ (ɪnˈdɛtɪd) *adj* (*postpositive*) **1** owing gratitude for help, favours, etc.; obligated. **2** owing money.

indebtedness (ɪnˈdɛtɪdnɪs) *n* **1** the state of being indebted. **2** the total of a person's debts.

indecency Ⓣ (ɪnˈdiːsənsɪ) *n, pl* **indecencies. 1** the state or quality of being indecent. **2** an indecent act, etc.

indecent Ⓣ (ɪnˈdiːsᵊnt) *adj* **1** offensive to standards of decency, esp. in sexual matters. **2** unseemly or improper (esp. in **indecent haste**).
▸**inˈdecently** *adv*

indecent assault *n* the offence of subjecting a person to a form of sexual activity, other than rape, against his or her will.

indecent exposure *n* the offence of indecently exposing one's body in public, esp. the genitals.

indecisive Ⓣ (ˌɪndɪˈsaɪsɪv) *adj* **1** (of a person) vacillating; irresolute. **2** not decisive or conclusive.
▸**ˌindeˈcision** *or* **ˌindeˈcisiveness** *n* ▸**ˌindeˈcisively** *adv*

indecorum Ⓣ (ˌɪndɪˈkɔːrəm) *n* lack of decorum; unseemliness.
▸**inˈdecorous** *adj*

indeed Ⓣ (ɪnˈdiːd) (*sentence connector*). **1** certainly; actually: *indeed, it may never happen.* ◆ *adv* **2** (intensifier): *that is indeed amazing.* **3** or rather; what is more: *a comfortable, indeed wealthy family.* ◆ *interj* **4** an expression of doubt, surprise, etc.

indef. *abbrev. for* indefinite.

indefatigable Ⓣ (ˌɪndɪˈfætɪgəbᵊl) *adj* unable to be tired out; unflagging. [C16: from L, from *fatīgāre* to tire]
▸**ˌindeˌfatigaˈbility** *n* ▸**ˌindeˈfatigably** *adv*

indefeasible (ˌɪndɪˈfiːzəbᵊl) *adj Law.* not liable to be annulled or forfeited.
▸**ˌindeˌfeasiˈbility** *n* ▸**ˌindeˈfeasibly** *adv*

indefensible Ⓣ (ˌɪndɪˈfɛnsəbᵊl) *adj* **1** not justifiable or excusable. **2** capable of being disagreed with; untenable. **3** incapable of defence against attack.
▸**ˌindeˌfensiˈbility** *n* ▸**ˌindeˈfensibly** *adv*

indefinite Ⓣ (ɪnˈdɛfɪnɪt) *adj* **1** not certain or determined; unsettled. **2**

THESAURUS

ing, astonishing, astounding, awe-inspiring, brilliant, extraordinary, far-out (*sl.*), great, marvellous, prodigious, sensational (*inf.*), superhuman, wonderful

incredulity *n* = **disbelief**, distrust, doubt, scepticism, unbelief

incredulous *adj* = **disbelieving**, distrustful, doubtful, doubting, dubious, mistrustful, sceptical, suspicious, unbelieving, unconvinced
Antonyms *adj* believing, credulous, gullible, naive, trusting, unsuspecting, wet behind the ears (*inf.*)

increment *n* **1, 2** = **increase**, accretion, accrual, accruement, addition, advancement, augmentation, enlargement, gain, step up, supplement

incriminate *vb* **1, 2** = **implicate**, accuse, arraign, blacken the name of, blame, charge, impeach, inculpate, indict, involve, point the finger at (*inf.*), stigmatize

incumbent *adj Formal* **1** = **obligatory**, binding, compulsory, mandatory, necessary

incur *vb* **1** = **earn**, arouse, bring (upon oneself), contract, draw, expose oneself to, gain, induce, lay oneself open to, meet with, provoke

incurable *adj* **1** = **fatal**, inoperable, irrecoverable, irremediable, remediless, terminal

incurious *adj* = **indifferent**, apathetic, pococurante, unconcerned, uninquiring, uninterested

incursion *n* **1** = **foray**, infiltration, inroad, invasion, irruption, penetration, raid

indebted *adj* **1** = **grateful**, beholden, in debt, obligated, obliged, under an obligation

indecency *n* **1** = **obscenity**, bawdiness, coarseness, crudity, foulness, grossness, immodesty, impropriety, impurity, indecorum, indelicacy, lewdness, licentiousness, outrageousness, pornography, smut, smuttiness, unseemliness, vileness, vulgarity
Antonyms *n* decency, decorum, delicacy, modesty, propriety, purity, seemliness

indecent *adj* **1** = **lewd**, blue, coarse, crude, dirty, filthy, foul, gross, immodest, improper, impure, indelicate, licentious, pornographic, salacious, scatological, smutty, vile **2** = **unbecoming**, ill-bred, improper, in bad taste, indecorous, offensive, outrageous, tasteless, unseemly, vulgar
Antonyms *adj* decent, decorous, delicate, modest, proper, pure, respectable, seemly, tasteful

indecision *n* **1** = **hesitation**, ambivalence, dithering (*chiefly Brit.*), doubt, hesitancy, indecisiveness, irresolution, shilly-shallying (*inf.*), uncertainty, vacillation, wavering

indecisive *adj* **1** = **hesitating**, dithering (*chiefly Brit.*), doubtful, faltering, in two minds (*inf.*), irresolute, pussyfooting (*inf.*), tentative, uncertain, undecided, undetermined, vacillating, wavering **2** = **inconclusive**, indefinite, indeterminate, unclear, undecided
Antonyms *adj* ≠ **hesitating:** certain, decided, determined, positive, resolute, unhesitating ≠ **inconclusive:** clear, conclusive, decisive, definite, determinate, final

indecorous *adj* = **improper**, boorish, churlish, coarse, ill-bred, immodest, impolite, indecent, rude, tasteless, uncivil, uncouth, undignified, unmannerly, unseemly, untoward

indeed *adv* **2** = **really**, actually, certainly, doubtlessly, in point of fact, in truth, positively, strictly, to be sure, truly, undeniably, undoubtedly, verily (*arch.*), veritably

indefatigable *adj* = **tireless**, assiduous, diligent, dogged, inexhaustible, patient, persevering, pertinacious, relentless, sedulous, unflagging, unremitting, untiring, unwearied, unwearying

indefensible *adj* **1** = **unforgivable**, faulty, inexcusable, insupportable, unjustifiable, unpardonable, untenable, unwarrantable, wrong
Antonyms *adj* defensible, excusable, forgivable, justifiable, legitimate, pardonable, supportable, tenable, warrantable

indefinite *adj* **1-3** = **unclear**, ambiguous, confused, doubtful, equivocal, evasive, general, ill-

without exact limits; indeterminate: *an indefinite number.* **3** vague or unclear. **4** in traditional logic, a proposition in which it is not stated whether the subject is universal or particular, as in *men are mortal.* ▸**in'definitely** *adv* ▸**in'definiteness** *n*

indefinite article *n Grammar.* a determiner that expresses nonspecificity of reference, such as *a, an,* or *some.*

indehiscent (ˌɪndɪˈhɪsᵊnt) *adj* (of fruits, etc.) not dehiscent; not opening to release seeds, etc. ▸**ˌinde'hiscence** *n*

indelible Ⓣ (ɪnˈdɛlɪbᵊl) *adj* **1** incapable of being erased or obliterated. **2** making indelible marks: *indelible ink.* [C16: from L, from IN-[1] + *delēre* to destroy] ▸**inˌdeli'bility** *or* **in'delibleness** *n* ▸**in'delibly** *adv*

indelicate Ⓣ (ɪnˈdɛlɪkɪt) *adj* **1** coarse, crude, or rough. **2** offensive, embarrassing, or tasteless. ▸**in'delicacy** *or* **in'delicateness** *n* ▸**in'delicately** *adv*

indemnify Ⓣ (ɪnˈdɛmnɪˌfaɪ) *vb* **indemnifies, indemnifying, indemnified.** *(tr)* **1** to secure against future loss, damage, or liability; give security for; insure. **2** to compensate for loss, etc.; reimburse. ▸**inˌdemnifi'cation** *n* ▸**in'demniˌfier** *n*

indemnity Ⓣ (ɪnˈdɛmnɪtɪ) *n, pl* **indemnities. 1** compensation for loss or damage; reimbursement. **2** protection or insurance against future loss or damage. **3** legal exemption from penalties incurred through one's acts or defaults. **4** *Canad.* the annual salary paid by the government to a member of Parliament or of a provincial legislature. [C15: from LL, from *indemnis* uninjured, from L IN-[1] + *damnum* damage]

indene (ˈɪndiːn) *n* a colourless liquid hydrocarbon obtained from coal tar and used in making synthetic resins. Formula: C_9H_8. [C20: from INDOLE + -ENE]

indent[1] Ⓣ *vb* (ɪnˈdɛnt). *(mainly tr)* **1** to place (written matter, etc.) in from the margin. **2** to cut (a document in duplicate) so that the irregular lines may be matched. **3** *Chiefly Brit.* (in foreign trade) to place an order for (foreign goods). **4** (when *intr,* foll. by *for, on,* or *upon*) *Chiefly Brit.* to make an order on (a source or supply) or for (something). **5** to notch (an edge, border, etc.); make jagged. **6** to bind (an apprentice, etc.) by indenture. ◆ *n* (ˈɪnˌdɛnt). *Chiefly Brit.* **7** (in foreign trade) an order for foreign merchandise. **8** an official order for goods. [C14: from OF *endenter,* from EN-[1] + *dent* tooth, from L *dēns*] ▸**in'denter** *or* **in'dentor** *n*

indent[2] *vb* (ɪnˈdɛnt). **1** *(tr)* to make a dent or depression in. ◆ *n* (ˈɪnˌdɛnt). **2** a dent or depression. [C15: from IN-[2] + DENT]

indentation Ⓣ (ˌɪndɛnˈteɪʃən) *n* **1** a hollowed, notched, or cut place, as on an edge or on a coastline. **2** a series of hollows, notches, or cuts. **3** the act of indenting or the condition of being indented. **4** Also: **indention, indent.** the leaving of space or the amount of space left between a margin and the start of an indented line.

indention (ɪnˈdɛnʃən) *n* another word for **indentation** (sense 4).

indenture (ɪnˈdɛntʃə) *n* **1** any deed, contract, or sealed agreement between two or more parties. **2** (formerly) a deed drawn up in duplicate, each part having correspondingly indented edges for identification and security. **3** *(often pl)* a contract between an apprentice and his master. **4** a less common word for **indentation.** ◆ *vb* **indentures, indenturing, indentured. 5** *(intr)* to enter into an agreement by indenture. **6** *(tr)* to bind (an apprentice, servant, etc.) by indenture. ▸**in'dentureˌship** *n*

independence Ⓣ (ˌɪndɪˈpɛndəns) *n* the state or quality of being independent. Also: **independency.**

independency (ˌɪndɪˈpɛndənsɪ) *n, pl* **independencies. 1** a territory or state free from the control of any other power. **2** another word for **independence.**

independent Ⓣ (ˌɪndɪˈpɛndənt) *adj* **1** free from control in action, judgment, etc.; autonomous. **2** not dependent on anything else for function, validity, etc.; separate. **3** not reliant on the support, esp. financial support, of others. **4** capable of acting for oneself or on one's own: *a very independent little girl.* **5** providing a large unearned sum towards one's support (esp. in **independent income, independent means**). **6** living on an unearned income. **7** *Maths.* (of a system of equations) not linearly dependent. See also **independent variable. 8** *Logic.* (of two or more propositions) unrelated. ◆ *n* **9** an independent person or thing. **10** a person who is not affiliated to or who acts independently of a political party. ▸**ˌinde'pendently** *adv*

Independent (ˌɪndɪˈpɛndənt) *Christianity.* ◆ *n* **1** (in England) a member of the Congregational Church. ◆ *adj* **2** of or relating to the Congregational Church.

independent clause *n Grammar.* a main or coordinate clause.

independent school *n* **1** (in Britain) a school that is neither financed nor controlled by the government or local authorities. **2** (in Australia) a school that is not part of the state system.

independent variable *n* a variable in a mathematical equation or statement whose value determines that of the dependent variable: in $y = f(x)$, x is the independent variable.

in-depth Ⓣ *adj* detailed and thorough: *an in-depth study.*

indescribable Ⓣ (ˌɪndɪˈskraɪbəbᵊl) *adj* beyond description; too intense, extreme, etc., for words. ▸**ˌindeˌscriba'bility** *n* ▸**ˌinde'scribably** *adv*

indestructible Ⓣ (ˌɪndɪˈstrʌktəbᵊl) *adj* incapable of being destroyed; very durable. ▸**ˌindeˌstructi'bility** *or* **ˌinde'structibleness** *n* ▸**ˌinde'structibly** *adv*

indeterminate Ⓣ (ˌɪndɪˈtɜːmɪnɪt) *adj* **1** uncertain in extent, amount, or nature. **2** not definite; inconclusive: *an indeterminate reply.* **3** unable to be predicted, calculated, or deduced. **4** *Maths.* **4a** having no numerical meaning, as 0/0. **4b** (of an equation) having more than one variable and an unlimited number of solutions. ▸**ˌinde'terminacy** *or* **ˌinde'terminateness** *n* ▸**ˌinde'terminately** *adv*

indeterminism (ˌɪndɪˈtɜːmɪˌnɪzəm) *n* the philosophical doctrine that behaviour is not entirely determined by motives. ▸**ˌinde'terminist** *n, adj* ▸**ˌindeˌtermin'istic** *adj*

index Ⓣ (ˈɪndɛks) *n, pl* **indexes** *or* **indices** (-dɪˌsiːz). **1** an alphabetical list of persons, subjects, etc., mentioned in a printed work, usually at the back, and indicating where they are referred to. **2** See **thumb index. 3** *Library science.* a systematic list of book titles or authors' names, giving cross-references and the location of each book; catalogue. **4** an indication, sign, or token. **5** a pointer, needle, or other indicator, as on an instrument. **6** *Maths.* **6a** another name for **exponent** (sense 4). **6b** a number or variable placed as a superscript to the left of a radical sign indicating the root to be extracted, as in $\sqrt[3]{8} = 2$. **7** a numerical scale by means of which levels of the cost of living can be compared with some base number. **8** a number or ratio indicating a specific characteristic, property, etc.: *refractive index.* **9** Also called: **fist.** a printer's mark, * used to indicate notes, paragraphs, etc. ◆ *vb (tr)* **10** to put an index in (a book). **11** to enter (a word, item, etc.) in an index. **12** to point out; indicate. **13** to make index-linked. **14** to move (a machine, etc.) so that an operation will be repeated at certain defined intervals. [C16: from L: pointer, hence forefinger, title, index, from *indicāre* to disclose, show; see INDICATE] ▸**'indexer** *n*

indexation (ˌɪndɛkˈseɪʃən) *or* **index-linking** *n* the act of making wages, interest rates, etc., index-linked.

index case *n Med.* the first case of a disease.

index finger *n* the finger next to the thumb. Also called: **forefinger.**

THESAURUS

defined, imprecise, indeterminate, indistinct, inexact, loose, obscure, oracular, uncertain, undefined, undetermined, unfixed, unknown, unlimited, unsettled, vague
Antonyms *adj* certain, clear, definite, determinate, distinct, exact, fixed, settled, specific

indefinitely *adv* **2** = **endlessly**, ad infinitum, continually, for ever, *sine die,* till the cows come home (*inf.*)

indelible *adj* **1** = **permanent**, enduring, indestructible, ineffaceable, ineradicable, inexpungible, inextirpable, ingrained, lasting
Antonyms *adj* eradicable, erasable, impermanent, removable, short-lived, temporary, washable

indelicacy *n* **1, 2** = **vulgarity**, bad taste, coarseness, crudity, grossness, immodesty, impropriety, indecency, obscenity, offensiveness, rudeness, smuttiness, suggestiveness, tastelessness

indelicate *adj* **1, 2** = **offensive**, blue, coarse, crude, embarrassing, gross, immodest, improper, indecent, indecorous, low, near the knuckle (*inf.*), obscene, off-colour, risqué, rude, suggestive, tasteless, unbecoming, unseemly, untoward, vulgar, X-rated (*inf.*)
Antonyms *adj* becoming, decent, decorous, delicate, modest, proper, refined, seemly

indemnify *vb* **1** = **insure**, endorse, guarantee, protect, secure, underwrite **2** = **compensate**, pay, reimburse, remunerate, repair, repay, requite, satisfy

indemnity *n* **1** = **compensation**, redress, reimbursement, remuneration, reparation, requital, restitution, satisfaction **2** = **insurance**, guarantee, protection, security **3** = **exemption**, immunity, impunity, privilege

indent[1] *vb* **3** = **order**, ask for, request, requisition **5** = **notch**, cut, dint, mark, nick, pink, scallop, score, serrate

indentation *n* **1** = **notch**, cut, dent, depression, dimple, dip, hollow, jag, nick, pit

independence *n* = **freedom**, autarchy, autonomy, home rule, liberty, self-determination, self-government, self-reliance, self-rule, self-sufficiency, separation, sovereignty
Antonyms *n* bondage, dependence, subjection, subjugation, subordination, subservience

independent *adj* **1** = **self-governing**, autarchic, autarchical, autonomous, decontrolled, nonaligned, self-determining, separated, sovereign **2** = **free**, absolute, liberated, separate, unconnected, unconstrained, uncontrolled, unrelated **3, 4** = **self-sufficient**, bold, individualistic, liberated, self-contained, self-reliant, self-supporting, unaided, unconventional
Antonyms *adj* ≠ **self-governing**: aligned, controlled, dependent, subject, submissive, subordinate, subservient, subsidiary ≠ **free**: controlled, dependent, restrained, subject

independently *adv* **3** = **separately**, alone, autonomously, by oneself, individually, on one's own, solo, unaided, under one's own steam

in-depth *adj* = **thorough**, comprehensive, extensive, intensive

indescribable *adj* = **unutterable**, beggaring description, beyond description, beyond words, incommunicable, indefinable, ineffable, inexpressible

indestructible *adj* = **permanent**, abiding, durable, enduring, everlasting, immortal, imperishable, incorruptible, indelible, indissoluble, lasting, nonperishable, unbreakable, unfading
Antonyms *adj* breakable, corruptible, destructible, fading, impermanent, mortal, perishable

indeterminate *adj* **1, 2** = **uncertain**, imprecise, inconclusive, indefinite, inexact, undefined, undetermined, unfixed, unspecified, unstipulated, vague
Antonyms *adj* certain, clear, conclusive, definite, determinate, exact, fixed, precise, specified, stipulated

index *n* **4** = **indication**, clue, guide, mark, sign, symptom, token

index fossil *n* a fossil species that characterizes and is used to delimit a geological zone. Also called: **zone fossil.**

index futures *pl n* a form of financial futures based on projected movements of a share price index, such as the Financial Times Stock Exchange 100 Share Index.

indexical (ɪn'dɛksɪkᵊl) *adj* **1** arranged as or relating to an index or indexes. ◆ *n* **2** Also called: **deictic.** *Logic, linguistics.* a term whose reference depends on the context of utterance, such as *I, you, here, now,* or *tomorrow.*

Index Librorum Prohibitorum *Latin.* ('ɪndɛks laɪ'brɔːrʊm prəʊˌhɪbɪ'tɔːrʊm) *n RC Church.* (formerly) an official list of proscribed books. Often called: **the Index.** [C17, lit.: list of forbidden books]

index-linked *adj* (of wages, interest rates, etc.) directly related to the cost-of-living index and rising or falling accordingly.

index number *n Statistics.* a statistic indicating the relative change occurring in the price or value of a commodity or in a general economic variable, with reference to a previous base period conventionally given the number 100.

Indiaman ('ɪndɪəmən) *n, pl* **Indiamen.** (formerly) a merchant ship engaged in trade with India.

Indian ('ɪndɪən) *n* **1** a native or inhabitant of the Republic of India, in S Asia, or a descendant of one. **2** an American Indian. **3** (*not in scholarly usage*) any of the languages of the American Indians. ◆ *adj* **4** of or relating to India, its inhabitants, or any of their languages. **5** of or relating to the American Indians or any of their languages.

Indian club *n* a bottle-shaped club, usually used in pairs by gymnasts, jugglers, etc.

Indian corn *n* another name for **maize** (sense 1).

Indian file *n* another term for **single file.**

Indian hemp *n* another name for **hemp**, esp. the variety *Cannabis indica*, from which several narcotic drugs are obtained.

Indian ink *or esp. US & Canad.* **India ink** ('ɪndɪə) *n* **1** a black pigment made from a mixture of lampblack and a binding agent such as gelatine or glue: usually formed into solid cakes and sticks. **2** a black liquid ink made from this pigment. ◆ Also called: **China ink, Chinese ink.**

Indian list *n Inf.* (in Canada) a list of persons to whom spirits may not be sold.

Indian meal *n* another name for **corn meal.**

Indian rope-trick *n* the supposed Indian feat of climbing an unsupported rope.

Indian summer *n* **1** a period of unusually warm weather in the late autumn. **2** a period of tranquillity or of renewed productivity towards the end of something, esp. a person's life. [orig. US: prob. so named because it was first noted in Amerind regions]

Indian tobacco *n* a poisonous North American plant with small pale bell-shaped blue flowers and rounded inflated seed capsules.

India paper *n* a thin soft opaque printing paper originally made in the Orient.

India rubber *n* another name for **rubber**[1] (sense 1).

Indic ('ɪndɪk) *adj* **1** denoting, belonging to, or relating to a branch of Indo-European consisting of certain languages of India, including Sanskrit, Hindi and Urdu. ◆ *n* **2** this group of languages. ◆ Also: **Indo-Aryan.**

indicate ❶ ('ɪndɪˌkeɪt) *vb* **indicates, indicating, indicated.** (*tr*) **1** (*may take a clause as object*) to be or give a sign or symptom of; imply: *cold hands indicate a warm heart.* **2** to point out or show. **3** (*may take a clause as object*) to state briefly; suggest. **4** (of instruments) to show a reading of. **5** (*usually passive*) to recommend or require: *surgery seems to be indicated for this patient.* [C17: from L *indicāre* to point out, from IN-[2] + *dicāre* to proclaim; cf. INDEX]
▸**'indiˌcatable** *adj* ▸**indicatory** (ɪn'dɪkətərɪ, -trɪ) *adj*

indication ❶ (ˌɪndɪ'keɪʃən) *n* **1** something that serves to indicate or suggest; sign: *an indication of foul play.* **2** the degree or quantity represented on a measuring instrument or device. **3** the action of indicating. **4** something that is indicated as advisable, necessary, or expedient.

indicative ❶ (ɪn'dɪkətɪv) *adj* **1** (*usually postpositive;* foll. by *of*) serving as a sign; suggestive: *indicative of trouble ahead.* **2** *Grammar.* denoting a mood of verbs used chiefly to make statements. ◆ *n* **3** *Grammar.* **3a** the indicative mood. **3b** a verb in the indicative mood. ◆ Abbrev.: **indic.**
▸**in'dicatively** *adv*

indicator ❶ ('ɪndɪˌkeɪtə) *n* **1** something that provides an indication, esp. of trends. See **economic indicator. 2** a device to attract attention, such as the pointer of a gauge or a warning lamp. **3** an instrument that displays certain operating conditions in a machine, such as a gauge showing temperature, etc. **4** a device that registers something, such as the movements of a lift, or that shows information, such as train departure times. **5** Also called: **blinker.** a device for indicating that a motor vehicle is about to turn left or right, esp. two pairs of lights that flash. **6** a delicate measuring instrument used to determine small differences in the height of mechanical components. **7** *Chem.* a substance used to indicate the completion of a chemical reaction, usually by a change of colour. **8** Also called: **indicator species.** *Ecology.* a plant or animal species that thrives only under particular environmental conditions and therefore indicates these conditions where it is found.

indices ('ɪndɪˌsiːz) *n* a plural of **index.**

indicia (ɪn'dɪʃɪə) *pl n, sing* **indicium** (-ʃɪəm). distinguishing markings or signs; indications. [C17: from L, pl of *indicium* a notice, from INDEX]
▸**in'dicial** *adj*

indict ❶ (ɪn'daɪt) *vb* (*tr*) to charge (a person) with crime, esp. formally in writing; accuse. [C14: alteration of *enditen* to INDITE]
▸**ˌindict'ee** *n* ▸**in'dicter** *or* **in'dictor** *n* ▸**in'dictable** *adj*

USAGE NOTE See at **indite.**

indictment ❶ (ɪn'daɪtmənt) *n Criminal law.* **1** a formal written charge of crime formerly referred to and presented on oath by a grand jury. **2** any formal accusation of crime. **3** the act of indicting or the state of being indicted.

indie ('ɪndɪ) *n Inf.* **a** an independent record company. **b** (*as modifier*): *the indie charts.*

indifference ❶ (ɪn'dɪfrəns, -fərəns) *n* **1** the fact or state of being indifferent; lack of care or concern. **2** lack of quality; mediocrity. **3** lack of importance; insignificance.

indifferent ❶ (ɪn'dɪfrənt, -fərənt) *adj* **1** (often foll. by *to*) showing no care or concern; uninterested: *he was indifferent to my pleas.* **2** unimportant; immaterial. **3a** of only average or moderate size, extent, quality, etc. **3b** not at all good; poor. **4** showing or having no preferences; impartial. [C14: from L *indifferēns* making no distinction]
▸**in'differently** *adv*

indifferentism (ɪn'dɪfrənˌtɪzəm, -fərən-) *n* systematic indifference, esp. in matters of religion.
▸**in'differentist** *n*

indigenous ❶ (ɪn'dɪdʒɪnəs) *adj* (when *postpositive,* foll. by *to*) **1** originating or occurring naturally (in a country, etc.); native. **2** innate (to); inherent (in). [C17: from L *indigenus,* from *indi-* in + *gignere* to beget]
▸**in'digenously** *adv* ▸**in'digenousness** *n*

indigent ❶ ('ɪndɪdʒənt) *adj* **1** so poor as to lack even necessities; very needy. **2** (usually foll. by *of*) *Arch.* lacking (in) or destitute (of). ◆ *n* **3** an impoverished person. [C14: from L *indigēre* to need, from *egēre* to lack]
▸**'indigence** *n* ▸**'indigently** *adv*

indigestible (ˌɪndɪ'dʒɛstəbᵊl) *adj* **1** incapable of being digested or difficult to digest. **2** difficult to understand or absorb mentally: *an indigestible book.*
▸**ˌindiˌgesti'bility** *n* ▸**ˌindi'gestibly** *adv*

indigestion ❶ (ˌɪndɪ'dʒɛstʃən) *n* difficulty in digesting food, accompanied by abdominal pain, heartburn, and belching.

indignant ❶ (ɪn'dɪgnənt) *adj* feeling or showing indignation. [C16: from L *indignārī* to be displeased with]
▸**in'dignantly** *adv*

THESAURUS

indicate *vb* **1 = signify**, add up to (*inf.*), bespeak, be symptomatic of, betoken, denote, evince, imply, manifest, point to, reveal, show, signal, suggest **2 = point out**, designate, point to, specify **4 = show**, display, express, mark, read, record, register

indicated *adj* **5 = recommended**, advisable, called-for, desirable, necessary, needed, suggested

indication *n* **1 = sign**, clue, evidence, explanation, forewarning, hint, index, inkling, intimation, manifestation, mark, note, omen, portent, signal, suggestion, symptom, warning

indicative *adj* **1 = suggestive**, exhibitive, indicatory, indicial, pointing to, significant, symptomatic

indicator *n* **1-3 = sign**, display, gauge, guide, index, mark, marker, meter, pointer, signal, signpost, symbol

indict *vb* **= charge**, accuse, arraign, impeach, prosecute, serve with a summons, summon, summons, tax

indictment *n* **1-3 = charge**, accusation, allegation, impeachment, prosecution, summons

indifference *n* **1 = disregard**, absence of feeling, aloofness, apathy, callousness, carelessness, coldness, coolness, detachment, disinterestedness, dispassion, heedlessness, inattention, lack of interest, negligence, nonchalance, stoicalness, unconcern **3 = irrelevance**, insignificance, triviality, unimportance
Antonyms *n* ≠ **disregard:** attention, care, commitment, concern, enthusiasm, heed, interest, regard

indifferent *adj* **1 = unconcerned**, aloof, apathetic, callous, careless, cold, cool, detached, distant, heedless, impervious, inattentive, regardless, uncaring, unimpressed, uninterested, unmoved, unresponsive, unsympathetic **2 = unimportant**, immaterial, insignificant, of no consequence **3a = mediocre**, average, fair, middling, moderate, no great shakes (*inf.*), ordinary, passable, perfunctory, so-so (*inf.*), undistinguished, uninspired **4 = impartial**, disinterested, dispassionate, equitable, neutral, nonaligned, nonpartisan, objective, unbiased, uninvolved, unprejudiced
Antonyms *adj* ≠ **unconcerned:** avid, compassionate, concerned, eager, enthusiastic, interested, keen, responsive, sensitive, susceptible, sympathetic ≠ **mediocre:** excellent, exceptional, fine, first-class, notable, remarkable

indigenous *adj* **1 = native**, aboriginal, autochthonous, home-grown, original

indigent *adj* **1 = destitute**, dirt-poor, down and out, down at heel (*inf.*), flat broke (*inf.*), impecunious, impoverished, in want, necessitous, needy, on one's uppers (*inf.*), on the breadline, penniless, penurious, poor, poverty-stricken, short, straitened, without two pennies to rub together (*inf.*)
Antonyms *adj* affluent, prosperous, rich, wealthy, well-off, well-to-do

indigestion *n* **= heartburn**, dyspepsia, dyspepsy, upset stomach

indignant *adj* **= resentful**, angry, annoyed, choked, disgruntled, exasperated, fuming (*inf.*), furious, heated, hot under the collar (*inf.*),

indignation ❶ (ˌɪndɪɡˈneɪʃən) *n* anger aroused by something felt to be unfair, unworthy, or wrong.

indignity ❶ (ɪnˈdɪɡnɪtɪ) *n, pl* **indignities.** injury to one's self-esteem or dignity; humiliation.

indigo (ˈɪndɪˌɡəʊ) *n, pl* **indigos** *or* **indigoes. 1** a blue vat dye originally obtained from plants but now made synthetically. **2** any of various leguminous tropical plants, such as the anil, that yield this dye. **3a** any of a group of colours that have the same blue-violet hue; a spectral colour. **3b** (*as adj*): *an indigo rug.* [C16: from Sp. *indico,* via L from Gk *Indikos* of India]
▸**indigotic** (ˌɪndɪˈɡɒtɪk) *adj*

indigo blue *n, adj* (**indigo-blue** *when prenominal*). the full name for **indigo** (the colour and the dye).

indirect ❶ (ˌɪndɪˈrɛkt) *adj* **1** deviating from a direct course or line; roundabout; circuitous. **2** not coming as a direct effect or consequence; secondary: *indirect benefits.* **3** not straightforward, open, or fair; devious or evasive.
▸ˌ**indiˈrectly** *adv* ▸ˌ**indiˈrectness** *n*

indirect costs *pl n* another name for **overheads.**

indirection (ˌɪndɪˈrɛkʃən) *n* **1** indirect procedure, courses, or methods. **2** lack of direction or purpose; aimlessness. **3** indirect dealing; deceit.

indirect lighting *n* reflected or diffused light from a concealed source.

indirect object *n Grammar.* a noun, pronoun, or noun phrase indicating the recipient or beneficiary of the action of a verb and its direct object, as *John* in the sentence *I bought John a newspaper.*

indirect proof *n Logic, maths.* proof of a conclusion by showing its negation to be self-contradictory. Cf. **direct** (sense 17).

indirect question *n* a question reported in indirect speech, as in *She asked why you came.*

indirect speech *or esp. US* **indirect discourse** *n* the reporting of something said or written by conveying what was meant rather than repeating the exact words, as in the sentence *He said I looked happy* as opposed to *He said to me, "You look happy."* Also called: **reported speech.**

indirect tax *n* a tax levied on goods or services rather than on individuals or companies.

indiscreet ❶ (ˌɪndɪˈskriːt) *adj* not discreet; imprudent or tactless.
▸ˌ**indisˈcreetly** *adv* ▸ˌ**indisˈcreetness** *n*

indiscrete (ˌɪndɪˈskriːt) *adj* not divisible or divided into parts.

indiscretion ❶ (ˌɪndɪˈskrɛʃən) *n* **1** the characteristic or state of being indiscreet. **2** an indiscreet act, remark, etc.

indiscriminate ❶ (ˌɪndɪˈskrɪmɪnɪt) *adj* **1** lacking discrimination or careful choice; random or promiscuous. **2** jumbled; confused.
▸ˌ**indisˈcriminately** *adv* ▸ˌ**indisˈcriminateness** *n* ▸ˌ**indisˌcrimiˈnation** *n*

indispensable ❶ (ˌɪndɪˈspɛnsəbᵊl) *adj* **1** absolutely necessary; essential. **2** not to be disregarded or escaped: *an indispensable role.* ◆ *n* **3** an indispensable person or thing.
▸ˌ**indisˌpensaˈbility** *or* ˌ**indisˈpensableness** *n* ▸ˌ**indisˈpensably** *adv*

indispose (ˌɪndɪˈspəʊz) *vb* **indisposes, indisposing, indisposed.** (*tr*) **1** to make unwilling or opposed; disincline. **2** to cause to feel ill. **3** to make unfit (for something or to do something).

indisposed ❶ (ˌɪndɪˈspəʊzd) *adj* **1** sick or ill. **2** unwilling. [C15: from L *indispositus* disordered]
▸**indisposition** (ˌɪndɪspəˈzɪʃən) *n*

indisputable ❶ (ˌɪndɪˈspjuːtəbᵊl) *adj* beyond doubt; not open to question.
▸ˌ**indisˌputaˈbility** *or* ˌ**indisˈputableness** *n* ▸ˌ**indisˈputably** *adv*

indissoluble ❶ (ˌɪndɪˈsɒljʊbᵊl) *adj* incapable of being dissolved or broken; permanent.
▸ˌ**indisˈsolubly** *adv*

indistinct ❶ (ˌɪndɪˈstɪŋkt) *adj* incapable of being clearly distinguished, as by the eyes, ears, or mind; not distinct.
▸ˌ**indisˈtinctly** *adv* ▸ˌ**indisˈtinctness** *n*

indistinguishable ❶ (ˌɪndɪˈstɪŋɡwɪʃəbᵊl) *adj* **1** (*often postpositive*; foll. by *from*) identical or very similar (to): *twins indistinguishable from one another.* **2** not easily perceptible; indiscernible.
▸ˌ**indisˌtinguishaˈbility** *or* ˌ**indisˈtinguishableness** *n* ▸ˌ**indisˈtinguishably** *adv*

indite (ɪnˈdaɪt) *vb* **indites, inditing, indited.** (*tr*) *Arch.* to write. [C14: from OF *enditer,* from L *indīcere* to declare, from IN-[2] + *dīcere* to say]
▸**inˈditement** *n* ▸**inˈditer** *n*

> **USAGE NOTE** *Indite* and *inditement* are sometimes wrongly used where *indict* and *indictment* are meant: *he was indicted* (not *indited*) *for fraud.*

indium (ˈɪndɪəm) *n* a rare soft silvery metallic element associated with zinc ores: used in alloys, electronics, and electroplating. Symbol: In; atomic no.: 49; atomic wt.: 114.82. [C19: NL, from INDIGO + -IUM]

individual ❶ (ˌɪndɪˈvɪdjʊəl) *adj* **1** of, relating to, characteristic of, or meant for a single person or thing. **2** separate or distinct, esp. from others of its kind; particular: *please mark the individual pages.* **3** characterized by unusual and striking qualities; distinctive. **4** *Obs.* indivisible; inseparable. ◆ *n* **5** a single person, esp. when regarded as distinct from others. **6** *Biol.* a single animal or plant, esp. as distinct from a species. **7** *Inf.* a person: *a most obnoxious individual.* [C15: from Med. L, from L *indīviduus* indivisible, from IN-[1] + *dīvidere* to DIVIDE]
▸ˌ**indiˈvidually** *adv*

individualism ❶ (ˌɪndɪˈvɪdjʊəˌlɪzəm) *n* **1** the principle of asserting one's independence and individuality; egoism. **2** an individual quirk. **3** another word for **laissez faire** (sense 1). **4** *Philosophy.* the doctrine that only individual things exist.
▸ˌ**indiˈvidualist** *n*

individuality ❶ (ˌɪndɪˌvɪdjʊˈælɪtɪ) *n, pl* **individualities. 1** distinctive or unique character or personality: *a work of great individuality.* **2** the qualities that distinguish one person or thing from another; identity. **3** the state or quality of being a separate entity; discreteness.

individualize *or* **individualise** (ˌɪndɪˈvɪdjʊəˌlaɪz) *vb* **individualizes, individualizing, individualized** *or* **individualises, individualising, individualised.** (*tr*) **1** to make or mark as individual or distinctive in character. **2** to consider or treat individually; particularize. **3** to make or modify so as to meet the special requirements of a person.
▸ˌ**indiˌvidualiˈzation** *or* ˌ**indiˌvidualiˈsation** *n* ▸ˌ**indiˈvidualˌizer** *or* ˌ**indiˈvidualˌiser** *n*

individuate (ˌɪndɪˈvɪdjʊˌeɪt) *vb* **individuates, individuating, individuated.** (*tr*) **1** to give individuality or an individual form to. **2** to distinguish from others of the same species or group; individualize.
▸ˌ**indiˈviduˌator** *n*

THESAURUS

in a huff, incensed, in high dudgeon, irate, livid (*inf.*), mad (*inf.*), miffed (*inf.*), peeved (*inf.*), provoked, riled, scornful, sore (*inf.*), up in arms (*inf.*), wrathful

indignation *n* = **resentment,** anger, exasperation, fury, ire (*literary*), pique, rage, righteous anger, scorn, umbrage, wrath

indignity *n* = **humiliation,** abuse, affront, contumely, dishonour, disrespect, injury, insult, obloquy, opprobrium, outrage, reproach, slap in the face (*inf.*), slight, snub

indirect *adj* **1** = **circuitous,** backhanded, circumlocutory, crooked, devious, long-drawn-out, meandering, oblique, periphrastic, rambling, roundabout, tortuous, wandering, winding, zigzag **2** = **incidental,** ancillary, collateral, contingent, secondary, subsidiary, unintended
Antonyms *adj* ≠ **circuitous:** direct, straight, straightforward, undeviating, uninterrupted

indiscreet *adj* = **tactless,** foolish, hasty, heedless, ill-advised, ill-considered, ill-judged, impolitic, imprudent, incautious, injudicious, naive, rash, reckless, undiplomatic, unthinking, unwise
Antonyms *adj* cautious, diplomatic, discreet, judicious, politic, prudent, tactful, wise

indiscretion *n* **2** = **mistake,** bloomer (*Brit. inf.*), boob (*Brit. sl.*), error, faux pas, folly, foolishness, gaffe, gaucherie, imprudence, lapse, rashness, recklessness, slip, slip of the tongue, tactlessness

indiscriminate *adj* **1** = **random,** aimless, careless, desultory, general, hit or miss (*inf.*), sweeping, uncritical, undiscriminating, unmethodical, unselective, unsystematic, wholesale **2** = **jumbled,** chaotic, confused, haphazard, higgledy-piggledy (*inf.*), mingled, miscellaneous, mixed, mongrel, motley, promiscuous, undistinguishable
Antonyms *adj* ≠ **random:** deliberate, discriminating, exclusive, methodical, selective, systematic

indispensable *adj* **1** = **essential,** crucial, imperative, key, necessary, needed, needful, requisite, vital
Antonyms *adj* dispensable, disposable, nonessential, superfluous, unimportant, unnecessary

indisposed *adj* **1** = **ill,** ailing, confined to bed, laid up (*inf.*), on the sick list (*inf.*), poorly (*inf.*), sick, under the weather, unwell **2** = **unwilling,** averse, disinclined, loath, reluctant
Antonyms *adj* ≠ **ill:** fine, fit, hardy, healthy, sound, well

indisposition *n* **1** = **illness,** ailment, ill health, sickness **2** = **reluctance,** aversion, disinclination, dislike, distaste, hesitancy, unwillingness

indisputable *adj* = **undeniable,** absolute, beyond doubt, certain, evident, incontestable, incontrovertible, indubitable, irrefutable, positive, sure, unassailable, unquestionable
Antonyms *adj* assailable, disputable, doubtful, indefinite, questionable, refutable, uncertain, vague

indissoluble *adj* = **permanent,** abiding, binding, enduring, eternal, fixed, imperishable, incorruptible, indestructible, inseparable, lasting, solid, unbreakable

indistinct *adj* = **unclear,** ambiguous, bleary, blurred, confused, dim, doubtful, faint, fuzzy, hazy, ill-defined, indefinite, indeterminate, indiscernible, indistinguishable, misty, muffled, obscure, out of focus, shadowy, undefined, unintelligible, vague, weak
Antonyms *adj* clear, defined, determinate, discernible, distinct, distinguishable, evident, intelligible

indistinguishable *adj* **1** = **identical,** alike, cut from the same cloth, like as two peas in a pod (*inf.*), (the) same, twin **2** = **imperceptible,** indiscernible, invisible, obscure

individual *adj* **1-3** = **personal,** characteristic, discrete, distinct, distinctive, exclusive, identical, idiosyncratic, own, particular, peculiar, personalized, proper, respective, separate, several, single, singular, special, specific, unique ◆ *n* **5** = **person,** being, body (*inf.*), character, creature, mortal, party, personage, soul, type, unit
Antonyms *adj* ≠ **personal:** collective, common, conventional, general, indistinct, ordinary, universal

individualism *n* **1** = **self-interest,** egocentricity, egoism, freethinking, independence, originality, self-direction, self-reliance

individualist *n* **1** = **maverick,** freethinker, independent, loner, lone wolf, nonconformist, original

individuality *n* **1** = **distinctiveness,** character, discreteness, distinction, originality, peculiarity, personality, separateness, singularity, uniqueness

individually *adv* **2** = **separately,** apart, independently, one at a time, one by one, personally, severally, singly

indivisible (ˌɪndɪˈvɪzəbəl) *adj* **1** unable to be divided. **2** *Maths.* leaving a remainder when divided by a given number.
▸ˌ**indiˌvisiˈbility** *n* ▸ˌ**indiˈvisibly** *adv*

Indo- (ˈɪndəʊ) *combining form.* denoting India or Indian: *Indo-European.*

indoctrinate ❶ (ɪnˈdɒktrɪˌneɪt) *vb* **indoctrinates, indoctrinating, indoctrinated.** (*tr*) **1** to teach (a person or group of people) systematically to accept doctrines, esp. uncritically. **2** *Rare.* to instruct.
▸**inˌdoctriˈnation** *n* ▸**inˈdoctriˌnator** *n*

Indo-European *adj* **1** denoting, belonging to, or relating to a family of languages that includes English: characteristically marked, esp. in the older languages, such as Latin, by inflection showing gender, number, and case. **2** denoting or relating to the hypothetical parent language of this family, primitive Indo-European. **3** denoting, belonging to, or relating to any of the peoples speaking these languages. ◆ *n* **4** the Indo-European family of languages. **5** the reconstructed hypothetical parent language of this family. ◆ Also (*obs.*): **Indo-Germanic.**

Indo-Iranian *adj* **1** of or relating to the Indic and Iranian branches of the Indo-European family of languages. ◆ *n* **2** this group of languages, sometimes considered as forming a single branch of Indo-European.

indole (ˈɪndəʊl) *or* **indol** (ˈɪndəʊl, -dɒl) *n* a white or yellowish crystalline heterocyclic compound extracted from coal tar and used in perfumery, medicine, and as a flavouring agent. [C19: from IND(IGO) + -OLE[1]]

indolent ❶ (ˈɪndələnt) *adj* **1** disliking work or effort; lazy; idle. **2** *Pathol.* causing little pain: *an indolent tumour.* **3** (esp. of a painless ulcer) slow to heal. [C17: from L *indolēns* not feeling pain, from IN-[1] + *dolēre* to grieve, cause distress]
▸ˈ**indolence** *n* ▸ˈ**indolently** *adv*

indomitable ❶ (ɪnˈdɒmɪtəbəl) *adj* (of courage, pride, etc.) difficult or impossible to defeat or subdue. [C17: from LL, from L *indomitus* untameable, from *domāre* to tame]
▸**inˌdomitaˈbility** *or* **inˈdomitableness** *n* ▸**inˈdomitably** *adv*

Indonesian (ˌɪndəʊˈniːzɪən) *adj* **1** of or relating to Indonesia, its people, or their language. ◆ *n* **2** a native or inhabitant of Indonesia.

indoor (ˈɪnˌdɔː) *adj* (*prenominal*) of, situated in, or appropriate to the inside of a house or other building: *an indoor pool; indoor amusements.*

indoors (ˌɪnˈdɔːz) *adv, adj* (*postpositive*) inside or into a house or other building.

indorse ❶ (ɪnˈdɔːs) *vb* **indorses, indorsing, indorsed.** a variant spelling of **endorse.**

indraught *or US* **indraft** (ˈɪnˌdrɑːft) *n* **1** the act of drawing or pulling in. **2** an inward flow, esp. of air.

indrawn (ˌɪnˈdrɔːn) *adj* **1** drawn or pulled in. **2** inward-looking or introspective.

indris (ˈɪndrɪs) *or* **indri** (ˈɪndrɪ) *n, pl* **indris. 1** a large Madagascan arboreal lemuroid primate with thick silky fur patterned in black, white, and fawn. **2 woolly indris.** a related nocturnal Madagascan animal with thick grey-brown fur and a long tail. [C19: from F: lemur, from native word *indry!* look! mistaken for the animal's name]

indubitable ❶ (ɪnˈdjuːbɪtəbəl) *adj* incapable of being doubted; unquestionable. [C18: from L, from IN-[1] + *dubitāre* to doubt]
▸**inˈdubitably** *adv*

induce ❶ (ɪnˈdjuːs) *vb* **induces, inducing, induced.** (*tr*) **1** (often foll. by an infinitive) to persuade or use influence on. **2** to cause or bring about. **3** *Med.* to initiate or hasten (labour), as by administering a drug to stimulate uterine contractions. **4** *Logic, obs.* to assert or establish (a general proposition, etc.) by induction. **5** to produce (an electromotive force or electrical current) by induction. **6** to transmit (magnetism) by induction. [C14: from L *indūcere* to lead in]
▸**inˈducer** *n* ▸**inˈducible** *adj*

inducement ❶ (ɪnˈdjuːsmənt) *n* **1** the act of inducing. **2** a means of inducing; persuasion; incentive. **3** *Law.* the introductory part that leads up to and explains the matter in dispute.

induct ❶ (ɪnˈdʌkt) *vb* (*tr*) **1** to bring in formally or install in an office, place, etc.; invest. **2** (foll. by *to* or *into*) to initiate in knowledge (of). **3** *US.* to enlist for military service. **4** *Physics.* another word for **induce** (senses 5, 6). [C14: from L *inductus* led in, p.p. of *indūcere* to introduce; see INDUCE]

inductance (ɪnˈdʌktəns) *n* **1** the property of an electric circuit as a result of which an electromotive force is created by a change of current in the same or in a neighbouring circuit. **2** a component, such as a coil, in an electrical circuit, the main function of which is to produce inductance.

induction ❶ (ɪnˈdʌkʃən) *n* **1** the act of inducting or state of being inducted. **2** the act of inducing. **3** (in an internal-combustion engine) the drawing in of mixed air and fuel from the carburettor to the cylinder. **4** *Logic.* **4a** a process of reasoning by which a general conclusion is drawn from a set of premises, based mainly on experience or experimental evidence. **4b** a conclusion reached by this process of reasoning. **5** the process by which electrical or magnetic properties are transferred, without physical contact, from one circuit or body to another. See also **inductance. 6** *Maths.* a method of proving a proposition P(*n*) by showing that it is true for all preceding values of *n* and for *n* + 1. **7a** a formal introduction or entry into an office or position. **7b** (*as modifier*): *induction course.* **8** *US.* the enlistment of a civilian into military service.
▸**inˈductional** *adj*

induction coil *n* **1** any coil of wire used to introduce inductance into a circuit. **2** another name for **ignition coil.**

induction heating *n* the heating of a conducting material as a result of the electric currents induced in it by an externally applied alternating magnetic field.

induction loop system *n* an electronic system enabling partially deaf people to hear dialogue and sound in theatres, cinemas, etc. Often shortened to **induction loop.**

induction motor *n* a type of electric motor in which an alternating supply fed to the windings of the stator creates a magnetic field that induces a current in the windings of the rotor. Rotation of the rotor results from the interaction of the magnetic field created by the rotor current with the field of the stator.

inductive (ɪnˈdʌktɪv) *adj* **1** relating to or operated by electrical or magnetic induction: *an inductive reactance.* **2** *Logic, maths.* of, relating to, or using induction: *inductive reasoning.* **3** serving to induce or cause.
▸**inˈductively** *adv* ▸**inˈductiveness** *n*

inductor (ɪnˈdʌktə) *n* **1** a person or thing that inducts. **2** another name for an **inductance** (sense 2).

indue (ɪnˈdjuː) *vb* **indues, induing, indued.** a variant spelling of **endue.**

indulge ❶ (ɪnˈdʌldʒ) *vb* **indulges, indulging, indulged. 1** (when *intr*, often foll. by *in*) to yield to or gratify (a whim or desire for): *to indulge in new clothes.* **2** (*tr*) to yield to the wishes of; pamper: *to indulge a child.* **3** (*tr*) to allow (oneself) the pleasure of something: *he indulged himself.* **4** (*intr*) *Inf.* to take alcoholic drink, esp. to excess. [C17: from L *indulgēre* to concede]
▸**inˈdulger** *n* ▸**inˈdulgingly** *adv*

indulgence ❶ (ɪnˈdʌldʒəns) *n* **1** the act of indulging or state of being indulgent. **2** a pleasure, habit, etc., indulged in; extravagance. **3** liberal or tolerant treatment. **4** something granted as a favour or privilege. **5** *RC Church.* a remission of the temporal punishment for sin after its guilt has been forgiven. **6** Also called: **Declaration of Indulgence.** a royal grant during the reigns of Charles II and James II of England giving Nonconformists and Roman Catholics a measure of religious freedom.

indulgent ❶ (ɪnˈdʌldʒənt) *adj* showing or characterized by indulgence.
▸**inˈdulgently** *adv*

induna (ɪnˈduːnə) *n* (in South Africa) a Black African overseer in a factory, mine, etc. [C20: from Zulu *nduna* an official]

indurate *vb* (ˈɪndjʊˌreɪt) **indurates, indurating, indurated. 1** to make or become hard or callous. **2** to make or become hardy. ◆ *adj* (ˈɪndjʊrɪt). **3** hardened, callous, or unfeeling. [C16: from L *indūrāre* to make hard; see ENDURE]
▸ˌ**induˈration** *n* ▸ˈ**induˌrative** *adj*

indusium (ɪnˈdjuːzɪəm) *n, pl* **indusia** (-zɪə). **1** a membranous outgrowth on the undersurface of fern leaves that protects the developing

THESAURUS

indoctrinate *vb* **1 = train,** brainwash, drill, ground, imbue, initiate, instruct, school, teach

indoctrination *n* **1 = training,** brainwashing, drilling, grounding, inculcation, instruction, schooling

indolence *n* **1 = idleness,** heaviness, inactivity, inertia, inertness, languidness, languor, laziness, lethargy, shirking, skiving (*Brit. sl.*), slacking, sloth, sluggishness, torpidity, torpor

indolent *adj* **1 = lazy,** good-for-nothing, idle, inactive, inert, lackadaisical, languid, lethargic, listless, lumpish, slack, slothful, slow, sluggish, torpid, workshy
Antonyms *adj* active, assiduous, busy, conscientious, diligent, energetic, industrious, vigorous

indomitable *adj* **= invincible,** bold, resolute, set, staunch, steadfast, unbeatable, unconquerable, unflinching, untameable, unyielding
Antonyms *adj* cowardly, faltering, feeble, shrinking, wavering, weak, yielding

indorse *see* **endorse**

indubitable *adj* **= certain,** evident, incontestable, incontrovertible, indisputable, irrefutable, obvious, open-and-shut, sure, unarguable, undeniable, undoubted, unquestionable, veritable

induce *vb* **1 = persuade,** actuate, convince, draw, encourage, get, impel, incite, influence, instigate, move, press, prevail upon, prompt, talk into **2 = cause,** bring about, effect, engender, generate, give rise to, lead to, occasion, produce, set in motion, set off
Antonyms *vb* curb, deter, discourage, dissuade, hinder, prevent, restrain, stop, suppress

inducement *n* **2 = incentive,** attraction, bait, carrot (*inf.*), cause, clarion call, come-on (*inf.*), consideration, encouragement, impulse, incitement, influence, lure, motive, reward, spur, stimulus, urge

induct *vb* **1 = install,** inaugurate, initiate, introduce, invest, swear in

induction *n* **1 = installation,** inauguration, initiation, institution, introduction, investiture **4b = inference,** conclusion, generalization

indulge *vb* **1 = gratify,** cater to, feed, give way to, pander to, regale, satiate, satisfy, treat oneself to, yield to **2 = spoil,** baby, coddle, cosset, favour, fawn on, foster, give in to, go along with, humour, mollycoddle, pamper, pet

indulgence *n* **1 = intemperance,** excess, fondness, immoderation, intemperateness, kindness, leniency, pampering, partiality, permissiveness, profligacy, profligateness, spoiling **2 = luxury,** extravagance, favour, privilege, treat **3 = tolerance,** courtesy, forbearance, goodwill, patience, understanding
Antonyms *n* ≠ **intemperance:** moderation, strictness, temperance, temperateness

indulgent *adj* **= lenient,** compliant, easygoing, favourable, fond, forbearing, gentle, gratifying, kind, kindly, liberal, mild, permissive, tender, tolerant, understanding
Antonyms *adj* austere, demanding, harsh, intolerant, rigorous, stern, strict, stringent, unmerciful

spores. **2** an enveloping membrane, such as the amnion. [C18: NL, from L: tunic, from *induere* to put on]
▸**in'dusial** *adj*

industrial (ɪn'dʌstrɪəl) *adj* **1** of, relating to, or derived from industry. **2** employed in industry: *the industrial workforce.* **3** relating to or concerned with workers in industry: *industrial conditions.* **4** used in industry: *industrial chemicals.*
▸**in'dustrially** *adv*

industrial action *n Brit.* any action, such as a strike or go-slow, taken by employees in industry to protest against working conditions, etc.

industrial archaeology *n* the study of industrial machines, works, etc. of the past.

industrial design *n* the art or practice of designing any object for manufacture.
▸**industrial designer** *n*

industrial diamond *n* a small often synthetic diamond, valueless as a gemstone, used in cutting tools, abrasives, etc.

industrial disease *n* any disease to which workers in a particular industry are prone.

industrial espionage *n* attempting to obtain trade secrets by dishonest means, as by telephone- or computer-tapping, infiltration of a competitor's workforce, etc.

industrial estate *n Brit.* another name for **trading estate.** US equivalent: **industrial park.**

industrialism (ɪn'dʌstrɪəˌlɪzəm) *n* an organization of society characterized by large-scale mechanized manufacturing industry rather than trade, farming, etc.

industrialist Ⓣ (ɪn'dʌstrɪəlɪst) *n* a person who has a substantial interest in the ownership or control of industrial enterprise.

industrialize *or* **industrialise** (ɪn'dʌstrɪəˌlaɪz) *vb* **industrializes, industrializing, industrialized** *or* **industrialises, industrialising, industrialised. 1** (*tr*) to develop industry on an extensive scale in (a country, region, etc.). **2** (*intr*) (of a country, region, etc.) to undergo the development of industry on an extensive scale.
▸**inˌdustriali'zation** *or* **inˌdustriali'sation** *n*

industrial medicine *n* the study and practice of the health care of employees of large organizations.

industrial relations *n* **1** (*functioning as pl*) relations between the employers and employees in an industrial enterprise. **2** (*functioning as sing*) the management of such relations.

Industrial Revolution *n* **the.** the transformation in the 18th and 19th centuries of Britain and other countries into industrial nations.

industrial tribunal *n* a tribunal that rules on disputes between employers and employees regarding unfair dismissal, redundancy, etc.

industrious Ⓣ (ɪn'dʌstrɪəs) *adj* hard-working, diligent, or assiduous.
▸**in'dustriously** *adv* ▸**in'dustriousness** *n*

industry Ⓣ ('ɪndəstrɪ) *n, pl* **industries. 1** organized economic activity concerned with manufacture, processing of raw materials, or construction. **2** a branch of commercial enterprise concerned with the output of a specified product: *the steel industry.* **3a** industrial ownership and management interests collectively. **3b** manufacturing enterprise collectively, as opposed to agriculture. **4** diligence; assiduity. [C15: from L *industria* diligence, from *industrius* active, from ?]

indwell (ɪn'dwɛl) *vb* **indwells, indwelling, indwelt. 1** (*tr*) (of a spirit, principle, etc.) to inhabit; suffuse. **2** (*intr*) to dwell; exist.
▸**in'dweller** *n*

-ine[1] *suffix forming adjectives.* **1** of, relating to, or belonging to: *saturnine.* **2** consisting of or resembling: *crystalline.* [from L *-īnus,* from Gk *-inos*]

-ine[2] *suffix forming nouns.* **1** indicating a halogen: *chlorine.* **2** indicating a nitrogenous organic compound, including amino acids, alkaloids, and certain other bases: *nicotine.* **3** Also: **-in.** indicating a chemical substance in certain nonsystematic names: *glycerine.* **4** indicating a mixture of hydrocarbons: *benzine.* **5** indicating feminine form: *heroine.* [via F from L *-ina* (from *-inus*) and Gk *-inē*]

inebriate Ⓣ *vb* (ɪn'iːbrɪˌeɪt), **inebriates, inebriating, inebriated.** (*tr*) **1** to make drunk; intoxicate. **2** to arouse emotionally; make excited. ◆ *n* (ɪn'iːbrɪɪt). **3** a person who is drunk, esp. habitually. ◆ *adj* (ɪn'iːbrɪɪt), *also* **inebriated. 4** drunk, esp. habitually. [C15: from L, from IN-[2] + *ēbriāre* to intoxicate, from *ēbrius* drunk]
▸**inˌebri'ation** *n* ▸**inebriety** (ˌɪnɪ'braɪɪtɪ) *n*

inedible (ɪn'ɛdɪbᵊl) *adj* not fit to be eaten.
▸**inˌedi'bility** *n*

ineducable (ɪn'ɛdjʊkəbᵊl) *adj* incapable of being educated, esp. on account of mental retardation.
▸**inˌeduca'bility** *n*

ineffable Ⓣ (ɪn'ɛfəbᵊl) *adj* **1** too great or intense to be expressed in words; unutterable. **2** too sacred to be uttered. **3** indescribable; indefinable. [C15: from L, from IN-[1] + *effābilis,* from *fārī* to speak]
▸**inˌeffa'bility** *or* **in'effableness** *n* ▸**in'effably** *adv*

ineffective Ⓣ (ˌɪnɪ'fɛktɪv) *adj* **1** having no effect. **2** incompetent or inefficient.
▸ˌ**inef'fectively** *adv* ▸ˌ**inef'fectiveness** *n*

ineffectual Ⓣ (ˌɪnɪ'fɛktʃʊəl) *adj* **1** having no effect or an inadequate effect. **2** lacking in power or forcefulness; impotent: *an ineffectual ruler.*
▸ˌ**inefˌfectu'ality** *or* ˌ**inef'fectualness** *n* ▸ˌ**inef'fectually** *adv*

inefficacious Ⓣ (ˌɪnɛfɪ'keɪʃəs) *adj* failing to produce the desired effect.
▸ˌ**ineffi'caciously** *adv* ▸**inefficacy** (ɪn'ɛfɪkəsɪ), ˌ**ineffi'caciousness,** *or* **inefficacity** (ˌɪnɛfɪ'kæsɪtɪ) *n*

inefficient Ⓣ (ˌɪnɪ'fɪʃənt) *adj* **1** unable to perform a task or function to the best advantage; wasteful or incompetent. **2** unable to produce the desired result.
▸ˌ**inef'ficiency** *n* ▸ˌ**inef'ficiently** *adv*

ineligible Ⓣ (ɪn'ɛlɪdʒəbᵊl) *adj* **1** (often foll. by *for* or an infinitive) not fit or qualified: *ineligible for a grant; ineligible to vote.* ◆ *n* **2** an ineligible person.
▸**inˌeligi'bility** *or* **in'eligibleness** *n* ▸**in'eligibly** *adv*

ineluctable (ˌɪnɪ'lʌktəbᵊl) *adj* (esp. of fate) incapable of being avoided; inescapable. [C17: from L, from IN-[1] + *ēluctārī* to escape, from *luctārī* to struggle]
▸ˌ**ineˌlucta'bility** *n* ▸ˌ**ine'luctably** *adv*

inept Ⓣ (ɪn'ɛpt) *adj* **1** awkward, clumsy, or incompetent. **2** not suitable, appropriate, or fitting; out of place. [C17: from L *ineptus,* from IN-[1] + *aptus* fitting]
▸**in'eptiˌtude** *n* ▸**in'eptly** *adv* ▸**in'eptness** *n*

inequable (ɪn'ɛkwəbᵊl) *adj* **1** uneven. **2** not uniform. **3** changeable.

inequality Ⓣ (ˌɪnɪ'kwɒlɪtɪ) *n, pl* **inequalities. 1** the state or quality of being unequal; disparity. **2** an instance of disparity. **3** lack of smoothness or regularity. **4** social or economic disparity. **5** *Maths.* **5a** a statement indicating that the value of one quantity or expression is not equal to another. **5b** the relation of being unequal. **6** *Astron.* a departure from uniform orbital motion.

inert Ⓣ (ɪn'ɜːt) *adj* **1** having no inherent ability to move or to resist motion. **2** inactive, lazy, or sluggish. **3** having only a limited ability to react chemically; unreactive. [C17: from L *iners* unskilled, from IN-[1] + *ars* skill; see ART[1]]
▸**in'ertly** *adv* ▸**in'ertness** *n*

THESAURUS

industrialist *n* = **capitalist**, baron, big businessman, boss, captain of industry, financier, magnate, manufacturer, producer, tycoon

industrious *adj* = **hard-working**, active, assiduous, busy, conscientious, diligent, energetic, laborious, persevering, persistent, productive, purposeful, sedulous, steady, tireless, zealous
Antonyms *adj* good-for-nothing, idle, indolent, lackadaisical, lazy, shiftless, slothful

industriously *adv* = **diligently**, assiduously, conscientiously, doggedly, hard, like a Trojan, nose to the grindstone (*inf.*), perseveringly, sedulously, steadily, without slacking

industry *n* **1** = **business**, commerce, commercial enterprise, manufacturing, production, trade **4** = **effort**, activity, application, assiduity, determination, diligence, labour, perseverance, persistence, tirelessness, toil, vigour, zeal

inebriate *vb* **1** = **intoxicate**, make drunk, stupefy **2** = **arouse**, animate, carry away, excite, exhilarate, fire, stimulate ◆ *n* **3** = **drunkard**, alcoholic, boozer, dipsomaniac, drunk, heavy drinker, lush (*sl.*), soak (*sl.*), sot, toper

inebriated *adj* **1** = **drunk**, blotto (*sl.*), half-cut (*inf.*), inebriate, in one's cups, intoxicated, legless (*inf.*), merry (*Brit. inf.*), paralytic (*inf.*), pissed (*taboo sl.*), plastered (*sl.*), rat-arsed (*taboo sl.*), smashed (*sl.*), tight (*inf.*), tipsy, under the influence (*inf.*)

inebriation *n* **1** = **drunkenness**, crapulence, inebriety, insobriety, intemperance, intoxication, sottishness

ineffable *adj* **1, 3** = **indescribable**, beyond words, incommunicable, indefinable, inexpressible, unspeakable, unutterable

ineffective *adj* **1** = **useless**, barren, bootless, feeble, fruitless, futile, idle, impotent, inadequate, ineffectual, inefficacious, inefficient, pathetic, unavailing, unproductive, vain, weak, worthless
Antonyms *adj* effective, efficacious, efficient, fruitful, potent, productive, useful, worthwhile

ineffectual *adj* **2** = **weak**, abortive, bootless, emasculate, feeble, fruitless, futile, idle, impotent, inadequate, incompetent, ineffective, inefficacious, inefficient, inept, lame, pathetic, powerless, unavailing, useless, vain

inefficacious *adj* = **ineffective**, abortive, futile, ineffectual, unavailing, unproductive, unsuccessful

inefficacy *n* = **ineffectiveness**, futility, inadequacy, ineffectuality, nonsuccess, unproductiveness, uselessness

inefficiency *n* **1** = **incompetence**, carelessness, disorganization, muddle, slackness, sloppiness

inefficient *adj* **1** = **incompetent**, cowboy (*inf.*), disorganized, feeble, incapable, ineffectual, inefficacious, inept, inexpert, slipshod, sloppy, wasteful, weak
Antonyms *adj* able, capable, competent, effective, efficient, expert, organized, skilled

ineligible *adj* **1** = **unqualified**, disqualified, incompetent (*Law*), objectionable, ruled out, unacceptable, undesirable, unequipped, unfit, unfitted, unsuitable

inept *adj* **1** = **incompetent**, awkward, bumbling, bungling, cack-handed (*inf.*), clumsy, cowboy (*inf.*), gauche, inexpert, maladroit, unhandy, unskilful, unworkmanlike **2** = **unsuitable**, absurd, improper, inappropriate, inapt, infelicitous, malapropos, meaningless, out of place, pointless, ridiculous, unfit
Antonyms *adj* ≠ **incompetent:** able, adroit, competent, dexterous, efficient, qualified, skilful, talented ≠ **unsuitable:** appropriate, apt, effectual, germane, sensible, suitable

ineptitude *n* **1** = **incompetence**, clumsiness, gaucheness, incapacity, inexpertness, unfitness, unhandiness **2** = **inappropriateness**, absurdity, pointlessness, uselessness

inequality *n* **1** = **disparity**, bias, difference, disproportion, diversity, imparity, irregularity, lack of balance, preferentiality, prejudice, unevenness

inert *adj* **2** = **inactive**, dead, dormant, dull, idle, immobile, inanimate, indolent, lazy, leaden, lifeless, motionless, passive, quiescent, slack, slothful, sluggish, slumberous (*chiefly poetic*), static, still, torpid, unmoving, unreactive, unresponsive

inert gas *n* **1** any of the unreactive gaseous elements helium, neon, argon, krypton, xenon, and radon. **2** (loosely) any gas, such as carbon dioxide, that is nonoxidizing.

inertia Ⓣ (ɪn'ɜːʃə, -ʃɪə) *n* **1** the state of being inert; disinclination to move or act. **2** *Physics.* **2a** the tendency of a body to preserve its state of rest or uniform motion unless acted upon by an external force. **2b** an analogous property of other physical quantities that resist change: *thermal inertia.*
▸**in'ertial** *adj*

inertial guidance *or* **navigation** *n* a method of controlling the flight path of a missile by instruments contained within it.

inertial mass *n* the mass of a body as determined by its momentum, as opposed to the extent to which it responds to the force of gravity. Cf. **gravitational mass.**

inertia-reel seat belt *n* a type of car seat belt in which the belt is free to unwind from a metal drum except when the drum locks as a result of rapid change of velocity.

inertia selling *n* the illegal practice of sending unrequested goods to householders, followed by a bill for the goods if they do not return them.

inescapable Ⓣ (ˌɪnɪ'skeɪpəbᵊl) *adj* incapable of being escaped or avoided.
▸ˌ**ines'capably** *adv*

inestimable Ⓣ (ɪn'ɛstɪməbᵊl) *adj* **1** not able to be estimated; immeasurable. **2** of immeasurable value.
▸**inˌestima'bility** *or* **in'estimableness** *n* ▸**in'estimably** *adv*

inevitable Ⓣ (ɪn'ɛvɪtəbᵊl) *adj* **1** unavoidable. **2** sure to happen; certain. ◆ *n* **3** (often preceded by *the*) something that is unavoidable. [C15: from L, from IN-[1] + *ēvītāre* to shun, from *vītāre* to avoid]
▸**inˌevita'bility** *or* **in'evitableness** *n* ▸**in'evitably** *adv*

inexcusable Ⓣ (ˌɪnɪk'skjuːzəbᵊl) *adj* not able to be excused or justified.
▸ˌ**inexˌcusa'bility** *or* ˌ**inex'cusableness** *n* ▸ˌ**inex'cusably** *adv*

inexhaustible Ⓣ (ˌɪnɪg'zɔːstəbᵊl) *adj* **1** incapable of being used up; endless. **2** incapable or apparently incapable of becoming tired; tireless.
▸ˌ**inexˌhausti'bility** *n* ▸ˌ**inex'haustibly** *adv*

inexorable Ⓣ (ɪn'ɛksərəbᵊl) *adj* **1** not able to be moved by entreaty or persuasion. **2** relentless. [C16: from L, from IN-[1] + *exōrāre* to prevail upon, from *ōrāre* to pray]
▸**inˌexora'bility** *n* ▸**in'exorably** *adv*

inexpensive Ⓣ (ˌɪnɪk'spɛnsɪv) *adj* not expensive; cheap.
▸ˌ**inex'pensively** *adv* ▸ˌ**inex'pensiveness** *n*

inexperience Ⓣ (ˌɪnɪk'spɪərɪəns) *n* lack of experience or of the knowledge and understanding derived from experience.
▸ˌ**inex'perienced** *adj*

inexpiable (ɪn'ɛkspɪəbᵊl) *adj* **1** incapable of being expiated; unpardonable. **2** *Arch.* implacable.
▸**in'expiableness** *n*

inexplicable Ⓣ (ˌɪnɪk'splɪkəbᵊl, ɪn'ɛksplɪkəbᵊl) *adj* not capable of explanation; unexplained.
▸ˌ**inexplica'bility** *n* ▸ˌ**inex'plicably** *adv*

in extenso *Latin.* (ɪn ɪk'stɛnsəʊ) *adv* at full length.

in extremis *Latin.* (ɪn ɪk'striːmɪs) *adv* **1** in extremity; in dire straits. **2** at the point of death. [lit.: in the furthest reaches]

inextricable Ⓣ (ˌɪnɛks'trɪkəbᵊl) *adj* **1** not able to be escaped from: *an inextricable dilemma.* **2** not able to be disentangled, etc.: *an inextricable knot.* **3** extremely involved or intricate.
▸ˌ**inextrica'bility** *or* ˌ**inex'tricableness** *n* ▸ˌ**inex'tricably** *adv*

inf. *abbrev. for:* **1** Also: **Inf.** infantry. **2** inferior. **3** infinitive. **4** informal. **5** information.

infallible Ⓣ (ɪn'fæləbᵊl) *adj* **1** not fallible; not liable to error. **2** not liable to failure; certain; sure: *an infallible cure.* ◆ *n* **3** a person or thing that is incapable of error or failure.
▸**inˌfalli'bility** *or* **in'fallibleness** *n* ▸**in'fallibly** *adv*

infamous Ⓣ ('ɪnfəməs) *adj* **1** having a bad reputation; notorious. **2** causing or deserving a bad reputation; shocking: *infamous conduct.*
▸**'infamously** *adv* ▸**'infamousness** *n*

infamy Ⓣ ('ɪnfəmɪ) *n, pl* **infamies. 1** the state or condition of being infamous. **2** an infamous act or event. [C15: from L *infāmis* of evil repute, from IN-[1] + *fāma* FAME]

infancy Ⓣ ('ɪnfənsɪ) *n, pl* **infancies. 1** the state or period of being an infant; childhood. **2** an early stage of growth or development. **3** infants collectively. **4** the period of life prior to attaining legal majority; minority nonage.

infant Ⓣ ('ɪnfənt) *n* **1** a child at the earliest stage of its life; baby. **2** *Law.* another word for **minor** (sense 9). **3** *Brit.* a young schoolchild. **4** a person who is beginning or inexperienced in an activity. **5** (*modifier*) **5a** of or relating to young children or infancy. **5b** designed or intended for young children. ◆ *adj* **6** in an early stage of development; nascent: *an infant science.* **7** *Law.* of or relating to the legal status of infancy. [C14: from L *infāns*, lit.: speechless, from IN-[1] + *fārī* to speak]
▸**'infantˌhood** *n*

infanta (ɪn'fæntə) *n* (formerly) **1** a daughter of a king of Spain or Portugal. **2** the wife of an infante. [C17: from Sp. or Port., fem of INFANTE]

infante (ɪn'fæntɪ) *n* (formerly) a son of a king of Spain or Portugal, esp. one not heir to the throne. [C16: from Sp. or Port., lit.: INFANT]

infanticide (ɪn'fæntɪˌsaɪd) *n* **1** the killing of an infant. **2** the practice of killing newborn infants, still prevalent in some primitive tribes. **3** a person who kills an infant.
▸**inˌfanti'cidal** *adj*

infantile Ⓣ ('ɪnfənˌtaɪl) *adj* **1** like a child in action or behaviour; childishly immature; puerile. **2** of, relating to, or characteristic of infants or infancy. **3** in an early stage of development.
▸**infantility** (ˌɪnfən'tɪlɪtɪ) *n*

infantile paralysis *n* a former name for **poliomyelitis.**

THESAURUS

Antonyms *adj* active, alive, alive and kicking, animated, energetic, full of beans (*inf.*), living, mobile, moving, reactive, responsive, vital

inertia *n* **1** = **inactivity**, apathy, deadness, disinclination to move, drowsiness, dullness, idleness, immobility, indolence, languor, lassitude, laziness, lethargy, listlessness, passivity, sloth, sluggishness, stillness, stupor, torpor, unresponsiveness
Antonyms *n* action, activity, animation, brio, energy, liveliness, vigour, vitality

inescapable *adj* = **unavoidable**, certain, destined, fated, ineluctable, ineludible (*rare*), inevitable, inexorable, sure

inestimable *adj* **1, 2** = **incalculable**, beyond price, immeasurable, invaluable, precious, priceless, prodigious

inevitability *n* **1, 2** = **certainty**, fate, ineluctability, inexorability *or* inexorableness, sureness, unavoidability *or* unavoidableness

inevitable *adj* **1, 2** = **unavoidable**, assured, certain, decreed, destined, fixed, ineluctable, inescapable, inexorable, necessary, ordained, settled, sure, unpreventable
Antonyms *adj* avoidable, escapable, evadable, preventable, uncertain

inevitably *adv* **1, 2** = **unavoidably**, as a necessary consequence, as a result, automatically, certainly, necessarily, of necessity, perforce, surely, willy-nilly

inexcusable *adj* = **unforgivable**, indefensible, inexpiable, outrageous, unjustifiable, unpardonable, unwarrantable
Antonyms *adj* defensible, excusable, forgivable, justifiable, pardonable

inexhaustible *adj* **1** = **endless**, bottomless, boundless, illimitable, infinite, limitless, measureless, never-ending, unbounded **2** = **tireless**, indefatigable, undaunted, unfailing, unflagging, untiring, unwearied, unwearying
Antonyms *adj* ≠ **endless:** bounded, exhaustible, finite, limitable, limited, measurable ≠ **tireless:** daunted, enervated, failing, flagging, tiring, wearied

inexorable *adj* **1** = **unrelenting**, adamant, cruel, hard, harsh, immovable, implacable, ineluctable, inescapable, inflexible, merciless, obdurate, pitiless, relentless, remorseless, severe, unappeasable, unbending, unyielding
Antonyms *adj* bending, flexible, lenient, movable, relenting, yielding

inexorably *adv* **1** = **relentlessly**, implacably, inevitably, irresistibly, remorselessly, unrelentingly

inexpensive *adj* = **cheap**, bargain, budget, economical, low-cost, low-priced, modest, reasonable
Antonyms *adj* costly, dear, exorbitant, expensive, high-priced, pricey, uneconomical

inexperience *n* = **unfamiliarity**, callowness, greenness, ignorance, newness, rawness, unexpertness

inexperienced *adj* = **immature**, amateur, callow, fresh, green, new, raw, unaccustomed, unacquainted, unfamiliar, unfledged, unpractised, unschooled, unseasoned, unskilled, untrained, untried, unused, unversed, wet behind the ears (*inf.*)
Antonyms *adj* experienced, familiar, knowledgeable, practised, seasoned, skilled, trained, versed

inexplicable *adj* = **unaccountable**, baffling, beyond comprehension, enigmatic, incomprehensible, inscrutable, insoluble, mysterious, mystifying, strange, unfathomable, unintelligible
Antonyms *adj* comprehensible, explainable, explicable, fathomable, intelligible, soluble, understandable

inextricably *adv* = **inseparably**, indissolubly, indistinguishably, intricately, irretrievably, totally

infallibility *n* **1** = **perfection**, faultlessness, impeccability, irrefutability, omniscience, supremacy, unerringness **2** = **reliability**, dependability, safety, sureness, trustworthiness

infallible *adj* **1** = **perfect**, faultless, impeccable, omniscient, unerring, unimpeachable **2** = **sure**, certain, dependable, foolproof, reliable, sure- fire (*inf.*), trustworthy, unbeatable, unfailing
Antonyms *adj* ≠ **perfect:** errant, fallible, human, imperfect, mortal ≠ **sure:** doubtful, dubious, uncertain, undependable, unreliable, unsure

infamous *adj* **1** = **notorious**, disreputable, ill-famed **2** = **shocking**, abominable, atrocious, base, detestable, disgraceful, dishonourable, egregious, flagitious, hateful, heinous, ignominious, iniquitous, loathsome, monstrous, nefarious, odious, opprobrious, outrageous, scandalous, scurvy, shameful, vile, villainous, wicked
Antonyms *adj* ≠ **notorious:** esteemed, glorious, honourable, noble, reputable, virtuous

infamy *n* **1** = **notoriety**, abomination, atrocity, discredit, disgrace, dishonour, disrepute, ignominy, obloquy, odium, opprobrium, outrageousness, scandal, shame, stigma, villainy

infancy *n* **1** = **early childhood**, babyhood **2** = **beginnings**, cradle, dawn, early stages, emergence, inception, origins, outset, start
Antonyms *n* ≠ **beginnings:** close, conclusion, death, end, expiration, finish, termination

infant *n* **1** = **baby**, ankle-biter, babe, babe in arms, bairn (*Scot.*), child, little one, neonate, newborn child, rug rat (*sl.*), sprog (*sl.*), suckling, toddler, tot, wean (*Scot.*) ◆ *adj* **6** = **early**, baby, dawning, developing, emergent, growing, immature, initial, nascent, newborn, unfledged, young

infantile *adj* **1** = **childish**, babyish, immature, puerile, tender, weak, young
Antonyms *adj* adult, developed, mature

infantilism (ɪnˈfæntɪˌlɪzəm) *n* **1** *Psychol.* a condition in which an older child or adult is mentally or physically undeveloped. **2** childish speech; baby talk.

infantry (ˈɪnfəntrɪ) *n, pl* **infantries. a** soldiers or units of soldiers who fight on foot with small arms. **b** (*as modifier*): *an infantry unit.* [C16: from It. *infanteria*, from *infante* boy, foot soldier; see INFANT]

infantryman (ˈɪnfəntrɪmən) *n, pl* **infantrymen.** a soldier belonging to the infantry.

infant school *n* (in England and Wales) a school for children aged between 5 and 7.

infarct (ɪnˈfɑːkt) *n* a localized area of dead tissue resulting from obstruction of the blood supply to that part. Also called: **infarction.** [C19: via NL from L *infarctus* stuffed into, from *farcīre* to stuff]
▸**inˈfarcted** *adj*

infatuate Ⓣ *vb* (ɪnˈfætjʊˌeɪt), **infatuates, infatuating, infatuated.** (*tr*) **1** to inspire or fill with foolish, shallow, or extravagant passion. **2** to cause to act foolishly. ◆ *n* (ɪnˈfætjʊɪt, -ˌeɪt). **3** *Literary.* a person who is infatuated. [C16: from L *infatuāre*, from IN-[2] + *fatuus* FATUOUS]
▸**inˌfatuˈation** *n*

infatuated Ⓣ (ɪnˈfætjʊˌeɪtɪd) *adj* (often foll. by *with*) possessed by a foolish or extravagant passion, esp. for another person.

infect Ⓣ (ɪnˈfɛkt) *vb* (*mainly tr*) **1** to cause infection in; contaminate (an organism, wound, etc.) with pathogenic microorganisms. **2** (*also intr*) to affect or become affected with a communicable disease. **3** to taint, pollute, or contaminate. **4** to affect, esp. adversely, as if by contagion. **5** (*also intr*) *Computing.* to affect or become affected with a computer virus. ◆ *adj* **6** *Arch.* contaminated or polluted with or as if with a disease; infected. [C14: from L *inficere* to dip into, stain, from *facere* to make]
▸**inˈfector** *or* **inˈfecter** *n*

infection Ⓣ (ɪnˈfɛkʃən) *n* **1** invasion of the body by pathogenic microorganisms. **2** the resulting condition in the tissues. **3** an infectious disease. **4** the act of infecting or state of being infected. **5** an agent or influence that infects. **6** persuasion or corruption, as by ideas, perverse influences, etc.

infectious Ⓣ (ɪnˈfɛkʃəs) *adj* **1** (of a disease) capable of being transmitted. **2** (of a disease) caused by microorganisms, such as bacteria, viruses, or protozoa. **3** causing or transmitting infection. **4** tending or apt to spread, as from one person to another: *infectious mirth.*
▸**inˈfectiously** *adv* ▸**inˈfectiousness** *n*

infectious hepatitis *n* any form of hepatitis caused by viruses. See **hepatitis A, hepatitis B, non-A, non-B hepatitis.**

infectious mononucleosis *n* an acute infectious disease, caused by a virus (**Epstein-Barr virus**), characterized by fever, sore throat, swollen and painful lymph nodes, and abnormal lymphocytes in the blood. Also called: **glandular fever.**

infective (ɪnˈfɛktɪv) *adj* **1** capable of causing infection. **2** a less common word for **infectious.**
▸**inˈfectively** *adv* ▸**inˈfectiveness** *n*

infelicity Ⓣ (ˌɪnfɪˈlɪsɪtɪ) *n, pl* **infelicities. 1** unhappiness; misfortune. **2** an instance of bad luck or mischance. **3** something, esp. a remark or expression, that is inapt or inappropriate.
▸**ˌinfeˈlicitous** *adj*

infer Ⓣ (ɪnˈfɜː) *vb* **infers, inferring, inferred.** (*when tr, may take a clause as object*) **1** to conclude (a state of affairs, supposition, etc.) by reasoning from evidence; deduce. **2** (*tr*) to have or lead to as a necessary or logical consequence; indicate. **3** (*tr*) to hint or imply. [C16: from L *inferre* to bring into, from *ferre* to bear, carry]
▸**inˈferable** *or* **inˈferrable** *adj* ▸**inˈferrer** *n*

USAGE NOTE The use of *infer* to mean *imply* is common in both speech and writing, but is regarded by many people as incorrect.

inference Ⓣ (ˈɪnfərəns, -frəns) *n* **1** the act or process of inferring. **2** an inferred conclusion, deduction, etc. **3** any process of reasoning from premises to a conclusion. **4** *Logic.* the specific mode of reasoning used.

inferential (ˌɪnfəˈrɛnʃəl) *adj* of, relating to, or derived from inference.
▸**ˌinferˈentially** *adv*

inferior Ⓣ (ɪnˈfɪərɪə) *adj* **1** lower in value or quality. **2** lower in rank, position, or status; subordinate. **3** not of the best; mediocre; commonplace. **4** lower in position; situated beneath. **5** (of a plant ovary) situated below the other floral parts. **6** *Astron.* **6a** orbiting between the sun and the earth: *an inferior planet.* **6b** lying below the horizon. **7** *Printing.* (of a character) printed at the foot of an ordinary character. ◆ *n* **8** an inferior person. **9** *Printing.* an inferior character. [C15: from L: lower, from *inferus* low]
▸**inferiority** (ɪnˌfɪərɪˈɒrɪtɪ) *n* ▸**inˈferiorly** *adv*

inferiority complex *n Psychiatry.* a disorder arising from the conflict between the desire to be noticed and the fear of being humiliated, characterized by aggressiveness or withdrawal into oneself.

infernal Ⓣ (ɪnˈfɜːnᵊl) *adj* **1** of or relating to an underworld of the dead. **2** deserving or befitting hell; diabolic; fiendish. **3** *Inf.* irritating; confounded. [C14: from LL, from *infernus* hell, from L (adj): lower, hellish; rel. to L *inferus* low]
▸**ˌinferˈnality** *n* ▸**inˈfernally** *adv*

infernal machine *n Arch.* an explosive device (usually disguised) or booby trap.

inferno (ɪnˈfɜːnəʊ) *n, pl* **infernos. 1** (*sometimes cap.*; usually preceded by *the*) hell; the infernal region. **2** any place or state resembling hell, esp. a conflagration. [C19: from It., from LL *infernus* hell]

infertile Ⓣ (ɪnˈfɜːtaɪl) *adj* **1** not capable of producing offspring; sterile. **2** (of land) not productive; barren.
▸**inˈfertilely** *adv* ▸**infertility** (ˌɪnfəˈtɪlɪtɪ) *n*

infest Ⓣ (ɪnˈfɛst) *vb* (*tr*) **1** to inhabit or overrun in unpleasantly large numbers. **2** (of parasites such as lice) to invade and live on or in (a host). [C15: from L *infestāre* to molest, from *infestus* hostile]
▸**ˌinfesˈtation** *n* ▸**inˈfester** *n*

infeudation (ˌɪnfjuːˈdeɪʃən) *n History.* **1** (in feudal society) the act of putting a vassal in possession of a fief. **2** the granting of tithes to laymen.

infidel Ⓣ (ˈɪnfɪdᵊl) *n* **1** a person who has no religious belief; unbeliever. ◆ *adj* **2** rejecting a specific religion, esp. Christianity or Islam. **3** of or relating to unbelievers or unbelief. [C15: from Med. L, from L (adj): unfaithful, from IN-[1] + *fidēlis* faithful; see FEALTY]

infidelity Ⓣ (ˌɪnfɪˈdɛlɪtɪ) *n, pl* **infidelities. 1** lack of faith or constancy, esp. sexual faithfulness. **2** lack of religious faith; disbelief. **3** an act or instance of disloyalty.

infield (ˈɪnˌfiːld) *n* **1** *Cricket.* the area of the field near the pitch. Cf. **outfield** (sense 1). **2** *Baseball.* the area of the playing field enclosed by the base lines. **3** *Agriculture.* the part of a farm nearest to the farm buildings.
▸**ˈinˌfielder** *n*

infighting (ˈɪnˌfaɪtɪŋ) *n* **1** *Boxing.* combat at close quarters in which proper blows are inhibited. **2** intense competition, as between members of an organization.
▸**ˈinˌfighter** *n*

infill (ˈɪnfɪl) *or* **infilling** (ˈɪnfɪlɪŋ) *n* **1** the act of filling or closing gaps, etc., in something, such as a row of buildings. **2** material used to fill a cavity, gap, hole, etc.

infiltrate Ⓣ (ˈɪnfɪlˌtreɪt) *vb* **infiltrates, infiltrating, infiltrated. 1** to undergo the process in which a fluid passes into the pores or interstices of a

THESAURUS

infatuate *vb* **1 = obsess,** befool, beguile, bewitch, captivate, delude, enchant, enrapture, fascinate, make a fool of, mislead, stupefy, sweep one off one's feet, turn (someone's) head

infatuated *adj* **= obsessed,** beguiled, besotted, bewitched, captivated, carried away, crazy about (*inf.*), enamoured, enraptured, fascinated, head over heels in love with, inflamed, intoxicated, possessed, smitten (*inf.*), spellbound, swept off one's feet, under the spell of

infatuation *n* **1 = obsession,** crush (*inf.*), fixation, folly, foolishness, madness, passion, thing (*inf.*)

infect *vb* **3 = contaminate,** affect, blight, corrupt, defile, influence, poison, pollute, spread to *or* among, taint, touch, vitiate

infection *n* **1-4 = contamination,** contagion, corruption, defilement, poison, pollution, septicity, virus

infectious *adj* **1, 3 = catching,** communicable, contagious, contaminating, corrupting, defiling, infective, pestilential, poisoning, polluting, spreading, transmittable, virulent, vitiating

infelicity *n* **1 = misfortune,** bad luck, misery, sadness, unhappiness, woe, wretchedness

infer *vb* **1 = deduce,** conclude, conjecture, derive, gather, presume, put two and two together, read between the lines, surmise, understand

inference *n* **2 = deduction,** assumption, conclusion, conjecture, consequence, corollary, illation (*rare*), presumption, reading, surmise

inferior *adj* **2 = lower,** junior, lesser, menial, minor, secondary, subordinate, subsidiary, under, underneath **3 = substandard,** bad, duff (*Brit. inf.*), imperfect, indifferent, low-grade, low-rent (*inf., chiefly US*), mean, mediocre, no great shakes (*inf.*), not a patch on, not much cop (*Brit. sl.*), of a sort *or* of sorts, poor, poorer, second-class, second-rate, shoddy, worse ◆ *n* **8 = underling,** junior, menial, subordinate
Antonyms *adj* ≠ **lower:** greater, higher, senior, superior, top ≠ **substandard:** excellent, fine, first-class

inferiority *n* **2 = subservience,** abasement, inferior status *or* standing, lowliness, subordination **3 = inadequacy,** badness, deficiency, imperfection, insignificance, meanness, mediocrity, shoddiness, unimportance, worthlessness
Antonyms *n* ≠ **subservience:** advantage, ascendancy, dominance, superiority ≠ **inadequacy:** eminence, excellence, superiority

infernal *adj* **1 = hellish,** chthonian, Hadean, lower, nether, Plutonian, Stygian, Tartarean (*literary*), underworld **2 = devilish,** accursed, damnable, damned, demonic, diabolical, fiendish, hellish, malevolent, malicious, satanic
Antonyms *adj* ≠ **hellish:** celestial, heavenly ≠ **devilish:** angelic, glorious, godlike, seraphic

infertile *adj* **1, 2 = barren,** infecund, nonproductive, sterile, unfruitful, unproductive
Antonyms *adj* fecund, fertile, fruitful, generative, productive

infertility *n* **1, 2 = sterility,** barrenness, infecundity, unfruitfulness, unproductiveness

infest *vb* **1 = overrun,** beset, flood, invade, penetrate, permeate, ravage, swarm, throng

infested *adj* **1 = overrun,** alive, beset, crawling, lousy, pervaded, plagued, ravaged, ridden, swarming, teeming

infidel *n* **1 = pagan,** atheist, freethinker, Gentile, giaour (*Turkish*), heathen, heretic, sceptic, unbeliever

infidelity *n* **1 = unfaithfulness,** adultery, bad faith, betrayal, cheating (*inf.*), disloyalty, duplicity, faithlessness, false-heartedness, falseness, perfidy

infiltrate *vb* **3 = penetrate,** creep in, filter through, insinuate oneself, make inroads (into), percolate, permeate, pervade, sneak in (*inf.*), work *or* worm one's way into

solid; permeate. **2** *Mil.* to pass undetected through (an enemy-held line or position). **3** to gain or cause to gain entrance or access surreptitiously: *they infiltrated the party structure.* ◆ *n* **4** something that infiltrates. [C18: from IN-[2] + FILTRATE]
▸ **,infil'tration** *n* ▸ **'infil,trative** *adj* ▸ **'infil,trator** *n*

infin. *abbrev. for* infinitive.

infinite ⓘ (ˈɪnfɪnɪt) *adj* **1a** having no limits or boundaries in time, space, extent, or magnitude. **1b** (*as n; preceded by the*): *the infinite.* **2** extremely or immeasurably great or numerous: *infinite wealth.* **3** all-embracing, absolute, or total: *God's infinite wisdom.* **4** *Maths.* having an unlimited or uncountable number of digits, factors, terms, etc.
▸ **'infinitely** *adv* ▸ **'infiniteness** *n*

infinitesimal ⓘ (ˌɪnfɪnɪˈtesɪməl) *adj* **1** infinitely or immeasurably small. **2** *Maths.* of, relating to, or involving a small change in the value of a variable that approaches zero as a limit. ◆ *n* **3** *Maths.* an infinitesimal quantity.
▸ **,infini'tesimally** *adv*

infinitesimal calculus *n* another name for **calculus** (sense 1).

infinitive (ɪnˈfɪnɪtɪv) *n Grammar.* a form of the verb not inflected for grammatical categories such as tense and person and used without an overt subject. In English, the infinitive usually consists of the word *to* followed by the verb.
▸ **infinitival** (ˌɪnfɪnɪˈtaɪvᵊl) *adj* ▸ **in'finitively** *or* **,infini'tivally** *adv*

infinitude (ɪnˈfɪnɪˌtjuːd) *n* **1** the state or quality of being infinite. **2** an infinite extent, quantity, degree, etc.

infinity ⓘ (ɪnˈfɪnɪtɪ) *n, pl* **infinities. 1** the state or quality of being infinite. **2** endless time, space, or quantity. **3** an infinitely or indefinitely great number or amount. **4** *Maths.* **4a** the concept of a value greater than any finite numerical value. **4b** the reciprocal of zero. **4c** the limit of an infinite sequence of numbers.

infirm ⓘ (ɪnˈfɜːm) *adj* **1a** weak in health or body, esp. from old age. **1b** (*as collective n; preceded by the*): *the infirm.* **2** lacking moral certainty; indecisive or irresolute. **3** not stable, sound, or secure: *an infirm structure.* **4** *Law.* (of a law, etc.) lacking legal force; invalid.
▸ **in'firmly** *adv* ▸ **in'firmness** *n*

infirmary (ɪnˈfɜːmərɪ) *n, pl* **infirmaries.** a place for the treatment of the sick or injured; hospital.

infirmity ⓘ (ɪnˈfɜːmɪtɪ) *n, pl* **infirmities. 1** the state or quality of being infirm. **2** physical weakness or debility; frailty. **3** a moral flaw or failing.

infix *vb* (ɪnˈfɪks, ˈɪnˌfɪks). **1** (*tr*) to fix firmly in. **2** (*tr*) to instil or inculcate. **3** *Grammar.* to insert (an affix) into the middle of a word. ◆ *n* (ˈɪnˌfɪks). **4** *Grammar.* an affix inserted into the middle of a word.
▸ **,infix'ation** *or* **infixion** (ɪnˈfɪkʃən) *n*

in flagrante delicto (ɪn fləˈgræntɪ dɪˈlɪktəʊ) *adv Chiefly law.* while committing the offence; red-handed. Also: **flagrante delicto.** [L, lit.: with the crime still blazing]

inflame ⓘ (ɪnˈfleɪm) *vb* **inflames, inflaming, inflamed. 1** to arouse or become aroused to violent emotion. **2** (*tr*) to increase or intensify; aggravate. **3** to produce inflammation in (a tissue, organ, or part) or (of a tissue, etc.) to become inflamed. **4** to set or be set on fire. **5** (*tr*) to cause to redden.
▸ **in'flamer** *n*

inflammable ⓘ (ɪnˈflæməbᵊl) *adj* **1** liable to catch fire; flammable. **2** readily aroused to anger or passion. ◆ *n* **3** something that is liable to catch fire.
▸ **in,flamma'bility** *or* **in'flammableness** *n* ▸ **in'flammably** *adv*

USAGE NOTE See at **flammable.**

inflammation ⓘ (ˌɪnfləˈmeɪʃən) *n* **1** the reaction of living tissue to injury or infection, characterized by heat, redness, swelling, and pain. **2** the act of inflaming or the state of being inflamed.

inflammatory ⓘ (ɪnˈflæmətərɪ, -trɪ) *adj* **1** characterized by or caused by inflammation. **2** tending to arouse violence, strong emotion, etc.
▸ **in'flammatorily** *adv*

inflatable (ɪnˈfleɪtəbᵊl) *n* **1** any of various large air-filled objects made of strong plastic or rubber. ◆ *adj* **2** capable of being inflated.

inflate ⓘ (ɪnˈfleɪt) *vb* **inflates, inflating, inflated. 1** to expand or cause to expand by filling with gas or air. **2** (*tr*) to cause to increase excessively; puff up; swell: *to inflate one's opinion of oneself.* **3** (*tr*) to cause inflation of (prices, money, etc.). **4** (*tr*) to raise in spirits; elate. **5** (*intr*) to undergo economic inflation. [C16: from L *inflāre* to blow into, from *flāre* to blow]
▸ **in'flatedly** *adv* ▸ **in'flatedness** *n* ▸ **in'flater** *or* **in'flator** *n*

inflation ⓘ (ɪnˈfleɪʃən) *n* **1** the act of inflating or state of being inflated. **2** *Econ.* a progressive increase in the general level of prices brought about by an expansion in demand or the money supply or by autonomous increases in costs. Cf. **reflation. 3** *Inf.* the rate of increase of prices. **4** *Astron.* a very fast expansion of the universe occurring immediately after the big bang, postulated in certain models of the universe (**inflationary universes**) to account for the present distribution of matter.
▸ **in'flationary** *adj*

inflationary spiral *n* a self-sustaining form of inflation in which a rise in prices generates a wage demand, causing a further price rise and a further wage demand.

inflationism (ɪnˈfleɪʃəˌnɪzəm) *n* the policy of inflation through expansion of the supply of money and credit.
▸ **in'flationist** *n, adj*

inflect (ɪnˈflɛkt) *vb* **1** *Grammar.* to change (the form of a word) by inflection. **2** (*tr*) to change (the voice) in tone or pitch; modulate. **3** (*tr*) to cause to deviate from a straight or normal line or course; bend. [C15: from L *inflectere* to curve round, alter, from *flectere* to bend]
▸ **in'flectedness** *n* ▸ **in'flective** *adj* ▸ **in'flector** *n*

inflection ⓘ *or* **inflexion** (ɪnˈflɛkʃən) *n* **1** modulation of the voice. **2** *Grammar.* a change in the form of a word, signalling change in such grammatical functions as tense, person, gender, number, or case. **3** an angle or bend. **4** the act of inflecting or the state of being inflected. **5** *Maths.* a change in curvature from concave to convex or vice versa.
▸ **in'flectional** *or* **in'flexional** *adj* ▸ **in'flectionally** *or* **in'flexionally** *adv*
▸ **in'flectionless** *or* **in'flexionless** *adj*

inflexible ⓘ (ɪnˈflɛksəbᵊl) *adj* **1** not flexible; rigid; stiff. **2** obstinate; unyielding. **3** without variation; unalterable; fixed. [C14: from L *inflexibilis*; see INFLECT]
▸ **in,flexi'bility** *or* **in'flexibleness** *n* ▸ **in'flexibly** *adv*

inflict ⓘ (ɪnˈflɪkt) *vb* (*tr*) **1** (often foll. by *on* or *upon*) to impose (something unwelcome, such as pain, oneself, etc.). **2** to deal out (blows, lashes, etc.). [C16: from L *inflīgere* to strike (something) against, dash against, from *flīgere* to strike]
▸ **in'flictable** *adj* ▸ **in'flicter** *or* **in'flictor** *n* ▸ **in'fliction** *n*

in-flight *adj* provided during flight in an aircraft: *in-flight entertainment.*

inflorescence (ˌɪnflɔːˈrɛsəns) *n* **1** the part of a plant that consists of the flower-bearing stalks. **2** the arrangement of the flowers on the stalks.

THESAURUS

infinite *adj* **1-3** = **never-ending**, absolute, all-embracing, bottomless, boundless, enormous, eternal, everlasting, illimitable, immeasurable, immense, inestimable, inexhaustible, interminable, limitless, measureless, numberless, perpetual, stupendous, total, unbounded, uncounted, untold, vast, wide, without end, without number
Antonyms *adj* bounded, circumscribed, finite, limited, measurable, restricted

infinitesimal *adj* **1** = **microscopic**, atomic, inappreciable, insignificant, minuscule, minute, negligible, teeny, teeny-weeny, tiny, unnoticeable, wee
Antonyms *adj* enormous, great, huge, infinite, large, vast

infinity *n* **1, 2** = **eternity**, boundlessness, endlessness, immensity, infinitude, perpetuity, vastness

infirm *adj* **1** = **frail**, ailing, debilitated, decrepit, doddering, doddery, enfeebled, failing, feeble, lame, weak **2** = **irresolute**, faltering, indecisive, insecure, shaky, unsound, unstable, vacillating, wavering, weak, wobbly
Antonyms *adj* ≠ **frail:** healthy, hearty, robust, sound, strong, sturdy, vigorous

infirmity *n* **1, 2** = **frailty**, debility, decrepitude, deficiency, feebleness, ill health, imperfection, sickliness, vulnerability **3** = **ailment**, defect, disorder, failing, fault, malady, sickness, weakness
Antonyms *n* ≠ **frailty:** health, soundness, stability, strength, vigour, wellness

inflame *vb* **1** = **enrage**, agitate, anger, arouse, embitter, exasperate, excite, fire, foment, heat, ignite, impassion, incense, infuriate, intoxicate, kindle, madden, make one's blood boil, provoke, rile, rouse, stimulate **2** = **aggravate**, exacerbate, exasperate, fan, increase, intensify, worsen
Antonyms *vb* allay, calm, cool, discourage, extinguish, pacify, quench, quiet, soothe, suppress

inflamed *adj* **3** = **sore**, angry, chafing, festering, fevered, heated, hot, infected, red, septic, swollen

inflammable *adj* **1** = **flammable**, combustible, incendiary

inflammation *n* **1** = **soreness**, burning, heat, painfulness, rash, redness, sore, tenderness

inflammatory *adj* **2** = **provocative**, anarchic, demagogic, explosive, fiery, incendiary, inflaming, instigative, insurgent, intemperate, like a red rag to a bull, rabble-rousing, rabid, riotous, seditious

inflate *vb* **1, 2** = **expand**, aerate, aggrandize, amplify, balloon, bloat, blow up, boost, dilate, distend, enlarge, escalate, exaggerate, increase, puff up *or* out, pump up, swell
Antonyms *vb* collapse, compress, contract, deflate, diminish, lessen, shrink

inflated *adj* **2** = **exaggerated**, bombastic, grandiloquent, ostentatious, overblown, swollen

inflation *n* **1** = **expansion**, aggrandizement, blowing up, distension, enhancement, enlargement, escalation, extension, increase, intensification, puffiness, rise, spread, swelling, tumefaction

inflection *n* **1** = **intonation**, accentuation, modulation **2** *Grammar* = **conjugation**, declension **3** = **bend**, angle, arc, arch, bow, crook, curvature

inflexibility *n* **1** = **rigidity**, hardness, immovability, inelasticity, stiffness, stringency **2** = **obstinacy**, fixity, intransigence, obduracy, steeliness

inflexible *adj* **1** = **inelastic**, hard, hardened, nonflexible, rigid, stiff, taut **2** = **obstinate**, adamant, brassbound, dyed-in-the-wool, firm, fixed, hard and fast, immovable, immutable, implacable, inexorable, intractable, iron, obdurate, relentless, resolute, rigorous, set, set in one's ways, steadfast, steely, stiff-necked, strict, stringent, stubborn, unadaptable, unbending, unchangeable, uncompromising, unyielding
Antonyms *adj* ≠ **inelastic:** elastic, flexible, lissom(e), pliable, pliant, supple, yielding ≠ **obstinate:** flexible, irresolute, movable, variable, yielding

inflict *vb* **1** = **impose**, administer, apply, deliver, exact, levy, mete *or* deal out, visit, wreak

infliction *n* **1** = **imposition**, administration, exaction, perpetration, wreaking

3 the process of flowering; blossoming. [C16: from NL, from LL, from *flōrescere* to bloom]
▸ˌinfloˈrescent *adj*

inflow (ˈɪnˌfləʊ) *n* **1** something, such as a liquid or gas, that flows in. **2** Also called: **inflowing.** the act of flowing in; influx.

influence ❶ (ˈɪnflʊəns) *n* **1** an effect of one person or thing on another. **2** the power of a person or thing to have such an effect. **3** power resulting from ability, wealth, position, etc. **4** a person or thing having influence. **5** *Astrol.* an ethereal fluid regarded as emanating from the stars and affecting a person's future. **6 under the influence.** *Inf.* drunk. ◆ *vb* **influences, influencing, influenced.** (*tr*) **7** to persuade or induce. **8** to have an effect upon (actions, events, etc.); affect. [C14: from Med. L *influentia* emanation of power from the stars, from L *influere* to flow into, from *fluere* to flow]
▸ˈinfluenceable *adj* ▸ˈinfluencer *n*

influent (ˈɪnflʊənt) *adj also* **inflowing. 1** flowing in. ◆ *n* **2** something flowing in, esp. a tributary. **3** *Ecology.* an organism that has a major effect on its community.

influential ❶ (ˌɪnflʊˈɛnʃəl) *adj* having or exerting influence.
▸ˌinfluˈentially *adv*

influenza (ˌɪnflʊˈɛnzə) *n* a highly contagious viral disease characterized by fever, muscular aches and pains, and inflammation of the respiratory passages. [C18: from It., lit.: INFLUENCE, hence, incursion, epidemic (first applied to influenza in 1743)]
▸ˌinfluˈenzal *adj*

influx ❶ (ˈɪnˌflʌks) *n* **1** the arrival or entry of many people or things. **2** the act of flowing in; inflow. **3** the mouth of a stream or river. [C17: from LL *influxus*, from *influere*; see INFLUENCE]

info (ˈɪnfəʊ) *n Inf.* short for **information.**

infold ❶ (ɪnˈfəʊld) *vb* (*tr*) a variant of **enfold.**

inform (ɪnˈfɔːm) *vb* **1** (*tr;* often foll. by *of* or *about*) to give information to; tell. **2** (*tr;* often foll. by *of* or *about*) to make conversant (with). **3** (*intr;* often foll. by *against* or *on*) to give information regarding criminals, to the police, etc. **4** (*tr*) to give form to. **5** (*tr*) to impart some essential or formative characteristic to. **6** (*tr*) to animate or inspire. [C14: from L *infōrmāre* to give form to, describe, from *fōrmāre* to FORM]
▸inˈformable *adj*

informal ❶ (ɪnˈfɔːməl) *adj* **1** not of a formal, official, or stiffly conventional nature. **2** appropriate to everyday life or use. **3** denoting or characterized by idiom, vocabulary, etc., appropriate to conversational language rather than to formal written language. **4** denoting a second-person pronoun in some languages used when the addressee is regarded as a friend or social inferior.
▸inˈformally *adv*

informality ❶ (ˌɪnfɔːˈmælɪtɪ) *n, pl* **informalities. 1** the condition or quality of being informal. **2** an informal act.

informal vote *n Austral. & NZ.* an invalid vote or ballot.

informant (ɪnˈfɔːmənt) *n* a person who gives information.

information ❶ (ˌɪnfəˈmeɪʃən) *n* **1** knowledge acquired through experience or study. **2** knowledge of specific and timely events or situations; news. **3** the act of informing or the condition of being informed. **4a** an office, agency, etc., providing information. **4b** (*as modifier*): *information service.* **5** a charge or complaint made before justices of the peace, usually on oath, to institute summary criminal proceedings. **6** *Computing.* **6a** the meaning given to data by the way it is interpreted. **6b** another word for **data** (sense 2).
▸ˌinforˈmational *adj*

information retrieval *n Computing.* the process of recovering information from stored data.

information superhighway *n* **1** the concept of a worldwide network of computers capable of transferring all types of digital information at high speed. **2** another name for the **Internet.** ◆ Also called: **information highway.**

information technology *n* the production, storage, and communication of information using computers, etc.

information theory *n* a collection of mathematical theories concerned with coding, transmitting, storing, retrieving, and decoding information.

informative ❶ (ɪnˈfɔːmətɪv) *or* **informatory** *adj* providing information; instructive.
▸inˈformatively *adv* ▸inˈformativeness *n*

informed ❶ (ɪnˈfɔːmd) *adj* **1** having much knowledge or education; learned or cultured. **2** based on information: an informed judgment.

informer ❶ (ɪnˈfɔːmə) *n* **1** a person who informs against someone, esp. a criminal. **2** a person who provides information.

infotainment (ˌɪnfəʊˈteɪnmənt) *n* (in television) the practice of presenting serious or instructive subjects in a style designed primarily to be entertaining. [C20: from INFO + (ENTER)TAINMENT]

infra- *prefix* below; beneath; after: *infrasonic.* [from L *infrā*]

infract ❶ (ɪnˈfrækt) *vb* (*tr*) to violate or break (a law, etc.). [C18: from L *infractus* broken off; see INFRINGE]
▸inˈfraction *n* ▸inˈfractor *n*

infra dig (ˈɪnfrə ˈdɪg) *adj* (*postpositive*) *Inf.* beneath one's dignity. [C19: from L *infrā dignitātem*]

infrangible (ɪnˈfrændʒɪbᵊl) *adj* **1** incapable of being broken. **2** not capable of being violated or infringed. [C16: from LL, from L IN-[1] + *frangere* to break]
▸inˌfrangiˈbility *or* inˈfrangibleness *n* ▸inˈfrangibly *adv*

infrared (ˌɪnfrəˈrɛd) *n* **1** the part of the electromagnetic spectrum with a longer wavelength than light but a shorter wavelength than radio waves. ◆ *adj* **2** of, relating to, using, or consisting of radiation lying within the infrared.

infrared astronomy *n* the study of radiations from space in the infrared region of the electromagnetic spectrum.

infrared photography *n* photography using film with an emulsion that is sensitive to infrared light, enabling it to be used in dark or misty conditions.

infrasound (ˈɪnfrəˌsaʊnd) *n* soundlike waves having a frequency below the audible range, i.e. below about 16 Hz.
▸**infrasonic** (ˌɪnfrəˈsɒnɪk) *adj*

infrastructure (ˈɪnfrəˌstrʌktʃə) *n* **1** the basic structure of an organization, system, etc. **2** the stock of fixed capital equipment in a country, including factories, roads, schools, etc., considered as a determinant of economic growth.

infrequent ❶ (ɪnˈfriːkwənt) *adj* rarely happening or present; only occasional.
▸inˈfrequency *or* inˈfrequence *n* ▸inˈfrequently *adv*

infringe ❶ (ɪnˈfrɪndʒ) *vb* **infringes, infringing, infringed. 1** (*tr*) to violate or break (a law, agreement, etc.). **2** (*intr;* foll. by *on* or *upon*) to encroach or trespass. [C16: from L *infringere* to break off, from *frangere* to break]
▸inˈfringement *n* ▸inˈfringer *n*

infundibular (ˌɪnfʌnˈdɪbjʊlə) *adj* funnel-shaped. [C18: from L *infundibulum* funnel]

infuriate ❶ *vb* (ɪnˈfjʊərɪˌeɪt), **infuriates, infuriating, infuriated. 1** (*tr*) to anger; annoy. ◆ *adj* (ɪnˈfjʊərɪɪt). **2** *Arch.* furious. [C17: from Med. L *infuriāre* (vb); see IN-[2], FURY]
▸inˈfuriˌating *adj* ▸inˈfuriˌatingly *adv*

infuse ❶ (ɪnˈfjuːz) *vb* **infuses, infusing, infused. 1** (*tr;* often foll. by *into*) to

THESAURUS

influence *n* **1** = **effect**, hold, magnetism, power, rule, spell, sway, weight **2** = **control**, ascendancy, authority, direction, domination, mastery **3** = **power**, bottom, clout (*inf.*), connections, good offices, importance, leverage, prestige, pull (*inf.*), weight ◆ *vb* **7** = **persuade**, arouse, dispose, incite, incline, induce, instigate, move, predispose, prompt, rouse **8** = **affect**, act *or* work upon, control, direct, guide, impact on, manipulate, modify, sway

influential *adj* = **important**, authoritative, controlling, effective, efficacious, forcible, guiding, instrumental, leading, meaningful, momentous, moving, persuasive, potent, powerful, significant, telling, weighty
Antonyms *adj* impotent, ineffective, ineffectual, powerless, unimportant, uninfluential, unpersuasive, weak

influx *n* = **arrival**, convergence, flow, incursion, inflow, inrush, inundation, invasion, rush

infold *see* **enfold**

inform *vb* **1** = **tell**, acquaint, advise, apprise, clue in (*inf.*), communicate, enlighten, give (someone) to understand, instruct, keep (someone) posted, leak to, let know, make conversant (with), notify, put (someone) in the picture (*inf.*), send word to, teach, tip off **3** = **betray**, blab, blow the whistle on (*inf.*), denounce, grass (*Brit. sl.*), incriminate, inculpate, let the cat out of the bag, rat (*inf.*), shop (*sl., chiefly Brit.*), sing (*sl., chiefly US*), snitch (*sl.*), spill the beans (*inf.*), squeal (*sl.*), tell all, tell on (*inf.*) **6** = **inspire**, animate, characterize, illuminate, imbue, permeate, suffuse, typify

informal *adj* **1-3** = **relaxed**, casual, colloquial, cosy, easy, familiar, natural, simple, unceremonious, unconstrained, unofficial
Antonyms *adj* ceremonious, constrained, conventional, formal, official, stiff

informality *n* **1** = **familiarity**, casualness, ease, lack of ceremony, naturalness, relaxation, simplicity

information *n* **1, 2** = **facts**, advice, blurb, counsel, data, dope (*inf.*), gen (*Brit. inf.*), info (*inf.*), inside story, instruction, intelligence, knowledge, latest (*inf.*), lowdown (*inf.*), material, message, news, notice, report, tidings, word

informative *adj* = **instructive**, chatty, communicative, edifying, educational, enlightening, forthcoming, gossipy, illuminating, newsy, revealing

informed *adj* **1** = **knowledgeable**, abreast, acquainted, *au courant*, *au fait*, briefed, conversant, enlightened, erudite, expert, familiar, genned up (*Brit. inf.*), in the know (*inf.*), in the loop, in the picture, keeping one's finger on the pulse, learned, posted, primed, reliable, up, up to date, versed, well-read

informer *n* **1** = **betrayer**, accuser, grass (*Brit. sl.*), Judas, nark (*Brit., Austral., & NZ sl.*), sneak, squealer (*sl.*), stool pigeon

infraction *n* = **violation**, breach, breaking, contravention, infringement, nonfulfilment, transgression, trespass

infrequent *adj* = **occasional**, few and far between, once in a blue moon, rare, sporadic, uncommon, unusual
Antonyms *adj* common, customary, frequent, habitual, often, regular, usual

infringe *vb* **1** = **break**, contravene, disobey, transgress, violate **2** *with* **on** *or* **upon** = **intrude on**, encroach on, trespass on

infringement *n* **1** = **contravention**, breach, infraction, noncompliance, nonobservance, transgression, trespass, violation

infuriate *vb* **1** = **enrage**, anger, be like a red rag to a bull, exasperate, gall, get one's back up, incense, irritate, madden, make one's blood boil, make one see red (*inf.*), make one's hackles rise, nark (*Brit., Austral., & NZ sl.*), provoke, put one's back up, rile
Antonyms *vb* appease, calm, mollify, pacify, placate, propitiate, soothe

infuriating *adj* **1** = **annoying**, exasperating, galling, irritating, maddening, mortifying, pestilential, provoking, vexatious

infuse *vb* **1** = **instil**, breathe into, engraft, impart to, implant, inculcate, inspire, introduce **3** = **soak**, brew, macerate, steep

instil or inculcate. **2** (*tr*; foll. by *with*) to inspire; emotionally charge. **3** to soak or be soaked so as to extract flavour or other properties. **4** *Rare.* (foll. by *into*) to pour. [C15: from L *infundere* to pour into]
▸inˈfuser *n*

infusible[1] (ɪnˈfjuːzəb(ə)l) *adj* not fusible; not easily melted; having a high melting point. [C16: from IN-[1] + FUSIBLE]
▸inˌfusiˈbility *or* **inˈfusibleness** *n*

infusible[2] (ɪnˈfjuːzəb(ə)l) *adj* capable of being infused. [C17: from INFUSE + -IBLE]
▸inˌfusiˈbility *or* **inˈfusibleness** *n*

infusion (ɪnˈfjuːʒən) *n* **1** the act of infusing. **2** something infused. **3** an extract obtained by soaking.
▸infusive (ɪnˈfjuːsɪv) *adj*

infusorian (ˌɪnfjuˈzɔːrɪən) *Obs.* ◆ *n* **1** any of the microscopic organisms, such as protozoans, found in infusions of organic material. ◆ *adj* **2** of or relating to infusorians. [C18: from NL *Infusoria* former class name; see INFUSE]
▸ˌinfuˈsorial *adj*

-ing[1] *suffix forming nouns.* **1** (*from verbs*) the action of, process of, result of, or something connected with the verb: *meeting; winnings.* **2** (*from other nouns*) something used in, consisting of, involving, etc.: *tubing; soldiering.* **3** (*from other parts of speech*): *an outing.* [OE *-ing, -ung*]

-ing[2] *suffix.* **1** forming the present participle of verbs: *walking; believing.* **2** forming participial adjectives: *a sinking ship.* **3** forming adjectives not derived from verbs: *swashbuckling.* [ME *-ing, -inde,* from OE *-ende*]

-ing[3] *suffix forming nouns.* a person or thing having a certain quality or being of a certain kind: *sweeting; whiting.* [OE *-ing*; rel. to ON *-ingr*]

ingather (ɪnˈgæðə) *vb* (*tr*) to gather together or in (a harvest, etc.).
▸inˈgatherer *n*

ingeminate (ɪnˈdʒɛmɪˌneɪt) *vb* **ingeminates, ingeminating, ingeminated.** (*tr*) *Rare.* to repeat; reiterate. [C16: from L *ingemināre* to redouble, from IN-[2] + *gemināre* to GEMINATE]

ingenious ❶ (ɪnˈdʒiːnjəs, -nɪəs) *adj* possessing or done with ingenuity; skilful or clever. [C15: from L, from *ingenium* natural ability; see ENGINE]
▸inˈgeniously *adv* **▸inˈgeniousness** *n*

ingénue (ˌænʒeɪˈnjuː) *n* an artless, innocent, or inexperienced girl or young woman. [C19: from F, fem of *ingénu* INGENUOUS]

ingenuity ❶ (ˌɪndʒɪˈnjuːɪtɪ) *n, pl* **ingenuities. 1** inventive talent; cleverness. **2** an ingenious device, act, etc. **3** *Arch.* frankness; candour. [C16: from L *ingenuitās* a freeborn condition, outlook consistent with such a condition, from *ingenuus* native, freeborn (see INGENUOUS); meaning infl. by INGENIOUS]

ingenuous ❶ (ɪnˈdʒɛnjʊəs) *adj* **1** naive, artless, or innocent. **2** candid; frank; straightforward. [C16: from L *ingenuus* freeborn, virtuous, from IN-[2] + *gignere* to beget]
▸inˈgenuously *adv* **▸inˈgenuousness** *n*

ingest (ɪnˈdʒɛst) *vb* (*tr*) to take (food or liquid) into the body. [C17: from L *ingerere* to put into, from IN-[2] + *gerere* to carry; see GEST]
▸inˈgestible *adj* **▸inˈgestion** *n* **▸inˈgestive** *adj*

ingle (ˈɪŋg(ə)l) *n Arch. or dialect.* a fire in a room or a fireplace. [C16: prob. from Scot. Gaelic *aingeal* fire]

inglenook (ˈɪŋg(ə)lˌnʊk) *n Brit.* a corner by a fireplace; chimney corner.

ingoing (ˈɪnˌgəʊɪŋ) *adj* going in; entering.

ingot (ˈɪŋgət) *n* a piece of cast metal obtained from a mould in a form suitable for storage, etc. [C14: ?from IN-[2] + OE *goten,* p.p. of *geotan* to pour]

ingraft ❶ (ɪnˈgrɑːft) *vb* a variant spelling of **engraft.**
▸inˈgraftment *or* **ˌingrafˈtation** *n*

ingrain ❶ *or* **engrain** *vb* (ɪnˈgreɪn). (*tr*) **1** to impress deeply on the mind or nature; instil. **2** *Arch.* to dye into the fibre of (a fabric). ◆ *adj* (ˈɪnˌgreɪn). **3** (of woven or knitted articles) made of dyed yarn or of fibre that is dyed before being spun into yarn. ◆ *n* (ˈɪnˌgreɪn). **4** a carpet made from ingrained yarn. [C18: from *dyed in grain* dyed with kermes through the fibre]

ingrained ❶ *or* **engrained** (ɪnˈgreɪnd) *adj* **1** deeply impressed or instilled. **2** (*prenominal*) complete or inveterate; utter. **3** (esp. of dirt) worked into or through the fibre, pores, etc.
▸ingrainedly *or* **engrainedly** (ɪnˈgreɪnɪdlɪ) *adv* **▸inˈgrainedness** *or* **enˈgrainedness** *n*

ingrate (ˈɪngreɪt, ɪnˈgreɪt) *Arch.* ◆ *n* **1** an ungrateful person. ◆ *adj* **2** ungrateful. [C14: from L *ingrātus* (adj), from IN-[1] + *grātus* GRATEFUL]
▸ˈingrately *adv*

ingratiate ❶ (ɪnˈgreɪʃɪˌeɪt) *vb* **ingratiates, ingratiating, ingratiated.** (*tr*; often foll. by *with*) to place (oneself) purposely in the favour (of another). [C17: from L, from IN-[2] + *grātia* grace, favour]
▸inˈgratiˌating *or* **inˈgratiatory** *adj* **▸inˈgratiˌatingly** *adv* **▸inˌgratiˈation** *n*

ingredient ❶ (ɪnˈgriːdɪənt) *n* a component of a mixture, compound, etc., esp. in cooking. [C15: from L *ingrediēns* going into, from *ingredī* to enter; see INGRESS]

ingress ❶ (ˈɪngrɛs) *n* **1** the act of going or coming in; an entering. **2** a way in; entrance. **3** the right or permission to enter. [C15: from L *ingressus,* from *ingredī* to go in, from *gradī* to step, go]
▸ingression (ɪnˈgrɛʃən) *n*

in-group *n Sociol.* a highly cohesive and relatively closed social group characterized by the preferential treatment reserved for its members.

ingrowing (ˈɪnˌgrəʊɪŋ) *adj* **1** (esp. of a toenail) growing abnormally into the flesh. **2** growing within or into.
▸ˈinˌgrowth *n*

ingrown (ˈɪnˌgrəʊn, ɪnˈgrəʊn) *adj* **1** (esp. of a toenail) grown abnormally into the flesh; covered by adjacent tissues. **2** grown within; native; innate.

inguinal (ˈɪŋgwɪn(ə)l) *adj Anat.* of or relating to the groin. [C17: from L *inguinālis,* from *inguen* groin]

ingulf ❶ (ɪnˈgʌlf) *vb* (*tr*) a variant of **engulf.**

ingurgitate (ɪnˈgɜːdʒɪˌteɪt) *vb* **ingurgitates, ingurgitating, ingurgitated.** to swallow (food, etc.) greedily or in excess. [C16: from L *ingurgitāre* to flood, from IN-[2] + *gurges* abyss]
▸inˌgurgiˈtation *n*

inhabit ❶ (ɪnˈhæbɪt) *vb* **inhabits, inhabiting, inhabited.** (*tr*) to live or dwell in; occupy. [C14: from L *inhabitāre,* from *habitāre* to dwell]
▸inˈhabitable *adj* **▸inˌhabitaˈbility** *n* **▸inˌhabiˈtation** *n*

inhabitant ❶ (ɪnˈhæbɪtənt) *n* a person or animal that is a permanent resident of a particular place or region.
▸inˈhabitancy *or* **inˈhabitance** *n*

inhalant (ɪnˈheɪlənt) *adj* **1** (esp. of a medicinal preparation) inhaled for its therapeutic effect. **2** inhaling. ◆ *n* **3** an inhalant medicinal preparation.

inhale ❶ (ɪnˈheɪl) *vb* **inhales, inhaling, inhaled.** to draw (breath, etc.) into the lungs; breathe in. [C18: from IN-[2] + L *halāre* to breathe]
▸ˌinhaˈlation *n*

inhaler (ɪnˈheɪlə) *n* **1** a device for breathing in therapeutic vapours, esp. one for relieving nasal congestion. **2** a person who inhales.

inhere (ɪnˈhɪə) *vb* **inheres, inhering, inhered.** (*intr*; foll. by *in*) to be an inseparable part (of). [C16: from L *inhaerēre* to stick in, from *haerēre* to stick]

inherent ❶ (ɪnˈhɪərənt, -ˈhɛr-) *adj* existing as an inseparable part; intrinsic.
▸inˈherently *adv*

inherit ❶ (ɪnˈhɛrɪt) *vb* **inherits, inheriting, inherited. 1** to receive (property, etc.) by succession or under a will. **2** (*intr*) to succeed as heir. **3** (*tr*) to possess (a characteristic) through genetic transmission. **4** (*tr*) to receive (a position, etc.) from a predecessor. [C14: from OF *enheriter,* from LL *inhērēditāre* to appoint an heir, from L *hērēs* HEIR]
▸inˈherited *adj* **▸inˈheritor** *n* **▸inˈheritress** *or* **inˈheritrix** *fem n*

inheritable (ɪnˈhɛrɪtəb(ə)l) *adj* **1** capable of being transmitted by hered-

THESAURUS

ingenious *adj* = **creative,** adroit, bright, brilliant, clever, crafty, dexterous, fertile, inventive, masterly, original, ready, resourceful, shrewd, skilful, subtle
Antonyms *adj* artless, clumsy, unimaginative, uninventive, unoriginal, unresourceful, unskilful

ingenuity *n* **1** = **originality,** adroitness, cleverness, faculty, flair, genius, gift, ingeniousness, inventiveness, knack, resourcefulness, sharpness, shrewdness, skill, turn
Antonyms *n* clumsiness, dullness, incompetence, ineptitude, ineptness

ingenuous *adj* **1, 2** = **naive,** artless, candid, childlike, frank, guileless, honest, innocent, open, plain, simple, sincere, trustful, trusting, unreserved, unsophisticated, unstudied
Antonyms *adj* artful, crafty, devious, insincere, reserved, sly, sophisticated, subtle, wily

ingenuousness *n* **1, 2** = **naivety,** artlessness, candour, frankness, guilelessness, innocence, openness, trustingness, unsuspiciousness
Antonyms *n* artfulness, craftiness, insincerity, slyness, sophistication, subterfuge, subtlety

ingraft *see* **engraft**

ingrain *vb* **1** = **fix,** embed, entrench, imbue, implant, impress, imprint, instil, root, sow the seeds

ingrained *adj* **1** = **fixed,** brassbound, constitutional, deep-rooted, deep-seated, fundamental, hereditary, inborn, inbred, inbuilt, indelible, ineradicable, inherent, in the blood, intrinsic, inveterate, rooted

ingratiate *vb* = **pander to,** be a yes man, blandish, crawl, curry favour, fawn, flatter, get in with, get on the right side of, grovel, insinuate oneself, keep (someone) sweet, lick (someone's) boots, play up to, rub (someone) up the right way (*inf.*), seek the favour (of someone), suck up to (*inf.*), toady, worm oneself into (someone's) favour

ingratiating *adj* = **sycophantic,** bootlicking (*inf.*), crawling, fawning, flattering, humble, obsequious, servile, timeserving, toadying, unctuous

ingredient *n* = **component,** constituent, element, part

ingress *n* **1-3** = **entrance,** access, admission, admittance, door, entrée, entry, right of entry, way in

ingulf *see* **engulf**

inhabit *vb* = **live,** abide, dwell, lodge, make one's home, occupy, people, populate, possess, reside, take up residence in, tenant

inhabitant *n* = **dweller,** aborigine, citizen, denizen, indigene, indweller, inmate, native, occupant, occupier, resident, tenant

inhabited *adj* = **populated,** colonized, developed, held, occupied, peopled, settled, tenanted

inhalation *n* = **breathing,** breath, inhaling, inspiration

inhale *vb* = **breathe in,** draw in, gasp, respire, suck in
Antonyms *vb* blow, breathe out, exhale, expire

inherent *adj* = **innate,** basic, congenital, connate, essential, hereditary, immanent, inborn, inbred, inbuilt, ingrained, inherited, in one's blood, instinctive, intrinsic, native, natural
Antonyms *adj* alien, extraneous, extrinsic, imposed, superficial, supplementary

inherit *vb* **1-4** = **be left,** accede to, be bequeathed, come into, fall heir to, succeed to

ity from one generation to a later one. **2** capable of being inherited. **3** *Rare.* having the right to inherit.
▸**in,herita'bility** *or* **in'heritableness** *n* ▸**in'heritably** *adv*

inheritance ⓘ (ɪn'hɛrɪtəns) *n* **1** *Law.* **1a** hereditary succession to an estate, title, etc. **1b** the right of an heir to succeed on the death of an ancestor. **1c** something that may legally be transmitted to an heir. **2** the act of inheriting. **3** something inherited; heritage. **4** the derivation of characteristics of one generation from an earlier one by heredity.

inheritance tax *n* **1** (in Britain) a tax introduced in 1986 to replace capital transfer tax, consisting of a percentage levied on that part of an inheritance exceeding a specified allowance. **2** (in the US) a state tax imposed on an inheritance according to its size and the relationship of the beneficiary to the deceased.

inhibit ⓘ (ɪn'hɪbɪt) *vb* **inhibits, inhibiting, inhibited.** (*tr*) **1** to restrain or hinder (an impulse, desire, etc.). **2** to prohibit, forbid, or prevent. **3** to stop, prevent, or decrease the rate of (a chemical reaction). [C15: from L *inhibēre* to restrain, from IN-[2] + *habēre* to have]
▸**in'hibitable** *adj* ▸**in'hibitive** *or* **in'hibitory** *adj*

inhibition ⓘ (,ɪnɪ'bɪʃən, ,ɪnhɪ-) *n* **1** the act of inhibiting or the condition of being inhibited. **2** *Psychol.* a mental state or condition in which the varieties of expression and behaviour of an individual become restricted. **3** the process of stopping or retarding a chemical reaction. **4** *Physiol.* the suppression of the function or action of an organ or part, as by stimulation of its nerve supply.

inhibitor (ɪn'hɪbɪtə) *n* **1** Also: **inhibiter.** a person or thing that inhibits. **2** a substance that retards or stops a chemical reaction. **3** *Biochem.* **3a** a substance that inhibits the action of an enzyme. **3b** a substance that inhibits a metabolic or physiological process: *a plant growth inhibitor.*

inhospitable ⓘ (ɪn'hɒspɪtəb[ə]l, ,ɪnhɒ'spɪt-) *adj* **1** not hospitable; unfriendly. **2** (of a region, an environment, etc.) lacking a favourable climate, terrain, etc.
▸**in'hospitableness** *n* ▸**in'hospitably** *adv*

in-house *adj, adv* within an organization or group: *an in-house job; the job was done in-house.*

inhuman ⓘ (ɪn'hju:mən) *adj* **1** Also: **inhumane** (,ɪnhju:'meɪn). lacking humane feelings, such as sympathy, understanding, etc.; cruel; brutal. **2** not human.
▸**,inhu'manely** *adv* ▸**in'humanly** *adv* ▸**in'humanness** *n*

inhumanity ⓘ (,ɪnhju:'mænɪtɪ) *n, pl* **inhumanities. 1** lack of humane qualities. **2** an inhumane act, decision, etc.

inhume ⓘ (ɪn'hju:m) *vb* **inhumes, inhuming, inhumed.** (*tr*) to inter; bury. [C17: from L, from IN-[2] + *humus* ground]
▸**,inhu'mation** *n* ▸**in'humer** *n*

inimical ⓘ (ɪ'nɪmɪk[ə]l) *adj* **1** adverse or unfavourable. **2** not friendly; hostile. [C17: from LL, from *inimīcus*, from IN-[1] + *amīcus* friendly; see ENEMY]
▸**in'imically** *adv* ▸**in'imicalness** *or* **in,imi'cality** *n*

inimitable ⓘ (ɪ'nɪmɪtəb[ə]l) *adj* incapable of being duplicated or imitated; unique.
▸**in,imita'bility** *or* **in'imitableness** *n* ▸**in'imitably** *adv*

iniquity ⓘ (ɪ'nɪkwɪtɪ) *n, pl* **iniquities. 1** lack of justice or righteousness; wickedness; injustice. **2** a wicked act; sin. [C14: from L, from *inīquus* unfair, from IN-[1] + *aequus* even, level; see EQUAL]
▸**in'iquitous** *adj* ▸**in'iquitously** *adv* ▸**in'iquitousness** *n*

initial ⓘ (ɪ'nɪʃəl) *adj* **1** of, at, or concerning the beginning. ◆ *n* **2** the first letter of a word, esp. a person's name. **3** *Printing.* a large letter set at the beginning of a chapter or work. **4** *Bot.* a cell from which tissues and organs develop by division and differentiation. ◆ *vb* **initials, initialling, initialled** *or US* **initials, initialing, initialed. 5** (*tr*) to sign with one's initials, esp. to indicate approval; endorse. [C16: from L *initiālis* of the beginning, from *initium* beginning, lit.: an entering upon, from *inīre* to go in]
▸**in'itialer** *or* **in'itialler** *n* ▸**in'itially** *adv*

initialize *or* **initialise** (ɪ'nɪʃə,laɪz) *vb* **initializes, initializing, initialized** *or* **initialises, initialising, initialised.** (*tr*) to assign an initial value to (a variable or storage location) in a computer program.
▸**in,itiali'zation** *or* **in,itiali'sation** *n*

initiate ⓘ *vb* (ɪ'nɪʃɪ,eɪt), **initiates, initiating, initiated.** (*tr*) **1** to begin or originate. **2** to accept (new members) into an organization such as a club, through often secret ceremonies. **3** to teach fundamentals to. ◆ *adj* (ɪ'nɪʃɪɪt, -,eɪt). **4** initiated; begun. ◆ *n* (ɪ'nɪʃɪɪt, -,eɪt). **5** a person who has been initiated, esp. recently. **6** a beginner; novice. [C17: from L *initiāre* (vb), from *initium;* see INITIAL]
▸**in'itiatory** *adj*

initiation ⓘ (ɪ,nɪʃɪ'eɪʃən) *n* **1** the act of initiating or the condition of being initiated. **2** the ceremony, often secret, initiating new members into an organization.

initiative ⓘ (ɪ'nɪʃɪətɪv, -'nɪʃətɪv) *n* **1** the first step or action of a matter; commencing move: *a peace initiative.* **2** the right or power to begin or initiate something: *he has the initiative.* **3** the ability or attitude required to begin or initiate something. **4** *Government.* the right of citizens to introduce legislation, etc., in a legislative body, as in Switzerland. **5 on one's own initiative.** without being prompted. ◆ *adj* **6** of or concerning initiation or serving to initiate; initiatory.
▸**in'itiatively** *adv*

initiator (ɪ'nɪʃɪ,eɪtə) *n* **1** a person or thing that initiates. **2** *Chem.* a substance that starts a chain reaction. **3** *Chem.* a very sensitive explosive used in detonators.

inject ⓘ (ɪn'dʒɛkt) *vb* (*tr*) **1** *Med.* to introduce (a fluid) into the body (of a person or animal) by means of a syringe. **2** (foll. by *into*) to introduce (a new aspect or element): *to inject humour into a scene.* **3** to interject (a comment, idea, etc.). [C17: from *injicere* to throw in, from *jacere* to throw]
▸**in'jectable** *adj* ▸**in'jector** *n*

injection ⓘ (ɪn'dʒɛkʃən) *n* **1** fluid injected into the body, esp. for medicinal purposes. **2** something injected. **3** the act of injecting. **4a** the act or process of introducing fluid under pressure, such as fuel into the combustion chamber of an engine. **4b** (*as modifier*): *injection moulding.*
▸**in'jective** *adj*

injunction ⓘ (ɪn'dʒʌŋkʃən) *n* **1** *Law.* an instruction or order issued by a court to a party to an action, esp. to refrain from some act. **2** a command, admonition, etc. **3** the act of enjoining. [C16: from LL, from L *injungere* to ENJOIN]
▸**in'junctive** *adj* ▸**in'junctively** *adv*

injure ⓘ ('ɪndʒə) *vb* **injures, injuring, injured.** (*tr*) **1** to cause physical or

THESAURUS

inheritance *n* **3** = **legacy**, bequest, birthright, heritage, patrimony

inheritor *n* **1** = **heir**, beneficiary, legatee, recipient, successor

inhibit *vb* **1** = **restrain**, arrest, bar, bridle, check, constrain, cramp (someone's) style (*inf.*), curb, debar, discourage, forbid, frustrate, hinder, hold back *or* in, impede, obstruct, prevent, prohibit, stem the flow, stop, throw a spanner in the works
Antonyms *vb* abet, allow, enable, encourage, further, let, permit, support

inhibited *adj* **1** = **shy**, constrained, frustrated, guarded, repressed, reserved, reticent, self-conscious, subdued, uptight (*inf.*), withdrawn
Antonyms *adj* free, natural, outgoing, relaxed, spontaneous, uninhibited, unreserved

inhibition *n* **1** = **shyness**, bar, block, check, embargo, hang-up (*inf.*), hindrance, interdict, mental blockage, obstacle, prohibition, reserve, restraint, restriction, reticence, self-consciousness

inhospitable *adj* **1** = **unfriendly**, cool, uncongenial, ungenerous, unkind, unreceptive, unsociable, unwelcoming, xenophobic **2** = **bleak**, bare, barren, desolate, empty, forbidding, godforsaken, hostile, lonely, sterile, unfavourable, uninhabitable
Antonyms *adj* ≠ **unfriendly:** amicable, friendly, generous, genial, gracious, hospitable, sociable, welcoming

inhuman *adj* **1** = **cruel**, animal, barbaric, barbarous, bestial, brutal, cold-blooded, diabolical, fiendish, heartless, inhumane, merciless, pitiless, remorseless, ruthless, savage, unfeeling, vicious
Antonyms *adj* charitable, compassionate, feeling, humane, merciful, sensitive, tender, warm-hearted

inhumanity *n* **1** = **cruelty**, atrocity, barbarism, brutality, brutishness, cold-bloodedness, cold-heartedness, hardheartedness, heartlessness, pitilessness, ruthlessness, unkindness, viciousness

inhumation *n* = **burial**, entombment, interment, sepulture

inimical *adj* **1, 2** = **hostile**, adverse, antagonistic, antipathetic, contrary, destructive, disaffected, harmful, hurtful, ill-disposed, injurious, noxious, opposed, oppugnant (*rare*), pernicious, repugnant, unfavourable, unfriendly, unwelcoming
Antonyms *adj* affable, amicable, congenial, favourable, friendly, good, helpful, kindly, sympathetic, welcoming

inimitable *adj* = **unique**, consummate, incomparable, matchless, nonpareil, peerless, supreme, unequalled, unexampled, unmatched, unparalleled, unrivalled, unsurpassable

iniquitous *adj* **1** = **wicked**, abominable, accursed, atrocious, base, criminal, evil, heinous, immoral, infamous, nefarious, reprehensible, reprobate, sinful, unjust, unrighteous, vicious

iniquity *n* **1, 2** = **wickedness**, abomination, baseness, crime, evil, evildoing, heinousness, infamy, injustice, misdeed, offence, sin, sinfulness, unrighteousness, wrong, wrongdoing
Antonyms *n* fairness, goodness, honesty, integrity, justice, morality, righteousness, uprightness, virtue

initial *adj* **1** = **first**, beginning, commencing, early, inaugural, inceptive, inchoate, incipient, introductory, opening, primary
Antonyms *adj* closing, concluding, ending, final, last, terminal, ultimate

initially *adv* **1** = **at first**, at *or* in the beginning, at the outset, at the start, first, firstly, in the early stages, originally, primarily, to begin with

initiate *vb* **1** = **begin**, break the ice, commence, get under way, inaugurate, institute, kick off (*inf.*), kick-start, launch, lay the foundations of, open, originate, pioneer, set going, set in motion, set the ball rolling, start **2** = **induct**, indoctrinate, instate, introduce, invest **3** = **instruct**, acquaint with, coach, familiarize with, teach, train ◆ *n* **6** = **novice**, beginner, convert, entrant, learner, member, probationer, proselyte, tyro

initiation *n* **1** = **introduction**, admission, baptism of fire, commencement, debut, enrolment, entrance, inauguration, inception, induction, installation, instatement, investiture

initiative *n* **1** = **first step**, advantage, beginning, commencement, first move, lead **3** = **resourcefulness**, ambition, drive, dynamism, enterprise, get-up-and-go, inventiveness, leadership, originality, push (*inf.*), resource

inject *vb* **1** = **vaccinate**, inoculate, jab (*inf.*), shoot (*inf.*) **2** = **introduce**, bring in, infuse, insert, instil, interject

injection *n* **1** = **vaccination**, inoculation, jab (*inf.*), shot (*inf.*), vaccine **2** = **introduction**, dose, infusion, insertion, interjection

injunction *n* **2** = **order**, admonition, command, dictate, exhortation, instruction, mandate, precept, ruling

injure *vb* **1** = **hurt**, abuse, blemish, blight, break, damage, deface, disable, harm, impair, mal-

mental harm or suffering to; hurt or wound. **2** to offend, esp. by an injustice. [C16: back formation from INJURY]
▸'**injurable** *adj* ▸'**injured** *adj* ▸'**injurer** *n*

injurious Ⓣ (ɪn'dʒʊərɪəs) *adj* **1** causing damage or harm; deleterious; hurtful. **2** abusive, slanderous, or libellous.
▸**in'juriously** *adv* ▸**in'juriousness** *n*

injury Ⓣ ('ɪndʒərɪ) *n, pl* **injuries. 1** physical damage or hurt. **2** a specific instance of this: *a leg injury.* **3** harm done to a reputation. **4** *Law.* a violation or infringement of another person's rights that causes him harm and is actionable at law. [C14: from L *injūria* injustice, wrong, from *injūriōsus* acting unfairly, wrongful, from IN-[1] + *jūs* right]

injury time *n Soccer, rugby, etc.* extra playing time added on to compensate for time spent attending to injured players during the match. Also called: **stoppage time.**

injustice Ⓣ (ɪn'dʒʌstɪs) *n* **1** the condition or practice of being unjust or unfair. **2** an unjust act.

ink (ɪŋk) *n* **1** a fluid or paste used for printing, writing, and drawing. **2** a dark brown fluid ejected into the water for self-concealment by an octopus or related mollusc. ◆ *vb (tr)* **3** to mark with ink. **4** to coat (a printing surface) with ink. [C13: from OF *enque,* from LL *encaustum* a purplish-red ink, from Gk *enkauston* purple ink, from *enkaustos* burnt in, from *enkaiein* to burn in; see EN-[2], CAUSTIC]
▸'**inker** *n*

Inkatha (ɪn'kɑːtə) *n* a South African political party; originally a Zulu organization founded in 1975 as a paramilitary group seeking nonracial democracy; won four seats in democratic multiracial elections in 1994. [C20: Zulu name for the grass coil used by Zulu women carrying loads on their heads]

inkblot ('ɪŋkˌblɒt) *n* a patch of ink accidentally or deliberately spilled. Ten such patches, of different shapes, are used in the Rorschach test.

ink-cap *n* any of several saprotrophic fungi whose caps disintegrate into a black inky fluid after the spores mature.

inkhorn ('ɪŋkˌhɔːn) *n* (formerly) a small portable container for ink, usually made from horn.

ink in *vb (adv)* **1** *(tr)* to use ink to go over pencil lines in (a drawing). **2** to apply ink to (a printing surface) in preparing to print from it. **3** to arrange or confirm definitely.

inkling Ⓣ ('ɪŋklɪŋ) *n* a slight intimation or suggestion; suspicion. [C14: prob. from *inclen* to hint at]

inkstand ('ɪŋkˌstænd) *n* a stand or tray on which are kept writing implements and containers for ink.

inkwell ('ɪŋkˌwɛl) *n* a small container for pen ink, often let into the surface of a desk.

inky ('ɪŋkɪ) *adj* **inkier, inkiest. 1** resembling ink, esp. in colour; dark or black. **2** of, containing, or stained with ink.
▸'**inkiness** *n*

INLA *abbrev. for* Irish National Liberation Army.

inlaid ('ɪnˌleɪd, ɪn'leɪd) *adj* **1** set in the surface, as a design in wood. **2** having such a design or inlay: *an inlaid table.*

inland Ⓣ *adj* ('ɪnlənd). **1** of or located in the interior of a country or region away from a sea or border. **2** *Chiefly Brit.* operating within a country or region; domestic; not foreign. ◆ *n* ('ɪnˌlænd, -lənd). **3** the interior of a country or region. ◆ *adv* ('ɪnˌlænd, -lənd). **4** towards or into the interior of a country or region.
▸'**inlander** *n*

Inland Revenue *n* (in Britain and New Zealand) a government board that administers and collects major direct taxes, such as income tax.

in-law *n* **1** a relative by marriage. ◆ *adj* **2** *(postpositive; in combination)* related by marriage: *a father-in-law.* [C19: back formation from *father-in-law,* etc.]

inlay *vb* (ɪn'leɪ), **inlays, inlaying, inlaid.** *(tr)* **1** to decorate (an article, esp. of furniture) by inserting pieces of wood, ivory, etc., into slots in the surface. ◆ *n* ('ɪnˌleɪ). **2** *Dentistry.* a filling inserted into a cavity and held in position by cement. **3** decoration made by inlaying. **4** an inlaid article, surface, etc.
▸'**in,layer** *n*

inlet Ⓣ *n* ('ɪnˌlɛt). **1** a narrow inland opening of the coastline. **2** an entrance or opening. **3** the act of letting someone or something in. **4** something let in or inserted. **5a** a passage or valve through which a substance, esp. a fluid, enters a machine. **5b** *(as modifier): an inlet valve.* ◆ *vb* (ɪn'lɛt), **inlets, inletting, inlet. 6** *(tr)* to insert or inlay.

inlier ('ɪnˌlaɪə) *n* an outcrop of rocks that is entirely surrounded by younger rocks.

in loco parentis *Latin.* (ɪn 'ləʊkəʊ pə'rɛntɪs) in place of a parent: said of a person acting in a parental capacity.

inly ('ɪnlɪ) *adv Poetic.* inwardly; intimately.

inmate ('ɪnˌmeɪt) *n* a person who is confined to an institution such as a prison or hospital.

in medias res *Latin.* (ɪn 'miːdɪˌæs 'reɪs) in or into the middle of events or a narrative. [lit.: into the midst of things, taken from a passage in Horace's *Ars Poetica*]

in memoriam (ɪn mɪ'mɔːrɪəm) in memory of: used in obituaries, epitaphs, etc. [L]

inmost ('ɪnˌməʊst) *adj* another word for **innermost.**

inn (ɪn) *n* a pub or small hotel providing food and accommodation.

innards Ⓣ ('ɪnədz) *pl n Inf.* **1** the internal organs of the body, esp. the viscera. **2** the interior parts of anything, esp. the working parts. [C19: colloquial var. of *inwards*]

innate Ⓣ (ɪ'neɪt, 'ɪneɪt) *adj* **1** existing from birth; congenital; inborn. **2** being an essential part of the character of a person or thing. **3** instinctive; not learned: *innate capacities.* **4** *Philosophy.* (of ideas) present in the mind before any experience and knowable by pure reason. [C15: from L, from *innascī* to be born in, from *nascī* to be born]
▸**in'nately** *adv* ▸**in'nateness** *n*

inner Ⓣ ('ɪnə) *adj (prenominal)* **1** being or located further inside: *an inner room.* **2** happening or occurring inside. **3** relating to the soul, mind, spirit, etc. **4** more profound or obscure; less apparent: *the inner meaning.* **5** exclusive or private: *inner regions of the party.* ◆ *n* **6** *Archery.* **6a** the red innermost ring on a target. **6b** a shot which hits this ring.
▸'**innerly** *adv* ▸'**innerness** *n*

inner bar *n* **the.** *Brit.* all Queen's or King's Counsel collectively.

inner child *n Psychol.* the part of the psyche that retains feelings as they were experienced in childhood.

inner city *n* **a** the parts of a city in or near its centre, esp. when associated with poverty, substandard housing, etc. **b** *(as modifier): inner-city schools.*

inner man *or (fem)* **inner woman** *n* **1** the mind or soul. **2** *Jocular.* the stomach or appetite.

innermost Ⓣ ('ɪnəˌməʊst) *adj* **1** being or located furthest within; central. **2** intimate; private.

inner tube *n* an inflatable rubber tube that fits inside a pneumatic tyre casing.

innervate ('ɪnɜːˌveɪt) *vb* **innervates, innervating, innervated.** *(tr)* **1** to supply nerves to (a bodily organ or part). **2** to stimulate (a bodily organ or part) with nerve impulses.
▸**ˌinner'vation** *n*

innings ('ɪnɪŋz) *n* **1** *(functioning as sing) Cricket, etc.* **1a** the batting turn of a player or team. **1b** the runs scored during such a turn. **2** *(sometimes sing)* a period of opportunity or action.

innkeeper Ⓣ ('ɪnˌkiːpə) *n* an owner or manager of an inn.

innocence Ⓣ ('ɪnəsəns) *n* the quality or state of being innocent. Archaic word: **innocency** ('ɪnəsənsɪ). [C14: from L *innocentia* harmlessness, from *innocēns* blameless, from IN-[1] + *nocēre* to hurt]

innocent Ⓣ ('ɪnəsənt) *adj* **1** not corrupted or tainted with evil; sinless; pure. **2** not guilty of a particular crime; blameless. **3** *(postpositive;* foll.

THESAURUS

treat, mar, ruin, spoil, tarnish, undermine, vitiate, weaken, wound, wrong

injured *adj* **1 = hurt,** broken, damaged, disabled, lamed, undermined, weakened, wounded **2 = wronged,** abused, blackened, blemished, defamed, ill-treated, maligned, maltreated, offended, tarnished, vilified

injurious *adj* **1 = harmful,** adverse, bad, baneful *(arch.)*, corrupting, damaging, deleterious, destructive, detrimental, disadvantageous, hurtful, iniquitous, maleficent, mischievous, noxious, pernicious, ruinous, unconducive, unhealthy, unjust, wrongful

injury *n* **1 = harm,** abuse, damage, detriment, disservice, evil, grievance, hurt, ill, injustice, mischief, ruin, trauma *(Pathology)*, wound, wrong

injustice *n* **1 = unfairness,** bias, discrimination, favouritism, inequality, inequity, iniquity, onesidedness, oppression, partiality, partisanship, prejudice, unjustness, unlawfulness, wrong
Antonyms *n* equality, equity, fairness, impartiality, justice, lawfulness, rectitude, right

inkling *n* **= suspicion,** clue, conception, faintest *or* foggiest idea, glimmering, hint, idea, indication, intimation, notion, suggestion, whisper

inland *adj* **1 = interior,** domestic, internal, upcountry

inlet *n* **1 = bay,** arm (of the sea), bight, cove, creek, firth *or* frith *(Scot.)*, fjord, sea loch *(Scot.)* **2 = bay,** entrance, ingress, passage

innards *pl n* **1 = intestines,** entrails, guts, insides *(inf.)*, inwards, viscera, vitals **2 = works,** guts *(inf.)*, mechanism

innate *adj* **1-3 = inborn,** congenital, connate, constitutional, essential, immanent, inbred, indigenous, ingrained, inherent, inherited, in one's blood, instinctive, intrinsic, intuitive, native, natural
Antonyms *adj* accidental, acquired, affected, assumed, cultivated, fostered, incidental, learned, nurtured, unnatural

inner *adj* **1, 2 = inside,** central, essential, interior, internal, intestinal, inward, middle **3 = mental,** emotional, psychological, spiritual **4 = hidden,** esoteric, intimate, personal, private, repressed, secret, unrevealed
Antonyms *adj* ≠ **inside:** exterior, external, outer, outside, outward ≠ **hidden:** exposed, obvious, overt, revealed, surface, unconcealed, unrepressed, visible

innermost *adj* **2 = deepest,** basic, buried, central, deep, essential, intimate, personal, private, secret

innkeeper *n* **= publican,** host *or* hostess, hotelier, landlord *or* landlady, mine host

innocence *n* **= guiltlessness,** blamelessness, chastity, clean hands, incorruptibility, inexperience, ingenuousness, inoffensiveness, naïveté, purity, righteousness, sinlessness, stainlessness, uprightness, virginity, virtue
Antonyms *n* ≠ **guiltlessness:** corruption, guilt, impurity, offensiveness, sinfulness, wrongness

innocent *adj* **1 = pure,** chaste, immaculate, impeccable, incorrupt, pristine, righteous, sinless, spotless, stainless, unblemished, unsullied, upright, virgin, virginal **2 = not guilty,** blameless, clear, faultless, guiltless, honest, in the clear, squeaky-clean, uninvolved, unoffending **3** *with* **of = lacking,** clear of, empty of, free from, ignorant, nescient, unacquainted with, unaware, unfamiliar with, untouched by **4 = harmless,** innocuous, inoffensive, unmalicious, unobjectionable, well-intentioned, well-meant **5 =**

by *of*) free (of); lacking: *innocent of all knowledge of history.* **4a** harmless or innocuous: *an innocent game.* **4b** not cancerous: *an innocent tumour.* **5** credulous, naive, or artless. **6** simple-minded; slow-witted. ◆ *n* **7** an innocent person, esp. a young child or an ingenuous adult. **8** a simple-minded person; simpleton.
▸ **ˈinnocently** *adv*

innocuous ⓣ (ɪˈnɒkjʊəs) *adj* having little or no adverse or harmful effect; harmless. [C16: from L *innocuus* harmless, from IN-[1] + *nocēre* to harm]
▸ **inˈnocuously** *adv* ▸ **inˈnocuousness** *or* **innocuity** (ˌɪnəˈkjuːɪtɪ) *n*

innominate bone (ɪˈnɒmɪnɪt) *n* either of the two bones that form the sides of the pelvis, consisting of the ilium, ischium, and pubis. Nontechnical name: **hipbone.**

innovate ⓣ (ˈɪnəˌveɪt) *vb* **innovates, innovating, innovated.** to invent or begin to apply (methods, ideas, etc.). [C16: from L *innovāre* to renew, from IN-[2] + *novāre* to make new, from *novus* new]
▸ **ˈinnoˌvative** *or* **ˈinnoˌvatory** *adj* ▸ **ˈinnoˌvator** *n*

innovation ⓣ (ˌɪnəˈveɪʃən) *n* **1** something newly introduced, such as a new method or device. **2** the act of innovating.
▸ **ˌinnoˈvational** *adj* ▸ **ˌinnoˈvationist** *n*

innuendo ⓣ (ˌɪnjʊˈendəʊ) *n, pl* **innuendos** *or* **innuendoes. 1** an indirect or subtle reference, esp. one made maliciously or indicating criticism or disapproval; insinuation. **2** *Law.* (in an action for defamation) an explanation of the construction put upon words alleged to be defamatory where this meaning is not apparent. [C17: from L, lit.: by hinting, from *innuere* to convey by a nod, from IN-[2] + *nuere* to nod]

Innuit (ˈɪnjuːɪt) *n* a variant spelling of **Inuit.**

innumerable ⓣ (ɪˈnjuːmərəbəl, ɪˈnjuːmrəbəl) *or* **innumerous** *adj* so many as to be uncountable; extremely numerous.
▸ **inˌnumeraˈbility** *or* **inˈnumerableness** *n* ▸ **inˈnumerably** *adv*

innumerate (ɪˈnjuːmərɪt) *adj* **1** having neither knowledge nor understanding of mathematics or science. ◆ *n* **2** an innumerate person.
▸ **inˈnumeracy** *n*

inoculate (ɪˈnɒkjʊˌleɪt) *vb* **inoculates, inoculating, inoculated. 1** to introduce (the causative agent of a disease) into the body in order to induce immunity. **2** (*tr*) to introduce (microorganisms, esp. bacteria) into (a culture medium). **3** (*tr*) to cause to be influenced or imbued, as with ideas. [C15: from L *inoculāre* to implant, from IN-[2] + *oculus* eye, bud]
▸ **inˌocuˈlation** *n* ▸ **inˈoculative** *adj* ▸ **inˈocuˌlator** *n*

inoculum (ɪˈnɒkjʊləm) *or* **inoculant** *n, pl* **inocula** (-lə) *or* **inoculants.** *Med.* the substance used in giving an inoculation. [C20: NL; see INOCULATE]

in-off *n Billiards.* a shot that goes into a pocket after striking another ball.

inoperable ⓣ (ɪnˈɒpərəbəl, -ˈɒprə-) *adj* **1** incapable of being implemented or operated. **2** *Surgery.* not suitable for operation without risk, esp. because of metastasis.
▸ **inˌoperaˈbility** *or* **inˈoperableness** *n* ▸ **inˈoperably** *adv*

inordinate ⓣ (ɪnˈɔːdɪnɪt) *adj* **1** exceeding normal limits; immoderate. **2** unrestrained, as in behaviour or emotion; intemperate. **3** irregular or disordered. [C14: from L *inordinātus* disordered, from IN-[1] + *ordināre* to put in order]
▸ **inˈordinacy** *or* **inˈordinateness** *n* ▸ **inˈordinately** *adv*

inorganic ⓣ (ˌɪnɔːˈgænɪk) *adj* **1** not having the structure or characteristics of living organisms; not organic. **2** relating to or denoting chemical compounds that do not contain carbon. **3** not having a system, structure, or ordered relation of parts; amorphous. **4** not resulting from or produced by growth; artificial.
▸ **ˌinorˈganically** *adv*

inorganic chemistry *n* the branch of chemistry concerned with the elements and all their compounds except those containing carbon.

inosculate (ɪnˈɒskjʊˌleɪt) *vb* **inosculates, inosculating, inosculated. 1** *Physiol.* (of small blood vessels) to communicate by anastomosis. **2** to unite or be united so as to be continuous; blend. **3** to intertwine or cause to intertwine. [C17: from IN-[2] + L *ōsculāre* to equip with an opening, from *ōsculum*, dim. of *ōs* mouth]
▸ **inˌoscuˈlation** *n*

inositol (ɪˈnəʊsɪˌtɒl) *n* a cyclic alcohol, one isomer of which (*i*-inositol) is present in yeast and is a growth factor for some organisms. [C19: from Gk *in-*, *is* sinew + -OSE[2] + -ITE[1] + -OL[1]]

inpatient (ˈɪnˌpeɪʃənt) *n* a patient living in the hospital where he is being treated.

in perpetuum *Latin.* (ɪn pɜːˈpɛtjʊəm) forever.

input (ˈɪnˌpʊt) *n* **1** the act of putting in. **2** that which is put in. **3** (*often pl*) a resource required for industrial production, such as capital goods, etc. **4** *Electronics.* the signal or current fed into a component or circuit. **5** *Computing.* the data fed into a computer from a peripheral device. **6** (*modifier*) of or relating to electronic, computer, or other input: *input program.* ◆ *vb* **inputs, inputting, input. 7** (*tr*) to insert (data) into a computer.

input/output *n Computing.* **1** the data or information passed into or out of a computer. **2** (*modifier*) concerned with or relating to such passage of data or information.

inquest ⓣ (ˈɪnˌkwest) *n* **1** an inquiry, esp. into the cause of an unexplained, sudden, or violent death, held by a coroner, in certain cases with a jury. **2** *Inf.* any inquiry or investigation. [C13: from Med. L, from L IN-[2] + *quaesītus* investigation, from *quaerere* to examine]

inquietude (ɪnˈkwaɪɪˌtjuːd) *n* restlessness, uneasiness, or anxiety.
▸ **inquiet** (ɪnˈkwaɪət) *adj* ▸ **inˈquietly** *adv*

inquiline (ˈɪnkwɪˌlaɪn) *n* **1** an animal that lives in close association with another animal without harming it. See also **commensal** (sense 1). ◆ *adj* **2** of or living as an inquiline. [C17: from L *inquilīnus* lodger, from IN-[2] + *colere* to dwell]
▸ **inquilinous** (ˌɪnkwɪˈlaɪnəs) *adj*

inquire ⓣ *or* **enquire** (ɪnˈkwaɪə) *vb* **inquires, inquiring, inquired** *or* **enquires, enquiring, enquired. 1a** to seek information (about); ask: *she inquired his age; she inquired about rates of pay.* **1b** (*intr;* foll. by *of*) to ask (a person) for information: *I'll inquire of my aunt when she is coming.* **2** (*intr;* often foll. by *into*) to make a search or investigation. [C13: from L *inquīrere*, from IN-[2] + *quaerere* to seek]
▸ **inˈquirer** *or* **enˈquirer** *n* ▸ **inˈquiry** *or* **enˈquiry** *n*

inquisition ⓣ (ˌɪnkwɪˈzɪʃən) *n* **1** the act of inquiring deeply or searchingly; investigation. **2** a deep or searching inquiry, esp. a ruthless official investigation in order to suppress revolt or root out the unorthodox. **3** an official inquiry, esp. one held by a jury before an officer of the Crown. [C14: from legal L *inquīsītiō*, from *inquīrere* to seek for; see INQUIRE]
▸ **ˌinquiˈsitional** *adj* ▸ **ˌinquiˈsitionist** *n*

Inquisition (ˌɪnkwɪˈzɪʃən) *n History.* a judicial institution of the Roman Catholic Church (1232–1820) founded to suppress heresy.

inquisitive ⓣ (ɪnˈkwɪzɪtɪv) *adj* **1** excessively curious, esp. about the affairs of others; prying. **2** eager to learn; inquiring.
▸ **inˈquisitively** *adv* ▸ **inˈquisitiveness** *n*

inquisitor (ɪnˈkwɪzɪtə) *n* **1** a person who inquires, esp. deeply, searchingly, or ruthlessly. **2** (*often cap.*) an official of the ecclesiastical court of the Inquisition.

inquisitorial (ɪnˌkwɪzɪˈtɔːrɪəl) *adj* **1** of, relating to, or resembling inquisition or an inquisitor. **2** offensively curious; prying. **3** *Law.* denoting criminal procedure in which one party is both prosecutor and judge, or in which the trial is held in secret. Cf. **accusatorial** (sense 2).
▸ **inˌquisiˈtorially** *adv* ▸ **inˌquisiˈtorialness** *n*

inquorate (ɪnˈkwɔːˌreɪt) *adj Brit.* not consisting of or being a quorum: *this meeting is inquorate.*

in re (ɪn ˈreɪ) *prep* in the matter of: used esp. in bankruptcy proceedings. [C17: from L]

INRI *abbrev. for* Iesus Nazarenus Rex Iudaeorum (the inscription placed over Christ's head during the Crucifixion). [L: Jesus of Nazareth, King of the Jews]

inro (ˈɪnrəʊ) *n, pl* **inro.** a set of small lacquer boxes formerly worn hung from the belt by Japanese men and used to carry medicines, seals, etc.

inroad ⓣ (ˈɪnˌrəʊd) *n* **1** an invasion or hostile attack; raid or incursion. **2** an encroachment or intrusion.

inrush (ˈɪnˌrʌʃ) *n* a sudden usually overwhelming inward flow or rush; influx.
▸ **ˈinˌrushing** *n, adj*

ins. *abbrev. for:* **1** inches. **2** insulated. **3** insurance.

THESAURUS

naive, artless, childlike, credulous, frank, guileless, gullible, ingenuous, open, simple, unsuspicious, unworldly, wet behind the ears (*inf.*) ◆ *n* **7** = **child**, babe (in arms) (*inf.*), greenhorn (*inf.*), ingénue *or* (*masc.*) ingénu
Antonyms *adj* ≠ **pure:** corrupt, dishonest, immoral, impure, sinful, wrong ≠ **not guilty:** blameworthy, culpable, guilty, responsible ≠ **harmless:** evil, harmful, iniquitous, malicious, offensive, wicked ≠ **naive:** artful, disingenuous, sophisticated, worldly

innocuous *adj* = **harmless**, innocent, innoxious, inoffensive, safe, unobjectionable

innovation *n* **2** = **modernization**, alteration, change, departure, introduction, modernism, newness, novelty, variation

innovative *adj* = **novel**, inventive, new, transformational, variational

innovator *n* = **modernizer**, changer, introducer, inventor, transformer

innuendo *n* **1** = **insinuation**, aspersion, hint, implication, imputation, intimation, overtone, suggestion, whisper

innumerable *adj* = **countless**, beyond number, incalculable, infinite, many, multitudinous, myriad, numberless, numerous, unnumbered, untold
Antonyms *adj* calculable, computable, finite, limited, measurable, numbered

inoperable *adj* **1** = **unworkable**, impracticable, impractical, nonviable, unrealistic

inordinate *adj* **1** = **excessive**, disproportionate, exorbitant, extravagant, immoderate, intemperate, preposterous, unconscionable, undue, unreasonable, unrestrained, unwarranted
Antonyms *adj* inhibited, moderate, reasonable, restrained, rightful, sensible, temperate

inorganic *adj* **1** = **artificial**, chemical, man-made, mineral

inquest *n* **2** = **inquiry**, inquisition, investigation, probe

inquire *vb* **1** = **ask**, query, question, request information, seek information **2** = **investigate**, examine, explore, inspect, look into, make inquiries, probe, research, scrutinize, search

inquiry *n* **1** = **question**, query **2** = **investigation**, examination, exploration, inquest, interrogation, probe, research, scrutiny, search, study, survey

inquisition *n* **1, 2** = **investigation**, cross-examination, examination, grilling (*inf.*), inquest, inquiry, questioning, quizzing, third degree (*inf.*)

inquisitive *adj* **1** = **curious**, inquiring, intrusive, nosy (*inf.*), nosy-parkering (*inf.*), peering, probing, prying, questioning, scrutinizing, snooping (*inf.*), snoopy (*inf.*)
Antonyms *adj* apathetic, incurious, indifferent, unconcerned, uninterested, unquestioning

inroad *n* **1** = **incursion**, advance, encroachment, foray, intrusion, invasion, irruption, onslaught, raid

insane Ⓣ (ɪnˈseɪn) *adj* **1a** mentally deranged; crazy; of unsound mind. **1b** (*as collective n; preceded by the*): *the insane*. **2** characteristic of a person of unsound mind: *an insane stare*. **3** irresponsible; very foolish; stupid.
▸**inˈsanely** *adv* ▸**inˈsaneness** *n*

insanitary Ⓣ (ɪnˈsænɪtərɪ, -trɪ) *adj* not sanitary; dirty or infected.

insanity Ⓣ (ɪnˈsænɪtɪ) *n, pl* **insanities. 1** relatively permanent disorder of the mind; state or condition of being insane. **2** utter folly; stupidity.

insatiable Ⓣ (ɪnˈseɪʃəbᵊl, -ʃɪə-) *or* **insatiate** (ɪnˈseɪʃɪɪt) *adj* not able to be satisfied; greedy or unappeasable.
▸**inˌsatiaˈbility** *or* **inˈsatiateness** *n* ▸**inˈsatiably** *or* **inˈsatiately** *adv*

inscape (ˈɪnskeɪp) *n* the essential inner nature of a person, object, etc. [C19: from IN-^{2} + *-scape*, as in LANDSCAPE; coined by Gerard Manley *Hopkins* (1844–89), E poet]

inscribe Ⓣ (ɪnˈskraɪb) *vb* **inscribes, inscribing, inscribed.** (*tr*) **1** to make, carve, or engrave (writing, letters, etc.) on (a surface such as wood, stone, or paper). **2** to enter (a name) on a list or in a register. **3** to sign one's name on (a book, etc.) before presentation to another person. **4** to draw (a geometric construction) inside another construction so that the two are in contact but do not intersect. [C16: from L *inscrībere*; see INSCRIPTION]
▸**inˈscribable** *adj* ▸**inˈscribableness** *n* ▸**inˈscriber** *n*

inscription Ⓣ (ɪnˈskrɪpʃən) *n* **1** something inscribed, esp. words carved or engraved on a coin, tomb, etc. **2** a signature or brief dedication in a book or on a work of art. **3** the act of inscribing. [C14: from L *inscriptiō* a writing upon, from *inscrībere* to write upon, from IN-^{2} + *scrībere* to write]
▸**inˈscriptional** *or* **inˈscriptive** *adj* ▸**inˈscriptively** *adv*

inscrutable Ⓣ (ɪnˈskruːtəbᵊl) *adj* mysterious or enigmatic; incomprehensible. [C15: from LL, from L IN-^{1} + *scrūtārī* to examine]
▸**inˌscrutaˈbility** *or* **inˈscrutableness** *n* ▸**inˈscrutably** *adv*

insect (ˈɪnsɛkt) *n* **1** any of a class of small air-breathing arthropods, having a body divided into head, thorax, and abdomen, three pairs of legs, and (in most species) two pairs of wings. **2** (loosely) any similar invertebrate, such as a spider, tick, or centipede. **3** a contemptible, loathsome, or insignificant person. [C17: from L *insectum* (animal that has been) cut into, insect, from *insecāre*, from IN-^{2} + *secāre* to cut]
▸**inˈsectile** *adj* ▸**ˈinsect-ˌlike** *adj*

insectarium (ˌɪnsɛkˈtɛərɪəm) *or* **insectary** (ɪnˈsɛktərɪ) *n, pl* **insectariums, insectaria** (-ˈtɛərɪə), *or* **insectaries.** a place where living insects are kept, bred, and studied.

insecticide (ɪnˈsɛktɪˌsaɪd) *n* a substance used to destroy insect pests.
▸**inˌsectiˈcidal** *adj*

insectivore (ɪnˈsɛktɪˌvɔː) *n* **1** any of an order of placental mammals, being typically small, with simple teeth, and feeding on invertebrates. The group includes shrews, moles, and hedgehogs. **2** any animal or plant that derives nourishment from insects.
▸**ˌinsecˈtivorous** *adj*

insecure Ⓣ (ˌɪnsɪˈkjʊə) *adj* **1** anxious or afraid; not confident or certain. **2** not adequately protected: *an insecure fortress*. **3** unstable or shaky.
▸**ˌinseˈcurely** *adv* ▸**ˌinseˈcureness** *n* ▸**ˌinseˈcurity** *n*

inselberg (ˈɪnzᵊlˌbɜːg) *n* an isolated rocky hill rising abruptly from a flat plain. [from G, from *Insel* island + *Berg* mountain]

inseminate (ɪnˈsɛmɪˌneɪt) *vb* **inseminates, inseminating, inseminated.** (*tr*) **1** to impregnate (a female) with semen. **2** to introduce (ideas or attitudes) into the mind of (a person or group). [C17: from L *insēmināre*, from IN-^{2} + *sēmināre* to sow, from *sēmen* seed]
▸**inˌsemiˈnation** *n* ▸**inˈsemiˌnator** *n*

insensate Ⓣ (ɪnˈsɛnseɪt, -sɪt) *adj* **1** lacking sensation or consciousness. **2** insensitive; unfeeling. **3** foolish; senseless.
▸**inˈsensately** *adv* ▸**inˈsensateness** *n*

insensible Ⓣ (ɪnˈsɛnsəbᵊl) *adj* **1** lacking sensation or consciousness. **2** (foll. by *of* or *to*) unaware (of) or indifferent (to): *insensible to suffering*. **3** thoughtless or callous. **4** a less common word for **imperceptible.**
▸**inˌsensiˈbility** *or* **inˈsensibleness** *n* ▸**inˈsensibly** *adv*

insensitive Ⓣ (ɪnˈsɛnsɪtɪv) *adj* **1** lacking sensitivity; unfeeling. **2** lacking physical sensation. **3** (*postpositive*; foll. by *to*) not sensitive (to) or affected (by): *insensitive to radiation*.
▸**inˈsensitively** *adv* ▸**inˈsensitiveness** *or* **inˌsensiˈtivity** *n*

insentient (ɪnˈsɛnʃɪənt) *adj* lacking consciousness or senses; inanimate.
▸**inˈsentience** *n*

inseparable Ⓣ (ɪnˈsɛpərəbᵊl, -ˈsɛprə-) *adj* incapable of being separated or divided.
▸**inˌseparaˈbility** *or* **inˈseparableness** *n* ▸**inˈseparably** *adv*

insert Ⓣ *vb* (ɪnˈsɜːt). (*tr*) **1** to put in or between; introduce. **2** to introduce into text, as in a newspaper; interpolate. ◆ *n* (ˈɪnsɜːt). **3** something inserted. **4** Also called: **inset. 4a** a folded section placed in another for binding in with a book. **4b** a printed sheet, esp. one bearing advertising, placed loose between the leaves of a book, periodical, etc. [C16: from L *inserere* to plant in, from IN-^{2} + *serere* to join]
▸**inˈsertable** *adj* ▸**inˈserter** *n*

insertion Ⓣ (ɪnˈsɜːʃən) *n* **1** the act of inserting or something that is inserted. **2** a word, sentence, correction, etc., inserted into text, such as a newspaper. **3** a strip of lace, embroidery, etc., between two pieces of material. **4** *Anat.* the point or manner of attachment of a muscle to the bone that it moves.
▸**inˈsertional** *adj*

in-service *adj* denoting training that is given to employees during the course of employment: *an in-service course*.

insessorial (ˌɪnsɛˈsɔːrɪəl) *adj* **1** (of feet or claws) adapted for perching. **2** (of birds) having insessorial feet. [C19: from NL *Insessōrēs* birds that perch, from L: perchers, from *insidēre* to sit upon]

inset *vb* (ɪnˈsɛt), **insets, insetting, inset. 1** (*tr*) to set or place in or within; insert. ◆ *n* (ˈɪnˌsɛt). **2** something inserted. **3** *Printing.* **3a** a small map or diagram set within the borders of a larger one. **3b** another name for **insert** (sense 4). **4** a piece of fabric inserted into a garment, as to shape it or for decoration.
▸**ˈinˌsetter** *n*

inshallah (ɪnˈʃælə) *sentence substitute. Islam.* if Allah wills it. [C19: from Ar.]

inshore (ˈɪnˈʃɔː) *adj* **1** in or on the water, but close to the shore: *inshore weather*. ◆ *adv, adj* **2** towards the shore from the water: *an inshore wind; we swam inshore*.

THESAURUS

insane *adj* **1** = **mad**, crackers (*Brit. sl.*), crazed, crazy, demented, deranged, mentally disordered, mentally ill, *non compos mentis*, nuts (*sl.*), off one's rocker (*sl.*), of unsound mind, out of one's mind, round the bend (*inf.*) **3** = **stupid**, bizarre, daft (*inf.*), fatuous, foolish, idiotic, impractical, inane, irrational, irresponsible, lunatic, preposterous, senseless
Antonyms *adj* logical, lucid, normal, practical, rational, reasonable, reasoned, sane, sensible, sound

insanitary *adj* = **unhealthy**, contaminated, dirtied, dirty, disease-ridden, feculent, filthy, impure, infected, infested, insalubrious, noxious, polluted, unclean, unhygienic
Antonyms *adj* clean, healthy, hygienic, pure, salubrious, unpolluted

insanity *n* **1** = **madness**, aberration, craziness, delirium, dementia, frenzy, mental derangement, mental disorder, mental illness **2** = **stupidity**, folly, irresponsibility, lunacy, preposterousness, senselessness
Antonyms *n* logic, lucidity, normality, rationality, reason, sanity, sense, soundness, wisdom

insatiable *adj* = **unquenchable**, edacious, gluttonous, greedy, insatiate, intemperate, quenchless, rapacious, ravenous, unappeasable, voracious
Antonyms *adj* appeasable, limited, quenchable, satiable, temperate

inscribe *vb* **1** = **carve**, cut, engrave, etch, impress, imprint **2** = **enrol**, engross, enlist, enter, record, register, write **3** = **dedicate**, address

inscription *n* **1** = **engraving**, label, legend, lettering, saying, words **2** = **dedication**

inscrutable *adj* = **enigmatic**, blank, deadpan, impenetrable, mysterious, poker-faced (*inf.*), sphinxlike, unfathomable, unreadable
Antonyms open, penetrable, readable, revealing, transparent

insecure *adj* **1** = **anxious**, afraid, uncertain, unconfident, unsure **2** = **unsafe**, dangerous, defenceless, exposed, hazardous, ill-protected, open to attack, perilous, unguarded, unprotected, unshielded, vulnerable, wide-open **3** = **unstable**, built upon sand, flimsy, frail, insubstantial, loose, on thin ice, precarious, rickety, rocky, shaky, unreliable, unsound, unsteady, weak, wobbly
Antonyms *adj* ≠ **anxious:** assured, certain, confident, decisive, secure ≠ **unsafe:** protected, safe, secure ≠ **unstable:** firm, reliable, secure, sound, stable, steady, substantial, sure

insecurity *n* **1** = **anxiety**, fear, uncertainty, unsureness, worry **2** = **vulnerability**, danger, defencelessness, hazard, peril, risk, uncertainty, weakness **3** = **unsteadiness**, dubiety, frailness, instability, precariousness, shakiness, uncertainty, unreliability, weakness
Antonyms *n* ≠ **anxiety:** assurance, certainty, confidence, security ≠ **vulnerability:** dependability, safety ≠ **unsteadiness:** firmness, reliability, security, stability, steadiness

insensate *adj* **1** = **lifeless**, anaesthetized, dead, inanimate, inert, insensible, insentient, numbed, out (*inf.*), unconscious **2** = **unfeeling**, hardened, imperceptive, impercipient, indifferent, insensitive, inured, obtuse, stolid, thick-skinned, thoughtless, unperceiving **3** = **foolish**, brainless, fatuous, mindless, senseless, stupid, thoughtless, unreasonable, witless

insensibility *n* **1** = **unconsciousness**, inertness, numbness **2** = **insensitivity**, apathy, callousness, dullness, indifference, inertia, lethargy, torpor

insensible *adj* **1** = **benumbed**, anaesthetized, dull, inert, insensate, numbed, torpid **2** = **unaware**, apathetic, callous, cold, deaf, hard-hearted, impassive, impervious, indifferent, oblivious, unaffected, unconscious, unfeeling, unmindful, unmoved, unresponsive, unsusceptible, untouched **4** = **imperceptible**, imperceivable, minuscule, negligible, unnoticeable
Antonyms *adj* ≠ **unaware:** affected, aware, conscious, feeling, mindful, responsive, sensible

insensibly *adv* **4** = **imperceptibly**, by degrees, gradually, invisibly, little by little, slightly, unnoticeably

insensitive *adj* **1** = **unfeeling**, callous, crass, hardened, imperceptive, indifferent, obtuse, tactless, thick-skinned, tough, uncaring, unconcerned, unresponsive, unsusceptible **3** *with* **to** = **unaffected by**, dead to, immune to, impervious to, proof against, unmoved by
Antonyms *adj* ≠ **unfeeling:** caring, concerned, perceptive, responsive, sensitive, sentient, susceptible, sympathetic, tactful, tender

inseparable *adj* = **indivisible**, conjoined, inalienable, indissoluble, inseverable

insert *vb* **1** = **enter**, embed, implant, infix, interject, interpolate, interpose, introduce, place, pop in (*inf.*), put, set, stick in, tuck in, work in
Antonyms *vb* delete, extract, pull out, remove, take out, withdraw

insertion *n* **1** = **inclusion**, addition, implant, insert, inset, interpolation, introduction, supplement

inside ➊ *n* ('ɪn'saɪd). **1** the interior; inner or enclosed part or surface. **2** the side of a path away from the road or adjacent to a wall. **3** (*also pl*) *Inf.* the internal organs of the body, esp. the stomach and bowels. **4 inside of.** in a period of time less than; within. **5 inside out.** with the inside facing outwards. **6 know (something) inside out.** to know thoroughly or perfectly. ◆ *prep* (ˌɪn'saɪd). **7** in or to the interior of; within or to within; on the inside of. ◆ *adj* ('ɪnˌsaɪd). **8** on or of an interior; on the inside: *an inside door.* **9** (*prenominal*) arranged or provided by someone within an organization or building, esp. illicitly: *the raid was an inside job; inside information.* ◆ *adv* (ˌɪn'saɪd). **10** within or to within a thing or place; indoors. **11** *Sl.* in or into prison.

USAGE NOTE See at **outside.**

inside job *n Inf.* a crime committed with the assistance of someone associated with the victim.

inside lane *n Athletics.* the inside, and therefore the shortest, route around a circular or oval multi-lane running track.

insider (ˌɪn'saɪdə) *n* **1** a member of a specified group. **2** a person with access to exclusive information.

insider dealing *or* **trading** *n* the illegal practice of a person on the Stock Exchange or in some branches of the Civil Service taking advantage of early confidential information in order to deal in shares for personal profit.
▸**insider dealer** *or* **trader** *n*

insidious ➊ (ɪn'sɪdɪəs) *adj* **1** stealthy, subtle, cunning, or treacherous. **2** working in a subtle or apparently innocuous way, but nevertheless deadly: *an insidious illness.* [C16: from L *insidiōsus* cunning, from *insidiae* an ambush, from *insidēre* to sit in]
▸**in'sidiously** *adv* ▸**in'sidiousness** *n*

insight ➊ ('ɪnˌsaɪt) *n* **1** the ability to perceive clearly or deeply; penetration. **2** a penetrating and often sudden understanding, as of a complex situation or problem. **3** *Psychol.* the capacity for understanding one's own or another's mental processes. **4** *Psychiatry.* the ability to understand one's own problems.
▸**'inˌsightful** *adj*

insignia ➊ (ɪn'sɪgnɪə) *n, pl* **insignias** *or* **insignia. 1** a badge or emblem of membership, office, or dignity. **2** a distinguishing sign or mark. [C17: from L: badges, from *insignis* distinguished by a mark, prominent, from IN-[2] + *signum* mark]

insignificant ➊ (ˌɪnsɪg'nɪfɪkənt) *adj* **1** having little or no importance; trifling. **2** almost or relatively meaningless. **3** small or inadequate: *an insignificant wage.* **4** not distinctive in character, etc.
▸ˌ**insig'nificance** *or* ˌ**insig'nificancy** *n* ▸ˌ**insig'nificantly** *adv*

insincere ➊ (ˌɪnsɪn'sɪə) *adj* lacking sincerity; hypocritical.
▸ˌ**insin'cerely** *adv* ▸**insincerity** (ˌɪnsɪn'serɪtɪ) *n*

insinuate ➊ (ɪn'sɪnjʊˌeɪt) *vb* **insinuates, insinuating, insinuated. 1** (*may take a clause as object*) to suggest by indirect allusion, hints, innuendo, etc. **2** (*tr*) to introduce subtly or deviously. **3** (*tr*) to cause (someone, esp. oneself) to be accepted by gradual approaches or manoeuvres. [C16: from L *insinuāre* to wind one's way into, from IN-[2] + *sinus* curve]
▸**in'sinuative** *or* **in'sinuatory** *adj* ▸**in'sinuˌator** *n*

insinuation ➊ (ɪnˌsɪnjʊ'eɪʃən) *n* **1** an indirect or devious hint or suggestion. **2** the act or practice of insinuating.

insipid ➊ (ɪn'sɪpɪd) *adj* **1** lacking spirit or interest; boring. **2** lacking taste; unpalatable. [C17: from L, from IN-[1] + *sapidus* full of flavour, SAPID]
▸ˌ**insi'pidity** *or* **in'sipidness** *n* ▸**in'sipidly** *adv*

insist ➊ (ɪn'sɪst) *vb* (when *tr, takes a clause as object;* when *intr,* usually foll. by *on* or *upon*) **1** to make a determined demand (for): *he insisted on his rights.* **2** to express a convinced belief (in) or assertion (of). [C16: from L *insistere* to stand upon, urge, from IN-[2] + *sistere* to stand]
▸**in'sister** *n* ▸**in'sistingly** *adv*

insistent ➊ (ɪn'sɪstənt) *adj* **1** making continual and persistent demands. **2** demanding notice or attention; compelling: *the insistent cry of a bird.*
▸**in'sistence** *or* **in'sistency** *n* ▸**in'sistently** *adv*

in situ *Latin.* (ɪn 'sɪtjuː) *adv, adj* (*postpositive*) in the natural, original, or appropriate position.

in so far as *or* **insofar as** (ˌɪnsəʊ'fɑː) *adv* to the degree or extent that.

insolation (ˌɪnsəʊ'leɪʃən) *n* **1** the quantity of solar radiation falling upon a body or planet, esp. per unit area. **2** exposure to the sun's rays. **3** another name for **sunstroke.**

insole ('ɪnˌsəʊl) *n* **1** the inner sole of a shoe or boot. **2** a loose additional inner sole used to give extra warmth or to make a shoe fit.

insolent ➊ ('ɪnsələnt) *adj* impudent or disrespectful. [C14: from L, from IN-[1] + *solēre* to be accustomed]
▸**'insolence** *n* ▸**'insolently** *adv*

insoluble ➊ (ɪn'sɒljʊbᵊl) *adj* **1** incapable of being dissolved; incapable of forming a solution, esp. in water. **2** incapable of being solved.
▸**inˌsolu'bility** *or* **in'solubleness** *n* ▸**in'solubly** *adv*

insolvent ➊ (ɪn'sɒlvənt) *adj* **1** having insufficient assets to meet debts and liabilities; bankrupt. **2** of or relating to bankrupts or bankruptcy. ◆ *n* **3** a person who is insolvent; bankrupt.
▸**in'solvency** *n*

insomnia ➊ (ɪn'sɒmnɪə) *n* chronic inability to fall asleep or to enjoy uninterrupted sleep. [C18: from L, from *insomnis* sleepless, from *somnus* sleep]
▸**in'somniˌac** *n, adj* ▸**in'somnious** *adj*

THESAURUS

inside *n* **1** = **interior**, contents, inner part **3** *plural Informal* = **stomach**, belly, bowels, entrails, gut, guts, innards (*inf.*), internal organs, viscera, vitals ◆ *adj* **8** = **inner**, innermost, interior, internal, intramural, inward **9** = **confidential**, classified, esoteric, exclusive, internal, limited, private, restricted, secret ◆ *adv* **10** = **indoors**, under cover, within
Antonyms *adj* ≠ **inner:** exterior, external, extramural, outer, outermost, outside, outward

insidious *adj* **1** = **stealthy**, artful, crafty, crooked, cunning, deceitful, deceptive, designing, disingenuous, duplicitous, guileful, intriguing, Machiavellian, slick, sly, smooth, sneaking, subtle, surreptitious, treacherous, tricky, wily
Antonyms *adj* artless, conspicuous, forthright, harmless, honest, ingenuous, obvious, open, sincere, straightforward, upright

insight *n* **1** = **understanding**, acumen, awareness, comprehension, discernment, intuition, intuitiveness, judgment, observation, penetration, perception, perspicacity, vision

insightful *adj* **1** = **perceptive**, astute, discerning, knowledgeable, observant, penetrating, perspicacious, sagacious, shrewd, understanding, wise

insignia *n* **1, 2** = **badge**, crest, decoration, distinguishing mark, earmark, emblem, ensign, symbol

insignificance *n* **1** = **unimportance**, immateriality, inconsequence, irrelevance, meaninglessness, negligibility, paltriness, pettiness, triviality, worthlessness
Antonyms *n* consequence, importance, matter, meaningfulness, relevance, significance, weight, worth

insignificant *adj* **1** = **unimportant**, flimsy, immaterial, inconsequential, inconsiderable, irrelevant, meagre, meaningless, measly, minor, negligible, nickel-and-dime (*US sl.*), nondescript, nonessential, not worth mentioning, nugatory, of no account, of no consequence, of no moment, paltry, petty, scanty, small potatoes, trifling, trivial
Antonyms *adj* consequential, considerable, essential, important, meaningful, momentous, relevant, significant, substantial, vital, weighty

insincere *adj* = **deceitful**, deceptive, devious, dishonest, disingenuous, dissembling, dissimulating, double-dealing, duplicitous, evasive, faithless, false, hollow, hypocritical, Janus-faced, lying, mendacious, perfidious, pretended, two-faced, unfaithful, untrue, untruthful, with tongue in cheek
Antonyms *adj* direct, earnest, faithful, genuine, honest, sincere, straightforward, true, truthful

insincerity *n* = **deceitfulness**, deviousness, dishonesty, disingenuousness, dissimulation, duplicity, faithlessness, hypocrisy, lip service, mendacity, perfidy, pretence, untruthfulness
Antonyms *n* directness, faithfulness, honesty, sincerity, truthfulness

insinuate *vb* **1** = **imply**, allude, hint, indicate, intimate, suggest **3** = **ingratiate**, curry favour, get in with, worm *or* work one's way in

insinuation *n* **1** = **implication**, allusion, aspersion, hint, innuendo, slur, suggestion

insipid *adj* **1** = **bland**, anaemic, banal, characterless, colourless, drab, dry, dull, flat, jejune, lifeless, limp, pointless, prosaic, spiritless, stale, stupid, tame, tedious, tiresome, trite, unimaginative, uninteresting, vapid, weak, wearisome, wishy-washy (*inf.*) **2** = **tasteless**, bland, flavourless, savourless, unappetizing, watered down, watery, wishy-washy (*inf.*)
Antonyms *adj* ≠ **bland:** colourful, engaging, exciting, interesting, lively, provocative, spirited, stimulating ≠ **tasteless:** appetizing, fiery, palatable, piquant, pungent, savoury, tasty

insipidity *n* **1** = **dullness**, banality, colourlessness, flatness, lack of imagination, pointlessness, staleness, tameness, tediousness, triteness, uninterestingness, vapidity **2** = **tastelessness**, blandness, flavourlessness, lack of flavour
Antonyms *n* ≠ **dullness:** animation, character, dynamism, gaiety, liveliness, spirit, vitality, vivacity

insist *vb* **1** = **demand**, be firm, brook no refusal, lay down the law, not take no for an answer, persist, press (someone), put one's foot down (*inf.*), require, stand firm, stand one's ground, take *or* make a stand, urge **2** = **assert**, asseverate, aver, claim, contend, hold, maintain, reiterate, repeat, swear, urge, vow

insistence *n* **1** = **persistence**, assertion, contention, demands, emphasis, importunity, insistency, pressing, reiteration, stress, urging

insistent *adj* **1** = **persistent**, demanding, dogged, emphatic, exigent, forceful, importunate, incessant, peremptory, persevering, pressing, unrelenting, urgent

insolence *n* = **rudeness**, abuse, audacity, backchat (*inf.*), boldness, cheek (*inf.*), chutzpah (*US & Canad. inf.*), contemptuousness, contumely, disrespect, effrontery, front, gall (*inf.*), impertinence, impudence, incivility, insubordination, offensiveness, pertness, uncivility
Antonyms *n* civility, courtesy, deference, esteem, mannerliness, politeness, respect, submission

insolent *adj* = **rude**, abusive, bold, brazen-faced, contemptuous, fresh (*inf.*), impertinent, impudent, insubordinate, insulting, pert, saucy, uncivil
Antonyms *adj* civil, courteous, deferential, mannerly, polite, respectful, submissive

insoluble *adj* **2** = **inexplicable**, baffling, impenetrable, indecipherable, mysterious, mystifying, obscure, unaccountable, unfathomable, unsolvable
Antonyms *adj* accountable, comprehensible, explicable, fathomable, penetrable, soluble, solvable

insolvency *n* **1** = **bankruptcy**, failure, liquidation, ruin

insolvent *adj* **1** = **bankrupt**, broke (*inf.*), failed, gone bust (*inf.*), gone to the wall, in queer street (*inf.*), in receivership, in the hands of the receivers, on the rocks (*inf.*), ruined

insomnia *n* = **sleeplessness**, wakefulness

insomuch (ˌɪnsəʊˈmʌtʃ) *adv* **1** (foll. by *as* or *that*) to such an extent or degree. **2** (foll. by *as*) because of the fact (that); inasmuch (as).

insouciant Ⓣ (ɪnˈsuːsɪənt) *adj* carefree or unconcerned; light-hearted. [C19: from F, from IN-[1] + *souciant* worrying, from *soucier* to trouble, from L *sollicitāre*]
▸**inˈsouciance** *n* ▸**inˈsouciantly** *adv*

inspan (ɪnˈspæn) *vb* **inspans, inspanning, inspanned.** (*tr*) *Chiefly S. African.* **1** to harness (animals) to (a vehicle); yoke. **2** to press (people) into service. [C19: from Afrik., from MDu. *inspannen,* from *spannen* to stretch]

inspect Ⓣ (ɪnˈspɛkt) *vb* (*tr*) **1** to examine closely, esp. for faults or errors. **2** to scrutinize officially (a document, military personnel on ceremonial parade, etc.). [C17: from L *inspicere, from specere* to look]
▸**inˈspectable** *adj* ▸**inˈspection** *n* ▸**inˈspective** *adj*

inspector Ⓣ (ɪnˈspɛktə) *n* **1** a person who inspects, esp. an official who examines for compliance with regulations, standards, etc. **2** a police officer ranking below a superintendent and above a sergeant.
▸**inˈspectoral** *or* **inspectorial** (ˌɪnspɛkˈtɔːrɪəl) *adj* ▸**inˈspectorˌship** *n*

inspectorate (ɪnˈspɛktərɪt) *n* **1** the office, rank, or duties of an inspector. **2** a body of inspectors. **3** a district under an inspector.

inspiration Ⓣ (ˌɪnspɪˈreɪʃən) *n* **1** stimulation or arousal of the mind, feelings, etc., to special activity or creativity. **2** the state or quality of being so stimulated or aroused. **3** someone or something that causes this state. **4** an idea or action resulting from such a state. **5** the act or process of inhaling; breathing in.

inspiratory (ɪnˈspaɪərətərɪ, -trɪ) *adj* of or relating to inhalation or the drawing in of air.

inspire Ⓣ (ɪnˈspaɪə) *vb* **inspires, inspiring, inspired. 1** to exert a stimulating or beneficial effect upon (a person, etc.); animate or invigorate. **2** (*tr; foll. by with* or *to; may take an infinitive*) to arouse (with a particular emotion or to a particular action); stir. **3** (*tr*) to prompt or instigate; give rise to. **4** (*tr; often passive*) to guide or arouse by divine influence or inspiration. **5** to take or draw (air, gas, etc.) into the lungs; inhale. **6** (*tr*) *Arch.* to breathe into or upon. [C14 (in the sense: to breathe upon, blow into): from L *inspīrāre,* from *spīrāre* to breathe]
▸**inˈspirable** *adj* ▸**inˈspirative** *adj* ▸**inˈspirer** *n* ▸**inˈspiringly** *adv*

inspirit (ɪnˈspɪrɪt) *vb* (*tr*) to fill with vigour; inspire.
▸**inˈspiriter** *n* ▸**inˈspiriting** *adj* ▸**inˈspiritment** *n*

inspissate (ɪnˈspɪseɪt) *vb* **inspissates, inspissating, inspissated.** *Arch.* to thicken, as by evaporation. [C17: from LL *inspissātus* thickened, from L, from *spissus* thick]
▸**ˌinspisˈsation** *n* ▸**ˈinspisˌsator** *n*

inst. *abbrev. for:* **1** instant (this month). **2** instantaneous. **3** instrumental.

Inst. *abbrev. for:* **1** Institute. **2** Institution.

instability Ⓣ (ˌɪnstəˈbɪlɪtɪ) *n, pl* **instabilities. 1** lack of stability or steadiness. **2** tendency to variable or unpredictable behaviour.

install Ⓣ *or* **instal** (ɪnˈstɔːl) *vb* **installs** *or* **instals, installing, installed.** (*tr*) **1** to place (equipment) in position and connect and adjust for use. **2** to transfer (computer software) from a distribution file to a permanent location on disk, and prepare it for its particular environment and application. **3** to put in a position, rank, etc. **4** to settle (a person, esp. oneself) in a position or state: *she installed herself in an armchair.* [C16: from Med. L *installāre,* from IN-[2] + *stallum* STALL[1]]
▸**inˈstaller** *n*

installation Ⓣ (ˌɪnstəˈleɪʃən) *n* **1** the act of installing or the state of being installed. **2** a large device, system, or piece of equipment that has been installed.

installment plan *or esp. Canad.* **instalment plan** *n* the US and Canad. name for **hire-purchase.**

instalment Ⓣ *or US* **installment** (ɪnˈstɔːlmənt) *n* **1** one of the portions into which a debt is divided for payment at specified intervals over a fixed period. **2** a portion of something that is issued, broadcast, or published in parts. [C18: from obs. *estallment,* prob. from OF *estaler* to fix, from *estal* something fixed, from OHG *stal* STALL[1]]

instance Ⓣ (ˈɪnstəns) *n* **1** a case or particular example. **2 for instance.** for or as an example. **3** a specified stage in proceedings; step (in **in the first, second,** etc., **instance**). **4** urgent request or demand (esp. in **at the instance of**). ◆ *vb* **instances, instancing, instanced.** (*tr*) **5** to cite as an example. [C14 (in the sense: case, example): from Med. L *instantia* example, (in the sense: urgency) from L: a being close upon, from *instāns* urgent; see INSTANT]

instant Ⓣ (ˈɪnstənt) *n* **1** a very brief time; moment. **2** a particular moment or point in time: *at the same instant.* **3 on the instant.** immediately; without delay. ◆ *adj* **4** immediate; instantaneous. **5** (esp. of foods) prepared or designed for preparation with very little time and effort: *instant coffee.* **6** urgent or imperative. **7** (*postpositive*) of the present month: *a letter of the 7th instant.* Abbrev.: **inst.** [C15: from L *instāns,* from *instāre* to be present, press closely, from IN-[2] + *stāre* to stand]

instantaneous Ⓣ (ˌɪnstənˈteɪnɪəs) *adj* **1** occurring with almost no delay; immediate. **2** happening or completed within a moment: *instantaneous death.*
▸**ˌinstanˈtaneously** *adv* ▸**ˌinstanˈtaneousness** *or* **instantaneity** (ɪnˌstæntəˈniːɪtɪ) *n*

instanter (ɪnˈstæntə) *adv Law.* without delay; the same day or within 24 hours. [C17: from L: urgently, from *instans* INSTANT]

instantly Ⓣ (ˈɪnstəntlɪ) *adv* **1** immediately; at once. **2** *Arch.* urgently or insistently.

instar (ˈɪnstɑː) *n* the stage in the development of an insect between any two moults. [C19: NL from L: image]

instate (ɪnˈsteɪt) *vb* **instates, instating, instated.** (*tr*) to place in a position or office; install.
▸**inˈstatement** *n*

instead Ⓣ (ɪnˈstɛd) *adv* **1** as a replacement, substitute, or alternative. **2 instead of.** (*prep*) in place of or as an alternative to. [C13: from *in stead* in place]

instep (ˈɪnˌstɛp) *n* **1** the middle section of the human foot, forming the arch between the ankle and toes. **2** the part of a shoe, stocking, etc., covering this. [C16: prob. from IN-[2] + STEP]

instigate Ⓣ (ˈɪnstɪˌgeɪt) *vb* **instigates, instigating, instigated.** (*tr*) **1** to bring about, as by incitement: *to instigate rebellion.* **2** to urge on to some drastic or unadvisable action. [C16: from L *instīgāre* to incite]
▸**ˌinstiˈgation** *n* ▸**ˈinstiˌgative** *adj* ▸**ˈinstiˌgator** *n*

THESAURUS

insouciance *n* = **nonchalance**, airiness, breeziness, carefreeness, jauntiness, lightheartedness

insouciant *adj* = **nonchalant**, airy, breezy, buoyant, carefree, casual, free and easy, gay, happy-go-lucky, jaunty, light-hearted, sunny, unconcerned, untroubled, unworried

inspect *vb* **1** = **examine**, audit, check, check out (*inf.*), eye, eyeball (*sl.*), give (something *or* someone) the once-over (*inf.*), go over *or* through, investigate, look over, oversee, recce (*sl.*), research, scan, scrutinize, search, superintend, supervise, survey, take a dekko at (*Brit. sl.*), vet, work over

inspection *n* **1** = **examination**, check, checkup, investigation, look-over, once-over (*inf.*), recce (*sl.*), review, scan, scrutiny, search, superintendence, supervision, surveillance, survey

inspector *n* **1** = **examiner**, auditor, censor, checker, critic, investigator, overseer, scrutineer, scrutinizer, superintendent, supervisor

inspiration *n* **1** = **revelation**, afflatus, arousal, awakening, creativity, elevation, encouragement, enthusiasm, exaltation, genius, illumination, insight, stimulation **3** = **influence**, muse, spur, stimulus
Antonyms *n* depressant, deterrent, discouragement, disenchantment

inspire *vb* **1** = **stimulate**, animate, be responsible for, encourage, enliven, fire *or* touch the imagination of, galvanize, gee up, hearten, imbue, influence, infuse, inspirit, instil, rouse, spark off, spur **2** = **arouse**, enkindle, excite, give rise to, produce, quicken, rouse, stir
Antonyms *vb* ≠ **stimulate:** daunt, deflate, depress, discourage, disenchant, dishearten, dispirit

inspiring *adj* **1** = **uplifting**, affecting, encouraging, exciting, exhilarating, heartening, moving, rousing, stimulating, stirring
Antonyms *adj* boring, depressing, discouraging, disheartening, dispiriting, dull, uninspiring

instability *n* **1, 2** = **unpredictability**, capriciousness, changeableness, disequilibrium, fickleness, fitfulness, fluctuation, fluidity, frailty, imbalance, impermanence, inconstancy, insecurity, irresolution, mutability, oscillation, precariousness, restlessness, shakiness, transience, unsteadiness, vacillation, variability, volatility, wavering, weakness
Antonyms *n* balance, constancy, equilibrium, permanence, predictability, resolution, security, stability, steadiness, strength

install *vb* **1** = **set up**, fix, lay, lodge, place, position, put in, station **3** = **induct**, establish, inaugurate, instate, institute, introduce, invest, set up **4** = **settle**, ensconce, position

installation *n* **1** = **setting up**, establishment, fitting, inauguration, instalment, placing, positioning **2** = **equipment**, machinery, plant, system

instalment *n* **1, 2** = **portion**, chapter, division, episode, part, repayment, section

instance *n* **1** = **example**, case, case in point, illustration, occasion, occurrence, precedent, situation, time **4** = **insistence**, application, behest, demand, entreaty, importunity, impulse, incitement, instigation, pressure, prompting, request, solicitation, urging ◆ *vb* **5** = **quote**, adduce, cite, mention, name, specify

instant *n* **1** = **second**, bat of an eye (*inf.*), flash, jiffy (*inf.*), moment, shake (*inf.*), split second, tick (*Brit. inf.*), trice, twinkling, twinkling of an eye (*inf.*), two shakes of a lamb's tail (*inf.*) **2** = **juncture**, moment, occasion, point, time ◆ *adj* **4** = **immediate**, direct, instantaneous, on-the-spot, prompt, quick, quickie (*inf.*), split-second, urgent **5** = **precooked**, convenience, fast, ready-mixed **6** = **urgent**, burning, exigent, imperative, importunate, pressing

instantaneous *adj* **1** = **immediate**, direct, instant, on-the-spot, prompt

instantaneously *adv* **1** = **immediately**, at once, forthwith, in a fraction of a second, instantly, in the same breath, in the twinkling of an eye (*inf.*), like a bat out of hell (*sl.*), like greased lightning (*inf.*), on the instant, on the spot, posthaste, promptly, pronto (*inf.*), straight away, then and there

instantly *adv* **1** = **immediately**, at once, directly, forthwith, instantaneously, instanter (*Law*), now, on the spot, posthaste, pronto (*inf.*), right away, right now, straight away, there and then, this minute, *tout de suite,* without delay

instead *adv* **1** = **rather**, alternatively, in lieu, in preference, on second thoughts, preferably **2 instead of** = **in place of**, as an alternative *or* equivalent to, in lieu of, rather than

instigate *vb* **1** = **provoke**, actuate, bring about, encourage, foment, get going, impel, incite, influence, initiate, kick-start, kindle, move, persuade, prod, prompt, rouse, set off, set on, spur, start, stimulate, stir up, trigger, urge, whip up
Antonyms *vb* discourage, repress, restrain, stop, suppress

instigation *n* **1** = **prompting**, behest, bidding, encouragement, incentive, incitement, urging

instigator *n* **2** = **ringleader**, agitator, firebrand, fomenter, goad, incendiary, inciter, leader, mischief-maker, motivator, prime mover, spur, stirrer (*inf.*), troublemaker

instil Ⓣ *or US* **instill** (ɪn'stɪl) *vb* **instils** *or US* **instills, instilling, instilled.** (*tr*) **1** to introduce gradually; implant or infuse. **2** *Rare.* to pour in or inject in drops. [C16: from L *instillāre* to pour in a drop at a time, from *stillāre* to drip]
▸**in'stiller** *n* ▸**in'stilment,** *US* **in'stillment,** *or* **ˌinstil'lation** *n*

instinct Ⓣ *n* ('ɪnstɪŋkt). **1** the innate capacity of an animal to respond to a given stimulus in a relatively fixed way. **2** inborn intuitive power. ◆ *adj* (ɪn'stɪŋkt). **3** (*postpositive; often foll. by with*) *Rare.* **3a** animated or impelled (by). **3b** imbued or infused (with). [C15: from L *instinctus* roused, from *instinguere* to incite]

instinctive Ⓣ (ɪn'stɪŋktɪv) *adj* **1** of, relating to, or resulting from instinct. **2** conditioned so as to appear innate: *an instinctive movement in driving.*
▸**in'stinctively** *adv*

instinctual (ɪn'stɪŋktjʊəl) *adj* of or pertaining to instinct.
▸**in'stinctually** *adv*

institute Ⓣ ('ɪnstɪˌtjuːt) *vb* **institutes, instituting, instituted.** (*tr*) **1** to organize; establish. **2** to initiate: *to institute a practice.* **3** to establish in a position or office; induct. ◆ *n* **4** an organization founded for particular work, such as education, promotion of the arts, or scientific research. **5** the building where such an organization is situated. **6** something instituted, esp. a rule, custom, or precedent. [C16: from L *instituere,* from *statuere* to place]
▸**'instiˌtutor** *or* **'instiˌtuter** *n*

institutes ('ɪnstɪˌtjuːts) *pl n* a digest or summary, esp. of laws.

institution Ⓣ (ˌɪnstɪ'tjuːʃən) *n* **1** the act of instituting. **2** an organization or establishment founded for a specific purpose, such as a hospital or college. **3** the building where such an organization is situated. **4** an established custom, law, or relationship in a society or community. **5** Also called: **institutional investor.** a large organization, such as an insurance company or pension fund, that has substantial sums to invest on a stock exchange. **6** *Inf.* a constant feature or practice: *Jones's drink at the bar was an institution.* **7** the appointment of an incumbent to an ecclesiastical office or pastoral charge.
▸**ˌinsti'tutionary** *adj*

institutional Ⓣ (ˌɪnstɪ'tjuːʃənᵊl) *adj* **1** of, relating to, or characteristic of institutions. **2** dull, routine, and uniform: *institutional meals.* **3** relating to principles or institutes, esp. of law.
▸**ˌinsti'tutionally** *adv* ▸**ˌinsti'tutionaˌlism** *n*

institutionalize *or* **institutionalise** (ˌɪnstɪ'tjuːʃənəˌlaɪz) *vb* **institutionalizes, institutionalizing, institutionalized** *or* **institutionalises, institutionalising, institutionalised. 1** (*tr; often passive*) to subject to the deleterious effects of confinement in an institution. **2** (*tr*) to place in an institution. **3** to make or become an institution.
▸**ˌinstiˌtutionali'zation** *or* **ˌinstiˌtutionali'sation** *n*

in-store *adj* available within a department store: *in-store banking facilities.*

instruct Ⓣ (ɪn'strʌkt) *vb* (*tr*) **1** to direct to do something; order. **2** to teach (someone) how to do (something). **3** to furnish with information; apprise. **4** *Law, chiefly Brit.* (esp. of a client to his solicitor or a solicitor to a barrister) to give relevant facts or information to. [C15: from L *instruere* to construct, equip, teach, from *struere* to build]
▸**in'structible** *adj*

instruction Ⓣ (ɪn'strʌkʃən) *n* **1** a direction; order. **2** the process or act of imparting knowledge; teaching; education. **3** *Computing.* a part of a program consisting of a coded command to the computer to perform a specified function.
▸**in'structional** *adj*

instructions Ⓣ (ɪn'strʌkʃənz) *pl n* **1** directions, orders, or recommended rules for guidance, use, etc. **2** *Law.* the facts and details relating to a case given by a client to his solicitor or by a solicitor to a barrister.

instructive Ⓣ (ɪn'strʌktɪv) *adj* serving to instruct or enlighten; conveying information.
▸**in'structively** *adv* ▸**in'structiveness** *n*

instructor Ⓣ (ɪn'strʌktə) *n* **1** someone who instructs; teacher. **2** *US & Canad.* a university teacher ranking below assistant professor.
▸**in'structorship** *n* ▸**instructress** (ɪn'strʌktrɪs) *fem n*

instrument Ⓣ *n* ('ɪnstrəmənt). **1** a mechanical implement or tool, esp. one used for precision work. **2** *Music.* any of various contrivances or mechanisms that can be played to produce musical tones or sounds. **3** an important factor or agency in something: *her evidence was an instrument in his arrest.* **4** *Inf.* a person used by another to gain an end; dupe. **5** a measuring device, such as a pressure gauge. **6a** a device or system for use in navigation or control, esp. of aircraft. **6b** (*as modifier*): *instrument landing.* **7** a formal legal document. ◆ *vb* ('ɪnstrəˌmɛnt). (*tr*) **8** another word for **orchestrate** (sense 1). **9** to equip with instruments. [C13: from L *instrūmentum* tool, from *instruere* to erect, furnish; see INSTRUCT]

instrumental Ⓣ (ˌɪnstrə'mɛntᵊl) *adj* **1** serving as a means or influence; helpful. **2** of, relating to, or characterized by an instrument. **3** played by or composed for musical instruments. **4** *Grammar.* denoting a case of nouns, etc. indicating the instrument used in performing an action, usually using the prepositions *with* or *by means of.* ◆ *n* **5** a piece of music composed for instruments rather than for voices. **6** *Grammar.* the instrumental case.
▸**ˌinstrumen'tality** *n* ▸**ˌinstru'mentally** *adv*

instrumentalist (ˌɪnstrə'mɛntəlɪst) *n* a person who plays a musical instrument.

instrumentation (ˌɪnstrəmɛn'teɪʃən) *n* **1** the instruments specified in a musical score or arrangement. **2** another word for **orchestration. 3** the study of the characteristics of musical instruments. **4** the use of instruments or tools.

instrument panel *or* **board** *n* **1** a panel on which instruments are mounted, as on a car. See also **dashboard. 2** an array of instruments, gauges, etc., mounted to display the condition or performance of a machine.

insubordinate Ⓣ (ˌɪnsə'bɔːdɪnɪt) *adj* **1** not submissive to authority; disobedient or rebellious. **2** not in a subordinate position or rank. ◆ *n* **3** an insubordinate person.
▸**ˌinsub'ordinately** *adv* ▸**ˌinsubˌordi'nation** *n*

insubstantial Ⓣ (ˌɪnsəb'stænʃəl) *adj* **1** not substantial; flimsy, tenuous, or slight. **2** imaginary; unreal.
▸**ˌinsubˌstanti'ality** *n* ▸**ˌinsub'stantially** *adv*

insufferable Ⓣ (ɪn'sʌfərəbᵊl) *adj* intolerable; unendurable.
▸**in'sufferableness** *n* ▸**in'sufferably** *adv*

THESAURUS

instil *vb* **1** = **introduce,** engender, engraft, imbue, implant, impress, inculcate, infix, infuse, insinuate, sow the seeds

instinct *n* **2** = **intuition,** aptitude, faculty, feeling, gift, gut feeling (*inf.*), gut reaction (*inf.*), impulse, knack, natural inclination, predisposition, proclivity, sixth sense, talent, tendency, urge

instinctive *adj* **1** = **inborn,** automatic, inherent, innate, instinctual, intuitional, intuitive, involuntary, mechanical, native, natural, reflex, spontaneous, unlearned, unpremeditated, unthinking, visceral
Antonyms *adj* acquired, calculated, considered, learned, mindful, premeditated, thinking, voluntary, willed

instinctively *adv* **1** = **intuitively,** automatically, by instinct, in one's bones, involuntarily, naturally, without thinking

institute *vb* **1-3** = **establish,** appoint, begin, bring into being, commence, constitute, enact, fix, found, induct, initiate, install, introduce, invest, launch, ordain, organize, originate, pioneer, put into operation, set in motion, settle, set up, start ◆ *n* **4, 5** = **society,** academy, association, college, conservatory, foundation, guild, institution, school, seat of learning, seminary **6** = **custom,** decree, doctrine, dogma, edict, law, maxim, precedent, precept, principle, regulation, rule, tenet
Antonyms *vb* ≠ **establish:** abandon, abolish, cancel, cease, discontinue, end, stop, suspend, terminate

institution *n* **1** = **creation,** constitution, enactment, establishment, formation, foundation, initiation, introduction, investiture, investment, organization **2, 3** = **establishment,** academy, college, foundation, hospital, institute, school, seminary, society, university **4** = **custom,** convention, fixture, law, practice, ritual, rule, tradition

institutional *adj* **2** = **routine,** cheerless, clinical, cold, drab, dreary, dull, forbidding, formal, impersonal, monotonous, regimented, uniform, unwelcoming **3** = **conventional,** accepted, bureaucratic, established, establishment (*inf.*), formal, organized, orthodox, societal

instruct *vb* **1** = **order,** bid, canon, charge, command, direct, enjoin, tell **2** = **teach,** coach, discipline, drill, educate, enlighten, ground, guide, inform, school, train, tutor **3** = **brief,** acquaint, advise, apprise, counsel, inform, notify, tell

instruction *n* **1** = **order,** briefing, command, demand, direction, directive, injunction, mandate, ruling **2** = **teaching,** apprenticeship, coaching, discipline, drilling, education, enlightenment, grounding, guidance, information, lesson(s), preparation, schooling, training, tuition, tutelage

instructions *pl n* **1** = **orders,** advice, directions, guidance, information, key, recommendations, rules

instructive *adj* = **informative,** cautionary, didactic, edifying, educational, enlightening, helpful, illuminating, instructional, revealing, useful

instructor *n* **1** = **teacher,** adviser, coach, demonstrator, exponent, guide, guru, handler, master *or* mistress, mentor, pedagogue, preceptor (*rare*), schoolmaster *or* schoolmistress, trainer, tutor

instrument *n* **1** = **tool,** apparatus, appliance, contraption (*inf.*), contrivance, device, gadget, implement, mechanism, utensil, waldo **3** = **means,** agency, agent, channel, factor, force, mechanism, medium, organ, vehicle **4** *Informal* = **puppet,** cat's-paw, dupe, pawn, tool

instrumental *adj* **1** = **active,** assisting, auxiliary, conducive, contributory, helpful, helping, influential, involved, of help *or* service, subsidiary, useful

insubordinate *adj* **1** = **disobedient,** contumacious, defiant, disorderly, fractious, insurgent, mutinous, rebellious, recalcitrant, refractory, riotous, seditious, turbulent, undisciplined, ungovernable, unruly
Antonyms *adj* compliant, deferential, disciplined, docile, obedient, orderly, submissive, subservient

insubordination *n* **1** = **disobedience,** defiance, indiscipline, insurrection, mutinousness, mutiny, rebellion, recalcitrance, revolt, riotousness, sedition, ungovernability
Antonyms *n* acquiescence, compliance, deference, discipline, docility, obedience, submission, subordination

insubstantial *adj* **1** = **flimsy,** feeble, frail, poor, slight, tenuous, thin, weak **2** = **imaginary,** chimerical, ephemeral, false, fanciful, idle, illusory, immaterial, incorporeal, unreal
Antonyms *adj* ≠ **flimsy:** firm, solid, strong, substantial, weighty

insufferable *adj* = **unbearable,** detestable, dreadful, impossible, insupportable, intolerable, more than flesh and blood can stand, outrageous, past bearing, too much, unendurable, unspeakable

insufficiency ➊ (ˌɪnsəˈfɪʃənsɪ) *n* **1** Also: **ˌinsufˈficience.** the state of being insufficient. **2** *Pathol.* failure in the functioning of an organ, tissue, etc.: *cardiac insufficiency.*

insufficient ➊ (ˌɪnsəˈfɪʃənt) *adj* not sufficient; inadequate or deficient.
▸**ˌinsufˈficiently** *adv*

insufflate (ˈɪnsʌˌfleɪt) *vb* **insufflates, insufflating, insufflated. 1** (*tr*) to breathe or blow (something) into (a room, area, etc.). **2** *Med.* to blow (air, medicated powder, etc.) into a body cavity. **3** (*tr*) to breathe or blow upon (someone or something) as a ritual or sacramental act.
▸**ˌinsufˈflation** *n* ▸**ˈinsufˌflator** *n*

insular ➊ (ˈɪnsjʊlə) *adj* **1** of, relating to, or resembling an island. **2** remote, detached, or aloof. **3** illiberal or narrow-minded. **4** isolated or separated. [C17: from LL, from L *insula* island]
▸**ˈinsularism** *or* **insularity** (ˌɪnsjʊˈlærɪtɪ) *n* ▸**ˈinsularly** *adv*

insulate ➊ (ˈɪnsjʊˌleɪt) *vb* **insulates, insulating, insulated.** (*tr*) **1** to prevent the transmission of electricity, heat, or sound to or from (a body or device) by surrounding with a nonconducting material. **2** to isolate or detach. [C16: from LL *insulātus* made into an island]

insulation (ˌɪnsjʊˈleɪʃən) *n* **1** Also: **insulant.** material used to insulate a body or device. **2** the act or process of insulating.

insulator (ˈɪnsjʊˌleɪtə) *n* any material or device that insulates, esp. a material with a very low electrical conductivity or thermal conductivity.

insulin (ˈɪnsjʊlɪn) *n* a protein hormone, secreted in the pancreas by the islets of Langerhans, that controls the concentration of glucose in the blood. [C20: from NL *insula* islet (of the pancreas) + -IN]

insult ➊ *vb* (ɪnˈsʌlt). (*tr*) **1** to treat, mention, or speak to rudely; offend; affront. ◆ *n* (ˈɪnsʌlt). **2** an offensive or contemptuous remark or action; affront; slight. **3** a person or thing producing the effect of an affront: *some television is an insult to intelligence.* **4** *Med.* an injury or trauma. [C16: from L *insultāre* to jump upon]
▸**inˈsulter** *n*

insuperable ➊ (ɪnˈsuːpərəbᵊl, -prəbᵊl, -ˈsjuː-) *adj* incapable of being overcome; insurmountable.
▸**inˌsuperaˈbility** *n* ▸**inˈsuperably** *adv*

insupportable ➊ (ˌɪnsəˈpɔːtəbᵊl) *adj* **1** incapable of being endured; intolerable; insufferable. **2** incapable of being supported or justified; indefensible.
▸**ˌinsupˈportableness** *n* ▸**ˌinsupˈportably** *adv*

insurance ➊ (ɪnˈʃʊərəns, -ˈʃɔː-) *n* **1a** the act, system, or business of providing financial protection against specified contingencies, such as death, loss, or damage. **1b** the state of having such protection. **1c** Also called: **insurance policy.** the policy providing such protection. **1d** the pecuniary amount of such protection. **1e** the premium payable in return for such protection. **f.** (*as modifier*): *insurance agent; insurance broker; insurance company.* **2** a means of protecting or safeguarding against risk or injury.

insure ➊ (ɪnˈʃʊə, -ˈʃɔː) *vb* **insures, insuring, insured. 1** (often foll. by *against*) to guarantee or protect (against risk, loss, etc.). **2** (often foll. by *against*) to issue (a person) with an insurance policy or take out an insurance policy (on): *his house was heavily insured against fire.* **3** a variant spelling (esp. US) of **ensure.** ◆ Also (rare) (for senses 1, 2): **ensure.**
▸**inˈsurable** *adj* ▸**inˌsuraˈbility** *n*

insured (ɪnˈʃʊəd, -ˈʃɔːd) *adj* **1** covered by insurance: *an insured risk.* ◆ *n* **2** the person, persons, or organization covered by an insurance policy.

insurer (ɪnˈʃʊərə, -ˈʃɔː-) *n* **1** a person or company offering insurance policies in return for premiums. **2** a person or thing that insures.

insurgence (ɪnˈsɜːdʒəns) *n* rebellion, uprising, or riot.

insurgent ➊ (ɪnˈsɜːdʒənt) *adj* **1** rebellious or in revolt, as against a government in power or the civil authorities. ◆ *n* **2** a person who takes part in an uprising or rebellion; insurrectionist. [C18: from L *insurgēns* rising upon or against, from *surgere* to rise]
▸**inˈsurgency** *n*

insurmountable ➊ (ˌɪnsəˈmaʊntəbᵊl) *adj* incapable of being overcome; insuperable.
▸**ˌinsurˌmountaˈbility** *or* **ˌinsurˈmountableness** *n* ▸**ˌinsurˈmountably** *adv*

insurrection ➊ (ˌɪnsəˈrɛkʃən) *n* the act or an instance of rebelling against a government in power or the civil authorities; insurgency. [C15: from LL *insurrectiō*, from *insurgere* to rise up]
▸**ˌinsurˈrectional** *adj* ▸**ˌinsurˈrectionary** *n, adj* ▸**ˌinsurˈrectionist** *n, adj*

int. *abbrev. for:* **1** interest. **2** interior. **3** internal. **4** Also: **Int.** international.

intact ➊ (ɪnˈtækt) *adj* untouched or unimpaired; left complete or perfect. [C15: from L *intactus* not touched, from *tangere* to touch]
▸**inˈtactness** *n*

intaglio (ɪnˈtɑːlɪˌəʊ) *n, pl* **intaglios** *or* **intagli** (-ljiː). **1** a seal, gem, etc., ornamented with a sunken or incised design. **2** the art or process of incised carving. **3** a design, figure, or ornamentation carved, engraved, or etched into the surface of the material used. **4** any of various printing techniques using an etched or engraved plate. **5** an incised die used to make a design in relief. [C17: from It., from *intagliare* to engrave, from *tagliare* to cut, from LL *tāliāre;* see TAILOR]
▸**intagliated** (ɪnˈtɑːlɪˌeɪtɪd) *adj*

intake (ˈɪnˌteɪk) *n* **1** a thing or a quantity taken in: *an intake of students.* **2** the act of taking in. **3** the opening through which fluid enters a duct or channel, esp. the air inlet of a jet engine. **4** a ventilation shaft in a mine. **5** a contraction or narrowing: *an intake in a garment.*

intangible ➊ (ɪnˈtændʒɪbᵊl) *adj* **1** incapable of being perceived by touch; impalpable. **2** imprecise or unclear to the mind: *intangible ideas.* **3** (of property or a business asset) saleable though not possessing intrinsic productive value. ◆ *n* **4** something that is intangible.
▸**inˌtangiˈbility** *n* ▸**inˈtangibly** *adv*

intarsia (ɪnˈtɑːsɪə) *or* **tarsia** *n* **1** a decorative mosaic of inlaid wood of a style developed in the Italian Renaissance. **2** (in knitting) **2a** an individually worked motif. **2b** the method of knitting blocks of colour in place to create such a pattern. [C19: changed from It. *intarsio*]

integer (ˈɪntɪdʒə) *n* **1** any rational number that can be expressed as the sum or difference of a finite number of units, as 1, 2, 3, etc. **2** an individual entity or whole unit. [C16: from L: untouched, from *tangere* to touch]

integral ➊ (ˈɪntɪgrəl, ɪnˈtɛgrəl) *adj* **1** (often foll. by *to*) being an essential part (of); intrinsic (to). **2** intact; entire. **3** formed of constituent parts; united. **4** *Maths.* **4a** of or involving an integral. **4b** involving or being an integer. ◆ *n* **5** *Maths.* the sum of a large number of infinitesimally small quantities, summed either between stated limits (**definite integral**) or in the absence of limits (**indefinite integral**). **6** a complete thing; whole.
▸**integrality** (ˌɪntɪˈgrælɪtɪ) *n* ▸**ˈintegrally** *adv*

integral calculus *n* the branch of calculus concerned with the determination of integrals (**integration**) and their application to the solution of differential equations.

integrand (ˈɪntɪˌgrænd) *n* a mathematical function to be integrated. [C19: from L: to be integrated]

integrant (ˈɪntəgrənt) *adj* **1** part of a whole; integral; constituent. ◆ *n* **2** an integrant part.

integrate ➊ *vb* (ˈɪntɪˌgreɪt), **integrates, integrating, integrated. 1** to make or be made into a whole; incorporate or be incorporated. **2** (*tr*) to designate (a school, park, etc.) for use by all races or groups; desegregate. **3** to amalgamate or mix (a racial or religious group) with an existing community. **4** *Maths.* to determine the integral of a function or variable. ◆ *adj* (ˈɪntɪgrɪt). **5** made up of parts; integrated. [C17: from L *integrāre;* see INTEGER]
▸**integrable** (ˈɪntəgrəbᵊl) *adj* ▸**ˌintegraˈbility** *n* ▸**ˌinteˈgration** *n* ▸**ˈinteˌgrative** *adj*

THESAURUS

Antonyms *adj* appealing, attractive, bearable, charming, disarming, pleasant

insufficiency *n* **1** = **shortage**, dearth, deficiency, inadequacy, inadequateness, lack, paucity, poverty, scantiness, scarcity, short supply, want

insufficient *adj* = **inadequate**, deficient, incapable, incommensurate, incompetent, lacking, scant, short, unfitted, unqualified
Antonyms *adj* adequate, ample, commensurate, competent, enough, plentiful, qualified, sufficient

insular *adj* **3** = **narrow-minded**, blinkered, circumscribed, closed, contracted, cut off, illiberal, inward-looking, isolated, limited, narrow, parish-pump, parochial, petty, prejudiced, provincial
Antonyms *adj* broad-minded, cosmopolitan, experienced, liberal, open-minded, tolerant, worldly

insulate *vb* **2** = **isolate**, close off, cocoon, cushion, cut off, protect, sequester, shield, wrap up in cotton wool

insult *vb* **1** = **offend**, abuse, affront, call names, give offence to, injure, miscall (*dialect*), outrage, put down, revile, slag (off) (*sl.*), slander, slight, snub ◆ *n* **2** = **abuse**, affront, aspersion, contumely, indignity, insolence, offence, outrage, put-down, rudeness, slap in the face (*inf.*), slight, snub
Antonyms *vb* ≠ **offend:** flatter, please, praise ◆ *n* ≠ **abuse:** compliment, flattery, honour

insulting *adj* **1** = **offensive**, abusive, affronting, contemptuous, degrading, disparaging, insolent, rude, scurrilous, slighting
Antonyms *adj* complimentary, deferential, flattering, laudatory, respectful

insuperable *adj* = **insurmountable**, impassable, invincible, unconquerable
Antonyms *adj* conquerable, possible, surmountable

insupportable *adj* **1** = **intolerable**, insufferable, past bearing, unbearable, unendurable **2** = **unjustifiable**, indefensible, untenable

insurance *n* **2** = **protection**, assurance, cover, coverage, guarantee, indemnification, indemnity, provision, safeguard, security, something to fall back on (*inf.*), warranty

insure *vb* **1** = **protect**, assure, cover, guarantee, indemnify, underwrite, warrant

insurgent *adj* **1** = **rebellious**, disobedient, insubordinate, insurrectionary, mutinous, revolting, revolutionary, riotous, seditious ◆ *n* **2** = **rebel**, insurrectionist, mutineer, resister, revolter, revolutionary, revolutionist, rioter

insurmountable *adj* = **insuperable**, hopeless, impassable, impossible, invincible, overwhelming, unconquerable

insurrection *n* = **rebellion**, coup, insurgency, mutiny, putsch, revolt, revolution, riot, rising, sedition, uprising

intact *adj* = **undamaged**, all in one piece, complete, entire, perfect, scatheless, sound, together, unbroken, undefiled, unharmed, unhurt, unimpaired, uninjured, unscathed, untouched, unviolated, virgin, whole
Antonyms *adj* broken, damaged, harmed, impaired, injured

intangible *adj* **1, 2** = **elusive**, airy, dim, ethereal, evanescent, impalpable, imperceptible, incorporeal, indefinite, invisible, shadowy, unreal, unsubstantial, vague

integral *adj* **1** = **essential**, basic, component, constituent, elemental, fundamental, indispensable, intrinsic, necessary, requisite **2** = **whole**, complete, entire, full, intact, undivided
Antonyms *adj* ≠ **essential:** inessential, unimportant, unnecessary ≠ **whole:** fractional

integrate *vb* **1** = **join**, accommodate, amalgamate, assimilate, blend, coalesce, combine,

DICTIONARY

integrated circuit *n* a very small electronic circuit consisting of an assembly of elements made from a chip of semiconducting material.

integrity ❶ (ɪnˈtɛgrɪtɪ) *n* **1** adherence to moral principles; honesty. **2** the quality of being unimpaired; soundness. **3** unity; wholeness. [C15: from L *integritās*; see INTEGER]

integument (ɪnˈtɛgjʊmənt) *n* any outer protective layer or covering, such as a cuticle, seed coat, rind, or shell. [C17: from L *integumentum*, from *tegere* to cover]
▸**inˌteguˈmental** *or* **inˌteguˈmentary** *adj*

intellect ❶ (ˈɪntɪˌlɛkt) *n* **1** the capacity for understanding, thinking, and reasoning. **2** a mind or intelligence, esp. a brilliant one: *his intellect is wasted on that job.* **3** *Inf.* a person possessing a brilliant mind; brain. [C14: from L *intellectus* comprehension, from *intellegere* to understand; see INTELLIGENCE]
▸**ˌintelˈlective** *adj* ▸**ˌintelˈlectively** *adv*

intellection (ˌɪntɪˈlɛkʃən) *n* **1** mental activity; thought. **2** an idea or thought.

intellectual ❶ (ˌɪntɪˈlɛktʃʊəl) *adj* **1** of or relating to the intellect. **2** appealing to or characteristic of people with a developed intellect: *intellectual literature.* **3** expressing or enjoying mental activity. ◆ *n* **4** a person who enjoys mental activity and has highly developed tastes in art, etc. **5** a person who uses his intellect. **6** a highly intelligent person.
▸**ˌintelˌlectuˈality** *or* **ˌintelˈlectualness** *n* ▸**ˌintelˈlectualˌize** *or* **ˌintelˈlectualˌise** *vb* ▸**ˌintelˈlectually** *adv*

intellectualism (ˌɪntɪˈlɛktʃʊəˌlɪzəm) *n* **1** development and exercise of the intellect. **2** *Philosophy.* the doctrine that reason is the ultimate criterion of knowledge.
▸**ˌintelˈlectualist** *n, adj* ▸**ˌintelˌlectualˈistic** *adj*

intellectual property *n* an intangible asset, such as a copyright or patent.

intelligence ❶ (ɪnˈtɛlɪdʒəns) *n* **1** the capacity for understanding; ability to perceive and comprehend meaning. **2** *Old-fashioned.* news; information. **3** military information about enemies, spies, etc. **4** a group or department that gathers or deals with such information. **5** (*often cap.*) an intelligent being, esp. one that is not embodied. **6** (*modifier*) of or relating to intelligence: *an intelligence network.* [C14: from L *intellegentia*, from *intellegere* to discern, lit.: to choose between, from INTER- + *legere* to choose]
▸**inˌtelliˈgential** *adj*

intelligence quotient *n* a measure of the intelligence of an individual. The quotient is derived by dividing an individual's mental age by his chronological age and multiplying the result by 100. Abbrev.: **IQ.**

intelligence test *n* any of a number of tests designed to measure a person's mental skills.

intelligent ❶ (ɪnˈtɛlɪdʒənt) *adj* **1** having or indicating intelligence; clever. **2** indicating high intelligence; perceptive: *an intelligent guess.* **3** (of computerized functions, weapons, etc.) able to initiate or modify action in the light of ongoing events. **4** (*postpositive;* foll. by *of*) *Arch.* having knowledge or information.
▸**inˈtelligently** *adv*

intelligent card *n* another name for **smart card.**

intelligentsia ❶ (ɪnˌtɛlɪˈdʒɛntsɪə) *n* (usually preceded by *the*) the educated or intellectual people in a society or community. [C20: from Russian *intelligentsiya*, from L *intellegentia* INTELLIGENCE]

intelligible ❶ (ɪnˈtɛlɪdʒəbᵊl) *adj* **1** able to be understood; comprehensible. **2** *Philosophy.* capable of being apprehended by the mind or intellect alone. [C14: from L *intellegibilis*; see INTELLECT]
▸**inˌtelligiˈbility** *n* ▸**inˈtelligibly** *adv*

intemperate ❶ (ɪnˈtɛmpərɪt, -prɪt) *adj* **1** consuming alcoholic drink habitually or to excess; immoderate. **2** unrestrained: *intemperate rage.* **3** extreme or severe: *an intemperate climate.*
▸**inˈtemperance** *or* **inˈtemperateness** *n* ▸**inˈtemperately** *adv*

intend ❶ (ɪnˈtɛnd) *vb* **1** (*may take a clause as object*) to propose or plan (something or to do something); have in mind; mean. **2** (*tr;* often foll. by *for*) to design or destine (for a certain purpose, person, etc.). **3** (*tr*) to mean to express or indicate: *what do his words intend?* **4** (*intr*) to have a purpose as specified; mean: *he intends well.* [C14: from L *intendere* to stretch forth, give one's attention to, from *tendere* to stretch]
▸**inˈtender** *n*

intendancy (ɪnˈtɛndənsɪ) *n* **1** the position or work of an intendant. **2** intendants collectively.

intendant (ɪnˈtɛndənt) *n* a senior administrator; superintendent or manager.

intended ❶ (ɪnˈtɛndɪd) *adj* **1** planned or future. ◆ *n* **2** *Inf.* a person whom one is to marry; fiancé or fiancée.

intense ❶ (ɪnˈtɛns) *adj* **1** of extreme force, strength, degree, or amount: *intense heat.* **2** characterized by deep or forceful feelings: *an intense person.* [C14: from L *intensus* stretched, from *intendere* to stretch out]
▸**inˈtensely** *adv* ▸**inˈtenseness** *n*

> **USAGE NOTE** *Intense* is sometimes wrongly used where *intensive* is meant: *the land is under intensive* (not *intense*) *cultivation. Intensely* is sometimes wrongly used where *intently* is meant: *he listened intently* (not *intensely*).

intensifier (ɪnˈtɛnsɪˌfaɪə) *n* **1** a person or thing that intensifies. **2** a word, esp. an adjective or adverb, that serves to intensify the meaning of the word or phrase that it modifies. **3** a substance, esp. one containing silver or uranium, used to increase the density of a photographic film or plate.

intensify ❶ (ɪnˈtɛnsɪˌfaɪ) *vb* **intensifies, intensifying, intensified. 1** to make or become intense or more intense. **2** (*tr*) to increase the density of (a photographic film or plate).
▸**inˌtensifiˈcation** *n*

intension (ɪnˈtɛnʃən) *n Logic.* the set of characteristics or properties that distinguish the referent or referents of a given word.
▸**inˈtensional** *adj*

intensity ❶ (ɪnˈtɛnsɪtɪ) *n, pl* **intensities. 1** the state or quality of being intense. **2** extreme force, degree, or amount. **3** *Physics.* **3a** a measure of field strength or of the energy transmitted by radiation. **3b** (of sound in a specified direction) the average rate of flow of sound energy for

THESAURUS

fuse, harmonize, incorporate, intermix, knit, meld, merge, mesh, unite
Antonyms *vb* disperse, divide, segregate, separate

integration *n* **1** = **assimilation**, amalgamation, blending, combining, commingling, fusing, harmony, incorporation, mixing, unification

integrity *n* **1** = **honesty**, candour, goodness, honour, incorruptibility, principle, probity, purity, rectitude, righteousness, uprightness, virtue **2, 3** = **soundness**, coherence, cohesion, completeness, unity, wholeness
Antonyms *n* ≠ **honesty:** corruption, deceit, dishonesty, disrepute, duplicity, immorality ≠ **soundness:** faultiness, flimsiness, fragility, uncertainty, unsoundness

intellect *n* **1** = **intelligence**, brains (*inf.*), judgment, mind, reason, sense, understanding **3** *Informal* = **thinker**, brain (*inf.*), egghead, genius, intellectual, intelligence, mind

intellectual *adj* **3** = **scholarly**, bookish, cerebral, highbrow, intelligent, mental, rational, studious, thoughtful ◆ *n* **4** = **academic**, bluestocking (*usually disparaging*), egghead (*inf.*), highbrow, thinker
Antonyms *adj* ≠ **scholarly:** ignorant, illiterate, material, physical, stupid, unintellectual, unlearned ◆ *n* ≠ **academic:** idiot, moron

intelligence *n* **1** = **understanding**, acumen, alertness, aptitude, brain power, brains (*inf.*), brightness, capacity, cleverness, comprehension, discernment, grey matter (*inf.*), intellect, mind, nous (*Brit. sl.*), penetration, perception, quickness, reason, sense, smarts (*sl., chiefly US*) **2** = **information**, advice, data, disclosure, facts, findings, gen (*Brit. inf.*), knowledge, low-down (*inf.*), news, notice, notification, report, rumour, tidings, tip-off, word
Antonyms *n* ≠ **understanding:** dullness, ignorance, stupidity ≠ **information:** concealment, misinformation

intelligent *adj* **1** = **clever**, acute, alert, apt, brainy (*inf.*), bright, discerning, enlightened, instructed, knowing, penetrating, perspicacious, quick, quick-witted, rational, sharp, smart, thinking, well-informed
Antonyms *adj* dim-witted, dull, foolish, ignorant, obtuse, stupid, unintelligent

intelligentsia *n* = **intellectuals**, eggheads (*inf.*), highbrows, illuminati, literati, masterminds, the learned

intelligibility *n* **1** = **clarity**, clearness, comprehensibility, distinctness, explicitness, lucidity, plainness, precision, simplicity

intelligible *adj* **1** = **understandable**, clear, comprehensible, distinct, lucid, open, plain
Antonyms *adj* confused, garbled, incomprehensible, puzzling, unclear, unintelligible

intemperance *n* **1** = **overindulgence**, crapulence, excess, extravagance, immoderation, inebriation, insobriety, intoxication, unrestraint

intemperate *adj* **1** = **excessive**, immoderate, incontinent, intoxicated, prodigal, profligate, self-indulgent **2** = **excessive**, extravagant, inordinate, over the top (*sl.*), passionate, unbridled, uncontrollable, ungovernable, unrestrained, violent **3** = **excessive**, extreme, severe, tempestuous, wild
Antonyms *adj* ≠ **excessive:** continent, disciplined, moderate, restrained, self-controlled, temperate

intend *vb* **1** = **plan**, aim, be resolved *or* determined, contemplate, determine, have in mind *or* view, mean, meditate, propose, purpose, scheme **2** *often with* **for** = **destine**, aim, consign, design, earmark, mark out, mean, set apart

intended *adj* **1** = **planned**, betrothed, destined, future, proposed ◆ *n* **2** *Informal* = **betrothed**, fiancé, fiancée, future wife *or* husband, husband- *or* wife-to-be

intense *adj* **1** = **extreme**, acute, agonizing, close, concentrated, deep, drastic, excessive, exquisite, fierce, forceful, great, harsh, intensive, powerful, profound, protracted, severe, strained, unqualified **2** = **passionate**, ardent, burning, consuming, eager, earnest, energetic, fanatical, fervent, fervid, fierce, flaming, forcible, heightened, impassioned, keen, speaking, vehement
Antonyms *adj* ≠ **extreme:** easy, gentle, mild, moderate, relaxed, slight ≠ **passionate:** casual, cool, indifferent, subdued, weak

intensely *adv* **1** = **strongly**, deeply, extremely, fiercely, passionately, profoundly, seriously (*inf.*)

intensify *vb* **1** = **increase**, add fuel to the flames (*inf.*), add to, aggravate, augment, boost, concentrate, deepen, emphasize, enhance, escalate, exacerbate, fan the flames of, heighten, magnify, quicken, redouble, reinforce, set off, sharpen, step up (*inf.*), strengthen, whet
Antonyms *vb* damp down, decrease, dilute, diminish, dull, lessen, minimize, weaken

intensity *n* **1** = **force**, ardour, concentration, depth, earnestness, emotion, energy, excess, extremity, fanaticism, fervency, fervour, fierceness, fire, intenseness, keenness, passion, potency, power, severity, strain, strength, tension, vehemence, vigour one period through unit area at right angles to the specified direction.

intensive ❶ (ɪn'tɛnsɪv) *adj* **1** of, relating to, or characterized by intensity: *intensive training.* **2** (*usually in combination*) using one factor of production proportionately more than others, as specified: *capital-intensive; labour-intensive.* **3** *Agriculture.* involving or farmed using large amounts of capital or labour to increase production from a particular area. Cf. **extensive** (sense 3). **4** denoting or relating to a grammatical intensifier. **5** denoting or belonging to a class of pronouns used to emphasize a noun or personal pronoun. **6** of or relating to intension. ◆ *n* **7** an intensifier or intensive pronoun or grammatical construction.
▸**in'tensively** *adv* ▸**in'tensiveness** *n*

intensive care *n* **1** extensive and continuous care provided for an acutely ill patient in a hospital. **2** the unit in which this care is provided; intensive-care unit.

intent ❶ (ɪn'tɛnt) *n* **1** something that is intended; aim; purpose; design. **2** the act of intending. **3** *Law.* the will or purpose with which one does an act. **4** implicit meaning; connotation. **5 to all intents and purposes.** for all practical purposes; virtually. ◆ *adj* **6** firmly fixed; determined; concentrated: *an intent look.* **7** (*postpositive;* usually foll. by *on* or *upon*) having the fixed intention (of); directing one's mind or energy (to): *intent on committing a crime.* [C13 (in the sense: intention): from LL *intentus* aim, from L: a stretching out; see INTEND]
▸**in'tently** *adv* ▸**in'tentness** *n*

intention ❶ (ɪn'tɛnʃən) *n* **1** a purpose or goal; aim: *it is his intention to reform.* **2** *Med.* a natural healing process in which the edges of a wound cling together with no tissue between (**first intention**), or in which the edges adhere with tissue between (**second intention**). **3** (*usually pl*) design or purpose with respect to a proposal of marriage (esp. in **honourable intentions**).

intentional ❶ (ɪn'tɛnʃən°l) *adj* **1** performed by or expressing intention; deliberate. **2** of or relating to intention or purpose.
▸**in,tention'ality** *n* ▸**in'tentionally** *adv*

inter ❶ (ɪn'tɜː) *vb* **inters, interring, interred.** (*tr*) to place (a body, etc.) in the earth; bury, esp. with funeral rites. [C14: from OF *enterrer,* from L IN-[2] + *terra* earth]

inter- *prefix* **1** between or among: *international.* **2** together, mutually, or reciprocally: *interdependent; interchange.* [from L]

interact (,ɪntər'ækt) *vb* (*intr*) to act on or in close relation with each other.

interaction (,ɪntə'ækʃən) *n* **1** a mutual or reciprocal action. **2** *Physics.* the transfer of energy between elementary particles, between a particle and a field, or between fields. See **fundamental interaction.**

interactive (,ɪntər'æktɪv) *adj* **1** allowing or relating to continuous two-way transfer of information between a user and the central point of a communication system, such as a computer or television. **2** (of two or more persons, forces, etc.) acting upon or in close relation with each other; interacting.

inter alia *Latin.* ('ɪntər 'eɪlɪə) *adv* among other things.

interbreed (,ɪntə'briːd) *vb* **interbreeds, interbreeding, interbred. 1** to breed within a single family or strain so as to produce particular characteristics in the offspring. **2** another term for **crossbreed** (sense 1).

interbroker dealer (,ɪntə'brəʊkə) *n Stock Exchange.* a specialist who matches the needs of different market makers and facilitates dealings between them.

intercalary (ɪn'tɜːkələrɪ) *adj* **1** (of a day, month, year, etc.) inserted in the calendar. **2** (of a particular year) having one or more days inserted. **3** inserted, introduced, or interpolated. [C17: from L *intercalārius;* see INTERCALATE]

intercalate (ɪn'tɜːkə,leɪt) *vb* **intercalates, intercalating, intercalated.** (*tr*) **1** to insert (one or more days) into the calendar. **2** to interpolate or insert. [C17: from L *intercalāre* to insert, proclaim that a day has been inserted, from INTER- + *calāre* to proclaim]
▸**in,terca'lation** *n* ▸**in'tercalative** *adj*

intercede ❶ (,ɪntə'siːd) *vb* **intercedes, interceding, interceded.** (*intr;* often foll. by *in*) to come between parties or act as mediator or advocate: *to intercede in the strike.* [C16: from L *intercēdere,* from INTER- + *cēdere* to move]
▸**,inter'ceder** *n*

intercensal (,ɪntə'sɛnsəl) *adj* (of population figures, etc.) estimated at a time between official censuses. [C19: from INTER- + *censal,* irregularly formed from CENSUS]

intercept ❶ *vb* (,ɪntə'sɛpt). (*tr*) **1** to stop, deflect, or seize on the way from one place to another; prevent from arriving or proceeding. **2** *Sport.* to seize or cut off (a pass) on its way from one opponent to another. **3** *Maths.* to cut off, mark off, or bound (some part of a line, curve, plane, or surface). ◆ *n* ('ɪntə,sɛpt). **4** *Maths.* **4a** a point at which two figures intersect. **4b** the distance from the origin to the point at which a line, curve, or surface cuts a coordinate axis. **5** *Sport, US & Canad.* the act of intercepting an opponent's pass. [C16: from L *intercipere* to seize before arrival, from INTER- + *capere* to take]
▸**,inter'ception** *n* ▸**,inter'ceptive** *adj*

interceptor *or* **intercepter** (,ɪntə'sɛptə) *n* **1** a person or thing that intercepts. **2** a fast highly manoeuvrable fighter aircraft used to intercept enemy aircraft.

intercession ❶ (,ɪntə'sɛʃən) *n* **1** the act or an instance of interceding. **2** the act of interceding or offering petitionary prayer to God on behalf of others. **3** such petitionary prayer. [C16: from L *intercessio;* see INTERCEDE]
▸**,inter'cessional** *or* **,inter'cessory** *adj* ▸**,inter'cessor** *n* ▸**,intercess'sorial** *adj*

interchange ❶ *vb* (,ɪntə'tʃeɪndʒ), **interchanges, interchanging, interchanged. 1** to change places or cause to change places; alternate; exchange; switch. ◆ *n* ('ɪntə,tʃeɪndʒ). **2** the act of interchanging; exchange or alternation. **3** a motorway junction of interconnecting roads and bridges designed to prevent streams of traffic crossing one another.
▸**,inter'changeable** *adj* ▸**,inter,changea'bility** *or* **,inter'changeableness** *n* ▸**,inter'changeably** *adv*

Intercity (,ɪntə'sɪtɪ) *adj* (in Britain) *Trademark.* denoting a fast train or passenger rail service, esp. between main towns.

intercom ('ɪntə,kɒm) *n Inf.* an internal telephone system for communicating within a building, aircraft, etc. [C20: short for INTERCOMMUNICATION]

intercommunicate (,ɪntəkə'mjuːnɪ,keɪt) *vb* **intercommunicates, intercommunicating, intercommunicated.** (*intr*) **1** to communicate mutually. **2** to interconnect, as two rooms, etc.
▸**,intercom'municable** *adj* ▸**,intercom,muni'cation** *n* ▸**,intercom'municative** *adj*

intercommunion (,ɪntəkə'mjuːnjən) *n* association between Churches, involving esp. mutual reception of Holy Communion.

intercontinental (,ɪntə,kɒntɪ'nɛnt°l) *adj* travelling between or linking continents.

interconvertible (,ɪntəkən'vɜːtɪb°l) *adj* (of two or more things) capable of being converted into each other.

intercostal (,ɪntə'kɒst°l) *adj Anat.* between the ribs: *intercostal muscles.* [C16: via NL from L INTER- + *costa* rib]

intercourse ❶ ('ɪntə,kɔːs) *n* **1** See **sexual intercourse. 2** communication or exchange between individuals; mutual dealings. [C15: from Med. L *intercursus* business, from L *intercurrere* to run between]

intercurrent (,ɪntə'kʌrənt) *adj* **1** occurring during or in between; intervening. **2** *Pathol.* (of a disease) occurring during the course of another disease.
▸**,inter'currence** *n*

interdependent (,ɪntədɪ'pɛndənt) *adj* (of two or more things) dependent on each other.

interdict ❶ *n* ('ɪntə,dɪkt). **1** *RC Church.* the exclusion of a person in a particular place from certain sacraments, although not from communion. **2** *Civil law.* any order made by a court or official prohibiting an act. **3** *Scots Law.* an order having the effect of an injunction. ◆ *vb* (,ɪntə'dɪkt). (*tr*) **4** to place under legal or ecclesiastical sanction; prohibit; forbid. **5** *Mil.* to destroy (an enemy's lines of communication) by firepower. [C13: from L *interdictum* prohibition, from *interdīcere* to forbid, from INTER- + *dīcere* to say]
▸**,inter'diction** *n* ▸**,inter'dictive** *or* **,inter'dictory** *adj* ▸**,inter'dictively** *adv* ▸**,inter'dictor** *n*

THESAURUS

intensive *adj* **1** = **concentrated,** all-out, comprehensive, demanding, exhaustive, in-depth, thorough, thoroughgoing

intent *n* **1** = **intention,** aim, design, end, goal, meaning, object, objective, plan, purpose **5 to all intents and purposes** = **virtually,** as good as, practically ◆ *adj* **6** = **intense,** absorbed, alert, attentive, committed, concentrated, earnest, engrossed, fixed, industrious, occupied, piercing, preoccupied, rapt, steadfast, steady, watchful, wrapped up **7** = **resolved,** bent, determined, eager, hellbent (*inf.*), resolute, set
Antonyms *n* ≠ **intention:** chance, fortune ◆ *adj* ≠ **intense:** casual, indifferent ≠ **resolved:** irresolute, unsteady, wavering

intention *n* **1** = **purpose,** aim, design, end, end in view, goal, idea, intent, meaning, object, objective, point, scope, target, view

intentional *adj* **1** = **deliberate,** calculated, designed, done on purpose, intended, meant, planned, prearranged, preconcerted, premeditated, purposed, studied, wilful
Antonyms *adj* accidental, inadvertent, unintentional, unplanned

intentionally *adv* **1** = **deliberately,** by design, designedly, on purpose, wilfully

intently *adv* **6** = **attentively,** closely, fixedly, hard, keenly, searchingly, steadily, watchfully

inter *vb* = **bury,** entomb, inhume, inurn, lay to rest, sepulchre

intercede *vb* = **mediate,** advocate, arbitrate, interpose, intervene, plead, speak

intercept *vb* **1** = **seize,** arrest, block, catch, check, cut off, deflect, head off, interrupt, obstruct, stop, take

intercession *n* **1** = **pleading,** advocacy, entreaty, good offices, intervention, mediation, plea, prayer, solicitation, supplication

intercessor *n* **1** = **mediator,** advocate, arbitrator, go-between, interceder, intermediary, middleman, negotiator, pleader

interchange *vb* **1** = **switch,** alternate, bandy, barter, exchange, reciprocate, swap, trade ◆ *n* **2** = **junction,** alternation, crossfire, exchange, give and take, intersection, reciprocation

interchangeable *adj* **1** = **identical,** commutable, equivalent, exchangeable, reciprocal, synonymous, the same, transposable

intercourse *n* **1** = **sexual intercourse,** carnal knowledge, coition, coitus, congress, copulation, intimacy, sex (*inf.*), sexual relations **2** = **communication,** association, commerce, communion, connection, contact, converse, correspondence, dealings, intercommunication, trade, traffic, truck

interdict *n* **2** = **ban,** disallowance, disqualification, interdiction, prohibition, taboo, veto ◆ *vb* **4** = **prohibit,** ban, bar, debar, disallow, forbid, outlaw, prevent, proscribe, veto

interdigitate (ˌɪntəˈdɪdʒɪˌteɪt) *vb* **interdigitates, interdigitating, interdigitated.** (*intr*) to interlock like the fingers of clasped hands. [C19: from INTER- + L *digitus* (see DIGIT) + -ATE[1]]

interdisciplinary (ˌɪntəˈdɪsɪˌplɪnərɪ) *adj* involving two or more academic disciplines.

interest Ⓣ (ˈɪntrɪst, -tərɪst) *n* **1** the sense of curiosity about or concern with something or someone. **2** the power of stimulating such a sense: *to have great interest.* **3** the quality of such stimulation. **4** something in which one is interested; a hobby or pursuit. **5** (*often pl*) benefit; advantage: *in one's own interest.* **6** (*often pl*) a right, share, or claim, esp. in a business or property. **7a** a charge for the use of credit or borrowed money. **7b** such a charge expressed as a percentage per time unit of the sum borrowed or used. **8** (*often pl*) a section of a community, etc., whose members have common aims: *the landed interest.* **9 declare an interest.** to make known one's connection, esp. a prejudicial connection, with an affair. ◆ *vb* (*tr*) **10** to arouse or excite the curiosity or concern of. **11** to cause to become involved in something; concern. [C15: from L: it concerns, from *interesse,* from INTER- + *esse* to be]

interested Ⓣ (ˈɪntrɪstɪd, -tərɪs-) *adj* **1** showing or having interest. **2** (*usually prenominal*) personally involved or implicated: *the interested parties met to discuss the business.*
▸ **ˈinterestedly** *adv* ▸ **ˈinterestedness** *n*

interesting Ⓣ (ˈɪntrɪstɪŋ, -tərɪs-) *adj* inspiring interest; absorbing.
▸ **ˈinterestingly** *adv* ▸ **ˈinterestingness** *n*

interest-rate futures *pl n* financial futures based on projected movements of interest rates.

interface Ⓣ *n* (ˈɪntəˌfeɪs). **1** *Physical chem.* a surface that forms the boundary between two liquids or chemical phases. **2** a common point or boundary between two things. **3** an electrical circuit linking one device, esp. a computer, with another. ◆ *vb* (ˌɪntəˈfeɪs), **interfaces, interfacing, interfaced. 4** (*tr*) to design or adapt the input and output configurations of (two electronic devices) so that they may work together compatibly. **5** to be an interface (with). **6** to be interactive (with).
▸ **interfacial** (ˌɪntəˈfeɪʃəl) *adj* ▸ **ˌinterˈfacially** *adv*

interfacing (ˈɪntəˌfeɪsɪŋ) *n* **1** a piece of fabric sewn beneath the facing of a garment, usually at the inside of the neck, armholes, etc., to give shape and firmness. **2** another name for **interlining.**

interfere Ⓣ (ˌɪntəˈfɪə) *vb* **interferes, interfering, interfered.** (*intr*) **1** (often foll. by *in*) to interpose, esp. meddlesomely or unwarrantedly; intervene. **2** (often foll. by *with*) to come between or into opposition; hinder. **3** (foll. by *with*) *Euphemistic.* to assault sexually. **4** to strike one against the other, as a horse's legs. **5** *Physics.* to cause or produce interference. [C16: from OF *s'entreferir* to collide, from *entre-* INTER- + *ferir* to strike, from L *ferīre*]
▸ **ˌinterˈfering** *adj*

interference Ⓣ (ˌɪntəˈfɪərəns) *n* **1** the act or an instance of interfering. **2** *Physics.* the process in which two or more coherent waves combine to form a resultant wave in which the displacement at any point is the vector sum of the displacements of the individual waves. **3** any undesired signal that tends to interfere with the reception of radio waves.
▸ **interferential** (ˌɪntəfəˈrɛnʃəl) *adj*

interferometer (ˌɪntəfəˈrɒmɪtə) *n Physics.* any acoustic, optical, or microwave instrument that uses interference patterns to make accurate measurements of wavelength, distance, etc.
▸ **interferometric** (ˌɪntəˌfɛrəˈmɛtrɪk) *adj* ▸ **ˌinterˌferoˈmetrically** *adv* ▸ **ˌinterferˈometry** *n*

interferon (ˌɪntəˈfɪərɒn) *n Biochem.* any of a family of proteins made by cells in response to virus infection that prevent the growth of the virus. [C20: from INTERFERE + -ON]

interfuse (ˌɪntəˈfjuːz) *vb* **interfuses, interfusing, interfused. 1** to diffuse or mix throughout or become so diffused or mixed; intermingle. **2** to blend or fuse or become blended or fused.
▸ **ˌinterˈfusion** *n*

intergovernmental (ˌɪntəˌgʌvənˈmɛntᵊl) *adj* conducted between or involving two or more governments.

interim Ⓣ (ˈɪntərɪm) *adj* **1** (*prenominal*) temporary, provisional, or intervening: *interim measures to deal with the emergency.* ◆ *n* **2** (usually preceded by *the*) the intervening time; the meantime (esp. in **in the interim**). ◆ *adv* **3** *Rare.* meantime. [C16: from L: meanwhile]

interior Ⓣ (ɪnˈtɪərɪə) *n* **1** a part, surface, or region that is inside or on the inside: *the interior of Africa.* **2** inner character or nature. **3** a film or scene shot inside a building, studio, etc. **4** a picture of the inside of a room or building, as in a painting or stage design. **5** the inside of a building or room, with respect to design and decoration. ◆ *adj* **6** of, situated on, or suitable for the inside; inner. **7** coming or acting from within; internal. **8** of or involving a nation's domestic affairs; internal. **9** (esp. of one's spiritual or mental life) secret or private; not observable. [C15: from L (adj), comp. of *inter* within]
▸ **inˈteriorly** *adv*

interior angle *n* an angle of a polygon contained between two adjacent sides.

interior decoration *n* **1** the colours, furniture, etc., of the interior of a house, etc. **2** Also called: **interior design.** the art or business of planning the interiors of houses, etc.
▸ **interior decorator** *n*

interiorize *or* **interiorise** (ɪnˈtɪərɪəˌraɪz) *vb* **interiorizes, interiorizing, interiorized** *or* **interiorises, interiorising, interiorised.** (*tr*) another word for **internalize.**

interj. *abbrev. for* interjection.

interject Ⓣ (ˌɪntəˈdʒɛkt) *vb* (*tr*) to interpose abruptly or sharply; interrupt with; throw in: *she interjected clever remarks.* [C16: from L *interjicere* to place between, from *jacere* to throw]
▸ **ˌinterˈjector** *n*

interjection Ⓣ (ˌɪntəˈdʒɛkʃən) *n* **1** the act of interjecting. **2** a word or phrase that is used in syntactic isolation and that expresses sudden emotion; expletive. Abbrev.: **interj.**
▸ **ˌinterˈjectional** *or* **ˌinterˈjectory** *adj* ▸ **ˌinterˈjectionally** *adv*

interlard (ˌɪntəˈlɑːd) *vb* (*tr*) **1** to scatter thickly in or between; intersperse: *to interlard one's writing with foreign phrases.* **2** to occur frequently in; be scattered in or through: *foreign phrases interlard his writings.*

interlay (ˌɪntəˈleɪ) *vb* **interlays, interlaying, interlaid.** (*tr*) to insert (layers) between; interpose.

interleaf (ˈɪntəˌliːf) *n, pl* **interleaves.** a blank leaf inserted between the leaves of a book.

interleave (ˌɪntəˈliːv) *vb* **interleaves, interleaving, interleaved.** (*tr*) **1** (often foll. by *with*) to intersperse (with), esp. alternately, as the illustrations in a book (with protective leaves). **2** to provide (a book) with blank leaves for notes, etc., or to protect illustrations.

interleukin (ˌɪntəˈluːkɪn) *n* a substance extracted from white blood cells that stimulates their activity against infection and may be used to combat some forms of cancer.

interline[1] (ˌɪntəˈlaɪn) *or* **interlineate** (ˌɪntəˈlɪnɪˌeɪt) *vb* **interlines, interlining, interlined** *or* **interlineates, interlineating, interlineated.** (*tr*) to write or print (matter) between the lines of (a text, book, etc.).
▸ **ˈinterˌlining** *or* **ˌinterˌlineˈation** *n*

interline[2] (ˌɪntəˈlaɪn) *vb* **interlines, interlining, interlined.** (*tr*) to provide (a part of a garment) with a second lining, esp. of stiffened material.
▸ **ˈinterˌliner** *n*

interlinear (ˌɪntəˈlɪnɪə) *or* **interlineal** *adj* **1** written or printed between lines of text. **2** written or printed with the text in different languages or versions on alternate lines.
▸ **ˌinterˈlinearly** *or* **ˌinterˈlineally** *adv*

interlining (ˈɪntəˌlaɪnɪŋ) *n* the material used to interline parts of garments, now often made of reinforced paper.

interlock *vb* (ˌɪntəˈlɒk). **1** to join or be joined firmly, as by a mutual interconnection of parts. ◆ *n* (ˈɪntəˌlɒk). **2** the act of interlocking or the state of being interlocked. **3** a device, esp. one operated electromechanically, used in a logic circuit to prevent an activity being initiated unless preceded by certain events. **4** a closely knitted fabric. ◆ *adj* **5** closely knitted.
▸ **ˈinterˌlocker** *n*

interlocutor (ˌɪntəˈlɒkjʊtə) *n* **1** a person who takes part in a conversa-

THESAURUS

interest *n* **1 = curiosity,** affection, attention, attentiveness, attraction, concern, notice, regard, suspicion, sympathy **2 = importance,** concern, consequence, moment, note, relevance, significance, weight **4 = hobby,** activity, diversion, leisure activity, pastime, preoccupation, pursuit, relaxation **5** *often plural* **= advantage,** benefit, boot (*dialect*), gain, good, profit **6 = stake,** authority, claim, commitment, influence, investment, involvement, participation, portion, right, share ◆ *vb* **10 = arouse one's curiosity,** amuse, attract, catch one's eye, divert, engross, fascinate, hold the attention of, intrigue, move, touch **11 = engage,** affect, concern, involve
Antonyms *n* ≠ **curiosity:** boredom, coolness, disinterest, dispassion, disregard, unconcern ≠ **importance:** inconsequence, insignificance, irrelevance, worthlessness ◆ *vb* ≠ **arouse one's curiosity:** bore, burden, irk, repel, tire, weary

interested *adj* **1 = curious,** affected, attentive, attracted, drawn, excited, fascinated, intent, into (*inf.*), keen, moved, responsive, stimulated **2 = involved,** biased, concerned, implicated, partial, partisan, predisposed, prejudiced
Antonyms *adj* ≠ **curious:** apathetic, bored, detached, inattentive, indifferent, unconcerned, uninterested, wearied

interesting *adj* **= intriguing,** absorbing, amusing, appealing, attractive, compelling, curious, engaging, engrossing, entertaining, gripping, pleasing, provocative, stimulating, stirring, suspicious, thought-provoking, unusual
Antonyms *adj* boring, dull, mind-numbing, tedious, tiresome, uninteresting

interface *n* **2 = connection,** border, boundary, frontier, link ◆ *vb* **5 = connect,** combine, couple, join together, link

interfere *vb* **1 = intrude,** butt in, get involved, intermeddle, intervene, meddle, poke one's nose in (*inf.*), put one's two cents in (*US sl.*), stick one's oar in (*inf.*), tamper **2** *often with* **with = conflict,** be a drag upon (*inf.*), block, clash, collide, cramp, frustrate, get in the way of, hamper, handicap, hinder, impede, inhibit, obstruct, trammel

interference *n* **1 = intrusion,** clashing, collision, intervention, meddlesomeness, meddling, obstruction, opposition, prying

interfering *adj* **1 = meddling,** interruptive, intrusive, meddlesome, obtrusive, prying

interim *adj* **1 = temporary,** acting, caretaker, improvised, intervening, makeshift, pro tem, provisional, stopgap ◆ *n* **2 = interval,** entr'acte, interregnum, meantime, meanwhile, respite

interior *n* **1 = inside,** bosom, centre, contents, core, heart, innards (*inf.*) ◆ *adj* **6, 7 = inside,** inner, internal, inward **8 = domestic,** home **9 = mental,** hidden, inner, intimate, personal, private, secret, spiritual
Antonyms *adj* ≠ **inside:** exterior, external, outer, outside, outward

interject *vb* **= interrupt with,** interpolate, interpose, introduce, put in, throw in

interjection *n* **1 = exclamation,** cry, ejaculation, interpolation, interposition

tion. **2** the man in the centre of a troupe of minstrels who engages the others in talk or acts as announcer. **3** *Scots Law.* a decree by a judge.
► **ˌinterˈlocutress, ˌinterˈlocutrice,** *or* **ˌinterˈlocutrix** *fem n*

interlocutory (ˌɪntəˈlɒkjʊtərɪ, -trɪ) *adj* **1** *Law.* pronounced during the course of proceedings; provisional: *an interlocutory injunction.* **2** interposed, as into a conversation, narrative, etc. **3** of, relating to, or characteristic of dialogue.
► **ˌinterˈlocutorily** *adv*

interloper ❶ (ˈɪntəˌləʊpə) *n* **1** an intruder. **2** a person who introduces himself into professional or social circles where he does not belong. **3** a person who interferes in matters that are not his concern. [C17: from INTER- + *loper*, from MDu. *loopen* to leap]
► **ˌinterˈlope** *vb (intr)*

interlude ❶ (ˈɪntəˌluːd) *n* **1** a period of time or different activity between longer periods, processes, or events; episode or interval. **2** *Theatre.* a short dramatic piece played separately or as part of a longer entertainment, common in 16th-century England. **3** a brief piece of music, dance, etc., given between the sections of another performance. [C14: from Med. L, from L INTER- + *lūdus* play]

intermarry (ˌɪntəˈmærɪ) *vb* **intermarries, intermarrying, intermarried.** *(intr)* **1** (of different races, religions, etc.) to become connected by marriage. **2** to marry within one's own family, clan, group, etc.
► **ˌinterˈmarriage** *n*

intermediary ❶ (ˌɪntəˈmiːdɪərɪ) *n, pl* **intermediaries. 1** a person who acts as a mediator or agent between parties. **2** something that acts as a medium or means. ◆ *adj* **3** acting as an intermediary. **4** situated, acting, or coming between.

intermediate ❶ *adj* (ˌɪntəˈmiːdɪɪt). **1** occurring or situated between two points, extremes, places, etc.; in between. **2** (of a class, course, etc.) suitable for learners with some degree of skill or competence. ◆ *n* (ˌɪntəˈmiːdɪɪt). **3** something intermediate. **4** a substance formed during one of the stages of a chemical process before the desired product is obtained. ◆ *vb* (ˌɪntəˈmiːdɪˌeɪt), **intermediates, intermediating, intermediated. 5** *(intr)* to act as an intermediary or mediator. [C17: from Med. L *intermediāre* to intervene, from L INTER- + *medius* middle]
► **ˌinterˈmediacy** *or* **ˌinterˈmediateness** *n* ► **ˌinterˈmediately** *adv* ► **ˌinterˌmediˈation** *n* ► **ˌinterˈmediˌator** *n*

intermediate-acting *adj* (of a drug) intermediate in its effects between long- and short-acting drugs. Cf. **long-acting, short-acting.**

intermediate frequency *n Electronics.* the frequency to which the signal carrier frequency is changed in a superheterodyne receiver and at which most of the amplification takes place.

intermediate-level waste *n* radioactive waste material, such as reactor components, that can be mixed with concrete and safely stored in steel drums in deep mines or beneath the seabed in concrete chambers. Cf. **high-level waste, low-level waste.**

intermediate vector boson *n Physics.* a hypothetical particle believed to mediate the weak interaction between elementary particles.

interment ❶ (ɪnˈtɜːmənt) *n* burial, esp. with ceremonial rites.

intermezzo (ˌɪntəˈmɛtsəʊ) *n, pl* **intermezzos** *or* **intermezzi** (-tsiː). **1** a short piece of instrumental music composed for performance between the acts or scenes of an opera, drama, etc. **2** an instrumental piece either inserted between two longer movements in an extended composition or intended for independent performance. [C19: from It., from LL *intermedium* interval; see INTERMEDIATE]

interminable ❶ (ɪnˈtɜːmɪnəbᵊl) *adj* endless or seemingly endless because of monotony or tiresome length.
► **inˈterminableness** *n* ► **inˈterminably** *adv*

intermission ❶ (ˌɪntəˈmɪʃən) *n* **1** an interval, as between parts of a film, etc. **2** a period between events or activities; pause. **3** the act of intermitting or the state of being intermitted. [C16: from L, from *intermittere* to INTERMIT]
► **ˌinterˈmissive** *adj*

intermit (ˌɪntəˈmɪt) *vb* **intermits, intermitting, intermitted.** to suspend (activity) or (of activity) to be suspended temporarily or at intervals. [C16: from L *intermittere* to leave off, from INTER- + *mittere* to send]
► **ˌinterˈmittor** *n*

intermittent ❶ (ˌɪntəˈmɪtᵊnt) *adj* occurring occasionally or at regular or irregular intervals; periodic.
► **ˌinterˈmittence** *or* **ˌinterˈmittency** *n* ► **ˌinterˈmittently** *adv*

intermix (ˌɪntəˈmɪks) *vb* **1** *(tr)* to mix (ingredients, liquids, etc.) together. **2** *(intr)* to become or have the capacity to become combined, joined, etc.

intermixture (ˌɪntəˈmɪkstʃə) *n* **1** the act of intermixing or state of being intermixed. **2** an additional ingredient.

intern ❶ *vb* **1** (ɪnˈtɜːn). *(tr)* to detain or confine within a country or a limited area, esp. during wartime. **2** (ˈɪntɜːn). *(intr) Chiefly US.* to serve or train as an intern. ◆ *n* (ˈɪntɜːn). **3** another word for **internee. 4** Also: **interne.** the approximate US and Canad. equivalent of **houseman. 5** Also: **interne.** *Chiefly US.* a student teacher. **6** Also: **interne.** *Chiefly US.* a student or recent graduate undergoing practical training in a working environment. [C19: from L *internus* internal]
► **inˈternment** *n* ► **ˈinternship** *or* **ˈinterneship** *n*

internal ❶ (ɪnˈtɜːnᵊl) *adj* **1** of, situated on, or suitable for the inside; inner. **2** coming or acting from within; interior. **3** involving the spiritual or mental life; subjective. **4** of or involving a nation's domestic as opposed to foreign affairs. **5** situated within, affecting, or relating to the inside of the body. ◆ *n* **6** *Euphemistic.* a medical examination of the vagina or uterus. [C16: from Med. L, from LL *internus* inward]
► **ˌinterˈnality** *or* **inˈternalness** *n* ► **inˈternally** *adv*

internal-combustion engine *n* a heat engine in which heat is supplied by burning the fuel in the working fluid (usually air).

internal energy *n* the thermodynamic property of a system that changes by an amount equal to the work done on the system when it suffers an adiabatic change.

internalize *or* **internalise** (ɪnˈtɜːnəˌlaɪz) *vb* **internalizes, internalizing, internalized** *or* **internalises, internalising, internalised.** *(tr) Psychol., sociol.* to make internal, esp. to incorporate within oneself (values, attitudes, etc.) through learning or socialization. Also: **interiorize.**
► **inˌternaliˈzation** *or* **inˌternaliˈsation** *n*

internal medicine *n* the branch of medical science concerned with the diagnosis and nonsurgical treatment of disorders of the internal structures of the body.

international ❶ (ˌɪntəˈnæʃənᵊl) *adj* **1** of, concerning, or involving two or more nations or nationalities. **2** established by, controlling, or legislating for several nations: *an international court.* **3** available for use by all nations: *international waters.* ◆ *n* **4** *Sport.* **4a** a contest between two national teams. **4b** a member of a national team.
► **ˌinterˌnationˈality** *n* ► **ˌinterˈnationally** *adv*

International (ˌɪntəˈnæʃənᵊl) *n* **1** any of several international socialist organizations, esp. **First International** (1864–76) and **Second International** (1889 until World War I). **2** a member of any of these organizations.

International Atomic Time *n* the scientific standard of time based on the SI unit, the second, used to synchronize the time standards of the major nations. Abbrev.: **TAI.**

International Bank for Reconstruction and Development *n* the official name for the **World Bank.**

International Court of Justice *n* a court established in the Hague, in the Netherlands, to settle disputes brought by nations that are parties to the Statute of the Court. Also called: **World Court.**

International Date Line *n* the line approximately following the 180° meridian from Greenwich on the east side of which the date is one day earlier than on the west.

internationalism (ˌɪntəˈnæʃənəˌlɪzəm) *n* **1** the ideal or practice of cooperation and understanding between nations. **2** the state or quality of being international.
► **ˌinterˈnationalist** *n*

internationalize *or* **internationalise** (ˌɪntəˈnæʃənəˌlaɪz) *vb* **internationalizes, internationalizing, internationalized** *or* **internationalises, internationalising, internationalised.** *(tr)* **1** to make international. **2** to put under international control.
► **ˌinterˌnationaliˈzation** *or* **ˌinterˌnationaliˈsation** *n*

international law *n* the body of rules generally recognized by civilized nations as governing their conduct towards each other.

International Modernism *n* See **International Style.**

International Phonetic Alphabet *n* a series of signs and letters for the representation of human speech sounds. It is based on the Roman alphabet but supplemented by modified signs or symbols from other writing systems.

International Practical Temperature Scale *n* a temperature scale adopted by international agreement in 1968 based on thermodynamic temperature and using experimental values to define 11 fixed points.

International Style *or* **Modernism** *n* an architectural style of the 1920s that used cubic forms, large windows, and modern materials.

International Telecommunications Union *n* a special agency of the United Nations, founded in 1947, that is responsible for the international allocation and registration of frequencies for communications and the regulation of telegraph, telephone, and radio services.

interne (ˈɪntɜːn) *n* a variant spelling of **intern** (senses 4, 5, 6).

THESAURUS

interloper *n* **1** = **trespasser**, gate-crasher (*inf.*), intruder, meddler, uninvited guest, unwanted visitor

interlude *n* **1** = **interval**, break, breathing space, delay, entr'acte, episode, halt, hiatus, intermission, pause, respite, rest, spell, stop, stoppage, wait

intermediary *n* **1** = **mediator**, agent, broker, entrepreneur, go-between, middleman

intermediate *adj* **1** = **middle**, halfway, in-between (*inf.*), intermediary, interposed, intervening, mean, mid, midway, transitional

interment *n* = **burial**, burying, funeral, inhumation, sepulture

interminable *adj* = **endless**, boundless, ceaseless, dragging, everlasting, immeasurable, infinite, limitless, long, long-drawn-out, long-winded, never-ending, perpetual, protracted, unbounded, unlimited, wearisome
Antonyms *adj* bounded, finite, limited, measurable, restricted, temporary

intermission *n* **1-3** = **interval**, break, breathing space, cessation, entr'acte, interlude, interruption, let-up (*inf.*), lull, pause, recess, respite, rest, stop, stoppage, suspense, suspension

intermittent *adj* = **periodic**, broken, discontinuous, fitful, irregular, occasional, punctuated, recurrent, recurring, spasmodic, sporadic, stop-go (*inf.*)
Antonyms *adj* continuous, steady, unceasing

intern *vb* **1** = **imprison**, confine, detain, hold, hold in custody

internal *adj* **1, 2** = **inner**, inside, interior **3** = **private**, intimate, subjective **4** = **domestic**, civic, home, in-house, intramural
Antonyms *adj* ≠ **inner:** exterior, external, outer, outermost, outside ≠ **private:** exposed, revealed, unconcealed

international *adj* **1-3** = **universal**, cosmopolitan, ecumenical, global, intercontinental, worldwide

internecine (ˌɪntəˈniːsaɪn) *adj* **1** mutually destructive or ruinous; maiming both or all sides: *internecine war.* **2** of or relating to slaughter or carnage; bloody. **3** of or involving conflict within a group or organization. [C17: from L, from *internecāre* to destroy, from *necāre* to kill]

internee (ˌɪntɜːˈniː) *n* a person who is interned, esp. an enemy citizen in wartime or a terrorism suspect.

Internet ❶ (ˈɪntəˌnet) *n* **the.** the single worldwide computer network that interconnects other computer networks, on which end-user services, such as World Wide Web sites or data archives, are located, enabling data and other information to be exchanged. Also called: the **Net.**

internist (ˈɪntɜːnɪst, ɪnˈtɜːnɪst) *n* a physician who specializes in internal medicine.

interpellate (ɪnˈtɜːpeˌleɪt) *vb* **interpellates, interpellating, interpellated.** (*tr*) *Parliamentary procedure.* (in European legislatures) to question (a member of the government) on a point of government policy, often interrupting the business of the day. [C16: from L *interpellāre* to disturb, from INTER- + *pellere* to push]
▸**inˌterpelˈlation** *n* ▸**inˈterpelˌlator** *n*

interpenetrate (ˌɪntəˈpenɪˌtreɪt) *vb* **interpenetrates, interpenetrating, interpenetrated. 1** to penetrate (something) thoroughly; pervade. **2** to penetrate each other or one another mutually.
▸**ˌinterˈpenetrable** *adj* ▸**ˌinterˈpenetrant** *adj* ▸**ˌinterˌpeneˈtration** *n* ▸**ˌinterˈpenetrative** *adj* ▸**ˌinterˈpenetratively** *adv*

interplay ❶ (ˈɪntəˌpleɪ) *n* reciprocal and mutual action and reaction, as in circumstances, events, or personal relations.

interpleader (ˌɪntəˈpliːdə) *n Law.* **1** a process by which a person holding money claimed by two or more parties and having no interest in it himself can require the claimants to litigate with each other. **2** a person who interpleads.

Interpol (ˈɪntəˌpɒl) *n acronym for* International Criminal Police Organization, an association of over 100 national police forces, devoted to fighting international crime.

interpolate ❶ (ɪnˈtɜːpəˌleɪt) *vb* **interpolates, interpolating, interpolated. 1** to insert or introduce (a comment, passage, etc.) into (a conversation, text, etc.). **2** to falsify or alter (a text, manuscript, etc.) by the later addition of (material, esp. spurious passages). **3** (*intr*) to make additions, interruptions, or insertions. **4** *Maths.* to estimate (a value of a function) between the values already known or determined. Cf. **extrapolate** (sense 1). [C17: from L *interpolāre* to give a new appearance to]
▸**inˈterpoˌlater** *or* **inˈterpoˌlator** *n* ▸**inˈterpolative** *adj*

interpose ❶ (ˌɪntəˈpəʊz) *vb* **interposes, interposing, interposed. 1** to put or place between or among other things. **2** to introduce (comments, questions, etc.) into a speech or conversation; interject. **3** to exert or use influence or action in order to alter or intervene in (a situation). [C16: from OF, from L *interpōnere,* from INTER- + *pōnere* to put]
▸**ˌinterˈposal** *n* ▸**ˌinterˈposer** *n* ▸**ˌinterpoˈsition** *n*

interpret ❶ (ɪnˈtɜːprɪt) *vb* **1** (*tr*) to clarify or explain the meaning of; elucidate. **2** (*tr*) to construe the significance or intention of. **3** (*tr*) to convey the spirit or meaning of (a poem, song, etc.) in performance. **4** (*intr*) to act as an interpreter; translate orally. [C14: from L *interpretārī,* from *interpres* negotiator, one who explains]
▸**inˈterpretable** *adj* ▸**inˌterpretaˈbility** *or* **inˈterpretableness** *n* ▸**inˈterpretably** *adv* ▸**inˈterpretive** *adj*

interpretation ❶ (ɪnˌtɜːprɪˈteɪʃən) *n* **1** the act or process of interpreting or explaining; elucidation. **2** the result of interpreting; an explanation. **3** a particular view of an artistic work, esp. as expressed by stylistic individuality in its performance. **4** explanation, as of a historical site, provided by the use of original objects, visual display material, etc.
▸**inˌterpreˈtational** *adj*

interpreter ❶ (ɪnˈtɜːprɪtə) *n* **1** a person who translates orally from one language into another. **2** a person who interprets the work of others. **3** *Computing.* a program that translates a statement in a source program to machine code and executes it before translating and executing the next statement.
▸**inˈterpretership** *n* ▸**inˈterpretress** *fem n*

interpretive centre *n* (at a historical site, etc.) a building that provides interpretation of the site through a variety of media, such as video displays and exhibitions, and, often, includes facilities such as refreshment rooms.

interregnum (ˌɪntəˈregnəm) *n, pl* **interregnums** *or* **interregna** (-nə). **1** an interval between two reigns, governments, etc. **2** any period in which a state lacks a ruler, government, etc. **3** a period of absence of some control, authority, etc. **4** a gap in a continuity. [C16: from L, from INTER- + *regnum* REIGN]
▸**ˌinterˈregnal** *adj*

interrelate (ˌɪntərɪˈleɪt) *vb* **interrelates, interrelating, interrelated.** to place in or come into a mutual or reciprocal relationship.
▸**ˌinterreˈlation** *n* ▸**ˌinterreˈlationˌship** *n*

interrogate ❶ (ɪnˈterəˌgeɪt) *vb* **interrogates, interrogating, interrogated.** to ask questions (of), esp. to question (a witness in court, spy, etc.) closely. [C15: from L *interrogāre,* from *rogāre* to ask]
▸**inˈterroˌgator** *n*

interrogation ❶ (ɪnˌterəˈgeɪʃən) *n* **1** the technique, practice, or an instance of interrogating. **2** a question or query. **3** *Telecomm.* the transmission of one or more triggering pulses to a transponder.
▸**inˌterroˈgational** *adj*

interrogation mark *n* a less common term for **question mark.**

interrogative ❶ (ˌɪntəˈrɒgətɪv) *adj* **1** asking or having the nature of a question. **2** denoting a form or construction used in asking a question. **3** denoting or belonging to a class of words, such as *which* and *whom,* that serve to question which individual referent is intended. ◆ *n* **4** an interrogative word, phrase, sentence, or construction. **5** a question mark.
▸**ˌinterˈrogatively** *adv*

interrogatory (ˌɪntəˈrɒgətərɪ, -trɪ) *adj* **1** expressing or involving a question. ◆ *n, pl* **interrogatories. 2** a question or interrogation.

interrupt ❶ (ˌɪntəˈrʌpt) *vb* **1** to break the continuity of (an action, event, etc.) or hinder (a person) by intrusion. **2** (*tr*) to cease to perform (some action). **3** (*tr*) to obstruct (a view, etc.). **4** to prevent or disturb (a conversation, discussion, etc.) by questions, interjections, or comment. [C15: from L *interrumpere,* from INTER- + *rumpere* to break]
▸**ˌinterˈruptible** *adj* ▸**ˌinterˈruptive** *adj* ▸**ˌinterˈruptively** *adv* ▸**ˌinterˈrupted** *adj*

interrupted screw *n* a screw with a slot cut into the thread, esp. one used in the breech of some guns permitting both engagement and release of the block by a partial turn of the screw.

interrupter *or* **interruptor** (ˌɪntəˈrʌptə) *n* **1** a person or thing that interrupts. **2** an electromechanical device for opening and closing an electric circuit.

interruption ❶ (ˌɪntəˈrʌpʃən) *n* **1** something that interrupts, such as a comment, question, or action. **2** an interval or intermission. **3** the act of interrupting or the state of being interrupted.

interscholastic (ˌɪntəskəˈlæstɪk) *adj* **1** (of sports events, competitions, etc.) occurring between two or more schools. **2** representative of various schools.

intersect ❶ (ˌɪntəˈsekt) *vb* **1** to divide, cut, or mark off by passing through or across. **2** (esp. of roads) to cross (each other). **3** *Maths.* (often foll. by *with*) to have one or more points in common (with another configuration). [C17: from L *intersecāre* to divide, from INTER- + *secāre* to cut]

intersection ❶ (ˌɪntəˈsekʃən, ˈɪntəˌsek-) *n* **1** a point at which things intersect, esp. a road junction. **2** the act of intersecting or the state of being intersected. **3** *Maths.* **3a** a point or set of points common to two or more geometric configurations. **3b** Also called: **product.** the set of elements that are common to two sets. **3c** the operation that yields that set from a pair of given sets.
▸**ˌinterˈsectional** *adj*

intersex (ˈɪntəˌseks) *n Zool.* an individual with characteristics intermediate between those of a male and a female.

intersexual (ˌɪntəˈseksjʊəl) *adj* **1** occurring or existing between the sexes. **2** relating to or being an intersex.
▸**ˌinterˌsexuˈality** *n* ▸**ˌinterˈsexually** *adv*

interspace *vb* (ˌɪntəˈspeɪs), **interspaces, interspacing, interspaced. 1** (*tr*) to make or occupy a space between. ◆ *n* (ˈɪntəˌspeɪs). **2** space between or among things.
▸**interspatial** (ˌɪntəˈspeɪʃəl) *adj* ▸**ˌinterˈspatially** *adv*

intersperse ❶ (ˌɪntəˈspɜːs) *vb* **intersperses, interspersing, interspersed.** (*tr*) **1** to scatter or distribute among, between, or on. **2** to diversify (some-

THESAURUS

Internet *n* = **information superhighway,** cyberspace, the net (*inf.*), the web (*inf.*), World Wide Web

interplay *n* = **interaction,** give-and-take, meshing, reciprocation, reciprocity

interpolate *vb* **1, 3** = **insert,** add, intercalate, introduce

interpose *vb* **2** = **interrupt,** insert, interject, introduce, put forth, put one's oar in **3** = **intervene,** come *or* place between, intercede, interfere, intermediate, intrude, mediate, step in

interpret *vb* **1, 2** = **explain,** adapt, clarify, construe, decipher, decode, define, elucidate, explicate, expound, make sense of, paraphrase, read, render, solve, spell out, take, throw light on, translate, understand

interpretation *n* **1, 2** = **explanation,** analysis, clarification, construction, diagnosis, elucidation, exegesis, explication, exposition, meaning, performance, portrayal, reading, rendering, rendition, sense, signification, translation, understanding, version

interpreter *n* **2** = **translator,** annotator, commentator, exponent, scholiast

interrogate *vb* = **question,** ask, catechize, cross-examine, cross-question, enquire, examine, give (someone) the third degree (*inf.*), grill (*inf.*), inquire, investigate, pump, put the screws on (*inf.*), quiz

interrogation *n* **1** = **questioning,** cross-examination, cross-questioning, examination, grilling (*inf.*), inquiry, inquisition, probing, third degree (*inf.*)

interrogative *adj* **1** = **questioning,** curious, inquiring, inquisitive, inquisitorial, quizzical

interrupt *vb* **1** = **intrude,** barge in (*inf.*), break in, break (someone's) train of thought, butt in, disturb, heckle, hinder, interfere (with), obstruct, punctuate, separate, sever **2** = **suspend,** break, break off, check, cut, cut off, cut short, delay, disconnect, discontinue, disjoin, disunite, divide, hold up, lay aside, stay, stop

interrupted *adj* **1, 2** = **disturbed,** broken, cut off, disconnected, discontinuous, incomplete, intermittent, uneven

interruption *n* **3** = **stoppage,** break, cessation, disconnection, discontinuance, disruption, dissolution, disturbance, disuniting, division, halt, hiatus, hindrance, hitch, impediment, intrusion, obstacle, obstruction, pause, separation, severance, stop, suspension

intersect *vb* **1** = **cross,** bisect, crisscross, cut, cut across, divide, meet

intersection *n* **1** = **junction,** crossing, crossroads, interchange

intersperse *vb* **1** = **scatter,** bestrew, interlard, intermix, pepper, sprinkle

thing) with other things scattered here and there. [C16: from L *interspargere,* from INTER- + *spargere* to sprinkle]
▸**interspersedly** (ˌɪntəˈspɜːsɪdlɪ) *adv* ▸**interspersion** (ˌɪntəˈspɜːʃən) *or* ˌ**interˈspersal** *n*

interstate (ˈɪntəˌsteɪt) *n US.* a motorway crossing between states.

interstellar (ˌɪntəˈstɛlə) *adj* between or among stars.

interstice (ɪnˈtɜːstɪs) *n* (*usually pl*) **1** a minute opening or crevice between things. **2** *Physics.* the space between adjacent atoms in a crystal lattice. [C17: from L *interstitium* interval, from *intersistere,* from INTER- + *sistere* to stand]

interstitial (ˌɪntəˈstɪʃəl) *adj* **1** of or relating to an interstice or interstices. **2** *Physics.* forming or occurring in an interstice: *an interstitial atom.* **3** *Anat., zool.* occurring in the spaces between organs, tissues, etc.: *interstitial cells.* ◆ *n* **4** *Chem.* an atom or ion situated in the interstices of a crystal lattice.
▸ˌ**interˈstitially** *adv*

intertrigo (ˌɪntəˈtraɪgəʊ) *n* chafing between two skin surfaces, as at the armpit. [C18: from INTER- + *-trigo,* from L *terere* to rub]

interval ❶ (ˈɪntəvəl) *n* **1** the period of time between two events, instants, etc. **2** the distance between two points, objects, etc. **3** a pause or interlude, as between periods of intense activity. **4** *Brit.* a short period between parts of a play, etc.; intermission. **5** *Music.* the difference of pitch between two notes, either sounded simultaneously or in succession as in a musical part. **6** the ratio of the frequencies of two sounds. **7 at intervals. 7a** occasionally or intermittently. **7b** with spaces between. [C13: from L *intervallum,* lit.: space between two palisades, from INTER- + *vallum* palisade]
▸**intervallic** (ˌɪntəˈvælɪk) *adj*

intervene ❶ (ˌɪntəˈviːn) *vb* **intervenes, intervening, intervened.** (*intr*) **1** (often foll. by *in*) to take a decisive or intrusive role (in) in order to determine events. **2** (foll. by *in* or *between*) to come or be (among or between). **3** (of a period of time) to occur between events or points in time. **4** (of an event) to disturb or hinder a course of action. **5** *Econ.* to take action to affect the market forces of an economy, esp. to maintain the stability of a currency. **6** *Law.* to interpose and become a party to a legal action between others, esp. in order to protect one's interests. [C16: from L *intervenīre* to come between]
▸ˌ**interˈvener** *or* ˌ**interˈvenor** *n*

intervention ❶ (ˌɪntəˈvɛnʃən) *n* **1** an act of intervening. **2** any interference in the affairs of others, esp. by one state in the affairs of another. **3** *Econ.* the action of a central bank in supporting the international value of a currency by buying large quantities of the currency to keep the price up. **4** *Commerce.* the action of the EU in buying up surplus produce when the market price drops to a certain value.

interventionist (ˌɪntəˈvɛnʃənɪst) *adj* **1** of, relating to, or advocating intervention, esp. in order to achieve a policy objective. ◆ *n* **2** a person or state that pursues a policy of intervention.

intervertebral disc (ˌɪntəˈvɜːtɪbrəl) *n* any of the cartilaginous discs between individual vertebrae, acting as shock absorbers.

interview ❶ (ˈɪntəˌvjuː) *n* **1** a conversation with or questioning of a person, usually conducted for television or a newspaper. **2** a formal discussion, esp. one in which an employer assesses a job applicant. ◆ *vb* **3** to conduct an interview with (someone). [C16: from OF *entrevue*]
▸ˌ**interviewˈee** *n* ▸ˈ**interˌviewer** *n*

inter vivos *Latin.* (ˈɪntə ˈviːvɒs) *adj Law.* between living people: *an inter vivos gift.*

interwar (ˌɪntəˈwɔː) *adj* of or happening in the period between World War I and World War II.

intestate (ɪnˈtɛsteɪt, -tɪt) *adj* **1a** (of a person) not having made a will. **1b** (of property) not disposed of by will. ◆ *n* **2** a person who dies without having made a will. [C14: from L *intestātus,* from IN-[1] + *testārī* to bear witness, make a will, from *testis* a witness]
▸**inˈtestacy** *n*

intestine ❶ (ɪnˈtɛstɪn) *n* the part of the alimentary canal between the stomach and the anus. See **large intestine, small intestine.** [C16: from L *intestīnum* gut, from *intestīnus* internal, from *intus* within]
▸**intestinal** (ɪnˈtɛstɪnᵊl, ˌɪntɛsˈtaɪnᵊl) *adj*

inti (ˈɪntɪ) *n* a former monetary unit of Peru. [C20: from Quechua]

intifada (ˌɪntɪˈfɑːdə) *n* the Palestinian uprising against Israel in the West Bank and Gaza Strip that started at the end of 1987. [C20: Ar., lit.: uprising]

intimacy ❶ (ˈɪntɪməsɪ) *n, pl* **intimacies. 1** close or warm friendship or understanding; personal relationship. **2** (*often pl*) *Euphemistic.* sexual relations.

intimate[1] ❶ (ˈɪntɪmɪt) *adj* **1** characterized by a close or warm personal relationship: *an intimate friend.* **2** deeply personal, private, or secret. **3** (*often postpositive;* foll. by *with*) *Euphemistic.* having sexual relations (with). **4** (*postpositive;* foll. by *with*) having a deep or unusual knowledge (of). **5** having a friendly, warm, or informal atmosphere: *an intimate nightclub.* **6** of or relating to the essential part or nature of something; intrinsic. ◆ *n* **7** a close friend. [C17: from L *intimus* very close friend, from (adj): innermost, from *intus* within]
▸ˈ**intimately** *adv* ▸ˈ**intimateness** *n*

intimate[2] ❶ (ˈɪntɪˌmeɪt) *vb* **intimates, intimating, intimated.** (*tr; may take a clause as object*) **1** to hint; suggest. **2** to proclaim; make known. [C16: from LL *intimāre* to proclaim, from L *intimus* innermost]
▸ˈ**intiˌmater** *n* ▸ˌ**intiˈmation** *n*

intimidate ❶ (ɪnˈtɪmɪˌdeɪt) *vb* **intimidates, intimidating, intimidated.** (*tr*) **1** to make timid or frightened; scare. **2** to discourage, restrain, or silence unscrupulously, as by threats. [C17: from Med. L *intimidāre,* from L IN-[2] + *timidus* fearful, from *timor* fear]
▸ˌ**inˈtimiˌdating** *adj* ▸**inˌtimiˈdation** *n* ▸**inˈtimiˌdator** *n*

intinction (ɪnˈtɪŋkʃən) *n Christianity.* the practice of dipping the Eucharistic bread into the wine at Holy Communion. [C16: from LL *intinctiō* a dipping in, from L *intingere,* from *tingere* to dip]

intitule (ɪnˈtɪtjuːl) *vb* **intitules, intituling, intituled.** (*tr*) *Parliamentary procedure.* (in Britain) to entitle (an Act). [C15: from OF *intituler,* from L *titulus* TITLE]

intl *abbrev. for* international.

into (ˈɪntuː; *unstressed* ˈɪntə) *prep* **1** to the interior or inner parts of: *to look into a case.* **2** to the middle or midst of so as to be surrounded by: *into the bushes.* **3** against; up against: *he drove into a wall.* **4** used to indicate the result of a change: *he changed into a monster.* **5** *Maths.* used to indicate a dividend: *three into six is two.* **6** *Inf.* interested or enthusiastically involved in: *I'm really into Freud.*

intonation ❶ (ˌɪntəʊˈneɪʃən) *n* **1** the sound pattern of phrases and sentences produced by pitch variation in the voice. **2** the act or manner of intoning. **3** an intoned, chanted, or monotonous utterance; incantation. **4** *Music.* the opening of a piece of plainsong, sung by a soloist. **5** *Music.* the capacity to play or sing in tune.
▸ˌ**intoˈnational** *adj*

intone ❶ (ɪnˈtəʊn) *or* **intonate** *vb* **intones, intoning, intoned** *or* **intonates, intonating, intonated. 1** to utter, recite, or sing (a chant, prayer, etc.) in a monotonous or incantatory tone. **2** (*intr*) to speak with a particular or characteristic intonation or tone. **3** to sing (the opening phrase of a psalm, etc.) in plainsong. [C15: from Med. L *intonare,* from IN-[2] + TONE]
▸**inˈtoner** *n*

in toto ❶ *Latin.* (ɪn ˈtəʊtəʊ) *adv* totally; entirely.

intoxicant (ɪnˈtɒksɪkənt) *n* **1** anything that causes intoxication. ◆ *adj* **2** causing intoxication.

intoxicate ❶ (ɪnˈtɒksɪˌkeɪt) *vb* **intoxicates, intoxicating, intoxicated.** (*tr*) **1**

THESAURUS

interval *n* **1-4** = **break,** delay, distance, entr'acte, gap, hiatus, interim, interlude, intermission, meantime, meanwhile, opening, pause, period, playtime, respite, rest, season, space, spell, term, time, wait

intervene *vb* **1** = **step in** (*inf.*), arbitrate, intercede, interfere, interpose oneself, intrude, involve oneself, mediate, put one's oar in, put one's two cents in (*US sl.*), take a hand (*inf.*)

intervention *n* **1** = **mediation,** agency, intercession, interference, interposition, intrusion

interview *n* **1** = **meeting,** audience, conference, consultation, dialogue, evaluation, oral (examination), press conference, talk ◆ *vb* **3** = **question,** examine, interrogate, sound out, talk to

interviewer *n* **3** = **questioner,** examiner, interlocutor, interrogator, investigator, reporter

intestinal *adj* = **abdominal,** coeliac, duodenal, gut (*inf.*), inner, stomachic, visceral

intestine *n* = **gut,** bowel

intimacy *n* **1** = **familiarity,** closeness, confidence, confidentiality, fraternization, understanding

Antonyms *n* alienation, aloofness, coldness, detachment, distance, estrangement, remoteness, separation

intimate[1] *adj* **1** = **close,** bosom, cherished, confidential, dear, friendly, near, nearest and dearest, thick (*inf.*), warm **2** = **private,** confidential, personal, privy, secret **4** = **detailed,** deep, exhaustive, experienced, first-hand, immediate, in-depth, penetrating, personal, profound, thorough **5** = **snug,** comfy (*inf.*), cosy, friendly, tête-à-tête, warm ◆ *n* **7** = **friend,** bosom friend, buddy (*inf.*), chum (*inf.*), close friend, comrade, confidant *or* confidante, (constant) companion, crony, homeboy (*sl., chiefly US*), mate (*inf.*), pal

Antonyms *adj* ≠ **close:** distant, remote, superficial ≠ **private:** known, open, public ◆ *n* ≠ **friend:** enemy, foe, stranger

intimate[2] *vb* **1** = **suggest,** allude, drop a hint, give (someone) to understand, hint, imply, indicate, insinuate, let it be known, tip (someone) the wink (*Brit. inf.*), warn **2** = **announce,** communicate, declare, impart, make known, remind, state

intimately[1] *adv* **1, 2** = **confidingly,** affectionately, closely, confidentially, familiarly, personally, tenderly, very well, warmly **4** = **in detail,** fully, inside out, thoroughly, through and through, to the core, very well

intimation[2] *n* **1** = **hint,** allusion, indication, inkling, insinuation, reminder, suggestion, warning **2** = **announcement,** communication, declaration, notice

intimidate *vb* **1** = **frighten,** alarm, appal, daunt, dishearten, dismay, dispirit, overawe, scare, subdue, terrify **2** = **threaten,** browbeat, bully, coerce, cow, lean on (*inf.*), scare off, terrorize, twist someone's arm (*inf.*)

intimidation *n* **2** = **bullying,** arm-twisting (*inf.*), browbeating, coercion, fear, menaces, pressure, terror, terrorization, threat(s)

intonation *n* **1** = **tone,** accentuation, cadence, inflection, modulation **3** = **incantation,** chant

intone *vb* **1** = **recite,** chant, croon, intonate, sing

in toto *adv* = **totally,** as a whole, completely, entirely, in its entirety, unabridged, uncut, wholly

intoxicate *vb* **1** = **go to one's head,** addle, befuddle, fuddle, inebriate, put (someone) under the table (*inf.*), stupefy **2** = **exhilarate,** elate, excite, go to one's head, inflame, make one's head spin, stimulate

intoxicated *adj* **1** = **drunk,** drunken, inebriated, in one's cups (*inf.*), legless (*inf.*), out of it (*sl.*), paralytic (*inf.*), pissed (*taboo sl.*), plastered (*sl.*), smashed (*sl.*), sozzled (*inf.*), three sheets in the wind (*inf.*), tight (*inf.*), tipsy, under the influence **2** = **euphoric,** dizzy, ecstatic, elated, en-

(of an alcoholic drink) to produce in (a person) a state ranging from euphoria to stupor; make drunk; inebriate. **2** to stimulate, excite, or elate so as to overwhelm. **3** (of a drug, etc.) to poison. [C16: from Med. L, from *intoxicāre* to poison, from L *toxicum* poison; see TOXIC]
▸**in'toxicable** *adj* ▸**in'toxi,cating** *adj* ▸**in'toxi,catingly** *adv*

intoxication ● (ɪn,tɒksɪ'keɪʃən) *n* **1** drunkenness; inebriation. **2** great elation. **3** the act of intoxicating. **4** poisoning.

intr. *abbrev. for* intransitive.

intra- *prefix* within; inside: *intrastate; intravenous.* [from L *intrā* within; see INTERIOR]

intractable ● (ɪn'træktəbᵊl) *adj* **1** difficult to influence or direct: *an intractable disposition.* **2** (of a problem, illness, etc.) difficult to solve, alleviate, or cure.
▸**in,tracta'bility** *or* **in'tractableness** *n* ▸**in'tractably** *adv*

intradermal (,ɪntrə'dɜ:məl) *adj* within the skin: *an intradermal injection.* Abbrevs. (esp. of an injection): **ID, i.d.**
▸**,intra'dermally** *adv*

intrados (ɪn'treɪdɒs) *n, pl* **intrados** *or* **intradoses.** *Archit.* the inner curve or surface of an arch. [C18: from F, from INTRA- + *dos* back, from L *dorsum*]

intramural (,ɪntrə'mjʊərəl) *adj Education, chiefly US & Canad.* operating within or involving those in a single establishment.
▸**,intra'murally** *adv*

intramuscular (,ɪntrə'mʌskjulə) *adj* within a muscle: *an intramuscular injection.* Abbrevs. (esp. of an injection): **IM, i.m.**
▸**,intra'muscularly** *adv*

intranet ('ɪntrə,nɛt) *n Computing.* an internal network that makes use of Internet technology. [C20: INTRA- + NET (sense 8), modelled on INTERNET]

intrans. *abbrev. for* intransitive.

intransigent ● (ɪn'trænsɪdʒənt) *adj* **1** not willing to compromise; obstinately maintaining an attitude. ◆ *n* **2** an intransigent person, esp. in politics. [C19: from Sp. *los intransigentes* the uncompromising (ones), a name adopted by certain political extremists, from IN-[1] + *transigir* to compromise, from L *transigere* to settle; see TRANSACT]
▸**in'transigence** *or* **in'transigency** *n* ▸**in'transigently** *adv*

intransitive (ɪn'trænsɪtɪv) *adj* **1a** denoting a verb that does not require a direct object: *"to faint" is an intransitive verb.* **1b** (*as n*) such a verb. **2** denoting an adjective or noun that does not require any particular noun phrase as a referent. **3** having the property that if it holds between one argument and a second, and between the second and a third, it must fail to hold between the first and third: *"being the mother of" is an intransitive relation.* ◆ Cf. **transitive.**
▸**in'transitively** *adv* ▸**in,transi'tivity** *or* **in'transitiveness** *n*

intrapreneur (,ɪntrəprə'nɜ:) *n* a person who while remaining within a larger organization uses entrepreneurial skills to develop a new product or line of business as a subsidiary of the organization. [C20: from INTRA- + (ENTRE)PRENEUR]

intrauterine (,ɪntrə'ju:tərаɪn) *adj* within the womb.

intrauterine device *n* a metal or plastic device, in the shape of a loop, coil, or ring, inserted into the uterus to prevent conception. Abbrev.: **IUD.**

intravenous (,ɪntrə'vi:nəs) *adj Anat.* within a vein: *an intravenous injection.* Abbrevs. (esp. of an injection): **IV, i.v.**
▸**,intra'venously** *adv*

in-tray *n* a tray for incoming papers, etc., requiring attention.

intrench ● (ɪn'trɛntʃ) *vb* a less common spelling of **entrench.**
▸**in'trencher** *n* ▸**in'trenchment** *n*

intrepid ● (ɪn'trɛpɪd) *adj* fearless; daring; bold. [C17: from L *intrepidus,* from IN-[1] + *trepidus* fearful]
▸**,intre'pidity** *n* ▸**in'trepidly** *adv*

intricate ● ('ɪntrɪkɪt) *adj* **1** difficult to understand; obscure; complex; puzzling. **2** entangled or involved: *intricate patterns.* [C15: from L *intrīcāre* to entangle, perplex, from IN-[2] + *trīcae* trifles, perplexities]
▸**'intricacy** *or* **'intricateness** *n* ▸**'intricately** *adv*

intrigue ● *vb* (ɪn'tri:g), **intrigues, intriguing, intrigued. 1** (*tr*) to make interested or curious. **2** (*intr*) to make secret plots or employ underhand methods; conspire. **3** (*intr; often foll. by with*) to carry on a clandestine love affair. ◆ *n* (ɪn'tri:g, 'ɪntri:g). **4** the act or an instance of secret plotting, etc. **5** a clandestine love affair. **6** the quality of arousing interest or curiosity; beguilement. [C17: from F *intriguer,* from It., from L *intrīcāre;* see INTRICATE]
▸**in'triguer** *n* ▸**in'triguingly** *adv*

intrinsic ● (ɪn'trɪnsɪk) *or* **intrinsical** *adj* **1** of or relating to the essential nature of a thing; inherent. **2** *Anat.* situated within or peculiar to a part: *intrinsic muscles.* [C15: from LL *intrinsecus* from L, inwardly, from *intrā* within + *secus* alongside]
▸**in'trinsically** *adv*

intro ('ɪntrəʊ) *n, pl* **intros.** *Inf.* short for **introduction.**

intro. *or* **introd.** *abbrev. for:* **1** introduction. **2** introductory.

intro- *prefix* in, into, or inward: *introvert.* [from L *intrō* inwardly, within]

introduce ● (,ɪntrə'dju:s) *vb* **introduces, introducing, introduced.** (*tr*) **1** (often foll. by *to*) to present (someone) by name (to another person). **2** (foll. by *to*) to cause to experience for the first time: *to introduce a visitor to beer.* **3** to present for consideration or approval, esp. before a legislative body: *to introduce a bill in parliament.* **4** to bring in; establish: *to introduce decimal currency.* **5** to present (a radio or television programme, etc.) verbally. **6** (foll. by *with*) to start: *he introduced his talk with some music.* **7** (often foll. by *into*) to insert or inject: *he introduced the needle into his arm.* **8** to place (members of a plant or animal species) in a new environment with the intention of producing a resident breeding population. [C16: from L *intrōdūcere* to bring inside]
▸**,intro'ducer** *n* ▸**,intro'ducible** *adj*

introduction ● (,ɪntrə'dʌkʃən) *n* **1** the act of introducing or fact of being introduced. **2** a presentation of one person to another or others. **3** a means of presenting a person to another person, such as a letter of introduction or reference. **4** a preliminary part, as of a book. **5** *Music.* an opening passage in a movement or composition that precedes the main material. **6** a basic or elementary work of instruction, reference, etc.

introductory ● (,ɪntrə'dʌktərɪ, -trɪ) *adj* serving as an introduction; preliminary; prefatory.

introit ('ɪntrɔɪt) *n RC Church, Church of England.* a short prayer said or sung as the celebrant is entering the sanctuary to celebrate Mass or Holy Communion. [C15: from Church L *introitus* introit, from L: entrance, from *introīre* to go in]
▸**in'troital** *adj*

THESAURUS

raptured, excited, exhilarated, high (*inf.*), infatuated, sent (*sl.*), stimulated

intoxicating *adj* **1 = alcoholic**, inebriant, intoxicant, spirituous, strong **2 = exciting**, exhilarating, heady, sexy (*inf.*), stimulating, thrilling

intoxication *n* **1 = drunkenness**, inebriation, inebriety, insobriety, tipsiness **2 = excitement**, delirium, elation, euphoria, exaltation, exhilaration, infatuation

intractability *n* **1 = obstinacy**, awkwardness, cantankerousness, contrariness, incorrigibility, indiscipline, indocility, mulishness, obduracy, perverseness, perversity, pig-headedness, stubbornness, uncooperativeness, ungovernability, waywardness

intractable *adj* **1 = difficult**, awkward, bullheaded, cantankerous, contrary, fractious, headstrong, intransigent, obdurate, obstinate, perverse, pig-headed, refractory, self-willed, stiff-necked, stubborn, unbending, uncooperative, undisciplined, ungovernable, unmanageable, unruly, unyielding, wayward, wild, wilful **2 = incurable**, insoluble

intransigent *adj* **1 = uncompromising**, hardline, immovable, intractable, obdurate, obstinate, stiff-necked, stubborn, tenacious, tough, unbending, unbudgeable, unyielding
Antonyms *adj* acquiescent, compliant, compromising, flexible, open-minded

intrenched *see* **entrenched**

intrepid *adj* **= fearless**, audacious, bold, brave, courageous, daring, dauntless, doughty, gallant, game (*inf.*), have-a-go (*inf.*), heroic, lion-hearted, nerveless, plucky, resolute, stalwart, stouthearted, unafraid, undaunted, unflinching, valiant, valorous
Antonyms *adj* afraid, cautious, cowardly, craven, daunted, faint-hearted, fearful, flinching, irresolute, timid

intrepidity *n* **= fearlessness**, audacity, boldness, bravery, courage, daring, dauntlessness, doughtiness, fortitude, gallantry, grit, guts (*inf.*), heroism, lion-heartedness, nerve, pluck, prowess, spirit, stoutheartedness, valour

intricacy *n* **1, 2 = complexity**, complication, convolutions, elaborateness, entanglement, intricateness, involution, involvement, knottiness, obscurity

intricate *adj* **1, 2 = complicated**, baroque, Byzantine, complex, convoluted, difficult, elaborate, fancy, involved, knotty, labyrinthine, obscure, perplexing, rococo, sophisticated, tangled, tortuous
Antonyms *adj* clear, easy, obvious, plain, simple, straightforward

intrigue *vb* **1 = interest**, arouse the curiosity of, attract, charm, fascinate, pique, rivet, tickle one's fancy, titillate **2 = plot**, connive, conspire, machinate, manoeuvre, scheme ◆ *n* **4 = plot**, cabal, chicanery, collusion, conspiracy, double-dealing, knavery, machination, manipulation, manoeuvre, ruse, scheme, sharp practice, stratagem, trickery, wile **5 = affair**, amour, intimacy, liaison, romance

intriguing *adj* **1 = interesting**, beguiling, compelling, diverting, exciting, fascinating, tantalizing, titillating

intrinsic *adj* **1 = inborn**, basic, built-in, central, congenital, constitutional, elemental, essential, fundamental, genuine, inbred, inherent, native, natural, radical, real, true, underlying
Antonyms *adj* acquired, added, appended, artificial, extraneous, extrinsic, incidental

intrinsically *adv* **1 = essentially**, as such, at heart, basically, by definition, constitutionally, fundamentally, in itself, per se

introduce *vb* **1 = present**, acquaint, do the honours, familiarize, make known, make the introduction **3 = bring up**, advance, air, broach, moot, offer, propose, put forward, recommend, set forth, submit, suggest, ventilate **4 = bring in**, begin, commence, establish, found, inaugurate, initiate, institute, launch, organize, pioneer, set up, start, usher in **6 = lead into**, announce, lead off, open, preface **7 = insert**, add, inject, interpolate, interpose, put in, throw in (*inf.*)

introduction *n* **1 = launch**, baptism, debut, establishment, first acquaintance, inauguration, induction, initiation, institution, pioneering, presentation **4, 5 = opening**, commencement, exordium, foreword, intro (*inf.*), lead-in, opening passage, opening remarks, overture, preamble, preface, preliminaries, prelude, proem, prolegomena, prolegomenon, prologue
Antonyms *n* ≠ **launch:** completion, elimination, termination ≠ **opening:** conclusion, end, epilogue

introductory *adj* **= preliminary**, early, elementary, first, inaugural, initial, initiatory, opening, precursory, prefatory, preparatory, starting
Antonyms *adj* closing, concluding, final, last, terminating

intromit (ˌɪntrəˈmɪt) *vb* **intromits, intromitting, intromitted.** (*tr*) *Rare.* to enter or insert. [C15: from L *intrōmittere* to send in]
▸ˌ**introˈmissible** *adj* ▸ˌ**introˈmission** *n* ▸ˌ**introˈmittent** *adj*

introspection ⓣ (ˌɪntrəˈspɛkʃən) *n* the examination of one's own thoughts, impressions, and feelings. [C17: from L *intrōspicere* to look within]
▸ˌ**introˈspective** *adj* ▸ˌ**introˈspectively** *adv*

introversion (ˌɪntrəˈvɜːʃən) *n Psychol.* the directing of interest inwards towards one's own thoughts and feelings rather than towards the external world or making social contacts.
▸ˌ**introˈversive** *or* ˌ**introˈvertive** *adj*

introvert ⓣ *n* (ˈɪntrəˌvɜːt). **1** *Psychol.* a person prone to introversion. ◆ *adj* (ˈɪntrəˌvɜːt). **2** Also: **introverted.** characterized by introversion. ◆ *vb* (ˌɪntrəˈvɜːt). **3** (*tr*) *Pathol.* to turn (a hollow organ or part) inside out. [C17: see INTRO-, INVERT]

intrude ⓣ (ɪnˈtruːd) *vb* **intrudes, intruding, intruded. 1** (often foll. by *into, on,* or *upon*) to put forward or interpose (oneself, one's views, something) abruptly or without invitation. **2** *Geol.* to force or thrust (molten magma) between solid rocks. [C16: from L *intrūdere* to thrust in]
▸**inˈtruder** *n* ▸**inˈtrudingly** *adv*

intrusion ⓣ (ɪnˈtruːʒən) *n* **1** the act or an instance of intruding; an unwelcome visit, etc.: *an intrusion on one's privacy.* **2a** the movement of magma into spaces in the overlying strata to form igneous rock. **2b** any igneous rock formed in this way. **3** *Property law.* an unlawful entry onto land by a stranger after determination of a particular estate of freehold.
▸**inˈtrusional** *adj*

intrusive ⓣ (ɪnˈtruːsɪv) *adj* **1** characterized by intrusion or tending to intrude. **2** (of igneous rocks) formed by intrusion. **3** *Phonetics.* relating to or denoting a speech sound that is introduced into a word or piece of connected speech for a phonetic reason.
▸**inˈtrusively** *adv* ▸**inˈtrusiveness** *n*

intrust ⓣ (ɪnˈtrʌst) *vb* a less common spelling of **entrust.**

intubate (ˈɪntjʊˌbeɪt) *vb* **intubates, intubating, intubated.** (*tr*) *Med.* to insert a tube into (a hollow organ).
▸ˌ**intuˈbation** *n*

intuit (ɪnˈtjuːɪt) *vb* **intuits, intuiting, intuited.** to know or discover by intuition.
▸**inˈtuitable** *adj*

intuition ⓣ (ˌɪntjʊˈɪʃən) *n* **1** knowledge or belief obtained neither by reason nor perception. **2** instinctive knowledge or belief. **3** a hunch or unjustified belief. [C15: from LL *intuitiō* a contemplation, from L *intuērī* to gaze upon, from *tuērī* to look at]
▸ˌ**intuˈitional** *adj* ▸ˌ**intuˈitionally** *adv*

intuitionism (ˌɪntjʊˈɪʃəˌnɪzəm) *or* **intuitionalism** *n Philosophy.* **1** the doctrine that knowledge is acquired primarily by intuition. **2** the theory that the solution to moral problems can be discovered by intuition. **3** the doctrine that external objects are known to be real by intuition.
▸ˌ**intuˈitionist** *or* ˌ**intuˈitionalist** *n*

intuitive ⓣ (ɪnˈtjuːɪtɪv) *adj* **1** resulting from intuition: *an intuitive awareness.* **2** of, characterized by, or involving intuition.
▸**inˈtuitively** *adv* ▸**inˈtuitiveness** *n*

intumesce (ˌɪntjʊˈmɛs) *vb* **intumesces, intumescing, intumesced.** (*intr*) to swell. [C18: from L *intumescere,* from *tumescere* to begin to swell, from *tumēre* to swell]
▸ˌ**intuˈmescence** *n*

intussusception (ˌɪntəssəˈsɛpʃən) *n* **1** *Pathol.* the telescoping of one section of the intestinal tract into a lower section. **2** *Biol.* growth in the surface area of a cell by the deposition of new particles between the existing particles of the cell wall. [C18: from L *intus* within + *susceptiō* a taking up]

Inuit *or* **Innuit** (ˈɪnjuːɪt) *n, pl* **Inuit, Inuits** *or* **Innuit, Innuits.** an Eskimo of North America or Greenland, as distinguished from one from Asia or the Aleutian Islands. [from Eskimo *inuit* people, pl of *inuk* a man]

Inuktitut (ɪˈnʊktɪˌtʊt) *n Canad.* the language of the Inuit; Eskimo. [from Eskimo *inuk* man + *titut* speech]

inunction (ɪnˈʌŋkʃən) *n* **1** the application of an ointment to the skin, esp. by rubbing. **2** the ointment so used. **3** the act of anointing; anointment. [C15: from L *inunguere* to anoint, from *unguere;* see UNCTION]

inundate ⓣ (ˈɪnʌnˌdeɪt) *vb* **inundates, inundating, inundated.** (*tr*) **1** to cover completely with water; overflow; flood; swamp. **2** to overwhelm, as if with a flood: *to be inundated with requests.* [C17: from L *inundāre,* from *unda* wave]
▸ˈ**inundant** *or* **inˈundatory** *adj* ▸ˌ**inunˈdation** *n* ▸ˈ**inunˌdator** *n*

inure ⓣ *or* **enure** (ɪˈnjʊə) *vb* **inures, inuring, inured** *or* **enures, enuring, enured. 1** (*tr; often passive;* often foll. by *to*) to cause to accept or become hardened to; habituate. **2** (*intr*) (esp. of a law, etc.) to come into operation; take effect. [C15 *enuren* to accustom, from *ure* use, from OF *euvre* custom, work, from L *opera* works]
▸**inˈurement** *or* **enˈurement** *n*

in utero *Latin.* (ɪn ˈjuːtərəʊ) *adv, adj* in the uterus.

inv. *abbrev. for:* **1** invented. **2** inventor. **3** invoice.

in vacuo *Latin.* (ɪn ˈvækjʊˌəʊ) *adv* in a vacuum.

invade ⓣ (ɪnˈveɪd) *vb* **invades, invading, invaded. 1** to enter (a country, territory, etc.) by military force. **2** (*tr*) to occupy in large numbers; overrun; infest. **3** (*tr*) to trespass or encroach upon (privacy, etc.). **4** (*tr*) to enter and spread throughout, esp. harmfully; pervade. [C15: from L *invādere,* from *vādere* to go]
▸**inˈvadable** *adj* ▸**inˈvader** *n*

invaginate *vb* (ɪnˈvædʒɪˌneɪt), **invaginates, invaginating, invaginated. 1** *Pathol.* to push one section of (a tubular organ or part) back into itself so that it becomes ensheathed. **2** (*intr*) (of the outer layer of an organism or part) to undergo this process. ◆ *adj* (ɪnˈvædʒɪnɪt, -ˌneɪt). **3** (of an organ or part) folded back upon itself. [C19: from Med. L *invāgīnāre,* from L IN-[2] + *vāgīna* sheath]
▸**inˈvaginable** *adj* ▸**inˌvagiˈnation** *n*

invalid[1] ⓣ (ˈɪnvəˌliːd, -lɪd) *n* **1a** a person suffering from disablement or chronic ill health. **1b** (*as modifier*): *an invalid chair.* ◆ *adj* **2** suffering from or disabled by injury, sickness, etc. ◆ *vb* (*tr*) **3** to cause to become an invalid; disable. **4** (*often passive;* usually foll. by *out*) *Chiefly Brit.* to require (a member of the armed forces) to retire from active service through wounds or illness. [C17: from L *invalidus* infirm, from IN-[1] + *validus* strong]
▸**invalidity** (ˌɪnvəˈlɪdɪtɪ) *n*

invalid[2] ⓣ (ɪnˈvælɪd) *adj* **1** not valid; having no cogency or legal force. **2** *Logic.* (of an argument) having a conclusion that does not follow from the premises. [C16: from Med. L *invalidus* without legal force; see INVALID[1]]
▸ˌ**invaˈlidity** *or* **inˈvalidness** *n* ▸**inˈvalidly** *adv*

invalidate ⓣ (ɪnˈvælɪˌdeɪt) *vb* **invalidates, invalidating, invalidated.** (*tr*) **1** to render weak or ineffective (an argument). **2** to take away the legal force or effectiveness of; annul (a contract).
▸**inˌvaliˈdation** *n* ▸**inˈvaliˌdator** *n*

invaluable ⓣ (ɪnˈvæljʊəbᵊl) *adj* having great value that is impossible to calculate; priceless.
▸**inˈvaluableness** *n* ▸**inˈvaluably** *adv*

Invar (ɪnˈvɑː) *n Trademark.* an alloy containing iron, nickel, and carbon. It has a very low coefficient of expansion and is used for the balance springs of watches, etc. [C20: shortened from INVARIABLE]

invariable ⓣ (ɪnˈvɛərɪəbᵊl) *adj* **1** not subject to alteration; unchanging. ◆ *n* **2** a mathematical quantity having an unchanging value; a constant.
▸**inˌvariaˈbility** *or* **inˈvariableness** *n* ▸**inˈvariably** *adv*

THESAURUS

introspection *n* = **self-examination,** brooding, heart-searching, introversion, navel-gazing (*sl.*), self-analysis

introspective *adj* = **inward-looking,** brooding, contemplative, inner-directed, introverted, meditative, pensive, subjective

introvert *adj* **2** = **introspective,** indrawn, inner-directed, introverted, inward-looking, self-centred, self-contained, withdrawn

intrude *vb* **1** = **interfere,** butt in, encroach, infringe, interrupt, meddle, obtrude, push in, put one's two cents in (*US sl.*), thrust oneself in *or* forward, trespass, violate

intruder *n* **1** = **trespasser,** burglar, gate-crasher (*inf.*), infiltrator, interloper, invader, prowler, raider, snooper (*inf.*), squatter, thief

intrusion *n* **1** = **invasion,** encroachment, infringement, interference, interruption, trespass, violation

intrusive *adj* **1** = **interfering,** disturbing, forward, impertinent, importunate, invasive, meddlesome, nosy (*inf.*), officious, presumptuous, pushy (*inf.*), uncalled-for, unwanted

intrust *see* **entrust**

intuition *n* **1-3** = **instinct,** discernment, hunch, insight, perception, presentiment, sixth sense

intuitive *adj* **1, 2** = **instinctive,** innate, instinctual, involuntary, spontaneous, unreflecting, untaught

intuitively *adv* **1, 2** = **instinctively,** automatically, innately, instinctually, involuntarily, spontaneously

inundate *vb* **1, 2** = **flood,** deluge, drown, engulf, glut, immerse, overflow, overrun, overwhelm, submerge, swamp

inundation *n* **1, 2** = **flood,** deluge, overflow, tidal wave, torrent

inured *adj* **1** = **accustomed,** annealed, case-hardened, desensitized, familiarized, habituated, hardened, strengthened, tempered, toughened, trained

invade *vb* **1** = **attack,** assail, assault, burst in, descend upon, encroach, infringe, make inroads, occupy, raid, violate **2** = **infest,** infect, overrun, overspread, penetrate, permeate, pervade, swarm over

invader *n* **1** = **attacker,** aggressor, alien, looter, plunderer, raider, trespasser

invalid[1] *n* **1** = **patient,** convalescent, valetudinarian ◆ *adj* **2** = **disabled,** ailing, bedridden, feeble, frail, ill, infirm, poorly (*inf.*), sick, sickly, valetudinarian, weak

invalid[2] *adj* **1, 2** = **null and void,** baseless, fallacious, false, ill-founded, illogical, inoperative, irrational, not binding, nugatory, null, unfounded, unscientific, unsound, untrue, void, worthless
Antonyms *adj* logical, operative, rational, solid, sound, true, valid, viable

invalidate *vb* **2** = **nullify,** abrogate, annul, cancel, overrule, overthrow, quash, render null and void, rescind, undermine, undo, weaken
Antonyms *vb* authorize, empower, ratify, sanction, strengthen, validate

invalidity[2] *n* **1, 2** = **falsity,** fallaciousness, fallacy, illogicality, inconsistency, irrationality, sophism, speciousness, unsoundness

invaluable *adj* = **precious,** beyond price, costly, inestimable, priceless, valuable, worth one's *or* its weight in gold
Antonyms *adj* cheap, rubbishy, valueless, worthless

invariable *adj* **1** = **regular,** changeless, consistent, constant, fixed, immutable, inflexible, rigid, set, unalterable, unchangeable, unchanging, unfailing, uniform, unvarying, unwavering
Antonyms *adj* alterable, changeable, changing, differing, flexible, inconsistent, irregular, uneven, variable, varying

invariably *adv* **1** = **consistently,** always, cus-

invariant (ɪnˈvɛərɪənt) *Maths.* ◆ *n* **1** an entity, quantity, etc., that is unaltered by a particular transformation of coordinates. ◆ *adj* **2** (of a relationship or a property of a function, configuration, or equation) unaltered by a particular transformation of coordinates.
▸**inˈvariance** *or* **inˈvariancy** *n*

invasion ⓘ (ɪnˈveɪʒən) *n* **1** the act of invading with armed forces. **2** any encroachment or intrusion: *an invasion of rats.* **3** the onset or advent of something harmful, esp. of a disease. **4** *Pathol.* the spread of cancer from its point of origin into surrounding tissues. **5** the movement of plants to an area to which they are not native.

invasive (ɪnˈveɪsɪv) *adj* **1** of or relating to an invasion, intrusion, etc. **2** (of surgery) involving making a relatively large incision in the body to gain access to the target of the surgery.

invective ⓘ (ɪnˈvɛktɪv) *n* **1** vehement accusation or denunciation, esp. of a bitterly abusive or sarcastic kind. ◆ *adj* **2** characterized by or using abusive language, bitter sarcasm, etc. [C15: from LL *invectīvus* reproachful, from L *invectus* carried in; see INVEIGH]
▸**inˈvectively** *adv* ▸**inˈvectiveness** *n*

inveigh (ɪnˈveɪ) *vb* (*intr;* foll. by *against*) to speak with violent or invective language; rail. [C15: from L *invehī*, lit.: to be carried in, hence, assail physically or verbally]
▸**inˈveigher** *n*

inveigle ⓘ (ɪnˈviːgᵊl, -ˈveɪ-) *vb* **inveigles, inveigling, inveigled.** (*tr;* often foll. by *into* or an infinitive) to lead (someone into a situation) or persuade (to do something) by cleverness or trickery; cajole. [C15: from OF *avogler* to blind, deceive, from *avogle* blind, from Med. L *ab oculis* without eyes]
▸**inˈveiglement** *n* ▸**inˈveigler** *n*

invent ⓘ (ɪnˈvɛnt) *vb* **1** to create or devise (new ideas, machines, etc.). **2** to make up (falsehoods, etc.); fabricate. [C15: from L *invenīre* to find, come upon]
▸**inˈventable** *adj*

invention ⓘ (ɪnˈvɛnʃən) *n* **1** the act or process of inventing. **2** something that is invented. **3** *Patent law.* the discovery or production of some new or improved process or machine. **4** creative power or ability; inventive skill. **5** *Euphemistic.* a fabrication; lie. **6** *Music.* a short piece consisting of two or three parts usually in imitative counterpoint.
▸**inˈventional** *adj* ▸**inˈventionless** *adj*

inventive ⓘ (ɪnˈvɛntɪv) *adj* **1** skilled or quick at contriving; ingenious; resourceful. **2** characterized by inventive skill: *an inventive programme of work.* **3** of or relating to invention.
▸**inˈventively** *adv* ▸**inˈventiveness** *n*

inventor ⓘ (ɪnˈvɛntə) *n* a person who invents, esp. as a profession.
▸**inˈventress** *fem n*

inventory ⓘ (ˈɪnvəntərɪ, -trɪ) *n, pl* **inventories. 1** a detailed list of articles, goods, property, etc. **2** (*often pl*) *Accounting, chiefly US.* **2a** the amount or value of a firm's current assets that consist of raw materials, work in progress, and finished goods; stock. **2b** such assets individually. ◆ *vb* **inventories, inventorying, inventoried. 3** (*tr*) to enter (items) in an inventory; make a list of. [C16: from Med. L *inventōrium;* see INVENT]
▸**ˈinventoriable** *adj* ▸**ˌinvenˈtorial** *adj* ▸**ˌinvenˈtorially** *adv*

Inverness (ˌɪnvəˈnɛs) *n* (*sometimes not cap.*) an overcoat with a removable cape. [C19: after *Inverness*, town in N Scotland]

inverse ⓘ (ɪnˈvɜːs, ˈɪnvɜːs) *adj* **1** opposite or contrary in effect, sequence, direction, etc. **2** *Maths.* **2a** (of a relationship) containing two variables such that an increase in one results in a decrease in the other. **2b** (of an element) operating on a specified member of a set to produce the identity of the set: *the additive inverse element of x is –x.* **3** (*usually prenominal*) upside-down; inverted: *in an inverse position.* ◆ *n* **4** *Maths.* an inverse element. [C17: from L *inversus*, from *invertere* to INVERT]
▸**inˈversely** *adv*

inverse function *n* a function whose independent variable is the dependent variable of a given trigonometric or hyperbolic function: *the inverse function of* sin *x* is arcsin *y* (*also written* $\sin^{-1}y$).

inversion ⓘ (ɪnˈvɜːʃən) *n* **1** the act of inverting or state of being inverted. **2** something inverted, esp. a reversal of order, mutual functions, etc.: *an inversion of their previous relationship.* **3** Also: **anastrophe.** *Rhetoric.* the reversal of a normal order of words, as in the phrase *weeping left she sorrowfully.* **4** *Chem.* **4a** the conversion of a dextrorotatory solution of sucrose into a laevorotatory solution of glucose and fructose by hydrolysis. **4b** any similar reaction in which the optical properties of the reactants are opposite to those of the products. **5** *Music.* **5a** the process or result of transposing the notes of a chord such that the root, originally in the bass, is placed in an upper part. **5b** the modification of an interval in which the higher note becomes the lower or the lower one the higher. **6** *Pathol.* abnormal positioning of an organ or part, as in being upside down or turned inside out. **7** *Psychiatry.* **7a** the adoption of the role or characteristics of the opposite sex. **7b** another word for **homosexuality. 8** *Meteorol.* an abnormal condition in which the layer of air next to the earth's surface is cooler than an overlying layer. **9** *Computing.* an operation by which each digit of a binary number is changed to the alternative digit, as *10110* to *01001.*
▸**inˈversive** *adj*

invert ⓘ *vb* (ɪnˈvɜːt). **1** to turn or cause to turn upside down or inside out. **2** (*tr*) to reverse in effect, sequence, direction, etc. **3** (*tr*) *Phonetics.* to turn (the tip of the tongue) up and back to pronounce (a speech sound). ◆ *n* (ˈɪnvɜːt). **4** *Psychiatry.* **4a** a person who adopts the role of the opposite sex. **4b** another word for **homosexual. 5** *Archit.* **5a** the lower inner surface of a drain, sewer, etc. **5b** an arch that is concave upwards, esp. one used in foundations. [C16: from L *invertere*, from IN-[2] + *vertere* to turn]
▸**inˈvertible** *adj* ▸**inˌvertiˈbility** *n*

invertase (ɪnˈvɜːteɪz) *n* an enzyme, occurring in the intestinal juice of animals and in yeasts, that hydrolyses sucrose to glucose and fructose.

invertebrate (ɪnˈvɜːtɪbrɪt, -ˌbreɪt) *n* **1** any animal lacking a backbone, including all species not classified as vertebrates. ◆ *adj also* **invertebral. 2** of, relating to, or designating invertebrates.

inverted comma *n* another term for **quotation mark.**

inverted mordent *n Music.* a melodic ornament consisting of the rapid alternation of a principal note with a note one degree higher.

inverter *or* **invertor** (ɪnˈvɜːtə) *n* any device for converting a direct current into an alternating current.

invert sugar *n* a mixture of fructose and glucose obtained by the inversion of sucrose.

invest ⓘ (ɪnˈvɛst) *vb* **1** (often foll. by *in*) to lay out (money or capital in an enterprise) with the expectation of profit. **2** (*tr;* often foll. by *in*) to devote (effort, resources, etc., to a project). **3** (*tr;* often foll. by *in* or *with*) *Arch. or ceremonial.* to clothe or adorn (in some garment, esp. the robes of an office). **4** (*tr;* often foll. by *in*) to install formally or ceremoniously (in an official position, rank, etc.). **5** (*tr;* foll. by *in* or *with*) to place (power, authority, etc., in) or provide (with power or authority): *to invest new rights in the monarchy.* **6** (*tr; usually passive;* foll. by *in* or *with*) to provide or endow (a person with qualities, characteristics, etc.). **7** (*tr;* foll. by *with*) *Usually poetic.* to cover or adorn, as if with a coat or garment: *when spring invests the trees with leaves.* **8** (*tr*) *Rare.* to surround with military forces; besiege. **9** (*intr;* foll. by *in*) *Inf.* to purchase; buy. [C16: from Med. L *investīre* to clothe, from L, from *vestīre*, from *vestis* a garment]
▸**inˈvestable** *or* **inˈvestible** *adj* ▸**inˈvestor** *n*

investigate ⓘ (ɪnˈvɛstɪˌgeɪt) *vb* **investigates, investigating, investigated.** to inquire into (a situation or problem, esp. a crime or death) thoroughly; examine systematically, esp. in order to discover the truth. [C16: from L *investīgāre* to search after, from IN-[2] + *vestīgium* track; see VESTIGE]
▸**inˈvestiˌgative** *or* **inˈvestigatory** *adj* ▸**inˈvestiˌgator** *n*

THESAURUS

tomarily, day in, day out, ever, every time, habitually, inevitably, on every occasion, perpetually, regularly, unfailingly, without exception

invasion *n* **1** = **attack**, aggression, assault, campaign, foray, incursion, inroad, irruption, offensive, onslaught, raid **2** = **intrusion**, breach, encroachment, infiltration, infraction, infringement, overstepping, usurpation, violation

invective *n* **1** = **abuse**, berating, billingsgate, castigation, censure, contumely, denunciation, diatribe, obloquy, philippic(s), reproach, revilement, sarcasm, tirade, tongue-lashing, vilification, vituperation

inveigle *n* = **coax**, allure, bamboozle (*inf.*), beguile, cajole, con (*sl.*), decoy, ensnare, entice, entrap, lead on, lure, manipulate, manoeuvre, persuade, seduce, sweet-talk (*inf.*), wheedle

invent *vb* **1** = **create**, coin, come up with (*inf.*), conceive, contrive, design, devise, discover, dream up (*inf.*), formulate, imagine, improvise, originate, think up **2** = **make up**, concoct, cook up (*inf.*), fabricate, feign, forge, manufacture, trump up

invention *n* **2** = **creation**, brainchild (*inf.*), contraption, contrivance, design, development, device, discovery, gadget, instrument, waldo **4** = **creativity**, coinage, creativeness, genius, imagination, ingenuity, inspiration, inventiveness, originality, resourcefulness **5** = **fiction**, deceit, fabrication, fake, falsehood, fantasy, fib (*inf.*), figment *or* product of (someone's) imagination, forgery, lie, prevarication, sham, story, tall story (*inf.*), untruth, urban legend, urban myth, yarn

inventive *adj* **1** = **creative**, fertile, gifted, ground-breaking, imaginative, ingenious, innovative, inspired, original, resourceful
Antonyms *adj* imitative, pedestrian, trite, unimaginative, uninspired, uninventive

inventor *n* = **creator**, architect, author, coiner, designer, father, framer, maker, originator

inventory *n* **1** = **list**, account, catalogue, file, record, register, roll, roster, schedule, stock book

inverse *adj* **1** = **opposite**, contrary, converse, inverted, reverse, reversed, transposed

inversion *n* **1** = **reversal**, contraposition, contrariety, transposal, transposition **2** = **opposite**, antipode, antithesis, contrary

invert *vb* **1, 2** = **overturn**, capsize, introvert, intussuscept (*Pathology*), invaginate (*Pathology*), overset, reverse, transpose, turn inside out, turn turtle, turn upside down, upset, upturn

invest *vb* **1** = **spend**, advance, devote, lay out, put in, sink **3** *Archaic* = **clothe**, array, bedeck, bedizen (*arch.*), deck, drape, dress, robe **4** = **install**, adopt, consecrate, enthrone, establish, inaugurate, induct, ordain **5** = **empower**, authorize, charge, license, sanction, vest **6** = **provide**, endow, endue, supply **8** = **besiege**, beleaguer, beset, enclose, lay siege to, surround

investigate *vb* = **examine**, consider, explore, go into, inquire into, inspect, look into, make inquiries, probe, put to the test, recce (*sl.*), research, scrutinize, search, sift, study, work over

investigation *n* = **examination**, analysis, exploration, fact finding, hearing, inquest, inquiry, inspection, probe, recce (*sl.*), research, review, scrutiny, search, study, survey

investigative *adj* = **fact-finding**, inspecting, investigating, research, researching

investigator *n* = **examiner**, gumshoe (*US sl.*),

DICTIONARY

investigation Ⓣ (ɪnˌvɛstɪˈgeɪʃən) *n* the act or process of investigating; a careful search or examination in order to discover facts, etc.

investiture Ⓣ (ɪnˈvɛstɪtʃə) *n* **1** the act of presenting with a title or with the robes and insignia of an office or rank. **2** (in feudal society) the formal bestowal of the possessory right to a fief.
▸**inˈvestitive** *adj*

investment Ⓣ (ɪnˈvɛstmənt) *n* **1a** the act of investing money. **1b** the amount invested. **1c** an enterprise, asset, etc., in which money is or can be invested. **2a** the act of investing effort, resources, etc. **2b** the amount invested. **3** *Biol.* the outer layer or covering of an organ, part, or organism. **4** a less common word for **investiture** (sense 1). **5** the act of investing or state of being invested, as with an official robe, specific quality, etc. **6** *Rare.* the act of besieging with military forces, works, etc.

investment analyst *n* a specialist in forecasting the prices of stocks and shares.

investment bond *n* a single-premium life-assurance policy in which a fixed sum is invested in an asset-backed fund.

investment trust *n* a financial enterprise that invests its subscribed capital in securities for its investors' benefit.

inveterate Ⓣ (ɪnˈvɛtərɪt) *adj* **1** long established, esp. so as to be deep-rooted or ingrained: *an inveterate feeling of hostility.* **2** (*prenominal*) confirmed in a habit or practice, esp. a bad one; hardened. [C16: from L *inveterātus* of long standing, from *inveterāre* to make old, from IN-[2] + *vetus* old]
▸**inˈveteracy** *n* ▸**inˈveterately** *adv*

invidious Ⓣ (ɪnˈvɪdɪəs) *adj* **1** incurring or tending to arouse resentment, unpopularity, etc.: *an invidious task.* **2** (of comparisons or distinctions) unfairly or offensively discriminating. [C17: from L *invidiōsus* full of envy, from *invidia* ENVY]
▸**inˈvidiously** *adv* ▸**inˈvidiousness** *n*

invigilate Ⓣ (ɪnˈvɪdʒɪˌleɪt) *vb* **invigilates, invigilating, invigilated.** (*intr*) **1** *Brit.* to watch examination candidates, esp. to prevent cheating. US word: **proctor. 2** *Arch.* to keep watch. [C16: from L *invigilāre* to watch over; see VIGIL]
▸**inˌvigiˈlation** *n* ▸**inˈvigiˌlator** *n*

invigorate Ⓣ (ɪnˈvɪgəˌreɪt) *vb* **invigorates, invigorating, invigorated.** (*tr*) to give vitality and vigour to; animate; brace; refresh: *to be invigorated by fresh air.* [C17: from IN-[2] + L *vigor* VIGOUR]
▸**inˈvigorˌating** *adj* ▸**inˌvigorˈation** *n* ▸**inˈvigorative** *adj* ▸**inˈvigorˌator** *n*

invincible Ⓣ (ɪnˈvɪnsəbᵊl) *adj* incapable of being defeated; unconquerable. [C15: from LL *invincibilis*, from L IN-[1] + *vincere* to conquer]
▸**inˌvinciˈbility** *or* **inˈvincibleness** *n* ▸**inˈvincibly** *adv*

inviolable Ⓣ (ɪnˈvaɪələbᵊl) *adj* that must not or cannot be transgressed, dishonoured, or broken; to be kept sacred: *an inviolable oath.*
▸**inˌviolaˈbility** *n* ▸**inˈviolably** *adv*

inviolate Ⓣ (ɪnˈvaɪəlɪt, -ˌleɪt) *adj* **1** free from violation, injury, disturbance, etc. **2** a less common word for **inviolable.**
▸**inˈviolacy** *or* **inˈviolateness** *n* ▸**inˈviolately** *adv*

invisible Ⓣ (ɪnˈvɪzəbᵊl) *adj* **1** not visible; not able to be perceived by the eye: *invisible rays.* **2** concealed from sight; hidden. **3** not easily seen or noticed: *invisible mending.* **4** kept hidden from public view; secret. **5** *Econ.* of or relating to services, such as insurance and freight, rather than goods: *invisible earnings.* ◆ *n* **6** *Econ.* an invisible item of trade; service.
▸**inˌvisiˈbility** *or* **inˈvisibleness** *n* ▸**inˈvisibly** *adv*

invitation Ⓣ (ˌɪnvɪˈteɪʃən) *n* **1a** the act of inviting, such as an offer of entertainment or hospitality. **1b** (*as modifier*): *an invitation race.* **2** the act of enticing or attracting; allurement.

invite Ⓣ *vb* (ɪnˈvaɪt), **invites, inviting, invited.** (*tr*) **1** to ask (a person) in a friendly or polite way (to do something, attend an event, etc.). **2** to make a request for, esp. publicly or formally: *to invite applications.* **3** to bring on or provoke; give occasion for: *you invite disaster by your actions.* **4** to welcome or tempt. ◆ *n* (ˈɪnvaɪt). **5** *Inf.* an invitation. [C16: from L *invitāre* to invite, entertain]
▸**inˈviter** *n*

inviting Ⓣ (ɪnˈvaɪtɪŋ) *adj* tempting; alluring; attractive.
▸**inˈvitingness** *n*

in vitro (ɪn ˈviːtrəʊ) *adv, adj* (of biological processes or reactions) made to occur outside the body of the organism in an artificial environment. [NL, lit.: in glass]

in vitro fertilization *n* a technique enabling some women who are unable to conceive to bear children. Egg cells removed from a woman's ovary are fertilized by sperm in vitro; some of the resulting fertilized egg cells are then implanted into her uterus. Abbrev.: **IVF.**

in vivo (ɪn ˈviːvəʊ) *adv, adj* (of biological processes or experiments) occurring or carried out in the living organism. [NL, lit.: in a living (thing)]

invocation Ⓣ (ˌɪnvəˈkeɪʃən) *n* **1** the act of invoking or calling upon some agent for assistance. **2** a prayer asking God for help, forgiveness, etc. **3** an appeal for inspiration from a Muse or deity at the beginning of a poem. **4a** the act of summoning a spirit from another world by ritual incantation or magic. **4b** the incantation used in this act.
▸ˌ**invoˈcational** *adj* ▸**invocatory** (ɪnˈvɒkətərɪ, -trɪ) *adj*

invoice (ˈɪnvɔɪs) *n* **1** a document issued by a seller to a buyer listing the goods or services supplied and stating the sum of money due. **2** *Rare.* a consignment of invoiced merchandise. ◆ *vb* **invoices, invoicing, invoiced. 3** (*tr*) **3a** to present (a customer, etc.) with an invoice. **3b** to list (merchandise sold) on an invoice. [C16: from earlier *invoyes*, from OF *envois*, pl. of *envoi* message; see ENVOY[1]]

invoke Ⓣ (ɪnˈvəʊk) *vb* **invokes, invoking, invoked.** (*tr*) **1** to call upon (an agent, esp. God or another deity) for help, inspiration, etc. **2** to put (a law, penalty, etc.) into use: *the union invoked the dispute procedure.* **3** to appeal to (an outside authority) for confirmation, corroboration, etc. **4** to implore or beg (help, etc.). **5** to summon (a spirit, etc.); conjure up. [C15: from L *invocāre* to appeal to, from *vocāre* to call]
▸**inˈvocable** *adj* ▸**inˈvoker** *n*

> **USAGE NOTE** *Invoke* is sometimes wrongly used where *evoke* is meant: *this proposal evoked* (not *invoked*) *a strong reaction.*

involucre (ˈɪnvəˌluːkə) *or* **involucrum** (ˌɪnvəˈluːkrəm) *n, pl* **involucres** *or* **involucra** (-krə). a ring of bracts at the base of an inflorescence. [C16 (in the sense: envelope): from NL *involucrum*, from L: wrapper, from *involvere* to wrap]
▸ˌ**invoˈlucral** *adj* ▸ˌ**invoˈlucrate** *adj*

involuntary Ⓣ (ɪnˈvɒləntərɪ, -trɪ) *adj* **1** carried out without one's conscious wishes; not voluntary; unintentional. **2** *Physiol.* (esp. of a movement or muscle) performed or acting without conscious control.
▸**inˈvoluntarily** *adv* ▸**inˈvoluntariness** *n*

involute *adj* (ˈɪnvəˌluːt), *also* **involuted. 1** complex, intricate, or involved. **2** *Bot.* (esp. of petals, leaves, etc., in bud) having margins that are rolled inwards. **3** (of certain shells) closely coiled so that the axis is obscured. ◆ *n* (ˈɪnvəˌluːt). **4** *Geom.* the curve described by the free end of a thread as it is wound around another curve, the **evolute,** such that its normals are tangential to the evolute. ◆ *vb* (ˌɪnvəˈluːt), **involutes, involuting, involuted. 5** (*intr*) to become involute. [C17: from L *involūtus*, from *involvere*; see INVOLVE]
▸ˈ**invoˌlutely** *adv* ▸ˌ**invoˈlutedly** *adv*

THESAURUS

inquirer, (private) detective, private eye (*inf.*), researcher, reviewer, sleuth

investiture *n* **1** = **installation**, admission, enthronement, inauguration, induction, instatement, investing, investment, ordination

investment *n* **1a** = **transaction**, investing, speculation, venture **1b** = **stake**, ante (*inf.*), contribution **6** = **siege**, beleaguering, besieging, blockading, surrounding

inveterate *adj* **1, 2** = **long-standing**, chronic, confirmed, deep-dyed (*usually derogatory*), deep-rooted, deep-seated, dyed-in-the-wool, entrenched, established, habitual, hard-core, hardened, incorrigible, incurable, ineradicable, ingrained, obstinate

invidious *adj* **1** = **undesirable**, hateful, thankless, unpleasant
Antonyms *adj* desirable, pleasant, pleasing

invigilate *vb* **1** = **watch over**, conduct, keep an eye on, oversee, preside over, run, superintend, supervise

invigorate *vb* = **refresh**, animate, brace, buck up (*inf.*), energize, enliven, exhilarate, fortify, freshen (up), galvanize, harden, liven up, nerve, pep up, perk up, put new heart into, quicken, rejuvenate, revitalize, stimulate, strengthen

invigorating *adj* = **refreshing**, bracing, energizing, exhilarating, fresh, healthful, rejuvenating, rejuvenative, restorative, salubrious, stimulating, tonic, uplifting

invincible *adj* = **unbeatable**, impregnable, indestructible, indomitable, inseparable, insuperable, invulnerable, unassailable, unconquerable, unsurmountable, unyielding
Antonyms *adj* assailable, beatable, conquerable, defenceless, fallible, powerless, unprotected, vulnerable, weak, yielding

inviolability *n* = **sanctity**, holiness, inalienability, inviolacy, invulnerability, sacredness

inviolable *adj* = **sacrosanct**, hallowed, holy, inalienable, sacred, unalterable

inviolate *adj* **1** = **intact**, entire, pure, sacred, stainless, unbroken, undefiled, undisturbed, unhurt, unpolluted, unstained, unsullied, untouched, virgin, whole
Antonyms *adj* abused, broken, defiled, polluted, stained, sullied, touched, violated

invisible *adj* **1** = **unseen**, imperceptible, indiscernible, out of sight, unperceivable **2** = **hidden**, concealed, disguised, inappreciable, inconspicuous, infinitesimal, microscopic
Antonyms *adj* ≠ **unseen:** discernible, distinct, obvious, perceptible, seen, visible

invitation *n* **1** = **request**, asking, begging, bidding, call, invite (*inf.*), solicitation, summons, supplication **2** = **inducement**, allurement, challenge, come-on (*inf.*), coquetry, enticement, glad eye, incitement, open door, overture, provocation, temptation

invite *vb* **1, 2** = **request**, ask, beg, bid, call, request the pleasure of (someone's) company, solicit, summon **3, 4** = **encourage**, allure, ask for (*inf.*), attract, bring on, court, draw, entice, lead, leave the door open to, provoke, solicit, tempt, welcome

inviting *adj* = **tempting**, alluring, appealing, attractive, beguiling, captivating, delightful, engaging, enticing, fascinating, intriguing, magnetic, mouthwatering, pleasing, seductive, warm, welcoming, winning
Antonyms *adj* disagreeable, offensive, off-putting (*Brit. inf.*), repellent, unappealing, unattractive, undesirable, uninviting, unpleasant

invocation *n* **1, 2** = **appeal**, beseeching, entreaty, petition, prayer, supplication

invoke *vb* **1, 3, 4** = **call upon**, adjure, appeal to, beg, beseech, conjure, entreat, implore, petition, pray, solicit, supplicate **2** = **apply**, call in, have recourse to, implement, initiate, put into effect, resort to, use

involuntary *adj* **1** = **unintentional**, automatic, blind, conditioned, instinctive, instinctual, reflex, spontaneous, unconscious, uncontrolled, unthinking
Antonyms *adj* calculated, deliberate, intentional, planned, purposed, volitional, voluntary, wilful

involution (ˌɪnvəˈluːʃən) *n* **1** the act of involving or complicating or the state of being involved or complicated. **2** something involved or complicated. **3** *Zool.* degeneration or structural deformation. **4** *Biol.* an involute formation or structure. **5** *Physiol.* reduction in size of an organ or part, as of the uterus following childbirth or as a result of ageing. **6** an algebraic operation in which a number, expression, etc., is raised to a specified power.
▸ˌ**invoˈlutional** *adj*

involve ❶ (ɪnˈvɒlv) *vb* **involves, involving, involved.** (*tr*) **1** to include or contain as a necessary part. **2** to have an effect on; spread to: *the investigation involved many innocent people.* **3** (*often passive; usually foll. by in or with*) to concern or associate significantly: *many people were involved in the crime.* **4** (*often passive*) to make complicated; tangle. **5** *Rare, often poetic.* to wrap or surround. **6** *Maths, obs.* to raise to a specified power. [C14: from L *involvere* to surround, from IN-[2] + *volvere* to roll]
▸**inˈvolvement** *n* ▸**inˈvolver** *n*

invulnerable ❶ (ɪnˈvʌlnərəbᵊl, -ˈvʌlnrəbᵊl) *adj* **1** incapable of being wounded, hurt, damaged, etc. **2** incapable of being damaged or captured: *an invulnerable fortress.*
▸**inˌvulneraˈbility** *or* **inˈvulnerableness** *n* ▸**inˈvulnerably** *adv*

inward ❶ (ˈɪnwəd) *adj* **1** going or directed towards the middle of or into something. **2** situated within; inside. **3** of, relating to, or existing in the mind or spirit: *inward meditation.* **4** of one's own country or a specific country: *inward investment.* ◆ *adv* **5** a variant of **inwards.** ◆ *n* **6** the inward part; inside.
▸ˈ**inwardness** *n*

inwardly ❶ (ˈɪnwədlɪ) *adv* **1** within the private thoughts or feelings; secretly. **2** not aloud: *to laugh inwardly.* **3** with reference to the inside or inner part; internally.

inwards *adv* (ˈɪnwədz), *also* **inward. 1** towards the interior or middle of something. **2** in, into, or towards the mind or spirit. ◆ *pl n* (ˈɪnədz). **3** a variant of **innards** (sense 1).

inweave (ɪnˈwiːv) *vb* **inweaves, inweaving, inwove** *or* **inweaved; inwoven** *or* **inweaved.** (*tr*) to weave together into or as if into a design, fabric, etc.

inwrap (ɪnˈræp) *vb* **inwraps, inwrapping, inwrapped.** a less common spelling of **enwrap.**

inwrought (ˌɪnˈrɔːt) *adj* **1** worked or woven into material, esp. decoratively. **2** *Rare.* blended with other things.

in-your-face *adj Sl.* aggressive and confrontational: *provocative in-your-face activism.*

Io *the chemical symbol for* ionium.

IOC *abbrev. for* International Olympic Committee.

iodic (aɪˈɒdɪk) *adj* of or containing iodine, esp. in the pentavalent state.

iodide (ˈaɪəˌdaɪd) *n* **1** a salt of hydriodic acid, containing the iodide ion, I^-. **2** a compound containing an iodine atom, such as methyl iodide (iodomethane).

iodine (ˈaɪəˌdiːn) *n* a bluish-black element of the halogen group that sublimates into a violet irritating gas. Its compounds are used in medicine and photography and in dyes. The radioisotope **iodine-131** is used in the treatment of thyroid disease. Symbol: I; atomic no.: 53; atomic wt.: 126.90. [C19: from F *iode,* from Gk *iōdēs* rust-coloured, but mistaken as violet-coloured, from *ion* violet]

iodize *or* **iodise** (ˈaɪəˌdaɪz) *vb* **iodizes, iodizing, iodized** *or* **iodises, iodising, iodised.** (*tr*) to treat or react with iodine or an iodine compound. Also: **iodate.**
▸ˌ**iodiˈzation** *or* ˌ**iodiˈsation** *n* ▸ˈ**ioˌdizer** *or* ˈ**ioˌdiser** *n*

iodoform (aɪˈɒdəˌfɔːm) *n* a yellow crystalline solid made by heating alcohol with iodine and an alkali: used as an antiseptic. Formula: CHI_3. Systematic name: **triiodomethane.**

iodopsin (ˌaɪəˈdɒpsɪn) *n* a violet light-sensitive pigment in the cones of the retina of the eye. See also **rhodopsin.**

IOM *abbrev. for* Isle of Man.

ion (ˈaɪən, -ɒn) *n* an electrically charged atom or group of atoms formed by the loss or gain of one or more electrons. See also **cation, anion.** [C19: from Gk, lit.: going, from *ienai* to go]

-ion *suffix forming nouns.* indicating an action, process, or state: *creation; objection.* Cf. **-ation, -tion.** [from L *-iōn-, -io*]

ion exchange *n* the process in which ions are exchanged between a solution and an insoluble solid, usually a resin. It is used to soften water.

ionic (aɪˈɒnɪk) *adj* of, relating to, or occurring in the form of ions.

Ionic (aɪˈɒnɪk) *adj* **1** of, denoting, or relating to one of the five classical orders of architecture, characterized by fluted columns and capitals with scroll-like ornaments. **2** of or relating to Ionia, on the coast of Asia Minor, its inhabitants or their dialect of Ancient Greek. ◆ *n* **3** one of four chief dialects of Ancient Greek; the dialect spoken in Ionia.

ionium (aɪˈəʊnɪəm) *n Obs.* a naturally occurring radioisotope of thorium with a mass number of 230. Symbol: Io [C20: from NL]

ionization *or* **ionisation** (ˌaɪənaɪˈzeɪʃən) *n* **a** the formation of ions as a result of a chemical reaction, high temperature, electrical discharge, or radiation. **b** (*as modifier*): *ionization temperature.*

ionize *or* **ionise** (ˈaɪəˌnaɪz) *vb* **ionizes, ionizing, ionized** *or* **ionises, ionising, ionised.** to change or become changed into ions.
▸ˈ**ionˌizable** *or* ˈ**ionˌisable** *adj* ▸ˈ**ionˌizer** *or* ˈ**ionˌiser** *n*

ionosphere (aɪˈɒnəˌsfɪə) *n* a region of the earth's atmosphere, extending from about 60 to 1000 km above the earth's surface, in which there is a high concentration of free electrons formed as a result of ionizing radiation entering the atmosphere from space.
▸**ionospheric** (aɪˌɒnəˈsfɛrɪk) *adj*

iota ❶ (aɪˈəʊtə) *n* **1** the ninth letter in the Greek alphabet (Ι, ι), a vowel or semivowel. **2** (*usually used with a negative*) a very small amount; jot (esp. in **not one** *or* **an iota**). [C16: via L from Gk, of Semitic origin]

IOU *n* a written promise or reminder to pay a debt. [C17: representing *I owe you*]

-ious *suffix forming adjectives from nouns.* characterized by or full of: *suspicious.* [from L *-ius* & *-iōsus* full of]

IOW *abbrev. for* Isle of Wight.

IPA *abbrev. for* International Phonetic Alphabet.

ipecacuanha (ˌɪpɪˌkækjuˈænə) *or* **ipecac** (ˈɪpɪˌkæk) *n* **1** a low-growing South American shrub. **2** a drug prepared from the dried roots of this plant, used as a purgative and emetic. [C18: from Port., from Amerind *ipekaaguéne,* from *ipeh* low + *kaa* leaves + *guéne* vomit]

ipomoea (ˌɪpəˈmɪə, ˌaɪ-) *n* **1** any tropical or subtropical plant, such as the morning-glory, sweet potato, and jalap, having trumpet-shaped flowers. **2** the dried root of a Mexican species which yields a cathartic resin. [C18: NL, from Gk *ips* worm + *homoios* like]

ippon (ˈɪpɒn) *n Judo & karate.* a winning point awarded in a sparring competition for a perfectly executed technique. [C20: Japanese, lit.: one point]

ipse dixit *Latin.* (ˈɪpseɪ ˈdɪksɪt) *n* an arbitrary and unsupported assertion. [C16, lit.: he himself said it]

ipso facto (ˈɪpsəʊ ˈfæktəʊ) *adv* by that very fact or act. [from L]

IQ *abbrev. for* intelligence quotient.

Ir *the chemical symbol for* iridium.

Ir. *abbrev. for:* **1** Ireland. **2** Irish.

ir- *prefix* a variant of **in-**[1] and **in-**[2] before *r.*

IRA *abbrev. for* Irish Republican Army.

irade (ɪˈrɑːde) *n* a written edict of a Muslim ruler. [C19: from Turkish: will, from Ar. *irādah*]

Iranian (ɪˈreɪnɪən) *n* **1** a native or inhabitant of Iran. **2** a branch of the Indo-European family of languages, including Persian. **3** the modern Persian language. ◆ *adj* **4** relating to or characteristic of Iran, its inhabitants, or their language; Persian. **5** belonging to or relating to the Iranian branch of Indo-European.

Iran-Iraq War *n* the indecisive war (1980–88) fought by Iran and Iraq, following the Iraqi invasion of disputed border territory in Iran. Also called: **Gulf War.**

Iraqi (ɪˈrɑːkɪ) *adj* **1** of or characteristic of Iraq, in SW Asia, its inhabitants, or their language. ◆ *n, pl* **Iraqis. 2** a native or inhabitant of Iraq.

irascible ❶ (ɪˈræsɪbᵊl) *adj* **1** easily angered; irritable. **2** showing irritability: *an irascible action.* [C16: from LL *īrascibilis,* from L *īra* anger]
▸**iˌrasciˈbility** *or* **iˈrascibleness** *n* ▸**iˈrascibly** *adv*

irate ❶ (aɪˈreɪt) *adj* **1** incensed with anger; furious. **2** marked by ex-

THESAURUS

involve *vb* **1** = **include**, comprehend, comprise, contain, cover, embrace, incorporate, number among, take in **3** = **concern**, affect, associate, compromise, connect, draw in, implicate, incriminate, inculpate, mix up (*inf.*), stitch up (*sl.*), touch **4** = **complicate**, embroil, enmesh, entangle, link, mire, mix up, snarl up, tangle

involved *adj* **3** = **concerned**, caught (up), implicated, in on (*inf.*), mixed up in *or* with, occupied, participating, taking part, up to one's ears in **4** = **complicated**, Byzantine, complex, confusing, convoluted, difficult, elaborate, intricate, knotty, labyrinthine, sophisticated, tangled, tortuous
Antonyms *adj* ≠ **complicated:** easy, easy-peasy (*sl.*), elementary, simple, simplified, straightforward, uncomplicated, unsophisticated

involvement *n* **3** = **connection**, association, commitment, concern, dedication, interest, participation, responsibility **4** = **complication**, complexity, difficulty, embarrassment, entanglement, imbroglio, intricacy, problem, ramification

invulnerability *n* **1, 2** = **safety**, impenetrability, inviolability, security, strength, unassailability, untouchability

invulnerable *adj* **1, 2** = **safe**, impenetrable, indestructible, insusceptible, invincible, proof against, secure, unassailable
Antonyms *adj* assailable, defenceless, insecure, susceptible, unprotected, vulnerable, weak

inward *adj* **1** = **incoming**, entering, inbound, inflowing, ingoing, inpouring, penetrating **2** = **internal**, inner, inside, interior **3** = **private**, confidential, hidden, inmost, innermost, personal, privy, secret
Antonyms *adj* ≠ **internal:** exterior, external, outer, outermost, outside, outward ≠ **private:** open, public

inwardly *adv* **1, 2** = **privately**, at heart, deep down, in one's head, in one's inmost heart, inside, secretly, to oneself, within

iota *n* **2** = **bit**, atom, grain, hint, jot, mite, particle, scintilla (*rare*), scrap, speck, tittle, trace, whit

irascibility *n* **1** = **bad temper**, asperity, cantankerousness, choler, crossness, edginess, fieriness, ill temper, impatience, irritability, irritation, petulance, shortness, snappishness, testiness, touchiness, uncertain temper

irascible *adj* **1** = **bad-tempered**, cantankerous, choleric, crabbed, cross, hasty, hot-tempered, irritable, peppery, petulant, quick-tempered, ratty (*Brit. & NZ inf.*), short-tempered, testy, tetchy, touchy

irate *adj* **1** = **angry**, angered, annoyed, choked, cross, enraged, exasperated, fuming (*inf.*), furious, hacked (off) (*US sl.*), hot under the collar (*inf.*), incandescent, incensed, indignant, in-

treme anger: *an irate letter.* [C19: from L *īrātus* enraged, from *īrascī* to be angry]
▸i'rately *adv*

IRBM *abbrev. for* intermediate-range ballistic missile.

ire ➊ ('aɪə) *n Literary.* anger; wrath. [C13: from OF, from L *īra*]
▸'ireful *adj* ▸'irefulness *n*

Ire. *abbrev. for* Ireland.

irenic, eirenic (aɪ'riːnɪk, -'ren-) *or* **irenical, eirenical** *adj* tending to conciliate or spromote peace. [C19: from Gk *eirēnikos*, from *eirēnē* peace]
▸i'renically *or* ei'renically *adv*

iridaceous (ˌɪrɪ'deɪʃəs, ˌaɪ-) *adj* of, relating to, or belonging to the family of monocotyledonous plants, including the iris, having swordlike leaves and showy flowers.

iridescent ➊ (ˌɪrɪ'des'nt) *adj* displaying a spectrum of colours that shimmer and change due to interference and scattering as the observer's position changes. [C18: from L *irid-* iris + -ESCENT]
▸ˌiri'descence *n* ▸ˌiri'descently *adv*

iridium (aɪ'rɪdɪəm, ɪ'rɪd-) *n* a very hard yellowish-white transition element that is the most corrosion-resistant metal known. It occurs in platinum ores and is used as an alloy with platinum. Symbol: Ir; atomic no.: 77; atomic wt.: 192.2. [C19: NL, from L *irid-* iris + -IUM; from its colourful appearance when dissolving in certain acids]

iris ('aɪrɪs) *n, pl* **irises** *or* **irides** ('aɪrɪˌdiːz, 'ɪrɪ-). **1** the coloured muscular diaphragm that surrounds and controls the size of the pupil of the eye. **2** Also called: **fleur-de-lys.** any iridaceous plant having brightly coloured flowers composed of three petals and three drooping sepals. **3** a poetic word for **rainbow. 4** short for **iris diaphragm.** [C14: from L: rainbow, iris (flower), crystal, from Gk]

iris diaphragm *n* an adjustable diaphragm that regulates the amount of light entering an optical instrument, esp. a camera.

Irish ➊ ('aɪrɪʃ) *adj* **1** of, relating to, or characteristic of Ireland, its people, their Celtic language, or their dialect of English. **2** *Inf. offens.* ludicrous or illogical. ◆ *n* **3 the Irish.** (*functioning as pl*) the natives or inhabitants of Ireland. **4** another name for **Irish Gaelic. 5** the dialect of English spoken in Ireland.

Irish coffee *n* hot coffee mixed with Irish whiskey and topped with double cream.

Irish Gaelic *n* the Goidelic language of the Celts of Ireland, now spoken mainly along the west coast; an official language of the Republic of Ireland since 1921.

Irishman ('aɪrɪʃmən) *or* (*fem*) **Irishwoman** *n, pl* **Irishmen** *or* **Irishwomen.** a native or inhabitant of Ireland.

Irish pipes *pl n* another name for **uillean pipes.**

Irish Republican Army *n* a militant organization of Irish nationalists founded with the aim of striving for a united independent Ireland by means of guerrilla warfare. Abbrev.: **IRA.**

Irish stew *n* a stew made of mutton, lamb, or beef, with potatoes, onions, etc.

Irish wolfhound *n* a large breed of hound with a rough thick coat.

iritis (aɪ'raɪtɪs) *n* inflammation of the iris of the eye.
▸iritic (aɪ'rɪtɪk) *adj*

irk ➊ (ɜːk) *vb* (*tr*) to irritate, vex, or annoy. [C13 *irken* to grow weary]

irksome ➊ ('ɜːksəm) *adj* causing vexation, annoyance, or boredom; troublesome or tedious.
▸'irksomely *adv* ▸'irksomeness *n*

IRO *abbrev. for:* **1** (in Britain) Inland Revenue Office. **2** International Refugee Organization.

iron ➊ ('aɪən) *n* **1a** a malleable ductile silvery-white ferromagnetic metallic element. It is widely used for structural and engineering purposes. Symbol: Fe; atomic no.: 26; atomic wt.: 55.847. Related adjs.: **ferric, ferrous.** Related prefix: **ferro-. 1b** (*as modifier*): *iron railings.* **2** any of certain tools or implements made of iron or steel, esp. for use when hot: *a grappling iron; a soldering iron.* **3** an appliance for pressing fabrics using dry heat or steam, esp. a small electrically heated device with a handle and a weighted flat bottom. **4** any of various golf clubs with metal heads, numbered from 1 to 10 according to the slant of the face. **5** a splintlike support for a malformed leg. **6** great hardness, strength, or resolve: *a will of iron.* **7 strike while the iron is hot.** to act at an opportune moment. ◆ *adj* **8** very hard, immovable, or implacable: *iron determination.* **9** very strong; extremely robust: *an iron constitution.* **10** cruel or unyielding: *he ruled with an iron hand.* ◆ *vb* **11** to smooth (clothes or fabric) by removing (creases or wrinkles) using a heated iron; press. **12** (*tr*) to furnish or clothe with iron. **13** (*tr*) *Rare.* to place (a prisoner) in irons. ◆ See also **iron out, irons.** [OE *īren*]
▸'ironer *n* ▸'ironless *adj* ▸'ironˌlike *adj*

Iron Age *n* **a** the period following the Bronze Age characterized by the extremely rapid spread of iron tools and weapons. **b** (*as modifier*): *an Iron-Age weapon.*

ironbark ('aɪənˌbɑːk) *n* any of several Australian eucalyptus trees that have hard rough bark.

ironbound ('aɪənˌbaʊnd) *adj* **1** bound with iron. **2** unyielding; inflexible. **3** (of a coast) rocky; rugged.

ironclad *adj* (ˌaɪən'klæd). **1** covered or protected with iron: *an ironclad warship.* **2** inflexible; rigid: *an ironclad rule.* ◆ *n* ('aɪənˌklæd). **3** a large wooden 19th-century warship with armoured plating.

Iron Curtain *n* **1** (formerly) **1a** the guarded border between the countries of the Soviet bloc and the rest of Europe. **1b** (*as modifier*): *Iron Curtain countries.* **2** (*sometimes not caps.*) any barrier that separates communities or ideologies.

iron hand *n* harsh or rigorous control; overbearing or autocratic force.

iron horse *n Arch.* a steam-driven railway locomotive.

ironic ➊ (aɪ'rɒnɪk) *or* **ironical** *adj* of, characterized by, or using irony.
▸i'ronically *adv* ▸i'ronicalness *n*

ironing ('aɪənɪŋ) *n* **1** the act of ironing washed clothes. **2** clothes, etc., that are to be or that have been ironed.

ironing board *n* a board, usually on legs, with a suitable covering on which to iron clothes.

iron lung *n* an airtight metal cylinder enclosing the entire body up to the neck and providing artificial respiration.

iron maiden *n* a medieval instrument of torture, consisting of a hinged case (often shaped in the form of a woman) lined with iron spikes, which was forcibly closed on the victim.

iron man *n Austral.* **1** an event at a surf carnival in which contestants compete at swimming, surfing, running, etc. **2** a participant in such an event.

ironmaster ('aɪənˌmɑːstə) *n Brit.* a manufacturer of iron.

ironmonger ('aɪənˌmʌŋgə) *n Brit.* a dealer in metal utensils, hardware, locks, etc. US and Canad. equivalent: **hardware dealer.**
▸'ironˌmongery *n*

iron out ➊ *vb* (*tr, adv*) **1** to smooth, using a heated iron. **2** to put right or settle (a problem or difficulty) as a result of negotiations or discussions. **3** *Austral. inf.* to knock unconscious.

iron pyrites ('paɪraɪts) *n* another name for **pyrite.**

iron rations *pl n* emergency food supplies, esp. for military personnel in action.

irons ➊ ('aɪənz) *pl n* **1** fetters or chains (often in **in** *or* **into irons**). **2 have several irons in the fire.** to be involved in many projects, etc.

ironsides ('aɪənˌsaɪdz) *n* **1** a person with great stamina or resistance. **2** an ironclad ship. **3** (*often cap.*) (in the English Civil War) **3a** the cavalry regiment trained and commanded by Oliver Cromwell. **3b** Cromwell's entire army.

ironstone ('aɪənˌstəʊn) *n* **1** any rock consisting mainly of an iron-bearing ore. **2** a tough durable earthenware.

ironware ('aɪənˌweə) *n* domestic articles made of iron.

ironwood ('aɪənˌwʊd) *n* **1** any of various trees, such as hornbeam, that have very hard wood. **2** a Californian rosaceous tree with very hard wood. **3** any of various other trees with hard wood, such as the mopani. **4** the wood of any of these trees.

ironwork ('aɪənˌwɜːk) *n* **1** work done in iron, esp. decorative work. **2** the craft or practice of working in iron.

ironworks ('aɪənˌwɜːks) *n* (*sometimes functioning as sing*) a building in which iron is smelted, cast, or wrought.

irony[1] ➊ ('aɪrənɪ) *n, pl* **ironies. 1** the humorous or mildly sarcastic use of words to imply the opposite of what they normally mean. **2** an instance of this, used to draw attention to some incongruity or irrationality. **3** incongruity between what is expected to be and what actually is, or a situation or result showing such incongruity. **4** See **dramatic irony. 5** *Philosophy.* See **Socratic irony.** [C16: from L, from Gk *eirōneia*, from *eirōn* dissembler, from *eirein* to speak]

irony[2] ('aɪənɪ) *adj* of, resembling, or containing iron.

Iroquois ('ɪrəˌkwɔɪ) *n* **1** (*pl* **Iroquois**) a member of a confederacy of North American Indian tribes formerly living in and around New York State. **2** any of the languages of these people.
▸Iro'quoian *adj*

irradiance (ɪ'reɪdɪəns) *n* the radiant flux incident on unit area of a surface. Also: **irradiation.** Cf. **illuminance.**

THESAURUS

furiated, irritated, livid, mad (*inf.*), piqued, provoked, riled, up in arms, worked up, wrathful

ire *n* = **anger**, annoyance, choler, displeasure, exasperation, fury, indignation, passion, rage, wrath

iridescent *adj* = **shimmering**, nacreous, opalescent, opaline, pearly, polychromatic, prismatic, rainbow-coloured, shot

Irish *adj* **1** = **Hibernian**, green

irk *vb* = **irritate**, aggravate (*inf.*), annoy, bug (*inf.*), gall, get one's back up, get on one's nerves (*inf.*), miff (*inf.*), nettle, peeve (*inf.*), provoke, put one's back up, put one's nose out of joint (*inf.*), put out (*inf.*), rile, rub one up the wrong way (*inf.*), ruffle, vex

irksome *adj* = **irritating**, aggravating, annoying, boring, bothersome, burdensome, disagreeable, exasperating, tedious, tiresome, troublesome, trying, uninteresting, unwelcome, vexatious, vexing, wearisome
Antonyms *adj* agreeable, enjoyable, gratifying, interesting, pleasant, pleasing, welcome

iron *modifier* **1b** = **ferrous**, chalybeate, ferric, irony ◆ *adj* **8-10** = **inflexible**, adamant, cruel, hard, heavy, immovable, implacable, indomitable, obdurate, rigid, robust, steel, steely, strong, tough, unbending, unyielding
Antonyms *adj* ≠ **inflexible**: bending, easy, flexible, light, malleable, pliable, soft, weak, yielding

ironic *adj* = **sarcastic**, double-edged, incongruous, mocking, mordacious, paradoxical, sardonic, satirical, scoffing, sneering, with tongue in cheek, wry

iron out *vb* **2** = **settle**, clear up, eliminate, eradicate, erase, expedite, get rid of, harmonize, put right, reconcile, resolve, simplify, smooth over, sort out, straighten out, unravel

irons *pl n* **1** = **chains**, bonds, fetters, gyves (*arch.*), manacles, shackles

irony[1] *n* **1, 2** = **sarcasm**, mockery, satire **3** = **paradox**, contrariness, incongruity

irradiate ❶ (ɪˈreɪdɪˌeɪt) *vb* **irradiates, irradiating, irradiated. 1** (*tr*) *Physics.* to subject to or treat with light or other electromagnetic radiation or with beams of particles. **2** (*tr*) to expose (food) to electromagnetic radiation to kill bacteria and retard deterioration. **3** (*tr*) to make clear or bright intellectually or spiritually; illumine. **4** a less common word for **radiate** (sense 1). **5** (*intr*) *Obs.* to become radiant.
▸**irˌradiˈation** *n* ▸**irˈradiative** *adj* ▸**irˈradiˌator** *n*

irrational ❶ (ɪˈræʃənᵊl) *adj* **1** inconsistent with reason or logic; illogical; absurd. **2** incapable of reasoning. **3a** *Maths.* (of an equation, etc.) containing one or more variables in irreducible radical form or raised to a fractional power: $\sqrt{(x^2 + 1)} = x^{5/3}$. **3b** (*as n*): *an irrational.*
▸**irˌrationˈality** *n* ▸**irˈrationally** *adv*

irrational number *n* any real number that cannot be expressed as the ratio of two integers, such as π.

irreclaimable (ˌɪrɪˈkleɪməbᵊl) *adj* not able to be reclaimed.
▸**ˌirreˌclaimaˈbility** *or* **ˌirreˈclaimableness** *n* ▸**ˌirreˈclaimably** *adv*

irreconcilable ❶ (ɪˈrɛkᵊnˌsaɪləbᵊl, ɪˌrɛkᵊnˈsaɪ-) *adj* **1** not able to be reconciled; uncompromisingly conflicting; incompatible. ◆ *n* **2** a person or thing that is implacably hostile or uncompromisingly opposed. **3** (*usually pl*) one of various principles, ideas, etc., that are incapable of being brought into agreement.
▸**irˌrecˌcilaˈbility** *or* **irˈreconˌcilableness** *n* ▸**irˈreconˌcilably** *adv*

irrecoverable ❶ (ˌɪrɪˈkʌvərəbᵊl, -ˈkʌvrə-) *adj* **1** not able to be recovered or regained. **2** not able to be remedied or rectified.
▸**ˌirreˈcoverableness** *n* ▸**ˌirreˈcoverably** *adv*

irrecusable (ˌɪrɪˈkjuːzəbᵊl) *adj* not able to be rejected or challenged, as evidence, etc.

irredeemable (ˌɪrɪˈdiːməbᵊl) *adj* **1** (of bonds, shares, etc.) without a date of redemption of capital; incapable of being bought back directly or paid off. **2** (of paper money) not convertible into specie. **3** (of a loss) not able to be recovered; irretrievable. **4** not able to be improved or rectified; irreparable.
▸**ˌirreˌdeemaˈbility** *or* **ˌirreˈdeemableness** *n* ▸**ˌirreˈdeemably** *adv*

irredentist (ˌɪrɪˈdɛntɪst) *n* **1** (*sometimes cap.*) a person, esp. a member of a 19th-century Italian association, who favours the acquisition of territory that was once part of his country or is considered to have been. ◆ *adj* **2** of or relating to irredentists or their policies. [C19: from It. *irredentista,* from *ir-* IN-[1] + *redento* redeemed, from L *redemptus* bought back; see REDEEM]
▸**ˌirreˈdentism** *n*

irreducible (ˌɪrɪˈdjuːsɪbᵊl) *adj* **1** not able to be reduced or lessened. **2** not able to be brought to a simpler or reduced form. **3** *Maths.* (of a polynomial) unable to be factorized into polynomials of lower degree, as $(x^2 + 1)$.
▸**ˌirreˌduciˈbility** *n* ▸**ˌirreˈducibly** *adv*

irrefragable (ɪˈrɛfrəgəbᵊl) *adj* not able to be denied or refuted. [C16: from LL *irrefrāgābilis,* from L *ir-* + *refrāgārī* to resist]
▸**irˌrefragaˈbility** *or* **irˈrefragableness** *n* ▸**irˈrefragably** *adv*

irrefrangible (ˌɪrɪˈfrændʒəbᵊl) *adj* **1** not to be broken or transgressed; inviolable. **2** *Physics.* incapable of being refracted.
▸**ˌirreˌfrangiˈbility** *or* **ˌirreˈfrangibleness** *n* ▸**ˌirreˈfrangibly** *adv*

irrefutable ❶ (ɪˈrɛfjʊtəbᵊl, ˌɪrɪˈfjuːtəbᵊl) *adj* impossible to deny or disprove; incontrovertible.
▸**irˌrefutaˈbility** *n* ▸**irˈrefutably** *adv*

irreg. *abbrev. for* irregular(ly).

irregular ❶ (ɪˈrɛgjʊlə) *adj* **1** lacking uniformity or symmetry; uneven in shape, position, arrangement, etc. **2** not occurring at expected or equal intervals: *an irregular pulse.* **3** differing from the normal or accepted practice or routine; unconventional. **4** (of the formation, inflections, or derivations of a word) not following the usual pattern of formation in a language. **5** of or relating to guerrillas or volunteers not belonging to regular forces: *irregular troops.* **6** (of flowers) having any of their petals differing in size, shape, etc. **7** *US.* (of merchandise) not up to the manufacturer's standards or specifications; imperfect. ◆ *n* **8** a soldier not in a regular army. **9** (*often pl*) *US.* imperfect or flawed merchandise.
▸**irˌreguˈlarity** *n* ▸**irˈregularly** *adv*

irrelevant ❶ (ɪˈrɛləvənt) *adj* not relating or pertinent to the matter at hand.
▸**irˈrelevance** *or* **irˈrelevancy** *n* ▸**irˈrelevantly** *adv*

irreligion ❶ (ˌɪrɪˈlɪdʒən) *n* **1** lack of religious faith. **2** indifference or opposition to religion.
▸**ˌirreˈligionist** *n* ▸**ˌirreˈligious** *adj* ▸**ˌirreˈligiously** *adv* ▸**ˌirreˈligiousness** *n*

irremediable ❶ (ˌɪrɪˈmiːdɪəbᵊl) *adj* not able to be remedied; incurable or irreparable.
▸**ˌirreˈmediableness** *n* ▸**ˌirreˈmediably** *adv*

irremissible (ˌɪrɪˈmɪsəbᵊl) *adj* **1** unpardonable; inexcusable. **2** that must be done, as through duty or obligation.
▸**ˌirreˌmissiˈbility** *or* **ˌirreˈmissibleness** *n* ▸**ˌirreˈmissibly** *adv*

irremovable (ˌɪrɪˈmuːvəbᵊl) *adj* not able to be removed.
▸**ˌirreˌmovaˈbility** *n* ▸**ˌirreˈmovably** *adv*

irreparable ❶ (ɪˈrɛpərəbᵊl, ɪˈrɛprəbᵊl) *adj* not able to be repaired or remedied; beyond repair.
▸**irˌreparaˈbility** *or* **irˈreparableness** *n* ▸**irˈreparably** *adv*

irreplaceable ❶ (ˌɪrɪˈpleɪsəbᵊl) *adj* not able to be replaced: *an irreplaceable antique.*
▸**ˌirreˈplaceably** *adv*

irrepressible ❶ (ˌɪrɪˈprɛsəbᵊl) *adj* not capable of being repressed, controlled, or restrained.
▸**ˌirreˌpressiˈbility** *or* **ˌirreˈpressibleness** *n* ▸**ˌirreˈpressibly** *adv*

irreproachable ❶ (ˌɪrɪˈprəʊtʃəbᵊl) *adj* not deserving reproach; blameless.
▸**ˌirreˌproachaˈbility** *or* **ˌirreˈproachableness** *n* ▸**ˌirreˈproachably** *adv*

irresistible ❶ (ˌɪrɪˈzɪstəbᵊl) *adj* **1** not able to be resisted or refused; overpowering: *an irresistible impulse.* **2** very fascinating or alluring: *an irresistible woman.*
▸**ˌirreˌsistiˈbility** *or* **ˌirreˈsistibleness** *n* ▸**ˌirreˈsistibly** *adv*

irresolute ❶ (ɪˈrɛzəˌluːt) *adj* lacking resolution; wavering; hesitating.
▸**irˈresoˌlutely** *adv* ▸**irˈresoˌluteness** *or* **irˌresoˈlution** *n*

THESAURUS

irradiate *vb* **3** = **light up**, brighten, cast light upon, enlighten, illume (*poetic*), illuminate, illumine, lighten, shine upon

irrational *adj* **1** = **illogical**, absurd, crackpot (*inf.*), crazy, foolish, injudicious, nonsensical, preposterous, silly, unreasonable, unreasoning, unsound, unthinking, unwise **2** = **senseless**, aberrant, brainless, crazy, demented, insane, mindless, muddle-headed, raving, unstable, wild
Antonyms *adj* ≠ **illogical**: circumspect, judicious, logical, rational, reasonable, sensible, sound, wise

irrationality *n* **1** = **senselessness**, absurdity, brainlessness, illogicality, insanity, lack of judgment, lunacy, madness, preposterousness, unreasonableness, unsoundness

irreconcilable *adj* **1** = **incompatible**, clashing, conflicting, diametrically opposed, incongruous, inconsistent, opposed

irrecoverable *adj* **1, 2** = **lost**, gone for ever, irreclaimable, irredeemable, irremediable, irreparable, irretrievable, unregainable, unsalvageable, unsavable

irrefutable *adj* = **undeniable**, apodeictic, apodictic, beyond question, certain, incontestable, incontrovertible, indisputable, indubitable, invincible, irrefragable, irresistible, sure, unanswerable, unassailable, unquestionable

irregular *adj* **1** = **uneven**, asymmetrical, broken, bumpy, craggy, crooked, elliptic, elliptical, holey, jagged, lopsided, lumpy, pitted, ragged, rough, serrated, unequal, unsymmetrical **2** = **variable**, desultory, disconnected, eccentric, erratic, fitful, fluctuating, fragmentary, haphazard, inconstant, intermittent, nonuniform, occasional, out of order, patchy, random, shifting, spasmodic, sporadic, uncertain, uneven, unmethodical, unpunctual, unsteady, unsystematic, wavering **3** = **unconventional**, abnormal, anomalous, capricious, disorderly, eccentric, exceptional, extraordinary, immoderate, improper, inappropriate, inordinate, odd, peculiar, queer, quirky, rum (*Brit. sl.*), unofficial, unorthodox, unsuitable, unusual ◆ *n* **8** = **guerrilla**, partisan, volunteer
Antonyms *adj* ≠ **uneven**: balanced, equal, even, regular, smooth, symmetrical ≠ **variable**: certain, invariable, methodical, punctual, reliable, steady, systematic ≠ **unconventional**: appropriate, conventional, normal, orthodox, proper, regular, standard, usual

irregularity *n* **1** = **unevenness**, asymmetry, bumpiness, crookedness, jaggedness, lack of symmetry, lopsidedness, lumpiness, patchiness, raggedness, roughness, spottiness **2** = **uncertainty**, confusion, desultoriness, disorderliness, disorganization, haphazardness, lack of method, randomness, unpunctuality, unsteadiness **3** = **abnormality**, aberration, anomaly, breach, deviation, eccentricity, freak, malfunction, malpractice, oddity, peculiarity, singularity, unconventionality, unorthodoxy

irregularly *adv* **2** = **erratically**, anyhow, by fits and starts, disconnectedly, eccentrically, fitfully, haphazardly, in snatches, intermittently, jerkily, now and again, occasionally, off and on, out of sequence, spasmodically, unevenly, unmethodically, unpunctually

irrelevance *n* = **inappropriateness**, inappositeness, inaptness, inconsequence, non sequitur
Antonyms *n* appositeness, appropriateness, aptness, consequence, pertinence, point, relevance, suitability

irrelevant *adj* = **unconnected**, beside the point, extraneous, immaterial, impertinent, inapplicable, inapposite, inappropriate, inapt, inconsequent, neither here nor there, unrelated
Antonyms *adj* applicable, apposite, appropriate, apt, connected, fitting, pertinent, related, relevant, suitable

irreligious *adj* **1** = **atheistic**, agnostic, freethinking, godless, pagan, sceptical, unbelieving **2** = **sacrilegious**, blasphemous, iconoclastic, impious, irreverent, profane, sinful, undevout, ungodly, unholy, unrighteous, wicked

irremediable *adj* = **incurable**, beyond redress, deadly, fatal, final, hopeless, irrecoverable, irredeemable, irreparable, irreversible, mortal, remediless, terminal

irreparable *adj* = **beyond repair**, incurable, irrecoverable, irremediable, irreplaceable, irretrievable, irreversible

irreplaceable *adj* = **indispensable**, invaluable, priceless, unique, vital

irrepressible *adj* = **ebullient**, boisterous, bubbling over, buoyant, effervescent, insuppressible, uncontainable, uncontrollable, unmanageable, unquenchable, unrestrainable, unstoppable

irreproachable *adj* = **blameless**, beyond reproach, faultless, guiltless, impeccable, inculpable, innocent, irreprehensible, irreprovable, perfect, pure, squeaky-clean, unblemished, unimpeachable

irresistible *adj* **1** = **overwhelming**, compelling, compulsive, imperative, overmastering, overpowering, potent, urgent **2** = **seductive**, alluring, beckoning, enchanting, fascinating, ravishing, tempting

irresolute *adj* = **indecisive**, doubtful, fickle, half-hearted, hesitant, hesitating, infirm, in two minds, tentative, undecided, undetermined,

irrespective ➊ (ˌɪrɪˈspɛktɪv) *adj* **1 irrespective of.** without taking account of; regardless of. ◆ *adv* **2** *Inf.* regardless; without due consideration: *he carried on with his plan irrespective.*
▸ ˌ**irreˈspectively** *adv*

irresponsible ➊ (ˌɪrɪˈspɒnsəbᵊl) *adj* **1** not showing or done with due care for the consequences of one's actions or attitudes; reckless. **2** not capable of bearing responsibility.
▸ ˌ**irreˌsponsiˈbility** *or* ˌ**irreˈsponsibleness** *n* ▸ ˌ**irreˈsponsibly** *adv*

irresponsive (ˌɪrɪˈspɒnsɪv) *adj* not responsive.
▸ ˌ**irreˈsponsively** *adv* ▸ ˌ**irreˈsponsiveness** *n*

irretrievable (ˌɪrɪˈtriːvəbᵊl) *adj* not able to be retrieved, recovered, or repaired.
▸ ˌ**irreˌtrievaˈbility** *n* ▸ ˌ**irreˈtrievably** *adv*

irreverence ➊ (ɪˈrɛvərəns, ɪˈrɛvrəns) *n* **1** lack of due respect or veneration; disrespect. **2** a disrespectful remark or act.
▸ **irˈreverent** *or* **irˌreveˈrential** *adj* ▸ **irˈreverently** *adv*

irreversible ➊ (ˌɪrɪˈvɜːsəbᵊl) *adj* **1** not able to be reversed: *the irreversible flow of time.* **2** not able to be revoked or repealed; irrevocable. **3** *Chem., physics.* capable of changing or producing a change in one direction only: *an irreversible reaction.*
▸ ˌ**irreˌversiˈbility** *or* ˌ**irreˈversibleness** *n* ▸ ˌ**irreˈversibly** *adv*

irrevocable ➊ (ɪˈrɛvəkəbᵊl) *adj* not able to be revoked, changed, or undone.
▸ **irˌrevocaˈbility** *or* **irˈrevocableness** *n* ▸ **irˈrevocably** *adv*

irrigate ➊ (ˈɪrɪˌgeɪt) *vb* **irrigates, irrigating, irrigated. 1** to supply (land) with water by means of artificial canals, etc., esp. to promote the growth of food crops. **2** *Med.* to bathe or wash out (a bodily part, cavity, or wound). **3** (*tr*) to make fertile, fresh, or vital by or as if by watering. [C17: from L *irrigāre,* from *rigāre* to moisten, conduct water]
▸ **ˈirrigable** *adj* ▸ ˌ**irriˈgation** *n* ▸ **ˈirriˌgative** *adj* ▸ **ˈirriˌgator** *n*

irritable ➊ (ˈɪrɪtəbᵊl) *adj* **1** quickly irritated; easily annoyed; peevish. **2** (of all living organisms) capable of responding to such stimuli as heat, light, and touch. **3** *Pathol.* abnormally sensitive.
▸ ˌ**irritaˈbility** *n* ▸ **ˈirritableness** *n* ▸ **ˈirritably** *adv*

irritable bowel syndrome *n Med.* a chronic condition of recurring abdominal pain with constipation or diarrhoea or both.

irritant (ˈɪrɪtənt) *adj* **1** causing irritation; irritating. ◆ *n* **2** something irritant.
▸ **ˈirritancy** *n*

irritate ➊ (ˈɪrɪˌteɪt) *vb* **irritates, irritating, irritated. 1** to annoy or anger (someone). **2** (*tr*) *Biol.* to stimulate (an organism or part) to respond in a characteristic manner. **3** (*tr*) *Pathol.* to cause (a bodily organ or part) to become excessively stimulated, resulting in inflammation, tenderness, etc. [C16: from L *irrītāre* to provoke]
▸ **ˈirriˌtator** *n*

irritation ➊ (ˌɪrɪˈteɪʃən) *n* **1** something that irritates. **2** the act of irritating or the condition of being irritated.
▸ **ˈirriˌtative** *adj*

irrupt (ɪˈrʌpt) *vb* (*intr*) **1** to enter forcibly or suddenly. **2** (of a plant or animal population) to enter a region suddenly and in very large numbers. **3** (of a population) to increase suddenly and greatly. [C19: from L *irrumpere* to rush into, invade, from *rumpere* to break, burst]
▸ **irˈruption** *n* ▸ **irˈruptive** *adj*

is (ɪz) *vb* (used with *he, she, it,* and with singular nouns) a form of the present tense (indicative mood) of **be.** [OE]

Is. *abbrev. for:* **1** Also: **Isa.** *Bible.* Isaiah. **2** Island(s) *or* Isle(s).

is- *combining form.* a variant of **iso-** before a vowel: *isentropic.*

ISA (ˈaɪsə) *n acronym for* individual savings account: a tax-free savings scheme introduced in the UK in 1999.

isagogics (ˌaɪsəˈgɒdʒɪks) *n* introductory studies, esp. in the history of the Bible. [C19: from L, from Gk, from *eisagein* to introduce, from *eis-* into + *agein* to lead]

isallobar (aɪˈsæləˌbɑː) *n* a line on a map connecting places with equal pressure changes.

isatin (ˈaɪsətɪn) *or* **isatine** (ˈaɪsəˌtiːn) *n* a yellowish-red crystalline compound soluble in hot water, used for the preparation of vat dyes. [C19: from L *isatis* woad + -IN]
▸ ˌ**isaˈtinic** *adj*

ISBN *abbrev. for* International Standard Book Number.

ischaemia *or* **ischemia** (ɪˈskiːmɪə) *n Pathol.* an inadequate supply of blood to an organ or part, as from an obstructed blood flow. [C19: from Gk *iskhein* to restrict, + -AEMIA]
▸ **ischaemic** *or* **ischemic** (ɪˈskɛmɪk) *adj*

ischium (ˈɪskɪəm) *n, pl* **ischia** (-kɪə). one of the three sections of the hipbone, situated below the ilium. [C17: from L: hip joint, from Gk *iskhion*]
▸ **ˈischial** *adj*

-ise *suffix forming verbs.* a variant of **-ize.**

USAGE NOTE See at **-ize.**

isentropic (ˌaɪsɛnˈtrɒpɪk) *adj* having or taking place at constant entropy.

-ish *suffix forming adjectives.* **1** of or belonging to a nationality: *Scottish.* **2** *Often derog.* having the manner or qualities of; resembling: *slavish; boyish.* **3** somewhat; approximately: *yellowish; sevenish.* **4** concerned or preoccupied with: *bookish.* [OE *-isc*]

isinglass (ˈaɪzɪŋˌglɑːs) *n* **1** a gelatine made from the air bladders of freshwater fish, used as a clarifying agent and adhesive. **2** another name for **mica.** [C16: from MDu. *huysenblase,* lit.: sturgeon bladder; infl. by E GLASS]

Isl. *abbrev. for:* **1** Island. **2** Isle.

Islam (ˈɪzlɑːm) *n* **1** Also called: **Islamism.** the religion of Muslims, teaching that there is only one God and that Mohammed is his prophet; Mohammedanism. **2a** Muslims collectively and their civilization. **2b** the countries where the Muslim religion is predominant. [C19: from Ar.: surrender (to God), from *aslama* to surrender]
▸ **Isˈlamic** *adj*

Islamist (ˈɪzˌləmɪst) *adj* **1** supporting or advocating Islamic fundamentalism. ◆ *n* **2** a supporter or advocate of Islamic fundamentalism.

Islamize *or* **Islamise** (ˈɪzləˌmaɪz) *vb* **Islamizes, Islamizing, Islamized** *or* **Islamises, Islamising, Islamised.** (*tr*) to convert or subject to the influence of Islam.
▸ ˌ**Islamiˈzation** *or* ˌ**Islamiˈsation** *n*

island ➊ (ˈaɪlənd) *n* **1** a mass of land that is surrounded by water and is smaller than a continent. **2** something isolated, detached, or surrounded: *a traffic island.* **3** *Anat.* a part, structure, or group of cells distinct in constitution from its immediate surroundings. ◆ Related adj: **insular.** ◆ *vb* (*tr*) *Rare.* **4** to cause to become an island. **5** to intersperse with islands. **6** to place on an island; insulate; isolate. [OE *īgland*]
▸ **ˈisland-ˌlike** *adj*

islander (ˈaɪləndə) *n* a native or inhabitant of an island.

THESAURUS

unsettled, unstable, unsteady, vacillating, wavering, weak
Antonyms *adj* decisive, determined, firm, fixed, resolute, resolved, settled, stable, stalwart, steadfast, steady, strong

irresoluteness *n* = **indecisiveness**, dithering (*chiefly Brit.*), faint-heartedness, half-heartedness, hesitancy, hesitation, infirmity (of purpose), shillyshallying (*inf.*), uncertainty, vacillation, wavering

irrespective *adj* **1 irrespective of** = **despite**, apart from, discounting, in spite of, notwithstanding, regardless of, without reference to, without regard to

irresponsible *adj* **1, 2** = **thoughtless**, careless, featherbrained, flighty, giddy, good-for-nothing, harebrained, harum-scarum, ill-considered, immature, reckless, scatterbrained, shiftless, undependable, unreliable, untrustworthy, wild
Antonyms *adj* careful, dependable, level-headed, mature, reliable, responsible, sensible, trustworthy

irreverence *n* **1** = **disrespect**, cheek (*inf.*), cheekiness (*inf.*), chutzpah (*US & Canad. inf.*), derision, flippancy, impertinence, impudence, lack of respect, mockery, sauce (*inf.*)

irreverent *adj* **1** = **disrespectful**, cheeky (*inf.*), contemptuous, derisive, flip (*inf.*), flippant, fresh (*inf.*), iconoclastic, impertinent, impious, impudent, mocking, sassy (*US inf.*), saucy, tongue-in-cheek
Antonyms *adj* awed, deferential, meek, pious, respectful, reverent, submissive

irreversible *adj* **1, 2** = **irrevocable**, final, incurable, irreparable, unalterable

irrevocable *adj* = **fixed**, changeless, fated, immutable, invariable, irremediable, irretrievable, irreversible, predestined, predetermined, settled, unalterable, unchangeable, unreversible

irrigate *vb* **1** = **water**, flood, inundate, moisten, wet

irritability *n* **1** = **bad temper**, ill humour, impatience, irascibility, peevishness, petulance, prickliness, testiness, tetchiness, touchiness
Antonyms *n* bonhomie, cheerfulness, complacence, good humour, patience

irritable *adj* = **bad-tempered**, cantankerous, choleric, crabbed, crabby, cross, crotchety (*inf.*), dyspeptic, edgy, exasperated, fiery, fretful, hasty, hot, ill-humoured, ill-tempered, irascible, out of humour, oversensitive, peevish, petulant, prickly, snappish, snappy, snarling, tense, testy, tetchy, touchy
Antonyms *adj* agreeable, calm, cheerful, complacent, composed, even-tempered, good-natured, imperturbable, patient, unexcitable

irritate *vb* **1** = **annoy**, anger, bother, enrage, exasperate, gall, get one's back up, get one's dander up (*inf.*), get on one's nerves (*inf.*), get under one's skin (*inf.*), harass, incense, inflame, infuriate, nark (*Brit., Austral., & NZ sl.*), needle (*inf.*), nettle, offend, pester, provoke, put one's back up, raise one's hackles, rankle with, rub up the wrong way (*inf.*), ruffle, try one's patience, vex **3** = **rub**, aggravate, chafe, fret, inflame, intensify, pain
Antonyms *vb* ≠ **annoy:** calm, comfort, gratify, mollify, placate, please, soothe

irritated *adj* **1** = **annoyed**, angry, bothered, cross, displeased, exasperated, flustered, harassed, impatient, irritable, nettled, out of humour, peeved (*inf.*), piqued, put out, ruffled, vexed

irritating *adj* **1** = **annoying**, displeasing, disquieting, disturbing, galling, infuriating, irksome, maddening, nagging, pestilential, provoking, thorny, troublesome, trying, upsetting, vexatious, worrisome
Antonyms *adj* agreeable, assuaging, calming, comforting, mollifying, pleasant, pleasing, quieting, soothing

irritation *n* **1** = **nuisance**, annoyance, drag (*inf.*), gall, goad, irritant, pain (*inf.*), pain in the neck (*inf.*), pest, provocation, tease, thorn in one's flesh **2** = **annoyance**, anger, crossness, displeasure, exasperation, ill humour, ill temper, impatience, indignation, irritability, resentment, shortness, snappiness, testiness, vexation, wrath
Antonyms *n* ≠ **annoyance:** calm, composure, ease, pleasure, quietude, satisfaction, serenity, tranquillity

island *n* **1** = **isle**, ait *or* eyot (*dialect*), atoll, cay *or* key, holm (*dialect*), inch (*Scot. & Irish*), islet

island universe *n* a former name for **galaxy.**

isle (aɪl) *n Poetic except when cap. and part of place name.* an island, esp. a small one. [C13: from OF, from L *insula* island]

islet ('aɪlɪt) *n* a small island. [C16: from OF *islette;* see ISLE]

islets *or* **islands of Langerhans** ('læŋə,hæns) *pl n* small groups of endocrine cells in the pancreas that secrete insulin. [C19: after Paul *Langerhans* (1847–88), G physician]

ism ('ɪzəm) *n Inf., often derog.* an unspecified doctrine, system, or practice.

-ism *suffix forming nouns.* **1** indicating an action, process, or result: *criticism.* **2** indicating a state or condition: *paganism.* **3** indicating a doctrine, system, or body of principles and practices: *Leninism; spiritualism.* **4** indicating behaviour or a characteristic quality: *heroism.* **5** indicating a characteristic usage, esp. of a language: *Scotticism.* **6** indicating prejudice on the basis specified: *sexism; ageism.* [from OF *-isme,* from L *-ismus,* from Gk *-ismos*]

Ismaili *or* **Isma'ili** (,ɪzmɑː'iːlɪ) *n Islam.* **1** a Shiah sect whose adherents believe that Ismail, son of the sixth imam, was the rightful seventh imam. **2** a member of this sect.

isn't ('ɪzᵊnt) *contraction of* is not.

ISO *abbrev. for:* **1** International Standards Organization. **2** Imperial Service Order (a Brit. decoration).

iso- *or before a vowel* **is-** *combining form.* **1** equal or identical: *isomagnetic.* **2** indicating that a chemical compound is an isomer of a specified compound: *isobutane.* [from Gk *isos* equal]

isobar ('aɪsəʊ,bɑː) *n* **1** a line on a map connecting places of equal atmospheric pressure, usually reduced to sea level for purposes of comparison, at a given time or period. **2** *Physics.* any of two or more atoms that have the same mass number but different atomic numbers. Cf. **isotope.** [C19: from Gk *isobarēs* of equal weight]
▸,**iso'baric** *adj* ▸**'isobar,ism** *n*

isobutene (,aɪsəʊ'bjuːtiːn) *n* a colourless gas used in the manufacture of synthetic rubber.

isocheim *or* **isochime** ('aɪsəʊ,kaɪm) *n* a line on a map connecting places with the same mean winter temperature. Cf. **isothere.** [C19: from ISO- + Gk *kheima* winter weather]
▸,**iso'cheimal** *or* ,**iso'chimal** *adj*

isochronal (aɪ'sɒkrənᵊl) *or* **isochronous** *adj* **1** having the same duration; equal in time. **2** occurring at equal time intervals; having a uniform period of vibration. [C17: from NL, from Gk *isokhronos,* from ISO- + *khronos* time]
▸**i'sochronally** *or* **i'sochronously** *adv* ▸**i'sochro,nism** *n*

isoclinal (,aɪsəʊ'klaɪnᵊl) *or* **isoclinic** (,aɪsəʊ'klɪnɪk) *adj* **1** sloping in the same direction and at the same angle. **2** *Geol.* (of folds) having limbs that are parallel to each other. ◆ *n* **3** Also: **isocline, isoclinal line.** an imaginary line connecting points on the earth's surface having equal angles of magnetic dip.

isocline ('aɪsəʊ,klaɪn) *n* **1** a series of rock strata with isoclinal folds. **2** another name for **isoclinal** (sense 3).

isodynamic (,aɪsəʊdaɪ'næmɪk) *adj Physics.* **1** having equal force or strength. **2** of or relating to an imaginary line on the earth's surface connecting points of equal magnetic intensity.

isogeotherm (,aɪsəʊ'dʒiːəʊ,θɜːm) *n* an imaginary line below the surface of the earth connecting points of equal temperature.
▸,**iso,geo'thermal** *or* ,**iso,geo'thermic** *adj*

isogloss ('aɪsəʊ,glɒs) *n* a line drawn on a map around the area in which a linguistic feature is to be found.
▸,**iso'glossal** *or* ,**iso'glottic** *adj*

isogonic (,aɪsəʊ'gɒnɪk) *or* **isogonal** (aɪ'sɒgənᵊl) *adj* **1** *Maths.* having, making, or involving equal angles. ◆ *n* **2** Also called: **isogonic line, isogonal line, isogone.** *Physics.* an imaginary line connecting points on the earth's surface having equal magnetic declination.

isohel ('aɪsəʊ,hɛl) *n* a line on a map connecting places with an equal period of sunshine. [C20: from ISO- + Gk *hēlios* sun]

isohyet (,aɪsəʊ'haɪɪt) *n* a line on a map connecting places having equal rainfall. [C19: from ISO- + *-hyet,* from Gk *huetos* rain]

isolate 🅣 *vb* ('aɪsə,leɪt), **isolates, isolating, isolated.** (*tr*) **1** to place apart; cause to be alone. **2** *Med.* to quarantine (a person or animal) having a contagious disease. **3** to obtain (a compound) in an uncombined form. **4** to obtain pure cultures of (bacteria, esp. those causing a particular disease). **5** *Electronics.* to prevent interaction between (circuits, components, etc.); insulate. ◆ *n* ('aɪsəlɪt). **6** an isolated person or group. [C19: back formation from *isolated,* via It. from L *insulātus,* lit.: made into an island]
▸**'isolable** *adj* ▸,**isola'bility** *n* ▸**'iso,lator** *n* ▸,**iso'lation** *n*

isolationism (,aɪsə'leɪʃə,nɪzəm) *n* **1** a policy of nonparticipation in or withdrawal from international affairs. **2** an attitude favouring such a policy.
▸,**iso'lationist** *n, adj*

isomer ('aɪsəmə) *n* **1** *Chem.* a compound that exhibits isomerism with one or more other compounds. **2** *Physics.* a nuclide that exhibits isomerism with one or more other nuclides.
▸**isomeric** (,aɪsə'mɛrɪk) *adj*

isomerism (aɪ'sɒmə,rɪzəm) *n* **1** the existence of two or more compounds having the same molecular formula but a different arrangement of atoms. **2** the existence of two or more nuclides having the same atomic numbers and mass numbers but different energy states.

isomerous (aɪ'sɒmərəs) *adj* (of flowers) having floral whorls with the same number of parts.

isometric (,aɪsəʊ'mɛtrɪk) *adj also* **isometrical. 1** having equal dimensions or measurements. **2** *Physiol.* of or relating to muscular contraction that does not produce shortening of the muscle. **3** (of a crystal or system of crystallization) having three mutually perpendicular equal axes. **4** (of a method of projecting a drawing in three dimensions) having the three axes equally inclined and all lines drawn to scale. ◆ *n* **5** Also called: **isometric drawing.** a drawing made in this way. [C19: from Gk *isometria*]
▸,**iso'metrically** *adv*

isometrics (,aɪsəʊ'mɛtrɪks) *n* (*functioning as sing*) physical exercise involving isometric contraction of muscles.

isomorphism (,aɪsəʊ'mɔː,fɪzəm) *n* **1** *Biol.* similarity of form, as in different generations of the same life cycle. **2** *Chem.* the existence of two or more substances of different composition in a similar crystalline form. **3** *Maths.* a one-to-one correspondence between the elements of two or more sets, such as those of Arabic and Roman numerals.
▸**'iso,morph** *n* ▸,**iso'morphic** *or* ,**iso'morphous** *adj*

isopleth ('aɪsəʊ,plɛθ) *n* a line on a map connecting places registering the same amount or ratio of some geographical, etc. phenomenon. [C20: from Gk *isoplēthēs* equal in number, from ISO- + *plēthos* multitude]

isopod ('aɪsəʊ,pɒd) *n* a crustacean, such as the woodlouse, in which the body is flattened.
▸**isopodan** (aɪ'sɒpədən) *or* **i'sopodous** *adj*

isoprene ('aɪsəʊ,priːn) *n* a colourless volatile liquid with a penetrating odour: used in making synthetic rubbers. Formula: $CH_2{:}C(CH_3)CH{:}CH_2$. Systematic name: **methylbuta-1,3-diene.** [C20: from ISO- + PR(OPYL) + -ENE]

isopteran (aɪ'sɒptərən) *n, pl* **isopterans** *or* **isoptera** (-tərə). **1** any of an order of insects having two pairs of wings equal in size: comprises the termites. ◆ *adj also* **isopterous. 2** of, relating to, or belonging to this order. [C19: from NL, from ISO- + Gk *pteron* wing]

ISO rating *n Photog.* a classification of film speed in which a doubling of the ISO number represents a doubling in sensitivity; for example, ISO 400 film requires half the exposure of ISO 200 under the same conditions. The system uses identical numbers to the obsolete ASA rating. [C20: from *I*nternational *S*tandards *O*rganization]

isosceles (aɪ'sɒsɪ,liːz) *adj* (of a triangle) having two sides of equal length. [C16: from LL, from Gk, from ISO- + *skelos* leg]

isoseismal (,aɪsəʊ'saɪzməl) *adj* **1** of or relating to equal intensity of earthquake shock. ◆ *n* **2** a line on a map connecting points at which earthquake shocks are of equal intensity. ◆ Also: **isoseismic.**

isostasy (aɪ'sɒstəsɪ) *n* the state of balance which sections of the earth's lithosphere are thought ultimately to achieve when the vertical forces upon them remain unchanged. If a section is loaded as by ice, it slowly subsides. If a section is reduced in mass, as by erosion, it slowly rises. [C19: ISO- + *-stasy,* from Gk *stasis* a standing]
▸**isostatic** (,aɪsəʊ'stætɪk) *adj*

isothere ('aɪsəʊ,θɪə) *n* a line on a map linking places of equal mean summer temperature. Cf. **isocheim.** [C19: from ISO- + Gk *theros* summer]
▸**isotheral** (aɪ'sɒθərəl) *adj*

isotherm ('aɪsəʊ,θɜːm) *n* **1** a line on a map linking places of equal temperature. **2** *Physics.* a curve on a graph that connects points of equal temperature. ◆ Also called: **isothermal, isothermal line.**

isothermal (,aɪsəʊ'θɜːməl) *adj* **1** (of a process or change) taking place at constant temperature. **2** of or relating to an isotherm. ◆ *n* **3** another word for **isotherm.**
▸,**iso'thermally** *adv*

isotonic (,aɪsəʊ'tɒnɪk) *adj* **1** *Physiol.* (of two or more muscles) having equal tension. **2** (of a drink) designed to replace the fluid and salts lost from the body during strenuous exercise. **3** Also: **isosmotic.** (of two solutions) having the same osmotic pressure, commonly having physiological osmotic pressure. Cf. **hypertonic, hypotonic.**
▸**isotonicity** (,aɪsəʊtəʊ'nɪsɪtɪ) *n*

isotope ('aɪsə,təʊp) *n* one of two or more atoms with the same atomic number that contain different numbers of neutrons. [C20: from ISO- + Gk *topos* place]
▸**isotopic** (,aɪsə'tɒpɪk) *adj* ▸,**iso'topically** *adv* ▸**isotopy** (aɪ'sɒtəpɪ) *n*

isotropic (,aɪsəʊ'trɒpɪk) *or* **isotropous** (aɪ'sɒtrəpəs) *adj* **1** having uniform physical properties in all directions. **2** *Biol.* not having predetermined axes: *isotropic eggs.*
▸,**iso'tropically** *adv* ▸**i'sotropy** *n*

ISP *abbrev. for* Internet service provider.

I-spy *n* a game in which one player specifies the initial letter of the name of an object that he can see, which the other players then try to guess.

Israeli (ɪz'reɪlɪ) *n, pl* **Israelis** *or* **Israeli. 1** a citizen or inhabitant of the

THESAURUS

isolate *vb* **1 = separate,** cut off, detach, disconnect, divorce, insulate, quarantine, segregate, sequester, set apart

isolated *adj* **1 = remote,** backwoods, hidden, incommunicado, in the middle of nowhere, lonely, off the beaten track, outlying, out-of-the-way, retired, secluded, solitary, unfrequented

isolation *n* **1 = separation,** aloofness, detachment, disconnection, exile, insularity, insulation, ivory tower, loneliness, quarantine, remoteness, retirement, seclusion, segregation, self-sufficiency, solitude, withdrawal state of Israel, in SW Asia. ◆ *adj* **2** of or relating to the state of Israel or its inhabitants.

Israelite ('ɪzrɪə,laɪt, -rə-) *n* **1** *Bible.* a member of the ethnic group claiming descent from Jacob; a Hebrew. **2** a member of any of various Christian sects who regard themselves as God's chosen people. **3** an archaic word for a **Jew.** [from *Israel*, the ancient kingdom of the Jews, at the SE end of the Mediterranean + -ITE[1]]

issuance ('ɪʃjuəns) *n* the act of issuing.

issue ❶ ('ɪʃju:) *n* **1** the act of sending or giving out something; supply; delivery. **2** something issued; an edition of stamps, a magazine, etc. **3** the number of identical items, such as banknotes or shares in a company, that become available at a particular time. **4** the act of emerging; outflow; discharge. **5** something flowing out, such as a river. **6** a place of outflow; outlet. **7** the descendants of a person; offspring; progeny. **8** a topic of interest or discussion. **9** an important subject requiring a decision. **10** an outcome or consequence; result. **11** *Pathol.* discharge from a wound. **12** *Law.* the matter remaining in dispute between the parties to an action after the pleadings. **13** the yield from or profits arising out of land or other property. **14 at issue. 14a** under discussion. **14b** in disagreement. **15 force the issue.** to compel decision on some matter. **16 join issue.** to join in controversy. **17 take issue.** to disagree. ◆ *vb* **issues, issuing, issued. 18** to come forth or emerge or cause to come forth or emerge. **19** to publish or deliver (a newspaper, magazine, etc.). **20** (*tr*) to make known or announce. **21** (*intr*) to originate or proceed. **22** (*intr*) to be a consequence; result. **23** (*intr*; foll. by *in*) to end or terminate. **24** (*tr*) (foll. by *with*) to supply officially (with). [C13: from OF *eissue* way out, from *eissir* to go out, from L *exīre*]
▸**'issuable** *adj* ▸**'issuer** *n*

issue price *n Stock Exchange.* the price at which a new issue of shares is offered to the public.

-ist *suffix.* **1** (*forming nouns*) a person who performs a certain action or is concerned with something specified: *motorist; soloist.* **2** (*forming nouns*) a person who practises in a specific field: *physicist.* **3** (*forming nouns and adjectives*) a person who advocates a particular doctrine, system, etc., or relating to such a person or the doctrine advocated: *socialist.* **4** (*forming nouns and adjectives*) a person characterized by a specified trait, tendency, etc., or relating to such a person or trait: *purist.* **5** (*forming nouns and adjectives*) a person who is prejudiced on the basis specified: *sexist; ageist.* [via OF from L *-ista, -istēs*, from Gk *-istēs*]

isthmian ('ɪsθmɪən) *adj* relating to or situated in an isthmus.

isthmus ❶ ('ɪsməs) *n, pl* **isthmuses** *or* **isthmi** (-maɪ). **1** a narrow strip of land connecting two relatively large land areas. **2** *Anat.* **2a** a narrow band of tissue connecting two larger parts of a structure. **2b** a narrow passage connecting two cavities. [C16: from L, from Gk *isthmos*]
▸**'isthmoid** *adj*

-istic *suffix forming adjectives.* equivalent to a combination of **-ist** and **-ic** but in some words having a less specific or literal application and sometimes a mildly pejorative force, as compared with corresponding adjectives ending in **-ist**: *communistic; impressionistic.* [from L *-isticus*, from Gk *istikos*]

istle ('ɪstlɪ) *or* **ixtle** *n* a fibre obtained from various tropical American agave and yucca trees used in making carpets, cord, etc. [C19: from Mexican Sp. *ixtle*, from Amerind *ichtli*]

it (ɪt) *pron* (*subjective or objective*) **1** refers to a nonhuman, animal, plant, or inanimate thing, or sometimes to a small baby: *it looks dangerous; give it a bone.* **2** refers to an unspecified or implied antecedent or to a previous or understood clause, phrase, etc.: *it is impossible; I knew it.* **3** used to represent human life or experience in respect of the present situation: *how's it going? I've had it; to brazen it out.* **4** used as a formal subject (or object), referring to a following clause, phrase, or word: *it helps to know the truth; I consider it dangerous to go on.* **5** used in the nominative as the formal grammatical subject of impersonal verbs: *it is raining; it hurts.* **6** (used as complement with *be*) *Inf.* the crucial or ultimate point: *the steering failed and I thought that was it.* ◆ *n* **7** (in children's games) the player whose turn it is to try to touch another. **8** *Inf.* **8a** sexual intercourse. **8b** sex appeal. **9** *Inf.* a desirable quality or ability: *he's really got it.* [OE *hit*]

IT *abbrev. for* information technology.

It. *abbrev. for:* **1** Italian. **2** Italy.

i.t.a. *or* **ITA** *abbrev. for* initial teaching alphabet, a partly phonetic alphabet used to teach reading.

ital. *abbrev. for* italic.

Ital. *abbrev. for:* **1** Italian. **2** Italy.

Italian (ɪ'tæljən) *n* **1** the official language of Italy and one of the official languages of Switzerland. **2** a native or inhabitant of Italy or a descendant of one. ◆ *adj* **3** relating to, denoting, or characteristic of Italy, its inhabitants, or their language.

Italianate (ɪ'tæljənɪt, -,neɪt) *or* **Italianesque** *adj* Italian in style or character.

italic (ɪ'tælɪk) *adj* **1** Also: **Italian.** of, relating to, or denoting a style of handwriting with the letters slanting to the right. **2** of, relating to, or denoting a style of printing type modelled on this, chiefly used to indicate emphasis, a foreign word, etc. Cf. **roman.** ◆ *n* **3** (*often pl*) italic type or print. [C16 (after an edition of Virgil (1501) printed in Venice and dedicated to Italy): from L *Italicus* of Italy, from Gk *Italikos*]

Italic (ɪ'tælɪk) *n* **1** a branch of the Indo-European family of languages that includes many of the ancient languages of Italy. ◆ *adj* **2** denoting, relating to, or belonging to this group of languages, esp. the extinct ones.

italicize *or* **italicise** (ɪ'tælɪ,saɪz) *vb* **italicizes, italicizing, italicized** *or* **italicises, italicising, italicised. 1** to print (textual matter) in italic type. **2** (*tr*) to underline (words, etc.) with a single line to indicate italics.
▸**i,talici'zation** *or* **i,talici'sation** *n*

ITC (in Britain) *abbrev. for* Independent Television Commission.

itch ❶ (ɪtʃ) *n* **1** an irritation or tickling sensation of the skin causing a desire to scratch. **2** a restless desire. **3** any skin disorder, such as scabies, characterized by intense itching. ◆ *vb* (*intr*) **4** to feel or produce an irritating or tickling sensation. **5** to have a restless desire (to do something). **6 have itchy feet.** to be restless; have a desire to travel. **7 itching palm.** a grasping nature; avarice. [OE *gīccean*]
▸**'itchy** *adj* ▸**'itchiness** *n*

-ite[1] *suffix forming nouns.* **1** a native or inhabitant of: *Israelite.* **2** a follower or advocate of; a supporter of a group: *Luddite; labourite.* **3** (in biology) indicating a division of a body or organ: *somite.* **4** indicating a mineral or rock: *nephrite; peridotite.* **5** indicating a commercial product: *vulcanite.* [via L *-ita* from Gk *-itēs* or directly from Gk]

-ite[2] *suffix forming nouns.* indicating a salt or ester of an acid having a name ending in *-ous: a nitrite is a salt of nitrous acid.* [from F, arbitrary alteration of -ATE[1]]

item ❶ *n* ('aɪtəm). **1** a thing or unit, esp. included in a list or collection. **2** *Book-keeping.* an entry in an account. **3** a piece of information, detail, or note: *a news item.* **4** *Inf.* two people having a romantic or sexual relationship. ◆ *vb* ('aɪtəm). **5** (*tr*) *Arch.* to itemize. ◆ *adv* ('aɪtem). **6** likewise; also. [C14 (adv) from L: in like manner]

itemize ❶ *or* **itemise** ('aɪtə,maɪz) *vb* **itemizes, itemizing, itemized** *or* **itemises, itemising, itemised.** (*tr*) to put on a list or make a list of.
▸**,itemi'zation** *or* **,itemi'sation** *n* ▸**'item,izer** *or* **'item,iser** *n*

iterate ('ɪtə,reɪt) *vb* **iterates, iterating, iterated.** (*tr*) to say or do again. [C16: from L *iterāre*, from *iterum* again]
▸**'iterant** *adj* ▸**,iter'ation** *n* ▸**'iterative** *adj*

itinerancy (ɪ'tɪnərənsɪ, aɪ-) *or* **itineracy** *n* **1** the act of itinerating. **2** *Chiefly Methodist Church.* the system of appointing a minister to a circuit of churches or chapels. **3** itinerants collectively.

itinerant ❶ (ɪ'tɪnərənt, aɪ-) *adj* **1** itinerating. **2** working for a short time in various places, esp. as a casual labourer. ◆ *n* **3** an itinerant worker or other person. [C16: from LL *itinerārī* to travel, from L *iter* a journey]
▸**i'tinerantly** *adv*

itinerary ❶ (aɪ'tɪnərərɪ, ɪ-) *n, pl* **itineraries. 1** a plan or line of travel; route. **2** a record of a journey. **3** a guidebook for travellers. ◆ *adj* **4** of or relating to travel or routes of travel.

itinerate (aɪ'tɪnə,reɪt, ɪ-) *vb* **itinerates, itinerating, itinerated.** (*intr*) to travel from place to place.
▸**i,tiner'ation** *n*

-itis *suffix forming nouns.* **1** indicating inflammation of a specified part: *tonsillitis.* **2** *Inf.* indicating a preoccupation with or imaginary condition of illness caused by: *computeritis; telephonitis.* [NL, from Gk, fem of *-itēs* belonging to]

it'll ('ɪtᵊl) *contraction of* it will *or* it shall.

ITO *abbrev. for* International Trade Organization.

-itol *suffix forming nouns.* indicating that certain chemical compounds

THESAURUS

issue *n* **1 = distribution**, circulation, delivery, dispersal, dissemination, granting, issuance, issuing, publication, sending out, supply, supplying **2 = edition**, copy, impression, instalment, number, printing **7 = children**, descendants, heirs, offspring, progeny, scions, seed (*chiefly Biblical*) **8, 9 = topic**, affair, argument, bone of contention, can of worms (*inf.*), concern, controversy, matter, matter of contention, point, point in question, problem, question, subject **10 = outcome**, conclusion, consequence, culmination, effect, end, end result, finale, pay-off (*inf.*), result, termination, upshot **14 at issue = under discussion**, at variance, controversial, in disagreement, in dispute, to be decided, unsettled **17 take issue = disagree**, challenge, dispute, object, oppose, raise an objection, take exception ◆ *vb* **18 = emerge**, arise, be a consequence of, come forth, emanate, flow, originate, proceed, rise, spring, stem **19 = give out**, circulate, deliver, distribute, emit, promulgate, publish, put in circulation, put out, release **20 = make known**, announce, broadcast
Antonyms *n* ≠ **distribution:** cancellation, recall ≠ **children:** parent, sire ≠ **outcome:** beginning, cause, inception, start ◆ *vb* ≠ **give out:** revoke, withdraw ≠ **emerge:** cause

isthmus *n* **1 = strip**, spit

itch *n* **1 = irritation**, itchiness, prickling, tingling **2 = desire**, craving, hankering, hunger, longing, lust, passion, restlessness, yearning, yen (*inf.*) ◆ *vb* **4 = prickle**, crawl, irritate, tickle, tingle **5 = long**, ache, burn, crave, hanker, hunger, lust, pant, pine, yearn

itching *adj* **5 = longing**, agog, aquiver, atremble, avid, burning, consumed with curiosity, eager, impatient, inquisitive, mad keen (*inf.*), raring, spoiling for

itchy *adj* **2 = impatient**, eager, edgy, fidgety, restive, restless, unsettled

item *n* **1 = detail**, article, aspect, component, consideration, entry, matter, particular, point, thing **3 = report**, account, article, bulletin, dispatch, feature, note, notice, paragraph, piece

itemize *vb* **= list**, count, detail, document, enumerate, instance, inventory, number, particularize, record, set out, specify

itinerant *adj* **1 = wandering**, ambulatory, Gypsy, journeying, migratory, nomadic, peripatetic, roaming, roving, travelling, unsettled, vagabond, vagrant, wayfaring
Antonyms *adj* established, fixed, resident, rooted, settled, stable

itinerary *n* **1 = schedule**, circuit, journey, line, programme, route, timetable, tour **3 = guidebook**, Baedeker, guide are alcohols containing two or more hydroxyl groups: *inisitol; sorbitol.* [from -ITE[2] + -OL[1]]

its (ɪts) *determiner* **a** of, belonging to, or associated in some way with it: *its left rear wheel; I can see its logical consequence.* **b** (*as pronoun*): *each town claims its is the best.*

it's (ɪts) *contraction of* it is *or* it has.

itself (ɪt'sɛlf) *pron* **1a** the reflexive form of **it**. **1b** (intensifier)*: even the money itself won't convince me.* **2** (*preceded by a copula*) its normal or usual self: *my cat doesn't seem itself these days.*

itsy-bitsy ('ɪtsɪ'bɪtsɪ) *or* **itty-bitty** ('ɪtɪ'bɪtɪ) *adj Inf.* very small; tiny. [C20: baby talk alteration of *little bit*]

ITU *abbrev. for:* **1** Intensive Therapy Unit. **2** International Telecommunications Union.

ITV (in Britain) *abbrev. for* Independent Television.

-ity *suffix forming nouns.* indicating state or condition: *technicality.* [from OF *-ite*, from L *-itās*]

IU *abbrev. for:* **1** immunizing unit. **2** international unit.

IU(C)D *abbrev. for* intrauterine (contraceptive) device.

-ium *or sometimes* **-um** *suffix forming nouns.* **1** indicating a metallic element: *platinum; barium.* **2** (in chemistry) indicating groups forming positive ions: *ammonium chloride; hydroxonium ion.* **3** indicating a biological structure: *syncytium.* [NL, from L, from Gk *-ion*, dim. suffix]

i.v. *abbrev. for:* **1** initial velocity. **2** Also: **IV**. intravenous(ly).

I've (aɪv) *contraction of* I have.

-ive *suffix.* **1** (*forming adjectives*) indicating a tendency, inclination, character, or quality: *divisive; festive; massive.* **2** (*forming nouns of adjectival origin*): *detective; expletive.* [from L *-īvus*]

IVF *abbrev. for* in vitro fertilization.

ivied ('aɪvɪd) *adj* covered with ivy.

Ivorian (aɪ'vɔːrɪən) *n* **1** a native or inhabitant of the Côte d'Ivoire. ◆ *adj* **2** of or relating to the Côte d'Ivoire or its inhabitants.

ivories ('aɪvərɪz, -vrɪz) *pl n Sl.* **1** the keys of a piano. **2** billiard balls. **3** another word for **teeth**. **4** another word for **dice**.

ivory ('aɪvərɪ, -vrɪ) *n, pl* **ivories**. **1a** a hard smooth creamy white variety of dentine that makes up a major part of the tusks of elephants and walruses. **1b** (*as modifier*): *ivory ornaments.* **2** a tusk made of ivory. **3a** a yellowish-white colour; cream. **3b** (*as adj*)*: ivory shoes.* **4** a substance resembling elephant tusk. **5** an ornament, etc., made of ivory. **6 black ivory.** *Obs.* Black slaves collectively. [C13: from OF, from L *evoreus* made of ivory, from *ebur* ivory]
▸'**ivory-,like** *adj*

ivory black *n* a black pigment obtained by grinding charred scraps of ivory in oil.

ivory nut *n* **1** the seed of the ivory palm, which contains an ivory-like substance used to make buttons, etc. **2** any similar seed from other palms. ◆ Also called: **vegetable ivory**.

ivory tower 🅣 ('tauə) *n* **a** seclusion or remoteness of attitude regarding problems, everyday life, etc. **b** (*as modifier*): *ivory-tower aestheticism.*
▸,**ivory-'towered** *adj*

ivorywood ('aɪvərɪ,wʊd) *n* **1** the yellowish-white wood of an Australian tree, used for engraving, inlaying, and turnery. **2** the tree itself.

IVR *abbrev. for* International Vehicle Registration.

ivy ('aɪvɪ) *n, pl* **ivies**. **1** a woody climbing or trailing plant having lobed evergreen leaves and black berry-like fruits. **2** any of various other climbing or creeping plants, such as poison ivy and ground ivy. [OE *īfig*]
▸'**ivy-,like** *adj*

IWW *abbrev. for* Industrial Workers of the World.

ixia ('ɪksɪə) *n* an iridaceous plant of southern Africa, having showy ornamental funnel-shaped flowers. [C18: NL from Gk *ixos* mistletoe]

ixtle ('ɪkstlɪ, 'ɪst-) *n* a variant spelling of **istle**.

izard ('ɪzəd) *n* (esp. in the Pyrenees) another name for **chamois**.

-ize *or* **-ise** *suffix forming verbs.* **1** to cause to become, resemble, or agree with: *legalize.* **2** to become; change into: *crystallize.* **3** to affect in a specified way; subject to: *hypnotize.* **4** to act according to some practice, principle, policy, etc.: *economize.* [from OF *-iser*, from LL *-izāre*, from Gk *-izein*]

> **USAGE NOTE** In Britain and the US *-ize* is the preferred ending for many verbs, but *-ise* is equally acceptable in British English. Certain words (chiefly those not formed by adding the suffix to an existing word) are, however, always spelt with *-ise* in both Britain and the US: *advertise, revise.*

THESAURUS

ivory tower *n* = **seclusion**, cloister, refuge, remoteness, retreat, sanctum, splendid isolation, unreality, world of one's own

ivory-towered *adj* = **withdrawn**, cloistered, far from the madding crowd, remote, retired, sequestered, sheltered

Jj

j *or* **J** (dʒeɪ) *n, pl* **j's, J's,** *or* **Js. 1** the tenth letter of the English alphabet. **2** a speech sound represented by this letter.

j *symbol for:* **1** *Maths.* the unit vector along the *y*-axis. **2** the imaginary number $\sqrt{-1}$.

J *symbol for:* **1** current density. **2** *Cards.* jack. **3** joule(s).

J. *abbrev. for:* **1** Journal. **2** (*pl* **JJ.**) Judge. **3** (*pl* **JJ.**) Justice.

jab Ⓣ (dʒæb) *vb* **jabs, jabbing, jabbed. 1** to poke or thrust sharply. **2** to strike with a quick short blow or blows. ◆ *n* **3** a sharp poke or stab. **4** a quick short blow. **5** *Inf.* an injection: *polio jabs.* [C19: orig. Scot. var. of JOB]
▸**'jabbing** *adj*

jabber Ⓣ ('dʒæbə) *vb* **1** to speak or say rapidly, incoherently, and without making sense; chatter. ◆ *n* **2** such talk. [C15: imit.]

jabberwocky ('dʒæbə,wɒkɪ) *n* nonsensical writing or speech. [C19: coined by Lewis Carroll as the title of a poem in *Through the Looking Glass* (1871)]

jabiru ('dʒæbɪ,ruː) *n* **1** a large white tropical American stork with a dark naked head and a dark bill. **2** Also called: **black-necked stork, policeman bird.** a large Australian stork, having a white plumage, dark green back and tail, and red legs. **3** another name for **saddlebill.** [C18: via Port., of Amerind origin]

jabot ('ʒæbəʊ) *n* a frill or ruffle on the breast or throat of a garment. [C19: from F: bird's crop, jabot]

jaçana (ˌʒɑːsə'nɑː, ˌdʒæ-) *n* a bird of tropical and subtropical marshy regions, having long legs and very long toes that enable walking on floating plants. [C18: from Port., of Amerind origin, from *jasanã*]

jacaranda (ˌdʒækə'rændə) *n* **1** a tropical American tree having fernlike leaves and pale purple flowers and widely cultivated in temperate areas of Australia. **2** the fragrant ornamental wood of this tree. **3** any of several related or similar trees or their wood. [C18: from Port., of Amerind origin, from *yacarandá*]

jacaré ('dʒækə,reɪ) *n* another name for **cayman.** [C18: from Port., of Amerind origin]

jacinth ('dʒæsɪnθ) *n* another name for **hyacinth** (sense 4). [C13: from Med. L *jacinthus*, from L *hyacinthus* plant, precious stone; see HYACINTH]

jack (dʒæk) *n* **1** a man or fellow. **2** a sailor. **3** the male of certain animals, esp. of the ass or donkey. **4** a mechanical or hydraulic device for exerting a large force, esp. to raise a heavy weight such as a motor vehicle. **5** any of several mechanical devices that replace manpower, such as a contrivance for rotating meat on a spit. **6** one of four playing cards in a pack, one for each suit; knave. **7** *Bowls.* a small usually white bowl at which the players aim with their own bowls. **8** *Electrical engineering.* a female socket with two or more terminals designed to receive a male plug (**jack plug**) that either makes or breaks the circuit or circuits. **9** a flag, esp. a small flag flown at the bow of a ship indicating the ship's nationality. **10** a part of the action of a harpsichord, consisting of a fork-shaped device on the end of a pivoted lever on which a plectrum is mounted. **11a** any of various tropical and subtropical fishes. **11b** an immature pike. **12** Also called: **jackstone.** one of the pieces used in the game of jacks. **13** *US.* a slang word for **money. 14 every man jack.** everyone without exception. **15 the jack.** *Austral. sl.* syphilis. ◆ *adj* **16** *Austral. sl.* tired or fed up (esp. in **be jack of something**). ◆ *vb* **17** (*tr*) to lift or push (an object) with a jack. ◆ See also **jack in, jack up.** [C16 *jakke*, var. of *Jankin*, dim. of *John*]

Jack (dʒæk) *n* **I'm all right, Jack.** *Brit. inf.* a remark indicating smug and complacent selfishness.

jackal ('dʒækɔːl) *n* **1** any of several African or S Asian mammals closely related to the dog, having long legs and pointed ears and muzzle: they are predators and carrion-eaters. **2** a person who does menial tasks for another. [C17: from Turkish, from Persian, from Sansk. *sṛgāla*]

jackanapes ('dʒækə,neɪps) *n* (*functioning as sing*) **1** a conceited impertinent person. **2** a mischievous child. **3** *Arch.* a monkey. [C16: var. of *Jakken-apes*, lit.: Jack of the ape, nickname of William de la Pole (1396–1450), first Duke of Suffolk, whose badge showed an ape's ball and chain]

jackass Ⓣ ('dʒæk,æs) *n* **1** a male donkey. **2** a fool. [C18: from JACK (male) + ASS[1]]

jackboot ('dʒæk,buːt) *n* **1** an all-leather military boot, extending up to or above the knee. **2** authoritarian rule or behaviour.
▸**'jack,booted** *adj*

jackdaw ('dʒæk,dɔː) *n* a large Eurasian bird, related to the crow, having a black and dark grey plumage: noted for its thieving habits. [C16: from JACK + *daw*, obs. name for jackdaw]

jackeroo *or* **jackaroo** (ˌdʒækə'ruː) *n, pl* **jackeroos** *or* **jackaroos.** *Austral. inf.* a novice on a sheep or cattle station. [C19: from JACK + (KANG)AROO]

jacket Ⓣ ('dʒækɪt) *n* **1** a short coat, esp. one that is hip-length and has a front opening and sleeves. **2** something that resembles this: *a life jacket.* **3** any exterior covering or casing, such as the insulating cover of a boiler. **4** See **dust jacket. 5a** the skin of a baked potato. **5b** (*as modifier*): *jacket potatoes.* **6** *Oil industry.* the support structure, esp. the legs, of an oil platform. ◆ *vb* **7** (*tr*) to put a jacket on (someone or something). [C15: from OF *jaquet* short jacket, from *jacque* peasant, from *Jacques* James]
▸**'jacketed** *adj*

Jack Frost *n* a personification of frost.

Jackie *or* **Jacky** ('dʒækɪ) *n, pl* **Jackies.** *Austral. offens. sl.* **1** a native Australian. **2** native Australians collectively. **3 sit up like Jackie.** to sit bolt upright, esp. cheekily.

jack in *vb* (*tr, adv*) *Sl.* to abandon or leave (an attempt or enterprise).

jack-in-office *n* a self-important petty official.

jack-in-the-box *n, pl* **jack-in-the-boxes** *or* **jacks-in-the-box.** a toy consisting of a figure on a compressed spring in a box, which springs out when the lid is opened.

Jack Ketch (kɛtʃ) *n Brit. arch.* a hangman. [C18: after *John Ketch* (died 1686), public executioner in England]

jackknife ('dʒæk,naɪf) *n, pl* **jackknives. 1** a knife with the blade pivoted to fold into a recess in the handle. **2** a former name for a type of dive in which the diver bends at the waist in midair; forward pike dive. ◆ *vb* **jackknifes, jackknifing, jackknifed.** (*intr*) **3** (of an articulated lorry) to go out of control in such a way that the trailer swings round at an angle to the tractor.

jack of all trades *n, pl* **jacks of all trades.** a person who undertakes many different kinds of work.

jack-o'-lantern *n* **1** a lantern made from a hollowed pumpkin, which has holes cut in it to represent a human face. **2** a will-o'-the-wisp.

jack plane *n* a carpenter's plane, usually with a wooden body, used for rough planing of timber.

jack plug *n* See **jack** (sense 8).

jackpot Ⓣ ('dʒæk,pɒt) *n* **1** any large prize, kitty, or accumulated stake that may be won in gambling. **2 hit the jackpot. 2a** to win a jackpot. **2b** *Inf.* to achieve great success, esp. through luck. [C20: prob. from JACK (playing card) + POT[1]]

jack rabbit *n* any of various W North American hares having long hind legs and large ears. [C19: shortened from *jackass-rabbit*, referring to its long ears]

Jack Robinson ('rɒbɪnsən) *n* **before you could** (*or* **can**) **say Jack Robinson.** extremely quickly or suddenly.

Jack Russell ('rʌsᵊl) *n* a small short-legged terrier having a white coat with tan, black, or lemon markings. [after John *Russell* (1795-1883), E clergyman who developed the breed]

jacks (dʒæks) *n* (*functioning as sing*) a game in which bone, metal, or plastic pieces (**jackstones**) are thrown and then picked up between bounces of a small ball or throws of another piece (the **jack**). [C19: shortened from *jackstones*, var. of *checkstones* pebbles]

jacksie *or* **jacksy** ('dʒæksɪ) *n, pl* **jacksies.** *Brit. sl.* the buttocks or anus. Also: **jaxie, jaxy.** [C19: ? from JACK]

jacksnipe ('dʒæk,snaɪp) *n, pl* **jacksnipe** *or* **jacksnipes.** a small Eurasian short-billed snipe.

jackstraws ('dʒæk,strɔːz) *n* (*functioning as sing*) another name for **spillikins.**

Jack Tar *n Now chiefly literary.* a sailor.

jack up Ⓣ *vb* (*adv*) **1** (*tr*) to increase (prices, salaries, etc.). **2** (*tr*) to raise an object, such as a car, with or as with a jack. **3** (*intr*) *Sl.* to inject oneself with a drug. **4** (*intr*) *Austral. inf.* to refuse to comply.

Jacobean (ˌdʒækə'bɪən) *adj* **1** *History.* relating to James I of England or to the period of his rule (1603–25). **2** of or relating to the style of furniture current at this time, characterized by the use of dark brown carved oak. **3** relating to or having the style of architecture used in England during this period. [C18: from NL, from *Jacōbus* James]

Jacobin ('dʒækəbɪn) *n* **1** a member of the most radical club founded during the French Revolution, which instituted the Reign of Terror. **2** an extreme political radical. **3** a French Dominican friar. ◆ *adj* **4** of or relating to the Jacobins or their policies. [C14: from OF, from Med. L

THESAURUS

jab *vb, n* **1, 3 = poke,** dig, lunge, nudge, prod, punch, stab, tap, thrust

jabber *vb* **1 = chatter,** babble, blather, blether, drivel, gabble, mumble, prate, rabbit (on) (*Brit. inf.*), ramble, run off at the mouth (*sl.*), tattle, waffle (*inf., chiefly Brit.*), yap (*inf.*)

jackass *n* **2 = fool,** blockhead, chump, coot, dolt, dork (*sl.*), idiot, imbecile, jerk (*sl., chiefly US & Canad.*), lamebrain (*inf.*), nerd *or* nurd (*sl.*), nincompoop, ninny, nitwit (*inf.*), numbskull *or* numskull, oaf (*sl.*), schmuck (*US sl.*), simpleton, twit (*inf., chiefly Brit.*), wally (*sl.*)

jacket *n* **3, 4 = covering,** case, casing, coat, envelope, folder, sheath, skin, wrapper, wrapping

jackpot *n* **1 = prize,** award, bonanza, kitty, pool, pot, pot of gold at the end of the rainbow, reward, winnings

jack up *vb* **1 = increase,** accelerate, augment, boost, escalate, inflate, put up, raise **2 = lift,** elevate, heave, hoist, lift up, raise, rear

Jacōbīnus, from LL *Jacōbus* James; the political club orig. met in the convent near the church of *St Jacques* in 1789]
▸ **ˌJacoˈbinic** *or* **ˌJacoˈbinical** *adj* ▸ **ˈJacobinism** *n*

Jacobite (ˈdʒækəˌbaɪt) *n Brit. history.* an adherent of James II after his overthrow in 1688, or of his descendants in their attempts to regain the throne. [C17: from LL *Jacōbus* James + -ITE[1]]
▸ **Jacobitic** (ˌdʒækəˈbɪtɪk) *adj*

Jacob's ladder *n* **1** *Old Testament.* the ladder reaching up to heaven that Jacob saw in a dream (Genesis 28:12–17). **2** a ladder made of wooden or metal steps supported by ropes or chains. **3** a North American plant with blue flowers and a ladder-like arrangement of leaves.

Jacob's staff *n* a medieval instrument for measuring heights and distances.

jaconet (ˈdʒækənɪt) *n* a light cotton fabric used for clothing, etc. [C18: from Urdu *jagannāthī*, from *Jagannāthpūrī*, India, where orig. made]

Jacquard (ˈdʒækɑːd, dʒəˈkɑːd) *n* **1** Also called: **Jacquard weave.** a fabric in which the design is incorporated into the weave. **2** Also called: **Jacquard loom.** the loom that produces this fabric. [C19: after Joseph M. *Jacquard* (1752–1834), F inventor]

jactation (dʒækˈteɪʃən) *n* **1** *Rare.* the act of boasting. **2** *Pathol.* another word for **jactitation.** [C16: from L *jactātiō* bragging, from *jactāre* to flourish, from *jacere* to throw]

jactitation (ˌdʒæktɪˈteɪʃən) *n* **1** the act of boasting. **2** a false assertion that one is married to another, formerly actionable at law. **3** *Pathol.* restless tossing in bed, characteristic of severe fevers. [C17: from Med. L, from L *jacitāre* to utter publicly, from *jactitāre* to toss about; see JACTATION]

Jacuzzi (dʒəˈkuːzɪ) *n Trademark.* **1** a device which swirls water in a bath. **2** a bath containing such a device. [C20: from *Candido* and *Roy Jacuzzi*, who developed and marketed it]

jade[1] (dʒeɪd) *n* **1** a semiprecious stone which varies in colour from white to green and is used for making ornaments and jewellery. **2a** the green colour of jade. **2b** (*as adj*): *a jade skirt.* [C18: from F, from It. *giada*, from obs. Sp. *piedra de ijada* colic stone (lit.: stone of the flank, because it was believed to cure renal colic)]

jade[2] ❶ (dʒeɪd) *n* **1** an old overworked horse. **2** *Derog., facetious.* a woman considered to be disreputable. ◆ *vb* **jades, jading, jaded. 3** to exhaust or make exhausted from work or use. [C14: from ?]
▸ **ˈjadish** *adj*

jaded ❶ (ˈdʒeɪdɪd) *adj* **1** exhausted or dissipated. **2** satiated.
▸ **ˈjadedly** *adv* ▸ **ˈjadedness** *n*

jadeite (ˈdʒeɪdaɪt) *n* a green or white mineral, a variety of jade, consisting of sodium aluminium silicate in monoclinic crystalline form.

j'adoube *French.* (ʒadub) *interj Chess.* an expression of an intention to touch a piece in order to adjust its placement rather than to make a move. [lit.: I adjust]

Jaffa (ˈdʒæfə, ˈdʒɑː-) *n* a large variety of orange, grown esp. in Israel, having a thick skin. [after *Jaffa*, port in W Israel (now part of Tel Aviv) where orig. cultivated]

jag[1] ❶ (dʒæg) *vb* **jags, jagging, jagged. 1** (*tr*) to cut unevenly. **2** *Austral.* to catch (fish) by impaling them on an unbaited hook. ◆ *n* **3** *Scot.* an informal word for **jab** (senses 3, 5). **4** a jagged notch or projection. [C14: from ?]

jag[2] ❶ (dʒæg) *n Sl.* **1a** intoxication from drugs or alcohol. **1b** a bout of drinking or drug taking. **2** a period of uncontrolled activity: *a crying jag.* [of unknown origin]

jagged ❶ (ˈdʒægɪd) *adj* having sharp projecting notches.
▸ **ˈjaggedly** *adv*

jaggy (ˈdʒægɪ) *adj* **jaggier, jaggiest. 1** a less common word for **jagged. 2** *Scot.* prickly.

jaguar (ˈdʒægjʊə) *n* a large feline mammal of S North America, Central America, and N South America, similar to the leopard but with larger spots on its coat. [C17: from Port., from Guarani *yaguara*]

jai alai (ˈhaɪ ˈlaɪ, ˈhaɪ əˌlaɪ) *n* a version of pelota played by two or four players. [via Sp. from Basque, from *jai* game + *alai* merry]

jail ❶ *or* **gaol** (dʒeɪl) *n* **1** a place for the confinement of persons convicted and sentenced to imprisonment or of persons awaiting trial. ◆ *vb* **2** (*tr*) to confine in prison. [C13: from OF *jaiole* cage, from Vulgar L *caveola* (unattested), from L *cavea* enclosure]

jailbird ❶ *or* **gaolbird** (ˈdʒeɪlˌbɜːd) *n* a person who is or has been confined to jail, esp. repeatedly; convict.

jailbreak *or* **gaolbreak** (ˈdʒeɪlˌbreɪk) *n* an escape from jail.

jailer ❶, **jailor,** *or* **gaoler** (ˈdʒeɪlə) *n* a person in charge of prisoners in a jail.

Jain (dʒaɪn) *or* **Jaina** (ˈdʒaɪnə) *n* **1** an adherent of Jainism. ◆ *adj* **2** of or relating to Jainism. [C19: from Hindi *jaina* saint, lit.: overcomer, from Sansk.]

Jainism (ˈdʒaɪˌnɪzəm) *n* an ancient Hindu religion, characterized by the belief that the material world is progressing endlessly in a series of cycles.
▸ **ˈJainist** *n, adj*

jake (dʒeɪk) *adj Austral. & NZ sl.* all right; fine: *she's jake.* [from ?]

jalap *or* **jalop** (ˈdʒæləp) *n* **1** a Mexican climbing plant. **2** the dried and powdered root of any of these plants, used as a purgative. [C17: from F, from Mexican Sp. *jalapa*]
▸ **jalapic** (dʒəˈlæpɪk) *adj*

jalapeño (dʒæləˈpiːnəʊ; *Spanish* xalaˈpenjo) *n, pl* **jalapeños.** a type of red capsicum with a hot taste used in Mexican cookery. [Mexican Sp.]

jalopy *or* **jaloppy** (dʒəˈlɒpɪ) *n, pl* **jalopies** *or* **jaloppies.** *Inf.* a dilapidated old car. [C20: from ?]

jalousie (ˈʒæluˌziː) *n* **1** a window blind or shutter constructed from angled slats of wood, etc. **2** a window made of angled slats of glass. [C19: from OF *gelosie* latticework screen]

jam[1] ❶ (dʒæm) *vb* **jams, jamming, jammed. 1** (*tr*) to cram or wedge into or against something: *to jam paper into an incinerator.* **2** (*tr*) to crowd or pack: *cars jammed the roads.* **3** to make or become stuck or locked. **4** (*tr*; often foll. by *on*) to activate suddenly (esp. in **jam on the brakes**). **5** (*tr*) to block; congest. **6** (*tr*) to crush or squeeze. **7** *Radio.* to prevent the clear reception of (radio communications) by transmitting other signals on the same frequency. **8** (*intr*) *Sl.* to play in a jam session. ◆ *n* **9** a crowd or congestion in a confined space: *a traffic jam.* **10** the act of jamming or the state of being jammed. **11** *Inf.* a predicament: *to help a friend out of a jam.* **12** See **jam session.** [C18: prob. imit.]
▸ **ˈjammer** *n*

jam[2] (dʒæm) *n* **1** a preserve containing fruit, which has been boiled with sugar until the mixture sets. **2** *Sl.* something desirable: *you want jam on it.* [C18: ?from JAM[1] (the act of squeezing)]

Jam. *Bible. abbrev. for* James.

Jamaican (dʒəˈmeɪkən) *adj* **1** of Jamaica, an island in the West Indies in the Caribbean Sea. ◆ *n* **2** a native or inhabitant of Jamaica or a descendant of one.

jamb *or* **jambe** (dʒæm) *n* a vertical side member of a doorframe, window frame, or lining. [C14: from OF *jambe* leg, jamb, from LL *gamba* hoof, from Gk *kampē* joint]

jamboree ❶ (ˌdʒæmbəˈriː) *n* **1** a large and often international gathering of Scouts. **2** a party or celebration. [C19: from ?]

jammy ❶ (ˈdʒæmɪ) *adj* **jammier, jammiest.** *Brit. sl.* **1** pleasant; desirable. **2** lucky.

jam-packed *adj* packed or filled to capacity.

jam session *n Sl.* an unrehearsed or improvised performance by jazz or rock musicians. [C20: prob. from JAM[1]]

Jan. *abbrev. for* January.

Jandal (ˈdʒændᵊl) *n NZ trademark.* a kind of sandal with a strip of material between the big toe and the other toes and over the foot.

jangle ❶ (ˈdʒæŋgᵊl) *vb* **jangles, jangling, jangled. 1** to sound or cause to sound discordantly, harshly, or unpleasantly. **2** (*tr*) to produce a jarring effect on: *the accident jangled his nerves.* **3** *Arch.* to wrangle. ◆ *n* **4** a harsh unpleasant ringing noise. **5** an argument or quarrel. [C13: from OF *jangler*, of Gmc origin]
▸ **ˈjangler** *n*

janissary (ˈdʒænɪsərɪ) *or* **janizary** (ˈdʒænɪzərɪ) *n, pl* **janissaries** *or* **janizaries.** an infantryman in the Turkish army, originally a member of the sovereign's guard, from the 14th to the 19th century. [C16: from F, from It., from Turkish *yeniçeri*, from *yeni* new + *çeri* soldiery]

janitor ❶ (ˈdʒænɪtə) *n* **1** *Scot., US, & Canad.* the caretaker of a building, esp. a school. **2** *Chiefly US & Canad.* a person employed to clean and maintain a building. [C17: L: doorkeeper, from *jānua* door, from *jānus* covered way]
▸ **janitorial** (ˌdʒænɪˈtɔːrɪəl) *adj*

THESAURUS

jade[2] *n* **2** *Derogatory, facetious* = **slut,** harridan, hussy, nag, shrew, slattern, trollop, vixen, wench

jaded *adj* **1** = **tired,** clapped out (*Austral. & NZ inf.*), exhausted, fagged (out) (*inf.*), fatigued, spent, tired-out, weary, zonked (*sl.*) **2** = **bored,** cloyed, dulled, glutted, gorged, sated, satiated, surfeited, tired
Antonyms *adj* ≠ **tired:** bright-eyed and bushy-tailed (*inf.*), fresh, refreshed ≠ **bored:** eager, enthusiastic, keen, life-loving, naive

jag[1] *n* **4** = **notch,** point, projection, protuberance, snag, spur, tooth

jag[2] *n* **1b** = **spree,** binge, bout, carousal, carouse, fit, orgy, period, spell

jagged *adj* = **uneven,** barbed, broken, cleft, craggy, denticulate, indented, notched, pointed, ragged, ridged, rough, serrated, snaggy, spiked, toothed
Antonyms *adj* glassy, level, regular, rounded, smooth

jail *n* **1** = **prison,** borstal, brig (*chiefly US*), calaboose (*US inf.*), can (*sl.*), clink (*sl.*), cooler (*sl.*), inside (*sl.*), jailhouse (*Southern US*), jug, lockup, nick (*Brit. sl.*), penitentiary (*US*), poky *or* pokey (*US & Canad. sl.*), quod (*sl.*), reformatory, slammer (*sl.*), stir (*sl.*) ◆ *vb* **2** = **imprison,** confine, detain, immure, impound, incarcerate, lock up, send down

jailbird *n* = **prisoner,** con (*sl.*), convict, felon, lag, malefactor, trusty

jailer *n* = **guard,** captor, keeper, screw (*sl.*), turnkey (*arch.*), warden, warder

jam[1] *vb* **1** = **pack,** cram, force, press, ram, squeeze, stuff, wedge **2** = **crowd,** crush, throng **5** = **congest,** block, cease, clog, halt, obstruct, stall, stick ◆ *n* **9** = **crush,** crowd, horde, mass, mob, multitude, pack, press, swarm, throng **11** *Informal* = **predicament,** bind, deep water, dilemma, fix (*inf.*), hole (*sl.*), hot water, pickle (*inf.*), plight, quandary, scrape (*inf.*), spot (*inf.*), strait, tight spot, trouble

jamboree *n* **2** = **festival,** beano (*Brit. sl.*), blast (*US sl.*), carnival, carousal, carouse, celebration, festivity, fête, frolic, hooley *or* hoolie (*chiefly Irish & NZ*), jubilee, merriment, party, rave (*Brit. sl.*), rave-up (*Brit. sl.*), revelry, spree

jammy *adj* **2** *Brit. slang* = **lucky,** favoured, fortunate

jangle *vb* **1** = **rattle,** chime, clank, clash, clatter, jingle, vibrate ◆ *n* **4** = **clash,** cacophony, clang, clangour, din, dissonance, jar, racket, rattle, reverberation
Antonyms *n* ≠ **clash:** harmoniousness, mellifluousness, quiet, silence

janitor *n* **1** = **caretaker,** concierge, custodian, doorkeeper, porter

Jansenism ('dʒænsə,nɪzəm) *n RC Church.* the doctrine of Cornelis Jansen and his disciples, who believed in predestination and denied free will.
▸'**Jansenist** *n, adj* ▸,**Jansen'istic** *adj*

jansky ('dʒænskɪ) *n, pl* **janskys.** (in radio astronomy) a unit used to measure the intensity of radio waves. Also called: **flux unit.** [C20: after Karl G. *Jansky* (1905–50), US electrical engineer]

January ('dʒænjʊərɪ) *n, pl* **Januaries.** the first month of the year, consisting of 31 days. [C14: from L *Jānuārius*]

japan (dʒə'pæn) *n* **1** a glossy black lacquer originally from the Orient, used on wood, metal, etc. **2** work decorated and varnished in the Japanese manner. ◆ *vb* **japans, japanning, japanned. 3** *(tr)* to lacquer with japan or any similar varnish.

Japanese (,dʒæpə'ni:z) *adj* **1** of or characteristic of Japan, its people, or their language. ◆ *n* **2** *(pl* **Japanese**) a native or inhabitant of Japan. **3** the official language of Japan.

Japanese stranglehold *n* a wrestling hold in which an opponent's arms exert pressure on his own windpipe.

jape (dʒeɪp) *n* **1** a jest or joke. ◆ *vb* **japes, japing, japed. 2** to joke or jest (about). [C14: ?from OF *japper* to yap, imit.]
▸'**japer** *n* ▸'**japery** *n*

Japlish ('dʒæplɪʃ) *n* the adoption and adaptation of English words into the Japanese language. [C20: from a blend of JAPANESE + ENGLISH]

japonica (dʒə'pɒnɪkə) *n* **1** Also called: **Japanese quince.** a Japanese shrub cultivated for its red flowers and yellowish fruit. **2** another name for the **camellia.** [C19: from NL, fem of *japonicus* Japanese, from *Japonia* Japan]

jar[1] ⓣ (dʒɑ:) *n* **1** a wide-mouthed container that is usually cylindrical, made of glass or earthenware, and without handles. **2** Also: **jarful.** the contents or quantity contained in a jar. **3** *Brit. inf.* a glass of beer. [C16: from OF *jarre, jarra,* from Ar. *jarrah* large earthen vessel]

jar[2] ⓣ (dʒɑ:) *vb* **jars, jarring, jarred. 1** to vibrate or cause to vibrate. **2** to make or cause to make a harsh discordant sound. **3** (often foll. by *on*) to have a disturbing or painful effect (on the nerves, mind, etc.). **4** *(intr)* to disagree; clash. ◆ *n* **5** a jolt or shock. **6** a harsh discordant sound. [C16: prob. imit.]
▸'**jarring** *adj* ▸'**jarringly** *adv*

jar[3] (dʒɑ:) *n* **on a** *(or* **the) jar.** (of a door) slightly open; ajar. [C17 (in the sense: turn): from earlier *char,* from OE *cierran* to turn]

jardinière (,ʒɑ:dɪ'njeə) *n* **1** an ornamental pot or trough for plants. **2** a garnish of fresh vegetables for a dish of meat. [C19: from F, fem of *jardinier* gardener, from *jardin* GARDEN]

jargon ⓣ ('dʒɑ:gən) *n* **1** specialized language concerned with a particular subject, culture, or profession. **2** language characterized by pretentious vocabulary or meaning. **3** gibberish. [C14: from OF, ? imit.]

jarl (jɑ:l) *n Medieval history.* a Scandinavian chieftain or noble. [C19: from ON]
▸'**jarldom** *n*

jarrah ('dʒærə) *n* an Australian eucalyptus tree that yields a valuable timber. [from Abor.]

jasmine ('dʒæsmɪn, 'dʒæz-) *n* **1** Also called: **jessamine.** any tropical or subtropical oleaceous shrub or climbing plant widely cultivated for their white, yellow, or red fragrant flowers. **2** any of several other shrubs with fragrant flowers, such as the Cape jasmine, yellow jasmine, and frangipani (**red jasmine**). [C16: from OF *jasmin,* from Ar., from Persian *yāsmīn*]

jaspé ('dʒæspeɪ) *adj* resembling jasper; variegated. [C19: from F, from *jasper* to marble]

jasper ('dʒæspə) *n* **1** an opaque impure form of quartz, red, yellow, brown, or dark green in colour, used as a gemstone and for ornamental decoration. **2** Also called: **jasper ware.** a dense hard stoneware. [C14: from OF *jaspe,* from L *jaspis,* from Gk *iaspis,* of Semitic origin]

jato ('dʒeɪtəʊ) *n, pl* **jatos.** *Aeronautics.* jet-assisted takeoff. [C20: from *j(et-)a(ssisted) t(ake)o(ff)*]

jaundice ('dʒɔ:ndɪs) *n* **1** Also called: **icterus.** yellowing of the skin due to the abnormal presence of bile pigments in the blood, as in hepatitis. **2** jealousy, envy, and ill humour. ◆ *vb* **jaundices, jaundicing, jaundiced. 3** to distort (the judgment, etc.) adversely: *jealousy had jaundiced his mind.* **4** *(tr)* to affect with or as if with jaundice. [C14: from OF *jaunisse,* from *jaune* yellow, from L *galbinus* yellowish]

jaunt ⓣ (dʒɔ:nt) *n* **1** a short pleasurable excursion; outing. ◆ *vb* **2** *(intr)* to go on such an excursion. [C16: from ?]

jaunting car *n* a light two-wheeled one-horse car, formerly widely used in Ireland.

jaunty ⓣ ('dʒɔ:ntɪ) *adj* **jauntier, jauntiest. 1** sprightly and cheerful: *a jaunty step.* **2** smart; trim: *a jaunty hat.* [C17: from F *gentil* noble; see GENTEEL]
▸'**jauntily** *adv* ▸'**jauntiness** *n*

Java ('dʒɑ:və) *n Trademark.* a programming language especially applicable to the World Wide Web. [C20: named after *Java* coffee, said to have been consumed in large quantities by the language's creators]

Java man ('dʒɑ:və) *n* a type of primitive man, *Homo erectus,* that lived in the middle Palaeolithic Age in Java.

Javanese (,dʒɑ:və'ni:z) *adj* **1** of or relating to the island of Java, in Indonesia. ◆ *n* **2** *(pl* **Javanese**) a native or inhabitant of Java. **3** the Malayo-Polynesian language of Java.

javelin ('dʒævlɪn) *n* **1** a long pointed spear thrown as a weapon or in competitive field events. **2 the javelin.** the event or sport of throwing the javelin. [C16: from OF *javeline,* var. of *javelot,* of Celtic origin]

jaw ⓣ (dʒɔ:) *n* **1** the part of the skull of a vertebrate that frames the mouth and holds the teeth. **2** the corresponding part of an invertebrate, esp. an insect. **3** a pair or either of a pair of hinged or sliding components of a machine or tool designed to grip an object. **4** *Sl.* **4a** impudent talk. **4b** idle conversation. **4c** a lecture. ◆ *vb* **5** *(intr) Sl.* **5a** to chat; gossip. **5b** to lecture. [C14: prob. from OF *joue* cheek]

jawbone ('dʒɔ:,bəʊn) *n* a nontechnical name for **mandible** or (less commonly) **maxilla.**

jawbreaker ('dʒɔ:,breɪkə) *n* **1** a device having hinged jaws for crushing rocks and ores. **2** *Inf.* a word that is hard to pronounce.
▸'**jaw,breaking** *adj*

jaws ⓣ (dʒɔ:z) *pl n* **1** the narrow opening of some confined place such as a gorge. **2 the jaws.** a dangerously close position: *the jaws of death.*

jay (dʒeɪ) *n* **1** a passerine bird related to the crow having a pinkish-brown body, blue-and-black wings, and a black-and-white crest. **2** a foolish or gullible person. [C13: from OF *jai,* from LL *gāius,* ?from name *Gāius*]

Jaycee ('dʒeɪ'si:) *n US, Canad., Austral., & NZ.* a young person who belongs to a junior chamber of commerce. [C20: from *J(unior) C(hamber)*]

jaywalk ('dʒeɪ,wɔ:k) *vb (intr)* to cross or walk in a street recklessly or illegally. [C20: from JAY (sense 2)]
▸'**jay,walker** *n* ▸'**jay,walking** *n*

jazz (dʒæz) *n* **1a** music of US Black origin, characterized by syncopated rhythms, solo and group improvisation, and a variety of harmonic idioms and instrumental techniques. **1b** *(as modifier): a jazz band.* **1c** *(in combination): a jazzman.* **2** *Sl.* rigmarole: *legal papers and all that jazz.* ◆ *vb* **3** *(intr)* to play or dance to jazz music. [C20: from ?]
▸'**jazzy** *adj* ▸'**jazzily** *adv* ▸'**jazziness** *n*

jazz up ⓣ *vb (tr, adv) Inf.* **1** to imbue (a piece of music) with jazz qualities, esp. by playing at a quicker tempo. **2** to make more lively or appealing.

JCB *n Trademark.* a type of construction machine with a hydraulically operated shovel on the front and an excavator arm on the back. [from the initials of *J*(oseph) *C*(yril) *B*(amford) (born 1916), its Brit. manufacturer]

jealous ⓣ ('dʒeləs) *adj* **1** suspicious or fearful of being displaced by a rival. **2** (often *postpositive* and foll. by *of*) resentful (of) or vindictive (towards). **3** (often *postpositive* and foll. by *of*) possessive and watchful in the protection (of): *jealous of one's reputation.* **4** characterized by or resulting from jealousy. **5** *Obsolete except in Biblical use.* demanding exclusive loyalty: *a jealous God.* [C13: from OF *gelos,* from Med. L, from LL *zēlus* emulation, from Gk *zēlos* ZEAL]
▸'**jealously** *adv*

jealousy ⓣ ('dʒeləsɪ) *n, pl* **jealousies.** the state or quality of being jealous.

jean (dʒi:n) *n* a tough twill-weave cotton fabric used for hard-wearing trousers, overalls, etc. [C16: short for *jean fustian,* from *Gene* Genoa]

Jean Baptiste *(French* ʒɑ̃batist) *n Canad. sl.* a French Canadian. [F: John the Baptist, traditional patron saint of French Canada]

jeans ⓣ (dʒi:nz) *pl n* trousers for casual wear, made esp. of denim or corduroy. [pl. of JEAN]

THESAURUS

jar[1] *n* **1 = pot,** amphora, carafe, container, crock, flagon, jug, pitcher, receptacle, urn, vase, vessel

jar[2] *vb* **1 = jolt,** agitate, bump, convulse, disturb, grate, rasp, rattle, rock, shake, vibrate **3 = irritate,** annoy, clash, discompose, gall, get on one's nerves *(inf.)*, grate, grind, irk, nark *(Brit., Austral., & NZ sl.)*, nettle, offend **4 = clash,** bicker, contend, disagree, interfere, oppose, quarrel, wrangle ◆ *n* **5 = jolt,** bump, convulsion, shock, vibration

jargon *n* **1 = parlance,** argot, cant, dialect, idiom, lingo *(inf.)*, patois, patter, slang, tongue, usage **3 = gobbledegook,** balderdash, bunkum *or* buncombe *(chiefly US)*, drivel, gabble, gibberish, Greek *(inf.)*, mumbo jumbo, nonsense, palaver, rigmarole, twaddle

jaundiced *adj* **3 = cynical,** preconceived, sceptical **3 = bitter,** biased, bigoted, distorted, envious, hostile, jealous, partial, prejudiced, resentful, spiteful, suspicious
Antonyms *adj* ≠ **cynical:** credulous, ingenuous, naive, optimistic ≠ **bitter:** open-minded, trusting, unbiased

jaunt *n* **1 = outing,** airing, excursion, expedition, promenade, ramble, stroll, tour, trip

jaunty *adj* **1, 2 = sprightly,** airy, breezy, buoyant, carefree, dapper, gay, high-spirited, lively, perky, self-confident, showy, smart, sparky, spruce, trim
Antonyms *adj* dignified, dull, lifeless, sedate, serious, staid

jaw *Slang n* **4b = chat,** chinwag *(Brit. inf.)*, conversation, gabfest *(inf., chiefly US & Canad.)*, gossip, natter, talk ◆ *vb* **5 = talk,** babble, chat, chatter, chew the fat *or* rag *(sl.)*, gossip, lecture, run off at the mouth *(sl.)*, spout

jaws *pl n* **1 = opening,** abyss, aperture, entrance, gates, ingress, maw, mouth, orifice

jazz up *vb* **= enliven,** animate, enhance, heighten, improve

jazzy *adj* **= flashy,** animated, fancy, gaudy, lively, smart, snazzy *(inf.)*, spirited, vivacious, wild, zestful

jealous *adj* **1, 3 = suspicious,** anxious, apprehensive, attentive, guarded, mistrustful, possessive, protective, solicitous, vigilant, wary, watchful, zealous **2, 4 = envious,** covetous, desirous, emulous, green, green-eyed, grudging, intolerant, invidious, resentful, rival
Antonyms *adj* ≠ **suspicious:** carefree, indifferent, trusting ≠ **envious:** satisfied

jealousy *n* **= envy,** covetousness, distrust, heart-burning, ill-will, mistrust, possessiveness, resentment, spite, suspicion

jeans *pl n* **= denims,** Levis *(Trademark)*

Jeep (dʒiːp) *n Trademark.* a small road vehicle with four-wheel drive. [C20: ?from *GP*, for *general-purpose (vehicle)*, infl. by Eugene the *Jeep*, creature in a comic strip by E. C. Segar]

jeepers *or* **jeepers creepers** (ˈdʒiːpəz ˈkriːpəz) *interj US sl.* a mild exclamation of surprise. [C20: euphemism for *Jesus*]

jeer Ⓣ (dʒɪə) *vb* **1** (often foll. by *at*) to laugh or scoff (at a person or thing). ◆ *n* **2** a remark or cry of derision. [C16: from ?]
▸ **ˈjeerer** *n* ▸ **ˈjeering** *adj, n* ▸ **ˈjeeringly** *adv*

jehad (dʒɪˈhæd) *n* a variant spelling of **jihad.**

Jehovah (dʒɪˈhəʊvə) *n Old Testament.* the personal name of God, revealed to Moses on Mount Horeb (Exodus 3). [C16: from Med. L, from Heb. YHVH YAHWEH]

Jehovah's Witness *n* a member of a Christian Church of American origin, the followers of which believe that the end of the present world system of government is near.

Jehu (ˈdʒiːhjuː) *n* **1** *Old Testament.* the successor to Ahab as king of Israel. **2** *Humorous.* a reckless driver.

jejune (dʒɪˈdʒuːn) *adj* **1** naive; unsophisticated. **2** insipid; dull. **3** lacking nourishment. [C17: from L *jējūnus* hungry, empty]
▸ **jeˈjunely** *adv* ▸ **jeˈjuneness** *n*

jejunum (dʒɪˈdʒuːnəm) *n* the part of the small intestine between the duodenum and the ileum. [C16: from L, from *jējūnus* empty; from the belief that the jejunum is empty after death]

Jekyll and Hyde (ˈdʒekᵊl; haɪd) *n* **a** a person with two distinct personalities, one good, the other evil. **b** (*as modifier*): *a Jekyll-and-Hyde personality.* [C19: after the principal character of Robert Louis Stevenson's novel *The Strange Case of Dr Jekyll and Mr Hyde* (1886)]

jell Ⓣ *or* **gel** (dʒel) *vb* **1** to make or become gelatinous; congeal. **2** (*intr*) to assume definite form: *his ideas have jelled.* [C19: back formation from JELLY[1]]

jellaba *or* **jellabah** (ˈdʒeləbə) *n* a variant spelling of **djellaba.**

jellies (ˈdʒelɪz) *pl n Brit. sl.* gelatine capsules of temazepam, dissolved and injected as a recreational drug. [C20: shortened from GELATINE]

jellify (ˈdʒelɪˌfaɪ) *vb* **jellifies, jellifying, jellified.** to make into or become jelly.
▸ **ˌjellifiˈcation** *n*

jelly[1] (ˈdʒelɪ) *n, pl* **jellies. 1** a fruit-flavoured clear dessert set with gelatine. **2** a preserve made from the juice of fruit boiled with sugar and used as jam. **3** a savoury food preparation set with gelatine or with gelatinous stock: *calf's-foot jelly.* ◆ *vb* **jellies, jellying, jellied. 4** to jellify. [C14: from OF *gelee* frost, jelly, from *geler* to set hard, from L, from *gelu* frost]
▸ **ˈjellied** *adj* ▸ **ˈjelly-ˌlike** *adj*

jelly[2] (ˈdʒelɪ) *n Brit.* a slang name for **gelignite.**

jelly baby *n Brit.* a small sweet made from a gelatinous substance formed to resemble a baby.

jellyfish (ˈdʒelɪˌfɪʃ) *n, pl* **jellyfish** *or* **jellyfishes. 1** any marine coelenterate having a gelatinous umbrella-shaped body with trailing tentacles. **2** *Inf.* a weak indecisive person.

jelly fungus *n* a fungus that grows on trees and has a jelly-like consistency when wet.

jemmy (ˈdʒemɪ) *or US* **jimmy** *n, pl* **jemmies** *or US* **jimmies. 1** a short steel crowbar used, esp. by burglars, for forcing doors and windows. ◆ *vb* **jemmies, jemmying, jemmied** *or US* **jimmies, jimmying, jimmied. 2** (*tr*) to prise (something) open with a jemmy. [C19: from the pet name for *James*]

jennet, genet, *or* **gennet** (ˈdʒenɪt) *n* a small Spanish riding horse. [C15: from OF *genet,* from Catalan *ginet,* horse used by the *Zenete,* from Ar. *Zanātah* the Zenete, a Moorish people renowned for their horsemanship]

jenny (ˈdʒenɪ) *n, pl* **jennies. 1** a machine for turning up the edge of a piece of sheet metal in preparation for making a joint. **2** the female of certain animals or birds, esp. a donkey, ass, or wren. **3** short for **spinning jenny. 4** *Billiards, etc.* an in-off. [C17: from name *Jenny,* dim. of *Jane*]

jeopardize Ⓣ *or* **jeopardise** (ˈdʒepəˌdaɪz) *vb* **jeopardizes, jeopardizing, jeopardized** *or* **jeopardises, jeopardising, jeopardised.** (*tr*) **1** to risk; hazard: *he jeopardized his job by being persistently unpunctual.* **2** to put in danger.

jeopardy Ⓣ (ˈdʒepədɪ) *n* (usually preceded by *in*) **1** danger of injury, loss, death, etc.: *his health was in jeopardy.* **2** *Law.* danger of being convicted and punished for a criminal offence. [C14: from OF *jeu parti,* lit.: divided game, hence uncertain issue, from *jeu* game, from L *jocus* joke, game + *partir* to divide]

jequirity (dʒɪˈkwɪrɪtɪ) *n, pl* **jequirities.** a tropical climbing plant with scarlet black-spotted seeds used as beads, and roots used as a substitute for liquorice. Also called: **Indian liquorice.** [C19: from Port. *jequiriti,* of Amerind origin, from *jekiriti*]

Jer. *Bible. abbrev. for* Jeremiah.

jerbil (ˈdʒɜːbɪl) *n* a variant spelling of **gerbil.**

jerboa (dʒɜːˈbəʊə) *n* any small nocturnal burrowing rodent inhabiting dry regions of Asia and N Africa, having long hind legs specialized for jumping. [C17: from NL, from Ar. *yarbū'*]

jeremiad (ˌdʒerɪˈmaɪəd) *n* a long mournful lamentation or complaint. [C18: from F *jérémiade,* referring to the Lamentations of Jeremiah in the Old Testament]

jerepigo (ˌdʒerɪˈpɪgəʊ) *n S. African.* a sweet white or red sherry-type wine. [from Port. *cheripiga* an adulterant of port wine]

jerk[1] Ⓣ (dʒɜːk) *vb* **1** to move or cause to move with an irregular or spasmodic motion. **2** to throw, twist, pull, or push (something) abruptly or spasmodically. **3** (*tr;* often foll. by *out*) to utter (words, etc.) in a spasmodic or breathless manner. ◆ *n* **4** an abrupt or spasmodic movement. **5** an irregular jolting motion: *the car moved with a jerk.* **6** (*pl*) Also called: **physical jerks.** *Brit. inf.* physical exercises. **7** *Sl., chiefly US & Canad.* a stupid or ignorant person. [C16: prob. var. of *yerk* to pull stitches tight]
▸ **ˈjerker** *n*

jerk[2] (dʒɜːk) *vb* (*tr*) **1** to preserve beef, etc., by cutting into thin strips and drying in the sun. ◆ *n* **2** Also called: **jerky.** jerked meat. [C18: back formation from *jerky,* from Sp. *charqui,* from Quechuan]

jerkin (ˈdʒɜːkɪn) *n* **1** a sleeveless short jacket worn by men or women. **2** a man's sleeveless fitted jacket, often made of leather, worn in the 16th and 17th centuries. [C16: from ?]

jerk off *or US* **jack off** *vb* (*adv often reflexive*) *Taboo sl.* (of a male) to masturbate.

jerky Ⓣ (ˈdʒɜːkɪ) *adj* **jerkier, jerkiest.** characterized by jerks.
▸ **ˈjerkily** *adv* ▸ **ˈjerkiness** *n*

jeroboam (ˌdʒerəˈbəʊəm) *n* a wine bottle holding the equivalent of four normal bottles. [C19: allusion to *Jeroboam,* a "mighty man of valour" (I Kings 11:28) who "made Israel to sin" (I Kings 14:16)]

jerry (ˈdʒerɪ) *n, pl* **jerries.** *Brit.* an informal word for **chamber pot.**

Jerry (ˈdʒerɪ) *n, pl* **Jerries.** *Brit. sl.* **1** a German, esp. a German soldier. **2** the Germans collectively.

jerry-build *vb* **jerry-builds, jerry-building, jerry-built.** (*tr*) to build (houses, flats, etc.) badly using cheap materials.
▸ **ˈjerry-ˌbuilder** *n*

jerry can *n* a flat-sided can with a capacity of between 4.5 and 5 gallons used for storing or transporting liquids, esp. motor fuel. [C20: from JERRY]

jersey (ˈdʒɜːzɪ) *n* **1** a knitted garment covering the upper part of the body. **2a** a machine-knitted slightly elastic cloth of wool, silk, nylon, etc., used for clothing. **2b** (*as modifier*): *a jersey suit.* **3** a football shirt. [C16: from *Jersey,* from the woollen sweaters worn by the fishermen]

Jersey (ˈdʒɜːzɪ) *n* a breed of dairy cattle producing milk with a high butterfat content, originating from the island of Jersey. [after *Jersey,* island in the English Channel]

Jerusalem artichoke (dʒəˈruːsələm) *n* **1** a North American sunflower widely cultivated for its underground edible tubers. **2** the tuber of this plant, which is eaten as a vegetable. [C17: by folk etymology from It. *girasole articiocco;* see GIRASOL]

jess (dʒes) *n Falconry.* a short leather strap, one end of which is permanently attached to the leg of a hawk or falcon. [C14: from OF *ges,* from L *jactus* a throw, from *jacere* to throw]
▸ **jessed** *adj*

jessamine (ˈdʒesəmɪn) *n* another name for **jasmine** (sense 1).

jessie (ˈdʒesɪ) *n Sl.* an effeminate, weak, or cowardly boy or man.

jest Ⓣ (dʒest) *n* **1** something done or said for amusement; joke. **2** playfulness; fun: *to act in jest.* **3** a jeer or taunt. **4** an object of derision. ◆ *vb* **5** to act or speak in an amusing or frivolous way. **6** to make fun of (a person or thing). [C13: var. of GEST]
▸ **ˈjesting** *adj, n* ▸ **ˈjestingly** *adv*

jester Ⓣ (ˈdʒestə) *n* a professional clown employed by a king or nobleman during the Middle Ages. [C17: from LL, vocative of JESUS]

Jesuit (ˈdʒezjʊɪt) *n* **1** a member of a Roman Catholic religious order (the **Society of Jesus**) founded by Ignatius Loyola in 1534 with the aim of defending Catholicism against the Reformation. **2** (*sometimes not cap.*) *Inf., offens.* a person given to subtle and equivocating arguments. [C16: from NL *Jēsuita,* from LL *Jēsus* + *-ita* -ITE[1]]
▸ **ˌJesuˈitical** *adj*

Jesus (ˈdʒiːzəs) *n* **1** Also called: **Jesus Christ, Jesus of Nazareth.** ?4 B.C.–?29 A.D., founder of Christianity and believed by Christians to be the Son

THESAURUS

jeer *vb* **1** = **mock,** banter, barrack, cock a snook at (*Brit.*), contemn (*formal*), deride, flout, gibe, heckle, hector, knock (*inf.*), ridicule, scoff, sneer, taunt ◆ *n* **2** = **mockery,** abuse, aspersion, boo, catcall, derision, gibe, hiss, hoot, obloquy, ridicule, scoff, sneer, taunt
Antonyms *vb* ≠ **mock:** acclaim, applaud, cheer, clap, praise ◆ *n* ≠ **mockery:** adulation, applause, cheers, encouragement, praise

jell *vb* **1** = **solidify,** congeal, harden, set, thicken **2** = **take shape,** come together, crystallize, finalize, form, materialize

jeopardize *vb* **1, 2** = **endanger,** chance, expose, gamble, hazard, imperil, risk, stake, venture

jeopardy *n* **1** = **danger,** endangerment, exposure, hazard, insecurity, liability, peril, pitfall, precariousness, risk, venture, vulnerability

jerk[1] *vb, n* **1, 2, 4, 5** = **tug,** jolt, lurch, pull, throw, thrust, tweak, twitch, wrench, yank

jerky *adj* = **bumpy,** bouncy, convulsive, fitful, jolting, jumpy, rough, shaky, spasmodic, tremulous, twitchy, uncontrolled
Antonyms *adj* flowing, frictionless, gliding, smooth

jerry-built *adj* = **ramshackle,** cheap, defective, faulty, flimsy, rickety, shabby, slipshod, thrown together, unsubstantial
Antonyms *adj* sturdy, substantial, well-built, well-constructed

jest *n* **1, 2** = **joke,** banter, bon mot, crack (*sl.*), fun, gag (*inf.*), hoax, jape, josh (*sl., chiefly US & Canad.*), play, pleasantry, prank, quip, sally, sport, wisecrack (*inf.*), witticism ◆ *vb* **5, 6** = **joke,** banter, chaff, deride, gibe, jeer, josh (*sl., chiefly US & Canad.*), kid (*inf.*), mock, quip, scoff, sneer, tease

jester *n* **1** = **clown,** buffoon, fool, harlequin, madcap, mummer, pantaloon, prankster, zany of God. ◆ *interj also* **Jesus wept. 2** used to express intense surprise, dismay, etc. [via L from Gk *Iēsous,* from Heb. *Yeshūa',* shortened from *Yehōshūa'* God is help]

Jesus freak *n Inf.* a vociferous Christian, esp. one who is evangelical and belongs to a community.

jet[1] ➊ (dʒɛt) *n* **1** a thin stream of liquid or gas forced out of a small aperture. **2** an outlet or nozzle for emitting such a stream. **3** a jet-propelled aircraft. ◆ *vb* **jets, jetting, jetted. 4** to issue or cause to issue in a jet: *water jetted from the hose.* **5** to transport or be transported by jet aircraft. [C16: from OF *jeter* to throw, from L *jactāre* to toss about]

jet[2] ➊ (dʒɛt) *n* **a** a hard black variety of lignite that takes a brilliant polish and is used for jewellery, etc. **b** (*as modifier*): *jet earrings.* [C14: from OF *jaiet,* from L, from Gk *lithos gagatēs* stone of Gagai, a town in Lycia, Asia Minor]

jet black *n* **a** a deep black colour. **b** (*as adj*): *jet-black hair.*

jeté (ʒə'teɪ) *n Ballet.* a step in which the dancer springs from one leg and lands on the other. [F, lit.: thrown, from *jeter;* see JET[1]]

jet engine *n* a gas turbine, esp. one fitted to an aircraft.

jet lag *n* a general feeling of fatigue, disorientation, or nausea often experienced by air travellers after long journeys.

jet-propelled *adj* **1** driven by jet propulsion. **2** *Inf.* very fast.

jet propulsion *n* **1** propulsion by means of a jet of fluid. **2** propulsion by means of a gas turbine, esp. when the exhaust gases provide the propulsive thrust.

jetsam ('dʒɛtsəm) *n* **1** that portion of the cargo of a vessel thrown overboard to lighten her, as during a storm. Cf. **flotsam** (sense 1). **2** another word for **flotsam** (sense 2). [C16: shortened from JETTISON]

jet set *n* **a** a rich and fashionable social set, the members of which travel widely for pleasure. **b** (*as modifier*): *jet-set travellers.*
▸**'jet-,setter** *n* ▸**'jet-,setting** *n, adj*

jet ski *Trademark. n* **1** a small self-propelled vehicle for one person resembling a scooter, which skims across water on a flat keel, and is steered by means of handlebars. ◆ *vb* **jet-ski, jet-skis, jet-skiing, jet-skied** *or* **jet ski'd.** (*intr*) **2** to ride a jet ski.
▸**jet skier** *n* ▸**jet skiing** *n*

jet stream *n* **1** *Meteorol.* a narrow belt of high-altitude winds moving east at high speeds. **2** the jet of exhaust gases produced by a gas turbine, etc.

jettison ➊ ('dʒɛtɪsᵊn, -zᵊn) *vb* **jettisons, jettisoning, jettisoned.** (*tr*) **1** to abandon: *to jettison old clothes.* **2** to throw overboard. ◆ *n* **3** another word for **jetsam** (sense 1). [C15: from OF, ult. from L *jactātiō* a tossing about]

jetton ('dʒɛtᵊn) *n* a counter or token, esp. a chip used in such gambling games as roulette. [C18: from F *jeton,* from *jeter* to cast up (accounts); see JET[1]]

jetty ➊ ('dʒɛtɪ) *n, pl* **jetties. 1** a structure built from a shore out into the water to direct currents or protect a harbour. **2** a landing pier; dock. [C15: from OF *jetee* projecting part, lit.: something thrown out, from *jeter* to throw]

jeu d'esprit (*French* ʒø dɛspri) *n, pl* ***jeux d'esprit*** (ʒø dɛspri). a light-hearted display of wit or cleverness, esp. in literature. [lit.: play of spirit]

Jew (dʒuː) *n* **1** a member of the Semitic people who are descended from the ancient Israelites. **2** a person whose religion is Judaism. [C12: from OF *juiu,* from L *jūdaeus,* from Gk *ioudaios,* from Heb., from *yehūdāh* Judah]

jewel ➊ ('dʒuːəl) *n* **1** a precious or semiprecious stone; gem. **2** a person or thing resembling a jewel in preciousness, brilliance, etc. **3** a gemstone used as a bearing in a watch. **4** a piece of jewellery. ◆ *vb* **jewels, jewelling, jewelled** *or US* **jewels, jeweling, jeweled. 5** (*tr*) to fit or decorate with a jewel or jewels. [C13: from OF *jouel,* ?from *jeu* game, from L *jocus*]

jewelfish ('dʒuːəl,fɪʃ) *n, pl* **jewelfish** *or* **jewelfishes.** a beautifully coloured and popular aquarium fish native to Africa.

jeweller *or US* **jeweler** ('dʒuːələ) *n* a person whose business is the cutting or setting of gemstones or the making or selling of jewellery.

jeweller's rouge *n* a finely powdered form of ferric oxide used as a metal polish.

jewellery ➊ *or US* **jewelry** ('dʒuːəlrɪ) *n* objects that are worn for personal adornment, such as rings, necklaces, etc., considered collectively.

Jewess ('dʒuːɪs) *n* a Jewish girl or woman.

jewfish ('dʒuː,fɪʃ) *n, pl* **jewfish** *or* **jewfishes. 1** any of various large dark fishes of warm or tropical seas. **2** *Austral.* a freshwater catfish. [C17: from ?]

Jewish ('dʒuːɪʃ) *adj* of or characteristic of Jews.
▸**'Jewishly** *adv* ▸**'Jewishness** *n*

Jew lizard *n* a large Australian lizard with spiny scales round its neck.

Jewry ('dʒʊərɪ) *n, pl* **Jewries. 1a** Jews collectively. **1b** the Jewish religion or culture. **2** a quarter of a town inhabited by Jews.

jew's-ear *n* a pinky-red fungus.

jew's-harp *n* a musical instrument consisting of a small lyre-shaped metal frame held between the teeth, with a steel tongue plucked with the finger.

Jezebel ('dʒɛzə,bɛl) *n* **1** *Old Testament.* the wife of Ahab, king of Israel. **2** (*sometimes not cap.*) a shameless or scheming woman.

jib[1] (dʒɪb) *n* **1** *Naut.* any triangular sail set forward of the foremast of a vessel. **2 cut of someone's jib.** someone's manner, style, etc. [C17: from ?]

jib[2] ➊ (dʒɪb) *vb* **jibs, jibbing, jibbed.** (*intr*) *Chiefly Brit.* **1** (often foll. by *at*) to be reluctant (to). **2** (of an animal) to stop short and refuse to go forwards. **3** *Naut.* a variant of **gybe.** [C19: from ?]
▸**'jibber** *n*

jib[3] (dʒɪb) *n* the projecting arm of a crane or the boom of a derrick. [C18: prob. based on GIBBET]

jib boom *n Naut.* a spar forming an extension of the bowsprit.

jibe[1] (dʒaɪb) *or* **jib** (dʒɪb) *vb* **jibes, jibing, jibed** *or* **jibs, jibbing, jibbed.** *n Naut.* a variant of **gybe.**

jibe[2] ➊ (dʒaɪb) *vb* **jibes, jibing, jibed.** a variant spelling of **gibe**[1].

jibe[3] (dʒaɪb) *vb* **jibes, jibing, jibed.** (*intr*) *Inf.* to agree; accord; harmonize. [C19: from ?]

jiffy ➊ ('dʒɪfɪ) *or* **jiff** *n, pl* **jiffies** *or* **jiffs.** *Inf.* a very short time: *wait a jiffy.* [C18: from ?]

Jiffy bag *n Trademark.* a large padded envelope.

jig ➊ (dʒɪg) *n* **1** any of several old rustic kicking and leaping dances. **2** a piece of music composed for or in the rhythm of this dance. **3** a mechanical device designed to hold and locate a component during machining. **4** *Angling.* any of various spinning lures that wobble when drawn through the water. **5** Also called: **jigger.** *Mining.* a device for separating ore or coal from waste material by agitation in water. ◆ *vb* **jigs, jigging, jigged. 6** to dance (a jig). **7** to jerk or cause to jerk up and down rapidly. **8** (often foll. by *up*) to fit or be fitted in a jig. **9** (*tr*) to drill or cut (a workpiece) in a jig. **10** (*tr*) *Mining.* to separate ore or coal from waste material using a jig. [C16: from ?]

jigger[1] ('dʒɪgə) *n* **1** a person or thing that jigs. **2** *Golf.* (formerly) a club, an iron, usually No. 4. **3** any of a number of mechanical devices having a vibratory motion. **4** a light lifting tackle used on ships. **5** a small glass, esp. for whisky. **6** *Billiards.* another word for **bridge**[1] (sense 11). **7** *NZ.* a light hand- or power-propelled vehicle used on railway lines.

jigger[2] *or* **jigger flea** ('dʒɪgə) *n* another name for the **chigoe** (sense 1).

jiggered ('dʒɪgəd) *adj* (*postpositive*) *Inf.* damned; blowed: *I'm jiggered if he'll get away with it.* [C19: prob. euphemism for *buggered;* see BUGGER]

jiggermast ('dʒɪgə,mɑːst) *n Naut.* any small mast on a sailing vessel.

jiggery-pokery ('dʒɪgərɪ'pəʊkərɪ) *n Inf., chiefly Brit.* dishonest or deceitful behaviour. [C19: from Scot. dialect *joukery-pawkery*]

jiggle ➊ ('dʒɪgᵊl) *vb* **jiggles, jiggling, jiggled. 1** to move or cause to move up and down or to and fro with a short jerky motion. ◆ *n* **2** a short jerky motion. [C19: frequentative of JIG]
▸**'jiggly** *adj*

jigsaw ('dʒɪg,sɔː) *n* **1** a mechanical saw with a fine steel blade for cutting intricate curves in sheets of material. **2** See **jigsaw puzzle.** [C19: from JIG (to jerk up and down rapidly) + SAW[1]]

jigsaw puzzle *n* a puzzle in which the player has to reassemble a picture that has been cut into irregularly shaped interlocking pieces.

jihad *or* **jehad** (dʒɪ'hæd) *n Islam.* a holy war against infidels undertaken by Muslims. [C19: from Ar. *jihād* a conflict]

jilt ➊ (dʒɪlt) *vb* **1** (*tr*) to leave or reject (a lover), esp. without previous warning. ◆ *n* **2** a woman who jilts a lover. [C17: from dialect *jillet* flighty girl, dim. of name *Gill*]

jim crow ('dʒɪm 'krəʊ) *n* (*often caps.*) *US.* **1a** the policy or practice of segregating Blacks. **1b** (*as modifier*): *jim-crow laws.* **2** a derogatory term for **Negro. 3** an implement for bending iron bars or rails. [C19: from *Jim Crow,* name of song used as the basis of an act by Thomas Rice (1808–60), US entertainer]
▸**'jim-'crowism** *n*

jimjams ('dʒɪm,dʒæmz) *pl n* **1** *Sl.* delirium tremens. **2** a state of nervous tension or anxiety. **3** *Inf.* pyjamas. [C19: whimsical formation based on JAM[1]]

jimmy ('dʒɪmɪ) *n, pl* **jimmies,** *vb* **jimmies, jimmying, jimmied.** a US variant of **jemmy.**

jingle ➊ ('dʒɪŋgᵊl) *vb* **jingles, jingling, jingled. 1** to ring or cause to ring lightly and repeatedly. **2** (*intr*) to sound in a manner suggestive of jin-

THESAURUS

jet[1] *n* **1** = **stream**, flow, fountain, gush, spout, spray, spring **2** = **nozzle**, atomizer, nose, rose, spout, sprayer, sprinkler ◆ *vb* **4** = **stream**, flow, gush, issue, rush, shoot, spew, spout, squirt, surge **5** = **fly**, soar, zoom

jet[2] *modifier* **b** = **black**, coal-black, ebony, inky, pitch-black, raven, sable

jet-setting *adj* = **fashionable**, cosmopolitan, high-society, rich, ritzy (*sl.*), sophisticated, trendsetting, trendy (*Brit. inf.*), well-off

jettison *vb* **1, 2** = **abandon**, discard, dump, eject, expel, heave, scrap, throw overboard, unload

jetty *n* **1, 2** = **pier**, breakwater, dock, groyne, mole, quay, wharf

jewel *n* **1** = **gemstone**, brilliant, ornament, precious stone, rock (*sl.*), sparkler (*inf.*), trinket **2** = **rarity**, charm, collector's item, find, gem, humdinger (*sl.*), masterpiece, paragon, pearl, prize, treasure, wonder

jewellery *n* = **jewels**, finery, gems, ornaments, precious stones, regalia, treasure, trinkets

jib[2] *vb* **1, 2** = **refuse**, balk, recoil, retreat, shrink, stop short

jibe[2] *see* **gibe**[1]

jiffy *n Informal* = **moment**, bat of an eye (*inf.*), flash, instant, second, split second, trice, twinkling

jig *vb* **6, 7** = **skip**, bob, bounce, caper, jiggle, jounce, prance, shake, twitch, wiggle, wobble

jiggle *vb* **1** = **jerk**, agitate, bounce, fidget, jig, jog, joggle, shake, shimmy, twitch, wiggle

jilt *vb* **1** = **reject**, abandon, betray, break with, coquette, deceive, desert, disappoint, discard, ditch (*sl.*), drop, forsake, leave (someone) in the lurch, throw over

jingle *vb* **1** = **ring**, chime, clatter, clink, jangle, rattle, tinkle ◆ *n* **3** = **rattle**, clang, clangour,

gling: *a jingling verse.* ◆ *n* **3** a sound of metal jingling. **4** a rhythmic verse, etc., esp. one used in advertising. [C16: prob. imit.]
▸ **'jingly** *adj*

jingo (ˈdʒɪŋɡəʊ) *n, pl* **jingoes. 1** a loud and bellicose patriot. **2** jingoism. **3 by jingo.** an exclamation of surprise. [C17: orig. ? euphemism for *Jesus;* applied to bellicose patriots after the use of *by Jingo!* in a 19th-cent. song]

jingoism Ⓣ (ˈdʒɪŋɡəʊˌɪzəm) *n* the belligerent spirit or foreign policy of jingoes.
▸ **'jingoist** *n, adj* ▸ **ˌjingo'istic** *adj*

jink (dʒɪŋk) *vb* **1** *(intr)* to move swiftly or turn in order to dodge. ◆ *n* **2** a jinking movement. [C18: of Scot. origin, imit. of swift movement]

jinker (ˈdʒɪŋkə) *n Austral.* a vehicle for transporting timber, consisting of a tractor and two sets of wheels for supporting the logs. [from ?]

jinks (dʒɪŋks) *pl n* boisterous or mischievous play (esp. in **high jinks**). [C18: from ?]

jinn (dʒɪn) *n (often functioning as sing)* the plural of **jinni.**

jinni, jinnee, *or* **djinni** (dʒɪˈniː) *n, pl* **jinn** *or* **djinn** (dʒɪn). a being or spirit in Muslim belief who could assume human or animal form and influence man by supernatural powers. [C17: from Ar.]

jinrikisha, jinricksha, *or* **jinrickshaw** (dʒɪnˈrɪkʃɔː) *n* another name for **rickshaw.** [C19: from Japanese, from *jin* man + *riki* power + *sha* carriage]

jinx Ⓣ (dʒɪŋks) *n* **1** an unlucky force, person, or thing. ◆ *vb* **2** *(tr)* to be or put a jinx on. [C20: ?from NL *Jynx,* genus name of the wryneck, from Gk *iunx* wryneck, a bird used in magic]

JIT *abbrev. for* just-in-time.

jitter Ⓣ (ˈdʒɪtə) *Inf.* ◆ *vb* **1** *(intr)* to be anxious or nervous. ◆ *n* **2 the jitters.** nervousness and anxiety. [C20: from ?]
▸ **'jittery** *adj* ▸ **'jitteriness** *n*

jitterbug (ˈdʒɪtəˌbʌɡ) *n* **1** a fast jerky American dance, usually to a jazz accompaniment, that was popular in the 1940s. **2** a person who dances the jitterbug. ◆ *vb* **jitterbugs, jitterbugging, jitterbugged. 3** *(intr)* to perform such a dance.

jiujitsu *or* **jiujutsu** (dʒuːˈdʒɪtsuː) *n* a variant spelling of **jujitsu.**

jive (dʒaɪv) *n* **1** a style of lively and jerky dance, popular esp. in the 1940s and 1950s. **2** *Sl., chiefly US.* **2a** misleading or deceptive talk. **2b** *(as modifier): jive talk.* ◆ *vb* **jives, jiving, jived. 3** *(intr)* to dance the jive. **4** *Sl., chiefly US.* to mislead; tell lies (to). [C20: from ?]
▸ **'jiver** *n*

job Ⓣ (dʒɒb) *n* **1** an individual piece of work or task. **2** an occupation. **3** an object worked on or a result produced from working. **4** a duty or responsibility: *her job was to cook the dinner.* **5** *Inf.* a difficult task or problem: *I had a job to contact him.* **6** a state of affairs: *make the best of a bad job.* **7** *Inf.* a particular type of something: *a four-wheel drive job.* **8** *Inf.* a crime, esp. a robbery. **9** *Computing.* a unit of work for a computer. **10 jobs for the boys.** jobs given to or created for allies or favourites. **11 just the job.** exactly what was required. **12 on the job.** actively engaged in one's employment. ◆ *vb* **jobs, jobbing, jobbed. 13** *(intr)* to work by the piece or at casual jobs. **14** to make a private profit out of (a public office, etc.). **15** *(intr; usually foll. by in)* **15a** to buy and sell (goods or services) as a middleman: *he jobs in government surplus.* **15b** *Brit.* to buy and sell stocks and shares as a stockjobber. **16** *Austral. sl.* to punch. [C16: from ?]
▸ **'jobless** *adj*

jobber (ˈdʒɒbə) *n* **1** *Brit.* short for **stockjobber** (sense 1). See also **market maker. 2** a person who jobs.

jobbery (ˈdʒɒbərɪ) *n* the practice of making private profit out of a public office.

jobbing (ˈdʒɒbɪŋ) *adj* working by the piece, not regularly employed: *a jobbing gardener.*

Jobcentre (ˈdʒɒbˌsɛntə) *n Brit.* any of a number of government offices usually having premises situated in or near the main shopping area of a town in which people seeking jobs can consult displayed advertisements.

Jobclub (ˈdʒɒbˌklʌb) *n* a group of unemployed people organized through a Jobcentre, which meets every weekday and is given advice on job seeking to increase its members' chances of finding employment.

job description *n* a formal description of the duties and responsibilities involved in a job, esp. as given to applicants for the job.

job lot *n* **1** a miscellaneous collection of articles sold as a lot. **2** a collection of cheap or trivial items.

job satisfaction *n* the extent to which the desires and hopes of a worker are fulfilled as a result of his work.

Job's comforter (dʒəʊbz) *n* a person who, while purporting to give sympathy, succeeds only in adding to distress. [from *Job* in the Old Testament (Job 16:1–5)]

jobseeker's allowance (ˈdʒɒbˌsiːkəz) *n* (in Britain) a National Insurance or social security payment for unemployed people; replaced unemployment benefit in 1996. Abbrev.: **JSA.**

job sharing *n* the division of a job between two or more people such that each covers the same job for complementary parts of the day or week.
▸ **job share** *n*

jobsworth (ˈdʒɒbzˌwɜːθ) *n Inf.* a person in a position of minor authority who invokes the letter of the law in order to avoid any action requiring initiative, cooperation, etc. [C20: from *it's more than my job's worth to…*]

jock (dʒɒk) *n Inf.* **1** short for **disc jockey. 2** short for **jockey. 3** short for **jockstrap.**

Jock (dʒɒk) *n* a slang word or term of address for a **Scot.**

jockey Ⓣ (ˈdʒɒkɪ) *n* **1** a person who rides horses in races, esp. as a profession. ◆ *vb* **2a** *(tr)* to ride (a horse) in a race. **2b** *(intr)* to ride as a jockey. **3** *(intr: often foll. by for)* to try to obtain an advantage by manoeuvring (esp. in **jockey for position**). **4** to trick or cheat (a person). [C16 (in the sense: lad): from name *Jock* + -EY]

jockstrap (ˈdʒɒkˌstræp) *n* an elasticated belt with a pouch worn by men, esp. athletes, to support the genitals. Also called: **athletic support.** [C20: from sl. *jock* penis + STRAP]

jocose Ⓣ (dʒəˈkəʊs) *adj* characterized by humour. [C17: from L *jocōsus* given to jesting, from *jocus* joke]
▸ **jo'cosely** *adv* ▸ **jocosity** (dʒəˈkɒsɪtɪ) *n*

jocular Ⓣ (ˈdʒɒkjʊlə) *adj* **1** characterized by joking and good humour. **2** meant lightly or humorously. [C17: from L *joculāris,* from *joculus* little JOKE]
▸ **jocularity** (ˌdʒɒkjʊˈlærɪtɪ) *n* ▸ **'jocularly** *adv*

jocund (ˈdʒɒkənd) *adj* of a humorous temperament; merry. [C14: from LL *jocundus,* from L *jūcundus* pleasant, from *juvāre* to please]
▸ **jocundity** (dʒəʊˈkʌndɪtɪ) *n* ▸ **'jocundly** *adv*

jodhpurs (ˈdʒɒdpəz) *pl n* riding breeches, loose-fitting around the thighs and tight-fitting from the knees to the ankles. [C19: from *Jodhpur,* town in NW India]

Joe Blake (ˌdʒəʊ ˈbleɪk) *n Austral. sl.* **1** a snake. **2 the Joe Blakes.** the DT's.

Joe Bloggs (ˈblɒɡz) *n Brit. sl.* an average or typical man. US, Canad., and Austral. equivalent: **Joe Blow.** See also **Joe Six-Pack.**

Joe Public *n Sl.* the general public.

joes (dʒəʊz) *pl n* **the.** *Austral. inf.* a fit of depression. [short for *the Joe Blakes*]

Joe Six-Pack *n US sl.* an average or typical man.

joey (ˈdʒəʊɪ) *n Austral. inf.* **1** a young kangaroo. **2** a young animal or child. [C19: from Abor.]

jog Ⓣ (dʒɒɡ) *vb* **jogs, jogging, jogged. 1** *(intr)* to run or move slowly or at a jog trot, esp. for physical exercise. **2** *(intr;* foll. by *on* or *along)* to continue in a plodding way. **3** *(tr)* to jar or nudge slightly. **4** *(tr)* to remind: *jog my memory.* ◆ *n* **5** the act of jogging. **6** a slight jar or nudge. **7** a jogging motion; trot. [C14: prob. var. of *shog* to shake]

jogger (ˈdʒɒɡə) *n* **1** a person who runs at a jog trot over some distance for exercise. **2** *NZ.* a cart with rubber tyres used on farms.

jogger's nipple *n Inf.* painful inflammation of the nipple, caused by friction with a garment when running for long distances.

jogging (ˈdʒɒɡɪŋ) *n* a slow run or trot, esp. as a keep-fit exercise.

joggle (ˈdʒɒɡᵊl) *vb* **joggles, joggling, joggled. 1** to shake or move (someone or something) with a slightly jolting motion. **2** *(tr)* to join or fasten (two pieces of building material) by means of a joggle. ◆ *n* **3** the act of joggling. **4** a slight irregular shake. **5** a joint between two pieces of building material by means of a projection on one piece that fits into a notch in the other. [C16: frequentative of JOG]
▸ **'joggler** *n*

jog trot *n* **1** an easy bouncy gait, esp. of a horse, midway between a walk and a trot. **2** a regular way of living or doing something.

john (dʒɒn) *n Chiefly US & Canad.* a slang word for **lavatory.** [C20: special use of the name]

THESAURUS

clink, reverberation, ringing, tinkle **4** = **song,** chorus, ditty, doggerel, limerick, melody, tune

jingoism *n* = **chauvinism,** belligerence, bigotry, flag-waving *(inf.),* hawkishness, insularity, xenophobia

jinx *n* **1** = **curse,** black magic, evil eye, hex *(US & Canad. inf.),* hoodoo *(inf.),* nemesis, plague, voodoo ◆ *vb* **2** = **curse,** bewitch, hex *(US & Canad. inf.)*

jitter *n* **2 the jitters** = **nerves,** anxiety, butterflies (in one's stomach), cold feet *(inf.),* fidgets, heebie-jeebies *(sl.),* nervousness, tenseness, the shakes *(inf.),* the willies *(inf.)*

jittery *adj* = **nervous,** agitated, anxious, fidgety, hyper *(inf.),* jumpy, neurotic, quivering, shaky, trembling, twitchy *(inf.),* wired *(sl.)*

Antonyms *adj* calm, composed, laid-back *(inf.),* relaxed, together *(sl.),* unfazed *(inf.),* unflustered

job *n* **1** = **task,** affair, assignment, charge, chore, concern, contribution, duty, enterprise, errand, function, pursuit, responsibility, role, stint, undertaking, venture, work **2** = **occupation,** activity, bread and butter *(inf.),* business, calling, capacity, career, craft, employment, function, livelihood, métier, office, position, post, profession, situation, trade, vocation **3** = **consignment,** allotment, assignment, batch, commission, contract, lot, output, piece, portion, product, share

jobless *adj* **2** = **unemployed,** idle, inactive, out of work, unoccupied

jockey *vb* **3** = **manoeuvre,** cajole, engineer, finagle *(inf.),* ingratiate, insinuate, manage, manipulate, negotiate, trim, wheedle

jocose *adj* = **humorous,** blithe, comical, droll, facetious, funny, jesting, jocular, jovial, joyous, merry, mischievous, playful, pleasant, sportive, teasing, waggish, witty

jocular *adj* **1, 2** = **humorous,** amusing, comical, droll, facetious, frolicsome, funny, jesting, jocose, jocund, joking, jolly, jovial, playful, roguish, sportive, teasing, waggish, whimsical, witty

Antonyms *adj* earnest, humourless, serious, solemn

jog *vb* **1** = **run,** canter, dogtrot, lope, trot **2** = **plod,** lumber, traipse *(inf.),* tramp, trudge **4** =

DICTIONARY

John Barleycorn *n Usually humorous.* the personification of alcoholic drink.

John Bull *n* **1** a personification of England or the English people. **2** a typical Englishman. [C18: name of a character intended to be representative of the English nation in *The History of John Bull* (1712) by John Arbuthnot]

John Doe *n* See **Doe.**

John Dory (ˈdɔːrɪ) *n* a European dory (the fish), having a deep compressed body and massive mobile jaws. [C18: from name *John* + DORY[1]; on the model of DOE]

John Hop *n Austral. sl.* a policeman. [rhyming sl. for COP[1]]

johnny (ˈdʒɒnɪ) *n, pl* **johnnies.** *Brit. inf.* (*often cap.*) a man or boy; chap.

Johnny Canuck (ˈdʒɒnɪ kəˈnʌk) *n Canad.* **1** an informal name for a **Canadian. 2** a personification of Canada.

Johnny-come-lately *n, pl* **Johnny-come-latelies** *or* **Johnnies-come-lately.** *Sl.* a brash newcomer, novice, or recruit.

Johnsonian (dʒɒnˈsəunɪən) *adj* of, relating to, or characteristic of Samuel Johnson, 18th-cent. English lexicographer, his works, or his style of writing.

John Thomas *n Sl.* a euphemistic name for **penis.**

joie de vivre Ⓣ *French.* (ʒwa də vivrə) *n* joy of living; enjoyment of life; ebullience.

join Ⓣ (dʒɔɪn) *vb* **1** to come or bring together. **2** to become a member of (a club, etc.). **3** (*intr;* often foll. by *with*) to become associated or allied. **4** (*intr;* usually foll. by *in*) to take part. **5** (*tr*) to meet (someone) as a companion. **6** (*tr*) to become part of. **7** (*tr*) to unite (two people) in marriage. **8** (*tr*) *Geom.* to connect with a straight line or a curve. **9 join hands. 9a** to hold one's own hands together. **9b** (of two people) to hold each other's hands. **9c** (usually foll. by *with*) to work together in an enterprise. ◆ *n* **10** a joint; seam. **11** the act of joining. ◆ See also **join up.** [C13: from OF, from L *jungere* to yoke]

joinder (ˈdʒɔɪndə) *n* **1** the act of joining, esp. in legal contexts. **2** *Law.* **2a** (in pleading) the stage at which the parties join issue (**joinder of issue**). **2b** the joining of two or more persons as coplaintiffs or codefendants (**joinder of parties**). [C17: from F *joindre* to JOIN]

joiner (ˈdʒɔɪnə) *n* **1** *Chiefly Brit.* a person skilled in making finished woodwork, such as windows and stairs. **2** a person or thing that joins. **3** *Inf.* a person who joins many clubs, etc.

joinery (ˈdʒɔɪnərɪ) *n* **1** the skill or craft of a joiner. **2** work made by a joiner.

joint Ⓣ (dʒɔɪnt) *n* **1** a junction of two or more parts or objects. **2** *Anat.* the junction between two or more bones. **3** the point of connection between movable parts in invertebrates. **4** the part of a plant stem from which a branch or leaf grows. **5** one of the parts into which a carcass of meat is cut by the butcher, esp. for roasting. **6** *Geol.* a crack in a rock along which no displacement has occurred. **7** *Sl.* **7a** a bar or nightclub. **7b** *Often facetious.* a dwelling or meeting place. **8** *Sl.* a cannabis cigarette. **9 out of joint. 9a** dislocated. **9b** out of order. ◆ *adj* **10** shared by or belonging to two or more: *joint property.* **11** created by combined effort. **12** sharing with others or with one another: *joint rulers.* ◆ *vb* (*tr*) **13** to provide with or fasten by a joint or joints. **14** to plane the edge of (a board, etc.) into the correct shape for a joint. **15** to cut or divide (meat, etc.) into joints.
▸ **ˈjointed** *adj* ▸ **ˈjointly** *adv*

joint account *n* a bank account registered in the name of two or more persons, any of whom may make deposits and withdrawals.

joint stock *n* capital funds held in common and usually divided into shares.

joint-stock company *n* **1** *Brit.* a business enterprise characterized by the sharing of ownership between shareholders, whose liability is limited. **2** *US.* a business enterprise whose owners are issued shares of transferable stock but do not enjoy limited liability.

jointure (ˈdʒɔɪntʃə) *n Law.* **a** a provision made by a husband for his wife by settling property upon her at marriage for her use after his death. **b** the property so settled. [C14: from OF, from L *junctūra* a joining]

join up *vb* (*adv*) **1** (*intr*) to become a member of a military or other organization; enlist. **2** (often foll. by *with*) to unite or connect.

joist (dʒɔɪst) *n* a beam made of timber, steel, or reinforced concrete, used in the construction of floors, roofs, etc. [C14: from OF *giste* beam supporting a bridge, from Vulgar L *jacitum* (unattested) support, from *jacēre* to lie]

jojoba (həuˈhəubə) *n* a shrub or small tree of SW North America having edible seeds containing a valuable oil that is used in cosmetics.

joke Ⓣ (dʒəuk) *n* **1** a humorous anecdote. **2** something that is said or done for fun. **3** a ridiculous or humorous circumstance. **4** a person or thing inspiring ridicule or amusement. **5 no joke.** something very serious. ◆ *vb* **jokes, joking, joked. 6** (*intr*) to tell jokes. **7** (*intr*) to speak or act facetiously. **8** to make fun of (someone). **9 joking apart.** seriously: said after there has been joking in a discussion. [C17: from L *jocus* a jest]
▸ **ˈjokey** *or* **ˈjoky** *adj* ▸ **ˈjokingly** *adv*

joker Ⓣ (ˈdʒəukə) *n* **1** a person who jokes, esp. in an obnoxious manner. **2** *Sl., often derog.* a person: *who does that joker think he is?* **3** an extra playing card in a pack, which in many card games can rank above any other card.

jollify Ⓣ (ˈdʒɒlɪˌfaɪ) *vb* **jollifies, jollifying, jollified.** to be or cause to be jolly.
▸ **ˌjollifiˈcation** *n*

jollity Ⓣ (ˈdʒɒlɪtɪ) *n, pl* **jollities.** the condition of being jolly.

jolly Ⓣ (ˈdʒɒlɪ) *adj* **jollier, jolliest. 1** full of good humour. **2** having or provoking gaiety and merrymaking. **3** pleasing. ◆ *adv* **4** *Brit.* (intensifier): *you're jolly nice.* ◆ *vb* **jollies, jollying, jollied.** (*tr*) *Inf.* **5** (often foll. by *up* or *along*) to try to make or keep (someone) cheerful. **6** to make good-natured fun of. [C14: from OF *jolif,* prob. from ON *jōl* YULE]
▸ **ˈjolliness** *n*

jolly boat *n* a small boat used as a utility tender for a vessel. [C18 *jolly* prob. from Danish *jolle* YAWL]

Jolly Roger *n* the traditional pirate flag, consisting of a white skull and crossbones on a black field.

jolt Ⓣ (dʒəult) *vb* **1** (*tr*) to bump against with a jarring blow. **2** to move in a jolting manner. **3** (*tr*) to surprise or shock. ◆ *n* **4** a sudden jar or blow. **5** an emotional shock. [C16: prob. blend of dialect *jot* to jerk & dialect *joll* to bump]

Jon. *Bible. abbrev. for* Jonah.

Jonah (ˈdʒəunə) *or* **Jonas** (ˈdʒəunəs) *n* **1** *Old Testament.* a Hebrew prophet who, having been thrown overboard from a ship was swallowed by a great fish and vomited onto dry land. **2** a person believed to bring bad luck to those around him.

jongleur (*French* ʒɔ̃glœr) *n* (in medieval France) an itinerant minstrel. [C18: from OF *jogleour,* from L *joculātor* jester]

jonquil (ˈdʒɒŋkwɪl) *n* a Eurasian variety of narcissus with long fragrant yellow or white short-tubed flowers. [C17: from F *jonquille,* from Sp. *junquillo,* dim. of *junco* reed]

jorum (ˈdʒɔːrəm) *n* a large drinking bowl or vessel or its contents. [C18: prob. after *Jorum,* who brought vessels of silver, gold, and brass to King David (II Samuel 8:10)]

josh (dʒɒʃ) *Sl., chiefly US & Canad.* ◆ *vb* **1** to tease (someone) in a bantering way. ◆ *n* **2** a teasing joke. [C19: ?from JOKE, infl. by BOSH]
▸ **ˈjosher** *n*

Josh. *Bible. abbrev. for* Joshua.

joss (dʒɒs) *n* a Chinese deity worshipped in the form of an idol. [C18: from pidgin E, from Port. *deos* god, from L *deus*]

joss house *n* a Chinese temple or shrine where an idol or idols are worshipped.

joss stick *n* a stick of dried perfumed paste, giving off a fragrant odour when burnt as incense.

jostle Ⓣ (ˈdʒɒsᵊl) *vb* **jostles, jostling, jostled. 1** to bump or push (someone) roughly. **2** to come or bring into contact. **3** to force (one's way) by pushing. ◆ *n* **4** the act of jostling. **5** a rough bump or push. [C14: see JOUST]

jot Ⓣ (dʒɒt) *vb* **jots, jotting, jotted. 1** (*tr;* usually foll. by *down*) to write a

THESAURUS

nudge, activate, arouse, prod, prompt, push, remind, shake, stimulate, stir, suggest

joie de vivre *n* = **enthusiasm,** ebullience, enjoyment, gaiety, gusto, joy, joyfulness, pleasure, relish, zest
Antonyms *n* apathy, depression, distaste

join *vb* **1, 7** = **connect,** accompany, add, adhere, annex, append, attach, cement, combine, couple, fasten, knit, link, marry, splice, tie, unite, yoke **2, 3** = **enrol,** affiliate with, associate with, enlist, enter, sign up **8** = **meet,** adjoin, border, border on, butt, conjoin, extend, reach, touch, verge on
Antonyms *vb* ≠ **connect:** detach, disconnect, disengage, disentangle, divide, separate, sever, unfasten ≠ **enrol:** leave, part, quit, resign

joint *n* **1** = **junction,** articulation, connection, hinge, intersection, juncture, knot, nexus, node, seam, union ◆ *adj* **10** = **shared,** collective, combined, communal, concerted, consolidated, cooperative, joined, mutual, united ◆ *vb* **13** = **join,** connect, couple, fasten, fit, unite **15** = **divide,** carve, cut up, dismember, dissect, segment, sever, sunder

jointly *adv* **10** = **collectively,** as one, in common, in conjunction, in league, in partnership, mutually, together, unitedly
Antonyms *adv* individually, separately, singly

joke *n* **1, 2** = **jest,** frolic, fun, gag (*inf.*), jape, josh (*sl., chiefly US & Canad.*), lark, play, prank, pun, quip, quirk, sally, sport, whimsy, wisecrack (*inf.*), witticism, yarn **4** = **laughing stock,** buffoon, butt, clown, simpleton, target ◆ *vb* **6-8** = **jest,** banter, chaff, deride, frolic, gambol, josh (*sl., chiefly US & Canad.*), kid (*inf.*), mock, play the fool, quip, ridicule, taunt, tease, wind up (*Brit. sl.*)

joker *n* **1** = **comedian,** buffoon, clown, comic, humorist, jester, kidder (*inf.*), prankster, trickster, wag, wit

jokey *adj* **1, 2** = **playful,** amusing, droll, facetious, funny, humorous, jesting, mischievous, nonserious, prankish, teasing, waggish, wisecracking
Antonyms *adj* dry, grave, humourless, solemn, straight-faced, unsmiling

jollification *n* = **festivity,** beano (*Brit. sl.*), carousal, celebration, jolly (*inf., chiefly Brit.*), knees-up (*Brit. inf.*), merrymaking, party, reception, shindig (*inf.*)

jollity *n* = **fun,** conviviality, gaiety, liveliness, merriment, merrymaking, mirth, revelry

jolly *adj* **1, 2** = **happy,** blithesome, carefree, cheerful, chirpy (*inf.*), convivial, festive, frolicsome, funny, gay, genial, gladsome (*arch.*), hilarious, jocund, jovial, joyful, joyous, jubilant, merry, mirthful, playful, sportive, sprightly
Antonyms *adj* doleful, down in the dumps (*inf.*), gaunt, grave, lugubrious, miserable, morose, saturnine, serious, solemn

jolt *vb* **1** = **jerk,** jar, jog, jostle, knock, push, shake, shove **3** = **surprise,** astonish, discompose, disturb, perturb, stagger, startle, stun, upset ◆ *n* **4** = **jerk,** bump, jar, jog, jump, lurch, quiver, shake, start **5** = **surprise,** blow, bolt from the blue, bombshell, reversal, setback, shock, thunderbolt, whammy (*inf., chiefly US*)

jostle *vb* **1, 3** = **push,** bump, butt, crowd, elbow, hustle, jog, joggle, jolt, press, scramble, shake, shove, squeeze, throng, thrust

jot *vb* **1** = **note down,** list, note, record, register, scribble, tally ◆ *n* **2** = **bit,** ace, atom, detail, frac-

brief note of. ◆ *n* 2 (*used with a negative*) a little bit (in **not care** (*or* **give**) **a jot**). [C16: from L *jota,* from Gk *iōta,* of Semitic origin]

jota (*Spanish* 'xota) *n* a Spanish dance in fast triple time. [Sp., prob. from OSp. *sota,* from *sotar* to dance, from L *saltāre*]

jotter ❶ ('dʒɒtə) *n* a small notebook.

jotting ('dʒɒtɪŋ) *n* something jotted down. [from ON, from *jötunn* giant + *heimr* world, HOME]

joual (ʒwɑ:l) *n* nonstandard Canadian French dialect, esp. as associated with ill-educated speakers. [from the pronunciation in this dialect of F *cheval* horse]

joule (dʒu:l) *n* the derived SI unit of work or energy; the work done when the point of application of a force of 1 newton is displaced through a distance of 1 metre in the direction of the force. Symbol: J [C19: after J. P. *Joule* (1818–89), E physicist]

jounce (dʒaʊns) *vb* **jounces, jouncing, jounced. 1** to shake or jolt or cause to shake or jolt. ◆ *n* **2** a shake; bump. [C15: prob. from dialect *joll* to bump + BOUNCE]

journal ❶ ('dʒɜ:nᵊl) *n* **1** a newspaper or periodical. **2** a book in which a daily record of happenings, etc., is kept. **3** an official record of the proceedings of a legislative body. **4** *Book-keeping.* one of several books in which transactions are initially recorded to facilitate subsequent entry in the ledger. **5** *Machinery.* the part of a shaft or axle in contact with or enclosed by a bearing. [C14: from OF: daily, from L *diurnālis;* see DIURNAL]

journal box *n Machinery.* a case enclosing or supporting a journal.

journalese (ˌdʒɜ:nᵊ'li:z) *n Derog.* a superficial style of writing regarded as typical of newspapers, etc.

journalism ('dʒɜ:nᵊˌlɪzəm) *n* **1** the profession or practice of reporting about, photographing, or editing news stories for one of the mass media. **2** newspapers and magazines collectively.

journalist ❶ ('dʒɜ:nᵊlɪst) *n* **1** a person whose occupation is journalism. **2** a person who keeps a journal.
▸ˌ**journa'listic** *adj* ▸ˌ**journa'listically** *adv*

journalize *or* **journalise** ('dʒɜ:nᵊˌlaɪz) *vb* **journalizes, journalizing, journalized** *or* **journalises, journalising, journalised.** to record (daily events) in a journal.
▸ˌ**journali'zation** *or* ˌ**journali'sation** *n*

journey ❶ ('dʒɜ:nɪ) *n* **1** a travelling from one place to another. **2a** the distance travelled in a journey. **2b** the time taken to make a journey. ◆ *vb* **3** (*intr*) to make a journey. [C13: from OF *journee* a day, a day's travelling, from L *diurnum* day's portion]
▸'**journeyer** *n*

journeyman ('dʒɜ:nɪmən) *n, pl* **journeymen. 1** a craftsman, artisan, etc., who is qualified to work at his trade in the employment of another. **2** a competent workman. [C15: from JOURNEY (in obs. sense: a day's work) + MAN]

joust ❶ (dʒaʊst) *History.* ◆ *n* **1** a combat between two mounted knights tilting against each other with lances. ◆ *vb* **2** (*intr;* often foll. by *against* or *with*) to encounter or engage in such a tournament: *he jousted with five opponents.* [C13: from OF, from *jouster* to fight on horseback, from Vulgar L *juxtāre* (unattested) to come together, from L *juxtā* close]
▸'**jouster** *n*

Jove (dʒəʊv) *n* **1** another name for **Jupiter**[1]. **2 by Jove.** an exclamation of surprise or excitement. [C14: from OL *Jovis* Jupiter]
▸'**Jovian** *n*

jovial ❶ ('dʒəʊvɪəl) *adj* having or expressing convivial humour. [C16: from L *joviālis* of (the planet) Jupiter, considered by astrologers to foster good humour]
▸**joviality** (ˌdʒəʊvɪ'ælɪtɪ) *n* ▸'**jovially** *adv*

jowl[1] (dʒaʊl) *n* **1** the jaw, esp. the lower one. **2** (*often pl*) a cheek. **3 cheek by jowl.** See **cheek.** [OE *ceafl* jaw]
▸**jowled** *adj*

jowl[2] (dʒaʊl) *n* **1** fatty flesh hanging from the lower jaw. **2** a similar fleshy part in animals, such as the dewlap of a bull. [OE *ceole* throat]

joy ❶ (dʒɔɪ) *n* **1** a deep feeling or condition of happiness or contentment. **2** something causing such a feeling. **3** an outward show of pleasure or delight. **4** *Brit. inf.* success; satisfaction: *I went for a loan, but got no joy.* ◆ *vb Chiefly poetic.* **5** (*intr*) to feel joy. **6** (*tr*) to gladden. [C13: from OF, from L *gaudium* joy, from *gaudēre* to be glad]

Joycean ('dʒɔɪsɪən) *adj* **1** of, relating to, or like, James Joyce (1882–1941), Irish writer, or his works. ◆ *n* **2** a student or admirer of Joyce or his works.

joyful ❶ ('dʒɔɪfʊl) *adj* **1** full of joy; elated. **2** expressing or producing joy: *a joyful look; a joyful occasion.*
▸'**joyfully** *adv* ▸'**joyfulness** *n*

joyless ❶ ('dʒɔɪlɪs) *adj* having or producing no joy or pleasure.
▸'**joylessly** *adv* ▸'**joylessness** *n*

joyous ❶ ('dʒɔɪəs) *adj* **1** having a happy nature or mood. **2** joyful.
▸'**joyously** *adv*

joyride ('dʒɔɪˌraɪd) *n* **1** a ride taken for pleasure in a car, esp. in a stolen car driven recklessly. ◆ *vb* **joy-ride, joy-rides, joy-riding, joy-rode, joy-ridden. 2** (*intr*) to take such a ride.
▸'**joyˌrider** *n* ▸'**joyriding** *n*

joystick ('dʒɔɪˌstɪk) *n* **1** *Inf.* the control stick of an aircraft, machine, etc. **2** *Computing.* a lever for controlling the movement of a cursor on a screen.

JP *abbrev. for* Justice of the Peace.

J/psi particle *n* a type of elementary particle thought to be formed from charmed quarks.

Jr *or* **jr** *abbrev. for* junior.

JSA (in Britain) *abbrev. for* jobseeker's allowance.

jubbah ('dʒʊbə) *n* a long loose outer garment with wide sleeves, worn by Muslim men and women, esp. in India. [C16: from Ar.]

jube (dʒu:b) *n Austral. & NZ inf.* any jelly-like sweet. [C20: shortened from JUJUBE]

jubilant ❶ ('dʒu:bɪlənt) *adj* feeling or expressing great joy. [C17: from L, from *jūbilāre* to give a joyful cry, from *jūbilum* a shout]
▸'**jubilance** *n* ▸'**jubilantly** *adv*

jubilate ('dʒu:bɪˌleɪt) *vb* **jubilates, jubilating, jubilated.** (*intr*) **1** to have or express great joy; rejoice. **2** to celebrate a jubilee. [C17: from L *jūbilāre;* see JUBILANT]

jubilation ❶ (ˌdʒu:bɪ'leɪʃən) *n* a feeling of great joy and celebration.

jubilee ❶ ('dʒu:bɪˌli:) *n* **1** a time or season for rejoicing. **2** a special anniversary, esp. a 25th or 50th one. **3** *RC Church.* a specially appointed period in which special indulgences are granted. **4** *Old Testament.* a year that was to be observed every 50th year, during which Hebrew slaves were to be liberated, etc. **5** a less common word for **jubilation.** [C14: from OF *jubile,* from LL *jubilaeus,* from LGk, from Heb. *yōbhēl* ram's horn, used for the proclamation of the year of jubilee]

Jud. *Bible. abbrev. for:* **1** Also: **Judg.** Judges. **2** Judith.

Judaic (dʒu:'deɪɪk) *adj* of or relating to the Jews or Judaism.
▸**Ju'daically** *adv*

Judaism ('dʒu:deɪˌɪzəm) *n* **1** the religion of the Jews, based on the Old Testament and the Talmud and having as its central point a belief in one God. **2** the religious and cultural traditions of the Jews.
▸ˌ**Juda'istic** *adj*

Judaize *or* **Judaise** ('dʒu:deɪˌaɪz) *vb* **Judaizes, Judaizing, Judaized** *or* **Judaises, Judaising, Judaised. 1** to conform or bring into conformity with Judaism. **2** (*tr*) to convert to Judaism.
▸ˌ**Judai'zation** *or* ˌ**Judai'sation** *n*

Judas ('dʒu:dəs) *n* **1** *New Testament.* the apostle who betrayed Jesus to his enemies for 30 pieces of silver (Luke 22:3–6, 47–48). **2** a person who betrays a friend; traitor.

Judas tree *n* small Eurasian leguminous tree with pinkish-purple flowers that bloom before the leaves appear.

judder ('dʒʌdə) *Inf., chiefly Brit.* ◆ *vb* **1** (*intr*) to shake or vibrate. ◆ *n* **2** abnormal vibration in a mechanical system. **3** a juddering motion. [prob. blend of JAR[2] + SHUDDER]

judge ❶ (dʒʌdʒ) *n* **1** a public official with authority to hear cases in a court of law and pronounce judgment upon them. **2** a person who is appointed to determine the result of contests or competitions. **3** a

THESAURUS

tion, grain, iota, mite, morsel, particle, scintilla, scrap, speck, tad (*inf., chiefly US*), tittle, trifle, whit

jotter *n* = **notebook**, Filofax (*Trademark*), notepad, pad

journal *n* **1** = **newspaper**, chronicle, daily, gazette, magazine, monthly, paper, periodical, record, register, review, tabloid, weekly, zine (*inf.*) **2** = **diary**, chronicle, commonplace book, daybook, log, record

journalist *n* **1** = **reporter**, broadcaster, columnist, commentator, contributor, correspondent, hack, journo (*sl.*), newsman *or* newswoman, newspaperman *or* newspaperwoman, pressman, scribe (*inf.*), stringer

journey *n* **1** = **trip**, excursion, expedition, jaunt, odyssey, outing, passage, peregrination, pilgrimage, progress, ramble, tour, travel, trek, voyage ◆ *vb* **3** = **travel**, fare, fly, go, peregrinate, proceed, ramble, range, roam, rove, tour, traverse, trek, voyage, wander, wend

joust *n* **1** = **duel**, combat, encounter, engagement, lists, match, passage of arms, set-to, tilt, tournament, tourney ◆ *vb* **2** = **cross swords**, break a lance, engage, enter the lists, fight, tilt, trade blows

jovial *adj* = **cheerful**, airy, animated, blithe, buoyant, cheery, convivial, cordial, gay, glad, happy, hilarious, jocose, jocund, jolly, jubilant, merry, mirthful
Antonyms *adj* antisocial, doleful, grumpy, morose, solemn, unfriendly

joviality *n* = **mirth**, fun, gaiety, glee, hilarity, jollity, merriment

joy *n* **1** = **delight**, bliss, ecstasy, elation, exaltation, exultation, felicity, festivity, gaiety, gladness, glee, hilarity, pleasure, rapture, ravishment, satisfaction, transport **2** = **treasure**, charm, delight, gem, jewel, pride, prize, treat, wonder
Antonyms *n* ≠ **delight:** despair, grief, misery, sorrow, tribulation, unhappiness ≠ **treasure:** bane

joyful *adj* **1** = **delighted**, blithesome, cock-a-hoop, elated, enraptured, floating on air, glad, gladsome (*arch.*), gratified, happy, jocund, jolly, jovial, jubilant, light-hearted, merry, on cloud nine (*inf.*), over the moon (*inf.*), pleased, rapt, satisfied

joyless *adj* = **unhappy**, cheerless, dejected, depressed, dismal, dispirited, downcast, down in the dumps (*inf.*), dreary, gloomy, miserable, sad

joyous *adj* **1, 2** = **joyful**, blithe, cheerful, festive, heartening, merry, rapturous

jubilant *adj* = **overjoyed**, cock-a-hoop, elated, enraptured, euphoric, excited, exuberant, exultant, glad, joyous, rejoicing, rhapsodic, thrilled, triumphal, triumphant
Antonyms *adj* despondent, doleful, downcast, melancholy, sad, sorrowful

jubilation *n* = **joy**, celebration, ecstasy, elation, excitement, exultation, festivity, jamboree, jubilee, triumph

jubilee *n* **1** = **celebration**, carnival, festival, festivity, fête, gala, holiday

judge *n* **1** = **magistrate**, beak (*Brit. sl.*), justice **2** = **referee**, adjudicator, arbiter, arbitrator, moder-

person qualified to comment critically: *a good judge of antiques.* **4** a leader of the peoples of Israel from Joshua's death to the accession of Saul. ◆ *vb* **judges, judging, judged. 5** to hear and decide upon (a case at law). **6** (*tr*) to pass judgment on. **7** (when *tr, may take a clause as object or an infinitive*) to decide (something) after inquiry. **8** to determine the result of (a contest or competition). **9** to appraise (something) critically. **10** (*tr; takes a clause as object*) to believe something to be the case. [C14: from OF, from L *jūdicāre* to pass judgment, from *jūdex* a judge]
▸**'judge,like** *adj* ▸**'judger** *n* ▸**'judgeship** *n*

judge advocate *n, pl* **judge advocates.** an officer who superintends proceedings at a military court martial.

judges' rules *pl n* (in English law) a set of rules, not legally binding, governing the behaviour of police towards suspects.

judgment ❶ *or* **judgement** ('dʒʌdʒmənt) *n* **1** the faculty of being able to make critical distinctions and achieve a balanced viewpoint. **2a** the verdict pronounced by a court of law. **2b** an obligation arising as a result of such a verdict, such as a debt. **2c** (*as modifier*): *a judgment debtor.* **3** the formal decision of one or more judges at a contest or competition. **4** a particular decision formed in a case in dispute or doubt. **5** an estimation: *a good judgment of distance.* **6** criticism or censure. **7 against one's better judgment.** contrary to a preferred course of action. **8 in someone's judgment.** in someone's opinion. **9 sit in judgment. 9a** to preside as judge. **9b** to assume the position of critic.

Judgment ('dʒʌdʒmənt) *n* **1** the estimate by God of the ultimate worthiness or unworthiness of the individual or of all mankind. **2** God's subsequent decision determining the final destinies of all individuals.

judgmental ❶ *or* **judgemental** (dʒʌdʒ'mentᵊl) *adj* of or denoting an attitude in which judgments about other people's conduct are made.

Judgment Day *n* the occasion of the Last Judgment by God at the end of the world. Also called: **Day of Judgment.** See **Last Judgment.**

judicatory ('dʒuːdɪkətərɪ) *adj* **1** of or relating to the administration of justice. ◆ *n* **2** a court of law. **3** the administration of justice.

judicature ('dʒuːdɪkətʃə) *n* **1** the administration of justice. **2** the office, function, or power of a judge. **3** the extent of authority of a court or judge. **4** a body of judges; judiciary. **5** a court of justice or such courts collectively.

judicial ❶ (dʒuː'dɪʃəl) *adj* **1** of or relating to the administration of justice. **2** of or relating to judgment in a court of law or to a judge exercising this function. **3** allowed or enforced by a court of law: *judicial separation.* **4** having qualities appropriate to a judge. **5** giving or seeking judgment. [C14: from L *jūdiciālis* belonging to the law courts, from *jūdicium* judgment, from *jūdex* a judge]
▸**ju'dicially** *adv*

judiciary (dʒuː'dɪʃɪərɪ) *adj* **1** of or relating to courts of law, judgment, or judges. ◆ *n, pl* **judiciaries. 2** the branch of the central authority in a state concerned with the administration of justice. **3** the system of courts in a country. **4** the judges collectively.

judicious ❶ (dʒuː'dɪʃəs) *adj* having or proceeding from good judgment.
▸**ju'diciously** *adv* ▸**ju'diciousness** *n*

judo ('dʒuːdəʊ) *n* **a** the modern sport derived from jujitsu, in which the object is to force an opponent to submit using the minimum of physical effort. **b** (*as modifier*): *a judo throw.* [Japanese, from *jū* gentleness + *dō* way]
▸**'judoist** *n*

Judy ('dʒuːdɪ) *n, pl* **Judies. 1** the wife of Punch in the children's puppet show *Punch and Judy.* See **Punch. 2** (*often not cap.*) *Brit. sl.* a girl.

jug ❶ (dʒʌg) *n* **1** a vessel for holding or pouring liquids, usually having a handle and a lip. US equivalent: **pitcher. 2** *Austral. & NZ.* a container in which water is boiled, esp. an electric kettle. **3** *US.* a large vessel with a narrow mouth. **4** Also called: **jugful.** the amount of liquid held by a jug. **5** *Brit. inf.* a glass of beer. **6** *Sl.* jail. ◆ *vb* **jugs, jugging, jugged. 7** to stew or boil (meat, esp. hare) in an earthenware container. **8** (*tr*) *Sl.* to put in jail. [C16: prob. from *Jug,* nickname from name *Joan*]

jugate ('dʒuːgeɪt, -gɪt) *adj* (esp. of compound leaves) having parts arranged in pairs. [C19: from NL *jugātus* (unattested), from L *jugum* a yoke]

juggernaut ('dʒʌgə,nɔːt) *n* **1** any terrible force, esp. one that demands complete self-sacrifice. **2** *Brit.* a very large heavy lorry. [C17: from Hindi, from Sansk. *Jagannātha* lord of the world: devotees supposedly threw themselves under a cart carrying *Juggernaut,* an idol of Krishna]

juggins ('dʒʌgɪnz) *n* (*functioning as sing*) *Brit. inf.* a silly person. [C19: special use of the surname *Juggins*]

juggle ❶ ('dʒʌgᵊl) *vb* **juggles, juggling, juggled. 1** to throw and catch (several objects) continuously so that most are in the air all the time. **2** to manipulate (facts, etc.) so as to give a false picture. **3** (*tr*) to keep (several activities) in progress, esp. with difficulty. ◆ *n* **4** an act of juggling. [C14: from OF *jogler* to perform as a jester, from L, from *jocus* a jest]
▸**'juggler** *n*

Jugoslav ('juːgəʊ,slɑːv) *n, adj* a variant spelling of **Yugoslav.**

jugular ('dʒʌgjʊlə) *adj* **1** of, relating to, or situated near the throat or neck. ◆ *n* **2** Also called: **jugular vein.** any of the large veins in the neck carrying blood to the heart from the head. [C16: from LL, from L *jugulum* throat]

juice ❶ (dʒuːs) *n* **1** any liquid that occurs naturally in or is secreted by plant or animal tissue: *the juice of an orange.* **2** *Inf.* **2a** petrol. **2b** electricity. **2c** alcoholic drink. **3** vigour or vitality. [C13: from OF *jus,* from L]
▸**'juiceless** *adj*

juice up *vb* (*tr, adv*) *US sl.* to make lively: *to juice up a party.*

juicy ❶ ('dʒuːsɪ) *adj* **juicier, juiciest. 1** full of juice. **2** provocatively interesting; spicy: *juicy gossip.* **3** profitable: *a juicy contract.*
▸**'juicily** *adv* ▸**'juiciness** *n*

jujitsu, jujutsu, *or* **jiujutsu** (dʒuː'dʒɪtsuː) *n* the traditional Japanese system of unarmed self-defence perfected by the samurai. See also **judo.** [C19: from Japanese, from *jū* gentleness + *jutsu* art]

juju ('dʒuːdʒuː) *n* **1** an object superstitiously revered by certain West African peoples and used as a charm or fetish. **2** the power associated with a juju. [C19: prob. from Hausa *djudju* evil spirit, fetish]

jujube ('dʒuːdʒuːb) *n* **1** any of several Old World spiny trees that have small yellowish flowers and dark red edible fruits. **2** the fruit of any of these trees. **3** a chewy sweet made of flavoured gelatine and sometimes medicated to soothe sore throats. [C14: from Med. L *jujuba,* modification of L *zīzyphum,* from Gk *zizuphon*]

jukebox ('dʒuːk,bɒks) *n* a coin-operated machine, usually found in pubs, clubs, etc., that contains records, CDs, or videos, which are played when selected by a customer. [C20: from Gullah (an African-American language) *juke* bawdy (as in *juke house* brothel) + BOX[1]]

jukskei ('jʊk,skeɪ) *n* a South African game in which a peg is thrown over a fixed distance at a stake driven into the ground. [from Afrik. *juk* yoke + *skei* pin]

julep ('dʒuːlɪp) *n* **1** a sweet drink, variously prepared and sometimes medicated. **2** *Chiefly US.* short for **mint julep.** [C14: from OF, from Ar. *julāb,* from Persian, from *gul* rose + *āb* water]

Julian calendar ('dʒuːljən, -lɪən) *n* the calendar introduced by Julius Caesar in 46 B.C., in which leap years occurred every fourth year and in every centenary year. Cf. **Gregorian calendar.**

julienne (,dʒuːlɪ'en) *adj* **1** (of vegetables) cut into thin shreds. ◆ *n* **2** a clear consommé to which such vegetables have been added. [F, from name *Jules, Julien,* or *Julienne*]

July (dʒuː'laɪ) *n, pl* **Julies.** the seventh month of the year, consisting of 31 days. [C13: from Anglo-F *julie,* from L *Jūlius,* after Gaius *Julius* Caesar, in whose honour it was named]

jumble ❶ ('dʒʌmbᵊl) *vb* **jumbles, jumbling, jumbled. 1** to mingle (objects, etc.) in a state of disorder. **2** (*tr; usually passive*) to remember in a confused form. ◆ *n* **3** a disordered mass, state, etc. **4** *Brit.* articles donated for a jumble sale. [C16: from ?]
▸**'jumbly** *adj*

jumble sale *n* a sale of miscellaneous articles, usually second-hand, in aid of charity. US and Canad. equivalent: **rummage sale.**

jumbo ❶ ('dʒʌmbəʊ) *n, pl* **jumbos. 1** *Inf.* **1a** a very large person or thing. **1b** (*as modifier*): *a jumbo box of detergent.* **2** See **jumbo jet.** [C19: after a famous elephant exhibited by P. T. Barnum, from Swahili *jumbe* chief]

jumbo jet *n Inf.* a type of large jet-propelled airliner that carries several hundred passengers.

jumbo pack *n* **1** the promotion of bulk sales of small unit items, such

THESAURUS

ator, umpire **3** = **critic**, appraiser, arbiter, assessor, authority, connoisseur, evaluator, expert ◆ *vb* **5** = **try**, adjudge, condemn, decree, doom, find, pass sentence, pronounce sentence, rule, sentence, sit **7, 8** = **adjudicate**, adjudge, arbitrate, ascertain, conclude, decide, determine, discern, distinguish, mediate, referee, umpire **9** = **consider**, appraise, appreciate, assess, criticize, esteem, estimate, evaluate, examine, rate, review, value

judgment *n* **1** = **sense**, acumen, common sense, discernment, discrimination, intelligence, penetration, percipience, perspicacity, prudence, sagacity, shrewdness, smarts (*sl., chiefly US*), taste, understanding, wisdom **2a** = **verdict**, arbitration, award, conclusion, decision, decree, determination, finding, order, result, ruling, sentence **5** = **opinion**, appraisal, assessment, belief, conviction, deduction, diagnosis, estimate, finding, valuation, view

judgmental *adj* = **condemnatory**, censorious, pharisaic, self-righteous

judicial *adj* **1-3** = **legal**, judiciary, juridical, official **4** = **discriminating**, distinguished, impartial, judgelike, magisterial, magistral

judicious *adj* = **sensible**, acute, astute, careful, cautious, circumspect, considered, diplomatic, discerning, discreet, discriminating, enlightened, expedient, informed, politic, prudent, rational, reasonable, sagacious, sage, sane, sapient, shrewd, skilful, sober, sound, thoughtful, well-advised, well-judged, wise
Antonyms *adj* imprudent, indiscreet, injudicious, tactless, thoughtless

jug *n* **1** = **container**, carafe, crock, ewer, jar, pitcher, urn, vessel

juggle *vb* **2** = **manipulate**, alter, change, disguise, doctor (*inf.*), falsify, fix (*inf.*), manoeuvre, misrepresent, modify, tamper with

juice *n* **1** = **liquid**, extract, fluid, liquor, nectar, sap, secretion, serum

juicy *adj* **1** = **moist**, lush, sappy, succulent, watery **2** = **interesting**, colourful, provocative, racy, risqué, sensational, spicy (*inf.*), suggestive, vivid

jumble *vb* **1** = **mix**, confound, confuse, disarrange, dishevel, disorder, disorganize, entangle, mistake, muddle, ravel, shuffle, tangle ◆ *n* **3** = **muddle**, chaos, clutter, confusion, disarrangement, disarray, disorder, farrago, gallimaufry, hodgepodge, hotchpotch (*US*), litter, medley, *mélange*, mess, miscellany, mishmash, mixture, pig's breakfast (*inf.*)

jumbo *modifier* **1b** = **giant**, elephantine, gigantic, ginormous (*inf.*), huge, humongous *or* humungous (*US sl.*), immense, large, mega (*inf.*), oversized
Antonyms *adj* baby, dwarf, micro, mini, pocket, tiny, wee

as confectionery, by packing several in one wrapping, usually with a unit price reduction. **2** such a package of items.

jumbuck ('dʒʌm,bʌk) *n Austral.* an informal word for **sheep.** [C19: from Abor.]

jump ➊ (dʒʌmp) *vb* **1** (*intr*) to leap or spring clear of the ground or other surface by using the muscles in the legs and feet. **2** (*tr*) to leap over or clear (an obstacle): *to jump a gap.* **3** (*tr*) to cause to leap over an obstacle: *to jump a horse over a hedge.* **4** (*intr*) to move or proceed hastily (into, onto, out of, etc.): *she jumped into a taxi.* **5** (*tr*) *Inf.* to board so as to travel illegally on: *he jumped the train as it was leaving.* **6** (*intr*) to parachute from an aircraft. **7** (*intr*) to jerk or start, as with astonishment, surprise, etc. **8** to rise or cause to rise suddenly or abruptly. **9** to pass or skip over (intervening objects or matter): *she jumped a few lines and then continued reading.* **10** (*intr*) to change from one thing to another, esp. from one subject to another. **11** *Draughts.* to capture (an opponent's piece) by moving one of one's own pieces over it to an unoccupied square. **12** (*intr*) *Bridge.* to bid in response to one's partner at a higher level than is necessary, to indicate a strong hand. **13** (*tr*) to come off (a track, etc.): *the locomotive jumped the rails.* **14** (*intr*) (of the stylus of a record player) to be jerked out of the groove. **15** (*intr*) *Sl.* to be lively: *the party was jumping.* **16** (*tr*) *Inf.* to attack without warning: *thieves jumped the old man.* **17** (*tr*) *Inf.* (of a driver or a motor vehicle) to pass through (a red traffic light) or move away from (traffic lights) before they change to green. **18 jump down someone's throat.** *Inf.* to address or reply to someone sharply. **19 jump ship.** to desert, esp. to leave a ship in which one is legally bound to serve. **20 jump the queue.** *Inf.* to obtain some advantage out of turn or unfairly. **21 jump to it.** *Inf.* to begin something quickly and efficiently. ◆ *n* **22** an act or instance of jumping. **23** a space, distance, or obstacle to be jumped or that has been jumped. **24** a descent by parachute from an aircraft. **25** *Sport.* any of several contests involving a jump: *the high jump.* **26** a sudden rise: *the jump in prices last month.* **27** a sudden or abrupt transition. **28** a sudden jerk or involuntary muscular spasm, esp. as a reaction of surprise. **29** a step or degree: *one jump ahead.* **30** *Draughts.* a move that captures an opponent's piece by jumping over it. **31** *Films.* **31a** a break in continuity in the normal sequence of shots. **31b** (*as modifier*): *a jump cut.* **32 on the jump.** *Inf., chiefly US & Canad.* **32a** in a hurry. **32b** busy. **33 take a running jump.** *Brit. inf.* a contemptuous expression of dismissal. ◆ See also **jump at, jump-off,** etc. [C16: prob. imit.]

jump at *vb* (*intr, prep*) to be glad to accept: *I would jump at the chance of going.*

jumped-up ➊ *adj Inf.* suddenly risen in significance, esp. when appearing arrogant.

jumper[1] ➊ ('dʒʌmpə) *n* **1** *Chiefly Brit.* a knitted or crocheted garment covering the upper part of the body. **2** the US and Canad. term for **pinafore dress.** [C19: from obs. *jump* man's loose jacket, var. of *jupe,* from OF, from Ar. *jubbah* long cloth coat]

jumper[2] ('dʒʌmpə) *n* **1** a boring tool that works by repeated impact, such as a steel bit in a drill used in boring rock. **2** Also called: **jumper cable, jumper lead.** a short length of wire used to make a connection, usually temporarily. **3** a person or animal that jumps.

jumping bean *n* a seed of any of several Mexican plants that contains a moth caterpillar whose movements cause it to jerk about.

jumping jack *n* a toy figure of a man with jointed limbs that can be moved by pulling attached strings.

jump jet *n Inf.* a fixed-wing jet aircraft that is capable of landing and taking off vertically.

jump jockey *n Brit. inf.* a jockey riding in a steeplechase, as opposed to racing on the flat.

jump leads (li:dz) *pl n* two heavy cables fitted with crocodile clips used to start a motor vehicle with a discharged battery by connecting the battery to an external battery.

jump-off *n* **1** an extra round in a showjumping contest when two or more horses are equal first, deciding the winner. ◆ *vb* **jump off. 2** (*intr, adv*) to engage in a jump-off.

jump on *vb* (*intr, prep*) *Inf.* to reprimand or attack suddenly and forcefully.

jump seat *n* **1** a folding seat on some aircraft for an additional crew member. **2** *Brit.* a folding seat in a motor vehicle.

jump-start *vb* **1** to start the engine of (a car) by pushing or rolling it and then engaging the gears or (of a car) to start in this way. ◆ *n* **2** the act of starting a car in this way. ◆ Also called (Brit.): **bump-start.**

jump suit *n* a one-piece garment of combined trousers and jacket or shirt.

jumpy ➊ ('dʒʌmpɪ) *adj* **jumpier, jumpiest. 1** nervous or apprehensive. **2** moving jerkily or fitfully.
▸'**jumpily** *adv* ▸'**jumpiness** *n*

Jun. *abbrev. for:* **1** June. **2** Also: **jun.** junior.

junco ('dʒʌŋkəʊ) *n, pl* **juncos** *or* **juncoes.** a North American bunting having a greyish plumage. [C18: from Sp.: a rush, from L *juncus* rush]

junction ➊ ('dʒʌŋkʃən) *n* **1** a place where several routes, lines, or roads meet, link, or cross each other: *a railway junction.* **2** a point on a motorway where traffic may leave or join it. **3** *Electronics.* **3a** a contact between two different metals or other materials: *a thermocouple junction.* **3b** a transition region in a semiconductor. **4** the act of joining or the state of being joined. [C18: from L *junctiō* a joining, from *jungere* to join]

junction box *n* an earthed enclosure within which wires or cables can be safely connected.

junction transistor *n* a bipolar transistor consisting of two p-n junctions combined to form either an n-p-n or a p-n-p transistor.

juncture ➊ ('dʒʌŋktʃə) *n* **1** a point in time, esp. a critical one (often in **at this juncture**). **2** *Linguistics.* the set of phonological features signalling a division between words, such as those that distinguish *a name* from *an aim.* **3** a less common word for **junction.**

June (dʒu:n) *n* the sixth month of the year, consisting of 30 days. [OE *iunius,* from L *junius,* prob. from *Junius* name of Roman gens]

jungle ('dʒʌŋgᵊl) *n* **1** an equatorial forest area with luxuriant vegetation. **2** any dense or tangled thicket or growth. **3** a place of intense or ruthless struggle for survival: *the concrete jungle.* **4** a type of fast electronic dance music, originating in the early 1990s, which combines elements of techno and ragga. [C18: from Hindi, from Sansk. *jāngala* wilderness]
▸'**jungly** *adj*

jungle fever *n* a serious malarial fever occurring in the East Indies.

jungle fowl *n* **1** any small gallinaceous bird of S and SE Asia, the males of which (**junglecock**) have an arched tail and a combed and wattled head. **2** *Austral.* any of several megapodes.

jungle juice *n Sl.* alcoholic liquor.

junior ➊ ('dʒu:njə) *adj* **1** lower in rank or length of service; subordinate. **2** younger in years. **3** of or relating to youth or childhood. **4** *Brit.* of schoolchildren between the ages of 7 and 11 approximately. **5** *US.* of or designating the third year of a four-year course at college or high school. ◆ *n* **6** *Law.* (in England) any barrister below the rank of Queen's Counsel. **7** a junior person. **8** *Brit.* a junior schoolchild. **9** *US.* a junior student. [C17: from L: younger, from *juvenis* young]

Junior ('dʒu:njə) *adj* being the younger: usually used after a name to distinguish the son from the father: *Charles Parker, Junior.* Abbrev.: **Jnr, Jr, Jun., Junr.**

junior common room *n* (in certain universities and colleges) a common room for the use of students.

junior lightweight *n* **a** a professional boxer weighing 126–130 pounds (57–59 kg). **b** (*as modifier*): *a junior-lightweight bout.*

junior middleweight *n* **a** a professional boxer weighing 147–154 pounds (66.5–70 kg). **b** (*as modifier*): *the junior-middleweight championship.*

junior school *n* (in England and Wales) a school for children aged between 7 and 11.

junior technician *n* a rank in the Royal Air Force comparable to that of private in the army.

junior welterweight *n* **a** a professional boxer weighing 135–140 pounds (61–63.5 kg). **b** (*as modifier*): *a junior-welterweight fight.*

juniper ('dʒu:nɪpə) *n* a coniferous shrub or small tree of the N hemisphere having purple berry-like cones. The cones of the **common** or **dwarf juniper** are used as a flavouring in making gin. [C14: from L *jūniperus,* from ?]

junk[1] ➊ (dʒʌŋk) *n* **1** discarded objects, etc., collectively. **2** *Inf.* **2a** rubbish generally. **2b** nonsense: *the play was absolute junk.* **3** *Sl.* any narcotic drug, esp. heroin. ◆ *vb* **4** (*tr*) *Inf.* to discard as junk. [C15 *jonke* old useless rope]

junk[2] (dʒʌŋk) *n* a sailing vessel used in Chinese waters and characterized by a very high poop, flat bottom, and square sails supported by battens. [C17: from Port. *junco,* from Javanese *jon*]

junk bond *n Finance.* a security that offers a high yield but often involves a high risk of default.

Junker ('jʊŋkə) *n* **1** *History.* any of the aristocratic landowners of Prussia. **2** an arrogant German army officer or official. **3** (formerly) a young German nobleman. [C16: from G, from OHG *junchērro* young lord]
▸'**Junkerdom** *n*

junket ('dʒʌŋkɪt) *n* **1** a sweet dessert made of flavoured milk set to a curd with rennet. **2** a feast. **3** an excursion, esp. one made for pleasure at public expense. ◆ *vb* **4** to have or entertain with a feast. **5** (*intr*) (of

THESAURUS

jump *vb* **1, 2** = **leap,** bounce, bound, caper, clear, gambol, hop, hurdle, skip, spring, vault **7** = **recoil,** flinch, jerk, start, wince **8** = **increase,** advance, ascend, boost, escalate, gain, hike, mount, rise, surge **9** = **miss,** avoid, digress, evade, omit, overshoot, skip, switch ◆ *n* **22** = **leap,** bound, buck, caper, hop, skip, spring, vault **23** = **hurdle,** barricade, barrier, fence, impediment, obstacle, rail **26** = **rise,** advance, augmentation, boost, increase, increment, upsurge, upturn **28** = **jolt,** jar, jerk, lurch, shock, start, swerve, twitch, wrench

jumped-up *adj Informal* = **conceited,** arrogant, cocky, immodest, insolent, overbearing, pompous, presumptuous, puffed up, self-opinionated, stuck-up, toffee-nosed, too big for one's boots *or* breeches

jumper[1] *n* **1** = **sweater,** jersey, pullover, woolly

jumpy *adj* **1** = **nervous,** agitated, anxious, apprehensive, fidgety, hyper (*inf.*), jittery (*inf.*), neurotic, on edge, restless, shaky, tense, timorous, twitchy (*inf.*), wired (*sl.*)
Antonyms *adj* calm, composed, laid-back (*inf.*), nerveless, together (*sl.*), unfazed (*inf.*), unflustered

junction *n* **1, 4** = **connection,** alliance, combination, coupling, joint, juncture, linking, seam, union

juncture *n* **1** = **moment,** conjuncture, contingency, crisis, crux, emergency, exigency, occasion, point, predicament, strait, time **3** = **junction,** bond, connection, convergence, edge, intersection, link, seam, weld

junior *adj* **1, 2** = **minor,** inferior, lesser, lower, secondary, subordinate, younger
Antonyms *adj* elder, higher-ranking, older, senior, superior

junk[1] *n* **1, 2a** = **rubbish,** clutter, debris, dreck (*sl.,*

a public official, etc.) to go on a junket. [C14 (in the sense: rush basket, hence custard served on rushes): from OF (dialect) *jonquette*, from *jonc* rush, from L *juncus* reed]
▸ **'junketing** *n*

junk food *n* food which is eaten in addition to or instead of regular meals, and which often has a low nutritional value.

junkie Ⓣ *or* **junky** ('dʒʌŋkɪ) *n, pl* **junkies.** an informal word for **drug addict.**

junk mail *n* unsolicited mail advertising goods or services.

junk shop *n* a shop selling miscellaneous second-hand goods and sometimes antiques.

junta Ⓣ ('dʒʌntə, 'hʊntə) *n* (*functioning as sing or pl*) **1** a group of military officers holding the power in a country, esp. after a coup d'état. **2** Also called: **junto.** a small group of men. **3** a legislative or executive council in some parts of Latin America. [C17: from Sp.: council, from L, from *jungere* to join]

junto ('dʒʊntəʊ) *n, pl* **juntos.** a variant of **junta** (sense 2). [C17]

Jupiter[1] ('dʒuːpɪtə) *n* (in Roman tradition) the king and ruler of the Olympian gods. Also called: **Jove.**

Jupiter[2] ('dʒuːpɪtə) *n* the largest of the planets and the fifth from the sun.

Jurassic (dʒʊ'ræsɪk) *adj* **1** of or formed in the second period of the Mesozoic era, during which dinosaurs and ammonites flourished. ◆ *n* **2 the.** the Jurassic period or rock system. [C19: from F *jurassique*, after the *Jura* (Mountains) in W central Europe]

jurat ('dʒʊəræt) *n* **1** *Law.* a statement at the foot of an affidavit, naming the parties, stating when, where, and before whom it was sworn, etc. **2** (in England) a municipal officer of the Cinque Ports. **3** (in France and the Channel Islands) a magistrate. [C16: from Med. L *jūrātus* one who has been sworn, from L *jūrāre* to swear]

juridical (dʒʊ'rɪdɪkᵊl) *adj* of or relating to law or to the administration of justice; legal. [C16: from L, from *iūs* law + *dicere* to say]
▸ **ju'ridically** *adv*

jurisdiction Ⓣ (ˌdʒʊərɪs'dɪkʃən) *n* **1** the right or power to administer justice and to apply laws. **2** the exercise or extent of such right or power. **3** authority in general. [C13: from L *jūrisdictiō* administration of justice, from *jus* law + DICTION]
▸ **ˌjuris'dictional** *adj*

jurisprudence (ˌdʒʊərɪs'pruːdᵊns) *n* **1** the science or philosophy of law. **2** a system or body of law. **3** a branch of law: *medical jurisprudence.* [C17: from L *jūris prūdentia*, from *jus* law + PRUDENCE]
▸ **jurisprudential** (ˌdʒʊərɪspruː'denʃəl) *adj*

jurist ('dʒʊərɪst) *n* a person versed in the science of law, esp. Roman or civil law. [C15: from F *juriste*, from Med. L *jūrista*]

juristic (dʒʊ'rɪstɪk) *or* **juristical** *adj* **1** of or relating to jurists. **2** of or characteristic of the study of law or the legal profession.

juror ('dʒʊərə) *n* **1** a member of a jury. **2** a person who takes an oath. [C14: from Anglo-F *jurour*, from OF *jurer* to take an oath, from L *jūrāre*]

jury[1] ('dʒʊərɪ) *n, pl* **juries. 1** a group of, usually, twelve people sworn to deliver a true verdict according to the evidence upon a case presented in a court of law. **2** a body of persons appointed to judge a competition and award prizes. [C14: from OF *juree*, from *jurer* to swear]

jury[2] ('dʒʊərɪ) *adj Chiefly naut.* (*in combination*) makeshift: *jury-rigged.* [C17: from ?]

jury box *n* an enclosure where the jury sits in court.

juryman ('dʒʊərɪmən) *or* (*fem*) **jurywoman** *n, pl* **jurymen** *or* **jurywomen.** a member of a jury.

jury-rigged *adj Chiefly naut.* set up in a makeshift manner.

just Ⓣ *adj* (dʒʌst). **1a** fair or impartial in action or judgment. **1b** (*as collective n; preceded by the*): *the just.* **2** conforming to high moral standards; honest. **3** consistent with justice: *a just action.* **4** rightly applied or given: *a just reward.* **5** legally valid; lawful: *a just inheritance.* **6** well-founded: *just criticism.* **7** correct or true: *a just account.* ◆ *adv* (dʒʌst; *unstressed* dʒəst). **8** used with forms of *have* to indicate an action performed in the very recent past: *I have just closed the door.* **9** at this very instant: *he's just coming in to land.* **10** no more than; only: *just an ordinary car.* **11** exactly: *that's just what I mean.* **12** barely: *he just got there in time.* **13 just about. 13a** at the point of starting (to do something). **13b** almost: *I've just about had enough.* **14 just a moment, second,** *or* **minute.** an expression requesting the hearer to wait or pause for a brief period of time. **15 just so.** arranged with precision. [C14: from L *jūstus* righteous, from *jūs* justice]
▸ **'justly** *adv* ▸ **'justness** *n*

> **USAGE NOTE** The use of *just* with *exactly* (*it's just exactly what they want*) is redundant and should be avoided: *it's exactly what they want.*

justice Ⓣ ('dʒʌstɪs) *n* **1** the quality or fact of being just. **2** *Ethics.* the principle of fairness that like cases should be treated alike. **3** the administration of law according to prescribed and accepted principles. **4** conformity to the law. **5** a judge of the Supreme Court of Judicature. **6** short for **justice of the peace. 7** good reason (esp. in **with justice**). **8 bring to justice.** to capture, try, and usually punish (a criminal, etc.). **9 do justice to. 9a** to show to full advantage. **9b** to show full appreciation of by action. **9c** to treat or judge fairly. **10 do oneself justice.** to make full use of one's abilities. [C12: from OF, from L *jūstitia*, from *justus* JUST]
▸ **'justiceˌship** *n*

justice of the peace *n* a lay magistrate whose function is to preserve the peace in his area and try summarily such cases as are within his jurisdiction.

justiciar (dʒʌ'stɪʃɪˌɑː) *n English legal history.* the chief political and legal officer from the time of William I to that of Henry III, who deputized for the king in his absence. Also called: **justiciary.**
▸ **jus'ticiarˌship** *n*

justiciary (dʒʌ'stɪʃɪərɪ) *adj* **1** of or relating to the administration of justice. ◆ *n, pl* **justiciaries. 2** an officer or administrator of justice; judge.

justifiable Ⓣ ('dʒʌstɪˌfaɪəbᵊl) *adj* capable of being justified.
▸ **ˌjustiˌfia'bility** *n* ▸ **'justiˌfiably** *adv*

justifiable homicide *n* lawful killing, as in the execution of a death sentence.

justification Ⓣ (ˌdʒʌstɪfɪ'keɪʃən) *n* **1** reasonable grounds for complaint, defence, etc. **2** proof, vindication, or exculpation. **3** *Christian theol.* **3a** the act of justifying. **3b** the process of being justified or the condition of having been justified.
▸ **'justifiˌcatory** *adj*

justify Ⓣ ('dʒʌstɪˌfaɪ) *vb* **justifies, justifying, justified.** (*mainly tr*) **1** (*often passive*) to prove or see to be just or valid; vindicate. **2** to show to be reasonable: *his behaviour justifies our suspicion.* **3** to declare or show to be free from blame or guilt. **4** *Law.* to show good reason in court for (some action taken). **5** (*also intr*) *Printing, computing.* to adjust the spaces between words in (a line of type or data) so that it is of the required length or (of a line of type or data) to fit exactly. **6a** *Protestant theol.* to declare righteous by the imputation of Christ's merits to the sinner. **6b** *RC theol.* to change from sinfulness to righteousness by the transforming effects of grace. **7** (*also intr*) *Law.* to prove (a person) to have sufficient means to act as surety, etc., or (of a person) to qualify to provide bail or surety. [C14: from OF *justifier*, from L *justificāre*, from *jūstus* JUST + *facere* to make]
▸ **'justiˌfier** *n*

Justinian Code (dʒʌ'stɪnɪən) *n* a compilation of Roman imperial law made by order of Justinian I (483–565 A.D.), Byzantine emperor.

just-in-time *adj* denoting or relating to an industrial method in which waste, queues, bottlenecks, etc., are eliminated or reduced by producing production-line components, etc., and by delivering materials just before they are needed. Abbrev.: **JIT.**

justle ('dʒʌsᵊl) *vb* **justles, justling, justled.** a less common word for **jostle.**

jut Ⓣ (dʒʌt) *vb* **juts, jutting, jutted. 1** (*intr;* often foll. by *out*) to stick out or overhang beyond the surface or main part. ◆ *n* **2** something that juts out. [C16: var. of JET[1]]
▸ **'jutting** *adj*

THESAURUS

chiefly US), leavings, litter, oddments, odds and ends, refuse, rummage, scrap, trash, waste

junkie *n* = **addict**, acidhead (*sl.*), cokehead (*sl.*), drug addict, druggie (*inf.*), head (*sl.*), mainliner (*sl.*), pill-popper (*sl.*), pothead (*sl.*), smackhead (*sl.*), user

junta *n* **2, 3** = **cabal**, assembly, camp, clique, combination, confederacy, convocation, coterie, council, crew, faction, gang, league, party, ring, schism, set

jurisdiction *n* **1** = **authority**, command, control, dominion, influence, power, prerogative, rule, say, sway **2** = **range**, area, bounds, circuit, compass, district, dominion, field, orbit, province, scope, sphere, zone

just *adj* **1, 2** = **fair**, blameless, conscientious, decent, equitable, fair-minded, good, honest, honourable, impartial, lawful, pure, right, righteous, unbiased, upright, virtuous **4, 6** = **fitting**, appropriate, apt, condign, deserved, due, justified, legitimate, merited, proper, reasonable, rightful, sensible, suitable, well-deserved **7** = **correct**, accurate, exact, faithful, normal, precise, proper, regular, sound, true ◆ *adv* **8** = **recently**, hardly, lately, only now, scarcely **10** = **merely**, at a push, at most, but, by the skin of one's teeth, no more than, nothing but, only, simply, solely **11** = **exactly**, absolutely, completely, entirely, perfectly, precisely **13 just about** = **practically**, all but, almost, around, close to, nearly, not quite, virtually, well-nigh
Antonyms *adj* ≠ **fair**: corrupt, devious, dishonest, inequitable, prejudiced, unfair, unjust, unlawful ≠ **fitting**: inappropriate, undeserved, unfit, unreasonable ≠ **correct**: untrue

justice *n* **1, 2** = **fairness**, equity, honesty, impartiality, integrity, justness, law, legality, legitimacy, reasonableness, rectitude, right **6** = **judge**, magistrate
Antonyms *n* ≠ **fairness**: dishonesty, favouritism, inequity, injustice, partiality, unfairness, unlawfulness, unreasonableness, wrong

justifiable *adj* = **reasonable**, acceptable, defensible, excusable, fit, lawful, legitimate, proper, right, sensible, sound, tenable, understandable, valid, vindicable, warrantable, well-founded
Antonyms *adj* arbitrary, capricious, indefensible, inexcusable, unreasonable, unwarranted

justification *n* **1** = **reason**, basis, defence, grounds, plea, warrant **2** = **explanation**, absolution, apology, approval, defence, exculpation, excuse, exoneration, extenuation, plea, rationalization, vindication

justify *vb* **1-3** = **explain**, absolve, acquit, approve, confirm, defend, establish, exculpate, excuse, exonerate, legalize, legitimize, maintain, substantiate, support, sustain, uphold, validate, vindicate, warrant

justly *adv* **1, 3, 4, 7** = **properly**, accurately, correctly, equally, equitably, fairly, honestly, impartially, lawfully

jut *vb* **1** = **stick out**, bulge, extend, impend, overhang, poke, project, protrude

DICTIONARY

jute (dʒuːt) *n* **1** either of two Old World tropical yellow-flowered herbaceous plants, cultivated for their strong fibre. **2** this fibre, used in making sacks, rope, etc. [C18: from Bengali *jhuto*, from Sansk. *jūta* braid of hair]

juv. *abbrev. for* juvenile.

juvenescence (ˌdʒuːvɪˈnɛsəns) *n* **1** youth or immaturity. **2** the act or process of growing from childhood to youth.
▸ **ˌjuveˈnescent** *adj*

juvenile ❶ (ˈdʒuːvɪˌnaɪl) *adj* **1** young, youthful, or immature. **2** suitable or designed for young people: *juvenile pastimes*. ◆ *n* **3** a juvenile person, animal, or plant. **4** an actor who performs youthful roles. **5** a book intended for young readers. [C17: from L *juvenīlis* youthful, from *juvenis* young]
▸ **ˈjuveˌnilely** *adv*

juvenile court *n* a court that deals with juvenile offenders and children beyond parental control or in need of care.

juvenile delinquency *n* antisocial or criminal conduct by juvenile delinquents.

juvenile delinquent *n* a child or young person guilty of some offence, act of vandalism, or antisocial behaviour and who may be brought before a juvenile court.

juvenilia (ˌdʒuːvɪˈnɪlɪə) *n* works of art, literature, or music produced in youth, before the artist, author, or composer has formed a mature style. [C17: from L, lit.: youthful things]

juxtapose ❶ (ˌdʒʌkstəˈpəʊz) *vb* **juxtaposes, juxtaposing, juxtaposed.** (*tr*) to place close together or side by side. [C19: back formation from *juxtaposition*, from L *juxta* next to + POSITION]
▸ **ˌjuxtapoˈsition** *n* ▸ **ˌjuxtapoˈsitional** *adj*

THESAURUS

juvenile *adj* **1 = young**, babyish, boyish, callow, childish, girlish, immature, inexperienced, infantile, jejune, puerile, undeveloped, unsophisticated, youthful ◆ *n* **3 = child**, adolescent, boy, girl, infant, minor, youth

Antonyms *adj* ≠ **young**: adult, grown-up, mature, responsible ◆ *n* ≠ **child**: adult, grown-up

juxtaposition *n* = **proximity**, adjacency, closeness, contact, contiguity, nearness, propinquity, vicinity

k *or* **K** (keɪ) *n, pl* **k's, K's,** *or* **Ks. 1** the 11th letter and 8th consonant of the English alphabet. **2** a speech sound represented by this letter, usually a voiceless velar stop, as in *kitten*.

k *symbol for:* **1** kilo(s). **2** *Maths.* the unit vector along the *z*-axis.

K *symbol for:* **1** Kelvin(s). **2** *Chess.* king. **3** *Chem.* potassium. [from NL *kalium*] **4** *Physics.* kaon. **5** *Currency.* **5a** kina. **5b** kip. **5c** kopeck. **5d** kwacha. **5e** kyat. **6** one thousand. [from KILO-] **7** *Computing.* **7a** a unit of 1024 words, bits, or bytes. **7b** (not in technical usage) 1000.

K *or* **K.** *abbrev. for* Köchel: indicating the serial number in the catalogue of the works of Mozart made by Ludwig von Köchel, 1800–77.

k. *abbrev. for:* **1** karat. **2** Also: **K.** king.

Kaaba *or* **Caaba** (ˈkɑːbə) *n* a cube-shaped building in Mecca, the most sacred Muslim pilgrim shrine, into which is built the black stone believed to have been given by Gabriel to Abraham. [from Ar. *ka'bah*, from *ka'b* cube]

kabaddi (kəˈbɑːdɪ) *n* a game played between two teams of seven players, in which individuals take turns to chase and try to touch members of the opposing team without being captured by them. [Tamil]

kabbala *or* **kabala** (kəˈbɑːlə) *n* variant spellings of **cabbala.**

kabuki (kæˈbuːkɪ) *n* a form of Japanese drama based on legends and characterized by elaborate costumes and the use of male actors. [Japanese, from *ka* singing + *bu* dancing + *ki* art]

Kabyle (kəˈbaɪl) *n* **1** (*pl* **Kabyles** *or* **Kabyle**) a member of a Berber people in Tunisia and Algeria. **2** the dialect of Berber spoken by this people. [C19: from Ar. *qabā'il*, pl. of *qabīlah* tribe]

kadi (ˈkɑːdɪ, ˈkeɪdɪ) *n, pl* **kadis.** a variant spelling of **cadi.**

Kaffir *or* **Kafir** (ˈkæfə) *n, pl* **Kaffirs** *or* **Kaffir, Kafirs** *or* **Kafir. 1** *Offens.* **1a** (in southern Africa) any Black African. **1b** (*as modifier*): *Kaffir farming.* **2** a former name for the **Xhosa** language. [C19: from Ar. *kāfir* infidel, from *kafara* to deny]

kaffir beer *n S. African.* beer made from sorghum (kaffir corn) or millet.

kaffirboom (ˈkæfəˌbuəm) *n* a S. African deciduous flowering tree. [from KAFFIR + Afrik. *boom* tree]

kaffir corn *n* a southern African variety of sorghum, cultivated in dry regions for its grain and as fodder. Sometimes shortened to **kaffir.**

Kafir (ˈkæfə) *n, pl* **Kafirs** *or* **Kafir. 1** a member of a people inhabiting E Afghanistan. **2** a variant spelling of **Kaffir.** [C19: from Ar.; see KAFFIR]

Kafkaesque (ˌkæfkəˈɛsk) *adj* of or like the writings of Franz Kafka (1883–1924), Czech novelist, esp. in having a nightmarish and dehumanized quality.

kaftan *or* **caftan** (ˈkæftæn) *n* **1** a long coatlike garment, usually with a belt, worn in the East. **2** an imitation of this, worn esp. by women, consisting of a loose dress with long wide sleeves. [C16: from Turkish *qaftān*]

kagoul (kəˈguːl) *n* a variant spelling of **cagoule.**

kahawai (ˈkɑːhəwaɪ, ˈkɑːwaɪ) *n* a New Zealand food and game fish. [from Maori]

kai (kaɪ) *n NZ inf.* food. [from Maori]

kaiak (ˈkaɪæk) *n* a variant spelling of **kayak.**

kail (keɪl) *n* a variant spelling of **kale.**

kai moana (məʊˈænə) *n NZ.* seafood. [Maori]

kainite (ˈkaɪnaɪt) *n* a white mineral consisting of potassium chloride and magnesium sulphate: a fertilizer and source of potassium salts. [C19: from G *Kainit*, from Gk *kainos* new + -ITE[1]]

Kaiser (ˈkaɪzə) *n* (*sometimes not cap.*) *History.* **1** any of the three German emperors. **2** *Obs.* any Austro-Hungarian emperor. [C16: from G, ult. from L *Caesar* emperor]

kaizen *Japanese.* (kaɪˈzɛn) *n* a philosophy of continuous improvement of working practices that underlies total quality management and just-in-time business techniques. [lit.: improvement]

kaka (ˈkɑːkə) *n* a New Zealand parrot with a long compressed bill. [C18: from Maori, ? imit. of its call]

kaka beak *n* a New Zealand shrub with beaklike red flowers. [from KAKA]

kakapo (ˈkɑːkəˌpəʊ) *n, pl* **kakapos.** a ground-living nocturnal parrot of New Zealand, resembling an owl. [C19: from Maori, lit.: night kaka]

kakemono (ˌkækɪˈməʊnəʊ) *n, pl* **kakemonos.** a Japanese paper or silk wall hanging, usually long and narrow, with a picture or inscription on it. [C19: from Japanese, from *kake* hanging + *mono* thing]

kala-azar (ˌkɑːləəˈzɑː) *n* a tropical infectious disease caused by a protozoan in the liver, spleen, etc. [C19: from Assamese *kālā* black + *āzār* disease]

Kalashnikov (kəˈlæʃnɪˌkɒf) *n* a Russian-made automatic rifle. See also **AK-47.** [C20: after Mikhail *Kalashnikov* (born 1919), its designer]

kale *or* **kail** (keɪl) *n* **1** a cultivated variety of cabbage with crinkled leaves. **2** *Scot.* a cabbage. ◆ Cf. **sea kale.** [OE *cāl*]

kaleidoscope ➊ (kəˈlaɪdəˌskəʊp) *n* **1** an optical toy for producing symmetrical patterns by multiple reflections in inclined mirrors enclosed in a tube. Loose pieces of coloured glass, paper, etc., are placed between transparent plates at the far end of the tube, which is rotated to change the pattern. **2** any complex pattern of frequently changing shapes and colours. [C19: from Gk *kalos* beautiful + *eidos* form + -SCOPE]

▸**kaleidoscopic** (kəˌlaɪdəˈskɒpɪk) *adj*

kalends (ˈkælɪndz) *pl n* a variant spelling of **calends.**

Kalevala (ˌkɑːləˈvɑːlə) *n Finnish legend.* **1** the land of the hero Kaleva, who performed legendary exploits. **2** the Finnish national epic in which these exploits are recounted. [Finnish, from *kaleva* of a hero + *-la* home]

kaleyard *or* **kailyard** (ˈkeɪlˌjɑːd; *Scot.* -ˌjard) *n Scot.* a vegetable garden. [C19: lit.: cabbage garden]

kaleyard school *or* **kailyard school** *n* a group of writers who depicted the homely aspects of life in the Scottish Lowlands. The best-known contributor was J. M. Barrie.

kalied (ˈkeɪlaɪd) *adj N English dialect.* drunk.

kalmia (ˈkælmɪə) *n* an evergreen North American ericaceous shrub having showy clusters of white or pink flowers. [C18: after Peter *Kalm* (1715–79), Swedish botanist and pupil of Linnaeus]

Kalmuck (ˈkælmʌk) *or* **Kalmyk** (ˈkælmɪk) *n* **1** (*pl* **Kalmucks, Kalmuck** *or* **Kalmyks, Kalmyk**) a member of a Mongoloid people of Buddhist tradition, who migrated from W China to Russia in the 17th century. **2** the language of this people.

kalong (ˈkɑːlɒŋ) *n* a fruit bat of the Malay Archipelago; a flying fox. [Javanese]

kalpa (ˈkælpə) *n* (in Hindu cosmology) a period in which the universe experiences a cycle of creation and destruction. [C18: Sansk.]

Kamasutra (ˌkɑːməˈsuːtrə) *n* **the.** an ancient Hindu text on erotic pleasure. [Sansk.: book on love, from *kāma* love + *sūtra* thread]

kame (keɪm) *n* an irregular mound or ridge of gravel, sand, etc., deposited by water derived from melting glaciers. [C19: Scot. & N English var. of COMB]

kamikaze ➊ (ˌkæmɪˈkɑːzɪ) *n* **1** (*often cap.*) (in World War II) one of a group of Japanese pilots who performed suicidal missions. **2** (*modifier*) (of an action) undertaken or (of a person) undertaking an action in the knowledge that it will result in the death of the person performing it in order to inflict maximum damage on an enemy: *a kamikaze attack.* **3** (*modifier*) extremely foolhardy and possibly self-defeating: *kamikaze prices.* [C20: from Japanese, from *kami* divine + *kaze* wind]

kamilaroi (ˈkæmələˌrɔɪ) *n* an Australian Aboriginal language formerly used in NW New South Wales.

Kamloops trout (ˈkæmluːps) *n* a variety of rainbow trout common in British Columbia.

kampong (ˈkæmpɒŋ) *n* (in Malaysia) a village. [C19: from Malay]

Kampuchean (ˌkæmpuˈtʃɪən) *adj, n* a former word for **Cambodian.**

Kanak (kəˈnæk) *n* a native or inhabitant of New Caledonia who seeks independence from France. [C20: from Hawaiian: man]

Kanaka (kəˈnækə) *n* **1** a native Hawaiian. **2** (*often not cap.*) *Austral.* any native of the South Pacific islands, esp. (formerly) one abducted to work in Australia. [C19: from Hawaiian: man]

Kanarese *or* **Canarese** (ˌkænəˈriːz) *n* **1** (*pl* **Kanarese** *or* **Canarese**) a member of a people of S India living chiefly in Kanara. **2** the language of this people.

kanban *Japanese.* (ˈkænbæn) *n* **1** a just-in-time manufacturing process in which the movements of materials through a process are recorded on specially designed cards. **2** any of the cards used for ordering materials in such a system. [lit.: advertisement hoarding]

kanga *or* **khanga** (ˈkæŋgə) *n* a piece of gaily decorated thin cotton cloth used as a woman's garment, originally in E Africa. [from Swahili]

kangaroo (ˌkæŋgəˈruː) *n, pl* **kangaroos. 1** a large herbivorous marsupial of Australia and New Guinea, having large powerful hind legs used for leaping, and a long thick tail. **2** (*usually pl*) *Stock Exchange.* an Australian share, esp. in mining, land, or a tobacco company. [C18: prob. from Abor.]

▸**ˌkangaˈroo-ˌlike** *adj*

kangaroo closure *n Parliamentary procedure.* a form of closure in which the chairman or speaker selects certain amendments for discussion and excludes others.

kangaroo court *n* an irregular court, esp. one set up by strikers to judge strikebreakers.

kangaroo paw *n* any of various Australian plants having green-and-red hairy flowers.

kangaroo rat *n* **1** a small leaping rodent related to the squirrels and inhabiting desert regions of North America, having a stocky body and very long hind legs and tail. **2** Also called: **kangaroo mouse.** any of several leaping Australian rodents.

THESAURUS

kaleidoscopic *adj* **2** = **changeable,** fluctuating, fluid, many-coloured, mobile, motley, mutable, unstable, variegated **2** = **complicated,** complex, confused, convoluted, disordered, intricate, jumbled, varied

kamikaze *modifier* **2, 3** = **self-destructive,** foolhardy, suicidal

kanji ('kændʒɪ) *n, pl* **kanji** *or* **kanjis. 1** a Japanese writing system using characters mainly derived from Chinese ideograms. **2** a character in this system. [Japanese, from Chinese *han* Chinese + *zi* character]

KANU ('kɑːnuː) *n acronym for* Kenya African National Union.

kaolin ('keɪəlɪn) *n* a fine white clay used for the manufacture of hard-paste porcelain and bone china and in medicine as a poultice. Also called: **china clay.** [C18: from F, from Chinese *Kaoling* Chinese mountain where supplies for Europe were first obtained]
▸ˌ**kao'linic** *adj* ▸'**kaolinˌize** *or* '**kaolinˌise** *vb*

kaon ('keɪɒn) *n* a meson that has a rest mass of about 996 or 964 electron masses. Also called: **K-meson.** [C20 *ka* representing the letter *k* + (MES)ON]

kapellmeister (kæ'pɛlˌmaɪstə) *n* a variant spelling of **capellmeister.**

kapok ('keɪpɒk) *n* a silky fibre obtained from the hairs covering the seeds of a tropical tree (**kapok tree**): used for stuffing pillows, etc. [C18: from Malay]

Kaposi's sarcoma (kæ'pəʊsɪz) *n* a form of skin cancer found in Africans and more recently in victims of AIDS. [C20: after Moritz Kohn *Kaposi* (1837–1902), Austrian dermatologist who first described the sores that characterize the disease]

kappa ('kæpə) *n* the tenth letter in the Greek alphabet (Κ, κ). [Gk, of Semitic origin]

kaput **T** (kæ'pʊt) *adj (postpositive) Inf.* ruined, broken, or not functioning. [C20: from G *kaputt* done for]

karabiner (ˌkærə'biːnə) *n Mountaineering.* a metal clip with a spring for attaching to a piton, belay, etc. Also called: **snaplink, krab.** [shortened from G *Karabinerhaken,* lit.: carbine hook]

karakul *or* **caracul** ('kærəkᵊl) *n* **1** a breed of sheep of central Asia having coarse black, grey, or brown hair: the lambs have soft curled hair. **2** the fur prepared from these lambs. ◆ See also **Persian lamb.** [C19: from Russian, from the name of a region in Bukhara where the sheep originated]

karaoke (ˌkɑːrə'əʊkɪ) *n* **a** an entertainment of Japanese origin in which people take it in turns to sing well-known songs over a prerecorded backing tape. **b** (*as modifier*): *a karaoke bar.* [from Japanese, from *kara* empty + *ōkesutora* orchestra]

karat ('kærət) *n* the usual US and Canad. spelling of **carat** (sense 2).

karate (kə'rɑːtɪ) *n* **a** a traditional Japanese system of unarmed combat, employing smashes, chops, kicks, etc., made with the hands, feet, elbows, or legs. **b** (*as modifier*): *karate chop.* [Japanese, lit.: empty hand]

karateka (kə'rɑːtɪˌkɑː) *n* a competitor or expert in karate. [Japanese; see KARATE]

Karitane (ˌkærɪ'tɑːne) *n NZ.* a nurse for babies; nanny. [from former child-care hospital at *Karitane,* New Zealand]

karma ('kɑːmə) *n* **1** *Hinduism, Buddhism.* the principle of retributive justice determining a person's state of life and the state of his reincarnations as the effect of his past deeds. **2** destiny or fate. **3** *Inf.* an aura or quality that a person, place, or thing is felt to have. [C19: from Sansk.: action, effect, from *karoti* he does]
▸'**karmic** *adj*

kaross (kə'rɒs) *n* a garment of skins worn by indigenous peoples in southern Africa. [C18: from Afrik. *karos,* ?from Du., from F *cuirasse* CUIRASS]

karri ('kɑːrɪ) *n, pl* **karris. 1** an Australian eucalyptus tree. **2** the durable dark red wood of this tree, used for construction, etc. [from Abor.]

karst (kɑːst) *n* (*modifier*) denoting the characteristic scenery of a limestone region, including underground streams, gorges, etc. [C19: G, from *Karst,* limestone plateau near Trieste]

kart (kɑːt) *n* a light low-framed vehicle with small wheels and engine used for recreational racing (**karting**). Also called: **go-cart, go-kart.**

karyo- *or* **caryo-** *combining form.* indicating the nucleus of a cell. [from NL, from Gk *karuon* kernel]

karyotype ('kærɪəˌtaɪp) *n* **1** the appearance of the chromosomes in a somatic cell of an individual or species, with reference to their number, size, shape, etc. ◆ *vb* **karyotypes, karyotyping, karyotyped.** (*tr*) **2** to determine the karyotype of (a cell).
▸**karyotypic** (ˌkærɪə'tɪpɪk) *or* ˌ**karyo'typical** *adj*

kasbah *or* **casbah** ('kæzbɑː) *n* (*sometimes cap.*) **1** the citadel of any of various North African cities. **2** the quarter in which a kasbah is located. [from Ar. *kaṣba* citadel]

kashruth *or* ***kashrut*** *Hebrew.* (kaʃ'ruːt) *n* **1** the condition of being fit for ritual use in general. **2** the system of dietary laws that requires ritual slaughter, the complete separation of milk and meat, and the prohibition of such foods as pig meat and shell fish. ◆ See also **kosher** (sense 1). [lit.: appropriateness]

kata ('kætə) *n* an exercise consisting of a sequence of the specific movements of a martial art, used in training and designed to show skill in technique. [C20: Japanese, lit.: shape, pattern]

kata- *prefix* a variant spelling of **cata-.**

katabatic (ˌkætə'bætɪk) *adj* (of winds) blowing downhill through having become denser with cooling.

katydid ('keɪtɪˌdɪd) *n* a green long-horned grasshopper living on the foliage of trees in North America. [C18: imit.]

kaumatua (kaʊ'mɑːtuːə) *n NZ.* a senior member of a tribe; elder. [Maori]

kauri ('kaʊrɪ) *n, pl* **kauris. 1** a New Zealand coniferous tree with oval leaves and round cones. **2** the wood or resin of this tree. [C19: from Maori]

kauri gum *n* the fossil resin of the kauri tree.

kava ('kɑːvə) *n* **1** a Polynesian shrub. **2** a drink prepared from the aromatic roots of this shrub. [C18: from Polynesian: bitter]

Kawasaki's disease (ˌkæwə'sækɪz) *n* a disease of children that causes a rash, fever, and swelling of the lymph nodes and often damages the heart muscle. [C20: after T. *Kawasaki,* Japanese physician who first described it]

kayak *or* **kaiak** ('kaɪæk) *n* **1** a canoe-like boat used by Eskimos, consisting of a frame covered with animal skins. **2** a fibreglass or canvas-covered canoe of similar design. [C18: from Eskimo]

kayo *or* **KO** ('keɪ'əʊ) *n, pl* **kayos,** *vb* **kayos, kayoing, kayoed.** *Boxing, sl.* another term for **knockout** or **knock out.** [C20: from the initial letters of *knock out*]

kazoo (kə'zuː) *n, pl* **kazoos.** a cigar-shaped musical instrument of metal or plastic with a membranous diaphragm of thin paper that vibrates with a nasal sound when the player hums into it. [C20: prob. imit.]

KB (in Britain) *abbrev. for:* **1** King's Bench. **2** *Computing.* kilobyte.

KBE *abbrev. for* Knight (Commander of the Order) of the British Empire.

kbyte *Computing. abbrev. for* kilobyte.

kc *abbrev. for* kilocycle.

KC (in Britain) *abbrev. for:* **1** King's Counsel. **2** Kennel Club.

kcal *abbrev. for* kilocalorie.

KCB *abbrev. for* Knight Commander of the Bath (a Brit. title).

KCMG *abbrev. for* Knight Commander (of the Order) of St Michael and St George (a Brit. title).

KE *abbrev. for* kinetic energy.

kea ('keə) *n* a large New Zealand parrot with a brownish-green plumage. [C19: from Maori, imit. of its call]

kebab (kə'bæb) *n* a dish consisting of small pieces of meat, tomatoes, onions, etc., grilled on skewers. Also called: **shish kebab.** [C17: from Ar. *kabāb* roast meat]

kecks *or* **keks** (kɛks) *pl n N English dialect.* trousers. [C19: from obs. *kicks* breeches]

kedge (kedʒ) *Naut.* ◆ *vb* **kedges, kedging, kedged. 1** to draw (a vessel) along by hauling in on the cable of a light anchor, or (of a vessel) to be drawn in this fashion. ◆ *n* **2** a light anchor, used esp. for kedging. [C15: from *caggen* to fasten]

kedgeree (ˌkedʒə'riː) *n Chiefly Brit.* a dish consisting of rice, cooked flaked fish, and hard-boiled eggs. [C17: from Hindi, from Sansk. *khiccā*]

keek (kiːk) *n, vb* a Scot. word for **peep**[1]. [C18: prob. from MDu. *kīken* to look]

keel[1] (kiːl) *n* **1** one of the main longitudinal structural members of a vessel to which the frames are fastened. **2 on an even keel.** well-balanced; steady. **3** any structure corresponding to or resembling the keel of a ship. **4** *Biol.* a ridgelike part; carina. ◆ *vb* **5** to capsize. ◆ See also **keel over.** [C14: from ON *kjölr*]

keel[2] (kiːl) *n Eastern English dialect.* **1** a flat-bottomed vessel, esp. one used for carrying coal. **2** a measure of coal. [C14 *kele,* from MDu. *kiel*]

keelage ('kiːlɪdʒ) *n* a fee charged by certain ports to allow a ship to dock.

keelhaul ('kiːlˌhɔːl) *vb* (*tr*) **1** to drag (a person) by a rope from one side of a vessel to the other through the water under the keel. **2** to rebuke harshly. [C17: from Du. *kielhalen;* see KEEL[1], HAUL]

keel over **T** *vb* (*adv*) **1** to turn upside down; capsize. **2** (*intr*) *Inf.* to collapse suddenly.

keelson ('kɛlsən, 'kiːl-) *or* **kelson** *n* a longitudinal beam fastened to the keel of a vessel for strength and stiffness. [C17: prob. from Low G *kielswin* keel swine, ult. of Scand. origin]

keen[1] **T** (kiːn) *adj* **1** eager or enthusiastic. **2** (*postpositive;* foll. by *on*) fond (of); devoted (to): *keen on golf.* **3** intellectually acute: *a keen wit.* **4** (of sight, smell, hearing, etc.) capable of recognizing fine distinctions. **5** having a sharp cutting edge or point. **6** extremely cold and penetrating: *a keen wind.* **7** intense or strong: *a keen desire.* **8** *Chiefly Brit.* extremely low so as to be competitive: *keen prices.* [OE *cēne*]
▸'**keenly** *adv* ▸'**keenness** *n*

keen[2] **T** (kiːn) *vb* (*intr*) **1** to lament the dead. ◆ *n* **2** a dirge or lament for the dead. [C19: from Irish Gaelic *caoine,* from OIrish *coīnim* I wail]
▸'**keener** *n*

THESAURUS

kaput *adj Informal* = **broken**, dead, defunct, destroyed, extinct, finished, ruined, undone, wrecked

keel over *vb* **1, 2** = **collapse**, black out, capsize, faint, founder, overturn, pass out, swoon (*literary*), topple over, upset

keen[1] *adj* **1, 2** = **eager**, ardent, avid, bright-eyed and bushy-tailed (*inf.*), devoted to, earnest, ebullient, enthusiastic, fervid, fierce, fond of, impassioned, intense, into (*inf.*), zealous **3** = **astute**, brilliant, canny, clever, discerning, discriminating, perceptive, perspicacious, quick, sagacious, sapient, sensitive, shrewd, wise **5** = **sharp**, acid, acute, biting, caustic, cutting, edged, finely honed, incisive, penetrating, piercing, pointed, razor-like, sardonic, satirical, tart, trenchant, vitriolic
Antonyms *adj* ≠ **eager:** apathetic, half-hearted, indifferent, laodicean, lukewarm, unenthusiastic, uninterested ≠ **astute:** dull, obtuse, unperceptive ≠ **sharp:** blunt, dull

keen[2] *vb* **1** = **lament**, bewail, grieve, mourn, wail, weep ◆ *n* **2** = **lament**, coronach (*Scot. & Irish*), dirge, lamentation, mourning, wailing, weeping

keenness *n* **1, 2** = **eagerness**, ardour, avidity, avidness, diligence, earnestness, ebullience, enthusiasm, fervour, impatience, intensity, pas-

keep Ⓣ (kiːp) *vb* **keeps, keeping, kept. 1** (*tr*) to have or retain possession of. **2** (*tr*) to have temporary possession or charge of: *keep my watch for me.* **3** (*tr*) to store in a customary place: *I keep my books in the desk.* **4** to remain or cause to remain in a specified state or condition: *keep ready.* **5** to continue or cause to continue: *keep in step.* **6** (*tr*) to have or take charge or care of: *keep the shop for me till I return.* **7** (*tr*) to look after or maintain for use, pleasure, etc.: *to keep chickens.* **8** (*tr*) to provide for the upkeep or livelihood of. **9** (*tr*) to support financially, esp. in return for sexual favours. **10** to confine or detain or be confined or detained. **11** to withhold or reserve or admit of withholding or reserving: *your news will keep.* **12** (*tr*) to refrain from divulging or violating: *to keep a secret.* **13** to preserve or admit of preservation. **14** (*tr;* sometimes foll. by *up*) to observe with due rites or ceremonies. **15** (*tr*) to maintain by writing regular records in: *to keep a diary.* **16** (when *intr*, foll. by *in, on, to,* etc.) to stay in, on, or at (a place or position): *keep to the path.* **17** (*tr*) to associate with (esp. in **keep bad company**). **18** (*tr*) to maintain in existence: *to keep court in the palace.* **19** (*tr*) *Chiefly Brit.* to have habitually in stock: *this shop keeps all kinds of wool.* **20 how are you keeping?** how are you? ◆ *n* **21** living or support. **22** *Arch.* charge or care. **23** Also called: **dungeon, donjon.** the main tower within the walls of a medieval castle or fortress. **24 for keeps.** *Inf.* **24a** permanently. **24b** for the winner or possessor to keep permanently. ◆ See also **keep at, keep away,** etc. [OE *cēpan* to observe]

keep at Ⓣ *vb* (*prep*) **1** (*intr*) to persist in. **2** (*tr*) to constrain (a person) to continue doing (a task).

keep away *vb* (*adv;* often foll. by *from*) to refrain or prevent from coming (near).

keep back Ⓣ *vb* (*adv;* often foll. by *from*) **1** (*tr*) to refuse to reveal or disclose. **2** to prevent or be prevented from advancing, entering, etc.

keep down *vb* (*adv, mainly tr*) **1** to repress. **2** to restrain or control: *he had difficulty keeping his anger down.* **3** to cause not to increase or rise. **4** (*intr*) to lie low. **5** not to vomit.

keeper Ⓣ ('kiːpə) *n* **1** a person in charge of animals, esp. in a zoo. **2** a person in charge of a museum, collection, or section of a museum. **3** a person in charge of other people, such as a warder in a jail. **4** See **goalkeeper, wicketkeeper, gamekeeper, park keeper. 5** a person who keeps something. **6** a bar placed across the poles of a permanent magnet to close the magnetic circuit when it is not in use.

keep fit *n* exercises designed to promote physical fitness if performed regularly.

keep from *vb* (*prep*) **1** (foll. by a gerund) to prevent or restrain (oneself or another); refrain or cause to refrain. **2** (*tr*) to protect or preserve from.

keeping Ⓣ ('kiːpɪŋ) *n* **1** conformity or harmony (esp. in **in** *or* **out of keeping**). **2** charge or care: *valuables in the keeping of a bank.*

keepnet ('kiːpˌnɛt) *n* a net strung on wire hoops and sealed at one end, suspended in water by anglers to keep alive the fish they have caught.

keep off *vb* **1** to stay or cause to stay at a distance (from). **2** (*prep*) not to eat or drink or to prevent from eating or drinking. **3** (*prep*) to avoid or cause to avoid (a topic).

keep on Ⓣ *vb* (*adv*) **1** to continue or persist in (doing something): *keep on running.* **2** (*tr*) to continue to wear. **3** (*tr*) to continue to employ: *the firm kept on only ten men.* **4** (*intr;* foll. by *about*) to persist in talking (about). **5** (*intr;* foll. by *at*) to nag (a person).

keep out *vb* (*adv*) **1** to remain or cause to remain outside. **2 keep out of. 2a** to remain or cause to remain unexposed to. **2b** to avoid or cause to avoid: *keep out of his way.*

keepsake Ⓣ ('kiːpˌseɪk) *n* a gift that evokes memories of a person or event.

keep to *vb* (*prep*) **1** to adhere to or stand by or cause to adhere to or stand by. **2** to confine or be confined to. **3 keep oneself to oneself.** to avoid the society of others. **4 keep to oneself. 4a** (*intr*) to avoid the society of others. **4b** (*tr*) to refrain from sharing or disclosing.

keep up Ⓣ *vb* (*adv*) **1** (*tr*) to maintain (prices, one's morale) at the present level. **2** (*intr;* often foll. by *with*) to maintain a pace or rate set by another. **3** (*intr;* often foll. by *with*) to remain informed: *to keep up with developments.* **4** (*tr*) to maintain in good condition. **5** (*tr*) to hinder (a person) from going to bed at night. **6 keep it up.** to continue a good performance. **7 keep up with.** to remain in contact with, esp. by letter. **8 keep up with (the Joneses).** *Inf.* to compete with (one's neighbours) in material possessions, etc.

kef (kɛf) *n* a variant spelling of **kif.**

keffiyeh (kɛ'fiːjə), **kaffiyeh,** *or* **kufiyah** *n* a cotton headdress worn by Arabs. [C19: from Ar., ?from LL *cofea* COIF]

keg Ⓣ (kɛg) *n* **1** a small barrel with a capacity of between five and ten gallons. **2** *Brit., Austral., & NZ.* an aluminium container in which beer is transported and stored. [C17: var. of ME *kag,* of Scand. origin]

keks (kɛks) *pl n* a variant spelling of **kecks.**

keloid ('kiːlɔɪd) *n Pathol.* a hard raised growth of scar tissue at the site of an injury. [C19: from Gk *khēlē* claw]

kelp (kɛlp) *n* **1** any large brown seaweed. **2** the ash of such seaweed, used as a source of iodine and potash. [C14: from ?]

kelpie[1] *or* **kelpy** ('kɛlpɪ) *n, pl* **kelpies.** an Australian breed of sheepdog having a coat of various colours and erect ears. [named after a particular specimen of the breed, c 1870]

kelpie[2] ('kɛlpɪ) *n* (in Scottish folklore) a water spirit in the form of a horse. [C18: prob. rel. to Scot. Gaelic *cailpeach* heifer, from ?]

kelson ('kɛlsən) *n* a variant spelling of **keelson.**

kelt (kɛlt) *n* a salmon that has recently spawned. [C14: from ?]

Kelt (kɛlt) *n* a variant spelling of **Celt.**

kelter ('kɛltə) *n* a variant of **kilter.**

kelvin ('kɛlvɪn) *n* the basic SI unit of thermodynamic temperature; the fraction 1/273.16 of the thermodynamic temperature of the triple point of water. Symbol: K [C20: after William Thomson *Kelvin,* 1st Baron Kelvin (1824–1907), Brit. physicist]

Kelvin scale *n* a thermodynamic temperature scale in which the zero is absolute zero. Originally the degree was equal to that on the Celsius scale but it is now defined so that the triple point of water is exactly 273.16 kelvins.

kempt (kɛmpt) *adj* (of hair) tidy; combed. See also **unkempt.** [C20: back formation from *unkempt;* orig. p.p. of dialect *kemb* to COMB]

ken Ⓣ (kɛn) *n* **1** range of knowledge (esp. in **beyond** *or* **in one's ken**). ◆ *vb* **kens, kenning, kenned** *or* **kent. 2** *Scot. & northern English dialect.* to know. **3** *Scot. & northern English dialect.* to understand. [OE *cennan*]

kendo ('kɛndəʊ) *n* the Japanese art of fencing with pliable bamboo staves or, sometimes, real swords. [Japanese, lit.: way of the sword, from *ken* sword + *do* way]

kennel ('kɛn^{ə}l) *n* **1** a hutlike shelter for a dog. US name: **doghouse. 2** (*usually pl*) an establishment where dogs are bred, trained, boarded, etc. **3** a hovel. **4** a pack of hounds. ◆ *vb* **kennels, kennelling, kennelled** *or US* **kennels, kenneling, kenneled. 5** to keep or stay in a kennel. [C14: from OF, from Vulgar L *canīle* (unattested), from L *canis* dog]

kenning ('kɛnɪŋ) *n* a conventional metaphoric name for something, esp. in Old Norse and Old English poetry. [C14: from ON, from *kenna;* see KEN]

kenspeckle ('kɛnˌspɛk^{ə}l) *adj Scot.* easily seen or recognized. [C18: from dialect *kenspeck,* of Scand. origin]

kepi ('keɪpiː) *n, pl* **kepis.** a military cap with a circular top and a horizontal peak. [C19: from F *képi,* from G (Swiss dialect) *käppi* a little cap, from *kappe* CAP]

Kepler's laws ('kɛpləz) *pl n* three laws of planetary motion published by Johannes Kepler (1571–1630), German astronomer, between 1609 and 1619. They deal with the shape of a planet's orbit, the constant velocity of the planet in orbit, and the relationship between the length of a planetary year and the distance from the sun.

kept (kɛpt) *vb* **1** the past tense and past participle of **keep. 2 kept woman.** *Censorious.* a woman maintained by a man as his mistress.

keratin ('kɛrətɪn) *n* a fibrous protein that occurs in the outer layer of the skin and in hair, nails, hooves, etc.

keratose ('kɛrəˌtəʊs, -ˌtəʊz) *adj* (esp. of certain sponges) having a horny skeleton. [C19: from Gk *keras* horn + -OSE[1]]

kerb *or US & Canad.* **curb** (kɜːb) *n* a line of stone or concrete forming an

THESAURUS

sion, zeal, zest **3** = **astuteness**, canniness, cleverness, discernment, insight, sagacity, sapience, sensitivity, shrewdness, wisdom **5** = **sharpness**, acerbity, harshness, incisiveness, mordancy, penetration, pungency, rigour, severity, sternness, trenchancy, unkindness, virulence

keep *vb* **1** = **retain**, conserve, control, hold, maintain, possess, preserve **2, 6** = **look after**, care for, defend, guard, maintain, manage, mind, operate, protect, safeguard, shelter, shield, tend, watch over **8** = **support**, board, feed, foster, maintain, nourish, nurture, provide for, provision, subsidize, sustain, victual **10** = **detain**, arrest, block, check, constrain, control, curb, delay, deter, hamper, hamstring, hinder, hold, hold back, impede, inhibit, keep back, limit, obstruct, prevent, restrain, retard, shackle, stall, withhold **14** = **comply with**, adhere to, celebrate, commemorate, fulfil, hold, honour, obey, observe, perform, respect, ritualize, solemnize **17** = **associate with**, accompany, consort with, fraternize with **19** = **store**, accumulate, amass, carry, deal in, deposit, furnish, garner, heap, hold, pile, place, stack, stock, trade in ◆ *n* **21** = **board**, food, livelihood, living, maintenance, means, nourishment, subsistence, support **23** = **tower**, castle, citadel, donjon, dungeon, fastness, stronghold
Antonyms *vb* ≠ **retain**: abandon, discard, give up, lose ≠ **detain**: free, liberate, release ≠ **comply with**: disregard, ignore

keep at *vb* **1** = **persist**, be steadfast, carry on, complete, continue, drudge, endure, finish, grind, labour, last, maintain, persevere, remain, slave, stay, stick, toil

keep back *vb* **1** = **suppress**, censor, conceal, hide, keep dark, keep under one's hat, reserve, withhold **2** = **restrain**, check, constrain, control, curb, delay, hold back, keep a tight rein on, limit, prohibit, restrict, retard, withhold

keeper *n* **2, 3** = **guardian**, attendant, caretaker, curator, custodian, defender, governor, guard, jailer *or* gaoler, overseer, preserver, steward, superintendent, warden, warder

keeping *n* **1** *As in* **in keeping with** = **agreement**, accord, balance, compliance, conformity, congruity, consistency, correspondence, harmony, observance, proportion **2** = **care**, aegis, auspices, charge, custody, guardianship, keep, maintenance, patronage, possession, protection, safekeeping, trust

keep on *vb* **1** = **continue**, carry on, endure, last, persevere, persist, prolong, remain

keepsake *n* = **souvenir**, emblem, favour, memento, relic, remembrance, reminder, symbol, token

keep up *vb* **1, 2** = **maintain**, balance, compete, contend, continue, emulate, keep pace, match, persevere, preserve, rival, sustain, vie

keg *n* **1** = **barrel**, cask, drum, firkin, hogshead, tun, vat

ken *n* **1** = **knowledge**, acquaintance, awareness, cognizance, comprehension, notice, understanding

edge between a pavement and a roadway. [C17: from OF *courbe* bent, from L *curvus;* see CURVE]
▸ **'kerbing** *n*

kerb crawling *n* the act of driving slowly beside the pavement seeking to entice someone into the car for sexual purposes.
▸ **kerb crawler** *n*

kerb drill *n* a pedestrian's procedure for crossing a road safely, esp. as taught to children.

kerbstone *or US & Canad.* **curbstone** ('kɜːbˌstəʊn) *n* one of a series of stones that form a kerb.

kerchief ❶ ('kɜːtʃɪf) *n* a piece of cloth worn over the head. [C13: from OF, from *covrir* to COVER + *chef* head]
▸ **'kerchiefed** *adj*

kerel ('kɛərəl) *n S. African.* a young man. [from Afrik. *kêrel;* cf. OE *ceorl*]

kerf (kɜːf) *n* the cut made by a saw, an axe, etc. [OE *cyrf* a cutting]

kerfuffle (kə'fʌfᵊl) *n Inf., chiefly Brit.* commotion; disorder. [from Scot. *curfuffle, carfuffle,* from Scot. Gaelic *car* twist, turn + *fuffle* to disarrange]

kermes ('kɜːmɪz) *n* **1** the dried bodies of female scale insects used as a red dyestuff. **2** a small evergreen Eurasian oak tree: the host plant of kermes scale insects. [C16: from F, from Ar. *qirmiz,* from Sansk. *krmija-* red dye, lit.: produced by a worm]

kermis *or* **kirmess** ('kɜːmɪs) *n* **1** (formerly, esp. in Holland and northern Germany) an annual country festival. **2** *US & Canad.* a similar event held to collect money for charity. [C16: from MDu., from *kerc* church + *misse* MASS; orig. a festival held to celebrate the dedication of a church]

kern[1] *or* **kerne** (kɜːn) *n* the part of the character on a piece of printer's type that projects beyond the body. [C17: from F *carne* corner of type, ult. from L *cardō* hinge]

kern[2] (kɜːn) *n* **1** a lightly armed foot soldier in medieval Ireland or Scotland. **2** *Arch.* a loutish peasant. [C14: from MIrish *cethern* band of foot soldiers, from *cath* battle]

kernel ❶ ('kɜːnᵊl) *n* **1** the edible seed of a nut or fruit within the shell or stone. **2** the grain of a cereal, esp. wheat, consisting of the seed in a hard husk. **3** the central or essential part of something. [OE *cyrnel* a little seed, from *corn* seed]
▸ **'kernel-less** *adj*

kerosene *or* **kerosine** ('kɛrəˌsiːn) *n* **1** another name (esp. US, Canad., Austral., & NZ) for **paraffin** (sense 1). **2** the general name for paraffin as a fuel for jet aircraft. [C19: from Gk *kēros* wax + -ENE]

> **USAGE NOTE** The spelling *kerosine* is now the preferred form in technical and industrial usage.

kersey ('kɜːzɪ) *n* a twilled woollen cloth with a cotton warp. [C14: prob. from *Kersey,* village in Suffolk]

kerseymere ('kɜːzɪˌmɪə) *n* a fine soft woollen cloth of twill weave. [C18: from KERSEY + *(cassi)mere,* var. of CASHMERE]

kestrel ('kɛstrəl) *n* any of several small falcons that feed on small mammals and tend to hover against the wind. [C15: changed from OF *cresserele,* from *cressele* rattle, from Vulgar L *crepicella* (unattested), from L, from *crepāre* to rustle]

ketch (kɛtʃ) *n* a two-masted sailing vessel, fore-and-aft rigged, with a tall mainmast. [C15 *cache,* prob. from *cacchen* to hunt; see CATCH]

ketchup ('kɛtʃəp), **catchup,** *or* **catsup** *n* any of various sauces containing vinegar: *tomato ketchup.* [C18: from Chinese *kōetsiap* brine of pickled fish, from *kōe* seafood + *tsiap* sauce]

ketone ('kiːtəʊn) *n* any of a class of compounds with the general formula R'COR, where R and R' are alkyl or aryl groups. [C19: from G, from *Aketon* ACETONE]
▸ **ketonic** (kɪ'tɒnɪk) *adj*

ketone body *n Biochem.* any of three compounds produced when fatty acids are broken down in the liver to provide a source of energy. Excess ketone bodies are present in the blood and urine of people unable to use glucose as an energy source, as in diabetes.

kettle ('kɛtᵊl) *n* **1** a metal container with a handle and spout for boiling water. **2** any of various metal containers for heating liquids, cooking fish, etc. **3** a large metal vessel designed to withstand high temperatures, used in various industrial processes such as refining and brewing. [C13: from ON *ketill,* ult. from L *catillus* a little pot, from *catīnus* pot]

kettledrum ('kɛtᵊlˌdrʌm) *n* a percussion instrument of definite pitch, consisting of a hollow bowl-like hemisphere covered with a skin or membrane, supported on a tripod. The pitch may be adjusted by means of screws, which alter the tension of the skin.
▸ **'kettleˌdrummer** *n*

kettle hole *n* a round hollow formed by the melting of a mass of buried ice.

kettle of fish *n* **1** a situation; state of affairs (often used ironically in **a pretty** *or* **fine kettle of fish**). **2** case; matter for consideration: *that's quite a different kettle of fish.*

key[1] ❶ (kiː) *n* **1** a metal instrument, usually of a specifically contoured shape, that is made to fit a lock and, when rotated, operates the lock's mechanism. **2** any instrument that is rotated to operate a valve, clock winding mechanism, etc. **3** a small metal peg or wedge inserted to prevent relative motion. **4** any of a set of buttons operating a typewriter, computer, etc. **5** any of the visible parts of the lever mechanism of a musical keyboard instrument that when depressed cause the instrument to sound. **6a** Also called: **tonality.** any of the 24 major and minor diatonic scales considered as a corpus of notes upon which a piece of music draws for its tonal framework. **6b** the main tonal centre in an extended composition: *a symphony in the key of F major.* **7** something that is crucial in providing an explanation or interpretation. **8** (*modifier*) of great importance: *a key issue.* **9** a means of achieving a desired end: *the key to happiness.* **10** a means of access or control: *Gibraltar is the key to the Mediterranean.* **11** a list of explanations of symbols, codes, etc. **12** a text that explains or gives information about a work of literature, art, or music. **13** *Electrical engineering.* a hand-operated switch that is pressed to transmit coded signals, esp. Morse code. **14** the grooving or scratching of a surface or the application of a rough coat of plaster, etc., to provide a bond for a subsequent finish. **15** pitch: *he spoke in a low key.* **16** a mood or style: *a poem in a melancholic key.* **17** short for **keystone** (sense 1). **18** *Bot.* any dry winged fruit, esp. that of the ash. ◆ *vb (mainly tr)* **19** (foll. by *to*) to harmonize (with): *to key one's actions to the prevailing mood.* **20** to adjust or fasten with a key or some similar device. **21** to provide with a key or keys. **22** (*also intr*) another word for **keyboard** (sense 3). **23** to include a distinguishing device in (an advertisement, etc.), so that responses to it can be identified. **24** (*also intr*) to groove, scratch, or apply a rough coat of plaster, etc., to (a surface) to provide a bond for a subsequent finish. ◆ See also **key in, key up.** [OE *cǣg*]
▸ **'keyless** *adj*

key[2] (kiː) *n* a variant spelling of **cay.**

keyboard ('kiːˌbɔːd) *n* **1a** a set of keys, usually hand-operated, as on a piano, typewriter, or typesetting machine. **1b** (*as modifier*): *a keyboard instrument.* **2** (*pl*) electronic keyboard instruments: *John plays keyboards for the band.* ◆ *vb* **3** (*tr*) to set (a text) in type by using a keyboard machine.
▸ **'keyˌboarder** *n*

key grip *n* the person in charge of moving and setting up camera tracks and scenery in a film or television studio.

keyhole ('kiːˌhəʊl) *n* an aperture in a door or a lock case through which a key may be passed to engage the lock mechanism.

keyhole surgery *n* surgery carried out through a very small incision.

key in ❶ *vb (tr, adv)* to enter (information or instructions) in a computer or other device by means of a keyboard or keypad.

key-man assurance *n* an assurance policy taken out, esp. by a small company, on the life of a senior executive whose death would create a serious loss.

key money *n* a fee payment required from a new tenant of a house or flat before he moves in.

keynote ❶ ('kiːˌnəʊt) *n* **1a** a central or determining principle in a speech, literary work, etc. **1b** (*as modifier*): *a keynote speech.* **2** the note upon which a scale or key is based; tonic. ◆ *vb* **keynotes, keynoting, keynoted.** (*tr*) **3** to deliver a keynote address to (a political convention, etc.).

keypad ('kiːˌpæd) *n* a small panel with a set of buttons for operating a teletext system, electronic calculator, etc.

key punch *n* **1** Also called: **card punch.** a device having a keyboard that is operated manually to transfer data onto punched cards, paper tape, etc. ◆ *vb* **key-punch. 2** to transfer (data) by using a key punch.

key signature *n Music.* a group of sharps or flats appearing at the beginning of each stave line to indicate the key in which a piece, section, etc., is to be performed.

key stage *n Brit. education.* any one of four broad age-group divisions (5–7; 7–11; 11–14; 14–16) to which each level of the National Curriculum applies.

keystone ❶ ('kiːˌstəʊn) *n* **1** the central stone at the top of an arch or the top stone of a dome or vault. **2** something that is necessary to connect other related things.

key up *vb (tr, adv)* to raise the intensity, excitement, tension, etc., of.

kg 1 *abbrev. for* keg. ◆ **2.** *symbol for* kilogram.

KG *abbrev. for* Knight of the Order of the Garter (a Brit. title).

KGB *abbrev. for* the former Soviet secret police, founded in 1954. [from Russian *Komitet gosudarstvennoi bezopasnosti* State Security Committee]

khaddar ('kɑːdə) *or* **khadi** ('kɑːdɪ) *n* a cotton cloth of plain weave, produced in India. [from Hindi *khādar*]

khaki ('kɑːkɪ) *n, pl* **khakis. 1** a dull yellowish-brown colour. **2a** a hard-wearing fabric of this colour, used esp. for military uniforms. **2b** (*as modifier*): *a khaki jacket.* [C19: from Urdu, from Persian: dusty, from *khāk* dust]

khalif ('keɪlɪf) *n* a variant spelling of **caliph.**

THESAURUS

kerchief *n* = **scarf,** babushka, headscarf, head-square, square

kernel *n* **3** = **essence,** core, germ, gist, grain, marrow, nub, pith, seed, substance

key[1] *n* **1** = **opener,** latchkey **7** = **answer,** clue, cue, explanation, guide, indicator, interpretation, lead, means, pointer, sign, solution, translation ◆ *modifier* **8** = **essential,** basic, chief, crucial, decisive, fundamental, important, leading, main, major, pivotal, principal
Antonyms *adj* ≠ **essential:** minor, secondary, subsidiary, superficial

key in *vb* = **type,** enter, input, keyboard

keynote *n* **1** = **heart,** centre, core, essence, gist, kernel, marrow, pith, substance, theme

keystone *n* **2** = **basis,** core, cornerstone, crux, fundament, ground, linchpin, mainspring, motive, principle, quoin, root, source, spring

Khalsa ('kælsə) *n* an order of the Sikh religion, founded (1699) by Guru Gobind Singh.

khan[1] (kɑːn) *n* **1a** (formerly) a title borne by medieval Chinese emperors and Mongol and Turkic rulers. **1b** such a ruler. **2** a title of respect borne by important personages in Afghanistan and central Asia. [C14: from OF, from Med. L, from Turkish *khān,* contraction of *khāqān* ruler]
▸**'khanate** *n*

khan[2] (kɑːn) *n* an inn in Turkey, etc.; caravanserai. [C14: via Ar. from Persian]

khedive (kɪ'diːv) *n* the viceroy of Egypt under Ottoman suzerainty (1867–1914). [C19: from F, from Turkish, from Persian *khidīw* prince]
▸**khe'dival** *or* **khe'divial** *adj*

Khmer (kmɛə) *n* **1** a member of a people of Cambodia, noted for a civilization that flourished from about 800 A.D. to about 1370. **2** the language of this people: the official language of Cambodia. ◆ *adj* **3** of or relating to this people or their language.
▸**'Khmerian** *adj*

Khoikhoi (kɔɪ'kɔɪ *or* xɔɪ'xɔɪ) *n* **1** a member of a Southern African people who formerly occupied the region around the Cape of Good Hope and are now almost extinct. **2** any of the languages of this people.

kHz *symbol for* kilohertz.

kiang (kɪ'æŋ) *n* a variety of the wild ass that occurs in Tibet and surrounding regions. [C19: from Tibetan *rkyan*]

kia ora (ˌkɪə 'ɔːrə) *sentence substitute. NZ.* greetings! good luck! [Maori, lit.: be well!]

kibble[1] ('kɪbᵊl) *n Brit.* a bucket used in wells or in mining for hoisting. [C17: from G *kübel,* ult. from Med. L *cuppa* CUP]

kibble[2] ('kɪbᵊl) *vb* **kibbles, kibbling, kibbled.** (*tr*) to grind into small pieces. [C18: from ?]

kibbutz (kɪ'bʊts) *n, pl* **kibbutzim** (ˌkɪbʊt'siːm). a collective agricultural settlement in modern Israel, owned and administered communally by its members. [C20: from Mod. Heb. *qibbūs* gathering, from Heb. *qibbūtz*]

kibe (kaɪb) *n* a chilblain, esp. an ulcerated one on the heel. [C14: prob. from Welsh *cibi,* from ?]

kiblah ('kɪblɑː) *n Islam.* the direction of Mecca, to which Muslims turn in prayer. [C18: from Ar. *qiblah* that which is placed opposite]

kibosh ('kaɪˌbɒʃ) *n* **put the kibosh on.** *Sl.* to put a stop to; prevent from continuing; halt. [C19: from ?]

kick Ⓣ (kɪk) *vb* **1** (*tr*) to drive or impel with the foot. **2** (*tr*) to hit with the foot or feet. **3** (*intr*) to strike out or thrash about with the feet, as in fighting or swimming. **4** (*intr*) to raise a leg high, as in dancing. **5** (of a gun, etc.) to recoil or strike in recoiling when fired. **6** (*tr*) *Rugby.* to make (a conversion or a drop goal) by means of a kick. **7** (*tr*) *Soccer.* to score (a goal) by a kick. **8** (*intr*) *Athletics.* to put on a sudden spurt. **9** (*intr*) to make a sudden violent movement. **10** (*intr;* sometimes foll. by *against*) *Inf.* to object or resist. **11** (*intr*) *Inf.* to be active and in good health (esp. in **alive and kicking**). **12** *Inf.* to change gear in (a car): *he kicked into third.* **13** (*tr*) *Inf.* to free oneself of (an addiction, etc.): *he tried to kick the habit.* **14 kick up one's heels.** *Inf.* to enjoy oneself without inhibition. ◆ *n* **15** a thrust or blow with the foot. **16** any of certain rhythmic leg movements used in swimming. **17** the recoil of a gun or other firearm. **18** *Inf.* exciting quality or effect (esp. in **get a kick out of, for kicks**). **19** *Athletics.* a sudden spurt, acceleration, or boost. **20** a sudden violent movement. **21** *Inf.* the sudden stimulating effect of strong alcoholic drink or certain drugs. **22** *Inf.* power or force. **23 kick in the teeth.** *Sl.* a humiliating rebuff. ◆ See also **kick about, kickback,** etc. [C14 *kiken,* ?from ON]
▸**'kickable** *adj*

kick about *or* **around** *vb* (*mainly adv*) *Inf.* **1** (*tr*) to treat harshly. **2** (*tr*) to discuss (ideas, etc.) informally. **3** (*intr*) to wander aimlessly. **4** (*intr*) to lie neglected or forgotten.

kickback Ⓣ ('kɪkˌbæk) *n* **1** a strong reaction. **2** part of an income paid to a person in return for an opportunity to make a profit, often by some illegal arrangement. ◆ *vb* **kick back.** (*adv*) **3** (*intr*) to have a strong reaction. **4** (*intr*) (esp. of a gun) to recoil. **5** to pay a kickback to (someone).

kick boxing *n* a martial art that resembles boxing but permits blows with the feet as well as punches.

kickdown ('kɪkˌdaʊn) *n* a method of changing gear in a car with automatic transmission, by fully depressing the accelerator.

kicker ('kɪkə) *n* **1** a person or thing that kicks. **2** *US & Canad. sl.* a hidden and disadvantageous factor.

kick in *vb* (*adv*) **1** (*intr*) to start or become activated. **2** (*tr*) *Chiefly Austral. & NZ inf.* to contribute.

kick off Ⓣ *vb* (*intr, adv*) **1** to start play in a game of football by kicking the ball from the centre of the field. **2** *Inf.* to commence (a discussion, job, etc.). ◆ *n* **kickoff. 3a** a place kick from the centre of the field in a game of football. **3b** the time at which the first such kick is due to take place.

kick on *vb* (*adv*) *Inf.* to continue.

kick out Ⓣ *vb* (*tr, adv*) *Inf.* to eject or dismiss.

kickshaw ('kɪkˌʃɔː) *or* **kickshaws** *n* **1** a valueless trinket. **2** *Arch.* a small exotic delicacy. [C16: back formation from *kickshaws,* by folk etymology from F *quelque chose* something]

kickstand ('kɪkˌstænd) *n* a short metal bar attached to the frame of a motorcycle or bicycle, which when kicked into a vertical position holds the stationary vehicle upright.

kick-start ('kɪkˌstɑːt) *vb* (*tr*) **1** to start (an engine, esp. of a motorcycle) by means of a pedal that is kicked downwards. **2** *Inf.* to make (something) active, functional, or productive again. ◆ *n* **3** an action or event resulting in the reactivation of something.
▸**'kick-ˌstarter** *n*

kick up *vb* (*adv*) *Inf.* to cause (trouble, etc.).

kick upstairs *vb* (*tr, adv*) *Inf.* to promote to a higher but effectively powerless position.

kid[1] Ⓣ (kɪd) *n* **1** the young of a goat or of a related animal, such as an antelope. **2** soft smooth leather made from the hide of a kid. **3** *Inf.* **3a** a young person; child. **3b** (*modifier*) younger or being still a child: *kid brother.* ◆ *vb* **kids, kidding, kidded. 4** (of a goat) to give birth to (young). [C12: from ON]
▸**'kiddishness** *n* ▸**'kidˌlike** *adj*

kid[2] Ⓣ (kɪd) *vb* **kids, kidding, kidded.** *Inf.* (sometimes foll. by *on* or *along*) **1** (*tr*) to tease or deceive for fun. **2** (*intr*) to behave or speak deceptively for fun. **3** (*tr*) to fool (oneself) into believing (something): *don't kid yourself that no-one else knows.* [C19: prob. from KID[1]]
▸**'kidder** *n* ▸**'kiddingly** *adv*

Kidderminster ('kɪdəˌmɪnstə) *n* a type of ingrain reversible carpet originally made at Kidderminster. [after *Kidderminster,* town in W central England]

kiddy *or* **kiddie** ('kɪdɪ) *n, pl* **kiddies.** *Inf.* an affectionate word for **child.**

kid glove *n* **1** a glove made of kidskin. **2 handle with kid gloves.** to treat with great tact or caution. ◆ *adj* **kidglove. 3** overdelicate. **4** diplomatic; tactful: *a kidglove approach.*

kidnap Ⓣ ('kɪdnæp) *vb* **kidnaps, kidnapping, kidnapped** *or US* **kidnaps, kidnaping, kidnaped.** (*tr*) to carry off and hold (a person), usually for ransom. [C17: KID[1] + obs. *nap* to steal; see NAB]
▸**'kidnapper** *n*

kidney ('kɪdnɪ) *n* **1** either of two bean-shaped organs at the back of the abdominal cavity in man. They filter waste products from the blood, which are excreted as urine. Related adj: **renal. 2** the corresponding organ in other animals. **3** the kidneys of certain animals used as food. **4** class, type, or disposition (esp. in **of the same** *or* **a different kidney**). [C14: from ?]

kidney bean *n* **1** any of certain bean plants having kidney-shaped seeds, esp. the scarlet runner. **2** the seed of any of these beans.

kidney machine *n* a machine carrying out the functions of a kidney, esp. used in haemodialysis.

kidney stone *n* **1** *Pathol.* a hard mass formed in the kidney, usually composed of oxalates, phosphates, and carbonates. **2** *Mineralogy.* another name for **nephrite.**

kidology (kɪ'dɒlədʒɪ) *n Brit. inf.* the practice of bluffing or deception. [C20: from KID[2] + *-ology* a science]

kidskin ('kɪdˌskɪn) *n* a soft smooth leather made from the hide of a young goat. Often shortened to **kid.**

kids' stuff *n Sl.* **1** something considered fit only for children. **2** something considered easy.

kidstakes ('kɪdˌsteɪks) *pl n Austral. inf.* pretence; nonsense: *cut the kidstakes!*

kie kie ('kiːɛ kiːɛ) *n* a New Zealand climbing plant with edible bracts. [from Maori]

kieselguhr ('kiːzᵊlˌgʊə) *n* an unconsolidated form of diatomite. [C19: from G *Kieselgur,* from *Kiesel* flint + *Gur* loose earthy deposit]

kif (kɪf, kiːf), **kef,** *or* **kief** (kiːf) *n* **1** another name for **marijuana. 2** any drug that when smoked is capable of producing a euphoric condition. **3** the euphoric condition produced by smoking marijuana. [C20: from Ar. *kayf* pleasure]

kike (kaɪk) *n US & Canad. sl.* an offensive word for **Jew.** [C20: prob. var. of *kiki,* reduplication of *-ki,* common name-ending among Jews from Slavic countries]

kilderkin ('kɪldəkɪn) *n* **1** an obsolete unit of liquid capacity equal to 16 or 18 Imperial gallons or of dry capacity equal to 16 or 18 wine gallons. **2** a cask capable of holding a kilderkin. [C14: from MDu. *kindekijn,* from *kintal* hundredweight, from Med. L *quintale*]

THESAURUS

kick *vb* **1, 2** = **boot**, punt, put the boot in(to) (*sl.*) **10** *Informal* = **resist**, complain, gripe (*inf.*), grumble, object, oppose, protest, rebel, spurn **13** *Informal* = **give up**, abandon, desist from, leave off, quit, stop ◆ *n* **18** *Informal* = **thrill**, buzz (*sl.*), enjoyment, excitement, fun, gratification, jollies (*sl.*), pleasure, stimulation **22** *Informal* = **pungency**, force, intensity, pep, power, punch, snap (*inf.*), sparkle, strength, tang, verve, vitality, zest

kickback *adj* **2** = **bribe**, cut (*inf.*), gift, graft (*inf.*), payment, payoff, recompense, reward, share, sop, sweetener (*sl.*)

kick off *vb* **2** *Informal* = **begin**, commence, get the show on the road, get under way, initiate, kick-start, open, start

kick out *vb Informal* = **dismiss**, discharge, eject, evict, expel, get rid of, give (someone) their marching orders, give the boot (*sl.*), oust, reject, remove, sack (*inf.*), show one the door, throw out on one's ear (*inf.*), toss out

kid[1] *n* **3a** *Informal* = **child**, ankle-biter (*Austral. sl.*), baby, bairn, boy, girl, infant, lad, lass, little one, rug rat (*US & Canad. inf.*), sprog (*sl.*), stripling, teenager, tot, youngster, youth

kid[2] *vb* **1, 2** *Informal* = **tease**, bamboozle, beguile, cozen, delude, fool, gull, hoax, hoodwink, jest, joke, mock, plague, pretend, rag (*Brit.*), ridicule, trick, wind up (*Brit. sl.*)

kidnap *vb* = **abduct**, capture, hijack, hold to ransom, remove, seize, steal

kilim (kɪ'li:m, 'ki:lɪm) *n* a pileless woven rug of intricate design made in the Middle East. [C19: from Turkish, from Persian *kilīm*]

kill (kɪl) *vb (mainly tr)* **1** *(also intr;* when *tr,* sometimes foll. by *off)* to cause the death of (a person or animal). **2** to put an end to: *to kill someone's interest.* **3** to occupy (time) by doing something unimportant, esp. while waiting for something. **4** to deaden (sound). **5** *Inf.* to tire out: *the effort killed him.* **6** *Inf.* to cause to suffer pain or discomfort: *my shoes are killing me.* **7** *Inf.* to quash or veto: *the bill was killed in the House of Lords.* **8** *Inf.* to switch off; stop. **9** *(also intr) Inf.* to overcome with attraction, laughter, surprise, etc.: *she was dressed to kill.* **10** *Tennis, squash, etc.* to hit (a ball) so hard or so accurately that the opponent cannot return it. **11** *Soccer.* to bring (a moving ball) under control. **12** **kill oneself.** *Inf.* to overexert oneself: *don't kill yourself.* **13** **kill two birds with one stone.** to achieve two results with one action. ◆ *n* **14** the act of causing death, esp. at the end of a hunt, bullfight, etc. **15** the animal or animals killed during a hunt. **16** *NZ.* a seasonal tally of the number of stock killed at a meatworks. **17** the destruction of a battleship, tank, etc. **18** **in at the kill.** present at the end of some undertaking. [C13 *cullen;* see QUELL]

killdeer ('kɪlˌdɪə) *n, pl* **killdeer** *or* **killdeers.** a large brown-and-white North American plover with two black breast bands. [C18: imit.]

killer ('kɪlə) *n* **1a** a person or animal that kills, esp. habitually. **1b** *(as modifier): a killer shark.* **2** something, esp. a task or activity, that is particularly taxing or exhausting. **3** *Austral. & NZ.* a farm animal selected to be killed for food.

killer bee *n* an African honeybee, or one of its hybrids originating in Brazil, that is extremely aggressive when disturbed.

killer cell *n* a type of white blood cell that is able to kill cells, such as cancer cells and cells infected with viruses.

killer whale *n* a predatory black-and-white toothed whale most common in cold seas.

killick ('kɪlɪk) *or* **killock** ('kɪlək) *n Naut.* a small anchor, esp. one made of a heavy stone. [C17: from ?]

killifish ('kɪlɪˌfɪʃ) *n, pl* **killifish** *or* **killifishes.** any of various chiefly American minnow-like fishes of fresh and brackish waters: used to control mosquitoes and as anglers' bait. [C19: from MDu. *kille* river + FISH]

killing ('kɪlɪŋ) *Inf.* ◆ *adj* **1** very tiring: *a killing pace.* **2** extremely funny. **3** causing death; fatal. ◆ *n* **4** the act of causing death; slaying. **5** a sudden stroke of success, usually financial, as in speculations on the stock market (esp. in **make a killing**).

killjoy ('kɪlˌdʒɔɪ) *n* a person who spoils other people's pleasure.

kiln (kɪln) *n* a large oven for burning, drying, or processing something, such as porcelain or bricks. [OE *cylen,* from LL *culīna* kitchen, from L *coquere* to COOK]

kilo ('ki:ləʊ) *n, pl* **kilos.** short for **kilogram** or **kilometre.**

kilo- *prefix* **1** denoting 10^3 (1000): *kilometre.* Symbol: k **2** (in computers) denoting 2^{10} (1024): *kilobyte:* in computer usage, *kilo-* is restricted to sizes of storage (e.g. *kilobit*) when it means 1024; in other computer contexts it retains its usual meaning of 1000. [from F, from Gk *khilioi* thousand]

kilobyte ('kɪləˌbaɪt) *n Computing.* 1024 bytes. Abbrev.: **KB, kbyte.** See also **kilo-** (sense 2).

kilocalorie ('kɪləʊˌkælərɪ) *n* another name for **Calorie.**

kilocycle ('kɪləʊˌsaɪkᵊl) *n* short for kilocycle per second: a former unit of frequency equal to 1 kilohertz.

kilogram ('kɪləʊˌgræm) *n* **1** one thousand grams. **2** the basic SI unit of mass, equal to the mass of the international prototype held by the *Bureau International des Poids et Mesures.* Symbol: kg

kilohertz ('kɪləʊˌhɜ:ts) *n* one thousand hertz; one thousand cycles per second. Symbol: kHz

kilolitre ('kɪləˌli:tə) *n* one thousand litres. Symbol: kl

kilometre *or US* **kilometer** ('kɪləˌmi:tə, kɪ'lɒmɪtə) *n* one thousand metres. Symbol: km
▸**kilometric** (ˌkɪləʊ'mɛtrɪk) *adj*

kiloton ('kɪləʊˌtʌn) *n* **1** one thousand tons. **2** an explosive power, esp. of a nuclear weapon, equal to the power of 1000 tons of TNT. Abbrev.: **kt.**

kilovolt ('kɪləʊˌvəʊlt) *n* one thousand volts. Symbol: kV

kilowatt ('kɪləʊˌwɒt) *n* one thousand watts. Symbol: kW

kilowatt-hour *n* a unit of energy equal to the work done by a power of 1000 watts in one hour. Symbol: kWh

kilt (kɪlt) *n* **1** a knee-length pleated skirt, esp. one in tartan, as worn by men in Highland dress. ◆ *vb (tr)* **2** to tuck (the skirt) up around one's body. **3** to put pleats in (cloth, etc.). [C18: of Scand. origin]
▸**'kilted** *adj*

kilter ('kɪltə) *or* **kelter** *n* working order (esp. in **out of kilter**). [C17: from ?]

kimberlite ('kɪmbəˌlaɪt) *n* an intrusive igneous rock consisting largely of peridotite and often containing diamonds. [C19: from *Kimberley,* city in South Africa, + -ITE[1]]

kimono (kɪ'məʊnəʊ) *n, pl* **kimonos.** a loose sashed ankle-length garment with wide sleeves, worn in Japan. [C19: from Japanese: clothing, from *kiru* to wear + *mono* thing]
▸**ki'monoed** *adj*

kin (kɪn) *n* **1** a person's relatives collectively. **2** a class or group with similar characteristics. **3** See **next of kin.** ◆ *adj* **4** *(postpositive)* related by blood. [OE *cyn*]

-kin *suffix forming nouns.* small: *lambkin.* [from MDu., of West Gmc origin]

kinaesthesia (ˌkɪnɪs'θi:zɪə) *or US* **kinesthesia** *n* the sensation by which bodily position, weight, muscle tension, and movement are perceived. [C19: from NL, from Gk *kinein* to move + AESTHESIA]
▸**kinaesthetic** *or US* **kinesthetic** (ˌkɪnɪs'θɛtɪk) *adj*

kincob ('kɪŋkɒb) *n* a fine silk fabric embroidered with threads of gold or silver, of a kind made in India. [C18: from Urdu *kimkhāb*]

kind[1] (kaɪnd) *adj* **1** having a friendly nature or attitude. **2** helpful to others or to another: *a kind deed.* **3** considerate or humane. **4** cordial; courteous (esp. in **kind regards**). **5** pleasant; mild: *a kind climate.* **6** *Inf.* beneficial or not harmful. [OE *gecynde* natural, native]

kind[2] (kaɪnd) *n* **1** a class or group having characteristics in common; sort; type: *two of a kind.* **2** an instance or example of a class or group, esp. a rudimentary one: *heating of a kind.* **3** essential nature or character: *the difference is one of kind rather than degree.* **4** *Arch.* nature; the natural order. **5** **in kind. 5a** (of payment) in goods or produce rather than in money. **5b** with something of the same sort: *to return an insult in kind.* [OE *gecynd* nature]

> **USAGE NOTE** The mixture of plural and singular constructions, although often used informally with *kind* and *sort,* should be avoided in serious writing: *children enjoy those kinds* (not *those kind*) *of stories; these sorts* (not *these sort*) *of distinctions are becoming blurred.*

kindergarten ('kɪndəˌgɑ:tᵊn) *n* a class or small school for young children, usually between the ages of four and six. [C19: from G, lit.: children's garden]

kind-hearted *adj* kindly, readily sympathetic.
▸ˌ**kind-'heartedly** *adv* ▸ˌ**kind-'heartedness** *n*

kindle ('kɪndᵊl) *vb* **kindles, kindling, kindled. 1** to set alight or start to burn. **2** to arouse or be aroused: *the project kindled his interest.* **3** to make or become bright. [C12: from ON *kynda,* infl. by ON *kyndill* candle]
▸**'kindler** *n*

kindling ('kɪndlɪŋ) *n* material for starting a fire, such as dry wood, straw, etc.

kindly ('kaɪndlɪ) *adj* **kindlier, kindliest. 1** having a sympathetic or warm-hearted nature. **2** motivated by warm and sympathetic feelings. **3** pleasant: *a kindly climate.* **4** *Arch.* natural; normal. ◆ *adv* **5** in a considerate or humane way. **6** with tolerance: *he kindly forgave my rudeness.* **7** cordially: *he greeted us kindly.* **8** please (often used to express

THESAURUS

kill *vb* **1** = **slay,** annihilate, assassinate, blow away *(sl., chiefly US),* bump off *(sl.),* butcher, destroy, dispatch, do away with, do in *(sl.),* eradicate, execute, exterminate, extirpate, knock off *(sl.),* liquidate, massacre, murder, neutralize, obliterate, slaughter, take out *(sl.),* take (someone's) life, waste *(inf.)* **7** *Informal* = **suppress,** cancel, cease, deaden, defeat, extinguish, halt, quash, quell, ruin, scotch, smother, stifle, still, stop, veto

killer *n* **1** = **assassin,** butcher, cut-throat, destroyer, executioner, exterminator, gunman, hit man *(sl.),* liquidator, murderer, slaughterer, slayer

killing *Informal adj* **1** = **tiring,** debilitating, enervating, exhausting, fatiguing, punishing **2** = **hilarious,** absurd, amusing, comical, ludicrous, uproarious **3** = **deadly,** death-dealing, deathly, fatal, lethal, mortal, murderous ◆ *n* **4** = **slaughter,** bloodshed, carnage, execution, extermination, fatality, homicide, manslaughter, massacre, murder, necktie party *(inf.),* slaying **5** = **bonanza,** bomb *(sl.),* cleanup *(inf.),* coup, gain, profit, success, windfall

killjoy *n* = **spoilsport,** dampener, damper, wet blanket *(inf.)*

kin *n* **1** = **family,** connections, kindred, kinsfolk, kinsmen, kith, people, relations, relatives

kind[1] *adj* **1, 3, 4** = **considerate,** affectionate, amiable, amicable, beneficent, benevolent, benign, bounteous, charitable, clement, compassionate, congenial, cordial, courteous, friendly, generous, gentle, good, gracious, humane, indulgent, kind-hearted, kindly, lenient, loving, mild, neighbourly, obliging, philanthropic, propitious, sympathetic, tender-hearted, thoughtful, understanding
Antonyms *adj* cruel, hard-hearted, harsh, heartless, merciless, severe, unkind, unsympathetic, vicious

kind[2] *n* **1** = **class,** brand, breed, family, genus, ilk, race, set, sort, species, stamp, type, variety **3** = **nature,** character, description, essence, habit, manner, mould, persuasion, sort, style, temperament, type

kind-hearted *adj* = **sympathetic,** altruistic, amicable, compassionate, considerate, generous, good-natured, gracious, helpful, humane, kind, tender, tender-hearted
Antonyms *adj* cold, cold-hearted, cruel, hard-hearted, harsh, heartless, selfish, severe, unkind, unsympathetic

kindle *vb* **1** = **set fire to,** fire, ignite, inflame, light **2** = **arouse,** agitate, animate, awaken, bestir, enkindle, exasperate, excite, foment, incite, induce, inflame, inspire, provoke, rouse, sharpen, stimulate, stir, thrill
Antonyms *vb* douse, extinguish, quell, quench

kindliness *n* **1, 2** = **kindness,** amiability, beneficence, benevolence, benignity, charity, compassion, friendliness, gentleness, humanity, kind-heartedness, sympathy

kindly *adj* **1, 2** = **benevolent,** affable, beneficial, benign, compassionate, cordial, favourable, genial, gentle, good-natured, hearty, helpful, kind, mild, pleasant, polite, sympathetic, warm ◆ *adv* **5, 7** = **benevolently,** agreeably, cordially, graciously, politely, tenderly, thoughtfully

impatience or formality): *will you kindly behave yourself!* **9** *Arch.* appropriately. **10 not take kindly to.** to react unfavourably towards.
▸**'kindliness** *n*

kindness ❶ ('kaɪndnɪs) *n* **1** the practice or quality of being kind. **2** a kind or helpful act.

kindred ❶ ('kɪndrɪd) *adj* **1** having similar or common qualities, origin, etc. **2** related by blood or marriage. **3 kindred spirit.** a person with whom one has something in common. ◆ *n* **4** relationship by blood. **5** similarity in character. **6** a person's relatives collectively. [C12 *kinred,* from KIN + *-red,* from OE *rǣden* rule, from *rǣdan* to rule]

kine (kaɪn) *n* (*functioning as pl*) an archaic word for cows or cattle. [OE *cȳna* of cows, from *cū* COW[1]]

kinematics (ˌkɪnɪ'mætɪks) *n* (*functioning as sing*) the study of the motion of bodies without reference to mass or force. [C19: from Gk *kinēma* movement; see CINEMA, -ICS]
▸**ˌkine'matic** *adj* ▸**ˌkine'matically** *adv*

kinematograph (ˌkɪnɪ'mætəˌgrɑːf) *n* a variant spelling of **cinematograph.**

kinesics (kɪ'niːsɪks) *n* (*functioning as sing*) the study of the role of body movements, such as winking, shrugging, etc., in communication.

kinesis (kɪ'niːsɪs, kaɪ-) *n Biol.* the nondirectional movement of an organism or cell in response to a stimulus, the rate of movement being dependent on the strength of the stimulus.

kinesthesia (ˌkɪnɪs'θiːzɪə) *n* the usual US spelling of **kinaesthesia.**

kinetic (kɪ'nɛtɪk) *adj* relating to or caused by motion. [C19: from Gk *kinētikos,* from *kinein* to move]
▸**ki'netically** *adv*

kinetic art *n* art, esp. sculpture, that moves or has moving parts.

kinetic energy *n* the energy of motion of a body equal to the work it would do if it were brought to rest. It is equal to the product of the increase of mass caused by motion times the square of the speed of light.

kinetics (kɪ'nɛtɪks, kaɪ-) *n* (*functioning as sing*) **1** another name for **dynamics** (sense 2). **2** the branch of mechanics, including both dynamics and kinematics, concerned with the study of bodies in motion. **3** the branch of dynamics that excludes the study of bodies at rest.

kinetic theory (of gases) *n* **the.** a theory of gases postulating that they consist of particles moving at random and undergoing elastic collisions.

kinfolk ('kɪnˌfəʊk) *pl n Chiefly US & Canad.* another word for **kinsfolk.**

king ❶ (kɪŋ) *n* **1** a male sovereign prince who is the official ruler of an independent state; monarch. Related adjs.: **royal, regal. 2a** a ruler or chief: *king of the fairies.* **2b** (*in combination*): *the pirate king.* **3** a person, animal, or thing considered as the best or most important of its kind. **4** any of four playing cards in a pack, one for each suit, bearing the picture of a king. **5** the most important chess piece. **6** *Draughts.* a piece that has moved entirely across the board and has been crowned, after which it may move backwards as well as forwards. **7 king of kings. 7a** God. **7b** a title of any of various oriental monarchs. ◆ *vb* (*tr*) **8** to make (someone) a king. **9 king it.** to act in a superior fashion. [OE *cyning*]
▸**'kingˌhood** *n* ▸**'kingˌlike** *adj*

kingbird ('kɪŋˌbɜːd) *n* any of several large American flycatchers.

kingbolt ('kɪŋˌbəʊlt) *or* **king rod** *n* **a** the pivot bolt that connects the body of a horse-drawn carriage to the front axle and provides the steering joint. **b** a similar bolt placed between a railway carriage and the bogies.

King Charles spaniel *n* a toy breed of spaniel with a short turned-up nose and a domed skull. [C17: after *Charles* II of England, who popularized the breed]

king cobra *n* a very large venomous tropical Asian snake that extends its neck into a hood when alarmed. Also called: **hamadryad.**

king crab *n* another name for the **horseshoe crab.**

kingcup ('kɪŋˌkʌp) *n Brit.* any of several yellow-flowered plants, esp. the marsh marigold.

kingdom ❶ ('kɪŋdəm) *n* **1** a territory, state, people, or community ruled or reigned over by a king or queen. **2** any of the three groups into which natural objects may be divided: the animal, plant, and mineral kingdoms. **3** *Biol.* any of the major categories into which living organisms are classified. Modern systems recognize five kingdoms: *Prokaryotae* (bacteria), *Protoctista* (algae, protozoans, etc.), *Fungi, Plantae,* and *Animalia.* **4** *Theol.* the eternal sovereignty of God. **5** an area of activity: *the kingdom of the mind.*

kingdom come *n* **1** the next world. **2** *Inf.* the end of the world (esp. in **until kingdom come**). **3** *Inf.* unconsciousness.

kingfish ('kɪŋˌfɪʃ) *n, pl* **kingfish** *or* **kingfishes. 1** a marine food and game fish occurring in warm American Atlantic coastal waters. **2** *Austral.* any of various types of trevally, mulloway, and barracouta. **3** any of various other large food fishes, esp. the Spanish mackerel.

kingfisher ('kɪŋˌfɪʃə) *n* a bird which has a greenish-blue and orange plumage, a large head, short tail, and long sharp bill, and feeds on fish. [C15: orig. *king's fisher*]

King James Version *or* **Bible** *n* **the.** another name for the **Authorized Version.**

kingklip ('kɪŋˌklɪp) *n* an edible eel-like marine fish. [from Afrik., from Du. *koning* king + *klip* rock]

kinglet ('kɪŋlɪt) *n* **1** *Often derog.* the king of a small or insignificant territory. **2** *US & Canad.* any of various small warblers having a black-edged yellow crown.

kingly ❶ ('kɪŋlɪ) *adj* **kinglier, kingliest. 1** appropriate to a king. **2** royal. ◆ *adv* **3** *Poetic or arch.* in a manner appropriate to a king.
▸**'kingliness** *n*

kingmaker ('kɪŋˌmeɪkə) *n* a person who has control over appointments to positions of authority.

king-of-arms *n, pl* **kings-of-arms. 1** the highest rank of heraldic officer. **2** a person holding this rank.

king of the castle *n Chiefly Brit.* a children's game in which each child attempts to stand alone on a mound by pushing other children off it.

king penguin *n* a large New Zealand subantarctic penguin.

kingpin ('kɪŋˌpɪn) *n* **1** the most important person in an organization. **2** Also called (Brit.): **swivel pin.** a pivot pin that provides a steering joint in a motor vehicle by securing the stub axle to the axle beam. **3** *Tenpin bowling.* the front pin in the triangular arrangement of the ten pins. **4** (in ninepins) the central pin in the diamond pattern of the nine pins.

king post *n* a vertical post connecting the apex of a triangular roof truss to the tie beam.

King's Bench *n* (when the sovereign is male) another name for **Queen's Bench.**

King's Counsel *n* (when the sovereign is male) another name for **Queen's Counsel.**

King's English *n* (esp. when the British sovereign is male) standard Southern British English.

king's evidence *n* (when the sovereign is male) another name for **queen's evidence.**

king's evil *n* **the.** *Pathol.* a former name for **scrofula.** [C14: from the belief that the king's touch would heal scrofula]

king's highway *n* (in Britain, esp. when the sovereign is male) any public road or right of way.

kingship ('kɪŋʃɪp) *n* **1** the position or authority of a king. **2** the skill of ruling as a king.

king-size *or* **king-sized** *adj* larger or longer than a standard size.

kinin ('kaɪnɪn) *n* **1** any of a group of polypeptides in the blood that cause dilation of the blood vessels. **2** *Bot.* another name for **cytokinin.** [C20: from Gk *kin(ēma)* motion + -IN]

kink ❶ (kɪŋk) *n* **1** a sharp twist or bend in a wire, rope, hair, etc. **2** a crick in the neck or similar muscular spasm. **3** a flaw or minor difficulty in some undertaking. **4** a flaw or idiosyncrasy of personality. [C17: from Du.: a curl in a rope]

kinkajou ('kɪŋkəˌdʒuː) *n* an arboreal fruit-eating mammal of Central and South America, with a long prehensile tail. Also called: **honey bear.** [C18: from F *quincajou,* from Algonquian]

kinky ❶ ('kɪŋkɪ) *adj* **kinkier, kinkiest. 1** *Sl.* given to unusual, abnormal, or deviant sexual practices. **2** *Inf.* exhibiting unusual idiosyncrasies of personality. **3** *Inf.* attractive or provocative in a bizarre way: *kinky clothes.* **4** tightly looped, as a wire or rope. **5** tightly curled, as hair.
▸**'kinkily** *adv* ▸**'kinkiness** *n*

kino ('kiːnəʊ) *n* a dark red resin obtained from various tropical plants, esp. an Indian leguminous tree, used as an astringent and in tanning. [C18: of West African origin]

kin selection *n Biol.* natural selection resulting from altruistic behaviour by animals towards members of the same species, esp. their offspring or other relatives.

kinsfolk ❶ ('kɪnzˌfəʊk) *pl n* one's family or relatives.

kinship ❶ ('kɪnʃɪp) *n* **1** blood relationship. **2** the state of having common characteristics.

THESAURUS

Antonyms *adj* ≠ **benevolent:** cruel, harsh, malevolent, malicious, mean, severe, spiteful, unkindly, unsympathetic ◆ *adv* ≠ **benevolently:** cruelly, harshly, malevolently, maliciously, meanly, spitefully, unkindly, unsympathetically

kindness *n* **1** = **goodwill**, affection, amiability, beneficence, benevolence, charity, clemency, compassion, decency, fellow-feeling, generosity, gentleness, goodness, grace, hospitality, humanity, indulgence, kindliness, magnanimity, patience, philanthropy, tenderness, tolerance, understanding **2** = **good deed**, aid, assistance, benefaction, bounty, favour, generosity, help, service
Antonyms *n* ≠ **goodwill:** animosity, callousness, cold-heartedness, cruelty, hard-heartedness, heartlessness, ill will, inhumanity, malevolence, malice, misanthropy, viciousness

kindred *adj* **1, 2** = **similar**, affiliated, akin, allied, cognate, congenial, corresponding, kin, like, matching, related ◆ *n* **4** = **relationship**, affinity, consanguinity **6** = **family**, connections, flesh, kin, kinsfolk, kinsmen, lineage, relations, relatives

king *n* **1, 2** = **ruler**, crowned head, emperor, majesty, monarch, overlord, prince, sovereign

kingdom *n* **1** = **country**, commonwealth, division, nation, province, realm, state, territory, tract **5** = **domain**, area, field, province, sphere, territory

kingly *adj* **2** = **royal**, imperial, monarchical, regal, sovereign

kink *n* **1** = **twist**, bend, coil, corkscrew, crimp, entanglement, frizz, knot, tangle, wrinkle **3** = **flaw**, complication, defect, difficulty, hitch, imperfection, knot, tangle **4** = **quirk**, crotchet, eccentricity, fetish, foible, idiosyncrasy, singularity, vagary, whim

kinky *adj* **1** *Slang* = **perverted**, degenerated, depraved, deviant, licentious, unnatural, warped **2** *Informal* = **weird**, bizarre, eccentric, odd, oddball (*inf.*), off-the-wall (*sl.*), outlandish, outré, peculiar, queer, quirky, strange, unconventional **4, 5** = **twisted**, coiled, crimped, curled, curly, frizzled, frizzy, tangled

kinsfolk *pl n* = **family**, connections, kin, kindred, kinsmen, relations, relatives

kinship *n* **1** = **relation**, blood relationship, con-

kinsman ❶ ('kɪnzmən) *n, pl* **kinsmen.** a blood relation or a relation by marriage.
▸ **'kins,woman** *fem n*

kiosk ❶ ('kiːɒsk) *n* **1** a small sometimes movable booth from which cigarettes, newspapers, sweets, etc., are sold. **2** *Chiefly Brit.* a telephone box. **3** (in Turkey, Iran, etc.) a light open-sided pavilion. [C17: from F *kiosque* bandstand, from Turkish, from Persian *kūshk* pavilion]

kip[1] (kɪp) *Brit. sl.* ◆ *n* **1** sleep or slumber: *to get some kip.* **2** a bed or lodging. ◆ *vb* **kips, kipping, kipped.** (*intr*) **3** to sleep or take a nap. **4** (foll. by *down*) to prepare for sleep. [C18: from ?]

kip[2] (kɪp) *or* **kipskin** *n* the hide of a young animal, esp. a calf or lamb. [C16: from MDu. *kipp*]

kip[3] (kɪp) *n Austral.* a small board used to spin the coins in two-up. [C19: from Brit. dialect *kep* to catch]

kipper ('kɪpə) *n* **1** a fish, esp. a herring, that has been cleaned, salted, and smoked. **2** a male salmon during the spawning season. ◆ *vb* **3** (*tr*) to cure (herrings or other fish) by salting and smoking. [OE *cypera,* ?from *coper* COPPER[1], referring to its colour]

kir (kɜː; *French* kir) *n* a drink made from dry white wine and cassis. [after Canon F. *Kir* (1876–1968), mayor of Dijon, who is said to have invented it]

kirby grip ('kɜːbɪ) *n Trademark.* a type of hairgrip with one straight and one wavy side.

kirk (kɜːk) *n* **1** a Scottish word for **church. 2** a Scottish church. [C12: from ON *kirkja,* from OE *cirice* CHURCH]

kirk session *n* the lowest court of the Presbyterian Church.

kirmess ('kɜːmɪs) *n* a variant spelling of **kermis.**

Kirsch (kɪəʃ) *or* **Kirschwasser** ('kɪəʃ,vɑːsə) *n* a brandy distilled from cherries, made chiefly in the Black Forest in Germany. [G *Kirschwasser* cherry water]

kirtle ('kɜːtᵊl) *n Arch.* **1** a woman's skirt or dress. **2** a man's coat. [OE *cyrtel,* prob. from *cyrtan* to shorten, ult. from L *curtus* cut short]

kismet ❶ ('kɪzmɛt, 'kɪs-) *n* **1** *Islam.* the will of Allah. **2** fate or destiny. [C19: from Turkish, from Persian *qismat,* from Ar. *qasama* he divided]

kiss ❶ (kɪs) *vb* **1** (*tr*) to touch with the lips or press the lips against as an expression of love, greeting, respect, etc. **2** (*intr*) to join lips with another person in an act of love or desire. **3** to touch (each other) lightly. **4** *Billiards.* (of balls) to touch (each other) lightly while moving. ◆ *n* **5** a caress with the lips. **6** a light touch. [OE *cyssan,* from *coss*]
▸ **'kissable** *adj*

kissagram ('kɪsə,græm) *n* a greetings service in which a person is employed to present greetings by kissing the person celebrating. [C20: blend of *kiss* and *telegram*]

kiss-and-tell *n* (*modifier*) denoting the practice of publicizing one's former sexual relationship with a celebrity, esp. in the tabloid press: *a kiss-and-tell interview.*

kiss curl *n Brit.* a circular curl of hair pressed flat against the cheek or forehead.

kisser ('kɪsə) *n* **1** a person who kisses, esp. in a way specified. **2** a slang word for **mouth** or **face.**

kissing gate *n* a gate set in a U- or V-shaped enclosure, allowing only one person to pass through at a time.

kiss of life *n* **the.** mouth-to-mouth resuscitation in which a person blows gently into the mouth of an unconscious person, allowing the lungs to deflate after each blow.

kist (kɪst) *n S. African.* a large wooden chest in which linen is stored, esp. one used to store a bride's trousseau. [from Afrik., from Du.: CHEST]

kit[1] ❶ (kɪt) *n* **1** a set of tools, supplies, etc., for use together or for a purpose: *a first-aid kit.* **2** the case or container for such a set. **3** a set of pieces of equipment sold ready to be assembled. **4a** clothing and other personal effects, esp. those of a traveller or soldier: *safari kit.* **4b** *Inf.* clothing in general (esp. in the phrase **get one's kit off**). ◆ See also **kit out.** [C14: from MDu. *kitte* tankard]

kit[2] (kɪt) *n NZ.* a string bag for shopping. [from Maori *kete*]

kitbag ('kɪt,bæg) *n* a canvas or other bag for a serviceman's kit.

kitchen ❶ ('kɪtʃɪn) *n* **a** a room or part of a building equipped for preparing and cooking food. **b** (*as modifier*): *a kitchen table.* [OE *cycene,* ult. from LL *coquīna,* from L *coquere* to COOK]

kitchen cabinet *n* a group of unofficial advisers to a political leader, esp. when considered to be more influential than the offical cabinet.

kitchenette (,kɪtʃɪ'nɛt) *n* a small kitchen or part of a room equipped for use as a kitchen.

kitchen garden *n* a garden where vegetables and sometimes also fruit are grown.

kitchen midden *n Archaeol.* the site of a large mound of domestic refuse marking a prehistoric settlement.

kitchen sink *n* **1** a sink in a kitchen for washing dishes, vegetables, etc. **2** (*modifier*) denoting a type of drama or painting of the 1950s depicting sordid reality.

kitchen tea *n Austral. & NZ.* a party held before a wedding to which guests bring items of kitchen equipment as wedding presents.

kitchenware ('kɪtʃɪn,wɛə) *n* pots and pans, knives, forks, spoons, etc., used in the kitchen.

kite (kaɪt) *n* **1** a light frame covered with a thin material flown in the wind at the end of a length of string. **2** *Brit. sl.* an aeroplane. **3** (*pl*) *Naut.* any of various light sails set in addition to the working sails of a vessel. **4** a bird of prey having a long forked tail and long broad wings and usually preying on small mammals and insects. **5** *Arch.* a person who preys on others. **6** *Commerce.* a negotiable paper drawn without any actual transaction or assets and designed to obtain money on credit, give an impression of affluence, etc. ◆ *vb* **kites, kiting, kited. 7** to issue (fictitious papers) to obtain credit or money. **8** (*intr*) to soar and glide. [OE *cȳta*]

Kite mark *n Brit.* the official mark of quality and reliability, in the form of a kite, on articles approved by the British Standards Institution.

kith (kɪθ) *n* **kith and kin.** one's friends and relations. [OE *cȳthth,* from *cūth;* see UNCOUTH]

kit out ❶ *or* **up** *vb* **kits, kitting, kitted.** (*tr, adv*) *Chiefly Brit.* to provide with (a kit of personal effects and necessities).

kitsch (kɪtʃ) *n* tawdry, vulgarized, or pretentious art, literature, etc., usually with popular appeal. [C20: from G]
▸ **'kitschy** *adj*

kitten ('kɪtᵊn) *n* **1** a young cat. **2 have kittens.** *Brit. inf.* to react with disapproval, anxiety, etc.: *she had kittens when she got the bill.* ◆ *vb* **3** (of cats) to give birth to (young). [C14: from OF *caton,* from CAT; prob. infl. by ME *kiteling*]

kittenish ('kɪtᵊnɪʃ) *adj* **1** like a kitten; lively. **2** (of a woman) flirtatious, esp. coyly flirtatious.

kittiwake ('kɪtɪ,weɪk) *n* either of two oceanic gulls having pale grey black-tipped wings and a square-cut tail. [C17: imit.]

kitty[1] ('kɪtɪ) *n, pl* **kitties.** a diminutive or affectionate name for a **kitten** or **cat.** [C18]

kitty[2] ('kɪtɪ) *n, pl* **kitties. 1** the pool of bets in certain gambling games. **2** any shared fund of money. **3** (in bowls) the jack. [C19: see KIT[1]]

kitty-cornered *adj* a variant of **cater-cornered.**

Kiwano (kɪ'wɑːnəʊ) *n, pl* **Kiwanos.** *Trademark.* an edible oval fruit of the passionflower family, having a golden spiky skin, juicy green pulp and many seeds.

kiwi ('kiːwiː) *n, pl* **kiwis. 1** a nocturnal flightless New Zealand bird having a long beak, stout legs, and weakly barbed feathers. **2** *Inf. except in NZ.* a New Zealander. **3** *NZ inf.* a lottery. [C19: from Maori, imit.: NZ sense from the *Golden Kiwi Lottery*]

kiwi fruit *n* the fuzzy edible fruit of an Asian climbing plant. Also called: **Chinese gooseberry.**

KKK *abbrev. for* Ku Klux Klan.

Klan (klæn) *n* (usually preceded by *the*) short for **Ku Klux Klan.**
▸ **'Klanism** *n*

klaxon ('klæksᵊn) *n* a type of loud horn formerly used on motor vehicles. [C20: former trademark]

Kleenex ('kliːnɛks) *n, pl* **Kleenex** *or* **Kleenexes.** *Trademark.* a kind of soft paper tissue, used esp. as a handkerchief.

Klein bottle (klaɪn) *n Maths.* a three-dimensional surface formed by inserting the smaller end of an open tapered tube through the surface of the tube and making this end stretch to fit the other end. [after Felix *Klein* (1849–1925), G mathematician]

kleptomania (,klɛptəʊ'meɪnɪə) *n Psychol.* a strong impulse to steal, esp. when there is no obvious motivation. [C19: *klepto-* from Gk, from *kleptein* to steal + -MANIA]
▸ **,klepto'mani,ac** *n*

klieg light (kliːg) *n* an intense carbon-arc light used in producing films. [C20: after John H. *Kliegl* (1869–1959) & his brother Anton (1872–1927), German-born American inventors]

klipspringer ('klɪp,sprɪŋə) *n* a small agile antelope inhabiting rocky regions of Africa south of the Sahara. [C18: from Afrik., from Du. *klip* rock + *springer,* from *springen* to SPRING]

kloof (kluːf) *n* a mountain pass or gorge in southern Africa. [C18: from Afrik., from MDu. *clove* a cleft]

klystron ('klɪstrɒn) *n* an electron tube for the amplification or generation of microwaves. [C20: *klys-,* from Gk *kluzein* to wash over + -TRON]

km *symbol for* kilometre.

K-meson *n* another name for **kaon.**

knack ❶ (næk) *n* **1** a skilful, ingenious, or resourceful way of doing something. **2** a particular talent or aptitude, esp. an intuitive one. [C14: prob. var. of *knak* sharp knock, imit.]

knacker ❶ ('nækə) *Brit.* ◆ *n* **1** a person who buys up old horses for slaughter. **2** a person who buys up old buildings and breaks them up

THESAURUS

sanguinity, kin, ties of blood **2** = **similarity**, affinity, alliance, association, bearing, connection, correspondence, relationship

kinsman *n* = **relative**, blood relative, fellow clansman, fellow tribesman, relation

kiosk *n* **1** = **booth**, bookstall, counter, newsstand, stall, stand

kismet *n* **2** = **fate**, destiny, fortune, karma, lot, portion, preordination, Providence

kiss *vb* **1, 2** = **osculate**, buss (*arch.*), canoodle (*sl.*), greet, neck (*inf.*), peck (*inf.*), salute, smooch (*inf.*) **3** = **brush**, caress, glance, graze, scrape, touch ◆ *n* **5** = **osculation**, buss, peck (*inf.*), smacker (*sl.*)

kit[1] *n* **1** = **equipment**, accoutrements, apparatus, effects, gear, impedimenta, implements, instruments, outfit, paraphernalia, provisions, rig, supplies, tackle, tools, trappings, utensils

kitchen *n* = **cookhouse**, galley, kitchenette

kit out *vb* = **equip**, accoutre, arm, deck out, fit out, fix up, furnish, outfit, provide with, supply

knack *n* **1, 2** = **skill**, ability, adroitness, aptitude, bent, capacity, dexterity, expertise, expertness, facility, flair, forte, genius, gift, handiness, ingenuity, propensity, quickness, skilfulness, talent, trick
Antonyms *n* awkwardness, clumsiness, disability, ineptitude

knackered *adj* **4** *Slang* = **exhausted**, all in (*sl.*),

for scrap. **3** *Irish sl.* a despicable person. ◆ *vb* **4** (*tr; usually passive*) *Sl.* to tire. [C16: prob. from *nacker* saddler, prob. of Scand. origin]
▸ **'knackery** *n*

knacker's yard *n Brit.* **1** a slaughterhouse for horses. **2** *Inf.* destruction because of being beyond all usefulness (esp. in the phrase **ready for the knacker's yard**).

knag (næg) *n* **1** a knot in wood. **2** a wooden peg. [C15: ?from Low G *knagge*]

knap (næp) *vb* **knaps, knapping, knapped.** (*tr*) *Dialect.* to hit or chip. [C15 (in the sense: to strike with a sharp sound): imit.]
▸ **'knapper** *n*

knapping hammer *n* a hammer used for breaking and shaping stones.

knapsack ('næp,sæk) *n* a canvas or leather bag carried strapped on the back or shoulder. [C17: from Low G, prob. from *knappen* to bite + *sack* bag]

knapweed ('næp,wi:d) *n* any of several plants having purplish thistle-like flowers. [C15 *knopwed*, from *knop* of Gmc origin + WEED]

knar (nɑ:) *n* a variant of **knur.** [C14 *knarre* rough stone, knot on a tree]

knave Ⓣ (neɪv) *n* **1** *Arch.* a dishonest man. **2** another word for **jack** (the playing card). **3** *Obs.* a male servant. [OE *cnafa*]
▸ **'knavish** *adj*

knavery Ⓣ ('neɪvərɪ) *n, pl* **knaveries. 1** a deceitful or dishonest act. **2** dishonest conduct; trickery.

knead Ⓣ (ni:d) *vb* (*tr*) **1** to work and press (a soft substance, such as bread dough) into a uniform mixture with the hands. **2** to squeeze or press with the hands. **3** to make by kneading. [OE *cnedan*]
▸ **'kneader** *n*

knee (ni:) *n* **1** the joint of the human leg connecting the tibia and fibula with the femur and protected in front by the patella. Technical name: **genu. 2a** the area surrounding and above this joint. **2b** (*modifier*) reaching or covering the knee: *knee socks.* **3** the upper surface of a sitting person's thigh: *the child sat on her mother's knee.* **4** a corresponding or similar part in other vertebrates. **5** the part of a garment that covers the knee. **6** anything resembling a knee in action or shape. **7** any of the hollow rounded protuberances that project upwards from the roots of the swamp cypress. **8 bend** *or* **bow the knee.** to kneel or submit. **9 bring someone to his knees.** to force someone into submission. ◆ *vb* **knees, kneeing, kneed. 10** (*tr*) to strike, nudge, or push with the knee. [OE *cnēow*]

kneecap ('ni:,kæp) *n* **1** *Anat.* a nontechnical name for **patella.** ◆ *vb* **kneecaps, kneecapping, kneecapped.** (*tr*) **2** (esp. of certain terrorist groups) to shoot (a person) in the kneecap.

knee-deep *adj* **1** so deep as to reach or cover the knees. **2** (*postpositive;* often foll. by *in*) **2a** sunk or covered to the knees: *knee-deep in sand.* **2b** deeply involved: *knee-deep in work.*

knee-high *adj* another word for **knee-deep** (sense 1).

kneehole ('ni:,həʊl) *n* a space for the knees, esp. under a desk.

knee jerk *n* **1** *Physiol.* an outward reflex kick of the lower leg caused by a sharp tap on the tendon just below the kneecap. ◆ *modifier.* **kneejerk. 2** made or occurring as a predictable and automatic response, without thought: *a kneejerk reaction.*

kneel Ⓣ (ni:l) *vb* **kneels, kneeling, knelt** *or* **kneeled. 1** (*intr*) to rest, fall, or support oneself on one's knees. ◆ *n* **2** the act or position of kneeling. [OE *cnēowlian;* see KNEE]
▸ **'kneeler** *n*

knees-up *n, pl* **knees-ups.** *Brit. inf.* a lively party. [C20: after popular song *Knees-up, Mother Brown!*]

knell Ⓣ (nɛl) *n* **1** the sound of a bell rung to announce a death or a funeral. **2** something that precipitates or indicates death or destruction. ◆ *vb* **3** (*intr*) to ring a knell. **4** (*tr*) to proclaim by or as if by a tolling bell. [OE *cnyll*]

knelt (nɛlt) *vb* a past tense and past participle of **kneel.**

Knesset ('knɛsɪt) *n* the representative assembly of Israel. [C20: Heb., lit.: gathering]

knew (nju:) *vb* the past tense of **know.**

knickerbocker glory ('nɪkə,bɒkə) *n* a rich confection consisting of layers of ice cream, jelly, cream, and fruit, served in a tall glass.

knickerbockers ('nɪkə,bɒkəz) *pl n* baggy breeches fastened with a band at the knee or above the ankle. Also called (US): **knickers.** [C19: regarded as the traditional dress of the Du. settlers in America; after Diedrich *Knickerbocker,* fictitious author of Washington Irving's *History of New York* (1809)]

knickers Ⓣ ('nɪkəz) *pl n* an undergarment for women covering the lower trunk and sometimes the thighs and having separate legs or leg-holes. [C19: contraction of KNICKERBOCKERS]

knick-knack Ⓣ *or* **nick-nack** ('nɪk,næk) *n* **1** a cheap ornament. **2** an ornamental article of furniture, dress, etc. [C17: by reduplication from *knack,* in obs. sense: toy]

knife Ⓣ (naɪf) *n, pl* **knives** (naɪvz). **1** a cutting instrument consisting of a sharp-edged blade of metal fitted into a handle or onto a machine. **2** a similar instrument used as a weapon. **3 have one's knife in someone.** to have a grudge against someone. **4 under the knife.** undergoing a surgical operation. ◆ *vb* **knifes, knifing, knifed.** (*tr*) **5** to stab or kill with a knife. **6** to betray or depose in an underhand way. [OE *cnīf*]
▸ **'knife,like** *adj*

knife edge *n* **1** the sharp cutting edge of a knife. **2** any sharp edge, esp. an arête. **3** a sharp-edged wedge of hard material on which the beam of a balance pivots. **4** a critical point.

knight (naɪt) *n* **1** (in medieval Europe) **1a** (originally) a person who served his lord as a mounted and heavily armed soldier. **1b** (later) a gentleman with the military and social standing of this rank. **2** (in modern times) a person invested by a sovereign with a nonhereditary rank and dignity usually in recognition of personal services, achievements, etc. **3** a chess piece, usually shaped like a horse's head. **4** a heroic champion of a lady or of a cause or principle. **5** a member of the Roman class below the senators. ◆ *vb* **6** (*tr*) to make (a person) a knight. [OE *cniht* servant]

knight errant *n, pl* **knights errant.** (esp. in medieval romance) a knight who wanders in search of deeds of courage, chivalry, etc.
▸ **knight errantry** *n*

knighthood ('naɪthʊd) *n* **1** the order, dignity, or rank of a knight. **2** the qualities of a knight.

knightly Ⓣ ('naɪtlɪ) *adj* of, relating to, resembling, or befitting a knight.
▸ **'knightliness** *n*

knight of the road *n Inf. or facetious.* **1** a tramp. **2** a commercial traveller. **3** a lorry driver.

Knights Hospitallers *pl n* a military Christian religious order founded about the time of the first crusade (1096–99).

Knight Templar *n, pl* **Knights Templars** *or* **Knights Templar.** another term for **Templar.**

kniphofia (nɪf'əʊfɪə) *n* the Latin name for **red-hot poker.** [C19: after Johann Hieronymus *Kniphof* (1704–63), G professor of medicine]

knit Ⓣ (nɪt) *vb* **knits, knitting, knitted** *or* **knit. 1** to make (a garment, etc.) by looping and entwining (wool) by hand by means of long eyeless needles (**knitting needles**) or by machine (**knitting machine**). **2** to join or be joined together closely. **3** to draw (the brows) together or (of the brows) to come together, as in frowning or concentrating. **4** (of a broken bone) to join together; heal. ◆ *n* **5a** a fabric made by knitting. **5b** (*in combination*): *a heavy knit.* [OE *cnyttan* to tie in]
▸ **'knitter** *n*

knitting ('nɪtɪŋ) *n* knitted work or the process of producing it.

knitwear ('nɪt,wɛə) *n* knitted clothes, esp. sweaters.

knives (naɪvz) *n* the plural of **knife.**

knob Ⓣ (nɒb) *n* **1** a rounded projection from a surface, such as a lump on a tree trunk. **2** a handle of a door, drawer, etc., esp. one that is rounded. **3** a round hill or knoll. ◆ *vb* **knobs, knobbing, knobbed. 4** (*tr*) to supply or ornament with knobs. **5** (*intr*) to bulge. [C14: from MLow G *knobbe* knot in wood]
▸ **'knobbly** *adj* ▸ **'knobby** *adj* ▸ **'knob,like** *adj*

knobkerrie ('nɒb,kɛrɪ), **knobkierie,** *or* **knobstick** *n* a stick with a round knob at the end, used as a club or missile by South African tribesmen. [C19: from Afrik., from *knop* knob, from MDu. *cnoppe* + *kierie* stick, from Khoikhoi *kirri*]

knock Ⓣ (nɒk) *vb* **1** (*tr*) to give a blow or push to. **2** (*intr*) to rap sharply with the knuckles, a hard object, etc.: *to knock at the door.* **3** (*tr*) to make or force by striking: *to knock a hole in the wall.* **4** (*intr;* usually foll. by *against*) to collide (with). **5** (*tr*) to bring into a certain condition by hitting: *to knock someone unconscious.* **6** (*tr*) *Inf.* to criticize adversely. **7** (*intr*) Also: **pink.** (of an internal-combustion engine) to emit a metallic noise as a result of faulty combustion. **8** (*intr*) (of a bearing, esp. one in

THESAURUS

beat (*sl.*), buggered (*Brit. sl.*), dead beat (*sl.*), dead tired, debilitated, dog-tired (*inf.*), done in (*inf.*), drained, enervated, prostrated, ready to drop, tired out, worn out, zonked (*sl.*)

knave *n* **1** *Archaic* = **rogue**, blackguard, bounder (*old-fashioned Brit. sl.*), cheat, rapscallion, rascal, reprobate, rotter (*sl., chiefly Brit.*), scallywag (*inf.*), scamp, scapegrace, scoundrel, scumbag (*sl.*), swindler, varlet (*arch.*), villain

knavery *n* **1, 2** = **dishonesty**, chicanery, corruption, deceit, deception, double-dealing, duplicity, fraud, imposture, rascality, roguery, trickery, villainy

knavish *adj* **1** *Archaic* = **dishonest**, deceitful, deceptive, dishonourable, fraudulent, lying, rascally, roguish, scoundrelly, tricky, unprincipled, unscrupulous, villainous

Antonyms *adj* honest, honourable, noble, principled, trustworthy

knead *vb* **1, 2** = **squeeze**, blend, form, manipulate, massage, mould, press, rub, shape, stroke, work

kneel *vb* **1** = **genuflect**, bow, bow down, curtsey, curtsy, get down on one's knees, kowtow, make obeisance, stoop

knell *n* **1** = **ringing**, chime, peal, sound, toll ◆ *vb* **3, 4** = **ring**, announce, chime, herald, peal, resound, sound, toll

knickers *pl n* = **underwear**, bloomers, briefs, drawers, panties, smalls

knick-knack *n* **1** = **trinket**, bagatelle, bauble, bibelot, bric-a-brac, gewgaw, gimcrack, kickshaw, plaything, trifle

knife *n* **1** = **blade**, cutter, cutting tool ◆ *vb* **5** = **cut**, impale, lacerate, pierce, slash, stab, wound

knightly *adj* = **chivalrous**, courageous, courtly, gallant, gracious, heroic, noble, valiant

knit *vb* **1, 2, 4** = **join**, affix, ally, bind, connect, contract, fasten, heal, interlace, intertwine, link, loop, mend, secure, tie, unite, weave **3** = **wrinkle**, crease, furrow, knot, pucker

knob *n* **1** = **lump**, boss, bulk, bump, bunch, hump, knot, knurl, nub, projection, protrusion, protuberance, snag, stud, swell, swelling, tumour

knock *vb* **1, 2** = **hit**, belt (*inf.*), buffet, chin (*sl.*), clap, cuff, deck, lay one on (*sl.*), punch, rap, slap, smack, smite (*arch.*), strike, thump, thwack **6** *Informal* = **criticize**, abuse, asperse, belittle, carp, cavil, censure, condemn, denigrate, deprecate, disparage, find fault, have a an engine) to emit a regular characteristic sound as a result of wear. **9** *Brit. sl.* to have sexual intercourse with (a person). **10 knock (a person) into the middle of next week.** *Inf.* to hit (a person) with a very heavy blow. **11 knock on the head. 11a** to daze or kill (a person) by striking on the head. **11b** to prevent the further development of (a plan). ◆ *n* **12a** a blow, push, or rap: *he gave the table a knock.* **12b** the sound so caused. **13** the sound of knocking in an engine or bearing. **14** *Inf.* a misfortune, rebuff, or setback. **15** *Inf.* criticism. ◆ See also **knock about, knock back,** etc. [OE *cnocian,* imit.]

knock about 🅣 *or* **around** *vb* **1** (*intr, adv*) to wander about aimlessly. **2** (*intr, prep*) to travel about, esp. as resulting in varied experience: *he's knocked about the world.* **3** (*intr, adv;* foll. by *with*) to associate. **4** (*tr, adv*) to treat brutally: *he knocks his wife about.* **5** (*tr, adv*) to consider or discuss informally. ◆ *adj* **knockabout. 6** tough; boisterous: *knockabout farce.*

knock back *vb* (*tr, adv*) *Inf.* **1** to drink, esp. quickly. **2** to cost. **3** to reject or refuse. **4** to shock; disconcert. ◆ *n* **knock-back. 5** *Sl.* a refusal or rejection. **6** *Prison sl.* failure to obtain parole.

knock down 🅣 *vb* (*tr, adv*) **1** to strike to the ground with a blow, as in boxing. **2** (in auctions) to declare (an article) sold. **3** to demolish. **4** to dismantle for ease of transport. **5** *Inf.* to reduce (a price, etc.). **6** *Austral. sl.* to spend (a cheque). **7** *Austral. sl.* to drink. ◆ *adj* **knockdown.** (*prenominal*) **8** powerful: *a knockdown blow.* **9** *Chiefly Brit.* cheap: *a knockdown price.* **10** easily dismantled: *knockdown furniture.*

knocker ('nɒkə) *n* **1** an object, usually made of metal, attached to a door by a hinge and used for knocking. **2** *Inf.* a person who finds fault or disparages. **3** (*usually pl*) *Sl.* a female breast. **4** a person or thing that knocks. **5 on the knocker.** *Inf.* promptly: *you pay on the knocker here.*

knocking copy *n* publicity material designed to denigrate a competing product.

knocking-shop *n Brit.* a slang word for **brothel.**

knock-knee *n* a condition in which the legs are bent inwards causing the knees to touch when standing.
▸ˌ**knock-'kneed** *adj*

knock off 🅣 *vb* (*mainly adv*) **1** (*intr, also prep*) *Inf.* to finish work: *we knocked off an hour early.* **2** (*tr*) *Inf.* to make or do hastily or easily: *to knock off a novel in a week.* **3** (*tr; also prep*) *Inf.* to reduce the price of (an article). **4** (*tr*) *Sl.* to kill. **5** (*tr*) *Sl.* to rob or steal: *to knock off a bank.* **6** (*tr*) *Sl.* to stop doing something, used as a command: *knock it off!*

knock-on *Rugby.* ◆ *n* **1** the infringement of playing the ball forward with the hand or arm. ◆ *vb* **knock on.** (*adv*) **2** to play (the ball) forward with the hand or arm.

knock-on effect *n* the indirect result of an action: *the number of redundancies was not great but there were as many again from the knock-on effect.*

knockout 🅣 ('nɒkˌaʊt) *n* **1** the act of rendering unconscious. **2** a blow that renders an opponent unconscious. **3a** a competition in which competitors are eliminated progressively. **3b** (*as modifier*): *a knockout contest.* **4** *Inf.* a person or thing that is overwhelmingly impressive or attractive: *she's a knockout.* ◆ *vb* **knock out.** (*tr, adv*) **5** to render unconscious, esp. by a blow. **6** *Boxing.* to defeat (an opponent) by a knockout. **7** to destroy or injure badly. **8** to eliminate, esp. in a knockout competition. **9** *Inf.* to overwhelm or amaze: *I was knocked out by that new song.* **10 knock the bottom out of.** *Inf.* to invalidate (an argument).

knockout drops *pl n Sl.* a drug secretly put into someone's drink to cause stupefaction. ◆ See also **Mickey Finn.**

knock up *vb* (*adv, mainly tr*) **1** Also: **knock together.** *Inf.* to assemble quickly: *to knock up a set of shelves.* **2** *Brit. inf.* to waken; rouse: *to knock someone up early.* **3** *Sl.* to make pregnant. **4** *Brit. inf.* to exhaust. **5** *Cricket.* to score (runs). **6** (*intr*) *Tennis, squash, etc.* to practise, esp. before a match. ◆ *n* **knock-up. 7** a practice session at tennis, squash, etc.

knoll 🅣 (nəʊl) *n* a small rounded hill. [OE *cnoll*]
▸'**knolly** *adj*

knot[1] 🅣 (nɒt) *n* **1** any of various fastenings formed by looping and tying a piece of rope, cord, etc., in upon itself or to another piece of rope. **2** a prescribed method of tying a particular knot. **3** a tangle, as in hair or string. **4** a decorative bow, as of ribbon. **5** a small cluster or huddled group. **6** a tie or bond: *the marriage knot.* **7** a difficult problem. **8a** a hard mass of wood where a branch joins the trunk of a tree. **8b** a cross section of this visible on a piece of timber. **9** a sensation of constriction, caused by tension or nervousness: *his stomach was tying itself in knots.* **10** *Pathol.* a lump of vessels or fibres formed in a part, as in a muscle. **11** a unit of velocity used by ships and aircraft, being one nautical mile (about 1.15 statute miles or 1.85 km) per hour. **12 at a rate of knots.** very fast. **13 tie (someone) in knots.** to completely perplex (someone). ◆ *vb* **knots, knotting, knotted. 14** (*tr*) to tie or fasten in a knot. **15** to form or cause to form into a knot. **16** (*tr*) to entangle or become entangled. **17** (*tr*) to make (an article or design) by tying thread in ornamental knots. [OE *cnotta*]
▸'**knotted** *adj* ▸'**knotter** *n* ▸'**knotless** *adj*

knot[2] (nɒt) *n* a small northern sandpiper with a short bill and grey plumage. [C15: from ?]

knot garden *n* (esp. formerly) a formal garden of intricate design.

knotgrass ('nɒtˌgrɑːs) *n* **1** Also called: **allseed.** a weed whose small green flowers produce numerous seeds. **2** any of several related plants.

knothole ('nɒtˌhəʊl) *n* a hole in a piece of wood where a knot has been.

knotty 🅣 ('nɒtɪ) *adj* **knottier, knottiest. 1** (of wood, rope, etc.) full of or characterized by knots. **2** extremely difficult or intricate.

knout (naʊt) *n* a stout whip used formerly in Russia as an instrument of punishment. [C17: from Russian *knut,* of Scand. origin]

know 🅣 (nəʊ) *vb* **knows, knowing, knew, known.** (*mainly tr*) **1** (*also intr; may take a clause as object*) to be or feel certain of the truth or accuracy of (a fact, etc.). **2** to be acquainted or familiar with: *she's known him five years.* **3** to have a familiarity or grasp of: *he knows French.* **4** (*also intr; may take a clause as object*) to understand, be aware of, or perceive (facts, etc.): *he knows the answer now.* **5** (foll. by *how*) to be sure or aware of (how to be or do something). **6** to experience, esp. deeply: *to know poverty.* **7** to be intelligent, informed, or sensible enough (to do something). **8** (*may take a clause as object*) to be able to distinguish or discriminate. **9** *Arch.* to have sexual intercourse with. **10 know what's what.** to know how one thing or things in general work. **11 you never know.** things are uncertain. ◆ *n* **12 in the know.** *Inf.* aware or informed. [OE *gecnāwan*]
▸'**knowable** *adj* ▸'**knower** *n*

know-all 🅣 *n Inf., disparaging.* a person who pretends or appears to know a great deal.

know-how 🅣 *n Inf.* **1** ingenuity, aptitude, or skill. **2** commercial and saleable knowledge of how to do a particular thing.

knowing 🅣 ('nəʊɪŋ) *adj* **1** suggesting secret knowledge. **2** wise, shrewd, or clever. **3** deliberate. ◆ *n* **4 there is no knowing.** one cannot tell.
▸'**knowingly** *adv* ▸'**knowingness** *n*

knowledge 🅣 ('nɒlɪdʒ) *n* **1** the facts or experiences known by a person or group of people. **2** the state of knowing. **3** consciousness or familiarity gained by experience or learning. **4** erudition or informed learning. **5** specific information about a subject. **6 to my knowledge. 6a** as I understand it. **6b** as I know.

knowledgeable 🅣 *or* **knowledgable** ('nɒlɪdʒəbᵊl) *adj* possessing or indicating much knowledge.
▸'**knowledgeably** *or* '**knowledgably** *adv*

THESAURUS

go (at) (*inf.*), lambast(e), run down, slag (off) (*sl.*), slam (*sl.*) ◆ *n* **12** = **blow,** belt (*inf.*), box, clip, clout (*inf.*), cuff, hammering, rap, slap, smack, thump **14** *Informal* = **setback,** defeat, failure, rebuff, rejection, reversal **15** *Informal* = **criticism,** blame, censure, condemnation, heat (*sl., chiefly US & Canad.*), slagging (off) (*sl.*), stick (*sl.*), stricture

knock about *vb* **1, 2** = **wander,** ramble, range, roam, rove, traipse, travel **4** = **hit,** abuse, batter, beat up (*inf.*), bruise, buffet, clobber, damage, hurt, lambast(e), maltreat, manhandle, maul, mistreat, strike, work over (*sl.*), wound ◆ *adj* **knockabout 6** = **boisterous,** farcical, harum-scarum, rambunctious (*inf.*), riotous, rollicking, rough-and-tumble, rumbustious, slapstick

knock down *vb* **1** = **demolish,** batter, clout (*inf.*), deck (*sl.*), destroy, fell, floor, level, pound, raze, smash, wallop (*inf.*), wreck

knock off *vb* **1** *Informal* = **stop work,** clock off, clock out, complete, conclude, finish, terminate **4** *Slang* = **kill,** assassinate, blow away (*sl., chiefly US*), bump off (*sl.*), do away with, do in (*sl.*), liquidate, murder, slay, take out (*sl.*), waste (*inf.*) **5** *Slang* = **steal,** blag (*sl.*), cabbage (*Brit. sl.*), filch, nick (*sl., chiefly Brit.*), pilfer, pinch, purloin, rob, thieve

knockout *n* **1, 2** = **killer blow,** *coup de grâce,* kayo (*sl.*), KO *or* K.O. (*sl.*) **4** *Informal* = **success,** hit, sensation, smash, stunner, triumph, winner

Antonyms *n* ≠ **success:** failure, flop (*inf.*), turkey (*inf.*)

knoll *n* = **hillock,** barrow, hill, hummock, mound, swell

knot[1] *n* **1** = **connection,** bond, bow, braid, joint, ligature, loop, rosette, tie **5** = **cluster,** aggregation, bunch, clump, collection, heap, mass, pile, tuft **5** = **group,** assemblage, band, circle, clique, company, crew (*inf.*), gang, pack, set, squad ◆ *vb* **14-16** = **tie,** bind, complicate, entangle, knit, loop, secure, tether, weave

knotty *adj* **1** = **knotted,** bumpy, gnarled, knobby, nodular, rough, rugged **2** = **puzzling,** baffling, complex, complicated, difficult, hard, intricate, mystifying, perplexing, problematical, thorny, tricky, troublesome

know *vb* **1, 4** = **understand,** apprehend, comprehend, experience, fathom, feel certain, ken (*Scot.*), learn, notice, perceive, realize, recognize, see, undergo **2, 3** = **be acquainted with,** associate with, be familiar with, fraternize with, have dealings with, have knowledge of, recognize **8** = **distinguish,** differentiate, discern, identify, make out, perceive, recognize, see, tell
Antonyms *vb* ≠ **understand:** misunderstand ≠ **be acquainted with:** be ignorant, be unfamiliar with

know-all *n Informal, disparaging* = **smart aleck** (*inf.*), clever-clogs (*inf.*), clever Dick, smarty (*inf.*), smarty-boots (*inf.*), smarty-pants (*inf.*), wiseacre, wise guy (*inf.*)

know-how *n* **1** *Informal* = **capability,** ability, adroitness, aptitude, craft, dexterity, experience, expertise, faculty, flair, ingenuity, knack, knowledge, proficiency, savoir-faire, skill, talent

knowing *adj* **1** = **meaningful,** eloquent, expressive, significant **2** = **cunning,** acute, astute, perceptive, sagacious, shrewd **2** = **well-informed,** clever, clued-up (*inf.*), competent, discerning, experienced, expert, intelligent, qualified, skilful **3** = **deliberate,** aware, conscious, intended, intentional
Antonyms *adj* ≠ **cunning:** ingenuous, naive, wet behind the ears (*inf.*) ≠ **well-informed:** ignorant, obtuse ≠ **deliberate:** accidental, unintentional

knowingly *adv* **3** = **deliberately,** consciously, intentionally, on purpose, purposely, wilfully, wittingly

knowledge *n* **3** = **understanding,** ability, apprehension, cognition, comprehension, consciousness, discernment, grasp, judgment, recognition **3** = **acquaintance,** cognizance, familiarity, information, intimacy, notice **4** = **learning,** education, enlightenment, erudition, instruction, intelligence, scholarship, schooling, science, tuition, wisdom
Antonyms ≠ **understanding:** misunderstanding, unawareness ≠ **acquaintance:** unfamiliarity *n* ≠ **learning:** ignorance, illiteracy

knowledgeable *adj* = **well-informed,** acquainted, *au courant, au fait,* aware, clued-up (*inf.*), cognizant, conscious, conversant, educated, erudite, experienced, familiar, intelli-

known ❶ (nəun) *vb* **1** the past participle of **know**. ◆ *adj* **2** identified: *a known criminal.*

knuckle ('nʌkᵊl) *n* **1** a joint of a finger, esp. that connecting a finger to the hand. **2** a joint of veal, pork, etc., consisting of the part of the leg below the knee joint. **3** **near the knuckle.** *Inf.* approaching indecency. ◆ *vb* **knuckles, knuckling, knuckled. 4** (*tr*) to rub or press with the knuckles. **5** (*intr*) to keep the knuckles on the ground while shooting a marble. ◆ See also **knuckle down, knuckle under.** [C14]
▸**'knuckly** *adj*

knucklebones ('nʌkᵊl,bəunz) *n* (*functioning as sing*) a less common name for **jacks** (the game).

knuckle down *vb* (*intr, adv*) *Inf.* to apply oneself diligently: *to knuckle down to some work.*

knuckle-duster *n* (*often pl*) a metal bar fitted over the knuckles, often with holes for the fingers, for inflicting injury by a blow with the fist.

knucklehead ('nʌkᵊl,hed) *n Inf.* a fool; idiot.
▸**'knuckle,headed** *adj*

knuckle under ❶ *vb* (*intr, adv*) to give way under pressure or authority; yield.

knur, knurr (nɜː), *or* **knar** *n* a knot or protuberance in a tree trunk or in wood. [C16 *knor;* cf. KNAR]

knurl *or* **nurl** (nɜːl) *vb* (*tr*) **1** to impress with a series of fine ridges or serrations. ◆ *n* **2** a small ridge, esp. one of a series. [C17: prob. from KNUR]

KO *or* **k.o.** ('keɪ'əu) *vb* **KO's, KO'ing, KO'd** *or* **k.o.'s, k.o.'ing, k.o.'d,** *n, pl* **KO's** *or* **k.o.'s.** a slang term for **knockout** or **knock out.**

koala *or* **koala bear** (kəu'ɑːlə) *n* a slow-moving Australian arboreal marsupial, having dense greyish fur and feeding on eucalyptus leaves. Also called (Austral.): **native bear.** [from Abor.]

koan ('kəuæn) *n* (in Zen Buddhism) a problem that admits no logical solution. [from Japanese]

kobold ('kɒbəuld) *n German myth.* **1** a mischievous household sprite. **2** a spirit that haunts mines. [C19: from G; see COBALT]

kochia ('kɒ'ʃiːə) *n* an annual plant with ornamental foliage that turns purple-red in late summer. [C19: after W.D.J. *Koch,* G botanist]

Kodiak bear *or* **Kodiak** ('kəudɪ,æk) *n* a large variety of the brown bear inhabiting the W coast of Alaska and neighbouring islands, esp. Kodiak.

koeksister ('kuk,sɪstə) *n S. African.* a plaited doughnut deep-fried and soaked in syrup. [Afrik. but possibly of Malay origin]

koel ('kəuəl) *n* any of several parasitic cuckoos of S and SE Asia and Australia. [C19: from Hindi, from Sansk. *kokila*]

koha ('kəuhə) *n NZ.* a gift or donation. [Maori]

kohl (kəul) *n* a cosmetic powder used, originally esp. in Muslim and Asian countries, to darken the area around the eyes. [C18: from Ar. *kohl;* see ALCOHOL]

kohlrabi (kəul'rɑːbɪ) *n, pl* **kohlrabies.** a cultivated variety of cabbage whose thickened stem is eaten as a vegetable. Also called: **turnip cabbage.** [C19: from G, from It. *cavoli rape* (pl), from *cavolo* cabbage (from L *caulis*) + *rapa* turnip (from L)]

koi (kɔɪ) *n* any of various ornamental forms of the common carp. [Japanese]

koine ('kɔɪniː) *n* a common language among speakers of different languages; lingua franca. [from Gk *koinē dialektos* common language]

Koine ('kɔɪniː) *n* (*sometimes not cap.*) **the.** the ancient Greek dialect that was the lingua franca of the empire of Alexander the Great and in Roman times.

kokanee (kəu'kænɪ) *n* a landlocked salmon of lakes in W North America: a variety of sockeye. [prob. from *Kokanee* Creek, in SE British Columbia]

kola ('kəulə) *n* a variant spelling of **cola.**

kola nut *n* a variant spelling of **cola nut.**

kolinsky (kə'lɪnskɪ) *n, pl* **kolinskies. 1** any of various Asian minks. **2** the rich tawny fur of this animal. [C19: from Russian *kolinsky* of *Kola,* in NW Russia]

kolkhoz (kɒl'hɔːz) *n* a Russian collective farm. [C20: from Russian, short for *kollektivnoe khozyaistvo* collective farm]

Kol Nidre (kɔːl 'nɪdreɪ) *n Judaism.* **1** the evening service with which Yom Kippur begins. **2** the opening prayer of that service. [Aramaic *kōl nidhrē* all the vows; the prayer's opening words]

komatik ('kəumætɪk) *n* a sledge having wooden runners and crossbars bound with rawhide, used by Eskimos. [C20: from Eskimo]

koodoo ('kuːduː) *n* a variant spelling of **kudu.**

kook (kuːk) *n US & Canad. inf.* an eccentric or foolish person. [C20: prob. from CUCKOO]
▸**'kooky** *or* **'kookie** *adj*

kookaburra ('kukə,bʌrə) *n* a large Australian kingfisher with a cackling cry. Also called: **laughing jackass.** [C19: from Abor.]

kopeck *or* **copeck** ('kəupɛk) *n* a monetary unit of Russia and Belarus worth one hundredth of a rouble: coins are still used as tokens for coin-operated machinery although the kopeck itself is virtually valueless. [Russian *kopeika,* from *kopye* lance]

koppie *or* **kopje** ('kɒpɪ) *n* (in southern Africa) a small isolated hill. [C19: from Afrik., from Du. *kopje,* lit.: a little head, from *kop* head]

kora ('kɔːrə) *n* a West African instrument with twenty-one strings, combining features of the harp and the lute.

Koran (kɔː'rɑːn) *n* the sacred book of Islam, believed by Muslims to be the infallible word of God dictated to Mohammed. Also: **Qur'an.** [C17: from Ar. *qur'ān* reading, book]
▸**Ko'ranic** *adj*

Korean (kə'riːən) *adj* **1** of or relating to Korea in SE Asia, its people, or their language. ◆ *n* **2** a native or inhabitant of Korea. **3** the official language of North and South Korea.

korfball ('kɔːf,bɔːl) *n* a game similar to basketball, in which each team consists of six men and six women. [C20: from Du. *korfbal* basketball]

korma ('kɔːmə) *n* an Indian dish consisting of meat or vegetables braised with stock, yogurt, or cream. [from Urdu]

Korsakoffian (,kɔːsə'kɒfɪən) *adj* **1** relating to or suffering from **Korsakoff's psychosis,** a mental illness involving severe confusion and inability to retain recent memories, usually caused by alcoholism. ◆ *n* **2** a person suffering from Korsakoff's psychosis. [C19: after Sergei *Korsakoff* (1854–1900), Russian neuropsychiatrist]

kosher ('kəuʃə) *adj* **1** *Judaism.* conforming to religious law; fit for use: esp. (of food) prepared in accordance with the dietary laws. **2** *Inf.* **2a** genuine or authentic. **2b** legitimate. [C19: from Yiddish, from Heb. *kāshēr* proper]

koto ('kəutəu) *n, pl* **kotos.** a Japanese stringed instrument. [Japanese]

kotuku ('kəutʊkuː) *n, pl* **kotuku.** *NZ.* a white heron having brilliant white plumage, black legs and yellow eyes and bill. [Maori]

kouprey ('kuːpreɪ) *n* a large wild member of the cattle tribe, of SE Asia, having a blackish-brown body and white legs: an endangered species. [C20: from F, from Cambodian, from Pali *gō* cow + Khmer *brai* forest]

kowhai ('kɔːwaɪ) *n, pl* **kowhais.** *NZ.* a small leguminous tree of New Zealand and Chile with clusters of yellow flowers. [C19: from Maori]

kowtow ❶ (,kau'tau) *vb* (*intr*) **1** to touch the forehead to the ground as a sign of deference: a former Chinese custom. **2** (*often foll. by to*) to be servile (towards). ◆ *n* **3** the act of kowtowing. [C19: from Chinese, from *k'o* to strike, knock + *t'ou* head]

Kr **1** *Currency. symbol for:* **1a** krona. **1b** krone. **2** *the chemical symbol for* krypton.

kr. *abbrev. for:* **1** krona. **2** krone.

kraal (krɑːl) *n S. African.* **1** a hut village in southern Africa, esp. one surrounded by a stockade. **2** an enclosure for livestock. [C18: from Afrik., from Port. *curral* pen]

kraft (krɑːft) *n* strong wrapping paper. [G: force]

krait (kraɪt) *n* any nonaggressive brightly coloured venomous snake of S and SE Asia. [C19: from Hindi *karait,* from ?]

kraken ('krɑːkən) *n* a legendary sea monster of gigantic size believed to dwell off the coast of Norway. [C18: from Norwegian, from ?]

krans (krɑːns) *n S. African.* a sheer rock face; precipice. [C18: from Afrik.]

kremlin ('krɛmlɪn) *n* the citadel of any Russian city. [C17: from obs. G *Kremelin,* from Russian *kreml*]

Kremlin ('krɛmlɪn) *n* **1** the 12th-century citadel in Moscow, containing the offices of the Russian government. **2** (formerly) the central government of the Soviet Union.

krill (krɪl) *n, pl* **krill.** any small shrimplike marine crustacean: the principal food of whalebone whales. [C20: from Norwegian *kril* young fish]

krimmer ('krɪmə) *n* a tightly curled light grey fur obtained from the skins of lambs from Crimea in the Ukraine. [C20: from G, from *Krim* Crimea]

Kriol ('kriːɒl) *n* a creole language used by Aboriginal communities in the northern regions of Australia, developed from Northern Territory pidgin.

kris (krɪs) *n* a Malayan and Indonesian stabbing or slashing knife with a scalloped edge. Also called: **crease, creese.** [C16: from Malay]

krona ('krəunə) *n, pl* **kronor** (-nə). the standard monetary unit of Sweden.

króna ('krəunə) *n, pl* **krónur** (-nə). the standard monetary unit of Iceland.

krone ('krəunə) *n, pl* **kroner** (-nə). **1** the standard monetary unit of Denmark. **2** the standard monetary unit of Norway. [C19: from Danish or Norwegian, ult. from L *corōna* CROWN]

Krugerrand ('kruːgə,rænd) *n* a one-ounce gold coin minted in South Africa for investment only. [C20: from Paul *Kruger* (1825–1904), Boer statesman, + RAND[1]]

krummhorn ('krʌm,hɔːn) *or* **crumhorn** *n* a medieval wind instrument consisting of an upward-curving tube blown through a double reed.

krypton ('krɪptɒn) *n* an inert gaseous element occurring in trace amounts in air and used in fluorescent lights and lasers. Symbol: Kr;

THESAURUS

gent, in the know (*inf.*), in the loop, learned, lettered, scholarly, understanding

known *adj* **2** = **famous**, acknowledged, admitted, avowed, celebrated, common, confessed, familiar, manifest, noted, obvious, patent, plain, popular, published, recognized, well-known

Antonyms *adj* closet (*inf.*), concealed, hidden, secret, unfamiliar, unknown, unrecognized, unrevealed

knuckle under *vb* = **give way**, accede, acquiesce, capitulate, cave in (*inf.*), give in, submit, succumb, surrender, yield

Antonyms *vb* be defiant, dig one's heels in (*inf.*), hold out (against), kick up (a fuss *or* stink), rebel, resist

kowtow *vb* **1** = **bow**, genuflect, kneel **2** = **grovel**, brown-nose, court, cringe, fawn, flatter, lick someone's boots, pander to, suck up to (*sl.*), toady, truckle atomic no.: 36; atomic wt.: 83.80. [C19: from Gk, from *kruptos* hidden]

krytron ('kraɪtrɒn) *n Electronics.* a type of fast electronic gas-discharge switch, used as a trigger in nuclear weapons.

Kshatriya ('kʃætrɪə) *n* a member of the second of the four main Hindu castes, the warrior caste. [C18: from Sansk., from *kshatra* rule]

kt *abbrev. for:* **1** karat. **2** *Naut.* knot.

Kt 1 Also: **knt.** *abbrev. for* Knight. **2** Also: **N.** *Chess. symbol for* knight.

kudos ❶ ('kju:dɒs) *n (functioning as sing)* acclaim, glory, or prestige. [C18: from Gk]

kudu *or* **koodoo** ('ku:du:) *n* either of two spiral-horned antelopes (**greater kudu** or **lesser kudu**), which inhabit the bush of Africa. [C18: from Afrik. *koedoe*, prob. from Khoi]

Ku Klux Klan (ˌku: klʌks 'klæn) *n* **1** a secret organization of White Southerners formed after the US Civil War to fight Black emancipation. **2** a secret organization of White Protestant Americans, mainly in the South, who use violence against Blacks, Jews, etc. [C19 *Ku Klux*, prob. based on Gk *kuklos* CIRCLE + *Klan* CLAN]
▸**Ku Klux Klanner** ('klænə) *n*

kukri ('kʊkrɪ) *n, pl* **kukris.** a knife with a curved blade that broadens towards the point, esp. as used by Gurkhas. [from Hindi]

kulak ('ku:læk) *n* (in Russia after 1906) a member of the class of peasants who became proprietors of their own farms. In 1929 Stalin initiated their liquidation. [C19: from Russian: fist, hence, tightfisted person]

kulfi ('kʊlfɪ) *n* an Indian dessert that resembles ice cream flavoured with nuts and cardamom seeds.

kumera *or* **kumara** ('ku:mərə) *n NZ.* the sweet potato. [from Maori]

kumiss *or* **koumiss** ('ku:mɪs) *n* a drink made from fermented mare's or other milk, drunk by certain Asian tribes. [C17: from Russian *kumys*]

kumite ('ku:mɪˌteɪ) *n Karate, etc.* freestyle sparring or fighting. [C20: Japanese, lit.: sparring]

kümmel ('kʊməl) *n* a German liqueur flavoured with aniseed and cumin. [C19: from G, from OHG *kumil*, prob. var. of *kumin* CUMIN]

kumquat *or* **cumquat** ('kʌmkwɒt) *n* **1** a small Chinese citrus tree. **2** the small round orange fruit of such a tree, with a sweet rind, used in preserves and confections. [C17: from Mandarin Chinese *chin chü* golden orange]

kung fu ('kʌŋ 'fu:) *n* a Chinese martial art combining principles of karate and judo. [from Chinese: martial art]

kurchatovium (ˌkɜ:tʃə'təʊvɪəm) *n* another name for **rutherfordium**, esp. as used in the former Soviet Union. [C20: from Russian, after I. V. *Kurchatov* (1903–60), Soviet physicist]

Kurd (kɜ:d) *n* a member of a nomadic people living chiefly in E Turkey, N Iraq, and W Iran.

Kurdish ('kɜ:dɪʃ) *n* **1** the language of the Kurds. ◆ *adj* **2** of or relating to the Kurds or their language.

kuri ('ku:rɪ) *n, pl* **kuris.** *NZ.* a mongrel dog. Also called: **goorie.** [Maori]

kurrajong *or* **currajong** ('kʌrəˌdʒɒŋ) *n* any of various Australian trees or shrubs, esp. one that yields a tough durable fibre. [C19: from Abor.]

kursaal ('kɜ:zəl) *n* a public room at a health resort. [from G, lit.: cure room]

kurtosis (kə'təʊsɪs) *n Statistics.* a measure of the concentration of a distribution around its mean. [from Gk, from *kurtos* arched]

kuru ('kʊru:) *n* a degenerative disease of the nervous system, restricted to certain tribes in New Guinea, marked by loss of muscular control and thought to be caused by a slow virus. [C20: from a native name]

kvass (kvɑ:s) *n* an alcoholic drink of low strength made in Russia and E Europe from cereals and stale bread. [C16: from Russian *kvas*]

kvetch (kvɛtʃ) *vb (intr) Sl., chiefly US.* to complain or grumble, esp. incessantly. [C20: from Yiddish *kvetshn*, lit.: to squeeze, press]

kW *abbrev. for* kilowatt.

kwacha ('kwɑ:tʃɑ:) *n* **1** the standard monetary unit of Zambia. **2** the standard monetary unit of Malawi. [from a native word in Zambia]

kwashiorkor (ˌkwæʃɪ'ɔ:kə) *n* severe malnutrition of infants and young children, resulting from dietary deficiency of protein. [C20: from native word in Ghana]

kWh *abbrev. for* kilowatt-hour.

KWIC (kwɪk) *n acronym for* key word in context (esp. in **KWIC index**).

KWOC (kwɒk) *n acronym for* key word out of context.

kyanite ('kaɪəˌnaɪt) *n* a variant spelling of **cyanite.**
▸**kyanitic** (ˌkaɪə'nɪtɪk) *adj*

kyanize *or* **kyanise** ('kaɪəˌnaɪz) *vb* **kyanizes, kyanizing, kyanized** *or* **kyanises, kyanising, kyanised.** *(tr)* to treat (timber) with corrosive sublimate to make it resistant to decay. [C19: after J.H. *Kyan* (died 1850), Brit. inventor of the process]
▸ˌ**kyani'zation** *or* ˌ**kyani'sation** *n*

kyle (kaɪl) *n Scot.* (esp. in place names) a narrow strait or channel: *Kyle of Lochalsh.* [C16: from Gaelic *caol* narrow]

kylie *or* **kiley** ('kaɪlɪ) *n Austral.* a boomerang that is flat on one side and convex on the other. [C19: from Abor.]

kyloe ('kaɪləʊ) *n* a breed of small long-horned long-haired beef cattle from NW Scotland. [C19: from ?]

kymograph ('kaɪməˌgrɑ:f) *n* a rotatable drum for holding paper on which a tracking stylus continuously records variations in sound waves, blood pressure, respiratory movements, etc. [C20: from Gk *kuma* wave + -GRAPH]
▸ˌ**kymo'graphic** *adj*

Kymric ('kɪmrɪk) *n, adj* a variant spelling of **Cymric.**

Kymry ('kɪmrɪ) *pl n* a variant spelling of **Cymry.**

kyphosis (kaɪ'fəʊsɪs) *n Pathol.* backward curvature of the thoracic spine, of congenital origin or resulting from injury or disease. [C19: from NL, from Gk *kuphōsis*, from *kuphos* humpbacked]
▸**kyphotic** (kaɪ'fɒtɪk) *adj*

Kyrgyz ('kɪəgɪz) *n* **1** *(pl* **Kyrgyz***)* a member of a Mongoloid people of central Asia, inhabiting Kyrgyzstan and a vast area of central Siberia. **2** the language of this people, belonging to the Turkic branch of the Altaic family. Also: **Kirghiz, Kirgiz.**

Kyrie eleison ('kɪrɪɪ ə'leɪsən) *n* **1** a formal invocation used in the liturgies of the Roman Catholic, Greek Orthodox, and Anglican Churches. **2** a musical setting of this. Often shortened to **Kyrie.** [C14: via LL from LGk *kurie, eleēson* Lord, have mercy]

kyu (kju:) *n Judo.* one of the student grades for inexperienced competitors. [from Japanese]

THESAURUS

kudos *n* = **prestige**, acclaim, applause, distinction, esteem, fame, glory, honour, laudation, notability, plaudits, praise, regard, renown, repute

Ll

l *or* **L** (ɛl) *n, pl* **l's, L's,** *or* **Ls. 1** the 12th letter of the English alphabet. **2** a speech sound represented by this letter. **3a** something shaped like an L. **3b** (*in combination*): *an L-shaped room.*

l *symbol for* litre.

L *symbol for:* **1** lambert(s). **2** large. **3** Latin. **4** (on British motor vehicles) learner driver. **5** *Physics.* length. **6** live. **7** Usually written: £, pound. [L *libra*]. **8** lire. **9** *Electronics.* inductor (in circuit diagrams). **10** *Physics.* **10a** latent heat. **10b** self-inductance. **11** the Roman numeral for 50. See **Roman numerals.**

L. *or* **l.** *abbrev. for:* **1** lake. **2** law. **3** leaf. **4** league. **5** left. **6** length. **7** (*pl* **LL** *or* **ll.**) line. **8** link. **9** low.

L. *abbrev. for:* **1** *Politics.* Liberal. **2** (in titles) Licentiate. **3** Linnaeus.

la[1] (lɑː) *n Music.* the syllable used in the fixed system of solmization for the note A. [C14: see GAMUT]

la[2] (lɔː) *interj* an exclamation of surprise or emphasis. [OE *lā* lo]

La *the chemical symbol for* lanthanum.

laager (ˈlɑːɡə) *n* **1** (in Africa) a camp, esp. one defended by a circular formation of wagons. **2** *Mil.* a place where armoured vehicles are parked. ◆ *vb* **3** to form (wagons) into a laager. **4** (*tr*) to park (armoured vehicles) in a laager. [C19: from Afrik. *lager,* via G from OHG *legar* bed, lair]

lab (læb) *n Inf.* short for **laboratory.**

lab. *abbrev. for:* **1** laboratory. **2** labour.

Lab. *abbrev. for:* **1** *Politics.* Labour. **2** Labrador.

label Ⓣ (ˈleɪbᵊl) *n* **1** a piece of paper, card, or other material attached to an object to identify it or give instructions or details concerning its ownership, use, nature, destination, etc.; tag. **2** a brief descriptive phrase or term given to a person, group, school of thought, etc.: *the label "Romantic" is applied to many different kinds of poetry.* **3** a word or phrase heading a piece of text to indicate or summarize its contents. **4** a trademark or company or brand name on certain goods, esp. on gramophone records. **5** *Computing.* a group of characters appended to a statement in a program to allow it to be identified. **6** *Chem.* a radioactive element used in a compound to trace the mechanism of a chemical reaction. ◆ *vb* **labels, labelling, labelled** *or US* **labels, labeling, labeled.** (*tr*) **7** to fasten a label to. **8** to mark with a label. **9** to describe or classify in a word or phrase: *to label someone a liar.* **10** to make (one or more atoms in a compound) radioactive, for use in determining the mechanism of a reaction. [C14: from OF, from Gmc]
▸**ˈlabeller** *n*

labia (ˈleɪbɪə) *n* the plural of **labium.**

labial (ˈleɪbɪəl) *adj* **1** of, relating to, or near lips or labia. **2** *Music.* producing sounds by the action of an air stream over a narrow liplike fissure, as in a flue pipe of an organ. **3** *Phonetics.* relating to a speech sound whose articulation involves movement or use of the lips. ◆ *n* **4** Also called: **labial pipe.** *Music.* an organ pipe with a liplike fissure. **5** *Phonetics.* a speech sound such as English *p* or *m,* whose articulation involves movement or use of the lips. [C16: from Med. L *labiālis,* from L *labium* lip]
▸**ˈlabially** *adv*

labiate (ˈleɪbɪˌeɪt, -ɪt) *n* **1** any plant of the family *Labiatae,* having square stems, aromatic leaves, and a two-lipped corolla: includes mint, thyme, sage, rosemary, etc. ◆ *adj* **2** of, relating to, or belonging to the family *Labiatae.* [C18: from NL *labiātus,* from L *labium* lip]

labile (ˈleɪbɪl) *adj Chem.* (of a compound) prone to chemical change. [C15: via LL *lābilis,* from L *lābī* to slide]
▸**lability** (ləˈbɪlɪtɪ) *n*

labiodental (ˌleɪbɪəʊˈdentᵊl) *Phonetics.* ◆ *adj* **1** pronounced by bringing the bottom lip into contact with the upper teeth, as for *f* in *fat, puff.* ◆ *n* **2** a labiodental consonant. [C17: from L LABIUM + DENTAL]

labium (ˈleɪbɪəm) *n, pl* **labia** (-bɪə). **1** a lip or liplike structure. **2** any one of the four lip-shaped folds of the female vulva, comprising an outer pair (**labia majora**) and an inner pair (**labia minora**). [C16: NL, from L.: lip]

laboratory (ləˈbɒrətərɪ, -trɪ; *US.* ˈlæbrəˌtɔːrɪ) *n, pl* **laboratories. 1a** a building or room equipped for conducting scientific research or for teaching practical science. **1b** (*as modifier*): *laboratory equipment.* **2** a place where chemicals or medicines are manufactured. ◆ Often shortened to **lab.** [C17: from Med. L *labōrātōrium* workshop, from L *labōrāre* to LABOUR]

Labor Day *n* **1** a public holiday in the US and Canada in honour of labour, held on the first Monday in September. **2** a public holiday in Australia, observed on different days in different states.

laborious Ⓣ (ləˈbɔːrɪəs) *adj* **1** involving great exertion or long effort. **2** given to working hard. **3** (of literary style, etc.) not fluent.
▸**laˈboriously** *adv* ▸**laˈboriousness** *n*

Labor Party *n* one of the chief political parties of Australia, generally supporting the interests of organized labour.

labour Ⓣ *or US & sometimes Canad.* **labor** (ˈleɪbə) *n* **1** productive work, esp. physical toil done for wages. **2a** the people, class, or workers involved in this, esp. in contrast to management, capital, etc. **2b** (*as modifier*): *labour relations.* **3a** difficult or arduous work or effort. **3b** (*in combination*): *labour-saving.* **4** a particular job or task, esp. of a difficult nature. **5a** the process or effort of childbirth or the time during which this takes place. **5b** (*as modifier*): *labour pain; labour ward.* ◆ *vb* **6** (*intr*) to perform labour; work. **7** (*intr; foll. by for, etc.*) to strive or work hard (for something). **8** (*intr; usually foll. by under*) to be burdened (by) or be at a disadvantage (because of): *to labour under a misapprehension.* **9** (*intr*) to make one's way with difficulty. **10** (*tr*) to deal with too persistently: *to labour a point.* **11** (*intr*) (of a woman) to be in labour. **12** (*intr*) (of a ship) to pitch and toss. [C13: via OF from L *labor*]

labour camp *n* **1** a penal colony involving forced labour. **2** a camp for migratory labourers.

Labour Day *n* a public holiday in many countries in honour of labour, usually held on May 1.

laboured Ⓣ *or US & sometimes Canad.* **labored** (ˈleɪbəd) *adj* **1** (of breathing) performed with difficulty. **2** showing effort; contrived; lacking grace or fluency.

labourer Ⓣ *or US & sometimes Canad.* **laborer** (ˈleɪbərə) *n* a person engaged in physical work, esp. unskilled work.

labour exchange *n Brit.* a former name for the **employment office.**

labour-intensive *adj* of or denoting a task, organization, industry, etc., in which a high proportion of the costs are due to wages, salaries, etc.

Labourite (ˈleɪbəˌraɪt) *n* an adherent of the Labour Party.

Labour Party *n* **1** a British political party, formed in 1900 as an amalgam of various trade unions and socialist groups, generally supporting the interests of organized labour and advocating democratic socialism and social equality. **2** any similar party in any of various other countries.

Labrador retriever (ˈlæbrəˌdɔː) *n* a powerfully-built variety of retriever with a short dense usually black or golden-brown coat. Often shortened to **Labrador.**

labret (ˈleɪbret) *n* a piece of bone, shell, etc., inserted into the lip as an ornament by certain peoples. [C19: from L *labrum* lip]

labrum (ˈleɪbrəm, ˈlæb-) *n, pl* **labra** (-brə). a lip or liplike part, such as the cuticular plate forming the upper lip of insects. [C19: NL, from L]

laburnum (ləˈbɜːnəm) *n* any tree or shrub of a Eurasian genus having clusters of yellow drooping flowers: all parts of the plant are poisonous. [C16: NL, from L]

labyrinth Ⓣ (ˈlæbərɪnθ) *n* **1** a mazelike network of tunnels, chambers, or paths, either natural or man-made. **2** any complex or confusing system of streets, passages, etc. **3** a complex or intricate situation. **4** any system of interconnecting cavities, esp. those comprising the internal ear. **5** *Electronics.* an enclosure behind a high-performance loudspeaker, consisting of a series of air chambers designed to absorb unwanted sound waves. [C16: via L from Gk *laburinthos,* from ?]

THESAURUS

label *n* **1** = **tag,** docket (*chiefly Brit.*), flag, marker, sticker, tally, ticket **2** = **epithet,** characterization, classification, description **4** = **brand,** company, mark, trademark ◆ *vb* **7, 8** = **tag,** docket, flag, mark, stamp, sticker, tally **9** = **describe,** brand, call, characterize, class, classify, define, designate, identify, name

laborious *adj* **1** = **hard,** arduous, backbreaking, burdensome, difficult, exhausting, fatiguing, herculean, onerous, strenuous, tiresome, tiring, toilsome, tough, uphill, wearing, wearisome **2** = **industrious,** assiduous, diligent, hard-working, indefatigable, painstaking, persevering, sedulous, tireless, unflagging **3** = **forced,** laboured, not fluent, ponderous, strained

Antonyms *adj* ≠ **hard:** easy, easy-peasy (*sl.*), effortless, light ≠ **forced:** natural, simple

labour *n* **1** = **work,** industry, toil **2a** = **workers,** employees, hands, labourers, workforce, workmen **3a** = **toil,** donkey-work, drudgery, effort, exertion, grind (*inf.*), industry, pains, painstaking, sweat (*inf.*), travail **4** = **chore,** job, task, undertaking **5a** = **childbirth,** contractions, delivery, labour pains, pains, parturition, throes, travail ◆ *vb* **6, 7** = **work,** drudge, endeavour, grind (*inf.*), peg along *or* away (*chiefly Brit.*), plod, plug along *or* away (*inf.*), slave, strive, struggle, sweat (*inf.*), toil, travail **8** *usually with* **under** = **be disadvantaged,** be a victim of, be burdened by, suffer **10** = **overemphasize,** dwell on, elaborate, go on about, make a federal case of (*US inf.*), make a production (out) of (*inf.*), overdo, strain

Antonyms *n* ≠ **toil:** ease, idleness, leisure, relaxation, repose, respite, rest ◆ *vb* ≠ **work:** relax, rest

laboured *adj* **1** = **difficult,** awkward, forced, heavy, stiff, strained **2** = **contrived,** affected, overdone, overwrought, ponderous, studied, unnatural

labourer *n* = **worker,** blue-collar worker, drudge, hand, labouring man, manual worker, navvy (*Brit. inf.*), unskilled worker, working man, workman

labyrinth *n* **3** = **maze,** coil, complexity, complication, convolution, entanglement, intricacy, jungle, knotty problem, perplexity, puzzle, riddle, snarl, tangle, windings

labyrinthine ❶ (ˌlæbəˈrɪnθaɪn) *adj* **1** of or relating to a labyrinth. **2** resembling a labyrinth in complexity.

lac[1] (læk) *n* a resinous substance secreted by certain insects (**lac insects**), used in the manufacture of shellac. [C16: from Du. *lak* or F *laque,* from Hindi *lākh* resin, ult. from Sansk. *lākshā*]

lac[2] (lɑːk) *n* a variant spelling of **lakh.**

laccolith (ˈlækəlɪθ) *or* **laccolite** (ˈlækəˌlaɪt) *n* a dome of igneous rock between two layers of older sedimentary rock. [C19: from Gk *lakkos* cistern + -LITH]

lace ❶ (leɪs) *n* **1** a delicate decorative fabric made from cotton, silk, etc., woven in an open web of different symmetrical patterns and figures. **2** a cord or string drawn through eyelets or around hooks to fasten a shoe or garment. **3** ornamental braid often used on military uniforms, etc. ◆ *vb* **laces, lacing, laced.** (*tr*) **4** to fasten (shoes, etc.) with a lace. **5** to draw (a cord or thread) through holes, eyes, etc., as when tying shoes. **6** to compress the waist of (someone), as with a corset. **7** to add a small amount of alcohol or drugs to (food or drink). **8** (*usually passive* and foll. by *with*) to streak or mark with lines or colours: *the sky was laced with red.* **9** to intertwine; interlace. **10** *Inf.* to give a sound beating to. [C13 *las,* from OF *laz,* from L *laqueus* noose]

lacebark (ˈleɪsbɑːk) *n* another name for **ribbonwood.**

lacerate ❶ *vb* (ˈlæsəˌreɪt), **lacerates, lacerating, lacerated.** (*tr*) **1** to tear (the flesh, etc.) jaggedly. **2** to hurt or harrow (the feelings, etc.). ◆ *adj* (ˈlæsəˌreɪt, -rɪt). **3** having edges that are jagged: *lacerate leaves.* [C16: from L *lacerāre* to tear, from *lacer* mangled]
▸ˌ**laceˈration** *n*

lace up *vb* **1** (*tr, adv*) to tighten or fasten (clothes or footwear) with laces. ◆ *adj* **lace-up. 2** (of footwear) to be fastened with laces. ◆ *n* **lace-up. 3** a lace-up shoe or boot.

lacewing (ˈleɪsˌwɪŋ) *n* any of various insects, esp. the green lacewings and brown lacewings, having lacy wings and preying on aphids and similar pests.

laches (ˈlætʃɪz) *n Law.* negligence or unreasonable delay in pursuing a legal remedy. [C14 *lachesse,* via OF *lasche* slack, from L *laxus* LAX]

Lachesis (ˈlækɪsɪs) *n Greek myth.* one of the three Fates. [via L from Gk, from *lakhesis* destiny, from *lakhein* to befall by lot]

lachrymal (ˈlækrɪməl) *adj* a variant spelling of **lacrimal.**

lachrymatory (ˈlækrɪmətərɪ, -trɪ) *n, pl* **lachrymatories. 1** a small vessel found in ancient tombs, formerly thought to hold the tears of mourners. ◆ *adj* **2** a variant spelling of **lacrimatory.**

lachrymose (ˈlækrɪˌməʊs) *adj* **1** given to weeping; tearful. **2** mournful; sad. [C17: from L, from *lacrima* a tear]
▸ˈ**lachryˌmosely** *adv*

lacing (ˈleɪsɪŋ) *n* **1** *Chiefly Brit.* a course of bricks, stone, etc., for strengthening a rubble or flint wall. **2** another word for **lace** (senses 2, 3). **3** *Inf.* a severe beating.

laciniate (ləˈsɪnɪˌeɪt, -ɪt) *or* **laciniated** *adj* **1** *Biol.* jagged: *a laciniate leaf.* **2** having a fringe. [C17: from L *lacinia* flap]
▸**laˌciniˈation** *n*

lack ❶ (læk) *n* **1** an insufficiency, shortage, or absence of something required or desired. **2** something that is required but is absent or in short supply. ◆ *vb* **3** (when *intr,* often foll. by *in* or *for*) to be deficient (in) or have need (of). [C12: rel. to MDu. *laken* to be wanting]

lackadaisical ❶ (ˌlækəˈdeɪzɪkᵊl) *adj* **1** lacking vitality and purpose. **2** lazy, esp. in a dreamy way. [C18: from earlier *lackadaisy*]
▸ˌ**lackaˈdaisically** *adv*

lackey ❶ (ˈlækɪ) *n* **1** a servile follower; hanger-on. **2** a liveried male servant or valet. **3** a person who is treated like a servant. ◆ *vb* **4** (when *intr,* often foll. by *for*) to act as a lackey (to). [C16: via F *laquais,* from OF, ?from Catalan *lacayo, alacayo*]

lacklustre ❶ *or US* **lackluster** (ˈlækˌlʌstə) *adj* lacking force, brilliance, or vitality.

laconic ❶ (ləˈkɒnɪk) *adj* (of a person's speech) using few words; terse. [C16: via L from Gk *Lakōnikos,* from *Lakōn* Laconian, Spartan; referring to the Spartans' terseness of speech]
▸**laˈconically** *adv*

lacquer (ˈlækə) *n* **1** a hard glossy coating made by dissolving cellulose derivatives or natural resins in a volatile solvent. **2** a black resinous substance, obtained from certain trees (**lacquer trees**), used to give a hard glossy finish to wooden furniture. **3** Also called: **hair lacquer.** a mixture of shellac and alcohol for spraying onto the hair to hold a style in place. **4** *Art.* decorative objects coated with such lacquer, often inlaid. ◆ *vb* (*tr*) **5** to apply lacquer to. [C16: from obs. F *lacre* sealing wax, from Port. *laca* LAC[1]]
▸ˈ**lacquerer** *n*

lacrimal, lachrymal, *or* **lacrymal** (ˈlækrɪməl) *adj* of or relating to tears or to the glands that secrete tears. [C16: from Med. L, from L *lacrima* a tear]

lacrimation (ˌlækrɪˈmeɪʃən) *n* the secretion of tears.

lacrimatory, lachrymatory, *or* **lacrymatory** (ˈlækrɪmətərɪ, -trɪ) *adj* of, causing, or producing tears.

lacrosse (ləˈkrɒs) *n* a ball game invented by American Indians, now played by two teams who try to propel a ball into each other's goal by means of long-handled pouched sticks (**lacrosse sticks**). [C19: Canad. F: the hooked stick, crosier]

lactam (ˈlæktæm) *n Chem.* any of a group of cyclic amides, derived from amino acids, having the characteristic group -CONH-. [C20: from LACTO- + AM(IDE)]

lactate[1] (ˈlækteɪt) *n* an ester or salt of lactic acid. [C18]

lactate[2] (lækˈteɪt) *vb* **lactates, lactating, lactated.** (*intr*) (of mammals) to produce or secrete milk.

lactation (lækˈteɪʃən) *n* **1** the secretion of milk from the mammary glands after parturition. **2** the period during which milk is secreted.

lacteal (ˈlæktɪəl) *adj* **1** of, relating to, or resembling milk. **2** (of lymphatic vessels) conveying or containing chyle. ◆ *n* **3** any of the lymphatic vessels conveying chyle from the small intestine to the thoracic duct. [C17: from L *lacteus* of milk, from *lac* milk]

lactescent (lækˈtɛsᵊnt) *adj* **1** (of plants and certain insects) secreting a milky fluid. **2** milky or becoming milky. [C18: from L, from *lactescēre* to become milky, from *lact-, lac* milk]
▸**lacˈtescence** *n*

lactic (ˈlæktɪk) *adj* relating to or derived from milk. [C18: from L *lact-, lac* milk]

lactic acid *n* a colourless syrupy carboxylic acid found in sour milk and many fruits and used as a preservative (**E270**) for foodstuffs. Formula: $CH_3CH(OH)COOH$. Systematic name: **2-hydroxypropanoic acid.**

lactiferous (lækˈtɪfərəs) *adj* producing, conveying, or secreting milk or a milky fluid. [C17: from L *lactifer,* from *lact-, lac* milk]

lacto- (ˈlæktəʊ) *or before a vowel* **lact-** *combining form.* indicating milk: *lactobacillus.* [from L *lact-, lac* milk]

lactose (ˈlæktəʊs, -təʊz) *n* a white crystalline sugar occurring in milk and used in pharmaceuticals and baby foods. Formula: $C_{12}H_{22}O_{11}$.

lacto-vegetarian *n* a vegetarian whose diet includes dairy produce.

lacuna (ləˈkjuːnə) *n, pl* **lacunae** (-niː) *or* **lacunas. 1** a gap or space, esp. in a book or manuscript. **2** *Biol.* a cavity or depression, such as any of the spaces in the matrix of bone. [C17: from L *lacūna* pool, cavity, from *lacus* lake]
▸**laˈcunose, laˈcunal, laˈcunar,** *or* **laˈcunary** *adj*

lacustrine (ləˈkʌstraɪn) *adj* **1** of or relating to lakes. **2** living or growing in or on the shores of a lake. [C19: from It. *lacustre,* from L *lacus* lake]

lacy ❶ (ˈleɪsɪ) *adj* **lacier, laciest.** made of or resembling lace.
▸ˈ**lacily** *adv* ▸ˈ**laciness** *n*

lad ❶ (læd) *n* **1** a boy or young man. **2** *Inf.* a familiar form of address for any male. **3** a lively or dashing man or youth (esp. in **a bit of a lad**). **4** *Brit.* a boy or man who looks after horses. [C13 *ladde;* ?from ON]

ladanum (ˈlædənəm) *n* a dark resinous juice obtained from various rockroses: used in perfumery. [C16: L from Gk, from *lēdon* rockrose]

ladder (ˈlædə) *n* **1** a portable framework of wood, metal, rope, etc., in the form of two long parallel members connected by rungs or steps fixed to them at right angles, for climbing up or down. **2** any hierarchy conceived of as having a series of ascending stages, levels, etc.: *the social ladder.* **3** Also called: **run.** *Chiefly Brit.* a line of connected stitches that have come undone in knitted material, esp. stockings. ◆ *vb* **4** *Chiefly Brit.* to cause a line of interconnected stitches in (stockings, etc.) to undo, as by snagging, or (of a stocking) to come undone in this way. [OE *hlǣdder*]

ladder back *n* a type of chair in which the back is constructed of horizontal slats between two uprights.

laddie (ˈlædɪ) *n Chiefly Scot.* a familiar term for a male, esp. a boy; lad.

laddish (ˈlædɪʃ) *adj Inf., usually derog.* characteristic of male adolescents or young men, esp. by being rowdy, macho, or immature: *laddish behaviour.*

lade (leɪd) *vb* **lades, lading, laded; laden** *or* **laded. 1** to put cargo or freight on board (a ship, etc.) or (of a ship, etc.) to take on cargo or freight. **2**

THESAURUS

labyrinthine *adj* **2** = **complex,** Byzantine, confused, convoluted, intricate, involved, knotty, mazelike, mazy, perplexing, puzzling, tangled, tortuous, winding

lace *n* **1** = **netting,** filigree, openwork, tatting **2** = **cord,** bootlace, shoelace, string, thong, tie ◆ *vb* **4** = **fasten,** attach, bind, close, do up, thread, tie **7** = **mix in,** add to, fortify, spike **9** = **intertwine,** interweave, twine

lacerate *vb* **1** = **tear,** claw, cut, gash, jag, maim, mangle, rend, rip, slash, wound **2** = **hurt,** afflict, distress, harrow, rend, torment, torture, wound

laceration *n* **1** = **cut,** gash, injury, mutilation, rent, rip, slash, tear, trauma (*Pathology*), wound

lack *n* **1** = **shortage,** absence, dearth, deficiency, deprivation, destitution, insufficiency, need, privation, scantiness, scarcity, shortcoming, shortness, want ◆ *vb* **3** = **need,** be deficient in, be short of, be without, miss, require, want
Antonyms *n* ≠ **shortage:** abundance, adequacy, excess, plentifulness, sufficiency, surplus ◆ *vb* ≠ **need:** enjoy, have, own, possess

lackadaisical *adj* **1** = **lethargic,** apathetic, dull, enervated, half-hearted, indifferent, languid, languorous, limp, listless, spiritless **2** = **lazy,** abstracted, dreamy, idle, indolent, inert
Antonyms *adj* ambitious, diligent, excited, inspired, spirited

lackey *n* **1** = **hanger-on,** creature, fawner, flatterer, flunky, instrument, menial, minion, parasite, pawn, sycophant, toady, tool, yes man **2** = **manservant,** attendant, cohort (*chiefly US*), flunky, footman, valet, varlet (*arch.*)

lacking *adj* **3** = **without,** defective, deficient, flawed, impaired, inadequate, minus, missing, needing, sans (*arch.*), wanting

lacklustre *adj* = **flat,** boring, dim, drab, dry, dull, leaden, lifeless, lustreless, muted, prosaic, sombre, unimaginative, uninspired, vapid

laconic *adj* = **terse,** brief, clipped, compact, concise, crisp, curt, monosyllabic, pithy, sententious, short, succinct, to the point
Antonyms *adj* long-winded, loquacious, rambling, verbose, voluble, wordy

lacy *adj* = **filigree,** delicate, fine, frilly, gauzy, gossamer, lace-like, meshy, net-like, open, sheer

lad *n* **1** = **boy,** chap (*inf.*), fellow, guy (*inf.*), juvenile, kid (*inf.*), laddie (*Scot.*), schoolboy, stripling, youngster, youth (*tr; usually passive* and foll. by *with*) to burden or oppress. **3** (*tr; usually passive* and foll. by *with*) to fill or load. **4** to remove (liquid) with or as if with a ladle. [OE *hladen* to load]

laden ➊ ('leɪdᵊn) *vb* **1** a past participle of **lade**. ◆ *adj* **2** weighed down with a load; loaded. **3** encumbered; burdened.

la-di-da ➊, **lah-di-dah**, *or* **la-de-da** (ˌlɑːdiːˈdɑː) *adj Inf.* affecting exaggeratedly genteel manners or speech. [C19: mockingly imit. of affected speech]

ladies *or* **ladies' room** *n* (*functioning as sing*) *Inf.* a women's public lavatory.

lading ('leɪdɪŋ) *n* a load; cargo; freight.

ladle ('leɪdᵊl) *n* **1** a long-handled spoon having a deep bowl for serving or transferring liquids. **2** a large bucket-shaped container for transferring molten metal. ◆ *vb* **ladles, ladling, ladled. 3** (*tr*) to serve out as with a ladle. [OE *hlædel*, from *hladan* to draw out]
▸ **'ladleful** *n*

ladle out *vb* (*tr, adv*) *Inf.* to distribute (money, gifts, etc.) generously.

lady ➊ ('leɪdɪ) *n, pl* **ladies. 1** a woman regarded as having the characteristics of a good family and high social position. **2a** a polite name for a woman. **2b** (*as modifier*): *a lady doctor.* **3** an informal name for **wife. 4 lady of the house.** the female head of the household. **5** *History.* a woman with proprietary rights and authority, as over a manor. [OE *hlǣfdīge*, from *hlāf* bread + *dīge* kneader, rel. to *dāh* dough]

Lady ('leɪdɪ) *n, pl* **Ladies. 1** (in Britain) a title of honour borne by various classes of women of the peerage. **2 my lady.** a term of address to holders of the title Lady. **3 Our Lady.** a title of the Virgin Mary.

ladybird ('leɪdɪˌbɜːd) *n* any of various small brightly coloured beetles, esp. one having red elytra with black spots. [C18: after Our *Lady*, the Virgin Mary]

lady bountiful *n* an ostentatiously charitable woman. [C19: after a character in George Farquhar's play *The Beaux' Stratagem* (1707)]

Lady Chapel *n* a chapel within a church or cathedral, dedicated to the Virgin Mary.

Lady Day *n* March 25, the feast of the Annunciation of the Virgin Mary. Also called: **Annunciation Day.**

lady-in-waiting *n, pl* **ladies-in-waiting.** a lady who attends a queen or princess.

lady-killer ➊ *n Inf.* a man who is, or believes he is, irresistibly fascinating to women.

ladylike ➊ ('leɪdɪˌlaɪk) *adj* like or befitting a lady in manners and bearing; refined and fastidious.

ladylove ('leɪdɪˌlʌv) *n Now rare.* a beloved woman.

Lady Macbeth strategy (mək'beθ) *n* a strategy in a takeover battle in which a third party makes a bid acceptable to the target company, appearing to act as a white knight but subsequently joining forces with the original (unwelcome) bidder. [C20: after *Lady Macbeth*, character in *Macbeth* (1605), a play by William Shakespeare]

lady mayoress *n Brit.* the wife of a lord mayor.

lady's bedstraw *n* a Eurasian plant with clusters of small yellow flowers.

lady's finger *n* another name for **bhindi.**

Ladyship ('leɪdɪʃɪp) *n* (preceded by *your* or *her*) a title used to address or refer to any peeress except a duchess.

lady's-slipper *n* any of various orchids having reddish or purple flowers.

lady's-smock *n* a N temperate plant with white or rose-pink flowers. Also called: **cuckooflower.**

laevo- *or US* **levo-** *combining form.* **1** on or towards the left: *laevorotatory.* **2** (in chemistry) denoting a laevorotatory compound. [from L *laevus* left]

laevorotation (ˌliːvəʊrəʊ'teɪʃən) *n* **1** a rotation to the left. **2** an anticlockwise rotation of the plane of polarization of plane-polarized light as a result of its passage through a crystal, liquid, or solution. ◆ Cf. **dextrorotation.**
▸ **laevorotatory** (ˌliːvəʊ'rəʊtətərɪ) *adj*

Laffer curve ('læfə) *n Econ.* a graph showing government tax revenue plotted against percentage tax rates; it illustrates that a cut in a high tax rate can increase government revenue. [C20: after Arthur *Laffer* (born 1940), US economist]

LAFTA ('læftə) *n acronym for* Latin American Free Trade Area, the name before 1981 of the Latin American Integration Association. See **LAIA.**

lag[1] ➊ (læg) *vb* **lags, lagging, lagged.** (*intr*) **1** (often foll. by *behind*) to hang (back) or fall (behind) in movement, progress, development, etc. **2** to fall away in strength or intensity. ◆ *n* **3** the act or state of slowing down or falling behind. **4** the interval of time between two events, esp. between an action and its effect. [C16: from ?]

lag[2] (læg) *Sl.* ◆ *n* **1** a convict or ex-convict (esp. in **old lag**). **2** a term of imprisonment. ◆ *vb* **lags, lagging, lagged. 3** (*tr*) to arrest or put in prison. [C19: from ?]

lag[3] (læg) *vb* **lags, lagging, lagged. 1** (*tr*) to cover (a pipe, cylinder, etc.) with lagging to prevent loss of heat. ◆ *n* **2** the insulating casing of a steam cylinder, boiler, etc. **3** a stave. [C17: of Scand. origin]

lagan ('lægᵊn) *n* goods or wreckage on the sea bed, sometimes attached to a buoy to permit recovery. [C16: from OF *lagan*, prob. of Gmc origin]

lager ('lɑːgə) *n* a light-bodied effervescent beer, fermented in a closed vessel using yeasts that sink to the bottom of the brew. [C19: from G *Lagerbier* beer for storing, from *Lager* storehouse]

lager lout *n* a rowdy or aggressive young drunk male.

laggard ➊ ('lægəd) *n* **1** a person who lags behind. ◆ *adj* **2** *Rare.* sluggish, slow, or dawdling.
▸ **'laggardly** *adj, adv* ▸ **'laggardness** *n*

lagging ('lægɪŋ) *n* **1** insulating material wrapped around pipes, boilers, etc., or laid in a roof loft, to prevent loss of heat. **2** the act or process of applying lagging.

lagomorph ('lægəʊˌmɔːf) *n* any placental mammal having two pairs of upper incisors specialized for gnawing, such as rabbits and hares. [C19: via NL from Gk *lagōs* hare; see -MORPH]

lagoon (lə'guːn) *n* **1** a body of water cut off from the open sea by coral reefs or sand bars. **2** any small body of water, esp. one adjoining a larger one. [C17: from It. *laguna*, from L *lacūna* pool; see LACUNA]

Lagrangian point (lə'greɪndʒɪən) *n Astron.* one of five points in the plane of revolution of two bodies in orbit around their common centre of gravity, at which a third body of negligible mass can remain in equilibrium with respect to the other two bodies. [after J. L. *Lagrange* (1736–1813), F mathematician and astronomer]

lah (lɑː) *n Music.* (in tonic sol-fa) the sixth note of any major scale; submediant. [C14: later variant of *la*; see GAMUT]

lahar ('lɑːhɑː) *n* a landslide of volcanic debris mixed with water down the sides of a volcano, usually precipitated by heavy rainfall. [C20: from Javanese: lava]

lah-di-dah (ˌlɑːdiː'dɑː) *adj, n Inf.* a variant spelling of **la-di-da.**

LAIA *abbrev. for* Latin American Integration Association (before 1981, known as the Latin American Free Trade Area). An economic group, its members are Argentina, Bolivia, Brazil, Chile, Colombia, Ecuador, Mexico, Paraguay, Peru, Uruguay, and Venezuela.

laic ('leɪɪk) *adj also* **laical. 1** of or involving the laity; secular. ◆ *n* **2** a rare word for **layman.** [C15: from LL *lāicus* LAY[3]]
▸ **'laically** *adv*

laicize *or* **laicise** ('leɪɪˌsaɪz) *vb* **laicizes, laicizing, laicized** *or* **laicises, laicising, laicised.** (*tr*) to withdraw clerical or ecclesiastical character or status from (an institution, building, etc.).
▸ ˌ**laici'zation** *or* ˌ**laici'sation** *n*

laid (leɪd) *vb* the past tense and past participle of **lay**[1].

laid-back ➊ *adj* relaxed in style or character; easy-going and unhurried.

laid paper *n* paper with a regular mesh impressed upon it.

Lailat-ul-Qadr (ˌleɪlætʊl'kɑːdə) *n* a night of study and prayer observed annually by Muslims to mark the communication of the Koran: it usually follows the 27th day of Ramadan. [from Ar.: night of determination]

lain (leɪn) *vb* the past participle of **lie**[2].

Laingian ('læŋɪən) *adj* **1** of or based on the theory of R. D. Laing (1927–89), Scottish psychiatrist, that mental illnesses can be responses to stress in family and social situations. ◆ *n* **2** a follower or adherent of Laing's teaching.

lair[1] ➊ (lɛə) *n* **1** the resting place of a wild animal. **2** *Inf.* a place of seclusion or hiding. ◆ *vb* **3** (*intr*) (esp. of a wild animal) to retreat to or rest in a lair. **4** (*tr*) to drive or place (an animal) in a lair. [OE *leger*]

lair[2] (lɛə) *Austral. sl.* ◆ *n* **1** a flashy man who shows off. ◆ *vb* **2** (*intr;* foll. by *up* or *around*) to behave or dress like a lair. [?from LEER]

laird (lɛəd) *n Scot.* a landowner, esp. of a large estate. [C15: Scot. var. of LORD]

laissez faire ➊ *or* **laisser faire** *French.* (ˌlɛseɪ 'fɛə) *n* **1a** Also called: **individualism.** the doctrine of unrestricted freedom in commerce, esp. for private interests. **1b** (*as modifier*): *a laissez-faire economy.* **2** indifference or noninterference, esp. in the affairs of others. [F, lit.: let (them) act]

THESAURUS

laden *adj* **2** = **loaded**, burdened, charged, encumbered, fraught, full, hampered, oppressed, taxed, weighed down, weighted

la-di-da *adj Informal* = **affected**, arty-farty (*inf.*), conceited, highfalutin (*inf.*), mannered, mincing, overrefined, posh (*inf., chiefly Brit.*), precious, pretentious, snobbish, snooty (*inf.*), stuck-up (*inf.*), toffee-nosed (*sl., chiefly Brit.*)

lady *n* **1** = **gentlewoman**, dame **2** = **woman**, female

lady-killer *n Informal* = **womanizer**, Casanova, Don Juan, heartbreaker, ladies' man, libertine, Lothario, philanderer, rake, roué, wolf (*inf.*)

ladylike *adj* = **refined**, courtly, cultured, decorous, elegant, genteel, modest, polite, proper, respectable, sophisticated, well-bred
Antonyms *adj* discourteous, ill-bred, ill-mannered, impolite, rude, uncultured, unladylike, unmannerly, unrefined

lag[1] *vb* **1** = **hang back**, be behind, dawdle, delay, drag (behind), drag one's feet (*inf.*), idle, linger, loiter, saunter, straggle, tarry, trail **2** = **flag**, decrease, diminish, ebb, fail, fall off, lose strength, slacken, wane

laggard *n* **1** = **straggler**, dawdler, idler, lingerer, loafer, loiterer, lounger, saunterer, skiver (*Brit. sl.*), slowcoach (*Brit. inf.*), slowpoke (*US & Canad. inf.*), sluggard, snail

laid-back *adj* = **relaxed**, at ease, casual, easy-going, easy-oasy (*sl.*), free and easy, together (*sl.*), unflappable (*inf.*), unhurried
Antonyms *adj* edgy, jittery (*inf.*), jumpy, keyed-up, nervous, on edge, tense, twitchy (*inf.*), uptight (*inf.*), wound-up (*inf.*)

lair[1] *n* **1** = **nest**, burrow, den, earth, form, hole, resting place **2** *Informal* = **hide-out**, den, refuge, retreat, sanctuary

laissez faire *n* **1a** = **nonintervention**, free enterprise, free trade, individualism, live and let live

laissez passer (ˌlɛseɪ ˈpæseɪ) *n* a permit allowing someone to pass, cross a frontier, etc. [F, lit.: let (them) pass]

laity (ˈleɪɪtɪ) *n* **1** laymen, as distinguished from clergymen. **2** all people not of a specific occupation. [C16: from LAY[3]]

lake[1] Ⓣ (leɪk) *n* **1** an expanse of water entirely surrounded by land and unconnected to the sea except by rivers or streams. Related adj: **lacustrine. 2** anything resembling this. **3** a surplus of a liquid commodity: *a wine lake.* [C13: *lac,* via OF from L *lacus* basin]

lake[2] (leɪk) *n* **1** a bright pigment produced by the combination of an organic colouring matter with an inorganic compound, usually a metallic salt, oxide, or hydroxide. **2** a red dye obtained by combining a metallic compound with cochineal. [C17: var. of LAC[1]]

Lake District *n* a region of lakes and mountains in NW England, in Cumbria. Also called: **Lakeland, the Lakes.**

lake dwelling *n* a dwelling, esp. in prehistoric villages, constructed on platforms supported by wooden piles driven into the bottom of a lake.
▸**lake dweller** *n*

Lakeland terrier (ˈleɪkˌlænd) *n* a wire-haired breed of terrier, originally from the Lake District.

Lake Poets *pl n* the English poets Wordsworth, Coleridge, and Southey, who lived in and drew inspiration from the Lake District at the beginning of the 19th century.

lake trout *n* a yellow-spotted char of the Great Lakes region of Canada.

lakh *or* **lac** (lɑːk) *n* (in India) the number 100 000, esp. referring to this sum of rupees. [C17: from Hindi *lākh,* ult. from Sansk. *lakshā* a sign]

-lalia *n combining form.* indicating a speech defect or abnormality: *echolalia.* [NL, from Gk *lalia* chatter, from *lalein* to babble]

Lallans (ˈlælənz) *or* **Lallan** (ˈlælən) *n* **1** a literary version of the variety of English spoken and written in the Lowlands of Scotland. **2** (*modifier*) of or relating to the Lowlands of Scotland or their dialects. [Scot. var. of *Lowlands*]

lallation (læˈleɪʃən) *n Phonetics.* a defect of speech consisting of the pronunciation of (r) as (l). [C17: from L *lallāre* to sing lullaby, imit.]

lam[1] Ⓣ (læm) *vb* **lams, lamming, lammed.** *Sl.* **1** (*tr*) to thrash or beat. **2** (*intr;* usually foll. by *into* or *out*) to make a sweeping stroke or blow. [C16: from Scand.]

lam[2] (læm) *n US & Canad. sl.* **1** a sudden flight or escape, esp. to avoid arrest. **2 on the lam.** making an escape. [C19: ? from LAM[1] (hence, to be off)]

Lam. *Bible. abbrev. for* Lamentations.

lama (ˈlɑːmə) *n* a priest or monk of Lamaism. [C17: from Tibetan *blama*]

Lamaism (ˈlɑːməˌɪzəm) *n* the Mahayana form of Buddhism of Tibet and Mongolia.
▸ˈ**Lamaist** *n, adj* ▸ˌ**Lamaˈistic** *adj*

Lamarckism (lɑːˈmɑːkɪzəm) *n* the theory of organic evolution proposed by Lamarck (1744–1829), French naturalist, based on the principle that characteristics of an organism modified during its lifetime are inheritable.

lamasery (ˈlɑːməsərɪ) *n, pl* **lamaseries.** a monastery of lamas. [C19: from F *lamaserie,* from LAMA + F *-serie,* from Persian *serāī* palace]

lamb Ⓣ (læm) *n* **1** the young of a sheep. **2** the meat of a young sheep. **3** a person, esp. a child, who is innocent, meek, good, etc. **4** a person easily deceived. ◆ *vb* **5** (*intr*) (of a ewe) to give birth. **6** (*intr*) (of a shepherd) to tend the ewes and newborn lambs at lambing time. [OE *lamb,* from Gmc]
▸ˈ**lamb,like** *adj*

Lamb (læm) *n* **the.** a title given to Christ in the New Testament.

lambada (læmˈbɑːdə) *n* **1** an erotic dance, originating in Brazil, performed by two people who hold each other closely and gyrate their hips in synchronized movements. **2** the music that accompanies the lambada, combining salsa, calypso, and reggae. [C20: from Port., lit.: the snapping of a whip]

lambast Ⓣ (læmˈbæst) *or* **lambaste** (læmˈbeɪst) *vb* **lambasts, lambasting, lambasted** *or* **lambastes, lambasting, lambasted.** (*tr*) **1** to beat or whip severely. **2** to reprimand or scold. [C17: ?from LAM[1] + BASTE[3]]

lambda (ˈlæmdə) *n* the 11th letter of the Greek alphabet (Λ, λ). [C14: from Gk, from Semitic]

lambent (ˈlæmbənt) *adj* **1** (esp. of a flame) flickering softly over a surface. **2** glowing with soft radiance. **3** (of wit or humour) light or brilliant. [C17: from the present participle of L *lambere* to lick]
▸ˈ**lambency** *n* ▸ˈ**lambently** *adv*

lambert (ˈlæmbət) *n* the cgs unit of illumination, equal to 1 lumen per square centimetre. Symbol: L [C20: after J. H. *Lambert* (1728–77), G mathematician & physicist]

lambing (ˈlæmɪŋ) *n* **1** the birth of lambs. **2** the shepherd's work of tending the ewes and newborn lambs at this time.

lambkin (ˈlæmkɪn) *n* **1** a small lamb. **2** a term of affection for a small endearing child.

lambrequin (ˈlæmbrɪkɪn, ˈlæmbə-) *n* **1** an ornamental hanging covering the edge of a shelf or the upper part of a window or door. **2** (*often pl*) a scarf worn over a helmet. [C18: from F, from Du. *lamperkin* (unattested), dim. of *lamper* veil]

Lambrusco (læmˈbruskəu) *n* **1** a red grape grown in Italy. **2** a sparkling red wine made in Italy from this grape. **3** a much less common white variety of this grape or wine.

lambskin (ˈlæmˌskɪn) *n* **1** the skin of a lamb, esp. with the wool still on. **2** a material or garment prepared from this skin.

lamb's lettuce *n* another name for **corn salad.**

lamb's tails *pl n* the pendulous catkins of the hazel tree.

lame Ⓣ (leɪm) *adj* **1** disabled or crippled in the legs or feet. **2** painful or weak: *a lame back.* **3** weak; unconvincing: *a lame excuse.* **4** not effective or enthusiastic: *a lame try.* **5** *US sl.* conventional or uninspiring. ◆ *vb* **lames, laming, lamed. 6** (*tr*) to make lame. [OE *lama*]
▸ˈ**lamely** *adv* ▸ˈ**lameness** *n*

lamé (ˈlɑːmeɪ) *n* a fabric of silk, cotton, or wool interwoven with threads of metal. [C20: from F, from OF *lame* gold or silver thread, thin plate, from L *lāmina* thin plate]

lame duck *n* **1** a person or thing that is disabled or ineffectual. **2** *Stock Exchange.* a speculator who cannot discharge his liabilities. **3** *US.* an elected official or body of officials remaining in office in the interval between the election and inauguration of a successor.

lamella (ləˈmɛlə) *n, pl* **lamellae** (-liː) *or* **lamellas.** a thin layer, plate, or membrane, esp. any of the calcified layers of which bone is formed. [C17: NL, from L, dim. of *lāmina* thin plate]
▸**laˈmellar, lamellate** (ˈlæmɪˌleɪt, -lɪt), *or* **lamellose** (ləˈmɛləus, ˈlæmɪˌləus) *adj*

lamellibranch (ləˈmɛlɪˌbræŋk) *n, adj* another word for **bivalve.** [C19: from NL *lamellibranchia* plate-gilled (animals)]

lamellicorn (ləˈmɛlɪˌkɔːn) *n* **1** any beetle having flattened terminal plates to the antennae, such as the scarabs and stag beetles. ◆ *adj* **2** designating antennae with platelike terminal segments. [C19: from NL *Lamellicornia* plate-horned (animals)]

lament Ⓣ (ləˈmɛnt) *vb* **1** to feel or express sorrow, remorse, or regret (for or over). ◆ *n* **2** an expression of sorrow. **3** a poem or song in which a death is lamented. [C16: from L *lāmentum*]
▸**laˈmenter** *n* ▸**laˈmentingly** *adv*

lamentable Ⓣ (ˈlæməntəbᵊl) *adj* **1** wretched, deplorable, or distressing. **2** an archaic word for **mournful.**
▸ˈ**lamentably** *adv*

lamentation Ⓣ (ˌlæmɛnˈteɪʃən) *n* **1** a lament; expression of sorrow. **2** the act of lamenting.

lamented (ləˈmɛntɪd) *adj* grieved for or regretted (often in **late lamented**): *our late lamented employer.*
▸**laˈmentedly** *adv*

lamina (ˈlæmɪnə) *n, pl* **laminae** (-ˌniː) *or* **laminas. 1** a thin plate, esp. of bone or mineral. **2** *Bot.* the flat blade of a leaf. [C17: NL, from L: thin plate]
▸ˈ**laminar** *or* **laminose** (ˈlæmɪˌnəus, -ˌnəuz) *adj*

laminar flow *n* nonturbulent motion of a fluid in which parallel layers have different velocities relative to each other.

laminate Ⓣ *vb* (ˈlæmɪˌneɪt), **laminates, laminating, laminated. 1** (*tr*) to make (material in sheet form) by bonding together two or more thin sheets. **2** to split or be split into thin sheets. **3** (*tr*) to beat, form, or press (material, esp. metal) into thin sheets. **4** (*tr*) to cover or overlay with a thin sheet of material. ◆ *n* (ˈlæmɪˌneɪt, -nɪt). **5** a material made by bonding together two or more sheets. ◆ *adj* (ˈlæmɪˌneɪt, -nɪt). **6** having or composed of lamina; laminated. [C17: from NL *lāminātus* plated]
▸ˈ**laminable** *adj* ▸ˌ**lamiˈnation** *n* ▸ˈ**lamiˌnator** *n*

laminated (ˈlæmɪˌneɪtɪd) *adj* **1** composed of many layers of plastic, wood, etc., bonded together. **2** covered with a thin protective layer of plastic, etc.

lamington (ˈlæmɪŋtən) *n Austral. & NZ.* a cube of sponge cake coated in chocolate and dried coconut. [C20 (in the earlier sense: a homburg hat): after Lady *Lamington,* wife of Baron Lamington, governor of Queensland (1896–1901)]

Lammas (ˈlæməs) *n* **1** *RC Church.* Aug. 1, held as a feast, commemorating St Peter's miraculous deliverance from prison. **2** Also called: **Lammas Day.** the same day formerly observed in England as a harvest festival. [OE *hlāfmæsse* loaf mass]

lammergeier *or* **lammergeyer** (ˈlæməˌgaɪə) *n* a rare vulture of S Eu-

THESAURUS

lake[1] *n* **1** = **pond**, lagoon, loch (*Scot.*), lough (*Irish*), mere, reservoir, tarn

lam[1] *vb Slang* **1** = **attack**, batter, beat, hit, knock, lambast(e), pelt, pound, strike, thrash

lambast *vb* **1** = **beat**, bludgeon, cosh (*Brit.*), cudgel, drub, flog, strike, thrash, whip **2** = **reprimand**, bawl out, berate, carpet (*inf.*), castigate, censure, chew out (*US & Canad. inf.*), excoriate, give a rocket (*Brit. & NZ inf.*), rap over the knuckles, read the riot act, rebuke, scold, slap on the wrist, tear into (*inf.*), tear (someone) off a strip (*Brit. inf.*), upbraid

lamblike *adj* **3** = **meek**, gentle, mild, passive, peaceable, submissive **4** = **innocent**, artless, childlike, guileless, naive, simple, trusting

lame *adj* **1** = **disabled**, crippled, defective, game, halt (*arch.*), handicapped, hobbling, limping **3, 4** = **unconvincing**, feeble, flimsy, inadequate, insufficient, pathetic, poor, thin, unsatisfactory, weak

lament *vb* **1** = **bemoan**, bewail, complain, deplore, grieve, mourn, regret, sorrow, wail, weep ◆ *n* **2** = **complaint**, keening, lamentation, moan, moaning, plaint, ululation, wail, wailing **3** = **dirge**, coronach, elegy, monody, requiem, threnody

lamentable *adj* **1** = **regrettable**, deplorable, distressing, grievous, gut-wrenching, harrowing, sorrowful, tragic, unfortunate, woeful, wretched

lamentation *n* **1, 2** = **sorrow**, dirge, grief, grieving, keening, lament, moan, mourning, plaint, sobbing, ululation, wailing, weeping

laminate *vb* **2** = **split**, exfoliate, flake, separate **4** = **cover**, coat, face, foliate, layer, stratify, veneer rope, Africa, and Asia, with dark wings, a pale breast, and black feathers around the bill. [C19: from G *Lämmergeier*, from *Lämmer* lambs + *Geier* vulture]

lamp (læmp) *n* **1a** any of a number of devices that produce illumination: *an electric lamp; a gas lamp; an oil lamp.* **1b** (*in combination*): *lampshade.* **2** a device for holding one or more electric light bulbs: *a table lamp.* **3** a vessel in which a liquid fuel is burned to supply illumination. **4** any of a variety of devices that produce radiation, esp. for therapeutic purposes: *an ultraviolet lamp.* [C13 *lampe*, via OF from L *lampas*, from Gk, from *lampein* to shine]

lampblack ('læmp,blæk) *n* a finely divided form of almost pure carbon produced by the incomplete combustion of organic compounds, such as natural gas, used in making carbon electrodes and dynamo brushes and as a pigment.

lamp chimney *n* a glass tube that surrounds the wick in an oil lamp.

lamplight ('læmp,laɪt) *n* the light produced by a lamp or lamps.

lamplighter ('læmp,laɪtə) *n* **1** (formerly) a person who lit and extinguished street lamps, esp. gas ones. **2** *Chiefly US & Canad.* any of various devices used to light lamps.

lampoon ❶ (læm'puːn) *n* **1** a satire in prose or verse ridiculing a person, literary work, etc. ◆ *vb* **2** (*tr*) to attack or satirize in a lampoon. [C17: from F *lampon*, ?from *lampons* let us drink (frequently used as a refrain in poems)]
▸**lam'pooner** *or* **lam'poonist** *n* ▸**lam'poonery** *n*

lamppost ('læmp,pəʊst) *n* a post supporting a lamp, esp. in a street.

lamprey ('læmprɪ) *n* any eel-like vertebrate having a round sucking mouth for clinging to and feeding on the blood of other animals. Also called: **lamper eel.** [C13: from OF *lampreie*, from LL *lamprēda*, from ?]

Lancashire ('læŋkə'ʃɪə) *n* a mild whitish-coloured cheese with a crumbly texture. [after *Lancashire*, a county in England]

Lancastrian (læŋ'kæstrɪən) *n* **1** a native or resident of Lancashire or Lancaster. **2** an adherent of the house of Lancaster in the Wars of the Roses. ◆ *adj* **3** of or relating to Lancashire or Lancaster. **4** of or relating to the house of Lancaster.

lance (lɑːns) *n* **1** a long weapon with a pointed head used by horsemen. **2** a similar weapon used for hunting, whaling, etc. **3** *Surgery.* another name for **lancet.** ◆ *vb* **lances, lancing, lanced.** (*tr*) **4** to pierce (an abscess or boil) with a lancet. **5** to pierce with or as with a lance. [C13 *launce*, from OF *lance*, from L *lancea*]

lance corporal *n* a noncommissioned army officer of the lowest rank.

lancelet ('lɑːnslɪt) *n* any of several marine animals closely related to the vertebrates: they burrow in sand. Also called: **amphioxus.** [C19: referring to the slender shape]

lanceolate ('lɑːnsɪə,leɪt, -lɪt) *adj* narrow and tapering to a point at each end: *lanceolate leaves.* [C18: from LL *lanceolātus*, from *lanceola* small LANCE]

lancer ('lɑːnsə) *n* **1** (formerly) a cavalryman armed with a lance. **2** a member of a regiment retaining such a title.

lancers ('lɑːnsəz) *n* (*functioning as sing*) **1** a quadrille for eight or sixteen couples. **2** a piece of music composed for or in the rhythm of this dance.

lancet ('lɑːnsɪt) *n* **1** Also called: **lance.** a pointed surgical knife with two sharp edges. **2** short for **lancet arch** or **lancet window.** [C15 *lancette*, from OF: small LANCE]

lancet arch *n* a narrow acutely pointed arch.

lancet window *n* a narrow window having a lancet arch.

lancewood ('lɑːns,wʊd) *n* a New Zealand tree with slender leaves showing different configurations in youth and maturity.

Lancs (læŋks) *abbrev. for* Lancashire.

land ❶ (lænd) *n* **1** the solid part of the surface of the earth as distinct from seas, lakes, etc. Related adj: **terrestrial. 2** ground, esp. with reference to its use, quality, etc. **3** rural or agricultural areas as contrasted with urban ones. **4** farming as an occupation or way of life. **5** *Law.* any tract of ground capable of being owned as property. **6a** a country, region, or area. **6b** the people of a country, etc. **7** *Econ.* the factor of production consisting of all natural resources. ◆ *vb* **8** to transfer (something) or go from a ship or boat to the shore: *land the cargo.* **9** (*intr*) to come to or touch shore. **10** (*intr*) (in Canada) to be legally admitted to the country, as an immigrant or **landed immigrant. 11** to come down or bring (something) down to earth after a flight or jump. **12** to come or bring to some point, condition, or state. **13** (*tr*) *Angling.* to retrieve (a hooked fish) from the water. **14** (*tr*) *Inf.* to win or obtain: *to land a job.* **15** (*tr*) *Inf.* to deliver (a blow). ◆ See also **land up.** [OE]
▸**'landless** *adj*

Land (*German* lant) *n*, *pl* ***Länder*** ('lɛndər). **1** any of the federal states of Germany. **2** any of the provinces of Austria. [G]

land agent *n* **1** a person who administers a landed estate and its tenancies. **2** a person who acts as an agent for the sale of land.
▸**land agency** *n*

landau ('lændɔː) *n* a four-wheeled carriage, usually horse-drawn, with two folding hoods over the passenger compartment. [C18: after *Landau* (a town in Germany), where first made]

landaulet (,lændɔː'lɛt) *n* **1** a small landau. **2** *US.* an early type of car with a folding hood over the passenger seats.

landed ('lændɪd) *adj* **1** owning land: *landed gentry.* **2** consisting of or including land: *a landed estate.*

landfall ('lænd,fɔːl) *n* **1** the act of sighting or nearing land, esp. from the sea. **2** the land sighted or neared.

landfill ('lænd,fɪl) *adj* of or denoting low-lying sites or tips being filled up with alternate layers of rubbish and earth.

landform ('lænd,fɔːm) *n Geol.* any natural feature of the earth's surface.

land girl *n* a girl or woman who does farm work, esp. in wartime.

landgrave ('lænd,greɪv) *n German history.* **1** (from the 13th century to 1806) a count who ruled over a specified territory. **2** (after 1806) the title of any of various sovereign princes. [C16: via G, from MHG *lantgrāve*, from *lant* land + *grāve* count]

land-holder *n* a person who owns or occupies land.
▸**'land-,holding** *adj, n*

landing ❶ ('lændɪŋ) *n* **1a** the act of coming to land, esp. after a flight or a sea voyage. **1b** (*as modifier*): *landing place.* **2** a place of disembarkation. **3** the floor area at the top of a flight of stairs.

landing craft *n Mil.* any small vessel designed for the landing of troops and equipment on beaches.

landing field *n* an area of land on which aircraft land and from which they take off.

landing gear *n* another name for **undercarriage.**

landing net *n Angling.* a loose long-handled net for lifting hooked fish from the water.

landing stage *n* a platform used for landing goods and passengers from a vessel.

landing strip *n* another name for **airstrip.**

landlady ('lænd,leɪdɪ) *n*, *pl* **landladies. 1** a woman who owns and leases property. **2** a woman who owns or runs a lodging house, pub, etc.

ländler (*German* 'lɛntlər) *n* **1** an Austrian country dance in which couples spin and clap. **2** a piece of music composed for or in the rhythm of this dance, in three-four time. [G, from dialect *Landl* Upper Austria]

land line *n* a telecommunications wire or cable laid over land.

landlocked ('lænd,lɒkt) *adj* **1** (esp. of lakes) completely surrounded by land. **2** (esp. of certain salmon) living in fresh water that is permanently isolated from the sea.

landlord ❶ ('lænd,lɔːd) *n* **1** a man who owns and leases property. **2** a man who owns or runs a lodging house, pub, etc.

landlubber ('lænd,lʌbə) *n Naut.* any person having no experience at sea.

landmark ❶ ('lænd,mɑːk) *n* **1** a prominent or well-known object in or feature of a particular landscape. **2** an important or unique decision, event, fact, discovery, etc. **3** a boundary marker.

landmass ('lænd,mæs) *n* a large continuous area of land, as opposed to seas or islands.

land mine *n Mil.* an explosive charge placed in the ground, usually detonated by stepping or driving on it.

land of milk and honey *n* **1** *Old Testament.* the fertile land promised to the Israelites by God (Ezekiel 20:6). **2** any fertile land, state, etc.

land of Nod *n* **1** *Old Testament.* a region to the east of Eden to which Cain went after he had killed Abel (Genesis 4:14). **2** an imaginary land of sleep.

landowner ('lænd,əʊnə) *n* a person who owns land.
▸**'land,owner,ship** *n* ▸**'land,owning** *n, adj*

land rail *n* another name for **corncrake.**

land reform *n* the redistributing of large agricultural holdings among the landless.

landscape ❶ ('lænd,skeɪp) *n* **1** an extensive area of land regarded as being visually distinct. **2** a painting, drawing, photograph, etc., depicting natural scenery. **3** the genre including such pictures. **4** the distinctive features of a given area of intellectual activity, regarded as an integrated whole. ◆ *adj* **5** *Printing.* **5a** (of an illustration in a book, magazine, etc.) of greater width than depth. Cf. **portrait** (sense 3). **5b** (of a page) carrying an illustration or table printed at right angles to the normal text. ◆ *vb* **landscapes, landscaping, landscaped. 6** (*tr*) to improve the natural features of (a garden, park, etc.), as by creating contoured features and planting trees. **7** (*intr*) to work as a landscape gardener. [C16 *landskip* (orig. a term in painting), from MDu. *lantscap* region]

landscape gardening *n* the art of laying out grounds in imitation of natural scenery. Also called: **landscape architecture.**
▸**landscape gardener** *n*

THESAURUS

lampoon *n* **1** = **satire**, burlesque, caricature, parody, pasquinade, send-up (*Brit. inf.*), skit, squib, takeoff (*inf.*) ◆ *vb* **2** = **ridicule**, burlesque, caricature, make fun of, mock, parody, pasquinade, satirize, send up (*Brit. inf.*), squib, take off (*inf.*)

land *n* **1** = **ground**, dry land, earth, terra firma **2** = **soil**, dirt, ground, loam **3** = **countryside**, farmland, rural districts **4** = **farming 5** *Law* = **property**, acres, estate, grounds, real property, realty **6a** = **country**, district, fatherland, motherland, nation, province, region, territory, tract ◆ *vb* **8, 9** = **arrive**, alight, berth, come to rest, debark, disembark, dock **11** = **touch down**, alight **14** *Informal* = **obtain**, acquire, gain, get, score (*sl.*), secure, win

landing *n* **1a** = **coming in**, arrival, disembarkation, disembarkment, touchdown **2** = **platform**, jetty, landing stage, quayside

landlord *n* **1** = **owner**, freeholder, lessor, proprietor **2** = **innkeeper**, host, hotelier, hotel-keeper

landmark *n* **1** = **feature**, monument **2** = **milestone**, crisis, turning point, watershed **3** = **boundary marker**, benchmark, cairn, milepost, signpost

landscape *n* **1** = **scenery**, countryside, outlook, panorama, prospect, scene, view, vista

landscapist ('lænd,skeɪpɪst) *n* a painter of landscapes.

landside ('lænd,saɪd) *n* **1** the part of an airport farthest from the aircraft, the boundary of which is the security check, customs, passport control, etc. Cf. **airside. 2** the part of a plough that slides along the face of the furrow wall on the opposite side to the mouldboard.

landslide ⓘ ('lænd,slaɪd) *n* **1** Also called: **landslip. 1a** the sliding of a large mass of rock material, soil, etc., down the side of a mountain or cliff. **1b** the material dislodged in this way. **2** an overwhelming electoral victory.

landsman ('lændzmən) *n, pl* **landsmen.** a person who works or lives on land, as distinguished from a seaman.

land up ⓘ *vb (adv, usually intr)* to arrive or cause to arrive at a final point or condition.

landward ('lændwəd) *adj* **1** lying, facing, or moving towards land. **2** in the direction of the land. ◆ *adv* **3** a variant of **landwards.**

landwards ('lændwədz) *or* **landward** *adv* towards land.

lane ⓘ (leɪn) *n* **1** a narrow road or way between buildings, hedges, fences, etc. **2a** any of the parallel strips into which the carriageway of a major road or motorway is divided. **2b** any narrow well-defined route or course for ships or aircraft. **3** one of the parallel strips into which a running track or swimming bath is divided for races. **4** the long strip of wooden flooring down which balls are bowled in a bowling alley. [OE *lane, lanu*]

lang. *abbrev. for* language.

Langerhans islets *or* **islands** ('læŋə,hæns) *pl n Anat.* See **islets of Langerhans.**

langlauf ('læŋ,lauf) *n* cross-country skiing. [G, lit.: long run]
▸**langläufer** ('læŋ,lɔɪfə) *n* ▸**langläufing** ('læŋ,lɔɪfɪŋ) *n*

langouste ('lɒŋguːst, lɒŋ'guːst) *n* another name for the **spiny lobster.** [F, from OProvençal *langosta,* ? from L *lōcusta* lobster, locust]

langoustine (,lɒŋguːs'tiːn) *n* a large prawn or small lobster. [from F, dim. of LANGOUSTE]

langsam ('læŋzæm) *adj Music.* slow. [G]

langsyne (,læŋ'saɪn) *Scot.* ◆ *adv* **1** long ago; long since. ◆ *n* **2** times long past, esp. those fondly remembered. [C16: Scot.: long since]

language ⓘ ('læŋgwɪdʒ) *n* **1** a system for the expression of thoughts, feelings, etc., by the use of spoken sounds or conventional symbols. **2** the faculty for the use of such systems, which is a distinguishing characteristic of man as compared with other animals. **3** the language of a particular nation or people. **4** any other means of communicating, such as gesture or animal sounds: *the language of love.* **5** the specialized vocabulary used by a particular group: *medical language.* **6** a particular manner or style of verbal expression: *your language is disgusting.* **7** *Computing.* See **programming language.** [C13: from OF *language,* ult. from L *lingua* tongue]

language laboratory *n* a room equipped with tape recorders, etc., for learning foreign languages.

langue (lɑːŋg) *n Linguistics.* language considered as an abstract system or a social institution, being the common possession of a speech community. [C19: from F: language]

langue d'oc *French.* (lɑ̃g dɔk) *n* the group of medieval French dialects spoken in S France: often regarded as including Provençal. [lit.: language of *oc* (form for the Provençal *yes*), ult. from L *hoc* this]

languid ⓘ ('læŋgwɪd) *adj* **1** without energy or spirit. **2** without interest or enthusiasm. **3** sluggish; inactive. [C16: from L *languidus,* from *languēre* to languish]
▸**'languidly** *adv* ▸**'languidness** *n*

languish ⓘ ('læŋgwɪʃ) *vb (intr)* **1** to lose or diminish in strength or energy. **2** (often foll. by *for*) to be listless with desire; pine. **3** to suffer deprivation, hardship, or neglect: *to languish in prison.* **4** to put on a tender, nostalgic, or melancholic expression. [C14 *languishen,* from OF *languiss-,* stem of *languir,* ult. from L *languēre*]
▸**'languishing** *adj* ▸**'languishingly** *adv* ▸**'languishment** *n*

languor ⓘ ('læŋgə) *n* **1** physical or mental laziness or weariness. **2** a feeling of dreaminess and relaxation. **3** oppressive silence or stillness. [C14 *langour,* via OF from L *languor,* from *languēre* to languish; the modern spelling is directly from L]
▸**'languorous** *adj*

langur (lʌŋ'guə) *n* any of various agile arboreal Old World monkeys of S and SE Asia having a long tail and long hair surrounding the face. [Hindi]

laniard ('lænjəd) *n* a variant spelling of **lanyard.**

laniary ('lænɪərɪ) *adj* **1** (esp. of canine teeth) adapted for tearing. ◆ *n, pl* **laniaries. 2** a tooth adapted for tearing. [C19: from L *lanius* butcher, from *laniāre* to tear]

laniferous (lə'nɪfərəs) *or* **lanigerous** (lə'nɪdʒərəs) *adj Biol.* bearing wool or fleecy hairs resembling wool. [C17: from L *lānifer,* from *lāna* wool]

lank ⓘ (læŋk) *adj* **1** long and limp. **2** thin or gaunt. [OE *hlanc* loose]
▸**'lankly** *adv* ▸**'lankness** *n*

lanky ⓘ ('læŋkɪ) *adj* **lankier, lankiest.** tall, thin, and loose-jointed.
▸**'lankily** *adv* ▸**'lankiness** *n*

lanner ('lænə) *n* **1** a large falcon of Mediterranean regions, N Africa, and S Asia. **2** *Falconry.* the female of this falcon. The male is called **lanneret.** [C15: from OF *(faucon) lanier* cowardly (falcon), from L *lanārius* wool worker, coward; referring to its sluggish flight and timid nature]

lanolin ('lænəlɪn) *or* **lanoline** ('lænəlɪn, -,liːn) *n* a yellowish viscous substance extracted from wool: used in some ointments. [C19: via G from L *lāna* wool + *oleum* oil; see -IN]

lantern ('læntən) *n* **1** a light with a transparent protective case. **2** a structure on top of a dome or roof having openings or windows to admit light or air. **3** the upper part of a lighthouse that houses the light. [C13: from L *lanterna,* from Gk *lamptēr* lamp, from *lampein* to shine]

lantern jaw *n* (when *pl,* refers to upper and lower jaw; when *sing,* usually to lower jaw) a long hollow jaw that gives the face a drawn appearance.
▸**'lantern-,jawed** *adj*

lantern slide *n* (formerly) a photographic slide for projection, used in a magic lantern.

lanthanide ('lænθə,naɪd) *or* **lanthanoid** ('lænθə,nɔɪd) *n* any of a class of 15 chemically related elements with atomic numbers from 57 (lanthanum) to 71 (lutetium).

lanthanum ('lænθənəm) *n* a silvery-white ductile metallic element of the lanthanide series: used in pyrophoric alloys, electronic devices, and in glass manufacture. Symbol: La; atomic no.: 57; atomic wt.: 138.91. [C19: NL, from Gk *lanthanein* to lie unseen]

lanthorn ('lænt,hɔːn, 'læntən) *n* an archaic word for **lantern.**

lanugo (lə'njuːgəʊ) *n, pl* **lanugos.** a layer of fine hairs, esp. the covering of the human fetus before birth. [C17: from L: down, from *lāna* wool]

lanyard *or* **laniard** ('lænjəd) *n* **1** a cord, esp. one worn around the neck, to hold a whistle, knife, etc. **2** a cord used in firing certain types of cannon. **3** *Naut.* a line for extending or tightening standing rigging. [C15 *lanyer,* from F *lanière,* from *lasne* strap, prob. of Gmc origin]

laodicean (,leɪəʊdɪ'sɪən) *adj* **1** lukewarm and indifferent, esp. in religious matters. ◆ *n* **2** a person having a lukewarm attitude towards religious matters. [C17: referring to the early Christians of Laodicea (Revelation 3:14–16)]

lap[1] (læp) *n* **1** the area formed by the upper surface of the thighs of a seated person. **2** Also called: **lapful.** the amount held in one's lap. **3** a protected place or environment: *in the lap of luxury.* **4** the part of one's clothing that covers the lap. **5 drop in someone's lap.** give someone the responsibility of. [OE *læppa* flap]

lap[2] ⓘ (læp) *n* **1** one circuit of a racecourse or track. **2** a stage or part of a journey, race, etc. **3a** an overlapping part or projection. **3b** the extent of overlap. **4** the length of material needed to go around an object. **5** a rotating disc coated with fine abrasive for polishing gemstones. ◆ *vb* **laps, lapping, lapped. 6** *(tr)* to wrap or fold (around or over): *he lapped a bandage around his wrist.* **7** *(tr)* to enclose or envelop in: *he lapped his wrist in a bandage.* **8** to place or lie partly or completely over or project beyond. **9** *(tr; usually passive)* to envelop or surround with comfort, love, etc.: *lapped in luxury.* **10** *(intr)* to be folded. **11** *(tr)* to overtake (an opponent) in a race so as to be one or more circuits ahead. **12** *(tr)* to polish or cut (a workpiece, gemstone, etc.) with a fine abrasive. [C13 (in the sense: to wrap): prob. from LAP[1]]
▸**'lapper** *n*

THESAURUS

landslide *n* **1** = **landslip,** avalanche, rockfall

land up *vb* = **end up,** arrive, lead, turn up, wind up

lane *n* **1** = **road,** aisle, alley, corridor, footpath, passageway, path, pathway, street, strip, way

language *n* **2** = **speech,** communication, conversation, discourse, expression, interchange, parlance, talk, utterance, verbalization, vocalization **3, 5** = **tongue,** argot, cant, dialect, idiom, jargon, lingo *(inf.),* lingua franca, patois, patter, speech, terminology, vernacular, vocabulary **6** = **style,** diction, expression, phraseology, phrasing, wording

languid *adj* **1** = **feeble,** drooping, faint, languorous, limp, pining, sickly, weak, weary **2** = **lazy,** indifferent, lackadaisical, languorous, listless, spiritless, unenthusiastic, uninterested **3** = **lethargic,** dull, heavy, inactive, inert, sluggish, torpid
Antonyms *adj* active, alive and kicking, energetic, strong, tireless, vigorous

languish *vb* **1** = **decline,** droop, fade, fail, faint, flag, sicken, waste, weaken, wilt, wither **2** *often with* **for** = **pine,** desire, eat one's heart out over, hanker, hunger, long, sigh, suspire, want, yearn **3** = **waste away,** be abandoned, be disregarded, be neglected, rot, suffer
Antonyms *vb* ≠ **decline, waste away:** bloom, flourish, prosper, thrive

languishing *adj* **1** = **fading,** declining, deteriorating, drooping, droopy, failing, flagging, sickening, sinking, wasting away, weakening, wilting, withering **2** = **lovesick,** dreamy, longing, lovelorn, melancholic, nostalgic, pensive, pining, soulful, tender, wistful, woebegone, yearning

languor *n* **1** = **lethargy,** apathy, debility, enervation, ennui, faintness, fatigue, feebleness, frailty, heaviness, inertia, lassitude, listlessness, torpor, weakness, weariness **2** = **relaxation,** dreaminess, drowsiness, indolence, laziness, lotus-eating, sleepiness, sloth **3** = **stillness,** calm, hush, lull, oppressiveness, silence

lank *adj* **1** = **limp,** dull, lifeless, long, lustreless, straggling **2** = **thin,** attenuated, emaciated, gaunt, lanky, lean, rawboned, scraggy, scrawny, skinny, slender, slim, spare

lanky *adj* = **gangling,** angular, bony, gaunt, loose-jointed, rangy, rawboned, scraggy, scrawny, spare, tall, thin, weedy *(inf.)*
Antonyms *adj* brawny, burly, chubby, fat, muscular, plump, portly, rotund, rounded, short, sinewy, stocky, stout

lap[2] *n* **1** = **circuit,** circle, course, distance, loop, orbit, round, tour ◆ *vb* **6, 7** = **wrap,** cover, enfold, envelop, fold, swaddle, swathe, turn, twist

lap[3] ❶ (læp) *vb* **laps, lapping, lapped. 1** (of small waves) to wash against (a shore, boat, etc.), usually with light splashing sounds. **2** (often foll. by *up*) (esp. of animals) to scoop (a liquid) into the mouth with the tongue. ◆ *n* **3** the act or sound of lapping. **4** a thin food for dogs or other animals. ◆ See also **lap up.** [OE *lapian*]
▸**'lapper** *n*

laparoscope ('læpərəˌskəʊp) *n* a medical instrument consisting of a tube that is inserted through the abdominal wall and illuminated to enable a doctor to view the internal organs. [C19 (applied to various instruments used to examine the abdomen) and C20 (in the specific modern sense): from Gk *lapara* (see LAPAROTOMY) + -SCOPE]
▸**ˌlapa'roscopy** *n*

laparotomy (ˌlæpə'rɒtəmɪ) *n, pl* **laparotomies.** surgical incision through the abdominal wall. [C19: from Gk *lapara* flank, from *laparos* soft + -TOMY]

lap dancing *n* a form of entertainment in which scantily dressed women dance erotically for individual members of the audience.

lap dissolve *n Films.* the technique of allowing the end of one scene to overlap the beginning of the next scene by fading out the former while fading in the latter.

lapdog ('læpˌdɒg) *n* a pet dog small and docile enough to be cuddled in the lap.

lapel (lə'pɛl) *n* the continuation of the turned or folded back collar on a suit, coat, jacket, etc. [C18: from LAP[1]]
▸**la'pelled** *adj*

lapheld ('læpˌhɛld) *adj* (esp. of a personal computer) small enough to be used on one's lap; portable.

lapidary ('læpɪdərɪ) *n, pl* **lapidaries. 1** a person whose business is to cut, polish, set, or deal in gemstones. ◆ *adj* **2** of or relating to gemstones or the work of a lapidary. **3** Also: **lapidarian** (ˌlæpɪ'dɛərɪən). engraved, cut, or inscribed in a stone or gemstone. **4** of sufficiently high quality to be engraved on a stone: *a lapidary inscription.* [C14: from L *lapidārius*, from *lapid-, lapis* stone]

lapillus (lə'pɪləs) *n, pl* **lapilli** (-laɪ). a small piece of lava thrown from a volcano. [C18: L: little stone]

lapis lazuli ('læpɪs 'læzjʊˌlaɪ) *n* **1** a brilliant blue mineral used as a gemstone. **2** the deep blue colour of lapis lazuli. [C14: from L *lapis* stone + Med. L *lazulī*, from Ar. *lāzaward*, from Persian *lāzhuward*, from ?]

lap joint *n* a joint made by placing one member over another and fastening them together. Also called: **lapped joint.**
▸**'lap-ˌjointed** *adj*

Laplace operator (læ'plæs; *French* laplas) *n Maths.* the operator $\partial^2/\partial x^2 + \partial^2/\partial y^2 + \partial^2/\partial z^2$, used in differential analysis. Symbol: ∇^2 [C19: after Pierre Simon *Laplace* (1749–1827), F mathematician]

lap of honour *n* a ceremonial circuit of a racing track, etc., by the winner of a race.

Lapp (læp) *n* **1** Also **Laplander.** a member of a nomadic people living chiefly in N Scandinavia and the Kola Peninsula of Russia. **2** the language of this people. ◆ *adj* **3** of or relating to this people or their language.
▸**'Lappish** *adj, n*

lappet ('læpɪt) *n* **1** a small hanging flap or piece of lace, etc. **2** *Zool.* a lobelike hanging structure, such as the wattle on a bird's head. [C16: from LAP[1] + -ET]

lapse ❶ (læps) *n* **1** a drop in standard of an isolated or temporary nature: *a lapse of justice.* **2** a break in occurrence, usage, etc.: *a lapse of five weeks between letters.* **3** a gradual decline or a drop to a lower degree, condition, or state: *a lapse from high office.* **4** a moral fall. **5** *Law.* the termination of some right, interest, or privilege, as by neglecting to exercise it or through failure of some contingency. **6** *Insurance.* the termination of coverage following a failure to pay the premiums. ◆ *vb* **lapses, lapsing, lapsed.** (*intr*) **7** to drop in standard or fail to maintain a norm. **8** to decline gradually or fall in status, condition, etc. **9** to be discontinued, esp. through negligence or other failure. **10** (usually foll. by *into*) to drift or slide (into a condition): *to lapse into sleep.* **11** (often foll. by *from*) to turn away (from beliefs or norms). **12** (of time) to slip away. [C15: from L *lāpsus* error, from *lābī* to glide]
▸**'lapsable** *or* **'lapsible** *adj* ▸**lapsed** *adj* ▸**'lapser** *n*

lapse rate *n* the rate of change of any meteorological factor with altitude, esp. atmospheric temperature.

laptop ('læpˌtɒp) *or* **laptop computer** *n* a personal computer that is small and light enough to be operated on the user's lap. Cf. **palmtop computer.**

lap up *vb* (*tr, adv*) **1** to eat or drink. **2** to relish or delight in: *he laps up horror films.* **3** to believe or accept eagerly and uncritically: *he laps up stories.*

lapwing ('læpˌwɪŋ) *n* any of several plovers, typically having a crested head, wattles, and spurs. Also called: **green plover, peewit.** [C17: altered form of OE *hlēapewince* plover]

larboard ('lɑːbəd) *n, adj Naut.* a former word for **port**[2]. [C14 *laddeborde* (changed to *larboard* by association with *starboard*), from *laden* to load + *borde* BOARD]

larceny ❶ ('lɑːsɪnɪ) *n, pl* **larcenies.** *Law.* (formerly) a technical word for **theft.** [C15: from OF *larcin*, from L *lātrocinium* robbery, from *latrō* robber]
▸**'larcenist** *or* **'larcener** *n* ▸**'larcenous** *adj*

larch (lɑːtʃ) *n* **1** any coniferous tree having deciduous needle-like leaves and egg-shaped cones. **2** the wood of any of these trees. [C16: from G *Lärche*, ult. from L *larix*]

lard (lɑːd) *n* **1** the rendered fat from a pig, used in cooking. ◆ *vb* (*tr*) **2** to prepare (lean meat, poultry, etc.) by inserting small strips of bacon or fat before cooking. **3** to cover or smear (foods) with lard. **4** to add extra material to (speech or writing); embellish. [C15: via OF from L *lāridum* bacon fat]
▸**'lardy** *adj*

larder ('lɑːdə) *n* a room or cupboard, used as a store for food. [C14: from OF *lardier*, from LARD]

lardon ('lɑːdⁿn) *or* **lardoon** (lɑː'duːn) *n* a strip of fat used in larding meat. [C15: from OF, from LARD]

lardy cake ('lɑːdɪ) *n Brit.* a rich sweet cake made of bread dough, lard, sugar, and dried fruit.

lares and penates ('lɛəriːz, 'lɑː-) *pl n* **1** *Roman myth.* **1a** household gods. **1b** statues of these gods kept in the home. **2** the valued possessions of a household. [from L]

large ❶ (lɑːdʒ) *adj* **1** having a relatively great size, quantity, extent, etc.; big. **2** of wide or broad scope, capacity, or range; comprehensive. **3** having or showing great breadth of understanding. ◆ *n* **4 at large. 4a** (esp. of a dangerous criminal or wild animal) free; not confined. **4b** roaming freely, as in a foreign country. **4c** as a whole; in general. **4d** in full detail; exhaustively. **4e ambassador at large.** See **ambassador** (sense 4). [C12 (orig.: generous): via OF from L *largus* ample]
▸**'largeness** *n*

large intestine *n* the part of the alimentary canal consisting of the caecum, colon, and rectum.

largely ❶ ('lɑːdʒlɪ) *adv* **1** principally; to a great extent. **2** on a large scale or in a large manner.

larger-than-life *adj* exceptionally striking or colourful.

large-scale ❶ *adj* **1** wide-ranging or extensive. **2** (of maps and models) constructed or drawn to a big scale.

largesse ❶ *or* **largess** (lɑː'dʒɛs) *n* **1** the generous bestowal of gifts, favours, or money. **2** the things so bestowed. **3** generosity of spirit or attitude. [C13: from OF, from LARGE]

larghetto (lɑː'gɛtəʊ) *Music.* ◆ *adj, adv* **1** to be performed moderately slowly. ◆ *n, pl* **larghettos. 2** a piece or passage to be performed in this way. [It.: dim. of LARGO]

largish ('lɑːdʒɪʃ) *adj* fairly large.

largo ('lɑːgəʊ) *Music.* ◆ *adj, adv* **1** to be performed slowly and broadly. ◆ *n, pl* **largos. 2** a piece or passage to be performed in this way. [C17: from It., from L *largus* large]

Lariam ('lærɪəm) *n Trademark.* a preparation of the drug mefloquine, used in the treatment and prevention of malaria.

lariat ('lærɪət) *n US & Canad.* **1** another word for **lasso. 2** a rope for tethering animals. [C19: from Sp. *la reata* the LASSO]

lark[1] (lɑːk) *n* **1** any brown bird of a predominantly Old World family of songbirds, esp. the skylark: noted for their singing. **2** short for **titlark.** [OE *lāwerce, lǣwerce*, of Gmc origin]

lark[2] ❶ (lɑːk) *Inf.* ◆ *n* **1** a carefree adventure or frolic. **2** a harmless piece of mischief. ◆ *vb* (*intr*) **3** (often foll. by *about*) to have a good time by frolicking. **4** to play a prank. [C19: orig. sl.]
▸**'larkish** *or* **'larky** *adj*

larkspur ('lɑːkˌspɜː) *n* any of various plants related to the delphinium,

THESAURUS

lap[3] *vb* **1 = ripple,** gurgle, plash, purl, slap, splash, swish, wash **2 = drink,** lick, sip, sup

lapse *n* **1 = mistake,** error, failing, fault, indiscretion, negligence, omission, oversight, slip **2 = interval,** break, breathing space, gap, intermission, interruption, lull, passage, pause **3 = drop,** backsliding, decline, descent, deterioration, fall, relapse ◆ *vb* **7, 8 = drop,** decline, degenerate, deteriorate, fail, fall, sink, slide, slip **9 = end,** become obsolete, become void, expire, run out, stop, terminate

lapsed *adj* **9 = expired,** discontinued, ended, finished, invalid, out of date, run out, unrenewed **11 = backsliding,** lacking faith, non-practising

larceny *n Law* **= theft,** burglary, misappropriation, pilfering, purloining, robbery, stealing

large *adj* **1 = big,** bulky, colossal, considerable, elephantine, enormous, giant, gigantic, ginormous (*inf.*), goodly, great, huge, humongous *or* humungous (*US sl.*), immense, jumbo (*inf.*), king-size, man-size, massive, mega (*sl.*), monumental, sizable *or* sizeable, substantial, tidy (*inf.*), vast **2 = comprehensive,** abundant, ample, broad, capacious, copious, extensive, full, generous, grand, grandiose, liberal, plentiful, roomy, spacious, sweeping, wide **4 at large: a = free,** at liberty, on the loose, on the run, roaming, unconfined **c = in general,** as a whole, chiefly, generally, in the main, mainly **d = at length,** considerably, exhaustively, greatly, in full detail

Antonyms *adj* ≠ **big:** inconsiderable, infinitesimal, little, minute, petty, short, slender, slight, slim, small, tiny, trivial ≠ **comprehensive:** brief, narrow, scanty, scarce, sparse, thin

largely *adv* **1 = mainly,** as a rule, by and large, chiefly, considerably, extensively, generally, mostly, predominantly, primarily, principally, to a great extent, widely

large-scale *adj* **1 = wide-ranging,** broad, extensive, far-reaching, global, sweeping, vast, wholesale, wide

largesse *n* **1 = generosity,** alms-giving, benefaction, bounty, charity, liberality, munificence, open-handedness, philanthropy **2 = gift,** bequest, bounty, donation, endowment, grant, present

lark[2] *Informal n* **1, 2 = prank,** antic, caper, escapade, fling, frolic, fun, gambol, game, jape, mischief, revel, rollick, romp, skylark, spree ◆

with spikes of blue, pink, or white irregular spurred flowers. [C16: LARK[1] + SPUR]

larn (lɑːn) *vb Not standard.* **1** *Facetious.* to learn. **2** (*tr*) to teach (someone) a lesson: *that'll larn you!* [C18: from a dialect form of LEARN]

larrigan ('lærɪgən) *n* a knee-high oiled leather moccasin boot worn by trappers, etc. [C19: from ?]

larrikin ('lærɪkɪn) *Austral. & NZ sl.* ◆ *n* **1** a mischievous person. **2** a hooligan. ◆ *adj* **3** mischievous: *larrikin wit.* [C19: from E dialect: a mischievous youth]

larrup ('lærəp) *vb* (*tr*) *Dialect.* to beat or flog. [C19: from ?]
▸**'larruper** *n*

Larry ('lærɪ) *n* **happy as Larry.** *Inf.* very happy.

larva ('lɑːvə) *n, pl* **larvae** (-viː). an immature free-living form of many animals that develops into a different adult form by metamorphosis. [C18: (C17 in the orig. L sense: ghost): NL]
▸**'larval** *adj*

laryngeal (ˌlærɪn'dʒiːəl, lə'rɪndʒɪəl) *or* **laryngal** (lə'rɪŋgəl) *adj* **1** of or relating to the larynx. **2** *Phonetics.* articulated at the larynx; glottal. [C18: from NL *laryngeus* of the LARYNX]

laryngitis (ˌlærɪn'dʒaɪtɪs) *n* inflammation of the larynx.
▸**laryngitic** (ˌlærɪn'dʒɪtɪk) *adj*

laryngo- *or before a vowel* **laryng-** *combining form.* indicating the larynx: *laryngoscope.*

laryngoscope (lə'rɪŋgəˌskəʊp) *n* a medical instrument for examining the larynx.
▸**ˌlaryn'goscopy** *n*

laryngotomy (ˌlærɪŋ'gɒtəmɪ) *n, pl* **laryngotomies.** surgical incision into the larynx to facilitate breathing.

larynx ('lærɪŋks) *n, pl* **larynges** (lə'rɪndʒiːz) *or* **larynxes.** a cartilaginous and muscular hollow organ forming part of the air passage to the lungs: in higher vertebrates it contains the vocal cords. [C16: from NL, from Gk *larunx*]

lasagne *or* **lasagna** (lə'zænjə, -'sæn-) *n* **1** a form of pasta consisting of wide flat sheets. **2** any of several dishes made from layers of lasagne and meat, cheese, etc. [from It. *lasagna*, from L *lasanum* cooking pot]

La Scala (læ 'skɑːlə) *n* the chief opera house in Italy, in Milan (opened 1776).

lascar ('læskə) *n* a sailor from the East Indies. [C17: from Urdu *lashkar* soldier, from Persian: the army]

lascivious ➊ (lə'sɪvɪəs) *adj* **1** lustful; lecherous. **2** exciting sexual desire. [C15: from LL *lascīviōsus*, from L *lascīvia* wantonness, from *lascīvus*]
▸**las'civiously** *adv* ▸**las'civiousness** *n*

lase (leɪz) *vb* **lases, lasing, lased.** (*intr*) (of a substance, such as carbon dioxide or ruby) to be capable of acting as a laser.

laser ('leɪzə) *n* **1** a source of high-intensity optical, infrared, or ultraviolet radiation produced as a result of stimulated emission maintained within a solid, liquid, or gaseous medium. The photons involved in the emission process all have the same energy and phase so that the laser beam is monochromatic and coherent, allowing it to be brought to a fine focus. **2** any similar source producing a beam of any electromagnetic radiation, such as infrared or microwave radiation. [C20: from *l*ight *a*mplification by *s*timulated *e*mission of *r*adiation]

laser printer *n* a quiet high-quality computer printer that uses a laser beam shining on a photoconductive drum to produce characters, which are then transferred to paper.

lash[1] ➊ (læʃ) *n* **1** a sharp cutting blow from a whip or other flexible object. **2** the flexible end or ends of a whip. **3** a cutting or hurtful blow to the feelings, as one caused by ridicule or scolding. **4** a forceful beating or impact, as of wind, rain, or waves against something. **5 have a lash at.** *Austral. & NZ inf.* to make an attempt at or take part in (something). **6** See **eyelash.** ◆ *vb* (*tr*) **7** to hit (a person or thing) sharply with a whip, rope, etc., esp. as punishment. **8** (of rain, waves, etc.) to beat forcefully against. **9** to attack with words, ridicule, etc. **10** to flick or wave sharply to and fro: *the panther lashed his tail.* **11** to urge or drive as with a whip: *to lash the audience into a violent mood.* ◆ See also **lash out.** [C14: ? imit.]
▸**'lasher** *n*

lash[2] ➊ (læʃ) *vb* (*tr*) to bind or secure with rope, string, etc. [C15: from OF *lachier*, ult. from L *laqueāre* to ensnare, from *laqueus* noose]

-lashed *adj* having eyelashes as specified: *long-lashed.*

lashing[1] ('læʃɪŋ) *n* **1** a whipping; flogging. **2** a scolding. **3** (*pl; usually* foll. by *of*) *Brit. inf.* large amounts; lots.

lashing[2] ('læʃɪŋ) *n* rope, cord, etc., used for binding or securing.

lash out *vb* (*intr, adv*) **1** to burst into or resort to verbal or physical attack. **2** *Brit. inf.* to be extravagant, as in spending.

lash-up *n* a temporary connection of equipment for experimental or emergency use.

lass ➊ (læs) *n* **1** a girl or young woman. **2** *Inf.* a familiar form of address for any female. [C13: from ?]

Lassa fever ('læsə) *n* a serious viral disease of Central West Africa, characterized by high fever and muscular pains. [from *Lassa*, the Nigerian village where it was first identified]

lassie ('læsɪ) *n Inf.* a little lass; girl.

lassitude ➊ ('læsɪˌtjuːd) *n* physical or mental weariness. [C16: from L *lassitūdō*, from *lassus* tired]

lasso (læ'suː, 'læsəʊ) *n, pl* **lassos** *or* **lassoes. 1** a long rope or thong with a running noose at one end, used (esp. in America) for roping horses, cattle, etc.; lariat. ◆ *vb* **lassos, lassoing, lassoed. 2** (*tr*) to catch as with a lasso. [C19: from Sp. *lazo*, ult. from L *laqueus* noose]
▸**las'soer** *n*

last[1] ➊ (lɑːst) *adj* (*often prenominal*) **1** being, happening, or coming at the end or after all others: *the last horse in the race.* **2** being or occurring just before the present; most recent: *last Thursday.* **3** only remaining: *one's last cigarette.* **4** most extreme; utmost. **5** least suitable, appropriate, or likely: *he was the last person I would have chosen.* **6** (esp. relating to the end of a person's life or of the world) final or ultimate: *last rites.* ◆ *adv* **7** after all others; at or in the end: *he came last.* **8** most recently: *he was last seen in the mountains.* **9** (*sentence modifier*) as the last or latest item. ◆ *n* **10 the last. 10a** a person or thing that is last. **10b** the final moment; end. **11** one's last moments before death. **12** the final appearance, mention, or occurrence: *we've seen the last of him.* **13 at last.** in the end; finally. **14 at long last.** finally, after difficulty, delay, or irritation. [var. of OE *latest*, *lætest*, sup. of LATE]

> **USAGE NOTE** Since *last* can mean either *after all others* or *most recent*, it is better to avoid using this word where ambiguity might arise as in *her last novel. Final* or *latest* should be used in such contexts to avoid ambiguity.

last[2] ➊ (lɑːst) *vb* **1** (when *intr*, often foll. by *for*) to remain in being (for a length of time); continue: *his hatred lasted for several years.* **2** to be sufficient for the needs of (a person) for (a length of time): *it will last us until Friday.* **3** (when *intr*, often foll. by *for*) to remain fresh, uninjured, or unaltered (for a certain time). ◆ See also **last out.** [OE *lǣstan*]
▸**'laster** *n*

last[3] (lɑːst) *n* **1** the wooden or metal form on which a shoe or boot is fashioned or repaired. ◆ *vb* **2** (*tr*) to fit (a shoe or boot) on a last. [OE *lǣste*, from *lāst* footprint]
▸**'laster** *n*

last-ditch ➊ *n* **a** a last resort or place of last defence. **b** (*as modifier*): *a last-ditch effort.*

last-gasp *n* (*modifier*) done in desperation at the last minute: *a last-gasp attempt to save the talks.*

lasting ➊ ('lɑːstɪŋ) *adj* permanent or enduring.
▸**'lastingly** *adv* ▸**'lastingness** *n*

Last Judgment *n* **the.** the occasion, after the resurrection of the dead at the end of the world, when, according to biblical tradition, God will decree the final destinies of all men according to the good and evil in their earthly lives. Also called: **the Last Day, Doomsday, Judgment Day.**

lastly ➊ ('lɑːstlɪ) *adv* **1** at the end or at the last point. ◆ *sentence connector.* **2** finally.

last name *n* another term for **surname.**

last out *vb* (*intr, adv*) **1** to be sufficient for one's needs: *how long will our supplies last out?* **2** to endure or survive: *some old people don't last out the winter.*

THESAURUS

vb **3** *often foll. by* **about** = **play**, caper, cavort, cut capers, frolic, gambol, have fun, make mischief, rollick, romp, sport

lascivious *adj* **1** = **lustful**, horny (*sl.*), lecherous, lewd, libidinous, licentious, prurient, randy (*inf., chiefly Brit.*), salacious, sensual, unchaste, voluptuous, wanton **2** = **bawdy**, blue, coarse, crude, dirty, indecent, obscene, offensive, pornographic, ribald, scurrilous, smutty, suggestive, vulgar, X-rated (*inf.*)

lash[1] *n* **1** = **blow**, hit, stripe, stroke, swipe (*inf.*) ◆ *vb* **7** = **whip**, beat, birch, chastise, flagellate, flog, horsewhip, lam (*sl.*), lambast(e), scourge, thrash **8** = **pound**, beat, buffet, dash, drum, hammer, hit, knock, lambast(e), larrup (*dialect*), punch, smack, strike **9** = **censure**, attack, belabour, berate, blast, castigate, criticize, flay, lambast(e), put down, ridicule, satirize, scold, slate (*inf., chiefly Brit.*), tear into (*inf.*), upbraid

lash[2] *vb* = **fasten**, bind, join, make fast, rope, secure, strap, tie

lass *n* **1** = **girl**, bird (*sl.*), chick (*sl.*), colleen (*Irish*), damsel, lassie (*inf.*), maid, maiden, miss, schoolgirl, wench (*facetious*), young woman

lassitude *n* = **weariness**, apathy, drowsiness, dullness, enervation, ennui, exhaustion, fatigue, heaviness, inertia, languor, lethargy, listlessness, prostration, sluggardliness, sluggishness, tiredness, torpor

last[1] *adj* **1** = **hindmost**, aftermost, at the end, rearmost **2** = **most recent**, latest **4, 6** = **final**, closing, concluding, extreme, furthest, remotest, terminal, ultimate, utmost ◆ *adv* **7** = **in** *or* **at the end**, after, behind, bringing up the rear, in the rear ◆ *n* **10b** = **end**, close, completion, conclusion, ending, finale, finish, termination **13 at last** = **finally**, at length, at the end of the day, eventually, in conclusion, in the end, in the fullness of time, ultimately
Antonyms *adj* ≠ **hindmost:** first, foremost, leading ≠ **final:** earliest, first, initial, introductory, opening

last[2] *vb* **1** = **continue**, abide, carry on, endure, hold on, hold out, keep, keep on, persist, remain, stand up, survive, wear
Antonyms *vb* cease, depart, die, end, expire, fade, fail, stop, terminate

last-ditch *n* **b** *as modifier* = **final**, all-out (*inf.*), desperate, frantic, heroic, straining, struggling

lasting *adj* = **continuing**, abiding, deep-rooted, durable, enduring, eternal, indelible, lifelong, long-standing, long-term, perennial, permanent, perpetual, unceasing, undying, unending
Antonyms *adj* ephemeral, fleeting, momentary, passing, short-lived, transient, transitory

lastly *adv, sentence connector* **1, 2** = **finally**, after

last post *n* (in the British military services) **1** a bugle call that orders men to retire for sleep. **2** a similar call sounded at military funerals.
last rites *pl n Christianity.* religious rites prescribed for those close to death.
Last Supper *n* **the.** the meal eaten by Christ with his disciples on the night before his Crucifixion.
lat. *abbrev. for* latitude.
Lat. *abbrev. for* Latin.
latah ('lɑːtə) *n* a psychological condition, observed esp. in Malaysian cultures, in which an individual, after experiencing a shock, becomes anxious and suggestible, often imitating the actions of another person. [C19: from Malay]
latch ❶ (lætʃ) *n* **1** a fastening for a gate or door that consists of a bar that may be slid or lowered into a groove, hole, etc. **2** a spring-loaded door lock that can be opened by a key from outside. **3** Also called: **latch circuit.** *Electronics.* a logic circuit that transfers the input states to the output states when signalled. ◆ *vb* **4** to fasten, fit, or be fitted as with a latch. [OE *læccan* to seize, of Gmc origin]
latchkey ('lætʃ,kiː) *n* **1** a key for an outside door or gate, esp. one that lifts a latch. **2** a supposed freedom from restrictions.
latchkey child *n* a child who has to let himself in at home on returning from school, as his parents are out at work.
latch on *vb* (*intr, adv;* often foll. by *to*) *Inf.* **1** to attach oneself (to). **2** to understand.
latchstring ('lætʃ,strɪŋ) *n* a length of string fastened to a latch and passed through a hole in the door so that it can be opened from the other side.
late ❶ (leɪt) *adj* **1** occurring or arriving after the correct or expected time: *the train was late.* **2** (*prenominal*) occurring at, scheduled for, or being at a relatively advanced time: *a late marriage.* **3** (*prenominal*) towards or near the end: *the late evening.* **4** at an advanced time in the evening or at night: *it was late.* **5** (*prenominal*) occurring or being just previous to the present time: *his late remarks on industry.* **6** (*prenominal*) having died, esp. recently: *my late grandfather.* **7** (*prenominal*) just preceding the present or existing person or thing; former: *the late manager of this firm.* **8 of late.** recently; lately. ◆ *adv* **9** after the correct or expected time: *he arrived late.* **10** at a relatively advanced age: *she married late.* **11** recently; lately: *as late as yesterday he was selling books.* **12 late in the day. 12a** at a late or advanced stage. **12b** too late. [OE *læt*]
▸**'lateness** *n*

> **USAGE NOTE** Since *late* can mean *deceased*, many people think it is better to avoid using this word to refer to the person who held a post or position before its present holder: *the previous* (not *the late*) *editor of The Times.*

lateen (lə'tiːn) *adj Naut.* denoting a rig with a triangular sail (**lateen sail**) bent to a yard hoisted to the head of a low mast, used esp. in the Mediterranean. [C18: from F *voile latine* Latin sail]
Late Greek *n* the Greek language from about the 3rd to the 8th centuries A.D.
Late Latin *n* the form of written Latin used from the 3rd to the 7th centuries A.D.
lately ❶ ('leɪtlɪ) *adv* in recent times; of late.
La Tène (læ 'tɛn) *adj* of or relating to a Celtic culture in Europe from about the 5th to the 1st centuries B.C., characterized by a distinctive type of curvilinear decoration. [C20: from *La Tène*, a part of Lake Neuchâtel, Switzerland, where remains of this culture were first discovered]
latent ❶ ('leɪtᵊnt) *adj* **1** potential but not obvious or explicit. **2** (of buds, spores, etc.) dormant. **3** *Pathol.* (esp. of an infectious disease) not yet revealed or manifest. **4** (of a virus) inactive in the host cell. **5** *Psychoanal.* relating to that part of a dream expressive of repressed desires: *latent content.* Cf. **manifest** (sense 2). [C17: from L *latēnt-*, from *latēre* to lie hidden]
▸**'latency** *n* ▸**'latently** *adv*
latent heat *n* (*no longer in technical usage*) the heat evolved or absorbed by unit mass (**specific latent heat**) or unit amount of substance (**molar latent heat**) when it changes phase without change of temperature.
latent image *n Photog.* the invisible image produced by the action of light, etc., on silver halide crystals suspended in the emulsion of a photographic material. It becomes visible after development.
later ❶ ('leɪtə) *adj, adv* **1** the comparative of **late.** ◆ *adv* **2** afterwards; subsequently.
lateral ❶ ('lætərəl) *adj* **1** of or relating to the side or sides: *a lateral blow.* ◆ *n* **2** a lateral object, part, passage, or movement. [C17: from L *laterālis*, from *latus* side]
▸**'laterally** *adv*
lateral thinking *n* a way of solving problems by employing unorthodox and apparently illogical means.
laterite ('lætə,raɪt) *n* any of a group of residual insoluble deposits of ferric and aluminium oxides: formed by weathering of rocks in tropical regions. [C19: from L *later* brick]
latest ❶ ('leɪtɪst) *adj, adv* **1** the superlative of **late.** ◆ *adj* **2** most recent, modern, or new: *the latest fashions.* ◆ *n* **3 at the latest.** no later than the time specified. **4 the latest.** *Inf.* the most recent fashion or development.
latex ('leɪtɛks) *n, pl* **latexes** *or* **latices** ('lætɪ,siːz). **1** a whitish milky fluid containing protein, starch, alkaloids, etc., that is produced by many plants. Latex from the rubber tree is used in the manufacture of rubber. **2** a suspension of synthetic rubber or plastic in water, used in the manufacture of synthetic rubber products, etc. [C19: NL, from L: liquid]
lath (lɑːθ) *n, pl* **laths** (lɑːðz, lɑːθs). **1** one of several thin narrow strips of wood used to provide a supporting framework for plaster, tiles, etc. **2** expanded sheet metal, wire mesh, etc., used to provide backing for plaster or rendering. **3** any thin strip of wood. ◆ *vb* **4** (*tr*) to attach laths to (a ceiling, roof, floor, etc.). [OE *lætt*]
lathe (leɪð) *n* **1** a machine for shaping or boring metal, wood, etc., in which the workpiece is turned about a horizontal axis against a fixed tool. ◆ *vb* **lathes, lathing, lathed. 2** (*tr*) to shape or bore (a workpiece) on a lathe. [? C15 *lath* a support, from ON]
lather ❶ ('lɑːðə) *n* **1** foam formed by the action of soap or a detergent in water. **2** foam formed by other liquid, such as the sweat of a horse. **3** *Inf.* a state of agitation. ◆ *vb* **4** to coat or become coated with lather. **5** (*intr*) to form a lather. [OE *lēathor* soap]
▸**'lathery** *adj*
lathi ('lɑːtɪ) *n, pl* **lathis.** a long heavy wooden stick used as a weapon in India, esp. by the police. [Hindi]
Latin ('lætɪn) *n* **1** the language of ancient Rome and the Roman Empire and of the educated in medieval Europe. Having originally been the language of Latium in W central Italy, belonging to the Italic branch of the Indo-European family, it later formed the basis of the Romance group. **2** a member of any of those peoples whose languages are derived from Latin. **3** an inhabitant of ancient Latium. ◆ *adj* **4** of or relating to the Latin language, the ancient Latins, or Latium. **5** characteristic of or relating to those peoples in Europe and Latin America whose languages are derived from Latin. **6** of or relating to the Roman Catholic Church. [OE *latin* and *læden* Latin, language, from L *Latīnus* of Latium]
Latin America *n* those areas of America whose official languages are Spanish and Portuguese, derived from Latin: South America, Central America, Mexico, and certain islands in the Caribbean.
▸**Latin American** *n, adj*
Latinate ('lætɪ,neɪt) *adj* (of writing, vocabulary, etc.) imitative of or derived from Latin.
Latinism ('lætɪ,nɪzəm) *n* a word, idiom, or phrase borrowed from Latin.
Latinist ('lætɪnɪst) *n* a person who studies or is proficient in Latin.
Latinize *or* **Latinise** ('lætɪ,naɪz) *vb* **Latinizes, Latinizing, Latinized** *or* **Latinises, Latinising, Latinised.** (*tr*) **1** to translate into Latin or Latinisms. **2** to cause to acquire Latin style or customs. **3** to bring Roman Catholic influence to bear upon (the form of religious ceremonies, etc.).
▸**,Latini'zation** *or* **,Latini'sation** *n* ▸**'Latin,izer** *or* **'Latin,iser** *n*
latish ('leɪtɪʃ) *adj, adv* rather late.
latitude ❶ ('lætɪ,tjuːd) *n* **1a** an angular distance measured in degrees north or south of the equator (latitude 0°). **1b** (*often pl*) a region considered with regard to its distance from the equator. **2** scope for freedom of action, thought, etc.; freedom from restriction: *his parents gave him a great deal of latitude.* [C14: from L *lātitūdō*, from *lātus* broad]
▸**,lati'tudinal** *adj* ▸**,lati'tudinally** *adv*
latitudinarian (,lætɪ,tjuːdɪ'nɛərɪən) *adj* **1** permitting or marked by freedom of attitude or behaviour, esp. in religious matters. ◆ *n* **2** a person with latitudinarian views. [C17: from L *lātitūdō* breadth, infl. in form by TRINITARIAN]

THESAURUS

all, all in all, at last, in conclusion, to conclude, to sum up, ultimately
latch *n* **1** = **fastening**, bar, bolt, catch, clamp, hasp, hook, lock, sneck (*dialect*) ◆ *vb* **4** = **fasten**, bar, bolt, lock, make fast, secure, sneck (*dialect*)
late *adj* **1** = **overdue**, behind, behindhand, belated, delayed, last-minute, slow, tardy, unpunctual **6** = **dead**, deceased, defunct, departed, ex-, former, old, past, preceding, previous ◆ *adv* **9** = **belatedly**, at the last minute, behindhand, behind time, dilatorily, slowly, tardily, unpunctually
Antonyms *adj* ≠ **overdue:** beforehand, early, prompt, punctual, seasoned, timely ≠ **dead:** alive, existing ◆ *adv* ≠ **belatedly:** beforehand, early, in advance
lately *adv* = **recently**, in recent times, just now, latterly, not long ago, of late
lateness *n* **1** = **delay**, advanced hour, belatedness, late date, retardation, tardiness, unpunctuality
latent *adj* **1** = **hidden**, concealed, dormant, immanent, inherent, invisible, lurking, potential, quiescent, secret, undeveloped, unexpressed, unrealized, unseen, veiled
Antonyms *adj* apparent, conspicuous, developed, evident, expressed, manifest, obvious, realized
later *adv* **2** = **afterwards**, after, by and by, in a while, in time, later on, next, subsequently, thereafter
lateral *adj* **1** = **sideways**, edgeways, flanking, side, sideward
latest *adj* **2** = **up-to-date**, current, fashionable, happening (*inf.*), in, modern, most recent, newest, now, up-to-the-minute, with it (*inf.*)
lather *n* **1** = **froth**, bubbles, foam, soap, soapsuds, suds **3** *Informal* = **fluster**, dither (*chiefly Brit.*), fever, flap (*inf.*), fuss, pother, state (*inf.*), stew (*inf.*), sweat, tizzy (*inf.*), twitter (*inf.*) ◆ *vb* **4** = **froth**, foam, soap
lathery *adj* **1** = **frothy**, bubbly, foamy, soapy, sudsy
latitude *n* **2** = **scope**, a free hand, elbowroom, freedom, indulgence, laxity, leeway, liberty, licence, play, room, space, unrestrictedness

▸ˌ**latiˌtudiˈnarianism** *n*

latria (ləˈtraɪə) *n RC Church, theol.* the adoration that may be offered to God alone. [C16: via L from Gk *latreia* worship]

latrine (ləˈtriːn) *n* a lavatory, as in a barracks, camp, etc. [C17: from F, from L *lātrīna*, shortened form of *lavātrīna* bath, from *lavāre* to wash]

-latry *n combining form.* indicating worship of or excessive veneration of: *idolatry; Mariolatry.* [from Gk *-latria*, from *latreia* worship]

▸**-latrous** *adj combining form.*

latter ❶ (ˈlætə) *adj* (*prenominal*) **1a** denoting the second or second mentioned of two: distinguished from *former*. **1b** (*as n; functioning as sing or pl*): *the latter is not important.* **2** near or nearer the end: *the latter part of a film.* **3** more advanced in time or sequence; later. [OE *lætra*]

> **USAGE NOTE** *The latter* should only be used to refer to the second of two items: *many people choose to go by hovercraft rather than use the ferry, but I prefer the latter.* The last of three or more items can be referred to as *the last-named.*

latter-day *adj* present-day; modern.

Latter-day Saint *n* a more formal name for a **Mormon**.

latterly ❶ (ˈlætəlɪ) *adv* recently; lately.

lattice ❶ (ˈlætɪs) *n* **1** Also called: **latticework**. an open framework of strips of wood, metal, etc., arranged to form an ornamental pattern. **2a** a gate, screen, etc., formed of such a framework. **2b** (*as modifier*): *a lattice window.* **3** something, such as a decorative or heraldic device, resembling such a framework. **4** an array of objects or points in a periodic pattern in two or three dimensions, esp. an array of atoms, ions, etc., in a crystal or an array of points indicating their positions in space. ◆ *vb* **lattices, latticing, latticed. 5** to make, adorn, or supply with a lattice or lattices. [C14: from OF *lattis*, from *latte* LATH]

▸ˈ**latticed** *adj*

Latvian (ˈlætvɪən) *adj* **1** of or relating to Latvia, a republic on the Gulf of Riga and the Baltic Sea. **2** of or relating to the people of Latvia or their language. ◆ *n* **3** a native or inhabitant of Latvia.

laud ❶ (lɔːd) *Literary.* ◆ *vb* **1** (*tr*) to praise or glorify. ◆ *n* **2** praise or glorification. [C14: vb from L *laudāre*; n from *laudēs*, pl. of L *laus* praise]

laudable ❶ (ˈlɔːdəbᵊl) *adj* deserving or worthy of praise; admirable; commendable.

▸ˈ**laudableness** *or* ˌ**laudaˈbility** *n* ▸ˈ**laudably** *adv*

laudanum (ˈlɔːdᵊnəm) *n* **1** a tincture of opium. **2** (formerly) any medicine of which opium was the main ingredient. [C16: NL, name chosen by Paracelsus (1493–1541), Swiss alchemist, for a preparation prob. containing opium]

laudation (lɔːˈdeɪʃən) *n* a formal word for **praise**.

laudatory ❶ (ˈlɔːdətərɪ, -trɪ) *or* **laudative** *adj* expressing or containing praise; eulogistic.

lauds (lɔːdz) *n* (*functioning as sing or pl*) *Chiefly RC Church.* the traditional morning prayer, constituting with matins the first of the seven canonical hours. [C14: see LAUD]

laugh ❶ (lɑːf) *vb* **1** (*intr*) to express or manifest emotion, esp. mirth or amusement, typically by expelling air from the lungs in short bursts to produce an inarticulate voiced noise, with the mouth open. **2** (*intr*) (esp. of certain mammals or birds) to make a noise resembling a laugh. **3** (*tr*) to utter or express with laughter: *he laughed his derision at the play.* **4** (*tr*) to bring or force (someone, esp. oneself) into a certain condition by laughter: *he laughed himself sick.* **5** (*intr*; foll. by *at*) to make fun (of); jeer (at). **6 laugh up one's sleeve.** to laugh or have grounds for amusement, self-satisfaction, etc., secretly. **7 laugh on the other side of one's face.** to show sudden disappointment or shame after appearing cheerful or confident. ◆ *n* **8** the act or an instance of laughing. **9** a manner of laughter. **10** *Inf.* a person or thing that causes laughter: *that holiday was a laugh.* **11 the last laugh.** the final success in an argument, situation, etc., after previous defeat. ◆ See also **laugh off**. [OE *læhan, hliehhen*]

▸ˈ**laugher** *n* ▸ˈ**laughing** *n, adj* ▸ˈ**laughingly** *adv*

laughable ❶ (ˈlɑːfəbᵊl) *adj* **1** producing scorn; ludicrous: *he offered me a laughable sum for the picture.* **2** arousing laughter.

▸ˈ**laughableness** *n* ▸ˈ**laughably** *adv*

laughing gas *n* another name for **nitrous oxide**.

laughing jackass *n* another name for the **kookaburra**.

laughing stock ❶ *n* an object of humiliating ridicule.

laugh off ❶ *vb* (*tr, adv*) to treat or dismiss lightly, esp. with stoicism.

laughter ❶ (ˈlɑːftə) *n* **1** the action of or noise produced by laughing. **2** the experience or manifestation of mirth, amusement, scorn, or joy. [OE *hleahtor*]

launch[1] ❶ (lɔːntʃ) *vb* **1** to move (a vessel) into the water. **2** to move (a newly built vessel) into the water for the first time. **3** (*tr*) **3a** to start off or set in motion: *to launch a scheme.* **3b** to put (a new product) on the market. **4** (*tr*) to propel with force. **5** to involve (oneself) totally and enthusiastically: *to launch oneself into work.* **6** (*tr*) to set (a missile, spacecraft, etc.) into motion. **7** (*intr*; foll. by *into*) to start talking or writing (about): *he launched into a story.* **8** (*intr*; usually foll. by *out*) to start (out) on a fresh course. ◆ *n* **9** an act or instance of launching. [C14: from Anglo-F *lancher*, from LL *lanceāre* to use a lance, hence, to set in motion. See LANCE]

▸ˈ**launcher** *n*

launch[2] (lɔːntʃ) *n* **1** a motor driven boat used chiefly as a transport boat. **2** the largest of the boats of a man-of-war. [C17: via Sp. *lancha* and Port. from Malay *lancharan* boat, from *lanchar* speed]

launch pad *or* **launching pad** *n* **1** a platform from which a spacecraft, rocket, etc., is launched. **2** an effective starting point for a career, enterprise, or campaign.

launch window *n* the limited period during which a spacecraft can be launched on a particular mission.

launder ❶ (ˈlɔːndə) *vb* **1** to wash and often also iron (clothes, linen, etc.). **2** (*intr*) to be capable of being laundered without shrinking, fading, etc. **3** (*tr*) to make (money illegally obtained) appear to be legally gained by passing it through foreign banks or legitimate enterprises. [C14 (n, meaning: a person who washes linen): changed from *lavender* washerwoman, from OF *lavandiere*, ult. from L *lavāre* to wash]

▸ˈ**launderer** *n*

Launderette (ˌlɔːndəˈrɛt, lɔːnˈdrɛt) *Brit. & NZ trademark.* a commercial establishment where clothes can be washed and dried, using coin-operated machines. Also called (US, Canad., and NZ): **Laundromat.**

laundress (ˈlɔːndrɪs) *n* a woman who launders clothes, sheets, etc., for a living.

laundry (ˈlɔːndrɪ) *n, pl* **laundries. 1** a place where clothes and linen are washed and ironed. **2** the clothes or linen washed and ironed. **3** the act of laundering. [C16: changed from C14 *lavendry*; see LAUNDER]

laundryman (ˈlɔːndrɪmən) *or* (*fem*) **laundrywoman** *n, pl* **laundrymen** *or* **laundrywomen. 1** a person who collects or delivers laundry. **2** a person who works in a laundry.

Laurasia (lɔːˈreɪʃə) *n* one of the two ancient supercontinents comprising what are now North America, Greenland, Europe, and Asia (excluding India). [C20: from NL *Laur(entia)* (referring to the ancient N American landmass, from *Laurentian* strata of the Canadian Shield) + *(Eur)asia*]

laureate (ˈlɔːrɪɪt) *adj* (*usually immediately postpositive*) **1** *Literary.* crowned with laurel leaves as a sign of honour. ◆ *n* **2** short for **poet laureate. 3** a person honoured with an award for art or science: *a Nobel laureate.* **4** *Rare.* a person honoured with the laurel crown or wreath. [C14: from L *laureātus*, from *laurea* LAUREL]

▸ˈ**laureateˌship** *n*

laurel ❶ (ˈlɒrəl) *n* **1** Also called: **bay, bay laurel, sweet bay, true laurel.** a small Mediterranean evergreen tree with glossy aromatic leaves, used for flavouring in cooking, and small blackish berries. **2** a similar and related tree of the Canary Islands and Azores. **3** short for **mountain laurel. 4 spurge laurel.** a European evergreen shrub, *Daphne laureola*, with glossy leaves and small green flowers. **5** (*pl*) a wreath of true laurel, worn on the head as an emblem of victory or honour in classical times. **6** (*pl*) honour, distinction, or fame. **7 look to one's laurels.** to be on guard against one's rivals. **8 rest on one's laurels.** to be satisfied with distinction won by past achievements and cease to strive for further achievements. ◆ *vb* **laurels, laurelling, laurelled** *or US* **laurels, laureling, laureled. 9** (*tr*) to crown with laurels. [C13 *lorer*, from OF *lorier* laurel tree, ult. from L *laurus*]

Laurentian (lɔːˈrɛnʃən) *adj* **1** Also: **Lawrentian.** of or resembling the style

THESAURUS

latter *adj* **1** = **second**, last, last-mentioned **2** = **concluding**, closing **3** = **later**
Antonyms *adj* ≠ **second**: antecedent, earlier, foregoing, former, preceding, previous, prior

latterly *adv* = **recently**, hitherto, lately, of late

lattice *n* **1** = **framework**, fretwork, grating, grid, grille, latticework, mesh, network, openwork, reticulation, tracery, trellis, web

laud *vb* **1** *Literary* = **praise**, acclaim, approve, celebrate, crack up (*inf.*), extol, glorify, honour, magnify (*arch.*), sing *or* sound the praises of

laudable *adj* = **praiseworthy**, admirable, commendable, creditable, estimable, excellent, meritorious, of note, worthy
Antonyms *adj* base, blameworthy, contemptible, ignoble, lowly, unworthy

laudatory *adj* = **eulogistic**, acclamatory, adulatory, approbatory, approving, commendatory, complimentary, panegyrical

laugh *vb* **1** = **chuckle**, be convulsed (*inf.*), be in stitches, be rolling in the aisles (*inf.*), bust a gut (*inf.*), chortle, crack up (*inf.*), crease up (*inf.*), giggle, guffaw, roar with laughter, snigger, split one's sides, titter **5 laugh at** = **make fun of**, belittle, deride, jeer, lampoon, make a mock of, mock, ridicule, scoff at, take the mickey (out of) (*inf.*), taunt ◆ *n* **8** = **chuckle**, belly laugh (*inf.*), chortle, giggle, guffaw, roar *or* shriek of laughter, snigger, titter **10** *Informal* = **joke**, card (*inf.*), caution (*inf.*), clown, comedian, comic, entertainer, hoot (*inf.*), humorist, lark, scream (*inf.*), wag, wit

laughable *adj* **1** = **ridiculous**, absurd, derisive, derisory, farcical, ludicrous, nonsensical, preposterous, risible, worthy of scorn **2** = **funny**, amusing, comical, diverting, droll, hilarious, humorous, mirthful

laughing stock *n* = **figure of fun**, Aunt Sally (*Brit.*), butt, everybody's fool, fair game, target, victim

laugh off *vb* = **disregard**, brush aside, dismiss, ignore, minimize, pooh-pooh, shrug off

laughter *n* **1** = **laughing**, cachinnation, chortling, chuckling, giggling, guffawing, tittering **2** = **amusement**, glee, hilarity, merriment, mirth

launch[1] *vb* **2, 6** = **propel**, cast, discharge, dispatch, fire, project, send off, set afloat, set in motion, throw **3** = **begin**, commence, embark upon, inaugurate, initiate, instigate, introduce, open, start ◆ *n* **9** = **start**, beginning, commencement, inauguration, initiation, instigation, introduction, opening, projection, propelling, sendoff

launder *vb* **1** = **wash**, clean, tub **3** = **process**, cook (*sl.*), doctor, manipulate

laurel *n* **6** *plural* = **glory**, acclaim, awards, Brownie points, commendation, credit, distincof D. H. or T. E. Lawrence. **2** of, relating to, or situated near the St Lawrence River.

Laurentian Shield *n* another name for the **Canadian Shield.** Also: **Laurentian Plateau.**

laurustinus (ˌlɔːrəˈstaɪnəs) *n* a Mediterranean shrub with glossy evergreen leaves and white or pink fragrant flowers. [C17: from NL, from L *laurus* laurel]

lav (læv) *n Brit. inf.* short for **lavatory.**

lava (ˈlɑːvə) *n* **1** magma emanating from volcanoes. **2** any extrusive igneous rock formed by the solidification of lava. [C18: from It., from L *lavāre* to wash]

lavabo (ləˈveɪbəʊ) *n, pl* **lavaboes** *or* **lavabos.** *Chiefly RC Church.* **1a** the ritual washing of the celebrant's hands after the offertory at Mass. **1b** (*as modifier*): *lavabo basin; lavabo towel.* **2** another name for **washbasin. 3** a trough for washing in a convent or monastery. [C19: from L: I shall wash, the opening of Psalm 26:6]

lavage (ˈlævɪdʒ, læˈvɑːʒ) *n Med.* the washing out of a hollow organ by flushing with water. [C19: via F, from L *lavāre* to wash]

lavatorial (ˌlævəˈtɔːrɪəl) *adj* characterized by excessive mention of the excretory functions; vulgar or scatological: *lavatorial humour.*

lavatory Ⓣ (ˈlævətərɪ, -trɪ) *n, pl* **lavatories. a** a sanitary installation for receiving and disposing of urine and faeces, consisting of a bowl fitted with a water-flushing device and connected to a drain. **b** a room containing such an installation. Also called: **toilet, water closet, WC.** [C14: from LL *lavātōrium,* from L *lavāre* to wash]

lavatory paper *n Brit.* another name for **toilet paper.**

lave (leɪv) *vb* **laves, laving, laved.** an archaic word for **wash.** [OE *lafian,* ?from L *lavāre* to wash]

lavender (ˈlævəndə) *n* **1** any of various perennial shrubs or herbaceous plants of the labiate family, esp. *Lavandula vera,* cultivated for its mauve or blue flowers and as the source of a fragrant oil (**oil of lavender**). **2** the dried parts of *L. vera,* used to perfume clothes. **3** a pale or light bluish-purple colour. **4** perfume scented with lavender. [C13 *lavendre,* via F from Med. L *lavendula,* from ?]

laver (ˈleɪvə) *n Old Testament.* a large basin of water used by the priests for ritual ablutions. [C14: from OF *laveoir,* from LL *lavātōrium* washing place]

lavish Ⓣ (ˈlævɪʃ) *adj* **1** prolific, abundant, or profuse. **2** generous; unstinting; liberal. **3** extravagant; prodigal; wasteful: *lavish expenditure.* ◆ *vb* **4** (*tr*) to give, expend, or apply abundantly, generously, or in profusion. [C15: adj use of *lavas* profusion, from OF *lavasse* torrent, from L *lavāre* to wash]
▸ˈ**lavisher** *n* ▸ˈ**lavishly** *adv* ▸ˈ**lavishness** *n*

law Ⓣ (lɔː) *n* **1** a rule or set of rules, enforceable by the courts regulating the relationship between the state and its subjects, and the conduct of subjects towards one another. **2a** a rule or body of rules made by the legislature. See **statute law. 2b** a rule or body of rules made by a municipal or other authority. See **bylaw. 3a** the condition and control enforced by such rules. **3b** (*in combination*): *lawcourt.* **4 law and order. 4a** the policy of strict enforcement of the law, esp. against crime and violence. **4b** (*as modifier*): *law-and-order candidate.* **5** a rule of conduct: *a law of etiquette.* **6** one of a set of rules governing a particular field of activity: *the laws of tennis.* **7 the law. 7a** the legal or judicial system. **7b** the profession or practice of law. **7c** *Inf.* the police or a policeman. **8** Also called: **law of nature.** a generalization based on a recurring fact or event. **9** the science or knowledge of law; jurisprudence. **10** the principles originating and formerly applied only in courts of common law. Cf. **equity** (sense 3). **11** a general principle, formula, or rule describing a phenomenon in mathematics, science, philosophy, etc.: *the laws of thermodynamics.* **12** Also called: **Law of Moses.** (*often cap.; preceded by the*) the body of laws contained in the first five books of the Old Testament. **13 go to law.** to resort to legal proceedings on some matter. **14 lay down the law.** to speak in an authoritative or dogmatic manner. ◆ Related adjs.: **judicial, juridical, legal.** [OE *lagu,* from ON]

law-abiding Ⓣ *adj* adhering more or less strictly to the laws: *a law-abiding citizen.*

law agent *n* (in Scotland) a solicitor entitled to appear for a client in any Sheriff Court.

lawbreaker Ⓣ (ˈlɔːˌbreɪkə) *n* a person who breaks the law.
▸ˈ**law,breaking** *n, adj*

law centre *n Brit.* an independent service financed by a local authority, which provides free legal advice and information to the general public.

lawful Ⓣ (ˈlɔːfʊl) *adj* allowed, recognized, or sanctioned by law; legal.
▸ˈ**lawfully** *adv* ▸ˈ**lawfulness** *n*

lawgiver (ˈlɔːˌgɪvə) *n* **1** the giver of a code of laws. **2** Also called: **lawmaker.** a maker of laws.
▸ˈ**law,giving** *n, adj*

lawks (lɔːks) *interj Brit.* an expression of surprise or dismay. [C18: var. of *Lord!,* prob. infl. in form by ALACK]

lawless Ⓣ (ˈlɔːlɪs) *adj* **1** without law. **2** disobedient to the law. **3** contrary to or heedless of the law. **4** uncontrolled; unbridled: *lawless rage.*
▸ˈ**lawlessly** *adv* ▸ˈ**lawlessness** *n*

Law Lords *pl n* (in Britain) members of the House of Lords who sit as the highest court of appeal.

lawn[1] (lɔːn) *n* a flat and usually level area of mown and cultivated grass. [C16: changed form of C14 *launde,* from OF *lande,* of Celtic origin]
▸ˈ**lawny** *adj*

lawn[2] (lɔːn) *n* a fine linen or cotton fabric, used for clothing. [C15: prob. from *Laon,* town in France where made]
▸ˈ**lawny** *adj*

lawn mower *n* a hand-operated or power-operated machine for cutting grass on lawns.

lawn tennis *n* **1** tennis played on a grass court. **2** the formal name for **tennis.**

law of averages *n* (popularly) the expectation that a possible event is bound to occur regularly with a frequency approximating to its probability.

law of supply and demand *n* the theory that the price of an article or service is determined by the interaction of supply and demand.

law of the jungle *n* a state of ruthless competition or self-interest.

law of thermodynamics *n* any of three principles governing the relationships between different forms of energy. The **first law** (conservation of energy) states that energy can be transformed but not destroyed. The **second law** states that in any irreversible process entropy always increases. The **third law** states that it is impossible to reduce the temperature of a system to absolute zero in a finite number of steps.

lawrencium (lɒˈrɛnsɪəm) *n* an element artificially produced from californium. Symbol: Lr; atomic no.: 103; half-life of most stable isotope, ^{256}Lr: 35 seconds. [C20: after Ernest O. *Lawrence* (1901–58), US physicist]

Lawrentian (lɔːˈrɛnʃən) *adj* a variant spelling of **Laurentian** (sense 1).

lawsuit Ⓣ (ˈlɔːˌsuːt) *n* a proceeding in a court of law brought by one party against another, esp. a civil action.

law term *n* **1** an expression or word used in law. **2** any of various periods of time appointed for the sitting of law courts.

lawyer Ⓣ (ˈlɔːjə, ˈlɔɪə) *n* a member of the legal profession, esp. a solicitor. [C14: from LAW]

lax Ⓣ (læks) *adj* **1** lacking firmness; not strict. **2** lacking precision or definition. **3** not taut. **4** *Phonetics.* (of a speech sound) pronounced with little muscular effort. [C14 (orig. used with reference to the bowels): from L *laxus* loose]
▸ˈ**laxly** *adv* ▸ˈ**laxity** *or* ˈ**laxness** *n*

laxative Ⓣ (ˈlæksətɪv) *n* **1** an agent stimulating evacuation of faeces. ◆ *adj* **2** stimulating evacuation of faeces. [C14 (orig.: relaxing): from Med. L *laxātīvus,* from L *laxāre* to loosen]

lay[1] Ⓣ (leɪ) *vb* **lays, laying, laid.** (*mainly tr*) **1** to put in a low or horizontal position; cause to lie: *to lay a cover on a bed.* **2** to place, put, or be in a

THESAURUS

tion, fame, honour, kudos, praise, prestige, recognition, renown, reward

lavatory *n* = **toilet**, bathroom, bog (*sl.*), can (*US & Canad. sl.*), cloakroom (*Brit.*), Gents *or* Ladies, head(s) (*Nautical sl.*), john (*sl., chiefly US & Canad.*), latrine, little boy's room *or* little girl's room (*inf.*), loo (*Brit. inf.*), powder room, privy, (public) convenience, washroom, water closet, W.C.

lavish *adj* **1** = **plentiful**, abundant, copious, exuberant, lush, luxuriant, opulent, profuse, prolific, sumptuous **2** = **generous**, bountiful, effusive, free, liberal, munificent, open-handed, unstinting **3** = **extravagant**, exaggerated, excessive, immoderate, improvident, intemperate, prodigal, thriftless, unreasonable, unrestrained, wasteful, wild ◆ *vb* **4** = **spend**, deluge, dissipate, expend, heap, pour, shower, squander, waste
Antonyms *adj* ≠ **plentiful:** frugal, meagre, miserly, scanty, stingy ≠ **generous:** cheap, miserly, parsimonious, stingy, tight-fisted ≠ **extravagant:** sparing, thrifty ◆ *vb* ≠ **spend:** begrudge, economize, stint, withhold

law *n* **1** = **constitution**, charter, code, jurisprudence **2** = **rule**, act, canon, code, command, commandment, covenant, decree, demand, edict, enactment, order, ordinance, regulation, statute **5, 6** = **principle**, axiom, canon, criterion, formula, precept, standard **14 lay down the law** = **dictate**, dogmatize, emphasize, pontificate

law-abiding *adj* = **obedient**, compliant, dutiful, good, honest, honourable, lawful, orderly, peaceable, peaceful

lawbreaker *n* = **criminal**, convict, crook (*inf.*), culprit, delinquent, felon (*formerly Criminal law*), miscreant, offender, sinner, transgressor, trespasser, villain, violater, wrongdoer

lawful *adj* = **legal**, allowable, authorized, constitutional, just, legalized, legitimate, licit, permissible, proper, rightful, valid, warranted
Antonyms *adj* banned, forbidden, illegal, illegitimate, illicit, prohibited, unauthorized, unlawful

lawless *adj* **1** = **anarchic**, chaotic, ungoverned **2, 3** = **disorderly**, insubordinate, insurgent, mutinous, rebellious, reckless, riotous, seditious, unruly **4** = **unrestrained**, wild
Antonyms *adj* ≠ **anarchic:** civilized, lawful, well-governed ≠ **disorderly:** compliant, disciplined, law-abiding, obedient, orderly ≠ **unrestrained:** restrained

lawlessness *n* **1** = **anarchy**, chaos, disorder, mobocracy, mob rule, ochlocracy, reign of terror

lawsuit *n* = **case**, action, argument, cause, contest, dispute, industrial tribunal, litigation, proceedings, prosecution, suit, trial

lawyer *n* = **legal adviser**, advocate, attorney, barrister, counsel, counsellor, solicitor

lax *adj* **1** = **slack**, careless, casual, easy-going, easy-oasy (*sl.*), lenient, neglectful, negligent, overindulgent, remiss, slapdash, slipshod **2** = **vague**, broad, general, imprecise, inaccurate, indefinite, inexact, nonspecific, shapeless **3** = **loose**, flabby, flaccid, slack, soft, yielding
Antonyms *adj* ≠ **slack:** conscientious, disciplined, firm, heedful, moral, rigid, scrupulous, severe, stern, strict, stringent ≠ **loose:** firm, rigid

laxative *n* **1** = **purgative**, aperient, cathartic, physic, purge, salts

lay[1] *vb* **1, 2** = **place**, deposit, establish, leave, plant, posit, put, set, set down, settle, spread **5** = **arrange**, dispose, locate, organize, position, particular state or position: *he laid his finger on his lips.* **3** (*intr*) *Dialect or not standard.* to be in a horizontal position; lie: *he often lays in bed all the morning.* **4** (sometimes foll. by *down*) to establish as a basis: *to lay a foundation for discussion.* **5** to place or dispose in the proper position: *to lay a carpet.* **6** to arrange (a table) for eating a meal. **7** to prepare (a fire) for lighting by arranging fuel in the grate. **8** (*also intr*) (of birds, esp. the domestic hen) to produce (eggs). **9** to present or put forward: *he laid his case before the magistrate.* **10** to impute or attribute: *all the blame was laid on him.* **11** to arrange, devise, or prepare: *to lay a trap.* **12** to place, set, or locate: *the scene is laid in London.* **13** to make (a bet) with (someone): *I lay you five to one on Prince.* **14** to cause to settle: *to lay the dust.* **15** to allay; suppress: *to lay a rumour.* **16** to bring down forcefully: *to lay a whip on someone's back.* **17** *Taboo sl.* to have sexual intercourse with. **18** to press down or make smooth: *to lay the nap of cloth.* **19** (*intr*) *Naut.* to move or go, esp. into a specified position or direction: *to lay close to the wind.* **20** **lay bare.** to reveal or explain: *he laid bare his plans.* **21** **lay hold of.** to seize or grasp. **22** **lay oneself open.** to make oneself vulnerable (to criticism, attack, etc.). **23** **lay open.** to reveal or disclose. ◆ *n* **24** the manner or position in which something lies or is placed. **25** *Taboo sl.* **25a** an act of sexual intercourse. **25b** a sexual partner. ◆ See also **lay aside, lay-by,** etc. [OE *lecgan*]

USAGE NOTE In careful English, the verb *lay* is used with an object and *lie* without one: *the soldier laid down his arms; the Queen laid a wreath; the book was lying on the table; he was lying on the floor.* In informal English, *lay* is frequently used for *lie*: *the book was laying on the table.* All careful writers and speakers observe the distinction even in informal contexts.

lay[2] (leɪ) *vb* the past tense of **lie**[2].

lay[3] ➊ (leɪ) *adj* **1** of, involving, or belonging to people who are not clergy. **2** nonprofessional or nonspecialist; amateur. [C14: from OF *lai*, from LL *lāicus*, ult. from Gk *laos* people]

lay[4] ➊ (leɪ) *n* **1** a ballad or short narrative poem, esp. one intended to be sung. **2** a song or melody. [C13: from OF *lai*, ? of Gmc origin]

layabout ➊ ('leɪəˌbaut) *n* a lazy person; loafer.

lay analyst *n* a person without medical qualifications who practises psychoanalysis.

lay aside ➊ *vb* (*tr, adv*) **1** to abandon or reject. **2** to store or reserve for future use.

lay brother *or* (*fem*) **lay sister** *n* a person who has taken the vows of a religious order but is not ordained and not bound to divine office.

lay-by ➊ *n* **1** *Brit.* a place for drivers to stop at the side of a main road. **2** *Naut.* an anchorage in a narrow waterway, away from the channel. **3** a small railway siding where rolling stock may be stored or parked. **4** *Austral. & NZ.* a system of payment whereby a buyer pays a deposit on an article, which is reserved for him until he has paid the full price. ◆ *vb* **lay by.** (*tr, adv*) **5** to set aside or save for future needs.

lay days *pl n* **1** *Commerce.* the number of days permitted for the loading or unloading of a ship without payment of demurrage. **2** *Naut.* the time during which a ship is kept from sailing because of loading, bad weather, etc.

lay down ➊ *vb* (*tr, adv*) **1** to place on the ground, etc. **2** to relinquish or discard: *to lay down one's life.* **3** to formulate (a rule, principle, etc.). **4** to build or begin to build: *the railway was laid down as far as Chester.* **5** to record (plans) on paper. **6** to convert (land) into pasture. **7** to store or stock: *to lay down wine.* **8** *Inf.* to wager or bet. **9** *Inf.* to record (tracks) in a studio.

layer ➊ ('leɪə) *n* **1** a thickness of some homogeneous substance, such as a stratum or a coating on a surface. **2** a laying hen. **3** *Horticulture.* a shoot or branch rooted during layering. ◆ *vb* **4** to form or make a layer of (something). **5** to take root or cause to take root by layering. [C14 *leyer, legger*, from LAY[1] + -ER[1]]

layering ('leɪərɪŋ) *n* **1** *Horticulture.* a method of propagation that induces a shoot to take root while it is still attached to the parent plant. **2** *Geol.* the banded appearance of certain igneous rocks, each band being of a different mineral composition.

layette (leɪ'ɛt) *n* a complete set of articles, including clothing, bedclothes, and other accessories, for a newborn baby. [C19: from F, from OF, from *laie*, from MDu. *laege* box]

lay figure *n* **1** an artist's jointed dummy, used in place of a live model, esp. for studying effects of drapery. **2** a person considered to be subservient or unimportant. [C18: from obs. *layman*, from Du. *leeman*, lit.: joint-man]

lay in ➊ *vb* (*tr, adv*) to accumulate and store: *we must lay in food for the party.*

lay into ➊ *vb* (*intr, prep*) *Inf.* **1** to attack forcefully. **2** to berate severely.

layman ➊ ('leɪmən) *or* (*fem*) **laywoman** *n, pl* **laymen** *or* **laywomen. 1** a person who is not a clergyman. **2** a person who does not have specialized or professional knowledge of a subject: *science for the layman.*

lay off ➊ *vb* **1** (*tr, adv*) to suspend from work with the intention of re-employing later: *the firm had to lay off 100 men.* **2** (*intr*) *Inf.* to leave (a person, thing, or activity) alone: *lay off me, will you!* **3** (*tr, adv*) to mark off the boundaries of. ◆ *n* **lay-off. 4** the act of suspending employees. **5** a period of imposed unemployment.

lay on ➊ *vb* (*tr, adv*) **1** to provide or supply: *to lay on entertainment.* **2** *Brit.* to install: *to lay on electricity.* **3** **lay it on.** *Sl.* **3a** to exaggerate, esp. when flattering. **3b** to charge an exorbitant price. **3c** to punish or strike harshly.

lay out ➊ *vb* (*tr, adv*) **1** to arrange or spread out. **2** to prepare (a corpse) for burial or cremation. **3** to plan or contrive. **4** *Inf.* to spend (money), esp. lavishly. **5** *Inf.* to knock unconscious. ◆ *n* **layout. 6** the arrangement or plan of something, such as a building. **7** the arrangement of written material, photographs, or other artwork on an advertisement or page in a book, newspaper, etc. **8** a preliminary plan indicating this. **9** a drawing showing the relative disposition of parts in a machine, etc. **10** the act of laying out. **11** something laid out.

lay over *US.* ◆ *vb* (*adv*) **1** (*tr*) to postpone for future action. **2** (*intr*) to make a temporary stop in a journey. ◆ *n* **layover. 3** a break in a journey, esp. in waiting for a connection.

lay reader *n* **1** *Church of England.* a person licensed by a bishop to conduct religious services other than the Eucharist. **2** *RC Church.* a layman chosen from among the congregation to read the epistle at Mass.

lay up ➊ *vb* (*tr, adv*) **1** to store or reserve for future use. **2** (*usually passive*) *Inf.* to incapacitate or confine through illness.

lazar ('læzə) *n* an archaic word for **leper.** [C14: via OF and Med. L, after *Lazarus*, beggar in Jesus' parable (Luke 16:19–31)]

lazaretto (ˌlæzə'rɛtəʊ), **lazaret,** *or* **lazarette** (ˌlæzə'rɛt) *n, pl* **lazarettos, lazarets,** *or* **lazarettes. 1** Also called: **glory hole.** *Naut.* a small locker at the stern of a boat or a storeroom between decks of a ship. **2** Also called: **lazar house, pesthouse.** (formerly) a hospital for persons with infectious diseases, esp. leprosy. [C16: It., from *lazzaro* LAZAR]

laze ➊ (leɪz) *vb* **lazes, lazing, lazed. 1** (*intr*) to be indolent or lazy. **2** (*tr*; often foll. by *away*) to spend (time) in indolence. ◆ *n* **3** the act or an instance of idling. [C16: back formation from LAZY]

lazy ➊ ('leɪzɪ) *adj* **lazier, laziest. 1** not inclined to work or exertion. **2** conducive to or causing indolence. **3** moving in a languid or sluggish manner: *a lazy river.* [C16: from ?]
▸ **'lazily** *adv* ▸ **'laziness** *n*

lazybones ➊ ('leɪzɪˌbəʊnz) *n Inf.* a lazy person.

lazy Susan *n* a revolving tray, often divided into sections, for holding condiments, etc.

lb *abbrev. for:* **1** pound (weight). [L *libra*] **2** *Cricket.* leg bye.

THESAURUS

set out **8** = **produce**, bear, deposit **9** = **put forward**, advance, bring forward, lodge, offer, present, submit **10** = **attribute**, allocate, allot, ascribe, assign, charge, impute **11** = **devise**, concoct, contrive, design, hatch, plan, plot, prepare, work out **13** = **bet**, gamble, give odds, hazard, risk, stake, wager **15** = **allay**, alleviate, appease, assuage, calm, quiet, relieve, soothe, still, suppress **20** **lay bare** = **reveal**, disclose, divulge, explain, expose, show, unveil **21** **lay hold of** = **grasp**, get, get hold of, grab, grip, seize, snatch

lay[3] *adj* **1** = **nonclerical**, laic, laical, secular **2** = **nonspecialist**, amateur, inexpert, nonprofessional

lay[4] *n* **1, 2** = **poem**, ballad, lyric, ode, song

layabout *n* = **idler**, couch potato (*sl.*), good-for-nothing, laggard, loafer, lounger, ne'er-do-well, shirker, skiver (*Brit. sl.*), vagrant, wastrel

lay aside *vb* **1** = **abandon**, cast aside, dismiss, postpone, put aside, put off, reject, shelve

lay-by *vb* **lay by 5** = **keep**, accumulate, collect, hoard, lay aside, lay in, salt away, save, stash (*inf.*), stockpile, store

lay down *vb* **2** = **sacrifice**, give up, relinquish, surrender, yield **3** = **stipulate**, affirm, assume, establish, formulate, ordain, postulate, prescribe

layer *n* **1** = **thickness**, bed, blanket, coat, coating, cover, covering, film, mantle, ply, row, seam, sheet, stratum, tier

lay in *vb* = **store (up)**, accumulate, amass, build up, collect, hoard, stockpile, stock up

lay into *vb* **1** *Informal* = **attack**, assail, belabour, go for the jugular, hit out at, lambast(e), let fly at, pitch into (*inf.*), set about

layman *n* **2** = **nonprofessional**, amateur, lay person, outsider

lay off *vb* **1** = **dismiss**, discharge, drop, give the boot to (*sl.*), let go, make redundant, oust, pay off **2** *Informal* = **stop**, belay (*Nautical*), cease, desist, get off someone's back (*inf.*), give it a rest (*inf.*), give over (*inf.*), give up, leave alone, leave off, let up, quit ◆ *n* **lay-off 4** = **unemployment**, discharge, dismissal

lay on *vb* **1** = **provide**, cater (for), furnish, give, purvey, supply **3a** **lay it on** *Slang* = **exaggerate**, butter up, flatter, overdo it, overpraise, soft-soap (*inf.*)

lay out *vb* **1** = **arrange**, design, display, exhibit, plan, spread out **4** *Informal* = **spend**, disburse, expend, fork out (*sl.*), invest, pay, shell out (*inf.*) **5** *Informal* = **knock out**, kayo (*sl.*), knock for six (*inf.*), knock unconscious, KO *or* K.O. (*sl.*) ◆ *n* **layout 6** = **arrangement**, design, draft, format, formation, geography, outline, plan

lay up *vb* **1** = **store up**, accumulate, amass, garner, hoard, keep, preserve, put away, save, treasure **2** *Informal* = **confine (to bed)**, hospitalize, incapacitate

laze *vb* **1** = **idle**, hang around, loaf, loll, lounge, stand around **2** *often with* **away** = **kill time**, fool away, fritter away, pass time, veg out (*sl., chiefly US*), waste time, while away the hours

laziness *n* **1** = **idleness**, dilatoriness, do-nothingness, inactivity, indolence, lackadaisicalness, slackness, sloth, slothfulness, slowness, sluggishness, tardiness

lazy *adj* **1** = **idle**, good-for-nothing, inactive, indolent, inert, remiss, shiftless, slack, slothful, slow, workshy **3** = **lethargic**, drowsy, languid, languorous, sleepy, slow-moving, sluggish, somnolent, torpid
Antonyms *adj* active, assiduous, diligent, energetic, industrious, quick, stimulated

lazybones *n Informal* = **idler**, couch potato (*sl.*), loafer, lounger, shirker, skiver (*Brit. sl.*), sleepyhead, slugabed, sluggard

LBO *abbrev. for* leveraged buyout.
lbw *Cricket. abbrev. for* leg before wicket.
lc *abbrev. for:* **1** left centre (of a stage, etc.). **2** loco citato. [L: in the place cited] **3** *Printing.* lower case.
L/C, l/c, *or* **lc** *abbrev. for* letter of credit.
LCD *abbrev. for:* **1** liquid-crystal display. **2** Also: **lcd.** lowest common denominator.
LCJ (in Britain) *abbrev. for* Lord Chief Justice.
lcm *or* **LCM** *abbrev. for* lowest common multiple.
L/Cpl *abbrev. for* lance corporal.
LD *abbrev. for* lethal dose (esp. in **LD$_{50}$**). See **median lethal dose.**
LDL *abbrev. for* low-density lipoprotein.
L-dopa (ˌɛlˈdəʊpə) *n* a substance occurring naturally in the body and used to treat Parkinson's disease. Also called: **levodopa.** [C20: from *L-d(ihydr)o(xy)p(henyl)a(lanine)*]
LDS *abbrev. for:* **1** Latter-day Saints. **2** laus Deo semper. [L: praise be to God forever] **3** (in Britain) Licentiate in Dental Surgery.
lea (liː) *n* **1** *Poetic.* a meadow or field. **2** land that has been sown with grass seed. [OE *lēah*]
LEA (in Britain) *abbrev. for* Local Education Authority.
leach ❶ (liːtʃ) *vb* **1** to remove or be removed from a substance by a percolating liquid. **2** to lose or cause to lose soluble substances by the action of a percolating liquid. ◆ *n* **3** the act or process of leaching. **4** a substance that is leached or the constituents removed by leaching. **5** a porous vessel for leaching. [C17: var. of obs. *letch* to wet, ?from OE *leccan* to water]
▸ **'leacher** *n*
lead[1] ❶ (liːd) *vb* **leads, leading, led. 1** to show the way to (an individual or a group) by going with or ahead: *lead the party into the garden.* **2** to guide or be guided by holding, pulling, etc.: *he led the horse by its reins.* **3** (*tr*) to cause to act, feel, think, or behave in a certain way; induce; influence: *he led me to believe that he would go.* **4** (when *intr*, foll. by *to*) (of a road, route, etc.) to serve as the means of reaching a place. **5** (*tr*) to go ahead so as to indicate (esp. in **lead the way**). **6** to guide, control, or direct: *to lead an army.* **7** (*tr*) to direct the course of or conduct (water, a rope, or wire, etc.) along or as if along a channel. **8** to initiate the action of (something); have the principal part in (something): *to lead a discussion.* **9** to go at the head of or have the top position in (something): *he leads his class in geography.* **10** (*intr;* foll. by *with*) to have as the first or principal item: *the newspaper led with the royal birth.* **11** *Music, Brit.* to play first violin in (an orchestra). **12** to direct and guide (one's partner) in a dance. **13** (*tr*) **13a** to pass or spend: *I lead a miserable life.* **13b** to cause to pass a life of a particular kind: *to lead a person a dog's life.* **14** (*intr;* foll. by *to*) to tend (to) or result (in): *this will only lead to misery.* **15** to initiate a round of cards by putting down (the first card) or to have the right to do this: *she led a diamond.* **16** (*intr*) *Boxing.* to make an offensive blow, esp. as one's habitual attacking punch. ◆ *n* **17a** the first, foremost, or most prominent place. **17b** (*as modifier*): *lead singer.* **18** example, precedence, or leadership: *the class followed the teacher's lead.* **19** an advance or advantage held over others: *the runner had a lead of twenty yards.* **20** anything that guides or directs; indication; clue. **21** another name for **leash. 22** the act or prerogative of playing the first card in a round of cards or the card so played. **23** the principal role in a play, film, etc., or the person playing such a role. **24a** the principal news story in a newspaper: *the scandal was the lead in the papers.* **24b** (*as modifier*): *lead story.* **25** *Music.* an important entry assigned to one part. **26** a wire, cable, or other conductor for making an electrical connection. **27** *Boxing.* **27a** one's habitual attacking punch. **27b** a blow made with this. **28** a deposit of metal or ore; lode. ◆ See also **lead off, lead on,** etc. [OE *lǣdan;* rel. to *līthan* to travel]
lead[2] (lɛd) *n* **1** a heavy toxic bluish-white metallic element that is highly malleable: used in alloys, accumulators, cable sheaths, paints, and as a radiation shield. Symbol: Pb; atomic no.: 82; atomic wt.: 207.2. **2** a lead weight suspended on a line used to take soundings of the depth of water. **3** lead weights or shot, as used in cartridges, fishing lines, etc. **4** a thin grooved strip of lead for holding small panes of glass or pieces of stained glass. **5** (*pl*) **5a** thin sheets or strips of lead used as a roof covering. **5b** a flat or low-pitched roof covered with such sheets. **6** Also called: **leading.** *Printing.* a thin strip of type metal used for spacing between lines. **7a** graphite used for drawing. **7b** a thin stick of this material, esp. the core of a pencil. **8** (*modifier*) of, consisting of, relating to, or containing lead. ◆ *vb* (*tr*) **9** to fill or treat with lead. **10** to surround, cover, or secure with lead or leads. **11** *Printing.* to space (type) by use of leads. [OE]
lead acetate (lɛd) *n* a white crystalline toxic solid used in dyeing cotton and in making varnishes and enamels. Formula: $Pb(CH_3COOH)_2$. Systematic name: **lead ethanoate.**
lead chromate (lɛd) *n Chem.* a yellow solid used as a pigment, as in chrome yellow. Formula: $PbCrO_4$.
leaded (ˈlɛdɪd) *adj* (of windows) composed of small panes of glass held in place by thin grooved strips of lead: *leaded lights.*
leaden ❶ (ˈlɛdᵊn) *adj* **1** heavy and inert. **2** laboured or sluggish: *leaden steps.* **3** gloomy, spiritless, or lifeless. **4** made partly or wholly of lead. **5** of a dull greyish colour: *a leaden sky.*
▸ **'leadenly** *adv* ▸ **'leadenness** *n*
leader ❶ (ˈliːdə) *n* **1** a person who rules, guides, or inspires others; head. **2** *Music.* **2a** Also called (esp. US and Canad.): **concertmaster.** the principal first violinist of an orchestra, who plays solo parts, and acts as the conductor's deputy and spokesman for the orchestra. **2b** *US.* a conductor or director of an orchestra or chorus. **3a** the leading horse or dog in a team. **3b** the first man on a climbing rope. **4** *Chiefly Brit.* the leading editorial in a newspaper. Also: **leading article. 5** *Angling.* another word for **trace**[2] (sense 2). **6** a strip of blank film or tape used to facilitate threading a projector, developing machine, etc. **7** (*pl*) *Printing.* rows of dots or hyphens used to guide the reader's eye across a page, as in a table of contents. **8** *Bot.* any of the long slender shoots that grow from the stem or branch of a tree. **9** *Brit.* a member of the Government having primary authority in initiating legislative business (esp. in **Leader of the House of Commons** and **Leader of the House of Lords**).
▸ **'leaderless** *adj*
leadership ❶ (ˈliːdəʃɪp) *n* **1** the position or function of a leader. **2** the period during which a person occupies the position of leader: *during her leadership very little was achieved.* **3a** the ability to lead. **3b** (*as modifier*): *leadership qualities.* **4** the leaders as a group of a party, union, etc.: *the union leadership is now very reactionary.*
lead-free (ˌlɛdˈfriː) *adj* See **unleaded.**
lead glass (lɛd) *n* glass that contains lead oxide as a flux.
lead-in (ˈliːdˌɪn) *n* **1** an introduction to a subject. **2** the connection between a radio transmitter, receiver, etc., and the aerial or transmission line.
leading[1] ❶ (ˈliːdɪŋ) *adj* **1** guiding, directing, or influencing. **2** (*prenominal*) principal or primary. **3** in the first position.
leading[2] (ˈlɛdɪŋ) *n Printing.* **1** the spacing between lines of photocomposed or digitized type. **2** another name for **lead**[2] (sense 6). ◆ Also called: **interlinear spacing.**
leading aircraftman (ˈliːdɪŋ) *n Brit. airforce.* the rank above aircraftman.
▸ **leading aircraftwoman** *fem n*
leading edge (ˈliːdɪŋ) *n* **1** the forward edge of a propeller blade, wing, or aerofoil. Cf. **trailing edge. 2** *Electrical engineering.* the part of a pulse signal that has an increasing amplitude. ◆ *modifier.* **leading-edge. 3** advanced; foremost: *leading-edge technology.*
leading light (ˈliːdɪŋ) *n* an important or outstanding person, esp. in an organization.
leading note (ˈliːdɪŋ) *n Music.* **1** another word for **subtonic. 2** (esp. in cadences) a note that tends most naturally to resolve to the note lying one semitone above it.
leading question (ˈliːdɪŋ) *n* a question phrased in a manner that tends to suggest the desired answer, such as *What do you think of the horrible effects of pollution?*
leading rating (ˈliːdɪŋ) *n* a rank in the Royal Navy comparable but junior to that of a corporal in the army.
leading reins *or US & Canad.* **leading strings** (ˈliːdɪŋ) *pl n* **1** straps or a harness and strap used to assist and control a child who is learning to walk. **2** excessive guidance or restraint.
lead monoxide (lɛd) *n* a poisonous insoluble oxide of lead existing in red and yellow forms: used in making glass, glazes, and cements, and as a pigment. Formula: PbO. Systematic name: **lead(II) oxide.**
lead off ❶ (liːd) *vb* (*adv*) **1** to initiate the action of (something); begin. ◆ *n* **lead-off. 2** an initial move or action.
lead on ❶ (liːd) *vb* (*tr, adv*) to lure or entice, esp. into trouble or wrongdoing.

THESAURUS

leach *vb* **1, 2** = **extract**, drain, filter, filtrate, lixiviate (*Chemistry*), percolate, seep, strain
lead[1] *vb* **1, 2** = **guide**, conduct, escort, pilot, precede, show the way, steer, usher **3** = **cause**, dispose, draw, incline, induce, influence, persuade, prevail, prompt **6** = **command**, direct, govern, head, manage, preside over, supervise **9** = **be ahead (of)**, blaze a trail, come first, exceed, excel, outdo, outstrip, surpass, transcend **13a** = **live**, experience, have, pass, spend, undergo **14** = **result in**, bring on, cause, conduce, contribute, produce, serve, tend ◆ *n* **17a** = **first place**, cutting edge, precedence, primacy, priority, supremacy, van, vanguard **18** = **example**, direction, guidance, leadership, model **19** = **advantage**, advance, edge, margin, start **20** = **clue**, guide, hint, indication, suggestion, tip, trace **23** = **leading role**, principal, protagonist, star part, title role ◆ *modifier* **24b** = **main**, chief, first, foremost, head, leading, most important, premier, primary, prime, principal
leaden *adj* **1** = **heavy**, burdensome, crushing, cumbersome, inert, lead, onerous, oppressive **2** = **laboured**, humdrum, plodding, sluggish, stiff, stilted, wooden **3** = **lifeless**, dismal, dreary, dull, gloomy, languid, listless, spiritless **5** = **grey**, dingy, greyish, lacklustre, louring *or* lowering, lustreless, overcast, sombre
leader *n* **1** = **principal**, boss (*inf.*), captain, chief, chieftain, commander, conductor, counsellor, director, guide, head, number one, ringleader, ruler, superior, torchbearer
Antonyms *n* adherent, disciple, follower, hanger-on, henchman, sidekick (*sl.*), supporter
leadership *n* **1** = **management**, administration, authority, command, control, direction, directorship, domination, guidance, influence, initiative, pre-eminence, running, superintendency, supremacy, sway
leading[1] *adj* **1, 2** = **principal**, chief, dominant, first, foremost, governing, greatest, highest, main, number one, outstanding, pre-eminent, primary, ruling, superior
Antonyms *adj* following, hindmost, incidental, inferior, lesser, minor, secondary, subordinate, superficial
lead off *vb* **1** = **begin**, commence, get going, get under way, inaugurate, initiate, kick off (*inf.*), open, set out, start, start the ball rolling (*inf.*)
lead on *vb* = **entice**, beguile, deceive, draw on, inveigle, lure, seduce, string along (*inf.*), tempt

lead pencil (lɛd) *n* a pencil containing a thin stick of a graphite compound.

lead poisoning (lɛd) *n* **1** acute or chronic poisoning by lead, characterized by abdominal pain, vomiting, convulsions, and coma. **2** *US sl.* death or injury resulting from being shot with bullets.

lead screw (li:d) *n* a threaded rod that drives the tool carriage in a lathe.

lead tetraethyl (lɛd) *n* another name for **tetraethyl lead.**

lead time (li:d) *n* **1** *Manufacturing, chiefly US.* the time between the design of a product and its production. **2** *Commerce.* the time from the placing of an order to the delivery of the goods.

lead up to ❶ (li:d) *vb* (*intr, adv + prep*) **1** to act as a preliminary or introduction to. **2** to approach (a topic) gradually or cautiously.

leaf ❶ (li:f) *n, pl* **leaves** (li:vz). **1** the main organ of photosynthesis and transpiration in higher plants, usually consisting of a flat green blade attached to the stem directly or by a stalk. **2** foliage collectively. **3 in leaf.** (of shrubs, trees, etc.) having a full complement of foliage leaves. **4** one of the sheets of paper in a book. **5** a hinged, sliding, or detachable part, such as an extension to a table. **6** metal in the form of a very thin flexible sheet: *gold leaf.* **7 take a leaf out of** (*or* **from**) **someone's book.** to imitate someone, esp. in one particular course of action. **8 turn over a new leaf.** to begin a new and improved course of behaviour. ◆ *vb* **9** (when *intr,* usually foll. by *through*) to turn (through pages, sheets, etc.) cursorily. **10** (*intr*) (of plants) to produce leaves. [OE]
▸ **'leafless** *adj* ▸ **'leaf,like** *adj*

leafage ('li:fɪdʒ) *n* a less common word for **foliage.**

leaflet ❶ ('li:flɪt) *n* **1** a printed and usually folded sheet of paper for distribution, usually free, esp. for advertising, giving information about a charity, etc. **2** any of the subdivisions of a compound leaf such as a fern leaf. **3** any small leaf or leaflike part. ◆ *vb* **leaflets, leafleting, leafleted. 4** to distribute leaflets (to).

leaf miner *n* **1** any of various insect larvae that bore into and feed on leaf tissue. **2** the adult insect of any of these larvae.

leaf mould *n* **1** a nitrogen-rich material consisting of decayed leaves, etc., used as a fertilizer. **2** any of various fungus diseases affecting the leaves of certain plants.

leaf spring *n* **1** one of a number of metal strips bracketed together in length to form a spring. **2** the compound spring so formed.

leafstalk ('li:f,stɔ:k) *n* the stalk attaching a leaf to a stem or branch. Technical name: **petiole.**

leafy ❶ ('li:fɪ) *adj* **leafier, leafiest. 1** covered with or having leaves. **2** resembling a leaf or leaves.
▸ **'leafiness** *n*

league[1] ❶ (li:g) *n* **1** an association or union of persons, nations, etc., formed to promote the interests of its members. **2** an association of sporting clubs that organizes matches between member teams. **3** a class, category, or level: *he is not in the same league.* **4 in league (with).** working or planning together with. **5** (*modifier*) of, involving, or belonging to a league: *a league game; a league table.* ◆ *vb* **leagues, leaguing, leagued. 6** to form or be formed into a league. [C15: from OF *ligue,* from It. *liga,* ult. from L *ligāre* to bind]

league[2] (li:g) *n* an obsolete unit of distance of varying length. It is commonly equal to 3 miles. [C14 *leuge,* from LL *leuga, leuca,* of Celtic origin]

league football *n* **1** Also called: **league.** *Chiefly Austral.* rugby league football. Cf. **rugby union. 2** *Austral.* an Australian Rules competition conducted within a league.

leaguer ('li:gə) *n Chiefly US & Canad.* a member of a league.

league table *n* **1** a list of sports clubs ranked in order according to their performance. **2** a comparison of performance in any sphere.

leak ❶ (li:k) *n* **1a** a crack, hole, etc., that allows the accidental escape or entrance of fluid, light, etc. **1b** such escaping or entering fluid, light, etc. **2 spring a leak.** to develop a leak. **3** something resembling this in effect: *a leak in the defence system.* **4** the loss of current from an electrical conductor because of faulty insulation, etc. **5** a disclosure of secret information. **6** the act or an instance of leaking. **7** a slang word for **urination.** ◆ *vb* **8** to enter or escape or allow to enter or escape through a crack, hole, etc. **9** (when *intr,* often foll. by *out*) to disclose (secret information) or (of secret information) to be disclosed. **10** (*intr*) a slang word for **urinate.** [C15: from ON]
▸ **'leaker** *n*

leakage ('li:kɪdʒ) *n* **1** the act or an instance of leaking. **2** something that escapes or enters by a leak. **3** *Physics.* an undesired flow of electric current, neutrons, etc.

leaky ❶ ('li:kɪ) *adj* **leakier, leakiest.** leaking or tending to leak.
▸ **'leakiness** *n*

leal (li:l) *adj Arch. or Scot.* loyal; faithful. [C13: from OF *leial,* from L *lēgālis* LEGAL; rel. to LOYAL]
▸ **'leally** *adv* ▸ **lealty** ('li:əltɪ) *n*

lean[1] ❶ (li:n) *vb* **leans, leaning, leaned** *or* **leant. 1** (foll. by *against, on,* or *upon*) to rest or cause to rest against a support. **2** to incline or cause to incline from a vertical position. **3** (*intr;* foll. by *to* or *towards*) to have or express a tendency or leaning. ◆ *n* **4** the condition of inclining from a vertical position. [OE *hleonian, hlinian*]

lean[2] ❶ (li:n) *adj* **1** (esp. of a person or animal) having no surplus flesh or bulk; not fat. **2** not bulky or full. **3** (of meat) having little or no fat. **4** not rich, abundant, or satisfying. **5** (of mixture of fuel and air) containing insufficient fuel and too much air. ◆ *n* **6** the part of meat that contains little or no fat. [OE *hlǣne,* of Gmc origin]
▸ **'leanly** *adv* ▸ **'leanness** *n*

lean-burn *adj* (esp. of an internal-combustion engine) designed to use a lean mixture of fuel and air in order to reduce petrol consumption and exhaust emissions.

leaning ❶ ('li:nɪŋ) *n* a tendency or inclination.

leant (lɛnt) *vb* a past tense and past participle of **lean**[1].

lean-to *n, pl* **lean-tos. 1** a roof that has a single slope adjoining a wall or building. **2** a shed or outbuilding with such a roof.

leap ❶ (li:p) *vb* **leaps, leaping, leapt** *or* **leaped. 1** (*intr*) to jump suddenly from one place to another. **2** (*intr;* often foll. by *at*) to move or react quickly. **3** (*tr*) to jump over. **4** to come into prominence rapidly: *the thought leapt into his mind.* **5** (*tr*) to cause (an animal, esp. a horse) to jump a barrier. ◆ *n* **6** the act of jumping. **7** a spot from which a leap was or may be made. **8** an abrupt change or increase. **9 a leap in the dark.** an action performed without knowledge of the consequences. **10 by leaps and bounds.** with unexpectedly rapid progress. [OE *hlēapan*]
▸ **'leaper** *n*

leapfrog ('li:p,frɒg) *n* **1** a children's game in which each player in turn leaps over the others' bent backs. ◆ *vb* **leapfrogs, leapfrogging, leapfrogged. 2a** (*intr*) to play leapfrog. **2b** (*tr*) to leap in this way over (something). **3** to advance or cause to advance by jumps or stages.

leap second *n* a second added to or removed from a scale for reckoning time on one particular occasion, to synchronize it with another scale.

leapt (lɛpt, li:pt) *vb* a past tense and past participle of **leap.**

leap year *n* a calendar year of 366 days, February 29 (**leap day**) being the additional day, that occurs every four years (those whose number is divisible by four) except for century years whose number is not divisible by 400.

learn ❶ (lɜ:n) *vb* **learns, learning, learned** (lɜ:nd) *or* **learnt. 1** (when *tr, may take a clause as object*) to gain knowledge of (something) or acquire skill in (some art or practice). **2** (*tr*) to commit to memory. **3** (*tr*) to gain by experience, example, etc. **4** (*intr;* often foll. by *of* or *about*) to become informed; know. **5** *Not standard.* to teach. [OE *leornian*]
▸ **'learnable** *adj* ▸ **'learner** *n*

learned ❶ ('lɜ:nɪd) *adj* **1** having great knowledge or erudition. **2** involving or characterized by scholarship. **3** (*prenominal*) a title applied in re-

THESAURUS

lead up to *vb* **1, 2** = **introduce,** approach, intimate, make advances, make overtures, pave the way, prepare for, prepare the way, work round to

leaf *n* **1** = **frond,** blade, bract, flag, needle, pad **4** = **page,** folio, sheet **8 turn over a new leaf** = **reform,** amend, begin anew, change, change one's ways, improve ◆ *vb* **9** *usually foll. by* **through** = **skim,** browse, flip, glance, riffle, thumb (through) **10** = **put out leaves,** bud, green, turn green

leaflet *n* **1** = **booklet,** advert (*Brit. inf.*), bill, brochure, circular, handbill, mailshot, pamphlet

leafy *adj* **1** = **green,** bosky (*literary*), in foliage, leafed, leaved, shaded, shady, springlike, summery, verdant, wooded

league[1] *n* **1** = **association,** alliance, band, coalition, combination, combine, compact, confederacy, confederation, consortium, federation, fellowship, fraternity, group, guild, order, partnership, union **3** *Informal* = **class,** ability group, category, level **4 in league (with)** = **collaborating,** allied, hand in glove, in cahoots (*inf.*), leagued ◆ *vb* **6** = **unite,** ally, amalgamate, associate, band, collaborate, combine, confederate, join forces

leak *n* **1a** = **hole,** aperture, chink, crack, crevice, fissure, opening, puncture **1b** = **leakage,** drip, leaking, oozing, percolation, seepage **5** = **disclosure,** divulgence ◆ *vb* **8** = **escape,** discharge, drip, exude, ooze, pass, percolate, seep, spill, trickle **9** = **disclose,** blow wide open (*sl.*), divulge, give away, let slip, let the cat out of the bag, make known, make public, pass on, reveal, spill the beans (*inf.*), tell

leaky *adj* = **leaking,** cracked, holey, not watertight, perforated, porous, punctured, split, waterlogged

lean[1] *vb* **1** = **rest,** be supported, prop, recline, repose **2** = **bend,** heel, incline, slant, slope, tilt, tip **3** = **tend,** be disposed to, be prone to, favour, gravitate towards, have a propensity, prefer

lean[2] *adj* **1** = **trim,** angular, bony, emaciated, gaunt, lank, rangy, scraggy, scrawny, skinny, slender, slim, spare, thin, unfatty, wiry **4** = **poor,** bare, barren, inadequate, infertile, meagre, pathetic, pitiful, scanty, sparse, unfruitful, unproductive

Antonyms *adj* ≠ **trim:** ample, brawny, burly, fat, full, obese, plump, portly ≠ **poor:** abundant, fertile, plentiful, profuse, rich

leaning *n* = **tendency,** aptitude, bent, bias, disposition, inclination, liking, partiality, penchant, predilection, proclivity, proneness, propensity, taste

leap *vb* **1** = **jump,** bounce, bound, caper, cavort, frisk, gambol, hop, skip, spring **2** = **rush,** arrive at, come to, form hastily, hasten, hurry, jump, reach **3** = **jump over,** clear, vault **4** = **increase,** advance, become prominent, escalate, gain attention, rocket, soar, surge ◆ *n* **6** = **jump,** bound, caper, frisk, hop, skip, spring, vault **8** = **rise,** change, escalation, increase, surge, upsurge, upswing

learn *vb* **1** = **master,** acquire, attain, become able, grasp, imbibe, pick up **2** = **memorize,** commit to memory, con (*arch.*), get off pat, get (something) word-perfect, learn by heart **4** = **discover,** ascertain, detect, determine, discern, find out, gain, gather, hear, suss (out) (*sl.*), understand

learned *adj* **1, 2** = **scholarly,** academic, cultured, erudite, experienced, expert, highbrow, intellectual, lettered, literate, skilled, versed, well-informed, well-read

Antonyms *adj* ignorant, illiterate, uneducated, unlearned

learner *n* **1** = **pupil,** apprentice, beginner, disci-

ferring to a member of the legal profession, esp. to a barrister: *my learned friend.*
▸ **'learnedly** *adv* ▸ **'learnedness** *n*

learning ❶ ('lɜːnɪŋ) *n* **1** knowledge gained by study; instruction or scholarship. **2** the act of gaining knowledge.

learning curve *n* a graphical representation of progress in learning: *I'm still only halfway up the learning curve.*

learnt (lɜːnt) *vb* a past tense and past participle of **learn.**

lease ❶ (liːs) *n* **1** a contract by which property is conveyed to a person for a specified period, usually for rent. **2** the instrument by which such property is conveyed. **3** the period of time for which it is conveyed. **4** a prospect of renewed health, happiness, etc.: *a new lease of life.* ◆ *vb* **leases, leasing, leased.** *(tr)* **5** to grant possession of (land, buildings, etc.) by lease. **6** to take a lease of (property); hold under a lease. [C15: via Anglo-F from OF *lais* (n), from *laissier* to let go, from L *laxāre* to loosen]
▸ **'leasable** *adj* ▸ **'leaser** *n*

leaseback ('liːs,bæk) *n* a transaction in which the buyer leases the property to the seller.

leasehold ('liːs,həʊld) *n* **1** land or property held under a lease. **2** the tenure by which such property is held. **3** *(modifier)* held under a lease.
▸ **'lease,holder** *n*

leash ❶ (liːʃ) *n* **1** a line or rope used to walk or control a dog or other animal; lead. **2** something resembling this in function: *he kept a tight leash on his emotions.* **3 straining at the leash.** eagerly impatient to begin something. ◆ *vb* **4** *(tr)* to control or secure as by a leash. [C13: from OF *laisse,* from *laissier* to loose (hence, to let a dog run on a leash), ult. from L *laxus* lax]

least ❶ (liːst) *determiner* **1a the.** the superlative of **little:** *you have the least talent of anyone.* **1b** *(as pronoun; functioning as sing): least isn't necessarily worst.* **2 at least. 2a** if nothing else: *you should at least try.* **2b** at the least. **3 at the least.** Also: **at least.** at the minimum: *at the least you should earn a hundred pounds.* **4 in the least.** *(usually used with a negative)* in the slightest degree; at all: *I don't mind in the least.* ◆ *adv* **5 the least.** superlative of **little:** *they travel the least.* ◆ *adj* **6** of very little importance. [OE *lǣst,* sup. of *lǣssa* less]

least common denominator *n* another name for **lowest common denominator.**

least common multiple *n* another name for **lowest common multiple.**

least squares *n* a method for determining the best value of an unknown quantity relating one or more sets of observations or measurements, esp. to find a curve that best fits a set of data.

leastways ('liːst,weɪz) *or US & Canad.* **leastwise** *adv Inf.* at least; anyway; at any rate.

least-worst *adj Inf.* bad but better than any available alternative: *a least-worst scenario.*

leather ('lɛðə) *n* **1a** a material consisting of the skin of an animal made smooth and flexible by tanning, removing the hair, etc. **1b** *(as modifier): leather goods.* **2** *(pl)* leather clothes, esp. as worn by motorcyclists. ◆ *vb (tr)* **3** to cover with leather. **4** to whip as with a leather strap. [OE *lether-* (in compound words)]

leatherjacket ('lɛðə,dʒækɪt) *n* **1** any of various tropical fishes having a leathery skin. **2** the greyish-brown tough-skinned larva of certain craneflies, which destroy the roots of grasses, etc.

leathern ('lɛðən) *adj Arch.* made of or resembling leather.

leatherneck ('lɛðə,nɛk) *n Sl.* a member of the US Marine Corps. [from the custom of facing the neckband of their uniform with leather]

leathery ❶ ('lɛðərɪ) *adj* having the appearance or texture of leather, esp. in toughness.
▸ **'leatheriness** *n*

leave[1] ❶ (liːv) *vb* **leaves, leaving, left.** *(mainly tr)* **1** *(also intr)* to go or depart (from a person or place). **2** to cause to remain behind, often by mistake, in a place: *he often leaves his keys in his coat.* **3** to cause to be or remain in a specified state: *paying the bill left him penniless.* **4** to renounce or abandon: *to leave a political movement.* **5** to refrain from consuming or doing something: *the things we have left undone.* **6** to result in; cause: *childhood problems often leave emotional scars.* **7** to entrust or commit: *leave the shopping to her.* **8** to pass in a specified direction: *flying out of the country, we left the cliffs on our left.* **9** to be survived by (members of one's family): *he leaves a wife and two children.* **10** to bequeath: *he left his investments to his children.* **11** *(tr)* to have as a remainder: *37 – 14 leaves 23.* **12** *Not standard.* to permit; let. **13 leave (someone) alone. 13a** Also: **let alone.** See **let**[1] (sense 6). **13b** to permit to stay or be alone. [OE *lǣfan;* rel. to *belīfan* to be left as a remainder] ◆ See also **leave off, leave out.**
▸ **'leaver** *n*

leave[2] ❶ (liːv) *n* **1** permission to do something: *he was granted leave to speak.* **2 by** *or* **with your leave.** with your permission. **3** permission to be absent, as from a place of work: *leave of absence.* **4** the duration of such absence: *ten days' leave.* **5** a farewell or departure (esp. in **take (one's) leave).** **6 on leave.** officially excused from work or duty. **7 take leave (of).** to say farewell (to). [OE *lēaf;* rel. to *alȳfan* to permit]

leave[3] (liːv) *vb* **leaves, leaving, leaved.** *(intr)* to produce or grow leaves.

leaved (liːvd) *adj* **a** having a leaf or leaves; leafed. **b** *(in combination): a five-leaved stem.*

leaven ❶ ('lɛvᵊn) *n also* **leavening. 1** any substance that produces fermentation in dough or batter, such as yeast, and causes it to rise. **2** a piece of such a substance kept to ferment a new batch of dough. **3** an agency or influence that produces a gradual change. ◆ *vb (tr)* **4** to cause fermentation in (dough or batter). **5** to pervade, causing a gradual change, esp. with some moderating or enlivening influence. [C14: via OF ult. from L *levāmen* relief, (hence, raising agent), from *levāre* to raise]

leave off ❶ *vb* **1** *(intr)* to stop; cease. **2** *(tr, adv)* to stop wearing or using.

leave out ❶ *vb (tr, adv)* **1** to cause to remain in the open. **2** to omit or exclude.

leaves (liːvz) *n* the plural of **leaf.**

leave-taking ❶ *n* the act of departing; a farewell.

leavings ❶ ('liːvɪŋz) *pl n* something remaining, such as food on a plate, residue, refuse, etc.

Lebensraum ('leɪbənz,raʊm) *n* territory claimed by a nation or state as necessary for survival or growth. [G, lit.: living space]

LEC (lɛk) *n acronym for* Local Enterprise Company. See **Training Agency.**

lech (lɛtʃ) *Inf.* ◆ *vb* **1** *(intr; usually foll. by after)* to behave lecherously (towards); lust (after). ◆ *n* **2** a lecherous act or indulgence. [C19: back formation from LECHER]

lecher ❶ ('lɛtʃə) *n* a promiscuous or lewd man. [C12: from OF *lecheor,* from *lechier* to lick, of Gmc origin]

lecherous ❶ ('lɛtʃərəs) *adj* characterized by or inciting lechery.
▸ **'lecherously** *adv*

lechery ❶ ('lɛtʃərɪ) *n, pl* **lecheries.** unrestrained and promiscuous sexuality.

lecithin ('lɛsɪθɪn) *n Biochem.* any of a group of phospholipids that are found in many plant and animal tissues, esp. egg yolk: used in making candles, cosmetics, and inks, and as an emulsifier and stabilizer **(E322)** in foods. Systematic name: **phosphatidycholine.** [C19: from Gk *lekithos* egg yolk]

lecky ('lɛkɪ) *n Brit. sl.* short for **electricity.**

Leclanché cell (lə'klɑːnʃeɪ) *n Electrical engineering.* a primary cell with a carbon anode, surrounded by crushed carbon and manganese dioxide in a porous container in an electrolyte of aqueous ammonium chloride into which a zinc cathode dips. [C19: after Georges *Leclanché* (1839–82), F engineer]

lectern ('lɛktən) *n* **1** a reading desk in a church. **2** any similar desk or

THESAURUS

ple, neophyte, novice, scholar, student, trainee, tyro
Antonyms *n* adept, coach, expert, grandmaster, guru, instructor, master, maven, mentor, past master, teacher, tutor, virtuoso, wizard

learning *n* **1** = **knowledge,** acquirements, attainments, culture, education, erudition, information, letters, literature, lore, research, scholarship, schooling, wisdom **2** = **study,** education, schooling, tuition

lease *vb* **5, 6** = **hire,** charter, let, loan, rent

leash *n* **1** = **lead,** rein, tether **2** = **restraint,** check, control, curb, hold ◆ *vb* **4** = **restrain,** check, control, curb, fasten, hold back, secure, suppress

least *determiner* **1** = **smallest,** feeblest, fewest, last, lowest, meanest, minimum, minutest, poorest, slightest, tiniest

leathery *adj* = **tough,** coriaceous, durable, hard, hardened, leatherlike, leathern *(arch.),* rough, rugged, wrinkled

leave[1] *vb* **1** = **depart,** abandon, abscond, decamp, desert, disappear, do a bunk *(Brit. sl.),* exit, flit *(inf.),* forsake, go, go away, make tracks, move, pull out, quit, relinquish, retire, set out, take off *(inf.),* withdraw **2** = **forget,** lay down, leave behind, mislay **4** = **renounce,** abandon, desert **5** = **give up,** cease, desist, drop, forbear, refrain, relinquish, stop **6** = **cause,** generate, produce, result in **7** = **entrust,** allot, assign, cede, commit, consign, give over, refer **10** = **bequeath,** demise, devise *(Law),* hand down, transmit, will
Antonyms *vb* ≠ **depart:** appear, arrive, come, emerge, stay ≠ **give up:** assume, continue, hold, persist, remove, retain

leave[2] *n* **1** = **permission,** allowance, authorization, concession, consent, dispensation, freedom, liberty, sanction **3, 4** = **holiday,** furlough, leave of absence, sabbatical, time off, vacation **5** = **departure,** adieu, farewell, goodbye, leave-taking, parting, retirement, withdrawal
Antonyms *n* ≠ **permission:** denial, prohibition, refusal, rejection ≠ **holiday:** duty ≠ **departure:** arrival, stay

leaven *n* **1, 2** = **yeast,** barm, ferment, leavening **3** = **catalyst,** influence, inspiration ◆ *vb* **4** = **ferment,** lighten, raise, work **5** = **stimulate,** elevate, imbue, inspire, permeate, pervade, quicken, suffuse

leave off *vb* **1** = **stop,** abstain, belay *(Nautical),* break off, cease, desist, discontinue, end, give over *(inf.),* give up, halt, kick *(inf.),* knock off *(inf.),* refrain

leave out *vb* **2** = **omit,** bar, cast aside, count out, disregard, except, exclude, ignore, neglect, overlook, reject

leave-taking *n* = **departure,** farewell, going, goodbye, leaving, parting, sendoff *(inf.),* valediction

leavings *pl n* = **leftovers,** bits, dregs, fragments, pieces, refuse, remains, remnants, residue, scraps, spoil, sweepings, waste

lecher *n* = **womanizer,** adulterer, Casanova, debauchee, dirty old man, Don Juan, fornicator, goat *(inf.),* lech *or* letch *(inf.),* libertine, profligate, rake, roué, satyr, seducer, sensualist, wanton, wolf *(inf.)*

lecherous *adj* = **lustful,** carnal, concupiscent, lascivious, lewd, libidinous, licentious, prurient, randy *(inf., chiefly Brit.),* raunchy *(sl.),* ruttish, salacious, unchaste, wanton
Antonyms *adj* prim, proper, prudish, puritanical, strait-laced, virginal, virtuous

lechery *n* = **lustfulness,** carnality, concupiscence, debauchery, lasciviousness, lecherousness, leching *(inf.),* lewdness, libertinism, libidinousness, licentiousness, lust, profligacy, prurience, rakishness, randiness *(inf., chiefly Brit.),* salaciousness, sensuality, wantonness, womanizing support. [C14: from OF *lettrun,* from LL *lectrum,* ult. from *legere* to read]

lectionary ('lɛkʃənərɪ) *n, pl* **lectionaries.** a book containing readings appointed to be read at divine services. [C15: from Church L *lectiōnārium,* from *lectio* a reading, from *legere* to read]

lector ('lɛktɔː) *n* **1** a lecturer or reader in certain universities. **2** *RC Church.* **2a** a person appointed to read lessons at certain services. **2b** (in convents or monastic establishments) a member of the community appointed to read aloud during meals. [C15: from L, from *legere* to read]

lecture Ⓣ ('lɛktʃə) *n* **1** a discourse on a particular subject given or read to an audience. **2** the text of such a discourse. **3** a method of teaching by formal discourse. **4** a lengthy reprimand or scolding. ◆ *vb* **lectures, lecturing, lectured. 5** to give or read a lecture (to an audience or class). **6** (*tr*) to reprimand at length. [C14: from Med. L *lectūra* reading, from *legere* to read]
▸ **'lecturer** *n* ▸ **'lectureship** *n*

led (lɛd) *vb* the past tense and past participle of **lead**[1].

LED *Electronics. abbrev. for* light-emitting diode.

lederhosen ('leɪdəˌhəuz[ə]n) *pl n* leather shorts with H-shaped braces, worn by men in Austria, Bavaria, etc. [G]

ledge Ⓣ (lɛdʒ) *n* **1** a narrow horizontal surface resembling a shelf and projecting from a wall, window, etc. **2** a layer of rock that contains an ore; vein. **3** a ridge of rock that lies beneath the surface of the sea. **4** a narrow shelflike projection on a cliff or mountain. [C14 *legge,* ?from *leggen* to LAY[1]]
▸ **'ledgy** *or* **ledged** *adj*

ledger ('lɛdʒə) *n* **1** *Book-keeping.* the principal book in which the commercial transactions of a company are recorded. **2** *Angling.* a wire trace that allows the weight to rest on the bottom and the bait to float freely. ◆ *vb* **3** (*intr*) *Angling.* to fish using a ledger. [C15 *legger* book retained in a specific place, prob. from *leggen* to LAY[1]]

ledger line *n Music.* a short line placed above or below the staff to accommodate notes representing pitches above or below the staff.

lee Ⓣ (liː) *n* **1** a sheltered part or side; the side away from the direction from which the wind is blowing. ◆ *adj* **2** (*prenominal*) *Naut.* on, at, or towards the side or part away from the wind: *on a lee shore.* Cf. **weather** (sense 4). [OE *hlēow* shelter]

leech[1] Ⓣ (liːtʃ) *n* **1** an annelid worm which has a sucker at each end of the body and feeds on the blood or tissues of other animals. **2** a person who clings to or preys on another person. **3a** an archaic word for **physician. 3b** (*in combination*): *leechcraft.* ◆ *vb* (*tr*) **4** to use leeches to suck the blood of (a person), as a method of medical treatment. [OE *lǣce, lœce*]

leech[2] (liːtʃ) *n Naut.* the after edge of a fore-and-aft sail or either of the vertical edges of a squaresail. [C15: of Gmc origin]

leek (liːk) *n* **1** a vegetable with a slender white bulb, cylindrical stem, and broad flat overlapping leaves. **2** a leek, or a representation of one, as a national emblem of Wales. [OE *lēac*]

leer Ⓣ (lɪə) *vb* **1** (*intr*) to give an oblique, sneering, or suggestive look or grin. ◆ *n* **2** such a look. [C16: ? verbal use of obs. *leer* cheek, from OE *hlēor*]
▸ **'leering** *adj, n* ▸ **'leeringly** *adv*

leery Ⓣ ('lɪərɪ) *adj* **leerier, leeriest. 1** *Now chiefly dialect.* knowing or sly. **2** *Sl.* (foll. by *of*) suspicious or wary. [C18: ?from obs. sense (to look askance) of LEER]
▸ **'leeriness** *n*

lees Ⓣ (liːz) *pl n* the sediment from an alcoholic drink. [C14: pl of obs. *lee,* from OF, prob. from Celtic]

leet (liːt) *n Scot.* a list of candidates for an office. [C15: ?from Anglo-F *litte,* var. of LIST[1]]

leeward ('liːwəd; *Naut.* 'luːəd) *Chiefly naut.* ◆ *adj* **1** of, in, or moving to the quarter towards which the wind blows. ◆ *n* **2** the point or quarter towards which the wind blows. **3** the side towards the lee. ◆ *adv* **4** towards the lee. ◆ Cf. **windward.**

lee wave *n Meteorol.* a stationary wave sometimes formed in an air stream on the leeward side of a hill or mountain range.

leeway Ⓣ ('liːˌweɪ) *n* **1** room for free movement within limits, as in action or expenditure. **2** sideways drift of a boat or aircraft.

left[1] Ⓣ (lɛft) *adj* **1** (*usually prenominal*) of or designating the side of something or someone that faces west when the front is turned towards the north. **2** (*usually prenominal*) worn on a left hand, foot, etc. **3** (*sometimes cap.*) of or relating to the political left. **4** (*sometimes cap.*) radical or progressive. ◆ *adv* **5** on or in the direction of the left. ◆ *n* **6** a left side, direction, position, area, or part. Related adjs.: **sinister, sinistral. 7** (*often cap.*) the supporters or advocates of varying degrees of social, political, or economic change, reform, or revolution. **8** *Boxing.* **8a** a blow with the left hand. **8b** the left hand. [OE *left* idle, weak, var. of *lyft-* (in *lyftādl* palsy, lit.: left-disease)]

left[2] (lɛft) *vb* the past tense and past participle of **leave**[1].

left-hand *adj* (*prenominal*) **1** of, relating to, located on, or moving towards the left. **2** for use by the left hand; left-handed.

left-handed Ⓣ *adj* **1** using the left hand with greater ease than the right. **2** performed with the left hand. **3** designed or adapted for use by the left hand. **4** awkward or clumsy. **5** ironically ambiguous: *a left-handed compliment.* **6** turning from right to left; anticlockwise. ◆ *adv* **7** with the left hand.
▸ **ˌleft-'handedly** *adv* ▸ **ˌleft-'handedness** *n* ▸ **ˌleft-'hander** *n*

leftist ('lɛftɪst) *adj* **1** of, tending towards, or relating to the political left or its principles. ◆ *n* **2** a person who supports or belongs to the political left.
▸ **'leftism** *n*

left-luggage office *n Brit.* a place at a railway station, etc., where luggage may be left for a small charge. US and Canad. name: **checkroom.**

leftover Ⓣ ('lɛftˌəuvə) *n* **1** (*often pl*) an unused portion or remnant, as of material or of cooked food. ◆ *adj* **2** left as an unused portion.

leftward ('lɛftwəd) *adj* **1** on or towards the left. ◆ *adv* **2** a variant of **leftwards.**

leftwards ('lɛftwədz) *or* **leftward** *adv* towards or on the left.

left wing Ⓣ *n* **1** (*often cap.*) the leftist faction of an assembly, party, group, etc.; the radical or progressive wing. **2** *Sport.* **2a** the left-hand side of the field of play from the point of view of either team facing its opponents' goal. **2b** a player positioned in this area in certain games. ◆ *adj* **left-wing. 3** of, belonging to, or relating to the political left wing.
▸ **ˌleft-'winger** *n*

lefty ('lɛftɪ) *n, pl* **lefties.** *Inf.* **1** a left-winger. **2** *Chiefly US & Canad.* a left-handed person.

leg Ⓣ (lɛg) *n* **1** either of the two lower limbs in humans, or any similar or analogous structure in animals that is used for locomotion or support. **2** this part of an animal, esp. the thigh, used for food: *leg of lamb.* **3** something similar to a leg in appearance or function, such as one of the four supporting members of a chair. **4** a branch, limb, or part of a forked or jointed object. **5** the part of a garment that covers the leg. **6** a section or part of a journey or course. **7** a single stage, lap, length, etc., in a relay race. **8** either the opposite or adjacent side of a right-angled triangle. **9** one of a series of games, matches, or parts of games. **10** *Austral. & NZ.* either one of two races on which a cumulative bet has been placed. **11** *Cricket.* **11a** the side of the field to the left of a right-handed batsman as he faces the bowler. **11b** (*as modifier*): *a leg slip; leg stump.* **12 not have a leg to stand on.** *Inf.* to have no reasonable or logical basis for an opinion or argument. **13 on his, its, etc., last legs.** (of a person or thing) worn out; exhausted. **14 pull (someone's) leg.** *Inf.* to tease, fool, or make fun of (someone). **15 shake a leg.** *Inf.* to hurry up: usually used in the imperative. **16 stretch one's legs.** to stand up or walk around, esp. after sitting for some time. ◆ *vb* **legs, legging, legged. 17 leg it.** *Inf.* to walk, run, or hurry. [C13: from ON *leggr,* from ?]

leg. *abbrev. for:* **1** legal. **2** legate. **3** legato. **4** legislation. **5** legislative. **6** legislature.

legacy Ⓣ ('lɛgəsɪ) *n, pl* **legacies. 1** a gift by will, esp. of money or personal property. **2** something handed down or received from an ancestor or predecessor. [C14 (meaning: office of a legate), C15 (meaning: bequest): from Med. L *lēgātia* commission; see LEGATE]

legal Ⓣ ('liːg[ə]l) *adj* **1** established by or founded upon law; lawful. **2** of or relating to law. **3** recognized, enforceable, or having a remedy at law

THESAURUS

lecture *n* **1** = **talk**, address, discourse, disquisition, harangue, instruction, lesson, speech **4** = **telling off** (*inf.*), castigation, censure, chiding, dressing-down (*inf.*), rebuke, reprimand, reproof, scolding, talking-to (*inf.*) ◆ *vb* **5** = **talk**, address, discourse, expound, give a talk, harangue, hold forth, speak, spout, teach **6** = **tell off** (*inf.*), admonish, bawl out (*inf.*), berate, carpet (*inf.*), castigate, censure, chew out, chide, give a rocket (*Brit. & NZ inf.*), read the riot act, reprimand, reprove, scold, tear into (*inf.*), tear (someone) off a strip (*Brit. inf.*)

ledge *n* **1, 3, 4** = **shelf**, mantle, projection, ridge, sill, step

lee *n* **1** = **shelter**, cover, protection, refuge, screen, shade, shadow, shield

leech[1] *n* **2** = **parasite**, bloodsucker (*inf.*), freeloader (*sl.*), hanger-on, ligger (*sl.*), sponger (*inf.*), sycophant

leer *vb, n* **1, 2** = **grin**, drool, eye, gloat, goggle, ogle, smirk, squint, stare, wink

leery *adj* **2** *Slang* = **wary**, careful, cautious, chary, distrustful, doubting, dubious, on one's guard, sceptical, shy, suspicious, uncertain, unsure

lees *pl n* = **sediment**, deposit, dregs, grounds, precipitate, refuse, settlings

leeway *n* **1** = **room**, elbowroom, latitude, margin, play, scope, space

left[1] *adj* **1** = **left-hand**, larboard (*Nautical*), port, sinistral **3, 4** = **socialist**, leftist, left-wing, liberal, progressive, radical

left-handed *adj* **4** = **awkward**, cack-handed (*inf.*), careless, clumsy, fumbling, gauche, maladroit **5** = **ambiguous**, backhanded, double-edged, enigmatic, equivocal, indirect, ironic, sardonic

leftover *n* **1** = **remnant**, leaving, oddment, remains, scrap ◆ *adj* **2** = **surplus**, excess, extra, remaining, uneaten, unused, unwanted

left wing *adj* **left-wing 3** = **socialist**, collectivist, communist, Marxist, radical, red (*inf.*)

leg *n* **1** = **limb**, lower limb, member, pin (*inf.*), stump (*inf.*) **3** = **support**, brace, prop, upright **6** = **stage**, lap, part, portion, section, segment, stretch **12 not have a leg to stand on** *Informal* = **have no basis**, be defenceless, be full of holes, be illogical, be invalid, be undermined, be vulnerable, lack support **13 on one's (its) last legs** = **worn out**, about to break down, about to collapse, at death's door, dying, exhausted, failing, giving up the ghost **14 pull someone's leg** *Informal* = **tease**, chaff, deceive, fool, have (someone) on, joke, kid (*inf.*), make fun of, poke fun at, rag, rib (*inf.*), trick, twit, wind up (*Brit. sl.*) **15 shake a leg** *Informal* = **hurry**, get a move on (*inf.*), get cracking (*inf.*), hasten, look lively (*inf.*), rush, stir one's stumps **16 stretch one's legs** = **take a walk**, exercise, go for a walk, move about, promenade, stroll, take the air ◆ *vb* **17 leg it** *Informal* = **run**, go on foot, hotfoot, hurry, skedaddle (*inf.*), walk

legacy *n* **1** = **bequest**, devise (*Law*), estate, gift, heirloom, inheritance **2** = **heritage**, birthright, endowment, inheritance, patrimony, throwback, tradition

legal *adj* **1** = **lawful**, allowable, allowed, authorized, constitutional, legalized, legitimate, licit,

rather than in equity. **4** relating to or characteristic of the profession of law. [C16: from L *lēgālis,* from *lēx* law]
▸ **'legally** *adv*

legal aid *n* financial assistance available to persons unable to meet the full cost of legal proceedings.

legalese (ˌliːgəˈliːz) *n* the conventional language in which legal documents are written.

legalism ⓣ (ˈliːgəˌlɪzəm) *n* strict adherence to the law, esp. the letter of the law rather than its spirit.
▸ **'legalist** *n, adj* ▸ **ˌlegal'istic** *adj*

legality ⓣ (lɪˈgælɪtɪ) *n, pl* **legalities. 1** the state or quality of being legal or lawful. **2** adherence to legal principles.

legalize ⓣ *or* **legalise** (ˈliːgəˌlaɪz) *vb* **legalizes, legalizing, legalized** *or* **legalises, legalising, legalised.** *(tr)* to make lawful or legal.
▸ **ˌlegali'zation** *or* **ˌlegali'sation** *n*

legal tender ⓣ *n* currency that a creditor must by law accept in redemption of a debt.

legate ⓣ (ˈlɛgɪt) *n* **1** a messenger, envoy, or delegate. **2** *RC Church.* an emissary representing the Pope. [OE, via OF from L *lēgātus* deputy, from *lēgāre* to delegate; rel. to *lēx* law]
▸ **'legateˌship** *n*

legatee ⓣ (ˌlɛgəˈtiː) *n* a person to whom a legacy is bequeathed.

legation ⓣ (lɪˈgeɪʃən) *n* **1** a diplomatic mission headed by a minister. **2** the official residence and office of a diplomatic minister. **3** the act of sending forth a diplomatic envoy. **4** the mission of a diplomatic envoy. **5** the rank or office of a legate. [C15: from L *lēgātiō,* from *lēgātus* LEGATE]

legato (lɪˈgɑːtəʊ) *Music.* ◆ *adj, adv* **1** to be performed smoothly and connectedly. ◆ *n, pl* **legatos. 2a** a style of playing with no perceptible gaps between notes. **2b** *(as modifier): a legato passage.* [C19: from It., lit.: bound]

leg before wicket *n Cricket.* a manner of dismissal on the grounds that a batsman has been struck on the leg by a bowled ball that otherwise would have hit the wicket. Abbrev.: **lbw.**

leg break *n Cricket.* a bowled ball that spins from leg to off on pitching.

legend ⓣ (ˈlɛdʒənd) *n* **1** a popular story handed down from earlier times whose truth has not been ascertained. **2** a group of such stories: *the Arthurian legend.* **3** a modern story that has the characteristics of a traditional tale. **4** a person whose fame or notoriety makes him a source of exaggerated or romanticized tales. **5** an inscription or title, as on a coin or beneath a coat of arms. **6** explanatory matter accompanying a table, map, chart, etc. [C14 (in the sense: a saint's life): from Med. L *legenda* passages to be read, from L *legere* to read]

legendary ⓣ (ˈlɛdʒəndərɪ, -drɪ) *adj* **1** of or relating to legend. **2** celebrated or described in a legend or legends. **3** very famous or notorious.

legerdemain ⓣ (ˌlɛdʒədəˈmeɪn) *n* **1** another name for **sleight of hand. 2** cunning deception or trickery. [C15: from OF: light of hand]

leger line (ˈlɛdʒə) *n* a variant spelling of **ledger line.**

legged (ˈlɛgɪd, lɛgd) *adj* **a** having a leg or legs. **b** *(in combination): three-legged; long-legged.*

leggiero (lɛdʒˈɛərəʊ) *adj, adv Music.* to be performed lightly and nimbly. [It.]

leggings (ˈlɛgɪŋz) *pl n* **1** an extra outer covering for the lower legs. **2** children's closefitting trousers, usually with a strap under the instep, worn for warmth in winter. **3** a fashion garment for women consiting of closefitting trousers.

leggy (ˈlɛgɪ) *adj* **leggier, leggiest. 1** having unusually long legs. **2** (of a woman) having long and shapely legs. **3** (of a plant) having an unusually long and weak stem.
▸ **'legginess** *n*

leghorn (ˈlɛgˌhɔːn) *n* **1** a type of Italian wheat straw that is woven into hats. **2** any hat made from this straw. [C19: after LEGHORN (Livorno), a port in W central Italy.]

Leghorn (lɛˈgɔːn) *n* a breed of domestic fowl.

legible ⓣ (ˈlɛdʒəbᵊl) *adj* (of handwriting, print, etc.) able to be read or deciphered. [C14: from LL *legibilis,* from L *legere* to read]
▸ **ˌlegi'bility** *n* ▸ **'legibly** *adv*

legion ⓣ (ˈliːdʒən) *n* **1** a unit in the ancient Roman army of infantry with supporting cavalry of three to six thousand men. **2** any large military force: *the French Foreign Legion.* **3** *(usually cap.)* an association of ex-servicemen: *the British Legion.* **4** *(often pl)* any very large number. ◆ *adj* **5** *(usually postpositive)* very numerous. [C13: from OF, from L *legio,* from *legere* to choose]

legionary (ˈliːdʒənərɪ) *adj* **1** of a legion. ◆ *n, pl* **legionaries. 2** a soldier belonging to a legion.

legionnaire (ˌliːdʒəˈnɛə) *n* *(often cap.)* a member of certain military forces or associations.

Legionnaire's disease (ˌliːdʒəˈnɛəz) *n* a serious, sometimes fatal, infection, caused by a bacterium (**legionella**), which has symptoms similar to those of pneumonia. [C20: after the outbreak at a meeting of the American Legion in Philadelphia in 1976]

legislate ⓣ (ˈlɛdʒɪsˌleɪt) *vb* **legislates, legislating, legislated. 1** *(intr)* to make or pass laws. **2** *(tr)* to bring into effect by legislation. [C18: back formation from LEGISLATOR]

legislation ⓣ (ˌlɛdʒɪsˈleɪʃən) *n* **1** the act or process of making laws. **2** the laws so made.

legislative ⓣ (ˈlɛdʒɪslətɪv) *adj* **1** of or relating to legislation. **2** having the power or function of legislating: *a legislative assembly.* **3** of or relating to a legislature.
▸ **'legislatively** *adv*

legislative assembly *n* *(often caps.)* **1** the bicameral legislature in 28 states of the US. **2** the chamber of the bicameral state legislatures in several Commonwealth countries, such as Australia. **3** the unicameral legislature in most Canadian provinces. **4** any assembly with legislative powers.

legislative council *n* *(often caps.)* **1** the upper chamber of certain bicameral legislatures, such as those of the Indian and Australian states (except Queensland). **2** the unicameral legislature of certain colonies or dependent territories. **3** (in the US) a committee of members of both chambers of a state legislature that discusses problems, constructs a legislative programme, etc.

legislator ⓣ (ˈlɛdʒɪsˌleɪtə) *n* **1** a person concerned with the making of laws. **2** a member of a legislature. [C17: from L *lēgis lātor,* from *lēx* law + *lātor* from *lātus,* p.p. of *ferre* to bring]

legislature ⓣ (ˈlɛdʒɪsˌleɪtʃə) *n* a body of persons vested with power to make and repeal laws.

legit (lɪˈdʒɪt) *Sl.* ◆ *adj* **1** short for **legitimate.** ◆ *n* **2** legitimate drama.

legitimate ⓣ *adj* (lɪˈdʒɪtɪmɪt). **1** born in lawful wedlock. **2** conforming to established standards of usage, behaviour, etc. **3** based on correct or acceptable principles of reasoning. **4** authorized by or in accordance with law. **5** of, relating to, or ruling by hereditary right: *a legitimate monarch.* **6** of or relating to a body of famous long-established plays as distinct from films, television, vaudeville, etc. ◆ *vb* (lɪˈdʒɪtɪˌmeɪt), **legitimates, legitimating, legitimated. 7** *(tr)* to make, pronounce, or show to be legitimate. [C15: from Med. L *lēgitimātus* made legal, from *lēx* law]
▸ **le'gitimacy** *n* ▸ **le'gitimately** *adv* ▸ **leˌgiti'mation** *n*

legitimist (lɪˈdʒɪtɪmɪst) *n* a monarchist who supports the rule of a legitimate dynasty or of its senior branch.
▸ **le'gitimism** *n*

legitimize ⓣ**, legitimise** (lɪˈdʒɪtɪˌmaɪz) *or* **legitimatize, legitimatise** (lɪˈdʒɪtɪməˌtaɪz) *vb* **legitimizes, legitimizing, legitimized; legitimises, le-**

THESAURUS

permissible, proper, rightful, sanctioned, valid **2, 4 = judicial**, forensic, judiciary, juridical

legalistic *adj* **= hairsplitting**, contentious, disputatious, literal, litigious, narrow, narrow-minded, polemical, strict

legality *n* **1 = lawfulness**, accordance with the law, admissibleness, legitimacy, permissibility, rightfulness, validity

legalize *vb* **= permit**, allow, approve, authorize, decriminalize, legitimate, legitimize, license, sanction, validate

legal tender *n* **= currency**, medium, money, payment, specie

legate *n* **1 = messenger**, ambassador, delegate, depute *(Scot.)*, deputy, emissary, envoy, nuncio

legatee *n* **= beneficiary**, heir, inheritor, recipient

legation *n* **1 = delegation**, consulate, diplomatic mission, embassy, envoys, ministry, representation

legend *n* **1, 3 = myth**, fable, fiction, folk tale, narrative, saga, story, tale, urban legend, urban myth **4 = celebrity**, big name, celeb *(inf.)*, luminary, marvel, megastar *(inf.)*, phenomenon, prodigy, spectacle, wonder **5 = inscription**, caption, device, motto **6 = key**, cipher, code, table of symbols

legendary *adj* **1, 2 = mythical**, apocryphal, fabled, fabulous, fanciful, fictitious, romantic, storied, traditional **3 = famous**, celebrated, famed, illustrious, immortal, renowned, well-known
Antonyms *adj* ≠ **mythical:** factual, genuine, historical ≠ **famous:** unknown

legerdemain *n* **1 = sleight of hand**, prestidigitation **2 = deception**, artfulness, artifice, chicanery, contrivance, craftiness, cunning, feint, hocus-pocus, manipulation, manoeuvring, subterfuge, trickery

legibility *n* **= readability**, clarity, decipherability, ease of reading, legibleness, neatness, plainness, readableness

legible *adj* **= readable**, bold, clear, decipherable, distinct, easily read, easy to read, neat, plain

legion *n* **1, 2 = army**, brigade, company, division, force, troop **4 = multitude**, drove, horde, host, mass, myriad, number, throng ◆ *adj* **5 = very many**, countless, multitudinous, myriad, numberless, numerous

legislate *vb* **1, 2 = make laws**, codify, constitute, enact, establish, ordain, pass laws, prescribe, put in force

legislation *n* **1 = lawmaking**, codification, enactment, prescription, regulation **2 = law**, act, bill, charter, measure, regulation, ruling, statute

legislative *adj* **1-3 = law-making**, congressional, judicial, juridical, jurisdictive, law-giving, ordaining, parliamentary

legislator *n* **1, 2 = lawmaker**, lawgiver, parliamentarian

legislature *n* **= parliament**, assembly, chamber, congress, diet, house, law-making body, senate

legitimate *adj* **2, 4, 5 = lawful**, acknowledged, authentic, authorized, genuine, kosher *(inf.)*, legal, legit *(sl.)*, licit, proper, real, rightful, sanctioned, statutory, true **4 = reasonable**, admissible, correct, just, justifiable, logical, sensible, valid, warranted, well-founded ◆ *vb* **7 = legitimize**, authorize, give the green light for, legalize, legitimatize, permit, pronounce lawful, sanction
Antonyms *adj* ≠ **lawful:** false, fraudulent, illegal, illegitimate, unlawful ≠ **reasonable:** unfair, unfounded, unjustified, unreasonable, unsound

legitimize *vb* **= legalize**, authorize, give the green light for, legitimate, permit, pronounce lawful, sanction gitimising, legitimised *or* legitimatizes, legitimatizing, legitimatized; legitimatises, legitimatising, legitimatised. (*tr*) to make legitimate; legalize. ▸le,gitimi'zation, le,gitimi'sation *or* le,gitimati,zation, le,gitimati'sation *n*

legless ('lɛglɪs) *adj* **1** without legs. **2** *Inf.* very drunk.

Lego ('lɛgəʊ) *n Trademark.* a construction toy consisting of plastic bricks and other components that fit together. [C20: from Danish *leg godt* play well]

leg-of-mutton *or* **leg-o'-mutton** *n* (*modifier*) (of a sail, sleeve, etc.) tapering sharply.

leg-pull *n Brit. inf.* a practical joke or mild deception.

legroom ('lɛg,ru:m) *n* room to move one's legs comfortably, as in a car.

leg rope *n Austral. & NZ.* a rope used to secure an animal by its hind leg.

leguan ('lɛgʊ,ɑ:n) *n* a large amphibious S African lizard. [C19: Du., from F *l'iguane* the iguana]

legume ('lɛgju:m, lɪ'gju:m) *n* **1** the long dry fruit produced by leguminous plants; a pod. **2** any of various table vegetables, esp. beans or peas. **3** any leguminous plant. [C17: from F *légume,* from L *legūmen* bean, from *legere* to pick (a crop)]

leguminous (lɪ'gju:mɪnəs) *adj* of, relating to, or belonging to any family of flowering plants having pods (or legumes) as fruits and root nodules enabling storage of nitrogen-rich material. [C17: from L *legūmen;* see LEGUME]

legwarmer ('lɛg,wɔ:mə) *n* one of a pair of garments resembling stockings without feet, often worn over jeans, tights, etc., or during exercise.

legwork ('lɛg,wɜ:k) *n Inf.* work that involves travelling on foot or as if on foot.

lei (leɪ) *n* (in Hawaii) a garland of flowers, worn around the neck. [from Hawaiian]

Leibnitzian (laɪb'nɪtsɪən) *adj* of the philosophy of Gottfried Leibnitz (1646–1716), German mathematician and philosopher, in which matter was conceived as existing in the form of independent units or monads, synchronized by pre-established harmony.

Leicester ('lɛstə) *n* a mild dark orange cheese similar to Cheddar but looser and more moist. [after *Leicester,* a county in England]

leishmaniasis (,li:ʃmə'naɪəsɪs) *or* **leishmaniosis** (li:ʃ,meɪnɪ'əʊsɪs, -,mæn-) *n* any disease, such as kala-azar, caused by protozoa of the genus *Leishmania.* [C20: NL, after Sir W. B. *Leishman* (1865-1926), Scot. bacteriologist]

leister ('li:stə) *n* **1** a spear with three or more prongs for spearing fish, esp. salmon. ◆ *vb* **2** (*tr*) to spear (a fish) with a leister. [C16: from Scand.]

leisure ❶ ('lɛʒə) *n* **1a** time or opportunity for ease, relaxation, etc. **1b** (*as modifier*): *leisure activities.* **2** ease or leisureliness. **3 at leisure. 3a** having free time. **3b** not occupied or engaged. **3c** without hurrying. **4 at one's leisure.** when one has free time. [C14: from OF *leisir;* ult. from L *licēre* to be allowed]
▸'**leisured** *adj*

leisure centre *n* a building designed to provide such leisure facilities as a library, sports hall, café, and rooms for meetings.

leisurely ❶ ('lɛʒəlɪ) *adj* **1** unhurried; relaxed. ◆ *adv* **2** without haste; in a relaxed way.
▸'**leisureliness** *n*

leitmotif ❶ *or* **leitmotiv** ('laɪtməʊ,ti:f) *n* **1** *Music.* a recurring short melodic phrase used, esp. in Wagnerian music dramas, to suggest a character, thing, etc. **2** an often repeated image or theme in a literary work. [C19: from G: leading motif]

lek (lɛk) *n* a small area in which birds of certain species, notably the black grouse, gather for sexual display and courtship. [C19: ?from dialect *lake* (vb) from OE *lácan* to frolic, fight, or ?from Swedish *leka* to play]

lekker ('lɛkə) *adj S. African sl.* **1** pleasing, enjoyable, or likeable. **2** tasty. [from Afrik., from Du.]

LEM (lɛm) *n acronym for* lunar excursion module.

lemma ('lɛmə) *n, pl* **lemmas** *or* **lemmata** (-mətə). **1** a subsidiary proposition, assumed to be valid, that is used in the proof of another proposition. **2** an argument or theme, esp. when used as the subject or title of a composition. **3** *Linguistics.* a word considered as its citation form together with all the inflected forms. [C16 (meaning: proposition), C17 (meaning: title, theme): via L from Gk: premise, from *lambanein* to take (for granted)]

lemming ('lɛmɪŋ) *n* **1** any of various volelike rodents of northern and arctic regions of Europe, Asia, and North America. **2** a member of any group following an unthinking course towards destruction. [C17: from Norwegian]
▸'**lemming-,like** *adj*

lemon ('lɛmən) *n* **1** a small Asian evergreen tree widely cultivated in warm and tropical regions for its edible fruits. Related adjs.: **citric, citrine, citrous. 2a** the yellow oval fruit of this tree, having juicy acidic flesh. **2b** (*as modifier*): *a lemon jelly.* **3** Also called: **lemon yellow. 3a** a greenish-yellow or pale yellow colour. **3b** (*as adj*): *lemon wallpaper.* **4** a distinctive tart flavour made from or in imitation of the lemon. **5** *Sl.* a person or thing considered to be useless or defective. [C14: from Med. L *lemōn-,* from Ar. *laymūn*]
▸'**lemony** *adj*

lemonade (,lɛmə'neɪd) *n* a drink made from lemon juice, sugar, and water or from carbonated water, citric acid, etc.

lemon balm *n* the full name of **balm.**

lemon cheese *or* **curd** *n* a soft spread made from lemons, sugar, eggs, and butter.

lemon grass *n* a perennial grass with a large flower spike: used in cooking and grown in tropical regions as the source of an aromatic oil (**lemon grass oil**).

lemon sole *n* a European flatfish with a variegated brown body: highly valued as a food fish.

lemon squash *n Brit.* a drink made from a sweetened lemon concentrate and water.

lemur ('li:mə) *n* **1** any of a family of Madagascan prosimian primates such as the ring-tailed lemur. They are typically arboreal, having foxy faces and long tails. **2** any similar or closely related animal, such as a loris or indris. [C18: NL, adapted from L *lemurēs* ghosts; so named for its ghost-like face and nocturnal habits]
▸**lemuroid** ('lɛmjʊ,rɔɪd) *n, adj*

lend ❶ (lɛnd) *vb* **lends, lending, lent. 1** (*tr*) to permit the use of (something) with the expectation of its return. **2** to provide (money) temporarily, often at interest. **3** (*intr*) to provide loans, esp. as a profession. **4** (*tr*) to impart or contribute (something, esp. some abstract quality): *her presence lent beauty.* **5 lend an ear.** to listen. **6 lend oneself** *or* **itself.** to possess the right characteristics or qualities for: *the novel lends itself to serialization.* [C15 *lende* (orig. the past tense), from OE *lǣnan,* from *lǣn* loan]
▸'**lender** *n*

lending library *n* **1** Also called (esp. US): **circulating library.** the department of a public library providing books for use outside the building. **2** a small commercial library.

lend-lease *n* (during World War II) the system organized by the US in 1941 by which equipment and services were provided for countries fighting Germany.

length ❶ (lɛŋkθ, lɛŋθ) *n* **1** the linear extent or measurement of something from end to end, usually being the longest dimension. **2** the extent of something from beginning to end, measured in some more or less regular units or intervals: *the book was 600 pages in length.* **3** a specified distance, esp. between two positions: *the length of a race.* **4** a period of time, as between specified limits or moments. **5** a piece or section of something narrow and long: *a length of tubing.* **6** the quality, state, or fact of being long rather than short. **7** (*usually pl*) the amount of trouble taken in pursuing or achieving something (esp. in **to great lengths**). **8** (*often pl*) the extreme or limit of action (esp. in **to any length(s)**). **9** *Prosody, phonetics.* the metrical quantity or temporal duration of a vowel or syllable. **10** the distance from one end of a rectangular swimming bath to the other. **11** *NZ inf.* the general idea; the main purpose. **12 at length. 12a** in depth; fully. **12b** eventually. **12c** interminably. [OE *lengthu*]

lengthen ❶ ('lɛŋkθən, 'lɛŋθən) *vb* to make or become longer.
▸'**lengthener** *n*

lengthways ('lɛŋkθ,weɪz, 'lɛŋθ-) *or* **lengthwise** *adv, adj* in, according to, or along the direction of length.

lengthy ❶ ('lɛŋkθɪ, 'lɛŋθɪ) *adj* **lengthier, lengthiest.** of relatively great or tiresome extent or duration.
▸'**lengthily** *adv* ▸'**lengthiness** *n*

THESAURUS

leisure *n* **1a** = **spare time**, breathing space, ease, freedom, free time, holiday, liberty, opportunity, pause, quiet, recreation, relaxation, respite, rest, retirement, spare moments, time off, vacation **3b at leisure** = **free**, available, not booked up, unengaged, unoccupied **4 at one's leisure** = **in one's own (good) time**, at an unhurried pace, at one's convenience, deliberately, unhurriedly, when it suits one, when one gets round to it (*inf.*), without hurry
Antonyms *n* ≠ **spare time:** business, duty, employment, labour, obligation, occupation, work

leisurely *adj* **1** = **unhurried**, comfortable, easy, gentle, laid-back, lazy, relaxed, restful, slow ◆ *adv* **2** = **unhurriedly**, at one's convenience, at one's leisure, comfortably, deliberately, easily, indolently, lazily, lingeringly, slowly, without haste
Antonyms *adj* ≠ **unhurried:** brisk, fast, hasty, hectic, hurried, quick, rapid, rushed ◆ *adv* ≠ **unhurriedly:** briskly, hastily, hurriedly, quickly, rapidly

leitmotif *n* **1** = **melody**, air, strain, theme **2** = **theme**, convention, device, idea, motif, phrase

lend *vb* **1, 2** = **loan**, accommodate one with, advance **4** = **give**, add, afford, bestow, confer, contribute, furnish, grant, hand out, impart, present, provide, supply **5 lend an ear** = **listen**, give ear, hearken (*arch.*), heed, take notice **6 lend oneself** *or* **itself** = **be appropriate**, be adaptable, be serviceable, fit, present opportunities for, suit

length *n* **1-3** = **distance**, extent, longitude, measure, reach, span **4** = **duration**, period, space, span, stretch, term **5** = **piece**, measure, portion, section, segment **6** = **lengthiness**, extensiveness, protractedness **12 at length: a** = **in detail**, completely, fully, in depth, thoroughly, to the full **b** = **at last**, at long last, eventually, finally, in the end **c** = **for a long time**, for ages, for hours, interminably

lengthen *vb* = **extend**, continue, draw out, elongate, expand, increase, make longer, prolong, protract, spin out, stretch
Antonyms *vb* abbreviate, abridge, curtail, cut, cut down, diminish, shorten, trim

lengthy *adj* = **long**, diffuse, drawn-out, extended, interminable, lengthened, long-drawn-out, long-winded, overlong, prolix, prolonged, protracted, tedious, verbose, very long
Antonyms *adj* brief, concise, condensed, limited, short, succinct, terse, to the point

lenient ➊ ('liːnɪənt) *adj* showing or characterized by mercy or tolerance. [C17: from L *lēnīre* to soothe, from *lēnis* soft]
▸ **'leniency** *or* **'lenience** *n* ▸ **'leniently** *adv*

Leninism ('lɛnɪˌnɪzəm) *n* the political and economic theories of Lenin (1870–1924), Russian statesman and Marxist theorist.
▸ **'Leninist** *n, adj*

lenitive ('lɛnɪtɪv) *adj* **1** soothing or alleviating pain or distress. ◆ *n* **2** a lenitive drug. [C16: from Med. L *lēnītīvus,* from L *lēnīre* to soothe]

lenity ('lɛnɪtɪ) *n, pl* **lenities.** the state or quality of being lenient. [C16: from L *lēnitās* gentleness, from *lēnis* soft]

leno ('liːnəʊ) *n, pl* **lenos. 1** (in textiles) a weave in which the warp yarns are twisted together in pairs between the weft or filling yarns. **2** a fabric of this weave. [C19: prob. from F *linon* lawn, from *lin* flax, from L *līnum*]

lens (lɛnz) *n* **1** a piece of glass or other transparent material, used to converge or diverge transmitted light and form optical images. **2** Also called: **compound lens.** a combination of such lenses for forming images or concentrating a beam of light. **3** a device that diverges or converges a beam of electromagnetic radiation, sound, or particles. **4** *Anat.* See **crystalline lens.** [C17: from L *lēns* lentil, referring to the similarity of a lens to the shape of a lentil]

lent (lɛnt) *vb* the past tense and past participle of **lend.**

Lent (lɛnt) *n Christianity.* the period of forty weekdays lasting from Ash Wednesday to Holy Saturday, observed as a time of penance and fasting commemorating Jesus' fasting in the wilderness. [OE *lencten, lengten* spring, lit.: lengthening (of hours of daylight)]

lentamente (ˌlɛntə'mɛnteɪ) *adv Music.* slowly. [It.]

lenten ('lɛntən) *adj* **1** (*often cap.*) of or relating to Lent. **2** *Arch. or literary.* spare, plain, or meagre: *lenten fare.*

lenticel ('lɛntɪˌsɛl) *n* any of numerous pores in the stem of a woody plant allowing exchange of gases between the plant and the exterior. [C19: from NL *lenticella,* from L *lenticula* dim. of *lēns* lentil]

lenticular (lɛn'tɪkjʊlə) *adj* **1** shaped like a biconvex lens. **2** of or concerned with a lens or lenses. **3** shaped like a lentil seed. [C17: from L *lenticulāris* like a LENTIL]

lentil ('lɛntɪl) *n* **1** a small annual leguminous plant of the Mediterranean region and W Asia, having edible convex seeds. **2** any of the seeds of this plant, which are cooked and eaten in soups, etc. [C13: from OF *lentille,* from L *lenticula,* dim. of *lēns* lentil]

lentivirus ('lɛntɪˌvaɪrəs) *n* another name for **slow virus.** [C20: NL, from L *lentus* slow + VIRUS]

lent lily *n* another name for the **daffodil.**

lento ('lɛntəʊ) *Music.* ◆ *adj, adv* **1** to be performed slowly. ◆ *n, pl* **lentos. 2** a movement or passage performed in this way. [C18: It., from L *lentus* slow]

Lent term *n* the spring term at Cambridge University and some other educational establishments.

Leo ('liːəʊ) *n, Latin genitive* **Leonis** (liː'əʊnɪs). **1** *Astron.* a zodiacal constellation in the N hemisphere, lying between Cancer and Virgo. **2** *Astrol.* Also called: the **Lion.** the fifth sign of the zodiac. The sun is in this sign between about July 23 and Aug. 22.

Leonid ('liːənɪd) *n, pl* **Leonids** *or* **Leonides** (lɪ'ɒnɪˌdiːz). any member of a meteor shower appearing to radiate from the constellation Leo. [C19: from NL *Leōnidēs,* from *leō* lion]

leonine ('liːəˌnaɪn) *adj* of, characteristic of, or resembling a lion. [C14: from L *leōnīnus,* from *leō* lion]

Leonine ('liːəˌnaɪn) *adj* **1** connected with one of the popes called Leo: an epithet applied to a district of Rome fortified by Pope Leo IV (**Leonine City**). **2 Leonine verse. 2a** a type of medieval hexameter or elegiac verse having internal rhyme. **2b** a type of English verse with internal rhyme.

leopard ('lɛpəd) *n* **1** Also called: **panther.** a large feline mammal of forests of Africa and Asia, usually having a tawny yellow coat with black rosette-like spots. **2** any of several similar felines, such as the snow leopard and cheetah. **3** *Heraldry.* a stylized leopard, painted as a lion with the face turned towards the front. [C13: from OF *lepart,* from LL, from LGk *leópardos,* from *leōn* lion + *pardos* PARD (the leopard was thought to be the result of cross-breeding)]
▸ **'leopardess** *fem n*

leotard ('lɪəˌtɑːd) *n* **1** a tight-fitting garment covering the body from the shoulders down to the thighs and worn by acrobats, ballet dancers, etc. **2** (*pl*) *US & Canad.* another name for **tights** (sense 1b). [C19: after Jules *Léotard,* F acrobat]

leper ➊ ('lɛpə) *n* **1** a person who has leprosy. **2** a person who is ignored or despised. [C14: via LL from Gk *lepra,* n. use of *lepros* scaly, from *lepein* to peel]

lepido- *or before a vowel* **lepid-** *combining form.* scale or scaly: *lepidopterous.* [from Gk *lepis* scale; see LEPER]

lepidopteran (ˌlɛpɪ'dɒptərən) *n, pl* **lepidopterans** *or* **lepidoptera** (-tərə). **1** any of a large order of insects typically having two pairs of wings covered with fragile scales: comprises the butterflies and moths. ◆ *adj also* **lepidopterous. 2** of, relating to, or belonging to this order. [C19: from NL, from LEPIDO- + Gk *pteron* wing]

lepidopterist ➊ (ˌlɛpɪ'dɒptərɪst) *n* a person who studies or collects moths and butterflies.

leprechaun ('lɛprəˌkɔːn) *n* (in Irish folklore) a mischievous elf, often believed to have a treasure hoard. [C17: from Irish Gaelic *leipreachān,* from MIrish *lūchorpān,* from *lū* small + *corp* body, from L *corpus* body]

leprosy ('lɛprəsɪ) *n Pathol.* a chronic infectious disease occurring mainly in tropical and subtropical regions, characterized by the formation of painful inflamed nodules beneath the skin and disfigurement and wasting of affected parts. [C16: from LEPROUS + -Y[3]]

leprous ('lɛprəs) *adj* **1** having leprosy. **2** relating to or resembling leprosy. [C13: from OF, from LL *leprosus,* from *lepra* LEPER]

-lepsy *or sometimes* **-lepsia** *n combining form.* indicating a seizure: *catalepsy.* [from NL *-lepsia,* from Gk, from *lēpsis* a seizure, from *lambanein* to seize]
▸ **-leptic** *adj combining form.*

leptodactylous (ˌlɛptəʊ'dæktɪləs) *adj Zool.* having slender digits.

lepton[1] ('lɛptɒn) *n, pl* **lepta** (-tə). **1** a Greek monetary unit worth one hundredth of a drachma. **2** a small coin of ancient Greece. [from Gk *lepton (nomisma)* small (coin)]

lepton[2] ('lɛptɒn) *n Physics.* any of a group of elementary particles and their antiparticles, such as an electron, muon, or neutrino, that participate in electromagnetic and weak interactions. [C20: from Gk *leptos* thin, from *lepein* to peel + -ON]

lepton number *n Physics.* a quantum number describing the behaviour of elementary particles, equal to the number of leptons present minus the number of antileptons. It is thought to be conserved in all processes.

leptospirosis (ˌlɛptəʊspaɪ'rəʊsɪs) *n* any of several infectious diseases caused by bacteria, transmitted to man by animals and characterized by jaundice, meningitis, and kidney failure. Also called: **Weil's disease.** [C20: from NL *Leptospira* (from Gk *leptos* thin + *speira* coil + -OSIS)]

lesbian ➊ ('lɛzbɪən) *n* **1** a female homosexual. ◆ *adj* **2** of or characteristic of lesbians. [C19: from the homosexuality attributed to Sappho (6th cent. B.C.), Gk poetess of *Lesbos*]
▸ **'lesbianism** *n*

lese-majesty ('liːz'mædʒɪstɪ) *n* **1** any of various offences committed against the sovereign power in a state; treason. **2** an attack on authority or position. [C16: from F *lèse majesté,* from L *laesa mājestās* wounded majesty]

lesion ➊ ('liːʒən) *n* **1** any structural change in a bodily part resulting from injury or disease. **2** an injury or wound. [C15: via OF from LL *laesiō* injury, from L *laedere* to hurt]

less ➊ (lɛs) *determiner* **1a** the comparative of **little** (sense 1): *less sugar; less spirit than before.* **1b** (*as pronoun; functioning as sing or pl*): *she has less than she needs; the less you eat, the less you want.* **2** (usually preceded by *no*) lower in rank or importance: *no less a man than the president.* **3 less of.** to a smaller extent or degree: *we see less of John these days; less of a success than I'd hoped.* ◆ *adv* **4** the comparative of *a little: she walks less than she should; less quickly; less beautiful.* ◆ *prep* **5** subtracting; minus: *three weeks less a day.* [OE *lǣssa* (adj), *lǣs* (adv, n)]

> **USAGE NOTE** *Less* should not be confused with *fewer. Less* refers strictly only to quantity and not to number: *there is less water than before. Fewer* means smaller in number: *there are fewer people than before.*

-less *suffix forming adjectives.* **1** without; lacking: *speechless.* **2** not able to (do something) or not able to be (done, performed, etc.): *countless.* [OE *-lēas,* from *lēas* lacking]

lessee (lɛ'siː) *n* a person to whom a lease is granted; a tenant under a lease. [C15: via Anglo-F from OF *lessé,* from *lesser* to LEASE]

lessen ➊ ('lɛsᵊn) *vb* **1** to make or become less. **2** (*tr*) to make little of.

lesser ➊ ('lɛsə) *adj* not as great in quantity, size, or worth.

lesser celandine *n* a Eurasian plant, related to the buttercup, having yellow flowers and heart-shaped leaves.

THESAURUS

leniency *n* = **mercy**, clemency, compassion, forbearance, gentleness, indulgence, lenity, mildness, moderation, pity, quarter, tenderness, tolerance

lenient *adj* = **merciful**, clement, compassionate, forbearing, forgiving, gentle, indulgent, kind, mild, sparing, tender, tolerant
Antonyms *adj* harsh, merciless, rigid, rigorous, severe, stern, strict, stringent

leper *n* **2** = **outcast**, pariah, untouchable

lepidopterist *n* = **butterfly collector**

lesbian *n* **1** = **dyke** (*sl.*), butch, tribade ◆ *adj* **2** = **homosexual**, butch (*sl.*), dykey, gay, sapphic, tribadic

lesion *n* **1, 2** = **injury**, abrasion, bruise, contusion, hurt, impairment, sore, trauma (*Pathology*), wound

less *determiner* **1** = **smaller**, shorter, slighter **2** = **inferior**, minor, secondary, subordinate ◆ *adv* **4** = **to a smaller extent**, barely, little, meagrely ◆ *prep* **5** = **minus**, excepting, lacking, subtracting, without

lessen *vb* **1** = **reduce**, abate, abridge, contract, curtail, decrease, de-escalate, degrade, die down, diminish, downsize, dwindle, ease, erode, grow less, lighten, lower, minimize, moderate, narrow, relax, shrink, slacken, slow down, weaken, wind down
Antonyms *vb* add to, augment, boost, enhance, enlarge, expand, increase, magnify, multiply, raise

lessening *n* **1** = **reduction**, abatement, contraction, curtailment, decline, decrease, de-escalation, diminution, dwindling, ebbing, erosion, let-up (*inf.*), minimization, moderation, petering out, shrinkage, slackening, slowing down, waning, weakening

lesser *adj* = **lower**, inferior, less important, minor, secondary, slighter, subordinate, under-
Antonyms *adj* greater, higher, major, primary, superior

lesser panda *n* See **panda** (sense 2).

lesson ❶ (ˈlɛsᵊn) *n* **1a** a unit, or single period of instruction in a subject; class: *an hour-long music lesson.* **1b** the content of such a unit. **2** material assigned for individual study. **3** something from which useful knowledge or principles can be learned; example. **4** the principles, knowledge, etc., gained. **5** a reprimand or punishment intended to correct. **6** a portion of Scripture appointed to be read at divine service. [C13: from OF *leçon,* from L *lēctiō,* from *legere* to read]

lessor (ˈlɛsɔː, lɛˈsɔː) *n* a person who grants a lease of property.

lest (lɛst) *conj* (*subordinating; takes a subjunctive vb*) **1** so as to prevent any possibility that: *keep down lest anyone see us.* **2** (*after vbs. or phrases expressing fear, worry, anxiety, etc.*) for fear that; in case: *he was alarmed lest she should find out.* [OE *the lǣste,* earlier *thȳ lǣs the,* lit.: whereby less that]

let[1] ❶ (lɛt) *vb* **lets, letting, let.** (*tr; usually takes an infinitive without to or an implied infinitive*) **1** to permit; allow: *she lets him roam around.* **2** (*imperative or dependent imperative*) **2a** used as an auxiliary to express a request, proposal, or command, or to convey a warning or threat: *let's get on; just let me catch you here again!* **2b** (in mathematical or philosophical discourse) used as an auxiliary to express an assumption or hypothesis: *let "a" equal "b".* **2c** used as an auxiliary to express resigned acceptance of the inevitable: *let the worst happen.* **3a** to allow the occupation of (accommodation) in return for rent. **3b** to assign (a contract for work). **4** to allow or cause the movement of (something) in a specified direction: *to let air out of a tyre.* **5 let alone.** (*conj*) much less; not to mention: *I can't afford wine, let alone champagne.* **6 let** *or* **leave alone** *or* **be.** refrain from annoying or interfering with: *let the poor cat alone.* **7 let go.** See **go** (sense 45). **8 let loose. 8a** to set free. **8b** *Inf.* to make (a sound or remark) suddenly: *he let loose a hollow laugh.* **8c** *Inf.* to discharge (rounds) from a gun or guns: *they let loose a couple of rounds of ammunition.* ◆ *n* **9** *Brit.* the act of letting property or accommodation. ◆ See also **let down, let off,** etc. [OE *lǣtan* to permit]

let[2] ❶ (lɛt) *n* **1** an impediment or obstruction (esp. in **without let or hindrance**). **2** *Tennis, squash, etc.* **2a** a minor infringement or obstruction of the ball, requiring a point to be replayed. **2b** the point so replayed. ◆ *vb* **lets, letting, letted** *or* **let. 3** (*tr*) *Arch.* to hinder; impede. [OE *lettan* to hinder, from *læt* late]

-let *suffix forming nouns.* **1** small or lesser: *booklet.* **2** an article of attire or ornament worn on a specified part of the body: *anklet.* [from OF *-elet,* from L *-āle,* from L *-ellus,* dim. suffix]

let down ❶ *vb* (*tr, mainly adv*) **1** (*also prep*) to lower. **2** to fail to fulfil the expectations of (a person); disappoint. **3** to undo, shorten, and resew (the hem) so as to lengthen (a dress, skirt, etc.). **4** to untie (long hair that is bound up) and allow to fall loose. **5** to deflate: *to let down a tyre.* ◆ *n* **letdown. 6** a disappointment.

lethal ❶ (ˈliːθəl) *adj* **1** able to cause or causing death. **2** of or suggestive of death. [C16: from L *lēthālis,* from *lētum* death]
▸**lethality** (liːˈθælɪtɪ) *n* ▸ˈ**lethally** *adv*

lethargy ❶ (ˈlɛθədʒɪ) *n, pl* **lethargies. 1** sluggishness, slowness, or dullness. **2** an abnormal lack of energy. [C14: from LL *lēthargīa,* from Gk *lēthargos* drowsy, from *lēthē* forgetfulness]
▸**lethargic** (lɪˈθɑːdʒɪk) *adj* ▸**leˈthargically** *adv*

Lethe (ˈliːθɪ) *n* **1** *Greek myth.* a river in Hades that caused forgetfulness in those who drank its waters. **2** forgetfulness. [C16: via L from Gk, from *lēthē* oblivion]
▸**Lethean** (lɪˈθiːən) *adj*

let off ❶ *vb* (*tr, mainly adv*) **1** (*also prep*) to allow to disembark or leave. **2** to explode or fire (a bomb, gun, etc.). **3** (*also prep*) to excuse from (work or other responsibilities): *I'll let you off for a week.* **4** *Inf.* to allow to get away without the expected punishment, work, etc. **5** to let (accommodation) in portions. **6** to release (liquid, air, etc.).

let on ❶ *vb* (*adv; when tr, takes a clause as object*) *Inf.* **1** to allow (something, such as a secret) to be known; reveal: *he never let on that he was married.* **2** (*tr*) to cause or encourage to be believed; pretend.

let out ❶ *vb* (*adv, mainly tr*) **1** to give vent to; emit: *to let out a howl.* **2** to allow to go or run free; release. **3** (*may take a clause as object*) to reveal (a secret). **4** to make available to tenants, hirers, or contractors. **5** to permit to flow out: *to let air out of the tyres.* **6** to make (a garment) larger, as by unpicking (the seams) and sewing nearer the outer edge. ◆ *n* **let-out. 7** a chance to escape.

let's (lɛts) *contraction of* let us: used to express a suggestion, command, etc., by the speaker to himself and his hearers.

Lett (lɛt) *n* a former name for a **Latvian.**

letter ❶ (ˈlɛtə) *n* **1** any of a set of conventional symbols used in writing or printing a language, each symbol being associated with a group of phonetic values; character of the alphabet. **2** a written or printed communication addressed to a person, company, etc., usually sent by post. **3** (often preceded by *the*) the strict legalistic or pedantic interpretation of the meaning of an agreement, document, etc.; exact wording as distinct from actual intention (esp. in **the letter of the law**). **4 to the letter. 4a** following the literal interpretation or wording exactly. **4b** attending to every detail. ◆ *vb* **5** to write or mark letters on (a sign, etc.), esp. by hand. **6** (*tr*) to set down or print using letters. [C13: from OF *lettre,* from L *littera* letter of the alphabet]
▸ˈ**letterer** *n*

letter bomb *n* an explosive device in an envelope, detonated when the envelope is opened.

letter box *n Chiefly Brit.* **1a** a slot through which letters, etc., are delivered to a building. **1b** a private box into which letters, etc., are delivered. **2** Also: **postbox.** a public box into which letters, etc., are put for collection.

lettered ❶ (ˈlɛtəd) *adj* **1** well educated in literature, the arts, etc. **2** literate. **3** of or characterized by learning or culture. **4** printed or marked with letters.

letterhead (ˈlɛtəˌhɛd) *n* a sheet of writing paper printed with one's address, name, etc.

lettering (ˈlɛtərɪŋ) *n* **1** the act, art, or technique of inscribing letters on to something. **2** the letters so inscribed.

letter of credit *n* a letter issued by a bank entitling the bearer to draw funds up to a specified maximum from that bank or its agencies.

letter of intent *n* a letter indicating that the writer has the serious intention of doing something, such as signing a contract, in the circumstances specified. It does not constitute either a promise or a contract.

letter of marque *or* **letters of marque** *n* (formerly) a licence granted by a state to a private citizen to arm a ship and seize merchant vessels of another nation. Also called: **letter of marque and reprisal.**

letter-perfect *adj* another term (esp. US) for **word-perfect.**

letterpress (ˈlɛtəˌprɛs) *n* **1a** a method of printing in which ink is transferred from raised surfaces to paper by pressure. **1b** matter so printed. **2** text matter as distinct from illustrations.

letters ❶ (ˈlɛtəz) *n* (*functioning as sing or pl*) **1** literary knowledge, ability, or learning: *a man of letters.* **2** literary culture in general. **3** an official title, degree, etc., indicated by an abbreviation: *letters after one's name.*

letters patent *pl n* See **patent** (senses 1, 4).

Lettish (ˈlɛtɪʃ) *n* another name for **Latvian** (sense 2).

lettuce (ˈlɛtɪs) *n* **1** any of various plants of the composite family cultivated in many varieties for their large edible leaves. **2** the leaves of any of these varieties, which are eaten in salads. **3** any of various plants that resemble true lettuce, such as lamb's lettuce. [C13: prob. from OF *laitues,* from L *lactūca,* from *lac-* milk, because of its milky juice]

let up ❶ *vb* (*intr, adv*) **1** to diminish, slacken, or stop. **2** (foll. by *on*) *Inf.* to be less harsh (towards someone). ◆ *n* **let-up. 3** *Inf.* a lessening or abatement.

leuco-, leuko- *or before a vowel* **leuc-, leuk-** *combining form.* white or lacking colour: *leucocyte; leukaemia.* [from Gk *leukos* white]

leucoblast *or esp. US* **leukoblast** (ˈluːkəʊˌblæst) *n* an immature leucocyte.

leucocyte *or esp. US* **leukocyte** (ˈluːkəˌsaɪt) *n* any of the various large

THESAURUS

lesson *n* **1a** = **class**, coaching, instruction, period, schooling, teaching, tutoring **2** = **exercise**, assignment, drill, homework, lecture, practice, reading, recitation, task **3, 4** = **example**, deterrent, exemplar, message, model, moral, precept **5** = **punishment**, admonition, censure, chiding, rebuke, reprimand, reproof, scolding, warning

let[1] *vb* **1** = **allow**, authorize, entitle, give leave, give permission, give the go-ahead, give the green light, give the O.K. *or* okay (*inf.*), grant, permit, sanction, suffer (*arch.*), tolerate, warrant **2** = **enable**, allow, cause, grant, make, permit **3** = **lease**, hire, rent

let[2] *n* **1** = **hindrance**, constraint, impediment, interference, obstacle, obstruction, prohibition, restriction

let down *vb* **2** = **disappoint**, disenchant, disillusion, dissatisfy, fail, fall short, leave in the lurch, leave stranded ◆ *n* **letdown 6** = **disappointment**, anticlimax, blow, comedown (*inf.*), disillusionment, frustration, setback, washout (*inf.*), whammy (*inf., chiefly US*)

lethal *adj* **1** = **deadly**, baneful, dangerous, deathly, destructive, devastating, fatal, mortal, murderous, noxious, pernicious, poisonous, virulent
Antonyms *adj* harmless, healthy, innocuous, safe, wholesome

lethargic *adj* **1, 2** = **sluggish**, apathetic, comatose, debilitated, drowsy, dull, enervated, heavy, inactive, indifferent, inert, languid, lazy, listless, sleepy, slothful, slow, somnolent, stupefied, torpid
Antonyms *adj* active, alert, animated, energetic, responsive, spirited, stimulated, vigorous

lethargy *n* **1, 2** = **sluggishness**, apathy, drowsiness, dullness, inaction, indifference, inertia, languor, lassitude, listlessness, sleepiness, sloth, slowness, stupor, torpidity, torpor
Antonyms *n* animation, brio, energy, life, liveliness, spirit, verve, vigour, vim, vitality, vivacity, zeal, zest

let off *vb* **2** = **fire**, detonate, discharge, explode **3, 4** = **excuse**, absolve, discharge, dispense, exempt, exonerate, forgive, pardon, release, spare **6** = **emit**, exude, give off, leak, release

let on *vb Informal* **1** = **reveal**, admit, disclose, divulge, give away, let the cat out of the bag (*inf.*), make known, say **2** = **pretend**, act, counterfeit, dissemble, dissimulate, feign, make believe, make out, profess, simulate

let out *vb* **1** = **emit**, give vent to, produce **2** = **release**, discharge, free, let go, liberate **3** = **reveal**, betray, blow wide open (*sl.*), disclose, leak, let fall, let slip, make known, take the wraps off

letter *n* **1** = **character**, sign, symbol **2** = **message**, acknowledgment, answer, billet (*arch.*), communication, dispatch, epistle, line, missive, note, reply **4a to the letter** = **precisely**, accurately, exactly, literally, strictly, word for word

lettered *adj* **1, 3** = **educated**, accomplished, cultivated, cultured, erudite, informed, knowledgeable, learned, scholarly, versed, well-educated, well-read

letters *pl n* **1, 2** = **learning**, culture, erudition, humanities, literature, scholarship

let up *vb* **1** = **stop**, abate, decrease, diminish, ease (up), moderate, relax, slacken, subside ◆ *n* **let-up 3** *Informal* = **lessening**, abatement, break,

unpigmented cells in the blood of vertebrates. Also called: **white blood cell, white (blood) corpuscle.**
▸**leucocytic** *or esp. US* **leukocytic** (ˌluːkəˈsɪtɪk) *adj*

leucoma (luːˈkəʊmə) *n Pathol.* a white opaque scar of the cornea.

leucotomy (luːˈkɒtəmɪ) *n, pl* **leucotomies.** the surgical operation of cutting some of the nerve fibres in the frontal lobes of the brain for treating intractable mental disorders.

leukaemia *or esp. US* **leukemia** (luːˈkiːmɪə) *n* an acute or chronic disease characterized by a gross proliferation of leucocytes, which crowd into the bone marrow, spleen, lymph nodes, etc., and suppress the blood-forming apparatus. [C19: from LEUCO- + Gk *haima* blood]

Lev. *Bible. abbrev. for* Leviticus.

levant (lɪˈvænt) *n* a type of leather made from the skins of goats, sheep, or seals, having a pattern of irregular creases. [C19: shortened from *Levant morocco* (type of leather)]

Levant (lɪˈvænt) *n* **the.** a former name for the area of the E Mediterranean now occupied by Lebanon, Syria, and Israel. [C15: from OF, from *lever* to raise (referring to the rising of the sun in the east), from L *levāre*]
▸**Levantine** (ˈlɛvənˌtaɪn) *adj, n*

levanter (lɪˈvæntə) *n (sometimes cap.)* **1** an easterly wind in the W Mediterranean area. **2** an inhabitant of the Levant.

levator (lɪˈveɪtə, -tɔː) *n Anat.* any of various muscles that raise a part of the body. [C17: NL, from L *levāre* to raise]

levee[1] (ˈlɛvɪ) *n US.* **1** an embankment alongside a river, produced naturally by sedimentation or constructed by man to prevent flooding. **2** an embankment that surrounds a field that is to be irrigated. **3** a landing place on a river; quay. [C18: from F, from Med. L *levāta* from L *levāre* to raise]

levee[2] ➊ (ˈlɛvɪ, ˈlɛveɪ) *n* **1** a formal reception held by a sovereign just after rising from bed. **2** (in Britain) a public court reception for men. [C17: from F, var. of *lever* a rising, from L *levāre* to raise]

level ➊ (ˈlɛvᵊl) *adj* **1** on a horizontal plane. **2** having a surface of completely equal height. **3** being of the same height as something else. **4** (of quantities to be measured, as in recipes) even with the top of the cup, spoon, etc. **5** equal to or even with (something or someone else). **6** not having or showing inconsistency or irregularities. **7** Also: **level-headed.** even-tempered; steady. **8 one's level best.** the best one can do. ◆ *vb* **levels, levelling, levelled** *or US* **levels, leveling, leveled. 9** *(tr;* sometimes foll. by *off)* to make (a surface) horizontal, level, or even. **10** to make (two or more people or things) equal, as in position or status. **11** *(tr)* to raze to the ground. **12** *(tr)* to knock (a person) down as by a blow. **13** *(tr)* to direct (a gaze, criticism, etc.) emphatically at someone. **14** *(intr;* often foll. by *with) Inf.* to be straightforward and frank. **15** *(intr;* foll. by *off* or *out)* to manoeuvre an aircraft into a horizontal flight path after a dive, climb, or glide. **16** (often foll. by *at)* to aim (a weapon) horizontally. ◆ *n* **17** a horizontal datum line or plane. **18** a device, such as a spirit level, for determining whether a surface is horizontal. **19** a surveying instrument used for measuring relative heights of land. **20** position or status in a scale of values. **21** amount or degree of progress; stage. **22** a specified vertical position; altitude. **23** a horizontal line or plane with respect to which measurement of elevation is based: *sea level.* **24** a flat even surface or area of land. **25** *Physics.* the ratio of the magnitude of a physical quantity to an arbitrary magnitude: *sound-pressure level.* **26 on the level.** *Inf.* sincere or genuine. [C14: from OF *livel,* from Vulgar L *lībellum* (unattested), from L *lībella,* dim. of *lībra* scales]
▸ˈ**leveller** *or US* ˈ**leveler** *n* ▸ˈ**levelly** *adv* ▸ˈ**levelness** *n*

level crossing *n Brit., Austral., & NZ.* a point at which a railway and a road cross, esp. one with barriers that close the road when a train is due to pass.

level-headed ➊ *adj* even-tempered, balanced, and reliable; steady.
▸ˌ**level-ˈheadedly** *adv* ▸ˌ**level-ˈheadedness** *n*

level of attainment *n Brit. education.* one of ten groupings, each with its own attainment criteria based on pupil age and ability, within which a pupil is assessed.

level pegging *Brit. inf.* ◆ *n* **1** equality between two contestants. ◆ *adj* **2** (of two contestants) equal.

level playing field *n* a situation in which none of the competing parties has an advantage at the outset of a competitive activity.

lever ➊ (ˈliːvə) *n* **1** a rigid bar pivoted about a fulcrum, used to transfer a force to a load and usually to provide a mechanical advantage. **2** any of a number of mechanical devices employing this principle. **3** a means of exerting pressure in order to accomplish something. ◆ *vb* **4** to prise or move (an object) with a lever. [C13: from OF *leveour,* from *lever* to raise, from L *levāre* from *levis* light]

leverage ➊ (ˈliːvərɪdʒ, -vrɪdʒ) *n* **1** the action of a lever. **2** the mechanical advantage gained by employing a lever. **3** strategic advantage. **4** power or influence: *the supermarket chains have greater leverage than single-outlet enterprises.* **5** the US word for **gearing** (sense 3). **6** the use made by a company of its limited assets to guarantee the substantial loans required to finance its business.

leveraged buyout (ˈliːvərɪdʒd, -vrɪdʒd) *n* a takeover bid in which a small company makes use of its limited assets, and those of the usually larger target company, to raise the loans required to finance the takeover. Abbrev.: **LBO.**

leveret (ˈlɛvərɪt, -vrɪt) *n* a young hare, esp. one less than one year old. [C15: from Norman F *levrete,* dim. of *levre,* from L *lepus* hare]

leviable (ˈlɛvɪəbᵊl) *adj* **1** (of taxes, etc.) liable to be levied. **2** (of goods, etc.) liable to bear a levy; taxable.

leviathan ➊ (lɪˈvaɪəθən) *n* **1** *Bible.* a monstrous beast, esp. a sea monster. **2** any huge or powerful thing. [C14: from LL, ult. from Heb. *liwyāthān,* from ?]

levigate (ˈlɛvɪˌgeɪt) *vb* **levigates, levigating, levigated.** *Chem.* **1** *(tr)* to grind into a fine powder or a smooth paste. **2** to form or cause to form a homogeneous mixture, as in the production of gels. **3** *(tr)* to suspend (fine particles) by grinding in a liquid, esp. as a method of separating fine from coarse particles. [C17: from L *lēvigāre,* from *lēvis* smooth]
▸ˌ**leviˈgation** *n*

Levi's (ˈliːvaɪz) *pl n Trademark.* jeans, usually blue and made of denim.

levitate (ˈlɛvɪˌteɪt) *vb* **levitates, levitating, levitated.** to rise or cause to rise and float in the air, without visible agency, usually attributed, esp. formerly, to supernatural intervention. [C17: from L *levis* light + *-tate,* as in *gravitate*]
▸ˌ**leviˈtation** *n* ▸ˈ**leviˌtator** *n*

levity ➊ (ˈlɛvɪtɪ) *n, pl* **levities. 1** inappropriate lack of seriousness. **2** fickleness or instability. **3** *Arch.* lightness in weight. [C16: from L *levitās* lightness, from *levis* light]

levodopa (ˌliːvəʊˈdəʊpə) *n* another name for **L-dopa.**

levy ➊ (ˈlɛvɪ) *vb* **levies, levying, levied.** *(tr)* **1** to impose and collect (a tax, tariff, fine, etc.). **2** to conscript troops for service. **3** to seize or attach (property) in accordance with the judgment of a court. ◆ *n, pl* **levies. 4a** the act of imposing and collecting a tax, tariff, etc. **4b** the money so raised. **5a** the conscription of troops for service. **5b** a person conscripted in this way. [C15: from OF *levée* a raising, from *lever,* from L *levāre* to raise]

lewd ➊ (luːd) *adj* characterized by or intended to excite crude sexual desire; obscene. [C14: from OE *lǣwde* ignorant]
▸ˈ**lewdly** *adv* ▸ˈ**lewdness** *n*

lewis (ˈluːɪs) *n* a lifting device for heavy stone blocks consisting of a number of curved pieces of metal fitting into a dovetailed recess cut into the stone. [C18: ?from the name of the inventor]

Lewis acid *n* a substance capable of accepting a pair of electrons from a base to form a covalent bond. Cf. **Lewis base.** [C20: after G. N. *Lewis* (1875–1946), US chemist]

Lewis base *n* a substance capable of donating a pair of electrons to an acid to form a covalent bond. Cf. **Lewis acid.** [C20: after G. N. *Lewis;* see LEWIS ACID]

Lewis gun *n* a light air-cooled gas-operated machine gun used chiefly in World Wars I and II. [C20: after I. N. *Lewis* (1858–1931), US soldier]

lewisite (ˈluːɪˌsaɪt) *n* a colourless oily poisonous liquid having a power-

THESAURUS

breathing space, cessation, interval, lull, pause, recess, remission, respite, slackening

levee[2] *n* **2** = **reception,** ceremony, entertainment, gathering, party

level *adj* **1** = **horizontal,** as flat as a pancake, flat, plane **2** = **even,** consistent, plain, smooth, uniform **5** = **equal,** aligned, balanced, commensurate, comparable, equivalent, even, flush, in line, neck and neck, on a line, on a par, proportionate **7** = **calm,** equable, even, even-tempered, stable, steady ◆ *vb* **9** = **flatten,** even off *or* out, make flat, plane, smooth **10** = **equalize,** balance, even up **11** = **destroy,** bulldoze, demolish, devastate, flatten, knock down, lay low, pull down, raze, tear down, wreck **14** *often foll. by* **with** *Informal* = **be honest,** be above board, be frank, be open, be straightforward, be up front (*sl.*), come clean (*inf.*), keep nothing back **16** = **direct,** aim, beam, focus, point, train ◆ *n* **17** = **flat surface,** horizontal, plane **20, 21** = **position,** achievement, degree, grade, rank, stage, standard, standing, status **22** = **height,** altitude, elevation, vertical position **26 on the level** *Informal* = **honest,** above board, fair, genuine, open, sincere, square, straight, straightforward, up front (*sl.*)
Antonyms *adj* ≠ **horizontal:** slanted, tilted, vertical ≠ **even:** bumpy, hilly, uneven, warped ≠ **equal:** above, below ◆ *vb* ≠ **destroy:** build, erect, raise

level-headed *adj* = **calm,** balanced, collected, composed, cool, dependable, even-tempered, reasonable, sane, self-possessed, sensible, steady, together (*sl.*), unflappable (*inf.*)

lever *n* **1** = **handle,** bar, crowbar, handspike, jemmy ◆ *vb* **4** = **prise,** force, jemmy, move, pry (*US*), raise

leverage *n* **4** = **influence,** ascendancy, authority, clout (*inf.*), pull (*inf.*), purchasing power, rank, weight

leviathan *n* **2** = **monster,** behemoth, colossus, hulk, mammoth, Titan, whale

levity *n* **1** = **frivolity,** facetiousness, flippancy, light-heartedness, silliness, triviality **2** = **fickleness,** flightiness, giddiness, light-mindedness, skittishness
Antonyms *n* earnestness, gravity, seriousness, solemnity

levy *vb* **1** = **impose,** charge, collect, demand, exact, gather, tax **2** = **conscript,** call, call up, mobilize, muster, press, raise, summon ◆ *n* **4a** = **imposition,** assessment, collection, exaction, gathering **4b** = **tax,** assessment, duty, excise, fee, imposition, impost, tariff, toll

lewd *adj* = **indecent,** bawdy, blue, dirty, impure, lascivious, libidinous, licentious, loose, lustful, obscene, pornographic, salacious, smutty, unchaste, vile, vulgar, wanton, wicked, X-rated (*inf.*)

lewdness *n* = **indecency,** bawdiness, carnality, crudity, debauchery, depravity, impurity, lasciviousness, lechery, licentiousness, lubricity, obscenity, pornography, profligacy, salaciousness, smut, smuttiness, unchastity, vulgarity, wantonness ful blistering action and used as a war gas. Formula: $ClCH{:}CHAsCl_2$. Systematic name: **1-chloro-2-dichloroarsinoethene.** [C20: after W. L. *Lewis* (1878–1943), US chemist]

lexeme ('lɛksiːm) *n Linguistics.* a minimal meaningful unit that cannot be understood from the meanings of its component morphemes. [C20: from LEX(ICON) + -EME]

lexical ('lɛksɪkᵊl) *adj* **1** of or relating to items of vocabulary in a language. **2** of or relating to a lexicon.
▸**'lexically** *adv*

lexicography (ˌlɛksɪ'kɒɡrəfɪ) *n* the process or profession of writing or compiling dictionaries.
▸**ˌlexi'cographer** *n* ▸**lexicographic** (ˌlɛksɪkə'ɡræfɪk) *or* **ˌlexico'graphical** *adj*

lexicon ❶ ('lɛksɪkən) *n* **1** a dictionary, esp. one of an ancient language such as Greek or Hebrew. **2** a list of terms relating to a particular subject. **3** the vocabulary of a language or of an individual. **4** *Linguistics.* the set of all the morphemes of a language. [C17: NL, from Gk *lexikon,* n use of *lexikos* relating to words, from Gk *lexis* word, from *legein* to speak]

lexigraphy (lɛk'sɪɡrəfɪ) *n* a system of writing in which each word is represented by a sign. [C19: from Gk *lexis* word + -GRAPHY]

lexis ('lɛksɪs) *n* the totality of vocabulary items in a language. [C20: from Gk *lexis* word]

ley (leɪ, liː) *n* **1** arable land temporarily under grass. **2** Also: **ley line.** a line joining two prominent points in the landscape, thought to be the line of a prehistoric track. [C14: var. of LEA]

Leyden jar ('laɪdᵊn) *n Physics.* an early type of capacitor consisting of a glass jar with the lower part of the inside and outside coated with tin foil. [C18: first made in Leiden (*Leyden*), city in the Netherlands]

lf *Printing. abbrev. for* light face.

LF *Radio. abbrev. for* low frequency.

LG *abbrev. for* Low German.

LGV (in Britain) *abbrev. for* large goods vehicle.

lh *or* **LH** *abbrev. for* left hand.

Li *the chemical symbol for* lithium.

liabilities (ˌlaɪə'bɪlɪtɪz) *pl n Accounting.* business obligations not discharged and shown as balanced against assets on the balance sheet.

liability ❶ (ˌlaɪə'bɪlɪtɪ) *n, pl* **liabilities. 1** the state of being liable. **2** a financial obligation. **3** a hindrance or disadvantage.

liable ❶ ('laɪəbᵊl) *adj* (*postpositive*) **1** legally obliged or responsible; answerable. **2** susceptible or exposed; subject. **3** probable or likely: *it's liable to happen soon.* [C15: ? via Anglo-F, from OF *lier* to bind, from L *ligāre*]

> **USAGE NOTE** The use of *liable to* to mean *likely to* was formerly considered incorrect, but is now acceptable.

liaise ❶ (lɪ'eɪz) *vb* **liaises, liaising, liaised.** (*intr;* usually foll. by *with*) to communicate and maintain contact (with). [C20: back formation from LIAISON]

liaison ❶ (lɪ'eɪzɒn) *n* **1** communication and contact between groups or units. **2** a secretive or adulterous sexual relationship. **3** the relationship between military units necessary to ensure unity of purpose. **4** (esp. in French) the pronunciation of a normally silent consonant at the end of a word immediately before another word commencing with a vowel, in such a way that the consonant is taken over as the initial sound of the following word, as in *ils ont* (ilzɔ̃). **5** any thickening for soups, sauces, etc., such as egg yolks or cream. [C17: via F from OF, from *lier* to bind, from L *ligāre*]

liana (lɪ'ɑːnə) *or* **liane** (lɪ'ɑːn) *n* any of various woody climbing plants of tropical forests. [C19: changed from earlier *liane* (through infl. of F *lier* to bind), from F, from ?]

liar ❶ ('laɪə) *n* a person who tells lies.

Lias ('laɪəs) *n* the lowest series of rocks of the Jurassic system. [C15 (referring to a kind of limestone), C19 (geological sense): from OF *liois,* ?from *lie* dregs, so called from its appearance]
▸**Liassic** (laɪ'æsɪk) *adj*

lib (lɪb) *n Inf., sometimes derog.* short for **liberation.**

lib. *abbrev. for:* **1** liber. [L: book] **2** librarian. **3** library.

Lib. *abbrev. for* Liberal.

libation (laɪ'beɪʃən) *n* **1a** the pouring-out of wine, etc., in honour of a deity. **1b** the liquid so poured out. **2** *Usually facetious.* an alcoholic drink. [C14: from L *lībātiō,* from *lībāre* to pour an offering of drink]

libel ❶ ('laɪbᵊl) *n* **1** *Law.* **1a** the publication of defamatory matter in permanent form, as by a written or printed statement, picture, etc. **1b** the act of publishing such matter. **2** any defamatory or unflattering representation or statement. **3** *Scots Law.* the formal statement of a charge. ◆ *vb* **libels, libelling, libelled** *or US* **libels, libeling, libeled.** (*tr*) **4** *Law.* to make or publish a defamatory statement or representation about (a person). **5** to misrepresent injuriously. [C13 (in the sense: written statement), hence C14 legal sense: a plaintiff's statement, via OF from L *libellus* a little book]
▸**'libeller** *or* **'libelist** *n* ▸**'libellous** *or* **'libelous** *adj*

liberal ❶ ('lɪbərəl, 'lɪbrəl) *adj* **1** relating to or having social and political views that favour progress and reform. **2** relating to or having policies or views advocating individual freedom. **3** giving and generous in temperament or behaviour. **4** tolerant of other people. **5** abundant; lavish: *a liberal helping of cream.* **6** not strict; free: *a liberal translation.* **7** of or relating to an education that aims to develop general cultural interests and intellectual ability. ◆ *n* **8** a person who has liberal ideas or opinions. [C14: from L *līberālis* of freedom, from *līber* free]
▸**'liberally** *adv* ▸**'liberalness** *n*

Liberal ('lɪbərəl, 'lɪbrəl) *n* **1** a member or supporter of a Liberal Party or Liberal Democrat party. ◆ *adj* **2** of or relating to a Liberal Party.

liberal arts *pl n* the fine arts, humanities, sociology, languages, and literature. Often shortened to **arts.**

Liberal Democrat *n* a member or supporter of the Liberal Democrats.

Liberal Democrats *pl n* (in Britain) a political party with centrist policies; established in 1988 as the Social and Liberal Democrats when the Liberal Party merged with the Social Democratic Party; renamed Liberal Democrats in 1989.

liberalism ❶ ('lɪbərəˌlɪzəm, 'lɪbrə-) *n* liberal opinions, practices, or politics.

liberality ❶ (ˌlɪbə'rælɪtɪ) *n, pl* **liberalities. 1** generosity; bounty. **2** the quality or condition of being liberal.

liberalize ❶ *or* **liberalise** ('lɪbərəˌlaɪz, 'lɪbrə-) *vb* **liberalizes, liberalizing, liberalized** *or* **liberalises, liberalising, liberalised.** to make or become liberal.
▸**ˌliberali'zation** *or* **ˌliberali'sation** *n* ▸**'liberalˌizer** *or* **'liberalˌiser** *n*

Liberal Party *n* **1** one of the former major political parties in Britain; in 1988 it merged with the Social Democratic Party to form the Social and Liberal Democrats; renamed the Liberal Democrats in 1989. **2** one of the major political parties in Australia, a conservative party, generally opposed to the Labor Party. **3** any other party supporting liberal policies.

liberal studies *n* (*functioning as sing*) *Brit.* a supplementary arts course for those specializing in scientific, technical, or professional studies.

liberate ❶ ('lɪbəˌreɪt) *vb* **liberates, liberating, liberated.** (*tr*) **1** to give liberty to; make free. **2** to release (something, esp. a gas) from chemical combination. **3** to release from occupation or subjugation by a foreign power. **4** to free from social prejudices or injustices. **5** *Euphemistic or facetious.* to steal.
▸**'liberˌator** *n*

liberated ('lɪbəˌreɪtɪd) *adj* **1** given liberty; freed; released. **2** released from occupation or subjugation by a foreign power. **3** (esp. in feminist theory) not bound by traditional sexual and social roles.

liberation ❶ (ˌlɪbə'reɪʃən) *n* **1** a liberating or being liberated. **2** the seek-

THESAURUS

lexicon *n* **1** = **dictionary**, wordbook **2** = **vocabulary**, glossary, word list

liability *n* **1** = **responsibility**, accountability, answerability, culpability, duty, obligation, onus **1** = **tendency**, likelihood, probability, proneness, susceptibility **2** = **debt**, arrear, debit, indebtedness, obligation **3** = **disadvantage**, albatross, burden, drag, drawback, encumbrance, handicap, hindrance, impediment, inconvenience, millstone, minus (*inf.*), nuisance

liable *adj* **1** = **responsible**, accountable, amenable, answerable, bound, chargeable, obligated **2** = **vulnerable**, exposed, open, subject, susceptible **3** = **likely**, apt, disposed, inclined, prone, tending

liaise *vb* = **communicate**, connect, hook up, interchange, intermediate, keep contact, link, mediate

liaison *n* **1** = **communication**, connection, contact, hook-up, interchange **2** = **affair**, amour, entanglement, fling, illicit romance, intrigue, love affair, romance

liar *n* = **falsifier**, fabricator, fibber, perjurer, prevaricator, storyteller (*inf.*)

libel *n* **2** = **defamation**, aspersion, calumny, denigration, obloquy, slander, smear, vituperation ◆ *vb* **5** = **defame**, blacken, calumniate, derogate, drag (someone's) name through the mud, malign, revile, slander, slur, smear, traduce, vilify

libellous *adj* **2** = **defamatory**, aspersive, calumniatory, calumnious, derogatory, false, injurious, malicious, maligning, scurrilous, slanderous, traducing, untrue, vilifying, vituperative

liberal *adj* **1, 2** = **progressive**, advanced, humanistic, latitudinarian, libertarian, politically correct *or* PC, radical, reformist, right-on (*inf.*) **3** = **generous**, altruistic, beneficent, bounteous, bountiful, charitable, free-handed, kind, openhanded, open-hearted, prodigal, unstinting **4** = **tolerant**, advanced, broad-minded, catholic, enlightened, high-minded, humanitarian, indulgent, magnanimous, permissive, politically correct *or* PC, right-on (*inf.*), unbiased, unbigoted, unprejudiced **5** = **abundant**, ample, bountiful, copious, handsome, lavish, munificent, plentiful, profuse, rich **6** = **flexible**, broad, free, general, inexact, lenient, loose, not close, not literal, not strict

Antonyms *adj* ≠ **progressive**: conservative, reactionary, right-wing ≠ **generous**: cheap, stingy ≠ **tolerant**: biased, bigoted, intolerant, prejudiced ≠ **abundant**: inadequate, limited, skimpy, small ≠ **flexible**: fixed, inflexible, literal, strict

liberalism *n* = **progressivism**, freethinking, humanitarianism, latitudinarianism, libertarianism, radicalism

liberality *n* **1** = **generosity**, altruism, beneficence, benevolence, bounty, charity, freehandedness, kindness, largesse *or* largess, munificence, open-handedness, philanthropy **2** = **broad-mindedness**, breadth, candour, catholicity, impartiality, latitude, liberalism, libertarianism, magnanimity, permissiveness, progressivism, toleration

liberalize *vb* = **relax**, ameliorate, broaden, ease, expand, extend, loosen, mitigate, moderate, modify, slacken, soften, stretch

liberate *vb* **1, 3** = **free**, deliver, discharge, disenthral, emancipate, let loose, let out, manumit, redeem, release, rescue, set free

Antonyms *vb* confine, detain, immure, imprison, incarcerate, intern, jail, lock up, put away

liberation *n* **1** = **freeing**, deliverance, emanci-

ing of equal status or just treatment for or on behalf of any group believed to be discriminated against: *women's liberation; animal liberation.* ▸ˌ**liber'ationist** *n, adj*

liberation theology *n* the belief that Christianity involves not only faith in the Church but a commitment to change social and political conditions where it is considered exploitation and oppression exist: applied esp. to South America.

libertarian (ˌlɪbə'tɛərɪən) *n* **1** a believer in freedom of thought, expression, etc. **2** a believer in the doctrine of free will. Cf. **determinism.** ◆ *adj* **3** of, relating to, or characteristic of a libertarian. [C18: from LIBERTY] ▸ˌ**liber'tarianism** *n*

libertine ❶ ('lɪbəˌtiːn, -ˌtaɪn) *n* **1** a morally dissolute person. ◆ *adj* **2** morally dissolute. [C14 (in the sense: freedman, dissolute person): from L *lībertīnus* freedman, from *lībertus* freed, from *līber* free] ▸'**liberˌtinage** *or* '**libertinˌism** *n*

liberty ❶ ('lɪbətɪ) *n, pl* **liberties. 1** the power of choosing, thinking, and acting for oneself; freedom from control or restriction. **2** the right or privilege of access to a particular place; freedom. **3** (*often pl*) a social action regarded as being familiar, forward, or improper. **4** (*often pl*) an action that is unauthorized: *he took liberties with the translation.* **5a** authorized leave granted to a sailor. **5b** (*as modifier*): *liberty man; liberty boat.* **6 at liberty.** free, unoccupied, or unrestricted. **7 take liberties (with).** to be overfamiliar or overpresumptuous. [C14: from OF *liberté,* from L *lībertās,* from *līber* free]

liberty bodice *n* a sleeveless vestlike undergarment covering the upper part of the body, formerly worn esp. by young children.

liberty hall *n* (*sometimes caps.*) *Inf.* a place or condition of complete liberty.

libidinous ❶ (lɪ'bɪdɪnəs) *adj* characterized by excessive sexual desire. ▸**li'bidinously** *adv* ▸**li'bidinousness** *n*

libido (lɪ'biːdəʊ) *n, pl* **libidos. 1** *Psychoanal.* psychic energy emanating from the id. **2** sexual urge or desire. [C20 (in psychoanalysis): from L: desire] ▸**libidinal** (lɪ'bɪdɪnᵊl) *adj* ▸**li'bidinally** *adv*

libra ('laɪbrə) *n, pl* **librae** (-briː). an ancient Roman unit of weight corresponding to 1 pound. [C14: from L, lit.: scales]

Libra ('liːbrə) *n, Latin genitive* **Librae** ('liːbriː). **1** *Astron.* a small faint zodiacal constellation in the S hemisphere, lying between Virgo and Scorpius. **2** Also called: the **Scales,** the **Balance.** *Astrol.* the seventh sign of the zodiac. The sun is in this sign between about Sept. 23 and Oct. 22.

librarian (laɪ'brɛərɪən) *n* a person in charge of or assisting in a library. ▸**li'brarianˌship** *n*

library ('laɪbrərɪ) *n, pl* **libraries. 1** a room or set of rooms where books and other literary materials are kept. **2** a collection of literary materials, films, CDs, etc., kept for borrowing or reference. **3** the building or institution that houses such a collection: *a public library.* **4** a set of books published as a series, often in a similar format. **5** *Computing.* a collection of standard programs and subroutines, usually stored on disk. **6** a collection of specific items for reference or checking against: *a library of genetic material.* [C14: from OF *librairie,* from Med. L *librāris,* n. use of L *librārius* relating to books, from *liber* book]

libration (laɪ'breɪʃən) *n* **1** the act of oscillating. **2** a real or apparent oscillation of the moon enabling approximately nine per cent of the surface facing away from earth to be seen. [C17: from L, from *librāre* to balance]

librettist (lɪ'brɛtɪst) *n* the author of a libretto.

libretto ❶ (lɪ'brɛtəʊ) *n, pl* **librettos** *or* **libretti** (-tiː). a text written for and set to music in an opera, etc. [C18: from It., dim. of *libro* book]

Librium ('lɪbrɪəm) *n Trademark.* a preparation of the drug chlordiazepoxide used as a tranquillizer. See also **benzodiazepine.**

Libyan ('lɪbɪən) *adj* **1** of or relating to Libya, a republic in N Africa, on the Mediterranean, its people, or its language. ◆ *n* **2** a native or inhabitant of Libya. **3** the extinct Hamitic language of ancient Libya.

lice (laɪs) *n* the plural of **louse.**

licence ❶ *or US* **license** ('laɪsəns) *n* **1** a certificate, tag, document, etc., giving official permission to do something. **2** formal permission or exemption. **3** liberty of action or thought; freedom. **4** intentional disregard of conventional rules to achieve a certain effect: *poetic licence.* **5** excessive freedom. [C14: via OF and Med. L *licentia* permission, from L: freedom, from *licet* it is allowed]

license ❶ ('laɪsəns) *vb* **licenses, licensing, licensed.** (*tr*) **1** to grant or give a licence for (something, such as the sale of alcohol). **2** to give permission to or for. ▸'**licensable** *adj* ▸'**licenser** *or* '**licensor** *n*

licensee (ˌlaɪsən'siː) *n* a person who holds a licence, esp. one to sell alcoholic drink.

licentiate (laɪ'sɛnʃɪɪt) *n* **1** a person who holds a formal attestation of competence to practise a certain profession. **2** a higher degree awarded by certain, chiefly European, universities. **3** a person who holds this degree. **4** *Chiefly Presbyterian Church.* a person holding a licence to preach. [C15: from Med. L *licentiātus,* from *licentiāre* to permit] ▸**li'centiateˌship** *n*

licentious ❶ (laɪ'sɛnʃəs) *adj* **1** sexually unrestrained or promiscuous. **2** *Now rare.* showing disregard for convention. [C16: from L *licentiōsus* capricious, from *licentia* LICENCE] ▸**li'centiously** *adv* ▸**li'centiousness** *n*

lichee (ˌlaɪ'tʃiː) *n* a variant spelling of **litchi.**

lichen ('laɪkən, 'lɪtʃən) *n* an organism that is formed by the symbiotic association of a fungus and an alga or cyanobacterium and occurs as crusty patches or bushy growths on tree trunks, bare ground, etc. Lichens are now classified as a phylum of fungi. [C17: via L from Gk *leikhēn,* from *leikhein* to lick] ▸'**lichened** *adj* ▸'**lichenous** *adj*

lich gate (lɪtʃ) *n* a variant spelling of **lych gate.**

licit ('lɪsɪt) *adj* a less common word for **lawful.** [C15: from L *licitus,* from *licēre* to be permitted] ▸'**licitly** *adv* ▸'**licitness** *n*

lick ❶ (lɪk) *vb* **1** (*tr*) to pass the tongue over, esp. in order to taste or consume. **2** to flicker or move lightly over or round (something): *the flames licked around the door.* **3** (*tr*) *Inf.* **3a** to defeat or vanquish. **3b** to flog or thrash. **3c** to be or do much better than. **4 lick into shape.** to put into a satisfactory condition. **5 lick one's wounds.** to retire after a defeat. ◆ *n* **6** an instance of passing the tongue over something. **7** a small amount: *a lick of paint.* **8** short for **salt lick. 9** *Inf.* a hit; blow. **10** *Sl.* a short musical phrase, usually on one instrument. **11** *Inf.* rate of movement; speed. **12 a lick and a promise.** something hastily done, esp. a hurried wash. [OE *liccian*] ▸'**licker** *n*

lickerish *or* **liquorish** ('lɪkərɪʃ) *adj Arch.* **1** lecherous or lustful. **2** greedy; gluttonous. **3** appetizing or tempting. [C16: changed from C13 *lickerous,* from OF *lechereus* lecherous; see LECHER]

lickety-split ('lɪkɪtɪ'splɪt) *adv US & Canad. inf.* very quickly; speedily. [C19: from LICK + SPLIT]

licking ❶ ('lɪkɪŋ) *n Inf.* **1** a beating. **2** a defeat.

lickspittle ('lɪkˌspɪtᵊl) *n* a flattering or servile person.

licorice ('lɪkərɪs) *n* the usual US and Canad. spelling of **liquorice.**

lictor ('lɪktə) *n* one of a group of ancient Roman officials, usually bearing fasces, who attended magistrates, etc. [C16 *lictor,* C14 *littour,* from L *ligāre* to bind]

lid (lɪd) *n* **1** a cover, usually removable or hinged, for a receptacle: *a*

THESAURUS

pation, enfranchisement, freedom, liberating, liberty, manumission, redemption, release, unfettering, unshackling

liberator *n* **1** = **deliverer**, emancipator, freer, manumitter, redeemer, rescuer, saviour

libertine *n* **1** = **reprobate**, debauchee, lech *or* letch (*inf.*), lecher, loose liver, profligate, rake, roué, seducer, sensualist, swinger (*sl.*), voluptuary, womanizer ◆ *adj* **2** = **promiscuous**, abandoned, corrupt, debauched, decadent, degenerate, depraved, dissolute, immoral, licentious, profligate, rakish, reprobate, voluptuous, wanton

liberty *n* **1** = **freedom**, autonomy, emancipation, immunity, independence, liberation, release, self-determination, sovereignty **2** = **permission**, authorization, blank cheque, carte blanche, dispensation, exemption, franchise, freedom, leave, licence, prerogative, privilege, right, sanction **3** = **impertinence**, disrespect, familiarity, forwardness, impropriety, impudence, insolence, overfamiliarity, presumption, presumptuousness **6 at liberty** = **free**, not confined, on the loose, unlimited, unoccupied, unrestricted

Antonyms *n* ≠ **freedom:** captivity, constraint, enslavement, imprisonment, restraint, slavery, tyranny ≠ **permission:** compulsion, duress, restriction

libidinous *adj* = **lustful**, carnal, concupiscent, debauched, impure, incontinent, lascivious, lecherous, lickerish (*arch.*), loose, prurient, randy (*inf., chiefly Brit.*), ruttish, salacious, sensual, unchaste, wanton, wicked

libretto *n* = **words**, book, lines, lyrics, script

licence *n* **1** = **certificate**, charter, permit, warrant **2, 3** = **permission**, a free hand, authority, authorization, blank cheque, carte blanche, dispensation, entitlement, exemption, immunity, leave, liberty, privilege, right **4** = **freedom**, independence, latitude, leeway, liberty **5** = **immoderation**, abandon, anarchy, disorder, excess, impropriety, indulgence, irresponsibility, lawlessness, laxity, profligacy, unruliness

Antonyms *n* ≠ **permission:** denial, prohibition, restriction ≠ **freedom:** constraint, restraint ≠ **immoderation:** moderation, strictness

license *vb* **1, 2** = **permit**, accredit, allow, authorize, certify, commission, empower, enable, entitle, give a blank cheque to, sanction, warrant

Antonyms *vb* ban, debar, disallow, forbid, outlaw, prohibit, proscribe, rule out, veto

licentious *adj* **1** = **promiscuous**, abandoned, debauched, disorderly, dissolute, immoral, impure, lascivious, lax, lewd, libertine, libidinous, lubricious (*literary*), lustful, profligate, sensual, uncontrollable, uncontrolled, uncurbed, unruly, wanton

Antonyms *adj* chaste, law-abiding, lawful, moral, principled, proper, scrupulous, virtuous

licentiousness *n* **1** = **promiscuity**, abandon, debauchery, dissipation, dissoluteness, lechery, lewdness, libertinism, libidinousness, lubricity, lust, lustfulness, profligacy, prurience, salaciousness, salacity, wantonness

lick *vb* **1** = **taste**, brush, lap, tongue, touch, wash **2** = **flicker**, dart, flick, ignite, kindle, play over, ripple, touch **3a** *Informal* = **beat**, best, blow out of the water (*sl.*), clobber (*sl.*), defeat, outdo, outstrip, overcome, rout, run rings around (*inf.*), surpass, tank (*sl.*), trounce, undo, vanquish, wipe the floor with (*inf.*) **3b** *Informal* = **thrash**, beat, clobber (*sl.*), flog, lambast(e), slap, spank, strike, wallop (*inf.*) ◆ *n* **7** = **dab**, bit, brush, little, sample, speck, stroke, taste, touch **11** *Informal* = **pace**, clip (*inf.*), rate, speed

licking *n Informal* **1** = **thrashing**, beating, drubbing, flogging, hiding (*inf.*), spanking, tanning (*sl.*), whipping **2** = **defeat**, beating, drubbing, pasting (*sl.*), trouncing

saucepan lid; a desk lid. **2** short for **eyelid. 3 put the lid on.** *Inf.* **3a** *Brit.* to be the final blow to. **3b** to curb, prevent, or discourage. [OE *hlid*]
► **'lidded** *adj* ► **'lidless** *adj*

lido ('li:dəʊ) *n, pl* **lidos.** *Brit.* a public place of recreation, including a swimming pool. [C20: after the *Lido,* island bathing beach near Venice, from L *litus* shore]

lie[1] ❶ (laɪ) *vb* **lies, lying, lied. 1** (*intr*) to speak untruthfully with intent to mislead or deceive. **2** (*intr*) to convey a false impression or practise deception: *the camera does not lie.* ◆ *n* **3** an untrue or deceptive statement deliberately used to mislead. **4** something that is deliberately intended to deceive. **5 give the lie to. 5a** to disprove. **5b** to accuse of lying. ◆ Related adj: **mendacious.** [OE *lyge* (n), *lēogan* (vb)]

lie[2] ❶ (laɪ) *vb* **lies, lying, lay, lain.** (*intr*) **1** (often foll. by *down*) to place oneself or be in a prostrate position, horizontal to the ground. **2** to be situated, esp. on a horizontal surface: *the pencil is lying on the desk; India lies to the south of Russia.* **3** to be buried: *here lies Jane Brown.* **4** (*copula*) to be and remain (in a particular state or condition): *to lie dormant.* **5** to stretch or extend: *the city lies before us.* **6** (usually foll. by *on* or *upon*) to rest or weigh: *my sins lie heavily on my mind.* **7** (usually foll. by *in*) to exist or consist inherently: *strength lies in unity.* **8** (foll. by *with*) **8a** to be or rest (with): *the ultimate decision lies with you.* **8b** *Arch.* to have sexual intercourse (with). **9** (of an action, claim, appeal, etc.) to subsist; be maintainable or admissible. **10** *Arch.* to stay temporarily. ◆ *n* **11** the manner, place, or style in which something is situated. **12** the hiding place or lair of an animal. **13 lie of the land. 13a** the topography of the land. **13b** the way in which a situation is developing. ◆ See also **lie down, lie in,** etc. [OE *licgan* akin to OHG *ligen* to lie, L *lectus* bed]

USAGE NOTE See at **lay**[1].

Liebig condenser ('li:bɪg) *n Chem.* a laboratory condenser consisting of a glass tube surrounded by a glass envelope through which cooling water flows. [C19: after Baron von *Liebig* (1803–73), G chemist]

lied (li:d; *German* li:t) *n, pl* **lieder** ('li:də; *German* 'li:dər). *Music.* any of various musical settings for solo voice and piano of a romantic or lyrical poem. [from G: song]

lie detector *n Inf.* a polygraph used esp. by a police interrogator to detect false or devious answers to questions, a sudden change in one or more involuntary physiological responses being considered a manifestation of guilt, fear, etc.

lie down *vb* (*intr, adv*) **1** to place oneself or be in a prostrate position in order to rest. **2** to accept without protest or opposition (esp. in **take something lying down**). ◆ *n* **lie-down. 3** a rest.

lief (li:f) *adv* **1** *Now rare.* gladly; willingly: *I'd as lief go today as tomorrow.* ◆ *adj* **2** *Arch.* **2a** ready; glad. **2b** dear; beloved. [OE *leof;* rel. to *lufu* love]

liege ❶ (li:dʒ) *adj* **1** (of a lord) owed feudal allegiance (esp. in **liege lord**). **2** (of a vassal or servant) owing feudal allegiance: *a liege subject.* **3** faithful; loyal. ◆ *n* **4** a liege lord. **5** a liegeman or true subject. [C13: from OF *lige,* from Med. L *līticus,* from *lītus, laetus* serf, of Gmc origin]

liegeman ('li:dʒ,mæn) *n, pl* **liegemen. 1** (formerly) a vassal. **2** a loyal follower.

lie in *vb* (*intr, adv*) **1** to remain in bed late in the morning. **2** to be confined in childbirth. ◆ *n* **lie-in. 3** a long stay in bed in the morning.

lien ('li:ən, li:n) *n Law.* a right to retain possession of another's property pending discharge of a debt. [C16: via OF from L *ligāmen* bond, from *ligāre* to bind]

lierne (lɪ'ɜ:n) *n Archit.* a short rib that connects the intersections of the primary ribs, esp. in Gothic vaulting. [C19: from F, ? rel. to *lier* to bind]

lie to *vb* (*intr, adv*) *Naut.* (of a vessel) to be hove to with little or no swinging.

lieu (lju:, lu:) *n* stead; place (esp. in **in lieu, in lieu of**). [C13: from OF, ult. from L *locus* place]

lieutenant (lɛf'tɛnənt; *US* lu:'tɛnənt) *n* **1** a military officer holding commissioned rank immediately junior to a captain. **2** a naval officer holding commissioned rank immediately junior to a lieutenant commander. **3** *US.* an officer in a police or fire department ranking immediately junior to a captain. **4** a person who holds an office in subordination to or in place of a superior. [C14: from OF, lit.: place-holding]
► **lieu'tenancy** *n*

lieutenant colonel *n* an officer holding commissioned rank immediately junior to a colonel in certain armies, air forces, and marine corps.

lieutenant commander *n* an officer holding commissioned rank in certain navies immediately junior to a commander.

lieutenant general *n* an officer holding commissioned rank in certain armies, air forces, and marine corps immediately junior to a general.

lieutenant governor *n* **1** a deputy governor. **2** (in the US) an elected official who acts as deputy to a state governor. **3** (in Canada) the representative of the Crown in a province: appointed by the federal government.

life ❶ (laɪf) *n, pl* **lives** (laɪvz). **1** the state or quality that distinguishes living beings or organisms from dead ones and from inorganic matter, characterized chiefly by metabolism, growth, and the ability to reproduce and respond to stimuli. Related adj: **animate. 2** the period between birth and death. **3** a living person or being: *to save a life.* **4** the time between birth and the present time. **5a** the remainder or extent of one's life. **5b** (*as modifier*): *a life sentence; life membership; life work.* **6** *Inf.* short for **life imprisonment. 7** the amount of time that something is active or functioning: *the life of a battery.* **8** a present condition, state, or mode of existence: *my life is very dull here.* **9a** a biography. **9b** (*as modifier*): *a life story.* **10** a characteristic state or mode of existence: *town life.* **11** the sum or course of human events and activities. **12** liveliness or high spirits: *full of life.* **13** a source of strength, animation, or vitality: *he was the life of the show.* **14** all living things, taken as a whole: *there is no life on Mars; plant life.* **15** (*modifier*) *Arts.* drawn or taken from a living model: *life drawing.* **16** (in certain games) one of a number of opportunities for participation. **17 a matter of life and death.** a matter of extreme urgency. **18 as large as life.** *Inf.* real and living. **19 for the life of me (him, her,** etc.) though trying desperately. **20 not on your life.** *Inf.* certainly not. **21 the life and soul.** *Inf.* a person regarded as the main source of merriment and liveliness: *the life and soul of the party.* **22 to the life.** (of a copy or image) resembling the original exactly. **23 true to life.** faithful to reality. [OE *līf*]

life assurance *n* a form of insurance providing for the payment of a specified sum to a named beneficiary on the death of the policyholder. Also called: **life insurance.**

life belt *n* a buoyant ring used to keep a person afloat when in danger of drowning.

lifeblood ❶ ('laɪf,blʌd) *n* **1** the blood, considered as vital to life. **2** the essential or animating force.

lifeboat ('laɪf,bəʊt) *n* **1** a boat used for rescuing people at sea, escaping from a sinking ship, etc. **2** *Inf.* a fund set up by the dealers in a market to rescue any member who may become insolvent as a result of a collapse in market prices.

life buoy *n* any of various kinds of buoyant device for keeping people afloat in an emergency.

life cycle *n* the series of changes occurring in an animal or plant between one stage and the identical stage in the next generation.

life expectancy *n* the statistically determined average number of years of life remaining after a specified age.

lifeguard ('laɪf,gɑ:d) *n* a person at a beach or pool to guard people against the risk of drowning.

life imprisonment *n* an indeterminate sentence always given for murder and as a maximum sentence in several other crimes. There is no remission, although the Home Secretary may order the prisoner's release on licence.

life jacket *n* an inflatable sleeveless jacket worn to keep a person afloat when in danger of drowning.

lifeless ❶ ('laɪflɪs) *adj* **1** without life; inanimate; dead. **2** not sustaining living organisms. **3** having no vitality or animation. **4** unconscious.
► **'lifelessly** *adv* ► **'lifelessness** *n*

lifelike ❶ ('laɪf,laɪk) *adj* closely resembling or representing life.
► **'life,likeness** *n*

lifeline ('laɪf,laɪn) *n* **1** a line thrown or fired aboard a vessel for hauling in a hawser for a breeches buoy. **2** a line by which a deep-sea diver is raised or lowered. **3** a single means of contact, communication, or support on which a person or an area, etc., relies.

lifelong ❶ ('laɪf,lɒŋ) *adj* lasting for or as if for a lifetime.

THESAURUS

lie[1] *vb* **1 = fib,** dissimulate, equivocate, fabricate, falsify, forswear oneself, invent, misrepresent, perjure, prevaricate, tell a lie, tell untruths ◆ *n* **3 = falsehood,** deceit, fabrication, falsification, falsity, fib, fiction, invention, mendacity, pork pie (*Brit. sl.*), porky (*Brit. sl.*), prevarication, untruth, white lie

lie[2] *vb* **1 = recline,** be prone, be prostrate, be recumbent, be supine, couch, loll, lounge, repose, rest, sprawl, stretch out **2 = be situated,** be, be found, be located, belong, be placed, exist, extend, remain **3 = be buried,** be interred **6** *usually with* **on** *or* **upon = weigh,** burden, oppress, press, rest **7** *usually with* **in = exist,** be present, consist, dwell, inhere, pertain

liege *n* **4 = feudal lord,** chieftain, master, overlord, seigneur, sovereign, superior, suzerain

life *n* **1 = being,** animation, breath, entity, growth, sentience, viability, vitality **2 = existence,** being, career, continuance, course, duration, lifetime, span, time **3 = person,** human, human being, individual, mortal, soul **9a = biography,** autobiography, career, confessions, history, life story, memoirs, story **10 = behaviour,** conduct, life style, way of life **11 = the human condition,** the school of hard knocks, the times, the world, this mortal coil, trials and tribulations, vicissitudes **12 = liveliness,** activity, animation, brio, energy, get-up-and-go (*inf.*), go (*inf.*), high spirits, oomph (*inf.*), pep, sparkle, spirit, verve, vigour, vitality, vivacity, zest **13 = spirit,** animating spirit, *élan vital,* essence, heart, lifeblood, soul, vital spark **14 = living things,** creatures, living beings, organisms, wildlife

lifeblood *n* **2 = animating force,** driving force, essence, guts (*inf.*), heart, inspiration, life, stimulus, vital spark

lifeless *adj* **1 = dead,** cold, deceased, defunct, extinct, inanimate, inert **2 = barren,** bare, desert, empty, sterile, uninhabited, unproductive, waste **3 = dull,** cold, colourless, flat, heavy, hollow, lacklustre, lethargic, listless, passive, pointless, slow, sluggish, spent, spiritless, static, stiff, torpid, wooden **4 = unconscious,** comatose, dead to the world (*inf.*), in a faint, inert, insensate, insensible, out cold, out for the count
Antonyms *adj* **≠ dead:** alive, alive and kicking, animate, live, living, vital **≠ dull:** active, animated, lively, spirited

lifelike *adj* **= realistic,** authentic, exact, faithful, graphic, natural, photographic, real, true-to-life, undistorted, vivid

lifelong *adj* **= long-lasting,** constant, deep-

life peer *n Brit.* a peer whose title lapses at his death.
life preserver *n* **1** *Brit.* a club or bludgeon, esp. one kept for self-defence. **2** *US & Canad.* a life belt or life jacket.
lifer ('laɪfə) *n Inf.* a prisoner sentenced to imprisonment for life.
life raft *n* a raft for emergency use at sea.
life-saver *n* **1** the saver of a person's life. **2** *Austral.* an expert swimmer, esp. a member of a surf life-saving club at a surfing beach, who rescues surfers or swimmers from drowning. **3** *Inf.* a person or thing that gives help in time of need.
▸ **'life-ˌsaving** *adj, n*
life science *n* any one of the branches of science concerned with the structure and behaviour of living organisms, such as biology, botany, zoology, physiology, or biochemistry.
life-size *or* **life-sized** *adj* representing actual size.
life span *n* the period of time during which a human being, animal, machine, etc., may be expected to live or function.
lifestyle ('laɪfˌstaɪl) *n* **1** a set of attitudes, habits, or possessions associated with a particular person or group. **2** such attitudes, etc., regarded as fashionable or desirable. **3** *NZ.* **3a** a luxurious semirural manner of living. **3b** *(as modifier): a lifestyle property.*
lifestyle business *n* a small business in which the owners are more anxious to pursue interests that reflect their lifestyle than to make more than a comfortable living.
life-support *adj* of, providing, or relating to the equipment or treatment necessary to keep a person alive.
lifetime Ⓣ ('laɪfˌtaɪm) *n* **1a** the length of time a person or animal is alive. **1b** *(as modifier): a lifetime supply.* **2** the length of time that something functions, is useful, etc. **3** Also called: **life.** *Physics.* the average time of existence of an unstable or reactive entity.
LIFO ('laɪfəʊ) *n acronym for* last in, first out (as an accounting principle in sorting stock). Cf. **FIFO.**
lift Ⓣ (lɪft) *vb* **1** to rise or cause to rise upwards from the ground or another support to a higher place: *to lift a sack.* **2** to move or cause to move upwards: *to lift one's eyes.* **3** *(tr)* to take hold of in order to carry or remove: *to lift something down from a shelf.* **4** *(tr)* to raise in status, spirituality, estimation, etc.: *his position lifted him from the common crowd.* **5** *(tr)* to revoke or rescind: *to lift tax restrictions.* **6** *(tr)* to take (plants or underground crops) out of the ground for transplanting or harvesting. **7** *(intr)* to disappear by lifting or as if by lifting: *the fog lifted.* **8** *(tr) Inf.* to take unlawfully or dishonourably; steal. **9** *(tr) Inf.* to plagiarize. **10** *(tr) Sl.* to arrest. **11** *(tr)* to perform a face-lift on. ◆ *n* **12** the act or an instance of lifting. **13** the power or force available or used for lifting. **14a** *Brit.* a platform, compartment, or cage raised or lowered in a vertical shaft to transport persons or goods in a building. US and Canad. word: **elevator. 14b** See **chairlift, ski lift. 15** the distance or degree to which something is lifted. **16** a ride in a car or other vehicle for part or all of a passenger's journey. **17** a rise in the height of the ground. **18** a rise in morale or feeling of cheerfulness usually caused by some specific thing or event. **19** the force required to lift an object. **20** a layer inserted in the heel of a shoe, etc., to give the wearer added height. **21** aid; help. **22** the component of the aerodynamic forces acting on a wing, etc., at right angles to the airflow and opposing gravity. [C13: from ON]
▸ **'lifter** *n*
liftoff ('lɪftˌɒf) *n* **1** the initial movement of a rocket from its launch pad. **2** the instant at which this occurs. ◆ *vb* **lift off. 3** *(intr, adv)* (of a rocket) to leave its launch pad.
lift pump *n* a pump that raises a fluid to a higher level. Cf. **force pump.**
lig (lɪg) *Brit. sl.* ◆ *n* **1** (esp. in the media) a function at which free entertainment and refreshments are available. ◆ *vb* **ligs, ligging, ligged. 2** *(intr)* to attend such a function; freeload. [C20: from ?]
▸ **'ligger** *n* ▸ **'ligging** *n*
ligament ('lɪgəmənt) *n* **1** *Anat.* any one of the bands of tough fibrous connective tissue that restrict movement in joints, connect various bones or cartilages, support muscles, etc. **2** any physical or abstract bond. [C14: from Med. L *ligāmentum,* from L (in the sense: bandage), from *ligāre* to bind]
ligand ('lɪgənd, 'laɪ-) *n Chem.* an atom, molecule, radical, or ion forming a complex with a central atom. [C20: from L *ligandum,* from *ligāre* to bind]
ligate ('laɪgeɪt) *vb* **ligates, ligating, ligated.** *(tr)* to tie up or constrict (something) with a ligature. [C16: from L *ligātus,* from *ligāre* to bind]
▸ **li'gation** *n*
ligature Ⓣ ('lɪgətʃə, -ˌtʃʊə) *n* **1** the act of binding or tying up. **2** something used to bind. **3** a link, bond, or tie. **4** *Surgery.* a thread or wire for tying around a vessel, duct, etc., as for constricting the flow of blood. **5** *Printing.* a character of two or more joined letters, such as ff, fi, fl, ffi. **6** *Music.* a slur or the group of notes connected by it. ◆ *vb* **ligatures, ligaturing, ligatured. 7** *(tr)* to bind with a ligature; ligate. [C14: from LL *ligātūra,* ult. from L *ligāre* to bind]
liger ('laɪgə) *n* the hybrid offspring of a female tiger and a male lion.
light[1] Ⓣ (laɪt) *n* **1** the medium of illumination that makes sight possible. **2** Also called: **visible radiation.** electromagnetic radiation that is capable of causing a visual sensation. See also **speed of light. 3** *(not in technical usage)* electromagnetic radiation that has a wavelength outside this range, esp. ultraviolet radiation: *ultraviolet light.* **4** the sensation experienced when electromagnetic radiation within the visible spectrum falls on the retina of the eye. **5** anything that illuminates, such as a lamp or candle. **6** See **traffic light. 7** a particular quality or type of light: *a good light for reading.* **8a** illumination from the sun during the day; daylight. **8b** the time this appears; daybreak; dawn. **9** anything that allows the entrance of light, such as a window or compartment of a window. **10** the condition of being visible or known (esp. in **bring** *or* **come to light**). **11** an aspect or view: *he saw it in a different light.* **12** mental understanding or spiritual insight. **13** a person considered to be an authority or leader. **14** brightness of countenance, esp. a sparkle in the eyes. **15a** the act of igniting or kindling something, such as a cigarette. **15b** something that ignites or kindles, esp. in a specified manner, such as a spark or flame. **15c** something used for igniting or kindling, such as a match. **16** See **lighthouse. 17 in (the) light of.** in view of; taking into account; considering. **18 see the light.** to acquire insight. **19 see the light (of day). 19a** to come into being. **19b** to come to public notice. **20 strike a light. 20a** *(vb)* to ignite something, esp. a match, by friction. **20b** *(interj) Brit.* an exclamation of surprise. ◆ *adj* **21** full of light; well-lighted. **22** (of a colour) reflecting or transmitting a large amount of light: *light yellow.* ◆ *vb* **lights, lighting, lighted** *or* **lit. 23** to ignite or cause to ignite. **24** (often foll. by *up*) to illuminate or cause to illuminate. **25** to make or become cheerful or animated. **26** *(tr)* to guide or lead by light. ◆ See also **lights**[1], **light up.** [OE *lēoht*]
▸ **'lightish** *adj* ▸ **'lightless** *adj*
light[2] Ⓣ (laɪt) *adj* **1** not heavy; weighing relatively little. **2** having relatively low density: *magnesium is a light metal.* **3** lacking sufficient weight; not agreeing with standard or official weights. **4** not great in degree, intensity, or number: *light rain.* **5** without burdens, difficulties, or problems; easily borne or done: *a light heart; light work.* **6** graceful, agile, or deft: *light fingers.* **7** not bulky or clumsy. **8** not serious or profound; entertaining: *light music; light verse.* **9** without importance or consequence; insignificant: *no light matter.* **10** frivolous or capricious. **11** loose in morals. **12** dizzy or unclear: *a light head.* **13** (of bread, cake, etc.) spongy or well leavened. **14** easily digested: *a light meal.* **15** relatively low in alcoholic content: *a light wine.* **16** (of a soil) having a crumbly texture. **17** (of a vessel, lorry, etc.) **17a** designed to carry light loads. **17b** not loaded. **18** carrying light arms or equipment: *light infantry.* **19** (of an industry) engaged in the production of small consumer goods using light machinery. **20** *Aeronautics.* (of an aircraft) having a maximum take-off weight less than 5670 kilograms (12 500 pounds). **21** *Chem.* (of an oil fraction obtained from coal tar) having a boiling range between about 100° and 210°C. **22** (of a railway) having

THESAURUS

rooted, enduring, for all one's life, for life, lasting, lifetime, long-standing, perennial, permanent, persistent
lifetime *n* **1a** = **existence,** all one's born days, career, course, day(s), life span, one's natural life, period, span, time
lift *vb* **1, 2** = **raise,** bear aloft, buoy up, draw up, elevate, heft, hoist, pick up, raise high, rear, upheave, uplift, upraise **4** = **exalt,** advance, ameliorate, boost, dignify, elevate, enhance, improve, promote, raise, upgrade **5** = **revoke,** annul, cancel, countermand, end, relax, remove, rescind, stop, terminate **7** = **disappear,** be dispelled, disperse, dissipate, vanish **8** *Informal* = **steal,** appropriate, blag, copy, crib *(inf.),* nick *(sl., chiefly Brit.),* pilfer, pinch *(inf.),* pirate, plagiarize, pocket, purloin, take, thieve ◆ *n* **14a** = **elevator** *(chiefly US)* **16** = **ride,** car ride, drive, run, transport **18** = **boost,** encouragement, fillip, gee-up, pick-me-up, reassurance, shot in the arm *(inf.),* uplift
Antonyms *vb* ≠ **raise:** dash, descend, drop, fall, hang, lower ≠ **exalt:** depress ≠ **revoke:** establish, impose ◆ *n* ≠ **boost:** blow, letdown
ligature *n* **2, 3** = **link,** band, bandage, binding, bond, connection, ligament, tie
light[1] *n* **1, 2** = **brightness,** blaze, brilliance, effulgence, flash, glare, gleam, glint, glow, illumination, incandescence, lambency, luminescence, luminosity, lustre, phosphorescence, radiance, ray, refulgence, scintillation, shine, sparkle **5** = **lamp,** beacon, bulb, candle, flare, lantern, lighthouse, star, taper, torch **8** = **daybreak,** broad day, cockcrow, dawn, daylight, daytime, morn *(poetic),* morning, sun, sunbeam, sunrise, sunshine **11** = **aspect,** angle, approach, attitude, context, interpretation, point of view, slant, vantage point, viewpoint **12** = **understanding,** awareness, comprehension, elucidation, explanation, illustration, information, insight, knowledge **13** = **shining example,** example, exemplar, guiding light, model, paragon **15b, c** = **match,** flame, lighter **17 in (the) light of** = **considering,** bearing in mind, because of, in view of, taking into account, with knowledge of ◆ *adj* **21** = **bright,** aglow, brilliant, glowing, illuminated, luminous, lustrous, shining, sunny, well-lighted, well-lit **22** = **pale,** bleached, blond, blonde, faded, fair, light-hued, light-toned, pastel ◆ *vb* **23** = **ignite,** fire, inflame, kindle, set a match to, torch **24** = **illuminate,** brighten, clarify, floodlight, flood with light, illumine, irradiate, lighten, light up, put on, switch on, turn on **25** = **cheer,** animate, brighten, irradiate, lighten
Antonyms *n* ≠ **brightness:** cloud, dark, darkness, dusk, obscurity, shade, shadow ≠ **understanding:** mystery ◆ *adj* ≠ **bright:** dark, dim, dusky, gloomy ≠ **pale:** dark, deep ◆ *vb* ≠ **ignite:** douse, extinguish, put out, quench ≠ **illuminate:** cloud, darken, dull
light[2] *adj* **1** = **insubstantial,** buoyant, delicate, flimsy, imponderous, lightsome, lightweight, portable, slight **3** = **underweight 4** = **weak,** faint, gentle, indistinct, mild, moderate, slight, soft **5** = **undemanding,** cushy *(inf.),* easy, effortless, manageable, moderate, simple, unexacting, untaxing **6** = **nimble,** agile, airy, graceful, light-footed, lithe, sprightly, sylphlike **8, 10** = **light-hearted,** amusing, diverting, entertaining, frivolous, funny, gay, humorous, pleasing, superficial, trifling, trivial, witty **9** = **insignificant,** inconsequential, inconsiderable, minute, scanty, slight, small, thin, tiny, trifling, trivial, unsubstantial, wee **12** = **dizzy,** giddy, light-headed, reeling, unsteady, volatile **14** = **digestible,** frugal, modest, not heavy, not rich, restricted, small **16** = **crumbly,** friable, loose,

a narrow gauge, or in some cases a standard gauge with speed or load restrictions not applied to a main line. **23** *Phonetics, prosody.* (of a syllable, vowel, etc.) unaccented or weakly stressed; short. **24 light on.** *Inf.* lacking a sufficient quantity of (something). **25 make light of.** to treat as insignificant or trifling. ◆ *adv* **26** a less common word for lightly. **27** with little equipment, baggage, etc.: *to travel light.* ◆ *vb* **lights, lighting, lighted** *or* **lit.** (*intr*) **28** (esp. of birds) to settle or land after flight. **29** to get down from a horse, vehicle, etc. **30** (foll. by *on* or *upon*) to come upon unexpectedly. **31** to strike or fall on: *the choice lighted on me.* ◆ See also **light into, light out, lights**[2]. [OE *lēoht*] ▸ **'lightish** *adj* ▸ **'lightly** *adv* ▸ **'lightness** *n*

light air *n* very light air movement of force one (1–3 mph) on the Beaufort scale.

light box *n* a light source contained in a box and covered with a diffuser, used for viewing photographic transparencies, negatives, etc.

light breeze *n* a very light wind of force two (4–7 mph) on the Beaufort scale.

light bulb *n* a glass bulb containing a gas at low pressure and enclosing a thin metal filament that emits light when an electric current is passed through it. Sometimes shortened to **bulb.**

light-emitting diode *n* a semiconductor that emits light when an electric current is applied to it: used in electronic calculators, digital watches, etc.

lighten[1] ❶ ('laɪtᵊn) *vb* **1** to become or make light. **2** (*intr*) to shine; glow. **3** (*intr*) (of lightning) to flash. **4** (*tr*) *Arch.* to cause to flash.

lighten[2] ❶ ('laɪtᵊn) *vb* **1** to make or become less heavy. **2** to make or become less burdensome or oppressive; mitigate. **3** to make or become more cheerful or lively.

lightening ('laɪtᵊnɪŋ) *n Obstetrics.* the sensation, experienced by many women late in pregnancy when the head of the fetus enters the pelvis, of a reduction in pressure on the diaphragm.

lighter[1] ('laɪtə) *n* **1** a small portable device for providing a naked flame to light cigarettes, etc. **2** a person or thing that ignites something.

lighter[2] ('laɪtə) *n* a flat-bottomed barge used for transporting cargo, esp. in loading or unloading a ship. [C15: prob. from MDu.]

lighterage ('laɪtərɪdʒ) *n* **1** the conveyance or loading and unloading of cargo by means of a lighter. **2** the charge for this service.

light face *n* **1** *Printing.* a weight of type characterized by light thin lines. ◆ *adj also* **light-faced. 2** (of type) having this weight.

light-fingered ❶ *adj* having nimble or agile fingers, esp. for thieving or picking pockets.

light flyweight *n* **1** an amateur boxer weighing not more than 48 kg (106 pounds). **2** an amateur wrestler weighing not more than 48 kg (106 pounds).

light-footed ❶ *adj* having a light or nimble tread. ▸ **,light-'footedly** *adv*

light-headed ❶ *adj* **1** frivolous. **2** giddy; feeling faint or slightly delirious. ▸ **,light-'headedly** *adv* ▸ **,light-'headedness** *n*

light-hearted ❶ *adj* cheerful or carefree in mood or disposition. ▸ **,light-'heartedly** *adv* ▸ **,light-'heartedness** *n*

light heavyweight *n* **1** Also (in Britain): **cruiserweight. 1a** a professional boxer weighing 160–175 pounds (72.5–79.5 kg). **1b** an amateur boxer weighing 75–81 kg (165–179 pounds). **2a** a professional wrestler weighing not more than 198 pounds (90 kg). **2b** an amateur wrestler weighing not more than 90 kg (198 pounds).

lighthouse ('laɪt,haʊs) *n* a fixed structure in the form of a tower equipped with a light visible to mariners for warning them of obstructions, etc.

lighting ('laɪtɪŋ) *n* **1** the act or quality of illumination or ignition. **2** the apparatus for supplying artificial light effects to a stage, film, or television set. **3** the distribution of light on an object or figure, as in painting, photography, etc.

lighting cameraman *n Films.* the person who designs and supervises the lighting of scenes to be filmed.

lighting-up time *n* the time when vehicles are required by law to have their lights on.

light into ❶ *vb* (*tr, prep*) *Inf.* to assail physically or verbally.

light middleweight *n* an amateur boxer weighing 67–71 kg (148–157 pounds).

lightness ('laɪtnɪs) *n* the attribute of an object or colour that enables an observer to judge the extent to which the object or colour reflects or transmits incident light.

lightning ('laɪtnɪŋ) *n* **1** a flash of light in the sky, occurring during a thunderstorm and caused by a discharge of electricity, either between clouds or between a cloud and the earth. **2** (*modifier*) fast and sudden: *a lightning raid.* [C14: var. of *lightening*]

lightning conductor *or* **rod** *n* a metal strip terminating in sharp points, attached to the highest part of a building, etc., to discharge the electric field before it can reach a dangerous level and cause a lightning strike.

light opera *n* another term for **operetta.**

light out ❶ *vb* (*intr, adv*) *Inf.* to depart quickly, as if being chased.

light pen *n Computer technol.* **a** a rodlike device which, when applied to the screen of a cathode-ray tube, can detect the time of passage of the illuminated spot across that point thus enabling a computer to determine the position on the screen being pointed at. **b** a penlike device, used to read bar codes, that emits light and determines the intensity of that light as reflected from a small area of an adjacent surface.

light pollution *n* the glow from street and domestic lighting that obscures the night sky and hinders the observation of faint stars.

light rail *n* a transport system using small trains or trams, often serving parts of a large metropolitan area.

lights[1] (laɪts) *pl n* a person's ideas, knowledge, or understanding: *he did it according to his lights.*

lights[2] (laɪts) *pl n* the lungs, esp. of sheep, bullocks, and pigs, used esp. for feeding pets. [C13: pl n use of LIGHT[2], referring to the light weight of the lungs]

light-sensitive *adj Physics.* (of a surface) having a photoelectric property, such as the ability to generate a current, change its electrical resistance, etc., when exposed to light.

lightship ('laɪt,ʃɪp) *n* a ship equipped as a lighthouse and moored where a fixed structure would prove impracticable.

light show *n* a kaleidoscopic display of moving lights, etc., projected onto a screen, esp. during pop concerts.

lightsome ('laɪtsəm) *adj Arch. or poetic.* **1** light-hearted or gay. **2** airy or buoyant. **3** not serious; frivolous.

lights out *n* **1** the time when those resident at an institution, such as soldiers in barracks or children at a boarding school, are expected to retire to bed. **2** a signal indicating this.

light table *n Printing.* a translucent surface of ground glass or a similar substance, illuminated from below and used for the examination of film, pages, etc.

light trap *n* any mechanical arrangement that allows some form of movement to take place while excluding light, such as a light-proof door or the lips of a film cassette.

light up *vb* (*adv*) **1** to light a cigarette, pipe, etc. **2** to illuminate or cause to illuminate. **3** to make or become cheerful or animated.

lightweight ❶ ('laɪt,weɪt) *adj* **1** of a relatively light weight. **2** not serious; trivial. ◆ *n* **3** a person or animal of a relatively light weight. **4a** a professional boxer weighing 130–135 pounds (59–61 kg). **4b** an amateur boxer weighing 57–60 kg (126–132 pounds). **5a** a professional wrestler weighing not more than 154 pounds (70 kg). **5b** an amateur wrestler weighing not more than 68 kg (150 pounds). **6** *Inf.* a person of little importance or influence.

light welterweight *n* an amateur boxer weighing 60–63.5 kg (132–140 pounds).

light year *n* a unit of distance used in astronomy, equal to the distance travelled by light in one year, i.e. 9.4607×10^{12} kilometres or 0.3066 parsecs.

THESAURUS

porous, sandy, spongy ◆ *vb* **28** = **settle**, alight, land, perch **30** *foll. by* **on** *or* **upon** = **come across**, chance upon, discover, encounter, find, happen upon, hit upon, stumble on

Antonyms *adj* ≠ **insubstantial:** heavy ≠ **weak:** forceful, strong ≠ **undemanding:** burdensome, strenuous ≠ **nimble:** clumsy ≠ **light-hearted:** serious, sombre ≠ **insignificant:** deep, profound, serious, weighty ≠ **digestible:** rich, substantial ≠ **crumbly:** hard, strong

lighten[1] *vb* **1, 2** = **brighten**, become light, gleam, illuminate, irradiate, light up, make bright, shine **3** = **flash**

lighten[2] *vb* **1** = **make lighter**, disburden, ease, reduce in weight, unload **2** = **ease**, allay, alleviate, ameliorate, assuage, facilitate, lessen, mitigate, reduce, relieve **3** = **cheer**, brighten, buoy up, elate, encourage, gladden, hearten, inspire, lift, perk up, revive

Antonyms *vb* ≠ **make lighter:** burden, encumber, handicap ≠ **ease:** aggravate, heighten, increase, intensify, make worse, worsen ≠ **cheer:** depress, oppress, sadden, weigh down

light-fingered *adj* = **thieving**, pilfering, pinching (*inf.*), stealing

light-footed *adj* = **nimble**, agile, graceful, sprightly, spry

light-headed *adj* **1** = **frivolous**, bird-brained (*inf.*), featherbrained, fickle, flighty, flippant, foolish, giddy, inane, shallow, silly, superficial, trifling **2** = **faint**, delirious, dizzy, giddy, hazy, vertiginous, woozy (*inf.*)

light-hearted *adj* = **carefree**, blithe, blithesome (*literary*), bright, cheerful, chirpy (*inf.*), effervescent, gay, genial, glad, gleeful, happy-go-lucky, insouciant, jocund, jolly, jovial, joyful, joyous, merry, playful, sunny, untroubled, upbeat (*inf.*)

Antonyms *adj* cheerless, dejected, depressed, despondent, gloomy, heavy-hearted, low, melancholy, morose, sad

light into *vb Informal* = **attack**, assail, belabour, clobber (*sl.*), lambast(e), lay into (*inf.*), let fly at, pitch into (*inf.*), sail into (*inf.*), set about, tear into (*inf.*)

lightless *adj* **1** = **dark**, dim, dusky, gloomy, inky, jet black, murky, pitch-black, pitch-dark, pitchy, Stygian, sunless, unilluminated, unlighted, unlit

lightly *adv* **4** = **moderately**, delicately, faintly, gently, slightly, softly, sparingly, sparsely, thinly **5** = **easily**, effortlessly, readily, simply **10** = **carelessly**, breezily, flippantly, frivolously, heedlessly, indifferently, slightingly, thoughtlessly

Antonyms *adv* ≠ **moderately:** abundantly, heavily, thickly ≠ **gently:** firmly, forcefully, heavily ≠ **easily:** arduously, awkwardly, slowly, with difficulty ≠ **carelessly:** carefully, earnestly, ponderously, seriously

light out *vb Informal* = **run away**, abscond, depart, do a bunk (*Brit. sl.*), do a runner (*sl.*), escape, fly the coop (*US & Canad. inf.*), make off, quit, scarper (*Brit. sl.*), skedaddle (*inf.*)

lightweight *adj* **2** = **unimportant**, inconsequential, insignificant, nickel-and-dime (*US sl.*), of no account, paltry, petty, slight, trifling, trivial, worthless

ligneous ('lɪgnɪəs) *adj* of or resembling wood. [C17: from L *ligneus*, from *lignum* wood]

lignin ('lɪgnɪn) *n* a complex polymer occurring in certain plant cell walls making the plant rigid. [C19: from L *lignum* wood + -IN]

lignite ('lɪgnaɪt) *n* a brown carbonaceous sedimentary rock with woody texture that consists of accumulated layers of partially decomposed vegetation: used as a fuel. Also called: **brown coal.**
▸**lignitic** (lɪg'nɪtɪk) *adj*

lignum vitae ('lɪgnəm 'vaɪtɪ) *n* **1** either of two tropical American trees having blue or purple flowers. **2** the heavy resinous wood of either of these trees. ◆ See also **guaiacum.** [NL, from LL, lit.: wood of life]

ligroin ('lɪgrəʊɪn) *n* a volatile fraction of petroleum: used as a solvent. [from ?]

likable ❶ *or* **likeable** ('laɪkəbᵊl) *adj* easy to like; pleasing.
▸'**likableness** *or* '**likeableness** *n*

like[1] ❶ (laɪk) *adj* **1** (*prenominal*) similar; resembling. ◆ *prep* **2** similar to; similarly to; in the manner of: *acting like a maniac; he's so like his father.* **3** used correlatively to express similarity: *like mother, like daughter.* **4** such as: *there are lots of games — like draughts, for instance.* ◆ *adv* **5** a dialect word for **likely.** ◆ *conj* **6** *Not standard.* as though; as if: *you look like you've just seen a ghost.* **7** in the same way as; in the same way that: *she doesn't dance like you do.* ◆ *n* **8** the equal or counterpart of a person or thing. **9 the like.** similar things: *dogs, foxes, and the like.* **10 the likes** (*or* **like**) **of.** people or things similar to (someone or something specified): *we don't want the likes of you around here.* [shortened from OE *gelīc*]

> **USAGE NOTE** The use of *like* to mean *such as* was formerly thought to be undesirable in formal writing, but has now become acceptable. It was also thought that *as* rather than *like* should be used to mean *in the same way that*, but now both *as* and *like* are acceptable: *they hunt and catch fish as/like their ancestors used to.* The use of *look like* and *seem like* before a clause, although very common, is thought by many people to be incorrect or non-standard: *it looks as though he won't come* (not *it looks like he won't come*).

like[2] ❶ (laɪk) *vb* **likes, liking, liked. 1** (*tr*) to find (something) enjoyable or agreeable or find it enjoyable or agreeable (to do something): *he likes boxing; he likes to hear music.* **2** (*tr*) to be fond of. **3** (*tr*) to prefer or wish (to do something): *we would like you to go.* **4** (*tr*) to feel towards; consider; regard: *how did she like it?* **5** (*intr*) to feel disposed or inclined; choose; wish. ◆ *n* **6** (*usually pl*) a favourable feeling, desire, preference, etc. (esp. in **likes and dislikes**). [OE *līcian*]

-like *suffix forming adjectives.* **1** resembling or similar to: *lifelike.* **2** having the characteristics of: *childlike.* [from LIKE[1] (prep)]

likelihood ❶ ('laɪklɪˌhʊd) *or* **likeliness** *n* **1** the condition of being likely or probable; probability. **2** something that is probable.

likely ❶ ('laɪklɪ) *adj* **1** (usually foll. by an infinitive) tending or inclined; apt: *likely to rain.* **2** probable: *a likely result.* **3** believable or feasible; plausible. **4** appropriate for a purpose or activity. **5** having good possibilities of success: *a likely candidate.* ◆ *adv* **6** probably or presumably. **7 as likely as not.** very probably. [C14: from ON *līkligr*]

> **USAGE NOTE** *Likely* as an adverb is preceded by another, intensifying adverb, as in *it will very likely rain* or *it will most likely rain.* Its use without an intensifier, as in *it will likely rain* is regarded as unacceptable by most users of British English, though it is common in colloquial US English.

like-minded ❶ *adj* agreeing in opinions, goals, etc.
▸ˌ**like-'mindedly** *adv* ▸ˌ**like-'mindedness** *n*

liken ❶ ('laɪkən) *vb* (*tr*) to see or represent as the same or similar; compare. [C14: from LIKE[1] (adj)]

likeness ❶ ('laɪknɪs) *n* **1** the condition of being alike; similarity. **2** a painted, carved, moulded, or graphic image of a person or thing. **3** an imitative appearance; semblance.

likewise ❶ ('laɪkˌwaɪz) *adv* **1** in addition; moreover; also. **2** in like manner; similarly.

liking ❶ ('laɪkɪŋ) *n* **1** the feeling of a person who likes; fondness. **2** a preference, inclination, or pleasure.

lilac ('laɪlək) *n* **1** any of various Eurasian shrubs or small trees of the olive family which have large sprays of purple or white fragrant flowers. **2a** a light or moderate purple colour. **2b** (*as adj*): *a lilac carpet.* [C17: via F from Sp., from Ar. *līlak*, changed from Persian *nīlak* bluish, from *nīl* blue]

liliaceous (ˌlɪlɪ'eɪʃəs) *adj* of, relating to, or belonging to a family of plants having showy flowers and a bulb or bulblike organ: includes the lily, tulip, bluebell, and onion. [C18: from LL *līliāceus*, from *līlium* lily]

Lilliputian ❶ (ˌlɪlɪ'pjuːʃɪən) *n* **1** a tiny person or being. ◆ *adj* **2** tiny; very small. **3** petty or trivial. [C18: from *Lilliput*, an imaginary country of tiny inhabitants in Swift's *Gulliver's Travels* (1726)]

Lilo ('laɪˌləʊ) *n, pl* **Lilos.** *Trademark.* a type of inflatable plastic or rubber mattress.

lilt ❶ (lɪlt) *n* **1** (in music) a jaunty rhythm. **2** a buoyant motion. ◆ *vb* (*intr*) **3** (of a melody) to have a lilt. **4** to move in a buoyant manner. [C14 *lulten*, from ?]
▸'**lilting** *adj*

lily ('lɪlɪ) *n, pl* **lilies. 1** any perennial plant of a N temperate genus, such as the tiger lily, having scaly bulbs and showy typically pendulous flowers. **2** the bulb or flower of any of these plants. **3** any of various similar or related plants, such as the water lily. [OE, from L *līlium;* rel. to Gk *leirion* lily]
▸'**lily-ˌlike** *adj*

lily-livered ❶ *adj* cowardly; timid.

lily of the valley *n, pl* **lilies of the valley.** a small liliaceous plant of Eurasia and North America cultivated for its spikes of fragrant white bell-shaped flowers.

lily-white ❶ *adj* **1** of a pure white: *lily-white skin.* **2** *Inf.* pure; irreproachable.

lima bean ('laɪmə, 'liː-) *n* **1** any of several varieties of the bean plant native to tropical America, cultivated for its flat pods containing pale green edible seeds. **2** the seed of such a plant. [C19: after *Lima*, Peru]

limb[1] ❶ (lɪm) *n* **1** an arm or leg, or the analogous part on an animal, such as a wing. **2** any of the main branches of a tree. **3** a branching or projecting section or member; extension. **4** a person or thing considered to be a member, part, or agent of a larger group or thing. **5** *Chiefly Brit.* a mischievous child (esp. in **limb of Satan**, etc.). **6 out on a limb. 6a** in a precarious or questionable position. **6b** *Brit.* isolated, esp. because of unpopular opinions. [OE *lim*]
▸'**limbless** *adj*

limb[2] (lɪm) *n* **1** the edge of the apparent disc of the sun, a moon, or a planet. **2** a graduated arc attached to instruments, such as the sextant, used for measuring angles. **3** *Bot.* the expanded part of a leaf, petal, or sepal. **4** Also called: **fold limb.** either of the sides of a geological fold. [C15: from L *limbus* edge]

limbed (lɪmd) *adj* **a** having limbs. **b** (*in combination*): *short-limbed; strong-limbed.*

limber[1] ❶ ('lɪmbə) *adj* **1** capable of being easily bent or flexed; pliant. **2** able to move or bend freely; agile. [C16: from ?]
▸'**limberness** *n*

limber[2] ('lɪmbə) *n* **1** part of a gun carriage, consisting of an axle, pole,

THESAURUS

Antonyms *adj* important, momentous, serious, significant, substantial, weighty

likable *adj* = **attractive**, agreeable, amiable, appealing, charming, engaging, friendly, genial, nice, pleasant, pleasing, sympathetic, winning, winsome

like[1] *adj* **1** = **similar**, akin, alike, allied, analogous, approximating, cognate, corresponding, equivalent, identical, parallel, relating, resembling, same ◆ *n* **8** = **equal**, counterpart, fellow, match, parallel, twin
Antonyms *adj* ≠ **similar:** contrasted, different, dissimilar, divergent, diverse, opposite, unlike ◆ *n* ≠ **equal:** opposite

like[2] *vb* **1, 2** = **enjoy**, admire, adore, appreciate, approve of, be fond of, be keen on, be partial to, cherish, delight in, dig (*sl.*), esteem, go for, hold dear, love, relish, revel in, take a shine to (*inf.*), take to **3, 5** = **wish**, care to, choose, choose to, desire, fancy, feel inclined, prefer, select, want ◆ *n* **6** *usually plural* = **preference**, cup of tea (*inf.*), favourite, liking, partiality, predilection
Antonyms *vb* ≠ **enjoy:** abominate, despise, detest, dislike, hate, loathe

likelihood *n* **1** = **probability**, chance, good chance, liability, likeliness, possibility, prospect, reasonableness, strong possibility

likely *adj* **1** = **inclined**, apt, disposed, liable, prone, tending **2** = **probable**, anticipated, expected, odds-on, on the cards, to be expected **3** = **plausible**, believable, credible, feasible, possible, reasonable, verisimilar **4** = **appropriate**, acceptable, agreeable, befitting, fit, pleasing, proper, qualified, suitable **5** = **promising**, fair, favourite, hopeful, up-and-coming ◆ *adv* **6** = **probably**, doubtlessly, in all probability, like as not (*inf.*), like enough (*inf.*), no doubt, presumably

like-minded *adj* = **agreeing**, compatible, *en rapport*, harmonious, in accord, in harmony, of one mind, of the same mind, unanimous

liken *vb* = **compare**, equate, juxtapose, match, mention in the same breath, parallel, relate, set beside

likeness *n* **1** = **resemblance**, affinity, correspondence, similarity, similitude **2** = **portrait**, copy, counterpart, delineation, depiction, effigy, facsimile, image, model, photograph, picture, replica, representation, reproduction, study **3** = **appearance**, form, guise, semblance

likewise *adv* **1** = **also**, besides, further, furthermore, in addition, moreover, too **2** = **similarly**, in like manner, in the same way

liking *n* **1** = **fondness**, affection, desire, love, soft spot **2** = **preference**, affinity, attraction, bent, bias, inclination, partiality, penchant, predilection, proneness, propensity, stomach, taste, tendency, thirst, weakness
Antonyms *n* abhorrence, aversion, dislike, hatred, loathing, repugnance

Lilliputian *n* **1** = **midget**, dwarf, homunculus, hop-o'-my-thumb, manikin, pygmy *or* pigmy, Tom Thumb ◆ *adj* **2** = **tiny**, baby, bantam, diminutive, dwarf, little, mini, miniature, minuscule, petite, pocket-sized, pygmy *or* pigmy, small, teensy-weensy, teeny, teeny-weeny, wee

lilt *n* **1** = **rhythm**, beat, cadence **2** = **swing**, sway

lily-livered *adj* = **cowardly**, abject, base, chicken (*sl.*), chicken-hearted, craven, faint-hearted, fearful, gutless (*inf.*), pusillanimous, scared, spineless, timid, timorous, yellow (*inf.*), yellow-bellied (*sl.*)

lily-white *adj* **1** = **pure white**, milk-white, white, white as snow, white-skinned **2** *Informal* = **innocent**, chaste, impeccable, irreproachable, pure, spotless, squeaky-clean, unsullied, untainted, untarnished, virgin, virtuous

limb[1] *n* **1** = **part**, appendage, arm, extension, extremity, leg, member, wing **2** = **branch**, bough, offshoot, projection, spur

limber[1] *adj* **1** = **pliant**, elastic, flexible, plas-

and two wheels. ◆ *vb* **2** (usually foll. by *up*) to attach the limber (to a gun, etc.). [C15 *lymour* shaft of a gun carriage, from ?]

limber up ⓘ *vb* (*intr, adv*) (esp. in sports) to exercise in order to be limber and agile.

limbic system ('lɪmbɪk) *n* the part of the brain concerned with basic emotion, hunger, and sex. [C19 *limbic*, from F, from *limbe*, from NL *limbus*, from L: border]

limbo[1] ('lɪmbəʊ) *n, pl* **limbos. 1** (*often cap.*) *Christianity.* the supposed abode of infants dying without baptism and the just who died before Christ. **2** an imaginary place for lost, forgotten, or unwanted persons or things. **3** an unknown intermediate place or condition between two extremes: *in limbo.* [C14: from Med. L *in limbo* on the border (of hell)]

limbo[2] ('lɪmbəʊ) *n, pl* **limbos.** a Caribbean dance in which dancers pass, while leaning backwards, under a bar. [C20: from ?]

Limburger ('lɪmˌbɜːgə) *n* a semihard white cheese of very strong smell and flavour. Also called: **Limburg cheese.**

lime[1] (laɪm) *n* **1** short for **quicklime, birdlime, slaked lime. 2** *Agriculture.* any of certain calcium compounds, esp. calcium hydroxide, spread as a dressing on lime-deficient land. ◆ *vb* **limes, liming, limed.** (*tr*) **3** to spread (twigs, etc.) with birdlime. **4** to spread a calcium compound upon (land) to improve plant growth. **5** to catch (animals, esp. birds) as with birdlime. **6** to whitewash (a wall, ceiling, etc.) with a mixture of lime and water (**limewash**). [OE *līm*]

lime[2] (laɪm) *n* **1** a small Asian citrus tree with stiff sharp spines and small round or oval greenish fruits. **2a** the fruit of this tree, having acid fleshy pulp rich in vitamin C. **2b** (*as modifier*): *lime juice.* ◆ *adj* **3** having the flavour of lime fruit. [C17: from F, from Ar. *līmah*]

lime[3] (laɪm) *n* a European linden tree planted in many varieties for ornament. [C17: changed from obs. *line*, from OE *lind* LINDEN]

limeade (ˌlaɪm'eɪd) *n* a drink made from sweetened lime juice and plain or carbonated water.

lime green *n* **a** a moderate greenish-yellow colour. **b** (*as adj*): *a lime-green dress.*

limekiln ('laɪmˌkɪln) *n* a kiln in which calcium carbonate is calcined to produce quicklime.

limelight ⓘ ('laɪmˌlaɪt) *n* **1 the.** a position of public attention or notice (esp. in **in the limelight**). **2a** a type of lamp, formerly used in stage lighting, in which light is produced by heating lime to white heat. **2b** Also called: **calcium light.** brilliant white light produced in this way.

limerick ('lɪmərɪk) *n* a form of comic verse consisting of five anapaestic lines. [C19: allegedly from *will you come up to Limerick?*, a refrain sung between nonsense verses at a party]

limestone ('laɪmˌstəʊn) *n* a sedimentary rock consisting mainly of calcium carbonate: used as a building stone and in making cement, lime, etc.

limewater ('laɪmˌwɔːtə) *n* **1** a clear colourless solution of calcium hydroxide in water, sometimes used in medicine as an antacid. **2** water that contains dissolved lime or calcium salts, esp. calcium carbonate or calcium sulphate.

limey ('laɪmɪ) *US, Canad., & Austral. sl.* ◆ *n* **1** a British person. **2** a British sailor or ship. ◆ *adj* **3** British. [abbrev. from C19 *lime-juicer*, because British sailors drank lime juice as a protection against scurvy]

limit ⓘ ('lɪmɪt) *n* **1** (*sometimes pl*) the ultimate extent, degree, or amount of something: *the limit of endurance.* **2** (*often pl*) the boundary or edge of a specific area: *the city limits.* **3** (*often pl*) the area of premises within specific boundaries. **4** the largest quantity or amount allowed. **5** *Maths.* **5a** a value to which a function approaches as the independent variable approaches a specified value or infinity. **5b** a value to which a sequence a_n approaches as n approaches infinity. **5c** the limit of a sequence of partial sums of a convergent infinite series. **6** *Maths.* one of the two specified values between which a definite integral is evaluated. **7 the limit.** *Inf.* a person or thing that is intolerably exasperating. ◆ *vb* **limits, limiting, limited.** (*tr*) **8** to restrict or confine, as to area, extent, time, etc. [C14: from L *līmes* boundary]
▸**'limitable** *adj* ▸**'limitless** *adj* ▸**'limitlessly** *adv* ▸**'limitlessness** *n*

limitary ('lɪmɪtərɪ, -trɪ) *adj* **1** of, involving, or serving as a limit. **2** restricted or limited.

limitation ⓘ (ˌlɪmɪ'teɪʃən) *n* **1** something that limits a quality or achievement. **2** the act of limiting or the condition of being limited. **3** *Law.* a certain period of time, legally defined, within which an action, claim, etc., must be commenced.

limited ⓘ ('lɪmɪtɪd) *adj* **1** having a limit; restricted; confined. **2** without fullness or scope; narrow. **3** (of governing powers, sovereignty, etc.) restricted or checked, by or as if by a constitution, laws, or an assembly: *limited government.* **4** *Chiefly Brit.* (of a business enterprise) owned by shareholders whose liability for the enterprise's debts is restricted.
▸**'limitedly** *adv* ▸**'limitedness** *n*

limited liability *n Brit.* liability restricted to the unpaid portion (if any) of the par value of the shares of a limited company.

limiter ('lɪmɪtə) *n* an electronic circuit that produces an output signal whose positive or negative amplitude, or both, is limited to some predetermined value above which the peaks become flattened. Also called: **clipper.**

limn (lɪm) *vb* (*tr*) **1** to represent in drawing or painting. **2** *Arch.* to describe in words. [C15: from OF *enluminer* to illumine (a manuscript) from L *inlūmināre* to brighten, from *lūmen* light]
▸**limner** ('lɪmnə) *n*

limnology (lɪm'nɒlədʒɪ) *n* the study of bodies of fresh water with reference to their plant and animal life, physical properties, geographical features, etc. [C20: from Gk *limnē* lake]
▸**limnological** (ˌlɪmnə'lɒdʒɪkᵊl) *adj* ▸**lim'nologist** *n*

limousine ('lɪməˌziːn, ˌlɪmə'ziːn) *n* any large and luxurious car, esp. one that has a glass division between the driver and passengers. [C20: from F, lit.: cloak (orig. one worn by shepherds in *Limousin*), hence later applied to the car]

limp[1] ⓘ (lɪmp) *vb* (*intr*) **1** to walk with an uneven step, esp. with a weak or injured leg. **2** to advance in a labouring or faltering manner. ◆ *n* **3** an uneven walk or progress. [C16: prob. a back formation from obs. *limphalt* lame, from OE *lemphealt*]
▸**'limper** *n* ▸**'limping** *adj, n*

limp[2] ⓘ (lɪmp) *adj* **1** not firm or stiff. **2** not energetic or vital. **3** (of the binding of a book) not stiffened with boards. [C18: prob. of Scand. origin]
▸**'limply** *adv* ▸**'limpness** *n*

limpet ('lɪmpɪt) *n* **1** any of numerous marine gastropods, such as the common limpet and keyhole limpet, that have a conical shell and are found clinging to rocks. **2** (*modifier*) relating to or denoting certain weapons that are attached to their targets by magnetic or adhesive properties and resist removal: *limpet mines.* [OE *lempedu*, from L *lepas*, from Gk]

limpid ⓘ ('lɪmpɪd) *adj* **1** clear or transparent. **2** (esp. of writings, style, etc.) free from obscurity. **3** calm; peaceful. [C17: from F *limpide*, from L *limpidus* clear]
▸**lim'pidity** *or* **'limpidness** *n* ▸**'limpidly** *adv*

limp-wristed ⓘ *adj* ineffectual; effete.

limy[1] ('laɪmɪ) *adj* **limier, limiest.** of, like, or smeared with birdlime.
▸**'liminess** *n*

limy[2] ('laɪmɪ) *adj* **limier, limiest.** of or tasting of lime (the fruit).

linage ('laɪnɪdʒ) *n* **1** the number of lines in a piece of written or printed matter. **2** payment for written material calculated according to the number of lines.

linchpin ⓘ *or* **lynchpin** ('lɪntʃˌpɪn) *n* **1** a pin placed transversely through an axle to keep a wheel in position. **2** a person or thing regarded as an essential or coordinating element: *the linchpin of the company.* [C14 *lynspin*, from OE *lynis*]

Lincoln green ('lɪŋkən) *n* **1a** a yellowish-green or brownish-green colour. **1b** (*as adj*): *a Lincoln-green suit.* **2** a cloth of this colour. [C16: after a green fabric formerly made at *Lincoln*, in E central England]

Lincs (lɪŋks) *abbrev. for* Lincolnshire.

linctus ('lɪŋktəs) *n, pl* **linctuses.** a syrupy medicinal preparation, taken to relieve coughs and sore throats. [C17 (in the sense: medicine to be licked with the tongue): from L, p.p. of *lingere* to lick]

lindane ('lɪndeɪn) *n* a white poisonous crystalline powder: used as an insecticide and weedkiller. [C20: after T. van der *Linden*, Du. chemist]

linden ('lɪndən) *n* any of various deciduous trees of a N temperate genus having heart-shaped leaves and small fragrant yellowish flow-

THESAURUS

tic, pliable, supple **2** = **agile**, graceful, lissom(e), lithe, loose-jointed, loose-limbed, supple

limber up *vb* = **loosen up**, exercise, get ready, prepare, warm up

limelight *n* **1** = **publicity**, attention, celebrity, fame, glare of publicity, prominence, public eye, public notice, recognition, stardom, the spotlight

limit *n* **1** = **end**, bound, breaking point, cutoff point, deadline, end point, furthest bound, greatest extent, termination, the bitter end, ultimate, utmost **2** = **boundary**, border, confines, edge, end, extent, frontier, pale, perimeter, periphery, precinct **4** = **maximum**, ceiling, check, curb, limitation, obstruction, restraint, restriction **7 the limit** *Informal* = **the last straw**, enough, it (*inf.*), the end ◆ *vb* **8** = **restrict**, bound, check, circumscribe, confine, curb, delimit, demarcate, fix, hem in, hinder, ration, restrain, specify, straiten

limitation *n* **1** = **restriction**, block, check, condition, constraint, control, curb, disadvantage, drawback, impediment, obstruction, qualification, reservation, restraint, snag

limited *adj* **1** = **restricted**, bounded, checked, circumscribed, confined, constrained, controlled, curbed, defined, finite, fixed, hampered, hemmed in **2** = **narrow**, cramped, diminished, inadequate, insufficient, minimal, reduced, restricted, scant, short, unsatisfactory
Antonyms *adj* ≠ **restricted:** boundless, limitless, unlimited, unrestricted

limitless *adj* **1** = **infinite**, boundless, countless, endless, illimitable, immeasurable, immense, inexhaustible, measureless, never-ending, numberless, unbounded, uncalculable, undefined, unending, unlimited, untold, vast

limp[1] *vb* **1** = **hobble**, falter, halt (*arch.*), hirple (*Scot.*), hop, shamble, shuffle ◆ *n* **3** = **lameness**, hirple (*Scot.*), hobble

limp[2] *adj* **1** = **floppy**, drooping, flabby, flaccid, flexible, lax, limber, loose, pliable, relaxed, slack, soft **2** = **weak**, debilitated, enervated, exhausted, lethargic, spent, tired, worn out
Antonyms *adj* ≠ **floppy:** firm, hard, rigid, solid, stiff, taut, tense, unyielding ≠ **weak:** hardy, powerful, robust, strong, sturdy, tough

limpid *adj* **1** = **clear**, bright, crystal-clear, crystalline, pellucid, pure, translucent, transparent **2** = **understandable**, clear, comprehensible, intelligible, lucid, perspicuous, unambiguous **3** = **calm**, peaceful, placid, quiet, serene, still, tranquil, unruffled, untroubled

limp-wristed *adj* = **ineffectual**, effete, feeble, impotent, inadequate, ineffective, inept, useless, weak

linchpin *n* **2** = **driving force**, chief, coordinator, cornerstone, director, principal ers: cultivated for timber and as shade trees. See also **lime**[3]. [C16: n use of obs. adj *linden,* from OE *linde* lime tree]

line[1] ● (laɪn) *n* **1** a narrow continuous mark, as one made by a pencil, pen, or brush across a surface. **2** such a mark cut into or raised from a surface. **3** a thin indented mark or wrinkle. **4** a straight or curved continuous trace having no breadth that is produced by a moving point. **5** *Maths.* **5a** any straight one-dimensional geometrical element whose identity is determined by two points. A **line segment** lies between any two points on a line. **5b** a set of points (x, y) that satisfies the equation $y = mx + c$, where m is the gradient and c is the intercept with the y-axis. **6** a border or boundary: *the county line.* **7** *Sport.* **7a** a white or coloured band indicating a boundary or division on a field, track, etc. **7b** a mark or imaginary mark at which a race begins or ends. **8** *American football.* **8a** See **line of scrimmage. 8b** the players arranged in a row on either side of the line of scrimmage at the start of each play. **9** a specified point of change or limit: *the dividing line between sanity and madness.* **10a** the edge or contour of a shape. **10b** the sum or type of such contours, characteristic of a style or design: *the line of a building.* **11** anything long, flexible, and thin, such as a wire or string: *a washing line; a fishing line.* **12** a telephone connection: *a direct line to New York.* **13** a conducting wire, cable, or circuit for making connections between pieces of electrical apparatus, such as a cable for electric-power transmission, telecommunications, etc. **14** a system of travel or transportation, esp. over agreed routes: *a shipping line.* **15** a company operating such a system. **16** a route between two points on a railway. **17** *Chiefly Brit.* a railway track, including the roadbed, sleepers, etc. **18** a course or direction of movement or advance: *the line of flight of a bullet.* **19** a course or method of action, behaviour, etc.: *take a new line with him.* **20** a policy or prescribed course of action or way of thinking (often in **bring** *or* **come into line**). **21** a field of study, interest, occupation, trade, or profession: *this book is in your line.* **22** alignment; true (esp. in **in line, out of line**). **23** one kind of product or article: *a nice line in hats.* **24** a row of persons or things: *a line of cakes on the conveyor belt.* **25** a chronological or ancestral series, esp. of people: *a line of prime ministers.* **26** a row of words printed or written across a page or column. **27** a unit of verse consisting of the number of feet appropriate to the metre being used and written or printed with the words in a single row. **28** a short letter; note: *just a line to say thank you.* **29** a piece of useful information or hint about something: *give me a line on his work.* **30** one of a number of narrow horizontal bands forming a television picture. **31** *Physics.* a narrow band in an electromagnetic spectrum, resulting from a transition in an atom of a gas. **32** *Music.* **32a** any of the five horizontal marks that make up the stave. **32b** the musical part or melody notated on one such set. **32c** a discernible shape formed by sequences of notes or musical sounds: *a meandering melodic line.* **32d** (in polyphonic music) a set of staves that are held together with a bracket or brace. **33** a defensive or fortified position, esp. one that marks the most forward position in war or a national boundary: *the front line.* **34** a formation adopted by a body or a number of military units when drawn up abreast. **35** the combatant forces of certain armies and navies, excluding supporting arms. **36a** the equator (esp. in **crossing the line**). **36b** any circle or arc on the terrestrial or celestial sphere. **37** a US and Canad. word for **queue. 38** *Sl.* a portion of a powdered drug for snorting. **39** *Sl.* something said for effect, esp. to solicit for money, sex, etc. **40 all along the line. 40a** at every stage in a series. **40b** in every detail. **41 draw the line (at).** to object (to) or set a limit (on): *her father draws the line at her coming in after midnight.* **42 get a line on.** *Inf.* to obtain information about. **43 hold the line. 43a** to keep a telephone line open. **43b** *Football.* to prevent the opponents from taking the ball forward. **43c** (of soldiers) to keep formation, as when under fire. **44 in line for.** in the running for; a candidate for: *he's in line for a directorship.* **45 in line with.** conforming to. **46 lay** *or* **put on the line. 46a** to pay money. **46b** to speak frankly and directly. **46c** to risk (one's career, reputation, etc.) on something. ◆ *vb* **lines, lining, lined. 47** *(tr)* to mark with a line or lines. **48** *(tr)* to draw or represent with a line or lines. **49** *(tr)* to be or put as a border to: *tulips lined the lawns.* **50** to place in or form a row, series, or alignment. ◆ See also **lines, line-up.** [C13: partly from OF *ligne,* ult. from L *līnea,* n. use of *līneus* flaxen, from *līnum* flax; partly from OE *līn,* ult. also from L *līnum* flax]

▸ **'linable** *or* **'lineable** *adj* ▸ **lined** *adj*

line[2] ● (laɪn) *vb* **lines, lining, lined.** *(tr)* **1** to attach an inside covering to (a garment, curtain, etc.), as for protection, to hide the seaming, or so that it should hang well. **2** to cover or fit the inside of: *to line the walls with books.* **3** to fill plentifully: *a purse lined with money.* [C14: ult. from L *līnum* flax, since linings were often of linen]

lineage[1] ● ('lɪnɪɪdʒ) *n* direct descent from an ancestor, esp. a line of descendants from one ancestor. [C14: from OF *lignage,* from L *līnea* LINE[1]]

lineage[2] ('laɪnɪdʒ) *n* a variant spelling of **linage.**

lineal ('lɪnɪəl) *adj* **1** being in a direct line of descent from an ancestor. **2** of, involving, or derived from direct descent. **3** a less common word for **linear.** [C14: via OF from LL *līneālis,* from L *līnea* LINE[1]]

▸ **'lineally** *adv*

lineament ● ('lɪnɪəmənt) *n* *(often pl)* **1** a facial outline or feature. **2** a distinctive feature. [C15: from L: line, from *līneāre* to draw a line]

linear ('lɪnɪə) *adj* **1** of, in, along, or relating to a line. **2** of or relating to length. **3** resembling, represented by, or consisting of a line or lines. **4** having one dimension. **5** designating a style in the arts, esp. painting, that obtains its effects through line rather than colour or light. **6** *Maths.* of or relating to the first degree: *a linear equation.* **7** narrow and having parallel edges: *a linear leaf.* **8** *Electronics.* **8a** (of a circuit, etc.) having an output that is directly proportional to input: *linear amplifier.* **8b** having components arranged in a line. [C17: from L *līneāris* of lines]

▸ **linearity** (ˌlɪnɪ'ærɪtɪ) *n* ▸ **'linearly** *adv*

linear accelerator *n* an accelerator in which charged particles are accelerated along a linear path by potential differences applied to a number of electrodes along their path.

Linear B *n* an ancient system of writing found on clay tablets and jars of the second millennium B.C. excavated in Crete and on the Greek mainland. The script is apparently a modified form of the earlier and hitherto undeciphered **Linear A** and is generally accepted as being an early representation of Mycenaean Greek.

linear measure *n* a unit or system of units for the measurement of length.

linear motor *n* a form of electric motor in which the stator and the rotor are linear and parallel. It can be used to drive a train, one part of the motor being in the locomotive, the other in the track.

linear programming *n Maths.* a technique used in economics, etc., for determining the maximum or minimum of a linear function of non-negative variables subject to constraints expressed as linear equalities or inequalities.

lineation (ˌlɪnɪ'eɪʃən) *n* **1** the act of marking with lines. **2** an arrangement of or division into lines.

line dancing *n* a form of dancing performed by rows of people to country and western music.

line drawing *n* a drawing made with lines only.

lineman ('laɪnmən) *n, pl* **linemen. 1** another name for **platelayer. 2** a person who does the chaining, taping, or marking of points for a surveyor. **3** *Austral. & NZ.* (formerly) the member of a beach life-saving team who controlled the line used to help drowning swimmers and surfers. **4** *American football.* a member of the row of players who start each down, positioned on either side of the line of scrimmage. **5** *US & Canad.* another word for **linesman** (sense 2).

line management *n* the managers in charge of specific functions and concerned in the day-to-day operations of a company.

linen ('lɪnɪn) *n* **1a** a hard-wearing fabric woven from the spun fibres of flax. **1b** *(as modifier): a linen tablecloth.* **2** yarn or thread spun from flax fibre. **3** clothes, sheets, tablecloths, etc., made from linen cloth or from cotton. [OE *linnen,* ult. from L *līnum* flax]

line of battle *n* a formation adopted by a military or naval force when preparing for action.

line of fire *n* the flight path of a missile discharged or to be discharged from a firearm.

line of force *n* a line in a field of force, such as an electric or magnetic field, for which the tangent at any point is the direction of the force at that point.

line of scrimmage *n American football.* an imaginary line, parallel to the goal lines, on which the ball is placed at the start of a down and on either side of which the offense and defense line up.

line-out *n Rugby Union.* the method of restarting play when the ball goes into touch, the forwards forming two parallel lines at right angles to the touchline and jumping for the ball when it is thrown in.

line printer *n* an electromechanical device that prints a line of characters at a time: used in printing and in computer systems.

liner[1] ('laɪnə) *n* **1** a passenger ship or aircraft, esp. one that is part of a commercial fleet. **2** See **freightliner. 3** Also called: **eyeliner.** a cosmetic

THESAURUS

line[1] *n* **1, 2** = **stroke,** band, bar, channel, dash, groove, mark, rule, score, scratch, streak, stripe, underline **3** = **wrinkle,** crease, crow's foot, furrow, mark **9** = **boundary,** border, borderline, demarcation, edge, frontier, limit, mark **10** = **outline,** configuration, contour, features, figure, profile, silhouette **11** = **string,** cable, cord, filament, rope, strand, thread, wire, wisp **18** = **trajectory,** axis, course, direction, path, route, track **19, 20** = **approach,** avenue, belief, course, course of action, ideology, method, policy, position, practice, procedure, scheme, system **21** = **occupation,** activity, area, bag *(sl.),* business, calling, department, employment, field, forte, interest, job, profession, province, pursuit, specialization, trade, vocation **24** = **row,** column, crocodile *(Brit.),* file, procession, queue, rank, sequence, series **25** = **lineage,** ancestry, breed, family, race, stock, strain, succession **28** = **note,** card, letter, message, postcard, report, word **29** = **clue,** hint, indication, information, lead **34** = **formation,** disposition, firing line, front, front line, position, trenches **41 draw the line** = **object,** lay down the law, prohibit, put one's foot down, restrict, set a limit **44 in line for** = **due for,** a candidate for, being considered for, in the running for, next in succession to, on the short list for **45 in line with** = **in accord,** in agreement, in conformity, in harmony, in step ◆ *vb* **47, 48** = **mark,** crease, cut, draw, furrow, inscribe, rule, score, trace, underline **49** = **border,** bound, edge, fringe, rank, rim, skirt, verge

line[2] *vb* **1, 2** = **cover,** ceil, face, interline **3** = **fill**

lineage[1] *n* = **descent,** ancestry, birth, breed, descendants, extraction, family, forebears, forefathers, genealogy, heredity, house, line, off- spring, pedigree, progeny, stock, succession

lineament *n, often plural* **1** = **features,** countenance, face, phiz *or* phizog *(sl., chiefly Brit.),* physiognomy, visage **2** = **configuration,** line, outline, trait

lined *adj* **1** = **ruled,** feint **3** = **wrinkled,** furrowed, wizened, worn used to outline the eyes. **4** a person or thing that uses lines, esp. in drawing or copying.

liner[2] ('laɪnə) *n* **1** a material used as a lining. **2** a person who supplies or fits linings.

lines ❶ (laɪnz) *pl n* **1** general appearance or outline: *a car with fine lines.* **2** a plan of procedure or construction: *built on traditional lines.* **3a** the spoken words of a theatrical presentation. **3b** the words of a particular role: *he forgot his lines.* **4** *Inf., chiefly Brit.* a marriage certificate: *marriage lines.* **5** a defensive position, row of trenches, or other fortification: *we broke through the enemy lines.* **6** a school punishment of writing the same sentence or phrase out a specified number of times. **7 read between the lines.** to understand or find an implicit meaning in addition to the obvious one.

linesman ('laɪnzmən) *n, pl* **linesmen. 1** an official who helps the referee or umpire in various sports, esp. by indicating when the ball has gone out of play. **2** *Chiefly Brit.* a person who installs, maintains, or repairs telephone or electric-power lines. US and Canad. name: **lineman.**

line-up ❶ *n* **1** a row or arrangement of people or things assembled for a particular purpose: *the line-up for the football match.* **2** the members of such a row or arrangement. **3** *US.* an identity parade. ◆ *vb* **line up.** (*adv*) **4** to form, put into, or organize a line-up. **5** (*tr*) to produce, organize, and assemble: *they lined up some questions.* **6** (*tr*) to align.

ling[1] (lɪŋ) *n, pl* **ling** *or* **lings. 1** any of several northern coastal food fishes having an elongated body with long fins. **2** another name for **burbot** (a fish). [C13: prob. from Low G]

ling[2] (lɪŋ) *n* another name for **heather.** [C14: from ON *lyng*]

ling. *abbrev. for* linguistics.

-ling[1] *suffix forming nouns.* **1** *Often disparaging.* a person or thing belonging to or associated with the group, activity, or quality specified: *nestling; underling.* **2** used as a diminutive: *duckling.* [OE *-ling,* of Gmc origin]

-ling[2] *suffix forming adverbs.* in a specified condition, manner, or direction: *darkling.* [OE *-ling,* adv. suffix]

lingam ('lɪŋgəm) *or* **linga** ('lɪŋgə) *n* the Hindu phallic image of the god Siva. [C18: from Sansk.]

linger ❶ ('lɪŋgə) *vb* (*mainly intr*) **1** to delay or prolong departure. **2** to go in a slow or leisurely manner; saunter. **3** to remain just alive for some time prior to death. **4** to persist or continue, esp. in the mind. **5** to be slow to act; dither. [C13 (northern dialect) *lengeren* to dwell, from *lengen* to prolong, from OE *lengan*]
▸'**lingerer** *n* ▸'**lingering** *adj* ▸'**lingeringly** *adv*

lingerie ('lænʒərɪ) *n* women's underwear and nightwear. [C19: from F, from *linge,* from L *līneus* linen, from *līnum* flax]

lingo ❶ ('lɪŋgəʊ) *n, pl* **lingoes.** *Inf.* any foreign or unfamiliar language, jargon, etc. [C17: ?from LINGUA FRANCA]

lingua franca ('lɪŋgwə 'fræŋkə) *n, pl* **lingua francas** *or* **linguae francae** ('lɪŋgwiː 'frænsiː). **1** a language used for communication among people of different mother tongues. **2** a hybrid language containing elements from several different languages used in this way. **3** any system of communication providing mutual understanding. [C17: It., lit.: Frankish tongue]

Lingua Franca *n* a particular lingua franca spoken from the Crusades to the 18th century in the ports of the Mediterranean, based on Italian, Spanish, French, Arabic, Greek, and Turkish.

lingual ('lɪŋgwəl) *adj* **1** *Anat.* of or relating to the tongue. **2a** *Rare.* of or relating to language or languages. **2b** (*in combination*): *polylingual.* **3** articulated with the tongue. ◆ *n* **4** a lingual consonant, such as Scots (r).
▸'**lingually** *adv*

linguiform ('lɪŋgwɪˌfɔːm) *adj* shaped like a tongue.

linguist ('lɪŋgwɪst) *n* **1** a person who is skilled in foreign languages. **2** a person who studies linguistics. [C16: from L *lingua* tongue]

linguistic (lɪŋ'gwɪstɪk) *adj* **1** of or relating to language. **2** of or relating to linguistics.
▸**lin'guistically** *adv*

linguistic atlas *n* an atlas showing the distribution of distinctive linguistic features.

linguistics (lɪŋ'gwɪstɪks) *n* (*functioning as sing*) the scientific study of language.

liniment ❶ ('lɪnɪmənt) *n* a medicated liquid, usually containing alcohol, camphor, and an oil, applied to the skin to relieve pain, stiffness, etc. [C15: from LL *linīmentum,* from *linere* to smear]

lining ('laɪnɪŋ) *n* **1** material used to line a garment, curtain, etc. **2** any material used as an interior covering.

link[1] ❶ (lɪŋk) *n* **1** any of the separate rings, loops, or pieces that connect or make up a chain. **2** something that resembles such a ring, loop, or piece. **3** a road, rail, air, or sea connection, as between two main routes. **4** a connecting part or episode. **5** a connecting piece in a mechanism. **6** Also called: **radio link.** a system of transmitters and receivers that connect two locations by means of radio and television signals. **7** a unit of length equal to one hundredth of a chain. 1 link of a Gunter's chain is equal to 7.92 inches, and of an engineer's chain to 1 foot. ◆ *vb* **8** (often foll. by *up*) to connect or be connected with or as if with links. **9** (*tr*) to connect by association, etc. [C14: from ON]

link[2] (lɪŋk) *n* (formerly) a torch used to light dark streets. [C16: ?from L *lychnus,* from Gk *lukhnos* lamp]

linkage ('lɪŋkɪdʒ) *n* **1** the act of linking or the state of being linked. **2** a system of interconnected levers or rods for transmitting or regulating the motion of a mechanism. **3** *Electronics.* the product of the total number of lines of magnetic flux and the number of turns in a coil or circuit through which they pass. **4** *Genetics.* the occurrence of two genes close together on the same chromosome so that they tend to be inherited as a single unit.

linkman ('lɪŋkmən) *n, pl* **linkmen.** a presenter of a television or radio programme, esp. a sports transmission, consisting of a number of outside broadcasts from different locations.

links (lɪŋks) *pl n* **1a** short for **golf links. 1b** (*as modifier*): *a links course.* See **golf course. 2** *Chiefly Scot.* undulating sandy ground near the shore. [OE *hlincas* pl. of *hlinc* ridge]

link-up *n* a joining or linking together of two factions, objects, etc.

linn (lɪn) *n Chiefly Scot.* **1** a waterfall or a pool at the foot of it. **2** a ravine or precipice. [C16: prob. from a confusion of two words, Scot. Gaelic *linne* pool and OE *hlynn* torrent]

Linnean *or* **Linnaean** (lɪ'niːən), -'neɪ-) *adj* **1** of or relating to Linnaeus (1707–78), Swedish botanist. **2** relating to the system of classification of plants and animals using binomial nomenclature.

linnet ('lɪnɪt) *n* a brownish Old World finch: the male has a red breast and forehead. [C16: from OF *linotte,* ult. from L *līnum* flax (because the bird feeds on flaxseeds)]

lino ('laɪnəʊ) *n* short for **linoleum.**

linocut ('laɪnəʊˌkʌt) *n* **1** a design cut in relief on linoleum mounted on a wooden block. **2** a print made from such a design.

linoleum (lɪ'nəʊlɪəm) *n* a sheet material made of hessian, jute, etc., coated with a mixture of powdered cork, linseed oil, rosin, and pigment, used as a floor covering. Often shortened to **lino.** [C19: from L *līnum* flax + *oleum* oil]

Linotype ('laɪnəʊˌtaɪp) *n* **1** *Trademark.* a typesetting machine, operated by a keyboard, that casts an entire line on one solid slug of metal. **2** type produced by such a machine.

linseed ('lɪnˌsiːd) *n* another name for **flaxseed.** [OE *līnsǣd,* from *līn* flax + *sǣd* seed]

linseed oil *n* a yellow oil extracted from seeds of the flax plant. It is used in making oil paints, printer's ink, linoleum, etc.

linsey-woolsey ('lɪnzɪ'wʊlzɪ) *n* **1** a thin rough fabric of linen warp and coarse wool or cotton filling. **2** a strange nonsensical mixture or confusion. [C15: prob. from *Lindsey,* village in Suffolk where first made + WOOL (with rhyming suffix *-sey*)]

lint (lɪnt) *n* **1** an absorbent cotton or linen fabric with the nap raised on one side, used to dress wounds, etc. **2** shreds of fibre, yarn, etc. [C14: prob. from L *linteus* made of linen, from *līnum* flax]
▸'**linty** *adj*

lintel ('lɪntᵊl) *n* a horizontal beam, as over a door or window. [C14: via OF prob. from LL *līmitāris* (unattested) of the boundary, infl. by *līminaris* of the threshold]

linter ('lɪntə) *n* **1** a machine for stripping the short fibres of ginned cotton seeds. **2** (*pl*) the fibres so removed.

lion ❶ ('laɪən) *n* **1** a large gregarious predatory feline mammal of open country in parts of Africa and India, having a tawny yellow coat and, in the male, a shaggy mane. Related adj: **leonine. 2** a conventionalized lion, the principal beast used as an emblem in heraldry. **3** a courageous, strong, or bellicose person. **4** a celebrity or idol who attracts much publicity and a large following. **5 the lion's share.** the largest portion. [OE *līo, lēo* (ME *lioun,* from Anglo-F *liun*), both from L *leo,* Gk *leōn*]
▸'**lioness** *fem n*

Lion ('laɪən) *n* **the.** the constellation Leo, the fifth sign of the zodiac.

lion-hearted ❶ *adj* very brave; courageous.

THESAURUS

lines *pl n* **1** = **outline,** appearance, configuration, contour, cut, shape, style **2** = **principle,** convention, example, model, pattern, plan, procedure **3** = **words,** part, script

line-up *n* **1, 2** = **arrangement,** array, row, selection, team ◆ *vb* **line up 4** = **queue up,** fall in, form ranks **5** = **produce,** assemble, come up with, lay on, obtain, organize, prepare, procure, secure **6** = **align,** arrange, array, marshal, order, range, regiment, sequence, straighten

linger *vb* **1** = **stay,** hang around, hang in the air, loiter, remain, stop, tarry, wait **3** = **hang on,** cling to life, die slowly, last, survive **4** = **continue,** abide, endure, persist, remain, stay **5** = **delay,** dally, dawdle, drag one's feet *or* heels, idle, lag, procrastinate, take one's time

lingering *adj* **3** = **slow,** dragging, long-drawn-out, protracted

lingo *n Informal* = **language,** argot, cant, dialect, idiom, jargon, patois, patter, speech, talk, tongue, vernacular

liniment *n* = **ointment,** balm, balsam, cream, embrocation, emollient, lotion, salve, unguent

link[1] *n* **1, 2** = **component,** constituent, division, element, member, part, piece **4** = **connection,** affiliation, affinity, association, attachment, bond, joint, knot, liaison, relationship, tie, tie-up ◆ *vb* **8** = **connect,** attach, bind, couple, fasten, join, tie, unite, yoke **9** = **associate,** bracket, connect, identify, relate
Antonyms *vb* ≠ **connect:** detach, disconnect, divide, separate, sever, split, sunder

lion *n* **3** = **hero,** brave person, champion, conqueror, fighter, warrior **4** = **celebrity,** big name, celeb (*inf.*), idol, luminary, megastar (*inf.*), notable, prodigy, star, superstar, V.I.P., wonder

lion-hearted *adj* = **brave,** bold, courageous, daring, dauntless, heroic, intrepid, resolute, stalwart, valiant, valorous
Antonyms *adj* abject, chicken-hearted, cowardly, craven, faint-hearted, gutless (*inf.*), lily-livered, pusillanimous, spineless, timorous, wimpish *or* wimpy (*inf.*), = **brave,** yellow (*inf.*)

lionize Ⓣ *or* **lionise** ('laɪə,naɪz) *vb* **lionizes, lionizing, lionized** *or* **lionises, lionising, lionised.** (*tr*) to treat as or make into a celebrity.
▸ **,lioni'zation** *or* **,lioni'sation** *n* ▸ **'lion,izer** *or* **'lion,iser** *n*

lip Ⓣ (lɪp) *n* **1** *Anat.* **1a** either of the two fleshy folds surrounding the mouth. Related adj: **labial. 1b** (*as modifier*): *lip salve.* **2** the corresponding part in animals, esp. mammals. **3** any structure resembling a lip, such as the rim of a crater, the margin of a gastropod shell, etc. **4** a nontechnical word for **labium. 5** *Sl.* impudent talk or backchat. **6 bite one's lip. 6a** to stifle one's feelings. **6b** to be annoyed or irritated. **7 keep a stiff upper lip.** to maintain one's courage or composure during a time of trouble. **8 lick** *or* **smack one's lips.** to anticipate or recall something with glee or relish. ◆ *vb* **lips, lipping, lipped. 9** (*tr*) to touch with the lip or lips. **10** (*tr*) to form or be a lip or lips for. **11** (*tr*) *Rare.* to murmur or whisper. **12** (*intr*) to use the lips in playing a wind instrument. [OE *lippa*]
▸ **'lipless** *adj* ▸ **'lip,like** *adj*

lipase ('laɪpeɪs, 'lɪpeɪs) *n* any of a group of fat-digesting enzymes produced in the stomach, pancreas, and liver. [C19: from Gk *lipos* fat + -ASE]

lip gloss *n* a cosmetic applied to the lips to give a sheen.

lipid *or* **lipide** ('laɪpɪd, 'lɪpɪd) *n Biochem.* any of a large group of organic compounds that are esters of fatty acids or closely related substances. They are important structural materials in living organisms. Former name: **lipoid.** [C20: from F *lipide,* from Gk *lipos* fat]

Lipizzaner *or* **Lippizaner** (,lɪpɪt'sɑːnə) *n* a breed of riding and carriage horse used by the Spanish Riding School in Vienna and nearly always grey in colour. [G, after *Lipizza,* near Trieste, where these horses were bred]

lipo- *or before a vowel* **lip-** *combining form.* fat or fatty: *lipoprotein.* [from Gk *lipos* fat]

lipogram ('lɪpəʊ,græm) *n* a piece of writing from which all words containing a particular letter have been deliberately omitted.

lipography (lɪ'pɒgrəfɪ) *n* the accidental omission of words or letters in writing. [C19: from Gk *lip-,* stem of *leipein* to omit + -GRAPHY]

lipoid ('lɪpɔɪd, 'laɪ-) *adj also* **lipoidal. 1** resembling fat; fatty. ◆ *n* **2** a fatlike substance, such as wax. **3** *Biochem.* a former name for **lipid.**

lipoprotein (,lɪpəʊ'prəʊtiːn, ,laɪ-) *n* any of a group of proteins to which a lipid molecule is attached, important in the transport of lipids in the bloodstream. See also **low-density lipoprotein.**

liposuction ('lɪpəʊ,sʌkʃən) *n* a cosmetic surgical operation in which subcutaneous fat is removed from the body by suction.

-lipped *adj* having a lip or lips as specified: *tight-lipped.*

Lippizaner (,lɪpɪt'sɑːnə) *n* a variant spelling of **Lipizzaner.**

lip-read ('lɪp,riːd) *vb* **lip-reads, lip-reading, lip-read** (-'rɛd). to interpret (words) by lip-reading.

lip-reading *n* a method used by the deaf to comprehend spoken words by interpreting movements of the speaker's lips. Also called: **speech-reading.**
▸ **'lip-,reader** *n*

lip service *n* insincere support or respect expressed but not practised.

lipstick ('lɪp,stɪk) *n* a cosmetic for colouring the lips, usually in the form of a stick.

lip-synch *or* **lip-sync** ('lɪp,sɪŋk) *vb* to mouth (prerecorded words) on television or film.

liq. *abbrev. for:* **1** liquid. **2** liquor.

liquefacient (,lɪkwɪ'feɪʃənt) *n* **1** a substance that liquefies or that causes liquefaction. ◆ *adj* **2** becoming or causing to become liquid. [C19: from L *liquefacere* to make LIQUID]

liquefied natural gas *n* a mixture of various gases, esp. methane, liquefied under pressure for transportation and used as an engine fuel. Abbrev.: **LNG.**

liquefied petroleum gas *n* a mixture of various petroleum gases, esp. propane and butane, stored as a liquid under pressure and used as an engine fuel. Abbrev.: **LPG** *or* **LP gas.**

liquefy Ⓣ ('lɪkwɪ,faɪ) *vb* **liquefies, liquefying, liquefied.** (esp. of a gas) to become or cause to become liquid. [C15: via OF from L *liquefacere* to make liquid]
▸ **liquefaction** (,lɪkwɪ'fækʃən) *n* ▸ **'lique,fiable** *adj* ▸ **'lique,fier** *n*

liquescent (lɪ'kwesᵊnt) *adj* (of a solid or gas) becoming or tending to become liquid. [C18: from L *liquescere*]
▸ **li'quescence** *or* **li'quescency** *n*

liqueur (lɪ'kjʊə; *French* likœr) *n* **1a** any of several highly flavoured sweetened spirits, such as Kirsch or Cointreau, intended to be drunk after a meal. **1b** (*as modifier*): *liqueur glass.* **2** a small hollow chocolate sweet containing liqueur. [C18: from F; see LIQUOR]

liquid Ⓣ ('lɪkwɪd) *n* **1** a substance in a physical state in which it does not resist change of shape but does resist change of size. Cf. **gas** (sense 1), **solid** (sense 1). **2** a substance that is a liquid at room temperature and atmospheric pressure. **3** *Phonetics.* a frictionless continuant, esp. (l) or (r). ◆ *adj* **4** of, concerned with, or being a liquid or having the characteristic state of liquids: *liquid wax.* **5** shining, transparent, or brilliant. **6** flowing, fluent, or smooth. **7** (of assets) in the form of money or easily convertible into money. [C14: via OF from L *liquidus,* from *liquēre* to be fluid]
▸ **li'quidity** *or* **'liquidness** *n* ▸ **'liquidly** *adv*

liquid air *n* air that has been liquefied by cooling: used in the production of pure oxygen, nitrogen, and as a refrigerant.

liquidambar (,lɪkwɪd'æmbə) *n* **1** a deciduous tree of Asia and North and Central America, with star-shaped leaves, and exuding a yellow aromatic balsam. **2** the balsam of this tree, used in medicine. [C16: NL, from L *liquidus* liquid + Med. L *ambar* AMBER]

liquidate Ⓣ ('lɪkwɪ,deɪt) *vb* **liquidates, liquidating, liquidated. 1** to settle or pay off (a debt, claim, etc.). **2a** to terminate the operations of (a commercial firm, bankrupt estate, etc.) by assessment of liabilities and appropriation of assets for their settlement. **2b** (of a commercial firm, etc.) to terminate operations in this manner. **3** (*tr*) to convert (assets) into cash. **4** (*tr*) to eliminate or kill.
▸ **'liqui,dator** *n*

liquidation (,lɪkwɪ'deɪʃən) *n* **1a** the process of terminating the affairs of a business firm, etc., by realizing its assets to discharge its liabilities. **1b** the state of a business firm, etc., having its affairs so terminated (esp. in **to go into liquidation**). **2** destruction; elimination.

liquid-crystal display *n* a flat-screen display used, for example, in portable computers, digital watches, and calculators, in which an array of liquid-crystal elements can be selectively activated to generate an image, by means of an electric field, which when applied to an element alters its optical properties.

liquidize *or* **liquidise** ('lɪkwɪ,daɪz) *vb* **liquidizes, liquidizing, liquidized** *or* **liquidises, liquidising, liquidised. 1** to make or become liquid; liquefy. **2** (*tr*) to pulverize (food) in a liquidizer so as to produce a fluid.

liquidizer *or* **liquidiser** ('lɪkwɪ,daɪzə) *n* a kitchen appliance with blades for puréeing vegetables, blending liquids, etc. Also called: **blender.**

liquid measure *n* a unit or system of units for measuring volumes of liquids or their containers.

liquid oxygen *n* the clear pale blue liquid state of oxygen produced by liquefying air and allowing the nitrogen to evaporate: used in rocket fuels. Also called: **lox.**

liquid paraffin *n* an oily liquid obtained by petroleum distillation and used as a laxative. Also called (esp. US and Canad.): **mineral oil.**

liquor Ⓣ ('lɪkə) *n* **1** any alcoholic drink, esp. spirits, or such drinks collectively. **2** any liquid substance, esp. that in which food has been cooked. **3** *Pharmacol.* a solution of a pure substance in water. **4 in liquor.** drunk. [C13: via OF from L, from *liquēre* to be liquid]

liquorice *or US & Canad.* **licorice** ('lɪkərɪs, -ərɪʃ) *n* **1** a perennial Mediterranean leguminous shrub. **2** the dried root of this plant, used as a laxative and in confectionery. **3** a sweet having a liquorice flavour. [C13: via Anglo-Norman and OF from LL *liquirītia,* from L *glycyrrhīza,* from Gk *glukurrhiza,* from *glukus* sweet + *rhiza* root]

lira ('lɪərə; *Italian* 'liːra) *n, pl* **lire** ('lɪərɪ; *Italian* 'liːre) *or* **liras. 1** the standard monetary unit of Italy and San Marino. **2** Also called: **pound.** the standard monetary unit of Turkey. **3** the standard monetary unit of Malta. [It., from L *lībra* pound]

liriodendron (,lɪrɪəʊ'dɛndrən) *n, pl* **liriodendrons** *or* **liriodendra** (-drə). a deciduous tulip tree of North America or a similar Chinese tree. [C18: NL, from Gk *leiron* lily + *dendron* tree]

lisle (laɪl) *n* **a** a strong fine cotton thread or fabric. **b** (*as modifier*): *lisle stockings.* [C19: after *Lisle* (now Lille), town in France where this thread was orig. manufactured]

lisp (lɪsp) *n* **1** the articulation of *s* and *z* like or nearly like the *th* sounds in English *thin* and *then* respectively. **2** the habit or speech defect of pronouncing *s* and *z* in this manner. **3** the sound of a lisp in pronunciation. ◆ *vb* **4** to use a lisp in the pronunciation of (speech). **5** to speak or pronounce imperfectly or haltingly. [OE *āwlispian,* from *wlisp* lisping (adj), imit.]
▸ **'lisper** *n* ▸ **'lisping** *adj, n* ▸ **'lispingly** *adv*

lissom Ⓣ *or* **lissome** ('lɪsəm) *adj* **1** supple in the limbs or body; lithe; flexible. **2** agile; nimble. [C19: var. of *lithesome,* LITHE + -SOME[1]]
▸ **'lissomly** *or* **'lissomely** *adv* ▸ **'lissomness** *or* **'lissomeness** *n*

list[1] Ⓣ (lɪst) *n* **1** an item-by-item record of names or things, usually written or printed one under the other. **2** *Computing.* a linearly ordered

THESAURUS

lionize *vb* = **idolize**, acclaim, adulate, aggrandize, celebrate, eulogize, exalt, fête, glorify, hero-worship, honour, make much of, mob

lip *n* 3 = **edge**, brim, brink, flange, margin, rim 5 *Slang* = **impudence**, backchat (*inf.*), cheek, effrontery, impertinence, insolence, rudeness, sauce (*inf.*) 8 **lick** *or* **smack one's lips** = **relish**, anticipate, delight in, drool over, enjoy, gloat over, savour, slaver over

liquefaction *n* = **melting**, deliquescence, dissolution, dissolving, fusion, thawing

liquefy *vb* = **melt**, deliquesce, dissolve, flux, fuse, liquesce, liquidize, run, thaw

liquid *n* 1 = **fluid**, juice, liquor, solution ◆ *adj* 4 = **fluid**, aqueous, flowing, liquefied, melted, molten, running, runny, thawed, wet 5 = **clear**, bright, brilliant, limpid, shining, translucent, transparent 6 = **smooth**, dulcet, flowing, fluent, mellifluent, mellifluous, melting, soft, sweet 7 = **convertible**, negotiable

liquidate *vb* 1 = **pay**, clear, discharge, honour, pay off, settle, square 2 = **dissolve**, abolish, annul, cancel, terminate 3 = **convert to cash**, cash, realize, sell off, sell up 4 = **kill**, annihilate, blow away, bump off (*sl.*), destroy, dispatch, do away with, do in (*sl.*), eliminate, exterminate, finish off, get rid of, murder, remove, wipe out (*inf.*)

liquor *n* 1 = **alcohol**, booze (*inf.*), drink, Dutch courage (*inf.*), grog, hard stuff (*inf.*), hooch *or* hootch (*inf., chiefly US & Canad.*), intoxicant, juice (*inf.*), spirits, strong drink 2 = **juice**, broth, extract, gravy, infusion, liquid, stock

lissom *adj* 1 = **supple**, flexible, limber, lithe, loose-jointed, loose-limbed, pliable, pliant, willowy 2 = **agile**, graceful, light, nimble

list[1] *n* 1 = **inventory**, catalogue, directory, file, index, invoice, leet (*Scot.*), listing, record, register, roll, schedule, series, syllabus, tabulation, tally ◆ *vb* 3, 4 = **itemize**, bill, book, catalogue, enrol, enter, enumerate, file, index, note, record, register, schedule, set down, tabulate, write down

data structure. ◆ *vb* **3** (*tr*) to make a list of. **4** (*tr*) to include in a list. **5** (*tr*) *Brit.* to declare to be a listed building. **6** (*tr*) *Stock Exchange.* to obtain an official quotation for (a security) so that it may be traded on the recognized market. **7** an archaic word for **enlist.** [C17: from F, ult. rel. to LIST[2]]
▸ **'listable** *adj* ▸ **'listing** *n*

list[2] (lɪst) *n* **1** a border or edging strip, esp. of cloth. **2** a less common word for **selvage.** ◆ *vb* (*tr*) **3** to border with or as if with a list or lists. ◆ See also **lists.** [OE *līst*]

list[3] ❶ (lɪst) *vb* **1** (esp. of ships) to lean over or cause to lean over to one side. ◆ *n* **2** the act or an instance of leaning to one side. [C17: from ?]

list[4] (lɪst) *Arch.* ◆ *vb* **1** to be pleasing to (a person). **2** (*tr*) to desire or choose. ◆ *n* **3** a liking or desire. [OE *lystan*]

list[5] (lɪst) *vb* an archaic or poetic word for **listen.** [OE *hlystan*]

listed building *n* (in Britain) a building officially recognized as having special historical or architectural interest and therefore protected from demolition or alteration.

listed company *n Stock Exchange.* a company whose shares are quoted on the main market of the London stock exchange.

listed security *n Stock Exchange.* a security that is quoted on the main market of the London stock exchange and appears in its *Official List of Securities*. Cf. **Third Market, Unlisted Securities Market.**

listen ❶ ('lɪsᵊn) *vb* (*intr*) **1** to concentrate on hearing something. **2** to take heed; pay attention: *I warned you but you wouldn't listen.* [OE *hlysnan*]
▸ **'listener** *n*

listen in *vb* (*intr, adv;* often foll. by *to*) **1** to listen to the radio. **2** to intercept radio communications. **3** to listen but not contribute (to a discussion), esp. surreptitiously.

listening post *n* **1** *Mil.* a forward position set up to obtain early warning of enemy movement. **2** any strategic position for obtaining information about another country or area.

lister ('lɪstə) *n US & Canad. agriculture.* a plough with a double mouldboard designed to throw soil to either side of a central furrow. [C19: from LIST[2]]

listeriosis (lɪˌstɪərɪ'əʊsɪs) *n* a serious form of food poisoning, caused by a bacterium (**listeria**). Its symptoms can include meningitis and in pregnant women it may cause damage to the fetus. [after Joseph *Lister* (1827–1912), E surgeon]

listless ❶ ('lɪstlɪs) *adj* having or showing no interest; lacking vigour or energy. [C15: from *list* desire + -LESS]
▸ **'listlessly** *adv* ▸ **'listlessness** *n*

list price *n* the selling price of merchandise as quoted in a catalogue or advertisement.

list renting *n* the practice of renting a list of potential customers to a direct-mail seller of goods or to the fund-raisers of a charity.

lists (lɪsts) *pl n* **1** *History.* **1a** the enclosed field of combat at a tournament. **1b** the barriers enclosing the field at a tournament. **2** any arena or scene of conflict, controversy, etc. **3 enter the lists.** to engage in a conflict, controversy, etc. [C14: pl of LIST[2] (border)]

lit (lɪt) *vb* **1** a past tense and past participle of **light**[1] (senses 23–26). **2** a past tense and past participle of **light**[2] (senses 28–31).

lit. *abbrev. for:* **1** literal(ly). **2** literary. **3** literature. **4** litre.

litany ❶ ('lɪtənɪ) *n, pl* **litanies. 1** *Christianity.* **1a** a form of prayer consisting of a series of invocations, each followed by an unvarying response. **1b the Litany.** the general supplication in this form in the Book of Common Prayer. **2** any tedious recital. [C13: via OF from Med. L *litanīa* from LGk *litaneia* prayer, ult. from Gk *litē* entreaty]

litchi, lichee, *or* **lychee** (ˌlaɪ'tʃiː) *n* **1** a Chinese tree cultivated for its round edible fruits. **2** the fruit of this tree, which has whitish juicy pulp. [C16: from Cantonese *lai chi*]

lite ('laɪt) *adj* **1** (of food and drink) containing few calories or little alcohol or fat. **2** denoting a more restrained or less extreme version of a person or thing: *reggae lite.* [C20: var. spelling of LIGHT[2]]

-lite *n combining form.* (in names of minerals) stone: *chrysolite.* [from F *-lite* or *-lithe,* from Gk *lithos* stone]

liter ('liːtə) *n* the US spelling of **litre.**

literacy ❶ ('lɪtərəsɪ) *n* **1** the ability to read and write. **2** the ability to use language proficiently.

literal ❶ ('lɪtərəl) *adj* **1** in exact accordance with or limited to the primary or explicit meaning of a word or text. **2** word for word. **3** dull, factual, or prosaic. **4** consisting of, concerning, or indicated by letters. **5** true; actual. ◆ *n* **6** Also called: **literal error.** a misprint or misspelling in a text. [C14: from LL *litterālis* concerning letters, from L *littera* letter]
▸ **'literalness** *or* **literality** (ˌlɪtə'rælɪtɪ) *n*

literalism ('lɪtərəˌlɪzəm) *n* **1** the disposition to take words and statements in their literal sense. **2** literal or realistic portrayal in art or literature.
▸ **'literalist** *n* ▸ **ˌliteral'istic** *adj*

literally ❶ ('lɪtərəlɪ) *adv* **1** in a literal manner. **2** (*intensifier*): *there were literally thousands of people.*

> **USAGE NOTE** The use of *literally* as an intensifier is common, esp. in informal contexts. In some cases, it provides emphasis without adding to the meaning: *the house was literally only five minutes walk away.* Often, however, its use results in absurdity: *the news was literally an eye-opener to me.* It is therefore best avoided in formal contexts.

literary ❶ ('lɪtərərɪ, 'lɪtrərɪ) *adj* **1** of, relating to, concerned with, or characteristic of literature or scholarly writing: *a literary style.* **2** versed in or knowledgeable about literature. **3** (of a word) formal; not colloquial. [C17: from L *litterārius* concerning reading & writing. See LETTER]
▸ **'literarily** *adv* ▸ **'literariness** *n*

literate ❶ ('lɪtərɪt) *adj* **1** able to read and write. **2** educated; learned. ◆ *n* **3** a literate person. [C15: from L *litterātus* learned. See LETTER]
▸ **'literately** *adv*

literati (ˌlɪtə'rɑːtiː) *pl n* literary or scholarly people. [C17: from L]

literature ❶ ('lɪtərɪtʃə, 'lɪtrɪ-) *n* **1** written material such as poetry, novels, essays, etc. **2** the body of written work of a particular culture or people: *Scandinavian literature.* **3** written or printed matter of a particular type or genre: *scientific literature.* **4** the art or profession of a writer. **5** *Inf.* printed matter on any subject. [C14: from L *litterātūra* writing; see LETTER]

lith. *abbrev. for:* **1** lithograph. **2** lithography.

Lith. *abbrev. for* Lithuania(n).

-lith *n combining form.* indicating stone or rock: *megalith.* [from Gk *lithos* stone]

litharge ('lɪθɑːdʒ) *n* another name for **lead monoxide.** [C14: via OF from L *lithargyrus,* from Gk, from *lithos* stone + *arguros* silver]

lithe ❶ (laɪð) *adj* flexible or supple. [OE (in the sense: gentle; C15: supple)]
▸ **'lithely** *adv* ▸ **'litheness** *n*

lithia ('lɪθɪə) *n* **1** another name for **lithium oxide. 2** lithium present in mineral waters as lithium salts. [C19: NL, ult. from Gk *lithos* stone]

lithic ('lɪθɪk) *adj* **1** of, relating to, or composed of stone. **2** *Pathol.* of or relating to a calculus or calculi. **3** of or containing lithium. [C18: from Gk *lithikos* stony]

-lithic *n and adj combining form.* relating to the use of stone implements in a specified cultural period: *Neolithic.* [from Gk *lithikos,* from *lithos* stone]

lithium ('lɪθɪəm) *n* a soft silvery element of the alkali metal series: the lightest known metal, used as an alloy hardener, as a reducing agent, and in batteries. Symbol: Li; atomic no.: 3; atomic wt.: 6.941. [C19: NL, from LITHO- + -IUM]

lithium carbonate *n* a white crystalline solid used in the treatment of manic-depressive illness and mania. Formula: Li_2CO_3.

lithium oxide *n* a white crystalline compound. It absorbs carbon dioxide and water vapour. Formula: Li_2O.

litho ('laɪθəʊ) *n, pl* **lithos,** *adj, adv* short for **lithography, lithograph, lithographic,** or **lithographically.**

litho- *or before a vowel* **lith-** *combining form.* stone: *lithograph.* [from L, from Gk, from *lithos* stone]

lithograph ('lɪθəˌgrɑːf) *n* **1** a print made by lithography. ◆ *vb* **2** (*tr*) to reproduce (pictures, text, etc.) by lithography.
▸ **lithographic** (ˌlɪθə'græfɪk) *adj* ▸ **ˌlitho'graphically** *adv*

lithography (lɪ'θɒgrəfɪ) *n* a method of printing from a metal or stone surface on which the printing areas are not raised but made ink-receptive as opposed to ink-repellent. [C18: from NL *lithographia*]
▸ **li'thographer** *n*

THESAURUS

list[3] *vb* **1** = **lean,** cant, careen, heel, heel over, incline, tilt, tip ◆ *n* **2** = **tilt,** cant, leaning, slant

listen *vb* **1** = **hear,** attend, be all ears, be attentive, give ear, hang on (someone's) words, hark, hearken (*arch.*), keep one's ears open, lend an ear, pin back one's ears (*inf.*), prick up one's ears **2** = **pay attention,** concentrate, do as one is told, give heed to, heed, mind, obey, observe, take notice

listless *adj* = **languid,** apathetic, enervated, heavy, impassive, inattentive, indifferent, indolent, inert, languishing, lethargic, lifeless, limp, sluggish, spiritless, supine, torpid, vacant
Antonyms *adj* active, alert, alive and kicking, attentive, energetic, full of beans (*inf.*), lively, sparky, spirited, wide-awake

listlessness *n* = **languor,** apathy, enervation, ennui, inattention, indifference, indolence, inertia, languidness, lethargy, lifelessness, sluggishness, spiritlessness, supineness, torpidity

litany *n* **1a** = **prayer,** invocation, petition, supplication **2** = **recital,** account, catalogue, enumeration, list, recitation, refrain, repetition, tale

literacy *n* **1, 2** = **education,** ability, articulacy, articulateness, cultivation, knowledge, learning, proficiency, scholarship

literal *adj* **1, 2** = **exact,** accurate, close, faithful, strict, verbatim, word for word **3** = **unimaginative,** boring, colourless, down-to-earth, dull, factual, matter-of-fact, prosaic, prosy, uninspired **4** = **actual,** bona fide, genuine, gospel, plain, real, simple, true, unexaggerated, unvarnished

literally *adv* **1** = **exactly,** actually, faithfully, plainly, precisely, really, simply, strictly, to the letter, truly, verbatim, word for word

literary *adj* **1, 2** = **scholarly,** bookish, erudite, formal, learned, lettered, literate, well-read

literate *adj* **1, 2** = **educated,** cultivated, cultured, erudite, informed, knowledgeable, learned, lettered, scholarly, well-informed, well-read

literature *n* **1, 2** = **writings,** letters, lore, written works **5** *Informal* = **information,** brochure, leaflet, mailshot, pamphlet

lithe *adj* = **supple,** flexible, limber, lissom(e), loose-jointed, loose-limbed, pliable, pliant

lithology (lɪ'θɒlədʒɪ) *n* **1** the physical characteristics of a rock, including colour, composition, and texture. **2** the study of rocks.
lithophyte ('lɪθəˌfaɪt) *n* **1** a plant that grows on stony ground. **2** an organism, such as a coral, that is partly composed of stony material.
lithosphere ('lɪθəˌsfɪə) *n* the rigid outer layer of the earth, comprising the earth's crust and the solid upper part of the mantle.
lithotomy (lɪ'θɒtəmɪ) *n, pl* **lithotomies.** the surgical removal of a calculus, esp. one in the urinary bladder. [C18: via LL from Gk]
lithotripsy ('lɪθəʊˌtrɪpsɪ) *n, pl* **-sies.** the use of ultrasound to pulverize kidney stones and gallstones *in situ.* [C20: from LITHO- + Gk *thruptein* to crush]
Lithuanian (ˌlɪθjʊ'eɪnɪən) *adj* **1** of, relating to, or characteristic of Lithuania, a republic on the Baltic Sea, its people, or their language. ◆ *n* **2** an official language of Lithuania. **3** a native or inhabitant of Lithuania.
litigable ('lɪtɪgəbᵊl) *adj Law.* that may be the subject of litigation.
litigant ❶ ('lɪtɪgənt) *n* **1** a party to a lawsuit. ◆ *adj* **2** engaged in litigation.
litigate ❶ ('lɪtɪˌgeɪt) *vb* **litigates, litigating, litigated. 1** to bring or contest (a claim, action, etc.) in a lawsuit. **2** (*intr*) to engage in legal proceedings. [C17: from L *lītigāre,* from *līt-,* stem of *līs* lawsuit + *agere* to carry on]
▸**'litiˌgator** *n*
litigation ❶ (ˌlɪtɪ'geɪʃən) *n* **1** the act or process of bringing or contesting a lawsuit. **2** a judicial proceeding or contest.
litigious ❶ (lɪ'tɪdʒəs) *adj* **1** excessively ready to go to law. **2** of or relating to litigation. **3** inclined to dispute or disagree. [C14: from L *lītigiōsus* quarrelsome, from *lītigium* strife]
▸**li'tigiously** *adv* ▸**li'tigiousness** *n*
litmus ('lɪtməs) *n* a soluble powder obtained from certain lichens. It turns red under acid conditions and blue under basic conditions. Absorbent paper treated with it (**litmus paper**) is used as an indicator. [C16: ?from Scand.]
litotes ('laɪtəʊˌtiːz) *n, pl* **litotes.** understatement for rhetorical effect, esp. using negation with a term in place of using an antonym of that term, as in "She was not a little upset" for "She was extremely upset". [C17: from Gk, from *litos* small]
litre *or US* **liter** ('liːtə) *n* **1** one cubic decimetre. **2** (formerly) the volume occupied by 1 kilogram of pure water. This is equivalent to 1.000 028 cubic decimetres or about 1.76 pints. [C19: from F, from Med. L *litra,* from Gk: a unit of weight]
LittD *or* **LitD** *abbrev. for* Doctor of Letters *or* Doctor of Literature. [L: *Litterarum Doctor*]
litter ❶ ('lɪtə) *n* **1a** small refuse or waste materials carelessly dropped, esp. in public places. **1b** (*as modifier*): *litter bin.* **2** a disordered or untidy condition or a collection of objects in this condition. **3** a group of offspring produced at one birth by a mammal such as a sow. **4** a layer of partly decomposed leaves, twigs, etc., on the ground in a wood or forest. **5** straw, hay, or similar material used as bedding, protection, etc., by animals or plants. **6** a means of conveying people, esp. sick or wounded people, consisting of a light bed or seat held between parallel sticks. **7** see **cat litter.** ◆ *vb* **8** to make (a place) untidy by strewing (refuse). **9** to scatter (objects, etc.) about or (of objects) to lie around or upon (anything) in an untidy fashion. **10** (of pigs, cats, etc.) to give birth to (offspring). **11** (*tr*) to provide (an animal or plant) with straw or hay for bedding, protection, etc. [C13 (in the sense: bed): via Anglo-F, ult. from L *lectus* bed]
littérateur (ˌlɪtərə'tɜː; *French* literatœr) *n* an author, esp. a professional writer. [C19: from F from L *litterātor* a grammarian]
litter lout *or US & Canad.* **litterbug** ('lɪtəˌbʌg) *n Sl.* a person who tends to drop refuse in public places.
little ❶ ('lɪtᵊl) *determiner* **1** (often preceded by *a*) **1a** a small quantity, extent, or duration of: *the little hope there is left; very little milk.* **1b** (*as pronoun*): *save a little for me.* **2** not much: *little damage was done.* **3 make little of.** to regard or treat as insignificant; dismiss. **4 not a little. 4a** very. **4b** a lot. **5 think little of.** to have a low opinion of. ◆ *adj* **6** of small or less than average size. **7** young: *a little boy.* **8** endearingly familiar; dear: *my husband's little ways.* **9** contemptible, mean, or disagreeable: *your filthy little mind.* ◆ *adv* **10** (usually preceded by *a*) in a small amount; to a small extent or degree; not a lot: *to laugh a little.* **11** (*used preceding a verb*) not at all, or hardly: *he little realized his fate.* **12** not much or often: *we go there very little now.* **13 little by little.** by small degrees. ◆ See also **less, lesser, least.** [OE *lȳtel*]
Little Bear *n* **the.** the English name for **Ursa Minor.**
Little Dipper *n* **the.** a US name for **Ursa Minor.**
little people *pl n Folklore.* small supernatural beings, such as elves or leprechauns.
little slam *n Bridge, etc.* the winning of all tricks except one. Cf. **grand slam.** Also called: **small slam.**
littoral ('lɪtərəl) *adj* **1** of or relating to the shore of a sea, lake, or ocean. ◆ *n* **2** a coastal or shore region. [C17: from LL *littorālis,* from *lītus* shore]
liturgical ❶ (lɪ'tɜːdʒɪkᵊl) *adj* **1** of or relating to public worship. **2** of or relating to the liturgy.
▸**li'turgically** *adv*
liturgy ❶ ('lɪtədʒɪ) *n, pl* **liturgies. 1** the forms of public services officially prescribed by a Church. **2** (*often cap.*) Also called: **Divine Liturgy.** *Chiefly Eastern Churches.* the Eucharistic celebration. **3** a particular order or form of public service laid down by a Church. [C16: via Med. L, from Gk *leitourgia,* from *leitourgos* minister, from *leit-* people + *ergon* work]
Liturgy of the Hours *n Christianity.* another name for **divine office.**
livable ❶ *or* **liveable** ('lɪvəbᵊl) *adj* **1** (of a room, house, etc.) suitable for living in. **2** worth living; tolerable. **3** (foll. by *with*) pleasant to live (with).
▸**'livableness, 'liveableness** *or* **ˌliva'bility, ˌlivea'bility** *n*
live[1] ❶ (lɪv) *vb* **lives, living, lived.** (*mainly intr*) **1** to show the characteristics of life; be alive. **2** to remain alive or in existence. **3** to exist in a specified way: *to live poorly.* **4** (usually foll. by *in* or *at*) to reside or dwell: *to live in London.* **5** (often foll. by *on*) to continue or last: *the pain still lives in her memory.* **6** (usually foll. by *by*) to order one's life (according to a certain philosophy, religion, etc.). **7** (foll. by *on, upon,* or *by*) to support one's style of life; subsist: *to live by writing.* **8** (foll. by *with*) to endure the effects (of a crime, mistake, etc.). **9** (foll. by *through*) to experience and survive: *he lived through the war.* **10** (*tr*) to pass or spend (one's life, etc.). **11** to enjoy life to the full: *he knows how to live.* **12** (*tr*) to put into practice in one's daily life; express: *he lives religion every day.* **13 live and let live.** to refrain from interfering in others' lives; be tolerant. ◆ See also **live down, live in,** etc. [OE *libban, lifian*]
live[2] ❶ (laɪv) *adj* **1** (*prenominal*) showing the characteristics of life. **2** (*usually prenominal*) of, relating to, or abounding in life: *the live weight of an animal.* **3** (*usually prenominal*) of current interest; controversial: *a live issue.* **4** actual: *a real live cowboy.* **5** *Inf.* full of life and energy. **6** (of a coal, ember, etc.) glowing or burning. **7** (esp. of a volcano) not extinct. **8** loaded or capable of exploding: *a live bomb.* **9** *Radio, television, etc.* transmitted or present at the time of performance, rather than being a recording: *a live show.* **10** (of a record) **10a** recorded in concert. **10b** recorded in one studio take. **11** connected to a source of electric power: *a live circuit.* **12** being in a state of motion or transmitting power. **13** acoustically reverberant. ◆ *adv* **14** during, at, or in the form of a live performance. [C16: from *on live* ALIVE]
-lived (-lɪvd) *adj* having or having had a life as specified: *short-lived.*
lived-in *adj* having a comfortable, natural, or homely appearance.
live down (lɪv) *vb* (*tr, adv*) to withstand the effects of (a crime, mistake, etc.) by waiting until others forget or forgive it.
live in (lɪv) *vb* (*intr, adv*) **1** (of an employee) to dwell at one's place of employment, as in a hotel, etc. ◆ *adj* **live-in. 2** resident: *a live-in nanny; a live-in lover.*
livelihood ❶ ('laɪvlɪˌhʊd) *n* occupation or employment.

THESAURUS

litigant *n* **1 = claimant,** contestant, disputant, litigator, party, plaintiff
litigate *vb* **1, 2 = sue,** contest at law, file a suit, go to court, go to law, institute legal proceedings, press charges, prosecute
litigation *n* **1, 2 = lawsuit,** action, case, contending, disputing, process, prosecution
litigious *adj* **3 = contentious,** argumentative, belligerent, disputatious, quarrelsome
litter *n* **1a = rubbish,** debris, detritus, fragments, garbage (*chiefly US*), grot (*sl.*), muck, refuse, shreds, trash **2 = jumble,** clutter, confusion, disarray, disorder, mess, scatter, untidiness **3 = brood,** family, offspring, progeny, young **4 = mulch 5 = bedding,** couch, floor cover, straw-bed **6 = stretcher,** palanquin ◆ *vb* **8 = clutter,** derange, disarrange, disorder, mess up **9 = scatter,** strew
little *determiner* **1 = bit,** dab, dash, fragment, hint, modicum, particle, pinch, small amount, snippet, speck, spot, tad (*inf., chiefly US*), taste, touch, trace, trifle ◆ *adj* **6 = small,** diminutive, dwarf, elfin, infinitesimal, Lilliputian, mini, miniature, minute, petite, pygmy *or* pigmy, short, slender, teensy-weensy, teeny-weeny, tiny, wee **7 = young,** babyish, immature, infant, junior, undeveloped **9 = mean,** base, cheap, illiberal, narrow-minded, petty, small-minded ◆ *adv* **11 = hardly,** barely, not much, not quite, only just **12 = rarely,** hardly ever, not often, scarcely, seldom **13 little by little = gradually,** bit by bit, by degrees, imperceptibly, piecemeal, progressively, slowly, step by step
Antonyms *n* ≠ **bit:** lot, many, much ◆ *adj* ≠ **small:** big, colossal, considerable, enormous, giant, ginormous (*inf.*), great, huge, immense, large, mega (*sl.*) ◆ *adv* ≠ **hardly:** certainly, much, surely ≠ **rarely:** always, much
liturgical *adj* **1 = ceremonial,** eucharistic, formal, ritual, sacramental, solemn
liturgy *n* **1 = ceremony,** celebration, form of worship, formula, rite, ritual, sacrament, service, services, worship
livable *adj* **1 = habitable,** adequate, comfortable, fit (for human habitation), inhabitable, satisfactory **2 = tolerable,** acceptable, bearable, endurable, passable, sufferable, supportable, worth living, worthwhile **3** *with* **with = congenial,** companionable, compatible, easy, easy to live with, harmonious, sociable
live[1] *vb* **1 = exist,** be, be alive, breathe, draw breath, have life **4 = dwell,** abide, hang out (*inf.*), inhabit, lodge, occupy, reside, settle, stay (*chiefly Scot.*) **5 = persist,** be permanent, be remembered, last, prevail, remain alive **7 = survive,** abide, continue, earn a living, endure, fare, feed, get along, lead, make ends meet, pass, remain, subsist, support oneself **11 = thrive,** be happy, enjoy life, flourish, luxuriate, make the most of life, prosper
live[2] *adj* **1 = living,** alive, animate, breathing, existent, quick (*arch.*), vital **3 = topical,** active, burning, controversial, current, hot, pertinent, pressing, prevalent, unsettled, vital **5** *Informal* **= lively,** active, alert, brisk, dynamic, earnest, energetic, sparky, vigorous, vivid, wide-awake **6 = burning,** active, alight, blazing, connected, glowing, hot, ignited, smouldering, switched on
livelihood *n* **= occupation,** bread and butter (*inf.*), employment, job, living, maintenance, means, (means of) support, (source of) income, subsistence, sustenance, work

livelong ⊕ (ˈlɪvˌlɒŋ) *adj Chiefly poetic.* **1** (of time) long or seemingly long (esp. in **all the livelong day**). **2** whole; entire.
lively ⊕ (ˈlaɪvlɪ) *adj* **livelier, liveliest. 1** full of life or vigour. **2** vivacious or animated, esp. when in company. **3** busy; eventful. **4** characterized by mental or emotional intensity; vivid. **5** having a striking effect on the mind or senses. **6** refreshing or invigorating: *a lively breeze.* **7** springy or bouncy or encouraging springiness: *a lively ball.* ◆ *adv* also **livelily. 8** in a brisk or lively manner: *step lively.*
▸ **ˈliveliness** *n*
liven ⊕ (ˈlaɪvᵊn) *vb* (usually foll. by *up*) to make or become lively; enliven.
▸ **ˈlivener** *n*
live oak (laɪv) *n* a hard-wooded evergreen oak of S North America: used for shipbuilding.
live out (lɪv) *vb* (*intr, adv*) (of an employee, as in a hospital or hotel) to dwell away from one's place of employment.
liver[1] (ˈlɪvə) *n* **1** a large highly vascular reddish-brown glandular organ in the human abdominal cavity. Its main function is the metabolic transformation of nutrients. It also secretes bile, stores glycogen, and detoxifies certain poisons. Related adj: **hepatic. 2** the corresponding organ in animals. **3** the liver of certain animals used as food. **4** a reddish-brown colour. [OE *lifer*]
liver[2] (ˈlɪvə) *n* a person who lives in a specified way: *a fast liver.*
liveried (ˈlɪvərɪd) *adj* (esp. of servants or footmen) wearing livery.
liverish ⊕ (ˈlɪvərɪʃ) *adj* **1** *Inf.* having a disorder of the liver. **2** disagreeable; peevish.
▸ **ˈliverishness** *n*
liver opal *n* a form of opal having a reddish-brown coloration.
Liverpudlian (ˌlɪvəˈpʌdlɪən) *n* **1** a native or inhabitant of Liverpool, in NW England. ◆ *adj* **2** of or relating to Liverpool. [C19: from *Liverpool,* with humorous alteration of *pool* to *puddle*]
liver salts *pl n* a preparation of mineral salts used to treat indigestion.
liver sausage *or esp. US* **liverwurst** (ˈlɪvəˌwɜːst) *n* a sausage containing liver.
liverwort (ˈlɪvəˌwɜːt) *n* any of a class of bryophyte plants growing in wet places and resembling green seaweeds or leafy mosses. [late OE *liferwyrt*]
livery ⊕ (ˈlɪvərɪ) *n, pl* **liveries. 1** the identifying uniform, badge, etc., of a member of a guild or one of the servants of a feudal lord. **2** a uniform worn by some menservants. **3** an individual or group that wears such a uniform. **4** distinctive dress or outward appearance. **5a** the stabling, keeping, or hiring out of horses for money. **5b** (*as modifier*): *a livery horse.* **6 at livery.** being kept in a livery stable. [C14: via Anglo-F from OF *livrée* allocation, from *livrer* to hand over, from L *līberāre* to set free]
livery company *n Brit.* one of the chartered companies of the City of London originating from the craft guilds.
liveryman (ˈlɪvərɪmən) *n, pl* **liverymen. 1** *Brit.* a member of a livery company. **2** a worker in a livery stable.
livery stable *n* a stable where horses are accommodated and from which they may be hired out.
lives (laɪvz) *n* the plural of **life.**
livestock (ˈlaɪvˌstɒk) *n* (*functioning as sing or pl*) cattle, horses, and similar animals kept for domestic use but not as pets, esp. on a farm.
live together (lɪv) *vb* (*intr, adv*) (esp. of an unmarried couple) to dwell in the same house or flat; cohabit.
live up (lɪv) *vb* **1** (*intr, adv;* foll. by *to*) to fulfil (an expectation, obligation, principle, etc.). **2 live it up.** *Inf.* to enjoy oneself, esp. flamboyantly.
live wire ⊕ (laɪv) *n* **1** *Inf.* an energetic or enterprising person. **2** a wire carrying an electric current.
live with (lɪv) *vb* (*tr, prep*) to dwell with (a person to whom one is not married).
livid ⊕ (ˈlɪvɪd) *adj* **1** (of the skin) discoloured, as from a bruise or contusion. **2** of a greyish tinge or colour. **3** *Inf.* angry or furious. [C17: via F from L *līvidus,* from *līvēre* to be black and blue]
▸ **ˈlividly** *adv* ▸ **ˈlividness** *or* **liˈvidity** *n*
living ⊕ (ˈlɪvɪŋ) *adj* **1a** possessing life; not dead. **1b** (*as collective n* preceded by *the*): *the living.* **2** having the characteristics of life (used esp. to distinguish organisms from nonliving matter). **3** currently in use or valid: *living language.* **4** seeming to be real: *a living image.* **5** (of animals or plants) existing in the present age. **6** presented by actors before a live audience: *living theatre.* **7** (*prenominal*) (intensifier): *the living daylights.* ◆ *n* **8** the condition of being alive. **9** the manner in which one conducts one's life: *fast living.* **10** the means, esp. the financial means, whereby one lives. **11** *Church of England.* another term for **benefice. 12** (*modifier*) of, involving, or characteristic of everyday life: *living area.* **13** (*modifier*) of or involving those now alive (esp. in **living memory**).
living death *n* a life or lengthy experience of constant misery.
living room *n* a room in a private house or flat used for relaxation and entertainment.
living wage *n* a wage adequate to maintain a person and his family in reasonable comfort.
living will *n* a document that states that a person who becomes terminally ill does not wish his or her life to be prolonged by artificial means such as a life-support machine.
lizard (ˈlɪzəd) *n* any of a group of reptiles typically having an elongated body, four limbs, and a long tail: includes the geckos, iguanas, chameleons, monitors, and slowworms. [C14: via OF from L *lacerta*]
LJ (in Britain) *abbrev. for* Lord Justice.
LL *abbrev. for:* **1** Late Latin. **2** Low Latin. **3** Lord Lieutenant.
ll. *abbrev. for* lines (of written matter).
llama (ˈlɑːmə) *n* **1** a domesticated South American cud-chewing mammal of the camel family, that is used as a beast of burden and is valued for its hair, flesh, and hide. **2** the cloth made from the wool of this animal. [C17: via Sp. from Amerind]
llano (ˈlɑːnəʊ; *Spanish* ˈʎano) *n, pl* **llanos** (-nəʊz; *Spanish* -nɔs). an extensive grassy treeless plain, esp. in South America. [C17: Sp., from L *plānum* level ground]
LLB *abbrev. for* Bachelor of Laws. [L: *Legum Baccalaureus*]
LLD *abbrev. for* Doctor of Laws. [L: *Legum Doctor*]
LLM *abbrev. for* Master of Laws. [L: *Legum Magister*]
Lloyd's (lɔɪdz) *n* an association of London underwriters, set up in the late 17th century. Originally concerned with marine insurance, it now underwrites a variety of insurance policies and publishes a daily list (**Lloyd's List**) of shipping information. [C17: after Edward *Lloyd* (died ?1726) at whose coffee house in London the underwriters orig. carried on their business]
lm *symbol for* lumen.
LMS (in Britain) *abbrev. for* local management of schools: the system of making each school responsible for controlling its total budget, after the budget has been calculated by the Local Education Authority.
LNG *abbrev. for* liquefied natural gas.
lo (ləʊ) *interj* look! see! (now often in **lo and behold**). [OE *lā*]
loach (ləʊtʃ) *n* a carplike freshwater fish of Eurasia and Africa, having a long narrow body with barbels around the mouth. [C14: from OF *loche,* from ?]
load ⊕ (ləʊd) *n* **1** something to be borne or conveyed; weight. **2a** the usual amount borne or conveyed. **2b** (*in combination*): *a carload.* **3** something that weighs down, oppresses, or burdens: *that's a load off my mind.* **4** a single charge of a firearm. **5** the weight that is carried by a structure. **6** *Electrical engineering, electronics.* **6a** a device that receives or dissipates the power from an amplifier, oscillator, generator, or some other source of signals. **6b** the power delivered by a machine, generator, circuit, etc. **7** the resistance overcome by an engine or motor when it is driving a machine, etc. **8** an external force applied to a component or mechanism. **9 a load of.** *Inf.* a quantity of: *a load of nonsense.* **10 get a load of.** *Inf.* pay attention to. **11 have a load on.** *US & Canad. sl.* to be intoxicated. ◆ *vb* (*mainly tr*) **12** (*also intr*) to place or receive (cargo, goods, etc.) upon (a ship, lorry, etc.). **13** to burden or oppress. **14** to supply in abundance: *load with gifts.* **15** to cause to be biased: *to load a question.* **16** (*also intr*) to put an ammunition charge into (a fire-

THESAURUS

liveliness *n* **1, 2** = **energy,** activity, animation, boisterousness, brio, briskness, dynamism, gaiety, quickness, smartness, spirit, sprightliness, vitality, vivacity
livelong *adj Chiefly poetic* **1** = **everlasting,** dragged out, long-drawn-out, unbroken **2** = **entire,** complete, full, whole
lively *adj* **1** = **vigorous,** active, agile, alert, alive and kicking, bright-eyed and bushy-tailed, brisk, chipper (*inf.*), chirpy (*inf.*), energetic, full of beans (*inf.*), full of pep (*inf.*), keen, nimble, perky, quick, sprightly, spry **2** = **animated,** blithe, blithesome, cheerful, chirpy (*inf.*), frisky, frolicsome, gay, merry, sparkling, sparky, spirited, upbeat (*inf.*), vivacious **3** = **busy,** astir, bustling, buzzing, crowded, eventful, moving, stirring **5** = **vivid,** bright, colourful, exciting, forceful **6** = **refreshing,** invigorating, stimulating
Antonyms *adj* ≠ **vigorous:** debilitated, disabled, inactive, slow, sluggish, torpid ≠ **animated:** apathetic, dull, lifeless, listless ≠ **busy:** dull, slow ≠ **vivid:** dull
liven *vb* = **stir,** animate, brighten, buck up (*inf.*), enliven, hot up (*inf.*), pep up, perk up, put life into, rouse, vitalize, vivify
liverish *adj* **1** *Informal* = **sick,** bilious, queasy **2** = **irritable,** crotchety (*inf.*), crusty, disagreeable, grumpy, ill-humoured, irascible, like a bear with a sore head, peevish, ratty (*Brit. & NZ inf.*), snappy, splenetic, tetchy
livery *n* **1, 2** = **costume,** attire, clothing, dress, garb, raiment (*arch. or poetic*), regalia, suit, uniform, vestments
live wire *n* **1** *Informal* = **dynamo,** ball of fire (*inf.*), go-getter (*inf.*), hustler (*US & Canad. sl.*), life and soul of the party, self-starter
livid *adj* **1** = **discoloured,** angry, black-and-blue, bruised, contused, purple **2** = **pale,** ashen, blanched, bloodless, doughy, greyish, leaden, pallid, pasty, wan, waxen **3** *Informal* = **angry,** as black as thunder, beside oneself, boiling, choked, cross, enraged, exasperated, fit to be tied (*sl.*), fuming, furious, hot under the collar (*inf.*), incandescent, incensed, indignant, infuriated, mad (*inf.*), outraged, pissed (*taboo sl.*), pissed off (*taboo sl.*)
Antonyms *adj* ≠ **angry:** assuaged, blissful, content, delighted, enchanted, forgiving, happy, mollified, overjoyed, pleased
living *adj* **1** = **alive,** active, alive and kicking, animated, breathing, existing, in the land of the living (*inf.*), lively, quick (*arch.*), strong, vigorous, vital **3** = **current,** active, contemporary, continuing, developing, extant, in use, ongoing, operative, persisting ◆ *n* **8** = **existence,** animation, being, existing, life, subsistence **9** = **lifestyle,** mode of living, way of life **10** = **livelihood,** bread and butter, job, maintenance, (means of) support, occupation, (source of) income, subsistence, sustenance, work **11** *Church of England* = **benefice,** incumbency, stipend
Antonyms *adj* ≠ **alive:** dead, deceased, defunct, departed, expired, late, lifeless, perished ≠ **current:** obsolescent, obsolete, out-of-date, vanishing
load *n* **1** = **cargo,** bale, consignment, freight, lading, shipment **3** = **burden,** affliction, alba-

arm). **17** *Photog.* to position (a film, cartridge, or plate) in (a camera). **18** to weight or bias (a roulette wheel, dice, etc.). **19** *Insurance.* to increase (a premium) to cover expenses, etc. **20** *Computing.* to transfer (a program) to a memory. **21** **load the dice. 21a** to add weights to dice in order to bias them. **21b** to arrange to have a favourable or unfavourable position. ◆ See also **loads.** [OE *lād* course; in meaning, infl. by LADE]
▸'**loader** *n*

loaded ❶ ('ləudɪd) *adj* **1** carrying a load. **2** (of dice, a roulette wheel, etc.) weighted or otherwise biased. **3** (of a question or statement) containing a hidden trap or implication. **4** charged with ammunition. **5** (of concrete) containing heavy metals, esp. iron or lead, for use in making radiation shields. **6** *Sl.* wealthy. **7** (*postpositive*) *Sl., chiefly US & Canad.* **7a** drunk. **7b** drugged.

loading ('ləudɪŋ) *n* **1** a load or burden; weight. **2** the addition of an inductance to electrical equipment, such as a transmission line or aerial, to improve its performance. **3** *Austral. & NZ.* a payment made in addition to a basic wage or salary to reward special skills, compensate for unfavourable conditions, etc.

load line *n* a pattern of lines painted on the hull of a ship, approximately midway between the bow and the stern, indicating the various levels that the water line should reach if the ship is properly loaded in different conditions.

loads (ləudz) *Inf.* ◆ *pl n* **1** (often foll. by *of*) a lot. ◆ *adv* **2** (intensifier): *loads better.*

loadstar ('ləud,stɑː) *n* a variant spelling of **lodestar.**

loadstone ('ləud,stəun) *n* a variant spelling of **lodestone.**

loaf[1] ❶ (ləuf) *n, pl* **loaves** (ləuvz). **1** a shaped mass of baked bread. **2** any shaped or moulded mass of food, such as sugar, cooked meat, etc. **3** *Sl.* the head; sense: *use your loaf!* [OE *hlāf*]

loaf[2] ❶ (ləuf) *vb* **1** (*intr*) to loiter or lounge around in an idle way. **2** (*tr*; foll. by *away*) to spend (time) idly: *he loafed away his life.* [C19: ? back formation from LOAFER]

loafer ❶ ('ləufə) *n* **1** a person who avoids work; idler. **2** *Chiefly US & Canad.* a moccasin-like shoe. [C19: ?from G *Landläufer* vagabond]

loam (ləum) *n* **1** rich soil consisting of a mixture of sand, clay, and decaying organic material. **2** a paste of clay and sand used for making moulds in a foundry, plastering walls, etc. ◆ *vb* **3** (*tr*) to cover, treat, or fill with loam. [OE *lām*]
▸'**loamy** *adj* ▸'**loaminess** *n*

loan ❶ (ləun) *n* **1** the act of lending: *the loan of a car.* **2** property lent, esp. money lent at interest for a period of time. **3** the adoption by speakers of one language of a form current in another language. **4** short for **loan word. 5 on loan.** lent out; borrowed. ◆ *vb* **6** to lend (something, esp. money). [C13 *loon, lan,* from ON *lān*]
▸'**loaner** *n*

loanback ('ləun,bæk) *n* **1** a facility offered by some life-assurance companies in which an individual can borrow from his pension fund. ◆ *vb* **loan back. 2** to make use of this facility.

Loan Council *n* (in Australia) a statutory body that controls borrowing by the states.

loan shark *n Inf.* a person who lends funds at illegal or exorbitant rates of interest.

loan translation *n* the adoption by one language of a phrase or compound word whose components are literal translations of the components of a corresponding phrase or compound in a foreign language: *English "superman" from German "Übermensch".* Also called: **calque.**

loan word *n* a word adopted, often in a modified form, from one language into another.

loath ❶ *or* **loth** (ləuθ) *adj* **1** (usually foll. by *to*) reluctant or unwilling. **2 nothing loath.** willing. [OE *lāth* (in the sense: hostile)]

loathe ❶ (ləuð) *vb* **loathes, loathing, loathed.** (*tr*) to feel strong hatred or disgust for. [OE *lāthiān,* from LOATH]
▸'**loather** *n*

loathing ❶ ('ləuðɪŋ) *n* abhorrence; disgust.

loathly[1] ('ləuθlɪ) *adv* with reluctance; unwillingly.

loathly[2] ('ləuðlɪ) *adj* an archaic word for **loathsome.**

loathsome ❶ ('ləuðsəm) *adj* causing loathing; abhorrent.
▸'**loathsomely** *adv* ▸'**loathsomeness** *n*

loaves (ləuvz) *n* the plural of **loaf**[1].

lob ❶ (lɒb) *Sport.* ◆ *n* **1** a ball struck in a high arc. **2** *Cricket.* a ball bowled in a slow high arc. ◆ *vb* **lobs, lobbing, lobbed. 3** to hit or kick (a ball) in a high arc. **4** to throw, esp. in a high arc. [C14: prob. from Low G, orig. in the sense: something dangling]

lobar ('ləubə) *adj* of, relating to, or affecting a lobe.

lobate ('ləubeɪt) *adj* **1** having or resembling lobes. **2** (of birds) having separate toes that are each fringed with a weblike lobe.
▸'**lobately** *adv* ▸**lo'bation** *n*

lobby ❶ ('lɒbɪ) *n, pl* **lobbies. 1** a room or corridor used as an entrance hall, vestibule, etc. **2** *Chiefly Brit.* a hall in a legislative building used for meetings between the legislators and members of the public. **3** Also called: **division lobby.** *Chiefly Brit.* one of two corridors in a legislative building in which members vote. **4** a group of persons who attempt to influence legislators on behalf of a particular interest. ◆ *vb* **lobbies, lobbying, lobbied. 5** to attempt to influence (legislators, etc.) in the formulation of policy. **6** (*intr*) to act in the manner of a lobbyist. **7** (*tr*) to apply pressure for the passage of (a bill, etc.). [C16: from Med. L *lobia* portico, from OHG *lauba* arbor, from *laub* leaf]
▸'**lobbyer** *n*

lobbyist ('lɒbɪɪst) *n* a person employed by a particular interest to lobby.
▸'**lobby,ism** *n*

lobe (ləub) *n* **1** any rounded projection forming part of a larger structure. **2** any of the subdivisions of a bodily organ or part, delineated by shape or connective tissue. **3** Also called: **ear lobe.** the fleshy lower part of the external ear. **4** any of the parts, not entirely separate from each other, into which a flattened plant part, such as a leaf, is divided. [C16: from LL *lobus,* from Gk *lobos* lobe of the ear or of the liver]

lobectomy (ləu'bɛktəmɪ) *n, pl* **lobectomies.** surgical removal of a lobe from any organ or gland in the body.

lobelia (ləu'biːlɪə) *n* any of a genus of plants having red, blue, white, or yellow five-lobed flowers with the three lower lobes forming a lip. [C18: from NL, after Matthias de *Lobel* (1538–1616), Flemish botanist]

loblolly ('lɒb,lɒlɪ) *n, pl* **loblollies.** a southern US pine tree with bright reddish-brown bark, green needle-like leaves, and reddish-brown cones. [C16: ?from dialect *lob* to boil + obs. dialect *lolly* thick soup]

lobola *or* **lobolo** (lɔː'bɔːlə, lə'bəu-) *n* (in southern Africa) an African custom by which a bridegroom's family makes a payment in cattle or cash to the bride's family shortly before the marriage. [from Nguni *ukulobola* to give the bride price]

lobotomy (ləu'bɒtəmɪ) *n, pl* **lobotomies. 1** surgical incision into a lobe of any organ. **2** Also called: **prefrontal leucotomy.** surgical interruption of one or more nerve tracts in the frontal lobe of the brain: used in the treatment of intractable mental disorders. [C20: from LOBE + -TOMY]

lobscouse ('lɒb,skaus) *n* a sailor's stew of meat, vegetables, and hardtack. [C18: ?from dialect *lob* to boil + *scouse* broth]

lobster ('lɒbstə) *n, pl* **lobsters** *or* **lobster. 1** any of several large marine decapod crustaceans occurring on rocky shores and having the first pair of limbs modified as large pincers. **2** any of several similar crustaceans, esp. the spiny lobster. **3** the flesh of any of these crustaceans, eaten as a delicacy. [OE *loppestre,* from *loppe* spider]

lobster pot *or* **trap** *n* a round basket or trap made of open slats used to catch lobsters.

lobule ('lɒbjuːl) *n* a small lobe or a subdivision of a lobe. [C17: from NL *lobulus,* from LL *lobus* LOBE]
▸**lobular** ('lɒbjulə) *or* **lobulate** ('lɒbjulɪt) *adj*

lobworm ('lɒb,wɜːm) *n* **1** another name for **lugworm. 2** a large earthworm used as bait in fishing. [C17: from obs. *lob* lump + WORM]

local ❶ ('ləuk[ə]l) *adj* **1** characteristic of or associated with a particular locality or area. **2** of, concerned with, or relating to a particular place or point in space. **3** *Med.* of, affecting, or confined to a limited area or part. **4** (of a train, bus, etc.) stopping at all stations or stops. ◆ *n* **5** a train, bus, etc., that stops at all stations or stops. **6** an inhabitant of a specified locality. **7** *Brit. inf.* a pub close to one's home or place of

THESAURUS

tross, encumbrance, incubus, millstone, onus, oppression, pressure, trouble, weight, worry ◆ *vb* **12 = fill**, cram, freight, heap, lade, pack, pile, stack, stuff **13 = burden**, encumber, hamper, oppress, saddle with, trouble, weigh down, worry **16 = make ready**, charge, prepare to fire, prime **21 load the dice = fix**, rig, set up

loaded *adj* **1 = laden**, burdened, charged, freighted, full, weighted **2 = biased**, weighted **3 = tricky**, artful, insidious, manipulative, prejudicial **4 = charged**, at the ready, primed, ready to shoot *or* fire **6** *Slang* **= rich**, affluent, flush, moneyed, rolling (*sl.*), wealthy, well-heeled (*inf.*), well off, well-to-do

loaf[1] *n* **2 = lump**, block, cake, cube, slab **3** *Slang* **= head**, block (*inf.*), chump (*Brit. sl.*), gumption (*Brit. inf.*), noddle (*inf., chiefly Brit.*), nous (*Brit. sl.*), sense

loaf[2] *vb* **1 = idle**, be indolent, laze, lie around, loiter, loll, lounge around, take it easy **2** *with* **away = fritter away**, kill time, pass time, veg out (*sl., chiefly US*), waste time, while away the hours

loafer *n* **1 = idler**, bum, couch potato (*sl.*), drone (*Brit.*), layabout, lazybones (*inf.*), lounger, ne'er-do-well, shirker, skiver (*Brit. sl.*), time-waster, wastrel

loan *n* **1, 2 = lending**, accommodation, advance, allowance, credit, mortgage, touch (*sl.*) ◆ *vb* **6 = lend**, accommodate, advance, allow, credit, let out

loath *adj* **1 = unwilling**, against, averse, backward, counter, disinclined, indisposed, opposed, reluctant, resisting
Antonyms *adj* anxious, avid, desirous, eager, enthusiastic, keen, willing

loathe *vb* **= hate**, abhor, abominate, despise, detest, dislike, execrate, feel repugnance towards, find disgusting, have a strong aversion to, not be able to bear *or* abide

loathing *n* **= hatred**, abhorrence, abomination, antipathy, aversion, detestation, disgust, execration, horror, odium, repugnance, repulsion, revulsion

loathsome *adj* **= hateful**, abhorrent, abominable, detestable, disgusting, execrable, horrible, nasty, nauseating, obnoxious, obscene, odious, offensive, repugnant, repulsive, revolting, vile, yucky *or* yukky (*sl.*)
Antonyms *adj* adorable, amiable, attractive, charming, delightful, enchanting, engaging, fetching, likable *or* likeable, lovable, lovely

lob *vb* **4 = throw**, fling, launch, lift, loft, pitch, shy, toss

lobby *n* **1 = corridor**, entrance hall, foyer, hall, hallway, passage, passageway, porch, vestibule **4 = pressure group** ◆ *vb* **5-7 = campaign**, bring pressure to bear, exert influence, influence, persuade, press, pressure, promote, pull strings (*Brit. inf.*), push, solicit votes, urge

local *adj* **1 = regional**, community, district, neighbourhood, parish, provincial ◆ *n* **6 = resident**, character (*inf.*), inhabitant, local yokel (*disparaging*), native

work. **8** *Med.* short for **local anaesthetic** (see **anaesthesia**). **9** *US & Canad.* an item of local interest in a newspaper. [C15: via OF from LL *locālis*, from L *locus* place]
▸'**locally** *adv* ▸'**localness** *n*

local anaesthetic *n Med.* See **anaesthesia.**

local authority *n Brit. & NZ.* the governing body of a county, district, etc. US equivalent: **local government.**

locale ❶ (ləʊ'kɑːl) *n* a place or area, esp. with reference to events connected with it. [C18: from F *local* (n use of adj); see LOCAL]

local government *n* **1** government of the affairs of counties, towns, etc., by locally elected political bodies. **2** the US equivalent of **local authority.**

Local Group *n Astron.* the cluster of galaxies to which the Galaxy and the Andromeda Galaxy belong.

localism ('ləʊkəˌlɪzəm) *n* **1** a pronunciation, phrase, etc., peculiar to a particular locality. **2** another word for **provincialism.**

locality ❶ (ləʊ'kælɪtɪ) *n, pl* **localities. 1** a neighbourhood or area. **2** the site or scene of an event. **3** the fact or condition of having a location or position in space.

localize ❶ *or* **localise** ('ləʊkəˌlaɪz) *vb* **localizes, localizing, localized** *or* **localises, localising, localised. 1** to make or become local in attitude, behaviour, etc. **2** (*tr*) to restrict or confine (something) to a particular area or part. **3** (*tr*) to assign or ascribe to a particular region.
▸'**localˌizable** *or* '**localˌisable** *adj* ▸ˌ**localiˈzation** *or* ˌ**localiˈsation** *n*

local loan *n* (in Britain) a loan issued by a local government authority.

local option *n* (esp. in Scotland, New Zealand, and the US) the privilege of a municipality, county, etc., to determine by referendum whether a particular activity, esp. the sale of liquor, shall be permitted there.

locate ❶ (ləʊ'keɪt) *vb* **locates, locating, located. 1** (*tr*) to discover the position, situation, or whereabouts of; find. **2** (*tr; often passive*) to situate or place: *located on the edge of the city.* **3** (*intr*) to become established or settled.
▸**lo'cater** *n*

location ❶ (ləʊ'keɪʃən) *n* **1** a site or position; situation. **2** the act or process of locating or the state of being located. **3** a place outside a studio where filming is done: *shot on location.* **4** (in South Africa) **4a** a Black African or Coloured township, usually located near a small town. **4b** (formerly) a Black African tribal reserve. **5** *Computing.* a position in a memory capable of holding a unit of information, such as a word, and identified by its address. [C16: from L *locatio,* from *locare* to place]

locative ('lɒkətɪv) *Grammar.* ◆ *adj* **1** (of a word or phrase) indicating place or direction. **2** denoting a case of nouns, etc., that refers to the place at which the action described by the verb occurs. ◆ *n* **3a** the locative case. **3b** a word or speech element in this case. [C19: LOCATE + -IVE, on the model of *vocative*]

loc. cit. (in textual annotation) *abbrev. for* loco citato. [L: in the place cited]

loch (lɒx, lɒk) *n* **1** a Scot. word for **lake**[1] (senses 1 and 2). **2** Also: **sea loch.** a long narrow bay or arm of the sea in Scotland. [C14: from Gaelic]

lochia ('lɒkɪə) *n* a vaginal discharge of cellular debris, mucus, and blood following childbirth. [C17: NL from Gk *lokhia,* from *lokhos* childbirth]
▸'**lochial** *adj*

loci ('ləʊsaɪ) *n* the plural of **locus.**

lock[1] ❶ (lɒk) *n* **1** a device fitted to a gate, door, drawer, lid, etc., to keep it firmly closed. **2** a similar device attached to a machine, vehicle, etc. **3a** a section of a canal or river that may be closed off by gates to control the water level and the raising and lowering of vessels that pass through it. **3b** (*as modifier*): *a lock gate; a lock keeper.* **4** the jamming, fastening, or locking together of parts. **5** *Brit.* the extent to which a vehicle's front wheels will turn to the right or left: *this car has a good lock.* **6** a mechanism that detonates the charge of a gun. **7 lock, stock, and barrel.** completely; entirely. **8** any wrestling hold in which a wrestler seizes a part of his opponent's body. **9** Also called: **lock forward.** *Rugby.* **9a** a player in the second row of the scrum. **9b** this position. **10** a gas bubble in a hydraulic system or a liquid bubble in a pneumatic system that stops the fluid flow in a pipe, capillary, etc.: *an air lock.* ◆ *vb* **11** to fasten (a door, gate, etc.) or (of a door, etc.) to become fastened with a lock, bolt, etc., so as to prevent entry or exit. **12** (*tr*) to secure (a building) by locking all doors, windows, etc. **13** to fix or become fixed together securely or inextricably. **14** to become or cause to become rigid or immovable: *the front wheels of the car locked.* **15** (when *tr, often passive*) to clasp or entangle (someone or each other) in a struggle or embrace. **16** (*tr*) to furnish (a canal) with locks. **17** (*tr*) to move (a vessel) through a system of locks. ◆ See also **lock out, lock up.** [OE *loc*]
▸'**lockable** *adj*

lock[2] ❶ (lɒk) *n* **1** a strand, curl, or cluster of hair. **2** a tuft or wisp of wool, cotton, etc. **3** (*pl*) *Chiefly literary.* hair, esp. when curly or fine. [OE *locc*]

locked-in syndrome *n* a condition in which a person is conscious but unable to move any part of the body except the eyes: results from damage to the brainstem.

locker ('lɒkə) *n* **1a** a small compartment or drawer that may be locked, as one of several in a gymnasium, etc., for clothes and valuables. **1b** (*as modifier*): *a locker room.* **2** a person or thing that locks.

locket ('lɒkɪt) *n* a small ornamental case, usually on a necklace or chain, that holds a picture, keepsake, etc. [C17: from F *loquet* latch, dim. of *loc* LOCK[1]]

lockjaw ('lɒkˌdʒɔː) *n Pathol.* a nontechnical name for **trismus** and (often) **tetanus.**

lock out ❶ *vb* (*tr, adv*) **1** to prevent from entering by locking a door. **2** to prevent (employees) from working during an industrial dispute, as by closing a factory. ◆ *n* **lockout. 3** the closing of a place of employment by an employer, in order to bring pressure on employees to agree to terms.

locksmith ('lɒkˌsmɪθ) *n* a person who makes or repairs locks.

lock step *n* a method of marching such that the men follow one another as closely as possible.

lock up ❶ *vb* (*adv*) **1** (*tr*) Also: **lock in, lock away.** to imprison or confine. **2** to lock or secure the doors, windows, etc., of (a building). **3** (*tr*) to keep or store securely: *secrets locked up in history.* **4** (*tr*) to invest (funds) so that conversion into cash is difficult. ◆ *n* **lockup. 5** the action or time of locking up. **6** a jail or block of cells. **7** *Brit.* a small shop with no attached quarters for the owner. **8** *Brit.* a garage or storage place separate from the main premises. **9** *Stock Exchange.* an investment that is intended to be held for a relatively long period. ◆ *adj* **lock-up. 10** *Brit. & NZ.* (of premises) without living quarters: *a lock-up shop.*

loco[1] ('ləʊkəʊ) *n, pl* **locos.** *Inf.* short for **locomotive.**

loco[2] ('ləʊkəʊ) *adj* **1** *Sl., chiefly US.* insane. **2** (of an animal) affected with loco disease. ◆ *n, pl* **locos. 3** *US.* short for **locoweed.** ◆ *vb* **locos, locoing, locoed.** (*tr*) **4** to poison with locoweed. **5** *US sl.* to make insane. [C19: via Mexican Sp. from Sp.: crazy]

loco[3] ('ləʊkəʊ) *adj* denoting a price for goods, esp. goods to be exported, that are in a place specified or known, the buyer being responsible for all transport charges from that place: *loco Bristol; a loco price.* [C20: from L *locō* from a place]

loco disease *n* a disease of cattle, sheep, and horses characterized by paralysis and faulty vision, caused by ingestion of locoweed.

locomotion ❶ (ˌləʊkə'məʊʃən) *n* the act, fact, ability, or power of moving. [C17: from L *locō* from a place, ablative of *locus* place + MOTION]

locomotive (ˌləʊkə'məʊtɪv) *n* **1a** Also called: **locomotive engine.** a self-propelled engine driven by steam, electricity, or diesel power and used for drawing trains along railway tracks. **1b** (*as modifier*): *a locomotive shed; a locomotive works.* ◆ *adj* **2** of or relating to locomotion. **3** moving or able to move, as by self-propulsion.

locomotor (ˌləʊkə'məʊtə) *adj* of or relating to locomotion. [C19: from L *locō* from a place + MOTOR (mover)]

locomotor ataxia *n Pathol.* another name for **tabes dorsalis.**

locoweed ('ləʊkəʊˌwiːd) *n* any of several perennial leguminous plants of W North America that cause loco disease in horses, cattle, and sheep.

loculus ('lɒkjʊləs) *n, pl* **loculi** ('lɒkjʊˌlaɪ). **1** *Bot.* any of the chambers of an ovary or anther. **2** *Biol.* any small cavity or chamber. [C19: NL, from L: compartment, from *locus* place]
▸'**locular** *adj*

locum tenens ('ləʊkəm 'tiːnenz) *n, pl* **locum tenentes** (tə'nentiːz). *Chiefly Brit.* a person who stands in temporarily for another member of the same profession, esp. for a physician, chemist, or clergyman. Often shortened to **locum.** [C17: Med. L: (someone) holding the place (of another)]

locus ('ləʊkəs) *n, pl* **loci. 1** (in many legal phrases) a place or area, esp. the place where something occurred. **2** *Maths.* a set of points or lines whose location satisfies or is determined by one or more specified conditions: *the locus of points equidistant from a given point is a circle.* **3** *Genetics.* the position of a particular gene on a chromosome. [C18: L]

locust ('ləʊkəst) *n* **1** any of numerous insects, related to the grasshopper, of warm and tropical regions of the Old World, which travel in vast swarms, stripping large areas of vegetation. **2** Also called: **locust tree.** a North American leguminous tree having prickly branches, hanging clusters of white fragrant flowers, and reddish-brown seed pods. **3** the yellowish durable wood of this tree. **4** any of several similar trees, such as the honey locust and carob. [C13 (the insect): from L *locusta;* applied to the tree (C17) because the pods resemble locusts]

locution ❶ (ləʊ'kjuːʃən) *n* **1** a word, phrase, or expression. **2** manner or style of speech. [C15: from L *locūtiō* an utterance, from *loquī* to speak]

THESAURUS

locale *n* = **site**, locality, location, locus, place, position, scene, setting, spot, venue

locality *n* **1** = **neighbourhood**, area, district, neck of the woods (*inf.*), region, vicinity **2** = **site**, locale, location, place, position, scene, setting, spot

localize *vb* **1, 2** = **restrict**, circumscribe, concentrate, confine, contain, delimit, delimitate, limit, restrain **3** = **ascribe**, assign, narrow down, pinpoint, specify

locate *vb* **1** = **find**, come across, detect, discover, lay one's hands on, pin down, pinpoint, run to earth *or* ground, track down, unearth **2, 3** = **place**, establish, fix, put, seat, set, settle, situate

location *n* **1** = **site**, bearings, locale, locus, place, point, position, situation, spot, venue, whereabouts

lock[1] *n* **1, 2** = **fastening**, bolt, clasp, padlock ◆ *vb* **11, 12** = **fasten**, bolt, close, latch, seal, secure, shut, sneck (*dialect*) **13** = **unite**, clench, engage, entangle, entwine, join, link, mesh **15** = **embrace**, clasp, clutch, encircle, enclose, grapple, grasp, hug, press

lock[2] *n* **1** = **strand**, curl, ringlet, tress, tuft

lock out *vb* **1** = **shut out**, ban, bar, debar, exclude, keep out, refuse admittance to

lock up *vb* **1** = **imprison**, cage, confine, detain, incarcerate, jail, put behind bars, shut up ◆ *n* **lockup 6** = **prison**, can (*sl.*), cell, cooler, jail *or* gaol, jug (*sl.*), police cell

locomotion *n* = **movement**, action, headway, motion, moving, progress, progression, travel, travelling

locution *n* **1** = **expression**, collocation, idiom, phrase, term, turn of speech, wording **2** = **man-**

lode (ləʊd) *n* **1** a deposit of valuable ore occurring between definite limits in the surrounding rock; vein. **2** a deposit of metallic ore filling a fissure in the surrounding rock. [OE *lād* course]

loden (ˈləʊdᵊn) *n* **1** a thick heavy waterproof woollen cloth with a short pile, used for coats. **2** a dark bluish-green colour, in which the cloth is often made. [G, from OHG *lodo* thick cloth]

lodestar Ⓣ *or* **loadstar** (ˈləʊdˌstɑː) *n* **1** a star, esp. the North Star, used in navigation or astronomy as a point of reference. **2** something that serves as a guide or model. [C14: lit.: guiding star]

lodestone Ⓣ *or* **loadstone** (ˈləʊdˌstəʊn) *n* **1a** magnetite that is naturally magnetic. **1b** a piece of this, which can be used as a magnet. **2** a person or thing regarded as a focus of attraction. [C16: lit.: guiding stone]

lodge Ⓣ (lɒdʒ) *n* **1** *Chiefly Brit.* a small house at the entrance to the grounds of a country mansion, usually occupied by a gatekeeper or gardener. **2** a house or cabin used occasionally, as for some seasonal activity. **3** (*cap. when part of a name*) a large house or hotel. **4** a room for the use of porters in a university, college, etc. **5** a local branch or chapter of certain societies. **6** the building used as the meeting place of such a society. **7** the dwelling place of certain animals, esp. beavers. **8** a hut or tent of certain North American Indian peoples. ◆ *vb* **lodges, lodging, lodged. 9** to provide or be provided with accommodation or shelter, esp. rented accommodation. **10** (*intr*) to live temporarily, esp. in rented accommodation. **11** to implant, embed, or fix or be implanted, embedded, or fixed. **12** (*tr*) to deposit or leave for safety, storage, etc. **13** (*tr*) to bring (a charge or accusation) against someone. **14** (*tr; often foll. by in or with*) to place (authority, power, etc.) in the control (of someone). [C15: from OF *loge*, ?from OHG *louba* porch]

lodger Ⓣ (ˈlɒdʒə) *n* a person who pays rent in return for accommodation in someone else's house.

lodging (ˈlɒdʒɪŋ) *n* **1** a temporary residence. **2** (*sometimes pl*) sleeping accommodation.

lodging house *n* a private home providing accommodation and meals for lodgers.

lodgings Ⓣ (ˈlɒdʒɪŋz) *pl n* a rented room or rooms, esp. in another person's house.

lodgment *or* **lodgement** (ˈlɒdʒmənt) *n* **1** the act of lodging or the state of being lodged. **2** a blockage or accumulation. **3** a small area gained and held in enemy territory.

loess (ˈləʊɪs) *n* a light-coloured fine-grained accumulation of clay and silt deposited by the wind. [C19: from G *Löss*, from Swiss G dialect *lösch* loose]
▸**loessial** (ləʊˈɛsɪəl) *adj*

loft (lɒft) *n* **1** the space inside a roof. **2** a gallery, esp. one for the choir in a church. **3** a room over a stable used to store hay. **4** *US.* an upper storey of a warehouse or factory. **5** a raised house or coop in which pigeons are kept. **6** *Sport.* **6a** (in golf) the angle from the vertical made by the club face to give elevation to a ball. **6b** elevation imparted to a ball. **6c** a lofting stroke or shot. ◆ *vb* (*tr*) **7** *Sport.* to strike or kick (a ball) high in the air. **8** to store or place in a loft. **9** *Golf.* to slant (the face of a golf club). [OE, from ON *lopt* air, ceiling]

lofty Ⓣ (ˈlɒftɪ) *adj* **loftier, loftiest. 1** of majestic or imposing height. **2** exalted or noble in character or nature. **3** haughty or supercilious. **4** elevated, eminent, or superior.
▸ˈ**loftily** *adv* ▸ˈ**loftiness** *n*

log[1] Ⓣ (lɒg) *n* **1a** a section of the trunk or a main branch of a tree, when stripped of branches. **1b** (*modifier*) constructed out of logs: *a log cabin.* **2a** a detailed record of a voyage of a ship or aircraft. **2b** a record of the hours flown by pilots and aircrews. **2c** a book in which these records are made; logbook. **3** a written record of information about transmissions kept by radio stations, amateur radio operators, etc. **4** Also called: **chip log.** a device consisting of a float with an attached line, formerly used to measure the speed of a ship. **5 like a log.** without stirring or being disturbed (in **sleep like a log**). ◆ *vb* **logs, logging, logged. 6** (*tr*) to fell the trees of (a forest, area, etc.) for timber. **7** (*tr*) to saw logs from (trees). **8** (*intr*) to work at the felling of timber. **9** (*tr*) to enter (a distance, event, etc.) in a logbook or log. **10** (*tr*) to travel (a specified distance or time) or move at (a specified speed). [C14: from ?]

log[2] (lɒg) *n* short for **logarithm.**

-log *n combining form.* a US variant of **-logue.**

logan (ˈləʊgən) *n Canad.* another name for **bogan** (a backwater).

loganberry (ˈləʊgənbərɪ, -brɪ) *n, pl* **loganberries. 1** a trailing prickly hybrid plant of the rose family, cultivated for its edible fruit. **2** the purplish-red acid fruit of this plant. [C19: after James H. *Logan* (1841–1928), American judge and horticulturalist who first grew it (1881)]

logarithm (ˈlɒgəˌrɪðəm) *n* the exponent indicating the power to which a fixed number, the base, must be raised to obtain a given number or variable. It is used esp. to simplify multiplication and division. Often shortened to **log.** [C17: from NL *logarithmus*, coined 1614 by John Napier (1550–1617), Scot. mathematician, from Gk *logos* ratio + *arithmos* number]
▸**logarithmic** (ˌlɒgəˈrɪðmɪk) *adj*

logarithmic function *n* **a** the mathematical function $y = \log x$. **b** a function that can be expressed in terms of this function.

logbook (ˈlɒgˌbʊk) *n* **1** a book containing the official record of trips made by a ship or aircraft. **2** *Brit.* a former name for **registration document.**

log chip *n Naut.* the wooden chip or float of a chip log. See **log**[1] (sense 4).

loge (ləʊʒ) *n* a small enclosure or box in a theatre or opera house. [C18: F; see LODGE]

logger (ˈlɒgə) *n* another word for **lumberjack.**

loggerhead Ⓣ (ˈlɒgəˌhɛd) *n* **1** Also called: **loggerhead turtle.** a large-headed turtle occurring in most seas. **2** a tool consisting of a large metal sphere attached to a long handle, used for warming liquids, melting tar, etc. **3** *Arch. or dialect.* a blockhead; dunce. **4 at loggerheads.** engaged in dispute or confrontation. [C16: prob. from dialect *logger* wooden block + HEAD]

loggia (ˈlɒdʒə, ˈlɒdʒɪə) *n, pl* **loggias** *or* **loggie** (-dʒɛ). a covered area on the side of a building. [C17: It., from F *loge.* See LODGE]

logging (ˈlɒgɪŋ) *n* the work of felling, trimming, and transporting timber.

logic Ⓣ (ˈlɒdʒɪk) *n* **1** the branch of philosophy concerned with analysing the patterns of reasoning by which a conclusion is properly drawn from a set of premises, without reference to meaning or context. **2** any formal system in which are defined axioms and rules of inference. **3** the system and principles of reasoning used in a specific field of study. **4** a particular method of argument or reasoning. **5** force or effectiveness in argument or dispute. **6** reasoned thought or argument, as distinguished from irrationality. **7** the relationship and interdependence of a series of events, facts, etc. **8** *Electronics, computing.* the principles underlying the units in a computer system that perform arithmetical and logical operations. See also **logic circuit.** [C14: from OF *logique* from Med. L *logica*, from Gk *logikos* concerning speech or reasoning]

logical Ⓣ (ˈlɒdʒɪkᵊl) *adj* **1** relating to, used in, or characteristic of logic: *logical connective.* **2** using, according to, or deduced from the principles of logic: *a logical conclusion.* **3** capable of or characterized by clear or valid reasoning. **4** reasonable or necessary because of facts, events, etc.: *the logical candidate.* **5** *Computing.* of, performed by, used in, or relating to the logic circuits in a computer.
▸ˌ**logiˈcality** *or* ˈ**logicalness** *n* ▸ˈ**logically** *adv*

logical form *n* the structure of an argument by virtue of which it can be shown to be formally valid.

logical positivism *or* **empiricism** *n* a philosophical theory holding that the only meaningful statements are those that are analytic or can be tested empirically. It therefore rejects theology, metaphysics, etc., as meaningless.

logic bomb *n Computing.* an unauthorized program that is inserted into a computer system; when activated it interferes with the operation of the computer.

logic circuit *n* an electronic circuit used in computers to perform a logical operation on its two or more input signals.

logician (lɒˈdʒɪʃən) *n* a person who specializes in or is skilled at logic.

logic programming *n* the study or implementation of computer programs capable of discovering or checking proofs of formal expressions or segments.

log in *Computing.* ◆ *vb* **1** Also: **log on.** to enter (an identification num-

THESAURUS

ner of speech, accent, articulation, diction, inflection, intonation, phrasing, style

lodestar *n* **2** = **guide**, beacon, model, par, pattern, signal, standard

lodestone *n* **2** = **focus**, beacon, focal point, lodestar, magnet

lodge *n* **1, 2** = **cabin**, chalet, cottage, gatehouse, house, hunting lodge, hut, shelter **5** = **society**, assemblage, association, branch, chapter, club, group **7** = **den**, haunt, lair, retreat ◆ *vb* **9** = **accommodate**, billet, entertain, harbour, put up, quarter, shelter **10** = **stay**, board, room, sojourn, stop **11** = **stick**, become fixed, catch, come to rest, imbed, implant **13** = **register**, file, lay, put on record, submit

lodger *n* = **tenant**, boarder, guest, paying guest, P.G., resident, roomer

lodgings *pl n* = **accommodation**, abode, apartments, boarding, digs (*Brit. inf.*), dwelling, habitation, quarters, residence, rooms, shelter

lofty *adj* **1** = **high**, elevated, raised, sky-high, soaring, tall, towering **2** = **noble**, dignified, distinguished, elevated, exalted, grand, illustrious, imposing, majestic, renowned, stately, sublime, superior **3** = **haughty**, arrogant, condescending, disdainful, high and mighty (*inf.*), lordly, patronizing, proud, snooty (*inf.*), supercilious, toffee-nosed (*sl., chiefly Brit.*)
Antonyms *adj* ≠ **high:** dwarfed, low, short, stunted ≠ **noble:** debased, degraded, humble, low, lowly, mean ≠ **haughty:** friendly, modest, unassuming, warm

log[1] *n* **1** = **stump**, block, bole, chunk, piece of timber, trunk **2** = **record**, account, chart, daybook, journal, listing, logbook, tally ◆ *vb* **6** = **chop**, cut, fell, hew **9** = **record**, book, chart, make a note of, note, register, report, set down, tally

loggerhead *n* **4 at loggerheads** = **quarrelling**, at daggers drawn, at each other's throats, at enmity, at odds, estranged, feuding, in dispute, opposed

logic *n* **1-3** = **science of reasoning**, argumentation, deduction, dialectics, ratiocination, syllogistic reasoning **6** = **reason**, good reason, good sense, sense, sound judgment **7** = **connection**, chain of thought, coherence, link, rationale, relationship

logical *adj* **1-3** = **rational**, clear, cogent, coherent, consistent, deducible, pertinent, reasonable, relevant, sound, valid, well-organized **4** = **reasonable**, judicious, most likely, necessary, obvious, plausible, sensible, wise
Antonyms *adj* ≠ **rational:** illogical, instinctive, irra-

ber, password, etc.) from a remote terminal to gain access to a multiaccess system. ◆ *n* **2** Also: **login.** the process by which a computer user logs in.

logistics ➊ (lɒˈdʒɪstɪks) *n (functioning as sing or pl)* **1** the science of the movement and maintenance of military forces. **2** the management of materials flow through an organization. **3** the detailed planning and organization of any large complex operation. [C19: from F *logistique*, from *loger* to LODGE]
▸**loˈgistical** *adj*

log jam *n Chiefly US & Canad.* **1** blockage caused by the crowding together of logs floating in a river. **2** a deadlock; standstill.

loglog (ˈlɒglɒg) *n* the logarithm of a logarithm (in equations, etc.).

logo (ˈləʊgəʊ, ˈlɒg-) *n, pl* **logos.** short for **logotype** (sense 2).

logo- *combining form.* indicating word or speech: *logogram.* [from Gk *logos* word, from *legein* to speak]

logogram (ˈlɒgəˌgræm) *n* single symbol representing an entire morpheme, word, or phrase, as for example the symbol (%) meaning *per cent.*

logorrhoea *or esp. US* **logorrhea** (ˌlɒgəˈrɪə) *n* uncontrollable or incoherent talkativeness.

logos (lɒgɒs) *n* **1** *Philosophy.* reason, regarded as the controlling principle of the universe. **2** *(cap.)* the divine Word; the second person of the Trinity. [C16: Gk: word, reason]

logotype (ˈlɒgəʊˌtaɪp) *n* **1** *Printing.* a piece of type with several uncombined characters cast on it. **2** Also called: **logo.** a trademark, company emblem, or similar device.

log out *Computing.* ◆ *vb* **1** Also: **log off.** to disconnect a remote terminal from a multiaccess system by entering (an identification number, password, etc.). ◆ *n* **2** Also: **logout.** the process by which a computer user logs out.

logroll (ˈlɒgˌrəʊl) *vb Chiefly US.* to use logrolling in order to procure the passage of (legislation).
▸**ˈlogˌroller** *n*

logrolling (ˈlɒgˌrəʊlɪŋ) *n* **1** *US.* the practice of undemocratic agreements between politicians involving mutual favours, the trading of votes, etc. **2** another name for **birling.** See **birl.**

-logue *or US* **-log** *n combining form.* indicating speech or discourse of a particular kind: *travelogue; monologue.* [from F, from Gk *-logos*]

logwood (ˈlɒgˌwʊd) *n* **1** a leguminous tree of the Caribbean and Central America. **2** the heavy reddish-brown wood of this tree, yielding a dye.

-logy *n combining form.* **1** indicating the science or study of: *musicology.* **2** indicating writing, discourse, or body of writings: *trilogy; phraseology; martyrology.* [from L *-logia*, from Gk, from *logos* word]
▸**-logical** *or* **-logic** *adj combining form.* ▸**-logist** *n combining form.*

loin (lɔɪn) *n* **1** *Anat.* the lower back and sides between the pelvis and the ribs. Related adj: **lumbar. 2** a cut of meat from this part of an animal. ◆ See also **loins.** [C14: from OF *loigne*, ?from Vulgar L *lumbra* (unattested), from L *lumbus* loin]

loincloth (ˈlɔɪnˌklɒθ) *n* a piece of cloth worn round the loins. Also called: **breechcloth.**

loins (lɔɪnz) *pl n* **1** the hips and the inner surface of the legs where they join the trunk of the body; crotch. **2** *Euphemistic.* the reproductive organs.

loiter ➊ (ˈlɔɪtə) *vb (intr)* to stand or act aimlessly or idly. [C14: ?from MDu. *löteren* to wobble]
▸**ˈloiterer** *n* ▸**ˈloitering** *n, adj*

loll ➊ (lɒl) *vb* **1** *(intr)* to lie, lean, or lounge in a lazy or relaxed manner. **2** to hang or allow to hang loosely. ◆ *n* **3** an act or instance of lolling. [C14: ? imit.]
▸**ˈloller** *n* ▸**ˈlolling** *adj*

Lollard (ˈlɒləd) *n English history.* a follower of John Wycliffe (?1330–84), English religious reformer, during the 14th, 15th, and 16th centuries. [C14: from MDu.; mutterer, from *lollen* to mumble (prayers)]
▸**ˈLollardism** *n*

lollipop (ˈlɒlɪˌpɒp) *n* **1** a boiled sweet or toffee stuck on a small wooden stick. **2** *Brit.* another word for **ice lolly.** [C18: ?from N. English dialect *lolly* the tongue + POP[1]]

lollipop man *or* **lady** *n Brit. inf.* a person who stops traffic by holding up a circular sign on a pole, to enable children to cross the road safely.

lollop (ˈlɒləp) *vb* **lollops, lolloping, lolloped.** *(intr) Chiefly Brit.* **1** to walk or run with a clumsy or relaxed bouncing movement. **2** a less common word for **lounge.** [C18: prob. from LOLL + *-op* as in GALLOP, to emphasize the contrast in meaning]

lollo rosso (ˈlɒləʊ ˈrɒsəʊ) *n* a variety of lettuce originating in Italy, having curly red-tipped leaves and a slightly bitter taste.

lolly (ˈlɒlɪ) *n, pl* **lollies. 1** an informal word for **lollipop. 2** *Brit.* short for **ice lolly. 3** *Brit., Austral. & NZ.* a slang word for **money. 4** *Austral. & NZ inf.* a sweet, esp. a boiled one. **5 do the** *(or* **one's) lolly.** *Austral. inf.* to lose one's temper. [shortened from LOLLIPOP]

Lombard (ˈlɒmbəd, -bɑːd, ˈlʌm-) *n* **1** a native or inhabitant of Lombardy, a region of N central Italy. **2** a member of an ancient Germanic people who settled in N Italy after 568 A.D. ◆ *adj* also **Lombardic. 3** of or relating to Lombardy or the Lombards.

Lombard Street *n* the British financial and banking world. [C16: from a street in London once occupied by Lombard bankers]

Lombardy poplar (ˈlɒmbədɪ, ˈlʌm-) *n* an Italian poplar tree with upwardly pointing branches giving it a columnar shape.

London pride (ˈlʌndən) *n* a type of saxifrage plant having a basal rosette of leaves and pinkish-white flowers.

lone ➊ (ləʊn) *adj (prenominal)* **1** unaccompanied; solitary. **2** single or isolated: *a lone house.* **3** a literary word for **lonely. 4** unmarried or widowed. [C14: from the mistaken division of ALONE into *a lone*]
▸**ˈloneness** *n*

lonely ➊ (ˈləʊnlɪ) *adj* **lonelier, loneliest. 1** unhappy as a result of being without companions. **2** causing or resulting from the state of being alone. **3** isolated, unfrequented, or desolate. **4** without companions; solitary.
▸**ˈloneliness** *n*

lonely hearts *adj (often caps.)* of or for people who wish to meet a congenial companion or marriage partner: *a lonely hearts advertisement.*

loner ➊ (ˈləʊnə) *n Inf.* a person who avoids the company of others or prefers to be alone.

lonesome ➊ (ˈləʊnsəm) *adj* **1** *Chiefly US & Canad.* another word for **lonely.** ◆ *n* **2 on** *or US* **by one's lonesome.** *Inf.* on one's own.
▸**ˈlonesomely** *adv* ▸**ˈlonesomeness** *n*

long[1] ➊ (lɒŋ) *adj* **1** having relatively great extent in space or duration in time. **2a** *(postpositive)* of a specified number of units in extent or duration: *three hours long.* **2b** *(in combination): a two-foot-long line.* **3** having or consisting of a relatively large number of items or parts: *a long list.* **4** having greater than the average or expected range, extent, or duration: *a long match.* **5** seeming to occupy a greater time than is really so: *she spent a long afternoon waiting.* **6** (of drinks) containing a large quantity of nonalcoholic beverage. **7** (of a garment) reaching to the wearer's ankles. **8** *Inf.* (foll. by *on*) plentifully supplied or endowed (with): *long on good ideas.* **9** *Phonetics.* (of a speech sound, esp. a vowel) **9a** of relatively considerable duration. **9b** (in popular usage) denoting the qualities of the five English vowels in such words as *mate, mete, mite, moat, moot,* and *mute.* **10** from end to end; lengthwise. **11** unlikely to win, happen, succeed, etc.: *a long chance.* **12** *Prosody.* **12a** denoting a vowel of relatively great duration. **12b** denoting a syllable containing such a vowel. **12c** carrying the emphasis. **13** *Finance.* having or characterized by large holdings of securities or commodities in anticipation of rising prices. **14** *Cricket.* (of a fielding position) near the boundary: *long leg.* **15 in the long run.** ultimately; after or over a period of time. ◆ *adv* **16** for a certain time or period: *how long will it last?* **17** for or during an extensive period of time: *long into the next year.* **18** at a distant time; quite a bit of time: *long before I met you; long ago.* **19** *Finance.* into a position with more security or commodity holdings than are required by sale contracts and therefore dependent on rising prices for profit: *to go long.* **20 as** *(or* **so) long as. 20a** for or during just the length of time that. **20b** inasmuch as; since. **20c** provided that; if. **21 no longer.** not any more; formerly but not now. ◆ *n* **22** a long time (esp. in **for long**). **23** a relatively long thing, such as a dash in Morse code. **24** *Phonetics.* a long vowel or syllable. **25** *Finance.* a person with large holdings of a security or commodity in expectation of a rise in its price; bull. **26 before long.** soon. **27 the long and the short of it.** the essential points or facts. ◆ See also **longs.** [OE *lang*]

long[2] ➊ (lɒŋ) *vb (intr;* foll. by *for* or an infinitive) to have a strong desire. [OE *langian*]

long. *abbrev. for* longitude.

long- *adv (in combination)* for or lasting a long time: *long-awaited; long-established; long-lasting.*

THESAURUS

tional, unorganized, unreasonable ≠ **reasonable:** illogical, implausible, unlikely, unreasonable

logistics *n* **3** = **organization**, coordination, engineering, management, masterminding, orchestration, plans, strategy

loiter *vb* = **linger**, dally, dawdle, delay, dilly-dally (*inf.*), hang about *or* around, idle, lag, loaf, loll, saunter, skulk, stroll

loll *vb* **1** = **lounge**, flop, lean, loaf, recline, relax, slouch, slump, sprawl **2** = **droop**, dangle, drop, flap, flop, hang, hang loosely, sag

lone *adj* **1** = **solitary**, by oneself, one, only, separate, separated, single, sole, unaccompanied **2** = **isolated**, deserted

loneliness *n* **1** = **solitude**, aloneness, forlornness, lonesomeness, solitariness **2** = **isolation**, desertedness, desolation, seclusion

lonely *adj* **1** = **abandoned**, destitute, estranged, forlorn, forsaken, friendless, lonesome, outcast **2, 4** = **solitary**, alone, apart, by oneself, companionless, isolated, lone, single, withdrawn **3** = **desolate**, deserted, godforsaken, isolated, off the beaten track (*inf.*), out-of-the-way, remote, secluded, sequestered, solitary, unfrequented, uninhabited
Antonyms *adj* ≠ **abandoned:** befriended, popular ≠ **solitary:** accompanied, together ≠ **desolate:** bustling, crowded, frequented, populous, teeming

loner *n Informal* = **individualist**, hermit, lone wolf, maverick, misanthrope, outsider, recluse, solitary

lonesome *adj* **1** *Chiefly U.S. & Canad.* = **lonely**, cheerless, companionless, deserted, desolate, dreary, forlorn, friendless, gloomy, isolated, lone

long[1] *adj* **1, 3, 4** = **elongated**, expanded, extended, extensive, far-reaching, lengthy, spread out, stretched **5** = **prolonged**, dragging, interminable, late, lengthy, lingering, long-drawn-out, protracted, slow, sustained, tardy
Antonyms *adj* ≠ **elongated:** compressed, contracted, little, short, small ≠ **prolonged:** abbreviated, abridged, brief, momentary, quick, short, short-lived

long[2] *vb* = **desire**, ache, covet, crave, dream of, eat one's heart out over, hanker, hunger, itch, lust, pine, set one's heart on, want, wish, yearn

long-acting *adj* (of a drug) slowly effective after initial dosage, but maintaining its effects over a long period of time. Cf. **intermediate-acting, short-acting.**

longboat ('lɒŋ,bəʊt) *n* the largest boat carried aboard a commercial sailing vessel.

longbow ('lɒŋ,bəʊ) *n* a large powerful hand-drawn bow, esp. as used in medieval England.

longcase clock ('lɒŋ,keɪs) *n* another name for **grandfather clock.**

longcloth ('lɒŋ,klɒθ) *n* a fine plain-weave cotton cloth made in long strips.

long-dated *adj* (of a gilt-edged security) having more than 15 years to run before redemption. Cf. **medium-dated, short-dated.**

long-day *adj* (of certain plants) able to mature and flower only if exposed to long periods of daylight. Cf. **short-day.**

long-distance *n* **1** (*modifier*) covering relatively long distances: *a long-distance driver.* **2** (*modifier*) (of telephone calls, lines, etc.) connecting points a relatively long way apart. **3** *Chiefly US & Canad.* a long-distance telephone call. **4** a long-distance telephone system or its operator. ◆ *adv* **5** by a long-distance telephone line: *he phoned long-distance.*

long-drawn-out ❶ *adj* overprolonged or extended.

longeron ('lɒndʒərən) *n* a main longitudinal structural member of an aircraft. [C20: from F: side support, ult. from L *longus* LONG[1]]

longevity (lɒn'dʒɛvɪtɪ) *n* **1** long life. **2** relatively long duration of employment, service, etc. [C17: from LL *longaevitās,* from L *longaevus* long-lived, from *longus* LONG[1] + *aevum* age]

long face *n* a disappointed, solemn, or miserable facial expression.
▸**,long-'faced** *adj*

longhand ('lɒŋ,hænd) *n* ordinary handwriting in which letters, words, etc., are set down in full, as opposed to typing or to shorthand.

long haul *n* **1** a journey over a long distance, esp. one involving the transport of goods. **2** a lengthy job.

long-headed *adj* astute; shrewd; sagacious.
▸**,long-'headedly** *adv* ▸**,long-'headedness** *n*

longhorn ('lɒŋ,hɔːn) *n* **1** a long-horned breed of beef cattle, formerly common in the southwestern US. **2** a British breed of beef cattle with long curved horns.

longing ❶ ('lɒŋɪŋ) *n* **1** a prolonged unfulfilled desire or need. ◆ *adj* **2** having or showing desire or need: *a longing look.*
▸**'longingly** *adv*

longish ('lɒŋɪʃ) *adj* rather long.

longitude ('lɒndʒɪ,tjuːd, 'lɒŋgɪ-) *n* distance in degrees east or west of the prime meridian at 0° measured by the angle between the plane of the prime meridian and that of the meridian through the point in question, or by the time difference. [C14: from L *longitūdō* length, from *longus* LONG[1]]

longitudinal (,lɒndʒɪ'tjuːdɪnəl, ,lɒŋgɪ-) *adj* **1** of or relating to longitude or length. **2** placed or extended lengthways.
▸**,longi'tudinally** *adv*

longitudinal wave *n* a wave that is propagated in the same direction as the displacement of the transmitting medium.

long johns *pl n Inf.* underpants with long legs.

long jump *n* an athletic contest in which competitors try to cover the farthest distance possible with a running jump from a fixed board or mark. US and Canad. equivalent: **broad jump.**

long leg *n Cricket.* **a** a fielding position on the leg side near the boundary almost directly behind the batsman's wicket. **b** a fielder in this position.

long-lived ❶ *adj* having long life, existence, or currency.
▸**,long-'livedness** *n*

long-off *n Cricket.* **a** a fielding position on the off side near the boundary almost directly behind the bowler. **b** a fielder in this position.

long-on *n Cricket.* **a** a fielding position on the leg side near the boundary almost directly behind the bowler. **b** a fielder in this position.

long-playing *adj* of or relating to an LP (long player).

long-range *adj* **1** of or extending into the future: *a long-range weather forecast.* **2** (of vehicles, aircraft, etc.) capable of covering great distances without refuelling. **3** (of weapons) made to be fired at a distant target.

longs (lɒŋz) *pl n* **1** full-length trousers. **2** long-dated gilt-edged securities. **3** unsold securities or commodities held in anticipation of rising prices.

longship ('lɒŋ,ʃɪp) *n* a narrow open vessel with oars and a square sail, used esp. by the Vikings.

longshore ('lɒŋ,ʃɔː) *adj* situated on, relating to, or along the shore. [C19: short form of *alongshore*]

longshore drift *n* the process whereby beach material is gradually shifted laterally.

longshoreman ('lɒŋ,ʃɔːmən) *n, pl* **longshoremen.** a US and Canad. word for **docker.**

long shot ❶ *n* **1** a competitor, as in a race, considered to be unlikely to win. **2** a bet against heavy odds. **3** an undertaking, guess, or possibility with little chance of success. **4** *Films, television.* a shot where the camera is or appears to be distant from the object to be photographed. **5 by a long shot.** by any means: *he still hasn't finished by a long shot.*

long-sighted *adj* **1** related to or suffering from hyperopia. **2** able to see distant objects in focus. **3** another term for **far-sighted.**
▸**,long-'sightedly** *adv* ▸**,long-'sightedness** *n*

long-standing ❶ *adj* existing for a long time.

long-suffering ❶ *adj* **1** enduring pain, unhappiness, etc., without complaint. ◆ *n* **2** long and patient endurance.
▸**,long-'sufferingly** *adv*

long suit *n* **1a** the longest suit in a hand of cards. **1b** a holding of four or more cards of a suit. **2** *Inf.* an outstanding advantage, personal quality, or talent.

long-term *adj* **1** lasting or extending over a long time: *long-term prospects.* **2** *Finance.* maturing after a long period: *a long-term bond.*

longtime ('lɒŋ,taɪm) *adj* of long standing.

long ton *n* the full name for **ton**[1] (sense 1).

longueur (*French* lɔ̃gœr) *n* a period of boredom or dullness. [lit.: length]

long vacation *n* the long period of holiday in the summer during which universities, law courts, etc., are closed.

long wave *n* **a** a radio wave with a wavelength greater than 1000 metres. **b** (*as modifier*): *a long-wave broadcast.*

longways ('lɒŋ,weɪz) *or US & Canad.* **longwise** *adv* another word for **lengthways.**

long weekend *n* a weekend holiday extended by a day or days on either side.

long-winded ❶ (,lɒŋ'wɪndɪd) *adj* **1** tiresomely long. **2** capable of energetic activity without becoming short of breath.
▸**,long-'windedly** *adv* ▸**,long-'windedness** *n*

lonicera (lɒ'nɪsərə) *n* See **honeysuckle.**

loo[1] (luː) *n, pl* **loos.** *Brit.* an informal word for **lavatory.** [C20: ?from F *lieux d'aisance* water closet]

loo[2] (luː) *n, pl* **loos. 1** a gambling card game. **2** a stake used in this game. [C17: shortened from *lanterloo,* via Du. from F *lanterelu,* orig. a nonsense word from the refrain of a popular song]

loofah ('luːfə) *n* the fibrous interior of the fruit of a type of gourd, which is dried and used as a bath sponge or for scrubbing. Also (esp. US): **loofa, luffa.** [C19: from NL *luffa,* from Ar. *lūf*]

look ❶ (lʊk) *vb* (*mainly intr*) **1** (often foll. by *at*) to direct the eyes (towards): *to look at the sea.* **2** (often foll. by *at*) to direct one's attention (towards): *let's look at the circumstances.* **3** (often foll. by *to*) to turn one's interests or expectations (towards): *to look to the future.* **4** (*copula*) to give the impression of being by appearance to the eye or mind; seem: *that looks interesting.* **5** to face in a particular direction: *the house looks north.* **6** to expect, hope, or plan (to do something): *I look to hear from you soon; he's looking to get rich.* **7** (foll. by *for*) **7a** to search or seek: *I looked for you everywhere.* **7b** to cherish the expectation (of); hope (for): *I look for success.* **8** (foll. by *to*) **8a** to be mindful (of): *to look to the promise one has made.* **8b** to have recourse (to): *look to your swords, men!* **9** (foll. by *into*) to carry out an investigation. **10** (*tr*) to direct a look at (someone) in a specified way: *she looked her rival up and down.* **11** (*tr*) to accord in appearance with (something): *to look one's age.* **12 look alive, lively, sharp,** *or* **smart.** to hurry up; get busy. **13 look here.** an expression used to attract someone's attention, add emphasis to a statement, etc. ◆ *n* **14** the act or an instance of looking: *a look of despair.* **15** a view or sight (of something): *let's have a look.* **16** (*often pl*) appearance to the eye or mind; aspect: *the look of innocence; I don't like the looks of this place.* **17**

THESAURUS

long-drawn-out *adj* = **prolonged**, dragged out, interminable, lengthy, marathon, overextended, overlong, protracted, spun out

longing *n* **1** = **desire**, ache, ambition, aspiration, coveting, craving, hankering, hope, hungering, itch, thirst, urge, wish, yearning, yen (*inf.*) ◆ *adj* **2** = **yearning**, anxious, ardent, avid, craving, desirous, eager, hungry, languishing, pining, wishful, wistful
Antonyms *n* ≠ **desire:** abhorrence, antipathy, apathy, disgust, disregard, indifference, loathing, revulsion, unconcern ◆ *adj* ≠ **yearning:** apathetic, cold, disgusted, hateful, indifferent, loathing, unconcerned, uninterested

long-lived *adj* = **long-lasting**, enduring, full of years, longevous, old as Methuselah

long shot *n* **1** = **outsider**, dark horse

long-standing *adj* = **established**, abiding, enduring, fixed, long-established, long-lasting, long-lived, time-honoured

long-suffering *adj* **1** = **uncomplaining**, easy-going, forbearing, forgiving, patient, resigned, stoical, tolerant

long-winded *adj* **1** = **rambling**, diffuse, discursive, garrulous, lengthy, long-drawn-out, overlong, prolix, prolonged, repetitious, tedious, tiresome, verbose, wordy
Antonyms *adj* brief, concise, crisp, curt, laconic, pithy, sententious, short, succinct, terse, to the point

look *vb* **1** = **see**, behold (*arch.*), check, check out (*inf.*), clock (*Brit. sl.*), examine, eye, eyeball (*sl.*), feast one's eyes upon, gaze, get a load of (*inf.*), glance, inspect, observe, peep, regard, scan, scrutinize, study, survey, take a dekko at (*Brit. sl.*), take a gander at (*inf.*), view, watch **2** = **consider**, contemplate **4** = **seem**, appear, display, evidence, exhibit, look like, make clear, manifest, present, seem to be, show, strike one as **5** = **face**, front, front on, give onto, overlook **7a** = **search**, forage, hunt, seek **7b** = **hope**, anticipate, await, expect, reckon on **9** *foll. by* **into** = **investigate**, check out, delve into, examine, explore, follow up, go into, inquire about, inspect, look over, make inquiries, probe, research, scrutinize, study ◆ *n* **14, 15** = **glimpse**, butcher's (*Brit. sl.*), examination, eyeful (*inf.*), gander (*inf.*), gaze, glance, inspection, look-see (*sl.*), observation, once-over (*inf.*), peek, review, shufti (*Brit. sl.*), sight, squint (*inf.*), survey, view **16** = **appearance**, air, aspect, bearing, cast, complexion, countenance, demeanour, effect, expression, face, fashion, guise, manner, mien (*literary*), semblance

style; fashion: *the new look for spring.* ◆ *sentence connector.* **18** an expression demanding attention or showing annoyance, determination, etc.: *look, I've had enough of this.* ◆ See also **look after, look back,** etc. [OE *lōcian*]
▸'**looker** *n*

USAGE NOTE See at **like.**

look after ❶ *vb* (*intr, prep*) **1** to take care of; be responsible for. **2** to follow with the eyes.
lookalike ❶ ('lʊkə,laɪk) *n* **a** a person or thing that is the double of another, often well-known, person or thing. **b** (*as modifier*): *a lookalike Minister; a lookalike newspaper.*
look back *vb* (*intr, adv*) **1** to cast one's mind to the past. **2 never look back**: to become increasingly successful: *after his first book was published, he never looked back.*
look down ❶ *vb* (*intr, adv;* foll. by *on* or *upon*) to express or show contempt or disdain (for).
look forward to ❶ *vb* (*intr, adv + prep*) to wait or hope for, esp. with pleasure.
look-in *Inf.* ◆ *n* **1** a chance to be chosen, participate, etc. **2** a short visit. ◆ *vb* **look in. 3** (*intr, adv;* often foll. by *on*) to pay a short visit.
looking glass *n* a mirror.
look on *vb* (*intr*) **1** (*adv*) to be a spectator at an event or incident. **2** (*prep*) Also: **look upon.** to consider or regard: *she looked on the whole affair as a joke.*
▸,**looker-'on** *n*
lookout ❶ ('lʊk,aʊt) *n* **1** the act of keeping watch against danger, etc. **2** a person or persons instructed or employed to keep such a watch, esp. on a ship. **3** a strategic point from which a watch is kept. **4** *Inf.* worry or concern: *that's his lookout.* **5** *Chiefly Brit.* outlook, chances, or view. ◆ *vb* **look out.** (*adv, mainly intr*) **6** to heed one's behaviour; be careful. **7** to be on the watch: *look out for my mother at the station.* **8** (*tr*) to search for and find. **9** (foll. by *on* or *over*) to face in a particular direction: *the house looks out over the moor.*
look over ❶ *vb* **1** (*intr, prep*) to inspect by making a tour of (a factory, house, etc.). **2** (*tr, adv*) to examine (a document, letter, etc.). ◆ *n* **look-over. 3** an inspection.
look-see *n Sl.* a brief inspection or look.
look up ❶ *vb* (*adv*) **1** (*tr*) to discover (something required to be known) by resorting to a work of reference, such as a dictionary. **2** (*intr*) to increase, as in quality or value: *things are looking up.* **3** (*intr;* foll. by *to*) to have respect (for): *I've always wanted a girlfriend I could look up to.* **4** (*tr*) to visit or make contact with (a person): *I'll look you up when I'm in town.*
loom[1] (lu:m) *n* an apparatus, worked by hand or mechanically (**power loom**), for weaving yarn into a textile. [C13 (meaning any kind of tool): var. of OE *gelōma* tool]
loom[2] ❶ (lu:m) *vb* (*intr*) **1** to come into view indistinctly with an enlarged and often threatening aspect. **2** (of an event) to seem ominously close. **3** (often foll. by *over*) (of large objects) to dominate or overhang. ◆ *n* **4** a rising appearance, as of something far away. [C16: ?from East Frisian *lomen* to move slowly]
loon[1] (lu:n) *n* the US and Canad. name for **diver** (the bird). [C17: of Scand. origin]
loon[2] (lu:n) *n* **1** *Inf.* a simple-minded or stupid person. **2** *Arch.* a person of low rank or occupation. [C15: from ?]
loony *or* **looney** ('lu:nɪ) *Sl.* ◆ *adj* **loonier, looniest. 1** lunatic; insane. **2** foolish or ridiculous. ◆ *n, pl* **loonies** *or* **looneys. 3** a foolish or insane person. **4** *Canad.* a Canadian dollar coin with a loon bird on one of its faces.
▸'**looniness** *n*
loony bin *n Sl.* a mental hospital or asylum.
loop ❶ (lu:p) *n* **1** the round or oval shape formed by a line, string, etc., that curves around to cross itself. **2** any round or oval-shaped thing that is closed or nearly closed. **3** an intrauterine contraceptive device in the shape of a loop. **4** *Electronics.* a closed electric or magnetic circuit through which a signal can circulate, as in a feedback control system. **5** a flight manoeuvre in which an aircraft flies one complete circle in the vertical plane. **6** Also called: **loop line.** *Chiefly Brit.* a railway branch line which leaves the main line and rejoins it after a short distance. **7** *Maths, physics.* a closed curve on a graph: *hysteresis loop.* **8** a continuous strip of cinematographic film. **9** *Computing.* a series of instructions in a program, performed repeatedly until some specified condition is satisfied. **10** a group of people to whom information is circulated (esp. in **in** *or* **out of the loop**). ◆ *vb* **11** (*tr*) to make a loop in or of (a line, string, etc.). **12** (*tr*) to fasten or encircle with a loop or something like a loop. **13** Also: **loop the loop.** to cause (an aircraft) to perform a loop or (of an aircraft) to perform a loop. **14** (*intr*) to move in loops or in a path like a loop. [C14 *loupe,* from ?]
▸'**looper** *n*
loophole ❶ ('lu:p,həʊl) *n* **1** an ambiguity, omission, etc., as in a law, by which one can avoid a penalty or responsibility. **2** a small gap or hole in a wall, esp. one in a fortified wall. ◆ *vb* **loopholes, loopholing, loopholed. 3** (*tr*) to provide with loopholes.
loopy ('lu:pɪ) *adj* **loopier, loopiest. 1** full of loops; curly or twisted. **2** *Inf.* slightly mad, crazy.
loose ❶ (lu:s) *adj* **1** free or released from confinement or restraint. **2** not close, compact, or tight in structure or arrangement. **3** not fitted or fitting closely: *loose clothing.* **4** not bundled, packaged, fastened, or put in a container: *loose nails.* **5** inexact; imprecise: *a loose translation.* **6** (of funds, cash, etc.) not allocated or locked away; readily available: *loose change.* **7a** (esp. of women) promiscuous or easy. **7b** (of attitudes, ways of life, etc.) immoral or dissolute. **8a** lacking a sense of responsibility or propriety: *loose talk.* **8b** (*in combination*): *loosetongued.* **9a** (of the bowels) emptying easily, esp. excessively. **9b** (of a cough) accompanied by phlegm, mucus, etc. **10** *Inf., chiefly US & Canad.* very relaxed; easy. ◆ *n* **11 the loose.** *Rugby.* the part of play when the forwards close round the ball in a ruck or loose scrum. **12 on the loose. 12a** free from confinement or restraint. **12b** *Inf.* on a spree. ◆ *adv* **13a** in a loose manner; loosely. **13b** (*in combination*): *loose-fitting.* ◆ *vb* **looses, loosing, loosed. 14** (*tr*) to set free or release, as from confinement, restraint, or obligation. **15** (*tr*) to unfasten or untie. **16** to make or become less strict, tight, firmly attached, compact, etc. **17** (when *intr,* often foll. by *off*) to let fly (a bullet, arrow, or other missile). [C13 (in the sense: not bound): from ON *lauss* free]
▸'**loosely** *adv* ▸'**looseness** *n*
loosebox ('lu:s,bɒks) *n* an enclosed stall with a door in which an animal can be confined.
loose cover *n* a fitted but easily removable cloth cover for a chair, sofa, etc.
loose end *n* **1** a detail that is left unsettled, unexplained, or incomplete. **2 at a loose end.** without purpose or occupation.
loose head *n Rugby.* the prop on the hooker's left in the front row of a scrum. Cf. **tight head.**
loose-jointed ❶ *adj* **1** supple and easy in movement. **2** loosely built; with ill-fitting joints.
▸,**loose-'jointedness** *n*
loose-leaf *adj* (of a binder, album, etc.) capable of being opened to allow removal and addition of pages.
loosen ❶ ('lu:sᵊn) *vb* **1** to make or become less tight, fixed, etc. **2** (often foll. by *up*) to make or become less firm, compact, or rigid. **3** (*tr*) to untie. **4** (*tr*) to let loose; set free. **5** (often foll. by *up*) to make or be-

THESAURUS

look after *vb* **1 = take care of,** attend to, care for, guard, keep an eye on, mind, nurse, protect, sit with, supervise, take charge of, tend, watch
lookalike *n* **a = double,** clone, dead ringer (*sl.*), exact match, living image, replica, ringer (*sl.*), spit (*inf., chiefly Brit.*), spitting image (*inf.*), twin
look down *vb, foll. by* **on** *or* **upon = disdain,** contemn, despise, hold in contempt, look down one's nose at (*inf.*), scorn, sneer, spurn, treat with contempt, turn one's nose up (at) (*inf.*)
look forward to *vb* **= anticipate,** await, count on, count the days until, expect, hope for, long for, look for, set one's heart on, wait for
lookout *n* **1 = watch,** guard, qui vive, readiness, vigil **2 = watchman,** guard, sentinel, sentry, vedette (*Military*) **3 = watchtower,** beacon, citadel, observation post, observatory, post, tower **4** *Informal* **= concern,** business, funeral (*inf.*), pigeon (*Brit. inf.*), worry **5** *Chiefly Brit.* **= prospect,** chances, future, likelihood, outlook, view ◆ *vb* **look out 6 = be careful,** be alert, be on guard, be on the qui vive, be vigilant, beware, keep an eye out, keep one's eyes open, keep one's eyes peeled, keep one's eyes skinned, pay attention, watch out
look over *vb* **1 = inspect,** cast an eye over, check, check out (*inf.*), examine, eyeball (*sl.*), monitor, take a dekko at (*Brit. sl.*), view **2 = look through,** cast an eye over, examine, flick through, peruse, scan
look up *vb* **1 = research,** find, hunt for, search for, seek out, track down **2 = improve,** ameliorate, come along, get better, perk up, pick up, progress, shape up (*inf.*), show improvement **3** *foll. by* **to = respect,** admire, defer to, esteem, have a high opinion of, honour, regard highly, revere **4 = visit,** call on, drop in on (*inf.*), go to see, look in on, pay a visit to
loom[2] *vb* **1 = appear,** become visible, bulk, emerge, hover, menace, take shape **2 = be imminent,** impend, threaten **3 = overhang,** dominate, hang over, mount, overshadow, overtop, rise, soar, tower
loop *n* **1, 2 = curve,** bend, circle, coil, convolution, curl, eyelet, hoop, kink, loophole, noose, ring, spiral, twirl, twist, whorl ◆ *vb* **11, 12 = twist,** bend, braid, circle, coil, connect, curl, curve round, encircle, fold, join, knot, roll, spiral, turn, wind round
loophole *n* **1 = let-out,** avoidance, escape, evasion, excuse, means of escape, plea, pretence, pretext, subterfuge **2 = opening,** aperture, knothole, slot
loose *adj* **1 = free,** floating, insecure, movable, released, unattached, unbound, unconfined, unfastened, unfettered, unrestricted, unsecured, untied, wobbly **3 = slack,** baggy, easy, hanging, loosened, not fitting, not tight, relaxed, slackened, sloppy **5 = vague,** diffuse, disconnected, disordered, ill-defined, imprecise, inaccurate, indefinite, indistinct, inexact, rambling, random **7 = promiscuous,** abandoned, debauched, disreputable, dissipated, dissolute, fast, immoral, lewd, libertine, licentious, profligate, unchaste, wanton **8 = careless,** heedless, imprudent, lax, negligent, rash, thoughtless, unmindful ◆ *vb* **14, 16 = free,** detach, disconnect, disengage, ease, let go, liberate, loosen, release, set free, slacken, unleash, unloose **15 = unfasten,** unbind, unbridle, undo, untie
Antonyms *adj* ≠ **free:** bound, curbed, fastened, fettered, restrained, secured, tethered, tied ≠ **slack:** tight ≠ **vague:** accurate, clear, concise, exact, precise ≠ **promiscuous:** chaste, disciplined, moral, virtuous ◆ *vb* ≠ **free:** bind, cage, capture, fasten, fetter, imprison, tether
loose-jointed *adj* **1 = supple,** agile, elastic, flexible, limber, lissom(e), lithe, pliable, pliant
loosen *vb* **1, 2 = slacken,** detach, let out, sepa-

come less strict, severe, etc. **6** (*tr*) to rid or relieve (the bowels) of constipation. [C14: from LOOSE]
▸**'loosener** *n*

loosestrife ('luːsˌstraɪf) *n* **1** any of a genus of plants, esp. the yellow-flowered yellow loosestrife. **2 purple loosestrife.** a purple-flowered marsh plant. [C16: LOOSE + STRIFE, an erroneous translation of L *lysimachia,* as if from Gk *lusimakhos* ending strife, instead of from the name of the supposed discoverer, *Lusimakhos*]

loot Ⓣ (luːt) *n* **1** goods stolen during pillaging, as in wartime, during riots, etc. **2** goods, money, etc., obtained illegally. **3** *Inf.* money or wealth. ◆ *vb* **4** to pillage (a city, etc.) during war or riots. **5** to steal (money or goods), esp. during pillaging. [C19: from Hindi *lūṭ*]
▸**'looter** *n*

lop[1] Ⓣ (lɒp) *vb* **lops, lopping, lopped.** (*tr;* usually foll. by *off*) **1** to sever (parts) from a tree, body, etc., esp. with swift strokes. **2** to cut out or eliminate from as excessive. ◆ *n* **3** a part or parts lopped off, as from a tree. [C15 *loppe* branches cut off]
▸**'lopper** *n*

lop[2] (lɒp) *vb* **lops, lopping, lopped. 1** to hang or allow to hang loosely. **2** (*intr*) to slouch about or move awkwardly. [C16: ? rel. to LOP[1]]

lope Ⓣ (ləʊp) *vb* **lopes, loping, loped. 1** (*intr*) (of a person) to move or run with a long swinging stride. **2** (*intr*) (of four-legged animals) to run with a regular bounding movement. **3** to cause (a horse) to canter with a long easy stride or (of a horse) to canter in this manner. ◆ *n* **4** a long steady gait or stride. [C15: from ON *hlaupa* to LEAP]

lop-eared *adj* (of animals) having ears that droop.

lopsided Ⓣ (ˌlɒp'saɪdɪd) *adj* **1** leaning to one side. **2** greater in weight, height, or size on one side.
▸**ˌlop'sidedly** *adv* ▸**ˌlop'sidedness** *n*

loquacious Ⓣ (lɒ'kweɪʃəs) *adj* characterized by or showing a tendency to talk a great deal. [C17: from L *loquāx* from *loquī* to speak]
▸**lo'quaciously** *adv* ▸**loquacity** (lɒ'kwæsɪtɪ) *or* **lo'quaciousness** *n*

loquat ('ləʊkwɒt, -kwæt) *n* **1** an ornamental evergreen tree of China and Japan, having reddish woolly branches, white flowers, and small yellow edible plumlike fruits. **2** the fruit of this tree. [C19: from Chinese (Cantonese) *lō kwat,* lit.: rush orange]

lor (lɔː) *interj Not standard.* an exclamation of surprise or dismay. [from LORD (interj.)]

loran ('lɔːrən) *n* a radio navigation system operating over long distances. Synchronized pulses are transmitted from widely spaced radio stations to aircraft or shipping, the time of arrival of the pulses being used to determine position. [C20: *lo(ng)-ra(nge) n(avigation)*]

lord Ⓣ (lɔːd) *n* **1** a person who has power or authority over others, such as a monarch or master. **2** a male member of the nobility, esp. in Britain. **3** (in medieval Europe) a feudal superior, esp. the master of a manor. **4** a husband considered as head of the household (archaic except in the facetious phrase **lord and master**). **5 my lord.** a respectful form of address used to a judge, bishop, or nobleman. ◆ *vb* **6** (*tr*) *Now rare.* to make a lord of (a person). **7** to act in a superior manner towards (esp. in **lord it over**). [OE *hlāford* bread keeper]
▸**'lordless** *adj* ▸**'lordˌlike** *adj*

Lord Ⓣ (lɔːd) *n* **1** a title given to God or Jesus Christ. **2** *Brit.* **2a** a title given to men of high birth, specifically to an earl, marquess, baron, or viscount. **2b** a courtesy title given to the younger sons of a duke or marquess. **2c** the ceremonial title of certain high officials or of a bishop or archbishop: *Lord Mayor.* ◆ *interj* **3** (*sometimes not cap.*) an exclamation of dismay, surprise, etc.: *Good Lord!*

Lord Chancellor *n Brit. government.* the cabinet minister who is head of the judiciary in England and Wales, and Speaker of the House of Lords.

Lord Chief Justice *n* the judge who is second only to the Lord Chancellor in the English legal hierarchy; president of one division of the High Court of Justice.

Lord High Chancellor *n* another name for the **Lord Chancellor.**

Lord Lieutenant *n* **1** (in Britain) the representative of the Crown in a county. **2** (formerly) the British viceroy in Ireland.

lordly Ⓣ ('lɔːdlɪ) *adj* **lordlier, lordliest. 1** haughty; arrogant; proud. **2** of or befitting a lord. ◆ *adv* **3** *Arch.* in the manner of a lord.
▸**'lordliness** *n*

Lord Mayor *n* the mayor in the City of London and in certain other important boroughs and large cities.

Lord of Misrule *n* (formerly, in England) a person appointed master of revels at a Christmas celebration. [translation of Hebrew: see BEELZEBUB]

lordosis (lɔː'dəʊsɪs) *n Pathol.* forward curvature of the lumbar spine. [C18: NL from Gk, from *lordos* bent backwards]
▸**lordotic** (lɔː'dɒtɪk) *adj*

Lord President of the Council *n* (in Britain) the cabinet minister who presides at meetings of the Privy Council.

Lord Privy Seal *n* (in Britain) the senior cabinet minister without official duties.

Lord Provost *n* the provost of one of the five major Scottish cities.

Lords (lɔːdz) *n* **the.** short for **House of Lords.**

Lord's (lɔːdz) *n* a cricket ground in N London; headquarters of the MCC.

lords-and-ladies *n* (*functioning as sing*) another name for **cuckoopint.**

Lord's Day *n* **the.** the Christian Sabbath; Sunday.

lordship ('lɔːdʃɪp) *n* the position or authority of a lord.

Lordship ('lɔːdʃɪp) *n* (preceded by *Your* or *His*) *Brit.* a title used to address or refer to a bishop, a judge of the high court, or any peer except a duke.

Lord's Prayer *n* **the.** the prayer taught by Jesus Christ to his disciples, as in Matthew 6:9–13, Luke 11:2–4. Also called: **Our Father, Paternoster** (esp. Latin version).

Lords Spiritual *pl n* the Anglican archbishops and senior bishops of England and Wales who are members of the House of Lords.

Lord's Supper *n* **the.** another term for **Holy Communion** (I Corinthians 11:20).

Lords Temporal *pl n* **the.** (in Britain) peers other than bishops in their capacity as members of the House of Lords.

lore Ⓣ (lɔː) *n* **1** collective knowledge or wisdom on a particular subject, esp. of a traditional nature. **2** knowledge or learning. [OE *lār;* rel. to *leornian* to LEARN]

lorgnette (lɔː'njɛt) *n* a pair of spectacles or opera glasses mounted on a handle. [C19: from F, from *lorgner* to squint, from OF *lorgne* squinting]

lorikeet ('lɒrɪˌkiːt, ˌlɒrɪ'kiːt) *n* any of various small lories, such as the varied lorikeet or rainbow lorikeet. [C18: from LORY + *-keet,* as in PARAKEET]

loris ('lɔːrɪs) *n, pl* **loris.** any of several omnivorous nocturnal slow-moving prosimian primates of S and SE Asia, esp. the slow loris and slender loris, having vestigial digits and no tails. [C18: from F; from ?]

lorn (lɔːn) *adj Poetic.* forsaken or wretched. [OE *loren,* p.p. of *-lēosan* to lose]

lorry ('lɒrɪ) *n, pl* **lorries. 1** a large motor vehicle designed to carry heavy loads, esp. one with a flat platform. US and Canad. name: **truck. 2 off the back of a lorry.** *Brit. inf.* a phrase used humorously to indicate that something has been dishonestly acquired. **3** any of various vehicles with a flat load-carrying surface, esp. one designed to run on rails. [C19: ? rel. to northern English dialect *lurry* to pull]

lory ('lɔːrɪ), **lowry,** *or* **lowrie** ('laʊrɪ) *n, pl* **lories** *or* **lowries.** any of various small brightly coloured parrots of Australia and Indonesia, having a brush-tipped tongue with which to feed on nectar and pollen. [C17: via Du. from Malay *lūrī,* var. of *nūrī*]

lose Ⓣ (luːz) *vb* **loses, losing, lost.** (*mainly tr*) **1** to part with or come to be without, as through theft, accident, negligence, etc. **2** to fail to keep or maintain: *to lose one's balance.* **3** to suffer the loss or deprivation of: *to lose a parent.* **4** to cease to have or possess. **5** to fail to get or make use of: *to lose a chance.* **6** (*also intr*) to fail to gain or win (a contest, game, etc.): *to lose the match.* **7** to fail to see, hear, perceive, or understand: *I lost the gist of his speech.* **8** to waste: *to lose money gambling.* **9** to wander from so as to be unable to find: *to lose one's way.* **10** to cause the loss of: *his delay lost him the battle.* **11** to allow to go astray or out of sight: *we lost him in the crowd.* **12** (*usually passive*) to absorb or engross: *he was lost in contemplation.* **13** (*usually passive*) to cause the death or destruction of: *two men were lost in the attack.* **14** to outdistance or elude: *he soon lost his pursuers.* **15** (*intr*) to decrease or depreciate in value or effectiveness: *poetry always loses in translation.* **16** (*also intr*) (of a timepiece) to run slow (by a specified amount). **17** (of a woman) to fail to give birth to (a viable baby), esp. as the result of a miscarriage.

THESAURUS

rate, work free, work loose **3** = **untie,** unbind, undo, unloose **4** = **free,** deliver, let go, liberate, release, set free **5** *often foll. by* **up** = **relax,** ease up *or* off, go easy, lessen, let up, lighten up (*sl.*), mitigate, moderate, soften, weaken

loot *n* **1, 2** = **plunder,** booty, goods, haul, prize, spoils, swag (*sl.*) ◆ *vb* **4** = **plunder,** despoil, pillage, raid, ransack, ravage, rifle, rob, sack

lop[1] *vb* **1, 2** = **cut,** chop, clip, crop, curtail, detach, dock, hack, prune, sever, shorten, trim, truncate

lope *vb* **1, 2** = **stride,** bound, canter, gallop, lollop, spring

lopsided *adj* **1** = **crooked,** askew, awry, cockeyed, out of true, skewwhiff (*Brit. inf.*), squint, tilting **2** = **unequal,** asymmetrical, disproportionate, off balance, one-sided, out of shape, unbalanced, uneven, warped

loquacious *adj* = **talkative,** babbling, blathering, chattering, chatty, gabby (*inf.*), garrulous, gossipy, voluble, wordy

loquacity *n* = **talkativeness,** babbling, chattering, chattiness, effusiveness, gabbling, garrulity, volubility

lord *n* **1** = **master,** commander, governor, king, leader, liege, monarch, overlord, potentate, prince, ruler, seigneur, sovereign, superior **2** = **nobleman,** earl, noble, peer, viscount ◆ *vb* **7** *As in* **lord it over** = **order around,** act big (*sl.*), be overbearing, boss around (*inf.*), domineer, play the lord, pull rank, put on airs, swagger

Lord *n* **1** = **Jesus Christ,** Christ, God, Jehovah, the Almighty, the Galilean, the Good Shepherd, the Nazarene

lordly *adj* **1** = **proud,** arrogant, condescending, despotic, dictatorial, disdainful, domineering, haughty, high and mighty (*inf.*), high-handed, hoity-toity (*inf.*), imperious, lofty, overbearing, patronizing, stuck-up (*inf.*), supercilious, toffee-nosed (*sl., chiefly Brit.*), tyrannical **2** = **noble,** aristocratic, dignified, exalted, gracious, grand, imperial, lofty, majestic, princely, regal, stately

lore *n* **1** = **traditions,** beliefs, doctrine, experience, folk-wisdom, mythos, saws, sayings, teaching, traditional wisdom, wisdom **2** = **learning,** erudition, know-how (*inf.*), knowledge, letters, scholarship

lose *vb* **1-4** = **mislay,** be deprived of, drop, fail to keep, forget, misplace, miss, suffer loss **5** = **forfeit,** fail, fall short, lose out on (*inf.*), miss, pass up (*inf.*), yield **6** = **be defeated,** be the loser, be worsted, come a cropper (*inf.*), come to grief, get the worst of, lose out, suffer defeat, take a licking (*inf.*) **7** = **stray from,** confuse, miss, wan-

18 lose it. *Sl.* to lose control of oneself or one's temper. [OE *losian* to perish]
▸**'losable** *adj*

lose out *vb Inf.* **1** (*intr, adv*) to be defeated or unsuccessful. **2 lose out on.** to fail to secure or make use of: *we lost out on the sale.*

loser 🅣 ('luːzə) *n* **1** a person or thing that loses. **2** *Inf.* a person or thing that seems destined to be taken advantage of, fail, etc.: *a born loser.*

losing ('luːzɪŋ) *adj* unprofitable; failing: *the business was a losing concern.*

losings ('luːzɪŋz) *pl n* losses, esp. in gambling.

loss 🅣 (lɒs) *n* **1** the act or an instance of losing. **2** the disadvantage or deprivation resulting from losing: *a loss of reputation.* **3** the person, thing, or amount lost: *a large loss.* **4** (*pl*) military personnel lost by death or capture. **5** (*sometimes pl*) the amount by which the costs of a business transaction or operation exceed its revenue. **6** *Insurance.* **6a** an occurrence of something that has been insured against, thus giving rise to a claim by a policyholder. **6b** the amount of the resulting claim. **7 at a loss. 7a** uncertain what to do; bewildered. **7b** rendered helpless (for lack of something): *at a loss for words.* **7c** with income less than outlay: *the firm was running at a loss.* [C14: n prob. formed from *lost,* p.p. of *losen* to perish, from OE *lōsian* to be destroyed, from *los* destruction]

loss adjuster *n Insurance.* a person qualified to adjust losses incurred through fire, theft, natural disaster, etc., to agree the loss and the compensation to be paid.

loss leader *n* an article offered below cost to attract customers.

lost 🅣 (lɒst) *adj* **1** unable to be found or recovered. **2** unable to find one's way or ascertain one's whereabouts. **3** confused, bewildered, or helpless: *he is lost in discussions of theory.* **4** (sometimes foll. by *on*) not utilized, noticed, or taken advantage of (by): *rational arguments are lost on her.* **5** no longer possessed or existing because of defeat, misfortune, or the passage of time: *a lost art.* **6** destroyed physically: *the lost platoon.* **7** (foll. by *to*) no longer available or open (to). **8** (foll. by *to*) insensible or impervious (to a sense of shame, justice, etc.). **9** (foll. by *in*) engrossed (in): *he was lost in his book.* **10** morally fallen: *a lost woman.* **11** damned: *a lost soul.*

Lost Generation *n* (*sometimes not cap.*) **1** the large number of talented young men killed in World War I. **2** the generation of writers, esp. American authors, active after World War I.

lot 🅣 (lɒt) *pron* **1** (*functioning as sing or pl; preceded by a*) a great number or quantity: *a lot to do; a lot of people.* ◆ *n* **2** a collection of objects, items, or people: *a nice lot of youngsters.* **3** portion in life; destiny; fortune: *it falls to my lot to be poor.* **4** any object, such as a straw or slip of paper, drawn from others at random to make a selection or choice (esp. in **draw** *or* **cast lots**). **5** the use of lots in making a selection or choice (esp. in **by lot**). **6** an assigned or apportioned share. **7** an item or set of items for sale in an auction. **8** *Chiefly US & Canad.* an area of land: *a parking lot.* **9** *Chiefly US & Canad.* a film studio. **10 a bad lot.** an unpleasant or disreputable person. **11 cast** *or* **throw in one's lot with.** to join with voluntarily and share the fortunes of. **12 the lot.** the entire amount or number. ◆ *adv* (preceded by *a*) *Inf.* **13** to a considerable extent, degree, or amount; very much: *to delay a lot.* **14** a great deal of the time or often: *to sing madrigals a lot.* ◆ *vb* **lots, lotting, lotted. 15** to draw lots for (something). **16** (*tr*) to divide (land, etc.) into lots. **17** (*tr*) another word for **allot.** ◆ See also **lots.** [OE *hlot*]

loth 🅣 (ləʊθ) *adj* a variant spelling of **loath.**

Lothario (ləʊ'θɑːrɪ,əʊ) *n, pl* **Lotharios.** (*sometimes not cap.*) a rake, libertine, or seducer. [C18: after a seducer in Nicholas Rowe's tragedy *The Fair Penitent* (1703)]

lotion 🅣 ('ləʊʃən) *n* a liquid preparation having a soothing, cleansing, or antiseptic action, applied to the skin, eyes, etc. [C14: via OF from L *lōtiō* a washing, from *lōtus* p.p. of *lavāre* to wash]

lots (lɒts) *Inf.* ◆ *pl n* **1** (often foll. by *of*) great numbers or quantities: *lots of people; to eat lots.* ◆ *adv* **2** a great deal. **3** (intensifier): *the journey is lots quicker by train.*

lottery 🅣 ('lɒtərɪ) *n, pl* **lotteries. 1** a game of chance in which tickets are sold, which may later qualify the holder for a prize. **2** an endeavour, the success of which is regarded as a matter of luck. [C16: from OF *loterie,* from MDu. *loterije*]

lotto ('lɒtəʊ) *n* **1** Also called: **housey-housey.** a children's game in which numbered discs are drawn at random and called out, while the players cover the corresponding numbers on cards, the winner being the first to cover all the numbers, a particular row, etc. Cf. **bingo. 2** *Austral.* a lottery with cash prizes based on this principle. [C18: from It., from OF *lot,* from Gmc]

lotus ('ləʊtəs) *n* **1** (in Greek mythology) a fruit that induces forgetfulness and a dreamy languor in those who eat it. **2** any of several water lilies of tropical Africa and Asia, esp. the **white lotus,** which was regarded as sacred in ancient Egypt. **3** a related plant which is the sacred lotus of India, China, and Tibet. **4** a representation of such a plant, common in Hindu, Buddhist, and ancient Egyptian art. **5** any of a genus of leguminous plants of the legume family of the Old World and North America, having yellow, pink, or white pealike flowers. ◆ Also (rare): **lotos.** [C16: via L from Gk *lōtos,* from Semitic]

lotus-eater *n Greek myth.* one of a people encountered by Odysseus in North Africa who lived in indolent forgetfulness, drugged by the fruit of the legendary lotus.

lotus position *n* a seated cross-legged position used in yoga, meditation, etc.

loud 🅣 (laʊd) *adj* **1** (of sound) relatively great in volume: *a loud shout.* **2** making or able to make sounds of relatively great volume: *a loud voice.* **3** clamorous, insistent, and emphatic: *loud protests.* **4** (of colours, designs, etc.) offensive or obtrusive to look at. **5** characterized by noisy, vulgar, and offensive behaviour. ◆ *adv* **6** in a loud manner. **7 out loud.** audibly, as distinct from silently. [OE *hlud*]
▸**'loudish** *adj* ▸**'loudly** *adv* ▸**'loudness** *n*

louden ('laudᵊn) *vb* to make or become louder.

loud-hailer *n* a portable loudspeaker having a built-in amplifier and microphone. Also (US and Canad.): **bullhorn.**

loudmouth 🅣 ('laʊd,maʊθ) *n Inf.* a person who brags or talks too loudly.
▸**loudmouthed** ('laʊd,maʊðd, -,maʊθt) *adj*

loudspeaker (,laʊd'spiːkə) *n* a device for converting audio-frequency signals into sound waves. Often shortened to **speaker.**

Lou Gehrig's disease (luː 'gerɪg) *n* another name for **amyotrophic lateral sclerosis.** [C20: named after *Lou Gehrig* (1903–41), US baseball player who suffered from it]

lough (lɒx, lɒk) *n* **1** an Irish word for **lake**[1] (senses 1 and 2). **2** a long narrow bay or arm of the sea in Ireland. [C14: from Irish *loch* lake]

louis d'or (,luːɪ 'dɔː) *n, pl* **louis d'or** (,luːɪz 'dɔː). **1** a former French gold coin worth 20 francs. **2** an old French coin minted in the reign of Louis XIII. ◆ Often shortened to **louis.** [C17: from F: golden louis, after Louis XIII]

lounge 🅣 (laʊndʒ) *vb* **lounges, lounging, lounged. 1** (*intr;* often foll. by *about* or *around*) to sit, lie, walk, or stand in a relaxed manner. **2** to pass (time) lazily or idly. ◆ *n* **3** a communal room in a hotel, ship, etc., used for waiting or relaxing in. **4** *Chiefly Brit.* a living room in a private house. **5** Also called: **lounge bar, saloon.** *Brit.* a more expensive bar in a pub or hotel. **6** a sofa or couch. **7** the act or an instance of lounging. [C16: from ?]

lounger ('laʊndʒə) *n* **1** a comfortable couch or extending chair designed for someone to relax on. **2** a loose comfortable leisure garment. **3** a person who lounges.

THESAURUS

der from **8** = **waste,** consume, deplete, dissipate, drain, exhaust, expend, lavish, misspend, squander, use up **14** = **elude,** dodge, duck, escape, evade, give someone the slip, lap, leave behind, outdistance, outrun, outstrip, overtake, pass, shake off, slip away, throw off

loser *n* **1, 2** = **failure,** also-ran, clinker (*sl., chiefly US*), dud (*inf.*), flop (*inf.*), lemon (*sl.*), no-hoper (*Austral. sl.*), underdog, washout (*inf.*)

loss *n* **1, 2** = **losing,** bereavement, defeat, deprivation, disappearance, drain, failure, forfeiture, misfortune, mislaying, privation, squandering, waste **3** = **damage,** cost, destruction, detriment, disadvantage, harm, hurt, impairment, injury, ruin **4** *plural* = **casualties,** dead, death toll, fatalities, number killed, number wounded **5** *sometimes plural* = **deficit,** debit, debt, deficiency, depletion, losings, shrinkage **7a at a loss** = **confused,** at one's wits' end, baffled, bewildered, helpless, nonplussed, perplexed, puzzled, stuck (*inf.*), stumped
Antonyms *n* ≠ **losing:** acquisition, finding, gain, preservation, reimbursement, saving, winning ≠ **damage:** advantage, recovery, restoration ≠ **deficit:** gain

lost *adj* **1** = **missing,** disappeared, forfeited, mislaid, misplaced, missed, strayed, vanished, wayward **2** = **off-course,** adrift, astray, at sea, disoriented, off-track **3** = **bewildered,** baffled, clueless (*sl.*), confused, helpless, ignorant, mystified, perplexed, puzzled **4** = **wasted,** consumed, dissipated, frittered away, misapplied, misdirected, misspent, misused, squandered **5** = **past,** bygone, dead, extinct, forgotten, gone, lapsed, obsolete, out-of-date, unremembered **6** = **wiped out,** abolished, annihilated, demolished, destroyed, devastated, eradicated, exterminated, obliterated, perished, ruined, wasted, wrecked **9** = **engrossed,** absent, absorbed, abstracted, distracted, dreamy, entranced, preoccupied, rapt, spellbound, taken up **10** = **fallen,** abandoned, corrupt, damned, depraved, dissolute, irreclaimable, licentious, profligate, unchaste, wanton

lot *pron* **1** = **plenty,** abundance, a great deal, heap(s), large amount, load(s) (*inf.*), masses (*inf.*), numbers, ocean(s), oodles (*inf.*), piles (*inf.*), quantities, reams (*inf.*), scores, stack(s) ◆ *n* **2** = **collection,** assortment, batch, bunch (*inf.*), consignment, crowd, group, quantity, set **3** = **destiny,** accident, chance, doom, fate, fortune, hazard, plight, portion **6** = **share,** allowance, cut (*inf.*), parcel, part, percentage, piece, portion, quota, ration **11 cast** *or* **throw in one's lot with** = **join with,** ally *or* align oneself with, join forces with, join fortunes with, make common cause with, support

loth *see* **loath**

lotion *n* = **cream,** balm, embrocation, liniment, salve, solution

lottery *n* **1** = **raffle,** draw, sweepstake **2** = **gamble,** chance, hazard, risk, toss-up (*inf.*), venture

loud *adj* **1-3** = **noisy,** blaring, blatant, boisterous, booming, clamorous, deafening, ear-piercing, ear-splitting, forte (*Music*), obstreperous, piercing, resounding, rowdy, sonorous, stentorian, strident, strong, thundering, tumultuous, turbulent, vehement, vociferous **4** = **garish,** brash, brassy, flamboyant, flashy, gaudy, glaring, lurid, naff (*Brit. sl.*), ostentatious, showy, tacky (*inf.*), tasteless, tawdry, vulgar **5** = **loud-mouthed** (*inf.*), brash, brazen, coarse, crass, crude, offensive, raucous, vulgar
Antonyms *adj* ≠ **noisy:** gentle, inaudible, low, low-pitched, quiet, silent, soft, soundless, subdued ≠ **garish:** conservative, dull, sober, sombre ≠ **loud-mouthed:** quiet, reserved, retiring, shy, unassuming

loudly *adv* **1-3** = **noisily,** at full volume, at the top of one's voice, clamorously, deafeningly, fortissimo (*Music*), lustily, shrilly, uproariously, vehemently, vigorously, vociferously

loudmouth *n Informal* = **bigmouth** (*sl.*), blowhard (*inf.*), blusterer, braggart, gasbag (*inf.*), swaggerer, windbag (*sl.*)

lounge *vb* **1** = **relax,** laze, lie about, loaf, loiter, loll, make oneself at home, recline, saunter,

lounge suit *n* a man's suit of matching jacket and trousers worn for the normal business day.

loupe (luːp) *n* a small magnifying glass used by jewellers, horologists, etc., worn in the eye socket. [C20: from F (formerly an imperfect precious stone), from OF, from ?]

lour Ⓣ *or* **lower** (ˈlaʊə) *vb* (*intr*) **1** (esp. of the sky, weather, etc.) to be overcast, dark, and menacing. **2** to scowl or frown. ◆ *n* **3** a menacing scowl or appearance. [C13 *louren* to scowl]
▸ **ˈlouring** *or* **ˈlowering** *adj*

lourie *or* **loerie** (ˈlaʊrɪ) *n* a type of African bird with bright plumage. [from Malay *luri*]

louse (laʊs) *n, pl* **lice. 1** a wingless bloodsucking insect, such as the head louse, body louse, and crab louse, all of which infest man. **2 biting** *or* **bird louse.** a wingless insect, such as the chicken louse: external parasites of birds and mammals, with biting mouthparts. **3** any of various similar but unrelated insects. **4** (*pl* **louses**) *Sl.* an unpleasant or mean person. ◆ *vb* **louses, lousing, loused.** (*tr*) **5** to remove lice from. **6** (foll. by *up*) *Sl.* to ruin or spoil. [OE *lūs*]

lousewort (ˈlaʊs,wɜːt) *n* any of various N temperate plants having spikes of white, yellow, or mauve flowers.

lousy Ⓣ (ˈlaʊzɪ) *adj* **lousier, lousiest. 1** *Sl.* very mean or unpleasant. **2** *Sl.* inferior or bad. **3** infested with lice. **4** (foll. by *with*) *Sl.* provided with an excessive amount (of): *he's lousy with money.*
▸ **ˈlousily** *adv* ▸ **ˈlousiness** *n*

lout Ⓣ (laʊt) *n* a crude or oafish person; boor. [C16: ? from OE *lūtan* to stoop]
▸ **ˈloutish** *adj*

louvre *or US* **louver** (ˈluːvə) *n* **1a** any of a set of horizontal parallel slats in a door or window, sloping outwards to throw off rain and admit air. **1b** Also called: **louvre boards.** the slats and frame supporting them. **2** *Archit.* a turret that allows smoke to escape. [C14: from OF *lovier*, from ?]
▸ **ˈlouvred** *or US* **ˈlouvered** *adj*

lovable Ⓣ *or* **loveable** (ˈlʌvəbᵊl) *adj* attracting or deserving affection.
▸ **ˌlovaˈbility, ˌloveaˈbility** *or* **ˈlovableness, ˈloveableness** *n* ▸ **ˈlovably** *or* **ˈloveably** *adv*

lovage (ˈlʌvɪdʒ) *n* a European umbelliferous plant with greenish-white flowers and aromatic fruits, which are used for flavouring food. [C14 *loveache*, from OF *luvesche*, from LL *levisticum*, from L *ligusticum*, lit.: Ligurian (plant)]

love Ⓣ (lʌv) *vb* **loves, loving, loved. 1** (*tr*) to have a great attachment to and affection for. **2** (*tr*) to have passionate desire, longing, and feelings for. **3** (*tr*) to like or desire (to do something) very much. **4** (*tr*) to make love to. **5** (*intr*) to be in love. ◆ *n* **6a** an intense emotion of affection, warmth, fondness, and regard towards a person or thing. **6b** (*as modifier*): *love story.* **7** a deep feeling of sexual attraction and desire. **8** wholehearted liking for or pleasure in something. **9** *Christianity.* God's benevolent attitude towards man. **10** Also: **my love.** a beloved person: used esp. as an endearment. **11** *Brit. inf.* a term of address, not necessarily for a person regarded as likable. **12** (in tennis, squash, etc.) a score of zero. **13 fall in love.** to become in love. **14 for love.** without payment. **15 for love or money.** (*used with a negative*) in any circumstances: *I would not eat a snail for love or money.* **16 for the love of.** for the sake of. **17 in love.** in a state of strong emotional attachment and usually sexual attraction. **18 make love (to). 18a** to have sexual intercourse (with). **18b** *Now arch.* to court. [OE *lufu*]

love affair Ⓣ *n* a romantic or sexual relationship, esp. temporary, between two people.

love apple *n* an archaic name for **tomato.**

lovebird (ˈlʌv,bɜːd) *n* any of several small African parrots often kept as cagebirds.

lovebite (ˈlʌv,baɪt) *n* a temporary red mark left on a person's skin by a partner's biting or sucking it during lovemaking.

love child *n Euphemistic.* an illegitimate child; bastard.

love-in-a-mist *n* an erect S European plant, cultivated as a garden plant, having finely cut leaves and white or pale blue flowers.

loveless Ⓣ (ˈlʌvlɪs) *adj* **1** without love: *a loveless marriage.* **2** receiving or giving no love.
▸ **ˈlovelessly** *adv* ▸ **ˈlovelessness** *n*

love-lies-bleeding *n* any of several plants having drooping spikes of small red flowers.

lovelock (ˈlʌv,lɒk) *n* a long lock of hair worn on the forehead.

lovelorn Ⓣ (ˈlʌv,lɔːn) *adj* miserable because of unrequited love or unhappiness in love.

lovely Ⓣ (ˈlʌvlɪ) *adj* **lovelier, loveliest. 1** very attractive or beautiful. **2** highly pleasing or enjoyable: *a lovely time.* **3** inspiring love; lovable. ◆ *n, pl* **lovelies. 4** *Sl.* a lovely woman.
▸ **ˈloveliness** *n*

lovemaking Ⓣ (ˈlʌv,meɪkɪŋ) *n* **1** sexual play and activity between lovers, esp. including sexual intercourse. **2** an archaic word for **courtship.**

love potion *n* any drink supposed to arouse sexual love in the one who drinks it.

lover Ⓣ (ˈlʌvə) *n* **1** a person, now esp. a man, who has an extramarital or premarital sexual relationship with another person. **2** (*often pl*) either of the two people involved in a love affair. **3a** someone who loves a specified person or thing: *a lover of music.* **3b** (*in combination*): *a music-lover; a cat-lover.*

love seat *n* a small upholstered sofa for two people.

lovesick Ⓣ (ˈlʌv,sɪk) *adj* pining or languishing because of love.
▸ **ˈloveˌsickness** *n*

lovey-dovey (ˌlʌvɪˈdʌvɪ) *adj* making an excessive or ostentatious display of affection.

loving Ⓣ (ˈlʌvɪŋ) *adj* feeling or showing love and affection.
▸ **ˈlovingly** *adv* ▸ **ˈlovingness** *n*

loving cup *n* **1** a large vessel, usually two-handled, out of which people drink in turn at a banquet. **2** a similar cup awarded to the winner of a competition.

low[1] Ⓣ (ləʊ) *adj* **1** having a relatively small distance from base to top;

THESAURUS

sprawl, take it easy **2** = **pass time**, dawdle, fritter time away, hang out (*inf.*), idle, kill time, potter, veg out (*sl., chiefly US*), waste time

lour *vb* **1** = **darken**, be brewing, blacken, cloud up *or* over, loom, menace, threaten **2** = **glower**, frown, give a dirty look, glare, look daggers, look sullen, scowl

louring *adj* **1** = **darkening**, black, clouded, cloudy, dark, forbidding, foreboding, gloomy, grey, heavy, menacing, ominous, overcast, threatening **2** = **glowering**, brooding, forbidding, frowning, grim, scowling, sullen, surly

lousy *adj* **1** *Slang* = **mean**, base, contemptible, despicable, dirty, hateful, low, rotten (*inf.*), vicious, vile **2** *Slang* = **inferior**, awful, bad, bush-league (*Austral. & NZ inf.*), dime-a-dozen (*inf.*), low-rent (*inf., chiefly US*), miserable, no good, not much cop (*Brit. sl.*), of a sort *or* of sorts, poor, poxy (*sl.*), rotten (*inf.*), second-rate, shoddy, slovenly, strictly for the birds (*inf.*), terrible, tinhorn (*US sl.*), two-bit (*US & Canad. sl.*) **3** = **lice-infested**, lice-infected, lice-ridden, pedicular, pediculous **4** *foll. by* **with** *Slang* = **well-supplied with**, amply supplied with, not short of, rolling in (*sl.*)

lout *n* = **oaf**, bear, boor, bumpkin, churl, clod, dolt, gawk, lubber, lummox (*inf.*), yahoo, yob *or* yobbo (*Brit. sl.*)

loutish *adj* = **oafish**, boorish, bungling, clodhopping (*inf.*), coarse, doltish, gawky, gross, ill-bred, ill-mannered, lubberly, lumpen (*inf.*), lumpish, rough, stolid, swinish, uncouth, unmannerly

lovable *adj* = **endearing**, adorable, amiable, attractive, captivating, charming, cuddly, cute, delightful, enchanting, engaging, fetching (*inf.*), likable *or* likeable, lovely, pleasing, sweet, winning, winsome
Antonyms *adj* abhorrent, abominable, detestable, hateful, loathsome, obnoxious, odious, offensive, revolting

love *vb* **1, 2** = **adore**, adulate, be attached to, be in love with, cherish, dote on, have affection for, hold dear, idolize, prize, think the world of, treasure, worship **3** = **enjoy**, appreciate, delight in, desire, fancy, have a weakness for, like, relish, savour, take pleasure in **4** = **make love to**, canoodle (*sl.*), caress, cuddle, embrace, fondle, kiss, neck (*inf.*), pet ◆ *n* **6a, 7** = **passion**, adoration, adulation, affection, amity, ardour, attachment, devotion, fondness, friendship, infatuation, liking, rapture, regard, tenderness, warmth **8** = **liking**, delight, devotion, enjoyment, fondness, inclination, partiality, relish, soft spot, taste, weakness **10** = **beloved**, angel, darling, dear, dearest, dear one, inamorata *or* inamorato, leman (*arch.*), loved one, lover, sweet, sweetheart, truelove **13 fall in love (with)** = **lose one's heart (to)**, become attached (to), become enamoured (of), become fond (of), become infatuated (with), be smitten (by), be taken (with), conceive an affection (for), fall (for) **14 for love** = **without payment**, for nothing, freely, free of charge, gratis, pleasurably **15 for love or money** = **by any means**, ever, under any conditions **17 in love** = **enamoured**, besotted, charmed, enraptured, infatuated, smitten
Antonyms *vb* ≠ **adore, enjoy:** abhor, abominate, detest, dislike, hate, scorn ◆ *n* ≠ **passion, liking:** abhorrence, abomination, animosity, antagonism, antipathy, aversion, bad blood, bitterness, detestation, disgust, dislike, hate, hatred, hostility, ill will, incompatibility, loathing, malice, repugnance, resentment, scorn ≠ **beloved:** enemy, foe

love affair *n* = **romance**, affair, *affaire de coeur*, amour, intrigue, liaison, relationship

loveless *adj* **2** = **unloving**, cold, cold-hearted, frigid, hard, heartless, icy, insensitive, unfeeling, unfriendly, unresponsive

lovelorn *adj* = **lovesick**, crossed in love, jilted, languishing, mooning, moping, pining, slighted, spurned, unrequited, yearning

lovely *adj* **1** = **beautiful**, admirable, adorable, amiable, attractive, captivating, charming, comely, enchanting, exquisite, graceful, handsome, pretty, sweet, winning **2** = **enjoyable**, agreeable, delightful, engaging, gratifying, nice, pleasant, pleasing
Antonyms *adj* ≠ **beautiful:** hideous, ugly, unattractive ≠ **enjoyable:** abhorrent, detestable, hateful, loathsome, odious, repellent, repugnant, revolting

lovemaking *n* **1** = **sexual intercourse**, act of love, carnal knowledge, coition, coitus, copulation, intercourse, intimacy, mating, nookie (*sl.*), rumpy-pumpy (*sl.*), sexual relations, sexual union *or* congress, the other (*inf.*)

lover *n* **1, 2** = **sweetheart**, admirer, beau, beloved, boyfriend *or* girlfriend, fancy bit (*sl.*), fancy man *or* fancy woman (*sl.*), fiancé *or* fiancée, flame (*inf.*), inamorata *or* inamorato, mistress, paramour, suitor, swain (*arch.*), toy boy

lovesick *adj* = **lovelorn**, desiring, languishing, longing, pining, yearning

loving *adj* = **affectionate**, amorous, ardent, cordial, dear, demonstrative, devoted, doting, fond, friendly, kind, solicitous, tender, warm, warm-hearted
Antonyms *adj* aloof, cold, contemptuous, cruel, detached, distasteful, hateful, hostile, indifferent, mean, scornful, unconcerned, unloving

low[1] *adj* **1** = **small**, little, short, squat, stunted **2** = **low-lying**, deep, depressed, ground-level, shallow, subsided, sunken **5** = **meagre**, depleted, insignificant, little, measly, paltry, reduced,

not tall or high: *a low hill; a low building.* **2a** situated at a relatively short distance above the ground, sea level, the horizon, or other reference position: *low cloud.* **2b** (*in combination*): *low-lying.* **3** of less than usual height, depth, or degree: *low temperature.* **4a** (of numbers) small. **4b** (of measurements) expressed in small numbers. **5a** involving or containing a relatively small amount of something: *a low supply.* **5b** (*in combination*): *low-pressure.* **6a** having little value or quality. **6b** (*in combination*): *low-grade.* **7** coarse or vulgar: *a low conversation.* **8a** inferior in culture or status. **8b** (*in combination*): *low-class.* **9** in a physically or mentally depressed or weakened state. **10** low-necked: *a low dress.* **11** with a hushed tone; quiet or soft: *a low whisper.* **12** of relatively small price or monetary value: *low cost.* **13** *Music.* relating to or characterized by a relatively low pitch. **14** (of latitudes) situated not far north or south of the equator. **15** having little or no money. **16** abject or servile. **17** unfavourable: *a low opinion.* **18** not advanced in evolution: *a low form of plant life.* **19** deep: *a low bow.* **20** *Phonetics.* of, relating to, or denoting a vowel whose articulation is produced by moving the back of the tongue away from the soft palate, such as for the *a* in English *father.* **21** (of a gear) providing a relatively low forward speed for a given engine speed. **22** (*usually cap.*) of or relating to the Low Church. ◆ *adv* **23** in a low position, level, degree, intensity, etc.: *to bring someone low.* **24** at a low pitch; deep: *to sing low.* **25** at a low price; cheaply: *to buy low.* **26** **lay low. 26a** to cause to fall by a blow. **26b** to overcome, defeat, or destroy. **27** **lie low. 27a** to keep or be concealed or quiet. **27b** to wait for a favourable opportunity. ◆ *n* **28** a low position, level, or degree: *an all-time low.* **29** an area of relatively low atmospheric pressure, esp. a depression. [C12 *lāh,* from ON *lāgr*]
▸ **'lowness** *n*

low[2] ❶ (ləʊ) *n also* **lowing. 1** the sound uttered by cattle; moo. ◆ *vb* **2** to make or express by a low or moo. [OE *hlōwan*]

low-alcohol *adj* (of beer or wine) containing only a small amount of alcohol. Cf. **alcohol-free.**

lowan ('ləʊən) *n* another name for **mallee fowl.** [from Abor.]

lowborn (,ləʊ'bɔːn) *or* **lowbred** (,ləʊ'brɛd) *adj Now rare.* of ignoble or common parentage.

lowbrow ('ləʊ,braʊ) *Disparaging.* ◆ *n* **1** a person who has uncultivated or nonintellectual tastes. ◆ *adj also* **lowbrowed. 2** of or characteristic of such a person.

Low Church *n* **1** the school of thought in the Church of England stressing evangelical beliefs and practices. ◆ *adj* **Low-Church. 2** of or relating to this school.

low comedy *n* comedy characterized by slapstick and physical action.

low-density lipoprotein *n* a lipoprotein that is the form in which cholesterol is transported in the bloodstream. High levels in the blood are associated with atheroma. Abbrev.: **LDL.**

low-down ❶ *Inf.* ◆ *adj* **1** mean, underhand, or despicable. ◆ *n* **low-down. 2 the.** information.

lower[1] ❶ ('ləʊə) *adj* **1** being below one or more other things: *the lower shelf.* **2** reduced in amount or value: *a lower price.* **3** *Maths.* (of a limit or bound) less than or equal to one or more numbers or variables. **4** (*sometimes cap.*) *Geol.* denoting the early part of a period, formation, etc.: *Lower Silurian.* ◆ *vb* **5** (*tr*) to cause to become low or on a lower level; bring, put, or cause to move down. **6** (*tr*) to reduce or bring down in estimation, dignity, value, etc.: *to lower oneself.* **7** to reduce or be reduced: *to lower one's confidence.* **8** (*tr*) to make quieter: *to lower the radio.* **9** (*tr*) to reduce the pitch of. **10** (*intr*) to diminish or become less. [C12 (comp. of LOW[1]); C17 (vb)]

lower[2] ❶ ('laʊə) *vb* a variant of **lour.**

lower case *n* **1** the bottom half of a compositor's type case, in which the small letters are kept. ◆ *adj* **lower-case. 2** of or relating to small letters. ◆ *vb* **lower-case, lower-cases, lower-casing, lower-cased. 3** (*tr*) to print with lower-case letters.

lower class *n* **1** the social stratum having the lowest position in the social hierarchy. ◆ *adj* **lower-class. 2** of or relating to the lower class. **3** inferior or vulgar.

lowerclassman (,ləʊ'klɑːsmən) *n, pl* **lowerclassmen.** *US.* a freshman or sophomore. Also called: **underclassman.**

lower deck *n* **1** the deck of a ship situated immediately above the hold. **2** *Inf.* the petty officers and seamen of a ship collectively.

lower house *n* one of the houses of a bicameral legislature: usually the larger and more representative. Also called: **lower chamber.**

lowermost ('ləʊə,məʊst) *adj* lowest.

lower regions *pl n* (usually preceded by *the*) hell.

lower world *n* **1** the earth as opposed to heaven. **2** another name for **hell.**

lowest common denominator *n* the smallest integer or polynomial that is exactly divisible by each denominator of a set of fractions. Abbrevs.: **lcd, LCD.** Also called: **least common denominator.**

lowest common multiple *n* the smallest number or quantity that is exactly divisible by each member of a set of numbers or quantities. Abbrevs.: **lcm, LCM.** Also called: **least common multiple.**

low frequency *n* a radio-frequency band or a frequency lying between 300 and 30 kilohertz.

Low German *n* a language of N Germany, spoken esp. in rural areas: more closely related to Dutch than to standard High German. Abbrev.: **LG.** Also called: **Plattdeutsch.**

low-key ❶ *or* **low-keyed** *adj* **1** having a low intensity or tone. **2** restrained or subdued. **3** (of a photograph, painting, etc.) having a predominance of dark grey tones or dark colours with few highlights. Cf. **high-key.**

lowland ('ləʊlənd) *n* **1** relatively low ground. **2** (*often pl*) a low generally flat region. ◆ *adj* **3** of or relating to a lowland or lowlands.
▸ **'lowlander** *n*

Lowland ('ləʊlənd) *adj* of or relating to the Lowlands of Scotland or the dialects of English spoken there.

Lowlands ('ləʊləndz) *pl n* **the.** a low generally flat region of central Scotland, around the Forth and Clyde valleys, separating the Southern Uplands from the Highlands.
▸ **'Lowlander** *n*

Low Latin *n* any form of Latin other than the classical, such as Medieval Latin.

low-level language *n* a computer programming language that is closer to machine language than to human language.

low-level waste *n* waste material contaminated by traces of radioactivity that can be disposed of in steel drums in concrete-lined trenches. Cf. **high-level waste, intermediate-level waste.**

lowlife ('ləʊ,laɪf) *n, pl* **lowlifes.** *Sl.* a member or members of the criminal underworld.

low-loader *n* a road or rail vehicle with a low platform for ease of access.

lowly ❶ ('ləʊlɪ) *adj* **lowlier, lowliest. 1** humble or low in position, rank, status, etc. **2** full of humility; meek. **3** simple, unpretentious, or plain. ◆ *adv* **4** in a low or lowly manner.
▸ **'lowliness** *n*

Low Mass *n* a Mass that has a simplified ceremonial form and is spoken rather than sung.

low-minded ❶ *adj* having a vulgar or crude mind and character.
▸ **,low-'mindedly** *adv* ▸ **,low-'mindedness** *n*

low-pass filter *n Electronics.* a filter that transmits all frequencies below a specified value, attenuating frequencies above this value.

low-pitched *adj* **1** pitched low in tone. **2** (of a roof) having sides with a shallow slope.

low-pressure *adj* **1** having, using, or involving a pressure below normal: *a low-pressure gas.* **2** relaxed or calm.

low profile *n* **1** a position or attitude characterized by a deliberate avoidance of prominence or publicity. ◆ *adj* **low-profile. 2** (of a tyre) wide in relation to its height.

low-rise *adj* **1** of or relating to a building having only a few storeys. ◆ *n* **2** such a building.

lowry *or* **lowrie** ('laʊrɪ) *n* variant spellings of **lory.**

THESAURUS

scant, small, sparse, trifling **6** = **inferior,** deficient, inadequate, low-grade, low-rent (*inf., chiefly US*), mediocre, pathetic, poor, puny, second-rate, shoddy, substandard, worthless **7** = **coarse,** common, crude, disgraceful, dishonourable, disreputable, gross, ill-bred, obscene, rough, rude, unbecoming, undignified, unrefined, vulgar **8a** = **lowly,** humble, lowborn, meek, obscure, plain, plebeian, poor, simple, unpretentious **9** = **dejected,** blue, brassed off (*Brit. sl.*), depressed, despondent, disheartened, dismal, down, downcast, down in the dumps (*inf.*), fed up, forlorn, gloomy, glum, miserable, morose, sad, sick as a parrot (*inf.*), unhappy **11** = **quiet,** gentle, hushed, muffled, muted, soft, subdued, whispered **12** = **inexpensive,** cheap, economical, moderate, modest, reasonable **16** = **contemptible,** abject, base, cowardly, dastardly, degraded, depraved, despicable, ignoble, mean, menial, nasty, scurvy, servile, sordid, unworthy, vile, vulgar ◆ *adv* **27a lie low** = **hide,** conceal oneself, go to earth, go underground, hide away, hide out, hole up, keep a low profile, keep out of sight, lurk, skulk, take cover

Antonyms *adj* ≠ **small:** tall, towering ≠ **low-lying:** elevated ≠ **meagre:** important, significant ≠ **dejected:** cheerful, elated, happy, high ≠ **quiet:** loud, noisy ≠ **contemptible:** brave, eminent, exalted, fine, grand, high-ranking, honourable, laudable, lofty, praiseworthy, superior, worthy

low[2] *n* **1** = **mooing,** bellow, bellowing, lowing, moo ◆ *vb* **2** = **moo,** bellow

low-down *Informal adj* **1** = **mean,** base, cheap, contemptible, despicable, low, nasty, reprehensible, scurvy, ugly, underhand ◆ *n* **lowdown 2** = **information,** dope (*inf.*), gen (*Brit. inf.*), info (*inf.*), inside story, intelligence

lower[1] *adj* **1** = **under,** inferior, junior, lesser, low-level, minor, secondary, second-class, smaller, subordinate **2** = **reduced,** curtailed, decreased, diminished, lessened, pared down ◆ *vb* **5** = **drop,** depress, fall, let down, make lower, sink, submerge, take down **6** = **demean,** abase, belittle, condescend, debase, degrade, deign, devalue, disgrace, downgrade, humble, humiliate, stoop **7** = **lessen,** abate, curtail, cut, decrease, diminish, minimize, moderate, reduce, slash **8** = **quieten,** soften, tone down

Antonyms *adj* ≠ **reduced:** enlarged, higher, increased ◆ *vb* ≠ **drop:** elevate, hoist, lift, raise ≠ **lessen:** amplify, augment, boost, enlarge, extend, increase, inflate, magnify, raise

lower[2] *see* **lour**

low-key *adj* **1, 2** = **subdued,** keeping a low profile, low-pitched, muffled, muted, played down, quiet, restrained, toned down, understated

lowly *adj* **1** = **lowborn,** ignoble, inferior, mean, obscure, plebeian, proletarian, subordinate **2** = **humble,** docile, dutiful, gentle, meek, mild, modest, submissive, unassuming **3** = **unpretentious,** average, common, homespun, modest, ordinary, plain, poor, simple

low-minded *adj* = **vulgar,** coarse, crude, dirty, disgusting, filthy, foul, gross, indecent, obscene, rude, smutty, uncouth

low-spirited Ⓣ *adj* depressed or dejected.
▸ **ˌlow-ˈspiritedly** *adv* ▸ **ˌlow-ˈspiritedness** *n*

low tech Ⓣ *n* **1** short for **low technology. 2** a style of interior design using items associated with low technology. ◆ *adj* **low-tech. 3** of or using low technology. **4** of or in the interior design style. ◆ Cf. **hi tech.**

low technology *n* simple unsophisticated technology that is limited to the production of basic necessities.

low-tension *adj* subjected to, carrying, or operating at a low voltage. Abbrev.: **LT.**

low tide *n* **1** the tide when it is at its lowest level or the time at which it reaches this. **2** a lowest point.

lowveld (ˈləʊˌfɛlt) *n* (in South Africa) name for the grasslands of the Transvaal province. [from Afrik. *laeveld*]

low water *n* **1** another name for **low tide. 2** the state of any stretch of water at its lowest level.

low-water mark *n* **1** the level reached at low tide. **2** the lowest point or level; nadir.

lox[1] (lɒks) *n* a kind of smoked salmon. [C19: from Yiddish *laks,* from MHG *lahs* salmon]

lox[2] (lɒks) *n* short for **liquid oxygen,** esp. when used as an oxidizer for rocket fuels.

loyal Ⓣ (ˈlɔɪəl) *adj* **1** showing allegiance. **2** faithful to one's country, government, etc. **3** of or expressing loyalty. [C16: from OF *loial, leial,* from L *lēgālis* LEGAL]
▸ **ˈloyally** *adv*

loyalist (ˈlɔɪəlɪst) *n* a patriotic supporter of his sovereign or government.
▸ **ˈloyalism** *n*

Loyalist (ˈlɔɪəlɪst) *n* **1** (in Northern Ireland) any of the Protestants wishing to retain Ulster's link with Britain. **2** (in North America) an American colonist who supported Britain during the War of American Independence. **3** (in Canada) short for **United Empire Loyalist. 4** (during the Spanish Civil War) a supporter of the republican government.

loyalty Ⓣ (ˈlɔɪəltɪ) *n, pl* **loyalties. 1** the state or quality of being loyal. **2** (*often pl*) allegiance.

loyalty card *n* a swipe card issued by a supermarket or chain store to a customer, used to record credit points awarded for money spent in the store.

lozenge Ⓣ (ˈlɒzɪndʒ) *n* **1** *Med.* a medicated tablet held in the mouth until it has dissolved. **2** *Geom.* another name for **rhombus. 3** *Heraldry.* a diamond-shaped charge. [C14: from OF *losange* of Gaulish origin]
▸ **ˈlozenged** *or* **ˈlozengy** *adj*

LP[1] *n* **1a** a long-playing gramophone record, usually 12 inches (30 cm) in diameter, designed to rotate at 33⅓ revolutions per minute. **1b** (*as modifier*): *an LP sleeve.* **2** long play: a slow-recording facility on a VCR which allows twice the length of material to be recorded on a tape from that of standard play.

LP[2] *abbrev. for:* **1** (in Britain) Lord Provost. **2** Also: **lp.** low pressure.

L/P *Printing abbrev. for* letterpress.

LPG *or* **LP gas** *abbrev. for* liquefied petroleum gas.

L-plate *n Brit.* a white rectangle with an "L" sign fixed to the back and front of a motor vehicle; a red "L" sign shows that the driver has not passed the driving test; a green "L" sign may be displayed by new drivers for up to a year after passing the driving test.

L'pool *abbrev. for* Liverpool.

Lr *the chemical symbol for* lawrencium.

LSD *n* lysergic acid diethylamide; a crystalline compound prepared from lysergic acid, used in experimental medicine and taken illegally as a hallucinogenic drug. Informal name: **acid.**

L.S.D., £.s.d., *or* **l.s.d.** (in Britain, esp. formerly) *abbrev. for* librae, solidi, denarii. [L: pounds, shillings, pence]

LSE *abbrev. for* London School of Economics.

LSO *abbrev. for* London Symphony Orchestra.

Lt *abbrev. for* Lieutenant.

Ltd *or* **ltd** *abbrev. for* limited (liability). US equivalent: **Inc.**

Lu *the chemical symbol for* lutetium.

luau (luːˈaʊ, ˈluːaʊ) *n* a feast of Hawaiian food. [from Hawaiian *lu'au*]

lubber Ⓣ (ˈlʌbə) *n* **1** a big, awkward, or stupid person. **2** short for **landlubber.** [C14 *lobre,* prob. from ON]
▸ **ˈlubberly** *adj, adv* ▸ **ˈlubberliness** *n*

lubber line *n* a mark on a ship's compass that designates the fore-and-aft axis of the vessel. Also called: **lubber's line.**

lubra (ˈluːbrə) *n Austral.* an Aboriginal woman. [C19: from Abor.]

lubricant (ˈluːbrɪkənt) *n* **1** a lubricating substance, such as oil. ◆ *adj* **2** serving to lubricate. [C19: from L *lūbricāns,* present participle of *lūbricāre*]

lubricate Ⓣ (ˈluːbrɪˌkeɪt) *vb* **lubricates, lubricating, lubricated. 1** (*tr*) to cover or treat with an oily substance so as to lessen friction. **2** (*tr*) to make greasy, slippery, or smooth. **3** (*intr*) to act as a lubricant. [C17: from L *lūbricāre,* from *lūbricus* slippery]
▸ **ˌlubriˈcation** *n* ▸ **ˈlubriˌcative** *adj* ▸ **ˈlubriˌcator** *n*

lubricity (luːˈbrɪsɪtɪ) *n* **1** *Formal or literary.* lewdness or salaciousness. **2** *Rare.* smoothness or slipperiness. [C15 (lewdness), C17 (slipperiness): from OF *lubricité,* from Med. L *lubricitās,* from L *lūbricus* slippery]
▸ **lubricious** (luːˈbrɪʃəs) *or* **lubricous** (ˈluːbrɪkəs) *adj*

luce (luːs) *n* another name for the **pike** (the fish). [C14: from OF *lus,* from LL *lūcius* pike]

lucent (ˈluːsᵊnt) *adj* brilliant, shining, or translucent. [C16: from L *lūcēns,* present participle of *lūcēre* to shine]
▸ **ˈlucency** *n* ▸ **ˈlucently** *adv*

lucerne (luːˈsɜːn) *n Brit.* another name for **alfalfa.**

lucid Ⓣ (ˈluːsɪd) *adj* **1** readily understood; clear. **2** shining or glowing. **3** of or relating to a period of normality between periods of insane behaviour. [C16: from L *lūcidus* full of light, from *lūx* light]
▸ **luˈcidity** *or* **ˈlucidness** *n* ▸ **ˈlucidly** *adv*

lucifer (ˈluːsɪfə) *n* a friction match: originally a trade name.

Lucifer (ˈluːsɪfə) *n* **1** the leader of the rebellion of the angels; Satan. **2** the planet Venus when it rises as the morning star. [OE, from L *Lūcifer* light-bearer, from *lūx* light + *ferre* to bear]

luck Ⓣ (lʌk) *n* **1** events that are beyond control and seem subject to chance; fortune. **2** success or good fortune. **3** something considered to bring good luck. **4 down on one's luck.** having little or no good luck to the point of suffering hardships. **5 no such luck.** *Inf.* unfortunately not. **6 try one's luck.** to attempt something that is uncertain. [C15: from MDu. *luc*]

luckless Ⓣ (ˈlʌklɪs) *adj* having no luck; unlucky.
▸ **ˈlucklessly** *adv* ▸ **ˈlucklessness** *n*

lucky Ⓣ (ˈlʌkɪ) *adj* **luckier, luckiest. 1** having or bringing good fortune. **2** happening by chance, esp. as desired.
▸ **ˈluckily** *adv* ▸ **ˈluckiness** *n*

lucky dip *n Brit., Austral., & NZ.* **1** a box filled with sawdust containing small prizes for which children search. **2** *Inf.* an undertaking of uncertain outcome.

lucrative Ⓣ (ˈluːkrətɪv) *adj* producing a profit; profitable. [C15: from OF *lucratif;* see LUCRE]
▸ **ˈlucratively** *adv* ▸ **ˈlucrativeness** *n*

lucre Ⓣ (ˈluːkə) *n Usually facetious.* money or wealth (esp. in **filthy lucre**). [C14: from L *lūcrum* gain]

lucubrate (ˈluːkjʊˌbreɪt) *vb* **lucubrates, lucubrating, lucubrated.** (*intr*) to write or study, esp. at night. [C17: from L *lūcubrāre* to work by lamplight]
▸ **ˈlucuˌbrator** *n*

lucubration (ˌluːkjʊˈbreɪʃən) *n* **1** laborious study, esp. at night. **2** (*often pl*) a solemn literary work.

lud (lʌd) *n Brit.* lord (in **my lud, m'lud**): used when addressing a judge in court.

Luddite (ˈlʌdaɪt) *n Brit. history.* **1** any of the textile workers opposed to mechanization, believing that its use led to unemployment, who organized machine-breaking between 1811 and 1816. **2** any opponent

THESAURUS

low-spirited *adj* = **depressed,** apathetic, blue, brassed off (*Brit. sl.*), dejected, despondent, dismal, down, down-hearted, down in the dumps (*inf.*), down in the mouth, fed up, gloomy, heavy-hearted, low, miserable, moody, sad, unhappy

low tech *adj* **low-tech 3** = **unsophisticated,** basic, simple
Antonyms *adj* high-tech *or* hi-tech, scientific, technical, technological

loyal *adj* **1-3** = **faithful,** attached, constant, dependable, devoted, dutiful, immovable, patriotic, staunch, steadfast, tried and true, true, true-blue, true-hearted, trustworthy, trusty, unswerving, unwavering
Antonyms *adj* disloyal, false, perfidious, traitorous, treacherous, unfaithful, untrustworthy

loyalty *n* **1, 2** = **faithfulness,** allegiance, constancy, dependability, devotion, fealty, fidelity, patriotism, reliability, staunchness, steadfastness, troth (*arch.*), true-heartedness, trueness, trustiness, trustworthiness

lozenge *n* **1** = **tablet,** cough drop, jujube, pastille

lubberly *adj* **1** = **oafish,** awkward, blundering, bungling, churlish, clodhopping (*inf.*), clownish, clumsy, coarse, crude, doltish, gawky, heavy-handed, loutish, lumbering, lumpen (*inf.*), lumpish, uncouth, ungainly

lubricate *vb* **1-3** = **oil,** grease, make slippery, make smooth, oil the wheels, smear, smooth the way

lucid *adj* **1** = **clear,** clear-cut, comprehensible, crystal clear, distinct, evident, explicit, intelligible, limpid, obvious, pellucid, plain, transparent **2** = **bright,** beaming, brilliant, effulgent, gleaming, luminous, radiant, resplendent, shining **3** = **clear-headed,** all there, *compos mentis,* in one's right mind, rational, reasonable, sane, sensible, sober, sound
Antonyms *adj* ≠ **clear:** ambiguous, clear as mud (*inf.*), confused, equivocal, incomprehensible, indistinct, muddled, unclear, unintelligible, vague ≠ **bright:** dull ≠ **clear-headed:** confused, irrational, muddled, unclear, unperceptive, vague

luck *n* **1** = **fortune,** accident, chance, destiny, fate, fortuity, hap (*arch.*), hazard **2** = **good fortune,** advantage, blessing, break (*inf.*), fluke, godsend, good luck, prosperity, serendipity, stroke, success, windfall

luckily *adv* **1** = **fortunately,** favourably, happily, opportunely, propitiously, providentially **2** = **by chance,** as it chanced, as luck would have it, fortuitously

luckless *adj* = **unlucky,** calamitous, cursed, disastrous, doomed, hapless, hopeless, ill-fated, ill-starred, jinxed, star-crossed, unfortunate, unhappy, unpropitious, unsuccessful

lucky *adj* **1** = **fortunate,** advantageous, blessed, charmed, favoured, jammy (*Brit. sl.*), on a roll (*inf.*), prosperous, serendipitous, successful **2** = **fortuitous,** adventitious, auspicious, opportune, propitious, providential, timely
Antonyms *adj* ≠ **fortunate:** bad, detrimental, ominous, unfavourable, unfortunate, unhappy, unlucky, unpromising ≠ **fortuitous:** unlucky, untimely

lucrative *adj* = **profitable,** advantageous, fat, fruitful, gainful, high-income, money-making, paying, productive, remunerative, well-paid

lucre *n Usually facetious* = **money,** gain, mammon, pelf, profit, riches, spoils, wealth of industrial change or innovation. ◆ *adj* **3** of or relating to the Luddites. [C19: alleged to be after Ned *Ludd,* an 18th-century Leicestershire workman, who destroyed industrial machinery]

ludicrous ❶ ('lu:dɪkrəs) *adj* absurd or incongruous to the point of provoking laughter. [C17: from L *lūdicrus* done in sport, from *lūdus* game]
▸**'ludicrously** *adv* ▸**'ludicrousness** *n*

ludo ('lu:dəʊ) *n Brit.* a simple board game in which players advance their counters by throwing dice. [C19: from L: I play]

luff (lʌf) *n* **1** *Naut.* the leading edge of a fore-and-aft sail. ◆ *vb* **2** *Naut.* to head (a sailing vessel) into the wind so that her sails flap. **3** *(intr) Naut.* (of a sail) to flap when the wind is blowing equally on both sides. **4** to move the jib of (a crane) in order to shift a load. [C13 (in the sense: steering gear): from OF *lof,* ?from MDu. *loef* peg of a tiller]

lug[1] ❶ (lʌg) *vb* **lugs, lugging, lugged. 1** to carry or drag (something heavy) with great effort. **2** *(tr)* to introduce (an irrelevant topic) into a conversation or discussion. ◆ *n* **3** the act or an instance of lugging. [C14: prob. from ON]

lug[2] (lʌg) *n* **1** a projecting piece by which something is connected, supported, or lifted. **2** a box or basket for vegetables or fruit. **3** *Inf. or Scot.* another word for **ear**[1]. **4** *Sl.* a man, esp. a stupid or awkward one. [C15 (Scots dialect) *lugge* ear]

lug[3] (lʌg) *n Naut.* short for **lugsail.**

luge (lu:ʒ) *n* **1** a racing toboggan on which riders lie on their backs, descending feet first. ◆ *vb* **luges, luging, luged. 2** *(intr)* to ride or race on a luge. [C20: from F]

Luger ('lu:gə) *n Trademark.* a German 9 mm calibre automatic pistol.

luggage ❶ ('lʌgɪdʒ) *n* suitcases, trunks, etc. [C16: ? from LUG[1], infl. in form by BAGGAGE]

luggage van *n Brit.* a railway carriage used to transport passengers' luggage, bicycles, etc.

lugger ('lʌgə) *n Naut.* a small working boat rigged with a lugsail. [C18: from LUGSAIL]

lughole ('lʌg,həʊl) *n Brit.* an informal word for **ear**[1]. See also **lug**[2] (sense 3).

lugsail ('lʌgsəl) *n Naut.* a four-sided sail bent and hoisted on a yard. [C17: ?from ME (now dialect) *lugge* pole, or from *lugge* ear]

lug screw *n* a small screw without a head.

lugubrious ❶ (lʊ'gu:brɪəs) *adj* excessively mournful; doleful. [C17: from L *lūgubris* mournful, from *lūgēre* to grieve]
▸**lu'gubriously** *adv* ▸**lu'gubriousness** *n*

lugworm ('lʌg,wɜ:m) *n* a worm living in burrows on sandy shores and having tufted gills: much used as bait. Sometimes shortened to **lug.** [C17: from ?]

lukewarm ❶ (,lu:k'wɔ:m) *adj* **1** (esp. of water) moderately warm; tepid. **2** having or expressing little enthusiasm or conviction. [C14 *luke* prob. from OE *hlēow* warm]
▸**,luke'warmly** *adv* ▸**,luke'warmness** *n*

lull ❶ (lʌl) *vb (tr)* **1** to soothe (a person or animal) by soft sounds or motions (esp. in **lull to sleep**). **2** to calm (someone or someone's fears, suspicions, etc.), esp. by deception. ◆ *n* **3** a short period of calm or diminished activity. [C14: ? imit. of crooning sounds; rel. to MLow G *lollen* to soothe, MDu. *lollen* to talk drowsily, mumble]

lullaby ❶ ('lʌlə,baɪ) *n, pl* **lullabies.** **1** a quiet song to lull a child to sleep. ◆ *vb* **lullabies, lullabying, lullabied. 2** *(tr)* to quiet or soothe as with a lullaby. [C16: ? a blend of LULL + GOODBYE]

lumbago (lʌm'beɪgəʊ) *n* pain in the lower back; backache. [C17: from LL, from L *lumbus* loin]

lumbar ('lʌmbə) *adj* of, near, or relating to the part of the body between the lowest ribs and the hipbones. [C17: from NL *lumbāris,* from L *lumbus* loin]

lumbar puncture *n Med.* insertion of a hollow needle into the lower spinal cord to withdraw cerebrospinal fluid, introduce drugs, etc.

lumber[1] ❶ ('lʌmbə) *n* **1** *Chiefly US & Canad.* **1a** logs; sawn timber. **1b** *(as modifier): the lumber trade.* **2** *Brit.* **2a** useless household articles that are stored away. **2b** *(as modifier): lumber room.* ◆ *vb* **3** *(tr)* to pile together in a disorderly manner. **4** *(tr)* to fill up or encumber with useless household articles. **5** *Chiefly US & Canad.* to convert (the trees) of (a forest) into marketable timber. **6** *(tr) Brit. inf.* to burden with something unpleasant, tedious, etc. [C17: ?from a n use of LUMBER[2]]
▸**'lumberer** *n* ▸**'lumbering** *n*

lumber[2] ❶ ('lʌmbə) *vb (intr)* **1** to move or proceed in an awkward heavy manner. **2** an obsolete word for **rumble.** [C14 *lomeren*]
▸**'lumbering** *adj*

lumberjack ('lʌmbə,dʒæk) *n* (esp. in North America) a person whose work involves felling trees, transporting the timber, etc. [C19: from LUMBER[1] + JACK (man)]

lumberjacket ('lʌmbə,dʒækɪt) *n* a boldly coloured, usually checked jacket in warm cloth.

lumberyard ('lʌmbə,jɑ:d) *n* the US and Canad word for **timberyard.**

lumen ('lu:mɪn) *n, pl* **lumens** *or* **lumina** (-mɪnə). **1** the derived SI unit of luminous flux; the flux emitted in a solid angle of 1 steradian by a point source having a uniform intensity of 1 candela. Symbol: lm **2** *Anat.* a passage, duct, or cavity in a tubular organ. **3** a cavity within a plant cell. [C19: NL, from L: light, aperture]
▸**'luminal** *adj*

luminance ('lu:mɪnəns) *n* **1** a state or quality of radiating or reflecting light. **2** a measure (in candelas per square metre) of the brightness of a point on a surface that is radiating or reflecting light. Symbol: *L* [C19: from L *lūmen* light]

luminary ❶ ('lu:mɪnərɪ) *n, pl* **luminaries.** **1** a person who enlightens or influences others. **2** a famous person. **3** *Literary.* something, such as the sun or moon, that gives off light. [C15: via OF, from L *lūmināre* lamp, from *lūmen* light]

luminesce (,lu:mɪ'nɛs) *vb* **luminesces, luminescing, luminesced.** *(intr)* to exhibit luminescence. [back formation from LUMINESCENT]

luminescence ❶ (,lu:mɪ'nɛsəns) *n Physics.* the emission of light at low temperatures by any process other than incandescence. [C19: from L *lūmen* light]
▸**,lumi'nescent** *adj*

luminous ❶ ('lu:mɪnəs) *adj* **1** radiating or reflecting light; shining; glowing: *luminous colours.* **2** *(not in technical use)* exhibiting luminescence: *luminous paint.* **3** full of light; well-lit. **4** (of a physical quantity in photometry) evaluated according to the visual sensation produced in an observer rather than by absolute energy measurements: *luminous intensity.* **5** easily understood; lucid; clear. **6** enlightening or wise. [C15: from L *lūminōsus* full of light, from *lūmen* light]
▸**luminosity** (,lu:mɪ'nɒsɪtɪ) *n* ▸**'luminously** *adv* ▸**'luminousness** *n*

luminous flux *n* a measure of the rate of flow of luminous energy, evaluated according to its ability to produce a visual sensation. It is measured in lumens.

luminous intensity *n* a measure of the amount of light that a point source radiates in a given direction.

lumme *or* **lummy** ('lʌmɪ) *interj Brit.* an exclamation of surprise or dismay. [C19: alteration of *Lord love me*]

lummox ('lʌməks) *n Inf.* a clumsy or stupid person. [C19: from ?]

lump[1] ❶ (lʌmp) *n* **1** a small solid mass without definite shape. **2** *Pathol.* any small swelling or tumour. **3** a collection of things; aggregate. **4** *Inf.* an awkward, heavy, or stupid person. **5 the lump.** *Brit.* self-employed workers in the building trade considered collectively. **6** *(modifier)* in the form of a lump or lumps: *lump sugar.* **7 a lump in one's throat.** a tight dry feeling in one's throat, usually caused by great emotion. **8 in the lump.** collectively; en masse. ◆ *vb* **9** *(tr; often foll. by together)* to collect into a mass or group. **10** *(intr)* to grow into lumps or become lumpy. **11** *(tr)* to consider as a single group, often without justification. **12** *(tr)* to make or cause lumps in or on. **13** *(intr; often foll. by along)* to move in a heavy manner. [C13: prob. rel. to early Du. *lompe* piece, Scand. dialect *lump* block, MHG *lumpe* rag]

lump[2] ❶ (lʌmp) *vb (tr) Inf.* to tolerate or put up with; endure (in **lump it**). [C16: from ?]

lumpectomy (lʌm'pɛktəmɪ) *n, pl* **lumpectomies.** the surgical removal of a tumour in a breast. [C20: from LUMP[1] + -ECTOMY]

lumpen ('lʌmpᵊn) *adj Inf.* stupid or unthinking. [from G *Lump* vagabond, infl. by *Lumpen* rags, as in LUMPENPROLETARIAT]

lumpenproletariat (,lʌmpən,prəʊlɪ'tɛərɪət) *n* (esp. in Marxist theory) the urban social group below the proletariat, consisting of criminals, tramps, etc. [G, lit.: ragged proletariat]

THESAURUS

ludicrous *adj* = **ridiculous,** absurd, comic, comical, crazy, droll, farcical, funny, incongruous, laughable, nonsensical, odd, outlandish, preposterous, silly, zany
Antonyms *adj* grave, logical, sad, sensible, serious, solemn

lug[1] **1** *vb* **1** = **carry,** drag, haul, heave, hump *(Brit. sl.),* pull, tow, yank

luggage *n* = **baggage,** bags, cases, gear, impedimenta, paraphernalia, suitcases, things, trunks

lugubrious *adj* = **gloomy,** dirgelike, dismal, doleful, dreary, funereal, melancholy, morose, mournful, sad, serious, sombre, sorrowful, woebegone, woeful

lukewarm *adj* **1** = **tepid,** blood-warm, warm **2** = **half-hearted,** apathetic, cold, cool, indifferent, phlegmatic, unconcerned, unenthusiastic, uninterested, unresponsive

lull *vb* **1** = **calm,** allay, hush, lullaby, pacify, quell, quiet, rock to sleep, soothe, still, subdue, tranquillize ◆ *n* **3** = **respite,** calm, calmness, hush, let-up *(inf.),* pause, quiet, silence, stillness, tranquillity

lullaby *n* **1** = **cradlesong,** berceuse

lumber[1] *n* **2** *Brit.* = **junk,** castoffs, clutter, discards, jumble, refuse, rubbish, trash, white elephants ◆ *vb* **6** *Brit. informal* = **burden,** encumber, impose upon, land, load, saddle

lumber[2] *vb* **1** = **plod,** clump, lump along, shamble, shuffle, stump, trudge, trundle, waddle

lumbering *adj* **1** = **awkward,** blundering, bovine, bumbling, clumsy, elephantine, heavy, heavy-footed, hulking, lubberly, overgrown, ponderous, ungainly, unwieldy

luminary *n* **2** = **celebrity,** big name, celeb *(inf.),* dignitary, leading light, lion, megastar *(inf.),* notable, personage, somebody, star, V.I.P., worthy

luminescent *adj* = **glowing,** Day-Glo, effulgent, fluorescent, luminous, phosphorescent, radiant, shining

luminous *adj* **1, 3** = **bright,** brilliant, glowing, illuminated, lighted, lit, luminescent, lustrous, radiant, resplendent, shining, vivid **5** = **clear,** evident, intelligible, lucid, obvious, perspicuous, plain, transparent

lump[1] *n* **1** = **piece,** ball, bunch, cake, chunk, clod, cluster, dab, gob, gobbet, group, hunk, mass, nugget, spot, wedge **2** *Pathology* = **swelling,** bulge, bump, growth, hump, protrusion, protuberance, tumescence, tumour ◆ *vb* **9** = **group,** aggregate, bunch, coalesce, collect, combine, conglomerate, consolidate, mass, pool, unite

lump[2] *vb Informal* = **put up with,** bear, brook, en-

lumpfish ('lʌmp,fɪʃ) *n, pl* **lumpfish** *or* **lumpfishes.** a North Atlantic fish having a globular body covered with tubercles, pelvic fins fused into a sucker, and an edible roe. Also called: **lumpsucker.** [C16 *lump* (now obs.) lumpfish, from MDu. *lumpe*, ? rel. to LUMP[1]]

lumpish ❶ ('lʌmpɪʃ) *adj* **1** resembling a lump. **2** stupid, clumsy, or heavy.
▸ **'lumpishly** *adv* ▸ **'lumpishness** *n*

lump sum *n* a relatively large sum of money, paid at one time, esp. in cash.

lumpy ❶ ('lʌmpɪ) *adj* **lumpier, lumpiest. 1** full of or having lumps. **2** (esp. of the sea) rough. **3** (of a person) heavy or bulky.
▸ **'lumpily** *adv* ▸ **'lumpiness** *n*

Luna ('luːnə) *n* the Roman goddess of the moon. [from L: moon]

lunacy ❶ ('luːnəsɪ) *n, pl* **lunacies. 1** (formerly) any severe mental illness. **2** foolishness.

luna moth *n* a large American moth having light green wings with a yellow crescent-shaped marking on each forewing. [C19: from the markings on its wings]

lunar ('luːnə) *adj* **1** of or relating to the moon. **2** occuring on or used on the moon: *lunar module*. **3** relating to, caused by, or measured by the position or orbital motion of the moon. [C17: from L *lūnāris*, from *lūna* the moon]

lunar eclipse *n* See **eclipse.**

lunar module *n* the module used to carry astronauts on a spacecraft to the surface of the moon and back to the spacecraft.

lunar month *n* See **month** (sense 6).

lunar year *n* See **year** (sense 6).

lunate ('luːneɪt) *or* **lunated** *adj Anat., bot.* shaped like a crescent. [C18: from L *lūnātus* crescent-shaped, from *lūna* moon]

lunatic ❶ ('luːnətɪk) *adj* **1** an archaic word for **insane. 2** foolish; eccentric. ◆ *n* **3** a person who is insane. [C13 (adj): via OF from LL *lūnāticus* crazy, moonstruck, from L *lūna* moon]

lunatic asylum *n Offens.* an institution for the mentally ill.

lunatic fringe *n* the members of a society who adopt views regarded as fanatical.

lunch (lʌntʃ) *n* **1** a meal eaten during the middle of the day. ◆ *vb* **2** (*intr*) to eat lunch. **3** (*tr*) to provide or buy lunch for. [C16: prob. short form of LUNCHEON]
▸ **'luncher** *n*

luncheon ('lʌntʃən) *n* a lunch, esp. a formal one. [C16: prob. var. of *nuncheon*, from ME *noneschench*, from *none* NOON + *schench* drink]

luncheon meat *n* a ground mixture of meat (often pork) and cereal, usually tinned.

luncheon voucher *n* a voucher worth a specified amount issued to employees and redeemable at a restaurant for food. Abbrev.: **LV.**

lunchroom ('lʌntʃ,ruːm, -,rʊm) *n US & Canad.* a room where lunch is served or where students, employees, etc., may eat lunches they bring.

lunette (luː'nɛt) *n* **1** anything that is shaped like a crescent. **2** an oval or circular opening to admit light in a dome. **3** a semicircular panel containing a window, mural, or sculpture. **4** a type of fortification like a detached bastion. **5** Also called: **lune.** *RC Church.* a case fitted with a bracket to hold the consecrated host. [C16: from F: crescent, from *lune* moon, from L *lūna*]

lung (lʌŋ) *n* **1** either one of a pair of spongy saclike respiratory organs within the thorax of higher vertebrates, which oxygenate the blood and remove its carbon dioxide. **2 at the top of one's lungs.** in one's loudest voice; yelling. [OE *lungen*]

lunge[1] ❶ (lʌndʒ) *n* **1** a sudden forward motion. **2** *Fencing.* a thrust made by advancing the front foot and straightening the back leg, extending the sword arm forwards. ◆ *vb* **lunges, lunging, lunged. 3** to move or cause to move with a lunge. **4** (*intr*) *Fencing.* to make a lunge. [C18: short form of obs. C17 *allonge*, from F *allonger* to stretch out (one's arm) from LL *ēlongāre* to lengthen]
▸ **'lunger** *n*

lunge[2] (lʌndʒ) *n* **1** a rope used in training or exercising a horse. ◆ *vb* **lunges, lunging, lunged. 2** to exercise or train (a horse) on a lunge. [C17: from OF *longe*, shortened from *allonge*, ult. from L *longus* long]

lungfish ('lʌŋ,fɪʃ) *n, pl* **lungfish** *or* **lungfishes.** a freshwater bony fish having an air-breathing lung, fleshy paired fins, and an elongated body.

lungwort ('lʌŋ,wɜːt) *n* **1** any of several Eurasian plants which have spotted leaves and clusters of blue or purple flowers: formerly used to treat lung diseases. **2** See **oyster plant.**

lunula ('luːnjʊlə) *n, pl* **lunulae** (-njʊ,liː). the white crescent-shaped area at the base of the human fingernail. Nontechnical name: **half-moon.** [C16: from L: small moon, from *lūna*]

Lupercalia (,luːpɜː'keɪlɪə) *n, pl* **Lupercalia** *or* **Lupercalias.** an ancient Roman festival of fertility, celebrated on Feb. 15. [L, from *Lupercālis* belonging to *Lupercus*, a Roman god of the flocks]
▸ **,Luper'calian** *adj*

lupin *or US* **lupine** ('luːpɪn) *n* a leguminous plant of North America, Europe, and Africa, with large spikes of brightly coloured flowers and flattened pods. [C14: from L *lupīnus* wolfish (see LUPINE); from the belief that the plant ravenously exhausted the soil]

lupine ('luːpaɪn) *adj* of, relating to, or resembling a wolf. [C17: from L *lupīnus*, from *lupus* wolf]

lupus ('luːpəs) *n* any of various ulcerative skin diseases. [C16: via Med. L from L: wolf; so called because it rapidly eats away the affected part]

lupus vulgaris (vʌl'gɛərɪs) *n* tuberculosis of the skin, esp. of the face. Sometimes shortened to **lupus.**

lurch[1] ❶ (lɜːtʃ) *vb* (*intr*) **1** to lean or pitch suddenly to one side. **2** to stagger. ◆ *n* **3** the act or an instance of lurching. [C19: from ?]

lurch[2] (lɜːtʃ) *n* **1 leave (someone) in the lurch.** to desert (someone) in trouble. **2** *Cribbage.* the state of a losing player with less than 30 points at the end of a game. [C16: from F *lourche* a game similar to backgammon, from *lourche* (adj) deceived, prob. of Gmc origin]

lurch[3] (lɜːtʃ) *vb* (*intr*) *Arch. or dialect.* to prowl suspiciously. [C15: ? a var. of LURK]

lurcher ('lɜːtʃə) *n* **1** a crossbred hunting dog, esp. one trained to hunt silently. **2** *Arch.* a person who prowls or lurks. [C16: from LURCH[3]]

lure ❶ (lʊə) *vb* **lures, luring, lured.** (*tr*) **1** (sometimes foll. by *away* or *into*) to tempt or attract by the promise of some type of reward. **2** *Falconry.* to entice (a hawk or falcon) from the air to the falconer by a lure. ◆ *n* **3** a person or thing that lures. **4** *Angling.* any of various types of brightly coloured artificial spinning baits. **5** *Falconry.* a feathered decoy to which small pieces of meat can be attached. [C14: from OF *loirre* falconer's lure, from Gmc]
▸ **'lurer** *n*

Lurex ('lʊərɛks) *n* **1** *Trademark.* a thin metallic thread coated with plastic. **2** fabric containing such thread, which makes it glitter.

lurgy ('lɜːgɪ) *n, pl* **lurgies.** *Facetious.* any undetermined illness. [C20: from ?]

lurid ❶ ('lʊərɪd) *adj* **1** vivid in shocking detail; sensational. **2** horrible in savagery or violence. **3** pallid in colour; wan. **4** glowing with an unnatural glare. [C17: from L *lūridus* pale yellow]
▸ **'luridly** *adv* ▸ **'luridness** *n*

lurk ❶ (lɜːk) *vb* (*intr*) **1** to move stealthily or be concealed, esp. for evil purposes. **2** to be present in an unobtrusive way; be latent. ◆ *n* **3** *Austral. & NZ sl.* a scheme for success. [C13: prob. frequentative of LOUR]
▸ **'lurker** *n*

lurking ('lɜːkɪŋ) *adj* lingering but almost unacknowledged: *a lurking suspicion.*

luscious ❶ ('lʌʃəs) *adj* **1** extremely pleasurable, esp. to the taste or smell. **2** very attractive. **3** *Arch.* cloying. [C15 *lucius, licius*, ? short for DELICIOUS]
▸ **'lusciously** *adv* ▸ **'lusciousness** *n*

lush[1] ❶ (lʌʃ) *adj* **1** (of vegetation) abounding in lavish growth. **2** (esp. of fruits) succulent and fleshy. **3** luxurious, elaborate, or opulent. [C15: prob. from OF *lasche* lazy, from L *laxus* loose]
▸ **'lushly** *adv* ▸ **'lushness** *n*

lush[2] (lʌʃ) *Sl.* ◆ *n* **1** a heavy drinker, esp. an alcoholic. **2** alcoholic drink. ◆ *vb* **3** *US & Canad.* to drink (alcohol) to excess. [C19: from ?]

lust ❶ (lʌst) *n* **1** a strong desire for sexual gratification. **2** a strong desire

THESAURUS

dure, hack (*sl.*), stand, suffer, take, thole (*N English dialect*), tolerate

lumpish *adj* **2** = **clumsy**, awkward, bungling, doltish, elephantine, gawky, heavy, lethargic, lumbering, oafish, obtuse, puddingy, stolid, stupid, ungainly

lumpy *adj* **1** = **bumpy**, clotted, curdled, full of lumps, grainy, granular, knobbly, uneven

lunacy *n* **1** = **insanity**, dementia, derangement, idiocy, madness, mania, psychosis **2** = **foolishness**, aberration, absurdity, craziness, folly, foolhardiness, idiocy, imbecility, madness, senselessness, stupidity, tomfoolery
Antonyms *n* ≠ **insanity:** reason, sanity ≠ **foolishness:** prudence, reason, sense

lunatic *adj* **1, 2** = **irrational**, as daft as a brush (*inf., chiefly Brit.*), barking (*sl.*), barking mad (*sl.*), barmy (*sl.*), bonkers (*sl., chiefly Brit.*), crack-brained, crackpot (*inf.*), crazy, daft, demented, deranged, insane, loopy (*inf.*), mad, maniacal, not the full shilling (*inf.*), nuts (*sl.*), off one's trolley (*sl.*), out to lunch (*inf.*), psychotic, unhinged, up the pole (*inf.*) ◆ *n* **3** = **madman**, headbanger (*inf.*), headcase (*inf.*), loony (*sl.*), maniac, nut (*sl.*), nutcase (*sl.*), nutter (*Brit. sl.*), psychopath

lunge[1] **1** *n* **1** = **spring**, charge, pounce, swing, swipe (*inf.*) **2** *Fencing* = **thrust**, cut, jab, pass, stab ◆ *vb* **3** = **spring**, bound, charge, dash, dive, fall upon, hit at, leap, pitch into (*inf.*), plunge, pounce, set upon, strike at **4** *Fencing* = **thrust**, cut, jab, stab

lurch[1] *vb* **1** = **tilt**, heave, heel, lean, list, pitch, rock, roll, wallow **2** = **stagger**, reel, stumble, sway, totter, weave

lure *vb* **1** = **tempt**, allure, attract, beckon, decoy, draw, ensnare, entice, inveigle, invite, lead on, seduce ◆ *n* **3** = **temptation**, allurement, attraction, bait, carrot (*inf.*), come-on (*inf.*), decoy, enticement, incentive, inducement, magnet, siren song

lurid *adj* **1** = **sensational**, exaggerated, graphic, melodramatic, shock-horror (*facetious*), shocking, startling, unrestrained, vivid, yellow (*of journalism*) **2** = **gruesome**, disgusting, ghastly, gory, grim, grisly, macabre, revolting, savage, violent **3** = **pallid**, ashen, ghastly, pale, sallow, wan **4** = **glaring**, bloody, fiery, flaming, glowering, intense, livid, overbright, sanguine
Antonyms *adj* ≠ **sensational:** breezy, carefree, controlled, factual, jaunty, light-hearted, mild ≠ **glaring:** pale, pastel, watery

lurk *vb* **1** = **hide**, conceal oneself, crouch, go furtively, lie in wait, move with stealth, prowl, skulk, slink, sneak, snoop

luscious *adj* **1** = **delicious**, appetizing, delectable, honeyed, juicy, mouth-watering, palatable, rich, savoury, scrumptious (*inf.*), succulent, sweet, toothsome, yummy (*sl.*)

lush[1] *adj* **1** = **abundant**, dense, flourishing, green, lavish, overgrown, prolific, rank, teeming, verdant **2** = **succulent**, fresh, juicy, ripe, tender **3** = **luxurious**, elaborate, extravagant, grand, lavish, opulent, ornate, palatial, plush (*inf.*), ritzy (*sl.*), sumptuous

lust *n* **1** = **lechery**, carnality, concupiscence, las-

or drive. ◆ *vb* **3** (*intr;* often foll. by *after* or *for*) to have a lust (for). [OE]
▸**'lustful** *adj* ▸**'lustfully** *adv* ▸**'lustfulness** *n*

lustral ('lʌstrəl) *adj* of or relating to a ceremony of purification. [C16: from L *lūstrālis* (adj) from LUSTRUM]

lustrate ('lʌstreɪt) *vb* **lustrates, lustrating, lustrated.** (*tr*) to purify by means of religious rituals or ceremonies. [C17: from L *lūstrāre* to brighten]
▸**lus'tration** *n*

lustre Ⓣ *or US* **luster** ('lʌstə) *n* **1** reflected light; sheen; gloss. **2** radiance or brilliance of light. **3** great splendour of accomplishment, beauty, etc. **4** a dress fabric of cotton and wool with a glossy surface. **5** a vase or chandelier from which hang cut-glass drops. **6** a drop-shaped piece of cut glass or crystal used as such a decoration. **7** a shiny metallic surface on some pottery and porcelain. **8** *Mineralogy.* the way in which light is reflected from the surface of a mineral. ◆ *vb* **lustres, lustring, lustred** *or US* **lusters, lustering, lustered. 9** to make, be, or become lustrous. [C16: from OF, from OIt. *lustro,* from L *lustrāre* to make bright]
▸**'lustreless** *or US* **'lusterless** *adj* ▸**'lustrous** *adj*

lustreware *or US* **lusterware** ('lʌstə,wɛə) *n* pottery with lustre decoration.

lustrum ('lʌstrəm) *or* **lustre** *n, pl* **lustrums, lustra** (-trə), *or* **lustres.** *Rare.* a period of five years. [C16: from L: ceremony of purification, from *lustrāre* to brighten, purify]

lusty Ⓣ ('lʌstɪ) *adj* **lustier, lustiest. 1** having or characterized by robust health. **2** strong or invigorating.
▸**'lustily** *adv* ▸**'lustiness** *n*

lute[1] (luːt) *n* an ancient plucked stringed instrument with a long fretted fingerboard and a body shaped like a sliced pear. [C14: from OF *lut,* from Ar. *al 'ūd,* lit.: the wood]

lute[2] (luːt) *n* **1** a mixture of cement and clay used to seal the joints between pipes, etc. **2** *Dentistry.* a thin layer of cement used to fix a crown or inlay in place on a tooth. ◆ *vb* **lutes, luting, luted. 3** (*tr*) to seal (a joint or surface) with lute. [C14: via OF ult. from L *lutum* clay]

lutein ('luːtɪɪn) *n* a xanthophyll pigment, occurring in plants, that has a light-absorbing function in photosynthesis. [C20: from L *lūteus* yellow + -IN]

luteinizing hormone ('luːtɪɪ,naɪzɪŋ) *n* a hormone secreted by the anterior lobe of the pituitary gland. In female vertebrates it stimulates ovulation, and in mammals it also induces corpus luteum formation. In male vertebrates it promotes maturation of the interstitial cells of the testes and stimulates androgen secretion. [C19: from L *lūteum* egg yolk, from *lūteus* yellow]

lutenist, lutanist, ('luːtənɪst) *or US & Canad.* (*sometimes*) **lutist** ('luːtɪst) *n* a person who plays the lute. [C17: from Med. L *lūtānista,* from *lūtāna,* apparently from OF *lut* LUTE[1]]

lutetium *or* **lutecium** (luˈtiːʃɪəm) *n* a silvery-white metallic element of the lanthanide series. Symbol: Lu; atomic no.: 71; atomic wt.: 174.97. [C19: NL, from L *Lūtētia* ancient name of Paris, home of G. Urbain (1872–1938), F chemist, who discovered it]

Lutheran ('luːθərən) *n* **1** a follower of Martin Luther (1483–1546), German leader of the Protestant Reformation, or a member of the Lutheran Church. ◆ *adj* **2** of or relating to Luther or his doctrines. **3** of or denoting any of the Churches that follow Luther's doctrines.
▸**'Lutheranism** *n*

Lutine bell ('luːtiːn, luː'tiːn) *n* a bell, taken from the ship *Lutine,* kept at Lloyd's in London and rung before important announcements, esp. the loss of a vessel.

lux (lʌks) *n, pl* **lux.** the derived SI unit of illumination equal to a luminous flux of 1 lumen per square metre. [C19: from L: light]

luxate ('lʌkseɪt) *vb* **luxates, luxating, luxated.** (*tr*) *Pathol.* to dislocate (a shoulder, knee, etc.). [C17: from L *luxāre* to displace, from *luxus* dislocated]
▸**lux'ation** *n*

luxe (lʌks, lʊks; *French* lyks) *n* See **de luxe.** [C16: from F from L *luxus* extravagance]

luxuriant Ⓣ (lʌg'zjʊərɪənt) *adj* **1** rich and abundant; lush. **2** very elaborate or ornate. **3** extremely productive or fertile. [C16: from L *luxuriāns,* present participle of *luxuriāre* to abound to excess]
▸**lux'uriance** *n* ▸**lux'uriantly** *adv*

> **USAGE NOTE** See at **luxurious.**

luxuriate Ⓣ (lʌg'zjʊərɪ,eɪt) *vb* **luxuriates, luxuriating, luxuriated.** (*intr*) **1** (foll. by *in*) to take voluptuous pleasure; revel. **2** to flourish profusely. **3** to live in a sumptuous way. [C17: from L *luxuriāre*]
▸**lux,uri'ation** *n*

luxurious Ⓣ (lʌg'zjʊərɪəs) *adj* **1** characterized by luxury. **2** enjoying or devoted to luxury. [C14: via OF from L *luxuriōsus* excessive]
▸**lux'uriously** *adv* ▸**lux'uriousness** *n*

> **USAGE NOTE** *Luxurious* is sometimes wrongly used where *luxuriant* is meant: *he had a luxuriant* (not *luxurious*) *moustache; the walls were covered with a luxuriant growth of wisteria.*

luxury Ⓣ ('lʌkʃərɪ) *n, pl* **luxuries. 1** indulgence in and enjoyment of rich and sumptuous living. **2** (*sometimes pl*) something considered an indulgence rather than a necessity. **3** something pleasant and satisfying: *the luxury of independence.* **4** (*modifier*) relating to, indicating, or supplying luxury: *a luxury liner.* [C14 (in the sense: lechery): via OF from L *luxuria* excess, from *luxus* extravagance]

LV *abbrev. for* luncheon voucher.

LW *abbrev. for:* **1** *Radio.* long wave. **2** low water.

lx *Physics. symbol for* lux.

LXX *symbol for* Septuagint.

-ly[1] *suffix forming adjectives.* **1** having the nature or qualities of: *godly.* **2** occurring at certain intervals; every: *daily.* [OE *-lic*]

-ly[2] *suffix forming adverbs.* in a certain manner; to a certain degree: *quickly; recently; chiefly.* [OE *-lice,* from *-lic* -LY[1]]

lyase ('laɪeɪz) *n* any enzyme that catalyses the separation of two parts of a molecule by the formation of a double bond between them. [C20: from Gk *lusis* a loosening + -ASE]

lycanthropy (laɪ'kænθrəpɪ) *n* **1** the supposed magical transformation of a human being into a wolf. **2** *Psychiatry.* a delusion in which a person believes that he is a wolf. [C16: from Gk *lukanthrōpia,* from *lukos* wolf + *anthrōpos* man]
▸**lycanthrope** ('laɪkən,θrəʊp) *n* ▸**lycanthropic** (,laɪkən'θrɒpɪk) *adj*

lycée ('liːseɪ) *n, pl* **lycées** (-seɪz). *Chiefly French.* a secondary school. [C19: F, from L: *Lyceum* a school in ancient Athens]

lyceum (laɪ'sɪəm) *n* (now chiefly in the names of buildings) **1** a public building for concerts, lectures, etc. **2** *US.* a cultural organization responsible for presenting concerts, lectures, etc.

lychee (,laɪ'tʃiː) *n* a variant spelling of **litchi.**

lych gate *or* **lich gate** (lɪtʃ) *n* a roofed gate to a churchyard, formerly used as a temporary shelter for the bier. [C15: *lich,* from OE *līc* corpse]

lychnis ('lɪknɪs) *n* any of a genus of plants having red, pink, or white five-petalled flowers: includes ragged robin. [C17: NL, via L, from Gk *lukhnis* a red flower]

lycopodium (,laɪkə'pəʊdɪəm) *n* **1** any of a genus of club moss resembling moss but having woody tissue and spore-bearing cones. **2** a flammable yellow powder from the spores of this plant, used in medicine and in making fireworks. [C18: NL, from Gk, from *lukos* wolf + *pous* foot]

Lycra ('laɪkrə) *n Trademark.* a type of synthetic elastic fabric and fibre used for tight-fitting garments, such as swimming costumes.

lyddite ('lɪdaɪt) *n* an explosive consisting chiefly of fused picric acid. [C19: after *Lydd,* town in Kent near which the first tests were made]

lye (laɪ) *n* **1** any solution obtained by leaching, such as the caustic solution obtained by leaching wood ash. **2** a concentrated solution of sodium hydroxide or potassium hydroxide. [OE *lēag*]

lying[1] Ⓣ ('laɪɪŋ) *vb* the present participle and gerund of **lie**[1].

THESAURUS

civiousness, lewdness, libido, licentiousness, pruriency, randiness (*inf., chiefly Brit.*), salaciousness, sensuality, the hots (*sl.*), wantonness **2 = desire**, appetence, appetite, avidity, covetousness, craving, cupidity, greed, longing, passion, thirst ◆ *vb* **3** *often foll. by* **after** *or* **for** = **desire**, be consumed with desire for, covet, crave, hunger for *or* after, lech after (*inf.*), need, slaver over, want, yearn

lustful *adj* **1 = lascivious**, carnal, concupiscent, craving, hankering, horny (*sl.*), hot-blooded, lecherous, lewd, libidinous, licentious, passionate, prurient, randy (*inf., chiefly Brit.*), raunchy (*sl.*), sensual, sexy (*inf.*), unchaste, wanton

lustily *adv* **2 = vigorously**, forcefully, hard, loudly, powerfully, strongly, with all one's might, with might and main

lustre *n* **1 = sparkle**, burnish, gleam, glint, glitter, gloss, glow, sheen, shimmer, shine **2 = radiance**, brightness, brilliance, dazzle, lambency, luminousness, resplendence **3 = glory**, distinction, fame, honour, illustriousness, prestige, renown

lustreless *adj* **1, 2 = dull**, colourless, dingy, drab, faded, flat, lacklustre, lifeless, matt, pale, tarnished, unpolished, washed out

lustrous *adj* **1, 2 = shining**, bright, burnished, dazzling, gleaming, glistening, glossy, glowing, luminous, radiant, shimmering, shiny, sparkling

lusty *adj* **1 = vigorous**, brawny, energetic, hale, healthy, hearty, in fine fettle, powerful, red-blooded (*inf.*), robust, rugged, stalwart, stout, strapping, strong, sturdy, virile

luxuriant *adj* **1 = abundant**, ample, copious, excessive, lavish, plenteous, plentiful, prodigal, profuse, superabundant **2 = elaborate**, baroque, corinthian, decorated, extravagant, fancy, festooned, flamboyant, florid, flowery, ornate, rococo, sumptuous **3 = fertile**, dense, exuberant, fecund, flourishing, fruitful, lush, overflowing, productive, prolific, rank, rich, riotous, teeming, thriving
Antonyms *adj* ≠ **abundant:** meagre, scanty, sparse, thin ≠ **elaborate:** plain, simple, unadorned

luxuriate *vb* **1 = enjoy**, bask, delight, flourish, indulge, relish, revel, wallow **2 = flourish**, abound, bloom, burgeon, grow, prosper, thrive **3 = live in luxury**, be in clover, have the time of one's life, live the life of Riley, take it easy

luxurious *adj* **1 = sumptuous**, comfortable, costly, de luxe, expensive, lavish, magnificent, opulent, plush (*inf.*), rich, ritzy (*sl.*), splendid, well-appointed **2 = pleasure-loving**, epicurean, pampered, self-indulgent, sensual, sybaritic, voluptuous
Antonyms *adj* ascetic, austere, deprived, economical, plain, poor, sparing, Spartan, thrifty

luxury *n* **1, 3 = pleasure**, bliss, comfort, delight, enjoyment, gratification, hedonism, indulgence, opulence, richness, satisfaction, voluptuousness, wellbeing **2 = extravagance**, extra, frill, indulgence, nonessential, treat
Antonyms *n* ≠ **pleasure:** austerity, deprivation, destitution, difficulty, discomfort, hardship, misery, poverty, privation, want ≠ **extravagance:** necessity, need

lying[1] *n* **1 = dishonesty**, deceit, dissimulation,

lying[2] ('laɪɪŋ) *vb* the present participle and gerund of **lie**[2].

lying-in *n, pl* **lyings-in.** confinement in childbirth.

lyke-wake ('laɪk,weɪk) *n Brit.* a watch held over a dead person, often with festivities. [C16: ?from ON]

Lyme disease (laɪm) *n* a disease of domestic animals and humans, caused by a spirochaete and transmitted by ticks, and affecting the joints, heart, and brain. [C20: after *Lyme*, Connecticut, the town where it was first identified in humans]

lymph (lɪmf) *n* the almost colourless fluid, containing chiefly white blood cells, that is collected from the tissues of the body and transported in the lymphatic system. [C17: from L *lympha* water, from earlier *limpa*, infl. in form by Gk *numphē* nymph]

lymphatic (lɪm'fætɪk) *adj* **1** of, relating to, or containing lymph. **2** of or relating to the lymphatic system. **3** sluggish or lacking vigour. ◆ *n* **4** a lymphatic vessel. [C17 (meaning: mad): from L *lymphāticus*. Original meaning ?from a confusion between *nymph* and LYMPH]

lymphatic system *n* an extensive network of capillary vessels that transports the interstitial fluid of the body as lymph to the venous blood circulation.

lymphatic tissue *n* tissue, such as the lymph nodes, tonsils, spleen, and thymus, that produces lymphocytes.

lymph gland *n* a former name for **lymph node.**

lymph node *n* any of numerous bean-shaped masses of tissue, situated along the course of lymphatic vessels, that help to protect against infection and are a source of lymphocytes.

lympho- *or before a vowel* **lymph-** *combining form.* indicating lymph or the lymphatic system: *lymphocyte.*

lymphocyte ('lɪmfəʊ,saɪt) *n* a type of white blood cell formed in lymphatic tissue.
▸**lymphocytic** (,lɪmfəʊ'sɪtɪk) *adj*

lymphoid ('lɪmfɔɪd) *adj* of or resembling lymph, or relating to the lymphatic system.

lymphoma (lɪm,fəʊmə) *n* cancer of the lymph nodes. Also called: **lymphosarcoma** (,lɪmfəʊsɑː'kəʊmə).

lynch (lɪntʃ) *vb* (*tr*) (of a mob) to punish (a person) for some supposed offence by hanging without a trial. [orig. *Lynch's law;* ? after Capt. William *Lynch* (1742–1820) of Virginia, USA]
▸'**lyncher** *n* ▸'**lynching** *n*

lynchet ('lɪntʃɪt) *n* a terrace or ridge formed in prehistoric or medieval times by ploughing a hillside. [OE *hlinc* ridge]

lynch law *n* the practice of punishing a person by mob action without a proper trial.

lynchpin ('lɪntʃ,pɪn) *n* a variant spelling of **linchpin.**

lynx (lɪŋks) *n, pl* **lynxes** *or* **lynx. 1** a feline mammal of Europe and North America, with grey-brown mottled fur, tufted ears, and a short tail. **2** the fur of this animal. **3 bay lynx.** another name for **bobcat. 4 desert lynx.** another name for **caracal.** [C14: via L from Gk *lunx*]
▸'**lynx,like** *adj*

lynx-eyed *adj* having keen sight.

Lyon King of Arms ('laɪən) *n* the chief herald of Scotland. Also called: **Lord Lyon.** [C14: archaic spelling of LION, referring to the figure on the royal shield]

lyrate ('laɪərɪt) *adj* **1** shaped like a lyre. **2** (of leaves) having a large terminal lobe and smaller lateral lobes. [C18: from NL *lyrātus, from* L *lyra* LYRE]

lyre ('laɪə) *n* an ancient Greek stringed instrument consisting of a resonating tortoise shell to which a crossbar was attached by two projecting arms. It was plucked with a plectrum and used for accompanying songs. [C13: via OF from L *lyra,* from Gk *lura*]

lyrebird ('laɪə,bɜːd) *n* either of two pheasant-like Australian birds: during courtship displays, the male spreads its tail into the shape of a lyre.

lyric ❶ ('lɪrɪk) *adj* **1** (of poetry) **1a** expressing the writer's personal feelings and thoughts. **1b** having the form and manner of a song. **2** of or relating to such poetry. **3** (of music) having songlike qualities. **4** (of a singing voice) having a light quality and tone. **5** intended for singing, esp. (in classical Greece) to the accompaniment of the lyre. ◆ *n* **6** a short poem of songlike quality. **7** (*pl*) the words of a popular song. ◆ Also (for senses 1–4): **lyrical.** [C16: from L *lyricus,* from Gk *lurikos,* from *lura* lyre]
▸'**lyrically** *adv* ▸'**lyricalness** *n*

lyrical ❶ ('lɪrɪkᵊl) *adj* **1** another word for **lyric** (senses 1–4). **2** enthusiastic; effusive.

lyricism ('lɪrɪ,sɪzəm) *n* **1** the quality or style of lyric poetry. **2** emotional outpouring.

lyricist ('lɪrɪsɪst) *n* **1** a person who writes the words for a song, opera, or musical play. **2** Also called: **lyrist.** a lyric poet.

lyse (laɪs, laɪz) *vb* **lyses, lysing, lysed.** to undergo or cause to undergo lysis.

lysergic acid diethylamide (lɪ'sɜːdʒɪk; daɪ,eθɪl'eɪmaɪd) *n* See **LSD.**

lysin ('laɪsɪn) *n* any of a group of antibodies that cause dissolution of cells.

lysis ('laɪsɪs) *n, pl* **lyses** (-siːz). **1** the destruction of cells by the action of a particular lysin. **2** *Med.* the gradual reduction in the symptoms of a disease. [C19: NL, from Gk, from *luein* to release]

-lysis *n combining form.* indicating a loosening, decomposition, or breaking down: *electrolysis; paralysis.* [from Gk, from *lusis* a loosening; see LYSIS]

Lysol ('laɪsɒl) *n Trademark.* a solution containing a mixture of cresols in water, used as an antiseptic and disinfectant.

-lyte *n combining form.* indicating a substance that can be decomposed or broken down: *electrolyte.* [from Gk *lutos* soluble, from *luein* to loose]

-lytic *adj combining form.* indicating a loosening or dissolving: *paralytic.* [from Gk, from *lusis;* see -LYSIS]

THESAURUS

double-dealing, duplicity, fabrication, falsity, fibbing, guile, mendacity, perjury, prevarication, untruthfulness ◆ *adj* **2** = **deceitful**, dishonest, dissembling, double-dealing, false, guileful, mendacious, perfidious, treacherous, two-faced, untruthful

Antonyms *adj* ≠ **deceitful**: candid, forthright, frank, honest, reliable, sincere, straight, straightforward, truthful, veracious

lyric *adj* **1** = **songlike**, expressive, lyrical, melodic, musical **3, 4** = **melodic**, clear, dulcet, flowing, graceful, light ◆ *n* **7** *plural* = **words**, book, libretto, text, words of a song

lyrical *adj* **2** = **enthusiastic**, carried away, ecstatic, effusive, emotional, expressive, impassioned, inspired, rapturous, rhapsodic

Mm

m *or* **M** (ɛm) *n, pl* **m's, M's,** *or* **Ms. 1** the 13th letter of the English alphabet. **2** a speech sound represented by this letter, as in *mat.*

m *symbol for:* **1** metre(s). **2** mile(s). **3** milli-. **4** minute(s).

M *symbol for:* **1** mach. **2** *Currency.* mark(s). **3** medium. **4** mega-. **5** million. **6** (in Britain) motorway. **7** *the Roman numeral for* 1000.

m. *abbrev. for:* **1** *Cricket.* maiden (over). **2** male. **3** mare. **4** married. **5** masculine. **6** meridian. **7** month.

M. *abbrev. for:* **1** Majesty. **2** Manitoba. **3** Master. **4** Medieval. **5** (in titles) Member. **6** million. **7** (*pl* **MM.** *or* **MM**) Also: **M** *French.* Monsieur. [F equivalent of *Mr*]

m- *prefix* short for **meta-** (sense 4).

M'- *prefix* a variant of **Mac-.**

ma (mɑː) *n* an informal word for **mother.**

MA *abbrev. for:* **1** Massachusetts. **2** Master of Arts. **3** Military Academy.

ma'am (mæm, mɑːm; *unstressed* məm) *n* short for **madam:** used as a title of respect, esp. for female royalty.

mac *or* **mack** (mæk) *n Brit. inf.* short for **mackintosh.**

Mac (mæk) *n Chiefly US & Canad.* an informal term of address to a man. [C20: abstracted from MAC-]

Mac-, Mc-, *or* **M'-** *prefix* (in surnames of Scottish or Irish Gaelic origin) son of: *MacDonald.* [from Goidelic *mac* son of]

macabre Ⓣ (məˈkɑːbə, -brə) *adj* gruesome; ghastly; grim. [C15: from OF *danse macabre* dance of death, prob. from *macabé* relating to the Maccabees, who were associated with death because of the doctrines and prayers for the dead in II Macc. (12:43–46)]

macadam (məˈkædəm) *n* a road surface made of compressed layers of small broken stones, esp. one that is bound together with tar or asphalt. [C19: after John *McAdam* (1756–1836), Scot. engineer, the inventor]

macadamia (ˌmækəˈdeɪmɪə) *n* **1** an Australian tree having clusters of small white flowers and edible nutlike seeds. **2 macadamia nut.** the seed. [C19: NL, after John *Macadam* (died 1865), Australian chemist]

macadamize *or* **macadamise** (məˈkædəˌmaɪz) *vb* **macadamizes, macadamizing, macadamized** *or* **macadamises, macadamising, macadamised.** (*tr*) to construct or surface (a road) with macadam.
▸**macˌadamiˈzation** *or* **macˌadamiˈsation** *n* ▸**macˈadamˌizer** *or* **macˈadamˌiser** *n*

macaque (məˈkɑːk) *n* any of various Old World monkeys of Asia and Africa. Typically the tail is short or absent and cheek pouches are present. [C17: from F, from Port. *macaco,* from W African *makaku,* from *kaku* monkey]

macaroni *or* **maccaroni** (ˌmækəˈrəʊnɪ) *n, pl* **macaronis, macaronies** *or* **maccaronis, maccaronies. 1** pasta tubes made from wheat flour. **2** (in 18th-century Britain) a dandy who affected foreign manners and style. [C16: from It. (dialect) *maccarone,* prob. from Gk *makaria* food made from barley]

macaroon (ˌmækəˈruːn) *n* a kind of sweet biscuit made of ground almonds, sugar, and egg whites. [C17: via F *macaron* from It. *maccarone* MACARONI]

Macassar oil (məˈkæsə) *n* an oily preparation formerly put on the hair to make it smooth and shiny. [C19: from *Makasar,* town in Indonesia]

macaw (məˈkɔː) *n* a large tropical American parrot having a long tail and brilliant plumage. [C17: from Port. *macau,* from ?]

Macc. *abbrev. for* Maccabees (books of the Apocrypha).

McCarthyism (məˈkɑːθɪˌɪzəm) *n Chiefly US.* **1** the practice of making unsubstantiated accusations of disloyalty or Communist leanings. **2** the use of unsupported accusations for any purpose. [C20: after Joseph *McCarthy* (1908–57), US senator]
▸**McˈCarthyist** *n, adj*

McCoy (məˈkɔɪ) *n Sl.* the genuine person or thing (esp. in **the real McCoy**). [C20: ? after Kid *McCoy,* professional name of Norman Selby (1873–1940), American boxer, who was called "the real McCoy" to distinguish him from another boxer of that name]

mace[1] (meɪs) *n* **1** a club, usually having a spiked metal head, used esp. in the Middle Ages. **2** a ceremonial staff carried by certain officials. **3** See **macebearer. 4** an early form of billiard cue. [C13: from OF, prob. from Vulgar L *mattea* (unattested); apparently rel. to L *mateola* mallet]

mace[2] (meɪs) *n* a spice made from the dried aril round the nutmeg seed. [C14: formed as a singular from OF *macis* (wrongly assumed to be pl), from L *macir* a spice]

macebearer (ˈmeɪsˌbɛərə) *n* a person who carries a mace in processions or ceremonies.

macedoine (ˌmæsɪˈdwɑːn) *n* **1** a mixture of diced vegetables. **2** a mixture of fruit in a syrup or in jelly. **3** any mixture; medley. [C19: from F, lit.: Macedonian, alluding to the mixture of nationalities in Macedonia]

macerate (ˈmæsəˌreɪt) *vb* **macerates, macerating, macerated. 1** to soften or separate or be softened or separated as a result of soaking. **2** to become or cause to become thin. [C16: from L *mācerāre* to soften]
▸**ˌmacerˈation** *n* ▸**ˈmacerˌator** *n*

MacGuffin (məˈgʌfɪn) *n* an object or event in a book or a film that serves as the impetus for the plot. [C20: coined (c. 1935) by Sir Alfred Hitchcock (1899–1980), Brit. film director]

Mach (mæk) *n* short for **Mach number.**

mach. *abbrev. for:* **1** machine. **2** machinery. **3** machinist.

machair (ˈmæxər) *n Scot.* (in the western Highlands and islands of Scotland) a strip of sandy grassy land just above the shore: used for grazing, etc. [C17: from Scot. Gaelic]

machete (məˈʃɛtɪ, -ˈtʃeɪ-) *n* a broad heavy knife used for cutting or as a weapon, esp. in parts of Central and South America. [C16 *macheto,* from Sp. *machete,* from *macho* club, ?from Vulgar L *mattea* (unattested) club]

Machiavellian Ⓣ (ˌmækɪəˈvɛlɪən) *adj* **1** of or relating to the alleged political principles of the Florentine statesman Machiavelli (1469–1527); cunning, amoral, and opportunist. ◆ *n* **2** a cunning, amoral, and opportunist person, esp. a politician.
▸**ˌMachiaˈvellianˌism** *n*

machicolate (məˈtʃɪkəʊˌleɪt) *vb* **machicolates, machicolating, machicolated.** (*tr*) to construct machicolations at the top of (a wall). [C18: from OF *machicoller,* ult. from Provençal *machacol,* from *macar* to crush + *col* neck]

machicolation (məˌtʃɪkəʊˈleɪʃən) *n* **1** (esp. in medieval castles) a projecting gallery or parapet having openings through which missiles could be dropped. **2** any such opening.

machinate (ˈmækɪˌneɪt) *vb* **machinates, machinating, machinated.** (*usually tr*) to contrive, plan, or devise (schemes, plots, etc.). [C17: from L *māchinārī* to plan, from *māchina* MACHINE]
▸**ˈmachiˌnator** *n*

machination Ⓣ (ˌmækɪˈneɪʃən) *n* **1** a plot or scheme. **2** the act of devising plots or schemes.

machine Ⓣ (məˈʃiːn) *n* **1** an assembly of interconnected components arranged to transmit or modify force in order to perform useful work. **2** a device for altering the magnitude or direction of a force, such as a lever or screw. **3** a mechanically operated device or means of transport, such as a car or aircraft. **4** any mechanical or electrical device that automatically performs tasks or assists in performing tasks. **5** any intricate structure or agency. **6** a mechanically efficient, rigid, or obedient person. **7** an organized body of people that controls activities, policies, etc. ◆ *vb* **machines, machining, machined. 8** (*tr*) to shape, cut, or remove (excess material) from (a workpiece) using a machine tool. **9** to use a machine to carry out a process on (something). [C16: via F from L *māchina* machine, from Doric Gk *makhana* pulley]
▸**maˈchinable** *or* **maˈchineable** *adj* ▸**maˌchinaˈbility** *n*

machine code *or* **language** *n* instructions for the processing of data in a binary, octal, or hexadecimal code that can be understood and executed by a computer.

machine-down time *n* a period during which a machine, computer, etc., is out of service, because it is out of order or being serviced.

machine gun *n* **1a** a rapid-firing automatic gun, using small-arms ammunition. **1b** (*as modifier*): *machine-gun fire.* ◆ *vb* **machine-gun, machine-guns, machine-gunning, machine-gunned. 2** (*tr*) to shoot or fire at with a machine gun.
▸**machine gunner** *n*

machine learning *n* a branch of artificial intelligence in which a computer generates rules underlying or based on raw data that has been fed into it.

machinery Ⓣ (məˈʃiːnərɪ) *n, pl* **machineries. 1** machines, machine parts, or machine systems collectively. **2** a particular machine system or set of machines. **3** a system similar to a machine.

machine shop *n* a workshop in which machine tools are operated.

machine tool *n* a power-driven machine, such as a lathe, for cutting, shaping, and finishing metals, etc.
▸**maˈchine-ˌtooled** *adj*

machinist (məˈʃiːnɪst) *n* **1** a person who operates machines to cut or process materials. **2** a maker or repairer of machines.

THESAURUS

macabre *adj* = **gruesome,** cadaverous, deathlike, deathly, dreadful, eerie, frightening, frightful, ghastly, ghostly, ghoulish, grim, grisly, hideous, horrid, morbid, unearthly, weird
Antonyms *adj* appealing, beautiful, charming, delightful, lovely, pleasant

Machiavellian *adj* **1** = **scheming,** amoral, artful, astute, crafty, cunning, cynical, deceitful, designing, double-dealing, foxy, intriguing, opportunist, perfidious, shrewd, sly, underhand, unscrupulous, wily

machination *n* **1** = **plot,** artifice, cabal, conspiracy, design, device, dodge, intrigue, manoeuvre, ploy, ruse, scheme, stratagem, trick

machine *n* **1-4** = **appliance,** apparatus, contraption, contrivance, device, engine, instrument, mechanism, tool **5** = **system,** agency, machinery, organization, party, setup (*inf.*), structure

machinery *n* **1, 2** = **equipment,** apparatus, gear, instruments, mechanism, tackle, tools, works **3** = **procedure,** agency, channels, machine, organization, structure, system

machismo (mæ'kɪzməʊ, -'tʃɪz-) *n* strong or exaggerated masculinity. [Mexican Sp., from Sp. *macho* male, from L *masculus* MASCULINE]

Mach number *n* (*often not cap.*) the ratio of the speed of a body in a particular medium to the speed of sound in that medium. Mach number 1 corresponds to the speed of sound. [C19: after Ernst *Mach* (1838–1916), Austrian physicist & philosopher]

macho ⓣ ('mætʃəʊ) *adj* **1** strongly or exaggeratedly masculine. ◆ *n, pl* **machos. 2** a strong virile man. [see MACHISMO]

mack (mæk) *n Brit. inf.* short for **mackintosh.**

mackerel ('mækrəl) *n, pl* **mackerel** *or* **mackerels. 1** a spiny-finned food fish occurring in northern coastal regions of the Atlantic and in the Mediterranean. It has a deeply forked tail and a greenish-blue body marked with wavy dark bands on the back. **2** any of various related fishes. [C13: from Anglo-F, from OF *maquerel,* from ?]

mackerel sky *n* a sky patterned with cirrocumulus or small altocumulus clouds. [from similarity to pattern on mackerel's back]

mackintosh *or* **macintosh** ('mækɪn,tɒʃ) *n* **1** a waterproof raincoat made of rubberized cloth. **2** such cloth. **3** any raincoat. [C19: after Charles *Macintosh* (1760–1843), who invented it]

McNaughten Rules *or* **McNaghten Rules** (mək'nɔːtᵊn) *pl n* (in English law) a set of rules established by the case of Regina v. McNaughten (1843) by which legal proof of criminal insanity depends on the accused being shown to be incapable of understanding what he has done.

macramé (mə'krɑːmɪ) *n* a type of ornamental work made by knotting and weaving coarse thread. [C19: via F & It. from Turkish *makrama* towel, from Ar. *migramah* striped cloth]

macro ('mækrəʊ) *n, pl* **macros. 1** *Photog.* a camera lens used for close-up photography. Also called: **macro lens. 2** *Computing.* a single computer instruction that initiates a set of instructions. Also called: **macro instruction.** [C20: from Gk *makros* large]

macro- *or before a vowel* **macr-** *combining form.* **1** large, long, or great in size or duration: *macroscopic.* **2** *Pathol.* indicating abnormal enlargement or overdevelopment: *macrocephaly.* [from Gk *makros* large]

macrobiotics (,mækrəʊbaɪ'ɒtɪks) *n* (*functioning as sing*) a dietary system which advocates whole grains and vegetables grown without chemical additives. [C20: from MACRO- + Gk *biotos* life + -ICS]
▸**,macrobi'otic** *adj*

macrocarpa (,mækrəʊ'kɑːpə) *n* a large Californian coniferous tree, used in New Zealand and elsewhere to form shelter belts on farms and for rough timber. [C19: from NL, from MACRO- + Gk *karpos* fruit]

macrocephaly (,mækrəʊ'sɛfəlɪ) *n* the condition of having an abnormally large head or skull.
▸**macrocephalic** (,mækrəʊsɪ'fælɪk) *or* **,macro'cephalous** *adj*

macroclimate ('mækrəʊ,klaɪmɪt) *n* the predominant climate over a large area.

macrocosm ('mækrə,kɒzəm) *n* a complex structure, such as the universe or society, regarded as an entirety. Cf. **microcosm.** [C16: via F & L from Gk *makros kosmos* great world]
▸**,macro'cosmic** *adj* ▸**,macro'cosmically** *adv*

macroeconomics (,mækrəʊ,iːkə'nɒmɪks, -,ɛk-) *n* (*functioning as sing*) the branch of economics concerned with aggregates, such as national income, consumption, and investment.
▸**,macro,eco'nomic** *adj*

macromolecule (,mækrəʊ'mɒlɪ,kjuːl) *n* any very large molecule, such as a protein or synthetic polymer.

macron ('mækrɒn) *n* a diacritical mark (ˉ) placed over a letter to represent a long vowel. [C19: from Gk *makron* something long, from *makros* long]

macropod ('mækrəʊ,pɒd) *n* any member of a family of marsupials consisting of the kangaroos and related animals.

macroscopic (,mækrəʊ'skɒpɪk) *adj* **1** large enough to be visible to the naked eye. **2** comprehensive; concerned with large units. [C19: see MACRO-, -SCOPIC]
▸**,macro'scopically** *adv*

macula ('mækjʊlə) *or* **macule** ('mækjuːl) *n, pl* **maculae** (-jʊ,liː) *or* **macules.** *Anat.* **1** a small spot or area of distinct colour, esp. the macula lutea. **2** any small discoloured spot or blemish on the skin, such as a freckle. [C14: from L]
▸**'macular** *adj* ▸**,macu'lation** *n*

macula lutea ('luːtɪə) *n, pl* **maculae luteae** ('luːtɪ,iː). a small yellowish oval-shaped spot on the retina of the eye, where vision is especially sharp. [NL, lit.: yellow spot]

macular degeneration *n* pathological changes in the macula lutea, resulting in loss of central vision: a common cause of blindness in the elderly.

mad ⓣ (mæd) *adj* **madder, maddest. 1** mentally deranged; insane. **2** senseless; foolish. **3** (often foll. by *at*) *Inf.* angry; resentful. **4** (foll. by *about, on,* or *over;* often *postpositive*) wildly enthusiastic (about) or fond (of). **5** extremely excited or confused; frantic: *a mad rush.* **6** temporarily overpowered by violent reactions, emotions, etc.: *mad with grief.* **7** (of animals) **7a** unusually ferocious: *a mad buffalo.* **7b** afflicted with rabies. **8 like mad.** *Inf.* with great energy, enthusiasm, or haste. ◆ *vb* **mads, madding, madded. 9** *US or arch.* to make or become mad; act or cause to act as if mad. [OE *gemǣded,* p.p. of *gemǣdan* to render insane]

madam ('mædəm) *n, pl* **madams** *or* (for sense 1) **mesdames. 1** a polite term of address for a woman, esp. one of relatively high social status. **2** a woman who runs a brothel. **3** *Brit. inf.* a precocious or pompous little girl. [C13: from OF *ma dame* my lady]

madame ('mædəm) *n, pl* **mesdames.** a married Frenchwoman: used as a title equivalent to *Mrs,* and sometimes extended to older unmarried women to show respect. [C17: from F; see MADAM]

madcap ⓣ ('mæd,kæp) *adj* **1** impulsive, reckless, or lively. ◆ *n* **2** an impulsive, reckless, or lively person.

mad cow disease *n* an informal name for **BSE.**

madden ⓣ ('mædᵊn) *vb* to make or become mad or angry.
▸**'maddening** *adj* ▸**'maddeningly** *adv*

madder ('mædə) *n* **1** a plant having small yellow flowers and a red fleshy root. **2** this root. **3** a dark reddish-purple dye formerly obtained from this root. **4** a red lake obtained from alizarin and an inorganic base; used as a pigment in inks and paints. [OE *mædere*]

madding ('mædɪŋ) *adj Arch.* **1** acting or behaving as if mad: *the madding crowd.* **2** making mad; maddening.
▸**'maddingly** *adv*

made (meɪd) *vb* **1** the past tense and past participle of **make.** ◆ *adj* **2** artificially produced. **3** (*in combination*) produced or shaped as specified: *handmade.* **4 get** *or* **have it made.** *Inf.* to be assured of success.

Madeira (mə'dɪərə) *n* a rich strong fortified white wine made on Madeira, a Portuguese island in the N Atlantic.

madeleine ('mædəlɪn, -,leɪn) *n* a small fancy sponge cake. [C19: ? after *Madeleine* Paulmier, F pastry cook]

mademoiselle (,mædmwə'zɛl) *n, pl* **mesdemoiselles. 1** a young unmarried French girl or woman: used as a title equivalent to *Miss.* **2** a French teacher or governess. [C15: F, from *ma* my + *demoiselle* DAMSEL]

made-up ⓣ *adj* **1** invented; fictional. **2** wearing make-up. **3** put together. **4** (of a road) surfaced with tarmac, concrete, etc.

madhouse ⓣ ('mæd,haʊs) *n Inf.* **1** a mental hospital or asylum. **2** a state of uproar or confusion.

madly ⓣ ('mædlɪ) *adv* **1** in an insane or foolish manner. **2** with great speed and energy. **3** *Inf.* extremely or excessively: *I love you madly.*

madman ⓣ ('mædmən) *or* (*fem*) **madwoman** *n, pl* **madmen** *or* **madwomen.** a person who is insane.

THESAURUS

macho *adj* **1** = **manly,** butch (*sl.*), chauvinist, he-man, masculine, virile

mad *adj* **1** = **insane,** aberrant, bananas (*sl.*), barking mad (*sl.*), barmy (*sl.*), batty (*sl.*), bonkers (*sl., chiefly Brit.*), crackers (*Brit. sl.*), crackpot (*inf.*), crazed, crazy (*inf.*), demented, deranged, distracted, doolally (*sl.*), frantic, frenzied, loony (*sl.*), loopy (*inf.*), lunatic, mental (*sl.*), *non compos mentis,* not right in the head, nuts (*sl.*), nutty (*sl.*), of unsound mind, out of one's mind, out to lunch (*inf.*), psychotic, rabid, raving, round the bend (*Brit. sl.*), round the twist (*Brit. sl.*), screwy (*inf.*), unbalanced, unhinged, unstable, up the pole (*inf.*) **2** = **foolish,** absurd, as daft as a brush (*inf., chiefly Brit.*), asinine, daft (*inf.*), foolhardy, imprudent, inane, irrational, ludicrous, nonsensical, preposterous, senseless, unreasonable, unsafe, unsound, wild **3** *Informal* = **angry,** ape (*sl.*), berserk, choked, cross, enraged, exasperated, fit to be tied (*sl.*), fuming, furious, incandescent, incensed, infuriated, irate, irritated, livid (*inf.*), raging, resentful, seeing red (*inf.*), wild, wrathful **4** = **enthusiastic,** ardent, avid, crazy (*inf.*), daft (*inf.*), devoted, dotty (*sl., chiefly Brit.*), enamoured, fanatical, fond, hooked, impassioned, infatuated, in love with, keen, nuts (*sl.*), wild, zealous **5** = **frenzied,** abandoned, agitated, boisterous, ebullient, energetic, excited, frenetic, full-on (*inf.*), gay, riotous, uncontrolled, unrestrained, wild **8 like mad** *Informal* = **energetically,** enthusiastically, excitedly, furiously, hell for leather, like greased lightning (*inf.*), like lightning, like nobody's business (*inf.*), like the clappers (*Brit. inf.*), madly, quickly, rapidly, speedily, unrestrainedly, violently, wildly, with might and main
Antonyms *adj* ≠ **insane:** rational, sane ≠ **foolish:** sensible, sound ≠ **angry:** appeased, calm, composed, cool, mollified ≠ **enthusiastic:** nonchalant, uncaring

madcap *adj* **1** = **reckless,** crackpot, crazy, foolhardy, hare-brained, heedless, hot-headed, ill-advised, imprudent, impulsive, lively, rash, thoughtless, wild ◆ *n* **2** = **daredevil,** hothead, tearaway, wild man

madden *vb* = **infuriate,** aggravate, annoy, craze, dement, derange, drive one crazy, enrage, exasperate, gall, get one's back up, get one's dander up (*inf.*), get one's goat (*sl.*), get one's hackles up, incense, inflame, irritate, make one's blood boil, make one see red (*inf.*), make one's hackles rise, provoke, put one's back up, raise one's hackles, unhinge, upset, vex
Antonyms *vb* appease, calm, mollify, pacify, soothe

made-up *adj* **1** = **false,** fabricated, fictional, imaginary, invented, make-believe, mythical, specious, trumped-up, unreal, untrue

madhouse *Informal n* **1** = **mental hospital,** funny farm (*facetious*), insane asylum, laughing academy (*US sl.*), loony bin (*sl.*), lunatic asylum, mental institution, nuthouse (*sl.*), psychiatric hospital, rubber room (*US sl.*) **2** = **chaos,** Babel, bedlam, pandemonium, turmoil, uproar

madly *adv* **1** = **insanely,** crazily, deliriously, dementedly, distractedly, frantically, frenziedly, hysterically, rabidly **1** = **foolishly,** absurdly, irrationally, ludicrously, nonsensically, senselessly, unreasonably, wildly **2** = **energetically,** excitedly, furiously, hastily, hell for leather, hotfoot, hurriedly, like greased lightning (*inf.*), like lightning, like mad (*inf.*), like nobody's business (*inf.*), like the clappers (*Brit. inf.*), quickly, rapidly, recklessly, speedily, violently, wildly **3** *Informal* = **passionately,** desperately, devotedly, exceedingly, excessively, extremely, intensely, to distraction

madman *n* = **lunatic,** headbanger (*inf.*), headcase (*inf.*), loony (*sl.*), maniac, mental case

madness ❶ ('mædnɪs) *n* **1** insanity; lunacy. **2** extreme anger, excitement, or foolishness. **3** a nontechnical word for **rabies.**

Madonna (mə'dɒnə) *n* **1** *Chiefly RC Church.* a designation of the Virgin Mary. **2** (*sometimes not cap.*) a picture or statue of the Virgin Mary. [C16: It., from *ma* my + *donna* lady]

Madonna lily *n* a perennial widely cultivated Mediterranean lily plant with white trumpet-shaped flowers.

madras ('mædrəs, mə'dræs) *n* **1** a strong fine cotton or silk fabric, usually with a woven stripe. **2** a medium-hot curry: *chicken madras.* [from *Madras,* city in S India]

madrepore (ˌmædrɪ'pɔː) *n* any coral of the genus *Madrepora,* many of which occur in tropical seas and form large coral reefs. [C18: via F from It. *madrepora* mother-stone]
▸ˌ**madre'poral, madreporic** (ˌmædrɪ'pɒrɪk), *or* ˌ**madre'porian** *adj*

madrigal ('mædrɪgᵊl) *n* **1** *Music.* a type of 16th- or 17th-century part song for unaccompanied voices, with an amatory or pastoral text. **2** a short love poem. [C16: from It., from Med. L *mātrīcāle* primitive, apparently from L *mātrīcālis,* from *matrix* womb]
▸'**madrigal**ˌ**esque** *adj* ▸**madrigalian** (ˌmædrɪ'gælɪən, -'geɪ-) *adj* ▸'**madrigalist** *n*

Maecenas (miː'siːnæs) *n* a wealthy patron of the arts. [after Gaius *Maecenas* (?70–8 B.C.), Roman statesman and patron of Horace and Virgil]

maelstrom ❶ ('meɪlstrəʊm) *n* **1** a large powerful whirlpool. **2** any turbulent confusion. [C17: from obs. Du. *maelstroom,* from *malen* to whirl round + *stroom* STREAM]

maenad ('miːnæd) *n* **1** *Classical history.* a woman participant in the orgiastic rites of Dionysus, Greek god of wine. **2** a frenzied woman. [C16: from L *Maenas,* from Gk *mainas* madwoman]
▸**mae'nadic** *adj*

maestoso (maɪ'stəʊsəʊ) *Music.* ◆ *adj, adv* **1** to be performed majestically. ◆ *n, pl* **maestosos. 2** a piece or passage directed to be played in this way. [C18: It.: majestic, from L *māiestās* MAJESTY]

maestro ❶ ('maɪstrəʊ) *n, pl* **maestri** (-trɪ) *or* **maestros. 1** a distinguished music teacher, conductor, or musician. **2** any master of an art: often used as a term of address. [C18: It.: master]

mae west (meɪ) *n Sl.* an inflatable life jacket, esp. as issued to the US armed forces. [C20: after *Mae West* (1892–1980), US actress, renowned for her large bust]

MAFF (in Britain) *abbrev. for* Ministry of Agriculture, Fisheries, and Food.

Mafia ('mæfɪə) *n* **1 the.** an international secret criminal organization founded in Sicily, and carried to the US by Italian immigrants. **2** any group considered to resemble the Mafia. [C19: from Sicilian dialect of It., lit.: hostility to the law, ?from Ar. *mahyah* bragging]

mafioso (ˌmæfɪ'əʊsəʊ) *n, pl* **mafiosos** *or* **mafiosi** (-sɪ). a person belonging to the Mafia.

mag. *abbrev. for:* **1** magazine. **2** magnesium. **3** magnetic. **4** magnetism. **5** magnitude.

magainin (mə'geɪnɪn) *n* any of a series of related substances with antibiotic properties, derived from the skins of frogs. [C20: from Heb. *magain* a shield]

magazine ❶ (ˌmægə'ziːn) *n* **1** a periodical paperback publication containing articles, fiction, photographs, etc. **2** a metal case holding several cartridges used in some firearms; it is removed and replaced when empty. **3** a building or compartment for storing weapons, explosives, military provisions, etc. **4** a stock of ammunition. **5** *Photog.* another name for **cartridge** (sense 3). **6** a rack for automatically feeding slides through a projector. **7** a TV or radio programme made up of a series of short nonfiction items. [C16: via F *magasin* from It. *magazzino,* from Ar. *makhāzin,* pl. of *makhzan* storehouse, from *khazana* to store away]

magdalen ('mægdəlɪn) *or* **magdalene** ('mægdəˌliːn) *n* **1** *Literary.* a reformed prostitute. **2** *Rare.* a reformatory for prostitutes. [from Mary *Magdalene* (New Testament), a woman from Magdala in Israel, often identified with the sinful woman of Luke 7:36–50]

Magdalenian (ˌmægdə'liːnɪən) *adj* **1** of or relating to the latest Palaeolithic culture in Europe, which ended about 10 000 years ago. ◆ *n* **2 the.** the Magdalenian culture. [C19: from F *magdalénien,* after *La Madeleine,* village in Dordogne, France, near which artefacts of the culture were found]

Magellanic cloud (ˌmægɪ'lænɪk) *n* either of two small irregular galaxies near the S celestial pole. Distances: 163 000 light years (Large Magellanic Cloud), 196 000 light years (Small Magellanic Cloud).

magenta (mə'dʒentə) *n* **1a** a deep purplish red. **1b** (*as adj*): *a magenta filter.* **2** another name for **fuchsin.** [C19: after *Magenta,* Italy, alluding to the blood shed in a battle there (1859)]

maggot ('mægət) *n* **1** the limbless larva of dipterous insects, esp. the housefly and blowfly. **2** *Rare.* a fancy or whim. [C14: from earlier *mathek;* rel. to ON *mathkr* worm, OE *matha,* OHG *mado* grub]

maggoty ('mægətɪ) *adj* **1** of, like, or ridden with maggots. **2** *Austral. sl.* angry.

magi ('meɪdʒaɪ) *pl n, sing* **magus** ('meɪgəs). **1** See **magus. 2 the three Magi.** the wise men from the East who came to do homage to the infant Jesus (Matthew 2:1–12). [see MAGUS]
▸**magian** ('meɪdʒɪən) *adj*

magic ❶ ('mædʒɪk) *n* **1** the art that, by use of spells, supposedly invokes supernatural powers to influence events; sorcery. **2** the practice of this art. **3** the practice of illusory tricks to entertain; conjuring. **4** any mysterious or extraordinary quality or power. **5 like magic.** very quickly. ◆ *adj also* **magical. 6** of or relating to magic. **7** possessing or considered to possess mysterious powers. **8** unaccountably enchanting. **9** *Inf.* wonderful; marvellous. ◆ *vb* **magics, magicking, magicked.** *(tr)* **10** to transform or produce by or as if by magic. **11** (foll. by *away*) to cause to disappear as if by magic. [C14: via OF *magique,* from Gk *magikē* witchcraft, from *magos* MAGUS]
▸'**magically** *adv*

magic bullet *n Inf.* any therapeutic agent, esp. one in the early stages of development, reputed to be very effective in treating a condition, such as a malignant tumour, by specifically targeting the diseased tissue.

magic eye *n* a miniature cathode-ray tube in some radio receivers, on the screen of which a pattern is displayed to assist tuning. Also called: **electric eye.**

magician ❶ (mə'dʒɪʃən) *n* **1** another term for **conjuror. 2** a person who practises magic. **3** a person with extraordinary skill, influence, etc.

magic lantern *n* an early type of slide projector.

magic mushroom *n Inf.* any of various types of fungi that contain a hallucinogenic substance.

magic realism *or* **magical realism** *n* a style of painting or writing that depicts images or scenes of surreal fantasy in a representational or realistic way.
▸**magic realist** *or* **magical realist** *n*

magic square *n* a square array of rows of integers arranged so that the sum of the integers is the same when taken vertically, horizontally, or diagonally.

Maginot line ('mæʒɪˌnəʊ) *n* **1** a line of fortifications built by France to defend its border with Germany prior to World War II; it proved ineffective. **2** any line of defence in which blind confidence is placed. [after André *Maginot* (1877–1932), F minister of war when the fortifications were begun in 1929]

magisterial ❶ (ˌmædʒɪ'stɪərɪəl) *adj* **1** commanding; authoritative. **2** domineering; dictatorial. **3** of or relating to a teacher or person of similar status. **4** of or relating to a magistrate. [C17: from LL *magisteriālis,* from *magister* master]
▸ˌ**magis'terially** *adv*

magistracy ('mædʒɪstrəsɪ) *or* **magistrature** ('mædʒɪstrəˌtjʊə) *n, pl* **magistracies** *or* **magistratures. 1** the office or function of a magistrate. **2** magistrates collectively. **3** the district under the jurisdiction of a magistrate.

magistral (mə'dʒɪstrəl) *adj* **1** *Pharmacol.* made up according to a special prescription. **2** of a master; masterly. [C16: from L *magistrālis,* from *magister* master]
▸**magistrality** (ˌmædʒɪ'strælɪtɪ) *n*

magistrate ❶ ('mædʒɪˌstreɪt, -strɪt) *n* **1** a public officer concerned with the administration of law. **2** another name for **justice of the peace.** [C17: from L *magistrātus,* from *magister* master]
▸'**magis**ˌ**trateship** *n*

magistrates' court *n* (in England) a court held before two or more justices of the peace or a stipendiary magistrate to deal with minor crimes, certain civil actions, and preliminary hearings.

Maglemosian *or* **Maglemosean** (ˌmæglə'məʊzɪən) *n* **1** the first Mesolithic culture of N Europe, dating from 8000 B.C. to about 5000 B.C. ◆ *adj* **2** designating or relating to this culture. [C20: after the site at *Maglemose,* Denmark, where the culture was first classified]

magma ('mægmə) *n, pl* **magmas** *or* **magmata** (-mətə). **1** a paste or suspension consisting of a finely divided solid dispersed in a liquid. **2** hot molten rock within the earth's crust which sometimes finds its way to the surface where it solidifies to form igneous rock. [C15: from L:

THESAURUS

(*sl.*), nut (*sl.*), nutcase (*sl.*), nutter (*Brit. sl.*), psycho (*sl.*), psychopath, psychotic

madness *n* **1 = insanity**, aberration, craziness, delusion, dementia, derangement, distraction, lunacy, mania, mental illness, psychopathy, psychosis **2 = anger**, exasperation, frenzy, fury, ire, rage, raving, wildness, wrath **2 = frenzy**, abandon, agitation, excitement, furore, intoxication, riot, unrestraint, uproar **2 = foolishness**, absurdity, daftness (*inf.*), folly, foolhardiness, idiocy, nonsense, preposterousness, wildness

maelstrom *n* **1 = whirlpool**, vortex **2 = turmoil**, bedlam, chaos, confusion, disorder, pandemonium, tumult, upheaval, uproar

maestro *n* **2 = master**, expert, genius, virtuoso

magazine *n* **1 = journal**, pamphlet, paper, periodical **3 = storehouse**, ammunition dump, arsenal, depot, powder room (*obs.*), store, warehouse

magic *n* **1, 2 = sorcery**, black art, enchantment, necromancy, occultism, sortilege, spell, theurgy, witchcraft, wizardry **3 = conjuring**, hocus-pocus, illusion, jiggery-pokery (*inf., chiefly Brit.*), jugglery, legerdemain, prestidigitation, sleight of hand, trickery **4 = charm**, allurement, enchantment, fascination, glamour, magnetism, power ◆ *adj* **8 = miraculous**, bewitching, charismatic, charming, enchanting, entrancing, fascinating, magnetic, marvellous, spellbinding

magician *n* **1, 2 = sorcerer**, archimage (*rare*), conjuror *or* conjuror, enchanter *or* enchantress, illusionist, necromancer, thaumaturge (*rare*), theurgist, warlock, witch, wizard **3 = miracle-worker**, genius, marvel, spellbinder, virtuoso, wizard, wonder-worker

magisterial *adj* **1 = authoritative**, commanding, imperious, lordly, masterful
Antonyms *adj* deferential, diffident, humble, servile, shy, submissive, subservient, wimpish *or* wimpy (*inf.*)

magistrate *n* **1, 2 = judge**, bailie, J.P., justice, justice of the peace, provost (*Scot.*)

dregs (of an ointment), from Gk: salve made by kneading, from *massein* to knead]
▸**magmatic** (mæg'mætɪk) *adj*

Magna Carta *or* **Magna Charta** ('mægnə 'kɑːtə) *n English history.* the charter granted by King John at Runnymede in 1215, recognizing the rights and privileges of the barons, church, and freemen. [Med. L: great charter]

magnanimity ❶ (ˌmægnə'nɪmɪtɪ) *n, pl* **magnanimities.** generosity. [C14: via OF from L *magnanimitās,* from *magnus* great + *animus* soul]

magnanimous ❶ (mæg'nænɪməs) *adj* generous and noble. [C16: from L *magnanimus* great-souled]
▸**mag'nanimously** *adv*

magnate ❶ ('mægneɪt, -nɪt) *n* **1** a person of power and rank, esp. in industry. **2** *History.* a great nobleman. [C15: back formation from earlier *magnates,* from LL: great men, from L *magnus* great]
▸**'magnate,ship** *n*

magnesia (mæg'niːʃə) *n* another name for **magnesium oxide.** [C14: via Med. L from Gk *Magnēsia,* of *Magnēs,* ancient mineral-rich region]
▸**mag'nesian** *or* **magnesic** (mæg'niːsɪk) *adj*

magnesium (mæg'niːzɪəm) *n* a light silvery-white metallic element of the alkaline earth series that burns with an intense white flame: used in light structural alloys, flashbulbs, flares, and fireworks. Symbol: Mg; atomic no.: 12; atomic wt.: 24.305. [C19: NL, from MAGNESIA]

magnesium oxide *n* a white tasteless substance used as an antacid and laxative and in refractory materials. Formula: MgO. Also called: **magnesia.**

magnet ('mægnɪt) *n* **1** a body that can attract certain substances, such as iron or steel, as a result of a magnetic field; a piece of ferromagnetic substance. See also **electromagnet. 2** a person or thing that exerts a great attraction. [C15: via L from Gk *magnēs,* shortened from *ho Magnēs lithos* the Magnesian stone. See MAGNESIA]

magnetic ❶ (mæg'netɪk) *adj* **1** of, producing, or operated by means of magnetism. **2** of or concerned with a magnet. **3** of or concerned with the magnetism of the earth: *the magnetic equator.* **4** capable of being magnetized. **5** exerting a powerful attraction: *a magnetic personality.*
▸**mag'netically** *adv*

magnetic constant *n* the magnetic permeability of free space; it has the value $4\pi \times 10^{-7}$ H m^{-1}.

magnetic declination *n* the angle that a compass needle makes with the direction of the geographical north pole at any given point on the earth's surface.

magnetic dip *or* **inclination** *n* another name for **dip** (sense 24).

magnetic dipole moment *n* a measure of the magnetic strength of a magnet or current-carrying coil, expressed as the torque produced when the magnet or coil is set with its axis perpendicular to unit magnetic field.

magnetic disk *n* another name for **disk** (sense 2).

magnetic equator *n* an imaginary line on the earth's surface, near the equator, at all points on which there is no magnetic dip.

magnetic field *n* a field of force surrounding a permanent magnet or a moving charged particle, in which another permanent magnet or moving charge experiences a force.

magnetic flux *n* a measure of the strength of a magnetic field over a given area, equal to the product of the area and the magnetic flux density through it. Symbol: ϕ

magnetic mine *n* a mine designed to explode when a magnetic field such as that generated by the metal of a ship's hull is detected.

magnetic needle *n* a slender magnetized rod used in certain instruments, such as the magnetic compass, for indicating the direction of a magnetic field.

magnetic north *n* the direction in which a compass needle points, at an angle (the declination) from the direction of true (geographic) north.

magnetic pick-up *n* a type of record-player pick-up in which the stylus moves an iron core in a coil, causing a changing magnetic field that produces the current.

magnetic pole *n* **1** either of two regions in a magnet where the magnetic induction is concentrated. **2** either of two variable points on the earth's surface towards which a magnetic needle points, where the lines of force of the earth's magnetic field are vertical.

magnetic resonance *n* the response by atoms, molecules, or nuclei subjected to a magnetic field to radio waves or other forms of energy: used in medicine for scanning (**magnetic resonance imaging**; abbrev.: **MRI**).

magnetic storm *n* a sudden severe disturbance of the earth's magnetic field, caused by emission of charged particles from the sun.

magnetic stripe *n* (across the back of various types of bank card, credit card, etc.) a dark stripe of magnetic material consisting of several tracks onto which information may be coded and which may be read or written to electronically.

magnetic tape *n* a long narrow plastic or metal strip coated or impregnated with iron oxide, chrome dioxide, etc., used to record sound or video signals or to store information in computing.

magnetism ❶ ('mægnɪˌtɪzəm) *n* **1** the property of attraction displayed by magnets. **2** any of a class of phenomena in which a field of force is caused by a moving electric charge. **3** the branch of physics concerned with magnetic phenomena. **4** powerful attraction.

magnetite ('mægnɪˌtaɪt) *n* a black magnetizable mineral that is an important source of iron.

magnetize *or* **magnetise** ('mægnɪˌtaɪz) *vb* **magnetizes, magnetizing, magnetized** *or* **magnetises, magnetising, magnetised.** (*tr*) **1** to make (a substance or object) magnetic. **2** to attract strongly.
▸**'magnet,izable** *or* **'magnet,isable** *adj* ▸**,magneti'zation** *or* **,magneti'sation** *n* ▸**'magnet,izer** *or* **'magnet,iser** *n*

magneto (mæg'niːtəʊ) *n, pl* **magnetos.** a small electric generator in which the magnetic field is produced by a permanent magnet, esp. one for providing the spark in an internal-combustion engine. [C19: short for *magnetoelectric generator*]

magneto- *combining form.* indicating magnetism or magnetic properties: *magnetosphere.*

magnetoelectricity (mægˌniːtəʊɪlek'trɪsɪtɪ) *n* electricity produced by the action of magnetic fields.
▸**mag,netoe'lectric** *or* **mag,netoe'lectrical** *adj*

magnetometer (ˌmægnɪ'tɒmɪtə) *n* any instrument for measuring the intensity or direction of a magnetic field, esp. the earth's field.
▸**,magne'tometry** *n*

magnetomotive (mægˌniːtəʊ'məʊtɪv) *adj* causing a magnetic flux.

magnetosphere (mæg'niːtəʊˌsfɪə) *n* the region surrounding a planet, such as the earth, in which the behaviour of charged particles is controlled by the planet's magnetic field.

magnetron ('mægnɪˌtrɒn) *n* a two-electrode electronic valve used with an applied magnetic field to generate high-power microwave oscillations, esp. for use in radar. [C20: from MAGNET + ELECTRON]

magnet school *n* a school that provides a focus on one subject area throughout its curriculum in order to attract, often from an early age, pupils who wish to specialize in this subject.

Magnificat (mæg'nɪfɪˌkæt) *n Christianity.* the hymn of the Virgin Mary (Luke 1:46-55), used as a canticle. [from the opening phrase, *Magnificat anima mea Dominum* (my soul doth magnify the Lord)]

magnification ❶ (ˌmægnɪfɪ'keɪʃən) *n* **1** the act of magnifying or the state of being magnified. **2** the degree to which something is magnified. **3** a magnified copy, photograph, drawing, etc., of something. **4** a measure of the ability of a lens or other optical instrument to magnify.

magnificence ❶ (mæg'nɪfɪsəns) *n* the quality of being magnificent. [C14: via F from L *magnificentia*]

magnificent ❶ (mæg'nɪfɪsᵊnt) *adj* **1** splendid or impressive in appearance. **2** superb or very fine. **3** (esp. of ideas) noble or elevated. [C16: from L *magnificentior,* irregular comp. of *magnificus* great in deeds, from *magnus* great + *facere* to do]
▸**mag'nificently** *adv*

magnifico (mæg'nɪfɪkəʊ) *n, pl* **magnificoes.** a magnate; grandee. [C16: It. from L *magnificus;* see MAGNIFICENT]

magnify ❶ ('mægnɪˌfaɪ) *vb* **magnifies, magnifying, magnified. 1** to increase, cause to increase, or be increased in apparent size, as through the action of a lens, microscope, etc. **2** to exaggerate or become exaggerated

THESAURUS

magnanimity *n* = **generosity**, beneficence, benevolence, big-heartedness, bountifulness, charitableness, high-mindedness, largesse *or* largess, munificence, nobility, openhandedness, selflessness, unselfishness

magnanimous *adj* = **generous**, beneficent, big, big-hearted, bountiful, charitable, free, great-hearted, handsome, high-minded, kind, kindly, munificent, noble, open-handed, selfless, ungrudging, unselfish, unstinting
Antonyms *adj* miserly, petty, resentful, selfish, small, unforgiving, vindictive

magnate *n* **1** = **tycoon**, baron, big cheese (*sl., old-fashioned*), big hitter (*inf.*), big noise (*inf.*), big shot (*inf.*), big wheel (*sl.*), bigwig (*inf.*), captain of industry, chief, fat cat (*sl., chiefly US*), heavy hitter (*inf.*), leader, Mister Big (*sl., chiefly US*), mogul, nabob (*inf.*), notable, plutocrat, V.I.P. **2** *History* = **aristocrat**, aristo (*inf.*), baron, bashaw, grandee, magnifico, nob (*sl., chiefly Brit.*), noble, notable, personage, prince

magnetic *adj* **5** = **attractive**, alluring, captivating, charismatic, charming, enchanting, entrancing, fascinating, hypnotic, irresistible, mesmerizing, seductive
Antonyms *adj* disagreeable, offensive, repellent, repulsive, unappealing, unattractive, unlikable *or* unlikeable, unpleasant

magnetism *n* **4** = **charm**, allure, appeal, attraction, attractiveness, captivatingness, charisma, draw, drawing power, enchantment, fascination, hypnotism, magic, mesmerism, power, pull, seductiveness, spell

magnification *n* **1, 3** = **increase**, aggrandizement, amplification, augmentation, blow-up (*inf.*), boost, build-up, deepening, dilation, enhancement, enlargement, exaggeration, expansion, heightening, inflation, intensification

magnificence *n* = **splendour**, brilliance, éclat, glory, gorgeousness, grandeur, luxuriousness, luxury, majesty, nobility, opulence, pomp, resplendence, stateliness, sublimity, sumptuousness

magnificent *adj* **1** = **splendid**, august, elegant, elevated, exalted, glorious, gorgeous, grand, grandiose, imposing, impressive, lavish, luxurious, majestic, noble, opulent, princely, regal, resplendent, rich, splendiferous (*facetious*), stately, striking, sublime, sumptuous, transcendent **2** = **excellent**, brilliant, divine (*inf.*), fine, outstanding, splendid, superb, superior
Antonyms *adj* bad, humble, ignoble, lowly, mean, modest, ordinary, petty, poor, trivial, undistinguished, unimposing

magnify *vb* **1** = **enlarge**, aggrandize, amplify, augment, blow up, boost, build up, deepen, dilate, expand, heighten, increase, intensify **2** = **overstate**, aggravate, blow up, blow up out of

in importance: *don't magnify your troubles.* **3** (*tr*) *Arch.* to glorify. [C14: via OF from L *magnificāre* to praise]
▸**'magni,fiable** *adj*

magnifying glass *or* **magnifier** *n* a convex lens used to produce an enlarged image of an object.

magniloquent ⓣ (mæg'nɪləkwənt) *adj* (of speech) lofty in style; grandiloquent. [C17: from L *magnus* great + *loquī* to speak]
▸**mag'niloquence** *n* ▸**mag'niloquently** *adv*

magnitude ⓣ ('mægnɪ,tjuːd) *n* **1** relative importance or significance: *a problem of the first magnitude.* **2** relative size or extent. **3** *Maths.* a number assigned to a quantity as a basis of comparison for the measurement of similar quantities. **4** Also called: **apparent magnitude.** *Astron.* the apparent brightness of a celestial body expressed on a numerical scale on which bright stars have a low value. **5** Also called: **earthquake magnitude.** *Geol.* a measure of the size of an earthquake based on the quantity of energy released. [C14: from L *magnitūdō* size, from *magnus* great]

magnolia (mæg'nəʊlɪə) *n* **1** any tree or shrub of the genus *Magnolia* of Asia and North America: cultivated for their white, pink, purple, or yellow showy flowers. **2** the flower of any of these plants. **3a** a very pale pinkish-white colour. **3b** (*as adj*): *magnolia walls.* [C18: NL, after Pierre *Magnol* (1638–1715), F botanist]

magnox ('mægnɒks) *n* an alloy consisting mostly of magnesium with small amounts of aluminium, used in fuel elements of nuclear reactors. [C20: from *mag(nesium) n(o) ox(idation)*]

magnox reactor *n* a nuclear reactor using carbon dioxide as the coolant, graphite as the moderator, and uranium cased in magnox as the fuel.

magnum ('mægnəm) *n, pl* **magnums.** a wine bottle holding the equivalent of two normal bottles (approximately 52 fluid ounces). [C18: from L: a big thing, from *magnus* large]

magnum opus *n* a great work of art or literature, esp. the greatest single work of an artist. [L]

magpie ('mæg,paɪ) *n* **1** any of various birds having a black-and-white plumage, long tail, and a chattering call. **2** any of various similar birds of Australia. **3** *Brit.* a person who hoards small objects. **4** a person who chatters. **5a** the outermost ring but one on a target. **5b** a shot that hits this ring. [C17: from *Mag,* dim. of *Margaret,* used to signify a chatterbox + PIE[2]]

maguey ('mægweɪ) *n* **1** any of various tropical American agave plants, esp. one that yields a fibre or is used in making an alcoholic beverage. **2** the fibre from any of these plants, used esp. for rope. [C16: Sp., of Amerind origin]

magus ('meɪgəs) *n, pl* **magi. 1** a Zoroastrian priest. **2** an astrologer, sorcerer, or magician of ancient times. [C14: from L, from Gk *magos,* from OPersian *magus* magician]

Magyar ('mægjɑː) *n* **1** (*pl* **Magyars**) a member of the predominant ethnic group of Hungary. **2** the Hungarian language. ◆ *adj* **3** of or relating to the Magyars or their language. **4** *Sewing.* of or relating to a style of sleeve cut in one piece with the bodice.

Mahabharata (,mɑːhə'bɑːrətə), **Mahabharatam,** *or* **Mahabharatum** (,mɑːhə'bɑːrətəm) *n* an epic Sanskrit poem of India of which the *Bhagavad-Gita* forms a part. [Sansk., from *mahā* great + *bhārata* story]

maharajah *or* **maharaja** (,mɑːhə'rɑːdʒə) *n* any of various Indian princes, esp. any of the rulers of the former native states. [C17: Hindi, from *mahā* great + RAJAH]

maharani *or* **maharanee** (,mɑːhə'rɑːniː) *n* **1** the wife of a maharajah. **2** a woman holding the rank of maharajah. [C19: from Hindi, from *mahā* great + RANI]

maharishi (,mɑːhə'riːʃɪ, mə'hɑːriːʃɪ) *n Hinduism.* a Hindu teacher of religious and mystical knowledge. [from Hindi, from *mahā* great + *rishi* sage]

mahatma (mə'hɑːtmə) *n* (*sometimes cap.*) **1** *Hinduism.* a Brahman sage. **2** *Theosophy.* an adept or sage. [C19: from Sansk. *mahātman,* from *mahā* great + *ātman* soul]

Mahayana (,mɑːhə'jɑːnə) *n* **a** a liberal Buddhist school of Tibet, China, and Japan, whose adherents seek enlightenment for all sentient beings. **b** (*as modifier*): *Mahayana Buddhism.* [from Sansk., from *mahā* great + *yāna* vehicle]

Mahdi ('mɑːdɪ) *n Islam.* any of a number of Muslim messiahs expected to convert all mankind to Islam by force. [Ar. *mahdīy* one who is guided, from *madā* to guide aright]
▸**'Mahdism** *n* ▸**'Mahdist** *n, adj*

mah jong *or* **mah-jongg** (,mɑː'dʒɒŋ) *n* a game of Chinese origin, usually played by four people, using tiles bearing various designs. [from Chinese, lit.: sparrows]

mahlstick ('mɔːl,stɪk) *n* a variant spelling of **maulstick.**

mahogany (mə'hɒgənɪ) *n, pl* **mahoganies. 1** any of various tropical American trees valued for their hard reddish-brown wood. **2** any of several trees with similar wood, such as African mahogany and Philippine mahogany. **3a** the wood of any of these trees. **3b** (*as modifier*): *a mahogany table.* **4a** a reddish-brown colour. **4b** (*as adj*): *mahogany skin.* [C17: from ?]

Mahometan (mə'hɒmɪtᵊn) *n, adj* a former word for **Muslim.**

mahonia (mə'həʊnɪə) *n* any evergreen shrub of the Asian and American genus *Mahonia:* cultivated for their ornamental spiny divided leaves and clusters of small yellow flowers. [C19: NL, after Bernard *McMahon* (died 1816), American botanist]

mahout (mə'haʊt) *n* (in India and the East Indies) an elephant driver or keeper. [C17: Hindi *mahāut,* from Sansk. *mahāmātra* of great measure, orig. a title]

mahseer ('mɑːsɪə) *n* any of various large freshwater Indian cyprinid fishes. [from Hindi]

maid ⓣ (meɪd) *n* **1** *Arch. or literary.* a young unmarried girl; maiden. **2a** a female servant. **2b** (*in combination*): *a housemaid.* **3** a spinster. [C12: form of MAIDEN]

maiden ⓣ ('meɪdᵊn) *n* **1** *Arch. or literary.* **1a** a young unmarried girl, esp. a virgin. **1b** (*as modifier*): *a maiden blush.* **2** *Horse racing.* **2a** a horse that has never won a race. **2b** (*as modifier*): *a maiden race.* **3** *Cricket.* See **maiden over. 4** (*modifier*) of or relating to an older unmarried woman: *a maiden aunt.* **5** (*modifier*) of or involving an initial experience or attempt: *a maiden voyage.* **6** (*modifier*) (of a person or thing) untried; unused. **7** (*modifier*) (of a place) never trodden, penetrated, or captured. [OE *mægden*]
▸**'maidenish** *adj* ▸**'maiden,like** *adj*

maidenhair fern *or* **maidenhair** ('meɪdᵊn,hɛə) *n* any of various ferns of tropical and warm regions, having delicate fan-shaped fronds with small pale green leaflets. [C15: from the hairlike appearance of its fronds]

maidenhair tree *n* another name for **ginkgo.**

maidenhead ('meɪdᵊn,hɛd) *n* **1** a nontechnical word for the **hymen. 2** virginity; maidenhood. [C13: from *maiden* + *-hed,* var. of -HOOD]

maidenhood ('meɪdᵊn,hʊd) *n* **1** the time during which a woman is a maiden or virgin. **2** the condition of being a maiden or virgin.

maidenly ⓣ ('meɪdᵊnlɪ) *adj* of or befitting a maiden.
▸**'maidenliness** *n*

maiden name *n* a woman's surname before marriage.

maiden over *n Cricket.* an over in which no runs are scored.

maid of honour *n* **1** *US & Canad.* the principal unmarried attendant of a bride. **2** *Brit.* a small tart with an almond-flavoured filling. **3** an unmarried lady attending a queen or princess.

maidservant ('meɪd,sɜːvənt) *n* a female servant.

maihem ('meɪhɛm) *n* a variant spelling of **mayhem.**

mail[1] ⓣ (meɪl) *n* **1** Also called (esp. Brit.): **post.** letters, packages, etc., that are transported and delivered by the post office. **2** the postal system. **3** a single collection or delivery of mail. **4** a train, ship, or aircraft that carries mail. **5** short for **electronic mail. 6** (*modifier*) of, involving, or used to convey mail: *a mail train.* ◆ *vb* (*tr*) **7** *Chiefly US & Canad.* to send by mail. **8** to contact (a person) by electronic mail. **9** to send (a message, document, etc.) by electronic mail. [C13: from OF *male* bag, prob. from OHG *malha* wallet]
▸**'mailable** *adj*

mail[2] (meɪl) *n* **1** a type of flexible armour consisting of riveted metal rings or links. **2** the hard protective shell of such animals as the turtle and lobster. ◆ *vb* **3** (*tr*) to clothe or arm with mail. [C14: from OF *maille* mesh, from L *macula* spot]

mailbag ('meɪl,bæg) *or* **mailsack** *n* a large bag for transporting or delivering mail.

mailbox ('meɪl,bɒks) *n* another name (esp. US and Canad.) for **letter box.**

mailing list *n* a register of names and addresses to which advertising matter, etc., is sent by post or electronic mail.

maillot (mæ'jəʊ) *n* **1** tights worn for ballet, gymnastics, etc. **2** a woman's swimsuit. **3** a jersey. [from F]

mailman ('meɪl,mæn) *n, pl* **mailmen.** *Chiefly US & Canad.* another name for **postman.**

mail merging *n Computing.* a software facility that can produce a large

THESAURUS

all proportion, dramatize, enhance, exaggerate, inflate, make a mountain out of a molehill, make a production (out) of (*inf.*), overdo, overemphasize, overestimate, overplay, overrate
Antonyms *vb* ≠ **enlarge:** decrease, diminish, lessen, lower, minimize, reduce, shrink ≠ **overstate:** belittle, deflate, denigrate, deprecate, disparage, understate

magniloquence *n* = **pomposity,** bombast, fustian, grandiloquence, loftiness, pretentiousness, turgidity

magniloquent *adj* = **pompous,** arty-farty (*inf.*), bombastic, declamatory, elevated, exalted, grandiloquent, high-flown, high-sounding, lofty, orotund, overblown, pretentious, rhetorical, sonorous, stilted, turgid

magnitude *n* **1** = **importance,** consequence, eminence, grandeur, greatness, mark, moment, note, significance, weight **2** = **size,** amount, amplitude, bigness, bulk, capacity, dimensions, enormity, expanse, extent, hugeness, immensity, intensity, largeness, mass, measure, proportions, quantity, space, strength, vastness, volume
Antonyms *n* ≠ **importance:** insignificance, triviality, unimportance ≠ **size:** meanness, smallness

maid *n* **1** *Archaic or literary* = **girl,** damsel, lass, lassie (*inf.*), maiden, miss, nymph (*poetic*), wench **2** = **servant,** abigail (*arch.*), handmaiden (*arch.*), housemaid, maidservant, serving-maid

maiden *n* **1** *Archaic or literary* = **girl,** damsel, lass, lassie (*inf.*), maid, miss, nymph (*poetic*), virgin, wench ◆ *adj* **5** = **first,** inaugural, initial, initiatory, introductory

maidenly *adj* = **modest,** chaste, decent, decorous, demure, gentle, girlish, pure, reserved, undefiled, unsullied, vestal, virginal, virtuous
Antonyms *adj* brazen, corrupt, defiled, depraved, dirty, immodest, immoral, impure, indecent, loose, promiscuous, shameless, sinful, unchaste, wanton, wicked

mail[1] *n* **1** = **letters,** correspondence, packages, parcels, post **2** = **postal service,** post, postal sys-

number of personalized letters by combining a file containing a list of names and addresses with one containing a single standard document.

mail order *n* **1** an order for merchandise sent by post. **2a** a system of buying and selling merchandise through the post. **2b** (*as modifier*): *a mail-order firm.*

mailshot ('meɪl,ʃɒt) *n* a circular, leaflet, or other advertising material sent by post, or the posting of such material to a large group of people at one time.

maim ❶ (meɪm) *vb* (*tr*) **1** to mutilate, cripple, or disable a part of the body of (a person or animal). **2** to make defective. [C14: from OF *mahaignier* to wound, prob. of Gmc origin]

mai mai (maɪ maɪ) *n NZ.* a duck shooter's shelter; hide. [probably from Australian Aboriginal *mia-mia* shelter]

main[1] ❶ (meɪn) *adj* (*prenominal*) **1** chief or principal. **2** sheer or utmost (esp. in **by main force**). **3** *Naut.* of, relating to, or denoting any gear, such as a stay or sail, belonging to the mainmast. ◆ *n* **4** a principal pipe, conduit, duct, or line in a system used to distribute water, electricity, etc. **5** (*pl*) **5a** the main distribution network for water, gas, or electricity. **5b** (*as modifier*): *mains voltage.* **6** the chief or most important part or consideration. **7** great strength or force (now esp. in **might and main**). **8** *Literary.* the open ocean. **9** *Arch.* short for **Spanish Main. 10** *Arch.* short for **mainland. 11 in** (*or* **for**) **the main.** on the whole; for the most part. [C13: from OE *mægen* strength]

main[2] (meɪn) *n* **1** a throw of the dice in dice games. **2** a cockfighting contest. **3** a match in archery, boxing, etc. [C16: from ?]

mainbrace ('meɪn,breɪs) *n Naut.* **1** a brace attached to the main yard. **2 splice the mainbrace.** See **splice.**

main clause *n Grammar.* a clause that can stand alone as a sentence.

mainframe ('meɪn,freɪm) *Computing.* ◆ *adj* **1** denoting a high-speed general-purpose computer, usually with a large store capacity. ◆ *n* **2** such a computer. **3** the central processing unit of a computer.

mainland ('meɪnlənd) *n* the main part of a landmass as opposed to an island or peninsula.
▸**'mainlander** *n*

main line *n* **1** *Railways.* **1a** the trunk route between two points, usually fed by branch lines. **1b** (*as modifier*): *a main-line station.* **2** *US.* a main road. ◆ *vb* **mainline, mainlines, mainlining, mainlined. 3** (*intr*) *Sl.* to inject a drug into a vein. ◆ *adj* **mainline. 4** having an important position.
▸**'main,liner** *n*

mainly ❶ ('meɪnlɪ) *adv* for the most part; to the greatest extent; principally.

main market *n* the market for trading in the listed securities of companies on the London stock exchange. Cf. **Third Market, Unlisted Securities Market.**

mainmast ('meɪn,mɑːst) *n Naut.* the chief mast of a sailing vessel with two or more masts.

mainsail ('meɪn,seɪl; *Naut.* 'meɪnsᵊl) *n Naut.* the largest and lowermost sail on the mainmast.

mainsheet ('meɪn,ʃiːt) *n Naut.* the line used to control the angle of the mainsail to the wind.

mainspring ❶ ('meɪn,sprɪŋ) *n* **1** the principal spring of a mechanism, esp. in a watch or clock. **2** the chief cause or motive of something.

mainstay ❶ ('meɪn,steɪ) *n* **1** *Naut.* the forestay that braces the mainmast. **2** a chief support.

mainstream ❶ ('meɪn,striːm) *n* **1** the main current (of a river, cultural trend, etc.). ◆ *adj* **2** of or relating to the style of jazz that lies between the traditional and the modern.

mainstream corporation tax *n* (in Britain) the balance of the corporation tax paid by a company for an accounting period after the advance corporation tax has been deducted.

mainstreeting ('meɪn,striːtɪŋ) *n Canad.* the practice of a politician walking about the streets of a town or city to gain votes and greet supporters.

maintain ❶ (meɪn'teɪn) *vb* (*tr*) **1** to continue or retain; keep in existence. **2** to keep in proper or good condition. **3** to enable (a person) to support a style of living: *the money maintained us for a month.* **4** (*takes a clause as object*) to state or assert. **5** to defend against contradiction; uphold: *she maintained her innocence.* **6** to defend against physical attack. [C13: from OF *maintenir,* ult. from L *manū tenēre* to hold in the hand]
▸**main'tainable** *adj* ▸**main'tainer** *n*

maintenance ❶ ('meɪntɪnəns) *n* **1** the act of maintaining or the state of being maintained. **2** a means of support; livelihood. **3** (*modifier*) of or relating to the maintaining of buildings, machinery, etc.: *maintenance man.* **4** *Law.* the interference in a legal action by a person having no interest in it, as by providing funds to continue the action. **5** *Law.* a provision ordered to be made by way of periodical payments or a lump sum, as for a spouse after a divorce. [C14: from OF; see MAINTAIN]

maintop ('meɪn,tɒp) *n* a top or platform at the head of the mainmast.

main-topmast *n Naut.* the mast immediately above the mainmast.

maintopsail (,meɪn'tɒpseɪl; *Naut.* ,meɪn'tɒpsᵊl) *n Naut.* a topsail on the mainmast.

main yard *n Naut.* a yard for a square mainsail.

maiolica (mə'jɒlɪkə) *n* a variant of **majolica.**

maisonette *or* **maisonnette** (,meɪzə'nɛt) *n* self-contained living accommodation often occupying two floors of a larger house and having its own outside entrance. [C19: from F, dim. of *maison* house]

mai tai ('maɪ ,taɪ) *n* a mixed drink consisting of rum, Curaçao, fruit juice, and grenadine. [C20: from ?]

maître d'hôtel (,mɛtrə dəʊ'tɛl) *n, pl* **maîtres d'hôtel. 1** a head waiter or steward. **2** the manager or owner of a hotel. [C16: from F: master of (the) hotel]

maize (meɪz) *n* **1** Also called: **sweet corn, Indian corn. 1a** a tall annual grass cultivated for its yellow edible grains, which develop on a spike. **1b** the grain of this plant, used for food, for fodder, and as a source of oil. **2a** a yellow colour. **2b** (*as adj*): *a maize gown.* [C16: from Sp. *maíz,* from Taino *mahiz*]

Maj. *abbrev. for* Major.

majestic ❶ (mə'dʒɛstɪk) *adj* having or displaying majesty or great dignity; grand; lofty.
▸**ma'jestically** *adv*

majesty ❶ ('mædʒɪstɪ) *n* **1** great dignity of bearing; loftiness; grandeur. **2** supreme power or authority. [C13: from OF, from L *mājestās;* rel. to L *major,* comp. of *magnus* great]

Majesty ('mædʒɪstɪ) *n, pl* **Majesties.** (preceded by *Your, His, Her,* or *Their*) a title used to address or refer to a sovereign or the wife or widow of a sovereign.

majolica (mə'dʒɒlɪkə, mə'jɒl-) *or* **maiolica** *n* a type of porous pottery glazed with bright metallic oxides. It was originally imported into Italy via Majorca and was extensively made in Renaissance Italy. [C16: from It., from LL *Mājorica* Majorca]

major ❶ ('meɪdʒə) *n* **1** *Mil.* an officer immediately junior to a lieutenant colonel. **2** a person who is superior in a group or class. **3** (often preceded by *the*) *Music.* a major key, chord, mode, or scale. **4** *US, Canad., Austral., & NZ.* **4a** the principal field of study of a student. **4b** a student who is studying a particular subject as his principal field: *a sociology major.* **5** a person who has reached the age of legal majority. **6** a principal or important record company, film company, etc. **7** *Logic.* a major term or premise. ◆ *adj* **8** larger in extent, number, etc. **9** of greater importance or priority. **10** very serious or significant. **11** main, chief, or principal. **12** of, involving, or making up a majority. **13** *Music.* **13a** (of a scale or mode) having notes separated by a whole tone, except for the third and fourth degrees, and seventh and eighth degrees, which are separated by a semitone. **13b** relating to or employing notes from the major scale: *a major key.* **13c** (*postpositive*) denoting a specified key or scale as being major: *C major.* **13d** denoting a

THESAURUS

tem ◆ *vb* **7** = **post**, dispatch, forward, send, send by mail *or* post

maim *vb* **1** = **cripple**, disable, hamstring, hurt, impair, incapacitate, injure, lame, mangle, mar, mutilate, put out of action, wound

main[1] *adj* **1** = **chief**, capital, cardinal, central, critical, crucial, essential, foremost, head, leading, major, necessary, outstanding, paramount, particular, predominant, pre-eminent, premier, primary, prime, principal, special, supreme, vital **2** *As in* **by main force** = **sheer**, absolute, brute, direct, downright, entire, mere, pure, undisguised, utmost, utter ◆ *n* **4** = **conduit**, cable, channel, duct, line, pipe **7** = **force**, effort, might, potency, power, puissance, strength **11 in the main** = **on the whole**, for the most part, generally, in general, mainly, mostly
Antonyms *adj* ≠ **chief:** auxiliary, dependent, insignificant, least, lesser, minor, secondary, subordinate, trivial, unimportant

mainly *adv* = **chiefly**, above all, first and foremost, for the most part, generally, in general, in the main, largely, mostly, most of all, on the whole, overall, predominantly, primarily, principally, substantially, to the greatest extent, usually

mainspring *n* **2** = **cause**, driving force, generator, impulse, incentive, inspiration, motivation, motive, origin, prime mover, source

mainstay *n* **2** = **pillar**, anchor, backbone, bulwark, buttress, chief support, linchpin, prop

mainstream *adj* **2** = **conventional**, accepted, central, core, current, established, general, orthodox, prevailing, received
Antonyms *adj* fringe, marginal, peripheral, unconventional, unorthodox

maintain *vb* **1** = **continue**, carry on, conserve, keep, keep up, nurture, perpetuate, preserve, prolong, retain, sustain, uphold **3** = **look after**, care for, finance, provide for, supply, support, take care of **4** = **assert**, affirm, allege, asseverate, aver, avow, claim, contend, declare, hold, insist, profess, state **5** = **support**, advocate, argue for, back, champion, defend, fight for, justify, plead for, stand by, take up the cudgels for, uphold, vindicate
Antonyms *vb* ≠ **continue:** abolish, break off, conclude, discontinue, drop, end, finish, give up, relinquish, suspend, terminate ≠ **assert:** disavow ≠ **support:** abandon, desert

maintenance *n* **1** = **continuation**, carrying-on, continuance, perpetuation, prolongation, retainment, support, sustainment, sustention **1** = **upkeep**, care, conservation, keeping, nurture, preservation, provision, repairs, supply **2, 5** = **allowance**, aliment, alimony, food, keep, livelihood, living, subsistence, support, sustenance, upkeep

majestic *adj* = **grand**, august, awesome, dignified, elevated, exalted, grandiose, imperial, imposing, impressive, kingly, lofty, magnificent, monumental, noble, pompous, princely, regal, royal, splendid, splendiferous (*facetious*), stately, sublime, superb
Antonyms *adj* humble, ignoble, lowly, mean, modest, ordinary, unassuming, undistinguished, unimposing

majesty *n* **1** = **grandeur**, augustness, awesomeness, dignity, exaltedness, glory, imposingness, impressiveness, kingliness, loftiness, magnificence, nobility, pomp, queenliness, royalty, splendour, state, stateliness, sublimity
Antonyms *n* disgrace, meanness, shame, triviality

major *adj* **8, 11** = **main**, better, bigger, chief, elder, greater, head, higher, larger, lead, leading, most, senior, superior, supreme, uppermost **9, 10** = **important**, critical, crucial,

chord or triad having a major third above the root. **13e** (in jazz) denoting a major chord with a major seventh added above the root. **14** *Logic.* constituting the major term or major premise of a syllogism. **15** *Chiefly US, Canad., Austral., & NZ.* of or relating to a student's principal field of study at a university, etc. **16** *Brit.* the elder: used after a schoolboy's surname if he has one or more younger brothers in the same school: *Price major.* **17** of full legal age. ◆ *vb* **18** (*intr;* usually foll. by *in*) *US, Canad., Austral., & NZ.* to do one's principal study (in a particular subject): *to major in English literature.* **19** (*intr;* usually foll. by *on*) to take or deal with as the main area of interest: *the book majors on peasant dishes.* [C15 (adj): from L, comp. of *magnus* great; C17 (n, in military sense): from F, short for SERGEANT MAJOR]
▸ **'majorship** *n*

major-domo (-'dəʊməʊ) *n, pl* **major-domos. 1** the chief steward or butler of a great household. **2** *Facetious.* a steward or butler. [C16: from Sp. *mayordomo,* from Med. L *mājor domūs* head of the household]

majorette (ˌmeɪdʒə'rɛt) *n* **1** one of a group of girls who practise formation marching and baton twirling. **2** See **drum majorette.**

major general *n Mil.* an officer immediately junior to a lieutenant general.
▸ **ˌmajor-'generalship** *or* **major-'generalcy** *n*

majority Ⓣ (mə'dʒɒrɪtɪ) *n, pl* **majorities. 1** the greater number or part of something. **2** (in an election) the number of votes or seats by which the strongest party or candidate beats the combined opposition or the runner-up. **3** the largest party or group that votes together in a legislative or deliberative assembly. **4** the time of reaching or state of having reached full legal age. **5** the rank, office, or commission of major. **6** *Euphemistic.* the dead (esp. in **join the majority, go** *or* **pass over to the majority**). **7** (*modifier*) of, involving, or being a majority: *a majority decision.* **8 in the majority.** forming or part of the greater number of something. [C16: from Med. L *mājoritās,* from MAJOR (adj)]

> **USAGE NOTE** *The majority of* can only refer to a number of things or people. When talking about an amount, *most of* should be used: *most of* (not *the majority of*) *the harvest was saved.*

major league *n US & Canad.* a league of highest classification in baseball, football, hockey, etc.

majorly ('meɪdʒəlɪ) *adv Sl., chiefly US & Canad.* very; extremely: *it was majorly important for us to do that.*

major orders *pl n RC Church.* the three higher degrees of holy orders: bishop, priest, and deacon.

major premise *n Logic.* the premise of a syllogism containing the predicate of its conclusion.

major term *n Logic.* the predicate of the conclusion of a syllogism.

majuscule ('mædʒəˌskjuːl) *n* **1** a large letter, either capital or uncial, used in printing or writing. ◆ *adj* **2** relating to, printed, or written in such letters. ◆ Cf. **minuscule.** [C18: via F from L *mājusculus,* dim. of *mājor* bigger]
▸ **majuscular** (mə'dʒʌskjʊlə) *adj*

make Ⓣ (meɪk) *vb* **makes, making, made.** (*mainly tr*) **1** to bring into being by shaping, changing, or combining materials, ideas, etc.; form or fashion. **2** to draw up, establish, or form: *to make one's will.* **3** to cause to exist, bring about, or produce: *don't make a noise.* **4** to cause, compel, or induce: *please make him go away.* **5** to appoint or assign: *they made him chairman.* **6** to constitute: *one swallow doesn't make a summer.* **7** (*also intr*) to come or cause to come into a specified state or condition: *to make merry.* **8** (*copula*) to be or become through development: *he will make a good teacher.* **9** to cause or ensure the success of: *your news has made my day.* **10** to amount to: *twelve inches make a foot.* **11** to serve as or be suitable for: *that piece of cloth will make a coat.* **12** to prepare or put into a fit condition for use: *to make a bed.* **13** to be the essential element in or part of: *charm makes a good salesman.* **14** to carry out, effect, or do. **15** (*intr;* foll. by *to, as if to,* or *as though to*) to act with the intention or with a show of doing something: *he made as if to hit her.* **16** to use for a specified purpose: *I will make this town my base.* **17** to deliver or pronounce: *to make a speech.* **18** to give information or an opinion: *what time do you make it?* **19** to cause to seem or represent as being. **20** to earn, acquire, or win for oneself: *to make friends.* **21** to engage in: *to make war.* **22** to traverse or cover (distance) by travelling: *we can make a hundred miles by nightfall.* **23** to arrive in time for: *he didn't make the first act of the play.* **24** *Cards.* **24a** to win a trick with (a specified card). **24b** to shuffle (the cards). **24c** *Bridge.* to fulfil (a contract) by winning the necessary number of tricks. **25** *Cricket.* to score (runs). **26** *Electronics.* to close (a circuit) permitting a flow of current. **27** (*intr*) to increase in depth: *the water in the hold was making a foot a minute.* **28** *Inf.* to gain a place or position on or in: *to make the headlines.* **29** *Inf., chiefly US.* to achieve the rank of. **30** *Taboo sl.* to seduce. **31 make a book.** to take bets on a race or another contest. **32 make a day, night,** etc., **of it.** to cause an activity to last a day, night, etc. **33 make do.** See **do**[1] (sense 32). **34 make eyes at.** to flirt with or ogle. **35 make it. 35a** *Inf.* to be successful in doing something. **35b** (foll. by *with*) *Taboo sl.* to have sexual intercourse. **36 make like.** *Sl., chiefly US & Canad.* **36a** to imitate. **36b** to pretend. ◆ *n* **37** brand, type, or style. **38** the manner or way in which something is made. **39** disposition or character; make-up. **40** the act or process of making. **41** the amount or number made. **42** *Cards.* a player's turn to shuffle. **43 on the make.** *Sl.* **43a** out for profit or conquest. **43b** in search of a sexual partner. ◆ See also **make away, make for,** etc. [OE *macian*]
▸ **'makable** *adj*

make away Ⓣ *vb* (*intr, adv*) **1** to depart in haste. **2 make away with. 2a** to steal or abduct. **2b** to kill, destroy, or get rid of.

make believe Ⓣ *vb* **makes believe, making believe, made believe. 1** to pretend or enact a fantasy. ◆ *n* **make-believe. 2a** a fantasy or pretence. **2b** (*as modifier*): *a make-believe world.*

make for Ⓣ *vb* (*intr, prep*) **1** to head towards. **2** to prepare to attack. **3** to help bring about.

make of *vb* (*tr, prep*) **1** to interpret as the meaning of. **2** to produce or construct from: *houses made of brick.* **3 make little, much,** etc., **of. 3a** to gain little, much, etc., benefit from. **3b** to attribute little, much, etc., significance to.

make off Ⓣ *vb* **1** (*intr, adv*) to go or run away in haste. **2 make off with.** to steal or abduct.

make out Ⓣ *vb* (*adv*) **1** (*tr*) to discern or perceive. **2** (*tr*) to understand or comprehend. **3** (*tr*) to write out: *he made out a cheque.* **4** (*tr*) to attempt to establish or prove: *he made me out to be a liar.* **5** (*intr*) to pretend: *he made out that he could cook.* **6** (*intr*) to manage or fare.

make over *vb* (*tr, adv*) **1** to transfer the title or possession of (property, etc.). **2** to renovate or remodel: *she made over the dress to fit her sister.* ◆ *n* **makeover. 3** a complete remodelling. **4** a series of alterations, including beauty treatments and new clothes, intended to make a significant improvement to a person's appearance.

maker Ⓣ ('meɪkə) *n* a person who executes a legal document, esp. one who signs a promissory note.

Maker Ⓣ ('meɪkə) *n* **1** a title given to God (as Creator). **2** (**go to**) **meet one's Maker.** to die.

THESAURUS

grave, great, mega (*sl.*), notable, outstanding, pre-eminent, radical, serious, significant, vital, weighty
Antonyms *adj* ≠ **main:** auxiliary, lesser, minor, secondary, smaller, subordinate ≠ **important:** inconsequential, insignificant, trivial, unimportant

majority *n* **1** = **most**, best part, bulk, greater number, mass, more, plurality, preponderance, superiority **4** = **adulthood**, manhood *or* womanhood, maturity, seniority

make *vb* **1** = **create**, assemble, build, compose, constitute, construct, fabricate, fashion, forge, form, frame, manufacture, mould, originate, produce, put together, shape, synthesize **2** = **enact**, draw up, establish, fix, form, frame, pass **3** = **produce**, accomplish, beget, bring about, cause, create, effect, engender, generate, give rise to, lead to, occasion **4** = **force**, cause, coerce, compel, constrain, dragoon, drive, impel, induce, oblige, press, pressurize, prevail upon, railroad (*inf.*), require **5** = **appoint**, assign, create, designate, elect, install, invest, nominate, ordain **6, 10** = **amount to**, add up to, compose, constitute, embody, form, represent **14** = **perform**, act, carry out, do, effect, engage in, execute, practise, prosecute **18** = **calculate**, estimate, gauge, judge, reckon, suppose, think **20** = **earn**, acquire, clear, gain, get, net, obtain, realize, secure, take in, win **23** = **get to**, arrive at, arrive in time for, attain, catch, meet, reach **35a make it** *Informal* = **succeed**, arrive (*inf.*), be successful, come through, crack it, cut it (*inf.*), get on, get somewhere, prosper, pull through, survive ◆ *n* **37, 38** = **brand**, build, character, composition, constitution, construction, cut, designation, form, kind, make-up, mark, model, shape, sort, structure, style, type, variety **39** = **nature**, cast of mind, character, disposition, frame of mind, humour, kidney, make-up, stamp, temper, temperament

make away *vb* **1** = **depart**, abscond, beat a hasty retreat, clear out (*inf.*), cut and run (*inf.*), decamp, do a runner (*sl.*), flee, fly, fly the coop (*US & Canad. inf.*), hook it (*sl.*), make off, run away *or* off, run for it (*inf.*), scoot, skedaddle (*inf.*), slope off **2a** *foll. by* **with** = **steal**, abduct, cabbage (*Brit. sl.*), carry off, cart off (*sl.*), filch, kidnap, knock off (*sl.*), make off with, nab (*inf.*), nick (*sl., chiefly Brit.*), pilfer, pinch (*inf.*), purloin, swipe (*sl.*) **2b** *foll. by* **with** = **kill**, blow away (*sl., chiefly US*), bump off (*sl.*), destroy, dispose of, do away with, do in (*sl.*), eliminate, get rid of, murder, rub out (*US sl.*)

make believe *vb* **1** = **pretend**, act as if *or* though, dream, enact, fantasize, imagine, play, play-act ◆ *n* **make-believe 2a** = **fantasy**, charade, dream, imagination, play-acting, pretence, unreality **2b** ◆ *modifier* = **imaginary**, dream, fantasized, fantasy, imagined, made-up, mock, pretend, pretended, sham, unreal
Antonyms *n* ≠ **fantasy:** actuality, fact, reality, truthfulness ◆ *adj* ≠ **imaginary:** authentic, genuine, real, unfeigned

make for *vb* **1** = **head for**, aim for, be bound for, head towards, proceed towards, steer (a course) for **2** = **attack**, assail, assault, fall on, fly at, go for, have a go at (*inf.*), lunge at, set upon **3** = **contribute to**, be conducive to, conduce to, facilitate, favour, promote

make off *vb* **1** = **flee**, abscond, beat a hasty retreat, bolt, clear out (*inf.*), cut and run (*inf.*), decamp, do a runner (*sl.*), fly, fly the coop (*US & Canad. inf.*), hook it (*sl.*), make away, run away *or* off, run for it (*inf.*), skedaddle (*inf.*), slope off **2 make off with** = **steal**, abduct, cabbage (*Brit. sl.*), carry off, cart off (*sl.*), filch, kidnap, knock off (*sl.*), make away with, nab (*inf.*), nick (*sl., chiefly Brit.*), pilfer, pinch (*inf.*), purloin, run away *or* off with, swipe (*sl.*)

make out *vb* **1** = **see**, descry, detect, discern, discover, distinguish, espy, perceive, recognize **2** = **understand**, comprehend, decipher, fathom, follow, grasp, perceive, realize, see, suss (out), work out **3** = **write out**, complete, draw up, fill in *or* out, inscribe **4** = **prove**, demonstrate, describe, represent, show **5** = **pretend**, assert, claim, let on, make as if *or* though **6** = **fare**, get on, manage, prosper, succeed, thrive

maker *n* = **manufacturer**, author, builder, constructor, director, fabricator, framer, producer

Maker *n* **1** = **God**, Creator

makeshift Ⓣ (ˈmeɪkˌʃɪft) *adj* **1** serving as a temporary or expedient means. ◆ *n* **2** something serving in this capacity.

make-up Ⓣ *n* **1** cosmetics, such as powder, lipstick, etc., applied to the face. **2a** the cosmetics, false hair, etc., used by an actor to adapt his appearance. **2b** the art or result of applying such cosmetics. **3** the manner of arrangement of the parts or qualities of someone or something. **4** the arrangement of type matter and illustrations on a page or in a book. **5** mental or physical constitution. ◆ *vb* **make up.** *(adv)* **6** *(tr)* to form or constitute: *these arguments make up the case for the defence.* **7** *(tr)* to devise, construct, or compose, sometimes with the intent to deceive: *to make up an excuse.* **8** *(tr)* to supply what is lacking or deficient in; complete: *these extra people will make up our total.* **9** *(tr)* to put in order, arrange, or prepare: *to make up a bed.* **10** *(intr;* foll. by *for)* to compensate or atone (for). **11** to settle (differences) amicably (often in **make it up**). **12** to apply cosmetics to (the face) to enhance one's appearance or for a theatrical role. **13** to assemble (type and illustrations) into (columns or pages). **14** *(tr)* to surface (a road) with tarmac, concrete, etc. **15 make up to.** *Inf.* **15a** to make friendly overtures to. **15b** to flirt with.

makeweight (ˈmeɪkˌweɪt) *n* **1** something put on a scale to make up a required weight. **2** an unimportant person or thing added to make up a lack.

making Ⓣ (ˈmeɪkɪŋ) *n* **1a** the act of a person or thing that makes or the process of being made. **1b** *(in combination): watchmaking.* **2 be the making of.** to cause the success of. **3 in the making.** in the process of becoming or being made. **4** something made or the quantity of something made at one time.

makings Ⓣ (ˈmeɪkɪŋz) *pl n* **1** potentials, qualities, or materials: *he had the makings of a leader.* **2** Also called: **rollings.** *Sl.* the tobacco and cigarette paper used for rolling a cigarette. **3** profits; earnings.

mako[1] (ˈmɑːkəʊ) *n, pl* **makos.** a blue-pointer game shark. [from Maori]

mako[2] (ˈmɑːkəʊ) *n, pl* **makos.** a small evergreen New Zealand tree. [from Maori]

Mal. *abbrev. for:* **1** *Bible.* Malachi. **2** Malay(an).

mal- *combining form.* bad or badly; wrong or wrongly; imperfect or defective: *maladjusted; malfunction.* [OF, from L *malus* bad, *male* badly]

malabsorption (mæləbˈsɔːpʃən) *n* a failure of absorption, esp. by the small intestine in coeliac disease, cystic fibrosis, etc.

malacca *or* **malacca cane** (məˈlækə) *n* **1** the stem of the rattan palm. **2** a walking stick made from this stem. [from *Malacca*, SW Peninsular Malaysia]

malachite (ˈmæləˌkaɪt) *n* a green mineral consisting of hydrated basic copper carbonate: a source of copper, also used for making ornaments. [C16: via OF from L *molochītēs*, from Gk *molokhitis* mallow-green stone, from *molokhē* mallow]

maladjustment Ⓣ (ˌmæləˈdʒʌstmənt) *n* **1** *Psychol.* a failure to meet the demands of society, such as coping with problems and social relationships. **2** faulty or bad adjustment.
▸ **ˌmaladˈjusted** *adj*

maladminister Ⓣ (ˌmæləd'mɪnɪstə) *vb (tr)* to administer badly, inefficiently, or dishonestly.
▸ **ˌmaladˌminisˈtration** *n*

maladroit Ⓣ (ˌmæləˈdrɔɪt) *adj* **1** clumsy; not dexterous. **2** tactless and insensitive. [C17: from F, from *mal* badly + ADROIT]
▸ **ˌmalaˈdroitly** *adv* ▸ **ˌmalaˈdroitness** *n*

malady Ⓣ (ˈmælədɪ) *n, pl* **maladies. 1** any disease or illness. **2** any unhealthy, morbid, or desperate condition. [C13: from OF, from Vulgar L *male habitus* (unattested) in poor condition, from L *male* badly + *habitus*, from *habēre* to have]

Málaga (ˈmæləgə) *n* a sweet fortified dessert wine from Málaga, a port in S Spain.

Malagasy (ˌmæləˈgæsɪ) *n* **1** *(pl* **Malagasy** *or* **Malagasies)** a native or inhabitant of Madagascar. **2** the official language of Madagascar. ◆ *adj* **3** of or relating to Madagascar, its people, or their language.

malaise Ⓣ (mæˈleɪz) *n* **1** a feeling of unease or depression. **2** a mild sickness, not symptomatic of any disease or ailment. **3** a complex of problems affecting a country, economy, etc.: *Bulgaria's economic malaise.* [C18: from OF, from *mal* bad + *aise* EASE]

malamute *or* **malemute** (ˈmæləˌmuːt) *n* an Alaskan Eskimo dog of the spitz type. [from the name of an Eskimo tribe]

malapropism (ˈmæləprɒpˌɪzəm) *n* **1** the unintentional misuse of a word by confusion with one of similar sound, esp. when creating a ridiculous effect, as in *under the affluence of alcohol.* **2** the habit of misusing words in this manner. [C18: after Mrs *Malaprop* in Sheridan's play *The Rivals* (1775), a character who misused words, from MALAPROPOS]

malapropos (ˌmælæprəˈpəʊ) *adj* **1** inappropriate or misapplied. ◆ *adv* **2** in an inappropriate way or manner. ◆ *n* **3** something inopportune or inappropriate. [C17: from F *mal à propos* not to the purpose]

malaria (məˈlɛərɪə) *n* an infectious disease characterized by recurring attacks of chills and fever, caused by the bite of an anopheles mosquito infected with any of certain protozoans. [C18: from It. *mala aria* bad air, from the belief that the disease was caused by the unwholesome air in swampy districts]
▸ **maˈlarial, maˈlarian,** *or* **maˈlarious** *adj*

malarkey *or* **malarky** (məˈlɑːkɪ) *n Sl.* nonsense; rubbish. [C20: from ?]

Malathion (ˌmæləˈθaɪɒn) *n Trademark.* an insecticide consisting of an organic phosphate. [C20: from *(diethyl)* MAL(EATE) + THIO- + -ON]

Malay (məˈleɪ) *n* **1** a member of a people living chiefly in Malaysia and Indonesia. **2** the language of this people. ◆ *adj* **3** of or relating to the Malays or their language.

Malayalam *or* **Malayalaam** (ˌmælɪˈɑːləm) *n* a language of SW India.

Malayan (məˈleɪən) *adj* **1** of or relating to Peninsular Malaysia in SE Asia. ◆ *n* **2** a native or inhabitant of Peninsular Malaysia.

Malayo-Polynesian *n* **1** Also called: **Austronesian.** a family of languages extending from Madagascar to the central Pacific. ◆ *adj* **2** of or relating to this family of languages.

Malaysian (məˈleɪzɪən) *adj* **1** of Malaysia in SE Asia. **2** a native or inhabitant of Malaysia.

malcontent Ⓣ (ˈmælkənˌtent) *adj* **1** disgusted or discontented. ◆ *n* **2** a person who is malcontent. [C16: from OF]

mal de mer *French.* (mal də mɛr) *n* seasickness.

male Ⓣ (meɪl) *adj* **1** of, relating to, or designating the sex producing gametes (spermatozoa) that can fertilize female gametes (ova). **2** of, relating to, or characteristic of a man. **3** for or composed of men or boys: *a male choir.* **4** (of gametes) capable of fertilizing an egg cell. **5** (of reproductive organs) capable of producing male gametes. **6** (of flowers) bearing stamens but lacking a functional pistil. **7** *Electronics, engineering.* having a projecting part or parts that fit into a female counterpart: *a male plug.* ◆ *n* **8** a male person, animal, or plant. [C14: via OF from L *masculus* MASCULINE]
▸ **ˈmaleness** *n*

maleate (ˈmælɪˌeɪt) *n* any salt or ester of maleic acid. [C19: from MALE(IC) ACID + -ATE[1]]

male chauvinism *n* the belief, held or alleged to be held by certain men, that men are superior to women.
▸ **male chauvinist** *n, adj*

malediction Ⓣ (ˌmælɪˈdɪkʃən) *n* **1** the utterance of a curse against someone or something. **2** a slanderous accusation or comment. [C15: from L *maledictiō* a reviling, from *male* ill + *dīcere* to speak]
▸ **ˌmaleˈdictive** *or* **ˌmaleˈdictory** *adj*

malefactor Ⓣ (ˈmælɪˌfæktə) *n* a criminal; wrongdoer. [C15: via OF from L, from *malefacere* to do evil]
▸ **ˈmaleˌfaction** *n*

maleficent (məˈlɛfɪsənt) *adj* causing evil or mischief; harmful or baleful. [C17: from L, from *maleficus* wicked, from *malum* evil]
▸ **maˈlefic** *adj* ▸ **maˈleficence** *n*

maleic acid (məˈleɪɪk) *n* a colourless soluble crystalline substance used to synthesize other compounds, such as polyester resins. Formula: HOOCCH:CHCOOH. Systematic name: **cis-butenedioic acid.** [C19: from F *maléique*, altered form of *malique;* see MALIC ACID]

male menopause *n* a period in a man's later middle age in which he

THESAURUS

makeshift *adj* **1** = **temporary**, expedient, jury, make-do, provisional, rough and ready, stopgap, substitute ◆ *n* **2** = **stopgap**, expedient, shift, substitute

make-up *n* **1, 2a** = **cosmetics**, face *(inf.)*, greasepaint *(Theatre)*, *maquillage*, paint *(inf.)*, powder, war paint *(inf., humorous)* **3** = **structure**, arrangement, assembly, composition, configuration, constitution, construction, form, format, formation, organization **5** = **nature**, build, cast of mind, character, constitution, disposition, figure, frame of mind, make, stamp, temper, temperament ◆ *vb* **make up 6** = **form**, compose, comprise, constitute **7** = **invent**, coin, compose, concoct, construct, cook up *(inf.)*, create, devise, dream up, fabricate, formulate, frame, hatch, manufacture, originate, trump up, write **8** = **complete**, fill, meet, supply **10** *foll. by* **for** = **compensate for**, atone for, balance, make amends for, offset, recompense, redeem, redress, requite **11** = **settle**, bury the hatchet, call it quits, come to terms, compose, forgive and forget, make peace, mend, reconcile, shake hands **15 make up to** *Informal* = **court**, chat up *(inf.)*, curry favour with, flirt with, make overtures to, woo

making *n* **1** = **creation**, assembly, building, composition, construction, fabrication, forging, manufacture, production **3 in the making** = **budding**, coming, emergent, growing, nascent, potential

makings *pl n* **1** = **beginnings**, capability, capacity, ingredients, materials, potential, potentiality, qualities

maladjusted *adj* **1** = **disturbed**, alienated, estranged, hung-up *(sl.)*, neurotic, unstable

maladministration *n* = **mismanagement**, blundering, bungling, corruption, dishonesty, incompetence, inefficiency, malfeasance *(Law)*, malpractice, misgovernment, misrule

maladroit *adj* **1** = **clumsy**, awkward, bungling, cack-handed *(inf.)*, ham-fisted *or* ham-handed *(inf.)*, inept, inexpert, unhandy, unskilful

malady *n* **1** = **disease**, affliction, ailment, complaint, disorder, ill, illness, indisposition, infirmity, lurgy *(inf.)*, sickness

malaise *n* **1, 2** = **unease**, angst, anxiety, depression, discomfort, disquiet, doldrums, enervation, illness, lassitude, melancholy, sickness, weakness

malcontent *adj* **1** = **discontented**, disaffected, disgruntled, disgusted, dissatisfied, dissentious, factious, ill-disposed, rebellious, resentful, restive, unhappy, unsatisfied ◆ *n* **2** = **troublemaker**, agitator, complainer, fault-finder, grouch *(inf.)*, grouser, grumbler, mischief-maker, rebel, stirrer *(inf.)*

male *adj* **1, 2** = **masculine**, manful, manlike, manly, virile
Antonyms *adj* camp *(inf.)*, effeminate, female, feminine, girlie, unmanly, wimpish *or* wimpy *(inf.)*, womanish, womanly

malediction *n* **1** = **curse**, anathema, damnation, damning, denunciation, execration, imprecation, malison *(arch.)*

malefactor *n* = **wrongdoer**, convict, criminal, crook *(inf.)*, culprit, delinquent, evildoer, felon, lawbreaker, miscreant, offender, outlaw, transgressor, villain may experience an identity crisis as he feels age overtake his sexual powers.

malevolent ❶ (məˈlɛvələnt) *adj* wishing or appearing to wish evil to others; malicious. [C16: from L *malevolens*, from *male* ill + *volens*, present participle of *velle* to wish]
▸**maˈlevolence** *n* ▸**maˈlevolently** *adv*

malfeasance (mælˈfiːzᵊns) *n Law.* the doing of a wrongful or illegal act, esp. by a public official. Cf. **misfeasance, nonfeasance.** [C17: from OF *mal faisant*, from *mal* evil + *faisant*, from *faire* to do, from L *facere*]
▸**malˈfeasant** *n, adj*

malformation ❶ (ˌmælfɔːˈmeɪʃən) *n* **1** the condition of being faulty or abnormal in form or shape. **2** *Pathol.* a deformity, esp. when congenital.
▸**malˈformed** *adj*

malfunction ❶ (mælˈfʌŋkʃən) *vb* **1** (*intr*) to function imperfectly or fail to function. ◆ *n* **2** failure to function or defective functioning.

malic acid (ˈmælɪk, ˈmeɪ-) *n* a colourless crystalline compound occurring in apples and other fruits. [C18 *malic*, via F *malique* from L *mālum* apple]

malice ❶ (ˈmælɪs) *n* **1** the desire to do harm or mischief. **2** evil intent. **3** *Law.* the state of mind with which an act is committed and from which the intent to do wrong may be inferred. [C13: via OF from L *malitia*, from *malus* evil]

malice aforethought *n Law.* **1** the predetermination to do an unlawful act, esp. to kill or seriously injure. **2** the intent with which an unlawful killing is effected, which must be proved for the crime to constitute murder.

malicious ❶ (məˈlɪʃəs) *adj* **1** characterized by malice. **2** motivated by wrongful, vicious, or mischievous purposes.
▸**maˈliciously** *adv* ▸**maˈliciousness** *n*

malign ❶ (məˈlaɪn) *adj* **1** evil in influence, intention, or effect. ◆ *vb* **2** (*tr*) to slander or defame. [C14: via OF from L *malīgnus* spiteful, from *malus* evil]
▸**maˈligner** *n* ▸**maˈlignly** *adv*

malignancy (məˈlɪgnənsɪ) *n, pl* **malignancies. 1** the state or quality of being malignant. **2** *Pathol.* a cancerous growth.

malignant ❶ (məˈlɪgnənt) *adj* **1** having or showing desire to harm others. **2** tending to cause great harm; injurious. **3** *Pathol.* (of a tumour) uncontrollable or resistant to therapy. [C16: from LL *malīgnāre* to behave spitefully, from L *malīgnus* MALIGN]
▸**maˈlignantly** *adv*

malignity ❶ (məˈlɪgnɪtɪ) *n, pl* **malignities. 1** the condition or quality of being malign or deadly. **2** (*often pl*) a malign or malicious act or feeling.

malines (məˈliːn) *n* **1** a type of silk net used in dressmaking. **2** another name for **Mechlin lace.** [C19: from F *Malines* (Mechelen), a Belgian city, where this lace was traditionally made]

malinger (məˈlɪŋgə) *vb* (*intr*) to pretend or exaggerate illness, esp. to avoid work. [C19: from F *malingre* sickly, ?from *mal* badly + OF *haingre* feeble]
▸**maˈlingerer** *n*

mall (mɔːl, mæl) *n* **1** a shaded avenue, esp. one open to the public. **2** short for **shopping mall.** [C17: after *the Mall*, in St James's Park, London]

mallard (ˈmælɑːd) *n, pl* **mallard** *or* **mallards.** a duck common over most of the N hemisphere, the male of which has a dark green head and reddish-brown breast: the ancestor of all domestic breeds of duck. [C14: from OF *mallart*, ?from *maslart* (unattested); see MALE, -ARD]

malleable ❶ (ˈmælɪəbᵊl) *adj* **1** (esp. of metal) able to be worked, hammered, or shaped under pressure or blows without breaking. **2** able to be influenced; pliable or tractable. [C14: via OF from Med. L *malleābilis*, from L *malleus* hammer]
▸ˌ**malleaˈbility** *or* (*less commonly*) ˈ**malleableness** *n* ▸ˈ**malleably** *adv*

mallee (ˈmæliː) *n* **1** any of several low shrubby eucalyptus trees in desert regions of Australia. **2** (usually preceded by *the*) *Austral. inf.* another name for the **bush** (sense 4). [C19: Abor.]

Mallee (ˈmæliː) *n* a region in NW Victoria, Australia.

mallee fowl *n* an Australian megapode.

malleolus (məˈliːələs) *n, pl* **malleoli** (-ˌlaɪ). either of two rounded bony projections, one on each side of the ankle. [C17: dim. of L *malleus* hammer]

mallet (ˈmælɪt) *n* **1** a tool resembling a hammer but having a large head of wood, copper, lead, leather, etc., used for driving chisels, beating sheet metal, etc. **2** a long stick with a head like a hammer used to strike the ball in croquet or polo. [C15: from OF *maillet* wooden hammer, dim. of *mail* MAUL (n)]

malleus (ˈmælɪəs) *n, pl* **mallei** (-lɪˌaɪ). the outermost and largest of the three small bones in the middle ear of mammals. See also **incus, stapes.** [C17: from L: hammer]

mallie (ˈmɔːlɪ) *n Inf., chiefly US.* a teenage girl who spends most of her spare time loitering in shopping malls.

mallow (ˈmæləʊ) *n* **1** any of several malvaceous plants of Europe, having purple, pink, or white flowers. **2** any of various related plants, such as the marsh mallow. [OE *mealuwe*, from L *malva*]

malm (mɑːm) *n* **1** a soft greyish limestone that crumbles easily. **2** a chalky soil formed from this. **3** an artificial mixture of clay and chalk used to make bricks. [OE *mealm-* (in compound words)]

malmsey (ˈmɑːmzɪ) *n* a sweet Madeira wine. [C15: from Med. L *Malmasia*, corruption of Gk *Monembasia*, Gk port from which the wine was shipped]

malnutrition (ˌmælnjuːˈtrɪʃən) *n* lack of adequate nutrition resulting from insufficient food, unbalanced diet, or defective assimilation.

malodorous ❶ (mælˈəʊdərəs) *adj* having a bad smell.

malpractice ❶ (mælˈpræktɪs) *n* **1** immoral, illegal, or unethical professional conduct or neglect of professional duty. **2** any instance of improper professional conduct.

malt (mɔːlt) *n* **1** cereal grain, such as barley, that is kiln-dried after it has germinated by soaking in water. **2** See **malt liquor, malt whisky.** ◆ *vb* **3** to make into or become malt. **4** to make (something, esp. liquor) with malt. [OE *mealt*]
▸ˈ**malty** *adj*

malted milk *n* **1** a soluble powder made from dehydrated milk and malted cereals. **2** a drink made from this powder.

Maltese (mɔːlˈtiːz) *adj* **1** of or relating to Malta, an island in the Mediterranean, its inhabitants, or their language. ◆ *n* **2** (*pl* **Maltese**) a native or inhabitant of Malta or a descendant of one. **3** the official language of Malta, a form of Arabic with borrowings from Italian, etc.

Maltese cross *n* a cross with triangular arms that taper towards the centre, sometimes having indented outer sides.

malt extract *n* a sticky substance obtained from an infusion of malt.

Malthusian (mælˈθjuːzɪən) *adj* **1** of or relating to the theory of T. R. Malthus (1766–1834), English economist, stating that increases in population tend to exceed increases in the means of subsistence and that therefore sexual restraint should be exercised. ◆ *n* **2** a supporter of this theory.
▸**Malˈthusianism** *n*

malting (ˈmɔːltɪŋ) *n* a building in which malt is made or stored. Also called: **malt house.**

malt liquor *n* any alcoholic drink brewed from malt.

maltose (ˈmɔːltəʊz) *n* a sugar formed by the enzymic hydrolysis of starch. [C19: from MALT + -OSE[2]]

maltreat ❶ (mælˈtriːt) *vb* (*tr*) to treat badly, cruelly, or inconsiderately. [C18: from F *maltraiter*]
▸**malˈtreater** *n* ▸**malˈtreatment** *n*

maltster (ˈmɔːltstə) *n* a person who makes or deals in malt.

malt whisky *n* whisky made from malted barley.

malvaceous (mælˈveɪʃəs) *adj* of, relating to, or belonging to a family of

THESAURUS

malevolence *n* = **malice**, hate, hatred, ill will, maliciousness, malignity, nastiness, rancour, spite, spitefulness, vengefulness, vindictiveness

malevolent *adj* = **spiteful**, baleful, evil-minded, hateful (*arch.*), hostile, ill-natured, maleficent, malicious, malign, malignant, pernicious, rancorous, vengeful, vicious, vindictive
Antonyms *adj* amiable, benevolent, benign, friendly, gracious, kind, warm-hearted

malformation *n* **1, 2** = **deformity**, crookedness, distortion, misshape, misshapenness

malformed *adj* **1, 2** = **misshapen**, abnormal, contorted, crooked, deformed, distorted, irregular, twisted

malfunction *vb* **1** = **break down**, develop a fault, fail, go wrong ◆ *n* **2** = **fault**, breakdown, defect, failure, flaw, glitch, impairment

malice *n* **1, 2** = **spite**, animosity, animus, bad blood, bitterness, enmity, evil intent, hate, hatred, ill will, malevolence, maliciousness, malignity, rancour, spitefulness, spleen, vengefulness, venom, vindictiveness

malicious *adj* **1, 2** = **spiteful**, baleful, bitchy (*inf.*), bitter, catty (*inf.*), evil-minded, hateful, ill-disposed, ill-natured, injurious, malevolent, malignant, mischievous, pernicious, rancorous, resentful, shrewish, vengeful, vicious
Antonyms *adj* amiable, benevolent, friendly, kind, warm-hearted

malign *adj* **1** = **evil**, bad, baleful, baneful, deleterious, destructive, harmful, hostile, hurtful, injurious, maleficent, malevolent, malignant, pernicious, vicious, wicked ◆ *vb* **2** = **disparage**, abuse, asperse, blacken (someone's name), calumniate, defame, denigrate, derogate, harm, injure, knock (*inf.*), libel, revile, rubbish (*inf.*), run down, slag (off) (*sl.*), slander, smear, speak ill of, traduce, vilify
Antonyms *adj* ≠ **evil:** agreeable, amiable, beneficial, benevolent, benign, friendly, good, harmless, honourable, innocuous, kind, moral, virtuous, warm-hearted, wholesome ◆ *vb* ≠ **disparage:** commend, compliment, extol, praise

malignant *adj* **1, 2** = **hostile**, baleful, bitter, destructive, harmful, hurtful, inimical, injurious, maleficent, malevolent, malicious, malign, of evil intent, pernicious, spiteful, vicious **3** *Pathol.* = **uncontrollable**, cancerous, dangerous, deadly, evil, fatal, irremediable, metastatic, virulent
Antonyms *adj* ≠ **hostile:** amicable, benevolent, benign, friendly, kind, warm-hearted

malignity *n* **1** = **deadliness**, balefulness, destructiveness, harmfulness, hurtfulness, perniciousness, virulence **2** = **malice**, animosity, animus, bad blood, bitterness, evil, hate, hatred, hostility, ill will, malevolence, maliciousness, rancour, spite, vengefulness, venom, viciousness, vindictiveness, wickedness

malleable *adj* **1** = **workable**, ductile, plastic, soft, tensile **2** = **manageable**, adaptable, biddable, compliant, governable, impressionable, pliable, tractable

malodorous *adj* = **smelly**, evil-smelling, fetid, foul-smelling, mephitic, nauseating, niffy, noisome, offensive, olid, putrid, rank, reeking, stinking

malpractice *n* **1** = **misconduct**, abuse, dereliction, misbehaviour, mismanagement, negligence

maltreat *vb* = **abuse**, bully, damage, handle roughly, harm, hurt, ill-treat, injure, mistreat

maltreatment *n* = **abuse**, bullying, harm, ill-treatment, ill-usage, injury, mistreatment, rough handling plants that includes mallow, cotton, okra, althaea, and abutilon. [C17: from L *malvāceus*, from *malva* MALLOW]

malversation (ˌmælvɜːˈseɪʃən) *n Rare.* professional or public misconduct. [C16: from F, from *malverser* to behave badly, from L *male versārī*]

mam (mæm) *n Inf. or dialect.* another word for **mother.**

mama *or esp. US* **mamma** (məˈmɑː) *n Old-fashioned.* an informal word for **mother.** [C16: reduplication of childish syllable *ma*]

mamba (ˈmæmbə) *n* any of various partly arboreal tropical African venomous snakes, esp. the **green** and **black mambas.** [from Zulu *im-amba*]

mambo (ˈmæmbəʊ) *n, pl* **mambos. 1** a modern Latin American dance, resembling the rumba. ◆ *vb* **2** (*intr*) to perform this dance. [American Sp., prob. from Haitian Creole: voodoo priestess]

Mameluke *or* **Mamaluke** (ˈmæmɪˌluːk) *n* **1** a member of a military class, originally of Turkish slaves, ruling in Egypt from about 1250 to 1517 and remaining powerful until 1811. **2** (in Muslim countries) a slave. [C16: via F, ult. from Ar. *mamlūk* slave, from *malaka* to possess]

mamilla *or US* **mammilla** (mæˈmɪlə) *n, pl* **mamillae** (-liː) *or US* **mammillae. 1** a nipple or teat. **2** any nipple-shaped prominence. [C17: from L, dim. of *mamma* breast]
▸ˈ**mamillary** *or US* ˈ**mammillary** *adj*

mamma (ˈmæmə) *n, pl* **mammae** (-miː). the milk-secreting organ of female mammals: the breast in women, the udder in cows, sheep, etc. [C17: from L: breast]
▸ˈ**mammary** *adj*

mammal (ˈmæməl) *n* any animal of the *Mammalia*, a large class of warm-blooded vertebrates having mammary glands in the female. [C19: via NL from L *mamma* breast]
▸**mammalian** (mæˈmeɪlɪən) *adj, n*

mammary gland *n* any of the milk-producing glands in mammals.

mammogram (ˈmæməʊˌɡræm) *n* an X-ray photograph of the breast.

mammography (mæˈmɒɡrəfɪ) *n* examination of the breasts by X-ray, esp. to detect early signs of cancer.

mammon (ˈmæmən) *n* riches or wealth regarded as a source of evil and corruption. [C14: via LL from New Testament Gk *mammōnas*, from Aramaic *māmōnā* wealth]
▸ˈ**mammonish** *adj* ▸ˈ**mammonism** *n* ▸ˈ**mammonist** *or* ˈ**mammonite** *n*

Mammon (ˈmæmən) *n Bible.* the personification of riches and greed in the form of a false god.

mammoth ❶ (ˈmæməθ) *n* **1** any large extinct elephant of the Pleistocene epoch, such as the **woolly mammoth**, having a hairy coat and long curved tusks. ◆ *adj* **2** of gigantic size or importance. [C18: from Russian *mamot*, from Tartar *mamont*, ?from *mamma* earth, because of a belief that the animal made burrows]

mammy *or* **mammie** (ˈmæmɪ) *n, pl* **mammies. 1** a child's word for **mother**[1] (senses 1–3). **2** *Chiefly southern US.* a Black woman employed as a nurse or servant to a White family.

man ❶ (mæn) *n, pl* **men. 1** an adult male human being, as distinguished from a woman. **2** (*modifier*) male; masculine: *a man child.* **3** a human being, considered as representative of mankind. **4** human beings collectively; mankind. **5** Also called: **modern man. 5a** a member of any of the living races of *Homo sapiens*, characterized by erect bipedal posture, a highly developed brain, and powers of articulate speech, abstract reasoning, and imagination. **5b** any extinct member of the species *Homo sapiens*, such as Cro-Magnon man. **6** a member of any of the extinct species of the genus *Homo*, such as Java man. **7** an adult male human being with qualities associated with the male, such as courage or virility: *be a man.* **8** manly qualities or virtues: *the man in him was outraged.* **9a** a subordinate, servant, or employee. **9b** (*in combination*): *the man-days required to complete a job.* **10** (*usually pl*) a member of the armed forces who does not hold commissioned, warrant, or noncommissioned rank (as in **officers and men**). **11** a member of a group, team, etc. **12** a husband, boyfriend, etc. **13** an expression used parenthetically to indicate an informal relationship between speaker and hearer. **14** a movable piece in various games, such as draughts. **15** a vassal of a feudal lord. **16** *S. African sl.* any person: used as a term of address. **17 as one man.** with unanimous action or response. **18 be one's own man.** to be independent or free. **19 he's your man.** he's the person needed. **20 man and boy.** from childhood. **21 sort out** *or* **separate the men from the boys.** to separate the experienced from the inexperienced. **22 to a man.** without exception. ◆ *interj* **23** *Inf.* an exclamation or expletive, often indicating surprise or pleasure. ◆ *vb* **mans, manning, manned.** (*tr*) **24** to provide with sufficient men for operation, defence, etc. **25** to take one's place at or near in readiness for action. [OE *mann*]

Man. *abbrev. for:* **1** Manila paper. **2** Manitoba.

-man *n combining form.* indicating a person who has a role, works in a place, or operates equipment as specified: *salesman; barman; cameraman.*

> **USAGE NOTE** The use of words ending in *-man* is avoided as implying a male in job advertisements, where sexual discrimination is illegal, and in many other contexts where a term that is not gender-specific is available, such as *salesperson, barperson, camera operator.*

mana (ˈmɑːnə) *n Anthropol.* **1** (in Polynesia, Melanesia, etc.) a concept of a life force associated with high social status and ritual power. **2** any power achieved by ritual means; prestige; authority. [of Polynesian origin]

man about town *n* a fashionable sophisticate, esp. one in a big city.

manacle ❶ (ˈmænəkᵊl) *n* **1** (*usually pl*) a shackle, handcuff, or fetter, used to secure the hands of a prisoner, convict, etc. ◆ *vb* **manacles, manacling, manacled.** (*tr*) **2** to put manacles on. **3** to confine or constrain. [C14: via OF from L *manicula*, dim. of *manus* hand]

manage ❶ (ˈmænɪdʒ) *vb* **manages, managing, managed.** (*mainly tr*) **1** (*also intr*) to be in charge (of); administer: *to manage a shop.* **2** to succeed in being able (to do something); contrive. **3** to have room, time, etc., for: *can you manage dinner tomorrow?* **4** to exercise control or domination over. **5** (*intr*) to contrive to carry on despite difficulties, esp. financial ones. **6** to wield or handle (a weapon). [C16: from It. *maneggiare* to train (esp. horses), ult. from L *manus* hand]

manageable ❶ (ˈmænɪdʒəbᵊl) *adj* able to be managed or controlled.
▸ˌ**manageaˈbility** *or* ˈ**manageableness** *n* ▸ˈ**manageably** *adv*

managed currency *n* a currency subject to governmental control with respect to the amount in circulation and rate of exchange.

managed fund *n* an investment managed by an insurance company to provide low-risk investments for the small investor.

management ❶ (ˈmænɪdʒmənt) *n* **1** the members of the executive or administration of an organization or business. **2** managers or employers collectively. **3** the technique, practice, or science of managing or controlling. **4** the skilful or resourceful use of materials, time, etc. **5** the specific treatment of a disease, etc.

management buyout *n* the purchase of a company by its managers, usually with outside backing from a bank or other institution.

management company *n* a company that manages a unit trust.

manager ❶ (ˈmænɪdʒə) *n* **1** a person who directs or manages an organization, industry, shop, etc. **2** a person who controls the business affairs of an actor, entertainer, etc. **3** a person who controls the training of a sportsman or team. **4** a person who has a talent for managing efficiently. **5** (in Britain) a member of either House of Parliament appointed to arrange a matter in which both Houses are concerned. **6** *Computing.* a computer program that organizes a resource, such as a set of files or a database.
▸ˈ**managership** *n*

manageress (ˌmænɪdʒəˈrɛs) *n* a woman who is in charge of a shop, department, etc.

managerial (ˌmænɪˈdʒɪərɪəl) *adj* of or relating to a manager or management.
▸ˌ**manaˈgerially** *adv*

managing (ˈmænɪdʒɪŋ) *adj* having administrative control or authority: *a managing director.*

mañana *Spanish.* (məˈnjɑːnə) *n, adv* **a** tomorrow. **b** some other and later time.

man-at-arms *n, pl* **men-at-arms.** a soldier, esp. a heavily armed mounted soldier in medieval times.

manatee (ˌmænəˈtiː) *n* a sirenian mammal occurring in tropical

THESAURUS

mammoth *adj* **2** = **colossal**, Brobdingnagian, elephantine, enormous, gargantuan, giant, gigantic, ginormous (*inf.*), huge, humongous *or* humungous (*US sl.*), immense, jumbo (*inf.*), massive, mega (*sl.*), mighty, monumental, mountainous, prodigious, stellar (*inf.*), stupendous, titanic, vast
Antonyms *adj* diminutive, insignificant, little, miniature, minute, puny, small, tiny, trivial

man *n* **1** = **male**, bloke (*Brit. inf.*), chap (*inf.*), gentleman, guy (*inf.*) **3** = **human**, adult, being, body, human being, individual, one, person, personage, somebody, soul **5** = **mankind**, Homo sapiens, humanity, humankind, human race, mortals, people **9** = **manservant**, attendant, follower, retainer, servant, valet **12** = **boyfriend**, beau, husband, lover, partner, significant other (*US inf.*), spouse **15** = **employee**, hand, hireling, liegeman, soldier, subject, subordinate, vassal, worker, workman **22 to a man** = **without exception**, bar none, every one, one and all, unanimously ◆ *vb* **24** = **staff**, crew, fill, furnish with men, garrison, occupy, people

manacle *n* **1** = **handcuff**, bond, chain, fetter, gyve (*arch.*), iron, shackle, tie ◆ *vb* **2** = **handcuff**, bind, chain, check, clap *or* put in irons, confine, constrain, curb, fetter, hamper, inhibit, put in chains, restrain, shackle, tie one's hands

manage *vb* **1** = **administer**, be in charge (of), call the shots, call the tune, command, concert, conduct, direct, govern, handle, manipulate, oversee, preside over, rule, run, superintend, supervise **2** = **succeed**, accomplish, arrange, bring about *or* off, contrive, cope with, crack it (*inf.*), cut it (*inf.*), deal with, effect, engineer **4, 6** = **handle**, control, dominate, govern, guide, influence, manipulate, operate, pilot, ply, steer, train, use, wield **5** = **cope**, carry on, fare, get along, get by (*inf.*), get on, get through, make do, make out, muddle through, shift, survive
Antonyms *vb* ≠ **succeed:** bodge (*inf.*), botch, fail, make a mess of, make a nonsense of, mismanage, muff, spoil

manageable *adj* = **easy**, convenient, handy, user-friendly, wieldy = **docile**, amenable, compliant, controllable, governable, submissive, tamable, tractable
Antonyms *adj* ≠ **easy:** demanding, difficult, hard ≠ **docile:** disobedient, headstrong, obstinate, refractory, stubborn, ungovernable, unruly, unyielding, wild

management *n* **1, 2** = **directors**, administration, board, bosses (*inf.*), directorate, employers, executive(s) **3** = **administration**, care, charge, command, conduct, control, direction, governance, government, guidance, handling, manipulation, operation, rule, running, superintendence, supervision

manager *n* **1-3** = **supervisor**, administrator, boss (*inf.*), comptroller, conductor, controller, coastal waters of America, the Caribbean, and Africa, having a prehensile upper lip and a broad flattened tail. [C16: via Sp. from Carib *Manattouï*]

manchester ('mæntʃɪstə) *n Austral. & NZ.* **1** goods, such as sheets and pillowcases, which are, or were originally, made of cotton. **2 manchester department.** a section of a store which sells such goods. [from *Manchester,* city of NW England, former centre of the textile trade]

manchineel (ˌmæntʃɪ'niːl) *n* a tropical American tree having fruit and milky highly caustic poisonous sap, which causes skin blisters. [C17: via F from Sp. MANZANILLA]

Manchu (mæn'tʃuː) *n* **1** (*pl* **Manchus** *or* **Manchu**) a member of a Mongoloid people of Manchuria, a region of NE China, who conquered China in the 17th century, establishing a dynasty that lasted until 1912. **2** the language of this people. ◆ *adj* **3** Also: **Ching.** of or relating to the dynasty of the Manchus. [from Manchu, lit.: pure]

manciple ('mænsɪpᵊl) *n* a steward who buys provisions, esp. in an Inn of Court. [C13: via OF from L *mancipium* purchase, from *manceps* purchaser, from *manus* hand + *capere* to take]

Mancunian (mæŋ'kjuːnɪən) *n* **1** a native or inhabitant of Manchester, a city in NW England. ◆ *adj* **2** of or relating to Manchester. [from Med. L *Mancunium* Manchester]

-mancy *n combining form.* indicating divination of a particular kind: *chiromancy.* [from OF *-mancie,* from L *-mantia,* from Gk *manteia* soothsaying]
▸**-mantic** *adj combining form.*

mandala ('mændələ, mæn'dɑːlə) *n Hindu & Buddhist art.* any of various designs symbolizing the universe, usually circular. [Sansk.: circle]

mandamus (mæn'deɪməs) *n, pl* **mandamuses.** *Law.* (formerly) a writ from (now an order of) a superior court commanding an inferior tribunal, public official, etc., to carry out a public duty. [C16: L, lit.: we command, from *mandāre*]

mandarin ('mændərɪn) *n* **1** (in the Chinese Empire) a member of a senior grade of the bureaucracy. **2** a high-ranking official whose powers are extensive and thought to be outside political control. **3** a person of standing and influence, as in literary or intellectual circles, esp. one regarded as conservative or reactionary. **4a** a small citrus tree cultivated for its edible fruit. **4b** the fruit, resembling the tangerine. [C16: from Port. via Malay from Sansk. *mantrin* counsellor, from *mantra* counsel]
▸**'mandarinate** *n*

Mandarin Chinese *or* **Mandarin** *n* the official language of China since 1917.

Mandarin collar *n* a high stiff round collar.

mandarin duck *n* an Asian duck, the male of which has a distinctive brightly coloured and patterned plumage and crest.

mandate ❶ *n* ('mændeɪt, -dɪt). **1** an official or authoritative instruction or command. **2** *Politics.* the support or commission given to a government and its policies or an elected representative and his policies through an electoral victory. **3** (*often cap.*) Also called: **mandated territory.** (formerly) any of the territories under the trusteeship of the League of Nations administered by one of its member states. **4a** *Roman law.* a contract by which one person commissions another to act for him gratuitously. **4b** *Contract law.* a contract under which a party entrusted with goods undertakes to perform gratuitously some service in respect of such goods. **4c** *Scots Law.* a contract by which a person is engaged to act in the management of the affairs of another. ◆ *vb* ('mændeɪt), **mandates, mandating, mandated.** (*tr*) **5** to assign (territory) to a nation under a mandate. **6** to delegate authority to. [C16: from L *mandātum* something commanded, from *mandāre* to command, ?from *manus* hand + *dāre* to give]
▸**'mandator** *n*

mandatory ❶ ('mændətərɪ, -trɪ) *adj* **1** having the nature or powers of a mandate. **2** obligatory; compulsory. **3** (of a state) having received a mandate over some territory. ◆ *n, pl* **mandatories.** *also* **mandatary. 4** a person or state holding a mandate.
▸**'mandatorily** *adv*

mandible ('mændɪbᵊl) *n* **1** the lower jawbone in vertebrates. **2** either of a pair of mouthparts in insects and other arthropods that are usually used for biting and crushing food. **3** *Ornithol.* either part of the bill, esp. the lower part. [C16: via OF from LL *mandibula* jaw, from *mandere* to chew]
▸**mandibular** (mæn'dɪbjʊlə) *adj* ▸**mandibulate** (mæn'dɪbjʊlɪt, -ˌleɪt) *n, adj*

mandolin *or* **mandoline** (ˌmændə'lɪn) *n* a plucked stringed instrument having four pairs of strings stretched over a small light body with a fretted fingerboard: usually played with a plectrum. [C18: via F from It. *mandolino,* dim. of *mandora* lute, ult. from Gk *pandoura* musical instrument with three strings]
▸**ˌmando'linist** *n*

mandrake ('mændreɪk) *or* **mandragora** (mæn'drægərə) *n* **1** a Eurasian plant with purplish flowers and a forked root. It was formerly thought to have magic powers and a narcotic was prepared from its root. **2** another name for the **May apple.** [C14: prob. via MDu. from L *mandragoras,* from Gk. The form *mandrake* was prob. adopted through folk etymology, because of the allegedly human appearance of the root and because *drake* (dragon) suggested magical powers]

mandrel *or* **mandril** ('mændrəl) *n* **1** a spindle on which a workpiece is supported during machining operations. **2** a shaft or arbor on which a machining tool is mounted. [C16: ? rel. to F *mandrin* lathe]

mandrill ('mændrɪl) *n* an Old World monkey of W Africa. It has a short tail and brown hair, and the ridged muzzle, nose, and hindquarters are red and blue. [C18: from MAN + DRILL[4]]

mane (meɪn) *n* **1** the long coarse hair that grows from the crest of the neck in such mammals as the lion and horse. **2** long thick human hair. [OE *manu*]
▸**maned** *adj*

manège *or* **manege** (mæ'neɪʒ) *n* **1** the art of training horses and riders. **2** a riding school. [C17: via F from It. *maneggio,* from *maneggiare* to MANAGE]

manes ('mɑːneɪz) *pl n* (*sometimes cap.*) (in Roman legend) **1** the spirits of the dead, often revered as minor deities. **2** (*functioning as sing*) the shade of a dead person. [C14: from L, prob.: the good ones, from OL *mānus* good]

maneuver (mə'nuːvə) *n, vb* the usual US spelling of **manoeuvre.**

man Friday *n* **1** a loyal male servant or assistant. **2** Also: **girl Friday, person Friday.** any factotum, esp. in an office. [after the native in Daniel Defoe's novel *Robinson Crusoe* (1719)]

manful ❶ ('mænfʊl) *adj* resolute, strong; manly.
▸**'manfully** *adv* ▸**'manfulness** *n*

mangabey ('mæŋgəˌbeɪ) *n* any of several large agile arboreal Old World monkeys of central Africa, having long limbs and tail. [C18: after a region in Madagascar]

manganese ('mæŋgəˌniːz) *n* a brittle greyish-white metallic element: used in making steel and ferromagnetic alloys. Symbol: Mn; atomic no.: 25; atomic wt.: 54.938. [C17: via F from It., prob. altered form of Med. L MAGNESIA]

mange (meɪndʒ) *n* an infectious disorder mainly affecting domestic animals, characterized by itching and loss of hair: caused by parasitic mites. [C14: from OF *mangeue* itch, from *mangier* to eat]

mangelwurzel ('mæŋgᵊlˌwɜːzᵊl) *or* **mangoldwurzel** ('mæŋgəʊldˌwɜːzᵊl) *n* a Eurasian variety of beet, cultivated as a cattle food, having a large yellowish root. [C18: from G *Mangoldwurzel,* from *Mangold* beet + *Wurzel* root]

manger ('meɪndʒə) *n* a trough or box in a stable, barn, etc., from which horses or cattle feed. [C14: from OF *maingeure* food trough, from *mangier* to eat, ult. from L *mandūcāre* to chew]

mangetout (ˌmɒnʒ'tuː) *n* a variety of garden pea in which the pod is also edible. Also called: **sugar pea.** [C20: from F lit.: eat all]

mangey ('meɪndʒɪ) *adj* **mangier, mangiest.** a variant spelling of **mangy.**

mangle[1] ❶ ('mæŋgᵊl) *vb* **mangles, mangling, mangled.** (*tr*) **1** to mutilate, disfigure, or destroy by cutting, crushing, or tearing. **2** to ruin, spoil, or mar. [C14: from Norman F *mangler,* prob. from OF *mahaignier* to maim]
▸**'mangled** *adj* ▸**'mangler** *n*

mangle[2] ('mæŋgᵊl) *n* **1** Also called: **wringer.** a machine for pressing or drying textiles, clothes, etc., consisting of two heavy rollers between which the cloth is passed. ◆ *vb* **mangles, mangling, mangled.** (*tr*) **2** to press or dry in a mangle. [C18: from Du. *mangel,* ult. from LL *manganum.* See MANGONEL]

mango ('mæŋgəʊ) *n, pl* **mangoes** *or* **mangos. 1** a tropical Asian evergreen tree, cultivated in the tropics for its fruit. **2** the ovoid edible fruit of this tree, having a smooth rind and sweet juicy flesh. [C16: via Port. from Malay *mangā,* from Tamil *mānkāy,* from *mān* mango tree + *kāy* fruit]

mangonel ('mæŋgəˌnel) *n History.* a war engine for hurling stones. [C13: via OF from Med. L *manganellus,* ult. from Gk *manganon*]

mangrove ('mæŋgrəʊv, 'mæn-) *n* any of various tropical evergreen trees or shrubs, having stiltlike intertwining aerial roots and forming dense thickets along coasts. [C17 *mangrow* (changed through infl. of *grove*), from Port. *mangue,* ult. from Taino]

mangy ❶ *or* **mangey** ('meɪndʒɪ) *adj* **mangier, mangiest. 1** having or caused by mange. **2** scruffy or shabby.
▸**'mangily** *adv* ▸**'manginess** *n*

THESAURUS

director, executive, gaffer (*inf., chiefly Brit.*), governor, head, organizer, overseer, proprietor, superintendent

mandate *n* **1, 2** = **command,** authority, authorization, bidding, canon, charge, commission, decree, directive, edict, fiat, injunction, instruction, order, precept, sanction, warrant

mandatory *adj* **2** = **compulsory,** binding, obligatory, required, requisite
Antonyms *adj* discretionary, nonbinding, noncompulsory, nonobligatory, optional, unnecessary, voluntary

manful *adj* = **brave,** bold, courageous, daring, determined, gallant, hardy, heroic, indomitable, intrepid, manly, noble, powerful, resolute, stalwart, stout, stout-hearted, strong, valiant, vigorous

manfully *adv* = **bravely,** boldly, courageously, desperately, determinedly, gallantly, hard, heroically, intrepidly, nobly, powerfully, resolutely, stalwartly, stoutly, strongly, valiantly, vigorously, with might and main

mangle[1] *vb* **1, 2** = **crush,** butcher, cripple, cut, deform, destroy, disfigure, distort, hack, lacerate, maim, mar, maul, mutilate, rend, ruin, spoil, tear, total (*sl.*), trash (*sl.*), wreck

mangy *adj* **2** = **scruffy,** dirty, grungy (*sl., chiefly US*), mean, moth-eaten, scabby (*inf.*), scuzzy (*sl., chiefly US*), seedy, shabby, shoddy, squalid
Antonyms *adj* attractive, choice, clean, de luxe, fine, splendid, spotless, superb, tidy, well-dressed, well-kempt, well-kept

manhandle Ⓣ (ˈmænˌhændəl, ˌmænˈhændəl) *vb* **manhandles, manhandling, manhandled.** (*tr*) **1** to handle or push (someone) about roughly. **2** to move or do by manpower rather than by machinery.

Manhattan (mænˈhætən, mən-) *n* a mixed drink consisting of four parts whisky, one part vermouth, and a dash of bitters. [after *Manhattan*, a borough of New York City, in the US]

manhole (ˈmænˌhəʊl) *n* **1** Also called: **inspection chamber.** a shaft with a removable cover that leads down to a sewer or drain. **2** a hole, usually with a detachable cover, through which a man can enter a boiler, tank, etc.

manhood Ⓣ (ˈmænhʊd) *n* **1** the state or quality of being a man or being manly. **2** men collectively. **3** the state of being human.

man-hour *n* a unit of work in industry, equal to the work done by one man in one hour.

manhunt (ˈmænˌhʌnt) *n* an organized search, usually by police, for a wanted man or fugitive.

mania Ⓣ (ˈmeɪnɪə) *n* **1** a mental disorder characterized by great excitement and occasionally violent behaviour. **2** obsessional enthusiasm or partiality. [C14: via LL from Gk: madness]

-mania *n combining form.* indicating extreme desire or pleasure of a specified kind or an abnormal excitement aroused by something: *kleptomania; nymphomania; pyromania.* [from MANIA]
▸**-maniac** *n and adj combining form.*

maniac Ⓣ (ˈmeɪnɪˌæk) *n* **1** a wild disorderly person. **2** a person who has a great craving or enthusiasm for something. **3** *Psychiatry, obs.* a person afflicted with mania. [C17: from LL *maniacus* belonging to madness, from Gk]

maniacal Ⓣ (məˈnaɪəkəl) *or* **maniac** *adj* **1** affected with or characteristic of mania. **2** characteristic of or befitting a maniac: *maniacal laughter.*
▸**maˈniacally** *adv*

manic (ˈmænɪk) *adj* **1** characterizing, denoting, or affected by mania. ◆ *n* **2** a person afflicted with mania. [C19: from Gk, from MANIA]

manic-depressive *Psychiatry.* ◆ *adj* **1** denoting a mental disorder characterized by an alternation between extreme euphoria and deep depression. ◆ *n* **2** a person afflicted with this disorder.

Manichaeism *or* **Manicheism** (ˈmænɪkiːˌɪzəm) *n* the system of religious doctrines taught by the Persian prophet Mani about the 3rd century A.D. It was based on a supposed primordial conflict between light and darkness or goodness and evil. [C14: from LL *Manichaeus*, from LGk *Manikhaios* of Mani]
▸**ˌManiˈchaean** *or* **ˌManiˈchean** *adj, n* ▸**ˈManichee** *n*

manicure (ˈmænɪˌkjʊə) *n* **1** care of the hands and fingernails, involving shaping the nails, removing cuticles, etc. **2** Also called: **manicurist.** a person who gives manicures, esp. as a profession. ◆ *vb* **manicures, manicuring, manicured. 3** to care for (the hands and fingernails) in this way. [C19: from F, from L *manus* hand + *cūra* care]

manifest Ⓣ (ˈmænɪˌfɛst) *adj* **1** easily noticed or perceived; obvious. **2** *Psychoanalysis.* of or relating to the ostensible elements of a dream: *manifest content.* Cf. **latent** (sense 5). ◆ *vb* **3** (*tr*) to show plainly; reveal or display. **4** (*tr*) to prove beyond doubt. **5** (*intr*) (of a disembodied spirit) to appear in visible form. ◆ *n* **6** a customs document containing particulars of a ship, its cargo, and its destination. **7a** a list of cargo, passengers, etc., on an aeroplane. **7b** a list of railway trucks or their cargo. [C14: from L *manifestus* plain, lit.: struck with the hand]
▸**ˈmaniˌfestable** *adj* ▸**ˈmaniˌfestly** *adv*

manifestation Ⓣ (ˌmænɪfɛˈsteɪʃən) *n* **1** the act of demonstrating; display. **2** the state of being manifested. **3** an indication or sign. **4** a public demonstration of feeling. **5** the materialization of a disembodied spirit.
▸**ˌmaniˈfestative** *adj*

manifesto (ˌmænɪˈfɛstəʊ) *n, pl* **manifestos** *or* **manifestoes.** a public declaration of intent, policy, aims, etc., as issued by a political party, government, or movement. [C17: from It., from *manifestare* to MANIFEST]

manifold Ⓣ (ˈmænɪˌfəʊld) *adj Formal.* **1** of several different kinds; multiple. **2** having many different forms, features, or elements. ◆ *n* **3** something having many varied parts, forms, or features. **4** a chamber or pipe with a number of inlets or outlets used to collect or distribute a fluid. In an internal-combustion engine the **inlet manifold** carries the vaporized fuel from the carburettor to the inlet ports and the **exhaust manifold** carries the exhaust gases away. ◆ *vb* (*tr*) **5** to duplicate (a page, book, etc.). **6** to make manifold; multiply. [OE *manigfeald.* See MANY, -FOLD]
▸**ˈmaniˌfoldly** *adv* ▸**ˈmaniˌfoldness** *n*

manikin *or* **mannikin** (ˈmænɪkɪn) *n* **1** a little man; dwarf or child. **2** an anatomical model of the body or a part of the body, esp. for use in medical or art instruction. **3** a variant of **mannequin.** [C17: from Du. *manneken*, dim. of MAN]

Manila (məˈnɪlə) *n* **1** a type of cigar made in Manila, chief port of the Philippines. **2** short for **Manila hemp** *or* **Manila paper.**

Manila hemp *or* **Manilla hemp** *n* a fibre obtained from the abaca plant, used for rope, paper, etc.

Manila paper *or* **Manilla paper** *n* a strong usually brown paper made from Manila hemp or similar fibres.

manilla (məˈnɪlə) *n* an early form of currency in W Africa in the pattern of a small bracelet. [from Sp.: bracelet, dim. of *mano* hand, from L *manus*]

man in the street *n* the typical or ordinary person.

manioc (ˈmænɪˌɒk) *or* **manioca** (ˌmænɪˈəʊkə) *n* another name for **cassava** (sense 1). [C16: from Tupi *mandioca*]

manipulate Ⓣ (məˈnɪpjʊˌleɪt) *vb* **manipulates, manipulating, manipulated. 1** (*tr*) to handle or use, esp. with some skill. **2** to control or influence (something or someone) cleverly, deviously, or skilfully. **3** to falsify (a bill, accounts, etc.) for one's own advantage. **4** (in physiotherapy) to examine or treat manually, as in loosening a joint. [C19: back formation from *manipulation*, from L *manipulus* handful]
▸**manipulability** (məˌnɪpjʊləˈbɪlɪtɪ) *n* ▸**maˈnipuˌlatable** *or* **maˈnipulable** *adj* ▸**maˌnipuˈlation** *n* ▸**maˈnipulative** *adj* ▸**maˈnipuˌlator** *n* ▸**maˈnipulatory** *adj*

Manitoban (ˌmænɪˈtəʊbən) *adj* **1** of or denoting Manitoba, a province of W Canada. ◆ *n* **2** a native or inhabitant of Manitoba.

manitou, manitu (ˈmænɪˌtuː), *or* **manito** (ˈmænɪˌtəʊ) *n, pl* **manitous, manitus, manitos** *or* **manitou, manitu, manito.** (among the Algonquian Indians) a deified spirit or force. [C17: of Amerind origin]

man jack *n Inf.* a single individual (in **every man jack, no man jack**).

mankind Ⓣ (ˌmænˈkaɪnd) *n* **1** human beings collectively; humanity. **2** men collectively, as opposed to womankind.

> **USAGE NOTE** Some people object to the use of *mankind* to refer to all human beings and prefer the term *humankind.*

manlike (ˈmænˌlaɪk) *adj* resembling or befitting a man.

manly Ⓣ (ˈmænlɪ) *adj* **manlier, manliest. 1** possessing qualities, such as vigour or courage, generally regarded as appropriate to or typical of a man; masculine. **2** characteristic of or befitting a man.
▸**ˈmanliness** *n*

man-made Ⓣ *adj* made by man; artificial.

manna (ˈmænə) *n* **1** *Old Testament.* the miraculous food which sustained the Israelites in the wilderness (Exodus 16:14–36). **2** any spiritual or divine nourishment. **3** a windfall (esp. in **manna from heaven**). **4** a sweet substance obtained from various plants, esp. from the **manna** or **flowering ash** of S Europe, used as a mild laxative. [OE via LL from Gk, from Heb. *mān*]

manned (mænd) *adj* **1** supplied or equipped with men, esp. soldiers. **2** (of spacecraft, etc.) having a human crew.

mannequin (ˈmænɪkɪn) *n* **1** a woman who wears the clothes displayed at a fashion show; model. **2** a life-size dummy of the human body used to fit or display clothes. [C18: via F from Du. *manneken* MANIKIN]

manner Ⓣ (ˈmænə) *n* **1** a way of doing or being. **2** a person's bearing and behaviour. **3** the style or customary way of doing or accomplish-

THESAURUS

manhandle *vb* **1** = **rough up**, handle roughly, knock about *or* around, maul, paw (*inf.*), pull, push **2** = **haul**, carry, heave, hump (*Brit. sl.*), lift, manoeuvre, pull, push, shove, tug

manhood *n* **1** = **manliness**, bravery, courage, determination, firmness, fortitude, hardihood, manfulness, masculinity, maturity, mettle, resolution, spirit, strength, valour, virility

mania *n* **1** = **madness**, aberration, craziness, delirium, dementia, derangement, disorder, frenzy, insanity, lunacy **2** = **obsession**, craving, craze, desire, enthusiasm, fad (*inf.*), fetish, fixation, partiality, passion, preoccupation, rage, thing (*inf.*)

maniac *n* **1, 3** = **madman** *or* **madwoman**, headbanger (*inf.*), headcase (*inf.*), loony (*sl.*), lunatic, nutcase (*sl.*), nutter (*Brit. sl.*), psycho (*sl.*), psychopath **2** = **fanatic**, enthusiast, fan, fiend (*inf.*), freak (*inf.*)

maniacal *adj* **1, 2** = **crazed**, berserk, crazy, demented, deranged, frenzied, insane, lunatic, mad, neurotic, nutty (*sl.*), psychotic, raving, unbalanced, wild

manifest *adj* **1** = **obvious**, apparent, blatant, bold, clear, conspicuous, distinct, evident, glaring, noticeable, open, palpable, patent, plain, salient, unmistakable, visible ◆ *vb* **3, 4** = **display**, declare, demonstrate, establish, evince, exhibit, expose, express, make plain, prove, reveal, set forth, show
Antonyms *adj* ≠ **obvious**: concealed, disguised, hidden, inconspicuous, indistinct, masked, suppressed, unapparent, vague, veiled ◆ *vb* ≠ **display**: conceal, cover, cover up, deny, hide, mask, obscure, refute

manifestation *n* **1, 3** = **display**, appearance, demonstration, disclosure, exhibition, exposure, expression, indication, instance, mark, materialization, revelation, show, sign, symptom, token

manifold *adj* **1, 2** *Formal* = **numerous**, abundant, assorted, copious, diverse, diversified, many, multifarious, multifold, multiple, multiplied, multitudinous, varied, various

manipulate *vb* **1** = **work**, employ, handle, operate, ply, use, wield **2** = **influence**, conduct, control, direct, do a number on (*chiefly US*), engineer, guide, manoeuvre, negotiate, steer, twist around one's little finger

mankind *n* **1** = **people**, Homo sapiens, humanity, humankind, human race, man

manliness *n* **1** = **virility**, boldness, bravery, courage, fearlessness, firmness, hardihood, heroism, independence, intrepidity, machismo, manfulness, manhood, masculinity, mettle, resolution, stoutheartedness, valour, vigour

manly *adj* **1** = **virile**, bold, brave, butch (*sl.*), courageous, daring, dauntless, fearless, gallant, hardy, heroic, macho, male, manful, masculine, muscular, noble, powerful, red-blooded, resolute, robust, stout-hearted, strapping, strong, valiant, valorous, vigorous, well-built
Antonyms *adj* camp (*inf.*), cowardly, craven, delicate, effeminate, faint-hearted, feeble, feminine, frail, girlie, ignoble, irresolute, sickly, soft, timid, unmanly, weak, wimpish *or* wimpy (*inf.*), womanish

man-made *adj* = **artificial**, ersatz, manufactured, mock, plastic (*sl.*), synthetic

manner *n* **1, 3** = **style**, approach, custom, fashion, form, genre, habit, line, means, method, ing something. **4** type or kind. **5** mannered style, as in art; mannerism. **6 in a manner of speaking.** in a way; so to speak. **7 to the manner born.** naturally fitted to a specified role or activity. [C12: via Norman F from OF *maniere,* from Vulgar L *manuāria* (unattested) a way of handling something, noun use of L *manuārius* belonging to the hand, from *manus* hand]

mannered ('mænəd) *adj* **1** having idiosyncrasies or mannerisms; affected. **2** (*in combination*) having manners as specified: *ill-mannered.*

mannerism ('mænə,rɪzəm) *n* **1** a distinctive and individual gesture or trait. **2** (*often cap.*) a principally Italian movement in art and architecture between the High Renaissance and Baroque periods (1520–1600), using distortion and exaggeration of human proportions, perspective, etc. **3** adherence to a distinctive or affected manner, esp. in art or literature.
▸**'mannerist** *n, adj* ▸**,manner'istic** *adj* ▸**,manner'istically** *adv*

mannerless ('mænəlɪs) *adj* having bad manners; boorish.
▸**'mannerlessness** *n*

mannerly ('mænəlɪ) *adj* **1** well-mannered; polite. ◆ *adv* **2** *Now rare.* with good manners; politely.
▸**'mannerliness** *n*

manners ('mænəz) *pl n* **1** social conduct. **2** a socially acceptable way of behaving.

mannikin ('mænɪkɪn) *n* a variant spelling of **manikin.**

mannish ('mænɪʃ) *adj* **1** (of a woman) displaying qualities regarded as typical of a man. **2** of or resembling a man.
▸**'mannishly** *adv* ▸**'mannishness** *n*

manoeuvre *or US* **maneuver** (mə'nu:və) *n* **1** a contrived, complicated, and possibly deceptive plan or action. **2** a movement or action requiring dexterity and skill. **3a** a tactic or movement of a military or naval unit. **3b** (*pl*) tactical exercises, usually on a large scale. **4** a planned movement of an aircraft in flight. **5** any change from the straight steady course of a ship. ◆ *vb* **manoeuvres, manoeuvring, manoeuvred** *or US* **manoeuvers, manoeuvering, manoeuvered. 6** (*tr*) to contrive or accomplish with skill or cunning. **7** (*intr*) to manipulate situations, etc., in order to gain some end. **8** (*intr*) to perform a manoeuvre or manoeuvres. **9** to move or deploy or be moved or deployed, as military units, etc. [C15: from F, from Med. L *manuopera* manual work, from L *manū operāre* to work with the hand]
▸**ma'noeuvrable** *or US* **ma'neuverable** *adj* ▸**ma,noeuvra'bility** *or US* **ma,neuvera'bility** *n* ▸**ma'noeuvrer** *or US* **ma'neuverer** *n* ▸**ma'noeuvring** *or US* **ma'neuvering** *n*

man of God *n* **1** a saint or prophet. **2** a clergyman.

man of straw *n* **1** a man who cannot be relied upon to honour his financial commitments, esp. because of his limited resources. **2** any weak or vulnerable man.

man-of-war *or* **man o' war** *n, pl* **men-of-war** *or* **men o' war. 1** a warship. **2** See **Portuguese man-of-war.**

man-of-war bird *or* **man-o'-war bird** *n* another name for **frigate bird.**

manometer (mə'nɒmɪtə) *n* an instrument for comparing pressures. [C18: from F *manomètre,* from Gk *manos* sparse + *metron* measure]
▸**manometric** (,mænəʊ'mɛtrɪk) *or* **,mano'metrical** *adj*

manor ('mænə) *n* **1** (in medieval Europe) the manor house of a lord and the lands attached to it. **2** a manor house. **3** a landed estate. **4** *Brit. sl.* a geographical area of operation, esp. of a local police force. [C13: from OF *manoir* dwelling, from *maneir* to dwell, from L *manēre* to remain]
▸**manorial** (mə'nɔ:rɪəl) *adj*

manor house *n* (esp. formerly) the house of the lord of a manor.

manpower ('mæn,paʊə) *n* **1** power supplied by men. **2** a unit of power based on the rate at which a man can work; roughly 75 watts. **3** the number of people needed or available for a job.

manqué *French.* ('mɒŋkeɪ) *adj* (*postpositive*) unfulfilled; potential; would-be: *the manager is an actor manqué.* [C19: lit.: having missed]

mansard ('mænsɑ:d, -səd) *n* a roof having two slopes on both sides and both ends, the lower slopes being steeper than the upper. Also called: **mansard roof.** [C18: from F *mansarde,* after François *Mansart* (1598–1666), F architect]

manse (mæns) *n* (in certain religious denominations) the house provided for a minister. [C15: from Med. L *mansus* dwelling, from p.p. of L *manēre* to stay]

manservant ('mæn,sɜ:vənt) *n, pl* **menservants.** a male servant, esp. a valet.

mansion ('mænʃən) *n* **1** Also called: **mansion house.** a large and imposing house. **2** a less common word for **manor house. 3** (*pl*) *Brit.* a block of flats. [C14: via OF from L *mansio* a remaining, from *mansus;* see MANSE]

Mansion House *n* **the. 1** the residence of the Lord Mayor of London. **2** the residence of the Lord Mayor of Dublin.

man-sized *adj* **1** of a size appropriate for or convenient for a man. **2** *Inf.* big; large.

manslaughter ('mæn,slɔ:tə) *n* **1** *Law.* the unlawful killing of one human being by another without malice aforethought. Cf. **murder. 2** (loosely) the killing of a human being.

manta ('mæntə) *n* **1** Also called: **manta ray, devilfish, devil ray.** any large ray (fish), having very wide winglike pectoral fins and feeding on plankton. **2** a rough cotton cloth made in Spain and Spanish America. **3** a piece of this used as a blanket or shawl. [Sp.: cloak, from Vulgar L; see MANTLE]

manteau ('mæntəʊ) *n, pl* **manteaus** (-təʊz) *or* **manteaux** (-təʊ). a cloak or mantle. [C17: via F from L *mantellum* MANTLE]

mantel ('mænt°l) *n* **1** a wooden, stone, or iron frame around the opening of a fireplace, together with its decorative facing. **2** Also called: **mantel shelf.** a shelf above this frame. [C15: from F, var. of MANTLE]

mantelet ('mænt°,lɛt) *or* **mantlet** *n* **1** a woman's short mantle, worn in the mid-19th century. **2** a portable bulletproof screen or shelter. [C14: from OF, dim. of *mantel* MANTLE]

mantelpiece ('mænt°l,pi:s) *n* **1** Also called: **mantel shelf, chimneypiece.** a shelf above a fireplace often forming part of the mantel. **2** another word for **mantel** (sense 1).

mantic ('mæntɪk) *adj* **1** of or relating to divination and prophecy. **2** having divining or prophetic powers. [C19: from Gk *mantikos* prophetic, from *mantis* seer]
▸**'mantically** *adv*

-mantic *adj combining form.* forming adjectives from nouns ending in **-mancy.**

mantilla (mæn'tɪlə) *n* a woman's lace or silk scarf covering the shoulders and head, worn esp. in Spain. [C18: Sp., dim. of *manta* cloak]

mantis ('mæntɪs) *n, pl* **mantises** *or* **mantes** (-ti:z). any carnivorous typically green insect of warm and tropical regions, having a long body and large eyes and resting with the first pair of legs raised as if in prayer. Also called: **praying mantis.** [C17: NL, from Gk: prophet, alluding to its praying posture]

mantissa (mæn'tɪsə) *n* the fractional part of a common logarithm representing the digits of the associated number but not its magnitude: *the mantissa of 2.4771 is .4771.* [C17: from L: something added]

mantle ('mænt°l) *n* **1** *Arch.* a loose wrap or cloak. **2** such a garment regarded as a symbol of someone's power or authority. **3** anything that covers completely or envelops. **4** a small dome-shaped or cylindrical mesh, used to increase illumination in a gas or oil lamp by becoming incandescent. **5** *Zool.* a protective layer of epidermis in molluscs and brachiopods that secretes a substance forming the shell. **6** *Ornithol.* the feathers of the folded wings and back, esp. when of a different colour from the remaining feathers. **7** *Geol.* the part of the earth between the crust and the core. **8** a less common spelling of **mantel.** ◆ *vb* **mantles, mantling, mantled. 9** (*tr*) to envelop or supply with a mantle. **10** (*tr*) to spread over or become spread over. **11** (*intr*) to blush; flush. [C13: via OF from L *mantellum,* dim. of *mantum* cloak]

mantle rock *n* the loose rock material, including glacial drift, soils, etc., that covers the bedrock and forms the land surface.

mantra ('mæntrə, 'mʌn-) *n* **1** *Hinduism.* any of those parts of the Vedic literature which consist of the metrical psalms of praise. **2** *Hinduism, Buddhism.* any sacred word or syllable used as an object of concentration. [C19: from Sansk., lit.: speech, instrument of thought, from *man* to think]

mantua ('mæntjʊə) *n* a woman's loose gown of the 17th and 18th centuries. [C17: changed from MANTEAU, through the infl. of *Mantua,* city in N Italy]

manual ('mænjʊəl) *adj* **1** of or relating to a hand or hands. **2** operated or done by hand. **3** physical, as opposed to mental or mechanical: *manual labour.* **4** by human labour rather than automatic or computer-aided means. ◆ *n* **5** a book, esp. of instructions or information. **6** *Music.* one of the keyboards played by hand on an organ. **7** *Mil.* the prescribed drill with small arms. [C15: via OF from L *manuālis,* from *manus* hand]
▸**'manually** *adv*

THESAURUS

mode, practice, procedure, process, routine, tack, tenor, usage, way, wont **2** = **behaviour,** air, appearance, aspect, bearing, comportment, conduct, demeanour, deportment, look, mien (*literary*), presence, tone **4** = **type,** brand, breed, category, form, kind, nature, sort, variety

mannered *adj* **1** = **affected,** artificial, arty-farty (*inf.*), posed, pretentious, pseudo (*inf.*), put-on, stilted
Antonyms *adj* genuine, honest, natural, real, sincere, unaffected, unpretentious

mannerism *n* **1** = **habit,** characteristic, foible, idiosyncrasy, peculiarity, quirk, trait, trick

mannerly *adj* **1** = **polite,** civil, civilized, courteous, decorous, genteel, gentlemanly, gracious, ladylike, polished, refined, respectful, well-behaved, well-bred, well-mannered
Antonyms *adj* boorish, discourteous, disrespectful, ill-mannered, impertinent, impolite, impudent, insolent, rude, unmannerly

manners *pl n* **1** = **behaviour,** bearing, breeding, carriage, comportment, conduct, demeanour, deportment **2** = **politeness,** ceremony, courtesy, decorum, etiquette, formalities, good form, polish, politesse, proprieties, protocol, p's and q's, refinement, social graces, the done thing

manoeuvre *n* **1** = **stratagem,** action, artifice, dodge, intrigue, machination, move, movement, plan, plot, ploy, ruse, scheme, subterfuge, tactic, trick **3** = **movement,** deployment, evolution, exercise, operation ◆ *vb* **6** = **manipulate,** contrive, devise, engineer, intrigue, machinate, manage, plan, plot, pull strings, scheme, wangle (*inf.*) **8** = **steer,** direct, drive, guide, handle, navigate, negotiate, pilot **9** = **move,** deploy, exercise

mansion *n* **1, 2** = **residence,** abode, dwelling, habitation, hall, manor, seat, villa

mantle *n* **1** *Archaic* = **cloak,** cape, hood, shawl, wrap **3** = **covering,** blanket, canopy, cloud, cover, curtain, envelope, pall, screen, shroud, veil ◆ *vb* **9** = **cover,** blanket, cloak, cloud, disguise, envelop, hide, mask, overspread, screen, shroud, veil, wrap

manual *adj* **2-4** = **hand-operated,** done by hand, human, physical ◆ *n* **5** = **handbook,** bible, guide, guidebook, instructions, workbook

manufactory (ˌmænjʊˈfæktərɪ, -trɪ) *n, pl* **manufactories.** an obsolete word for **factory.** [C17: from obs. *manufact;* see MANUFACTURE]

manufacture ➊ (ˌmænjʊˈfæktʃə) *vb* **manufactures, manufacturing, manufactured. 1** to process or make (a product) from a raw material, esp. as a large-scale operation using machinery. **2** (*tr*) to invent or concoct. ◆ *n* **3** the production of goods, esp. by industrial processes. **4** a manufactured product. **5** the creation or production of anything. [C16: from obs. *manufact* handmade, from LL *manūfactus,* from L *manus* hand + *facere* to make]
▸ˌ**manu'facturing** *n, adj*

manufacturer ➊ (ˌmænjʊˈfæktʃərə) *n* a person or business concern that manufactures goods or owns a factory.

manuka (ˈmɑːnʊkə) *n* a New Zealand tree with strong elastic wood and aromatic leaves. Also called: **tea tree.** [from Maori]

manumit ➊ (ˌmænjʊˈmɪt) *vb* **manumits, manumitting, manumitted.** (*tr*) to free from slavery, servitude, etc.; emancipate. [C15: from L *manūmittere* to release, from *manū* from one's hand + *ēmittere* to send away]
▸**manumission** (ˌmænjʊˈmɪʃən) *n*

manure ➊ (məˈnjʊə) *n* **1** animal excreta, usually with straw, etc., used to fertilize land. **2** *Chiefly Brit.* any material, esp. chemical fertilizer, used to fertilize land. ◆ *vb* **manures, manuring, manured. 3** (*tr*) to spread manure upon (fields or soil). [C14: from Med. L *manuopera* manual work; see MANOEUVRE]
▸**ma'nurer** *n*

manus (ˈmeɪnəs) *n, pl* **manus. 1** *Anat.* the wrist and hand. **2** the corresponding part in other vertebrates. [C19: L: hand]

manuscript (ˈmænjʊˌskrɪpt) *n* **1** a book or other document written by hand. **2** the original handwritten or typed version of a book, article, etc., as submitted by an author for publication. **3** handwriting, as opposed to printing. [C16: from Med. L *manūscriptus,* from L *manus* hand + *scribere* to write]

Manx (mæŋks) *adj* **1** of or relating to the Isle of Man (an island in the Irish Sea), its inhabitants, their language, or their dialect of English. ◆ *n* **2** an almost extinct language of the Isle of Man, closely related to Scottish Gaelic. **3 the Manx.** (*functioning as pl*) the people of the Isle of Man. [C16: earlier *Maniske,* of Scand. origin, from *Mana* Isle of Man + *-iske* -ISH]

Manx cat *n* a short-haired tailless variety of cat, believed to originate on the Isle of Man.

Manxman (ˈmæŋksmən) *or* (*fem*) **Manxwoman** (ˈmæŋksˌwʊmən) *n, pl* **Manxmen** *or* **Manxwomen.** a native or inhabitant of the Isle of Man.

many ➊ (ˈmɛnɪ) *determiner* **1** (sometimes preceded by *a great* or *a good*) **1a** a large number of: *many times.* **1b** (*as pron; functioning as pl*): *many are seated already.* **2** (foll. by *a, an,* or *another,* and a sing noun) each of a considerable number of: *many a man.* **3** (preceded by *as, too, that,* etc.) **3a** a great number of: *as many apples as you like.* **3b** (*as pron; functioning as pl*): *I have as many as you.* ◆ *n* **4 the many.** the majority of mankind, esp. the common people. [OE *manig*]

many-sided *adj* having many sides, aspects, etc.
▸ˌ**many-'sidedness** *n*

many-valued logic *n* any of various logics in which the truth-values that a proposition may have are not restricted to truth and falsity.

manzanilla (ˌmænzəˈnɪlə) *n* a very dry pale sherry. [C19: from Sp.: camomile (referring to its bouquet)]

Maoism (ˈmaʊɪzəm) *n* Marxism-Leninism as interpreted by Mao Tse-tung (1893–1976), Chinese statesman: distinguished by its theory of guerrilla warfare and its emphasis on the revolutionary potential of the peasantry.
▸**'Maoist** *n, adj*

Maori (ˈmaʊrɪ) *n* **1** (*pl* **Maoris** *or* **Maori**) a member of the people of Polynesian origin living in New Zealand and the Cook Islands since before the arrival of European settlers. **2** the language of this people, belonging to the Malayo-Polynesian family. ◆ *adj* **3** of or relating to this people or their language.
▸**'Maoriˌland** *n*

map (mæp) *n* **1** a diagrammatic representation of the earth's surface or part of it, showing the geographical distributions, positions, etc., of features such as roads, towns, relief, rainfall, etc. **2** a diagrammatic representation of the stars or of the surface of a celestial body. **3** a maplike drawing of anything. **4** *Maths.* another name for **function** (sense 5). **5** a slang word for **face** (sense 1). **6 off the map.** no longer important; out of existence (esp. in **wipe off the map**). **7 put on the map.** to make (a town, company, etc.) well-known. ◆ *vb* **maps, mapping, mapped.** (*tr*) **8** to make a map of. **9** *Maths.* to represent or transform (a function, figure, set, etc.). ◆ See also **map out.** [C16: from Med. L *mappa* (*mundi*) map (of the world), from L *mappa* cloth]

maple (ˈmeɪpᵊl) *n* **1** any tree or shrub of a N temperate genus, having winged seeds borne in pairs and lobed leaves. **2** the hard wood of any of these trees, used for furniture and flooring. **3** the flavour of the sap of the sugar maple. ◆ See also **sugar maple.** [C14: from OE *mapel-,* as in *mapeltrēow* maple tree]

maple leaf *n* the leaf of the maple tree, the national emblem of Canada.

maple sugar *n US & Canad.* sugar made from the sap of the sugar maple.

maple syrup *n Chiefly US & Canad.* a very sweet syrup made from the sap of the sugar maple.

map out *vb* (*tr, adv*) to plan or design.

mapping (ˈmæpɪŋ) *n Maths.* another name for **function** (sense 5).

map projection *n* a means of representing or a representation of a globe or celestial sphere or part of it on a flat map.

maquette (mæˈkɛt) *n* a sculptor's small preliminary model or sketch. [C20: from F, from It. *macchietta* a little sketch, from *macchiare,* from L *macula* blemish]

maquis (mɑːˈkiː) *n, pl* **maquis** (-ˈkiː). **1** shrubby, mostly evergreen, vegetation found in coastal regions of the Mediterranean. **2** (*often cap.*) **2a** the French underground movement that fought against the German occupying forces in World War II. **2b** a member of this movement. [C20: from F, from It. *macchia* thicket, from L *macula* spot]

mar ➊ (mɑː) *vb* **mars, marring, marred.** (*tr*) to cause harm to; spoil or impair. [OE *merran*]
▸**'marrer** *n*

mar. *abbrev. for:* **1** maritime. **2** married.

Mar. *abbrev. for* March.

marabou (ˈmærəˌbuː) *n* **1** a large black-and-white African carrion-eating stork. **2** a down feather of this bird, used to trim garments. [C19: from F, from Ar. *murābit* MARABOUT: the stork is considered a holy bird in Islam]

marabout (ˈmærəˌbuː) *n* **1** a Muslim holy man or hermit of North Africa. **2** a shrine of the grave of a marabout. [C17: via F & Port. *marabuto,* from Ar. *murābit*]

maraca (məˈrækə) *n* a percussion instrument, usually one of a pair, consisting of a gourd or plastic shell filled with dried seeds, pebbles, etc. [C20: Brazilian Port., of Amerind origin]

marae (məˈraɪ) *n* **1** *NZ.* a traditional Maori tribal meeting place, originally one in the open air, now frequently a purpose-built building. **2** (in Polynesia) an open-air place of worship. [from Maori]

maranta (mɑːˈræntə) *n* any of various tropical monocotyledons with ornamental leaves. [C19: after B. *Maranta* 16th-century Venetian botanist]

marasca (məˈræskə) *n* a European cherry tree with red acid-tasting fruit. [C19: from It., var. of *amarasca,* ult. from L *amārus* bitter]

maraschino (ˌmærəˈskiːnəʊ, -ˈʃiːnəʊ) *n* a liqueur made from marasca cherries, having a taste like bitter almonds. [C18: from It.; see MARASCA]

maraschino cherry *n* a cherry preserved in maraschino or an imitation of this liqueur.

marasmus (məˈræzməs) *n Pathol.* general emaciation, esp. of infants, thought to be associated with severe malnutrition or impaired utilization of nutrients. [C17: from NL, from Gk *marasmos,* from *marainein* to waste]
▸**ma'rasmic** *adj*

marathon (ˈmærəθən) *n* **1** a race on foot of 26 miles 385 yards (42.195 kilometres). **2a** any long or arduous task, etc. **2b** (*as modifier*): *a marathon effort.* [referring to the feat of the messenger who ran more than 20 miles from Marathon to Athens to bring the news of victory in 490 B.C.]

marathon group *n* (in psychotherapy) an encounter group that lasts for many hours or days.

maraud ➊ (məˈrɔːd) *vb* to wander or raid in search of plunder. [C18: from F *marauder* to prowl, from *maraud* vagabond]
▸**ma'rauder** *n* ▸**ma'rauding** *adj*

marble (ˈmɑːbᵊl) *n* **1a** a hard crystalline metamorphic rock resulting from the recrystallization of a limestone. **1b** (*as modifier*): *a marble bust.* **2** a block or work of art of marble. **3** a small round glass or stone ball used in playing marbles. ◆ *vb* **marbles, marbling, marbled. 4** (*tr*) to mottle with variegated streaks in imitation of marble. [C12: via OF from L *marmor,* from Gk *marmaros,* rel. to Gk *marmairein* to gleam]
▸**'marbled** *adj*

marbles (ˈmɑːbᵊlz) *n* **1** (*functioning as sing*) a game in which marbles are rolled at one another, similar to bowls. **2** (*functioning as pl*) *Inf.* wits: *to lose one's marbles.*

marbling (ˈmɑːblɪŋ) *n* **1** a mottled effect or pattern resembling marble.

THESAURUS

manufacture *vb* **1** = **make,** assemble, build, compose, construct, create, fabricate, forge, form, mass-produce, mould, process, produce, put together, shape, turn out **2** = **concoct,** cook up (*inf.*), devise, fabricate, hatch, invent, make up, think up, trump up ◆ *n* **3, 5** = **making,** assembly, construction, creation, fabrication, mass-production, produce, production

manufacturer *n* = **maker,** builder, constructor, creator, fabricator, factory-owner, industrialist, producer

manumission *n* = **freeing,** deliverance, emancipation, enfranchisement, liberation, release, unchaining

manure *n* **1, 2** = **compost,** droppings, dung, excrement, fertilizer, muck, ordure

many *determiner* **1a** = **numerous,** abundant, copious, countless, divers (*arch.*), frequent, innumerable, manifold, multifarious, multifold, multitudinous, myriad, profuse, sundry, umpteen (*inf.*), varied, various ◆ *n* **4 the many** = **the masses,** the crowd, (the) hoi polloi, the majority, the multitude, the people, the rank and file

mar *vb* = **spoil,** blemish, blight, blot, damage, deface, detract from, disfigure, harm, hurt, impair, injure, maim, mangle, mutilate, ruin, scar, stain, sully, taint, tarnish, vitiate
Antonyms *vb* adorn, ameliorate, better, embellish, improve, ornament

maraud *vb* = **raid,** despoil, forage, foray, harry, loot, pillage, plunder, ransack, ravage, sack

marauder *n* = **raider,** bandit, brigand, buccaneer, corsair, freebooter, mosstrooper, outlaw, pillager, pirate, plunderer, ravager, robber, sea wolf

2 such an effect obtained by transferring floating colours from a gum solution. 3 the streaks of fat in lean meat.

Marburg disease ('mɑːbɜːg) *n* a severe, sometimes fatal, viral disease of vervet (green) monkeys, which may be transmitted to humans. Also called: **green monkey disease.** [C20: after *Marburg*, German city in which the first human cases were recorded]

marc (mɑːk) *n* 1 the remains of grapes or other fruit that have been pressed for wine-making. 2 a brandy distilled from these. [C17: from F, from OF *marchier* to trample (grapes)]

marcasite ('mɑːkəˌsaɪt) *n* 1 a metallic pale yellow mineral consisting of iron pyrites in crystalline form used in jewellery. 2 a cut and polished form of steel or any white metal used for making jewellery. [C15: from Med. L *marcasīta*, from Ar. *marqashītā*, ?from Persian]

marcato (mɑː'kɑːtəʊ) *adj, adv Music.* with each note heavily accented. [from It.: marked]

march[1] ❶ (mɑːtʃ) *vb* 1 (*intr*) to walk or proceed with stately or regular steps, usually in a procession or military formation. 2 (*tr*) to make (a person or group) proceed. 3 (*tr*) to traverse or cover by marching. ◆ *n* 4 the act or an instance of marching. 5 a regular stride. 6 a long or exhausting walk. 7 advance; progression (of time, etc.). 8 a distance or route covered by marching. 9 a piece of music, as for a march. 10 **steal a march on.** to gain an advantage over, esp. by a secret enterprise or trick. [C16: from OF *marchier* to tread, prob. of Gmc origin]
▸ **'marcher** *n*

march[2] ❶ (mɑːtʃ) *n* 1 a frontier, border, or boundary or the land lying along it, often of disputed ownership. ◆ *vb* 2 (*intr*; *often foll. by upon or with*) to share a common border (with). [C13: from OF *marche*, of Gmc origin]

March (mɑːtʃ) *n* the third month of the year, consisting of 31 days. [from OF, from L *Martius* (month) of Mars]

Marches ('mɑːtʃɪz) *n* **the.** 1 the border area between England and Wales or Scotland, both characterized by continual feuding (13th–16th centuries). 2 any of various other border regions.

March hare *n* a hare during its breeding season in March, noted for its wild and excitable behaviour (esp. in **mad as a March hare**).

marching orders *pl n* 1 military orders, esp. to infantry, giving instructions about a march, its destination, etc. 2 *Inf.* any dismissal, esp. notice of dismissal from employment.

marchioness ('mɑːʃənɪs, ˌmɑːʃə'nes) *n* 1 the wife or widow of a marquis. 2 a woman who holds the rank of marquis. [C16: from Med. L *marchionissa*, fem. of *marchiō* MARQUIS]

marchpane ('mɑːtʃˌpeɪn) *n* an archaic word for **marzipan.** [C15: from F]

Mardi Gras ('mɑːdɪ 'grɑː) *n* the festival of Shrove Tuesday, celebrated in some cities with great revelry. [F: fat Tuesday]

Marduk ('mɑːdʊk) *n* the chief god of the Babylonian pantheon.

mare[1] (mɛə) *n* the adult female of a horse or zebra. [C12: from OE, of Gmc origin]

mare[2] ('mɑːreɪ, -rɪ) *n, pl* **maria.** 1 (*cap. when part of a name*) any of a large number of huge dry plains on the surface of the moon, visible as dark markings and once thought to be seas. 2 a similar area on the surface of Mars. [from L: sea]

mare's-nest ('mɛəzˌnest) *n* 1 a discovery imagined to be important but proving worthless. 2 a disordered situation.

mare's-tail ('mɛəzˌteɪl) *n* 1 a wisp of trailing cirrus cloud, indicating strong winds at high levels. 2 an erect pond plant with minute flowers and crowded whorls of narrow leaves.

margaric (mɑː'gærɪk) *or* **margaritic** *adj* of or resembling pearl. [C19: from Gk *margaron* pearl]

margarine (ˌmɑːdʒə'riːn, ˌmɑːgə-) *n* a substitute for butter, prepared from vegetable and animal fats with added small amounts of milk, salt, vitamins, colouring matter, etc. [C19: from MARGARIC]

marge[1] (mɑːdʒ) *n Brit. inf.* short for **margarine.**

marge[2] (mɑːdʒ) *n Arch.* a margin. [C16: from F]

margin ❶ ('mɑːdʒɪn) *n* 1 an edge or rim, and the area immediately adjacent to it; border. 2 the blank space surrounding the text on a page. 3 a vertical line on a page delineating this space. 4 an additional amount or one beyond the minimum necessary: *a margin of error.* 5 *Chiefly Austral.* a payment made in addition to a basic wage, esp. for special skill or responsibility. 6 a bound or limit. 7 the amount by which one thing differs from another. 8 *Commerce.* the profit on a transaction. 9 *Econ.* the minimum return below which an enterprise becomes unprofitable. 10 *Finance.* collateral deposited by a client with a broker as security. ◆ Also (archaic): **margent** ('mɑːdʒənt). ◆ *vb* (*tr*) 11 to provide with a margin; border. 12 *Finance.* to deposit a margin upon. [C14: from L *margō* border]

marginal ❶ ('mɑːdʒɪnᵊl) *adj* 1 of, in, on, or constituting a margin. 2 close to a limit, esp. a lower limit: *marginal legal ability.* 3 not considered central or important; insignificant. 4 *Econ.* relating to goods or services produced and sold at the margin of profitability: *marginal cost.* 5 *Politics, chiefly Brit. & NZ.* of or designating a constituency in which elections tend to be won by small margins: *a marginal seat.* 6 designating agricultural land on the margin of cultivated zones. ◆ *n* 7 *Politics, chiefly Brit. & NZ.* a marginal constituency.
▸ **marginality** (ˌmɑːdʒɪ'nælɪtɪ) *n* ▸ **'marginally** *adv*

marginalia (ˌmɑːdʒɪ'neɪlɪə) *pl n* notes in the margin of a book, manuscript, or letter. [C19: NL, noun (neuter pl) from *margināIis* marginal]

marginate ('mɑːdʒɪˌneɪt) *vb* **marginates, marginating, marginated.** 1 (*tr*) to provide with a margin or margins. ◆ *adj* 2 *Biol.* having a margin of a distinct colour or form. [C18: from L *margināre*]
▸ **ˌmargin'ation** *n*

margrave ('mɑːˌgreɪv) *n* a German nobleman ranking above a count. Margraves were originally counts appointed to govern frontier provinces, but all eventually became princes of the Holy Roman Empire. [C16: from MDu. *markgrave*, lit.: count of the MARCH[2]]
▸ **margravate** ('mɑːgrəvɪt) *n*

margravine ('mɑːgrəˌviːn) *n* 1 the wife or widow of a margrave. 2 a woman who holds the rank of margrave. [C17: from MDu., fem of MARGRAVE]

marguerite (ˌmɑːgə'riːt) *n* 1 a cultivated garden plant whose flower heads have white or pale yellow rays around a yellow disc. 2 any of various related plants with daisy-like flowers. [C19: from F: daisy, pearl, from L, from Gk, from *margaron*]

maria ('mɑːrɪə) *n* the plural of **mare**[2].

mariachi (ˌmɑːrɪ'ɑːtʃɪ) *n* a small ensemble of street musicians in Mexico. [C20: from Mexican Sp.]

marigold ('mærɪˌgəʊld) *n* 1 any of various tropical American plants cultivated for their yellow or orange flower heads and strongly scented foliage. 2 any of various similar or related plants, such as the marsh marigold. [C14: from *Mary* (the Virgin) + GOLD]

marijuana ❶ *or* **marihuana** (ˌmærɪ'hwɑːnə) *n* 1 the dried leaves and flowers of the hemp plant, used for its euphoric effects, esp. in cigarettes. See also **cannabis.** 2 another name for **hemp** (the plant). [C19: from Mexican Sp.]

marimba (mə'rɪmbə) *n* a Latin American percussion instrument consisting of a set of hardwood plates placed over tuned metal resonators, played with two soft-headed sticks in each hand. [C18: of West African origin]

marina (mə'riːnə) *n* an elaborate docking facility for yachts and other pleasure boats. [C19: via It. & Sp. from L: MARINE]

marinade *n* (ˌmærɪ'neɪd). 1 a spiced liquid mixture of oil, wine, vinegar, etc., in which meat or fish is soaked before cooking. 2 meat or fish soaked in this. ◆ *vb* ('mærɪˌneɪd), **marinades, marinading, marinaded.** 3 a variant of **marinate.** [C17: from F, from Sp., from *marinar* to MARINATE]

marinate ('mærɪˌneɪt) *vb* **marinates, marinating, marinated.** to soak in marinade. [C17: prob. from It. *marinato*, from *marinare* to pickle, ult. from L *marīnus* MARINE]
▸ **ˌmari'nation** *n*

marine ❶ (mə'riːn) *adj* (*usually prenominal*) 1 of, found in, or relating to the sea. 2 of or relating to shipping, navigation, etc. 3 of or relating to a body of seagoing troops: *marine corps.* 4 of or relating to a government department concerned with maritime affairs. 5 used or adapted for use at sea. ◆ *n* 6 shipping and navigation in general. 7 (*cap. when part of a name*) a member of a marine corps or similar body. 8 a picture of a ship, seascape, etc. 9 **tell it to the marines.** *Inf.* an expression of disbelief. [C15: from OF *marin*, from L *marīnus*, from *mare* sea]

mariner ❶ ('mærɪnə) *n* a formal or literary word for **seaman.** [C13: from Anglo-F, ult. from L *marīnus* MARINE]

Mariolatry (ˌmɛərɪ'ɒlətrɪ) *n Derog.* devotion to the Virgin Mary, considered as excessive.
▸ **ˌMari'olater** *n* ▸ **ˌMari'olatrous** *adj*

marionette (ˌmærɪə'nɛt) *n* a puppet or doll whose jointed limbs are moved by strings. [C17: from F, from *Marion*, dim. of *Marie* Mary + -ETTE]

Marist ('mɛərɪst) *n RC Church.* a member of the Society of Mary, a religious congregation founded in 1824. [C19: from F *Mariste*, from *Marie* Mary (the Virgin)]

marital ❶ ('mærɪtᵊl) *adj* 1 of or relating to marriage. 2 of or relating to a husband. [C17: from L *marītālis*, from *marītus* married (adj), husband (n)]
▸ **'maritally** *adv*

maritime ❶ ('mærɪˌtaɪm) *adj* 1 of or relating to navigation, shipping, etc. 2 of, relating to, near, or living near the sea. 3 (of a climate) having small temperature differences between summer and winter. [C16: from L *maritimus*, from *mare* sea]

THESAURUS

march[1] *vb* 1 = **walk**, file, footslog, pace, parade, stalk, stride, strut, tramp, tread ◆ *n* 5 = **stride**, gait, pace, step 6 = **walk**, hike, routemarch, tramp, trek 7 = **progress**, advance, development, evolution, progression

march[2] *n* 1 *plural* = **borders**, borderland, boundaries, confines, frontiers, limits, march- lands

margin *n* 1, 6 = **edge**, border, bound, boundary, brim, brink, confine, limit, perimeter, periphery, rim, side, verge 4 = **room**, allowance, compass, elbowroom, extra, latitude, leeway, play, scope, space, surplus

marginal *adj* 1 = **borderline**, bordering, on the edge, peripheral 3 = **insignificant**, low, minimal, minor, negligible, slight, small

marijuana *n* 1 = **cannabis**, bhang, blow (*sl.*), charas, chronic (*US sl.*), dope (*sl.*), ganja, grass (*sl.*), hash (*sl.*), hashish, hemp, kif, leaf (*sl.*), mary jane (*US sl.*), pot (*sl.*), sinsemilla, smoke (*inf.*), stuff (*sl.*), tea (*US sl.*), wacky baccy (*sl.*), weed (*sl.*)

marine *adj* 1, 2 = **nautical**, maritime, naval, ocean-going, oceanic, pelagic, saltwater, sea, seafaring, seagoing, thalassic

mariner *n* = **sailor**, bluejacket, gob, hand, Jack Tar, matelot (*sl., chiefly Brit.*), navigator, salt, sea dog, seafarer, seafaring man, seaman, tar

marital *adj* 1 = **matrimonial**, conjugal, connubial, married, nuptial, spousal, wedded

maritime *adj* 1 = **nautical**, marine, naval, oceanic, sea, seafaring 2 = **coastal**, littoral, seaside

Maritimer ('mærɪ,taɪmə) *n* a native or inhabitant of the Maritime Provinces of Canada, consisting of the provinces of New Brunswick, Nova Scotia, Prince Edward Island, and usually Newfoundland.

marjoram ('mɑːdʒərəm) *n* **1** Also called: **sweet marjoram.** an aromatic Mediterranean plant with sweet-scented leaves, used for seasoning food and in salads. **2** Also called: **wild marjoram, pot marjoram, origan.** a similar and related European plant. See also **oregano.** [C14: via OF *majorane,* from Med. L *marjorana*]

mark[1] ➊ (mɑːk) *n* **1** a visible impression, stain, etc., on a surface, such as a spot or scratch. **2** a sign, symbol, or other indication that distinguishes something. **3** a cross or other symbol made instead of a signature. **4** a written or printed sign or symbol, as for punctuation. **5** a letter, number, or percentage used to grade academic work. **6** a thing that indicates position or directs; marker. **7** a desired or recognized standard: *up to the mark.* **8** an indication of some quality, feature, or prowess. **9** quality or importance: *a person of little mark.* **10** a target or goal. **11** impression or influence. **12** one of the temperature settings on a gas oven: *gas mark 5.* **13** *Sl.* a suitable victim, esp. for swindling. **14** (*often cap.*) (in trade names) a model, brand, or type. **15** *Naut.* one of the intervals distinctively marked on a sounding lead. **16** *Rugby.* an action in which a player within his own 22 m line catches a forward kick by an opponent and shouts "mark", which entitles him to a free kick. **17** *Australian Rules football.* **17a** a catch of the ball from a kick of at least 10 yards, after which a free kick is taken. **17b** the spot where this occurs. **18** (in medieval England and Germany) a piece of land held in common by the free men of a community. **19 the mark.** *Boxing.* the middle of the stomach. **20 make one's mark.** to succeed or achieve recognition. **21 on your mark** *or* **marks.** a command given to runners in a race to prepare themselves at the starting line. ◆ *vb* **22** to make or receive (a visible impression, trace, or stain) on (a surface). **23** (*tr*) to characterize or distinguish. **24** (often foll. by *off* or *out*) to set boundaries or limits (on). **25** (*tr*) to select, designate, or doom by or as if by a mark: *a marked man.* **26** (*tr*) to put identifying or designating labels, stamps, etc., on, esp. to indicate price. **27** (*tr*) to pay heed or attention to: *mark my words.* **28** to observe; notice. **29** to grade or evaluate (scholastic work). **30** *Football, etc.* to stay close to (an opponent) to hamper his play. **31** to keep (score) in some games. **32 mark time. 32a** to move the feet alternately as in marching but without advancing. **32b** to act in a mechanical and routine way. **32c** to halt progress temporarily. ◆ See also **markdown, mark-up.** [OE *mearc* mark]
▸**'marker** *n*

mark[2] (mɑːk) *n* **1** See **Deutschmark, markka, Reichsmark, Ostmark. 2** a former monetary unit and coin in England and Scotland worth two thirds of a pound sterling. **3** a silver coin of Germany until 1924. [OE *marc* unit of weight of precious metal, ?from the marks on metal bars; apparently of Gmc origin and rel. to MARK[1]]

markdown ('mɑːk,daʊn) *n* **1** a price reduction. ◆ *vb* **mark down. 2** (*tr, adv*) to reduce in price.

marked ➊ (mɑːkt) *adj* **1** obvious, evident, or noticeable. **2** singled out, esp. as the target of attack: *a marked man.* **3** *Linguistics.* distinguished by a specific feature, as in phonology. For example, of the two phonemes /t/ and /d/, the /d/ is marked because it exhibits the feature of voice.
▸**markedly** ('mɑːkɪdlɪ) *adv* ▸**'markedness** *n*

market ➊ ('mɑːkɪt) *n* **1a** an event or occasion, usually held at regular intervals, at which people meet to buy and sell merchandise. **1b** (*as modifier*): *market day.* **2** a place at which a market is held. **3** a shop that sells a particular merchandise: *an antique market.* **4** the trading or selling opportunities provided by a particular group of people: *the foreign market.* **5** demand for a particular product or commodity. **6** See **stock market. 7** See **market price, market value. 8 be in the market for.** to wish to buy or acquire. **9 on the market.** available for purchase. **10 seller's** (*or* **buyer's**) **market.** a market characterized by excess demand (or supply) and thus favourable to sellers (or buyers). **11 the market.** business or trade in a commodity as specified: *the sugar market.* ◆ *vb* **markets, marketing, marketed. 12** (*tr*) to offer or produce for sale. **13** (*intr*) to buy or deal in a market. [C12: from L *mercātus,* from *mercārī* to trade, from *merx* merchandise]
▸**'marketable** *adj* ▸**'marketer** *n*

marketeer (,mɑːkɪ'tɪə) *n* **1** *Brit.* a supporter of the EU and of Britain's membership of it. **2** a marketer.

market forces *pl n* the effect of supply and demand on trading within a free market.

market garden *n Chiefly Brit.* an establishment where fruit and vegetables are grown for sale.
▸**market gardener** *n* ▸**market gardening** *n*

marketing ('mɑːkɪtɪŋ) *n* the provision of goods or services to meet consumer needs.

market maker *n* a dealer in securities on the London stock exchange, who buys and sells as a principal and since 1986 can also deal directly with the public.

marketplace ('mɑːkɪt,pleɪs) *n* **1** a place where a public market is held. **2** any centre where ideas, etc., are exchanged. **3** the commercial world of buying and selling.

market price *n* the prevailing price, as determined by supply and demand, at which goods, services, etc., may be bought or sold.

market research *n* the study of influences upon customer behaviour and the analysis of market characteristics and trends.

market-test *vb* (*tr*) to put (a section of a public-sector enterprise) out to tender, often as a prelude to full-scale privatization.

market town *n Chiefly Brit.* a town that holds a market, esp. an agricultural centre.

market value *n* the amount obtainable on the open market for the sale of property, financial assets, or goods and services.

markhor ('mɑːkɔː) *or* **markhoor** ('mɑːkʊə) *n, pl* **markhors, markhor** *or* **markhoors, markhoor.** a large wild Himalayan goat with large spiralled horns. [C19: from Persian, lit.: snake-eater]

marking ('mɑːkɪŋ) *n* **1** a mark or series of marks. **2** the arrangement of colours on an animal, plant, etc. **3** assessment and correction of pupils' or students' written work by teachers.

markka ('mɑːkɑː, -kə) *n, pl* **markkaa** (-kɑː). the standard monetary unit of Finland. [Finnish; see MARK[2]]

marksman ➊ ('mɑːksmən) *n, pl* **marksmen. 1** a person skilled in shooting. **2** a serviceman selected for his skill in shooting.
▸**'marksmanship** *n*

mark-up *n* **1** an amount added to the cost of a commodity to provide the seller with a profit. **2a** an increase in the price of a commodity. **2b** the amount of this. ◆ *vb* **mark up.** (*tr, adv*) **3** to add a percentage for profit, etc., to the cost of (a commodity). **4** to increase the price of.

marl (mɑːl) *n* **1** a fine-grained sedimentary rock consisting of clay minerals, calcium carbonate, and silt: used as a fertilizer. ◆ *vb* **2** (*tr*) to fertilize (land) with marl. [C14: via OF, from LL *margila,* dim. of L *marga*]
▸**'marly** *adj*

marlin ('mɑːlɪn) *n, pl* **marlin** *or* **marlins.** any of several large food and game fishes of warm and tropical seas, having a very long upper jaw. [C20: from MARLINESPIKE, from shape of the beak]

marline *or* **marlin** ('mɑːlɪn) *n Naut.* a light rope, usually tarred, made of two strands laid left-handed. [C15: from Du. *marlijn,* from *marren* to tie + *lijn* line]

marlinespike *or* **marlinspike** ('mɑːlɪn,spaɪk) *n Naut.* a pointed metal tool used in separating strands of rope, etc.

marlite ('mɑːlaɪt) *or* **marlstone** ('mɑːl,stəʊn) *n* a type of marl that is resistant to the decomposing action of air.

marmalade ('mɑːmə,leɪd) *n* a preserve made by boiling the pulp and rind of citrus fruits, esp. oranges, with sugar. [C16: via F from Port. *marmelada,* from *marmelo* quince, from L, from Gk *melimēlon,* from *meli* honey + *mēlon* apple]

marmite ('mɑːmaɪt) *n* a large cooking pot. [from F: pot]

Marmite ('mɑːmaɪt) *n Trademark.* a yeast and vegetable extract used as a spread, flavouring, etc.

marmoreal (mɑː'mɔːrɪəl) *adj* of, relating to, or resembling marble. [C18: from L *marmoreus,* from *marmor* marble]

marmoset ('mɑːmə,zɛt) *n* **1** any of various small South American monkeys having long hairy tails. **2 pygmy marmoset.** a related form: the smallest monkey, inhabiting tropical forests of the Amazon. [C14: from OF *marmouset* grotesque figure, from ?]

marmot ('mɑːmət) *n* **1** any of various burrowing rodents of Europe, Asia, and North America. They are heavily built and have coarse fur. **2 prairie marmot.** another name for **prairie dog.** [C17: from F *marmotte,* ? ult. from L *mūr-* (stem of *mūs*) mouse + *montis* of the mountain]

marocain ('mærə,keɪn) *n* **1** a fabric of ribbed crepe. **2** a garment made from this fabric. [C20: from F *maroquin* Moroccan]

maroon[1] ➊ (mə'ruːn) *vb* (*tr*) **1** to abandon ashore, esp. on an island. **2** to isolate without resources. ◆ *n* **3** a descendant of a group of runaway slaves living in the remoter areas of the Caribbean or Guyana.

THESAURUS

mark[1] *n* **1** = **spot**, blemish, blot, blotch, bruise, dent, impression, line, nick, pock, scar, scratch, smirch, smudge, splotch, stain, streak **2** = **sign**, badge, blaze, brand, characteristic, device, earmark, emblem, evidence, feature, flag, hallmark, impression, incision, index, indication, label, note, print, proof, seal, signet, stamp, symbol, symptom, token **7** = **criterion**, level, measure, norm, par, standard, yardstick **9** = **influence**, consequence, dignity, distinction, eminence, fame, importance, notability, note, notice, prestige, quality, regard, standing **10** = **target**, aim, end, goal, object, objective, purpose **20 make one's mark** = **succeed**, achieve recognition, be a success, find a place in the sun, get on in the world, make a success of oneself, make good, make it, make something of oneself, prosper ◆ *vb* **22** = **scar**, blemish, blot, blotch, brand, bruise, dent, impress, imprint, nick, scratch, smirch, smudge, splotch, stain, streak **23** = **distinguish**, betoken, denote, evince, exemplify, illustrate, show **26** = **characterize**, brand, flag, identify, label, stamp **27, 28** = **observe**, attend, hearken, mind, note, notice, pay attention, pay heed, regard, remark, watch **29** = **grade**, appraise, assess, correct, evaluate

marked *adj* **1** = **noticeable**, apparent, blatant, clear, considerable, conspicuous, decided, distinct, dramatic, evident, manifest, notable, noted, obvious, outstanding, patent, prominent, pronounced, remarkable, salient, signal, striking

Antonyms *adj* concealed, doubtful, dubious, hidden, imperceptible, inconspicuous, indistinct, insignificant, obscure, unclear, unnoticeable, vague

markedly *adv* **1** = **noticeably**, clearly, considerably, conspicuously, decidedly, distinctly, evidently, greatly, manifestly, notably, obviously, outstandingly, patently, remarkably, seriously (*inf.*), signally, strikingly, to a great extent

market *n* **1, 2** = **fair**, bazaar, mart ◆ *vb* **12** = **sell**, offer for sale, retail, vend

marksman *n* **1** = **sharpshooter**, crack shot (*inf.*), deadeye, dead shot (*inf.*), good shot

maroon[1] *vb* **1** = **abandon**, cast ashore, cast away, desert, leave, leave high and dry (*inf.*), strand

[C17 (applied to fugitive slaves): from American Sp. *cimarrón* wild, lit.: dwelling on peaks, from Sp. *cima* summit]

maroon[2] (mə'ru:n) *n* **1a** a dark red to purplish-red colour. **1b** (*as adj*): *a maroon carpet.* **2** an exploding firework, esp. one used as a warning signal. [C18: from F, lit.: chestnut]

Marq. *abbrev. for:* **1** Marquess. **2** Marquis.

marque (mɑ:k) *n* **1** a brand of product, esp. of a car. **2** See **letter of marque.** [from F, from *marquer* to MARK[1]]

marquee (mɑ:'ki:) *n* **1** a large tent used for entertainment, exhibition, etc. **2** Also called: **marquise.** *Chiefly US & Canad.* a canopy over the entrance to a theatre, hotel, etc. [C17 (orig. an officer's tent): invented sing form of MARQUISE, erroneously taken to be pl]

marquess ('mɑ:kwɪs) *n* **1** (in the British Isles) a nobleman ranking between a duke and an earl. **2** See **marquis.**

marquetry *or* **marqueterie** ('mɑ:kɪtrɪ) *n, pl* **marquetries** *or* **marqueteries.** a pattern of inlaid veneers of wood, brass, ivory, etc., used chiefly as ornamentation in furniture. [C16: from OF, from *marqueter* to inlay, from *marque* MARK[1]]

marquis ('mɑ:kwɪs, mɑ:'ki:) *n, pl* **marquises** *or* **marquis.** (in various countries) a nobleman ranking above a count, corresponding to a British marquess. The title of marquis is often used in place of that of marquess. [C14: from OF *marchis,* lit.: count of the march, from *marche* MARCH[2]]

marquise (mɑ:'ki:z) *n* **1** (in various countries) another word for **marchioness. 2a** a gemstone, esp. a diamond, cut in a pointed oval shape and usually faceted. **2b** a piece of jewellery, esp. a ring, set with such a stone or with an oval cluster of stones. **3** another name for **marquee** (sense 2). [C18: from F, fem of MARQUIS]

marquisette (ˌmɑ:kɪ'zɛt, -kwɪ-) *n* a leno-weave fabric of cotton, silk, etc. [C20: from F, dim. of MARQUISE]

marram grass ('mærəm) *n* any of several grasses that grow on sandy shores: often planted to stabilize sand dunes. [C17 *marram,* from ON *marálmr,* from *marr* sea + *hálmr* HAULM]

marri ('mærɪ) *n* a species of eucalyptus of Western Australia, widely cultivated for its coloured flowers. [C19: from Abor.]

marriage Ⓣ ('mærɪdʒ) *n* **1** the state or relationship of being husband and wife. **2a** the legal union or contract made by a man and woman to live as husband and wife. **2b** (*as modifier*): *marriage certificate.* **3** the ceremony formalizing this union; wedding. **4** a close or intimate union, relationship, etc. [C13: from OF; see MARRY[1], -AGE]

marriageable ('mærɪdʒəbᵊl) *adj* (esp. of women) suitable for marriage, usually with reference to age.

▸ˌ**marriagea'bility** *n*

marriage guidance *n* advice given to couples who have problems in their married life.

married Ⓣ ('mærɪd) *adj* **1** having a husband or wife. **2** joined in marriage. **3** of or involving marriage or married persons. **4** closely or intimately united. ◆ *n* **5** (*usually pl*) a married person (esp. in **young marrieds**).

marrons glacés *French.* (marɔ̃ glase) *pl n* chestnuts cooked in syrup and glazed.

marrow Ⓣ ('mærəʊ) *n* **1** the fatty network of connective tissue that fills the cavities of bones. **2** the vital part; essence. **3** *Brit.* short for **vegetable marrow.** [OE *mærg*]

▸'**marrowy** *adj*

marrowbone ('mærəʊˌbəʊn) *n* **a** a bone containing edible marrow. **b** (*as modifier*): *marrowbone jelly.*

marrowfat ('mærəʊˌfæt) *or* **marrow pea** *n* **1** any of several varieties of pea plant that have large seeds. **2** the seed of such a plant.

marry[1] Ⓣ ('mærɪ) *vb* **marries, marrying, married. 1** to take (someone as one's husband or wife) in marriage. **2** (*tr*) to join or give in marriage. **3** to unite closely or intimately. **4** (*tr;* sometimes foll. by *up*) to fit together or align (two things); join. **5** (*tr*) *Naut.* to match up (the strands of ropes) before splicing. [C13: from OF *marier,* from L *marītāre,* from *marītus* married (man), ?from *mās* male]

marry[2] ('mærɪ) *interj Arch.* an exclamation of surprise, anger, etc. [C14: euphemistic for the Virgin *Mary*]

marry off *vb* (*tr, adv*) to find a husband or wife for (a person, esp. one's son or daughter).

Mars[1] (mɑ:z) *n* the Roman god of war.

Mars[2] (mɑ:z) *n* the fourth planet from the sun.

Marsala (mɑ:'sɑ:lə) *n* a dark sweet dessert wine from Marsala, a port in Sicily.

Marseillaise (ˌmɑ:seɪ'jeɪz, -sə'leɪz) *n* **the.** the French national anthem. [C18: from F (*chanson*) *marseillaise* song of Marseilles (first sung in Paris by the battalion of Marseilles)]

marseille (mɑ:'seɪl) *or* **marseilles** (mɑ:'seɪlz) *n* a strong cotton fabric with a raised pattern, used for bedspreads, etc. [C18: from *Marseille quilting,* made in Marseilles]

marsh Ⓣ (mɑ:ʃ) *n* low poorly drained land that is sometimes flooded and often lies at the edge of lakes, etc. Cf. **swamp** (sense 1). [OE *merisc*]

marshal Ⓣ ('mɑ:ʃəl) *n* **1** (in some armies and air forces) an officer of the highest rank. **2** (in England) an officer who accompanies a judge on circuit and performs secretarial duties. **3** (in the US) **3a** a Federal court officer assigned to a judicial district whose functions are similar to those of a sheriff. **3b** (in some states) the chief police or fire officer. **4** an officer who organizes or conducts ceremonies, parades, etc. **5** Also called: **knight marshal.** (formerly in England) an officer of the royal family or court, esp. one in charge of protocol. ◆ *vb* **marshals, marshalling, marshalled** *or US* **marshals, marshaling, marshaled.** (*tr*) **6** to arrange in order: *to marshal the facts.* **7** to assemble and organize (troops, vehicles, etc.) prior to onward movement. **8** to guide or lead, esp. in a ceremonious way. **9** to combine (coats of arms) on one shield. [C13: from OF *mareschal;* rel. to OHG *marahscalc,* from *marah* horse + *scalc* servant]

▸'**marshalcy** *or* '**marshalship** *n*

marshalling yard *n Railways.* a place or depot where railway wagons are shunted and made up into trains.

Marshal of the Royal Air Force *n* a rank in the Royal Air Force comparable to that of a field marshal in the army.

marsh fever *n* another name for **malaria.**

marsh gas *n* a hydrocarbon gas largely composed of methane formed when organic material decays in the absence of air.

marshmallow (ˌmɑ:ʃ'mæləʊ) *n* **1** a spongy sweet containing gum arabic or gelatine, sugar, etc. **2** a sweetened paste or confection made from the root of the marsh mallow.

marsh mallow *n* a malvaceous plant that grows in salt marshes and has pale pink flowers. The roots yield a mucilage formerly used to make marshmallows.

marsh marigold *n* a yellow-flowered plant that grows in swampy places.

marshy Ⓣ ('mɑ:ʃɪ) *adj* **marshier, marshiest.** of, involving, or like a marsh.

▸'**marshiness** *n*

marsupial (mɑ:'sju:pɪəl, -'su:-) *n* **1** any mammal of an order in which the young are born in an immature state and continue development in the marsupium. The order occurs mainly in Australia and South and Central America and includes the opossums and kangaroos. ◆ *adj* **2** of, relating to, or belonging to marsupials. **3** of or relating to a marsupium. [C17: see MARSUPIUM]

marsupium (mɑ:'sju:pɪəm, -'su:-) *n, pl* **marsupia** (-pɪə). an external pouch in most female marsupials within which the newly born offspring complete their development. [C17: NL, from L: purse, from Gk, dim. of *marsipos*]

mart (mɑ:t) *n* a market or trading centre. [C15: from MDu.: MARKET]

martagon *or* **martagon lily** ('mɑ:təgən) *n* a Eurasian lily plant cultivated for its mottled purplish-red flowers with reflexed petals. [C15: from F, from Turkish *martağān* a type of turban]

Martello tower (mɑ:'tɛləʊ) *n* a small circular tower for coastal defence. [C18: after Cape *Mortella* in Corsica, where the British navy captured a tower of this type in 1794]

marten ('mɑ:tɪn) *n, pl* **martens** *or* **marten. 1** any of several agile arboreal mammals of Europe, Asia, and North America, having bushy tails and golden-brown to blackish fur. See also **pine marten. 2** the highly valued fur of these animals. ◆ See also **sable** (sense 1). [C15: from MDu. *martren,* from OF (*peau*) *martrine* skin of a marten, from *martre,* prob. of Gmc origin]

martial Ⓣ ('mɑ:ʃəl) *adj* of, relating to, or characteristic of war, soldiers, or the military life. [C14: from L *martiālis* of MARS[1]]

▸'**martialism** *n* ▸'**martialist** *n* ▸'**martially** *adv*

martial art *n* any of various philosophies of self-defence and techniques of single combat, such as judo or karate, originating in the Far East.

martial law *n* rule of law maintained by the military in the absence of civil law.

Martian ('mɑ:ʃən) *adj* **1** of, occurring on, or relating to the planet Mars. ◆ *n* **2** an inhabitant of Mars, esp. in science fiction.

martin ('mɑ:tɪn) *n* any of various birds of the swallow family, having a square or slightly forked tail. See also **house martin.** [C15: ?from St *Martin,* bishop of Tours & patron saint of France, because the birds were believed to migrate at the time of Martinmas]

martinet Ⓣ (ˌmɑ:tɪ'nɛt) *n* a person who maintains strict discipline, esp. in a military force. [C17: from F, from General *Martinet,* drillmaster under Louis XIV]

martingale ('mɑ:tɪnˌgeɪl) *n* **1** a strap from the reins to the girth of a horse, preventing it from carrying its head too high. **2** any gambling system in which the stakes are raised, usually doubled, after each loss.

THESAURUS

marriage *n* **1, 3** = **wedding,** espousal, match, matrimony, nuptial rites, nuptials, wedding ceremony, wedlock **4** = **union,** alliance, amalgamation, association, confederation, coupling, link, merger

married *adj* **1, 2** = **wedded,** hitched (*sl.*), joined, one, spliced (*inf.*), united, wed **3** = **marital,** conjugal, connubial, husbandly, matrimonial, nuptial, spousal, wifely

marrow *n* **2** = **core,** cream, essence, gist, heart, kernel, pith, quick, quintessence, soul, spirit, substance

marry[1] *vb* **1** = **wed,** become man and wife, espouse, get hitched (*sl.*), get spliced (*inf.*), plight one's troth (*old-fashioned*), take the plunge (*inf.*), take to wife, tie the knot (*inf.*), walk down the aisle (*inf.*), wive (*arch.*) **3** = **unite,** ally, bond, join, knit, link, match, merge, splice, tie, unify, yoke

marsh *n* = **swamp,** bog, fen, morass, moss (*Scot. & N English dialect*), quagmire, slough

marshal *vb* **6, 7** = **arrange,** align, array, assemble, collect, deploy, dispose, draw up, gather, group, line up, muster, order, organize, rank, sequence **8** = **conduct,** escort, guide, lead, shepherd, usher

marshy *adj* = **swampy,** boggy, fenny, miry, paludal, quaggy, spongy, waterlogged, wet

martial *adj* = **military,** bellicose, belligerent, brave, heroic, soldierly, warlike

martinet *n* = **disciplinarian,** drillmaster, stickler

3 *Naut.* a chain or cable running from a jib boom to the stern or stem. [C16: from F, from ?]

martini (mɑːˈtiːnɪ) *n* **1** (*often cap.*) *Trademark.* an Italian vermouth. **2** a cocktail of gin and vermouth. [C19 (sense 2): ?from the name of the inventor]

Martinmas (ˈmɑːtɪnməs) *n* the feast of St Martin on Nov. 11; a quarter day in Scotland.

martyr ❶ (ˈmɑːtə) *n* **1** a person who suffers death rather than renounce his religious beliefs. **2** a person who suffers greatly or dies for a cause, belief, etc. **3** a person who suffers from poor health, misfortune, etc.: *a martyr to rheumatism.* ◆ *vb also* **ˈmartyrize** *or* **martyrise.** (*tr*) **4** to kill as a martyr. **5** to make a martyr of. [OE *martir,* from Church L *martyr,* from LGk *martur-, martus* witness]
▸**ˈmartyrdom** *n* ▸**ˌmartyriˈzation** *or* **ˌmartyriˈsation** *n*

martyrology (ˌmɑːtəˈrɒlədʒɪ) *n, pl* **martyrologies. 1** an official list of martyrs. **2** *Christianity.* the study of the lives of the martyrs. **3** a historical account of the lives of martyrs.
▸**ˌmartyrˈologist** *n*

marvel ❶ (ˈmɑːvᵊl) *vb* **marvels, marvelling, marvelled** *or US* **marvels, marveling, marveled. 1** (when *intr,* often foll. by *at* or *about;* when *tr, takes a clause as object*) to be filled with surprise or wonder. ◆ *n* **2** something that causes wonder. **3** *Arch.* astonishment. [C13: from OF *merveille,* from LL *mīrābilia,* from L *mīrābilis* from *mīrārī* to wonder at]

marvellous ❶ *or US* **marvelous** (ˈmɑːvᵊləs) *adj* **1** causing great wonder, surprise, etc.; extraordinary. **2** improbable or incredible. **3** excellent; splendid.
▸**ˈmarvellously** *or US* **ˈmarvelously** *adv* ▸**ˈmarvellousness** *or US* **ˈmarvelousness** *n*

marvel-of-Peru *n, pl* **marvels-of-Peru.** another name for **four-o'clock** (the plant). [C16: first found in Peru]

Marxism (ˈmɑːksɪzəm) *n* the economic and political theory and practice originated by Karl Marx (1818–83) and Friedrich Engels (1820–95), German political philosophers. It holds that actions and human institutions are economically determined, that the class struggle is the basic agency of historical change, and that capitalism will ultimately be superseded by communism.
▸**ˈMarxist** *n, adj*

Marxism-Leninism *n* the modification of Marxism by Lenin stressing that imperialism is the highest form of capitalism.
▸**ˈMarxist-ˈLeninist** *n, adj*

marzipan (ˈmɑːzɪˌpæn) *n* **1** a paste made from ground almonds, sugar, and egg whites, used to coat fruit cakes or moulded into sweets. **2** (*modifier*) *Inf.* of or relating to the stratum of middle managers in a financial institution or other business: *marzipan layer job losses.* [C19: via G from It. *marzapane*]

-mas *n combining form.* indicating a Christian festival: *Christmas; Michaelmas.* [from MASS]

Masai (ˈmɑːsaɪ, mɑːˈsaɪ) *n* **1** (*pl* **Masais** *or* **Masai**) a member of a Nilotic people, formerly noted as warriors, living chiefly in Kenya and Tanzania. **2** the language of this people.

masc. *abbrev. for* masculine.

mascara (mæˈskɑːrə) *n* a cosmetic for darkening the eyelashes. [C20: from Sp.: mask]

mascarpone (ˌmæskəˈpəʊnɪ) *n* an Italian soft cream cheese. [from It. from dialect *mascherpa* ricotta]

mascon (ˈmæskɒn) *n* any of several lunar regions of high gravity. [C20: from MAS(S) + CON(CENTRATION)]

mascot (ˈmæskət) *n* a person, animal, or thing considered to bring good luck. [C19: from F *mascotte,* from Provençal *mascotto* charm, from *masco* witch]

masculine ❶ (ˈmæskjʊlɪn) *adj* **1** possessing qualities or characteristics considered typical of or appropriate to a man; manly. **2** unwomanly. **3** *Grammar.* denoting a gender of nouns that includes all kinds of referents as well as some male animate referents. **4** *Prosody.* denoting an ending consisting of a single stressed syllable. **5** *Prosody.* denoting a rhyme between pairs of single final stressed syllables. [C14: via F from L *masculīnus,* from *masculus* male, from *mās* a male]
▸**ˈmasculinely** *adv* ▸**ˌmascuˈlinity** *n*

masculinize *or* **masculinise** (ˈmæskjʊlɪˌnaɪz) *vb* **masculinizes, masculinizing, masculinized** *or* **masculinises, masculinising, masculinised.** to make or become masculine, esp. to cause (a woman) to show male secondary characteristics as a result of taking steroids.
▸**ˌmasculiniˈzation** *or* **ˌmasculiniˈsation** *n*

maser (ˈmeɪzə) *n* a device for amplifying microwaves, working on the same principle as a laser. [C20: *m(icrowave) a(mplification by) s(timulated) e(mission of) r(adiation)*]

mash (mæʃ) *n* **1** a soft pulpy mass or consistency. **2** *Agriculture.* a feed of bran, meal, or malt mixed with water and fed to horses, cattle, or poultry. **3** (esp. in brewing) a mixture of mashed malt grains and hot water, from which malt is extracted. **4** *Brit. inf.* mashed potatoes. ◆ *vb* (*tr*) **5** to beat or crush into a mash. **6** to steep (malt grains) in hot water in order to extract malt. **7** *Scot. & N English dialect.* to brew (tea). [OE *mǣsc-* (in compound words)]
▸**mashed** *adj* ▸**ˈmasher** *n*

mashie *or* **mashy** (ˈmæʃɪ) *n, pl* **mashies.** *Golf.* (formerly) an iron for lofting shots, usually No. 5. [C19: ?from F *massue* club, ult. from L *mateola* mallet]

mask ❶ (mɑːsk) *n* **1** any covering for the whole or a part of the face worn for amusement, protection, disguise, etc. **2** a fact, action, etc., that conceals something. **3** another name for **masquerade. 4** a likeness of a face or head, either sculpted or moulded, such as a death mask. **5** an image of a face worn by an actor, esp. in classical drama, in order to symbolize a character. **6** a variant spelling of **masque. 7** *Surgery.* a sterile gauze covering for the nose and mouth worn to minimize the spread of germs. **8** *Sport.* a protective covering for the face worn for fencing, ice hockey, etc. **9** a carving in the form of a face or head, used as an ornament. **10** a device placed over the nose and mouth to facilitate or prevent inhalation of a gas. **11** *Photog.* a shield of paper, paint, etc., placed over an area of unexposed photographic surface to stop light falling on it. **12** the face or head of an animal, such as a fox. **13** *Rare.* a person wearing a mask. ◆ *vb* **14** to cover with or put on a mask. **15** (*tr*) to conceal; disguise: *to mask an odour.* **16** (*tr*) to cover; protect. **17** (*tr*) *Photog.* to shield a particular area of (an unexposed photographic surface) to prevent or reduce the action of light there. [C16: from It. *maschera,* ult. from Ar. *maskharah* clown, from *sakhira* mockery]
▸**masked** *adj* ▸**ˈmasker** *n*

masked ball *n* a ball at which masks are worn.

masking tape *n* an adhesive tape used to protect surfaces surrounding an area to be painted.

maskinonge (ˈmæskəˌnɒndʒ) *n* another name for **muskellunge.**

masochism (ˈmæsəˌkɪzəm) *n* **1** *Psychiatry.* an abnormal condition in which pleasure, esp. sexual pleasure, is derived from pain or from humiliation, domination, etc., by another person. **2** a tendency to take pleasure from one's own suffering. Cf. **sadism.** [C19: after Leopold von Sacher *Masoch* (1836–95), Austrian novelist, who described it]
▸**ˈmasochist** *n, adj* ▸**ˌmasoˈchistic** *adj* ▸**ˌmasoˈchistically** *adv*

mason (ˈmeɪsᵊn) *n* **1** a person skilled in building with stone. **2** a person who dresses stone. ◆ *vb* **3** (*tr*) to construct or strengthen with masonry. [C13: from OF *masson,* of Frankish origin; ? rel. to OE *macian* to make]

Mason (ˈmeɪsᵊn) *n* short for **Freemason.**

Mason-Dixon Line (-ˈdɪksən) *n* in the US, the state boundary between Maryland and Pennsylvania: surveyed between 1763 and 1767 by Charles Mason and Jeremiah Dixon; popularly regarded as the dividing line between North and South.

masonic (məˈsɒnɪk) *adj* **1** (*often cap.*) of or relating to Freemasons or Freemasonry. **2** of or relating to masons or masonry.
▸**maˈsonically** *adv*

Masonite (ˈmeɪsənaɪt) *n Austral. trademark.* a kind of dark brown hardboard.

masonry (ˈmeɪsənrɪ) *n, pl* **masonries. 1** the craft of a mason. **2** work that is built by a mason; stonework or brickwork. **3** (*often cap.*) short for **Freemasonry.**

masque *or* **mask** (mɑːsk) *n* **1** a dramatic entertainment of the 16th to 17th centuries, consisting of pantomime, dancing, dialogue, and song. **2** the words and music for this. **3** short for **masquerade.** [C16: var. of MASK]

masquerade ❶ (ˌmæskəˈreɪd) *n* **1** a party or other gathering at which the guests wear masks and costumes. **2** the disguise worn at such a function. **3** a pretence or disguise. ◆ *vb* **masquerades, masquerading, masqueraded.** (*intr*) **4** to participate in a masquerade; disguise oneself. **5** to dissemble. [C16: from Sp. *mascarada,* from *mascara* MASK]
▸**ˌmasquerˈader** *n*

mass ❶ (mæs) *n* **1** a large coherent body of matter without a definite shape. **2** a collection of the component parts of something. **3** a large

THESAURUS

martyrdom *n* **1, 2** = **persecution**, agony, anguish, ordeal, suffering, torment, torture
Antonyms *n* bliss, ecstasy, happiness, joy

marvel *vb* **1** = **wonder**, be amazed, be awed, be filled with surprise, gape, gaze, goggle ◆ *n* **2** = **wonder**, genius, miracle, phenomenon, portent, prodigy, whizz (*inf.*)

marvellous *adj* **1** = **amazing**, astonishing, astounding, breathtaking, brilliant, extraordinary, jaw-dropping, miraculous, phenomenal, prodigious, remarkable, sensational (*inf.*), singular, spectacular, stupendous, wondrous (*arch. or literary*) **3** = **excellent**, awesome, brill (*inf.*), cracking (*Brit. inf.*), divine (*inf.*), fabulous (*inf.*), fantastic (*inf.*), glorious, great (*inf.*), jim-dandy (*sl.*), magnificent, sensational (*inf.*), smashing (*inf.*), sovereign, splendid, stupendous, super (*inf.*), superb, terrific (*inf.*), topping (*Brit. sl.*), wonderful
Antonyms *adj* ≠ **amazing**: believable, commonplace, credible, everyday, ordinary ≠ **excellent**: awful, bad, terrible

masculine *adj* **1** = **male**, manful, manlike, manly, mannish, virile **1** = **strong**, bold, brave, butch (*sl.*), gallant, hardy, macho, muscular, powerful, red-blooded (*inf.*), resolute, robust, stout-hearted, strapping, vigorous, well-built

mask *n* **1** = **visor**, domino, false face, vizard (*arch.*) **2** = **disguise**, blind, camouflage, cloak, concealment, cover, cover-up, façade, front, guise, screen, semblance, show, veil, veneer ◆ *vb* **15** = **disguise**, camouflage, cloak, conceal, cover, hide, obscure, screen, veil

masquerade *n* **1** = **masked ball**, costume ball, fancy dress party, mask, masked party, mummery, revel **2, 3** = **pretence**, cloak, cover, cover-up, deception, disguise, dissimulation, front (*inf.*), guise, imposture, mask, pose, put-on (*sl.*), screen, subterfuge ◆ *vb* **4, 5** = **pose**, disguise, dissemble, dissimulate, impersonate, mask, pass oneself off, pretend (to be)

mass *n* **1** = **piece**, block, chunk, concretion, hunk, lump **2** = **collection**, aggregate, body, entirety, sum, sum total, totality, whole **2** = **lot**, accumulation, aggregation, assemblage, batch, bunch, collection, combination, conglomeration, heap, load, pile, quantity, rick, stack **3** =

amount or number, as of people. **4** the main part or majority. **5 in the mass.** in the main; collectively. **6** the size of a body; bulk. **7** *Physics.* a physical quantity expressing the amount of matter in a body. It is a measure of a body's resistance to changes in velocity (**inertial mass**) and also of the force experienced in a gravitational field (**gravitational mass**). **8** (in painting, drawing, etc.) an area of unified colour, shade, or intensity, usually denoting a solid form or plane. ◆ (*modifier*) **9** done or occurring on a large scale: *mass hysteria.* **10** consisting of a mass or large number, esp. of people: *a mass meeting.* ◆ *vb* **11** to form (people or things) or (of people or things) to join together into a mass. ◆ See also **masses.** [C14: from OF *masse,* from L *massa* that which forms a lump, from Gk *maza* barley cake]

Mass (mæs, mɑːs) *n* **1** (in the Roman Catholic Church and certain Protestant Churches) the celebration of the Eucharist. See also **High Mass, Low Mass. 2** a musical setting of those parts of the Eucharistic service sung by choir or congregation. [OE *mæsse,* from Church L *missa,* ult. from L *mittere* to send away; ?from the concluding dismissal in the Roman Mass, *Ite, missa est* Go, it is the dismissal]

massacre ➊ (ˈmæsəkə) *n* **1** the wanton or savage killing of large numbers of people, as in battle. **2** *Inf.* an overwhelming defeat, as in a game. ◆ *vb* **massacres, massacring, massacred.** (*tr*) **3** to kill indiscriminately or in large numbers. **4** *Inf.* to defeat overwhelmingly. [C16: from OF]

massage ➊ (ˈmæsɑːʒ, -sɑːdʒ) *n* **1** the act of kneading, rubbing, etc., parts of the body to promote circulation, suppleness, or relaxation. ◆ *vb* **massages, massaging, massaged.** (*tr*) **2** to give a massage to. **3** to treat (stiffness, etc.) by a massage. **4** to manipulate (statistics, etc.) to produce a desired result; doctor. **5 massage (someone's) ego.** to boost (someone's) sense of self-esteem by flattery. [C19: from F, from *masser* to rub]

massasauga (ˌmæsəˈsɔːgə) *n* a North American venomous snake that has a horny rattle at the end of the tail. [C19: after the *Missisauga* River, Ontario, Canada, where it was first found]

mass defect *n Physics.* the amount by which the mass of a particular nucleus is less than the total mass of its constituent particles.

massé *or* **massé shot** (ˈmæsɪ) *n Billiards.* a stroke made by hitting the cue ball off centre with the cue held nearly vertically, esp. so as to make the ball move in a curve. [C19: from F, from *masser,* from *masse* sledgehammer, from OF *mace* MACE[1]]

masses ➊ (ˈmæsɪz) *pl n* **1** (preceded by *the*) the body of common people. **2** (often foll. by *of*) *Inf., chiefly Brit.* great numbers or quantities: *masses of food.*

masseur (mæˈsɜː) *or* (*fem*) **masseuse** (mæˈsɜːz) *n* a person who gives massages, esp. as a profession. [C19: from F *masser* to MASSAGE]

massif (ˈmæsiːf) *n* a mass of rock or a series of connected masses forming a mountain range. [C19: from F, noun use of *massif* MASSIVE]

massive ➊ (ˈmæsɪv) *adj* **1** (of objects) large in mass; bulky, heavy, and usually solid. **2** impressive or imposing. **3** relatively intensive or large; considerable: *a massive dose.* **4** *Geol.* **4a** (of igneous rocks) having no stratification, cleavage, etc.; homogeneous. **4b** (of sedimentary rocks) arranged in thick poorly defined strata. **5** *Mineralogy.* without obvious crystalline structure. [C15: from F *massif,* from *masse* MASS]
▸ˈ**massively** *adv* ▸ˈ**massiveness** *n*

mass-market *adj* of, for, or appealing to a large number of people; popular: *mass-market paperbacks.*

mass media *pl n* the means of communication that reach large numbers of people, such as television, newspapers, magazines, and radio.

mass noun *n* a noun that refers to an extended substance rather than to each of a set of objects, e.g., *water* as opposed to *lake.* In English when used indefinitely they are characteristically preceded by *some* rather than *a* or *an;* they do not have normal plural forms. Cf. **count noun.**

mass number *n* the total number of neutrons and protons in the nucleus of a particular atom.

mass observation *n* (*sometimes cap.*) *Chiefly Brit.* the study of the social habits of people through observation, interviews, etc.

mass-produce *vb* **mass-produces, mass-producing, mass-produced.** (*tr*) to manufacture (goods) to a standardized pattern on a large scale by means of extensive mechanization and division of labour.
▸ˌ**mass-proˈduced** *adj* ▸ˌ**mass-proˈducer** *n* ▸**mass production** *n*

mass spectrometer *or* **spectroscope** *n* an instrument in which ions, produced from a sample, are separated by electric or magnetic fields according to their ratios of charge to mass. A record is produced (**mass spectrum**) of the types of ion present and their amounts.

mast[1] (mɑːst) *n* **1** *Naut.* any vertical spar for supporting sails, rigging, flags, etc., above the deck of a vessel. **2** any sturdy upright pole used as a support. **3 before the mast.** *Naut.* as an apprentice seaman. ◆ *vb* **4** (*tr*) *Naut.* to equip with a mast or masts. [OE *mæst;* rel. to MDu. *mast* & L *mālus* pole]

mast[2] (mɑːst) *n* the fruit of forest trees, such as beech, oak, etc., used as food for pigs. [OE *mæst;* rel. to OHG *mast* food]

mastaba *or* **mastabah** (ˈmæstəbə) *n* a mudbrick superstructure above tombs in ancient Egypt. [from Ar.: bench]

mast cell *n* any of a number of cells in connective tissue that release heparin, histamine, and serotonin during inflammation and allergic reactions.

mastectomy (mæˈstɛktəmɪ) *n, pl* **mastectomies.** the surgical removal of a breast.

master ➊ (ˈmɑːstə) *n* **1** the man in authority, such as the head of a household, the employer of servants, or the owner of slaves or animals. **2a** a person with exceptional skill at a certain thing. **2b** (*as modifier*): *a master thief.* **3** (*often cap.*) a great artist, esp. an anonymous but influential one. **4a** a person who has complete control of a situation, etc. **4b** an abstract thing regarded as having power or influence: *they regarded fate as the master of their lives.* **5a** a workman or craftsman fully qualified to practise his trade and to train others. **5b** (*as modifier*): *master carpenter.* **6a** an original copy, stencil, tape, etc., from which duplicates are made. **6b** (*as modifier*): *master copy.* **7** a player of a game, esp. chess or bridge, who has won a specified number of tournament games. **8** the principal of some colleges. **9** a highly regarded teacher or leader. **10** a graduate holding a master's degree. **11** the chief executive officer aboard a merchant ship. **12** a person presiding over a function, organization, or institution. **13** *Chiefly Brit.* a male teacher. **14** an officer of the Supreme Court of Judicature subordinate to a judge. **15** the superior person or side in a contest. **16** (*often cap.*) the heir apparent of a Scottish viscount or baron. ◆ (*modifier*) **17** overall or controlling: *master plan.* **18** designating a device or mechanism that controls others: *master switch.* **19** main; principal: *master bedroom.* ◆ *vb* (*tr*) **20** to become thoroughly proficient in. **21** to overcome; defeat. **22** to rule or control as master. [OE *magister* teacher, from L]

Master (ˈmɑːstə) *n* **1** a title of address for a boy. **2** a term of address, esp. as used by disciples addressing or referring to a religious teacher. **3** an archaic equivalent of **Mr.**

master aircrew *n* a warrant rank in the Royal Air Force, equal to but before a warrant officer.

master-at-arms *n, pl* **masters-at-arms.** the senior rating in a naval unit responsible for discipline and police duties.

master builder *n* **1** a person skilled in the design and construction of buildings, esp. before the foundation of the profession of architecture. **2** a self-employed builder who employs labour.

masterclass (ˈmɑːstəˌklɑːs) *n* a session of tuition by an expert, esp. a musician, for exceptional students, usually given in public or on television.

masterful ➊ (ˈmɑːstəfʊl) *adj* **1** having or showing mastery. **2** fond of playing the master; imperious.
▸ˈ**masterfully** *adv* ▸ˈ**masterfulness** *n*

> **USAGE NOTE** The use of *masterful* to mean *masterly* as in *a masterful performance,* although common, is considered incorrect by many people.

master key *n* a key that opens all the locks of a set. Also called: **passkey.**

THESAURUS

crowd, assemblage, band, body, bunch (*inf.*), group, horde, host, lot, mob, number, throng, troop **4** = **majority**, body, bulk, greater part, lion's share, preponderance **6** = **size**, bulk, dimension, greatness, magnitude ◆ *modifier* **9, 10** = **large-scale**, extensive, general, indiscriminate, pandemic, popular, wholesale, widespread ◆ *vb* **11** = **gather**, accumulate, amass, assemble, collect, congregate, foregather, mob, muster, rally, swarm, throng

massacre *n* **1** = **slaughter**, annihilation, blood bath, butchery, carnage, extermination, holocaust, killing, mass slaughter, murder ◆ *vb* **3** = **slaughter**, annihilate, blow away (*sl., chiefly US*), butcher, cut to pieces, exterminate, kill, mow down, murder, slay, take out (*sl.*), wipe out

massage *n* **1** = **rub-down**, acupressure, kneading, manipulation, reflexology, rubbing, shiatsu ◆ *vb* **2** = **rub down**, knead, manipulate, rub

masses *pl n* **1** *preceded by* **the** = **the multitude**, the commonalty, the common people, the crowd, (the) hoi polloi

massive *adj* **1, 2** = **huge**, big, bulky, colossal, elephantine, enormous, extensive, gargantuan, gigantic, ginormous (*inf.*), great, heavy, hefty, hulking, humongous *or* humungous (*US sl.*), immense, imposing, impressive, mammoth, mega (*sl.*), monster, monumental, ponderous, solid, stellar (*inf.*), substantial, titanic, vast, weighty, whacking (*inf.*), whopping (*inf.*)
Antonyms *adj* frail, light, little, minute, petty, slight, small, thin, tiny, trivial

master *n* **1** = **head**, boss (*inf.*), captain, chief, commander, controller, director, employer, governor, lord, manager, overlord, overseer, owner, principal, ruler, skipper (*inf.*), superintendent **2a** = **expert**, ace (*inf.*), adept, dab hand (*Brit. inf.*), doyen, genius, grandmaster, maestro, maven (*US*), past master, pro (*inf.*), virtuoso, wizard ◆ *modifier* **2b** = **expert**, adept, crack (*inf.*), masterly, proficient, skilful, skilled ◆ *n* **9** = **teacher**, guide, guru, instructor, pedagogue, preceptor, schoolmaster, spiritual leader, swami, torchbearer, tutor ◆ *modifier* **17, 19** = **main**, chief, controlling, foremost, grand, great, leading, predominant, prime, principal ◆ *vb* **20** = **learn**, acquire, become proficient in, get the hang of (*inf.*), grasp **21** = **overcome**, bridle, check, conquer, curb, defeat, lick, overpower, quash, quell, subdue, subjugate, suppress, tame, triumph over, vanquish **22** = **control**, command, direct, dominate, govern, manage, regulate, rule
Antonyms *n* ≠ **head:** crew, servant, slave, subject ≠ **expert:** amateur, novice ≠ **teacher:** student ◆ *modifier* ≠ **expert:** amateurish, clumsy, incompetent, inept, novice, unaccomplished, unskilled, untalented ≠ **main:** lesser, minor ◆ *vb* ≠ **overcome:** cave in (*inf.*), give in, surrender, yield

masterful *adj* **1** = **skilful**, adept, adroit, clever, consummate, crack (*inf.*), deft, dexterous, excellent, expert, exquisite, fine, finished, first-rate, masterly, skilled, superior, superlative, supreme, world-class **2** = **domineering**, arrogant, authoritative, bossy (*inf.*), despotic, dictatorial, high-handed, imperious, magisterial, overbearing, overweening, peremptory, self-willed, tyrannical

masterly ➊ (ˈmɑːstəlɪ) *adj* of the skill befitting a master.
▸ˈ**masterliness** *n*

master mason *n* **1** see **master** (sense 5a). **2** a Freemason who has reached the rank of third degree.

mastermind ➊ (ˈmɑːstəˌmaɪnd) *vb* **1** (*tr*) to plan and direct (a complex undertaking). ◆ *n* **2** a person of great intelligence or executive talent, esp. one who directs an undertaking.

Master of Arts *n* a degree, usually postgraduate and in a nonscientific subject, or the holder of this degree. Abbrev.: **MA**.

master of ceremonies *n* a person who presides over a public ceremony, formal dinner, or entertainment, introducing the events, performers, etc.

Master of Science *n* a postgraduate degree, usually in science, or the holder of this degree. Abbrev.: **MSc**.

Master of the Rolls *n* (in England) a judge of the court of appeal: the senior civil judge in the country and the Keeper of the Records at the Public Record Office.

masterpiece ➊ (ˈmɑːstəˌpiːs) *or* (*less commonly*) **masterwork** (ˈmɑːstəˌwɜːk) *n* **1** an outstanding work or performance. **2** the most outstanding piece of work of a creative artist, craftsman, etc. [C17: cf. Du. *meesterstuk*, G *Meisterstück*, a sample of work submitted to a guild by a craftsman in order to qualify for the rank of master]

masterstroke (ˈmɑːstəˌstrəʊk) *n* an outstanding piece of strategy, skill, talent, etc.

mastery ➊ (ˈmɑːstərɪ) *n, pl* **masteries. 1** full command or understanding of a subject. **2** outstanding skill; expertise. **3** the power of command; control. **4** victory or superiority.

masthead (ˈmɑːstˌhɛd) *n* **1** *Naut.* the head of a mast. **2** the name of a newspaper or periodical, its proprietors, staff, etc., printed at the top of the front page. ◆ *vb* (*tr*) **3** to send (a sailor) to the masthead as a punishment. **4** to raise (a sail) to the masthead.

mastic (ˈmæstɪk) *n* **1** an aromatic resin obtained from the mastic tree and used as an astringent and to make varnishes and lacquers. **2 mastic tree.** a small Mediterranean evergreen tree that yields the resin mastic. **3** any of several putty-like substances used as a filler, adhesive, or seal in wood, plaster, or masonry. **4** a liquor flavoured with mastic gum. [C14: via OF from LL *mastichum*, from L from Gk *mastikhē* resin used as chewing gum]

masticate ➊ (ˈmæstɪˌkeɪt) *vb* **masticates, masticating, masticated. 1** to chew (food). **2** to reduce (materials such as rubber) to a pulp by crushing, grinding, or kneading. [C17: from LL *masticāre*, from Gk *mastikhan* to grind the teeth]
▸ˌ**mastiˈcation** *n* ▸ˈ**mastiˌcator** *n*

masticatory (ˈmæstɪkətərɪ, -trɪ) *adj* **1** of, relating to, or adapted to chewing. ◆ *n, pl* **masticatories. 2** a medicinal substance chewed to increase the secretion of saliva.

mastiff (ˈmæstɪf) *n* a breed of large powerful short-haired dog, usually fawn or brindled. [C14: from OF, ult. from L *mansuētus* tame]

mastitis (mæˈstaɪtɪs) *n* inflammation of a breast or an udder.

masto- *or before a vowel* **mast-** *combining form.* indicating the breast, mammary glands, or something resembling a breast or nipple: *mastodon; mastoid.* [from Gk *mastos* breast]

mastodon (ˈmæstəˌdɒn) *n* an extinct elephant-like mammal common in Pliocene times. [C19: from NL, lit.: breast-tooth, referring to the nipple-shaped projections on the teeth]

mastoid (ˈmæstɔɪd) *adj* **1** shaped like a nipple or breast. **2** designating or relating to a nipple-like process of the temporal bone behind the ear. ◆ *n* **3** the mastoid process. **4** *Inf.* mastoiditis.

mastoiditis (ˌmæstɔɪˈdaɪtɪs) *n* inflammation of the mastoid process.

masturbate ➊ (ˈmæstəˌbeɪt) *vb* **masturbates, masturbating, masturbated.** to stimulate the genital organs of (oneself or another) to achieve sexual pleasure. [C19: from L *masturbārī*, from ?; formerly thought to be derived from *manus* hand + *stuprāre* to defile]
▸ˌ**masturˈbation** *n* ▸ˈ**masturˌbator** *n* ▸**masturbatory** (ˈmæstəˌbeɪtərɪ) *adj*

mat[1] (mæt) *n* **1** a thick flat piece of fabric used as a floor covering, a place to wipe one's shoes, etc. **2** a smaller pad of material used to protect a surface from the heat, scratches, etc., of an object placed upon it. **3** a large piece of thick padded material put on the floor as a surface for wrestling, judo, etc. **4** any surface or mass that is densely interwoven or tangled: *a mat of weeds.* ◆ *vb* **mats, matting, matted. 5** to tangle or weave or become tangled or woven into a dense mass. **6** (*tr*) to cover with a mat or mats. [OE *matte*]

mat[2] (mæt) *n* **1** a border of cardboard, cloth, etc., placed around a picture as a frame or between picture and frame. ◆ *adj* **2** having a dull, lustreless, or roughened surface. ◆ *vb* **mats, matting, matted.** (*tr*) **3** to furnish (a picture) with a mat. **4** to give (a surface) a mat finish. ◆ Also (for senses 2 & 4): **matt.** [C17: from F, lit.: dead]

mat[3] (mæt) *n Printing, inf.* short for **matrix** (senses 4 and 5).

mat. *abbrev. for* matinée.

matador (ˈmætədɔː) *n* **1** the principal bullfighter who kills the bull. **2** (in some card games) one of the highest cards. **3** a game played with dominoes in which the dots on adjacent halves must total seven. [C17: from Sp., from *matar* to kill]

matagouri (ˌmætəˈguːrɪ) *n* a New Zealand thorny bush which forms thickets in open country. Also called: **wild Irishman.** [from Maori *tumatakuru*]

matai (ˈmɑːtaɪ) *n* a New Zealand tree, the black pine, the wood of which is used as building timber. Also called: **black pine.** [from Maori]

match[1] ➊ (mætʃ) *n* **1** a formal game or sports event in which people, teams, etc., compete. **2** a person or thing able to provide competition for another: *she's met her match.* **3** a person or thing that resembles, harmonizes with, or is equivalent to another in a specified respect. **4** a person or thing that is an exact copy or equal of another. **5a** a partnership between a man and a woman, as in marriage. **5b** an arrangement for such a partnership. **6** a person regarded as a possible partner, as in marriage. ◆ *vb* (*mainly tr*) **7** to fit (parts) together. **8** (*also intr; sometimes foll. by up*) to resemble, harmonize with, or equal (one another or something else). **9** (sometimes foll. by *with* or *against*) to compare in order to determine which is the superior. **10** (often foll. by *to* or *with*) to adapt so as to correspond with: *to match hope with reality.* **11** (often foll. by *with* or *against*) to arrange a competition between. **12** to find a match for. **13** *Electronics.* to connect (two circuits) so that their impedances are equal, to produce a maximum transfer of energy. [OE *gemæcca* spouse]
▸ˈ**matchable** *adj* ▸ˈ**matching** *adj*

match[2] (mætʃ) *n* **1** a thin strip of wood or cardboard tipped with a chemical that ignites by friction on a rough surface or a surface coated with a suitable chemical (see **safety match**). **2** a length of cord or wick impregnated with a chemical so that it burns slowly. It is used to fire cannons, explosives, etc. [C14: from OF *meiche*, ?from L *myxa* wick, from Gk *muxa* lamp nozzle]

matchboard (ˈmætʃˌbɔːd) *n* a long flimsy board tongued and grooved for lining work.

matchbox (ˈmætʃˌbɒks) *n* a small box for holding matches.

match-fit *adj Sport.* in good physical condition for competing in a match.

matchless ➊ (ˈmætʃlɪs) *adj* unequalled; incomparable; peerless.
▸ˈ**matchlessly** *adv*

matchlock (ˈmætʃˌlɒk) *n* **1** an obsolete type of gunlock igniting the powder by means of a slow match. **2** a gun having such a lock.

matchmaker (ˈmætʃˌmeɪkə) *n* **1** a person who brings together suitable partners for marriage. **2** a person who arranges competitive matches.
▸ˈ**matchˌmaking** *n, adj*

match play *n Golf.* scoring according to the number of holes won and lost. Cf. **Stableford, stroke play.**
▸**match player** *n*

match point *n* **1** *Tennis, squash, etc.* the final point needed to win a match. **2** *Bridge.* the unit used for scoring in tournaments.

matchstick (ˈmætʃˌstɪk) *n* **1** the wooden part of a match. ◆ *adj* **2** made with or as if with matchsticks. **3** (esp. of drawn figures) thin and straight: *matchstick men.*

matchwood (ˈmætʃˌwʊd) *n* **1** wood suitable for making matches. **2** splinters or fragments.

mate[1] ➊ (meɪt) *n* **1** the sexual partner of an animal. **2** a marriage part-

THESAURUS

Antonyms *adj* ≠ **skilful:** amateurish, clumsy, incompetent, inept, unaccomplished, unskilled, untalented ≠ **domineering:** irresolute, meek, spineless, weak, wimpish *or* wimpy (*inf.*)

masterly *adj* = **skilful**, adept, adroit, clever, consummate, crack (*inf.*), dexterous, excellent, expert, exquisite, fine, finished, first-rate, masterful, skilled, superior, superlative, supreme, world-class

mastermind *vb* **1** = **plan**, be the brains behind (*inf.*), conceive, devise, direct, manage, organize ◆ *n* **2** = **organizer**, architect, authority, brain(s) (*inf.*), brainbox, director, engineer, genius, intellect, manager, planner, virtuoso

masterpiece *n* **1, 2** = **classic**, *chef-d'oeuvre*, jewel, magnum opus, master work, *pièce de résistance, tour de force*

mastery *n* **1** = **understanding**, command, comprehension, familiarity, grasp, grip, knowledge **2** = **expertise**, ability, acquirement, attainment, cleverness, deftness, dexterity, finesse, know-how (*inf.*), proficiency, prowess, skill, virtuosity **3, 4** = **control**, ascendancy, authority, command, conquest, domination, dominion, pre-eminence, rule, superiority, supremacy, sway, triumph, upper hand, victory, whip hand

masticate *vb* **1** = **chew**, champ, crunch, eat, munch

masturbation *n* = **self-abuse**, autoeroticism, onanism, playing with oneself (*sl.*), wanking (*taboo sl.*)

match[1] *n* **1** = **game**, bout, competition, contest, head-to-head, test, trial **2** = **equal**, competitor, counterpart, equivalent, peer, rival **3** = **companion**, complement, counterpart, equal, equivalent, fellow, mate, tally **4** = **replica**, copy, dead ringer (*sl.*), double, duplicate, equal, lookalike, ringer (*sl.*), spit (*inf., chiefly Brit.*), spit and image (*inf.*), spitting image (*inf.*), twin **5** = **marriage**, affiliation, alliance, combination, couple, duet, item (*inf.*), pair, pairing, partnership, union ◆ *vb* **7** = **pair**, ally, combine, couple, join, link, marry, mate, unite, yoke **8, 10** = **correspond**, accompany, accord, adapt, agree, blend, coordinate, fit, go with, harmonize, suit, tally, tone with **9** = **rival**, compare, compete, contend, emulate, equal, measure up to, oppose, pit against, vie

matching *adj* **8** = **identical**, analogous, comparable, coordinating, corresponding, double, duplicate, equal, equivalent, like, paired, parallel, same, toning, twin
Antonyms *adj* different, disparate, dissimilar, distinct, divergent, diverse, nonparallel, other, unequal, unlike

matchless *adj* = **unequalled**, consummate, exquisite, incomparable, inimitable, peerless, perfect, superlative, supreme, unique, unmatched, unparalleled, unrivalled, unsurpassed
Antonyms *adj* average, common, commonplace, comparable, equalled, everyday, excelled, inferior, lesser, mediocre, no great shakes (*inf.*), ordinary, second-class, surpassed

mate[1] *n* **2** = **partner**, better half (*humorous*), husband *or* wife, significant other (*US inf.*), spouse **3a** *Informal, chiefly Brit., Austral., & N.Z.* = **friend**, ner. **3a** *Inf., chiefly Brit., Austral. & NZ.* a friend, usually of the same sex: often used to any male in direct address. **3b** (*in combination*) an associate, colleague, fellow sharer, etc.: *a classmate.* **4** one of a pair of matching items. **5** *Naut.* **5a** short for **first mate. 5b** any officer below the master on a commercial ship. **6** (in some trades) an assistant: *a plumber's mate.* ◆ *vb* **mates, mating, mated. 7** to pair (a male and female animal) or (of animals) to pair for reproduction. **8** to marry or join in marriage. **9** (*tr*) to join as a pair. [C14: from MLow G; rel. to OE *gemetta* table-guest, from *mete* MEAT]

mate[2] (meɪt) *n, vb* **mates, mating, mated.** *Chess.* See **checkmate.**

maté *or* **mate** ('mɑːteɪ) *n* **1** an evergreen tree cultivated in South America for its leaves, which contain caffeine. **2** a stimulating milky beverage made from the dried leaves of this tree. ◆ Also called: **Paraguay tea, yerba, yerba maté.** [C18: from American Sp. (orig. referring to the vessel in which the drink was brewed), from Quechua *máti* gourd]

matelot, matlo, *or* **matlow** ('mætləʊ) *n Sl., chiefly Brit.* a sailor. [C20: from F]

mater ('meɪtə) *n Brit. sl.* a word for **mother**[1]: often used facetiously. [C16: from L]

material ❶ (mə'tɪərɪəl) *n* **1** the substance of which a thing is made or composed; component or constituent matter. **2** facts, notes, etc., that a finished work may be based on or derived from. **3** cloth or fabric. **4** a person who has qualities suitable for a given occupation, training, etc.: *that boy is university material.* ◆ *adj* **5** of, relating to, or composed of physical substance: *material possessions.* **6** of, relating to, or affecting economic or physical wellbeing: *material ease.* **7** of or concerned with physical rather than spiritual interests. **8** of great import or consequence: *material benefit.* **9** (often foll. by *to*) relevant. **10** *Philosophy.* of or relating to matter as opposed to form. ◆ See also **materials.** [C14: via F from LL *māteriālis,* from L *māteria* MATTER]
▸ **ma,teri'ality** *n*

material implication *n Logic.* a form of implication in which the proposition "if A then B" is true except when A is true and B is false.

materialism (mə'tɪərɪə,lɪzəm) *n* **1** interest in and desire for money, possessions, etc., rather than spiritual or ethical values. **2** *Philosophy.* the doctrine that matter is the only reality and that the mind, the emotions, etc., are merely functions of it. Cf. **idealism, dualism. 3** *Ethics.* the rejection of any religious or supernatural account of things.
▸ **ma'terialist** *n* ▸ **ma,terial'istic** *adj* ▸ **ma,terial'istically** *adv*

materialize ❶ *or* **materialise** (mə'tɪərɪə,laɪz) *vb* **materializes, materializing, materialized** *or* **materialises, materialising, materialised. 1** (*intr*) to become fact; actually happen. **2** to invest or become invested with a physical shape or form. **3** to cause (a spirit, as of a dead person) to appear in material form or (of a spirit) to appear in such form. **4** (*intr*) to take shape; become tangible.
▸ **ma,teriali'zation** *or* **ma,teriali'sation** *n* ▸ **ma'terial,izer** *or* **ma'terial,iser** *n*

materially ❶ (mə'tɪərɪəlɪ) *adv* **1** to a significant extent; considerably. **2** with respect to material objects. **3** *Philosophy.* with respect to substance as distinct from form.

materials (mə'tɪərɪəlz) *pl n* the equipment necessary for a particular activity.

materia medica (mə'tɪərɪə 'mɛdɪkə) *n* **1** the branch of medical science concerned with the study of drugs used in the treatment of disease. **2** the drugs used in the treatment of disease. [C17: from Med. L: medical matter]

materiel ❶ *or* **matériel** (mə,tɪərɪ'ɛl) *n* the materials and equipment of an organization, esp. of a military force. [C19: from F: MATERIAL]

maternal ❶ (mə'tɜːnᵊl) *adj* **1** of, relating to, or characteristic of a mother. **2** related through the mother's side of the family: *his maternal uncle.* [C15: from Med. L *māternālis,* from L *māternus,* from *māter* mother]
▸ **ma'ternalism** *n* ▸ **ma,ternal'istic** *adj* ▸ **ma'ternally** *adv*

maternity ❶ (mə'tɜːnɪtɪ) *n* **1** motherhood. **2** the characteristics associated with motherhood; motherliness. **3** (*modifier*) relating to pregnant women or women at the time of childbirth: *a maternity ward.*

mateship ('meɪtʃɪp) *n Austral.* friendly egalitarian comradeship.

mate's rates *pl n NZ inf.* discounted or preferential rates of payment offered to a friend or colleague: *he got the job done cheaply by a plumber friend at mate's rates.*

matey ❶ *or* **maty** ('meɪtɪ) *Brit. inf.* ◆ *adj* **1** friendly or intimate. ◆ *n* **2** friend or fellow: usually used in direct address.
▸ **'mateyness** *or* **'matiness** *n*

math (mæθ) *n US & Canad. inf.* short for **mathematics.** Brit. equivalent: **maths.**

mathematical (,mæθə'mætɪkᵊl) *or* **mathematic** *adj* **1** of, used in, or relating to mathematics. **2** characterized by or using the precision of mathematics. **3** using, determined by, or in accordance with the principles of mathematics.
▸ **,mathe'matically** *adv*

mathematical logic *n* symbolic logic, esp. when concerned with the foundations of mathematics.

mathematician (,mæθəmə'tɪʃən) *n* an expert or specialist in mathematics.

mathematics (,mæθə'mætɪks) *n* **1** (*functioning as sing*) a group of related sciences, including algebra, geometry, and calculus, concerned with the study of number, quantity, shape, and space and their interrelationships by using a specialized notation. **2** (*functioning as sing or pl*) mathematical operations and processes involved in the solution of a problem or study of some scientific field. [C14 *mathematik* (n), via L from Gk (adj), from *mathēma* a science; rel. to *manthanein* to learn]

maths (mæθs) *n* (*functioning as sing*) *Brit. inf.* short for **mathematics.** US and Canad. equivalent: **math.**

Matilda (mə'tɪldə) *n Austral. inf.* **1** a bushman's swag. **2 waltz Matilda.** to travel as a bushman carrying one's swag. [C20: from the Christian name]

matin, mattin ('mætɪn), *or* **matinal** *adj* of or relating to matins. [C14: see MATINS]

matinée ('mætɪ,neɪ) *n* a daytime, esp. afternoon, performance of a play, concert, etc. [C19: from F; see MATINS]

matinée coat *or* **jacket** *n* a short coat for a baby.

matins *or* **mattins** ('mætɪnz) *n* (*functioning as sing or pl*) **1a** *Chiefly RC Church.* the first of the seven canonical hours of prayer. **1b** the service of morning prayer in the Church of England. **2** *Literary.* a morning song, esp. of birds. [C13: from OF, ult. from L *mātūtīnus* of the morning, from *Mātūta* goddess of dawn]

matlo *or* **matlow** ('mætləʊ) *n* variant spellings of **matelot.**

matrass ('mætrəs) *n Chem., obs.* a long-necked glass flask, used for distilling, dissolving substances, etc. [C17: from F, ? rel. to L *mētiri* to measure]

matri- *combining form.* mother or motherhood: *matriarchy.* [from L *māter* mother]

matriarch ('meɪtrɪ,ɑːk) *n* **1** a woman who dominates an organization, community, etc. **2** the female head of a tribe or family. **3** a very old or venerable woman. [C17: from MATRI- + -ARCH, by false analogy with PATRIARCH]
▸ **'matri,archal** *or* **'matri,archic** *adj*

matriarchy ('meɪtrɪ,ɑːkɪ) *n, pl* **matriarchies. 1** a form of social organization in which a female is head of the family or society, and descent and kinship are traced through the female line. **2** any society dominated by women.

matric (mə'trɪk) *n Brit.* short for **matriculation** (see **matriculate**).

matrices ('meɪtrɪ,siːz, 'mæ-) *n* a plural of **matrix.**

matricide ('mætrɪ,saɪd, 'meɪ-) *n* **1** the act of killing one's own mother. **2** a person who kills his mother. [C16: from L *mātricīdium* (the act), *mātrīcīda* (the agent). See MATRI-, -CIDE]
▸ **,matri'cidal** *adj*

matriculate (mə'trɪkju,leɪt) *vb* **matriculates, matriculating, matriculated. 1** to enrol or be enrolled in an institution, esp. a college or university. **2** (*intr*) to attain the academic standard required for a course at such an institution. [C16: from Med. L *mātrīculāre* to register, from *mātrīcula,* dim. of *matrix* list]
▸ **ma,tricu'lation** *n*

matrilineal (,mætrɪ'lɪnɪəl, ,meɪ-) *adj* relating to descent or kinship through the female line.

matrimony ❶ ('mætrɪmənɪ) *n, pl* **matrimonies. 1** the state or condition of being married. **2** the ceremony of marriage. **3a** a card game in which the king and queen together are a winning combination. **3b** such a combination. [C14: via Norman F from L *mātrimōnium* wedlock, from *māter* mother]
▸ **,matri'monial** *adj*

matrix ('meɪtrɪks, 'mæ-) *n, pl* **matrices** *or* **matrixes. 1** a substance, situation, or environment in which something has its origin, takes form, or is enclosed. **2** the intercellular substance of bone, cartilage, connective tissue, etc. **3** the rock in which fossils, pebbles, etc., are embedded. **4** *Printing.* **4a** a metal mould for casting type. **4b** a papier-mâché or plastic mould impressed from the forme and used for stereotyping. **5** a mould used in the production of gramophone records. **6** a bed of perforated material placed beneath a workpiece in a

THESAURUS

buddy (*inf.*), china (*Brit. sl.*), chum (*inf.*), cock (*Brit. inf.*), comrade, crony, homeboy (*sl., chiefly US*), pal (*inf.*) **3b** = **colleague**, associate, companion, compeer, co-worker, fellow-worker **4** = **double**, companion, fellow, match, twin **6** = **assistant**, helper, subordinate ◆ *vb* **7** = **pair**, breed, copulate, couple **8** = **marry**, match, wed **9** = **join**, couple, match, pair, yoke

material *n* **1** = **substance**, body, constituents, element, matter, stuff **2** = **information**, data, evidence, facts, notes, work **3** = **cloth**, fabric, stuff ◆ *adj* **5, 7** = **physical**, bodily, concrete, corporeal, fleshly, nonspiritual, palpable, substantial, tangible, worldly **8** = **important**, consequential, essential, grave, indispensable, key, meaningful, momentous, serious, significant, vital, weighty **9** = **relevant**, applicable, apposite, apropos, germane, pertinent

materialize *vb* **1, 4** = **occur**, appear, come about, come into being, come to pass, happen, take place, take shape, turn up

materially *adv* **1** = **significantly**, considerably, essentially, gravely, greatly, much, seriously, substantially
Antonyms *adv* barely, hardly, insignificantly, little, scarcely, superficially, unsubstantially

materiel *n* = **equipment**, accoutrements, apparatus, gear, hardware, machinery, materials, stores, supplies, tackle, tools

maternal *adj* **1** = **motherly**

maternity *n* **1, 2** = **motherhood**, motherliness

matey *adj* **1** *Brit. informal* = **friendly**, amiable, buddy-buddy (*sl., chiefly US & Canad.*), chummy (*inf.*), clubby, companionable, comradely, hail-fellow-well-met, intimate, pally (*inf.*), palsy-walsy (*inf.*), sociable, thick (*inf.*)

matrimonial *adj* **1, 2** = **marital**, conjugal, connubial, hymeneal, married, nuptial, spousal, wedded, wedding

matrimony *n* **1, 2** = **marriage**, marital rites, nuptials, wedding ceremony, wedlock press or stamping machine against which the punch operates. **7** *Maths.* a rectangular array of elements set out in rows and columns, used to facilitate the solution of problems, such as transformation of coordinates. **8** *Obs.* the womb. [C16: from L: womb, female animal used for breeding, from *māter* mother]

matron ('meɪtrən) *n* **1** a married woman regarded as staid or dignified. **2** a woman in charge of the domestic or medical arrangements in an institution. **3** *US.* a wardress in a prison. **4** *Brit.* the administrative head of the nursing staff in a hospital. Official name: **nursing officer.** [C14: via OF from L *mātrōna,* from *māter* mother]
▸**'matronal** *or* **'matronly** *adj* ▸**'matron,hood** *or* **'matronship** *n*

matron of honour *n, pl* **matrons of honour.** a married woman serving as chief attendant to a bride.

matt *or* **matte** (mæt) *adj, vb* **matts, matting, matted** *or* **mattes, matting, matted.** variant spellings of **mat**^{2} (senses 2 & 4).

Matt. *Bible. abbrev. for* Matthew.

mattamore ('mætə,mɔː) *n* a subterranean storehouse or dwelling. [C17: from F, from Ar. *matmurā,* from *tamara* to store, bury]

matted ⓣ ('mætɪd) *adj* **1** tangled into a thick mass. **2** covered with or formed of matting.

matter ⓣ ('mætə) *n* **1** that which makes up something, esp. a physical object; material. **2** substance that occupies space and has mass, as distinguished from substance that is mental, spiritual, etc. **3** substance of a specified type: *vegetable matter.* **4** (sometimes foll. by *of* or *for*) thing; affair; concern; question: *a matter of taste.* **5** a quantity or amount: *a matter of a few pence.* **6** the content of written or verbal material as distinct from its style or form. **7** (*used with a negative*) importance; consequence. **8** *Philosophy.* (in the writings of Aristotle and the Scholastics) that which is itself formless but can receive form and become substance. **9** *Philosophy.* (in the Cartesian tradition) one of two basic modes of existence, the other being mind. **10** *Printing.* **10a** type set up. **10b** copy to be set in type. **11** a secretion or discharge, such as pus. **12** *Law.* **12a** something to be proved. **12b** statements or allegations to be considered by a court. **13 for that matter.** as regards that. **14 no matter. 14a** regardless of; irrespective of: *no matter what the excuse, you must not be late.* **14b** (*sentence substitute*) it is unimportant. **15 the matter.** wrong; the trouble: *there's nothing the matter.* ◆ *vb* (*intr*) **16** to be of consequence or importance. **17** to form and discharge pus. [C13 (n), C16 (vb): from L *māteria* cause, substance, esp. wood, or a substance that produces something else]

matter of course *n* **1** an event or result that is natural or inevitable. ◆ *adj* **matter-of-course. 2** (*usually postpositive*) occurring as a matter of course. **3** accepting things as inevitable or natural: *a matter-of-course attitude.*

matter of fact ⓣ *n* **1** a fact that is undeniably true. **2** *Law.* a statement of facts the truth of which the court must determine on the basis of the evidence before it. **3 as a matter of fact.** actually; in fact. ◆ *adj* **matter-of-fact. 4** unimaginative or emotionless: *he gave a matter-of-fact account of the murder.*

matting^1 ('mætɪŋ) *n* **1** a coarsely woven fabric, usually made of a natural fibre such as straw or hemp and used as a floor covering, packing material, etc. **2** the act or process of making mats. **3** material for mats.

matting^2 ('mætɪŋ) *n* **1** another word for **mat**^{2} (sense 1). **2** the process of producing a mat finish.

mattins ('mætɪnz) *n* a variant spelling of **matins.**

mattock ('mætək) *n* a type of large pick that has one end of its blade shaped like an adze, used for loosening soil, cutting roots, etc. [OE *mattuc,* from ?; rel. to L *mateola* club, mallet]

mattress ('mætrɪs) *n* **1** a large flat pad with a strong cover, filled with straw, foam rubber, etc., and often incorporating coiled springs, used as a bed or as part of a bed. **2** a woven mat of brushwood, poles, etc., used to protect an embankment, dyke, etc., from scour. **3** a concrete or steel raft or slab used as a foundation or footing. [C13: via OF from It. *materasso,* from Ar. *almatrah* place where something is thrown]

maturate ('mætjʊ,reɪt, 'mætʃʊ-) *vb* **maturates, maturating, maturated. 1** to mature or bring to maturity. **2** a less common word for **suppurate.**
▸**,matu'ration** *n* ▸**maturative** (mə'tjʊərətɪv, mə'tʃʊə-) *adj*

mature ⓣ (mə'tjʊə, -'tʃʊə) *adj* **1** relatively advanced physically, mentally, etc.; grown-up. **2** (of plans, theories, etc.) fully considered; perfected. **3** due or payable: *a mature debenture.* **4** *Biol.* **4a** fully developed or differentiated: *a mature cell.* **4b** fully grown; adult: *a mature animal.* **5** (of fruit, wine, cheese, etc.) ripe or fully aged. ◆ *vb* **matures, maturing, matured. 6** to make or become mature. **7** (*intr*) (of notes, bonds, etc.) to become due for payment or repayment. [C15: from L *mātūrus* early, developed]
▸**ma'turely** *adv* ▸**ma'tureness** *n*

mature student *n* a student at a college or university who has passed the usual age for formal education.

maturity ⓣ (mə'tjʊərɪtɪ, -'tʃʊə-) *n* **1** the state or quality of being mature; full development. **2** *Finance.* **2a** the date upon which a bond, note, etc., becomes due for repayment. **2b** the state of a bill, note, etc., when due.

matutinal (,mætjʊ'taɪn^{ə}l) *adj* of, occurring in, or during the morning. [C17: from LL *mātūtīnālis,* from L *Mātūta* goddess of the dawn]

matzo, matzoh ('mætsəʊ) *or* **matza, matzah** ('mætsə) *n, pl* **matzos, matzohs, matzas, matzahs,** *or* **matzoth** (*Hebrew* ma'tsɔt). a large very thin biscuit of unleavened bread, traditionally eaten during Passover. [from Heb. *matsāh*]

maudlin ⓣ ('mɔːdlɪn) *adj* foolishly tearful or sentimental, as when drunk. [C17: from ME *Maudelen* Mary Magdalene, typically portrayed as a tearful penitent]

maugre *or* **mauger** ('mɔːgə) *prep Obs.* in spite of. [C13 (meaning: ill will): from OF *maugre,* lit.: bad pleasure]

maul ⓣ (mɔːl) *vb* (*tr*) **1** to handle clumsily; paw. **2** to batter or lacerate. ◆ *n* **3** a heavy two-handed hammer. **4** *Rugby.* a loose scrum. [C13: from OF *mail,* from L *malleus* hammer]
▸**'mauler** *n*

maulstick *or* **mahlstick** ('mɔːl,stɪk) *n* a long stick used by artists to steady the hand holding the brush. [C17: partial translation of Du. *maalstok,* from obs. *malen* to paint + *stok* STICK^1]

maunder ('mɔːndə) *vb* (*intr*) to move, talk, or act aimlessly or idly. [C17: ?from obs. *maunder* to beg, from L *mendīcāre*]

maundy ('mɔːndɪ) *n, pl* **maundies.** *Christianity.* the ceremonial washing of the feet of poor persons in commemoration of Jesus' washing of his disciples' feet. [C13: from OF *mandé* something commanded, from L, ult. from Christ's words: *Mandātum novum dō vōbīs* A new commandment give I unto you]

Maundy money *n* specially minted coins distributed by the British sovereign on the Thursday before Easter (**Maundy Thursday**).

mausoleum (,mɔːsə'lɪəm) *n, pl* **mausoleums** *or* **mausolea** (-'lɪə). a large stately tomb. [C16: via L from Gk *mausōleion,* the tomb of *Mausolus,* king of Caria; built at Halicarnassus in the 4th cent. B.C.]

mauve (məʊv) *n* **1a** any of various pale to moderate pinkish-purple or bluish-purple colours. **1b** (*as adj*): *a mauve flower.* **2** a reddish-purple aniline dye. [C19: from F, from L *malva* MALLOW]

maven *or* **mavin** ('meɪvən) *n US.* an expert or connoisseur. [C20: from Yiddish, from Heb. *mevin* understanding]

maverick ⓣ ('mævərɪk) *n* **1** (in the US and Canada) an unbranded animal, esp. a stray calf. **2a** a person of independent or unorthodox views. **2b** (*as modifier*): *a maverick politician.* [C19: after Samuel A. *Maverick* (1803–70), Texas rancher, who did not brand his cattle]

mavis ('meɪvɪs) *n* a popular name for the **song thrush.** [C14: from OF *mauvis* thrush; from ?]

maw ⓣ (mɔː) *n* **1** the mouth, throat, crop, or stomach of an animal, esp. of a voracious animal. **2** *Inf.* the mouth or stomach of a greedy person. [OE *maga*]

mawkish ⓣ ('mɔːkɪʃ) *adj* **1** falsely sentimental, esp. in a weak or maudlin way. **2** nauseating or insipid. [C17: from obs. *mawk* MAGGOT + -ISH]
▸**'mawkishly** *adv* ▸**'mawkishness** *n*

max (mæks) *n Inf.* **1** the most significant, highest, furthest, or greatest thing. **2 to the max.** to the ultimate extent.

max. *abbrev. for* maximum.

maxi ('mæksɪ) *adj* **1a** (of a garment) reaching the ankle. **1b** (*as n*): *she wore a maxi.* **1c** (*in combination*): *a maxidress.* **2** large or considerable. [C20: from MAXIMUM]

maxilla (mæk'sɪlə) *n, pl* **maxillae** (-liː). **1** the upper jawbone in vertebrates. **2** any member of one or two pairs of mouthparts in insects and other arthropods. [C17: NL, from L: jaw]

THESAURUS

matted *adj* **1** = **tangled,** knotted, tousled, uncombed

matter *n* **1-3** = **substance,** body, material, stuff **4** = **situation,** affair, business, concern, episode, event, incident, issue, occurrence, proceeding, question, subject, thing, topic, transaction **5** = **amount,** quantity, sum **6** = **content,** argument, purport, sense, subject, substance, text, thesis **7** = **importance,** consequence, import, moment, note, significance, weight **11** = **pus,** discharge, purulence, secretion **15 the matter** = **problem,** complication, difficulty, distress, trouble, upset, worry ◆ *vb* **16** = **be important,** be of consequence, carry weight, count, have influence, make a difference, mean something, signify

matter-of-fact *adj* **4** = **unsentimental,** deadpan, down-to-earth, dry, dull, emotionless, flat, lifeless, mundane, plain, prosaic, sober, unembellished, unimaginative, unvarnished

mature *adj* **1, 2, 5** = **grown-up,** adult, complete, fit, full-blown, full-grown, fully fledged, grown, matured, mellow, of age, perfect, prepared, ready, ripe, ripened, seasoned ◆ *vb* **6** = **develop,** age, become adult, bloom, blossom, come of age, grow up, maturate, mellow, perfect, reach adulthood, ripen, season
Antonyms *adj* ≠ **grown-up:** adolescent, childish, green, immature, incomplete, juvenile, puerile, undeveloped, unfinished, unperfected, unripe, young, youthful

maturity *n* **1** = **adulthood,** completion, experience, full bloom, full growth, fullness, majority, manhood *or* womanhood, maturation, matureness, perfection, ripeness, wisdom
Antonyms *n* childishness, excitability, immaturity, imperfection, incompletion, irresponsibility, juvenility, puerility, youthfulness

maudlin *adj* = **sentimental,** lachrymose, mawkish, mushy (*inf.*), overemotional, slushy (*inf.*), soppy (*Brit. inf.*), tearful, weepy (*inf.*)

maul *vb* **1** = **ill-treat,** abuse, batter, beat, beat up (*inf.*), handle roughly, knock about *or* around, manhandle, molest, pummel, rough up, thrash, work over (*sl.*) **2** = **tear,** claw, lacerate, mangle

maverick *n* **2a** = **rebel,** dissenter, dissentient, eccentric, heretic, iconoclast, individualist, nonconformist, protester, radical ◆ *modifier* **2b** = **rebel,** dissenting, eccentric, heretical, iconoclastic, individualistic, nonconformist, radical
Antonyms *n* ≠ **rebel:** Babbitt (*US*), conventionalist, stick-in-the-mud (*inf.*), traditionalist, yes man

maw *n* **1** = **stomach,** craw, crop, gullet, jaws, mouth, throat

mawkish *adj* **1** = **sentimental,** emotional, feeble, gushy (*inf.*), maudlin, mushy, schmaltzy (*sl.*), slushy (*inf.*), soppy (*Brit. inf.*), three-hankie (*inf.*)

▸**max'illary** *adj*
maxim ❶ ('mæksɪm) *n* a brief expression of a general truth, principle, or rule of conduct. [C15: via F from Med. L, from *maxima,* in the phrase *maxima prōpositio* basic axiom (lit.: greatest proposition)]
maxima ('mæksɪmə) *n* a plural of **maximum.**
maximal ('mæksɪməl) *adj* of, relating to, or achieving a maximum; being the greatest or best possible.
▸**'maximally** *adv*
maximin ('mæksɪˌmɪn) *n* **1** *Maths.* the highest of a set of minimum values. **2** (in game theory, etc.) the procedure of choosing the strategy that most benefits the least advantaged member of a group. Cf. **minimax.** [C20: from MAXI(MUM) + MIN(IMUM)]
maximize *or* **maximise** ('mæksɪˌmaɪz) *vb* **maximizes, maximizing, maximized** *or* **maximises, maximising, maximised.** *(tr)* to make as high or great as possible; increase to a maximum.
▸ˌ**maximi'zation** *or* ˌ**maximi'sation** *n* ▸**'maxiˌmizer** *or* **'maxiˌmiser** *n*
maximum ❶ ('mæksɪməm) *n, pl* **maximums** *or* **maxima. 1** the greatest possible amount, degree, etc. **2** the highest value of a variable quantity. ◆ *adj* **3** of, being, or showing a maximum or maximums. ◆ Abbrev.: **max.** [C18: from L: greatest (neuter form used as noun), from *magnus* great]
maxwell ('mækswəl) *n* the cgs unit of magnetic flux equal to the flux through one square centimetre normal to a field of one gauss. It is equivalent to 10^{-8} weber. Symbol: Mx [C20: after J. C. *Maxwell* (1831–79), Scot. physicist]
may[1] (meɪ) *vb past* **might.** (takes an infinitive without *to* or an implied infinitive) used as an auxiliary: **1** to indicate that permission is requested by or granted to someone: *he may go.* **2** (often foll. by *well*) to indicate possibility: *the rope may break.* **3** to indicate ability or capacity, esp. in questions: *may I help you?* **4** to express a strong wish: *long may she reign.* **5** to indicate result or purpose: used only in clauses introduced by *that* or *so that: he writes so that the average reader may understand.* **6** another word for **might**[1]. **7** to express courtesy in a question: *whose child may this little girl be?* **8 be that as it may.** in spite of that: a sentence connector conceding the possible truth of a previous statement and introducing an adversative clause: *be that as it may, I still think he should come.* **9 come what may.** whatever happens. **10 that's as may be.** (foll. by a clause introduced by *but*) that may be so. [OE *mæg,* from *magan*]

> **USAGE NOTE** It was formerly considered correct to use *may* rather than *can* when referring to permission, as in: *you may use the laboratory for your experiments,* but this use of *may* is now almost entirely restricted to polite questions such as: *may I open the window?* The use of *may* with *if* in constructions such as *your analysis may have been more credible if...*is generally regarded as incorrect, *might* being preferred: *your analysis might have been more credible if...*

may[2] *or* **may tree** (meɪ) *n* a Brit. name for **hawthorn.** [C16: from MAY]
May (meɪ) *n* the fifth month of the year, consisting of 31 days. [from OF, from L *Maius* (month) of *Maia,* Roman goddess]
Maya ('maɪə) *n* **1** (*pl* **Maya** *or* **Mayas**) Also called: **Mayan.** a member of an American Indian people of Yucatán, Belize, and N Guatemala, once having an advanced civilization. **2** the language of this people.
May apple *n* **1** an American plant with edible yellowish egg-shaped fruit. **2** the fruit.
maybe ❶ ('meɪˌbi:) *adv* **1** perhaps. ◆ *sentence substitute.* **2** possibly; neither yes nor no.
May beetle *or* **bug** *n* another name for **cockchafer.**
Mayday ('meɪˌdeɪ) *n* the international radiotelephone distress signal. [C20: phonetic spelling of F *m'aidez* help me]
May Day *n* the first day of May, traditionally a celebration of the coming of spring: in some countries now observed as a holiday in honour of workers.
mayest ('meɪɪst) *vb* a variant of **mayst.**
mayflower ('meɪˌflauə) *n* **1** any of various plants that bloom in May. **2** *Brit.* another name for **hawthorn, cowslip,** or **marsh marigold.**
Mayflower ('meɪˌflauə) *n* **the.** the ship in which the Pilgrim Fathers sailed from Plymouth to America in 1620.
mayfly ('meɪˌflaɪ) *n, pl* **mayflies.** any of an order of short-lived insects having large transparent wings.
mayhap ('meɪˌhæp) *adv* an archaic word for **perhaps.** [C16: shortened from *it may hap*]
mayhem ❶ *or* **maihem** ('meɪhɛm) *n* **1** *Law.* the wilful and unlawful infliction of injury upon a person, esp. (formerly) the injuring or removing of a limb rendering him less capable of defending himself against attack. **2** any violent destruction or confusion. [C15: from Anglo-F *mahem* injury, of Gmc origin]
Maying ('meɪɪŋ) *n* the traditional celebration of May Day.
mayn't ('meɪənt, meɪnt) *contraction of* may not.
mayonnaise (ˌmeɪə'neɪz) *n* a thick creamy sauce made from egg yolks, oil, and vinegar or lemon juice. [C19: from F, ? from *mahonnais* of Mahón, a port in Minorca]
mayor (mɛə) *n* the civic head of a municipal corporation in many countries. Scot. equivalent: **provost.** [C13: from OF *maire,* from L *maior* greater]
▸**'mayoral** *adj* ▸**'mayorship** *n*
mayoralty ('mɛərəltɪ) *n, pl* **mayoralties.** the office or term of office of a mayor. [C14: from OF *mairalté*]
mayoress ('mɛərɪs) *n* **1** *Chiefly Brit.* the wife of a mayor. **2** a female mayor.
maypole ('meɪˌpəul) *n* a tall pole around which people dance during May-Day celebrations.
May queen *n* a girl chosen, esp. for her beauty, to preside over May-Day celebrations.
mayst (meɪst) *or* **mayest** *vb Arch.* (used with *thou* or its relative equivalent) a singular form of the present tense of **may**[1].
mayweed ('meɪˌwi:d) *n* **1** Also called: **dog fennel, stinking mayweed.** a widespread Eurasian weedy plant having evil-smelling leaves and daisy-like flower heads. **2 scentless mayweed.** a similar and related plant, with scentless leaves. [C16: changed from OE *mægtha* mayweed + WEED]
maze ❶ (meɪz) *n* **1** a complex network of paths or passages, esp. one with high hedges in a garden, designed to puzzle those walking through it. **2** a similar system represented diagrammatically as a pattern of lines. **3** any confusing network of streets, paths, etc. **4** a state of confusion. ◆ *vb* **mazes, mazing, mazed. 5** an archaic or dialect word for **amaze.** [C13: see AMAZE]
▸**'mazement** *n* ▸**'mazy** *adj*
mazurka *or* **mazourka** (mə'zɜ:kə) *n* **1** a Polish national dance in triple time. **2** a piece of music composed for this dance. [C19: from Polish: (dance) of *Mazur* (Mazovia) province in Poland]
Mb *Computing. abbrev. for* megabyte.
MB *abbrev. for* Bachelor of Medicine.
MBA *abbrev. for* Master of Business Administration.
mbaqanga (ᵊmbɑ:'kæŋgə) *n* a style of Black popular music of urban South Africa. [C20: ? from Zulu *umbaqanga* mixture]
MBE *abbrev. for* Member of the Order of the British Empire (a Brit. title).
mbira (ᵊm'bi:rə) *n* an African musical instrument consisting of tuned metal strips attached to a resonating box, which are plucked with the thumbs. Also called: **thumb piano.** [Bantu]
MC *abbrev. for:* **1** Master of Ceremonies. **2** (in the US) Member of Congress. **3** (in Britain) Military Cross.
Mc- *prefix* a variant of **Mac-**. For entries beginning with this prefix, see under **Mac-**.
MCC (in Britain) *abbrev. for* Marylebone Cricket Club.
MCh *abbrev. for* Master of Surgery. [L *Magister Chirurgiae*]
MCP *Inf. abbrev. for* male chauvinist pig.
Md *the chemical symbol for* mendelevium.
MD *abbrev. for:* **1** Doctor of Medicine. [from L *Medicinae Doctor*] **2** Managing Director. **3** mentally deficient.
MDMA *abbrev. for* 3,4-methylenedioxymethamphetamine. See **ecstasy** (sense 4).
MDS See **MMDS.**
MDT (in the US and Canada) *abbrev. for* Mountain Daylight Time.
me[1] (mi:; *unstressed* mɪ) *pron (objective)* **1** refers to the speaker or writer: *that shocks me.* ◆ *n* **2** *Inf.* the personality of the speaker or writer or something that expresses it: *the real me.* [OE *mē* (dative)]

> **USAGE NOTE** It was formerly regarded as correct to use *I, he, she,* etc. rather than *me, him, her,* after the verb *to be,* as in: *it is I who told him.* Since both *I* and *me* can sound strange in a sentence like this, it is better to use a different construction: *I am the one who told him.* The use of a possessive before an *-ing* form of a verb was formerly thought to be preferable to using *me,* etc., but now both forms are acceptable: *he didn't like my/me having a job of my own.*

me[2] (mi:) *n* a variant spelling of **mi** (sense 2).
ME *abbrev. for:* **1** Marine Engineer. **2** Mechanical Engineer. **3** Methodist Episcopal. **4** Middle English. **5** Mining Engineer. **6** (in titles) Most Excellent. **7** myalgic encephalomyelitis.
mea culpa *Latin.* ('meɪɑ: 'kulpɑ:) an acknowledgment of guilt. [lit.: my fault]
mead[1] (mi:d) *n* an alcoholic drink made by fermenting a solution of honey, often with spices added. [OE *meodu*]
mead[2] (mi:d) *n* an archaic or poetic word for **meadow.** [OE *mæd*]
meadow ❶ ('mɛdəu) *n* **1** an area of grassland, often used for hay or for

THESAURUS

maxim *n* = **saying,** adage, aphorism, apophthegm, axiom, byword, dictum, gnome, motto, proverb, rule, saw

maximum *n* **1, 2** = **top,** apogee, ceiling, crest, extremity, height, most, peak, pinnacle, summit, upper limit, utmost, uttermost, zenith ◆ *adj* **3** = **greatest,** highest, maximal, most, paramount, supreme, topmost, utmost

Antonyms *n* ≠ **top:** bottom, minimum ◆ *adj* ≠ **greatest:** least, lowest, minimal

maybe *adv* **1** = **perhaps,** it could be, mayhap (*arch.*), peradventure (*arch.*), perchance (*arch.*), possibly

mayhem *n* **2** = **chaos,** commotion, confusion, destruction, disorder, fracas, havoc, trouble, violence

maze *n* **1-3** = **labyrinth,** convolutions, intricacy, meander **4** = **web,** bewilderment, confusion, imbroglio, mesh, perplexity, puzzle, snarl, tangle, uncertainty

meadow *n* **1** = **field,** grassland, lea (*poetic*), ley, pasture

grazing of animals. **2** a low-lying piece of grassland, often boggy and near a river. [OE *mædwe,* from *mæd* MEAD²]
▸ **'meadowy** *adj*

meadow grass *n* a perennial grass that grows in meadows and similar places in N temperate regions.

meadow saffron *n* another name for **autumn crocus.**

meadowsweet ('mɛdəʊ,swiːt) *n* **1** a Eurasian plant with dense heads of small fragrant cream-coloured flowers. **2** any of several related North American plants. See also **spiraea.**

meagre ❶ *or US* **meager** ('miːgə) *adj* **1** deficient in amount, quality, or extent. **2** thin or emaciated. **3** lacking in richness or strength. [C14: from OF *maigre,* from L *macer* lean, poor]
▸ **'meagrely** *adv* ▸ **'meagreness** *n*

meal¹ ❶ (miːl) *n* **1a** any of the regular occasions, such as breakfast, lunch, dinner, etc., when food is served and eaten. **1b** (*in combination*): *mealtime.* **2** the food served and eaten. **3 make a meal of.** *Inf.* to perform (a task) with unnecessarily great effort. [OE *mǣl* measure, set time, meal]

meal² (miːl) *n* **1** the edible part of a grain or pulse (excluding wheat) ground to a coarse powder. **2** *Scot.* oatmeal. **3** *Chiefly US.* maize flour. [OE *melu*]

mealie *or* **mielie** ('miːlɪ) *n* (*often pl*) a S. African word for **maize.** [C19: from Afrik. *milie,* from Port. *milho,* from L *milium* millet]

mealie-meal *n S. African.* meal made from finely ground maize.

meals-on-wheels *n* (*functioning as sing*) a service taking hot meals to the elderly, infirm, etc., in their own homes.

meal ticket *n Sl.* a person, situation, etc., providing a source of livelihood or income. [from orig. US sense of ticket entitling holder to a meal]

mealworm ('miːl,wɜːm) *n* the larva of various beetles feeding on stored foods, esp. meal and flour.

mealy ('miːlɪ) *adj* **mealier, mealiest. 1** resembling meal; powdery. **2** containing or consisting of meal or grain. **3** sprinkled or covered with meal or similar granules. **4** (esp. of horses) spotted; mottled. **5** pale in complexion. **6** short for **mealy-mouthed.**
▸ **'mealiness** *n*

mealy bug *n* any of various plant-eating insects coated with a powdery waxy secretion: some species are pests of citrus fruits and greenhouse plants.

mealy-mouthed ❶ *adj* hesitant or afraid to speak plainly; not outspoken. [C16: from MEALY (in the sense: soft, soft-spoken)]

mean¹ ❶ (miːn) *vb* **means, meaning, meant.** (*mainly tr*) **1** (*may take a clause as object or an infinitive*) to intend to convey or express. **2** (*may take a clause as object or an infinitive*) to intend: *she didn't mean to hurt it.* **3** (*may take a clause as object*) to say or do in all seriousness: *the boss means what he says.* **4** (*often passive;* often foll. by *for*) to destine or design (for a certain person or purpose): *she was meant for greater things.* **5** (*may take a clause as object*) to denote or connote; signify; represent. **6** (*may take a clause as object*) to produce; cause: *the weather will mean long traffic delays.* **7** (*may take a clause as object*) to foretell; portend: *those dark clouds mean rain.* **8** to have the importance of: *money means nothing to him.* **9** (*intr*) to have the intention of behaving or acting (esp. in **mean well** *or* **mean ill**). [OE *mænan*]

> **USAGE NOTE** In standard English, *mean* should not be followed by *for* when expressing intention: *I didn't mean this to happen* (not *I didn't mean for this to happen*).

mean² ❶ (miːn) *adj* **1** *Chiefly Brit.* miserly, ungenerous, or petty. **2** despicable, ignoble, or callous: *a mean action.* **3** poor or shabby: *a mean abode.* **4** *Inf., chiefly US & Canad.* bad-tempered; vicious. **5** *Inf.* ashamed: *he felt mean about not letting the children stay out late.* **6** *Sl.* excellent; skilful: *he plays a mean trombone.* **7 no mean. 7a** of high quality: *no mean performer.* **7b** difficult: *no mean feat.* [C12: from OE *gemǣne* common]
▸ **'meanly** *adv* ▸ **'meanness** *n*

mean³ ❶ (miːn) *n* **1** the middle point, state, or course between limits or extremes. **2** moderation. **3** *Maths.* **3a** the second and third terms of a proportion, as *b* and *c* in $a/b = c/d$. **3b** another name for **average** (sense 2). **4** *Statistics.* a statistic obtained by multiplying each possible value of a variable by its probability and then taking the sum or integral over the range of the variable. ◆ *adj* **5** intermediate or medium in size, quantity, etc. **6** occurring halfway between extremes or limits; average. [C14: via Anglo-Norman from OF *moien,* from LL *mediānus* MEDIAN]

meander ❶ (mɪ'ændə) *vb* (*intr*) **1** to follow a winding course. **2** to wander without definite aim or direction. ◆ *n* **3** (*often pl*) a curve or bend, as in a river. **4** (*often pl*) a winding course or movement. **5** an ornamental pattern, esp. as used in ancient Greek architecture. [C16: from L *maeander,* from Gk *Maiandros* the River Maeander, now the River Menderes in SW Turkey]
▸ **me'andering** *adj*

mean deviation *n Statistics.* **1** the difference between an observed value of a variable and its mean. **2** Also called: **mean deviation from the mean** (*or* **median**), **average deviation.** a measure of dispersion derived by computing the mean of the absolute values of the differences between observed values of a variable and the variable's mean.

meanie *or* **meany** ('miːnɪ) *n Inf.* **1** *Chiefly Brit.* a miserly or stingy person. **2** *Chiefly US.* a nasty ill-tempered person.

meaning ❶ ('miːnɪŋ) *n* **1** the sense or significance of a word, sentence, symbol, etc.; import. **2** the purpose behind speech, action, etc. **3** the inner, symbolic, or true interpretation, value, or message. **4** valid content; efficacy. ◆ *adj* **5** expressive of some sense, intention, criticism, etc.: *a meaning look.* ◆ See also **well-meaning.**

meaningful ❶ ('miːnɪŋfʊl) *adj* **1** having great meaning or validity. **2** eloquent; expressive: *a meaningful silence.*
▸ **'meaningfully** *adv* ▸ **'meaningfulness** *n*

meaningless ❶ ('miːnɪŋlɪs) *adj* futile or empty of meaning.
▸ **'meaninglessly** *adv* ▸ **'meaninglessness** *n*

mean lethal dose *n* another term for **median lethal dose.**

mean life *n Physics.* the average time of existence of an unstable or reactive entity, such as a nucleus, elementary particle, etc.

means ❶ (miːnz) *n* **1** (*functioning as sing or pl*) the medium, method, or instrument used to obtain a result or achieve an end: *a means of com-*

THESAURUS

meagre *adj* **1** = **insubstantial**, deficient, exiguous, inadequate, little, measly, paltry, pathetic, poor, puny, scant, scanty, scrimpy, short, skimpy, slender, slight, small, spare, sparse **2** = **thin**, bony, emaciated, gaunt, hungry, lank, lean, scraggy, scrawny, skinny, starved, underfed

meal¹ *n* **1, 2** = **repast**, board, spread (*inf.*)

mealy-mouthed *adj* = **hesitant**, afraid, doubtful, equivocal, euphemistic, indirect, mincing, overdelicate, prim, reticent

mean¹ *vb* **1, 5** = **signify**, betoken, connote, convey, denote, drive at, express, hint at, imply, indicate, purport, represent, say, spell, stand for, suggest, symbolize **2** = **intend**, aim, aspire, contemplate, design, desire, have in mind, plan, propose, purpose, set out, want, wish **4** = **destine**, design, fate, fit, make, match, predestine, preordain, suit **6** = **result in**, bring about, cause, engender, entail, give rise to, involve, lead to, necessitate, produce **7** = **foretell**, adumbrate, augur, betoken, foreshadow, herald, portend, presage, promise

mean² *adj* **1** = **miserly**, beggarly, close (*inf.*), mercenary, mingy, near (*inf.*), niggardly, parsimonious, penny-pinching, penurious, selfish, skimpy, stingy, tight, tight-arsed (*taboo sl.*), tight as a duck's arse (*taboo sl.*), tight-assed (*US taboo sl.*), tight-fisted, ungenerous **2** = **dishonourable**, abject, base, callous, contemptible, degenerate, degraded, despicable, disgraceful, hard-hearted, ignoble, low-minded, narrow-minded, petty, scurvy, shabby, shameful, sordid, vile, wretched **3** = **shabby**, beggarly, contemptible, down-at-heel, grungy (*sl., chiefly US*), insignificant, low-rent (*inf., chiefly US*), miserable, paltry, poor, run-down, scruffy, scuzzy (*sl., chiefly US*), seedy, sordid, squalid, tawdry, wretched **4** = **malicious**, bad-tempered, cantankerous, churlish, disagreeable, hostile, ill-tempered, nasty, rude, sour, unfriendly, unpleasant
Antonyms *adj* ≠ **miserly:** altruistic, big, bountiful, generous, munificent, prodigal, unselfish ≠ **dishonourable:** good, honourable, praiseworthy ≠ **shabby:** attractive, choice, de luxe, excellent, first-rate, pleasing, superb, superior ≠ **malicious:** compassionate, gentle, humane, kind, liberal, sympathetic, warm-hearted

mean³ *n* **1** = **average**, balance, compromise, happy medium, median, middle, middle course *or* way, midpoint, norm ◆ *adj* **5, 6** = **average**, intermediate, medial, median, medium, middle, middling, normal, standard

meander *vb* **1** = **wind**, snake, turn, zigzag **2** = **wander**, ramble, stravaig (*Scot. & N English dialect*), stray, stroll ◆ *n* **3, 4** = **curve**, bend, coil, loop, turn, twist, zigzag

meandering *adj* **1, 2** = **winding**, anfractuous, circuitous, convoluted, indirect, roundabout, serpentine, snaking, tortuous, wandering
Antonyms *adj* direct, straight, straightforward, undeviating

meaning *n* **1** = **sense**, connotation, denotation, drift, explanation, gist, implication, import, interpretation, message, purport, significance, signification, substance, upshot, value **2** = **purpose**, aim, design, end, goal, idea, intention, object, plan, point, trend **4** = **force**, effect, efficacy, point, thrust, use, usefulness, validity, value, worth ◆ *adj* **5** = **expressive**, eloquent, meaningful, pointed, pregnant, speaking, suggestive

meaningful *adj* **1** = **significant**, important, material, purposeful, relevant, serious, useful, valid, worthwhile **2** = **expressive**, eloquent, meaning, pointed, pregnant, speaking, suggestive
Antonyms *adj* ≠ **significant:** inconsequential, insignificant, meaningless, senseless, superficial, trivial, unimportant, useless, worthless

meaningless *adj* = **pointless**, aimless, empty, futile, hollow, inane, inconsequential, insignificant, insubstantial, nonsensical, nugatory, purposeless, senseless, trifling, trivial, useless, vain, valueless, worthless
Antonyms *adj* consequential, deep, evident, important, meaningful, obvious, purposeful, sensible, significant, useful, valuable, worthwhile

meanness *n* **1** = **miserliness**, minginess (*Brit. inf.*), niggardliness, parsimony, penuriousness, selfishness, stinginess, tight-fistedness **2** = **pettiness**, abjectness, baseness, degeneracy, degradation, despicableness, disgracefulness, dishonourableness, ignobility, low-mindedness, narrow-mindedness, scurviness, shabbiness, shamefulness, sordidness, vileness, wretchedness **3** = **shabbiness**, beggarliness, contemptibleness, insignificance, paltriness, pettiness, poorness, scruffiness, seediness, sordidness, squalor, tawdriness, wretchedness **4** = **malice**, bad temper, cantankerousness, churlishness, disagreeableness, hostility, ill temper, maliciousness, nastiness, rudeness, sourness, unfriendliness, unpleasantness

means *n* **1** = **method**, agency, avenue, channel, course, expedient, instrument, measure, medium, mode, process, way ◆ *pl n* **2** = **money**, affluence, capital, estate, fortune, funds, income, property, resources, riches, substance, wealth, wherewithal **4 by all means** = **certainly**, abso-

munication. 2 (*functioning as pl*) resources or income. 3 (*functioning as pl*) considerable wealth or income: *a man of means.* 4 **by all means.** without hesitation or doubt; certainly. 5 **by means of.** with the use or help of. 6 **by no manner of means.** definitely not. 7 **by no** (*or* **not by any**) **means.** on no account; in no way.

means test *n* the checking of a person's income to determine whether he qualifies for financial or social aid from a government.

mean sun *n* an imaginary sun moving along the celestial equator at a constant speed and completing its annual course in the same time as the sun takes to move round the ecliptic at a varying speed. It is used in the measurement of mean solar time.

meant (mɛnt) *vb* the past tense and past participle of **mean**[1].

meantime ➊ ('miːnˌtaɪm) *or* **meanwhile** ('miːnˌwaɪl) *n* 1 the intervening time or period (esp. in **in the meantime**). ◆ *adv* 2 during the intervening time or period. 3 at the same time, esp. in another place.

mean time *or* **mean solar time** *n* the times, at a particular place, measured in terms of the passage of the mean sun, giving 24-hour days (mean solar days) throughout a year.

meany ('miːnɪ) *n, pl* **meanies.** a variant of **meanie.**

measles ('miːzəlz) *n* (*functioning as sing*) 1 a highly contagious viral disease common in children, characterized by fever, profuse nasal discharge of mucus, conjunctivitis, and a rash of small red spots. See also **German measles.** 2 a disease of cattle, sheep, and pigs, caused by infestation with tapeworm larvae. [C14: from MLow G *masele* spot on the skin; infl. by ME *mesel* leper, from L *misellus,* dim. of *miser* wretched]

measly ➊ ('miːzlɪ) *adj* **measlier, measliest.** 1 *Inf.* meagre in quality or quantity. 2 (of meat) infested with tapeworm larvae. 3 having or relating to measles. [C17: see MEASLES]

measurable ➊ ('mɛʒərəbᵊl) *adj* able to be measured; perceptible or significant.
▸ **'measurably** *adv*

measure ➊ ('mɛʒə) *n* 1 the extent, quantity, amount, or degree of something, as determined by measurement or calculation. 2 a device for measuring distance, volume, etc., such as a graduated scale or container. 3 a system of measurement: *metric measure.* 4 a standard used in a system of measurements. 5 a specific or standard amount of something: *a measure of grain; full measure.* 6 a basis or standard for comparison. 7 reasonable or permissible limit or bounds: *within measure.* 8 degree or extent (often in **in some measure, in a measure,** etc.): *a measure of freedom.* 9 (*often pl*) a particular action intended to achieve an effect. 10 a legislative bill, act, or resolution. 11 *Music.* another word for **bar**[1] (sense 15). 12 *Prosody.* poetic rhythm or cadence; metre. 13 a metrical foot. 14 *Poetic.* a melody or tune. 15 the act of measuring; measurement. 16 *Arch.* a dance. 17 *Printing.* the width of a page or column of type. 18 **for good measure.** as an extra precaution or beyond requirements. 19 **made to measure.** (of clothes) made to fit an individual purchaser. ◆ *vb* **measures, measuring, measured.** 20 (*tr;* often foll. by *up*) to determine the size, amount, etc., of by measurement. 21 (*intr*) to make a measurement. 22 (*tr*) to estimate or determine. 23 (*tr*) to function as a measurement of: *the ohm measures electrical resistance.* 24 (*tr*) to bring into competition or conflict with: *he measured his strength against that of his opponent.* 25 (*intr*) to be as specified in extent, amount, etc.: *the room measures six feet.* 26 (*tr*) to travel or move over as if measuring. ◆ See also **measure up.** [C13: from OF, from L *mēnsūra,* from *mēnsus,* p.p. of *mētīrī* to measure]

measured ➊ ('mɛʒəd) *adj* 1 determined by measurement. 2 slow or stately. 3 carefully considered; deliberate.
▸ **'measuredly** *adv*

measureless ➊ ('mɛʒəlɪs) *adj* limitless, vast, or infinite.
▸ **'measurelessly** *adv*

measurement ➊ ('mɛʒəmənt) *n* 1 the act or process of measuring. 2 an amount, extent, or size determined by measuring. 3 a system of measures based on a particular standard.

measures ('mɛʒəz) *pl n* rock strata that are characterized by a particular type of sediment or deposit: *coal measures.*

measure up ➊ *vb* 1 (*adv*) to determine the size of (something) by measurement. 2 **measure up to.** to fulfil (expectations, standards, etc.).

measuring jug *n* a graduated jug used in cooking to measure ingredients.

measuring worm *n* the larva of a geometrid moth: it moves in a series of loops. Also called: **inchworm.**

meat ➊ (miːt) *n* 1 the flesh of mammals used as food. 2 anything edible, esp. flesh with the texture of meat: *crab meat.* 3 food, as opposed to drink. 4 the essence or gist. 5 an archaic word for **meal**[1] (senses 1 and 2). 6 **meat and drink.** a source of pleasure. [OE *mete*]
▸ **'meatless** *adj*

meatball ('miːtˌbɔːl) *n* 1 minced beef, shaped into a ball before cooking. 2 *US & Canad. sl.* a stupid or boring person.

meatus (mɪ'eɪtəs) *n, pl* **meatuses** *or* **meatus.** *Anat.* a natural opening or channel, such as the canal leading from the outer ear to the eardrum. [C17: from L: passage, from *meāre* to pass]

meaty ➊ ('miːtɪ) *adj* **meatier, meatiest.** 1 of, relating to, or full of meat. 2 heavily built; fleshy or brawny. 3 full of import or interest: *a meaty discussion.*
▸ **'meatily** *adv* ▸ **'meatiness** *n*

Mecca *or* **Mekka** ('mɛkə) *n* 1 a city in W Saudi Arabia: birthplace of Mohammed; the holiest city of Islam. 2 (*sometimes not cap.*) a place that attracts many visitors.

Meccano (mɪ'kɑːnəʊ) *n Trademark.* a construction set of miniature metal parts from which mechanical models can be made.

mech. *abbrev. for:* 1 mechanical. 2 mechanics. 3 mechanism.

mechanic (mɪ'kænɪk) *n* a person skilled in maintaining or operating machinery, motors, etc. [C14: from L *mēchanicus,* from Gk, from *mēkhanē* MACHINE]

mechanical ➊ (mɪ'kænɪkᵊl) *adj* 1 made, performed, or operated by or as if by a machine or machinery. 2 concerned with machines or machinery. 3 relating to or controlled or operated by physical forces. 4 of or concerned with mechanics. 5 (of a gesture, etc.) automatic; lacking thought, feeling, etc. 6 *Philosophy.* accounting for phenomena by physically determining forces.
▸ **me'chanicalism** *n* ▸ **me'chanically** *adv* ▸ **me'chanicalness** *n*

mechanical advantage *n* the ratio of the working force exerted by a mechanism to the applied effort.

mechanical drawing *n* a drawing to scale of a machine, machine component, architectural plan, etc., from which dimensions can be taken.

mechanical engineering *n* the branch of engineering concerned with the design, construction, and operation of machines.

mechanical equivalent of heat *n Physics.* a factor for converting units of energy into heat units.

mechanician (ˌmɛkə'nɪʃən) *or* **mechanist** *n* a person skilled in making machinery and tools; technician.

mechanics (mɪ'kænɪks) *n* 1 (*functioning as sing*) the branch of science, divided into statics, dynamics, and kinematics, concerned with the equilibrium or motion of bodies in a particular frame of reference. 2 (*functioning as sing*) the science of designing, constructing, and operating machines. 3 the working parts of a machine. 4 the technical aspects of something.

mechanism ➊ ('mɛkəˌnɪzəm) *n* 1 a system or structure of moving parts that performs some function, esp. in a machine. 2 something resem-

THESAURUS

lutely, definitely, doubtlessly, of course, positively, surely 5 **by means of = by way of,** by dint of, through, using, utilizing, via, with the aid of 7 **by no means = in no way,** absolutely not, definitely not, not at all, not in the least, not in the slightest, not the least bit, no way, on no account

meantime *adv* 2, 3 = **at the same time,** concurrently, for now, for the duration, for the moment, for then, in the interim, in the interval, in the intervening time, in the meantime, in the meanwhile, simultaneously

measly *adj* 1 *Informal* = **meagre,** beggarly, contemptible, mean, mingy (*Brit. inf.*), miserable, miserly, niggardly, paltry, pathetic, petty, pitiful, poor, puny, scanty, skimpy, stingy, ungenerous

measurable *adj* = **quantifiable,** assessable, computable, determinable, gaugeable, material, mensurable, perceptible, quantitative, significant

measure *n* 1 = **quantity,** allotment, allowance, amount, amplitude, capacity, degree, extent, magnitude, portion, proportion, quota, range, ration, reach, scope, share, size 2 = **gauge,** metre, rule, scale, yardstick 6 = **standard,** criterion, example, model, norm, par, test, touchstone, yardstick 7 = **limit,** bounds, control, limitation, moderation, restraint 9 *often plural* = **action,** act, course, deed, expedient, manoeuvre, means, procedure, proceeding, step 10 = **law,** act, bill, enactment, resolution, statute 12, 13 = **rhythm,** beat, cadence, foot, metre, verse 18 **for good measure = in addition,** as a bonus, besides, into the bargain, to boot ◆ *vb* 20-22 = **quantify,** appraise, assess, calculate, calibrate, compute, determine, estimate, evaluate, gauge, judge, mark out, rate, size, sound, survey, value, weigh

measured *adj* 1 = **quantified,** exact, gauged, modulated, precise, predetermined, regulated, standard, verified 2 = **steady,** dignified, even, leisurely, regular, sedate, slow, solemn, stately, unhurried 3 = **considered,** calculated, deliberate, grave, planned, premeditated, reasoned, sober, studied, well-thought-out

measureless *adj* = **infinite,** beyond measure, boundless, endless, immeasurable, immense, incalculable, inestimable, limitless, unbounded, vast

measurement *n* 1 = **calculation,** appraisal, assessment, calibration, computation, estimation, evaluation, judgment, mensuration, metage, survey, valuation 2 = **size,** amount, amplitude, area, capacity, depth, dimension, extent, height, length, magnitude, volume, weight, width

measure up *vb* 2 **measure up to = fulfil the expectations,** be adequate, be capable, be equal to, be fit, be suitable, be suited, come up to scratch (*inf.*), come up to standard, compare, equal, fit *or* fill the bill, make the grade (*inf.*), match, meet, rival

meat *n* 1-3 = **food,** aliment, cheer, chow (*inf.*), comestibles, eats (*sl.*), fare, flesh, grub (*sl.*), nosh (*sl.*), nourishment, nutriment, provender, provisions, rations, subsistence, sustenance, viands, victuals 4 = **gist,** core, essence, heart, kernel, marrow, nub, nucleus, pith, point, substance

meaty *adj* 2 = **brawny,** beefy (*inf.*), burly, fleshy, heavily built, heavy, husky (*inf.*), muscular, solid, strapping, sturdy 3 = **interesting,** meaningful, pithy, profound, rich, significant, substantial

mechanical *adj* 1 = **automatic,** automated, machine-driven 5 = **unthinking,** automatic, cold, cursory, dead, emotionless, habitual, impersonal, instinctive, involuntary, lacklustre, lifeless, machine-like, matter-of-fact, perfunctory, routine, spiritless, unconscious, unfeeling
Antonyms *adj* ≠ **automatic:** manual ≠ **unthinking:** conscious, genuine, sincere, thinking, voluntary, warm, wholehearted

mechanism *n* 1 = **workings,** action, components, gears, innards (*inf.*), machinery, motor, bling a machine in the arrangement and working of its parts. **3** any mechanical device or part of such a device. **4** a process or technique: *the mechanism of novel writing.* **5** *Philosophy.* the doctrine that human action can be explained in purely physical terms. **6** *Psychoanal.* **6a** the ways in which psychological forces interact and operate. **6b** a structure having an influence on the behaviour of a person, such as a defence mechanism.

mechanistic (ˌmɛkəˈnɪstɪk) *adj* **1** *Philosophy.* of or relating to the theory of mechanism. **2** *Maths.* of or relating to mechanics.
▸ **ˈmechanist** *n* ▸ **ˌmechaˈnistically** *adv*

mechanize *or* **mechanise** (ˈmɛkəˌnaɪz) *vb* **mechanizes, mechanizing, mechanized** *or* **mechanises, mechanising, mechanised.** (*tr*) **1** to equip (a factory, industry, etc.) with machinery. **2** to make mechanical, automatic, or monotonous. **3** to equip (an army, etc.) with motorized or armoured vehicles.
▸ **ˌmechaniˈzation** *or* **ˌmechaniˈsation** *n* ▸ **ˈmechaˌnizer** *or* **ˈmechaˌniser** *n*

mechanoreceptor (ˌmɛkənəʊrɪˈsɛptə) *n Physiol.* a sensory receptor, as in the skin, that is sensitive to a mechanical stimulus, such as pressure.

mechanotherapy (ˌmɛkənəʊˈθɛrəpɪ) *n* the treatment of disorders or injuries by means of mechanical devices, esp. devices that provide exercise for bodily parts.

Mechlin lace (ˈmɛklɪn) *n* bobbin lace characterized by patterns outlined by heavier thread, made at Mechlin, English name for Mechelen, a city in N Belgium.

meconium (mɪˈkəʊnɪəm) *n* the first faeces of a newborn infant. [C17: from NL, from L: poppy juice, from Gk, from *mēkōn* poppy]

meconopsis (ˌmiːkənˈɒpsɪs) *n* any of various mainly Asiatic poppies. [C19: from Gk *mēkōn* poppy + -OPSIS]

Med (mɛd) *n Inf.* the Mediterranean region.

MEd *abbrev. for* Master of Education.

med. *abbrev. for:* **1** medical. **2** medicine. **3** medieval. **4** medium.

médaillons (*French* medajɔ̃) *pl n Cookery.* small round pieces of meat, fish, vegetables, etc. Also called: **medallions.**

medal (ˈmɛdᵊl) *n* a small flat piece of metal bearing an inscription or image, given as an award or commemoration of some outstanding event, etc. [C16: from F *médaille,* prob. from It. *medaglia,* ult. from L *metallum* METAL]

medallion (mɪˈdæljən) *n* **1** a large medal. **2** an oval or circular decorative device resembling a medal, usually bearing a portrait or relief moulding, used in architecture and textile design. [C17: from F, from It., from *medaglia* MEDAL]

medallist *or US* **medalist** (ˈmɛdᵊlɪst) *n* **1** a designer, maker, or collector of medals. **2** *Chiefly sport.* a recipient of a medal or medals.

medal play *n Golf.* another name for **stroke play.**

meddle 🅣 (ˈmɛdᵊl) *vb* **meddles, meddling, meddled.** (*intr*) **1** (usually foll. by *with*) to interfere officiously or annoyingly. **2** (usually foll. by *in*) to involve oneself unwarrantedly. [C14: from OF *medler,* ult. from L *miscēre* to mix]
▸ **ˈmeddler** *n* ▸ **ˈmeddling** *adj*

meddlesome 🅣 (ˈmɛdᵊlsəm) *adj* intrusive or meddling.
▸ **ˈmeddlesomely** *adv* ▸ **ˈmeddlesomeness** *n*

Mede (miːd) *n* a member of an Indo-European people who established an empire in SW Asia in the 7th and 6th centuries B.C.
▸ **ˈMedian** *n, adj*

media (ˈmiːdɪə) *n* **1** a plural of **medium. 2** the means of communication that reach large numbers of people, such as television, newspapers, and radio. ◆ *adj* **3** of or relating to the mass media: *media hype.*

> **USAGE NOTE** When *media* refers to the mass media, it is sometimes treated as a singular form, as in: *the media has shown great interest in these events.* Many people think this use is incorrect and that *media* should always be treated as a plural form: *the media have shown great interest in these events.*

mediaeval (ˌmɛdɪˈiːvᵊl) *adj* a variant spelling of **medieval.**

media event *n* an event that is staged for or exploited by the mass media.

medial (ˈmiːdɪəl) *adj* **1** of or situated in the middle. **2** ordinary or average in size. **3** *Maths.* relating to an average. **4** another word for **median** (senses 1, 2). [C16: from LL *mediālis,* from *medius* middle]
▸ **ˈmedially** *adv*

median (ˈmiːdɪən) *adj* **1** of, relating to, situated in, or directed towards the middle. **2** *Statistics.* of or relating to the median. ◆ *n* **3** a middle point, plane, or part. **4** *Geom.* **4a** a straight line joining one vertex of a triangle to the midpoint of the opposite side. **4b** a straight line joining the midpoints of the nonparallel sides of a trapezium. **5** *Statistics.* the middle value in a frequency distribution, below and above which lie values with equal total frequencies. **6** *Statistics.* the middle number or average of the two middle numbers in an ordered sequence of numbers. [C16: from L *mediānus,* from *medius* middle]
▸ **ˈmedianly** *adv*

median lethal dose *or* **mean lethal dose** *n* **1** the amount of a drug or other substance that, when administered to a group of experimental animals, will kill 50 per cent of the group in a specified time. **2** the amount of ionizing radiation that will kill 50 per cent of a population in a specified time. ◆ Abbrev.: **LD_{50}**.

mediant (ˈmiːdɪənt) *n Music.* **a** the third degree of a major or minor scale. **b** (*as modifier*): *a mediant chord.* [C18: from It. *mediante,* from LL *mediāre* to be in the middle]

mediastinum (ˌmiːdɪəˈstaɪnəm) *n, pl* **mediastina** (-nə). *Anat.* **1** a membrane between two parts of an organ or cavity such as the pleural tissue between the two lungs. **2** the part of the thoracic cavity that lies between the lungs, containing the heart, trachea, etc. [C16: from Medical L, neuter of Med. L *mediastīnus* median, from L: low grade of servant, from *medius* mean]
▸ **ˌmediasˈtinal** *adj*

mediate 🅣 *vb* (ˈmiːdɪˌeɪt), **mediates, mediating, mediated. 1** (*intr;* usually foll. by *between* or *in*) to intervene (between parties or in a dispute) in order to bring about agreement. **2** to bring about (an agreement) between parties in a dispute. **3** to resolve (differences) by mediation. **4** (*intr*) to be in an intermediate position. **5** (*tr*) to serve as a medium for causing (a result) or transferring (objects, information, etc.). ◆ *adj* (ˈmiːdɪɪt). **6** occurring as a result of or dependent upon mediation. [C16: from LL *mediāre* to be in the middle]
▸ **ˈmediately** *adv* ▸ **ˈmediˌator** *n*

mediation 🅣 (ˌmiːdɪˈeɪʃən) *n* the act of mediating; intercession between people, states, etc. in an attempt to reconcile disputed matters.

Medibank (ˈmɛdɪbæŋk) *n* (in Australia), a government-run health insurance scheme.

medic[1] (ˈmɛdɪk) *n Inf.* a doctor, medical orderly, or medical student. [C17: from MEDICAL]

medic[2] (ˈmɛdɪk) *n* the usual US spelling of **medick.**

medicable (ˈmɛdɪkəbᵊl) *adj* potentially able to be treated or cured medically.

medical (ˈmɛdɪkᵊl) *adj* **1** of or relating to the science of medicine or to the treatment of patients by drugs, etc., as opposed to surgery. ◆ *n* **2** *Inf.* a medical examination. [C17: from Med. L *medicālis,* from L *medicus* physician, surgeon, from *mederī* to heal]
▸ **ˈmedically** *adv*

medical certificate *n* **1** a document stating the result of a satisfactory medical examination. **2** a doctor's certificate giving evidence of a person's unfitness for work.

medical jurisprudence *n* another name for **forensic medicine.**

medicament (mɪˈdɪkəmənt, ˈmɛdɪ-) *n* a medicine or remedy. [C16: via F from L *medicāmentum,* from *medicāre* to cure]

medicate (ˈmɛdɪˌkeɪt) *vb* **medicates, medicating, medicated.** (*tr*) **1** to cover or impregnate (a wound, etc.) with an ointment, etc. **2** to treat (a patient) with a medicine. **3** to add a medication to (a bandage, shampoo, etc.). [C17: from L *medicāre* to heal]
▸ **ˈmedicative** *adj*

medication (ˌmɛdɪˈkeɪʃən) *n* **1** treatment with drugs or remedies. **2** a drug or remedy.

medicinal 🅣 (meˈdɪsɪnᵊl) *adj* **1** relating to or having therapeutic properties. ◆ *n* **2** a medicinal substance.
▸ **meˈdicinally** *adv*

medicine 🅣 (ˈmɛdɪsɪn, ˈmɛdsɪn) *n* **1** any drug or remedy for use in treating, preventing, or alleviating the symptoms of disease. **2** the science of preventing, diagnosing, alleviating, or curing disease. **3** any nonsurgical branch of medical science. **4** the practice or profession of medicine. **5** something regarded by primitive people as having magical or remedial properties. **6 a taste** (*or* **dose**) **of one's own medicine.** an unpleasant experience in retaliation for a similar unkind or aggressive act. **7 take one's medicine.** to accept a deserved punishment. [C13: via OF from L *medicīna* (*ars*) (art) of healing, from *medicus* doctor, from *mederī* to heal]

medicine ball *n* a heavy ball used for physical training.

medicine man *n* (among certain peoples, esp. North American Indians) a person believed to have supernatural powers of healing; a magician or sorcerer.

medick *or US* **medic** (ˈmɛdɪk) *n* any of various small plants having yellow or purple flowers and trifoliate leaves. [C15: from L *mēdica,* from Gk *mēdikē* (*poa*) Median (grass), a type of clover]

medico (ˈmɛdɪˌkəʊ) *n, pl* **medicos.** *Inf.* a doctor or medical student. [C17: via It. from L *medicus*]

THESAURUS

works **3** = **machine**, apparatus, appliance, contrivance, device, instrument, structure, system, tool **4** = **process**, agency, execution, functioning, means, medium, method, methodology, operation, performance, procedure, system, technique, way, workings

meddle *vb* **1, 2** = **interfere**, butt in, intermeddle, interpose, intervene, intrude, pry, put one's oar in, put one's two cents in (*US sl.*), stick one's nose in (*inf.*), tamper

meddlesome *adj* = **interfering**, intermeddling, intruding, intrusive, meddling, mischievous, officious, prying

mediate *vb* **1-3** = **intervene**, act as middleman, arbitrate, bring to an agreement, bring to terms, conciliate, intercede, interpose, make peace between, moderate, reconcile, referee, resolve, restore harmony, settle, step in (*inf.*), umpire

mediation *n* = **arbitration**, conciliation, good offices, intercession, interposition, intervention, reconciliation

mediator *n* **1-3** = **negotiator**, advocate, arbiter, arbitrator, go-between, honest broker, interceder, intermediary, judge, middleman, moderator, peacemaker, referee, umpire

medicinal *adj* **1** = **therapeutic**, analeptic, curative, healing, medical, remedial, restorative, roborant, sanative

medicine *n* **1** = **remedy**, cure, drug, medicament, medication, nostrum, physic

medieval Ⓣ *or* **mediaeval** (ˌmɛdɪˈiːvᵊl) *adj* **1** of, relating to, or in the style of the Middle Ages. **2** *Inf.* old-fashioned; primitive. [C19: from NL *medium aevum* the middle age]

Medieval Greek *n* the Greek language from the 7th century A.D. to shortly after the sacking of Constantinople in 1204. Also called: **Middle Greek, Byzantine Greek.**

medievalism *or* **mediaevalism** (ˌmɛdɪˈiːvəˌlɪzəm) *n* **1** the beliefs, life, or style of the Middle Ages or devotion to those. **2** a belief, custom, or point of style copied or surviving from the Middle Ages.

medievalist *or* **mediaevalist** (ˌmɛdɪˈiːvəlɪst) *n* a student or devotee of the Middle Ages.

Medieval Latin *n* the Latin language as used throughout Europe in the Middle Ages.

mediocre Ⓣ (ˌmiːdɪˈəʊkə) *adj Often derog.* average or ordinary in quality. [C16: via F from L *mediocris* moderate, lit.: halfway up the mountain, from *medius* middle + *ocris* stony mountain]

mediocrity Ⓣ (ˌmiːdɪˈɒkrɪtɪ, ˌmɛd-) *n, pl* **mediocrities. 1** the state or quality of being mediocre. **2** a mediocre person or thing.

Medit. *abbrev. for* Mediterranean.

meditate Ⓣ (ˈmɛdɪˌteɪt) *vb* **meditates, meditating meditated. 1** (*intr;* foll. by *on* or *upon*) to think about something deeply. **2** (*intr*) to reflect deeply on spiritual matters, esp. as a religious act. **3** (*tr*) to plan, consider, or think of doing (something). [C16: from L *meditārī* to reflect upon]
▸**ˈmeditative** *adj* ▸**ˈmeditatively** *adv* ▸**ˈmediˌtator** *n*

meditation Ⓣ (ˌmɛdɪˈteɪʃən) *n* **1** the act of meditating; reflection. **2** contemplation of spiritual matters, esp. as a religious practice.

Mediterranean (ˌmɛdɪtəˈreɪnɪən) *n* **1** short for the **Mediterranean Sea,** the sea between S Europe, N Africa, and SW Asia. **2** a native or inhabitant of a Mediterranean country. ◆ *adj* **3** of, relating to, situated or dwelling near the Mediterranean Sea. **4** denoting a postulated subdivision of the Caucasoid race, characterized by slender build and dark complexion. **5** *Meteorol.* (of a climate) characterized by hot summers and relatively warm winters when most of the annual rainfall occurs. **6** (*often not cap.*) *Obs.* situated in the middle of a landmass; inland. [C16: from L *mediterrāneus,* from *medius* middle + *-terrāneus,* from *terra* land]

medium Ⓣ (ˈmiːdɪəm) *adj* **1** midway between extremes; average. ◆ *n, pl* **media** *or* **mediums. 2** an intermediate or middle state, degree, or condition; mean: *the happy medium.* **3** an intervening substance or agency for transmitting or producing an effect; vehicle. **4** a means or agency for communicating or diffusing information, news, etc., to the public. **5** a person supposedly used as a spiritual intermediary between the dead and the living. **6** the substance in which specimens of animals and plants are preserved or displayed. **7** *Biol.* Also called: **culture medium.** a nutritive substance in which cultures of bacteria or fungi are grown. **8** the substance or surroundings in which an organism naturally lives or grows. **9** *Art.* **9a** the category of a work of art, as determined by its materials and methods of production. **9b** the materials used in a work of art. **10** any solvent in which pigments are mixed and thinned. [C16: from L: neuter sing of *medius* middle]

USAGE NOTE See at **media.**

medium-dated *adj* (of a gilt-edged security) having between five and fifteen years to run before redemption. Cf. **long-dated, short-dated.**

medium frequency *n* a radio-frequency band or radio frequency lying between 3000 and 300 kilohertz. Abbrev: **MF.**

medium wave *n* **a** a radio wave with a wavelength between 100 and 1000 metres. **b** (*as modifier*): *a medium-wave broadcast.*

medlar (ˈmɛdlə) *n* **1** a small Eurasian tree. **2** its fruit, which resembles the crab apple and is not edible until it has begun to decay. [C14: from OF *medlier,* from L *mespilum* medlar fruit, from Gk *mespilon*]

medley Ⓣ (ˈmɛdlɪ) *n* **1** a mixture of various types or elements. **2** a musical composition consisting of various tunes arranged as a continuous whole. **3** Also called: **medley relay. 3a** *Swimming.* a race in which a different stroke is used for each length. **3b** *Athletics.* a relay race in which each leg has a different distance. [C14: from OF *medlee,* from *medler* to mix, quarrel]

medulla (mɪˈdʌlə) *n, pl* **medullas** *or* **medullae** (-liː). **1** *Anat.* **1a** the innermost part of an organ or structure. **1b** short for **medulla oblongata. 2** *Bot.* another name for **pith** (sense 4). [C17: from L: marrow, prob. from *medius* middle]
▸**meˈdullary** *or* **meˈdullar** *adj*

medulla oblongata (ˌɒblɒŋˈgɑːtə) *n, pl* **medulla oblongatas** *or* **medullae oblongatae** (mɪˈdʌliː ˌɒblɒŋˈgɑːtiː). the lower stalklike section of the brain, continuous with the spinal cord, containing control centres for the heart and lungs. [C17: NL: oblong-shaped medulla]

medusa (mɪˈdjuːzə) *n, pl* **medusas** *or* **medusae** (-ziː). another name for **jellyfish** (sense 1). [C18: from the likeness of its tentacles to the snaky locks of *Medusa,* the Gorgon]
▸**meˈdusoid** *adj, n*

meed (miːd) *n Arch.* a recompense; reward. [OE: wages]

meek Ⓣ (miːk) *adj* **1** patient, long-suffering, or submissive; humble. **2** spineless or spiritless; compliant. [C12: rel. to ON *mjūkr* amenable]
▸**ˈmeekly** *adv* ▸**ˈmeekness** *n*

meerkat (ˈmɪəˌkæt) *n* any of several South African mongooses, esp. the slender-tailed meerkat or suricate, which has a lemur-like face and four-toed feet. [C19: from Du.: sea-cat]

meerschaum (ˈmɪəʃəm) *n* **1** a white, yellowish, or pink compact earthy mineral consisting of hydrated magnesium silicate: used to make tobacco pipes and as a building stone. **2** a tobacco pipe having a bowl made of this mineral. [C18: from G *Meerschaum* lit.: sea foam]

meet[1] Ⓣ (miːt) *vb* **meets, meeting, met. 1** (sometimes foll. by *up* or (US) *with*) to come together (with), either by design or by accident; encounter. **2** to come into or be in conjunction or contact with (something or each other). **3** (*tr*) to come to or be at the place of arrival of: *to meet a train.* **4** to make the acquaintance of or be introduced to (someone or each other). **5** to gather in the company of (someone or each other). **6** to come into the presence of (someone or each other) as opponents. **7** (*tr*) to cope with effectively; satisfy: *to meet someone's demands.* **8** (*tr*) to be apparent to (esp. in **meet the eye**). **9** (*tr*) to return or counter: *to meet a blow with another.* **10** to agree with (someone or each other): *we met him on the price he suggested.* **11** (*tr;* sometimes foll. by *with*) to experience; suffer: *he met his death in a road accident.* **12** (*intr*) to occur together: *courage and kindliness met in him.* ◆ *n* **13** the assembly of hounds, huntsmen, etc., prior to a hunt. **14** a meeting, esp. a sports meeting. [OE *mētan*]
▸**ˈmeeter** *n*

meet[2] (miːt) *adj Arch.* proper, fitting, or correct. [C13: from var. of OE *gemǣte*]
▸**ˈmeetly** *adv*

meeting Ⓣ (ˈmiːtɪŋ) *n* **1** an act of coming together; encounter. **2** an assembly or gathering. **3** a conjunction or union. **4** a sporting competition, as of athletes, or of horse racing.

meeting house *n* the place in which certain religious groups, esp. Quakers, hold their meetings for worship.

mefloquine (ˈmɛfləʊˌkwiːn) *n* a synthetic drug administered orally to prevent or treat malaria. [C20]

mega (ˈmɛgə) *adj Sl.* extremely good, great, or successful. [C20: prob. independent use of MEGA-]

mega- *combining form.* **1** denoting 10^6: *megawatt.* Symbol: M **2** (in com-

THESAURUS

medieval *adj* **1 = Gothic 2** *Informal* **= old-fashioned,** antediluvian, antiquated, antique, archaic, primitive, unenlightened

mediocre *adj* **= second-rate,** average, banal, bog-standard (*Brit. & Irish sl.*), commonplace, fair to middling (*inf.*), indifferent, inferior, insignificant, mean, medium, middling, no great shakes (*inf.*), ordinary, passable, pedestrian, run-of-the-mill, so-so (*inf.*), tolerable, undistinguished, uninspired, vanilla (*sl.*)
Antonyms *adj* distinctive, distinguished, excellent, extraordinary, fine, incomparable, superb, superior, unexcelled, unique, unrivalled, unsurpassed

mediocrity *n* **1 = insignificance,** commonplaceness, indifference, inferiority, meanness, ordinariness, poorness, unimportance **2 = nonentity,** cipher, lightweight (*inf.*), nobody, second-rater

meditate *vb* **1, 2 = reflect,** be in a brown study, cogitate, consider, contemplate, deliberate, muse, ponder, ruminate, study, think **3 = plan,** consider, contemplate, design, devise, have in mind, intend, mull over, purpose, scheme, think over

meditation *n* **1 = reflection,** brown study, cerebration, cogitation, concentration, contemplation, musing, pondering, reverie, ruminating, rumination, study, thought

meditative *adj* **1 = reflective,** cogitative, contemplative, deliberative, pensive, ruminative, studious, thoughtful

medium *adj* **1 = average,** fair, intermediate, mean, medial, median, mediocre, middle, middling, midway ◆ *n* **2 = middle,** average, centre, compromise, mean, middle course, middle ground, middle path, middle way, midpoint **2 = means,** agency, avenue, channel, form, instrument, instrumentality, mode, organ, vehicle, way **5 = spiritualist,** channeller, spiritist **8 = environment,** atmosphere, conditions, element, habitat, influences, milieu, setting, surroundings
Antonyms *adj* ≠ **average:** curious, distinctive, extraordinary, extreme, uncommon, unique, unusual, utmost

medley *n* **1 = mixture,** assortment, confusion, farrago, gallimaufry, hodgepodge, hotchpotch, jumble, *mélange,* miscellany, mishmash, mixed bag (*inf.*), olio, omnium-gatherum, pastiche, patchwork, potpourri, salmagundi

meek *adj* **1 = submissive,** acquiescent, compliant, deferential, docile, forbearing, gentle, humble, long-suffering, mild, modest, patient, peaceful, soft, timid, unassuming, unpretentious, yielding **2 = spineless,** boneless, resigned, spiritless, tame, unresisting, weak, weak-kneed (*inf.*), wimpish *or* wimpy (*inf.*)
Antonyms *adj* arrogant, bold, bossy, domineering, feisty (*inf., chiefly US & Canad.*), forward, immodest, overbearing, presumptuous, pretentious, proud, self-assertive, spirited, wilful

meekness *n* **1 = submissiveness,** acquiescence, compliance, deference, docility, forbearance, gentleness, humbleness, humility, long-suffering, lowliness, mildness, modesty, patience, peacefulness, resignation, softness, submission, timidity **2 = spinelessness,** resignation, spiritlessness, tameness, weakness

meet[1] *vb* **1 = encounter,** bump into, chance on, come across, confront, contact, find, happen on, run across, run into **1 = gather,** assemble, collect, come together, congregate, convene, foregather, muster, rally **2 = converge,** abut, adjoin, come together, connect, cross, intersect, join, link up, touch, unite **7 = fulfil,** answer, carry out, come up to, comply with, cope with, discharge, equal, gratify, handle, match, measure up to, perform, satisfy **11 = experience,** bear, encounter, endure, face, go through, suffer, undergo
Antonyms *vb* ≠ **encounter:** avoid, elude, escape, miss ≠ **gather:** adjourn, disperse, scatter ≠ **converge:** diverge ≠ **fulfil:** fail, fall short, renege

meeting *n* **1 = encounter,** assignation, confron-

puter technology) denoting 2^{20} (1 048 576): *megabyte.* **3** large or great: *megalith.* **4** *Inf.* greatest: *megastar.* [from Gk *megas* huge, powerful]

megabit ('mɛgəˌbɪt) *n Computing.* **1** one million bits. **2** 2^{20} bits.

megabuck ('mɛgəˌbʌk) *n US & Canad. sl.* a million dollars.

megacephaly (ˌmɛgə'sɛfəlɪ) *or* **megalocephaly** *n* the condition of having an unusually large head or cranial capacity.
▸**megacephalic** (ˌmɛgəsɪ'fælɪk), ˌ**mega'cephalous,** ˌ**megaloce'phalic,** *or* ˌ**megalo'cephalous** *adj*

megacycle ('mɛgəˌsaɪkᵊl) *n* a former unit of frequency equal to one million cycles per second; megahertz.

megadeath ('mɛgəˌdɛθ) *n* the death of a million people, esp. in a nuclear war or attack.

megafauna ('mɛgəˌfɔːnə) *n* the component of the fauna of a region or period that comprises the larger terrestrial animals.

megaflop ('mɛgəˌflɒp) *n Computing.* a measure of processing speed, consisting of a million floating-point operations a second. [C20: from MEGA- + *flo(ating) p(oint)*]

megahertz ('mɛgəˌhɜːts) *n, pl* **megahertz.** one million hertz. Former name: **megacycle.**

megalith ('mɛgəlɪθ) *n* a stone of great size, esp. one forming part of a prehistoric monument.
▸ˌ**mega'lithic** *adj*

megalo- *or before a vowel* **megal-** *combining form.* indicating greatness or abnormal size: *megalopolis.* [from Gk *megas* great]

megalomania (ˌmɛgələʊ'meɪnɪə) *n* **1** a mental illness characterized by delusions of grandeur, power, wealth, etc. **2** *Inf.* a lust or craving for power.
▸ˌ**megalo'maniac** *adj, n* ▸**megalomaniacal** (ˌmɛgələʊmə'naɪəkᵊl) *adj*

megalopolis (ˌmɛgə'lɒpəlɪs) *n* an urban complex, usually comprising several large towns. [C20: MEGALO- + Gk *polis* city]
▸**megalopolitan** (ˌmɛgələ'pɒlɪtᵊn) *adj, n*

megalosaur ('mɛgələʊˌsɔː) *n* any very large Jurassic or Cretaceous bipedal carnivorous dinosaur. [C19: from NL *megalosaurus,* from MEGALO- + Gk *sauros* lizard]

megaphone ('mɛgəˌfəʊn) *n* a funnel-shaped instrument used to amplify the voice. See also **loud-hailer.**
▸**megaphonic** (ˌmɛgə'fɒnɪk) *adj*

megapode ('mɛgəˌpəʊd) *n* any of various ground-living gallinaceous birds of Australia, New Guinea, and adjacent islands. Their eggs incubate in mounds of sand, rotting vegetation, etc., by natural heat.

megathere ('mɛgəˌθɪə) *n* any of various gigantic extinct American sloths, common in late Cenozoic times. [C19: from NL *megathērium,* from MEGA- + *-there,* from Gk *thērion* wild beast]

megaton ('mɛgəˌtʌn) *n* **1** one million tons. **2** an explosive power, esp. of a nuclear weapon, equal to the power of one million tons of TNT.

Me generation *n* **the.** the generation, originally in the 1970s, characterized by self-absorption; in the 1980s, characterized by material greed.

Megger ('mɛgə) *n Trademark.* an instrument that generates a high voltage in order to test the resistance of insulation, etc.

megilp *or* **magilp** (mə'gɪlp) *n* an oil-painting medium of linseed oil mixed with mastic varnish or turpentine. [C18: from ?]

megohm ('mɛgˌəʊm) *n* one million ohms.

megrim ('miːgrɪm) *n Arch.* **1** a caprice. **2** a migraine. **3** (*pl*) *Rare.* a fit of depression. **4** (*pl*) a disease of horses and cattle; staggers. [C14: see MIGRAINE]

meibomian gland (maɪ'bəʊmɪən) *n* any of the small sebaceous glands in the eyelid, beneath the conjunctiva. [C19: after H. *Meibom* (1638–1700), G anatomist]

meiosis (maɪ'əʊsɪs) *n, pl* **meioses** (-ˌsiːz). **1** a type of cell division in which a nucleus divides into four daughter nuclei, each containing half the chromosome number of the parent nucleus. **2** *Rhetoric.* another word for **litotes.** [C16: via NL from Gk, from *meioun* to diminish, from *meiōn* less]
▸**meiotic** (maɪ'ɒtɪk) *adj* ▸**mei'otically** *adv*

Meistersinger ('maɪstəˌsɪŋə) *n, pl* **Meistersinger** *or* **Meistersingers.** a member of one of the German guilds organized to compose and perform poetry and music, esp. in the 15th and 16th centuries. [C19: from G *Meistersinger* master singer]

meitnerium (ˌmaɪt'nɛərɪəm) *n* a synthetic element produced in small quantities by high-energy ion bombardment. Symbol: Mt; atomic no.: 109. [C20: from Lise *Meitner* (1878–1968), Austrian physicist]

Mekka ('mɛkə) *n* a variant spelling of **Mecca.**

melaleuca (ˌmɛlə'luːkə) *n* any shrub or tree of the mostly Australian genus *Melaleuca,* found in sandy or swampy regions. [C19: NL from Gk *melas* black + *leukos* white, from its black trunk and white branches]

melamine ('mɛləˌmiːn) *n* **1** a colourless crystalline compound used in making synthetic resins. Formula: $C_3N_6H_6$. **2** a resin produced from melamine (**melamine resin**) or a material made from this resin. [C19: from G *Melamin,* from *Melam* distillate of ammonium thiocyanate, with *-am* representing *ammonia*]

melancholia (ˌmɛlən'kəʊlɪə) *n* a former name for **depression** (sense 3).
▸ˌ**melan'choliˌac** *adj, n*

melancholy **T** ('mɛlənkəlɪ) *n, pl* **melancholies.** **1** a tendency to gloominess or depression. **2** a sad thoughtful state of mind. **3** *Arch.* **3a** a gloomy character. **3b** one of the four bodily humours; black bile. ◆ *adj* **4** characterized by, causing, or expressing sadness, dejection, etc. [C14: via OF from LL *melancholia,* from Gk, from *melas* black + *kholē* bile]
▸'**melanˌcholic** *adj, n*

Melanesian (ˌmɛlə'niːʒən, -ʒɪən) *adj* **1** of or relating to Melanesia (a division of islands in the Pacific), its people, or their languages. ◆ *n* **2** a native or inhabitant of Melanesia: generally Negroid with frizzy hair and small stature. **3** a group or branch of languages spoken in Melanesia.

melange **T** *or* **mélange** (meɪ'lɑːnʒ) *n* a mixture; confusion. [C17: from F *mêler* to mix]

melanin ('mɛlənɪn) *n* any of a group of black or dark brown pigments present in the hair, skin, and eyes of man and animals: produced in excess in certain skin diseases and in melanomas.

melanism ('mɛləˌnɪzəm) *n* **1** the condition in man and animals of having dark-coloured or black skin, feathers, etc. **2** another name for **melanosis.**
▸ˌ**mela'nistic** *adj*

melano- *or before a vowel* **melan-** *combining form.* black or dark: *melanin; melanism; melanoma.* [from Gk *melas* black]

melanoma (ˌmɛlə'nəʊmə) *n, pl* **melanomas** *or* **melanomata** (-mətə). *Pathol.* a malignant tumour composed of melanin-containing cells, occurring esp. in the skin, often as a result of excessive exposure to sunlight.

melanosis (ˌmɛlə'nəʊsɪs) *or* **melanism** ('mɛləˌnɪzəm) *n Pathol.* a skin condition characterized by excessive deposits of melanin.
▸**melanotic** (ˌmɛlə'nɒtɪk) *adj*

Melba ('mɛlbə) *n* **do a Melba.** *Austral. sl.* to make repeated farewell appearances. [C20: after Dame Nellie *Melba* (1861–1931), Austral. operatic soprano]

Melba toast *n* very thin crisp toast. [C20: after Dame Nellie *Melba*]

meld[1] (mɛld) *vb* to blend or become blended; combine. [C20: blend of MELT + WELD[1]]

meld[2] (mɛld) *vb* **1** (in some card games) to declare or lay down (cards), which then score points. ◆ *n* **2** the act of melding. **3** a set of cards for melding. [C19: from G *melden* to announce]

melee **T** *or* **mêlée** ('mɛleɪ) *n* a noisy riotous fight or brawl. [C17: from F *mêlée,* from *mêler* to mix]

meliorate ('miːlɪəˌreɪt) *vb* **meliorates, meliorating, meliorated.** a variant of **ameliorate.**
▸ˌ**melio'ration** *n* ▸**meliorative** ('miːlɪərətɪv) *adj, n*

melisma (mɪ'lɪzmə) *n, pl* **melismata** (-mətə) *or* **melismas.** *Music.* an expressive vocal phrase or passage consisting of several notes sung to one syllable. [C19: from Gk: melody]

melliferous (mɪ'lɪfərəs) *or* **mellific** (mɪ'lɪfɪk) *adj* forming or producing honey. [C17: from L *mellifer,* from *mel* honey + *ferre* to bear]

mellifluous **T** (mɪ'lɪfluəs) *or* **mellifluent** *adj* (of sounds or utterances) smooth or honeyed; sweet. [C15: from LL *mellifluus,* from L *mel* honey + *fluere* to flow]
▸**mel'lifluously** *adv* ▸**mel'lifluousness** *or* **mel'lifluence** *n*

mellow **T** ('mɛləʊ) *adj* **1** (esp. of fruits) full-flavoured; sweet; ripe. **2** (esp. of wines) well-matured. **3** (esp. of colours or sounds) soft or rich. **4** kind-hearted, esp. through maturity or old age. **5** genial, as through the effects of alcohol. **6** (of soil) soft and loamy. ◆ *vb* **7** to make or become mellow. **8** (foll. by *out*) to become calm and relaxed or (esp. of a drug) to have a calming and relaxing effect on (someone). [C15: ?from OE *meru* soft (as through ripeness)]
▸'**mellowness** *n*

melodeon *or* **melodion** (mɪ'ləʊdɪən) *n Music.* **1** a type of small accordion. **2** a type of keyboard instrument similar to the harmonium. [C19: from G, from *Melodie* melody]

melodic (mɪ'lɒdɪk) *adj* **1** of or relating to melody. **2** of or relating to a part in a piece of music. **3** melodious.
▸**me'lodically** *adv*

THESAURUS

tation, engagement, introduction, rendezvous, tryst **2** = **conference**, assembly, audience, company, conclave, congregation, congress, convention, convocation, gathering, get-together (*inf.*), meet, powwow, rally, reunion, session **3** = **convergence**, concourse, confluence, conjunction, crossing, intersection, junction, union

melancholy *n* **1, 2** = **sadness**, blues, dejection, depression, despondency, gloom, gloominess, low spirits, misery, pensiveness, sorrow, the hump (*Brit. inf.*), unhappiness, woe ◆ *adj* **4** = **sad**, blue, dejected, depressed, despondent, disconsolate, dismal, dispirited, doleful, down, downcast, downhearted, gloomy, glum, heavy-hearted, joyless, low, low-spirited, lugubrious, melancholic, miserable, moody, mournful, pensive, sombre, sorrowful, unhappy, woebegone, woeful
Antonyms *n* ≠ **sadness:** delight, gladness, happiness, joy, pleasure ◆ *adj* ≠ **sad:** blithe, bright, cheerful, gay, glad, happy, jolly, joyful, joyous, light-hearted, lively, merry, sunny

melange *n* = **mixture**, assortment, confusion, farrago, gallimaufry, hodge-podge, hotchpotch, jumble, medley, miscellany, mishmash, mix, mixed bag (*inf.*), pastiche, potpourri, salmagundi

melee *n* = **fight**, affray (*Law*), battle royal, brawl, broil, donnybrook, fracas, fray, free-for-all (*inf.*), ruckus (*inf.*), ruction (*inf.*), rumpus, scrimmage, scuffle, set-to (*inf.*), shindig (*inf.*), shindy (*inf.*), skirmish, stramash (*Scot.*), tussle

mellifluous *adj* = **sweet**, dulcet, euphonious, honeyed, mellow, silvery, smooth, soft, soothing, sweet-sounding

mellow *adj* **1, 2** = **ripe**, delicate, full-flavoured, juicy, mature, perfect, rich, soft, sweet, well-matured **3** = **tuneful**, dulcet, euphonic, full, mellifluous, melodious, rich, rounded, smooth, sweet, well-tuned **5** = **relaxed**, cheerful, cordial, elevated, expansive, genial, half-tipsy, happy,

melodic minor scale *n Music.* a minor scale modified from the natural by the sharpening of the sixth and seventh when taken in ascending order and the restoration of their original pitches when taken in descending order.

melodious ❶ (mɪˈləudɪəs) *adj* **1** having a tune that is pleasant to the ear. **2** of or relating to melody; melodic.
▸**meˈlodiously** *adv* ▸**meˈlodiousness** *n*

melodist (ˈmɛlədɪst) *n* **1** a composer of melodies. **2** a singer.

melodize *or* **melodise** (ˈmɛləˌdaɪz) *vb* **melodizes, melodizing, melodized** *or* **melodises, melodising, melodised. 1** *(tr)* to provide with a melody. **2** *(tr)* to make melodious. **3** *(intr)* to sing or play melodies.
▸ˈ**meloˌdizer** *or* ˈ**meloˌdiser** *n*

melodrama ❶ (ˈmɛləˌdrɑːmə) *n* **1** a play, film, etc., characterized by extravagant action and emotion. **2** (formerly) a romantic drama characterized by sensational incident, music, and song. **3** overdramatic emotion or behaviour. [C19: from F *mélodrame,* from Gk *melos* song + *drame* DRAMA]
▸**melodramatist** (ˌmɛləˈdræmətɪst) *n* ▸**melodramatic** (ˌmɛlədrəˈmætɪk) *adj* ▸ˌ**melodraˈmatics** *pl n* ▸ˌ**melodraˈmatically** *adv*

melody ❶ (ˈmɛlədɪ) *n, pl* **melodies. 1** *Music.* **1a** a succession of notes forming a distinctive sequence; tune. **1b** the horizontally represented aspect of the structure of a piece of music. Cf. **harmony** (sense 4b). **2** sounds that are pleasant because of tone or arrangement, esp. words of poetry. [C13: from OF, from LL *melōdia,* from Gk *melōidia,* from *melos* song + *aoidein* to sing]

melon (ˈmɛlən) *n* **1** any of several varieties of trailing plants (see **muskmelon, watermelon**), cultivated for their edible fruit. **2** the fruit of any of these plants, which has a hard rind and juicy flesh. [C14: via OF from LL *mēlo,* form of *mēlopepō,* from Gk, from *mēlon* apple + *pepōn* gourd]

Melpomene (melˈpɒmɪnɪ) *n Greek myth.* The Muse of tragedy.

melt ❶ (mɛlt) *vb* **melts, melting, melted; melted** *or* **molten. 1** to liquefy (a solid) or (of a solid) to become liquefied, as a result of the action of heat. **2** to become or make liquid; dissolve. **3** (often foll. by *away*) to disappear; fade. **4** (foll. by *down*) to melt (metal scrap) for reuse. **5** (often foll. by *into*) to blend or cause to blend gradually. **6** to make or become emotional or sentimental; soften. ◆ *n* **7** the act or process of melting. **8** something melted or an amount melted. [OE *meltan* to digest]
▸ˈ**meltable** *adj* ▸ˈ**melter** *n* ▸ˈ**meltingly** *adv*

meltdown (ˈmɛltˌdaun) *n* **1** (in a nuclear reactor) the melting of the fuel rods as a result of a defect in the cooling system, with the possible escape of radiation. **2** *Inf.* a sudden disastrous failure with potential for widespread harm, as a stock-exchange crash. **3** *Inf.* the process or state of irreversible breakdown or decline: *the community is slowly going into meltdown.*

melting point *n* the temperature at which a solid turns into a liquid.

melting pot *n* **1** a pot in which metals or other substances are melted, esp. in order to mix them. **2** an area in which many races, ideas, etc., are mixed.

melton (ˈmɛltən) *n* a heavy smooth woollen fabric with a short nap. Also called: **melton cloth.** [C19: from *Melton Mowbray,* Leicestershire, a former centre for making this]

meltwater (ˈmɛltˌwɔːtə) *n* melted snow or ice.

mem. *abbrev. for:* **1** member. **2** memoir. **3** memorandum. **4** memorial.

member ❶ (ˈmɛmbə) *n* **1** a person who belongs to a club, political party, etc. **2** any individual plant or animal in a taxonomic group. **3** any part of an animal body, such as a limb. **4** any part of a plant, such as a petal, root, etc. **5** *Maths, logic.* any individual object belonging to a set or logical class. **6** a component part of a building or construction. [C13: from L *membrum* limb, part]
▸ˈ**memberless** *adj*

Member (ˈmɛmbə) *n (sometimes not cap.)* **1** short for **Member of Parliament. 2** short for **Member of Congress. 3** a member of some other legislative body.

Member of Congress *n* a member of the US Congress, esp. of the House of Representatives.

Member of Parliament *n* a member of the House of Commons or similar legislative body, as in many Commonwealth countries.

membership ❶ (ˈmɛmbəʃɪp) *n* **1** the members of an organization collectively. **2** the state of being a member.

membrane (ˈmɛmbreɪn) *n* **1** any thin pliable sheet of material. **2** a pliable sheetlike usually fibrous tissue that covers, lines, or connects plant and animal organs or cells. [C16: from L *membrāna* skin covering a part of the body, from *membrum* MEMBER]
▸**membranous** (ˈmɛmbrənəs) *or* **membraneous** (mɛmˈbreɪnɪəs) *adj*

memento ❶ (mɪˈmɛntəu) *n, pl* **mementos** *or* **mementoes.** something that reminds one of past events; a souvenir. [C15: from L, imperative of *meminisse* to remember]

memento mori (ˈmɔːriː) *n, pl* **memento mori.** an object, such as a skull, intended to remind people of death. [C16: L: remember you must die]

memo (ˈmɛməu, ˈmiːməu) *n, pl* **memos.** short for **memorandum.**

memoir ❶ (ˈmɛmwɑː) *n* **1** a biography or historical account, esp. one based on personal knowledge. **2** an essay, as on a specialized topic. [C16: from F, from L *memoria* MEMORY]
▸ˈ**memoirist** *n*

memoirs ❶ (ˈmɛmwɑːz) *pl n* **1** a collection of reminiscences about a period, series of events, etc., written from personal experience or special sources. **2** an autobiographical record. **3** a record, as of transactions of a society, etc.

memorabilia (ˌmɛmərəˈbɪlɪə) *pl n, sing* **memorabile** (-ˈræbɪlɪ). **1** memorable events or things. **2** objects connected with famous people or events. [C17: from L, from *memorābilis* MEMORABLE]

memorable ❶ (ˈmɛmərəbᵊl) *adj* worth remembering or easily remembered. [C15: from L *memorābilis,* from *memorāre* to recall, from *memor* mindful]
▸ˌ**memoraˈbility** *n* ▸ˈ**memorably** *adv*

memorandum ❶ (ˌmɛməˈrændəm) *n, pl* **memorandums** *or* **memoranda** (-də). **1** a written statement, record, or communication. **2** a note of things to be remembered. **3** an informal diplomatic communication. **4** *Law.* a short written summary of the terms of a transaction. ◆ Often (esp. for senses 1, 2) shortened to **memo.** [C15: from L: (something) to be remembered]

memorial ❶ (mɪˈmɔːrɪəl) *adj* **1** serving to preserve the memory of the dead or a past event. **2** of or involving memory. ◆ *n* **3** something serving as a remembrance. **4** a written statement of facts submitted to a government, authority, etc., in conjunction with a petition. **5** an informal diplomatic paper. [C14: from LL *memoriāle* a reminder, neuter of *memoriālis*]
▸**meˈmorially** *adv*

memorialize *or* **memorialise** (mɪˈmɔːrɪəˌlaɪz) *vb* **memorializes, memorializing, memorialized** *or* **memorialises, memorialising, memorialised.** *(tr)* **1** to honour or commemorate. **2** to present or address a memorial to.

memorize ❶ *or* **memorise** (ˈmɛməˌraɪz) *vb* **memorizes, memorizing, memorized** *or* **memorises, memorising, memorised.** *(tr)* to commit to memory; learn so as to remember.

memory ❶ (ˈmɛmərɪ) *n, pl* **memories. 1a** the ability of the mind to store and recall past sensations, thoughts, knowledge, etc.: *he can do it from memory.* **1b** the part of the brain that appears to have this function. **2** the sum of everything retained by the mind. **3** a particular recollection of an event, person, etc. **4** the time over which recollection extends: *within his memory.* **5** commemoration or remembrance: *in memory of our leader.* **6** the state of being remembered, as after death. **7** a part of a computer in which information is stored for immediate use by the central processing unit. Cf. **RAM**[1]. [C14: from OF *memorie,* from L *memoria,* from *memor* mindful]

memsahib (ˈmɛmˌsɑːɪb, -hɪb) *n* (formerly, in India) a term of respect used for a European married woman. [C19: from MA'AM + SAHIB]

men (mɛn) *n* the plural of **man.**

menace ❶ (ˈmɛnɪs) *vb* **menaces, menacing, menaced. 1** to threaten with

THESAURUS

jolly, jovial, merry ◆ *vb* **7** = **mature**, develop, improve, perfect, ripen, season, soften, sweeten
Antonyms *adj* ≠ **ripe:** green, immature, raw, sour, unripe

melodious *adj* **1, 2** = **musical**, concordant, dulcet, euphonic, euphonious, harmonious, melodic, silvery, sweet-sounding, sweet-toned, tuneful
Antonyms *adj* cacophonous, discordant, grating, harsh, unharmonious, unmelodic, unmelodious, unmusical, untuneful

melodramatic *adj* **1, 3** = **theatrical**, actorly, actressy, blood-and-thunder, extravagant, hammy *(inf.)*, histrionic, overdramatic, overemotional, sensational, stagy

melody *n* **1** = **tune**, air, descant, music, refrain, song, strain, theme **2** = **tunefulness**, euphony, harmony, melodiousness, music, musicality

melt *vb* **1, 2** = **dissolve**, deliquesce, diffuse, flux, fuse, liquefy, soften, thaw **3** *often foll. by* **away** = **disappear**, disperse, dissolve, evanesce, evaporate, fade, vanish **6** = **soften**, disarm, mollify, relax, touch

member *n* **1** = **representative**, associate, fellow **3** = **limb**, appendage, arm, component, constituent, element, extremity, leg, organ, part, portion

membership *n* **1** = **members**, associates, body, fellows **2** = **participation**, belonging, enrolment, fellowship

memento *n* = **souvenir**, keepsake, memorial, relic, remembrance, reminder, token, trophy

memoir *n* **1, 2** = **account**, biography, essay, journal, life, monograph, narrative, record, register

memoirs *pl n* **1, 2** = **autobiography**, diary, experiences, journals, life, life story, memories, recollections, reminiscences

memorable *adj* = **noteworthy**, catchy, celebrated, distinguished, extraordinary, famous, historic, illustrious, important, impressive, momentous, notable, remarkable, signal, significant, striking, unforgettable
Antonyms *adj* commonplace, forgettable, insignificant, ordinary, trivial, undistinguished, unimportant, unimpressive, unmemorable

memorandum *n* **1, 2** = **note**, communication, jotting, memo, message, minute, reminder

memorial *adj* **1** = **commemorative**, monumental ◆ *n* **3** = **monument**, cairn, memento, plaque, record, remembrance, souvenir **4** = **petition**, address, memorandum, statement

memorize *vb* = **remember**, commit to memory, con *(arch.)*, get by heart, learn, learn by heart, learn by rote

memory *n* **1** = **recall**, recollection, remembrance, reminiscence, retention **5** = **commemoration**, honour, remembrance **6** = **reputation**, celebrity, fame, glory, name, renown, repute

menace *vb* **1** = **threaten**, alarm, bode ill, browbeat, bully, frighten, impend, intimidate, loom, lour *or* lower, terrorize, utter threats to ◆ *n* **2** *Literary* = **threat**, commination, intimidation, scare, warning **3** = **danger**, hazard, jeopardy, peril **4** *Informal* = **nuisance**, annoyance, pest, plague, troublemaker

menacing *adj* **1** = **threatening**, alarming, baleful, dangerous, forbidding, frightening, intimi-

violence, danger, etc. ◆ *n* 2 *Literary.* a threat. 3 something menacing; a source of danger. 4 *Inf.* a nuisance. [C13: ult. rel. to L *minax* threatening, from *minārī* to threaten]
▸ **'menacer** *n* ▸ **'menacing** *adj* ▸ **'menacingly** *adv*

ménage (meɪ'nɑːʒ) *n* the persons of a household. [C17: from F, from Vulgar L (unattested) *mansiōnāticum* household]

ménage à trois *French.* (menaʒ a trwa) *n, pl* ***ménages à trois*** (menaʒ a trwa). a sexual arrangement involving a married couple and the lover of one of them. [lit.: household of three]

menagerie (mɪ'nædʒərɪ) *n* 1 a collection of wild animals kept for exhibition. 2 the place where such animals are housed. [C18: from F: household management, which formerly included care of domestic animals]

mend ❶ (mɛnd) *vb* 1 (*tr*) to repair (something broken or unserviceable). 2 to improve or undergo improvement; reform (often in **mend one's ways**). 3 (*intr*) to heal or recover. 4 (*intr*) (of conditions) to improve; become better. ◆ *n* 5 the act of repairing. 6 a mended area, esp. on a garment. 7 **on the mend.** becoming better, esp. in health. [C12: from AMEND]
▸ **'mendable** *adj* ▸ **'mender** *n*

mendacity ❶ (mɛn'dæsɪtɪ) *n, pl* **mendacities.** 1 the tendency to be untruthful. 2 a falsehood. [C17: from LL *mendācitās*, from L *mendāx* untruthful]
▸ **mendacious** (mɛn'deɪʃəs) *adj* ▸ **men'daciously** *adv*

mendelevium (ˌmɛndɪ'liːvɪəm) *n* a transuranic element artificially produced by bombardment of einsteinium. Symbol: Md; atomic no.: 101; half-life of most stable isotope, ^{258}Md: 60 days (approx.). [C20: after D. I. *Mendeleyev* (1843–1907), Russian chemist who devised the first form of periodic table]

Mendel's laws *pl n* the principles of heredity proposed by Gregor Mendel (1822–84), Austrian monk and botanist. The **Law of Segregation** states that each hereditary character is determined by a pair of units in the reproductive cells: the pairs separate during meiosis so that each gamete carries only one unit of each pair. The **Law of Independent Assortment** states that the separation of the units of each pair is not influenced by that of any other pair.

mendicant ('mɛndɪkənt) *adj* 1 begging. 2 (of a member of a religious order) dependent on alms for sustenance. ◆ *n* 3 a mendicant friar. 4 a less common word for **beggar.** [C16: from L *mendīcāre*, from *mendīcus* beggar, from *mendus* flaw]
▸ **'mendicancy** *or* **mendicity** (mɛn'dɪsɪtɪ) *n*

meneer (mə'nɪə) *n* a S. African title of address equivalent to *sir* when used alone or *Mr* when placed before a name. [Afrik.]

menfolk ('mɛnˌfəʊk) *pl n* men collectively, esp. the men of a particular family.

menhaden (mɛn'heɪdᵊn) *n, pl* **menhaden.** a marine North American fish: source of fishmeal, fertilizer, and oil. [C18: from Algonquian; prob. rel. to another Amerind word, *munnawhatteaúg* fertilizer]

menhir ('mɛnhɪə) *n* a single standing stone, dating from prehistoric times. [C19: from Breton *men* stone + *hir* long]

menial ❶ ('miːnɪəl) *adj* 1 consisting of or occupied with work requiring little skill, esp. domestic duties. 2 of, involving, or befitting servants. 3 servile. ◆ *n* 4 a domestic servant. 5 a servile person. [C14: from Anglo-Norman *meignial*, from OF *meinie* household]

meninges (mɪ'nɪndʒiːz) *pl n, sing* **meninx** ('miːnɪŋks). the three membranes (**dura mater, arachnoid, pia mater**) that envelop the brain and spinal cord. [C17: from Gk, pl of *meninx* membrane]
▸ **meningeal** (mɪ'nɪndʒɪəl) *adj*

meningitis (ˌmɛnɪn'dʒaɪtɪs) *n* inflammation of the membranes that surround the brain or spinal cord, caused by infection.
▸ **meningitic** (ˌmɛnɪn'dʒɪtɪk) *adj*

meningococcus (meˌnɪŋgəʊ'kɒkəs) *n, pl* **meningococci** (-'kɒksaɪ). the bacterium that causes cerebrospinal meningitis.
▸ **meˌningo'coccal** *adj*

meniscus (mɪ'nɪskəs) *n, pl* **menisci** (-'nɪsaɪ) *or* **meniscuses.** 1 the curved upper surface of a liquid standing in a tube, produced by the surface tension. 2 a crescent-shaped lens; a concavo-convex or convexo-concave lens. [C17: from NL, from Gk *mēniskos* crescent, dim. of *mēnē* moon]
▸ **me'niscoid** *adj*

Mennonite ('mɛnəˌnaɪt) *n* a member of a Protestant sect that rejects infant baptism and Church organization, and in most cases refuses military service, public office, and the taking of oaths. [C16: from G *Mennonit*, after *Menno* Simons (1496–1561), Frisian religious leader]
▸ **'Mennonitism** *n*

meno ('mɛnəʊ) *adv Music.* to be played less quickly, less softly, etc. [from It., from L *minus* less]

meno- *combining form.* menstruation. [from Gk *mēn* month]

menopause ('mɛnəʊˌpɔːz) *n* the period during which a woman's menstrual cycle ceases, normally at an age of 45 to 50. [C19: from F, from Gk *mēn* month + *pausis* halt]
▸ **ˌmeno'pausal** *adj*

menorah (mɪ'nɔːrə) *n Judaism.* 1 a seven-branched candelabrum used in the Temple and now an emblem of Judaism and the badge of the state of Israel. 2 a similar lamp lit during the Chanukah festival. [from Heb.: candlestick]

menorrhagia (ˌmɛnɔː'reɪdʒɪə) *n* excessive bleeding during menstruation.

menorrhoea (ˌmɛnə'rɪə) *n* normal bleeding in menstruation.

menses ('mɛnsiːz) *n* (*functioning as sing or pl*) 1 another name for **menstruation.** 2 the period of time during which one menstruation occurs. 3 the matter discharged during menstruation. [C16: from L, pl of *mensis* month]

Menshevik ('mɛnʃɪvɪk) *or* **Menshevist** *n* a member of the moderate wing of the Russian Social Democratic Party. Cf. **Bolshevik.** [C20: from Russian, lit.: minority, from *menshe* less, from *malo* few]
▸ **'Mensheˌvism** *n*

menstruate ('mɛnstrʊˌeɪt) *vb* **menstruates, menstruating, menstruated.** (*intr*) to undergo menstruation. [C17: from L *menstruāre*, from *mensis* month]

menstruation ❶ (ˌmɛnstrʊ'eɪʃən) *n* the approximately monthly discharge of blood and cellular debris from the uterus by nonpregnant women from puberty to the menopause.
▸ **'menstrual** *or* **'menstruous** *adj*

menstruum ('mɛnstrʊəm) *n, pl* **menstruums** *or* **menstrua** (-strʊə). a solvent, esp. one used in the preparation of a drug. [C17 (meaning: solvent), C14 (menstrual discharge): from Med. L, from L *mēnstruus* monthly, from *mēnsis* month; from alchemical comparison between a base metal being transmuted into gold and the supposed action of the menses]

mensurable ('mɛnsjʊrəbᵊl, -ʃə-) *adj* a less common word for **measurable.** [C17: from LL *mēnsūrābilis*, from *mēnsūra* MEASURE]
▸ **ˌmensura'bility** *n*

mensural ('mɛnʃərəl) *adj* 1 of or involving measure. 2 *Music.* of or relating to music in which notes have fixed values. [C17: from LL *mēnsūrālis*, from *mēnsūra* MEASURE]

mensuration (ˌmɛnʃə'reɪʃən) *n* 1 the study of the measurement of geometric magnitudes such as length. 2 the act or process of measuring.
▸ **mensurative** ('mɛnʃərətɪv) *adj*

-ment *suffix forming nouns, esp. from verbs.* 1 indicating state, condition, or quality: *enjoyment.* 2 indicating the result or product of an action: *embankment.* 3 indicating process or action: *management.* [from F, from L *-mentum*]

mental ❶ ('mɛntᵊl) *adj* 1 of or involving the mind. 2 occurring only in the mind: *mental arithmetic.* 3 affected by mental illness: *a mental patient.* 4 concerned with mental illness: *a mental hospital.* 5 *Sl.* insane. [C15: from LL *mentālis*, from L *mēns* mind]
▸ **'mentally** *adv*

mental deficiency *n Psychiatry.* a less common term for **mental retardation.**

mental handicap *n* any intellectual disability resulting from injury to the brain or from abnormal neurological development.
▸ **mentally handicapped** *adj*

mental healing *n* the healing of a disorder by mental concentration or suggestion.

mental illness *n* any of various disorders in which a person's thoughts, emotions, or behaviour are so abnormal as to cause suffering to himself, herself, or other people.

mentalism ('mɛntᵊˌlɪzəm) *n Philosophy.* the doctrine that mind is the fundamental reality and that objects of knowledge exist only as aspects of the subject's consciousness.
▸ **ˌmental'istic** *adj*

mentality ❶ (mɛn'tælɪtɪ) *n, pl* **mentalities.** 1 the state or quality of men-

THESAURUS

dating, intimidatory, looming, louring *or* lowering, minacious, minatory, ominous
Antonyms *adj* auspicious, encouraging, favourable, promising

mend *vb* 1 = **repair**, cure, darn, fix, heal, patch, rectify, refit, reform, remedy, renew, renovate, restore, retouch 2 = **improve**, ameliorate, amend, better, correct, emend, rectify, reform, revise 3 = **heal**, convalesce, get better, recover, recuperate ◆ *n* 6 = **repair**, darn, patch, stitch 7 **on the mend** = **convalescent**, convalescing, getting better, improving, recovering, recuperating

mendacious *adj* 1 = **lying**, deceitful, deceptive, dishonest, duplicitous, fallacious, false, fraudulent, insincere, perfidious, perjured, untrue, untruthful
Antonyms *adj* genuine, honest, true, truthful

mendacity *n* 1, 2 = **lying**, deceit, deceitfulness, dishonesty, distortion, duplicity, falsehood, falsification, fraudulence, insincerity, inveracity, lie, mendaciousness, misrepresentation, perfidy, perjury, untruth, untruthfulness

menial *adj* 1 = **unskilled**, boring, dull, humdrum, low-status, routine 3 = **humble**, abject, base, degrading, demeaning, fawning, grovelling, ignoble, ignominious, low, lowly, mean, obsequious, servile, slavish, sorry, subservient, sycophantic, vile ◆ *n* 4 = **servant**, attendant, dogsbody (*inf.*), domestic, drudge, flunky, labourer, lackey, serf, skivvy (*chiefly Brit.*), slave, underling, varlet (*arch.*), vassal
Antonyms *adj* ≠ **humble**: aristocratic, autocratic, bossy, dignified, domineering, elevated, haughty, high, noble, overbearing, proud ◆ *n* ≠ **servant**: boss, chief, commander, lord, master, superior

menstruation *n* = **period**, catamenia (*Physiology*), courses (*Physiology*), the curse (*inf.*), flow (*inf.*), menses, menstrual cycle, monthly (*inf.*)

mental *adj* 1 = **intellectual**, cerebral 5 *Slang* = **insane**, deranged, disturbed, lunatic, mad, mentally ill, not right in the head, psychiatric, psychotic, round the bend (*Brit. sl.*), unbalanced, unstable

mentality *n* 2 = **attitude**, cast of mind, character, disposition, frame of mind, make-up, outlook, personality, psychology, turn of mind, way of thinking

mentally *adv* 1 = **in the mind**, in one's head,

tal or intellectual ability. **2** a way of thinking; mental inclination or character.
mental lexicon *n* the store of words in a person's mind.
mental reservation *n* a tacit withholding of full assent or an unexpressed qualification made when taking an oath, making a statement, etc.
mental retardation *n Psychiatry.* the condition of having a low intelligence quotient (below 70).
menthol ('mɛnθɒl) *n* an organic compound found in peppermint oil and used as an antiseptic, in inhalants, and as an analgesic. Formula: $C_{10}H_{19}OH$. [C19: from G, from L *mentha* MINT[1]]
mentholated ('mɛnθəˌleɪtɪd) *adj* containing, treated with, or impregnated with menthol.
mention ❶ ('mɛnʃən) *vb (tr)* **1** to refer to or speak about briefly or incidentally. **2** to acknowledge or honour. **3 not to mention (something).** to say nothing of (something too obvious to mention). ◆ *n* **4** a recognition or acknowledgment. **5** a slight reference or allusion. **6** the act of mentioning. [C14: via OF from L *mentiō* a calling to mind, from *mēns* mind]
▸'**mentionable** *adj*
mentor ❶ ('mɛntɔː) *n* a wise or trusted adviser or guide. [C18: from *Mentor,* adviser of Telemachus in the Odyssey]
mentoring ('mɛntərɪŋ) *n* (in business) the practice of assigning a junior member of staff to the care of a more experienced person who assists him in his career.
menu ❶ ('mɛnjuː) *n* **1** a list of dishes served at a meal or that can be ordered in a restaurant. **2** a list of options displayed on a visual display unit from which the operator selects an action to be carried out. [C19: from F *menu* small, detailed (list), from L *minūtus* MINUTE[2]]
menuetto (mɛnjuˈɛtəʊ) *n, pl* **menuettos.** *Music.* another term for **minuet.** [from It.]
meow, miaou, miaow (mɪˈaʊ, mjaʊ), *or* **miaul** (mɪˈaʊl, mjaʊl) *vb* **1** *(intr)* (of a cat) to make a characteristic crying sound. ◆ *interj* **2** an imitation of this sound.
MEP (in Britain) *abbrev. for* Member of the European Parliament.
mepacrine ('mɛpəkrɪn) *n Brit.* a drug formerly widely used to treat malaria. [C20: from ME(THYL) + PA(LUDISM + A)CR(ID)INE]
meperidine (məˈpɛrɪˌdiːn, -dɪn) *n* the US name for **pethidine.** [C20: from METHYL + PIPERIDINE]
Mephistopheles (ˌmɛfɪˈstɒfɪˌliːz) *or* **Mephisto** (məˈfɪstəʊ) *n* a devil in medieval mythology and the one to whom Faust sold his soul in German legend.
▸**Mephistophelean** *or* **Mephistophelian** (ˌmɛfɪstəˈfiːlɪən) *adj*
mephitic (mɪˈfɪtɪk) *or* **mephitical** *adj* **1** poisonous; foul. **2** foul-smelling; putrid. [C17: from LL *mephīticus* pestilential]
meprobamate (məˈprəʊbəˌmeɪt, ˌmɛprəʊˈbæmeɪt) *n* a white bitter powder used as a tranquillizer. [C20: from ME(THYL) + PRO(PYL + *car)bamate* a salt or ester of an amide of carbonic acid]
-mer *suffix forming nouns. Chem.* denoting a substance of a particular class: *monomer; polymer.* [from Gk *meros* part]
mercantile ❶ ('mɜːkənˌtaɪl) *adj* **1** of, relating to, or characteristic of trade or traders; commercial. **2** of or relating to mercantilism. [C17: from F, from It., from *mercante* MERCHANT]
mercantilism ('mɜːkəntɪˌlɪzəm) *n Econ.* a theory prevalent in Europe during the 17th and 18th centuries asserting that the wealth of a nation depends on possession of precious metals and therefore that a government must maximize foreign trade surplus and foster national commercial interests, a merchant marine, the establishment of colonies, etc.
▸'**mercantilist** *n, adj*
mercaptan (mɜːˈkæptæn) *n* another name (not in technical use) for **thiol.** [C19: from G, from Med. L *mercurium captans,* lit.: seizing quicksilver]
Mercator projection *n* a conformal map projection on which parallels and meridians form a rectangular grid, scale being exaggerated with increasing distance from the equator. Also called: **Mercator's projection.** [C17: after G. *Mercator,* Latinized name of G. Kremer (1512–94), Flemish cartographer]
mercenary ❶ ('mɜːsɪnərɪ, -sɪnrɪ) *adj* **1** influenced by greed or desire for gain. **2** of or relating to a mercenary or mercenaries. ◆ *n, pl* **mercenaries. 3** a man hired to fight for a foreign army, etc. **4** *Rare.* any person who works solely for pay. [C16: from L *mercēnārius,* from *mercēs* wages]
mercer ('mɜːsə) *n Brit.* a dealer in textile fabrics and fine cloth. [C13: from OF *mercier* dealer, from Vulgar L, from L *merx* wares]
▸'**mercery** *n*
mercerize *or* **mercerise** ('mɜːsəˌraɪz) *vb* **mercerizes, mercerizing, mercerized** *or* **mercerises, mercerising, mercerised.** *(tr)* to treat (cotton yarn) with an alkali to increase its strength and reception to dye and impart a lustrous silky appearance. [C19: after John *Mercer* (1791–1866), E maker of textiles]
merchandise ❶ *n* ('mɜːtʃənˌdaɪs, -ˌdaɪz). **1** commercial goods; commodities. ◆ *vb* ('mɜːtʃənˌdaɪz), **merchandises, merchandising, merchandised. 2** to engage in the commercial purchase and sale of (goods or services); trade. [C13: from OF; see MERCHANT]
merchandising ('mɜːtʃənˌdaɪzɪŋ) *n* **1** the selection and display of goods in a retail outlet. **2** commercial goods, esp. ones issued to exploit the popularity of a pop group, sporting event, etc.
merchant ❶ ('mɜːtʃənt) *n* **1** a person engaged in the purchase and sale of commodities for profit; trader. **2** *Chiefly Scot., US, & Canad.* a person engaged in retail trade. **3** (esp. in historical contexts) any trader. **4** *Derog.* a person dealing or involved in something undesirable: *a gossip merchant.* **5** *(modifier)* **5a** of the merchant navy: *a merchant sailor.* **5b** of or concerned with trade: *a merchant ship.* ◆ *vb* **6** *(tr)* to conduct trade in; deal in. [C13: from OF, prob. from Vulgar L, from L *mercārī* to trade, from *merx* wares]
merchantable ❶ ('mɜːtʃəntəbᵊl) *adj* suitable for trading.
merchant bank *n Brit.* a financial institution engaged primarily in accepting foreign bills, advising companies on flotations and takeovers, underwriting new issues, hire-purchase finance, making long-term loans to companies, and managing investment portfolios, funds, and trusts.
▸**merchant banker** *n*
merchantman ('mɜːtʃəntmən) *n, pl* **merchantmen.** a merchant ship.
merchant navy *or* **marine** *n* the ships or crew engaged in a nation's commercial shipping.
Mercian ('mɜːʃɪən) *adj* **1** of or relating to Mercia, an Anglo-Saxon kingdom in England, or its dialect. ◆ *n* **2** the dialect of Old and Middle English spoken in Mercia. **3** a native or inhabitant of Mercia.
merciful ❶ ('mɜːsɪfʊl) *adj* showing or giving mercy; compassionate.
▸'**mercifully** *adv* ▸'**mercifulness** *n*
merciless ❶ ('mɜːsɪlɪs) *adj* without mercy; pitiless, cruel, or heartless.
▸'**mercilessly** *adv* ▸'**mercilessness** *n*
mercurial ❶ (mɜːˈkjʊərɪəl) *adj* **1** of, like, containing, or relating to mercury. **2** volatile; lively: *a mercurial temperament.* **3** *(sometimes cap.)* of, like, or relating to the god or the planet Mercury. ◆ *n* **4** *Med.* any salt of mercury for use as a medicine. [C14: from L *mercuriālis*]
▸**merˌcuriˈality** *n* ▸**merˈcurially** *adv*
mercuric (mɜːˈkjʊərɪk) *adj* of or containing mercury in the divalent state; denoting a mercury(II) compound.
mercuric chloride *n* a white poisonous crystalline substance used as a pesticide, antiseptic, and preservative for wood. Formula: $HgCl_2$. Systematic name: **mercury(II) chloride.**
Mercurochrome (məˈkjʊərəˌkrəʊm) *n Trademark.* a solution of a crystalline compound, used as topical antibacterial agent.
mercurous ('mɜːkjʊrəs) *adj* of or containing mercury in the monovalent state; denoting a mercury(I) compound.
mercury ('mɜːkjʊrɪ) *n, pl* **mercuries. 1** Also called: **quicksilver.** a heavy silvery-white toxic liquid metallic element: used in thermometers, barometers, mercury-vapour lamps, and dental amalgams. Symbol: Hg; atomic no.: 80; atomic wt.: 200.59. **2** any plant of the genus *Mercurialis.* **3** *Arch.* a messenger or courier. [C14: from L *Mercurius,* messenger of Jupiter, god of commerce; rel. to *merx* merchandise]
Mercury[1] ('mɜːkjʊrɪ) *n Roman myth.* the messenger of the gods.
Mercury[2] ('mɜːkjʊrɪ) *n* the second smallest planet and the nearest to the sun.
mercury-vapour lamp *n* a lamp in which an electric discharge through mercury vapour is used to produce a greenish-blue light.

THESAURUS

intellectually, inwardly, psychologically, rationally, subjectively
mention *vb* **1 = refer to,** acknowledge, adduce, allude to, bring up, broach, call attention to, cite, communicate, declare, disclose, divulge, hint at, impart, intimate, make known, name, point out, recount, report, reveal, speak about *or* of, state, tell, touch upon **3 not to mention = to say nothing of,** as well as, besides, not counting ◆ *n* **4 = acknowledgment,** citation, recognition, tribute **5 = reference,** allusion, announcement, indication, notification, observation, remark
mentor *n* **= guide,** adviser, coach, counsellor, guru, instructor, teacher, tutor
menu *n* **1 = bill of fare,** *carte du jour,* tariff (*chiefly Brit.*)
mercantile *adj* **1 = commercial,** marketable, trade, trading
mercenary *adj* **1 = greedy,** acquisitive, avaricious, bribable, covetous, grasping, money-grubbing (*inf.*), sordid, venal **2 = hired,** bought, paid, venal ◆ *n* **3 = hireling,** condottiere (*History*), free companion (*History*), freelance (*History*), soldier of fortune
Antonyms *adj* ≠ **greedy:** altruistic, benevolent, generous, idealistic, liberal, munificent, philanthropic, unselfish
merchandise *n* **1 = goods,** commodities, produce, products, staples, stock, stock in trade, truck, vendibles, wares ◆ *vb* **2 = trade,** buy and sell, deal in, distribute, do business in, market, retail, sell, traffic in, vend
merchant *n* **1 = tradesman,** broker, dealer, purveyor, retailer, salesman, seller, shopkeeper, supplier, trader, trafficker, vendor, wholesaler
merchantable *adj* **= saleable,** marketable, tradable, vendible
merciful *adj* **= compassionate,** beneficent, benignant, clement, forbearing, forgiving, generous, gracious, humane, kind, lenient, liberal, mild, pitying, soft, sparing, sympathetic, tender-hearted
Antonyms *adj* cruel, hard-hearted, inhumane, merciless, pitiless, uncompassionate, unfeeling
merciless *adj* **= cruel,** barbarous, callous, fell (*arch.*), hard, hard-hearted, harsh, heartless, implacable, inexorable, inhumane, pitiless, relentless, ruthless, severe, unappeasable, unfeeling, unforgiving, unmerciful, unpitying, unsparing, unsympathetic
mercurial *adj* **2 = lively,** active, capricious, changeable, erratic, fickle, flighty, gay, impulsive, inconstant, irrepressible, light-hearted, mobile, quicksilver, spirited, sprightly, temperamental, unpredictable, unstable, variable, volatile
Antonyms *adj* consistent, constant, dependable, predictable, reliable, stable, steady, unchanging

mercy ➊ ('mɜːsɪ) *n, pl* **mercies. 1** compassionate treatment of or attitude towards an offender, adversary, etc., who is in one's power or care; clemency; pity. **2** the power to show mercy. **3** a relieving or welcome occurrence or state of affairs. **4 at the mercy of.** in the power of. [C12: from OF, from L *mercēs* recompense, from *merx* goods]

mercy flight *n* an aircraft flight to bring a seriously ill or injured person to hospital from an isolated community.

mercy killing *n* another term for **euthanasia.**

mere[1] ➊ (mɪə) *adj* being nothing more than something specified: *a mere child.* [C15: from L *merus* pure]
►**'merely** *adv*

mere[2] (mɪə) *n* **1** *Dialect or arch.* a lake or marsh. **2** *Obs.* the sea or an inlet of it. [OE *mere* sea, lake]

mere[3] ('mɛrɪ) *n* a short flat Maori striking weapon. [from Maori]

-mere *n combining form.* indicating a part or division. [from Gk *meros* part]
►**meric** *adj combining form.*

meretricious ➊ (ˌmɛrɪ'trɪʃəs) *adj* **1** superficially or garishly attractive. **2** insincere. **3** *Arch.* of, like, or relating to a prostitute. [C17: from L *merētrīcius*, from *merētrix* prostitute, from *merēre* to earn money]
►ˌ**mere'triciously** *adv* ►ˌ**mere'triciousness** *n*

merganser (mɜː'gænsə) *n, pl* **mergansers** *or* **merganser.** any of several typically crested large marine diving ducks, having a long slender hooked bill with serrated edges. [C18: from NL, from L *mergus* waterfowl, from *mergere* to plunge + *anser* goose]

merge ➊ (mɜːdʒ) *vb* **merges, merging, merged. 1** to meet and join or cause to meet and join. **2** to blend or cause to blend; fuse. [C17: from L *mergere* to plunge]
►**'mergence** *n*

merger ➊ ('mɜːdʒə) *n* **1** *Commerce.* the combination of two or more companies. **2** *Law.* the absorption of an estate, interest, offence, etc., into a greater one. **3** the act of merging or the state of being merged.

meridian ➊ (mə'rɪdɪən) *n* **1a** one of the imaginary lines joining the north and south poles at right angles to the equator, designated by degrees of longitude from 0° at Greenwich to 180°. **1b** the great circle running through both poles. **2** *Astron.* the great circle on the celestial sphere passing through the north and south celestial poles and the zenith and nadir of the observer. **3** the peak; zenith: *the meridian of his achievements.* **4** (in acupuncture, etc.) any of the channels through which vital energy is believed to circulate round the body. **5** *Obs.* noon. ◆ *adj* **6** along or relating to a meridian. **7** of or happening at noon. **8** relating to the peak of something. [C14: from L *merīdiānus* of midday, from *merīdiēs* midday, from *medius* MID[1] + *diēs* day]

meridional (mə'rɪdɪənᵊl) *adj* **1** along, relating to, or resembling a meridian. **2** characteristic of or located in the south, esp. of Europe. ◆ *n* **3** an inhabitant of the south, esp. of France. [C14: from LL *merīdiōnālis* southern; see MERIDIAN]

meringue (mə'ræŋ) *n* **1** stiffly beaten egg whites mixed with sugar and baked. **2** a small cake or shell of this mixture, often filled with cream. [C18: from F, from ?]

merino (mə'riːnəʊ) *n, pl* **merinos. 1** a breed of sheep originating in Spain. **2** the long fine wool of this sheep. **3** the yarn made from this wool, often mixed with cotton. ◆ *adj* **4** made from merino wool. [C18: from Sp., from ?]

meristem ('mɛrɪˌstɛm) *n* a plant tissue responsible for growth, whose cells divide and differentiate to form the tissues and organs of the plant. [C19: from Gk *meristos* divided, from *merizein*, from *meris* portion]
►**meristematic** (ˌmɛrɪstɪ'mætɪk) *adj*

merit ➊ ('mɛrɪt) *n* **1** worth or superior quality; excellence. **2** (*often pl*) a deserving or commendable quality or act. **3** *Christianity.* spiritual credit granted or received for good works. **4** the fact or state of deserving; desert. ◆ *vb* **merits, meriting, merited. 5** (*tr*) to be worthy of; deserve. [C13: via OF from L *meritum* reward, from *merēre* to deserve]
►**'merited** *adj* ►**'meritless** *adj*

meritocracy (ˌmɛrɪ'tɒkrəsɪ) *n, pl* **meritocracies. 1** rule by persons chosen for their superior talents or intellect. **2** the persons constituting such a group. **3** a social system formed on such a basis.
►**meritocratic** (ˌmɛrɪtə'krætɪk) *adj*

meritorious ➊ (ˌmɛrɪ'tɔːrɪəs) *adj* praiseworthy; showing merit. [C15: from L *meritōrius* earning money]
►ˌ**meri'toriously** *adv* ►ˌ**meri'toriousness** *n*

merits ('mɛrɪts) *pl n* **1** the actual and intrinsic rights and wrongs of an issue, esp. in a law case. **2 on its (his, her,** etc.**) merits.** on the intrinsic qualities or virtues.

merle *or* **merl** (mɜːl) *n Scot.* another name for the (European) **blackbird.** [C15: via OF from L *merula*]

merlin ('mɜːlɪn) *n* a small falcon that has a dark plumage with a black-barred tail. [C14: from OF *esmerillon*, from *esmeril*, of Gmc origin]

mermaid ('mɜːˌmeɪd) *n* an imaginary sea creature fabled to have a woman's head and upper body and a fish's tail. [C14: from MERE[2] + MAID]

merman ('mɜːˌmæn) *n, pl* **mermen.** a male counterpart of the mermaid. [C17: see MERMAID]

-merous *adj combining form.* (in biology) having a certain number or kind of parts. [from Gk *meros* part]

Merovingian (ˌmɛrəʊ'vɪndʒɪən) *adj* **1** of or relating to a Frankish dynasty which ruled Gaul and W Germany from about 500 to 751 A.D. ◆ *n* **2** a member or supporter of this dynasty. [C17: from F, from Med. L *Merovingi* offspring of *Merovaeus*, L form of *Merowig*, traditional founder of the line]

merriment ➊ ('mɛrɪmənt) *n* gaiety, fun, or mirth.

merry ➊ ('mɛrɪ) *adj* **merrier, merriest. 1** cheerful; jolly. **2** very funny; hilarious. **3** *Brit. inf.* slightly drunk. **4 make merry.** to revel; be festive. **5 play merry hell with.** *Inf.* to disturb greatly; disrupt. [OE *merige* agreeable]
►**'merrily** *adv* ►**'merriness** *n*

merry-andrew (-'ændruː) *n* a joker, clown, or buffoon. [C17: from ?]

merry-go-round *n* **1** another name for **roundabout** (sense 1). **2** a whirl of activity.

merrymaking ➊ ('mɛrɪˌmeɪkɪŋ) *n* fun, revelry, or festivity.
►**'merryˌmaker** *n*

merrythought ('mɛrɪˌθɔːt) *n Brit.* a less common word for **wishbone.**

mesa ('meɪsə) *n* a flat tableland with steep edges, common in the southwestern US. [from Sp.: table]

mésalliance (me'zælɪəns) *n* a marriage with a person of lower social status. [C18: from F: MISALLIANCE]

mescal (mɛ'skæl) *n* **1** Also called: **peyote.** a spineless globe-shaped cactus of Mexico and the southwestern US. Its button-like tubercles (**mescal buttons**) are chewed by certain Indian tribes for their hallucinogenic effects. **2** a colourless alcoholic spirit distilled from the fermented juice of certain agave plants. [C19: from American Sp., from Nahuatl *mexcalli* the liquor, from *metl* MAGUEY + *ixcalli* stew]

mescaline *or* **mescalin** ('mɛskəˌliːn, -lɪn) *n* a hallucinogenic drug derived from mescal buttons.

mesdames ('meɪˌdæm) *n* the plural of **madame** and **madam** (sense 1).

mesdemoiselles (ˌmeɪdmwə'zɛl) *n* the plural of **mademoiselle.**

meseems (mɪ'siːmz) *vb* (*tr; takes a clause as object*) *Arch.* it seems to me.

mesembryanthemum (mɪzˌɛmbrɪ'ænθɪməm) *n* any of a genus of plants with succulent leaves and bright flowers with rayed petals which typically open at midday. [C18: NL, from Gk *mesēmbria* noon + *anthemon* flower]

mesencephalon (ˌmɛsɛn'sɛfəˌlɒn) *n* the part of the brain that develops from the middle portion of the embryonic neural tube. Nontechnical name: **midbrain.**

mesentery ('mɛsəntərɪ, 'mɛz-) *n, pl* **mesenteries.** the double layer of peritoneum that is attached to the back wall of the abdominal cavity

THESAURUS

mercy *n* **1 = compassion,** benevolence, charity, clemency, favour, forbearance, forgiveness, grace, kindness, leniency, pity, quarter **3 = blessing,** benison (*arch.*), boon, godsend, piece of luck, relief **4 at the mercy of = in the power of,** defenceless against, exposed to, in the clutches of, naked before, open to, prey to, subject to, threatened by, unprotected against, vulnerable to
Antonyms *n* ≠ **compassion:** brutality, cruelty, harshness, inhumanity, pitilessness, severity

mere[1] *adj* **= simple,** absolute, bare, common, complete, entire, nothing more than, plain, pure, pure and simple, sheer, stark, unadulterated, unmitigated, unmixed, utter

meretricious *adj* **1 = trashy,** flashy, garish, gaudy, gimcrack, plastic (*sl.*), showy, tawdry, tinsel **2 = false,** bogus, counterfeit, deceitful, hollow, insincere, mock, phoney *or* phony (*inf.*), pseudo (*inf.*), put-on, sham, specious, spurious

merge *vb* **1, 2 = combine,** amalgamate, become lost in, be swallowed up by, blend, coalesce, consolidate, converge, fuse, incorporate, intermix, join, meet, meld, melt into, mingle, mix, tone with, unite
Antonyms *vb* detach, diverge, divide, part, separate, sever

merger *n* **1, 3 = union,** amalgamation, coalition, combination, consolidation, fusion, incorporation

meridian *n* **3, 5 = peak,** acme, apex, apogee, climax, crest, culmination, high noon, high-water mark, pinnacle, summit, zenith

merit *n* **1 = worth,** advantage, asset, excellence, good, goodness, integrity, quality, strong point, talent, value, virtue, worthiness **4 = claim,** credit, desert, due, right ◆ *vb* **5 = deserve,** be entitled to, be worthy of, earn, have a claim to, have a right to, have coming to one, incur, rate, warrant

merited *adj* **5 = deserved,** appropriate, condign, earned, entitled, just, justified, rightful, rightly due, warranted

meritorious *adj* **= praiseworthy,** admirable, commendable, creditable, deserving, excellent, exemplary, good, honourable, laudable, right, righteous, virtuous, worthy
Antonyms *adj* discreditable, dishonourable, ignoble, unchivalrous, undeserving, unexceptional, ungenerous, unpraiseworthy

merriment *n* **= fun,** amusement, conviviality, festivity, frolic, gaiety, glee, hilarity, jocularity, jollity, joviality, laughter, levity, liveliness, merrymaking, mirth, revelry, sport

merry *adj* **1 = cheerful,** blithe, blithesome, carefree, chirpy (*inf.*), convivial, festive, frolicsome, fun-loving, gay, genial, glad, gleeful, happy, jocund, jolly, joyful, joyous, light-hearted, mirthful, rollicking, sportive, upbeat (*inf.*), vivacious **2 = comical,** amusing, comic, facetious, funny, hilarious, humorous, jocular, mirthful **3** *Brit. informal* **= tipsy,** elevated (*inf.*), happy, mellow, squiffy (*Brit. inf.*), tiddly (*sl., chiefly Brit.*) **4 make merry = have fun,** carouse, celebrate, enjoy oneself, feast, frolic, have a good time, make whoopee (*inf.*), revel
Antonyms *adj* ≠ **cheerful:** dejected, dismal, down in the dumps (*inf.*), gloomy, miserable, sad, unhappy

merrymaking *n* **= festivity,** carousal, carouse, celebration, conviviality, fun, gaiety, hooley *or* hoolie (*chiefly Irish & NZ*), jollification, merriment, party, revelry

and supports most of the small intestine. [C16: from NL *mesenterium, from* MESO- + Gk *enteron* intestine]
▸,**mesen'teric** *adj* ▸**mesenteritis** (mɛsˌɛntəˈraɪtɪs) *n*

mesh ❶ (mɛʃ) *n* **1** a network; net. **2** an open space between the strands of a network. **3** (*often pl*) the strands surrounding these spaces. **4** anything that ensnares, or holds like a net. **5** the engagement of teeth on interacting gearwheels: *the gears are in mesh.* ◆ *vb* **6** to entangle or become entangled. **7** (of gear teeth) to engage or cause to engage. **8** (*intr; often foll. by with*) to coordinate (with). **9** to work or cause to work in harmony. [C16: prob. from Du. *maesche*]

mesial (ˈmiːzɪəl) *adj Anat.* another word for **medial** (sense 1). [C19: from MESO- + -IAL]

mesmerism (ˈmɛzməˌrɪzəm) *n Psychol.* **1** a hypnotic state induced by the operator's imposition of his will on that of the patient. **2** an early doctrine concerning this. [C19: after F. A. *Mesmer* (1734–1815), Austrian physician]
▸**mesmeric** (mɛzˈmɛrɪk) *adj* ▸**'mesmerist** *n*

mesmerize ❶ *or* **mesmerise** (ˈmɛzməˌraɪz) *vb* **mesmerizes, mesmerizing, mesmerized** *or* **mesmerises, mesmerising, mesmerised.** (*tr*) **1** to hold (someone) as if spellbound. **2** a former word for **hypnotize.**
▸,**mesmeri'zation** *or* ,**mesmeri'sation** *n* ▸**'mesmer,izer** *or* **'mesmer,iser** *n*

mesne (miːn) *adj Law.* **1** intermediate or intervening: *a mesne assignment of property.* **2 mesne profits.** rents or profits accruing during the rightful owner's exclusion from his land. [C15: from legal F *meien* in the middle]

meso- *or before a vowel* **mes-** *combining form.* middle or intermediate: *mesomorph.* [from Gk *misos* middle]

mesoblast (ˈmɛsəʊˌblæst) *n* another name for **mesoderm.**
▸,**meso'blastic** *adj*

mesocarp (ˈmɛsəʊˌkɑːp) *n* the middle layer of the pericarp of a fruit, such as the flesh of a peach.

mesocephalic (ˌmɛsəʊsɪˈfælɪk) *Anat.* ◆ *adj* **1** having a medium-sized head. ◆ *n* **2** an individual with such a head.
▸**mesocephaly** (ˌmɛsəʊˈsɛfəlɪ) *n*

mesoderm (ˈmɛsəʊˌdɜːm) *n* the middle germ layer of an animal embryo, giving rise to muscle, blood, bone, connective tissue, etc.
▸,**meso'dermal** *or* ,**meso'dermic** *adj*

Mesolithic (ˌmɛsəʊˈlɪθɪk) *n* **1** the period between the Palaeolithic and the Neolithic, in Europe from about 12 000 to 3000 B.C. ◆ *adj* **2** of or relating to the Mesolithic.

mesomorph (ˈmɛsəʊˌmɔːf) *n* a type of person having a muscular body build with a relatively prominent underlying bone structure.

mesomorphic (ˌmɛsəʊˈmɔːfɪk) *adj* **1** *Chem.* existing in or concerned with an intermediate state of matter between a true liquid and a true solid. **2** relating to or being a mesomorph. ◆ Also: **mesomorphous.**
▸,**meso'morphism** *n*

meson (ˈmiːzɒn) *n* any of a group of elementary particles that has a rest mass between those of an electron and a proton, and an integral spin. [C20: from MESO- + -ON]
▸**me'sonic** *or* **'mesic** *adj*

mesophyte (ˈmɛsəʊˌfaɪt) *n* any plant that grows in surroundings receiving an average supply of water.

mesosphere (ˈmɛsəʊˌsfɪə) *n* the atmospheric layer lying between the stratosphere and the thermosphere.

Mesozoic (ˌmɛsəʊˈzəʊɪk) *adj* **1** of, denoting, or relating to an era of geological time that began 225 000 000 years ago and lasted about 155 000 000 years. ◆ *n* **2 the.** the Mesozoic era.

mesquite *or* **mesquit** (mɛˈskiːt, ˈmɛskiːt) *n* any of various small trees, esp. a tropical American variety, whose sugary pods (**mesquite beans**) are used as animal fodder. [C19: from Mexican Sp., from Nahautl *mizquitl*]

mess ❶ (mɛs) *n* **1** a state of confusion or untidiness, esp. if dirty or unpleasant. **2** a chaotic or troublesome state of affairs; muddle. **3** *Inf.* a dirty or untidy person or thing. **4** *Arch.* a portion of food, esp. soft or semiliquid food. **5** a place where service personnel eat or take recreation. **6** a group of people, usually servicemen, who eat together. **7** the meal so taken. ◆ *vb* **8** (*tr; often foll. by up*) to muddle or dirty. **9** (*intr*) to make a mess. **10** (*intr; often foll. by with*) to interfere; meddle. **11** (*intr; often foll. by with or together*) *Mil.* to group together, esp. for eating. [C13: from OF *mes* dish of food, from LL *missus* course (at table), from L *mittere* to send forth]

mess about ❶ *or* **around** *vb* (*adv*) **1** (*intr*) to occupy oneself trivially; potter. **2** (when *intr*, often foll. by *with*) to interfere or meddle (with). **3** (*intr; sometimes foll. by with*) *Chiefly US.* to engage in adultery.

message ❶ (ˈmɛsɪdʒ) *n* **1** a communication, usually brief, from one person or group to another. **2** an implicit meaning, as in a work of art. **3** a formal communiqué. **4** an inspired communication of a prophet or religious leader. **5** a mission; errand. **6 get the message.** *Inf.* to understand. ◆ *vb* **messages, messaging, messaged. 7** (*tr*) to send as a message. [C13: from OF, from Vulgar L *missāticum* (unattested) something sent, from L *missus*, p.p. of *mittere*]

messages (ˈmɛsɪdʒɪz) *pl n Scot. & NE English dialect.* household shopping.

message stick *n* a stick bearing carved symbols, carried by a native Australian as identification.

messenger ❶ (ˈmɛsɪndʒə) *n* **1** a person who takes messages from one person or group to another. **2** a person who runs errands. **3** a carrier of official dispatches; courier. [C13: from OF *messagier*, from MESSAGE]

messenger RNA *n Biochem.* a form of RNA, transcribed from a single strand of DNA, that carries genetic information required for protein synthesis from DNA to the ribosomes.

mess hall *n* a military dining room.

Messiah (mɪˈsaɪə) *n* **1** *Judaism.* the awaited king of the Jews, to be sent by God to free them. **2** Jesus Christ, when regarded in this role. **3** an exceptional or hoped-for liberator of a country or people. [C14: from OF *Messie*, ult. from Heb. *māshīah* anointed]
▸**Mes'siahship** *n* ▸**Messianic** *or* **messianic** (ˌmɛsɪˈænɪk) *adj*

Messier catalogue (ˈmɛsɪˌeɪ) *n Astronomy.* a catalogue of 103 nonstellar objects, such as nebulae and galaxies, prepared in 1781–86. An object is referred to by its number in this catalogue, for example the Andromeda Galaxy is referred to as *M31.* [C18: after Charles *Messier* (1730–1817), F astronomer]

messieurs (ˈmɛsəz) *n* the plural of **monsieur.**

mess jacket *n* a waist-length jacket, worn by officers in the mess for formal dinners.

mess kit *n Mil.* **1** *Brit.* formal evening wear for officers. **2** Also called: **mess gear.** eating utensils used esp. in the field.

messmate (ˈmɛsˌmeɪt) *n* a person with whom one shares meals in a mess, esp. in the army.

Messrs (ˈmɛsəz) *n* the plural of **Mr.** [C18: abbrev. from F *messieurs*, pl. of MONSIEUR]

messy ❶ (ˈmɛsɪ) *adj* **messier, messiest.** dirty, confused, or untidy.
▸**'messily** *adv* ▸**'messiness** *n*

mestizo (mɛˈstiːzəʊ, mɪ-) *n, pl* **mestizos** *or* **mestizoes.** a person of mixed parentage, esp. the offspring of a Spanish American and an American Indian. [C16: from Sp., ult. from L *miscēre* to mix]
▸**mestiza** (mɛˈstiːzə) *fem n*

mestranol (ˈmɛstrəˌnɒl, -ˌnəʊl) *n* a synthetic oestrogen used in combination with progesterones as an oral contraceptive. [C20: from M(ETHYL) + (O)ESTR(OGEN) + (*pregn*)*an*(*e*) + -OL]

met (mɛt) *vb* the past tense and past participle of **meet**[1].

met. *abbrev. for:* **1** meteorological. **2** meteorology. **3** metropolitan.

meta- *or sometimes before a vowel* **met-** *prefix* **1** indicating change or alternation: *metabolism; metamorphosis.* **2** (of an academic discipline) concerned with the concepts and results of that discipline: *metamathematics.* **3** occurring or situated behind or after: *metaphysics.* **4** (*often in italics*) denoting that an organic compound contains a benzene ring with substituents in the 1,3-positions: *meta-cresol.* Abbrev.: *m-*. **5** denoting an isomer, polymer, or compound related to a specified compound: *metaldehyde.* **6** denoting an oxyacid that is the least hydrated form of the anhydride or a salt of such an acid: *metaphosphoric acid.* [from Gk (prep)]

metabolism (mɪˈtæbəˌlɪzəm) *n* **1** the sum total of the chemical processes that occur in living organisms, resulting in growth, production of energy, elimination of waste, etc. **2** the sum total of the chemical processes affecting a particular substance in the body: *carbohydrate metabolism.* [C19: from Gk *metabolē* change, from *metaballein*, from META- + *ballein* to throw]
▸**metabolic** (ˌmɛtəˈbɒlɪk) *adj* ▸,**meta'bolically** *adv*

metabolize *or* **metabolise** (mɪˈtæbəˌlaɪz) *vb* **metabolizes, metabolizing, metabolized** *or* **metabolises, metabolising, metabolised.** to produce or be produced by metabolism.

metacarpus (ˌmɛtəˈkɑːpəs) *n, pl* **metacarpi** (-paɪ). **1** the skeleton of the hand between the wrist and the fingers, consisting of five long bones. **2** the corresponding bones in other vertebrates.
▸,**meta'carpal** *adj, n*

metacentre *or US* **metacenter** (ˈmɛtəˌsɛntə) *n* the intersection of a vertical line through the centre of buoyancy of a floating body at

THESAURUS

mesh *n* **1** = **net**, netting, network, plexus, reticulation, tracery, web **4** = **trap**, entanglement, snare, tangle, toils, web ◆ *vb* **6** = **entangle**, catch, enmesh, ensnare, net, snare, tangle, trap **8, 9** = **engage**, combine, come together, connect, coordinate, dovetail, fit together, harmonize, interlock, knit

mesmerize *vb* **1, 2** = **entrance**, absorb, captivate, enthral, fascinate, grip, hold spellbound, hypnotize, magnetize, spellbind

mess *n* **1** = **disorder**, bodge (*inf.*), botch, chaos, clutter, confusion, dirtiness, disarray, disorganization, grot (*sl.*), hash, hodgepodge (*US*), hotchpotch, jumble, litter, mishmash, shambles, state, turmoil, untidiness **2** = **difficulty**, deep water, dilemma, fine kettle of fish (*inf.*), fix (*inf.*), hole (*inf.*), hot water (*inf.*), imbroglio, jam (*inf.*), mix-up, muddle, perplexity, pickle (*inf.*), plight, predicament, spot (*inf.*), stew (*inf.*), tight spot ◆ *vb* **8, 9** *often with* **up** = **dirty**, befoul, besmirch, botch, bungle, clutter, disarrange, dishevel, foul, litter, make a hash of (*inf.*), make a nonsense of, muck up (*Brit. sl.*), muddle, pollute, scramble **10** *often with* **with** = **interfere**, fiddle (*inf.*), meddle, play, tamper, tinker

mess about *vb* **1** = **potter**, amuse oneself, dabble, fool (about *or* around), footle (*inf.*), muck about (*inf.*), play about *or* around, trifle **2** = **meddle**, fiddle (*inf.*), fool (about *or* around), interfere, play, tamper, tinker, toy

message *n* **1, 3** = **communication**, bulletin, communiqué, dispatch, intimation, letter, memorandum, missive, note, notice, tidings, word **2** = **point**, idea, import, meaning, moral, purport, theme **5** = **errand**, commission, job, mission, task **6 get the message** = **understand**, catch on (*inf.*), comprehend, get it, get the point, see, take the hint, twig (*Brit. inf.*)

messenger *n* **1-3** = **courier**, agent, bearer, carrier, delivery boy, emissary, envoy, errand- boy, go-between, harbinger, herald, runner

messy *adj* = **untidy**, chaotic, cluttered, confused, dirty, dishevelled, disordered, disorganized, grubby, littered, muddled, shambolic, sloppy (*inf.*), slovenly, unkempt

equilibrium with a vertical line through the centre of buoyancy when the body is tilted.
▸ˌmeta'centric *adj*

metage ('miːtɪdʒ) *n* **1** the official measuring of weight or contents. **2** a charge for this. [C16: from METE[1]]

metal ('mɛtᵊl) *n* **1a** any of a number of chemical elements, such as iron or copper, that are often lustrous ductile solids, have basic oxides, form positive ions, and are good conductors of heat and electricity. **1b** an alloy, such as brass or steel, containing one or more of these elements. **2** the substance of glass in a molten state or as the finished product. **3** short for **road metal. 4** *Inf.* short for **heavy metal. 5** *Heraldry.* gold or silver. **6** the basic quality of a person or thing; stuff. **7** *(pl)* the rails of a railway. ◆ *adj* **8** made of metal. ◆ *vb* **metals, metalling, metalled** *or US* **metals, metaling, metaled.** *(tr)* **9** to fit or cover with metal. **10** to make or mend (a road) with road metal. [C13: from L *metallum* mine, product of a mine, from Gk *metallon*]
▸'metalled *adj*

metal. *or* **metall.** *abbrev. for:* **1** metallurgical. **2** metallurgy.

metalanguage ('mɛtəˌlæŋgwɪdʒ) *n* a language or system of symbols used to discuss another language or system. Cf. **object language.**

metal detector *n* a device that gives an audible or visual signal when its search head comes close to a metallic object embedded in food, buried in the ground, etc.

metallic (mɪ'tælɪk) *adj* **1** of, concerned with, or consisting of metal or a metal. **2** suggestive of a metal: *a metallic click; metallic lustre.* **3** *Chem.* (of a metal element) existing in the free state rather than in combination: *metallic copper.*

metallic soap *n* any one of a number of salts or esters containing a metal, such as aluminium, calcium, magnesium, iron, and zinc. They are used as bases for ointments, fungicides, fireproofing and waterproofing agents, and dryers for paints and varnishes.

metalliferous (ˌmetᵊ'lɪfərəs) *adj* containing a metallic element. [C17: from L *metallifer* yielding metal, from *metallum* metal + *ferre* to bear]

metallize, metallise, *or US* **metalize** ('mɛtəˌlaɪz) *vb* **metallizes, metallizing, metallized; metallises, metallising, metallised** *or US* **metalizes, metalizing, metalized.** *(tr)* to make metallic or to coat or treat with metal.
▸ˌmetalli'zation, metalli'sation, *or US* ˌmetali'zation *n*

metallography (ˌmɛtə'lɒgrəfɪ) *n* the branch of metallurgy concerned with the composition and structure of metals and alloys.
▸metallographic (mɪˌtælə'græfɪk) *adj*

metalloid ('mɛtəˌlɔɪd) *n* **1** a nonmetallic element, such as arsenic or silicon, that has some of the properties of a metal. ◆ *adj also* ˌ**metal'loidal. 2** of or being a metalloid. **3** resembling a metal.

metallurgy (mɛ'tælədʒɪ) *n* the scientific study of the extraction, refining, alloying, and fabrication of metals and of their structure and properties.
▸metallurgic (ˌmɛtə'lɜːdʒɪk) *or* ˌmetal'lurgical *adj* ▸metallurgist (mɛ'tælədʒɪst, 'mɛtəˌlɜːdʒɪst) *n*

metal tape *n* a magnetic recording tape coated with pure iron: it gives enhanced recording quality.

metalwork ('mɛtᵊlˌwɜːk) *n* **1** the craft of working in metal. **2** work in metal or articles made from metal.

metalworking ('mɛtᵊlˌwɜːkɪŋ) *n* the processing of metal to change its shape, size, etc.
▸'metalˌworker *n*

metamere ('mɛtəˌmɪə) *n* one of the similar body segments into which earthworms, crayfish, and similar animals are divided longitudinally.
▸metameral (mɪ'tæmərəl) *adj*

metamerism (mɪ'tæməˌrɪzəm) *n* **1** Also called: **(metameric) segmentation.** the division of an animal into metameres. **2** *Chem.* a type of isomerism in which molecular structures differ by the attachment of different groups to the same atom.
▸metameric (ˌmɛtə'mɛrɪk) *adj*

metamict ('mɛtəˌmɪkt) *adj* of or denoting the amorphous state of a substance that has lost its crystalline structure as a result of the radioactivity of uranium or thorium within it.
▸ˌmetaˌmicti'zation *or* ˌmetaˌmicti'sation *n*

metamorphic (ˌmɛtə'mɔːfɪk) *or* **metamorphous** *adj* **1** relating to or resulting from metamorphosis or metamorphism. **2** (of rocks) altered considerably from the original structure and composition by pressure and heat.

metamorphism (ˌmɛtə'mɔːfɪzəm) *n* **1** the process by which metamorphic rocks are formed. **2** a variant of **metamorphosis.**

metamorphose ➊ (ˌmɛtə'mɔːfəʊz) *vb* **metamorphoses, metamorphosing, metamorphosed.** to undergo or cause to undergo metamorphosis or metamorphism.

metamorphosis ➊ (ˌmɛtə'mɔːfəsɪs) *n, pl* **metamorphoses** (-ˌsiːz). **1** a complete change of physical form or substance. **2** a complete change of character, appearance, etc. **3** a person or thing that has undergone metamorphosis. **4** *Zool.* the rapid transformation of a larva into an adult that occurs in certain animals, for example the stage between chrysalis and butterfly. [C16: via L from Gk: transformation, from META- + *morphē* form]

metaphor ➊ ('mɛtəfə, -ˌfɔː) *n* a figure of speech in which a word or phrase is applied to an object or action that it does not literally denote in order to imply a resemblance, for example *he is a lion in battle.* Cf. **simile.** [C16: from L, from Gk *metaphora,* from *metapherein* to transfer, from META- + *pherein* to bear]
▸metaphoric (ˌmɛtə'fɒrɪk) *or* ˌmeta'phorical *adj* ▸ˌmeta'phorically *adv*

metaphrase ('mɛtəˌfreɪz) *n* **1** a literal translation. ◆ *vb* **metaphrases, metaphrasing, metaphrased.** *(tr)* **2** to alter or manipulate the wording of. **3** to translate literally. [C17: from Gk *metaphrazein* to translate]

metaphrast ('mɛtəˌfræst) *n* a person who metaphrases, esp. one who changes the form of a text, as by rendering verse into prose. [C17: from Med. Gk *metaphrastēs* translator]
▸ˌmeta'phrastic *or* ˌmeta'phrastical *adj* ▸ˌmeta'phrastically *adv*

metaphysic (ˌmɛtə'fɪzɪk) *n* the system of first principles and assumptions underlying an inquiry or philosophical theory.

metaphysical ➊ (ˌmɛtə'fɪzɪkᵊl) *adj* **1** of or relating to metaphysics. **2** (of a statement or theory) having an empirical form but in fact immune from empirical testing. **3** (popularly) abstract, abstruse, or unduly theoretical. **4** incorporeal; supernatural.
▸ˌmeta'physically *adv*

Metaphysical (ˌmɛtə'fɪzɪkᵊl) *adj* **1** denoting or relating to certain 17th-century poets who combined intense feeling with elaborate imagery. ◆ *n* **2** a poet of this group.

metaphysics (ˌmɛtə'fɪzɪks) *n (functioning as sing)* **1** the branch of philosophy that deals with first principles, esp. of being and knowing. **2** the philosophical study of the nature of reality. **3** (popularly) abstract or subtle discussion or reasoning. [C16: from Med. L, from Gk *ta meta ta phusika* the things after the physics, from the arrangement of subjects treated in the works of Aristotle]
▸metaphysician (ˌmɛtəfɪ'zɪʃən) *or* metaphysicist (ˌmɛtə'fɪzɪsɪst) *n*

metapsychology (ˌmɛtəsaɪ'kɒlədʒɪ) *n Psychol.* **1** the study of philosophical questions, such as the relation between mind and body, that go beyond the laws of experimental psychology. **2** any attempt to state the general laws of psychology. **3** another word for **parapsychology.**
▸metapsychological (ˌmɛtəˌsaɪkə'lɒdʒɪkᵊl) *adj*

metastable (ˌmɛtə'steɪbᵊl) *adj Physics.* (of a body or system) having a state of apparent equilibrium although capable of changing to a more stable state.
▸ˌmetasta'bility *n*

metastasis (mɪ'tæstəsɪs) *n, pl* **metastases** (-ˌsiːz). *Pathol.* the spreading of a disease organism, esp. cancer cells, from one part of the body to another. [C16: via L from Gk: transition]
▸metastatic (ˌmɛtə'stætɪk) *adj* ▸ˌmeta'statically *adv*

metastasize *or* **metastasise** (mɪ'tæstəˌsaɪz) *vb* **metastasizes, metastasizing, metastasized** *or* **metastasises, metastasising, metastasised.** *(intr) Pathol.* (esp. of cancer cells) to spread to a new site in the body via blood or lymph vessels.

metatarsus (ˌmɛtə'tɑːsəs) *n, pl* **metatarsi** (-saɪ). **1** the skeleton of the human foot between the toes and the tarsus, consisting of five long bones. **2** the corresponding skeletal part in other vertebrates.
▸ˌmeta'tarsal *adj, n*

metathesis (mɪ'tæθəsɪs) *n, pl* **metatheses** (-ˌsiːz). the transposition of two sounds or letters in a word. [C16: from LL, from Gk, from *metatithenai* to transpose]
▸metathetic (ˌmɛtə'θɛtɪk) *or* ˌmeta'thetical *adj*

metazoan (ˌmɛtə'zəʊən) *n* **1** any multicellular animal: includes all animals except sponges. ◆ *adj also* **metazoic. 2** of or relating to the metazoans. [C19: from NL *Metazoa;* see META-, -ZOA]

mete[1] ➊ (miːt) *vb* **metes, meting, meted.** *(tr)* **1** (usually foll. by *out*) *Formal.* to distribute or allot (something, often unpleasant). **2** *Poetic, dialect.* to measure. [OE *metan*]

mete[2] (miːt) *n Rare.* a mark, limit, or boundary (esp. in **metes and bounds**). [C15: from OF, from L *mēta* goal, turning post (in race)]

metempsychosis (ˌmɛtəmsaɪ'kəʊsɪs) *n, pl* **metempsychoses** (-siːz). the migration of a soul from one body to another. [C16: via LL from Gk, from *metempsukhousthai,* from META- + *-em-* in + *psukhē* soul]
▸ˌmetempsy'chosist *n*

meteor ('miːtɪə) *n* **1** a very small meteoroid that has entered the earth's atmosphere. **2** Also called: **shooting star, falling star.** the bright streak of light appearing in the sky due to the incandescence of such a body heated by friction at its surface. [C15: from Med. L *meteōrum,* from Gk *meteōron,* from *meteōros* lofty, from *meta-* (intensifier) + *aeirein* to raise]

meteoric ➊ (ˌmiːtɪ'ɒrɪk) *adj* **1** of, formed by, or relating to meteors. **2**

THESAURUS

Antonyms *adj* clean, meticulous, neat, ordered, orderly, shipshape, smart, squeaky-clean, tidy

metamorphose *vb* = **transform,** alter, be reborn, change, convert, mutate, remake, remodel, reshape, transfigure, translate, transmogrify (*jocular*), transmute, transubstantiate

metamorphosis *n* **1, 2** = **transformation,** alteration, change, changeover, conversion, mutation, rebirth, transfiguration, translation, transmogrification (*jocular*), transmutation, transubstantiation

metaphor *n* = **figure of speech,** allegory, analogy, emblem, image, symbol, trope

metaphorical *adj* = **figurative,** allegorical, emblematic, emblematical, symbolic, tropical (*Rhetoric*)

metaphysical *adj* **1** = **philosophical,** basic, esoteric, essential, eternal, fundamental, general, ideal, intellectual, profound, speculative, spiritual, subjective, universal **3** = **abstract,** abstruse, deep, high-flown, oversubtle, recondite, theoretical, transcendental **4** = **supernatural,** immaterial, impalpable, incorporeal, intangible, spiritual, unreal, unsubstantial

mete[1] *vb* **1, 2** = **distribute,** administer, allot, apportion, assign, deal, dispense, divide, dole, measure, parcel, portion, ration, share

meteoric *adj* **2** = **spectacular,** brief, brilliant, dazzling, ephemeral, fast, flashing, fleeting,

like a meteor in brilliance, speed, or transience. 3 *Rare.* of weather; meteorological.
▸ ˌ**mete'orically** *adv*

meteorism ('miːtɪəˌrɪzəm) *n Med.* another name for **tympanites.**

meteorite ('miːtɪəˌraɪt) *n* a rocklike object consisting of the remains of a meteoroid that has fallen on earth.
▸**meteoritic** (ˌmiːtɪə'rɪtɪk) *adj*

meteoroid ('miːtɪəˌrɔɪd) *n* any of the small celestial bodies that are thought to orbit the sun. When they enter the earth's atmosphere, they become visible as meteors.
▸ ˌ**meteor'oidal** *adj*

meteorol. *or* **meteor.** *abbrev for:* 1 meteorological. 2 meteorology.

meteorology (ˌmiːtɪə'rɒlədʒɪ) *n* the study of the earth's atmosphere, esp. of weather-forming processes and weather forecasting. [C17: from Gk; see METEOR, -LOGY]
▸**meteorological** (ˌmiːtɪərə'lɒdʒɪkᵊl) *or* ˌ**meteoro'logic** *adj* ▸ ˌ**meteoro'logically** *adv* ▸ ˌ**meteor'ologist** *n*

meteor shower *n* a transient rain of meteors occurring at regular intervals and coming from a particular region in the sky.

meter[1] ('miːtə) *n* 1 any device that measures and records a quantity, such as of gas, current, voltage, etc., that has passed through it during a specified period. 2 See **parking meter.** ◆ *vb (tr)* 3 to measure (a rate of flow) with a meter. [C19: see METE[1]]

meter[2] ('miːtə) *n* the US spelling of **metre**[1].

meter[3] ('miːtə) *n* the US spelling of **metre**[2].

-meter *n combining form.* 1 indicating an instrument for measuring: *barometer.* 2 *Prosody.* indicating a verse having a specified number of feet: *pentameter.* [from Gk *metron* measure]

Meth. *abbrev. for* Methodist.

meth- *combining form.* indicating a chemical compound derived from methane or containing methyl groups: *methacrylic acid.*

methacrylic acid (ˌmeθə'krɪlɪk) *n* a colourless crystalline water-soluble substance used in the manufacture of acrylic resins.

methadone ('meθəˌdəʊn) *or* **methadon** ('meθəˌdɒn) *n* a narcotic analgesic drug similar to morphine and formerly thought to be less habit-forming. [C20: from *(di)meth(yl)* + A(MINO) + *d(iphenyl)* + -ONE]

methamphetamine (ˌmeθæm'fetəmiːn, -mɪn) *n* a variety of amphetamine used for its stimulant action. [C20: from METH- + AMPHETAMINE]

methanal ('meθəˌnæl) *n* the systematic name for **formaldehyde.**

methane ('miːθeɪn) *n* a colourless odourless flammable gas, the main constituent of natural gas: used as a fuel. Formula: CH_4.

methane series *n* another name for **alkane series.**

methanoic acid ('meθəˌnəʊɪk) *n* the systematic name for **formic acid.**

methanol ('meθəˌnɒl) *n* a colourless volatile poisonous liquid compound used as a solvent and fuel. Formula: CH_3OH. Also called: **methyl alcohol, wood alcohol.** [C20: from METHANE + -OL[1]]

methinks (mɪ'θɪŋks) *vb past* **methought.** *(tr; takes a clause as object) Arch.* it seems to me.

metho ('meθəʊ) *n Austral. inf.* 1 another name for **methylated spirits.** 2 *(pl* **methos**) a drinker of methylated spirits.

method ❶ ('meθəd) *n* 1 a way of proceeding or doing something, esp. a systematic or regular one. 2 orderliness of thought, action, etc. 3 *(often pl)* the techniques or arrangement of work for a particular field or subject. [C16: via F from L, from Gk *methodos,* lit.: a going after, from *meta-* after + *hodos* way]

Method ('meθəd) *n (sometimes not cap.)* **a** a technique of acting in which the actor bases his role on the inner motivation of the character played. **b** *(as modifier): a Method actor.*

methodical ❶ (mɪ'θɒdɪkᵊl) *or (less commonly)* **methodic** *adj* characterized by method or orderliness; systematic.
▸**me'thodically** *adv*

Methodism ('meθəˌdɪzəm) *n* the system and practices of the Methodist Church.

Methodist ('meθədɪst) *n* 1 a member of any of the Nonconformist denominations that derive from the system of faith and practice initiated by John Wesley and his followers. ◆ *adj also* ˌ**Method'istic** *or* ˌ**Method'istical.** 2 of or relating to Methodism or the Church embodying it (the **Methodist Church**).

methodize *or* **methodise** ('meθəˌdaɪz) *vb* **methodizes, methodizing, methodized** *or* **methodises, methodising, methodised.** *(tr)* to organize according to a method; systematize
▸ '**methodˌizer** *or* '**methodˌiser** *n*

methodology (ˌmeθə'dɒlədʒɪ) *n, pl* **methodologies.** 1 the system of methods and principles used in a particular discipline. 2 the branch of philosophy concerned with the science of method.
▸**methodological** (ˌmeθədə'lɒdʒɪkᵊl) *adj* ▸ ˌ**methodo'logically** *adv* ▸ ˌ**method'ologist** *n*

methought (mɪ'θɔːt) *vb Arch.* the past tense of **methinks.**

meths (meθs) *n Chiefly Brit., Austral., & NZ.* an informal name for **methylated spirits.**

methyl ('miːθaɪl, 'meθɪl) *n* 1 *(modifier)* of, consisting of, or containing the monovalent group of atoms CH_3. 2 a compound in which methyl groups are bound directly to a metal atom. [C19: from F *méthyle,* back formation from METHYLENE]
▸**methylic** (mə'θɪlɪk) *adj*

methyl acetate *n* a colourless volatile flammable liquid ester used as a solvent, esp. in paint removers. Formula: CH_3COOCH_3. Systematic name: **methyl ethanoate.**

methyl alcohol *n* another name for **methanol.**

methylate ('meθɪˌleɪt) *vb* **methylates, methylating, methylated.** *(tr)* to mix with methanol.

methylated spirits *n (functioning as sing or pl)* alcohol that has been denatured by the addition of methanol and pyridine and a violet dye. Also: **methylated spirit.**

methyl chloride *n* a colourless gas with an ether-like odour, used as a refrigerant and anaesthetic. Formula: CH_3Cl. Systematic name: **chloromethane.**

methylene ('meθɪˌliːn) *n (modifier)* of, consisting of, or containing the divalent group of atoms $=CH_2$: *a methylene group or radical.* [C19: from F *méthylène,* from Gk *methu* wine + *hulē* wood + -ENE: orig. referring to a substance distilled from wood]

methylene dichloride *n* the traditional name for **dichloromethane.**

methylphenol (ˌmiːθaɪl'fiːnɒl) *n* the systematic name for **cresol.**

meticulous ❶ (mɪ'tɪkjʊləs) *adj* very precise about details; painstaking. [C16 (meaning: timid): from L *meticulōsus* fearful, from *metus* fear]
▸**me'ticulously** *adv* ▸**me'ticulousness** *n*

métier ❶ ('metɪeɪ) *n* 1 a profession or trade. 2 a person's strong point or speciality. [C18: from F, ult. from L *ministerium* service]

Métis (me'tiːs) *n, pl* **Métis** (-'tiːs, -'tiːz). a person of mixed parentage, esp. the offspring of a French Canadian and a North American Indian. [C19: from F, from Vulgar L *mixtīcius* (unattested) of mixed race]
▸**Métisse** (me'tiːs) *fem n*

metol ('miːtɒl) *n* a colourless soluble organic substance used, in the form of its sulphate, as a photographic developer. [C20: from G, arbitrary coinage]

Metonic cycle (mɪ'tɒnɪk) *n* a cycle of 235 synodic months after which the phases of the moon recur on the same day of the month. [C17: after *Meton,* 5th-cent. B.C. Athenian astronomer]

metonymy (mɪ'tɒnɪmɪ) *n, pl* **metonymies.** the substitution of a word referring to an attribute for the thing that is meant, e.g. *the crown,* used to refer to a monarch. Cf. **synecdoche.** [C16: from LL, from Gk, from *meta-* (indicating change) + *onoma* name]
▸**metonymical** (ˌmetə'nɪmɪkᵊl) *or* ˌ**meto'nymic** *adj*

metope ('metəʊp, 'metəpɪ) *n Archit.* a square space between triglyphs in a Doric frieze. [C16: via L from Gk, from *meta* between + *opē* one of the holes for the beam-ends]

metre[1] *or US* **meter** ('miːtə) *n* 1 a metric unit of length equal to approximately 1.094 yards. 2 the basic SI unit of length; the length of the path travelled by light in free space during a time interval of 1/299 792 458 of a second. Symbol: m [C18: from F; see METRE[2]]

metre[2] *or US* **meter** ('miːtə) *n* 1 *Prosody.* the rhythmic arrangement of syllables in verse, usually according to the number and kind of feet in a line. 2 *Music.* another word (esp. US) for **time** (sense 22). [C14: from L *metrum,* from Gk *metron* measure]

metre-kilogram-second *n* See **mks units.**

metric ('metrɪk) *adj* of or relating to the metre or metric system.

metrical ('metrɪkᵊl) *or* **metric** *adj* 1 of or relating to measurement. 2 of or in poetic metre.
▸ '**metrically** *adv*

metricate ('metrɪˌkeɪt) *vb* **metricates, metricating, metricated.** to convert (a measuring system, instrument, etc.) from nonmetric to metric units.
▸ ˌ**metri'cation** *n*

metric system *n* any decimal system of units based on the metre. For scientific purposes SI units are used.

metric ton *n* another name (not in technical use) for **tonne.**

metro ('metrəʊ) *or* **métro** *French.* (metro) *n, pl* **metros.** an underground, or largely underground, railway system in certain cities, such as that in Paris. [C20: from F, *chemin de fer métropolitain* metropolitan railway]

Metro ('metrəʊ) *n Canad.* a metropolitan city administration, esp. Metropolitan Toronto.

metronome ('metrəˌnəʊm) *n* a device which indicates the tempo of music by producing a clicking sound from a pendulum with an adjustable period of swing. [C19: from Gk *metron* measure + *nomos* law]
▸**metronomic** (ˌmetrə'nɒmɪk) *adj*

metronymic (ˌmetrəʊ'nɪmɪk) *adj* 1 (of a name) derived from the name

THESAURUS

momentary, overnight, rapid, speedy, sudden, swift, transient
Antonyms *adj* gradual, lengthy, long, prolonged, slow, steady, unhurried

method *n* 1 = **manner**, approach, arrangement, course, fashion, form, mode, modus operandi, plan, practice, procedure, process, programme, routine, rule, scheme, style, system, technique, way 2 = **orderliness**, design, form, order, organization, pattern, planning, purpose, regularity, structure, system

methodical *adj* = **orderly**, businesslike, deliberate, disciplined, efficient, meticulous, neat, ordered, organized, painstaking, planned, precise, regular, structured, systematic, tidy, well-regulated
Antonyms *adj* casual, chaotic, confused, disordered, disorderly, haphazard, irregular, random, unmethodical

meticulous *adj* = **thorough**, detailed, exact, fastidious, fussy, microscopic, painstaking, particular, perfectionist, precise, punctilious, scrupulous, strict
Antonyms *adj* careless, haphazard, imprecise, inexact, loose, negligent, slapdash, sloppy

métier *n* 1 = **profession**, calling, craft, line, occupation, pursuit, trade, vocation 2 = **strong point**, forte, long suit (*inf.*), speciality, specialty, strong suit of the mother or other female ancestor. ◆ *n* **2** a metronymic name. [C19: from Gk *mētronumikos*, from *mētēr* mother + *onoma* name]

metropolis ❶ (mɪ'trɒpəlɪs) *n, pl* **metropolises. 1** the main city, esp. of a country or region. **2** a centre of activity. **3** the chief see in an ecclesiastical province. [C16: from LL from Gk, from *mētēr* mother + *polis* city]

metropolitan (ˌmɛtrə'pɒlɪtən) *adj* **1** of or characteristic of a metropolis. **2** constituting a city and its suburbs. **3** of, relating to, or designating an ecclesiastical metropolis. **4** of or belonging to the home territories of a country, as opposed to overseas territories: *metropolitan France*. ◆ *n* **5a** *Eastern Churches*. the head of an ecclesiastical province, ranking between archbishop and patriarch. **5b** *Church of England*. an archbishop. **5c** *RC Church*. an archbishop or bishop having authority over the dioceses in his province.
▸ˌ**metro'politanism** *n*

metropolitan county *n* (in England) any of the six conurbations established as units in the new local government system in 1974; the metropolitan county councils were abolished in 1986.

metropolitan district *n* (in England since 1974) any of the districts that make up the metropolitan counties of England: since 1986 they have functioned as unitary authorities.

metrorrhagia (ˌmiːtrɔː'reɪdʒɪə, ˌmɛt-) *n* abnormal bleeding from the uterus. [C19: NL, from Gk *mētra* womb + *-rrhagia* a breaking forth]

-metry *n combining form*. indicating the process or science of measuring: *geometry*. [from OF *-metrie*, from L, ult. from Gk *metron* measure]
▸**-metric** *adj combining form*.

mettle ❶ ('mɛtᵊl) *n* **1** courage; spirit. **2** character. **3 on one's mettle.** roused to making one's best efforts. [C16: orig. var. of METAL]

mettled ('mɛtᵊld) *or* **mettlesome** ('mɛtᵊlsəm) *adj* courageous, spirited, or valiant.

MeV *symbol for* million electronvolts (10^6 electronvolts).

mevrou (mə'frəʊ) *n* a S. African title of address equivalent to *Mrs* when placed before a surname or *madam* when used alone. [Afrik.]

mew[1] (mjuː) *vb* **1** (*intr*) (esp. of a cat) to make a characteristic high-pitched cry. ◆ *n* **2** such a sound. [C14: imit.]

mew[2] (mjuː) *n* any seagull, esp. the common gull. [OE *mǣw*]

mew[3] (mjuː) *n* **1** a room or cage for hawks, esp. while moulting. ◆ *vb* (*tr*) **2** (often foll. by *up*) to confine (hawks or falcons) in a shelter, cage, etc. **3** to confine; conceal. [C14: from OF *mue*, from *muer* to moult, from L *mūtāre* to change]

mewl ❶ (mjuːl) *vb* **1** (*intr*) (esp. of a baby) to cry weakly; whimper. ◆ *n* **2** such a cry. [C17: imit.]

mews (mjuːz) *n* (*functioning as sing or pl*) *Chiefly Brit.* **1** a yard or street lined by buildings originally used as stables but now often converted into dwellings. **2** the buildings around a mews. [C14: pl of MEW[3], orig. referring to royal stables built on the site of hawks' mews at Charing Cross in London]

Mex. *abbrev. for:* **1** Mexican. **2** Mexico.

Mexican ('mɛksɪkən) *adj* **1** of or relating to Mexico, in Central America. ◆ *n* **2** a native or inhabitant of Mexico or a descendant of one.

Mexican wave *n* the rippling effect produced when the spectators in successive sections of a sports stadium stand up while raising their arms and then sit down. [C20: first seen at the World Cup in Mexico in 1986]

MEZ *abbrev. for* Central European Time. [from G *Mitteleuropäische Zeit*]

mezcal (mɛ'skæl) *n* a variant spelling of **mescal.**

mezcaline ('mɛskəˌliːn) *n* a variant spelling of **mescaline.**

mezuzah (mə'zuzə) *n, pl* **mezuzahs** *or* **mezuzoth** (*Hebrew* məzu'zɔt). *Judaism.* **1** a piece of parchment inscribed with biblical passages and fixed to the doorpost of a Jewish house. **2** a metal case for such a parchment, sometimes worn as an ornament. [from Heb., lit.: doorpost]

mezzanine ('mɛzəˌniːn, 'mɛtsəˌniːn) *n* **1** Also called: **mezzanine floor.** an intermediate storey, esp. a low one between the ground and first floor of a building. **2** *Theatre, US & Canad.* the first balcony. **3** *Theatre, Brit.* a room or floor beneath the stage. ◆ *adj* **4** often shortened to **mezz.** of or relating to an intermediate stage in a financial process: *mezzanine funding*. [C18: from F, from It., dim. of *mezzano* middle, from L *mediānus* MEDIAN]

mezzo ('mɛtsəʊ) *adv Music.* moderately; quite: *mezzo piano*. [C19: from It., lit.: half, from L *medius* middle]

mezzo-soprano *n, pl* **mezzo-sopranos. 1** a female voice intermediate between a soprano and contralto. **2** a singer with such a voice.

mezzotint ('mɛtsəʊˌtɪnt) *n* **1** a method of engraving a copper plate by scraping and burnishing the roughened surface. **2** a print made from a plate so treated. ◆ *vb* **3** (*tr*) to engrave (a copper plate) in this fashion. [C18: from It. *mezzotinto* half tint]

mf *Music. symbol for* mezzo forte. [It.: moderately loud]

MF *abbrev. for:* **1** *Radio.* medium frequency. **2** Middle French.

mfd *abbrev. for* manufactured.

mfg *abbrev. for* manufacturing.

MFH *Hunting. abbrev. for* Master of Foxhounds.

mfr *abbrev. for:* **1** manufacture. **2** manufacturer.

mg *symbol for* milligram.

Mg *the chemical symbol for* magnesium.

M. Glam *abbrev. for* Mid Glamorgan.

Mgr *abbrev. for:* **1** manager. **2** Monseigneur. **3** Monsignor.

MHA (in Australia) *abbrev. for* Member of the House of Assembly.

MHG *abbrev. for* Middle High German.

mho (məʊ) *n, pl* **mhos.** the former name for **siemens.** [C19: formed by reversing the letters of OHM (first used by Lord Kelvin)]

MHR (in the US and Australia) *abbrev. for* Member of the House of Representatives.

MHz *symbol for* megahertz.

mi (miː) *n Music.* **1** the syllable used in the fixed system of solmization for the note E. **2** Also: **me.** (in tonic sol-fa) the third degree of any major scale; a mediant. [C14: see GAMUT]

MI *abbrev. for:* **1** Michigan. **2** Military Intelligence.

mi. *abbrev. for* mile.

MI5 *abbrev. for* Military Intelligence, section five; a former official and current popular name for the counterintelligence agency of the British Government.

MI6 *abbrev. for* Military Intelligence, section six; a former official and current popular name for the intelligence and espionage agency of the British Government.

miaou *or* **miaow** (mɪ'aʊ, mjaʊ) *vb, interj* variant spellings of **meow.**

miasma (mɪ'æzmə) *n, pl* **miasmata** (-mətə) *or* **miasmas. 1** an unwholesome or foreboding atmosphere. **2** pollution in the atmosphere, esp. noxious vapours from decomposing organic matter. [C17: NL, from Gk: defilement, from *miainein* to defile]
▸**mi'asmal** *or* **miasmatic** (ˌmiːæz'mætɪk) *adj*

Mic. *Bible. abbrev. for* Micah.

mica ('maɪkə) *n* any of a group of minerals consisting of hydrous silicates of aluminium, potassium, etc., in monoclinic crystalline form, occurring in igneous and metamorphic rock. Because of their resistance to electricity and heat they are used as dielectrics, in heating elements, etc. Also called: **isinglass.** [C18: from L: crumb]
▸**micaceous** (maɪ'keɪʃəs) *adj*

mice (maɪs) *n* the plural of **mouse.**

micelle, micell (mɪ'sɛl), *or* **micella** (mɪ'sɛlə) *n Chem.* **a** a charged aggregate of molecules of colloidal size in a solution. **b** any molecular aggregate of colloidal size. [C19: from NL *micella*, dim. of L *mīca* crumb]

Mich. *abbrev. for:* **1** Michaelmas. **2** Michigan.

Michaelmas ('mɪkᵊlməs) *n* Sept. 29, the feast of St Michael the archangel; in England, Ireland, and Wales, one of the four quarter days.

Michaelmas daisy *n Brit.* any of various composite plants that have small autumn-blooming purple, pink, or white flowers.

Michaelmas term *n* the autumn term at Oxford and Cambridge Universities, the Inns of Court, and some other educational establishments.

Mick (mɪk) *n* (*sometimes not cap.*) **1** Also: **Mickey.** *Derog.* a slang name for an **Irishman** or a **Roman Catholic. 2** *Austral.* the tails side of a coin. [C19: from nickname for *Michael*]

mickey *or* **micky** ('mɪkɪ) *n Inf.* **take the mickey (out of).** to tease. [C20: from ?]

Mickey Finn *n Sl.* **a** a drink containing a drug to make the drinker unconscious. **b** the drug itself. ◆ Often shortened to **Mickey.** [C20: from ?]

mickle ('mɪkᵊl) *or* **muckle** ('mʌkᵊl) *Arch. or Scot. & N English dialect.* ◆ *adj* **1** great or abundant. ◆ *adv* **2** much; greatly. ◆ *n* **3** a great amount, esp. in the proverb, *many a little makes a mickle*. **4** *Scot.* a small amount, esp. in the proverb *mony a mickle makes a muckle*. [C13 *mikel*, from ON *mikell*, replacing OE *micel* MUCH]

micro ('maɪkrəʊ) *adj* **1** very small. ◆ *n, pl* **micros. 2** short for **microcomputer, microprocessor, microwave oven.**

micro- *or* **micr-** *combining form.* **1** small or minute: *microdot*. **2** involving the use of a microscope: *microscopy*. **3** indicating a method or instrument for dealing with small quantities: *micrometer*. **4** (in pathology) indicating abnormal smallness or underdevelopment: *microcephaly*. **5** denoting 10^{-6}: *microsecond*. Symbol: μ [from Gk *mikros* small]

microbe ❶ ('maɪkrəʊb) *n* any microscopic organism, esp. a disease-causing bacterium. [C19: from F, from MICRO- + Gk *bios* life]
▸**mi'crobial** *or* **mi'crobic** *adj*

microbiology (ˌmaɪkrəʊbaɪ'ɒlədʒɪ) *n* the branch of biology involving the study of microorganisms.
▸**microbiological** (ˌmaɪkrəʊˌbaɪə'lɒdʒɪkᵊl) *or* ˌ**micro**ˌ**bio'logic** *adj*
▸ˌ**micro**ˌ**bio'logically** *adv* ▸ˌ**microbi'ologist** *n*

microcephaly (ˌmaɪkrəʊ'sɛfəlɪ) *n* the condition of having an abnormally small head or cranial capacity.
▸**microcephalic** (ˌmaɪkrəʊsɪ'fælɪk) *adj, n* ▸ˌ**micro'cephalous** *adj*

microchemistry (ˌmaɪkrəʊ'kɛmɪstrɪ) *n* chemical experimentation with minute quantities of material.
▸ˌ**micro'chemical** *adj*

microchip ('maɪkrəʊˌtʃɪp) *n* another word for **chip** (sense 7).

microcircuit ('maɪkrəʊˌsɜːkɪt) *n* a miniature electronic circuit, esp. one in which a number of permanently connected components are contained in one small chip of semiconducting material. See **integrated circuit.**
▸ˌ**micro'circuitry** *n*

microclimate ('maɪkrəʊˌklaɪmɪt) *n Ecology.* the atmospheric conditions affecting an individual or a small group of organisms, esp. when they differ from the climate of the rest of the community.

THESAURUS

metropolis *n* **1** = **city**, capital

mettle *n* **1** = **courage**, ardour, boldness, bravery, daring, fire, fortitude, gallantry, gameness, grit, guts (*inf.*), hardihood, heart, indomitability, life, nerve, pluck, resolution, resolve, spirit, spunk (*inf.*), valour, vigour **2** = **character**, calibre, disposition, kidney, make-up, nature, quality, stamp, temper, temperament

mewl *vb* **1** = **whimper**, blubber, cry, grizzle (*inf., chiefly Brit.*), pule, snivel, whine, whinge (*inf.*)

microbe *n* = **microorganism**, bacillus, bacterium, bug (*inf.*), germ, virus

▸**microclimatic** (ˌmaɪkrəʊklaɪˈmætɪk) *adj* ▸**ˌmicroˌclimaˈtology** *n*
microcomputer (ˌmaɪkrəʊkəmˈpjuːtə) *n* a computer in which the central processing unit is contained in one or more silicon chips.
microcosm (ˈmaɪkrəʊˌkɒzəm) *or* **microcosmos** (ˌmaɪkrəʊˈkɒzmɒs) *n* **1** a miniature representation of something. **2** man regarded as epitomizing the universe. ◆ Cf. **macrocosm.** [C15: via Med. L from Gk *mikros kosmos* little world]
▸**ˌmicroˈcosmic** *or* **ˌmicroˈcosmical** *adj*
microdot (ˈmaɪkrəʊˌdɒt) *n* **1** a greatly reduced photographic copy (about the size of a pinhead) of a document, etc., used esp. in espionage. **2** a tiny tablet containing LSD.
microeconomics (ˌmaɪkrəʊˌiːkəˈnɒmɪks, -ˌɛkə-) *n* (*functioning as sing*) the branch of economics concerned with particular commodities, firms, or individuals and the economic relationships between them.
▸**ˌmicroˌecoˈnomic** *adj*
microelectronics (ˌmaɪkrəʊɪlɛkˈtrɒnɪks) *n* (*functioning as sing*) the branch of electronics concerned with microcircuits.
microfiche (ˈmaɪkrəʊˌfiːʃ) *n* a sheet of film, usually the size of a filing card, on which books, newspapers, documents, etc., can be recorded in miniaturized form. [C20: from F, from MICRO- + *fiche* small card]
microfilm (ˈmaɪkrəʊˌfɪlm) *n* **1** a strip of film on which books, documents, etc., can be recorded in miniaturized form. ◆ *vb* **2** to photograph (a page, document, etc.) on microfilm.
microgravity (ˈmaɪkrəʊˌgrævɪtɪ) *n* gravitational effects operating, or apparently operating, in a localized region, as in a spacecraft under conditions of weightlessness.
microhabitat (ˌmaɪkrəʊˈhæbɪtæt) *n Ecology.* the smallest part of the environment that supports a distinct flora and fauna, such as a fallen log in a forest.
microlight *or* **microlite** (ˈmaɪkrəʊˌlaɪt) *n* a small private aircraft carrying no more than two people, with a wing area not less than 10 square metres: used in pleasure flying and racing.
microlith (ˈmaɪkrəʊˌlɪθ) *n Archaeol.* a small Mesolithic flint tool which formed part of a hafted tool.
▸**ˌmicroˈlithic** *adj*
micrometer (maɪˈkrɒmɪtə) *n* **1** any of various instruments or devices for the accurate measurement of distances or angles. **2** Also called: **micrometer gauge, micrometer calliper.** a type of gauge for the accurate measurement of small distances, thicknesses, etc. The gap between its measuring faces is adjusted by a fine screw (**micrometer screw**).
▸**micrometric** (ˌmaɪkrəʊˈmɛtrɪk) *or* **ˌmicroˈmetrical** *adj* ▸**miˈcrometry** *n*
microminiaturization *or* **microminiaturisation** (ˌmaɪkrəʊˌmɪnɪtʃəraɪˈzeɪʃən) *n* the production and application of very small components and the circuits and equipment in which they are used.
micron (ˈmaɪkrɒn) *n, pl* **microns** *or* **micra** (-krə). a unit of length equal to 10^{-6} metre. It is being replaced by the micrometre, the equivalent SI unit. [C19: NL, from Gk *mikros* small]
Micronesian (ˌmaɪkrəʊˈniːʒən, -ʒɪən) *adj* **1** of or relating to Micronesia (a division of islands in the Pacific), its inhabitants, or their languages. ◆ *n* **2** a native or inhabitant of Micronesia or a descendant of one. **3** a group of languages spoken in Micronesia.
microorganism (ˌmaɪkrəʊˈɔːgəˌnɪzəm) *n* any organism, such as a bacterium, of microscopic size.
microphone (ˈmaɪkrəˌfəʊn) *n* a device used in sound-reproduction systems for converting sound into electrical energy.
▸**microphonic** (ˌmaɪkrəˈfɒnɪk) *adj*
microprint (ˈmaɪkrəʊˌprɪnt) *n* a greatly reduced photographic copy of print, read by a magnifying device. It is used in order to reduce the size of large books, etc.
microprocessor (ˌmaɪkrəʊˈprəʊsɛsə) *n Computing.* a single integrated circuit performing the basic functions of the central processing unit in a small computer.
microscope (ˈmaɪkrəˌskəʊp) *n* **1** an optical instrument that uses a lens or combination of lenses to produce a magnified image of a small, close object. **2** any instrument, such as the electron microscope, for producing a magnified visual image of a small object.
microscopic ❶ (ˌmaɪkrəˈskɒpɪk) *or* (*less commonly*) **microscopical** *adj* **1** not large enough to be seen with the naked eye but visible under a microscope. **2** very small; minute. **3** of, concerned with, or using a microscope.
▸**ˌmicroˈscopically** *adv*
microscopy (maɪˈkrɒskəpɪ) *n* **1** the study, design, and manufacture of microscopes. **2** investigation by use of a microscope.
▸**microscopist** (maɪˈkrɒskəpɪst) *n*
microsecond (ˈmaɪkrəʊˌsɛkənd) *n* one millionth of a second.
microstructure (ˈmaɪkrəʊˌstrʌktʃə) *n* structure on a microscopic scale, esp. the structure of an alloy as observed by etching, polishing, and observation under a microscope.
microsurgery (ˌmaɪkrəʊˈsɜːdʒərɪ) *n* intricate surgery performed on cells, tissues, etc., using a specially designed operating microscope and miniature precision instruments.
microswitch (ˈmaɪkrəʊˌswɪtʃ) *n Electrical engineering.* a switch that operates by small movements of a lever.
microtome (ˈmaɪkrəʊˌtəʊm) *n* an instrument used for cutting thin sections for microscopical examination.
▸**microtomy** (maɪˈkrɒtəmɪ) *n*
microwave (ˈmaɪkrəʊˌweɪv) *n* **1a** electromagnetic radiation in the wavelength range 0.3 to 0.001 metres: used in radar, cooking, etc. **1b** (*as modifier*): *microwave oven.* **2** short for **microwave oven.** ◆ *vb* **microwaves, microwaving, microwaved.** (*tr*) **3** to cook in a microwave oven.
microwave background *n* a background of microwave electromagnetic radiation discovered in space in 1965, believed to have emanated from the big bang with which the universe began.
microwave detector *n NZ.* a device for recording the speed of a motorist.
microwave oven *n* an oven in which food is cooked by microwaves. Often shortened to **micro, microwave.**
microwave spectroscopy *n* a type of spectroscopy in which information is obtained on the structure and chemical bonding of molecules and crystals by measurements of the wavelengths of microwaves emitted or absorbed by the sample.
▸**microwave spectroscope** *n*
micturate (ˈmɪktjʊˌreɪt) *vb* **micturates, micturating, micturated.** (*intr*) a less common word for **urinate.** [C19: from L *micturīre* to desire to urinate, from *mingere* to urinate]
▸**micturition** (ˌmɪktjʊˈrɪʃən) *n*
mid[1] (mɪd) *adj* **1** *Phonetics.* of, relating to, or denoting a vowel whose articulation lies approximately halfway between high and low, such as *e* in English *bet.* ◆ *n* **2** an archaic word for **middle.** [C12 *midre* (inflected form of *midd*, unattested)]
mid[2] *or* **'mid** (mɪd) *prep* a poetic word for **amid.**
mid- *combining form.* indicating a middle part, point, time, or position: *midday; mid-April; mid-Victorian.* [OE; see MIDDLE, MID[1]]
midair (ˌmɪdˈɛə) *n* **a** some point above ground level, in the air. **b** (*as modifier*): *a midair collision of aircraft.*
mid-Atlantic *adj* characterized by a blend of British and American styles, elements, etc.: *a mid-Atlantic accent.*
midbrain (ˈmɪdˌbreɪn) *n* the nontechnical name for **mesencephalon.**
midday ❶ (ˈmɪdˈdeɪ) *n* **a** the middle of the day; noon. **b** (*as modifier*): *a midday meal.*
middelskot (ˈmɪdəlˌskɒt) *n* (in South Africa) an intermediate payment to a farmers' cooperative for a crop or wool clip. [from Afrik. *middel* middle + *skot* payment]
midden (ˈmɪdən) *n* **1a** *Arch. or dialect.* a dunghill or pile of refuse. **1b** *Dialect.* a dustbin. **2** See **kitchen midden.** [C14: from ON]
middle ❶ (ˈmɪdəl) *adj* **1** equally distant from the ends or periphery of something; central. **2** intermediate in status, situation, etc. **3** located between the early and late parts of a series, time sequence, etc. **4** not extreme, esp. in size; medium. **5** (esp. in Greek and Sanskrit grammar) denoting a voice of verbs expressing reciprocal or reflexive action. **6** (*usually cap.*) (of a language) intermediate between the earliest and the modern forms. ◆ *n* **7** an area or point equal in distance from the ends or periphery or in time between the early and late parts. **8** an intermediate part or section, such as the waist. **9** *Grammar.* the middle voice. **10** *Logic.* See **middle term. 11** *Cricket.* a position on the batting crease in alignment with the middle stumps on which a batsman may take guard. ◆ *vb* **middles, middling, middled.** (*tr*) **12** to place in the middle. **13** *Naut.* to fold in two. **14** *Cricket.* to hit (the ball) with the middle of the bat. [OE *middel*]
middle age *n* the period of life between youth and old age, usually (in man) considered to occur approximately between the ages of 40 and 60.
▸**ˌmiddle-ˈaged** *adj*
Middle Ages *n* **the.** *European history.* **1** (broadly) the period from the deposition of the last W Roman emperor in 476 A.D. to the Italian Renaissance (or the fall of Constantinople in 1453). **2** (narrowly) the period from about 1000 A.D. to the 15th century. Cf. **Dark Ages.**
Middle America *n* **1** the territories between the US and South America: Mexico, Central America, and the Antilles. **2** the US middle class, esp. those groups that are politically conservative.
▸**Middle American** *adj, n*
middle-and-leg *n Cricket.* a position on the batting crease in alignment with the middle and leg stumps on which a batsman may take guard.
middle-and-off *n Cricket.* a position on the batting crease in alignment with the middle and off stumps on which a batsman may take guard.
middlebrow (ˈmɪdəlˌbraʊ) *Disparaging.* ◆ *n* **1** a person with conventional tastes and limited cultural appreciation. ◆ *adj also* **middlebrowed. 2** of or appealing to middlebrows.
middle C *n Music.* the note written on the first ledger line below the treble staff or the first ledger line above the bass staff.
middle class ❶ *n* **1** Also called: **bourgeoisie.** a social stratum between the lower and upper classes. It consists of businessmen, professional people, etc., along with their families, and is marked by bourgeois values. ◆ *adj* **middle-class. 2** of, relating to, or characteristic of the middle class.

THESAURUS

microscopic *adj* **2** = **tiny**, imperceptible, infinitesimal, invisible, minuscule, minute, negligible, teensy-weensy, teeny-weeny
Antonyms *adj* enormous, gigantic, ginormous (*inf.*), great, huge, immense, large, vast

midday *n* = **noon**, noonday, noontide, noontime, twelve noon, twelve o'clock

middle *adj* **1-4** = **central**, halfway, inner, inside, intermediate, intervening, mean, medial, median, medium, mid ◆ *n* **7** = **centre**, focus, halfway point, heart, mean, midpoint, mid-section, midst, thick **8** = **waist**, midriff, midsection

middle class *adj* **middle-class 2** = **bourgeois**, conventional, petit-bourgeois, suburban, traditional

middle ear *n* the sound-conducting part of the ear, containing the malleus, incus, and stapes.

Middle East *n* **1** (loosely) the area around the E Mediterranean, esp. Israel and the Arab countries from Turkey to North Africa and eastwards to Iran. **2** (formerly) the area extending from the Tigris and Euphrates to Myanmar.
▸**Middle Eastern** *adj*

Middle England *n* a characterization of a predominantly middle-class, middle-income section of British society living mainly in suburban and rural England.

Middle English *n* the English language from about 1100 to about 1450.

middle game *n Chess.* the central phase between the opening and the endgame.

Middle High German *n* High German from about 1200 to about 1500.

Middle Low German *n* Low German from about 1200 to about 1500.

middleman 🅣 ('mɪdᵊl,mæn) *n, pl* **middlemen. 1** a trader engaged in the distribution of goods from producer to consumer. **2** an intermediary.

middlemost ('mɪdᵊl,məʊst) *adj* another word for **midmost.**

middle name *n* **1** a name between a person's first name and surname. **2** a characteristic quality for which a person is known: *caution is my middle name.*

middle-of-the-road *adj* **1** not extreme, esp. in political views; moderate. **2** of, denoting, or relating to popular music having a wide general appeal.

middle passage *n* **the.** *History.* the journey across the Atlantic Ocean from the W coast of Africa to the Caribbean: the longest part of the journey of the slave ships.

middle school *n* (in England and Wales) a school for children aged between 8 or 9 and 12 or 13.

middle term *n Logic.* the term that appears in both minor and major premises but not in the conclusion of a syllogism.

middle watch *n Naut.* the watch between midnight and 4 a.m.

middleweight ('mɪdᵊl,weɪt) *n* **1a** a professional boxer weighing 154–160 pounds (70–72.5 kg). **1b** an amateur boxer weighing 71–75 kg (157–165 pounds). **2a** a professional wrestler weighing 166–176 pounds (76–80 kg). **2b** an amateur wrestler weighing 75–82 kg (162–180 pounds).

Middle West *n* another name for the **Midwest.**
▸**Middle Western** *adj* ▸**Middle Westerner** *n*

middling 🅣 ('mɪdlɪŋ) *adj* **1** mediocre in quality, size, etc.; neither good nor bad, esp. in health (often in **fair to middling**). ◆ *adv* **2** *Inf.* moderately: *middling well.* [C15 (N English & Scot.): from MID[1] + -LING[2]]
▸'**middlingly** *adv*

Middx. *abbrev. for* Middlesex.

middy ('mɪdɪ) *n, pl* **middies. 1** *Inf.* short for **midshipman. 2** *Austral.* **2a** a glass of middling size, used for beer. **2b** the measure of beer it contains.

midfield (,mɪd'fi:ld) *n Soccer.* **a** the general area between the two opposing defences. **b** (*as modifier*): *a midfield player.*

midge (mɪdʒ) *n* **1** a mosquito-like dipterous insect occurring in dancing swarms, esp. near water. **2** a small or diminutive person or animal. [OE *mycge*]
▸'**midgy** *adj*

midget 🅣 ('mɪdʒɪt) *n* **1** a dwarf whose skeleton and features are of normal proportions. **2a** something small of its kind. **2b** (*as modifier*): *a midget car.* [C19: from MIDGE + -ET]

midgut ('mɪd,gʌt) *n* **1** the middle part of the digestive tract of vertebrates, including the small intestine. **2** the middle part of the digestive tract of arthropods.

mid-heavyweight *n* **a** a professional wrestler weighing 199–209 pounds (91–95 kg). **b** an amateur wrestler weighing 91–100 kg (199–220 pounds).

midi ('mɪdɪ) *adj* (formerly) **a** (of a skirt, coat, etc.) reaching to below the knee or midcalf. **b** (*as n*): *she wore her new midi.* [C20: from MID-, on the model of MINI]

MIDI ('mɪdɪ) *n* (*modifier*) a generally accepted specification for the external control of electronic musical instruments: *a MIDI synthesizer; a MIDI system.* [C20: from *m(usical) i(nstrument) d(igital) i(nterface)*]

midi- *combining form.* of medium or middle size, length, etc.: *midibus; midi system.*

midinette (,mɪdɪ'net) *n* a Parisian seamstress or salesgirl in a clothes shop. [C20: from F, from *midi* noon + *dinette* light meal; the girls had time for only a snack at midday]

midiron ('mɪd,aɪən) *n Golf.* a club, usually a No. 5, 6, or 7 iron, used for medium-length approach shots.

midi system *n* a complete set of hi-fi sound equipment designed as a single unit that is more compact than the standard equipment.

midland ('mɪdlənd) *n* **a** the central or inland part of a country. **b** (*as modifier*): *a midland region.*

Midlands ('mɪdləndz) *n* (*functioning as pl or sing*) **the.** the central counties of England: characterized by manufacturing industries.
▸'**Midlander** *n*

midlife crisis *n* a crisis that may be experienced in middle age involving frustration, panic, and feelings of pointlessness, sometimes resulting in radical and often ill-advised changes of lifestyle.

midmost ('mɪd,məʊst) *adj, adv* in the middle or midst.

midnight 🅣 ('mɪd,naɪt) *n* **1a** the middle of the night; 12 o'clock at night. **1b** (*as modifier*): *the midnight hour.* **2 burn the midnight oil.** to work or study late into the night.

midnight sun *n* the sun visible at midnight during the summer inside the Arctic and Antarctic circles.

mid-off *n Cricket.* the fielding position on the off side closest to the bowler.

mid-on *n Cricket.* the fielding position on the on side closest to the bowler.

midpoint ('mɪd,pɔɪnt) *n* **1** the point on a line that is at an equal distance from either end. **2** a point in time halfway between the beginning and end of an event.

midrib ('mɪd,rɪb) *n* the main vein of a leaf, running down the centre of the blade.

midriff ('mɪdrɪf) *n* **1a** the middle part of the human body, esp. between waist and bust. **1b** (*as modifier*): *midriff bulge.* **2** *Anat.* another name for the **diaphragm** (sense 1). **3** the part of a woman's garment covering the midriff. [OE *midhrif*, from MID[1] + *hrif* belly]

midship ('mɪd,ʃɪp) *Naut.* ◆ *adj* **1** in, of, or relating to the middle of a vessel. ◆ *n* **2** the middle of a vessel.

midshipman ('mɪd,ʃɪpmən) *n, pl* **midshipmen.** a probationary rank held by young naval officers under training, or an officer holding such a rank.

midships ('mɪd,ʃɪps) *adv, adj Naut.* See **amidships.**

midst[1] 🅣 (mɪdst) *n* **1 in our midst.** among us. **2 in the midst of.** surrounded or enveloped by; at a point during. [C14: back formation from *amiddes* AMID]

midst[2] (mɪdst) *prep Poetic.* See **amid.**

midsummer ('mɪd'sʌmə) *n* **1a** the middle or height of the summer. **1b** (*as modifier*): *a midsummer carnival.* **2** another name for **summer solstice.**

Midsummer's Day *or* **Midsummer Day** *n* June 24, the feast of St John the Baptist; in England, Ireland, and Wales, one of the four quarter days. See also **summer solstice.**

midterm ('mɪd'tɜ:m) *n* **1a** the middle of a term in a school, university, etc. **1b** (*as modifier*): *midterm exam.* **2** *US politics.* **2a** the middle of a term of office, esp. of a presidential term, when congressional and local elections are held. **2b** (*as modifier*): *midterm elections.* **3a** the middle of the gestation period. **3b** (*as modifier*): *midterm pregnancy.* See **term** (sense 6).

mid-Victorian *adj* **1** *Brit. history.* of or relating to the middle period of the reign of Queen Victoria (1837–1901). ◆ *n* **2** a person of the mid-Victorian era.

midway 🅣 ('mɪd,weɪ *or, for adv, n* ,mɪd'weɪ) *adj* **1** in or at the middle of the distance; halfway. ◆ *adv* **2** to the middle of the distance. ◆ *n* **3** *Obs.* a middle place, way, etc.

midweek ('mɪd'wi:k) *n* **a** the middle of the week. **b** (*as modifier*): *a midweek holiday.*

Midwest ('mɪd'west) *or* **Middle West** *n* the N central part of the US; the states from Ohio westwards that border on the Great Lakes, and often the upper Mississippi and Missouri valleys.
▸'**Mid'western** *adj* ▸'**Mid'westerner** *n*

mid-wicket *n Cricket.* the fielding position on the on side, midway between square leg and mid-on.

midwife ('mɪd,waɪf) *n, pl* **midwives** (-,waɪvz). a person qualified to deliver babies and to care for women before, during, and after childbirth. [C14: from OE *mid* with + *wif* woman]

midwifery ('mɪd,wɪfərɪ) *n* the training, art, or practice of a midwife; obstetrics.

midwinter ('mɪd'wɪntə) *n* **1a** the middle or depth of the winter. **1b** (*as modifier*): *a midwinter festival.* **2** another name for **winter solstice.**

midyear ('mɪd'jɪə) *n* the middle of the year.

mien 🅣 (mi:n) *n Literary.* a person's manner, bearing, or appearance. [C16: prob. var. of obs. *demean* appearance; rel. to F *mine* aspect]

mifepristone (mɪ'feprɪ,stəʊn) *n* See **abortion pill.**

miff 🅣 (mɪf) *Inf.* ◆ *vb* **1** to take offence or to offend. ◆ *n* **2** a petulant mood. **3** a petty quarrel. [C17: ? an imitative expression of bad temper]
▸'**miffy** *adj*

might[1] (maɪt) *vb* (takes an implied infinitive or an infinitive without *to*) used as an auxiliary: **1** making the past tense or subjunctive mood

THESAURUS

middleman *n* **1, 2** = **intermediary**, broker, distributor, entrepreneur, go-between

middling *adj* **1** = **mediocre**, indifferent, run-of-the-mill, so-so (*inf.*), tolerable, unexceptional, unremarkable **1** = **moderate**, adequate, all right, average, bog-standard (*Brit. & Irish sl.*), fair, medium, modest, O.K. *or* okay (*inf.*), ordinary, passable, serviceable

midget *n* **1** = **dwarf**, gnome, homuncule, homunculus, manikin, pygmy *or* pigmy, shrimp (*inf.*), Tom Thumb ◆ *modifier* **2b** = **tiny**, baby, dwarf, Lilliputian, little, miniature, pocket, pygmy *or* pigmy, small, teensy-weensy, teeny-weeny

midnight *n* **1** = **twelve o'clock**, dead of night, middle of the night, the witching hour, twelve o'clock at night

midst[1] *n* **2 in the midst of** = **among**, amidst, during, enveloped by, in the middle of, in the thick of, surrounded by

midway *adj, adv* **1, 2** = **halfway**, betwixt and between, in the middle

mien *n Literary* = **demeanour**, air, appearance, aspect, aura, bearing, carriage, countenance, deportment, look, manner, presence

miffed *adj* **1** *Informal* = **upset**, aggrieved, annoyed, displeased, hacked (off) (*US sl.*), hurt, in of **may**[1]: *he might have come.* **2** (often foll. by *well*) expressing possibility: *he might well come.* In this sense *might* looks to the future and functions as a weak form of *may*. See **may**[1] (sense 2). [OE *mihte*]

USAGE NOTE See at **may**[1].

might[2] ❶ (maɪt) *n* **1** power, force, or vigour, esp. of a great or supreme kind. **2** physical strength. **3** (**with**) **might and main.** See **main**[1] (sense 7). [OE *miht*]

mighty ❶ ('maɪtɪ) *adj* **mightier, mightiest. 1a** having or indicating might; powerful or strong. **1b** (*as collective n; preceded by the*): *the mighty.* **2** very large; vast. **3** very great in extent, importance, etc. ◆ *adv* **4** *Inf., chiefly US & Canad.* (intensifier): *mighty tired.*
▸**'mightily** *adv* ▸**'mightiness** *n*

mignon ('mɪnjɒn) *adj* small and pretty; dainty. [C16: from F, from OF *mignot* dainty]
▸**mignonne** ('mɪnjɒn) *fem n*

mignonette (ˌmɪnjə'nɛt) *n* **1** any of various mainly Mediterranean plants, such as **garden mignonette**, that have spikes of small greenish-white flowers. **2** a type of fine pillow lace. **3a** a greyish-green colour. **3b** (*as adj*): *mignonette ribbons.* [C18: from F, dim. of MIGNON]

migraine ('miːgreɪn, 'maɪ-) *n* a throbbing headache usually affecting only one side of the head and commonly accompanied by nausea and visual disturbances. [C18: (earlier form, C14 *mygrame* MEGRIM): from F, from LL *hēmicrānia* pain in half of the head, from Gk, from HEMI- + *kranion* CRANIUM]
▸**'migrainous** *adj*

migrant ❶ ('maɪgrənt) *n* **1** a person or animal that moves from one region, place, or country to another. **2** an itinerant agricultural worker. ◆ *adj* **3** moving from one region, place, or country to another; migratory.

migrate ❶ (maɪ'greɪt) *vb* **migrates, migrating, migrated.** (*intr*) **1** to go from one place to settle in another, esp. in a foreign country. **2** (of birds, fishes, etc.) to journey between different habitats at specific times of the year. [C17: from L *migrāre* to change one's abode]
▸**mi'grator** *n*

migration ❶ (maɪ'greɪʃən) *n* **1** the act or an instance of migrating. **2** a group of people, birds, etc., migrating in a body. **3** *Chem.* a movement of atoms, ions, or molecules, such as the motion of ions in solution under the influence of electric fields.
▸**mi'grational** *adj*

migratory ❶ ('maɪgrətərɪ, -trɪ) *adj* **1** of or characterized by migration. **2** nomadic; itinerant.

mihrab ('miːræb, -rəb) *n Islam.* the niche in a mosque showing the direction of Mecca. [from Ar.]

mikado (mɪ'kɑːdəʊ) *n, pl* **mikados.** (*often cap.*) *Arch.* the Japanese emperor. [C18: from Japanese, from *mi-* honourable + *kado* gate]

mike (maɪk) *n Inf.* short for **microphone.**

mil (mɪl) *n* **1** a unit of length equal to one thousandth of an inch. **2** a unit of angular measure, used in gunnery, equal to one six-thousand-four-hundredth of a circumference. **3** *Photog.* short for millimetre: *35-mil film.* [C18: from L *millēsimus* thousandth]

mil. *abbrev. for:* **1** military. **2** militia.

milady *or* **miladi** (mɪ'leɪdɪ) *n, pl* **miladies.** (formerly) a continental title used for an English gentlewoman.

milch (mɪltʃ) *n* **1** (*modifier*) (esp. of cattle) yielding milk. **2 milch cow.** *Inf.* a source of easy income, esp. a person. [C13: from OE *-milce* (in compounds); rel. to OE *melcan* to milk]

mild ❶ (maɪld) *adj* **1** (of a taste, sensation, etc.) not powerful or strong; bland. **2** gentle or temperate in character, climate, behaviour, etc. **3** not extreme; moderate. **4** feeble; unassertive. ◆ *n* **5** *Brit.* draught beer, of darker colour than bitter and flavoured with fewer hops. [OE *milde*]
▸**'mildly** *adv* ▸**'mildness** *n*

mildew ('mɪlˌdjuː) *n* **1** any of various diseases of plants that affect mainly the leaves and are caused by parasitic fungi. **2** any fungus causing this. **3** another name for **mould**[2]. ◆ *vb* **4** to affect or become affected with mildew. [OE *mildēaw*, from *mil-* honey + *dēaw* DEW]
▸**'milˌdewy** *adj*

mild steel *n* any of a class of strong tough steels that contain a low quantity of carbon.

mile (maɪl) *n* **1** Also called: **statute mile.** a unit of length used in the UK, the US, and certain other countries, equal to 1760 yards. 1 mile is equivalent to 1.60934 kilometres. **2** See **nautical mile. 3** the Roman mile, equivalent to 1620 yards. **4** (*often pl*) *Inf.* a great distance; great deal: *he missed by a mile.* **5** a race extending over a mile. ◆ *adv* **6 miles.** (intensifier): *that's miles better.* [OE *mīl*, from L *mīlia* (*passuum*) a thousand (paces)]

mileage *or* **milage** ('maɪlɪdʒ) *n* **1** a distance expressed in miles. **2** the total number of miles that a motor vehicle has travelled. **3** allowance for travelling expenses, esp. as a fixed rate per mile. **4** the number of miles a motor vehicle will travel on one gallon of fuel. **5** *Inf.* use, benefit, or service provided by something. **6** *Inf.* grounds, substance, or weight: *some mileage in their arguments.*

mileometer *or* **milometer** (maɪ'lɒmɪtə) *n* a device that records the number of miles that a bicycle or motor vehicle has travelled.

milepost ('maɪlˌpəʊst) *n* **1** *Horse racing.* a marking post on a racecourse a mile before the finishing line. **2** *Chiefly US & Canad.* a signpost that shows the distance in miles to or from a place.

miler ('maɪlə) *n* an athlete, horse, etc., that runs or specializes in races of one mile.

milestone ('maɪlˌstəʊn) *n* **1** a stone pillar that shows the distance in miles to or from a place. **2** a significant event in life, history, etc.

milfoil ('mɪlˌfɔɪl) *n* **1** another name for **yarrow. 2** See **water milfoil.** [C13: from OF, from L *milifolium*, from *mille* thousand + *folium* leaf]

miliaria (ˌmɪlɪ'ɛərɪə) *n* an acute itching eruption of the skin, caused by blockage of the sweat glands. [C19: from NL, from L *miliārius* MILIARY]

miliary ('mɪljərɪ) *adj* **1** resembling or relating to millet seeds. **2** (of a disease or skin eruption) characterized by small lesions resembling millet seeds: *miliary fever.* [C17: from L *miliārius*, from *milium* MILLET]

milieu ❶ ('miːljɜː; *French* miljø) *n, pl* **milieux** (-ljɜː, -ljɜːz; *French* -ljø) *or* **milieus.** (miljø). surroundings, location, or setting. [C19: from F, from *mi-* MID[1] + *lieu* place]

militant ❶ ('mɪlɪtənt) *adj* **1** aggressive or vigorous, esp. in the support of a cause. **2** warring; engaged in warfare. ◆ *n* **3** a militant person. [C15: from L *mīlitāre* to be a soldier, from *mīles* soldier]
▸**'militancy** *n* ▸**'militantly** *adv*

militarism ('mɪlɪtəˌrɪzəm) *n* **1** military spirit; pursuit of military ideals. **2** domination by the military, esp. on a political level. **3** a policy of maintaining a strong military organization in aggressive preparedness for war.
▸**'militarist** *n*

militarize *or* **militarise** ('mɪlɪtəˌraɪz) *vb* **militarizes, militarizing, militarized** *or* **militarises, militarising, militarised.** (*tr*) **1** to convert to military use. **2** to imbue with militarism.
▸**ˌmilitari'zation** *or* **ˌmilitari'sation** *n*

military ❶ ('mɪlɪtərɪ, -trɪ) *adj* **1** of or relating to the armed forces, warlike matters, etc. **2** of or characteristic of soldiers. ◆ *n, pl* **militaries** *or* **military. 3** (preceded by *the*) the armed services, esp. the army. [C16: via F from L *mīlitāris*, from *mīles* soldier]
▸**mili'tarily** *adv*

military police *n* a corps within an army that performs police and disciplinary duties.
▸**military policeman** *n*

militate ❶ ('mɪlɪˌteɪt) *vb* **militates, militating, militated.** (*intr;* usually foll. by *against* or *for*) (of facts, etc.) to have influence or effect: *the evidence militated against his release.* [C17: from L *mīlitātus*, from *mīlitāre* to be a soldier]

USAGE NOTE See at **mitigate.**

THESAURUS

a huff, irked, irritated, narked (*Brit., Austral., & NZ sl.*), nettled, offended, piqued, put out, resentful, vexed

might[2] *n* **1, 2** = **power**, ability, capability, capacity, clout (*inf.*), efficacy, efficiency, energy, force, potency, prowess, puissance, strength, sway, valour, vigour

mighty *adj* **1** = **powerful**, doughty, forceful, hardy, indomitable, lusty, manful, potent, puissant, robust, stalwart, stout, strapping, strong, sturdy, vigorous **2** = **great**, bulky, colossal, elephantine, enormous, gigantic, ginormous (*inf.*), grand, huge, humongous *or* humungous (*US sl.*), immense, large, massive, mega (*sl.*), monumental, prodigious, stellar (*inf.*), stupendous, titanic, towering, tremendous, vast
Antonyms *adj* ≠ **powerful:** feeble, impotent, weak, weedy (*inf.*), wimpish *or* wimpy (*inf.*) ≠ **great:** small, tiny, unimposing, unimpressive

migrant *n* **1, 2** = **wanderer**, drifter, emigrant, gypsy, immigrant, itinerant, nomad, rover, tinker, transient, traveller, vagrant ◆ *adj* **3** = **travelling**, drifting, gypsy, immigrant, itinerant, migratory, nomadic, roving, shifting, transient, vagrant, wandering

migrate *vb* **1** = **move**, drift, emigrate, journey, roam, rove, shift, travel, trek, voyage, wander

migration *n* **1** = **wandering**, emigration, journey, movement, roving, shift, travel, trek, voyage

migratory *adj* **2** = **nomadic**, gypsy, itinerant, migrant, peripatetic, roving, shifting, transient, travelling, unsettled, vagrant, wandering

mild *adj* **1** = **bland**, smooth **2** = **gentle**, amiable, calm, compassionate, docile, easy, easy-going, easy-oasy (*sl.*), equable, forbearing, forgiving, indulgent, kind, meek, mellow, merciful, moderate, pacific, peaceable, placid, pleasant, serene, soft, tender **2** = **temperate**, balmy, calm, clement, moderate, tranquil, warm
Antonyms *adj* ≠ **gentle:** harsh, powerful, severe, sharp, strong, unkind, unpleasant, violent ≠ **temperate:** bitter, cold, fierce, harsh, rough, stormy, violent, wild

mildness *n* **1, 2** = **gentleness**, blandness, calmness, clemency, docility, forbearance, indulgence, kindness, leniency, lenity, meekness, mellowness, moderation, placidity, smoothness, softness, temperateness, tenderness, tranquillity, warmth

milieu *n* = **surroundings**, background, element, environment, locale, location, *mise en scène*, scene, setting, sphere

militant *adj* **1** = **aggressive**, active, assertive, combative, vigorous **2** = **warring**, belligerent, combating, contending, embattled, fighting, in arms ◆ *n* **3** = **activist**, partisan **3** = **warrior**, belligerent, combatant, fighter, gladiator
Antonyms *adj* ≠ **aggressive, warring:** concessive, pacific, pacifist, peaceful

military *adj* **1, 2** = **warlike**, armed, martial, soldierlike, soldierly ◆ *n* **3** = **armed forces**, army, forces, services

militate *vb, foll. by* **against** = **counteract**, be detrimental to, conflict with, contend with, count against, counter, oppose, resist, tell against,

militia ❶ (mɪˈlɪʃə) *n* **1** a body of citizen (as opposed to professional) soldiers. **2** an organization containing men enlisted for service in emergency only. [C16: from L: soldiery, from *mīles* soldier]
▸**miˈlitiaman** *n*

milk ❶ (mɪlk) *n* **1a** a whitish fluid secreted by the mammary glands of mature female mammals and used for feeding their young until weaned. **1b** the milk of cows, goats, etc., used by man as a food or in the production of butter, cheese, etc. **2** any similar fluid in plants, such as the juice of a coconut. **3** a milklike pharmaceutical preparation, such as milk of magnesia. **4 cry over spilt milk.** to lament something that cannot be altered. ◆ *vb* **5** to draw milk from the udder of (an animal). **6** (*intr*) (of animals) to yield milk. **7** (*tr*) to draw off or tap in small quantities: *to milk the petty cash.* **8** (*tr*) to extract as much money, help, etc., as possible from: *to milk a situation of its news value.* **9** (*tr*) to extract venom, sap, etc., from. [OE *milc*]
▸**ˈmilker** *n*

milk-and-water ❶ *adj* (**milk and water** *when postpositive*). weak, feeble, or insipid.

milk bar *n* **1** a snack bar at which milk drinks and light refreshments are served. **2** (in Australia) a shop selling, in addition to milk, basic provisions and other items.

milk chocolate *n* chocolate that has been made with milk, having a creamy taste.

milk float *n Brit.* a small motor vehicle used to deliver milk to houses.

milk leg *n* inflammation and thrombosis of the femoral vein following childbirth, characterized by painful swelling of the leg.

milkmaid (ˈmɪlkˌmeɪd) *n* a girl or woman who milks cows.

milkman (ˈmɪlkmən) *n, pl* **milkmen.** a man who delivers or sells milk.

milk of magnesia *n* a suspension of magnesium hydroxide in water, used as an antacid and laxative.

milk pudding *n Chiefly Brit.* a pudding made by boiling or baking milk with a grain, esp. rice.

milk round *n Brit.* **1** a route along which a milkman regularly delivers milk. **2** a regular series of visits, esp. as made by recruitment officers from industry to universities.

milk run *n Aeronautics, inf.* a routine and uneventful flight. [C20: from a milkman's safe and regular routine]

milk shake *n* a cold frothy drink made of milk, flavouring, and sometimes ice cream, whisked or beaten together.

milksop ❶ (ˈmɪlkˌsɒp) *n* a feeble or ineffectual man or youth.

milk sugar *n* another name for **lactose.**

milk tooth *n* any of the first teeth to erupt; a deciduous tooth. Also called: **baby tooth.**

milkwort (ˈmɪlkˌwɜːt) *n* any of several plants having small blue, pink, or white flowers. They were formerly believed to increase milk production in nursing women.

milky ❶ (ˈmɪlkɪ) *adj* **milkier, milkiest. 1** resembling milk, esp. in colour or cloudiness. **2** of or containing milk. **3** spiritless or spineless.
▸**ˈmilkily** *adv* ▸**ˈmilkiness** *n*

Milky Way *n* **the.** the diffuse band of light stretching across the night sky that consists of millions of faint stars, nebulae, etc., and forms part of the Galaxy. [C14: translation of L *via lactea*]

mill ❶ (mɪl) *n* **1** a building in which grain is crushed and ground to make flour. **2** a building fitted with machinery for processing materials, manufacturing goods, etc.; factory. **3** a machine that processes materials, manufactures goods, etc., by performing a continuous or repetitive operation, such as a machine to grind flour, pulverize solids, or press fruit. **4** a machine that tools or polishes metal. **5** a small machine for grinding solids: *a pepper mill.* **6** a system, institution, etc., that influences people or things in the manner of a factory: *the educational mill.* **7** an unpleasant experience; ordeal (esp. in **go** *or* **be put through the mill**). **8** a fist fight. ◆ *vb* **9** (*tr*) to grind, press, or pulverize in or as if in a mill. **10** (*tr*) to process or produce in or with a mill. **11** to cut or roll (metal) with or as if with a milling machine. **12** (*tr*) to groove or flute the edge of (a coin). **13** (*intr;* often foll. by *about* or *around*) to move about in a confused manner. **14** *Arch. sl.* to fight, esp. with the fists. [OE *mylen* from LL *molīna* a mill, from L *mola* mill, from *molere* to grind]
▸**ˈmillable** *adj* ▸**milled** *adj*

millboard (ˈmɪlˌbɔːd) *n* strong pasteboard, used esp. in book covers. [C18: from *milled board*]

milldam (ˈmɪlˌdæm) *n* a dam built in a stream to raise the water level sufficiently for it to turn a millwheel.

millefeuille *French.* (milfœj) *n Brit.* a small iced cake made of puff pastry filled with jam and cream. [lit.: thousand leaves]

millefleurs (ˈmiːlˌflɜː) *n* (*functioning as sing*) a design of stylized floral patterns, used in textiles, paperweights, etc. [F: thousand flowers]

millenarian (ˌmɪlɪˈnɛərɪən) *adj* **1** of or relating to a thousand or to a thousand years. **2** of or relating to the millennium or millenarianism. ◆ *n* **3** an adherent of millenarianism.

millenarianism (ˌmɪlɪˈnɛərɪəˌnɪzəm) *n* **1** *Christianity.* the belief in a future millennium during which Christ will reign on earth: based on Revelation 20:1–5. **2** any belief in a future period of ideal peace and happiness.

millenary (mɪˈlɛnərɪ) *n, pl* **millenaries. 1** a sum or aggregate of one thousand. **2** another word for a **millennium.** ◆ *adj, n* **3** another word for **millenarian.** [C16: from LL *millēnārius* containing a thousand, from L *mille* thousand]

millennium (mɪˈlɛnɪəm) *n, pl* **millennia** (-nɪə) *or* **millenniums. 1 the.** *Christianity.* the period of a thousand years of Christ's awaited reign upon earth. **2** a period or cycle of one thousand years. **3** a time of peace and happiness, esp. in the distant future. [C17: from NL, from L *mille* thousand + *annus* year]
▸**milˈlennial** *adj* ▸**milˈlennialist** *n*

millennium bug *n Computing.* any software problem arising from the change in date at the start of the 21st century.

millepede (ˈmɪlɪˌpiːd) *or* **milleped** *n* variants of **millipede.**

millepore (ˈmɪlɪˌpɔː) *n* any of a genus of tropical colonial coral-like hydrozoans, having a calcareous skeleton. [C18: from NL, from L *mille* thousand + *porus* hole]

miller (ˈmɪlə) *n* **1** a person who keeps, operates, or works in a mill, esp. a corn mill. **2** another name for **milling machine. 3** a person who operates a milling machine.

miller's thumb *n* any of several small freshwater European fishes having a flattened body. [C15: from the alleged likeness of the fish's head to a thumb]

millesimal (mɪˈlɛsɪməl) *adj* **1a** denoting a thousandth. **1b** (*as n*): *a millesimal.* **2** of, consisting of, or relating to a thousandth. [C18: from L *millēsimus*]

millet (ˈmɪlɪt) *n* **1** a cereal grass cultivated for grain and animal fodder. **2a** an Indian annual grass cultivated for grain and forage, having pale round shiny seeds. **2b** the seed of this plant. **3** any of various similar or related grasses. [C14: via OF from L *milium*]

milli- *prefix* denoting 10^{-3}: *millimetre.* Symbol: m [from F, from L *mille* thousand]

milliard (ˈmɪlɪˌɑːd, ˈmɪljɑːd) *n Brit.* (no longer in technical use) a thousand million. US & Canad. equivalent: **billion.** [C19: from F]

millibar (ˈmɪlɪˌbɑː) *n* a cgs unit of atmospheric pressure equal to 10^{-3} bar, 100 newtons per square metre or 0.7500617 millimetre of mercury.

milligram *or* **milligramme** (ˈmɪlɪˌgræm) *n* one thousandth of a gram. [C19: from F]

millilitre *or US* **milliliter** (ˈmɪlɪˌliːtə) *n* one thousandth of a litre.

millimetre *or US* **millimeter** (ˈmɪlɪˌmiːtə) *n* one thousandth of a metre.

millimicron (ˈmɪlɪˌmaɪkrɒn) *n Obs.* one thousand-millionth of a metre; nanometre.

milliner (ˈmɪlɪnə) *n* a person who makes or sells women's hats. [C16: orig. *Milaner,* a native of *Milan,* at that time famous for its fancy goods]

millinery (ˈmɪlɪnərɪ, -ɪnrɪ) *n* **1** hats, trimmings, etc., sold by a milliner. **2** the business or shop of a milliner.

milling (ˈmɪlɪŋ) *n* **1** the act or process of grinding, pressing, or crushing in a mill. **2** the grooves or fluting on the edge of a coin, etc.

milling machine *n* a machine tool in which a horizontal arbor or vertical spindle rotates a cutting tool above a horizontal table.

million (ˈmɪljən) *n, pl* **millions** *or* **million. 1** the cardinal number that is the product of 1000 multiplied by 1000. **2** a numeral, 1 000 000, 10^6, $\overline{M}$, etc., representing this number. **3** (*often pl*) *Inf.* an extremely large but unspecified number or amount: *I have millions of things to do.* ◆ *determiner* **4** (preceded by *a* or by a numeral) **4a** amounting to a million: *a million light years.* **4b** (*as pron*): *I can see a million.* [C17: via OF from early It. *millione,* from *mille* thousand, from L]

millionaire (ˌmɪljəˈnɛə) *n* a person whose assets are worth at least a million of the standard monetary units of his or her country.
▸**ˌmillionˈairess** *fem n*

millionth (ˈmɪljənθ) *n* **1a** one of 1 000 000 equal parts of something. **1b** (*as modifier*): *a millionth part.* **2** one of 1 000 000 equal divisions of a scientific quantity. **3** the fraction one divided by 1 000 000. ◆ *adj* **4** (*usually prenominal*) **4a** being the ordinal number of 1 000 000 in numbering or counting order, etc. **4b** (*as n*): *the millionth to be manufactured.*

millipede, millepede (ˈmɪlɪˌpiːd), *or* **milleped** (ˈmɪlɪˌpɛd) *n* any of various terrestrial herbivorous arthropods, having a cylindrical segmented body, each segment of which bears two pairs of legs. [C17: from L, from *mille* thousand + *pēs* foot]

millisecond (ˈmɪlɪˌsɛkənd) *n* one thousandth of a second.

millpond (ˈmɪlˌpɒnd) *n* **1** a pool formed by damming a stream to provide water to turn a mill-wheel. **2** any expanse of calm water.

millrace (ˈmɪlˌreɪs) *or* **millrun** *n* **1** the current of water that turns a millwheel. **2** the channel for this water.

THESAURUS

weigh against *foll. by* **for** = **promote**, advance, aid, further, help

militia *n* **1, 2** = **reserve(s)**, fencibles (*History*), National Guard (*US*), Territorial Army (*Brit.*), trainband (*History*), yeomanry (*History*)

milk *vb* **5, 9** = **siphon**, drain, draw off, express, extract, let out, press, tap **8** = **exploit**, bleed, drain, extract, impose on, pump, take advantage of, use, wring

milk-and-water *adj* = **weak**, feeble, innocuous, insipid, jejune, nerdy *or* nurdy (*sl.*), vapid, weedy (*inf.*), wimpish *or* wimpy (*inf.*), wishy-washy (*inf.*)
Antonyms *adj* effective, energetic, forceful, healthy, strong

milksop *n* = **weakling**, chinless wonder (*Brit. inf.*), coward, dastard (*arch.*), jessie (*Scot. sl.*), namby-pamby, sissy, wimp (*inf.*)

milky *n* **1** = **white**, alabaster, clouded, cloudy, milk-white, opaque, whitish

mill *n* **2** = **factory**, foundry, plant, shop, works **3** = **grinder**, crusher ◆ *vb* **9** = **grind**, comminute, crush, granulate, grate, pound, powder, press, pulverize **13** = **swarm**, crowd, seethe, throng

Mills bomb (mɪlz) *n* a type of high-explosive hand grenade. [C20: after Sir William *Mills* (1856–1932), Brit. inventor]

millstone ❶ (ˈmɪlˌstəʊn) *n* **1** one of a pair of heavy flat disc-shaped stones that are rotated one against the other to grind grain. **2** a heavy burden, such as a responsibility or obligation.

millstream (ˈmɪlˌstriːm) *n* a stream of water used to turn a millwheel.

millwheel (ˈmɪlˌwiːl) *n* a wheel, esp. a waterwheel, that drives a mill.

millwork (ˈmɪlˌwɜːk) *n* work done in a mill.

millwright (ˈmɪlˌraɪt) *n* a person who designs, builds, or repairs grain mills or mill machinery.

milometer (maɪˈlɒmɪtə) *n* a variant spelling of **mileometer.**

milord (mɪˈlɔːd) *n* (formerly) a continental title used for an English gentleman. [C19: via F from E *my lord*]

milt (mɪlt) *n* **1** the testis of a fish. **2** the spermatozoa and seminal fluid produced by a fish. **3** *Rare.* the spleen, esp. of fowls and pigs. ◆ *vb* **4** to fertilize (fish roe) with milt, esp. artificially. [OE *milte* spleen; in the sense: fish sperm, prob. from MDu. *milte*]
▸**ˈmilter** *n*

mim (mɪm) *adj Dialect.* prim, modest, or demure. [C17: ? imit. of lip-pursing]

mime ❶ (maɪm) *n* **1** the theatrical technique of expressing an idea or mood or portraying a character entirely by gesture and bodily movement without the use of words. **2** Also called: **mime artist.** a performer specializing in this. **3** a dramatic presentation using such a technique. **4** (in the classical theatre) **4a** a comic performance with exaggerated gesture and physical action. **4b** an actor in such a performance. ◆ *vb* **mimes, miming, mimed. 5** to express (an idea, etc.) in actions or gestures without speech. **6** (of singers or musicians) to perform as if singing a song or playing a piece of music that is actually prerecorded. [OE *mīma,* from L *mīmus* mimic actor, from Gk *mimos* imitator]
▸**ˈmimer** *n*

Mimeograph (ˈmɪmɪəˌgrɑːf) *n* **1** *Trademark.* an office machine for printing multiple copies of text or line drawings from a stencil. **2** a copy produced by this. ◆ *vb* **3** to print copies from (a prepared stencil) using this machine.

mimesis (mɪˈmiːsɪs) *n* **1** *Art, literature.* the imitative representation of nature or human behaviour. **2** *Biol.* another name for **mimicry** (sense 2). **3** *Rhetoric.* representation of another person's alleged words in a speech. [C16: from Gk, from *mimeisthai* to imitate]

mimetic (mɪˈmetɪk) *adj* **1** of, resembling, or relating to mimesis or imitation, as in art, etc. **2** *Biol.* of or exhibiting mimicry.
▸**miˈmetically** *adv*

mimic ❶ (ˈmɪmɪk) *vb* **mimics, mimicking, mimicked.** (*tr*) **1** to imitate (a person, a manner, etc.), esp. for satirical effect; ape. **2** to take on the appearance of: *certain flies mimic wasps.* **3** to copy closely or in a servile manner. ◆ *n* **4** a person or an animal, such as a parrot, that is clever at mimicking. **5** an animal that displays mimicry. ◆ *adj* **6** of, relating to, or using mimicry. **7** simulated, make-believe, or mock. [C16: from L *mīmicus,* from Gk *mimikos,* from *mimos* MIME]
▸**ˈmimicker** *n*

mimicry ❶ (ˈmɪmɪkrɪ) *n, pl* **mimicries. 1** the act or art of copying or imitating closely; mimicking. **2** the resemblance shown by one animal species to another, which protects it from predators.

MIMinE *abbrev. for* Member of the Institute of Mining Engineers.

mimosa (mɪˈməʊsə, -zə) *n* any of various tropical shrubs or trees having ball-like clusters of typically yellow flowers and leaves that are often sensitive to touch or light. See also **sensitive plant.** [C18: from NL, prob. from L *mīmus* MIME, because the plant's sensitivity to touch imitates the similar reaction of animals]

mimulus (ˈmɪmjʊləs) *n* any of a genus of flowering plants of temperate regions. See **monkey flower.** [C19: Med. L, from L *mimus* MIME, alluding to masklike flowers]

min. *abbrev. for:* **1** mineralogy. **2** minimum. **3** mining. **4** minute *or* minutes.

Min. *abbrev. for:* **1** Minister. **2** Ministry.

minaret (ˌmɪnəˈret, ˈmɪnəˌret) *n* a slender tower of a mosque having one or more balconies. [C17: from F, from Turkish, from Ar. *manārat* lamp, from *nār* fire]
▸**ˌminaˈreted** *adj*

minatory (ˈmɪnətərɪ, -trɪ) *or* **minatorial** *adj* threatening or menacing. [C16: from LL *minātōrius,* from L *minārī* to threaten]

mince ❶ (mɪns) *vb* **minces, mincing, minced. 1** (*tr*) to chop, grind, or cut into very small pieces. **2** (*tr*) to soften or moderate: *I didn't mince my words.* **3** (*intr*) to walk or speak in an affected dainty manner. ◆ *n* **4** *Chiefly Brit.* minced meat. [C14: from OF *mincier,* ult. from LL *minūtia;* see MINUTIAE]
▸**ˈmincer** *n*

mincemeat (ˈmɪnsˌmiːt) *n* **1** a mixture of dried fruit, spices, etc., used esp. for filling pies. **2 make mincemeat of.** *Inf.* to defeat completely.

mince pie *n* a small round pastry tart filled with mincemeat.

mincing ❶ (ˈmɪnsɪŋ) *adj* (of a person) affectedly elegant in gait, manner, or speech.
▸**ˈmincingly** *adv*

mind ❶ (maɪnd) *n* **1** the human faculty to which are ascribed thought, feelings, intention, etc. **2** intelligence or the intellect, esp. as opposed to feelings or wishes. **3** recollection or remembrance: *it comes to mind.* **4** the faculty of original or creative thought; imagination: *it's all in the mind.* **5** a person considered as an intellectual being: *great minds.* **6** condition, state, or manner of feeling or thought: *his state of mind.* **7** an inclination, desire, or purpose: *I have a mind to go.* **8** attention or thoughts: *keep your mind on your work.* **9** a sound mental state; sanity (esp. in **out of one's mind**). **10** (in Cartesian philosophy) one of two basic modes of existence, the other being matter. **11 blow someone's mind.** *Sl.* **11a** (of a drug) to alter someone's mental state. **11b** to astound or surprise someone. **12 change one's mind.** to alter one's decision or opinion. **13 in** *or* **of two minds.** undecided; wavering. **14 give (someone) a piece of one's mind.** to criticize or censure (someone) frankly or vehemently. **15 make up one's mind.** to decide (something or to do something). **16 on one's mind.** in one's thoughts. ◆ *vb* **17** (when *tr, may take a clause as object*) to take offence at: *do you mind if I smoke?* **18** to pay attention to (something); heed; notice: *to mind one's own business.* **19** (*tr; takes a clause as object*) to make certain; ensure: *mind you tell her.* **20** (*tr*) to take care of; have charge of: *to mind the shop.* **21** (when *tr, may take a clause as object*) to be cautious or careful about (something): *mind how you go.* **22** (*tr*) to obey (someone or something); heed: *mind your father!* **23** to be concerned (about); be troubled (about): *never mind about your hat.* **24** (*tr; passive; takes an infinitive*) to be intending or inclined (to do something): *clearly he was not minded to finish the story.* **25 mind you.** an expression qualifying a previous statement: *Dogs are nice. Mind you, I don't like all dogs.* ◆ Related adj: **mental.** ◆ See also **mind out.** [OE *gemynd* mind]

mind-bending *adj Inf.* **1** Also: **mind-blowing.** altering one's state of consciousness, esp. as a result of taking drugs. **2** reaching the limit of credibility: *they offered a mind-bending salary.* ◆ *n* **3** the process of brainwashing.

mind-boggling *adj Inf.* astonishing; bewildering.

minded (ˈmaɪndɪd) *adj* **1** having a mind, inclination, intention, etc., as specified: *politically minded.* **2** (*in combination*): *money-minded.*

minder (ˈmaɪndə) *n* **1** someone who looks after someone or something. **2** short for **childminder. 3** *Sl.* an aide to someone in public life who keeps control of press and public relations. **4** *Sl.* someone acting as a bodyguard or assistant, esp. in the criminal underworld.

mindful ❶ (ˈmaɪndfʊl) *adj* (usually *postpositive* and foll. by *of*) keeping aware; heedful: *mindful of your duty.*
▸**ˈmindfully** *adv* ▸**ˈmindfulness** *n*

mindless ❶ (ˈmaɪndlɪs) *adj* **1** stupid or careless. **2** requiring little or no intellectual effort.
▸**ˈmindlessly** *adv* ▸**ˈmindlessness** *n*

mind-numbing *adj* extremely boring and uninspiring.
▸**ˈmind-ˌnumbingly** *adv*

mind out ❶ *vb* (*intr, adv*) *Brit.* to be careful or pay attention.

THESAURUS

millstone *n* **1 = grindstone,** quernstone **2 = burden,** affliction, albatross, dead weight, drag, encumbrance, load, weight

mime *n* **1 = dumb show,** gesture, mummery, pantomime ◆ *vb* **5 = act out,** gesture, pantomime, represent, simulate

mimic *vb* **1 = imitate,** ape, caricature, do (*inf.*), impersonate, parody, take off (*inf.*) **2 = resemble,** echo, look like, mirror, simulate, take on the appearance of ◆ *n* **4 = imitator,** caricaturist, copycat (*inf.*), impersonator, impressionist, parodist, parrot ◆ *adj* **6, 7 = imitative,** echoic, imitation, make-believe, mimetic, mock, sham, simulated

mimicry *n* **1 = imitation,** apery, burlesque, caricature, copying, imitating, impersonation, impression, mimicking, mockery, parody, take-off (*inf.*)

mince *vb* **1 = cut,** chop, crumble, grind, hash **2** *As in* **mince one's words = tone down,** diminish, euphemize, extenuate, hold back, moderate, palliate, soften, spare, weaken **3 = posture,** attitudinize, give oneself airs, ponce (*sl.*), pose

mincing *adj* **= affected,** arty-farty (*inf.*), camp (*inf.*), dainty, effeminate, foppish, lah-di-dah (*inf.*), nice, niminy-piminy, poncy (*sl.*), precious, pretentious, sissy

mind *n* **1 = brain,** head, imagination, psyche **2 = intelligence,** brain(s), grey matter (*inf.*), intellect, mentality, ratiocination, reason, sense, spirit, understanding, wits **3 = memory,** recollection, remembrance **5 = thinker,** brain, brainbox, genius, intellect, intellectual **6 = attitude,** belief, feeling, judgment, opinion, outlook, point of view, sentiment, thoughts, view, way of thinking **7 = intention,** bent, desire, disposition, fancy, inclination, leaning, notion, purpose, tendency, urge, will, wish **8 = attention,** concentration, thinking, thoughts **9 = sanity,** judgment, marbles (*inf.*), mental balance, rationality, reason, senses, wits **13 in** *or* of two minds **= undecided,** dithering (*chiefly Brit.*), hesitant, shillyshallying (*inf.*), swithering (*Scot.*), uncertain, unsure, vacillating, wavering **15 make up one's mind = decide,** choose, come to a decision, determine, make a decision, reach a decision, resolve, settle ◆ *vb* **17 = take offence,** be affronted, be bothered, care, disapprove, dislike, look askance at, object, resent **18, 22 = pay attention,** adhere to, attend, comply with, follow, heed, listen to, mark, note, notice, obey, observe, pay heed to, regard, respect, take heed, watch **19 = be sure,** ensure, make certain **20 = guard,** attend to, have charge of, keep an eye on, look after, take care of, tend, watch **21 = be careful,** be cautious, be on (one's) guard, be wary, take care, watch

mindful *adj* **= aware,** alert, alive to, attentive, careful, chary, cognizant, conscious, heedful, regardful, respectful, sensible, thoughtful, wary, watchful
Antonyms *adj* heedless, inattentive, incautious, mindless, oblivious, thoughtless, unaware

mindless *adj* **1 = unthinking,** asinine, braindead (*inf.*), brutish, careless, foolish, forgetful, gratuitous, heedless, idiotic, imbecilic, inane, inattentive, moronic, neglectful, negligent, oblivious, obtuse, stupid, thoughtless, unintel-

mind-reader *n* a person seemingly able to discern the thoughts of another.
▸ **'mind-,reading** *n*
mind-set *n* the ideas and attitudes with which a person approaches a situation, esp. when these are seen as being difficult to alter.
mind's eye ❶ *n* the visual memory or the imagination.
mine[1] (maɪn) *pron* **1** something or someone belonging to or associated with me: *mine is best.* **2 of mine.** belonging to or associated with me. ◆ *determiner* **3** (*preceding a vowel*) an archaic word for **my:** *mine eyes; mine host.* [OE *mīn*]
mine[2] ❶ (maɪn) *n* **1** a system of excavations made for the extraction of minerals, esp. coal, ores, or precious stones. **2** any deposit of ore or minerals. **3** a lucrative source or abundant supply: *a mine of information.* **4** a device containing explosive designed to destroy ships, vehicles, or personnel, usually laid beneath the ground or in water. **5** a tunnel dug to undermine a fortification, etc. ◆ *vb* **mines, mining, mined. 6** to dig into (the earth) for (minerals). **7** to make (a hole, tunnel, etc.) by digging or boring. **8** to place explosive mines in position below the surface of (the sea or land). **9** to undermine (a fortification, etc.) by digging mines. **10** another word for **undermine.** [C13: from OF, prob. of Celtic origin]
mine detector *n* an instrument designed to detect explosive mines.
▸ **mine detection** *n*
mine dump *n S. African.* a large mound of residue esp. from gold-mining operations.
minefield ('maɪn,fi:ld) *n* **1** an area of ground or water containing explosive mines. **2** a subject, situation, etc., beset with hidden problems.
minelayer ('maɪn,leɪə) *n* a warship or aircraft designed for the carrying and laying of mines.
miner ❶ ('maɪnə) *n* **1** a person who works in a mine. **2** any of various insects or insect larvae that bore into and feed on plant tissues. See also **leaf miner. 3** *Austral.* any of several honeyeaters.
mineral ('mɪnərəl, 'mɪnrəl) *n* **1** any of a class of naturally occurring solid inorganic substances with a characteristic crystalline form and a homogeneous chemical composition. **2** any inorganic matter. **3** any substance obtained by mining, esp. a metal ore. **4** (*often pl*) *Brit.* short for **mineral water. 5** *Brit.* a soft drink containing carbonated water and flavourings. ◆ *adj* **6** of, relating to, containing, or resembling minerals. [C15: from Med. L *minerāle* (n), from *minerālis* (adj); rel. to *minera* mine, ore, from ?]
mineral. *abbrev. for* mineralogy *or* mineralogical.
mineralize *or* **mineralise** ('mɪnərə,laɪz) *vb* **mineralizes, mineralizing, mineralized** *or* **mineralises, mineralising, mineralised.** (*tr*) **1a** to impregnate (organic matter, water, etc.) with a mineral substance. **1b** to convert (such matter) into a mineral; petrify. **2** (of gases, vapours, etc., in magma) to transform (a metal) into an ore.
▸ **,minerali'zation** *or* **,minerali'sation** *n* ▸ **'mineral,izer** *or* **'mineral,iser** *n*
mineralogy (,mɪnə'rælədʒɪ) *n* the branch of geology concerned with the study of minerals.
▸ **mineralogical** (,mɪnərə'lɒdʒɪkᵊl) *or* **,minera'logic** *adj* ▸ **,miner'alogist** *n*
mineral oil *n Brit.* any oil of mineral origin, esp. petroleum.
mineral water *n* water containing dissolved mineral salts or gases, usually having medicinal properties.
mineral wool *n* a fibrous material made by blowing steam or air through molten slag and used for packing and insulation.
miner's right *n Austral.* a licence to prospect for and mine gold, etc.
minestrone (,mɪnɪ'strəʊnɪ) *n* a soup made from a variety of vegetables and pasta. [from It., from *minestrare* to serve]
minesweeper ('maɪn,swi:pə) *n* a naval vessel equipped to clear mines.
▸ **'mine,sweeping** *n*
Ming (mɪŋ) *n* **1** the imperial dynasty of China from 1368 to 1644. ◆ *adj* **2** of or relating to Chinese porcelain from the Ming dynasty.
mingle ❶ ('mɪŋgᵊl) *vb* **mingles, mingling, mingled. 1** to mix or cause to mix. **2** (*intr; often foll. by with*) to come into close association. [C15: from OE *mengan* to mix]
▸ **'mingler** *n*
mingy ('mɪndʒɪ) *adj* **mingier, mingiest.** *Brit. inf.* miserly, stingy, or niggardly. [C20: prob. a blend of MEAN[2] + STINGY[1]]
mini ('mɪnɪ) *adj* **1** (of a woman's dress, skirt, etc.) very short; thigh-length. **2** (*prenominal*) small; miniature. ◆ *n, pl* **minis. 3** something very small of its kind, esp. a small car or a miniskirt.
mini- *combining form.* smaller or shorter than the standard size: *minibus; miniskirt.* [C20: from MINIATURE & MINIMUM]
miniature ❶ ('mɪnɪtʃə) *n* **1** a model, copy, or representation on a very small scale. **2** anything that is very small of its kind. **3** a very small painting, esp. a portrait. **4** an illuminated decoration in a manuscript. **5 in miniature.** on a small scale. ◆ *adj* **6** greatly reduced in size, etc. **7** on a small scale; minute. [C16: from It., from Med. L, from *miniāre* to paint red (in illuminating manuscripts), from *minium* red lead]
▸ **'miniaturist** *n*
miniaturize *or* **miniaturise** ('mɪnɪtʃə,raɪz) *vb* **miniaturizes, miniaturizing, miniaturized** *or* **miniaturises, miniaturising, miniaturised.** (*tr*) to make or construct (something, esp. electronic equipment) on a very small scale; reduce in size.
▸ **,miniaturi'zation** *or* **,miniaturi'sation** *n*
minibar ('mɪnɪ,bɑ:) *n* a selection of drinks and confectionery provided in a hotel room and charged to the guest's bill if used.
minibus ('mɪnɪ,bʌs) *n* a small bus able to carry approximately ten passengers.
minicab ('mɪnɪ,kæb) *n Brit.* a small saloon car used as a taxi.
minicomputer (,mɪnɪkəm'pju:tə) *n* a small comparatively cheap digital computer.
minim ('mɪnɪm) *n* **1** a unit of fluid measure equal to one sixtieth of a drachm. It is approximately equal to one drop. Symbol: **M 2.** *Music.* a note having the time value of half a semibreve. **3** a small or insignificant thing. **4** a downward stroke in calligraphy. [C15 (*Music.*): from L *minimus* smallest]
minimal art *n* abstract painting or sculpture in which expressiveness and illusion are minimized by the use of simple geometric shapes, flat colour, and arrangements of ordinary objects.
▸ **minimal artist** *n*
minimalism ('mɪnɪmə,lɪzəm) *n* **1** another name for **minimal art. 2** a type of music based on simple elements and avoiding elaboration or embellishment. **3** design or style in which the simplest and fewest elements are used to create the maximum effect.
▸ **'minimalist** *adj, n*
minimax ('mɪnɪ,mæks) *n* **1** *Maths.* the lowest of a set of maximum values. **2** (in game theory, etc.) the procedure of choosing the strategy that least benefits the most advantaged member of a group. Cf. **maximin.** [C20: from MINI(MUM) + MAX(IMUM)]
minimize ❶ *or* **minimise** ('mɪnɪ,maɪz) *vb* **minimizes, minimizing, minimized** *or* **minimises, minimising, minimised.** (*tr*) **1** to reduce to or estimate at the least possible degree or amount. **2** to rank or treat at less than the true worth; belittle.
▸ **,minimi'zation** *or* **,minimi'sation** *n* ▸ **'mini,mizer** *or* **'mini,miser** *n*
minimum ❶ ('mɪnɪməm) *n, pl* **minimums** *or* **minima** (-mə). **1** the least possible amount, degree, or quantity. **2** the least amount recorded, allowed, or reached. **3** (*modifier*) being the least possible, recorded, allowed, etc.: *minimum age.* ◆ *adj* **4** of or relating to a minimum or minimums. [C17: from L: smallest thing, from *minimus* least]
▸ **'minimal** *adj* ▸ **'minimally** *adv*
minimum lending rate *n* (in Britain) the minimum rate at which the Bank of England would lend to discount houses between 1971 and 1981, after which it was replaced by the less formal base rate.
minimum wage *n* the lowest wage that an employer is permitted to pay by law or union contract.
mining ('maɪnɪŋ) *n* **1** the act, process, or industry of extracting coal, ores, etc., from the earth. **2** *Mil.* the process of laying mines.
minion ❶ ('mɪnjən) *n* **1** a favourite or dependant, esp. a servile or fawning one. **2** a servile agent. [C16: from F *mignon,* from OF *mignot,* of Gaulish origin]
minipill ('mɪnɪ,pɪl) *n* a low-dose oral contraceptive containing progesterone only.
miniseries ('mɪnɪ,sɪəri:z) *n, pl* **miniseries.** a television programme in several parts that is shown on consecutive days for a short period.
miniskirt ('mɪnɪ,skɜ:t) *n* a very short skirt, originally in the 1960s, one at least four inches above the knee. Often shortened to **mini.**

THESAURUS

ligent, unmindful, witless **2** = **mechanical,** automatic, brainless
Antonyms *adj* ≠ **unthinking:** attentive, aware, considerate, intelligent, mindful, reasonable, reasoning, sane, sensitive, thinking
mind out *vb Brit* = **be careful,** be on one's guard, beware, keep one's eyes open, look out, pay attention, take care, watch
mind's eye *n* = **imagination,** head, memory, mind, recollection, remembrance
mine[2] *n* **1, 2** = **pit,** coalfield, colliery, deposit, excavation, lode, shaft, vein **3** = **source,** abundance, fund, hoard, reserve, stock, store, supply, treasury, wealth ◆ *vb* **6, 7** = **dig up,** delve, dig for, excavate, extract, hew, quarry, unearth **8** = **lay mines in** *or* **under,** sow with mines **10** = **tunnel,** sap, subvert, undermine, weaken
miner *n* **1** = **coalminer,** collier (*Brit.*), pitman (*Brit.*)
mingle *vb* **1** = **mix,** admix, alloy, blend, coalesce, combine, commingle, compound, intermingle, intermix, interweave, join, marry, meld, merge, unite **2** = **associate,** circulate, consort, fraternize, hang about *or* around, hang out (*inf.*), hobnob, rub shoulders (*inf.*), socialize
Antonyms *vb* ≠ **mix:** detach, dissolve, divide, part, separate ≠ **associate:** avoid, dissociate, estrange
miniature *adj* **6, 7** = **small,** baby, diminutive, dwarf, Lilliputian, little, midget, mini, minuscule, minute, pocket, pygmy *or* pigmy, reduced, scaled-down, teensy-weensy, teeny-weeny, tiny, toy, wee
Antonyms *adj* big, enlarged, enormous, giant, gigantic, ginormous (*inf.*), great, huge, immense, large, mega (*sl.*), oversize
minimal *adj* **1, 2** = **minimum,** least, least possible, littlest, nominal, slightest, smallest, token
minimize *vb* **1** = **reduce,** abbreviate, attenuate, curtail, decrease, diminish, downsize, miniaturize, prune, shrink **2** = **play down,** belittle, decry, deprecate, depreciate, discount, disparage, make light *or* little of, underestimate, underrate
Antonyms *vb* ≠ **reduce:** augment, enlarge, expand, extend, heighten, increase, magnify ≠ **play down:** boast about, elevate, enhance, exalt, praise, vaunt
minimum *n* **1, 2** = **least,** bottom, depth, lowest, nadir, slightest ◆ *adj* **4** = **least,** least possible, littlest, lowest, minimal, slightest, smallest
Antonyms *adj* ≠ **least:** greatest, highest, largest, maximum, most
minion *n* **1, 2** = **follower,** bootlicker, cohort (*chiefly US*), creature, darling, dependant, favourite, flatterer, flunky, hanger-on, henchman, hireling, lackey, lickspittle, myrmidon, parasite, pet, sycophant, toady, underling, yes man

minister Ⓣ ('mɪnɪstə) *n* **1** (esp. in Presbyterian and some Nonconformist Churches) a member of the clergy. **2** a head of a government department. **3** any diplomatic agent accredited to a foreign government or head of state. **4** Also called: **minister plenipotentiary.** another term for **envoy**[1] (sense 1). **5** Also called: **minister resident.** a diplomat ranking after an envoy. **6** a person who attends to the needs of others, esp. in religious matters. **7** a person who acts as the agent or servant of a person or thing. ◆ *vb* **8** (*intr;* often foll. by *to*) to attend to the needs (of); take care (of). **9** (*tr*) *Arch.* to provide; supply. [C13: via OF from L: servant; rel. to *minus* less]

ministerial (ˌmɪnɪ'stɪərɪəl) *adj* **1** of or relating to a minister of religion or his office. **2** of or relating to a government minister or ministry. **3** (*often cap.*) of or supporting the ministry against the opposition. **4** *Law.* relating to or possessing delegated executive authority. **5** acting as an agent or cause; instrumental.
▸ˌ**minis'terially** *adv*

minister of state *n* **1** (in the British Parliament) a minister, usually below cabinet rank, appointed to assist a senior minister. **2** any government minister.

Minister of the Crown *n Brit.* any Government minister of cabinet rank.

minister plenipotentiary *n, pl* **ministers plenipotentiary.** another term for **envoy**[1] (sense 1).

ministrant ('mɪnɪstrənt) *adj* **1** ministering or serving as a minister. ◆ *n* **2** a person who ministers. [C17: from L *ministrans,* from *ministrāre* to wait upon]

ministration Ⓣ (ˌmɪnɪ'streɪʃən) *n* **1** the act or an instance of serving or giving aid. **2** the act or an instance of ministering religiously. [C14: from L *ministrātiō,* from *ministrāre* to wait upon]
▸**ministrative** ('mɪnɪstrətɪv) *adj*

ministry Ⓣ ('mɪnɪstrɪ) *n, pl* **ministries. 1a** the profession or duties of a minister of religion. **1b** the performance of these duties. **2** ministers of religion or government ministers considered collectively. **3** the tenure of a minister. **4a** a government department headed by a minister. **4b** the buildings of such a department. [C14: from L *ministerium* service; see MINISTER]

miniver ('mɪnɪvə) *n* white fur, used in ceremonial costumes. [C13: from OF *menu vair,* from *menu* small + *vair* variegated fur]

mink (mɪŋk) *n, pl* **mink** *or* **minks. 1** any of several mammals of Europe, Asia, and North America, having slightly webbed feet. **2** their highly valued fur, esp. that of the American mink. **3** a garment made of this, esp. a woman's coat or stole. [C15: from ON]

minneola (ˌmɪnɪ'əʊlə) *n* a juicy citrus fruit that is a cross between a tangerine and a grapefruit. [C20: ?from *Mineola,* Texas]

minnesinger ('mɪnɪˌsɪŋə) *n* one of the German lyric poets and musicians of the 12th to 14th centuries. [C19: from G *Minnesinger* love-singer]

minnow ('mɪnəʊ) *n, pl* **minnows** *or* **minnow. 1** a small slender European freshwater cyprinid fish. **2** a small or insignificant person. [C15: rel. to OE *myne* minnow]

Minoan (mɪ'nəʊən) *adj* **1** of or denoting the Bronze Age culture of Crete from about 3000 B.C. to about 1100 B.C. ◆ *n* **2** a Cretan belonging to the Minoan culture. [C19: after *Minos* in Gk myth, king of Crete, from the excavations of his supposed palace at Knossos]

minor Ⓣ ('maɪnə) *adj* **1** lesser or secondary in amount, importance, etc. **2** of or relating to the minority. **3** below the age of legal majority. **4** *Music.* **4a** (of a scale) having a semitone between the second and third and fifth and sixth degrees (**natural minor**). **4b** (of a key) based on the minor scale. **4c** (*postpositive*) denoting a specified key based on the minor scale: *C minor.* **4d** (of an interval) reduced by a semitone from the major. **4e** (of a chord, esp. a triad) having a minor third above the root. **f.** (esp. in jazz) of or relating to a chord built upon a minor triad and containing a minor seventh: *a minor ninth.* **5** *Logic.* (of a term or premise) having less generality or scope than another term or proposition. **6** *US education.* of or relating to an additional secondary subject taken by a student. **7** (*immediately postpositive*) *Brit.* the younger or junior: sometimes used after the surname of a schoolboy if he has an older brother in the same school. ◆ *n* **8** a person or thing that is lesser or secondary. **9** a person below the age of legal majority. **10** *US & Canad. education.* a subsidiary subject. **11** *Music.* a minor key, chord, mode, or scale. **12** *Logic.* a minor term or premise. ◆ *vb* **13** (*intr;* usually foll. by *in*) *US education.* to take a minor. [C13: from L: less, smaller]

minor axis *n* the shorter or shortest axis of an ellipse or ellipsoid.

minority (maɪ'nɒrɪtɪ, mɪ-) *n, pl* **minorities. 1** the smaller of two parts, factions, or groups. **2** a group that is different racially, politically, etc., from a larger group of which it is a part. **3a** the state of being a minor. **3b** the period during which a person is below legal age. **4** (*modifier*) relating to or being a minority: *a minority opinion.* [C16: from Med. L *minōritās,* from L MINOR]

minor league *n US & Canad.* any professional league in baseball other than a major league.

minor orders *pl n RC Church.* the four lower degrees of holy orders, namely porter, exorcist, lector, and acolyte.

minor premise *n Logic.* the premise of a syllogism containing the subject of its conclusion.

minor term *n Logic.* the subject of the conclusion of a syllogism.

minster ('mɪnstə) *n Brit.* any of certain cathedrals and large churches, usually originally connected to a monastery. [OE *mynster,* prob. from Vulgar L *monisterium* (unattested), var. of Church L *monastērium* MONASTERY]

minstrel Ⓣ ('mɪnstrəl) *n* **1** a medieval musician who performed songs or recited poetry with instrumental accompaniment. **2** a performer in a minstrel show. **3** *Arch. or poetic.* any poet, musician, or singer. [C13: from OF *menestral,* from LL *ministeriālis* an official, from L MINISTER]

minstrel show *n* a theatrical entertainment consisting of songs, dances, etc., performed by actors wearing black face make-up.

minstrelsy ('mɪnstrəlsɪ) *n, pl* **minstrelsies. 1** the art of a minstrel. **2** the poems, music, or songs of a minstrel. **3** a troupe of minstrels.

mint[1] (mɪnt) *n* **1** any N temperate plant of a genus having aromatic leaves. The leaves of some species are used for seasoning and flavouring. See also **peppermint, spearmint. 2** a sweet flavoured with mint. [OE *minte,* from L *mentha,* from Gk *minthē*]
▸'**minty** *adj*

mint[2] Ⓣ (mɪnt) *n* **1** a place where money is coined by governmental authority. **2** a very large amount of money. ◆ *adj* **3** (of coins, postage stamps, etc.) in perfect condition as issued. **4 in mint condition.** in perfect condition; as if new. ◆ *vb* **5** to make (coins) by stamping metal. **6** (*tr*) to invent (esp. phrases or words). [OE *mynet* coin, from L *monēta* money, mint, from the temple of Juno *Monēta,* used as a mint in ancient Rome]
▸'**minter** *n*

mintage ('mɪntɪdʒ) *n* **1** the process of minting. **2** the money minted. **3** a fee paid for minting a coin. **4** an official impression stamped on a coin.

mint julep *n Chiefly US.* a long drink consisting of bourbon whiskey, crushed ice, sugar, and sprigs of mint.

minuend ('mɪnjʊˌend) *n* the number from which another number, the **subtrahend,** is to be subtracted. [C18: from L *minuendus* (*numerus*) (the number) to be diminished]

minuet (ˌmɪnjʊ'ɛt) *n* **1** a stately court dance of the 17th and 18th centuries in triple time. **2** a piece of music composed for or in the rhythm of this dance. [C17: from F *menuet* dainty, from *menu* small]

minus ('maɪnəs) *prep* **1** reduced by the subtraction of: *four minus two* (written 4 – 2). **2** *Inf.* deprived of; lacking: *minus the trimmings.* ◆ *adj* **3a** indicating or involving subtraction: *a minus sign.* **3b** Also: **negative.** having a value or designating a quantity less than zero: *a minus number.* **4** involving a disadvantage, harm, etc.: *a minus factor.* **5** (*postpositive*) *Education.* slightly below the standard of a particular grade: *a B minus.* **6** denoting a negative electric charge. ◆ *n* **7** short for **minus sign. 8** a negative quantity. **9** a disadvantage, loss, or deficit. **10** *Inf.* something detrimental or negative. ◆ Mathematical symbol: – [C15: from L, neuter of MINOR]

minuscule Ⓣ ('mɪnəˌskjuːl) *n* **1** a lower-case letter. **2** writing using such letters. **3** a small cursive 7th-century style of lettering. ◆ *adj* **4** relating to, printed in, or written in small letters. Cf. **majuscule. 5** very small. **6** (of letters) lower-case. [C18: from F, from L (*littera*) *minuscula* very small (letter), dim. of MINOR]
▸**minuscular** (mɪ'nʌskjʊlə) *adj*

minus sign *n* the symbol –, indicating subtraction or a negative quantity.

minute[1] Ⓣ ('mɪnɪt) *n* **1** a period of time equal to 60 seconds; one sixtieth of an hour. **2** Also called: **minute of arc.** a unit of angular measure equal to one sixtieth of a degree. Symbol: ′. **3** any very short period of time; moment. **4** a short note or memorandum. **5** the distance that can be travelled in a minute: *it's only two minutes away.* **6 up to the minute** (**up-to-the-minute** *when prenominal*). the very latest or newest. ◆ *vb* **minutes, minuting, minuted.** (*tr*) **7** to record in minutes: *to minute a meeting.* **8**

THESAURUS

minister *n* **1** = **clergyman,** chaplain, churchman, cleric, divine, ecclesiastic, padre (*inf.*), parson, pastor, preacher, priest, rector, vicar **2, 3** = **official,** administrator, ambassador, cabinet member, delegate, diplomat, envoy, executive, office-holder, plenipotentiary **7** = **assistant,** agent, aide, lieutenant, servant, subordinate, underling ◆ *vb* **8** = **attend,** accommodate, administer, answer, be solicitous of, cater to, pander to, serve, take care of, tend

ministration *n* **1** = **help,** aid, assistance, favour, patronage, relief, service, succour, support

ministry *n* **1** = **the priesthood,** holy orders, the church, the pulpit **4a** = **department,** administration, bureau, cabinet, council, government, office, quango

minor *adj* **1, 7** = **small,** inconsequential, inconsiderable, inferior, insignificant, junior, lesser, light, negligible, nickel-and-dime (*US sl.*), paltry, petty, secondary, slight, smaller, subordinate, trifling, trivial, unimportant, younger
Antonyms *adj* appreciable, consequential, considerable, essential, grand, great, heavy, important, major, profound, serious, significant, substantial, superior, vital, weighty

minstrel *n* **1-3** = **musician,** bard, harper, jongleur, singer, songstress, troubadour

mint[2] *n* **2** = **fortune,** bomb (*Brit. sl.*), bundle (*sl.*), heap (*inf.*), King's ransom, million, packet (*sl.*), pile (*inf.*) ◆ *adj* **3** = **perfect,** brand-new, excellent, first-class, fresh, unblemished, undamaged, untarnished ◆ *vb* **5** = **make,** cast, coin, produce, punch, stamp, strike **6** = **invent,** coin, construct, devise, fabricate, fashion, forge, make up, produce, think up

minuscule *adj* **6** = **tiny,** diminutive, fine, infinitesimal, Lilliputian, little, microscopic, miniature, minute, teensy-weensy, teeny-weeny, very small

minute[1] *n* **1** = **sixty seconds,** sixtieth of an hour **3** = **moment,** flash, instant, jiffy (*inf.*), second, shake (*inf.*), tick (*Brit. inf.*), trice **6 up to the minute** = **latest,** all the rage, in, modish, (most) fashionable, newest, now (*inf.*), smart, stylish,

to time in terms of minutes. ◆ See also **minutes.** [C14: from OF, from Med. L *minūta,* n. use of L *minūtus* MINUTE[2]]
▸**minutely** ('mɪnɪtlɪ) *adv*

minute[2] Ⓣ (maɪ'nju:t) *adj* **1** very small; diminutive; tiny. **2** unimportant; petty. **3** precise or detailed. [C15: from L *minūtus,* p.p. of *minuere* to diminish]
▸**mi'nuteness** *n* ▸**mi'nutely** *adv*

minute gun ('mɪnɪt) *n* a gun fired at one-minute intervals as a sign of distress or mourning.

minute hand ('mɪnɪt) *n* the pointer on a timepiece that indicates minutes.

Minuteman ('mɪnɪt,mæn) *n, pl* **Minutemen. 1** (*sometimes not cap.*) (in the War of American Independence) a colonial militiaman who promised to be ready to fight at one minute's notice. **2** a US three-stage intercontinental ballistic missile.

minutes Ⓣ ('mɪnɪts) *pl n* an official record of the proceedings of a meeting, conference, etc.

minute steak ('mɪnɪt) *n* a small piece of steak that can be cooked quickly.

minutiae Ⓣ (mɪ'nju:ʃɪ,i:) *pl n, sing* **minutia** (-ʃɪə). small, precise, or trifling details. [C18: pl of LL *minūtia* smallness, from L *minūtus* MINUTE[2]]

minx Ⓣ (mɪŋks) *n* a bold, flirtatious, or scheming woman. [C16: from ?]

Miocene ('maɪə,si:n) *adj* **1** of or denoting the fourth epoch of the Tertiary period. ◆ *n* **2 the.** this epoch or rock series. [C19: Gk *meiōn* less + -CENE]

miosis *or* **myosis** (maɪ'əʊsɪs) *n, pl* **mioses** (-si:z) *or* **myoses. 1** excessive contraction of the pupil of the eye. **2** a variant spelling of **meiosis** (sense 1). [C20: from Gk *muein* to shut the eyes + -OSIS]
▸**miotic** *or* **myotic** (maɪ'ɒtɪk) *adj, n*

MIP *abbrev. for:* **1** monthly investment plan. **2** maximum investment plan: an endowment assurance policy designed to produce maximum profits.

Mir (mɪə) *n* the Russian (formerly Soviet) orbiting space station. [Russian]

miracle Ⓣ ('mɪrək^{ə}l) *n* **1** an event contrary to the laws of nature and attributed to a supernatural cause. **2** any amazing or wonderful event. **3** a marvellous example of something: *a miracle of engineering.* **4** short for **miracle play. 5** (*modifier*) being or seeming a miracle: *a miracle cure.* [C12: from L *mīrāculum,* from *mīrārī* to wonder at]

miracle play *n* a medieval play based on a biblical story or the life of a saint. Cf. **mystery play.**

miraculous Ⓣ (mɪ'rækjʊləs) *adj* **1** of, like, or caused by a miracle; marvellous. **2** surprising. **3** having the power to work miracles.
▸**mi'raculously** *adv* ▸**mi'raculousness** *n*

mirage Ⓣ (mɪ'rɑ:ʒ) *n* **1** an image of a distant object or sheet of water, often inverted or distorted, caused by atmospheric refraction by hot air. **2** something illusory. [C19: from F, from (*se*) *mirer* to be reflected]

mire Ⓣ ('maɪə) *n* **1** a boggy or marshy area. **2** mud, muck, or dirt. ◆ *vb* **mires, miring, mired. 3** to sink or cause to sink in a mire. **4** (*tr*) to make dirty or muddy. **5** (*tr*) to involve, esp. in difficulties. [C14: from ON *mýrr*]

mirepoix (mɪə'pwɑ:) *n* a mixture of sautéed root vegetables used as a base for braising meat or for various sauces. [F, prob. after Duke of *Mirepoix,* 18th-cent. F general]

mirk (mɜ:k) *n* a variant spelling of **murk.**
▸**'mirky** *adj* ▸**'mirkily** *adv* ▸**'mirkiness** *n*

mirror Ⓣ ('mɪrə) *n* **1** a surface, such as polished metal or glass coated with a metal film, that reflects an image of an object placed in front of it. **2** such a reflecting surface mounted in a frame. **3** any reflecting surface. **4** a thing that reflects or depicts something else. ◆ *vb* **5** (*tr*) to reflect, represent, or depict faithfully: *he mirrors his teacher's ideals.* [C13: from OF from *mirer* to look at, from L *mīrārī* to wonder at]

mirror ball *n* a large revolving ball covered with small pieces of mirror glass so that it reflects light in changing patterns: used in discos and ballrooms.

mirror carp *n* a variety of carp with a smooth shiny body surface.

mirror image *n* **1** an image as observed in a mirror. **2** an object that corresponds to another but has left and right reversed as if seen in a mirror.

mirror writing *n* backward writing that forms a mirror image of normal writing.

mirth Ⓣ (mɜ:θ) *n* laughter, gaiety, or merriment. [OE *myrgth*]
▸**'mirthful** *adj* ▸**'mirthfulness** *n* ▸**'mirthless** *adj* ▸**'mirthlessness** *n*

MIRV (mɜ:v) *n acronym for* multiple independently targeted re-entry vehicle: a missile that has several warheads, each one being directed to a different enemy target.

mis- *prefix* **1** wrong or bad; wrongly or badly: *misunderstanding; misfortune; mistreat; mislead.* **2** lack of; not: *mistrust.* [OE *mis(se)*-]

misadventure Ⓣ (,mɪsəd'ventʃə) *n* **1** an unlucky event; misfortune. **2** *Law.* accidental death not due to crime or negligence.

misalliance (,mɪsə'laɪəns) *n* an unsuitable alliance or marriage.
▸**,misal'ly** *vb*

misanthrope Ⓣ ('mɪzən,θrəʊp) *or* **misanthropist** (mɪ'zænθrəpɪst) *n* a person who dislikes or distrusts other people or mankind in general. [C17: from Gk *mīsanthrōpos,* from *misos* hatred + *anthrōpos* man]
▸**misanthropic** (,mɪzən'θrɒpɪk) *or* **,misan'thropical** *adj* ▸**misanthropy** (mɪ'zænθrəpɪ) *n*

misapply Ⓣ (,mɪsə'plaɪ) *vb* **misapplies, misapplying, misapplied.** (*tr*) **1** to apply wrongly or badly. **2** another word for **misappropriate.**
▸**misapplication** (,mɪsæplɪ'keɪʃən) *n*

misapprehend Ⓣ (,mɪsæprɪ'hend) *vb* (*tr*) to misunderstand.
▸**misapprehension** (,mɪsæprɪ'henʃən) *n* ▸**,misappre'hensive** *adj* ▸**,misappre'hensiveness** *n*

misappropriate Ⓣ (,mɪsə'prəʊprɪ,eɪt) *vb* **misappropriates, misappropriating, misappropriated.** (*tr*) to appropriate for a wrong or dishonest use; embezzle or steal.
▸**,misap,propri'ation** *n*

misbecome (,mɪsbɪ'kʌm) *vb* **misbecomes, misbecoming, misbecame, misbecome.** (*tr*) to be unbecoming to or unsuitable for.

misbegotten Ⓣ (,mɪsbɪ'gɒt^{ə}n) *adj* **1** unlawfully obtained. **2** badly conceived, planned, or designed. **3** *Literary and dialect.* illegitimate; bastard.

misbehave Ⓣ (,mɪsbɪ'heɪv) *vb* **misbehaves, misbehaving, misbehaved.** to behave (oneself) badly.
▸**,misbe'haver** *n* ▸**misbehaviour** *or US* **misbehavior** (,mɪsbɪ'heɪvjə) *n*

THESAURUS

trendiest, trendy (*Brit. inf.*), up to date, vogue, with it (*inf.*)

minute[2] *adj* **1** = **small**, diminutive, fine, infinitesimal, Lilliputian, little, microscopic, miniature, minuscule, slender, teensy-weensy, teeny-weeny, tiny **2** = **negligible**, inconsiderable, paltry, petty, picayune (*US*), piddling (*inf.*), puny, slight, trifling, trivial, unimportant **3** = **precise**, close, critical, detailed, exact, exhaustive, meticulous, painstaking, punctilious
Antonyms *adj* ≠ **small:** enormous, generous, gigantic, ginormous (*inf.*), grand, great, huge, immense, mega (*sl.*), monstrous ≠ **negligible:** important, major, significant, vital ≠ **precise:** careless, haphazard, imprecise, inexact, loose, quick, rough, superficial

minutely *adv* **3** = **precisely**, closely, critically, exactly, exhaustively, in detail, meticulously, painstakingly, with a fine-tooth comb

minutes *pl n* = **record**, memorandum, notes, proceedings, transactions, transcript

minutiae *pl n* = **details**, finer points, ins and outs, niceties, particulars, subtleties, trifles, trivia

minx *n* = **flirt**, baggage, coquette, hoyden, hussy, jade, tomboy, wanton

miracle *n* **1** = **wonder**, marvel, phenomenon, prodigy, thaumaturgy

miraculous *adj* **1, 3** = **wonderful**, amazing, astonishing, astounding, extraordinary, incredible, inexplicable, magical, marvellous, phenomenal, preternatural, prodigious, superhuman, supernatural, thaumaturgic, unaccountable, unbelievable, wondrous (*arch. or literary*)
Antonyms *adj* awful, bad, banal, common, commonplace, everyday, normal, ordinary, run-of-the-mill, terrible, unexceptional, unremarkable, usual

mirage *n* **1, 2** = **illusion**, hallucination, optical illusion, phantasm

mire *n* **1** = **swamp**, bog, marsh, morass, quagmire **2** = **mud**, dirt, gloop (*inf.*), grot (*sl.*), muck, ooze, slime, slob (*Irish*) ◆ *vb* **3** = **bog down**, flounder, sink, stick in the mud **4** = **begrime**, besmirch, bespatter, cake, dirty, muddy, soil **5** = **entangle**, catch up, enmesh, involve

mirror *n* **1, 2** = **looking-glass**, glass, reflector, speculum ◆ *vb* **5** = **reflect**, copy, depict, echo, emulate, follow, represent, show

mirth *n* = **merriment**, amusement, cheerfulness, festivity, frolic, fun, gaiety, gladness, glee, hilarity, jocularity, jollity, joviality, joyousness, laughter, levity, merrymaking, pleasure, rejoicing, revelry, sport

mirthful *adj* = **merry**, amused, amusing, blithe, cheerful, cheery, festive, frolicsome, funny, gay, glad, gladsome (*arch.*), happy, hilarious, jocund, jolly, jovial, laughable, light-hearted, playful, sportive, uproarious, vivacious
Antonyms *adj* dejected, depressed, despondent, dismal, down in the dumps (*inf.*), gloomy, grave, lugubrious, melancholy, miserable, morose, sad, saturnine, sedate, serious, solemn, sombre, sorrowful, unhappy

misadventure *n* **1** = **misfortune**, accident, bad break (*inf.*), bad luck, bummer (*sl.*), calamity, catastrophe, debacle, disaster, failure, ill fortune, ill luck, mischance, mishap, reverse, setback

misanthrope *n* = **cynic**, egoist, egotist, mankind-hater, misanthropist

misanthropic *adj* = **antisocial**, cynical, egoistic, inhumane, malevolent, unfriendly, unsociable

misanthropy *n* = **cynicism**, egoism, hatred of mankind, inhumanity, malevolence

misapply *vb* **1, 2** = **misuse**, abuse, misappropriate, misemploy, pervert

misapprehend *vb* = **misunderstand**, get hold of the wrong end of the stick, get one's lines crossed, get the wrong idea *or* impression, misconceive, misconstrue, misinterpret, misread, mistake

misapprehension *n* = **misunderstanding**, delusion, error, fallacy, false belief, false impression, misconception, misconstruction, misinterpretation, misreading, mistake, wrong idea *or* impression

misappropriate *vb* = **steal**, defalcate (*Law*), embezzle, misapply, misspend, misuse, peculate, pocket, swindle

misbegotten *adj* **1** = **ill-gotten**, dishonest, disreputable, illicit, purloined, shady (*inf.*), stolen, unlawful, unrespectable **2** = **ill-conceived**, abortive, hare-brained, ill-advised, poorly thought-out **3** *Literary and dialect* = **illegitimate**, bastard, born out of wedlock, natural, spurious (*rare*)

misbehave *vb* = **be naughty**, act up (*inf.*), be bad, be insubordinate, carry on (*inf.*), get up to mischief (*inf.*), muck about (*Brit. sl.*)
Antonyms *vb* act correctly, be good, behave, conduct oneself properly, mind one's manners, mind one's p's and q's, toe the line

misbehaviour *n* = **misconduct**, acting up (*inf.*), bad behaviour, impropriety, incivility, in-

misbelief 🅣 (ˌmɪsbɪˈliːf) *n* a false or unorthodox belief.
▸ˌ**misbeˈliever** *n*
misc. *abbrev. for:* **1** miscellaneous. **2** miscellany.
miscalculate 🅣 (ˌmɪsˈkælkjʊˌleɪt) *vb* **miscalculates, miscalculating, miscalculated.** (*tr*) to calculate wrongly.
▸ˌ**miscalcuˈlation** *n*
miscall (ˌmɪsˈkɔːl) *vb* (*tr*) **1** to call by the wrong name. **2** *Dialect.* to abuse or malign.
▸ˌ**misˈcaller** *n*
miscarriage 🅣 (mɪsˈkærɪdʒ) *n* **1** (*also* ˈmɪskær-). spontaneous expulsion of a fetus from the womb, esp. prior to the 20th week of pregnancy. **2** an act of mismanagement or failure: *a miscarriage of justice.* **3** *Brit.* the failure of freight to reach its destination.
miscarry 🅣 (mɪsˈkærɪ) *vb* **miscarries, miscarrying, miscarried.** (*intr*) **1** to expel a fetus prematurely from the womb; abort. **2** to fail. **3** *Brit.* (of freight, mail, etc.) to fail to reach a destination.
miscast (ˌmɪsˈkɑːst) *vb* **miscasts, miscasting, miscast.** (*tr*) **1** to cast badly. **2** (*often passive*) **2a** to cast (a role) in (a play, film, etc.) inappropriately: *Falstaff was miscast.* **2b** to assign an inappropriate role to: *he was miscast as Othello.*
miscegenation (ˌmɪsɪdʒɪˈneɪʃən) *n* interbreeding of races, esp. where differences of pigmentation are involved. [C19: from L *miscēre* to mingle + *genus* race]
miscellanea (ˌmɪsəˈleɪnɪə) *pl n* a collection of miscellaneous items, esp. literary works. [C16: from L: neuter pl of *miscellāneus* MISCELLANEOUS]
miscellaneous 🅣 (ˌmɪsəˈleɪnɪəs) *adj* **1** composed of or containing a variety of things; mixed. **2** having varied capabilities, sides, etc. [C17: from L *miscellāneus,* from *miscellus* mixed, from *miscēre* to mix]
▸ˌ**miscelˈlaneously** *adv* ▸ˌ**miscelˈlaneousness** *n*
miscellany 🅣 (mɪˈsɛlənɪ; *US* ˈmɪsəˌleɪnɪ) *n, pl* **miscellanies. 1** a mixed assortment of items. **2** (*sometimes pl*) a miscellaneous collection of items, esp. essays, poems, etc. [C16: from F *miscellanées* (pl) MISCELLANEA]
▸**miscellanist** (mɪˈsɛlənɪst) *n*
mischance 🅣 (mɪsˈtʃɑːns) *n* **1** bad luck. **2** a stroke of bad luck.
mischief 🅣 (ˈmɪstʃɪf) *n* **1** wayward but not malicious behaviour, usually of children, that causes trouble, irritation, etc. **2** a playful inclination to behave in this way or to tease or disturb. **3** injury or harm caused by a person or thing. **4** a person, esp. a child, who is mischievous. **5** a source of trouble, difficulty, etc. [C13: from OF *meschief,* from *meschever* to meet with calamity; from *mes-* MIS- + *chever,* from *chef* end]
mischievous 🅣 (ˈmɪstʃɪvəs) *adj* **1** inclined to acts of mischief. **2** teasing; slightly malicious. **3** causing or intended to cause harm.
▸ˈ**mischievously** *adv* ▸ˈ**mischievousness** *n*
miscible (ˈmɪsɪbᵊl) *adj* capable of mixing: *miscible with water.* [C16: from Med. L *miscibilis,* from L *miscēre* to mix]
▸ˌ**misciˈbility** *n*
misconceive 🅣 (ˌmɪskənˈsiːv) *vb* **misconceives, misconceiving, misconceived.** to have the wrong idea; fail to understand.
▸ˌ**misconˈceiver** *n*
misconception 🅣 (ˌmɪskənˈsɛpʃən) *n* a false or mistaken view, opinion, or attitude.
misconduct 🅣 *n* (mɪsˈkɒndʌkt). **1** behaviour, such as adultery or professional negligence, that is regarded as immoral or unethical. ◆ *vb* (ˌmɪskənˈdʌkt). (*tr*) **2** to conduct (oneself) in such a way. **3** to manage (something) badly.
misconstrue 🅣 (ˌmɪskənˈstruː) *vb* **misconstrues, misconstruing, misconstrued.** (*tr*) to interpret mistakenly.
▸ˌ**misconˈstruction** *n*
miscreant 🅣 (ˈmɪskrɪənt) *n* **1** a wrongdoer or villain. **2** *Arch.* an unbeliever or heretic. ◆ *adj* **3** evil or villainous. **4** *Arch.* unbelieving or heretical. [C14: from OF *mescreant* unbelieving, from *mes-* MIS- + *creant,* ult. from L *credere* to believe]
miscue (ˌmɪsˈkjuː) *n* **1** *Billiards, etc.* a faulty stroke in which the cue tip slips off the cue ball or misses it. **2** *Inf.* a blunder or mistake. ◆ *vb* **miscues, miscuing, miscued.** (*intr*) **3** *Billiards.* to make a miscue. **4** *Theatre.* to fail to answer one's cue.
miscue analysis *n Brit. education.* analysis of the errors a pupil makes while reading.
misdate (mɪsˈdeɪt) *vb* **misdates, misdating, misdated.** (*tr*) to date (a letter, event, etc.) wrongly.
misdeal (ˌmɪsˈdiːl) *vb* **misdeals, misdealing, misdealt. 1** (*intr*) to deal out cards incorrectly. ◆ *n* **2** a faulty deal.
▸ˌ**misˈdealer** *n*
misdeed 🅣 (ˌmɪsˈdiːd) *n* an evil or illegal action.
misdemean (ˌmɪsdɪˈmiːn) *vb* a rare word for **misbehave.**
misdemeanour 🅣 *or US* **misdemeanor** (ˌmɪsdɪˈmiːnə) *n* **1** *Criminal law.* (formerly) an offence generally less heinous than a felony. **2** any minor offence or transgression.
misdirect (ˌmɪsdɪˈrɛkt) *vb* (*tr*) **1** to give (a person) wrong directions or instructions. **2** to address (a letter, parcel, etc.) wrongly.
▸ˌ**misdiˈrection** *n*
misdoubt (mɪsˈdaʊt) *vb* an archaic word for **doubt** or **suspect.**
mise en scène *French.* (miz ɑ̃ sɛn) *n* **1a** the arrangement of properties, scenery, etc., in a play. **1b** the objects so arranged; stage setting. **2** the environment of an event.
miser 🅣 (ˈmaɪzə) *n* **1** a person who hoards money or possessions, often living miserably. **2** a selfish person. [C16: from L: wretched]
miserable 🅣 (ˈmɪzərəbᵊl) *adj* **1** unhappy or depressed; wretched. **2** causing misery, discomfort, etc.: *a miserable life.* **3** contemptible: *a miserable villain.* **4** sordid or squalid: *miserable living conditions.* **5** mean; stingy. [C16: from OF, from L *miserābilis,* from *miserārī* to pity, from *miser* wretched]
▸ˈ**miserableness** *n* ▸ˈ**miserably** *adv*
misère (mɪˈzɛə) *n* **1** a call in solo whist, etc. declaring a hand that will win no tricks. **2** a hand that will win no tricks. [C19: from F: misery]
Miserere (ˌmɪzəˈrɛərɪ, -ˈrɪərɪ) *n* the 51st psalm, the Latin version of which begins "Miserere mei, Deus" ("Have mercy on me, O God").
misericord *or* **misericorde** (mɪˈzɛrɪˌkɔːd) *n* **1** a ledge projecting from the underside of the hinged seat of a choir stall in a church, on which the occupant can support himself while standing. **2** *Christianity.* **2a** a relaxation of certain monastic rules for infirm or aged monks or nuns. **2b** a monastery or room where this can be enjoyed. **3** a medieval dagger used to give the death stroke to a wounded foe. [C14: from OF, from L *misericordia* compassion, from *miserēre* to pity + *cor* heart]

THESAURUS

discipline, insubordination, mischief, misdeeds, misdemeanour, monkey business (*inf.*), naughtiness, rudeness, shenanigans (*inf.*)
misbelief *n* = **delusion,** error, fallacy, false belief, heresy, unorthodoxy
miscalculate *vb* = **misjudge,** blunder, calculate wrongly, err, get (it) wrong, go wrong, make a mistake, overestimate, overrate, slip up, underestimate, underrate
miscarriage *n* **1** = **spontaneous abortion,** miss (*inf.*) **2** = **failure,** botch (*inf.*), breakdown, error, misadventure, mischance, misfire, mishap, mismanagement, nonsuccess, perversion, thwarting, undoing
miscarry *vb* **1** = **abort 2** = **fail,** come to grief, come to nothing, fall through, gang agley (*Scot.*), go amiss, go astray, go awry, go pear-shaped (*inf.*), go wrong, misfire
miscellaneous *adj* **1** = **mixed,** assorted, confused, diverse, diversified, farraginous, heterogeneous, indiscriminate, jumbled, manifold, many, mingled, motley, multifarious, multiform, promiscuous, sundry, varied, various
miscellany *n* **1, 2** = **assortment,** anthology, collection, diversity, farrago, gallimaufry, hotchpotch, jumble, medley, *mélange,* mixed bag, mixture, omnium-gatherum, potpourri, salmagundi, variety
mischance *n* **1, 2** = **misfortune,** accident, bad break, bad luck, bummer (*sl.*), calamity, contretemps, disaster, ill chance, ill fortune, ill luck, infelicity, misadventure, mishap
mischief *n* **1** = **misbehaviour,** devilment, impishness, monkey business (*inf.*), naughtiness, pranks, roguery, roguishness, shenanigans (*inf.*), trouble, waywardness **3** = **harm,** damage, detriment, disadvantage, disruption, evil, hurt, injury, misfortune, trouble **4** = **rogue,** devil, imp, monkey, nuisance, pest, rascal, scallywag (*inf.*), scamp, tyke (*inf.*), villain
mischievous *adj* **1, 2** = **naughty,** arch, bad, badly behaved, exasperating, frolicsome, impish, playful, puckish, rascally, roguish, sportive, teasing, troublesome, vexatious, wayward **3** = **malicious,** bad, damaging, deleterious, destructive, detrimental, evil, harmful, hurtful, injurious, malignant, pernicious, sinful, spiteful, troublesome, vicious, wicked
misconceive *vb* = **misunderstand,** fail to understand, get one's lines crossed, get the wrong idea (about), misapprehend, misconstrue, misjudge, mistake
misconception *n* = **delusion,** error, fallacy, misapprehension, misconstruction, mistaken belief, misunderstanding, wrong end of the stick, wrong idea
misconduct *n* **1** = **immorality,** delinquency, dereliction, impropriety, malfeasance (*Law*), malpractice, malversation (*rare*), misbehaviour, misdemeanour, mismanagement, naughtiness, rudeness, transgression, unethical behaviour, wrongdoing ◆ *vb* **2, 3** = **mismanage,** behave badly, botch (up), bungle, err, make a mess of, misdirect, sin
misconstruction *n* = **misinterpretation,** false interpretation, misapprehension, misreading, mistake, mistaken *or* false impression, misunderstanding, wrong idea
misconstrue *vb* = **misinterpret,** get a false impression, get one's lines crossed, make a wrong interpretation, misapprehend, misconceive, misjudge, misread, mistake, mistranslate, misunderstand, take the wrong way (*inf.*)
miscreant *n* **1** = **wrongdoer,** blackguard, caitiff (*arch.*), criminal, evildoer, knave, malefactor, rascal, reprobate, rogue, scoundrel, sinner, vagabond, villain ◆ *adj* **3** = **wicked,** corrupt, criminal, depraved, evil, iniquitous, nefarious, rascally, reprehensible, reprobate, scoundrelly, unprincipled, vicious, villainous
misdeed *n* = **offence,** crime, fault, misconduct, misdemeanour, sin, transgression, trespass, villainy, wrong
misdemeanour *n* **2** = **offence,** fault, infringement, misbehaviour, misconduct, misdeed, peccadillo, transgression, trespass
miser *n* **1** = **hoarder,** cheapskate (*inf.*), churl (*arch.*), curmudgeon, hunks (*rare*), niggard, penny-pincher (*inf.*), screw (*sl.*), Scrooge, skinflint
miserable *adj* **1** = **unhappy,** afflicted, broken-hearted, crestfallen, dejected, depressed, desolate, despondent, disconsolate, dismal, distressed, doleful, down, downcast, down in the dumps (*inf.*), down in the mouth (*inf.*), forlorn, gloomy, heartbroken, low, melancholy, mournful, sorrowful, woebegone, wretched **3** = **despicable,** abject, bad, contemptible, deplorable, detestable, disgraceful, lamentable, low, mean, pathetic, piteous, pitiable, scurvy, shabby, shameful, sordid, sorry, squalid, vile, worthless, wretched

miserly ➊ ('maɪzəlɪ) *adj* of or resembling a miser; avaricious.
▸**'miserliness** *n*

misery ➊ ('mɪzərɪ) *n, pl* **miseries. 1** intense unhappiness, suffering, etc. **2** a cause of such unhappiness, etc. **3** squalid or poverty-stricken conditions. **4** *Brit. inf.* a person who is habitually depressed: *he is such a misery.* [C14: via Anglo-Norman from L *miseria,* from *miser* wretched]

misfeasance (mɪs'fiːzəns) *n Law.* the improper performance of an act that is lawful in itself. Cf. **malfeasance, nonfeasance.** [C16: from OF *mesfaisance,* from *mesfaire* to perform misdeeds]

misfile (ˌmɪs'faɪl) *vb* **misfiles, misfiling, misfiled.** to file (papers, records, etc.) wrongly.

misfire ➊ (ˌmɪs'faɪə) *vb* **misfires, misfiring, misfired.** (*intr*) **1** (of a firearm or its projectile) to fail to fire or explode as expected. **2** (of a motor engine or vehicle, etc.) to fail to fire at the appropriate time. **3** to fail to operate or occur as intended. ◆ *n* **4** the act or an instance of misfiring.

misfit ➊ *n* ('mɪsˌfɪt). **1** a person not suited to a particular social environment. **2** something that does not fit or fits badly. ◆ *vb* (ˌmɪs'fɪt), **misfits, misfitting, misfitted.** (*intr*) **3** to fail to fit or be fitted.

misfortune ➊ (mɪs'fɔːtʃən) *n* **1** evil fortune; bad luck. **2** an unfortunate or disastrous event.

misgive (mɪs'gɪv) *vb* **misgives, misgiving, misgave, misgiven.** to make or be apprehensive or suspicious.

misgiving ➊ (mɪs'gɪvɪŋ) *n* (*often pl*) a feeling of uncertainty, apprehension, or doubt.

misguide (ˌmɪs'gaɪd) *vb* **misguides, misguiding, misguided.** (*tr*) to guide or direct wrongly or badly.

misguided ➊ (ˌmɪs'gaɪdɪd) *adj* foolish or unreasonable, esp. in action or behaviour.
▸ˌ**mis'guidedly** *adv*

mishandle ➊ (ˌmɪs'hændᵊl) *vb* **mishandles, mishandling, mishandled.** (*tr*) to handle or treat badly or inefficiently.

mishap ➊ ('mɪshæp) *n* **1** an unfortunate accident. **2** bad luck.

mishit *Sport.* ◆ *n* ('mɪsˌhɪt). **1** a faulty shot or stroke. ◆ *vb* (ˌmɪs'hɪt), **mishits, mishitting, mishit. 2** to hit (a ball) with a faulty stroke.

mishmash ➊ ('mɪʃˌmæʃ) *n* a confused collection or mixture. [C15: reduplication of MASH]

Mishna ('mɪʃnə) *n, pl* **Mishnayoth** (mɪʃ'nɑːjəʊt). *Judaism.* a compilation of precepts collected in the late second century A.D. It forms the earlier part of the Talmud. [C17: from Heb., from *shānāh* to repeat]
▸**Mishnaic** (mɪʃ'neɪɪk) *or* **'Mishnic** *adj*

misinform ➊ (ˌmɪsɪn'fɔːm) *vb* (*tr*) to give incorrect information to.
▸**misinformation** (ˌmɪsɪnfə'meɪʃən) *n*

misinterpret ➊ (ˌmɪsɪn'tɜːprɪt) *vb* (*tr*) to interpret badly, misleadingly, or incorrectly.
▸ˌ**misinˌterpre'tation** *n* ▸ˌ**misin'terpreter** *n*

misjudge ➊ (mɪs'dʒʌdʒ) *vb* **misjudges, misjudging, misjudged.** to judge (a person or persons) wrongly or unfairly.
▸**mis'judger** *n* ▸**mis'judgment** *or* **mis'judgement** *n*

mislay ➊ (mɪs'leɪ) *vb* **mislays, mislaying, mislaid.** (*tr*) **1** to lose (something) temporarily, esp. by forgetting where it is. **2** to lay (something) badly.

mislead ➊ (mɪs'liːd) *vb* **misleads, misleading, misled.** (*tr*) **1** to give false or confusing information to. **2** to lead or guide in the wrong direction.
▸**mis'leader** *n* ▸**mis'leading** *adj*

mismarriage (mɪs'mærɪdʒ) *n* a marriage to an unsuitable partner.

mismatch ➊ (ˌmɪs'mætʃ) *vb* **1** to match badly, esp. in marriage. ◆ *n* **2** a bad match.

misname (mɪs'neɪm) *vb* **misnames, misnaming, misnamed.** (*tr*) to call by a wrong or inappropriate name.

misnomer (ˌmɪs'nəʊmə) *n* **1** an incorrect or unsuitable name for a person or thing. **2** the act of referring to a person by the wrong name. [C15: via Anglo-Norman from OF *mesnommer* to misname, from L *nōmināre* to call by name]

miso- *or before a vowel* **mis-** *combining form.* indicating hatred: *misogyny.* [from Gk *misos* hatred]

misogamy (mɪ'sɒgəmɪ, maɪ-) *n* hatred of marriage.
▸**mi'sogamist** *n*

misogyny (mɪ'sɒdʒɪnɪ, maɪ-) *n* hatred of women. [C17: from Gk, from MISO- + *gunē* woman]
▸**mi'sogynist** *n* ▸**mi'sogynous** *or* **miˌsogy'nistic** *adj*

misplace ➊ (ˌmɪs'pleɪs) *vb* **misplaces, misplacing, misplaced.** (*tr*) **1** to put (something) in the wrong place, esp. to lose (something) temporarily by forgetting where it was placed. **2** (*often passive*) to bestow (trust, affection, etc.) unadvisedly.
▸ˌ**mis'placement** *n*

misplaced modifier *n Grammar.* a participle intended to modify a noun but having the wrong grammatical relationship to it, for example *having left* in the sentence *Having left Europe for good, Peter's future seemed bleak.*

misplay (ˌmɪs'pleɪ) *vb* **1** (*tr*) to play badly or wrongly in games or sports. ◆ *n* **2** a wrong or unskilful play.

misprint ➊ *n* ('mɪsˌprɪnt). **1** an error in printing, made through damaged type, careless reading, etc. ◆ *vb* (ˌmɪs'prɪnt). **2** (*tr*) to print (a letter) incorrectly.

misprision[1] (mɪs'prɪʒən) *n* **a** a failure to inform the authorities of the commission of an act of treason. **b** the deliberate concealment of the commission of a felony. [C15: via Anglo-F from OF *mesprision* error, from *mesprendre* to mistake, from *mes-* MIS- + *prendre* to take]

misprision[2] (mɪs'prɪʒən) *n Arch.* **1** contempt. **2** failure to appreciate the value of something. [C16: from MISPRIZE]

misprize *or* **misprise** (mɪs'praɪz) *vb* **misprizes, misprizing, misprized** *or* **misprises, misprising, misprised.** to fail to appreciate the value of; disparage. [C15: from OF *mesprisier,* from *mes-* MIS- + *prisier* to PRIZE[2]]

mispronounce (ˌmɪsprə'naʊns) *vb* **mispronounces, mispronouncing, mispronounced.** to pronounce (a word) wrongly.
▸**mispronunciation** (ˌmɪsprəˌnʌnsɪ'eɪʃən) *n*

misproportion (ˌmɪsprə'pɔːʃən) *n* a lack of due proportion.

misquote ➊ (ˌmɪs'kwəʊt) *vb* **misquotes, misquoting, misquoted.** to quote (a text, speech, etc.) inaccurately.
▸ˌ**misquo'tation** *n*

misread (ˌmɪs'riːd) *vb* **misreads, misreading, misread** (-'rɛd). (*tr*) **1** to read incorrectly. **2** to misinterpret.

THESAURUS

Antonyms *adj* ≠ **unhappy:** cheerful, happy ≠ **despicable:** admirable, good, respectable

miserliness *n* = **meanness**, avarice, cheeseparing, churlishness, close- *or* tightfistedness, covetousness, graspingness, minginess (*Brit. inf.*), nearness, niggardliness, parsimony, penny-pinching (*inf.*), penuriousness, stinginess

miserly *adj* = **mean**, avaricious, beggarly, close, close-fisted, covetous, grasping, illiberal, mingy (*Brit. inf.*), near, niggardly, parsimonious, penny-pinching (*inf.*), penurious, sordid, stingy, tightfisted, ungenerous
Antonyms *adj* charitable, extravagant, generous, prodigal, unselfish

misery *n* **1** = **unhappiness**, agony, anguish, depression, desolation, despair, discomfort, distress, gloom, grief, hardship, melancholy, sadness, sorrow, suffering, torment, torture, woe, wretchedness **2** = **misfortune**, affliction, bitter pill (*inf.*), burden, calamity, catastrophe, curse, disaster, hardship, load, ordeal, sorrow, trial, tribulation, trouble, woe **3** = **poverty**, destitution, indigence, need, penury, privation, sordidness, squalor, want, wretchedness **4** *Brit. informal* = **moaner**, grouch (*inf.*), killjoy, pessimist, prophet of doom, sourpuss (*inf.*), spoilsport, wet blanket (*inf.*), wowser (*Austral. & NZ sl.*)
Antonyms *n* ≠ **unhappiness:** comfort, contentment, ease, enjoyment, happiness, joy, pleasure ≠ **poverty:** luxury

misfire *vb* **1, 3** = **fail**, fail to go off, fall through, go pear-shaped (*inf.*), go phut (*inf.*), go wrong, miscarry

misfit *n* **1** = **nonconformist**, eccentric, fish out of water (*inf.*), oddball (*inf.*), square peg (in a round hole) (*inf.*)

misfortune *n* **1** = **bad luck**, adversity, evil fortune, hard luck, ill luck, infelicity **2** = **mishap**, accident, affliction, blow, bummer (*sl.*), calamity, disaster, evil chance, failure, hardship, harm, loss, misadventure, mischance, misery, reverse, setback, stroke of bad luck, tragedy, trial, tribulation, trouble, whammy (*inf., chiefly US*)
Antonyms *n* fortune, good luck, relief

misgiving *n* = **unease**, anxiety, apprehension, distrust, doubt, dubiety, hesitation, qualm, reservation, scruple, suspicion, trepidation, uncertainty, worry

misguided *adj* = **unwise**, deluded, erroneous, foolish, ill-advised, imprudent, injudicious, misled, misplaced, mistaken, uncalled-for, unreasonable, unwarranted

mishandle *vb* = **mismanage**, bodge (*inf.*), botch, bungle, make a hash of (*inf.*), make a mess of, make a nonsense of, mess up (*inf.*), muff, screw (up) (*inf.*)

mishap *n* **1, 2** = **accident**, adversity, bad luck, calamity, contretemps, disaster, evil chance, evil fortune, hard luck, ill fortune, ill luck, infelicity, misadventure, mischance, misfortune

mishmash *n* = **jumble**, farrago, gallimaufry, hash, hotchpotch, medley, potpourri, salmagundi

misinform *vb* = **mislead**, deceive, give (someone) a bum steer (*inf., chiefly US*), give (someone) duff gen (*Brit. inf.*), misdirect, misguide

misinterpret *vb* = **misunderstand**, distort, falsify, get wrong, misapprehend, misconceive, misconstrue, misjudge, misread, misrepresent, mistake, pervert

misjudge *vb* = **miscalculate**, be wrong about, get the wrong idea about, overestimate, overrate, underestimate, underrate

mislay *vb* **1** = **lose**, be unable to find, be unable to put *or* lay one's hand on, forget the whereabouts of, lose track of, misplace, miss

mislead *vb* **1** = **deceive**, beguile, bluff, delude, fool, give (someone) a bum steer (*inf., chiefly US*), hoodwink, lead astray, misdirect, misguide, misinform, pull the wool over (someone's) eyes (*inf.*), take for a ride (*inf.*), take in (*inf.*)

misleading *adj* **1** = **confusing**, ambiguous, casuistical, deceitful, deceptive, delusive, delusory, disingenuous, evasive, false, sophistical, specious, spurious, tricky (*inf.*), unstraightforward
Antonyms *adj* candid, clear, correct, direct, explicit, frank, genuine, honest, obvious, open, plain, simple, sincere, straightforward, true, truthful

mismatched *adj* **1** = **incompatible**, clashing, discordant, disparate, ill-assorted, incongruous, irregular, misallied, unreconcilable, unsuited

misplace *vb* **1** = **lose**, be unable to find, be unable to put *or* lay one's hand on, forget the whereabouts of, lose track of, misfile, mislay, miss, put in the wrong place **2** = **place wrongly**, place unwisely

misprint *n* **1** = **mistake**, corrigendum, erratum, literal, printing error, typo (*inf.*), typographical error

misquote *vb* = **misrepresent**, distort, falsify, garble, mangle, misreport, misstate, muddle, pervert, quote *or* take out of context, twist

misrepresent ❶ (ˌmɪsrɛprɪˈzɛnt) *vb* (*tr*) to represent wrongly or inaccurately.
▸ˌ**misrepresen'tation** *n* ▸ˌ**misrepre'sentative** *adj*

misrule ❶ (ˌmɪsˈruːl) *vb* **misrules, misruling, misruled.** 1 (*tr*) to govern inefficiently or without justice. ◆ *n* 2 inefficient or unjust government. 3 disorder.

miss[1] ❶ (mɪs) *vb* 1 to fail to reach, hit, meet, find, or attain (some aim, target, etc.). 2 (*tr*) to fail to attend or be present for: *to miss an appointment.* 3 (*tr*) to fail to see, hear, understand, or perceive. 4 (*tr*) to lose, overlook, or fail to take advantage of: *to miss an opportunity.* 5 (*tr*) to leave out; omit: *to miss an entry in a list.* 6 (*tr*) to discover or regret the loss or absence of: *she missed him.* 7 (*tr*) to escape or avoid (something, esp. a danger), usually narrowly: *he missed death by inches.* ◆ *n* 8 a failure to reach, hit, etc. 9 **give (something) a miss.** *Inf.* to avoid (something): *give the pudding a miss.* ◆ See also **miss out**. [OE *missan* (meaning: to fail to hit)]

miss[2] ❶ (mɪs) *n Inf.* an unmarried woman or girl. [C17: from MISTRESS]

Miss (mɪs) *n* a title of an unmarried woman or girl, usually used before the surname or sometimes alone in direct address. [C17: shortened from MISTRESS]

missal (ˈmɪsᵊl) *n RC Church.* a book containing the prayers, rites, etc., of the Masses for a complete year. [C14: from Church L *missale* (n), from *missālis* concerning the MASS]

misshape *vb* (ˌmɪsˈʃeɪp), **misshapes, misshaping, misshaped; misshaped** *or* **misshapen.** 1 (*tr*) to shape badly; deform. ◆ *n* (ˈmɪsˌʃeɪp). 2 something that is badly shaped.

misshapen ❶ (ˌmɪsˈʃeɪpᵊn) *adj* badly shaped; deformed.
▸ˌ**mis'shapenness** *n*

missile ❶ (ˈmɪsaɪl) *n* 1 any object or weapon that is thrown at a target or shot from an engine, gun, etc. 2 a rocket-propelled weapon that flies either in a fixed trajectory (**ballistic missile**) or in a trajectory controlled during flight (**guided missile**). [C17: from L *missilis*, from *mittere* to send]

missilery *or* **missilry** (ˈmɪsaɪlrɪ) *n* 1 missiles collectively. 2 the design, operation, or study of missiles.

missing ❶ (ˈmɪsɪŋ) *adj* 1 not present; absent or lost. 2 not able to be traced and not known to be dead: *nine men were missing after the attack.* 3 **go missing.** to become lost or disappear.

missing link *n* 1 (*sometimes cap.*; usually preceded by *the*) a hypothetical extinct animal, formerly thought to be intermediate between the anthropoid apes and man. 2 any missing section or part in a series.

mission ❶ (ˈmɪʃən) *n* 1 a specific task or duty assigned to a person or group of people. 2 a person's vocation (often in **mission in life**). 3 a group of persons representing or working for a particular country, business, etc., in a foreign country. 4 a special embassy sent to a foreign country for a specific purpose. 5a a group of people sent by a religious body, esp. a Christian church, to a foreign country to do religious and social work. 5b the campaign undertaken by such a group. 6a a building in which missionary work is performed. 6b the area assigned to a particular missionary. 7 the dispatch of aircraft or spacecraft to achieve a particular task. 8 a charitable centre that offers shelter or aid to the destitute or underprivileged. 9 (*modifier*) of or relating to an ecclesiastical mission: *a mission station.* ◆ *vb* 10 (*tr*) to direct a mission to or establish a mission in (a given region). [C16: from L *missiō*, from *mittere* to send]

missionary ❶ (ˈmɪʃənərɪ) *n, pl* **missionaries.** 1 a member of a religious mission. ◆ *adj* 2 of or relating to missionaries: *missionary work.* 3 resulting from a desire to convert people to one's own beliefs: *missionary zeal.*

missionary position *n Inf.* a position for sexual intercourse in which the man lies on top of the woman and they are face to face. [C20: from the belief that missionaries advocated this as the proper position to primitive peoples among whom it was unknown]

Mississippian (ˌmɪsɪˈsɪpɪən) *adj* 1 of or relating to the state of Mississippi in the US, or the Mississippi river. 2 (in North America) of or denoting the lower of two subdivisions of the Carboniferous period (see also **Pennsylvanian** (sense 2)). ◆ *n* 3 an inhabitant or native of the state of Mississippi. 4 **the.** the Mississippian period or rock system.

missive ❶ (ˈmɪsɪv) *n* 1 a formal or official letter. 2 a formal word for **letter.** [C15: from Med. L *missivus*, from *mittere* to send]

miss out *vb* (*adv*) 1 (*tr*) to leave out; overlook. 2 (*intr*; often foll. by *on*) to fail to experience: *you missed out on the celebrations.*

misspell (ˌmɪsˈspɛl) *vb* **misspells, misspelling, misspelt** *or* **misspelled.** to spell (a word or words) wrongly.

misspelling (ˌmɪsˈspɛlɪŋ) *n* a wrong spelling.

misspend ❶ (ˌmɪsˈspɛnd) *vb* **misspends, misspending, misspent.** to spend thoughtlessly or wastefully.

misstep ❶ (ˌmɪsˈstɛp) *n* 1 a false step. 2 an error.

missus *or* **missis** (ˈmɪsɪz, -ɪs) *n* 1 (usually preceded by *the*) *Inf.* one's wife or the wife of the person addressed or referred to. 2 an informal term of address for a woman. [C19: spoken version of MISTRESS]

missy (ˈmɪsɪ) *n, pl* **missies.** *Inf.* an affectionate or disparaging form of address to a young girl.

mist ❶ (mɪst) *n* 1 a thin fog resulting from condensation in the air near the earth's surface. 2 *Meteorol.* such an atmospheric condition with a horizontal visibility of 1–2 kilometres. 3 a fine spray of liquid, such as that produced by an aerosol container. 4 condensed water vapour on a surface. 5 something that causes haziness or lack of clarity, such as a film of tears. ◆ *vb* 6 to cover or be covered with or as if with mist. [OE]

mistake ❶ (mɪˈsteɪk) *n* 1 an error or blunder in action, opinion, or judgment. 2 a misconception or misunderstanding. ◆ *vb* **mistakes, mistaking, mistook, mistaken.** 3 (*tr*) to misunderstand; misinterpret: *she mistook his meaning.* 4 (*tr*; foll. by *for*) to take (for), interpret (as), or confuse (with): *she mistook his directness for honesty.* 5 (*tr*) to choose badly or incorrectly: *he mistook his path.* 6 (*intr*) to make a mistake. [C13 (meaning: to do wrong, err): from ON *mistaka* to take erroneously]
▸**mis'takable** *adj*

mistaken ❶ (mɪˈsteɪkən) *adj* 1 (*usually predicative*) wrong in opinion, judgment, etc.: *a mistaken viewpoint.* 2 arising from error in opinion, judgment, etc.
▸**mis'takenly** *adv* ▸**mis'takenness** *n*

mister (ˈmɪstə) (*sometimes cap.*) ◆ *n* 1 an informal form of address for a man. 2 *Mil.* the official form of address for subordinate or senior warrant officers. 3 *Naval.* the official form of address for all officers in a merchant ship, other than the captain. 4 *Brit.* the form of address for a surgeon. 5 the form of address for officials holding certain positions: *mister chairman.* ◆ *vb* 6 (*tr*) *Inf.* to call (someone) mister. [C16: var. of MASTER]

Mister (ˈmɪstə) *n* the full form of **Mr.**

misterioso (mɪˌstɛrɪˈəʊsəʊ) *adv Music.* in a mysterious manner; mysteriously. [It.]

mistigris (ˈmɪstɪgriː) *n* 1 the joker or a blank card used as a wild card in a variety of draw poker. 2 the game. [C19: from F: jack of clubs, game in which this card was wild]

mistime ❶ (ˌmɪsˈtaɪm) *vb* **mistimes, mistiming, mistimed.** (*tr*) to time (an action, utterance, etc.) wrongly.

mistle thrush *or* **missel thrush** (ˈmɪsᵊl) *n* a large European thrush with a brown back and spotted breast, noted for feeding on mistletoe berries. [C18: from OE *mistel* MISTLETOE]

mistletoe (ˈmɪsᵊlˌtəʊ) *n* 1 a Eurasian evergreen shrub with waxy white

THESAURUS

misrepresent *vb* = **distort**, belie, disguise, falsify, garble, misinterpret, misstate, pervert, twist

misrule *n* 2 = **mismanagement**, bad government, maladministration, misgovernment 3 = **disorder**, anarchy, chaos, confusion, lawlessness, tumult, turmoil

miss[1] *vb* 1-5 = **omit**, be late for, blunder, err, fail, fail to grasp, fail to notice, forego, lack, leave out, let go, let slip, lose, miscarry, mistake, overlook, pass over, pass up, skip, slip, trip 6 = **long for**, feel the loss of, hunger for, need, pine for, want, wish, yearn for 7 = **avoid**, escape, evade ◆ *n* 8 = **mistake**, blunder, error, failure, fault, loss, omission, oversight, want

miss[2] *n Informal* = **girl**, damsel, lass, lassie (*inf.*), maid, maiden, schoolgirl, spinster, young lady

misshapen *adj* 1 = **deformed**, contorted, crippled, crooked, distorted, grotesque, ill-made, ill-proportioned, malformed, twisted, ugly, ungainly, unshapely, unsightly, warped, wry

missile *n* 1, 2 = **rocket**, projectile, weapon

missing *adj* 1, 2 = **absent**, astray, gone, lacking, left behind, left out, lost, mislaid, misplaced, not present, nowhere to be found, unaccounted-for, wanting
Antonyms *adj* accounted for, at hand, available, here, in attendance, on hand, present, there, to hand

mission *n* 1, 2 = **task**, aim, assignment, business, calling, charge, commission, duty, errand, goal, job, office, operation, purpose, pursuit, quest, trust, undertaking, vocation, work 3-5 = **delegation**, commission, deputation, embassy, legation, ministry, task force

missionary *n* 1 = **evangelist**, apostle, converter, preacher, propagandist, proselytizer

missive *n* 1 = **letter**, communication, dispatch, epistle, memorandum, message, note, report

misspent *adj* = **wasted**, dissipated, idle, imprudent, misapplied, prodigal, profitless, squandered, thrown away
Antonyms *adj* active, fruitful, industrious, meaningful, profitable, unwasted, useful, worthwhile

misstep *n* 1, 2 = **slip**, bad move, blunder, error, false step, faux pas, gaffe, indiscretion, lapse, mistake, slip-up (*inf.*), stumble, trip, wrong move

mist *n* 1 = **fog**, cloud, condensation, dew, drizzle, film, haar (*Eastern Brit.*), haze, smog, smur *or* smir (*Scot.*), spray, steam, vapour ◆ *vb* 6 = **steam (up)**, becloud, befog, blear, blur, cloud, film, fog, obscure

mistake *n* 1, 2 = **error**, bloomer (*Brit. inf.*), blunder, boob (*Brit. sl.*), boo-boo (*inf.*), clanger (*inf.*), erratum, error of judgment, false move, fault, faux pas, gaffe, goof (*inf.*), howler (*inf.*), inaccuracy, miscalculation, misconception, misstep, misunderstanding, oversight, slip, slip-up (*inf.*), solecism ◆ *vb* 4 = **misunderstand**, get wrong, misapprehend, misconceive, misconstrue, misinterpret, misjudge, misread 5 = **confuse with**, accept as, confound, misinterpret as, mix up with, take for 6 = **miscalculate**, be wide of *or* be off the mark, be wrong, blunder, boob (*Brit. sl.*), drop a clanger (*inf.*), err, goof (*inf.*), misjudge, put one's foot in it (*inf.*), slip up (*inf.*)

mistaken *adj* 1, 2 = **wrong**, barking up the wrong tree (*inf.*), erroneous, fallacious, false, faulty (*inf.*), inaccurate, inappropriate, incorrect, in the wrong, misguided, misinformed, misled, off base (*US & Canad. inf.*), off beam (*inf.*), off target, off the mark, unfounded, unsound, way off beam (*inf.*), wide of the mark
Antonyms *adj* accurate, correct, logical, right, sound, true

mistakenly *adv* 1, 2 = **incorrectly**, by mistake, erroneously, fallaciously, falsely, inaccurately, inappropriately, in error, misguidedly, wrongly

mistimed *adj* = **inopportune**, badly timed, ill-timed, inconvenient, unseasonable, unsynchronized, untimely berries: grows as a partial parasite on various trees: used as a Christmas decoration. **2** any of several similar and related American plants. [OE *misteltān,* from *mistel* mistletoe + *tān* twig; rel. to ON *mistilteinn*]

mistook (mɪ'stʊk) *vb* the past tense of **mistake.**

mistral ('mɪstrəl, mɪ'strɑːl) *n* a strong cold dry wind that blows through the Rhône valley and S France to the Mediterranean coast, mainly in the winter. [C17: via F from Provençal, from L *magistrālis* MAGISTRAL]

mistreat ⓣ (ˌmɪs'triːt) *vb* (*tr*) to treat badly.
▸ˌ**mis'treatment** *n*

mistress ⓣ ('mɪstrɪs) *n* **1** a woman who has a continuing extramarital sexual relationship with a man, esp. a married man. **2** a woman in a position of authority, ownership, or control. **3** a woman having control over something specified: *mistress of her own destiny.* **4** *Chiefly Brit.* short for **schoolmistress. 5** an archaic or dialect word for **sweetheart.** [C14: from OF; see MASTER, -ESS]

Mistress ('mɪstrɪs) *n* an archaic or dialect title equivalent to **Mrs.**

Mistress of the Robes *n* (in Britain) a lady of high rank in charge of the Queen's wardrobe.

mistrial (mɪs'traɪəl) *n* **1** a trial made void because of some error. **2** *US.* an inconclusive trial, as when a jury cannot agree on a verdict.

mistrust ⓣ (ˌmɪs'trʌst) *vb* **1** to have doubts or suspicions about (someone or something). ◆ *n* **2** distrust.
▸ˌ**mis'trustful** *adj* ▸ˌ**mis'trustfully** *adv* ▸ˌ**mis'trustfulness** *n*

misty ⓣ ('mɪstɪ) *adj* **mistier, mistiest. 1** consisting of or resembling mist. **2** obscured as by mist. **3** indistinct; blurred.
▸'**mistily** *adv* ▸'**mistiness** *n*

misunderstand ⓣ (ˌmɪsʌndə'stænd) *vb* **misunderstands, misunderstanding, misunderstood.** to fail to understand properly.

misunderstanding ⓣ (ˌmɪsʌndə'stændɪŋ) *n* **1** a failure to understand properly. **2** a disagreement.

misunderstood ⓣ (ˌmɪsʌndə'stʊd) *adj* not properly or sympathetically understood: *a misunderstood adolescent.*

misuse ⓣ *n* (ˌmɪs'juːs), *also* **misusage. 1** erroneous, improper, or unorthodox use: *misuse of words.* **2** cruel or inhumane treatment. ◆ *vb* (ˌmɪs'juːz), **misuses, misusing, misused.** (*tr*) **3** to use wrongly. **4** to treat badly or harshly.
▸ˌ**mis'user** *n*

mite[1] (maɪt) *n* any of numerous small terrestrial or aquatic free-living or parasitic arachnids. [OE *mīte*]

mite[2] (maɪt) *n* **1** a very small particle, creature, or object. **2** a very small contribution or sum of money. See also **widow's mite. 3** a former Flemish coin of small value. **4 a mite.** *Inf.* somewhat: *he's a mite foolish.* [C14: from MLow G, MDu. *mīte*]

Mithraism ('mɪθreɪˌɪzəm) *or* **Mithraicism** (mɪθ'reɪɪˌsɪzəm) *n* the ancient religion of Mithras, the Persian god of light.
▸**Mithraic** (mɪθ'reɪɪk) *adj* ▸'**Mithraist** *n, adj*

mithridatism ('mɪθrɪdeɪˌtɪzəm) *n* immunity to large doses of poison by prior ingestion of gradually increased doses.
▸**mithridatic** (ˌmɪθrɪ'dætɪk, -'deɪ-) *adj*

mitigate ⓣ ('mɪtɪˌgeɪt) *vb* **mitigates, mitigating, mitigated.** to make or become less severe or harsh; moderate. [C15: from L *mītigāre,* from *mītis* mild + *agere* to make]
▸'**mitigable** *adj* ▸ˌ**miti'gation** *n* ▸'**mitiˌgative** *or* '**mitiˌgatory** *adj* ▸'**mitiˌgator** *n*

> **USAGE NOTE** *Mitigate* is sometimes wrongly used where *militate* is meant: *his behaviour militates* (not *mitigates*) *against his chances of promotion.*

mitochondrion (ˌmaɪtəʊ'kɒndrɪən) *n, pl* **mitochondria** (-drɪə). a small spherical or rodlike body, in the cytoplasm of most cells: contains enzymes responsible for energy production. [C19: NL, from Gk *mitos* thread + *khondrion* small grain]

mitosis (maɪ'təʊsɪs, mɪ-) *n* a method of cell division, in which the nucleus divides into daughter nuclei, each containing the same number of chromosomes as the parent nucleus. [C19: from NL, from Gk *mitos* thread]
▸**mitotic** (maɪ'tɒtɪk, mɪ-) *adj*

mitral ('maɪtrəl) *adj* **1** of or like a mitre. **2** *Anat.* of or relating to the mitral valve.

mitral valve *n* the valve between the left atrium and the left ventricle of the heart.

mitre *or US* **miter** ('maɪtə) *n* **1** *Christianity.* the liturgical headdress of a bishop or abbot, consisting of a tall pointed cleft cap with two bands hanging down at the back. **2** Also called: **mitre joint.** a corner joint formed by cutting bevels of equal angles at the ends of each piece of material. **3** a bevelled surface of a mitre joint. ◆ *vb* **mitres, mitring, mitred** *or US* **miters, mitering, mitered.** (*tr*) **4** to make a mitre joint between (two pieces of material). **5** to confer a mitre upon: *a mitred abbot.* [C14: from OF, from L *mitra,* from Gk: turban]

mitre box *n* an open-ended box with sides slotted to guide a saw in cutting mitre joints.

mitt (mɪt) *n* **1** any of various glovelike hand coverings, such as one that does not cover the fingers. **2** short for **mitten** (sense 1). **3** *Baseball.* a large round thickly padded leather mitten worn by the catcher. **4** (*often pl*) a slang word for **hand. 5** *Sl.* a boxing glove. [C18: from MITTEN]

mitten ('mɪtᵊn) *n* **1** a glove having one section for the thumb and a single section for the other fingers. Sometimes shortened to **mitt. 2** *Sl.* a boxing glove. [C14: from OF *mitaine,* from ?]

mittimus ('mɪtɪməs) *n, pl* **mittimuses.** *Law.* a warrant of commitment to prison or a command to a jailer to hold someone in prison. [C15: from L: we send, the first word of such a command]

mix ⓣ (mɪks) *vb* **1** (*tr*) to combine or blend (ingredients, liquids, objects, etc.) together into one mass. **2** (*intr*) to become or have the capacity to become combined, joined, etc.: *some chemicals do not mix.* **3** (*tr*) to form (something) by combining constituents: *to mix cement.* **4** (*tr;* often foll. by *in* or *into*) to add as an additional element (to a mass or compound): *to mix flour into a batter.* **5** (*tr*) to do at the same time: *to mix study and pleasure.* **6** (*tr*) to consume (different alcoholic drinks) in close succession. **7** to come or cause to come into association socially: *Pauline mixed well.* **8** (*intr;* often foll. by *with*) to go together; complement. **9** (*tr*) to crossbreed (differing strains of plants or breeds of livestock), esp. more or less at random. **10** *Music.* to balance and adjust (individual performers' parts) to make an overall sound by electronic means. **11 mix it.** *Inf.* to cause mischief or trouble, often for a person named: *she tried to mix it for John.* ◆ *n* **12** the act or an instance of mixing. **13** the result of mixing; mixture. **14** a mixture of ingredients, esp. one commercially prepared for making a cake, bread, etc. **15** *Inf.* a state of confusion. **16** *Music.* the sound produced by mixing. ◆ See also **mix-up.** [C15: back formation from *mixt* mixed, via OF from L *mixtus,* from *miscēre* to mix]
▸'**mixable** *adj*

mixed ⓣ (mɪkst) *adj* **1** formed or blended together by mixing. **2** composed of different elements, races, sexes, etc.: *a mixed school.* **3** consisting of conflicting elements, thoughts, attitudes, etc.: *mixed feelings.* **4** *Maths.* (of a number) consisting of the sum of an integer and a fraction or a decimal fraction, as 5½ or 17.43.
▸**mixedness** ('mɪksɪdnɪs) *n*

THESAURUS

mistreat *vb* = **abuse**, brutalize, handle roughly, harm, ill-treat, ill-use, injure, knock about *or* around, maltreat, manhandle, maul, misuse, molest, rough up, wrong

mistreatment *n* = **abuse**, brutalization, harm, ill-treatment, ill-usage, injury, maltreatment, manhandling, mauling, misuse, molestation, rough handling, roughing up, unkindness

mistress *n* **1** = **lover**, concubine, doxy (*arch.*), fancy bit (*sl.*), fancy woman (*sl.*), floozy (*sl.*), girlfriend, inamorata, kept woman, ladylove (*rare*), paramour

mistrust *vb* **1** = **doubt**, apprehend, beware, be wary of, distrust, fear, have doubts about, suspect ◆ *n* **2** = **suspicion**, apprehension, distrust, doubt, dubiety, fear, misgiving, scepticism, uncertainty, wariness

mistrustful *adj* **2** = **suspicious**, apprehensive, cautious, chary, cynical, distrustful, doubtful, dubious, fearful, hesitant, leery (*sl.*), nervous, sceptical, uncertain, wary
Antonyms *adj* certain, definite, positive, sure, unafraid

misty *adj* **1-3** = **foggy**, bleary, blurred, cloudy, dark, dim, fuzzy, hazy, indistinct, murky, nebulous, obscure, opaque, overcast, unclear, vague
Antonyms *adj* bright, clear, distinct, lucid, obvious, plain, sunny, well-defined

misunderstand *vb* = **misinterpret**, be at cross-purposes, get (it) wrong, get one's lines crossed, get one's wires crossed, get the wrong end of the stick, get the wrong idea (about), misapprehend, misconceive, misconstrue, mishear, misjudge, misread, miss the point (of), mistake

misunderstanding *n* **1** = **mistake**, error, false impression, misapprehension, misconception, misconstruction, misinterpretation, misjudgment, misreading, mix-up, wrong idea **2** = **disagreement**, argument, breach, conflict, difference, difficulty, discord, dissension, falling-out (*inf.*), quarrel, rift, rupture, squabble, variance

misunderstood *adj* = **misjudged**, misconstrued, misheard, misinterpreted, misread, unappreciated, unrecognized

misuse *n* **1** = **waste**, abuse, barbarism, catachresis, corruption, desecration, dissipation, malapropism, misapplication, misemployment, misusage, perversion, profanation, solecism, squandering **2** = **mistreatment**, abuse, cruel treatment, exploitation, harm, ill-treatment, ill-usage, inhumane treatment, injury, maltreatment, manhandling, rough handling ◆ *vb* **3** = **waste**, abuse, corrupt, desecrate, dissipate, misapply, misemploy, pervert, profane, prostitute, squander **4** = **mistreat**, abuse, brutalize, exploit, handle roughly, harm, ill-treat, ill-use, injure, maltreat, manhandle, maul, molest, wrong
Antonyms *vb* ≠ **waste**: appreciate, prize, treasure, use ≠ **mistreat**: cherish, honour, respect

mitigate *vb* = **ease**, abate, allay, appease, assuage, blunt, calm, check, diminish, dull, extenuate, lessen, lighten, moderate, modify, mollify, pacify, palliate, placate, quiet, reduce the force of, remit, soften, soothe, subdue, take the edge off, temper, tone down, tranquillize, weaken
Antonyms *vb* aggravate, augment, enhance, heighten, increase, intensify, strengthen

mitigation *n* = **relief**, abatement, allaying, alleviation, assuagement, diminution, easement, extenuation, moderation, mollification, palliation, remission

mix *vb* **1-3** = **combine**, alloy, amalgamate, associate, blend, coalesce, commingle, commix, compound, cross, fuse, incorporate, intermingle, interweave, join, jumble, meld, merge, mingle, put together, unite **7** = **socialize**, associate, come together, consort, fraternize, hang out (*inf.*), hobnob, join, mingle ◆ *n* **13** = **mixture**, alloy, amalgam, assortment, blend, combination, compound, fusion, medley, meld, mixed bag

mixed *adj* **1** = **combined**, alloyed, amalgamated, blended, composite, compound, fused, incorporated, joint, mingled, united **2** = **varied**, assorted, cosmopolitan, diverse, diversified, heterogeneous, manifold, miscellaneous, mot-

mixed bag *n Inf.* something composed of diverse elements, characteristics, people, etc.

mixed blessing *n* an event, situation, etc., having both advantages and disadvantages.

mixed doubles *pl n Tennis.* a doubles game with a man and a woman as partners on each side.

mixed economy *n* an economic system in which the public and private sectors coexist.

mixed farming *n* combined arable and livestock farming (on **mixed farms**).

mixed marriage *n* a marriage between persons of different races or religions.

mixed metaphor *n* a combination of incongruous metaphors, as *when the Nazi jackboots sing their swan song.*

mixed-up ❶ *adj* in a state of mental confusion.

mixer ('mɪksə) *n* **1** a person or thing that mixes. **2** *Inf.* **2a** a person considered in relation to his ability to mix socially. **2b** a person who creates trouble for others. **3** a kitchen appliance, usually electrical, used for mixing foods, etc. **4** a drink such as ginger ale, fruit juice, etc., used in preparing cocktails. **5** *Electronics.* a device in which two or more input signals are combined to give a single output signal.

mixer tap *n* a tap in which hot and cold water supplies have a joint outlet but are controlled separately.

mixture ❶ ('mɪkstʃə) *n* **1** the act of mixing or state of being mixed. **2** something mixed; a result of mixing. **3** *Chem.* a substance consisting of two or more substances mixed together without any chemical bonding between them. **4** *Pharmacol.* a liquid medicine in which an insoluble compound is suspended in the liquid. **5** *Music.* an organ stop that controls several ranks of pipes. **6** the mixture of petrol vapour and air in an internal-combustion engine. [C16: from L *mixtūra*, from *mixtus*, p.p. of *miscere* to mix]

mix-up ❶ *n* **1** a confused condition or situation. **2** *Inf.* a fight. ◆ *vb* **mix up.** (*tr, adv*) **3** to make into a mixture. **4** to confuse or confound: *Tom mixes John up with Bill.* **5** (*often passive*) to put (someone) into a state of confusion: *I'm all mixed up.* **6** (foll. by *in* or *with; usually passive*) to involve (in an activity or group, esp. one that is illegal): *mixed up in the drugs racket.*

mizzen *or* **mizen** ('mɪz°n) *Naut.* ◆ *n* **1** a sail set on a mizzenmast. **2** short for **mizzenmast.** ◆ *adj* **3** of or relating to a mizzenmast: *a mizzen staysail.* [C15: from F *misaine*, from It. *mezzana*, *mezzano* middle]

mizzenmast *or* **mizenmast** ('mɪz°nˌmɑːst; *Naut.* 'mɪz°nməst) *n Naut.* (on a vessel with three or more masts) the third mast from the bow.

mizzle[1] ('mɪz°l) *vb* **mizzles, mizzling, mizzled,** *n* a dialect word for **drizzle.** [C15: ?from Low G *miseln* to drizzle]
▸'**mizzly** *adj*

mizzle[2] ('mɪz°l) *vb* **mizzles, mizzling, mizzled.** (*intr*) *Brit. sl.* to decamp. [C18: from ?]

mk *Currency. symbol for:* **1** mark. **2** markka.

mks units *pl n* a metric system of units based on the metre, kilogram, and second as the units of length, mass, and time; it forms the basis of the SI units.

mkt *abbrev. for* market.

ml *symbol for:* **1** mile. **2** millilitre.

ML *abbrev. for* Medieval Latin.

MLA *abbrev. for:* **1** Member of the Legislative Assembly. **2** Modern Language Association (of America).

MLC (in Australia and India) *abbrev. for* Member of the Legislative Council.

MLitt *abbrev. for* Master of Letters. [L *Magister Litterarum*]

Mlle *or* **Mlle.** *pl* **Mlles** *or* **Mlles.** the French equivalent of **Miss.** [from F *Mademoiselle*]

MLR *abbrev. for* minimum lending rate.

mm *symbol for* millimetre.

MM **1** the French equivalent of **Messrs.** [from F *Messieurs*] **2** *abbrev. for* Military Medal.

MMC (formerly in Britain) *abbrev. for* Monopolies and Mergers Commission.

MMDS *abbrev. for* multipoint microwave distribution system: a radio alternative to cable television. Sometimes shortened to **MDS.**

Mme *pl* **Mmes** the French equivalent of **Mrs.** [from F *Madame, Mesdames*]

MMP *abbrev. for* mixed member proportional: a system of proportional representation, used in Germany and New Zealand.

MMR *n* a combined vaccine against measles, mumps, and rubella, given to very young children.

MMus *abbrev. for* Master of Music.

Mn *the chemical symbol for* manganese.

MNA (in Canada) *abbrev. for* Member of the National Assembly (of Quebec).

mnemonic (nɪ'mɒnɪk) *adj* **1** aiding or meant to aid one's memory. **2** of or relating to memory or mnemonics. ◆ *n* **3** something, such as a verse, to assist memory. [C18: from Gk *mnēmonikos*, from *mnēmōn* mindful, from *mnasthai* to remember]
▸**mne'monically** *adv*

mnemonics (nɪ'mɒnɪks) *n* (*usually functioning as sing*) **1** the art or practice of improving or of aiding the memory. **2** a system of rules to aid the memory.

mo (məʊ) *n Inf.* **1** *Chiefly Brit.* short for **moment** (sense 1) (esp. in **half a mo**). **2** *Austral.* short for **moustache** (sense 1).

Mo *the chemical symbol for* molybdenum.

MO *abbrev. for:* **1** Missouri. **2** Medical Officer.

m.o. *or* **MO** *abbrev. for:* **1** mail order. **2** money order.

-mo *suffix forming nouns.* (in bookbinding) indicating book size by specifying the number of leaves formed by folding one sheet of paper: *16mo* or *sixteenmo.* [abstracted from DUODECIMO]

moa ('məʊə) *n* any of various recently extinct large flightless birds of New Zealand (see **ratite**). [C19: from Maori]

moa hunter *n NZ.* an anthropologists' term for an early Maori.

moan ❶ (məʊn) *n* **1** a low prolonged mournful sound expressive of suffering or pleading. **2** any similar mournful sound, esp. that made by the wind. **3** *Inf.* a grumble or complaint. ◆ *vb* **4** to utter (words, etc.) in a low mournful manner. **5** (*intr*) to make a sound like a moan. **6** (*usually intr*) *Inf.* to grumble or complain. [C13: rel. to OE *mǣnan* to grieve over]
▸'**moaner** *n* ▸'**moanful** *adj* ▸'**moaning** *n, adj*

moat (məʊt) *n* **1** a wide water-filled ditch surrounding a fortified place, such as a castle. ◆ *vb* **2** (*tr*) to surround with or as if with a moat. [C14: from OF *motte* mound]

mob ❶ (mɒb) *n* **1a** a riotous or disorderly crowd of people; rabble. **1b** (*as modifier*): *mob law.* **2** *Often derog.* a group or class of people, animals, or things. **3** *Often derog.* the masses. **4** *Sl.* a gang of criminals. **5** *Austral. & NZ.* a large number of anything. **6** *Austral. & NZ.* a flock or herd of animals. **7** **mobs of.** *Austral. & NZ inf.* lots of. ◆ *vb* **mobs, mobbing, mobbed.** (*tr*) **8** to attack in a group resembling a mob. **9** (of a group of animals of a prey species) to harass (a predator). **10** to surround, esp. in order to acclaim. **11** to crowd into (a building, etc.). [C17: shortened from L *mōbile vulgus* the fickle populace]

mobcap ('mɒbˌkæp) *n* a woman's large cotton cap with a pouched crown, worn esp. during the 18th century. [C18: from obs. *mob* woman, esp. loose-living, + CAP]

mobile ❶ ('məʊbaɪl) *adj* **1** having freedom of movement; movable. **2** changing quickly in expression: *a mobile face.* **3** *Sociol.* (of individuals or social groups) moving within and between classes, occupations, and localities. **4** (of military forces) able to move freely and quickly. **5** (*postpositive*) *Inf.* having transport available: *are you mobile?* ◆ *n* **6a** a sculpture suspended in midair with delicately balanced parts that are set in motion by air currents. **6b** (*as modifier*): *mobile sculpture.* **7** short for **mobile phone.** [C15: via OF from L *mōbilis*, from *movēre* to move]
▸**mobility** (məʊ'bɪlɪtɪ) *n*

-mobile (məʊˌbiːl) *suffix forming nouns.* indicating a vehicle designed for a particular person or purpose: *Popemobile.*

mobile home *n* living quarters mounted on wheels and capable of being towed by a motor vehicle.

mobile phone *n* a portable telephone that works by means of a cellular radio system.

mobilize ❶ *or* **mobilise** ('məʊbɪˌlaɪz) *vb* **mobilizes, mobilizing, mobilized** *or* **mobilises, mobilising, mobilised. 1** to prepare for war or another emergency by organizing (national resources, the armed services, etc.). **2** (*tr*) to organize for a purpose. **3** (*tr*) to put into motion or use.
▸'**mobiˌlizable** *or* '**mobiˌlisable** *adj* ▸**ˌmobili'zation** *or* **ˌmobili'sation** *n*

THESAURUS

ley **2** = **crossbred**, hybrid, interbred, interdenominational, mongrel **3** = **uncertain**, ambivalent, equivocal, indecisive
Antonyms *adj* ≠ **combined:** isolated, pure, straight, unmixed ≠ **varied:** homogeneous, unmixed ≠ **crossbred:** pure

mixed-up *adj* = **confused**, at sea, bewildered, distraught, disturbed, maladjusted, muddled, perplexed, puzzled, upset

mixture *n* **2** = **blend**, admixture, alloy, amalgam, amalgamation, association, assortment, brew, combine, composite, compound, concoction, conglomeration, cross, fusion, hotchpotch, jumble, medley, *mélange*, meld, miscellany, mix, mixed bag (*inf.*), potpourri, salmagundi, union, variety

mix-up *n* **1** = **confusion**, disorder, fankle (*Scot.*), jumble, mess, mistake, misunderstanding, muddle, snarl-up (*inf., chiefly Brit.*), tangle ◆ *vb* **mix up 3** = **combine**, blend, commix, mix **4** = **confuse**, confound, muddle **5** = **bewilder**, confuse, disturb, fluster, muddle, perplex, puzzle, throw into confusion, unnerve, upset **6** = **entangle**, embroil, implicate, involve, rope in

moan *n* **1, 2** = **groan**, lament, lamentation, sigh, sob, sough, wail, whine **3** *Informal* = **grumble**, beef, bitch (*sl.*), complaint, gripe (*inf.*), grouch (*inf.*), grouse, kvetch (*US sl.*), protest, whine ◆ *vb* **4, 5** = **groan**, bemoan, bewail, deplore, grieve, keen, lament, mourn, sigh, sob, sough, whine **6** *Informal* = **grumble**, beef (*sl.*), bitch (*sl.*), bleat, carp, complain, gripe (*inf.*), groan, grouch (*inf.*), grouse, moan and groan, whine, whinge (*inf.*)

mob *n* **1** = **crowd**, assemblage, body, collection, drove, flock, gang, gathering, herd, horde, host, mass, multitude, pack, press, swarm, throng **2** *Often derogatory* = **gang**, class, company, crew (*inf.*), group, lot, set, troop **3** *Often derogatory* = **masses**, *canaille*, commonalty, great unwashed (*inf. & derogatory*), hoi polloi, rabble, riffraff, scum ◆ *vb* **8, 10** = **surround**, crowd around, jostle, overrun, set upon, swarm around **11** = **crowd into**, cram into, crowd, fill, fill to overflowing, jam, pack

mobile *adj* **1** = **movable**, ambulatory, itinerant, locomotive, migrant, motile, moving, peripatetic, portable, travelling, wandering **2** = **changeable**, animated, ever-changing, expressive

mobilize *vb* **1, 2** = **prepare**, activate, animate, call to arms, call up, get *or* make ready, marshal, muster, organize, put in motion, rally, ready

Möbius strip ('mɜːbɪəs) *n Maths.* a one-sided continuous surface, formed by twisting a long narrow rectangular strip of material through 180° and joining the ends. [C19: after August *Möbius* (1790–1868), G mathematician]

mobocracy (mɒ'bɒkrəsɪ) *n, pl* **mobocracies. 1** rule or domination by a mob. **2** the mob that rules.

mobster ('mɒbstə) *n* a US slang word for **gangster.**

moccasin ('mɒkəsɪn) *n* **1** a shoe of soft leather, esp. deerskin, worn by North American Indians. **2** any soft shoe resembling this. **3** short for **water moccasin.** [C17: of Amerind origin]

moccasin flower *n* any of several North American orchids with a pink solitary flower. See also **lady's-slipper, cypripedium.**

mocha ('mɒkə) *n* **1** a dark brown coffee originally imported from the port of Mocha in Arabia. **2** a flavouring made from coffee and chocolate. **3** a soft glove leather, made from goatskin or sheepskin. **4a** a dark brown colour. **4b** (*as adj*): *mocha shoes.*

mock ➊ (mɒk) *vb* **1** (when *intr*, often foll. by *at*) to behave with scorn or contempt (towards); show ridicule (for). **2** (*tr*) to imitate, esp. in fun; mimic. **3** (*tr*) to deceive, disappoint, or delude. **4** (*tr*) to defy or frustrate. ◆ *n* **5** the act of mocking. **6** a person or thing mocked. **7** a counterfeit; imitation. **8** (*often pl*) *Inf.* (in England and Wales) school examinations taken as practice before public exams. ◆ *adj* (*prenominal*) **9** sham or counterfeit. **10** serving as an imitation or substitute, esp. for practice purposes: *a mock battle.* ◆ See also **mock-up.** [C15: from OF *mocquer*]
▸**'mocker** *n* ▸**'mocking** *n, adj* ▸**'mockingly** *adv*

mockers ('mɒkəz) *pl n Inf.* **put the mockers on.** to ruin the chances of success of. [C20: ?from MOCK]

mockery ➊ ('mɒkərɪ) *n, pl* **mockeries. 1** ridicule, contempt, or derision. **2** a derisive action or comment. **3** an imitation or pretence, esp. a derisive one. **4** a person or thing that is mocked. **5** a person, thing, or action that is inadequate.

mock-heroic *adj* **1** (of a literary work, esp. a poem) imitating the style of heroic poetry in order to satirize an unheroic subject. ◆ *n* **2** burlesque imitation of the heroic style.

mockingbird ('mɒkɪŋˌbɜːd) *n* any of various American songbirds, noted for their ability to mimic the song of other birds.

mock orange *n* **1** Also called: **syringa, philadelphus.** a shrub with white fragrant flowers resembling those of the orange. **2** an Australian shrub with white flowers and dark shiny leaves.

mock turtle soup *n* an imitation turtle soup made from a calf's head.

mock-up *n* **1** a working full-scale model of a machine, apparatus, etc., for testing, research, etc. **2** a layout of printed matter. ◆ *vb* **mock up. 3** (*tr, adv*) to build or make a mock-up of.

mod[1] (mɒd) *n Brit.* **a** a member of a group of teenagers, originally in the mid-1960s, noted for their clothes-consciousness. **b** a member of a revived group of this type in the late 1970s and early 1980s. [C20: from MODERNIST]

mod[2] (mɒd) *n* an annual Highland Gaelic meeting with musical and literary competitions. [C19: from Gaelic *mōd* assembly, from ON]

MOD (in Britain) *abbrev. for* Ministry of Defence.

mod. *abbrev. for:* **1** moderate. **2** moderato. **3** modern.

modal ('məʊdᵊl) *adj* **1** of or relating to mode or manner. **2** *Grammar.* (of a verb form or auxiliary verb) expressing a distinction of mood, such as that between possibility and actuality. **3** qualifying, or expressing a qualification of, the truth of some statement. **4** *Metaphysics.* of or relating to the form of a thing as opposed to its attributes, substance, etc. **5** *Music.* of or relating to a mode. **6** of or relating to a statistical mode.
▸**mo'dality** *n* ▸**'modally** *adv*

modal logic *n* **1** the logical study of such philosophical concepts as necessity, possibility, contingency, etc. **2** the logical study of concepts whose formal properties resemble certain moral, epistemological, and psychological concepts.

mod cons *pl n Inf.* modern conveniences; the usual installations of a modern house, such as hot water, heating, etc.

mode ➊ (məʊd) *n* **1** a manner or way of doing, acting, or existing. **2** the current fashion or style. **3** *Music.* **3a** any of the various scales of notes within one octave, esp. any of the twelve natural diatonic scales taken in ascending order used in plainsong, folk song, and art music until 1600. **3b** (in the music of classical Greece) any of the descending diatonic scales from which the liturgical modes evolved. **3c** either of the two main scale systems in music since 1600: *major mode; minor mode.* **4** *Logic, linguistics.* another name for **mood**[2]. **5** *Philosophy.* a complex combination of ideas which is not simply the sum of its component ideas. **6** that one of a range of values that has the highest frequency as determined statistically. [C14: from L *modus* manner]

model ➊ ('mɒdᵊl) *n* **1a** a representation, usually on a smaller scale, of a device, structure, etc. **1b** (*as modifier*): *a model train.* **2a** a standard to be imitated. **2b** (*as modifier*): *a model wife.* **3** a representative form, style, or pattern. **4** a person who poses for a sculptor, painter, or photographer. **5** a person who wears clothes to display them to prospective buyers; mannequin. **6** a preparatory sculpture in clay, wax, etc., from which the finished work is copied. **7** a design or style of a particular product. ◆ *vb* **models, modelling, modelled** *or US* **models, modeling, modeled. 8** to make a model of (something or someone). **9** to form in clay, wax, etc.; mould. **10** to display (clothing and accessories) as a mannequin. **11** to plan or create according to a model or models. [C16: from OF *modelle,* from It., from L *modulus,* dim. of *modus* MODE]
▸**'modeller** *or US* **'modeler** *n*

modelling *or US* **modeling** ('mɒdᵊlɪŋ) *n* **1** the act or an instance of making a model. **2** the practice or occupation of a person who models clothes. **3** a technique in psychotherapy in which the therapist encourages the patient to model his behaviour on his own.

modem ('məʊdɛm) *n Computing.* a device for connecting two computers by a telephone line, consisting of a modulator that converts computer signals into audio signals and a corresponding demodulator. [C20: from *mo(dulator) dem(odulator)*]

moderate ➊ *adj* ('mɒdərɪt). **1** not extreme or excessive. **2** not violent; mild or temperate. **3** of average quality or extent: *moderate success.* ◆ *n* ('mɒdərɪt). **4** a person who holds moderate views, esp. in politics. ◆ *vb* ('mɒdəˌreɪt). **moderates, moderating, moderated. 5** to become or cause to become less extreme or violent. **6** (when *intr*, often foll. by *over*) to preside over a meeting, discussion, etc. **7** *Physics.* to slow down (neutrons), esp. by using a moderator. [C14: from L *moderātus,* from *moderārī* to restrain]

moderate breeze *n* a wind of force 4 on the Beaufort scale, reaching speeds of 13 to 18 mph.

moderation ➊ (ˌmɒdə'reɪʃən) *n* **1** the state or an instance of being moderate. **2** the act of moderating. **3 in moderation.** within moderate or reasonable limits.

moderato (ˌmɒdə'rɑːtəʊ) *adv Music.* **1** at a moderate tempo. **2** a direction indicating that the tempo specified is to be used with restraint: *allegro moderato.* [It.]

moderator ('mɒdəˌreɪtə) *n* **1** a person or thing that moderates. **2** *Presbyterian Church.* a minister appointed to preside over a Church court, synod, or general assembly. **3** a presiding officer at a public or legislative assembly. **4** a material, such as heavy water, used for slowing down neutrons in nuclear reactors. **5** an examiner at Oxford or Cambridge Universities in first public examinations. **6** (in Britain and New Zealand) one who is responsible for consistency of standards in the grading of some public examinations.
▸**'moderˌatorship** *n*

modern ➊ ('mɒdən) *adj* **1** of, involving, or befitting the present or a re-

THESAURUS

mock *vb* **1 = laugh at,** chaff, deride, flout, insult, jeer, laugh to scorn, make a monkey out of, make fun of, poke fun at, ridicule, scoff, scorn, show contempt for, sneer, take the mickey (out of) (*inf.*), taunt, tease, wind up (*Brit. sl.*) **2 = mimic,** ape, burlesque, caricature, counterfeit, do (*inf.*), imitate, lampoon, parody, satirize, send up (*Brit. inf.*), take off (*inf.*), travesty **3 = deceive,** belie, cheat, delude, disappoint, dupe, elude, fool, let down, mislead **4 = foil,** defeat, defy, disappoint, frustrate, thwart ◆ *n* **6 = laughing stock,** Aunt Sally (*Brit.*), butt, dupe, fool, jest, sport, travesty ◆ *adj* **9 = imitation,** artificial, bogus, counterfeit, dummy, ersatz, fake, faked, false, feigned, forged, fraudulent, phoney *or* phony (*inf.*), pretended, pseudo (*inf.*), sham, spurious
Antonyms *vb* ≠ **laugh at:** encourage, praise, respect, revere ◆ *adj* ≠ **imitation:** authentic, genuine, natural, real, sincere, true, unfeigned

mockery *n* **1 = derision,** contempt, contumely, disdain, disrespect, gibes, insults, jeering, ridicule, scoffing, scorn **2, 3 = parody,** burlesque, caricature, deception, farce, imitation, lampoon, mimicry, pretence, send-up (*Brit. inf.*), sham, spoof (*inf.*), take-off (*inf.*), travesty **5 = farce,** apology (*inf.*), disappointment, joke, laughing stock, letdown

mocking *adj* **1 = scornful,** contemptuous, contumelious, derisive, derisory, disdainful, disrespectful, insulting, irreverent, sarcastic, sardonic, satiric, satirical, scoffing, taunting

mode *n* **1 = method,** approach, condition, course, custom, fashion, form, manner, plan, practice, procedure, process, quality, rule, state, style, system, technique, vein, way **2 = fashion,** craze, look, rage, style, trend, vogue

model *n* **1a = representation,** copy, dummy, facsimile, image, imitation, miniature, mock-up, replica ◆ *modifier* **1b = imitation,** copy, dummy, facsimile, miniature ◆ *n* **2a = pattern,** archetype, design, epitome, example, exemplar, gauge, ideal, lodestar, mould, norm, original, par, paradigm, paragon, prototype, standard, type ◆ *modifier* **2b = ideal,** archetypal, exemplary, illustrative, paradigmatic, perfect, standard, typical ◆ *n* **4 = sitter,** poser, subject **5 = mannequin,** supermodel **7 = version,** configuration, design, form, kind, mark, mode, stamp, style, type, variety ◆ *vb* **8, 9 = shape,** carve, cast, design, fashion, form, mould, sculpt, stamp **10 = show off,** display, sport (*inf.*), wear **11 = base,** pattern, plan
Antonyms *modifier* ≠ **ideal:** deficient, flawed, impaired, imperfect

moderate *adj* **1, 2 = mild,** calm, controlled, cool, deliberate, equable, gentle, judicious, limited, middle-of-the-road, modest, peaceable, reasonable, restrained, sober, steady, temperate **3 = average,** fair, fairish, fair to middling (*inf.*), indifferent, mediocre, medium, middling, ordinary, passable, so-so (*inf.*), unexceptional ◆ *vb* **5 = lessen,** abate, allay, appease, assuage, calm, clear the air, control, curb, decrease, diminish, ease, mitigate, modulate, pacify, play down, quiet, regulate, relax, repress, restrain, soften, soft-pedal (*inf.*), subdue, tame, temper, tone down **6 = arbitrate,** chair, judge, mediate, preside, referee, take the chair
Antonyms *adj* ≠ **mild:** extreme, intemperate, ruffled, unreasonable, wild ≠ **average:** excessive, extreme, immoderate, inordinate, unusual ◆ *vb* ≠ **lessen:** heighten, increase, intensify

moderation *n* **1 = restraint,** calmness, composure, coolness, equanimity, fairness, judiciousness, justice, justness, mildness, moderateness, reasonableness, sedateness, temperance **3 in moderation = moderately,** within limits, within reason

modern *adj* **1 = current,** contemporary, fresh,

cent time; contemporary. **2** of, relating to, or characteristic of contemporary styles or schools of art, literature, music, etc., esp. those of an experimental kind. **3** belonging or relating to the period in history from the end of the Middle Ages to the present. ◆ *n* **4** a contemporary person. [C16: from OF, from LL *modernus*, from *modō* (adv) just recently, from *modus* MODE]
▸**mo'dernity** *or* **'modernness** *n*

modern apprenticeship *n* an arrangement that allows a school-leaver to gain vocational qualifications while being trained in a job.

Modern English *n* the English language since about 1450.

Modern Hebrew *n* the official language of Israel; a revived form of ancient Hebrew.

modernism ('mɒdəˌnɪzəm) *n* **1** modern tendencies, thoughts, etc., or the support of these. **2** something typical of contemporary life or thought. **3** a 20th-century divergence in the arts from previous traditions, esp. in architecture. See **International Style.** **4** (*cap.*) *RC Church.* the movement at the end of the 19th and beginning of the 20th centuries that sought to adapt doctrine to modern thought.
▸**'modernist** *n, adj* ▸**ˌmodern'istic** *adj* ▸**ˌmodern'istically** *adv*

modernize ❶ *or* **modernise** ('mɒdəˌnaɪz) *vb* **modernizes, modernizing, modernized** *or* **modernises, modernising, modernised.** **1** (*tr*) to make modern in appearance or style. **2** (*intr*) to adopt modern ways, ideas, etc.
▸**ˌmoderni'zation** *or* **ˌmoderni'sation** *n* ▸**'modernˌizer** *or* **'modernˌiser** *n*

modern pentathlon *n* an athletic contest consisting of five different events: horse riding with jumps, fencing with electric épée, freestyle swimming, pistol shooting, and cross-country running.

modest ❶ ('mɒdɪst) *adj* **1** having or expressing a humble opinion of oneself or one's accomplishments or abilities. **2** reserved or shy. **3** not ostentatious or pretentious. **4** not extreme or excessive. **5** decorous or decent. [C16: via OF from L *modestus* moderate, from *modus* MODE]
▸**'modestly** *adv*

modesty ❶ ('mɒdɪstɪ) *n, pl* **modesties.** the quality or condition of being modest.

modicum ❶ ('mɒdɪkəm) *n* a small amount or portion. [C15: from L: a little way, from *modicus* moderate]

modification ❶ (ˌmɒdɪfɪ'keɪʃən) *n* **1** the act of modifying or the condition of being modified. **2** something modified. **3** a small change or adjustment. **4** *Grammar.* the relation between a modifier and the word or phrase that it modifies.
▸**'modifiˌcatory** *or* **'modifiˌcative** *adj*

modifier ('mɒdɪˌfaɪə) *n* **1** Also called: **qualifier.** *Grammar.* a word or phrase that qualifies the sense of another word; for example, the noun *alarm* is a modifier of *clock* in *alarm clock* and the phrase *every day* is an adverbial modifier of *walks* in *he walks every day.* **2** a person or thing that modifies.

modify ❶ ('mɒdɪˌfaɪ) *vb* **modifies, modifying, modified.** (*mainly tr*) **1** to change the structure, character, intent, etc., of. **2** to make less extreme or uncompromising. **3** *Grammar.* (of a word or phrase) to bear the relation of modifier to (another word or phrase). **4** *Linguistics.* to change (a vowel) by umlaut. **5** (*intr*) to be or become modified. [C14: from OF *modifier*, from L *modificāre* to limit, from *modus* measure + *facere* to make]
▸**'modiˌfiable** *adj*

modish ❶ ('məʊdɪʃ) *adj* in the current fashion or style.
▸**'modishly** *adv* ▸**'modishness** *n*

modiste (məʊ'diːst) *n* a fashionable dressmaker or milliner. [C19: from F, from *mode* fashion]

modular ('mɒdjʊlə) *adj* of, consisting of, or resembling a module or modulus.

modulate ❶ ('mɒdjʊˌleɪt) *vb* **modulates, modulating, modulated.** **1** (*tr*) to change the tone, pitch, or volume of. **2** (*tr*) to adjust or regulate the degree of. **3** *Music.* **3a** to change or cause to change from one key to another. **3b** (often foll. by *to*) to make or become in tune (with a pitch, key, etc.). **4** *Physics, electronics.* to superimpose the amplitude, frequency, phase, etc., of a wave or signal onto another wave or signal or onto an electron beam. [C16: from L *modulātus* in due measure, melodious, from *modulārī*, from *modus* measure]
▸**ˌmodu'lation** *n* ▸**'moduˌlator** *n*

module ('mɒdjuːl) *n* **1** a standard unit of measure, esp. one used to coordinate the dimensions of buildings and components. **2** a standard self-contained unit or item, such as an assembly of electronic components, or a standardized piece of furniture, that can be used in combination with other units. **3** *Astronautics.* any of several self-contained separable units making up a spacecraft or launch vehicle, each of which has one or more specified tasks. **4** *Education.* a short course of study that together with other such courses counts towards a qualification. [C16: from L *modulus*, dim. of *modus* MODE]

modulus ('mɒdjʊləs) *n, pl* **moduli** (-ˌlaɪ). **1** *Physics.* a coefficient expressing a specified property of a specified substance. See **modulus of elasticity.** **2** *Maths.* another name for the **absolute value** of a complex number. **3** *Maths.* the number by which a logarithm to one base is multiplied to give the corresponding logarithm to another base. **4** *Maths.* an integer that can be divided exactly into the difference between two other integers: *7 is a modulus of 25 and 11.* [C16: from L, dim. of *modus* measure]

modulus of elasticity *n* the ratio of the stress applied to a body or substance to the resulting strain within the elastic limit. Also called: **elastic modulus.**

modus operandi ❶ ('məʊdəs ˌɒpə'rændiː, -'rændaɪ) *n, pl* **modi operandi** ('məʊdiː ˌɒpə'rændiː, 'məʊdaɪ ˌɒpə'rændaɪ). procedure; method of operating. [C17: from L]

modus vivendi ('məʊdəs vɪ'vendiː, -'vendaɪ) *n, pl* **modi vivendi** ('məʊdiː vɪ'vendiː, 'məʊdaɪ vɪ'vendaɪ). a working arrangement between conflicting interests; practical compromise. [C19: from L: way of living]

mog (mɒg) *or* **moggy** *n, pl* **mogs** *or* **moggies.** *Brit.* a slang name for **cat**[1]. [C20: dialect, orig. a pet name for a cow]

Mogadon ('mɒgəˌdɒn) *n Trademark.* a minor tranquillizer used to treat insomnia.

mogul ❶ ('məʊgʌl, məʊ'gʌl) *n* an important or powerful person. [C18: from MOGUL]

Mogul ('məʊgʌl, məʊ'gʌl) *n* **1** a member of the Muslim dynasty of Indian emperors established in 1526. **2** a Muslim Indian, Mongol, or Mongolian. ◆ *adj* **3** of or relating to the Moguls or their empire. [C16: from Persian *mughul* Mongolian]

mogul skiing *n* an event in which skiers descend a slope covered in mounds of snow, making two jumps during their descent. [C20: *mogul* ? from G dialect *Mugl* hillock or hummock]

MOH (in Britain) *abbrev. for* Medical Officer of Health.

mohair ('məʊˌhɛə) *n* **1** Also called: **angora.** the long soft silky hair of the Angora goat. **2a** a fabric made from the yarn of this hair and cotton or wool. **2b** (*as modifier*): *a mohair suit.* [C16: (infl. by *hair*), ult. from Ar. *mukhayyar*, lit.: choice]

Moham. *abbrev. for* Mohammedan.

Mohammedan (məʊ'hæmɪdᵊn) *n, adj* another word (not in Muslim use) for **Muslim.**

Mohammedanism (məʊ'hæmɪdᵊˌnɪzəm) *n* another word (not in Muslim use) for **Islam.**

Mohawk ('məʊhɔːk) *n* **1** (*pl* **Mohawks** *or* **Mohawk**) a member of a North American Indian people formerly living along the Mohawk River. **2** the Iroquoian language of this people.

mohican (məʊ'hiːkən) *n* a punk hairstyle in which the head is shaved at the sides and the remaining strip of hair is worn stiffly erect and sometimes brightly coloured.

moidore ('mɔɪdɔː) *n* a former Portuguese gold coin. [C18: from Port. *moeda de ouro* money of gold]

moiety ('mɔɪɪtɪ) *n, pl* **moieties.** **1** a half. **2** one of two parts or divisions of something. [C15: from OF *moitié*, from L *mediētās* middle, from *medius*]

moil (mɔɪl) *Arch. or dialect.* ◆ *vb* **1** to moisten or soil or become moist, soiled, etc. **2** (*intr*) to toil or drudge (esp. in **toil and moil**). ◆ *n* **3** toil; drudgery. **4** confusion. [C14 (to moisten; later: to work hard in unpleasantly wet conditions) from OF *moillier*, ult. from L *mollis* soft]

moire (mwɑː) *n* a fabric, usually silk, having a watered effect. [C17: from F, earlier *mouaire*, from MOHAIR]

moiré ('mwɑːreɪ) *adj* **1** having a watered or wavelike pattern. ◆ *n* **2** such a pattern, impressed on fabrics by means of engraved rollers. **3** any fabric having such a pattern; moire. **4** Also: **moiré pattern.** a pattern

THESAURUS

late, latest, neoteric (*rare*), new, newfangled, novel, present, present-day, recent, up-to-date, up-to-the-minute, with it (*inf.*)
Antonyms *adj* ancient, antiquated, archaic, former, obsolete, old, old-fashioned, old hat, outmoded, passé, past, square (*inf.*), uncool (*sl.*)

modernity *n* **1** = **novelty**, contemporaneity, currency, freshness, innovation, newness, recentness

modernize *vb* **1, 2** = **update**, bring up to date, face-lift, make over, rebrand, rejuvenate, remake, remodel, renew, renovate, revamp

modest *adj* **1-3** = **unpretentious**, bashful, blushing, coy, demure, diffident, discreet, humble, meek, quiet, reserved, reticent, retiring, self-conscious, self-effacing, shy, simple, unassuming **4** = **moderate**, fair, limited, middling, ordinary, small, unexceptional

modesty *n* = **reserve**, bashfulness, coyness, decency, demureness, diffidence, discreetness, humbleness, humility, lack of pretension, meekness, propriety, quietness, reticence, self-effacement, shyness, simplicity, timidity, unobtrusiveness, unpretentiousness
Antonyms *n* arrogance, assurance, boastfulness, boldness, conceit, confidence, egotism, extravagance, forwardness, haughtiness, immodesty, indecency, ostentation, presumption, pretentiousness, pride, showiness, vanity

modicum *n* = **little**, atom, bit, crumb, dash, drop, fragment, grain, inch, iota, mite, ounce, particle, pinch, scrap, shred, small amount, speck, tad (*inf., chiefly US*), tinge, touch

modification *n* **1, 3** = **change**, adjustment, alteration, modulation, mutation, qualification, refinement, reformation, restriction, revision, variation

modify *vb* **1** = **change**, adapt, adjust, alter, convert, recast, redo, refashion, reform, remodel, reorganize, reshape, revise, rework, transform, tweak (*inf.*), vary **2** = **tone down**, abate, ease, lessen, limit, lower, moderate, qualify, reduce, relax, restrain, restrict, soften, temper

modish *adj* = **fashionable**, à la mode, all the rage, chic, contemporary, current, hip (*sl.*), in, now (*inf.*), smart, stylish, trendy (*Brit. inf.*), up-to-the-minute, vogue, voguish, with it (*inf.*)

modulate *vb* **2** = **adjust**, attune, balance, harmonize, inflect, regulate, tone, tune, vary

modus operandi *n* = **procedure**, method, operation, practice, praxis, process, system, technique, way

mogul *n* = **tycoon**, baron, bashaw, big gun (*inf.*), big hitter, big noise (*inf.*), big shot (*inf.*), big wheel (*sl.*), heavy hitter (*inf.*), lord, magnate, nabob (*inf.*), notable, personage, potentate, V.I.P.

seen when two geometrical patterns, such as grids, are visually superimposed. [C17: from F, from *moire* MOHAIR]

Moism ('məʊ,ɪzəm) *n* the religious and ethical teaching of Mo-Zi (?470–?391 B.C.), Chinese philosopher, and his followers, emphasizing universal love, ascetic self-discipline, and obedience to the will of Heaven.

moist ❶ (mɔɪst) *adj* **1** slightly damp or wet. **2** saturated with or suggestive of moisture. [C14: from OF, ult. rel. to L *mūcidus* musty]
▸**'moistly** *adv* ▸**'moistness** *n*

moisten ❶ ('mɔɪsᵊn) *vb* to make or become moist.

moisture ❶ ('mɔɪstʃə) *n* water or other liquid diffused as vapour or condensed on or in objects.

moisturize *or* **moisturise** ('mɔɪstʃə,raɪz) *vb* **moisturizes, moisturizing, moisturized** *or* **moisturises, moisturising, moisturised.** (*tr*) to add moisture to (the air, the skin, etc.).
▸**'moistur,izer** *or* **'moistur,iser** *n*

mojo ('məʊdʒəʊ) *n, pl* **mojos** *or* **mojoes.** *US sl.* **1** an amulet, charm, or magic spell. **2** the art of casting magic spells. [C20: of W African origin]

moke (məʊk) *n Brit. sl.* a donkey. [C19: from ?]

mol *Chem. symbol for* mole³.

mol. *abbrev. for:* **1** molecular. **2** molecule.

molal ('məʊləl) *adj Chem.* of or consisting of a solution containing one mole of solute per thousand grams of solvent. [C20: from MOLE³ + -AL¹]

molar¹ ('məʊlə) *n* **1** any of the 12 grinding teeth in man. **2** a corresponding tooth in other mammals. ◆ *adj* **3** of or relating to any of these teeth. **4** used for or capable of grinding. [C16: from L *molāris*, from *mola* millstone]

molar² ('məʊlə) *adj* **1** (of a physical quantity) per unit amount of substance: *molar volume.* **2** (not recommended in technical usage) (of a solution) containing one mole of solute per litre of solution. [C19: from L *mōlēs* a mass]

molasses (mə'læsɪz) *n* (*functioning as sing*) **1** the thick brown uncrystallized bitter syrup obtained from sugar during refining. **2** the US and Canad. name for **treacle** (sense 1). [C16: from Port. *melaço*, from LL *mellāceum* must, from L *mel* honey]

mold (məʊld) *n, vb* the US spelling of **mould.**

moldboard ('məʊld,bɔːd) *n* the US spelling of **mouldboard.**

molder ('məʊldə) *vb* the US spelling of **moulder.**

molding ('məʊldɪŋ) *n* the US spelling of **moulding.**

moldy ('məʊldɪ) *adj* the US spelling of **mouldy.**

mole¹ (məʊl) *n Pathol.* a nontechnical name for **naevus.** [OE *māl*]

mole² (məʊl) *n* **1** any small burrowing mammal of a family of Europe, Asia, and North and Central America. They have velvety, typically dark fur and forearms specialized for digging. **2** *Inf.* a spy who has infiltrated an organization and become a trusted member of it. [C14: from MDu. *mol*, of Gmc origin]

mole³ (məʊl) *n* the basic SI unit of amount of substance; the amount that contains as many elementary entities as there are atoms in 0.012 kilogram of carbon-12. The entity may be an atom, a molecule, an ion, a radical, etc. Symbol: mol. See **gram molecule.** [C20: from G *Mol*, short for *Molekül* MOLECULE]

mole⁴ ❶ (məʊl) *n* **1** a breakwater. **2** a harbour protected by a breakwater. [C16: from F *môle*, from L *mōlēs* mass]

Molech ('məʊlɛk) *n Old Testament.* a variant of **Moloch.**

molecular (məʊ'lɛkjʊlə, mə-) *adj* of or relating to molecules.
▸**mo'lecularly** *adv*

molecular biology *n* the study of the structure and function of biological molecules, esp. nucleic acids and proteins.

molecular formula *n* a chemical formula indicating the numbers and types of atoms in a molecule: *H_2SO_4 is the molecular formula of sulphuric acid.*

molecular genetics *n* (*functioning as sing*) the study of the molecular constitution of genes and chromosomes.

molecular weight *n* the former name for **relative molecular mass.**

molecule ❶ ('mɒlɪ,kjuːl) *n* **1** the simplest unit of a chemical compound that can exist, consisting of two or more atoms held together by chemical bonds. **2** a very small particle. [C18: via F from NL *mōlēcula*, dim. of L *mōlēs* mass]

molehill ('məʊl,hɪl) *n* **1** the small mound of earth thrown up by a burrowing mole. **2 make a mountain out of a molehill.** to exaggerate an unimportant matter out of all proportion.

moleskin ('məʊl,skɪn) *n* **1** the dark grey dense velvety pelt of a mole, used as a fur. **2** a hard-wearing cotton fabric of twill weave. **3** (*modifier*): *a moleskin waistcoat.*

molest ❶ (mə'lɛst) *vb* (*tr*) **1** to disturb or annoy by malevolent interference. **2** to accost or attack, esp. with the intention of assaulting sexually. [C14: from L *molestāre* to annoy, from *molestus* troublesome, from *mōlēs* mass]
▸**molestation** (,məʊlɛ'steɪʃən) *n* ▸**mo'lester** *n*

moll (mɒl) *n Sl.* **1** the female accomplice of a gangster. **2** a prostitute. [C17: from *Moll*, familiar form of *Mary*]

mollify ❶ ('mɒlɪ,faɪ) *vb* **mollifies, mollifying, mollified.** (*tr*) **1** to pacify; soothe. **2** to lessen the harshness or severity of. [C15: from OF *mollifier*, via LL, from L *mollis* soft + *facere* to make]
▸**'molli,fiable** *adj* ▸**,mollifi'cation** *n* ▸**'molli,fier** *n*

mollusc *or US* **mollusk** ('mɒləsk) *n* any of various invertebrates having a soft unsegmented body and often a shell, secreted by a fold of skin (the mantle). The group includes the gastropods (snails, slugs, etc.), bivalves (clams, mussels, etc.), and cephalopods (squid, octopuses, etc.). [C18: via NL from L *molluscus*, from *mollis* soft]
▸**molluscan** *or US* **molluskan** (mɒ'lʌskən) *adj, n* ▸**mollusc-like** *or US* **mollusk-like** *adj*

molly¹ ('mɒlɪ) *n, pl* **mollies.** any of various brightly coloured tropical or subtropical American freshwater fishes. [C19: from NL *Mollienisia*, from Comte F. N. *Mollien* (1758–1850), F statesman]

molly² ('mɒlɪ) *n, pl* **mollies.** *Irish inf.* an effeminate, weak, or cowardly boy or man. [C18: perhaps from *Molly*, pet name for *Mary*]

mollycoddle ❶ ('mɒlɪ,kɒdᵊl) *vb* **mollycoddles, mollycoddling, mollycoddled.** **1** (*tr*) to treat with indulgent care; pamper. ◆ *n* **2** a pampered person. [C19: from MOLLY² + CODDLE]

Moloch ('məʊlɒk) *or* **Molech** ('məʊlɛk) *n Old Testament.* a Semitic deity to whom parents sacrificed their children.

Molotov cocktail ('mɒlə,tɒf) *n* an elementary incendiary weapon, usually a bottle of petrol with a short delay fuse or wick; petrol bomb. [C20: after V. M. *Molotov* (1890–1986), Soviet statesman]

molt (məʊlt) *vb, n* the usual US spelling of **moult.**
▸**'molter** *n*

molten ('məʊltən) *adj* **1** liquefied; melted. **2** made by having been melted: *molten casts.* ◆ *vb* **3** the past participle of **melt.**

molto ('mɒltəʊ) *adv Music.* very: *allegro molto; molto adagio.* [from It., from L *multum* (adv) much]

mol. wt. *abbrev. for* molecular weight.

moly ('məʊlɪ) *n, pl* **molies.** **1** *Greek myth.* a magic herb given by Hermes to Odysseus to nullify the spells of Circe. **2** a variety of wild garlic of S Europe having yellow flowers. [C16: from L *mōly*, from Gk *mōlu*]

molybdenite (mɒ'lɪbdɪ,naɪt) *n* a soft grey mineral consisting of molybdenum sulphide in hexagonal crystalline form with rhenium as an impurity. Formula: MoS_2.

molybdenum (mɒ'lɪbdɪnəm) *n* a very hard silvery-white metallic element occurring principally in molybdenite: used in alloys, esp. to harden and strengthen steels. Symbol: Mo; atomic no.: 42; atomic wt.: 95.94. [C19: from NL, from L *molybdaena* galena, from Gk, from *molubdos* lead]

mom (mɒm) *n Chiefly US & Canad.* an informal word for **mother¹.**

moment ❶ ('məʊmənt) *n* **1** a short indefinite period of time. **2** a specific instant or point in time: *at that moment the phone rang.* **3 the moment.** the present point of time: *at the moment it's fine.* **4** import, significance, or value: *a man of moment.* **5** *Physics.* **5a** a tendency to produce motion, esp. rotation about a point or axis. **5b** the product of a physical quantity, such as force or mass, and its distance from a fixed reference point. See also **moment of inertia.** [C14: from OF, from L *mōmentum*, from *movēre* to move]

momentarily ❶ ('məʊməntərɪlɪ, -trɪlɪ, ,məʊmən'tærɪlɪ) *adv* **1** for an instant; temporarily. **2** from moment to moment; every instant. **3** *US & Canad.* very soon. ◆ Also (for senses 1, 2): **momently.**

momentary ❶ ('məʊməntərɪ, -trɪ) *adj* **1** lasting for only a moment; temporary. **2** *Rare.* occurring or present at each moment.
▸**'momentariness** *n*

moment of inertia *n* the tendency of a body to resist angular acceleration, expressed as the sum of the products of the mass of each particle in the body and the square of its perpendicular distance from the axis of rotation.

moment of truth *n* **1** a moment when a person or thing is put to the test. **2** the point in a bullfight when the matador is about to kill the bull.

THESAURUS

moist *adj* **1, 2 = damp,** clammy, dampish, dank, dewy, dripping, drizzly, humid, not dry, rainy, soggy, wet, wettish

moisten *vb* **= dampen,** bedew, damp, humidify, lick, moisturize, soak, water, wet

moisture *n* **= damp,** dampness, dankness, dew, humidity, liquid, perspiration, sweat, water, wateriness, wetness

mole⁴ *n* **1 = breakwater,** dike, dyke, embankment, groyne, jetty, pier, sea wall

molecule *n* **2 = particle,** atom, iota, jot, mite, mote, speck

molest *vb* **1 = annoy,** abuse, afflict, badger, beset, bother, bug (*inf.*), disturb, harass, harry, hector, irritate, persecute, pester, plague, tease, torment, upset, vex, worry **2 = abuse,** accost, assail, attack, harm, hurt, ill-treat, injure, interfere with, maltreat, manhandle

mollify *vb* **1 = pacify,** appease, calm, compose, conciliate, placate, pour oil on troubled waters, propitiate, quell, quiet, soothe, sweeten **2 = soften,** abate, allay, assuage, blunt, curb, cushion, ease, lessen, lull, mitigate, moderate, modify, relieve, temper, tone down, tranquillize

mollycoddle *vb* **1 = pamper,** baby, coddle, cosset, indulge, pet, ruin, spoil

moment *n* **1 = instant,** bat of an eye (*inf.*), flash, jiffy (*inf.*), minute, no time, second, shake (*inf.*), split second, tick (*Brit. inf.*), trice, twinkling, two shakes (*inf.*), two shakes of a lamb's tail (*inf.*) **2 = time,** hour, instant, juncture, point, point in time, stage **4 = importance,** concern, consequence, gravity, import, seriousness, significance, substance, value, weight, weightiness, worth

momentarily *adv* **1 = briefly,** for a little while, for a minute, for a moment, for an instant, for a second, for a short time, for a short while, for the nonce, temporarily

momentary *adj* **1 = short-lived,** brief, ephemeral, evanescent, fleeting, flying, fugitive, hasty, passing, quick, short, temporary, transitory

Antonyms *adj* lasting, lengthy, long-lived, permanent

momentous ⓣ (məʊ'mɛntəs) *adj* of great significance.
▸**mo'mentously** *adv* ▸**mo'mentousness** *n*

momentum ⓣ (məʊ'mɛntəm) *n, pl* **momenta** (-tə) *or* **momentums. 1** *Physics.* the product of a body's mass and its velocity. **2** the impetus of a body resulting from its motion. **3** driving power or strength. [C17: from L: movement; see MOMENT]

momma ('mɒmə) *n Chiefly US.* **1** an informal or childish word for **mother**[1]. **2** *Inf.* a buxom and voluptuous woman.

mon. *abbrev. for* monetary.

Mon. *abbrev. for* Monday.

mon- *combining form.* a variant of **mono-** before a vowel.

monad ('mɒnæd, 'məʊ-) *n* **1** (*pl* **monads** *or* **monades** (-əˌdiːz)). *Philosophy.* any fundamental singular metaphysical entity, esp. if autonomous. **2** a single-celled organism. **3** an atom, ion, or radical with a valency of one. ◆ Also (for senses 1, 2): **monas.** [C17: from LL *monas,* from Gk: unit, from *monos* alone]
▸**monadic** (mɒ'nædɪk) *adj*

monadelphous (ˌmɒnə'dɛlfəs) *adj* **1** (of stamens) having united filaments forming a tube around the style. **2** (of flowers) having monadelphous stamens. [C19: from MONO- + Gk *adelphos* brother]

monadnock (mə'nædnɒk) *n* a residual hill of hard rock in an otherwise eroded area. [C19: after Mount *Monadnock,* New Hampshire, US]

monandrous (mɒ'nændrəs) *adj* **1** having only one male sexual partner over a period of time. **2** (of plants) having flowers with only one stamen. **3** (of flowers) having only one stamen. [C19: from MONO- + -ANDROUS]
▸**mo'nandry** *n*

monarch ⓣ ('mɒnək) *n* **1** a sovereign head of state, esp. a king, queen, or emperor, who rules usually by hereditary right. **2** a supremely powerful or pre-eminent person or thing. **3** Also called: **milkweed.** a large migratory orange-and-black butterfly that feeds on the milkweed plant. [C15: from LL *monarcha,* from Gk; see MONO-, -ARCH]
▸**monarchal** (mɒ'nɑːkᵊl) *or* **mo'narchial** *adj* ▸**mo'narchical** *or* **mo'narchic** *adj* ▸**'monarchism** *n* ▸**'monarchist** *n, adj* ▸**ˌmonar'chistic** *adj*

monarchy ⓣ ('mɒnəkɪ) *n, pl* **monarchies. 1** a form of government in which supreme authority is vested in a single and usually hereditary figure, such as a king. **2** a country reigned over by a monarch.

monarda (mɒ'nɑːdə) *n* any of various mintlike North American plants. [C19: from NL, after N. *Monardés* (1493–1588), Sp. botanist]

monastery ⓣ ('mɒnəstərɪ) *n, pl* **monasteries.** the residence of a religious community, esp. of monks, living in seclusion from secular society and bound by religious vows. [C15: from Church L *monastērium,* ult. from Gk *monazein* to live alone, from *monos* alone]
▸**monasterial** (ˌmɒnə'stɪərɪəl) *adj*

monastic ⓣ (mə'næstɪk) *adj* **1** of or relating to monasteries or monks, nuns, etc. **2** resembling this sort of life. ◆ *n* **3** a person committed to this way of life, esp. a monk.

monasticism (mə'næstɪˌsɪzəm) *n* the monastic system, movement, or way of life.

monatomic (ˌmɒnə'tɒmɪk) *or* **monoatomic** (ˌmɒnəʊə'tɒmɪk) *adj Chem.* **1** (of an element) having or consisting of single atoms. **2** (of a compound or molecule) having only one atom or group that can be replaced in a chemical reaction.

monaural (mɒ'nɔːrəl) *adj* **1** relating to, having, or hearing with only one ear. **2** another word for **monophonic.**
▸**mon'aurally** *adv*

monazite ('mɒnəˌzaɪt) *n* a yellow to reddish-brown mineral consisting of a phosphate of thorium, cerium, and lanthanum in monoclinic crystalline form. [C19: from G, from Gk *monazein* to live alone, so called because of its rarity]

Monday ('mʌndɪ) *n* the second day of the week; first day of the working week. [OE *mōnandæg* moon's day, translation of LL *lūnae diēs*]

monecious (mɒ'niːʃəs) *adj* a variant spelling of **monoecious.**

Monel metal *or* **Monell metal** (mɒ'nel) *n Trademark.* any of various silvery corrosion-resistant alloys. [C20: after A. *Monell* (died 1921), president of the International Nickel Co., New York, which introduced the alloys]

monetarism ('mʌnɪtəˌrɪzəm) *n* **1** the theory that inflation is caused by an excess quantity of money in an economy. **2** an economic policy based on this theory and on a belief in the efficiency of free market forces.
▸**'monetarist** *n, adj*

monetary ⓣ ('mʌnɪtərɪ, -trɪ) *adj* **1** of or relating to money or currency. **2** of or relating to monetarism. [C19: from LL *monētārius,* from L *monēta* MONEY]
▸**'monetarily** *adv*

monetize *or* **monetise** ('mʌnɪˌtaɪz) *vb* **monetizes, monetizing, monetized** *or* **monetises, monetising, monetised.** (*tr*) **1** to establish as legal tender. **2** to give a legal value to (a coin).
▸**ˌmoneti'zation** *or* **ˌmoneti'sation** *n*

money ⓣ ('mʌnɪ) *n* **1** a medium of exchange that functions as legal tender. **2** the official currency, in the form of banknotes, coins, etc., issued by a government or other authority. **3** a particular denomination or form of currency: *silver money.* **4** (*Law or arch. pl* **moneys** *or* **monies**) a pecuniary sum or income. **5** an unspecified amount of paper currency or coins: *money to lend.* **6 for one's money.** in one's opinion. **7 in the money.** *Inf.* well-off; rich. **8 one's money's worth.** full value for the money one has paid for something. **9 put money on.** to place a bet on. ◆ Related adj: **pecuniary.** [C13: from OF *moneie,* from L *monēta;* see MINT[2]]

moneybags ('mʌnɪˌbægz) *n* (*functioning as sing*) *Inf.* a very rich person.

moneychanger ('mʌnɪˌtʃeɪndʒə) *n* **1** a person engaged in the business of exchanging currencies or money. **2** *Chiefly US.* a machine for dispensing coins.

moneyed ⓣ *or* **monied** ('mʌnɪd) *adj* **1** having a great deal of money; rich. **2** arising from or characterized by money.

money-grubbing *adj Inf.* seeking greedily to obtain money.
▸**'money-ˌgrubber** *n*

moneylender ('mʌnɪˌlɛndə) *n* a person who lends money at interest as a living.
▸**'moneyˌlending** *adj, n*

moneymaker ⓣ ('mʌnɪˌmeɪkə) *n* **1** a person who is intent on accumulating money. **2** a person or thing that is or might be profitable.
▸**'moneyˌmaking** *adj, n*

money of account *n* another name (esp. US and Canad.) for **unit of account.**

money-spinner *n Inf.* an enterprise, idea, person, or thing that is a source of wealth.

money supply *n* the total amount of money in a country's economy at a given time, which can be calculated in various ways.

monger ('mʌŋgə) *n* **1** (*in combination except in archaic use*) a trader or dealer: *ironmonger.* **2** (*in combination*) a promoter of something: *warmonger.* [OE *mangere,* ult. from L *mangō* dealer]
▸**'mongering** *n, adj*

mongol ('mɒŋgᵊl) *n* (not in technical use) a person affected by Down's syndrome.

Mongol ('mɒŋgɒl, -gᵊl) *n* another word for **Mongolian.**

mongolian (mɒŋ'gəʊlɪən) *adj* (not in technical use) of, relating to, or affected by Down's syndrome.

Mongolian (mɒŋ'gəʊlɪən) *adj* **1** of or relating to Mongolia, a country in Central Asia, its people, or their language. ◆ *n* **2** a native or inhabitant of Mongolia. **3** the language of Mongolia.

Mongolic (mɒŋ'gɒlɪk) *n* **1** a branch or subfamily of the Altaic family of languages, including Mongolian and Kalmuck. **2** another word for **Mongoloid.**

mongolism ('mɒŋgəˌlɪzəm) *n Pathol.* a former name (not in technical use) for **Down's syndrome.** [C20: the condition produces facial features similar to those of the Mongoloid peoples]

mongoloid ('mɒŋgəˌlɔɪd) *adj* (not in technical use) **1** relating to or characterized by Down's syndrome. ◆ *n* **2** a person affected by Down's syndrome.

Mongoloid ('mɒŋgəˌlɔɪd) *adj* **1** of or relating to a major racial group of mankind, characterized by yellowish complexion, straight black hair, slanting eyes, short nose, and scanty facial hair, including most of the peoples of Asia, the Eskimos, and the North American Indians. ◆ *n* **2** a member of this group.

mongoose ('mɒŋˌguːs) *n, pl* **mongooses.** any of various small predatory mammals occurring in Africa and from S Europe to SE Asia, typically having a long tail and brindled coat. [C17: from Marathi (a language of India) *mangūs*]

mongrel ⓣ ('mʌŋgrəl) *n* **1** a plant or animal, esp. a dog, of mixed or unknown breeding. **2** *Derog.* a person of mixed race. ◆ *adj* **3** of mixed origin, breeding, character, etc. [C15: from obs. *mong* mixture]
▸**'mongrelism** *n* ▸**'mongreˌlize** *or* **'mongreˌlise** *vb* ▸**ˌmongreli'zation** *or* **ˌmongreli'sation** *n* ▸**'mongrelly** *adj*

THESAURUS

momentous *adj* = **significant**, consequential, critical, crucial, decisive, earth-shaking (*inf.*), fateful, grave, historic, important, of moment, pivotal, serious, vital, weighty
Antonyms *adj* inconsequential, insignificant, trifling, trivial, unimportant

momentum *n* **2, 3** = **impetus**, drive, energy, force, power, propulsion, push, strength, thrust

monarch *n* **1** = **ruler**, crowned head, emperor *or* empress, king, potentate, prince *or* princess, queen, sovereign

monarchy *n* **1** = **sovereignty**, absolutism, autocracy, despotism, kingship, monocracy, royalism **2** = **kingdom**, empire, principality, realm

monastery *n* = **abbey**, cloister, convent, friary, house, nunnery, priory, religious community

monastic *adj* **1, 2** = **monkish**, ascetic, austere, celibate, cenobitic, cloistered, cloistral, coenobitic, contemplative, conventual, eremitic, hermit-like, monachal, recluse, reclusive, secluded, sequestered, withdrawn

monetary *adj* **1** = **financial**, budgetary, capital, cash, fiscal, pecuniary

money *n* **1, 2** = **cash**, banknotes, brass (*N English dialect*), bread, capital, coin, currency, dibs (*sl.*), dosh (*Brit. & Austral. sl.*), dough (*sl.*), filthy lucre (*facetious*), funds, hard cash, legal tender, lolly (*Brit. sl.*), loot (*inf.*), moolah (*sl.*), necessary (*inf.*), needful (*inf.*), pelf (*contemptuous*), readies (*inf.*), rhino (*Brit. sl.*), riches, shekels (*inf.*), silver, specie, spondulicks (*sl.*), tin (*sl.*), wealth **7 in the money** *Informal* = **rich**, affluent, flush (*inf.*), in clover (*inf.*), loaded (*sl.*), on Easy Street (*inf.*), prosperous, rolling (*sl.*), wealthy, well-heeled (*inf.*), well-off, well-to-do

moneyed *adj* **1** = **rich**, affluent, flush (*inf.*), loaded (*sl.*), prosperous, wealthy, well-heeled (*inf.*), well-off, well-to-do

moneymaking *adj* **1, 2** = **profitable**, gainful, going, lucrative, paying, remunerative, successful, thriving

mongrel *n* **1** = **hybrid**, bigener (*Biology*), cross, crossbreed, half-breed, mixed breed ◆ *adj* **3** =

'mongst (mʌŋst) *prep Poetic.* short for **amongst.**
monied ('mʌnɪd) *adj* a less common spelling of **moneyed.**
monies ('mʌnɪz) *n Law, arch.* a plural of **money.**
moniker *or* **monicker** ('mɒnɪkə) *n Sl.* a person's name or nickname. [C19: from Shelta *munnik,* altered from Irish Gaelic *ainm* name]
monism ('mɒnɪzəm) *n* **1** *Philosophy.* the doctrine that reality consists of only one basic substance or element, such as mind or matter. Cf. **dualism** (sense 2), **pluralism** (sense 4). **2** the attempt to explain anything in terms of one principle only.
▸**'monist** *n, adj* ▸**mo'nistic** *adj*
monition (məʊ'nɪʃən) *n* **1** a warning or caution; admonition. **2** *Christianity.* a formal notice from a bishop or ecclesiastical court requiring a person to refrain from committing a specific offence. [C14: via OF from L *monitiō,* from *monēre* to warn]
monitor ❶ ('mɒnɪtə) *n* **1** a person or piece of equipment that warns, checks, controls, or keeps a continuous record of something. **2** *Education.* **2a** a senior pupil with various supervisory duties, etc. **2b** a pupil assisting a teacher in classroom organization, etc. **3** a television set used to display certain kinds of information in a television studio, airport, etc. **4a** a loudspeaker used in a recording studio to determine quality or balance. **4b** a loudspeaker used on stage to enable musicians to hear themselves. **5** any of various large predatory lizards inhabiting warm regions of Africa, Asia, and Australia. **6** (formerly) a small heavily armoured warship used for coastal assault. ◆ *vb* **7** to act as a monitor of. **8** (*tr*) to observe or record (the activity or performance of) (an engine or other device). **9** (*tr*) to check (the technical quality of) (a radio or television broadcast). [C16: from L, from *monēre* to advise]
▸**monitorial** (,mɒnɪ'tɔːrɪəl) *adj* ▸**'monitorship** *n* ▸**'monitress** *fem n*
monitory ('mɒnɪtərɪ, -trɪ) *adj also* **monitorial. 1** warning or admonishing. ◆ *n, pl* **monitories. 2** *Rare.* a letter containing a monition.
monk ❶ (mʌŋk) *n* a male member of a religious community bound by vows of poverty, chastity, and obedience. Related adj: **monastic.** [OE *munuc,* from LL *monachus,* from LGk: solitary (man), from Gk *monos* alone]
▸**'monkish** *adj*
monkey ❶ ('mʌŋkɪ) *n* **1** any of numerous long-tailed primates excluding lemurs, tarsiers, etc.: see **Old World monkey, New World monkey. 2** any primate except man. **3** a naughty or mischievous person, esp. a child. **4** the head of a pile-driver (**monkey engine**) or of some similar mechanical device. **5** *US & Canad. sl.* an addict's dependence on a drug (esp. in **have a monkey on one's back**). **6** *Sl.* a butt of derision; someone made to look a fool (esp. in **make a monkey of**). **7** *Sl.* (esp. in bookmaking) £500. **8** *US & Canad. sl.* $500. ◆ *vb* **9** (*intr;* usually foll. by *around, with,* etc.) to meddle, fool, or tinker. **10** (*tr*) *Rare.* to imitate; ape. [C16: ?from Low G; cf. MLow G *Moneke,* name of the ape's son in the tale of Reynard the Fox]
monkey business ❶ *n Inf.* mischievous, suspect, or dishonest behaviour or acts.
monkey flower *n* any of various plants of the genus *Mimulus,* cultivated for their yellow or red flowers.
monkey jacket *n* a short close-fitting jacket, esp. a waist-length jacket similar to a mess jacket.
monkey nut *n Brit.* another name for a **peanut.**
monkey puzzle *n* a South American coniferous tree having branches shaped like a candelabrum and stiff sharp leaves. Also called: **Chile pine.**
monkey's wedding *n S. African inf.* a combination of rain and sunshine. [from ?]
monkey tricks *or US* **monkey shines** *pl n Inf.* mischievous behaviour or acts.
monkey wrench *n* a wrench with adjustable jaws.
monkfish ('mʌŋk,fɪʃ) *n, pl* **monkfish** *or* **monkfishes. 1** any of various angler fishes. **2** another name for **angelfish** (sense 3).
monk's cloth *n* a heavy cotton fabric of basket weave, used mainly for bedspreads.
monkshood ('mʌŋkshʊd) *n* any of several poisonous N temperate plants that have hooded blue-purple flowers.
mono ('mɒnəʊ) *adj* **1** short for **monophonic.** ◆ *n* **2** monophonic sound.
mono- *or before a vowel* **mon-** *combining form.* **1** one; single: *monorail.* **2** indicating that a chemical compound contains a single specified atom or group: *monoxide.* [from Gk *monos*]
monoacid (,mɒnəʊ'æsɪd), **monacid, monoacidic** (,mɒnəʊə'sɪdɪk), *or* **monacidic** *adj Chem.* (of a base) capable of reacting with only one molecule of a monobasic acid; having only one hydroxide ion per molecule.
monobasic (,mɒnəʊ'beɪsɪk) *adj Chem.* (of an acid, such as hydrogen chloride) having only one replaceable hydrogen atom per molecule.
monocarpic (,mɒnəʊ'kɑːpɪk) *or* **monocarpous** *adj* (of some flowering plants) producing fruit only once before dying.
monochromatic (,mɒnəʊkrəʊ'mætɪk) *or* **monochroic** (,mɒnəʊ'krəʊɪk) *adj* (of light or other electromagnetic radiation) having only one wavelength.
monochromator (,mɒnəʊ'krəʊm,eɪtə) *n Physics.* a device that isolates a single wavelength of radiation.
monochrome ('mɒnə,krəʊm) *n* **1** a black-and-white photograph or transparency. **2** *Photog.* black-and-white. **3a** a painting, drawing, etc., done in a range of tones of a single colour. **3b** the technique or art of this. **4** (*modifier*) executed in or resembling monochrome: *a monochrome print.* ◆ *adj* **5** devoid of any distinctive or stimulating characteristics. ◆ Also called (for senses 3, 4): **monotint.** [C17: via Med. L from Gk *monokhrōmos* of one colour]
▸**,mono'chromic** *adj* ▸**'mono,chromist** *n*
monocle ('mɒnək^əl) *n* a lens for correcting defective vision of one eye, held in position by the facial muscles. [C19: from F, from LL, from MONO- + *oculus* eye]
▸**'monocled** *adj*
monocline ('mɒnəʊ,klaɪn) *n* a fold in stratified rocks in which the strata are inclined in the same direction from the horizontal. [C19: from MONO- + Gk *klīnein* to lean]
▸**,mono'clinal** *adj, n*
monoclinic (,mɒnəʊ'klɪnɪk) *adj Crystallog.* relating to or belonging to the crystal system characterized by three unequal axes, one pair of which are not at right angles to each other. [C19: from MONO- + Gk *klīnein* to lean]
monoclinous (,mɒnəʊ'klaɪnəs, 'mɒnəʊ,klaɪnəs) *adj* (of flowering plants) having the male and female reproductive organs on the same flower. Cf. **diclinous.** [C19: from MONO- + Gk *klīne* bed]
▸**'mono,clinism** *n*
monoclonal antibody (,mɒnəʊ'kləʊn^əl) *n* an antibody, produced by a single clone of cells grown in culture, that is both pure and specific and capable of proliferating indefinitely: used in diagnosis, therapy, and biotechnology.
monocotyledon (,mɒnəʊ,kɒtɪ'liːd^ən) *n* any of various flowering plants having a single embryonic seed leaf, leaves with parallel veins, and flowers with parts in threes: includes grasses, lilies, palms, and orchids. Cf. **dicotyledon.**
▸**,mono,coty'ledonous** *adj*
monocracy (mɒ'nɒkrəsɪ) *n, pl* **monocracies.** government by one person.
▸**monocrat** ('mɒnə,kræt) *n* ▸**,mono'cratic** *adj*
monocular (mɒ'nɒkjʊlə) *adj* having or intended for the use of only one eye. [C17: from LL *monoculus* one-eyed]
▸**mo'nocularly** *adv*
monoculture ('mɒnəʊ,kʌltʃə) *n* the continuous growing of one type of crop.
monocycle ('mɒnə,saɪk^əl) *n* another name for **unicycle.**
monocyte ('mɒnəʊ,saɪt) *n* the largest type of white blood cell that acts as part of the immune system by engulfing particles, such as invading microorganisms.
monody ('mɒnədɪ) *n, pl* **monodies. 1** (in Greek tragedy) an ode sung by a single actor. **2** any poem of lament for someone's death. **3** *Music.* a style of composition consisting of a single vocal part, usually with accompaniment. [C17: via LL from Gk *monōidia,* from MONO- + *aeidein* to sing]
▸**monodic** (mɒ'nɒdɪk) *adj* ▸**'monodist** *n*
monoecious (mɒ'niːʃəs) *adj* **1** (of some flowering plants) having the male and female reproductive organs in separate flowers on the same plant. **2** (of some animals and lower plants) hermaphrodite. [C18: from NL *monoecia,* from MONO- + Gk *oikos* house]
monofilament (,mɒnə'fɪləmənt) *or* **monofil** ('mɒnəfɪl) *n* synthetic thread or yarn composed of a single strand rather than twisted fibres.
monogamy (mɒ'nɒgəmɪ) *n* **1** the state or practice of having only one husband or wife over a period of time. **2** *Zool.* the practice of having only one mate. [C17: via F from LL *monogamia,* from Gk; see MONO- + -GAMY]
▸**mo'nogamist** *n* ▸**mo'nogamous** *adj*
monogenesis (,mɒnəʊ'dʒɛnɪsɪs) *or* **monogeny** (mɒ'nɒdʒɪnɪ) *n* **1** the hypothetical descent of all organisms from a single cell. **2** asexual reproduction in animals. **3** the direct development of an ovum into an organism resembling the adult. **4** the hypothetical descent of all human beings from a single pair of ancestors.
monogram ('mɒnə,græm) *n* a design of one or more letters, esp. initials, on clothing, stationery, etc. [C17: from LL *monogramma,* from Gk; see MONO-, -GRAM]
▸**monogrammatic** (,mɒnəgrə'mætɪk) *adj*
monograph ('mɒnə,grɑːf) *n* **1** a paper, book, or other work concerned with a single subject or aspect of a subject. ◆ *vb* **monographs, monographing, monographed.** (*tr*) **2** to write a monograph on.
▸**monographer** (mɒ'nɒgrəfə) *or* **mo'nographist** *n* ▸**,mono'graphic** *adj*
monogyny (mɒ'nɒdʒɪnɪ) *n* the custom of having only one female sexual partner over a period of time.
▸**mo'nogynous** *adj*
monohull ('mɒnəʊ,hʌl) *n* a sailing vessel with a single hull.

THESAURUS

hybrid, bastard, crossbred, half-breed, of mixed breed

monitor *n* **1, 2** = **watchdog**, guide, invigilator, overseer, prefect, supervisor ◆ *vb* **7, 8** = **check**, follow, keep an eye on, keep tabs on, keep track of, observe, oversee, record, scan, supervise, survey, watch

monk *n* = **friar** (*loosely*), brother, monastic, religious

monkey *n* **1, 2** = **simian**, jackanapes (*arch.*), primate **3** = **rascal**, devil, imp, mischief maker, pickle, rogue, scamp ◆ *vb* **9** *with* **around** *or* **about with** = **fool**, fiddle (*inf.*), interfere, meddle, mess, play, tamper, tinker, trifle

monkey business *n Informal* = **mischief**, carry-on (*inf., chiefly Brit.*), clowning, horseplay, monkey tricks, pranks, shenanigans (*inf.*), skylarking (*inf.*), tomfoolery = **dishonesty**, chicanery, funny business, hanky-panky (*inf.*), skulduggery (*inf.*), trickery

monokini ('mɒnəʊ,kiːnɪ) *n* a woman's one-piece bathing garment usually equivalent to the bottom half of a bikini. [C20: from MONO- + BIKINI (as if *bikini* were from BI-)]

monolayer ('mɒnəʊ,leɪə) *n* a single layer of atoms or molecules adsorbed on a surface. Also called: **molecular film.**

monolingual (,mɒnəʊ'lɪŋgwəl) *adj* knowing or expressed in only one language.

monolith 🅣 ('mɒnəlɪθ) *n* **1** a large block of stone or anything that resembles one in appearance, intractability, etc. **2** a statue, obelisk, column, etc., cut from one block of stone. **3** a large hollow foundation piece sunk as a caisson and filled with concrete. [C19: via F from Gk *monolithos* made from a single stone]
▸**,mono'lithic** *adj*

monologue 🅣 ('mɒnə,lɒg) *n* **1** a long speech made by one actor in a play, film, etc., esp. when alone. **2** a dramatic piece for a single performer. **3** any long speech by one person, esp. when interfering with conversation. [C17: via F from Gk *monologos* speaking alone]
▸**monologic** (,mɒnə'lɒdʒɪk) *or* **,mono'logical** *adj* ▸**monologist** ('mɒnə,lɒgɪst) *n* ▸**monologize** *or* **monologise** (mɒ'nɒlədʒaɪz) *vb*

USAGE NOTE See at **soliloquy.**

monomania (,mɒnəʊ'meɪnɪə) *n* an excessive mental preoccupation with one thing, idea, etc.
▸**,mono'mani,ac** *n, adj* ▸**monomaniacal** (,mɒnəʊmə'naɪəkəl) *adj*

monomark ('mɒnəmɑːk) *n Brit.* a series of letters or figures to identify goods, personal articles, etc.

monomer ('mɒnəmə) *n Chem.* a compound whose molecules can join together to form a polymer.
▸**monomeric** (,mɒnə'merɪk) *adj*

monometallism (,mɒnəʊ'metə,lɪzəm) *n* **1** the use of one metal, esp. gold or silver, as the sole standard of value and currency. **2** the economic policies supporting a monometallic standard.
▸**monometallic** (,mɒnəʊmɪ'tælɪk) *adj* ▸**,mono'metallist** *n*

monomial (mɒ'nəʊmɪəl) *n* **1** *Maths.* an expression consisting of a single term, such as *5ax.* ◆ *adj* **2** consisting of a single algebraic term. [C18: MONO- + (BIN)OMIAL]

monomorphic (,mɒnəʊ'mɔːfɪk) *or* **monomorphous** *adj* **1** (of an individual organism) showing little or no change in structure during the entire life history. **2** (of a species) existing or having parts that exist in only one form. **3** (of a chemical compound) having only one crystalline form.

mononucleosis (,mɒnəʊ,njuːklɪ'əʊsɪs) *n* **1** *Pathol.* the presence of a large number of monocytes in the blood. **2** See **infectious mononucleosis.**

monophonic (,mɒnəʊ'fɒnɪk) *adj* **1** Also: **monaural.** (of a system of broadcasting, recording, or reproducing sound) using only one channel between source and loudspeaker. Sometimes shortened to **mono.** Cf. **stereophonic. 2** *Music.* of or relating to a style of musical composition consisting of a single melodic line.

monophthong ('mɒnəf,θɒŋ) *n* a simple or pure vowel. [C17: from Gk *monophthongos,* from MONO- + *thongos* sound]

Monophysite (mɒ'nɒfɪ,saɪt) *n Christianity.* a person who holds that there is only one nature in the person of Christ, which is primarily divine with human attributes. [C17: via Church L from LGk, from MONO- + *phusis* nature]
▸**Monophysitic** (,mɒnəʊfɪ'sɪtɪk) *adj*

monoplane ('mɒnəʊ,pleɪn) *n* an aeroplane with only one pair of wings. Cf. **biplane.**

monopole ('mɒnə,pəʊl) *n Physics.* **1** an electric charge or magnetic pole considered in isolation. **2** Also called: **magnetic monopole.** a hypothetical elementary particle postulated in certain theories of particle physics to exist as an isolated north or south magnetic pole.

monopolize 🅣 *or* **monopolise** (mə'nɒpə,laɪz) *vb* **monopolizes, monopolizing, monopolized** *or* **monopolises, monopolising, monopolised.** (*tr*) **1** to have, control, or make use of fully, excluding others. **2** to obtain, maintain, or exploit a monopoly of (a market, commodity, etc.).
▸**mo,nopoli'zation** *or* **mo,nopoli'sation** *n* ▸**mo'nopo,lizer** *or* **mo'nopo,liser** *n*

monopoly (mə'nɒpəlɪ) *n, pl* **monopolies. 1** exclusive control of the market supply of a product or service. **2a** an enterprise exercising this control. **2b** the product or service so controlled. **3** *Law.* the exclusive right granted to a person, company, etc., by the state to purchase, manufacture, use, or sell some commodity or to trade in a specified area. **4** exclusive control, possession, or use of something. [C16: from LL, from Gk *monopōlion,* from MONO- + *pōlein* to sell]
▸**mo'nopolist** *n* ▸**mo,nopo'listic** *adj*

Monopoly (mə'nɒpəlɪ) *n Trademark.* a board game for two to six players who throw dice to advance their tokens, the object being to acquire the property on which their tokens land.

monorail ('mɒnəʊ,reɪl) *n* a single-rail railway, often elevated and with suspended cars.

monosaccharide (,mɒnəʊ'sækə,raɪd) *n* a simple sugar, such as glucose or fructose, that does not hydrolyse to yield other sugars.

monoski ('mɒnəʊ,skiː) *n* a wide ski on which the skier stands with both feet.
▸**'mono,skier** *n* ▸**'mono,skiing** *n*

monosodium glutamate (,mɒnəʊ'səʊdɪəm 'gluːtə,meɪt) *n* a white crystalline substance that has little flavour itself but enhances protein flavours: used as a food additive.

monostable (,mɒnəʊ'steɪbəl) *adj Physics.* (of an electronic circuit) having only one stable state but able to pass into a second state in response to an input pulse.

monosyllabic (,mɒnəsɪ'læbɪk) *adj* **1** (of a word) containing only one syllable. **2** characterized by monosyllables; curt.
▸**,monosyl'labically** *adv*

monosyllable ('mɒnə,sɪləbəl) *n* a word of one syllable, esp. one used as a sentence.

monoterpene ('mɒnə,tɜːpiːn) *n Chem.* an isoprene unit, C_5H_8, forming a terpene.

monotheism ('mɒnəʊθɪ,ɪzəm) *n* the belief or doctrine that there is only one God.
▸**'mono,theist** *n, adj* ▸**,monothe'istic** *adj* ▸**,monothe'istically** *adv*

monotint ('mɒnə,tɪnt) *n* another word for **monochrome** (senses 3, 4).

monotone ('mɒnə,təʊn) *n* **1** a single unvaried pitch level in speech, sound, etc. **2** utterance, etc., without change of pitch. **3** lack of variety in style, expression, etc. ◆ *adj* **4** unvarying.

monotonous 🅣 (mə'nɒtənəs) *adj* **1** tedious, esp. because of repetition. **2** in unvarying tone.
▸**mo'notonously** *adv* ▸**mo'notonousness** *n*

monotony 🅣 (mə'nɒtənɪ) *n, pl* **monotonies. 1** wearisome routine; dullness. **2** lack of variety in pitch or cadence.

monotreme ('mɒnəʊ,triːm) *n* any mammal of a primitive order of Australia and New Guinea, having a single opening (cloaca) for the passage of eggs or sperm, faeces, and urine. The group contains only the echidnas and the platypus. [C19: via NL from MONO- + Gk *trēma* hole]
▸**monotrematous** (,mɒnəʊ'triːmətəs) *adj*

monotype ('mɒnə,taɪp) *n* **1** a single print made from a metal or glass plate on which a picture has been painted. **2** *Biol.* a monotypic genus or species.

Monotype ('mɒnə,taɪp) *n* **1** *Trademark.* any of various typesetting systems, esp. originally one in which each character was cast individually from hot metal. **2** type produced by such a system.

monotypic (,mɒnəʊ'tɪpɪk) *adj* **1** (of a genus or species) consisting of only one type of animal or plant. **2** of or relating to a monotype.

monounsaturated (,mɒnəʊʌn'sætʃə,reɪtɪd) *adj* of or relating to a class of vegetable oils, such as olive oil, the molecules of which have long chains of carbon atoms containing only one double bond. See also **polyunsaturated.**

monovalent (,mɒnəʊ'veɪlənt) *adj Chem.* **a** having a valency of one. **b** having only one valency. ◆ Also: **univalent.**
▸**,mono'valence** *or* **,mono'valency** *n*

monoxide (mɒ'nɒksaɪd) *n* an oxide that contains one oxygen atom per molecule.

Monseigneur *French.* (mɔ̃sɛɲœr) *n, pl* **Messeigneurs** (mesɛɲœr). a title given to French bishops, prelates, and princes. [lit.: my lord]

monsieur (məs'jɜː) *n, pl* **messieurs.** a French title of address equivalent to *sir* when used alone or *Mr* before a name. [lit.: my lord]

Monsignor (mɒn'siːnjə) *n, pl* **Monsignors** *or* **Monsignori** (*Italian* monsiɲ'ɲoːri). *RC Church.* an ecclesiastical title attached to certain offices. [C17: from It., from F MONSEIGNEUR]

monsoon (mɒn'suːn) *n* **1** a seasonal wind of S Asia from the southwest in summer and from the northeast in winter. **2** the rainy season when the SW monsoon blows, from about April to October. **3** any wind that changes direction with the seasons. [C16: from obs. Du. *monssoen,* from Port., from Ar. *mawsim* season]
▸**mon'soonal** *adj*

mons pubis ('mɒnz 'pjuːbɪs) *n, pl* **montes pubis** ('mɒntiːz). the fatty flesh in human males over the junction of the pubic bones. Cf. **mons veneris.** [C17: NL: hill of the pubes]

monster 🅣 ('mɒnstə) *n* **1** an imaginary beast, usually made up of various animal or human parts. **2** a person, animal, or plant with a marked deformity. **3** a cruel, wicked, or inhuman person. **4a** a very large person, animal, or thing. **4b** (*as modifier*): *a monster cake.* [C13: from OF *monstre,* from L *monstrum* portent, from *monēre* to warn]

monstera (mɒn'stɪərə) *n* any of various tropical evergreen climbing plants. [from ?]

THESAURUS

monolithic *adj* **1 = huge,** colossal, giant, gigantic, immovable, impenetrable, imposing, intractable, massive, monumental, solid, substantial, undifferentiated, undivided, unitary

monologue *n* **1, 3 = speech,** harangue, lecture, sermon, soliloquy

monopolize *vb* **1, 2 = control,** corner, corner the market in, dominate, engross, exercise *or* have a monopoly of, hog (*sl.*), keep to oneself, take over, take up

monotonous *adj* **1, 2 = tedious,** all the same, boring, colourless, droning, dull, flat, ho-hum (*inf.*), humdrum, mind-numbing, plodding, repetitious, repetitive, samey (*inf.*), soporific, tiresome, toneless, unchanging, uniform, uninflected, unvaried, wearisome
Antonyms *adj* animated, enjoyable, entertaining, enthralling, exciting, exhilarating, interesting, lively, sexy (*inf.*), stimulating

monotony *n* **1 = tedium,** boredom, colourlessness, dullness, flatness, humdrumness, monotonousness, repetitiousness, repetitiveness, routine, sameness, tediousness, tiresomeness, uniformity, wearisomeness

monster *n* **2 = freak,** abortion, lusus naturae, miscreation, monstrosity, mutant, teratism **3 = brute,** barbarian, beast, bogeyman, demon, devil, fiend, ghoul, ogre, savage, villain **4a = giant,** behemoth, Brobdingnagian, colossus, leviathan, mammoth, titan ◆ *modifier* **4b = huge,**

monstrance ('mɒnstrəns) *n RC Church.* a receptacle in which the consecrated Host is exposed for adoration. [C16: from Med. L *mōnstrantia,* from L *mōnstrāre* to show]

monstrosity 🅣 (mɒn'strɒsɪtɪ) *n, pl* **monstrosities.** **1** an outrageous or ugly person or thing; monster. **2** the state or quality of being monstrous.

monstrous 🅣 ('mɒnstrəs) *adj* **1** abnormal, hideous, or unnatural in size, character, etc. **2** (of plants and animals) abnormal in structure. **3** outrageous, atrocious, or shocking. **4** huge. **5** of, relating to, or resembling a monster.
▸**'monstrously** *adv* ▸**'monstrousness** *n*

mons veneris ('mɒnz 'venərɪs) *n, pl* **montes veneris** ('mɒntiːz). the fatty flesh in human females over the junction of the pubic bones. Cf. **mons pubis.** [C17: NL: hill of Venus]

montage (mɒn'tɑːʒ) *n* **1** the art or process of composing pictures of miscellaneous elements, such as other pictures or photographs. **2** such a composition. **3** a method of film editing by juxtaposition or partial superimposition of several shots to form a single image. **4** a film sequence of this kind. [C20: from F, from *monter* to MOUNT[1]]

montane ('mɒnteɪn) *adj* of or inhabiting mountainous regions. [C19: from L *montānus,* from *mons* MOUNTAIN]

montbretia (mɒn'briːʃə) *n* any plant of an African genus related to the iris with ornamental orange or yellow flowers. [C19: NL, after A. F. E. Coquebert de *Montbret* (1780–1801), F botanist]

monte ('mɒntɪ) *n* a gambling card game of Spanish origin. [C19: from Sp.: mountain, hence pile of cards]

Montessori method (ˌmɒntɪ'sɔːrɪ) *n* a method of nursery education in which children are provided with facilities for practical play and allowed to develop at their own pace. [C20: after Maria *Montessori* (1870–1952), It. educationalist]

month 🅣 (mʌnθ) *n* **1** one of the twelve divisions (**calendar months**) of the calendar year. **2** a period of time extending from one date to a corresponding date in the next calendar month. **3** a period of four weeks or of 30 days. **4** the period of time (**solar month**) taken by the moon to return to the same longitude after one complete revolution around the earth; 27.321 58 days (approximately 27 days, 7 hours, 43 minutes, 4.5 seconds). **5** the period of time (**sidereal month**) taken by the moon to make one complete revolution around the earth, measured between two successive conjunctions with a particular star; 27.321 66 days (approximately 27 days, 7 hours, 43 minutes, 11 seconds). **6** Also called: **lunation.** the period of time (**lunar** or **synodic month**) taken by the moon to make one complete revolution around the earth, measured between two successive new moons; 29.530 59 days (approximately 29 days, 12 hours, 44 minutes, 3 seconds). [OE *mōnath*]

monthly ('mʌnθlɪ) *adj* **1** occurring, done, appearing, payable, etc., once every month. **2** lasting or valid for a month. ◆ *adv* **3** once a month. ◆ *n, pl* **monthlies.** **4** a book, periodical, magazine, etc., published once a month. **5** *Inf.* a menstrual period.

monument 🅣 ('mɒnjʊmənt) *n* **1** an obelisk, statue, building, etc., erected in commemoration of a person or event. **2** a notable building or site, esp. one preserved as public property. **3** a tomb or tombstone. **4** a literary or artistic work regarded as commemorative of its creator or a particular period. **5** *US.* a boundary marker. **6** an exceptional example: *his lecture was a monument of tedium.* [C13: from L *monumentum,* from *monēre* to remind]

monumental 🅣 (ˌmɒnjʊ'mentᵊl) *adj* **1** like a monument, esp. in large size, endurance, or importance. **2** of, relating to, or being a monument. **3** *Inf.* (intensifier): *monumental stupidity.*
▸**ˌmonu'mentally** *adv*

moo (muː) *vb* **1** (*intr*) (of a cow, bull, etc.) to make a characteristic deep long sound; low. ◆ *interj* **2** an instance or imitation of this sound.

mooch (muːtʃ) *vb Sl.* **1** (*intr; often with around*) to loiter or walk aimlessly. **2** (*intr*) to lurk; skulk. **3** (*tr*) to cadge. **4** (*tr*) *Chiefly US & Canad.* to steal. [C17: ?from OF *muchier* to skulk]
▸**'moocher** *n*

mood[1] 🅣 (muːd) *n* **1** a temporary state of mind or temper: *a cheerful mood.* **2** a sullen or gloomy state of mind, esp. when temporary: *she's in a mood.* **3** a prevailing atmosphere or feeling. **4 in the mood.** in a favourable state of mind. [OE *mōd* mind, feeling]

mood[2] (muːd) *n* **1** *Grammar.* a category of the verb or verbal inflections that expresses semantic and grammatical differences, including such forms as the indicative, subjunctive, and imperative. **2** *Logic.* one of the possible arrangements of the syllogism, classified by whether the component propositions are universal or particular and affirmative or negative. ◆ Also called: **mode.** [C16: from MOOD[1], infl. in meaning by MODE]

moody 🅣 ('muːdɪ) *adj* **moodier, moodiest.** **1** sullen, sulky, or gloomy. **2** temperamental or changeable.
▸**'moodily** *adv* ▸**'moodiness** *n*

Moog (muːg, məʊg) *n Music, trademark.* a type of synthesizer. [C20: after Robert *Moog* (born 1934), US engineer]

mooi (mɔɪ) *adj S. African sl.* pleasing; nice. [from Afrik.]

mooli ('muːlɪ) *n* a type of large white radish. [E African native name]

moolvie *or* **moolvi** ('muːlviː) *n* (esp. in India) a Muslim doctor of the law, teacher, or learned man: also used as a title of respect. [C17: from Urdu, from Ar. *mawlawīy;* cf. MULLAH]

Moomba ('muːmbə) *n* an annual carnival that takes place in Melbourne, Australia, in March. [from Abor. *moom* buttocks, anus; *moomba* orig. thought to be Abor. word meaning "Let's get together and have fun"]

moon 🅣 (muːn) *n* **1** the natural satellite of the earth. **2** the face of the moon as it is seen during its revolution around the earth, esp. at one of its phases: *new moon; full moon.* **3** any natural satellite of a planet. **4** moonlight. **5** something resembling a moon. **6** a month, esp. a lunar one. **7 over the moon.** *Inf.* extremely happy; ecstatic. ◆ *vb* **8** (when *tr,* often foll. by *away;* when *intr,* often foll. by *around*) to be idle in a listless way, as if in love, or to idle (time) away. **9** (*intr*) *Sl.* to expose one's buttocks to passers-by. [OE *mōna*]
▸**'moonless** *adj*

moonbeam ('muːnˌbiːm) *n* a ray of moonlight.

mooncalf ('muːnˌkɑːf) *n, pl* **mooncalves** (-ˌkɑːvz). **1** a born fool; dolt. **2** a person who idles time away.

moon-faced *adj* having a round face.

moonlight ('muːnˌlaɪt) *n* **1** light from the sun received on earth after reflection by the moon. **2** (*modifier*) illuminated by the moon: *a moonlight walk.* ◆ *vb* **moonlights, moonlighting, moonlighted.** **3** (*intr*) *Inf.* to work at a secondary job, esp. at night and illegally.
▸**'moonˌlighter** *n*

moonlight flit *n Brit. inf.* a hurried departure at night, esp. from rented accommodation to avoid payments of rent owed. Often shortened to **moonlight.**

moonlit ('muːnlɪt) *adj* illuminated by the moon.

moonquake ('muːnˌkweɪk) *n* a light tremor of the moon, detected on the moon's surface.

moonscape ('muːnˌskeɪp) *n* the general surface of the moon or a representation of it.

moonshine 🅣 ('muːnˌʃaɪn) *n* **1** another word for **moonlight** (sense 1). **2** *US & Canad.* illegally distilled or smuggled whisky. **3** foolish talk or thought.

moonshot ('muːnˌʃɒt) *n* the launching of a spacecraft, rocket, etc., to the moon.

THESAURUS

Brobdingnagian, colossal, elephantine, enormous, gargantuan, giant, gigantic, ginormous (*inf.*), humongous *or* humungous (*US sl.*), immense, jumbo (*inf.*), mammoth, massive, mega (*sl.*), monstrous, stellar (*inf.*), stupendous, titanic, tremendous

monstrosity *n* **1** = **eyesore,** abortion, freak, horror, lusus naturae, miscreation, monster, mutant, ogre, teratism **2** = **hideousness,** abnormality, atrocity, dreadfulness, evil, frightfulness, heinousness, hellishness, horror, loathsomeness, obscenity

monstrous *adj* **1** = **unnatural,** abnormal, dreadful, enormous, fiendish, freakish, frightful, grotesque, gruesome, hellish, hideous, horrendous, horrible, miscreated, obscene, teratoid, terrible **3** = **outrageous,** atrocious, cruel, devilish, diabolical, disgraceful, egregious, evil, fiendish, foul, heinous, horrifying, infamous, inhuman, intolerable, loathsome, odious, satanic, scandalous, shocking, vicious, villainous **4** = **huge,** colossal, elephantine, enormous, gargantuan, giant, gigantic, ginormous (*inf.*), great, humongous *or* humungous (*US sl.*), immense, mammoth, massive, mega (*sl.*), prodigious, stellar (*inf.*), stupendous, titanic, towering, tremendous, vast
Antonyms *adj* ≠ **unnatural:** appealing, attractive, beautiful, delightful, lovely, natural, normal, ordinary, pleasant ≠ **outrageous:** admirable, decent, fine, good, honourable, humane, kind, merciful, mild ≠ **huge:** diminutive, insignificant, little, meagre, miniature, minute, puny, slight, small, tiny

month *n* **1, 3** = **four weeks,** moon, thirty days

monument *n* **1, 3** = **memorial,** cairn, cenotaph, commemoration, gravestone, headstone, marker, mausoleum, obelisk, pillar, shrine, statue, tombstone

monumental *adj* **1** = **important,** awe-inspiring, awesome, classic, enduring, enormous, epoch-making, historic, immortal, lasting, majestic, memorable, outstanding, prodigious, significant, stupendous, unforgettable **2** = **commemorative,** cyclopean, funerary, memorial, monolithic, statuary **3** *Informal* = **immense,** catastrophic, colossal, egregious, gigantic, great, horrible, indefensible, massive, staggering, terrible, tremendous, unforgivable, whopping (*inf.*)
Antonyms *adj* ≠ **important:** ephemeral, inconsequential, insignificant, modest, negligible, ordinary, trivial, undistinguished, unimportant, unimpressive, unremarkable ≠ **immense:** average, insignificant, mild, petty, slight, small, tiny, trivial

mood[1] *n* **1** = **state of mind,** disposition, frame of mind, humour, spirit, temper, tenor, vein **2** = **depression,** bad temper, bate (*Brit. sl.*), blues, doldrums, dumps (*inf.*), fit of pique, grumps (*inf.*), low spirits, melancholy, sulk, the hump (*Brit. inf.*), the sulks, wax (*inf., chiefly Brit.*) **4 in the mood** = **inclined,** disposed (towards), eager, favourable, interested, in the (right) frame of mind, keen, minded, willing

moody *adj* **1** = **gloomy,** broody, crestfallen, dismal, doleful, dour, downcast, down in the dumps (*inf.*), down in the mouth (*inf.*), frowning, glum, in the doldrums, introspective, lugubrious, melancholy, miserable, mopy, morose, out of sorts (*inf.*), pensive, sad, saturnine, sullen **2** = **changeable,** capricious, erratic, faddish, fickle, fitful, flighty, impulsive, inconstant, mercurial, temperamental, unpredictable, unstable, unsteady, volatile
Antonyms *adj* ≠ **gloomy:** amiable, cheerful, gay, happy, optimistic ≠ **changeable:** constant, stable, steady

moon *n* **1, 3** = **satellite** ◆ *vb* **8** = **idle,** daydream, languish, mooch (*sl.*), mope, waste time

moonshine *n* **1** = **moonlight,** moonbeams **2** *US & Canad.* = **bootleg,** hooch *or* hootch (*inf., chiefly US & Canad.*), poteen **3** = **nonsense,** blather, blether, bunk (*inf.*), bunkum *or* buncombe (*chiefly US*), claptrap (*inf.*), foolish talk, guff (*sl.*),

moonstone ('mu:n,stəʊn) *n* a gem variety of orthoclase or albite that is white and translucent.
moonstruck ('mu:n,strʌk) *or* **moonstricken** ('mu:n,strɪkən) *adj* deranged or mad.
moony ('mu:nɪ) *adj* **moonier, mooniest. 1** *Inf.* dreamy or listless. **2** of or like the moon.
moor[1] ❶ (mʊə, mɔ:) *n* a tract of unenclosed ground, usually covered with heather, coarse grass, bracken, and moss. [OE *mōr*]
moor[2] ❶ (mʊə, mɔ:) *vb* **1** to secure (a ship, boat, etc.) with cables or ropes. **2** (of a ship, boat, etc.) to be secured in this way. **3** (not in technical usage) a less common word for **anchor** (senses 7 and 8). [C15: of Gmc origin; rel. to OE *mǣrelsrāp* rope for mooring]
▸**moorage** ('mʊərɪdʒ) *n*
Moor (mʊə, mɔ:) *n* a member of a Muslim people of North Africa, of mixed Arab and Berber descent. [C14: via OF from L *Maurus*, from Gk *Mauros*, ?from Berber]
▸**'Moorish** *adj*
moorcock ('mʊə,kɒk, 'mɔ:-) *n* the male of the red grouse.
moorhen ('mʊə,hen, 'mɔ:-) *n* **1** a bird of the rail family, inhabiting ponds, lakes, etc., having a black plumage, red bill, and a red shield above the bill. **2** the female of the red grouse.
mooring ('mʊərɪŋ, 'mɔ:-) *n* **1** a place for mooring a vessel. **2** a permanent anchor with a floating buoy, to which vessels can moor.
moorings ('mʊərɪŋz, 'mɔ:-) *pl n* **1** *Naut.* the ropes, anchors, etc., used in mooring a vessel. **2** (*sometimes sing*) something that provides security or stability.
Moorish idol *n* a tropical marine spiny-finned fish that is common around coral reefs. It has a deeply compressed body with yellow and black stripes.
moorland ('mʊələnd) *n Brit.* an area of moor.
moose (mu:s) *n, pl* **moose.** a large North American deer having large flattened palmate antlers: also occurs in Europe and Asia where it is called an elk. [C17: of Amerind origin]
moot ❶ (mu:t) *adj* **1** subject or open to debate: *a moot point.* ◆ *vb* **2** (*tr*) to suggest or bring up for debate. **3** (*intr*) to plead or argue hypothetical cases, as an academic exercise or as training for law students. ◆ *n* **4** a discussion or debate of a hypothetical case or point, held as an academic activity. **5** (in Anglo-Saxon England) an assembly dealing with local legal and administrative affairs. [OE *gemōt*]
moot court *n* a mock court trying hypothetical legal cases.
mop ❶ (mɒp) *n* **1** an implement with a wooden handle and a head made of twists of cotton or a piece of synthetic sponge, used for polishing or washing floors, or washing dishes. **2** something resembling this, such as a tangle of hair. ◆ *vb* **mops, mopping, mopped.** (*tr*) **3** (often foll. by *up*) to clean or soak up as with a mop. ◆ See also **mop up.** [C15 *mappe*, ult. from L *mappa* napkin]
mopani *or* **mopane** (mɒ'pɑ:nɪ) *n* **1** a leguminous tree, native to southern Africa, that is highly resistant to drought and produces very hard wood. **2** Also called: **mopani worm.** an edible caterpillar that feeds on mopani leaves. [C19: from Bantu]
mope ❶ (məʊp) *vb* **mopes, moping, moped.** (*intr*) **1** to be gloomy or apathetic. **2** to move or act in an aimless way. ◆ *n* **3** a gloomy person. [C16: ?from obs. *mope* fool & rel. to *mop* grimace]
▸**'moper** *n* ▸**'mopy** *adj*
moped ('məʊped) *n* a light motorcycle not over 50cc. [C20: from MOTOR + PEDAL[1]]
mopes (məʊps) *pl n* **the.** low spirits.
mopoke ('məʊ,pəʊk) *n* **1** a small spotted owl of Australia and New Zealand. In Australia the tawny frogmouth is often wrongly identified as the mopoke. **2** *Austral. & NZ sl.* a slow or lugubrious person. ◆ Also called: **morepork.** [C19: imit. of the bird's cry]
moppet ('mɒpɪt) *n* a less common word for **poppet** (sense 1). [C17: from obs. *mop* rag doll; from ?]
mop up ❶ *vb* (*tr, adv*) **1** to clean with a mop. **2** *Inf.* to complete (a task, etc.). **3** *Mil.* to clear (remaining enemy forces) after a battle, as by killing, taking prisoner, etc.
moquette (mɒ'ket) *n* a thick velvety fabric used for carpets, upholstery, etc. [C18: from F; from ?]
MOR *abbrev. for* middle-of-the-road: used esp. in radio programming.
Mor. *abbrev. for* Morocco.
mora *or* **morra** ('mɔ:rə) *n* a guessing game played with the fingers, esp. in Italy and China. [C18: from It. *mora*]
moraine (mɒ'reɪn) *n* a mass of debris, carried by glaciers and forming ridges and mounds when deposited. [C18: from F, from Savoy dialect *morena*, from ?]
▸**mo'rainal** *or* **mo'rainic** *adj*
moral ❶ ('mɒrəl) *adj* **1** concerned with or relating to human behaviour, esp. the distinction between good and bad or right and wrong behaviour: *moral sense.* **2** adhering to conventionally accepted standards of conduct. **3** based on a sense of right and wrong according to conscience: *moral courage; moral law.* **4** having psychological rather than tangible effects: *moral support.* **5** having the effects but not the appearance of (victory or defeat): *a moral victory.* **6** having a strong probability: *a moral certainty.* ◆ *n* **7** the lesson to be obtained from a fable or event. **8** a concise truth; maxim. **9** (*pl*) principles of behaviour in accordance with standards of right and wrong. **10** *Austral. sl.* a certainty: *a moral to win.* [C14: from L *mōrālis* relating to morals or customs, from *mōs* custom]
▸**'morally** *adv*
morale ❶ (mɒ'rɑ:l) *n* the degree of mental or moral confidence of a person or group. [C18: morals, from F, n use of MORAL (adj)]
moralist ('mɒrəlɪst) *n* **1** a person who seeks to regulate the morals of others. **2** a person who lives in accordance with moral principles.
▸**,moral'istic** *adj* ▸**,moral'istically** *adv*
morality ❶ (mə'rælɪtɪ) *n, pl* **moralities. 1** the quality of being moral. **2** conformity, or degree of conformity, to conventional standards of moral conduct. **3** a system of moral principles. **4** an instruction or lesson in morals. **5** short for **morality play.**
morality play *n* a type of drama between the 14th and 16th centuries concerned with the conflict between personified virtues and vices.
moralize *or* **moralise** ('mɒrə,laɪz) *vb* **moralizes, moralizing, moralized** *or* **moralises, moralising, moralised. 1** (*intr*) to make moral pronouncements. **2** (*tr*) to interpret or explain in a moral sense. **3** (*tr*) to improve the morals of.
▸**,morali'zation** *or* **,morali'sation** *n* ▸**'moral,izer** *or* **'moral,iser** *n*
moral majority *n* a presumed majority of people believed to be in favour of a stricter code of public morals. [C20: after *Moral Majority*, a right-wing US religious organization, based on SILENT MAJORITY]
moral philosophy *n* the branch of philosophy dealing with ethics.
Moral Rearmament *n* a worldwide movement for moral and spiritual renewal founded by Frank Buchman in 1938. Also called: **Buchmanism.** Former name: **Oxford Group.**
moral theology *n* the branch of theology dealing with ethics.
morass ❶ (mə'ræs) *n* **1** a tract of swampy low-lying land. **2** a disordered or muddled situation or circumstance, esp. one that impedes progress. [C17: from Du. *moeras*, ult. from OF *marais* MARSH]
moratorium ❶ (,mɒrə'tɔ:rɪəm) *n, pl* **moratoria** (-rɪə) *or* **moratoriums. 1** a legally authorized postponement of the fulfilment of an obligation. **2** an agreed suspension of activity. [C19: NL, from LL *morātōrius* dilatory, from *mora* delay]
Moravian (mə'reɪvɪən, mɒ-) *adj* **1** of or relating to Moravia, a region of the Czech Republic, its people, or their dialect of Czech. **2** of or relating to the Moravian Church. ◆ *n* **3** the Moravian dialect. **4** a native or inhabitant of Moravia. **5** a member of the Moravian Church.
▸**Mo'ravianism** *n*
moray (mɒ'reɪ) *n, pl* **morays.** a voracious marine coastal eel marked with brilliant colours. [C17: from Port. *moréia*, from L *mūrēna*, from Gk *muraina*]
morbid ❶ ('mɔ:bɪd) *adj* **1** having an unusual interest in death or unpleasant events. **2** gruesome. **3** relating to or characterized by disease. [C17: from L *morbidus* sickly, from *morbus* illness]
▸**mor'bidity** *n* ▸**'morbidly** *adv* ▸**'morbidness** *n*
morbid anatomy *n* the branch of medical science concerned with the study of the structure of diseased organs and tissues.
morbific (mɔ:'bɪfɪk) *adj* causing disease.

THESAURUS

havers (*Scot.*), hogwash, hot air (*inf.*), rubbish, stuff and nonsense, tarradiddle, tosh (*sl., chiefly Brit.*), trash, tripe (*inf.*), twaddle
moor[1] *n* = **moorland**, fell (*Brit.*), heath, muir (*Scot.*)
moor[2] *vb* **1-3** = **tie up**, anchor, berth, dock, fasten, fix, lash, make fast, secure
moot *adj* **1** = **debatable**, arguable, at issue, contestable, controversial, disputable, doubtful, open, open to debate, undecided, unresolved, unsettled ◆ *vb* **2** = **bring up**, broach, introduce, propose, put forward, suggest, ventilate
mop *n* **1** = **squeegee**, sponge, swab **2** = **mane**, shock, tangle, thatch ◆ *vb* **3** = **clean**, soak up, sponge, swab, wash, wipe
mope *vb* **1** = **brood**, be apathetic, be dejected, be down in the mouth (*inf.*), be gloomy, eat one's heart out, fret, hang around, have a long face, idle, languish, moon, pine, pout, sulk, waste time, wear a long face
mop up *vb* **1** = **clean up**, mop, soak up, sponge, swab, wash, wipe **3** *Military* = **finish off**, account for, clean out, clear, eliminate, neutralize, pacify, round up, secure
moral *adj* **1** = **ethical 2, 3** = **good**, blameless, chaste, decent, ethical, high-minded, honest, honourable, incorruptible, innocent, just, meritorious, noble, principled, proper, pure, right, righteous, upright, upstanding, virtuous ◆ *n* **7** = **lesson**, meaning, message, point, significance **8** = **motto**, adage, aphorism, apophthegm, epigram, gnome, maxim, proverb, saw, saying **9** *plural* = **morality**, behaviour, conduct, ethics, habits, integrity, manners, mores, principles, scruples, standards
Antonyms *adj* ≠ **good:** amoral, dishonest, dishonourable, immoral, improper, sinful, unethical, unfair, unjust, wrong
morale *n* = **confidence**, esprit de corps, heart, mettle, self-esteem, spirit, temper
morality *n* **1** = **integrity**, chastity, decency, ethicality, ethicalness, goodness, honesty, justice, principle, rectitude, righteousness, rightness, uprightness, virtue **3** = **standards**, conduct, ethics, habits, ideals, manners, moral code, morals, mores, philosophy, principles
morass *n* **1** = **marsh**, bog, fen, marshland, moss (*Scot. & N English dialect*), quagmire, slough, swamp **2** = **mess**, chaos, confusion, jam, mix-up, muddle, quagmire, tangle
moratorium *n* **1, 2** = **postponement**, freeze, halt, respite, standstill, stay, suspension
morbid *adj* **1** = **unwholesome**, brooding, funereal, ghoulish, gloomy, grim, melancholy, pessimistic, sick, sombre, unhealthy **2** = **gruesome**, dreadful, ghastly, grisly, hideous, horrid, macabre **3** = **diseased**, ailing, deadly, infected, malignant, pathological, sick, sickly, unhealthy, unsound
Antonyms *adj* ≠ **unwholesome:** bright, cheerful, happy, healthy, wholesome ≠ **diseased:** healthy, salubrious

mordant Ⓣ ('mɔːdᵊnt) *adj* **1** sarcastic or caustic. **2** having the properties of a mordant. **3** pungent. ◆ *n* **4** a substance used before the application of a dye, possessing the ability to fix colours. **5** an acid or other corrosive fluid used to etch lines on a printing plate. [C15: from OF: biting, from *mordre* to bite, from L *mordēre*]
▸**'mordancy** *n* ▸**'mordantly** *adv*

mordent ('mɔːdᵊnt) *n Music.* a melodic ornament consisting of the rapid alternation of a note with a note one degree lower than it. [C19: from G, from It. *mordente,* from *mordere* to bite]

more Ⓣ (mɔː) *determiner* **1a** the comparative of **much** or **many:** *more joy than you know; more sausages.* **1b** (*as pron; functioning as sing or pl*): *he has more than she has; even more are dying.* **2a** additional; further: *no more bananas.* **2b** (*as pron; functioning as sing or pl*): *I can't take any more; more than expected.* **3 more of.** to a greater extent or degree: *we see more of Sue; more of a nuisance.* ◆ *adv* **4** used to form the comparative of some adjectives and adverbs: *a more believable story; more quickly.* **5** the comparative of **much:** *people listen to the radio more now.* **6 more or less. 6a** as an estimate; approximately. **6b** to an unspecified extent or degree: *the party was ruined, more or less.* [OE *māra*]

USAGE NOTE See at **most.**

moreish *or* **morish** ('mɔːrɪʃ) *adj Inf.* (of food) causing a desire for more.

morel (mɒ'rɛl) *n* an edible fungus in which the mushroom has a pitted cap. [C17: from F *morille,* prob. of Gmc origin]

morello (mə'rɛləʊ) *n, pl* **morellos.** a variety of small very dark sour cherry. [C17: ?from Med. L *amārellum,* dim. of L *amārus* bitter, but also infl. by It. *morello* blackish]

morendo (mɒ'rɛndəʊ) *adv Music.* gradually dying away. [It.: dying]

moreover Ⓣ (mɔː'rəʊvə) *sentence connector.* in addition to what has already been said.

morepork ('mɔːˌpɔːk) *n* another name, esp. in New Zealand, for **mopoke.**

mores ('mɔːreɪz) *pl n* the customs and conventions embodying the fundamental values of a group or society. [C20: from L, pl of *mōs* custom]

morganatic (ˌmɔːgə'nætɪk) *adj* of or designating a marriage between a person of high rank and a person of low rank, by which the latter is not elevated to the higher rank and any issue have no rights to the succession of the higher party's titles, property, etc. [C18: from Med. L *mātrimōnium ad morganāticum* marriage based on the morning-gift (a token present after consummation representing the husband's only liability); *morganātica,* ult. from OHG *morgan* morning]
▸**ˌmorga'natically** *adv*

morgen ('mɔːgən) *n* **1** a South African unit of area, equal to about two acres or 0.8 hectare. **2** a unit of area, formerly used in Prussia and Scandinavia, equal to about two thirds of an acre. [C17: from Du.: morning, a morning's ploughing]

morgue Ⓣ (mɔːg) *n* **1** another word for **mortuary. 2** *Inf.* a room or file containing clippings, etc., used for reference in a newspaper. [C19: from F *le Morgue,* a Paris mortuary]

moribund Ⓣ ('mɒrɪˌbʌnd) *adj* **1** near death. **2** without force or vitality. [C18: from L, from *morī* to die]
▸**ˌmori'bundity** *n* ▸**'moriˌbundly** *adv*

Morisco (mə'rɪskəʊ) *or* **Moresco** (mə'rɛskəʊ) *n, pl* **Moriscos, Moriscoes** *or* **Morescos, Morescoes. 1** a Spanish Moor. **2** a morris dance. ◆ *adj* **3** another word for **Moorish;** see **Moor.** [C16: from Sp., from *Moro* MOOR]

morish ('mɔːrɪʃ) *adj* a variant spelling of **moreish.**

Mormon ('mɔːmən) *n* **1** a member of the Church of Jesus Christ of Latter-day Saints, founded in 1830 in New York by Joseph Smith. **2** a prophet whose supposed revelations were recorded by Joseph Smith in the Book of Mormon. ◆ *adj* **3** of or relating to the Mormons, their Church, or their beliefs.
▸**'Mormonism** *n*

morn (mɔːn) *n* a poetic word for **morning.** [OE *morgen*]

mornay ('mɔːneɪ) *adj* (*often immediately postpositive*) denoting a cheese sauce: *eggs mornay.* [? after Philippe de *Mornay* (1549–1623), F Huguenot leader]

morning Ⓣ ('mɔːnɪŋ) *n* **1** the first part of the day, ending at noon. **2** sunrise; daybreak; dawn. **3** the beginning or early period. **4 the morning after.** *Inf.* the aftereffects of excess, esp. a hangover. **5** (*modifier*) of, used in, or occurring in the morning: *morning coffee.* [C13 *morwening,* from MORN, on the model of EVENING]

morning-after pill *n* an oral contraceptive that is effective if taken some hours after intercourse.

morning dress *n* formal day dress for men, comprising a cutaway frock coat (**morning coat**), usually with grey trousers and top hat.

morning-glory *n, pl* **morning-glories.** any of various mainly tropical plants of the convolvulus family, with trumpet-shaped blue, pink, or white flowers, which close in late afternoon.

mornings ('mɔːnɪŋz) *adv Inf.* in the morning, esp. regularly, or during every morning.

morning sickness *n* nausea occurring shortly after rising: a symptom of pregnancy.

morning star *n* a planet, usually Venus, seen just before sunrise. Also called: **daystar.**

Moro ('mɔːrəʊ) *n* **1** (*pl* **Moros** *or* **Moro**) a member of a group of predominantly Muslim peoples of the S Philippines. **2** the language of these peoples. [C19: via Sp. from L *Maurus* MOOR]

Moroccan (mə'rɒkən) *adj* **1** of or denoting Morocco, a kingdom in NW Africa, or its inhabitants, their customs, etc. ◆ *n* **2** a native or inhabitant of Morocco or a descendant of one.

morocco (mə'rɒkəʊ) *n* a fine soft leather made from goatskins, used for bookbinding, shoes, etc. [C17: after *Morocco,* kingdom in NW Africa, where it was orig. made]

moron Ⓣ ('mɔːrɒn) *n* **1** a foolish or stupid person. **2** a person having an intelligence quotient of between 50 and 70. [C20: from Gk *mōros* foolish]
▸**moronic** (mə'rɒnɪk) *adj* ▸**mo'ronically** *adv* ▸**'moronism** *or* **mo'ronity** *n*

morose Ⓣ (mə'rəʊs) *adj* ill-tempered or gloomy. [C16: from L *mōrōsus* peevish, from *mōs* custom, will]
▸**mo'rosely** *adv* ▸**mo'roseness** *n*

-morph *n combining form.* indicating shape, form, or structure of a specified kind: *ectomorph.* [from Gk *-morphos,* from *morphē* shape]
▸**-morphic** *or* **-morphous** *adj combining form.* ▸**-morphy** *n combining form.*

morpheme ('mɔːfiːm) *n Linguistics.* a speech element having a meaning or grammatical function that cannot be subdivided into further such elements. [C20: from F, from Gk *morphē* form, on the model of PHONEME]
▸**mor'phemic** *adj* ▸**mor'phemically** *adv*

morphine ('mɔːfiːn) *or* **morphia** ('mɔːfɪə) *n* an alkaloid extracted from opium: used in medicine as an anaesthetic and sedative. [C19: from F, from *Morpheus,* in Gk myth the god of sleep & dreams]

morphing ('mɔːfɪŋ) *n* a computer technique used for graphics and in films, in which one image is gradually transformed into another. [C20: from METAMORPHOSIS]

morphogenesis (ˌmɔːfəʊ'dʒɛnɪsɪs) *n* **1** the development of form in an organism during its growth. **2** the evolutionary development of form in an organism or part of an organism.
▸**morphogenetic** (ˌmɔːfəʊdʒɪ'nɛtɪk) *adj*

morphology (mɔː'fɒlədʒɪ) *n* **1** the branch of biology concerned with the form and structure of organisms. **2** the form and structure of words in a language. **3** the form and structure of anything.
▸**morphologic** (ˌmɔːfə'lɒdʒɪk) *or* **ˌmorpho'logical** *adj* ▸**ˌmorpho'logically** *adv* ▸**mor'phologist** *n*

Morris chair ('mɒrɪs) *n* an armchair with an adjustable back. [C19: after William *Morris* (1834–96), Brit. writer, painter, & craftsman]

morris dance *n* any of various old English folk dances usually performed by men (**morris men**) adorned with bells and often representing characters from folk tales. Often shortened to **morris.** [C15 *moreys daunce* Moorish dance]
▸**morris dancing** *n*

morro ('mɒrəʊ) *n, pl* **morros** (-rəʊz). a rounded hill or promontory. [from Sp.]

morrow ('mɒrəʊ) *n* (usually preceded by *the*) *Arch. or poetic.* **1** the next day. **2** the period following a specified event. **3** the morning. [C13 *morwe,* from OE *morgen* morning]

Morse code *n* (mɔːs) *n* a telegraph code used internationally for transmitting messages. Letters, numbers, etc., are represented by groups of shorter dots and longer dashes, or by groups of the corresponding sounds. [C19: after Samuel *Morse* (1791–1872), US inventor]

morsel Ⓣ ('mɔːsᵊl) *n* **1** a small slice or mouthful of food. **2** a small piece;

THESAURUS

mordant *adj* **1** = **sarcastic,** acerbic, acid, acrimonious, astringent, biting, caustic, cutting, edged, harsh, incisive, mordacious, pungent, scathing, sharp, stinging, trenchant, venomous, vitriolic, waspish **2, 3** = **corrosive,** acid, acidic, caustic, pungent, vitriolic

more *determiner* **1, 2** = **extra,** added, additional, fresh, further, new, new-found, other, spare, supplementary ◆ *adv* **4, 5** = **to a greater extent,** better, further, longer

moreover *sentence connector* = **furthermore,** additionally, also, as well, besides, further, in addition, into the bargain, likewise, to boot, too, what is more, withal (*literary*)

morgue *n* **1** = **mortuary**

moribund *adj* **1** = **dying,** at death's door, breathing one's last, doomed, fading fast, failing, (having) one foot in the grave, *in extremis,* near death, near the end, on one's deathbed, on one's last legs **2** = **declining,** at a standstill, forceless, obsolescent, on its last legs, on the way out, stagnant, stagnating, standing still, waning, weak

morning *n* **1, 2** = **dawn,** a.m., break of day, daybreak, forenoon, morn (*poetic*), morrow (*arch.*), sunrise

moron *n* **1** = **fool,** airhead (*sl.*), ass, berk (*Brit. sl.*), blockhead, bonehead (*sl.*), chump, coot, cretin, dolt, dope (*inf.*), dork (*sl.*), dummy (*sl.*), dunce, dunderhead, fathead (*inf.*), halfwit, idiot, imbecile, mental defective, muttonhead (*sl.*), nerd *or* nurd (*sl.*), nitwit (*inf.*), numbskull *or* numskull, oaf, pillock (*Brit. sl.*), schmuck (*US sl.*), simpleton, thickhead, twit (*inf., chiefly Brit.*), wally (*sl.*)

moronic *adj* **1** = **idiotic,** asinine, Boeotian, braindead (*inf.*), brainless, cretinous, dimwitted (*inf.*), doltish, foolish, gormless (*Brit. inf.*), half-witted, imbecilic, mentally defective, mindless, muttonheaded (*sl.*), retarded, simple, stupid, thick, unintelligent

morose *adj* = **sullen,** blue, churlish, crabbed, crabby, cross, crusty, depressed, dour, down, down in the dumps (*inf.*), gloomy, glum, grouchy, gruff, ill-tempered, in a bad mood, low, melancholy, miserable, moody, mournful, perverse, pessimistic, saturnine, sour, sulky, surly, taciturn
Antonyms *adj* amiable, blithe, cheerful, chirpy (*inf.*), friendly, gay, genial, good-humoured, good-natured, happy, pleasant, sweet

morsel *n* **1, 2** = **piece,** bit, bite, crumb, fraction, fragment, grain, mouthful, nibble, part, scrap, bit. **3** *Irish inf.* a term of endearment for a child. [C13: from OF, from *mors* a bite, from L *morsus*, from *mordēre* to bite]

mortal ❶ ('mɔːtᵊl) *adj* **1** (of living beings, esp. human beings) subject to death. **2** of or involving life or the world. **3** ending in or causing death; fatal: *a mortal blow.* **4** deadly or unrelenting: *a mortal enemy.* **5** of or like the fear of death: *mortal terror.* **6** great or very intense: *mortal pain.* **7** conceivable or possible: *there was no mortal reason to go.* **8** *Sl.* long and tedious: *for three mortal hours.* ◆ *n* **9** a mortal being. **10** *Inf.* a person: *a mean mortal.* [C14: from L *mortālis*, from *mors* death]
▸ **'mortally** *adv*

mortality ❶ (mɔː'tælɪtɪ) *n, pl* **mortalities. 1** the condition of being mortal. **2** great loss of life, as in war or disaster. **3** the number of deaths in a given period. **4** mankind; humanity.

mortal sin *n Christianity.* a sin regarded as involving total loss of grace.

mortar ('mɔːtə) *n* **1** a mixture of cement or lime or both with sand and water, used as a bond between bricks or stones or as a covering on a wall. **2** a cannon having a short barrel and relatively wide bore that fires low-velocity shells in high trajectories. **3** a vessel, usually bowl-shaped, in which substances are pulverized with a pestle. ◆ *vb* (*tr*) **4** to join (bricks or stones) or cover (a wall) with mortar. **5** to fire on with mortars. [C13: from L *mortārium* basin in which mortar is mixed; in some senses, via OF *mortier* substance mixed inside such a vessel]

mortarboard ('mɔːtə,bɔːd) *n* **1** a black tasselled academic cap with a flat square top. **2** a small square board with a handle on the underside for carrying mortar.

mortgage ('mɔːgɪdʒ) *n* **1** an agreement under which a person borrows money to buy property, esp. a house, and the lender may take possession of the property if the borrower fails to repay the money. **2** the deed affecting such an agreement. **3** the loan obtained under such an agreement: *a mortgage of £48000.* **4** a regular payment of money borrowed under such an agreement: *a mortgage of £347 per month.* ◆ *vb* **mortgages, mortgaging, mortgaged.** (*tr*) **4** to convey (property) by mortgage. **5** *Inf.* to pledge. [C14: from OF, lit.: dead pledge]
▸ **'mortgageable** *adj*

mortgagee (,mɔːgɪ'dʒiː) *n Law.* the party to a mortgage who makes the loan.

mortgagor (,mɔːgɪ'dʒɔː) *or* **mortgager** *n Property law.* a person who borrows money by mortgaging his property to the lender as security.

mortician (mɔː'tɪʃən) *n Chiefly US.* another word for **undertaker.** [C19: from MORTUARY + *-ician*, as in *physician*]

mortification ❶ (,mɔːtɪfɪ'keɪʃən) *n* **1** a feeling of humiliation. **2** something causing this. **3** *Christianity.* the practice of mortifying the senses. **4** another word for **gangrene.**

mortify ❶ ('mɔːtɪ,faɪ) *vb* **mortifies, mortifying, mortified. 1** (*tr*) to humiliate or cause to feel shame. **2** (*tr*) *Christianity.* to subdue and bring under control by self-denial, disciplinary exercises, etc. **3** (*intr*) to undergo tissue death or become gangrenous. [C14: via OF from Church L *mortificāre* to put to death, from L *mors* death + *facere* to do]
▸ **'morti,fier** *n* ▸ **'morti,fying** *adj*

mortise *or* **mortice** ('mɔːtɪs) *n* **1** a slot or recess cut into a piece of wood, stone, etc., to receive a matching projection (tenon) of another piece, or a mortise lock. ◆ *vb* **mortises, mortising, mortised** *or* **mortices, morticing, morticed.** (*tr*) **2** to cut a slot or recess in (a piece of wood, stone, etc.). **3** to join (two pieces of wood, stone, etc.) by means of a mortise and tenon. [C14: from OF *mortoise*, ?from Ar. *murtazza* fastened in position]

mortise lock *n* a lock set into a mortise in a door so that the mechanism of the lock is enclosed by the door.

mortmain ('mɔːt,meɪn) *n Law.* the state or condition of lands, buildings, etc., held inalienably, as by an ecclesiastical or other corporation. [C15: from OF *mortemain*, from Med. L *mortua manus* dead hand, inalienable ownership]

mortuary ❶ ('mɔːtjʊərɪ) *n, pl* **mortuaries. 1** Also called: **morgue.** a building where dead bodies are kept before cremation or burial. ◆ *adj* **2** of or relating to death or burial. [C14 (as n, a funeral gift to a parish priest): via Med. L *mortuārium* (n) from L *mortuārius* of the dead]

morwong ('mɔː,wɒŋ) *n* a food fish of Australasian coastal waters. [from Abor.]

moryah (mɒr'jæ) *interj Irish.* an exclamation of annoyance, disbelief, etc. [from Irish Gaelic *Mar dhea* forsooth]

mosaic (mə'zeɪɪk) *n* **1** a design or decoration made up of small pieces of coloured glass, stone, etc. **2** the process of making a mosaic. **3a** a mottled yellowing that occurs in the leaves of plants affected with any of various virus diseases. **3b** Also called: **mosaic disease.** any of the diseases, such as **tobacco mosaic**, that produce this discoloration. **4** a light-sensitive surface on a television camera tube, consisting of a large number of granules of photoemissive material. [C16: via F & It. from Med. L, from LGk: mosaic work, from Gk: of the Muses, from *mousa* MUSE]
▸ **mosaicist** (mə'zeɪɪsɪst) *n*

Mosaic (məʊ'zeɪɪk) *adj* of or relating to Moses or the laws and traditions ascribed to him.

Mosaic law *n Bible.* the laws ascribed to Moses and contained in the Pentateuch.

moschatel (,mɒskə'tɛl) *n* a small N temperate plant with greenish-white musk-scented flowers. Also called: **townhall clock, five-faced bishop.** [C18: via F from It. *moscatella*, dim. of *moscato* MUSK]

Moselle (məʊ'zɛl) *n* (*sometimes not cap.*) a German white wine from the Moselle valley.

mosey ('məʊzɪ) *vb* (*intr*) *Inf.* (often foll. by *along* or *on*) to amble. [C19: from ?]

Moslem ('mɒzləm) *n, pl* **Moslems** *or* **Moslem.** *adj* a variant of **Muslim.**
▸ **Moslemic** (mɒz'lɛmɪk) *adj* ▸ **'Moslemism** *n*

mosque (mɒsk) *n* a Muslim place of worship. [C14: earlier *mosquee*, from OF via It. *moschea*, ult. from Ar. *masjid* temple]

mosquito (mə'skiːtəʊ) *n, pl* **mosquitoes** *or* **mosquitos.** any dipterous insect of the family Culicidae: the females have a long proboscis adapted for piercing the skin of man and animals to suck their blood. See also **aedes, anopheles, culex.** [C16: from Sp., dim. of *mosca* fly, from L *musca*]

mosquito net *or* **netting** *n* a fine curtain or net to keep mosquitoes out.

moss (mɒs) *n* **1** any of a class of plants, typically growing in dense mats on trees, rocks, moist ground, etc. **2** a clump or growth of any of these plants. **3** any of various similar but unrelated plants, such as Spanish moss and reindeer moss. **4** *Scot. & N English.* a peat bog or marsh. [OE *mos* swamp]
▸ **'moss,like** *adj* ▸ **'mossy** *adj* ▸ **'mossiness** *n*

moss agate *n* a variety of chalcedony with dark greenish mossy markings.

mossie ('mɒsɪ) *n* another name for the **Cape sparrow.** [Afrik.]

mosso ('mɒsəʊ) *adv Music.* to be performed with rapidity. [It., p.p. of *muovere* to MOVE]

moss rose *n* a variety of rose that has a mossy stem and calyx and fragrant pink flowers.

moss stitch *n* a knitting stitch made up of alternate plain and purl stitches.

mosstrooper ('mɒs,truːpə) *n* a raider in the Borders of England and Scotland in the mid-17th century. [C17 *moss*, in dialect sense: bog]

most (məʊst) *determiner* **1a** a great majority of; nearly all: *most people like eggs.* **1b** (*as pron; functioning as sing or pl*): *most of them don't know; most of it is finished.* **2 the most. 2a** the superlative of **many** and **much:** *you have the most money; the most apples.* **2b** (*as pron*): *the most he can afford is two pounds.* **3 at (the) most.** at the maximum: *that girl is four at the most.* **4 make the most of.** to use to the best advantage: *she makes the most of her accent.* ◆ *adv* **5 the most.** used to form the superlative of some adjectives and adverbs: *he suffered the most terribly of all.* **6** the superlative of **much:** *people welcome a drink most after work.* **7** (intensifier): *a most absurd story.* [OE *māst* or *mǣst*, whence ME *moste*, *mēst*]

> **USAGE NOTE** *More* and *most* should be distinguished when used in comparisons. *More* applies to cases involving two people, objects, etc., *most* to cases involving three or more: *John is the more intelligent of the two; he is the most intelligent of the students.*

-most *suffix. forming the superlative degree of some adjectives and adverbs: hindmost; uppermost.* [OE *-mǣst*, *-mest*, orig. a sup. suffix, later mistakenly taken as from *mǣst* (adv) most]

mostly ❶ ('məʊstlɪ) *adv* **1** almost entirely; chiefly. **2** on many or most occasions; usually.

Most Reverend *n* (in Britain) a courtesy title applied to Anglican and Roman Catholic archbishops.

THESAURUS

segment, slice, snack, *soupçon*, tad (*inf., chiefly US*), taste, titbit

mortal *adj* **1, 2** = **human**, corporeal, earthly, ephemeral, impermanent, passing, sublunary, temporal, transient, worldly **3** = **fatal**, deadly, death-dealing, destructive, killing, lethal, murderous, terminal **4** = **unrelenting**, bitter, deadly, implacable, irreconcilable, out-and-out, remorseless, sworn, to the death **6** = **great**, agonizing, awful, dire, enormous, extreme, grave, intense, serious, severe, terrible ◆ *n* **9, 10** = **human being**, being, body, earthling, human, individual, man, person, woman

mortality *n* **1** = **humanity**, ephemerality, impermanence, temporality, transience **2** = **killing**, bloodshed, carnage, death, destruction, fatality, loss of life

mortification *n* **1** = **humiliation**, abasement, annoyance, chagrin, discomfiture, dissatisfaction, embarrassment, loss of face, shame, vexation **3** *Christianity* = **discipline**, abasement, chastening, control, denial, subjugation **4** = **gangrene**, corruption, festering, necrosis, putrescence

mortified *adj* **1** = **humiliated**, abashed, affronted, annoyed, ashamed, chagrined, chastened, confounded, crushed, deflated, discomfited, displeased, embarrassed, given a showing-up (*inf.*), humbled, made to eat humble pie (*inf.*), pissed (*taboo sl.*), pissed off (*taboo sl.*), put down, put out (*inf.*), put to shame, rendered speechless, shamed, vexed **2** *Christianity* = **disciplined**, abased, chastened, conquered, controlled, crushed, subdued **3** = **gangrenous**, decayed, necrotic, rotted

mortify *vb* **1** = **humiliate**, abase, abash, affront, annoy, chagrin, chasten, confound, crush, deflate, disappoint, discomfit, displease, embarrass, humble, make (someone) eat humble pie (*inf.*), put down, put to shame, shame, take (someone) down a peg (*inf.*), vex **2** *Christianity* = **discipline**, abase, chasten, control, deny, subdue **3** = **putrefy**, become gangrenous, corrupt, deaden, die, fester, gangrene, necrose

mortuary *n* **1** = **morgue**, funeral home (*US*), funeral parlour

mostly *adv* **1, 2** = **generally**, above all, almost

mot (məʊ) *n* short for **bon mot.** [C16: via F from Vulgar L *muttum* (unattested) utterance, from L *muttum,* from *muttīre* to mutter]

MOT (in New Zealand and, formerly, in Britain) *abbrev. for:* **1** Ministry of Transport. **2** *Brit.* MOT test: a compulsory annual test for all road vehicles over a certain age, which require a valid **MOT certificate.**

mote Ⓣ (məʊt) *n* a tiny speck. [OE *mot*]

motel (məʊˈtɛl) *n* a roadside hotel for motorists. [C20: from *motor* + *hotel*]

motet (məʊˈtɛt) *n* a polyphonic choral composition used as an anthem in the Roman Catholic service. [C14: from OF, dim. of *mot* word; see MOT]

moth (mɒθ) *n* any of numerous insects that typically have stout bodies with antennae of various shapes (but not clubbed), including large brightly coloured species, such as hawk moths, and small inconspicuous types, such as the clothes moths. Cf. **butterfly** (sense 1). [OE *moththe*]

mothball (ˈmɒθ,bɔːl) *n* **1** a small ball of camphor or naphthalene used to repel clothes moths in stored clothing, etc. **2 put in mothballs.** to postpone work on (a project, activity, etc.). ◆ *vb* (*tr*) **3** to prepare (a ship) for a long period of storage by sealing with plastic. **4** to take (a factory, etc.) out of operation but maintain it for future use. **5** to postpone work on (a project, activity, etc.).

moth-eaten Ⓣ *adj* **1** decayed, decrepit, or outdated. **2** eaten away by or as if by moths.

mother[1] Ⓣ (ˈmʌðə) *n* **1a** a female who has given birth to offspring. **1b** (*as modifier*): *a mother bird.* **2** (*often cap., esp. as a term of address*) a person's own mother. **3** a female substituting in the function of a mother. **4** (*often cap.*) *Chiefly arch.* a term of address for an old woman. **5a** motherly qualities, such as maternal affection: *it appealed to the mother in her.* **5b** (*as modifier*): *mother love.* **5c** (*in combination*): *mothercraft.* **6a** a female or thing that creates, nurtures, protects, etc., something. **6b** (*as modifier*): *mother church; mother earth.* **7** a title given to certain members of female religious orders. **8** (*modifier*) native or innate: *mother wit.* **9 the mother of all...** *Inf.* the greatest example of its kind: *the mother of all parties.* ◆ *vb* (*tr*) **10** to give birth to or produce. **11** to nurture, protect, etc. as a mother. [OE *mōdor*]
▸ **ˈmotherless** *adj*

mother[2] (ˈmʌðə) *n* a stringy slime containing various bacteria that forms on the surface of liquids undergoing fermentation. Also called: **mother of vinegar.** [C16: ?from MOTHER[1], but cf. Sp. *madre* scum, Du. *modder* dregs, MLow G *modder* decaying object, *mudde* sludge]

Mother Carey's chicken (ˈkɛərɪz) *n* another name for **stormy petrel.** [from ?]

mother country *n* **1** the original country of colonists or settlers. **2** a person's native country.

Mother Goose *n* the imaginary author of a collection of nursery rhymes. [C18: translated from F *Contes de ma mère l'Oye* (1697), a collection of tales by Charles Perrault (1628–1703)]

motherhood (ˈmʌðə,hʊd) *n* **1** the state of being a mother. **2** the qualities characteristic of a mother.

Mothering Sunday (ˈmʌðərɪŋ) *n Brit.* the fourth Sunday in Lent, when mothers traditionally receive presents from their children. Also called: **Mother's Day.**

mother-in-law *n, pl* **mothers-in-law.** the mother of one's wife or husband.

motherland (ˈmʌðə,lænd) *n* a person's native country.

mother lode *n Mining.* the principal lode in a system.

motherly Ⓣ (ˈmʌðəlɪ) *adj* of or resembling a mother, esp. in warmth or protectiveness.
▸ **ˈmotherliness** *n*

mother-of-pearl *n* a hard iridescent substance that forms the inner layer of the shells of certain molluscs, such as the oyster. It is used to make buttons, etc. Also called: **nacre.**

Mother's Day *n* **1** *US & Canad.* the second Sunday in May, observed as a day in honour of mothers. **2** See **Mothering Sunday.**

mother ship *n* a ship providing facilities and supplies for a number of small vessels.

mother superior *n, pl* **mother superiors** *or* **mothers superior.** the head of a community of nuns.

mother tongue *n* **1** the language first learned by a child. **2** a language from which another has evolved.

mother wit Ⓣ *n* native practical intelligence; common sense.

mothproof (ˈmɒθ,pruːf) *adj* **1** (esp. of clothes) chemically treated so as to repel clothes moths. ◆ *vb* **2** (*tr*) to make (clothes, etc.) mothproof.

mothy (ˈmɒθɪ) *adj* **mothier, mothiest. 1** moth-eaten. **2** containing moths; full of moths.

motif Ⓣ (məʊˈtiːf) *n* **1** a distinctive idea, esp. a theme elaborated on in a piece of music, literature, etc. **2** Also called: **motive.** a recurring shape in a design. **3** a single decoration, such as a symbol or name on a jumper, sweatshirt, etc. [C19: from F; see MOTIVE]

motile (ˈməʊtaɪl) *adj* capable of moving spontaneously and independently. [C19: from L *mōtus* moved, from *movēre* to move]
▸ **motility** (məʊˈtɪlɪtɪ) *n*

motion Ⓣ (ˈməʊʃən) *n* **1** the process of continual change in the physical position of an object; movement. **2** a movement or action, esp. of part of the human body; a gesture. **3a** the capacity for movement. **3b** a manner of movement, esp. walking; gait. **4** a mental impulse. **5** a formal proposal to be discussed and voted on in a debate, meeting, etc. **6** *Law.* an application made to a judge or court for an order or ruling necessary to the conduct of legal proceedings. **7** *Brit.* **7a** the evacuation of the bowels. **7b** excrement. **8a** part of a moving mechanism. **8b** the action of such a part. **9 go through the motions. 9a** to act or perform the task (of doing something) mechanically or without sincerity. **9b** to mimic the action (of something) by gesture. **10 in motion.** operational or functioning (often in **set in motion, set the wheels in motion**). ◆ *vb* **11** (when *tr, may take a clause as object or an infinitive*) to signal or direct (a person) by a movement or gesture. [C15: from L *mōtiō* a moving, from *movēre* to move]
▸ **ˈmotionless** *adj*

motion picture *n* a US and Canad. term for **film** (sense 1).

motivate Ⓣ (ˈməʊtɪ,veɪt) *vb* **motivates, motivating, motivated.** (*tr*) to give incentive to.
▸ **,motiˈvation** *n*

motivational research (,məʊtɪˈveɪʃənᵊl) *n* the application of psychology to the study of consumer behaviour, esp. the planning of advertising and sales campaigns. Also called: **motivation research.**

motive Ⓣ (ˈməʊtɪv) *n* **1** the reason for a certain course of action, whether conscious or unconscious. **2** a variant of **motif** (sense 2). ◆ *adj* **3** of or causing motion: *a motive force.* **4** of or acting as a motive; motivating. ◆ *vb* **motives, motiving, motived.** (*tr*) **5** to motivate. [C14: from OF *motif,* from LL *mōtīvus* (adj) moving, from L *mōtus,* p.p. of *movēre* to move]
▸ **ˈmotiveless** *adj*

motive power *n* **1** any source of energy used to produce motion. **2** the means of supplying power to an engine, vehicle, etc.

mot juste *French.* (mo ʒyst) *n, pl* **mots justes** (mo ʒyst). the appropriate word or expression.

motley Ⓣ (ˈmɒtlɪ) *adj* **1** made up of elements of varying type, quality, etc. **2** multicoloured. ◆ *n* **3** a motley collection. **4** the particoloured attire of a jester. [C14: ?from *mot* speck]

moto (ˈməʊtəʊ) *n Music.* movement. [It.]

motocross (ˈməʊtə,krɒs) *n* **1** cross-country motorcycle racing across rough ground. **2** another name for **rallycross.** [C20: from MOTO(R) + CROSS(-COUNTRY)]

motor (ˈməʊtə) *n* **1a** the engine, esp. an internal-combustion engine, of a vehicle. **1b** (*as modifier*): *a motor scooter.* **2** Also called: **electric motor.** a machine that converts electrical energy into mechanical energy. **3** any device that converts another form of energy into mechanical energy to produce motion. **4a** *Chiefly Brit.* a car. **4b** (*as modifier*): *motor spares.* ◆ *adj* **5** producing or causing motion. **6** *Physiol.* **6a** of or relating to nerves or neurons that carry impulses that cause muscles to

THESAURUS

entirely, as a rule, chiefly, customarily, for the most part, largely, mainly, most often, on the whole, particularly, predominantly, primarily, principally, usually

mote *n* = **speck,** atom, grain, mite, particle, spot

moth-eaten *adj* **1** = **decayed,** antiquated, decrepit, dilapidated, grungy (*sl., chiefly US*), obsolete, outdated, outworn, ragged, scuzzy (*sl., chiefly US*), seedy, shabby, stale, tattered, threadbare, worn-out

mother[1] *n* **1, 2** = **parent,** dam, ma, mater, mom (*US inf.*), mum (*Brit. inf.*), mummy (*Brit. inf.*), old lady (*inf.*), old woman (*inf.*) ◆ *modifier* **8** = **native,** connate, inborn, innate, natural ◆ *vb* **10** = **give birth to,** bear, bring forth, drop, produce **11** = **nurture,** care for, cherish, nurse, protect, raise, rear, tend

motherly *adj* = **maternal,** affectionate, caring, comforting, fond, gentle, kind, loving, protective, sheltering, tender, warm

mother wit *n* = **common sense,** brains, gumption (*Brit. inf.*), horse sense, judgment, native intelligence, nous (*Brit. sl.*), savvy (*sl.*), smarts (*sl., chiefly US*)

motif *n* **1** = **theme,** concept, idea, leitmotif, subject **2, 3** = **design,** decoration, form, ornament, shape

motion *n* **1** = **movement,** action, change, flow, kinesis, locomotion, mobility, motility, move, passage, passing, progress, travel **2** = **gesture,** gesticulation, sign, signal, wave **5** = **proposal,** proposition, recommendation, submission, suggestion **10 in motion** = **moving,** afoot, functioning, going, in progress, on the go (*inf.*), on the move (*inf.*), operational, travelling, under way, working ◆ *vb* **11** = **gesture,** beckon, direct, gesticulate, nod, signal, wave

motionless *adj* **1** = **still,** at a standstill, at rest, calm, fixed, frozen, halted, immobile, inanimate, inert, lifeless, paralysed, standing, static, stationary, stock-still, transfixed, unmoved, unmoving
Antonyms *adj* active, agitated, animated, frantic, lively, mobile, moving, restless, travelling

motivate *vb* = **inspire,** actuate, arouse, bring, cause, draw, drive, get going, give incentive to, impel, induce, inspirit, instigate, lead, move, persuade, prod, prompt, provoke, set off, set on, stimulate, stir, trigger

motivation *n* = **inspiration,** ambition, desire, drive, hunger, interest, wish = **incentive,** carrot and stick, impulse, incitement, inducement, inspiration, instigation, motive, persuasion, reason, spur, stimulus

motive *n* **1** = **reason,** cause, design, ground(s), incentive, incitement, inducement, influence, inspiration, intention, mainspring, motivation, object, occasion, purpose, rationale, spur, stimulus, the why and wherefore, thinking ◆ *adj* **3, 4** = **moving,** activating, driving, impelling, motivating, operative, prompting

motley *adj* **1** = **miscellaneous,** assorted, disparate, dissimilar, diversified, heterogeneous, mingled, mixed, unlike, varied **2** = **multicoloured,** chequered, parti-coloured, polychromatic, polychrome, polychromous, rainbow, variegated
Antonyms *adj* ≠ **miscellaneous:** homogeneous,

contract. **6b** of or relating to movement or to muscles that induce movement. ◆ *vb* **7** (*intr*) to travel by car. **8** (*tr*) *Brit.* to transport by car. **9** (*intr*) *Inf.* to move fast; make good progress. [C16: from L *mōtor* a mover, from *movēre* to move]

motorbicycle (ˈməʊtəˌbaɪsɪkᵊl) *n* **1** a motorcycle. **2** a moped.

motorbike (ˈməʊtəˌbaɪk) *n* a less formal name for **motorcycle.**

motorboat (ˈməʊtəˌbəʊt) *n* any boat powered by a motor.

motorbus (ˈməʊtəˌbʌs) *n* a bus driven by an internal-combustion engine.

motorcade (ˈməʊtəˌkeɪd) *n* a parade of cars. [C20: from MOTOR + CAVALCADE]

motorcar (ˈməʊtəˌkɑː) *n* **1** a more formal word for **car. 2** a self-propelled electric railway car.

motorcycle (ˈməʊtəˌsaɪkᵊl) *n* **1** Also called: **motorbike.** a two-wheeled vehicle that is driven by a petrol engine. ◆ *vb* **motorcycles, motorcycling, motorcycled.** (*intr*) **2** to ride on a motorcycle.
▸**ˈmotorˌcyclist** *n*

motorist (ˈməʊtərɪst) *n* a driver of a car.

motorize *or* **motorise** (ˈməʊtəˌraɪz) *vb* **motorizes, motorizing, motorized** *or* **motorises, motorising, motorised.** (*tr*) **1** to equip with a motor. **2** to provide (military units) with motor vehicles.
▸**ˌmotoriˈzation** *or* **ˌmotoriˈsation** *n*

motorman (ˈməʊtəmən) *n, pl* **motormen. 1** the driver of an electric train. **2** the operator of a motor.

motormouth (ˈməʊtəˌmaʊθ) *n Sl.* a garrulous person.

motor scooter *n* a light motorcycle with small wheels and an enclosed engine. Often shortened to **scooter.**

motor vehicle *n* a road vehicle driven esp. by an internal-combustion engine.

motorway (ˈməʊtəˌweɪ) *n Brit., Austral., & NZ.* a main road for fast-moving traffic, having separate carriageways for vehicles travelling in opposite directions.

Motown (ˈməʊˌtaʊn) *n Trademark.* music combining rhythm and blues and pop, or gospel rhythms and modern ballad harmony. [C20: from *Motown Records* of Detroit, from *Mo(tor) Town,* nickname for Detroit, centre of the US car industry]

motte (mɒt) *n History.* a mound on which a castle was erected. [C14: see MOAT]

MOT test *n* (in Britain) See **MOT** (sense 2).

mottle Ⓣ (ˈmɒtᵊl) *vb* **mottles, mottling, mottled. 1** (*tr*) to colour with streaks or blotches of different shades. ◆ *n* **2** a mottled appearance, as of the surface of marble. [C17: back formation from MOTLEY]
▸**ˈmottled** *adj*

motto Ⓣ (ˈmɒtəʊ) *n, pl* **mottoes** *or* **mottos. 1** a short saying expressing the guiding maxim or ideal of a family, organization, etc., esp. when part of a coat of arms. **2** a verse or maxim contained in a paper cracker. **3** a quotation prefacing a book or chapter of a book. [C16: via It. from L *muttum* utterance]

moue *French.* (mu) *n* a pouting look.

moufflon (ˈmuːflɒn) *n* a wild short-fleeced mountain sheep of Corsica and Sardinia. [C18: via F from Romance *mufrone,* from LL *mufrō*]

mouillé (ˈmwiːeɪ) *adj Phonetics.* palatalized, as in the sounds represented by Spanish *ll* or *ñ,* (pronounced as (ʎ) and (ɲ)), or French *ll* (representing a (j) sound). [C19: from F, p.p. of *mouiller* to moisten, from L *mollis* soft]

moujik (ˈmuːʒɪk) *n* a variant spelling of **muzhik.**

mould[1] Ⓣ *or US* **mold** (məʊld) *n* **1** a shaped cavity used to give a definite form to fluid or plastic material. **2** a frame on which something may be constructed. **3** something shaped in or made on a mould. **4** shape, form, design, or pattern. **5** specific nature, character, or type. ◆ *vb* (*tr*) **6** to make in a mould. **7** to shape or form, as by using a mould. **8** to influence or direct: *to mould opinion.* **9** to cling to: *the skirt moulds her figure.* **10** *Metallurgy.* to make (a material) into a mould used in casting. [C13 (n): from OF *modle,* from L *modulus* a small measure]
▸**ˈmouldable** *or US* **ˈmoldable** *adj* ▸**ˈmoulder** *or US* **ˈmolder** *n*

mould[2] Ⓣ *or US* **mold** (məʊld) *n* **1** a coating or discoloration caused by various fungi that develop in a damp atmosphere on the surface of food, fabrics, etc. **2** any of the fungi that cause this growth. ◆ *vb* **3** to become or cause to become covered with this growth. ◆ Also called: **mildew.** [C15: dialect (N English) *mowlde* mouldy, from p.p. of *moulen* to become mouldy, prob. from ON]

mould[3] Ⓣ *or US* **mold** (məʊld) *n* loose soil, esp. when rich in organic matter. [OE *molde*]

mouldboard *or US* **moldboard** (ˈməʊldˌbɔːd) *n* the curved blade of a plough, which turns over the furrow.

moulder Ⓣ *or US* **molder** (ˈməʊldə) *vb* (often foll. by *away*) to crumble or cause to crumble, as through decay. [C16: verbal use of MOULD[3]]

moulding *or US* **molding** (ˈməʊldɪŋ) *n* **1** *Archit.* **1a** a shaped outline, esp. one used on cornices, etc. **1b** a shaped strip made of wood, stone, etc. **2** something moulded.

mouldy Ⓣ *or US* **moldy** (ˈməʊldɪ) *adj* **mouldier, mouldiest** *or US* **moldier, moldiest. 1** covered with mould. **2** stale or musty, esp. from age or lack of use. **3** *Sl.* boring; dull.
▸**ˈmouldiness** *or US* **ˈmoldiness** *n*

moult *or US* **molt** (məʊlt) *vb* **1** (of birds, mammals, arthropods, etc.) to shed (feathers, hair, or cuticle) in order that new growth can take place. ◆ *n* **2** the periodic process of moulting. [C14 *mouten,* from OE *mūtian,* as in *bimūtian* to exchange for, from L *mūtāre* to change]
▸**ˈmoulter** *or US* **ˈmolter** *n*

mound Ⓣ (maʊnd) *n* **1** a raised mass of earth, debris, etc. **2** any heap or pile. **3** a small natural hill. **4** an artificial ridge of earth, stone, etc., as used for defence. ◆ *vb* **5** (often foll. by *up*) to gather into a mound; heap. **6** (*tr*) to cover or surround with a mound: *to mound a grave.* [C16: earthwork, ?from OE *mund* hand, hence defence]

Mound Builder *n* a member of a group of prehistoric inhabitants of the Mississippi region of the US, who built altar mounds, barrows, etc.

mound-builder *n* another name for **megapode.**

mount[1] Ⓣ (maʊnt) *vb* **1** to go up (a hill, stairs, etc.); climb. **2** to get up on (a horse, a platform, etc.). **3** (*intr;* often foll. by *up*) to increase; accumulate: *excitement mounted.* **4** (*tr*) to fix onto a backing, setting, or support: *to mount a photograph; to mount a slide.* **5** (*tr*) to provide with a horse for riding, or to place on a horse. **6** (of male animals) to climb onto (a female animal) for copulation. **7** (*tr*) to prepare (a play, etc.) for production. **8** (*tr*) to plan and organize (a campaign, etc.). **9** (*tr*) to prepare (a skeleton, etc.) for exhibition as a specimen. **10** (*tr*) to place or carry (weapons) in such a position that they can be fired. **11 mount guard.** See **guard.** ◆ *n* **12** a backing, setting, or support onto which something is fixed. **13** the act or manner of mounting. **14** a horse for riding. **15** a slide used in microscopy. [C16: from OF *munter,* from Vulgar L *montāre* (unattested) from L *mons* MOUNT[2]]
▸**ˈmountable** *adj* ▸**ˈmounter** *n*

mount[2] (maʊnt) *n* a mountain or hill: used in literature and (when cap.) in proper names: *Mount Everest.* [OE *munt,* from L *mons* mountain, but infl. in ME by OF *mont*]

mountain Ⓣ (ˈmaʊntɪn) *n* **1a** a natural upward projection of the earth's surface, higher and steeper than a hill. **1b** (*as modifier*): *mountain scenery.* **1c** (*in combination*): *a mountaintop.* **2** a huge heap or mass: *a mountain of papers.* **3** anything of great quantity or size. **4** a surplus of a commodity, esp. in the European Union: *a butter mountain.* [C13: from OF *montaigne,* ult. from L *montānus,* from *mons* mountain]

mountain ash *n* **1** any of various trees, such as the European mountain ash or rowan, having clusters of small white flowers and bright red berries. **2** any of several Australian eucalyptus trees, such as *Eucalyptus regnans.*

mountain avens *n* See **avens** (sense 2).

mountain bike *n* a type of sturdy bicycle with at least 16 gears, straight handlebars, and heavy-duty tyres.

mountain cat *n* any of various wild feline mammals, such as the bobcat, lynx, or puma.

mountaineer (ˌmaʊntɪˈnɪə) *n* **1** a person who climbs mountains. **2** a person living in a mountainous area. ◆ *vb* **3** (*intr*) to climb mountains.
▸**ˌmountainˈeering** *n*

mountain goat *n* any wild goat inhabiting mountainous regions.

mountain laurel *n* any of various ericaceous shrubs or trees of E North America having leathery poisonous leaves and clusters of pink or white flowers. Also called: **calico bush.**

mountain lion *n* another name for **puma.**

THESAURUS

similar, uniform ≠ **multicoloured:** monochromatic, plain, self-coloured, solid

mottled *adj* **1** = **blotchy,** brindled, chequered, dappled, flecked, freckled, marbled, piebald, pied, speckled, spotted, stippled, streaked, tabby, variegated

motto *n* **1** = **saying,** adage, byword, cry, dictum, formula, gnome, maxim, precept, proverb, rule, saw, slogan, tag-line, watchword

mould[1] *n* **1** = **cast,** die, form, matrix, pattern, shape, stamp **2, 4** = **design,** brand, build, configuration, construction, cut, fashion, form, format, frame, kind, line, make, pattern, shape, stamp, structure, style **5** = **nature,** calibre, character, ilk, kidney, kind, quality, sort, stamp, type ◆ *vb* **6, 7** = **shape,** carve, cast, construct, create, fashion, forge, form, make, model, sculpt, stamp, work **8** = **influence,** affect, control, direct, form, make, shape

mould[2] *n* **1, 2** = **fungus,** blight, mildew, mouldiness, mustiness

mould[3] *n* = **soil,** dirt, earth, humus, loam

moulder *vb* = **decay,** break down, crumble, decompose, disintegrate, perish, rot, waste

mouldy *adj* **1, 2** = **stale,** bad, blighted, decaying, fusty, mildewed, musty, rotten, rotting, spoiled

mound *n* **1, 2** = **heap,** bing (*Scot.*), drift, pile, rick, stack **3** = **hill,** bank, dune, embankment, hillock, knoll, rise **4** = **earthwork,** bulwark, motte (*History*), rampart

mount[1] *vb* **1** = **ascend,** clamber up, climb, escalade, go up, make one's way up, scale **2** = **get (up) on,** bestride, climb onto, climb up on, get astride, jump on **3** = **increase,** accumulate, build, escalate, grow, intensify, multiply, pile up, swell **4** = **display,** frame, set, set off **4** = **fit,** emplace, install, place, position, put in place, set up **7** = **stage,** exhibit, get up, prepare, produce, put on **8** = **launch,** deliver, prepare, ready, set in motion, stage ◆ *n* **12** = **backing,** base, fixture, foil, frame, mounting, setting, stand, support **14** = **horse,** steed (*literary*)
Antonyms *vb* ≠ **ascend:** descend, drop, go down, make one's way down ≠ **get (up) on:** climb down from, climb off, dismount, get down from, get off, jump off ≠ **increase:** contract, decline, decrease, diminish, dwindle, fall, lessen, lower, reduce, shrink, wane

mountain *n* **1** = **peak,** alp, ben (*Scot.*), berg (*S. Afr.*), elevation, eminence, fell (*Brit.*), height, mount, Munro **2** = **heap,** abundance, mass, mound, pile, stack, ton

mountainous ➊ ('maʊntɪnəs) *adj* **1** of or relating to mountains: *a mountainous region.* **2** like a mountain, esp. in size or impressiveness.

mountain sickness *n* nausea, headache, and shortness of breath caused by climbing to high altitudes. Also called: **altitude sickness.**

mountebank ➊ ('maʊntɪ,bæŋk) *n* **1** (formerly) a person who sold quack medicines in public places. **2** a charlatan; fake. ◆ *vb* **3** (*intr*) to play the mountebank. [C16: from It. *montambanco* a climber on a bench, from *montare* to MOUNT[1] + *banco* BENCH]
▸ ,**mounte'bankery** *n*

mounted ('maʊntɪd) *adj* **1** riding horses: *mounted police.* **2** provided with a support, backing, etc.

Mountie *or* **Mounty** ('maʊntɪ) *n, pl* **Mounties.** *Inf.* a member of the Royal Canadian Mounted Police. [from MOUNTED]

mounting ('maʊntɪŋ) *n* another word for **mount**[1] (sense 12).

mounting-block *n* a block of stone formerly used to aid a person when mounting a horse.

mourn ➊ (mɔːn) *vb* **1** to feel or express sadness for the death or loss of (someone or something). **2** (*intr*) to observe the customs of mourning, as by wearing black. [OE *murnan*]
▸ '**mourner** *n*

mournful ➊ ('mɔːnfʊl) *adj* **1** evoking grief; sorrowful. **2** gloomy; sad.
▸ '**mournfully** *adv* ▸ '**mournfulness** *n*

mourning ➊ ('mɔːnɪŋ) *n* **1** the act or feelings of one who mourns; grief. **2** the conventional symbols of grief, such as the wearing of black. **3** the period of time during which a death is officially mourned. ◆ *adj* **4** of or relating to mourning.
▸ '**mourningly** *adv*

mourning band *n* a piece of black material, esp. an armband, worn to indicate mourning.

mourning dove *n* a brown North American dove with a plaintive song.

mouse *n* (maʊs), *pl* **mice** (maɪs). **1** any of numerous small long-tailed rodents that are similar to but smaller than rats. See also **fieldmouse, harvest mouse, house mouse. 2** any of various related rodents, such as the jumping mouse. **3** a quiet, timid, or cowardly person. **4** *Computing.* a hand-held device used to control cursor movements and computing functions without keying. **5** *Sl.* a black eye. ◆ *vb* (maʊz), **mouses, mousing, moused. 6** to stalk and catch (mice, etc.). **7** (*intr*) to go about stealthily. [OE *mūs*]
▸ '**mouse,like** *adj*

mouser ('maʊzə, 'maʊsə) *n* a cat or other animal that is used to catch mice.

mousetrap ('maʊs,træp) *n* **1** any trap for catching mice, esp. one with a spring-loaded metal bar that is released by the taking of the bait. **2** *Brit. inf.* cheese of indifferent quality.

moussaka *or* **mousaka** (mʊ'sɑːkə) *n* a dish originating in the Balkan States, consisting of meat, aubergines, and tomatoes, topped with cheese sauce. [C20: from Mod. Gk]

mousse (muːs) *n* **1** a light creamy dessert made with eggs, cream, fruit, etc., set with gelatine. **2** a similar dish made from fish or meat. **3** short for **styling mousse.** [C19: from F: froth]

mousseline (*French* muslin) *n* **1** a fine fabric made of rayon or silk. **2** a type of fine glass. [C17: F: MUSLIN]

moustache *or US* **mustache** (mə'stɑːʃ) *n* **1** the unshaved growth of hair on the upper lip. **2** a similar growth of hair or bristles (in animals). **3** a mark like a moustache. [C16: via F from It. *mostaccio*, ult. from Doric Gk *mustax* upper lip]
▸ **mous'tached** *or US* **mus'tached** *adj*

moustache cup *n* a cup with a partial cover to protect a drinker's moustache.

Mousterian (muː'stɪərɪən) *n* **1** a culture characterized by flint flake tools and associated with Neanderthal man, dating from before 70 000–32 000 B.C. ◆ *adj* **2** of or relating to this culture. [C20: from F *moustérien*, from archaeological finds of the same period in the cave of *Le Moustier*, Dordogne, France]

mousy ➊ *or* **mousey** ('maʊsɪ) *adj* **mousier, mousiest. 1** resembling a mouse, esp. in hair colour. **2** shy or ineffectual. **3** infested with mice.
▸ '**mousily** *adv* ▸ '**mousiness** *n*

mouth ➊ *n* (maʊθ), *pl* **mouths** (maʊðz). **1** the opening through which many animals take in food and issue vocal sounds. **2** the system of organs surrounding this opening, including the lips, tongue, teeth, etc. **3** the visible part of the lips on the face. **4** a person regarded as a consumer of food: *four mouths to feed.* **5** a particular manner of speaking: *a foul mouth.* **6** *Inf.* boastful, rude, or excessive talk: *he is all mouth.* **7** the point where a river issues into a sea or lake. **8** the opening of a container, such as a jar. **9** the opening of a cave, tunnel, volcano, etc. **10** that part of the inner lip of a horse on which the bit acts. **11** a pout; grimace. **12 down in** *or* **at the mouth.** in low spirits. ◆ *vb* (maʊð). **13** to speak or say (something) insincerely, esp. in public. **14** (*tr*) to form (words) with movements of the lips but without speaking. **15** (*tr*) to take (something) into the mouth or to move (something) around inside the mouth. **16** (*intr;* usually foll. by *at*) to make a grimace. [OE *mūth*]
▸ **mouther** ('maʊðə) *n*

mouthful ➊ ('maʊθ,fʊl) *n, pl* **mouthfuls. 1** as much as is held in the mouth at one time. **2** a small quantity, as of food. **3** a long word or phrase that is difficult to say. **4** *Brit. inf.* an abusive response.

mouth organ *n* another name for **harmonica.**

mouthpart ('maʊθ,pɑːt) *n* any of the paired appendages in arthropods that surround the mouth and are specialized for feeding.

mouthpiece ➊ ('maʊθ,piːs) *n* **1** the part of a wind instrument into which the player blows. **2** the part of a telephone receiver into which a person speaks. **3** the part of a container forming its mouth. **4** a person who acts as a spokesman, as for an organization. **5** a publication expressing the official views of an organization.

mouthwash ('maʊθ,wɒʃ) *n* a medicated solution for gargling and cleansing the mouth.

mouthy ('maʊðɪ) *adj* **mouthier, mouthiest.** bombastic; excessively talkative.

mouton ('muːtɒn) *n* sheepskin processed to resemble the fur of another animal, esp. beaver or seal. [from F: sheep]

movable ➊ *or* **moveable** ('muːvəb[ə]l) *adj* **1** able to be moved; not fixed. **2** (esp. of Easter) varying in date from year to year. **3** (usually spelt **moveable**) *Law.* denoting or relating to personal property as opposed to realty. ◆ *n* **4** (*often pl*) a movable article, esp. a piece of furniture.
▸ ,**mova'bility** *or* '**movableness** *n* ▸ '**movably** *adv*

move ➊ (muːv) *vb* **moves, moving, moved. 1** to go or take from one place to another; change in position. **2** (*usually intr*) to change (one's dwelling, place of business, etc.). **3** to be or cause to be in motion; stir. **4** (*intr*) (of machines, etc.) to work or operate. **5** (*tr*) to cause (to do something); prompt. **6** (*intr*) to begin to act: *move soon or we'll lose the order.* **7** (*intr*) to associate oneself with a specified social circle: *to move in exalted spheres.* **8** (*intr*) to make progress. **9** (*tr*) to arouse affection, pity, or compassion in; touch. **10** (in board games) to change the position of (a piece) or (of a piece) to change position. **11** (*intr*) (of merchandise) to be disposed of by being bought. **12** (when *tr, often takes a clause as object;* when *intr,* often foll. by *for*) to suggest (a proposal) formally, as in debating or parliamentary procedure. **13** (*intr;* usually foll. by *on* or *along*) to go away or to another place; leave. **14** to cause (the bowels) to evacuate or (of the bowels) to be evacuated. ◆ *n* **15** the act of moving; movement. **16** one of a sequence of actions, usually part of a plan; manoeuvre. **17** the act of moving one's residence, place of business, etc. **18** (in board games) **18a** a player's turn to move his piece. **18b** a manoeuvre of a piece. **19 get a move on.** *Inf.* **19a** to get started. **19b** to hurry up. **20 on the move. 20a** travelling from place to

THESAURUS

mountainous *adj* **1** = **high**, alpine, highland, rocky, soaring, steep, towering, upland **2** = **huge**, daunting, enormous, gigantic, great, hulking, immense, mammoth, mighty, monumental, ponderous, prodigious
Antonyms *adj* ≠ **huge:** diminutive, insignificant, little, minute, petty, puny, small, tiny, trivial, weak

mountebank *n* **1, 2** = **charlatan**, cheat, chiseller (*inf.*), confidence trickster, con man (*inf.*), fake, fraud, fraudster, hustler (*US inf.*), impostor, phoney *or* phony (*inf.*), pretender, quack, rogue, swindler

mourn *vb* **1, 2** = **grieve**, bemoan, bewail, deplore, keen, lament, miss, rue, sorrow, wail, wear black, weep

mournful *adj* **1** = **sad**, afflicting, calamitous, deplorable, distressing, grievous, harrowing, lamentable, melancholy, painful, piteous, plaintive, sorrowful, tragic, unhappy, woeful **2** = **dismal**, brokenhearted, cheerless, desolate, disconsolate, downcast, down in the dumps (*inf.*), funereal, gloomy, grief-stricken, grieving, heartbroken, heavy, heavy-hearted, joyless, lugubrious, melancholy, miserable, rueful, sad, sombre, unhappy, woeful
Antonyms *adj* ≠ **sad:** agreeable, cheerful, fortunate, happy, lucky, pleasant, satisfying ≠ **dismal:** bright, cheerful, chirpy (*inf.*), genial, happy, jolly, joyful, light-hearted, sunny, upbeat (*inf.*)

mourning *n* **1** = **grieving**, bereavement, grief, keening, lamentation, weeping, woe **2** = **black**, sackcloth and ashes, weeds, widow's weeds

mousy *adj* **1** = **brownish**, colourless, drab, dull, indeterminate, plain **2** = **shy**, diffident, ineffectual, quiet, self-effacing, timid, timorous, unassertive

mouth *n* **1, 3** = **lips**, chops (*sl.*), gob (*sl., especially Brit.*), jaws, maw, trap (*sl.*), yap (*sl.*) **6** *Informal* = **boasting**, braggadocio, bragging, empty talk, gas (*inf.*), hot air (*sl.*), idle talk **6** *Informal* = **insolence**, backchat, cheek (*inf.*), impudence, lip (*sl.*), rudeness, sauce (*inf.*) **8, 9** = **opening**, aperture, cavity, crevice, door, entrance, gateway, inlet, lips, orifice, rim **12 down in** *or* **at the mouth** = **depressed**, blue, crestfallen, dejected, disheartened, dispirited, down, downcast, down in the dumps (*inf.*), in low spirits, melancholy, miserable, sad, sick as a parrot (*inf.*), unhappy

mouthful *n* **2** = **taste**, bit, bite, drop, forkful, little, morsel, sample, sip, spoonful, sup, swallow

mouthpiece *n* **4** = **spokesperson**, agent, delegate, representative, spokesman *or* spokeswoman **5** = **publication**, journal, organ, periodical

movable *adj* **1** = **portable**, detachable, mobile, not fixed, portative, transferable, transportable ◆ *n* **4** *often plural* = **furniture**, belongings, chattels, effects, gear, goods, possessions, property, stuff (*inf.*), things (*inf.*)

move *vb* **1** = **go**, advance, budge, change position, drift, march, proceed, progress, shift, stir, walk **1** = **change**, carry, shift, switch, transfer, transport, transpose **2** = **relocate**, change residence, flit, go away, leave, migrate, move house, pack one's bags (*inf.*), quit, remove **3** = **drive**, activate, impel, motivate, operate, prod, propel, push, set going, shift, shove, start, turn **5** = **prompt**, actuate, cause, give rise to, impel, incite, induce, influence, inspire, instigate, lead, motivate, persuade, rouse, stimulate, urge **9** = **touch**, affect, agitate, excite, impress, make an impression on, tug at (someone's) heartstrings (*often facetious*) **12** = **propose**, advocate, put forward, recommend, suggest, urge ◆ *n* **15, 16, 18** = **action**, act, deed, manoeuvre, measure, motion, movement, ploy, place. **20b** advancing; succeeding. **20c** very active; busy. [C13: from Anglo-F *mover*, from L *movēre*]

move in *vb* (*mainly adv*) **1** (*also prep*) Also (when *prep*): **move into.** to occupy or take possession of (a new residence, place of business, etc.). **2** (*intr; often foll. by on*) *Inf.* to creep close (to), as in preparing to capture. **3** (*intr; often foll. by on*) *Inf.* to try to gain power or influence (over).

movement ('mu:vmənt) *n* **1a** the act, process, or result of moving. **1b** an instance of moving. **2** the manner of moving. **3a** a group of people with a common ideology. **3b** the organized action of such a group. **4** a trend or tendency. **5** the driving and regulating mechanism of a watch or clock. **6** (*often pl*) a person's location and activities during a specific time. **7a** the evacuation of the bowels. **7b** the matter evacuated. **8** *Music.* a principal self-contained section of a symphony, sonata, etc. **9** tempo or pace, as in music or literature. **10** *Fine arts.* the appearance of motion in painting, sculpture, etc. **11** *Prosody.* the rhythmic structure of verse. **12** a positional change by one or a number of military units. **13** a change in the market price of a security or commodity.

mover ('mu:və) *n* **1** *Inf.* a person, business, idea, etc., that is advancing or progressing. **2** a person or thing that moves. **3** a person who moves a proposal, as in a debate. **4** *US & Canad.* a removal firm or a person who works for one.

movers and shakers *pl n Inf.* the people with power and influence in a particular field of activity. [C20: ? from the line "We are the movers and shakers of the world for ever" in 'Ode' by Arthur O'Shaughnessy (1844–81), Brit. poet]

movie ('mu:vɪ) *n* **a** an informal word for **film** (sense 1). **b** (*as modifier*): *movie ticket.*

moving ('mu:vɪŋ) *adj* **1** arousing or touching the emotions. **2** changing or capable of changing position. **3** causing motion.
▸**'movingly** *adv*

moving staircase *or* **stairway** *n* less common terms for **escalator** (sense 1).

mow (məʊ) *vb* **mows, mowing, mowed; mowed** *or* **mown. 1** to cut down (grass, crops, etc.), with a hand implement or machine. **2** (*tr*) to cut the growing vegetation of (a field, lawn, etc.). [OE *māwan*]
▸**'mower** *n*

mow down *vb* (*tr, adv*) to kill in large numbers, esp. by gunfire.

mown (məʊn) *vb* a past participle of **mow.**

mozzarella (ˌmɒtsə'relə) *n* a moist white curd cheese originally made in Italy from buffalo milk. [from It., dim. of *mozza* a type of cheese, from *mozzare* to cut off]

mp 1 *abbrev. for* melting point. **2** *Music. symbol for* mezzo piano. [It.: moderately soft]

MP *abbrev. for:* **1** (in Britain, Canada, etc.) Member of Parliament. **2** (in Britain) Metropolitan Police. **3** Military Police. **4** Mounted Police.

mpg *abbrev. for* miles per gallon.

mph *abbrev. for* miles per hour.

MPhil *or* **MPh** *abbrev. for* Master of Philosophy.

MPP (in Canada) *abbrev. for* Member of Provincial Parliament.

Mr ('mɪstə) *n, pl* **Messrs.** a title used before a man's name or before some office that he holds: *Mr Jones; Mr President.* [C17: abbrev. of MISTER]

MR *abbrev. for:* **1** (in Britain) Master of the Rolls. **2** motivation(al) research.

MRC (in Britain) *abbrev. for* Medical Research Council.

MRI *abbrev. for* magnetic resonance imaging.

m-RNA *abbrev. for* messenger RNA.

MRP *abbrev. for* manufacturers' recommended price.

Mrs ('mɪsɪz) *n, pl* **Mrs** *or* **Mesdames.** a title used before the name or names of a married woman. [C17: orig. abbrev. of MISTRESS]

MRSA *abbrev. for* methicillin-resistant *Staphylococcus aureus*: a bacterium that enters the skin through open wounds to cause septicaemia and is extremely resistant to most antibiotics. It has been responsible for outbreaks of untreatable infections among patients in hospitals.

Ms (mɪz, məs) *n* a title substituted for **Mrs** or **Miss** to avoid making a distinction between married and unmarried women.

MS *abbrev. for:* **1** Master of Surgery. **2** (on gravestones, etc.) memoriae sacrum. [L: sacred to the memory of] **3** multiple sclerosis.

MS. *or* **ms.** *pl* **MSS.** *or* **mss.** *abbrev. for* manuscript.

MSc *abbrev. for* Master of Science.

MS-DOS (ɛm'ɛs'dɒs) *n Trademark, computing.* a type of disk operating system. [C20: from *M(icro)s(oft)*, the company that developed it, + DOS]

MSF (in Britain) *abbrev. for* Manufacturing, Science, and Finance Union.

MSG *abbrev. for* monosodium glutamate.

Msgr *abbrev. for* Monsignor.

MST *abbrev. for* Mountain Standard Time.

Mt *or* **mt** *abbrev. for:* **1** mount: *Mt Everest.* **2** Also: **mtn.** mountain.

MTech *abbrev. for* Master of Technology.

mtg *abbrev. for:* **1** meeting. **2** Also: **mtge.** mortgage.

MTV *abbrev. for* music television: a US music channel that operates 24 hours a day.

mu (mju:) *n* the 12th letter in the Greek alphabet (Μ, μ).

much (mʌtʃ) *determiner* **1a** (*usually used with a negative*) a great quantity or degree of: *there isn't much honey left.* **1b** (*as pron*): *much has been learned from this.* **2 a bit much.** *Inf.* rather excessive. **3 make much of. 3a** (*used with a negative*) to make sense of: *he couldn't make much of her babble.* **3b** to give importance to: *she made much of this fact.* **3c** to pay flattering attention to: *the reporters made much of the film star.* **4 not much of.** not to any appreciable degree or extent: *he's not much of an actor really.* **5 not up to much.** *Inf.* of a low standard: *this beer is not up to much.* ◆ *adv* **6** considerably: *they're much better now.* **7** practically; nearly (esp. in **much the same**). **8** (*usually used with a negative*) often; a great deal: *it doesn't happen much in this country.* **9** (**as**) **much as.** even though; although: *much as I'd like to, I can't come.* ◆ See also **more, most.** [OE *mycel*]

muchness ('mʌtʃnɪs) *n* **1** *Arch. or inf.* magnitude. **2 much of a muchness.** *Brit.* very similar.

mucilage ('mju:sɪlɪdʒ) *n* **1** a sticky preparation, such as gum or glue, used as an adhesive. **2** a complex glutinous carbohydrate secreted by certain plants. [C14: via OF from LL *mūcilāgo* mouldy juice, from L, from *mucēre* to be mouldy]
▸**mucilaginous** (ˌmju:sɪ'lædʒɪnəs) *adj*

muck (mʌk) *n* **1** farmyard dung or decaying vegetable matter. **2** an organic soil rich in humus and used as a fertilizer. **3** dirt or filth. **4** *Sl., chiefly Brit.* rubbish. **5 make a muck of.** *Sl., chiefly Brit.* to ruin or spoil. ◆ *vb* (*tr*) **6** to spread manure upon (fields, etc.). **7** to soil or pollute. **8** (usually foll. by *up*) *Brit. sl.* to ruin or spoil. **9** (often foll. by *out*) to clear muck from. [C13: prob. from ON]
▸**'mucky** *adj*

muck about *vb Brit. sl.* **1** (*intr*) to waste time; misbehave. **2** (when *intr*, foll. by *with*) to interfere (with), annoy, or waste the time (of).

mucker ('mʌkə) *n Brit. sl.* **a** a friend; mate. **b** a coarse person.
▸**'muckerish** *adj*

muck in *vb* (*intr, adv*) *Brit. sl.* to share duties, work, etc. (with other people).

muckrake ('mʌkˌreɪk) *vb* **muckrakes, muckraking, muckraked.** (*intr*) to seek out and expose scandal, esp. concerning public figures.
▸**'muckˌraker** *n* ▸**'muckˌraking** *n*

mucksweat ('mʌkˌswet) *n Brit. inf.* profuse sweat or a state of profuse sweating.

mucous ('mju:kəs) *adj* of, resembling, or secreting mucus. [C17: from L *mūcōsus* slimy, from MUCUS]
▸**mucosity** (mju:'kɒsɪtɪ) *n*

> **USAGE NOTE** The noun *mucus* is often misspelled as *mucous. Mucous* can only be correctly used as an adjective.

THESAURUS

shift, step, stratagem, stroke, turn **17 = transfer**, change of address, flit, flitting (*Scot. & N English dialect*), migration, relocation, removal, shift **19 get a move on = speed up**, get cracking (*inf.*), get going, hurry (up), make haste, shake a leg (*inf.*), step on it (*inf.*), stir oneself **20 on the move: a = in transit**, journeying, moving, on the road (*inf.*), on the run, on the wing, travelling, under way, voyaging **b, c = active**, advancing, astir, going forward, moving, progressing, stirring, succeeding

Antonyms *vb* ≠ **prompt:** deter, discourage, dissuade, prevent, stop

movement *n* **1, 2 = motion**, act, action, activity, advance, agitation, change, development, displacement, exercise, flow, gesture, manoeuvre, move, moving, operation, progress, progression, shift, steps, stir, stirring, transfer **3 = group**, camp, campaign, crusade, drive, faction, front, grouping, organization, party **4 = trend**, current, drift, flow, swing, tendency **5 = workings**, action, innards (*inf.*), machinery, mechanism, works **8** *Music* **= section**, division, part, passage **9, 11 = rhythm**, beat, cadence, measure (*Prosody*), metre, pace, swing, tempo

movie *n* **1 = film**, feature, flick (*sl.*), motion picture, moving picture (*US*), picture

moving *adj* **1 = emotional**, affecting, arousing, emotive, exciting, impelling, impressive, inspiring, pathetic, persuasive, poignant, stirring, touching **2 = mobile**, motile, movable, portable, running, unfixed

Antonyms *adj* ≠ **emotional:** unemotional, unexciting, unimpressive, uninspiring ≠ **mobile:** fixed, immobile, immovable, stationary, still, unmoving

mow *vb* **1, 2 = cut**, crop, scythe, shear, trim

mow down *vb* **= massacre**, blow away (*sl., chiefly US*), butcher, cut down, cut to pieces, shoot down, slaughter

much *determiner* **1a = great**, abundant, a lot of, ample, considerable, copious, plenteous, plenty of, sizable *or* sizeable, substantial ◆ *pron* **1b = a lot**, a good deal, a great deal, an appreciable amount, heaps (*inf.*), loads (*inf.*), lots (*inf.*), plenty ◆ *adv* **6, 8 = greatly**, a great deal, a lot, considerably, decidedly, exceedingly, frequently, indeed, often, regularly

Antonyms *determiner* ≠ **great:** inadequate, insufficient, little, scant ◆ *pron* ≠ **a lot:** hardly anything, little, next to nothing, not a lot, not much, practically nothing, very little ◆ *adv* ≠ **greatly:** barely, hardly, infrequently, irregularly, not a lot, not much, occasionally, only just, rarely, scarcely, seldom, slightly

muck *n* **1 = manure**, dung, ordure **3 = dirt**, crap (*sl.*), crud (*sl.*), filth, grot (*sl.*), gunge (*inf.*), gunk (*inf.*), mire, mud, ooze, scum, sewage, shit (*taboo sl.*), slime, slob (*Irish*), sludge **5 make a muck of** *Slang, chiefly Brit.* **= spoil**, blow (*sl.*), botch, bungle, make a mess of, make a nonsense of, make a pig's ear of (*inf.*), mar, mess up, muff, ruin ◆ *vb* **8** *usually foll. by* **up** *Brit. slang* **= ruin**, blow (*sl.*), bodge (*inf.*), botch, bungle, make a mess of, make a muck of (*sl.*), make a nonsense of, make a pig's ear of (*inf.*), mar, mess up, muff, spoil

mucky *adj* **3 = dirty**, begrimed, bespattered, filthy, grimy, messy, mud-caked, muddy, soiled, sticky

mucous *adj* **= slimy**, glutinous, gummy, mucilaginous, viscid, viscous

mucous membrane *n* a mucus-secreting membrane that lines body cavities or passages that are open to the external environment.

mucus ('mju:kəs) *n* the slimy protective secretion of the mucous membranes. [C17: from L: nasal secretions; cf. *mungere* to blow the nose]

USAGE NOTE See at **mucous**.

mud ❶ (mʌd) *n* **1** a fine-grained soft wet deposit that occurs on the ground after rain, at the bottom of ponds, etc. **2** *Inf.* slander or defamation. **3 clear as mud.** *Inf.* not at all clear. **4 here's mud in your eye.** *Inf.* a humorous drinking toast. **5 (someone's) name is mud.** *Inf.* (someone) is disgraced. **6 throw** (*or* **sling**) **mud at.** *Inf.* to slander; vilify. ◆ *vb* **muds, mudding, mudded. 7** (*tr*) to soil or cover with mud. [C14: prob. from MLow G *mudde*]

mud bath *n* **1** a medicinal bath in heated mud. **2** a dirty or muddy occasion, state, etc.

mudbrick ('mʌd,brɪk) *n* a brick made with mud.

muddle ❶ ('mʌdᵊl) *vb* **muddles, muddling, muddled.** (*tr*) **1** (often foll. by *up*) to mix up (objects, items, etc.). **2** to confuse. **3** *US.* to mix or stir (alcoholic drinks, etc.). ◆ *n* **4** a state of physical or mental confusion. [C16: ?from MDu. *moddelen* to make muddy]
▸ **'muddled** *adj* ▸ **'muddler** *n* ▸ **'muddling** *adj, n*

muddleheaded (,mʌdᵊl'hɛdɪd) *adj* mentally confused or vague.
▸ **,muddle'headedness** *n*

muddle through ❶ *vb* (*intr, adv*) *Chiefly Brit.* to succeed in spite of lack of organization.

muddy ❶ ('mʌdɪ) *adj* **muddier, muddiest. 1** covered or filled with mud. **2** not clear or bright: *muddy colours.* **3** cloudy: *a muddy liquid.* **4** (esp. of thoughts) confused or vague. ◆ *vb* **muddies, muddying, muddied. 5** to become or cause to become muddy.
▸ **'muddily** *adv* ▸ **'muddiness** *n*

mudfish ('mʌd,fɪʃ) *n, pl* **mudfish** *or* **mudfishes.** any of various fishes, such as the bowfin, that live at the muddy bottoms of rivers, lakes, etc.

mud flat *n* a tract of low muddy land that is covered at high tide and exposed at low tide.

mudflow ('mʌd,fləʊ) *n Geol.* a flow of soil mixed with water down a steep unstable slope.

mudguard ('mʌd,gɑ:d) *n* a curved part of a motorcycle, bicycle, etc., attached above the wheels to reduce the amount of water or mud thrown up by them. US and Canad. name: **fender.**

mud hen *n* any of various birds that frequent marshes, esp. the coots, rails, etc.

mudlark ('mʌd,lɑ:k) *n* **1** (formerly) a person who made a living by picking up odds and ends in the mud of tidal rivers. **2** *Sl., now rare.* a street urchin. **3** *Austral. sl.* a racehorse that runs well on a wet or muddy course.

mud map *n Austral.* **1** a rough map drawn on the ground with a stick. **2** any rough sketch map.

mudpack ('mʌd,pæk) *n* a cosmetic astringent paste containing fuller's earth.

mud puppy *n* an aquatic North American salamander having persistent larval features.

mudskipper ('mʌd,skɪpə) *n* any of various gobies that occur in tropical coastal regions of Africa and Asia and can move on land by means of their strong pectoral fins.

mudslinging ('mʌd,slɪŋɪŋ) *n* casting malicious slurs on an opponent, esp. in politics.
▸ **'mud,slinger** *n*

mudstone ('mʌd,stəʊn) *n* a dark grey clay rock similar to shale.

mud turtle *n* any of various small turtles that inhabit muddy rivers in North and Central America.

muesli ('mju:zlɪ) *n* a mixture of rolled oats, nuts, fruit, etc., usually eaten with milk. [Swiss G, from G *Mus* mush, purée + *-li,* dim. suffix]

muezzin (mu:'ɛzɪn) *n Islam.* the official of a mosque who calls the faithful to prayer from the minaret. [C16: from Ar. *mu'adhdhin*]

muff[1] (mʌf) *n* an open-ended cylinder of fur or cloth into which the hands are placed for warmth. [C16: prob. from Du. *mof,* ult. from F *mouffle* MUFFLE[1]]

muff[2] ❶ (mʌf) *vb* **1** to perform (an action) awkwardly. **2** (*tr*) to bungle (a shot, catch, etc.). ◆ *n* **3** any unskilful play, esp. a dropped catch. **4** any bungled action. **5** a bungler. [C19: from ?]

muffin ('mʌfɪn) *n* **1** *Brit.* a thick round baked yeast roll, usually toasted and served with butter. **2** *US & Canad.* a small cup-shaped sweet bread roll, usually eaten hot with butter. [C18: ?from Low G *muffen* cakes]

muffin man *n Brit.* (formerly) an itinerant seller of muffins.

muffle[1] ❶ ('mʌfᵊl) *vb* **muffles, muffling, muffled.** (*mainly tr*) **1** (*also intr;* often foll. by *up*) to wrap up (the head) in a scarf, cloak, etc., esp. for warmth. **2** (*also intr*) to deaden (a sound or noise), esp. by wrapping. **3** to prevent (the expression of something) by (someone). ◆ *n* **4** something that muffles. **5** a kiln with an inner chamber for firing porcelain, enamel, etc. [C15: prob. from OF; cf. OF *moufle* mitten, *emmouflé* wrapped up]

muffle[2] ('mʌfᵊl) *n* the fleshy hairless part of the upper lip and nose in ruminants and some rodents. [C17: from F *mufle,* from ?]

muffler ('mʌflə) *n* **1** a thick scarf, collar, etc. **2** the US and Canad. name for **silencer** (sense 1).

mufti ('mʌftɪ) *n* civilian dress, esp. as worn by a person who normally wears a military uniform. [C19: ?from MUFTI]

Mufti ('mʌftɪ) *n, pl* **Muftis.** a Muslim legal expert and adviser on the law of the Koran. [C16: from Ar. *muftī,* from *aftā* to give a (legal) decision]

mug[1] ❶ (mʌg) *n* **1** a drinking vessel with a handle, usually cylindrical and made of earthenware. **2** Also called: **mugful.** the quantity held by a mug or its contents. [C16: prob. of Scand. origin]

mug[2] ❶ (mʌg) *n* **1** *Sl.* a person's face or mouth. **2** *Brit. sl.* a gullible person, esp. one who is swindled easily. **3 a mug's game.** a worthless activity. ◆ *vb* **mugs, mugging, mugged. 4** (*tr*) *Inf.* to attack or rob (someone) violently. [C18: ?from MUG[1], since drinking vessels were sometimes modelled into the likeness of a face]
▸ **'mugger** *n*

muggins ('mʌgɪnz) *n* (*functioning as sing*) **1** *Brit. sl.* **1a** a simpleton. **1b** a title used humorously to refer to oneself as a dupe or victim. **2** a card game. [C19: prob. from the surname *Muggins*]

muggy ❶ ('mʌgɪ) *adj* **muggier, muggiest.** (of weather, air, etc.) unpleasantly warm and humid. [C18: dialect *mug* drizzle, prob. of Scand. origin]
▸ **'mugginess** *n*

mug shot *n Inf.* a photograph of a person's face, esp. one resembling a police-file picture.

mug up ❶ *vb* (*adv*) *Brit. sl.* to study (a subject) hard, esp. for an exam. [C19: from ?]

Muhammadan *or* **Muhammedan** (mu'hæmədᵊn) *n, adj* another word (not in Muslim use) for **Muslim.**

mujaheddin *or* **mujahedeen** (,mu:dʒəhə'di:n) *pl n* (preceded by *the; sometimes cap.*) (in Afghanistan and Iran) fundamentalist Muslim guerrillas. In Afghanistan in 1992 the mujaheddin overthrew the government but were unable to agree on a new constitution and were themselves overthrown by the Taliban militia in 1996. [C20: from Ar. *mujāhidīn* fighters, ult. from JIHAD]

mukluk ('mʌklʌk) *n* a soft boot, usually of sealskin, worn by Eskimos. [from Eskimo *muklok* large seal]

mulatto (mju:'lætəʊ) *n, pl* **mulattos** *or* **mulattoes. 1** a person having one Black and one White parent. ◆ *adj* **2** of a light brown colour; tawny. [C16: from Sp. *mulato* young mule, var. of *mulo* MULE[1]]

mulberry ('mʌlbərɪ, -brɪ) *n, pl* **mulberries. 1** a tree having edible blackberry-like fruit, such as the white mulberry, the leaves of which are used to feed silkworms. **2** the fruit of any of these trees. **3** any of several similar or related trees. **4a** a dark purple colour. **4b** (*as adj*): *a mulberry dress.* [C14: from L *mōrum,* from Gk *moron;* rel. to OE *mōrberie*]

mulch (mʌltʃ) *n* **1** half-rotten vegetable matter, peat, etc., used to prevent soil erosion or enrich the soil. ◆ *vb* **2** (*tr*) to cover (the surface of land) with mulch. [C17: from obs. *mulch* soft; rel. to OE *mylisc* mellow]

mulct (mʌlkt) *vb* (*tr*) **1** to cheat or defraud. **2** to fine (a person). ◆ *n* **3** a fine or penalty. [C15: via F from L *multa* a fine]

mule[1] (mju:l) *n* **1** the sterile offspring of a male donkey and a female

THESAURUS

mud *n* **1** = **dirt**, clay, gloop (*inf.*), mire, ooze, silt, slime, slob (*Irish*), sludge

muddle *vb* **1** = **jumble**, confuse, disarrange, disorder, disorganize, make a mess of, mess, mix up, ravel, scramble, spoil, tangle **2** = **confuse**, befuddle, bewilder, confound, daze, disorient, perplex, stupefy ◆ *n* **4** = **confusion**, chaos, clutter, daze, disarray, disorder, disorganization, fankle (*Scot.*), hodgepodge (*US*), hotchpotch, jumble, mess, mix-up, perplexity, pig's breakfast (*inf.*), plight, predicament, ravel, tangle

muddled *adj* **1** = **jumbled**, chaotic, confused, disarrayed, disordered, disorganized, higgledy-piggledy (*inf.*), messy, mixed-up, scrambled, tangled **2** = **bewildered**, at sea, befuddled, confused, dazed, disoriented, perplexed, stupefied, vague
Antonyms *adj* ≠ **jumbled:** cut-and-dried (*inf.*), orderly, organized

muddle through *vb Chiefly Brit.* = **scrape by**, cope, get along, get by, make it, manage, manage somehow

muddy *adj* **1** = **dirty**, bespattered, clarty (*Scot. & N English dialect*), grimy, mucky, mud-caked, soiled **1** = **boggy**, marshy, miry, quaggy, swampy **2** = **dull**, blurred, dingy, flat, lustreless, smoky, unclear, washed-out **3** = **cloudy**, dirty, foul, impure, opaque, turbid **4** = **confused**, fuzzy, hazy, indistinct, muddled, unclear, vague, woolly ◆ *vb* **5** = **smear**, begrime, bespatter, cloud, dirty, smirch, soil

muff[2] *vb* **1, 2** = **botch**, bodge (*inf.*), bungle, fluff (*inf.*), make a mess of, make a muck of (*inf.*), make a nonsense of, make a pig's ear of (*inf.*), mess up, mismanage, spoil

muffle[1] *vb* **1** = **wrap up**, cloak, conceal, cover, disguise, envelop, hood, mask, shroud, swaddle, swathe **2** = **deaden**, dull, gag, hush, muzzle, quieten, silence, soften, stifle, suppress

muffled *adj* **2** = **indistinct**, dim, dull, faint, muted, stifled, strangled, subdued, suppressed

mug[1] *n* **1** = **cup**, beaker, flagon, jug, pot, stein, tankard, toby jug

mug[2] *n* **1** *Slang* = **face**, clock (*Brit. sl.*), countenance, dial (*sl.*), features, kisser (*sl.*), mush (*Brit. sl.*), phiz *or* phizog (*Brit. sl.*), puss (*sl.*), visage **2** *Brit. slang* = **fool**, charlie (*Brit. inf.*), chump (*inf.*), easy *or* soft touch (*sl.*), gull (*arch.*), innocent, mark (*sl.*), muggins (*Brit. sl.*), simpleton, sucker (*sl.*) ◆ *vb* **4** *Informal* = **attack**, assail, assault, beat up, do over (*Brit., Austral., & NZ sl.*), duff up (*Brit. sl.*), hold up, lay into (*inf.*), put the boot in (*sl.*), rob, set about *or* upon, steam (*inf.*), work over (*sl.*)

muggy *adj* = **humid**, clammy, close, damp, moist, oppressive, sticky, stuffy, sultry

mug up *vb Brit. slang* = **study**, bone up on (*inf.*), burn the midnight oil (*inf.*), cram (*inf.*), get up (*inf.*), swot (*Brit. inf.*)

horse, used as a beast of burden. **2** any hybrid animal: *a mule canary.* **3** Also called: **spinning mule.** a machine that spins cotton into yarn and winds the yarn on spindles. **4** *Inf.* an obstinate or stubborn person. [C13: from OF *mul,* from L *mūlus* ass, mule]

mule[2] (mjuːl) *n* a backless shoe or slipper. [C16: from OF from L *mulleus* a magistrate's shoe]

muleta (mjuːˈletə) *n* the small cape attached to a stick used by the matador during a bullfight. [Sp.: small mule, crutch, from *mula* MULE[1]]

muleteer (ˌmjuːlɪˈtɪə) *n* a person who drives mules.

mulga (ˈmʌlgə) *n Austral.* **1** any of various Australian acacia shrubs. **2** scrub comprised of a dense growth of acacia. **3** *Inf.* the outback; bush. [from Abor.]

muliebrity (ˌmjuːlɪˈɛbrɪtɪ) *n* **1** the condition of being a woman. **2** femininity. [C16: via LL from L *muliēbris* womanly, from *mulier* woman]

mulish Ⓣ (ˈmjuːlɪʃ) *adj* stubborn; obstinate.
▸ **ˈmulishly** *adv* ▸ **ˈmulishness** *n*

mull[1] Ⓣ (mʌl) *vb (tr)* (often foll. by *over*) to study or ponder. [C19: prob. from MUDDLE]

mull[2] (mʌl) *vb (tr)* to heat (wine, ale, etc.) with sugar and spices. [C17: from ?]
▸ **mulled** *adj*

mull[3] (mʌl) *n* a light muslin fabric of soft texture. [C18: earlier *mulmull,* from Hindi *malmal*]

mull[4] (mʌl) *n Scot.* a promontory. [C14: rel. to Gaelic *maol,* Icelandic *múli*]

mullah *or* **mulla** (ˈmʌlə, ˈmʊlə) *n* (formerly) a Muslim scholar, teacher, or religious leader: also used as a title of respect. [C17: from Turkish *molla,* Persian & Hindi *mulla,* from Ar. *mawlā* master]

mullein (ˈmʌlɪn) *n* any of various Mediterranean herbaceous plants such as the common mullein or Aaron's rod, typically having tall spikes of yellow flowers and broad hairy leaves. [C15: from OF *moleine,* prob. from OF *mol* soft, from L *mollis*]

muller (ˈmʌlə) *n* a flat heavy implement of stone or iron used to grind material against a slab of stone, etc. [C15: prob. from *mullen* to grind to powder]

mullet (ˈmʌlɪt) *n* any of various teleost food fishes such as the grey mullet or red mullet. [C15: via OF from L *mullus,* from Gk *mullos*]

mulligatawny (ˌmʌlɪgəˈtɔːnɪ) *n* a curry-flavoured soup of Anglo-Indian origin, made with meat stock. [C18: from Tamil *milakutanni,* from *milaku* pepper + *tanni* water]

mullion (ˈmʌlɪən) *n* **1** a vertical member between the casements or panes of a window. ◆ *vb* **2** *(tr)* to furnish (a window, screen, etc.) with mullions. [C16: var. of ME *munial,* from OF *moinel,* from ?]

mullock (ˈmʌlək) *n Austral.* **1** waste material from a mine. **2 poke mullock at.** *Inf.* to ridicule. [C14: rel. to OE *myl* dust, ON *mylja* to crush]

mulloway (ˈmʌləˌweɪ) *n* a large Australian marine food fish. [C19: from ?]

multangular (mʌlˈtæŋgjʊlə) *or* **multiangular** *adj* having many angles.

multi- *combining form.* **1** many or much: *multimillion.* **2** more than one: *multistorey.* [from L *multus* much, many]

multicultural (ˌmʌltɪˈkʌltʃərəl) *adj* consisting of, relating to, or designed for the cultures of several different races.
▸ **ˌmultiˈculturalˌism** *n*

multifactorial (ˌmʌltɪfækˈtɔːrɪəl) *adj* having many separate factors, causes, components, etc.: *multifactorial disease; multifactorial inheritance.*

multifarious Ⓣ (ˌmʌltɪˈfɛərɪəs) *adj* having many parts of great variety. [C16: from LL *multifārius* manifold, from L *multifāriam* on many sides]
▸ **ˌmultiˈfariously** *adv* ▸ **ˌmultiˈfariousness** *n*

multiflora rose (ˌmʌltɪˈflɔːrə) *n* an Asian climbing shrubby rose having clusters of small fragrant flowers.

multiform (ˈmʌltɪˌfɔːm) *adj* having many forms.
▸ **ˌmultiˈformity** *n*

multigym (ˈmʌltɪˌdʒɪm) *n* an exercise apparatus incorporating a variety of weights, used for toning the muscles.

multilateral (ˌmʌltɪˈlætərəl, -ˈlætrəl) *adj* **1** of or involving more than two nations or parties: *a multilateral pact.* **2** having many sides.
▸ **ˌmultiˈlaterally** *adv*

multilingual (ˌmʌltɪˈlɪŋgwəl) *adj* **1** able to speak more than two languages. **2** written or expressed in more than two languages.

multimedia (ˌmʌltɪˈmiːdɪə) *adj* **1** of or relating to the combined use of such media as television, slides, etc. **2** *Computing.* of or relating to any of various systems that can manipulate data in a variety of forms, such as sound, graphics, or text.

multimillionaire (ˌmʌltɪˌmɪljəˈnɛə) *n* a person with a fortune of several million pounds, dollars, etc.

multinational (ˌmʌltɪˈnæʃənᵊl) *adj* **1** (of a large business company) operating in several countries. ◆ *n* **2** such a company.

multipack (ˈmʌltɪˌpæk) *n* a form of packaging of foodstuffs, etc., that contains several units and is offered at a price below that of the equivalent number of units.

multiparous (mʌlˈtɪpərəs) *adj* (of certain species of mammal) producing many offspring at one birth. [C17: from NL *multiparus*]

multipartite (ˌmʌltɪˈpɑːtaɪt) *adj* **1** divided into many parts or sections. **2** *Government.* a less common word for **multilateral.**

multiparty (ˌmʌltɪˈpɑːtɪ) *adj* of or relating to a state, political system, etc., in which more than one political party is permitted: *multiparty democracy.*

multiple Ⓣ (ˈmʌltɪpᵊl) *adj* **1** having or involving more than one part, individual, etc. **2** *Electronics, US & Canad.* (of a circuit) having a number of conductors in parallel. ◆ *n* **3** the product of a given number or polynomial and any other one: *6 is a multiple of 2.* **4** short for **multiple store.** [C17: via F from LL *multiplus,* from L MULTIPLEX]
▸ **ˈmultiply** *adv*

multiple-choice *adj* having a number of possible given answers out of which the correct one must be chosen.

multiple personality *n Psychiatry.* a mental disorder in which an individual's personality appears to have become separated into two or more distinct personalities. Nontechnical name: **split personality.**

multiple sclerosis *n* a chronic progressive disease of the central nervous system, resulting in speech and visual disorders, tremor, muscular incoordination, partial paralysis, etc.

multiple store *n* one of several retail enterprises under the same ownership and management. Also called: **multiple shop.**

multiplex (ˈmʌltɪˌplɛks) *n* **1** *Telecomm.* **1a** the use of a common communications channel for sending two or more messages or signals. **1b** *(as modifier): a multiplex transmitter.* **2a** a purpose-built complex containing a number of cinemas and usually a restaurant or bar. **2b** *(as modifier): a multiplex cinema.* ◆ *adj* **3** a less common word for **multiple.** ◆ *vb* **4** to send (messages or signals) or (of messages and signals) to be sent by multiplex. [C16: from L: having many folds, from MULTI- + *plicāre* to fold]

multiplicand (ˌmʌltɪplɪˈkænd) *n* a number to be multiplied by another number, the **multiplier.** [C16: from L *multiplicandus,* gerund of *multiplicāre* to MULTIPLY]

multiplication (ˌmʌltɪplɪˈkeɪʃən) *n* **1** a mathematical operation, the inverse of division, in which the product of two or more numbers or quantities is calculated. Usually written $a \times b$, $a.b$, ab. **2** the act of multiplying or state of being multiplied. **3** the act or process in animals, plants, or people, of reproducing or breeding.

multiplication sign *n* the symbol ×, placed between numbers to be multiplied.

multiplication table *n* one of a group of tables giving the results of multiplying two numbers together.

multiplicity Ⓣ (ˌmʌltɪˈplɪsɪtɪ) *n, pl* **multiplicities. 1** a large number or great variety. **2** the state of being multiple.

multiplier (ˈmʌltɪˌplaɪə) *n* **1** a person or thing that multiplies. **2** the number by which another number, the **multiplicand,** is multiplied. **3** *Physics.* any instrument, such as a photomultiplier, for increasing an effect. **4** *Econ.* the ratio of the total change in income (resulting from successive rounds of spending) to an initial autonomous change in expenditure.

multiply Ⓣ (ˈmʌltɪˌplaɪ) *vb* **multiplies, multiplying, multiplied. 1** to increase or cause to increase in number, quantity, or degree. **2** *(tr)* to combine (two numbers or quantities) by multiplication. **3** *(intr)* to increase in number by reproduction. [C13: from OF *multiplier,* from L *multiplicāre* to multiply, from *multus* much, many + *plicāre* to fold]
▸ **ˈmultiˌpliable** *or* **multiplicable** (ˈmʌltɪˌplɪkəbᵊl) *adj*

multiprocessor (ˌmʌltɪˈprəʊsɛsə) *n Computing.* a number of central processing units linked together to enable parallel processing to take place.

multipurpose vehicle *n* a large car, similar to a van, designed to carry up to eight passengers. Abbrev.: **MPV.**

multiskilling (ˈmʌltɪˌskɪlɪŋ) *n* the practice of training employees to do a number of different tasks.

multistage (ˈmʌltɪˌsteɪdʒ) *adj* **1** (of a rocket or missile) having several stages, each of which can be jettisoned after it has burnt out. **2** (of a turbine, compressor, or supercharger) having more than one rotor. **3** (of any process or device) having more than one stage.

multistorey (ˌmʌltɪˈstɔːrɪ) *adj* **1** (of a building) having many storeys. ◆ *n* **2** a multistorey car park.

multitrack (ˈmʌltɪˌtræk) *adj* (in sound recording) using tape containing two or more tracks, usually four to twenty-four.

multitude Ⓣ (ˈmʌltɪˌtjuːd) *n* **1** a large gathering of people. **2 the.** the common people. **3** a large number. **4** the state or quality of being numerous. [C14: via OF from L *multitūdō*]

THESAURUS

mulish *adj* = **stubborn,** bull-headed, cross-grained, difficult, headstrong, inflexible, intractable, intransigent, obstinate, perverse, pig-headed, recalcitrant, refractory, rigid, self-willed, stiff-necked, unreasonable, wilful

mull[1] *vb* = **ponder,** consider, contemplate, deliberate, examine, meditate, muse on, reflect on, review, ruminate, study, think about, think over, turn over in one's mind, weigh

multifarious *adj* = **diverse,** different, diversified, legion, manifold, many, miscellaneous, multiform, multiple, multitudinous, numerous, sundry, varied, variegated

multiple *adj* **1** = **many,** collective, manifold, multitudinous, numerous, several, sundry, various

multiplicity *n* **1** = **number,** abundance, array, diversity, heaps (*inf.*), host, loads (*inf.*), lot, lots (*inf.*), mass, myriad, oodles (*inf.*), piles (*inf.*), profusion, scores, stacks, tons, variety

multiply *vb* **1** = **increase,** accumulate, augment, build up, expand, extend, proliferate, spread **3** = **reproduce,** breed, propagate
Antonyms *vb* ≠ **increase:** abate, decline, decrease, diminish, lessen, reduce

multitude *n* **1, 3** = **mass,** army, assemblage, assembly, collection, concourse, congregation,

multitudinous ❶ (ˌmʌltɪˈtjuːdɪnəs) *adj* **1** very numerous. **2** *Rare.* great in extent, variety, etc. **3** *Poetic.* crowded.
▸ˌ**multiˈtudinously** *adv* ▸ˌ**multiˈtudinousness** *n*

multi-user *adj* (of a computer) capable of being used by several people at once.

multivalent (ˌmʌltɪˈveɪlənt) *adj* another word for **polyvalent.**
▸ˌ**multiˈvalency** *n*

mum[1] (mʌm) *n Chiefly Brit.* an informal word for **mother.** [C19: a child's word]

mum[2] ❶ (mʌm) *adj* **1** keeping information, etc., to oneself; silent. ◆ *n* **2 mum's the word.** (*interj*) silence or secrecy is to be observed. [C14: suggestive of closed lips]

mum[3] (mʌm) *vb* **mums, mumming, mummed.** (*intr*) to act in a mummer's play. [C16: verbal use of MUM[2]]

mumble (ˈmʌmbᵊl) *vb* **mumbles, mumbling, mumbled. 1** to utter indistinctly, as with the mouth partly closed. **2** *Rare.* to chew (food) ineffectually. ◆ *n* **3** an indistinct or low utterance or sound. [C14 *momelen,* from MUM[2]]
▸ˈ**mumbler** *n* ▸ˈ**mumbling** *adj* ▸ˈ**mumblingly** *adv*

mumbo jumbo ❶ (ˈmʌmbəʊ) *n, pl* **mumbo jumbos. 1** foolish religious reverence, ritual, or incantation. **2** meaningless or unnecessarily complicated language. **3** an object of superstitious awe or reverence. [C18: prob. from W African *mama dyumbo,* name of a tribal god]

mu meson (mjuː) *n* a former name for **muon.**

mummer (ˈmʌmə) *n* **1** one of a group of masked performers in a folk play or mime. **2** *Humorous or derog.* an actor. [C15: from OF *momeur,* from *momer* to mime]

Mummerset (ˈmʌməsɪt, -ˌset) *n* an imitation West Country accent used in drama. [C20: from *mummer* + (*Somer*)*set,* county in SW England]

mummery (ˈmʌmərɪ) *n, pl* **mummeries. 1** a performance by mummers. **2** hypocritical or ostentatious ceremony.

mummify (ˈmʌmɪˌfaɪ) *vb* **mummifies, mummifying, mummified. 1** (*tr*) to preserve (a body) as a mummy. **2** (*intr*) to dry up; shrivel.
▸ˌ**mummifiˈcation** *n*

mummy[1] (ˈmʌmɪ) *n, pl* **mummies. 1** an embalmed or preserved body, esp. as prepared for burial in ancient Egypt. **2** a mass of pulp. **3** a dark brown pigment. [C14: from OF *momie,* from Med. L, from Ar.: asphalt, from Persian *mūm* wax]

mummy[2] (ˈmʌmɪ) *n, pl* **mummies.** *Chiefly Brit.* a child's word for **mother**[1] (senses 1–3). [C19: var. of MUM[1]]

mumps (mʌmps) *n* (*functioning as sing or pl*) **1** an acute contagious viral disease of the parotid salivary glands, characterized by swelling of the affected parts, fever, and pain beneath the ear. **2** sulks. [C16: from *mump* to grimace]
▸ˈ**mumpish** *adj*

mumsy ❶ (ˈmʌmzɪ) *adj* **mumsier, mumsiest.** homely or drab.
▸ˈ**mumsiness** *n*

mun. *abbrev. for* municipal.

munch ❶ (mʌntʃ) *vb* to chew (food) steadily, esp. with a crunching noise. [C14 *monche,* imit.]

mundane ❶ (mʌnˈdeɪn, ˈmʌndeɪn) *adj* **1** everyday, ordinary, or banal. **2** relating to the world or worldly matters. [C15: from F *mondain,* via LL, from L *mundus* world]
▸**munˈdanely** *adv* ▸**munˈdaneness** *n*

mung bean (mʌŋ) *n* **1** an E Asian bean plant grown for forage and as the source of bean sprouts for cookery. **2** the seed of this plant. [C20: from *mung,* changed from *mungo,* from Tamil *mūngu,* from Sansk. *mudga*]

municipal ❶ (mjuːˈnɪsɪpᵊl) *adj* of or relating to a town, city, or borough or its local government. [C16: from L *mūnicipium* a free town, from *mūniceps* citizen, from *mūnia* responsibilities + *capere* to take]
▸**muˈnicipally** *adv*

municipality ❶ (mjuːˌnɪsɪˈpælɪtɪ) *n, pl* **municipalities. 1** a city, town, or district enjoying local self-government. **2** the governing body of such a unit.

municipalize *or* **municipalise** (mjuːˈnɪsɪpəˌlaɪz) *vb* **municipalizes, municipalizing, municipalized** *or* **municipalises, municipalising, municipalised.** (*tr*) **1** to bring under municipal ownership or control. **2** to make a municipality of.
▸**muˌnicipaliˈzation** *or* **muˌnicipaliˈsation** *n*

munificent ❶ (mjuːˈnɪfɪsənt) *adj* **1** (of a person) generous; bountiful. **2** (of a gift) liberal. [C16: back formation from L *mūnificentia* liberality, from *mūnificus,* from *mūnus* gift + *facere* to make]
▸**muˈnificence** *n* ▸**muˈnificently** *adv*

muniments (ˈmjuːnɪmənts) *pl n Law.* the title deeds and other documentary evidence relating to the title to land. [C15: via OF from L *munire* to defend]

munition (mjuːˈnɪʃən) *vb* (*tr*) to supply with munitions. [C16: via F from L *mūnītiō* fortification, from *mūnīre* to fortify]

munitions (mjuːˈnɪʃənz) *pl n* (*sometimes sing*) military equipment and stores, esp. ammunition.

Munro (mʌnˈrəʊ) *n, pl* **Munros.** *Mountaineering.* any separate mountain peak over 3000 feet high: originally used of Scotland only but now sometimes extended to other parts of the British Isles. [C20: after Hugh Thomas *Munro* (1856–1919), who listed these in 1891]

muntjac *or* **muntjak** (ˈmʌntˌdʒæk) *n* any small Asian deer typically having a chestnut-brown coat and small antlers. [C18: prob. from Javanese *mindjangan* deer]

muon (ˈmjuːɒn) *n* a positive or negative elementary particle with a mass 207 times that of an electron. It was originally called the **mu meson.** [C20: short for MU MESON]
▸**muˈonic** *adj*

mural (ˈmjʊərəl) *n* **1** a large painting on a wall. ◆ *adj* **2** of or relating to a wall. [C15: from L *mūrālis,* from *mūrus* wall]
▸ˈ**muralist** *n*

murder ❶ (ˈmɜːdə) *n* **1** the unlawful premeditated killing of one human being by another. Cf. **manslaughter. 2** *Inf.* something dangerous, difficult, or unpleasant: *driving around London is murder.* **3 cry blue murder.** *Inf.* to make an outcry. **4 get away with murder.** *Inf.* to escape censure; do as one pleases. ◆ *vb* (*mainly tr*) **5** (*also intr*) to kill (someone) unlawfully with premeditation or during the commission of a crime. **6** to kill brutally. **7** *Inf.* to destroy; ruin. **8** *Inf.* to defeat completely; beat decisively: *the home team murdered their opponents.* [OE *morthor*]
▸ˈ**murderer** *n* ▸ˈ**murderess** *fem n*

murderous ❶ (ˈmɜːdərəs) *adj* **1** intending, capable of, or guilty of murder. **2** *Inf.* very dangerous or difficult: *a murderous road.*
▸ˈ**murderously** *adv* ▸ˈ**murderousness** *n*

murex (ˈmjʊəreks) *n, pl* **murices** (ˈmjʊərɪˌsiːz). any of a genus of spiny-shelled marine gastropods: formerly used as a source of the dye Tyrian purple. [C16: from L *mūrex* purple fish]

muriatic acid (ˌmjʊərɪˈætɪk) *n* a former name for **hydrochloric acid.** [C17: from L *muriāticus* pickled, from *muria* brine]

murk *or* **mirk** (mɜːk) *n* **1** gloomy darkness. ◆ *adj* **2** an archaic variant of **murky.** [C13: prob. from ON *myrkr* darkness]

murky ❶ *or* **mirky** (ˈmɜːkɪ) *adj* **murkier, murkiest** *or* **mirkier, mirkiest. 1** gloomy or dark. **2** cloudy or impenetrable, as with smoke or fog. **3** *Inf.* obscure and suspicious; shady: *she had a murky past.*
▸ˈ**murkily** *or* ˈ**mirkily** *adv* ▸ˈ**murkiness** *or* ˈ**mirkiness** *n*

THESAURUS

crowd, great number, horde, host, legion, lot, lots (*inf.*), mob, myriad, sea, swarm, throng **2 the multitude** = **public,** commonalty, common people, herd, hoi polloi, mob, populace, proletariat, rabble

multitudinous *adj* **1** = **numerous,** abounding, abundant, considerable, copious, countless, great, infinite, innumerable, legion, manifold, many, myriad, profuse, teeming, very numerous

mum[2] *adj* **1** = **silent,** closemouthed, dumb, mute, quiet, secretive, tight-lipped, uncommunicative, unforthcoming ◆ *n* **2 mum's the word** = **keep silent,** don't let on, don't tell a soul, keep quiet, keep (something) secret, keep (something) to oneself, keep (something) under one's hat, play dumb, say nothing, tell no-one

mumbo jumbo *n* **1** = **superstition,** abracadabra, chant, charm, conjuration, hocus-pocus, incantation, magic, rite, ritual, spell **2** = **gibberish,** cant, claptrap (*inf.*), double talk, gobbledegook (*inf.*), Greek (*inf.*), humbug, jargon, nonsense, rigmarole

mumsy *adj* = **homely,** dowdy, drab, fogeyish, frumpy *or* frumpish, old-fashioned, plain, square (*inf.*), unfashionable, unglamorous, unsophisticated
Antonyms *adj* attractive, beautiful, chic, elegant, fashionable, glamorous, modern, modish, smart, sophisticated, well-dressed

munch *vb* = **chew,** champ, chomp, crunch, masticate, scrunch

mundane *adj* **1** = **ordinary,** banal, commonplace, day-to-day, everyday, humdrum, prosaic, routine, vanilla (*sl.*), workaday **2** = **earthly,** fleshly, human, material, mortal, secular, sublunary, temporal, terrestrial, worldly
Antonyms *adj* ≠ **ordinary:** dramatic, exciting, extraordinary, ground-breaking, imaginative, interesting, left-field (*inf.*), novel, original, special, uncommon, unusual ≠ **earthly:** ethereal, heavenly, spiritual, unworldly

municipal *adj* = **civic,** borough, city, community, public, town, urban

municipality *n* **1** = **town,** borough, burgh (*Scot.*), city, district, township, urban community

munificence *n* **1, 2** = **generosity,** beneficence, benevolence, big-heartedness, bounteousness, bounty, generousness, largesse *or* largess, liberality, magnanimousness, openhandedness, philanthropy

munificent *adj* **1, 2** = **generous,** beneficent, benevolent, big-hearted, bounteous, bountiful, free-handed, lavish, liberal, magnanimous, open-handed, philanthropic, princely, rich, unstinting
Antonyms *adj* cheap, mean, miserly, parsimonious, small, stingy

murder *n* **1** = **killing,** assassination, bloodshed, butchery, carnage, homicide, manslaughter, massacre, slaying **2** *Informal* = **agony,** an ordeal, a trial, danger, difficulty, hell (*inf.*), misery, trouble ◆ *vb* **5, 6** = **kill,** assassinate, blow away (*sl., chiefly US*), bump off (*sl.*), butcher, destroy, dispatch, do in (*inf.*), do to death, eliminate (*sl.*), hit (*sl.*), massacre, rub out (*US sl.*), slaughter, slay, take out (*sl.*), take the life of, waste (*inf.*) **7** *Informal* = **ruin,** abuse, destroy, mangle, mar, misuse, spoil **8** *Informal* = **beat decisively,** blow out of the water (*sl.*), cream (*sl., chiefly US*), defeat utterly, drub, hammer (*inf.*), lick (*inf.*), make mincemeat of (*inf.*), slaughter, stuff (*sl.*), tank (*sl.*), thrash, wipe the floor with (*inf.*)

murderer *n* **1** = **killer,** assassin, butcher, cut-throat, hit man (*sl.*), homicide, slaughterer, slayer

murderous *adj* **1** = **deadly,** barbarous, bloodthirsty, bloody, brutal, cruel, cut-throat, death-dealing, destructive, devastating, fatal, fell (*arch.*), ferocious, internecine, lethal, sanguinary, savage, slaughterous, withering **2** *Informal* = **unpleasant,** arduous, dangerous, difficult, exhausting, harrowing, hellish (*inf.*), killing (*inf.*), sapping, strenuous

murky *adj* **1, 2** = **dark,** cheerless, cloudy, dim,

murmur ⓘ ('mɜːmə) *n* **1** a continuous low indistinct sound, as of distant voices. **2** an indistinct utterance: *a murmur of satisfaction.* **3** a complaint; grumble: *he made no murmur at my suggestion.* **4** *Med.* any abnormal soft blowing sound heard usually over the chest (**heart murmur**). ◆ *vb* **murmurs, murmuring, murmured. 5** to utter (something) in a murmur. **6** (*intr*) to complain. [C14: as n, from L *murmur;* vb. via OF *murmurer* from L *murmurāre* to rumble]
▸**'murmurer** *n* ▸**'murmuring** *n, adj* ▸**'murmuringly** *adv* ▸**'murmurous** *adj*

murphy ('mɜːfɪ) *n, pl* **murphies.** a dialect or informal word for **potato.** [C19: from the common Irish surname *Murphy*]

murrain ('mʌrɪn) *n* **1** any plaguelike disease in cattle. **2** *Arch.* a plague. [C14: from OF *morine,* from *morir* to die, from L *morī*]

Murray cod *n* ('mʌrɪ) a large greenish Australian freshwater food fish. [after *Murray* River in SE Australia]

murther ('mɜːðə) *n, vb* an archaic word for **murder.**
▸**'murtherer** *n*

mus. *abbrev. for:* **1** museum. **2** music. **3** musical.

MusB *or* **MusBac** *abbrev. for* Bachelor of Music.

muscadine ('mʌskədɪn, -ˌdaɪn) *n* **1** a woody climbing plant of the southeastern US. **2** the musk-scented purple grape produced by this plant: used to make wine. [C16: from MUSCATEL]

muscae volitantes ('mʌsiː vɒlɪ'tæntiːz) *pl n Pathol.* moving black specks or threads seen before the eyes, caused by opaque fragments floating in the vitreous humour or a defect in the lens. [C18: NL: flying flies]

muscat ('mʌskət, -kæt) *n* **1** any of various grapevines that produce sweet white grapes used for making wine or raisins. **2** another name for **muscatel** (sense 1). [C16: via OF from Provençal, from *musc* MUSK]

muscatel (ˌmʌskə'tɛl) *or* **muscadel** *n* **1** Also called: **muscat.** a rich sweet wine made from muscat grapes. **2** the grape or raisin from a muscat vine. [C14: from OF *muscadel,* from OProvençal, from *moscadel,* from *muscat* musky]

muscle ⓘ ('mʌsᵊl) *n* **1** a tissue composed of bundles of elongated cells capable of contraction and relaxation to produce movement in an organ or part. **2** an organ composed of muscle tissue. **3** strength or force. ◆ *vb* **muscles, muscling, muscled. 4** (*intr;* often foll. by *in, on,* etc.) *Inf.* to force one's way (in). [C16: from Medical L *musculus* little mouse, from the imagined resemblance of some muscles to mice]
▸**'muscly** *adj*

muscle-bound *adj* **1** having overdeveloped and inelastic muscles. **2** lacking flexibility.

muscleman ('mʌsᵊlˌmæn) *n, pl* **musclemen. 1** a man with highly developed muscles. **2** a henchman employed by a gangster to intimidate or use violence upon victims.

Muscovite ('mʌskəˌvaɪt) *n* **1** a native or inhabitant of Moscow. ◆ *adj* **2** an archaic word for **Russian.**

Muscovy duck ('mʌskəvɪ) *or* **musk duck** *n* a large crested widely domesticated South American duck, having a greenish-black plumage with white markings and a large red caruncle on the bill. [C17: orig. *musk duck,* a name later mistakenly associated with *Muscovy,* an arch. name for Russia]

muscular ⓘ ('mʌskjʊlə) *adj* **1** having well-developed muscles; brawny. **2** of, relating to, or consisting of muscle. [C17: from NL *muscularis,* from *musculus* MUSCLE]
▸**muscularity** (ˌmʌskjʊ'lærɪtɪ) *n* ▸**'muscularly** *adv*

muscular dystrophy *n* a genetic disease characterized by progressive deterioration and wasting of muscle fibres.

musculature ('mʌskjʊlətʃə) *n* **1** the arrangement of muscles in an organ or part. **2** the total muscular system of an organism.

MusD *or* **MusDoc** *abbrev. for* Doctor of Music.

muse[1] ⓘ (mjuːz) *vb* **muses, musing, mused. 1** (when *intr,* often foll. by *on* or *about*) to reflect (about) or ponder (on), usually in silence. **2** (*intr*) to gaze thoughtfully. ◆ *n* **3** a state of abstraction. [C14: from OF *muser,* ?from *mus* snout, from Med. L *mūsus*]

muse[2] (mjuːz) *n* (often preceded by *the*) a goddess that inspires a creative artist, esp. a poet. [C14: from OF, from L *Mūsa,* from Gk *Mousa* a Muse]

Muse (mjuːz) *n Greek myth.* any of nine sister goddesses, each of whom was regarded as the protectress of a different art or science.

musette (mjuː'zɛt) *n* **1** a type of bagpipe popular in France during the 17th and 18th centuries. **2** a dance, originally accompanied by a musette. [C14: from OF, dim. of *muse* bagpipe]

museum (mjuː'zɪəm) *n* a building where objects of historical, artistic, or scientific interest are exhibited and preserved. [C17: via L from Gk *Mouseion* home of the Muses, from *Mousa* MUSE]

museum piece *n* **1** an object of sufficient age or interest to be kept in a museum. **2** *Inf.* a person or thing regarded as antiquated.

mush[1] ⓘ (mʌʃ) *n* **1** a soft pulpy mass or consistency. **2** *US.* a thick porridge made from corn meal. **3** *Inf.* cloying sentimentality. [C17: from obs. *moose* porridge; prob. rel. to MASH]

mush[2] (mʌʃ) *Canad.* ◆ *interj* **1** an order to dogs in a sled team to start up or go faster. ◆ *vb* **2** to travel by or drive a dogsled. ◆ *n* **3** a journey with a dogsled. [C19: ?from imperative of F *marcher* to advance]

mushroom ⓘ ('mʌʃruːm, -rʊm) *n* **1a** the fleshy spore-producing body of any of various fungi, typically consisting of a cap at the end of a stem. Some species, such as the field mushroom, are edible. Cf. **toadstool. 1b** (*as modifier*): *mushroom soup.* **2a** something resembling a mushroom in shape or rapid growth. **2b** (*as modifier*): *mushroom expansion.* ◆ *vb* (*intr*) **3** to grow rapidly: *demand mushroomed overnight.* **4** to assume a mushroom-like shape. [C15: from OF *mousseron,* from LL *mussiriō,* from ?]

mushroom cloud *n* the large mushroom-shaped cloud produced by a nuclear explosion.

mushy ⓘ ('mʌʃɪ) *adj* **mushier, mushiest. 1** soft and pulpy. **2** *Inf.* excessively sentimental or emotional.
▸**'mushily** *adv* ▸**'mushiness** *n*

music ('mjuːzɪk) *n* **1** an art form consisting of sequences of sounds in time, esp. tones of definite pitch organized melodically, harmonically and rhythmically. **2** the sounds so produced, esp. by singing or musical instruments. **3** written or printed music, such as a score or set of parts. **4** any sequence of sounds perceived as pleasing or harmonious. **5 face the music.** *Inf.* to confront the consequences of one's actions. [C13: via OF from L *mūsica,* from Gk *mousikē* (*tekhnē*) (art) belonging to the Muses, from *Mousa* MUSE]

musical ⓘ ('mjuːzɪkᵊl) *adj* **1** of, relating to, or used in music. **2** harmonious; melodious: *musical laughter.* **3** talented in or fond of music. **4** involving or set to music. ◆ *n* **5** Also called: **musical comedy.** a light romantic play or film having dialogue interspersed with songs and dances.
▸**ˌmusi'cality** *n* ▸**'musically** *adv*

musical box *or* **music box** *n* a mechanical instrument that plays tunes by means of pins on a revolving cylinder striking the tuned teeth of a comblike metal plate, contained in a box.

musical chairs *n* (*functioning as sing*) **1** a party game in which players walk around chairs while music is played, there being one more player than chairs. Whenever the music stops, the player who fails to find a chair is eliminated. **2** any situation involving several people in a series of interrelated changes.

music centre *n* a single hi-fi unit containing a turntable, amplifier, radio, cassette player, and compact disc player.

music drama *n* **1** an opera in which the musical and dramatic elements are of equal importance and strongly interfused. **2** the genre of such operas. [C19: from G *Musikdrama,* coined by Wagner to describe his later operas]

music hall *n Chiefly Brit.* **1** a variety entertainment consisting of songs, comic turns, etc. US and Canad. name: **vaudeville. 2** a theatre at which such entertainments are staged.

musician (mjuː'zɪʃən) *n* a person who plays or composes music, esp. as a profession.
▸**mu'sicianly** *adj* ▸**mu'sicianship** *n*

musicology (ˌmjuːzɪ'kɒlədʒɪ) *n* the scholarly study of music.
▸**musicological** (ˌmjuːzɪkə'lɒdʒɪkᵊl) *adj* ▸**ˌmusi'cologist** *n*

music paper *n* paper ruled or printed with a stave for writing music.

musique concrète *French.* (myzik kõkrɛt) *n* another term for **concrete music.**

musk (mʌsk) *n* **1** a strong-smelling glandular secretion of the male musk deer, used in perfumery. **2** a similar substance produced by certain other animals, such as the civet and otter, or manufactured synthetically. **3** a North American plant which has yellow flowers and was formerly cultivated for its musky scent. **4** the smell of musk or a similar heady smell. **5** (*modifier*) containing or resembling musk: *musk oil.* [C14: from LL *muscus,* from Gk, from Persian, prob. from Sansk. *mushká* scrotum (from the appearance of the musk deer's musk bag), dim. of *mūsh* MOUSE]

THESAURUS

dismal, dreary, dull, dusky, foggy, gloomy, grey, impenetrable, misty, nebulous, obscure, overcast
Antonyms *adj* bright, cheerful, clear, distinct, sunny

murmur *n* **1, 2** = **drone**, babble, buzzing, humming, mumble, muttering, purr, rumble, susurrus (*literary*), undertone, whisper, whispering **3** = **complaint**, beef (*sl.*), gripe (*inf.*), grouse, grumble, moan (*inf.*), word ◆ *vb* **5** = **mumble**, babble, buzz, drone, hum, mutter, purr, rumble, speak in an undertone, whisper **6** = **grumble**, beef (*sl.*), carp, cavil, complain, gripe (*inf.*), grouse, moan (*inf.*)

muscle *n* **1** = **tendon**, muscle tissue, sinew, thew **3** = **strength**, brawn, clout (*inf.*), force, forcefulness, might, potency, power, stamina, sturdiness, weight ◆ *vb* **4** *often foll. by* **in** *Informal* = **impose oneself**, butt in, elbow one's way in, force one's way in

muscular *adj* **1** = **strong**, athletic, beefy (*inf.*), brawny, husky (*inf.*), lusty, powerful, powerfully built, robust, sinewy, stalwart, strapping, sturdy, thickset, vigorous, well-knit

muse[1] *vb* **1** = **ponder**, be in a brown study, be lost in thought, brood, cogitate, consider, contemplate, deliberate, dream, meditate, mull over, reflect, ruminate, speculate, think, think over, weigh

mush[1] *n* **1** = **pulp**, dough, mash, pap, paste **3** *Informal* = **sentimentality**, corn (*inf.*), mawkishness, schmaltz (*sl.*), slush (*inf.*)

mushroom *vb* **3** = **expand**, boom, burgeon, flourish, grow rapidly, increase, luxuriate, proliferate, shoot up, spread, spring up, sprout

mushy *adj* **1** = **soft**, doughy, pappy, paste-like, pulpy, semi-liquid, semi-solid, slushy, squashy, squelchy, squidgy (*inf.*) **2** *Informal* = **sentimental**, corny (*sl.*), maudlin, mawkish, saccharine, schmaltzy (*sl.*), sloppy (*inf.*), slushy (*inf.*), sugary, syrupy, three-hankie (*inf.*), weepy, wet (*Brit. inf.*)

musical *adj* **1, 2** = **melodious**, dulcet, euphonic, euphonious, harmonious, lilting, lyrical, melodic, sweet-sounding, tuneful
Antonyms *adj* discordant, grating, harsh, unmelodious, unmusical

musing *n* **1** = **thinking**, absent-mindedness, abstraction, brown study, cerebration, cogitation, contemplation, day-dreaming, dreaming, in-

musk deer *n* a small central Asian mountain deer. The male secretes musk.

musk duck *n* **1** another name for **Muscovy duck. 2** a duck inhabiting swamps, lakes, and streams in Australia. The male emits a musky odour.

muskeg ('mʌsˌkɛg) *n Chiefly Canad.* **1** undrained boggy land. **2** a bog or swamp of this nature. [C19: of Amerind origin: grassy swamp]

muskellunge ('mʌskəˌlʌndʒ) *or* **maskinonge** ('mæskɪˌnɒndʒ) *n, pl* **muskellunges** *or* **muskellunge, maskinonges** *or* **maskinonge.** a large North American freshwater game fish, related to the pike. Often shortened (informally) to **musky** or **muskie.** [C18 *maskinunga,* of Amerind origin]

musket ('mʌskɪt) *n* a long-barrelled muzzle-loading shoulder gun used between the 16th and 18th centuries by infantry soldiers. [C16: from F *mousquet,* from It. *moschetto* arrow, earlier: sparrow hawk, from *moscha* a fly, from L *musca*]

musketeer (ˌmʌskɪ'tɪə) *n* (formerly) a soldier armed with a musket.

musketry ('mʌskɪtrɪ) *n* **1** muskets or musketeers collectively. **2** the technique of using small arms.

muskmelon ('mʌskˌmɛlən) *n* **1** any of several varieties of the melon, such as the cantaloupe and honeydew. **2** the fruit of any of these melons, having ribbed or warty rind and sweet yellow, white, orange, or green flesh with a musky aroma.

musk ox *n* a large bovid mammal, which has a dark shaggy coat, short legs, and widely spaced downward-curving horns, and emits a musky smell: now confined to the tundras of Canada and Greenland.

muskrat ('mʌskˌræt) *n, pl* **muskrats** *or* **muskrat. 1** a North American beaver-like amphibious rodent, closely related to but larger than the voles. **2** the brown fur of this animal. ◆ Also called: **musquash.**

musk rose *n* a Mediterranean rose, cultivated for its white musk-scented flowers.

musky ('mʌskɪ) *adj* **muskier, muskiest.** resembling the smell of musk; having a heady or pungent sweet aroma.
▸**'muskiness** *n*

Muslim ('mʊzlɪm, 'mʌz-) *or* **Moslem** *n, pl* **Muslims** *or* **Muslim, Moslems** *or* **Moslem. 1** a follower of the religion of Islam. ◆ *adj* **2** of or relating to Islam, its doctrines, culture, etc. ◆ Also (but not in Muslim use): **Mohammedan, Muhammadan.** [C17: from Ar., lit.: one who surrenders]
▸**'Muslimism** *or* **'Moslemism** *n*

muslin ('mʌzlɪn) *n* a fine plain-weave cotton fabric. [C17: from F *mousseline,* from It., from Ar. *mawṣilīy* of Mosul (Iraq), where it was first produced]

muso ('mju:zəʊ) *n, pl* **musos.** *Sl.* **1** *Brit. derog.* a musician, esp. a pop musician, regarded as being overconcerned with technique rather than musical content or expression. **2** *Austral.* any musician, esp. a professional one.

musquash ('mʌskwɒʃ) *n* another name for **muskrat,** esp. the fur. [C17: of Amerind origin]

muss (mʌs) *US & Canad. inf.* ◆ *vb* **1** (*tr;* often foll. by *up*) to make untidy; rumple. ◆ *n* **2** a state of disorder; muddle. [C19: prob. a blend of MESS + FUSS]
▸**'mussy** *adj*

mussel ('mʌsᵊl) *n* **1** any of various marine bivalves, esp. the edible mussel, having a dark slightly elongated shell and living attached to rocks, etc. **2** any of various freshwater bivalves, attached to rocks, sand, etc., having a flattened oval shell (a source of mother-of-pearl). [OE *muscle,* from Vulgar L *muscula* (unattested), from L *musculus,* dim. of *mūs* mouse]

Mussulman ('mʌsᵊlmən) *n pl* **Mussulmans.** an archaic word for **Muslim.** [C16: from Persian *Musulmān* (pl) from Ar. *Muslimūn,* pl. of MUSLIM]

must[1] ❶ (mʌst; *unstressed* məst, məs) *vb* (takes an infinitive without *to* or an implied infinitive) used as an auxiliary: **1** to express obligation or compulsion: *you must pay your dues.* In this sense, *must* does not form a negative. If used with a negative infinitive it indicates obligatory prohibition. **2** to indicate necessity: *I must go to the bank tomorrow.* **3** to indicate the probable correctness of a statement: *he must be there by now.* **4** to indicate inevitability: *all good things must come to an end.* **5** to express resolution: **5a** on the part of the speaker: *I must finish this.* **5b** on the part of another or others: *let him get drunk if he must.* **6** (used emphatically) to express conviction or certainty on the part of the speaker: *you must be joking.* **7** (foll. by *away*) used with an implied verb of motion to express compelling haste: *I must away.* ◆ *n* **8** an essential or necessary thing: *strong shoes are a must for hill walking.* [OE *mōste,* p.t. of *mōtan* to be allowed, be obliged to]

must[2] (mʌst) *n* the pressed juice of grapes or other fruit ready for fermentation. [OE, from L *mustum* new wine, from *mustus* newborn]

must[3] ❶ (mʌst) *n* mustiness or mould. [C17: back formation from MUSTY]

mustache (mə'stɑ:ʃ) *n* the US spelling of **moustache.**
▸**mus'tached** *adj*

mustachio (mə'stɑ:ʃɪˌəʊ) *n, pl* **mustachios.** (*often pl*) *Often humorous.* a moustache, esp. when bushy or elaborately shaped. [C16: from Sp. *mostacho* & It. *mostaccio*]
▸**mus'tachioed** *adj*

mustang ('mʌstæŋ) *n* a small breed of horse, often wild or half wild, found in the southwestern US. [C19: from Mexican Sp. *mestengo,* from *mesta* a group of stray animals]

mustard ('mʌstəd) *n* **1** any of several Eurasian plants, esp. black mustard and white mustard, having yellow flowers and slender pods: cultivated for their pungent seeds. **2** a paste made from the powdered seeds of any of these plants and used as a condiment. **3a** a brownish-yellow colour. **3b** (*as adj*): *a mustard carpet.* **4** *Sl., chiefly US.* zest or enthusiasm. [C13: from OF *moustarde,* from L *mustum* MUST[2], since the original was made by adding must]

mustard and cress *n* seedlings of white mustard and garden cress, used in salads, etc.

mustard gas *n* an oily liquid vesicant compound used in chemical warfare. Its vapour causes blindness and burns.

mustard plaster *n Med.* a mixture of powdered black mustard seeds applied to the skin for its counterirritant effects.

musteline ('mʌstɪˌlaɪn, -lɪn) *adj* of or belonging to a family of typically predatory mammals, including weasels, ferrets, badgers, skunks, and otters. [C17: from L *mustēlīnus,* from *mustēla* weasel]

muster ❶ ('mʌstə) *vb* **1** to call together (numbers of men) for duty, inspection, etc., or (of men) to assemble in this way. **2 muster in** *or* **out.** *US.* to enlist into or discharge from military service. **3** (*tr;* sometimes foll. by *up*) to summon or gather: *to muster one's arguments; to muster up courage.* **4** (*tr*) *Austral. & NZ.* to round up (stock). ◆ *n* **5** an assembly of military personnel for duty, etc. **6** a collection, assembly, or gathering. **7** *Austral. & NZ.* the act of rounding up stock. **8 pass muster.** to be acceptable. [C14: from OF *moustrer,* from L *monstrāre* to show, from *monstrum* portent]

musth *or* **must** (mʌst) *n* (often preceded by *in*) a state of frenzied sexual excitement in the males of certain large mammals, esp. elephants. [C19: from Urdu *mast,* from Persian: drunk]

musty ❶ ('mʌstɪ) *adj* **mustier, mustiest. 1** smelling or tasting old, stale, or mouldy. **2** old-fashioned, dull, or hackneyed: *musty ideas.* [C16: ? var. of obs. *moisty*]
▸**'mustily** *adv* ▸**'mustiness** *n*

mutable ❶ ('mju:təbᵊl) *adj* able to or tending to change. [C14: from L *mūtābilis* fickle, from *mūtāre* to change]
▸**ˌmuta'bility** *or* (*less commonly*) **'mutableness** *n* ▸**'mutably** *adv*

mutagen ('mju:tədʒən) *n* a substance that can induce genetic mutation. [C20: from MUTATION + -GEN]
▸**mutagenic** (ˌmju:tə'dʒɛnɪk) *adj*

mutagenesis (ˌmju:tə'dʒɛnɪsɪs) *n Genetics.* the origin and development of a mutation. [C20: from MUTA(TION) + -GENESIS]

mutant ('mju:tᵊnt) *n* **1** Also called: **mutation.** an animal, organism, or gene that has undergone mutation. ◆ *adj* **2** of, undergoing, or resulting from mutation. [C20: from L *mutāre* to change]

mutate (mju:'teɪt) *vb* **mutates, mutating, mutated.** to undergo or cause to undergo mutation. [C19: from L *mūtātus,* p.p. of *mūtāre* to change]

mutation ❶ (mju:'teɪʃən) *n* **1** the act or process of mutating; change; alteration. **2** a change or alteration. **3** a change in the chromosomes or genes of a cell which may affect the structure and development of the resultant offspring. **4** another word for **mutant** (sense 1). **5** a physical characteristic of an individual resulting from this type of chromosomal change. **6** *Phonetics.* **6a** (in Germanic languages) another name for **umlaut. 6b** (in Celtic languages) a phonetic change in certain initial consonants caused by a preceding word.
▸**mu'tational** *adj* ▸**mu'tationally** *adv*

mutatis mutandis *Latin.* (mu:'tɑ:tɪs mu:'tændɪs) the necessary changes having been made.

mutch (mʌtʃ) *n* a close-fitting linen cap formerly worn by women and children in Scotland. [C15: from MDu. *mutse* cap, from Med. L *almucia* AMICE]

mute ❶ (mju:t) *adj* **1** not giving out sound or speech; silent. **2** unable to speak; dumb. **3** unspoken or unexpressed. **4** *Law.* (of a person arraigned on indictment) refusing to answer a charge. **5** *Phonetics.* another word for **plosive. 6** (of a letter in a word) silent. ◆ *n* **7** a person who is unable to speak. **8** *Law.* a person who refuses to plead. **9** any of various devices used to soften the tone of stringed or brass instru-

THESAURUS

trospection, meditation, navel gazing (*sl.*), reflection, reverie, rumination, woolgathering

must[1] *n* **8** = **necessity,** duty, essential, fundamental, imperative, necessary thing, obligation, prerequisite, requirement, requisite, *sine qua non*

must[3] *n* = **mould,** decay, fetor, fustiness, mildew, mouldiness, mustiness, rot

muster *vb* **1, 3** = **assemble,** call together, call up, collect, come together, congregate, convene, convoke, enrol, gather, group, marshal, meet, mobilize, rally, round up, summon ◆ *n* **6** = **assembly,** assemblage, collection, concourse, congregation, convention, convocation, gathering, meeting, mobilization, rally, roundup **8 pass muster** = **be acceptable,** be *or* come up to scratch, fill the bill (*inf.*), make the grade, measure up, qualify

musty *adj* **1** = **stale,** airless, dank, decayed, frowsty, fusty, mildewed, mildewy, mouldy, old, smelly, stuffy **2** = **old-fashioned,** ancient, antediluvian, antiquated, banal, clichéd, dull, hackneyed, hoary, moth-eaten, obsolete, stale, threadbare, trite, worn-out

Antonyms *adj* ≠ **old-fashioned:** current, exciting, fashionable, fresh, imaginative, interesting, lively, modern, modish, new, novel, original, unusual, up-to-date, with it (*inf.*)

mutability *n* = **change,** alteration, evolution, metamorphosis, transition, variation, vicissitude

mutable *adj* = **changeable,** adaptable, alterable, changing, fickle, flexible, inconsistent, inconstant, irresolute, uncertain, undependable, unreliable, unsettled, unstable, unsteady, vacillating, variable, volatile, wavering

mutation *n* **1, 2** = **change,** alteration, deviation, evolution, metamorphosis, modification, transfiguration, transformation, variation **4** = **mutant,** anomaly, deviant

mute *adj* **1-3** = **silent,** aphasiac, aphasic, aphonic, dumb, mum, speechless, unex-

ments. **10** *Phonetics.* a plosive consonant. **11** a silent letter. **12** an actor in a dumb show. **13** a hired mourner. ◆ *vb* **mutes, muting, muted.** (*tr*) **14** to reduce the volume of (a musical instrument) by means of a mute, soft pedal, etc. **15** to subdue the strength of (a colour, tone, lighting, etc.). [C14 *muwet* from OF *mu,* from L *mūtus* silent]
▸**'mutely** *adv* ▸**'muteness** *n*

mute swan *n* a Eurasian swan with a pure white plumage and an orange-red bill.

muti ('muːtɪ) *n S. African inf.* medicine, esp. herbal. [from Zulu *umuthi* tree, medicine]

mutilate ❶ ('mjuːtɪˌleɪt) *vb* **mutilates, mutilating, mutilated.** (*tr*) **1** to deprive of a limb, essential part, etc.; maim. **2** to expurgate, damage, etc. (a text, book, etc.). [C16: from L *mutilāre* to cut off; rel. to *mutilus* maimed]
▸**ˌmutiˈlation** *n* ▸**'mutiˌlative** *adj* ▸**'mutiˌlator** *n*

mutineer (ˌmjuːtɪˈnɪə) *n* a person who mutinies.

mutinous ❶ ('mjuːtɪnəs) *adj* **1** openly rebellious. **2** characteristic or indicative of mutiny.
▸**'mutinously** *adv* ▸**'mutinousness** *n*

mutiny ❶ ('mjuːtɪnɪ) *n, pl* **mutinies. 1** open rebellion against constituted authority, esp. by seamen or soldiers against their officers. ◆ *vb* **mutinies, mutinying, mutinied. 2** (*intr*) to engage in mutiny. [C16: from obs. *mutine,* from OF *mutin* rebellious, from *meute* mutiny, ult. from L *movēre* to move]

mutism ('mjuːˌtɪzəm) *n* **1** the state of being mute. **2** *Psychiatry.* **2a** a refusal to speak. **2b** the lack of development of speech.

mutt ❶ (mʌt) *n Sl.* **1** an inept, ignorant, or stupid person. **2** a mongrel dog; cur. [C20: from MUTTONHEAD]

mutter ❶ ('mʌtə) *vb* **1** to utter (something) in a low and indistinct tone. **2** (*intr*) to grumble or complain. **3** (*intr*) to make a low continuous murmuring sound. ◆ *n* **4** a muttered sound or complaint. [C14 *moteren*]
▸**'muttering** *n, adj*

mutton ('mʌtᵊn) *n* **1** the flesh of sheep, esp. of mature sheep, used as food. **2 mutton dressed as lamb.** an older woman dressed up to look young. [C13 *moton* sheep, from OF, from Med. L *multō,* of Celtic origin]
▸**'muttony** *adj*

mutton bird *n* any of several shearwaters, having a dark plumage with greyish underparts. In New Zealand, applied to one collected for food, esp. by Maoris. [C19: from the taste of its flesh]

mutton chop *n* a piece of mutton from the loin.

muttonchops ('mʌtᵊnˌtʃɒps) *pl n* side whiskers trimmed in the shape of chops.

muttonhead ('mʌtᵊnˌhɛd) *n Sl.* a stupid or ignorant person; fool.
▸**'muttonˌheaded** *adj*

mutual ❶ ('mjuːtʃʊəl) *adj* **1** experienced or expressed by each of two or more people about the other; reciprocal: *mutual distrust.* **2** *Inf.* common to or shared by both: *a mutual friend.* **3** denoting an insurance company, etc., in which the policyholders share the profits and expenses and there are no shareholders. See also **mutual insurance.** [C15: from OF *mutuel,* from L *mūtuus* reciprocal (orig.: borrowed); rel. to *mūtāre* to change]
▸**mutuality** (ˌmjuːtʃʊˈælɪtɪ) *n* ▸**'mutually** *adv*

> **USAGE NOTE** The use of *mutual* to mean *common to or shared by two or more parties* was formerly considered incorrect, but is now acceptable. Tautologous use of *mutual* should be avoided: *cooperation* (not *mutual cooperation*) *between the two countries.*

mutual induction *n* the production of an electromotive force in a circuit by a current change in a second circuit magnetically linked to the first.

mutual insurance *n* a system of insurance by which all policyholders become company members under contract to pay premiums into a common fund out of which claims are paid. See also **mutual** (sense 3).

mutuel ('mjuːtʃʊəl) *n* short for **pari-mutuel.**

muu-muu ('muːˌmuː) *n* a loose brightly coloured dress worn by women in Hawaii. [from Hawaiian]

Muzak ('mjuːzæk) *n Trademark.* recorded light music played in shops, restaurants, factories, etc.

muzhik *or* **moujik** ('muːʒɪk) *n* a Russian peasant, esp. under the tsars. [C16: from Russian: peasant]

muzzle ❶ ('mʌzᵊl) *n* **1** the projecting part of the face, usually the jaws and nose, of animals such as the dog and horse. **2** a guard or strap fitted over an animal's nose and jaws to prevent it biting or eating. **3** the front end of a gun barrel. ◆ *vb* **muzzles, muzzling, muzzled.** (*tr*) **4** to prevent from being heard or noticed. **5** to put a muzzle on (an animal). [C15 *mosel,* from OF *musel,* dim. of *muse* snout, from Med. L *mūsus,* from ?]
▸**'muzzler** *n*

muzzle-loader *n* a firearm receiving its ammunition through the muzzle.
▸**'muzzle-ˌloading** *adj*

muzzle velocity *n* the velocity of a projectile as it leaves a firearm's muzzle.

muzzy ('mʌzɪ) *adj* **muzzier, muzziest. 1** blurred or hazy. **2** confused or befuddled. [C18: from ?]
▸**'muzzily** *adv* ▸**'muzziness** *n*

MVO (in Britain) *abbrev. for* Member of the Royal Victorian Order.

MW 1 *symbol for* megawatt. **2** *Radio. abbrev. for* medium wave.

Mx *Physics. symbol for* maxwell.

my (maɪ) *determiner* **1** of, belonging to, or associated with the speaker or writer (me): *my own ideas.* **2** used in various forms of address: *my lord.* ◆ *interj* **3** an exclamation of surprise, awe, etc.: *my, how you've grown!* [C12 *mī,* var. of OE *mīn* when preceding a word beginning with a consonant]

> **USAGE NOTE** See at **me**[1].

myalgia (maɪˈældʒɪə) *n* pain in a muscle or a group of muscles. [C19: from MYO- + -ALGIA]

myalgic encephalomyelitis (maɪˈældʒɪk ɛnˌsɛfələʊˌmaɪɪˈlaɪtɪs) *n* a former name for **chronic fatigue syndrome.** Abbrev.: **ME.**

myalism ('maɪəˌlɪzəm) *n* a kind of witchcraft practised esp. in the Caribbean. [C19: from *myal,* prob. West African]

myall ('maɪəl) *n* **1** any of several Australian acacias having hard scented wood. **2** a native Australian living independently of society. [C19: Abor. name]

mycelium (maɪˈsiːlɪəm) *n, pl* **mycelia** (-lɪə). the vegetative body of fungi: a mass of branching filaments (hyphae). [C19 (lit.: nail of fungus): from MYCO- + Gk *hēlos* nail]
▸**myˈcelial** *adj*

Mycenaean (ˌmaɪsɪˈniːən) *adj* **1** of or relating to ancient Mycenae, a city in S Greece, or its inhabitants. **2** of or relating to the Aegean civilization of Mycenae (1400 to 1100 B.C.).

-mycete *n combining form.* indicating a member of a class of fungi: *myxomycete.* [from NL *-mycetes,* from Gk *mukētes,* pl. of *mukēs* fungus]

myco- *or before a vowel* **myc-** *combining form.* indicating fungus: *mycology.* [from Gk *mukēs* fungus]

mycology (maɪˈkɒlədʒɪ) *n* the branch of biology concerned with the study of fungi.
▸**mycological** (ˌmaɪkəˈlɒdʒɪkᵊl) *or* ˌ**mycoˈlogic** *adj* ▸**myˈcologist** *n*

mycoplasma (ˌmaɪkəʊˈplæzmə) *n* any one of a genus of prokaryotic microorganisms some species of which cause disease (**mycoplasmosis**) in animals and humans.

mycorrhiza *or* **mycorhiza** (ˌmaɪkəˈraɪzə) *n, pl* **mycorrhizae** (-ziː) *or* **mycorrhizas, mycorhizae** *or* **mycorhizas.** an association of a fungus and a plant in which the fungus lives within or on the outside of the plant's roots forming a symbiotic or parasitic relationship. [C19: from MYCO- + Gk *rhiza* root]
▸ˌ**mycorˈrhizal** *or* ˌ**mycoˈrhizal** *adj*

mycosis (maɪˈkəʊsɪs) *n* any infection or disease caused by fungus.
▸**mycotic** (maɪˈkɒtɪk) *adj*

mycotoxin (ˌmaɪkəˈtɒksɪn) *n* any of various toxic substances produced by fungi, some of which may affect food.
▸ˌ**mycotoxˈology** *n*

mycotrophic (ˌmaɪkəʊˈtrɒfɪk) *adj Bot.* (of a plant) symbiotic with a fungus, esp. a mycorrhizal fungus.
▸**mycotrophy** (maɪˈkɒtrəfɪ) *n*

myelin ('maɪɪlɪn) *or* **myeline** ('maɪɪˌliːn) *n* a white tissue forming an insulating sheath (**myelin sheath**) around certain nerve fibres. Damage to the myelin sheath causes neurological disease, as in multiple sclerosis.

myelitis (ˌmaɪɪˈlaɪtɪs) *n* inflammation of the spinal cord or of the bone marrow.

myeloma (ˌmaɪəˈləʊmə) *n, pl* **myelomas** *or* **myelomata** (-mətə). a usually malignant tumour of the bone marrow.

mynah *or* **myna** ('maɪnə) *n* any of various tropical Asian starlings,

THESAURUS

pressed, unspeaking, unspoken, voiceless, wordless ◆ *vb* **14, 15** = **muffle,** dampen, deaden, lower, moderate, soften, soft-pedal, subdue, tone down, turn down

mutilate *vb* **1** = **maim,** amputate, butcher, cripple, cut to pieces, cut up, damage, disable, disfigure, dismember, hack, injure, lacerate, lame, mangle **2** = **distort,** adulterate, bowdlerize, butcher, censor, cut, damage, expurgate, hack, mar, spoil

mutinous *adj* **1** = **rebellious,** bolshie (*Brit. inf.*), contumacious, disobedient, insubordinate, insurgent, refractory, revolutionary, riotous, seditious, subversive, turbulent, ungovernable, unmanageable, unruly

mutiny *n* **1** = **rebellion,** defiance, disobedience, insubordination, insurrection, refusal to obey orders, resistance, revolt, revolution, riot, rising, strike, uprising ◆ *vb* **2** = **rebel,** be insubordinate, defy authority, disobey, refuse to obey orders, resist, revolt, rise up, strike

mutt *n Slang* **1** = **fool,** berk (*Brit. sl.*), coot, dolt, dunderhead, idiot, ignoramus, imbecile (*inf.*), jerk (*sl., chiefly US & Canad.*), moron, nerd *or* nurd (*sl.*), numbskull *or* numskull, prat (*sl.*), thickhead, twit (*inf., chiefly Brit.*), wally (*sl.*) **2** = **mongrel,** cur, dog

mutter *vb* **1, 2** = **grumble,** complain, grouch (*inf.*), grouse, mumble, murmur, rumble

mutual *adj* **1, 2** = **shared,** common, communal, correlative, interactive, interchangeable, interchanged, joint, reciprocal, reciprocated, requited, returned

muzzle *n* **1** = **jaws,** mouth, nose, snout **2** = **gag,** guard ◆ *vb* **4, 5** = **suppress,** censor, choke, curb, gag, restrain, silence, stifle some of which can mimic human speech. [C18: from Hindi *mainā*, from Sansk. *madana*]

Mynheer (mə'nɪə) *n* a Dutch title of address equivalent to *Sir* when used alone or to *Mr* before a name. [C17: from Du. *mijnheer* my lord]

myo- *or before a vowel* **my-** *combining form.* muscle: *myocardium.* [from Gk *mus* MUSCLE]

myocardium (ˌmaɪəʊ'kɑːdɪəm) *n, pl* **myocardia** (-dɪə). the muscular tissue of the heart. [C19: *myo-* + *cardium*, from Gk *kardia* heart]
▸ˌ**myo'cardial** *adj*

myology (maɪ'ɒlədʒɪ) *n* the branch of medical science concerned with muscles.

myope ('maɪəʊp) *n* any person afflicted with myopia. [C18: via F from Gk *muōps*; see MYOPIA]

myopia Ⓣ (maɪ'əʊpɪə) *n* inability to see distant objects clearly because the images are focused in front of the retina; short-sightedness. [C18: via NL from Gk *muōps* short-sighted, from *mūein* to close (the eyes), + *ōps* eye]
▸**myopic** (maɪ'ɒpɪk) *adj* ▸**my'opically** *adv*

myosin ('maɪəsɪn) *n* the chief protein of muscle. [C19: from MYO- + -OSE² + -IN]

myosotis (ˌmaɪə'səʊtɪs) *n* any plant of the genus *Myosotis*. See **forget-me-not.** [C18: NL from Gk *muosōtis* mouse-ear (referring to its furry leaves), from *mus* mouse + *ous* ear]

myriad Ⓣ ('mɪrɪəd) *adj* **1** innumerable. ◆ *n* (*also used in pl*) **2** a large indefinite number. **3** *Arch.* ten thousand. [C16: via LL from Gk *murias* ten thousand]

myriapod ('mɪrɪəˌpɒd) *n* **1** any of a group of terrestrial arthropods having a long segmented body and many walking limbs, such as the centipedes and millipedes. ◆ *adj* **2** of, relating to, or belonging to this group. [C19: from NL *Myriapoda*. See MYRIAD, -POD]

Myrmidon ('mɜːmɪˌdɒn, -dᵊn) *n* **1** *Greek myth.* one of a race of people who were led against Troy by Achilles. **2** (*often not cap.*) a follower or henchman.

myrobalan (maɪ'rɒbələn, mɪ-) *n* **1** the dried plumlike fruit of various tropical trees used in dyeing, tanning, ink, and medicine. **2** a dye extracted from this fruit. [C16: via L from Gk *murobalanos*, from *muron* ointment + *balanos* acorn]

myrrh (mɜː) *n* **1** any of several trees and shrubs of Africa and S Asia that exude an aromatic resin. **2** the resin obtained from such a plant, used in perfume, incense, and medicine. [OE *myrre*, via L from Gk *murrha*, ult. from Akkadian *murrū*]

myrtle ('mɜːtᵊl) *n* an evergreen shrub or tree, esp. a S European shrub with pink or white flowers and aromatic blue-black berries. [C16: from Med. L *myrtilla*, from L *myrtus*, from Gk *murtos*]

myself (maɪ'sɛlf) *pron* **1a** the reflexive form of *I* or *me*. **1b** (intensifier): *I myself know of no answer.* **2** (*preceded by a copula*) my usual self: *I'm not myself today.* **3** *Not standard.* used instead of *I* or *me* in compound noun phrases: *John and myself are voting together.*

mysterious Ⓣ (mɪ'stɪərɪəs) *adj* **1** characterized by or indicative of mystery. **2** puzzling, curious.
▸**mys'teriously** *adv* ▸**mys'teriousness** *n*

mystery¹ Ⓣ ('mɪstərɪ, -trɪ) *n, pl* **mysteries. 1** an unexplained or inexplicable event, phenomenon, etc. **2** a person or thing that arouses curiosity or suspense because of an unknown, obscure, or enigmatic quality. **3** the state or quality of being obscure, inexplicable, or enigmatic. **4** a story, film, etc., which arouses suspense and curiosity because of facts concealed. **5** *Christianity.* any truth that is divinely revealed but otherwise unknowable. **6** *Christianity.* a sacramental rite, such as the Eucharist, or (*when pl*) the consecrated elements of the Eucharist. **7** (*often pl*) any rites of certain ancient Mediterranean religions. **8** short for **mystery play.** [C14: via L from Gk *mustērion* secret rites]

mystery² ('mɪstərɪ) *n, pl* **mysteries.** *Arch.* **1** a trade, occupation, or craft. **2** a guild of craftsmen. [C14: from Med. L *mistērium*, from L *ministerium* occupation, from *minister* official]

mystery play *n* (in the Middle Ages) a type of drama based on the life of Christ. Cf. **miracle play.**

mystery tour *n* an excursion to an unspecified destination.

mystic Ⓣ ('mɪstɪk) *n* **1** a person who achieves mystical experience or an apprehension of divine mysteries. ◆ *adj* **2** another word for **mystical.** [C14: via L from Gk *mustikos*, from *mustēs* mystery initiate; rel. to *muein* to initiate into sacred rites]

mystical ('mɪstɪkᵊl) *adj* **1** relating to or characteristic of mysticism. **2** *Christianity.* having a divine or sacred significance that surpasses human apprehension. **3** having occult or metaphysical significance.
▸**'mystically** *adv*

mysticism ('mɪstɪˌsɪzəm) *n* **1** belief in or experience of a reality surpassing normal human understanding or experience. **2** a system of contemplative prayer and spirituality aimed at achieving direct intuitive experience of the divine. **3** obscure or confused belief or thought.

mystify Ⓣ ('mɪstɪˌfaɪ) *vb* **mystifies, mystifying, mystified.** (*tr*) **1** to confuse, bewilder, or puzzle. **2** to make obscure. [C19: from F *mystifier*, from *mystère* MYSTERY¹ or *mystique* MYSTIC]
▸ˌ**mystifi'cation** *n* ▸**'mystiˌfying** *adj*

mystique Ⓣ (mɪ'stiːk) *n* an aura of mystery, power, and awe that surrounds a person or thing. [C20: from F (adj): MYSTIC]

myth Ⓣ (mɪθ) *n* **1a** a story about superhuman beings of an earlier age, usually of how natural phenomena, social customs, etc., came into existence. **1b** another word for **mythology** (senses 1, 3). **2** a person or thing whose existence is fictional or unproven. [C19: via LL from Gk *muthos* fable]

myth. *abbrev. for:* **1** mythological. **2** mythology.

mythical Ⓣ ('mɪθɪkᵊl) *or* **mythic** *adj* **1** of or relating to myth. **2** imaginary or fictitious.
▸**'mythically** *adv*

mythicize *or* **mythicise** ('mɪθɪˌsaɪz) *vb* **mythicizes, mythicizing, mythicized** *or* **mythicises, mythicising, mythicised.** (*tr*) to make into or treat as a myth.
▸**'mythicist** *n*

mytho- *combining form.* myth: *mythopoeia.*

mythologize *or* **mythologise** (mɪ'θɒləˌdʒaɪz) *vb* **mythologizes, mythologizing, mythologized** *or* **mythologises, mythologising, mythologised. 1** to tell, study, or explain (myths). **2** (*intr*) to create or make up myths. **3** (*tr*) to convert into a myth.
▸**my'tholoˌgizer** *or* **my'tholoˌgiser** *n*

mythology Ⓣ (mɪ'θɒlədʒɪ) *n, pl* **mythologies. 1** a body of myths, esp. one associated with a particular culture, person, etc. **2** a body of stories about a person, institution, etc. **3** myths collectively. **4** the study of myths.
▸**mythological** (ˌmɪθə'lɒdʒɪkᵊl) *adj* ▸**my'thologist** *n*

mythomania (ˌmɪθəʊ'meɪnɪə) *n Psychiatry.* the tendency to lie or exaggerate, occurring in some mental disorders.
▸ˌ**mytho'maniˌac** *n, adj*

mythopoeia (ˌmɪθəʊ'piːə) *n* the composition or making of myths. [C19: from Gk, ult. from *muthos* myth + *poiein* to make]
▸ˌ**mytho'poeic** *adj*

mythos ('maɪθɒs, 'mɪθɒs) *n, pl* **mythoi** (-θɔɪ). **1** the complex of beliefs, values, attitudes, etc., characteristic of a specific group or society. **2** another word for **myth** or **mythology.**

myxo ('mɪksəʊ) *n Austral. sl.* myxomatosis.

myxo- *or before a vowel* **myx-** *combining form.* mucus or slime: *myxomatosis.* [from Gk *muxa*]

myxoedema *or US* **myxedema** (ˌmɪksɪ'diːmə) *n* a disease resulting from underactivity of the thyroid gland characterized by puffy eyes, face, and hands and mental sluggishness. See also **cretinism.**

myxoma (mɪk'səʊmə) *n, pl* **myxomas** *or* **myxomata** (-mətə). a tumour composed of mucous connective tissue, usually situated in subcutaneous tissue.
▸**myxomatous** (mɪk'sɒmətəs) *adj*

myxomatosis (ˌmɪksəmə'təʊsɪs) *n* an infectious and usually fatal viral disease of rabbits characterized by swelling of the mucous membranes and formation of skin tumours.

myxomycete (ˌmɪksəʊmaɪ'siːt) *n* a slime mould, esp. a slime mould of the phylum *Myxomycota* (division *Myxomycetes* in traditional classifications).

myxovirus ('mɪksəʊˌvaɪrəs) *n* any of a group of viruses that cause influenza, mumps, etc.

THESAURUS

myopic *adj* = **short-sighted**, near-sighted

myriad *adj* **1** = **innumerable**, a thousand and one, countless, immeasurable, incalculable, multitudinous, untold ◆ *n* **2** = **multitude**, a million, army, flood, horde, host, millions, mountain, scores, sea, swarm, thousands

mysterious *adj* **1** = **secretive**, cloak-and-dagger, covert, furtive **2** = **strange**, abstruse, arcane, baffling, concealed, cryptic, curious, Delphic, enigmatic, hidden, impenetrable, incomprehensible, inexplicable, inscrutable, insoluble, mystical, mystifying, obscure, perplexing, puzzling, recondite, secret, sphinxlike, uncanny, unfathomable, unknown, veiled, weird
Antonyms *adj* apparent, clear, manifest, open, plain

mystery¹ *n* **1** = **puzzle**, cloak and dagger, closed book, conundrum, enigma, problem, question, riddle, secrecy, secret, teaser

mystic *adj* **2** = **supernatural**, abstruse, arcane, cabalistic, cryptic, enigmatical, esoteric, hidden, inscrutable, metaphysical, mysterious, nonrational, occult, otherworldly, paranormal, preternatural, transcendental

mystify *vb* **1** = **puzzle**, baffle, bamboozle (*inf.*), be all Greek to (*inf.*), beat (*sl.*), befog, bewilder, confound, confuse, elude, escape, flummox, nonplus, perplex, stump

mystique *n* = **fascination**, awe, charisma, charm, glamour, magic, spell

myth *n* **1a** = **legend**, allegory, fable, fairy story, fiction, folk tale, parable, saga, story, tradition, urban legend, urban myth

mythical *adj* **1** = **legendary**, allegorical, chimerical, fabled, fabulous, fairy-tale, mythological, storied **2** = **imaginary**, fabricated, fanciful, fantasy, fictitious, invented, made-up, make-believe, nonexistent, pretended, unreal, untrue

mythological *adj* **1** = **legendary**, fabulous, folkloric, heroic, mythic, mythical, traditional

mythology *n* **1-3** = **legend**, folklore, folk tales, lore, mythos, myths, stories, tradition

Nn

n *or* **N** (ɛn) *n, pl* **n's, N's,** *or* **Ns. 1** the 14th letter of the English alphabet. **2** a speech sound represented by this letter.

n[1] *symbol for:* **1** neutron. **2** *Optics.* index of refraction. **3** nano-.

n[2] (ɛn) *determiner* an indefinite number (of): *there are n objects in a box.*

N *symbol for:* **1** Also: **kt.** *Chess.* knight. **2** newton(s). **3** *Chem.* nitrogen. **4** North. **5** noun. **6** (*in combination*) nuclear: *N-power; N-plant.*

n. *abbrev. for:* **1** neuter. **2** new. **3** nominative. **4** noon. **5** note. **6** noun. **7** number.

N. *abbrev. for:* **1** National(ist). **2** Navy. **3** New. **4** Norse.

Na *the chemical symbol for* sodium. [L *natrium*]

NA *abbrev. for* North America.

NAAFI *or* **Naafi** (ˈnæfɪ) *n* **1** *acronym for* Navy, Army, and Air Force Institutes: an organization providing canteens, shops, etc., for British military personnel at home or overseas. **2** a canteen, shop, etc., run by this organization.

naartjie (ˈnɑːtʃɪ) *n S. African.* a tangerine. [from Afrik., from Tamil]

nab ⓣ (næb) *vb* **nabs, nabbing, nabbed.** (*tr*) *Inf.* **1** to arrest (a criminal, etc.). **2** to seize suddenly; snatch. [C17: ? of Scand. origin]

nabla (ˈnæblə) *n Maths.* another name for **del.** [C19: from Gk: stringed instrument, because it is shaped like a harp]

nabob (ˈneɪbɒb) *n* **1** *Inf.* a rich or important man. **2** (formerly) a European who made a fortune in India. **3** another name for a **nawab.** [C17: from Port. *nababo,* from Hindi *nawwāb;* see NAWAB]

NAC *abbrev. for* National Advisory Council.

nacelle (nəˈsɛl) *n* a streamlined enclosure on an aircraft, not part of the fuselage, to accommodate an engine, passengers, crew, etc. [C20: from F: small boat, from LL *nāvicella,* a dim. of L *nāvis* ship]

nacho (ˈnɑːtʃəʊ) *n, pl* **nachos.** a Mexican snack consisting of a piece of tortilla topped with melted cheese.

NACODS (ˈneɪkɒdz) *n* (in Britain) *acronym for* National Association of Colliery Overmen, Deputies, and Shotfirers.

nacre (ˈneɪkə) *n* the technical name for **mother-of-pearl.** [C16: via F from OIt. *naccara,* from Ar. *naqqārah* shell, drum]
▸ˈ**nacred** *adj*

nacreous (ˈneɪkrɪəs) *adj* relating to, consisting of, or having the lustre of mother-of-pearl.

NACRO *or* **Nacro** (ˈnækrəʊ) *n* (in Britain) *acronym for* National Association for the Care and Resettlement of Offenders.

nadir ⓣ (ˈneɪdɪə, ˈnæ-) *n* **1** the point on the celestial sphere directly below an observer and diametrically opposite the zenith. **2** the lowest point; depths. [C14: from OF, from Ar. *nazīr as-samt,* lit.: opposite the zenith]

nae (neɪ) *or* **na** (nɑː) a Scot. word for **no**[2] or **not.**

naevus ⓣ *or US* **nevus** (ˈniːvəs) *n, pl* **naevi** *or US* **nevi** (-vaɪ). any pigmented blemish on the skin; birthmark or mole. [C19: from L; rel. to (*g*)*natus* born, produced by nature]
▸ˈ**naevoid** *or US* ˈ**nevoid** *adj*

naff ⓣ (næf) *adj Brit. sl.* inferior; in poor taste. [C19: ?from back slang on *fan,* short for FANNY]
▸ˈ**naffness** *n*

naff off *sentence substitute. Brit sl.* a forceful expression of dismissal or contempt.

nag[1] ⓣ (næg) *vb* **nags, nagging, nagged. 1** to scold or annoy constantly. **2** (when *intr,* often foll. by *at*) to be a constant source of discomfort or worry (to). ◆ *n* **3** a person, esp. a woman, who nags. [C19: of Scand. origin]
▸ˈ**nagger** *n*

nag[2] ⓣ (næg) *n* **1** *Often derog.* a horse. **2** a small riding horse. [C14: of Gmc origin]

nagana (nəˈgɑːnə) *n* a disease of hoofed animals of central and southern Africa, transmitted by tsetse flies. [from Zulu *u-nakane*]

Nah. *Bible. abbrev. for* Nahum.

NAHT (in Britain) *abbrev. for* National Association of Head Teachers.

Nahuatl (ˈnɑːwɑːtᵊl, nɑːˈwɑːtᵊl) *n* **1** (*pl* **Nahuatl** *or* **Nahuatls**) a member of one of a group of Central American and Mexican Indian peoples including the Aztecs. **2** the language of these peoples.

naiad ⓣ (ˈnaɪæd) *n, pl* **naiads** *or* **naiades** (-əˌdiːz). **1** *Greek myth.* a nymph dwelling in a lake, river, or spring. **2** the aquatic larva of the dragonfly, mayfly, and related insects. **3** Also called: **water nymph.** a submerged aquatic plant, having narrow leaves and small flowers. [C17: via L from Gk *nāias* water nymph; rel. to *náein* to flow]

naïf (nɑːˈiːf) *adj, n* a less common word for **naive.**

nail ⓣ (neɪl) *n* **1** a fastening device, usually made of metal, having a point at one end and a head at the other. **2** anything resembling such a device in function or shape. **3** the horny plate covering part of the dorsal surface of the fingers or toes. Related adj: **ungual. 4** the claw of a mammal, bird, or reptile. **5** a unit of length, formerly used for measuring cloth, equal to two and a quarter inches. **6 hit the nail on the head.** to do or say something correct or telling. **7 on the nail.** (of payments) at once. ◆ *vb* (*tr*) **8** to attach with or as if with nails. **9** *Inf.* to arrest, catch, or seize. **10** *Inf.* to hit or bring down, as with a shot. **11** *Inf.* to expose or detect (a lie or liar). **12** to fix (one's eyes, attention, etc.) on. **13** to stud with nails. [OE *nægl*]
▸ˈ**nailer** *n*

nail-biting *n* **1** the act or habit of biting one's fingernails. **2a** anxiety or tension. **2b** (*as modifier*): *nail-biting suspense.*

nail bomb *n* an explosive device containing nails, used by terrorists to cause serious injuries in crowded situations.

nailbrush (ˈneɪlˌbrʌʃ) *n* a small stiff-bristled brush for cleaning the fingernails.

nailfile (ˈneɪlˌfaɪl) *n* a small file of metal or of board coated with emery, used to trim the nails.

nail polish *or* **varnish** *or esp. US* **enamel** *n* a quick-drying cosmetic lacquer applied to colour the nails or make them shiny or esp. both.

nail set *or* **punch** *n* a punch for driving the head of a nail below or flush with the surrounding surface.

nainsook (ˈneɪnsʊk, ˈnæn-) *n* a light soft plain-weave cotton fabric. [C19: from Hindi, from *nain* eye + *sukh* delight]

naira (ˈnaɪrə) *n* the standard monetary unit of Nigeria. [C20: altered from *Nigeria*]

naive ⓣ**, naïve** (nɑːˈiːv, naɪˈiːv), *or* **naïf** *adj* **1** having or expressing innocence and credulity; ingenuous. **2** lacking developed powers of reasoning or criticism: *a naive argument.* **3** another word for **primitive** (sense 5). ◆ *n* **4** a person who is naive, esp. in artistic style. See **primitive** (sense 10). [C17: from F fem of *naïf,* from OF: native, spontaneous, from L *nātīvus* NATIVE]
▸**naˈively, naˈïvely,** *or* **naˈïfly** *adv* ▸**naˈiveness, naˈïveness,** *or* **naˈïfness** *n*

naivety ⓣ (naɪˈiːvtɪ), **naiveté,** *or* **naïveté** (ˌnɑːiːvˈteɪ) *n, pl* **naiveties, naivetés** *or* **naïvetés. 1** the state or quality of being naive. **2** a naive act or statement.

naked ⓣ (ˈneɪkɪd) *adj* **1** having the body unclothed; undressed. **2** having no covering; exposed: *a naked flame.* **3** with no qualification or concealment: *the naked facts.* **4** unaided by any optical instrument (esp. in **the naked eye**). **5** (usually foll. by *of*) destitute: *naked of weapons.* **6** (of animals) lacking hair, feathers, scales, etc. **7** *Law.* **7a** unsupported by authority: *a naked contract.* **7b** lacking some essential condition to render valid; incomplete. [OE *nacod*]
▸ˈ**nakedly** *adv* ▸ˈ**nakedness** *n*

naked ladies *n* (*functioning as sing*) another name for **autumn crocus.**

THESAURUS

nab *vb* **1** = **arrest,** apprehend, capture, catch, catch in the act, collar (*inf.*), feel one's collar (*sl.*), lift (*sl.*), nail (*inf.*), nick (*sl., chiefly Brit.*) **2** = **seize,** grab, snatch

nadir *n* **2** = **bottom,** depths, lowest point, minimum, rock bottom, zero
Antonyms *n* acme, apex, climax, crest, height, high point, peak, pinnacle, summit, top, vertex, zenith

naevus *n* = **birthmark,** mole

naff *adj Brit. slang* = **bad,** crappy (*sl.*), duff (*Brit. inf.*), inferior, low-grade, low-quality, poor, poxy (*sl.*), rubbishy, second-rate, shabby, shoddy, substandard, trashy, twopenny-halfpenny, valueless, worthless
Antonyms *adj* excellent, exceptional, fine, first-class, first-rate, high-quality, superior

nag[1] *vb* **1** = **annoy,** badger, bend someone's ear (*inf.*), be on one's back (*sl.*), berate, breathe down someone's neck, chivvy, harass, harry, hassle (*inf.*), henpeck, irritate, nark (*Brit., Austral., & NZ sl.*), pester, plague, scold, torment, upbraid ◆ *n* **3** = **scold,** harpy, shrew, tartar, termagant, virago

nag[2] *n* **1** = **horse,** hack, jade, plug (*US*)

nagging *adj* **1** = **critical,** irritating, on someone's back (*inf.*), scolding, shrewish **2** = **distressing,** continuous, painful, persistent, worrying

naiad *n* **1** = **nymph,** Oceanid (*Greek myth*), sprite, undine, water nymph

nail *vb* **8** = **fasten,** attach, beat, fix, hammer, join, pin, secure, tack

naive *adj* **1** = **innocent,** artless, as green as grass, callow, candid, childlike, confiding, credulous, frank, green, guileless, gullible, ingenuous, jejune, natural, open, simple, trusting, unaffected, unpretentious, unsophisticated, unsuspicious, unworldly, wet behind the ears (*inf.*)
Antonyms *adj* ≠ **innocent:** artful, disingenuous, experienced, sly, sophisticated, urbane, worldly, worldly-wise

naivety *n* **1** = **innocence,** artlessness, callowness, candour, credulity, frankness, guilelessness, inexperience, ingenuousness, naturalness, openness, simplicity

naked *adj* **1** = **nude,** bare, buck naked (*sl.*), denuded, disrobed, divested, exposed, in one's birthday suit (*inf.*), in the altogether, in the buff (*inf.*), naked as the day one was born (*inf.*), starkers (*inf.*), stripped, unclothed, uncovered, undraped, undressed, without a stitch on (*inf.*) **3** = **undisguised,** blatant, evident, manifest, open, overt, patent, plain, simple, stark, unadorned, unconcealed, unexaggerated, unmistakable, unqualified, unvarnished
Antonyms *adj* ≠ **nude:** clothed, concealed, covered, dressed, wrapped up ≠ **undisguised:** concealed, disguised

nakedness *n* **1** = **nudity,** bareness, undress **3** = **openness,** plainness, simplicity, starkness

naked lady *n* a pink orchid found in Australia and New Zealand.
NALGO (ˈnælgəʊ) *n* (formerly, in Britain) *acronym for* National and Local Government Officers' Association.
Nam *or* **'Nam** (næm) *n US inf.* short for Vietnam (referring to the Vietnam War).
namby-pamby Ⓣ (ˌnæmbɪˈpæmbɪ) *adj* **1** sentimental or prim in a weak insipid way. **2** clinging, feeble, or spineless. ◆ *n, pl* **namby-pambies. 3** a person who is namby-pamby. [C18: a nickname of Ambrose Phillips (died 1749), whose pastoral verse was ridiculed for being insipid]
name Ⓣ (neɪm) *n* **1** a word or term by which a person or thing is commonly and distinctively known. **2** mere outward appearance as opposed to fact: *he was ruler in name only.* **3** a word or phrase descriptive of character, usually abusive: *to call a person names.* **4** reputation, esp., if unspecified, good reputation: *he's made quite a name for himself.* **5a** a famous person or thing: *a name in the advertising world.* **5b** *Chiefly US & Canad. (as modifier): a name product.* **6** a member of Lloyd's who provides part of the capital of a syndicate and shares in its profits or losses but does not arrange its business. **7 in the name of. 7a** for the sake of. **7b** by the authority of. **8 name of the game. 8a** anything that is significant or important. **8b** normal conditions, circumstances, etc.: *in gambling, losing money's the name of the game.* **9 to one's name.** belonging to one: *I haven't a penny to my name.* ◆ *vb* **names, naming, named.** *(tr)* **10** to give a name to. **11** to refer to by name; cite: *he named three French poets.* **12** to fix or specify: *they have named a date for the meeting.* **13** to appoint or nominate: *he was named Journalist of the Year.* **14** *(tr)* to ban (an MP) from the House of Commons by mentioning him formally by name as being guilty of disorderly conduct. **15 name names.** to cite people, esp. in order to blame or accuse them. **16 name the day.** to choose the day for an event, esp. one's wedding. [OE *nama,* rel. to L *nomen,* Gk *noma*]
▸**ˈnamable** *or* **ˈnameable** *adj*
name-calling *n* verbal abuse.
namecheck (ˈneɪmˌtʃɛk) *vb (tr)* **1** to mention (someone) specifically by name. ◆ *n* **2** a specific mention of someone's name, for example on a radio programme.
name day *n* **1** *RC Church.* the feast day of a saint whose name one bears. **2** another name for **ticket day.**
name-dropping *n Inf.* the practice of referring frequently to famous people, esp. as though they were intimate friends, in order to impress others.
▸**ˈname-ˌdropper** *n*
nameless Ⓣ (ˈneɪmlɪs) *adj* **1** without a name. **2** indescribable: *a nameless horror seized him.* **3** too unpleasant or disturbing to be mentioned: *nameless atrocities.*
▸**ˈnamelessness** *n*
namely Ⓣ (ˈneɪmlɪ) *adv* that is to say.
nameplate (ˈneɪmˌpleɪt) *n* a small panel on or next to the door of a room or building, bearing the occupant's name and profession.
namesake (ˈneɪmˌseɪk) *n* a person or thing named after another, or with the same name as another. [C17: prob. describing people connected *for the name's sake*]
nametape (ˈneɪmˌteɪp) *n* a tape bearing the owner's name and attached to an article.
nan (næn), **nana,** *or* **nanna** (ˈnænə) *n* a child's word for **grandmother.**
nana (ˈnɑːnə) *n* **1** *Sl.* a fool. **2 do one's nana.** *Austral. sl.* to become very angry. **3 off one's nana.** *Austral. sl.* mad; insane. [C19: prob. from BANANA]
nan bread *or* **naan** (nɑːn) *n* (in Indian cookery) a slightly leavened bread in a large flat leaf shape. [from Hindi]
nancy (ˈnænsɪ) *n, pl* **nancies.** an effeminate or homosexual boy or man. Also called: **nance, nancy boy.** [C20: from the girl's name *Nancy*]
NAND circuit *or* **gate** (nænd) *n Electronics.* a computer logic circuit having two or more input wires and one output wire that has an output signal if one or more of the input signals are at a low voltage. Cf. **OR circuit.** [C20: from *not* + AND; see NOT CIRCUIT, AND CIRCUIT]
nankeen (næŋˈkiːn) *or* **nankin** (ˈnænkɪn) *n* **1** a hard-wearing buff-coloured cotton fabric. **2a** a pale greyish-yellow colour. **2b** *(as adj): a nankeen carpet.* [C18: after *Nanking,* China, where it originated]
nanny (ˈnænɪ) *n, pl* **nannies. 1** a nurse or nursemaid for children. **2a** any person or thing regarded as treating people like children, esp. by being overprotective. **2b** *(as modifier): the nanny state.* **3** a child's word for **grandmother.** ◆ *vb* **nannies, nannying, nannied. 4** *(intr)* to nurse or look after someone else's children. **5** *(tr)* to be overprotective towards. [C19: child's name for a nurse]
nannygai (ˈnænɪˌgaɪ) *n, pl* **nannygais.** an edible red Australian sea fish. [from Abor.]
nanny goat *n* a female goat.
nano- *combining form.* denoting 10^{-9}: *nanometre; nanosecond.* Symbol: n [from L *nānus* dwarf, from Gk *nanos*]
nanotechnology (ˌnænəʊtɛkˈnɒlədʒɪ) *n* a branch of technology dealing with the manufacture of objects with dimensions of less than 100 thousand-millionths of a metre and the manipulation of individual molecules and atoms.
Nansen bottle (ˈnænsən) *n* an instrument used by oceanographers for obtaining samples of sea water from a desired depth. [C19: after F. *Nansen* (1861–1930), Norwegian arctic explorer & statesman]
nap[1] Ⓣ (næp) *vb* **naps, napping, napped.** *(intr)* **1** to sleep for a short while; doze. **2** to be inattentive or off guard (esp. in **catch someone napping**). ◆ *n* **3** a short light sleep; doze. [OE *hnappian*]
nap[2] Ⓣ (næp) *n* **1a** the raised fibres of velvet or similar cloth. **1b** the direction in which these fibres lie. **2** any similar downy coating. **3** *Austral. inf.* blankets; bedding. ◆ *vb* **naps, napping, napped. 4** *(tr)* to raise the nap of (velvet, etc.) by brushing. [C15: prob. from MDu. *noppe*]
nap[3] (næp) *n* **1** Also called: **napoleon.** a card game similar to whist, usually played for stakes. **2** a call in this game, undertaking to win all five tricks. **3** *Horse racing.* a tipster's choice for a certain winner. **4 nap hand.** a position in which there is a very good chance of success if a risk is taken. ◆ *vb* **naps, napping, napped.** *(tr)* **5** *Horse racing.* to name (a horse) as likely to win a race. [C19: from NAPOLEON, the card game]
napalm (ˈneɪpɑːm, ˈnæ-) *n* **1** a thick and highly incendiary liquid, usually consisting of petrol gelled with aluminium soaps, used in firebombs, flame-throwers, etc. ◆ *vb* **2** *(tr)* to attack with napalm. [C20: from NA(PHTHENE) + *palm(itate)* salt of PALMITIC ACID]
nape (neɪp) *n* the back of the neck. [C13: from ?]
napery (ˈneɪpərɪ) *n Scot. & Arch.* household linen, esp. table linen. [C14: from OF *naperie,* from *nape* tablecloth, from L *mappa*]
naphtha (ˈnæfθə, ˈnæp-) *n* a distillation product from coal tar or petroleum: used as a solvent and in petrol. [C16: via L from Gk, from Iranian]
naphthalene (ˈnæfθəˌliːn, ˈnæp-) *n* a white crystalline hydrocarbon with a characteristic penetrating odour, used in mothballs and in dyes, explosives, etc. Formula: $C_{10}H_8$. [C19: from NAPHTHA + ALCOHOL + -ENE]
▸**naphthalic** (næfˈθælɪk, næp-) *adj*
naphthene (ˈnæfθiːn, ˈnæp-) *n* any of various cyclic methylene hydrocarbons found in petroleum. [C20: from NAPHTHA + -ENE]
naphthol (ˈnæfθɒl, ˈnæp-) *n* a white crystalline solid having two isomeric forms, used in dyes and as an antioxidant. Formula: $C_{10}H_7OH$. [C19: from NAPHTHA + -OL[1]]
Napierian logarithm (nəˈpɪərɪən, neɪ-) *n* another name for **natural logarithm.**
Napier's bones (ˈneɪpɪəz) *pl n* a set of graduated rods formerly used for multiplication and division. [C17: based on a method invented by John *Napier* (1550–1617), Scot. mathematician]
napkin Ⓣ (ˈnæpkɪn) *n* **1** Also called: **table napkin.** a usually square piece of cloth or paper used while eating to protect the clothes, wipe the mouth, etc.; serviette. **2** *Rare.* a small piece of cloth. **3** a more formal name for **nappy**[1]. **4** a less common term for **sanitary towel.** [C15: from OF, from *nape* tablecloth, from L *mappa* cloth]
napoleon (nəˈpəʊlɪən) *n* **1** a former French gold coin worth 20 francs. **2** *Cards.* the full name for **nap**[3] (sense 1). [C19: from F *napoléon,* after Napoleon I, Emperor of the French (1804–15)]
Napoleonic (nəˌpəʊlɪˈɒnɪk) *adj* relating to or characteristic of Napoleon I (1769–1821), Emperor of the French (1804–15), or his era.
nappe (næp) *n* **1** a large sheet or mass of rock, originally a recumbent fold, that has been thrust from its original position by earth movements. **2** the sheet of water that flows over a dam or weir. **3** *Geom.* either of the two parts into which a cone is divided by the vertex. [C20: from F: tablecloth]
nappy[1] (ˈnæpɪ) *n, pl* **nappies.** *Brit.* a piece of soft towelling or a disposable material wrapped around a baby in order to absorb its urine or excrement. Also called: **napkin.** US and Canad. name: **diaper.** [C20: changed from NAPKIN]
nappy[2] (ˈnæpɪ) *adj* **nappier, nappiest. 1** having a nap; downy; fuzzy. **2** (of beer) **2a** having a head; frothy. **2b** strong or heady.
nappy rash *n Brit.* (in babies) any irritation to the skin around the genitals, anus, or buttocks, usually caused by contact with urine or excrement. Formal name: **napkin rash.** US and Canad. name: **diaper rash.**
narc (nɑːk) *n US sl.* a narcotics agent.
narcissism Ⓣ (ˈnɑːsɪˌsɪzəm) *or* **narcism** (ˈnɑːsɪzəm) *n* **1** an exceptional

THESAURUS

namby-pamby *adj* **1** = **prim,** mawkish, niminy-piminy, prissy *(inf.)*, sentimental **2** = **feeble,** anaemic, colourless, insipid, spineless, vapid, weak, weedy *(inf.)*, wimpish *or* wimpy *(inf.)*, wishy-washy *(inf.)*
name *n* **1, 3** = **title,** appellation, cognomen, denomination, designation, epithet, handle *(sl.)*, moniker *or* monicker *(sl.)*, nickname, sobriquet, term **4** = **reputation,** character, credit ◆ *vb* **10** = **call,** baptize, christen, denominate, dub, entitle, label, style, term **11** = **mention,** cite, identify, specify **12** = **fix,** choose, specify **13** = **nominate,** appoint, choose, commission, designate, select
named *adj* **10** = **called,** baptized, christened, denominated, dubbed, entitled, known as, labelled, styled, termed **11** = **mentioned,** cited, identified, specified **13** = **nominated,** appointed, chosen, commissioned, designated, picked, selected, singled out
nameless *adj* **1** = **anonymous,** innominate, undesignated, unnamed, untitled **2** = **indescribable,** ineffable, inexpressible **3** = **unspeakable,** abominable, horrible, unmentionable, unutterable
namely *adv* = **specifically,** i.e., that is to say, to wit, viz.
nap[1] *vb* **1** = **sleep,** catnap, doze, drop off *(inf.)*, drowse, kip *(Brit. sl.)*, nod, nod off *(inf.)*, rest, snooze *(inf.)*, zizz *(Brit. inf.)* ◆ *n* **3** = **sleep,** catnap, forty winks *(inf.)*, kip *(Brit. sl.)*, rest, shuteye *(sl.)*, siesta, zizz *(Brit. inf.)*
nap[2] *n* **1** = **weave,** down, fibre, grain, pile, shag
napkin *n* **1** = **serviette,** cloth
narcissism *n* **1** = **egotism,** self-admiration, self-love, vanity

interest in or admiration for oneself, esp. one's physical appearance. **2** sexual satisfaction derived from contemplation of one's own physical endowments. [C19: after *Narcissus*, a beautiful youth in Gk myth., who fell in love with his reflection in a pool]
▸**'narcissist** *n* ▸**,narcis'sistic** *adj*

narcissus (nɑː'sɪsəs) *n, pl* **narcissuses** *or* **narcissi** (-'sɪsaɪ). a plant of a Eurasian genus whose yellow, orange, or white flowers have a crown surrounded by spreading segments. [C16: via L from Gk *nárkissos*, ?from *narkē* numbness, because of narcotic properties attributed to the plant]

narco- *or sometimes before a vowel* **narc-** *combining form.* **1** indicating numbness or torpor: *narcolepsy.* **2** connected with or derived from illicit drug production: *narcoeconomies.* [from Gk *narkē* numbness]

narcoanalysis (,nɑːkəʊə'nælɪsɪs) *n* psychoanalysis of a patient in a trance induced by a narcotic drug.

narcolepsy ('nɑːkə,lepsɪ) *n Pathol.* a rare condition characterized by sudden episodes of deep sleep.
▸**,narco'leptic** *adj*

narcosis (nɑː'kəʊsɪs) *n* unconsciousness induced by narcotics or general anaesthetics.

narcosynthesis (,nɑːkəʊ'sɪnθɪsɪs) *n* a method of treating severe personality disorders by working with the patient while he is under the influence of a barbiturate drug.

narcotic ❶ (nɑː'kɒtɪk) *n* **1** any of a group of drugs, such as opium and morphine, that produce numbness and stupor. **2** anything that relieves pain or induces sleep, mental numbness, etc. **3** any illegal drug. ◆ *adj* **4** of or relating to narcotics or narcotics addicts. **5** of or relating to narcosis. [C14: via Med. L from Gk *narkōtikós*, from *narkoūn* to numb, from *narkē* numbness]
▸**nar'cotically** *adv*

narcotism ('nɑːkə,tɪzəm) *n* stupor or addiction induced by narcotic drugs.

narcotize *or* **narcotise** ('nɑːkə,taɪz) *vb* **narcotizes, narcotizing, narcotized** *or* **narcotises, narcotising, narcotised.** (*tr*) to place under the influence of a narcotic drug.
▸**,narcoti'zation** *or* **,narcoti'sation** *n*

nard (nɑːd) *n* **1** another name for **spikenard. 2** any of several plants whose aromatic roots were formerly used in medicine. [C14: via L from Gk *nárdos*, ? ult. from Sansk. *nalada* Indian spikenard]

nardoo ('nɑːduː) *n* (in Australia) **1** any of certain cloverlike ferns that grow in swampy areas. **2** the spores of such a plant, used as food. [C19: from Abor.]

nares ('nɛəriːz) *pl n, sing* **naris** ('nɛərɪs). *Anat.* the technical name for the nostrils. [C17: from L; rel. to OE *nasu*, L *nāsus* nose]
▸**'narial** *adj*

narghile, nargile, *or* **nargileh** ('nɑːgɪlɪ, -,leɪ) *n* another name for **hookah.** [C19: from F *narguilé*, from Persian *nārgīleh* a pipe having a bowl made of coconut shell, from *nārgīl* coconut]

nark ❶ (nɑːk) *Sl.* ◆ *n* **1** *Brit., Austral., & NZ.* an informer or spy: *copper's nark.* **2** *Brit.* someone who complains in an irritating or whining manner. ◆ *vb* **3** *Brit., Austral., & NZ.* to annoy, upset, or irritate. **4** (*intr*) *Brit., Austral., & NZ.* to inform or spy, esp. for the police. **5** (*intr*) *Brit.* to complain irritatingly. [C19: prob. from Romany *nāk* nose]

narky ('nɑːkɪ) *adj* **narkier, narkiest.** *Sl.* irritable, complaining, or sarcastic.

Narraganset (,nærə'gænsɪt) *n* **1** (*pl* **Narraganset** *or* **Narragansets**) a member of a North American Indian people formerly living in Rhode Island. **2** the language of this people, belonging to the Algonquian family.

narrate ❶ (nə'reɪt) *vb* **narrates, narrating, narrated. 1** to tell (a story); relate. **2** to speak in accompaniment of (a film, etc.). [C17: from L *narrāre* to recount, from *gnārus* knowing]
▸**nar'ratable** *adj* ▸**nar'rator** *n*

narration ❶ (nə'reɪʃən) *n* **1** the act or process of narrating. **2** a narrated account or story.

narrative ❶ ('nærətɪv) *n* **1** an account or story, as of events, experiences, etc. **2** the part of a literary work, etc., that relates events. **3** the process or technique of narrating. ◆ *adj* **4** telling a story: *a narrative poem.* **5** of or relating to narration: *narrative art.*

narrow ❶ ('nærəʊ) *adj* **1** small in breadth, esp. in comparison to length. **2** limited in range or extent. **3** limited in outlook. **4** limited in means or resources. **5** barely adequate or successful (esp. in **a narrow escape**). **6** painstakingly thorough: *a narrow scrutiny.* **7** *Finance.* denoting an assessment of liquidity as including notes and coins in circulation with the public, banks' till money, and banks' balances: *narrow money.* Cf. **broad** (sense 12). **8** *Phonetics.* another word for **tense**[1] (sense 4). ◆ *vb* **9** to make or become narrow. **10** (often foll. by *down*) to limit or restrict. ◆ *n* **11** a narrow place, esp. a pass or strait. ◆ See also **narrows.** [OE *nearu*]
▸**'narrowly** *adv* ▸**'narrowness** *n*

narrowboat ('nærəʊ,bəʊt) *n* a long bargelike boat with a beam of 2.1 metres (7 feet), used on canals.

narrow gauge *n* **1** a railway track with a smaller distance between the lines than the standard gauge of 56½ inches. ◆ *adj* **narrow-gauge. 2** of or denoting a railway with a narrow gauge.

narrow-minded ❶ *adj* having a biased or illiberal viewpoint; bigoted, intolerant, or prejudiced.
▸**,narrow-'mindedness** *n*

narrows ❶ ('nærəʊz) *pl n* a narrow part of a strait, river, current, etc.

narthex ('nɑːθeks) *n* **1** a portico at the west end of a church, esp. one at right angles to the nave. **2** a rectangular entrance hall between the porch and nave of a church. [C17: via L from Med. Gk: enclosed porch (earlier: box), from Gk *narthēx* giant fennel, the stems of which were used to make boxes]

narwhal, narwal ('nɑːwəl), *or* **narwhale** ('nɑː,weɪl) *n* an arctic toothed whale having a black-spotted whitish skin and, in the male, a long spiral tusk. [C17: of Scand. origin; cf. Danish, Norwegian *narhval*, from ON *nāhvalr*, from *nār* corpse + *hvalr* whale]

nary ('nɛərɪ) *adv Dialect or inf.* not; never: *nary a man was left.* [C19: var. of *ne'er a* never a]

NASA ('næsə) *n* (in the US) *acronym for* National Aeronautics and Space Administration.

nasal ('neɪzᵊl) *adj* **1** of the nose. **2** *Phonetics.* pronounced with the soft palate lowered allowing air to escape via the nasal cavity. ◆ *n* **3** a nasal speech sound, such as English *m, n,* or *ng.* [C17: from F from LL *nāsālis*, from L *nāsus* nose]
▸**nasality** (neɪ'zælɪtɪ) *n* ▸**'nasally** *adv*

nasalize *or* **nasalise** ('neɪzᵊ,laɪz) *vb* **nasalizes, nasalizing, nasalized** *or* **nasalises, nasalising, nasalised.** (*tr*) to pronounce nasally.
▸**,nasali'zation** *or* **,nasali'sation** *n*

nascent ('næsᵊnt, 'neɪ-) *adj* starting to grow or develop; being born. [C17: from L *nascēns*, present participle of *nāscī* to be born]
▸**'nascency** *n*

nascent hydrogen *n Chem.* hydrogen produced in a reactive form within the reaction mixture.

naso- *combining form.* nose: *nasopharynx.* [from L *nāsus* nose]

nasogastric (,neɪzəʊ'gæstrɪk) *adj Anat.* of or relating to the nose and stomach: *a nasogastric tube.*

nastic movement ('næstɪk) *n* a response of plant parts that is independent of the direction of the external stimulus, such as the opening of buds caused by an alteration in light intensity. [C19 *nastic*, from Gk *nastos* close-packed, from *nassein* to press down]

nasturtium (nə'stɜːʃəm) *n* a plant having round leaves and yellow, red, or orange trumpet-shaped spurred flowers. [C17: from L: kind of cress, from *nāsus* nose + *tortus* twisted; because the pungent smell causes one to wrinkle one's nose]

nasty ❶ ('nɑːstɪ) *adj* **nastier, nastiest. 1** unpleasant or repugnant. **2** dangerous or painful: *a nasty wound.* **3** spiteful or ill-natured. **4** obscene or indecent. ◆ *n, pl* **nasties. 5** an offensive or unpleasant person or thing:

THESAURUS

narcotic *n* **1 = drug,** anaesthetic, analgesic, anodyne, opiate, painkiller, sedative, tranquillizer ◆ *adj* **5 = sedative,** analgesic, calming, dulling, hypnotic, Lethean, numbing, painkilling, somnolent, soporific, stupefacient, stupefactive, stupefying

nark *vb* **3 = annoy,** aggravate (*inf.*), bother, bug, exasperate, gall, get on one's nerves (*inf.*), irk, irritate, miff (*inf.*), nettle, peeve, pique, provoke, rile

narrate *vb* **1 = tell,** chronicle, describe, detail, recite, recount, rehearse, relate, repeat, report, set forth, unfold

narration *n* **1 = telling,** description, explanation, reading, recital, rehearsal, relation, storytelling, voice-over (*in film*)

narrative *n* **1 = story,** account, chronicle, detail, history, report, statement, tale

narrator *n* **1 = storyteller,** annalist, author, bard, chronicler, commentator, raconteur, reciter, relater, reporter, writer

narrow *adj* **1 = thin,** attenuated, fine, slender, slim, spare, tapering **2 = limited,** circumscribed, close, confined, constricted, contracted, cramped, incapacious, meagre, near, pinched, restricted, scanty, straitened, tight **3 = insular,** biased, bigoted, dogmatic, illiberal, intolerant, narrow-minded, partial, prejudiced, puritan, reactionary, small-minded ◆ *vb* **9 = tighten,** circumscribe, constrict, diminish, limit, reduce, simplify, straiten
Antonyms *adj* ≠ **thin:** broad, wide ≠ **limited:** ample, big, broad, generous, open, spacious, wide ≠ **insular:** broad-minded, generous, liberal, receptive, tolerant

narrowly *adv* **5 = just,** barely, by a whisker *or* hair's-breadth, by the skin of one's teeth, only just, scarcely **6 = painstakingly,** carefully, closely, scrutinizingly

narrow-minded *adj* **= intolerant,** biased, bigoted, conservative, hidebound, illiberal, insular, opinionated, parochial, petty, prejudiced, provincial, reactionary, short-sighted, small-minded, strait-laced
Antonyms *adj* broad-minded, catholic, cosmopolitan, freethinking, indulgent, open-minded, permissive, tolerant, unprejudiced

narrows *pl n* **= channel,** gulf, passage, sound, straits

nastiness *n* **1 = squalor,** defilement, dirtiness, filth, filthiness, foulness, impurity, pollution, uncleanliness **3 = unpleasantness,** disagreeableness, malice, meanness, offensiveness, spitefulness **4 = obscenity,** indecency, licentiousness, pollution, porn (*inf.*), pornography, ribaldry, smuttiness

nasty *adj* **1 = objectionable,** dirty, disagreeable, disgusting, filthy, foul, grotty (*sl.*), horrible, loathsome, malodorous, mephitic, nauseating, noisome, obnoxious, odious, offensive, polluted, repellent, repugnant, sickening, unappetizing, unpleasant, vile, yucky *or* yukky (*sl.*) **2 = painful,** bad, critical, dangerous, serious, severe **3 = spiteful,** abusive, annoying, bad-tempered, despicable, disagreeable, distasteful, malicious, mean, unpleasant, vicious, vile **4 = obscene,** blue, foul, gross, impure, indecent, lascivious, lewd, licentious, pornographic, ribald, smutty
Antonyms *adj* ≠ **objectionable:** admirable, agreeable, enjoyable, nice, pleasant, sweet ≠ **spiteful:**

a video nasty. [C14: from ?; prob. rel. to Swedish dialect *nasket* & Du. *nestig* dirty]
▸**'nastily** *adv* ▸**'nastiness** *n*

NAS/UWT (in Britain) *abbrev. for* National Association of Schoolmasters/Union of Women Teachers.

nat. *abbrev. for:* **1** national. **2** native. **3** natural.

natal ('neɪtᵊl) *adj* of or relating to birth. [C14: from L *nātālis* of one's birth, from *nātus,* from *nascī* to be born]

natant ('neɪtᵊnt) *adj* floating or swimming. [C18: from L *natāns,* present participle of *natāre* to swim]

natation (nə'teɪʃən) *n* a literary word for **swimming.** [C16: from L *natātiō* a swimming, from *natāre* to swim]

natatory (nə'teɪtərɪ) *or* **natatorial** (ˌnætə'tɔːrɪəl) *adj* of or relating to swimming. [C18: from LL *natātōrius,* from L *natāre* to swim]

natch (nætʃ) *sentence substitute. Inf.* short for **naturally.**

nates ('neɪtiːz) *pl n, sing* **natis** (-tɪs). a technical word for the **buttocks.** [C17: from L]

NATFHE (in Britain) *abbrev. for* National Association of Teachers in Further and Higher Education.

natheless ('neɪθlɪs) *or* **nathless** ('næθlɪs) *Arch. sentence connector.* nonetheless. [OE *nāthylǣs,* from *nā* never + *thӯ* for that + *lǣs* less]

nation ❶ ('neɪʃən) *n* **1** an aggregation of people or peoples of one or more cultures, races, etc., organized into a single state: *the Australian nation.* **2** a community of persons not constituting a state but bound by common descent, language, history, etc.: *the French-Canadian nation.* [C13: via OF from L *nātiō* birth, tribe, from *nascī* to be born]
▸**'nationˌhood** *n*

national ❶ ('næʃənᵊl) *adj* **1** of or relating to a nation as a whole. **2** characteristic of a particular nation: *the national dress of Poland.* ◆ *n* **3** a citizen or subject. **4** a national newspaper.
▸**'nationally** *adv*

national anthem *n* a patriotic song adopted by a nation for use on public occasions.

national assistance *n* (formerly, in Britain) a weekly allowance paid to individuals of various groups by the state to bring their incomes up to minimum levels established by law. Now replaced by income support.

national bank *n* **1** (in the US) a commercial bank incorporated under a Federal charter and legally required to be a member of the Federal Reserve System. **2** a bank operated by a government.

national call *n Brit.* a telephone call made to a number within the country but outside the local area.

National Curriculum *n* (in England and Wales) the curriculum of subjects taught in state schools from 1989. The ten foundation subjects are: English, maths, and science (the core subjects); art, design and technology, geography, history, music, physical education, and a foreign language. Pupils are assessed at four stages. Abbrev.: **NC.**

national debt *n* the total outstanding borrowings of a nation's central government.

National Economic Development Council *n* a former advisory body on economic policy in Britain, composed of representatives of government, management, and trade unions: abolished in 1992. Abbrevs.: **NEDC,** (inf.) **Neddy.**

National Enterprise Board *n* a public corporation established in 1975 to help the economy of the UK. In 1981 it merged with the National Research and Development Council to form the British Technology Group. Abbrev.: **NEB.**

National Football *n* (in Australia) another name for **Australian Rules.**

National Front *n* an extreme right-wing British political party founded in 1967.

national grid *n Brit.* **1** a network of high-voltage electric power lines linking major electric power stations. **2** the metric coordinate system used in ordnance survey maps.

National Guard *n* **1** (*sometimes not cap.*) the armed force that was established in France in 1789 and existed intermittently until 1871. **2** (in the US) a state military force that can be called into federal service by the president.

National Health Service *n* (in Britain) the system of national medical services since 1948, financed mainly by taxation. Abbrev.: **NHS.**

national hunt *n Brit.* (*often caps.*) **a** the racing of horses on racecourses with jumps. **b** (*as modifier*): *a National Hunt jockey.*

national income *n Econ.* the total of all incomes accruing over a specified period to residents of a country.

national insurance *n* (in Britain) state insurance based on weekly contributions from employees and employers and providing payments to the unemployed, the sick, the retired, etc., as well as medical services.

nationalism ❶ ('næʃənəˌlɪzəm) *n* **1** a sentiment based on common cultural characteristics that binds a population and often produces a policy of national independence. **2** loyalty to one's country; patriotism. **3** exaggerated or fanatical devotion to a national community.
▸**'nationalist** *n, adj* ▸**ˌnational'istic** *adj*

nationality ❶ (ˌnæʃə'nælɪtɪ) *n, pl* **nationalities. 1** the fact of being a citizen of a particular nation. **2** a body of people sharing common descent, history, language, etc.; a nation. **3** a national group: *30 different nationalities are found in this city.* **4** national character. **5** the fact of being a nation; national status.

nationalize *or* **nationalise** ('næʃənəˌlaɪz) *vb* **nationalizes, nationalizing, nationalized** *or* **nationalises, nationalising, nationalised.** (*tr*) **1** to put (an industry, resources, etc.) under state control. **2** to make national in character or status. **3** a less common word for **naturalize.**
▸**ˌnationali'zation** *or* **ˌnationali'sation** *n*

national park *n* an area of countryside for public use designated by a national government as being of notable scenic, environmental, or historical importance.

National Party *n* **1** (in New Zealand) the more conservative of the two main political parties. **2** (in Australia) a political party drawing its main support from rural areas. Former name: **National Country Party. 3** (in South Africa) a political party composed mainly of centre-to-right-wing Afrikaners. It ruled from 1948 until 1994, when South Africa's first multiracial elections were won by the African National Congress.

National Savings Bank *n* (in Britain) a government savings bank, run through the Post Office.

national service *n Chiefly Brit.* compulsory military service.

National Socialism *n German history.* the doctrines and practices of the Nazis, involving the supremacy of Hitler as Führer, anti-Semitism, state control of the economy, and national expansion.
▸**National Socialist** *n, adj*

national superannuation *n NZ.* a government pension given on the attainment of a specified age; old age pension.

National Trust *n* **1** (in Britain) an organization concerned with the preservation of historic buildings and areas of the countryside of great beauty. **2** (in Australia) a similar organization in each of the states.

nationwide ❶ ('neɪʃənˌwaɪd) *adj* covering or available to the whole of a nation; national.

native ❶ ('neɪtɪv) *adj* **1** relating or belonging to a person by virtue of conditions existing at birth: *a native language.* **2** natural or innate: *a native strength.* **3** born in a specified place: *a native Indian.* **4** (when *postpositive,* foll. by *to*) originating in: *kangaroos are native to Australia.* **5** relating to the indigenous inhabitants of a country: *the native art of the New Guinea Highlands.* **6** (of metals) found naturally in the elemental form; not chemically combined as in an ore. **7** unadulterated by civilization, artifice, or adornment; natural. **8** *Arch.* related by birth or race. **9 go native.** (of a settler) to adopt the lifestyle of the local population, esp. when it appears less civilized. ◆ *n* **10** (usually foll. by *of*) a person born in a particular place: *a native of Geneva.* **11** (usually foll. by *of*) a species of animal or plant originating in a particular place. **12** a member of an indigenous people of a country, esp. a non-White people, as opposed to colonial immigrants. [C14: from L *nātīvus* innate, natural, from *nascī* to be born]
▸**'natively** *adv* ▸**'nativeness** *n*

Native American *n* another name for an **American Indian.**

native bear *n* an Australian name for **koala.**

native-born *adj* born in the country or area indicated.

native companion *n* (in Australia) another name for **brolga.**

native dog *n Austral.* a dingo.

nativity ❶ (nə'tɪvɪtɪ) *n, pl* **nativities.** birth or origin. [C14: from LL *nātīvitas* birth; see NATIVE]

Nativity ❶ (nə'tɪvɪtɪ) *n* **1** the birth of Christ. **2** the feast of Christmas as a commemoration of this. **3a** an artistic representation of the circumstances of the birth of Christ. **3b** (*as modifier*): *a Nativity play.*

NATO *or* **Nato** ('neɪtəʊ) *n acronym for* North Atlantic Treaty Organization: an international organization established (1949) for purposes of collective security.

natron ('neɪtrən) *n* a whitish or yellow mineral that consists of hydrated sodium carbonate and occurs in saline deposits and salt lakes. [C17: via F & Sp. from Ar. *natrūn,* from Gk *nitron* NITRE]

NATSOPA (næt'səʊpə) *n* (formerly, in Britain) *acronym for* National Society of Operative Printers, Graphical and Media Personnel.

natter ❶ ('nætə) *Chiefly Brit. inf.* ◆ *vb* **1** (*intr*) to talk idly and at length; chatter. ◆ *n* **2** prolonged idle chatter. [C19: from *gnatter* to grumble, imit.]

THESAURUS

decent, kind, nice, pleasant, sweet ≠ **obscene:** clean, decent

nation *n* **1** = **country,** commonwealth, community, people, population, race, realm, society, state, tribe

national *adj* **1** = **nationwide,** civil, countrywide, governmental, public, state, widespread **2** = **domestic,** internal, social ◆ *n* **3** = **citizen,** inhabitant, native, resident, subject

nationalism *n* **2, 3** = **patriotism,** allegiance, chauvinism, fealty, jingoism, loyalty, nationality

nationalistic *adj* **2, 3** = **patriotic,** chauvinistic, jingoistic, loyal, xenophobic

nationality *n* **2, 3** = **race,** ethnic group, nation

nationwide *adj* = **national,** countrywide, general, overall, widespread

native *adj* **1** = **local,** domestic, home, home-grown, home-made, indigenous, mother, vernacular **2** = **inborn,** built-in, congenital, endemic, hereditary, immanent, inbred, ingrained, inherent, inherited, innate, instinctive, intrinsic, inveterate, natal, natural **5** = **indigenous,** aboriginal, autochthonous ◆ *n* **10** = **inhabitant,** citizen, countryman, dweller, national, resident **12** = **aborigine,** autochthon

nativity *n* = **birth,** delivery, parturition
Antonyms *n* death, demise, dying, expiration

Nativity *n* **3** = **crèche,** manger scene

natter *vb* **1** = **gossip,** blather, blether, chatter, chew the fat *or* rag (*sl.*), gabble, jabber, jaw (*sl.*), prate, prattle, rabbit (on) (*Brit. inf.*), talk, talk idly, witter (*inf.*) ◆ *n* **2** = **gossip,** blather, blether, chat, chinwag (*Brit. inf.*), chitchat, confab-

natterjack ('nætəˌdʒæk) *n* a European toad having a greyish-brown body marked with reddish warty processes. [C18: from ?]

natty ⓘ ('nætɪ) *adj* **nattier, nattiest.** *Inf.* smart; spruce; dapper. [C18: from obs. *netty*, from *net* NEAT[1]]
▸**'nattily** *adv* ▸**'nattiness** *n*

natural ⓘ ('nætʃrəl) *adj* **1** of, existing in, or produced by nature: *natural science; natural cliffs.* **2** in accordance with human nature. **3** as is normal or to be expected: *the natural course of events.* **4** not acquired; innate: *a natural gift for sport.* **5** being so through innate qualities: *a natural leader.* **6** not supernatural or strange: *natural phenomena.* **7** genuine or spontaneous. **8** lifelike: *she looked more natural without make-up.* **9** not affected by man; wild: *in the natural state this animal is not ferocious.* **10** being or made from organic material; not synthetic: *a natural fibre like cotton.* **11** born out of wedlock. **12** not adopted but rather related by blood: *her natural parents.* **13** *Music.* **13a** not sharp or flat. **13b** (*postpositive*) denoting a note that is neither sharp nor flat. **13c** (of a key or scale) containing no sharps or flats. **14** based on the principles and findings of human reason rather than on revelation: *natural religion.* ◆ *n* **15** *Inf.* a person or thing regarded as certain to qualify for success, selection, etc.: *the horse was a natural for first place.* **16** *Music.* **16a** Also called (US): **cancel.** an accidental cancelling a previous sharp or flat. Usual symbol: ♮ **16b** a note affected by this accidental. **17** *Obs.* an imbecile; idiot.
▸**'naturalness** *n*

natural childbirth *n* a method of childbirth characterized by the absence of anaesthetics, in which the expectant mother is given special breathing and relaxing exercises.

natural gas *n* a gaseous mixture, consisting mainly of methane, trapped below ground; used extensively as a fuel.

natural history *n* **1** the study of animals and plants in the wild state. **2** the sum of these phenomena in a given place or at a given time.
▸**natural historian** *n*

natural immunity *n* immunity with which an individual is born, which has a genetic basis.

naturalism ⓘ ('nætʃrəˌlɪzəm) *n* **1** a movement, esp. in art and literature, advocating detailed realistic and factual description. **2** the belief that all religious truth is based not on revelation but rather on the study of natural causes and processes. **3** *Philosophy.* a scientific account of the world in terms of causes and natural forces. **4** action or thought caused by natural instincts.

naturalist ⓘ ('nætʃrəlɪst) *n* **1** a person who is versed in or interested in botany or zoology. **2** a person who advocates or practises naturalism.

naturalistic ⓘ (ˌnætʃrə'lɪstɪk) *adj* **1** of or reproducing nature in effect or characteristics. **2** of or characteristic of naturalism. **3** of naturalists.
▸ˌ**natural'istically** *adv*

naturalize ⓘ *or* **naturalise** ('nætʃrəˌlaɪz) *vb* **naturalizes, naturalizing, naturalized** *or* **naturalises, naturalising, naturalised. 1** (*tr*) to give citizenship to (a person of foreign birth). **2** to be or cause to be adopted in another place, as a word, custom, etc. **3** (*tr*) to introduce (a plant or animal from another region) and cause it to adapt to local conditions. **4** (*intr*) (of a plant or animal) to adapt successfully to a foreign environment. **5** (*tr*) to make natural or more lifelike.
▸ˌ**naturali'zation** *or* ˌ**naturali'sation** *n*

natural language *n* a language that has evolved naturally as a means of communication among people, as opposed to an invented language or a code.

natural logarithm *n* a logarithm to the base e. Usually written $\log_e$ or ln. Also called: **Napierian logarithm.**

naturally ⓘ ('nætʃrəlɪ) *adv* **1** in a natural way. **2** instinctively. ◆ *adv, sentence substitute.* **3** of course; surely.

natural number *n* any of the numbers 0 ,1, 2, 3, 4,... that can be used to count the members of a set; the non-negative integers.

natural philosophy *n* physical science, esp. physics.
▸**natural philosopher** *n*

natural resources *pl n* naturally occurring materials such as coal, fertile land, etc.

natural science *n* the sciences that are involved in the study of the physical world and its phenomena, including biology, physics, chemistry, and geology.

natural selection *n* a process resulting in the survival of those individuals from a population of animals or plants that are best adapted to the prevailing environmental conditions.

natural theology *n* the attempt to derive theological truth, and esp. the existence of God, from empirical facts by reasoned argument. Cf. **revealed religion.**

natural wastage *n* the loss of employees, etc., through not replacing those who retire or resign rather than dismissal or redundancy.

nature ⓘ ('neɪtʃə) *n* **1** fundamental qualities; identity or essential character. **2** (*often cap.*) the whole system of the existence, forces, and events of all physical life that are not controlled by man. **3** plant and animal life, as distinct from man. **4** a wild primitive state untouched by man. **5** natural unspoilt countryside. **6** disposition or temperament. **7** desires or instincts governing behaviour. **8** the normal biological needs of the body. **9** sort; character. **10 against nature.** unnatural or immoral. **11 by nature.** essentially or innately. **12 call of nature.** *Inf.* the need to urinate or defecate. **13 from nature.** using natural models in drawing, painting, etc. **14 in** (*or* **of**) **the nature of.** essentially the same as; by way of. [C13: via OF from L *nātūra*, from *nātus*, p.p. of *nascī* to be born]

nature reserve *n* an area of land that is protected and managed in order to preserve its flora and fauna.

nature study *n* the study of the natural world, esp. animals and plants, by direct observation at an elementary level.

nature trail *n* a path through countryside designed and usually signposted to draw attention to natural features of interest.

naturism ⓘ ('neɪtʃəˌrɪzəm) *n* another name for **nudism.**
▸**'naturist** *n, adj*

naturopathy (ˌnætʃə'rɒpəθɪ) *n* the treatment of illness by stimulating natural healing, esp. by herbal remedies, manipulation, etc.
▸**'naturoˌpath** *n* ▸ˌ**naturo'pathic** *adj*

naught ⓘ (nɔːt) *n* **1** *Arch. or literary.* nothing; ruin or failure. **2** a variant spelling (esp. US) of **nought. 3 set at naught.** to disregard or scorn; disdain. ◆ *adv* **4** *Arch. or literary.* not at all: *it matters naught.* ◆ *adj* **5** *Obs.* worthless, ruined, or wicked. [OE *nāwiht*, from *nā* NO[1] + *wiht* thing, person]

naughty ⓘ ('nɔːtɪ) *adj* **naughtier, naughtiest. 1** (esp. of children) mischievous or disobedient. **2** mildly indecent; titillating. [C14: (orig.: needy, poor): from NAUGHT]
▸**'naughtily** *adv* ▸**'naughtiness** *n*

nauplius ('nɔːplɪəs) *n, pl* **nauplii** (-plɪˌaɪ). the larva of many crustaceans, having a rounded unsegmented body with three pairs of limbs. [C19: from L: type of shellfish, from Gk *Nauplios*, one of the sons of the Greek god Poseidon]

nausea ⓘ ('nɔːzɪə, -sɪə) *n* **1** the sensation that precedes vomiting. **2** a feeling of revulsion. [C16: via L from Gk: seasickness, from *naus* ship]

nauseate ⓘ ('nɔːzɪˌeɪt, -sɪ-) *vb* **nauseates, nauseating, nauseated. 1** (*tr*) to arouse feelings of disgust or revulsion in. **2** to feel or cause to feel sick.
▸**'nauseˌating** *adj*

nauseous ⓘ ('nɔːzɪəs, -sɪəs) *adj* **1** causing nausea. **2** distasteful; repulsive.
▸**'nauseously** *adv* ▸**'nauseousness** *n*

nautch *or* **nauch** (nɔːtʃ) *n* an intricate traditional Indian dance performed by professional dancing girls. [C18: from Hindi *nāc*, from Sansk., from *nṛtyati* he acts or dances]

THESAURUS

ulation, conversation, gab (*inf.*), gabble, gabfest (*inf., chiefly US & Canad.*), jabber, jaw (*sl.*), prattle, talk

natty *adj Informal* = **smart**, chic, crucial (*sl.*), dapper, elegant, fashionable, neat, snazzy (*inf.*), spruce, stylish, trendy (*Brit. inf.*), trim, well-dressed, well-turned-out

natural *adj* **3** = **normal**, common, everyday, legitimate, logical, ordinary, regular, typical, usual **4** = **innate**, characteristic, congenital, essential, immanent, inborn, indigenous, inherent, in one's blood, instinctive, intuitive, natal, native **7** = **unaffected**, artless, candid, frank, genuine, ingenuous, open, real, simple, spontaneous, unpretentious, unsophisticated, unstudied **10** = **pure**, organic, plain, unbleached, unmixed, unpolished, unrefined, whole
Antonyms *adj* ≠ **normal:** abnormal, irregular, out of the ordinary, strange, untypical ≠ **unaffected:** affected, artificial, assumed, counterfeit, feigned, phoney *or* phony (*inf.*), unnatural ≠ **pure:** manufactured, processed, synthetic, unnatural

naturalism *n* **1** = **realism**, factualism, verisimilitude

naturalist *n* **1** = **biologist**, botanist, ecologist, zoologist **2** = **realist**, factualist

naturalistic *adj* **2** = **realistic**, factualistic, kitchen sink, lifelike, photographic, real-life, representational, true-to-life, vérité, warts and all (*inf.*)

naturalize *vb* **1** = **acclimatize**, enfranchise, grant citizenship **2** = **adopt**, adapt **3** = **acclimate**, accustom, adapt, domesticate, familiarize, habituate

naturally *adv* **1** = **genuinely**, as anticipated, customarily, informally, normally, simply, spontaneously, typically, unaffectedly, unpretentiously ◆ *sentence substitute* **3** = **of course**, absolutely, as a matter of course, certainly

naturalness *n* **7** = **spontaneousness**, artlessness, candidness, frankness, genuineness, ingenuousness, openness, realism, simpleness, simplicity, unaffectedness, unpretentiousness, unsophisticatedness, unstudiedness **10** = **purity**, plainness, pureness, wholeness

nature *n* **1** = **make-up**, attributes, character, complexion, constitution, essence, features, quality, traits **2** = **creation**, cosmos, earth, environment, universe, world **5** = **country**, countryside, landscape, scenery **6** = **temperament**, disposition, humour, mood, outlook, temper **9** = **kind**, category, description, sort, species, style, type, variety

naturist *n* = **nudist**

naught *n Archaic or literary* **1** = **nothing**, nil, nothingness, nought, zero

naughty *adj* **1** = **disobedient**, annoying, bad, exasperating, fractious, impish, misbehaved, mischievous, perverse, playful, refractory, roguish, sinful, teasing, wayward, wicked, worthless **2** = **obscene**, bawdy, blue, improper, lewd, off-colour, ribald, risqué, smutty, vulgar, X-rated (*inf.*)
Antonyms *adj* ≠ **disobedient:** good, obedient, polite, proper, seemly, well-behaved, well-mannered ≠ **obscene:** polite, proper

nausea *n* **1** = **sickness**, biliousness, qualm(s), queasiness, retching, squeamishness, vomiting **2** = **disgust**, abhorrence, aversion, loathing, odium, repugnance, revulsion

nauseate *vb* **1, 2** = **sicken**, disgust, gross out (*US sl.*), horrify, offend, repel, repulse, revolt, turn one's stomach

nauseous *adj* **1, 2** = **sickening**, abhorrent, detestable, disgusting, distasteful, loathsome, nauseating, offensive, repugnant, repulsive, revolting, yucky *or* yukky (*sl.*)

nautical ❶ (ˈnɔːtɪkᵊl) *adj* of or involving ships, navigation, or seamen. [C16: from L *nauticus,* from Gk *nautikos,* from *naus* ship]
▸ **ˈnautically** *adv*

nautical mile *n* **1** Also called **international nautical mile, air mile.** a unit of length, used esp. in navigation, equivalent to the average length of a minute of latitude, and corresponding to a latitude of 45°, i.e. 1852 m (6076.12 ft). **2** a former British unit of length equal to 1853.18 m (6080 ft), which was replaced by the international nautical mile in 1970. Former name: **geographical mile.** Cf. **sea mile.**

nautilus (ˈnɔːtɪləs) *n, pl* **nautiluses** *or* **nautili** (-ˌlaɪ). **1** any of a genus of cephalopod molluscs, esp. the pearly nautilus. **2** short for **paper nautilus.** [C17: via L from Gk *nautilos* sailor, from *naus* ship]

NAV *abbrev. for* net asset value.

Navaho *or* **Navajo** (ˈnævəˌhəʊ) *n* **1** (*pl* **Navaho, Navahos, Navahoes** *or* **Navajo, Navajos, Navajoes**) a member of a North American Indian people of Arizona, New Mexico, and Utah. **2** the language of this people. [C18: from Sp. *Navajó* pueblo, from Tena *Navahu* large planted field]

naval ❶ (ˈneɪvᵊl) *adj* **1** of, characteristic of, or having a navy. **2** of or relating to ships; nautical. [C16: from L *nāvālis,* from *nāvis* ship]

naval architecture *n* the designing of ships.
▸ **naval architect** *n*

Navaratri (ˌnævəˈrɑːtrɪ) *n* an annual Hindu festival celebrated over nine days in September–October. It commemorates the slaying of demons by Rama and the goddess Durga. Also called: **Durga Puja.** [from Sansk. *navaratri* nine nights]

navarin (ˈnævərɪn) *n* a stew of mutton or lamb with root vegetables. [from F]

nave[1] (neɪv) *n* the central space in a church, extending from the narthex to the chancel and often flanked by aisles. [C17: via Med. L from L *nāvis* ship, from the similarity of shape]

nave[2] (neɪv) *n* the central block or hub of a wheel. [OE *nafu, nafa*]

navel ❶ (ˈneɪvᵊl) *n* **1** the scar in the centre of the abdomen, usually forming a slight depression, where the umbilical cord was attached. Technical name: **umbilicus.** Related adj: **umbilical. 2** a central part or point. [OE *nafela*]

navel orange *n* a sweet orange that has at its apex a navel-like depression enclosing an underdeveloped secondary fruit.

navelwort (ˈneɪvᵊlˌwɜːt) *n* another name for **pennywort** (sense 1).

navicular (nəˈvɪkjʊlə) *Anat.* ◆ *adj* **1** shaped like a boat. ◆ *n* **2** a small boat-shaped bone of the wrist or foot. [C16: from LL *nāviculāris,* from L *nāvicula,* dim. of *nāvis* ship]

navigable ❶ (ˈnævɪgəbᵊl) *adj* **1** wide, deep, or safe enough to be sailed through: *a navigable channel.* **2** capable of being steered: *a navigable raft.*
▸ **ˌnavigaˈbility** *n* ▸ **ˈnavigably** *adv*

navigate ❶ (ˈnævɪˌgeɪt) *vb* **navigates, navigating, navigated. 1** to direct or plot the path or position of (a ship, an aircraft, etc.). **2** (*tr*) to travel over, through, or on in a boat, aircraft, etc. **3** *Inf.* to direct (oneself) carefully or safely: *he navigated his way to the bar.* **4** (*intr*) (of a passenger in a motor vehicle) to give directions to the driver; point out the route. [C16: from L *nāvigāre* to sail, from *nāvis* ship + *agere* to drive]

navigation ❶ (ˌnævɪˈgeɪʃən) *n* **1** the skill or process of plotting a route and directing a ship, aircraft, etc., along it. **2** the act or practice of navigating: *dredging made navigation of the river possible.*
▸ **ˌnaviˈgational** *adj*

navigator ❶ (ˈnævɪˌgeɪtə) *n* **1** a person who performs navigation. **2** (esp. formerly) a person who explores by ship. **3** an instrument for assisting a pilot to navigate an aircraft.

navvy ❶ (ˈnævɪ) *n, pl* **navvies.** *Brit. inf.* a labourer on a building site, etc. [C19: from *navigator* builder of a *navigation* (in the sense: canal)]

navy ❶ (ˈneɪvɪ) *n, pl* **navies. 1** the warships and auxiliary vessels of a nation or ruler. **2** (*often cap.*) the branch of a country's armed services comprising such ships, their crews, and all their supporting services. **3** short for **navy blue. 4** *Arch. or literary.* a fleet of ships. [C14: via OF from Vulgar L *nāvia* (unattested) ship, from L *nāvis* ship]

navy blue *n* **a** a dark greyish-blue colour. **b** (*as adj*): *a navy-blue suit.* [C19: from the colour of the British naval uniform]

Navy List *n* (in Britain) an official list of all commissioned officers of the Royal Navy.

navy yard *n* a naval shipyard, esp. in the US.

nawab (nəˈwɑːb) *n* (formerly) a Muslim ruling prince or powerful landowner in India. [C18: from Hindi *nawwāb,* from Ar. *nuwwāb,* pl. of *na'ib* viceroy]

nay (neɪ) *sentence substitute.* **1** a word for **no**[1]: archaic or dialectal except in voting by voice. ◆ *n* **2** a person who votes in the negative. ◆ *adv* **3** (*sentence modifier*) *Arch.* an emphatic form of **no**[1]. [C12: from ON *nei,* from *ne* not + *ei* ever]

Nazarene (ˌnæzəˈriːn) *n* **1** an early name for a **Christian** (Acts 24:5) or (when preceded by *the*) for **Jesus Christ. 2** a member of one of several groups of Jewish-Christians found principally in Syria. ◆ *adj* **3** of Nazareth in N Israel, or the Nazarenes.

Nazarite (ˈnæzəˌraɪt) *or* **Nazirite** *n* a religious ascetic of ancient Israel. [C16: from L *Nazaraeus,* from Heb. *nāzar* to consecrate + -ITE[1]]

Nazi (ˈnɑːtsɪ) *n, pl* **Nazis. 1** a member of the fascist National Socialist German Workers' Party, which seized political control in Germany in 1933. ◆ *adj* **2** characteristic of or relating to the Nazis. [C20: from G, phonetic spelling of the first two syllables of *Nationalsozialist* National Socialist]
▸ **Nazism** (ˈnɑːtˌsɪzəm) *or* **Naziism** (ˈnɑːtsɪˌɪzəm) *n*

Nb *the chemical symbol for* niobium.

NB *abbrev. for* New Brunswick.

NB, N.B., nb, *or* **n.b.** *abbrev. for* nota bene. [L: note well]

NBA *abbrev. for* Net Book Agreement.

NC *or* **N.C.** *abbrev. for:* **1** North Carolina. **2** *Brit. education.* National Curriculum.

NCB (in Britain) *abbrev. for* National Coal Board: now British Coal.

NCC (in Britain) *abbrev. for:* **1** Nature Conservancy Council. **2** *Brit. education.* National Curriculum Council: a statutory organization responsible for the content of the National Curriculum.

NCO *abbrev. for* noncommissioned officer.

NCU (in Britain) *abbrev. for* National Communications Union.

nd *abbrev. for* no date.

Nd *the chemical symbol for* neodymium.

NDP *abbrev. for:* **1** net domestic product. **2** (in Canada) New Democratic Party.

NDT (in Canada) *abbrev. for* Newfoundland Daylight Time.

Ne *the chemical symbol for* neon.

NE 1 *symbol for* northeast(ern). **2** *abbrev. for* Nebraska. **3** Also: **N.E.** *abbrev. for* New England.

ne- *combining form.* a variant of **neo-,** esp. before a vowel: *Nearctic.*

Neanderthal man (nɪˈændəˌtɑːl) *n* a type of primitive man occurring throughout much of Europe in late Palaeolithic times. They are not thought to be ancestors of modern humans. [C19: from the anthropological findings (1857) in the Neandertal, a valley near Düsseldorf, Germany]

neap (niːp) *adj* **1** of, relating to, or constituting a neap tide. ◆ *n* **2** short for **neap tide.** [OE, as in *nēpflōd* neap tide, from ?]

Neapolitan (ˌnɪəˈpɒlɪtᵊn) *n* **1** a native or inhabitant of Naples, a city in SW Italy. ◆ *adj* **2** of or relating to Naples. [C15: from L *Neāpolītānus,* ult. from Gk *Neapolis* new town]

Neapolitan ice cream *n* ice cream with several layers of different colours and flavours.

neap tide *n* either of the tides that occur at the first or last quarter of the moon when the tide-generating forces of the sun and moon oppose each other and produce the smallest rise and fall in tidal level. Cf. **spring tide** (sense 1).

near ❶ (nɪə) *prep* **1** at or to a place or time not far away from; close to. ◆ *adv* **2** at or to a place or time not far away; close by. **3** short for **nearly** (sense 1): *I was damn near killed.* ◆ *adj* **4** (*postpositive*) at or in a place not far away. **5** (*prenominal*) only just successful or only just failing: *a near thing.* **6** (*postpositive*) *Inf.* miserly, mean. **7** (*prenominal*) closely connected or intimate: *a near relation.* ◆ *vb* **8** to come or draw close (to). ◆ *n* **9** Also called: **nearside. 9a** the left side of a horse, vehicle, etc. **9b** (*as modifier*): *the near foreleg.* [OE *nēar* (adv), comp. of *nēah* close]
▸ **ˈnearness** *n*

nearby ❶ *adj* (ˈnɪəˌbaɪ), *adv* (ˌnɪəˈbaɪ). not far away; close at hand.

Nearctic (nɪˈɑːktɪk) *adj* of a zoogeographical region consisting of North America, north of the tropic of Cancer, and Greenland.

Near East *n* **1** another term for the **Middle East. 2** (formerly) the Balkan States and the area of the Ottoman Empire.

near gale *n Meteorol.* a wind of force seven on the Beaufort scale or from 32-38 mph.

nearly ❶ (ˈnɪəlɪ) *adv* **1** almost. **2 not nearly.** nowhere near: *not nearly enough.* **3** closely: *the person most nearly concerned.*

near-market *n* (*modifier*) (of scientific research, etc.) very close to being commercially exploitable.

near miss *n* **1** a bomb, shell, etc., that does not exactly hit the target. **2** any attempt or shot that just fails to be successful. **3** an incident in which two aircraft, etc., narrowly avoid collision.

THESAURUS

nautical *adj* = **maritime,** marine, naval, oceanic, seafaring, seagoing, yachting

naval *adj* **2** = **nautical,** marine, maritime, oceanic

navel *n* **1** = **umbilicus,** bellybutton (*inf.*), omphalos **2** = **centre,** central point, hub, middle

navigable *adj* **1** = **passable,** clear, negotiable, traversable, unobstructed **2** = **sailable,** controllable, dirigible, steerable

navigate *vb* **1** = **direct,** drive, guide, handle, manoeuvre, pilot, plan, plot, sail, skipper, steer **2** = **travel,** cross, cruise, journey, voyage

navigation *n* **1, 2** = **sailing,** cruising, helmsmanship, pilotage, seamanship, steering, voyaging

navigator *n* **1** = **pilot,** mariner, seaman

navvy *n Brit. informal* = **labourer,** ganger, worker, workman

navy *n* **1** = **fleet,** argosy (*arch.*), armada, flotilla, warships

near *adj* **4** = **close,** adjacent, adjoining, a hop, skip and a jump away (*inf.*), alongside, at close quarters, beside, bordering, close by, contiguous, just round the corner, nearby, neighbouring, proximate, touching, within sniffing distance (*inf.*) **6** *Informal* = **mean,** close-fisted, miserly, niggardly, parsimonious, stingy, tight-fisted, ungenerous **7** = **intimate,** akin, allied, attached, connected, dear, familiar, related
Antonyms *adj* ≠ **close:** distant, far, faraway, far-flung, far-off, far-removed, outlying, out-of-the-way, remote, removed ≠ **intimate:** distant, remote

nearby *adj* = **neighbouring,** adjacent, adjoining, convenient, handy ◆ *adv* = **close at hand,** at close quarters, just round the corner, not far away, proximate, within reach, within sniffing distance (*inf.*)

nearly *adv* **1** = **almost,** about, all but, approaching, approximately, as good as, just about, not quite, practically, roughly, virtually, well-nigh

near point *n Optics.* the nearest point to the eye at which an object remains in focus.

nearside ('nɪəˌsaɪd) *n* **1** (usually preceded by *the*) *Chiefly Brit.* **1a** the side of a vehicle, etc., nearer the kerb. **1b** (*as modifier*): *the nearside door.* **2a** the left side of an animal, etc. **2b** (*as modifier*): *the nearside flank.*

near-sighted Ⓣ (ˌnɪə'saɪtɪd) *adj* relating to or suffering from myopia. ▸**ˌnear-'sightedly** *adv*

near thing Ⓣ *n Inf.* an event or action whose outcome is nearly a failure, success, disaster, etc.

neat[1] Ⓣ (niːt) *adj* **1** clean, tidy, and orderly. **2** liking or insisting on order and cleanliness. **3** smoothly or competently done; efficient: *a neat job.* **4** pat or slick: *his excuse was suspiciously neat.* **5** (of alcoholic drinks, etc.) undiluted. **6** (of language) concise and well-phrased. **7** *Sl., chiefly US & Canad.* pleasing; admirable; excellent. [C16: from OF *net,* from L *nitidus* clean, from *nitēre* to shine] ▸**'neatly** *adv* ▸**'neatness** *n*

neat[2] (niːt) *n, pl* **neat.** *Arch. or dialect.* a domestic bovine animal. [OE *neat*]

neaten Ⓣ ('niːtᵊn) *vb* (*tr*) to make neat; tidy.

neath *or* **'neath** (niːθ) *prep Arch.* short for **beneath.**

neat's-foot oil *n* a yellow oil obtained by boiling the feet and shinbones of cattle.

neb (nɛb) *n Arch. or dialect.* **1** the peak of a cap. **2** the beak of a bird or the nose or snout of an animal. **3** the projecting end of anything. [OE *nebb*]

NEB *abbrev. for:* **1** New English Bible. **2** National Enterprise Board.

nebula ('nɛbjʊlə) *n, pl* **nebulae** (-ˌliː) *or* **nebulas. 1** *Astron.* a diffuse cloud of particles and gases visible either as a hazy patch of light (either an **emission** or **reflection nebula**) or an irregular dark region (**dark nebula**). **2** *Pathol.* opacity of the cornea. [C17: from L: mist, cloud] ▸**'nebular** *adj*

nebular hypothesis *n* the theory that the solar system evolved from nebular matter.

nebulize *or* **nebulise** ('nɛbjʊˌlaɪz) *vb* **nebulizes, nebulizing, nebulized** *or* **nebulises, nebulising, nebulized.** (*tr*) to convert (a liquid) into a fine mist or spray; atomize. ▸**ˌnebuli'zation** *or* **ˌnebuli'sation** *n*

nebulizer *or* **nebuliser** ('nɛbjʊˌlaɪzə) *n* a device for converting a drug in liquid form into a mist or fine spray which is inhaled through a mask to provide medication for the respiratory system.

nebulosity (ˌnɛbjʊ'lɒsɪtɪ) *n, pl* **nebulosities. 1** the state of being nebulous. **2** *Astron.* a nebula.

nebulous Ⓣ ('nɛbjʊləs) *adj* **1** lacking definite form, shape, or content; vague or amorphous. **2** of a nebula. **3** *Rare.* misty or hazy. ▸**'nebulousness** *n*

NEC *abbrev. for* National Executive Committee.

necessaries ('nɛsɪsərɪz) *pl n* (*sometimes sing*) what is needed; essential items: *the necessaries of life.*

necessarily Ⓣ ('nɛsɪsərɪlɪ, ˌnɛsɪ'sɛrɪlɪ) *adv* **1** as an inevitable or natural consequence. **2** as a certainty: *he won't necessarily come.*

necessary Ⓣ ('nɛsɪsərɪ) *adj* **1** needed to achieve a certain desired result; required. **2** inevitable: *the necessary consequences of your action.* **3** *Logic.* **3a** (of a statement, formula, etc.) true under all interpretations. **3b** (of a proposition) determined to be true by its meaning, so that its denial would be self-contradictory. Cf. **sufficient** (sense 2). **4** *Rare.* compelled, as by necessity or law; not free. ◆ *n* **5** (preceded by *the*) *Inf.* the money required for a particular purpose. **6 do the necessary.** *Inf.* to do something that is necessary in a particular situation. ◆ See also **necessaries.** [C14: from L *necessārius* indispensable, from *necesse* unavoidable]

necessitarianism (nɪˌsɛsɪ'tɛərɪəˌnɪzəm) *n Philosophy.* another word for **determinism.** ▸**neˌcessi'tarian** *n, adj*

necessitate Ⓣ (nɪ'sɛsɪˌteɪt) *vb* **necessitates, necessitating, necessitated.** (*tr*) **1** to cause as an unavoidable result. **2** (*usually passive*) to compel or require (someone to do something).

necessitous Ⓣ (nɪ'sɛsɪtəs) *adj* very needy; destitute; poverty-stricken.

necessity Ⓣ (nɪ'sɛsɪtɪ) *n, pl* **necessities. 1** (*sometimes pl*) something needed; prerequisite: *necessities of life.* **2** a condition or set of circumstances that inevitably requires a certain result: *it is a matter of necessity to wear formal clothes when meeting the Queen.* **3** the state or quality of being obligatory or unavoidable. **4** urgent requirement, as in an emergency. **5** poverty or want. **6** *Rare.* compulsion through laws of nature; fate. **7** *Logic.* the property of being necessary. **8 of necessity.** inevitably.

neck (nɛk) *n* **1** the part of an organism connecting the head with the body. **2** the part of a garment around the neck. **3** something resembling a neck in shape or position: *the neck of a bottle.* **4** *Anat.* a constricted portion of an organ or part. **5** a narrow strip of land; peninsula or isthmus. **6** a strait or channel. **7** the part of a violin, cello, etc., that extends from the body to the tuning pegs and supports the fingerboard. **8** a solid block of lava from an extinct volcano, exposed after erosion of the surrounding rock. **9** the length of a horse's head and neck taken as an approximate distance by which one horse beats another in a race: *to win by a neck.* **10** *Archit.* the narrow band at the top of the shaft of a column. **11** *Inf.* impudence or cheek. **12 get it in the neck.** *Inf.* to be reprimanded or punished severely. **13 neck and neck.** absolutely level in a race or competition. **14 neck of the woods.** *Inf.* a particular area: *what brings you to this neck of the woods?* **15 neck or nothing.** at any cost. **16 save one's** *or* **someone's neck.** *Inf.* to escape from or help someone else to escape from a difficult or dangerous situation. **17 stick one's neck out.** *Inf.* to risk criticism, ridicule, etc., by speaking one's mind. ◆ *vb* **18** (*intr*) *Inf.* to kiss or fondle someone or one another passionately. [OE *hnecca*]

neckband ('nɛkˌbænd) *n* a band around the neck of a garment as finishing, decoration, or a base for a collar.

neckcloth Ⓣ ('nɛkˌklɒθ) *n* a large ornamental usually white cravat worn formerly by men.

neckerchief ('nɛkətʃɪf, -ˌtʃiːf) *n* a piece of ornamental cloth, often square, worn round the neck. [C14: from NECK + KERCHIEF]

necking ('nɛkɪŋ) *n Inf.* the activity of kissing and embracing lovingly.

necklace ('nɛklɪs) *n* **1** a chain, band, or cord, often bearing beads, pearls, jewels, etc., worn around the neck as an ornament, esp. by women. **2** (in South Africa) **2a** a tyre soaked in petrol, placed round a person's neck, and set on fire in order to burn the person to death. **2b** (*as modifier*): *necklace victims.* ◆ *vb* **necklaces, necklacing, necklaced.** (*tr*) **3** (in South Africa) to kill (a person) by means of a necklace.

neckline ('nɛkˌlaɪn) *n* the shape or position of the upper edge of a dress, blouse, etc.

necktie ('nɛkˌtaɪ) *n* the US name for **tie** (sense 10).

neckwear ('nɛkˌwɛə) *n* articles of clothing, such as ties, scarves, etc., worn round the neck.

necro- *or before a vowel* **necr-** *combining form.* indicating death, a dead body, or dead tissue: *necrosis.* [from Gk *nekros* corpse]

necrobiosis (ˌnɛkrəʊbaɪ'əʊsɪs) *n Physiol.* the normal degeneration and death of cells.

necrolatry (nɛ'krɒlətrɪ) *n* the worship of the dead.

necrology (nɛ'krɒlədʒɪ) *n, pl* **necrologies. 1** a list of people recently dead. **2** a less common word for **obituary.** ▸**necrological** (ˌnɛkrə'lɒdʒɪkᵊl) *adj*

necromancy Ⓣ ('nɛkrəʊˌmænsɪ) *n* **1** the art of supposedly conjuring up the dead, esp. in order to obtain from them knowledge of the future. **2** black magic; sorcery. [C13: (sense 1) ult. from Gk

THESAURUS

nearness *n* **4** = **closeness**, accessibility, availability, contiguity, handiness, juxtaposition, propinquity, proximity, vicinity **6** *Informal* = **meanness**, niggardliness, parsimony, stinginess **7** = **intimacy**, dearness, familiarity

near-sighted *adj* = **short-sighted**, myopic

near thing *n Informal* = **narrow escape**, close shave (*inf.*), near miss

neat[1] *adj* **1, 2** = **tidy**, accurate, dainty, fastidious, methodical, nice, orderly, shipshape, smart, spick-and-span, spruce, straight, systematic, trim, uncluttered **3** = **efficient**, adept, adroit, agile, apt, clever, deft, dexterous, effortless, elegant, expert, graceful, handy, nimble, practised, precise, skilful, stylish, well-judged **5** = **undiluted**, pure, straight, unmixed
Antonyms *adj* ≠ **tidy:** clumsy, cluttered, disarrayed, disorderly, disorganized, messy, slobby (*inf.*), sloppy (*inf.*), untidy ≠ **efficient:** awful, bad, clumsy, incompetent, inefficient, inelegant, terrible

neaten *vb* = **tidy up**, arrange, clean up, groom, put to rights, straighten out *or* up, tidy, trim

neatly *adv* **1, 2** = **tidily**, accurately, daintily, fastidiously, methodically, nicely, smartly, sprucely, systematically **3** = **elegantly**, adeptly, adroitly, agilely, aptly, cleverly, deftly, dexterously, efficiently, effortlessly, expertly, gracefully, handily, nimbly, precisely, skilfully, stylishly

neatness *n* **1, 2** = **tidiness**, accuracy, daintiness, fastidiousness, methodicalness, niceness, nicety, orderliness, smartness, spruceness, straightness, trimness **3** = **elegance**, adeptness, adroitness, agility, aptness, cleverness, deftness, dexterity, efficiency, effortlessness, expertness, grace, gracefulness, handiness, nimbleness, preciseness, precision, skilfulness, skill, style, stylishness

nebulous *adj* **1** = **vague**, ambiguous, amorphous, cloudy, confused, dim, hazy, imprecise, indefinite, indeterminate, indistinct, misty, murky, obscure, shadowy, shapeless, uncertain, unclear, unformed

necessarily *adv* **1** = **inevitably**, accordingly, automatically, by definition, compulsorily, consequently, incontrovertibly, ineluctably, inexorably, irresistibly, naturally, *nolens volens,* of course, of necessity, perforce, willy-nilly **2** = **certainly**, undoubtedly

necessary *adj* **1** = **needed**, compulsory, *de rigueur,* essential, imperative, indispensable, mandatory, needful, obligatory, required, requisite, vital **2** = **certain**, fated, inescapable, inevitable, inexorable, unavoidable
Antonyms *adj* ≠ **needed:** dispensable, expendable, inessential, nonessential, superfluous, unnecessary ≠ **certain:** unnecessary

necessitate *vb* **1, 2** = **compel**, call for, coerce, constrain, demand, entail, force, impel, make necessary, oblige, require

necessitous *adj* = **needy**, destitute, distressed, impecunious, impoverished, indigent, penniless, penurious, poor, poverty-stricken

necessity *n* **1** *sometimes plural* = **essentials**, exigencies, fundamentals, indispensables, needs, requirements **2** = **essential**, desideratum, fundamental, necessary, need, prerequisite, requirement, requisite, *sine qua non,* want **3** = **inevitability**, compulsion, destiny, fate, inexorableness, obligation **4** = **needfulness**, demand, exigency, indispensability, need, requirement **5** = **poverty**, destitution, extremity, indigence, need, penury, privation

neckcloth *n* = **neckerchief**, cravat, kerchief, scarf

necromancer *n* **2** = **magician**, black magician, diviner, enchanter, enchantress, sorcerer, sorceress, warlock, witch, wizard

necromancy *n* **2** = **magic**, black art, black

nekromanteia, from *nekros* corpse; (sense 2) from Med. L *nigromantia,* from L *niger* black, which replaced *necro-* through folk etymology]
▸ ˈ**necroˌmancer** *n* ▸ ˌ**necroˈmantic** *adj*

necrophilia (ˌnɛkrəʊˈfɪlɪə) *n* sexual attraction for or sexual intercourse with dead bodies. Also called: **necromania, necrophilism.**
▸**necrophile** (ˈnɛkrəʊˌfaɪl) *n* ▸ ˌ**necroˈphilic** *adj*

necropolis ➊ (nɛˈkrɒpəlɪs) *n, pl* **necropolises** *or* **necropoleis** (-ˌleɪs). a burial site or cemetery. [C19: from Gk, from *nekros* dead + *polis* city]

necropsy (ˈnɛkrɒpsɪ) *or* **necroscopy** (nɛˈkrɒskəpɪ) *n, pl* **necropsies** *or* **necroscopies.** another name for **autopsy.** [C19: from Gk *nekros* dead body + *opsis* sight]

necrosis (nɛˈkrəʊsɪs) *n* **1** the death of one or more cells in the body, usually within a localized area, as from an interruption of the blood supply. **2** death of plant tissue due to disease, frost, etc. [C17: NL, from Gk *nekrōsis,* from *nekroun* to kill, from *nekros* corpse]
▸**necrotic** (nɛˈkrɒtɪk) *adj*

nectar (ˈnɛktə) *n* **1** a sugary fluid produced in the nectaries of flowers and collected by bees. **2** *Classical myth.* the drink of the gods. Cf. **ambrosia** (sense 1). **3** any delicious drink. [C16: via L from Gk *nektar*]
▸ ˈ**nectarous** *adj*

nectarine (ˈnɛktərɪn) *n* **1** a variety of peach tree. **2** the smooth-skinned fruit of this tree. [C17: apparently from NECTAR]

nectary (ˈnɛktərɪ) *n, pl* **nectaries.** any of various structures secreting nectar that occur in the flowers, leaves, stipules, etc., of a plant. [C18: from NL *nectarium,* from NECTAR]

ned (nɛd) *n Scot. sl.* a hooligan. [from ?]

NEDC *abbrev. for* National Economic Development Council. Also (inf.): **Neddy** (ˈnɛdɪ).

neddy (ˈnɛdɪ) *n, pl* **neddies.** a child's word for a **donkey.** [C18: from *Ned,* pet form of *Edward*]

née *or* **nee** (neɪ) *adj* indicating the maiden name of a married woman: *Mrs Bloggs née Blandish.* [C19: from F: p.p. (fem) of *naître* to be born, from L *nascī*]

need ➊ (niːd) *vb* **1** (*tr*) to be in want of: *to need money.* **2** (*tr*) to be obliged: *to need to do more work.* **3** (takes an infinitive without *to*) used as an auxiliary to express necessity or obligation and does not add *-s* when used with *he, she, it,* and singular nouns: *need he go?* **4** (*intr*) *Arch.* to be essential to: *there needs no reason for this.* ◆ *n* **5** the fact or an instance of feeling the lack of something: *he has need of a new coat.* **6** a requirement: *the need for vengeance.* **7** necessity or obligation: *no need to be frightened.* **8** distress: *a friend in need.* **9** poverty or destitution. ◆ See also **needs.** [OE *nēad, nied*]

needful ➊ (ˈniːdfʊl) *adj* **1** necessary; required. **2** *Arch.* poverty-stricken. ◆ *n* **3 the needful.** *Inf.* what is necessary, esp. money.
▸ ˈ**needfulness** *n*

needle ➊ (ˈniːdᵊl) *n* **1** a pointed slender piece of metal with a hole in it through which thread is passed for sewing. **2** a somewhat larger rod with a point at one end, used in knitting. **3** a similar instrument with a hook at one end for crocheting. **4** a small thin pointed device, esp. one made of stainless steel, used to transmit the vibrations from a gramophone record to the pick-up. Cf. **stylus** (sense 3). **5** *Med.* the long hollow pointed part of a hypodermic syringe, which is inserted into the body. **6** *Surgery.* a pointed instrument, often curved, for suturing, puncturing, or ligating. **7** a long narrow stiff leaf in which water loss is greatly reduced: *pine needles.* **8** any slender sharp spine. **9** a pointer on the scale of a measuring instrument. **10** short for **magnetic needle.** **11** a sharp pointed instrument used in engraving. **12** anything long and pointed, such as an obelisk. **13** *Inf.* **13a** anger or intense rivalry, esp. in a sporting encounter. **13b** (*as modifier*): *a needle match.* **14 have** *or* **get the needle.** *Brit. inf.* to feel dislike, nervousness, or annoyance: *she got the needle after he had refused her invitation.* ◆ *vb* **needles, needling, needled.** (*tr*) **15** *Inf.* to goad or provoke, as by constant criticism. **16** to sew, embroider, or prick (fabric) with a needle. [OE *nǣdl*]

needlecord (ˈniːdᵊlˌkɔːd) *n* a corduroy fabric with narrow ribs.

needlepoint (ˈniːdᵊlˌpɔɪnt) *n* **1** embroidery done on canvas with various stitches so as to resemble tapestry. **2** another name for **point lace.**

needless ➊ (ˈniːdlɪs) *adj* not required; unnecessary.
▸ ˈ**needlessly** *adv* ▸ ˈ**needlessness** *n*

needle time *n* the limited time allocated by a radio channel to the broadcasting of music from records.

needlewoman (ˈniːdᵊlˌwʊmən) *n, pl* **needlewomen.** a woman who does needlework; seamstress.

needlework ➊ (ˈniːdᵊlˌwɜːk) *n* sewing and embroidery.

needs (niːdz) *adv* **1** (preceded or foll. by *must*) of necessity: *we must needs go.* ◆ *pl n* **2** what is required; necessities: *his needs are modest.*

needy ➊ (ˈniːdɪ) *adj* **needier, neediest. a** in need of practical or emotional support; distressed. **b** (*as collective n; preceded by the*): *the needy.*

ne'er (nɛə) *adv* a poetic contraction of **never.**

ne'er-do-well ➊ *n* **1** an improvident, irresponsible, or lazy person. ◆ *adj* **2** useless; worthless: *your ne'er-do-well schemes.*

nefarious ➊ (nɪˈfɛərɪəs) *adj* evil; wicked; sinful. [C17: from L *nefārius,* from *nefās* unlawful deed, from *nē* not + *fās* divine law]
▸**neˈfariously** *adv* ▸**neˈfariousness** *n*

neg. *abbrev. for* negative(ly).

negate ➊ (nɪˈgeɪt) *vb* **negates, negating, negated.** (*tr*) **1** to nullify; invalidate. **2** to contradict. [C17: from L *negāre,* from *neg-,* var. of *nec* not + *aio* I say]
▸**neˈgator** *or* **neˈgater** *n*

negation ➊ (nɪˈgeɪʃən) *n* **1** the opposite or absence of something. **2** a negative thing or condition. **3** the act of negating. **4** *Logic.* a proposition that is the denial of another proposition and is true only if the original proposition is false.

negative ➊ (ˈnɛgətɪv) *adj* **1** expressing a refusal or denial: *a negative answer.* **2** lacking positive qualities, such as enthusiasm or optimism. **3** showing opposition or resistance. **4** measured in a direction opposite to that regarded as positive. **5** *Biol.* indicating movement or growth away from a stimulus: *negative geotropism.* **6** *Med.* indicating absence of the disease or condition for which a test was made. **7** another word for **minus** (senses 3b, 4). **8** *Physics.* **8a** (of an electric charge) having the same polarity as the charge of an electron. **8b** (of a body, system, ion, etc.) having a negative electric charge; having an excess of electrons. **9** short for **electronegative.** **10** of or relating to a photographic negative. **11** *Logic.* (of a categorial proposition) denying the satisfaction by the subject of the predicate, as in *some men are irrational; no pigs have wings.* ◆ *n* **12** a statement or act of denial or refusal. **13** a negative thing. **14** *Photog.* a piece of photographic film or a plate, previously exposed and developed, showing an image that, in black-and-white photography, has a reversal of tones. **15** *Physics.* a negative object, such as a terminal or a plate in a voltaic cell. **16** a sentence or other linguistic element with a negative meaning, as the English word *not.* **17** a quantity less than zero. **18** *Logic.* a negative proposition. **19 in the negative.** indicating denial or refusal. ◆ *vb* **negatives, negativing, negatived.** (*tr*) **20** to deny; negate. **21** to show to be false; disprove. **22** to refuse consent to or approval of: *the proposal was negatived.*
▸ ˈ**negatively** *adv* ▸ ˈ**negativeness** *or* ˌ**negaˈtivity** *n*

negative equity *n* the state of holding a property the value of which is less than the amount of mortgage still unpaid.

negative feedback *n* See **feedback.**

negative resistance *n* a characteristic of certain electronic components in which an increase in the applied voltage increases the resistance, producing a proportional decrease in current.

negative sign *n* the symbol (–) used to indicate a negative quantity or a subtraction.

negativism (ˈnɛgətɪvˌɪzəm) *n* **1** a tendency to be unconstructively critical. **2** any sceptical or derisive system of thought.
▸ ˈ**negativist** *n, adj*

neglect ➊ (nɪˈglɛkt) *vb* (*tr*) **1** to fail to give due care, attention, or time to: *to neglect a child.* **2** to fail (to do something) through carelessness:

THESAURUS

magic, demonology, divination, enchantment, sorcery, voodoo, witchcraft, witchery, wizardry

necropolis *n* = **cemetery**, burial ground, churchyard, God's acre, graveyard

need *vb* **1** = **lack**, miss, want ◆ *n* **5** = **lack**, inadequacy, insufficiency, paucity, shortage **6, 7** = **requirement**, demand, necessity, obligation **9** = **poverty**, deprivation, destitution, distress, extremity, impecuniousness, indigence, neediness, penury, privation

needed *adj* **1** = **necessary**, called for, desired, lacked, required, wanted

needful *adj* **1** = **necessary**, essential, indispensable, needed, required, requisite, stipulated, vital

needle *vb* **15** *Informal* = **irritate**, aggravate (*inf.*), annoy, bait, be on one's back (*sl.*), gall, get in one's hair (*inf.*), get on one's nerves (*inf.*), get under one's skin (*inf.*), goad, harass, hassle (*inf.*), irk, nag, nark (*Brit., Austral., & NZ sl.*), nettle, pester, provoke, rile, ruffle, sting

needless *adj* = **unnecessary**, causeless, excessive, gratuitous, groundless, nonessential, pointless, redundant, superfluous, uncalled-for, undesired, unwanted, useless

Antonyms *adj* beneficial, essential, obligatory, required, useful

needlework *n* = **embroidery**, fancywork, needlecraft, sewing, stitching, tailoring

needy *adj* **a** = **poor**, deprived, destitute, dirt-poor, disadvantaged, down at heel (*inf.*), impecunious, impoverished, indigent, on the breadline (*inf.*), penniless, poverty-stricken, underprivileged

Antonyms *adj* affluent, comfortable, moneyed, prosperous, rich, wealthy, well-off, well-to-do

ne'er-do-well *n* **1** = **layabout**, black sheep, good-for-nothing, idler, loafer, loser, skiver (*Brit. sl.*), wastrel

nefarious *adj* = **wicked**, abominable, atrocious, base, criminal, depraved, detestable, dreadful, evil, execrable, foul, heinous, horrible, infamous, infernal, iniquitous, monstrous, odious, opprobrious, shameful, sinful, vicious, vile, villainous

Antonyms *adj* admirable, good, honest, honourable, just, noble, praiseworthy, upright, virtuous

negate *vb* **1** = **invalidate**, abrogate, annul, cancel, countermand, neutralize, nullify, obviate, repeal, rescind, retract, reverse, revoke, void, wipe out **2** = **deny**, contradict, disallow, disprove, gainsay (*arch. or literary*), oppose, rebut, refute

Antonyms *vb* ≠ **deny**: affirm, assert, attest, avouch, avow, certify, confirm, declare, maintain, pronounce, ratify, state, swear, testify

negation *n* **1** = **denial**, antithesis, antonym, contradiction, contrary, converse, counterpart, disavowal, disclaimer, inverse, opposite, rejection, renunciation, reverse **3** = **cancellation**, neutralization, nullification

negative *adj* **1** = **contradictory**, contrary, denying, dissenting, opposing, recusant, refusing, rejecting, resisting **2** = **pessimistic**, colourless, cynical, gloomy, jaundiced, neutral, unenthusiastic, uninterested, weak **3** = **antagonistic**, contrary, uncooperative, unwilling ◆ *n* **12** = **contradiction**, denial, refusal

Antonyms *adj* ≠ **contradictory**: affirmative, approving, assenting, concurring, positive ≠ **pessimistic**: cheerful, enthusiastic, optimistic, positive

neglect *vb* **2** = **forget**, be remiss, evade, let slide, omit, pass over, procrastinate, shirk, skimp **3** = **disregard**, contemn, discount, disdain, ignore, leave alone, overlook, pass by, rehe neglected to tell her. **3** to disregard. ◆ *n* **4** lack of due care or attention; negligence: *the child starved through neglect.* **5** the act or an instance of neglecting or the state of being neglected. [C16: from L *neglegere,* from *nec* not + *legere* to select]

neglectful ➊ (nɪ'glɛktfʊl) *adj* (when *postpositive,* foll. by *of*) careless; heedless.

negligee *or* **negligée** ('nɛglɪˌʒeɪ) *n* **1** a woman's light dressing gown, esp. one that is lace-trimmed. **2** a thin and revealing woman's nightdress. **3** (formerly) any informal women's attire. [C18: from F *négligée,* p.p. (fem) of *négliger* to NEGLECT]

negligence ➊ ('nɛglɪdʒəns) *n* **1** the state of being negligent. **2** a negligent act. **3** *Law.* a civil wrong whereby the defendant is in breach of a legal duty of care, resulting in injury to the plaintiff.

negligent ➊ ('nɛglɪdʒənt) *adj* **1** lacking attention, care, or concern; neglectful. **2** careless or nonchalant.
▸**'negligently** *adv*

negligible ➊ ('nɛglɪdʒəbᵊl) *adj* so small, unimportant, etc., as to be not worth considering.
▸**'negligibly** *adv*

negotiable ➊ (nɪ'gəʊʃəbᵊl) *adj* **1** able to be negotiated. **2** (of a bill of exchange, promissory note, etc.) legally transferable in title from one party to another.
▸**neˌgotia'bility** *n*

negotiable instrument *n* a legal document, such as a cheque or bill of exchange, that is freely negotiable.

negotiate ➊ (nɪ'gəʊʃɪˌeɪt) *vb* **negotiates, negotiating, negotiated. 1** to talk (with others) to achieve (an agreement, etc.). **2** (*tr*) to succeed in passing round or over. **3** (*tr*) *Finance.* **3a** to transfer (a negotiable commercial paper) to another in return for value received. **3b** to sell (financial assets). **3c** to arrange for (a loan). [C16: from L *negōtiārī* to do business, from *negōtium* business, from *nec* not + *ōtium* leisure]
▸**neˌgoti'ation** *n* ▸**ne'gotiˌator** *n*

Negress ('ni:grɪs) *n* a female Black person.

Negrillo (nɪ'grɪləʊ) *n, pl* **Negrillos** *or* **Negrilloes.** a member of a dwarfish Negroid race of central and southern Africa. [C19: from Sp., dim. of *negro* black]

Negrito (nɪ'gri:təʊ) *n, pl* **Negritos** *or* **Negritoes.** a member of any of various dwarfish Negroid peoples of SE Asia and Melanesia. [C19: from Sp., dim. of *negro* black]

negritude ('ni:grɪˌtju:d, 'nɛg-) *n* **1** the fact of being a Negro. **2** awareness and cultivation of the Negro heritage, values, and culture. [C20: from F, from *nègre* NEGRO]

Negro ('ni:grəʊ) *Old-fashioned.* ◆ *n, pl* **Negroes. 1** a member of any of the dark-skinned indigenous peoples of Africa and their descendants elsewhere. ◆ *adj* **2** relating to or characteristic of Negroes. [C16: from Sp. or Port.: black, from L *niger*]
▸**'Negroˌism** *n*

Negroid ('ni:grɔɪd) *adj* **1** denoting, relating to, or belonging to one of the major racial groups of mankind, characterized by brown-black skin, tightly curled hair, a short nose, and full lips. ◆ *n* **2** a member of this racial group.

negus ('ni:gəs) *n, pl* **neguses.** a hot drink of port and lemon juice, usually spiced and sweetened. [C18: after Col. Francis *Negus* (died 1732), its E inventor]

Negus ('ni:gəs) *n, pl* **Neguses.** *History.* a title of the emperor of Ethiopia. [from Amharic: king]

Neh. *Bible. abbrev. for* Nehemiah.

neigh (neɪ) *n* **1** the high-pitched cry of a horse. ◆ *vb* **2** to make a neigh or utter with a sound like a neigh. [OE *hnǣgan*]

neighbour ➊ *or US* **neighbor** ('neɪbə) *n* **1** a person who lives near or next to another. **2a** a person or thing near or next to another. **2b** (*as modifier*): *neighbour states.* ◆ *vb* **3** (when *intr,* often foll. by *on*) to be or live close to. [OE *nēahbūr,* from *nēah* NIGH + *būr, gebūr* dweller; see BOOR]
▸**'neighbouring** *or US* **'neighboring** *adj*

neighbourhood ➊ *or US* **neighborhood** ('neɪbəˌhʊd) *n* **1** the immediate environment; surroundings. **2** a district where people live. **3** the people in a particular area. **4** *Maths.* the set of all points whose distance from a given point is less than a specified value. **5** (*modifier*) living or situated in and serving the needs of a local area: *a neighbourhood community worker.* **6 in the neighbourhood of.** approximately.

neighbourhood watch *n* a scheme in which members of a community agree to take joint responsibility for keeping a watch on each other's property, as a way of preventing crime.

neighbourly ➊ *or US* **neighborly** ('neɪbəlɪ) *adj* kind, friendly, or sociable, as befits a neighbour.
▸**'neighbourliness** *or US* **'neighborliness** *n*

neither ('naɪðə, 'ni:ðə) *determiner* **1a** not one nor the other (of two). **1b** (*as pronoun*): *neither can win.* ◆ *conj* **2** (*coordinating*) **2a** (used preceding alternatives joined by *nor*) not: *neither John nor Mary nor Joe went.* **2b** another word for **nor** (sense 2). ◆ *adv* (*sentence modifier*) **3** *Not standard.* another word for **either** (sense 4). [C13 (lit.: *ne either* not either): changed from OE *nāwther,* from *nāhwæther,* from *nā* not + *hwæther* which of two]

> **USAGE NOTE** A verb following a compound subject that uses *neither...(nor)* should be in the singular if both subjects are in the singular: *neither Jack nor John has done the work.*

nekton ('nɛktɒn) *n* the population of free-swimming animals that inhabits the middle depths of a sea or lake. [C19: via G from Gk *nēkton* a swimming thing, from *nēkhein* to swim]

nelly ('nɛlɪ) *n* **not on your nelly.** (*sentence substitute*). *Brit. sl.* certainly not.

nelson ('nɛlsən) *n* any wrestling hold in which a wrestler places his arm or arms under his opponent's arm or arms from behind and exerts pressure with the palms of his hands on the back of his opponent's neck. [C19: from a proper name]

nematic (nɪ'mætɪk) *adj Chem.* (of a substance) existing in or having a mesomorphic state in which a linear orientation of the molecules causes anisotropic properties. [C20: NEMAT(O)- (referring to the threadlike chains of molecules in liquid) + -IC]

nemato- *or before a vowel* **nemat-** *combining form.* indicating a threadlike form: *nematocyst.* [from Gk *nēma* thread]

nematocyst ('nɛmətəˌsɪst, nɪ'mætə-) *n* a structure in coelenterates, such as jellyfish, consisting of a capsule containing a hollow coiled thread that can sting or paralyse.

nematode ('nɛməˌtəʊd) *n* any of a class of unsegmented worms having a tough outer cuticle, including the hookworm and filaria. Also called: **nematode worm, roundworm.**

Nembutal ('nɛmbjʊˌtɑ:l) *n* a trademark for **pentobarbitone sodium.**

nemertean (nɪ'mɜ:tɪən) *or* **nemertine** ('nɛməˌtaɪn) *n* **1** any of a class of soft flattened ribbon-like marine worms having an eversible threadlike proboscis. ◆ *adj* **2** of or belonging to the *Nemertea.* [C19: via NL from Gk *Nēmertēs* a NEREID]

nemesia (nɪ'mi:ʒə) *n* any plant of a southern African genus cultivated for their brightly coloured flowers. [C19: NL, from Gk *nemesion,* name of a plant resembling this]

Nemesis ➊ ('nɛmɪsɪs) *n* **1** *Greek myth.* the goddess of retribution and vengeance. **2** (*pl* **Nemeses** (-ˌsi:z)). (*sometimes not cap.*) any agency of retribution and vengeance. [C16: via L from Gk: righteous wrath, from *nemein* to distribute what is due]

nemophila (nɛ'mɒfɪlə) *n* an annual trailing plant with blue flowers. [from Gk *nemos* grove + *philos* loving]

neo- *or sometimes before a vowel* **ne-** *combining form.* **1** (*sometimes cap.*) new, recent, or a modern form: *neoclassicism; neocolonialism.* **2** (*usually cap.*) the most recent subdivision of a geological period: *Neogene.* [from Gk *neos* new]

neoclassicism (ˌni:əʊ'klæsɪˌsɪzəm) *n* **1** a late 18th- and early 19th-century style in architecture and art, based on classical models. **2** *Music.* a movement of the 1920s that sought to avoid the emotionalism of late romantic music.
▸**neoclassical** (ˌni:əʊ'klæsɪkᵊl) *or* ˌ**neo'classic** *adj*

neocolonialism (ˌni:əʊkə'ləʊnɪəˌlɪzəm) *n* (in the modern world) political control by an outside power of a country that is in theory independent, esp. through the domination of its economy.

THESAURUS

buff, scorn, slight, spurn, turn one's back on ◆ *n* **4** = **negligence,** carelessness, default, dereliction, failure, forgetfulness, laxity, laxness, neglectfulness, oversight, remissness, slackness, slovenliness
Antonyms *vb* ≠ **disregard:** appreciate, attend to, notice, observe, regard, remember, value ◆ *n* ≠ **negligence, disregard:** attention, care, consideration, notice, regard, respect

neglected *adj* **1** = **abandoned,** derelict, overgrown **3** = **disregarded,** unappreciated, underestimated, undervalued

neglectful *adj* = **careless,** disregardful, heedless, inattentive, indifferent, lax, negligent, remiss, thoughtless, uncaring, unmindful

negligence *n* **1, 2** = **carelessness,** default, dereliction, disregard, failure, forgetfulness, heedlessness, inadvertence, inattention, inattentiveness, indifference, laxity, laxness, neglect, omission, oversight, remissness, shortcoming, slackness, thoughtlessness

negligent *adj* **1, 2** = **careless,** cursory, disregardful, forgetful, heedless, inadvertent, inattentive, indifferent, neglectful, nonchalant, offhand, regardless, remiss, slack, slapdash, slipshod, thoughtless, unmindful, unthinking
Antonyms *adj* attentive, careful, considerate, mindful, painstaking, rigorous, thorough, thoughtful

negligible *adj* = **insignificant,** imperceptible, inconsequential, minor, minute, nickel-and-dime (*US sl.*), petty, small, trifling, trivial, unimportant
Antonyms *adj* important, noteworthy, significant, vital

negotiable *adj* **1** = **debatable,** discussable *or* discussible **2** = **transactional,** transferable

negotiate *vb* **1** = **deal,** adjudicate, arbitrate, arrange, bargain, conciliate, confer, consult, contract, cut a deal, debate, discuss, handle, manage, mediate, parley, settle, transact, work out **2** = **get round,** clear, cross, get over, get past, pass, pass through, surmount

negotiation *n* **1** = **bargaining,** arbitration, debate, diplomacy, discussion, mediation, transaction, wheeling and dealing (*inf.*)

negotiator *n* **1** = **mediator,** adjudicator, ambassador, arbitrator, delegate, diplomat, honest broker, intermediary, moderator

neighbourhood *n* **1, 2** = **district,** community, confines, environs, locale, locality, precincts, proximity, purlieus, quarter, region, surroundings, vicinity

neighbouring *adj* **3** = **nearby,** abutting, adjacent, adjoining, bordering, connecting, contiguous, near, nearest, next, surrounding
Antonyms *adj* distant, far, far-off, remote

neighbourly *adj* = **helpful,** amiable, civil, companionable, considerate, friendly, genial, harmonious, hospitable, kind, obliging, sociable, social, well-disposed

Nemesis *n* **2** *sometimes not cap.* = **retribution,** destiny, destruction, fate, vengeance

▸ ˌneocoˈlonialist *n, adj*

Neo-Darwinism (ˌniːəʊˈdɑːwɪnˌɪzəm) *n* a modern theory of evolution that relates Darwinism to the occurrence of inheritable variation by genetic mutation.

neodymium (ˌniːəʊˈdɪmɪəm) *n* a toxic silvery-white metallic element of the lanthanide series. Symbol: Nd; atomic no.: 60; atomic wt.: 144.24. [C19: NL; see NEO- + DIDYMIUM]

neogothic (ˌniːəʊˈgɒθɪk) *n* another name for **Gothic Revival.**

Neolithic (ˌniːəˈlɪθɪk) *n* **1** the cultural period that was characterized by primitive farming and the use of polished stone and flint tools and weapons. ◆ *adj* **2** relating to this period.

neologism ➊ (nɪˈɒləˌdʒɪzəm) *or* **neology** *n, pl* **neologisms** *or* **neologies. 1** a newly coined word, or a phrase or familiar word used in a new sense. **2** the practice of using or introducing neologisms. [C18: via F from NEO- + *-logism,* from Gk *logos* word]

▸ neˈologist *n*

neologize *or* **neologise** (nɪˈɒləˌdʒaɪz) *vb* **neologizes, neologizing, neologized** *or* **neologises, neologising, neologised.** (*intr*) to invent or use neologisms.

neomycin (ˌniːəʊˈmaɪsɪn) *n* an antibiotic obtained from the bacterium *Streptomyces fradiae,* administered in the treatment of skin and eye infections. [C20: from NEO- + Gk *mukēs* fungus + -IN]

neon (ˈniːɒn) *n* **1** a colourless odourless rare gaseous element occurring in trace amounts in the atmosphere: used in illuminated signs and lights. Symbol: Ne; atomic no.: 10; atomic wt.: 20.179. **2** (*modifier*) of or illuminated by neon: *neon sign.* [C19: via NL from Gk *neon* new]

neonatal (ˌniːəʊˈneɪtᵊl) *adj* occurring in or relating to the first few weeks of life in human babies.

▸ ˈneoˌnate *n*

neon light *n* a glass bulb or tube containing neon at low pressure that gives a pink or red glow when a voltage is applied.

neophyte ➊ (ˈniːəʊˌfaɪt) *n* **1** a person newly converted to a religious faith. **2** a novice in a religious order. **3** a beginner. [C16: via Church L from New Testament Gk *neophutos* recently planted, from *neos* new + *phuton* a plant]

neoplasm (ˈniːəʊˌplæzəm) *n Pathol.* any abnormal new growth of tissue; tumour.

Neo-Platonism (ˌniːəʊˈpleɪtəˌnɪzəm) *n* a philosophical system which was developed in the 3rd century A.D. as a synthesis of Platonic, Pythagorean, and Aristotelian elements.

▸ **Neo-Platonic** (ˌniːəʊpləˈtɒnɪk) *adj* ▸ ˌ**Neo-**ˈ**Platonist** *n, adj*

neoprene (ˈniːəʊˌpriːn) *n* a synthetic rubber obtained by the polymerization of chloroprene, a colourless liquid derivative of butadiene, resistant to oil and ageing and used in waterproof products. [C20: from NEO- + PR(OPYL) + -ENE]

neoteny (nɪˈɒtənɪ) *n* the persistence of larval or fetal features in the adult form of an animal. [C19: from NL *neotenia,* from Gk NEO- + *teinein* to stretch]

neoteric (ˌniːəʊˈtɛrɪk) *Rare.* ◆ *adj* **1** belonging to a new fashion or trend; modern. ◆ *n* **2** a new writer or philosopher. [C16: via LL from Gk *neōterikos* young, fresh, from *neoteros* younger, more recent, from *neos* new, recent]

Nepali (nɪˈpɔːlɪ) *n* **1** the official language of Nepal, also spoken in Sikkim and parts of India. **2** (*pl* **Nepali** *or* **Nepalis**) a native or inhabitant of Nepal; a Nepalese. ◆ *adj* **3** of or relating to Nepal, its inhabitants, or their language; Nepalese.

nepenthe (nɪˈpɛnθɪ) *or* **nepenthes** (nɪˈpɛnθiːz) *n* a drug that ancient writers referred to as a means of forgetting grief or trouble. [C16: via L from Gk *nēpenthes* sedative made from a herb, from *nē-* not + *penthos* grief]

nepeta (ˈnɛpɛtə, nəˈpetə) *n* any of a genus of plants found in N temperate regions. It includes catmint. [from L]

nephew (ˈnɛvjuː, ˈnɛf-) *n* a son of one's sister or brother. [C13: from OF *neveu,* from L *nepōs*]

nephology (nɪˈfɒlədʒɪ) *n* the study of clouds. [C19: from Gk *nephos* cloud + -LOGY]

nephridium (nɪˈfrɪdɪəm) *n, pl* **nephridia** (-ɪə). a simple excretory organ of many invertebrates, consisting of a tube through which waste products pass to the exterior. [C19: NL: little kidney]

nephrite (ˈnɛfraɪt) *n* a tough fibrous mineral: a variety of jade. Also called: **kidney stone.** [C18: via G from Gk *nephros* kidney; it was thought to help in kidney disorders]

nephritic (nɪˈfrɪtɪk) *adj* **1** of or relating to the kidneys. **2** relating to or affected with nephritis.

nephritis (nɪˈfraɪtɪs) *n* inflammation of a kidney.

nephro- *or before a vowel* **nephr-** *combining form.* kidney or kidneys: *nephritis.* [from Gk *nephros*]

nephrology (nɪˈfrɒlədʒɪ) *n* the branch of medicine concerned with diseases of the kidney.

▸ neˈphrologist *n*

nephron (ˈnɛfrɒn) *n* one of the units of the kidney that secretes urine, via ducts, into the ureter.

nephroscope (ˈnɛfrəˌskəʊp) *n* a tubular medical instrument inserted through an incision in the skin to enable examination of a kidney.

▸ **nephroscopy** (nɪˈfrɒskəpɪ) *n*

ne plus ultra *Latin.* (ˈneɪ ˈplʊs ˈʊltrɑː) *n* the extreme or perfect point or state. [lit.: not more beyond (that is, go no further), allegedly a warning to sailors inscribed on the Pillars of Hercules at Gibraltar]

nepotism ➊ (ˈnɛpəˌtɪzəm) *n* favouritism shown to relatives or close friends by those with power. [C17: from It. *nepotismo,* from *nepote* NEPHEW, from the former papal practice of granting favours to nephews or other relatives]

▸ ˈnepotist *n*

Neptune[1] (ˈnɛptjuːn) *n* the Roman god of the sea. Greek counterpart: **Poseidon.**

Neptune[2] (ˈnɛptjuːn) *n* the eighth planet from the sun, having two satellites, Triton and Nereid.

neptunium (nɛpˈtjuːnɪəm) *n* a silvery metallic element synthesized in the production of plutonium and occurring in trace amounts in uranium ores. Symbol: Np; atomic no.: 93; half-life of most stable isotope, ^{237}Np: 2.14×10^6 years. [C20: from NEPTUNE[2], the planet beyond Uranus, because neptunium is beyond uranium in the periodic table]

NERC *abbrev. for* Natural Environment Research Council.

nerd ➊ *or* **nurd** (nɜːd) *n Sl.* **1** a boring or unpopular person, esp. one obsessed with something specified: *computer nerd.* **2** a stupid and feeble person. [C20: from ?]

▸ ˈ**nerdish** *or* ˈ**nurdish** *adj* ▸ ˈ**nerdy** *or* ˈ**nurdy** *adj*

Nereid (ˈnɪərɪɪd) *n, pl* **Nereides** (nəˈriːəˌdiːz). *Greek myth.* any of 50 sea nymphs who were the daughters of the sea god Nereus. [C17: via L from Gk]

nerine (nɪˈraɪnɪ; *S. African* nəˈriːn) *n* any of a genus of bulbous plants native to South Africa and grown elsewhere as greenhouse plants for their pink, red, or orange flowers: includes the Guernsey lily. [after the water nymph *Nerine* in Roman myth]

neroli oil *or* **neroli** (ˈnɪərəlɪ) *n* a brown oil distilled from the flowers of various orange trees: used in perfumery. [C17: after Anne Marie de la Tremoïlle of *Neroli,* French-born It. princess believed to have discovered it]

nervate (ˈnɜːveɪt) *adj* (of leaves) having veins.

nervation (nɜːˈveɪʃən) *or* **nervature** (ˈnɜːvətʃə) *n* a less common word for **venation.**

nerve ➊ (nɜːv) *n* **1** any of the cordlike bundles of fibres that conduct impulses between the brain or spinal cord and another part of the body. **2** bravery or steadfastness. **3 lose one's nerve.** to become timid, esp. failing to perform some audacious act. **4** *Inf.* effrontery; impudence. **5** muscle or sinew (often in **strain every nerve**). **6** a vein in a leaf or an insect's wing. ◆ *vb* **nerves, nerving, nerved.** (*tr*) **7** to give courage to (oneself); steel (oneself). **8** to provide with nerve or nerves. ◆ See also **nerves.** [C16: from L *nervus;* rel. to Gk *neuron*]

nerve block *n* induction of anaesthesia in a specific part of the body by injecting a local anaesthetic close to the sensory nerves that supply it.

nerve cell *n* another name for **neurone.**

nerve centre *n* **1** a group of nerve cells associated with a specific function. **2** a principal source of control over any complex activity.

nerve fibre *n* a threadlike extension of a nerve cell; axon.

nerve gas *n* any of various poisonous gases that have a paralysing effect on the central nervous system that can be fatal.

nerve impulse *n* the electrical wave transmitted along a nerve fibre, usually following stimulation of the nerve-cell body.

nerveless ➊ (ˈnɜːvlɪs) *adj* **1** calm and collected. **2** listless or feeble.

▸ ˈ**nervelessly** *adv*

nerve-racking ➊ *or* **nerve-wracking** *adj* very distressing, exhausting, or harrowing.

nerves ➊ (nɜːvz) *pl n Inf.* **1** the imagined source of emotional control: *my nerves won't stand it.* **2** anxiety, tension, or imbalance: *she's all nerves.* **3 get on one's nerves.** to irritate or upset one.

nervine (ˈnɜːviːn) *adj* **1** having a soothing effect upon the nerves. ◆ *n* **2** a nervine agent. [C17: from NL *nervīnus,* from L *nervus* NERVE]

THESAURUS

neologism *n* **1** = **new word**, buzz word (*inf.*), coinage, new phrase, nonce word, vogue word

neophyte *n* **1** = **catechumen**, proselyte **2** = **novitiate**, novice **3** = **beginner**, amateur, apprentice, disciple, learner, novice, probationer, pupil, recruit, student, trainee, tyro

nepotism *n* = **favouritism**, bias, partiality, patronage, preferential treatment

nerd *n* **1** *Slang* = **bore**, anorak (*inf.*), geek (*inf.*), obsessive, trainspotter (*inf.*) **2** = **fool**, booby, divvy (*Brit. sl.*), drip (*inf.*), plonker (*sl.*), prat (*sl.*), sap (*sl.*), schmuck (*US sl.*), simpleton, sucker (*sl.*), twit (*inf., chiefly Brit.*), wally (*sl.*), weed, wimp (*inf.*)

nerve *n* **2** = **bravery**, balls (*taboo sl.*), bottle (*Brit. sl.*), coolness, courage, daring, determination, endurance, energy, face (*inf.*), fearlessness, firmness, force, fortitude, gameness, grit, guts (*inf.*), hardihood, intrepidity, mettle, might, pluck, resolution, spirit, spunk (*inf.*), steadfastness, vigour, will **4** *Informal* = **impudence**, audacity, boldness, brass neck (*Brit. inf.*), brazenness, cheek (*inf.*), chutzpah (*US & Canad. inf.*), effrontery, front, gall, impertinence, insolence, neck (*inf.*), sassiness (*US sl.*), sauce (*inf.*), temerity ◆ *vb* **7** = **brace (oneself)**, embolden (oneself), encourage (oneself), fortify (oneself), gee (oneself) up, hearten (oneself), invigorate (oneself), steel (oneself), strengthen (oneself)

nerveless *adj* **1** = **calm**, collected, composed, controlled, cool, impassive, imperturbable, self-possessed, unemotional **2** = **feeble**, debilitated, enervated, spineless, weak

nerve-racking *adj* = **tense**, annoying, difficult, distressing, frightening, gut-wrenching, harassing, harrowing, maddening, stressful, trying, worrying

nerves *pl n* **2** = **tension**, anxiety, butterflies (in one's stomach) (*inf.*), cold feet (*inf.*), fretfulness, heebie-jeebies (*sl.*), imbalance, nervousness, strain, stress, worry

nervous ◐ ('nɜːvəs) *adj* **1** very excitable or sensitive; highly strung. **2** (often foll. by *of*) apprehensive or worried. **3** of or containing nerves: *nervous tissue.* **4** affecting the nerves or nervous tissue: *a nervous disease.* **5** *Arch.* vigorous or forceful.
▸'**nervously** *adv* ▸'**nervousness** *n*

nervous breakdown ◐ *n* any mental illness not primarily of organic origin, in which the patient ceases to function properly, often accompanied by severely impaired concentration, anxiety, insomnia, and lack of self-esteem.

nervous system *n* the sensory and control apparatus of animals, consisting of a network of neurones.

nervure ('nɜːvjʊə) *n* **1** *Entomol.* any of the chitinous rods that form the framework of an insect's wing; vein. **2** *Bot.* any of the veins of a leaf. [C19: from F; see NERVE, -URE]

nervy ◐ ('nɜːvɪ) *adj* **nervier, nerviest. 1** *Brit. inf.* tense or apprehensive. **2** having or needing bravery or endurance. **3** *US & Canad. inf.* brash or cheeky. **4** *Arch.* muscular; sinewy.

nescience ('nɛsɪəns) *n* a formal or literary word for **ignorance.** [C17: from LL *nescientia,* from L *nescīre* to be ignorant of, from *ne* not + *scīre* to know]
▸'**nescient** *adj*

ness (nɛs) *n Arch.* a promontory or headland. [OE *næs* headland]

-ness *suffix forming nouns chiefly from adjectives and participles.* indicating state, condition, or quality: *greatness; selfishness.* [OE *-nes,* of Gmc origin]

nest ◐ (nɛst) *n* **1** a place or structure in which birds, fishes, etc., lay eggs or give birth to young. **2** a number of animals of the same species occupying a common habitat: *an ants' nest.* **3** a place fostering something undesirable: *a nest of thievery.* **4** a cosy or secluded place. **5** a set of things, usually of graduated sizes, designed to fit together: *a nest of tables.* ♦ *vb* **6** (*intr*) to make or inhabit a nest. **7** (*intr*) to hunt for birds' nests. **8** (*tr*) to place in a nest. **9** *Computing.* to position data within other data at different ranks or levels so that the different levels of data can be used or accessed recursively. [OE]

nest egg ◐ *n* **1** a fund of money kept in reserve; savings. **2** a natural or artificial egg left in a nest to induce hens to lay their eggs in it.

nestle ◐ ('nɛsᵊl) *vb* **nestles, nestling, nestled. 1** (*intr;* often foll. by *up* or *down*) to snuggle, settle, or cuddle closely. **2** (*intr*) to be in a sheltered position; lie snugly. **3** (*tr*) to shelter or place snugly or partly concealed, as in a nest. [OE *nestlian*]

nestling ◐ ('nɛstlɪŋ, 'nɛslɪŋ) *n* **a** a young bird not yet fledged. **b** (*as modifier*): *a nestling thrush.* [C14: from NEST + -LING[1]]

net[1] ◐ (nɛt) *n* **1** an openwork fabric of string, wire, etc.; mesh. **2** a device made of net, used to protect or enclose things or to trap animals. **3** a thin light mesh fabric used for curtains, etc. **4** a plan, strategy, etc., intended to trap or ensnare: *the murderer slipped through the police net.* **5** *Tennis, badminton, etc.* **5a** a strip of net that divides the playing area into two equal parts. **5b** a shot that hits the net. **6** the goal in soccer, hockey, etc. **7** (*often pl*) *Cricket.* **7a** a pitch surrounded by netting, used for practice. **7b** a practice session in a net. **8** *Inf.* (*often cap.*) short for **Internet. 9** another word for **network** (sense 2). ♦ *vb* **nets, netting, netted. 10** (*tr*) to ensnare. **11** (*tr*) to shelter or surround with a net. **12** (*intr*) *Tennis, badminton, etc.* to hit a shot into the net. **13** to make a net out of (rope, string, etc.). [OE *net;* rel. to Gothic *nati,* Du. *net*]

net[2] ◐ *or* **nett** (nɛt) *adj* **1** remaining after all deductions, as for taxes, expenses, losses, etc.: *net profit.* Cf. **gross** (sense 2). **2** (of weight) after deducting tare. **3** final; conclusive (esp. in **net result**). ♦ *n* **4** net income, profits, weight, etc. ♦ *vb* **nets, netting, netted. 5** (*tr*) to yield or earn as clear profit. [C14: clean, neat, from F *net* NEAT[1]]

net asset value *n* the total value of the assets of an organization less its liabilities and capital charges. Abbrev.: **NAV.**

netball ('nɛt,bɔːl) *n* a game for two teams of seven players (usually women) played on a hard court. Points are scored by shooting the ball through a net hanging from a ring at the top of a pole.

Net Book Agreement *n* a former (until 1995) agreement between UK publishers and booksellers that prohibited booksellers from reducing the price of books. Abbrev.: **NBA.**

net domestic product *n Econ.* the gross domestic product minus an allowance for the depreciation of capital goods. Abbrev.: **NDP.**

nether ◐ ('nɛðə) *adj* below, beneath, or underground: *nether regions.* [OE *niothera, nithera,* lit.: further down, from *nither* down]

nethermost ('nɛðə,məʊst) *adj* **the.** farthest down; lowest.

nether world ◐ *n* **1** the underworld. **2** hell. ♦ Also called: **nether regions.**

netiquette ('nɛtɪ,kɛt) *n* the informal code of behaviour on the Internet. [C20: from NET(WORK) + (ET)IQUETTE]

net national product *n* gross national product minus an allowance for the depreciation of capital goods. Abbrev.: **NNP.**

net present value *n Accounting.* an assessment of the long-term profitability of a project made by adding together all the revenue it can be expected to achieve over its whole life and deducting all the costs involved. Abbrev.: **NPV.**

net profit *n* gross profit minus all operating costs not included in the calculation of gross profit, esp. wages, overheads, and depreciation.

net realizable value *n* the net value of an asset if it were to be sold. Abbrev.: **NRV.**

net statutory income *n* (in Britain) the total taxable income of a person for the tax assessment year, after the deduction of personal allowances.

netsuke ('nɛtsʊkɪ) *n* (in Japan) a carved toggle, esp. of wood or ivory, originally used to tether a medicine box, purse, etc., worn dangling from the waist. [C19: from Japanese]

nett (nɛt) *adj, n, vb* a variant spelling of **net**[2].

netting ('nɛtɪŋ) *n* any netted fabric or structure.

nettle ◐ ('nɛtᵊl) *n* **1** a plant having serrated leaves with stinging hairs and greenish flowers. **2** any of various other plants with stinging hairs or spines. **3** any of various plants that resemble nettles, such as the dead-nettle. **4 grasp the nettle.** to attempt something with boldness and courage. ♦ *vb* **nettles, nettling, nettled.** (*tr*) **5** to bother; irritate. **6** to sting as a nettle does. [OE *netele*]

nettle rash *n* a nontechnical name for **urticaria.**

network ◐ ('nɛt,wɜːk) *n* **1** an interconnected group or system: *a network of shops.* **2** a system of intersecting lines, roads, veins, etc. **3** another name for **net**[1] (sense 1) or **netting. 4** *Radio & TV.* a group of broadcasting stations that all transmit the same programme simultaneously. **5** *Computing.* a system of interconnected computer systems, terminals, and other equipment. **6** *Electronics.* a system of interconnected components or circuits. ♦ *vb* **7** *Radio & TV.* to broadcast over a network. **8** (of computers, terminals, etc.) to connect or be connected. **9** (*intr*) to form business contacts through informal social meetings.

neume *or* **neum** (njuːm) *n Music.* one of a series of notational symbols used before the 14th century. [C15: from Med. L *neuma* group of notes sung on one breath, from Gk *pneuma* breath]

neural ('njʊərəl) *adj* of or relating to a nerve or the nervous system.
▸'**neurally** *adv*

neural chip *n* another name for **neurochip.**

neural computer *n* another name for **neurocomputer.**

neuralgia (njʊ'rældʒə) *n* severe spasmodic pain caused by damage to or malfunctioning of a nerve and often following the course of the nerve.
▸**neu'ralgic** *adj*

neural tube *n* the embryonic brain and spinal cord in mammals. Incomplete development results in **neural-tube defects,** such as spina bifida, in a newborn baby.

neurasthenia (,njʊərəs'θiːnɪə) *n* (no longer in technical use) a neurosis characterized by extreme lassitude and inability to cope with any but the most trivial tasks.

neuritis (njʊ'raɪtɪs) *n* inflammation of a nerve or nerves, often accompanied by pain and loss of function in the affected part.
▸**neuritic** (njʊ'rɪtɪk) *adj*

neuro- *or before a vowel* **neur-** *combining form.* indicating a nerve or the nervous system: *neurology.* [from Gk *neuron* nerve; rel. to L *nervus*]

neurobiology (,njʊərəʊbaɪ'ɒlədʒɪ) *n* the study of the anatomy, physiology, and biochemistry of the nervous system.
▸,**neurobi'ologist** *n*

neurochip ('njʊərəʊ,tʃɪp) *n Computing.* a semiconductor chip designed for use in an electronic neural network. Also called: **neural chip.**

neurocomputer ('njʊərəʊkəm,pjuːtə) *n* a type of computer designed

THESAURUS

nervous *adj* **1, 2 = apprehensive**, agitated, anxious, edgy, excitable, fearful, fidgety, flustered, hesitant, highly strung, hyper (*inf.*), hysterical, jittery (*inf.*), jumpy, nervy (*Brit. inf.*), neurotic, on edge, ruffled, shaky, tense, timid, timorous, twitchy (*inf.*), uneasy, uptight (*inf.*), weak, wired (*sl.*), worried
Antonyms *adj* bold, calm, confident, constant, cool, equable, even, laid-back (*inf.*), peaceful, relaxed, steady, together (*sl.*), unfazed (*inf.*)

nervous breakdown *n* **= collapse**, breakdown, crack-up (*inf.*), nervous disorder, neurasthenia (*obs.*)

nervousness *n* **1, 2 = anxiety**, agitation, disquiet, excitability, fluster, perturbation, tension, timidity, touchiness, tremulousness, worry

nervy *adj* **1** *Brit. informal* **= anxious**, agitated, excitable, fidgety, jittery (*inf.*), jumpy, nervous, on edge, restless, tense, twitchy (*inf.*), wired (*sl.*)

nest *n* **3 = hotbed**, breeding-ground, den **4 = refuge**, den, haunt, hideaway, resort, retreat, snuggery

nest egg *n* **1 = reserve**, cache, deposit, fall-back, fund(s), savings, store

nestle *vb* **1 = snuggle**, cuddle, curl up, huddle, nuzzle

nestling *n* **a = chick**, fledgling

net[1] *n* **1 = mesh**, lacework, lattice, netting, network, openwork, reticulum, tracery, web ♦ *vb* **10 = catch**, bag, capture, enmesh, ensnare, entangle, nab (*inf.*), trap

net[2] *adj* **1 = take-home**, after taxes, clear, final **2 = conclusive**, closing, final ♦ *vb* **5 = earn**, accumulate, bring in, clear, gain, make, realize, reap

nether *adj* **= lower**, basal, below, beneath, bottom, inferior, Stygian, under, underground

nether world *n* **1 = underworld**, Hades, infernal regions, nether regions **2 = hell**

nettle *vb* **5 = irritate**, aggravate, annoy, exasperate, fret, gall, get on one's nerves (*inf.*), harass, hassle (*inf.*), incense, nark (*Brit., Austral., & NZ sl.*), pique, provoke, ruffle, sting, tease, vex

nettled *adj* **5 = irritated**, aggrieved, angry, annoyed, chafed, choked, cross, exasperated, galled, hacked (off) (*US sl.*), harassed, huffy, incensed, irritable, peeved, peevish, piqued, provoked, put out, ratty (*Brit. & NZ inf.*), riled, ruffled, stung, teased, tetchy, touchy, vexed

network *n* **1, 2 = system**, arrangement, channels, circuitry, complex, convolution, grid, grill, interconnections, labyrinth, lattice, maze, mesh, net, nexus, organization, plexus, structure, tracks, web to mimic the action of the human brain by use of an electronic neural network. Also called: **neural computer**.

neuroendocrine (ˌnjʊərəʊˈɛndəʊˌkraɪn) *adj* of, relating to, or denoting the dual control of certain body functions by both nervous and hormonal stimulation: *neuroendocrine system.*

neuroglia (njʊˈrɒglɪə) *n* another name for **glia**.

neurohormone (ˈnjʊərəʊˌhɔːməʊn) *n* a hormone, such as noradrenaline, that is produced by specialized nervous tissue rather than by endocrine glands.

neurolemma (ˌnjʊərəʊˈlɛmə) *n* the thin membrane that forms a sheath around nerve fibres. [C19: NL, from NEURO- + Gk *eilēma* covering]

neurology (njʊˈrɒlədʒɪ) *n* the study of the anatomy, physiology, and diseases of the nervous system.
▸**neurological** (ˌnʊərəˈlɒdʒɪkˡl) *adj*

neuromuscular (ˌnjʊərəʊˈmʌskjʊlə) *adj* of, relating to, or affecting nerves and muscles.

neurone (ˈnjʊərəʊn) *or* **neuron** (ˈnjʊərɒn) *n* a cell specialized to conduct nerve impulses: consists of a cell body, axon, and dendrites. Also called: **nerve cell**.
▸**neuˈronal** *adj* ▸**neuronic** (njʊˈrɒnɪk) *adj*

neuropathology (ˌnjʊərəʊpəˈθɒlədʒɪ) *n* the study of diseases of the nervous system.

neuropathy (njʊˈrɒpəθɪ) *n* any disease of the nervous system.
▸**neuropathic** (ˌnjʊərəʊˈpæθɪk) *adj* ▸**ˌneuroˈpathically** *adv*

neurophysiology (ˌnjʊərəʊˌfɪzɪˈɒlədʒɪ) *n* the study of the functions of the nervous system.
▸**neurophysiological** (ˌnjʊərəʊˌfɪzɪəˈlɒdʒɪkˡl) *adj*

neuropterous (njʊˈrɒptərəs) *or* **neuropteran** *adj* of or belonging to an order of insects having two pairs of large much-veined wings and biting mouthparts. [C18: from NL *Neuroptera*, from NEURO- + Gk *pteron* wing]

neuroscience (ˈnjʊərəʊsaɪəns) *n* the study of the anatomy, physiology, and biochemistry of the nervous system.

neurosis Ⓣ (njʊˈrəʊsɪs) *n, pl* **neuroses** (-siːz). a relatively mild mental disorder, characterized by hysteria, anxiety, depression, or obsessive behaviour.

neurosurgery (ˌnjʊərəʊˈsɜːdʒərɪ) *n* the branch of surgery concerned with the nervous system.
▸**ˌneuroˈsurgical** *adj*

neurotic Ⓣ (njʊˈrɒtɪk) *adj* **1** of or afflicted by neurosis. ◆ *n* **2** a person who is afflicted with a neurosis or who tends to be emotionally unstable.
▸**neuˈrotically** *adv* ▸**neuˈrotiˌcism** *n*

neurotomy (njʊˈrɒtəmɪ) *n, pl* **neurotomies**. the surgical cutting of a nerve.

neurotransmitter (ˌnjʊərəʊtrænzˈmɪtə) *n* a chemical by which a nerve cell communicates with another nerve cell or with a muscle.

neuter Ⓣ (ˈnjuːtə) *adj* **1** *Grammar.* **1a** denoting or belonging to a gender of nouns which do not specify the sex of their referents. **1b** (*as n*): *German "Mädchen" (meaning "girl") is a neuter.* **2** (of animals and plants) having nonfunctional, underdeveloped, or absent reproductive organs. **3** giving no indication of sex. ◆ *n* **4** a sexually underdeveloped female insect, such as a worker bee. **5** a castrated animal. ◆ *vb* **6** (*tr*) to castrate (an animal). [C14: from L, from *ne* not + *uter* either (of two)]

neutral Ⓣ (ˈnjuːtrəl) *adj* **1** not siding with any party to a war or dispute. **2** of or belonging to a neutral party, country, etc. **3** of no distinctive quality or type. **4** (of a colour) **4a** having no hue; achromatic. **4b** dull, but harmonizing with most other colours. **5** a less common term for **neuter** (sense 2). **6** *Chem.* neither acidic nor alkaline. **7** *Physics.* having zero charge or potential. **8** *Phonetics.* (of a vowel) articulated with the tongue relaxed in mid-central position: *"about" begins with a neutral vowel.* ◆ *n* **9** a neutral person, nation, etc. **10** a citizen of a neutral state. **11** the position of the controls of a gearbox that leaves the transmission disengaged. [C16: from L *neutrālis*; see NEUTER]
▸**ˈneutrally** *adv*

neutralism (ˈnjuːtrəˌlɪzəm) *n* (in international affairs) the policy of noninvolvement or nonalignment with power blocs.
▸**ˈneutralist** *n*

neutrality Ⓣ (njuːˈtrælɪtɪ) *n* **1** the state of being neutral. **2** the condition of being chemically or electrically neutral.

neutralize Ⓣ *or* **neutralise** (ˈnjuːtrəˌlaɪz) *vb* **neutralizes, neutralizing, neutralized** *or* **neutralises, neutralising, neutralised.** (*mainly tr*) **1** (*also intr*) to render or become neutral by counteracting, mixing, etc. **2** (*also intr*) to make or become electrically or chemically neutral. **3** to exclude (a country) from warfare or alliances by international agreement: *the great powers neutralized Belgium in the 19th century.*
▸**ˌneutraliˈzation** *or* **ˌneutraliˈsation** *n* ▸**ˈneutralˌizer** *or* **ˈneutralˌiser** *n*

neutretto (njuːˈtrɛtəʊ) *n, pl* **neutrettos.** *Physics.* **1** the neutrino associated with the muon. **2** (formerly) any of various hypothetical neutral particles. [C20: from NEUTR(INO) + diminutive suffix *-etto*]

neutrino (njuːˈtriːnəʊ) *n, pl* **neutrinos.** *Physics.* a stable elementary particle with zero rest mass and spin ½ that travels at the speed of light. [C20: from It., dim. of *neutrone* NEUTRON]

neutron (ˈnjuːtrɒn) *n Physics.* a neutral elementary particle with approximately the same mass as a proton. In the nucleus of an atom it is stable but when free it decays. [C20: from NEUTRAL, on the model of ELECTRON]

neutron bomb *n* a type of nuclear weapon designed to cause little blast or long-lived radioactive contamination. The neutrons destroy all life in the target area. Technical name: **enhanced radiation weapon.**

neutron gun *n Physics.* a device used for producing a beam of fast neutrons.

neutron number *n* the number of neutrons in the nucleus of an atom. Symbol: *N*

neutron star *n* a star, composed solely of neutrons, that has collapsed under its own gravity.

névé (ˈneveɪ) *n* a mass of porous ice, formed from snow, that has not yet become frozen into glacier ice. [C19: from Swiss F *névé* glacier, from LL *nivātus* snow-cooled, from *nix* snow]

never Ⓣ (ˈnɛvə) *adv, sentence substitute.* **1** at no time; not ever. **2** certainly not; by no means; in no case. ◆ *sentence substitute.* **3** Also: **well I never!** surely not! [OE *nǣfre*, from *ne* not + *ǣfre* EVER]

> **USAGE NOTE** In informal speech and writing, *never* can be used instead of *not* with the simple past tenses of certain verbs, for emphasis (*I never said that; I never realized how clever he was*), but this usage should be avoided in serious writing.

nevermore (ˌnɛvəˈmɔː) *adv Literary.* never again.

never-never Ⓣ *Inf.* ◆ *n* **1** *Brit.* the hire-purchase system of buying. **2** *Austral.* remote desert country. ◆ *adj* **3** imaginary; idyllic (esp. in **never-never land**).

nevertheless Ⓣ (ˌnɛvəðəˈlɛs) *sentence connector.* in spite of that; however; yet.

new Ⓣ (njuː) *adj* **1a** recently made or brought into being. **1b** (*as collective n; preceded by the*): *the new.* **2** of a kind never before existing; novel: *a new concept in marketing.* **3** recently discovered: *a new comet.* **4** markedly different from what was before: *the new liberalism.* **5** (often foll. by *to* or *at*) recently introduced (to); inexperienced (in) or unaccustomed (to): *new to this neighbourhood.* **6** (*cap. in names or titles*) more or most recent of things with the same name: *the New Testament.* **7** (*prenominal*) fresh; additional: *send some new troops.* **8** (often foll. by *to*) unknown: *this is new to me.* **9** (of a cycle) beginning or occurring again: *a new year.* **10** (*prenominal*) (of crops) harvested early. **11** changed, esp. for the better: *she returned a new woman.* **12** up-to-date; fashionable. ◆ *adv* (*usually in combination*) **13** recently, freshly: *new-laid eggs.* **14** anew; again. ◆ See also **news.** [OE *nīowe*]
▸**ˈnewness** *n*

New Age *n* **1a** a philosophy, originating in the late 1980s, characterized by a belief in alternative medicine, astrology, spiritualism, etc. **1b** (*as modifier*): *New Age therapies.* **2** short for **New Age music.**

New Age music *or* **New Age** *n* a type of gentle melodic popular music originating in the US in the late 1980s, which takes in elements of jazz, folk, and classical music and is played largely on synthesizers and acoustic instruments.

New Australian *n* an Australian name for a recent immigrant, esp. one from Europe.

THESAURUS

neurosis *n* = **obsession**, abnormality, affliction, derangement, deviation, instability, maladjustment, mental disturbance, mental illness, phobia, psychological *or* emotional disorder

neurotic *adj* **1** = **unstable**, abnormal, anxious, compulsive, deviant, disordered, distraught, disturbed, hyper (*inf.*), maladjusted, manic, nervous, obsessive, overwrought, twitchy (*inf.*), unhealthy
Antonyms *adj* calm, laid-back (*inf.*), level-headed, normal, rational, sane, stable, together (*sl.*), well-adjusted, well-balanced

neuter *vb* **6** = **castrate**, doctor (*inf.*), dress, emasculate, fix (*inf.*), geld, spay

neutral *adj* **1** = **unbiased**, disinterested, dispassionate, even-handed, impartial, indifferent, nonaligned, nonbelligerent, noncombatant, noncommittal, nonpartisan, sitting on the fence, unaligned, uncommitted, undecided, uninvolved, unprejudiced **4** = **indeterminate**, achromatic, colourless, dull, indistinct, indistinguishable, intermediate, toneless, undefined
Antonyms *adj* ≠ **unbiased:** active, belligerent, biased, decided, interested, interfering, partial, participating, positive, prejudiced

neutrality *n* **1** = **impartiality**, detachment, disinterestedness, nonalignment, noninterference, nonintervention, noninterventionism, noninvolvement, nonpartisanship

neutralize *vb* **1** = **counteract**, cancel, compensate for, counterbalance, frustrate, invalidate, negate, nullify, offset, undo

never *adv* **1** = **at no time 2** = **not at all**, not for love nor money (*inf.*), not on your life (*inf.*), not on your nelly (*Brit. sl.*), no way, on no account, under no circumstances
Antonyms *adv* ≠ **at no time:** always, aye (*Scot.*), constantly, continually, every time, forever, perpetually, without exception

never-never *n Informal* **1** = **hire-purchase** (*Brit.*), H.P. (*Brit.*)

nevertheless *sentence connector* = **nonetheless**, but, even so, (even) though, however, notwithstanding, regardless, still, yet

new *adj* **2** = **modern**, advanced, all-singing, all-dancing, contemporary, current, fresh, ground-breaking, happening (*inf.*), latest, modernistic, modish, newfangled, novel, original, recent, state-of-the-art, topical, ultramodern, unknown, unused, unusual, up-to-date, virgin **4** = **changed**, altered, improved, modernized, rebranded, redesigned, renewed **7** = **extra**, added, more, supplementary
Antonyms *adj* ≠ **modern:** aged, ancient, antiquated, antique, hackneyed, old, old-fashioned, outmoded, passé, stale, trite

newborn ('njuːˌbɔːn) *adj* **1** recently or just born. **2** (of hope, faith, etc.) reborn.
new brutalism *n* another name for **brutalism.**
New Canadian *n Canad.* a recent immigrant to Canada.
new chum *n* **1** *Austral.* a novice in any activity. **2** *Austral. & NZ inf.* (formerly) a recent British immigrant.
newcomer ❶ ('njuːˌkʌmə) *n* a person who has recently arrived or started to participate in something.
New Country *n* a style of country music of the late 1980s characterized by down-to-earth lyrics.
newel ('njuːəl) *n* **1** the central pillar of a winding staircase, esp. one that is made of stone. **2** Also called: **newel post.** the post at the top or bottom of a flight of stairs that supports the handrail. [C14: from OF *nouel* knob, from Med. L *nōdellus*, dim. of *nōdus* NODE]
New English Bible *n* a new translation of the Bible made between 1962 and 1970.
newfangled ❶ ('njuːˈfæŋgᵊld) *adj* newly come into existence or fashion, esp. excessively modern. [C14 *newefangel* liking new things, from *new* + *-fangel*, from OE *fōn* to take]
new-found *adj* newly or recently discovered: *new-found confidence.*
newish ('njuːɪʃ) *adj* fairly new.
new issue *n Stock Exchange.* an issue of shares being offered to the public for the first time.
New Jerusalem *n Christianity.* heaven.
New Journalism *n* a style of journalism using techniques borrowed from fiction to portray a situation or event as vividly as possible.
New Latin *n* the form of Latin used since the Renaissance, esp. for scientific nomenclature.
New Look *n* **the.** a fashion in women's clothes introduced in 1947, characterized by long full skirts.
newly ❶ ('njuːlɪ) *adv* **1** recently. **2** again; anew: *newly raised hopes.* **3** in a new manner; differently: *a newly arranged hairdo.*
newlywed ('njuːlɪˌwɛd) *n* (*often pl*) a recently married person.
New Man *n* **the.** a type of modern man who allows the caring side of his nature to show by being supportive and by sharing child care and housework.
new maths *n* (*functioning as sing*) *Brit.* an approach to mathematics in which the basic principles of set theory are introduced at an elementary level.
new moon *n* the moon when it appears as a narrow waxing crescent.
news ❶ (njuːz) *n* (*functioning as sing*) **1** important or interesting recent happenings. **2** information about such events, as in the mass media. **3 the news.** a presentation, such as a radio broadcast, of information of this type. **4** interesting or important information not previously known. **5** a person, fashion, etc., widely reported in the mass media: *she is news in the film world.* [C15: from ME *newes*, pl. of *newe* new (adj), a model of OF *noveles* or Med. L *nova* new things]
▸ **'newsless** *adj*
news agency *n* an organization that collects news reports for newspapers, etc. Also called: **press agency.**
newsagent ('njuːzˌeɪdʒənt) *or US* **newsdealer** *n* a shopkeeper who sells newspapers, stationery, etc.
newscast ('njuːzˌkɑːst) *n* a radio or television broadcast of the news. [C20: from NEWS + (BROAD)CAST]
▸ **'newsˌcaster** *n*
news conference *n* another term for **press conference.**
newsflash ('njuːzˌflæʃ) *n* a brief item of important news, often interrupting a radio or television programme.
newsgroup ('njuːzˌgruːp) *n Computing.* a forum where subscribers exchange information about a specific subject by electronic mail.
newsletter ('njuːzˌlɛtə) *n* **1** Also called: **news-sheet.** a printed periodical bulletin circulated to members of a group. **2** *History.* a written or printed account of the news.
newsmonger ('njuːzˌmʌŋgə) *n Old-fashioned.* a gossip.
newspaper ('njuːzˌpeɪpə) *n* a weekly or daily publication consisting of folded sheets and containing articles on the news, features, reviews, and advertisements. Often shortened to **paper.**
newspaperman ('njuːzˌpeɪpəˌmæn) *n, pl* **newspapermen. 1** a person who works for a newspaper as a reporter or editor. **2** the owner or proprietor of a newspaper. **3** a person who sells newspapers in the street.
newspeak ('njuːˌspiːk) *n* the language of bureaucrats and politicians, regarded as deliberately ambiguous and misleading. [C20: from *1984*, a novel by George Orwell]
newsprint ('njuːzˌprɪnt) *n* an inexpensive wood-pulp paper used for newspapers.
newsreader ('njuːzˌriːdə) *n* a news announcer on radio or television.
newsreel ('njuːzˌriːl) *n* a short film with a commentary presenting current events.
newsroom ('njuːzˌruːm, -ˌrʊm) *n* a room in a newspaper office, television station, etc., where news is received and prepared for publication or broadcasting.
newsstand ('njuːzˌstænd) *n* a portable stand or stall from which newspapers are sold.
New Style *n* the present method of reckoning dates using the Gregorian calendar.
news vendor *n* a person who sells newspapers.
newsworthy ❶ ('njuːzˌwɜːðɪ) *adj* sufficiently interesting to be reported in a news bulletin, etc.
newsy ('njuːzɪ) *adj* **newsier, newsiest.** full of news, esp. gossipy or personal news.
newt (njuːt) *n* any of various small semiaquatic amphibians having a long slender body and tail and short feeble legs. [C15: from *a newt*, a mistaken division of *an ewt; ewt*, from OE *eveta* EFT]
New Testament *n* a collection of writings composed soon after Christ's death and added to the Jewish writings of the Old Testament to make up the Christian Bible.
newton ('njuːtᵊn) *n* the derived SI unit of force that imparts an acceleration of 1 metre per second per second to a mass of 1 kilogram. Symbol: N [C20: after Sir Isaac *Newton* (1643–1727), E scientist]
Newtonian telescope (njuːˈtəʊnɪən) *n* a type of astronomical reflecting telescope in which light is reflected from a large concave mirror onto a plane mirror, and through a hole in the side of the body of the telescope to form an image.
Newton's law of gravitation *n* the principle that two particles attract each other with forces directly proportional to the product of their masses divided by the square of the distance between them.
Newton's laws of motion *pl n* three laws of mechanics describing the motion of a body. **The first law** states that a body remains at rest or in uniform motion unless acted upon by a force. **The second law** states that a body's rate of change of momentum is proportional to the force causing it. **The third law** states that when a force acts on a body an equal and opposite force acts simultaneously on another body.
new town *n* (in Britain) a town planned as a complete unit and built with government sponsorship, esp. to accommodate overspill population.
new wave *n* a movement in art, politics, etc., that consciously breaks with traditional ideas, esp. **the New Wave,** a movement in the French cinema of the 1960s, characterized by a fluid use of the camera.
New World *n* **the.** the Americas; the western hemisphere.
New World monkey *n* any of a family of monkeys of Central and South America, many of which are arboreal and have a prehensile tail.
New Year *n* the first day or days of the year in various calendars, usually a holiday.
New Year's Day *n* January 1, celebrated as a holiday in many countries. Often shortened to (US and Canad. inf.) **New Year's.**
New Year's Eve *n* the evening of Dec. 31. See also **Hogmanay.**
New Zealander (ˈziːləndə) *n* **1** a native or inhabitant of New Zealand. **2** in earlier usage, a Maori.
next ❶ (nɛkst) *adj* **1** immediately following: *the next patient to be examined.* **2** immediately adjoining: *the next room.* **3** closest to in degree: *the next-best thing.* **4 the next (Sunday) but one.** the (Sunday) after the next. ◆ *adv* **5** at a time immediately to follow: *the patient to be examined next.* **6 next to. 6a** adjacent to: *the house next to ours.* **6b** following in degree: *next to your mother, who do you love most?* **6c** almost: *next to impossible.* ◆ *prep* **7** *Arch.* next to. [OE *nēhst*, sup. of *nēah* NIGH]
next door *adj* (**next-door** *when prenominal*), *adv* at or to the adjacent house, flat, etc.
next of kin *n* a person's closest relative.
nexus ❶ ('nɛksəs) *n, pl* **nexus. 1** a means of connection; link; bond. **2** a connected group or series. [C17: from L, from *nectere* to bind]
Nez Percé ('nɛz 'pɜːs) *n* **1** (*pl* **Nez Percés** ('pɜːsɪz) *or* **Nez Percé**) a member of a North American Indian people of the Pacific coast. **2** the language of this people. [F, lit. pierced nose]
NF (in Britain) *abbrev. for* National Front.
Nfld. *or* **NF.** *abbrev. for* Newfoundland.
NFU (in Britain) *abbrev. for* National Farmers' Union.
NG *abbrev. for:* **1** (in the US) National Guard. **2** New Guinea. **3** Also: **ng.** no good.
NGA (formerly, in Britain) *abbrev. for* National Graphical Association.
ngaio ('naɪəʊ) *n, pl* **ngaios.** a small evergreen New Zealand tree. [from Maori]
ngati ('nɑːtiː) *n, pl* **ngati.** *NZ.* a tribe or clan. [from Maori]
NHI (in Britain) *abbrev. for* National Health Insurance.
NHS (in Britain) *abbrev. for* National Health Service.
Ni *the chemical symbol for* nickel.

THESAURUS

newcomer *n* = **novice**, alien, arrival, beginner, foreigner, immigrant, incomer, Johnny-come-lately (*inf.*), outsider, parvenu, settler, stranger
newfangled *adj* = **new**, all-singing, all- dancing, contemporary, fashionable, gimmicky, modern, new-fashioned, novel, recent, state-of-the-art
Antonyms *adj* antiquated, dated, obsolete, old-fashioned, outmoded, out-of-date, passé
newly *adv* **1** = **recently**, just, lately, latterly **2** = **anew**, freshly
newness *n* **2** = **novelty**, freshness, innovation, originality
news *n* **1, 2, 4** = **information**, account, advice, bulletin, buzz, communiqué, dirt (*US sl.*), disclosure, dispatch, exposé, gen (*Brit. inf.*), gossip, hearsay, intelligence, latest (*inf.*), leak, news flash, release, report, revelation, rumour, scandal, scuttlebutt (*US sl.*), statement, story, tidings, word
newsworthy *adj* = **interesting**, arresting, important, notable, noteworthy, remarkable, significant, stimulating
next *adj* **1** = **following**, consequent, ensuing, later, subsequent, succeeding **2** = **nearest**, adjacent, adjoining, closest, neighbouring ◆ *adv* **5** = **afterwards**, closely, following, later, subsequently, thereafter
nexus *n* **1** = **connection**, bond, joining, junction, link, tie

NI *abbrev. for:* **1** (in Britain) National Insurance. **2** Northern Ireland. **3** (in New Zealand) North Island.

niacin ('naɪəsɪn) *n* another name for **nicotinic acid.** [C20: from NI(COTINIC) AC(ID) + -IN]

nib (nɪb) *n* **1** the writing point of a pen, esp. an insertable tapered metal part. **2** a point, tip, or beak. **3** (*pl*) crushed cocoa beans. ◆ *vb* **nibs, nibbing, nibbed.** (*tr*) **4** to provide with a nib. **5** to sharpen the nib of. [C16 (in the sense: beak): from ?]

nibble Ⓣ ('nɪbᵊl) *vb* **nibbles, nibbling, nibbled.** (when *intr*, often foll. by *at*) **1** (esp. of animals) to take small repeated bites (of). **2** to take dainty or tentative bites: *to nibble at a cake.* **3** to bite (at) gently. ◆ *n* **4** a small mouthful. **5** an instance of nibbling. [C15: rel. to Low G *nibbelen*]
▸**'nibbler** *n*

niblick ('nɪblɪk) *n Golf.* (formerly) a club giving a great deal of lift. [C19: from ?]

nibs (nɪbz) *n* **his nibs.** *Sl.* a mock title used of someone in authority. [C19: from ?]

NICAM ('naɪkæm) *n acronym for* near-instantaneous companded audio multiplex: a technique for coding audio signals into digital form.

nice Ⓣ (naɪs) *adj* **1** pleasant: *a nice day.* **2** kind or friendly: *a nice gesture of help.* **3** good or satisfactory: *they made a nice job of it.* **4** subtle or discriminating: *a nice point in the argument.* **5** precise; skilful: *a nice fit.* **6** *Now rare.* fastidious; respectable: *he was not too nice about his methods.* **7** *Obs.* **7a** foolish or ignorant. **7b** delicate. **7c** shy; modest. **7d** wanton. [C13 (orig.: foolish): from OF *nice* simple, silly, from L *nescius,* from *nescīre* to be ignorant]
▸**'nicely** *adv* ▸**'niceness** *n* ▸**'nicish** *adj*

nice-looking *adj Inf.* attractive in appearance; pretty or handsome.

nicety Ⓣ ('naɪsɪtɪ) *n, pl* **niceties. 1** a subtle point: *a nicety of etiquette.* **2** (*usually pl*) a refinement or delicacy: *the niceties of first-class travel.* **3** subtlety, delicacy, or precision. **4 to a nicety.** with precision.

niche Ⓣ (nɪtʃ, niːʃ) *n* **1** a recess in a wall, esp. one that contains a statue, etc. **2** a position particularly suitable for the person occupying it: *he found his niche in politics.* **3** (*modifier*) relating to or aimed at a small specialized group or market: *shampoo shops and other niche retailing ventures.* **4** *Ecology.* the status of a plant or animal within its community, which determines its activities, relationships with other organisms, etc. ◆ *vb* **niches, niching, niched. 5** (*tr*) to place (a statue) in a niche; ensconce (oneself). [C17: from F, from OF *nichier* to nest, from Vulgar L *nīdicāre* (unattested), from L *nīdus* NEST]

Nichrome ('naɪ,krəʊm) *n Trademark.* any of various alloys containing nickel, iron, and chromium, used in electrical heating elements, furnaces, etc.

nick Ⓣ (nɪk) *n* **1** a small notch or indentation. **2** *Brit. sl.* a prison or police station. **3 in good nick.** *Inf.* in good condition. **4 in the nick of time.** just in time. ◆ *vb* **5** (*tr*) to chip or cut. **6** *Sl., chiefly Brit.* **6a** to steal. **6b** to arrest. **7** (*intr;* often foll. by *off*) *Inf.* to depart rapidly. **8 nick (someone) for.** *US & Canad. sl.* to defraud (someone) to the extent of. **9** to divide and reset (the tail muscles of a horse) to give the tail a high carriage. **10** (*tr*) to guess, catch, etc., exactly. [C15: ? changed from C14 *nocke* NOCK]

nickel ('nɪkᵊl) *n* **1** a malleable silvery-white metallic element that is corrosion-resistant: used in alloys, in electroplating, and as a catalyst in organic synthesis. Symbol: Ni; atomic no.: 28; atomic wt.: 58.71. **2** a US or Canadian coin worth five cents. ◆ *vb* **nickels, nickelling, nickelled** *or US* **nickels, nickeling, nickeled. 3** (*tr*) to plate with nickel. [C18: from G *Kupfernickel* niccolite, lit.: copper demon; it was mistakenly thought to contain copper]

nickelodeon (,nɪkə'ləʊdɪən) *n US.* **1** an early form of jukebox. **2** (formerly) a Pianola, esp. one operated by inserting a five-cent piece. [C20: from NICKEL + (MEL)ODEON]

nickel plate *n* a thin layer of nickel deposited on a surface, usually by electrolysis.

nickel silver *n* any of various white alloys containing copper, zinc, and nickel: used in making tableware, etc. Also called: **German silver.**

nickel steel *n Engineering.* steel containing between 0.5 and 6.0 per cent nickel to increase its strength.

nicker[1] ('nɪkə) *vb* (*intr*) **1** (of a horse) to neigh softly. **2** to snigger. [C18: ?from NEIGH]

nicker[2] ('nɪkə) *n, pl* **nicker.** *Brit. sl.* a pound sterling. [C20: from ?]

nick-nack ('nɪk,næk) *n* a variant spelling of **knick-knack.**

nickname Ⓣ ('nɪk,neɪm) *n* **1** a familiar, pet, or derisory name given to a person, animal, or place. **2** a shortened or familiar form of a person's name: *Joe is a nickname for Joseph.* ◆ *vb* **nicknames, nicknaming, nicknamed. 3** (*tr*) to call by a nickname. [C15 *a nekename,* mistaken division of *an ekename* an additional name]

Nicol prism ('nɪkᵊl) *n* two prisms of Iceland spar or calcite cut at specified angles and cemented together, to produce plane-polarized light. [C19: after William *Nicol* (?1768–1851), Scot. physicist, its inventor]

nicotiana (nɪ,kəʊʃɪ'ɑːnə) *n* a plant of an American and Australian genus, having white, yellow, or purple fragrant flowers. Also called: **tobacco plant.** [C16: see NICOTINE]

nicotinamide (,nɪkə'tɪnə,maɪd) *n* the amide of nicotinic acid: a component of the vitamin B complex. Formula: $C_6H_6ON_2$.

nicotine ('nɪkə,tiːn) *n* a colourless oily acrid toxic liquid that turns yellowish-brown in air and light: the principal alkaloid in tobacco. [C19: from F, from NL *herba nicotiana* Nicot's plant, after J. *Nicot* (1530-1600), F diplomat who introduced tobacco into France]
▸**'nico,tined** *adj* ▸**nicotinic** (,nɪkə'tɪnɪk) *adj*

nicotinic acid *n* a vitamin of the B complex that occurs in milk, liver, yeast, etc. Lack of it in the diet leads to the disease pellagra.

nicotinism ('nɪkətiː,nɪzəm) *n Pathol.* a toxic condition of the body caused by nicotine.

nictitate ('nɪktɪ,teɪt) *or* **nictate** ('nɪkteɪt) *vb* **nictitates, nictitating, nictitated** *or* **nictates, nictating, nictated.** a technical word for **blink.** [C19: from Med. L *nictitāre* to wink repeatedly, from L *nictāre* to blink]
▸**,nicti'tation** *or* **nic'tation** *n*

nictitating membrane *n* (in reptiles, birds, and some mammals) a thin fold of skin beneath the eyelid that can be drawn across the eye.

nidicolous (nɪ'dɪkələs) *adj* (of young birds) remaining in the nest some time after hatching. [C19: from L *nīdus* nest + *colere* to inhabit]

nidifugous (nɪ'dɪfjʊgəs) *adj* (of young birds) leaving the nest very soon after hatching. [C19: from L *nīdus* nest + *fugere* to flee]

nidify ('nɪdɪ,faɪ) *or* **nidificate** ('nɪdɪfɪ,keɪt) *vb* **nidifies, nidifying, nidified** *or* **nidificates, nidificating, nidificated.** (*intr*) (of birds) to make or build a nest. [C17: from L *nīdificāre,* from *nīdus* a nest + *facere* to make]
▸**,nidifi'cation** *n*

niece (niːs) *n* a daughter of one's sister or brother. [C13: from OF: niece, granddaughter, ult. from L *neptis* granddaughter]

niello (nɪ'ɛləʊ) *n, pl* **nielli** (-lɪ) *or* **niellos. 1** a black compound of sulphur and silver, lead, or copper used to incise a design on a metal surface. **2** this process. **3** an object decorated with niello. [C19: from It. from L *nigellus* blackish, from *niger* black]

niff (nɪf) *Brit. sl.* ◆ *n* **1** a bad smell. ◆ *vb* (*intr*) **2** to stink. [C20: ?from SNIFF]
▸**'niffy** *adj*

nifty Ⓣ ('nɪftɪ) *adj* **niftier, niftiest.** *Inf.* **1** pleasing, apt, or stylish. **2** quick; agile. [C19: from ?]
▸**'niftily** *adv* ▸**'niftiness** *n*

nigella (naɪ'dʒɛlə) *n* another name for **love-in-a-mist.**

Nigerian (naɪ'dʒɪərɪən) *n* **1** a native or inhabitant of Nigeria, a country in West Africa. **2** of Nigeria, its people, culture, etc.

niggard Ⓣ ('nɪgəd) *n* **1** a stingy person. ◆ *adj* **2** *Arch.* miserly. [C14: ?from ON]

niggardly Ⓣ ('nɪgədlɪ) *adj* **1** stingy. **2** meagre: *a niggardly salary.* ◆ *adv* **3** stingily; grudgingly.
▸**'niggardliness** *n*

nigger ('nɪgə) *n Derog.* **1** another name for a Negro. **2** a member of any

THESAURUS

nibble *vb* **1-3 = bite,** eat, gnaw, munch, nip, peck, pick at ◆ *n* **4 = snack,** bite, crumb, morsel, peck, *soupçon,* taste, titbit

nice *adj* **1 = pleasant,** agreeable, attractive, charming, delightful, good, pleasurable **2 = kind,** amiable, commendable, courteous, friendly, likable *or* likeable, polite, prepossessing, refined, well-mannered **4 = subtle,** accurate, careful, delicate, discriminating, exact, exacting, fine, meticulous, precise, rigorous, scrupulous, strict **5 = neat,** exact, fine, precise, tidy, trim
Antonyms *adj* ≠ **pleasant:** awful, disagreeable, dreadful, miserable, unpleasant ≠ **kind:** disagreeable, mean, unfriendly, unkind, unpleasant, vulgar ≠ **subtle:** careless, rough, sloppy (*inf.*), vague ≠ **neat:** coarse, crude, rough, shabby, sloppy (*inf.*)

nicely *adv* **1 = pleasantly,** acceptably, agreeably, attractively, charmingly, delightfully, pleasingly, pleasurably, well **2 = kindly,** amiably, commendably, courteously, likably, politely, prepossessingly **4 = subtly,** accurately, carefully, delicately, exactingly, exactly, finely, meticulously, precisely, rigorously, scrupulously, strictly **5 = neatly,** finely, precisely, tidily, trimly
Antonyms *adv* ≠ **pleasantly:** unattractively, unpleasantly ≠ **subtly:** carelessly, sloppily (*inf.*) ≠ **neatly:** sloppily (*inf.*)

niceness *n* **1, 2 = kindness,** agreeableness, amiability, attractiveness, charm, courtesy, delightfulness, friendliness, good manners, goodness, likableness *or* likeableness, pleasantness, pleasurableness, politeness, refinement **4 = precision,** accuracy, care, carefulness, delicacy, discrimination, exactingness, exactitude, exactness, fineness, meticulosity, meticulousness, preciseness, rigorousness, rigour, scrupulousness, strictness, subtleness, subtlety **5 = neatness,** daintiness, fineness, tidiness

nicety *n* **1, 2 = subtlety,** delicacy, distinction, nuance, refinement **3 = precision,** accuracy, exactness, fastidiousness, finesse, meticulousness, minuteness

niche *n* **1 = alcove,** corner, hollow, nook, opening, recess **2 = position,** calling, pigeonhole (*inf.*), place, slot (*inf.*), vocation

nick *n* **1 = cut,** chip, dent, mark, notch, scar, score, scratch, snick ◆ *vb* **5 = cut,** chip, damage, dent, mark, notch, scar, score, scratch, snick **6a** *Slang* **= steal,** finger (*sl.*), knock off (*sl.*), pilfer, pinch (*inf.*), snitch (*sl.*), swipe (*sl.*)

nickname *n* **1 = pet name,** epithet, familiar name, handle (*sl.*), label, moniker *or* monicker (*sl.*), sobriquet **2 = diminutive**

nifty *adj Informal* **1 = pleasing,** apt, attractive, chic, clever, enjoyable, excellent, neat, sharp, smart, spruce, stylish **2 = quick,** agile, deft

niggard *n* **1 = miser,** cheapskate (*inf.*), meanie *or* meany, penny-pincher (*inf.*), screw (*sl.*), Scrooge, skinflint

niggardliness *n* **1 = miserliness,** avarice, avariciousness, closeness, covetousness, frugality, grudgingness, meanness, mercenariness, nearness (*inf.*), parsimony, penuriousness, sordidness, sparingness, stinginess, thrift, tightfistedness, ungenerousness **2 = paltriness,** beggarliness, inadequacy, insufficiency, meagreness, meanness, miserableness, scantiness, skimpiness, smallness, wretchedness

niggardly *adj* **1 = stingy,** avaricious, close, covetous, frugal, grudging, mean, mercenary, miserly, near (*inf.*), parsimonious, penurious, dark-skinned race. **3 nigger in the woodpile.** a hidden cause of trouble. [C18: from C16 dialect *neeger,* from F *nègre,* from Sp. NEGRO]

niggle ● ('nɪgᵊl) *vb* **niggles, niggling, niggled. 1** (*intr*) to find fault continually. **2** (*intr*) to be preoccupied with details; fuss. **3** (*tr*) to irritate; worry. ◆ *n* **4** a trivial objection or complaint. **5** a slight feeling as of misgiving, uncertainty, etc. [C16: from Scand.]
▸**'niggler** *n* ▸**'niggly** *adj*

niggling ● ('nɪglɪŋ) *adj* **1** petty. **2** fussy. **3** irritating. **4** requiring painstaking work. **5** persistently troubling.

nigh ● (naɪ) *adj, adv, prep* an archaic, poetic, or dialect word for **near.** [OE *nēah, nēh*]

night ● (naɪt) *n* **1** the period of darkness that occurs each 24 hours, as distinct from day. **2** (*modifier*) of, occurring, working, etc., at night: *a night nurse.* **3** this period considered as a unit: *four nights later they left.* **4** the period between sunset and retiring to bed; evening. **5** the time between bedtime and morning. **6** the weather at night: *a clear night.* **7** the activity or experience of a person during a night. **8** (*sometimes cap.*) any evening designated for a special observance or function. **9** nightfall or dusk. **10** a state or period of gloom, ignorance, etc. **11 make a night of it.** to celebrate for most of the night. ◆ Related adj: **nocturnal.** ◆ See also **nights.** [OE *niht*]

night blindness *n Pathol.* a nontechnical term for **nyctalopia.**
▸**'night-ˌblind** *adj*

nightcap ('naɪtˌkæp) *n* **1** a bedtime drink. **2** a soft cap formerly worn in bed.

nightclothes ('naɪtˌkləʊðz) *pl n* clothes worn in bed.

nightclub ('naɪtˌklʌb) *n* a place of entertainment open until late at night, usually offering food, drink, a floor show, dancing, etc.

nightdress ('naɪtˌdrɛs) *n Brit.* a loose dress worn in bed by women. Also called: **nightgown, nightie.**

nightfall ● ('naɪtˌfɔːl) *n* the approach of darkness; dusk.

night fighter *n* an interceptor aircraft used for operations at night.

nightgown ('naɪtˌgaʊn) *n* **1** another name for **nightdress. 2** a man's nightshirt.

nighthawk ('naɪtˌhɔːk) *n* **1** any of various nocturnal American birds. **2** *Inf.* another name for **night owl.**

nightie *or* **nighty** ('naɪtɪ) *n, pl* **nighties.** *Inf.* short for **nightdress.**

nightingale ('naɪtɪŋˌgeɪl) *n* a brownish European songbird with a broad reddish-brown tail: well known for its musical song, usually heard at night. [OE *nihtegale,* from NIGHT + *galan* to sing]

nightjar ('naɪtˌdʒɑː) *n* any of a family of nocturnal birds which have large eyes and feed on insects. [C17: NIGHT + JAR², so called from its discordant cry]

night latch *n* a door lock operated by means of a knob on the inside and a key on the outside.

nightlife ('naɪtˌlaɪf) *n* social life or entertainment taking place at night.

night-light *n* a dim light burning at night, esp. for children.

nightlong ('naɪtˌlɒŋ) *adj, adv* throughout the night.

nightly ● ('naɪtlɪ) *adj* **1** happening or relating to each night. **2** happening at night. ◆ *adv* **3** at night or each night.

nightmare ● ('naɪtˌmɛə) *n* **1** a terrifying or deeply distressing dream. **2a** an event or condition resembling a terrifying dream. **2b** (*as modifier*): *a nightmare drive.* **3** a thing that is feared. **4** (formerly) an evil spirit supposed to suffocate sleeping people. [C13 (meaning: incubus; C16: bad dream): from NIGHT + OE *mare, mære* evil spirit, from Gmc]
▸**'nightˌmarish** *adj*

night owl *or* **nighthawk** *n Inf.* a person who is or prefers to be up and about late at night.

nights (naɪts) *adv Inf.* at night, esp. regularly: *he works nights.*

night safe *n* a safe built into the outside wall of a bank, in which customers can deposit money at times when the bank is closed.

night school *n* an educational institution that holds classes in the evening.

nightshade ('naɪtˌʃeɪd) *n* any of various solanaceous plants, such as deadly nightshade and black nightshade. [OE *nihtscada,* apparently NIGHT + SHADE, referring to the poisonous or soporific qualities of these plants]

night shift *n* **1** a group of workers who work a shift during the night. **2** the period worked.

nightshirt ('naɪtˌʃɜːt) *n* a loose knee-length or longer shirtlike garment worn in bed.

nightspot ('naɪtˌspɒt) *n* an informal word for **nightclub.**

night-time *n* the time from sunset to sunrise; night as distinct from day.

night watch *n* **1** a watch or guard kept at night, esp. for security. **2** the period of time the watch is kept. **3** a night watchman.

night watchman *n* **1** Also called: **night watch.** a person who keeps guard at night on a factory, public building, etc. **2** *Cricket.* a batsman sent in to bat to play out time when a wicket has fallen near the end of a day's play.

nightwear ('naɪtˌwɛə) *n* apparel worn in bed or before retiring to bed; pyjamas, etc.

nigrescent (naɪ'grɛsᵊnt) *adj* blackish; dark. [C18: from L *nigrescere* to grow black, from *niger* black]
▸**ni'grescence** *n*

nihilism ● ('naɪɪˌlɪzəm) *n* **1** a complete denial of all established authority and institutions. **2** *Philosophy.* an extreme form of scepticism that systematically rejects all values, belief in existence, etc. **3** a revolutionary doctrine of destruction for its own sake. **4** the practice of terrorism. [C19: from L *nihil* nothing]
▸**'nihilist** *n, adj* ▸**ˌnihil'istic** *adj* ▸**nihility** (naɪ'hɪlɪtɪ) *n*

nihil obstat ('naɪhɪl 'ɒbstæt) the phrase used by a Roman Catholic censor to declare publication inoffensive to faith or morals. [L, lit.: nothing hinders]

-nik *suffix forming nouns.* denoting a person associated with a specified state or quality: *beatnik.* [C20: from Russian *-nik,* as in SPUTNIK, and infl. by Yiddish *-nik* (agent suffix)]

Nikkei Stock Average ('nɪkeɪ) *n* an index of share prices based on an average of 225 equities quoted on the Tokyo Stock Exchange. [C20: from *Nik(on) Kei(zai Shimbun),* a Japanese newspaper group]

nil ● (nɪl) *n* nothing: used esp. in the scoring of certain games. [C19: from L]

Nile green (naɪl) *n* **a** a pale bluish-green colour. **b** (*as adj*): *a Nile-green dress.*

nilgai ('nɪlgaɪ) *or* **nilghau** ('nɪlgɔː) *n, pl* **nilgai, nilgais** *or* **nilghau, nilghaus.** a large Indian antelope, the male of which has small horns. [C19: from Hindi *nīlgāw,* from Sansk. *nīla* blue + *go* bull]

Nilotic (naɪ'lɒtɪk) *adj* **1** of the Nile. **2** of or belonging to a Negroid pastoral people inhabiting the S Sudan, parts of Kenya and Uganda, and neighbouring countries. **3** relating to the group of languages spoken by the Nilotic peoples. [C17: via L from Gk *Neilotikós,* from *Neilos* the River Nile]

nimble ● ('nɪmbᵊl) *adj* **1** agile, quick, and neat in movement. **2** alert; acute. [OE *næmel* quick to grasp, & *numol* quick at seizing, both from *niman* to take]
▸**'nimbleness** *n* ▸**'nimbly** *adv*

nimbostratus (ˌnɪmbəʊ'streɪtəs, -'strɑːtəs) *n, pl* **nimbostrati** (-taɪ). a dark rain-bearing stratus cloud.

nimbus ● ('nɪmbəs) *n, pl* **nimbi** (-baɪ) *or* **nimbuses. 1a** a dark grey rain-bearing cloud. **1b** (*in combination*): *cumulonimbus clouds.* **2a** an emanation of light surrounding a saint or deity. **2b** a representation of this emanation. **3** a surrounding aura. [C17: from L: cloud]

NIMBY ('nɪmbɪ) *n acronym for* not in my back yard: a person who objects to the occurrence of something if it will affect them or take place in their locality.

Nimrod ('nɪmrɒd) *n* **1** a hunter famous for his prowess (Genesis 10:8–9). **2** a person dedicated to or skilled in hunting.

nincompoop ● ('nɪnkəmˌpuːp, 'nɪŋ-) *n* a stupid person; fool; idiot. [C17: from ?]

nine (naɪn) *n* **1** the cardinal number that is the sum of one and eight. **2** a numeral, 9, IX, etc., representing this number. **3** something repre-

THESAURUS

Scrooge-like, sordid, sparing, stinging, tight-fisted, ungenerous **2** = **paltry**, beggarly, inadequate, insufficient, meagre, mean, measly, miserable, pathetic, scant, scanty, skimpy, small, wretched

Antonyms *adj* ≠ **stingy:** bountiful, generous, lavish, liberal, munificent, prodigal ≠ **paltry:** abundant, ample, bountiful, copious, generous, handsome, liberal, plentiful, profuse

niggle *vb* **2** = **criticize**, carp, cavil, find fault, fuss **3** = **worry**, annoy, irritate, rankle

niggling *adj* **1, 2** = **petty**, cavilling, finicky, fussy, insignificant, minor, nit-picking (*inf.*), pettifogging, picky (*inf.*), piddling (*inf.*), quibbling, trifling, unimportant **3, 5** = **persistent**, gnawing, irritating, troubling, worrying

nigh *adj* = **near**, adjacent, adjoining, approximate, at hand, bordering, close, contiguous, imminent, impending, next, upcoming ◆ *adv* = **near**, about, almost, approximately, close, practically

night *n* **1** = **darkness**, dark, dead of night, hours of darkness, night-time, night watches

nightfall *n* = **evening**, dusk, eve, eventide, gloaming (*Scot. or poetic*), sundown, sunset, twilight, vespers

Antonyms *n* aurora (*poetic*), cockcrow, dawn, dawning, daybreak, daylight, morning, sunrise

nightly *adv* **1** = **every night**, each night, night after night, nights (*inf.*) ◆ *adj* **2** = **nocturnal**, night-time ◆ *adv* **3** = **by night**, after dark, at night, in the night, nights (*inf.*), nocturnally

nightmare *n* **1** = **bad dream**, hallucination, incubus, night terror, succubus **2** = **ordeal**, hell on earth, horror, torment, trial, tribulation

nightmarish *adj* **2** = **frightening**, agonizing, alarming, creepy, disturbing, harrowing, horrible, Kafkaesque, scaring, terrifying, unreal

nihilism *n* **1, 2** = **nonbelief**, abnegation, agnosticism, atheism, denial, disbelief, rejection, renunciation, repudiation, scepticism **3, 4** = **lawlessness**, anarchy, disorder, terrorism

nihilist *n* **1, 2** = **nonbeliever**, agnostic, atheist, cynic, disbeliever, pessimist, sceptic **3, 4** = **anarchist**, agitator, extremist, revolutionary, terrorist

nil *n* = **nothing**, duck, love, naught, *nihil,* none, zero, zilch (*sl.*)

nimble *adj* **1** = **agile**, active, brisk, deft, dexterous, lively, nippy (*Brit. inf.*), proficient, prompt, quick, ready, sprightly, spry, swift **2** = **alert**, bright (*inf.*), quick-witted, smart

Antonyms *adj* ≠ **agile:** awkward, clumsy, dull, heavy, inactive, indolent, lethargic, slow

nimbleness *n* **1** = **agility**, adroitness, alacrity, dexterity, finesse, grace, lightness, nippiness (*Brit. inf.*), skill, sprightliness, spryness **2** = **alertness**, smartness

nimbly *adv* **1** = **quickly**, actively, agilely, briskly, deftly, dexterously, easily, fast, fleetly, hotfoot, posthaste, proficiently, promptly, pronto (*inf.*), readily, sharply, smartly, speedily, spryly, swiftly **2** = **alertly**, acutely, quick-wittedly

nimbus *n* **1a** = **cloud 2** = **halo**, aura, aureole, corona, glow, irradiation **3** = **atmosphere**, ambience, aura

nincompoop *n* = **idiot**, berk (*Brit. sl.*), blockhead, charlie (*Brit. inf.*), chump, coot, dimwit (*inf.*), divvy (*sl.*), dolt, dork (*sl.*), dunce, fathead senting, represented by, or consisting of nine units, such as a playing card with nine symbols on it. **4** Also: **nine o'clock.** nine hours after noon or midnight: *the play starts at nine.* **5 dressed (up) to the nines.** *Inf.* elaborately dressed. **6 999** (in Britain) the telephone number of the emergency services. **7 nine to five.** normal office hours: *a nine-to-five job.* ◆ *determiner* **8a** amounting to nine: *nine days.* **8b** (*as pronoun*): *nine are ready.* [OE *nigon*]

nine-days wonder *n* something that arouses great interest but only for a short period.

ninefold ('naɪn,fəʊld) *adj* **1** equal to or having nine times as many or as much. **2** composed of nine parts. ◆ *adv* **3** by nine times as much.

ninepins ('naɪn,pɪnz) *n* **1** (*functioning as sing*) another name for **skittles.** **2** (*sing*) one of the pins used in this game.

nineteen ('naɪn'ti:n) *n* **1** the cardinal number that is the sum of ten and nine. **2** a numeral, 19, XIX, etc., representing this number. **3** something represented by, representing, or consisting of 19 units. **4 talk nineteen to the dozen.** to talk incessantly. ◆ *determiner* **5a** amounting to nineteen: *nineteen pictures.* **5b** (*as pronoun*): *only nineteen voted.* [OE *nigontīne*]

nineteenth (,naɪn'ti:nθ) *adj* **1** (*usually prenominal*) **1a** coming after the eighteenth in numbering, position, etc.; being the ordinal number of *nineteen.* Often written: 19th. **1b** (*as n*): *the nineteenth was rainy.* ◆ *n* **2a** one of 19 equal parts of something. **2b** (*as modifier*): *a nineteenth part.* **3** the fraction equal to one divided by 19 (1/19).

nineteenth hole *n Golf, sl.* the bar in a golf clubhouse. [C20: from its being the next objective after a standard 18-hole round]

ninetieth ('naɪntɪɪθ) *adj* **1** (*usually prenominal*) **1a** being the ordinal number of *ninety* in numbering, position, etc. Often written: 90th. **1b** (*as n*): *ninetieth in succession.* ◆ *n* **2a** one of 90 equal parts of something. **2b** (*as modifier*): *a ninetieth part.* **3** the fraction one divided by 90 (1/90).

ninety ('naɪntɪ) *n, pl* **nineties. 1** the cardinal number that is the product of ten and nine. **2** a numeral, 90, XC, etc., representing this number. **3** something represented by, representing, or consisting of 90 units. ◆ *determiner* **4a** amounting to ninety: *ninety times.* **4b** (*as pronoun*): *at least ninety are missing.* [OE *nigontig*]
▸ **'ninetieth** *adj, n*

ninja ('nɪndʒə) *n, pl* **ninja** *or* **ninjas.** (*sometimes cap.*) a person skilled in **ninjutsu,** a Japanese martial art characterized by stealthy movement and camouflage. [Japanese]

ninny ('nɪnɪ) *n, pl* **ninnies.** a dull-witted person. [C16: ?from *an innocent* simpleton]

ninth (naɪnθ) *adj* **1** (*usually prenominal*) **1a** coming after the eighth in order, position, etc.; being the ordinal number of *nine.* Often written: 9th. **1b** (*as n*): *ninth in line.* ◆ *n* **2a** one of nine equal parts. **2b** (*as modifier*): *a ninth part.* **3** the fraction one divided by nine (1/9). **4** *Music.* an interval of one octave plus a second. ◆ *adv* **5** Also: **ninthly.** after the eighth person, position, event, etc. [OE *nigotha*]

niobium (naɪ'əʊbɪəm) *n* a ductile white superconductive metallic element that occurs principally in the black mineral columbite and tantalite. Symbol: Nb; atomic no.: 41; atomic wt.: 92.906. Former name: **columbium.** [C19: from NL, from *Niobe* (daughter of Tantalus); because it occurred in TANTALITE]

nip[1] ❶ (nɪp) *vb* **nips, nipping, nipped.** (*mainly tr*) **1** to compress, as between a finger and the thumb; pinch. **2** (often foll. by *off*) to remove by clipping, biting, etc. **3** (when *intr*, often foll. by *at*) to give a small sharp bite (to): *the dog nipped at his heels.* **4** (esp. of the cold) to affect with a stinging sensation. **5** to harm through cold: *the frost nipped the young plants.* **6** to check or destroy the growth of (esp. in **nip in the bud**). **7** (*intr;* foll. by *along, up, out,* etc.) *Brit. inf.* to hurry; dart. **8** *Sl., chiefly US & Canad.* to snatch. ◆ *n* **9** a pinch, snip, etc. **10** severe frost or cold: *the first nip of winter.* **11 put the nips in.** *Austral. & NZ sl.* to exert pressure on someone, esp. in order to extort money. **12** *Arch.* a taunting remark. **13 nip and tuck.** *US & Canad.* neck and neck. [C14: from ON]

nip[2] ❶ (nɪp) *n* **1** a small drink of spirits; dram. ◆ *vb* **nips, nipping, nipped.** **2** to drink spirits, esp. habitually in small amounts. [C18: from *nipperkin* a vessel holding a half-pint or less, from ?]

nipper ❶ ('nɪpə) *n* **1** a person or thing that nips. **2** the large pincer-like claw of a lobster, crab, etc. **3** *Inf., chiefly Brit. & Austral.* a small child. **4** *Austral.* a type of small prawn used as bait.

nippers ('nɪpəz) *pl n* an instrument or tool, such as a pair of pliers, for snipping or squeezing.

nipple ❶ ('nɪpᵊl) *n* **1** the small conical projection in the centre of each breast, which in women contains the outlet of the milk ducts. **2** something resembling a nipple in shape or function. **3** Also called: **grease nipple.** a small drilled bush, usually screwed into a bearing, through which grease is introduced. [C16: from earlier *neble, nible,* ?from NEB, NIB]

nipplewort ('nɪpᵊl,wɜ:t) *n* an annual Eurasian plant with pointed oval leaves and small yellow flower heads.

nippy ❶ ('nɪpɪ) *adj* **nippier, nippiest. 1** (of weather) frosty or chilly. **2** *Brit. inf.* **2a** quick; nimble; active. **2b** (of a motor vehicle) small and relatively powerful. **3** (of dogs) inclined to bite.
▸ **'nippily** *adv*

NIREX ('naɪrɛks) *n acronym for* Nuclear Industry Radioactive Waste Executive.

nirvana ❶ (nɪə'vɑ:nə, nɜ:-) *n Buddhism & Hinduism.* final release from the cycle of reincarnation attained by extinction of all desires and individual existence, culminating (in Buddhism) in absolute blessedness, or (in Hinduism) in absorption into Brahman. [C19: from Sansk.: extinction, from *nir-* out + *vāti* it blows]

Nisei ('ni:seɪ) *n* a native-born citizen of the United States or Canada whose parents were Japanese immigrants. [Japanese, lit.: second generation]

nisi ('naɪsaɪ) *adj* (*postpositive*) *Law.* (of a court order) coming into effect on a specified date unless cause is shown why it should not: *a decree nisi.* [C19: from: unless, if not]

Nissen hut ('nɪsᵊn) *n* a military shelter of semicircular cross section, made of corrugated steel sheet. [C20: after Lt Col. Peter *Nissen* (1871–1930), British mining engineer, its inventor]

nit[1] (nɪt) *n* **1** the egg of a louse, esp. adhering to human hair. **2** the larva of a louse. [OE *hnitu*]

nit[2] (nɪt) *n* a unit of luminance equal to 1 candela per square metre. [C20: from L *nitor* brightness]

nit[3] (nɪt) *n Inf., chiefly Brit.* short for **nitwit.**

nit[4] (nɪt) *n* a unit of information equal to 1.44 bits. Also called: **nepit.** [C20: from *N(apierian dig)it*]

nit[5] (nɪt) *n* **keep nit.** *Austral. inf.* to keep watch, esp. during illegal activity. [C19: from *nix!* a shout of warning]
▸ **'nit-,keeper** *n*

nit-picking ❶ *Inf.* ◆ *n* **1** a concern with insignificant details, esp. with the intention of finding fault. ◆ *adj* **2** showing such a concern; fussy. [C20: from NIT[1] + PICK[1]]
▸ **'nit-,picker** *n*

nitrate ('naɪtreɪt) *n* **1** any salt or ester of nitric acid. **2** a fertilizer containing nitrate salts. ◆ *vb* **nitrates, nitrating, nitrated. 3** (*tr*) to treat with nitric acid or a nitrate. **4** to convert or be converted into a nitrate.
▸ **ni'tration** *n*

nitre *or US* **niter** ('naɪtə) *n* another name for **potassium nitrate** or **sodium nitrate.** [C14: via OF from L *nitrum,* prob. from Gk *nitron*]

nitric ('naɪtrɪk) *adj* of or containing nitrogen.

nitric acid *n* a colourless corrosive liquid important in the manufacture of fertilizers, explosives, and many other chemicals. Formula: HNO_3. Former name: **aqua fortis.**

nitric oxide *n* a colourless reactive gas. Formula: NO. Systematic name: **nitrogen monoxide.**

nitride ('naɪtraɪd) *n* a compound of nitrogen with a more electropositive element.

nitrification (,naɪtrɪfɪ'keɪʃən) *n* **1** the oxidation of the ammonium compounds in dead organic material into nitrites and nitrates by soil nitrobacteria, making nitrogen available to plants. **2** the addition of a nitro group to an organic compound.

nitrify ('naɪtrɪ,faɪ) *vb* **nitrifies, nitrifying, nitrified.** (*tr*) **1** to treat or cause to react with nitrogen. **2** to treat (soil) with nitrates. **3** (of nitrobacteria) to convert (ammonium compounds) into nitrates by oxidation.
▸ **'nitri,fiable** *adj*

nitrite ('naɪtraɪt) *n* any salt or ester of nitrous acid.

nitro- *or before a vowel* **nitr-** *combining form.* **1** indicating that a chemical compound contains a nitro group, $-NO_2$: *nitrobenzene.* **2** indicating that a chemical compound is a nitrate ester: *nitrocellulose.* [from Gk *nitron* NATRON]

nitrobacteria (,naɪtrəʊbæk'tɪərɪə) *pl n, sing* **nitrobacterium** (-'tɪərɪəm). soil bacteria that are involved in nitrification.

nitrobenzene (,naɪtrəʊ'bɛnzi:n) *n* a yellow oily liquid compound, used as a solvent and in the manufacture of aniline. Formula: $C_6H_5NO_2$.

nitrocellulose (,naɪtrəʊ'sɛlju,ləʊs) *n* another name (not in chemical usage) for **cellulose nitrate.**

nitrogen ('naɪtrədʒən) *n* a colourless odourless relatively unreactive gaseous element that forms 78 per cent of the air and is an essential constituent of proteins and nucleic acids. Symbol: N; atomic no.: 7; atomic wt.: 14.0067.

nitrogen cycle *n* the natural circulation of nitrogen by living organisms. Nitrates in the soil, derived from dead organic matter by bacterial action, are absorbed and synthesized into complex organic compounds by plants and reduced to nitrates again when the plants and the animals feeding on them die and decay.

nitrogen dioxide *n* a red-brown poisonous gas that is an intermediate in the manufacture of nitric acid, a nitrating agent, and an oxidizer for rocket fuels. Formula: NO_2.

nitrogen fixation *n* **1** the conversion of atmospheric nitrogen into nitrogen compounds by certain bacteria in the root nodules of le-

THESAURUS

(*inf.*), fool, jerk (*sl., chiefly US & Canad.*), lamebrain (*inf.*), nerd *or* nurd (*sl.*), ninny, nitwit (*inf.*), numbskull *or* numskull, oaf, pillock (*Brit. sl.*), prat (*sl.*), prick (*sl.*), schmuck (*US sl.*), simpleton, twit (*inf., chiefly Brit.*), wally (*sl.*)

nip[1] *vb* **1 = pinch,** catch, compress, grip, snag, squeeze, tweak, twitch **3 = bite,** nibble, snap **6 = thwart,** check, frustrate

nip[2] *n* **1 = dram,** draught, drop, finger, mouthful, peg (*Brit.*), portion, shot (*inf.*), sip, snifter (*inf.*), *soupçon,* sup, swallow, taste

nipper *n* **2 = pincer,** claw **3** *Informal* **= child,** ankle-biter (*Austral. sl.*), baby, boy, girl, infant, kid (*inf.*), little one, rug rat (*sl.*), sprog (*sl.*), tot

nipple *n* **1 = teat,** boob (*sl.*), breast, dug, mamilla, pap, papilla, tit, udder

nippy *adj* **1 = chilly,** biting, nipping, sharp, stinging **2a** *Brit. informal* **= quick,** active, agile, fast, nimble, spry

nirvana *n* **= paradise,** bliss, joy, peace, serenity, tranquillity

nit-picking *adj* **2 = fussy,** captious, carping, cavilling, finicky, hairsplitting, pedantic, pettifogging, quibbling gumes. **2** a process in which atmospheric nitrogen is converted into a nitrogen compound, used esp. for fertilizer.

nitrogenize *or* **nitrogenise** (naɪ'trɒdʒɪˌnaɪz) *vb* **nitrogenizes, nitrogenizing, nitrogenized** *or* **nitrogenises, nitrogenising, nitrogenised.** to combine or treat with nitrogen or a nitrogen compound.
▸**niˌtrogeni'zation** *or* **niˌtrogeni'sation** *n*

nitrogen monoxide *n* the systematic name for **nitric oxide.**

nitrogen mustard *n* any of a class of organic compounds resembling mustard gas in their molecular structure: important in the treatment of cancer.

nitrogenous (naɪ'trɒdʒɪnəs) *adj* containing nitrogen or a nitrogen compound.

nitroglycerine (ˌnaɪtrəʊ'glɪsəriːn) *or* **nitroglycerin** (ˌnaɪtrəʊ'glɪsəˌrɪn) *n* a pale yellow viscous explosive liquid made from glycerol and nitric and sulphuric acids. Formula: $CH_2NO_3CHNO_3CH_2NO_3$. Also called: **trinitroglycerine.**

nitromethane (ˌnaɪtrəʊ'miːθeɪn) *n* an oily colourless liquid obtained from methane and used as a solvent and rocket fuel.

nitrous ('naɪtrəs) *adj* of, derived from, or containing nitrogen, esp. in a low valency state. [C17: from L *nitrōsus* full of natron]

nitrous acid *n* a weak monobasic acid known only in solution and in the form of nitrite salts. Formula: HNO_2. Systematic name: **dioxonitric(III) acid.**

nitrous oxide *n* a colourless gas with a sweet smell: used as an anaesthetic in dentistry. Formula: N_2O. Also called: **laughing gas.** Systematic name: **dinitrogen oxide.**

nitty ('nɪtɪ) *adj* **nittier, nittiest.** infested with nits.

nitty-gritty Ⓣ ('nɪtɪ'grɪtɪ) *n* **the.** *Inf.* the basic facts of a matter, situation, etc.; the core. [C20: ? rhyming compound from GRIT]

nitwit Ⓣ ('nɪtˌwɪt) *n Inf.* a foolish or dull person. [C20: ?from NIT[1] + WIT[1]]

nix[1] (nɪks) *Inf.* ◆ *sentence substitute.* **1** another word for **no**[1]. ◆ *n* **2** a refusal. **3** nothing. [C18: from G, inf. form of *nichts* nothing]

nix[2] (nɪks) *or* (*fem*) **nixie** ('nɪksɪ) *n Germanic myth.* a water sprite, usually unfriendly to humans. [C19: from G *Nixe*, from OHG *nihhus*]

NMR *abbrev. for* nuclear magnetic resonance.

NNE *symbol for* north-northeast.

NNP *abbrev. for* net national product.

NNW *symbol for* north-northwest.

no[1] Ⓣ (nəʊ) *sentence substitute.* **1** used to express denial, disagreement, refusal, etc. ◆ *n, pl* **noes** *or* **nos. 2** an answer or vote of *no.* **3 not take no for an answer.** to continue in a course of action, etc., despite refusals. **4** (*often pl*) a person who votes in the negative. **5 the noes have it.** there is a majority of votes in the negative. [OE *nā*, from *ne* not, no + *ā* ever]

no[2] (nəʊ) *determiner* **1** not any, not a, or not one: *there's no money left; no card in the file.* **2** not at all: *she's no youngster.* **3** (foll. by comparative adjectives and adverbs) not: *no less than forty; no taller than a child.* [OE *nā*, from *nān* NONE]

No[1] *or* **Noh** (nəʊ) *n, pl* **No** *or* **Noh.** the stylized classic drama of Japan, developed in the 15th century or earlier, using music, dancing, and themes from religious stories or myths. [from Japanese *nō* talent, from Chinese *neng*]

No[2] *the chemical symbol for* nobelium.

no' (no, nəʊ) *adv Scot.* not.

No. *abbrev. for:* **1** north(ern). **2** Also: **no.** (*pl* **Nos.** *or* **nos.**) number. [from L *numero* the ablative of *numerus* number]

n.o. *Cricket. abbrev. for* not out.

no-account *adj* **1** worthless; good-for-nothing. ◆ *n* **2** a worthless person.

nob[1] (nɒb) *n Cribbage.* **1** the jack of the suit turned up. **2 one for his nob.** the call made with this jack, scoring one point. [C19: from ?]

nob[2] Ⓣ (nɒb) *n Sl., chiefly Brit.* a person of wealth or social distinction. [C19: from ?]

no-ball *n* **1** *Cricket.* an illegal ball, as for overstepping the crease, for which the batting side scores a run, and from which the batsman can only be out by being run out. **2** *Rounders.* an illegal ball, esp. one bowled too high or too low. ◆ *interj* **3** *Cricket, rounders.* a call by the umpire indicating a no-ball.

nobble Ⓣ ('nɒbᵊl) *vb* **nobbles, nobbling, nobbled.** (*tr*) *Brit. sl.* **1** to disable (a racehorse), esp. with drugs. **2** to win over or outwit (a person) by underhand means. **3** to suborn (a person, esp. a juror) by threats, bribery, etc. **4** to steal. **5** to grab. **6** to kidnap. [C19: from *nobbler*, from a false division of *an hobbler* (one who hobbles horses) as *a nobbler*]

nobelium (nəʊ'biːlɪəm) *n* a transuranic element produced artificially from curium. Symbol: No; atomic no.: 102; half-life of most stable isotope, ^{255}No: 180 seconds (approx.). [C20: NL, after *Nobel* Institute, Stockholm, where it was discovered]

Nobel prize (nəʊ'bel) *n* a prize for outstanding contributions to chemistry, physics, physiology or medicine, literature, economics, and peace that may be awarded annually; established 1901. [C20: after Alfred *Nobel* (1833–96), Swedish chemist and philanthropist]

nobility Ⓣ (nəʊ'bɪlɪtɪ) *n, pl* **nobilities. 1** a privileged class whose titles are conferred by descent or royal decree. **2** the quality of being good; dignity: *nobility of mind.* **3** (in the British Isles) the class of people holding the title of dukes, marquesses, earls, viscounts, or barons and their feminine equivalents; peerage.

nobilmente (ˌnəʊbɪl'mɛnteɪ) *adj, adv Music.* to be performed in a noble manner. [It.]

noble Ⓣ ('nəʊbᵊl) *adj* **1** of or relating to a hereditary class with special status, often derived from a feudal period. **2** of or characterized by high moral qualities; magnanimous: *a noble deed.* **3** having dignity or eminence; illustrious. **4** imposing; magnificent: *a noble avenue of trees.* **5** superior; excellent: *a noble strain of horses.* **6** *Chem.* **6a** (of certain elements) chemically unreactive. **6b** (of certain metals, esp. copper, silver, and gold) resisting oxidation. ◆ *n* **7** a person belonging to a privileged class whose status is usually indicated by a title. **8** (in the British Isles) a person holding the title of duke, marquess, earl, viscount, or baron, or a feminine equivalent. **9** a former British gold coin having the value of one third of a pound. [C13: via OF from L *nōbilis*, orig., capable of being known, hence well-known, from *noscere* to know]
▸**'nobleness** *n* ▸**'nobly** *adv*

nobleman ('nəʊbᵊlmən) *or* (*fem*) **noblewoman** *n, pl* **noblemen** *or* **noblewomen.** a person of noble rank, title, or status; peer; aristocrat.

noble savage *n* (in romanticism) an idealized view of primitive man.

noblesse oblige (nəʊ'bles əʊ'bliːʒ) *n Often ironic.* the supposed obligation of nobility to be honourable and generous. [F, lit.: nobility obliges]

nobody Ⓣ ('nəʊbədɪ) *pron* **1** no person; no-one. ◆ *n, pl* **nobodies. 2** an insignificant person.

> **USAGE NOTE** See at **everyone.**

nock (nɒk) *n* **1** a notch on an arrow that fits on the bowstring. **2** either of the grooves at each end of a bow that hold the bowstring. ◆ *vb* (*tr*) **3** to fit (an arrow) on a bowstring. [C14: rel. to Swedish *nock* tip]

no-claims bonus *n* a reduction on an insurance premium, esp. one covering a motor vehicle, if no claims have been made within a specified period. Also called: **no-claim bonus.**

noctambulism (nɒk'tæmbjʊˌlɪzəm) *or* **noctambulation** *n* another word for **somnambulism.** [C19: from L *nox* night + *ambulāre* to walk]

noctilucent (ˌnɒktɪ'luːsᵊnt) *adj* shining at night, usually of very thin high altitude clouds observable in the summer twilight sky. [from L, from *nox* night + *lūcēre* to shine]

noctuid ('nɒktjʊɪd) *n* any of a large family of nocturnal moths that includes the underwings. [C19: via NL from L *noctua* night owl, from *nox* night]

noctule ('nɒktjuːl) *n* any of several large Old World insectivorous bats. [C18: prob. from LL *noctula* small owl, from L *noctua* night owl]

nocturnal Ⓣ (nɒk'tɜːnᵊl) *adj* **1** of, used during, occurring in, or relating to the night. **2** (of animals) active at night. **3** (of plants) having flowers that open at night and close by day. [C15: from LL *nocturnālis*, from L *nox* night]
▸**ˌnoctur'nality** *n* ▸**noc'turnally** *adv*

nocturne ('nɒktɜːn) *n* **1** a short, dreamy, and melodic piece of music, esp. one for the piano. **2** a painting of a night scene.

nod Ⓣ (nɒd) *vb* **nods, nodding, nodded. 1** to lower and raise (the head) briefly, as to indicate agreement, etc. **2** (*tr*) to express by nodding: *she nodded approval.* **3** (*intr*) (of flowers, trees, etc.) to sway or bend forwards and back. **4** (*intr*) to let the head fall forwards through drowsiness; be almost asleep. **5** (*intr*) to be momentarily careless: *even Homer*

THESAURUS

nitty-gritty *n Informal* = **basics**, bottom line, brass tacks (*inf.*), core, crux, essence, essentials, facts, fundamentals, gist, heart of the matter, ins and outs, nuts and bolts, reality, substance

nitwit *n Informal* = **fool**, dimwit, divvy (*sl.*), dork (*sl.*), dummy (*sl.*), halfwit, lamebrain (*inf.*), nincompoop, ninny, oaf, simpleton

no[1] *sentence substitute* **1** = **never**, nay, not at all, no way ◆ *n* **2** = **refusal**, denial, negation, rejection, veto **4** = **objector**, dissenter, dissident, protester
Antonyms *sentence substitute* ≠ **never:** certainly, of course, yes ◆ *n* ≠ **refusal:** acceptance, assent, consent

nob[2] *n Slang* = **aristocrat**, aristo (*inf.*), big hitter (*inf.*), big shot (*inf.*), bigwig (*inf.*), celeb (*inf.*), fat cat (*sl., chiefly US*), heavy hitter (*inf.*), nabob (*inf.*), toff (*Brit. sl.*), V.I.P.

nobble *vb* **1** *Brit. slang* = **disable**, handicap, incapacitate, weaken **2, 3** *Brit. slang* = **bribe**, get at, influence, intimidate, outwit, win over **4** *Brit. slang* = **steal**, filch, knock off (*sl.*), nick (*sl., chiefly Brit.*), pilfer, pinch (*inf.*), purloin, snitch (*sl.*), swipe (*sl.*) **5** *Brit. slang* = **grab**, get hold of, take

nobility *n* **1, 3** = **aristocracy**, elite, high society, lords, nobles, patricians, peerage, ruling class, upper class **2** = **integrity**, honour, incorruptibility, uprightness, virtue

noble *adj* **1** = **aristocratic**, blue-blooded, gentle (*arch.*), highborn, lordly, patrician, titled **2** = **worthy**, generous, honourable, magnanimous, upright, virtuous **3, 4, 5** = **impressive**, august, dignified, distinguished, elevated, eminent, excellent, grand, great, imposing, lofty, splendid, stately, superb ◆ *n* **7, 8** = **lord**, aristo (*inf.*), aristocrat, nobleman, peer
Antonyms ≠ **aristocratic:** base, humble, ignoble, lowborn, lowly, peasant, plebeian, vulgar *adj* ≠ **worthy:** contemptible, despicable, dishonest, selfish ≠ **impressive:** base, humble, ignoble, insignificant, lowly, mean, modest, plain ◆ *n* ≠ **lord:** commoner, peasant, serf

nobody *pron* **1** = **no-one** ◆ *n* **2** = **nonentity**, cipher, lightweight (*inf.*), menial, nothing (*inf.*)
Antonyms *n* ≠ **nonentity:** big name, big noise (*inf.*), big shot (*sl.*), celeb (*inf.*), celebrity, megastar (*inf.*), personage, star, superstar, V.I.P.

nocturnal *adj* **1** = **nightly**, night, night-time, of the night

nod *vb* **1** = **acknowledge**, bob, bow, dip, duck, gesture, indicate, salute, signal **2** = **agree**, assent, concur, show agreement **4** = **sleep**, be sleepy, doze, droop, drowse, kip (*Brit. sl.*), nap, slump, zizz (*Brit. inf.*) ◆ *n* **7** = **gesture**, acknowl-

sometimes nods. **6 nodding acquaintance.** a slight, casual, or superficial knowledge (of a subject or person). ◆ *n* **7** a quick down-and-up movement of the head, as in assent, command, etc. **8 on the nod.** *Inf.* agreed, as in committee, without formal procedure. **9** See **land of Nod.** ◆ See also **nod off.** [C14 *nodde,* from ?]
▸ **'nodding** *adj, n*

noddle[1] ('nɒdᵊl) *n Inf., chiefly Brit.* the head or brains: *use your noddle!* [C15: from ?]

noddle[2] ('nɒdᵊl) *vb* **noddles, noddling, noddled.** *Inf., chiefly Brit.* to nod (the head), as through drowsiness. [C18: from NOD]

noddy[1] ('nɒdɪ) *n, pl* **noddies. 1** any of several tropical terns, typically having a dark plumage. **2** a fool or dunce. [C16: ? n use of obs. *noddy* foolish, drowsy, ?from NOD (vb); the bird is so called because it allows itself to be caught by hand]

noddy[2] ('nɒdɪ) *n, pl* **noddies.** *(usually pl) Television.* film footage of an interviewer's reactions to comments made by an interviewee, used in editing the interview after it has been recorded. [C20: from NOD]

node Ⓣ (nəʊd) *n* **1** a knot, swelling, or knob. **2** the point on a plant stem from which the leaves or lateral branches grow. **3** *Physics.* a point at which the amplitude of one of the two kinds of displacement in a standing wave has zero or minimum value. **4** Also called: **crunode.** *Maths.* a point at which two branches of a curve intersect. **5** *Maths., linguistics.* one of the objects of which a graph or a tree consists. **6** *Astron.* either of the two points at which the orbit of a body intersects the plane of the ecliptic. **7** *Anat.* any natural bulge or swelling, such as those along the course of a lymphatic vessel (**lymph node**). **8** *Computing.* an interconnection point on a computer network. [C16: from L *nōdus* knot]
▸ **'nodal** *adj*

nod off *vb (intr, adv) Inf.* to fall asleep.

nodule ('nɒdjuːl) *n* **1** a small knot, lump, or node. **2** any of the knoblike outgrowths on the roots of clover and other legumes that contain bacteria involved in nitrogen fixation. **3** a small rounded lump of rock or mineral substance, esp. in a matrix of different rock material. [C17: from L *nōdulus,* from *nōdus* knot]
▸ **'nodular, 'nodulose,** *or* **'nodulous** *adj*

Noel *or* **Noël** (nəʊ'el) *n* (in carols, etc.) another word for **Christmas.** [C19: from F, from L *nātālis* a birthday]

noetic (nəʊ'etɪk) *adj* of or relating to the mind. [C17: from Gk *noētikos,* from *noein* to think]

nog *or* **nogg** (nɒg) *n* **1** Also called: **flip.** a drink, esp. an alcoholic one, containing beaten egg. **2** *East Anglian dialect.* strong local beer. [C17 (orig.: a strong beer): from ?]

noggin Ⓣ ('nɒgɪn) *n* **1** a small quantity of spirits. **2** a small mug. **3** *Inf.* the head. [C17: from ?]

no-go area *n* a district in a town that is barricaded off, usually by a paramilitary organization, which the police, army, etc., can only enter by force.

Noh (nəʊ) *n* a variant spelling of **No**[1].

noir (nwɑː) *adj* (of a film) showing characteristics of a *film noir,* in plot or style. [C20: from French, lit.: black]

noise Ⓣ (nɔɪz) *n* **1** a sound, esp. one that is loud or disturbing. **2** loud shouting; clamour; din. **3** any undesired electrical disturbance in a circuit, etc. **4** undesired or irrelevant elements in a visual image: *removing noise from pictures.* **5** *(pl)* conventional comments or sounds conveying a reaction: *sympathetic noises.* **6 make a noise.** to talk a great deal or complain (about). ◆ *vb* **noises, noising, noised. 7** *(tr;* usually foll. by *abroad* or *about)* to spread (news, gossip, etc.). [C13: from OF, from L: NAUSEA]

noiseless Ⓣ ('nɔɪzlɪs) *adj* making little or no sound.
▸ **'noiselessly** *adv* ▸ **'noiselessness** *n*

noise pollution *n* annoying or harmful noise in an environment.

noisette (nwɑː'zet) *adj* **1** flavoured with hazelnuts. **2** nutbrown, as butter browned over heat. ◆ *n* **3** a small round or oval piece of meat. **4** a hazelnut chocolate. [from F: hazelnut]

noisome Ⓣ ('nɔɪsəm) *adj* **1** (esp. of smells) offensive. **2** harmful or noxious. [C14: from obs. *noy,* var. of ANNOY + -SOME[1]]
▸ **'noisomeness** *n*

noisy Ⓣ ('nɔɪzɪ) *adj* **noisier, noisiest. 1** making a loud or constant noise. **2** full of or characterized by noise.
▸ **'noisily** *adv* ▸ **'noisiness** *n*

nolens volens *Latin.* ('nəʊlenz 'vəʊlenz) *adv* whether willing or unwilling.

nolle prosequi ('nɒlɪ 'prɒsɪˌkwaɪ) *n Law.* an entry made on the court record when the plaintiff or prosecutor undertakes not to continue the action or prosecution. [L: do not pursue]

nomad Ⓣ ('nəʊmæd) *n* **1** a member of a people or tribe who move from place to place to find pasture and food. **2** a wanderer. [C16: via F from L *nomas* wandering shepherd, from Gk]
▸ **no'madic** *adj* ▸ **'nomadism** *n*

no-man's-land *n* **1** land between boundaries, esp. an unoccupied zone between opposing forces. **2** an unowned or unclaimed piece of land. **3** an ambiguous area of activity.

nom de guerre ('nɒm də 'geə) *n, pl* **noms de guerre** ('nɒm də 'geə). an assumed name. [F, lit.: war name]

nom de plume Ⓣ ('nɒm də 'pluːm) *n, pl* **noms de plume** ('nɒm də 'pluːm). another term for **pen name.** [F]

nomenclature Ⓣ (nəʊ'menklətʃə; *US.* 'nəʊmənˌkleɪtʃər) *n* the terminology used in a particular science, art, activity, etc. [C17: from L *nōmenclātūra* list of names]

nominal Ⓣ ('nɒmɪnᵊl) *adj* **1** in name only; theoretical: *the nominal leader.* **2** minimal in comparison with real worth; token: *a nominal fee.* **3** of, constituting, or giving a name. **4** *Grammar.* of or relating to a noun or noun phrase. ◆ *n* **5** *Grammar.* a noun, noun phrase, or syntactically similar structure. [C15: from L *nōminālis,* from *nōmen* name]
▸ **'nominally** *adv*

nominalism ('nɒmɪnᵊˌlɪzəm) *n* the philosophical theory that the variety of objects to which a single general name, such as *dog,* applies have nothing in common other than that name.
▸ **'nominalist** *n*

nominal value *n* another name for **par value.**

nominate Ⓣ ('nɒmɪˌneɪt) *vb* **nominates, nominating, nominated.** *(mainly tr)* **1** to propose as a candidate, esp. for an elective office. **2** to appoint to an office or position. **3** to name (someone) to act on one's behalf, esp. to conceal one's identity. **4** *(intr) Austral.* to stand as a candidate in an election. [C16: from L *nōmināre* to call by name, from *nōmen* name]
▸ **ˌnomi'nation** *n* ▸ **'nomiˌnator** *n*

nominative ('nɒmɪnətɪv) *adj* **1** *Grammar.* denoting a case of nouns and pronouns in inflected languages that is used esp. to identify the subject of a finite verb. **2** appointed rather than elected to a position, office, etc. ◆ *n* **3** *Grammar.* **3a** the nominative case. **3b** a word or speech element in the nominative case. [C14: from L *nōminātīvus* belonging to naming, from *nōmen* name]
▸ **nominatival** (ˌnɒmɪnə'taɪvᵊl) *adj*

nominee Ⓣ (ˌnɒmɪ'niː) *n* **1** a person who is nominated to an office or as a candidate. **2a** a person or organization named to act on behalf of someone else, esp. to conceal the identity of the nominator. **2b** *(as modifier): nominee shareholder.* [C17: from NOMINATE + -EE]

nomogram ('nɒməˌgræm, 'nəʊmə-) *or* **nomograph** *n* an arrangement of two linear or logarithmic scales such that an intersecting straight line enables intermediate values or values on a third scale to be read off. [C20: from Gk *nomos* law + -GRAM]

-nomy *n combining form.* indicating a science or the laws governing a certain field of knowledge: *agronomy; economy.* [from Gk *-nomia* law]
▸ **-nomic** *adj combining form.*

non- *prefix* **1** indicating negation: *nonexistent.* **2** indicating refusal or failure: *noncooperation.* **3** indicating exclusion from a specified class: *nonfiction.* **4** indicating lack or absence: *nonobjective; nonevent.* [from L *nōn* not]

nonaddictive (ˌnɒnə'dɪktɪv) *adj* (of a drug, etc.) not causing addiction.

nonage ('nəʊnɪdʒ) *n* **1** *Law.* the state of being under any of various ages at which a person may legally enter into certain transactions, such as marrying, etc. **2** any period of immaturity.

nonagenarian (ˌnəʊnədʒɪ'neərɪən) *n* **1** a person who is from 90 to 99 years old. ◆ *adj* **2** of, relating to, or denoting a nonagenarian. [C19: from L *nōnāgēnārius,* from *nōnāginta* ninety]

nonaggression (ˌnɒnə'greʃən) *n* **a** restraint of aggression, esp. between states. **b** *(as modifier): a nonaggression pact.*

nonagon ('nɒnəˌgɒn) *n* a polygon having nine sides.
▸ **nonagonal** (nɒn'ægənᵊl) *adj*

nonalcoholic (ˌnɒnˌælkə'hɒl'ɪk) *adj* (of a drink, etc.) not containing alcohol.

THESAURUS

edgment, beck, greeting, indication, salute, sign, signal

node *n* **1** = **nodule,** bud, bump, burl, growth, knob, knot, lump, protuberance, swelling

noggin *n* **1** = **dram,** nip, tot **2** = **mug,** cup **3** *Informal* = **head,** bean *(US & Canad. sl.),* block *(inf.),* bonce *(Brit. sl.),* conk *(sl.),* dome *(sl.),* noddle *(inf., chiefly Brit.),* nut *(sl.)*

noise *n* **1, 2** = **sound,** babble, blare, clamour, clatter, commotion, cry, din, fracas, hubbub, outcry, pandemonium, racket, row, rumpus, talk, tumult, uproar ◆ *vb* **7** = **report,** advertise, bruit, circulate, gossip, publicize, repeat, rumour

noiseless *adj* = **silent,** hushed, inaudible, mute, muted, quiet, soundless, still

noisome *adj* **1** = **offensive,** disgusting, fetid, foul, malodorous, mephitic, niffy, putrid, reeking, smelly, stinking **2** = **harmful,** bad, baneful *(arch.),* deleterious, hurtful, injurious, noxious, pernicious, pestiferous, pestilential, poisonous, unhealthy, unwholesome

noisy *adj* **1, 2** = **loud,** boisterous, cacophonous, chattering, clamorous, deafening, ear-splitting, obstreperous, piercing, riotous, strident, tumultuous, turbulent, uproarious, vociferous
Antonyms *adj* hushed, quiet, silent, still, subdued, tranquil, tuneful

nomad *n* **2** = **wanderer,** drifter, itinerant, rambler, rover, vagabond

nomadic *adj* **1** = **migratory,** migrant, pastoral **2** = **wandering,** itinerant, peripatetic, roaming, roving, travelling, vagrant

nom de plume *n* = **pseudonym,** alias, assumed name, nom de guerre, pen name

nomenclature *n* = **terminology,** classification, codification, locution, phraseology, taxonomy, vocabulary

nominal *adj* **1** = **so-called,** formal, ostensible, pretended, professed, purported, self-styled, *soi-disant,* supposed, theoretical, titular **2** = **small,** inconsiderable, insignificant, minimal, symbolic, token, trifling, trivial

nominate *vb* **1** = **propose,** present, recommend, submit, suggest **2** = **appoint,** assign, choose, commission, designate, elect, elevate, empower, name, select

nomination *n* **1** = **proposal,** recommendation, suggestion **2** = **appointment,** choice, designation, election, selection

nominee *n* **1** = **candidate,** aspirant, contestant, entrant, favourite, protégé, runner

nonaligned ❶ (ˌnɒnəˈlaɪnd) *adj* (of states, etc.) not part of a major alliance or power bloc.
▸ˌ**nonaˈlignment** *n*

non-A, non-B hepatitis *n* a form of viral hepatitis, not caused by the agents responsible for hepatitis A and hepatitis B, that is commonly transmitted by infected blood transfusions. The causative virus has been isolated. Also called: **hepatitis C.**

nonce (nɒns) *n* the present time or occasion (now only in **for the nonce**). [C12: from *for the nonce*, a mistaken division of *for then anes*, from *then* dative singular of *the* + *anes* ONCE]

nonce word *n* a word coined for a single occasion.

nonchalant ❶ (ˈnɒnʃələnt) *adj* casually unconcerned or indifferent; uninvolved. [C18: from F, from *nonchaloir* to lack warmth, from NON- + *chaloir* from L *calēre* to be warm]
▸ˈ**nonchalance** *n*

non-com (ˈnɒnˌkɒm) *n* short for **noncommissioned officer.**

noncombatant ❶ (nɒnˈkɒmbətənt) *n* **1** a civilian in time of war. **2** a member of the armed forces whose duties do not include fighting, such as a chaplain or surgeon.

noncommissioned officer (ˌnɒnkəˈmɪʃənd) *n* (in the armed forces) a person, such as a sergeant or corporal, who is appointed from the ranks as a subordinate officer.

noncommittal ❶ (ˌnɒnkəˈmɪtᵊl) *adj* not involving or revealing commitment to any particular opinion or action.

non compos mentis ❶ *Latin.* (ˈnɒn ˈkɒmpəs ˈmɛntɪs) *adj* mentally incapable of managing one's own affairs; of unsound mind. [L: not in control of one's mind]

nonconformist ❶ (ˌnɒnkənˈfɔːmɪst) *n* **1** a person who does not conform to generally accepted patterns of behaviour or thought. ◆ *adj* **2** of or characterized by behaviour that does not conform to accepted patterns.
▸ˌ**nonconˈformity** *or* ˌ**nonconˈformism** *n*

Nonconformist (ˌnɒnkənˈfɔːmɪst) *n* **1** a member of a Protestant denomination that dissents from an Established Church, esp. the Church of England. ◆ *adj* **2** of, relating to, or denoting Nonconformists.
▸ˌ**Nonconˈformity** *or* ˌ**Nonconˈformism** *n*

noncontributory (ˌnɒnkənˈtrɪbjʊtərɪ) *adj* **1** denoting an insurance or pension scheme for employees, the premiums of which are paid by the employer. **2** (of a state benefit) not dependent on national insurance contributions.

nondenominational (ˌnɒndɪˌnɒmɪˈneɪʃənᵊl) *adj* not restricted with regard to religious denomination.

nondescript ❶ (ˈnɒndɪˌskrɪpt) *adj* **1** having no outstanding features. ◆ *n* **2** a nondescript person or thing. [C17: from NON- + L *dēscriptus*, p.p. of *dēscribere* to copy]

nondomiciled (nɒnˈdɒmɪˌsaɪld) *adj* of, relating to, or denoting a person who is not domiciled in his country of origin.

none[1] ❶ (nʌn) *pron* **1** not any of a particular class: *none of my letters has arrived.* **2** no-one; nobody: *there was none to tell the tale.* **3** not any (of): *none of it looks edible.* **4 none other.** no other person: *none other than the Queen herself.* **5 none the.** (*foll. by a comparative adj*) in no degree: *she was none the worse for her ordeal.* **6 none too.** not very: *he was none too pleased.* [OE *nān*, lit.: not one]

> **USAGE NOTE** *None* is a singular pronoun and should be used with a singular form of a verb: *none of the students has* (not *have*) a car.

none[2] (nəʊn) *n* another word for **nones.**

nonentity ❶ (nɒnˈɛntɪtɪ) *n, pl* **nonentities. 1** an insignificant person or thing. **2** a nonexistent thing. **3** the state of not existing; nonexistence.

nones (nəʊnz) *n* (*functioning as sing or pl*) **1** (in the Roman calendar) the ninth day before the ides of each month: the seventh day of March, May, July, and October, and the fifth of each other month. **2** *Chiefly RC Church.* the fifth of the seven canonical hours of the divine office, originally fixed at the ninth hour of the day, about 3 p.m. [OE *nōn*, from L *nōna hora* ninth hour, from *nōnus* ninth]

nonesuch *or* **nonsuch** (ˈnʌnˌsʌtʃ) *n Arch.* a matchless person or thing; nonpareil.

nonet (nəʊˈnɛt) *n* **1** a piece of music for nine instruments or voices. **2** a group of nine singers or instrumentalists.

nonetheless ❶ (ˌnʌnðəˈlɛs) *sentence connector.* despite that; however; nevertheless.

non-Euclidean geometry *n* the branch of modern geometry in which certain axioms of Euclidean geometry are denied.

nonevent ❶ (ˌnɒnɪˈvɛnt) *n* a disappointing or insignificant occurrence, esp. one predicted to be important.

nonexecutive director (ˌnɒnɪgˈzɛkjʊtɪv) *n* a director of a commercial company who is not a full-time employee of the company.

nonexistent ❶ (ˌnɒnɪgˈzɪstənt) *adj* **1** not having being or reality. **2** not present under specified conditions or in a specified place.
▸**nonexˈistence** *n*

nonfeasance (nɒnˈfiːzᵊns) *n Law.* a failure to act when under an obligation to do so. Cf. **malfeasance, misfeasance.** [C16: from NON- + *feasance* (obs.) doing, from F *faisance*, from *faire* to do, L *facere*]

nonferrous (nɒnˈfɛrəs) *adj* **1** denoting any metal other than iron. **2** not containing iron.

nonflammable (nɒnˈflæməbᵊl) *adj* incapable of burning or not easily set on fire.

nonfunctional (ˌnɒnˈfʌŋkʃənᵊl) *adj* not having a function.

nong (nɒŋ) *n Austral. sl.* a stupid or incompetent person. [C19: ?from obs. E dialect *nigmenog* silly fellow, from ?]

nonillion (nəʊˈnɪljən) *n* **1** (in Britain, France, and Germany) the number represented as one followed by 54 zeros (10^{54}). **2** (in the US and Canada) the number represented as one followed by 30 zeros (10^{30}). Brit. word: **quintillion.** [C17: from F, from L *nōnus* ninth, on the model of MILLION]

nonintervention (ˌnɒnɪntəˈvɛnʃən) *n* refusal to intervene, esp. the abstention by a state from intervening in the affairs of other states or in its own internal disputes.

noninvasive (ˌnɒnɪnˈveɪsɪv) *adj* (of medical treatment) not involving the making of a relatively large incision in the body or the insertion of instruments, etc., into the patient.

nonjudgmental (ˌnɒndʒʌdʒˈmɛntᵊl) *adj* avoiding moral judgments, esp. relating to the conduct of others.

nonjuror (nɒnˈdʒʊərə) *n* a person who refuses to take an oath, as of allegiance.

Nonjuror (nɒnˈdʒʊərə) *n* any of a group of clergy in England and Scotland who declined to take the oath of allegiance to William and Mary in 1689.

nonlinear (ˌnɒnˈlɪnɪə) *adj* not linear, esp. with regard to dimension.

nonmetal (nɒnˈmɛtᵊl) *n* any of a number of chemical elements that have acidic oxides and are poor conductors of heat and electricity.
▸ˌ**nonmeˈtallic** *adj*

nonmoral (nɒnˈmɒrəl) *adj* not involving morality or ethics; neither moral nor immoral.

nonobjective (ˌnɒnəbˈdʒɛktɪv) *adj* of or designating an art movement in which things are depicted in an abstract or purely formalized way.

no-nonsense (ˌnəʊˈnɒnsəns) *adj* sensible, practical, and straightforward: *a severe no-nonsense look.*

nonpareil (ˈnɒnpərəl, ˌnɒnpəˈreɪl) *n* a person or thing that is unsurpassed; peerless example. [C15: from F, from NON- + *pareil* similar]

nonpersistent (ˌnɒnpəˈsɪstənt) *adj* (of pesticides) breaking down rapidly after application; not persisting in the environment.

non-person *n* a person regarded as nonexistent or unimportant; a nonentity.

nonplus ❶ (nɒnˈplʌs) *vb* **nonplusses, nonplussing, nonplussed** *or US* **nonpluses, nonplusing, nonplused. 1** (*tr*) to put at a loss; confound. ◆ *n, pl* **nonpluses. 2** a state of utter perplexity prohibiting action or speech. [C16: from L *nōn plūs* no further]

nonprofessional (ˌnɒnprəˈfɛʃənᵊl) *adj* **1** not professional in status. ◆ *n* **2** a person who is not a professional.

THESAURUS

nonaligned *adj* = **neutral**, impartial, uncommitted, undecided

nonchalance *n* = **indifference**, calm, composure, cool (*sl.*), equanimity, imperturbability, sang-froid, self-possession, unconcern

nonchalant *adj* = **casual**, airy, apathetic, blasé, calm, careless, collected, cool, detached, dispassionate, indifferent, insouciant, laid-back (*inf.*), offhand, unconcerned, unemotional, unfazed (*inf.*), unperturbed
Antonyms *adj* anxious, caring, concerned, involved, worried

noncombatant *n* **1** = **civilian**, neutral, nonbelligerent

noncommittal *adj* = **evasive**, ambiguous, careful, cautious, circumspect, discreet, equivocal, guarded, indefinite, neutral, politic, reserved, tactful, temporizing, tentative, unrevealing, vague, wary

non compos mentis *adj* = **insane**, crazy, deranged, mentally ill, of unsound mind, unbalanced, unhinged
Antonyms *adj* all there (*inf.*), *compos mentis*, in one's right mind, lucid, mentally sound, rational, sane

nonconformist *n* **1** = **maverick**, dissenter, dissentient, eccentric, heretic, iconoclast, individualist, protester, radical, rebel
Antonyms *n* Babbitt (*US*), conventionalist, stick-in-the-mud (*inf.*), traditionalist, yes man

nonconformity *n* = **dissent**, eccentricity, heresy, heterodoxy, unconventionality

nondescript *adj* **1** = **ordinary**, bog-standard, characterless, common or garden (*inf.*), commonplace, dull, featureless, indeterminate, mousy, run-of-the-mill, undistinguished, unexceptional, uninspiring, uninteresting, unmemorable, unremarkable, vague, vanilla (*inf.*)
Antonyms *adj* distinctive, extraordinary, memorable, remarkable, unique, unusual

none[1] *pron* **1** = **not any**, not one **2** = **no-one**, nobody **3** = **no part**, bugger all (*sl.*), nil, not a bit, nothing, zero, zilch (*sl., chiefly US & Canad.*)

nonentity *n* **1** = **nobody**, cipher, lightweight (*inf.*), mediocrity, small fry, unimportant person

nonetheless *sentence connector* = **nevertheless**, despite that, even so, however, in spite of that, yet

nonevent *n* = **flop** (*inf.*), disappointment, dud (*inf.*), failure, fiasco, washout

nonexistent *adj* **1** = **imaginary**, chimerical, fancied, fictional, hallucinatory, hypothetical, illusory, imagined, insubstantial, legendary, mythical, unreal
Antonyms *adj* actual, existent, existing, genuine, real, true, veritable

nonplus *vb* **1** = **take aback**, astonish, astound, baffle, bewilder, confound, confuse, discomfit, disconcert, discountenance, dismay, dumb-

non-profit-making *adj* not yielding a profit, esp. because organized or established for some other reason: *a non-profit-making organization.*

nonproliferation (ˌnɒnprəˌlɪfəˈreɪʃən) *n* **a** limitation of the production or spread of something, esp. nuclear or chemical weapons. **b** (*as modifier*): *a nonproliferation treaty.*

non-pros (ˌnɒnˈprɒs) *n* **1** short for **non prosequitur.** ◆ *vb* **non-prosses, non-prossing, non-prossed. 2** (*tr*) to enter a judgment of non prosequitur against (a plaintiff).

non prosequitur (ˈnɒn prəʊˈsɛkwɪtə) *n Law.* (formerly) a judgment in favour of a defendant when the plaintiff failed to take the necessary steps in an action within the time allowed. [L, lit.: he does not prosecute]

nonracial (ˌnɒnˈreɪʃəl) *adj* not involving race or racial factors.

nonrepresentational (ˌnɒnreprɪzɛnˈteɪʃənᵊl) *adj Art.* another word for **abstract.**

nonresident (nɒnˈrɛzɪdənt) *n* **1** a person who is not residing in the place implied or specified. **2** a British person employed abroad for a minimum of one year, who is exempt from UK income tax provided that he does not spend more than 90 days in the UK during that tax year. ◆ *adj* **3** not residing in the place specified.
▸**nonˈresidence** *or* **nonˈresidency** *n* ▸**ˌnonresiˈdential** *adj*

nonresistant (ˌnɒnrɪˈzɪstənt) *adj* **1** incapable of resisting something, such as a disease; susceptible. **2** *History.* (esp. in 17th-century England) practising passive obedience to royal authority even when its commands were unjust.

nonrestrictive (ˌnɒnrɪˈstrɪktɪv) *adj* **1** not limiting. **2** *Grammar.* denoting a relative clause that is not restrictive. Cf. **restrictive** (sense 2).

nonsense ❶ (ˈnɒnsəns) *n* **1** something that has or makes no sense; unintelligible language; drivel. **2** conduct or action that is absurd. **3** foolish behaviour: *she'll stand no nonsense.* **4** things of little or no value; trash. ◆ *interj* **5** an exclamation of disagreement.
▸**nonsensical** (nɒnˈsɛnsɪkᵊl) *adj* ▸**nonˈsensically** *adv* ▸**nonˈsensicalness** *or* **nonˌsensiˈcality** *n*

nonsense verse *n* verse in which the sense is nonexistent or absurd.

non sequitur (ˈnɒn ˈsɛkwɪtə) *n* **1** a statement having little or no relevance to what preceded it. **2** *Logic.* a conclusion that does not follow from the premises. [L, lit.: it does not follow]

nonsmoker (nɒnˈsməʊkə) *n* **1** a person who does not smoke. **2** a train compartment in which smoking is forbidden.
▸**nonˈsmoking** *adj*

nonspecific urethritis *n* inflammation of the urethra as a result of a sexually transmitted infection that cannot be traced to a specific cause. Abbrev.: **NSU.**

nonstandard (nɒnˈstændəd) *adj* **1** denoting or characterized by idiom, vocabulary, etc., that is not regarded as correct and acceptable by educated native speakers of a language; not standard. **2** deviating from a given standard.

nonstarter ❶ (nɒnˈstɑːtə) *n* **1** a horse that fails to run in a race for which it has been entered. **2** a person or thing that has little chance of success.

nonstick (ˈnɒnˈstɪk) *adj* (of saucepans, etc.) coated with a substance that prevents food sticking to them.

nonstop ❶ (ˈnɒnˈstɒp) *adj, adv* done without pause or interruption: *a nonstop flight.*

nonsuch (ˈnʌnˌsʌtʃ) *n* a variant spelling of **nonesuch.**

nonsuit (nɒnˈsuːt) *Law.* ◆ *n* **1** an order of a judge dismissing a suit when the plaintiff fails to show he has a good cause of action or fails to produce any evidence. ◆ *vb* **2** (*tr*) to order the dismissal of the suit of (a person).

nontechnical (ˌnɒnˈtɛknɪkᵊl) *adj* **1** not technical in nature. **2** (of a person) not having technical knowledge or aptitude.

non troppo (ˈnɒn ˈtrɒpəʊ) *adv Music.* (preceded by a direction, esp. a tempo marking) not to be observed too strictly (esp. in **allegro ma non troppo, adagio ma non troppo**). [It.]

non-U (nɒnˈjuː) *adj Brit. inf.* (esp. of language) not characteristic of or used by the upper class.

nonunion (nɒnˈjuːnjən) *adj* **1** not belonging or related to a trade union: *nonunion workers.* **2** not favouring or employing union labour: *a nonunion shop.* **3** not produced by union labour.

nonvoter (nɒnˈvəʊtə) *n* **1** a person who does not vote. **2** a person not eligible to vote.

nonvoting (nɒnˈvəʊtɪŋ) *adj* **1** of or relating to a nonvoter. **2** *Finance.* (of shares, etc.) not entitling the holder to vote at company meetings.

noodle[1] (ˈnuːdᵊl) *n* (*often pl*) pasta in the form of ribbons or fine strands. [C18: from G *Nudel* from ?]

noodle[2] (ˈnuːdᵊl) *n* **1** *US & Canad. sl.* the head. **2** a simpleton. [C18: ? a blend of NODDLE[1] & NOODLE[1]]

nook ❶ (nʊk) *n* **1** a corner or narrow recess. **2** a secluded or sheltered place. [C13: from ?]

nooky *or* **nookie** (ˈnʊkɪ) *n Sl.* lovemaking.

noon ❶ (nuːn) *n* **1** the middle of the day; 12 o'clock. **2** *Poetic.* the most important part; culmination. [OE *nōn,* from L *nōna* (*hōra*) ninth hour (orig. 3 p.m., the ninth hour from sunrise)]

noonday (ˈnuːnˌdeɪ) *n* the middle of the day; noon.

no-one *or* **no one** *pron* no person; nobody.

> **USAGE NOTE** See at **everyone.**

noontime (ˈnuːnˌtaɪm) *or* **noontide** *n* the middle of the day; noon.

noose (nuːs) *n* **1** a loop in the end of a rope, such as a lasso or hangman's halter, usually tied with a slipknot. **2** something that restrains or traps. **3 put one's head in a noose.** to bring about one's own downfall. ◆ *vb* **nooses, noosing, noosed.** (*tr*) **4** to secure as in a noose. **5** to make a noose of or in. [C15: ?from Provençal *nous,* from L *nōdus* NODE]

no-par *adj* (of securities) without a par value.

nor (nɔː; *unstressed* nə) *conj* (*coordinating*) **1** (used to join alternatives, the first of which is preceded by *neither*) and not: *neither measles nor mumps.* **2** (foll. by a verb) (and) not…either: *they weren't talented — nor were they particularly funny.* **3** *Poetic.* neither: *nor wind nor rain.* [C13: contraction of OE *nōther,* from *nāhwæther* NEITHER]

Nor. *abbrev. for:* **1** Norman. **2** north. **3** Norway. **4** Norwegian.

noradrenaline (ˌnɔːrəˈdrɛnəlɪn, -liːn) *or* **noradrenalin** *n* a hormone secreted by the adrenal medulla, increasing blood pressure and heart rate. US name: **norepinephrine.**

NOR circuit *or* **gate** (nɔː) *n Computing.* a logic circuit having two or more input wires and one output wire that has a high-voltage output signal only if all input signals are at a low voltage. Cf. **AND circuit.** [C20: from NOR; the action performed is similar to the operation of the conjunction *nor* in logic]

nordic (ˈnɔːdɪk) *adj Skiing.* of competitions in cross-country racing and ski-jumping. Cf. **alpine** (sense 4).

Nordic (ˈnɔːdɪk) *adj* of or belonging to a subdivision of the Caucasoid race typified by the tall blond blue-eyed long-headed inhabitants of Scandinavia. [C19: from F *nordique,* from *nord* NORTH]

norepinephrine (ˌnɔːrɛpɪˈnɛfrɪn, -riːn) *n* the US name for **noradrenaline.**

Norfolk jacket (ˈnɔːfək) *n* a man's single-breasted belted jacket with one or two chest pockets and a box pleat down the back. [C19: worn in *Norfolk* for duck shooting]

noria (ˈnɔːrɪə) *n* a water wheel with buckets attached to its rim for raising water from a stream into irrigation canals, etc. [C18: via Sp. from Ar. *nāʿūra,* from *naʿara* to creak]

nork (nɔːk) *n* (*usually pl*) *Austral. taboo sl.* a female breast. [C20: from ?]

norm ❶ (nɔːm) *n* **1** an average level of achievement or performance, as of a group. **2** a standard of achievement or behaviour that is required, desired, or designated as normal. [C19: from L *norma* carpenter's square]

normal ❶ (ˈnɔːmᵊl) *adj* **1** usual; regular; common; typical: *the normal level.* **2** constituting a standard: *if we take this as normal.* **3** *Psychol.* **3a** being within certain limits of intelligence, ability, etc. **3b** conforming to the conventions of one's group. **4** (of laboratory animals) maintained in a natural state for purposes of comparison with animals treated with drugs, etc. **5** *Chem.* (of a solution) containing a number of grams equal to the equivalent weight of the solute in each litre of solvent. **6** *Geom.* another word for **perpendicular** (sense 1). ◆ *n* **7** the usual, average, or typical state, degree, form, etc. **8** anything that is normal. **9** *Geom.* a perpendicular line or plane. [C16: from L *normālis* conforming to the carpenter's square, from *norma* NORM]
▸**normality** (nɔːˈmælɪtɪ) *or esp. US* ˈ**normalcy** *n*

THESAURUS

found, embarrass, faze, flummox, mystify, perplex, puzzle, stump, stun

nonsense *n* **1** = **rubbish,** balderdash, bilge (*inf.*), bosh (*inf.*), bunk (*inf.*), bunkum *or* buncombe (*chiefly US*), claptrap (*inf.*), cobblers (*Brit. taboo sl.*), crap (*sl.*), double Dutch (*Brit. inf.*), drivel, garbage (*inf.*), gibberish, hogwash, hokum (*sl., chiefly US & Canad.*), hot air (*inf.*), jest, moonshine, piffle (*inf.*), poppycock (*inf.*), rot, tommyrot, tosh (*sl., chiefly Brit.*), trash, tripe (*inf.*), twaddle, waffle (*inf., chiefly Brit.*) **2, 3** = **foolishness,** absurdity, fatuity, folly, idiocy, inanity, ludicrousness, ridiculousness, senselessness, silliness, stupidity
Antonyms *n* ≠ **rubbish:** fact, reality, reason, sense, truth ≠ **foolishness:** seriousness, wisdom

nonsensical *adj* **1** = **senseless,** incomprehensible, meaningless **2** = **foolish,** absurd, asinine, crazy, inane, irrational, ludicrous, ridiculous, silly

nonstarter *n* **2** = **dead loss,** dud (*inf.*), lemon (*inf.*), loser, no-hoper (*inf.*), turkey (*inf.*), washout (*inf.*), waste of space *or* time

nonstop *adj* = **continuous,** ceaseless, constant, direct, endless, incessant, interminable, relentless, steady, unbroken, unending, unfaltering, uninterrupted, unremitting ◆ *adv* = **continuously,** ceaselessly, constantly, directly, endlessly, incessantly, interminably, perpetually, relentlessly, steadily, unbrokenly, unendingly, unfalteringly, uninterruptedly, unremittingly, without stopping
Antonyms *adj* ≠ **continuous:** broken, discontinuous, fitful, intermittent, irregular, occasional, periodic, punctuated, recurrent, spasmodic, sporadic, stop-go (*inf.*)

nook *n* **1** = **niche,** alcove, cavity, corner, cranny, crevice, cubbyhole, hide-out, inglenook (*Brit.*), opening, recess, retreat

noon *n* **1** = **midday,** high noon, noonday, noontide, noontime, twelve noon

norm *n* **2** = **standard,** average, benchmark, criterion, mean, measure, model, par, pattern, rule, type, yardstick

normal *adj* **1, 2** = **usual,** accustomed, acknowledged, average, bog-standard (*Brit. & Irish sl.*), common, conventional, habitual, natural, ordinary, popular, regular, routine, run-of-the-mill, standard, typical **3a** = **sane,** rational, reasonable, well-adjusted
Antonyms *adj* ≠ **usual:** abnormal, exceptional, irregular, peculiar, rare, remarkable, singular, uncommon, unnatural, unusual

normality *n* **1, 2** = **regularity,** accustomedness, averageness, commonness, commonplaceness, conventionality, habitualness, naturalness, ordinariness, popularity, routineness, typicality,

normal curve *n Statistics.* a symmetrical bell-shaped curve representing the probability density function of a normal distribution.
normal distribution *n Statistics.* a continuous distribution of a random variable with its mean, median, and mode equal.
normalize *or* **normalise** ('nɔːmə,laɪz) *vb* **normalizes, normalizing, normalized** *or* **normalises, normalising, normalised.** *(tr)* **1** to bring or make into the normal state. **2** to bring into conformity with a standard. **3** to heat (steel) above a critical temperature and allow it to cool in air to relieve internal stresses; anneal.
▸**,normali'zation** *or* **,normali'sation** *n*
normally ❶ ('nɔːməlɪ) *adv* **1** as a rule; usually; ordinarily. **2** in a normal manner.
Norman ('nɔːmən) *n* **1** (in the Middle Ages) a member of the people of Normandy in N France, descended from the 10th-century Scandinavian conquerors of the country and the native French. **2** a native or inhabitant of Normandy. **3** another name for **Norman French.** ◆ *adj* **4** of or characteristic of the Normans, esp. the Norman kings of England and the Norman people living in England, or their dialect of French. **5** of or characteristic of Normandy. **6** denoting or having the style of Romanesque architecture used in Britain from the Norman Conquest until the 12th century, characterized by the rounded arch, massive masonry walls, etc.
Norman Conquest *n* the invasion and settlement of England by the Normans, following the Battle of Hastings (1066).
Norman French *n* the medieval Norman and English dialect of Old French.
normative ❶ ('nɔːmətɪv) *adj* **1** implying, creating, or prescribing a norm or standard, as in language: *normative grammar.* **2** expressing value judgments as contrasted with stating facts.
Norn[1] (nɔːn) *n Norse myth.* any of the three virgin goddesses of fate. [C18: ON]
Norn[2] (nɔːn) *n* the medieval Norse language of the Orkneys, Shetlands, and parts of N Scotland. [C17: from ON *norrœna* Norwegian, from *northr* north]
Norse (nɔːs) *adj* **1** of ancient and medieval Scandinavia or its inhabitants. **2** of or characteristic of Norway. ◆ *n* **3a** the N group of Germanic languages, spoken in Scandinavia. **3b** any one of these languages, esp. in their ancient or medieval forms. **4 the Norse.** *(functioning as pl)* **4a** the Norwegians. **4b** the Vikings.
Norseman ('nɔːsmən) *n, pl* **Norsemen.** another name for a **Viking.**
north ❶ (nɔːθ) *n* **1** one of the four cardinal points of the compass, at 0° or 360°, that is 90° from east and west and 180° from south. **2** the direction along a meridian towards the North Pole. **3** the direction in which a compass needle points; magnetic north. **4 the north.** *(often cap.)* any area lying in or towards the north. **5** *(usually cap.) Cards.* the player or position at the table corresponding to north on the compass. ◆ *adj* **6** in, towards, or facing the north. **7** (esp. of the wind) from the north. ◆ *adv* **8** in, to, or towards the north. [OE]
North (nɔːθ) *n* **the. 1** the northern area of England, generally regarded as reaching the southern boundaries of Yorkshire, Derbyshire, and Cheshire. **2** (in the US) the states north of the Mason-Dixon Line that were known as the Free States during the Civil War. **3** the northern part of North America, esp. Alaska, the Yukon and the Northwest Territories. **4** the countries of the world that are economically and technically advanced. ◆ *adj* **5** of or denoting the northern part of a specified country, area, etc.
Northants (nɔː'θænts) *abbrev. for* Northamptonshire.
northbound ('nɔːθ,baʊnd) *adj* going or leading towards the north.
north by east *n* one point on the compass east of north.
north by west *n* one point on the compass west of north.
North Country *n* (usually preceded by *the*) **1** another name for **North** (sense 1). **2** another name for **North** (sense 3).
Northd *abbrev. for* Northumberland.
northeast (,nɔːθ'iːst; *Naut.* ,nɔːr'iːst) *n* **1** the point of the compass or direction midway between north and east. **2** *(often cap.;* usually preceded by *the)* any area lying in or towards this direction. ◆ *adj also* **northeastern. 3** *(sometimes cap.)* of or denoting the northeastern part of a specified country, area, etc.: *northeast Lincolnshire.* **4** in, towards, or facing the northeast. **5** (esp. of the wind) from the northeast. ◆ *adv* **6** in, to, or towards the northeast.
▸**,north'easternmost** *adj*
Northeast (,nɔːθ'iːst) *n* (usually preceded by *the*) the northeastern part of England, esp. Northumberland, Durham, and the Tyneside area.
northeast by east *n* one point on the compass east of northeast.
northeast by north *n* one point on the compass north of northeast.
northeaster (,nɔːθ'iːstə; *Naut.* ,nɔːr'iːstə) *n* a strong wind or storm from the northeast.
northeasterly (,nɔːθ'iːstəlɪ; *Naut.* ,nɔːr'iːstəlɪ) *adj, adv* **1** in, towards, or (esp. of a wind) from the northeast. ◆ *n, pl* **northeasterlies. 2** a wind or storm from the northeast.
northeastward (,nɔːθ'iːstwəd; *Naut.* ,nɔːr'iːstwəd) *adj* **1** towards or (esp. of a wind) from the northeast. ◆ *n* **2** a direction towards or area in the northeast.
▸**,north'eastwardly** *adj, adv*
norther ('nɔːðə) *n Chiefly southern US.* a wind or storm from the north.
northerly ('nɔːðəlɪ) *adj* **1** of or situated in the north. ◆ *adv, adj* **2** towards the north. **3** from the north: *a northerly wind.* ◆ *n, pl* **northerlies. 4** a wind from the north.
▸**'northerliness** *n*
northern ('nɔːðən) *adj* **1** in or towards the north. **2** (esp. of winds) proceeding from the north. **3** *(sometimes cap.)* of or characteristic of the north or North.
Northerner ('nɔːðənə) *n (sometimes not cap.)* a native or inhabitant of the north of any specified region, esp. England, the US, or the far north of Canada.
northern hemisphere *n (often caps.)* that half of the globe lying north of the equator.
northern lights *pl n* another name for **aurora borealis.**
northernmost ('nɔːðən,məʊst) *adj* situated or occurring farthest north.
northing ('nɔːθɪŋ, -ðɪŋ) *n* **1** *Navigation.* movement or distance covered in a northerly direction, esp. as expressed in the resulting difference in latitude. **2** *Astron.* a north or positive declination.
Northland ('nɔːθlənd) *n* **1** the peninsula containing Norway and Sweden. **2** (in Canada) the far north.
▸**'Northlander** *n*
Northman ('nɔːθmən) *n, pl* **Northmen.** another name for a **Viking.**
north-northeast *n* **1** the point on the compass or the direction midway between north and northeast. ◆ *adj, adv* **2** in, from, or towards this direction.
north-northwest *n* **1** the point on the compass or the direction midway between northwest and north. ◆ *adj, adv* **2** in, from, or towards this direction.
North Pole *n* **1** the northernmost point on the earth's axis, at a latitude of 90°N, characterized by very low temperatures. **2** Also called: **north celestial pole.** *Astron.* the point of intersection of the earth's extended axis and the northern half of the celestial sphere. **3** *(usually not cap.)* the pole of a freely suspended magnet, which is attracted to the earth's magnetic North Pole.
North-Sea gas *n* (in Britain) natural gas obtained from deposits below the North Sea.
North Star ❶ *n* **the.** another name for **Polaris.**
northward ('nɔːθwəd; *Naut.* 'nɔːðəd) *adj* **1** moving, facing, or situated towards the north. ◆ *n* **2** the northward part, direction, etc. ◆ *adv also* **northwards. 3** towards the north.
northwest (,nɔːθ'wɛst; *Naut.* ,nɔː'wɛst) *n* **1** the point of the compass or direction midway between north and west. **2** *(often cap.;* usually preceded by *the)* any area lying in or towards this direction. ◆ *adj also* **northwestern. 3** *(sometimes cap.)* of or denoting the northwestern part of a specified country, area, etc.: *northwest Greenland.* ◆ *adj, adv* **4** in, to, or towards the northwest.
▸**,north'westernmost** *adj*
Northwest (,nɔːθ'wɛst) *n* (usually preceded by *the*) the northwestern part of England, esp. Lancashire and the Lake District.
northwest by north *n* one point on the compass north of northwest.
northwest by west *n* one point on the compass south of northwest.
northwester (,nɔːθ'wɛstə; *Naut.* ,nɔː'wɛstə) *n* a strong wind or storm from the northwest.
northwesterly (,nɔːθ'wɛstəlɪ; *Naut.* ,nɔː'wɛstəlɪ) *adj, adv* **1** in, towards, or (esp. of a wind) from the northwest. ◆ *n, pl* **northwesterlies. 2** a wind or storm from the northwest.
Northwest Territories *pl n* the part of Canada north of the provinces and east of the Yukon Territory.
northwestward (,nɔːθ'wɛstwəd; *Naut.* ,nɔː'wɛstwəd) *adj* **1** towards or (esp. of a wind) from the northwest. ◆ *n* **2** a direction towards or area in the northwest.
▸**,north'westwardly** *adj, adv*
Norw. *abbrev. for:* **1** Norway. **2** Norwegian.
Norway lobster ('nɔː,weɪ) *n* a European lobster fished for food.
Norway rat *n* the common brown rat.
Norway spruce *n* a European spruce tree having drooping branches and dark green needle-like leaves.
Norwegian (nɔː'wiːdʒən) *adj* **1** of or characteristic of Norway, its language, or its people. ◆ *n* **2** any of the various North Germanic languages of Norway. **3** a native or inhabitant of Norway.
Nos. *or* **nos.** *abbrev. for* numbers.
nose ❶ (nəʊz) *n* **1** the organ of smell and entrance to the respiratory tract, consisting of a prominent structure divided into two hair-lined air passages. Related adj: **nasal. 2** the sense of smell itself: in animals, the ability to follow trails by scent (esp. in **a good nose**). **3** the scent, aroma, bouquet of something, esp. wine. **4** instinctive skill in discovering things (sometimes in **follow one's nose**): *he had a nose for good news stories.* **5** any part resembling a nose in form or function, such as a nozzle or spout. **6** the forward part of a vehicle, aircraft, etc. **7** narrow margin of victory (in **(win) by a nose**). **8 cut off one's nose to spite one's**

THESAURUS

usualness **3** = **sanity**, adjustment, balance, rationality, reason
normally *adv* **1** = **usually**, as a rule, commonly, generally, habitually, ordinarily, regularly, typically
normative *adj* **1** = **standardizing**, controlling, normalizing, prescriptive, regularizing, regulating
north *adj* **6,7** = **northern**, Arctic, boreal, northerly, polar ◆ *adv* **8** = **northward(s)**, northerly
North Star *n* = **Pole Star**, lodestar, Polaris
nose *n* **1** = **snout**, beak, bill, conk, hooter *(sl.)*, neb *(arch. or dialect)*, proboscis, schnozzle *(sl., chiefly US)*, snitch *(sl.)* ◆ *vb* **23** = **ease forward**, nudge, nuzzle, push, shove **24** = **pry**, meddle, snoop *(inf.)*

face. to carry out a vengeful action that hurts oneself more than another. **9 get up (someone's) nose.** *Inf.* to annoy or irritate (someone). **10 keep one's nose clean.** to stay out of trouble. **11 lead by the nose.** to make (someone) do unquestioningly all one wishes; dominate. **12 look down one's nose at.** *Inf.* to be disdainful of. **13 nose to tail.** (of vehicles) moving or standing very close behind one another. **14 on the nose.** *Sl.* **14a** (in horse-race betting) to win only: *I bet twenty pounds on the nose on that horse.* **14b** *Chiefly US & Canad.* precisely; exactly. **14c** *Austral.* bad or bad-smelling. **15 pay through the nose.** *Inf.* to pay an exorbitant price. **16 put someone's nose out of joint.** *Inf.* to thwart or offend someone. **17 rub someone's nose in it.** *Inf.* to remind someone unkindly of a failing or error. **18 turn up one's nose (at).** *Inf.* to behave disdainfully (towards). **19 with one's nose in the air.** haughtily. ◆ *vb* **noses, nosing, nosed. 20** (*tr*) (esp. of horses, dogs, etc.) to rub, touch, or sniff with the nose; nuzzle. **21** to smell or sniff (wine, etc.). **22** (*intr; usually foll. by after or for*) to search (for) by or as if by scent. **23** to move or cause to move forwards slowly and carefully: *we nosed the car into the garage.* **24** (*intr;* foll. by *into, around, about,* etc.) to pry or snoop (into) or meddle (in). [OE *nosu*]
▸**'noseless** *adj* ▸**'nose,like** *adj*

nosebag ('nəuz,bæg) *n* a bag, fastened around the head of a horse and covering the nose, in which feed is placed.

noseband ('nəuz,bænd) *n* the detachable part of a horse's bridle that goes around the nose.

nosebleed ('nəuz,bli:d) *n* bleeding from the nose as the result of injury, etc.

nose cone *n* the conical forward section of a missile, spacecraft, etc., designed to withstand high temperatures, esp. during re-entry into the earth's atmosphere.

nose dive ❶ *n* **1** a sudden plunge with the nose or front pointing downwards, esp. of an aircraft. **2** *Inf.* a sudden drop or sharp decline: *prices took a nose dive.* ◆ *vb* **nose-dive, nose-dives, nose-diving, nose-dived.** (*intr*) **3** to perform a nose dive.

nose flute *n* (esp. in the South Sea Islands) a type of flute blown through the nose.

nosegay ❶ ('nəuz,geɪ) *n* a small bunch of flowers; posy. [C15: from NOSE + *gay* (arch.) toy]

nose job *n Sl.* a surgical remodelling of the nose for cosmetic reasons.

nosepiece ('nəuz,pi:s) *n* **1** a piece of armour to protect the nose. **2** the connecting part of a pair of spectacles that rests on the nose; bridge. **3** the part of a microscope to which one or more objective lenses are attached. **4** a less common word for **noseband.**

nose rag *n Sl.* a handkerchief.

nose ring *n* a ring fixed through the nose, as for leading a bull.

nose wheel *n* a wheel fitted to the forward end of a vehicle, esp. the landing wheel under the nose of an aircraft.

nosey ('nəuzɪ) *adj* a variant spelling of **nosy.**

nosh ❶ (nɒʃ) *Sl.* ◆ *n* **1** food or a meal. ◆ *vb* **2** to eat. [C20: from Yiddish; cf. G *naschen* to nibble]

no-show *n* a person who fails to take up a reserved seat, place, etc., without having cancelled it.

nosh-up *n Brit. sl.* a large and satisfying meal.

no-side *n Rugby.* the end of a match, signalled by the referee's whistle.

nosocomial (,nɒsə'kəumɪəl) *adj* of or denoting an infection that originates in a hospital. [C19: from Gk *nosokomos* one that tends the sick, from *nosos* disease + *komein* to tend]

nosology (nɒ'sɒlədʒɪ) *n* the branch of medicine concerned with the classification of diseases. [C18: from Gk *nosos* disease]
▸**nosological** (,nɒsə'lɒdʒɪkᵊl) *adj*

nostalgia ❶ (nɒ'stældʒə, -dʒɪə) *n* **1** a yearning for past circumstances, events, etc. **2** the evocation of this emotion, as in a book, film, etc. **3** homesickness. [C18: NL, from Gk *nostos a* return home + -ALGIA]
▸**nos'talgic** *adj* ▸**nos'talgically** *adv*

nostoc ('nɒstɒk) *n* a gelatinous cyanobacterium occurring in moist places. [C17: NL, coined by Paracelsus (1493–1541) Swiss physician]

nostril ('nɒstrɪl) *n* either of the two external openings of the nose. See **nares.** [OE *nosthyrl,* from *nosu* NOSE + *thyrel* hole]

nostro account ('nɒstrəu) *n* a bank account conducted by a British bank with a foreign bank, usually in the foreign currency. Cf. **vostro account.**

nostrum ❶ ('nɒstrəm) *n* **1** a patent or quack medicine. **2** a favourite remedy. [C17: from L: our own (make), from *noster* our]

nosy ❶ *or* **nosey** ('nəuzɪ) *adj* **nosier, nosiest.** *Inf.* prying or inquisitive.
▸**'nosily** *adv* ▸**'nosiness** *n*

nosy parker *n Inf.* a prying person. [C20: arbitrary use of surname *Parker*]

not (nɒt) *adv* **1a** used to negate the sentence, phrase, or word that it modifies: *I will not stand for it.* **1b** (*in combination*): *they cannot go.* **2 not that.** (*conj*) Also (arch.): **not but what.** which is not to say or suppose that: *I expect to lose the game — not that I mind.* ◆ *sentence substitute.* **3** used to indicate denial or refusal: *certainly not.* [C14 *not,* var. of *nought* nothing, from OE *nāwiht,* from *nā* no + *wiht* creature, thing]

nota bene *Latin.* ('nəutə 'bi:nɪ) note well; take note. Abbrevs.: **NB, N.B., nb, n.b.**

notability ❶ (,nəutə'bɪlɪtɪ) *n, pl* **notabilities. 1** the quality of being notable. **2** a distinguished person.

notable ❶ ('nəutəbᵊl) *adj* **1** worthy of being noted or remembered; remarkable; distinguished. ◆ *n* **2** a notable person. [C14: via OF from L *notābilis,* from *notāre* to NOTE]
▸**'notably** *adv*

notarize *or* **notarise** ('nəutə,raɪz) *vb* **notarizes, notarizing, notarized** *or* **notarises, notarising, notarised.** (*tr*) *US.* to attest to (a document, etc.), as a notary.

notary ('nəutərɪ) *n, pl* **notaries. 1** a notary public. **2** (formerly) a clerk licensed to prepare legal documents. **3** *Arch.* a clerk or secretary. [C14: from L *notārius* clerk, from *nota* a mark, note]
▸**notarial** (nəu'tεərɪəl) *adj* ▸**'notaryship** *n*

notary public *n, pl* **notaries public.** a public official, usually a solicitor, who is legally authorized to administer oaths, attest and certify certain documents, etc.

notation ❶ (nəu'teɪʃən) *n* **1** any series of signs or symbols used to represent quantities or elements in a specialized system, such as music or mathematics. **2** the act or process of notating. **3** a note or record. [C16: from L *notātiō,* from *notāre* to NOTE]
▸**no'tational** *adj*

notch ❶ (nɒtʃ) *n* **1** a V-shaped cut or indentation; nick. **2** a nick made in a tally stick. **3** *US & Canad.* a narrow gorge. **4** *Inf.* a step or level (esp. in **a notch above**). ◆ *vb* (*tr*) **5** to cut or make a notch in. **6** to record with or as if with a notch. **7** (usually foll. by *up*) *Inf.* to score or achieve: *the team notched up its fourth win.* [C16: from incorrect division of *an otch* (as *a notch*), from OF *oche* notch, from L *obsecāre,* from *secāre* to cut]

NOT circuit *or* **gate** (nɒt) *n Computing.* a logic circuit that has a high-voltage output signal if the input signal is low, and vice versa: used extensively in computing. Also called: **inverter, negator.** [C20: the action performed on electrical signals is similar to the operation of *not* in logical constructions]

note ❶ (nəut) *n* **1** a brief record in writing, esp. a jotting for future reference. **2** a brief informal letter. **3** a formal written communication, esp. from one government to another. **4** a short written statement giving any kind of information. **5** a critical comment, explanatory statement, or reference in a book. **6** short for **banknote. 7** a characteristic atmosphere: *a note of sarcasm.* **8** a distinctive vocal sound, as of a species of bird or animal. **9** any of a series of graphic signs representing the pitch and duration of a musical sound. **10** Also called (esp. US and Canad.): **tone.** a musical sound of definite fundamental frequency or pitch. **11** a key on a piano, organ, etc. **12** a sound used as a signal or warning: *the note to retreat was sounded.* **13** short for **promissory note. 14** *Arch. or poetic.* a melody. **15 of note. 15a** distinguished or famous. **15b** important: *nothing of note.* **16 strike the right** (*or* **a false**) **note.** to behave appropriately (or inappropriately). **17 take note.** (often foll. by *of*) to pay attention (to). ◆ *vb* **notes, noting, noted.** (*tr; may take a clause as object*) **18** to notice; perceive. **19** to pay close attention to: *they noted every movement.* **20** to make a written note of: *she noted the date in her diary.* **21** to remark upon: *I note that you do not wear shoes.* **22** to write down (music, a melody, etc.) in notes. **23** to take (an unpaid or dishonoured bill of exchange) to a notary public to re-present the bill and if it is still unaccepted or unpaid to note the circumstances in a register. See

THESAURUS

nose dive *vb* **nose-dive 3** = **drop,** dive, plummet, plunge

nosegay *n* = **posy,** bouquet

nosh *Slang n* **1** = **food,** aliment, chow (*inf.*), comestibles, eats (*sl.*), fare, feed, grub (*sl.*), meal, repast, sustenance, tack (*inf.*), viands, victuals, vittles (*obs. or dialect*) ◆ *vb* **2** = **eat,** consume, scoff (*sl.*)

nostalgia *n* **1** = **reminiscence,** longing, pining, regret, regretfulness, remembrance, wistfulness, yearning **3** = **homesickness**

nostalgic *adj* **1** = **sentimental,** emotional, longing, maudlin, regretful, wistful **2** = **homesick**

nostrum *n* **1** = **patent medicine,** cure-all, elixir, panacea, quack medicine, sovereign cure **2** = **remedy,** cure, drug, medicine, potion, specific, treatment

nosy *adj* = **inquisitive,** curious, eavesdropping, interfering, intrusive, meddlesome, prying, snooping (*inf.*)

notability *n* **1** = **fame,** celebrity, distinction, eminence, esteem, renown **2** = **celebrity,** big name, celeb (*inf.*), dignitary, megastar (*inf.*), notable, personage, V.I.P., worthy

notable *adj* **1** = **remarkable,** celebrated, conspicuous, distinguished, eminent, evident, extraordinary, famous, manifest, marked, memorable, noteworthy, noticeable, notorious, outstanding, pre-eminent, pronounced, rare, renowned, salient, striking, uncommon, unusual, well-known ◆ *n* **2** = **celebrity,** big name, celeb (*inf.*), dignitary, luminary, megastar (*inf.*), notability, personage, V.I.P., worthy

Antonyms *adj* ≠ **remarkable:** anonymous, concealed, hidden, imperceptible, obscure, unknown, vague

notably *adv* **1** = **particularly,** conspicuously, distinctly, especially, markedly, noticeably, outstandingly, remarkably, seriously (*inf.*), signally, strikingly, uncommonly

notation *n* **1** = **signs,** characters, code, script, symbols, system **2** = **noting,** jotting, notating **3** = **note,** record

notch *n* **1** = **cut,** cleft, incision, indentation, mark, nick, score **4** *Informal* = **level,** cut (*inf.*), degree, grade, step ◆ *vb* **5** = **cut,** indent, mark, nick, score, scratch **7** *usually with* **up** = **register,** achieve, gain, make, score

note *n* **1** = **record,** jotting, minute, remark, reminder **2** = **message,** communication, epistle, letter, memo, memorandum **5** = **annotation,** comment, gloss **15 of note** = **famous,** distinguished, eminent, prestigious, renowned **17 take note** = **notice,** heed, observe, regard ◆ *vb* **18** = **see,** notice, observe, perceive **20** = **mark,** denote, indicate, record, register **21** = **mention,** remark

protest (sense 9). **24** a less common word for **annotate.** [C13: via OF from L *nota* sign]
▸'**noteless** *adj*

notebook ➊ ('nəʊtˌbʊk) *n* a book for recording notes or memoranda.

notebook computer *n* a portable computer smaller than a laptop model, often approximately the size of a sheet of A4 paper.

notecase ('nəʊtˌkeɪs) *n* a less common word for **wallet** (sense 1).

noted ➊ ('nəʊtɪd) *adj* **1** celebrated; famous. **2** of special significance; noticeable.
▸'**notedly** *adv*

notelet ('nəʊtlɪt) *n* a folded card with a printed design on the front, for writing a short letter.

notepaper ('nəʊtˌpeɪpə) *n* paper for writing letters; writing paper.

noteworthy ➊ ('nəʊtˌwɜːðɪ) *adj* worthy of notice; notable.
▸'**noteˌworthiness** *n*

nothing ➊ ('nʌθɪŋ) *pron* **1** (*indefinite*) no thing; not anything: *I can give you nothing.* **2** no part or share: *to have nothing to do with this crime.* **3** a matter of no importance: *it doesn't matter, it's nothing.* **4** indicating the absence of anything perceptible; nothingness. **5** indicating the absence of meaning, value, worth, etc.: *to amount to nothing.* **6** zero quantity; nought. **7 be nothing to. 7a** not to concern or be significant to (someone). **7b** to be not nearly as good, etc., as. **8 have** *or* **be nothing to do with.** to have no connection with. **9 nothing but.** not something other than; only. **10 nothing doing.** *Inf.* an expression of dismissal, refusal, etc. **11 nothing if not.** at the very least; certainly. **12 nothing less than** *or* **nothing short of.** downright; truly. **13 there's nothing to it.** it is very simple, easy, etc. **14 think nothing of. 14a** to regard as easy or natural. **14b** to have no compunction about. **14c** to have a very low opinion of. ◆ *adv* **15** in no way; not at all: *he looked nothing like his brother.* ◆ *n* **16** *Inf.* a person or thing of no importancee.**17 sweet nothings.** words of endearment or affection. [OE *nāthing, nān thing,* from *nān* NONE[1] + THING]

> **USAGE NOTE** *Nothing* normally takes a singular verb, but when *nothing but* is followed by a plural form of a noun, a plural verb is usually used: *it was a large room where nothing but souvenirs were sold.*

nothingness ➊ ('nʌθɪŋnɪs) *n* **1** the state of being nothing; nonexistence. **2** absence of consciousness or life. **3** complete insignificance. **4** something that is worthless.

notice ➊ ('nəʊtɪs) *n* **1** observation; attention: *to escape notice.* **2 take notice.** to pay attention. **3 take no notice of.** to ignore or disregard. **4** a warning; announcement. **5** a displayed placard or announcement giving information. **6** advance notification of intention to end an arrangement, contract, etc., as of employment (esp. in **give notice**). **7 at short notice.** with notification only a little in advance. **8** *Chiefly Brit.* dismissal from employment. **9** interested, or polite attention: *she was beneath his notice.* **10** a theatrical or literary review: *the play received very good notices.* ◆ *vb* **notices, noticing, noticed. 11** to become aware (of); perceive; note. **12** (*tr*) to point out or remark upon. **13** (*tr*) to pay polite or interested attention to. **14** (*tr*) to acknowledge (an acquaintance, etc.). [C15: via OF from L *notitia* fame, from *nōtus* known]

noticeable ➊ ('nəʊtɪsəbᵊl) *adj* easily seen or detected; perceptible.
▸'**noticeably** *adv*

notice board *n* a board on which notices, advertisements, bulletins, etc., are displayed. US and Canad. name: **bulletin board.**

notifiable ('nəʊtɪˌfaɪəbᵊl) *adj* **1** denoting certain infectious diseases of humans, such as tuberculosis, outbreaks of which must be reported to the public health authorities. **2** denoting certain infectious diseases of animals, such as BSE and rabies, outbreaks of which must be reported to the appropriate veterinary authority.

notification ➊ (ˌnəʊtɪfɪ'keɪʃən) *n* **1** the act of notifying. **2** a formal announcement. **3** something that notifies; a notice.

notify ➊ ('nəʊtɪˌfaɪ) *vb* **notifies, notifying, notified.** (*tr*) **1** to tell. **2** *Chiefly Brit.* to make known; announce. [C14: from OF *notifier,* from L *notificāre,* from *nōtus* known + *facere* to make]
▸'**notiˌfier** *n*

notion ➊ ('nəʊʃən) *n* **1** a vague idea; impression. **2** an idea, concept, or opinion. **3** an inclination or whim. ◆ See also **notions.** [C16: from L *nōtiō* a becoming acquainted (with), examination (of), from *noscere* to know]

notional ➊ ('nəʊʃənᵊl) *adj* **1** expressing or consisting of ideas. **2** not evident in reality; hypothetical or imaginary: *a notional tax credit.* **3** characteristic of a notion, esp. in being speculative or abstract. **4** *Grammar.* **4a** (of a word) having lexical meaning. **4b** another word for **semantic.**
▸'**notionally** *adv*

notions ('nəʊʃənz) *pl n Chiefly US & Canad.* pins, cotton, ribbon, etc., used for sewing; haberdashery.

notochord ('nəʊtəˌkɔːd) *n* a fibrous longitudinal rod in all embryo and some adult chordate animals, immediately above the gut, that supports the body. [C19: from Gk *nōton* the back + CHORD[1]]

notorious ➊ (nəʊ'tɔːrɪəs) *adj* **1** well-known for some bad quality, deed, etc.; infamous. **2** *Rare.* generally known or widely acknowledged. [C16: from Med. L *notōrius* well-known, from *nōtus* known]
▸**notoriety** (ˌnəʊtə'raɪɪtɪ) *n* ▸**no'toriously** *adv*

notornis (nəʊ'tɔːnɪs) *n* a rare flightless rail of New Zealand. [C19: NL, from Gk *notos* south + *ornis* bird]

not proven ('prəʊvᵊn) *adj* (*postpositive*) a third verdict available to Scottish courts, returned when there is insufficient evidence against the accused to convict.

no-trump *Cards.* ◆ *n also* **no-trumps. 1** a bid or contract to play without trumps. ◆ *adj also* **no-trumper. 2** (of a hand) suitable for playing without trumps.

Notts (nɒts) *abbrev. for* Nottinghamshire.

notwithstanding ➊ (ˌnɒtwɪθ'stændɪŋ) *prep* **1** (*often immediately postpositive*) in spite of; despite. ◆ *conj* **2** (*subordinating*) although. ◆ *sentence connector.* **3** nevertheless.

nougat ('nuːgɑː) *n* a hard chewy pink or white sweet containing chopped nuts, cherries, etc. [C19: via F from Provençal *nogat,* from *noga* nut, from L *nux* nut]

nought ➊ (nɔːt) *n also* **naught, ought, aught. 1** another name for **zero:** used esp. in numbering. ◆ *n, adj, adv* **2** a variant spelling of **naught.** [OE *nōwiht,* from *ne* not, no + *ōwiht* something]

noughts and crosses *n* (*functioning as sing*) a game in which two players, one using a nought, "O", the other a cross, "X", alternately mark squares formed by two pairs of crossed lines, the winner being the first to get three of his symbols in a row. US and Canad. term: **tick-tack-toe,** (US) **crisscross.**

noun (naʊn) *n* **a** a word or group of words that refers to a person, place, or thing. **b** (*as modifier*): *a noun phrase.* Abbrev.: **N, n.** Related adj: **nominal.** [C14: via Anglo-F from L *nōmen* NAME]
▸'**nounal** *adj*

nourish ➊ ('nʌrɪʃ) *vb* (*tr*) **1** to provide with the materials necessary for life and growth. **2** to encourage (an idea, etc.); foster: *to nourish resentment.* [C14: from OF *norir,* from L *nūtrīre* to feed]
▸'**nourisher** *n* ▸'**nourishing** *adj*

nourishment ➊ ('nʌrɪʃmənt) *n* **1** the act or state of nourishing. **2** a substance that nourishes; food.

nous (naʊs) *n* **1** *Metaphysics.* mind or reason, esp. regarded as the principle governing all things. **2** *Brit. sl.* common sense. [C17: from Gk: mind]

nouveau *or before a plural noun* **nouveaux** ('nuːvəʊ) *adj* (*prenominal*) *Facetious or derog.* having recently become the thing specified: *a nouveau hippy.* [C20: F, lit.: new; on the model of NOUVEAU RICHE]

nouveau riche ➊ (riːʃ) *n, pl* **nouveaux riches** (riːʃ). (often preceded by *the*)

THESAURUS

notebook *n* = **jotter,** diary, exercise book, Filofax (*Trademark*), journal, memorandum book, notepad, record book

noted *adj* **1** = **famous,** acclaimed, celebrated, conspicuous, distinguished, eminent, illustrious, notable, prominent, recognized, renowned, well-known
Antonyms *adj* infamous, obscure, undistinguished, unknown

noteworthy *adj* = **remarkable,** exceptional, extraordinary, important, notable, outstanding, significant, unusual
Antonyms *adj* commonplace, insignificant, normal, ordinary, pedestrian, run-of-the-mill, unexceptional, unremarkable

nothing *pron* **3** = **trifle,** bagatelle, **4** = **nothingness,** emptiness, nonexistence, nullity, void **6** = **nought,** naught, nil, zero ◆ *n* **14 think nothing of: a** = **consider unimportant,** regard as routine **b** have no hesitation about **c** set no store by

nothingness *n* **1** = **oblivion,** nihility, nonbeing, nonexistence, nullity **3** = **insignificance,** unimportance, worthlessness

notice *n* **1** = **interest,** cognizance, consideration, heed, note, observation, regard **4** = **announcement,** advice, communication, instruction, intelligence, intimation, news, notification, order, warning **5** = **advertisement,** announcement, poster, sign **9** = **attention,** civility, respect **10** = **review,** comment, criticism ◆ *vb* **11** = **observe,** behold (*arch. or literary*), detect, discern, distinguish, eyeball (*sl.*), heed, mark, mind, note, perceive, remark, see, spot
Antonyms *n* ≠ **interest:** disregard, ignorance, neglect, omission, oversight ◆ *vb* ≠ **observe:** disregard, ignore, neglect, overlook

noticeable *adj* = **obvious,** appreciable, blatant, bold, clear, conspicuous, distinct, evident, manifest, observable, perceptible, plain, salient, striking, unmistakable

notification *n* **1** = **notifying,** advice, alert, information, intelligence, telling, warning **2** = **announcement,** declaration, message, notice, publication, statement

notify *vb* **1** = **inform,** acquaint, advise, alert, apprise, tell, warn **2** = **announce,** declare, make known, publish

notion *n* **1, 2** = **idea,** apprehension, belief, concept, conception, impression, inkling, judgment, knowledge, opinion, sentiment, understanding, view **3** = **whim,** caprice, desire, fancy, impulse, inclination, wish

notional *adj* **1, 3** = **conceptual,** abstract, ideal, unreal, visionary **2** = **hypothetical,** fanciful, imaginary, speculative, theoretical
Antonyms *adj* actual, factual, genuine, real

notoriety *n* **1** = **scandal,** dishonour, disrepute, infamy, obloquy, opprobrium

notorious *adj* **1** = **infamous,** dishonourable, disreputable, opprobrious, scandalous

notoriously *adv* **1** = **infamously,** dishonourably, disreputably, opprobriously, scandalously

notwithstanding *prep* **1** = **despite,** in spite of ◆ *conj* **2** = **although,** (even) though, though ◆ *sentence connector* **3** = **nevertheless,** however, nonetheless, yet

nought *n* **1** = **zero,** naught, nil, nothing

nourish *vb* **1** = **feed,** furnish, nurse, nurture, supply, sustain **2** = **encourage,** comfort, cultivate, foster, maintain, promote, support

nourishing *adj* **1** = **nutritious,** beneficial, healthful, health-giving, nutritive, wholesome

nourishment *n* **2** = **food,** aliment, diet, nutriment, nutrition, sustenance, tack (*inf.*), viands, victuals, vittles (*obs. or dialect*)

nouveau riche *n* = **new-rich,** arriviste, parvenu, upstart a person who has acquired wealth recently and is regarded as vulgarly ostentatious or lacking in social graces. [C19: from F lit.: new rich]

nouvelle cuisine ('nu:vel kwi:'zi:n; *French* nuvɛl kɥizin) *n* a style of cooking based on presenting small attractively arranged helpings of lightly cooked fresh ingredients. [C20: F, lit.: new cookery]

Nov. *abbrev. for* November.

nova ('nəʊvə) *n, pl* **novae** (-vi:) *or* **novas.** a variable star that undergoes a cataclysmic eruption, observed as a sudden large increase in brightness with a subsequent decline over months or years; it is a close binary system with one component a white dwarf. [C19: NL *nova* (*stella*) new (star), from L *novus* new]

novel[1] **T** ('nɒv°l) *n* **1** an extended fictional work in prose dealing with character, action, thought, etc., esp. in the form of a story. **2 the novel.** the literary genre represented by novels. [C15: from OF *novelle,* from L *novella* (*narrātiō*) new (story); see NOVEL[2]]

novel[2] **T** ('nɒv°l) *adj* of a kind not seen before; fresh; new; original: *a novel suggestion.* [C15: from L *novellus,* dim. of *novus* new]

novelette (ˌnɒvə'lɛt) *n* **1** an extended prose narrative or short novel. **2** a novel that is regarded as slight, trivial, or sentimental. **3** a short piece of lyrical music, esp. for piano.

novelettish (ˌnɒvə'lɛtɪʃ) *adj* characteristic of a novelette; trite or sentimental.

novelist ('nɒvəlɪst) *n* a writer of novels.

novelistic (ˌnɒvə'lɪstɪk) *adj* of or characteristic of novels, esp. in style or method of treatment.

novella (nəʊ'vɛlə) *n, pl* **novellas** *or* **novelle** (-leɪ). **1** a short narrative tale, esp. one having a satirical point, such as those in Boccaccio's *Decameron.* **2** a short novel. [C20: from It.; see NOVEL[1]]

novelty **T** ('nɒv°ltɪ) *n, pl* **novelties. 1a** the quality of being new and interesting. **1b** (*as modifier*): *novelty value.* **2** a new or unusual experience. **3** (*often pl*) a small usually cheap new ornament or trinket. [C14: from OF *novelté;* see NOVEL[2]]

November (nəʊ'vɛmbə) *n* the eleventh month of the year, consisting of 30 days. [C13: via OF from L: ninth month (the Roman year orig. began in March), from *novem* nine]

novena (nəʊ'vi:nə) *n, pl* **novenas** *or* **novenae** (-ni:). *RC Church.* a devotion consisting of prayers or services on nine consecutive days. [C19: from Med. L, from L *novem* nine]

novice **T** ('nɒvɪs) *n* **1a** a person who is new to or inexperienced in a certain task, situation, etc.; beginner; tyro. **1b** (*as modifier*): *novice driver.* **2** a probationer in a religious order. **3** a racehorse that has not won a specified number of races. [C14: via OF from L *novīcius,* from *novus* new]

novitiate **T** *or* **noviciate** (nəʊ'vɪʃɪɪt, -ˌeɪt) *n* **1** the state of being a novice, esp. in a religious order, or the period for which this lasts. **2** the part of a religious house where the novices live. [C17: from F *noviciat,* from L *novīcius* NOVICE]

Novocaine ('nəʊvəˌkeɪn) *n* a trademark for **procaine hydrochloride.** See **procaine.**

now **T** (naʊ) *adv* **1** at or for the present time. **2** immediately. **3** in these times; nowadays. **4** given the present circumstances: *now we'll have to stay to the end.* **5** (preceded by *just*) very recently: *he left just now.* **6** (often preceded by *just*) very soon: *he is leaving just now.* **7 (every) now and again** *or* **then.** occasionally; on and off. **8 now now!** an exclamation used to rebuke or pacify someone. ◆ *conj* **9** (*subordinating;* often foll. by *that*) seeing that: *now you're in charge, things will be better.* ◆ *sentence connector.* **10a** used as a hesitation word: *now, I can't really say.* **10b** used for emphasis: *now listen to this.* **10c** used at the end of a command: *run along, now.* ◆ *n* **11** the present time: *now is the time to go.* ◆ *adj* **12** *Inf.* of the moment; fashionable: *the now look.* [OE *nū*]

nowadays **T** ('naʊəˌdeɪz) *adv* in these times. [C14: from NOW + *adays* from OE *a* on + *daeges* genitive of DAY]

noway ('nəʊˌweɪ) *adv* **1** not at all. ◆ *sentence substitute.* **no way. 2** used to make an emphatic refusal, denial, etc.

Nowel *or* **Nowell** (nəʊ'ɛl) *n* archaic spellings of **Noel.**

nowhere ('nəʊwɛə) *adv* **1** in, at, or to no place; not anywhere. **2 get nowhere (fast).** *Inf.* to fail completely to make any progress. **3 nowhere near.** far from; not nearly. ◆ *n* **4** a nonexistent or insignificant place. **5 middle of nowhere.** a completely isolated place.

no-win *adj* offering no possibility of a favourable outcome (esp. in a **no-win situation**).

nowise ('nəʊˌwaɪz) *adv* in no manner; not at all.

nowt (naʊt) *n N English.* a dialect word for **nothing.** [from NAUGHT]

noxious **T** ('nɒkʃəs) *adj* poisonous or harmful. [C17: from L *noxius* harmful, from *noxa* injury]

▸**'noxiously** *adv* ▸**'noxiousness** *n*

nozzle ('nɒz°l) *n* a projecting pipe or spout from which fluid is discharged. [C17 *nosle, nosel,* dim. of NOSE]

Np *the chemical symbol for* neptunium.

NP *or* **np.** *abbrev. for* Notary Public.

NPA *abbrev. for* Newspaper Publishers' Association.

NPD *Commerce. abbrev. for* new product development.

NPL *abbrev. for* National Physical Laboratory.

NPV *abbrev. for:* **1** net present value. **2** no par value.

NRV *abbrev. for* net realizable value.

NS *abbrev. for:* **1** New Style (method of reckoning dates). **2** Nova Scotia. **3** Nuclear Ship.

NSAID *abbrev. for* nonsteroidal anti-inflammatory drug: any of a class of drugs, including aspirin and ibuprofen, used for treating rheumatic diseases.

NSB (in Britain) *abbrev. for* National Savings Bank.

NSC (in Britain) *abbrev. for* National Safety Council.

NSG *Brit. education. abbrev. for* nonstatutory guidelines: practical nonmandatory advice and information on the implementation of the National Curriculum.

NSPCC (in Britain) *abbrev. for* National Society for the Prevention of Cruelty to Children.

NST (in Canada) abbrev. for Newfoundland Standard Time.

NSU *abbrev. for* nonspecific urethritis.

NSW *abbrev. for* New South Wales.

NT *abbrev. for:* **1** (in Britain) National Trust. **2** New Testament. **3** Northern Territory. **4** no-trump.

-n't *contraction of* not: used as an enclitic after *be* and *have* when they function as main verbs and after auxiliary verbs or verbs operating syntactically as auxiliaries: *can't; don't; isn't.*

nth (ɛnθ) *adj* **1** *Maths.* of or representing an unspecified ordinal number, usually the greatest in a series: *the nth power.* **2** *Inf.* being the last or most extreme of a long series: *for the nth time.* **3 to the nth degree.** *Inf.* to the utmost extreme.

NTP *abbrev. for* normal temperature and pressure. Also: **STP.**

nt. wt. *or* **nt wt** *abbrev. for* net weight.

n-type *adj* **1** (of a semiconductor) having more conduction electrons than mobile holes. **2** associated with or resulting from the movement of electrons in a semiconductor.

nu (nju:) *n* the 13th letter in the Greek alphabet (Ν, ν), a consonant. [from Gk, of Semitic origin]

nuance **T** (nju:'ɑ:ns, 'nju:ɑ:ns) *n* a subtle difference in colour, meaning, tone, etc. [C18: from F, from *nuer* to show light and shade, ult. from L *nūbēs* a cloud]

nub **T** (nʌb) *n* **1** a small lump or protuberance. **2** a small piece or chunk. **3** the point or gist: *the nub of a story.* [C16: var. of *knub,* from MLow G *knubbe* KNOB]

▸**'nubbly** *or* **'nubby** *adj*

nubble ('nʌb°l) *n* a small lump. [C19: dim. of NUB]

nubile **T** ('nju:baɪl) *adj* (of a girl) **1** ready or suitable for marriage by virtue of age or maturity. **2** sexually attractive. [C17: from L *nūbilis,* from *nūbere* to marry]

▸**nubility** (nju:'bɪlɪtɪ) *n*

nucha ('nju:kə) *n, pl* **nuchae** (-ki:). *Zool., anat.* the back or nape of the neck. [C14: from Med. L, from Ar.: spinal marrow]

▸**'nuchal** *adj*

nuclear ('nju:klɪə) *adj* **1** of or involving the nucleus of an atom: *nuclear fission.* **2** *Biol.* of, relating to, or contained within the nucleus of a cell: *a nuclear membrane.* **3** of, forming, or resembling any other kind of nucleus. **4** of or operated by energy from fission or fusion of atomic nuclei: *a nuclear weapon.* **5** involving or possessing nuclear weapons: *nuclear war.*

nuclear bomb *n* a bomb whose force is due to uncontrolled nuclear fusion or nuclear fission.

nuclear chemistry *n* the branch of chemistry concerned with nuclear reactions.

nuclear energy *n* energy released during a nuclear reaction as a result of fission or fusion. Also called: **atomic energy.**

THESAURUS

novel[1] *n* **1** = **story,** fiction, narrative, romance, tale

novel[2] *adj* = **new,** different, fresh, groundbreaking, innovative, left-field (*inf.*), original, rare, singular, strange, uncommon, unfamiliar, unusual
Antonyms *adj* ancient, common, customary, familiar, habitual, old-fashioned, ordinary, run-of-the-mill, traditional, usual

novelty *n* **1** = **newness,** freshness, innovation, oddity, originality, strangeness, surprise, unfamiliarity, uniqueness **3** = **trinket,** bagatelle, bauble, curiosity, gadget, gewgaw, gimmick, knick-knack, memento, souvenir, trifle

novice *n* **1** = **beginner,** amateur, apprentice, convert, learner, neophyte, newcomer, proselyte, pupil, trainee, tyro **2** = **novitiate,** probationer
Antonyms *n* ≠ **beginner:** ace, doyen, expert, grandmaster, guru, master, maven, old hand, professional, teacher

novitiate *n* **1** = **probation,** apprenticeship, training

now *adv* **2** = **immediately,** at once, instanter (*Law*), instantly, presently (*Scot. & US*), promptly, straightaway **3** = **nowadays,** any more, at the moment, these days **7 (every) now and again** *or* **then** = **occasionally,** at times, from time to time, infrequently, intermittently, on and off, once in a while, on occasion, sometimes, sporadically

nowadays *adv* = **now,** any more, at the moment, in this day and age, these days, today

noxious *adj* = **harmful,** baneful (*arch.*), corrupting, deadly, deleterious, destructive, detrimental, foul, hurtful, injurious, insalubrious, noisome, pernicious, pestilential, poisonous, unhealthy, unwholesome
Antonyms *adj* innocuous, innoxious, inoffensive, nontoxic, not dangerous, safe, unobjectionable

nuance *n* = **subtlety,** degree, distinction, gradation, graduation, hint, nicety, refinement, shade, shadow, suggestion, suspicion, tinge, touch, trace

nub *n* **1** = **knob,** bulge, bump, knot, lump, node, protuberance, swelling **3** = **gist,** core, crux, essence, heart, kernel, nucleus, pith, point

nubile *adj* **1** = **marriageable,** ripe (*inf.*)

nuclear family *n Sociol., anthropol.* a primary social unit consisting of parents and their offspring.

nuclear fission *n* the splitting of an atomic nucleus into approximately equal parts, either spontaneously or as a result of the impact of a particle usually with an associated release of energy. Sometimes shortened to **fission.**

nuclear fuel *n* a fuel that provides nuclear energy, used in nuclear submarines, etc.

nuclear fusion *n* a reaction in which two nuclei combine to form a nucleus with the release of energy. Sometimes shortened to **fusion.**

nuclear magnetic resonance *n* a technique for determining the magnetic moments of nuclei by subjecting a substance to high-frequency radiation and a large magnetic field. It is used for determining structure, esp. in body scanning. Abbrev.: **NMR.**

nuclear medicine *n* the branch of medicine concerned with the use of radionuclides in the diagnosis and treatment of disease.

nuclear physics *n* (*functioning as sing*) the branch of physics concerned with the structure and behaviour of the nucleus and the particles of which it consists.

nuclear power *n* power, esp. electrical or motive, produced by a nuclear reactor. Also called: **atomic power.**

nuclear reaction *n* a process in which the structure and energy content of an atomic nucleus is changed by interaction with another nucleus or particle.

nuclear reactor *n* a device in which a nuclear reaction is maintained and controlled for the production of nuclear energy. Sometimes shortened to **reactor.**

nuclear waste *n* another name for **radioactive waste.**

nuclear winter *n* a period of low temperatures and little light that has been suggested would occur after a nuclear war.

nuclease ('nju:klɪ,eɪz) *n* any of a group of enzymes that hydrolyse nucleic acids to simple nucleotides.

nucleate *adj* ('nju:klɪɪt, -,eɪt). **1** having a nucleus. ◆ *vb* ('nju:klɪ,eɪt), **nucleates, nucleating, nucleated.** (*intr*) **2** to form a nucleus.

nuclei ('nju:klɪ,aɪ) *n* a plural of **nucleus.**

nucleic acid (nju:'kli:ɪk, -'kleɪ-) *n Biochem.* any of a group of complex compounds with a high molecular weight that are vital constituents of all living cells. See also **RNA, DNA.**

nucleo- *or before a vowel* **nucle-** *combining form.* **1** nucleus or nuclear. **2** nucleic acid. [from Latin *nucleus* kernel, from *nux* nut]

nucleolus (,nju:klɪ'əʊləs) *n, pl* **nucleoli** (-laɪ). a small rounded body within a resting cell nucleus that contains RNA and proteins and is involved in protein synthesis. Also called: **nucleole.** [C19: from L, dim. of NUCLEUS]
▸,**nucle'olar** *adj*

nucleon ('nju:klɪ,ɒn) *n* a proton or neutron, esp. one present in an atomic nucleus.

nucleonics (,nju:klɪ'ɒnɪks) *n* (*functioning as sing*) the branch of physics concerned with the applications of nuclear energy.
▸,**nucle'onic** *adj* ▸,**nucle'onically** *adv*

nucleon number *n* the number of nucleons in an atomic nucleus; mass number.

nucleophile ('nju:klɪə,faɪl) *n* a molecule or ion that can donate electrons.
▸**nucleophilic** (,nju:klɪə'fɪlɪk) *adj*

nucleoside ('nju:klɪə,saɪd) *n Biochem.* a compound containing a purine or pyrimidine base linked to a sugar (usually ribose or deoxyribose).

nucleotide ('nju:klɪə,taɪd) *n Biochem.* a compound consisting of a nucleoside linked to phosphoric acid.

nucleus ❶ ('nju:klɪəs) *n, pl* **nuclei** *or* **nucleuses. 1** a central or fundamental thing around which others are grouped; core. **2** a centre of growth or development; basis: *the nucleus of an idea.* **3** *Biol.* the spherical or ovoid compartment of a cell that contains the chromosomes and associated molecules that control the characteristics and growth of the cell. **4** *Astron.* the central portion in the head of a comet, consisting of small solid particles of ice and frozen gases. **5** *Physics.* the positively charged dense region at the centre of an atom, composed of protons and neutrons, about which electrons orbit. **6** *Chem.* a fundamental group of atoms in a molecule serving as the base structure for related compounds. [C18: from L: kernel, from *nux* nut]

nuclide ('nju:klaɪd) *n* a species of atom characterized by its atomic number and its mass number. [C20: from NUCLEO- + *-ide*, from Gk *eidos* shape]

nude ❶ (nju:d) *adj* **1** completely undressed. **2** having no covering; bare; exposed. **3** *Law.* **3a** lacking some essential legal requirement. **3b** (of a contract, etc.) made without consideration and void unless under seal. ◆ *n* **4** the state of being naked (esp. in **in the nude**). **5** a naked figure, esp. in painting, sculpture, etc. [C16: from L *nūdus*]
▸'**nudely** *adv*

nudge ❶ (nʌdʒ) *vb* **nudges, nudging, nudged.** (*tr*) **1** to push (someone) gently, esp. with the elbow, to get attention; jog. **2** to push slowly or lightly: *as I drove out, I just nudged the gatepost.* ◆ *n* **3** a gentle poke or push. [C17: ?from Scand.]
▸'**nudger** *n*

nudibranch ('nju:dɪ,bræŋk) *n* a marine gastropod of an order characterized by a shell-less, often beautifully coloured, body bearing external gills. Also called: **sea slug.** [C19: from L *nudus* naked + *branche*, from L *branchia* gills]

nudism ('nju:dɪzəm) *n* the practice of nudity, esp. for reasons of health, etc.
▸'**nudist** *n, adj*

nudity ❶ ('nju:dɪtɪ) *n, pl* **nudities.** the state or fact of being nude; nakedness.

nugatory ❶ ('nju:gətərɪ, -trɪ) *adj* **1** of little value. **2** not valid: *a nugatory law.* [C17: from L *nūgātōrius*, from *nūgārī* to jest, from *nūgae* trifles]

nugget ❶ ('nʌgɪt) *n* **1** a small piece or lump, esp. of gold in its natural state. **2** something small but valuable or excellent. [C19: from ?]

nuggety ('nʌgɪtɪ) *adj* **1** of or resembling a nugget. **2** *Austral. & NZ inf.* (of a person) thickset; stocky.

nuisance ❶ ('nju:səns) *n* **1a** a person or thing that causes annoyance or bother. **1b** (*as modifier*): *nuisance calls.* **2** *Law.* something unauthorized that is obnoxious or injurious to the community at large or to an individual, esp. in relation to his ownership of property. **3 nuisance value.** the usefulness of a person's or thing's capacity to cause difficulties or irritation. [C15: via OF from *nuire* to injure, from L *nocēre*]

NUJ (in Britain) *abbrev. for* National Union of Journalists.

nuke (nju:k) *Sl., chiefly US.* ◆ *vb* **nukes, nuking, nuked.** (*tr*) **1** to attack or destroy with nuclear weapons. ◆ *n* **2** a nuclear bomb.

null ❶ (nʌl) *adj* **1** without legal force; invalid; (esp. in **null and void**). **2** without value or consequence; useless. **3** lacking distinction; characterless. **4** nonexistent; amounting to nothing. **5** *Maths.* **5a** quantitatively zero. **5b** relating to zero. **5c** (of a set) having no members. **6** *Physics.* involving measurement in which conditions are adjusted so that an instrument has a zero reading, as with a Wheatstone bridge. [C16: from L *nullus* none, from *ne* not + *ullus* any]

nullah ('nʌlɑ:) *n* a stream or drain. [C18: from Hindi *nālā*]

null hypothesis *n Statistics.* the residual hypothesis if the alternative hypothesis tested against it fails to achieve a predetermined significance level.

nullify ❶ ('nʌlɪ,faɪ) *vb* **nullifies, nullifying, nullified.** (*tr*) **1** to render legally void or of no effect. **2** to render ineffective or useless; cancel out. [C16: from LL *nullificāre* to despise, from L *nullus* of no account + *facere* to make]
▸,**nullifi'cation** *n*

nullity ❶ ('nʌlɪtɪ) *n, pl* **nullities. 1** the state of being null. **2** a null or legally invalid act or instrument. **3** something null, ineffective, characterless, etc. [C16: from Med. L *nullitās*, from L *nullus* no, not any]

NUM (in Britain) *abbrev. for* National Union of Mineworkers.

num. *abbrev. for:* **1** number. **2** numeral.

Num. *Bible. abbrev. for* Numbers.

numb ❶ (nʌm) *adj* **1** deprived of feeling through cold, shock, etc. **2** unable to move; paralysed. ◆ *vb* **3** (*tr*) to make numb; deaden, shock, or paralyse. [C15 *nomen*, lit.: taken (with paralysis), from OE *niman* to take]
▸'**numbly** *adv* ▸'**numbness** *n*

numbat ('nʌm,bæt) *n* a small Australian marsupial having a long snout and tongue and strong claws for hunting and feeding on termites. [C20: from Abor.]

number ❶ ('nʌmbə) *n* **1** a concept of quantity that is or can be derived from a single unit, the sum of a collection of units, or zero. Every number occupies a unique position in a sequence, enabling it to be used in counting. See also **cardinal number, ordinal number. 2** the symbol used to represent a number; numeral. **3** a numeral or string of numerals used to identify a person or thing: *a telephone number.* **4** the person or thing so identified or designated: *she was number seven in the race.* **5** sum or quantity: *a large number of people.* **6** one of a series, as of a maga-

THESAURUS

nucleus *n* **1 = centre**, basis, core, focus, heart, kernel, nub, pivot

nude *adj* **1 = naked**, *au naturel*, bare, buck naked (*sl.*), disrobed, exposed, in one's birthday suit (*inf.*), in the altogether (*inf.*), in the buff (*inf.*), naked as the day one was born (*inf.*), starkers (*inf.*), stark-naked, stripped, unclad, unclothed, uncovered, undraped, undressed, without a stitch on (*inf.*)
Antonyms *adj* attired, clothed, covered, dressed

nudge *vb, n* **1, 3 = push**, bump, dig, elbow, jog, poke, prod, shove, touch

nudity *n* **= nakedness**, bareness, deshabille, nudism, undress

nugatory *adj* **1 = trivial**, insignificant, trifling, valueless, worthless **2 = invalid**, bootless, futile, ineffectual, inoperative, null and void, unavailing, useless, vain

nugget *n* **1 = lump**, chunk, clump, hunk, mass, piece

nuisance *n* **1a = problem**, annoyance, bore, bother, drag, gall, hassle (*inf.*), inconvenience, infliction, irritation, offence, pain in the neck, pest, plague, trouble, vexation
Antonyms *n* benefit, blessing, delight, happiness, joy, pleasure, satisfaction

null *adj* **1 = invalid**, inoperative, void **2 = useless**, ineffectual, powerless, vain, valueless, worthless **3 = characterless 4 = nonexistent**

nullify *vb* **1 = invalidate**, abolish, abrogate, annul, countervail, render null and void, repeal, rescind, revoke, veto, void **2 = cancel out**, bring to naught, counteract, negate, neutralize, obviate
Antonyms *vb* ≠ **invalidate:** authorize, confirm, endorse, ratify, validate

nullity *n* **1 = worthlessness**, characterlessness, ineffectualness, invalidity, nonexistence, powerlessness, uselessness, valuelessness, voidness

numb *adj* **1 = unfeeling**, benumbed, dead, deadened, frozen, immobilized, insensible, insensitive, paralysed, stupefied, torpid ◆ *vb* **3 = deaden**, benumb, dull, freeze, immobilize, paralyse, stun, stupefy
Antonyms *adj* ≠ **unfeeling:** feeling, responsive, sensitive, sentient

number *n* **2 = numeral**, character, count, digit, figure, integer **5 = sum**, aggregate, amount, zine; issue. **7a** a self-contained piece of pop or jazz music. **7b** a self-contained part of an opera or other musical score. **8** a group of people, esp. an exclusive group: *he was not one of our number.* **9** *Sl.* a person, esp. a sexually attractive girl: *who's that nice little number?* **10** *Inf.* an admired article: *that little number is by Dior.* **11** a grammatical category for the variation in form of nouns, pronouns, and any words agreeing with them, depending on how many persons or things are referred to. **12 any number of.** several or many. **13 by numbers.** *Mil.* (of a drill procedure, etc.) performed step by step, each move being made on the call of a number. **14 get** *or* **have someone's number.** *Inf.* to discover a person's true character or intentions. **15 one's number is up.** *Brit. inf.* one is finished; one is ruined or about to die. **16 without** *or* **beyond number.** innumerable. ◆ *vb* (*mainly tr*) **17** to assign a number to. **18** to add up to; total. **19** (*also intr*) to list (items) one by one; enumerate. **20** (*also intr*) to put or be put into a group, category, etc.: *they were numbered among the worst hit.* **21** to limit the number of: *his days were numbered.* [C13: from OF *nombre,* from L *numerus*]

number crunching *n Computing.* the large-scale processing of numerical data.

numbered account *n Banking.* an account identified only by a number, esp. one in a Swiss bank that could contain funds illegally obtained.

numberless ❶ (ˈnʌmbəlɪs) *adj* **1** too many to be counted; countless. **2** not containing numbers.

number one *n* **1** the first in a series or sequence. **2** an informal phrase for **oneself, myself,** etc.: *to look after number one.* **3** *Inf.* the most important person; chief: *he's number one in the organization.* **4** *Inf.* the bestselling pop record in any one week. ◆ *adj* **5** first in importance, urgency, quality, etc.: *number one priority.*

numberplate (ˈnʌmbəˌpleɪt) *n* a plate mounted on the front and back of a motor vehicle bearing the registration number. Usual US term: **license plate,** (Canad.) **licence plate.**

numbers game *or* **racket** *n US.* an illegal lottery in which money is wagered on a certain combination of digits appearing at the beginning of a series of numbers published in a newspaper, as in share prices or sports results. Often shortened to **numbers.**

Number Ten *n* 10 Downing Street, the British prime minister's official London residence.

number theory *n* the study of integers, their properties, and the relationship between integers.

numbfish (ˈnʌmˌfɪʃ) *n, pl* **numbfish** *or* **numbfishes.** any of several electric rays. [C18: so called because it numbs its victims]

numbles (ˈnʌmbᵊlz) *pl n Arch.* the heart, lungs, liver, etc., of a deer or other animal. [C14: from OF *nombles,* pl. of *nomble* thigh muscle of a deer, changed from L *lumbulus,* dim. of *lumbus* loin]

numbskull ❶ *or* **numskull** (ˈnʌmˌskʌl) *n* a stupid person; dolt.

numen (ˈnju:mɛn) *n, pl* **numina** (-mɪnə). **1** (esp. in ancient Roman religion) a deity or spirit presiding over a thing or place. **2** a guiding principle, force, or spirit. [C17: from L: a nod (indicating a command), divine power]

numerable (ˈnju:mərəbᵊl) *adj* able to be numbered or counted.
▸ˈ**numerably** *adv*

numeral ❶ (ˈnju:mərəl) *n* **1** a symbol or group of symbols used to express a number: for example, *6* (*Arabic*), *VI* (*Roman*), *110* (*binary*). ◆ *adj* **2** of, consisting of, or denoting a number. [C16: from LL *numerālis* belonging to number, from L *numerus*]

numerate *adj* (ˈnju:mərɪt). **1** able to use numbers, esp. in arithmetical operations. ◆ *vb* (ˈnju:məˌreɪt), **numerates, numerating, numerated.** (*tr*) **2** to read (a numerical expression). **3** a less common word for **enumerate.** [C18 (vb): from L *numerus* number + -ATE[1], by analogy with *literate*]
▸**numeracy** (ˈnju:mərəsɪ) *n*

numeration (ˌnju:məˈreɪʃən) *n* **1** the writing, reading, or naming of numbers. **2** a system of numbering.
▸ˈ**numerative** *adj*

numerator (ˈnju:məˌreɪtə) *n* **1** *Maths.* the dividend of a fraction: the numerator of 7/8 is 7. Cf. **denominator. 2** a person or thing that numbers; enumerator.

numerical (nju:ˈmɛrɪkᵊl) *or* **numeric** *adj* **1** of, relating to, or denoting a number or numbers. **2** measured or expressed in numbers: *numerical value.*
▸**nuˈmerically** *adv*

numerology (ˌnju:məˈrɒlədʒɪ) *n* the study of numbers and of their supposed influence on human affairs.
▸**numerological** (ˌnju:mərəˈlɒdʒɪkᵊl) *adj*

numerous ❶ (ˈnju:mərəs) *adj* **1** being many. **2** consisting of many parts: *a numerous collection.*
▸ˈ**numerously** *adv* ▸ˈ**numerousness** *n*

numinous ❶ (ˈnju:mɪnəs) *adj* **1** denoting, being, or relating to a numen; divine. **2** arousing spiritual or religious emotions. **3** mysterious or awe-inspiring. [C17: from L *numin-,* NUMEN + -OUS]

numismatics (ˌnju:mɪzˈmætɪks) *n* (*functioning as sing*) the study or collection of coins, medals, etc. Also called: ˌ**numismaˈtology.** [C18: from F *numismatique,* from L *nomisma,* from Gk: piece of currency, from *nomizein* to have in use, from *nomos* use]
▸ˌ**numisˈmatic** *adj* ▸ˌ**numisˈmatically** *adv*

nummulite (ˈnʌmjʊˌlaɪt) *n* any of a family of large fossil protozoans common in Tertiary times. [C19: from NL, from L *nummulus,* from *nummus* coin]

numpty (ˈnʌmptɪ) *n, pl* **numpties.** *Scot. inf.* a foolish or ignorant person.

numskull (ˈnʌmˌskʌl) *n* a variant spelling of **numbskull.**

nun (nʌn) *n* a female member of a religious order. [OE *nunne,* from Church L *nonna,* from LL: form of address used for an elderly woman]
▸ˈ**nunhood** *n* ▸ˈ**nunlike** *adj*

nun buoy *n Naut.* a buoy, conical at the top, marking the right side of a channel leading into a harbour: green in British waters but red in US waters. [C18: from obs. *nun* child's spinning top + BUOY]

Nunc Dimittis (ˈnʌŋk dɪˈmɪtɪs, ˈnʊŋk) *n* **1** the Latin name for the Canticle of Simeon (Luke 2:29–32). **2** a musical setting of this. [from the opening words (Vulgate): now let depart]

nunciature (ˈnʌnsɪətʃə) *n* the office or term of office of a nuncio. [C17: from It. *nunziatura;* see NUNCIO]

nuncio ❶ (ˈnʌnʃɪˌəʊ, -sɪ-) *n, pl* **nuncios.** *RC Church.* a diplomatic representative of the Holy See. [C16: via It. from L *nuntius* messenger]

nunnery ❶ (ˈnʌnərɪ) *n, pl* **nunneries.** the convent or religious house of a community of nuns.

NUPE (ˈnju:pɪ) *n* (formerly, in Britain) *acronym for* National Union of Public Employees.

nuptial ❶ (ˈnʌpʃəl, -tʃəl) *adj* **1** relating to marriage; conjugal: *nuptial vows.* **2** *Zool.* of or relating to mating: *the nuptial flight of a queen bee.* [C15: from L *nuptiālis,* from *nuptiae* marriage, from *nubere* to marry]
▸ˈ**nuptially** *adv*

nuptials ❶ (ˈnʌpʃəlz, -tʃəlz) *pl n* (*sometimes sing*) a marriage ceremony; wedding.

NUR (formerly, in Britain) *abbrev. for* National Union of Railwaymen.

nurd a variant spelling of **nerd.**

nurse ❶ (nɜ:s) *n* **1** a person, often a woman, who is trained to tend the sick and infirm, assist doctors, etc. **2** short for **nursemaid. 3** a woman employed to breast-feed another woman's child; wet nurse. **4** a worker in a colony of social insects that takes care of the larvae. ◆ *vb* **nurses, nursing, nursed.** (*mainly tr*) **5** (*also intr*) to tend (the sick). **6** (*also intr*) to feed (a baby) at the breast. **7** to try to cure (an ailment). **8** to clasp fondly: *she nursed the child in her arms.* **9** to look after (a child) as one's employment. **10** to harbour; preserve: *to nurse a grudge.* **11** to give special attention to, esp. in order to promote goodwill: *to nurse a difficult constituency.* **12** *Billiards.* to keep (the balls) together for a series of cannons. [C16: from earlier *norice,* OF *nourice,* from LL *nūtrīcia,* from L *nūtrīcius* nourishing, from *nūtrīre* to nourish]

nursemaid (ˈnɜ:sˌmeɪd) *or* **nurserymaid** *n* a woman employed to look after someone else's children. Often shortened to **nurse.**

nursery ❶ (ˈnɜ:srɪ) *n, pl* **nurseries. 1** a room in a house set apart for children. **2** a place where plants, young trees, etc., are grown commercially. **3** an establishment providing daycare for babies and young children; crèche. **4** anywhere serving to foster or nourish new ideas, etc. **5** Also called: **nursery cannon.** *Billiards.* **5a** a series of cannons with the three balls adjacent to a cushion, esp. near a corner pocket. **5b** a cannon in such a series.

nurseryman (ˈnɜ:srɪmən) *n, pl* **nurserymen.** a person who owns or works in a nursery in which plants are grown.

nursery rhyme *n* a short traditional verse or song for children, such as *Little Jack Horner.*

nursery school *n* a school for young children, usually from three to five years old.

nursery slopes *pl n* gentle slopes used by beginners in skiing.

THESAURUS

total **6** = **issue**, copy, edition, imprint, printing **8** = **quantity**, collection, company, crowd, horde, many, multitude, throng ◆ *vb* **18** = **calculate**, account, add, compute, count, include, reckon, tell, total **19** = **list**, enumerate
Antonyms *n* ≠ **quantity:** insufficiency, lack, scantiness, scarcity, shortage, want ◆ *vb* ≠ **calculate:** conjecture, guess, theorize

numbered *adj* **20** = **included**, categorized, contained, counted, designated, fixed, specified **21** = **limited**, limited in number

numberless *adj* **1** = **infinite**, countless, endless, innumerable, multitudinous, myriad, unnumbered, untold

numbness *n* **1** = **deadness**, dullness, insensibility, insensitivity, stupefaction, torpor, unfeelingness

numbskull *n* = **fool**, berk, blockhead, bonehead (*sl.*), buffoon, clot (*Brit. inf.*), coot, dimwit (*inf.*), dipstick (*Brit. sl.*), divvy (*sl.*), dolt, dope (*inf.*), dork (*sl.*), dullard, dummy (*sl.*), dunce, dunderhead, fathead (*inf.*), jerk (*sl., chiefly US & Canad.*), lamebrain (*inf.*), nerd *or* nurd (*sl.*), nitwit (*inf.*), oaf, pillock (*Brit. sl.*), prat (*sl.*), prick (*sl.*), schmuck (*US sl.*), simpleton, thickhead, twit (*inf.*), wally (*sl.*)

numeral *n* **1** = **number**, character, cipher, digit, figure, integer, symbol

numerous *adj* **1** = **many**, abundant, copious, plentiful, profuse, several, thick on the ground
Antonyms *adj* few, not many, scarcely any

numinous *adj* **1-3** = **holy**, awe-inspiring, divine, heavenly, mysterious, religious, spiritual, supernatural

nuncio *n* = **ambassador**, envoy, legate, messenger

nunnery *n* = **convent**, abbey, cloister, house, monastery

nuptial *adj* **1** = **marital**, bridal, conjugal, connubial, hymeneal (*poetic*), matrimonial, wedded, wedding

nuptials *pl n* = **wedding**, espousal (*arch.*), marriage, matrimony

nurse *vb* **5** = **look after**, care for, minister to, tend, treat **6** = **breast-feed**, feed, nourish, nurture, suckle, wet-nurse **10** = **foster**, cherish, cultivate, harbour, keep alive, preserve

nursery *n* **3** = **crèche**, kindergarten, playgroup

nursery stakes *pl n* a race for two-year-old horses.

nurse shark *n* any of various sharks having an external groove on each side of the head between the mouth and nostril. [C15 *nusse fisshe* (later infl. in spelling by NURSE), ?from a division of obs. *an huss* shark, dogfish (from ?) as *a nuss*]

nursing ('nɜːsɪŋ) *n* **1a** the practice or profession of caring for the sick and injured. **1b** (*as modifier*): *a nursing home.*

nursing home *n* a private hospital or residence for aged or infirm persons.

nursing officer *n* (in Britain) the official name for **matron** (sense 4).

nursling *or* **nurseling** ('nɜːslɪŋ) *n* a child or young animal that is being suckled, nursed, or fostered.

nurture ❶ ('nɜːtʃə) *n* **1** the act or process of promoting the development, etc., of a child. **2** something that nourishes. ◆ *vb* **nurtures, nurturing, nurtured.** (*tr*) **3** to feed or support. **4** to educate or train. [C14: from OF *norriture,* from L *nūtrīre* to nourish]
▸**'nurtural** *adj* ▸**'nurturer** *n*

NUS (in Britain) *abbrev. for:* **1** (formerly) National Union of Seamen. **2** National Union of Students.

nut ❶ (nʌt) *n* **1** a dry one-seeded indehiscent fruit that usually possesses a woody wall. **2** (*not in technical use*) any similar fruit, such as the walnut, having a hard shell and an edible kernel. **3** the edible kernel of such a fruit. **4** *Sl.* an eccentric or mad person. **5** *Sl.* the head. **6 do one's nut.** *Brit. sl.* to be extremely angry. **7 off one's nut.** *Sl.* mad or foolish. **8** a person or thing that presents difficulties (esp. in **a tough nut to crack**). **9** a small square hexagonal block, usually metal, with a threaded hole through the middle for screwing on the end of a bolt. **10** Also called (US and Canad.): **frog.** *Music.* **10a** the ridge at the upper end of the fingerboard of a violin, cello, etc., over which the strings pass to the tuning pegs. **10b** the end of a violin bow that is held by the player. **11** a small usually gingery biscuit. **12** *Brit.* a small piece of coal. ◆ *vb* **nuts, nutting, nutted. 13** (*intr*) to gather nuts. ◆ See also **nuts.** [OE *hnutu*]

NUT (in Britain) *abbrev. for* National Union of Teachers.

nutant ('njuːtᵊnt) *adj Bot.* having the apex hanging down. [C18: from L *nūtāre* to nod]

nutation (njuː'teɪʃən) *n* **1** *Astron.* a periodic variation in the precession of the earth's axis causing the earth's poles to oscillate about their mean position. **2** the spiral growth of a shoot or similar plant organ, caused by variation in the growth rate in different parts. **3** the act of nodding. [C17: from L *nutātiō,* from *nūtāre* to nod]

nutbrown ('nʌt'braʊn) *adj* reddish-brown.

nutcase ('nʌt,keɪs) *n Sl.* an insane or very foolish person.

nutcracker ('nʌt,krækə) *n* **1** (*often pl*) a device for cracking the shells of nuts. **2** either an Old World bird or a North American bird (**Clark's nutcracker**) having speckled plumage and feeding on nuts, seeds, etc.

nutgall ('nʌt,gɔːl) *n* a nut-shaped gall caused by gall wasps on the oak and other trees.

nuthatch ('nʌt,hætʃ) *n* a songbird having strong feet and bill, and feeding on insects, seeds, and nuts. [C14 *notehache,* from *note* nut + *hache* hatchet, from its habit of splitting nuts]

nuthouse ('nʌt,haʊs) *n Sl.* a mental hospital.

nutmeg ('nʌt,mɛg) *n* **1** an East Indian evergreen tree cultivated in the tropics for its hard aromatic seed. See also **mace**[2]. **2** the seed of this tree, used as a spice. ◆ *vb* **nutmegs, nutmegging, nutmegged.** (*tr*) **3** *Brit. sport inf.* to kick or hit the ball between the legs of (an opposing player). [C13: from OF *nois muguede,* from OProvençal *noz muscada* musk-scented nut, from L *nux* NUT + *muscus* MUSK]

nutria ('njuːtrɪə) *n* another name for **coypu,** esp. the fur. [C19: from Sp., var. of *lutria,* ult. from L *lūtra* otter]

nutrient ('njuːtrɪənt) *n* **1** any of the mineral substances that are absorbed by the roots of plants. **2** any substance that nourishes an animal. ◆ *adj* **3** providing or contributing to nourishment. [C17: from L *nūtrīre* to nourish]

nutriment ❶ ('njuːtrɪmənt) *n* any material providing nourishment. [C16: from L *nūtrīmentum,* from *nūtrīre* to nourish]
▸**nutrimental** (,njuːtrɪ'mentᵊl) *adj*

nutrition ❶ (njuː'trɪʃən) *n* **1** a process in animals and plants involving the intake and assimilation of nutrient materials. **2** the act or process of nourishing. **3** the study of nutrition, esp. in humans. [C16: from LL *nūtrītiō,* from *nūtrīre* to nourish]
▸**nu'tritional** *adj* ▸**nu'tritionist** *n*

nutritious ❶ (njuː'trɪʃəs) *adj* nourishing. [C17: from L *nūtrīcius,* from *nūtrix* NURSE]
▸**nu'tritiously** *adv* ▸**nu'tritiousness** *n*

nutritive ('njuːtrɪtɪv) *adj* **1** providing nourishment. **2** of, concerning, or promoting nutrition. ◆ *n* **3** a nutritious food.

nuts ❶ (nʌts) *adj* **1** a slang word for **insane. 2** (foll. by *about* or *on*) *Sl.* extremely fond (of) or enthusiastic (about). ◆ *interj* **3** *Sl.* an expression of contempt, refusal, or defiance.

nuts and bolts ❶ *pl n Inf.* the essential or practical details.

nutshell ('nʌt,ʃel) *n* **1** the shell around the kernel of a nut. **2 in a nutshell.** in essence; briefly.

nutter ('nʌtə) *n Brit. sl.* a mad or eccentric person.

nutty ('nʌtɪ) *adj* **nuttier, nuttiest. 1** containing nuts. **2** resembling nuts. **3** a slang word for **insane. 4** (foll. by *over* or *about*) *Inf.* extremely enthusiastic (about).
▸**'nuttiness** *n*

nux vomica ('nʌks 'vɒmɪkə) *n* **1** an Indian tree with orange-red berries containing poisonous seeds. **2** any of the seeds of this tree, which contain strychnine and other poisonous alkaloids. **3** a medicine manufactured from the seeds of this tree, formerly used as a heart stimulant. [C16: from Med. L: vomiting nut]

nuzzle ❶ ('nʌzᵊl) *vb* **nuzzles, nuzzling, nuzzled. 1** to push or rub gently with the nose or snout. **2** (*intr*) to nestle; lie close. **3** (*tr*) to dig out with the snout. [C15 *nosele,* from NOSE (n)]

NVQ *abbrev. for* National Vocational Qualification.

NW *symbol for* northwest(ern).

NWMP (in Canada) *abbrev. for* North West Mounted Police.

NWT *abbrev. for* Northwest Territories (of Canada).

NY *or* **N.Y.** *abbrev. for* New York (city or state).

nyala ('njɑːlə) *n, pl* **nyala** *or* **nyalas. 1** a spiral-horned southern African antelope with a fringe of white hairs along the length of the back and neck. **2 mountain nyala.** a similar Ethiopian animal lacking the white crest. [from Zulu]

NYC *abbrev. for* New York City.

nyctalopia (,nɪktə'ləʊpɪə) *n* inability to see normally in dim light. Nontechnical name: **night blindness.** [C17: via LL from Gk *nuktálōps,* from *nux* night + *alaos* blind + *ōps* eye]

nyctitropism (nɪk'tɪtrə,pɪzəm) *n* a tendency of some plant parts to assume positions at night that are different from their daytime positions. [C19: *nyct-,* from Gk *nukt-, nux* night + -TROPISM]

nye (naɪ) *n* a flock of pheasants. Also called: **nide, eye.** [C15: from OF *ni,* from L *nīdus* nest]

nylon ('naɪlɒn) *n* **1** a class of synthetic polyamide materials of which monofilaments are used for bristles, etc., and fibres can be spun into yarn. **2** yarn or cloth made of nylon, used for clothing, stockings, etc. [C20: orig. a trademark]

nylons ('naɪlɒnz) *pl n* stockings made of nylon.

nymph ❶ (nɪmf) *n* **1** *Myth.* a spirit of nature envisaged as a beautiful maiden. **2** *Chiefly poetic.* a beautiful young woman. **3** the larva of insects such as the dragonfly. It resembles the adult, apart from having underdeveloped wings, and develops without a pupal stage. [C14: via OF from L, from Gk *numphē*]
▸**'nymphal** *or* **nymphean** ('nɪmfɪən)*adj* ▸**'nymphlike** *adj*

nympha ('nɪmfə) *n, pl* **nymphae** (-fiː). *Anat.* either one of the labia minora. [C17: from L: bride]

nymphet ('nɪmfɪt) *n* a young girl who is sexually precocious and desirable. [C17 (meaning: a young nymph): dim. of NYMPH]

nympho ('nɪmfəʊ) *n, pl* **nymphos.** *Inf.* short for **nymphomaniac.**

nympholepsy ('nɪmfə,lepsɪ) *n, pl* **nympholepsies.** a state of violent emotion, esp. when associated with a desire for something that one cannot have. [C18: from Gk *numpholēptos* caught by nymphs, from *numphē* nymph + *lambanein* to seize]
▸**'nympho,lept** *n* ▸**,nympho'leptic** *adj*

nymphomania (,nɪmfə'meɪnɪə) *n* a neurotic compulsion in women to have sexual intercourse with many men without being able to have lasting relationships with them. [C18: NL, from Gk *numphē* nymph + -MANIA]
▸**,nympho'maniac** *n, adj*

nystagmus (nɪ'stægməs) *n* involuntary movement of the eye comprising a smooth drift followed by a flick back. [C19: NL, from Gk *nustagmos*]
▸**nys'tagmic** *adj*

NZ *or* **N. Zeal.** *abbrev. for* New Zealand.

NZBC (formerly) *abbrev. for* New Zealand Broadcasting Commission.

NZEF (in New Zealand) *abbrev. for* New Zealand Expeditionary Force, the New Zealand army that served 1914-18. **2NZEF** refers to the Second New Zealand Expeditionary Force, in World War II.

THESAURUS

nurture *n* **1** = **development,** discipline, education, instruction, rearing, training, upbringing **2** = **food,** diet, nourishment ◆ *vb* **3** = **nourish,** feed, nurse, support, sustain, tend **4** = **develop,** bring up, cultivate, discipline, educate, instruct, rear, school, train
Antonyms *vb* ≠ **develop, nourish:** deprive, disregard, ignore, neglect, overlook

nut *n* **1-3** = **kernel,** pip, seed, stone **4** *Slang* = **madman,** crackpot, crank (*inf.*), eccentric, headbanger (*inf.*), headcase (*inf.*), loony (*sl.*), lunatic, maniac, nutcase (*sl.*), nutter (*Brit. sl.*), oddball (*inf.*), psycho (*sl.*) **5** *Slang* = **head,** brain, mind, reason, senses

nutriment *n* = **food,** aliment, diet, foodstuff, nourishment, nutrition, subsistence, support, sustenance

nutrition *n* **1, 2** = **nourishment,** nutriment, sustenance

nutritious *adj* = **nourishing,** alimental, alimentative, beneficial, healthful, health-giving, invigorating, nutritive, strengthening, wholesome

nuts *adj* **1** *Slang* = **insane,** bananas (*sl.*), barking mad (*sl.*), batty (*sl.*), crazy, demented, deranged, doolally (*sl.*), eccentric, irrational, loony (*sl.*), loopy (*inf.*), mad, not the full shilling (*inf.*), nutty (*sl.*), off one's trolley (*sl.*), out to lunch (*inf.*), psycho (*sl.*), psychopathic, up the pole (*inf.*)

nuts and bolts *pl n Informal* = **essentials,** basics, details, fundamentals, ins and outs, nitty-gritty (*inf.*), practicalities

nuzzle *vb* **2** = **snuggle,** burrow, cuddle, fondle, nestle, nudge, pet

nymph *n* **1** = **sylph,** dryad, hamadryad, naiad, Oceanid (*Greek myth*), oread **2** *Chiefly poetic* = **girl,** damsel, lass, maid, maiden

Oo

o *or* **O** (əʊ) *n, pl* **o's, O's,** *or* **Os. 1** the 15th letter and fourth vowel of the English alphabet. **2** any of several speech sounds represented by this letter, as in *code, pot, cow,* or *form.* **3** another name for **nought.**
O[1] *symbol for:* **1** *Chem.* oxygen. **2** a human blood type of the ABO group. **3** Old.
O[2] (əʊ) *interj* **1** a variant of **oh. 2** an exclamation introducing an invocation, entreaty, wish, etc.: *O God! O for the wings of a dove!*
o. *abbrev. for:* **1** octavo. **2** old. **3** only. **4** order. **5** *Pharmacol.* pint. [from L *octarius*]
O. *abbrev. for:* **1** Ocean. **2** octavo. **3** old.
o' (ə) *prep Inf. or arch.* shortened form of **of:** *a cup o' tea.*
O'- *prefix* (in surnames of Irish Gaelic origin) descendant of: *O'Corrigan.* [from Irish Gaelic *ó, ua* descendant]
-o *suffix forming nouns.* indicating a diminutive or slang abbreviation: *wino.*
oaf Ⓣ (əʊf) *n* a stupid or loutish person. [C17: var. of OE *ælf* ELF]
►**'oafish** *adj* ►**'oafishness** *n*
oak (əʊk) *n* **1** any deciduous or evergreen tree or shrub having acorns as fruits and lobed leaves. **2a** the wood of any of these trees, used esp. as building timber and for making furniture. **2b** (*as modifier*): *an oak table.* **3** any of various trees that resemble the oak, such as the poison oak. **4** the leaves of an oak tree, worn as a garland. [OE *āc*]
oak apple *or* **gall** *n* any of various brownish round galls on oak trees, containing the larvae of certain wasps.
oaken ('əʊkən) *adj* made of the wood of the oak.
Oaks (əʊks) *n* (*functioning as sing*) **the.** a horse race for fillies held annually at Epsom since 1779: one of the classics of English flat racing. [named after an estate near Epsom]
oakum ('əʊkəm) *n* loose fibre obtained by unravelling old rope, used esp. for caulking seams in wooden ships. [OE *ācuma,* var. of *ācumba,* lit.: off-combings, from *ā-* off + *-cumba,* from *cemban* to COMB]
O & M *abbrev. for* organization and method (in studies of working methods).
OAP (in Britain) *abbrev. for* old age pension *or* pensioner.
oar (ɔː) *n* **1** a long shaft of wood for propelling a boat by rowing, having a broad blade that is dipped into and pulled against the water. **2** short for **oarsman. 3 stick** *or* **put one's oar in.** to interfere or interrupt. ◆ *vb* **4** to row or propel with or as if with oars. [OE *ār,* of Gmc origin]
►**'oarless** *adj* ►**'oarˌlike** *adj*
oarfish ('ɔːˌfɪʃ) *n, pl* **oarfish** *or* **oarfishes.** a very long ribbonfish with long slender ventral fins. [C19: referring to the flattened oarlike body]
oarlock ('ɔːˌlɒk) *n* the usual US and Canad. word for **rowlock.**
oarsman ('ɔːzmən) *n, pl* **oarsmen.** a man who rows, esp. one who rows in a racing boat.
►**'oarsmanship** *n*
OAS *abbrev. for:* **1** *Organisation de l'Armée Secrète;* an organization which opposed Algerian independence by acts of terrorism. **2** Organization of American States.
oasis Ⓣ (əʊ'eɪsɪs) *n, pl* **oases** (-iːz). **1** a fertile patch in a desert occurring where the water table approaches or reaches the ground surface. **2** a place of peace, safety, or happiness. [C17: via L from Gk, prob. from Egyptian]
oast (əʊst) *n Chiefly Brit.* **1** a kiln for drying hops. **2** Also called: **oast house.** a building containing such kilns, usually having a conical or pyramidal roof. [OE *āst*]
oat (əʊt) *n* **1** an erect annual grass grown in temperate regions for its edible seed. **2** (*usually pl*) the seeds or fruits of this grass. **3** any of various other grasses such as the wild oat. **4** *Poetic.* a flute made from an oat straw. **5 feel one's oats.** *US & Canad. inf.* **5a** to feel exuberant. **5b** to feel self-important. **6 sow one's (wild) oats.** to indulge in adventure or promiscuity during youth. [OE *āte,* from ?]
oatcake ('əʊtˌkeɪk) *n* a crisp brittle unleavened biscuit made of oatmeal.
oaten ('əʊtᵊn) *adj* made of oats or oat straw.
oath Ⓣ (əʊθ) *n, pl* **oaths** (əʊðz). **1** a solemn pronouncement to affirm the truth of a statement or to pledge a person to some course of action. **2** the form of such a pronouncement. **3** an irreverent or blasphemous expression, esp. one involving the name of a deity; curse. **4 my oath.** *Austral. sl.* certainly; yes indeed. **5 on, upon,** *or* **under oath. 5a** under the obligation of an oath. **5b** *Law.* having sworn to tell the truth, usually with one's hand on the Bible. **6 take an oath.** to declare formally with a pledge, esp. before giving evidence. [OE *āth*]
oatmeal ('əʊtˌmiːl) *n* **1** meal ground from oats, used for making porridge, oatcakes, etc. **2a** a greyish-yellow colour. **2b** (*as adj*): *an oatmeal coat.*
OAU *abbrev. for* Organization of African Unity.
OB *Brit. abbrev. for:* **1** Old Boy. **2** outside broadcast.
ob. *abbrev. for:* **1** (on tombstones, etc.) obiit. [L: he (or she) died] **2** obiter. [L: incidentally; in passing] **3** oboe.
ob- *prefix* inverse or inversely: *obovate.* [from OF, from L *ob.* In compound words from L, *ob-* (and *oc-, of-, op-*) indicates: to, towards (*object*); against (*oppose*); away from (*obsolete*); before (*obstetric*); and is used as an intensifier (*oblong*)]
Obad. *Bible. abbrev. for* Obadiah.
obbligato *or* **obligato** (ˌɒblɪ'gɑːtəʊ) *Music.* ◆ *adj* **1** not to be omitted in performance ◆ *n, pl* **obbligatos, obbligati** (-tiː) *or* **obligatos, obligati** (-tiː). **2** an essential part in a score: *with oboe obbligato.* [C18: from It., from *obbligare* to OBLIGE]
obconic (ɒb'kɒnɪk) *or* **obconical** *adj Bot.* (of a fruit) shaped like a cone and attached at the pointed end.
obcordate (ɒb'kɔːdeɪt) *adj Bot.* heart-shaped and attached at the pointed end: *obcordate leaves.*
obdurate Ⓣ ('ɒbdjʊrɪt) *adj* **1** not easily moved by feelings or supplication; hardhearted. **2** impervious to persuasion. [C15: from L *obdūrāre* to make hard, from *ob-* (intensive) + *dūrus* hard]
►**'obduracy** *or* **'obdurateness** *n* ►**'obdurately** *adv*
OBE *abbrev. for* Officer of the Order of the British Empire (a Brit. title).
obeah ('əʊbɪə) *n* **1** a kind of witchcraft practised by some West Indians. **2** a charm used in this. [of W African origin]
obedience Ⓣ (ə'biːdɪəns) *n* **1** the condition or quality of being obedient. **2** the act or an instance of obeying; dutiful or submissive behaviour. **3** the authority vested in a Church or similar body. **4** the collective group of persons submitting to this authority.
obedient Ⓣ (ə'biːdɪənt) *adj* obeying or willing to obey. [C13: from OF, from L *oboediens,* present participle of *oboedīre* to OBEY]
►**o'bediently** *adv*
obeisance Ⓣ (əʊ'beɪsəns) *n* **1** an attitude of deference or homage. **2** a gesture expressing obeisance. [C14: from OF *obéissant,* present participle of *obéir* to OBEY]
►**o'beisant** *adj*
obelisk Ⓣ ('ɒbɪlɪsk) *n* **1** a stone pillar having a square or rectangular cross section and sides that taper towards a pyramidal top. **2** *Printing.* another name for **dagger** (sense 2). [C16: via L from Gk *obeliskos* a little spit, from *obelos* spit]
►**ˌobe'liscal** *adj* ►**ˌobe'liskoid** *adj*
obelus ('ɒbɪləs) *n, pl* **obeli** (-laɪ). **1** a mark (— or ÷) used in ancient documents to indicate spurious words or passages. **2** another name for **dagger** (sense 2). [C14: via LL from Gk *obelos* spit]
obese Ⓣ (əʊ'biːs) *adj* excessively fat or fleshy; corpulent. [C17: from L *obēsus,* from *ob-* (intensive) + *edere* to eat]
►**o'besity** *or* **o'beseness** *n*

THESAURUS

oaf *n* = **dolt,** blockhead, brute, dummy (*sl.*), dunce, fathead (*inf.*), fool, goon, halfwit, idiot, imbecile, jerk (*sl., chiefly US & Canad.*), lout, lummox (*inf.*), moron, nerd *or* nurd (*sl.*), nincompoop, nitwit (*inf.*), numbskull *or* numskull, sap (*sl.*), schmuck (*US sl.*), simpleton, twit (*inf., chiefly Brit.*)
Antonyms *n* brain (*inf.*), egghead (*inf.*), genius, intellect, smart aleck (*inf.*), wiseacre

oafish *adj* = **stupid,** bovine, brutish, dense, dim, dim-witted (*inf.*), doltish, dozy (*Brit. inf.*), dull, dumb (*inf.*), loutish, lubberly, lumbering, moronic, obtuse, slow on the uptake (*inf.*), thick
Antonyms *adj* acute, brainy (*inf.*), bright, clever, intelligent, quick-witted, sharp, smart

oasis *n* **2** = **haven,** island, refuge, resting place, retreat, sanctuary, sanctum

oath *n* **1** = **promise,** affirmation, avowal, bond, pledge, sworn statement, vow, word **3** = **swearword,** blasphemy, curse, cuss (*inf.*), expletive, imprecation, malediction, profanity, strong language

obdurate *adj* **1, 2** = **stubborn,** adamant, callous, dogged, firm, fixed, hard, hard-hearted, harsh, immovable, implacable, indurate (*rare*), inexorable, inflexible, iron, mulish, obstinate, perverse, pig-headed, relentless, stiff-necked, unbending, unfeeling, unimpressible, unrelenting, unshakable, unyielding
Antonyms *adj* amenable, biddable, compliant, flexible, malleable, pliant, soft-hearted, submissive, tender, tractable, yielding

obedience *n* **1** = **submissiveness,** accordance, acquiescence, agreement, assent, compliance, conformability, deference, docility, dutifulness, duty, observance, respect, reverence, submission, subservience, tractability
Antonyms *n* defiance, disobedience, insubordination, obstinacy, recalcitrance, stubbornness, wilfulness

obedient *adj* = **submissive,** acquiescent, amenable, biddable, compliant, deferential, docile, duteous, dutiful, law-abiding, observant, regardful, respectful, subservient, tractable, under control, well-trained, yielding
Antonyms *adj* arrogant, contrary, disobedient, disrespectful, intractable, obdurate, obstinate, rebellious, stubborn, undutiful, ungovernable, unmanageable, unruly, wayward

obeisance *n* **1** = **respect,** deference, homage, reverence, salutation **2** = **bow,** bending of the knee, curtsy *or* curtsey, genuflection, kowtow, salaam

obelisk *n* **1** = **column,** monolith, monument, needle, pillar, shaft

obese *adj* = **fat,** corpulent, Falstaffian, fleshy, gross, heavy, outsize, overweight, paunchy, plump, podgy, portly, roly-poly, rotund, stout, tubby, well-upholstered (*inf.*)

obey ⓘ (əˈbeɪ) *vb* **1** to carry out (instructions or orders); comply with (demands). **2** to behave or act in accordance with (one's feelings, whims, etc.). [C13: from OF *obéir,* from L *oboedīre,* from *ob-* towards + *audīre* to hear]
▸**oˈbeyer** *n*

obfuscate ⓘ (ˈɒbfʌsˌkeɪt) *vb* **obfuscates, obfuscating, obfuscated.** (*tr*) **1** to obscure or darken. **2** to perplex or bewilder. [C16: from L *ob-* (intensive) + *fuscāre* to blacken, from *fuscus* dark]
▸**ˌobfusˈcation** *n* ▸**ˈobfusˌcatory** *adj*

obi (ˈəʊbɪ) *n, pl* **obis** *or* **obi.** a broad sash tied in a large flat bow at the back, worn as part of the Japanese national costume. [C19: from Japanese]

obit (ˈɒbɪt, ˈəʊbɪt) *n Inf.* **1** short for **obituary. 2** a memorial service.

obiter dictum (ˈɒbɪtə ˈdɪktəm, ˈəʊ-) *n, pl* **obiter dicta** (ˈdɪktə). **1** *Law.* an observation by a judge on some point of law not directly in issue in the case before him. **2** any comment or remark made in passing. [L: something said in passing]

obituary (əˈbɪtjʊərɪ) *n, pl* **obituaries.** a published announcement of a death, often accompanied by a short biography of the dead person. [C18: from Med. L *obituārius,* from L *obīre* to fall]
▸**oˈbituarist** *n*

obj. *abbrev. for:* **1** objection. **2** *Grammar.* object(ive).

object[1] ⓘ (ˈɒbdʒɪkt) *n* **1** a tangible and visible thing. **2** a person or thing seen as a focus for feelings, thought, etc. **3** an aim or objective. **4** *Inf.* a ridiculous or pitiable person, spectacle, etc. **5** *Philosophy.* that towards which cognition is directed as contrasted with the thinking subject. **6** *Grammar.* a noun, pronoun, or noun phrase whose referent is the recipient of the action of a verb. See also **direct object, indirect object. 7** *Grammar.* a noun, pronoun, or noun phrase that is governed by a preposition. **8** *Computing.* a self-contained identifiable component of a software system or design. **9 no object.** not a hindrance or obstacle: *money is no object.* [C14: from LL *objectus* something thrown before (the mind), from L *obicere;* see OBJECT[2]]

object[2] ⓘ (əbˈdʒɛkt) *vb* **1** (*tr; takes a clause as object*) to state as an objection. **2** (*intr;* often foll. by *to*) to raise or state an objection (to); present an argument (against). [C15: from L *obicere,* from *ob-* against + *jacere* to throw]
▸**obˈjector** *n*

object glass *n Optics.* another name for **objective** (sense 10).

objectify (əbˈdʒɛktɪˌfaɪ) *vb* **objectifies, objectifying, objectified.** (*tr*) to represent concretely; present as an object.
▸**obˌjectifiˈcation** *n*

objection ⓘ (əbˈdʒɛkʃən) *n* **1** an expression or feeling of opposition or dislike. **2** a cause for such an expression or feeling. **3** the act of objecting.

objectionable ⓘ (əbˈdʒɛkʃənəbᵊl) *adj* unpleasant, offensive, or repugnant.
▸**obˌjectionaˈbility** *or* **obˈjectionableness** *n* ▸**obˈjectionably** *adv*

objective ⓘ (əbˈdʒɛktɪv) *adj* **1** existing independently of perception or an individual's conceptions. **2** undistorted by emotion or personal bias. **3** of or relating to actual and external phenomena as opposed to thoughts, feelings, etc. **4** *Med.* (of disease symptoms) perceptible to persons other than the individual affected. **5** *Grammar.* denoting a case of nouns and pronouns, esp. in languages having only two cases, that is used to identify the direct object of a finite verb or preposition. See also **accusative. 6** of or relating to a goal or aim. ◆ *n* **7** the object of one's endeavours; goal; aim. **8** an actual phenomenon; reality. **9** *Grammar.* the objective case. **10** Also called: **object glass.** *Optics.* the lens or combination of lenses nearest to the object in an optical instrument. ◆ Abbrev.: **obj.** Cf. **subjective.**
▸**objectival** (ˌɒbdʒɛkˈtaɪvəl) *adj* ▸**obˈjectively** *adv* ▸**ˌobjecˈtivity** *or* (*less commonly*) **obˈjectiveness** *n*

objectivism (əbˈdʒɛktɪˌvɪzəm) *n* **1** the tendency to stress what is objective. **2** the philosophical doctrine that reality is objective, and that sense data correspond with it.
▸**obˈjectivist** *n, adj* ▸**obˌjectivˈistic** *adj*

object language *n* a language described by another language. Cf. **metalanguage.**

object lesson *n* a convincing demonstration of some principle or ideal.

object program *n* a computer program translated from the equivalent source program into machine language by the compiler or assembler.

object relations theory *n* a form of psychoanalytic theory postulating that people relate to others in order to develop themselves.

objet d'art *French.* (ɔbʒɛ dar) *n, pl* ***objets d'art*** (ɔbʒɛ dar). a small object considered to be of artistic worth. [F: object of art]

objurgate (ˈɒbdʒəˌgeɪt) *vb* **objurgates, objurgating, objurgated.** (*tr*) to scold or reprimand. [C17: from L *objurgāre,* from *ob-* against + *jurgāre* to scold]
▸**ˌobjurˈgation** *n* ▸**ˈobjurˌgator** *n* ▸**objurgatory** (ɒbˈdʒɜːgətərɪ, -trɪ) *adj*

obl. *abbrev. for:* **1** oblique. **2** oblong.

oblate[1] (ˈɒbleɪt) *adj* having an equatorial diameter of greater length than the polar diameter: *the earth is an oblate sphere.* Cf. **prolate.** [C18: from NL *oblātus* lengthened, from L *ob-* towards + *lātus,* p.p. of *ferre* to bring]

oblate[2] (ˈɒbleɪt) *n* a person dedicated to a monastic or religious life. [C19: from F *oblat,* from Med. L *oblātus,* from L *offerre* to OFFER]

oblation (ɒˈbleɪʃən) *n* **1** *Christianity.* the offering of the Eucharist to God. **2** any offering made for religious or charitable purposes. [C15: from Church L *oblātiō;* see OBLATE[2]]
▸**oblatory** (ˈɒblətərɪ, -trɪ) *or* **obˈlational** *adj*

obligate (ˈɒblɪˌgeɪt) *vb* **obligates, obligating, obligated. 1** to compel, constrain, or oblige morally or legally. **2** (in the US) to bind (property, funds, etc.) as security. ◆ *adj* **3** compelled, bound, or restricted. **4** *Biol.* able to exist under only one set of environmental conditions. [C16: from L *obligāre* to OBLIGE]
▸**ˈobligable** *adj* ▸**obˈligative** *adj* ▸**ˈobliˌgator** *n*

obligation ⓘ (ˌɒblɪˈgeɪʃən) *n* **1** a moral or legal requirement; duty. **2** the act of obligating or the state of being obligated. **3** *Law.* **3a** a written contract containing a penalty. **3b** an instrument acknowledging indebtedness to secure the repayment of money borrowed. **4** a person or thing to which one is bound morally or legally. **5** a service or favour for which one is indebted.

obligato (ˌɒblɪˈgɑːtəʊ) *adj, n Music.* a variant spelling of **obbligato.**

obligatory ⓘ (ɒˈblɪgətərɪ, -trɪ) *adj* **1** required to be done, obtained, possessed, etc. **2** of the nature of or constituting an obligation.
▸**obˈligatorily** *adv*

oblige ⓘ (əˈblaɪdʒ) *vb* **obliges, obliging, obliged. 1** (*tr; often passive*) to bind or constrain (someone to do something) by legal, moral, or physical means. **2** (*tr; usually passive*) to make indebted or grateful (to someone) by doing a favour. **3** to do a service or favour to (someone): *she obliged the guests with a song.* [C13: from OF *obliger,* from L *obligāre,* from *ob-* towards + *ligāre* to bind]
▸**oˈbliger** *n*

obligee (ˌɒblɪˈdʒiː) *n* a person in whose favour an obligation, contract, or bond is created; creditor.

THESAURUS

Antonyms *adj* emaciated, gaunt, lean, scraggy, skeletal, skinny, slender, thin

obesity *n* = **fatness,** beef (*inf.*), bulk, corpulence, *embonpoint,* fleshiness, grossness, overweight, portliness, stoutness, tubbiness, weight problem
Antonyms *n* emaciation, gauntness, leanness, skinniness, slenderness, thinness

obey *vb* **1** = **carry out,** abide by, act upon, adhere to, be ruled by, comply, conform, discharge, do what is expected, embrace, execute, follow, fulfil, heed, keep, mind, observe, perform, respond, serve
Antonyms *vb* ≠ **carry out:** contravene, defy, disobey, disregard, ignore, transgress, violate

obfuscate *vb* **2** = **confuse,** befog, bewilder, cloud, darken, muddy the waters, obscure, perplex

object[1] *n* **1** = **thing,** article, body, entity, fact, item, phenomenon, reality **2** = **target,** butt, focus, recipient, victim **3** = **purpose,** aim, design, end, end in view, end purpose, goal, idea, intent, intention, motive, objective, point, reason, the why and wherefore

object[2] *vb* **2** = **protest,** argue against, demur, draw the line (at something), expostulate, oppose, raise objections, take exception
Antonyms *vb* accept, acquiesce, agree, approve, assent, comply, concur, consent, like, take on board, welcome

objection *n* **1** = **protest,** cavil, censure, counter-argument, demur, doubt, exception, niggle (*inf.*), opposition, remonstrance, scruple
Antonyms *n* acceptance, affirmation, agreement, approbation, assent, endorsement, support

objectionable *adj* = **unpleasant,** abhorrent, beyond the pale, deplorable, disagreeable, dislikable *or* dislikeable, displeasing, distasteful, exceptionable, indecorous, insufferable, intolerable, noxious, obnoxious, offensive, regrettable, repugnant, unacceptable, undesirable, unseemly, unsociable
Antonyms *adj* acceptable, agreeable, desirable, likable *or* likeable, pleasant, pleasing, welcome

objective *adj* **2** = **unbiased,** detached, disinterested, dispassionate, equitable, even-handed, fair, impartial, impersonal, judicial, just, open-minded, uncoloured, unemotional, uninvolved, unprejudiced ◆ *n* **7** = **purpose,** aim, ambition, aspiration, design, end, end in view, goal, Holy Grail (*inf.*), intention, mark, object, target
Antonyms *adj* ≠ **unbiased:** biased, personal, prejudiced, subjective, unfair, unjust

objectively *adv* **2** = **impartially,** disinterestedly, dispassionately, even-handedly, with an open mind, with objectivity *or* impartiality, without fear or favour

objectivity *n* **2** = **impartiality,** detachment, disinterest, disinterestedness, dispassion, equitableness, impersonality
Antonyms *n* bent, bias, partiality, predisposition, prejudice, subjectivity

obligation *n* **1** = **duty,** accountability, accountableness, burden, charge, compulsion, culpability, liability, must, onus, pigeon (*inf.*), requirement, responsibility, trust **3** = **contract,** agreement, bond, commitment, debt, engagement, promise, understanding

obligatory *adj* **1, 2** = **compulsory,** binding, coercive, *de rigueur,* enforced, essential, imperative, mandatory, necessary, required, requisite, unavoidable
Antonyms *adj* discretionary, elective, noncompulsory, optional, voluntary

oblige *vb* **1** = **compel,** bind, coerce, constrain, dragoon, force, impel, make, necessitate, obligate, railroad (*inf.*), require **2, 3** = **do (someone) a favour** *or* **a kindness,** accommodate, benefit, favour, gratify, indulge, please, put oneself out for, serve
Antonyms *vb* ≠ **do (someone) a favour** *or* **a kindness:** bother, discommode, disoblige, disrupt, inconvenience, put out, trouble

obliged *adj* **1** = **bound,** compelled, forced, required, under an obligation, under compulsion, without any option **2** = **grateful,** appreciative, beholden, gratified, indebted, in (someone's) debt, thankful

obliging ➊ (əˈblaɪdʒɪŋ) *adj* ready to do favours; agreeable; kindly.
▸**oˈbligingly** *adv* ▸**oˈbligingness** *n*

obligor (ˌɒblɪˈgɔː) *n* a person who binds himself by contract to perform some obligation; debtor.

oblique ➊ (əˈbliːk) *adj* **1** at an angle; slanting; sloping. **2** *Geom.* **2a** (of lines, planes, etc.) neither perpendicular nor parallel to one another or to another line, plane, etc. **2b** not related to or containing a right angle. **3** indirect or evasive. **4** *Grammar.* denoting any case of nouns, pronouns, etc., other than the nominative and vocative. **5** *Biol.* having asymmetrical sides or planes: *an oblique leaf.* ◆ *n* **6** something oblique, esp. a line. **7** another name for **solidus** (sense 1). ◆ *vb* **obliques, obliquing, obliqued.** (*intr*) **8** to take or have an oblique direction. **9** (of a military formation) to move forward at an angle. [C15: from OF, from L *oblīquus,* from ?]
▸**oˈbliquely** *adv* ▸**oˈbliqueness** *n* ▸**obliquity** (əˈblɪkwɪtɪ) *n*

oblique angle *n* an angle that is not a right angle or any multiple of a right angle.

obliterate ➊ (əˈblɪtəˌreɪt) *vb* **obliterates, obliterating, obliterated.** (*tr*) to destroy every trace of; wipe out completely. [C16: from L *oblitterāre* to erase, from *ob-* out + *littera* letter]
▸**oˌbliteˈration** *n* ▸**oˈbliterative** *adj* ▸**oˈbliterˌator** *n*

oblivion ➊ (əˈblɪvɪən) *n* **1** the condition of being forgotten or disregarded. **2** *Law.* amnesty; pardon. [C14: via OF from L *oblīviō* forgetfulness, from *oblīviscī* to forget]

oblivious ➊ (əˈblɪvɪəs) *adj* (foll. by *of* or *to*) unaware or forgetful.
▸**obˈliviously** *adv* ▸**obˈliviousness** *n*

> **USAGE NOTE** It was formerly considered incorrect to use *oblivious* to mean *unaware*, but this use is now acceptable.

oblong (ˈɒbˌlɒŋ) *adj* **1** having an elongated, esp. rectangular, shape. ◆ *n* **2** a figure or object having this shape. [C15: from L *oblongus,* from *ob-* (intensive) + *longus* LONG[1]]

obloquy ➊ (ˈɒbləkwɪ) *n, pl* **obloquies. 1** defamatory or censorious statements, esp. when directed against one person. **2** disgrace brought about by public abuse. [C15: from L *obloquium* contradiction, from *ob-* against + *loquī* to speak]

obnoxious ➊ (əbˈnɒkʃəs) *adj* **1** extremely unpleasant. **2** *Obs.* exposed to harm, injury, etc. [C16: from L *obnoxius,* from *ob-* to + *noxa* injury, from *nocēre* to harm]
▸**obˈnoxiously** *adv* ▸**obˈnoxiousness** *n*

oboe (ˈəʊbəʊ) *n* **1** a woodwind instrument consisting of a conical tube fitted with a mouthpiece having a double reed. It has a penetrating nasal tone. **2** a person who plays this instrument in an orchestra. ◆ Arch. form: **hautboy.** [C18: via It. *oboe,* phonetic approximation to F *haut bois,* lit.: high wood (referring to its pitch)]
▸**ˈoboist** *n*

oboe d'amore (dɑːˈmɔːreɪ) *n* a type of oboe pitched a minor third lower than the oboe itself: used chiefly in baroque music.

obs. *abbrev. for:* **1** observation. **2** obsolete.

obscene ➊ (əbˈsiːn) *adj* **1** offensive or outrageous to accepted standards of decency or modesty. **2** *Law.* (of publications, etc.) having a tendency to deprave or corrupt. **3** disgusting; repellent. [C16: from L *obscēnus* inauspicious]
▸**obˈscenely** *adv*

obscenity ➊ (əbˈsɛnɪtɪ) *n, pl* **obscenities. 1** the state or quality of being obscene. **2** an obscene act, statement, word, etc.

obscurant (əbˈskjʊərənt) *n* an opposer of reform and enlightenment.
▸**obscurantism** (ˌɒbskjʊəˈrænˌtɪzəm) *n* ▸**ˌobscuˈrantist** *n, adj*

obscure ➊ (əbˈskjʊə) *adj* **1** unclear. **2** indistinct, vague, or indefinite. **3** inconspicuous or unimportant. **4** hidden, secret, or remote. **5** (of a vowel) reduced to a neutral vowel (ə). **6** gloomy, dark, clouded, or dim. ◆ *vb* **obscures, obscuring, obscured.** (*tr*) **7** to make unclear, vague, or hidden. **8** to cover or cloud over. **9** *Phonetics.* to pronounce (a vowel) so that it becomes a neutral sound represented by (ə). [C14: via OF from L *obscūrus* dark]
▸**obscuration** (ˌɒbskjʊˈreɪʃən) *n* ▸**obˈscurely** *adv* ▸**obˈscureness** *n*

obscurity ➊ (əbˈskjʊərɪtɪ) *n, pl* **obscurities. 1** the state or quality of being obscure. **2** an obscure person or thing.

obsequies ➊ (ˈɒbsɪkwɪz) *pl n, sing* **obsequy.** funeral rites. [C14: via Anglo-Norman from Med. L *obsequiae* (infl. by L *exsequiae*), from *obsequium* compliance]

obsequious ➊ (əbˈsiːkwɪəs) *adj* **1** obedient or attentive in an ingratiating or servile manner. **2** *Now rare.* submissive or compliant. [C15: from L *obsequiōsus* compliant, from *obsequi* to follow]
▸**obˈsequiously** *adv* ▸**obˈsequiousness** *n*

observance ➊ (əbˈzɜːvəns) *n* **1** recognition of or compliance with a law, custom, practice, etc. **2** a ritual, ceremony, or practice, esp. of a religion. **3** observation or attention. **4** the degree of strictness of a religious order in following its rule. **5** *Arch.* respectful or deferential attention.

observant ➊ (əbˈzɜːvənt) *adj* **1** paying close attention to detail; watchful or heedful. **2** adhering strictly to rituals, ceremonies, laws, etc.
▸**obˈservantly** *adv*

THESAURUS

obliging *adj* = **cooperative**, accommodating, agreeable, amiable, civil, complaisant, considerate, courteous, eager to please, friendly, good-natured, helpful, kind, polite, willing
Antonyms *adj* discourteous, disobliging, inconsiderate, rude, sullen, surly, unaccommodating, uncooperative, unhelpful, unobliging

oblique *adj* **1** = **slanting**, angled, aslant, at an angle, atilt, inclined, slanted, sloped, sloping, tilted **3** = **indirect**, backhanded, circuitous, circumlocutory, evasive, implied, roundabout, sidelong
Antonyms *adj* ≠ **indirect**: blunt, candid, direct, downright, forthright, frank, open, straightforward

obliquely *adv* **1** = **at an angle**, aslant, aslope, diagonally, slantwise **3** = **indirectly**, circuitously, evasively, in a roundabout manner *or* way, not in so many words

obliterate *vb* = **destroy**, annihilate, blot out, blow sky-high, cancel, delete, destroy root and branch, efface, eradicate, erase, expunge, extirpate, root out, wipe from *or* off the face of the earth, wipe out
Antonyms *vb* build, construct, create, establish, form, formulate, generate, make

obliteration *n* = **annihilation**, blotting out, deletion, effacement, elimination, eradication, erasure, expunction, extirpation, rooting out, sponging out, wiping out
Antonyms *n* building, construction, creation, establishment, formation, generation, making

oblivion *n* **1** = **neglect**, abeyance, disregard, forgetfulness, (waters of) Lethe

oblivious *adj* = **unaware**, blind, careless, deaf, disregardful, forgetful, heedless, ignorant, inattentive, insensible, neglectful, negligent, regardless, unconcerned, unconscious, unmindful, unobservant
Antonyms *adj* alert, attentive, aware, conscious, heedful, mindful, observant, watchful

obloquy *n* **1** = **abuse**, animadversion, aspersion, attack, bad press, blame, calumny, censure, character assassination, contumely, criticism, defamation, detraction, invective, opprobrium, reproach, slander, stick (*sl.*), vilification **2** = **disgrace**, discredit, disfavour, dishonour, humiliation, ignominy, ill fame, ill repute, infamy, odium, shame, stigma

obnoxious *adj* **1** = **offensive**, abhorrent, abominable, detestable, disagreeable, disgusting, dislikable *or* dislikeable, foul, hateable, hateful, horrid, insufferable, loathsome, nasty, nauseating, objectionable, obscene, odious, repellent, reprehensible, repugnant, repulsive, revolting, sickening, unpleasant
Antonyms *adj* agreeable, amiable, charming, congenial, delightful, likable *or* likeable, pleasant, pleasing

obscene *adj* **1** = **indecent**, bawdy, blue, coarse, dirty, filthy, foul, gross, immodest, immoral, improper, impure, lewd, licentious, loose, offensive, pornographic, prurient, ribald, salacious, scabrous, shameless, smutty, suggestive, unchaste, unwholesome, X-rated (*inf.*) **3** = **disgusting**, atrocious, evil, heinous, loathsome, outrageous, shocking, sickening, vile, wicked
Antonyms *adj* ≠ **indecent**: chaste, decent, decorous, inoffensive, modest, proper, pure, refined, respectable, seemly

obscenity *n* **1** = **indecency**, bawdiness, blueness, coarseness, dirtiness, filthiness, foulness, grossness, immodesty, impropriety, impurity, indelicacy, lewdness, licentiousness, pornography, prurience, salacity, smut, smuttiness, suggestiveness, vileness **2** = **swearword**, four-letter word, profanity, vulgarism
Antonyms *n* ≠ **indecency**: chastity, decency, decorum, delicacy, innocence, modesty, propriety, purity

obscure *adj* **1, 2** = **vague**, abstruse, ambiguous, arcane, clear as mud (*inf.*), concealed, confusing, cryptic, deep, Delphic, doubtful, enigmatic, esoteric, hazy, hidden, incomprehensible, indefinite, intricate, involved, mysterious, occult, opaque, recondite, unclear **3** = **little-known**, humble, inconspicuous, inglorious, lowly, minor, nameless, out-of-the-way, remote, undistinguished, unheard-of, unhonoured, unimportant, unknown, unnoted, unseen, unsung **6** = **dark**, blurred, clouded, cloudy, dim, dusky, faint, gloomy, indistinct, murky, obfuscated, shadowy, shady, sombre, tenebrous, unlit, veiled ◆ *vb* **7** = **conceal**, cover, disguise, hide, muddy, obfuscate, screen, throw a veil over, veil **8** = **cover**, adumbrate, bedim, befog, block, block out, blur, cloak, cloud, darken, dim, dull, eclipse, mask, overshadow, shade, shroud
Antonyms *adj* ≠ **vague**: apparent, clear, definite, distinct, evident, explicit, intelligible, lucid, manifest, obvious, plain, prominent, straightforward, transparent, unmistakable ≠ **little-known**: celebrated, distinguished, eminent, familiar, famous, illustrious, important, major, prominent, renowned, significant, well-known, widely-known ≠ **dark**: bright, clear, sharp, transparent, well-defined ◆ *vb* ≠ **conceal**: clarify, disclose, explain, explicate, expose, interpret, reveal, show ≠ **cover**: expose, reveal, uncover, unmask, unveil

obscurity *n* **1** = **indistinctness**, dimness, haze, impenetrableness, incomprehensibility, inconspicuousness, insignificance, murkiness, shadows, unimportance, vagueness
Antonyms *n* ≠ **indistinctness**: clarity, clearness, comprehensibility, explicitness, lucidity, obviousness

obsequies *pl n* = **funeral rites**, burial, burial service, exequies, funeral, last offices

obsequious *adj* **1** = **sycophantic**, abject, cringing, deferential, fawning, flattering, grovelling, ingratiating, mealy-mouthed, menial, servile, slavish, smarmy (*Brit. inf.*), submissive, toadying, unctuous

obsequiously *adv* **1** = **ingratiatingly**, abjectly, cringingly, deferentially, fawningly, on one's knees, servilely, slavishly, smarmily (*Brit. inf.*), sycophantically, unctuously

observable *adj* **1** = **noticeable**, apparent, appreciable, blatant, clear, detectable, discernible, evident, obvious, open, patent, perceivable, perceptible, recognizable, visible

observance *n* **1** = **carrying out**, adherence to, celebration, compliance, discharge, fulfilment, heeding, honouring, notice, observation, performance **2** = **ritual**, ceremonial, ceremony, custom, fashion, form, formality, practice, rite, service, tradition
Antonyms *n* ≠ **carrying out**: disdain, disregard, evasion, heedlessness, inattention, neglect, nonobservance, omission, oversight

observant *adj* **1** = **attentive**, alert, eagle-eyed,

observation ⓣ (ˌɒbzəˈveɪʃən) *n* **1** the act of observing or the state of being observed. **2** a comment or remark. **3** detailed examination of phenomena prior to analysis, diagnosis, or interpretation: *the patient was under observation.* **4** the facts learned from observing. **5** *Navigation.* **5a** a sight taken with an instrument to determine the position of an observer relative to that of a given heavenly body. **5b** the data so taken.
▸ˌ**obserˈvational** *adj* ▸ˌ**obserˈvationally** *adv*

observatory (əbˈzɜːvətərɪ, -trɪ) *n, pl* **observatories. 1** an institution or building specially designed and equipped for observing meteorological and astronomical phenomena. **2** any building or structure providing an extensive view of its surroundings.

observe ⓣ (əbˈzɜːv) *vb* **observes, observing, observed. 1** (*tr; may take a clause as object*) to see; perceive; notice: *we have observed that you steal.* **2** (when *tr, may take a clause as object*) to watch (something) carefully; pay attention to (something). **3** to make observations of (something), esp. scientific ones. **4** (when *intr*, usually foll. by *on* or *upon;* when *tr, may take a clause as object*) to make a comment or remark: *the speaker observed that times had changed.* **5** (*tr*) to abide by, keep, or follow (a custom, tradition, etc.). [C14: via OF from L *observāre,* from *ob-* to + *servāre* to watch]
▸**obˈservable** *adj* ▸**obˈserver** *n*

obsess ⓣ (əbˈsɛs) *vb* **1** (*tr;* when passive, foll. by *with* or *by*) to preoccupy completely; haunt. **2** (*intr*, usually foll. by *on* or *over*) to brood obsessively. [C16: from L *obsessus* besieged, p.p. of *obsidēre,* from *ob-* in front of + *sedēre* to sit]
▸**obˈsessive** *adj, n* ▸**obˈsessively** *adv* ▸**obˈsessiveness** *n*

obsession ⓣ (əbˈsɛʃən) *n* **1** *Psychiatry.* a persistent idea or impulse, often associated with anxiety and mental illness. **2** a persistent preoccupation, idea, or feeling. **3** the act of obsessing or the state of being obsessed.
▸**obˈsessional** *adj* ▸**obˈsessionally** *adv*

obsidian (ɒbˈsɪdɪən) *n* a dark glassy volcanic rock formed by very rapid solidification of lava. Also called: **Iceland agate.** [C17: from L *obsidiānus,* erroneous transcription of *obsiānus* (*lapis*) (stone of) *Obsius,* (in Pliny) the discoverer of a stone resembling obsidian]

obsolesce (ˌɒbsəˈlɛs) *vb* **obsolesces, obsolescing, obsolesced.** (*intr*) to become obsolete.

obsolescent ⓣ (ˌɒbsəˈlɛsᵊnt) *adj* becoming obsolete or out of date. [C18: from L *obsolescere;* see OBSOLETE]
▸ˌ**obsoˈlescence** *n*

obsolete ⓣ (ˈɒbsəˌliːt, ˌɒbsəˈliːt) *adj* **1** out of use or practice; not current. **2** out of date; unfashionable or outmoded. **3** *Biol.* (of parts, organs, etc.) vestigial; rudimentary. [C16: from L *obsolētus* worn out, p.p. of *obsolēre* (unattested), from *ob-* opposite to + *solēre* to be used]
▸ˈ**obsoˌletely** *adv* ▸ˈ**obsoˌleteness** *n*

> **USAGE NOTE** The word *obsoleteness* is hardly ever used, *obsolescence* standing as the noun form for both *obsolete* and *obsolescent.*

obstacle ⓣ (ˈɒbstəkᵊl) *n* **1** a person or thing that opposes or hinders something. **2** *Brit.* a fence or hedge used in showjumping. [C14: via OF from L *obstāculum,* from *obstāre,* from *ob-* against + *stāre* to stand]

obstacle race *n* a race in which competitors have to negotiate various obstacles.

obstetric (ɒbˈstɛtrɪk) *or* **obstetrical** *adj* of or relating to childbirth or obstetrics. [C18: via NL from L *obstetrīcius,* from *obstetrix* a midwife, lit.: woman who stands opposite, from *obstāre* to stand in front of; see OBSTACLE]
▸**obˈstetrically** *adv*

obstetrician (ˌɒbstɪˈtrɪʃən) *n* a physician who specializes in obstetrics.

obstetrics (ɒbˈstɛtrɪks) *n* (*functioning as sing*) the branch of medicine concerned with childbirth and the treatment of women before and after childbirth.

obstinacy ⓣ (ˈɒbstɪnəsɪ) *n, pl* **obstinacies. 1** the state or quality of being obstinate. **2** an obstinate act, attitude, etc.

obstinate ⓣ (ˈɒbstɪnɪt) *adj* **1** adhering fixedly to a particular opinion, attitude, course of action, etc. **2** self-willed or headstrong. **3** difficult to subdue or alleviate; persistent: *an obstinate fever.* [C14: from L *obstinātus,* p.p. of *obstināre* to persist in, from *ob-* (intensive) + *stin-,* var. of *stare* to stand]
▸ˈ**obstinately** *adv*

obstreperous ⓣ (əbˈstrɛpərəs) *adj* noisy or rough, esp. in resisting restraint or control. [C16: from L, from *obstrepere,* from *ob-* against + *strepere* to roar]
▸**obˈstreperously** *adv* ▸**obˈstreperousness** *n*

obstruct ⓣ (əbˈstrʌkt) *vb* (*tr*) **1** to block (a road, passageway, etc.) with an obstacle. **2** to make (progress or activity) difficult. **3** to impede or block a clear view of. [C17: L *obstructus* built against, p.p. of *obstruere,* from *ob-* against + *struere* to build]
▸**obˈstructive** *adj, n* ▸**obˈstructively** *adv* ▸**obˈstructiveness** *n* ▸**obˈstructor** *n*

obstruction ⓣ (əbˈstrʌkʃən) *n* **1** a person or thing that obstructs. **2** the act or an instance of obstructing. **3** delay of business, esp. in a legislature by means of procedural devices. **4** *Sport.* the act of unfairly impeding an opposing player.
▸**obˈstructional** *adj*

obstructionist (əbˈstrʌkʃənɪst) *n* a person who deliberately obstructs business, etc., esp. in a legislature.
▸**obˈstructionism** *n*

obtain ⓣ (əbˈteɪn) *vb* **1** (*tr*) to gain possession of; acquire; get. **2** (*intr*) to

THESAURUS

heedful, mindful, obedient, perceptive, quick, sharp-eyed, submissive, vigilant, watchful, wide-awake
Antonyms *adj* distracted, dreamy, heedless, inattentive, indifferent, negligent, preoccupied, unobservant, vague

observation *n* **1 = study,** attention, cognition, consideration, examination, experience, information, inspection, knowledge, monitoring, notice, review, scrutiny, surveillance, watching **2 = comment,** annotation, finding, note, obiter dictum, opinion, pronouncement, reflection, remark, thought, utterance

observe *vb* **1 = see,** detect, discern, discover, espy, note, notice, perceive, spot, witness **2 = watch,** behold (*arch. or literary*), check, check out (*inf.*), contemplate, eye, get a load of, keep an eye on (*inf.*), keep tabs on (*inf.*), keep track of, keep under observation, look at, monitor, pay attention to, regard, scrutinize, study, survey, take a dekko at (*Brit. sl.*), view **4 = remark,** animadvert, comment, declare, mention, note, opine, say, state **5 = carry out,** abide by, adhere to, comply, conform to, follow, fulfil, heed, honour, keep, mind, obey, perform, respect
Antonyms *vb* ≠ **carry out:** disregard, ignore, miss, neglect, omit, overlook, violate

observer *n* **2 = spectator,** beholder, bystander, commentator, eyewitness, fly on the wall, looker-on, onlooker, spotter, viewer, watcher, witness

obsess *vb* **1 = preoccupy,** bedevil, be on one's mind, be uppermost in one's thoughts, consume, dominate, engross, grip, haunt, monopolize, plague, possess, prey on one's mind, rule, torment

obsessed *adj* **1 = preoccupied,** beset, dominated, gripped, hag-ridden, haunted, having a one-track mind, hung up on (*sl.*), immersed in, infatuated, in the grip of, troubled
Antonyms *adj* aloof, apathetic, detached, disinterested, impassive, indifferent, uncaring, unconcerned

obsession *n* **1, 2 = preoccupation,** addiction, bee in one's bonnet (*inf.*), complex, enthusiasm, fetish, fixation, hang-up (*inf.*), *idée fixe,* infatuation, mania, phobia, ruling passion, thing (*inf.*)

obsessive *adj* **1 = compulsive,** besetting, consuming, fixed, gripping, haunting, tormenting, unforgettable

obsolescent *adj* **= becoming obsolete,** ageing, declining, dying out, not with it (*inf.*), on the decline, on the wane, on the way out, past its prime, waning

obsolete *adj* **2 = out of date,** anachronistic, ancient, antediluvian, antiquated, antique, archaic, bygone, dated, *démodé,* discarded, disused, extinct, musty, old, old-fashioned, old hat, out, outmoded, out of fashion, out of the ark (*inf.*), outworn, passé, past it, superannuated, *vieux jeu*
Antonyms *adj* à la mode, contemporary, current, fashionable, in, in vogue, modern, new, present day, trendy (*Brit. inf.*), up-to-date

obstacle *n* **1 = difficulty,** bar, barrier, block, check, hindrance, hitch, hurdle, impediment, interference, interruption, obstruction, snag, stumbling block
Antonyms *n* advantage, aid, asset, assistance, benefit, crutch, help, support

obstinacy *n* **1 = stubbornness,** doggedness, firmness, inflexibility, intransigence, mulishness, obduracy, perseverance, persistence, pertinacity, pig-headedness, resoluteness, tenacity, wilfulness
Antonyms *n* compliance, cooperativeness, docility, flexibility, meekness, submissiveness, tractability

obstinate *adj* **1, 2 = stubborn,** contumacious, cussed, determined, dogged, firm, headstrong, immovable, inflexible, intractable, intransigent, mulish, opinionated, persistent, pertinacious, perverse, pig-headed, recalcitrant, refractory, self-willed, steadfast, stiff-necked, strong-minded, tenacious, unyielding, wilful
Antonyms *adj* amenable, biddable, complaisant, compliant, docile, flexible, irresolute, manageable, obedient, submissive, tractable, undecided, wavering

obstreperous *adj* **= unruly,** boisterous, clamorous, disorderly, loud, noisy, out of control, out of hand, rackety, rampaging, raucous, restive, riotous, rip-roaring (*inf.*), roistering, roisterous, rough, rowdy, stroppy (*Brit. sl.*), tempestuous, tumultuous, turbulent, uncontrolled, undisciplined, unmanageable, uproarious, vociferous, wild
Antonyms *adj* calm, controlled, disciplined, docile, gentle, orderly, peaceful, placid, quiet

obstruct *vb* **1-3 = block,** arrest, bar, barricade, bring to a standstill, bung, check, choke, clog, cumber, curb, cut off, frustrate, get in the way of, hamper, hamstring, hide, hinder, hold up, impede, inhibit, interfere with, interrupt, mask, obscure, prevent, restrict, retard, shield, shut off, slow down, stop, thwart, trammel
Antonyms *vb* abet, advance, aid, assist, encourage, favour, further, gee up, help, promote, support

obstruction *n* **1 = obstacle,** bar, barricade, barrier, block, blockage, check, difficulty, hazard, hindrance, impediment, occlusion, snag, stop, stoppage, trammel
Antonyms *n* aid, assistance, cooperation, encouragement, favour, furtherance, geeing-up, help, support

obstructive *adj* **2 = unhelpful,** awkward, blocking, delaying, difficult, hindering, inhibiting, preventative, restrictive, stalling, uncooperative
Antonyms *adj* cooperative, encouraging, favourable, helpful, obliging, supportive

obtain *vb* **1 = get,** achieve, acquire, attain, come by, earn, gain, get hold of, get one's

be customary, valid, or accepted: *a new law obtains in this case.* [C15: via OF from L *obtinēre* to take hold of]
▸**ob'tainable** *adj* ▸**ob,taina'bility** *n* ▸**ob'tainer** *n* ▸**ob'tainment** *n*

obtrude (əb'tru:d) *vb* **obtrudes, obtruding, obtruded. 1** to push (oneself, one's opinions, etc.) on others in an unwelcome way. **2** (*tr*) to push out or forward. [C16: from L *obtrūdere,* from *ob-* against + *trūdere* to push forward]
▸**ob'truder** *n* ▸**obtrusion** (əb'tru:ʒən) *n*

obtrusive ➊ (əb'tru:sɪv) *adj* **1** obtruding or tending to obtrude. **2** sticking out; protruding; noticeable.
▸**ob'trusively** *adv* ▸**ob'trusiveness** *n*

obtuse ➊ (əb'tju:s) *adj* **1** mentally slow or emotionally insensitive. **2** *Maths.* (of an angle) lying between 90° and 180°. **3** not sharp or pointed. **4** indistinctly felt, heard, etc.; dull: *obtuse pain.* **5** (of a leaf or similar flat part) having a rounded or blunt tip. [C16: from L *obtūsus* dulled, p.p. of *obtundere* to beat down]
▸**ob'tusely** *adv* ▸**ob'tuseness** *n*

obverse ('ɒbvɜ:s) *adj* **1** facing or turned towards the observer. **2** forming or serving as a counterpart. **3** (of leaves) narrower at the base than at the top. ◆ *n* **4** a counterpart or complement. **5** *Logic.* a proposition derived from another by replacing the original predicate by its negation and changing the proposition from affirmative to negative or vice versa, as *no sum is correct* from *every sum is incorrect.* **6** the side of a coin that bears the main design or device. [C17: from L *obversus* turned towards, p.p. of *obvertere*]
▸**ob'versely** *adv*

obvert (ɒb'vɜ:t) *vb* (*tr*) **1** *Logic.* to deduce the obverse of (a proposition). **2** *Rare.* to turn so as to show the main or other side. [C17: from L *obvertere* to turn towards]
▸**ob'version** *n*

obviate ➊ ('ɒbvɪ,eɪt) *vb* **obviates, obviating, obviated.** (*tr*) to avoid or prevent (a need or difficulty). [C16: from LL *obviātus* prevented, p.p. of *obviāre;* see OBVIOUS]
▸**,obvi'ation** *n*

> **USAGE NOTE** Only things which have not yet occurred can be *obviated.* For example, one can *obviate* a possible future difficulty, but not one which already exists.

obvious ➊ ('ɒbvɪəs) *adj* **1** easy to see or understand; evident. **2** exhibiting motives, feelings, intentions, etc., clearly or without subtlety. **3** naive or unsubtle: *the play was rather obvious.* [C16: from L *obvius,* from *obviam* in the way]
▸**'obviously** *adv* ▸**'obviousness** *n*

OC *abbrev. for* Officer Commanding.

Oc. *abbrev. for* Ocean.

o/c *abbrev. for* overcharge.

ocarina (,ɒkə'ri:nə) *n* an egg-shaped wind instrument with a protruding mouthpiece and six to eight finger holes, producing an almost pure tone. [C19: from It.: little goose, from *oca* goose, ult. from L *avis* bird]

Occam's razor *n* a variant spelling of **Ockham's razor.**

occas. *abbrev. for* occasional(ly).

occasion ➊ (ə'keɪʒən) *n* **1** (sometimes foll. by *of*) the time of a particular happening or event. **2** (sometimes foll. by *for*) a reason or cause (to do or be something); grounds: *there was no occasion to complain.* **3** an opportunity (to do something); chance. **4** a special event, time, or celebration: *the party was quite an occasion.* **5 on occasion.** every so often. **6 rise to the occasion.** to have the courage, wit, etc., to meet the special demands of a situation. **7 take occasion.** to avail oneself of an opportunity (to do something). ◆ *vb* **8** (*tr*) to bring about, esp. incidentally or by chance. [C14: from L *occāsiō* a falling down, from *occidere* to fall]

occasional ➊ (ə'keɪʒən^{ə}l) *adj* **1** taking place from time to time; not frequent or regular. **2** of, for, or happening on special occasions. **3** serving as an occasion (for something).
▸**oc'casionally** *adv*

occasional table *n* a small table with no regular use.

occident ('ɒksɪdənt) *n* a literary or formal word for **west.** Cf. **orient.** [C14: via OF from L *occidere* to fall (with reference to the setting sun)]
▸**,occi'dental** *adj*

Occident ('ɒksɪdənt) *n* (usually preceded by *the*) **1** the countries of Europe and America. **2** the western hemisphere.
▸**,Occi'dental** *adj, n*

occipital (ɒk'sɪpɪt^{ə}l) *adj* **1** of or relating to the back of the head or skull. ◆ *n* **2** short for **occipital bone.** [See OCCIPUT]

occipital bone *n* the bone that forms the back part of the skull and part of its base.

occipital lobe *n* the posterior portion of each cerebral hemisphere, concerned with the interpretation of visual sensory impulses.

occiput ('ɒksɪ,pʌt) *n, pl* **occiputs** *or* **occipita** (ɒk'sɪpɪtə). the back part of the head or skull. [C14: from L, from *ob-* at the back of + *caput* head]

occlude ➊ (ə'klu:d) *vb* **occludes, occluding, occluded. 1** (*tr*) to block or stop up (a passage or opening); obstruct. **2** (*tr*) to prevent the passage of. **3** (*tr*) *Chem.* (of a solid) to incorporate (a substance) by absorption or adsorption. **4** *Meteorol.* to form or cause to form an occluded front. **5** *Dentistry.* to produce or cause to produce occlusion, as in chewing. [C16: from L *occlūdere,* from *ob-* (intensive) + *claudere* to close]
▸**oc'cludent** *adj*

occluded front *n Meteorol.* the line or plane occurring where the cold front of a depression has overtaken the warm front, raising the warm sector from ground level. Also called: **occlusion.**

occlusion (ə'klu:ʒən) *n* **1** the act of occluding or the state of being occluded. **2** *Meteorol.* another term for **occluded front. 3** *Dentistry.* the normal position of the teeth when the jaws are closed.
▸**oc'clusive** *adj*

occult ➊ *adj* (ɒ'kʌlt, 'ɒkʌlt). **1a** of or characteristic of mystical or supernatural phenomena or influences. **1b** (*as n*): *the occult.* **2** beyond ordinary human understanding. **3** secret or esoteric. ◆ *vb* (ɒ'kʌlt). **4** *Astron.* (of a celestial body) to hide (another celestial body) from view by occultation or (of a celestial body) to become hidden by occultation. **5** to hide or become hidden or shut off from view. **6** (*intr*) (of lights, esp. in lighthouses) to shut off at regular intervals. [C16: from L *occultus,* p.p. of *occulere,* from *ob-* over, up + *-culere,* rel. to *celāre* to conceal]
▸**'occul,tism** *n* ▸**'occultist** *n* ▸**oc'cultness** *n*

occultation (,ɒkʌl'teɪʃən) *n* the temporary disappearance of one celestial body as it moves out of sight behind another body.

occupancy ➊ ('ɒkjupənsɪ) *n, pl* **occupancies. 1** the act of occupying; possession of a property. **2** *Law.* the possession and use of property by or without agreement and without any claim to ownership. **3** *Law.* the act of taking possession of unowned property, esp. land, with the intent of thus acquiring ownership. **4** the condition or fact of being an occupant, esp. a tenant. **5** the period of time during which one is an occupant, esp. of property.

THESAURUS

hands on, land, procure, score (*sl.*), secure **2** = **exist,** be in force, be prevalent, be the case, hold, prevail, stand
Antonyms *vb* ≠ **get:** forfeit, forgo, give up, hand over, lose, relinquish, renounce, surrender

obtainable *adj* **1** = **available,** achievable, at hand, attainable, on tap (*inf.*), procurable, ready, realizable, to be had

obtrusive *adj* **1** = **pushy** (*inf.*), forward, importunate, interfering, intrusive, meddling, nosy, officious, prying **2** = **noticeable,** blatant, obvious, prominent, protruding, protuberant, sticking out
Antonyms *adj* ≠ **pushy:** bashful, decorous, diffident, modest, reserved, reticent, retiring, shy, unassuming ≠ **noticeable:** concealed, covert, hidden, inconspicuous, low-key, muted, unnoticeable, unobtrusive

obtrusively *adv* **1** = **pushily,** blatantly, bluntly, boldly, crassly, importunately, obviously, officiously

obtuse *adj* **1** = **stupid,** boneheaded (*sl.*), dense, dopey (*inf.*), dull, dull-witted, dumb, imperceptive, insensitive, retarded, slow, slow on the uptake (*inf.*), stolid, thick, thick-skinned, uncomprehending, unintelligent **3** = **blunt,** rounded
Antonyms *adj* ≠ **stupid:** astute, bright, clever, keen, quick, sensitive, sharp, shrewd, smart

obviate *vb* = **preclude,** anticipate, avert, counter, counteract, do away with, prevent, remove, render unnecessary

obvious *adj* **1** = **evident,** apparent, blatant, bold, clear, clear as a bell, conspicuous, cut-and-dried (*inf.*), distinct, indisputable, manifest, much in evidence, noticeable, open, open-and-shut, overt, palpable, patent, perceptible, plain, pronounced, recognizable, right under one's nose (*inf.*), salient, self-evident, self-explanatory, staring one in the face (*inf.*), sticking out a mile (*inf.*), straightforward, transparent, unconcealed, undeniable, undisguised, unmistakable, unsubtle, visible
Antonyms *adj* ambiguous, clear as mud (*inf.*), concealed, dark, hidden, imperceptible, inconspicuous, indistinct, invisible, obscure, unapparent, unclear, vague

obviously *adv* **1** = **clearly,** certainly, distinctly, manifestly, needless to say, of course, palpably, patently, plainly, undeniably, unmistakably, unquestionably, without doubt

occasion *n* **1, 3** = **time,** chance, convenience, incident, moment, occurrence, opening, opportunity, window **2** = **reason,** call, cause, excuse, ground(s), inducement, influence, justification, motive, prompting, provocation **4** = **event,** affair, celebration, experience, happening, occurrence ◆ *vb* **8** = **cause,** bring about, create, effect, elicit, engender, evoke, generate, give rise to, induce, influence, inspire, lead to, move, originate, persuade, produce, prompt, provoke

occasional *adj* **1** = **infrequent,** casual, desultory, incidental, intermittent, irregular, odd, rare, sporadic, uncommon
Antonyms *adj* constant, continual, customary, frequent, habitual, incessant, regular, routine, usual

occasionally *adv* **1** = **sometimes,** at intervals, at times, (every) now and then, every so often, from time to time, irregularly, now and again, off and on, on and off, once in a while, on occasion, periodically
Antonyms *adv* constantly, continually, continuously, frequently, habitually, often, regularly, routinely

occlude *vb* **1** = **block,** bung, choke, clog, close, fill, hinder, obstruct, plug, seal, shut, stop up

occult *adj* **1** = **supernatural,** abstruse, arcane, cabbalistic, esoteric, magical, mysterious, mystic, mystical, preternatural, recondite **3** = **secret,** concealed, hidden, invisible, obscure, unknown, unrevealed, veiled
Antonyms *adj* ≠ **secret:** apparent, blatant, evident, exposed, manifest, obvious, open, overt, plain, revealed, visible

occultism *n* **1** = **black magic,** diabolism, magic, sorcery, supernaturalism, the black arts, witchcraft

occupancy *n* **1** = **tenancy,** habitation, hold-

occupant ❶ (ˈɒkjʊpənt) *n* **1** a person, thing, etc., holding a position or place. **2** *Law.* a person who has possession of something, esp. an estate, house, etc.; tenant. **3** *Law.* a person who acquires by occupancy the title to something previously without an owner.

occupation ❶ (ˌɒkjʊˈpeɪʃən) *n* **1** a person's regular work or profession; job. **2** any activity on which time is spent by a person. **3** the act of occupying or the state of being occupied. **4** the control of a country by a foreign military power. **5** the period of time that a nation, place, or position is occupied. **6** (*modifier*) for the use of the occupier of a particular property: *occupation road.*
▸ˌ**occuˈpational** *adj*

occupational psychology *n* the scientific study of mental or emotional problems associated with the working environment.

occupational therapy *n Med.* treatment of people with physical, emotional, or social problems, using purposeful activity to help them overcome or learn to deal with their problems.

occupation groupings *pl n* a system of classifying people according to occupation, based originally on information obtained by government census and subsequently developed by market research. The classifications are used by the advertising industry to identify potential markets. The groups are **A, B, C1, C2, D,** and **E.**

occupier (ˈɒkjʊˌpaɪə) *n* **1** *Brit.* a person who is in possession or occupation of a house or land. **2** a person or thing that occupies.

occupy ❶ (ˈɒkjʊˌpaɪ) *vb* **occupies, occupying, occupied.** (*tr*) **1** to live or be established in (a house, flat, office, etc.). **2** (*often passive*) to keep (a person) busy or engrossed. **3** (*often passive*) to take up (time or space). **4** to take and hold possession of, esp. as a demonstration: *students occupied the college buildings.* **5** to fill or hold (a position or rank). [C14: from OF *occuper,* from L *occupāre* to seize hold of]

occur ❶ (əˈkɜː) *vb* **occurs, occurring, occurred.** (*intr*) **1** to happen; take place; come about. **2** to be found or be present; exist. **3** (foll. by *to*) to be realized or thought of (by); suggest itself (to). [C16: from L *occurrere* to run up to]

> **USAGE NOTE** It is usually regarded as incorrect to talk of pre-arranged events *occurring* or *happening*: *the wedding took place* (not *occurred* or *happened*) *in the afternoon.*

occurrence ❶ (əˈkʌrəns) *n* **1** something that occurs; a happening; event. **2** the act or an instance of occurring: *a crime of frequent occurrence.*
▸**ocˈcurrent** *adj*

ocean (ˈəʊʃən) *n* **1** a very large stretch of sea, esp. one of the five oceans of the world, the Atlantic, Pacific, Indian, Arctic, and Antarctic. **2** the body of salt water covering approximately 70 per cent of the earth's surface. **3** a huge quantity or expanse: *an ocean of replies.* **4** *Literary.* the sea. [C13: via OF from L *ōceanus,* from *Oceanus,* Gk god of the stream believed to flow round the earth]

oceanarium (ˌəʊʃəˈnɛərɪəm) *n, pl* **oceanariums** *or* **oceanaria** (-ɪə). a large saltwater aquarium for marine life.

ocean-going *adj* (of a ship, boat, etc.) suited for travel on the open ocean.

oceanic (ˌəʊʃɪˈænɪk) *adj* **1** of or relating to the ocean. **2** living in the depths of the ocean beyond the continental shelf at a depth exceeding 200 metres: *oceanic fauna.* **3** huge or overwhelming.

Oceanid (əʊˈsɪənɪd) *n, pl* **Oceanids** *or* **Oceanides** (ˌəʊsɪˈænɪˌdiːz). *Greek myth.* an ocean nymph.

oceanography (ˌəʊʃəˈnɒgrəfɪ, ˌəʊʃɪə-) *n* the branch of science dealing with the physical, chemical, geological, and biological features of the oceans.
▸ˌ**oceanˈographer** *n* ▸**oceanographic** (ˌəʊʃənəˈgræfɪk, ˌəʊʃɪə-) *or* ˌ**oceanoˈgraphical** *adj*

oceanology (ˌəʊʃəˈnɒlədʒɪ, ˌəʊʃɪə-) *n* the study of the sea, esp. of its economic geography.

ocellus (ɒˈsɛləs) *n, pl* **ocelli** (-laɪ). **1** the simple eye of insects and some other invertebrates, consisting basically of light-sensitive cells. **2** any eyelike marking in animals, such as the eyespot on the tail feather of a peacock. [C19: via NL from L: small eye, from *oculus* eye]
▸**oˈcellar** *adj* ▸**ocellate** (ˈɒsɪˌleɪt) *or* ˈ**ocelˌlated** *adj* ▸ˌ**ocelˈlation** *n*

ocelot (ˈɒsɪˌlɒt, ˈəʊ-) *n* a feline mammal inhabiting Central and South America and having a dark-spotted buff-brown coat. [C18: via F from Nahuatl *ocelotl* jaguar]

och (ɒx) *interj Scot. & Irish.* an expression of surprise, contempt, disagreement, etc.

oche (ˈɒkɪ) *n Darts.* the mark or ridge on the floor behind which a player must stand to throw. [from ?]

ochlocracy (ɒkˈlɒkrəsɪ) *n, pl* **ochlocracies.** rule by the mob; mobocracy. [C16: via F, from Gk *okhlokratia,* from *okhlos* mob + *kratos* power]
▸**ochlocrat** (ˈɒkləˌkræt) *n* ▸ˌ**ochloˈcratic** *adj*

ochone (ɒˈxəʊn) *interj Scot. & Irish.* an expression of sorrow or regret. [from Gaelic *ochóin*]

ochre *or US* **ocher** (ˈəʊkə) *n* **1** any of various natural earths containing ferric oxide, silica, and alumina: used as yellow or red pigments. **2a** a moderate yellow-orange to orange colour. **2b** (*as adj*): *an ochre dress.* ◆ *vb* **ochres, ochring, ochred** *or US* **ochers, ochering, ochered. 3** (*tr*) to colour with ochre. [C15: from OF *ocre,* from L *ōchra,* from Gk *ōkhros* pale yellow]
▸**ochreous** (ˈəʊkrɪəs, ˈəʊkərəs), **ochrous** (ˈəʊkrəs), **ochry** (ˈəʊkərɪ, ˈəʊkrɪ) *or US* ˈ**ocherous,** ˈ**ochery** *adj*

-ock *suffix forming nouns.* indicating smallness: *hillock.* [OE *-oc, -uc*]

ocker (ˈɒkə) *Austral. sl.* ◆ *n* **1** (*often cap.*) an uncultivated or boorish Australian. ◆ *adj* **2** typical of such a person. [C20: after an Australian TV character]

Ockham's *or* **Occam's razor** (ˈɒkəmz) *n* a maxim, attributed to William of Occam, English nominalist philosopher (died ?1349), stating that in explaining something assumptions must not be needlessly multiplied.

o'clock (əˈklɒk) *adv* **1** used after a number from one to twelve to indicate the hour of the day or night. **2** used after a number to indicate direction or position relative to the observer, twelve o'clock being directly ahead and other positions being obtained by comparisons with a clock face. [C18: abbrev. for *of the clock*]

OCR *abbrev. for* optical character reader *or* recognition.

oct. *abbrev. for* octavo.

Oct. *abbrev. for* October.

oct- *combining form.* a variant of **octo-** before a vowel.

octa- *combining form.* a variant of **octo-.**

octad (ˈɒktæd) *n* **1** a group or series of eight. **2** *Chem.* an element with a valency of eight. [C19: from Gk *oktās,* from *oktō* eight]
▸**ocˈtadic** *adj*

octagon (ˈɒktəgən) *n* a polygon having eight sides. [C17: via L from Gk *oktagōnos* having eight angles]
▸**octagonal** (ɒkˈtægənᵊl) *adj*

octahedron (ˌɒktəˈhiːdrən) *n, pl* **octahedrons** *or* **octahedra** (-drə). a solid figure having eight plane faces.

octal notation *or* **octal** (ˈɒktəl) *n Computing.* a number system having a base 8, one octal digit being equivalent to a group of three bits.

octane (ˈɒkteɪn) *n* a liquid hydrocarbon found in petroleum. Formula: C_8H_{18}.

octane number *or* **rating** *n* a measure of the antiknock quality of a petrol expressed as a percentage.

octant (ˈɒktənt) *n* **1** *Maths.* **1a** any of the eight parts into which the three planes containing the Cartesian coordinate axes divide space. **1b** an eighth part of a circle. **2** *Astron.* the position of a celestial body when it is at an angular distance of 45° from another body. **3** an instrument used for measuring angles, similar to a sextant but having a graduated arc of 45°. [C17: from L *octans* half quadrant, from *octo* eight]

octavalent (ˌɒktəˈveɪlənt) *adj Chem.* having a valency of eight.

octave (ˈɒktɪv) *n* **1a** the interval between two musical notes one of which has twice the pitch of the other and lies eight notes away from it counting inclusively along the diatonic scale. **1b** one of these two notes, esp. the one of higher pitch. **1c** (*as modifier*): *an octave leap.* **2** *Prosody.* a rhythmic group of eight lines of verse. **3** (ˈɒkteɪv). **3a** a feast day and the seven days following. **3b** the final day of this period. **4** the eighth of eight basic positions in fencing. **5** any set or series of eight. ◆ *adj* **6** consisting of eight parts. [C14: (orig.: eighth day) via OF from Med. L *octāva diēs* eighth day (after a festival), from L *octo* eight]

octavo (ɒkˈteɪvəʊ) *n, pl* **octavos. 1** a book size resulting from folding a sheet of paper of a specified size to form eight leaves: *demi-octavo.* Often written: **8vo, 8°. 2** a book of this size. [C16: from NL *in octavo* in an eighth (of a sheet)]

octennial (ɒkˈtɛnɪəl) *adj* **1** occurring every eight years. **2** lasting for eight years. [C17: from L *octennium,* from *octo* eight + *annus* year]
▸**ocˈtennially** *adv*

octet (ɒkˈtɛt) *n* **1** any group of eight, esp. singers or musicians. **2** a piece

THESAURUS

ing, inhabitancy, occupation, possession, residence, tenure, term, use

occupant *n* **1** = **inhabitant,** addressee, denizen, holder, incumbent, indweller, inmate, lessee, occupier, resident, tenant, user

occupation *n* **1** = **profession,** activity, business, calling, craft, employment, job, line (of work), post, pursuit, trade, vocation, walk of life, work **3** = **possession,** control, holding, occupancy, residence, tenancy, tenure, use **4** = **invasion,** conquest, foreign rule, seizure, subjugation

occupied *adj* **1** = **inhabited,** full, lived-in, peopled, settled, tenanted **2** = **busy,** employed, engaged, hard at it (*inf.*), tied up (*inf.*), working **3** = **in use,** engaged, full, taken, unavailable
Antonyms *adj* ≠ **inhabited:** deserted, empty, tenantless, uninhabited, unoccupied, untenanted, vacant

occupy *vb* **1** = **live in,** be established in, be in residence in, dwell in, ensconce oneself in, establish oneself in, inhabit, own, possess, reside in, stay in (*Scot.*), tenant **2** *often passive* = **take up,** absorb, amuse, busy, divert, employ, engage, engross, entertain, hold the attention of, immerse, interest, involve, keep busy *or* occupied, monopolize, preoccupy, tie up **3, 5** = **fill,** cover, hold, permeate, pervade, take up, use, utilize **4** = **invade,** capture, garrison, hold, keep, overrun, seize, take over, take possession of
Antonyms *vb* ≠ **live in:** abandon, depart, desert, evacuate, quit, vacate ≠ **invade:** retreat, withdraw

occur *vb* **1** = **happen,** arise, befall, betide, chance, come about, come off (*inf.*), come to pass (*arch.*), crop up (*inf.*), eventuate, materialize, result, take place, turn up (*inf.*) **2** = **exist,** appear, be found, be met with, be present, develop, manifest itself, obtain, show itself **3** *with* **to** = **come to mind,** come to one, cross one's mind, dawn on, enter one's head, offer itself, present itself, spring to mind, strike one, suggest itself

occurrence *n* **1** = **incident,** adventure, affair, circumstance, episode, event, happening, instance, proceeding, transaction of music composed for such a group. **3** *Prosody.* another word for **octave** (sense 2). **4** *Chem.* a stable group of eight electrons. ◆ Also (for senses 1, 2, 3): **octette.** [C19: from L *octo* eight, on the model of DUET]

octillion (ɒkˈtɪljən) *n* **1** (in Britain and Germany) the number represented as one followed by 48 zeros (10^{48}). **2** (in the US, Canada, and France) the number represented as one followed by 27 zeros (10^{27}). [C17: from F, on the model of MILLION]
▸**ocˈtillionth** *adj, n*

octo-, octa-, *or before a vowel* **oct-** *combining form.* eight: *octosyllabic; octagon.* [from L *octo,* Gk *oktō*]

October (ɒkˈtəʊbə) *n* the tenth month of the year, consisting of 31 days. [OE, from L, from *octo* eight, since it was orig. the eighth month in Roman reckoning]

Octobrist (ɒkˈtəʊbrɪst) *n* a member of a Russian political party favouring the constitutional reforms granted in a manifesto issued by Nicholas II in Oct. 1905.

octocentenary (ˌɒktəʊsɛnˈtiːnərɪ) *n, pl* **octocentenaries.** an 800th anniversary.

octogenarian (ˌɒktəʊdʒɪˈnɛərɪən) *n* **1** a person who is from 80 to 89 years old. ◆ *adj* **2** of or relating to an octogenarian. [C19: from L *octōgēnārius* containing eighty, from *octōgēnī* eighty each]

octopus (ˈɒktəpəs) *n, pl* **octopuses.** **1** a cephalopod mollusc having a soft oval body with eight long suckered tentacles and occurring at the sea bottom. **2** a powerful influential organization, etc., with far-reaching effects, esp. harmful ones. [C18: via NL from Gk *oktōpous* having eight feet]

octoroon *or* **octaroon** (ˌɒktəˈruːn) *n* a person having one quadroon and one White parent and therefore having one-eighth Black blood. Cf. **quadroon.** [C19: OCTO- + *-roon* as in QUADROON]

octosyllable (ˈɒktəˌsɪləbᵊl) *n* **1** a line of verse composed of eight syllables. **2** a word of eight syllables.
▸**octosyllabic** (ˌɒktəʊsɪˈlæbɪk) *adj*

octroi (ˈɒktrwɑː) *n* **1** (in some European countries, esp. France) a duty on goods brought into certain towns. **2** the place where it is collected. **3** the officers responsible for its collection. [C17: from F *octroyer* to concede, from Med. L *auctorizāre* to AUTHORIZE]

octuple (ˈɒktjʊpᵊl) *n* **1** a quantity or number eight times as great as another. ◆ *adj* **2** eight times as much or as many. **3** consisting of eight parts. ◆ *vb* **octuples, octupling, octupled.** **4** (*tr*) to multiply by eight. [C17: from L *octuplus,* from *octo* eight + *-plus* as in *duplus* double]

ocular (ˈɒkjʊlə) *adj* **1** of or relating to the eye. ◆ *n* **2** another name for **eyepiece.** [C16: from L *oculāris* from *oculus* eye]
▸**ˈocularly** *adv*

ocularist (ˈɒkjʊlərɪst) *n* a person who makes artificial eyes.

oculate (ˈɒkjʊlɪt) *adj Zool.* **1** having eyes. **2** relating to or resembling eyes: *oculate markings.*

oculist (ˈɒkjʊlɪst) *n Med.* a former term for **ophthalmologist.** [C17: via F from L *oculus* eye]

od (ɒd, əʊd), **odyl,** *or* **odyle** (ˈɒdɪl) *n Arch.* a hypothetical force formerly thought to be responsible for many natural phenomena, such as magnetism, light, and hypnotism. [C19: coined by Baron Karl von Reichenbach (1788–1869), G scientist]
▸**ˈodic** *adj*

OD[1] (ˌəʊˈdiː) *Inf.* ◆ *n* **1** an overdose of a drug. ◆ *vb* **OD's, OD'ing, OD'd.** (*intr*) **2** to take an overdose of a drug. [C20: from *o(ver)d(ose)*]

OD[2] *abbrev. for:* **1** Officer of the Day. **2** Also: **o.d.** *Mil.* olive drab. **3** Also: **O/D** *Banking.* **3a** on demand. **3b** overdrawn. **4** ordnance datum. **5** outside diameter.

ODA (in Britain) *abbrev. for* Overseas Development Administration.

odalisque *or* **odalisk** (ˈəʊdəlɪsk) *n* a female slave or concubine. [C17: via F, changed from Turkish *ōdalik,* from *ōdah* room + *-lik,* n. suffix]

odd Ⓣ (ɒd) *adj* **1** unusual or peculiar in appearance, character, etc. **2** occasional, incidental, or random: *odd jobs.* **3** leftover or additional: *odd bits of wool.* **4a** not divisible by two. **4b** represented or indicated by a number that is not divisible by two: *graphs are on odd pages.* Cf. **even**[1] (sense 7). **5** being part of a matched pair or set when the other or others are missing: *an odd sock.* **6** (*in combination*) used to designate an indefinite quantity more than the quantity specified in round numbers: *fifty-odd pounds.* **7** out-of-the-way or secluded: *odd corners.* **8** **odd man out.** a person or thing excluded from others forming a group, unit, etc. ◆ *n* **9** *Golf.* **9a** one stroke more than the score of one's opponent. **9b** a handicap of one stroke. **10** a thing or person that is odd in sequence or number. ◆ See also **odds.** [from ON *oddi* triangle, point]
▸**ˈoddly** *adv* ▸**ˈoddness** *n*

oddball (ˈɒdˌbɔːl) *Inf.* ◆ *n* **1** Also: **odd bod, odd fish.** a strange or eccentric person or thing. ◆ *adj* **2** strange or peculiar.

Oddfellow (ˈɒdˌfɛləʊ) *n* a member of a secret benevolent and fraternal association founded in England in the 18th century.

oddity Ⓣ (ˈɒdɪtɪ) *n, pl* **oddities.** **1** an odd person or thing. **2** an odd quality or characteristic. **3** the condition of being odd.

odd-jobman *or* **odd-jobber** *n* a person who does casual work, esp. domestic repairs.

oddment Ⓣ (ˈɒdmənt) *n* **1** (*often pl*) an odd piece or thing; leftover. **2** *Printing.* **2a** pages that do not make a complete signature. **2b** any individual part of a book excluding the main text.

odd pricing *n* pricing goods in such a way as to imply that a bargain is being offered, as £5.99 instead of £6.

odds Ⓣ (ɒdz) *pl n* **1** (foll. by *on* or *against*) the probability, expressed as a ratio, that a certain event will take place: *the odds against the outsider are a hundred to one.* **2** the amount, expressed as a ratio, by which the wager of one better is greater than that of another: *he was offering odds of five to one.* **3** the likelihood that a certain state of affairs will be so: *the odds are that he is drunk.* **4** an equalizing allowance, esp. one given to a weaker side in a contest. **5** the advantage that one contender is judged to have over another. **6** *Brit.* a significant difference (esp. in **it makes no odds**). **7** **at odds.** on bad terms. **8** **give** *or* **lay odds.** to offer a bet with favourable odds. **9** **over the odds. 9a** more than is expected, necessary, etc. **9b** unfair or excessive. **10** **take odds.** to accept a bet with favourable odds. **11** **what's the odds?** *Brit. inf.* what difference does it make?

odds and ends Ⓣ *pl n* miscellaneous items or articles.

odds-on *adj* **1** (of a horse, etc.) rated at even money or less to win. **2** regarded as more or most likely to win, succeed, happen, etc.

ode (əʊd) *n* **1** a lyric poem, typically addressed to a particular subject, with lines of varying lengths and complex rhythms. **2** (formerly) a poem meant to be sung. [C16: via F from LL *ōda,* from Gk *ōidē,* from *aeidein* to sing]

-ode[1] *n combining form.* denoting resemblance: *nematode.* [from Gk *-ōdēs,* from *eidos* shape]

-ode[2] *n combining form.* denoting a path or way: *electrode.* [from Gk *-odos,* from *hodos* a way]

odeum (ˈəʊdɪəm) *n, pl* **odea** (ˈəʊdɪə). (esp. in ancient Greece and Rome) a building for musical performances. Also called: **odeon.** [C17: from L, from Gk *ōideion,* from *ōidē* ODE]

odious Ⓣ (ˈəʊdɪəs) *adj* offensive; repugnant. [C17: from L; see ODIUM]
▸**ˈodiousness** *n*

odium Ⓣ (ˈəʊdɪəm) *n* **1** the dislike accorded to a hated person or thing. **2** hatred; repugnance. [C17: from L; rel. to *ōdī* I hate, Gk *odussasthai* to be angry]

odometer (ɒˈdɒmɪtə, əʊ-) *n* the usual US and Canad. name for **mileometer.** [C18 *hodometer,* from Gk *hodos* way + -METER]
▸**oˈdometry** *n*

-odont *adj and n combining form.* -toothed: *acrodont.* [from Gk *odōn* tooth]

odonto- *or before a vowel* **odont-** *combining form.* indicating a tooth or teeth: *odontology.* [from Gk *odōn* tooth]

odontoglossum (ɒˌdɒntəˈglɒsəm) *n* a tropical American epiphytic orchid having clusters of brightly coloured flowers.

odontology (ˌɒdɒnˈtɒlədʒɪ) *n* the branch of science concerned with the anatomy, development, and diseases of teeth.
▸**odontological** (ɒˌdɒntəˈlɒdʒɪkᵊl) *adj* ▸**ˌodonˈtologist** *n*

odoriferous (ˌəʊdəˈrɪfərəs) *adj* having or emitting an odour, esp. a fragrant one.
▸**ˌodorˈiferously** *adv* ▸**ˌodorˈiferousness** *n*

odoriphore (əʊˈdɒrɪˌfɔː) *n Chem.* the group of atoms in an odorous molecule responsible for its odour.

odorous Ⓣ (ˈəʊdərəs) *adj* having or emitting a characteristic smell or odour.
▸**ˈodorously** *adv* ▸**ˈodorousness** *n*

THESAURUS

odd *adj* **1 = unusual,** abnormal, atypical, bizarre, curious, deviant, different, eccentric, exceptional, extraordinary, fantastic, freak, freakish, funny, irregular, kinky (*inf.*), left-field (*inf.*), off-the-wall (*sl.*), outlandish, out of the ordinary, outré, peculiar, quaint, queer, rare, remarkable, singular, strange, uncanny, uncommon, unconventional, weird, whimsical **2 = occasional,** casual, fragmentary, incidental, irregular, miscellaneous, periodic, random, seasonal, sundry, varied, various **3 = spare,** leftover, lone, remaining, single, solitary, surplus, unconsumed, uneven, unmatched, unpaired ◆ *n* **8 odd man out = misfit,** exception, freak, maverick, nonconformist, outsider, square peg in a round hole (*inf.*)
Antonyms *adj* ≠ **unusual:** common, customary, familiar, natural, normal, ordinary, regular, typical, unexceptional, unremarkable, usual ≠ **occasional:** habitual, permanent, regular, steady ≠ **spare:** even, matched, paired

oddity *n* **1 = misfit,** card (*inf.*), crank (*inf.*), fish out of water, loose cannon, maverick, nut (*sl.*), oddball (*inf.*), rara avis, screwball (*sl., chiefly US & Canad.*), weirdo *or* weirdie (*inf.*) **2 = irregularity,** abnormality, anomaly, eccentricity, freak, idiosyncrasy, kink, peculiarity, phenomenon, quirk, rarity **3 = strangeness,** abnormality, bizarreness, eccentricity, extraordinariness, freakishness, incongruity, oddness, outlandishness, peculiarity, queerness, singularity, unconventionality, unnaturalness

oddment *n* **1 = leftover,** bit, butt, end, end of a line, fag end, fragment, off cut, remnant, scrap, shred, sliver, snippet, stub, tail end

odds *pl n* **1, 3 = probability,** balance, chances, likelihood **5 = advantage,** allowance, edge, lead, superiority **6** *Brit.* **= difference,** disparity, dissimilarity, distinction **7 at odds = in conflict,** at daggers drawn, at loggerheads, at sixes and sevens, at variance, in disagreement, in opposition to, not in keeping, on bad terms, out of line

odds and ends *pl n* **= scraps,** bits, bits and pieces, debris, leavings, litter, oddments, remnants, rubbish, sundry *or* miscellaneous items

odious *adj* **= offensive,** abhorrent, abominable, detestable, disgusting, execrable, foul, hateful, horrible, horrid, loathsome, obnoxious, obscene, repellent, repugnant, repulsive, revolting, unpleasant, vile, yucky *or* yukky (*sl.*)
Antonyms *adj* agreeable, charming, congenial, delightful, enchanting, enjoyable, pleasant, pleasing, winsome

odium *n* **1, 2 = hatred,** abhorrence, antipathy, censure, condemnation, detestation, disapprobation, disapproval, discredit, disfavour, disgrace, dishonour, dislike, disrepute, execration, infamy, obloquy, opprobrium, reprobation, shame

odorous *adj* **= scented,** aromatic, balmy, fra-

odour 🅣 *or US* **odor** ('əudə) *n* **1** the property of a substance that gives it a characteristic scent or smell. **2** a pervasive quality about something: *an odour of dishonesty.* **3** repute or regard (in **in good odour, in bad odour**). **4** *Arch.* a sweet-smelling fragrance. [C13: from OF *odur,* from L *odor*]
▸**'odourless** *or US* **'odorless** *adj*

Odyssey 🅣 ('ɒdɪsɪ) *n* **1** a Greek epic poem, attributed to Homer, describing the ten-year homeward wanderings of Odysseus, a mythical Greek hero, after the fall of Troy. **2** (*often not cap.*) any long eventful journey.
▸**Odyssean** (ˌɒdɪ'siːən) *adj*

Oe *symbol for* oersted.

OE *abbrev. for* Old English (language).

OECD *abbrev. for* Organization for Economic Cooperation and Development.

OED *abbrev. for* Oxford English Dictionary.

oedema *or* **edema** (ɪ'diːmə) *n, pl* **oedemata** *or* **edemata** (-mətə). **1** *Pathol.* an excessive accumulation of serous fluid in the intercellular spaces of tissue. **2** *Bot.* an abnormal swelling in a plant caused by parenchyma or an accumulation of water in the tissues. [C16: via NL from Gk *oidēma,* from *oidein* to swell]
▸**oedematous, edematous** (ɪ'dɛmətəs) *or* **oe'demaˌtose, e'demaˌtose** *adj*

Oedipus complex ('iːdɪpəs) *n Psychoanal.* the repressed sexual feeling of a child, esp. a male child, for its parent of the opposite sex combined with a rivalry with the parent of the same sex. [C20: after *Oedipus,* a legendary king who unknowingly killed his father and married his mother]
▸**'oedipal** *or* **ˌoedi'pean** *adj*

OEEC *abbrev. for* Organization for European Economic Cooperation. It was superseded by the OECD in 1961.

OEM *abbrev. for* original equipment manufacturer: a computer company whose products are made by combining basic parts supplied by others to meet a customer's needs.

oenology *or* **enology** (iː'nɒlədʒɪ) *n* the study of wine. [C19: from Gk *oinos* wine + -LOGY]
▸**oenological** *or* **enological** (ˌiːnə'lɒdʒɪkᵊl) *adj* ▸**oe'nologist** *or* **e'nologist** *n*

oenothera (iː'nɒθərə) *n* any of various hardy biennial or herbaceous perennial plants having yellow flowers. Also called: **evening primrose.** [from Gk *oinothēras,* ?from *onothēras* a plant whose roots smell of wine]

o'er (ɔː, əuə) *prep, adv* a poetic contraction of **over.**

oersted ('ɜːstɛd) *n* the cgs unit of magnetic field strength; the field strength that would cause a unit magnetic pole to experience a force of 1 dyne in free space. It is equivalent to 79.58 amperes per metre. Symbol. Oe [C20: after H. C. *Oersted* (1777–1851), Danish physicist who discovered electromagnetism]

oesophagus *or US* **esophagus** (iː'sɒfəgəs) *n, pl* **oesophagi** *or US* **esophagi** (-ˌgaɪ). the part of the alimentary canal between the pharynx and the stomach; gullet. [C16: via NL from Gk *oisophagos,* from *oisein,* future infinitive of *pherein* to carry + *-phagos,* from *phagein* to eat]
▸**oesophageal** *or US* **esophageal** (iːˌsɒfə'dʒiːəl) *adj*

oestradiol (ˌiːstrə'daɪɒl, ˌɛstrə-) *or US* **estradiol** *n* the most potent oestrogenic horome secreted by the mammalian ovary: synthesized and used to treat oestrogen deficiency and cancer of the breast. [C20: from NL, from OESTRIN + DI-[1] + -OL[1]]

oestrin ('iːstrɪn) *n* an obsolete term for **oestrogen.** [C20: from OESTR(US) + -IN]

oestrogen ('iːstrədʒən, 'ɛstrə-) *or US* **estrogen** *n* any of several hormones that induce oestrus, stimulate changes in the female reproductive organs, and promote development of female secondary sexual characteristics. [C20: from OESTRUS + -GEN]
▸**oestrogenic** (ˌiːstrə'dʒɛnɪk, ˌɛstrə-) *or US* **estrogenic** (ˌɛstrə'dʒɛnɪk, ˌiːstrə-) *adj* ▸**ˌoestro'genically** *or US* **ˌestro'genically** *adv*

oestrous cycle ('iːstrəs) *n* a hormonally controlled cycle of activity of the reproductive organs in many female mammals.

oestrus ('iːstrəs, 'ɛstrəs) *or US* **estrus, estrum** ('ɛstrəm, 'iːstrəm) *n* a regularly occurring period of sexual receptivity in most female mammals, except humans, during which ovulation occurs and copulation can take place; heat. [C17: from L *oestrus* gadfly, hence frenzy, from Gk *oistros*]
▸**'oestrous, 'oestral** *or US* **'estrous, 'estral** *adj*

oeuvre *French.* (œvrə) *n* **1** a work of art, literature, music, etc. **2** the total output of a writer, painter, etc. [ult. from L *opera,* pl. of *opus* work]

of (ɒv; *unstressed* əv) *prep* **1** used with a verbal noun or gerund to link it with a following noun that is either the subject or the object of the verb embedded in the gerund: *the breathing of a fine swimmer* (subject); *the breathing of clean air* (object). **2** used to indicate possession, origin, or association: *the house of my sister; to die of hunger.* **3** used after words or phrases expressing quantities: *a pint of milk.* **4** constituted by, containing, or characterized by: *a family of idiots; a rod of iron; a man of some depth.* **5** used to indicate separation, as in time or space: *within a mile of the town; within ten minutes of the beginning of the concert.* **6** used to mark apposition: *the city of Naples; a speech on the subject of archaeology.* **7** about; concerning: *speak to me of love.* **8** used in passive constructions to indicate the agent: *he was beloved of all.* **9** *Inf.* used to indicate a day or part of a period of time when some activity habitually occurs: *I go to the pub of an evening.* **10** *US.* before the hour of: *a quarter of nine.* [OE (as prep & adv); rel. to L *ab*]

> **USAGE NOTE** See at **off.**

OF *abbrev. for* Old French (language).

off 🅣 (ɒf) *prep* **1** used to indicate actions in which contact is absent, as between an object and a surface: *to lift a cup off the table.* **2** used to indicate the removal of something that is appended to or in association with something else: *to take the tax off potatoes.* **3** out of alignment with: *we are off course.* **4** situated near to or leading away from: *just off the High Street.* **5** not inclined towards: *I've gone off you.* ◆ *adv* **6** (*particle*) so as to be deactivated or disengaged: *turn off the radio.* **7** (*particle*) **7a** so as to get rid of: *sleep off a hangover.* **7b** so as to be removed from, esp. as a reduction: *he took ten per cent off.* **8** spent away from work or other duties: *take the afternoon off.* **9a** on a trip, journey, or race: *I saw her off at the station.* **9b** (*particle*) so as to be completely absent, used up, or exhausted: *this stuff kills off all vermin.* **10** out from the shore or land: *the ship stood off.* **11a** out of contact; at a distance: *the ship was 10 miles off.* **11b** out of the present location: *the girl ran off.* **12** away in the future: *August is less than a week off.* **13** (*particle*) so as to be no longer taking place: *the match has been rained off.* **14** (*particle*) removed from contact with something, as clothing from the body: *the girl took all her clothes off.* **15** offstage: *noises off.* **16 off and on.** intermittently; from time to time: *he comes here off and on.* **17 off with.** (*interj*) a command or an exhortation to remove or cut off (something specified): *off with his head; off with that coat.* ◆ *adj* **18** not on; no longer operative: *the off position on the dial.* **19** (*postpositive*) not taking place; cancelled or postponed: *the meeting is off.* **20** in a specified condition regarding money, provisions, etc.: *well off; how are you off for bread?* **21** unsatisfactory or disappointing: *his performance was rather off; an off year for good tennis.* **22** (*postpositive*) in a condition as specified: *I'd be better off without this job.* **23** (*postpositive*) no longer on the menu: *haddock is off.* **24** (*postpositive*) (of food or drink) having gone bad, sour, etc.: *this milk is off.* ◆ *n* **25** *Cricket.* **25a** the part of the field on that side of the pitch to which the batsman presents his bat when taking strike. **25b** (*in combination*) a fielding position in this part of the field: *mid-off.* **25c** (*as modifier*): *the off stump.* [orig. var. of OF; fully distinguished from it in the 17th cent.]

> **USAGE NOTE** In standard English, *off* is not followed by *of: he stepped off* (not *off of*) *the platform.*

off. *abbrev. for:* **1** offer. **2** office. **3** officer. **4** official.

offal ('ɒfᵊl) *n* **1** the edible internal parts of an animal, such as the heart, liver, and tongue. **2** dead or decomposing organic matter. **3** refuse; rubbish. [C14: from OFF + FALL, referring to parts fallen or cut off]

off-balance-sheet reserve *n Accounting.* a sum of money or an asset that should appear on a company's balance but does not; hidden reserve.

offbeat 🅣 ('ɒfˌbiːt) *n* **1** *Music.* any of the normally unaccented beats in a bar, such as the second and fourth beats in a bar of four-four time. ◆ *adj* **2a** unusual, unconventional, or eccentric. **2b** (*as n*): *he liked the offbeat in fashion.*

off break *n Cricket.* a bowled ball that spins from off to leg on pitching.

off-Broadway *adj* **1** designating the kind of experimental, low-budget, or noncommercial productions associated with theatre outside the Broadway area in New York. **2** (of theatres) not located on Broadway.

off colour 🅣 *adj* (**off-colour** *when prenominal*). **1** *Chiefly Brit.* slightly ill; unwell. **2** indecent or indelicate; risqué.

offcut ('ɒfˌkʌt) *n* a piece of paper, wood, fabric, etc., remaining after the main pieces have been cut; remnant.

offence 🅣 *or US* **offense** (ə'fɛns) *n* **1** a violation or breach of a law, rule, etc. **2** any public wrong or crime. **3** annoyance, displeasure, or resentment. **4 give offence (to).** to cause annoyance or displeasure (to). **5 take offence.** to feel injured, humiliated, or offended. **6** a source of annoyance, displeasure, or anger. **7** attack; assault. **8** *Arch.* injury or harm.

THESAURUS

grant, odoriferous, perfumed, redolent, sweet-smelling

odour *n* **1** = **smell,** aroma, bouquet, essence, fragrance, niff (*Brit. sl.*), perfume, redolence, scent, stench, stink **2** = **quality,** air, atmosphere, aura, emanation, flavour, spirit

Odyssey *n* **2** *often not cap.* = **journey,** crusade, peregrination, pilgrimage, quest, trek, voyage

off *adv* **8-11** = **away,** apart, aside, elsewhere, out **16 off and on** = **occasionally,** (every) now and again, every once in a while, from time to time, intermittently, now and then, on and off, sometimes, sporadically ◆ *adj* **19** = **cancelled,** absent, finished, gone, inoperative, postponed, unavailable **21** = **substandard,** bad, below par, disappointing, disheartening, displeasing, low-quality, mortifying, poor, quiet, slack, unrewarding, unsatisfactory **24** = **bad,** decomposed, high, mouldy, rancid, rotten, sour, turned

offbeat *adj* **2** = **unusual,** bizarre, Bohemian, eccentric, far-out (*sl.*), idiosyncratic, left-field (*inf.*), novel, oddball (*inf.*), off-the-wall (*sl.*), outré, rum (*Brit. sl.*), strange, uncommon, unconventional, unorthodox, way-out (*inf.*), weird

Antonyms *adj* common, conventional, normal, ordinary, orthodox, run-of-the-mill, stereotyped, traditional, unoriginal, usual

off colour *adj* **1** = **ill,** green about the gills, not up to par, off form, out of sorts, peaky, peely-wally (*Scot.*), poorly (*inf.*), queasy, run down, sick, under par, under the weather (*inf.*), unwell, washed out

offence *n* **1, 2** = **crime,** breach of conduct, delinquency, fault, lapse, misdeed, misdemeanour, peccadillo, sin, transgression, trespass, wrong, wrongdoing **3** = **annoyance,** anger, displeasure, hard feelings, huff, indignation, ire (*literary*), needle (*inf.*), pique, resentment, um-

offend ❶ (əˈfɛnd) *vb* **1** to hurt the feelings, sense of dignity, etc., of (a person, etc.). **2** (*tr*) to be disagreeable to; disgust: *the smell offended him.* **3** (*intr except in archaic uses*) to break (a law). [C14: via OF *offendre* to strike against, from L *offendere*]
▸**ofˈfender** *n* ▸**ofˈfending** *adj*

offensive ❶ (əˈfɛnsɪv) *adj* **1** unpleasant or disgusting, as to the senses. **2** causing anger or annoyance; insulting. **3** for the purpose of attack rather than defence. ◆ *n* **4** (usually preceded by *the*) an attitude or position of aggression. **5** an assault, attack, or military initiative, esp. a strategic one.
▸**ofˈfensively** *adv* ▸**ofˈfensiveness** *n*

offer ❶ (ˈɒfə) *vb* **1** to present (something, someone, oneself, etc.) for acceptance or rejection. **2** (*tr*) to present as part of a requirement: *she offered English as a second subject.* **3** (*tr*) to provide or make accessible: *this stream offers the best fishing.* **4** (*intr*) to present itself: *if an opportunity should offer.* **5** (*tr*) to show or express willingness or the intention (to do something). **6** (*tr*) to put forward (a proposal, opinion, etc.) for consideration. **7** (*tr*) to present for sale. **8** (*tr*) to propose as payment; bid or tender. **9** (when *tr*, often foll. by *up*) to present (a prayer, sacrifice, etc.) as or during an act of worship. **10** (*tr*) to show readiness for: *to offer battle.* **11** (*intr*) *Arch.* to make a proposal of marriage. ◆ *n* **12** something, such as a proposal or bid, that is offered. **13** the act of offering or the condition of being offered. **14** a proposal of marriage. **15 on offer.** for sale at a reduced price. [OE, from L *offerre* to present, from *ob-* to + *ferre* to bring]

offer document *n* a document sent by a person or firm making a takeover bid to the shareholders of the target company, giving details of the offer that has been made and, usually, reasons for accepting it.

offering ❶ (ˈɒfərɪŋ) *n* **1** something that is offered. **2** a contribution to the funds of a religious organization. **3** a sacrifice, as of an animal, to a deity.

offertory (ˈɒfətərɪ) *n, pl* **offertories.** *Christianity.* **1** the oblation of the bread and wine at the Eucharist. **2** the offerings of the worshippers at this service. **3** the prayers said or sung while the worshippers' offerings are being brought to the altar during the **offertory procession.** [C14: from Church L *offertōrium* place appointed for offerings, from L *offerre* to OFFER]

offhand ❶ (ˌɒfˈhænd) *adj also* **offhanded,** *adv* **1** without care, thought, attention, or consideration; sometimes, brusque or ungracious: *an offhand manner.* **2** without preparation or warning; impromptu.
▸ˌ**offˈhandedly** *adv* ▸ˌ**offˈhandedness** *n*

office ❶ (ˈɒfɪs) *n* **1a** a room or rooms in which business, professional duties, clerical work, etc., are carried out. **1b** (*as modifier*): *office furniture; an office boy.* **2** (*often pl*) the building or buildings in which the work of an organization, such as a business, is carried out. **3** a commercial or professional business: *the architect's office approved the plans.* **4** the group of persons working in an office: *it was a happy office until she came.* **5** (*cap. when part of a name*) a department of the national government: *the Home Office.* **6** (*cap. when part of a name*) **6a** a governmental agency, esp. of the Federal government in the US. **6b** a subdivision of such an agency: *Office of Science and Technology.* **7a** a position of trust, responsibility, or duty, esp. in a government or organization: *to seek office.* **7b** (*in combination*): *an office-holder.* **8** duty or function: *the office of an administrator.* **9** (*often pl*) a minor task or service: *domestic offices.* **10** (*often pl*) an action performed for another, usually a beneficial action: *through his good offices.* **11** a place where tickets, information, etc., can be obtained: *a ticket office.* **12** *Christianity.* **12a** (*often pl*) a ceremony or service, prescribed by ecclesiastical authorities, esp. one for the dead. **12b** *RC Church.* the official daily service. **12c** short for **divine office.** **13** (*pl*) the parts of a house or estate where work is done, goods are stored, etc. **14** (*usually pl*) *Brit., euphemistic.* a lavatory (esp. in **usual offices**). **15 in** (*or* **out of**) **office.** (of a government) in (*or* out of) power. **16 the office.** a hint or signal. [C13: via OF from L *officium* service, duty, from *opus* work, service + *facere* to do]

office block *n* a large building designed to provide office accommodation.

office boy *n* a male office junior.

office junior *n* a young person, esp. a school-leaver, employed in an office for running errands and doing other minor jobs.

officer ❶ (ˈɒfɪsə) *n* **1** a person in the armed services who holds a position of responsibility, authority, and duty. **2** See **police officer.** **3** (on a non-naval ship) any person, including the captain and mate, who holds a position of authority and responsibility: *radio officer; engineer officer.* **4** a person appointed or elected to a position of responsibility or authority in a government, society, etc. **5** a government official: *a customs officer.* **6** (in the Order of the British Empire) a member of the grade below commander. ◆ *vb* (*tr*) **7** to furnish with officers. **8** to act as an officer over (some section, group, organization, etc.).

officer of the day *n* a military officer whose duty is to take charge of the security of the unit or camp for a day. Also called: **orderly officer.**

official ❶ (əˈfɪʃəl) *adj* **1** of or relating to an office, its administration, or its duration. **2** sanctioned by, recognized by, or derived from authority: *an official statement.* **3** having a formal ceremonial character: *an official dinner.* ◆ *n* **4** a person who holds a position in an organization, government department, etc., esp. a subordinate position.
▸**ofˈficially** *adv*

officialdom (əˈfɪʃəldəm) *n* **1** the outlook or behaviour of officials, esp. those rigidly adhering to regulations; bureaucracy. **2** officials or bureaucrats collectively.

officialese (əˌfɪʃəˈliːz) *n* language characteristic of official documents, esp. when verbose or pedantic.

Official Receiver *n* an officer appointed by the Department of Trade and Industry to receive the income and manage the estate of a bankrupt. See also **receiver** (sense 2).

officiant (əˈfɪʃɪənt) *n* a person who presides and officiates at a religious ceremony.

officiate ❶ (əˈfɪʃɪˌeɪt) *vb* **officiates, officiating, officiated.** (*intr*) **1** to hold the position, responsibility, or function of an official. **2** to conduct a religious or other ceremony. [C17: from Med. L *officiāre,* from L *officium;* see OFFICE]
▸**ofˌficiˈation** *n* ▸**ofˈficiˌator** *n*

officious ❶ (əˈfɪʃəs) *adj* **1** unnecessarily or obtrusively ready to offer advice or services. **2** *Diplomacy.* informal or unofficial. [C16: from L *officiōsus* kindly, from *officium* service; see OFFICE]
▸**ofˈficiously** *adv* ▸**ofˈficiousness** *n*

offing ❶ (ˈɒfɪŋ) *n* **1** the part of the sea that can be seen from the shore. **2 in the offing.** likely to occur soon.

offish (ˈɒfɪʃ) *adj Inf.* aloof or distant in manner.
▸ˈ**offishly** *adv* ▸ˈ**offishness** *n*

THESAURUS

brage, wounded feelings, wrath **4** *As in* **give offence** = **insult**, affront, displeasure, harm, hurt, indignity, injury, injustice, outrage, put-down (*sl.*), slight, snub **5 take offence** = **be offended**, be disgruntled, get riled, go into a huff, resent, take the huff, take the needle (*inf.*), take umbrage

offend *vb* **1** = **insult**, affront, annoy, cut to the quick, disgruntle, displease, fret, gall, give offence, hurt (someone's) feelings, irritate, miff (*inf.*), outrage, pain, pique, provoke, put down, put (someone's) back up, rile, slight, snub, tread on (someone's) toes (*inf.*), upset, vex, wound **2** = **disgust**, be disagreeable to, gross out (*US sl.*), make (someone) sick, nauseate, repel, repulse, sicken, turn (someone) off (*inf.*)
Antonyms *vb* ≠ **insult:** appease, assuage, conciliate, delight, mollify, placate, please, soothe

offended *adj* **1** = **resentful**, affronted, disgruntled, displeased, huffy, in a huff, miffed (*inf.*), outraged, pained, piqued, put out (*inf.*), smarting, stung, upset

offender *n* **3** = **criminal**, crook, culprit, delinquent, lawbreaker, malefactor, miscreant, sinner, transgressor, villain, wrongdoer

offensive *adj* **1** = **disgusting**, abominable, detestable, disagreeable, grisly, loathsome, nasty, nauseating, noisome, obnoxious, odious, repellent, revolting, sickening, unpalatable, unpleasant, unsavoury, vile, yucky *or* yukky (*sl.*) **2** = **insulting**, abusive, annoying, detestable, discourteous, displeasing, disrespectful, embarrassing, impertinent, insolent, irritating, objectionable, rude, uncivil, unmannerly **3** = **attacking**, aggressive, invading ◆ *n* **4** *As in* **on the offensive** = **aggression**, advance, attack, invasion, the warpath (*inf.*) **5** = **attack**, campaign, drive, onslaught, push (*inf.*)
Antonyms *adj* ≠ **disgusting:** agreeable, attractive, captivating, charming, delightful, pleasant ≠ **insulting:** civil, conciliatory, courteous, deferential, polite, respectful ≠ **attacking:** defensive ◆ *n* ≠ **aggression:** defensive

offer *vb* **1, 7, 8** = **proffer**, bid, extend, give, hold out, put on the market, put under the hammer, put up for sale, tender **3** = **provide**, afford, furnish, make available, place at (someone's) disposal, present, purvey, show **5** = **volunteer**, be at (someone's) service, come forward, offer one's services **6** = **propose**, advance, extend, move, put forth, put forward, submit, suggest ◆ *n* **12** = **proposal**, attempt, bid, endeavour, essay, overture, proposition, submission, suggestion, tender
Antonyms *vb* ≠ **proffer:** refuse, retract, revoke, take back, withdraw, withhold

offering *n* **2** = **contribution**, donation, gift, hand-out, present, subscription, widow's mite **3** = **sacrifice**, oblation

offhand *adj* **1** = **casual**, abrupt, aloof, brusque, careless, cavalier, couldn't-care-less, curt, glib, informal, offhanded, perfunctory, take-it-or-leave-it (*inf.*), unceremonious, unconcerned, uninterested ◆ *adv* **2** = **impromptu**, ad lib, extempore, just like that (*inf.*), off the cuff (*inf.*), off the top of one's head (*inf.*), without preparation
Antonyms *adj* ≠ **casual:** attentive, careful, grave, intent, planned, premeditated, prepared, responsible, serious, thoughtful

office *n* **7, 8** = **post**, appointment, business, capacity, charge, commission, duty, employment, function, obligation, occupation, place, responsibility, role, service, situation, station, trust, work

officer *n* **4** = **official**, agent, appointee, bureaucrat, dignitary, executive, functionary, office-holder, public servant, representative

official *adj* **2** = **authorized**, accredited, authentic, authoritative, bona fide, certified, endorsed, ex cathedra, ex officio, formal, legitimate, licensed, proper, sanctioned, signed and sealed, straight from the horse's mouth (*inf.*) ◆ *n* **4** = **officer**, agent, bureaucrat, executive, functionary, office bearer, representative
Antonyms *adj* ≠ **authorized:** casual, doubtful, dubious, informal, unauthorized, unofficial, unreliable

officiate *vb* **1** = **preside**, chair, conduct, emcee (*inf.*), manage, oversee, serve, superintend

officious *adj* **1** = **interfering**, bustling, dictatorial, forward, impertinent, inquisitive, intrusive, meddlesome, meddling, mischievous, obtrusive, opinionated, overbusy, overzealous, pragmatical (*rare*), pushy (*inf.*), self-important
Antonyms *adj* aloof, detached, indifferent, reserved, reticent, retiring, shy, taciturn, unforthcoming, withdrawn

offing *n* **2 in the offing** = **imminent**, close at hand, coming up, hovering, in prospect, in the immediate future, in the wings, on the horizon, on the way, upcoming

off key Ⓣ *adj* (**off-key** *when prenominal*), *adv* **1** *Music.* **1a** not in the correct key. **1b** out of tune. **2** out of keeping; discordant.

off-licence *n Brit.* **1** a shop or a counter in a pub or hotel where alcoholic drinks are sold for consumption elsewhere. US equivalents: **package store, liquor store. 2** a licence permitting such sales.

off limits *adj* (**off-limits** *when prenominal*). **1** *US, chiefly mil.* not to be entered; out of bounds. ◆ *adv* **2** in or into an area forbidden by regulations.

off line *adj* (**off-line** *when prenominal*). **1** of or concerned with a part of a computer system not connected to the central processing unit but controlled by a computer storage device. Cf. **on line. 2** disconnected from a computer; switched off.

off-load Ⓣ *vb (tr)* to get rid of (something unpleasant), as by delegation to another.

off message *adj* (**off-message** *when prenominal*) (esp. of a politician) not following the official line of his or her party.

off-peak *adj* of or relating to services as used outside periods of intensive use.

off-piste *adj* of or relating to skiing on virgin snow off the regular runs.

off-putting Ⓣ *adj Brit. inf.* arousing reluctance or aversion.

off-road *adj* **1** denoting the use of a vehicle away from public roads, esp. on rough terrain: *off-road motorcycling.* **2** (of a vehicle) designed or built for off-road use.

off-roader *n* a motor vehicle designed for use away from public roads, esp. on rough terrain.

off-sales *pl n Brit.* sales of alcoholic drink for consumption off the premises by a pub or an off-licence attached to a pub.

off season *adj* (**off-season** *when prenominal*). **1** denoting or occurring during a period of little activity in a trade or business. ◆ *n* **2** such a period. ◆ *adv* **3** in an off-season period.

offset Ⓣ *n* (ˈɒfˌsɛt). **1** something that counterbalances or compensates for something else. **2a** a printing method in which the impression is made onto an intermediate surface, such as a rubber blanket, which transfers it to the paper. **2b** (*modifier*) relating to, involving, or printed by offset: *offset letterpress.* **3** another name for **set off. 4** *Bot.* a short runner in certain plants that produces roots and shoots at the tip. **5** a ridge projecting from a range of hills or mountains. **6** a narrow horizontal or sloping surface formed where a wall is reduced in thickness towards the top. **7** *Surveying.* a measurement of distance to a point at right angles to a survey line. ◆ *vb* (ˌɒfˈsɛt), **offsets, offsetting, offset. 8** *(tr)* to counterbalance or compensate for. **9** *(tr)* to print (text, etc.) using the offset process. **10** *(tr)* to construct an offset in (a wall). **11** *(intr)* to project or develop as an offset.

offshoot Ⓣ (ˈɒfˌʃuːt) *n* **1** a shoot or branch growing from the main stem of a plant. **2** something that develops or derives from a principal source or origin.

offshore (ˌɒfˈʃɔː) *adj, adv* **1** from, away from, or at some distance from the shore. ◆ *adj* **2** sited or conducted at sea: *offshore industries.* **3** based or operating abroad: *offshore banking; offshore fund.*

offside *adj, adv* (ˌɒfˈsaɪd). **1** *Sport.* (in football, etc.) in a position illegally ahead of the ball when it is played. Cf. **onside.** ◆ *n* (ˈɒfˈsaɪd). **2** (usually preceded by *the*) *Chiefly Brit.* **2a** the side of a vehicle, etc., nearest the centre of the road. **2b** (*as modifier*): *the offside passenger door.*

off-sider (ˌɒfˈsaɪdə) *n Austral. & NZ.* a partner or assistant.

offspring Ⓣ (ˈɒfˌsprɪŋ) *n* **1** the immediate descendant or descendants of a person, animal, etc.; progeny. **2** a product, outcome, or result.

offstage (ˈɒfˈsteɪdʒ) *adj, adv* out of the view of the audience; off the stage.

off-the-peg *adj* (of clothing) ready to wear; not produced especially for the person buying.

off the shelf *adv* **1** from stock and readily available: *you can have this model off the shelf.* ◆ *adj* (**off-the-shelf** *when prenominal*). **2** of or relating to a product that is readily available: *an off-the-shelf model.* **3** of or denoting a company that has been registered with the Registrar of Companies for the sole purpose of being sold.

off-the-wall *adj* (**off the wall** *when postpositive*). *Sl.* new or unexpected in an unconventional or eccentric way. [C20: ?from the use of the phrase in handball and squash to describe a shot that is unexpected]

off-white *n* **1** a colour consisting of white with a tinge of grey or yellow. ◆ *adj* **2** of such a colour: *an off-white coat.*

oft (ɒft) *adv* short for **often** (archaic or poetic except in combinations such as **oft-repeated** and **oft-recurring**). [OE *oft;* rel. to OHG *ofto*]

OFT (in Britain) *abbrev. for* Office of Fair Trading.

Oftel (ˈɒfˌtɛl) *n* (in Britain) *acronym for* Office of Telecommunications: a government body set up in 1984 to supervise telecommunications activities in the UK, and to protect the interests of the consumers.

often Ⓣ (ˈɒfᵊn) *adv* **1** frequently or repeatedly; much of the time. Arch. equivalents: **ˈoftenˌtimes, ˈoftˌtimes. 2 as often as not.** quite frequently. **3 every so often.** at intervals. **4 more often than not.** in more than half the instances. ◆ *adj* **5** *Arch.* repeated; frequent. [C14: var. of OFT before vowels and *h*]

ogee (ˈəʊdʒiː) *n Archit.* **1** Also called: **talon.** a moulding having a cross section in the form of a letter S. **2** short for **ogee arch.** [C15: prob. var. of OGIVE]

ogee arch *n Archit.* a pointed arch having an S-shaped curve on both sides. Sometimes shortened to **ogee.**

Ogen melon (ˈəʊgɛn) *n* a variety of small melon with sweet pale orange flesh. [C20: after a kibbutz in Israel where it was first developed]

ogham *or* **ogam** (ˈɒgəm) *n* an ancient alphabetical writing system used by the Celts in Britain, consisting of straight lines drawn or carved perpendicular to or at an angle to another long straight line. [C17: from OIrish *ogom,* from ?, but associated with the name *Ogma,* legendary inventor of this alphabet]

ogive (ˈəʊdʒaɪv, əʊˈdʒaɪv) *n* **1** a diagonal rib or groin of a Gothic vault. **2** another name for **lancet arch.** [C17: from OF, from ?]
▸**oˈgival** *adj*

ogle Ⓣ (ˈəʊgᵊl) *vb* **ogles, ogling, ogled. 1** to look at (someone) amorously or lustfully. **2** *(tr)* to stare or gape at. ◆ *n* **3** a flirtatious or lewd look. [C17: prob. from Low G *oegeln,* from *oegen* to look at]
▸**ˈogler** *n*

O grade *n* (formerly, in Scotland). **1a** the basic level of the Scottish Certificate of Education, now replaced by **Standard Grade. 1b** (*as modifier*): *O-grade history.* **2** a pass in a subject at O grade: *she has ten O grades.*

ogre Ⓣ (ˈəʊgə) *n* **1** (in folklore) a giant, usually given to eating human flesh. **2** any monstrous or cruel person. [C18: from F, ?from L *Orcus,* god of the infernal regions]
▸**ˈogreish** *adj* ▸**ˈogress** *fem n*

oh (əʊ) *interj* an exclamation expressive of surprise, pain, pleasure, etc.

OHG *abbrev. for* Old High German.

ohm (əʊm) *n* the derived SI unit of electrical resistance; the resistance between two points on a conductor when a constant potential difference of 1 volt between them produces a current of 1 ampere. Symbol: Ω [C19: after Georg Simon *Ohm* (1787–1854), G physicist]
▸**ˈohmage** *n*

ohmmeter (ˈəʊmˌmiːtə) *n* an instrument for measuring electrical resistance.

OHMS (in Britain and the Commonwealth) *abbrev. for* On Her (*or* His) Majesty's Service.

Ohm's law (əʊmz) *n* the principle that the electric current passing through a conductor is directly proportional to the potential difference across it. The constant of proportionality is the resistance of the conductor.

oho (əʊˈhəʊ) *interj* an exclamation expressing surprise, exultation, or derision.

-oic *suffix forming adjectives.* indicating that a chemical compound is a carboxylic acid: *ethanoic acid.*

-oid *suffix forming adjectives and associated nouns.* indicating likeness, resemblance, or similarity: *anthropoid.* [from Gk *-oeidēs* resembling, from *eidos* form]

-oidea *suffix forming plural proper nouns.* forming the names of zoological classes or superfamilies: *Canoidea.* [from NL, from L *-oīdēs* -OID]

oil Ⓣ (ɔɪl) *n* **1** any of a number of viscous liquids with a smooth sticky feel. They are usually flammable, insoluble in water, soluble in organic solvents, and are obtained from plants and animals, from mineral deposits, and by synthesis. See also **essential oil. 2a** another name for **petroleum. 2b** (*as modifier*): *an oil engine; an oil rig.* **3a** any of a number of substances usually derived from petroleum and used for lubrication. **3b** (*in combination*): *an oilcan.* **3c** (*as modifier*): *an oil pump.* **4** Also called: **fuel oil.** a petroleum product used as a fuel in domestic heating, marine engines, etc. **5** *Brit.* **5a** paraffin, esp. when used as a domestic fuel. **5b** (*as modifier*): *an oil lamp.* **6** any substance of a consistency resembling that of oil: *oil of vitriol.* **7** the solvent, usually linseed oil, with which pigments are mixed to make artists' paints. **8a** (*often pl*) oil colour or paint. **8b** (*as modifier*): *an oil painting.* **9** an oil painting. **10** *Austral. & NZ sl.* facts or news. **11 strike oil. 11a** to discover petroleum while drilling for it. **11b** *Inf.* to become very rich or successful. ◆ *vb (tr)* **12** to lubricate, smear, polish, etc., with oil or an oily substance. **13 oil one's tongue.** *Inf.* to speak flatteringly or glibly. **14 oil someone's palm.**

THESAURUS

off key *adj* **1, 2 = out of tune,** discordant, dissonant, inharmonious, jarring, out of keeping

off-load *vb* **= get rid of,** disburden, discharge, dump, jettison, lighten, shift, take off, transfer, unburden, unload, unship

off-putting *adj Brit. informal* **= discouraging,** daunting, discomfiting, disconcerting, dismaying, dispiriting, disturbing, formidable, frustrating, intimidating, unnerving, unsettling, upsetting

offset *n* **1 = counterbalance,** balance, compensation, counterweight, equipoise ◆ *vb* **8 = cancel out,** balance out, compensate for, counteract, counterbalance, counterpoise, countervail, make up for, neutralize

offshoot *n* **1 = outgrowth,** branch, limb, scion, sprout **2 = by-product,** adjunct, appendage, development, spin-off

offspring *n* **1 = children,** brood, descendants, family, fry, heirs, issue, kids (*inf.*), progeny, scions, seed (*chiefly Biblical*), spawn, successors, young
Antonyms *n* ancestor, begetter, forebear, forefather, forerunner, parent, predecessor, procreator, progenitor

often *adv* **1 = frequently,** again and again, generally, many a time, much, oft (*arch. or poetic*), oftentimes (*arch.*), ofttimes (*arch.*), over and over again, repeatedly, time after time, time and again
Antonyms *adv* hardly ever, infrequently, irregularly, never, now and then, occasionally, rarely, scarcely, seldom

ogle *vb* **1 = leer,** eye up (*inf.*), gawp at (*Brit. sl.*), give the glad eye (*inf.*), give the once-over (*inf.*), lech *or* letch after (*inf.*), make sheep's eyes at (*inf.*)

ogre *n* **1, 2 = monster,** bogey, bogeyman, bugbear, demon, devil, giant, spectre

oil *vb* **12 = lubricate,** grease

Inf. to bribe someone. **15 oil the wheels.** to make things run smoothly. [C12: from OF *oile,* from L *oleum* (olive) oil, from *olea* olive tree, from Gk *elaia* OLIVE]
▸ **'oiler** *n* ▸ **'oil-,like** *adj*

oil cake *n* stock feed consisting of compressed cubes made from the residue of the crushed seeds of oil-bearing crops such as linseed.

oilcan ('ɔɪl,kæn) *n* a container with a long nozzle for applying lubricating oil to machinery.

oilcloth ('ɔɪl,klɒθ) *n* **1** waterproof material made by treating one side of a cotton fabric with a drying oil or a synthetic resin. **2** another name for **linoleum.**

oil drum *n* a metal drum used to contain or transport oil.

oilfield ('ɔɪl,fi:ld) *n* an area containing reserves of petroleum, esp. one that is already being exploited.

oilfired ('ɔɪl,faɪəd) *adj* (of central heating, etc.) using oil as fuel.

oilgas ('ɔɪl,gæs) *n* a gaseous mixture of hydrocarbons used as a fuel, obtained by the destructive distillation of mineral oils.

oilman ('ɔɪlmən) *n, pl* **oilmen. 1** a person who owns or operates oil wells. **2** a person who sells oil.

oil minister *n* a government official in charge of or representing the interests of an oil-producing country.

oil of cloves *n* another name for **clove oil.**

oil of vitriol *n* another name for **sulphuric acid.**

oil paint *n* paint made of pigment ground in oil, usually linseed oil.

oil painting *n* **1** a picture painted with oil paints. **2** the art or process of painting with oil paints. **3 he's** *or* **she's no oil painting.** *Inf.* he *or* she is not good-looking.

oil palm *n* a tropical African palm tree, the fruits of which yield palm oil.

oil rig *n* See **rig** (sense 6).

oil sand *n* a sandstone impregnated with hydrocarbons, esp. such deposits in Alberta, Canada.

oil-seed rape *n* another name for **rape**[2].

oil shale *n* a carbonaceous rock from which oil can be extracted.

oilskin ('ɔɪl,skɪn) *n* **1a** a cotton fabric treated with oil and pigment to make it waterproof. **1b** (*as modifier*): *an oilskin hat.* **2** (*often pl*) a protective outer garment of this fabric.

oil slick *n* a mass of floating oil covering an area of water.

oilstone ('ɔɪl,stəʊn) *n* a stone with a fine grain lubricated with oil and used for sharpening cutting tools. See also **whetstone.**

oil well *n* a boring into the earth or sea bed for the extraction of petroleum.

oily ❶ ('ɔɪlɪ) *adj* **oilier, oiliest. 1** soaked in or smeared with oil or grease. **2** consisting of, containing, or resembling oil. **3** flatteringly servile or obsequious.
▸ **'oilily** *adv* ▸ **'oiliness** *n*

oink (ɔɪŋk) *interj* an imitation or representation of the grunt of a pig.

ointment ❶ ('ɔɪntmənt) *n* **1** a fatty or oily medicated preparation applied to the skin to heal or protect. **2** a similar substance used as a cosmetic. [C14: from OF *oignement,* from L *unguentum* UNGUENT]

Oireachtas ('ɛrəkθəs) *n* the parliament of the Republic of Ireland. [Irish Gaelic: assembly, from OIrish *airech* nobleman]

Ojibwa (əʊ'dʒɪbwə) *n* **1** (*pl* **Ojibwas** *or* **Ojibwa**) a member of a North American Indian people living west of Lake Superior. **2** the language of this people.

O.K. ❶ (,əʊ'keɪ) *Inf.* ◆ *sentence substitute.* **1** an expression of approval or agreement. ◆ *adj* (*usually postpositive*), *adv* **2** in good or satisfactory condition. ◆ *vb* **O.K.s, O.K.ing** (,əʊ'keɪɪŋ), **O.K.ed** (,əʊ'keɪd). **3** (*tr*) to approve or endorse. ◆ *n, pl* **O.K.s. 4** approval or agreement. ◆ Also: **okay.** [C19: ?from *o(ll) k(orrect),* jocular alteration of *all correct*]

okapi (əʊ'kɑ:pɪ) *n, pl* **okapis** *or* **okapi.** a ruminant mammal of the forests of central Africa, having a reddish-brown coat with horizontal white stripes on the legs, and small horns. [C20: from a Central African word]

okay (,əʊ'keɪ) *sentence substitute, adj, adv, vb, n* a variant spelling of **O.K.**

okra ('əʊkrə) *n* **1** an annual plant of the Old World tropics, with yellow-and-red flowers and edible oblong green pods. **2** the pod of this plant, eaten in soups, stews, etc. See also **gumbo** (sense 1). [C18: of West African origin]

-ol[1] *suffix forming nouns.* denoting a chemical compound containing a hydroxyl group, esp. alcohols and phenols: *ethanol; quinol.* [from ALCOHOL]

-ol[2] *n combining form.* (not used systematically) a variant of **-ole**[1].

old ❶ (əʊld) *adj* **1** having lived or existed for a relatively long time: *an old man; an old tradition; an old house.* **2a** of or relating to advanced years or a long life: *old age.* **2b** (*as collective n;* preceded by *the*): *the old.* **2c old and young.** people of all ages. **3** decrepit or senile. **4** worn with age or use: *old clothes; an old car.* **5a** (*postpositive*) having lived or existed for a specified period: *a child who is six years old.* **5b** (*in combination*): *a six-year-old child.* **5c** (*as n in combination*): *a six-year-old.* **6** (*cap. when part of a name or title*) earlier or earliest of two or more things with the same name: *the old edition; the Old Testament.* **7** (*cap. when part of a name*) designating the form of a language in which the earliest known records are written: *Old English.* **8** (*prenominal*) familiar through long acquaintance or repetition: *an old friend; an old excuse.* **9** practised; hardened: *old in cunning.* **10** (*prenominal;* often preceded by *good*) cherished; dear: used as a term of affection or familiarity: *good old George.* **11** *Inf.* (with any of several nouns) used as a familiar form of address to a person: *old thing; old bean; old stick.* **12** skilled through long experience (esp. in **an old hand**). **13** out of date; unfashionable. **14** remote or distant in origin or time of origin: *an old culture.* **15** (*prenominal*) former; previous: *my old house was small.* **16a** (*prenominal*) established for a relatively long time: *an old member.* **16b** (*in combination*): *old-established.* **17** sensible, wise, or mature: *old beyond one's years.* **18** (intensifier) (esp. in **a high old time, any old thing, any old how,** etc.). **19 good old days.** an earlier period of time regarded as better than the present. **20 little old.** *Inf.* indicating affection, esp. humorous affection. **21 the old one** (*or* **gentleman**). *Inf.* a jocular name for **Satan.** ◆ *n* **22** an earlier or past time: *in days of old.* [OE *eald*]
▸ **'oldish** *adj* ▸ **'oldness** *n*

old age pension *n* a former name for **retirement pension.**
▸ **old age pensioner** *n*

Old Bailey ('beɪlɪ) *n* the Central Criminal Court of England.

Old Bill (bɪl) *n* (*functioning as pl,* preceded by *the*) *Brit. sl.* policemen collectively. [C20: ?from the World War I cartoon of a soldier with a drooping moustache]

old boy *n* **1** (*sometimes caps.*) *Brit.* a male ex-pupil of a school. **2** *Inf., chiefly Brit.* **2a** a familiar name used to refer to a man. **2b** an old man.

old boy network *n Brit. inf.* the appointment to power of former pupils of the same small group of public schools or universities.

Old Contemptibles *pl n* the British expeditionary force to France in 1914. [from the Kaiser's alleged reference to them as a "contemptible little army"]

old country *n* the country of origin of an immigrant or an immigrant's ancestors.

Old Dart *n* **the.** *Austral. sl.* Britain, esp. England. [C19: from ?]

olden ('əʊldᵊn) *adj* an archaic or poetic word for **old** (often in **in olden days** and **in olden times**).

Old English *n* **1** Also called: **Anglo-Saxon.** the English language from the time of the earliest Saxon settlements in the fifth century A.D. to about 1100. Abbrev.: **OE. 2** *Printing.* a Gothic typeface commonly used in England up to the 18th century.

Old English sheepdog *n* a breed of large bobtailed sheepdog with a profuse shaggy coat.

older ('əʊldə) *adj* **1** the comparative of **old. 2** Also (of people): **elder.** of greater age.

old-fashioned ❶ *adj* **1** belonging to, characteristic of, or favoured by former times; outdated: *old-fashioned ideas.* **2** favouring or adopting the dress, manners, fashions, etc., of a former time. **3** *Scot. & N English dialect.* old for one's age: *an old-fashioned child.* ◆ *n* **4** a cocktail containing spirit, bitters, fruit, etc.

Old French *n* the French language in its earliest forms, from about the 9th century up to about 1400. Abbrev.: **OF.**

old girl *n* **1** (*sometimes caps.*) *Brit.* a female ex-pupil of a school. **2** *Inf., chiefly Brit.* **2a** a familiar name used to refer to a woman. **2b** an old woman.

Old Glory *n* a nickname for the flag of the United States of America.

THESAURUS

oily *adj* **1, 2** = **greasy,** fatty, oiled, oleaginous, smeary, swimming **3** = **obsequious,** flattering, fulsome, glib, hypocritical, plausible, servile, smarmy (*Brit. inf.*), smooth, unctuous

ointment *n* **1** = **lotion,** balm, cerate, cream, embrocation, emollient, liniment, salve, unguent

O.K. *sentence substitute* **1** = **all right,** agreed, right, roger, very good, very well, yes ◆ *adj* **2** = **fine,** acceptable, accurate, adequate, all right, approved, convenient, correct, fair, good, in order, middling, not bad (*inf.*), passable, permitted, satisfactory, so-so (*inf.*), tolerable, up to scratch (*inf.*) ◆ *vb* **3** = **approve,** agree to, authorize, consent to, endorse, entitle, give one's consent to, give the go-ahead, give the green light, give the thumbs up (*inf.*), pass, rubber-stamp (*inf.*), sanction, say yes to ◆ *n* **4** = **approval,** agreement, approbation, assent, authorization, consent, endorsement, go-ahead (*inf.*), green light, permission, sanction, say-so (*inf.*), seal of approval
Antonyms *adj* ≠ **fine:** displeasing, inaccurate, inadequate, incorrect, not up to scratch (*inf.*), poor, unacceptable, unsatisfactory, unsuitable

old *adj* **1-3** = **aged,** advanced in years, ancient, decrepit, elderly, full of years, getting on, grey, grey-haired, grizzled, hoary, mature, over the hill (*inf.*), past it, past one's prime, patriarchal, senescent, senile, venerable **4** = **worn-out,** crumbling, done **8, 9, 12** = **long-established,** age-old, experienced, familiar, hardened, of long standing, practised, skilled, time-honoured, traditional, versed, veteran, vintage **13** = **out of date,** antediluvian, antiquated, antique, cast-off, cobwebby, dated, decayed, hackneyed, obsolete, old-fashioned, outdated, outmoded, out of the ark (*inf.*), passé, stale, superannuated, timeworn, unfashionable, unoriginal **14** = **early,** aboriginal, antique, archaic, bygone, immemorial, of old, of yore, olden (*arch.*), original, primeval, primitive, primordial, pristine, remote **15** = **former,** earlier, erstwhile, ex-, one-time, previous, quondam
Antonyms *adj* ≠ **aged:** immature, juvenile, young, youthful ≠ **out of date:** current, fashionable, modern, modish, new, novel, recent, up-to-date

old-fashioned *adj* **1** = **out of date,** ancient, antiquated, archaic, behind the times, cobwebby, corny (*sl.*), dated, dead, *démodé,* fusty, musty, not with it (*inf.*), obsolescent, obsolete, oldfangled, (old-)fogeyish, old hat, old-time, outdated, outmoded, out of style, out of the ark (*inf.*), passé, past, square (*inf.*), superannuated, unfashionable
Antonyms *adj* chic, contemporary, current, fashionable, happening (*inf.*), modern, modish, trendy (*Brit. inf.*), up-to-date, voguish, with it (*inf.*)

old gold *n* **a** a dark yellow colour, sometimes with a brownish tinge. **b** *(as adj): an old-gold carpet.*

old guard *n* **1** a group that works for a long-established or old-fashioned cause or principle. **2** the conservative element in a political party or other group. [C19: after Napoleon's imperial guard]

old hat *adj (postpositive)* old-fashioned or trite.

Old High German *n* a group of West Germanic dialects that eventually developed into modern German; High German up to about 1200. Abbrev.: **OHG.**

oldie ('əʊldɪ) *n Inf.* an old joke, song, film, person, etc.

Old Irish *n* the Celtic language of Ireland up to about 900 A.D.

old lady *n* an informal term for **mother** or **wife.**

Old Latin *n* the Latin language before the classical period, up to about 100 B.C.

Old Low German *n* the Saxon and Low Franconian dialects of German up to about 1200; the old form of modern Low German and Dutch. Abbrev.: **OLG.**

old maid *n* **1** a woman regarded as unlikely ever to marry; spinster. **2** *Inf.* a prim, fastidious, or excessively cautious person. **3** a card game in which players try to avoid holding the unpaired card at the end of the game.
▸ **ˌold-'maidish** *adj*

old man *n* **1** an informal term for **father** or **husband.** **2** *(sometimes caps.) Inf.* a man in command, such as an employer, foreman, or captain of a ship. **3** *Sometimes facetious.* an affectionate term used in addressing a man. **4** Also called: **southernwood.** an aromatic shrubby wormwood of S Europe, having drooping yellow flowers. **5** *Christianity.* the unregenerate aspect of human nature.

old man's beard *n* any of various plants having white feathery seed heads, esp. traveller's joy and Spanish moss.

old master *n* **1** one of the great European painters of the period 1500 to 1800. **2** a painting by one of these.

old moon *n* a phase of the moon lying between last quarter and new moon, when it appears as a waning crescent.

Old Nick (nɪk) *n Inf.* a jocular name for **Satan.**

Old Norse *n* the language or group of dialects of medieval Scandinavia and Iceland from about 700 to about 1350. Abbrev.: **ON.**

Old Pretender *n* **James Francis Edward Stewart**, 1688–1766, son of James II and pretender to the British throne.

Old Prussian *n* the former language of the non-German Prussians, belonging to the Baltic branch of the Indo-European family: extinct by 1700.

old rose *n* **a** a greyish-pink colour. **b** *(as adj): old-rose gloves.*

Old Saxon *n* the Saxon dialect of Low German up to about 1200, from which modern Low German is derived. Abbrev.: **OS.**

old school *n* **1** *Chiefly Brit.* one's former school. **2** a group of people favouring traditional ideas or conservative practices.

old school tie *n* **1** *Brit.* a distinctive tie that indicates which school the wearer attended. **2** the attitudes, loyalties, values, etc., associated with British public schools.

Old South *n* the American South before the Civil War.

oldster ('əʊldstə) *n Inf.* an older person.

old style *n Printing.* a type style reviving the characteristics of **old face,** a type style that originated in the 18th century and was characterized by having little contrast between thick and thin strokes.

Old Style *n* the former method of reckoning dates using the Julian calendar. Cf. **New Style.**

Old Testament *n* the collection of books comprising the sacred Scriptures of the Hebrews; the first part of the Christian Bible.

old-time Ⓣ *adj (prenominal)* of or relating to a former time; old-fashioned: *old-time dancing.*

old-timer *n* **1** a person who has been in a certain place, occupation, etc., for a long time. **2** *US.* an old man.

old wives' tale *n* a belief, usually superstitious or erroneous, passed on by word of mouth as a piece of traditional wisdom.

old woman Ⓣ *n* **1** an informal term for **mother** or **wife.** **2** a timid, fussy, or cautious person.
▸ **ˌold-'womanish** *adj*

Old World *n* that part of the world that was known before the discovery of the Americas; the eastern hemisphere.

old-world Ⓣ *adj* of or characteristic of former times, esp., in Europe, quaint or traditional.

Old World monkey *n* any monkey such as a macaque, baboon, or mandrill, which has nostrils that are close together and a nonprehensile tail.

-ole[1] *or* **-ol** *n combining form.* **1** denoting an organic unsaturated compound containing a 5-membered ring: *thiazole.* **2** denoting an aromatic organic ether: *anisole.* [from L *oleum* oil, from Gk *elaion,* from *elaia* olive]

-ole[2] *suffix of nouns.* indicating something small: *arteriole.* [from L *-olus,* dim. suffix]

oleaceous (ˌəʊlɪ'eɪʃəs) *adj* of, relating to, or belonging to a family of trees and shrubs which includes the ash, jasmine, privet, lilac, and olive. [C19: via NL from L *olea* OLIVE; see also OIL]

oleaginous Ⓣ (ˌəʊlɪ'ædʒɪnəs) *adj* **1** resembling or having the properties of oil. **2** containing or producing oil. [C17: from L *oleāginus, from olea* OLIVE; see also OIL]

oleander (ˌəʊlɪ'ændə) *n* a poisonous evergreen Mediterranean shrub or tree with fragrant white, pink, or purple flowers. Also called: **rosebay.** [C16: from Med. L, var. of *arodandrum,* ?from L RHODODENDRON]

oleate ('əʊlɪˌeɪt) *n* any salt or ester of oleic acid.

oleic acid (əʊ'liːɪk) *n* a colourless oily liquid unsaturated acid occurring, as the glyceride, in almost all natural fats; used in making soaps, ointments, cosmetics, and lubricating oils. Formula: $CH_3(CH_2)_7CH{:}CH(CH_2)_7COOH$. Systematic name: ***cis*-9-octadecenoic acid.** [C19 *oleic,* from L *oleum* oil + -IC]

olein ('əʊlɪɪn) *n* another name for **triolein.** [C19: from F *oléine,* from L *oleum* oil + -IN]

oleo- *combining form.* oil: *oleomargarine.* [from L *oleum* OIL]

oleomargarine (ˌəʊlɪəʊˌmɑːdʒə'riːn) *or* **oleomargarin** (ˌəʊlɪəʊ'mɑːdʒərɪn) *n* another name (esp. US) for **margarine.**

oleoresin (ˌəʊlɪəʊ'rezɪn) *n* **1** a semisolid mixture of a resin and essential oil, obtained from certain plants. **2** *Pharmacol.* a liquid preparation of resins and oils, obtained by extraction from plants.
▸ **ˌoleo'resinous** *adj*

oleum ('əʊlɪəm) *n, pl* **olea** ('əʊlɪə) *or* **oleums.** another name for **fuming sulphuric acid.** [from L: oil, referring to its oily consistency]

O level *n Brit.* **1a** the former basic (ordinary) level of the General Certificate of Education. **1b** *(as modifier): O-level maths.* **2** a pass in a particular subject at O level: *he has eight O levels.*

olfaction (ɒl'fækʃən) *n* **1** the sense of smell. **2** the act or function of smelling.

olfactory (ɒl'fæktərɪ, -trɪ) *adj* **1** of or relating to the sense of smell. ◆ *n, pl* **olfactories.** **2** *(usually pl)* an organ or nerve concerned with the sense of smell. [C17: from L *olfactus,* p.p. of *olfacere,* from *olere* to smell + *facere* to make]

OLG *abbrev. for* Old Low German.

oligarch ('ɒlɪˌgɑːk) *n* a member of an oligarchy.

oligarchy ('ɒlɪˌgɑːkɪ) *n, pl* **oligarchies.** **1** government by a small group of people. **2** a state or organization so governed. **3** a small body of individuals ruling such a state. **4** *Chiefly US.* a small clique of private citizens who exert a strong influence on government. [C16: via Med. L from Gk *oligarkhia,* from *oligos* few + -ARCHY]
▸ **ˌoli'garchic** *or* **ˌoli'garchical** *adj*

oligo- *or before a vowel* **olig-** *combining form.* indicating a few or little: *oligopoly.* [from Gk *oligos* little, few]

Oligocene ('ɒlɪgəʊˌsiːn, ɒ'lɪg-) *adj* **1** of, denoting, or formed in the third epoch of the Tertiary period. ◆ *n* **2 the.** the Oligocene epoch or rock series. [C19: OLIGO- + -CENE]

oligochaete ('ɒlɪgəʊˌkiːt) *n* **1** any freshwater or terrestrial annelid worm having bristles borne singly along the length of the body: includes the earthworms. ◆ *adj* **2** of or relating to this type of worm. [C19: from NL from OLIGO- + Gk *khaitē* long hair]

oligopoly (ˌɒlɪ'gɒpəlɪ) *n, pl* **oligopolies.** *Econ.* a market situation in which control over the supply of a commodity is held by a small number of producers. [C20: from OLIGO- + Gk *pōlein* to sell]
▸ **ˌoliˌgopo'listic** *adj*

oligospermia (ˌɒlɪgəʊ'spɜːmɪə) *n* the condition of having less than the normal number of spermatozoa in the semen: a cause of infertility in men.

oligotrophic (ˌɒlɪgəʊ'trɒfɪk) *adj* (of lakes and similar habitats) poor in nutrients and plant life and rich in oxygen. [C20: from OLIGO- + Gk *trophein* to nourish + -IC]
▸ **oligotrophy** (ˌɒlɪ'gɒtrəfɪ) *n*

olio ('əʊlɪˌəʊ) *n, pl* **olios.** **1** a dish of many different ingredients. **2** a miscellany or potpourri. [C17: from Sp. *olla* stew, from L: jar]

olivaceous (ˌɒlɪ'veɪʃəs) *adj* of an olive colour.

olive ('ɒlɪv) *n* **1** an evergreen oleaceous tree of the Mediterranean region having white fragrant flowers and edible fruits that are black when ripe. **2** the fruit of this plant, eaten as a relish and used as a source of olive oil. **3** the wood of the olive tree, used for ornamental work. **4a** a yellow-green colour like that of an unripe olive. **4b** *(as adj): an olive coat.* ◆ *adj* **5** of, relating to, or made of the olive tree, its wood, or its fruit. [C13: via OF from L *oliva,* rel. to Gk *elaia* olive tree]

olive branch *n* **1** a branch of an olive tree used to symbolize peace. **2** any offering of peace or conciliation.

olive crown *n* (esp. in ancient Greece and Rome) a garland of olive leaves awarded as a token of victory.

olive drab *n US.* **1a** a dull but fairly strong greyish-olive colour. **1b** *(as adj): an olive-drab jacket.* **2** cloth or clothes in this colour, esp. the uniform of the US Army.

olive green *n* **a** a colour that is greener, stronger, and brighter than olive; deep yellowish-green. **b** *(as adj): an olive-green coat.*

olive oil *n* a yellow to yellowish-green oil pressed from ripe olive fruits and used in cooking, medicines, etc.

olivine ('ɒlɪˌviːn, ˌɒlɪ'viːn) *n* any of a group of hard glassy olive-green

THESAURUS

old-time *adj* = **old-fashioned**, ancient, antique, bygone, former, past, vintage

old-womanish *adj* **2** = **fussy,** finicky, niggly, niminy-piminy, old-maidish (*inf.*), overcautious, overparticular, pernickety (*inf.*), prim, prudish, strait-laced, timid, timorous

old-world *adj* = **traditional,** archaic, ceremonious, chivalrous, courtly, gallant, old-fashioned, picturesque, quaint

oleaginous *adj* **1** = **oily,** adipose, fat, fatty, greasy, sebaceous, unguinous (*obs.*)

minerals consisting of magnesium iron silicate in crystalline form. [C18: from G, after its colour]

olla ('ɒlə) *n* **1** a cooking pot. **2** short for **olla podrida.** [Sp., from L *olla,* var. of *aulla* pot]

olla podrida ('ɒlə pɒ'driːdə) *n* **1** a Spanish dish, consisting of a stew with beans, sausages, etc. **2** an assortment; miscellany. [Sp., lit.: rotten pot]

Olmec ('ɒlmɛk) *n, pl* **Olmecs** *or* **Olmec. 1** a member of an ancient Central American Indian people who inhabited the S Gulf Coast of Mexico. ◆ *adj* **2** of or relating to this people.

ology ('ɒlədʒɪ) *n, pl* **ologies.** *Inf.* a science or other branch of knowledge. [C19: abstracted from words such as *theology, biology,* etc.; see -LOGY]

-ology *n combining form.* See **-logy.**

oloroso (ˌɒlə'rəusəu) *n, pl* **olorosos.** a full-bodied golden-coloured sweet sherry. [from Sp.: fragrant]

Olympiad (ə'lɪmpɪˌæd) *n* **1** a staging of the modern Olympic Games. **2** the four-year period between consecutive celebrations of the Olympic Games; a unit of ancient Greek chronology dating back to 776 B.C. **3** an international contest in chess, bridge, etc.

Olympian Ⓣ (ə'lɪmpɪən) *adj* **1** of or relating to Mount Olympus or to the classical Greek gods. **2** majestic or godlike in manner or bearing. **3** of or relating to ancient Olympia, a plain in Greece, or its inhabitants. ◆ *n* **4** a god of Mount Olympus. **5** an inhabitant of ancient Olympia. **6** *Chiefly US.* a competitor in the Olympic Games.

Olympic (ə'lɪmpɪk) *adj* **1** of or relating to the Olympic Games. **2** of or relating to ancient Olympia.

Olympic Games *n* (*functioning as sing or pl*) **1** the greatest Panhellenic festival, held every fourth year in honour of Zeus at ancient Olympia, consisting of games and festivities. **2** Also called: **the Olympics.** the modern revival of these games, consisting of international athletic and sporting contests held every four years in a selected country.

OM *abbrev. for* Order of Merit (a Brit. title).

-oma *n combining form.* indicating a tumour: *carcinoma.* [from Gk *-ōma*]

omasum (əu'meɪsəm) *n, pl* **omasa** (-sə). another name for **psalterium.** [C18: from L: bullock's tripe]

ombre *or US* **omber** ('ɒmbə) *n* an 18th-century card game. [C17: from Sp. *hombre* man, referring to the player who attempts to win the stakes]

ombudsman ('ɒmbudzmən) *n, pl* **ombudsmen.** an official who investigates citizens' complaints against the government or its servants. Also called (Brit.): **Parliamentary Commissioner.** See also **Financial Ombudsman.** [C20: from Swedish: commissioner]

-ome *n combining form.* denoting a mass or part of a specified kind: *rhizome.* [var. of -OMA]

omega ('əumɪgə) *n* **1** the 24th and last letter of the Greek alphabet (Ω, ω). **2** the ending or last of a series. [C16: from Gk *ō mega* big o]

omega minus *n* an unstable negatively charged elementary particle, classified as a baryon, that has a mass 3276 times that of the electron.

omelette *or esp. US* **omelet** ('ɒmlɪt) *n* a savoury or sweet dish of beaten eggs cooked in fat. [C17: from F *omelette,* changed from *alumette,* from *alumelle* sword blade, changed by mistaken division from *la lemelle,* from L (see LAMELLA); apparently from the flat shape of the omelette]

omen Ⓣ ('əumən) *n* **1** a phenomenon or occurrence regarded as a sign of future happiness or disaster. **2** prophetic significance. ◆ *vb* **3** (*tr*) to portend. [C16: from L]

omentum (əu'mentəm) *n, pl* **omenta** (-tə). *Anat.* a double fold of peritoneum connecting the stomach with other abdominal organs. [C16: from L: membrane, esp. a caul, from ?]

omertà *Italian.* (omer'ta) *n* a conspiracy of silence.

omicron (əu'maɪkrɒn, 'ɒmɪkrɒn) *n* the 15th letter in the Greek alphabet (Ο, ο). [from Gk *ō mikron* small o]

ominous Ⓣ ('ɒmɪnəs) *adj* **1** foreboding evil. **2** serving as or having significance as an omen. [C16: from L *ōminōsus,* from OMEN]
▸'**ominously** *adv* ▸'**ominousness** *n*

omission Ⓣ (əu'mɪʃən) *n* **1** something that has been omitted or neglected. **2** the act of omitting or the state of having been omitted. [C14: from L *omissiō,* from *omittere* to OMIT]
▸**o'missive** *adj*

omit Ⓣ (əu'mɪt) *vb* **omits, omitting, omitted.** (*tr*) **1** to neglect to do or include. **2** to fail (to do something). [C15: from L *omittere,* from *ob-* away + *mittere* to send]
▸**omissible** (əu'mɪsɪbᵊl) *adj* ▸**o'mitter** *n*

omni- *combining form.* all or everywhere: *omnipresent.* [from L *omnis* all]

omnibus ('ɒmnɪˌbʌs, -bəs) *n, pl* **omnibuses. 1** a formal word for **bus** (sense 1). **2** Also called: **omnibus volume.** a collection of works by one author or several works on a similar topic, reprinted in one volume. **3** Also called: **omnibus edition.** a television or radio programme consisting of two or more episodes of a serial broadcast earlier in the week. ◆ *adj* **4** (*prenominal*) of, dealing with, or providing for many different things or cases. [C19: from L, lit.: for all, dative pl of *omnis* all]

omnicompetent (ˌɒmnɪ'kɒmpɪtənt) *adj* able to judge or deal with all matters.
▸ˌ**omni'competence** *n*

omnidirectional (ˌɒmnɪdɪ'rɛkʃənᵊl, -daɪ-) *adj* (of an antenna) capable of transmitting and receiving radio signals equally in any direction of the horizontal plane.

omnifarious (ˌɒmnɪ'fɛərɪəs) *adj* of many or all varieties or forms. [C17: from LL *omnifārius,* from L *omnis* all + *-farius* doing]
▸ˌ**omni'fariously** *adv* ▸ˌ**omni'fariousness** *n*

omnific (ɒm'nɪfɪk) *or* **omnificent** (ɒm'nɪfɪsənt) *adj Rare.* creating all things. [C17: via Med. L from L *omni-* + *-ficus,* from *facere* to do]
▸**om'nificence** *n*

omnipotent Ⓣ (ɒm'nɪpətənt) *adj* **1** having very great or unlimited power. ◆ *n* **2 the Omnipotent.** an epithet for God. [C14: via OF from L *omnipotens* all-powerful, from OMNI- + *potens,* from *posse* to be able]
▸**om'nipotence** *n* ▸**om'nipotently** *adv*

omnipresent (ˌɒmnɪ'prɛzᵊnt) *adj* (esp. of a deity) present in all places at the same time.
▸ˌ**omni'presence** *n*

omniscient Ⓣ (ɒm'nɪsɪənt) *adj* **1** having infinite knowledge or understanding. **2** having very great or seemingly unlimited knowledge. [C17: from Med. L *omnisciens,* from L OMNI- + *scīre* to know]
▸**om'niscience** *n* ▸**om'nisciently** *adv*

omnium-gatherum ('ɒmnɪəm'gæðərəm) *n Often facetious.* a miscellaneous collection. [C16: from L *omnium* of all, + Latinized form of E *gather*]

omnivorous (ɒm'nɪvərəs) *adj* **1** eating any type of food indiscriminately. **2** taking in or assimilating everything, esp. with the mind. [C17: from L *omnivorus* all-devouring, from OMNI- + *vorāre* to eat greedily]
▸'**omniˌvore** *n* ▸**om'nivorously** *adv* ▸**om'nivorousness** *n*

omphalos ('ɒmfəˌlɒs) *n* **1** (in the ancient world) a sacred conical object, esp. a stone. The famous omphalos at Delphi was assumed to mark the centre of the earth. **2** the central point. **3** *Literary.* another word for **navel.** [Gk: navel]

on Ⓣ (ɒn) *prep* **1** in contact or connection with the surface of; at the upper surface of: *an apple on the ground; a mark on the tablecloth.* **2** attached to: *a puppet on a string.* **3** carried with: *I've no money on me.* **4** in the immediate vicinity of; close to or along the side of: *a house on the sea.* **5** within the time limits of (a day or date): *he arrived on Thursday.* **6** being performed upon or relayed through the medium of: *what's on the television?* **7** at the occasion of: *on his retirement.* **8** used to indicate support, subsistence, contingency, etc.: *he lives on bread.* **9a** regularly taking (a drug): *she's on the pill.* **9b** addicted to: *he's on heroin.* **10** by means of (something considered as a mode of transport) (esp. in **on foot, on horseback,** etc.). **11** in the process or course of: *on a journey; on strike.* **12** concerned with or relating to: *a programme on archaeology.* **13** used to indicate the basis or grounds, as of a statement or action: *I have it on good authority.* **14** against: used to indicate opposition: *they marched on the city at dawn.* **15** used to indicate a meeting or encounter: *he crept up on her.* **16** (used with an adj preceded by *the*) indicating the manner or way in which an action is carried out: *on the sly; on the cheap.* **17** staked or wagered as a bet upon: *ten pounds on that horse.* **18** *Inf.* charged to: *the drinks are on me.* ◆ *adv* (*often used as a particle*) **19** in the position or state required for the commencement or sustained continuation, as of a mechanical operation: *the radio's been on all night.* **20** attached to, surrounding, or placed in contact with something: *the child had nothing on.* **21** arranged: *we've nothing on for tonight.* **22** in a manner indicating continuity, persistence, etc.: *don't keep on about it; the play went on all afternoon.* **23** in a direction towards something, esp. forward: *we drove on towards London; march on!* **24 on and off.** intermittently; from time to time. **25 on and on.** without ceasing; continually. ◆ *adj* **26** functioning; operating: *the on position on a radio.* **27** (*postpositive*) *Inf.* performing, as on stage, etc.: *I'm on in five minutes.* **28** definitely taking place: *the match is on for Friday.* **29** tolerable or practicable, acceptable, etc.: *your plan just isn't on.* **30** *Cricket.* (of a bowler) bowling. **31 on at.** *Inf.* nagging: *she was always on at her husband.* ◆ *n* **32**

THESAURUS

Olympian *adj* **2** = **majestic**, elevated, exalted, glorious, godlike, lofty, rarefied, splendid, sublime

omen *n* **1** = **sign**, augury, foreboding, foretoken, indication, portent, premonition, presage, prognostic, prognostication, straw in the wind, warning, writing on the wall

ominous *adj* **1** = **threatening**, baleful, dark, fateful, forbidding, foreboding, inauspicious, menacing, minatory, portentous, premonitory, sinister, unpromising, unpropitious
Antonyms *adj* auspicious, encouraging, favourable, promising, propitious

omission *n* **2** = **exclusion**, default, failure, forgetfulness, gap, lack, leaving out, neglect, noninclusion, oversight
Antonyms *n* addition, inclusion, incorporation, insertion

omit *vb* **1, 2** = **leave out**, disregard, drop, eliminate, exclude, fail, forget, give (something) a miss (*inf.*), leave (something) undone, let (something) slide, miss (out), neglect, overlook, pass over, skip
Antonyms *vb* add, enter, include, incorporate, insert, put in

omnipotence *n* **1** = **supremacy**, divine right, invincibility, mastery, sovereignty, supreme power, undisputed sway
Antonyms *n* frailty, impotence, inability, inferiority, powerlessness, vulnerability, weakness

omnipotent *adj* **1** = **almighty**, all-powerful, supreme
Antonyms *adj* feeble, frail, impotent, incapable, inferior, powerless, vulnerable, weak

omniscient *adj* **1** = **all-knowing**, all-seeing, all-wise

on *adv* **24 on and off** = **occasionally**, by fits and starts, discontinuously, (every) now and again, fitfully, from time to time, intermittently, now and then, off and on, sometimes, spasmodically

Cricket. **32a** (*modifier*) relating to or denoting the leg side of a cricket field or pitch: *an on drive.* **32b** (*in combination*) used to designate certain fielding positions on the leg side: *mid-on.* [OE *an, on*]

ON *abbrev. for:* **1** Old Norse. **2** Ontario.

-on *suffix forming nouns.* **1** indicating a chemical substance: *interferon.* **2** (in physics) indicating an elementary particle or quantum: *electron; photon.* **3** (in chemistry) indicating an inert gas: *neon; radon.* **4** (in biochemistry) a molecular unit: *codon; operon.* [from ION]

onager ('ɒnədʒə) *n, pl* **onagri** (-ˌgraɪ) *or* **onagers. 1** a Persian variety of the wild ass. **2** an ancient war engine for hurling stones, etc. [C14: from LL: military engine for stone throwing, from L: wild ass, from Gk *onagros,* from *onos* ass + *agros* field]

onanism ('əʊnəˌnɪzəm) *n* **1** the withdrawal of the penis from the vagina before ejaculation. **2** masturbation. [C18: after *Onan,* son of Judah; see Genesis 38:9]
▸'**onanist** *n, adj* ▸ˌ**onan'istic** *adj*

ONC (in Britain) *abbrev. for* Ordinary National Certificate.

once ❶ (wʌns) *adv* **1** one time; on one occasion or in one case. **2** at some past time: *I could speak French once.* **3** by one step or degree (of relationship): *a cousin once removed.* **4** (*in conditional clauses, negatives, etc.*) ever; at all: *if you once forget it.* **5** multiplied by one. **6 once and away. 6a** conclusively. **6b** occasionally. **7 once and for all.** conclusively; for the last time. **8 once in a while.** occasionally; now and then. **9 once or twice** *or* **once and again.** a few times. **10 once upon a time.** used to begin fairy tales and children's stories. ◆ *conj* **11** (*subordinating*) as soon as; if ever: *once you begin, you'll enjoy it.* ◆ *n* **12** one occasion or case: *you may do it, this once.* **13 all at once. 13a** suddenly. **13b** simultaneously. **14 at once. 14a** immediately. **14b** simultaneously. **15 for once.** this time, if (or but) at no other time. [C12 *ones, anes,* adverbial genitive of *on, an* ONE]

once-over *n Inf.* **1** a quick examination or appraisal. **2** a quick but comprehensive piece of work. **3** a violent beating or thrashing (esp. in **give (a person** or **thing) the** (or **a**) **once-over**).

oncer ('wʌnsə) *n* **1** *Brit. sl.* (formerly) a one-pound note. **2** *Austral. sl.* a person elected to Parliament who can only expect to serve one term. **3** *Austral. & NZ.* something which happens only once. [C20: from ONCE]

oncogene ('ɒŋkəʊˌdʒiːn) *n* any of several genes, present in all cells, that when abnormally activated can cause cancer. [C20: from Gk *onkos* mass, tumour + GENE]
▸**oncogenic** (ˌɒŋkəʊ'dʒenɪk) *adj*

oncoming ❶ ('ɒnˌkʌmɪŋ) *adj* **1** coming nearer in space or time; approaching. ◆ *n* **2** the approach or onset: *the oncoming of winter.*

oncost ('ɒnˌkɒst) *n Brit.* **1** another word for **overhead** (sense 5). **2** (*sometimes pl*) another word for **overheads.**

OND (in Britain) *abbrev. for* Ordinary National Diploma.

on dit *French* (ɔ̃ di) *n, pl* **on dits** (ɔ̃ di). a rumour; piece of gossip. [lit.: it is said, they say]

one (wʌn) *determiner* **1a** single; lone; not two or more. **1b** (*as pron*)*: one is enough for now; one at a time.* **1c** (*in combination*): *one-eyed.* **2a** distinct from all others; only; unique: *one girl in a million.* **2b** (*as pron*)*: one of a kind.* **3a** a specified (person, item, etc.) as distinct from another or others of its kind: *raise one hand and then the other.* **3b** (*as pron*)*: which one is correct?* **4** a certain, indefinite, or unspecified (time); some: *one day you'll be sorry.* **5** *Inf.* an emphatic word for **a** or **an**[1]: *it was one hell of a fight.* **6** a certain (person): *one Miss Jones was named.* **7 (all) in one.** combined; united. **8 all one. 8a** all the same. **8b** of no consequence: *it's all one to me.* **9 at one.** (often foll. by *with*) in a state of agreement or harmony. **10 be made one.** to become married. **11 many a one.** many people. **12 neither one thing nor the other.** indefinite, undecided, or mixed. **13 never a one.** none. **14 one and all.** everyone, without exception. **15 one by one.** one at a time; individually. **16 one or two.** a few. **17 one way and another.** on balance. **18 one with another.** on average. ◆ *pron* **19** an indefinite person regarded as typical of every person: *one can't say any more than that.* **20** any indefinite person: used as the subject of a sentence to form an alternative grammatical construction to that of the passive voice: *one can catch fine trout in this stream.* **21** *Arch.* an unspecified person: *one came to him.* ◆ *n* **22** the smallest natural number and the first cardinal number; unity. **23** a numeral (1, I, i, etc.) representing this number. **24** *Inf.* a joke or story (esp. in **the one about**). **25** something representing, represented by, or consisting of one unit. **26** Also: **one o'clock.** one hour after noon or midnight. **27** a blow or setback (esp. in **one in the eye for**). **28 the Evil one.** Satan. **29 the Holy One** *or* **the One above.** God. ◆ Related prefixes: **mono-, uni-.** [OE *ān*]

-one *suffix forming nouns.* indicating that a chemical compound is a ketone: *acetone.* [arbitrarily from Gk *-ōnē,* fem. patronymic suffix, but ? infl. by *-one* in OZONE]

one another *pron* the reflexive form of plural pronouns when the action, attribution, etc., is reciprocal: *they kissed one another; knowing one another.* Also: **each other.**

one-armed bandit *n Inf.* a fruit machine operated by pulling down a lever at one side.

one-horse ❶ *adj* **1** drawn by or using one horse. **2** (*prenominal*) *Inf.* small or obscure: *a one-horse town.*

one-liner *n Inf.* a short joke or witty remark.

one-man *adj* consisting of or done by or for one man: *a one-man band; a one-man show.*

oneness ('wʌnnɪs) *n* **1** the state or quality of being one; singleness. **2** the state of being united; agreement. **3** uniqueness. **4** sameness.

one-night stand *n* **1** a performance given only once at any one place. **2** *Inf.* a sexual encounter lasting only one evening or night.

one-off *n Brit.* **a** something that is carried out or made only once. **b** (*as modifier*)*: a one-off job.*

one-on-one *adj* another term for **one-to-one** (sense 2).

one-parent family *n* another term for **single-parent family.**

one-piece *adj* **1** (of a garment, esp. a bathing costume) consisting of one piece. ◆ *n* **2** a garment, esp. a bathing costume, consisting of one piece.

onerous ❶ ('ɒnərəs, 'əʊ-) *adj* **1** laborious or oppressive. **2** *Law.* (of a contract, etc.) having or involving burdens or obligations. [C14: from L *onerōsus* burdensome, from *onus* load]
▸'**onerously** *adv* ▸'**onerousness** *n*

oneself (wʌn'sɛlf) *pron* **1a** the reflexive form of *one.* **1b** (intensifier): *one doesn't do that oneself.* **2** (*preceded by a copula*) one's normal or usual self: *one doesn't feel oneself after such an experience.*

one-sided ❶ *adj* **1** considering or favouring only one side of a matter, problem, etc. **2** having all the advantage on one side: *a one-sided boxing match.* **3** larger or more developed on one side. **4** having, existing on, or occurring on one side only.
▸ˌ**one-'sidedly** *adv* ▸ˌ**one-'sidedness** *n*

one-step *n* an early 20th-century ballroom dance with long quick steps, the precursor of the foxtrot.

one-stop *adj* having or providing a range of related services or goods in one place: *a one-stop shop.*

One Thousand Guineas *n* See **Thousand Guineas.**

one-time ❶ *adj* (*prenominal*) at some time in the past; former.

one-to-one *adj* **1** (of two or more things) corresponding exactly. **2** denoting a relationship or encounter in which someone is involved with only one other person: *one-to-one tuition.* **3** *Maths.* involving the pairing of each member of one set with only one member of another set, without remainder.

one-track ❶ *adj* **1** *Inf.* obsessed with one idea, subject, etc. **2** having or consisting of a single track.

one-up *adj Inf.* having an advantage or lead over someone or something.
▸ˌ**one-'upmanship** *n*

one-way *adj* **1** moving or allowing travel in one direction only: *one-way traffic; a one-way bus ticket.* **2** entailing no reciprocal obligation, action, etc.: *a one-way agreement.*

ongoing ❶ ('ɒnˌgəʊɪŋ) *adj* **1** actually in progress: *ongoing projects.* **2** continually moving forward; developing. **3** remaining in existence; continuing.

onion ('ʌnjən) *n* **1** an alliaceous plant having greenish-white flowers: cultivated for its rounded edible bulb. **2** the bulb of this plant, consisting of concentric layers of white succulent leaf bases with a pungent odour and taste. **3 know one's onions.** *Brit. sl.* to be fully acquainted with a subject. [C14: via Anglo-Norman from OF *oignon,* from L *unio* onion]
▸'**oniony** *adj*

onionskin ('ʌnjənˌskɪn) *n* a glazed translucent paper.

on line *adj* (**on-line** *when prenominal*). of or concerned with a peripheral device that is directly connected to and controlled by the central processing unit of a computer. Cf. **off line.**

onlooker ❶ ('ɒnˌlʊkə) *n* a person who observes without taking part.
▸'**onˌlooking** *adj*

only ❶ ('əʊnlɪ) *adj* (*prenominal*) **1 the.** being single or very few in number: *the only men left in town were too old to bear arms.* **2** (of a child) having no siblings. **3** unique by virtue of being superior to anything else; peerless. **4 one and only. 4a** (*adj*) incomparable; unique. **4b** (*as n*) the ob-

THESAURUS

once *adv* **1** = **at one time,** formerly, in the old days, in the past, in times gone by, in times past, long ago, once upon a time, previously **7 once and for all** = **for the last time,** conclusively, decisively, finally, for all time, for good, permanently, positively, with finality **8 once in a while** = **occasionally,** at intervals, at times, every now and then, from time to time, now and again, on occasion, sometimes ◆ *n* **14 at once: a** = **immediately,** directly, forthwith, instantly, now, right away, straight away, this (very) minute, without delay, without hesitation **b** = **simultaneously,** at *or* in one go (*inf.*), at the same time, together

oncoming *adj* **1** = **approaching,** advancing, forthcoming, imminent, impending, looming, onrushing, upcoming

one-horse *adj* **2** *Informal* = **small,** backwoods, inferior, minor, obscure, petty, quiet, sleepy, slow, small-time (*inf.*), tinpot (*Brit. inf.*), unimportant

onerous *adj* **1** = **difficult,** backbreaking, burdensome, crushing, demanding, exacting, exhausting, exigent, formidable, grave, hard, heavy, laborious, oppressive, responsible, taxing, weighty
Antonyms *adj* cushy (*inf.*), easy, effortless, facile, light, painless, simple, trifling, undemanding, unexacting, untaxing

one-sided *adj* **1** = **biased,** coloured, discriminatory, inequitable, lopsided, partial, partisan, prejudiced, unequal, unfair, unjust
Antonyms *adj* equal, equitable, fair, impartial, just, unbiased, uncoloured, unprejudiced

one-time *adj* = **former,** erstwhile, ex-, late, previous, quondam, sometime

one-track *adj* **1** *Informal* = **obsessed,** fanatical, fixated, monomaniacal, single-track

ongoing *adj* **1-3** = **in progress,** advancing, continuous, current, developing, evolving, extant, growing, progressing, successful, unfinished, unfolding

onlooker *n* = **observer,** bystander, eyewitness, looker-on, spectator, viewer, watcher, witness

only *adj* **1** = **sole,** exclusive, individual, lone, one ject of all one's love: *you are my one and only.* ◆ *adv* **5** without anyone or anything else being included; alone: *you have one choice only; only a genius can do that.* **6** merely or just: *it's only Henry.* **7** no more or no greater than: *we met only an hour ago.* **8** used in conditional clauses introduced by *if* to emphasize the impossibility of the condition ever being fulfilled: *if I had only known, this would never have happened.* **9** not earlier than; not...until: *I only found out yesterday.* **10 if only** *or* **if...only.** an expression used to introduce a wish, esp. one felt to be unrealizable. **11 only if.** never...except when. **12 only too. 12a** (intensifier): *he was only too pleased to help.* **12b** most regrettably (esp. in **only too true**). ◆ *sentence connector.* **13** but; however: used to introduce an exception or condition: *you may play outside: only don't go into the street.* [OE *ānlīc,* from *ān* ONE + *-līc* -LY[1]]

USAGE NOTE In informal English, *only* is often used as a sentence connector: *I would have phoned you, only I didn't know your number.* This use should be avoided in formal writing: *I would have phoned you if I'd known your number.* In formal speech and writing, *only* is placed directly before the word or words that it modifies: *she could interview only three applicants in the morning.* In all but the most formal contexts, however, it is generally regarded as acceptable to put *only* before the verb: *she could only interview three applicants in the morning.* Care must be taken not to create ambiguity, esp. in written English, in which intonation will not, as it does in speech, help to show to which item in the sentence *only* applies. A sentence such as *she only drinks tea in the afternoon* is capable of two interpretations and is therefore better rephrased either as *she drinks only tea in the afternoon* (i.e. no other drink) or *she drinks tea only in the afternoon* (i.e. at no other time).

o.n.o. *abbrev. for* or near(est) offer.

onomastics (ˌɒnəˈmæstɪks) *n* (*functioning as sing*) the study of proper names, esp. of their origins. [from Gk *onomastikos,* from *onomazein* to name, from *onoma* NAME]

onomatopoeia ❶ (ˌɒnəˌmætəˈpiːə) *n* **1** the formation of words whose sound is imitative of the sound of the noise or action designated, such as *hiss.* **2** the use of such words for poetic or rhetorical effect. [C16: via LL from Gk *onoma* name + *poiein* to make]
▸**ˌonoˌmatoˈpoeic** *or* **onomatopoetic** (ˌɒnəˌmætəpəʊˈetɪk) *adj* ▸**ˌonoˌmatoˈpoeically** *or* **ˌonoˌmatopoˈetically** *adv*

onrush ❶ (ˈɒnˌrʌʃ) *n* a forceful forward rush or flow.

onset ❶ (ˈɒnˌset) *n* **1** an attack; assault. **2** a start; beginning.

onshore (ˈɒnˈʃɔː) *adj, adv* **1** towards the land: *an onshore gale.* **2** on land; not at sea.

onside (ˌɒnˈsaɪd) *adj, adv* **1** *Football, etc.* (of a player) in a legal position, as when behind the ball or with a required number of opponents between oneself and the opposing team's goal line. Cf. **offside.** ◆ *adj* **2** taking one's part or side; working towards the same goal (esp. in **get someone onside**).

onslaught ❶ (ˈɒnˌslɔːt) *n* a violent attack. [C17: from MDu. *aenslag,* from *aan* ON + *slag* a blow]

Ont. *abbrev. for* Ontario.

Ontarian (ɒnˈtɛərɪən) *or* **Ontarioan** (ɒnˈtɛərɪˌəʊən) *adj* **1** of or denoting Ontario, a province of central Canada. ◆ *n* **2** a native or inhabitant of Ontario.

onto *or* **on to** (ˈɒntʊ; *unstressed* ˈɒntə) *prep* **1** to a position that is on: *step onto the train.* **2** having become aware of (something illicit or secret): *the police are onto us.* **3** into contact with: *get onto the factory.*

USAGE NOTE *Onto* is now generally accepted as a word in its own right. *On to* is still used, however, where *on* is considered to be part of the verb: *he moved on to a different town* as contrasted with *he jumped onto the stage.*

onto- *combining form.* existence or being: *ontogeny; ontology.* [from LGk, from *ōn* (stem *ont-*) being, present participle of *einai* to be]

ontogeny (ɒnˈtɒdʒənɪ) *or* **ontogenesis** (ˌɒntəˈdʒenɪsɪs) *n* the entire sequence of events involved in the development of an individual organism. Cf. **phylogeny.**
▸**ontogenic** (ˌɒntəˈdʒenɪk) *or* **ontogenetic** (ˌɒntədʒɪˈnetɪk) *adj* ▸**ˌontoˈgenically** *or* **ˌontogeˈnetically** *adv*

ontology (ɒnˈtɒlədʒɪ) *n* **1** *Philosophy.* the branch of metaphysics that deals with the nature of being. **2** *Logic.* the set of entities presupposed by a theory.
▸**ˌontoˈlogical** *adj* ▸**ˌontoˈlogically** *adv*

onus ❶ (ˈəʊnəs) *n, pl* **onuses.** a responsibility, task, or burden. [C17: L: burden]

onward (ˈɒnwəd) *adj* **1** directed or moving forwards, onwards, etc. ◆ *adv* **2** a variant of **onwards.**

onwards ❶ (ˈɒnwədz) *or* **onward** *adv* at or towards a point or position ahead, in advance, etc.

onychophoran (ˌɒnɪˈkɒfərən) *n* a wormlike invertebrate having a segmented body and short unjointed limbs, and breathing by means of tracheae. [from NL *Onychophora,* from Gk *onukh-* claw + -PHORE]

-onym *n combining form.* indicating a name or word: *pseudonym.* [from Gk *-onumon,* from var. of *onoma* name]

onyx (ˈɒnɪks) *n* **1** a variety of chalcedony with alternating black-and-white parallel bands, used as a gemstone. **2** a variety of calcite used as an ornamental stone; onyx marble. [C13: from L, from Gk: fingernail (so called from its veined appearance)]

ONZ *abbrev. for* Order of New Zealand.

oo- *or* **oö-** *combining form.* egg or ovum: *oosperm.* [from Gk *ōion* EGG[1]]

oocyte (ˈəʊəˌsaɪt) *n* an immature female germ cell that gives rise to an ovum after two meiotic divisions.

oodles (ˈuːdᵊlz) *pl n Inf.* great quantities: *oodles of money.* [C20: from ?]

oogamy (əʊˈɒgəmɪ) *n* sexual reproduction involving a small motile male gamete and a large much less motile female gamete.
▸**oˈogamous** *adj*

Ookpik (ˈuːkpɪk) *n Canad. trademark.* a sealskin doll resembling an owl, first made in 1963 by an Inuit and used abroad as a symbol of Canadian handicrafts. [from Eskimo *ukpik* a snowy owl]

oolite (ˈəʊəˌlaɪt) *n* any sedimentary rock, esp. limestone, consisting of tiny spherical concentric grains within a fine matrix. [C18: from F, from NL *oolitēs,* lit.: egg stone; prob. a translation of G *Rogenstein* roe stone]
▸**oolitic** (ˌəʊəˈlɪtɪk) *adj*

oolith (ˈəʊəˌlɪθ) *n* any of the tiny spherical grains of sedimentary rock of which oolite is composed.

oology (əʊˈɒlədʒɪ) *n* the branch of ornithology concerned with the study of birds' eggs.
▸**oological** (ˌəʊəˈlɒdʒɪkᵊl) *adj* ▸**oˈologist** *n*

oolong (ˈuːˌlɒŋ) *n* a kind of dark tea, grown in China, that is partly fermented before being dried. [C19: from Chinese *wu lung,* from *wu* black + *lung* dragon]

oomiak *or* **oomiac** (ˈuːmɪˌæk) *n* a variant of **umiak.**

oompah (ˈuːmˌpɑː) *n* a representation of the sound made by a deep brass instrument, esp. in military band music.

oomph (ʊmf) *n Inf.* **1** enthusiasm, vigour, or energy. **2** sex appeal. [C20: from ?]

oops (ʊps, uːps) *interj* an exclamation of surprise or of apology as when someone drops something or makes a mistake.

ooze[1] ❶ (uːz) *vb* **oozes, oozing, oozed. 1** (*intr*) to flow or leak out slowly, as through small holes. **2** to emit (moisture, etc.). **3** (*tr*) to overflow with: *to ooze charm.* **4** (*intr;* often foll. by *away*) to disappear or escape gradually. ◆ *n* **5** a slow flowing or leaking. **6** an infusion of vegetable matter, such as oak bark, used in tanning. [OE *wōs* juice]

ooze[2] ❶ (uːz) *n* **1** a soft thin mud found at the bottom of lakes and rivers. **2** a fine-grained marine deposit consisting of the hard parts of planktonic organisms. **3** muddy ground, esp. of bogs. [OE *wāse* mud]

oozy[1] ❶ (ˈuːzɪ) *adj* **oozier, ooziest.** moist or dripping.

oozy[2] ❶ (ˈuːzɪ) *adj* **oozier, ooziest.** of, resembling, or containing mud; slimy.
▸**ˈoozily** *adv* ▸**ˈooziness** *n*

OP *abbrev. for:* **1** Ordo Praedicatorum (the Dominicans). [L: Order of Preachers] **2** organophosphate.

op. *abbrev. for:* **1** opera. **2** operation. **3** operator. **4** optical. **5** opposite. **6** opus.

o.p. *or* **O.P.** *abbrev. for* out of print.

opacity ❶ (əʊˈpæsɪtɪ) *n, pl* **opacities. 1** the state or quality of being opaque. **2** the degree to which something is opaque. **3** an opaque object or substance. **4** obscurity of meaning; unintelligibility.

opah (ˈəʊpə) *n* a large soft-finned deep-sea teleost fish having a deep, brilliantly coloured body. Also called: **moonfish, kingfish.** [C18: of West African origin]

opal (ˈəʊpᵊl) *n* an amorphous form of hydrated silicon dioxide that can be of almost any colour. It is used as a gemstone. [C16: from L *opalus,* from Gk *opallios,* from Sansk. *upala* precious stone]
▸**ˈopal-ˌlike** *adj*

opalescent ❶ (ˌəʊpəˈlesᵊnt) *adj* having or emitting an iridescence like that of an opal.
▸**ˌopaˈlesce** *vb* ▸**ˌopalˈescence** *n*

THESAURUS

and only, single, solitary, unique ◆ *adv* **5-7** = **merely**, at most, barely, exclusively, just, purely, simply

onomatopoeic *adj* **1** = **imitative**, echoic, onomatopoetic

onrush *n* = **surge**, charge, flood, flow, onset, onslaught, push, rush, stampede, stream

onset *n* **1** = **attack**, assault, charge, onrush, onslaught **2** = **beginning**, inception, kick-off (*inf.*), outbreak, start
Antonyms *n* ≠ **beginning:** conclusion, culmination, end, ending, finish, outcome, termination, wind-up

onslaught *n* = **attack**, assault, blitz, charge, offensive, onrush, onset
Antonyms *n* defensive, escape, flight, recession, retreat, rout, stampede, withdrawal

onus *n* = **burden**, liability, load, obligation, responsibility, task
Antonyms *n* easement, exemption, exoneration, liberation, pardon, release, relief, remission

onwards *adv* = **ahead**, beyond, forth, forward, in front, on

ooze[1] *vb* **1, 2** = **seep**, bleed, discharge, drain, dribble, drip, drop, emit, escape, exude, filter, leach, leak, overflow with, percolate, strain, sweat, weep

ooze[2] *n* **1** = **mud**, alluvium, gloop (*inf.*), mire, muck, silt, slime, slob (*Irish*), sludge

oozy[1] *adj* = **moist**, dripping, sweaty, weeping

oozy[2] *adj* = **slimy**, miry, mucky, sloppy, sludgy

opacity *n* **1** = **opaqueness**, cloudiness, density, dullness, filminess, impermeability, milkiness, murkiness, obscurity

opalescent *adj* = **iridescent**, lustrous, nacre-

opal glass *n* glass that is opalescent or white, made by the addition of fluorides.

opaline ('əupəˌlaɪn) *adj* **1** opalescent. ◆ *n* **2** an opaque or semiopaque whitish glass.

opaque ❶ (əu'peɪk) *adj* **1** not transmitting light; not transparent or translucent. **2** not reflecting light; lacking lustre or shine; dull. **3** hard to understand; unintelligible. **4** unintelligent; dense. ◆ *n* **5** *Photog.* an opaque pigment used to block out areas on a negative. ◆ *vb* **opaques, opaquing, opaqued.** (*tr*) **6** to make opaque. **7** *Photog.* to block out areas on (a negative), using an opaque. [C15: from L *opācus* shady]
▸**o'paquely** *adv* ▸**o'paqueness** *n*

op art (ɒp) *n* a style of abstract art chiefly concerned with the exploitation of optical effects such as the illusion of movement. [C20 *op*, short for *optical*]

op. cit. (in textual annotations) *abbrev. for* opere citato. [L: in the work cited]

ope (əup) *vb* **opes, oping, oped,** *adj* an archaic or poetic word for **open.**

OPEC ('əupɛk) *n acronym for* Organization of Petroleum-Exporting Countries.

open ❶ ('əupᵊn) *adj* **1** not closed or barred. **2** affording free passage, access, view, etc.; not blocked or obstructed. **3** not sealed, fastened, or wrapped. **4** having the interior part accessible: *an open drawer.* **5** extended, expanded, or unfolded: *an open flower.* **6** ready for business. **7** able to be obtained; available: *the position is no longer open.* **8** unobstructed by buildings, trees, etc.: *open countryside.* **9** free to all to join, enter, use, visit, etc.: *an open competition.* **10** unengaged or unoccupied: *the doctor has an hour open for you to call.* **11** See **open season. 12** not decided or finalized: *an open question.* **13** ready to entertain new ideas; not biased or prejudiced. **14** unreserved or candid. **15** liberal or generous: *an open hand.* **16** extended or eager to receive (esp. in **with open arms**). **17** exposed to view; blatant: *open disregard of the law.* **18** liable or susceptible: *you will leave yourself open to attack.* **19** (of climate or seasons) free from frost; mild. **20** free from navigational hazards, such as ice, sunken ships, etc. **21** having large or numerous spacing or apertures: *open ranks.* **22** full of small openings or gaps; porous: *an open texture.* **23** *Music.* **23a** (of a string) not stopped with the finger. **23b** (of a pipe, such as an organ pipe) not closed at either end. **23c** (of a note) played on such a string or pipe. **24** *Commerce.* **24a** in operation; active: *an open account.* **24b** unrestricted; unlimited: *open credit; open insurance cover.* **25** See **open cheque. 26** (of a return ticket) not specifying a date for travel. **27** *Sport.* (of a goal, court, etc.) unguarded or relatively unprotected. **28** (of a wound) exposed to the air. **29** (esp. of the large intestine) free from obstruction. **30** undefended and of no military significance: *an open city.* **31** *Phonetics.* **31a** denoting a vowel pronounced with the lips relatively wide apart. **31b** denoting a syllable that does not end in a consonant, as in *pa.* **32** *Maths.* (of a set) containing points whose neighbourhood consists of other points of the same set. **33** *Computing.* designed to an internationally agreed standard in order to allow communication between computers, irrespective of size, manufacturer, etc. ◆ *vb* **34** to move from a closed or fastened position: *to open a window.* **35** (when *intr*, foll. by *on* or *onto*) to render, be, or become accessible or unobstructed: *to open a road; to open a parcel.* **36** (*intr*) to come into or appear in view: *the lake opened before us.* **37** to extend or unfold or cause to extend or unfold: *to open a newspaper.* **38** to disclose or uncover or be disclosed or uncovered: *to open one's heart.* **39** to cause (the mind) to become receptive or (of the mind) to become receptive. **40** to operate or cause to operate: *to open a shop.* **41** (when *intr*, sometimes foll. by *out*) to make or become less compact or dense in structure: *to open ranks.* **42** to set or be set in action; start: *to open the batting.* **43** (*tr*) to arrange for (a bank account, etc.), usually by making an initial deposit. **44** to turn to a specified point in (a book, etc.): *open at page one.* **45** *Law.* to make the opening statement in (a case before a court of law). **46** (*intr*) *Cards.* to bet, bid, or lead first on a hand. ◆ *n* **47** (often preceded by *the*) any wide or unobstructed space or expanse, esp. of land or water. **48** See **open air. 49** *Sport.* a competition which anyone may enter. **50 bring** (*or* **come**) **into the open.** to make (*or* become) evident or public. ◆ See also **open up.** [OE]
▸**'openable** *adj* ▸**'opener** *n* ▸**'openly** *adv* ▸**'openness** *n*

open air ❶ *n* **a** the place or space where the air is unenclosed; the outdoors. **b** (*as modifier*): *an open-air concert.*

open-and-shut ❶ *adj* easily decided or solved; obvious: *an open-and-shut case.*

opencast mining ('əupᵊnˌkɑːst) *n Brit.* mining by excavating from the surface. Also called: (esp. US) **strip mining,** (Austral. and NZ) **open cut mining.** [C18: from OPEN + arch. *cast* ditch, cutting]

open chain *n* a chain of atoms in a molecule that is not joined at its ends into the form of a ring.

open cheque *n* an uncrossed cheque that can be cashed at the drawee bank.

open circuit *n* an incomplete electrical circuit in which no current flows.

Open College *n* **the.** (in Britain) a college of art founded in 1987 for mature students studying foundation courses in arts and crafts by television programmes, written material, and tutorials.

open day *n* an occasion on which an institution, such as a school, is open for inspection by the public.

open door *n* **1** a policy or practice by which a nation grants opportunities for trade to all other nations equally. **2** free and unrestricted admission. ◆ *adj* **open-door. 3** open to all; accessible.

open-ended *adj* **1** without definite limits, as of duration or amount: *an open-ended contract.* **2** denoting a question, esp. one on a questionnaire, that cannot be answered "yes", "no", or "don't know".

open-eyed *adj* **1** with the eyes wide open, as in amazement. **2** watchful; alert.

open-faced *adj* **1** having an ingenuous expression. **2** (of a watch) having no lid or cover other than the glass.

open-handed ❶ *adj* generous.
▸**ˌopen-'handedly** *adv* ▸**ˌopen-'handedness** *n*

open-hearted *adj* **1** kindly and warm. **2** disclosing intentions and thoughts clearly; candid.
▸**ˌopen-'heartedness** *n*

open-hearth furnace *n* (esp. formerly) a steel-making reverbatory furnace in which pig iron and scrap are contained in a shallow hearth and heated by producer gas.

open-heart surgery *n* surgical repair of the heart during which the blood circulation is often maintained mechanically.

open house *n* **1** a US and Canad. name for **at-home. 2 keep open house.** to be always ready to receive guests.

opening ❶ ('əupənɪŋ) *n* **1** the act of making or becoming open. **2** a vacant or unobstructed space, esp. one that will serve as a passageway; gap. **3** *Chiefly US.* a tract in a forest in which trees are scattered or absent. **4** the first part or stage of something. **5a** the first performance of something, esp. a theatrical production. **5b** (*as modifier*): *the opening night.* **6** a specific or formal sequence of moves at the start of any of certain games, esp. chess or draughts. **7** an opportunity or chance. **8** *Law.* the preliminary statement made by counsel to the court or jury.

opening batsman *n Cricket.* one of the two batsmen beginning an innings.

THESAURUS

ous, opaline, pearly, prismatic, rainbow-hued, shot

opaque *adj* **2** = **cloudy**, clouded, dim, dull, filmy, hazy, impenetrable, lustreless, muddied, muddy, murky, obfuscated, turbid **3** = **incomprehensible**, abstruse, baffling, cryptic, difficult, enigmatic, obscure, unclear, unfathomable, unintelligible
Antonyms *adj* ≠ **cloudy:** bright, clear, crystal clear, limpid, lucid, pellucid, transparent, transpicuous ≠ **incomprehensible:** clear, crystal clear, lucid

open *adj* **1-3** = **unclosed**, agape, ajar, gaping, revealed, unbarred, uncovered, unfastened, unlocked, unobstructed, unsealed, yawning **5** = **extended**, expanded, spread out, unfolded, unfurled **8** = **unenclosed**, airy, bare, clear, exposed, extensive, free, not built-up, rolling, spacious, sweeping, uncluttered, uncrowded, unfenced, unsheltered, wide, wide-open **9, 10** = **accessible**, available, free, free to all, general, nondiscriminatory, public, unconditional, unengaged, unoccupied, unqualified, unrestricted, up for grabs (*inf.*), vacant **12** = **unresolved**, arguable, debatable, moot, undecided, unsettled, up in the air, yet to be decided **13** = **objective**, disinterested, free, impartial, receptive, unbiased, uncommitted, unprejudiced **14** = **frank**, above board, artless, candid, fair, guileless, honest, ingenuous, innocent, natural, sincere, transparent, unreserved **15** = **generous**, bounteous, bountiful, liberal, munificent, prodigal **17** = **obvious**, apparent, avowed, barefaced, blatant, bold, clear, conspicuous, downright, evident, flagrant, frank, manifest, noticeable, overt, plain, unconcealed, undisguised, visible **18** = **unprotected**, an easy target, at the mercy of, defenceless, exposed, liable, susceptible, undefended, unfortified, vulnerable **22** = **gappy**, filigree, fretted, holey, honeycombed, lacy, loose, openwork, porous, spongy ◆ *vb* **34** = **unfasten**, clear, crack, throw wide, unbar, unblock, unclose, uncork, uncover, undo, unlock, unseal, untie, unwrap **37** = **unfold**, expand, spread (out), unfurl, unroll **38** = **disclose**, divulge, exhibit, explain, lay bare, pour out, show, uncover **42** = **start**, begin, begin business, commence, get *or* start the ball rolling, inaugurate, initiate, kick off (*inf.*), launch, set in motion, set up shop
Antonyms *adj* ≠ **unclosed:** closed, fastened, locked, sealed, shut ≠ **unenclosed:** bounded, confined, covered, crowded, enclosed, limited, obstructed, restricted ≠ **accessible:** inaccessible, private, protected, restricted ≠ **objective:** biased, partial, prejudiced ≠ **frank:** artful, cunning, introverted, reserved, secretive, sly, withdrawn ≠ **obvious:** covert, disguised, hidden, secret, veiled ≠ **unprotected:** defended, protected ◆ *vb* ≠ **unfasten:** block, close, fasten, lock, obstruct, seal, shut ≠ **unfold:** fold ≠ **start:** close, conclude, end, finish, terminate

open-air *modifier* = **outdoor**, alfresco

open-and-shut *adj* = **straightforward**, foregone, noncontroversial, obvious, simple

open-handed *adj* = **generous**, bountiful, free, lavish, liberal, munificent, prodigal, unstinting
Antonyms *adj* avaricious, close-fisted, grasping, grudging, mean, miserly, parsimonious, penny-pinching (*inf.*), penurious, stingy, tight-fisted

opening *n* **1, 4** = **beginning**, birth, commencement, dawn, inauguration, inception, initiation, kickoff (*inf.*), launch, launching, onset, opening move, outset, overture, start **2** = **hole**, aperture, breach, break, chink, cleft, crack, fissure, gap, interstice, orifice, perforation, rent, rupture, slot, space, split, vent **7** = **opportunity**, break (*inf.*), chance, look-in (*inf.*), occasion, place, vacancy, window
Antonyms *n* ≠ **beginning:** cessation, close, completion, conclusion, culmination, ending, finale, finish, termination, winding up (*inf.*) ≠ **hole:** blockage, closing, closure, obstruction, occlusion, plug, seal, stoppage

openly *adv* **14** = **candidly**, face to face, forthrightly, frankly, overtly, plainly, straight from the shoulder (*inf.*), unhesitatingly, unreservedly **17** = **blatantly**, brazenly, flagrantly, in full view, in public, publicly, shamelessly, unabashedly, unashamedly, wantonly, without pretence

opening time *n Brit.* the time at which public houses can legally start selling alcoholic drinks.
open learning *n* a system of further education on a flexible part-time basis.
open letter *n* a letter, esp. one of protest, addressed to a person but also made public, as through the press.
open market *n* **a** a market in which prices are determined by supply and demand, there are no barriers to entry, and trading is not restricted to a specific area. **b** *(as modifier): open-market value.*
open marriage *n* a marriage in which the partners agree to pursue separate social and sexual lives.
open-minded Ⓣ *adj* having a mind receptive to new ideas, arguments, etc.; unprejudiced.
▸ **ˌopen-ˈmindedness** *n*
open-mouthed *adj* **1** having an open mouth, esp. in surprise. **2** greedy or ravenous. **3** clamorous or vociferous.
open-plan *adj* having no or few dividing walls between areas: *an open-plan office floor.*
open position *n Commerce.* a situation in which a dealer in commodities, securities, or currencies has either unsold stock or uncovered sales.
open prison *n* a penal establishment in which the prisoners are trusted to serve their sentences and so do not need to be locked up.
open punctuation *n* punctuation which has relatively few semicolons, commas, etc. Cf. **close punctuation.**
open question *n* **1** a matter which is undecided. **2** a question that cannot be answered with "yes" or "no" but requires a developed answer.
open-reel *adj* another term for **reel-to-reel.**
open season *n* a specified period of time in the year when it is legal to hunt or kill game or fish protected at other times by law.
open secret *n* something that is supposed to be secret but is widely known.
open sesame *n* a very successful means of achieving a result. [from the magical words used in the *Arabian Nights' Entertainments* to open the robbers' den]
open shop *n* an establishment in which persons are employed irrespective of their membership or nonmembership of a trade union.
open slather *n* See **slather.**
Open University *n* **the.** (in Britain) a university founded in 1969 for mature students studying by television and radio lectures, correspondence courses, local counselling, and summer schools.
open up *vb (adv)* **1** *(intr)* to start firing a gun or guns. **2** *(intr)* to speak freely or without restraint. **3** *(intr) Inf.* (of a motor vehicle) to accelerate. **4** *(tr)* to render accessible: *the motorway opened up the remote areas.* **5** *(intr)* to make or become more exciting or lively: *the game opened up after half-time.*
open verdict *n* a finding by a coroner's jury of death without stating the cause.
openwork (ˈəupᵊnˌwɜːk) *n* ornamental work, as of metal or embroidery, having a pattern of openings or holes.
opera[1] (ˈɒpərə, ˈɒprə) *n* **1** an extended dramatic work in which music constitutes a dominating feature. **2** the branch of music or drama represented by such works. **3** the score, libretto, etc., of an opera. **4** a theatre where opera is performed. [C17: via It. from L: work, a work, pl of *opus* work]
opera[2] (ˈɒpərə) *n* a plural of **opus.**
operable (ˈɒpərəbᵊl, ˈɒprə-) *adj* **1** capable of being treated by a surgical operation. **2** capable of being operated. **3** capable of being put into practice.
▸ **ˌoperaˈbility** *n* ▸ **ˈoperably** *adv*
opéra bouffe (ˈɒpərə ˈbuːf) *n, pl* **opéras bouffes** (ˈɒpərə ˈbuːf). a type of light or satirical opera common in France during the 19th century. [F: comic opera]
opera buffa (ˈbuːfə) *n, pl* **opera buffas.** comic opera, esp. that originating in Italy during the 18th century. [It.: comic opera]
opéra comique (kɒˈmiːk) *n, pl* **opéras comiques.** (ˈɒpərə kɒˈmiːk). a type of opera current in France during the 19th century and characterized by spoken dialogue. [F: comic opera: it originated in satirical parodies of grand opera]
opera glasses *pl n* small low-powered binoculars used by audiences in theatres, etc.
opera hat *n* a collapsible top hat operated by a spring.
opera house *n* a theatre designed for opera.
operand (ˈɒpəˌrænd) *n* a quantity or function upon which a mathematical or logical operation is performed. [C19: from L *operandum* (something) to be worked upon, from *operārī* to work]
operant (ˈɒpərənt) *adj* **1** producing effects; operating. ◆ *n* **2** a person or thing that operates. **3** *Psychol.* any response by an organism that is not directly caused by stimulus.
opera seria (ˈsɪərɪə) *n, pl* **opera serias.** a type of opera current in 18th-century Italy based on a serious plot, esp. a mythological tale. [It.: serious opera]
operate Ⓣ (ˈɒpəˌreɪt) *vb* **operates, operating, operated. 1** to function or cause to function. **2** *(tr)* to control the functioning of. **3** to manage, direct, run, or pursue (a business, system, etc.). **4** *(intr)* to perform a surgical operation (upon a person or animal). **5** *(intr)* to produce a desired effect. **6** *(tr; usually foll. by on)* to treat or process in a particular or specific way. **7** *(intr)* to conduct military or naval operations. **8** *(intr)* to deal in securities on a stock exchange. [C17: from L *operārī* to work]
operatic (ˌɒpəˈrætɪk) *adj* **1** of or relating to opera. **2** histrionic or exaggerated.
▸ **ˌoperˈatically** *adv*
operating budget *n Accounting.* a forecast of the sales revenue, production costs, overheads, cash flow, etc., of an organization, used to monitor its trading activities, usually for one year.
operating cycle *n* the time taken by a firm to convert its raw materials into finished goods and thereafter sell them and collect payment.
operating system *n* the set of software controlling a computer.
operating theatre *n* a room in which surgical operations are performed.
operation Ⓣ (ˌɒpəˈreɪʃən) *n* **1** the act, process, or manner of operating. **2** the state of being in effect, in action, or operative (esp. in **in** *or* **into operation**). **3** a process, method, or series of acts, esp. of a practical or mechanical nature. **4** *Surgery.* any manipulation of the body or one of its organs or parts to repair damage, arrest the progress of a disease, remove foreign matter, etc. **5a** a military or naval action, such as a campaign, manoeuvre, etc. **5b** *(cap. and prenominal when part of a name): Operation Crossbow.* **6** *Maths.* any procedure, such as addition, in which one or more numbers or quantities are operated upon according to specific rules. **7** a commercial or financial transaction.
operational Ⓣ (ˌɒpəˈreɪʃənᵊl) *adj* **1** of or relating to an operation. **2** in working order and ready for use. **3** *Mil.* capable of, needed in, or actually involved in operations.
▸ **ˌoperˈationally** *adv*
operationalism (ˌɒpəˈreɪʃənəˌlɪzəm) *or* **operationism** (ˌɒpəˈreɪʃəˌnɪzəm) *n Philosophy.* the theory that scientific terms are defined by the experimental operations which determine their applicability.
▸ **ˌoperˌationalˈistic** *adj*
operations research *n* the analysis of problems in business and industry involving quantitative techniques. Also called: **operational research.**
operative Ⓣ (ˈɒpərətɪv) *adj* **1** in force, effect, or operation. **2** exerting force or influence. **3** producing a desired effect; significant: *the operative word.* **4** of or relating to a surgical procedure. ◆ *n* **5** a worker, esp. one with a special skill. **6** *US.* a private detective.
▸ **ˈoperatively** *adv* ▸ **ˈoperativeness** *or* **ˌoperaˈtivity** *n*
operator Ⓣ (ˈɒpəˌreɪtə) *n* **1** a person who operates a machine, instrument, etc., esp. a telephone switchboard. **2** a person who owns or operates an industrial or commercial establishment. **3** a speculator, esp. one who operates on currency or stock markets. **4** *Inf.* a person who manipulates affairs and other people. **5** *Maths.* any symbol, term, letter, etc., used to indicate or express a specific operation or process, such as ∫ (the integral operator).
operculum (əʊˈpɜːkjʊləm) *n, pl* **opercula** (-lə) *or* **operculums. 1** *Zool.* **1a** the hard bony flap covering the gill slits in fishes. **1b** the bony plate in certain gastropods covering the opening of the shell when the body is withdrawn. **2** *Biol. & Bot.* any other covering or lid in various organisms. [C18: via NL from L: lid, from *operīre* to cover]
▸ **oˈpercular** *or* **operculate** (əʊˈpɜːkjʊlɪt, -ˌleɪt) *adj*
operetta (ˌɒpəˈrɛtə) *n* a type of comic or light-hearted opera. [C18: from It.: a small OPERA[1]]
▸ **ˌoperˈettist** *n*

THESAURUS

Antonyms *adv* covertly, furtively, in camera, privately, quietly, secretly, slyly, surreptitiously
open-minded *adj* = **unprejudiced**, broad, broad-minded, catholic, dispassionate, enlightened, free, impartial, liberal, reasonable, receptive, tolerant, unbiased, undogmatic
Antonyms *adj* assertive, biased, bigoted, dogmatic, intolerant, narrow-minded, opinionated, pig-headed, prejudiced, uncompromising
openness *n* **14** = **frankness**, artlessness, candidness, candour *or* (*US*) candor, freedom, freeness, guilelessness, honesty, ingenuousness, naturalness, open-heartedness, sincerity *or* sincereness, transparency, unreservedness
operate *vb* **1** = **work**, act, be in action, be in business, function, go, perform, run **2** = **handle**, be in charge of, manage, manoeuvre, use, work **4** = **perform surgery**
Antonyms *vb* ≠ **work:** break down, conk out (*inf.*), cut out (*inf.*), fail, falter, halt, seize up, stall, stop
operation *n* **1** = **procedure**, action, affair, course, exercise, motion, movement, performance, process, use, working **2 in operation** = **in action**, effective, functioning, going, in business, in force, operative **4** = **surgery 5** = **manoeuvre**, assault, campaign, exercise **7** = **undertaking**, affair, business, deal, enterprise, proceeding, transaction
operational *adj* **2** = **working**, functional, going, in working order, operative, prepared, ready, up and running, usable, viable, workable
Antonyms *adj* broken, ineffective, inoperative, kaput (*inf.*), nonfunctional, on the blink (*sl.*), out of order
operative *adj* **1** = **in force**, active, current, effective, efficient, functional, functioning, in business, in operation, operational, serviceable, standing, workable **2, 3** = **relevant**, crucial, important, indicative, influential, key, significant ◆ *n* **5** = **worker**, artisan, employee, hand, labourer, machinist, mechanic
Antonyms *adj* ≠ **in force:** ineffective, inefficient, inoperative, nonfunctional, powerless, unusable, unworkable
operator *n* **1** = **worker**, conductor, driver, handler, mechanic, operative, practitioner, skilled employee, technician **2** = **manager**, administrator, contractor, dealer, director, speculator, trader **4** *Informal* = **manipulator**, Machiavellian,

ophicleide (ˈɒfɪˌklaɪd) *n Music.* an obsolete keyed wind instrument of bass pitch. [C19: from F *ophicléide,* from Gk *ophis* snake + *kleis* key]

ophidian (əʊˈfɪdɪən) *adj* **1** snakelike. **2** of, relating to, or belonging to the suborder of reptiles that comprises the snakes. ◆ *n* **3** any reptile of this suborder; a snake. [C19: from NL *Ophidia,* name of suborder, from Gk *ophidion,* from *ophis* snake]

ophthalmia (ɒfˈθælmɪə) *n* inflammation of the eye, often including the conjunctiva. [C16: via LL from Gk, from *ophthalmos* eye; see OPTIC]

ophthalmic (ɒfˈθælmɪk) *adj* of or relating to the eye.

ophthalmic optician *n* See **optician.**

ophthalmo- *or before a vowel* **ophthalm-** *combining form.* indicating the eye or the eyeball. [from Gk *ophthalmos* EYE]

ophthalmology (ˌɒfθælˈmɒlədʒɪ) *n* the branch of medicine concerned with the eye and its diseases.
▸**ophthalmological** (ɒfˌθælməˈlɒdʒɪkᵊl) *adj* ▸ˌ**ophthalˈmologist** *n*

ophthalmoscope (ɒfˈθælməˌskəʊp) *n* an instrument for examining the interior of the eye.
▸**ophthalmoscopic** (ɒfˌθælməˈskɒpɪk) *adj*

-opia *n combining form.* indicating a visual defect or condition: *myopia.* [from Gk, from *ōps* eye]
▸**-opic** *adj combining form.*

opiate Ⓣ *n* (ˈəʊpɪɪt). **1** any of various narcotic drugs containing opium. **2** any other narcotic or sedative drug. **3** something that soothes, deadens, or induces sleep. ◆ *adj* (ˈəʊpɪɪt). **4** containing or consisting of opium. **5** inducing relaxation; soporific. ◆ *vb* (ˈəʊpɪˌeɪt), **opiates, opiating, opiated.** (*tr*) *Rare.* **6** to treat with an opiate. **7** to dull or deaden. [C16: from Med. L *opiātus,* from L *opium* OPIUM]

opine Ⓣ (əʊˈpaɪn) *vb* **opines, opining, opined.** (when *tr, usually takes a clause as object*) to hold or express an opinion: *he opined that it was a mistake.* [C16: from L *opīnārī*]

opinion Ⓣ (əˈpɪnjən) *n* **1** judgment or belief not founded on certainty or proof. **2** the prevailing or popular feeling or view: *public opinion.* **3** evaluation, impression, or estimation of the value or worth of a person or thing. **4** an evaluation or judgment given by an expert: *a medical opinion.* **5** the advice given by counsel on a case submitted to him for his view on the legal points involved. **6 a matter of opinion.** a point open to question. **7 be of the opinion (that).** to believe (that). [C13: via OF from L *opīniō* belief, from *opīnārī* to think]

opinionated Ⓣ (əˈpɪnjəˌneɪtɪd) *adj* holding obstinately and unreasonably to one's own opinions; dogmatic.
▸**oˈpinionˌatedly** *adv* ▸**oˈpinionˌatedness** *n*

opinionative (əˈpɪnjənətɪv) *adj Rare.* **1** of or relating to opinion. **2** another word for **opinionated.**
▸**oˈpinionatively** *adv* ▸**oˈpinionativeness** *n*

opinion poll *n* another term for a **poll** (sense 3).

opioid (ˈəʊpɪˌɔɪd) *n* any of a group of substances that resemble morphine in their physiological or pharmacological effects, esp. in their pain-relieving properties.

opium (ˈəʊpɪəm) *n* **1** an addictive narcotic drug extracted from the seed capsules of the opium poppy: used in medicine as an analgesic and hypnotic. **2** something having a tranquillizing or stupefying effect. [C14: from L: poppy juice, from Gk *opion,* dim. of *opos,* juice of a plant]

opium poppy *n* a poppy of SW Asia, with greyish-green leaves and typically white or reddish flowers: widely cultivated as a source of opium.

opossum (əˈpɒsəm) *n, pl* **opossums** *or* **opossum. 1** a thick-furred marsupial, esp. the **common opossum** of North and South America, having an elongated snout and a hairless prehensile tail. **2** *Austral. & NZ.* any of various similar animals, esp. a phalanger. ◆ Often shortened to **possum.** [C17: from Algonquian *aposoum*]

opp. *abbrev. for:* **1** opposed. **2** opposite.

opponent Ⓣ (əˈpəʊnənt) *n* **1** a person who opposes another in a contest, battle, etc. **2** *Anat.* an opponent muscle. ◆ *adj* **3** opposite, as in position. **4** *Anat.* (of a muscle) bringing two parts into opposition. **5** opposing; contrary. [C16: from L *oppōnere* to oppose]
▸**opˈponency** *n*

opportune Ⓣ (ˈɒpəˌtjuːn) *adj* **1** occurring at a time that is suitable or advantageous. **2** fit or suitable for a particular purpose or occurrence. [C15: via OF from L *opportūnus,* from *ob-* to + *portus* harbour (orig.: coming to the harbour, obtaining timely protection)]
▸ˈ**opporˌtunely** *adv* ▸ˈ**opporˌtuneness** *n*

opportunist Ⓣ (ˌɒpəˈtjuːnɪst) *n* **1** a person who adapts his actions, responses, etc., to take advantage of opportunities, circumstances, etc. ◆ *adj* **2** taking advantage of opportunities and circumstances in this way.
▸ˌ**opporˈtunism** *n*

opportunistic (ˌɒpətjʊˈnɪstɪk) *adj* **1** of or characterized by opportunism. **2** *Med.* (of an infection) caused by any microorganism that is harmless to a healthy person but debilitates a person whose immune system has been weakened.

opportunity Ⓣ (ˌɒpəˈtjuːnɪtɪ) *n, pl* **opportunities. 1** a favourable, appropriate, or advantageous combination of circumstances. **2** a chance or prospect.

opportunity shop *n Austral. & NZ.* a shop selling used goods for charitable funds.

opposable (əˈpəʊzəbᵊl) *adj* **1** capable of being opposed. **2** Also: **apposable.** (of the thumb of primates, esp. man) capable of being moved into a position facing the other digits so as to be able to touch the ends of each. **3** capable of being placed opposite something else.
▸**opˌposaˈbility** *n* ▸**opˈposably** *adv*

oppose Ⓣ (əˈpəʊz) *vb* **opposes, opposing, opposed. 1** (*tr*) to fight against, counter, or resist strongly. **2** (*tr*) to be hostile or antagonistic to; be against. **3** (*tr*) to place or set in opposition; contrast or counterbalance. **4** (*tr*) to place opposite or facing. **5** (*intr*) to be or act in opposition. [C14: via OF from L *oppōnere,* from *ob-* against + *pōnere* to place]
▸**opˈposer** *n* ▸**opˈposing** *adj* ▸**oppositive** (əˈpɒzɪtɪv) *adj*

opposite Ⓣ (ˈɒpəzɪt, -sɪt) *adj* **1** situated or being on the other side or at each side of something between. **2** facing or going in contrary directions: *opposite ways.* **3** diametrically different in character, tendency, belief, etc. **4** *Bot.* **4a** (of leaves) arranged in pairs on either side of the stem. **4b** (of parts of a flower) arranged opposite the middle of another part. **5** *Maths.* (of a side in a triangle) facing a specified angle. Abbrev.: **opp.** ◆ *n* **6** a person or thing that is opposite; antithesis. ◆ *prep* **7** Also: **opposite to.** facing; corresponding to (something on the other side of a division). **8** as a co-star with: *she played opposite Olivier.* ◆ *adv* **9** on opposite sides: *she lives opposite.*
▸ˈ**oppositely** *adv* ▸ˈ**oppositeness** *n*

opposite number *n* a person holding an equivalent and corresponding position on another side or situation.

opposition Ⓣ (ˌɒpəˈzɪʃən) *n* **1** the act of opposing or the state of being opposed. **2** hostility, unfriendliness, or antagonism. **3** a person or group antagonistic or opposite in aims to another. **4a** (usually preceded by *the*) a political party or group opposed to the ruling party or government. **4b** (*cap. as part of a name, esp. in Britain and Commonwealth countries*): *Her Majesty's Loyal Opposition.* **4c in opposition.** (of a political party) opposing the government. **5** a position facing or opposite another. **6** something that acts as an obstacle to some course or progress. **7** *Astron.* the position of an outer planet or the moon when it is in line with the earth as seen from the sun and is approximately at its nearest to the earth. **8** *Astrol.* an exact aspect of 180° be-

THESAURUS

machinator, mover, shyster (*sl., chiefly US*), smart aleck (*inf.*), wheeler-dealer (*inf.*), wire-puller, worker

opiate *n* 2, 3 = **narcotic**, anodyne, bromide, downer, drug, nepenthe, pacifier, sedative, soporific, tranquillizer

opine *vb* = **give as one's opinion**, believe, conceive, conclude, conjecture, declare, judge, presume, say, suggest, suppose, surmise, think, venture, volunteer, ween (*poetic*)

opinion *n* 1 = **belief**, assessment, conception, conjecture, estimation, feeling, idea, impression, judgment, mind, notion, persuasion, point of view, sentiment, theory, view **6 matter of opinion** = **debatable point**, matter of judgment, moot point, open question **7 be of the opinion** = **believe**, be convinced, be under the impression, conclude, consider, hold, judge, reckon, suppose, surmise, think

opinionated *adj* = **dogmatic**, adamant, biased, bigoted, bull-headed, cocksure, dictatorial, doctrinaire, inflexible, obdurate, obstinate, overbearing, pig-headed, prejudiced, self-assertive, single-minded, stubborn, uncompromising
Antonyms *adj* broad-minded, compliant, compromising, dispassionate, flexible, open-minded, receptive, tolerant, unbiased, unbigoted, unprejudiced

opponent *n* 1 = **adversary**, antagonist, challenger, competitor, contestant, disputant, dissentient, enemy, foe, opposer, rival, the opposition
Antonyms *n* accomplice, ally, associate, colleague, friend, helper, mate, supporter

opportune *adj* 1, 2 = **timely**, advantageous, appropriate, apt, auspicious, convenient, falling into one's lap, favourable, felicitous, fit, fitting, fortunate, happy, lucky, proper, propitious, seasonable, suitable, well-timed
Antonyms *adj* inappropriate, inconvenient, inopportune, unfavourable, unfortunate, unsuitable, untimely

opportunism *n* 2 = **expediency**, exploitation, Machiavellianism, making hay while the sun shines (*inf.*), pragmatism, realism, *Realpolitik*, striking while the iron is hot (*inf.*), trimming, unscrupulousness

opportunity *n* 1 = **chance**, break, convenience, hour, look-in (*inf.*), moment, occasion, opening, scope, time, window

oppose *vb* 1 = **fight**, bar, block, check, combat, confront, contradict, counter, counterattack, defy, face, fly in the face of, hinder, obstruct, prevent, resist, set one's face against, speak against, stand up to, take a stand against, take issue with, take on, thwart, withstand **3** = **counterbalance**, compare, contrast, match, pit *or* set against, play off
Antonyms *vb* ≠ **fight**: advance, advocate, aid, back, defend, espouse, help, promote, support

opposed *adj* 2 = **against**, antagonistic, anti (*inf.*), antipathetic, antithetical, at daggers drawn, averse, clashing, conflicting, contra (*inf.*), contrary, dissentient, hostile, incompatible, inimical, in opposition, opposing, opposite

opposing *adj* 2 = **conflicting**, antagonistic, antipathetic, clashing, combatant, contrary, enemy, hostile, incompatible, irreconcilable, opposed, opposite, rival, warring

opposite *adj* 1 = **facing**, corresponding, fronting **3** = **different**, adverse, antagonistic, antithetical, conflicting, contradictory, contrary, contrasted, diametrically opposed, differing, diverse, hostile, inconsistent, inimical, irreconcilable, opposed, poles apart, reverse, unlike ◆ *n* **6** = **reverse**, antithesis, contradiction, contrary, converse, inverse, the other extreme, the other side of the coin (*inf.*)
Antonyms *adj* ≠ **different**: alike, consistent, corresponding, identical, like, matching, same, similar, uniform

opposition *n* 2 = **hostility**, antagonism,

tween two planets, etc., an orb of 8° being allowed. **9** *Logic.* the relation between propositions having the same subject and predicate but differing in quality, quantity, or both, as with *all men are wicked; no men are wicked; some men are not wicked.*
▸**ˌoppoˈsitional** *adj* ▸**ˌoppoˈsitionist** *n* ▸**ˌoppoˈsitionless** *adj*

oppress Ⓣ (əˈpres) *vb* (*tr*) **1** to subjugate by cruelty, force, etc. **2** to afflict or torment. **3** to lie heavy on (the mind, etc.). [C14: via OF from Med. L *oppressāre,* from L *opprimere,* from *ob-* against + *premere* to press]
▸**opˈpressing** *adj* ▸**opˈpression** *n* ▸**opˈpressor** *n*

oppressive Ⓣ (əˈpresɪv) *adj* **1** cruel, harsh, or tyrannical. **2** heavy, constricting, or depressing.
▸**opˈpressively** *adv* ▸**opˈpressiveness** *n*

opprobrious Ⓣ (əˈprəubrɪəs) *adj* **1** expressing scorn, disgrace, or contempt. **2** shameful or infamous.
▸**opˈprobriously** *adv* ▸**opˈprobriousness** *n*

opprobrium Ⓣ (əˈprəubrɪəm) *n* **1** the state of being abused or scornfully criticized. **2** reproach or censure. **3** a cause of disgrace or ignominy. [C17: from L *ob-* against + *probrum* a shameful act]

oppugn Ⓣ (əˈpjuːn) *vb* (*tr*) to call into question; dispute. [C15: from L *oppugnāre,* from *ob-* against + *pugnāre* to fight, from *pugnus* clenched fist]
▸**opˈpugner** *n*

opsin (ˈɒpsɪn) *n* the protein that together with retinene makes up the purple visual pigment rhodopsin. [C20: back formation from RHODOPSIN]

-opsis *n combining form.* indicating a specified appearance or resemblance: *meconopsis.* [from Gk *opsis* sight]

opsonin (ˈɒpsənɪn) *n* a constituent of blood serum that renders bacteria more susceptible to ingestion by phagocytes. [C20: from Gk *opsōnion* victuals]
▸**opsonic** (ɒpˈsɒnɪk) *adj*

opt Ⓣ (ɒpt) *vb* (when *intr,* foll. by *for*) to show preference (for) or choose (to do something). See also **opt in, opt out.** [C19: from F *opter,* from L *optāre* to choose]

opt. *abbrev. for:* **1** *Grammar.* optative. **2** optical. **3** optician. **4** optimum. **5** optional.

optative (ˈɒptətɪv) *adj* **1** indicating or expressing choice or wish. **2** *Grammar.* denoting a mood of verbs in Greek and Sanskrit expressing a wish. ◆ *n* **3** *Grammar.* **3a** the optative mood. **3b** a verb in this mood. [C16: via F *optatif,* from LL *optātīvus,* from L *optāre* to desire]

optic (ˈɒptɪk) *adj* **1** of or relating to the eye or vision. **2** a less common word for **optical.** ◆ *n* **3** an informal word for **eye**[1]. **4** *Brit., trademark.* a device attached to an inverted bottle for dispensing measured quantities of liquid. [C16: from Med. L *opticus,* from Gk *optikos,* from *optos* visible; rel. to *ōps* eye]

optical (ˈɒptɪkᵊl) *adj* **1** of, relating to, producing, or involving light. **2** of or relating to the eye or to the sense of sight; optic. **3** (esp. of a lens) aiding vision or correcting a visual disorder.
▸**ˈoptically** *adv*

optical activity *n* the ability of substances that are optical isomers to rotate the plane of polarization of a transmitted beam of plane-polarized light.

optical character reader *n* a computer peripheral device enabling letters, numbers, or other characters usually printed on paper to be optically scanned and input to a storage device, such as magnetic tape. The device uses the process of **optical character recognition.** Abbrev. (for both *reader* and *recognition*): **OCR.**

optical crown *n* an optical glass of low dispersion and relatively low refractive index.

optical disc *n Computing.* an inflexible disc on which information is stored in digital form by laser technology. Also called: **video disc.**

optical fibre *n* a communications cable consisting of a thin glass fibre in a protective sheath. Light transmitted along the fibre may be modulated with vision, sound, or data signals. See also **fibre optics.**

optical flint *n* an optical glass of high dispersion and high refractive index containing lead oxide, used in the manufacture of lenses, artificial gems, and cut glass.

optical glass *n* any of several types of clear homogeneous glass of known refractive index used in the construction of lenses, etc.

optical isomerism *n* isomerism of chemical compounds in which the two isomers differ only in that their molecules are mirror images of each other.
▸**optical isomer** *n*

optical scanner *n* a computer peripheral device enabling printed material, including characters and diagrams, to be scanned and converted into a form that can be stored in a computer. See also **optical character reader.**

optician (ɒpˈtɪʃən) *n* a general name used to refer to: **a** an **ophthalmic optician.** one qualified to examine the eyes and prescribe and supply spectacles and contact lenses. **b** a **dispensing optician.** one who supplies and fits spectacle frames and lenses, but is not qualified to prescribe lenses.

optics (ˈɒptɪks) *n* (*functioning as sing*) the branch of science concerned with vision and the generation, nature, propagation, and behaviour of electromagnetic light.

optimal (ˈɒptɪməl) *adj* another word for **optimum** (sense 2).

optimism Ⓣ (ˈɒptɪˌmɪzəm) *n* **1** the tendency to expect the best in all things. **2** hopefulness; confidence. **3** the doctrine of the ultimate triumph of good over evil. **4** the philosophical doctrine that this is the best of all possible worlds. ◆ Cf. **pessimism.** [C18: from F *optimisme,* from L *optimus* best, sup. of *bonus* good]
▸**ˈoptimist** *n* ▸**ˌoptiˈmistic** *adj* ▸**ˌoptiˈmistically** *adv*

optimize *or* **optimise** (ˈɒptɪˌmaɪz) *vb* **optimizes, optimizing, optimized** *or* **optimises, optimising, optimised. 1** (*tr*) to take full advantage of. **2** (*tr*) to plan or carry out (an economic activity) with maximum efficiency. **3** (*intr*) to be optimistic. **4** (*tr*) to write or modify (a computer program) to achieve maximum efficiency.
▸**ˌoptimiˈzation** *or* **ˌoptimiˈsation** *n*

optimum Ⓣ (ˈɒptɪməm) *n, pl* **optima** (-mə) *or* **optimums. 1** a condition, degree, amount, or compromise that produces the best possible result. ◆ *adj* **2** most favourable or advantageous; best: *optimum conditions.* [C19: from L: the best (thing), from *optimus* best; see OPTIMISM]

optimum population *n Econ.* a population that is sufficiently large to provide an adequate workforce with minimal unemployment.

opt in *vb* (*intr, adv*) to choose to be involved in or part of a scheme, etc.

option Ⓣ (ˈɒpʃən) *n* **1** the act or an instance of choosing or deciding. **2** the power or liberty to choose. **3** an exclusive opportunity, usually for a limited period, to buy something at a future date: *a six-month option on the Canadian rights to this book.* **4** *Commerce.* the right to buy (**call option**) or sell (**put option**) a fixed quantity of a commodity, security, foreign exchange, etc., at a fixed price at a specified date in the future. See also **traded option. 5** something chosen; choice. **6 keep** (*or* **leave**) **one's options open.** not to commit oneself. **7 soft option.** an easy alternative. ◆ *vb* **8** (*tr*) to obtain or grant an option on: *the BBC have optioned her latest novel.* [C17: from L *optiō* free choice, from *optāre* to choose]

optional Ⓣ (ˈɒpʃənᵊl) *adj* possible but not compulsory; left to personal choice.
▸**ˈoptionally** *adv*

option money *n Commerce.* the price paid for buying an option.

THESAURUS

competition, contrariety, counteraction, disapproval, obstruction, obstructiveness, prevention, resistance, unfriendliness **3 = opponent**, antagonist, competition, foe, other side, rival
Antonyms *n* ≠ **hostility:** agreement, approval, assent, collaboration, concurrence, cooperation, friendliness, responsiveness

oppress *vb* **1 = subjugate**, abuse, crush, harry, maltreat, overpower, overwhelm, persecute, rule with an iron hand, subdue, suppress, trample underfoot, tyrannize over, wrong **2, 3 = depress**, afflict, burden, dispirit, harass, lie *or* weigh heavy upon, sadden, take the heart out of, torment, vex
Antonyms *vb* ≠ **subjugate:** deliver, emancipate, free, liberate, loose, release, set free ≠ **depress:** unburden

oppressed *adj* **1 = downtrodden**, abused, browbeaten, burdened, disadvantaged, enslaved, harassed, henpecked, maltreated, misused, prostrate, slave, subject, tyrannized, underprivileged
Antonyms *adj* advantaged, exalted, favoured, honoured, liberated, privileged

oppression *n* **1 = subjugation**, abuse, brutality, calamity, cruelty, hardship, harshness, injury, injustice, iron hand, maltreatment, misery, persecution, severity, subjection, suffering, tyranny
Antonyms *n* benevolence, clemency, compassion, goodness, humaneness, justice, kindness, mercy, sympathy, tenderness

oppressive *adj* **1 = tyrannical**, brutal, burdensome, cruel, despotic, grinding, harsh, heavy, inhuman, onerous, overbearing, overwhelming, repressive, severe, unjust **2 = stifling**, airless, close, heavy, muggy, overpowering, stuffy, suffocating, sultry, torrid
Antonyms *adj* ≠ **tyrannical:** encouraging, gentle, humane, just, lenient, merciful, propitious, soft

oppressor *n* **1 = persecutor**, autocrat, bully, despot, harrier, intimidator, iron hand, scourge, slave-driver, taskmaster, tormentor, tyrant

opprobrious *adj* **1 = contemptuous**, abusive, calumniatory, contumelious, damaging, defamatory, hateful, insolent, insulting, invective, offensive, scandalous, scurrilous, vitriolic, vituperative **2 = shameful**, abominable, contemptible, despicable, dishonourable, disreputable, hateful, ignominious, infamous, notorious, reprehensible

opprobrium *n* **1, 2 = disgrace**, calumny, censure, contumely, discredit, disfavour, dishonour, disrepute, ignominy, ill repute, infamy, obloquy, odium, reproach, scurrility, shame, slur, stigma

oppugn *vb* **= dispute**, argue, assail, attack, call into question, cast doubt on, combat, oppose, resist, withstand

opt *vb, often with* **for = choose**, decide (on), elect, exercise one's discretion (in favour of), go for, make a selection, plump for, prefer
Antonyms *vb* decide against, dismiss, eliminate, exclude, preclude, reject, rule out, turn down

optimistic *adj* **1 = idealistic**, disposed to take a favourable view, seen through rose-coloured spectacles, Utopian **2 = hopeful**, assured, bright, buoyant, buoyed up, can-do (*inf.*), cheerful, confident, encouraged, expectant, looking on the bright side, positive, rosy, sanguine
Antonyms *adj* ≠ **hopeful:** bleak, cynical, despairing, despondent, downhearted, fatalistic, gloomy, glum, hopeless, pessimistic, resigned

optimum *adj* **2 = ideal**, A1 *or* A-one (*inf.*), best, choicest, flawless, highest, most favourable *or* advantageous, optimal, peak, perfect, superlative
Antonyms *adj* inferior, least, lowest, minimal, poorest, worst

option *n* **1, 5 = choice**, alternative, election, preference, selection

optional *adj* **= voluntary**, discretionary, elective, extra, noncompulsory, open, possible, up to the individual

optometrist (ɒpˈtɒmɪtrɪst) *n* a person who is qualified to examine the eyes and prescribe and supply spectacles and contact lenses. Also called (esp. Brit.): **ophthalmic optician.**

optometry (ɒpˈtɒmɪtrɪ) *n* the science or practice of testing visual acuity and prescribing corrective lenses.
▸**optometric** (ˌɒptəˈmɛtrɪk) *adj*

optophone (ˈɒptəˌfəʊn) *n* a device for blind people that converts printed words into sounds.

opt out *vb* **1** (*intr, adv; often foll. by of*) to choose not to be involved (in) or part (of). ◆ *n* **opt-out. 2** the act of opting out, esp. of a local-authority administration: *opt-outs by hospitals and schools.*

opulent Ⓣ (ˈɒpjʊlənt) *adj* **1** having or indicating wealth. **2** abundant or plentiful. [C17: from L *opulens,* from *opēs* (pl) wealth]
▸ˈ**opulence** *or* (*less commonly*) ˈ**opulency** *n* ▸ˈ**opulently** *adv*

opuntia (ɒˈpʌnʃɪə) *n* a cactus, esp. the prickly pear, having fleshy branched stems and green, red, or yellow flowers. [C17: NL, from L *Opuntia* (*herba*) the Opuntian (plant), from *Opus,* ancient town of Locris, Greece]

opus Ⓣ (ˈəʊpəs) *n, pl* **opuses** *or* **opera. 1** an artistic composition, esp. a musical work. **2** (*often cap.*) (usually followed by a number) a musical composition by a particular composer, generally catalogued in order of publication: *Beethoven's opus 61.* Abbrev.: **op.** [C18: from L: a work]

Opus Dei (ˈəʊpəs ˈdeɪiː) *n* **1** another name for **divine office. 2** an international Roman Catholic organization founded in Spain in 1928 by Josemaria Escrivá de Balaguer (1902–75), to spread Christian principles.

or[1] (ɔː; *unstressed* ə) *conj* (*coordinating*) **1** used to join alternatives. **2** used to join rephrasings of the same thing: *twelve, or a dozen.* **3** used to join two alternatives when the first is preceded by *either* or *whether: either yes or no.* **4 one or two, four or five,** etc. a few. **5** a poetic word for **either** or **whether,** as the first element in correlatives, with *or* also preceding the second alternative. [C13: contraction of *other,* changed (through infl. of EITHER) from OE *oththe*]

or[2] (ɔː) *adj* (*usually postpositive*) *Heraldry.* of the metal gold. [C16: via F from L *aurum* gold]

OR *abbrev. for:* **1** operational research. **2** Oregon. **3** *Mil.* other ranks.

-or[1] *suffix forming nouns from verbs.* a person or thing that does what is expressed by the verb: *actor; conductor; generator; sailor.* [via OF *-eur, -eor,* from L *-or* or *-ātor*]

-or[2] *suffix forming nouns.* **1** indicating state, condition, or activity: *terror; error.* **2** the US spelling of **-our.**

ora (ˈɔːrə) *n* the plural of **os**[2].

orache *or esp. US* **orach** (ˈɒrɪtʃ) *n* any of several herbaceous plants or small shrubs of the goosefoot family, esp. **garden orache,** which is cultivated as a vegetable. They have typically greyish-green lobed leaves and inconspicuous flowers. [C15: from OF *arache,* from L *atriplex,* from Gk *atraphaxus,* from ?]

oracle Ⓣ (ˈɒrəkᵊl) *n* **1** a prophecy revealed through the medium of a priest or priestess at the shrine of a god. **2** a shrine at which an oracular god is consulted. **3** an agency through which a prophecy is transmitted. **4** any person or thing believed to indicate future action with infallible authority. [C14: via OF from L *ōrāculum,* from *ōrāre* to request]

Oracle (ˈɒrəkᵊl) *n Trademark.* the Teletext system operated by ITV. See **Teletext.** [C20: acronym of *o*(*ptional*) *r*(*eception of*) *a*(*nnouncements by*) *c*(*oded*) *l*(*ine*) *e*(*lectronics*)]

oracular Ⓣ (ɒˈrækjʊlə) *adj* **1** of or relating to an oracle. **2** wise and prophetic. **3** mysterious or ambiguous.
▸**oˈracularly** *adv*

oracy (ˈɔːrəsɪ) *n* the capacity to express oneself in and understand speech. [C20: from L *or-, os* mouth, by analogy with *literacy*]

oral Ⓣ (ˈɔːrəl, ˈɒrəl) *adj* **1** spoken or verbal. **2** relating to, affecting, or for use in the mouth: *an oral thermometer.* **3** denoting a drug to be taken by mouth: *an oral contraceptive.* **4** of, relating to, or using spoken words. **5** *Psychoanal.* relating to a stage of psychosexual development during which the child's interest is concentrated on the mouth. ◆ *n* **6** an examination in which the questions and answers are spoken rather than written. [C17: from LL *ōrālis,* from L *ōs* face]
▸ˈ**orally** *adv*

oral history *n* the memories of living people about events or social conditions in their earlier lives taped and preserved as historical evidence.

oral hygiene *n* the maintenance of healthy teeth and gums by brushing, etc. Also called: **dental hygiene.**

oral society *n* a society that has not developed literacy.

orange (ˈɒrɪndʒ) *n* **1** any of several citrus trees, esp. **sweet orange** and the Seville orange, cultivated in warm regions for their round edible fruit. **2a** the fruit of any of these trees, having a yellowish-red bitter rind and segmented juicy flesh. **2b** (*as modifier*): *orange peel.* **3** the hard wood of any of these trees. **4** any of a group of colours, such as that of the skin of an orange, that lie between red and yellow in the visible spectrum. **5** a dye or pigment producing these colours. **6** orange cloth or clothing: *dressed in orange.* **7** any of several trees or herbaceous plants that resemble the orange, such as mock orange. ◆ *adj* **8** of the colour orange. [C14: via OF *auranja,* from Ar. *nāranj,* from Persian, from Sansk. *nāranga*]

orangeade (ˌɒrɪndʒˈeɪd) *n* an effervescent or still orange-flavoured drink.

orange blossom *n* the flowers of the orange tree, traditionally worn by brides.

Orangeman (ˈɒrɪndʒmən) *n, pl* **Orangemen.** a member of a society founded in Ireland (1795) to uphold Protestantism. [C18: after William, prince of *Orange,* later William III]

Orangeman's Day *n* the 12th of July, celebrated by Protestants in Northern Ireland and elsewhere, to commemorate the anniversary of the Battle of the Boyne (1690).

orange pekoe *n* a superior grade of black tea growing in India and Sri Lanka.

orange roughy (ˈrʌfɪ) *n* a marine food fish of S Pacific waters.

orangery (ˈɒrɪndʒərɪ, -dʒrɪ) *n, pl* **orangeries.** a building, such as a greenhouse, in which orange trees are grown.

orange stick *n* a small stick used to clean the fingernails and cuticles.

orangewood (ˈɒrɪndʒˌwʊd) *n* **a** the hard fine-grained yellowish wood of the orange tree. **b** (*as modifier*): *an orangewood table.*

orang-utan (ɔːˌræŋuːˈtæn, ˌɔːræŋˈuːtæn) *or* **orang-utang** (ɔːˌræŋuːˈtæŋ, ˌɔːræŋˈuːtæŋ) *n* a large anthropoid ape of the forests of Sumatra and Borneo, with shaggy reddish-brown hair and strong arms. Sometimes shortened to **orang.** [C17: from Malay *orang hutan,* from *ōrang* man + *hūtan* forest]

orate Ⓣ (ɔːˈreɪt) *vb* **orates, orating, orated.** (*intr*) **1** to make or give an oration. **2** to speak pompously and lengthily.

oration Ⓣ (ɔːˈreɪʃən) *n* **1** a formal public declaration or speech. **2** any rhetorical, lengthy, or pompous speech. [C14: from L *ōrātiō* speech, harangue, from *ōrāre* to plead, pray]

orator Ⓣ (ˈɒrətə) *n* **1** a public speaker, esp. one versed in rhetoric. **2** a person given to lengthy or pompous speeches. **3** *Obs.* the plaintiff in a cause of action in chancery.

oratorio (ˌɒrəˈtɔːrɪəʊ) *n, pl* **oratorios.** a dramatic but unstaged musical composition for soloists, chorus, and orchestra, based on a religious theme. [C18: from It., lit.: ORATORY[2], referring to the Church of the Oratory at Rome where musical services were held]

oratory[1] Ⓣ (ˈɒrətərɪ, -trɪ) *n* **1** the art of public speaking. **2** rhetorical skill or style. [C16: from L (*ars*) *ōrātōria* (the art of) public speaking]
▸ˌ**oraˈtorical** *adj* ▸ˌ**oraˈtorically** *adv*

oratory[2] (ˈɒrətərɪ, -trɪ) *n, pl* **oratories.** a small room or secluded place, set apart for private prayer. [C14: from Anglo-Norman, from Church L *ōrātōrium* place of prayer, from *ōrāre* to plead, pray]

orb Ⓣ (ɔːb) *n* **1** (in regalia) an ornamental sphere surmounted by a cross. **2** a sphere; globe. **3** *Poetic.* another word for **eye**[1] (sense 1). **4** *Obs. or poetic.* **4a** a celestial body, esp. the earth or sun. **4b** the orbit of a celestial body. ◆ *vb* **5** to make or become circular or spherical. **6** (*tr*) an archaic word for **encircle.** [C16: from L *orbis* circle, disc]

orbicular (ɔːˈbɪkjʊlə), **orbiculate,** *or* **orbiculated** *adj* **1** circular or spherical. **2** (of a leaf or similar flat part) circular or nearly circular.
▸**orbicularity** (ɔːˌbɪkjʊˈlærɪtɪ) *n* ▸**orˈbicularly** *adv*

orbit Ⓣ (ˈɔːbɪt) *n* **1** *Astron.* the curved path followed by a planet, satellite, etc., in its motion around another celestial body. **2** a range or field of action or influence; sphere. **3** the bony cavity containing the eyeball; eye socket. **4** *Zool.* **4a** the skin surrounding the eye of a bird. **4b** the hollow in which lies the eye or eyestalk of an insect. **5** *Physics.*

THESAURUS

Antonyms *adj* compulsory, *de rigueur,* mandatory, obligatory, required

opulence *n* **1 = wealth,** affluence, Easy Street (*inf.*), fortune, lavishness, luxuriance, luxury, prosperity, riches, richness, sumptuousness **2 = abundance,** copiousness, cornucopia, fullness, plenty, profusion, richness, superabundance
Antonyms *n* ≠ **wealth:** impecuniousness, indigence, lack, penury, poverty, privation, want ≠ **abundance:** dearth, lack, paucity, scantiness, scarcity, want

opulent *adj* **1 = rich,** affluent, lavish, luxurious, moneyed, prosperous, sumptuous, wealthy, well-heeled (*inf.*), well-off, well-to-do **2 = abundant,** copious, lavish, luxuriant, plentiful, profuse, prolific
Antonyms *adj* ≠ **rich:** broke (*inf.*), destitute, down and out, indigent, moneyless, needy, on the rocks, penurious, poor, poverty-stricken

opus *n* **1 = work,** brainchild, composition, creation, *oeuvre,* piece, production

oracle *n* **1 = prophecy,** answer, augury, divination, divine utterance, prediction, prognostication, revelation, vision **3 = prophet,** augur, Cassandra, seer, sibyl, soothsayer **4 = authority,** adviser, guru, high priest, horse's mouth, mastermind, mentor, pundit, source, wizard

oracular *adj* **1 = prophetic,** auspicious, foreboding, ominous, portentous, prescient, sibylline **2 = wise,** authoritative, dictatorial, dogmatic, grave, positive, sage, significant, venerable **3 = mysterious,** ambiguous, arcane, cryptic, Delphic, equivocal, obscure, two-edged

oral *adj* **1 = spoken,** verbal, viva voce, vocal

orate *vb* **1, 2 = make a speech,** declaim, discourse, hold forth, pontificate, speak, speechify, talk

oration *n* **1 = speech,** address, declamation, discourse, harangue, homily, lecture, spiel (*inf.*)

orator *n* **1 = public speaker,** Cicero, declaimer, lecturer, rhetorician, speaker, spellbinder

oratorical *adj* **2 = rhetorical,** bombastic, Ciceronian, declamatory, eloquent, grandiloquent, high-flown, magniloquent, silver-tongued, sonorous

oratory[1] *n* **1, 2 = eloquence,** declamation, elocution, grandiloquence, public speaking, rhetoric, speechifying, speech-making, spieling (*inf.*)

orb *n* **2 = sphere,** ball, circle, globe, ring, round

orbit *n* **1 = path,** circle, course, cycle, ellipse, revolution, rotation, track, trajectory **2 = sphere of influence,** ambit, compass, course, domain, influence, range, reach, scope, sphere, sweep ◆ *vb* **7 = circle,** circumnavigate, encircle, revolve around

the path of an electron around the nucleus of an atom. **6 go into orbit.** *Inf.* to reach an extreme and often uncontrolled state: *when he realized the price he nearly went into orbit.* ◆ *vb* **7** to move around (a body) in a curved path. **8** (*tr*) to send (a satellite, spacecraft, etc.) into orbit. **9** (*intr*) to move in or as if in an orbit. [C16: from L *orbita* course, from *orbis* circle]
▸ **'orbitally** *adv*

orbital ('ɔːbɪtəl) *adj* **1** of or denoting an orbit. **2** (of a motorway or major road) circling a large city. ◆ *n* **3** the region around an atomic nucleus, or around two nuclei in a molecule, within which an electron moves. **4** an orbital road.

orbital velocity *n* the velocity required by a spacecraft to enter and maintain a given orbit.

orc (ɔːk) *n* **1** any of various whales, such as the killer and grampus. **2** a mythical monster. [C16: via L *orca*, ?from Gk *orux* whale]

Orcadian (ɔː'keɪdɪən) *n* **1** a native or inhabitant of the Orkneys, a group of islands off the N coast of Scotland. ◆ *adj* **2** of or relating to the Orkneys. [from L *Orcades* the Orkney Islands]

orchard ('ɔːtʃəd) *n* **1** an area of land devoted to the cultivation of fruit trees. **2** a collection of fruit trees especially cultivated. [OE *orceard, ortigeard*, from *ort-*, from L *hortus* garden + *geard* YARD[2]]

orchestra ('ɔːkɪstrə) *n* **1** a large group of musicians, esp. one whose members play a variety of different instruments. **2** a group of musicians, each playing the same type of instrument. **3** Also called: **orchestra pit.** the space reserved for musicians in a theatre, immediately in front of or under the stage. **4** *Chiefly US & Canad.* the stalls in a theatre. **5** (in ancient Greek theatre) the semicircular space in front of the stage. [C17: via L from Gk: the space in the theatre for the chorus, from *orkheisthai* to dance]
▸ **orchestral** (ɔː'kɛstrəl) *adj* ▸ **or'chestrally** *adv*

orchestrate ❶ ('ɔːkɪˌstreɪt) *vb* **orchestrates, orchestrating, orchestrated.** (*tr*) **1** to score or arrange (a piece of music) for orchestra. **2** to arrange, organize, or build up for special or maximum effect.
▸ **ˌorches'tration** *n* ▸ **'orchesˌtrator** *n*

orchid ('ɔːkɪd) *n* a terrestrial or epiphytic plant having flowers of unusual shapes and beautiful colours, usually with one petal larger than the other two. The flowers are specialized for pollination by certain insects. [C19: from NL *Orchideae*; see ORCHIS]

orchidectomy (ˌɔːkɪ'dɛktəmɪ) *n, pl* **orchidectomies.** the surgical removal of one or both testes. [C19: from Gk *orkhis* testicle + -ECTOMY]

orchil ('ɔːkɪl, -tʃɪl) *or* **archil** *n* **1** a purplish dye obtained by treating various lichens with aqueous ammonia. **2** the lichens yielding this dye. [C15: from OF *orcheil*, from ?]

orchis ('ɔːkɪs) *n* **1** a N temperate terrestrial orchid having fleshy tubers and spikes of typically pink flowers. **2** any of various temperate or tropical orchids such as the fringed orchis. [C16: via L from Gk *orkhis* testicle; so called from the shape of its roots]

OR circuit *or* **gate** (ɔː) *n Computing.* a logic circuit having two or more input wires and one output wire that gives a high-voltage output signal if one or more input signals are at a high voltage: used extensively as a basic circuit in computing. [C20: from its similarity to the function of *or* in logical constructions]

ord. *abbrev. for:* **1** order. **2** ordinal. **3** ordinance. **4** ordinary.

ordain ❶ (ɔː'deɪn) *vb* (*tr*) **1** to consecrate (someone) as a priest; confer holy orders upon. **2** (*may take a clause as object*) to decree, appoint, or predestine irrevocably. **3** (*may take a clause as object*) to order, establish, or enact with authority. [C13: from Anglo-Norman *ordeiner*, from LL *ordināre*, from L *ordo* ORDER]
▸ **or'dainer** *n* ▸ **or'dainment** *n*

ordeal ❶ (ɔː'diːl) *n* **1** a severe or trying experience. **2** *History.* a method of trial in which the innocence of an accused person was determined by subjecting him to physical danger, esp. by fire or water. [OE *ordāl, ordēl* verdict]

order ❶ ('ɔːdə) *n* **1** a state in which all components or elements are arranged logically, comprehensibly, or naturally. **2** an arrangement or disposition of things in succession; sequence: *alphabetical order.* **3** an established or customary method or state, esp. of society. **4** a peaceful or harmonious condition of society: *order reigned in the streets.* **5** (*often pl*) a class, rank, or hierarchy: *the lower orders.* **6** *Biol.* any of the taxonomic groups into which a class is divided and which contains one or more families. **7** an instruction that must be obeyed; command. **8a** a commission or instruction to produce or supply something in return for payment. **8b** the commodity produced or supplied. **8c** (*as modifier*): *order form.* **9** a procedure followed by an assembly, meeting, etc. **10** (*cap. when part of a name*) a body of people united in a particular aim or purpose. **11** (*usually cap.*) Also called: **religious order.** a group of persons who bind themselves by vows in order to devote themselves to the pursuit of religious aims. **12** (*often pl*) another name for **holy orders, major orders,** or **minor orders. 13** *History.* a society of knights constituted as a fraternity, such as the Knights Templars. **14a** a group of people holding a specific honour for service or merit, conferred on them by a sovereign or state. **14b** the insignia of such a group. **15a** any of the five major classical styles of architecture classified by the style of columns and entablatures used. **15b** any style of architecture. **16** *Christianity.* **16a** the sacrament by which bishops, priests, etc., have their offices conferred upon them. **16b** any of the degrees into which the ministry is divided. **16c** the office of an ordained Christian minister. **17** *Maths.* **17a** the number of times a function must be differentiated to obtain a given derivative. **17b** the order of the highest derivative in a differential equation. **17c** the number of rows or columns in a determinant or square matrix. **17d** the number of members of a finite group. **18** *Mil.* (often preceded by *the*) the dress, equipment, or formation directed for a particular purpose or undertaking: *battle order.* **19 a tall order.** something difficult, demanding, or exacting. **20 in order. 20a** in sequence. **20b** properly arranged. **20c** appropriate or fitting. **21 in order that.** (*conj*) with the purpose that; so that. **22 in order to.** (*prep*; foll. by an infinitive) so that it is possible to: *to eat in order to live.* **23 keep order.** to maintain or enforce order. **24 of** *or* **in the order of.** having an approximately specified size or quantity. **25 on order.** having been ordered but not having been delivered. **26 out of order. 26a** not in sequence. **26b** not working. **26c** not following the rules or customary procedure. **27 to order. 27a** according to a buyer's specifications. **27b** on request or demand. ◆ *vb* **28** (*tr*) to give a command to (a person or animal to do or be something). **29** to request (something) to be supplied or made, esp. in return for payment. **30** (*tr*) to instruct or command to move, go, etc. (to a specified place): *they ordered her into the house.* **31** (*tr; may take a clause as object*) to authorize; prescribe: *the doctor ordered a strict diet.* **32** (*tr*) to arrange, regulate, or dispose (articles, etc.) in their proper places. **33** (*tr*) (of fate) to will; ordain. ◆ *interj* **34** an exclamation demanding that orderly behaviour be restored. [C13: from OF *ordre*, from L *ordō*]
▸ **'orderer** *n*

order-driven *adj* denoting an electronic market system, esp. for stock exchanges, in which prices are determined by the publication of orders to buy or sell. Cf. **quote-driven.**

order in council *n* (in Britain) a decree of the Cabinet, usually made under the authority of a statute: in theory a decree of the sovereign and Privy Council.

orderly ❶ ('ɔːdəlɪ) *adj* **1** in order, properly arranged, or tidy. **2** obeying or appreciating method, system, and arrangement. **3** *Mil.* of or relating to orders: *an orderly book.* ◆ *n, pl* **orderlies. 4** *Med.* a male hospital attendant. **5** *Mil.* a junior rank detailed to carry orders or perform minor tasks for a more senior officer.
▸ **'orderliness** *n*

orderly room *n Mil.* a room in the barracks of a battalion or company used for general administrative purposes.

order of magnitude *n* a numerical value expressed to the nearest power of ten.

Order of Merit *n Brit.* an order conferred on civilians and servicemen for eminence in any field.

order of the day *n* **1** the general directive of a commander in chief or the specific instructions of a commanding officer. **2** *Inf.* the pre-

THESAURUS

orchestrate *vb* **1** = **score,** arrange **2** = **organize,** arrange, concert, coordinate, integrate, present, put together, set up, stage-manage

ordain *vb* **1** = **appoint,** anoint, call, consecrate, destine, elect, frock, invest, nominate **2** = **predestine,** fate, foreordain, intend, predetermine **3** = **order,** decree, demand, dictate, enact, enjoin, establish, fix, lay down, legislate, prescribe, pronounce, rule, set, will

ordeal *n* **1** = **hardship,** affliction, agony, anguish, baptism of fire, nightmare, suffering, test, torture, trial, tribulation(s), trouble(s)
Antonyms *n* bliss, delight, elation, enjoyment, gladness, happiness, joy, pleasure

order *n* **1** = **tidiness,** arrangement, harmony, method, neatness, orderliness, organization, pattern, plan, propriety, regularity, symmetry, system **2** = **sequence,** arrangement, array, categorization, classification, codification, disposal, disposition, grouping, layout, line, line-up, ordering, placement, progression, series, setup (*inf.*), structure, succession **4** = **peace,** calm, control, discipline, law, law and order, quiet, tranquillity **5** = **class,** caste, degree, grade, hierarchy, pecking order (*inf.*), position, rank, status **6** = **kind,** breed, sort, taxonomic group, type **7** = **instruction,** behest, canon, command, decree, dictate, direction, directive, injunction, law, mandate, ordinance, precept, regulation, rule, say-so (*inf.*), stipulation **8a** = **request,** application, booking, commission, requisition, reservation **10** = **society,** association, brotherhood, community, company, fraternity, guild, league, lodge, organization, sect, sisterhood, sodality, union **20 in order: b** = **arranged,** in sequence, neat, orderly, shipshape **c** = **appropriate,** acceptable, called for, correct, fitting, O.K. *or* okay (*inf.*), right, suitable **26 out of order: b** = **broken,** broken-down, bust (*inf.*), in disrepair, inoperative, kaput (*inf.*), nonfunctional, on the blink (*sl.*), out of commission, U.S. (*inf.*), wonky (*Brit. sl.*) **c** = **improper,** indecorous, not cricket (*inf.*), not done, not on (*inf.*), out of place, out of turn, uncalled-for, wrong ◆ *vb* **28** = **command,** adjure, bid, charge, decree, demand, direct, enact, enjoin, instruct, ordain, prescribe, require **29** = **request,** apply for, book, contract for, engage, reserve, send away for **31** = **prescribe,** authorize, call for, demand **32** = **arrange,** adjust, align, catalogue, class, classify, conduct, control, dispose, group, lay out, manage, marshal, neaten, organize, put to rights, regulate, sequence, set in order, sort out, systematize, tabulate, tidy
Antonyms *n* ≠ **tidiness:** chaos, clutter, confusion, disarray, disorder, jumble, mess, muddle, pandemonium, shambles ◆ *vb* ≠ **arrange:** clutter, confuse, disarrange, disorder, disturb, jumble up, mess up, mix up, muddle, scramble

orderly *adj* **1** = **well-organized,** businesslike, in apple-pie order (*inf.*), in order, methodical, neat, regular, scientific, shipshape, systematic, systematized, tidy, trim, well-regulated **2** = **well-behaved,** controlled, decorous, disciplined, law-abiding, nonviolent, peaceable, quiet, restrained
Antonyms *adj* ≠ **well-organized:** chaotic, disorderly, disorganized, higgledy-piggledy (*inf.*), messy, sloppy, unsystematic ≠ **well-behaved:** disorderly, riotous, uncontrolled, undisciplined

scribed or only thing offered or available. **3** (in Parliament) any item of public business ordered to be considered on a specific day. **4** an agenda or programme.

Order of the Garter *n* See **Garter.**

order paper *n* a list indicating the order in which business is to be conducted, esp. in Parliament.

ordinal ('ɔːdɪnᵊl) *adj* **1** denoting a certain position in a sequence of numbers. **2** of, relating to, or characteristic of an order in biological classification. ◆ *n* **3** short for **ordinal number. 4** a book containing the forms of services for the ordination of ministers. **5** *RC Church.* a service book.

ordinal number *n* a number denoting relative position in a sequence, such as *first, second, third.* Sometimes shortened to **ordinal.**

ordinance ❶ ('ɔːdɪnəns) *n* an authoritative regulation, decree, law, or practice. [C14: from OF *ordenance,* from L *ordināre* to set in order]

ordinarily ❶ ('ɔːdᵊnrɪlɪ) *adv* in ordinary, normal, or usual practice; usually; normally.

ordinary ❶ ('ɔːdᵊnrɪ) *adj* **1** of common or established type or occurrence. **2** familiar, everyday, or unexceptional. **3** uninteresting or commonplace. **4** having regular or ex officio jurisdiction: *an ordinary judge.* **5** *Maths.* (of a differential equation) containing two variables only and derivatives of one of the variables with respect to the other. ◆ *n, pl* **ordinaries. 6** a common or average situation, amount, or degree (esp. in **out of the ordinary**). **7** a normal or commonplace person or thing. **8** *Civil law.* a judge who exercises jurisdiction in his own right. **9** (*usually cap.*) an ecclesiastic, esp. a bishop, holding an office to which certain jurisdictional powers are attached. **10** *RC Church.* **10a** the parts of the Mass that do not vary from day to day. **10b** a prescribed form of divine service, esp. the Mass. **11** the US name for **penny-farthing. 12** *Heraldry.* any of several conventional figures, such as the bend, and the cross, commonly charged upon shields. **13** *History.* a clergyman who visited condemned prisoners. **14** *Brit. obs.* **14a** a meal provided regularly at a fixed price. **14b** the inn, etc., providing such meals. **15 in ordinary.** *Brit.* (used esp. in titles) in regular service or attendance: *physician in ordinary to the sovereign.* [C16 (adj) & C13 (some n senses): ult. from L *ordinārius* orderly, from *ordō* order]

Ordinary level *n* a formal name for **O level.**

ordinary rating *n* a rank in the Royal Navy comparable to that of a private in the army.

ordinary seaman *n* a seaman of the lowest rank, being insufficiently experienced to be an able-bodied seaman.

ordinary shares *pl n Brit.* shares representing part of the capital issued by a company, entitling their holders to a share in the profits and the net assets. US equivalent: **common stock.** Cf. **preference shares.**

ordinate ('ɔːdɪnɪt) *n* the vertical or *y*-coordinate of a point in a two-dimensional system of Cartesian coordinates. Cf. **abscissa.** [C16: from NL (*linea*) *ordināte* (*applicāta*) (line applied) in an orderly manner, from *ordināre* to arrange in order]

ordination (ˌɔːdɪ'neɪʃən) *n* **1a** the act of conferring holy orders. **1b** the reception of holy orders. **2** the condition of being ordained or regulated. **3** an arrangement or order.

ordnance ❶ ('ɔːdnəns) *n* **1** cannon or artillery. **2** military supplies; munitions. **3 the.** a department of an army or government dealing with military supplies. [C14: var. of ORDINANCE]

ordnance datum *n* mean sea level calculated from observation taken at Newlyn, Cornwall, and used as the official basis for height calculation on British maps. Abbrev.: **OD.**

Ordnance Survey *n* the official map-making body of the British or Irish government.

Ordovician (ˌɔːdəʊ'vɪʃɪən) *adj* **1** of, denoting, or formed in the second period of the Palaeozoic era, between the Cambrian and Silurian periods. ◆ *n* **2 the.** the Ordovician period or rock system. [C19: from L *Ordovices,* ancient Celtic tribe in N Wales]

ordure ('ɔːdjʊə) *n* excrement; dung. [C14: via OF, from *ord* dirty, from L *horridus* shaggy]

ore (ɔː) *n* any naturally occurring mineral or aggregate of minerals from which economically important constituents, esp. metals, can be extracted. [OE *ār, ōra*]

öre ('øːrə) *n, pl* **öre.** a Scandinavian monetary unit worth one hundredth of a Swedish krona and (**øre**) one hundredth of a Danish and Norwegian krone.

oread ('ɔːrɪˌæd) *n Greek myth.* a mountain nymph. [C16: via L from Gk *Oreias,* from *oros* mountain]

oregano (ˌɒrɪ'gɑːnəʊ) *n* **1** a Mediterranean variety of wild marjoram (*Origanum vulgare*), with pungent leaves. **2** the dried powdered leaves of this plant, used to season food. [C18: American Sp., from Sp., from L *orīganum,* from Gk *origanon* an aromatic herb, ? marjoram]

orfe (ɔːf) *n* a small slender European cyprinoid fish, occurring in two colour varieties, namely the **silver orfe** and the **golden orfe,** popular aquarium fishes. [C17: from G; rel. to L *orphus,* Gk *orphos* the sea perch]

organ ❶ ('ɔːgən) *n* **1a** Also called: **pipe organ.** a large complex musical keyboard instrument in which sound is produced by means of a number of pipes arranged in sets or stops, supplied with air from a bellows. **1b** (*as modifier*): *organ stop; organ loft.* **2** any instrument, such as a harmonium, in which sound is produced in this way. **3** a fully differentiated structural and functional unit, such as a kidney or a root, in an animal or plant. **4** an agency or medium of communication, esp. a periodical issued by a specialist group or party. **5** an instrument with which something is done or accomplished. **6** a euphemistic word for **penis.** [C13: from OF *organe,* from L *organum* implement, from Gk *organon* tool]

organdie *or esp. US* **organdy** ('ɔːgəndɪ) *n, pl* **organdies.** a fine and slightly stiff cotton fabric used for dresses, etc. [C19: from F *organdi,* from ?]

organelle (ˌɔːgə'nɛl) *n* a structural and functional unit in a cell or unicellular organism. [C20: from NL *organella,* from L *organum;* see ORGAN]

organ-grinder *n* a street musician playing a hand organ for money.

organic ❶ (ɔː'gænɪk) *adj* **1** of, relating to, or derived from living plants and animals. **2** of or relating to animal or plant constituents or products having a carbon basis. **3** of or relating to one or more organs of an animal or plant. **4** of, relating to, or belonging to the class of chemical compounds that are formed from carbon: *an organic compound.* **5** constitutional in the structure of something; fundamental; integral. **6** of or characterized by the coordination of integral parts; organized. **7** of or relating to the essential constitutional laws regulating the government of a state: *organic law.* **8** of, relating to, or grown with the use of fertilizers or pesticides deriving from animal or vegetable matter, rather than from chemicals. ◆ *n* **9** any substance, such as a fertilizer or pesticide, that is derived from animal or vegetable matter rather than from chemicals.
▸**or'ganically** *adv*

organic chemistry *n* the branch of chemistry concerned with the compounds of carbon.

organism ❶ ('ɔːgəˌnɪzəm) *n* **1** any living animal or plant, including any bacterium or virus. **2** anything resembling a living creature in structure, behaviour, etc.
▸**ˌorgan'ismal** *or* **ˌorgan'ismic** *adj* ▸**ˌorgan'ismally** *adv*

organist ('ɔːgənɪst) *n* a person who plays the organ.

organization ❶ *or* **organisation** (ˌɔːgənaɪ'zeɪʃən) *n* **1** the act of organizing or the state of being organized. **2** an organized structure or whole. **3** a business or administrative concern united and constructed for a particular end. **4** a body of administrative officials, as of a government department, etc. **5** order, tidiness, or system; method.
▸**ˌorgani'zational** *or* **ˌorgani'sational** *adj*

organizational psychology *n* the study of the structure of an organization and of the ways in which the people in it interact, usually undertaken in order to improve the organization.

organize ❶ *or* **organise** ('ɔːgəˌnaɪz) *vb* **organizes, organizing, organized** *or* **organises, organising, organised. 1** to form (parts or elements of something) into a structured whole; coordinate. **2** (*tr*) to arrange methodically or in order. **3** (*tr*) to provide with an organic structure. **4** (*tr*) to

THESAURUS

ordinance *n* = **rule**, canon, command, decree, dictum, edict, enactment, fiat, law, order, precept, regulation, ruling, statute

ordinarily *adv* = **usually**, as a rule, commonly, customarily, generally, habitually, in general, in the general run (of things), in the usual way, normally
Antonyms *adv* hardly ever, infrequently, occasionally, rarely, scarcely, seldom, uncommonly

ordinary *adj* **1, 2** = **usual**, accustomed, common, conventional, customary, down-to-earth, established, everyday, familiar, habitual, household, normal, prevailing, quotidian, regular, routine, settled, simple, standard, stock, typical, unexceptional, unpretentious, wonted **3** = **commonplace**, banal, common or garden (*inf.*), homespun, humble, humdrum, modest, mundane, pedestrian, plain, prosaic, run-of-the-mill, stereotyped, unmemorable, unremarkable, workaday ◆ *n* **6 out of the ordinary** = **unusual**, atypical, distinguished, exceptional, exciting, extraordinary, high-calibre, imaginative, important, impressive, inspired, noteworthy, outstanding, rare, remarkable, significant, special, striking, superior, uncommon
Antonyms *adj* ≠ **commonplace, average:** distinguished, exceptional, extraordinary, important, impressive, inspired, notable, novel, outstanding, rare, significant, superior, uncommon, unconventional, unique, unusual

ordnance *n* **1, 2** = **weapons**, arms, artillery, big guns, cannon, guns, materiel, munitions

organ *n* **3** = **part**, element, member, process, structure, unit **4** = **medium**, agency, channel, forum, journal, means, mouthpiece, newspaper, paper, periodical, publication, vehicle, voice **5** = **instrument**, device, implement, tool

organic *adj* **1** = **natural**, animate, biological, biotic, live, living **5** = **integral**, anatomical, constitutional, fundamental, immanent, inherent, innate, structural **6** = **systematic**, integrated, methodical, ordered, organized, structured

organism *n* **1** = **creature**, animal, being, body, entity, living thing, structure

organization *n* **1** = **management**, assembling, assembly, construction, coordination, direction, disposal, formation, forming, formulation, making, methodology, organizing, planning, regulation, running, standardization, structuring **2** = **structure**, arrangement, chemistry, composition, configuration, conformation, constitution, design, format, framework, grouping, make-up, method, organism, pattern, plan, system, unity, whole **3** = **group**, association, body, combine, company, concern, confederation, consortium, corporation, federation, institution, league, outfit (*inf.*), syndicate

organize *vb* **1** = **plan**, arrange, be responsible for, constitute, construct, coordinate, establish, form, frame, get going, get together, lay the foundations of, lick into shape, look after, marshal, put together, run, see to (*inf.*), set up, shape, straighten out, take care of **2** = **put in order**, arrange, catalogue, classify, codify, dispose, group, pigeonhole, systematize, tabulate
Antonyms *vb* ≠ **plan:** confuse, derange, disrupt,

enlist (the workers) of (a factory, etc.) in a trade union. 5 (*intr*) to join or form an organization or trade union. 6 (*tr*) *Inf.* to put (oneself) in an alert and responsible frame of mind. [C15: from Med. L *organizare*, from L *organum* ORGAN]
▸**'organ,izer** *or* **'organ,iser** *n*

organometallic (ɔː,gænəʊmɪ'tælɪk) *adj* of, concerned with, or being an organic compound with one or more metal atoms in its molecules.

organon ('ɔːgə,nɒn) *or* **organum** *n, pl* **organa** (-nə), **organons** *or* **organa, organums.** 1 *Epistemology.* a system of logical or scientific rules, esp. that of Aristotle. 2 *Arch.* a sense organ, regarded as an instrument for acquiring knowledge. [C16: from Gk: implement; see ORGAN]

organophosphate (ɔː,gænəʊ'fɒsfeɪt) *n* any of a group of organic compounds containing phosphorus and used as a pesticide.

organotin (ɔːgænəʊ'tɪn) *adj* 1 of, concerned with, or being an organic compound with one or more tin atoms in its molecules. ◆ *n* 2 such a compound used as a pesticide, formerly believed to decompose safely, now found to be toxic in the food chain.

organza (ɔː'gænzə) *n* a thin stiff fabric of silk, cotton, nylon, rayon, etc. [C20: from ?]

orgasm Ⓣ ('ɔːgæzəm) *n* 1 the most intense point during sexual excitement. 2 *Rare.* intense or violent excitement. [C17: from NL *orgasmus*, from Gk *orgasmos*, from *organ* to mature, swell]
▸**or'gasmic** *or* **or'gastic** *adj*

orgeat ('ɔːʒɑː) *n* a drink made from barley or almonds, and orangeflower water. [C18: via F, from *orge* barley, from L *hordeum*]

orgy Ⓣ ('ɔːdʒɪ) *n, pl* **orgies.** 1 a wild gathering marked by promiscuous sexual activity, excessive drinking, etc. 2 an act of immoderate or frenzied indulgence. 3 (*often pl*) secret religious rites of Dionysus, Bacchus, etc., marked by drinking, dancing, and songs. [C16: from F *orgies*, from L *orgia*, from Gk: nocturnal festival]
▸**,orgi'astic** *adj*

oribi ('ɒrɪbɪ) *n, pl* **oribi** *or* **oribis.** a small African antelope of the grasslands and bush south of the Sahara, with fawn-coloured coat and, in the male, ridged spikelike horns. [C18: from Afrik., prob. from Khoikhoi *arab*]

oriel window ('ɔːrɪəl) *n* a bay window, esp. one that is supported by one or more brackets or corbels. Sometimes shortened to **oriel.** [C14: from OF *oriol* gallery, ?from Med. L *auleolum* niche]

orient Ⓣ *n* ('ɔːrɪənt). 1 *Poetic.* another word for **east.** Cf. **occident.** 2 *Arch.* the eastern sky or the dawn. 3a the iridescent lustre of a pearl. 3b (*as modifier*): *orient pearls.* 4 a pearl of high quality. ◆ *adj* ('ɔːrɪənt). 5 *Now chiefly poetic.* oriental. 6 *Arch.* (of the sun, stars, etc.) rising. ◆ *vb* ('ɔːrɪ,ɛnt). 7 to adjust or align (oneself or something else) according to surroundings or circumstances. 8 (*tr*) to position or set (a map, etc.) with reference to the compass or other specific directions. 9 (*tr*) to build (a church) with the chancel end facing in an easterly direction. [C18: via F from L *oriēns* rising (sun), from *orīrī* to rise]

Orient ('ɔːrɪənt) *n* (usually preceded by *the*) 1 the countries east of the Mediterranean. 2 the eastern hemisphere.

oriental (,ɔːrɪ'ɛntᵊl) *adj* another word for **eastern.**

Oriental (,ɔːrɪ'ɛntᵊl) *adj* 1 (*sometimes not cap.*) of or relating to the Orient. 2 of or denoting a region consisting of southeastern Asia from India to Borneo, Java, and the Philippines. ◆ *n* 3 (*sometimes not cap.*) an inhabitant, esp. a native, of the Orient.

Orientalism (,ɔːrɪ'ɛntə,lɪzəm) *n* 1 knowledge of or devotion to the Orient. 2 an Oriental quality, style, or trait.
▸**,Ori'entalist** *n* ▸**,Ori,ental'istic** *adj*

orientate ('ɔːrɪɛn,teɪt) *vb* **orientates, orientating, orientated.** another word for **orient** (senses 7, 8, 9).

orientation Ⓣ (,ɔːrɪɛn'teɪʃən) *n* 1 the act or process of orienting or the state of being oriented. 2 positioning with relation to the compass or other specific directions. 3 the adjustment or alignment of oneself or one's ideas to surroundings or circumstances. 4 Also called: **orientation course.** *Chiefly US & Canad.* 4a a course, lecture, etc., introducing a new situation or environment. 4b (*as modifier*): *an orientation talk.* 5 *Psychol.* the knowledge of one's own temporal, social, and practical circumstances. 6 the siting of a church on an east-west axis.
▸**,orien'tational** *adj*

-oriented *suffix forming adjectives.* geared or directed towards: *sports-oriented.*

orienteer (,ɔːrɪɛn'tɪə) *vb* (*intr*) 1 to take part in orienteering. ◆ *n* 2 a person who takes part in orienteering.

orienteering (,ɔːrɪɛn'tɪərɪŋ) *n* a sport in which contestants race on foot over a course consisting of checkpoints found with the aid of a map and a compass. [C20: from Swedish *orientering*]

orifice Ⓣ ('ɒrɪfɪs) *n Chiefly technical.* an opening or mouth into a cavity; vent; aperture. [C16: via F from LL *ōrificium*, from L *ōs* mouth + *facere* to make]

oriflamme ('ɒrɪ,flæm) *n* a scarlet flag adopted as the national banner of France in the Middle Ages. [C15: via OF, from L *aurum* gold + *flamma* flame]

orig. *abbrev. for:* 1 origin. 2 original(ly).

origami (,ɒrɪ'gɑːmɪ) *n* the art or process, originally Japanese, of paper folding. [from Japanese, from *ori* a fold + *kami* paper]

origan ('ɒrɪgən) *n* another name for **marjoram** (sense 2). [C16: from L *orīganum*, from Gk *origanon* an aromatic herb]

origanum (,ɒrɪ'gɑːnəm) *n* See **oregano.**

origin Ⓣ ('ɒrɪdʒɪn) *n* 1 a primary source; derivation. 2 the beginning of something; first part. 3 (*often pl*) ancestry or parentage; birth; extraction. 4 *Anat.* 4a the end of a muscle, opposite its point of insertion. 4b the beginning of a nerve or blood vessel or the site where it first starts to branch out. 5 *Maths.* 5a the point of intersection of coordinate axes or planes. 5b the point whose coordinates are all zero. 6 *Commerce.* the country from which a commodity or product originates: *shipment from origin.* [C16: from F *origine*, from L *orīgō* beginning]

original Ⓣ (ə'rɪdʒɪnᵊl) *adj* 1 of or relating to an origin or beginning. 2 fresh and unusual; novel. 3 able to think of or carry out new ideas or concepts. 4 being that from which a copy, translation, etc., is made. ◆ *n* 5 the first and genuine form of something, from which others are derived. 6 a person or thing used as a model in art or literature. 7 a person whose way of thinking is unusual or creative. 8 the first form or occurrence of something.
▸**o'riginally** *adv*

originality Ⓣ (ə,rɪdʒɪ'nælɪtɪ) *n, pl* **originalities.** 1 the quality or condition of being original. 2 the ability to create or innovate.

original sin *n* a state of sin held to be innate in mankind as the descendants of Adam.

originate Ⓣ (ə'rɪdʒɪ,neɪt) *vb* **originates, originating, originated.** 1 to come or bring into being. 2 (*intr*) *US & Canad.* (of a bus, train, etc.) to begin its journey at a specified point.
▸**o,rigi'nation** *n* ▸**o'rigi,nator** *n*

O-ring *n* a rubber ring used in machinery as a seal against oil, air, etc.

oriole ('ɔːrɪ,əʊl) *n* 1 a tropical Old World songbird, such as the **golden oriole,** having a long pointed bill and a mostly yellow-and-black plumage. 2 an American songbird, esp. the Baltimore oriole, with a typical male plumage of black with either orange or yellow. [C18: from Med. L *oryolus*, from L *aureolus*, dim. of *aureus*, from *aurum* gold]

Orion (ə'raɪən) *n* a conspicuous constellation containing two first-magnitude stars (Betelgeuse and Rigel) and a distant bright emission nebula (the **Orion Nebula**).

orison ('ɒrɪzᵊn) *n Literary.* another word for **prayer**[1] (senses 1 and 2). [C12: from OF *oreison*, from LL *ōrātiō*, from L: speech, from *ōrāre* to speak]

Oriya (ɒ'riːə) *n* 1 (*pl* **Oriya**) a member of a people of India living chiefly

THESAURUS

upset ≠ **put in order:** disorganize, jumble, mix up, muddle, scramble

orgasm *n* 1 = **climax**

orgiastic *adj* 1 = **wild,** abandoned, bacchanalian, bacchic, debauched, depraved, Dionysian, dissolute, frenetic, riotous, Saturnalian, wanton

orgy *n* 1 = **revel,** bacchanal, bacchanalia, carousal, carouse, debauch, revelry, Saturnalia 2 = **spree,** binge (*inf.*), bout, excess, indulgence, overindulgence, splurge, surfeit

orient *vb* 7 = **adjust,** acclimatize, adapt, align, familiarize, find one's feet (*inf.*), get one's bearings, get the lie of the land, orientate

orientation *n* 1 = **adjustment,** acclimatization, adaptation, assimilation, breaking in, familiarization, introduction, settling in 2 = **position,** bearings, coordination, direction, location, sense of direction

orifice *n* = **opening,** aperture, cleft, hole, mouth, perforation, pore, rent, vent

origin *n* 1 = **root,** base, basis, cause, derivation, *fons et origo*, font (*poetic*), fount, fountain, fountainhead, occasion, provenance, roots, source, spring, wellspring 2 = **beginning,** birth, commencement, creation, dawning, early stages, emergence, foundation, genesis, inauguration, inception, launch, origination, outset, start 3 = **ancestry,** beginnings, birth, descent, extraction, family, heritage, lineage, parentage, pedigree, stirps, stock
Antonyms *n* ≠ **beginning:** conclusion, culmination, death, end, expiry, finale, finish, outcome, termination

original *adj* 1 = **first,** aboriginal, autochthonous, commencing, earliest, early, embryonic, infant, initial, introductory, opening, primary, primitive, primordial, pristine, rudimentary, starting 2 = **new,** fresh, groundbreaking, innovative, innovatory, novel, seminal, unconventional, unprecedented, untried, unusual 3 = **creative,** fertile, imaginative, ingenious, inventive, resourceful 4 = **authentic,** archetypal, first, first-hand, genuine, master, primary, prototypical ◆ *n* 5 = **prototype,** archetype, master, model, paradigm, pattern, precedent, standard, type 7 = **character,** card (*inf.*), case (*inf.*), eccentric, nonconformist, nut (*sl.*), oddball (*inf.*), oddity, queer fish (*Brit. inf.*)
Antonyms *adj* ≠ **first:** final, last, latest ≠ **new:** antiquated, banal, commonplace, conventional, familiar, normal, old, old-fashioned, ordinary, stale, standard, stock, traditional, typical, unimaginative, unoriginal, usual ≠ **authentic:** borrowed, copied, secondary, unoriginal ◆ *n* ≠ **prototype:** copy, imitation, replica, reproduction

originality *n* 2 = **novelty,** boldness, break with tradition, cleverness, creativeness, creative spirit, creativity, daring, freshness, imagination, imaginativeness, individuality, ingenuity, innovation, innovativeness, inventiveness, new ideas, newness, resourcefulness, unconventionality, unorthodoxy
Antonyms *n* conformity, conventionality, imitativeness, normality, orthodoxy, regularity, staleness, traditionalism

originally *adv* 1 = **initially,** at first, at the outset, at the start, by birth, by derivation, by origin, first, in the beginning, in the first place, to begin with

originate *vb* 1 = **begin,** arise, be born, come, conceive, create, derive, develop, emanate, emerge, evolve, flow, generate, initiate, issue, proceed, result, rise, set in motion, set up, spring, start, stem
Antonyms *vb* cease, conclude, end, finish, terminate, wind up

originator *n* 1 = **creator,** architect, author, father *or* mother, founder, generator, innovator, inventor, maker, pioneer, prime mover in Orissa. 2 the state language of Orissa, belonging to the Indo-European family.

Orlon ('ɔːlɒn) *n Trademark.* a crease-resistant acrylic fibre or fabric used for clothing, etc.

orlop *or* **orlop deck** ('ɔːlɒp) *n Naut.* (in a vessel with four or more decks) the lowest deck. [C15: from Du. *overloopen* to spill]

ormer ('ɔːmə) *n* 1 Also called: **sea-ear.** an edible marine gastropod mollusc that has an ear-shaped shell perforated with holes and occurs near the Channel Islands. 2 any other abalone. [C17: from F, apparently from L *auris* ear + *mare* sea]

ormolu ('ɔːmə,luː) *n* **1a** a gold-coloured alloy of copper, tin, or zinc used to decorate furniture, etc. **1b** (*as modifier*): *an ormolu clock.* 2 gold prepared for gilding. [C18: from F *or moulu* ground gold]

ornament ⓣ *n* ('ɔːnəmənt). 1 anything that enhances the appearance of a person or thing. 2 decorations collectively: *she was totally without ornament.* 3 a small decorative object. 4 something regarded as a source of pride or beauty. 5 *Music.* any of several decorations, such as the trill, etc. ◆ *vb* ('ɔːnə,mɛnt). (*tr*) 6 to decorate with or as if with ornaments. 7 to serve as an ornament to. [C14: from L *ornāmentum,* from *ornāre* to adorn]

▸ **,ornamen'tation** *n*

ornamental ⓣ (,ɔːnə'mentᵊl) *adj* 1 of value as an ornament; decorative. 2 (of a plant) used to decorate houses, gardens, etc. ◆ *n* 3 a plant cultivated for show or decoration.

▸ **,orna'mentally** *adv*

ornate ⓣ (ɔː'neɪt) *adj* 1 heavily or elaborately decorated. 2 (of style in writing, etc.) over-embellished; flowery. [C15: from L *ornāre* to decorate]

▸ **or'nately** *adv* ▸ **or'nateness** *n*

ornery ('ɔːnərɪ) *adj US & Canad. dialect or inf.* 1 stubborn or vile-tempered. 2 low; treacherous: *an ornery trick.* 3 ordinary. [C19: alteration of ORDINARY]

▸ **'orneriness** *n*

ornitho- *or before a vowel* **ornith-** *combining form.* bird or birds. [from Gk *ornis, ornith-* bird]

ornithology (,ɔːnɪ'θɒlədʒɪ) *n* the study of birds.

▸ **ornithological** (,ɔːnɪθə'lɒdʒɪkᵊl) *adj* ▸ **,ornitho'logically** *adv* ▸ **,orni'thologist** *n*

ornithorhynchus (,ɔːnɪθəʊ'rɪŋkəs) *n* the technical name for **duck-billed platypus.** [C19: NL, from ORNITHO- + Gk *rhunkhos* bill]

oro-[1] *combining form.* mountain: *orogeny.* [from Gk *oros*]

oro-[2] *combining form.* oral; mouth: *oromaxillary.* [from L, from *ōs*]

orogeny (ɒ'rɒdʒɪnɪ) *or* **orogenesis** (,ɒrəʊ'dʒenɪsɪs) *n* the formation of mountain ranges.

▸ **orogenic** (,ɒrəʊ'dʒenɪk) *or* **orogenetic** (,ɒrəʊdʒɪ'netɪk) *adj*

orotund ('ɒrəʊ,tʌnd) *adj* 1 (of the voice) resonant; booming. 2 (of speech or writing) bombastic; pompous. [C18: from L *ore rotundo* with rounded mouth]

orphan ('ɔːfən) *n* **1a** a child, one or both of whose parents are dead. **1b** (*as modifier*): *an orphan child.* ◆ *vb* 2 (*tr*) to deprive of one or both parents. [C15: from LL *orphanus,* from Gk *orphanos*]

orphanage ('ɔːfənɪdʒ) *n* 1 an institution for orphans and abandoned children. 2 the state of being an orphan.

Orphean ('ɔːfɪən) *adj* 1 of or relating to Orpheus, a poet and lyre-player in Greek mythology. 2 melodious or enchanting.

Orphic ('ɔːfɪk) *adj* 1 of or relating to Orpheus or Orphism, a mystery religion of ancient Greece. 2 (*sometimes not cap.*) mystical or occult.

▸ **'Orphically** *adv*

orpine ('ɔːpaɪn) *or* **orpin** ('ɔːpɪn) *n* a succulent perennial N temperate plant with toothed leaves and heads of small purplish-white flowers. [C14: from OF, apparently from *orpiment,* a yellow mineral (? referring to the yellow flowers of a related species)]

orrery ('ɒrərɪ) *n, pl* **orreries.** a mechanical model of the solar system in which the planets can be moved at the correct relative velocities around the sun. [C18: orig. made for Charles Boyle, Earl of *Orrery*]

orris[1] *or* **orrice** ('ɒrɪs) *n* 1 any of various irises that have fragrant rhizomes. 2 Also: **orrisroot.** the rhizome of such a plant, prepared and used as perfume. [C16: var. of IRIS]

orris[2] ('ɒrɪs) *n* a kind of lace made of gold or silver, used esp. in the 18th century. [from Old French *orfreis,* from L *auriphrygium* Phrygian gold]

orthicon ('ɔːθɪ,kɒn) *n* a television camera tube in which an optical image produces a corresponding electrical charge pattern on a mosaic surface that is scanned from behind by an electron beam. The resulting discharge of the mosaic provides the output signal current. See also **image orthicon.** [C20: from ORTHO- + ICON(OSCOPE)]

ortho- *or before a vowel* **orth-** *combining form.* 1 straight or upright: *orthorhombic.* 2 perpendicular or at right angles: *orthogonal.* 3 correct or right: *orthodontics.* 4 (*often in italics*) denoting an organic compound containing a benzene ring with substituents attached to adjacent carbon atoms (the 1,2- positions). 5 denoting an oxyacid regarded as the highest hydrated form of the anhydride or a salt of such an acid: *orthophosphoric acid.* 6 denoting a diatomic substance in which the spins of the two atoms are parallel: *orthohydrogen.* [from Gk *orthos* straight, upright]

orthochromatic (,ɔːθəʊkrəʊ'mætɪk) *adj Photog.* of or relating to an emulsion giving a rendering of relative light intensities of different colours that corresponds approximately to the colour sensitivity of the eye, esp. one that is insensitive to red light. Sometimes shortened to **ortho.**

▸ **orthochromatism** (,ɔːθəʊ'krəʊmə,tɪzəm) *n*

orthoclase ('ɔːθəʊ,kleɪs, -,kleɪz) *n* a white or coloured feldspar mineral consisting of an aluminium silicate of potassium in monoclinic crystalline form.

orthodontics (,ɔːθəʊ'dɒntɪks) *or* **orthodontia** (,ɔːθəʊ'dɒntɪə) *n* (*functioning as sing*) the branch of dentistry concerned with preventing or correcting irregularities of the teeth.

▸ **,ortho'dontic** *adj* ▸ **,ortho'dontist** *n*

orthodox ⓣ ('ɔːθə,dɒks) *adj* 1 conforming with established standards, as in religion, behaviour, or attitudes. 2 conforming to the Christian faith as established by the early Church. [C16: via Church L from Gk *orthodoxos,* from *orthos* correct + *doxa* belief]

▸ **'ortho,doxy** *n*

Orthodox ('ɔːθə,dɒks) *adj* 1 of or relating to the Orthodox Church of the East. 2 (*sometimes not cap.*) of or relating to Orthodox Judaism.

Orthodox Church *n* 1 the collective body of those Eastern Churches that were separated from the western Church in the 11th century and are in communion with the Greek patriarch of Constantinople. 2 any of these Churches.

Orthodox Judaism *n* a form of Judaism characterized by traditional interpretation and strict observance of the Mosaic Law.

orthoepy ('ɔːθəʊ,ɛpɪ) *n* the study of correct or standard pronunciation. [C17: from Gk *orthoepeia,* from ORTHO- straight + *epos* word]

▸ **orthoepic** (,ɔːθəʊ'ɛpɪk) *adj* ▸ **,ortho'epically** *adv*

orthogenesis (,ɔːθəʊ'dʒenɪsɪs) *n* 1 *Biol.* **1a** evolution of a group of organisms in a particular direction, which is generally predetermined. **1b** the theory that proposes such a development. 2 the theory that there is a series of stages through which all cultures pass in the same order.

▸ **orthogenetic** (,ɔːθəʊdʒɪ'netɪk) *adj* ▸ **,orthoge'netically** *adv*

orthogonal (ɔː'θɒgənᵊl) *adj* relating to, consisting of, or involving right angles; perpendicular.

▸ **or'thogonally** *adv*

orthographic (,ɔːθə'græfɪk) *or* **orthographical** *adj* of or relating to spelling.

▸ **,ortho'graphically** *adv*

orthography (ɔː'θɒgrəfɪ) *n, pl* **orthographies.** 1 a writing system. **2a** spelling considered to be correct. **2b** the principles underlying spelling. 3 the study of spelling.

▸ **or'thographer** *or* **or'thographist** *n*

orthopaedics *or US* **orthopedics** (,ɔːθəʊ'piːdɪks) *n* (*functioning as sing*) 1 the branch of surgery concerned with disorders of the spine and joints and the repair of deformities of these parts. 2 **dental orthopaedics.** another name for **orthodontics.**

▸ **,ortho'paedic** *or US* **,ortho'pedic** *adj* ▸ **,ortho'paedist** *or US* **,ortho'pedist** *n*

orthopteran (ɔː'θɒptərən) *n, pl* **orthoptera** (-tərə). 1 Also: **orthopteron** (*pl* **orthoptera**). any orthopterous insect. ◆ *adj* 2 another word for **orthopterous.**

orthopterous (ɔː'θɒptərəs) *adj* of, relating to, or belonging to a large order of insects, including crickets, locusts, and grasshoppers, having leathery forewings and membranous hind wings.

orthoptic (ɔː'θɒptɪk) *adj* relating to normal binocular vision.

orthoptics (ɔː'θɒptɪks) *n* (*functioning as sing*) the science or practice of correcting defective vision, as by exercises to strengthen weak eye muscles.

▸ **or'thoptist** *n*

orthorhombic (,ɔːθəʊ'rɒmbɪk) *adj Crystallog.* relating to the crystal system characterized by three mutually perpendicular unequal axes.

ortolan ('ɔːtələn) *n* 1 a brownish Old World bunting regarded as a delicacy. 2 any of various other small birds eaten as delicacies, esp. the bobolink. [C17: via F from L *hortulānus,* from *hortulus,* dim. of *hortus* garden]

THESAURUS

ornament *n* 3 = **decoration,** accessory, adornment, bauble, embellishment, festoon, frill, furbelow, garnish, gewgaw, knick-knack, trimming, trinket 4 = **leading light,** flower, honour, jewel, pride, treasure ◆ *vb* 6 = **decorate,** adorn, beautify, bedizen (*arch.*), brighten, deck, dress up, embellish, festoon, garnish, gild, grace, prettify, prink, trim

ornamental *adj* 1 = **decorative,** attractive, beautifying, embellishing, for show, showy

ornamentation *n* 6 = **decoration,** adornment, elaboration, embellishment, embroidery, frills, ornateness

ornate *adj* 1, 2 = **elaborate,** aureate, baroque, beautiful, bedecked, busy, convoluted, decorated, elegant, fancy, florid, flowery, fussy, high-wrought, ornamented, overelaborate, rococo

Antonyms *adj* austere, bare, basic, ordinary, plain, severe, simple, spartan, stark, subdued, unadorned, unfussy

orthodox *adj* 1 = **established,** accepted, approved, conformist, conventional, correct, customary, doctrinal, kosher (*inf.*), official, received, sound, traditional, true, well-established

Antonyms *adj* eccentric, heretical, left-field (*inf.*), liberal, nonconformist, novel, off-the-wall (*sl.*), original, radical, unconventional, unorthodox, unusual

orthodoxy *n* 1 = **conformity,** authenticity, authoritativeness, authority, conformism, conventionality, devotion, devoutness, faithfulness, inflexibility, received wisdom, soundness, traditionalism

Antonyms *n* flexibility, heresy, heterodoxy, impiety, nonconformism, nonconformity, unconventionality

-ory[1] *suffix forming nouns.* **1** indicating a place for: *observatory.* **2** something having a specified use: *directory.* [via OF *-orie,* from L *-ōrium, -ōria*]

-ory[2] *suffix forming adjectives.* of or relating to; characterized by; having the effect of: *contributory.* [via OF *-orie,* from L *-ōrius*]

oryx ('ɒrɪks) *n, pl* **oryxes** *or* **oryx.** any large African antelope of the genus *Oryx,* typically having long straight nearly upright horns. [C14: via L from Gk *orux* stonemason's axe, used also of the pointed horns of an antelope]

os[1] (ɒs) *n, pl* **ossa** ('ɒsə). *Anat.* the technical name for **bone.** [C16: from L: bone]

os[2] (ɒs) *n, pl* **ora.** *Anat., zool.* a mouth or mouthlike part or opening. [C18: from L]

Os *the chemical symbol for* osmium.

OS *abbrev. for:* **1** Old Saxon (language). **2** Old Style. **3** Ordinary Seaman. **4** (in Britain) Ordnance Survey. **5** outsize.

Osage orange (əʊ'seɪdʒ) *n* **1** a North American thorny tree, grown for hedges and ornament. **2** the warty orange-like fruit of this plant. [from *Osage* Amerind tribe]

Oscar ('ɒskə) *n* any of several small gold statuettes awarded annually in the US for outstanding achievements in films. Official name: **Academy Award.** [C20: said to have been named after a remark made by a secretary that it reminded her of her uncle Oscar]

oscillate ❶ ('ɒsɪˌleɪt) *vb* **oscillates, oscillating, oscillated. 1** (*intr*) to move or swing from side to side regularly. **2** (*intr*) to waver between opinions, courses of action, etc. **3** *Physics.* to undergo or produce or cause to undergo or produce oscillation. [C18: from L *oscillāre* to swing]

oscillating universe theory *n* the theory that the universe is oscillating between periods of expansion and contraction.

oscillation ❶ (ˌɒsɪ'leɪʃən) *n* **1** *Statistics, physics.* **1a** regular fluctuation in value, position, or state about a mean value, such as the variation in an alternating current. **1b** a single cycle of such a fluctuation. **2** the act or process of oscillating.
▸**oscillatory** ('ɒsɪlətərɪ, -trɪ) *adj*

oscillator ('ɒsɪˌleɪtə) *n* **1** a circuit or instrument for producing an alternating current or voltage of a required frequency. **2** any instrument for producing oscillations. **3** a person or thing that oscillates.

oscillogram (ɒ'sɪləˌgræm) *n* the recording obtained from an oscillograph or the trace on an oscilloscope screen.

oscillograph (ɒ'sɪləˌgrɑːf) *n* a device for producing a graphical record of the variation of an oscillating quantity, such as an electric current.
▸**oscillographic** (ɒˌsɪlə'græfɪk) *adj* ▸**oscillography** (ˌɒsɪ'lɒgrəfɪ) *n*

oscilloscope (ɒ'sɪləˌskəʊp) *n* an instrument for producing a representation of a rapidly changing quantity on the screen of a cathode-ray tube.

oscine ('ɒsaɪn, 'ɒsɪn) *adj* of, relating to, or belonging to the suborder of passerine birds that includes most of the songbirds. [C17: via NL from L *oscen* singing bird]

oscitancy ('ɒsɪtənsɪ) *or* **oscitance** *n, pl* **oscitancies** *or* **oscitances. 1** the state of being drowsy, lazy, or inattentive. **2** the act of yawning. ◆ Also called: **oscitation.** [C17: from L *oscitāre* to yawn]
▸**'oscitant** *adj*

oscular ('ɒskjʊlə) *adj* **1** *Zool.* of or relating to a mouthlike aperture, esp. of a sponge. **2** of or relating to the mouth or to kissing.

osculate ('ɒskjʊˌleɪt) *vb* **osculates, osculating, osculated. 1** *Usually humorous.* to kiss. **2** (*intr*) (of an organism) to be intermediate between two taxonomic groups. **3** *Geom.* to touch in osculation. [C17: from L *ōsculārī* to kiss]

osculation (ˌɒskjʊ'leɪʃən) *n* **1** *Maths.* Also called: **tacnode.** a point at which two branches of a curve have a common tangent, each branch extending in both directions of the tangent. **2** *Rare.* the act of kissing.
▸**osculatory** ('ɒskjʊlətərɪ, -trɪ) *adj*

-ose[1] *suffix forming adjectives.* possessing; resembling: *grandiose.* [from L *-ōsus;* see -OUS]

-ose[2] *suffix forming nouns.* **1** indicating a carbohydrate, esp. a sugar: *lactose.* **2** indicating a decomposition product of protein: *albumose.* [from GLUCOSE]

osier ('əʊzɪə) *n* **1** any of various willow trees, whose flexible branches or twigs are used for making baskets, etc. **2** a twig or branch from such a tree. **3** any of several North American dogwoods, esp. the red osier. [C14: from OF, prob. from Med. L *auseria,* ? of Gaulish origin]

-osis *suffix forming nouns.* **1** indicating a process or state: *metamorphosis.* **2** indicating a diseased condition: *tuberculosis.* Cf. **-iasis. 3** indicating the formation or development of something: *fibrosis.* [from Gk, suffix used to form nouns from verbs with infinitives in *-oein* or *-oun*]

Osmanli (ɒz'mænlɪ) *adj* **1** of or relating to the Ottoman Empire. ◆ *n* **2** (formerly) a subject of the Ottoman Empire. [C19: from Turkish, from *Osman* I (1259–1326), Turkish Sultan]

osmiridium (ˌɒzmɪ'rɪdɪəm) *n* a very hard corrosion-resistant white or grey natural alloy of osmium and iridium: used in pen nibs, etc. [C19: from OSM(IUM) + IRIDIUM]

osmium ('ɒzmɪəm) *n* a very hard brittle bluish-white metal, the heaviest known element, occurring with platinum and alloyed with iridium in osmiridium. Symbol: Os; atomic no.: 76; atomic wt.: 190.2. [C19: from Gk *osmē* smell, from its penetrating odour]

osmoregulation (ˌɒzməʊˌrɛgjʊ'leɪʃən) *n Zool.* the adjustment of the osmotic pressure of a cell or organism in relation to the surrounding fluid.

osmose ('ɒzməʊs, -məʊz, 'ɒs-) *vb* **osmoses, osmosing, osmosed.** to undergo or cause to undergo osmosis. [C19 (n): abstracted from the earlier terms *endosmose* and *exosmose;* rel. to Gk *ōsmos* push]

osmosis (ɒz'məʊsɪs, ɒs-) *n* **1** the tendency of the solvent of a less concentrated solution of dissolved molecules to pass through a semipermeable membrane into a more concentrated solution until both solutions are of the same concentration. **2** diffusion through any membrane or porous barrier, as in dialysis. **3** gradual or unconscious assimilation or adoption, as of ideas. [C19: Latinized form from OSMOSE, from Gk *ōsmos* push]
▸**osmotic** (ɒz'mɒtɪk, ɒs-) *adj* ▸**os'motically** *adv*

osmotic pressure *n* the pressure necessary to prevent osmosis into a given solution when the solution is separated from the pure solvent by a semipermeable membrane.

osmunda (ɒz'mʌndə) *or* **osmund** ('ɒzmənd) *n* any of a genus of ferns having large spreading fronds. [C13: from OF *osmonde,* from ?]

osprey ('ɒsprɪ, -preɪ) *n* **1** a large broad-winged fish-eating diurnal bird of prey, with a dark back and whitish head and underparts. Often called (US and Canad.): **fish hawk. 2** any of the feathers of various other birds, used esp. as trimming for hats. [C15: from OF *ospres,* apparently from L *ossifraga,* lit.: bone-breaker, from *os* bone + *frangere* to break]

ossein ('ɒsɪɪn) *n* a protein that forms the organic matrix of bone. [C19: from L *osseus* bony, from *os* bone]

osseous ('ɒsɪəs) *adj* consisting of or containing bone, bony. [C17: from L *osseus,* from *os* bone]
▸**'osseously** *adv*

ossify ❶ ('ɒsɪˌfaɪ) *vb* **ossifies, ossifying, ossified. 1** to convert or be converted into bone. **2** (*intr*) (of habits, attitudes, etc.) to become inflexible. [C18: from F *ossifier,* from L *os* bone + *facere* to make]
▸**ˌossifi'cation** *n* ▸**'ossiˌfier** *n*

ossuary ('ɒsjʊərɪ) *n, pl* **ossuaries.** any container for the burial of human bones, such as an urn or vault. [C17: from LL *ossuārium,* from L *os* bone]

osteal ('ɒstɪəl) *adj* **1** of or relating to bone or to the skeleton. **2** composed of bone; osseous. [C19: from Gk *osteon* bone]

osteitis (ˌɒstɪ'aɪtɪs) *n* inflammation of a bone.
▸**osteitic** (ˌɒstɪ'ɪtɪk) *adj*

ostensible ❶ (ɒ'stɛnsɪbᵊl) *adj* **1** apparent; seeming. **2** pretended. [C18: via F from Med. L *ostensibilis,* from L *ostendere* to show, from *ob-* before + *tendere* to extend]
▸**osˌtensi'bility** *n* ▸**os'tensibly** *adv*

ostensive (ɒ'stɛnsɪv) *adj* **1** obviously or manifestly demonstrative. **2** (of a definition) giving examples of objects to which a word or phrase is properly applied. **3** a less common word for **ostensible.** [C17: from LL *ostentīvus,* from L *ostendere* to show; see OSTENSIBLE]
▸**os'tensively** *adv*

ostentation ❶ (ˌɒstɛn'teɪʃən) *n* pretentious, showy, or vulgar display.
▸**ˌosten'tatious** *adj* ▸**ˌosten'tatiously** *adv* ▸**ˌosten'tatiousness** *n*

osteo- *or before a vowel* **oste-** *combining form.* indicating bone or bones. [from Gk *osteon*]

osteoarthritis (ˌɒstɪəʊɑː'θraɪtɪs) *n* chronic inflammation of the joints, esp. those that bear weight, with pain and stiffness.
▸**osteoarthritic** (ˌɒstɪəʊɑː'θrɪtɪk) *adj, n*

osteology (ˌɒstɪ'ɒlədʒɪ) *n* the study of the structure and function of bones.
▸**osteological** (ˌɒstɪə'lɒdʒɪkᵊl) *adj* ▸**ˌosteo'logically** *adv* ▸**ˌoste'ologist** *n*

osteoma (ˌɒstɪ'əʊmə) *n, pl* **osteomata** (-mətə) *or* **osteomas.** a benign tumour composed of bone or bonelike tissue.

osteomalacia (ˌɒstɪəʊmə'leɪʃɪə) *n* a disease characterized by softening of the bones, resulting from a deficiency of vitamin D and of calcium and phosphorus. [C19: from NL, from OSTEO- + Gk *malakia* softness]
▸**ˌosteoma'lacial** *or* **osteomalacic** (ˌɒstɪəʊmə'læsɪk) *adj*

THESAURUS

oscillate *vb* **1, 2 = fluctuate,** seesaw, sway, swing, vacillate, vary, vibrate, waver
Antonyms *vb* commit oneself, decide, determine, purpose, resolve, settle

oscillation *n* **2 = swing,** fluctuation, instability, seesawing, vacillation, variation, wavering

ossified *adj* **2 = hardened,** fixed, fossilized, frozen, indurated (*rare*), inflexible, petrified, rigid, rigidified, solid

ossify *vb* **2 = harden,** fossilize, freeze, indurate (*rare*), petrify, solidify, stiffen

ostensible *adj* **1, 2 = apparent,** alleged, avowed, exhibited, manifest, outward, plausible, pretended, professed, purported, seeming, so-called, specious, superficial, supposed

ostensibly *adv* **1 = apparently,** for the ostensible purpose of, on the face of it, on the surface, professedly, seemingly, supposedly, to all intents and purposes

ostentation *n* **= display,** affectation, boasting, exhibitionism, flamboyance, flashiness, flaunting, flourish, pageantry, parade, pomp, pretension, pretentiousness, show, showiness, showing off (*inf.*), swank (*inf.*), vaunting, window-dressing
Antonyms *n* humility, inconspicuousness, modesty, plainness, reserve, simplicity, unpretentiousness

ostentatious *adj* **= pretentious,** boastful, brash, conspicuous, crass, dashing, extravagant, flamboyant, flash (*inf.*), flashy, flaunted, gaudy, loud, obtrusive, pompous, showy, swanky (*inf.*), vain, vulgar
Antonyms *adj* conservative, inconspicuous, low-key, modest, plain, reserved, simple, sombre

osteomyelitis (ˌɒstɪəʊˌmaɪɪˈlaɪtɪs) *n* inflammation of bone marrow, caused by infection.

osteopathy (ˌɒstɪˈɒpəθɪ) *n* a system of healing based on the manipulation of bones or other parts of the body.
▸ˈ**osteoˌpath** *n* ▸**osteopathic** (ˌɒstɪəˈpæθɪk) *adj* ▸ˌ**osteoˈpathically** *adv*

osteoplasty (ˈɒstɪəˌplæstɪ) *n, pl* **osteoplasties.** the branch of surgery concerned with bone repair or bone grafting.

osteoporosis (ˌɒstɪəʊpɔːˈrəʊsɪs) *n* porosity and brittleness of the bones caused by loss of calcium from the bone matrix. [C19: from OSTEO- + PORE[2] + -OSIS]
▸**osteoporotic** (ˌɒstɪəʊpɔːˈrɒtɪk) *adj*

ostinato (ˌɒstɪˈnɑːtəʊ) *n, pl* **ostinatos. a** a continuously reiterated musical phrase. **b** (*as modifier*): *an ostinato passage.* [It.: from L *obstinātus* OBSTINATE]

ostler *or* **hostler** (ˈɒslə) *n Arch.* a stableman, esp. one at an inn. [C15: var. of *hostler*, from HOSTEL]

Ostmark (ˈɒstmɑːk; *German* ˈɔstmark) *n* (formerly) the standard monetary unit of East Germany, divided into 100 pfennigs. [G, lit.: east mark]

ostracize ➊ *or* **ostracise** (ˈɒstrəˌsaɪz) *vb* **ostracizes, ostracizing, ostracized** *or* **ostracises, ostracising, ostracised.** (*tr*) **1** to exclude or banish (a person) from a particular group, society, etc. **2** (in ancient Greece) to punish by temporary exile. [C17: from Gk *ostrakizein* to select someone for banishment by voting on potsherds, from *ostrakon* potsherd]
▸ˈ**ostracism** *n* ▸ˈ**ostraˌcizable** *or* ˈ**ostraˌcisable** *adj* ▸ˈ**ostraˌcizer** *or* ˈ**ostraˌciser** *n*

ostrich (ˈɒstrɪtʃ) *n, pl* **ostriches** *or* **ostrich. 1** a fast-running flightless African bird that is the largest living bird with stout two-toed feet and dark feathers, except on the naked head, neck, and legs. **2 American ostrich.** another name for **rhea. 3** a person who refuses to recognize the truth, reality, etc. [C13: from OF *ostrice*, from L *avis* bird + LL *struthio* ostrich, from Gk *strouthion*]

OT *abbrev. for:* **1** occupational therapy. **2** Old Testament. **3** overtime.

otalgia (əʊˈtældʒɪə, -dʒə) *n* the technical name for **earache.**

OTC (in Britain) *abbrev. for:* **1** Officers' Training Corps. **2** over-the-counter.

OTE *abbrev. for* on target earnings: referring to the salary a salesman should be able to achieve.

other ➊ (ˈʌðə) *determiner* **1a** (when used before a singular noun, usually preceded by *the*) the remaining (one or ones in a group of which one or some have been specified): *I'll read the other sections of the paper later.* **1b the other.** (*as pron; functioning as sing*): *one walks while the other rides.* **2** (a) different (one or ones from that or those already specified or understood): *no other man but you.* **3** additional; further: *there are no other possibilities.* **4** (preceded by *every*) alternate; two: *it buzzes every other minute.* **5 other than. 5a** apart from; besides: *a lady other than his wife.* **5b** different from: *he couldn't be other than what he is.* Archaic form: **other from. 6 no other.** *Arch.* nothing else: *I can do no other.* **7 or other.** (preceded by a phrase or word with *some*) used to add vagueness to the preceding pronoun, noun, or noun phrase: *he's somewhere or other.* **8 other things being equal.** conditions being the same or unchanged. **9 the other day, night,** etc. a few days, nights, etc., ago. **10 the other thing.** an unexpressed alternative. ◆ *pron* **11** another: *show me one other.* **12** (*pl*) additional or further ones. **13** (*pl*) other people or things. **14 the others.** the remaining ones (of a group). ◆ *adv* **15** (usually used with a negative and foll. by *than*) otherwise; differently: *they couldn't behave other than they do.* [OE *ōther*]
▸ˈ**otherness** *n*

> **USAGE NOTE** See at **otherwise.**

other-directed *adj* guided by values derived from external influences.

other ranks *pl n* (*rarely sing*) *Chiefly Brit.* (in the armed forces) all those who do not hold a commissioned rank.

otherwise ➊ (ˈʌðəˌwaɪz) *sentence connector.* **1** or else; if not, then: *go home — otherwise your mother will worry.* ◆ *adv* **2** differently: *I wouldn't have thought otherwise.* **3** in other respects: *an otherwise hopeless situation.* ◆ *adj* **4** (*predicative*) of an unexpected nature; different: *the facts are otherwise.* ◆ *pron* **5** something different in outcome: *success or otherwise.* [C14: from OE *on ōthre wīsan* in other manner]

> **USAGE NOTE** The expression *otherwise than* means *in any other way than* and should not be followed by an adjective: *no-one taught by this method can be other than* (not *otherwise than*) *successful; you are not allowed to use the building otherwise than as a private dwelling.*

other world *n* the spirit world or afterlife.

otherworldly (ˌʌðəˈwɜːldlɪ) *adj* **1** of or relating to the spiritual or imaginative world. **2** impractical or unworldly.
▸ˌ**otherˈworldliness** *n*

Othman (ˈɒθmən, ɒθˈmɑːn) *adj, n* a variant of **Ottoman.**

otic (ˈəʊtɪk, ˈɒtɪk) *adj* of or relating to the ear. [C17: from Gk *ōtikos*, from *ous* ear]

-otic *suffix forming adjectives.* **1** relating to or affected by: *sclerotic.* **2** causing: *narcotic.* [from Gk *-ōtikos*]

otiose (ˈəʊtɪˌəʊs, -ˌəʊz) *adj* **1** serving no useful purpose: *otiose language.* **2** *Rare.* indolent; lazy. [C18: from L *ōtiōsus* leisured, from *ōtium* leisure]
▸**otiosity** (ˌəʊtɪˈɒsɪtɪ) *or* ˈ**otiˌoseness** *n*

otitis (əʊˈtaɪtɪs) *n* inflammation of the ear.

oto- *or before a vowel* **ot-** *combining form.* indicating the ear. [from Gk *ous*, *ōt-* ear]

otolaryngology (ˌəʊtəʊˌlærɪŋˈgɒlədʒɪ) *n* another name for **otorhinolaryngology.**
▸**otolaryngological** (ˌəʊtəʊləˌrɪŋgəˈlɒdʒɪkᵊl) *adj* ▸ˌ**otoˌlarynˈgologist** *n*

otolith (ˈəʊtəʊˌlɪθ) *n* any of the granules of calcium carbonate in the inner ear of vertebrates. Movement of otoliths, caused by a change in the animal's position, stimulates sensory hair cells, which convey information to the brain.
▸ˌ**otoˈlithic** *adj*

otology (əʊˈtɒlədʒɪ) *n* the branch of medicine concerned with the ear.
▸**otological** (ˌəʊtəˈlɒdʒɪkᵊl) *adj* ▸**oˈtologist** *n*

otorhinolaryngology (ˌəʊtəʊˌraɪnəʊˌlærɪŋˈgɒlədʒɪ) *n* the branch of medicine concerned with the ear, nose, and throat. Sometimes called **otolaryngology.**

otoscope (ˈəʊtəʊˌskəʊp) *n* a medical instrument for examining the external ear.
▸**otoscopic** (ˌəʊtəʊˈskɒpɪk) *adj*

OTT *Sl. abbrev. for* over the top: see **top**[1] (sense 16b).

ottava rima (əʊˈtɑːvə ˈriːmə) *n Prosody.* a stanza form consisting of eight iambic pentameter lines, rhyming a b a b a b c c. [It.: eighth rhyme]

otter (ˈɒtə) *n, pl* **otters** *or* **otter. 1** a freshwater carnivorous mammal, esp. the **Eurasian otter,** typically having smooth fur, a streamlined body, and webbed feet. **2** the fur of this animal. **3** a type of fishing tackle consisting of a weighted board to which hooked and baited lines are attached. [OE *otor*]

otter hound *n* a large rough-coated dog of a breed formerly used for otter hunting.

ottoman (ˈɒtəmən) *n, pl* **ottomans. 1a** a low padded seat, usually armless, sometimes in the form of a chest. **1b** a cushioned footstool. **2** a corded fabric. [C17: from F *ottomane*, fem. of OTTOMAN]

Ottoman (ˈɒtəmən) *or* **Othman** (ˈɒθmən) *adj* **1** *History.* of or relating to the Ottomans or the Ottoman Empire. **2** denoting or relating to the Turkish language. ◆ *n, pl* **Ottomans** *or* **Othmans. 3** a member of a Turkish people who invaded the Near East in the late 13th century. [C17: from F, via Med. L, from Ar. *Othmānī* Turkish, from Turkish *Othman* or *Osman* I (1259–1326), Turkish Sultan]

Ottoman Empire *n* the former Turkish empire in Europe, Asia, and Africa, which lasted from the late 13th century until the end of World War I.

ou (əʊ) *n S. African. sl.* a man, bloke, or chap. [from Afrik., ?from Du.]

OU *abbrev. for:* **1** the Open University. **2** Oxford University.

ouananiche (ˌwɑːnəˈniːʃ) *n* a landlocked variety of the Atlantic salmon found in lakes in SE Canada. [from Canad. F, of Amerind origin, from *wananish*, dim. of *wanans* salmon]

oubaas (ˈəʊˌbɑːs) *n S. African.* a man in authority. [from Afrik., from Du. *oud* old + *baas* boss]

oubliette (ˌuːblɪˈɛt) *n* a dungeon, the only entrance to which is through the top. [C19: from F, from *oublier* to forget]

ouch (aʊtʃ) *interj* an exclamation of sharp sudden pain.

ought[1] (ɔːt) *vb* (foll. by *to; takes an infinitive or implied infinitive*) used as an auxiliary: **1** to indicate duty or obligation: *you ought to pay.* **2** to express prudent expediency: *you ought to be more careful with your money.* **3** (usually with reference to future time) to express probability or expectation: *you ought to finish this by Friday.* **4** to express a desire or wish on the part of the speaker: *you ought to come next week.* [OE *āhte*, p.t. of *āgan* to OWE]

> **USAGE NOTE** In correct English, *ought* is not used with *did* or *had. I ought not to do it,* not *I didn't ought to do it; I ought not to have done it,* not *I hadn't ought to have done it.*

ought[2] (ɔːt) *pron, adv* a variant spelling of **aught.**

ought[3] (ɔːt) *n* a less common word for **nought** (zero). [C19: mistaken division of *a nought* as *an ought*; see NOUGHT]

Ouija board (ˈwiːdʒə) *n Trademark.* a board on which are marked the letters of the alphabet. Answers to questions are spelt out by a pointer and are supposedly formed by spirits. [C19: from F *oui* yes + G *ja* yes]

ouma (ˈəʊmɑː) *n S. African.* **1** grandmother, esp. in titular use with her surname. **2** *Sl.* any elderly woman. [from Afrik., from Du. *oma* grandmother]

THESAURUS

ostracism *n* **1 = exclusion,** avoidance, banishment, boycott, cold-shouldering, exile, expulsion, isolation, rejection
Antonyms *n* acceptance, admission, approval, inclusion, invitation, reception, welcome

ostracize *vb* **1 = exclude,** avoid, banish, blackball, blacklist, boycott, cast out, cold-shoulder, excommunicate, exile, expatriate, expel, give (someone) the cold shoulder, reject, send to Coventry, shun, snub
Antonyms *vb* accept, admit, approve, embrace, greet, include, invite, receive, welcome

other *determiner* **2 = different,** contrasting, dissimilar, distinct, diverse, remaining, separate, unrelated, variant **3 = additional,** added, alternative, auxiliary, extra, further, more, spare, supplementary

otherwise *sentence connector* **1 = or else,** if not, or then ◆ *adv* **2 = differently,** any other way, contrarily

ounce[1] ❶ (auns) *n* **1** a unit of weight equal to one sixteenth of a pound (avoirdupois). Abbrev.: **oz.** **2** a unit of weight equal to one twelfth of a Troy or Apothecaries' pound; 1 ounce is equal to 480 grains. **3** short for **fluid ounce.** **4** a small portion or amount. [C14: from OF *unce*, from L *uncia* a twelfth]

ounce[2] (auns) *n* another name for **snow leopard.** [C18: from OF *once*, by mistaken division of *lonce* as if *l'once*, from L LYNX]

oupa ('əupɑː) *n S. African.* **1** grandfather, esp. in titular use with surname. **2** *Sl.* any elderly man. [Afrik.]

our ('auə) *determiner* **1** of, belonging to, or associated in some way with us: *our best vodka; our parents are good to us.* **2** belonging to or associated with all people or people in general: *our nearest planet is Venus.* **3** a formal word for *my* used by editors or other writers, and monarchs. [OE *ūre* (genitive pl), from US]

-our *suffix forming nouns.* indicating state, condition, or activity: *behaviour; labour.* [in OF *-eur*, from L *-or*, n. suffix]

Our Father *n* another name for the **Lord's Prayer,** taken from its opening words.

ours ('auəz) *pron* **1** something or someone belonging to or associated with us: *ours have blue tags.* **2** **of ours.** belonging to or associated with us.

ourself (auə'sɛlf) *pron Arch.* a variant of **myself,** formerly used by monarchs or editors.

ourselves (auə'sɛlvz) *pron* **1a** the reflexive form of *we* or *us.* **1b** (intensifier): *we ourselves will finish it.* **2** (*preceded by a copula*) our usual selves: *we are ourselves when we're together.* **3** *Not standard.* used instead of *we* or *us* in compound noun phrases: *other people and ourselves.*

-ous *suffix forming adjectives.* **1** having or full of: *dangerous; spacious.* **2** (in chemistry) indicating that an element is chemically combined in the lower of two possible valency states: *ferrous.* Cf. **-ic** (sense 2). [from OF, from L *-ōsus* or *-us*, Gk *-os*, adj. suffixes]

ousel ('uːzᵊl) *n* a variant spelling of **ouzel.**

oust ❶ (aust) *vb* (*tr*) **1** to force out of a position or place; supplant or expel. **2** *Property law.* to deprive (a person) of the possession of land, etc. [C16: from Anglo-Norman *ouster*, from L *obstāre* to withstand]

ouster ('austə) *n Property law.* the act of dispossessing of freehold property; eviction.

out ❶ (aut) *adv* (*when predicative, can in some senses be regarded as adj*) **1** (*often used as a particle*) at or to a point beyond the limits of some location; outside: *get out at once.* **2** (*particle*) used to indicate exhaustion or extinction: *the sugar's run out; put the light out.* **3** not in a particular place, esp., not at home. **4** public; revealed: *the secret is out.* **5** on sale or on view to the public: *the book is being brought out next May.* **6** (of the sun, stars, etc.) visible. **7** in flower: *the roses are out now.* **8** not in fashion, favour, or current usage. **9** not or not any longer worth considering: *that plan is out.* **10** not allowed: *smoking on duty is out.* **11** (of a fire or light) no longer burning or providing illumination. **12** not working: *the radio's out.* **13** Also: **out on strike.** on strike. **14** (of a jury) withdrawn to consider a verdict in private. **15** (*particle*) out of consciousness: *she passed out.* **16** (*particle*) used to indicate a burst of activity as indicated by the verb: *fever broke out.* **17** (*particle*) used to indicate obliteration of an object: *the graffiti was painted out.* **18** (*particle*) used to indicate an approximate drawing or description: *chalk out.* **19** at or to the fullest length or extent: *spread out.* **20** loudly; clearly: *calling out.* **21** desirous of or intent on (something or doing something): *I'm out for as much money as I can get.* **22** (*particle*) used to indicate a goal or object achieved at the end of the action specified by the verb: *he worked it out.* **23** (*preceded by a superlative*) existing: *the friendliest dog out.* **24** an expression in signalling, radio, etc., to indicate the end of a transmission. **25** used up; exhausted: *our supplies are completely out.* **26** worn into holes: *out at the elbows.* **27** inaccurate, deficient, or discrepant: *out by six pence.* **28** not in office or authority. **29** completed or concluded, as of time: *before the year is out.* **30** *Obs.* (of a young woman) in or into society: *Lucinda had a large party when she came out.* **31** *Sport.* denoting the state in which a player is caused to discontinue active participation, esp. in some specified role. **32** **out of.** **32a** at or to a point outside: *out of his reach.* **32b** away from; not in: *stepping out of line; out of focus.* **32c** because of; motivated by: *out of jealousy.* **32d** from (a material or source): *made out of plastic.* **32e** not or no longer having any of (a substance, material, etc.): *we're out of sugar.* **32f** no longer in a specified state or condition: *out of work; out of practice.* **32g** (of a horse) born of. ◆ *adj* **33** directed or indicating direction outwards: *the out tray.* **34** (of an island) remote from the mainland. **35** *Inf.* not concealing one's homosexuality. ◆ *prep* **36** *Nonstandard or US.* out of; out through: *he ran out the door.* ◆ *interj* **37a** an exclamation of dismissal, reproach, etc. **37b** (in wireless telegraphy) an expression used to signal that the speaker is signing off. **38** **out with it.** a command to make something known immediately, without missing any details. ◆ *n* **39** *Chiefly US.* a method of escape from a place, difficult situation, etc. **40** *Baseball.* an instance of causing a batter to be out by fielding. ◆ *vb* **41** (*tr*) to put or throw out. **42** (*intr*) to be made known or effective despite efforts to the contrary (esp. in **the truth will out**). **43** (*tr*) *Inf.* (of homosexuals) to expose (a public figure) as being a fellow homosexual. **44** *Inf.* to expose something secret, embarrassing, or unknown about (a person): *he was eventually outed as a talented goal scorer.* [OE *ūt*]

> **USAGE NOTE** The use of *out* as a preposition, though common in American English, is regarded as incorrect in British English: *he climbed out of* (not *out*) *a window; he went out through the door.*

out- *prefix* **1** excelling or surpassing in a particular action: *outlast; outlive.* **2** indicating an external location or situation away from the centre: *outpost; outpatient.* **3** indicating emergence, an issuing forth, etc.: *outcrop; outgrowth.* **4** indicating the result of an action: *outcome.*

outage ('autɪdʒ) *n* **1** a quantity of goods missing or lost after storage or shipment. **2** a period of power failure, machine stoppage, etc.

out and away *adv* by far.

out-and-out ❶ *adj* (*prenominal*) thoroughgoing; complete.

outback ('aut,bæk) *n* **a** the remote bush country of Australia. **b** (*as modifier*): *outback life.*

outbalance (,aut'bæləns) *vb* **outbalances, outbalancing, outbalanced.** another word for **outweigh.**

outboard ('aut,bɔːd) *adj* **1** (of a boat's engine) portable, with its own propeller, and designed to be attached externally to the stern. **2** in a position away from, or further away from, the centre line of a vessel or aircraft, esp. outside the hull or fuselage. ◆ *adv* **3** away from the centre line of a vessel or aircraft, esp. outside the hull or fuselage. ◆ *n* **4** an outboard motor.

outbound ('aut,baund) *adj* going out; outward bound.

outbrave (,aut'breɪv) *vb* **outbraves, outbraving, outbraved.** (*tr*) **1** to surpass in bravery. **2** to confront defiantly.

outbreak ❶ ('aut,breɪk) *n* a sudden, violent, or spontaneous occurrence, esp. of disease or strife.

outbuilding ('aut,bɪldɪŋ) *n* a building separate from a main building; outhouse.

outburst ❶ ('aut,bɜːst) *n* **1** a sudden and violent expression of emotion. **2** an explosion or eruption.

outcast ❶ ('aut,kɑːst) *n* **1** a person who is rejected or excluded from a social group. **2** a vagabond or wanderer. **3** anything thrown out or rejected. ◆ *adj* **4** rejected, abandoned, or discarded; cast out.

outcaste ('aut,kɑːst) *n* **1** a person who has been expelled from a caste. **2** a person having no caste. ◆ *vb* **outcastes, outcasting, outcasted.** **3** (*tr*) to cause (someone) to lose his caste.

outclass ❶ (,aut'klɑːs) *vb* (*tr*) **1** to surpass in class, quality, etc. **2** to defeat easily.

outcome ❶ ('aut,kʌm) *n* something that follows from an action or situation; result; consequence.

outcrop *n* ('aut,krɒp). **1** part of a rock formation or mineral vein that appears at the surface of the earth. **2** an emergence; appearance. ◆ *vb* (,aut'krɒp), **outcrops, outcropping, outcropped.** **3** (*intr*) (of rock strata, mineral veins, etc.) to protrude through the surface of the earth.

outcry ❶ *n* ('aut,kraɪ), *pl* **outcries.** **1** a widespread or vehement protest. **2** clamour; uproar. **3** *Commerce.* a method of trading in which dealers shout out bids and offers at a prearranged meeting: *sale by open outcry.* ◆ *vb* (,aut'kraɪ), **outcries, outcrying, outcried.** (*tr*) **4** to cry louder or make more noise than (someone or something).

outdated ❶ (,aut'deɪtɪd) *adj* old-fashioned or obsolete.

outdo ❶ (,aut'duː) *vb* **outdoes, outdoing, outdid, outdone.** (*tr*) to surpass or exceed in performance.

THESAURUS

ounce[1] *n* **4** = **shred**, atom, crumb, drop, grain, iota, particle, scrap, speck, trace, whit

oust *vb* **1** = **expel**, depose, disinherit, dislodge, displace, dispossess, eject, evict, relegate, throw out, topple, turn out, unseat

out *adj* **1, 3** = **away**, abroad, absent, elsewhere, gone, not at home, outside **2, 11** = **extinguished**, at an end, cold, dead, doused, ended, exhausted, expired, finished, used up **8** = **old-fashioned**, antiquated, behind the times, dated, dead, *démodé*, old hat, passé, square (*inf.*), unfashionable **10** = **not allowed**, impossible, not on (*inf.*), ruled out, unacceptable
Antonyms *adj* ≠ **old-fashioned:** à la mode, fashionable, in, in fashion, latest, modern, trendy (*Brit. inf.*), up-to-date, with it (*inf.*)

out-and-out *adj* = **absolute**, arrant, complete, consummate, deep-dyed (*usually derogatory*), downright, dyed-in-the-wool, outright, perfect, thorough, thoroughgoing, total, unmitigated, unqualified, utter

outbreak *n* = **eruption**, burst, epidemic, explosion, flare-up, flash, outburst, rash, spasm, upsurge

outburst *n* **1** = **outpouring**, access, attack, discharge, eruption, explosion, fit of temper, flare-up, gush, outbreak, paroxysm, spasm, storm, surge

outcast *n* **1** = **pariah**, castaway, derelict, displaced person, exile, leper, *persona non grata*, refugee, reprobate, untouchable, wretch

outclass *vb* **1** = **surpass**, be a cut above (*inf.*), beat, eclipse, exceed, excel, leave *or* put in the shade, leave standing (*inf.*), outdistance, outdo, outrank, outshine, outstrip, overshadow, run rings around (*inf.*)

outcome *n* = **result**, aftereffect, aftermath, conclusion, consequence, end, end result, issue, payoff (*inf.*), sequel, upshot

outcry *n* **1, 2** = **protest**, clamour, commotion, complaint, cry, exclamation, howl, hue and cry, hullaballoo, noise, outburst, scream, screech, uproar, yell

outdated *adj* = **old-fashioned**, antiquated, antique, archaic, behind the times, *démodé*, obsolete, outmoded, out of date, out of style, out of the ark (*inf.*), passé, unfashionable
Antonyms *adj* à la mode, all the rage, contemporary, current, fashionable, in vogue, modern, modish, stylish, trendy (*Brit. inf.*), up-to-date, with it (*inf.*)

outdo *vb* = **surpass**, beat, be one up on, best, eclipse, exceed, excel, get the better of, go one better than (*inf.*), outclass, outdistance, outfox, outjockey, outmanoeuvre, outshine, outsmart

outdoor ❶ (ˈaʊtˈdɔː) *adj (prenominal)* taking place, existing, or intended for use in the open air: *outdoor games; outdoor clothes*. Also: **out-of-door.**
outdoors (ˌaʊtˈdɔːz) *adv* **1** Also: **out-of-doors.** in the open air; outside. ◆ *n* **2** the world outside or far away from human habitation.
outer ❶ (ˈaʊtə) *adj (prenominal)* **1** being or located on the outside; external. **2** further from the middle or central part. ◆ *n* **3** *Archery*. **3a** the white outermost ring on a target. **3b** a shot that hits this ring. **4** *Austral. & NZ.* the unsheltered part of the spectator area at a sports ground. **5 on the outer.** *Austral. & NZ.* excluded or neglected.
outer bar *n* (in England) a collective name for junior barristers who plead from outside the bar of the court.
outermost (ˈaʊtəˌməʊst) *adj* furthest from the centre or middle; outmost.
outer space *n* any region of space beyond the atmosphere of the earth.
outfall (ˈaʊtˌfɔːl) *n* the end of a river, sewer, drain, etc., from which it discharges.
outfield (ˈaʊtˌfiːld) *n* **1** *Cricket.* the area of the field relatively far from the pitch; the deep. Cf. **infield** (sense 1). **2** *Baseball.* **2a** the area of the playing field beyond the lines connecting first, second, and third bases. **2b** the positions of the left fielder, centre fielder, and right fielder taken collectively. **3** *Agriculture.* farmland most distant from the farmstead.
▸ **ˈoutˌfielder** *n*
outfit ❶ (ˈaʊtˌfɪt) *n* **1** a set of articles or equipment for a particular task, etc. **2** a set of clothes, esp. a carefully selected one. **3** *Inf.* any group or association regarded as a cohesive unit, such as a military company, etc. ◆ *vb* **outfits, outfitting, outfitted. 4** to furnish or be furnished with an outfit, equipment, etc.
▸ **ˈoutˌfitter** *n*
outflank (ˌaʊtˈflæŋk) *vb (tr)* **1** to go around the flank of (an opposing army, etc.). **2** to get the better of.
outflow ❶ (ˈaʊtˌfləʊ) *n* **1** anything that flows out, such as liquid, money, etc. **2** the amount that flows out. **3** the act or process of flowing out.
outfox (ˌaʊtˈfɒks) *vb (tr)* to surpass in guile or cunning.
outgeneral (ˌaʊtˈdʒɛnərəl) *vb* **outgenerals, outgeneralling, outgeneralled** *or US* **outgenerals, outgeneraling, outgeneraled.** *(tr)* to surpass in generalship.
outgo *vb* (ˌaʊtˈgəʊ), **outgoes, outgoing, outwent, outgone. 1** *(tr)* to exceed or outstrip. ◆ *n* (ˈaʊtˌgəʊ). **2** cost; outgoings; outlay. **3** something that goes out; outflow.
outgoing ❶ (ˈaʊtˌgəʊɪŋ) *adj* **1** departing; leaving. **2** retiring from office. **3** friendly and sociable. ◆ *n* **4** the act of going out.
outgoings ❶ (ˈaʊtˌgəʊɪŋz) *pl n* expenditure.
outgrow (ˌaʊtˈgrəʊ) *vb* **outgrows, outgrowing, outgrew, outgrown.** *(tr)* **1** to grow too large for (clothes, shoes, etc.). **2** to lose (a habit, idea, reputation, etc.) in the course of development or time. **3** to grow larger or faster than.
outgrowth ❶ (ˈaʊtˌgrəʊθ) *n* **1** a thing growing out of a main body. **2** a development, result, or consequence. **3** the act of growing out.
outgun (ˌaʊtˈgʌn) *vb* **outguns, outgunning, outgunned.** *(tr)* **1** to surpass in fire power. **2** to surpass in shooting. **3** *Inf.* to surpass or excel.
outhouse (ˈaʊtˌhaʊs) *n* a building near to, but separate from, a main building; outbuilding.
outing ❶ (ˈaʊtɪŋ) *n* **1** a short outward and return journey; trip; excursion. **2** *Inf.* the naming by homosexuals of other prominent homosexuals, often against their will.
outjockey (ˌaʊtˈdʒɒkɪ) *vb (tr)* to outwit by deception.
outlandish ❶ (aʊtˈlændɪʃ) *adj* **1** grotesquely unconventional in appearance, habits, etc. **2** *Arch.* foreign.
▸ **outˈlandishly** *adv* ▸ **outˈlandishness** *n*
outlast ❶ (ˌaʊtˈlɑːst) *vb (tr)* to last longer than.
outlaw ❶ (ˈaʊtˌlɔː) *n* **1** (formerly) a person excluded from the law and deprived of its protection. **2** any fugitive from the law, esp. a habitual transgressor. ◆ *vb (tr)* **3** to put (a person) outside the law and deprive of its protection. **4** to ban.
▸ **ˈoutˌlawry** *n*
outlay ❶ *n* (ˈaʊtˌleɪ). **1** an expenditure of money, effort, etc. ◆ *vb* (ˌaʊtˈleɪ), **outlays, outlaying, outlaid. 2** *(tr)* to spend (money, etc.).
outlet ❶ (ˈaʊtlɛt, -lɪt) *n* **1** an opening or vent permitting escape or release. **2a** a market for a product or service. **2b** a commercial establishment retailing the goods of a particular producer or wholesaler. **3** a channel that drains a body of water. **4** a point in a wiring system from which current can be taken to supply electrical devices.
outlier (ˈaʊtˌlaɪə) *n* **1** an outcrop of rocks that is entirely surrounded by older rocks. **2** a person, thing, or part situated away from a main or related body. **3** a person who lives away from his place of work, duty, etc.
outline ❶ (ˈaʊtˌlaɪn) *n* **1** a preliminary or schematic plan, draft, etc. **2** *(usually pl)* the important features of a theory, work, etc. **3** the line by which an object or figure is or appears to be bounded. **4a** a drawing or manner of drawing consisting only of external lines. **4b** *(as modifier)*: *an outline map*. ◆ *vb* **outlines, outlining, outlined.** *(tr)* **5** to draw or display the outline of. **6** to give the main features or general idea of.
outlive ❶ (ˌaʊtˈlɪv) *vb* **outlives, outliving, outlived.** *(tr)* **1** to live longer than (someone). **2** to live beyond (a date or period): *he outlived the century*. **3** to live through (an experience).
outlook ❶ (ˈaʊtˌlʊk) *n* **1** a mental attitude or point of view. **2** the probable or expected condition or outcome of something: *the weather outlook*. **3** the view from a place. **4** view or prospect. **5** the act or state of looking out.
outlying ❶ (ˈaʊtˌlaɪɪŋ) *adj* distant or remote from the main body or centre, as of a town or region.
outmanoeuvre ❶ *or US* **outmaneuver** (ˌaʊtməˈnuːvə) *vb* **outmanoeuvres, outmanoeuvring, outmanoeuvred** *or US* **outmaneuvers, outmaneuvering, outmaneuvered.** *(tr)* to secure a strategic advantage over by skilful manoeuvre.
outmoded ❶ (ˌaʊtˈməʊdɪd) *adj* no longer fashionable or widely accepted.
▸ **ˌoutˈmodedly** *adv* ▸ **ˌoutˈmodedness** *n*
outmost (ˈaʊtˌməʊst) *adj* another word for **outermost.**
out of bounds ❶ *adj (postpositive), adv* **1** (often foll. by *to*) not to be entered (by); barred (to). **2** outside specified or prescribed limits.
out of date ❶ *adj* (**out-of-date** *when prenominal*), *adv* no longer valid, current, or fashionable; outmoded.
out-of-door *adj (prenominal)* another term for **outdoor.**
out-of-doors *adv, adj (postpositive)* in the open air; outside. Also: **outdoors.**

THESAURUS

(*inf.*), overcome, run rings around (*inf.*), score points off, top, transcend
outdoor *adj* = **open-air**, alfresco, out-of-door(s), outside
Antonyms *adj* indoor, inside, interior, within
outer *adj* **1** = **external**, exposed, exterior, outlying, outside, outward, peripheral, remote, superficial, surface
Antonyms *adj* central, closer, inner, inside, interior, internal, inward, nearer
outfit *n* **2** = **costume**, accoutrements, clothes, ensemble, garb, gear (*inf.*), get-up (*inf.*), kit, rigout (*inf.*), suit, threads (*sl.*), togs (*inf.*), trappings **3** *Informal* = **group**, clique, company, corps, coterie, crew, firm, organization, set, setup (*inf.*), squad, team, unit ◆ *vb* **4** = **equip**, accoutre, appoint, fit out, furnish, kit out, provision, stock, supply, turn out
outfitter *n* **4** = **clothier**, costumier, couturier, dressmaker, haberdasher (*US*), modiste, tailor
outflow *n* **1** = **discharge**, drainage, ebb, effluence, efflux, effusion, emanation, emergence, gush, issue, jet, outfall, outpouring, rush, spout
outgoing *adj* **1, 2** = **leaving**, departing, ex-, former, last, past, retiring, withdrawing **3** = **sociable**, approachable, communicative, cordial, demonstrative, easy, expansive, extrovert, friendly, genial, gregarious, informal, open, sympathetic, unreserved, warm
Antonyms *adj* ≠ **leaving:** arriving, entering, incoming ≠ **sociable:** austere, cold, indifferent, reserved, retiring, withdrawn
outgoings *pl n* = **expenses**, costs, expenditure, outlay, overheads
outgrowth *n* **1** = **offshoot**, bulge, excrescence, node, outcrop, process, projection, protuberance, scion, shoot, sprout **2** = **product**, by-product, consequence, derivative, development, emergence, issue, result, spin-off, yield
outing *n* **1** = **trip**, excursion, expedition, jaunt, pleasure trip, spin (*inf.*)
outlandish *adj* **1** = **strange**, alien, barbarous, bizarre, eccentric, exotic, fantastic, far-out, foreign, freakish, grotesque, left-field (*inf.*), outré, preposterous, queer, unheard-of, weird
Antonyms *adj* banal, commonplace, everyday, familiar, humdrum, mundane, normal, ordinary, usual, well-known
outlast *vb* = **outlive**, endure beyond, outstay, outwear, survive
outlaw *n* **1** = **bandit**, brigand, desperado, footpad (*arch.*), fugitive, highwayman, marauder, outcast, pariah, robber ◆ *vb* **3** = **put a price on (someone's) head 4** = **forbid**, ban, banish, bar, condemn, disallow, embargo, exclude, interdict, make illegal, prohibit, proscribe
Antonyms *vb* ≠ **forbid:** allow, approve, authorize, consent, endorse, legalise, permit, sanction, support
outlay *n* **1** = **expenditure**, cost, disbursement, expenses, investment, outgoings, spending
outlet *n* **1** = **opening**, avenue, channel, duct, egress, exit, orifice, release, safety valve, vent, way out **2** = **shop**, market, store
outline *n* **1** = **draft**, drawing, frame, framework, layout, lineament(s), plan, rough, skeleton, sketch, tracing **2** = **summary**, bare facts, main features, recapitulation, résumé, rough idea, rundown, synopsis, thumbnail sketch **3** = **shape**, configuration, contour, delineation, figure, form, profile, silhouette ◆ *vb* **5** = **trace**, delineate, draft, plan, rough out, sketch in **6** = **summarize**, adumbrate, delineate, sketch
outlive *vb* **1-3** = **survive**, come through, endure beyond, live through, outlast
outlook *n* **1** = **attitude**, angle, frame of mind, perspective, point of view, slant, standpoint, viewpoint, views **2** = **prospect**, expectations, forecast, future **3** = **view**, aspect, panorama, prospect, scene, vista
outlying *adj* = **remote**, backwoods, distant, far-flung, in the middle of nowhere, outer, out-of-the-way, peripheral, provincial
outmanoeuvre *vb* = **outwit**, circumvent, get the better of, outdo, outflank, outfox, outgeneral, outjockey, outsmart (*inf.*), run rings round (*inf.*), steal a march on (*inf.*)
outmoded *adj* = **old-fashioned**, anachronistic, antediluvian, antiquated, antique, archaic, behind the times, bygone, dated, *démodé*, fossilized, obsolescent, obsolete, old-time, out, out-of-date, out of style, out of the ark (*inf.*), outworn, passé, square (*inf.*), superannuated, superseded, unfashionable, unusable
Antonyms *adj* all the rage, fashionable, fresh, in vogue, latest, modern, modish, new, recent, usable
out of bounds *adj, adv* **1, 2** = **forbidden** (*chiefly US military*), banned, barred, off-limits, prohibited, taboo
out of date *adj* = **old-fashioned**, antiquated, archaic, dated, discarded, elapsed, expired, extinct, invalid, lapsed, obsolete, outmoded, out of the ark (*inf.*), outworn, passé, stale, superannuated, superseded, unfashionable

out of pocket *adj* (**out-of-pocket** *when prenominal*). **1** (*postpositive*) having lost money, as in a commercial enterprise. **2** without money to spend. **3** (*prenominal*) (of expenses) unbudgeted and paid for in cash.
out of the way ❶ *adj* (**out-of-the-way** *when prenominal*). **1** distant from more populous areas. **2** uncommon or unusual.
outpace (ˌaʊtˈpeɪs) *vb* **outpaces, outpacing, outpaced.** (*tr*) **1** to go faster than (someone). **2** to surpass or outdo (something or someone) in growth, development. etc.
outpatient (ˈaʊtˌpeɪʃənt) *n* a nonresident hospital patient. Cf. **inpatient.**
outperform (ˌaʊtpəˈfɔːm) *vb* (*tr*) to outdo or surpass in a specified field or activity.
outplacement (ˈaʊtˌpleɪsmənt) *n* a service that offers counselling and careers advice, esp. to redundant executives, which is paid for by their previous employer.
outpoint (ˌaʊtˈpɔɪnt) *vb* (*tr*) to score more points than.
outport (ˈaʊtˌpɔːt) *n* **1** *Chiefly Brit.* a subsidiary port built in deeper water than the original port. **2** *Canad.* a small fishing village of Newfoundland.
outpost (ˈaʊtˌpəʊst) *n* **1** *Mil.* **1a** a position stationed at a distance from the area occupied by a major formation. **1b** the troops assigned to such a position. **2** an outlying settlement or position.
outpour *n* (ˈaʊtˌpɔː). **1** the act of flowing or pouring out. **2** something that pours out. ◆ *vb* (ˌaʊtˈpɔː). **3** to pour or cause to pour out freely or rapidly.
outpouring ❶ (ˈaʊtˌpɔːrɪŋ) *n* **1** a passionate or exaggerated outburst; effusion. **2** another word for **outpour** (senses 1, 2).
output ❶ (ˈaʊtˌpʊt) *n* **1** the act of production or manufacture. **2** the amount produced, as in a given period: *a weekly output.* **3** the material produced, manufactured, etc. **4** *Electronics.* **4a** the power, voltage, or current delivered by a circuit or component. **4b** the point at which the signal is delivered. **5** the power, energy, or work produced by an engine or a system. **6** *Computing.* **6a** the information produced by a computer. **6b** the operations and devices involved in producing this information. **7** (*modifier*) of or relating to electronic or computer output: *output signal.* ◆ *vb* **outputs, outputting, outputted** *or* **output. 8** (*tr*) *Computing.* to cause (data) to be emitted as output.
outrage ❶ (ˈaʊtˌreɪdʒ) *n* **1** a wantonly vicious or cruel act. **2** a gross violation of decency, morality, honour, etc. **3** profound indignation, anger, or hurt, caused by such an act. ◆ *vb* **outrages, outraging, outraged.** (*tr*) **4** to cause profound indignation, anger, or resentment in. **5** to offend grossly. **6** to commit an act of wanton viciousness, cruelty, or indecency on. **7** a euphemistic word for **rape**[1]. [C13 (meaning: excess): via F from *outré* beyond, from L *ultrā*]
outrageous ❶ (aʊtˈreɪdʒəs) *adj* **1** being or having the nature of an outrage. **2** grossly offensive to decency, authority, etc. **3** violent or unrestrained in behaviour or temperament. **4** extravagant or immoderate. ▸**outˈrageously** *adv* ▸**outˈrageousness** *n*
outrank (ˌaʊtˈræŋk) *vb* (*tr*) **1** to be of higher rank than. **2** to take priority over.
outré ❶ (ˈuːtreɪ) *adj* deviating from what is usual or proper. [C18: from F, p.p. of *outrer* to pass beyond]
outride (ˌaʊtˈraɪd) *vb* **outrides, outriding, outrode, outridden.** (*tr*) **1** to outdo by riding faster, farther, or better than. **2** (of a vessel) to ride out (a storm).
outrider ❶ (ˈaʊtˌraɪdə) *n* **1** a person who goes in advance to investigate, discover a way, etc.; scout. **2** a person who rides in front of or beside a carriage, esp. as an attendant or guard. **3** *US.* a mounted herdsman.
outrigger (ˈaʊtˌrɪgə) *n* **1** a framework for supporting a pontoon outside and parallel to the hull of a boat to provide stability. **2** a boat equipped with such a framework, esp. one of the canoes of the South Pacific. **3** any projecting framework attached to a boat, aircraft, building, etc., to act as a support. **4** *Rowing.* another name for **rigger** (sense 2). [C18: from OUT- + RIG + -ER[1]]
outright ❶ *adj* (ˈaʊtˌraɪt). (*prenominal*) **1** without qualifications or limitations: *outright ownership.* **2** complete; total. **3** straightforward; direct. ◆ *adv* (ˌaʊtˈraɪt). **4** without restrictions. **5** without reservation or concealment: *ask outright.* **6** instantly: *he was killed outright.*
outrush (ˈaʊtˌrʌʃ) *n* a flowing or rushing out.
outset ❶ (ˈaʊtˌsɛt) *n* a start; beginning (esp. in **from** (*or* **at**) **the outset**).
outside ❶ *prep* (ˌaʊtˈsaɪd). **1** (sometimes foll. by *of*) on or to the exterior of: *outside the house.* **2** beyond the limits of. **3** apart from; other than: *no-one knows outside you.* ◆ *adj* (ˈaʊtˌsaɪd). **4** (*prenominal*) situated on the exterior: *an outside lavatory.* **5** remote; unlikely. **6** not a member of. **7** the greatest possible or probable (prices, odds, etc.). **8** (of a road lane, esp. in a dual carriageway or motorway) situated nearer or nearest to the central reservation, for use by faster or overtaking vehicles. ◆ *adv* (ˌaʊtˈsaɪd). **9** outside a specified thing or place; out of doors. **10** *Sl.* not in prison. ◆ *n* (ˈaʊtˈsaɪd). **11** the external side or surface. **12** the external appearance or aspect. **13** (of a pavement, etc.) the side nearest the road or away from a wall. **14** *Sport.* an outside player, as in football. **15** (*pl*) the outer sheets of a ream of paper. **16** *Canad.* (in the north) the settled parts of Canada. **17 at the outside.** *Inf.* at the most or at the greatest extent: *two days at the outside.*

> **USAGE NOTE** The use of *outside of* and *inside of*, although fairly common, is generally thought to be incorrect or nonstandard: *she waits outside* (not *outside of*) *the school.*

outside broadcast *n Radio, television.* a broadcast not made from a studio.
outside director *n* a director of a company who is not employed by that company but is often employed by a holding or associated company.
outsider ❶ (ˌaʊtˈsaɪdə) *n* **1** a person or thing excluded from or not a member of a set, group, etc. **2** a contestant, esp. a horse, thought unlikely to win in a race. **3** *Canad.* a person who does not live in the Arctic regions.
outsize ❶ (ˈaʊtˌsaɪz) *adj* **1** Also: **outsized.** very large or larger than normal. ◆ *n* **2** something outsize, such as a garment or person. **3** (*modifier*) relating to or dealing in outsize clothes: *an outsize shop.*
outskirts ❶ (ˈaʊtˌskɜːts) *pl n* (*sometimes sing*) outlying or bordering areas, districts, etc., as of a city.
outsmart ❶ (ˌaʊtˈsmɑːt) *vb* (*tr*) *Inf.* to get the better of; outwit.
outspan *S. African.* ◆ *n* (ˈaʊtˌspæn). **1** an area on a farm kept available for travellers to rest and refresh animals, etc. **2** the act of unharnessing or unyoking. ◆ *vb* (ˌaʊtˈspæn), **outspans, outspanning, outspanned. 3** to unharness or unyoke (animals). [C19: partial translation of Afrik. *uitspan*, from *uit* out + *spannen* to stretch]
outspoken ❶ (ˌaʊtˈspəʊkən) *adj* **1** candid or bold in speech. **2** said or expressed with candour or boldness.

THESAURUS

Antonyms *adj* contemporary, current, fashionable, in, new, now (*inf.*), trendy (*Brit. inf.*), up to date, valid
out of the way *adj* **1** = **remote**, distant, farflung, inaccessible, isolated, lonely, obscure, off the beaten track, outlying, secluded, unfrequented **2** = **unusual**, abnormal, curious, exceptional, extraordinary, odd, outlandish, out of the ordinary, peculiar, strange, uncommon
Antonyms *adj* ≠ **remote:** accessible, close, convenient, frequented, handy, near, nearby, proximate, reachable, within sniffing distance (*inf.*)
outpouring *n* **1, 2** = **stream**, cascade, debouchment, deluge, effluence, efflux, effusion, emanation, flow, flux, issue, outflow, spate, spurt, torrent
output *n* **1** = **production**, achievement, manufacture, product, productivity, yield
outrage *n* **1** = **atrocity**, barbarism, enormity, evil, inhumanity **2** = **violation**, abuse, affront, desecration, indignity, injury, insult, offence, profanation, rape, ravishing, sacrilege, shock, violence **3** = **indignation**, anger, fury, hurt, resentment, shock, wrath ◆ *vb* **5** = **offend**, affront, incense, infuriate, madden, make one's blood boil, scandalize, shock **6** = **abuse**, defile, desecrate, injure, insult, maltreat **7** = **rape**, ravage, ravish, violate
outrageous *adj* **1-3** = **atrocious**, abominable, barbaric, beastly, disgraceful, egregious, flagrant, heinous, horrible, infamous, inhuman, iniquitous, nefarious, offensive, scandalous, shocking, unspeakable, villainous, violent, wicked **4** = **unreasonable**, excessive, exorbitant, extravagant, immoderate, over the top (*sl.*), preposterous, scandalous, shocking, steep (*inf.*)
Antonyms *adj* ≠ **atrocious:** just, mild, minor, tolerable, trivial ≠ **unreasonable:** equitable, fair, moderate, reasonable
outré *adj* = **eccentric**, bizarre, extravagant, fantastic, freakish, freaky (*sl.*), grotesque, indecorous, kinky (*inf.*), left-field (*inf.*), odd, off-the-wall (*sl.*), outlandish, rum (*Brit. sl.*), unconventional, way-out (*inf.*), weird
outrider *n* **1, 2** = **escort**, advance guard, advance man, attendant, bodyguard, guard, harbinger, herald, precursor, scout, squire
outright *adj* **1, 2** = **absolute**, arrant, complete, consummate, deep-dyed (*usually derogatory*), downright, out-and-out, perfect, pure, thorough, thoroughgoing, total, unconditional, undeniable, unmitigated, unqualified, utter, wholesale **3** = **direct**, definite, flat, straight- forward, unequivocal, unqualified ◆ *adv* **4** = **absolutely**, completely, straightforwardly, thoroughly, to the full, without hesitation, without restraint **5** = **openly**, explicitly, overtly **6** = **instantly**, at once, cleanly, immediately, instantaneously, on the spot, straight away, there and then, without more ado
outset *n* = **beginning**, commencement, early days, inauguration, inception, kickoff (*inf.*), onset, opening, start, starting point
Antonyms *n* closing, completion, conclusion, consummation, end, finale, finish, termination
outside *adj* **4** = **external**, exterior, extramural, extraneous, extreme, out, outdoor, outer, outermost, outward, surface **5** = **remote**, distant, faint, marginal, negligible, slight, slim, small, unlikely ◆ *n* **11** = **exterior**, façade, face, front, skin, surface, topside
Antonyms *adj* ≠ **external:** in, indoor, inner, innermost, inside, interior, internal, intramural, inward
outsider *n* **1** = **interloper**, alien, foreigner, incomer, intruder, newcomer, nonmember, odd one out, outlander, stranger
outsize *adj* **1** = **extra-large**, enormous, gargantuan, giant, gigantic, huge, immense, jumbo (*inf.*), large, mammoth, monster, oversized
Antonyms *adj* baby, dwarf, micro, mini, pocket, tiny, undersized
outskirts *pl n* = **edge**, borders, boundary, environs, faubourgs, periphery, purlieus, suburbia, suburbs, vicinity
outsmart *vb Informal* = **outwit**, deceive, dupe, get the better of, go one better than (*inf.*), make a fool of (*inf.*), outfox, outjockey, outmanoeuvre, outperform, outthink, pull a fast one on (*inf.*), put one over on (*inf.*), run rings round (*inf.*), trick
outspoken *adj* **1, 2** = **forthright**, abrupt, blunt, candid, direct, downright, explicit, frank, free, free-spoken, open, plain-spoken, round, unceremonious, undissembling, unequivocal, unreserved
Antonyms *adj* diplomatic, gracious, judicious, reserved, reticent, tactful

outspread ❶ *vb* (ˌaʊtˈsprɛd), **outspreads, outspreading, outspread. 1** to spread out. ◆ *adj* (ˈaʊtˈsprɛd). **2** spread or stretched out. **3** scattered or diffused widely. ◆ *n* (ˈaʊtˌsprɛd). **4** a spreading out.

outstanding ❶ (ˌaʊtˈstændɪŋ) *adj* **1** superior; excellent. **2** prominent, remarkable, or striking. **3** unsettled, unpaid, or unresolved. **4** (of shares, bonds, etc.) issued and sold. **5** projecting or jutting upwards or outwards.
▸ **ˌoutˈstandingly** *adv*

outstare (ˌaʊtˈstɛə) *vb* **outstares, outstaring, outstared.** (*tr*) **1** to outdo in staring. **2** to disconcert by staring.

outstation (ˈaʊtˌsteɪʃən) *n* a station or post at a distance from the base station or in a remote region.

outstay (ˌaʊtˈsteɪ) *vb* (*tr*) **1** to stay longer than. **2** to stay beyond (a limit). **3 outstay one's welcome.** See **overstay** (sense 2).

outstretch (ˌaʊtˈstrɛtʃ) *vb* (*tr*) **1** to extend or expand; stretch out. **2** to stretch or extend beyond.

outstrip ❶ (ˌaʊtˈstrɪp) *vb* **outstrips, outstripping, outstripped.** (*tr*) **1** to surpass in a sphere of activity, competition, etc. **2** to be or grow greater than. **3** to go faster than and leave behind.

outtake (ˈaʊtˌteɪk) *n* an unreleased take from a recording session, film, or television programme.

out-tray *n* (in an office, etc.) a tray for outgoing correspondence, documents, etc.

outturn (ˈaʊtˌtɜːn) *n* another word for **output** (sense 2).

outvote (ˌaʊtˈvəʊt) *vb* **outvotes, outvoting, outvoted.** (*tr*) to defeat by a majority of votes.

outward ❶ (ˈaʊtwəd) *adj* **1** of or relating to what is apparent or superficial. **2** of or relating to the outside of the body. **3** belonging or relating to the external, as opposed to the mental, spiritual, or inherent. **4** of, relating to, or directed towards the outside or exterior. **5 the outward man. 5a** *Theol.* the body as opposed to the soul. **5b** *Facetious.* clothing. ◆ *adv* **6** (of a ship) away from port. **7** a variant of **outwards.** ◆ *n* **8** the outward part; exterior.
▸ **ˈoutwardness** *n*

Outward Bound movement *n Trademark.* (in Britain) a scheme to provide adventure training for young people.

outwardly ❶ (ˈaʊtwədlɪ) *adv* **1** in outward appearance. **2** with reference to the outside or outer surface; externally.

outwards (ˈaʊtwədz) *or* **outward** *adv* towards the outside; out.

outwear (ˌaʊtˈwɛə) *vb* **outwears, outwearing, outwore, outworn.** (*tr*) **1** to use up or destroy by wearing. **2** to last or wear longer than. **3** to outlive, outgrow, or develop beyond. **4** to deplete or exhaust in strength, determination, etc.

outweigh ❶ (ˌaʊtˈweɪ) *vb* (*tr*) **1** to prevail over; overcome. **2** to be more important or significant than. **3** to be heavier than.

outwit ❶ (ˌaʊtˈwɪt) *vb* **outwits, outwitting, outwitted.** (*tr*) to get the better of by cunning or ingenuity.

outwith (ˌaʊtˈwɪθ) *prep Scot.* outside; beyond.

outwork *n* (ˈaʊtˌwɜːk). **1** (*often pl*) defences which lie outside main defensive works. **2** work done away from the factory, etc., by which it has been commissioned. ◆ *vb* (ˌaʊtˈwɜːk). (*tr*) **3** to work better, harder, etc., than. **4** to work out to completion.
▸ **ˈoutˌworker** *n*

ouzel *or* **ousel** (ˈuːzᵊl) *n* **1** short for **water ouzel.** See **dipper** (sense 2). **2** an archaic name for the (European) **blackbird.** [OE *ōsle*]

ouzo (ˈuːzəʊ) *n, pl* **ouzos.** a strong aniseed-flavoured spirit from Greece. [Mod. Gk *ouzon,* from ?]

ova (ˈəʊvə) *n* the plural of **ovum.**

oval ❶ (ˈəʊvᵊl) *adj* **1** having the shape of an ellipse or ellipsoid. ◆ *n* **2** anything that is oval in shape, such as a sports ground. **3** *Austral.* **3a** an Australian Rules ground. **3b** any sports field. [C16: from Med. L *ōvālis,* from L *ōvum* egg]
▸ **ˈovally** *adv* ▸ **ˈovalness** *or* **ovality** (əʊˈvælɪtɪ) *n*

ovariectomy (əʊˌvɛərɪˈɛktəmɪ) *n, pl* **ovariectomies.** *Surgery.* surgical removal of an ovary or ovarian tumour.

ovary (ˈəʊvərɪ) *n, pl* **ovaries. 1** either of the two female reproductive organs, which produce ova and secrete oestrogen hormones. **2** the corresponding organ in vertebrate and invertebrate animals. **3** *Bot.* the hollow basal region of a carpel containing one or more ovules. [C17: from NL *ōvārium,* from L *ōvum* egg]
▸ **ovarian** (əʊˈvɛərɪən) *adj*

ovate (ˈəʊveɪt) *adj* **1** shaped like an egg. **2** (esp. of a leaf) shaped like the longitudinal section of an egg, with the broader end at the base. [C18: from L *ōvātus* egg-shaped]
▸ **ˈovately** *adv*

ovation ❶ (əʊˈveɪʃən) *n* **1** an enthusiastic reception, esp. one of prolonged applause. **2** a victory procession less glorious than a triumph awarded to a Roman general. [C16: from L *ovātiō* rejoicing, from *ovāre* to exult]
▸ **oˈvational** *adj*

oven (ˈʌvᵊn) *n* **1** an enclosed heated compartment or receptacle for baking or roasting food. **2** a similar device, usually lined with a refractory material, used for drying substances, firing ceramics, heat-treating, etc. ◆ *vb* **3** (*tr*) to cook in an oven. [OE *ofen*]
▸ **ˈoven-ˌlike** *adj*

ovenable (ˈʌvᵊnəbᵊl) *adj* suitable for cooking in or using in an oven.

ovenbird (ˈʌvᵊnˌbɜːd) *n* **1** any of numerous small brownish South American passerine birds that build oven-shaped clay nests. **2** a common North American warbler that has an olive-brown striped plumage with an orange crown and builds a cup-shaped nest on the ground.

oven-ready *adj* (of various foods) bought already prepared so that they are ready to be cooked in the oven.

ovenware (ˈʌvᵊnˌwɛə) *n* heat-resistant dishes in which food can be both cooked and served.

over ❶ (ˈəʊvə) *prep* **1** directly above; on the top of; via the top or upper surface of: *over one's head.* **2** on or to the other side of: *over the river.* **3** during; through or throughout (a period of time). **4** in or throughout all parts of: *to travel over England.* **5** throughout the whole extent of: *over the racecourse.* **6** above; in preference to. **7** by the agency of (an instrument of telecommunication): *over the radio.* **8** more than: *over a century ago.* **9** on the subject of; about: *an argument over nothing.* **10** while occupied in: *discussing business over golf.* **11** having recovered from the effects of. **12 over and above.** added to; in addition to. ◆ *adv* **13** in a state, condition, situation, or position that is placed or put over something: *to climb over.* **14** (*particle*) so as to cause to fall: *knocking over a policeman.* **15** at or to a point across intervening space, water, etc. **16** throughout a whole area: *the world over.* **17** (*particle*) from beginning to end, usually cursorily: *to read a document over.* **18** throughout a period of time: *stay over for this week.* **19** (esp. in signalling and radio) it is now your turn to speak, act, etc. **20** more than is expected or usual: *not over well.* **21 over again.** once more. **22 over against. 22a** opposite to. **22b** contrasting with. **23 over and over.** (often foll. by *again*) repeatedly. ◆ *adj* **24** (*postpositive*) finished; no longer in progress. ◆ *adv, adj* **25** remaining; surplus (often in **left over**). ◆ *n* **26** *Cricket.* **26a** a series of six balls bowled by a bowler from the same end of the pitch. **26b** the play during this. [OE *ofer*]

over- *prefix* **1** excessive or excessively; beyond an agreed or desirable limit: *overcharge; overdue.* **2** indicating superior rank: *overseer.* **3** indicating location or movement above: *overhang.* **4** indicating movement downwards: *overthrow.*

overage (ˌəʊvərˈeɪdʒ) *adj* beyond a specified age.

overall ❶ *adj* (ˈəʊvərˌɔːl). (*prenominal*) **1** from one end to the other. **2** including or covering everything: *the overall cost.* ◆ *adv* (ˌəʊvərˈɔːl). **3** in general; on the whole. ◆ *n* (ˈəʊvərˌɔːl). **4** *Brit.* a protective work garment usually worn over ordinary clothes. **5** (*pl*) hard-wearing work trousers with a bib and shoulder straps or jacket attached.

overarch (ˌəʊvərˈɑːtʃ) *vb* (*tr*) to form an arch over.

THESAURUS

outspread *vb* **1** = **outstretch**, expand, extend, fan out, open, open wide, spread out, unfold, unfurl ◆ *adj* **2** = **outstretched**, expanded, extended, fanlike, fanned out, flared, open, opened up, unfolded, unfurled, wide-open

outstanding *adj* **1** = **excellent**, celebrated, distinguished, eminent, exceptional, great, important, impressive, meritorious, pre-eminent, special, stellar (*inf.*), superior, superlative, well-known **2** = **conspicuous**, arresting, eye-catching, marked, memorable, notable, noteworthy, prominent, salient, signal, striking **3** = **unpaid**, due, ongoing, open, owing, payable, pending, remaining, uncollected, unresolved, unsettled
Antonyms *adj* ≠ **excellent**: dull, inferior, insignificant, mediocre, no great shakes (*inf.*), ordinary, pedestrian, run-of-the-mill, unexceptional, unimpressive

outstrip *vb* **1** = **surpass**, beat, better, eclipse, exceed, excel, get ahead of, knock spots off (*inf.*), leave behind, leave standing (*inf.*), lose, outclass, outdo, outperform, outshine, overtake, run rings around (*inf.*), top, transcend **3** = **outdistance**, outpace, outrun, shake off

outward *adj* **1** = **apparent**, evident, exterior, external, noticeable, observable, obvious, ostensible, outer, outside, perceptible, superficial, surface, visible
Antonyms *adj* inner, inside, interior, internal, invisible, inward, obscure, unnoticeable

outwardly *adv* **1** = **apparently**, as far as one can see, externally, officially, on the face of it, on the surface, ostensibly, professedly, seemingly, superficially, to all appearances, to all intents and purposes, to the eye

outweigh *vb* **1** = **override**, cancel (out), compensate for, eclipse, make up for, outbalance, overcome, predominate, preponderate, prevail over, take precedence over, tip the scales

outwit *vb* = **outsmart** (*inf.*), cheat, circumvent, deceive, defraud, dupe, get the better of, gull, make a fool *or* monkey of, outfox, outjockey, outmanoeuvre, outthink, put one over on (*inf.*), run rings round (*inf.*), swindle, take in (*inf.*)

oval *adj* **1** = **elliptical**, egg-shaped, ellipsoidal, ovate, oviform, ovoid

ovation *n* **1** = **applause**, acclaim, acclamation, big hand, cheering, cheers, clapping, laudation, plaudits, tribute
Antonyms *n* abuse, booing, catcalls, derision, heckling, jeers, jibes, mockery, ridicule

over *prep* **1** = **on top of**, above, on, superior to, upon **8** = **more than**, above, exceeding, in excess of **12 over and above** = **in addition to**, added to, as well as, besides, let alone, not to mention, on top of, plus ◆ *adv* **13** = **above**, aloft, on high, overhead **23 over and over (again)** = **repeatedly**, ad nauseam, again and again, frequently, often, time and again ◆ *adj* **24** = **finished**, accomplished, ancient history (*inf.*), at an end, by, bygone, closed, completed, concluded, done (with), ended, gone, past, settled, up (*inf.*) **25** = **extra**, remaining, superfluous, surplus, unused

overall *adj* **2** = **total**, all-embracing, blanket, complete, comprehensive, general, global, inclusive, long-range, long-term, overarching, umbrella ◆ *adv* **3** = **in general**, generally speaking, in (the) large, in the long term, on the whole

overarching (ˌəʊvərˈɑːtʃɪŋ) *adj* overall; all-encompassing: *an overarching concept.*

overarm (ˈəʊvərˌɑːm) *adj* **1** *Sport, esp. cricket.* bowled, thrown, or performed with the arm raised above the shoulder. ◆ *adv* **2** with the arm raised above the shoulder.

overawe Ⓣ (ˌəʊvərˈɔː) *vb* **overawes, overawing, overawed.** (*tr*) to subdue, restrain, or overcome by affecting with a feeling of awe.

overbalance Ⓣ *vb* (ˌəʊvəˈbæləns), **overbalances, overbalancing, overbalanced. 1** to lose or cause to lose balance. **2** (*tr*) another word for **outweigh.** ◆ *n* (ˈəʊvəˌbæləns). **3** excess of weight, value, etc.

overbear (ˌəʊvəˈbɛə) *vb* **overbears, overbearing, overbore, overborne. 1** (*tr*) to dominate or overcome. **2** (*tr*) to press or bear down with weight or physical force. **3** to produce (fruit, etc.) excessively.

overbearing Ⓣ (ˌəʊvəˈbɛərɪŋ) *adj* **1** domineering or dictatorial in manner or action. **2** of particular or overriding importance or significance.
► ˌ**overˈbearingly** *adv*

overblown Ⓣ (ˌəʊvəˈbləʊn) *adj* **1** overdone or excessive. **2** bombastic; turgid: *overblown prose.* **3** (of flowers) past the stage of full bloom.

overboard (ˈəʊvəˌbɔːd) *adv* **1** from on board a vessel into the water. **2 go overboard.** *Inf.* **2a** to be extremely enthusiastic. **2b** to go to extremes. **3 throw overboard.** to reject or abandon.

overbook (ˌəʊvəˈbʊk) *vb* (*tr, also absol.*) to make more reservations than there are places, tickets, etc., available.

overbuild (ˌəʊvəˈbɪld) *vb* **overbuilds, overbuilding, overbuilt.** (*tr*) **1** to build over or on top of. **2** to erect too many buildings in (an area). **3** to build too large or elaborately.

overburden *vb* (ˌəʊvəˈbɜːdᵊn). **1** (*tr*) to load with excessive weight, work, etc. ◆ *n* (ˈəʊvəˌbɜːdᵊn). **2** an excessive burden or load. **3** *Geol.* the sedimentary rock material that covers coal seams, mineral veins, etc.
► ˌ**overˈburdensome** *adj*

overcast Ⓣ *adj* (ˈəʊvəˌkɑːst). **1** covered over or obscured, esp. by clouds. **2** *Meteorol.* (of the sky) cloud-covered. **3** gloomy or melancholy. **4** sewn over by overcasting. ◆ *vb* (ˌəʊvəˈkɑːst), **overcasts, overcasting, overcast. 5** to sew (an edge, as of a hem) with long stitches passing successively over the edge. ◆ *n* (ˈəʊvəˌkɑːst). **6** *Meteorol.* the state of the sky when it is cloud-covered.

overcharge Ⓣ *vb* (ˌəʊvəˈtʃɑːdʒ), **overcharges, overcharging, overcharged. 1** to charge too much. **2** (*tr*) to fill or load beyond capacity. **3** *Literary.* another word for **exaggerate.** ◆ *n* (ˈəʊvəˌtʃɑːdʒ). **4** an excessive price or charge. **5** an excessive load.

overcloud (ˌəʊvəˈklaʊd) *vb* **1** to make or become covered with clouds. **2** to make or become dark or dim.

overcoat (ˈəʊvəˌkəʊt) *n* a warm heavy coat worn over the outer clothes in cold weather.

overcome Ⓣ (ˌəʊvəˈkʌm) *vb* **overcomes, overcoming, overcame, overcome. 1** (*tr*) to get the better of in a conflict. **2** (*tr; often passive*) to render incapable or powerless by laughter, sorrow, exhaustion, etc. **3** (*tr*) to surmount obstacles, objections, etc. **4** (*intr*) to be victorious.

overcrop (ˌəʊvəˈkrɒp) *vb* **overcrops, overcropping, overcropped.** (*tr*) to exhaust (land) by excessive cultivation.

overdo Ⓣ (ˌəʊvəˈduː) *vb* **overdoes, overdoing, overdid, overdone.** (*tr*) **1** to take or carry too far; do to excess. **2** to exaggerate, overelaborate, or overplay. **3** to cook or bake too long. **4 overdo it** *or* **things.** to overtax one's strength, capacity, etc.

overdose *n* (ˈəʊvəˌdəʊs). **1** (esp. of drugs) an excessive dose. ◆ *vb* (ˌəʊvəˈdəʊs), **overdoses, overdosing, overdosed. 2** to take an excessive dose or give an excessive dose to.
► ˌ**overˈdosage** *n*

overdraft (ˈəʊvəˌdrɑːft) *n* **1** a deficit in a bank or building-society cheque account caused by withdrawing more money than is credited to it. **2** the amount of this deficit.

overdraw (ˌəʊvəˈdrɔː) *vb* **overdraws, overdrawing, overdrew, overdrawn. 1** to draw on (a bank account) in excess of the credit balance. **2** (*tr*) to exaggerate in describing or telling.

overdress *vb* (ˌəʊvəˈdrɛs). **1** to dress (oneself or another) too elaborately or finely. ◆ *n* (ˈəʊvəˌdrɛs). **2** a dress that may be worn over a jumper, blouse, etc.

overdrive *n* (ˈəʊvəˌdraɪv). **1** a very high gear in a motor vehicle used at high speeds to reduce wear. ◆ *vb* (ˌəʊvəˈdraɪv), **overdrives, overdriving, overdrove, overdriven. 2** (*tr*) to drive too hard or too far; overwork or overuse.

overdub (in multitrack recording) ◆ *vb* (ˌəʊvəˈdʌb), **overdubs, overdubbing, overdubbed. 1** to add (new sound) on a spare track or tracks. ◆ *n* (ˈəʊvəˌdʌb). **2** the blending of various layers of sound in one recording by this method.

overdue Ⓣ (ˌəʊvəˈdjuː) *adj* past the time specified, required, or preferred for arrival, occurrence, payment, etc.

overestimate *vb* (ˌəʊvərˈɛstɪˌmeɪt), **overestimates, overestimating, overestimated. 1** (*tr*) to estimate too highly. ◆ *n* (ˌəʊvərˈɛstɪmɪt). **2** an estimate that is too high.
► ˌ**overˌestiˈmation** *n*

overexpose (ˌəʊvərɪksˈpəʊz) *vb* **overexposes, overexposing, overexposed.** (*tr*) **1** to expose too much or for too long. **2** *Photog.* to expose (a film, etc.) for too long or with too bright a light.
► ˌ**overexˈposure** *n*

overflow Ⓣ *vb* (ˌəʊvəˈfləʊ), **overflows, overflowing, overflowed** *or (formerly)* **overflown. 1** to flow or run over (a limit, brim, etc.). **2** to fill or be filled beyond capacity so as to spill or run over. **3** (*intr; usually foll. by with*) to be filled with happiness, tears, etc. **4** (*tr*) to spread or cover over; flood or inundate. ◆ *n* (ˈəʊvəˌfləʊ). **5** overflowing matter, esp. liquid. **6** any outlet that enables surplus liquid to be discharged or drained off. **7** the amount by which a limit, capacity, etc., is exceeded.

overfold (ˈəʊvəˌfəʊld) *n Geol.* a fold in the form of an anticline in which one limb is more steeply inclined than the other.

overfunding (ˈəʊvəˌfʌndɪŋ) *n* (in Britain) a government policy in which it sells more of its securities than would be required to finance public spending, with the object of absorbing surplus funds to curb inflation.

overgrow (ˌəʊvəˈgrəʊ) *vb* **overgrows, overgrowing, overgrew, overgrown. 1** (*tr*) to grow over or across (an area, path, etc.). **2** (*tr*) to choke or supplant by a stronger growth. **3** (*tr*) to grow too large for. **4** (*intr*) to grow beyond normal size.
► ˈ**overˌgrowth** *n*

overhand (ˈəʊvəˌhænd) *adj* **1** thrown or performed with the hand raised above the shoulder. **2** sewn with thread passing over two edges in one direction. ◆ *adv* **3** with the hand above the shoulder; overarm. **4** with shallow stitches passing over two edges. ◆ *vb* **5** to sew (two edges) overhand.

overhang Ⓣ *vb* (ˌəʊvəˈhæŋ), **overhangs, overhanging, overhung. 1** to project or extend beyond (a surface, building, etc.). **2** (*tr*) to hang or be suspended over. **3** (*tr*) to menace, threaten, or dominate. ◆ *n* (ˈəʊvəˌhæŋ). **4** a formation, object, etc., that extends beyond or hangs over something, such as an outcrop of rock overhanging a mountain face. **5** the amount or extent of projection.

overhaul Ⓣ *vb* (ˌəʊvəˈhɔːl). (*tr*) **1** to examine carefully for faults, necessary repairs, etc. **2** to make repairs or adjustments to (a car, machine, etc.). **3** to overtake. ◆ *n* (ˈəʊvəˌhɔːl). **4** a thorough examination and repair.

THESAURUS

overawe *vb* = **intimidate**, abash, alarm, browbeat, cow, daunt, frighten, scare, terrify
Antonyms *vb* bolster, buoy up, cheer up, comfort, console, hearten, reassure

overbalance *vb* **1** = **topple over**, capsize, keel over, lose one's balance, lose one's footing, overset, overturn, slip, take a tumble, tip over, tumble, turn turtle, upset

overbearing *adj* **1** = **dictatorial**, arrogant, autocratic, bossy (*inf.*), cavalier, despotic, dogmatic, domineering, haughty, high-handed, imperious, lordly, magisterial, officious, oppressive, overweening, peremptory, supercilious, superior, tyrannical
Antonyms *adj* deferential, humble, modest, self-effacing, submissive, unassertive, unassuming

overblown *adj* **1** = **excessive**, disproportionate, fulsome, immoderate, inflated, overdone, over the top, undue **2** = **grandiloquent**, aureate, bombastic, euphuistic, florid, flowery, fustian, magniloquent, pompous, turgid, windy

overcast *adj* **1** = **cloudy**, clouded, clouded over, darkened, dismal, dreary, dull, grey, hazy, leaden, louring *or* lowering, murky, sombre, sunless, threatening
Antonyms *adj* bright, brilliant, clear, cloudless, fine, sunny, unclouded

overcharge *vb* **1** = **cheat**, clip (*sl.*), diddle (*inf.*), do (*sl.*), fleece, rip off (*sl.*), rook (*sl.*), short-change, skin (*sl.*), sting (*inf.*), surcharge **2** = **overload**, burden, oppress, overburden, overtask, overtax, strain, surfeit **3** *Literary* = **exaggerate**, embellish, embroider, hyperbolize, lay it on thick (*inf.*), overstate

overcome *vb* **1** = **conquer**, beat, best, be victorious, blow out of the water (*sl.*), bring (someone) to their knees (*inf.*), clobber (*sl.*), come out on top (*inf.*), crush, defeat, get the better of, lick (*inf.*), make mincemeat of (*inf.*), master, overpower, overthrow, overwhelm, prevail, rise above, subdue, subjugate, surmount, survive, triumph over, undo, vanquish, weather, wipe the floor with (*inf.*), worst

overdo *vb* **1, 2** = **exaggerate**, be intemperate, belabour, carry too far, do to death (*inf.*), gild the lily, go overboard (*inf.*), go to extremes, lay it on thick (*inf.*), not know when to stop, overindulge, overplay, overreach, overstate, overuse, overwork, run riot **4 overdo it** = **overwork**, bite off more than one can chew, burn the candle at both ends (*inf.*), drive oneself, go too far, have too many irons in the fire, overburden oneself, overload oneself, overtax one's strength, overtire oneself, strain *or* overstrain oneself, wear oneself out
Antonyms *vb* ≠ **exaggerate:** belittle, disparage, minimize, play down, underplay, underrate, understate, underuse, undervalue

overdone *adj* **1, 2** = **excessive**, beyond all bounds, exaggerated, fulsome, hyped, immoderate, inordinate, overelaborate, preposterous, too much, undue, unnecessary **3** = **overcooked**, burnt, burnt to a cinder, charred, dried up, spoiled
Antonyms *adj* ≠ **excessive:** belittled, minimized, moderated, played down, underdone, underplayed, understated

overdue *adj* = **late**, behindhand, behind schedule, behind time, belated, late in the day, long delayed, not before time (*inf.*), owing, tardy, unpunctual
Antonyms *adj* ahead of time, beforehand, early, in advance, in good time, punctual

overflow *vb* **1, 2** = **spill**, brim over, bubble over, discharge, fall over, pour out, pour over, run over, run with, shower, slop over, spray, surge, teem, well over **4** = **flood**, cover, deluge, drown, inundate, soak, submerge, swamp ◆ *n* **5** = **surplus**, discharge, flash flood, flood, flooding, inundation, overabundance, spill, spilling over

overflowing *adj* **1** = **plentiful**, abounding, bountiful, brimful, copious, profuse, rife, superabundant, swarming, teeming, thronged
Antonyms *adj* deficient, inadequate, insufficient, lacking, missing, scarce, wanting

overhang *vb* **1** = **project**, beetle, bulge, cast a shadow, extend, impend, jut, loom, protrude, stick out, threaten

overhaul *vb* **1** = **check**, do up (*inf.*), examine,

overhead ⓣ *adj* ('əʊvə,hɛd). **1** situated or operating above head height or some other reference level. **2** (*prenominal*) inclusive: *the overhead price included meals.* ◆ *adv* (,əʊvə'hɛd). **3** over or above head height, esp. in the sky. ◆ *n* ('əʊvə,hɛd). **4a** a stroke in racket games played from above head height. **4b** (*as modifier*): *an overhead smash.* **5** (*modifier*) of, concerned with, or resulting from overheads: *overhead costs.*

overhead camshaft *n* a type of camshaft situated above the cylinder head in an internal-combustion engine.

overhead projector *n* a projector that throws an enlarged image of a transparency onto a surface above and behind the person using it.

overheads ⓣ ('əʊvə,hɛdz) *pl n* business expenses, such as rent, that are not directly attributable to any department or product and can therefore be assigned only arbitrarily.

overhead-valve engine *n* a type of internal-combustion engine in which the inlet and exhaust valves are in the cylinder head above the pistons. US name: **valve-in-head engine.**

overhear (,əʊvə'hɪə) *vb* **overhears, overhearing, overheard.** (*tr*) to hear (a person, remark, etc.) without the knowledge of the speaker.

overheat (,əʊvə'hi:t) *vb* **1** to make or become excessively hot. **2** (*tr; often passive*) to make very agitated, irritated, etc. **3** (*intr*) (of an economy) to tend towards inflation, often as a result of excessive growth in demand. **4** (*tr*) to cause (an economy) to tend towards inflation. ◆ *n* **5** the condition of being overheated.

overjoy ⓣ (,əʊvə'dʒɔɪ) *vb* (*tr*) to give great delight to.
▸**,over'joyed** *adj*

overkill ('əʊvə,kɪl) *n* **1** the capability to deploy more weapons, esp. nuclear weapons, than is necessary to ensure military advantage. **2** any capacity or treatment that is greater than that required or appropriate.

overland ('əʊvə,lænd) *adj* (*prenominal*), *adv* **1** over or across land. ◆ *vb* **2** *Austral.* (formerly) to drive (cattle or sheep) overland.
▸**'over,lander** *n*

overlap *vb* (,əʊvə'læp), **overlaps, overlapping, overlapped. 1** (of two things) to extend or lie partly over (each other). **2** to cover and extend beyond (something). **3** (*intr*) to coincide partly in time, subject, etc. ◆ *n* ('əʊvə,læp). **4** a part that overlaps or is overlapped. **5** the amount, length, etc., overlapping. **6** *Geol.* the horizontal extension of the lower beds in a series of rock strata beyond the upper beds.

overlay ⓣ *vb* (,əʊvə'leɪ), **overlays, overlaying, overlaid.** (*tr*) **1** to lay or place over or upon (something else). **2** (often foll. by *with*) to cover, overspread, or conceal (with). **3** (foll. by *with*) to cover (a surface) with an applied decoration: *ebony overlaid with silver.* **4** to achieve the correct printing pressure all over (a forme or plate) by adding to the appropriate areas of the packing. ◆ *n* ('əʊvə,leɪ). **5** something that is laid over something else; covering. **6** an applied decoration or layer, as of gold leaf. **7** a transparent sheet giving extra details to a map or diagram over which it is designed to be placed. **8** *Printing.* material, such as paper, used to overlay a forme or plate.

overleaf (,əʊvə'li:f) *adv* on the other side of the page.

overlie (,əʊvə'laɪ) *vb* **overlies, overlying, overlay, overlain.** (*tr*) **1** to lie or rest upon. Cf. **overlay. 2** to kill (a baby or newborn animal) by lying upon it.

overlong (,əʊvə'lɒŋ) *adj, adv* too or excessively long.

overlook ⓣ *vb* (,əʊvə'lʊk). (*tr*) **1** to fail to notice or take into account. **2** to disregard deliberately or indulgently. **3** to afford a view of from above: *the house overlooks the bay.* **4** to rise above. **5** to look at carefully. **6** to cast the evil eye upon (someone). ◆ *n* ('əʊvə,lʊk). *US.* **7** a high place affording a view. **8** an act of overlooking.

overlord ('əʊvə,lɔ:d) *n* a supreme lord or master.
▸**'over,lordship** *n*

overly ⓣ ('əʊvəlɪ) *adv* too; excessively.

overman *vb* (,əʊvə'mæn), **overmans, overmanning, overmanned. 1** (*tr*) to supply with an excessive number of men. ◆ *n* ('əʊvə,mæn), *pl* **overmen. 2** a man who oversees others. **3** a superman.

overmaster (,əʊvə'mɑ:stə) *vb* (*tr*) to overpower.

overmatch *Chiefly US.* ◆ *vb* (,əʊvə'mætʃ). (*tr*) **1** to be more than a match for. **2** to match with a superior opponent. ◆ *n* ('əʊvə,mætʃ). **3** a person superior in ability. **4** a match in which one contestant is superior.

overmuch (,əʊvə'mʌtʃ) *adv, adj* **1** too much; very much. ◆ *n* **2** an excessive amount.

overnice (,əʊvə'naɪs) *adj* too fastidious, precise, etc.

overnight *adv* (,əʊvə'naɪt). **1** for the duration of the night. **2** in or as if in the course of one night; suddenly: *the situation changed overnight.* ◆ *adj* ('əʊvə,naɪt). (*usually prenominal*) **3** done in, occurring in, or lasting the night: *an overnight stop.* **4** staying for one night. **5** for use during a single night. **6** occurring in or as if in the course of one night; sudden: *an overnight victory.*

overpass *n* ('əʊvə,pɑ:s). **1** another name for **flyover** (sense 1). ◆ *vb* (,əʊvə'pɑ:s). (*tr*) *Now rare.* **2** to pass over, through, or across. **3** to exceed. **4** to ignore.

overplay (,əʊvə'pleɪ) *vb* **1** (*tr*) to exaggerate the importance of. **2** to act or behave in an exaggerated manner. **3 overplay one's hand.** to overestimate the worth or strength of one's position.

overpower ⓣ (,əʊvə'paʊə) *vb* (*tr*) **1** to conquer or subdue by superior force. **2** to have such a strong effect on as to make helpless or ineffective. **3** to supply with more power than necessary.
▸**,over'powering** *adj*

overprice (,əʊvə'praɪs) *vb* **overprices, overpricing, overpriced.** (*tr*) to ask too high a price for.

overprint *vb* (,əʊvə'prɪnt). **1** (*tr*) to print (additional matter or another colour) on a sheet of paper. ◆ *n* ('əʊvə,prɪnt). **2** additional matter or another colour printed onto a previously printed sheet. **3** additional matter applied to a finished postage stamp by printing, stamping, etc.

overqualified (,əʊvə'kwɒlɪfaɪd) *adj* having more managerial experience or academic qualifications than required for a particular job.

overrate ⓣ (,əʊvə'reɪt) *vb* **overrates, overrating, overrated.** (*tr*) to assess too highly.

overreach ⓣ (,əʊvə'ri:tʃ) *vb* **1** (*tr*) to defeat or thwart (oneself) by attempting to do or gain too much. **2** (*tr*) to aim for but miss by going too far. **3** to get the better of (a person) by trickery. **4** (*tr*) to reach beyond or over. **5** (*intr*) to reach or go too far. **6** (*intr*) (of a horse) to strike the back of a forefoot with the edge of the opposite hind foot.

overreact (,əʊvərɪ'ækt) *vb* (*intr*) to react excessively to something.
▸**,overre'action** *n*

override ⓣ *vb* (,əʊvə'raɪd), **overrides, overriding, overrode, overridden.** (*tr*) **1** to set aside or disregard with superior authority or power. **2** to supersede or annul. **3** to dominate or vanquish by or as if by trampling down. **4** to take manual control of (a system that is usually under automatic control). **5** to extend or pass over, esp. to overlap. **6** to ride (a horse, etc.) too hard. **7** to ride over. ◆ *n* ('əʊvə,raɪd). **8** a device that can override an automatic control.

overrider ('əʊvə,raɪdə) *n* either of two attachments fitted to the bumper of a motor vehicle to prevent it interlocking with that of another vehicle.

overriding ⓣ (,əʊvə'raɪdɪŋ) *adj* taking precedence.

overrule ⓣ (,əʊvə'ru:l) *vb* **overrules, overruling, overruled.** (*tr*) **1** to disallow the arguments of (a person) by the use of authority. **2** to rule or decide against (an argument, decision, etc.). **3** to prevail over, dominate, or influence. **4** to exercise rule over.

overrun ⓣ *vb* (,əʊvə'rʌn), **overruns, overrunning, overran, overrun. 1** (*tr*) to swarm or spread over rapidly. **2** to run over (something); overflow. **3**

THESAURUS

inspect, recondition, re-examine, repair, restore, service, survey **3** = **overtake**, catch up with, draw level with, get ahead of, pass ◆ *n* **4** = **checkup**, check, examination, going-over (*inf.*), inspection, reconditioning, service

overhead *adj* **1** = **aerial**, overhanging, roof, upper ◆ *adv* **3** = **above**, aloft, atop, in the sky, on high, skyward, up above, upward
Antonyms *adv* ≠ **above:** below, beneath, downward, underfoot, underneath

overheads *pl n* = **running costs**, burden, oncosts, operating costs

overjoyed *adj* = **delighted**, cock-a-hoop, deliriously happy, elated, euphoric, floating on air, happy as a lark, in raptures, joyful, jubilant, on cloud nine (*inf.*), only too happy, over the moon (*inf.*), rapt, rapturous, thrilled, tickled pink (*inf.*), transported
Antonyms *adj* crestfallen, dejected, disappointed, downcast, down in the dumps (*inf.*), heartbroken, miserable, sad, unhappy, woebegone

overlay *vb* **2, 3** = **cover**, adorn, blanket, inlay, laminate, ornament, overspread, superimpose, veneer ◆ *n* **5, 6** = **covering**, adornment, appliqué, decoration, ornamentation, veneer

overlook *vb* **1** = **miss**, disregard, fail to notice, forget, leave out of consideration, leave undone, neglect, omit, pass, slight, slip up on **2** = **ignore**, blink at, condone, disregard, excuse, forgive, let bygones be bygones, let one off with, let pass, let ride, make allowances for, pardon, turn a blind eye to, wink at **3** = **have a view of**, afford a view of, command a view of, front on to, give upon, look over *or* out on
Antonyms *vb* ≠ **miss:** discern, heed, mark, note, notice, observe, perceive, regard, spot

overly *adv* = **excessively**, exceedingly, immoderately, inordinately, over, too, unduly, very much

overpower *vb* **1** = **overwhelm**, beat, clobber, conquer, crush, defeat, get the upper hand over, immobilize, knock out, lick (*inf.*), make mincemeat of (*inf.*), master, overcome, overthrow, quell, subdue, subjugate, vanquish

overpowering *adj* **2** = **overwhelming**, compelling, compulsive, extreme, forceful, invincible, irrefutable, irresistible, nauseating, powerful, sickening, strong, suffocating, telling, unbearable, uncontrollable

overrate *vb* = **overestimate**, assess too highly, exaggerate, make too much of, overpraise, overprize, oversell, overvalue, rate too highly, think *or* expect too much of, think too highly of

overreach *vb* **1 overreach oneself** = **try to be too clever**, be hoist with one's own petard, bite off more than one can chew, defeat one's own ends, go too far **3** = **trick**, cheat, circumvent, deceive, defraud, dupe, gull (*arch.*), outsmart (*inf.*), outwit, swindle, victimize

override *vb* **1, 2** = **overrule**, annul, cancel, countermand, discount, disregard, ignore, nullify, outweigh, quash, reverse, ride roughshod over, set aside, supersede, take no account of, trample underfoot, upset

overriding *adj* = **predominant**, cardinal, compelling, determining, dominant, final, major, mother of all (*inf.*), number one, overruling, paramount, pivotal, prevailing, primary, prime, ruling, supreme, ultimate
Antonyms *adj* immaterial, inconsequential, insignificant, irrelevant, minor, negligible, paltry, petty, trifling, trivial, unimportant

overrule *vb* **1** = **reverse**, alter, annul, cancel, countermand, disallow, invalidate, make null and void, outvote, override, overturn, recall, repeal, rescind, revoke, rule against, set aside, veto **3** = **influence**, bend to one's will, control, direct, dominate, govern, prevail over, sway
Antonyms *vb* ≠ **reverse:** allow, approve, consent to, endorse, pass, permit, sanction

overrun *vb* **1** = **spread over**, choke, infest, inundate, overflow, overgrow, permeate, ravage, to extend or run beyond a limit. **4** (*intr*) (of an engine) to run with a closed throttle at a speed dictated by that of the vehicle it drives. **5** (*tr*) to print (a book, journal, etc.) in a greater quantity than ordered. **6** (*tr*) *Printing.* to transfer (set type) from one column, line, or page, to another. **7** (*tr*) *Arch.* to run faster than. ◆ *n* ('əuvəˌrʌn). **8** the act or an instance of overrunning. **9** the amount or extent of overrunning. **10** the number of copies of a publication in excess of the quantity ordered.

overseas *adv* (ˌəuvə'si:z). **1** beyond the sea; abroad. ◆ *adj* ('əuvə'si:z). **2** of, to, in, from, or situated in countries beyond the sea. **3** Also: **oversea.** of or relating to passage over the sea. ◆ *n* (ˌəuvə'si:z). **4** (*functioning as sing*) *Inf.* a foreign country or foreign countries collectively.

overseas territory *n* See **United Kingdom overseas territory.**

oversee (ˌəuvə'si:) *vb* **oversees, overseeing, oversaw, overseen.** (*tr*) **1** to watch over and direct; supervise. **2** to watch secretly or accidentally. **3** *Arch.* to scrutinize; inspect.

overseer Ⓣ ('əuvəˌsi:ə) *n* **1** a person who oversees others, esp. workmen. **2** *Brit. history.* a minor official of a parish attached to the poorhouse.

oversell (ˌəuvə'sel) *vb* **oversells, overselling, oversold.** **1** (*tr*) to sell more of (a commodity, etc.) than can be supplied. **2** to use excessively aggressive methods in selling (commodities). **3** (*tr*) to exaggerate the merits of.

overset (ˌəuvə'set) *vb* **oversets, oversetting, overset.** (*tr*) **1** to disturb or upset. **2** *Printing.* to set (type or copy) in excess of the space available.

oversew ('əuvəˌsəu, ˌəuvə'səu) *vb* **oversews, oversewing, oversewed; oversewn** *or* **oversewed.** to sew (two edges) with close stitches that pass over them both.

oversexed (ˌəuvə'sekst) *adj* having an excessive preoccupation with sexual activity.

overshadow Ⓣ (ˌəuvə'ʃædəu) *vb* (*tr*) **1** to render insignificant or less important in comparison. **2** to cast a shadow or gloom over.

overshoe ('əuvəˌʃu:) *n* a protective shoe worn over an ordinary shoe.

overshoot *vb* (ˌəuvə'ʃu:t), **overshoots, overshooting, overshot.** **1** to shoot or go beyond (a mark or target). **2** (of an aircraft) to fly or taxi too far along a runway. **3** (*tr*) to pass swiftly over or down over, as water over a wheel. ◆ *n* ('əuvəˌʃu:t). **4** an act or instance of overshooting. **5** the extent of such overshooting.

overshot ('əuvəˌʃɒt) *adj* **1** having or designating an upper jaw that projects beyond the lower jaw. **2** (of a water wheel) driven by a flow of water that passes over the wheel.

oversight Ⓣ ('əuvəˌsaɪt) *n* **1** an omission or mistake, esp. one made through failure to notice something. **2** supervision.

oversize *adj* (ˌəuvə'saɪz). **1** Also: **oversized.** larger than the usual size. ◆ *n* ('əuvəˌsaɪz). **2** a size larger than the usual or proper size. **3** something that is oversize.

overskirt ('əuvəˌskɜ:t) *n* an outer skirt, esp. one that reveals a decorative underskirt.

overspend *vb* (ˌəuvə'spend), **overspends, overspending, overspent.** **1** to spend in excess of (one's desires or what one can afford or is allocated). **2** (*tr; usually passive*) to wear out; exhaust. ◆ *n* ('əuvəˌspend). **3** the amount by which someone or something is overspent.

overspill *n* ('əuvəˌspɪl). **1a** something that spills over or is in excess. **1b** (*as modifier*): *overspill population.* ◆ *vb* (ˌəuvə'spɪl), **overspills, overspilling, overspilt** *or* **overspilled.** **2** (*intr*) to overflow.

overspread (ˌəuvə'spred) *vb* (*tr*) **overspreads, overspreading, overspread.** to extend or spread over.

overstate (ˌəuvə'steɪt) *vb* **overstates, overstating, overstated.** (*tr*) to state too strongly; exaggerate or overemphasize.
▸ˌ**over'statement** *n*

overstay (ˌəuvə'steɪ) *vb* (*tr*) **1** to stay beyond the time, limit, or duration of. **2 overstay** *or* **outstay one's welcome.** to stay (at a party, etc.), longer than pleases the host or hostess.

overstep (ˌəuvə'step) *vb* **oversteps, overstepping, overstepped.** (*tr*) to go beyond (a certain or proper limit).

overstrung (ˌəuvə'strʌŋ) *adj* **1** too highly strung; tense. **2** (of a piano) having two sets of strings crossing each other at an oblique angle.

overstuff (ˌəuvə'stʌf) *vb* (*tr*) **1** to force too much into. **2** to cover (furniture, etc.) entirely with upholstery.

oversubscribe (ˌəuvəsəb'skraɪb) *vb* **oversubscribes, oversubscribing, oversubscribed.** (*tr; often passive*) to subscribe or apply for in excess of available supply.
▸ˌ**oversub'scription** *n*

overt Ⓣ ('əuvɜ:t, əu'vɜ:t) *adj* **1** open to view; observable. **2** *Law.* open; deliberate. [C14: via OF, from *ovrir* to open, from L *aperīre*]
▸'**overtly** *adv*

overtake Ⓣ (ˌəuvə'teɪk) *vb* **overtakes, overtaking, overtook, overtaken.** **1** *Chiefly Brit.* to move past (another vehicle or person) travelling in the same direction. **2** (*tr*) to pass or do better than, after catching up with. **3** (*tr*) to come upon suddenly or unexpectedly: *night overtook him.* **4** (*tr*) to catch up with; draw level with.

overtax (ˌəuvə'tæks) *vb* (*tr*) **1** to tax too heavily. **2** to impose too great a strain on.

over-the-counter *adj* **1** (of a stock exchange dealing) conducted between brokers in areas for which no official market prices are quoted. **2** (of a medicinal drug) able to be sold without prescription. Cf. **POM.** ◆ Abbrev.: **OTC.**

overthrow Ⓣ *vb* (ˌəuvə'θrəu), **overthrows, overthrowing, overthrew, overthrown.** **1** (*tr*) to effect the downfall or destruction of (a ruler, institution, etc.), esp. by force. **2** (*tr*) to throw or turn over. **3** to throw (something, esp. a ball) too far. ◆ *n* ('əuvəˌθrəu). **4** downfall; destruction. **5** *Cricket.* **5a** a ball thrown back too far by a fielder. **5b** a run scored because of this.

overthrust ('əuvəˌθrʌst) *n Geol.* a reverse fault in which the rocks on the upper surface of a fault plane have moved over the rocks on the lower surface.

overtime *n* ('əuvəˌtaɪm). **1a** work at a regular job done in addition to regular working hours. **1b** (*as modifier*): *overtime pay.* **2** the rate of pay established for such work. **3** time in excess of a set period. **4** *Sport, US & Canad.* extra time. ◆ *adv* ('əuvəˌtaɪm). **5** beyond the regular or stipulated time. ◆ *vb* (ˌəuvə'taɪm), **overtimes, overtiming, overtimed.** **6** (*tr*) to exceed the required time for (a photographic exposure, etc.).

overtone Ⓣ ('əuvəˌtəun) *n* **1** (*often pl*) additional meaning or nuance: *overtones of despair.* **2** *Music, acoustics.* any of the tones, with the exception of the fundamental, that constitute a musical sound and contribute to its quality.

overture Ⓣ ('əuvəˌtjuə) *n* **1** *Music.* **1a** a piece of orchestral music that is played at the beginning of an opera or oratorio, often containing the main musical themes of the work. **1b** a one-movement orchestral piece, usually having a descriptive or evocative title. **2** (*often pl*) a proposal, act, or gesture initiating a relationship, negotiation, etc. **3** something that introduces what follows. ◆ *vb* **overtures, overturing, overtured.** (*tr*) **4** to make or present an overture to. **5** to introduce with an overture. [C14: via OF from LL *apertūra* opening, from L *aperīre* to open]

overturn Ⓣ *vb* (ˌəuvə'tɜ:n). **1** to turn or cause to turn from an upright or normal position. **2** (*tr*) to overthrow or destroy. **3** (*tr*) to invalidate; reverse. ◆ *n* ('əuvəˌtɜ:n). **4** the act of overturning or the state of being overturned.

overuse Ⓣ *vb* (ˌəuvə'ju:z), **overuses, overusing, overused.** **1** (*tr*) to use excessively. ◆ *n* (ˌəuvə'ju:s) **2** excessive use.

overview ('əuvəˌvju:) *n* a general survey.

overweening Ⓣ (ˌəuvə'wi:nɪŋ) *adj* **1** (of a person) excessively arrogant or presumptuous. **2** (of opinions, appetites, etc.) excessive; immoderate. [C14: from OVER + *weening* from OE *wēnan* WEEN]
▸ˌ**over'weeningness** *n*

overweight Ⓣ *adj* (ˌəuvə'weɪt). **1** weighing more than is usual, allowed, or healthy. ◆ *n* ('əuvəˌweɪt). **2** extra or excess weight. ◆ *vb*

THESAURUS

spread like wildfire, surge over, swarm over **3** = **exceed**, go beyond, overshoot, run over *or* on

overseer *n* **1** = **supervisor**, boss, chief, foreman, gaffer (*inf., chiefly Brit.*), manager, master, super (*inf.*), superintendent, superior

overshadow *vb* **1** = **outshine**, dominate, dwarf, eclipse, excel, leave *or* put in the shade, outweigh, rise above, steal the limelight from, surpass, take precedence over, throw into the shade, tower above **2** = **spoil**, blight, cast a gloom upon, cloud, darken, mar, put a damper on, ruin, take the edge off, take the pleasure *or* enjoyment out of, temper

oversight *n* **1** = **mistake**, blunder, carelessness, delinquency, error, fault, inattention, lapse, laxity, neglect, omission, slip **2** = **supervision**, administration, care, charge, control, custody, direction, handling, inspection, keeping, management, superintendence, surveillance

overt *adj* **1** = **open**, apparent, blatant, bold, manifest, observable, obvious, patent, plain, public, unconcealed, undisguised, visible
Antonyms *adj* concealed, covert, disguised, hidden, hush-hush (*inf.*), invisible, secret, surreptitious, underhand

overtake *vb* **1, 2** = **pass**, get past, leave behind, outdistance, outdo, outstrip, overhaul **3** = **befall**, catch unprepared, come upon, engulf, happen, hit, overwhelm, strike, take by surprise **4** = **catch up with**, draw level with

overthrow *vb* **1** = **defeat**, abolish, beat, bring down, conquer, crush, depose, dethrone, do away with, master, oust, overcome, overpower, overwhelm, subdue, subjugate, topple, unseat, vanquish ◆ *n* **4** = **downfall**, defeat, deposition, destruction, dethronement, discomfiture, disestablishment, displacement, dispossession, end, fall, ousting, prostration, rout, ruin, subjugation, subversion, suppression, undoing, unseating
Antonyms *vb* ≠ **defeat:** defend, guard, keep, maintain, preserve, protect, restore, support, uphold ◆ *n* ≠ **downfall:** defence, preservation, protection

overtone *n* **1** *often plural* = **hint**, association, connotation, flavour, implication, innuendo, intimation, nuance, sense, suggestion, undercurrent

overture *n* **1a** *Music* = **introduction**, opening, prelude **2** *often plural* = **approach**, advance, conciliatory move, invitation, offer, opening move, proposal, proposition, signal, tender
Antonyms *n* ≠ **introduction:** coda, finale ≠ **approach:** rebuke, rejection, withdrawal

overturn *vb* **1** = **tip over**, capsize, keel over, knock over *or* down, overbalance, reverse, spill, topple, tumble, upend, upset, upturn **2, 3** = **overthrow**, abolish, annul, bring down, countermand, depose, destroy, invalidate, obviate, repeal, rescind, reverse, set aside, unseat

overused *adj* **1** = **hackneyed**, cliché'd, platitudinous, played out, stale, stereotyped, threadbare, tired, unoriginal, worn (out)

overweening *adj* **1** = **arrogant**, cavalier, cocksure, cocky, conceited, egotistical, haughty, high and mighty (*inf.*), high-handed, insolent, lordly, opinionated, pompous, presumptuous, proud, self-confident, supercilious, uppish (*Brit. inf.*), vain, vainglorious **2** = **excessive**, blown up out of all proportion, extravagant, immoderate
Antonyms *adj* ≠ **arrogant:** deferential, diffident, hesitant, modest, self-conscious, self-effacing, timid, unassuming, unobtrusive

overweight *adj* **1** = **fat**, ample, bulky, buxom, chubby, chunky, corpulent, fleshy, gross,

(ˌəʊvəˈweɪt). (*tr*) **3** to give too much emphasis or consideration to. **4** to add too much weight to. **5** to weigh down.

overwhelm ❶ (ˌəʊvəˈwɛlm) *vb* (*tr*) **1** to overpower the thoughts, emotions, or senses of. **2** to overcome with irresistible force. **3** to cover over or bury completely. **4** to weigh or rest upon overpoweringly. ▸ˌ**overˈwhelming** *adj*

overwind (ˌəʊvəˈwaɪnd) *vb* **overwinds, overwinding, overwound.** (*tr*) to wind (a watch, etc.) beyond the proper limit.

overwork ❶ *vb* (ˌəʊvəˈwɜːk). (*mainly tr*) **1** (*also intr*) to work too hard or too long. **2** to use too much: *to overwork an excuse.* **3** to decorate the surface of. ◆ *n* (ˈəʊvəˌwɜːk). **4** excessive or excessively tiring work.

overwrite (ˌəʊvəˈraɪt) *vb* **overwrites, overwriting, overwrote, overwritten. 1** to write (something) in an excessively ornate style. **2** to write too much about (someone or something). **3** to write on top of (other writing). **4** to record on a storage medium, such as a magnetic disk, thus destroying what was originally recorded there.

overwrought ❶ (ˌəʊvəˈrɔːt) *adj* **1** full of nervous tension; agitated. **2** too elaborate; fussy: *an overwrought style.* **3** (*often postpositive* and foll. by *with*) with the surface decorated or adorned.

ovi- *or* **ovo-** *combining form.* egg or ovum: *oviform; ovoviviparous.* [from L *ōvum*]

oviduct (ˈɒvɪˌdʌkt, ˈəʊ-) *n* the tube through which ova are conveyed from an ovary. Also called (in mammals): **Fallopian tube.** ▸**oviducal** (ˌɒvɪˈdjuːkˈl, ˌəʊ-) *or* ˌ**oviˈductal** *adj*

oviform (ˈəʊvɪˌfɔːm) *adj Biol.* shaped like an egg.

ovine (ˈəʊvaɪn) *adj* of, relating to, or resembling a sheep. [C19: from LL *ovīnus,* from L *ovis* sheep]

oviparous (əʊˈvɪpərəs) *adj* (of fishes, reptiles, birds, etc.) producing eggs that hatch outside the body of the mother. Cf. **ovoviviparous, viviparous** (sense 1). ▸**oviparity** (ˌəʊvɪˈpærɪtɪ) *n* ▸**oˈviparously** *adv*

ovipositor (ˌəʊvɪˈpɒzɪtə) *n* **1** the egg-laying organ of most female insects, consisting of a pair of specialized appendages at the end of the abdomen. **2** a similar organ in certain female fishes, formed by an extension of the edges of the genital opening. [C19:from OVI- + L *positor,* from *ponere* to place] ▸ˌ**oviˈposit** *vb* (*intr*)

ovoid (ˈəʊvɔɪd) *adj* **1** egg-shaped. ◆ *n* **2** something that is ovoid.

ovoviviparous (ˌəʊvəʊvaɪˈvɪpərəs) *adj* (of certain reptiles, fishes, etc.) producing eggs that hatch within the body of the mother. Cf. **oviparous, viviparous** (sense 1). ▸**ovoviviparity** (ˌəʊvəʊˌvaɪvɪˈpærɪtɪ) *n*

ovulate (ˈɒvjʊˌleɪt) *vb* **ovulates, ovulating, ovulated.** (*intr*) to produce or discharge eggs from an ovary. [C19: from OVULE] ▸ˌ**ovuˈlation** *n*

ovulation method *n* another name for **Billings method.**

ovule (ˈɒvjuːl) *n* **1** a small body in seed-bearing plants that contains the egg cell and develops into the seed after fertilization. **2** *Zool.* an immature ovum. [C19: via F from Med. L *ōvulum* a little egg, from L *ōvum* egg] ▸ˈ**ovular** *adj*

ovum (ˈəʊvəm) *n, pl* **ova.** an unfertilized female gamete; egg cell. [from L: egg]

ow (aʊ) *interj* an exclamation of pain.

owe ❶ (əʊ) *vb* **owes, owing, owed.** (*mainly tr*) **1** to be under an obligation to pay (someone) to the amount of. **2** (*intr*) to be in debt: *he still owes for his house.* **3** (often foll. by *to*) to have as a result (of). **4** to feel the need or obligation to do, give, etc. **5** to hold or maintain in the mind or heart (esp. in **owe a grudge**). [OE *āgan* to have (C12: to have to)]

Owen gun (ˈəʊɪn) *n* a type of simple recoil-operated sub-machine-gun first used by Australian forces in World War II. [after E. E. *Owen* (1915–49), its Austral. inventor]

owing ❶ (ˈəʊɪŋ) *adj* **1** (*postpositive*) owed; due. **2 owing to.** because of or on account of.

owl (aʊl) *n* **1** a nocturnal bird of prey having large front-facing eyes, a small hooked bill, soft feathers, and a short neck. **2** any of various breeds of owl-like fancy domestic pigeon. **3** a person who looks or behaves like an owl, esp. in having a solemn manner. [OE *ūle*] ▸ˈ**owlish** *adj* ▸ˈ**owl-ˌlike** *adj*

owlet (ˈaʊlɪt) *n* a young or nestling owl.

own ❶ (əʊn) *determiner* (*preceded by a possessive*) **1a** (intensifier): *John's own idea.* **1b** (*as pron*): *I'll use my own.* **2** on behalf of oneself or in relation to oneself: *he is his own worst enemy.* **3 come into one's own. 3a** to become fulfilled: *she really came into her own when she got divorced.* **3b** to receive what is due to one. **4 hold one's own.** to maintain one's situation or position, esp. in spite of opposition or difficulty. **5 on one's own. 5a** without help. **5b** by oneself; alone. ◆ *vb* **6** (*tr*) to have as one's possession. **7** (when *intr,* often foll. by *up, to,* or *up to*) to confess or admit; acknowledge. **8** (*tr; takes a clause as object*) *Now rare.* to concede: *I own that you are right.* [OE *āgen,* orig. p.p. of *āgan* to have. See OWE] ▸ˈ**owner** *n* ▸ˈ**ownership** *n*

own brand *n* a product which displays the name of the retailer rather than the producer.

owner-occupier *n* someone who has bought or is buying the house in which he lives.

own goal *n* **1** *Soccer.* a goal scored by a player accidentally playing the ball into his own team's net. **2** *Inf.* any action that results in disadvantage to the person who took it or to his associates.

ox (ɒks) *n, pl* **oxen. 1** an adult castrated male of any domesticated species of cattle used for draught work and meat. **2** any bovine mammal, esp. any of the domestic cattle. [OE *oxa*]

oxalic acid (ɒkˈsælɪk) *n* a colourless poisonous crystalline acid found in many plants: used as a bleach and a cleansing agent for metals. Formula: $(COOH)_2$. Recommended name: **ethanedioic acid.** [C18: from F *oxalique,* from L *oxalis* garden sorrel; see OXALIS]

oxalis (ˈɒksəlɪs, ɒkˈsælɪs) *n* a plant having clover-like leaves which contain oxalic acid and white, pink, red, or yellow flowers. See also **wood sorrel.** [C18: via L from Gk: sorrel, sour wine, from *oxus* acid, sharp]

oxblood (ˈɒksˌblʌd) *or* **oxblood red** *adj* of a dark reddish-brown colour.

oxbow (ˈɒksˌbəʊ) *n* **1** a U-shaped piece of wood fitted under and around the neck of a harnessed ox and attached to the yoke. **2** Also called: **oxbow lake.** a small curved lake lying on the flood plain of a river and constituting the remnant of a former meander.

Oxbridge (ˈɒksˌbrɪdʒ) *n* **a** the British universities of Oxford and Cambridge, esp. considered as ancient and prestigious academic institutions, bastions of privilege and superiority, etc. **b** (*as modifier*): *Oxbridge graduates.*

oxen (ˈɒksən) *n* the plural of **ox.**

oxeye (ˈɒksˌaɪ) *n* **1** a Eurasian composite plant having daisy-like flower heads with yellow rays and dark centres. **2** any of various North American plants having daisy-like flowers. **3 oxeye daisy.** a type of hardy perennial chrysanthemum.

ox-eyed *adj* having large round eyes, like those of an ox.

Oxfam (ˈɒksˌfæm) *n acronym for* Oxford Committee for Famine Relief.

Oxford (ˈɒksfəd) *n* (*sometimes not cap.*) **1** a type of stout laced shoe with a low heel. **2** a lightweight fabric of plain or twill weave used for men's shirts, etc. [from *Oxford,* city in S England]

Oxford bags *pl n* trousers with very wide baggy legs.

Oxford blue *n* **1a** a dark blue colour. **1b** (*as adj*): *an Oxford-blue scarf.* **2** a person who has been awarded a blue from Oxford University.

Oxford Movement *n* a movement within the Church of England that began at Oxford in 1833. It affirmed the continuity of the Church with early Christianity and strove to restore the High-Church ideals of the 17th century. Also called: **Tractarianism.**

oxidant (ˈɒksɪdənt) *n* a substance that acts or is used as an oxidizing agent. Also called (esp. in rocketry): **oxidizer.**

oxidation (ˌɒksɪˈdeɪʃən) *n* **a** the act or process of oxidizing. **b** (*as modifier*): *an oxidation state.* ▸ˈ**oxiˌdate** *vb* ▸ˌ**oxiˈdational** *adj* ▸ˈ**oxiˌdative** *adj*

oxidation-reduction *n* **a** a reversible chemical process usually involving the transfer of electrons, in which one reaction is an oxidation

THESAURUS

heavy, hefty, huge, massive, obese, outsize, plump, podgy, portly, stout, tubby (*inf.*)
Antonyms *adj* emaciated, gaunt, lean, pinched, scraggy, scrawny, skinny, thin, underweight

overwhelm *vb* **1 = overcome,** bowl over (*inf.*), confuse, devastate, knock (someone) for six (*inf.*), make mincemeat of, overpower, prostrate, render speechless, stagger, sweep (someone) off his *or* her feet, take (someone's) breath away **2 = destroy,** crush, cut to pieces, massacre, overpower, overrun, rout **3 = submerge,** bury, crush, deluge, engulf, flood, inundate, snow under, swamp

overwhelming *adj* **1 = overpowering,** breathtaking, crushing, devastating, invincible, irresistible, shattering, stunning, towering, uncontrollable, vast, vastly superior
Antonyms *adj* commonplace, incidental, insignificant, negligible, paltry, resistible, trivial, unimportant

overwork *vb* **1 = strain (oneself),** burn the candle at both ends, burn the midnight oil, drive into the ground, exhaust (oneself), fatigue (oneself), overstrain (oneself), overtax (oneself), sweat (*inf.*), wear (oneself) out, weary (oneself), work one's fingers to the bone

overwrought *adj* **1 = agitated,** beside oneself, distracted, excited, frantic, in a state, keyed up, on edge, overexcited, overworked, strung out (*inf.*), tense, uptight (*inf.*), wired (*sl.*), worked up (*inf.*), wound up (*inf.*) **2 = overelaborate,** baroque, busy, contrived, florid, flowery, fussy, overdone, overembellished, overornate, rococo
Antonyms *adj* ≠ **agitated:** calm, collected, controlled, cool, dispassionate, emotionless, impassive, self-contained, unfazed (*inf.*), unmoved

owe *vb* **1, 2 = be in debt,** be beholden (to), be in arrears, be obligated *or* indebted, be under an obligation (to)

owing *adj* **1 = unpaid,** due, outstanding, overdue, owed, payable, unsettled **2 owing to = because of,** as a result of, on account of

own *determiner* **2 = personal,** individual, particular, private **4 hold one's own = keep up,** compete, do well, hold fast, hold out, keep one's end up, keep one's head above water, keep pace, maintain one's position, stand firm, stand one's ground, stay put, stick to one's guns (*inf.*) **5 on one's own: a = alone,** by one's own efforts, independently, off one's own bat, singly, (standing) on one's own two feet, unaided, unassisted, under one's own steam **b** by oneself, left to one's own devices, on one's tod (*Brit. sl.*) ◆ *vb* **6 = possess,** be in possession of, be responsible for, enjoy, have, hold, keep, retain **7 = acknowledge,** admit, allow, allow to be valid, avow, concede, confess, disclose, go along with, grant, recognize

owner *n* **6 = possessor,** holder, landlord *or* landlady, lord, master *or* mistress, proprietor, proprietress, proprietrix

ownership *n* **6 = possession,** dominion, proprietary rights, proprietorship, right of possession, title and the reverse reaction is a reduction. **b** (*as modifier*): *an oxidation-reduction reaction.* ◆ Also: **redox.**

oxide ('ɒksaɪd) *n* **1** any compound of oxygen with another element. **2** any organic compound in which an oxygen atom is bound to two alkyl groups; an ether. [C18: from F, from *ox(ygène)* + *(ac)ide*]

oxidize *or* **oxidise** ('ɒksɪ,daɪz) *vb* **oxidizes, oxidizing, oxidized** *or* **oxidises, oxidising, oxidised. 1** to undergo or cause to undergo a chemical reaction with oxygen, as in formation of an oxide. **2** to form or cause to form a layer of metal oxide, as in rusting. **3** to lose or cause to lose hydrogen atoms. **4** to undergo or cause to undergo a decrease in the number of electrons.
▸,**oxidi'zation** *or* ,**oxidi'sation** *n*

oxidizing agent *n Chem.* a substance that oxidizes another substance, being itself reduced in the process.

oxlip ('ɒks,lɪp) *n* **1** a Eurasian woodland plant, with small drooping pale yellow flowers. **2** a similar and related plant that is a natural hybrid between the cowslip and primrose. [OE *oxanslyppe*, lit.: ox's slippery dropping; see SLIP[3]]

oxo acid ('ɒksəʊ) *n* another name for **oxyacid.**

Oxon *abbrev. for* Oxfordshire. [from L *Oxonia*]

Oxon. *abbrev. for* (in degree titles, etc.) of Oxford. [from L *Oxoniensis*]

Oxonian (ɒk'səʊnɪən) *adj* **1** of or relating to Oxford or Oxford University. ◆ *n* **2** a member of Oxford University. **3** an inhabitant or native of Oxford.

oxpecker ('ɒks,pɛkə) *n* either of two African starlings, having flattened bills with which they obtain food from the hides of cattle. Also called: **tick-bird.**

oxtail ('ɒks,teɪl) *n* the skinned tail of an ox, used esp. in soups and stews.

oxter ('əʊkstə) *n Scot., Irish, & N English dialect.* the armpit. [C16: from OE *oxta*]

oxtongue ('ɒks,tʌŋ) *n* **1** any of various Eurasian composite plants having oblong bristly leaves and clusters of dandelion-like flowers. **2** any of various other plants having bristly tongue-shaped leaves. **3** the tongue of an ox, braised or boiled as food.

oxy-[1] *combining form.* denoting something sharp; acute: *oxytone.* [from Gk, from *oxus*]

oxy-[2] *combining form.* containing or using oxygen: *oxyacetylene.*

oxyacetylene (,ɒksɪə'sɛtɪ,liːn) *n* **a** a mixture of oxygen and acetylene; used in torches for cutting or welding metals at high temperatures. **b** (*as modifier*): *an oxyacetylene burner.*

oxyacid (,ɒksɪ'æsɪd) *n* any acid that contains oxygen with the acidic hydrogen atoms bound to oxygen atoms. Also called: **oxo acid.**

oxygen ('ɒksɪdʒən) *n* **a** a colourless odourless highly reactive gaseous element: the most abundant element in the earth's crust. Symbol: O; atomic no.: 8; atomic wt.: 15.9994. **b** (*as modifier*): *an oxygen mask.*
▸**oxygenic** (,ɒksɪ'dʒɛnɪk) *or* **oxygenous** (ɒk'sɪdʒɪnəs) *adj*

oxygenate ('ɒksɪdʒɪ,neɪt) *or* **oxygenize, oxygenise** *vb* **oxygenates, oxygenating, oxygenated** *or* **oxygenizes, oxygenizing, oxygenized; oxygenises, oxygenising, oxygenised.** to enrich or be enriched with oxygen: *to oxygenate blood.*
▸,**oxygen'ation** *n* ▸'**oxygen,izer** *or* '**oxygen,iser** *n*

oxygen tent *n Med.* a transparent enclosure covering a bedridden patient, into which oxygen is released to help maintain respiration.

oxyhaemoglobin (,ɒksɪ,hiːməʊ'gləʊbɪn) *n Biochem.* the bright red product formed when oxygen from the lungs combines with haemoglobin in the blood.

oxyhydrogen (,ɒksɪ'haɪdrɪdʒən) *n* **a** a mixture of hydrogen and oxygen used to provide an intense flame for welding. **b** (*as modifier*): *an oxyhydrogen blowpipe.*

oxymoron (,ɒksɪ'mɔːrɒn) *n, pl* **oxymora** (-'mɔːrə). *Rhetoric.* an epigrammatic effect, by which contradictory terms are used in conjunction: *living death.* [C17: via NL from Gk *oxumōron*, from *oxus* sharp + *mōros* stupid]

oyer and terminer ('ɔɪə; 'tɜːmɪnə) *n* **1** *English law.* (formerly) a commission issued to judges to try cases on assize. **2** the court in which such a hearing was held. [C15: from Anglo-Norman, from *oyer* to hear + *terminer* to judge]

oyez *or* **oyes** (əʊ'jɛs, -'jɛz) *sentence substitute.* **1** a cry, usually uttered three times, by a public crier or court official for silence and attention before making a proclamation. ◆ *n* **2** such a cry. [C15: via Anglo-Norman from OF *oiez!* hear!]

-oyl *suffix of nouns* (in chemistry) indicating an acyl group or radical: *ethanoyl, methanoyl.* [C20: from O(XYGEN) + -YL]

oyster ('ɔɪstə) *n* **1a** an edible marine bivalve mollusc having a rough irregularly shaped shell and occurring on the sea bed, mostly in coastal waters. **1b** (*as modifier*): *oyster farm; oyster knife.* **2** any of various similar and related molluscs, such as the pearl oyster and the saddle oyster. **3** the oyster-shaped piece of dark meat in the hollow of the pelvic bone of a fowl. **4** something from which advantage, delight, profit, etc., may be derived: *the world is his oyster.* **5** *Inf.* a very uncommunicative person. ◆ *vb* **6** (*intr*) to dredge for, gather, or raise oysters. [C14 *oistre*, from OF *uistre*, from L *ostrea*, from Gk *ostreon*; rel. to Gk *osteon* bone, *ostrakon* shell]

oyster bed *n* a place, esp. on the sea bed, where oysters breed and grow naturally or are cultivated for food or pearls. Also called: **oyster bank, oyster park.**

oystercatcher ('ɔɪstə,kætʃə) *n* a shore bird having a black or black-and-white plumage and a long stout laterally compressed red bill.

oyster crab *n* any of several small soft-bodied crabs that live as commensals in the mantles of oysters.

oyster plant *n* **1** another name for **salsify** (sense 1). **2** Also called: **sea lungwort.** a prostrate coastal plant with clusters of blue flowers.

oz *or* **oz.** *abbrev. for* ounce. [from It. *onza*]

Oz (ɒz) *n Austral. sl.* Australia.

Ozalid ('ɒzəlɪd) *n* **1** *Trademark.* a method of duplicating type matter, illustrations, etc., when printed on translucent paper. **2** a reproduction produced by this method.

ozocerite *or* **ozokerite** (əʊ'zəʊkə,raɪt) *n* a brown or greyish wax that occurs associated with petroleum and is used for making candles and waxed paper. [C19: from G *Ozokerit*, from Gk *ozein* odour + *kēros* beeswax]

ozone ('əʊzəʊn, əʊ'zəʊn) *n* **1** a colourless gas with a chlorine-like odour, formed by an electric discharge in oxygen: a strong oxidizing agent, used in bleaching, sterilizing water, purifying air, etc. Formula: O_3. Technical name: **trioxygen. 2** *Inf.* clean bracing air, as found at the seaside. [C19: from G *Ozon*, from Gk: smell]
▸**ozonic** (əʊ'zɒnɪk) *or* '**ozonous** *adj*

ozone-friendly *adj* not harmful to the ozone layer; using substances that do not produce gases harmful to the ozone layer: *an ozone-friendly refrigerator.*

ozone layer *n* the region of the stratosphere with the highest concentration of ozone molecules, which by absorbing high-energy solar ultraviolet radiation protects organisms on earth. Also called: **ozonosphere.**

ozonize *or* **ozonise** ('əʊzəʊ,naɪz) *vb* **ozonizes, ozonizing, ozonized** *or* **ozonises, ozonising, ozonised.** (*tr*) **1** to convert (oxygen) into ozone. **2** to treat (a substance) with ozone.
▸,**ozoni'zation** *or* ,**ozoni'sation** *n* ▸'**ozo,nizer** *or* '**ozo,niser** *n*

ozonosphere (əʊ'zəʊnə,sfɪə, -'zɒnə-) *n* another name for **ozone layer.**

Pp

p *or* **P** (piː) *n, pl* **p's, P's,** *or* **Ps. 1** the 16th letter of the English alphabet. **2** a speech sound represented by this letter. **3 mind one's p's and q's.** to be careful to behave correctly and use polite or suitable language.

p *symbol for:* **1** (in Britain) penny *or* pence. **2** *Music.* piano: an instruction to play quietly. **3** *Physics.* pico-. **4** *Physics.* **4a** momentum. **4b** proton. **4c** pressure.

P *symbol for:* **1** *Chem.* phosphorus. **2** *Physics.* **2a** parity. **2b** poise. **2c** power. **2d** pressure. **3** (on road signs) parking. **4** *Chess.* pawn. **5** *Currency.* **5a** peseta. **5b** peso. **6** (of a medicine or drug) available only from a chemist's shop, but not requiring a prescription to obtain it.

p. *abbrev. for:* **1** (*pl* **pp.**) page. **2** part. **3** participle. **4** past. **5** per. **6** pint. **7** pipe. **8** population. **9** post. [L: after] **10** pro. [L: in favour of; for]

p- *prefix* short for **para-**[1] (sense 6).

pa (pɑː) *n* an informal word for **father.**

Pa 1 *the chemical symbol for* protactinium. **2** *symbol for* pascal.

PA *abbrev. for:* **1** personal assistant. **2** *Mil.* Post Adjutant. **3** power of attorney. **4** press agent. **5** Press Association. **6** private account. **7** public-address system. **8** publicity agent. **9** Publishers Association. **10** purchasing agent. **11** *Insurance.* particular average.

p.a. *abbrev. for* per annum. [L: yearly]

pabulum (ˈpæbjʊləm) *n Rare.* **1** food. **2** food for thought, esp. when bland or dull. [C17: from L, from *pascere* to feed]

PABX (in Britain) *abbrev. for* private automatic branch exchange. See also **PBX.**

paca (ˈpɑːkə, ˈpækə) *n* a large burrowing rodent of Central and South America, having white-spotted brown fur. [C17: from Sp., from Amerind]

pace[1] 🅣 (peɪs) *n* **1a** a single step in walking. **1b** the distance covered by a step. **2** a measure of length equal to the average length of a stride, approximately 3 feet. **3** speed of movement, esp. of walking or running. **4** rate or style of proceeding at some activity: *to live at a fast pace.* **5** manner or action of stepping, walking, etc.; gait. **6** any of the manners in which a horse or other quadruped walks or runs. **7** a manner of moving, sometimes developed in the horse, in which the two legs on the same side are moved at the same time. **8 keep pace with.** to proceed at the same speed as. **9 put (someone) through his paces.** to test the ability of (someone). **10 set the pace.** to determine the rate at which a group runs or walks or proceeds at some other activity. ◆ *vb* **paces, pacing, paced. 11** (*tr*) to set or determine the pace for, as in a race. **12** (often foll. by *about, up and down,* etc.) to walk with regular slow or fast paces, as in boredom, agitation, etc.: *to pace the room.* **13** (*tr;* often foll. by *out*) to measure by paces: *to pace out the distance.* **14** (*intr*) to walk with slow regular strides. **15** (*intr*) (of a horse) to move at the pace (the specially developed gait). [C13: via OF from L *passūs* step, from *pandere* to extend (the legs as in walking)]

pace[2] (ˈpeɪsɪ; *Latin* ˈpɑːke) *prep* with due deference to: used to acknowledge politely someone who disagrees. [C19: from L, from *pāx* peace]

PACE (peɪs) *n* (in England and Wales) *acronym for* Police and Criminal Evidence Act.

pace bowler *n Cricket.* a bowler who characteristically delivers the ball rapidly.

pacemaker (ˈpeɪsˌmeɪkə) *n* **1** a person, horse, vehicle, etc., used in a race or speed trial to set the pace. **2** a person, organization, etc., regarded as being the leader in a particular activity. **3** Also called: **cardiac pacemaker.** a small area of specialized tissue within the wall of the heart whose spontaneous electrical activity initiates and controls the heartbeat. **4** Also called: **artificial pacemaker.** an electronic device to assume the functions of the natural cardiac pacemaker.

pacer (ˈpeɪsə) *n* **1** a horse trained to move at a special gait. **2** another word for **pacemaker** (sense 1).

pacesetter (ˈpeɪsˌsetə) *n* another word for **pacemaker** (senses 1, 2).

paceway (ˈpeɪsˌweɪ) *n Austral.* a racecourse for trotting and pacing.

pachisi (pəˈtʃiːzɪ) *n* an Indian game somewhat resembling backgammon, played on a cruciform board using six cowries as dice. [C18: from Hindi, from *pacīs* twenty-five (the highest throw)]

pachyderm (ˈpækɪˌdɜːm) *n* any very large thick-skinned mammal, such as an elephant, rhinoceros, or hippopotamus. [C19: from F *pachyderme,* from Gk *pakhudermos,* from *pakhus* thick + *derma* skin]
▸ **ˌpachyˈdermatous** *adj*

pacific 🅣 (pəˈsɪfɪk) *adj* **1** tending or conducive to peace; conciliatory. **2** not aggressive. **3** free from conflict; peaceful. [C16: from OF, from L *pācificus,* from *pāx* peace + *facere* to make]
▸ **paˈcifically** *adv*

Pacific (pəˈsɪfɪk) *n* **1 the.** short for **Pacific Ocean.** ◆ *adj* **2** of or relating to the Pacific Ocean or its islands.

Pacific Ocean *n* the world's largest and deepest ocean, lying between Asia and Australia and North and South America.

Pacific rim *n* the regions, countries, etc. that lie on the western shores of the Pacific Ocean, esp. in the context of their developing manufacturing capacity and consumer markets.

pacifier (ˈpæsɪˌfaɪə) *n* **1** a person or thing that pacifies. **2** *US & Canad.* a baby's dummy or teething ring.

pacifism 🅣 (ˈpæsɪˌfɪzəm) *n* **1** the belief that violence of any kind is unjustifiable and that one should not participate in war, etc. **2** the belief that international disputes can be settled by arbitration rather than war.
▸ **ˈpacifist** *n, adj*

pacify 🅣 (ˈpæsɪˌfaɪ) *vb* **pacifies, pacifying, pacified.** (*tr*) **1** to calm the anger or agitation of; mollify. **2** to restore to peace or order. [C15: from OF *pacifier;* see PACIFIC]
▸ **ˈpaciˌfiable** *adj* ▸ **pacification** (ˌpæsɪfɪˈkeɪʃən) *n*

pack[1] 🅣 (pæk) *n* **1a** a bundle or load, esp. one carried on the back. **1b** (*as modifier*): *a pack animal.* **2** a collected amount of anything. **3** a complete set of similar things, esp. a set of 52 playing cards. **4** a group of animals of the same kind, esp. hunting animals: *a pack of hounds.* **5** any group or band that associates together, esp. for criminal purposes. **6** any group or set regarded dismissively: *a pack of fools; a pack of lies.* **7** *Rugby.* the forwards of a team. **8** the basic organizational unit of Cub Scouts and Brownie Guides. **9** *US & Canad.* same as **packet** (sense 1). **10** short for **pack ice. 11** the quantity of something, such as food, packaged for preservation. **12** *Med.* a sheet or blanket, either damp or dry, for wrapping about the body, esp. for its soothing effect. **13** another name for **rucksack** *or* **backpack. 14** Also called: **face pack.** a cream treatment that cleanses and tones the skin. **15** a parachute folded and ready for use. **16 go to the pack.** *Austral. & NZ inf.* to fall into a worse state or condition. **17** *Computing.* another name for **deck** (sense 4). ◆ *vb* **18** to place or arrange (articles) in (a container), such as clothes in a suitcase. **19** (*tr*) to roll up into a bundle. **20** (when *passive,* often foll. by *out*) to press tightly together; cram: *the audience packed into the foyer; the hall was packed out.* **21** to form (snow, ice, etc.) into a hard compact mass or (of snow, etc.) to become compacted. **22** (*tr*) to press in or cover tightly. **23** (*tr*) to load (a horse, donkey, etc.) with a burden. **24** (often foll. by *off* or *away*) to send away or go away, esp. hastily. **25** (*tr*) to seal (a joint) by inserting a layer of compressible material between the faces. **26** (*tr*) *Med.* to treat with a pack. **27** (*tr*) *Sl.* to be capable of inflicting (a blow, etc.): *he packs a mean punch.* **28** (*tr*) *US inf.* to carry or wear habitually: *he packs a gun.* **29** (*tr;* often foll. by *in, into, to,* etc.) *US, Canad., & NZ.* to carry (goods, etc.), esp. on the back. **30 send packing.** *Inf.* to dismiss peremptorily. ◆ See also **pack in, pack up.** [C13: from ?]
▸ **ˈpackable** *adj*

pack[2] (pæk) *vb* (*tr*) to fill (a legislative body, committee, etc.) with one's own supporters: *to pack a jury.* [C16: ? changed from PACT]

package 🅣 (ˈpækɪdʒ) *n* **1** any wrapped or boxed object or group of objects. **2a** a proposition, offer, or thing for sale in which separate items are offered together as a unit. **2b** (*as modifier*): *a package holiday; a package deal.* **3** the act or process of packing or packaging. **4** *Computing.* a set of programs designed for a specific type of problem. **5** the usual US and Canad. word for **packet** (sense 1). ◆ *vb* **packages, packaging, packaged.** (*tr*) **6** to wrap in or put into a package. **7** to design and produce a

THESAURUS

pace[1] *n* **1, 5 = step,** gait, measure, stride, tread, walk **3, 4 = speed,** clip (*inf.*), lick, momentum, motion, movement, progress, rate, tempo, time, velocity ◆ *vb* **12 = stride,** march, patrol, pound, walk back and forth, walk up and down **13** *often foll. by* **out = measure,** count, determine, mark out, step

pacific *adj* **1 = peacemaking,** appeasing, conciliatory, diplomatic, irenic, pacificatory, placatory, propitiatory **2 = nonaggressive,** dovelike, dovish, friendly, gentle, mild, nonbelligerent, nonviolent, pacifist, peaceable, peace-loving **3 = peaceful,** at peace, calm, halcyon, placid, quiet, serene, smooth, still, tranquil, unruffled
Antonyms *adj* **≠ nonaggressive:** aggressive, antagonistic, belligerent, hostile, nonconciliatory, pugnacious, unforgiving, unfriendly, violent, warlike

pacifist *n* **1, 2 = peace lover,** conchie (*inf.*), conscientious objector, dove, passive resister, peacemonger, peacenik (*inf.*), satyagrahi

pacify *vb* **1 = calm,** allay, ameliorate, appease, assuage, clear the air, compose, conciliate, make peace, moderate, mollify, placate, pour oil on troubled waters, propitiate, quiet, restore harmony, smooth down *or* over, smooth one's ruffled feathers, soften, soothe, still, tranquillize **2 = quell,** chasten, crush, impose peace, put down, repress, silence, subdue, tame

pack[1] *n* **1 = bundle,** back pack, bale, burden, fardel (*arch.*), kit, kitbag, knapsack, load, parcel, rucksack, truss **4, 5 = group,** assemblage, band, bunch, collection, company, crew, crowd, deck, drove, flock, gang, herd, lot, mob, set, troop **9 = packet,** package ◆ *vb* **18, 19 = package,** batch, bundle, burden, load, store, stow **20, 22 = cram,** charge, compact, compress, crowd, fill, jam, mob, press, ram, stuff, tamp, throng, wedge **24** *often foll. by* **off** *or* **away = send away,** bundle out, dismiss, hustle out, send packing (*inf.*), send someone about his business **30** *Informal* **send packing = send away,** discharge, dismiss, give the bird (*inf.*), give the brushoff (*sl.*), send about his *or* her business, send away with a flea in his *or* her ear (*inf.*)

package *n* **1 = parcel,** box, carton, container, packet **2 = unit,** amalgamation, combination, package for (retail goods). **8** to group (separate items) together as a single unit. **9** to compile (complete books) for a publisher to market. ▸ **'packager** *n*

packaging Ⓣ ('pækɪdʒɪŋ) *n* **1** the box or wrapping in which a product is offered for sale. **2** the presentation of a person, product, etc., to the public in a way designed to build up a favourable image.

pack drill *n* a military punishment of marching about carrying a full pack of equipment.

packer ('pækə) *n* **1** a person or company whose business is to pack goods, esp. food: *a meat packer.* **2** a person or machine that packs.

packet Ⓣ ('pækɪt) *n* **1** a small or medium-sized container of cardboard, paper, etc., often together with its contents: *a packet of biscuits.* Usual US and Canad. word: **package, pack. 2** a small package; parcel. **3** Also called: **packet boat.** a boat that transports mail, passengers, goods, etc., on a fixed short route. **4** *Sl.* a large sum of money: *to cost a packet.* **5** *Computing.* a unit into which a larger piece of data is broken down for more efficient transmission. ◆ *vb* **6** (*tr*) to wrap up in a packet or as a packet. [C16: from OF *pacquet,* from *pacquer* to pack, from ODu. *pak* a pack]

packhorse ('pæk,hɔːs) *n* a horse used to transport goods, equipment, etc.

pack ice *n* a large area of floating ice, consisting of pieces that have become massed together.

pack in Ⓣ *vb* (*tr, adv*) *Brit. & NZ inf.* to stop doing (something) (esp. in **pack it in**).

packing ('pækɪŋ) *n* **1a** material used to cushion packed goods. **1b** (*as modifier*): *a packing needle.* **2** the packaging of foodstuffs. **3** any substance or material used to make joints watertight or gastight.

pack rat *n* a rat of W North America, having a long tail that is furry in some species.

packsaddle ('pæk,sædᵊl) *n* a saddle hung with packs, equipment, etc., used on a pack animal.

packthread ('pæk,θrɛd) *n* a strong twine for sewing or tying up packages.

pack up Ⓣ *vb* (*adv*) **1** to put (things) away in a proper or suitable place. **2** *Inf.* to give up (an attempt) or stop doing (something). **3** (*intr*) (of an engine, etc.) to fail to operate; break down.

pact Ⓣ (pækt) *n* an agreement or compact between two or more parties, nations, etc. [C15: from OF *pacte,* from L *pactum,* from *pacīscī* to agree]

pad[1] Ⓣ (pæd) *n* **1** a thick piece of soft material used to make something comfortable, give it shape, or protect it. **2** Also called: **stamp pad, ink pad.** a block of firm absorbent material soaked with ink for transferring to a rubber stamp. **3** Also called: **notepad, writing pad.** a number of sheets of paper fastened together along one edge. **4** a flat piece of stiff material used to back a piece of blotting paper. **5a** the fleshy cushion-like underpart of the foot of a cat, dog, etc. **5b** any of the parts constituting such a structure. **6** any of various level surfaces or flat-topped structures, such as a launch pad. **7** the large flat floating leaf of the water lily. **8** *Sl.* a person's residence. ◆ *vb* **pads, padding, padded.** (*tr*) **9** to line, stuff, or fill out with soft material, esp. in order to protect or shape. **10** (often foll. by *out*) to inflate with irrelevant or false information: *to pad out a story.* [C16: from ?]

pad[2] Ⓣ (pæd) *vb* **pads, padding, padded. 1** (*intr;* often foll. by *along, up,* etc.) to walk with a soft or muffled tread. **2** (when *intr,* often foll. by *around*) to travel (a route, etc.) on foot, esp. at a slow pace; tramp: *to pad around the country.* ◆ *n* **3** a dull soft sound, esp. of footsteps. [C16: ?from MDu. *paden,* from *pad* PATH]

padded cell *n* a room, esp. one in a mental hospital, with padded surfaces in which violent inmates are placed.

padding Ⓣ ('pædɪŋ) *n* **1** any soft material used to pad clothes, etc. **2** superfluous material put into a speech or written work to pad it out; waffle. **3** inflated or false entries in a financial account, esp. an expense account.

paddle[1] Ⓣ ('pædᵊl) *n* **1** a short light oar with a flat blade at one or both ends, used without a rowlock. **2** Also called: **float.** a blade of a water wheel or paddle wheel. **3** a period of paddling: *to go for a paddle upstream.* **4a** a paddle wheel used to propel a boat. **4b** (*as modifier*): *a paddle steamer.* **5** any of various instruments shaped like a paddle and used for beating, mixing, etc. **6** a table-tennis bat. **7** the flattened limb of a seal, turtle, etc., specialized for swimming. ◆ *vb* **paddles, paddling, paddled. 8** to propel (a canoe, etc.) with a paddle. **9 paddle one's own canoe. 9a** to be self-sufficient. **9b** to mind one's own business. **10** (*tr*) to stir or mix with or as if with a paddle. **11** to row (a boat) steadily, but not at full pressure. **12** (*intr*) to swim with short rapid strokes, like a dog. **13** (*tr*) *US & Canad. inf.* to spank. [C15: from ?] ▸ **'paddler** *n*

paddle[2] Ⓣ ('pædᵊl) *vb* **paddles, paddling, paddled.** (*mainly intr*) **1** to walk or play barefoot in shallow water, mud, etc. **2** to dabble the fingers, hands, or feet in water. **3** to walk unsteadily, like a baby. **4** (*tr*) *Arch.* to fondle with the fingers. ◆ *n* **5** the act of paddling in water. [C16: from ?] ▸ **'paddler** *n*

paddle wheel *n* a large wheel fitted with paddles, turned by an engine to propel a vessel.

paddock ('pædək) *n* **1** a small enclosed field, often for grazing or training horses. **2** (in horse racing) the enclosure in which horses are paraded and mounted before a race. **3** *Austral. & NZ.* any area of fenced land. [C17: var. of dialect *parrock,* from OE *pearruc* enclosure, of Gmc origin. See PARK]

paddy[1] ('pædɪ) *n, pl* **paddies. 1** Also called: **paddy field.** a field planted with rice. **2** rice as a growing crop or when harvested but not yet milled. [from Malay *pādī*]

paddy[2] Ⓣ ('pædɪ) *n, pl* **paddies.** *Brit. inf.* a fit of temper. [C19: from *Paddy* inf. name for an Irishman]

pademelon *or* **paddymelon** ('pædɪ,mɛlən) *n* a small wallaby of coastal scrubby regions of Australia. [C19: of Abor. origin]

padlock ('pæd,lɒk) *n* **1** a detachable lock having a hinged or sliding shackle, which can be used to secure a door, lid, etc., by passing the shackle through rings or staples. ◆ *vb* **2** (*tr*) to fasten as with a padlock. [C15 *pad,* from ?]

padre ('pɑːdrɪ) *n Inf.* (*sometimes cap.*) **1** father: used to address or refer to a priest. **2** a chaplain to the armed forces. [via Sp. or It. from L *pater* father]

padsaw ('pæd,sɔː) *n* a small narrow saw used for cutting curves. [C19: from PAD[1] (in the sense: a handle that can be fitted to various tools) + SAW[1]]

paean Ⓣ *or US* (*sometimes*) **pean** ('piːən) *n* **1** a hymn sung in ancient Greece in thanksgiving to a deity. **2** any song of praise. **3** enthusiastic praise: *the film received a paean from the critics.* [C16: via L from Gk *paiān* hymn to Apollo, from his title *Paiān,* the physician of the gods]

paediatrician *or esp. US* **pediatrician** (,piːdɪə'trɪʃən) *n* a medical practitioner who specializes in paediatrics.

paediatrics *or esp. US* **pediatrics** (,piːdɪ'ætrɪks) *n* (*functioning as sing*) the branch of medical science concerned with children and their diseases. ▸ **,paedi'atric** *or esp. US* **,pedi'atric** *adj*

paedo-, *before a vowel* **paed-,** *or esp. US* **pedo-, ped-** *combining form.* indicating a child or children: *paedophilia.* [from Gk *pais, paid-* child]

paedomorphosis (,piːdə'mɔːfəsɪs) *n* the resemblance of adult animals to the young of their ancestors.

paedophilia *or esp. US* **pedophilia** (,piːdəʊ'fɪlɪə) *n* the condition of being sexually attracted to children. ▸ **paedophile** *or esp. US* **pedophile** ('piːdəʊ,faɪl) *or* **,paedo'phili,ac** *or esp. US* **,pedo'phili,ac** *n, adj*

paella (paɪ'ɛlə) *n, pl* **paellas** (-ləz). **1** a Spanish dish made from rice, shellfish, chicken, and vegetables. **2** the pan in which a paella is cooked. [from Catalan, from OF *paelle,* from L *patella* small pan]

paeony ('piːənɪ) *n, pl* **paeonies.** a variant spelling of **peony.**

pagan Ⓣ ('peɪgən) *n* **1** a member of a group professing any religion other than Christianity, Judaism, or Islam. **2** a person without any religion; heathen. ◆ *adj* **3** of or relating to pagans. **4** heathen; irreligious. [C14: from Church L *pāgānus* civilian (hence, not a soldier of Christ), from L: villager, from *pāgus* village] ▸ **'pagandom** *n* ▸ **'paganish** *adj* ▸ **'paganism** *n*

paganize *or* **paganise** ('peɪgə,naɪz) *vb* **paganizes, paganizing, paganized** *or*

THESAURUS

entity, whole ◆ *vb* **6** = **pack**, batch, box, parcel (up), wrap, wrap up

packaging *n* **1** = **wrapping**, box, casing, packing **2** = **outward** *or* **external appearance**, appearance, exterior, facade, image, PR (*inf.*), presentation, surface show, window dressing

packed *adj* **20, 22** = **full**, brimful, bursting at the seams, chock-a-block, chock-full, congested, cram-full, crammed, crowded, filled, hoatching (*Scot.*), jammed, jam-packed, loaded *or* full to the gunwales, overflowing, overloaded, packed like sardines, seething, swarming

Antonyms *adj* deserted, empty, uncongested, uncrowded

packet *n* **1, 2** = **package**, bag, carton, container, parcel, poke (*dialect*), wrapper, wrapping **4** *Slang* = **fortune**, big bucks (*inf., chiefly US*), big money, bomb, bundle (*sl.*), king's ransom (*inf.*), lot(s), megabucks (*US & Canad. sl.*), mint, pile (*inf.*), pot(s) (*inf.*), pretty penny (*inf.*), small fortune, tidy sum (*inf.*)

pack in *vb Brit. & N.Z. informal* = **stop**, cease, chuck (*inf.*), desist, give up *or* over, jack in, kick (*inf.*), leave off

pack up *vb* **1** = **put away**, store, tidy up **2** *Informal* = **stop**, call it a day, call it a night (*inf.*), finish, give up, pack in (*Brit. inf.*) **3** = **break down**, conk out (*inf.*), fail, give out, stall, stop

pact *n* = **agreement**, alliance, arrangement, bargain, bond, compact, concord, concordat, contract, convention, covenant, deal, league, protocol, treaty, understanding

pad[1] *n* **1** = **cushion**, buffer, protection, stiffening, stuffing, wad **3** = **notepad**, block, jotter, tablet, writing pad **5** = **paw**, foot, sole **8** *Slang* = **home**, apartment, flat, hang-out (*inf.*), place, quarters, room ◆ *vb* **9** = **pack**, cushion, fill, line, protect, shape, stuff **10** *often foll. by* **out** = **lengthen**, amplify, augment, eke, elaborate, fill out, flesh out, inflate, protract, spin out, stretch

pad[2] *vb* **1** = **sneak**, creep, go barefoot, pussyfoot (*inf.*), steal **2** = **walk**, hike, march, plod, traipse (*inf.*), tramp, trek, trudge

padding *n* **1** = **filling**, packing, stuffing, wadding **2** = **waffle** (*inf., chiefly Brit.*), hot air, prolixity, verbiage, verbosity, wordiness

paddle[1] *n* **1** = **oar**, scull, sweep ◆ *vb* **8** = **row**, oar, propel, pull, scull

paddle[2] *vb* **1** = **wade**, plash, slop, splash (about) **2** = **dabble**, stir

paddy[2] *n Brit. informal* = **temper**, bate, fit of temper, passion, rage, tantrum, tiff, wax (*inf., chiefly Brit.*)

paean *n* **1** = **hymn**, anthem, psalm, thanksgiving **2, 3** = **praise**, encomium, eulogy, hymn of praise, ovation, panegyric, rave review (*inf.*)

pagan *n* **1, 2** = **heathen**, Gentile, idolater, infidel, polytheist, unbeliever ◆ *adj* **3, 4** = **heathen**, Gentile, heathenish, idolatrous, infidel, irreligious, polytheistic

paganises, paganising, paganised. to become pagan or convert to paganism.

page[1] Ⓣ (peɪdʒ) *n* **1** one side of one of the leaves of a book, newspaper, etc., or the written or printed matter it bears. **2** such a leaf considered as a unit. **3** an episode, phase, or period: *a glorious page in the revolution.* **4** a screenful of information from a website, teletext service, etc., displayed on a television monitor or visual display unit. ◆ *vb* **pages, paging, paged. 5** another word for **paginate.** [C15: via OF from L *pāgina*]

page[2] Ⓣ (peɪdʒ) *n* **1** a boy employed to run errands, carry messages, etc., for the guests in a hotel, club, etc. **2** a youth in attendance at official functions or ceremonies, esp. weddings. **3** *Medieval history.* **3a** a boy in training for knighthood in personal attendance on a knight. **3b** a youth in the personal service of a person of rank. ◆ *vb* **pages, paging, paged.** (*tr*) **4** to call out the name of (a person), esp. by a loudspeaker system, so as to give him a message. **5** to call (a person) by an electronic device, such as a bleeper. **6** to act as a page to or attend as a page. [C13: via OF from It. *paggio,* prob. from Gk *paidion* boy, from *pais* child]

pageant Ⓣ (ˈpædʒənt) *n* **1** an elaborate colourful display portraying scenes from history, etc. **2** any magnificent or showy display, procession, etc. [C14: from Med. L *pāgina* scene of a play, from L: PAGE[1]]

pageantry Ⓣ (ˈpædʒəntrɪ) *n, pl* **pageantries. 1** spectacular display or ceremony. **2** *Arch.* pageants collectively.

pageboy (ˈpeɪdʒˌbɔɪ) *n* **1** a smooth medium-length hairstyle with the ends of the hair curled under. **2** a less common word for **page**[2].

pager (ˈpeɪdʒə) *n* an electronic device, capable of receiving short messages, used by people who need to be contacted urgently.

page-three *n modifier Brit.* denoting a scantily dressed attractive girl, as photographed on page three of some tabloid newspapers.

page-turner *n* a very exciting or interesting book. [C20: from the notion that a reader cannot stop turning the pages]

paginate (ˈpædʒɪˌneɪt) *vb* **paginates, paginating, paginated.** (*tr*) to number the pages of (a book, manuscript, etc.) in sequence. Cf. **foliate.**
▸ˌ**pagiˈnation** *n*

pagoda (pəˈɡəʊdə) *n* an Indian or Far Eastern temple, esp. a tower, usually pyramidal and having many storeys. [C17: from Port. *pagode,* ult. from Sansk. *bhagavatī* divine]

pagoda tree *n* a Chinese leguminous tree with ornamental white flowers.

paid (peɪd) *vb* **1** the past tense and past participle of **pay**[1]. **2 put paid to.** *Chiefly Brit. & NZ.* to end or destroy: *breaking his leg put paid to his hopes of running in the Olympics.*

paid-up *adj* **1** having paid the required fee to be a member of an organization, etc. **2** denoting a security in which all the instalments have been paid; fully paid: *a paid-up share.* **3** denoting all the money that a company has received from its shareholders: *the paid-up capital.* **4** denoting an endowment assurance policy on which the payment of premiums has stopped and the surrender value has been used to purchase a new single-premium policy.

pail (peɪl) *n* **1** a bucket, esp. one made of wood or metal. **2** Also called: **pailful.** the quantity that fills a pail. [OE *pægel*]

paillasse (ˈpælɪˌæs, ˌpælɪˈæs) *n* a variant spelling (esp. US) of **palliasse.**

pain Ⓣ (peɪn) *n* **1** the sensation of acute physical hurt or discomfort caused by injury, illness, etc. **2** emotional suffering or mental distress. **3 on pain of.** subject to the penalty of. **4** Also called: **pain in the neck.** *Inf.* a person or thing that is a nuisance. ◆ *vb* (*tr*) **5** to cause (a person) hurt, grief, anxiety, etc. **6** *Inf.* to annoy; irritate. ◆ See also **pains.** [C13: from OF *peine,* from L *poena* punishment, grief, from Gk *poinē* penalty]
▸ˈ**painless** *adj*

pained Ⓣ (peɪnd) *adj* having or expressing pain or distress, esp. mental or emotional distress.

painful Ⓣ (ˈpeɪnfʊl) *adj* **1** causing pain; distressing: *a painful duty.* **2** affected with pain. **3** tedious or difficult. **4** *Inf.* extremely bad.
▸ˈ**painfully** *adv* ▸ˈ**painfulness** *n*

painkiller Ⓣ (ˈpeɪnˌkɪlə) *n* **1** an analgesic drug or agent. **2** anything that relieves pain.

pains Ⓣ (peɪnz) *pl n* **1** care or trouble (esp. in **take pains, be at pains to**). **2** painful sensations experienced during contractions in childbirth; labour pains.

painstaking Ⓣ (ˈpeɪnzˌteɪkɪŋ) *adj* extremely careful, esp. as to fine detail.
▸ˈ**painsˌtakingly** *adv* ▸ˈ**painsˌtakingness** *n*

paint Ⓣ (peɪnt) *n* **1** a substance used for decorating or protecting a surface, esp. a mixture consisting of a solid pigment suspended in a liquid that dries to form a hard coating. **2** a dry film of paint on a surface. **3** *Inf.* face make-up, such as rouge. **4** short for **greasepaint.** ◆ *vb* **5** to make (a picture) of (a figure, landscape, etc.) with paint applied to a surface such as canvas. **6** to coat (a surface, etc.) with paint, as in decorating. **7** (*tr*) to apply (liquid, etc.) onto (a surface): *she painted the cut with antiseptic.* **8** (*tr*) to apply make-up onto (the face, lips, etc.). **9** (*tr*) to describe vividly in words. **10 paint the town red.** *Inf.* to celebrate uninhibitedly. [C13: from OF *peint* painted, from *peindre* to paint, from L *pingere* to paint]
▸ˈ**painty** *adj*

paintball game (ˈpeɪntˌbɔːl) *n* a game in which teams of players simulate a military skirmish, shooting each other with paint pellets that explode on impact.

paintbox (ˈpeɪntˌbɒks) *n* a box containing a tray of dry watercolour paints.

paintbrush (ˈpeɪntˌbrʌʃ) *n* a brush used to apply paint.

painted lady *n* a migratory butterfly with pale brownish-red mottled wings.

painter[1] (ˈpeɪntə) *n* **1** a person who paints surfaces as a trade. **2** an artist who paints pictures.
▸ˈ**painterly** *adj*

painter[2] (ˈpeɪntə) *n* a line attached to the bow of a boat for tying it up. [C15: prob. from OF *penteur* strong rope]

painting (ˈpeɪntɪŋ) *n* **1** the art of applying paints to canvas, etc. **2** a picture made in this way. **3** the act of applying paint to a surface.

paint stripper *or* **remover** *n* a liquid, often caustic, used to remove paint from a surface.

paintwork (ˈpeɪntˌwɜːk) *n* a surface, such as wood or a car body, that is painted.

pair Ⓣ (pɛə) *n, pl* **pairs** *or* (*functioning as sing or pl*) **pair. 1** two identical or similar things matched for use together: *a pair of socks.* **2** two persons, animals, things, etc., used or grouped together: *a pair of horses; a pair of scoundrels.* **3** an object considered to be two identical or similar things joined together: *a pair of trousers.* **4** two people joined in love or marriage. **5** a male and a female animal of the same species kept for breeding purposes. **6** *Parliament.* **6a** two opposed members who both agree not to vote on a specified motion. **6b** the agreement so made. **7** two playing cards of the same rank or denomination. **8** one member of a matching pair: *I can't find the pair to this glove.* ◆ *vb* **9** (often foll. by *off*) to arrange or fall into groups of twos. **10** to group or be grouped in matching pairs. **11** to join or be joined in marriage; mate or couple. **12** (when *tr, usually passive*) *Parliament.* to form or cause to form a pair. [C13: from OF *paire,* from L *paria* equal (things), from *pār* equal]

> **USAGE NOTE** Like other collective nouns, *pair* takes a singular or a plural verb according to whether it is seen as a unit or as a collection of two things: *the pair are said to dislike each other; a pair of good shoes is essential.*

THESAURUS

page[1] *n* **1 = folio,** leaf, sheet, side **3 = period,** chapter, episode, epoch, era, event, incident, phase, point, stage, time ◆ *vb* **5 = paginate,** foliate, number

page[2] *n* **1, 3 = attendant,** bellboy (*US*), footboy, pageboy, servant, squire ◆ *vb* **4, 5 = call,** announce, call out, preconize, seek, send for, summon

pageant *n* **1, 2 = show,** display, extravaganza, parade, procession, ritual, spectacle, tableau

pageantry *n* **1 = spectacle,** display, drama, extravagance, glamour, glitter, grandeur, magnificence, parade, pomp, show, showiness, splash (*inf.*), splendour, state, theatricality

pain *n* **1 = hurt,** ache, cramp, discomfort, irritation, pang, smarting, soreness, spasm, suffering, tenderness, throb, throe (*rare*), trouble, twinge **2 = suffering,** affliction, agony, anguish, bitterness, distress, grief, hardship, heartache, misery, torment, torture, tribulation, woe, wretchedness **4** *Informal* **= nuisance,** aggravation, annoyance, bore, bother, drag (*inf.*), gall, headache (*inf.*), irritation, pain in the neck (*inf.*), pest, vexation ◆ *vb* **5 = hurt,** ail, chafe, discomfort, harm, inflame, injure, smart, sting, throb **5 = distress,** afflict, aggrieve, agonize, cut to the quick, disquiet, grieve, hurt, sadden, torment, torture, vex, worry, wound **6** *Informal* **= irritate,** annoy, exasperate, gall, harass, nark (*Brit., Austral., & NZ sl.*), rile, vex

pained *adj* **= distressed,** aggrieved, anguished, hurt, injured, miffed (*inf.*), offended, reproachful, stung, unhappy, upset, worried, wounded

painful *adj* **1 = distressing,** afflictive, disagreeable, distasteful, grievous, saddening, unpleasant **1, 2 = sore,** aching, agonizing, excruciating, harrowing, hurting, inflamed, raw, smarting, tender, throbbing **3 = difficult,** arduous, hard, laborious, severe, tedious, troublesome, trying, vexatious **4** *Informal* **= terrible,** abysmal, awful, dire, dreadful, excruciating, extremely bad
Antonyms *adj* ≠ **distressing:** agreeable, enjoyable, pleasant, satisfying ≠ **sore:** comforting, painless, relieving, soothing ≠ **difficult:** a piece of cake (*inf.*), easy, effortless, interesting, short, simple, straightforward, undemanding

painfully *adv* **1-4 = distressingly,** alarmingly, clearly, deplorably, dreadfully, excessively, markedly, sadly, unfortunately, woefully

painkiller *n* **1 = analgesic,** anaesthetic, anodyne, drug, palliative, remedy, sedative

painless *adj* **= simple,** easy, effortless, fast, no trouble, pain-free, quick, trouble-free

pains *pl n* **1 = trouble,** assiduousness, bother, care, diligence, effort, industry, labour, special attention **2 = contractions,** birth-pangs, childbirth, labour

painstaking *adj* **= thorough,** assiduous, careful, conscientious, diligent, earnest, exacting, hard-working, industrious, meticulous, persevering, punctilious, scrupulous, sedulous, strenuous, thoroughgoing
Antonyms *adj* careless, half-hearted, haphazard, heedless, lazy, negligent, slapdash, slipshod, thoughtless

paint *n* **1 = colouring,** colour, dye, emulsion, pigment, stain, tint **3, 4** *Informal* **= make-up,** cosmetics, face, greasepaint, *maquillage,* war paint (*inf.*) ◆ *vb* **5 = depict,** catch a likeness, delineate, draw, figure, picture, portray, represent, sketch **6, 7 = coat,** apply, colour, cover, daub, decorate, slap on (*inf.*) **9 = describe,** bring to life, capture, conjure up a vision, depict, evoke, make one see, portray, put graphically, recount, tell vividly **10 paint the town red** *Informal* **= celebrate,** carouse, go on a binge (*inf.*), go on a spree, go on the town, live it up (*inf.*), make merry, make whoopee (*inf.*), revel

pair *n* **1, 2, 4, 5 = couple,** brace, combination, doublet, duo, match, matched set, span, twins, two of a kind, twosome, yoke ◆ *vb* **9-11 = cou-**

paisley ('peɪzlɪ) *n* **1** a pattern of small curving shapes with intricate detailing. **2** a soft fine wool fabric traditionally printed with this pattern. **3** a shawl made of this fabric, popular in the late 19th century. **4** (*modifier*) of or decorated with this pattern: *a paisley scarf.* [C19: after *Paisley*, town in Scotland]

pajamas (pə'dʒɑːməz) *pl n* the US spelling of **pyjamas.**

pakeha ('pɑːkɪ,hɑː) *n NZ.* a European, as distinct from a Maori: *Maori and pakeha.* [from Maori]

Paki ('pækɪ) *Brit. sl., offens.* ◆ *n, pl* **Pakis. 1** a Pakistani or person of Pakistani descent. ◆ *adj* **2** Pakistani or of Pakistani descent.

Pakistani (,pɑːkɪ'stɑːnɪ) *adj* **1** of or relating to Pakistan, a country in the Indian subcontinent. ◆ *n, pl* **Pakistanis. 2** a native or inhabitant of Pakistan or a descendant of one.

pakora (pə'kɔːrə) *n* an Indian dish consisting of pieces of vegetable, chicken, etc., dipped in spiced batter and deep-fried. [C20: from Hindi]

pal ❶ (pæl) *Inf.* ◆ *n* **1** a close friend; comrade. ◆ *vb* **pals, palling, palled. 2** (*intr;* usually foll. by *with*) to associate as friends. [C17: from E Gypsy: brother, ult. from Sansk. *bhrātar* BROTHER]

PAL (pæl) *n acronym for* phase alternation line: a colour-television broadcasting system used generally in Europe.

palace ('pælɪs) *n* (*cap. when part of a name*) **1** the official residence of a reigning monarch. **2** the official residence of various high-ranking people, as of an archbishop. **3** a large and richly furnished building resembling a royal palace. [C13: from OF *palais*, from L *Palātium* Palatine, the site of the palace of the emperors in Rome]

paladin ('pælədɪn) *n* **1** one of the legendary twelve peers of Charlemagne's court. **2** a knightly champion. [C16: via F from It. *paladino*, from L *palātīnus* imperial official]

palaeo-, *before a vowel* **palae-** *or esp. US* **paleo-, pale-** *combining form.* old, ancient, or prehistoric: *palaeography.* [from Gk *palaios* old]

palaeobotany *or US* **paleobotany** (,pælɪəʊ'bɒtənɪ) *n* the study of fossil plants.
▸ **,palaeo'botanist** *or US* **,paleo'botanist** *n*

Palaeocene *or US* **Paleocene** ('pælɪəʊ,siːn) *adj* **1** of, denoting, or formed in the first epoch of the Tertiary period. ◆ *n* **2 the.** the Palaeocene epoch or rock series. [C19: from F, from *paléo* PALAEO- + Gk *kainos* new]

palaeoclimatology *or US* **paleoclimatology** (,pælɪəʊ,klaɪmə'tɒlədʒɪ) *n* the study of climates of the geological past.
▸ **,palaeo,clima'tologist** *or US* **,paleo,clima'tologist** *n*

palaeoecology *or US* **paleoecology** (,pælɪəʊɪ'kɒlədʒɪ) *n* the study of fossil animals and plants in order to deduce their ecology and the environment conditions in which they lived.
▸ **,palaeo,eco'logical** *or US* **,paleo,eco'logical** *adj* ▸ **,palaeoe'cologist** *or US* **,paleoe'cologist** *n*

palaeography *or US* **paleography** (,pælɪ'ɒgrəfɪ) *n* **1** the study of the handwritings of the past, and often the manuscripts, etc., so that they may be dated, read, etc. **2** a handwriting of the past.
▸ **,palae'ographer** *or US* **,pale'ographer** *n* ▸**palaeographic** (,pælɪəʊ'græfɪk), **,palaeo'graphical** *or US* **,paleo'graphic, ,paleo'graphical** *adj*

Palaeolithic *or US* **Paleolithic** (,pælɪəʊ'lɪθɪk) *n* **1** the period of the emergence of primitive man and the manufacture of unpolished chipped stone tools, about 2.5 million to 3 million years ago. ◆ *adj* **2** (*sometimes not cap.*) of or relating to this period.

palaeomagnetism *or US* **paleomagnetism** (,pælɪəʊ'mægnɪtɪzəm) *n* the study of the fossil magnetism in rocks, used to determine the past configuration of the earth's constituents.

palaeontology *or US* **paleontology** (,pælɪɒn'tɒlədʒɪ) *n* the study of fossils to determine the structure and evolution of extinct animals and plants and the age and conditions of deposition of the rock strata in which they are found. [C19: from PALAEO- + ONTO- + -LOGY]
▸**palaeontological** *or US* **paleontological** (,pælɪ,ɒntə'lɒdʒɪkᵊl) *adj* ▸ **,palaeon'tologist** *or US* **,paleon'tologist** *n*

Palaeozoic (,pælɪəʊ'zəʊɪk) *adj* **1** of, denoting, or relating to an era of geological time that began 600 million years ago with the Cambrian period and lasted about 375 million years until the end of the Permian period. ◆ *n* **2 the.** the Palaeozoic era. [C19: from PALAEO- + Gk *zōē* life + -IC]

palanquin *or* **palankeen** (,pælən'kiːn) *n* a covered litter, formerly used in the Orient, carried on the shoulders of four men. [C16: from Port. *palanquim*, from Prakrit *pallanka*, from Sansk. *paryanka* couch]

palatable ❶ ('pælətəbᵊl) *adj* **1** pleasant to taste. **2** acceptable or satisfactory.
▸ **,palata'bility** *or* **'palatableness** *n* ▸ **'palatably** *adv*

palatal ('pælətᵊl) *adj* **1** Also: **palatine.** of or relating to the palate. **2** *Phonetics.* of, relating to, or denoting a speech sound articulated with the blade of the tongue touching the hard palate. ◆ *n* **3** Also called: **palatine.** the bony plate that forms the palate. **4** *Phonetics.* a palatal speech sound, such as (j).
▸ **'palatally** *adv*

palatalize *or* **palatalise** ('pælətə,laɪz) *vb* **palatalizes, palatalizing, palatalized** *or* **palatalises, palatalising, palatalised.** (*tr*) to pronounce (a speech sound) with the blade of the tongue touching the palate.
▸ **,palatali'zation** *or* **,palatali'sation** *n*

palate ❶ ('pælɪt) *n* **1** the roof of the mouth, separating the oral and nasal cavities. See **hard palate, soft palate. 2** the sense of taste: *she had no palate for the wine.* **3** relish or enjoyment. [C14: from L *palātum*, ? of Etruscan origin]

USAGE NOTE Avoid confusion with **palette** or **pallet.**

palatial ❶ (pə'leɪʃəl) *adj* of, resembling, or suitable for a palace; sumptuous.
▸**pa'latially** *adv*

palatinate (pə'lætɪnɪt) *n* a territory ruled by a palatine prince or noble or count palatine.

palatine[1] ('pælə,taɪn) *adj* **1** (of an individual) possessing royal prerogatives in a territory. **2** of or relating to a count palatine, county palatine, palatinate, or palatine. **3** of or relating to a palace. ◆ *n* **4** *Feudal history.* the lord of a palatinate. **5** any of various important officials at the late Roman, Merovingian, or Carolingian courts. [C15: via F from L *palātīnus* belonging to the palace, from *palātium;* see PALACE]

palatine[2] ('pælə,taɪn) *adj* **1** of the palate. ◆ *n* **2** either of two bones forming the hard palate. [C17: from F *palatin*, from L *palātum* palate]

palaver ❶ (pə'lɑːvə) *n* **1** tedious or time-consuming business, esp. when of a formal nature: *all the palaver of filling in forms.* **2** confused talk and activity; hubbub. **3** (often used humorously) a conference. **4** *Now rare.* talk intended to flatter or persuade. ◆ *vb* **5** (*intr*) (often used humorously) to have a conference. **6** (*intr*) to talk confusedly. **7** (*tr*) to flatter or cajole. [C18: from Port. *palavra* talk, from L *parabola* PARABLE]

pale[1] ❶ (peɪl) *adj* **1** lacking brightness or colour: *pale morning light.* **2** (of a colour) whitish. **3** dim or wan: *the pale stars.* **4** feeble: *a pale effort.* ◆ *vb* **pales, paling, paled. 5** to make or become pale or paler; blanch. **6** (*intr;* often foll. by *before*) to lose superiority (in comparison to): *her beauty paled before that of her hostess.* [C13: from OF *palle*, from L *pallidus*, from *pallēre* to look wan]
▸ **'palely** *adv* ▸ **'paleness** *n* ▸ **'palish** *adj*

pale[2] ❶ (peɪl) *n* **1** a wooden post or strip used as an upright member in a fence. **2** an enclosing barrier, esp. a fence made of pales. **3** an area enclosed by a pale. **4** *Heraldry.* a vertical stripe, usually in the centre of a shield. **5 beyond the pale.** outside the limits of social convention. [C14: from OF *pal*, from L *pālus* stake]

paleface ('peɪl,feɪs) *n* a derogatory term for a White person, said to have been used by North American Indians.

paleo- *or before a vowel* **pale-** *combining form.* variants (esp. US) of **palaeo-.**

Palestine Liberation Organization ('pælɪ,staɪn) *n* an organization founded in 1964 with the aim of creating a state for Palestinian Arabs. In 1993 it signed a peace agreement with Israel, which granted Palestinian autonomy in the Gaza Strip and West Bank. Abbrev.: **PLO.**

Palestinian (,pælɪ'stɪnɪən) *adj* **1a** of or relating to Palestine, an area of the Middle East between the Jordan River and the Mediterranean, or to the former (1922–48) British mandatory territory in this region. **1b** of or relating to the native Arab population of Palestine or their descendants. ◆ *n* **2** a Palestinian Arab, esp. one now living in the Palestinian Administered Territories, Israel, Jordan, Lebanon, or as a refugee from Israeli-occupied territory.

Palestinian National Authority *n* the authority formed in 1994 to govern the Palestinian Administered Territories. Abbrev.: **PNA.**

palette ('pælɪt) *n* **1** Also: **pallet.** a flat piece of wood, plastic, etc., used by artists as a surface on which to mix their paints. **2** the range of colours characteristic of a particular artist, painting, or school of painting: *a*

THESAURUS

ple, bracket, join, marry, match (up), mate, pair off, put together, team, twin, wed, yoke

pal *n* **1** *Informal* = **friend**, boon companion, buddy, chum (*inf.*), cock (*Brit. inf.*), companion, comrade, crony, homeboy (*sl., chiefly US*), mate (*inf.*)

palatable *adj* **1** = **delicious**, appetizing, delectable, luscious, mouthwatering, savoury, tasty, toothsome **2** = **acceptable**, agreeable, attractive, enjoyable, fair, pleasant, satisfactory
Antonyms *adj* ≠ **delicious:** bland, flat, insipid, stale, tasteless, unappetizing, unpalatable

palate *n* **2** = **taste**, appetite, heart, stomach **3** = **enjoyment**, appreciation, gusto, liking, relish, zest

palatial *adj* = **magnificent**, de luxe, gorgeous, grand, grandiose, illustrious, imposing, luxurious, majestic, opulent, plush (*inf.*), regal, spacious, splendid, splendiferous (*facetious*), stately, sumptuous

palaver *n* **1** = **fuss**, business (*inf.*), carry-on (*inf., chiefly Brit.*), pantomime (*inf., chiefly Brit.*), performance (*inf.*), procedure, rigmarole, song and dance (*Brit. inf.*), to-do **2** = **prattle**, babble, blather, blether, chatter, hubbub, natter (*Brit.*), tongue-wagging, yak (*sl.*) **3** = **conference**, colloquy, confab (*inf.*), discussion, get-together (*inf.*), parley, powwow, session ◆ *vb* **5** = **confer**, confab (*inf.*), discuss, go into a huddle (*inf.*), parley, powwow, put heads together **6** = **prattle**, blather, blether, chatter, gabble, jabber, jaw (*sl.*), natter (*Brit.*), yak (*sl.*)

pale[1] *adj* **1, 2** = **white**, anaemic, ashen, ashy, bleached, bloodless, colourless, faded, light, like death warmed up (*inf.*), pallid, pasty, sallow, wan, washed-out, whitish **4** = **poor**, feeble, inadequate, pathetic, thin, weak ◆ *vb* **5** = **become pale**, blanch, go white, lose colour, whiten **6** = **fade**, decrease, dim, diminish, dull, grow dull, lessen, lose lustre
Antonyms *adj* ≠ **white:** blooming, florid, flushed, glowing, rosy-cheeked, rubicund, ruddy, sanguine

pale[2] *n* **1** = **post**, paling, palisade, picket, slat, stake, upright **2** = **barrier**, barricade, fence, palisade, railing **3** = **boundary**, border, bounds, confines, district, limits, region, territory **5 beyond the pale** = **unacceptable**, forbidden, improper, inadmissible, indecent, irregular, not done, out of line, unseemly, unspeakable, unsuitable *restricted palette.* **3** the available range of colours or patterns that can be displayed by a computer on a visual display unit. [C17: from F, dim. of *pale* shovel, from L *pala* spade]

> **USAGE NOTE** Avoid confusion with **palate** or **pallet**.

palette *or* **pallet knife** *n* a spatula with a thin flexible blade used in painting and cookery.

palfrey (ˈpɔːlfrɪ) *n Arch.* a light saddle horse, esp. ridden by women. [C12: from OF *palefrei,* from Med. L, from LL *paraverēdus,* from Gk *para* beside + L *verēdus* light fleet horse, of Celtic origin]

Pali (ˈpɑːlɪ) *n* an ancient language of India derived from Sanskrit; the language of the Buddhist scriptures. [C19: from Sansk. *pāli-bhāsa,* from *pāli* canon + *bhāsa* language, of Dravidian origin]

palimony (ˈpælɪmənɪ) *n US.* alimony awarded to a nonmarried partner after the break-up of a long-term relationship. [C20: from PAL + ALIMONY]

palimpsest (ˈpælɪmpˌsɛst) *n* **1** a manuscript on which two or more texts have been written, each one being erased to make room for the next. ◆ *adj* **2** (of a text) written on a palimpsest. **3** (of a document, etc.) used as a palimpsest. [C17: from L *palimpsestus,* from Gk *palimpsēstos,* from *palin* again + *psēstos* rubbed smooth]

palindrome (ˈpælɪnˌdrəʊm) *n* a word or phrase the letters of which, when taken in reverse order, read the same: *able was I ere I saw Elba.* [C17: from Gk *palindromos* running back again]
▸**palindromic** (ˌpælɪnˈdrɒmɪk) *adj*

paling (ˈpeɪlɪŋ) *n* **1** a fence made of pales. **2** pales collectively. **3** a single pale. **4** the act of erecting pales.

palisade Ⓣ (ˌpælɪˈseɪd) *n* **1** a strong fence made of stakes driven into the ground, esp. for defence. **2** one of the stakes used in such a fence. ◆ *vb* **palisades, palisading, palisaded. 3** (*tr*) to enclose with a palisade. [C17: via F from OProvençal *palissada,* ult. from L *pālus* stake]

pall[1] Ⓣ (pɔːl) *n* **1** a cloth covering, usually black, spread over a coffin or tomb. **2** a coffin, esp. during the funeral ceremony. **3** a dark heavy covering; shroud: *the clouds formed a pall over the sky.* **4** a depressing or oppressive atmosphere: *her bereavement cast a pall on the party.* **5** *Heraldry.* a Y-shaped bearing. **6** *Christianity.* a small square linen cloth with which the chalice is covered at the Eucharist. ◆ *vb* **7** (*tr*) to cover or depress with a pall. [OE *pæll,* from L *pallium* cloak]

pall[2] Ⓣ (pɔːl) *vb* **1** (*intr;* often foll. by *on*) to become boring, insipid, or tiresome (to): *history classes palled on me.* **2** to cloy or satiate, or become cloyed or satiated. [C14: var. of APPAL]

Palladian (pəˈleɪdɪən) *adj* denoting, relating to, or having the style of architecture created by Andrea Palladio. [C18: after Andrea *Palladio* (1508–80), It. architect]
▸**Palˈladian,ism** *n*

palladium[1] (pəˈleɪdɪəm) *n* a ductile malleable silvery-white element of the platinum metal group: used as a catalyst and, alloyed with gold, in jewellery, etc. Symbol: Pd; atomic no.: 46; atomic wt.: 106.4. [C19: after the asteroid *Pallas,* at the time (1803) a recent discovery]

palladium[2] (pəˈleɪdɪəm) *n* something believed to ensure protection; safeguard. [C17: after the *Palladium,* a statue of Pallas Athena, Gk goddess of wisdom]

pallbearer (ˈpɔːlˌbɛərə) *n* a person who carries or escorts the coffin at a funeral.

pallet[1] (ˈpælɪt) *n* a straw-filled mattress or bed. [C14: from Anglo-Norman *paillet,* from OF *paille* straw, from L *palea* straw]

> **USAGE NOTE** Avoid confusion with **palate** or **palette**.

pallet[2] (ˈpælɪt) *n* **1** an instrument with a handle and a flat, sometimes flexible, blade used by potters for shaping. **2** a portable platform for storing and moving goods. **3** *Horology.* the locking lever that engages and disengages to give impulses to the balance. **4** a variant spelling of **palette** (sense 1). **5** *Music.* a flap valve that opens to allow air from the wind chest to enter an organ pipe, causing it to sound. [C16: from OF *palette* a little shovel, from L *pala* spade]

palletize *or* **palletise** (ˈpæləˌtaɪz) *vb* **palletizes, palletizing, palletized** *or* **palletises, palletising, palletised.** (*tr*) to store or transport (goods) on pallets.
▸ˌ**palletiˈzation** *or* ˌ**palletiˈsation** *n*

palliasse *or esp. US* **paillasse** (ˈpælɪˌæs, ˌpælɪˈæs) *n* a straw-filled mattress; pallet. [C18: from F *paillasse,* from It. *pagliaccio,* ult. from L *palea* PALLET[1]]

palliate (ˈpælɪˌeɪt) *vb* **palliates, palliating, palliated.** (*tr*) **1** to lessen the severity of (pain, disease, etc.) without curing; alleviate. **2** to cause (an offence, etc.) to seem less serious; extenuate. [C16: from LL *palliāre* to cover up, from L *pallium* a cloak]
▸ˌ**palliˈation** *n*

palliative (ˈpælɪətɪv) *adj* **1** relieving without curing. ◆ *n* **2** something that palliates, such as a sedative drug.
▸ˈ**palliatively** *adv*

pallid Ⓣ (ˈpælɪd) *adj* lacking colour, brightness, or vigour: *a pallid complexion; a pallid performance.* [C17: from L *pallidus,* from *pallēre* to be PALE[1]]
▸ˈ**pallidly** *adv* ▸ˈ**pallidness** *or* **palˈlidity** *n*

pall-mall (ˈpælˈmæl) *n Obs.* **1** a game in which a ball is driven by a mallet along an alley and through an iron ring. **2** the alley itself. [C17: from obs. F, from It. *pallamaglio,* from *palla* ball + *maglio* mallet]

pallor Ⓣ (ˈpælə) *n* a pale condition, esp. when unnatural: *fear gave his face a deathly pallor.* [C17: from L: whiteness (of the skin), from *pallēre* to be PALE[1]]

pally Ⓣ (ˈpælɪ) *adj* **pallier, palliest.** *Inf.* on friendly terms.

palm[1] Ⓣ (pɑːm) *n* **1** the inner part of the hand from the wrist to the base of the fingers. **2** a linear measure based on the breadth or length of a hand, equal to three to four inches (7.5 to 10 centimetres) or seven to ten inches (17.5 to 25 centimetres) respectively. **3** the part of a glove that covers the palm. **4a** one side of the blade of an oar. **4b** the face of the fluke of an anchor. **5** a flattened part of the antlers of certain deer. **6 in the palm of one's hand.** at one's mercy or command. ◆ *vb* (*tr*) **7** to conceal in or about the hand, as in sleight-of-hand tricks, etc. ◆ See also **palm off.** [C14 *paume,* via OF from L *palma*]
▸**palmar** (ˈpælmə) *adj*

palm[2] Ⓣ (pɑːm) *n* **1** any treelike plant of a tropical and subtropical family having a straight unbranched trunk crowned with large pinnate or palmate leaves. **2** a leaf or branch of any of these trees, a symbol of victory, success, etc. **3** merit or victory. [OE, from L *palma,* from the likeness of its spreading fronds to a hand; see PALM[1]]
▸**palmaceous** (pælˈmeɪʃəs) *adj*

palmate (ˈpælmeɪt, -mɪt) *or* **palmated** *adj* **1** shaped like an open hand: *palmate antlers.* **2** *Bot.* having five lobes that spread out from a common point: *palmate leaves.* **3** (of most water birds) having three toes connected by a web.

palmer (ˈpɑːmə) *n* (in medieval Europe) **1** a pilgrim bearing a palm branch as a sign of his visit to the Holy Land. **2** any pilgrim. [C13: from OF *palmier,* from Med. L, from L *palma* PALM[2]]

palmetto (pælˈmɛtəʊ) *n, pl* **palmettos** *or* **palmettoes.** any of several small chiefly tropical palms with fan-shaped leaves. [C16: from Sp. *palmito* a little PALM[2]]

palmistry (ˈpɑːmɪstrɪ) *n* the process or art of telling fortunes, etc., by the configuration of lines and bumps on a person's hand. Also called: **chiromancy.** [C15 *pawmestry,* from *paume* PALM[1]; the second element is unexplained]
▸ˈ**palmist** *n*

palmitic acid (pælˈmɪtɪk) *n* a white crystalline solid that is a saturated fatty acid: used in the manufacture of soap and candles. Formula: $C_{15}H_{31}COOH$. Systematic name: **hexadecanoic acid.** [C19: from F]

palm off Ⓣ *vb* (*tr, adv;* often foll. by *on*) **1** to offer, sell, or spend fraudulently: *to palm off a counterfeit coin.* **2** to divert in order to be rid of: *I palmed the unwelcome visitor off on John.*

palm oil *n* an oil obtained from the fruit of certain palms, used as an edible fat and in soap, etc.

Palm Sunday *n* the Sunday before Easter commemorating Christ's triumphal entry into Jerusalem.

palmtop computer (ˈpɒːmˌtɒp) *n* a computer that is small enough to be held in the hand. Often shortened to **palmtop.** Cf. **laptop computer.**

palmy Ⓣ (ˈpɑːmɪ) *adj* **palmier, palmiest. 1** prosperous, flourishing, or luxurious: *a palmy life.* **2** covered with, relating to, or resembling palms.

palmyra (pælˈmaɪrə) *n* a tall tropical Asian palm with large fan-shaped leaves used for thatching and weaving. [C17: from Port. *palmeira* palm tree; ? infl. by *Palmyra,* city in Syria]

palomino (ˌpæləˈmiːnəʊ) *n, pl* **palominos.** a golden horse with a white mane and tail. [American Sp., from Sp.: dovelike, from L, from *palumbēs* ring dove]

palp (pælp) *or* **palpus** (ˈpælpəs) *n, pl* **palps** *or* **palpi** (ˈpælpaɪ). either of a pair of sensory appendages that arise from the mouthparts of crustaceans and insects. [C19: from F, from L *palpus* a touching]

palpable Ⓣ (ˈpælpəbᵊl) *adj* **1** (*usually prenominal*) easily perceived by the senses or the mind; obvious: *a palpable lie.* **2** capable of being touched;

THESAURUS

palisade *n* **1 = fence,** bulwark, defence, enclosure, paling, stockade

pall[1] *n* **1, 3 = cloud,** mantle, shadow, shroud, veil **4 = gloom,** check, damp, damper, dismay, melancholy

pall[2] *vb* **1, 2 = become boring,** become dull, become tedious, cloy, glut, jade, satiate, sicken, surfeit, tire, weary

pallid *adj* **= pale,** anaemic, ashen, ashy, cadaverous, colourless, like death warmed up (*inf.*), pasty, sallow, wan, waxen, wheyfaced, whitish **= insipid,** anaemic, bloodless, colourless, lifeless, spiritless, sterile, tame, tired, uninspired, vapid

pallor *n* **= paleness,** ashen hue, bloodlessness, lack of colour, pallidness, wanness, whiteness

pally *adj Informal* **= friendly,** affectionate, buddy-buddy (*sl., chiefly US & Canad.*), chummy, close, familiar, intimate, palsy-walsy (*inf.*), thick as thieves (*inf.*)

palm[1] *n* **1 = hand,** hook, mitt (*sl.*), paw (*inf.*) **6 in the palm of one's hand = in one's power,** at one's mercy, in one's clutches, in one's control

palm[2] *n* **3 = victory,** bays, crown, fame, glory, honour, laurels, merit, prize, success, triumph, trophy

palm off *vb* **1 = fob off,** foist off, pass off **2** *often foll. by* **on = foist on,** force upon, impose upon, thrust upon, unload upon

palmy *adj* **1 = prosperous,** flourishing, fortunate, glorious, golden, halcyon, happy, joyous, luxurious, thriving, triumphant

palpable *adj* **1 = obvious,** apparent, blatant, clear, conspicuous, evident, manifest, open, patent, plain, salient, unmistakable, visible **2 =**

tangible. [C14: from LL *palpābilis* that may be touched, from L *palpāre* to touch]
▸ ˌpalpaˈbility *n* ▸ ˈpalpably *adv*

palpate (ˈpælpeɪt) *vb* **palpates, palpating, palpated.** (*tr*) *Med.* to examine (an area of the body) by the sense of touch. [C19: from L *palpāre* to stroke]
▸ palˈpation *n*

palpebral (ˈpælpɪbrəl) *adj* of or relating to the eyelid. [C19: from LL, from L *palpebra* eyelid]

palpitate ● (ˈpælpɪˌteɪt) *vb* **palpitates, palpitating, palpitated.** (*intr*) **1** (of the heart) to beat rapidly. **2** to flutter or tremble. [C17: from L *palpitāre* to throb, from *palpāre* to stroke]
▸ ˈpalpitant *adj* ▸ ˌpalpiˈtation *n*

palsy ● (ˈpɔːlzɪ) *Pathol.* ◆ *n, pl* **palsies. 1** paralysis, esp. of a specified type: *cerebral palsy.* ◆ *vb* **palsies, palsying, palsied.** (*tr*) **2** to paralyse. [C13 *palesi,* from OF *paralisie,* from L PARALYSIS]
▸ ˈpalsied *adj*

palter (ˈpɔːltə) *vb* (*intr*) **1** to act or talk insincerely. **2** to haggle. [C16: from ?]

paltry ● (ˈpɔːltrɪ) *adj* **paltrier, paltriest. 1** insignificant; meagre. **2** worthless or petty. [C16: from Low Gmc *palter, paltrig* ragged]
▸ ˈpaltrily *adv* ▸ ˈpaltriness *n*

paludal (pəˈljuːdᵊl) *adj Rare.* **1** of or relating to marshes. **2** malarial. [C19: from L *palus* marsh]

paludism (ˈpæljʊˌdɪzəm) *n* a less common word for **malaria.** [C19: from L *palus* marsh]

palynology (ˌpælɪˈnɒlədʒɪ) *n* the study of living and fossil pollen grains and plant spores. [C20: from Gk *palunein* to scatter + -LOGY]
▸ **palynological** (ˌpælɪnəˈlɒdʒɪkᵊl) *adj* ▸ ˌpalyˈnologist *n*

pampas (ˈpæmpəz) *n* (*functioning as sing or more often pl*) **a** the extensive grassy plains of temperate South America, esp. in Argentina. **b** (*as modifier*): *pampas dwellers.* [C18: from American Sp. *pampa* (sing), from Amerind *bamba* plain]
▸ **pampean** (ˈpæmpɪən, pæmˈpiːən) *adj*

pampas grass (ˈpæmpəs, -pəz) *n* any of various large South American grasses, widely cultivated for their large feathery silver-coloured flower branches.

pamper ● (ˈpæmpə) *vb* (*tr*) **1** to treat with affectionate and usually excessive indulgence; coddle; spoil. **2** *Arch.* to feed to excess. [C14: of Gmc origin]
▸ ˈpamperer *n*

pamphlet ● (ˈpæmflɪt) *n* **1** a brief publication generally having a paper cover; booklet. **2** a brief treatise, often on a subject of current interest, in pamphlet form. [C14 *pamflet,* from Med. L *Pamphilus* title of a 12th-century amatory poem from Gk *Pamphilos* proper name]

pamphleteer (ˌpæmflɪˈtɪə) *n* **1** a person who writes or issues pamphlets. ◆ *vb* **2** (*intr*) to write or issue pamphlets.

Pamphylia (pæmˈfɪlɪə) *n* an area on the S coast of ancient Asia Minor.

pan[1] ● (pæn) *n* **1a** a wide metal vessel used in cooking. **1b** (*in combination*): *saucepan.* **2** Also called: **panful.** the amount such a vessel will hold. **3** any of various similar vessels used in industry, etc. **4** a dish used esp. by gold prospectors for separating gold from gravel by washing and agitating. **5** either of the two dishlike receptacles on a balance. **6** Also called: **lavatory pan.** *Brit.* the bowl of a lavatory. **7a** a natural or artificial depression in the ground where salt can be obtained by the evaporation of brine. **7b** a natural depression containing water or mud. **8** See **hardpan, brainpan. 9** a small cavity containing priming powder in the locks of old guns. **10** a hard substratum of soil. ◆ *vb* **pans, panning, panned. 11** (when *tr,* often foll. by *off* or *out*) to wash (gravel) in a pan to separate particles of (valuable minerals) from it. **12** (*intr;* often foll. by *out*) (of gravel, etc.) to yield valuable minerals by this process. **13** (*tr*) *Inf.* to criticize harshly: *the critics panned his new play.* ◆ See also **pan out.** [OE *panne*]

pan[2] ● (pæn) *vb* **pans, panning, panned. 1** to move (a film camera) or (of a film camera) to be moved so as to follow a moving object or obtain a panoramic effect. ◆ *n* **2** the act of panning. [C20: shortened from PANORAMIC]

pan- *combining form.* **1** all or every: *panchromatic.* **2** including or relating to all parts or members: *Pan-American; pantheistic.* [from Gk *pan,* neuter of *pas* all]

panacea ● (ˌpænəˈsɪə) *n* a remedy for all diseases or ills. [C16: via L from Gk *panakeia,* from *pan* all + *akēs* remedy]
▸ ˌpanaˈcean *adj*

panache ● (pəˈnæʃ, -ˈnɑːʃ) *n* **1** a dashing manner; swagger: *he rides with panache.* **2** a plume on a helmet. [C16: via F from OIt. *pennacchio,* from LL *pinnāculum* feather, from L *pinna* feather]

panada (pəˈnɑːdə) *n* a mixture of flour, water, etc., or of breadcrumbs soaked in milk, used as a thickening. [C16: from Sp., from *pan* bread, from L *pānis*]

Panama hat (ˌpænəˈmɑː) *n* (*sometimes not cap.*) a hat made of the plaited leaves of a palmlike plant of Central and South America. Often shortened to **panama** or **Panama.**

Pan-American *adj* of, relating to, or concerning North, South, and Central America collectively or the advocacy of political or economic unity among American countries.
▸ ˈPan-Aˈmericanˌism *n*

panatella (ˌpænəˈtɛlə) *n* a long slender cigar. [American Sp. *panetela* long slim biscuit, from It. *panatella* small loaf, from *pane* bread, from L *pānis*]

pancake (ˈpænˌkeɪk) *n* **1** a thin flat cake made from batter and fried on both sides. **2** a stick or flat cake of compressed make-up. **3** Also called: **pancake landing.** an aircraft landing made by levelling out a few feet from the ground and then dropping onto it. ◆ *vb* **pancakes, pancaking, pancaked. 4** to cause (an aircraft) to make a pancake landing or (of an aircraft) to make a pancake landing.

Pancake Day *n* another name for **Shrove Tuesday.** See **Shrovetide.**

panchromatic (ˌpænkrəʊˈmætɪk) *adj Photog.* (of an emulsion or film) made sensitive to all colours.
▸ **panchromatism** (pænˈkrəʊməˌtɪzəm) *n*

pancosmism (pænˈkɒzˌmɪzəm) *n* the philosophical doctrine that the material universe is all that exists.

pancreas (ˈpæŋkrɪəs) *n* a large elongated glandular organ, situated behind the stomach, that secretes insulin and pancreatic juice. [C16: via NL from Gk *pankreas,* from PAN- + *kreas* flesh]
▸ **pancreatic** (ˌpæŋkrɪˈætɪk) *adj*

pancreatic juice *n* the clear alkaline secretion of the pancreas that is released into the duodenum and contains digestive enzymes.

pancreatin (ˈpæŋkrɪətɪn) *n* the powdered extract of the pancreas of certain animals, used in medicine as an aid to the digestion.

panda (ˈpændə) *n* **1** Also called: **giant panda.** a large black-and-white herbivorous bearlike mammal, related to the raccoons and inhabiting the high mountain bamboo forests of China. **2 lesser** *or* **red panda.** a closely related smaller animal resembling a raccoon, of the mountain forests of S Asia, having a reddish-brown coat and ringed tail. [C19: via F from a native Nepalese word]

panda car *n Brit.* a police patrol car. [C20: so called because its blue-and-white markings resemble the black-and-white markings of the giant panda]

pandanus (pænˈdeɪnəs) *n, pl* **pandanuses.** any of various Old World tropical palmlike plants having leaves and roots yielding a fibre used for making mats, etc. [C19: via NL from Malay *pandan*]

pandect (ˈpændɛkt) *n* **1** a treatise covering all aspects of a particular subject. **2** (*often pl*) the complete body of laws of a country; legal code, esp. the digest of Roman civil law made in the 6th century by order of Justinian. [C16: via LL from Gk *pandektēs* containing everything, from PAN- + *dektēs* receiver]

pandemic (pænˈdɛmɪk) *adj* **1** (of a disease) affecting persons over a wide geographical area; extensively epidemic. ◆ *n* **2** a pandemic disease. [C17: from LL *pandēmus,* from Gk *pandēmos* general, from PAN- + *demos* the people]

pandemonium ● (ˌpændɪˈməʊnɪəm) *n* **1** wild confusion; uproar. **2** a place of uproar and chaos. [C17: coined by Milton for the capital of hell in *Paradise Lost,* from PAN- + Gk *daimōn* DEMON]

pander ● (ˈpændə) *vb* **1** (*intr;* foll. by *to*) to give gratification (to weaknesses or desires). **2** (*arch.* when tr) to act as a go-between in a sexual intrigue (for). ◆ *n also* **panderer. 3** a person who caters for vulgar desires. **4** a person who procures a sexual partner for another; pimp. [C16 (n): from *Pandare* Pandarus, in legend, the procurer of Cressida for Troilus]

pandit (ˈpʌndɪt; *spelling pron* ˈpændɪt) *n Hinduism.* a variant of **pundit** (sense 3).

P & L *abbrev. for* profit and loss.

THESAURUS

tangible, concrete, material, real, solid, substantial, touchable

palpitate *vb* **1, 2 = beat**, flutter, pitapat, pitter-patter, pound, pulsate, pulse, quiver, shiver, throb, tremble, vibrate

palsied *adj* **2 = paralysed**, arthritic, atonic (*Pathology*), crippled, debilitated, disabled, helpless, paralytic, rheumatic, sclerotic, shaking, shaky, spastic, trembling

paltry *adj* **1, 2 = insignificant**, base, beggarly, contemptible, crappy (*sl.*), derisory, despicable, inconsiderable, low, meagre, mean, measly, Mickey Mouse (*sl.*), minor, miserable, petty, piddling (*inf.*), pitiful, poor, poxy (*sl.*), puny, slight, small, sorry, trifling, trivial, two-penny-halfpenny (*Brit. inf.*), unimportant, worthless, wretched

Antonyms *adj* consequential, considerable, essential, grand, important, major, mega (*sl.*), significant, valuable

pamper *vb* **1 = spoil**, baby, cater to one's every whim, coddle, cosset, fondle, gratify, humour, indulge, mollycoddle, pander to, pet, wait on (someone) hand and foot

pamphlet *n* **1 = booklet**, brochure, circular, folder, leaflet, tract

pan[1] *n* **1 = pot**, container, saucepan, vessel ◆ *vb* **11 = sift out**, look for, search for, separate, wash **13** *Informal* **= criticize**, blast, censure, flay, hammer (*Brit. inf.*), knock (*inf.*), lambast(e), put down, roast (*inf.*), rubbish (*inf.*), slag (off) (*sl.*), slam (*sl.*), slate (*inf.*), tear into (*inf.*)

pan[2] *vb* **1 = move**, follow, scan, sweep, swing, track, traverse

panacea *n* **= cure-all**, catholicon, elixir, nostrum, sovereign remedy, universal cure

panache *n* **1 = style**, a flourish, brio, dash, élan, flair, flamboyance, spirit, swagger, verve

pandemonium *n* **1 = uproar**, babel, bedlam, chaos, clamour, commotion, confusion, din, hubbub, hue and cry, hullabaloo, racket, ruckus (*inf.*), ruction (*inf.*), rumpus, tumult, turmoil

Antonyms *n* arrangement, calm, hush, order, peace, peacefulness, quietude, repose, stillness, tranquillity

pander *vb* **1** *foll. by* **to = indulge**, cater to, fawn on, gratify, play up to (*inf.*), please, satisfy ◆ *n* **4** *Chiefly archaic* **= pimp**, go-between, mack (*sl.*), ponce (*sl.*), procurer, white-slaver, whoremaster (*arch.*)

P & O *abbrev. for* the Peninsular and Oriental Steam Navigation Company.
p & p *Brit. abbrev. for* postage and packing.
pane (peɪn) *n* **1** a sheet of glass in a window or door. **2** a panel of a window, door, wall, etc. **3** a flat section or face, as of a cut diamond. [C13: from OF *pan* portion, from L *pannus* rag]
panegyric (ˌpænɪˈdʒɪrɪk) *n* a formal public commendation; eulogy. [C17: via F & L from Gk, from *panēguris* public gathering]
▸ **ˌpaneˈgyrical** *adj* ▸ **ˌpaneˈgyrically** *adv* ▸ **ˌpaneˈgyrist** *n* ▸ **panegyrize** *or* **panegyrise** (ˈpænɪdʒɪˌraɪz) *vb*
panel (ˈpænᵊl) *n* **1** a flat section of a wall, door, etc. **2** any distinct section of something formed from a sheet of material, esp. of a car body. **3** a piece of material inserted in a skirt, etc. **4a** a group of persons selected to act as a team in a quiz, to discuss a topic before an audience, etc. **4b** (*as modifier*): *a panel game.* **5** *Law.* **5a** a list of persons summoned for jury service. **5b** the persons on a jury. **6** *Scots Law.* a person accused of a crime. **7a** a thin board used as a surface or backing for an oil painting. **7b** a painting done on such a surface. **8** any picture with a length much greater than its breadth. **9** See **instrument panel. 10** *Brit.* (formerly) **10a** a list of patients insured under the National Health Insurance Scheme. **10b** a list of medical practitioners available for consultation by these patients. ◆ *vb* **panels, panelling, panelled** *or US* **panels, paneling, paneled.** (*tr*) **11** to furnish or decorate with panels. **12** *Law.* **12a** to empanel (a jury). **12b** (in Scotland) to bring (a person) to trial; indict. [C13: from OF: portion, from *pan* piece of cloth, from L *pannus*]
panel beater *n* a person who beats out the bodywork of motor vehicles, etc.
panelling *or US* **paneling** (ˈpænᵊlɪŋ) *n* **1** panels collectively, as on a wall or ceiling. **2** material used for making panels.
panellist *or US* **panelist** (ˈpænᵊlɪst) *n* a member of a panel, esp. on radio or television.
panel pin *n* a slender nail with a narrow head.
panel saw *n* a saw with a long narrow blade for cutting thin wood.
panel van *n Austral. & NZ.* a small van.
Pan-European *adj* of or relating to all European countries or the advocacy of political or economic unity among European countries.
pang ❶ (pæŋ) *n* a sudden brief sharp feeling, as of loneliness, physical pain, or hunger. [C16: var. of earlier *prange,* of Gmc origin]
panga (ˈpæŋgə) *n* a broad heavy knife of E Africa. [from a native E African word]
pangolin (pæŋˈgəʊlɪn) *n* a mammal of tropical Africa, S Asia, and Indonesia, having a scaly body and a long snout for feeding on ants and termites. Also called: **scaly anteater.** [C18: from Malay *peng-gōling,* from *gōling* to roll over; from its ability to roll into a ball]
Pan Gu (ˈpænˈguː) *or* **P'an Ku** *n* 32–92 A.D., Chinese historian and court official, noted for his history of the Han dynasty: died in prison.
panhandle[1] (ˈpænˌhændᵊl) *n* (*sometimes cap.*) (in the US) a narrow strip of land that projects from one state into another.
panhandle[2] (ˈpænˌhændᵊl) *vb* **panhandles, panhandling, panhandled.** *US inf.* to beg from (passers-by). [C19: prob. a back formation from *panhandler* a person who begs with a pan]
▸ **ˈpanˌhandler** *n*
Panhellenic (ˌpænheˈlɛnɪk) *adj* of or relating to all the Greeks or all Greece.
panic ❶ (ˈpænɪk) *n* **1** a sudden overwhelming feeling of terror or anxiety, esp. one affecting a whole group of people. **2** (*modifier*) of or resulting from such terror: *panic measures.* **3** (*modifier*) for use in an emergency: *panic stations; panic button.* ◆ *vb* **panics, panicking, panicked. 4** to feel or cause to feel panic. [C17: from F *panique,* from NL, from Gk *panikos* emanating from *Pan,* Gk god of the fields, considered as the source of irrational fear]
▸ **ˈpanicky** *adj*
panic attack *n* an episode of acute and disabling anxiety associated with such physical symptoms as hyperventilation and sweating.
panic button *n* a button or switch that operates a safety device or alarm, for use in an emergency.
panic disorder *n Psychiatry.* a condition in which a person experiences recurrent panic attacks.
panic grass *n* any of various grasses, such as millet, grown in warm and tropical regions for fodder and grain. [C15 *panic,* from L *pānicum,* prob. a back formation from *pānicula* PANICLE]
panicle (ˈpænɪkᵊl) *n* a compound raceme, as in the oat. [C16: from L *pānicula* tuft, dim. of *panus* thread, ult. from Gk *penos* web]
▸ **ˈpanicled** *adj* ▸ **paniculate** (pəˈnɪkjʊˌleɪt, -lɪt) *adj*
panic-stricken ❶ *or* **panic-struck** *adj* affected by panic.
panjandrum (pænˈdʒændrəm) *n* a pompous self-important official or person of rank. [C18: after a character in a nonsense work (1755) by S. Foote, E playwright]
pan loaf *n Scot.* a loaf of bread with a light crust all the way round. Often shortened to **pan.**
pannage (ˈpænɪdʒ) *n Arch.* **1** the right to pasture pigs in a forest. **2** payment for this. **3** acorns, beech mast, etc., on which pigs feed. [C13: from OF *pasnage,* ult. from L *pastion-, pastiō* feeding, from *pascere* to feed]
pannier (ˈpænɪə) *n* **1** a large basket, esp. one of a pair slung over a beast of burden. **2** one of a pair of bags slung either side of the back wheel of a motorcycle, etc. **3** (esp. in the 18th century) **3a** a hooped framework to distend a woman's skirt. **3b** one of two puffed-out loops of material worn drawn back onto the hips. [C13: from OF *panier,* from L *pānārium* basket for bread, from *pānis* bread]
pannikin (ˈpænɪkɪn) *n Chiefly Brit.* a small metal cup or pan. [C19: from PAN[1] + -KIN]
pannikin boss *n Austral. sl.* a minor overseer.
panoply ❶ (ˈpænəplɪ) *n, pl* **panoplies. 1** a complete or magnificent array. **2** the entire equipment of a warrior. [C17: via F from Gk, from PAN- + *hopla* armour]
▸ **ˈpanoplied** *adj*
panoptic (pænˈɒptɪk) *adj* taking in all parts, aspects, etc., in a single view; all-embracing. [C19: from Gk *panoptēs* seeing everything]
panorama ❶ (ˌpænəˈrɑːmə) *n* **1** an extensive unbroken view in all directions. **2** a wide or comprehensive survey of a subject. **3** a large extended picture of a scene, unrolled before spectators a part at a time so as to appear continuous. **4** another name for **cyclorama.** [C18: from PAN- + Gk *horāma* view]
▸ **panoramic** (ˌpænəˈræmɪk) *adj* ▸ **ˌpanoˈramically** *adv*
pan out ❶ *vb* (*intr, adv*) *Inf.* to work out; result.
panpipes (ˈpænˌpaɪps) *pl n* (*often sing; often cap.*) a number of reeds or whistles of graduated lengths bound together to form a musical wind instrument. Also called: **pipes of Pan, syrinx.**
pansy (ˈpænzɪ) *n, pl* **pansies. 1** a garden plant having flowers with rounded velvety petals, white, yellow, or purple in colour. See also **wild pansy. 2** *Sl.* an effeminate or homosexual man or boy. [C15: from OF *pensée* thought, from *penser* to think, from L *pensāre*]
pant ❶ (pænt) *vb* **1** to breathe with noisy deep gasps, as when out of breath from exertion. **2** to say (something) while breathing thus. **3** (*intr;* often foll. by *for*) to have a frantic desire (for). **4** (*intr*) to throb rapidly. ◆ *n* **5** the act or an instance of panting. **6** a short deep gasping noise. [C15: from OF *pantaisier,* from Gk *phantasioun* to have visions, from *phantasia* FANTASY]
pantalets *or* **pantalettes** (ˌpæntəˈlɛts) *pl n* **1** long drawers extending below the skirts: worn during the 19th century. **2** ruffles for the ends of such drawers. [C19: dim. of PANTALOONS]
pantaloon (ˌpæntəˈluːn) *n* **1** (in pantomime) an absurd old man, the butt of the clown's tricks. **2** (*usually cap.*) (in commedia dell'arte) a lecherous old merchant dressed in pantaloons. [C16: from F *Pantalon,* from It. *Pantalone,* prob. from *San Pantaleone,* a fourth-century Venetian saint]
pantaloons (ˌpæntəˈluːnz) *pl n* **1** *History.* **1a** men's tight-fitting trousers fastened below the calf or under the shoe. **1b** children's trousers resembling these. **2** *Inf.* any trousers, esp. baggy ones.
pantechnicon (pænˈtɛknɪkən) *n Brit.* **1** a large van, esp. one used for furniture removals. **2** a warehouse where furniture is stored. [C19: from PAN- + Gk *tekhnikon* relating to the arts, from *tekhnē* art; orig. a London bazaar, later used as a furniture warehouse]
pantheism (ˈpænθɪˌɪzəm) *n* **1** the doctrine that regards God as identical with the material universe or the forces of nature. **2** readiness to worship all gods.
▸ **ˈpantheist** *n* ▸ **ˌpantheˈistic** *or* **ˌpantheˈistical** *adj* ▸ **ˌpantheˈistically** *adv*
pantheon (ˈpænθɪən) *n* **1** (esp. in ancient Greece or Rome) a temple to all the gods. **2** all the gods of a religion. **3** a building commemorating a nation's dead heroes. [C14: via L from Gk *Pantheion,* from PAN- + *-theios* divine, from *theos* god]
panther (ˈpænθə) *n, pl* **panthers** *or* **panther. 1** another name for **leopard** (sense 1), esp. the black variety (**black panther**). **2** *US & Canad.* any of various related animals, esp. the puma. [C14: from OF *pantère,* from L *panthēra,* from Gk *panthēr*]
panties (ˈpæntɪz) *pl n* a pair of women's or children's underpants.
pantihose (ˈpæntɪˌhəʊz) *pl n* See **panty hose.**
pantile (ˈpænˌtaɪl) *n* a roofing tile, with an S-shaped cross section, so

THESAURUS

pang *n* = **twinge,** ache, agony, anguish, discomfort, distress, gripe, pain, prick, spasm, stab, sting, stitch, throe (*rare*), wrench
panic *n* **1** = **fear,** agitation, alarm, consternation, dismay, fright, horror, hysteria, scare, terror ◆ *vb* **4** = **go to pieces,** become hysterical, be terror-stricken, have kittens (*inf.*), lose one's bottle (*Brit. sl.*), lose one's nerve, overreact **4** = **alarm,** put the wind up (someone) (*inf.*), scare, startle, terrify, unnerve
panicky *adj* **1** = **frightened,** afraid, agitated, distressed, fearful, frantic, frenzied, hysterical, in a flap (*inf.*), in a tizzy (*inf.*), jittery (*inf.*), nervous, windy (*sl.*), worked up, worried
Antonyms *adj* calm, collected, composed, confident, cool, imperturbable, self-controlled, together (*sl.*), unexcitable, unfazed (*inf.*), unflappable, unruffled
panic-stricken *adj* = **frightened,** aghast, agitated, alarmed, appalled, fearful, frenzied, frightened to death, horrified, horror-stricken, hysterical, in a cold sweat (*inf.*), panicky, petrified, scared, scared stiff, startled, terrified, terror-stricken, unnerved
panoply *n* **1** = **array,** attire, dress, garb, get-up (*inf.*), insignia, raiment (*arch. or poetic*), regalia, show, trappings, turnout
panorama *n* **1** = **view,** bird's-eye view, prospect, scenery, scenic view, vista **2** = **survey,** overall picture, overview, perspective
panoramic *adj* **1, 2** = **wide,** all-embracing, bird's-eye, comprehensive, extensive, far-reaching, general, inclusive, overall, scenic, sweeping
pan out *vb Informal* = **work out,** come out, come to pass (*arch.*), culminate, eventuate, happen, result, turn out
pant *vb* **1** = **puff,** blow, breathe, gasp, heave, huff, palpitate, throb, wheeze **3** *with* **for** = **long,** ache, covet, crave, desire, eat one's heart out over, hanker after, hunger, pine, set one's heart

that the downward curve of one tile overlaps the upward curve of the next. [C17: from PAN[1] + TILE]

pantisocracy (ˌpæntɪˈsɒkrəsɪ) *n, pl* **pantisocracies.** a community, social group, etc., in which all have rule and everyone is equal. [C18: (coined by Robert Southey, E poet) from Gk, from PANTO- + *isos* equal + -CRACY]

panto (ˈpæntəʊ) *n, pl* **pantos.** *Brit. inf.* short for **pantomime** (sense 1).

panto- *or before a vowel* **pant-** *combining form.* all: *pantisocracy; pantograph; pantomime.* [from Gk *pant-, pas*]

pantograph (ˈpæntəˌgrɑːf) *n* **1** an instrument consisting of pivoted levers for copying drawings, maps, etc., to any scale. **2** a sliding type of current collector, esp. a diamond-shaped frame mounted on a train roof in contact with an overhead wire. **3** a device used to suspend a studio lamp so that its height can be adjusted.
▸**pantographic** (ˌpæntəˈgræfɪk) *adj*

pantomime (ˈpæntəˌmaɪm) *n* **1** (in Britain) a kind of play performed at Christmas time characterized by farce, music, lavish sets, stock roles, and topical jokes. **2** a theatrical entertainment in which words are replaced by gestures and bodily actions. **3** action without words as a means of expression. **4** *Inf., chiefly Brit.* a confused or farcical situation. ◆ *vb* **pantomimes, pantomiming, pantomimed. 5** another word for **mime.** [C17: via L from Gk *pantomīmos*]
▸**pantomimic** (ˌpæntəˈmɪmɪk) *adj* ▸**pantomimist** (ˈpæntəˌmaɪmɪst) *n*

pantothenic acid (ˌpæntəˈθenɪk) *n* an oily acid that is a vitamin of the B complex: occurs widely in animal and vegetable foods. [C20: from Gk *pantothen* from every side]

pantry (ˈpæntrɪ) *n, pl* **pantries.** a small room in which provisions, cooking utensils, etc., are kept; larder. [C13: via Anglo-Norman from OF *paneterie* store for bread, ult. from L *pānis* bread]

pants ➊ (pænts) *pl n* **1** *Brit.* an undergarment covering the body from the waist to the thighs or knees. **2** the usual US and Canad. name for **trousers. 3 bore, scare,** etc., **the pants off.** *Inf.* to bore, scare, etc., extremely. [C19: shortened from *pantaloons*]

panty girdle (ˈpæntɪ) *n* a foundation garment with a crotch, often of lighter material than a girdle.

panty hose *pl n* the US name for **tights** (sense 1). Also (Canad. and NZ) **pantyhose,** (Austral.) **pantihose.**

panzer (ˈpænzə; *German* ˈpantsər) *n* **1** (*modifier*) of or relating to the fast mechanized armoured units employed by the German army in World War II: *a panzer attack.* **2** a vehicle belonging to a panzer unit, esp. a tank. **3** (*pl*) armoured troops. [C20: from G, from MHG, from OF *panciere* coat of mail, from L *pantex* PAUNCH]

pap[1] ➊ (pæp) *n* **1** any soft or semiliquid food, esp. for babies or invalids; mash. **2** worthless or oversimplified ideas, etc.; drivel. **3** *S. African.* maize porridge. [C15: from MLow G *pappe,* via Med. L from L *pappāre* to eat]

pap[2] (pæp) *n* **1** *Arch. or Scot. & N English dialect.* a nipple or teat. **2** something resembling a breast, such as one of a pair of rounded hilltops. [C12: from ON, imit. of a sucking sound]

papa (pəˈpɑː) *n Old-fashioned.* an informal word for **father.** [C17: from F, a children's word for father]

papacy (ˈpeɪpəsɪ) *n, pl* **papacies. 1** the office or term of office of a pope. **2** the system of government in the Roman Catholic Church that has the pope as its head. [C14: from Med. L *pāpātia,* from *pāpa* POPE]

papain (pəˈpeɪɪn, -ˈpaɪɪn) *n* an enzyme occurring in the unripe fruit of the papaya tree: used as a meat tenderizer and in medicine as an aid to protein digestion. [C19: from PAPAYA]

papal (ˈpeɪpᵊl) *adj* of or relating to the pope or the papacy.
▸ˈ**papally** *adv*

paparazzo (ˌpæpəˈrætsəʊ) *n, pl* **paparazzi** (-ˈrætsiː). a freelance photographer who specializes in candid camera shots of famous people. [C20: from It.]

papaver (pæˈpɑːvə) *n* any of a genus of hardy annual or perennial plants with showy flowers; poppy. [L: poppy]

papaveraceous (pəˌpeɪvəˈreɪʃəs) *adj* of or relating to a family of plants having large showy flowers and a cylindrical seed capsule with pores beneath the lid: includes the poppies and greater celandine. [C19: from NL, from L *papāver* poppy]

papaverine (pəˈpævəˌriːn, -rɪn) *n* a white crystalline alkaloid found in opium and used to treat coronary spasms and certain types of colic. [C19: from L *papāver* poppy]

papaw (pəˈpɔː) *or* **pawpaw** *n* **1** Also called: **custard apple. 1a** a bush or small tree of Central North America, having small fleshy edible fruit. **1b** the fruit of this tree. **2** another name for **papaya.** [C16: from Sp. PAPAYA]

papaya (pəˈpaɪə) *n* **1** a Caribbean evergreen tree with a crown of large dissected leaves and large green hanging fruit. **2** the fruit of this tree, having a yellow sweet edible pulp and small black seeds. ◆ Also called: **papaw, pawpaw.** [C15 *papaye,* from Sp. *papaya,* of Amerind origin]

paper ➊ (ˈpeɪpə) *n* **1** a substance made from cellulose fibres derived from rags, wood, etc., and formed into flat thin sheets suitable for writing on, decorating walls, wrapping, etc. **2** a single piece of such material, esp. if written or printed on. **3** (*usually pl*) documents for establishing the identity of the bearer. **4** (*pl*) Also called: **ship's papers.** official documents relating to a ship. **5** (*pl*) collected diaries, letters, etc. **6** See **newspaper, wallpaper. 7** *Government.* See **white paper, green paper. 8** a lecture or treatise on a specific subject. **9** a short essay. **10a** a set of examination questions. **10b** the student's answers. **11** *Commerce.* See **commercial paper. 12** *Theatre sl.* a free ticket. **13 on paper.** in theory, as opposed to fact. ◆ *adj* **14** made of paper: *paper cups do not last long.* **15** thin like paper: *paper walls.* **16** (*prenominal*) existing only as recorded on paper but not yet in practice: *paper expenditure.* **17** taking place in writing: *paper battles.* ◆ *vb* **18** to cover (walls) with wallpaper. **19** (*tr*) to cover or furnish with paper. **20** (*tr*) *Theatre sl.* to fill (a performance, etc.) by giving away free tickets (esp. in **paper the house**). ◆ See also **paper over.** [C14: from L PAPYRUS]
▸ˈ**paperer** *n* ▸ˈ**papery** *adj*

paperback (ˈpeɪpəˌbæk) *n* **1** a book or edition with covers made of flexible card. ◆ *adj* **2** of or denoting a paperback or publication of paperbacks. ◆ *vb* **3** (*tr*) to publish a paperback edition of a book.

paperbark (ˈpeɪpəˌbɑːk) *n* any of several Australian trees of swampy regions, having papery bark that can be peeled off in thin layers.

paperboy (ˈpeɪpəˌbɔɪ) *n* a boy employed to deliver newspapers, etc.
▸ˈ**paperˌgirl** *fem n*

paper chase *n* a former type of cross-country run in which a runner laid a trail of paper for others to follow.

paperclip (ˈpeɪpəˌklɪp) *n* a clip for holding sheets of paper together, esp. one of bent wire.

paper-cutter *n* a machine for cutting paper, usually a blade mounted over a table.

paperhanger (ˈpeɪpəˌhæŋə) *n* a person who hangs wallpaper as an occupation.

paperknife (ˈpeɪpəˌnaɪf) *n, pl* **paperknives.** a knife with a comparatively blunt blade for opening sealed envelopes, etc.

paper money *n* paper currency issued by the government or the central bank as legal tender and which circulates as a substitute for specie.

paper mulberry *n* a small E Asian tree, the inner bark of which was formerly used for making paper in Japan. See also **tapa.**

paper nautilus *n* a cephalopod mollusc of warm and tropical seas, having a papery external spiral shell. Also called: **argonaut.**

paper over *vb* (*tr, adv*) to conceal (something controversial or unpleasant) (esp. in **paper over the cracks**).

paper tape *n* a strip of paper for recording information in the form of rows of either six or eight holes, some or all of which are punched to produce a combination used as a discrete code symbol, formerly used in computers, telex machines, etc. US equivalent: **perforated tape.**

paper tiger *n* a nation, institution, etc., that appears powerful but is in fact weak or insignificant. [C20: translation of a Chinese phrase first applied to the US]

paperweight (ˈpeɪpəˌweɪt) *n* a small heavy object to prevent loose papers from scattering.

paperwork (ˈpeɪpəˌwɜːk) *n* clerical work, such as the writing of reports or letters.

Paphian (ˈpeɪfɪən) *adj* **1** of or relating to Paphos, a village in SW Cyprus. **2** of or relating to Aphrodite, who was worshipped at Paphos. **3** *Literary.* of sexual love.

papier-mâché (ˌpæpjeɪˈmæʃeɪ) *n* **1** a hard strong substance made of paper pulp or layers of paper mixed with paste, size, etc., and moulded when moist. ◆ *adj* **2** made of papier-mâché. [C18: from F, lit.: chewed paper]

papilionaceous (pəˌpɪlɪəˈneɪʃəs) *adj* of, relating to, or belonging to a family of leguminous plants having irregular flowers: includes peas, beans, clover, alfalfa, gorse, and broom. [C17: from NL, from L *pāpiliō* butterfly]

papilla (pəˈpɪlə) *n, pl* **papillae** (-liː). **1** the small projection of tissue at the base of a hair, tooth, or feather. **2** any similar protuberance. [C18: from L: nipple]
▸**paˈpillary** *or* ˈ**papillate** *adj*

papilloma (ˌpæpɪˈləʊmə) *n, pl* **papillomata** (-mətə) *or* **papillomas.** *Pathol.* a benign tumour forming a rounded mass. [C19: from PAPILLA + -OMA]

papillon (ˈpæpɪˌlɒn) *n* a breed of toy dog with large ears. [F: butterfly, from L *pāpiliō*]

papillote (ˈpæpɪˌləʊt) *n* **1** a paper frill around cutlets, etc. **2 en papillote** (ɑ̃ papijɔt). (of food) cooked in oiled greaseproof paper or foil. [C18: from F PAPILLON]

papist (ˈpeɪpɪst) *n, adj* (*often cap.*) *Usually disparaging.* another term for **Roman Catholic.** [C16: from F *papiste,* from Church L *pāpa* POPE]
▸**paˈpistical** *or* **paˈpistic** *adj* ▸ˈ**papistry** *n*

papoose (pəˈpuːs) *n* **1** an American Indian baby. **2** a pouchlike bag

THESAURUS

on, sigh, suspire (*arch. or poetic*), thirst, want, yearn ◆ *n* **6** = **puff,** gasp, huff, wheeze

pants *pl n* **1** *Brit.* = **underpants,** boxer shorts, briefs, drawers, knickers, panties, Y-fronts (*Trademark*) **2** *U.S. & Canad.* = **trousers,** slacks

pap[1] *n* **1** = **mush,** baby food, mash, pulp **2** = **rubbish,** drivel, trash, trivia

paper *n* **3** *usually plural* = **documents,** certificates, deeds, instruments, records **5** *usually plural* = **letters,** archive, diaries, documents, dossier, file, records **6** = **newspaper,** blat, daily, gazette, journal, news, organ, rag (*inf.*) **8** = **essay,** analysis, article, assignment, composition, critique, dissertation, examination, monograph, report, script, study, thesis, treatise **13 on paper** = **in theory,** ideally, in the abstract, theoretically ◆ *adj* **14, 15** = **disposable,** cardboard, flimsy, insubstantial, paper-thin, papery, thin ◆ *vb* **18, 19** = **wallpaper,** cover with paper, hang, line, paste up

papery *adj* **15** = **thin,** flimsy, fragile, frail, insubstantial, light, lightweight, paperlike, paper-thin, wafer-thin used for carrying a baby, worn on the back. [C17: from Algonquian *papoos*]

pappus (ˈpæpəs) *n, pl* **pappi** (ˈpæpaɪ). a ring of fine feathery hairs surrounding the fruit in composite plants, such as the thistle. [C18: via NL from Gk *pappos* old man, old man's beard, hence: pappus, down]
▸ **ˈpappose** *or* **ˈpappous** *adj*

paprika (ˈpæprɪkə, pæˈpriː-) *n* **1** a mild powdered seasoning made from a sweet variety of red pepper. **2** the fruit or plant from which this seasoning is obtained. [C19: via Hungarian from Serbian, from *papar* PEPPER]

Pap test *or* **smear** (pæp) *n Med.* **1** another name for **cervical smear. 2** a similar test for precancerous cells in organs other than the cervix. ◆ Also called: **Papanicolaou smear.** [C20: after George *Papanicolaou* (1883–1962), US anatomist, who devised it]

papule (ˈpæpjuːl) *or* **papula** (ˈpæpjulə) *n, pl* **papules** *or* **papulae** (-juˌliː). *Pathol.* a small solid usually round elevation of the skin. [C19: from L *papula* pustule]
▸ **ˈpapular** *adj*

papyrology (ˌpæpɪˈrɒlədʒɪ) *n* the study of ancient papyri.
▸ **ˌpapyˈrologist** *n*

papyrus (pəˈpaɪrəs) *n, pl* **papyri** (-raɪ) *or* **papyruses. 1** a tall aquatic plant of S Europe and N and central Africa. **2** a kind of paper made from the stem pith of this plant, used by the ancient Egyptians, Greeks, and Romans. **3** an ancient document written on this paper. [C14: via L from Gk *papūros* reed used in making paper]

par ❶ (pɑː) *n* **1** an accepted standard, such as an average (esp. in **up to par**). **2** a state of equality (esp. in **on a par with**). **3** *Finance.* the established value of the unit of one national currency in terms of the unit of another. **4** *Commerce.* **4a** See **par value. 4b** equality between the current market value of a share, bond, etc., and its face value, indicated by **at par; above** (*or* **below**) **par** indicates that the market value is above (or below) face value. **5** *Golf.* a standard score for a hole or course that a good player should make: *par for the course was 72.* ◆ *adj* **6** average or normal. **7** (*usually prenominal*) of or relating to par: *par value.* [C17: from L *pār* equal]

par. *abbrev. for:* **1** paragraph. **2** parallel. **3** parenthesis. **4** parish.

Par. *abbrev. for* Paraguay.

para (ˈpærə) *n Inf.* **1a** a soldier in an airborne unit. **1b** an airborne unit. **2** a paragraph.

para-[1] *or before a vowel* **par-** *prefix* **1** beside; near: *parameter.* **2** beyond: *parapsychology.* **3** resembling: *paratyphoid fever.* **4** defective; abnormal: *paranoia.* **5** (*usually in italics*) denoting that an organic compound contains a benzene ring with substituents attached to atoms that are directly opposite (the 1,4- positions): *paracresol.* **6** denoting an isomer, polymer, or compound related to a specified compound: *paraldehyde.* **7** denoting the form of a diatomic substance in which the spins of the two constituent atoms are antiparallel: *parahydrogen.* [from Gk *para* (prep) alongside, beyond]

para-[2] *combining form.* indicating an object that acts as a protection against something: *parachute; parasol.* [via F from It. *para-*, from *parare* to defend, ult. from L *parāre* to prepare]

para-aminobenzoic acid (əˌmaɪnəubenˈzəuɪk, -ˌmiː-) *n Biochem.* an acid present in yeast and liver: used in the manufacture of dyes and pharmaceuticals.

parabasis (pəˈræbəsɪs) *n, pl* **parabases** (-ˌsiːz). (in classical Greek comedy) an address by the chorus. [C19: from Gk, from *parabanein* to step forward]

parabiosis (ˌpærəbaɪˈəusɪs) *n* **1** the natural union of two individuals, such as Siamese twins. **2** a similar union induced for experimental or therapeutic purposes. [C20: from PARA-[1] + Gk *biōsis* manner of life, from *bios* life]
▸ **parabiotic** (ˌpærəbaɪˈɒtɪk) *adj*

parable ❶ (ˈpærəbᵊl) *n* **1** a short story that uses familiar events to illustrate a religious or ethical point. **2** any of the stories of this kind told by Jesus Christ. [C14: from OF *parabole*, from L *parabola* comparison, from Gk *parabolē* analogy, from *paraballein* to throw alongside]

parabola (pəˈræbələ) *n* a conic section formed by the intersection of a cone by a plane parallel to its side. [C16: via NL from Gk *parabolē* a setting alongside; see PARABLE]

parabolic[1] (ˌpærəˈbɒlɪk) *adj* **1** of, relating to, or shaped like a parabola. **2** shaped like a paraboloid: *a parabolic mirror.*

parabolic[2] ❶ (ˌpærəˈbɒlɪk) *or* **parabolical** *adj* of or like a parable.
▸ **ˌparaˈbolically** *adv*

parabolic aerial *n* a formal name for **dish aerial.**

paraboloid (pəˈræbəˌlɔɪd) *n* a geometric surface whose sections parallel to two coordinate planes are parabolic and whose sections parallel to the third plane are either elliptical or hyperbolic.
▸ **paˌraboˈloidal** *adj*

paracetamol (ˌpærəˈsiːtəˌmɒl, -ˈsetə-) *n* a mild analgesic drug. [C20: from *para-acetamidophenol*]

parachronism (pəˈrækrəˌnɪzəm) *n* an error in dating, esp. by giving too late a date. [C17: from PARA-[1] + *-chronism*, as in ANACHRONISM]

parachute (ˈpærəˌʃuːt) *n* **1** a device used to retard the fall of a person or package from an aircraft, consisting of a large fabric canopy connected to a harness. ◆ *vb* **parachutes, parachuting, parachuted. 2** (of troops, supplies, etc.) to land or cause to land by parachute from an aircraft. [C18: from F, from PARA-[2] + *chute* fall]
▸ **ˈparaˌchutist** *n*

Paraclete (ˈpærəˌkliːt) *n Christianity.* the Holy Ghost as comforter or advocate. [C15: via OF from Church L *Paraclētus*, from LGk *Paraklētos* advocate, from Gk *parakalein* to summon help]

parade ❶ (pəˈreɪd) *n* **1** an ordered, esp. ceremonial, march or procession, as of troops being reviewed. **2** Also called: **parade ground.** a place where military formations regularly assemble. **3** a visible show or display: *to make a parade of one's grief.* **4** a public promenade or street of shops. **5** a successive display of things or people. **6 on parade. 6a** on display. **6b** showing oneself off. ◆ *vb* **parades, parading, paraded. 7** (when *intr*, often foll. by *through* or *along*) to walk or march, esp. in a procession. **8** (*tr*) to exhibit or flaunt: *he was parading his medals.* **9** (*tr*) to cause to assemble in formation, as for a military parade. **10** (*intr*) to walk about in a public place. [C17: from F: a making ready, a boasting display]
▸ **paˈrader** *n*

paradiddle (ˈpærəˌdɪdᵊl) *n* a group of four drumbeats played with alternate sticks in the pattern right-left-right-right or left-right-left-left. [C20: imit.]

paradigm ❶ (ˈpærəˌdaɪm) *n* **1** the set of all the inflected forms of a word. **2** a pattern or model. **3** (in the philosophy of science) a general conception of the nature of scientific endeavour within which a given enquiry is undertaken. [C15: via F & L from Gk *paradeigma* pattern, from *paradeiknunai* to compare]
▸ **paradigmatic** (ˌpærədɪgˈmætɪk) *adj*

paradisal ❶ (ˌpærəˈdaɪsᵊl), **paradisiacal** (ˌpærədɪˈsaɪəkᵊl), *or* **paradisiac** (ˌpærəˈdɪsɪˌæk) *adj* of, relating to, or resembling paradise.

paradise ❶ (ˈpærəˌdaɪs) *n* **1** heaven as the ultimate abode or state of the righteous. **2** *Islam.* the sensual garden of delights that the Koran promises the faithful after death. **3** Also called: **limbo.** (according to some theologians) the intermediate abode or state of the just prior to the Resurrection of Jesus. **4** the Garden of Eden. **5** any place or condition that fulfils all one's desires or aspirations. **6** a park in which foreign animals are kept. [OE, from Church L *paradīsus*, from Gk *paradeisos* garden, of Persian origin]

paradise duck *n* a New Zealand duck with bright plumage.

paradox ❶ (ˈpærəˌdɒks) *n* **1** a seemingly absurd or self-contradictory statement that is or may be true: *religious truths are often expressed in paradox.* **2** a self-contradictory proposition, such as *I always tell lies.* **3** a person or thing exhibiting apparently contradictory characteristics. **4** an opinion that conflicts with common belief. [C16: from LL *paradoxum*, from Gk *paradoxos* opposed to existing notions]
▸ **ˌparaˈdoxical** *adj* ▸ **ˌparaˈdoxically** *adv*

paradoxical sleep *n Physiol.* sleep that appears deep but is characterized by a brain wave pattern similar to that of wakefulness, rapid eye movements, and heavier breathing.

paraffin (ˈpærəfɪn) *n* **1** Also called: **paraffin oil,** (esp. US, Canad., Austral., & NZ) **kerosene.** a liquid mixture consisting mainly of alkane hydrocarbons, used as an aircraft fuel, in domestic heaters, and as a solvent. **2** another name for **alkane. 3** See **paraffin wax. 4** See **liquid paraffin.** ◆ *vb* (*tr*) **5** to treat with paraffin. [C19: from G, from L *parum* too little + *affinis* adjacent; so called from its chemical inertia]

paraffin wax *n* a white insoluble odourless waxlike solid consisting mainly of alkane hydrocarbons, used in candles, waterproof paper, and as a sealant. Also called: **paraffin.**

paragliding (ˈpærəˌglaɪdɪŋ) *n* the sport of cross-country gliding using a specially designed parachute shaped like flexible wings. The parachutist glides from an aeroplane to a predetermined landing area.

paragon ❶ (ˈpærəgən) *n* a model of excellence; pattern: *a paragon of virtue.* [C16: via F from OIt. *paragone* comparison, from Med. Gk *parakonē*, from PARA-[1] + *akonē* whetstone]

paragraph ❶ (ˈpærəˌgrɑːf) *n* **1** (in a piece of writing) one of a series of subsections each usually devoted to one idea and each marked by the

THESAURUS

par *n* **1 = average,** level, mean, median, norm, standard, usual **2 = equivalence,** balance, equal footing, equality, equilibrium, parity

parable *n* **1 = lesson,** allegory, exemplum, fable, moral tale, story

parabolic[2] *adj* **= allegorical,** figurative, metaphoric, symbolic

parade *n* **1 = procession,** array, cavalcade, ceremony, column, march, pageant, review, spectacle, train **3 = show,** array, display, exhibition, flaunting, ostentation, pomp, spectacle, vaunting ◆ *vb* **7 = march,** defile, process **8 = flaunt,** air, brandish, display, exhibit, make a show of, show, show off (*inf.*), strut, swagger, vaunt

paradigm *n* **2 = model,** archetype, example, exemplar, ideal, norm, original, pattern, prototype

paradisal *adj* **= heavenly,** blessed, blissful, celestial, divine, Elysian, glorious, golden, out of this world (*inf.*), utopian

paradise *n* **1 = heaven,** City of God, divine abode, Elysian fields, garden of delights, Happy Valley (*Islam*), heavenly kingdom, Olympus (*poetic*), Promised Land, Zion (*Christianity*) **4 = Garden of Eden,** Eden **5 = bliss,** delight, felicity, heaven, seventh heaven, utopia

paradox *n* **1, 2 = contradiction,** absurdity, ambiguity, anomaly, enigma, inconsistency, mystery, oddity, puzzle

paradoxical *adj* **1, 2 = contradictory,** absurd, ambiguous, baffling, confounding, enigmatic, equivocal, illogical, impossible, improbable, inconsistent, oracular, puzzling, riddling

paragon *n* **= model,** apotheosis, archetype, criterion, cynosure, epitome, exemplar, ideal, jewel, masterpiece, nonesuch (*arch.*), nonpareil, norm, paradigm, pattern, prototype, quintessence, standard

paragraph *n* **1 = section,** clause, item, notice, part, passage, portion, subdivision

beginning of a new line, indention, etc. **2** *Printing.* the character ¶, used to indicate the beginning of a new paragraph. **3** a short article, etc., in a newspaper. ◆ *vb (tr)* **4** to form into paragraphs. **5** to express or report in a paragraph. [C16: from Med. L *paragraphus,* from Gk *paragraphos* line drawing attention to part of a text, from *paragraphein* to write beside]
▸**paragraphic** (ˌpærəˈgræfɪk) *adj*

paragraphia (ˌpærəˈgrɑːfɪə) *n Psychiatry.* the habitual writing of a different word or letter from the one intended, often the result of a mental disorder. [C20: from NL; see PARA-[1], -GRAPH]

Paraguayan (ˈpærəˌgwaɪən) *adj* **1** of or relating to Paraguay, a republic in South America. ◆ *n* **2** a native or inhabitant of Paraguay or a descendant of one.

Paraguay tea (ˈpærəˌgwaɪ) *n* another name for **maté**.

parahydrogen (ˌpærəˈhaɪdrədʒən) *n Chem.* the form of molecular hydrogen in which the nuclei of the two atoms in each molecule spin in opposite directions.

parakeet *or* **parrakeet** (ˈpærəˌkiːt) *n* any of numerous small long-tailed parrots. [C16: from Sp. *periquito* & OF *paroquet* parrot, from ?]

paraldehyde (pəˈrældɪˌhaɪd) *n* a colourless liquid that is a cyclic trimer of acetaldehyde: used as a hypnotic.

paralipsis (ˌpærəˈlɪpsɪs) *or* **paraleipsis** (ˌpærəˈlaɪpsɪs) *n, pl* **paralipses** *or* **paraleipses** (-siːz). a rhetorical device in which an idea is emphasized by the pretence that it is too obvious to discuss, as in *there are many practical drawbacks, not to mention the cost.* [C16: via LL from Gk: neglect, from *paraleipein* to leave aside]

parallax (ˈpærəˌlæks) *n* **1** an apparent change in the position of an object resulting from a change in position of the observer. **2** *Astron.* the angle subtended at a celestial body, esp. a star, by the radius of the earth's orbit. [C17: via F from NL *parallaxis,* from Gk: change, from *parallassein* to change]
▸**parallactic** (ˌpærəˈlæktɪk) *adj*

parallel ❶ (ˈpærəˌlɛl) *adj* (when *postpositive,* usually foll. by *to*) **1** separated by an equal distance at every point; never touching or intersecting: *parallel walls.* **2** corresponding; similar: *parallel situations.* **3** *Music.* Also: **consecutive.** (of two or more parts or melodies) moving in similar motion but keeping the same interval apart throughout: *parallel fifths.* **4** *Grammar.* denoting syntactic constructions in which the constituents of one construction correspond to those of the other. **5** *Computing.* operating on several items of information, instructions, etc., simultaneously. ◆ *n* **6** *Maths.* one of a set of parallel lines, planes, etc. **7** an exact likeness. **8** a comparison. **9** Also called: **parallel of latitude.** any of the imaginary lines around the earth parallel to the equator, designated by degrees of latitude. **10** *Electronics.* **10a** an arrangement of two or more electrical components connected between two points in a circuit so that the same voltage is applied to each (esp. in **in parallel**). Cf. **series** (sense 6). **10b** *(as modifier): a parallel circuit.* **11** *Printing.* the character (‖) used as a reference mark. ◆ *vb* **parallels, paralleling, paralleled.** *(tr)* **12** to make parallel. **13** to supply a parallel to. **14** to be a parallel to or correspond with: *your experience parallels mine.* [C16: via F & L from Gk *parallēlos* alongside one another, from PARA-[1] + *allēlos* one another]

parallel bars *pl n Gymnastics.* a pair of wooden bars on uprights used for various exercises.

parallelepiped (ˌpærəˌlɛlɪˈpaɪpɛd) *or* **parallelepipedon** (ˌpærəˌlɛlɪˈpaɪpɪdən) *n* a geometric solid whose six faces are parallelograms. [C16: from Gk, from *parallēlos* PARALLEL + *epipedon* plane surface, from EPI- + *pedon* ground]

paralleling (ˈpærəˌlɛlɪŋ) *n* a form of trading in which companies buy highly priced goods in a market in which the prices are low in order to be able to sell them in a market in which the prices are higher.

parallelism (ˈpærəˌlɛlɪzəm) *n* **1** the state of being parallel. **2** *Grammar.* the repetition of a syntactic construction in successive sentences for rhetorical effect. **3** *Philosophy.* the doctrine that mental and physical processes are regularly correlated but are not casually connected, so that, for example, pain always accompanies, but is not caused by, a pinprick.

parallelogram (ˌpærəˈlɛləˌgræm) *n* a quadrilateral whose opposite sides are parallel and equal in length. [C16: via F from LL, from Gk *parallēlogrammon,* from *parallēlos* PARALLEL + *grammē* line]

parallelogram rule *n Maths, physics.* a rule for finding the resultant of two vectors by constructing a parallelogram with two adjacent sides representing the magnitudes and directions of the vectors, the diagonal through the point of intersection of the vectors representing their resultant.

parallel processing *n* the performance by a computer system of two or more simultaneous operations.

parallel ruler *n Engineering.* a drawing instrument in which two parallel edges are connected so that they remain parallel, although the distance between them can be varied.

paralogism (pəˈræləˌdʒɪzəm) *n* **1** *Logic, psychol.* an argument that is unintentionally invalid. Cf. **sophism. 2** any invalid argument or conclusion. [C16: via LL from Gk *paralogismos,* from *paralogizesthai* to argue fallaciously, from PARA-[1] + *-logizesthai,* ult. from *logos* word]
▸**paˈralogist** *n*

Paralympian (ˌpærəˈlɪmpɪən) *n* a competitor in the Paralympics.

Paralympics (ˌpærəˈlɪmpɪks) *n* **the.** *(functioning as sing or pl)* a sporting event, modelled on the Olympic Games, held solely for disabled competitors. Also called: **the Parallel Olympics.** [C20: from PARALLEL + OLYMPICS]

paralyse ❶ *or US* **paralyze** (ˈpærəˌlaɪz) *vb* **paralyses, paralysing, paralysed** *or US* **paralyzes, paralyzing, paralyzed.** *(tr)* **1** *Pathol.* to affect with paralysis. **2** *Med.* to render (a part of the body) insensitive to pain, touch, etc. **3** to make immobile; transfix. [C19: from F *paralyser,* from *paralysie* PARALYSIS]
▸ˌ**paralyˈsation** *or US* ˌ**paralyˈzation** *n* ▸ˈ**paraˌlyser** *or US* ˈ**paraˌlyzer** *n*

paralysis ❶ (pəˈrælɪsɪs) *n, pl* **paralyses** (-ˌsiːz). **1** *Pathol.* **1a** impairment or loss of voluntary muscle function or of sensation (**sensory paralysis**) in a part or area of the body. **1b** a disease characterized by such impairment or loss; palsy. **2** cessation or impairment of activity: *paralysis of industry by strikes.* [C16: via L from Gk *paralusis;* see PARA-[1], -LYSIS]

paralytic ❶ (ˌpærəˈlɪtɪk) *adj* **1** of, relating to, or of the nature of paralysis. **2** afflicted with or subject to paralysis. **3** *Brit. inf.* very drunk. ◆ *n* **4** a person afflicted with paralysis.

paramagnetism (ˌpærəˈmægnɪˌtɪzəm) *n Physics.* a weakly magnetic condition of substances with a relative permeability just greater than unity: used in some special low temperature techniques.
▸**paramagnetic** (ˌpærəmægˈnɛtɪk) *adj*

paramatta *or* **parramatta** (ˌpærəˈmætə) *n* a lightweight twill-weave dress fabric of wool with silk or cotton, now used esp. for rubber-proofed garments. [C19: after *Parramatta,* New South Wales, Australia, where orig. produced]

paramecium (ˌpærəˈmiːsɪəm) *n, pl* **paramecia** (-sɪə). any of a genus of freshwater protozoa having an oval body covered with cilia and a ventral groove for feeding. [C18: NL, from Gk *paramēkēs* elongated, from PARA-[1] + *mēkos* length]

paramedic (ˌpærəˈmɛdɪk) *n* **1** a person, such as a laboratory technician, who supplements the work of the medical profession. **2** a member of an ambulance crew trained in a number of life-saving skills, including infusion and cardiac care.
▸ˌ**paraˈmedical** *adj*

parameter ❶ (pəˈræmɪtə) *n* **1** an arbitrary constant that determines the specific form of a mathematical expression, such as *a* and *b* in $y = ax^2 + b$. **2** a characteristic constant of a statistical population, such as its variance or mean. **3** *Inf.* any constant or limiting factor: *a designer must work within the parameters of budget and practicality.* [C17: from NL; see PARA-[1], -METER]
▸**parametric** (ˌpærəˈmɛtrɪk) *adj*

parametric amplifier *n* a type of high-frequency amplifier in which energy is transferred to the input signal through a circuit with a varying reactance.

paramilitary (ˌpærəˈmɪlɪtərɪ, -trɪ) *adj* **1** denoting or relating to a group of personnel with military structure functioning either as a civil force or in support of military forces. **2** denoting or relating to a force with military structure conducting armed operations against a ruling power.

paramount ❶ (ˈpærəˌmaʊnt) *adj* of the greatest importance or significance. [C16: via Anglo-Norman from OF *paramont,* from *par* by + *-amont* above, from L *ad montem* to the mountain]
▸ˈ**paraˌmountcy** *n* ▸ˈ**paraˌmountly** *adv*

paramour ❶ (ˈpærəˌmʊə) *n* **1** *Now usually derog.* a lover, esp. adulterous. **2** an archaic word for **beloved.** [C13: from OF, lit.: through love]

parang (ˈpɑːræŋ) *n* a Malay short stout straight-edged knife used in Borneo. [C19: from Malay]

paranoia ❶ (ˌpærəˈnɔɪə) *n* **1** a mental disorder characterized by any of several types of delusions, as of grandeur or persecution. **2** *Inf.* intense

THESAURUS

parallel *adj* **1** = **equidistant,** aligned, alongside, coextensive, side by side **2** = **matching,** akin, analogous, complementary, correspondent, corresponding, like, resembling, similar, uniform ◆ *n* **7** = **equivalent,** analogue, complement, corollary, counterpart, duplicate, equal, likeness, match, twin **8** = **similarity,** analogy, comparison, correlation, correspondence, likeness, parallelism, resemblance ◆ *vb* **14** = **correspond,** agree, be alike, chime with, compare, complement, conform, correlate, equal, keep pace (with), match
Antonyms *adj* ≠ **matching:** different, dissimilar, divergent, non-parallel, unlike ◆ *n* ≠ **equivalent:** opposite, reverse ≠ **similarity:** difference, dissimilarity, divergence ◆ *vb* ≠ **correspond:** be unlike, differ, diverge

paralyse *vb* **1** = **disable,** cripple, debilitate, incapacitate, lame **2, 3** = **immobilize,** anaesthetize, arrest, benumb, freeze, halt, numb, petrify, stop dead, stun, stupefy, transfix

paralysis *n* **1** = **immobility,** palsy, paresis (*Pathology*) **2** = **standstill,** arrest, breakdown, halt, inactivity, shutdown, stagnation, stoppage

paralytic *adj* **2** = **paralysed,** crippled, disabled, immobile, immobilized, incapacitated, lame, numb, palsied **3** *Brit. informal* = **drunk,** bevvied (*dialect*), blitzed (*sl.*), blotto (*sl.*), flying (*sl.*), inebriated, intoxicated, legless (*inf.*), pie-eyed (*sl.*), plastered (*sl.*), sloshed (*sl.*), smashed (*sl.*), stoned (*sl.*), tired and emotional (*euphemistic*), wasted (*sl.*), wrecked (*sl.*)

parameter *n* **3** *Informal* = **limit,** constant, criterion, framework, guideline, limitation, restriction, specification

paramount *adj* = **principal,** capital, cardinal, chief, dominant, eminent, first, foremost, main, outstanding, predominant, pre-eminent, primary, prime, superior, supreme
Antonyms *adj* inferior, insignificant, least, minor, negligible, secondary, slight, subordinate, trifling, unimportant

paramour *n Now usually derogatory* = **lover,** beau, concubine, courtesan, fancy bit (*sl.*),

fear or suspicion, esp. when unfounded. [C19: via NL from Gk: frenzy, from *paranoos* distraught, from PARA-[1] + *noos* mind]
▸ **'para,noid, paranoiac** (,pærə'nɔɪk) *or* **paranoic** (,pærə'nəʊɪk) *adj, n*

paranormal (,pærə'nɔːməl) *adj* **1** beyond normal explanation. ◆ *n* **2** **the.** paranormal happenings generally.

parapente ('pærə,pɒnt) *n* **1** another name for **paraskiing. 2** the form of parachute used in this sport. [C20: from PARA(CHUTE) + F *pente* slope]

parapet ('pærəpɪt, -,pɛt) *n* **1** a low wall or railing along the edge of a balcony, roof, etc. **2** *Mil.* a rampart, mound of sandbags, etc., in front of a trench giving protection from fire. [C16: from It. *parapetto*, lit.: chest-high wall, from L *pectus* breast]

paraph ('pærəf) *n* a flourish after a signature, originally to prevent forgery. [C14: via F from Med. L *paraphus*, var. of *paragraphus* PARAGRAPH]

paraphernalia ❶ (,pærəfə'neɪlɪə) *pl n* (*sometimes functioning as sing*) **1** miscellaneous articles or equipment. **2** *Law.* (formerly) articles of personal property given to a married woman by her husband and regarded in law as her possessions. [C17: via Med. L from L *parapherna* personal property of a married woman, apart from her dowry, from Gk, from PARA-[1] + *phernē* dowry, from *pherein* to carry]

paraphrase ❶ ('pærə,freɪz) *n* **1** an expression of a statement or text in other words. ◆ *vb* **paraphrases, paraphrasing, paraphrased. 2** to put into other words; restate. [C16: via F from L *paraphrasis*, from Gk, from *paraphrazein* to recount]
▸ **paraphrastic** (,pærə'fræstɪk) *adj*

paraplegia (,pærə'pliːdʒə) *n Pathol.* paralysis of the lower half of the body, usually as the result of disease or injury of the spine. [C17: via NL from Gk: a blow on one side, from PARA-[1] + *plēssein* to strike]
▸ **,para'plegic** *adj, n*

parapraxis (,pærə'præksɪs) *n, pl* **parapraxes** (-'præksiːz) *Psychoanal.* a minor error in action, such as a slip of the tongue. [C20: from PARA-[1] + Gk *praxis* a deed]

parapsychology (,pærəsaɪ'kɒlədʒɪ) *n* the study of mental phenomena, such as telepathy, which are beyond the scope of normal physical explanation.
▸ **,parapsy'chologist** *n*

Paraquat ('pærə,kwɒt) *n Trademark.* a yellow extremely poisonous weedkiller.

parascending ('pærə,sɛndɪŋ) *n* a sport in which a parachutist, starting from ground level, is towed by a vehicle until he is airborne and then descends in the normal way.

paraselene (,pærəsɪ'liːnɪ) *n, pl* **paraselenae** (-niː). a bright image of the moon on a lunar halo. Also called: **mock moon.** [C17: NL, from PARA-[1] + Gk *selēnē* moon]

parasite ❶ ('pærə,saɪt) *n* **1** an animal or plant that lives in or on another (the host) from which it obtains nourishment. **2** a person who habitually lives at the expense of others; sponger. [C16: via L from Gk *parasitos* one who lives at another's expense, from PARA-[1] + *sitos* grain]
▸ **parasitic** (,pærə'sɪtɪk) *or* **,para'sitical** *adj* ▸ **,para'sitically** *adv* ▸ **'parasi,tism** *n*

parasitize *or* **parasitise** ('pærəsɪ,taɪz) *vb* **parasitizes, parasitizing, parasitized** *or* **parasitises, parasitising, parasitised.** (*tr*) **1** to infest with parasites. **2** to live on (another organism) as a parasite.
▸ **,parasiti'zation** *or* **,parasiti'sation** *n*

parasitoid ('pærəsɪ,tɔɪd) *n Zool.* an animal, esp. an insect, that is parasitic as a larva but becomes free-living when adult.

parasitology (,pærəsaɪ'tɒlədʒɪ) *n* the branch of biology that is concerned with the study of parasites.
▸ **,parasit'ologist** *n*

paraskiing ('pærə,skiːɪŋ) *n* the sport of jumping off high mountains wearing skis and a light parachute composed of inflatable fabric tubes that form a semirigid wing. Also called: **parapente.**

parasol ('pærə,sɒl) *n* an umbrella used for protection against the sun; sunshade. [C17: via F from It. *parasole*, from PARA-[2] + *sole* sun, from L *sōl*]

parasuicide (,pærə'suːɪ,saɪd) *n* an attempt to inflict an injury on oneself, not motivated by a desire to die.

parasympathetic (,pærə,sɪmpə'θɛtɪk) *adj Anat., Physiol.* of or relating to the division of the autonomic nervous system that acts by slowing the heartbeat, constricting the bronchi of the lungs, stimulating the smooth muscles of the digestive tract, etc. Cf. **sympathetic** (sense 4).

parasynthesis (,pærə'sɪnθɪsɪs) *n* formation of words by compounding a phrase and adding an affix, as *light-headed, light* + *head* with the affix *-ed.*
▸ **parasynthetic** (,pærəsɪn'θɛtɪk) *adj*

parataxis (,pærə'tæksɪs) *n* the juxtaposition of clauses without the use of a conjunction, as *None of my friends stayed—they all left early.* [C19: NL from Gk, from *paratassein*, lit.: to arrange side by side]
▸ **paratactic** (,pærə'tæktɪk) *adj*

parathion (,pærə'θaɪɒn) *n* a toxic oil used as an insecticide. [from PARA-[1] + Gk *theion* sulphur]

parathyroid gland (,pærə'θaɪrɔɪd) *n* any one of the small egg-shaped endocrine glands situated near or embedded within the thyroid gland.

paratroops ('pærə,truːps) *pl n* troops trained and equipped to be dropped by parachute into a battle area. Also called: **paratroopers.**

paratyphoid fever (,pærə'taɪfɔɪd) *n* a disease resembling but less severe than typhoid fever, caused by bacteria of the genus *Salmonella.*

paravane ('pærə,veɪn) *n* a torpedo-shaped device towed from the bow of a vessel so that the cables will cut the anchors of any moored mines. [C20: from PARA-[2] + VANE]

par avion *French.* (par avjɔ̃) *adv* by aeroplane: used in labelling mail sent by air.

parazoan (,pærə'zəʊən) *n, pl* **parazoa** (-'zəʊə). any multicellular invertebrate of a division of the animal kingdom, the sponges. [C19: from *parazoa*, on the model of *protozoa* & *metazoa*, from PARA-[1] + Gk *zōon* animal]

parboil ('pɑː,bɔɪl) *vb* (*tr*) **1** to boil until partially cooked. **2** to subject to uncomfortable heat. [C15: from OF *parboillir*, from LL *perbullīre* to boil thoroughly (see PER-, BOIL[1]); modern meaning due to confusion of *par-* with *part*]

parbuckle ('pɑː,bʌkᵊl) *n* **1** a rope sling for lifting or lowering a heavy cylindrical object, such as a cask. ◆ *vb* **parbuckles, parbuckling, parbuckled. 2** (*tr*) to raise or lower (an object) with such a sling. [C17 *parbunkel*: from ?]

parcel ❶ ('pɑːsᵊl) *n* **1** something wrapped up; package. **2** a group of people or things having some common characteristic. **3** a quantity of some commodity offered for sale; lot. **4** a distinct portion of land. ◆ *vb* **parcels, parcelling, parcelled** *or US* **parcels, parceling, parceled.** (*tr*) **5** (often foll. by *up*) to make a parcel of; wrap up. **6** (often foll. by *out*) to divide (up) into portions. [C14: from OF *parcelle*, from L *particula* PARTICLE]

parch ❶ (pɑːtʃ) *vb* **1** to deprive or be deprived of water; dry up: *the sun parches the fields.* **2** (*tr; usually passive*) to make very thirsty. **3** (*tr*) to roast (corn, etc.) lightly. [C14: from ?]

Parcheesi (pɑː'tʃiːzɪ) *n Trademark.* a board game derived from the ancient game of pachisi.

parchment ('pɑːtʃmənt) *n* **1** the skin of certain animals, such as sheep, treated to form a durable material, as for manuscripts. **2** a manuscript, etc., made of this material. **3** a type of stiff yellowish paper resembling parchment. [C13: from OF *parchemin*, via L from Gk *pergamēnē*, from *Pergamēnos* of Pergamum (where parchment was made); OF *parchemin* was infl. by *parche* leather, from L *Parthica* (*pellis*) Parthian (leather)]

pard (pɑːd) *n Arch.* a leopard or panther. [C13: via OF from L *pardus*, from Gk *pardos*]

pardon ❶ ('pɑːdᵊn) *vb* (*tr*) **1** to excuse or forgive (a person) for (an offence, mistake, etc.): *to pardon someone; to pardon a fault.* ◆ *n* **2** forgiveness. **3a** release from punishment for an offence. **3b** the warrant granting such release. **4** a Roman Catholic indulgence. ◆ *sentence substitute.* **5** Also: **pardon me, I beg your pardon. 5a** sorry; excuse me. **5b** what did you say? [C13: from OF, from Med. L *perdōnum*, from *perdōnāre* to forgive freely, from L *per* (intensive) + *dōnāre* to grant]
▸ **'pardonable** *adj* ▸ **'pardonably** *adv*

pardoner ('pɑːdᵊnə) *n* (before the Reformation) a person licensed to sell ecclesiastical indulgences.

pare ❶ (pɛə) *vb* **pares, paring, pared.** (*tr*) **1** to peel (the outer layer) from (something). **2** to cut the edges from (the nails). **3** to decrease bit by bit. [C13: from OF *parer* to adorn, from L *parāre* to make ready]
▸ **'parer** *n*

paregoric (,pærə'gɒrɪk) *n* a medicine consisting of opium, benzoic

THESAURUS

fancy man (*sl.*), fancy woman (*sl.*), inamorata, inamorato, kept woman, mistress

paranoid *adj* **1** = **mentally ill**, deluded, disturbed, manic, neurotic, obsessive, paranoiac, psychotic, unstable **2** *Informal* = **suspicious**, apprehensive, fearful, nervous, worried

paraphernalia *n* **1** = **equipment**, accoutrements, apparatus, appurtenances, baggage, belongings, effects, equipage, gear, impedimenta, material, stuff, tackle, things, trappings

paraphrase *n* **1** = **rewording**, interpretation, rehash, rendering, rendition, rephrasing, restatement, translation, version ◆ *vb* **2** = **reword**, express in other words *or* one's own words, interpret, rehash, render, rephrase, restate

parasite *n* **2** = **sponger** (*inf.*), bloodsucker (*inf.*), cadger, drone (*Brit.*), hanger-on, leech, scrounger (*inf.*), sponge (*inf.*)

parasitic *adj* **2** = **scrounging** (*inf.*), bloodsucking (*inf.*), cadging, leechlike, sponging (*inf.*)

parcel *n* **1** = **package**, bundle, carton, pack, packet **2** = **group**, band, batch, bunch, collection, company, crew, crowd, gang, lot, pack **4** = **plot**, piece of land, property, tract ◆ *vb* **5** *often foll. by* **up** = **wrap**, do up, pack, package, tie up **6** *often foll. by* **out** = **distribute**, allocate, allot, apportion, carve up, deal out, dispense, divide, dole out, mete out, portion, share out, split up

parch *vb* **1, 2** = **dry up**, blister, burn, dehydrate, desiccate, evaporate, make thirsty, scorch, sear, shrivel, wither

parched *adj* **1, 2** = **dried out** *or* **up**, arid, dehydrated, drouthy (*Scot.*), dry, scorched, shrivelled, thirsty, torrid, waterless, withered

pardon *vb* **1** = **forgive**, absolve, acquit, amnesty, condone, exculpate, excuse, exonerate, free, let off (*inf.*), liberate, overlook, release, remit, reprieve ◆ *n* **2, 3** = **forgiveness**, absolution, acquittal, allowance, amnesty, condonation, discharge, excuse, exoneration, grace, indulgence, mercy, release, remission, reprieve
Antonyms *vb* ≠ **forgive:** admonish, blame, castigate, censure, chasten, chastise, condemn, discipline, excoriate, fine, penalize, punish, rebuke ◆ *n* ≠ **forgiveness:** condemnation, guilt, penalty, punishment, redress, retaliation, retribution, revenge, vengeance

pardonable *adj* **1** = **forgivable**, allowable, condonable, excusable, minor, not serious, permissible, understandable, venial

pare *vb* **1, 2** = **peel**, clip, cut, shave, skin, trim **3** = **cut back**, crop, cut, decrease, dock, lop, prune, reduce, retrench, shear acid, and camphor, formerly widely used to relieve diarrhoea and coughing. [C17 (meaning: relieving pain): via LL from Gk *parēgoros* relating to soothing speech, from PARA-[1] (beside) + *agora* assembly]

pareira (pə'rɛərə) *n* the root of a South American climbing plant, used as a diuretic, tonic, and as a source of curare. [C18: from Port. *pareira brava,* lit.: wild vine]

parenchyma (pə'rɛŋkɪmə) *n* **1** a soft plant tissue consisting of simple thin-walled cells: constitutes the greater part of fruits, stems, roots, etc. **2** animal tissue that constitutes the essential part of an organ as distinct from the blood vessels, connective tissue, etc. [C17: via NL from Gk *parenkhuma* something poured in beside, from PARA-[1] + *enkhuma* infusion]
▸**parenchymatous** (ˌpærɛŋ'kɪmətəs) *adj*

parent (ˈpɛərənt) *n* **1** a father or mother. **2** a person acting as a father or mother; guardian. **3** *Rare.* an ancestor. **4** a source or cause. **5** an organism or organization that has produced one or more organisms similar to itself. **6** *Physics, chem.* a precursor, such as a nucleus or compound, of a derived entity. [C15: via OF from L *parens* parent, from *parere* to bring forth]
▸**pa'rental** *adj* ▸**'parenthood** *n*

parentage (ˈpɛərəntɪdʒ) *n* **1** ancestry. **2** derivation from a particular origin.

parent company *n* a company that owns a number of subsidiary companies.

parenteral (pæ'rɛntərəl) *adj Med.* **1** (esp. of the route by which a drug is administered) by means other than through the digestive tract, esp. by injection. **2** designating a drug to be injected. [C20: from PARA-[1] + ENTERO- + -AL[1]]

parenthesis (pə'rɛnθɪsɪs) *n, pl* **parentheses** (-ˌsiːz). **1** a phrase, often explanatory or qualifying, inserted into a passage with which it is not grammatically connected, and marked off by brackets, dashes, etc. **2** Also called: **bracket.** either of a pair of characters, ( ), used to enclose such a phrase or as a sign of aggregation in mathematical or logical expressions. **3** an interlude; interval. **4 in parenthesis.** inserted as a parenthesis. [C16: via LL from Gk: something placed in besides, from *parentithenai,* from PARA-[1] + EN-[2] + *tithenai* to put]
▸**parenthetic** (ˌpærən'θɛtɪk) *or* ˌ**paren'thetical** *adj* ▸ˌ**paren'thetically** *adv*

parenthesize *or* **parenthesise** (pə'rɛnθɪˌsaɪz) *vb* **parenthesizes, parenthesizing, parenthesized** *or* **parenthesises, parenthesising, parenthesised.** (*tr*) **1** to place in parentheses. **2** to insert as a parenthesis. **3** to intersperse (a speech, writing, etc.) with parentheses.

parenting (ˈpɛərəntɪŋ) *n* all the skills and experience of bringing up children.

parent teacher association *n* a social group of the parents of children at a school and their teachers formed in order to foster better understanding between them and to organize fund-raising activities on behalf of the school.

parergon (pə'rɛəgɒn) *n, pl* **parerga** (-gə). work that is not one's main employment. [C17: from L, from Gk, from PARA-[1] + *ergon* work]

paresis (pə'riːsɪs, ˈpærɪsɪs) *n, pl* **pareses** (-ˌsiːz). *Pathol.* incomplete or slight paralysis of motor functions. [C17: via NL from Gk: a relaxation, from *parienai* to let go]
▸**paretic** (pə'rɛtɪk) *adj*

par excellence *French.* (par ɛkselɑ̃s; *English* pɑːr ˈɛksələns) *adv* to a degree of excellence; beyond comparison. [F, lit.: by (way of) excellence]

parfait (pɑːˈfeɪ) *n* a rich frozen dessert made from eggs and cream, fruit, etc. [from F: PERFECT]

parget (ˈpɑːdʒɪt) *n* **1** Also called: **pargeting. 1a** plaster, mortar, etc., used to line chimney flues or cover walls. **1b** plasterwork that has incised ornamental patterns. ◆ *vb* (*tr*). **2** to cover or decorate with parget. [C14: from OF *pargeter* to throw over, from *par* PER- + *geter* to throw]

parhelic circle *n Meteorol.* a luminous band at the same altitude as the sun, parallel to the horizon, caused by reflection of the sun's rays by ice crystals in the atmosphere.

parhelion (pɑːˈhiːlɪən) *n, pl* **parhelia** (-lɪə). one of several bright spots on the parhelic circle or solar halo, caused by the diffraction of light by ice crystals in the atmosphere. Also called: **mock sun.** [C17: via L from Gk *parēlion,* from PARA-[1] (beside) + *hēlios* sun]
▸**par'helic** *or* **parheliacal** (ˌpɑːhɪˈlaɪək°l) *adj*

pariah (pəˈraɪə, ˈpærɪə) *n* **1** a social outcast. **2** (formerly) a member of a low caste in South India. [C17: from Tamil *paraiyan* drummer, from *parai* drum: members were drummers at festivals]

pariah dog *n* another term for **pye-dog.**

parietal (pəˈraɪɪt°l) *adj* **1** *Anat., biol.* of or forming the walls of a bodily cavity: *the parietal bones of the skull.* **2** of or relating to the side of the skull. **3** (of plant ovaries) having ovules attached to the walls. **4** *US.* living or having authority within a college. ◆ *n* **5** a parietal bone. [C16: from LL *parietālis,* from L *pariēs* wall]

parietal lobe *n* the portion of each cerebral hemisphere concerned with the perception of sensations of touch, temperature, and taste and with muscular movements.

pari-mutuel (ˌpærɪˈmjuːtʃʊəl) *n, pl* **pari-mutuels** *or* **paris-mutuels** (ˌpærɪˈmjuːtʃʊəlz). a system of betting in which those who have bet on the winners of a race share in the total amount wagered less a percentage for the management. [C19: from F, lit.: mutual wager]

paring (ˈpɛərɪŋ) *n* (*often pl*) something pared or cut off.

pari passu *Latin.* (ˌpærɪ ˈpæsuː, ˈpɑːrɪ) *adv Usually legal.* with equal speed or progress.

Paris Club (ˈpærɪs) *n* another name for **Group of Ten.**

Paris Commune *n French history.* the council established in Paris in the spring of 1871 in opposition to the National Assembly and esp. to the peace negotiated with Prussia following the Franco-Prussian War.

Paris green *n* an emerald-green poisonous substance used as a pigment and insecticide.

parish (ˈpærɪʃ) *n* **1** a subdivision of a diocese, having its own church and a clergyman. **2** the churchgoers of such a subdivision. **3** (in England and, formerly, Wales) the smallest unit of local government. **4** (in Louisiana) a county. **5** (in Quebec and New Brunswick, Canada) a subdivision of a county. **6** the people living in a parish. **7 on the parish.** *History.* receiving parochial relief. [C13: from OF *paroisse,* from Church L, from LGk, from *paroikos* Christian, sojourner, from Gk: neighbour, from PARA-[1] (beside) + *oikos* house]

parish clerk *n* a person designated to assist in various church duties.

parish council *n* (in England and, formerly, Wales) the administrative body of a parish. See **parish** (sense 3).

parishioner (pəˈrɪʃənə) *n* a member of a particular parish.

parish pump *adj* of only local interest; parochial.

parish register *n* a book in which the births, baptisms, marriages, and deaths in a parish are recorded.

parity (ˈpærɪtɪ) *n, pl* **parities. 1** equality of rank, pay, etc. **2** close or exact analogy or equivalence. **3** *Finance.* the amount of a foreign currency equivalent to a specific sum of domestic currency. **4** equality between prices of commodities or securities in two separate markets. **5** *Physics.* **5a** a property of a physical system characterized by the behaviour of the sign of its wave function when reflected in space. The wave function either remains unchanged (**even parity**) or changes in sign (**odd parity**). **5b** a quantum number describing this property, equal to +1 for even parity systems and –1 for odd parity systems. Symbol: *P* **6** *Maths.* a relationship between two integers. If both are odd or both even they have the same parity; if one is odd and one even they have different parity. [C16: from LL *pāritās;* see PAR]

parity check *n* a check made of computer data to ensure that the total number of bits of value 1 (or 0) in each unit of information remains odd or even after transfer between a peripheral device and the memory or vice versa.

park (pɑːk) *n* **1** a large area of land preserved in a natural state for recreational use by the public. **2** a piece of open land for public recreation in a town. **3** a large area of land forming a private estate. **4** an area designed to accommodate a number of related enterprises: *a business park.* **5** *US & Canad.* a playing field or sports stadium. **6 the park.** *Brit. inf.* a soccer pitch. **7** a gear selector position on the automatic transmission of a motor vehicle that acts as a parking brake. **8** the area in which the equipment and supplies of a military formation are assembled. ◆ *vb* **9** to stop and leave (a vehicle) temporarily. **10** to manoeuvre (a motor vehicle) into a space for it to be left: *try to park without hitting the kerb.* **11** *Stock Exchange.* to register (securities) in the name of another or of nominees in order to conceal their real ownership. **12** (*tr*) *Inf.* to leave or put somewhere: *park yourself in front of the fire.* **13** (*intr*) *Mil.* to arrange equipment in a park. **14** (*tr*) to enclose in or as a park. [C13: from OF *parc,* from Med. L *parricus* enclosure, from Gmc]

parka (ˈpɑːkə) *n* a warm weatherproof coat with a hood, originally worn by Eskimos. [C19: from Aleutian: skin]

parkin (ˈpɑːkɪn) *n* (in Britain and New Zealand) moist spicy ginger cake usually containing oatmeal. [C19: from ?]

parking lot *n* the US and Canad. term for **car park.**

parking meter *n* a timing device, usually coin-operated, that indicates how long a vehicle may be left parked.

parking orbit *n* an orbit around the earth or moon in which a spacecraft can be placed temporarily in order to prepare for the next step in its programme.

parking ticket *n* a summons served for a parking offence.

Parkinson's disease (ˈpɑːkɪnsənz) *n* a progressive chronic disorder of the central nervous system characterized by impaired muscular coor-

THESAURUS

parent *n* **1** = **father** *or* **mother**, begetter, procreator, progenitor, sire **4** = **source**, architect, author, cause, creator, forerunner, origin, originator, prototype, root, wellspring

parentage *n* **1, 2** = **family**, ancestry, birth, derivation, descent, extraction, line, lineage, origin, paternity, pedigree, race, stirps, stock

parenthetical *adj* **1** = **interposed**, bracketed, by-the-way, explanatory, extraneous, extrinsic, incidental, in parenthesis, inserted, qualifying

parenthetically *adv* **1** = **incidentally**, by the bye, by the way, by way of explanation, in parenthesis, in passing

parenthood *n* **1** = **fatherhood** *or* **motherhood**, baby *or* child care, bringing up, child rearing, fathering *or* mothering, nurturing, parenting, rearing, upbringing

pariah *n* **1** = **outcast**, exile, leper, outlaw, undesirable, unperson, untouchable

paring *n* = **clipping**, flake, fragment, peel, peeling, rind, shaving, shred, skin, slice, sliver, snippet

parish *n* **1, 2** = **community**, church, churchgoers, congregation, flock, fold, parishioners

parity *n* **1, 2** = **equality**, consistency, equal terms, equivalence, par, parallelism, quits (*inf.*), uniformity, unity

park *n* **1-3** = **parkland**, estate, garden, grounds, pleasure garden, recreation ground, woodland ◆ *vb* **9, 10** = **leave**, manoeuvre, position, station dination and tremor. Often shortened to **Parkinson's**. Also called: **Parkinsonism**. [C19: after James *Parkinson* (1755–1824), Brit. surgeon, who first described it]

Parkinson's law *n* the notion, expressed facetiously as a law of economics, that work expands to fill the time available for its completion. [C20: after C. N. *Parkinson* (1909–93), Brit. historian and writer, who formulated it]

park keeper *n* (in Britain) an official who patrols and supervises a public park.

parkland ('pɑːkˌlænd) *n* grassland with scattered trees.

parky ('pɑːkɪ) *adj* **parkier, parkiest.** (*usually postpositive*) *Brit. inf.* (of the weather) chilly; cold. [C19: ?from PERKY]

Parl. *abbrev. for:* **1** Parliament. **2** Also: **parl.** parliamentary.

parlance ⓣ ('pɑːləns) *n* a particular manner of speaking, esp. when specialized; idiom: *political parlance.* [C16: from OF, from *parler* to talk, via Med. L from LL *parabola* speech]

parlando (pɑː'lændəʊ) *adj, adv Music.* to be performed as though speaking. [It.: speaking]

parley ⓣ ('pɑːlɪ) *n* **1** a discussion, esp. between enemies under a truce to decide terms of surrender, etc. ◆ *vb* **2** (*intr*) to discuss, esp. with an enemy. [C16: from F, from *parler* to talk, from Med. L *parabolāre,* from LL *parabola* speech]

parliament ⓣ ('pɑːləmənt) *n* **1** an assembly of the representatives of a political nation or people, often the supreme legislative authority. **2** any legislative or deliberative assembly, conference, etc. [C13: from Anglo-L *parliamentum,* from OF *parlement,* from *parler* to speak; see PARLEY]

Parliament ⓣ ('pɑːləmənt) *n* **1** the highest legislative authority in Britain, consisting of the House of Commons, which exercises effective power, the House of Lords, and the sovereign. **2** a similar legislature in another country or state. **3** any of the assemblies of such a body created by a general election and royal summons and dissolved before the next election.

parliamentarian (ˌpɑːləmen'tɛərɪən) *n* **1** an expert in parliamentary procedures. ◆ *adj* **2** of or relating to a parliament.

parliamentary ⓣ (ˌpɑːlə'mɛntərɪ) *adj* (*sometimes cap.*) **1** of or proceeding from a parliament or Parliament: *a parliamentary decree.* **2** conforming to the procedures of a parliament or Parliament: *parliamentary conduct.* **3** having a parliament or Parliament.

Parliamentary Commissioner *or in full* **Parliamentary Commissioner for Administration** *n* (in Britain) the official name for **ombudsman** (sense 2).

parliamentary private secretary *n* (in Britain) a backbencher in Parliament who assists a minister. Abbrev.: **PPS.**

parliamentary secretary *n* a member of Parliament appointed to assist a minister of the Crown with his departmental responsibilities.

parlour ⓣ *or US* **parlor** ('pɑːlə) *n* **1** *Old-fashioned.* a living room, esp. one kept tidy for the reception of visitors. **2** a small room for guests away from the public rooms in an inn, club, etc. **3** *Chiefly US, Canad., & NZ.* a room or shop equipped as a place of business: *a billiard parlor.* **4** a building equipped for the milking of cows. [C13: from Anglo-Norman *parlur,* from OF *parleur* room in convent for receiving guests, from *parler* to speak; see PARLEY]

parlous ⓣ ('pɑːləs) *Arch. or humorous.* ◆ *adj* **1** dangerous or difficult. **2** cunning. ◆ *adv* **3** extremely. [C14 *perlous,* var. of PERILOUS]
▸**'parlously** *adv*

Parmesan cheese (ˌpɑːmɪ'zæn, 'pɑːmɪzən) *n* a hard dry cheese used grated, esp. on pasta dishes and soups. [C16: from F, from It. *parmegiano* of Parma, town in Italy]

Parnassus (pɑː'næsəs) *n* **1 Mount.** a mountain in central Greece: in ancient times sacred to Apollo and the Muses. **2a** the world of poetry. **2b** a centre of poetic or other creative activity.
▸**Par'nassian** *adj*

parochial ⓣ (pə'rəʊkɪəl) *adj* **1** narrow in outlook or scope; provincial. **2** of or relating to a parish. [C14: via OF from Church L *parochiālis;* see PARISH]
▸**pa'rochialˌism** *n* ▸**pa'rochially** *adv*

parody ⓣ ('pærədɪ) *n, pl* **parodies. 1** a musical, literary, or other composition that mimics the style of another composer, author, etc., in a humorous or satirical way. **2** something so badly done as to seem an intentional mockery; travesty. ◆ *vb* **parodies, parodying, parodied. 3** (*tr*) to make a parody of. [C16: via L from Gk *paroidiā* satirical poem, from PARA-[1] + *ōidē* song]
▸**parodic** (pə'rɒdɪk) *or* **pa'rodical** *adj* ▸**'parodist** *n*

parol ('pærəl, pə'rəʊl) *Law.* ◆ *n* **1** an oral statement; word of mouth (now only in **by parol**). ◆ *adj* **2a** (of a contract, lease, etc.) made orally or in writing but not under seal. **2b** expressed or given by word of mouth: *parol evidence.* [C15: from OF *parole* speech; see PAROLE]

parole (pə'rəʊl) *n* **1a** the freeing of a prisoner before his sentence has expired, on the condition that he is of good behaviour. **1b** the duration of such conditional release. **2** a promise given by a prisoner, as to be of good behaviour if granted liberty or partial liberty. **3** *Linguistics.* language as manifested in the individual speech acts of particular speakers. **4 on parole.** conditionally released from detention. ◆ *vb* **paroles, paroling, paroled.** (*tr*) **5** to place (a person) on parole. [C17: from OF, from *parole d'honneur* word of honour; *parole* from LL *parabola* speech]
▸**parolee** (pəˌrəʊ'liː) *n*

paronomasia (ˌpærənəʊ'meɪzɪə) *n Rhetoric.* a play on words, esp. a pun. [C16: via L from Gk, from *paronomazein* to make a change in naming, from PARA-[1] (besides) + *onomazein* to name, from *onoma* a name]

parotid (pə'rɒtɪd) *adj* **1** relating to or situated near the parotid gland. ◆ *n* **2** See **parotid gland.** [C17: via F, via L from Gk *parōtis,* from PARA-[1] (near) + *-ōtis,* from *ous* ear]

parotid gland *n* a large salivary gland, in man situated in front of and below each ear.

parotitis (ˌpærə'taɪtɪs) *n* inflammation of the parotid gland. See also **mumps.**

-parous *adj combining form.* giving birth to: *oviparous.* [from L *-parus,* from *parere* to bring forth]

paroxysm ⓣ ('pærəkˌsɪzəm) *n* **1** an uncontrollable outburst: *a paroxysm of giggling.* **2** *Pathol.* **2a** a sudden attack or recurrence of a disease. **2b** any fit or convulsion. [C17: via F from Med. L *paroxysmus* annoyance, from Gk, from *paroxunein* to goad, from PARA-[1] (intensifier) + *oxunein* to sharpen, from *oxus* sharp]
▸**ˌparox'ysmal** *adj*

parquet ('pɑːkeɪ, -kɪ) *n* **1** a floor covering of pieces of hardwood fitted in a decorative pattern; parquetry. **2** Also called: **parquet floor.** a floor so covered. **3** *US.* the stalls of a theatre. ◆ *vb* (*tr*) **4** to cover a floor with parquet. [C19: from OF: small enclosure, from *parc* enclosure; see PARK]

parquetry ('pɑːkɪtrɪ) *n* a geometric pattern of inlaid pieces of wood, esp. as used to cover a floor.

parr (pɑː) *n, pl* **parrs** *or* **parr.** a salmon up to two years of age. [C18: from ?]

parrakeet ('pærəˌkiːt) *n* a variant spelling of **parakeet.**

parramatta (ˌpærə'mætə) *n* a variant spelling of **paramatta.**

parricide ('pærɪˌsaɪd) *n* **1** the act of killing either of one's parents. **2** a person who kills his or her parent. [C16: from L *parricīdium* murder of a parent or relative, & from *parricīda* one who murders a relative, from *parri-* (rel. to Gk *pēos* kinsman) + -CIDE]
▸**ˌparri'cidal** *adj*

parrot ⓣ ('pærət) *n* **1** any of several related tropical and subtropical birds having a short hooked bill, bright plumage, and an ability to mimic sounds. **2** a person who repeats or imitates the words or actions of another. **3 sick as a parrot.** *Usually facetious.* extremely disappointed. ◆ *vb* **parrots, parroting, parroted. 4** (*tr*) to repeat or imitate without understanding. [C16: prob. from F *paroquet,* from ?]

parrot-fashion ⓣ *adv Inf.* without regard for meaning; by rote: *she learned it parrot-fashion.*

parrot fever *or* **disease** *n* another name for **psittacosis.**

parrotfish ('pærətˌfɪʃ) *n, pl* **parrotfish** *or* **parrotfishes.** a brightly coloured tropical marine percoid fish having parrot-like jaws.

parry ⓣ ('pærɪ) *vb* **parries, parrying, parried. 1** to ward off (an attack, etc.) by blocking or deflecting, as in fencing. **2** (*tr*) to evade (questions, etc.), esp. adroitly. ◆ *n, pl* **parries. 3** an act of parrying. **4** a skilful evasion, as of a question. [C17: from F *parer* to ward off, from L *parāre* to prepare]

parse (pɑːz) *vb* **parses, parsing, parsed.** *Grammar.* to assign constituent structure to (a sentence or the words in a sentence). [C16: from L *pars* (*ōrātionis*) part (of speech)]

parsec ('pɑːˌsɛk) *n* a unit of astronomical distance equivalent to

THESAURUS

parlance *n* = **language**, idiom, jargon, lingo (*inf.*), manner of speaking, phraseology, -speak, speech, talk, tongue

parley *n* **1** = **discussion**, colloquy, confab (*inf.*), conference, congress, council, dialogue, meeting, palaver, powwow, seminar, talk(s) ◆ *vb* **2** = **discuss**, confabulate, confer, deliberate, negotiate, palaver, powwow, speak, talk

parliament *n* **1, 2** = **assembly**, congress, convention, convocation, council, diet, legislature, senate, talking shop (*inf.*)

Parliament *n* **1** = **Houses of Parliament**, Mother of Parliaments, the House, the House of Commons and the House of Lords, Westminster

parliamentary *adj* **1** = **governmental**, congressional, deliberative, law-giving, lawmaking, legislative

parlour *n* **1** *Old-fashioned* = **sitting room**, best room, drawing room, front room, living room, lounge, reception room

parlous *adj* **1** *Archaic or humorous* = **dangerous**, chancy (*inf.*), desperate, difficult, dire, hairy (*sl.*), hazardous, perilous, risky

parochial *adj* **1** = **provincial**, insular, inward-looking, limited, narrow, narrow-minded, parish-pump, petty, restricted, small-minded
Antonyms *adj* all-embracing, broad, broad-minded, cosmopolitan, international, liberal, national, universal, world-wide

parochialism *n* **1** = **provincialism**, insularity, limitedness, localism, narrow-mindedness, narrowness, restrictedness, small-mindedness

parody *n* **1** = **takeoff** (*inf.*), burlesque, caricature, imitation, lampoon, satire, send-up, skit, spoof (*inf.*) **2** = **travesty**, apology, caricature, farce, mockery ◆ *vb* **3** = **take off** (*inf.*), burlesque, caricature, do a takeoff of (*inf.*), lampoon, mimic, poke fun at, satirize, send up (*Brit. inf.*), spoof (*inf.*), travesty

paroxysm *n* **1, 2** = **outburst**, attack, convulsion, eruption, fit, flare-up (*inf.*), seizure, spasm

parrot *n* **2** = **mimic**, copycat (*inf.*), imitator, (little) echo ◆ *vb* **4** = **repeat**, copy, echo, imitate, mimic, reiterate

parrot-fashion *n Informal* = **by rote**, mechanically, mindlessly

parry *vb* **1** = **ward off**, block, deflect, fend off, hold at bay, rebuff, repel, repulse, stave off **2** = **evade**, avoid, circumvent, dodge, duck (*inf.*), fence, fight shy of, shun, sidestep

3.0857 × 10^{16} metres or 3.262 light years. [C20: from PARALLAX + SECOND[2]]

Parsee *or* **Parsi** (ˌpɑːˈsiː, ˈpɑːˌsiː) *n* an adherent of a Zoroastrian religion, the practitioners of which were driven out of Persia by the Muslims in the eighth century A.D. It is now found chiefly in western India. [C17: from Persian *Pārsī* a Persian, from OPersian *Pārsa* Persia]
▸**ˈParseeˌism** *or* **ˈParsiˌism** *n*

parser (ˈpɑːzə) *n Computing.* a program that interprets ordinary language typed into a computer by recognizing key words or analysing sentence structure and then translating it into the appropriate machine language.

parsimony ❶ (ˈpɑːsɪmənɪ) *n* extreme care in spending; niggardliness. [C15: from L *parcimōnia,* from *parcere* to spare]
▸**parsimonious** (ˌpɑːsɪˈməʊnɪəs) *adj* ▸**ˌparsiˈmoniously** *adv*

parsley (ˈpɑːslɪ) *n* **1** a S European umbelliferous plant, widely cultivated for its curled aromatic leaves, which are used in cooking. **2** any of various similar and related plants, such as fool's-parsley and cow parsley. [C14 *persely,* from OE *petersilie* + OF *persil, peresil,* both ult. from L *petroselīnum* rock parsley, from Gk, from *petra* rock + *selinon* parsley]

parsnip (ˈpɑːsnɪp) *n* **1** an umbelliferous plant cultivated for its long whitish root. **2** the root of this plant, eaten as a vegetable. [C14: from OF *pasnaie,* from L *pastināca,* from *pastināre* to dig, from *pastinum* two-pronged tool for digging]

parson ❶ (ˈpɑːsᵊn) *n* **1** a parish priest in the Church of England. **2** any clergyman. [C13: from Med. L *persōna* parish priest, from L: personage; see PERSON]

parsonage (ˈpɑːsᵊnɪdʒ) *n* the residence of a parson, as provided by the parish.

parson bird *n* another name for **tui.**

parson's nose *n* the fatty extreme end portion of the tail of a fowl when cooked.

part ❶ (pɑːt) *n* **1** a piece or portion of a whole. **2** an integral constituent of something: *dancing is part of what we teach.* **3** an amount less than the whole; bit: *they only recovered part of the money.* **4** one of several equal divisions: *mix two parts flour to one part water.* **5** an actor's role in a play. **6** a person's proper role or duty: *everyone must do his part.* **7** (*often pl*) region; area: *you're well known in these parts.* **8** *Anat.* any portion of a larger structure. **9** a component that can be replaced in a machine, etc. **10** the US, Canad., and Austral. word for **parting** (sense 1). **11** *Music.* one of a number of separate melodic lines which is assigned to one or more instrumentalists or singers. **12 for one's part.** as far as one is concerned. **13 for the most part.** generally. **14 in part.** to some degree; partly. **15 of many parts.** having many different abilities. **16 on the part of.** on behalf of. **17 part and parcel.** an essential ingredient. **18 play a part. 18a** to pretend to be what one is not. **18b** to have something to do with; be instrumental. **19 take in good part.** to respond to (teasing, etc.) with good humour. **20 take part in.** to participate in. **21 take someone's part.** to support one person in an argument, etc. ◆ *vb* **22** to divide or separate from one another; take or come apart: *to part the curtains; the seams parted when I washed the dress.* **23** to go away or cause to go away from one another: *the couple parted amicably.* **24** (*intr;* foll. by *from*) to leave; say goodbye to. **25** (*intr;* foll. by *with*) to relinquish, esp. reluctantly: *I couldn't part with my teddy bear.* **26** (*tr;* foll. by *from*) to cause to relinquish, esp. reluctantly: *he's not easily parted from his cash.* **27** (*intr*) to split; separate: *the path parts here.* **28** (*tr*) to arrange (the hair) in such a way that a line of scalp is left showing. **29** (*intr*) *Euphemistic.* to die. **30** (*intr*) *Arch.* to depart. ◆ *adv* **31** to some extent; partly. ◆ See also **parts.** [C13: via OF from L *partīre* to divide, from *pars* a part]

part. *abbrev. for:* **1** participle. **2** particular.

partake ❶ (pɑːˈteɪk) *vb* **partakes, partaking, partook, partaken.** (*mainly intr*) **1** (foll. by *in*) to have a share; participate. **2** (foll. by *of*) to take or receive a portion, esp. of food or drink. **3** (foll. by *of*) to suggest or have some of the quality (of): *music partaking of sadness.* [C16: back formation from *partaker,* earlier *part taker,* based on L *particeps* participant]
▸**parˈtaker** *n*

> **USAGE NOTE** *Partake of* is sometimes wrongly used as if it were a synonym for *eat* or *drink.* Correctly, one can only *partake of* food or drink which is available for several people to share.

parterre (pɑːˈtɛə) *n* **1** a formally patterned flower garden. **2** the pit of a theatre. [C17: from F, from *par* along + *terre* ground]

parthenogenesis (ˌpɑːθɪnəʊˈdʒɛnɪsɪs) *n* a type of reproduction, occurring in some insects and flowers, in which the unfertilized ovum develops directly into a new individual. [C19: from Gk *parthenos* virgin + *genesis* birth]
▸**parthenogenetic** (ˌpɑːθɪˌnəʊdʒɪˈnɛtɪk) *adj*

Parthian shot (ˈpɑːθɪən) *n* a hostile remark or gesture delivered while departing. [from the custom of archers from Parthia, an ancient Asian empire, who shot their arrows backwards while retreating]

partial ❶ (ˈpɑːʃəl) *adj* **1** relating to only a part; not general or complete: *a partial eclipse.* **2** biased: *a partial judge.* **3** (*postpositive;* foll. by *to*) having a particular liking (for). **4** *Maths.* designating or relating to an operation in which only one of a set of independent variables is considered at a time. ◆ *n* **5** Also called: **partial tone.** *Music, acoustics.* any of the component tones of a single musical sound. **6** *Maths.* a partial derivative. [C15: from OF *parcial,* from LL *partiālis* incomplete, from L *pars* part]
▸**ˈpartially** *adv* ▸**ˈpartialness** *n*

> **USAGE NOTE** See at **partly.**

partial derivative *n* the derivative of a function of two or more variables with respect to one of the variables, the other or others being considered constant. Written $\partial f/\partial x$.

partiality ❶ (ˌpɑːʃɪˈælɪtɪ) *n, pl* **partialities. 1** favourable bias. **2** (usually foll. by *for*) liking or fondness. **3** the state of being partial.

partible (ˈpɑːtəbᵊl) *adj* (esp. of property or an inheritance) divisible; separable. [C16: from LL *partibilis,* from *part-, pars* part]

participate ❶ (pɑːˈtɪsɪˌpeɪt) *vb* **participates, participating, participated.** (*intr;* often foll. by *in*) to take part, be or become actively involved, or share (in). [C16: from L *participāre,* from *pars* part + *capere* to take]
▸**parˈticipant** *adj, n* ▸**parˌticiˈpation** *n* ▸**parˈticiˌpator** *n* ▸**parˈticipatory** *adj*

participle (ˈpɑːtɪsɪpᵊl) *n* a nonfinite form of verbs, in English and other languages, used adjectivally and in the formation of certain compound tenses. See also **present participle, past participle.** [C14: via OF from L *participium,* from *particeps,* from *pars* part + *capere* to take]
▸**participial** (ˌpɑːtɪˈsɪpɪəl) *adj* ▸**ˌpartiˈcipially** *adv*

particle ❶ (ˈpɑːtɪkᵊl) *n* **1** an extremely small piece of matter; speck. **2** a very tiny amount; iota: *it doesn't make a particle of difference.* **3** a function word, esp. (in certain languages) a word belonging to an uninflected class having grammatical function: *"up" is sometimes regarded as an adverbial particle.* **4** a common affix, such as *re-, un-,* or *-ness.* **5**

THESAURUS

parsimonious *adj* = **mean,** cheeseparing, close, close-fisted, frugal, grasping, miserable, miserly, near (*inf.*), niggardly, penny-pinching (*inf.*), penurious, saving, scrimpy, skinflinty, sparing, stingy, stinting, tightfisted
Antonyms *adj* extravagant, generous, lavish, munificent, open-handed, spendthrift, wasteful

parsimony *n Formal* = **meanness,** frugality, miserliness, nearness (*inf.*), niggardliness, penny-pinching (*inf.*), stinginess, tightness

parson *n* **1, 2** = **clergyman,** churchman, cleric, divine, ecclesiastic, incumbent, man of God, man of the cloth, minister, pastor, preacher, priest, rector, reverend (*inf.*), vicar

part *n* **1** = **piece,** bit, fraction, fragment, lot, particle, portion, scrap, section, sector, segment, share, slice **2** = **component,** branch, constituent, department, division, element, ingredient, limb, member, module, organ, piece, unit **5** = **role,** character, lines **6** = **duty,** bit, business, capacity, charge, function, involvement, office, place, responsibility, role, say, share, task, work **7** *often plural* = **region,** airt (*Scot.*), area, district, neck of the woods, neighbourhood, quarter, territory, vicinity **13 for the most part** = **mainly,** chiefly, generally, in the main, largely, mostly, on the whole, principally **14 in part** = **partly,** a little, in some measure, partially, slightly, somewhat, to a certain extent, to some degree **16 on the part of** = **on behalf of,** for the sake of, in support of, in the name of **20 take part in** = **participate in,** associate oneself with, be instrumental in, be involved in, have a hand in, join in, partake in, play a part in, put one's twopence-worth in, take a hand in ◆ *vb* **22** = **divide,** break, cleave, come apart, detach, disconnect, disjoin, dismantle, disunite, rend, separate, sever, split, tear **23, 24** = **leave,** break up, depart, go, go away, go (their) separate ways, part company, quit, say goodbye, separate, split up, take one's leave, withdraw **25** *foll. by* **with** = **give up,** abandon, discard, forgo, let go of, relinquish, renounce, sacrifice, surrender, yield
Antonyms *n* ≠ **piece:** bulk, entirety, mass, totality, whole ◆ *vb* ≠ **divide:** adhere, close, combine, hold, join, stick, unite ≠ **leave:** appear, arrive, come, gather, remain, show up (*inf.*), stay, turn up

partake *vb* **1** *foll. by* **in** = **participate in,** engage in, enter into, share in, take part in **2** *foll. by* **of** = **consume,** eat, receive, share, take

partial *adj* **1** = **incomplete,** fragmentary, imperfect, limited, uncompleted, unfinished **2** = **biased,** discriminatory, influenced, interested, one-sided, partisan, predisposed, prejudiced, tendentious, unfair, unjust **3 be partial to** = **have a liking for,** be fond of, be keen on, be taken with, care for, have a soft spot for, have a weakness for
Antonyms *adj* ≠ **incomplete:** complete, entire, finished, full, total, whole ≠ **biased:** impartial, objective, unbiased, unprejudiced

partiality *n* **2** = **bias,** favouritism, partisanship, predisposition, preference, prejudice **3** = **liking,** affinity, fondness, inclination, love, penchant, predilection, predisposition, preference, proclivity, taste, weakness
Antonyms *n* ≠ **bias:** disinterest, equity, fairness, impartiality, objectivity ≠ **liking:** abhorrence, antipathy, aversion, disgust, disinclination, dislike, distaste, loathing, revulsion

partially *adv* **1** = **partly,** fractionally, halfway, incompletely, in part, moderately, not wholly, piecemeal, somewhat, to a certain extent *or* degree

participant *n* = **participator,** associate, contributor, member, partaker, party, player, shareholder, stakeholder

participate *vb* = **take part,** be a participant, be a party to, be involved in, engage in, enter into, get in on the act, have a hand in, join in, partake, perform, share
Antonyms *vb* abstain, boycott, forgo, forsake, forswear, opt out, pass up, refrain from, take no part of

participation *n* = **taking part,** assistance, contribution, involvement, joining in, partaking, partnership, sharing in

particle *n* **1, 2** = **bit,** atom, crumb, grain, iota, jot, mite, molecule, mote, piece, scrap, shred, speck, tittle, whit

Physics. a body with finite mass that can be treated as having negligible size, and internal structure. **6** See **elementary particle.** [C14: from L *particula* a small part, from *pars* part]

particle accelerator *n* a machine for accelerating charged elementary particles to very high energies, used in nuclear physics.

particle physics *n* the study of fundamental particles and their properties. Also called: **high-energy physics.**

parti-coloured (ˈpɑːtɪˌkʌləd) *adj* having different colours in different parts; variegated. [C16 *parti*, from (obs.) *party* of more than one colour, from OF: striped, from L *partīre* to divide]

particular ❶ (pəˈtɪkjʊlə) *adj* **1** (*prenominal*) of or belonging to a single or specific person, thing, category, etc.; specific; special: *the particular demands of the job.* **2** (*prenominal*) exceptional or marked: *a matter of particular importance.* **3** (*prenominal*) relating to or providing specific details or circumstances: *a particular account.* **4** exacting or difficult to please, esp. in details; fussy. **5** (of the solution of a differential equation) obtained by giving specific values to the arbitrary constants in a general equation. **6** *Logic.* (of a proposition) affirming or denying something about only some members of a class of objects, as in *some men are not wicked.* Cf. **universal** (sense 9). ◆ *n* **7** a separate distinct item that helps to form a generalization: opposed to *general.* **8** (*often pl*) an item of information; detail: *complete in every particular.* **9 in particular.** especially or exactly. [C14: from OF *particuler*, from LL *particulāris* concerning a part, from L *particula* PARTICLE]
▸**parˈticularly** *adv*

particular average *n Insurance.* partial damage to or loss of a ship or its cargo affecting only the shipowner or one cargo owner. Abbrev.: **PA.** Cf. **general average.**

particularism (pəˈtɪkjʊləˌrɪzəm) *n* **1** exclusive attachment to the interests of one group, class, sect, etc. **2** the principle of permitting each state in a federation the right to further its own interests. **3** *Christian theol.* the doctrine that divine grace is restricted to the elect.
▸**parˈticularist** *n, adj*

particularity ❶ (pəˌtɪkjʊˈlærɪtɪ) *n, pl* **particularities. 1** (*often pl*) a specific circumstance: *the particularities of the affair.* **2** great attentiveness to detail; fastidiousness. **3** the quality of being precise: *a description of great particularity.* **4** the state or quality of being particular as opposed to general; individuality.

particularize ❶ *or* **particularise** (pəˈtɪkjʊləˌraɪz) *vb* **particularizes, particularizing, particularized** *or* **particularises, particularising, particularised. 1** to treat in detail; give details (about). **2** (*intr*) to go into detail.
▸**parˌticulariˈzation** *or* **parˌticulariˈsation** *n*

particulate (pɑːˈtɪkjʊlɪt, -ˌleɪt) *n* **1** a substance consisting of separate particles. ◆ *adj* **2** of or made up of separate particles.

parting ❶ (ˈpɑːtɪŋ) *n* **1** *Brit.* the line of scalp showing when sections of hair are combed in opposite directions. US, Canad., and Austral. equivalent: **part. 2** the act of separating or the state of being separated. **3a** a departure or leave-taking, esp. one causing a final separation. **3b** (*as modifier*): *a parting embrace.* **4** a place or line of separation or division. **5** a euphemism for **death.** ◆ *adj* (*prenominal*) **6** *Literary.* departing: *the parting day.* **7** serving to divide or separate.

partisan ❶ *or* **partizan** (ˌpɑːtɪˈzæn, ˈpɑːtɪˌzæn) *n* **1** an adherent or devotee of a cause, party, etc. **2** a member of an armed resistance group within occupied territory. ◆ *adj* **3** of, relating to, or characteristic of a partisan. **4** excessively devoted to one party, faction, etc.; one-sided. [C16: via F from OIt. *partigiano*, from *parte* faction, from L *pars* part]
▸**ˌpartiˈsanship** *or* **ˌpartiˈzanship** *n*

partita (pɑːˈtiːtə) *n, pl* **partite** (-teɪ) *or* **partitas** *Music.* a type of suite. [It.: divided (piece), from L *partīre* to divide]

partite (ˈpɑːtaɪt) *adj* **1** (*in combination*) composed of or divided into a specified number of parts: *bipartite.* **2** (esp. of plant leaves) divided almost to the base to form two or more parts. [C16: from L *partīre* to divide]

partition ❶ (pɑːˈtɪʃən) *n* **1** a division into parts; separation. **2** something that separates, such as a large screen dividing a room in two. **3** a part or share. **4** *Property law.* a division of property, esp. realty, among joint owners. ◆ *vb* (*tr*) **5** (often foll. by *off*) to separate or apportion into sections: *to partition a room off with a large screen.* **6** *Property law.* to divide (property, esp. realty) among joint owners. [C15: via OF from L *partītiō*, from *partīre* to divide]
▸**parˈtitioner** *or* **parˈtitionist** *n*

partitive (ˈpɑːtɪtɪv) *adj* **1** *Grammar.* indicating that a noun involved in a construction refers only to a part of what it otherwise refers to. The phrase *some of the butter* is a partitive construction. **2** serving to separate or divide into parts. ◆ *n* **3** *Grammar.* a partitive linguistic element or feature. [C16: from Med. L *partītīvus* serving to divide, from L *partīre* to divide]
▸**ˈpartitively** *adv*

partly ❶ (ˈpɑːtlɪ) *adv* not completely.

> **USAGE NOTE** *Partly* and *partially* are to some extent interchangeable, but *partly* should be used when referring to a part or parts of something: *the building is partly* (not *partially*) *of stone,* while *partially* is preferred for the meaning *to some extent: his mother is partially* (not *partly*) *sighted.*

partner ❶ (ˈpɑːtnə) *n* **1** an ally or companion: *a partner in crime.* **2** a member of a partnership. **3** one of a pair of dancers or players on the same side in a game: *my bridge partner.* **4** either member of a couple in a relationship. ◆ *vb* **5** to be or cause to be a partner (of). [C14: var. (infl. by PART) of *parcener* one who shares equally with another, from OF *parçonier*, ult. from L *partīre* to divide]

partnership ❶ (ˈpɑːtnəʃɪp) *n* **1a** a contractual relationship between two or more persons carrying on a joint business venture. **1b** the deed creating such a relationship. **1c** the persons associated in such a relationship. **2** the state or condition of being a partner.

part of speech *n* a class of words sharing important syntactic or semantic features; a group of words in a language that may occur in similar positions or fulfil similar functions in a sentence. The chief parts of speech in English are noun, pronoun, adjective, determiner, adverb, verb, preposition, conjunction, and interjection.

parton (ˈpɑːˌtɒn) *n Physics.* a hypothetical elementary particle postulated as a constituent of neutrons and protons. [from PART + -ON]

partook (pɑːˈtʊk) *vb* the past tense of **partake.**

partridge (ˈpɑːtrɪdʒ) *n, pl* **partridges** *or* **partridge.** any of various small Old World game birds of the pheasant family, esp. the common or European partridge. [C13: from OF *perdriz*, from L *perdix*, from Gk]

parts ❶ (pɑːts) *pl n* **1** personal abilities or talents: *a man of many parts.* **2** short for **private parts.**

part song *n* **1** a song composed in harmonized parts. **2** (*in more technical usage*) a piece of homophonic choral music in which the topmost part carries the melody.

part-time *adj* **1** occupying less than the full time normally associated with an activity: *a part-time job.* ◆ *adv* **part time. 2** on a part-time basis: *he works part time.* ◆ Cf. **full-time.**
▸**ˌpart-ˈtimer** *n*

parturient (pɑːˈtjʊərɪənt) *adj* **1** of or relating to childbirth. **2** giving birth. **3** producing a new idea, etc. [C16: via L *parturīre*, from *parere* to bring forth]
▸**parˈturiency** *n*

parturition (ˌpɑːtjʊˈrɪʃən) *n* the act or process of giving birth. [C17: from LL *parturītiō*, from *parturīre* to be in labour]

THESAURUS

particular *adj* **1** = **specific**, distinct, exact, express, peculiar, precise, special **2** = **special**, especial, exceptional, marked, notable, noteworthy, remarkable, singular, uncommon, unusual **3** = **detailed**, blow-by-blow, circumstantial, itemized, minute, painstaking, precise, selective, thorough **4** = **fussy**, choosy (*inf.*), critical, dainty, demanding, discriminating, exacting, fastidious, finicky, meticulous, nice (*rare*), overnice, pernickety (*inf.*), picky (*inf.*) ◆ *n* **8** *often plural* = **detail**, circumstance, fact, feature, item, specification **9 in particular** = **especially**, distinctly, exactly, expressly, particularly, specifically
Antonyms *adj* ≠ **specific:** general, imprecise, indefinite, indistinct, inexact, unspecified, vague ≠ **fussy:** casual, easy, easy to please, indiscriminate, negligent, slack, sloppy, uncritical

particularity *n* **1** *often plural* = **circumstance**, detail, fact, instance, item, point **2, 3** = **meticulousness**, accuracy, carefulness, choosiness (*inf.*), detail, fastidiousness, fussiness, precision, thoroughness **4** = **individuality**, characteristic, distinctiveness, feature, idiosyncrasy, peculiarity, property, singularity, trait

particularize *vb* **1, 2** = **specify**, detail, enumerate, give details, itemize, spell out, stipulate

particularly *adv* **1** = **specifically**, distinctly, especially, explicitly, expressly, in particular **2** = **especially**, decidedly, exceptionally, markedly, notably, outstandingly, peculiarly, singularly, surprisingly, uncommonly, unusually

parting *n* **1** = **division**, breaking, detachment, divergence, partition, rift, rupture, separation, split **3** = **going**, adieu, departure, farewell, goodbye, leave-taking, valediction ◆ *adj* **6** *Literary* = **farewell**, departing, final, last, valedictory

partisan *n* **1** = **supporter**, adherent, backer, champion, devotee, disciple, follower, stalwart, upholder, votary **2** = **underground fighter**, guerrilla, irregular, resistance fighter ◆ *adj* **3** = **underground**, guerrilla, irregular, resistance **4** = **prejudiced**, biased, factional, interested, one-sided, partial, sectarian, tendentious
Antonyms *n* ≠ **supporter:** adversary, contender, critic, detractor, foe, knocker (*inf.*), leader, opponent, rival ◆ *adj* ≠ **prejudiced:** bipartisan, broad-minded, disinterested, impartial, non-partisan, unbiased, unprejudiced

partition *n* **1** = **division**, dividing, segregation, separation, severance, splitting **2** = **screen**, barrier, divider, room divider, wall **3** = **allotment**, apportionment, distribution, portion, rationing out, share ◆ *vb* **5** = **separate**, divide, fence off, screen, wall off **5** = **divide**, apportion, cut up, parcel out, portion, section, segment, separate, share, split up, subdivide

partly *adv* = **partially**, halfway, incompletely, in part, in some measure, not fully, relatively, slightly, somewhat, to a certain degree *or* extent, up to a certain point
Antonyms *adv* completely, entirely, fully, in full, totally, wholly

partner *n* **1, 3** = **companion**, accomplice, ally, associate, bedfellow, collaborator, colleague, comrade, confederate, copartner, helper, mate, participant, team-mate **4** = **spouse**, bedfellow, better half (*Brit. inf.*), consort, helpmate, her indoors (*Brit. sl.*), husband *or* wife, mate, significant other (*US inf.*)

partnership *n* **1** = **company**, alliance, association, combine, conglomerate, cooperative, corporation, firm, house, society, union **2** = **cooperation**, companionship, connection, copartnership, fellowship, interest, participation, sharing

parts *pl n* **1** = **talents**, abilities, accomplishments, attributes, calibre, capabilities, endowments, faculties, genius, gifts, intellect, intelligence

part work *n Brit.* a series of magazines issued weekly or monthly, which are designed to be bound together to form a complete book.

party ➊ ('pɑːtɪ) *n, pl* **parties. 1a** a social gathering for pleasure, often held as a celebration. **1b** (*as modifier*): *party spirit.* **1c** (*in combination*): *partygoer.* **2** a group of people associated in some activity: *a rescue party.* **3a** (*often cap.*) a group of people organized together to further a common political aim, etc. **3b** (*as modifier*): *party politics.* **4** a person, esp. one entering into a contract. **5** the person or persons taking part in legal proceedings: *a party to the action.* **6** *Inf., humorous.* a person. ◆ *vb* **parties, partying, partied.** (*intr*) **7** *Inf.* to celebrate; revel. ◆ *adj* **8** *Heraldry.* (of a shield) divided vertically into two colours, metals, or furs. [C13: from OF *partie* part, from L *partīre* to divide; see PART]

party line *n* **1** a telephone line serving two or more subscribers. **2** the policies or dogma of a political party, etc.

party list *n* (*modifier*) of or relating to a system of voting in which people vote for a party rather than for a candidate. Parties are assigned the number of seats that reflects their share of the vote. See **proportional representation.**

party pooper ('puːpə) *n Inf.* a person whose behaviour or personality spoils other people's enjoyment. [C20: orig. US]

party wall *n Property law.* a wall separating two properties or pieces of land and over which each of the adjoining owners has certain rights.

par value *n* the value imprinted on the face of a share certificate or bond and used to assess dividend, capital ownership, or interest.

parvenu ➊ *or* (*fem*) **parvenue** ('pɑːvəˌnjuː) *n* **1** a person who, having risen socially or economically, is considered to be an upstart. ◆ *adj* **2** of or characteristic of a parvenu. [C19: from F, from *parvenir* to attain, from L *pervenīre,* from *per* through + *venīre* to come]

parvovirus ('pɑːvəʊˌvaɪrəs) *n* any of a group of viruses characterized by their very small size, each of which is specific to a particular species, as for example canine parvovirus. [C20: NL, from L *parvus* little + VIRUS]

pas (pɑː) *n, pl* **pas.** a dance step or movement, esp. in ballet. [C18: from F, lit.: step]

pascal ('pæskᵊl) *n* the derived SI unit of pressure; the pressure exerted on an area of 1 square metre by a force of 1 newton; equivalent to 10 dynes per square centimetre or 1.45×10^{-4} pound per square inch. Symbol: Pa [C20: after B. *Pascal* (1623–62), F mathematician & scientist]

PASCAL ('pæsˌkæl) *n* a high-level computer-programming language developed as a teaching language.

Pascal's triangle *n* a triangle consisting of rows of numbers; the apex is 1 and each row starts and ends with 1, other numbers being obtained by adding together the two numbers on either side in the row above: used to calculate probabilities. [C17: after B. *Pascal*; see PASCAL]

paschal ('pæskᵊl) *adj* **1** of or relating to **Passover** (sense 1). **2** of or relating to **Easter.** [C15: from OF *pascal,* via Church L from Heb. *pesakh* Passover]

Paschal Lamb *n* **1** (*sometimes not caps.*) *Old Testament.* the lamb killed and eaten on the first day of the Passover. **2** Christ regarded as this sacrifice.

pas de basque (ˌpɑː də 'bɑː) *n, pl* **pas de basque.** a dance step performed usually on the spot and used esp. in reels and jigs. [from F, lit.: Basque step]

pas de deux (*French* pɑddø) *n, pl* **pas de deux.** *Ballet.* a sequence for two dancers. [F: step for two]

pash (pæʃ) *n Sl.* infatuation. [C20: from PASSION]

pasha *or* **pacha** ('pɑːʃə, 'pæʃə) *n* (formerly) a high official of the Ottoman Empire or the modern Egyptian kingdom: placed after a name when used as a title. [C17: from Turkish *paşa*]

pashm ('pæʃəm) *n* the underfur of various Tibetan animals, esp. goats, used for Cashmere shawls. [from Persian, lit.: wool]

Pashto, Pushto ('pʌʃtəʊ), *or* **Pushtu** *n* **1** a language of Afghanistan and NW Pakistan. **2** (*pl* **Pashto** *or* **Pashtos, Pashtu** *or* **Pashtus; Pushto** *or* **Pushtos, Pushtu** *or* **Pushtus**) a speaker of the Pashto language; a Pathan. ◆ *adj* **3** denoting or relating to this language or a speaker of it.

paso doble ('pæsəʊ 'dəʊbleɪ) *n, pl* **paso dobles** *or* **pasos dobles. 1** a modern ballroom dance in fast duple time. **2** a piece of music composed for or in the rhythm of this dance. [Sp.: double step]

pas op ('pɑːs ˌɒp) *interj S. African.* beware. [Afrik.]

pasqueflower ('pɑːskˌflaʊə) *n* **1** a small purple-flowered plant of N and Central Europe and W Asia. **2** any of several related North American plants. [C16: from F *passefleur,* from *passer* to excel + *fleur* flower; changed to *pasqueflower* Easter flower, because it blooms at Easter]

pasquinade (ˌpæskwɪ'neɪd) *n* an abusive lampoon or satire, esp. one posted in a public place. [C17: from It. *Pasquino* name given to an ancient Roman statue disinterred in 1501, which was annually posted with satirical verses]

pass ➊ (pɑːs) *vb* **1** to go onwards or move by or past (a person, thing, etc.). **2** to run, extend, or lead through, over, or across (a place): *the route passes through the city.* **3** to go through or cause to go through (an obstacle or barrier): *to pass a needle through cloth.* **4** to move or cause to move onwards or over: *he passed his hand over her face.* **5** (*tr*) to go beyond or exceed: *this victory passes all expectation.* **6** to gain or cause to gain an adequate mark or grade in (an examination, course, etc.). **7** (often foll. by *away* or *by*) to elapse or allow to elapse: *we passed the time talking.* **8** (*intr*) to take place or happen: *what passed at the meeting?* **9** to speak or exchange or be spoken or exchanged: *angry words passed between them.* **10** to spread or cause to spread: *we passed the news round the class.* **11** to transfer or exchange or be transferred or exchanged: *the bomb passed from hand to hand.* **12** (*intr*) to undergo change or transition: *to pass from joy to despair.* **13** (when *tr,* often foll. by *down*) to transfer or be transferred by inheritance: *the house passed to the younger son.* **14** to agree to or be agreed to by a legislative body, etc.: *the assembly passed 10 resolutions.* **15** (*tr*) (of a legislative measure) to undergo (a procedural stage) and be agreed: *the bill passed the committee stage.* **16** (when *tr,* often foll. by *on* or *upon*) to pronounce (judgment, findings, etc.): *the court passed sentence.* **17** to go or allow to go without comment or censure: *the insult passed unnoticed.* **18** (*intr*) to opt not to exercise a right, as by not answering a question or not making a bid or a play in card games. **19** to discharge (urine, etc.) from the body. **20** (*intr*) to come to an end or disappear: *his anger soon passed.* **21** (*intr;* usually foll. by *for* or *as*) to be likely to be mistaken for (someone or something else): *you could easily pass for your sister.* **22** (*intr;* foll. by *away, on,* or *over*) *Euphemistic.* to die. **23** *Sport.* to hit, kick, or throw (the ball, etc.) to another player. **24 bring to pass.** *Arch.* to cause to happen. **25 come to pass.** *Arch.* to happen. ◆ *n* **26** the act of passing. **27** a route through a range of mountains where there is a gap between peaks. **28** a permit, licence, or authorization to do something without restriction. **29a** a document allowing entry to and exit from a military installation. **29b** a document authorizing leave of absence. **30** *Brit.* **30a** the passing of a college or university examination to a satisfactory standard but not as high as honours. **30b** (*as modifier*): *a pass degree.* **31** a dive, sweep, or bombing or landing run by an aircraft. **32** a motion of the hand or of a wand as part of a conjuring trick. **33** *Inf.* an attempt to invite sexual intimacy (esp. in **make a pass at**). **34** a state of affairs, esp. a bad one (esp. in **a pretty pass**). **35** *Sport.* the transfer of a ball, etc., from one player to another. **36** *Fencing.* a thrust or lunge. **37** *Bridge, etc.* the act of passing (making no bid). ◆ *sentence substitute.* **38** *Bridge, etc.* a call indicating that a player has no bid to make. ◆ See also **pass off, pass out,** etc. [C13: from OF *passer* to pass, surpass, from L *passūs* step]

pass. *abbrev. for:* **1** passive. **2** passenger. **3** passage.

passable ➊ ('pɑːsəbᵊl) *adj* **1** adequate, fair, or acceptable. **2** (of an obstacle) capable of being crossed. **3** (of currency) valid for circulation. **4** (of a proposed law) able to be enacted.
▸ **'passableness** *n* ▸ **'passably** *adv*

passacaglia (ˌpæsə'kɑːljə) *n* **1** an old Spanish dance in slow triple time. **2** a slow instrumental piece characterized by a series of variations on a

THESAURUS

party *n* **1** = **get-together** (*inf.*), at-home, bash (*inf.*), beano (*Brit. sl.*), celebration, do (*inf.*), festivity, function, gathering, hooley *or* hoolie (*chiefly Irish & NZ*), knees-up (*Brit. inf.*), rave (*Brit. sl.*), rave-up (*Brit. sl.*), reception, shindig (*inf.*), social, social gathering, soirée **2** = **group**, band, body, bunch (*inf.*), company, crew, detachment (*Military*), gang, gathering, squad, team, unit **3** = **faction**, alliance, association, cabal, camp, clique, coalition, combination, confederacy, coterie, grouping, league, schism, set, side **4** = **person**, individual, somebody, someone **5** = **litigant**, contractor (*Law*), defendant, participant, plaintiff

parvenu *n* **1** = **upstart**, arriviste, *nouveau riche*, social climber ◆ *adj* **2** = **upstart**, *nouveau riche*

pass *vb* **1, 7** = **go by** *or* **past**, depart, elapse, flow, go, lapse, leave, move, move onwards, proceed, roll, run **5** = **exceed**, beat, excel, go beyond, outdistance, outdo, outstrip, overtake, surmount, surpass, transcend **6** = **qualify**, answer, come up to scratch, do, get through, graduate, pass muster, succeed, suffice, suit **7** = **spend**, beguile, devote, employ, experience, fill, occupy, suffer, undergo, while away **8** = **happen**, befall, come up, develop, fall out, occur, take place **11** = **give**, convey, deliver, exchange, hand, kick, let have, reach, send, throw, transfer, transmit **14** = **approve**, accept, adopt, authorize, decree, enact, establish, legislate, ordain, ratify, sanction, validate **16** = **pronounce**, declare, deliver, express, utter **17** = **ignore**, disregard, miss, neglect, not heed, omit, overlook, skip (*inf.*) **19** = **excrete**, crap (*taboo sl.*), defecate, discharge, eliminate, empty, evacuate, expel, shit (*taboo sl.*), void **20** = **end**, blow over, cease, die, disappear, dissolve, dwindle, ebb, evaporate, expire, fade, go, melt away, terminate, vanish, wane **21** *with* **for** *or* **as** = **be mistaken for**, be accepted as, be regarded as, be taken for, impersonate, serve as **22** *foll. by* **away**, **on** *or* **over** *Euphemistic* = **die**, buy it (*US sl.*), croak (*sl.*), decease, depart (this life), expire, kick the bucket (*sl.*), peg out (*inf.*), pop one's clogs (*inf.*), shuffle off this mortal coil, snuff it (*inf.*) ◆ *n* **27** = **gap**, canyon, col, defile, gorge, ravine, route **28, 29** = **licence**, authorization, identification, identity card, passport, permission, permit, safe-conduct, ticket, warrant **33** *Informal As in* **make a pass at** = **advances**, approach, overture, play (*inf.*), proposition, suggestion **34** *As in* **a pretty pass** = **predicament**, condition, juncture, pinch, plight, situation, stage, state, state of affairs, straits
Antonyms *vb* ≠ **go by** *or* past: bring *or* come to a standstill, cease, halt, pause, stop ≠ **qualify:** be inadequate, be inferior to, be unsuccessful, come a cropper (*inf.*), fail, lose, suffer defeat ≠ **approve:** ban, disallow, invalidate, overrule, prohibit, refuse, reject, veto ≠ **ignore:** acknowledge, heed, note, notice, observe, pay attention to

passable *adj* **1** = **adequate**, acceptable, admissible, allowable, all right, average, fair, fair enough, mediocre, middling, moderate, not too bad, ordinary, presentable, so-so (*inf.*), tolerable, unexceptional **2** = **clear**, crossable, navigable, open, traversable, unobstructed
Antonyms *adj* ≠ **adequate:** A1 *or* A-one (*inf.*), exceptional, extraordinary, first-class, inadequate, inadmissible, marvellous, outstanding, superb, tops (*sl.*), unacceptable, unsatisfactory ≠ **clear:** blocked, closed, impassable, obstructed, sealed off, unnavigable

passably *adv* **1** = **well enough**, acceptably, adequately, after a fashion, fairly, moderately, particular theme played over a repeated bass part. [C17: earlier *passacalle,* from Sp. *pasacalle* street dance, from *paso* step + *calle* street]

passage Ⓣ ('pæsɪdʒ) *n* **1** a channel, opening, etc., through or by which a person or thing may pass. **2** *Music.* a section or division of a piece, movement, etc. **3** a way, as in a hall or lobby. **4** a section of a written work, speech, etc. **5** a journey, esp. by ship. **6** the act or process of passing from one place, condition, etc., to another: *passage of a gas through a liquid.* **7** the permission, right, or freedom to pass: *to be denied passage through a country.* **8** the enactment of a law by a legislative body. **9** *Rare.* an exchange, as of blows, words, etc. [C13: from OF from *passer* to PASS]

passageway Ⓣ ('pæsɪdʒ,weɪ) *n* a way, esp. one in or between buildings; passage.

pass band *n* the band of frequencies that is transmitted with maximum efficiency through a circuit, filter, etc.

passbook ('pɑːs,bʊk) *n* **1** a book for keeping a record of withdrawals from and payments into a building society. **2** another name for **bankbook. 3** *S. African.* an official document to identify the bearer, his race, residence, and employment.

passé Ⓣ ('pɑːseɪ, 'pæseɪ) *adj* **1** out-of-date: *passé ideas.* **2** past the prime; faded: *a passé society beauty.* [C18: from F, p.p. of *passer* to PASS]

passenger Ⓣ ('pæsɪndʒə) *n* **1a** a person travelling in a car, train, boat, etc., not driven by him. **1b** *(as modifier): a passenger seat.* **2** *Chiefly Brit.* a member of a group or team who is not participating fully in the work. [C14: from OF *passager* passing, from PASSAGE]

passenger pigeon *n* a gregarious North American pigeon, now extinct.

passe-partout (ˌpæspɑː'tuː) *n* **1** a mounting for a picture in which strips of gummed paper bind together the glass, picture, and backing. **2** the gummed paper used for this. **3** a mat on which a photograph, etc., is mounted. **4** something that secures entry everywhere, esp. a master key. [C17: from F, lit.: pass everywhere]

passepied (pɑːs'pjeɪ) *n, pl* **passepieds** (-'pjeɪ). **1** a lively minuet in triple time, popular in the 17th century. **2** a piece of music composed for or in the rhythm of this dance. [C17: from F: pass foot]

passer-by Ⓣ *n, pl* **passers-by.** a person who is passing or going by, esp. on foot.

passerine ('pæsəˌraɪn, -ˌriːn) *adj* **1** of, relating to, or belonging to an order of birds characterized by the perching habit: includes the larks, finches, starlings, etc. ◆ *n* **2** any bird belonging to this order. [C18: from L *passer* sparrow]

passim *Latin.* ('pæsɪm) *adv* here and there; throughout: used to indicate that what is referred to occurs frequently in the work cited.

passing Ⓣ ('pɑːsɪŋ) *adj* **1** transitory or momentary: *a passing fancy.* **2** cursory or casual in action or manner: *a passing reference.* ◆ *adv, adj* **3** *Arch.* to an extreme degree: *the events were passing strange.* ◆ *n* **4** a place where or means by which one may pass, cross, ford, etc. **5** a euphemistic word for **death. 6 in passing.** by the way; incidentally.

passing bell *n* a bell rung to announce a death or a funeral. Also called: **death knell.**

passing note *or US* **passing tone** *n* a nonharmonic note through which a melody passes from one harmonic note to the next.

passion Ⓣ ('pæʃən) *n* **1** ardent love or affection. **2** intense sexual love. **3** a strong affection or enthusiasm for an object, concept, etc.: *a passion for poetry.* **4** any strongly felt emotion, such as love, hate, envy, etc. **5** an outburst of anger: *he flew into a passion.* **6** the object of an intense desire, ardent affection, or enthusiasm. **7** an outburst expressing intense emotion: *he burst into a passion of sobs.* **8** the sufferings and death of a Christian martyr. [C12: via F from Church L *passiō* suffering, from L *patī* to suffer]
▸'**passional** *adj* ▸'**passionless** *adj*

Passion ('pæʃən) *n* **1** the sufferings of Christ from the Last Supper to his death on the cross. **2** any of the four Gospel accounts of this. **3** a musical setting of this: *the St Matthew Passion.*

passionate Ⓣ ('pæʃənɪt) *adj* **1** manifesting or exhibiting intense sexual feeling or desire. **2** capable of, revealing, or characterized by intense emotion. **3** easily roused to anger; quick-tempered.
▸'**passionately** *adv*

passionflower ('pæʃən,flaʊə) *n* any plant of a tropical American genus cultivated for their red, yellow, greenish, or purple showy flowers: some species have edible fruit. [C17: from alleged resemblance betweeen parts of the flower and the instruments of the Crucifixion]

passion fruit *n* the edible fruit of any of various passionflowers, esp. granadilla.

Passion play *n* a play depicting the Passion of Christ.

passive Ⓣ ('pæsɪv) *adj* **1** not active or not participating perceptibly in an activity, organization, etc. **2** unresisting and receptive to external forces; submissive. **3** affected or acted upon by an external object or force. **4** *Grammar.* denoting a voice of verbs in sentences in which the grammatical subject is the recipient of the action described by the verb, as *was broken* in the sentence *The glass was broken by a boy.* **5** *Chem.* (of a substance, esp. a metal) apparently chemically unreactive. **6** *Electronics, telecomm.* **6a** capable only of attenuating a signal: *a passive network.* **6b** not capable of amplifying a signal or controlling a function: *a passive communications satellite.* **7** *Finance.* (of a bond, share, debt, etc.) yielding no interest. ◆ *n* **8** *Grammar.* **8a** the passive voice. **8b** a passive verb. [C14: from L *passīvus* susceptible of suffering, from *patī* to undergo]
▸'**passively** *adv* ▸**pas'sivity** *or* '**passiveness** *n*

passive resistance *n* resistance to a government, law, etc., without violence, as by fasting, demonstrating, or refusing to cooperate.

passive smoking *n* the inhalation of smoke from other people's cigarettes by a nonsmoker.

passkey ('pɑːs,kiː) *n* **1** any of various keys, esp. a latchkey. **2** another term for **master key** or **skeleton key.**

pass law *n* (formerly, in South Africa) a law restricting the movement of Black Africans.

pass off Ⓣ *vb (adv)* **1** to be or cause to be accepted in a false character: *he passed the fake diamonds off as real.* **2** *(intr)* to come to a gradual end; disappear: *eventually the pain passed off.* **3** *(intr)* to take place: *the meeting passed off without disturbance.* **4** *(tr)* to set aside or disregard: *I managed to pass off his insult.*

pass out Ⓣ *vb (adv)* **1** *(intr) Inf.* to become unconscious; faint. **2** *(intr) Brit.* (esp. of an officer cadet) to qualify for a military commission, etc. **3** *(tr)* to distribute.

pass over Ⓣ *vb* **1** *(tr, adv)* to take no notice of; disregard: *they passed me over in the last round of promotions.* **2** *(intr, prep)* to disregard (something bad or embarrassing).

Passover ('pɑːs,əʊvə) *n* **1** an eight-day Jewish festival celebrated in commemoration of the passing over or sparing of the Israelites in Egypt (Exodus 12). **2** another term for the **Paschal Lamb.** [C16: from *pass over,* translation of Heb. *pesah,* from *pāsah* to pass over]

THESAURUS

pretty much, rather, relatively, somewhat, tolerably

passage *n* **1** = **way,** alley, avenue, channel, course, lane, opening, path, road, route, thoroughfare **3** = **corridor,** aisle, doorway, entrance, entrance hall, exit, hall, hallway, lobby, passageway, vestibule **4** = **extract,** clause, excerpt, paragraph, piece, quotation, reading, section, sentence, text, verse **5** = **journey,** crossing, tour, trek, trip, voyage **6** = **movement,** advance, change, conversion, flow, motion, passing, progress, progression, transit, transition **7** = **safe-conduct,** allowance, authorization, freedom, permission, right, visa, warrant **8** = **establishment,** acceptance, enactment, legalization, legislation, passing, ratification

passageway *n* = **corridor,** aisle, alley, cut, entrance, exit, hall, hallway, lane, lobby, passage, wynd *(Scot.)*

passé *adj* **1** = **out-of-date,** antiquated, dated, *démodé,* obsolete, old-fashioned, old hat, outdated, outmoded, outworn, unfashionable

passenger *n* **1** = **traveller,** fare, hitchhiker, pillion rider, rider

passer-by *n* = **bystander,** onlooker, witness

passing *adj* **1** = **momentary,** brief, ephemeral, fleeting, short, short-lived, temporary, transient, transitory **2** = **superficial,** casual, cursory, glancing, hasty, quick, shallow, short, slight ◆ *n* **5** = **end,** death, decease, demise, finish, loss, termination **6 in passing** = **incidentally,** accidentally, by the bye, by the way, en passant, on the way

passion *n* **1, 2** = **love,** adoration, affection, ardour, attachment, concupiscence, desire, fondness, infatuation, itch, keenness, lust, the hots *(sl.)* **3** = **mania,** bug *(inf.),* craving, craze, enthusiasm, fancy, fascination, idol, infatuation, obsession **5, 7** = **rage,** anger, fit, flare-up *(inf.),* frenzy, fury, indignation, ire, outburst, paroxysm, resentment, storm, vehemence, wrath
Antonyms *n* ≠ **emotion:** apathy, calmness, coldness, coolness, frigidity, hate, indifference, unconcern

passionate *adj* **1** = **loving,** amorous, ardent, aroused, desirous, erotic, hot, lustful, sensual, sexy *(inf.),* steamy *(inf.),* wanton **2** = **emotional,** ablaze, animated, ardent, eager, enthusiastic, excited, fervent, fervid, fierce, flaming, frenzied, heartfelt, impassioned, impetuous, impulsive, intense, strong, vehement, warm, wild, zealous **3** = **quick-tempered,** choleric, excitable, fiery, hot-headed, hot-tempered, irascible, irritable, peppery, stormy, tempestuous, violent
Antonyms *adj* ≠ **loving:** cold, frigid, passionless, unloving, unresponsive ≠ **emotional:** apathetic, calm, cold, half-hearted, indifferent, languorous, nonchalant, subdued, unemotional, unenthusiastic ≠ **quick-tempered:** agreeable, calm, easy-going, even-tempered, nonviolent, placid, unexcitable

passionately *adv* **1** = **lovingly,** amorously, ardently, desirously, erotically, hot-bloodedly, libidinously, lustfully, sensually, sexily *(inf.),* steamily *(inf.),* with passion **2** = **emotionally,** animatedly, ardently, eagerly, enthusiastically, excitedly, fervently, fervidly, fiercely, frenziedly, impetuously, impulsively, intensely, strongly, vehemently, warmly, wildly, with all one's heart, zealously **3** = **furiously,** angrily, excitably, fierily, hot-headedly, irascibly, stormily, tempestuously, violently
Antonyms *adv* ≠ **lovingly:** coldly, frigidly, unlovingly, unresponsively ≠ **emotionally:** apathetically, calmly, coldly, half-heartedly, indifferently, nonchalantly, unemotionally, unenthusiastically ≠ **furiously:** calmly, placidly, unexcitably

passive *adj* **1, 2** = **submissive,** acquiescent, compliant, docile, enduring, inactive, inert, lifeless, long-suffering, nonviolent, patient, quiescent, receptive, resigned, unassertive, uninvolved, unresisting
Antonyms *adj* active, alive, assertive, bossy *(inf.),* defiant, domineering, energetic, feisty *(inf., chiefly US & Canad.),* impatient, involved, lively, rebellious, spirited, violent, zippy *(inf.)*

pass off *vb* **1** = **fake,** counterfeit, feign, make a pretence of, palm off **2** = **come to an end,** die away, disappear, fade out, vanish **3** = **take place,** be completed, go off, happen, occur, turn out

pass out *vb* **1** *Informal* = **faint,** become unconscious, black out *(inf.),* drop, flake out *(inf.),* keel over *(inf.),* lose consciousness, swoon *(literary)* **2** = **hand out,** deal out, distribute, dole out

pass over *vb* **1, 2** = **disregard,** discount, forget,

passport (ˈpɑːspɔːt) *n* **1** an official document issued by a government, identifying an individual, granting him permission to travel abroad, and requesting the protection of other governments for him. **2** a quality, asset, etc., that gains a person admission or acceptance. [C15: from F *passeport,* from *passer* to PASS + PORT[1]]

pass up Ⓣ *vb (tr, adv) Inf.* to let go by; ignore: *I won't pass up this opportunity.*

password Ⓣ (ˈpɑːsˌwɜːd) *n* **1** a secret word, phrase, etc., that ensures admission by proving identity, membership, etc. **2** an action, quality, etc., that gains admission or acceptance. **3** *Computing.* a sequence of characters used to gain access to a computer system.

past Ⓣ (pɑːst) *adj* **1** completed, finished, and no longer in existence: *past happiness.* **2** denoting or belonging to the time that has elapsed at the present moment: *the past history of the world.* **3** denoting a specific unit of time that immediately precedes the present one: *the past month.* **4** (*prenominal*) denoting a person who has held an office or position; former: *a past president.* **5** *Grammar.* denoting any of various tenses of verbs that are used in describing actions, events, or states that have been begun or completed at the time of utterance. ♦ *n* **6 the past.** the period of time that has elapsed: *forget the past.* **7** the history, experience, or background of a nation, person, etc. **8** an earlier period of someone's life, esp. one regarded as disreputable. **9** *Grammar.* **9a** a past tense. **9b** a verb in a past tense. ♦ *adv* **10** at a time before the present; ago: *three years past.* **11** on or onwards: *I greeted him but he just walked past.* ♦ *prep* **12** beyond in time: *it's past midnight.* **13** beyond in place or position: *the library is past the church.* **14** moving beyond: *he walked past me.* **15** beyond or above the reach, limit, or scope of: *his foolishness is past comprehension.* **16 past it.** *Inf.* unable to perform the tasks one could do when one was younger. **17 not put it past someone.** to consider someone capable of (the action specified). [C14: from *passed,* p.p. of PASS]

> **USAGE NOTE** The past participle of *pass* is sometimes wrongly spelt *past*: *the time for recrimination has passed* (not *past*).

pasta (ˈpæstə) *n* any of several variously shaped edible preparations made from a flour and water dough, such as spaghetti. [It., from LL: PASTE]

paste Ⓣ (peɪst) *n* **1** a mixture of a soft or malleable consistency, such as toothpaste. **2** an adhesive made from water and flour or starch, used for joining pieces of paper, etc. **3** a preparation of food, such as meat, that has been pounded to a creamy mass, for spreading on bread, etc. **4** any of various sweet doughy confections: *almond paste.* **5** dough, esp. for making pastry. **6a** a hard shiny glass used for making imitation gems. **6b** an imitation gem made of this glass. **7** the combined ingredients of porcelain. See also **hard paste, soft paste.** ♦ *vb* **pastes, pasting, pasted.** (*tr*) **8** (often foll. by *on* or *onto*) to attach as by using paste: *he pasted posters onto the wall.* **9** (usually foll. by *with*) to cover (a surface) with paper, etc.: *he pasted the wall with posters.* **10** *Sl.* to thrash or beat; defeat. [C14: via OF from LL *pasta* dough, from Gk *pastē* barley porridge, from *passein* to sprinkle]

pasteboard (ˈpeɪstˌbɔːd) *n* **1** a stiff board formed from layers of paper or pulp pasted together. ♦ *adj* **2** flimsy or fake.

pastel Ⓣ (ˈpæstᵊl, pæˈstɛl) *n* **1a** a substance made of ground pigment bound with gum. **1b** a crayon of this. **1c** a drawing done in such crayons. **2** the medium or technique of pastel drawing. **3** a pale delicate colour. ♦ *adj* **4** (of a colour) pale; delicate: *pastel blue.* [C17: via F from It. *pastello,* from LL *pastellus* woad, dim. of *pasta* PASTE]
▸ **ˈpastelist** *or* **ˈpastellist** *n*

pastern (ˈpæstən) *n* the part of a horse's foot between the fetlock and the hoof. [C14: from OF *pasturon,* from *pasture* a hobble, from L *pāstōrius* of a shepherd, from PASTOR]

paste-up *n Printing.* a sheet of paper or board on which are pasted artwork, proofs, etc., for photographing prior to making a plate.

pasteurism (ˈpæstəˌrɪzəm, -stjə-, ˈpɑː-) *n Med.* a method of securing immunity from rabies or of treating patients with other viral infections by the serial injection of progressively more virulent suspensions of the causative virus. Also called: **Pasteur treatment.** [C19: after Louis *Pasteur* (1822–95), F chemist & bacteriologist]

pasteurization *or* **pasteurisation** (ˌpæstəraɪˈzeɪʃən, -stjə-, ˌpɑː-) *n* the process of heating beverages, such as milk, beer, wine, or cider, or solid foods, such as cheese or crab meat, to destroy harmful microorganisms.

pasteurize *or* **pasteurise** (ˈpæstəˌraɪz, -stjə-, ˈpɑː-) *vb* **pasteurizes, pasteurizing, pasteurized** *or* **pasteurises, pasteurising, pasteurised.** (*tr*) to subject (milk, beer, etc.) to pasteurization.
▸ **ˈpasteurˌizer** *or* **ˈpasteurˌiser** *n*

pastiche Ⓣ (pæˈstiːʃ) *or* **pasticcio** (pæˈstɪtʃəʊ) *n, pl* **pastiches** *or* **pasticcios. 1** a work of art that mixes styles, materials, etc. **2** a work of art that imitates the style of another artist or period. [C19: F *pastiche,* It. *pasticcio,* lit.: piecrust (hence, something blended) from LL *pasta* PASTE]

pastille Ⓣ *or* **pastil** (ˈpæstɪl) *n* **1** a small flavoured or medicated lozenge. **2** an aromatic substance burnt to fumigate the air. [C17: via F from L *pastillus* small loaf, from *pānis* bread]

pastime Ⓣ (ˈpɑːsˌtaɪm) *n* an activity or entertainment which makes time pass pleasantly.

past master Ⓣ *n* **1** a person with talent for, or experience in, a particular activity. **2** a person who has held the office of master in a guild, etc.

pastor Ⓣ (ˈpɑːstə) *n* **1** a clergyman or priest in charge of a congregation. **2** a person who exercises spiritual guidance over a number of people. **3** a S Asian starling having a black head and wings and a pale pink body. [C14: from L: shepherd, from *pascere* to feed]
▸ **ˈpastorship** *n*

pastoral Ⓣ (ˈpɑːstərəl) *adj* **1** of, characterized by, or depicting rural life, scenery, etc. **2** (of a literary work) dealing with an idealized form of rural existence. **3** (of land) used for pasture. **4** of or relating to a clergyman or priest in charge of a congregation or his duties as such. **5** of or relating to shepherds, their work, etc. **6** of or relating to a teacher's responsibility for the personal, as distinct from the educational, development of pupils. ♦ *n* **7** a literary work or picture portraying rural life, esp. in an idealizing way. **8** *Music.* a variant spelling of **pastorale. 9a** a letter from a clergyman to the people under his charge. **9b** the letter of a bishop to the clergy or people of his diocese. **9c** Also called: **pastoral staff.** the crosier carried by a bishop. [C15: from L, from PASTOR]
▸ **ˈpastoralism** *n* ▸ **ˈpastorally** *adv*

pastorale (ˌpæstəˈrɑːl) *n, pl* **pastorales.** *Music.* **1** a composition evocative of rural life, sometimes with a droning accompaniment. **2** a musical play based on a rustic story. [C18: It., from L: PASTORAL]

pastoralist (ˈpɑːstərəlɪst) *n Austral.* a grazier raising sheep, cattle, etc., on a large scale.

pastorate (ˈpɑːstərɪt) *n* **1** the office or term of office of a pastor. **2** a body of pastors.

pastourelle (ˌpɑːstuːˈrɛl) *n Music.* **1** a pastoral piece of music. **2** one of the figures in a quadrille. [C19: from F: little shepherdess]

past participle *n* a participial form of verbs used to modify a noun that is logically the object of a verb, also used in certain compound tenses and passive forms of the verb.

past perfect *Grammar.* ♦ *adj* **1** denoting a tense of verbs used in relating past events where the action had already occurred at the time of the action of a main verb that is itself in a past tense. In English this is a compound tense formed with *had* plus the past participle. ♦ *n* **2a** the past perfect tense. **2b** a verb in this tense.

pastrami (pəˈstrɑːmɪ) *n* highly seasoned smoked beef. [from Yiddish, from Romanian *pastramă,* from *păstra* to preserve]

pastry (ˈpeɪstrɪ) *n, pl* **pastries. 1** a dough of flour, water, and fat. **2** baked foods, such as tarts, made with this dough. **3** an individual cake or pastry pie. [C16: from PASTE]

pasturage (ˈpɑːstʃərɪdʒ) *n* **1** the business of grazing cattle. **2** another word for **pasture.**

pasture Ⓣ (ˈpɑːstʃə) *n* **1** land covered with grass or herbage and grazed by or suitable for grazing by livestock. **2** the grass or herbage growing on it. ♦ *vb* **pastures, pasturing, pastured. 3** (*tr*) to cause (livestock) to graze or (of livestock) to graze (a pasture). [C13: via OF from LL *pāstūra,* from *pascere* to feed]

pasty[1] Ⓣ (ˈpeɪstɪ) *adj* **pastier, pastiest. 1** of or like the colour, texture, etc., of paste. **2** (esp. of the complexion) pale or unhealthy-looking.
▸ **ˈpastily** *adv* ▸ **ˈpastiness** *n*

THESAURUS

ignore, not dwell on, omit, overlook, pass by, take no notice of

pass up *vb Informal* = **miss**, abstain, decline, forgo, give (something) a miss (*inf.*), ignore, let slip, let (something) go by, neglect, refuse, reject

password *n* **1** = **signal**, countersign, key word, open sesame, watchword

past *adj* **1** = **over**, accomplished, completed, done, elapsed, ended, extinct, finished, forgotten, gone, over and done with, spent **2, 4** = **former**, ancient, bygone, early, erstwhile, foregoing, late, long-ago, olden, preceding, previous, prior, quondam, recent ♦ *n* **6 the past** = **former times**, antiquity, days gone by, days of yore, good old days, history, long ago, olden days, old times, times past, yesteryear (*literary*) **7** = **background**, experience, history, life, past life ♦ *prep* **12, 13** = **after**, beyond, farther than, later than, outside, over, subsequent to **14** = **beyond**, across, by, on, over

Antonyms *adj* ≠ **former**: arrived, begun, coming, future, now, present ♦ *n* ≠ **former times**: future, now, present, time to come, today, tomorrow

paste *n* **2** = **adhesive**, cement, glue, gum, mucilage ♦ *vb* **8** = **stick**, cement, fasten, fix, glue, gum

pastel *adj* **3** = **pale**, delicate, light, muted, soft, soft-hued

Antonyms *adj* bright, deep, rich, strong, vibrant, vivid

pastiche *n* **1** = **medley**, blend, farrago, gallimaufry, hotchpotch, *mélange,* miscellany, mixture, motley

pastille *n* **1** = **lozenge**, cough drop, jujube, tablet, troche (*Medical*)

pastime *n* = **activity**, amusement, distraction, diversion, entertainment, game, hobby, leisure, play, recreation, relaxation, sport

past master *n* **1** = **expert**, ace, artist, dab hand (*Brit. inf.*), old hand, virtuoso, wizard

pastor *n* **1** = **clergyman**, churchman, divine, ecclesiastic, minister, parson, priest, rector, vicar

pastoral *adj* **1** = **rustic**, agrestic, Arcadian, bucolic, country, georgic (*literary*), idyllic, rural, simple **4** = **ecclesiastical**, clerical, ministerial, priestly

pasture *n* **1, 2** = **grassland**, grass, grazing, grazing land, lea (*poetic*), meadow, pasturage, shieling (*Scot.*)

pasty[1] *adj* **1** = **sticky**, doughy, glutinous, mucilaginous, starchy **2** = **pale**, anaemic, like death warmed up (*inf.*), pallid, sallow, sickly, unhealthy, wan, wheyfaced

pasty[2] ('pæstɪ) *n, pl* **pasties.** a round of pastry folded over a filling of meat, vegetables, etc. [C13: from OF *pastée,* from LL *pasta* dough]

PA system *n* See **public-address system.**

pat[1] Ⓣ (pæt) *vb* **pats, patting, patted. 1** to hit (something) lightly with the palm of the hand or some other flat surface: *to pat a ball.* **2** to slap (a person or animal) gently, esp. on the back, as an expression of affection, congratulation, etc. **3** (*tr*) to shape, smooth, etc., with a flat instrument or the palm. **4** (*intr*) to walk or run with light footsteps. **5 pat (someone) on the back.** *Inf.* to congratulate. ◆ *n* **6** a light blow with something flat. **7** a gentle slap. **8** a small mass of something: *a pat of butter.* **9** the sound of patting. **10 pat on the back.** *Inf.* a gesture or word indicating approval. [C14: ? imit.]

pat[2] Ⓣ (pæt) *adv* **1** Also: **off pat.** exactly or fluently memorized: *he recited it pat.* **2** opportunely or aptly. **3 stand pat. 3a** *Chiefly US & Canad.* to refuse to abandon a belief, decision, etc. **3b** (in poker, etc.) to play without adding new cards to the hand dealt. ◆ *adj* **4** exactly right; apt: *a pat reply.* **5** too exactly fitting; glib: *a pat answer to a difficult problem.* **6** exactly right: *a pat hand in poker.* [C17: ? adv use ("with a light stroke") of PAT[1]]

pat[3] (pæt) *n* **on one's pat.** *Austral. inf.* alone. [C20: rhyming slang, from *Pat* Malone]

pat. *abbrev. for* patent(ed).

patagium (pə'teɪdʒɪəm) *n, pl* **patagia** (-dʒɪə). **1** a web of skin in bats and gliding mammals that functions as a wing. **2** a membranous fold of skin connecting a bird's wing to the shoulder. [C19: NL, from L, from Gk *patageion* gold border on a tunic]

patch Ⓣ (pætʃ) *n* **1** a piece of material used to mend a garment, etc., or to make patchwork, a sewn-on pocket, etc. **2a** a small plot of land. **2b** its produce: *a patch of cabbages.* **3** *Med.* **3a** a protective covering for an injured eye. **3b** any protective dressing. **4** an imitation beauty spot made of black silk, etc., worn esp. in the 18th century. **5** an identifying piece of fabric worn on the shoulder of a uniform. **6** a small contrasting section: *a patch of cloud in the blue sky.* **7** a scrap; remnant. **8 a bad patch.** a difficult or troubled time. **9 not a patch on.** not nearly as good as. ◆ *vb* (*tr*) **10** to mend or supply (a garment, etc.) with a patch or patches. **11** to put together or produce with patches. **12** (of material) to serve as a patch to. **13** (often foll. by *up*) to mend hurriedly or in a makeshift way. **14** (often foll. by *up*) to make (up) or settle (a quarrel, etc.). **15** to connect (electric circuits) together temporarily by means of a patch board. [C16 *pacche,* ?from F *pieche* PIECE]
▸**'patcher** *n*

patch board *or* **panel** *n* a device with a large number of sockets into which electrical plugs can be inserted to form many different temporary circuits: used in telephone exchanges, computer systems, etc. Also called: **plugboard.**

patchouli *or* **patchouly** ('pætʃʊlɪ, pə'tʃu:lɪ) *n, pl* **patchoulis** *or* **patchoulies. 1** any of several Asiatic trees, the leaves of which yield a heavy fragrant oil. **2** the perfume made from this oil. [C19: from Tamil *paccilai,* from *paccu* green + *ilai* leaf]

patch pocket *n* a pocket on the outside of a garment.

patch test *n Med.* a test to detect an allergic reaction by applying small amounts of a suspected substance to the skin.

patchwork Ⓣ ('pætʃ,wɜ:k) *n* **1** needlework done by sewing pieces of different materials together. **2** something made up of various parts.

patchy Ⓣ ('pætʃɪ) *adj* **patchier, patchiest. 1** irregular in quality, occurrence, intensity, etc.: *a patchy essay.* **2** having or forming patches.
▸**'patchily** *adv* ▸**'patchiness** *n*

pate (peɪt) *n* the head, esp. with reference to baldness or (in facetious use) intelligence. [C14: from ?]

pâté ('pæteɪ) *n* **1** a spread of finely minced liver, poultry, etc., served usually as an hors d'oeuvre. **2** a savoury pie. [C18: from F: PASTE]

pâté de foie gras (pɑte də fwa grɑ) *n, pl* **pâtés de foie gras** (pɑte). a smooth rich paste made from the liver of a specially fattened goose. [F: pâté of fat liver]

patella (pə'telə) *n, pl* **patellae** (-li:). *Anat.* a small flat triangular bone in front of and protecting the knee joint. Nontechnical name: **kneecap.** [C17: from L, from *patina* shallow pan]
▸**pa'tellar** *adj*

paten ('pætən) *n* a plate, usually made of silver or gold, esp. for the bread in the Eucharist. [C13: from OF *patene,* from Med. L, from L *patina* pan]

patency ('peɪtənsɪ) *n* the condition of being obvious.

patent Ⓣ ('peɪtənt, 'pætənt) *n* **1a** a government grant to an inventor assuring him the sole right to make, use, and sell his invention for a limited period. **1b** a document conveying such a grant. **2** an invention, privilege, etc., protected by a patent. **3a** an official document granting a right. **3b** any right granted by such a document. ◆ *adj* **4** open or available for inspection (esp. in **letters patent, patent writ**). **5** ('peɪtənt). obvious: *their scorn was patent to everyone.* **6** concerning protection, appointment, etc., of or by a patent or patents. **7** proprietary. **8** (esp. of a bodily passage or duct) being open or unobstructed. ◆ *vb* (*tr*) **9** to obtain a patent for. **10** to grant by a patent. [C14: via OF from L *patēre* to lie open; n use, short for *letters patent,* from Med. L *litterae patentes* letters lying open (to public inspection)]
▸**'patentable** *adj* ▸**,paten'tee** *n* ▸**,paten'tor** *n*

USAGE NOTE The pronunciation "'pætənt" is heard in *letters patent* and *Patent Office* and is the usual US pronunciation for all senses. In Britain "'pætənt" is sometimes heard for senses 1, 2, and 3, but "peɪtənt" is commoner and is regularly used in collocations like *patent leather.*

patent leather ('peɪtənt) *n* leather processed with lacquer to give a hard glossy surface.

patently ('peɪtəntlɪ) *adv* obviously.

patent medicine ('peɪtənt) *n* a medicine with a patent, available without a prescription.

Patent Office ('pætənt) *n* a government department that issues patents.

Patent Rolls ('pætənt) *pl n* (in Britain) the register of patents issued.

pater ('peɪtə) *n Brit. sl.* another word for **father:** now chiefly used facetiously. [from L]

paterfamilias (,peɪtəfə'mɪlɪ,æs) *n, pl* **patresfamilias** (,pɑ:treɪzfə'mɪlɪ,æs). the male head of a household. [L: father of the family]

paternal Ⓣ (pə'tɜ:nəl) *adj* **1** relating to or characteristic of a father; fatherly. **2** (*prenominal*) related through the father: *his paternal grandfather.* **3** inherited or derived from the male parent. [C17: from LL *paternālis,* from L *pater* father]
▸**pa'ternally** *adv*

paternalism (pə'tɜ:nə,lɪzəm) *n* the attitude or policy of a government or other authority that manages the affairs of a country, company, etc., in the manner of a father, esp. in usurping individual responsibility.
▸**pa'ternalist** *n, adj* ▸**pa,ternal'istic** *adj* ▸**pa,ternal'istically** *adv*

paternity Ⓣ (pə'tɜ:nɪtɪ) *n* **1a** the fact or state of being a father. **1b** (*as modifier*): *a paternity suit; paternity leave.* **2** descent or derivation from a father. **3** authorship or origin. [C15: from LL *paternitās,* from L *pater* father]

paternoster (,pætə'nɒstə) *n* **1** *RC Church.* the beads at the ends of each decade of the rosary at which the Paternoster is recited. **2** a type of fishing tackle in which short lines and hooks are attached at intervals to the main line. **3** a type of lift in which platforms are attached to continuous chains: passengers enter while it is moving. [L, lit.: our father (from the opening of the Lord's Prayer)]

Paternoster (,pætə'nɒstə) *n* (*sometimes not cap.*) *RC Church.* **1** the Lord's Prayer, esp. in Latin. **2** the recital of this as an act of devotion.

Paterson's curse ('pætəsənz) *n* an Australian name for **viper's bugloss.**

path Ⓣ (pɑ:θ) *n, pl* **paths** (pɑ:ðz). **1** a road or way, esp. a narrow trodden track. **2** a surfaced walk, as through a garden. **3** the course or direction in which something moves: *the path of a whirlwind.* **4** a course of conduct: *the path of virtue.* [OE *pæth*]
▸**'pathless** *adj*

path. *abbrev. for:* **1** pathological. **2** pathology.

-path *n combining form.* **1** denoting a person suffering from a specified disease or disorder: *neuropath.* **2** denoting a practitioner of a particular method of treatment: *osteopath.* [back formation from -PATHY]

Pathan (pə'tɑ:n) *n* a member of the Pashto-speaking people of Afghanistan, NW Pakistan, and elsewhere. [C17: from Hindi]

pathetic Ⓣ (pə'θetɪk) *adj* **1** evoking or expressing pity, sympathy, etc. **2** distressingly inadequate: *the old man sat huddled before a pathetic fire.* **3** *Brit. sl.* ludicrously or contemptibly uninteresting or worthless. **4** *Obs.* of or affecting the feelings. [C16: from F *pathétique,* via LL from Gk *pathētikos* sensitive, from *pathos* suffering]
▸**pa'thetically** *adv*

pathetic fallacy *n* (in literature) the presentation of inanimate objects in nature as possessing human feelings.

THESAURUS

pat[1] *vb* **1, 2 = stroke,** caress, dab, fondle, pet, slap, tap, touch ◆ *n* **6, 7 = stroke,** clap, dab, light blow, slap, tap **8 = lump,** cake, dab, portion, small piece

pat[2] *adv* **1 = perfectly,** exactly, faultlessly, flawlessly, off pat, precisely ◆ *adj* **5 = glib,** automatic, easy, facile, ready, simplistic, slick, smooth

patch *n* **1 = reinforcement,** piece of material **2 = plot,** area, ground, land, tract **6 = spot,** bit, scrap, shred, small piece, stretch ◆ *vb* **10 = mend,** cover, fix, reinforce, repair, sew up **14** *often foll. by* **up = settle,** bury the hatchet, conciliate, make friends, placate, restore, settle differences, smooth

patchwork *n* **2 = mixture,** confusion, hash, hotchpotch, jumble, medley, mishmash, pastiche

patchy *adj* **1 = uneven,** bitty, erratic, fitful, inconstant, irregular, random, sketchy, spotty, variable, varying
Antonyms *adj* constant, even, regular, unbroken, unvarying

patent *n* **1-3 = copyright,** invention, licence ◆ *adj* **5 = obvious,** apparent, blatant, clear, conspicuous, downright, evident, flagrant, glaring, indisputable, manifest, open, palpable, transparent, unconcealed, unequivocal, unmistakable

paternal *adj* **1 = fatherly,** benevolent, concerned, fatherlike, protective, solicitous, vigilant **3 = patrilineal,** patrimonial

paternity *n* **1 = fatherhood,** fathership **2 = parentage,** descent, extraction, family, lineage **3 = origin,** authorship, derivation, source

path *n* **1 = way,** footpath, footway, pathway, road, towpath, track, trail, walkway (*chiefly US*) **2 = walk,** avenue **3 = course,** avenue, direction, passage, procedure, road, route, track, way

pathetic *adj* **1 = sad,** affecting, distressing, gut-wrenching, harrowing, heartbreaking, heart-rending, melting, moving, pitiable, plaintive, poignant, tender, touching **2 = inadequate,** deplorable, feeble, lamentable, meagre, measly, miserable, paltry, petty, pitiful, poor, puny, sorry, woeful **3** *Brit. slang* **= worthless,** crummy (*sl.*), poxy, rubbishy, trashy, uninteresting, useless

pathfinder Ⓣ ('pɑːθˌfaɪndə) *n* **1** a person who makes or finds a way, esp. through unexplored areas or fields of knowledge. **2** an aircraft or parachutist that indicates a target area by dropping flares, etc. **3** a radar device used for navigation or homing onto a target.

pathfinder prospectus *n* a prospectus regarding the flotation of a new company that contains only sufficient details to test the market reaction.

patho- *or before a vowel* **path-** *combining form.* disease: *pathology.* [from Gk *pathos* suffering]

pathogen ('pæθəˌdʒɛn) *n* any agent that can cause disease.
▸**ˌpatho'genic** *adj*

pathogenesis (ˌpæθə'dʒɛnɪsɪs) *or* **pathogeny** (pə'θɒdʒɪnɪ) *n* the development of a disease.
▸**pathogenetic** (ˌpæθədʒɪ'nɛtɪk) *adj*

pathological (ˌpæθə'lɒdʒɪk^{ə}l) *or (less commonly)* **pathologic** *adj* **1** of or relating to pathology. **2** relating to, involving, or caused by disease. **3** *Inf.* compulsively motivated: *a pathological liar.*
▸**ˌpatho'logically** *adv*

pathology (pə'θɒlədʒɪ) *n, pl* **pathologies. 1** the branch of medicine concerned with the cause, origin, and nature of disease, including the changes occurring as a result of disease. **2** the manifestations of disease, esp. changes occurring in tissues or organs.
▸**pa'thologist** *n*

pathos Ⓣ ('peɪθɒs) *n* **1** the quality or power, esp. in literature or speech, of arousing feelings of pity, sorrow, etc. **2** a feeling of sympathy or pity. [C17: from Gk: suffering]

pathway ('pɑːθˌweɪ) *n* **1** a path. **2** *Biochem.* a chain of reactions associated with a particular metabolic process.

-pathy *n combining form.* **1** indicating feeling or perception: *telepathy.* **2** indicating disease: *psychopathy.* **3** indicating a method of treating disease: *osteopathy.* [from Gk *patheia* suffering; see PATHOS]
▸**-pathic** *adj combining form.*

patience Ⓣ ('peɪʃəns) *n* **1** tolerant and even-tempered perseverance. **2** the capacity for calmly enduring pain, trying situations, etc. **3** *Chiefly Brit.* any of various card games for one player only. US word: **solitaire.** [C13: via OF from L *patientia* endurance, from *patī* to suffer]

patient Ⓣ ('peɪʃənt) *adj* **1** enduring trying circumstances with even temper. **2** tolerant; understanding. **3** capable of accepting delay with equanimity. **4** persevering or diligent: *a patient worker.* ◆ *n* **5** a person who is receiving medical care. [C14: see PATIENCE]
▸**'patiently** *adv*

patina[1] ('pætɪnə) *n, pl* **patinas. 1** a film formed on the surface of a metal, esp. the green oxidation of bronze or copper. **2** any fine layer on a surface: *a patina of frost.* **3** the sheen on a surface caused by much handling. [C18: from It.: coating, from L: PATINA[2]]

patina[2] ('pætɪnə) *n, pl* **patinae** (-ˌniː). a broad shallow dish used in ancient Rome. [from L, from Gk *patanē* platter]

patio ('pætɪˌəʊ) *n, pl* **patios. 1** an open inner courtyard, esp. one in a Spanish or Spanish-American house. **2** an area adjoining a house, esp. one that is paved. [C19: from Sp.: courtyard]

patisserie (pə'tiːsərɪ) *n* **1** a shop where fancy pastries are sold. **2** such pastries. [C18: F, from *pâtissier* pastry cook, ult. from LL *pasta* PASTE]

Patna rice ('pætnə) *n* a variety of long-grain rice, used for savoury dishes. [after *Patna,* city in NE India]

patois Ⓣ ('pætwɑː) *n, pl* **patois** ('pætwɑːz). **1** a regional dialect of a language, usually considered substandard. **2** the jargon of a particular group. [C17: from OF: rustic speech, ?from *patoier* to handle awkwardly, from *patte* paw]

pat. pend. *abbrev. for* patent pending.

patri- *combining form.* father: *patricide; patriarch.* [from L *pater,* Gk *patēr* father]

patrial ('peɪtrɪəl) *n* (in Britain, formerly) a person having by statute the right of abode in the United Kingdom. [C20: from L *patria* native land]

patriarch Ⓣ ('peɪtrɪˌɑːk) *n* **1** the male head of a tribe or family. **2** a very old or venerable man. **3** *Bible.* **3a** any of a number of persons regarded as the fathers of the human race. **3b** any of the three ancestors of the Hebrew people: Abraham, Isaac, or Jacob. **3c** any of Jacob's twelve sons, regarded as the ancestors of the twelve tribes of Israel. **4** *Early Christian Church.* the bishop of one of several principal sees, esp. those of Rome, Antioch, and Alexandria. **5** *Eastern Orthodox Church.* the bishops of the four ancient principal sees of Constantinople, Antioch, Alexandria, and Jerusalem, and also of Russia, Rumania, and Serbia. **6** *RC Church.* **6a** a title given to the pope. **6b** a title given to a number of bishops, esp. of the Uniat Churches, indicating their rank as immediately below that of the pope. **7** the oldest or most venerable member of a group, community, etc. **8** a person regarded as the founder of a community, tradition, etc. [C12: via OF from Church L *patriarcha*]
▸**ˌpatri'archal** *adj*

patriarchate ('peɪtrɪˌɑːkɪt) *n* the office, jurisdiction, province, or residence of a patriarch.

patriarchy ('peɪtrɪˌɑːkɪ) *n, pl* **patriarchies. 1** a form of social organization in which a male is the head of the family and descent, kinship, and title are traced through the male line. **2** any society governed by such a system.

patrician Ⓣ (pə'trɪʃən) *n* **1** a member of the hereditary aristocracy of ancient Rome. **2** (in medieval Europe) a member of the upper class in numerous Italian republics and German free cities. **3** an aristocrat. **4** a person of refined conduct, tastes, etc. ◆ *adj* **5** (esp. in ancient Rome) of, relating to, or composed of patricians. **6** aristocratic. [C15: from OF *patricien,* from L *patricius* noble, from *pater* father]

patricide ('pætrɪˌsaɪd) *n* **1** the act of killing one's father. **2** a person who kills his father.
▸**ˌpatri'cidal** *adj*

patrilineal (ˌpætrɪ'lɪnɪəl) *adj* tracing descent, kinship, or title through the male line.

patrimony ('pætrɪmənɪ) *n, pl* **patrimonies. 1** an inheritance from one's father or other ancestor. **2** the endowment of a church. [C14 *patrimoyne,* from OF, from L *patrimonium* paternal inheritance]
▸**patrimonial** (ˌpætrɪ'məʊnɪəl) *adj*

patriot Ⓣ ('peɪtrɪət, 'pæt-) *n* a person who vigorously supports his country and its way of life. [C16: via F from LL *patriōta,* from Gk *patriōtēs,* from *patris* native land; rel. to Gk *patēr* father; cf. L *pater* father, *patria* fatherland]
▸**patriotic** (ˌpætrɪ'ɒtɪk) *adj* ▸**ˌpatri'otically** *adv*

Patriot ('peɪtrɪət) *n* a US surface-to-air missile system with multiple launch stations and the capability to track multiple targets by radar.

patriotism Ⓣ ('pætrɪəˌtɪzəm) *n* devotion to one's own country and concern for its defence.

patristic (pə'trɪstɪk) *or* **patristical** *adj* of or relating to the Fathers of the Church, their writings, or the study of these.
▸**pa'tristics** *n (functioning as sing)*

patrol Ⓣ (pə'trəʊl) *n* **1** the action of going round a town, etc., at regular intervals for purposes of security or observation. **2** a person or group that carries out such an action. **3** a military detachment with the mission of security or combat with enemy forces. **4** a division of a troop of Scouts or Guides. ◆ *vb* **patrols, patrolling, patrolled. 5** to engage in a patrol of (a place). [C17: from F *patrouiller,* from *patouiller* to flounder in mud, from *patte* paw]
▸**pa'troller** *n*

patrol car *n* a police car used for patrolling streets and motorways.

patrology (pə'trɒlədʒɪ) *n* **1** the study of the writings of the Fathers of the Church. **2** a collection of such writings. [C17: from Gk *patr-, patēr* father + -LOGY]
▸**pa'trologist** *n*

patrol wagon *n* the usual US, Austral., and NZ term for **Black Maria.**

patron[1] Ⓣ ('peɪtrən) *n* **1** a person who sponsors or aids artists, charities, etc.; protector or benefactor. **2** a customer of a shop, hotel, etc., esp. a regular one. **3** See **patron saint.** [C14: via OF from L *patrōnus* protector, from *pater* father]
▸**'patroness** *fem n*

patron[2] (patrɔ̃) *n* the owner of a restaurant, hotel. etc., esp. of a French one. [F]

patronage Ⓣ ('pætrənɪdʒ) *n* **1a** the support given or custom brought by a patron. **1b** the position of a patron. **2** (in politics) **2a** the practice of making appointments to office, granting contracts, etc. **2b** the favours, etc., so distributed. **3a** a condescending manner. **3b** any kindness done in a condescending way.

patronize Ⓣ *or* **patronise** ('pætrəˌnaɪz) *vb* **patronizes, patronizing, patron-**

THESAURUS

Antonyms *adj* ≠ **sad:** amusing, comical, droll, entertaining, funny, laughable, ludicrous, ridiculous

pathfinder *n* **1** = **pioneer,** discoverer, explorer, guide, scout, trailblazer

pathos *n* **1** = **sadness,** pitiableness, pitifulness, plaintiveness, poignancy

patience *n* **1** = **forbearance,** calmness, composure, cool (*sl.*), equanimity, even temper, imperturbability, restraint, serenity, sufferance, tolerance, toleration **2** = **endurance,** constancy, fortitude, long-suffering, perseverance, persistence, resignation, stoicism, submission

Antonyms *n* ≠ **forbearance:** agitation, exasperation, excitement, impatience, irritation, nervousness, passion, restlessness

patient *adj* **1** = **long-suffering,** calm, composed, enduring, persevering, persistent, philosophical, quiet, resigned, self-possessed, serene, stoical, submissive, uncomplaining, untiring **2** = **forbearing,** accommodating, even-tempered, forgiving, indulgent, lenient, mild, tolerant, understanding ◆ *n* **5** = **sick person,** case, invalid, sufferer

patois *n* **1** = **dialect 2** = **jargon,** argot, cant, lingo (*inf.*), patter, slang, vernacular

patriarch *n* **1** = **father,** paterfamilias, sire **2** = **elder,** grandfather, greybeard, old man

patrician *n* **3** = **aristocrat,** aristo, childe (*arch.*), noble, nobleman, peer ◆ *adj* **6** = **aristocratic,** blue-blooded, gentle (*arch.*), highborn, high-class, lordly, noble

patriot *n* = **nationalist,** chauvinist, flag-waver (*inf.*), jingo, lover of one's country, loyalist

patriotic *adj* = **nationalistic,** chauvinistic, flag-waving (*inf.*), jingoistic, loyal

patriotism *n* = **nationalism,** flag-waving (*inf.*), jingoism, love of one's country, loyalty

patrol *n* **1** = **policing,** guarding, protecting, rounds, safeguarding, vigilance, watching **2** = **guard,** garrison, patrolman, sentinel, watch, watchman ◆ *vb* **5** = **police,** cruise, guard, inspect, keep guard, keep watch, make the rounds, pound, range, safeguard, walk the beat

patron[1] *n* **1** = **supporter,** advocate, angel (*inf.*), backer, benefactor, champion, defender, friend, guardian, helper, philanthropist, protagonist, protector, sponsor **2** = **customer,** buyer, client, frequenter, habitué, shopper

patronage *n* **1a** = **support,** aid, assistance, backing, benefaction, championship, encouragement, espousal, help, promotion, sponsorship **1a** = **custom,** business, clientele, commerce, trade, trading, traffic **3a** = **condescension,** deigning, disdain, patronizing, stooping

patronize *vb* **1** = **talk down to,** be lofty with, look down on, treat as inferior, treat conde-

ized *or* **patronises, patronising, patronised. 1** to behave or treat in a condescending way. **2** (*tr*) to act as a patron by sponsoring or bringing trade to.
▸ **'patron,izer** *or* **'patron,iser** *n* ▸ **'patron,izing** *or* **'patron,ising** *adj* ▸ **'patron,izingly** *or* **'patron,isingly** *adv*

patron saint *n* a saint regarded as the particular guardian of a country, person, etc.

patronymic (,pætrə'nɪmɪk) *adj* **1** (of a name) derived from the name of its bearer's father or ancestor. ◆ *n* **2** a patronymic name. [C17: via LL from Gk *patronumikos*, from *patēr* father + *onoma* NAME]

patroon (pə'truːn) *n US.* a Dutch land holder in New Netherland and New York with manorial rights in the colonial era. [C18: from Du.: PATRON[1]]

patsy ('pætsɪ) *n, pl* **patsies.** *Sl., chiefly US & Canad.* **1** a person who is easily cheated, victimized, etc. **2** a scapegoat. [C20: from ?]

patten ('pæt°n) *n* a wooden clog or sandal on a raised wooden platform or metal ring. [C14: from OF *patin*, prob. from *patte* paw]

patter[1] ❶ ('pætə) *vb* **1** (*intr*) to walk or move with quick soft steps. **2** to strike with or make a quick succession of light tapping sounds. ◆ *n* **3** a quick succession of light tapping sounds, as of feet: *the patter of mice.* [C17: from PAT[1]]

patter[2] ❶ ('pætə) *n* **1** the glib rapid speech of comedians, etc. **2** quick idle talk; chatter. **3** the jargon of a particular group, etc.; lingo. ◆ *vb* **4** (*intr*) to speak glibly and rapidly. **5** to repeat (prayers, etc.) in a mechanical or perfunctory manner. [C14: from L *pater* in *Pater Noster* Our Father]

pattern ❶ ('pæt°n) *n* **1** an arrangement of repeated or corresponding parts, decorative motifs, etc. **2** a decorative design: *a paisley pattern.* **3** a style: *various patterns of cutlery.* **4** a plan or diagram used as a guide in making something: *a paper pattern for a dress.* **5** a standard way of moving, acting, etc.: *traffic patterns.* **6** a model worthy of imitation: *a pattern of kindness.* **7** a representative sample. **8** a wooden or metal shape or model used in a foundry to make a mould. ◆ *vb* (*tr*) **9** (often foll. by *after* or *on*) to model. **10** to arrange as or decorate with a pattern. [C14 *patron*, from Med. L *patrōnus* example, from L: PATRON[1]]

patty ('pætɪ) *n, pl* **patties. 1** a small cake of minced food. **2** a small pie. [C18: from F PÂTÉ]

patu ('pɑːtuː) *n, pl* **patus.** *NZ.* a short Maori club, now ceremonial only. [from Maori]

patulous ('pætjʊləs) *adj Bot.* spreading widely or expanded: *patulous branches.* [C17: from L *patulus* open, from *patēre* to lie open]

paua ('pɑːʊɑ) *n* an edible abalone of New Zealand, having an iridescent shell used for jewellery, etc. [from Maori]

paucity ❶ ('pɔːsɪtɪ) *n* **1** insufficiency; dearth. **2** smallness of number; fewness. [C15: from L *paucitās* scarcity, from *paucus* few]

Pauli exclusion principle ('pɔːlɪ) *n Physics.* the principle that two identical fermions cannot occupy the same quantum state in a body, such as an atom; sometimes shortened to **exclusion principle.** [C20: after Wolfgang *Pauli* (1900–58), US physicist]

Pauline ('pɔːlaɪn) *adj* relating to Saint Paul or his doctrines.

Paul Jones (pɔːl dʒəʊnz) *n* an old-time dance in which partners are exchanged. [C19: after John Paul *Jones* (1747–92), US naval commander in the War of Independence]

paulownia (pɔː'ləʊnɪə) *n* a tree of a Japanese genus, esp. one having large heart-shaped leaves and clusters of purplish or white flowers. [C19: NL, after Anna *Paulovna*, daughter of Paul I of Russia]

paunch ❶ (pɔːntʃ) *n* **1** the belly or abdomen, esp. when protruding. **2** another name for **rumen.** ◆ *vb* (*tr*) **3** to stab in the stomach; disembowel. [C14: from Anglo-Norman *paunche*, from OF *pance*, from L *panticēs* (pl) bowels]
▸ **'paunchy** *adj* ▸ **'paunchiness** *n*

pauper ❶ ('pɔːpə) *n* **1** a person who is extremely poor. **2** (formerly) a person supported by public charity. [C16: from L: poor]
▸ **'pauper,ism** *n*

pauperize ❶ *or* **pauperise** ('pɔːpə,raɪz) *vb* **pauperizes, pauperizing, pauperized** *or* **pauperises, pauperising, pauperised.** (*tr*) to make a pauper of; impoverish.

pause ❶ (pɔːz) *vb* **pauses, pausing, paused.** (*intr*) **1** to cease an action temporarily. **2** to hesitate; delay: *she replied without pausing.* ◆ *n* **3** a temporary stop or rest, esp. in speech or action; short break. **4** *Prosody.* another word for **caesura. 5** Also called: **fermata.** *Music.* a continuation of a note or rest beyond its normal length. Usual symbol: 𝄐 **6 give pause to.** to cause to hesitate. [C15: from L *pausa* pause, from Gk *pausis*, from *pauein* to halt]

pav (pæv) *n Austral. & NZ inf.* short for **pavlova.**

pavane *or* **pavan** (pə'vɑːn, 'pæv°n) *n* **1** a slow and stately dance of the 16th and 17th centuries. **2** a piece of music composed for or in the rhythm of this dance. [C16 *pavan*, via F from Sp. *pavana*, from OIt. *padovana* Paduan (dance), from *Padova* Padua]

pave ❶ (peɪv) *vb* **paves, paving, paved.** (*tr*) **1** to cover (a road, etc.) with a firm surface suitable for travel, as with paving stones or concrete. **2** to serve as the material for a pavement or other hard layer: *bricks paved the causeway.* **3** (often foll. by *with*) to cover with a hard layer (of): *shelves paved with marble.* **4** to prepare or make easier (esp. in **pave the way**). [C14: from OF *paver*, from L *pavīre* to ram down]
▸ **'paver** *n*

pavement ('peɪvmənt) *n* **1** a hard-surfaced path for pedestrians alongside and a little higher than a road. US and Canad. word: **sidewalk. 2** the material used in paving. [C13: from L *pavīmentum* hard floor, from *pavīre* to beat hard]

pavilion (pə'vɪljən) *n* **1** *Brit.* a building at a sports ground, esp. a cricket pitch, in which players change, etc. **2** a summerhouse or other decorative shelter. **3** a building or temporary structure, esp. one that is open and ornamental, for housing exhibitions, etc. **4** a large ornate tent, esp. one with a peaked top, as used by medieval armies. **5** one of a set of buildings that together form a hospital or other large institution. ◆ *vb* (*tr*) *Literary.* **6** to place as in a pavilion: *pavilioned in splendour.* **7** to provide with a pavilion or pavilions. [C13: from OF *pavillon* canopied structure, from L *pāpiliō* butterfly, tent]

paving ('peɪvɪŋ) *n* **1** a paved surface; pavement. **2** material used for a pavement.

pavlova (pæv'ləʊvə) *n* a meringue cake topped with whipped cream and fruit. [C20: after Anna *Pavlova* (1885–1931), Russian ballerina]

Pavlovian (pæv'ləʊvɪən) *adj* **1** of or relating to the work of Ivan Pavlov (1849–1936), Soviet physiologist, on conditioned reflexes. **2** (of a reaction or response) automatic; involuntary.

paw ❶ (pɔː) *n* **1** any of the feet of a four-legged mammal, bearing claws or nails. **2** *Inf.* a hand, esp. one that is large, clumsy, etc. ◆ *vb* **3** to scrape or contaminate with the paws or feet. **4** (*tr*) *Inf.* to touch or caress in a clumsy, rough, or overfamiliar manner. [C13: via OF from Gmc]

pawky ('pɔːkɪ) *adj* **pawkier, pawkiest.** *Dialect or Scot.* having a dry wit. [C17: from Scot. *pawk* trick, from ?]
▸ **'pawkily** *adv* ▸ **'pawkiness** *n*

pawl (pɔːl) *n* a pivoted lever shaped to engage with a ratchet to prevent motion in a particular direction. [C17: ?from Du. *pal* pawl]

pawn[1] ❶ (pɔːn) *vb* (*tr*) **1** to deposit (an article) as security for the repayment of a loan, esp. from a pawnbroker. **2** to stake: *to pawn one's honour.* ◆ *n* **3** an article deposited as security. **4** the condition of being so deposited (esp. in **in pawn**). **5** a person or thing that is held as a security. **6** the act of pawning. [C15: from OF *pan* security, from L *pannus* cloth, apparently because clothing was often left as a surety]
▸ **'pawnage** *n*

pawn[2] ❶ (pɔːn) *n* **1** a chess man of the lowest theoretical value. **2** a person, group, etc., manipulated by another. [C14: from Anglo-Norman *poun*, from OF, from Med. L *pedō* infantryman, from L *pēs* foot]

pawnbroker ('pɔːn,brəʊkə) *n* a dealer licensed to lend money at a spec-

THESAURUS

scendingly, treat like a child **2** = **support**, assist, back, befriend, foster, fund, help, maintain, promote, sponsor, subscribe to **2** = **be a customer** *or* **client of**, buy from, deal with, do business with, frequent, shop at, trade with

patronizing *adj* **1** = **condescending**, contemptuous, disdainful, gracious, haughty, lofty, snobbish, stooping, supercilious, superior, toffee-nosed (*sl., chiefly Brit.*)
Antonyms *adj* deferential, humble, obsequious, respectful, servile

patter[1] *vb* **1** = **walk lightly**, scurry, scuttle, skip, tiptoe, trip **2** = **tap**, beat, pat, pelt, pitapat, pitter-patter, rat-a-tat, spatter ◆ *n* **3** = **tapping**, pattering, pitapat, pitter-patter

patter[2] *n* **1** = **spiel** (*inf.*), line, monologue, pitch **2** = **chatter**, gabble, jabber, nattering, prattle, yak (*sl.*) **3** = **jargon**, argot, cant, lingo (*inf.*), patois, slang, vernacular ◆ *vb* **4** = **chatter**, babble, blab, hold forth, jabber, prate, rattle off, rattle on, spiel (*inf.*), spout (*inf.*), tattle

pattern *n* **1, 2** = **design**, arrangement, decoration, decorative design, device, figure, motif, ornament **3** = **type**, kind, shape, sort, style, variety **4** = **plan**, design, diagram, guide, instructions, original, stencil, template **6** = **model**, archetype, criterion, cynosure, example, exemplar, guide, norm, original, par, paradigm, paragon, prototype, standard **7** = **sample**, example, specimen ◆ *vb* **9** = **model**, copy, emulate, follow, form, imitate, mould, order, shape, style **10** = **decorate**, design, trim

paucity *n* **1, 2** *Formal* = **scarcity**, dearth, deficiency, fewness, insufficiency, lack, meagreness, paltriness, poverty, rarity, scantiness, shortage, slenderness, slightness, smallness, sparseness, sparsity

paunch *n* **1** = **belly**, abdomen, beer-belly (*inf.*), corporation (*inf.*), middle-age spread (*inf.*), pot, potbelly, spare tyre (*Brit. sl.*), spread (*inf.*)

pauper *n* **1** = **down-and-out**, bankrupt, beggar, have-not, indigent, insolvent, mendicant, poor person

pauperism *n* **1** = **poverty**, beggary, destitution, impecuniousness, indigence, mendicancy, need, neediness, pennilessness, penury, privation, want

pauperize *vb* = **impoverish**, bankrupt, beggar, break, bust (*inf.*), cripple financially, reduce to beggary, ruin

pause *vb* **1, 2** = **stop briefly**, break, cease, delay, deliberate, desist, discontinue, halt, have a breather (*inf.*), hesitate, interrupt, rest, take a break, wait, waver ◆ *n* **3** = **stop**, break, breather (*inf.*), breathing space, caesura, cessation, delay, discontinuance, entr'acte, gap, halt, hesitation, interlude, intermission, interruption, interval, let-up (*inf.*), lull, respite, rest, stay, stoppage, wait
Antonyms *vb* ≠ **stop briefly**: advance, continue, proceed, progress ◆ *n* ≠ **stop**: advancement, continuance, progression

pave *vb* **1** = **cover**, asphalt, concrete, flag, floor, macadamize, surface, tar, tile

paw *vb* **4** *Informal* = **manhandle**, grab, handle roughly, maul, molest

pawn[1] *vb* **1, 2** = **hock** (*inf., chiefly US*), deposit, gage (*arch.*), hazard, mortgage, pledge, pop (*inf.*), stake, wager ◆ *n* **3** = **security**, assurance, bond, collateral, gage, guarantee, guaranty, pledge

pawn[2] *n* **2** = **tool**, cat's-paw, creature, dupe, instrument, plaything, puppet, stooge (*sl.*), toy ified rate of interest on the security of movable personal property, which can be sold if the loan is not repaid within a specified period. ► 'pawn,broking *n*

pawnshop ('pɔːn,ʃɒp) *n* the premises of a pawnbroker.

pawn ticket *n* a receipt for goods pawned.

pawpaw ('pɔː,pɔː) *n* another name for **papaw** or **papaya.**

pax (pæks) *n* **1** *Chiefly RC Church.* **1a** the kiss of peace. **1b** a small metal or ivory plate, formerly used to convey the kiss of peace from the celebrant at Mass to those attending it. ◆ *interj* **2** *Brit. school sl.* a call signalling an end to hostilities or claiming immunity from the rules of a game. [L: peace]

PAX (in Britain) *abbrev. for* private automatic exchange.

pay[1] Ⓣ (peɪ) *vb* **pays, paying, paid. 1** to discharge (a debt, obligation, etc.) by giving or doing something: *he paid his creditors.* **2** (when *intr*, often foll. by *for*) to give (money, etc.) to (a person) in return for goods or services: *they pay their workers well; they pay by the hour.* **3** to give or afford (a person, etc.) a profit or benefit: *it pays one to be honest.* **4** (*tr*) to give or bestow (a compliment, regards, attention, etc.). **5** (*tr*) to make (a visit or call). **6** (*intr*; often foll. by *for*) to give compensation or make amends. **7** (*tr*) to yield a return of: *the shares pay 15 per cent.* **8** *Austral. inf.* to acknowledge or accept (something) as true, just, etc. **9 pay one's way. 9a** to contribute one's share of expenses. **9b** to remain solvent without outside help. ◆ *n* **10a** money given in return for work or services; a salary or wage. **10b** (*as modifier*): *a pay slip; a pay claim.* **11** paid employment (esp. in **in the pay of**). **12** (*modifier*) requiring the insertion of money before or during use: *a pay phone.* **13** (*modifier*) rich enough in minerals to be profitably worked: *pay gravel.* ◆ See also **pay back, pay for,** etc. [C12: from OF *payer*, from L *pācāre* to appease (a creditor), from *pāx* peace] ► '**payer** *n*

pay[2] (peɪ) *vb* **pays, paying, payed.** (*tr*) *Naut.* to caulk (the seams of a wooden vessel) with pitch or tar. [C17: from OF *peier*, from L *picāre*, from *pix* pitch]

payable Ⓣ ('peɪəbᵊl) *adj* **1** (often foll. by *on*) to be paid: *payable on the third of each month.* **2** that is capable of being paid. **3** capable of being profitable. **4** (of a debt, etc.) imposing an obligation on the debtor to pay, esp. at once.

pay-and-display *adj* denoting a car-parking system in which a motorist buys a permit to park for a specified period, usually from a coin-operated machine, and displays the permit on or near the windscreen of his or her car so that it can be seen by a parking attendant.

pay back Ⓣ *vb* (*tr, adv*) **1** to retaliate against: *to pay someone back for an insult.* **2** to give or do (something equivalent) in return for a favour, insult, etc. **3** to repay (a loan, etc.).

pay bed *n* an informal name for **private pay bed.**

payday ('peɪ,deɪ) *n* the day on which wages or salaries are paid.

pay dirt *n Chiefly US.* **1** soil, gravel, ore, etc. that contains sufficient minerals to make it worthwhile mining. **2 hit** (*or* **strike**) **pay dirt.** *Inf.* to become wealthy, successful, etc.

PAYE (in Britain and New Zealand) *abbrev. for* pay as you earn; a system by which income tax levied on wage and salary earners is paid by employers directly to the government.

payee (peɪ'iː) *n* the person to whom a cheque, money order, etc., is made out.

pay for Ⓣ *vb* (*prep*) **1** to make payment for. **2** (*intr*) to suffer or be punished, as for a mistake, wrong decision, etc.

paying guest *n* a euphemism for **lodger.**

payload ('peɪ,ləʊd) *n* **1** that part of a cargo earning revenue. **2a** the passengers, cargo, or bombs carried by an aircraft. **2b** the equipment carried by a rocket, satellite, or spacecraft. **3** the explosive power of a warhead, bomb, etc., carried by a missile or aircraft.

paymaster ('peɪ,mɑːstə) *n* an official of a government, business, etc., responsible for the payment of wages and salaries.

payment Ⓣ ('peɪmənt) *n* **1** the act of paying. **2** a sum of money paid. **3** something given in return; punishment or reward.

paynim ('peɪnɪm) *n Arch.* **1** a heathen or pagan. **2** a Muslim. [C13: from OF *paienime*, from LL *pāgānismus* paganism, from *pāgānus* PAGAN]

pay off Ⓣ *vb* **1** (*tr, adv*) to pay all that is due in wages, etc., and discharge from employment. **2** (*tr, adv*) to pay the complete amount of (a debt, bill, etc.). **3** (*intr, adv*) to turn out to be profitable, effective, etc.: *the gamble paid off.* **4** (*tr, adv* or *intr, prep*) to take revenge on (a person) or for (a wrong done): *to pay someone off for an insult.* **5** (*tr, adv*) *Inf.* to give a bribe to. ◆ *n* **payoff. 6** the final settlement, esp. in retribution. **7** *Inf.* the climax, consequence, or outcome of events, a story, etc. **8** the final payment of a debt, salary, etc. **9** the time of such a payment. **10** *Inf.* a bribe.

payola (peɪ'əʊlə) *n Inf.* **1** a bribe given to secure special treatment, esp. to a disc jockey to promote a commercial product. **2** the practice of paying or receiving such bribes. [C20: from PAY[1] + *-ola*, as in PIANOLA]

pay out Ⓣ *vb* (*adv*) **1** to distribute (money, etc.); disburse. **2** (*tr*) to release (a rope) gradually, hand over hand. ◆ *n* **payout. 3** a sum of money paid out.

pay-per-view *n* **a** a system of television broadcasting by which subscribers pay for each programme they wish to receive. **b** (*as modifier*): *a pay-per-view channel.*

payphone ('peɪ,fəʊn) *n* a public telephone operated by coins or a phonecard.

payroll ('peɪ,rəʊl) *n* **1** a list of employees, specifying the salary or wage of each. **2a** the total of these amounts or the actual money equivalent. **2b** (*as modifier*): *a payroll tax.*

payt *abbrev. for* payment.

pay up *vb* (*adv*) to pay (money) promptly, in full, or on demand.

Pb *the chemical symbol for* lead. [from NL *plumbum*]

PB *Athletics abbrev. for* personal best.

PBS *US abbrev. for* Public Broadcasting Service.

PBX (in Britain) *abbrev. for* private branch exchange; a telephone system that handles the internal and external calls of a building, firm, etc.

pc *abbrev. for:* **1** per cent. **2** postcard. **3** (in prescriptions) post cibum. [L: after meals]

PC *abbrev. for:* **1** personal computer. **2** Parish Council(lor). **3** (in Britain) Police Constable. **4** politically correct. **5** (in Britain) Privy Council(lor). **6** (in Canada) Progressive Conservative.

pc. *abbrev. for:* **1** (*pl* **pcs.**) piece. **2** price.

PCB *abbrev. for* polychlorinated biphenyl; any of a group of compounds in which chlorine atoms replace the hydrogen atoms in biphenyl: used in electrical insulators and in the manufacture of plastics; a toxic pollutant.

PCC (in Britain) *abbrev. for* Press Complaints Commission.

PCP *n Trademark.* phencyclidine; a depressant drug used illegally as a hallucinogen.

PCV (in Britain) *abbrev. for* passenger carrying vehicle.

pd *abbrev. for:* **1** paid. **2** Also: **PD.** per diem. **3** potential difference.

Pd *the chemical symbol for* palladium.

PDR *abbrev. for* price-dividend ratio.

P-D ratio *n* short for **price-dividend ratio.**

PDSA (in Britain) *abbrev. for* People's Dispensary for Sick Animals.

PDT (in the US and Canada) *abbrev. for* Pacific Daylight Time.

PE *abbrev. for:* **1** physical education. **2** potential energy. **3** Presiding Elder. **4** Also: **p.e.** printer's error. **5** *Statistics.* probable error. **6** Protestant Episcopal.

pea (piː) *n* **1** an annual climbing plant with small white flowers and long green pods containing edible green seeds: cultivated in temperate regions. **2** the seed of this plant, eaten as a vegetable. **3** any of several other leguminous plants, such as the sweet pea. [C17: from PEASE (incorrectly assumed to be a pl)]

peace Ⓣ (piːs) *n* **1a** the state existing during the absence of war. **1b** (*as modifier*): *peace negotiations.* **2** (*often cap.*) a treaty marking the end of a war. **3** a state of harmony between people or groups. **4** law and order within a state: *a breach of the peace.* **5** absence of mental anxiety (often in **peace of mind**). **6** a state of stillness, silence, or serenity. **7 at peace. 7a** in a state of harmony or friendship. **7b** in a state of serenity. **7c** dead: *the old lady is at peace now.* **8 hold** *or* **keep one's peace.** to keep silent. **9 keep the peace.** to maintain law and order. ◆ *vb* **peaces, peacing, peaced. 10** (*intr*) *Obs. except as an imperative.* to be or become silent or still. ◆ *modifier* **11** denoting a person or thing symbolizing support for international peace: *peace women.* [C12: from OF *pais*, from L *pāx*]

peaceable Ⓣ ('piːsəbᵊl) *adj* **1** inclined towards peace. **2** tranquil; calm. ► '**peaceableness** *n* ► '**peaceably** *adv*

Peace Corps *n* an agency of the US government that sends volunteers to developing countries to work on educational projects, etc.

peace dividend *n* additional money available to a government from

THESAURUS

pay[1] *vb* **1, 2** = **reimburse**, clear, compensate, cough up (*inf.*), discharge, foot, give, honour, liquidate, meet, offer, recompense, remit, remunerate, render, requite, reward, settle, square up **3** = **benefit**, be advantageous, be worthwhile, repay, serve **3** = **be profitable**, be remunerative, make a return, make money, provide a living **4** = **give**, bestow, extend, grant, hand out, present, proffer, render **7** = **yield**, bring in, produce, profit, return ◆ *n* **10** = **wages**, allowance, compensation, earnings, emoluments, fee, hand-out, hire, income, meed (*arch.*), payment, recompense, reimbursement, remuneration, reward, salary, stipend, takings

payable *adj* **1, 4** = **due**, mature, obligatory, outstanding, owed, owing, receivable, to be paid

pay back *vb* **1** = **get even with** (*inf.*), get one's own back, hit back, reciprocate, recompense, retaliate, settle a score with **3** = **repay**, refund, reimburse, return, settle up, square

pay for *vb* **2** = **suffer**, answer for, atone, be punished, compensate, get one's deserts, make amends, suffer the consequences

payment *n* **1** = **paying**, defrayal, discharge, outlay, remittance, settlement **2** = **remittance**, advance, deposit, instalment, portion, premium **2** = **wage**, fee, hire, remuneration, reward

pay off *vb* **1** = **settle**, clear, discharge, liquidate, pay in full, square **1** = **dismiss**, discharge, fire, lay off, let go, sack (*inf.*) **3** = **succeed**, be effective, be profitable, be successful, work **4** = **get even with** (*inf.*), pay back, retaliate, settle a score **5** *Informal* = **bribe**, buy off, corrupt, get at, grease the palm of (*sl.*), oil (*inf.*), suborn ◆ *n* **payoff 6** = **retribution**, conclusion, day of reckoning, final reckoning, judgment, reward, settlement **7** *Informal* = **outcome**, climax, clincher (*inf.*), consequence, culmination, finale, moment of truth, punch line, result, the crunch (*inf.*), upshot

pay out *vb* **1** = **spend**, cough up (*inf.*), disburse, expend, fork out *or* over *or* up (*sl.*), lay out (*inf.*), shell out (*inf.*)

peace *n* **1, 2** = **truce**, armistice, cessation of hostilities, conciliation, pacification, treaty **3** = **harmony**, accord, agreement, amity, concord **5** = **serenity**, calm, composure, contentment, placidity, relaxation, repose **6** = **stillness**, calm, calmness, hush, peacefulness, quiet, quietude, repose, rest, silence, tranquillity

peaceable *adj* **1** = **peace-loving**, amiable, amicable, conciliatory, dovish, friendly, gentle, cuts in defence expenditure because of the end of a period of hostilities.

peaceful Ⓣ ('pi:sfʊl) *adj* **1** not in a state of war or disagreement. **2** calm; tranquil. **3** not involving violence: *peaceful picketing.* **4** of, relating to, or in accord with a time of peace. **5** inclined towards peace.
▸ **'peacefully** *adv* ▸ **'peacefulness** *n*

peacekeeping ('pi:sˌki:pɪŋ) *n* **a** the maintenance of peace, esp. the prevention of further fighting between hostile forces. **b** (*as modifier*): *a UN peacekeeping force.*

peacemaker Ⓣ ('pi:sˌmeɪkə) *n* a person who establishes peace, esp. between others.
▸ **'peaceˌmaking** *n*

peace offering *n* **1** something given to an adversary in the hope of procuring or maintaining peace. **2** *Judaism.* a sacrificial meal shared between the offerer and Jehovah.

peace pipe *n* a long decorated pipe smoked by North American Indians, esp. as a token of peace. Also called: **calumet.**

peace sign *n* a gesture made with the palm of the hand outwards and the index and middle fingers raised in a V.

peacetime ('pi:sˌtaɪm) *n* **a** a period without war; time of peace. **b** (*as modifier*): *a peacetime agreement.*

peach[1] (pi:tʃ) *n* **1** a small tree with pink flowers and rounded edible fruit: cultivated in temperate regions. **2** the soft juicy fruit of this tree, which has a downy reddish-yellow skin, yellowish-orange sweet flesh, and a single stone. **3a** a pinkish-yellow to orange colour. **3b** (*as adj*): *a peach dress.* **4** *Inf.* a person or thing that is especially pleasing. [C14 *peche,* from OF, from Med. L *persica,* from L *Persicum mālum* Persian apple]

peach[2] (pi:tʃ) *vb* (*intr*) *Sl.* to inform against an accomplice. [C15: var. of earlier *apeche,* from F, from LL *impedicāre* to entangle; see IMPEACH]

peach brandy *n* (esp. in S. Africa) a coarse brandy made from fermented peaches.

peach Melba *n* a dessert made of halved peaches, vanilla ice cream, and raspberries. [C20: after Dame Nellie MELBA]

peachy ('pi:tʃɪ) *adj* **peachier, peachiest. 1** of or like a peach, esp. in colour or texture. **2** *Inf.* excellent; fine.
▸ **'peachiness** *n*

peacock ('pi:ˌkɒk) *n, pl* **peacocks** *or* **peacock. 1** a male peafowl, having a crested head and a very large fanlike tail marked with blue and green eyelike spots. **2** another name for **peafowl. 3** a vain strutting person. ◆ *vb* **4** to display (oneself) proudly. [C14 *pecok, pe-* from OE *pāwa* (from L *pāvō* peacock) + COCK[1]]
▸ **'peaˌcockish** *adj* ▸ **'peaˌhen** *fem n*

peacock blue *n* **a** a greenish-blue colour. **b** (*as adj*): *a peacock-blue car.*

peafowl ('pi:ˌfaʊl) *n, pl* **peafowls** *or* **peafowl.** either of two large pheasants of India and Ceylon and of SE Asia. The males (see **peacock** (sense 1)) have a characteristic bright plumage.

pea green *n* **a** a yellowish-green colour. **b** (*as adj*): *a pea-green teapot.*

pea jacket *or* **peacoat** ('pi:ˌkəʊt) *n* a sailor's short heavy woollen overcoat. [C18: from Du. *pijjekker, from pij* coat of coarse cloth + *jekker* jacket]

peak[1] Ⓣ (pi:k) *n* **1** a pointed end, edge, or projection: *the peak of a roof.* **2** the pointed summit of a mountain. **3** a mountain with a pointed summit. **4** the point of greatest development, strength, etc.: *the peak of his career.* **5a** a sharp increase followed by a sharp decrease: *a voltage peak.* **5b** the maximum value of this quantity. **5c** (*as modifier*): *peak voltage.* **6** Also called: **visor.** a projecting piece on the front of some caps. **7** *Naut.* **7a** the extreme forward (**forepeak**) or aft (**afterpeak**) part of the hull. **7b** (of a fore-and-aft quadrilateral sail) the after uppermost corner. **7c** the after end of a gaff. ◆ *vb* **8** to form or reach or cause to form or reach a peak. **9** (*tr*) *Naut.* to set (a gaff) or tilt (oars) vertically. ◆ *adj* **10** of or relating to a period of greatest use or demand: *peak viewing hours.* [C16: ?from PIKE[2], infl. by BEAK[1]]

peak[2] Ⓣ (pi:k) *vb* (*intr*) to become wan, emaciated, or sickly. [C16: from ?]
▸ **'peaky** *or* **'peakish** *adj*

peaked (pi:kt) *adj* having a peak; pointed.

peak load *n* the maximum load on an electrical power-supply system.

peal Ⓣ (pi:l) *n* **1** a loud prolonged usually reverberating sound, as of bells, thunder, or laughter. **2** *Bell-ringing.* a series of changes rung in accordance with specific rules. **3** (*not in technical usage*) the set of bells in a belfry. ◆ *vb* **4** (*intr*) to sound with a peal or peals. **5** (*tr*) to give forth loudly and sonorously. **6** (*tr*) to ring (bells) in peals. [C14 *pele,* var. of *apele* APPEAL]

peanut ('pi:ˌnʌt) *n* **a** a leguminous plant widely cultivated for its edible seeds. **b** the edible nutlike seed of this plant, used for food and as a source of oil. Also called: **groundnut, monkey nut.** ◆ See also **peanuts.**

peanut butter *n* a brownish oily paste made from peanuts.

peanuts ('pi:ˌnʌts) *n Sl.* a trifling amount of money.

pear (peə) *n* **1** a widely cultivated tree, having white flowers and edible fruits. **2** the sweet gritty-textured juicy fruit of this tree, which has a globular base and tapers towards the apex. **3** the wood of this tree, used for making furniture. **4 go pear-shaped.** *Inf.* to go wrong: *the plan started to go pear-shaped.* [OE *pere,* ult. from L *pirum*]

pearl[1] (pɜ:l) *n* **1** a hard smooth lustrous typically rounded structure occurring on the inner surface of the shell of a clam or oyster around an invading particle such as a sand grain; much valued as a gem. **2** any artificial gem resembling this. **3** See **mother-of-pearl. 4** a person or thing that is like a pearl, esp. in beauty or value. **5** a pale greyish-white colour, often with a bluish tinge. ◆ *adj* **6** of, made of, or set with pearl or mother-of-pearl. **7** having the shape or colour of a pearl. ◆ *vb* **8** (*tr*) to set with or as if with pearls. **9** to shape into or assume a pearl-like form or colour. **10** (*intr*) to dive or search for pearls. [C14: from OF, from Vulgar L *pernula* (unattested), from L *perna* sea mussel]

pearl[2] (pɜ:l) *n, vb* a variant spelling of **purl**[1] (senses 2, 3, 5).

pearl ash *n* the granular crystalline form of potassium carbonate.

pearl barley *n* barley ground into small round grains, used esp. in soups and stews.

pearly Ⓣ ('pɜ:lɪ) *adj* **pearlier, pearliest. 1** resembling a pearl, esp. in lustre. **2** decorated with pearls or mother-of-pearl. ◆ *n, pl* **pearlies.** *Brit.* **3** a London costermonger or his wife who wear on ceremonial occasions a traditional dress of dark clothes covered with pearl buttons. **4** (*pl*) the clothes or the buttons themselves.
▸ **'pearliness** *n*

Pearly Gates *pl n Inf.* the entrance to heaven.

pearly king *or* (*fem*) **pearly queen** *n* the London costermonger whose ceremonial clothes display the most lavish collection of pearl buttons.

pearly nautilus *n* any of several cephalopod molluscs of warm and tropical seas, having a partitioned pale pearly external shell with brown stripes. Also called: **chambered nautilus.**

pearmain ('peəˌmeɪn) *n* any of several varieties of apple having a red skin. [C15: from OF *permain* a type of pear, ?from L *Parmēnsis* of Parma]

peart (pɪət) *adj Dialect.* lively; spirited; brisk. [C15: var. of PERT]
▸ **'peartly** *adv*

peasant Ⓣ ('pɛzənt) *n* **1** a member of a class of low social status that depends on either cottage industry or agricultural labour as a means of subsistence. **2** *Inf.* a person who lives in the country; rustic. **3** *Inf.* an uncouth or uncultured person. [C15: from Anglo-F, from OF *païsant,* from *païs* country, from L *pāgus* rural area]

peasantry ('pɛzəntrɪ) *n* peasants as a class.

pease (pi:z) *n, pl* **pease.** *Arch. or dialect.* another word for **pea.** [OE *peose,* via LL from L *pisa* peas, pl of *pisum,* from Gk *pison*]

peasecod *or* **peascod** ('pi:zˌkɒd) *n Arch.* the pod of a pea plant. [C14: from PEASE + COD[2]]

pease pudding *n* (esp. in Britain) a dish of split peas that have been soaked and boiled.

peashooter ('pi:ˌʃu:tə) *n* a tube through which dried peas are blown, used as a toy weapon.

peasouper (ˌpi:'su:pə) *n* **1** *Inf., chiefly Brit.* dense dirty yellowish fog. **2** *Canad.* a disparaging name for a **French Canadian.**

peat (pi:t) *n* **a** a compact brownish deposit of partially decomposed vegetable matter saturated with water: found in uplands and bogs and used as a fuel (when dried) and as a fertilizer. **b** (*as modifier*): *peat bog.* [C14: from Anglo-L *peta,* ?from Celtic]
▸ **'peaty** *adj*

peat moss *n* any of various mosses, esp. sphagnum, that grow in wet places and decay to form peat. See also **sphagnum.**

pebble ('pɛbəl) *n* **1** a small smooth rounded stone, esp. one worn by the action of water. **2a** a transparent colourless variety of rock crystal, used for making certain lenses. **2b** such a lens. **3** (*modifier*) *Inf.* (of a lens or of spectacles) thick, with a high degree of magnification or distortion. **4a** a grainy irregular surface, esp. on leather. **4b** leather having such a surface. ◆ *vb* **pebbles, pebbling, pebbled.** (*tr*) **5** to cover with pebbles. **6** to impart a grainy surface to (leather). [OE *papolstān,* from *papol-* (? imit.) + *stān* stone]
▸ **'pebbly** *adj*

THESAURUS

inoffensive, mild, nonbelligerent, pacific, peaceful, placid, unwarlike **2 = calm**, balmy, peaceful, quiet, restful, serene, still, tranquil, undisturbed

peaceful *adj* **1 = at peace**, amicable, free from strife, friendly, harmonious, nonviolent, on friendly *or* good terms, without hostility **2 = calm**, gentle, placid, quiet, restful, serene, still, tranquil, undisturbed, unruffled, untroubled **5 = peace-loving**, conciliatory, irenic, pacific, peaceable, placatory, unwarlike
Antonyms *adj* **≠ at peace:** antagonistic, bitter, hostile, unfriendly, violent, warring, wartime **≠ calm:** agitated, disquieted, disturbed, loud, nervous, noisy, raucous, restless, upset **≠ peace-loving:** belligerent, warlike

peacemaker *n* **= mediator**, appeaser, arbitrator, conciliator, pacifier, peacemonger

peak[1] *n* **1, 2 = point**, aiguille, apex, brow, crest, pinnacle, summit, tip, top **4 = high point**, acme, apogee, climax, crown, culmination, maximum point, *ne plus ultra,* zenith ◆ *vb* **8 = culminate**, be at its height, climax, come to a head, reach its highest point, reach the zenith

peaky *adj* **= off colour**, emaciated, green about the gills, ill, in poor shape, like death warmed up (*inf.*), pale, peelie-wally (*Scot.*), pinched, poorly (*inf.*), sick, sickly, under the weather (*inf.*), unwell, wan

peal *n* **1, 2 = ring**, blast, carillon, chime, clamour, clang, clap, crash, resounding, reverberation, ringing, roar, rumble, sound, tintinnabulation ◆ *vb* **5, 6 = ring**, chime, crack, crash, resonate, resound, reverberate, roar, roll, rumble, sound, toll

pearly *adj* **1 = silvery**, creamy, ivory, milky **1 = iridescent**, margaric, margaritic, mother-of-pearl, nacreous, opalescent

peasant *n* **1 = rustic**, churl, countryman, hind (*obs.*), son of the soil, swain (*arch.*) **2** *Informal* **= boor**, churl, country bumpkin, hayseed (*US & Canad. inf.*), hick (*inf., chiefly US & Canad.*), lout, provincial, yokel

pebble dash *n Brit.* a finish for external walls consisting of small stones embedded in plaster.
pec (pɛk) *n* (*usually pl*) *Inf.* short for **pectoral muscle.**
pecan (pɪˈkæn, ˈpiːkən) *n* **1** a hickory tree of the southern US having deeply furrowed bark and edible nuts. **2** the smooth oval nut of this tree, which has a sweet oily kernel. [C18: from Algonquian *paccan*]
peccable (ˈpɛkəbᵊl) *adj* liable to sin. [C17: via F from Med. L *peccābilis*, from L *peccāre* to sin]
peccadillo ⓘ (ˌpɛkəˈdɪləʊ) *n, pl* **peccadilloes** *or* **peccadillos.** a petty sin or fault. [C16: from Sp., from *pecado* sin, from L *peccātum*, from *peccāre* to transgress]
peccant (ˈpɛkənt) *adj Rare.* **1** guilty of an offence; corrupt. **2** violating or disregarding a rule; faulty. **3** producing disease; morbid. [C17: from L *peccans*, from *peccāre* to sin]
▸ˈ**peccancy** *n*
peccary (ˈpɛkərɪ) *n, pl* **peccaries** *or* **peccary.** either of two piglike mammals of forests of southern North America, Central and South America. [C17: from Carib]
peck[1] (pɛk) *n* **1** a unit of dry measure equal to 8 quarts or one quarter of a bushel. **2** a container used for measuring this quantity. **3** a large quantity or number. [C13: from Anglo-Norman, from ?]
peck[2] ⓘ (pɛk) *vb* **1** (when *intr*, sometimes foll. by *at*) to strike with the beak or with a pointed instrument. **2** (*tr*; sometimes foll. by *out*) to dig (a hole, etc.) by pecking. **3** (*tr*) (of birds) to pick up (corn, worms, etc.) by pecking. **4** (*intr*; often foll. by *at*) to nibble or pick (at one's food). **5** *Inf.* to kiss (a person) quickly and lightly. **6** (*intr*; foll. by *at*) to nag. ◆ *n* **7** a quick light blow, esp. from a bird's beak. **8** a mark made by such a blow. **9** *Inf.* a quick light kiss. [C14: from ?]
pecker (ˈpɛkə) *n Brit. sl.* spirits (esp. in **keep one's pecker up**).
pecking order *n* **1** Also called: **peck order.** a natural hierarchy in a group of gregarious birds, such as domestic fowl. **2** any hierarchical order, as among people in a particular group.
peckish (ˈpɛkɪʃ) *adj Inf., chiefly Brit.* feeling slightly hungry. [C18: from PECK[2]]
pecten (ˈpɛktɪn) *n, pl* **pectens** *or* **pectines** (-tɪˌniːz). **1** a comblike structure in the eye of birds and reptiles, consisting of a network of blood vessels projecting inwards from the retina. **2** any other comblike part or organ. [C18: from L: a comb, from *pectere* to comb]
pectin (ˈpɛktɪn) *n Biochem.* any of the acidic polysaccharides that occur in ripe fruit and vegetables: used in the manufacture of jams because of their ability to solidify to a gel. [C19: from Gk *pēktos* congealed, from *pegnuein* to set]
▸ˈ**pectic** *or* ˈ**pectinous** *adj*
pectoral (ˈpɛktərəl) *adj* **1** of or relating to the chest, breast, or thorax: *pectoral fins.* **2** worn on the breast or chest: *a pectoral medallion.* ◆ *n* **3** a pectoral organ or part, esp. a muscle or fin. **4** a medicine for disorders of the chest or lungs. **5** anything worn on the chest or breast for decoration or protection. [C15: from L *pectorālis*, from *pectus* breast]
▸ˈ**pectorally** *adv*
pectoral fin *n* either of a pair of fins, situated just behind the head in fishes, that help to control the direction of movement during locomotion.
pectoral muscle *n* either of two large chest muscles (**pectoralis major** and **pectoralis minor**), that assist in movements of the shoulder and upper arm.
peculate (ˈpɛkjʊˌleɪt) *vb* **peculates, peculating, peculated.** to appropriate or embezzle (public money, etc.). [C18: from L *pecūlārī*, from *pecūlium* private property (orig., cattle); see PECULIAR]
▸ˌ**pecuˈlation** *n* ▸ˈ**pecuˌlator** *n*
peculiar ⓘ (pɪˈkjuːlɪə) *adj* **1** strange or unusual; odd: *a peculiar idea.* **2** distinct from others; special. **3** (*postpositive*; foll. by *to*) belonging characteristically or exclusively (to): *peculiar to North America.* [C15: from L *pecūliāris* concerning private property, from *pecūlium*, lit.: property in cattle, from *pecus* cattle]
▸**peˈculiarly** *adv*
peculiarity ⓘ (pɪˌkjuːlɪˈærɪtɪ) *n, pl* **peculiarities. 1** a strange or unusual habit or characteristic. **2** a distinguishing trait, etc., that is characteristic of a particular person; idiosyncrasy. **3** the state or quality of being peculiar.
pecuniary ⓘ (pɪˈkjuːnɪərɪ) *adj* **1** of or relating to money. **2** *Law.* (of an offence) involving a monetary penalty. [C16: from L *pecūniāris*, from *pecūnia* money]
▸**peˈcuniarily** *adv*
pecuniary advantage *n Law.* financial advantage that is dishonestly obtained by deception and that constitutes a criminal offence.
-ped *or* **-pede** *n combining form.* foot or feet: *quadruped; centipede.* [from L *pēs*, *ped-* foot]
pedagogue ⓘ *or US* (*sometimes*) **pedagog** (ˈpɛdəˌgɒg) *n* **1** a teacher or educator. **2** a pedantic or dogmatic teacher. [C14: from L *paedagōgus*, from Gk *paidagōgos* slave who looked after his master's son, from *pais* boy + *agōgos* leader]
▸ˌ**pedaˈgogic** *or* ˌ**pedaˈgogical** *adj* ▸ˌ**pedaˈgogically** *adv*
pedagogy (ˈpɛdəˌgɒgɪ, -ˌgɒdʒɪ, -ˌgəʊdʒɪ) *n* the principles, practice, or profession of teaching.
pedal[1] (ˈpɛdᵊl) *n* **1a** any foot-operated lever, esp. one of the two levers that drive the chainwheel of a bicycle, the foot brake, clutch control, or accelerator of a car, one of the levers on an organ controlling deep bass notes, or one of the levers on a piano used to mute or sustain tone. **1b** (*as modifier*): *a pedal cycle.* ◆ *vb* **pedals, pedalling, pedalled** *or US* **pedals, pedaling, pedaled. 2** to propel (a bicycle, etc.) by operating the pedals. **3** (*intr*) to operate the pedals of an organ, piano, etc. **4** to work (pedals of any kind). [C17: from L *pedālis*; see PEDAL[2]]
pedal[2] (ˈpiːdᵊl) *adj* of or relating to the foot or feet. [C17: from L *pedālis*, from *pēs* foot]
pedal point (ˈpɛdᵊl) *n Music.* a sustained bass note, over which the other parts move bringing changing harmonies. Often shortened to **pedal.**
pedal steel guitar (ˈpɛdᵊl) *n* a floor-mounted multineck steel guitar with each set of strings tuned to a different open chord and foot pedals to raise or lower the pitch.
pedant ⓘ (ˈpɛdᵊnt) *n* **1** a person who relies too much on academic learning or who is concerned chiefly with insignificant detail. **2** *Arch.* a schoolmaster or teacher. [C16: via OF from It. *pedante* teacher]
▸**pedantic** (pɪˈdæntɪk) *adj* ▸**peˈdantically** *adv*
pedantry ⓘ (ˈpɛdᵊntrɪ) *n, pl* **pedantries.** the habit or an instance of being a pedant, esp. in the display of useless knowledge or minute observance of petty rules or details.
pedate (ˈpɛdeɪt) *adj* **1** (of a plant leaf) deeply divided into several lobes. **2** *Zool.* having or resembling a foot: *a pedate appendage.* [C18: from L *pedātus* equipped with feet, from *pēs* foot]
peddle ⓘ (ˈpɛdᵊl) *vb* **peddles, peddling, peddled. 1** to go from place to place selling (goods, esp. small articles). **2** (*tr*) to sell (illegal drugs, esp. narcotics). **3** (*tr*) to advocate (ideas, etc.) persistently: *to peddle a new philosophy.* [C16: back formation from PEDLAR]
peddler (ˈpɛdlə) *n* **1** a person who sells illegal drugs, esp. narcotics. **2** the usual US spelling of **pedlar.**
pederasty *or* **paederasty** (ˈpɛdəˌræstɪ) *n* homosexual relations between men and boys. [C17: from NL *paederastia*, from Gk, from *pais* boy + *erastēs* lover, from *eran* to love]
▸ˈ**pederˌast** *or* ˈ**paederˌast** *n* ▸ˌ**pederˈastic** *or* ˌ**paederˈastic** *adj*
pedestal ⓘ (ˈpɛdɪstᵊl) *n* **1** a base that supports a column, statue, etc. **2** a position of eminence or supposed superiority (esp. in **place, put,** *or* **set on a pedestal**). [C16: from F *piédestal*, from OIt. *piedestallo*, from *pie* foot + *di* of + *stallo* a stall]
pedestrian ⓘ (pɪˈdɛstrɪən) *n* **1a** a person travelling on foot; walker. **1b** (*as modifier*): *a pedestrian precinct.* ◆ *adj* **2** dull; commonplace: *a pedestrian style of writing.* [C18: from L *pedester*, from *pēs* foot]
pedestrian crossing *n Brit.* a path across a road marked as a crossing for pedestrians.
pedestrianize *or* **pedestrianise** (pɪˈdɛstrɪəˌnaɪz) *vb* **pedestrianizes, pedestrianizing, pedestrianized** *or* **pedestrianises, pedestrianising, pedestrianised.** (*tr*) to convert (a street, etc.) into an area for the use of pedestrians only.
▸**peˌdestrianiˈzation** *or* **peˌdestrianiˈsation** *n*
pedi- *combining form.* indicating the foot: *pedicure.* [from L *pēs*, *ped-* foot]
pedicab (ˈpɛdɪˌkæb) *n* a pedal-operated tricycle, available for hire in

THESAURUS

peccadillo *n* = **misdeed**, error, indiscretion, infraction, lapse, misdemeanour, petty sin, slip, trifling fault

peck[2] *vb, n* **1-9** = **pick**, bite, dig, hit, jab, kiss, nibble, poke, prick, strike, tap

peculiar *adj* **1** = **odd**, abnormal, bizarre, curious, eccentric, exceptional, extraordinary, far-out, freakish, funny, offbeat, off-the-wall (*sl.*), outlandish, out-of-the-way, outré, quaint, queer, singular, strange, uncommon, unconventional, unusual, weird **2, 3** = **specific**, appropriate, characteristic, distinct, distinctive, distinguishing, endemic, idiosyncratic, individual, local, particular, personal, private, restricted, special, unique
Antonyms *adj* ≠ **odd**: commonplace, conventional, expected, familiar, ordinary, usual ≠ **specific**: common, general, indistinctive, unspecific

peculiarity *n* **1, 3** = **eccentricity**, abnormality, bizarreness, foible, freakishness, idiosyncrasy, mannerism, oddity, odd trait, queerness, quirk **2** = **characteristic**, attribute, distinctiveness, feature, mark, particularity, property, quality, singularity, speciality, trait

pecuniary *adj* **1** = **monetary**, commercial, financial, fiscal

pedagogue *n* **1, 2** = **teacher**, dogmatist, dominie (*Scot.*), educator, instructor, master *or* mistress, pedant, schoolmaster *or* schoolmistress

pedant *n* **1** = **hairsplitter**, casuist, doctrinaire, dogmatist, literalist, nit-picker (*inf.*), pedagogue, pettifogger, precisian, quibbler, scholastic, sophist

pedantic *adj* **1** = **hairsplitting**, abstruse, academic, bookish, didactic, donnish, erudite, formal, fussy, nit-picking (*inf.*), overnice, particular, pedagogic, picky (*inf.*), pompous, precise, priggish, punctilious, scholastic, schoolmasterly, sententious, stilted

pedantry *n* = **hairsplitting**, bookishness, finicality, overnicety, pedagogism, pettifoggery, pomposity, punctiliousness, quibbling, sophistry, stuffiness

peddle *vb* **1, 2** = **sell**, flog (*sl.*), hawk, huckster, market, push (*inf.*), sell door to door, trade, vend

pedestal *n* **1** = **support**, base, dado (*Architecture*), foot, foundation, mounting, pier, plinth, socle, stand

pedestrian *n* **1** = **walker**, footslogger, foot-traveller ◆ *adj* **2** = **dull**, banal, boring, commonplace, flat, ho-hum (*inf.*), humdrum, mediocre, mundane, no great shakes (*inf.*), ordinary, plodding, prosaic, run-of-the-mill, unimaginative, uninspired, uninteresting
Antonyms *n* ≠ **walker**: driver, motorist ◆ *adj* ≠ **dull**: exciting, fascinating, imaginative, important, interesting, noteworthy, outstanding, remarkable, significant

some Asian countries, with an attached seat for one or two passengers.

pedicel ('pɛdɪˌsɛl) *n* **1** the stalk bearing a single flower of an inflorescence. **2** Also called: **peduncle.** *Biol.* any short stalk bearing an organ or organism. ◆ Also called: **pedicle.** [C17: from NL *pedicellus,* from L *pedīculus,* from *pēs* foot]
▸**pedicellate** (pɪ'dɪsɪˌleɪt) *adj*

pediculosis (pɪˌdɪkjʊ'ləʊsɪs) *n Pathol.* the state of being infested with lice. [C19: via NL from L *pedīculus* louse]
▸**pediculous** (pɪ'dɪkjʊləs) *adj*

pedicure ('pɛdɪˌkjʊə) *n* treatment of the feet, either by a medical expert or a cosmetician. [C19: via F from L *pēs* foot + *curāre* to care for]

pedigree Ⓣ ('pɛdɪˌgriː) *n* **1a** the line of descent of a purebred animal. **1b** (*as modifier*): *a pedigree bull.* **2** a document recording this. **3** a genealogical table, esp. one indicating pure ancestry. [C15: from OF *pie de grue* crane's foot, alluding to the spreading lines used in a genealogical chart]
▸**'pediˌgreed** *adj*

pediment ('pɛdɪmənt) *n* a low-pitched gable, esp. one that is triangular as used in classical architecture. [C16: from obs. *periment,* ? workman's corruption of PYRAMID]
▸**ˌpedi'mental** *adj*

pedipalp ('pɛdɪˌpælp) *n* either member of the second pair of head appendages of arachnids: specialized for feeding, locomotion, etc. [C19: from NL *pedipalpi,* from L *pēs* foot + *palpus* palp]

pedlar Ⓣ *or esp. US* **peddler** ('pɛdlə) *n* a person who peddles; hawker. [C14: changed from *peder,* from *ped, pedde* basket, from ?]

pedo- *or before a vowel* **ped-** a variant (esp. US) of **paedo-.**

pedology (pɪ'dɒlədʒɪ) *n* the study of soils. [C20: from Gk *pedon* ground, earth + -OLOGY]

pedometer (pɪ'dɒmɪtə) *n* a device that records the number of steps taken in walking and hence the distance travelled.

peduncle (pɪ'dʌŋkᵊl) *n* **1** the stalk of a plant bearing an inflorescence or solitary flower. **2** *Anat., pathol.* any stalklike structure. **3** *Biol.* another name for **pedicel** (sense 2). [C18: from NL *pedunculus,* from L *pedīculus* little foot]
▸**peduncular** (pɪ'dʌŋkjʊlə) *or* **pedunculate** (pɪ'dʌŋkjʊlɪt, -ˌleɪt) *adj*

pee (piː) *Inf.* ◆ *vb* **pees, peeing, peed. 1** (*intr*) to urinate. ◆ *n* **2** urine. **3** the act of urinating. [C18: euphemistic for PISS, based on the initial letter]

peek Ⓣ (piːk) *vb* **1** (*intr*) to glance quickly or furtively. ◆ *n* **2** such a glance. [C14 *pike,* rel. to M Du *kiken* to peek]

peekaboo ('piːkəˌbuː) *n* **1** a game for young children, in which one person hides his face and suddenly reveals it and cries "peekaboo". ◆ *adj* **2** (of a garment) made of fabric that is sheer or patterned with small holes. [C16: from PEEK + BOO]

peel[1] Ⓣ (piːl) *vb* **1** (*tr*) to remove (the skin, rind, etc.) of (a fruit, egg, etc.). **2** (*intr*) (of paint, etc.) to be removed from a surface, esp. by weathering. **3** (*intr*) (of a surface) to lose its outer covering of paint, etc., esp. by weathering. **4** (*intr*) (of a person or part of the body) to shed skin in flakes or (of skin) to be shed in flakes, esp. as a result of sunburn. ◆ *n* **5** the skin or rind of a fruit, etc. ◆ See also **peel off.** [OE *pilian* to strip off the outer layer, from L *pilāre* to make bald, from *pilus* a hair]
▸**'peeler** *n*

peel[2] (piːl) *n* a long-handled shovel used by bakers for moving bread in an oven. [C14 *pele,* from OF, from L *pāla* spade, from *pangere* to drive in]

peel[3] (piːl) *n Brit.* a fortified tower of the 16th century on the borders of Scotland. [C14 (fence made of stakes): from OF *piel* stake, from L *pālus*]

peeler ('piːlə) *n Irish & obs. Brit. sl.* another word for **policeman.** [C19: from the founder of the police force, Sir Robert *Peel* (1788–1850), Brit. statesman & prime minister]

peeling ('piːlɪŋ) *n* a strip of skin, rind, bark, etc., that has been peeled off: *a potato peeling.*

peel off *vb* (*adv*) **1** to remove or be removed by peeling. **2** (*intr*) *Sl.* to undress. **3** (*intr*) (of an aircraft) to turn away as by banking, and leave a formation.

peen (piːn) *n* **1** the end of a hammer head opposite the striking face, often rounded or wedge-shaped. ◆ *vb* **2** (*tr*) to strike with the peen of a hammer or a stream of metal shot. [C17: var. of *pane,* ?from F *panne,* ult. from L *pinna* point]

peep[1] Ⓣ (piːp) *vb* (*intr*) **1** to look furtively or secretly, as through a small aperture or from a hidden place. **2** to appear partially or briefly: *the sun peeped through the clouds.* ◆ *n* **3** a quick or furtive look. **4** the first appearance: *the peep of dawn.* [C15: var. of PEEK]

peep[2] Ⓣ (piːp) *vb* (*intr*) **1** (esp. of young birds) to utter shrill small noises. **2** to speak in a weak voice. ◆ *n* **3** a peeping sound. [C15: imit.]

peeper ('piːpə) *n* **1** a person who peeps. **2** (*often pl*) a slang word for **eye**[1] (sense 1).

peephole Ⓣ ('piːpˌhəʊl) *n* a small aperture, as in a door for observing callers before opening.

Peeping Tom *n* a man who furtively observes women undressing; voyeur. [C19: after the tailor who, according to legend, peeped at Lady Godiva when she rode naked through Coventry]

peepshow ('piːpˌʃəʊ) *n* **1** Also called: **raree show.** a box with a peephole through which a series of pictures can be seen. **2** a booth from which a viewer can see a live nude model for a fee.

peepul ('piːpᵊl) *or* **pipal** *n* an Indian tree resembling the banyan: regarded as sacred by Buddhists. Also called: **bo tree.** [C18: from Hindi *pīpal,* from Sansk. *pippala*]

peer[1] Ⓣ (pɪə) *n* **1** a member of a nobility; nobleman. **2** a person who holds any of the five grades of the British nobility: duke, marquess, earl, viscount, and baron. See also **life peer. 3** a person who is an equal in social standing, rank, age, etc.: *to be tried by one's peers.* [C14 (in sense 3): from OF *per,* from L *pār* equal]

peer[2] Ⓣ (pɪə) *vb* (*intr*) **1** to look intently with or as if with difficulty: *to peer into the distance.* **2** to appear partially or dimly: *the sun peered through the fog.* [C16: from Flemish *pieren* to look with narrowed eyes]

peerage Ⓣ ('pɪərɪdʒ) *n* **1** the whole body of peers; aristocracy. **2** the position, rank, or title of a peer. **3** (esp. in the British Isles) a book listing the peers and giving their genealogy.

peeress ('pɪərɪs) *n* **1** the wife or widow of a peer. **2** a woman holding the rank of a peer in her own right.

peer group *n* a social group composed of individuals of approximately the same age.

peerless Ⓣ ('pɪəlɪs) *adj* having no equals; matchless.

peeve Ⓣ (piːv) *Inf.* ◆ *vb* **peeves, peeving, peeved. 1** (*tr*) to irritate; vex; annoy. ◆ *n* **2** something that irritates; vexation. [C20: back formation from PEEVISH]
▸**peeved** *adj*

peevish Ⓣ ('piːvɪʃ) *adj* fretful or irritable. [C14: from ?]
▸**'peevishly** *adv* ▸**'peevishness** *n*

peewee ('piːwiː) *n* a small black-and-white Australian bird with long thin legs. [imit.]

peewit *or* **pewit** ('piːwɪt) *n* another name for **lapwing.** [C16: imit. of its call]

peg Ⓣ (pɛg) *n* **1** a small cylindrical pin or dowel used to join two parts together. **2** a pin pushed or driven into a surface: used to mark scores, define limits, support coats, etc. **3** any of several pins on a violin, etc., which can be turned so as to tune strings wound around them. **4** Also called: **clothes peg.** *Brit., Austral., & NZ.* a split or hinged pin for fastening wet clothes to a line to dry. US and Canad. equivalent: **clothespin. 5** *Brit.* a small drink of wine or spirits. **6** an opportunity or pretext for doing something: *a peg on which to hang a theory.* **7** *Inf.* a level of self-esteem, importance, etc. (esp. in **bring** *or* **take down a peg**). **8** *Inf.* See **peg leg. 9 off the peg.** *Chiefly Brit.* (of clothes) ready-to-wear, as opposed to tailor-made. ◆ *vb* **pegs, pegging, pegged. 10** (*tr*) to knock or insert a peg into. **11** (*tr*) to secure with pegs: *to peg a tent.* **12** (*tr*) to mark (a

THESAURUS

pedigree *n* **1a, 3** = **lineage,** ancestry, blood, breed, derivation, descent, extraction, family, family tree, genealogy, heritage, line, race, stemma, stirps, stock ◆ *modifier* **1b** = **purebred,** full-blooded, thoroughbred

pedlar *n* = **seller,** cheap-jack (*inf.*), colporteur, door-to-door salesman, duffer (*dialect*), hawker, huckster, vendor

peek *vb* **1** = **glance,** eyeball (*sl.*), keek (*Scot.*), look, peep, peer, snatch a glimpse, sneak a look, spy, take a look, take *or* have a gander (*inf.*) ◆ *n* **2** = **glance,** blink, butcher's (*Brit. sl.*), gander (*inf.*), glim (*Scot.*), glimpse, keek (*Scot.*), look, look-see (*sl.*), peep, shufti (*Brit. sl.*)

peel[1] *vb* **1, 2, 4** = **skin,** decorticate, desquamate, flake off, pare, scale, strip off ◆ *n* **5** = **skin,** epicarp, exocarp, peeling, rind

peep[1] *vb* **1** = **peek,** eyeball (*sl.*), keek (*Scot.*), look, look from hiding, look surreptitiously, peer, sneak a look, spy, steal a look **2** = **appear briefly,** emerge, peer out, show partially ◆ *n* **3** = **look,** butcher's, gander (*inf.*), glim (*Scot.*), glimpse, keek (*Scot.*), look-see (*sl.*), peek

peep[2] *vb, n* **1-3** = **tweet,** cheep, chirp, chirrup, pipe, squeak, twitter

peephole *n* = **spyhole,** aperture, chink, crack, crevice, fissure, hole, keyhole, opening, pinhole, slit

peer[1] *n* **1, 2** = **noble,** aristo (*inf.*), aristocrat, baron, count, duke, earl, lord, marquess, marquis, nobleman, viscount **3** = **equal,** coequal, compeer, fellow, like, match

peer[2] *vb* **1** = **squint,** gaze, inspect, peep, scan, scrutinize, snoop, spy **2** = **appear,** become visible, emerge, peep out

peerage *n* **1** = **aristocracy,** lords and ladies, nobility, peers, titled classes

peerless *adj* = **unequalled,** beyond compare, excellent, incomparable, matchless, nonpareil, outstanding, second to none, superlative, unique, unmatched, unparalleled, unrivalled, unsurpassed
Antonyms *adj* commonplace, inferior, mediocre, no great shakes (*inf.*), ordinary, poor, second-rate

peeve *Informal vb* **1** = **irritate,** annoy, bother, bug (*inf.*), exasperate, gall, get (*inf.*), get on one's nerves, irk, nark (*Brit., Austral., & NZ sl.*), nettle, pique, provoke, rile, rub (up) the wrong way, vex ◆ *n* **2** = **irritation,** annoyance, bother, gripe (*inf.*), nuisance, pest, sore point, vexation

peeved *adj* **1** = **irritated,** annoyed, exasperated, galled, hacked (off) (*US sl.*), irked, nettled, piqued, put out, riled, sore, upset, vexed

peevish *adj* = **irritable,** acrimonious, cantankerous, captious, childish, churlish, crabbed, cross, crotchety (*inf.*), crusty, fractious, fretful, grumpy, huffy, ill-natured, ill-tempered, liverish, pettish, petulant, querulous, short-tempered, shrewish, snappy, splenetic, sulky, sullen, surly, testy, tetchy, touchy, waspish, whingeing (*inf.*)
Antonyms *adj* affable, agreeable, cheerful, cheery, easy-going, even-tempered, genial, good-natured, happy, merry, pleasant, sweet

peg *vb* **11** = **fasten,** attach, fix, join, make fast, secure **14** *Chiefly Brit.* *with* **along** *or* **away** = **work at,** apply oneself to, beaver away, keep at it, keep going, keep on, persist, plod along, plug away at (*inf.*), stick to it, work away **15** = **fix,** control, freeze, limit, set, stabilize score) with pegs, as in some card games. **13** (*tr*) *Inf.* to throw (stones, etc.) at a target. **14** (*intr; foll. by away, along, etc.*) *Chiefly Brit.* to work steadily: *he pegged away at his job for years.* **15** (*tr*) to stabilize (the price of a commodity, an exchange rate, etc.). [C15: from Low Gmc *pegge*]

pegboard ('pɛɡˌbɔːd) *n* **1** a board having a pattern of holes into which small pegs can be fitted, used for playing certain games or keeping a score. **2** another name for **solitaire** (sense 1). **3** hardboard perforated by a pattern of holes in which articles may be hung, as for display.

peg leg *n Inf.* **1** an artificial leg, esp. one made of wood. **2** a person with an artificial leg.

pegmatite ('pɛɡməˌtaɪt) *n* any of a class of coarse-grained intrusive igneous rocks consisting chiefly of quartz and feldspar. [C19: from Gk *pegma* something joined together]

peg out *vb* (*adv*) **1** (*intr*) *Inf.* to collapse or die. **2** (*intr*) *Cribbage.* to score the point that wins the game. **3** (*tr*) to mark or secure with pegs: *to peg out one's claims to a piece of land.*

peg top *n* a child's spinning top, usually made of wood with a metal centre pin.

peg-top *adj* (of skirts, trousers, etc.) wide at the hips then tapering off towards the ankle.

PEI *abbrev. for* Prince Edward Island.

peignoir ('peɪnwɑː) *n* a woman's dressing gown. [C19: from F, from *peigner* to comb, since the garment was worn while the hair was combed]

pejoration (ˌpiːdʒə'reɪʃən) *n* **1** semantic change whereby a word acquires unfavourable connotations. **2** the process of worsening.

pejorative ❶ (pɪ'dʒɒrətɪv, 'piːdʒər-) *adj* **1** (of words, expressions, etc.) having an unpleasant or disparaging connotation. ◆ *n* **2** a pejorative word, etc. [C19: from F *péjoratif*, from LL *pējōrātus*, p.p. of *pējōrāre* to make worse, from L *pēior* worse]
▸**pe'joratively** *adv*

pekan ('pɛkən) *n* another name for **fisher** (the animal). [C18: from Canad. F *pékan*, from Amerind]

peke (piːk) *n Inf.* a Pekingese dog.

Pekingese (ˌpiːkɪŋ'iːz) *or* **Pekinese** (ˌpiːkə'niːz) *n* **1** (*pl* **Pekingese** *or* **Pekinese**) a small breed of pet dog with a profuse straight coat, curled plumed tail, and short wrinkled muzzle. **2** the dialect of Mandarin Chinese spoken in Beijing (formerly Peking). **3** (*pl* **Pekingesese**) a native or inhabitant of Beijing (formerly Peking), in NE China. ◆ *adj* **4** of Beijing (formerly Peking) or its inhabitants.

Peking man (piː'kɪŋ) *n* an early type of man, of the Lower Palaeolithic age, remains of which were found in a cave near Beijing (formerly Peking).

pekoe ('piːkəʊ) *n* a high-quality tea made from the downy tips of the young buds of the tea plant. [C18: from Chinese *peh ho*, from *peh* white + *ho* down]

pelage ('pɛlɪdʒ) *n* the coat of a mammal, consisting of hair, wool, fur, etc. [C19: via F from OF *pel* animal's coat, from L *pilus* hair]

Pelagianism (pɛ'leɪdʒɪəˌnɪzəm) *n Christianity.* a heretical doctrine, first formulated by Pelagius, a 5th-century British monk, that rejected the concept of original sin.
▸**Pe'lagian** *n, adj*

pelagic (pɛ'lædʒɪk) *adj* **1** of or relating to the open sea: *pelagic whaling.* **2** (of marine life) occurring in the upper waters of open sea. [C17: from L *pelagicus*, from *pelagus*, from Gk *pelagos* sea]

pelargonium (ˌpɛlə'ɡəʊnɪəm) *n* any plant of a chiefly southern African genus having circular or lobed leaves and red, pink, or white aromatic flowers: includes many cultivated geraniums. [C19: via NL from Gk *pelargos* stork, on the model of GERANIUM; from the likeness of the seed vessels to a stork's bill]

pelf (pɛlf) *n Contemptuous.* money or wealth; lucre. [C14: from OF *pelfre* booty]

pelham ('pɛləm) *n* a horse's bit for a double bridle, less severe than a curb but more severe than a snaffle. [prob. from the name *Pelham*]

pelican ('pɛlɪkən) *n* any aquatic bird of a tropical and warm water family. They have a long straight flattened bill, with a distensible pouch for engulfing fish. [OE *pellican*, from LL *pelicānus*, from Gk *pelekān*]

pelican crossing *n* a type of road crossing with a pedestrian-operated traffic-light system. [C20: from *pe(destrian) li(ght) con(trolled) crossing*, with *-con* adapted to *-can* of *pelican*]

pelisse (pɛ'liːs) *n* **1** a fur-trimmed cloak. **2** a loose coat, usually fur-trimmed, worn esp. by women in the early 19th century. [C18: via OF from Med. L *pellicia* cloak, from L *pellis* skin]

pellagra (pə'leɪɡrə, -'læ-) *n Pathol.* a disease caused by a dietary deficiency of nicotinic acid, characterized by scaling of the skin, inflammation of the mouth, diarrhoea, mental impairment, etc. [C19: via It. from *pelle* skin + *-agra*, from Gk *agra* paroxysm]
▸**pel'lagrous** *adj*

pellet ('pɛlɪt) *n* **1** a small round ball, esp. of compressed matter. **2a** an imitation bullet used in toy guns. **2b** a piece of small shot. **3** a stone ball formerly used in a catapult. **4** *Ornithol.* a mass of undigested food that is regurgitated by birds of prey. **5** a small pill. ◆ *vb* (*tr*) **6** to strike with pellets. **7** to make or form into pellets. [C14: from OF *pelote*, from Vulgar L *pilota* (unattested), from L *pila* ball]

pellitory ('pɛlɪtərɪ, -trɪ) *n, pl* **pellitories.** **1** any of various plants of a S and W European genus, esp. wall pellitory, that grow in crevices and have long narrow leaves and small pink flowers. **2** **pellitory of Spain.** a small Mediterranean plant, the root of which contains an oil formerly used to relieve toothache. [C16 *peletre*, from OF *piretre*, from L, from Gk *purethron*, from *pur* fire, from the hot pungent taste of the root]

pell-mell ❶ ('pɛl'mɛl) *adv* **1** in a confused headlong rush: *the hounds ran pell-mell into the yard.* **2** in a disorderly manner: *the things were piled pell-mell in the room.* ◆ *adj* **3** disordered; tumultuous: *a pell-mell rush for the exit.* ◆ *n* **4** disorder; confusion. [C16: from OF *pesle-mesle*, jingle based on *mesler* to MEDDLE]

pellucid ❶ (pɛ'luːsɪd) *adj* **1** transparent or translucent. **2** extremely clear in style and meaning. [C17: from L *pellūcidus*, var. of *perlūcidus*, from *perlūcēre* to shine through]
▸ˌ**pellu'cidity** *or* **pel'lucidness** *n* ▸**pel'lucidly** *adv*

pelmet ('pɛlmɪt) *n* an ornamental drapery or board fixed above a window to conceal the curtain rail. [C19: prob. from F *palmette* palm-leaf decoration on cornice moulding]

pelota (pə'lɒtə) *n* any of various games played in Spain, Spanish America, SW France, etc., by two players who use a basket strapped to their wrists or a wooden racket to propel a ball against a specially marked wall. [C19: from Sp.: ball, from OF *pelote*; see PELLET]

peloton ('pɛləˌtɒn) *n* the main field of riders in a cycling race. [C20: F, lit.: pack]

pelt[1] ❶ (pɛlt) *vb* **1** (*tr*) to throw (missiles, etc.) at (a person, etc.). **2** (*tr*) to hurl (insults, etc.) at (a person, etc.). **3** (*intr; foll. by along, etc.*) to hurry. **4** (*intr*) to rain heavily. ◆ *n* **5** a blow. **6** speed (esp. in **at full pelt**). [C15: from ?]

pelt[2] ❶ (pɛlt) *n* **1** the skin of a fur-bearing animal, esp. when it has been removed from the carcass. **2** the hide of an animal, stripped of hair. [C15: ? back formation from PELTRY]

peltate ('pɛlteɪt) *adj* (of leaves) having the stalk attached to the centre of the lower surface. [C18: from L *peltātus* equipped with a *pelta* small shield]

peltry ('pɛltrɪ) *n, pl* **peltries.** the pelts of animals collectively. [C15: from OF *peleterie* collection of pelts, from L *pilus* hair]

pelvic fin *n* either of a pair of fins attached to the pelvic girdle of fishes that help to control the direction of movement during locomotion.

pelvic inflammatory disease *n* inflammation of a woman's womb, Fallopian tubes, or ovaries as a result of infection. Abbrev.: **PID.**

pelvimetry (pɛl'vɪmɪtrɪ) *n Obstetrics.* measurement of the dimensions of the female pelvis.

pelvis ('pɛlvɪs) *n, pl* **pelvises** *or* **pelves** (-viːz). **1** the large funnel-shaped structure at the lower end of the trunk of most vertebrates. **2** Also called: **pelvic girdle.** the bones that form this structure. **3** any anatomical cavity or structure shaped like a funnel or cup. [C17: from L: basin]
▸**'pelvic** *adj*

pemmican *or* **pemican** ('pɛmɪkən) *n* a small pressed cake of shredded dried meat, pounded into paste, used originally by Native Americans and now chiefly for emergency rations. [C19: from Amerind *pimikân*, from *pimii* grease]

pemphigus ('pɛmfɪɡəs, pɛm'faɪ-) *n Pathol.* any of a group of blistering skin diseases. [C18: via NL from Gk *pemphix* bubble]

pen[1] ❶ (pɛn) *n* **1** an implement for writing or drawing using ink, formerly consisting of a sharpened and split quill, and now of a metal nib attached to a holder. See also **ballpoint, fountain pen.** **2** the writing end of such an implement; nib. **3** style of writing. **4** **the pen.** writing as an occupation. ◆ *vb* **pens, penning, penned.** **5** (*tr*) to write or compose. [OE *pinne*, from LL *penna* (quill) pen, from L: feather]

pen[2] ❶ (pɛn) *n* **1** an enclosure in which domestic animals are kept. **2** any place of confinement. **3** a dock for servicing submarines, esp. having a bombproof roof. ◆ *vb* **pens, penning, penned** *or* **pent.** **4** (*tr*) to enclose in a pen. [OE *penn*]

pen[3] (pɛn) *n US & Canad. inf.* short for **penitentiary** (sense 1).

pen[4] (pɛn) *n* a female swan. [C16: from ?]

PEN (pɛn) *n acronym for* International Association of Poets, Playwrights, Editors, Essayists, and Novelists.

Pen. *abbrev. for* Peninsula.

penal ❶ ('piːnᵊl) *adj* **1** of, relating to, constituting, or prescribing punishment. **2** used or designated as a place of punishment: *a penal institution.* [C15: from LL *poenālis* concerning punishment, from L *poena* penalty]
▸**'penally** *adv*

THESAURUS

pejorative *adj* **1** = **derogatory**, belittling, debasing, deprecatory, depreciatory, detractive, detractory, disparaging, negative, slighting, uncomplimentary, unpleasant

pell-mell *adv* **1** = **helter-skelter**, full tilt, hastily, heedlessly, hurriedly, impetuously, posthaste, precipitously, rashly, recklessly ◆ *adj* **2** = **disorderly**, chaotic, confused, disorganized, haphazard, tumultuous

pellucid *adj* **1** = **transparent**, bright, clear, crystalline, glassy, limpid, translucent **2** = **clear**, comprehensible, limpid, lucid, perspicuous, plain, straightforward, unambiguous

pelt[1] *vb* **1** = **throw**, assail, batter, beat, belabour, bombard, cast, hurl, pepper, pummel, shower, sling, strike, thrash, wallop (*inf.*) **3** = **rush**, belt (*sl.*), burn rubber (*inf.*), career, charge, dash, hurry, run fast, shoot, speed, stampede, tear, whizz (*inf.*) **4** = **pour**, bucket down (*inf.*), rain cats and dogs (*inf.*), rain hard, teem

pelt[2] *n* **1, 2** = **coat**, fell, hide, skin

pen[1] *vb* **5** = **write**, commit to paper, compose, draft, draw up, jot down

pen[2] *n* **1** = **enclosure**, cage, coop, corral (*chiefly US & Canad.*), fold, hutch, pound, sty ◆ *vb* **4** = **enclose**, cage, confine, coop up, fence in, hedge, hem in, hurdle, impound, mew (up), pound, shut up *or* in

penal *adj* **1** = **disciplinary**, corrective, penalizing, punitive, retributive

penal code *n* the codified body of the laws that relate to crime and its punishment.

penalize ➊ *or* **penalise** ('pi:nə,laɪz) *vb* **penalizes, penalizing, penalized** *or* **penalises, penalising, penalised.** (*tr*) **1** to impose a penalty on (someone), as for breaking a law or rule. **2** to inflict a disadvantage on. **3** *Sport.* to award a free stroke, point, or penalty against (a player or team). **4** to declare (an act) legally punishable.
▸,**penali'zation** *or* ,**penali'sation** *n*

penalty ➊ ('pen^{ə}ltɪ) *n, pl* **penalties. 1** a legal or official punishment, such as a term of imprisonment. **2** some other form of punishment, such as a fine or forfeit for not fulfilling a contract. **3** loss, suffering, or other misfortune occurring as a result of one's own action, error, etc. **4** *Sport, games, etc.* a handicap awarded against a player or team for illegal play, such as a free shot at goal by the opposing team. [C16: from Med. L *poenālitās* penalty; see PENAL]

penalty area *n* another name for **penalty box** (sense 1).

penalty box *n* **1** *Soccer.* a rectangular area in front of the goal, within which a penalty is awarded for a serious foul by the defending team. **2** *Ice hockey.* a bench for players serving time penalties.

penalty corner *n Hockey.* a free hit from the goal line taken by the attacking side. Also called: **short corner.**

penalty rates *pl n Austral. & NZ.* rates of pay for employees working outside normal hours.

penalty shoot-out *n* **1** *Soccer.* a method of deciding the winner of a drawn match, in which players from each team attempt to score with a penalty kick. **2** a similar method of resolving a tie in hockey, ice hockey, polo, etc.

penance ➊ ('penəns) *n* **1** voluntary self-punishment to atone for a sin, crime, etc. **2** a feeling of regret for one's wrongdoings. **3** *Christianity.* a punishment usually consisting of prayer, fasting, etc., imposed by church authority as a condition of absolution. **4** *RC Church.* a sacrament in which repentant sinners are absolved on condition of confession of their sins to a priest and of performing a penance. ◆ *vb* **penances, penancing, penanced. 5** (*tr*) (of ecclesiastical authorities) to impose a penance upon (a sinner). [C13: via OF from L *paenitentia* repentance]

penates (pə'nɑ:ti:z) *pl n* See **lares and penates.**

pence (pens) *n* a plural of **penny.**

> **USAGE NOTE** Since the decimalization of British currency and the introduction of the abbreviation **p,** as in *10p, 85p,* etc., the abbreviation has tended to replace *pence* in speech, as in *4p* (,fɔ:'pi:), *12p* (,twelv'pi:), etc.

penchant ➊ ('pɒŋʃɒn) *n* strong inclination or liking; bent or taste. [C17: from F, from *pencher* to incline, from L *pendēre* to be suspended]

pencil ('pens^{ə}l) *n* **1** a thin cylindrical instrument used for writing, drawing, etc., consisting of a rod of graphite or other marking substance usually encased in wood and sharpened. **2** something similar in shape or function: *a styptic pencil.* **3** a narrow set of lines or rays, such as light rays, diverging from or converging to a point. **4** *Rare.* an artist's individual style. **5** a type of artist's brush. ◆ *vb* **pencils, pencilling, pencilled** *or US* **pencils, penciling, penciled.** (*tr*) **6** to draw, colour, or write with a pencil. **7** to mark with a pencil. [C14: from OF *pincel,* from L *pēnicillus* painter's brush, from *pēniculus* a little tail]
▸'**penciller** *or US* '**penciler** *n*

pend (pend) *vb* (*intr*) to await judgment or settlement. [C15: from L *pendēre* to hang]

pendant ('pendənt) *n* **1a** an ornament that hangs from a piece of jewellery. **1b** a necklace with such an ornament. **2** a hanging light, esp. a chandelier. **3** a carved ornament that is suspended from a ceiling or roof. ◆ *adj* **4** a variant spelling of **pendent.** [C14: from OF, from *pendre* to hang, from L *pendēre* to hang down]

pendent ('pendənt) *adj* **1** dangling. **2** jutting. **3** (of a grammatical construction) incomplete. **4** a less common word for **pending.** ◆ *n* **5** a variant spelling of **pendant.** [C15: from OF *pendant,* from *pendre* to hang; see PENDANT]
▸'**pendency** *n*

pendentive (pen'dentɪv) *n* any of four triangular sections of vaulting with concave sides, positioned at a corner of a rectangular space to support a dome. [C18: from F *pendentif,* from L *pendens* hanging, from *pendere* to hang]

pending ➊ ('pendɪŋ) *prep* **1** while waiting for. ◆ *adj* (*postpositive*) **2** not yet decided, confirmed, or finished. **3** imminent: *these developments have been pending for some time.*

pendragon (pen'drægən) *n* a supreme war chief or leader of the ancient Britons. [Welsh, lit.: head dragon]

pendulous ➊ ('pendjʊləs) *adj* hanging downwards, esp. so as to swing from side to side. [C17: from L *pendulus,* from *pendēre* to hang down]
▸'**pendulously** *adv* ▸'**pendulousness** *n*

pendulum ('pendjʊləm) *n* **1** a body mounted so that it can swing freely under the influence of gravity. **2** such a device used to regulate a clock mechanism. **3** something that changes fairly regularly: *the pendulum of public opinion.* [C17: from L *pendulus* PENDULOUS]

peneplain *or* **peneplane** ('pi:nɪ,pleɪn) *n* a relatively flat land surface produced by erosion. [C19: from L *paene* almost + PLAIN[1]]

penetrant ('penɪtrənt) *adj* **1** sharp; penetrating. ◆ *n* **2** *Chem.* a substance that lowers the surface tension of a liquid and thus causes it to penetrate or be absorbed more easily. **3** a person or thing that penetrates.

penetrate ➊ ('penɪ,treɪt) *vb* **penetrates, penetrating, penetrated. 1** to find or force a way into or through (something); pierce; enter. **2** to diffuse through (a substance, etc.); permeate. **3** (*tr*) to see through: *their eyes could not penetrate the fog.* **4** (*tr*) (of a man) to insert the penis into the vagina of (a woman). **5** (*tr*) to grasp the meaning of (a principle, etc.). **6** (*intr*) to be understood: *his face lit up as the new idea penetrated.* [C16: from L *penetrāre*]
▸'**penetrable** *adj* ▸,**penetra'bility** *n* ▸'**pene,trator** *n*

penetrating ➊ ('penɪ,treɪtɪŋ) *adj* tending to or able to penetrate: *a penetrating mind; a penetrating voice.*
▸'**pene,tratingly** *adv*

penetration ➊ (,penɪ'treɪʃən) *n* **1** the act or an instance of penetrating. **2** the ability or power to penetrate. **3** keen insight or perception. **4** *Mil.* an offensive manoeuvre that breaks through an enemy's defensive position. **5** Also called: **market penetration.** the proportion of the total number of potential purchasers of a product or service who either are aware of its existence or actually buy it.

pen friend *n* a person with whom one exchanges letters, often a person in another country whom one has not met. Also called: **pen pal.**

penguin ('peŋgwɪn) *n* a flightless marine bird of cool southern, esp. Antarctic, regions: they have wings modified as flippers, webbed feet, and feathers lacking barbs. [C16: ?from Welsh *pen gwyn,* from *pen* head + *gwyn* white]

penicillin (,penɪ'sɪlɪn) *n* any of a group of antibiotics with powerful action against bacteria: originally obtained from the fungus *Penicillium.* [C20: from PENICILLIUM]

penicillium (,penɪ'sɪlɪəm) *n, pl* **penicilliums** *or* **penicillia** (-'sɪlɪə). any saprophytic fungus of the genus *Penicillium,* which commonly grow as a green or blue mould on stale food. [C19: NL, from L *pēnicillus* tuft of hairs; from the appearance of the sporangia of this fungus]

penillion *or* **pennillion** (pɪ'nɪlɪən) *pl n, sing* **penill** (pɪ'nɪl). the Welsh art or practice of singing poetry in counterpoint to a traditional melody played on the harp. [from Welsh: verses]

peninsula (pɪ'nɪnsjʊlə) *n* a narrow strip of land projecting into a sea or lake from the mainland. [C16: from L, lit.: almost an island, from *paene* almost + *insula* island]
▸**pen'insular** *adj*

> **USAGE NOTE** The noun *peninsula* is sometimes confused with the adjective *peninsular: the Iberian peninsula* (not *peninsular*).

penis ➊ ('pi:nɪs) *n, pl* **penises** *or* **penes** (-ni:z). the male organ of copulation in higher vertebrates, also used for urine excretion in many mammals. [C17: from L: penis]
▸**penile** ('pi:naɪl) *adj*

penitent ➊ ('penɪtənt) *adj* **1** feeling regret for one's sins; repentant. ◆ *n* **2** a person who is penitent. **3** *Christianity.* **3a** a person who repents

THESAURUS

penalize *vb* **1-3** = **punish**, award a penalty against (*Sport*), correct, discipline, handicap, impose a penalty on, inflict a handicap on, put at a disadvantage

penalty *n* **1, 2** = **punishment**, disadvantage, fine, forfeit, forfeiture, handicap, mulct, price, retribution

penance *n* **1** = **atonement**, mortification, penalty, punishment, reparation, sackcloth and ashes

penchant *n* = **liking**, affinity, bent, bias, disposition, fondness, inclination, leaning, partiality, predilection, predisposition, proclivity, proneness, propensity, taste, tendency, turn

pending *adj* **2, 3** = **undecided**, awaiting, forthcoming, hanging fire, imminent, impending, in the balance, in the offing, undetermined, unsettled, up in the air

pendulous *adj* = **hanging**, dangling, drooping, pendent, sagging, swaying, swinging

penetrable *adj* **1, 2, 5** = **clear**, accessible, comprehensible, fathomable, intelligible, open, passable, permeable, pervious, porous

penetrate *vb* **1** = **pierce**, bore, enter, go through, impale, perforate, prick, probe, stab **2** = **permeate**, diffuse, enter, get in, infiltrate, make inroads (into), pervade, seep, suffuse **5** = **grasp**, comprehend, decipher, discern, fathom, figure out (*inf.*), get to the bottom of, suss (out) (*sl.*), understand, unravel, work out **6** = **be understood**, affect, become clear, come across, get through to, impress, touch

penetrating *adj* **1** = **sharp**, biting, carrying, harsh, intrusive, pervasive, piercing, shrill, stinging, strong **5** = **perceptive**, acute, astute, critical, discerning, discriminating, incisive, intelligent, keen, perspicacious, profound, quick, sagacious, searching, sharp, sharp-witted, shrewd
Antonyms *adj* ≠ **sharp:** blunt, dull, mild, sweet ≠ **perceptive:** apathetic, dull, indifferent, obtuse, shallow, stupid, uncomprehending, unperceptive

penetration *n* **1** = **piercing**, entrance, entry, incision, inroad, invasion, perforation, puncturing **3** = **perception**, acuteness, astuteness, discernment, insight, keenness, perspicacity, sharpness, shrewdness, wit

penis *n* = **phallus**, cock (*taboo sl.*), dick (*taboo sl.*), dong (*sl.*), John Thomas (*taboo sl.*), knob (*Brit. taboo sl.*), member, organ, pizzle (*arch. & dialect*), plonker (*sl.*), prick (*taboo sl.*), tool (*taboo sl.*), willie *or* willy (*Brit. inf.*)

penitence *n* **1** = **repentance**, compunction, contrition, regret, remorse, ruefulness, self-reproach, shame, sorrow

penitent *adj* **1** = **repentant**, abject, apologetic, atoning, conscience-stricken, contrite, regretful, remorseful, rueful, sorrowful, sorry

his sins and seeks forgiveness for them. **3b** *RC Church.* a person who confesses his sins and submits to a penance. [C14: from Church L *paenitēns* regretting, from *paenitēre* to repent, from ?]
▸ **'penitence** *n* ▸ **'penitently** *adv*

penitential (ˌpɛnɪ'tɛnʃəl) *adj* **1** of, showing, or constituting penance. ◆ *n* **2** *Chiefly RC Church.* a book or compilation of instructions for confessors. **3** a less common word for **penitent** (senses 2, 3).
▸ **ˌpeni'tentially** *adv*

penitentiary (ˌpɛnɪ'tɛnʃərɪ) *n, pl* **penitentiaries. 1** (in the US and Canada) a state or federal prison. Also (US and Canad. inf.): **pen. 2** *RC Church.* **2a** a cardinal who presides over a tribunal that decides all matters affecting the sacrament of penance. **2b** this tribunal itself. ◆ *adj* **3** another word for **penitential** (sense 1). **4** *US & Canad.* (of an offence) punishable by imprisonment in a penitentiary. [C15 (meaning also: an officer dealing with penances): from Med. L *poenitentiārius*, from L *paenitēns* PENITENT]

penknife ('pɛnˌnaɪf) *n, pl* **penknives.** a small knife with one or more blades that fold into the handle; pocketknife.

penman ('pɛnmən) *n, pl* **penmen. 1** a person skilled in handwriting. **2** a person who writes by hand in a specified way: *a bad penman.* **3** an author. **4** *Rare.* a scribe.

penmanship Ⓣ ('pɛnmənʃɪp) *n* style or technique of writing by hand.

penna ('pɛnə) *n, pl* **pennae** (-niː). *Ornithol.* any large feather that has a vane and forms part of the main plumage of a bird. [L: feather]

pen name Ⓣ *n* an author's pseudonym. Also called: **nom de plume.**

pennant Ⓣ ('pɛnənt) *n* **1** a type of pennon, esp. one flown from vessels as identification or for signalling. **2** *Chiefly US, Canad., & Austral.* **2a** a flag serving as an emblem of championship in certain sports. **2b** (*as modifier*): *pennant cricket.* [C17: prob. a blend of PENDANT & PENNON]

pennate ('pɛneɪt) *adj Biol.* **1** having feathers, wings, or winglike structures. **2** another word for **pinnate.** [C19: from L *pennātus*, from *penna* wing]

penni ('pɛnɪ) *n, pl* **penniä** (-nɪə) *or* **pennis.** a Finnish monetary unit worth one hundredth of a markka. [Finnish, from Low G *pennig* PENNY]

penniless Ⓣ ('pɛnɪlɪs) *adj* very poor; almost totally without money.
▸ **'pennilessly** *adv* ▸ **'pennilessness** *n*

pennon ('pɛnən) *n* **1** a long flag, often tapering and divided at the end, originally a knight's personal flag. **2** a small tapering or triangular flag borne on a ship or boat. **3** a poetic word for **wing.** [C14: via OF ult. from L *penna* feather]

Pennsylvania Dutch (ˌpɛnsɪl'veɪnɪə) *n* **1** a dialect of German spoken in E Pennsylvania. **2** (preceded by *the; functioning as pl*) a group of German-speaking people in E Pennsylvania, descended from 18th-century settlers from SW Germany and Switzerland.

Pennsylvanian (ˌpɛnsɪl'veɪnɪən) *adj* **1** of the state of Pennsylvania, in the US. **2** (in North America) of, denoting, or formed in the upper of two divisions of the Carboniferous period. ◆ *n* **3** an inhabitant or native of the state of Pennsylvania. **4** (preceded by *the*) the Pennsylvanian period or rock system.

penny ('pɛnɪ) *n, pl* **pennies** *or* **pence** (pɛns). **1** Also called: **new penny.** *Brit.* a bronze coin having a value equal to one hundredth of a pound. Abbrev.: **p. 2** *Brit.* (before 1971) a bronze or copper coin having a value equal to one twelfth of a shilling. Abbrev.: **d. 3** a monetary unit of the Republic of Ireland worth one hundredth of a pound. **4** (*pl* **pennies**) *US & Canad.* a cent. **5** a coin of similar value, as used in several other countries. **6** (*used with a negative*) *Inf., chiefly Brit.* the least amount of money: *I don't have a penny.* **7 a pretty penny.** *Inf.* a considerable sum of money. **8 spend a penny.** *Brit. inf.* to urinate. **9 the penny dropped.** *Inf., chiefly Brit.* the explanation of something was finally realized. [OE *penig, pening*]

penny arcade *n Chiefly US.* a public place with various coin-operated machines for entertainment.

Penny Black *n* the first adhesive postage stamp, issued in Britain in 1840.

penny-dreadful *n, pl* **penny-dreadfuls.** *Brit. inf.* a cheap, often lurid book or magazine.

penny-farthing *n Brit.* an early type of bicycle with a large front wheel and a small rear wheel, the pedals being on the front wheel.

penny-pinching Ⓣ *adj* **1** excessively careful with money; miserly. ◆ *n* **2** miserliness.
▸ **'penny-ˌpincher** *n*

pennyroyal (ˌpɛnɪ'rɔɪəl) *n* **1** a Eurasian plant with hairy leaves and small mauve flowers, yielding an aromatic oil used in medicine. **2** a similar and related plant of E North America. [C16: var. of Anglo-Norman *puliol real*, from OF *pouliol* (from L *pūleium* pennyroyal) + *real* ROYAL]

penny shares *pl n Stock Exchange.* securities with a low market price, esp. less than 20p, enabling small investors to purchase a large number for a relatively small outlay.

pennyweight ('pɛnɪˌweɪt) *n* a unit of weight equal to 24 grains or one twentieth of an ounce (Troy).

penny whistle *n* a type of flageolet with six finger holes, esp. a cheap metal one. Also called: **tin whistle.**

penny-wise *adj* **1** greatly concerned with saving small sums of money. **2 penny-wise and pound-foolish.** careful about trifles but wasteful in large ventures.

pennywort ('pɛnɪˌwɜːt) *n* **1** a Eurasian rock plant with whitish-green tubular flowers and rounded leaves. **2** a marsh plant of Europe and North Africa, having circular leaves and greenish-pink flowers. **3** any of various other plants with rounded penny-like leaves.

pennyworth Ⓣ ('pɛnɪˌwɜːθ) *n* **1** the amount that can be bought for a penny. **2** a small amount: *he hasn't got a pennyworth of sense.*

penology (piː'nɒlədʒɪ) *n* **1** the branch of the social sciences concerned with the punishment of crime. **2** the science of prison management. [C19: from Gk *poinē* punishment]
▸ **penological** (ˌpiːnə'lɒdʒɪkᵊl) *adj* ▸ **pe'nologist** *n*

pen pal *n* another name for **pen friend.**

penpusher ('pɛnˌpʊʃə) *n* a person who writes a lot, esp. a clerk involved with boring paperwork.
▸ **'penˌpushing** *adj, n*

pension[1] Ⓣ ('pɛnʃən) *n* **1** a regular payment made by the state to people over a certain age to enable them to subsist without having to work. **2** a regular payment made by an employer to former employees after they retire. **3** any regular payment made by way of patronage, or in recognition of merit, service, etc.: *a pension paid to a disabled soldier.* ◆ *vb* **4** (*tr*) to grant a pension to. [C14: via OF from L *pēnsiō* a payment, from *pendere* to pay]
▸ **'pensionable** *adj* ▸ **'pensionary** *adj* ▸ **'pensioner** *n*

pension[2] *French.* (pɑ̃sjɔ̃) *n* (in France and some other countries) a relatively cheap boarding house. [C17: from F; extended meaning of *pension* grant; see PENSION[1]]

pensioneer trustee (ˌpɛnʃə'nɪə) *n* (in Britain) a person authorized by the Inland Revenue to oversee the management of a pension fund.

pension off *vb* (*tr, adv*) **1** to cause to retire from a job and pay a pension to. **2** to discard, because of age: *to pension off submarines.*

pensive Ⓣ ('pɛnsɪv) *adj* **1** deeply or seriously thoughtful, often with a tinge of sadness. **2** expressing or suggesting pensiveness. [C14: from OF *pensif*, from *penser* to think, from L *pensāre* to consider]
▸ **'pensively** *adv* ▸ **'pensiveness** *n*

penstemon (pɛn'stiːmən) *n* a variant (esp. US) of **pentstemon.**

penstock ('pɛnˌstɒk) *n* **1** a conduit that supplies water to a hydroelectric power plant. **2** a channel bringing water from the head gates to a water wheel. **3** a sluice for controlling water flow. [C17: from PEN[2] + STOCK]

pent (pɛnt) *vb* a past tense and past participle of **pen**[2] (sense 4).

penta- *or before a vowel* **pent-** *combining form.* five: *pentagon; pentode.* [from Gk *pente*]

pentacle ('pɛntəkᵊl) *n* another name for **pentagram.** [C16: from It. *pentacolo* something having five corners]

pentad ('pɛntæd) *n* **1** a group or series of five. **2** the number or sum of five. **3** a period of five years. **4** *Chem.* a pentavalent element, atom, or radical. **5** *Meteorol.* a period of five days. [C17: from Gk *pentas* group of five]

pentadactyl (ˌpɛntə'dæktɪl) *adj* (of the limbs of amphibians, reptiles, birds, and mammals) having a hand or foot bearing five digits.

pentagon ('pɛntəˌgɒn) *n* a polygon having five sides.
▸ **pentagonal** (pɛn'tægənᵊl) *adj*

Pentagon ('pɛntəˌgɒn) *n* **1** the five-sided building in Arlington, Virginia, that houses the headquarters of the US Department of Defense. **2** the military leadership of the US.

pentagram ('pɛntəˌgræm) *n* **1** a star-shaped figure with five points. **2** such a figure used by the Pythagoreans, black magicians, etc. ◆ Also called: **pentacle, pentangle.**

pentahedron (ˌpɛntə'hiːdrən) *n, pl* **pentahedrons** *or* **pentahedra** (-drə). a solid figure having five plane faces.
▸ **ˌpenta'hedral** *adj*

pentamerous (pɛn'tæmərəs) *adj* consisting of five parts, esp. (of flowers) having the petals, sepals, and other parts arranged in groups of five.

pentameter (pɛn'tæmɪtə) *n* **1** a verse line consisting of five metrical feet. **2** (in classical prosody) a verse line consisting of two dactyls, one

THESAURUS

Antonyms *adj* callous, impenitent, remorseless, unrepentant

penmanship *n* = **handwriting,** calligraphy, chirography, fist (*inf.*), hand, longhand, script, writing

pen name *n* = **pseudonym,** allonym, nom de plume

pennant *n* **1** = **flag,** banderole, banner, burgee, ensign, jack, pennon, streamer

penniless *adj* = **poor,** bankrupt, broke (*inf.*), cleaned out (*sl.*), destitute, down and out, down at heel, flat broke (*inf.*), impecunious, impoverished, indigent, moneyless, necessitous, needy, on one's uppers, on the breadline, penurious, poverty-stricken, ruined, short, skint (*Brit. sl.*), stony-broke (*Brit. sl.*), strapped (*sl.*), without a penny to one's name
Antonyms *adj* affluent, filthy rich, loaded (*sl.*), rich, rolling (*sl.*), wealthy, well-heeled (*inf.*)

penny-pincher *n* **1** = **miser,** meany (*inf.*), niggard, pinchpenny, screw (*sl.*), Scrooge, skinflint

penny-pinching *adj* **1** = **miserly,** cheeseparing, close, frugal, mean, near (*inf.*), niggardly, scrimping, Scrooge-like, stingy, tightfisted
Antonyms *adj* generous, kind, liberal, munificent, open-handed, prodigal, unstinting

pennyworth *n* **2** = **bit,** crumb, jot, little, mite, modicum, particle, scrap, small amount, tittle

pension[1] *n* **1-3** = **allowance,** annuity, benefit, superannuation

pensioner *n* **1, 2** = **senior citizen,** O.A.P., retired person

pensive *adj* **1** = **thoughtful,** blue (*inf.*), cogitative, contemplative, dreamy, grave, in a brown study (*inf.*), meditative, melancholy, mournful, musing, preoccupied, reflective, ruminative, sad, serious, sober, solemn, sorrowful, wistful
Antonyms *adj* active, carefree, cheerful, frivolous, gay, happy, joyous, light-hearted

stressed syllable, two dactyls, and a final stressed syllable. ◆ *adj* **3** designating a verse line consisting of five metrical feet.

pentamidine (pɛnˈtæmɪˌdiːn, -dɪn) *n* a drug used to treat protozoal infections, esp. pneumonia caused by *Pneumocystis carinii* in AIDS patients.

pentane (ˈpɛnteɪn) *n* an alkane hydrocarbon having three isomers, esp. the isomer with a straight chain of carbon atoms (*n*-pentane) which is a colourless flammable liquid used as a solvent.

pentangle (ˈpɛnˌtæŋgᵊl) *n* another name for **pentagram.**

pentanoic acid (ˌpɛntəˈnəʊɪk) *n* a colourless liquid carboxylic acid used in making perfumes, flavourings, and pharmaceuticals. Formula: $CH_3(CH_2)_3COOH$. Former name: **valeric acid.**

Pentateuch (ˈpɛntəˌtjuːk) *n* the first five books of the Old Testament. [C16: from Church L *pentateuchus,* from Gk PENTA- + *teukhos* tool (in LGk: scroll)]
▸ˌ**Penta'teuchal** *adj*

pentathlon (pɛnˈtæθlən) *n* an athletic contest consisting of five different events. [C18: from Gk *pentathlon,* from PENTA- + *athlon* contest]

pentatomic (ˌpɛntəˈtɒmɪk) *adj Chem.* having five atoms in the molecule.

pentatonic scale (ˌpɛntəˈtɒnɪk) *n Music.* any of several scales consisting of five notes.

pentavalent (ˌpɛntəˈveɪlənt) *adj Chem.* having a valency of five. Also: **quinquevalent.**

pentazocine (pɛnˈtæzəʊˌsiːn) *n* a powerful synthetic opiate used in medical practice as an analgesic.

Pentecost (ˈpɛntɪˌkɒst) *n* **1** a Christian festival occurring on Whit Sunday commemorating the descent of the Holy Ghost on the apostles. **2** *Judaism.* the harvest festival, celebrated on the fiftieth day after the second day of Passover. Hebrew name: **Shavuot.** [OE, from Church L, from Gk *pentēkostē* fiftieth]

Pentecostal (ˌpɛntɪˈkɒstᵊl) *adj* **1** (*usually prenominal*) of or relating to any of various Christian groups that emphasize the charismatic aspects of Christianity and adopt a fundamental attitude to the Bible. **2** of or relating to Pentecost or the influence of the Holy Spirit. ◆ *n* **3** a member of a Pentecostal Church.
▸ˌ**Pente'costalist** *n, adj*

penthouse (ˈpɛntˌhaʊs) *n* **1** a flat or maisonette built onto the top floor or roof of a block of flats. **2** a construction on the roof of a building, esp. one used to house machinery, etc. **3** a shed built against a building, esp. one that has a sloping roof. [C14 *pentis* (later *penthouse*), from OF *apentis,* from LL *appendicium* appendage, from L *appendere* to hang from; see APPEND]

pentobarbitone sodium (ˌpɛntəˈbɑːbɪˌtəʊn) *n* a barbiturate drug used in medicine as a sedative and hypnotic.

pentode (ˈpɛntəʊd) *n* **1** an electronic valve having five electrodes: a cathode, anode, and three grids. **2** (*modifier*) (of a transistor) having three terminals at the base or gate. [C20: from PENTA- + Gk *hodos* way]

Pentothal sodium (ˈpɛntəˌθæl) *n* a trademark for **thiopentone sodium.**

pentstemon (pɛntˈstiːmən) *or esp. US* **penstemon** *n* any plant of a North American genus having white, pink, red, blue, or purple flowers with five stamens, one of which is sterile. [C18: NL, from PENTA- + Gk *stēmōn* thread (here: stamen)]

pent-up ❶ *adj* not released; repressed: *pent-up emotions.*

pentyl acetate (ˈpɛntaɪl, -tɪl) *n* a colourless combustible liquid used as a solvent for paints, in the extraction of penicillin, in photographic film, and as a flavouring. Formula: $C_2H_5OOCCH_3$. Also called: **amyl acetate.**

penult (ˈpɛnʌlt, pɪˈnʌlt) *n* the last syllable but one in a word. [C16: L *paenultima syllaba,* from *paene ultima* almost the last]

penultimate (pɪˈnʌltɪmɪt) *adj* **1** next to the last. ◆ *n* **2** anything next to last, esp. a penult.

penumbra (pɪˈnʌmbrə) *n, pl* **penumbrae** (-briː) *or* **penumbras. 1** a fringe region of half shadow resulting from the partial obstruction of light by an opaque object. **2** *Astron.* the lighter and outer region of a sunspot. **3** *Painting.* the area in which light and shade blend. [C17: via NL from L *paene* almost + *umbra* shadow]
▸**pe'numbral** *adj*

penurious ❶ (pɪˈnjʊərɪəs) *adj* **1** niggardly with money. **2** lacking money or means. **3** scanty.
▸**pe'nuriously** *adv* ▸**pe'nuriousness** *n*

penury ❶ (ˈpɛnjʊrɪ) *n* **1** extreme poverty. **2** extreme scarcity. [C15: from L *pēnūria* dearth, from ?]

peon[1] (ˈpiːən, ˈpiːɒn) *n* **1** a Spanish-American farm labourer or unskilled worker. **2** (formerly, in Spanish America) a debtor compelled to work off his debts. **3** any very poor person. [C19: from Sp. *peón* peasant, from Med. L *pedō* man who goes on foot, from L *pēs* foot]
▸'**peonage** *n*

peon[2] (pjuːn, ˈpiːən, ˈpiːɒn) *n* (in India, Sri Lanka, etc., esp. formerly) **1** a messenger or attendant, esp. in an office. **2** a native policeman. **3** a foot soldier. [C17: from Port. *peão* orderly; see PEON[1]]

peony *or* **paeony** (ˈpiːənɪ) *n, pl* **peonies** *or* **paeonies. 1** any of a genus of shrubs and plants of Eurasia and North America, having large pink, red, white, or yellow flowers. **2** the flower of any of these plants. [OE *peonie,* from L *paeōnia,* from Gk *paiōnia;* rel. to *paiōnios* healing, from *paiōn* physician]

people ❶ (ˈpiːpᵊl) *n* (*usually functioning as pl*) **1** persons collectively or in general. **2** a group of persons considered together: *blind people.* **3** (*pl* **peoples**) the persons living in a country and sharing the same nationality: *the French people.* **4** one's family: *he took her home to meet his people.* **5** persons loyal to someone powerful: *the king's people accompanied him in exile.* **6 the people. 6a** the mass of persons without special distinction, privileges, etc. **6b** the body of persons in a country, etc., esp. those entitled to vote. ◆ *vb* **peoples, peopling, peopled. 7** (*tr*) to provide with or as if with people or inhabitants. [C13: from OF *pople,* from L *populus*]

USAGE NOTE See at **person.**

people carrier *n* another name for **multipurpose vehicle.**

people mover *n* **1** any of various automated forms of transport for large numbers of passengers over short distances, such as a moving pavement, driverless cars, etc. **2** another name for **multipurpose vehicle.**

people's democracy *n* (in Communist ideology) a country or government in transition from bourgeois democracy to socialism.

people's front *n* a less common term for **popular front.**

pep ❶ (pɛp) *n* **1** high spirits, energy, or vitality. ◆ *vb* **peps, pepping, pepped. 2** (*tr;* usually foll. by *up*) to liven by imbuing with new vigour. [C20: short for PEPPER]

PEP (pɛp) *n acronym for* **1** personal equity plan: a method of saving in the UK with certain tax advantages, in which investments up to a fixed annual value can be purchased. ◆ *abbrev. for* **2** political and economic planning.

peperomia (ˌpɛpərˈəʊmɪə) *n* any of a genus of tropical plants cultivated for their ornamental foliage. [C19: NL from Gk *peperi* pepper + *omoros* similar]

peplum (ˈpɛpləm) *n, pl* **peplums** *or* **pepla** (-lə). a flared ruffle attached to the waist of a jacket, bodice, etc. [C17: from L: full upper garment, from Gk *peplos* shawl]

pepo (ˈpiːpəʊ) *n, pl* **pepos.** the fruit of any of various plants, such as the melon, cucumber, and pumpkin, having a firm rind, fleshy watery pulp, and numerous seeds. [C19: from L: pumpkin, from Gk *pepōn* edible gourd, from *peptein* to ripen]

pepper ❶ (ˈpɛpə) *n* **1** a woody climbing plant, *Piper nigrum,* of the East Indies, having small black berry-like fruits. **2** the dried fruit of this plant, which is ground to produce a sharp hot condiment. See also **black pepper, white pepper. 3** any of various other plants of the genus *Piper.* **4** Also called: **capsicum.** any of various tropical plants, the fruits of which are used as a vegetable and a condiment. See also **sweet pepper, red pepper, cayenne pepper. 5** the fruit of any of these capsicums, which has a mild or pungent taste. **6** the condiment made from the fruits of any of these plants. ◆ *vb* (*tr*) **7** to season with pepper. **8** to sprinkle liberally; dot: *his prose was peppered with alliteration.* **9** to pelt with small missiles. [OE *piper,* from L, from Gk *peperi*]

pepper-and-salt *adj* **1** (of cloth, etc.) marked with a fine mixture of black and white. **2** (of hair) streaked with grey.

peppercorn (ˈpɛpəˌkɔːn) *n* **1** the small dried berry of the pepper plant. **2** something trifling.

peppercorn rent *n* a rent that is very low or nominal.

pepper mill *n* a small hand mill used to grind peppercorns.

peppermint (ˈpɛpəˌmɪnt) *n* **1** a temperate mint plant with purple or white flowers and downy leaves, which yield a pungent oil. **2** the oil from this plant, which is used as a flavouring. **3** a sweet flavoured with peppermint.

pepperoni (ˌpɛpəˈrəʊnɪ) *n* a highly seasoned dry sausage of pork and beef spiced with pepper, used esp. on pizza. [C20: from It. *peperoni,* pl of *peperone* cayenne pepper]

pepper pot *n* **1** a small container with perforations in the top for sprinkling pepper. **2** a West Indian stew of meat, etc., highly seasoned with an extract of bitter cassava.

THESAURUS

pent-up *adj* = **suppressed,** bottled up, bridled, checked, constrained, curbed, held back, inhibited, repressed, smothered, stifled

penurious *adj* **1** = **mean,** cheeseparing, close, close-fisted, frugal, grudging, miserly, near (*inf.*), niggardly, parsimonious, skimping, stingy, tightfisted, ungenerous **2** = **poor,** destitute, down and out, down at heel, impecunious, impoverished, indigent, needy, on the breadline, penniless, poverty-stricken **3** = **meagre,** beggarly, deficient, inadequate, miserable, miserly, paltry, pathetic, poor, scanty

penury *n* **1** = **poverty,** beggary, destitution, indigence, need, pauperism, privation, straitened circumstances, want **2** = **scarcity,** dearth, deficiency, lack, paucity, scantiness, shortage, sparseness

people *pl n* **1** = **persons,** human beings, humanity, humans, mankind, men and women, mortals **3** = **nation,** citizens, community, folk, inhabitants, population, public **4** = **family,** clan, race, tribe **6a the people** = **the public,** the commonalty, the crowd, the general public, the grass roots, the herd, (the) hoi polloi, the masses, the mob, the multitude, the plebs, the populace, the proles (*derogatory sl., chiefly Brit.*), the proletariat, the rabble, the rank and file ◆ *vb* **7** = **inhabit,** colonize, occupy, populate, settle

pep *n* **1** = **energy,** animation, brio, get-up-and-go (*inf.*), gusto, high spirits, life, liveliness, spirit, verve, vigour, vim (*sl.*), vitality, vivacity, zip (*inf.*) ◆ *vb* **2** *usually foll. by* **up** = **enliven,** animate, exhilarate, inspire, invigorate, jazz up (*inf.*), quicken, stimulate, vitalize, vivify

pepper *n* **6** = **seasoning,** flavour, spice ◆ *vb* **8** = **sprinkle,** bespatter, dot, fleck, spatter, speck, stipple, stud **9** = **pelt,** bombard, riddle, scatter, shower

pepper tree *n* any of several evergreen trees of a chiefly South American genus having yellowish-white flowers and bright red ornamental fruits.

peppery ➊ ('pɛpərɪ) *adj* **1** flavoured with or tasting of pepper. **2** quick-tempered; irritable. **3** full of bite and sharpness: *a peppery speech.*
▸ **'pepperiness** *n*

pep pill *n Inf.* a tablet containing a stimulant drug.

peppy ('pɛpɪ) *adj* **peppier, peppiest.** *Inf.* full of vitality; bouncy or energetic.
▸ **'peppily** *adv* ▸ **'peppiness** *n*

pepsin ('pɛpsɪn) *n* an enzyme produced in the stomach, which, when activated by acid, splits proteins into peptones. [C19: via G from Gk *pepsis,* from *peptein* to digest]

pep talk *n Inf.* an enthusiastic talk designed to increase confidence, production, cooperation, etc.

peptic ('pɛptɪk) *adj* **1** of, relating to, or promoting digestion. **2** of, relating to, or caused by pepsin or the action of the digestive juices. [C17: from Gk *peptikos* capable of digesting, from *peptein* to digest]

peptic ulcer *n Pathol.* an ulcer of the mucous membrane lining those parts of the alimentary tract exposed to digestive juices. It can occur in the oesophagus, the stomach, the duodenum, the jejunum, or in the ileum.

peptide ('pɛptaɪd) *n* any of a group of compounds consisting of two or more amino acids linked by chemical bonding between their respective carboxyl and amino groups.

peptide bond *n Biochem.* a chemical amide linkage, -NH-CO-, formed by the condensation of the amino group of one amino acid with the carboxyl group of another.

peptone ('pɛptəʊn) *n Biochem.* any of a group of compounds that form an intermediary group in the digestion of proteins to amino acids. [C19: from G *Pepton,* from Gk *pepton* something digested, from *peptein* to digest]
▸ **peptonic** (pɛp'tɒnɪk) *adj*

per (pɜː; *unstressed* pə) *determiner* **1** for every: *three pence per pound.* ◆ *prep* **2** (esp. in some Latin phrases) by; through. **3 as per.** according to: *as per specifications.* **4 as per usual.** *Inf.* as usual. [C15: from L: by, for each]

per. *abbrev. for:* **1** period. **2** person.

per- *prefix* **1** through: *pervade.* **2** throughout: *perennial.* **3** away, beyond: *perfidy.* **4** (*intensifier*): *perfervid.* **5** indicating that a chemical compound contains a high proportion of a specified element: *peroxide.* **6** indicating that a chemical element is in a higher than usual state of oxidation: *permanganate.* [from L *per* through]

peracid (pɜː'ræsɪd) *n* an acid, such as perchloric acid ($HClO_4$), in which the element forming the acid radical exhibits its highest valency.

peradventure (pərəd'vɛntʃə, ˌpɜːr-) *Arch.* ◆ *adv* **1** by chance; perhaps. ◆ *n* **2** chance or doubt. [C13: from OF *par aventure* by chance]

perambulate (pə'ræmbjʊˌleɪt) *vb* **perambulates, perambulating, perambulated. 1** to walk about (a place). **2** (*tr*) to walk round in order to inspect. [C16: from L *perambulāre* to traverse, from *per-* through + *ambulāre* to walk]
▸ **perˌambu'lation** *n* ▸ **perambulatory** (pə'ræmbjʊlətərɪ, -trɪ) *adj*

perambulator (pə'ræmbjʊˌleɪtə) *n* a formal word for **pram**[1].

per annum (pər 'ænəm) *adv* every year or by the year. [L]

P-E ratio *abbrev. for* price-earnings ratio.

percale (pə'keɪl, -'kɑːl) *n* a close-textured woven cotton fabric, used esp. for sheets. [C17: via F from Persian *pargālah* piece of cloth]

per capita (pə 'kæpɪtə) *adj, adv* of or for each person. [L, lit.: according to heads]

perceive ➊ (pə'siːv) *vb* **perceives, perceiving, perceived. 1** to become aware of (something) through the senses; recognize or observe. **2** (*tr; may take a clause as object*) to come to comprehend; grasp. [C13: from OF *perçoivre,* from L *percipere* to seize entirely]
▸ **per'ceivable** *adj* ▸ **per'ceivably** *adv*

per cent (pə 'sɛnt) *adv* **1** Also: **per centum.** in or for every hundred. Symbol: % ◆ *n also* **percent. 2** a percentage or proportion. **3** (*often pl*) securities yielding a rate of interest as specified: *he bought three percents.* [C16: from Med. L *per centum* out of every hundred]

percentage (pə'sɛntɪdʒ) *n* **1** proportion or rate per hundred parts. **2** *Commerce.* the interest, tax, commission, or allowance on a hundred items. **3** any proportion in relation to the whole. **4** *Inf.* profit or advantage.

percentile (pə'sɛntaɪl) *n* one of 99 actual or notional values of a variable dividing its distribution into 100 groups with equal frequencies. Also called: **centile.**

percept ('pɜːsɛpt) *n* **1** a concept that depends on recognition by the senses, such as sight, of some external object or phenomenon. **2** an object or phenomenon that is perceived. [C19: from L *perceptum,* from *percipere* to PERCEIVE]

perceptible ➊ (pə'sɛptəbᵊl) *adj* able to be perceived; noticeable or recognizable.
▸ **perˌcepti'bility** *n* ▸ **per'ceptibly** *adv*

perception ➊ (pə'sɛpʃən) *n* **1** the act or the effect of perceiving. **2** insight or intuition gained by perceiving. **3** the ability or capacity to perceive. **4** way of perceiving; view. **5** the process by which an organism detects and interprets the external world by means of the sensory receptors. [C15: from L *perceptiō* comprehension; see PERCEIVE]
▸ **per'ceptional** *adj* ▸ **perceptual** (pə'sɛptjʊəl) *adj*

perceptive ➊ (pə'sɛptɪv) *adj* **1** quick at perceiving; observant. **2** perceptual. **3** able to perceive.
▸ **per'ceptively** *adv* ▸ **per'ceptiveness** *or* **ˌpercep'tivity** *n*

perch[1] ➊ (pɜːtʃ) *n* **1** a pole, branch, or other resting place above ground on which a bird roosts. **2** a similar resting place for a person or thing. **3** another name for **rod** (sense 7). ◆ *vb* **4** (usually foll. by *on*) to alight, rest, or cause to rest on or as if on a perch: *the bird perched on the branch; the cap was perched on his head.* [C13 *perche* stake, from OF, from L *pertica* long staff]

perch[2] (pɜːtʃ) *n, pl* **perch** *or* **perches. 1** any of a family of freshwater spiny-finned teleost fishes of Europe and North America: valued as food and game fishes. **2** any of various similar or related fishes. [C13: from OF *perche,* from L *perca,* from Gk *perkē*]

perchance ➊ (pə'tʃɑːns) *adv Arch. or poetic.* **1** perhaps; possibly. **2** by chance; accidentally. [C14: from Anglo-F *par chance*]

Percheron ('pɜːʃəˌrɒn) *n* a compact heavy breed of carthorse. [C19: from F, from *le Perche,* region of NW France, where the breed originated]

perchloric acid (pə'klɔːrɪk) *n* a colourless syrupy oxyacid of chlorine containing a greater proportion of oxygen than chloric acid. It is a powerful oxidizing agent. Formula: $HClO_4$. Systematic name: **chloric(VII) acid.**

percipient ➊ (pə'sɪpɪənt) *adj* **1** able to perceive. **2** perceptive. ◆ *n* **3** a person who perceives. [C17: from L *percipiens* observing, from *percipere* to grasp]
▸ **per'cipience** *n* ▸ **per'cipiently** *adv*

percolate ➊ *vb* ('pɜːkəˌleɪt), **percolates, percolating, percolated. 1** to cause (a liquid) to pass through a fine mesh, porous substance, etc., or (of a liquid) to pass through a fine mesh, etc.; trickle: *rain percolated through the roof.* **2** to permeate; penetrate gradually: *water percolated the road.* **3** to make (coffee) or (of coffee) to be made in a percolator. ◆ *n* ('pɜːkəlɪt, -ˌleɪt). **4** a product of percolation. [C17: from L *percolāre,* from PER- + *cōlāre* to strain, from *cōlum* a strainer; see COLANDER]
▸ **percolable** ('pɜːkələbᵊl) *adj* ▸ **ˌperco'lation** *n*

percolator ('pɜːkəˌleɪtə) *n* a kind of coffeepot in which boiling water is forced up through a tube and filters down through the coffee grounds into a container.

per contra ('pɜː 'kɒntrə) *adv* on the contrary. [from L]

percuss (pə'kʌs) *vb* (*tr*) **1** to strike sharply or suddenly. **2** *Med.* to tap on (a body surface) with the fingertips or a special hammer to aid diagnosis. [C16: from L *percutere,* from *per-* through + *quatere* to shake]
▸ **per'cussor** *n*

percussion ➊ (pə'kʌʃən) *n* **1** the act, an instance, or an effect of percussing. **2** *Music.* the family of instruments in which sound arises from the striking of materials with sticks or hammers. **3** *Music.* instruments of this family constituting a section of an orchestra, etc. **4** *Med.* the act of percussing a body surface. **5** the act of exploding a percussion cap. [C16: from L *percussiō,* from *percutere* to hit; see PERCUSS]
▸ **per'cussive** *adj* ▸ **per'cussively** *adv* ▸ **per'cussiveness** *n*

percussion cap *n* a detonator consisting of a paper or thin metal cap containing material that explodes when struck.

percussion instrument *n* any of various musical instruments that

THESAURUS

peppery *adj* **1 = hot,** fiery, highly seasoned, piquant, pungent, spicy **2 = irritable,** choleric, hot-tempered, irascible, quick-tempered, snappish, testy, touchy, vitriolic, waspish **3 = sharp,** astringent, biting, caustic, incisive, sarcastic, stinging, trenchant, vitriolic
Antonyms *adj* ≠ **hot:** bland, insipid, mild, tasteless, vapid

perceive *vb* **1 = see,** be aware of, behold, descry, discern, discover, distinguish, espy, make out, note, notice, observe, recognize, remark, spot **2 = understand,** appreciate, apprehend, comprehend, conclude, deduce, feel, gather, get (*inf.*), get the message, get the picture, grasp, know, learn, realize, see, sense, suss (out) (*sl.*)

perceptible *adj* **= visible,** apparent, appreciable, blatant, clear, conspicuous, detectable, discernible, distinct, evident, noticeable, observable, obvious, palpable, perceivable, recognizable, tangible
Antonyms *adj* concealed, hidden, imperceptible, inconspicuous, indiscernible, invisible, unapparent, undetectable, unnoticeable

perception *n* **1, 2 = understanding,** apprehension, awareness, conception, consciousness, discernment, feeling, grasp, idea, impression, insight, notion, observation, recognition, sensation, sense, taste

perceptive *adj* **1 = observant,** acute, alert, astute, aware, discerning, insightful, intuitive, penetrating, percipient, perspicacious, quick, responsive, sensitive, sharp
Antonyms *adj* dull, indifferent, insensitive, obtuse, slow-witted, stupid, thick

perch[1] *n* **1, 2 = resting place,** branch, pole, post, roost ◆ *vb* **4 = sit,** alight, balance, land, rest, roost, settle

perchance *adv Archaic or poetic* **1, 2 = perhaps,** by chance, for all one knows, haply (*arch.*), maybe, mayhap (*arch.*), peradventure (*arch.*), possibly, probably

percipient *adj* **1, 2 = perceptive,** alert, alive, astute, aware, bright (*inf.*), discerning, discriminating, intelligent, observant, penetrating, perspicacious, quick-witted, sharp, wide-awake

percolate *vb* **1-3 = filter,** drain, drip, exude, filtrate, leach, ooze, penetrate, perk (*of coffee, inf.*), permeate, pervade, seep, strain, transfuse

percussion *n* **1 = impact,** blow, brunt, bump, clash, collision, concussion, crash, jolt, knock, shock, smash, thump produce a sound when their resonating surfaces are struck directly, as with a stick or mallet, or by leverage action.

percussionist (pəˈkʌʃənɪst) *n Music.* a person who plays any of several percussion instruments.

percutaneous (ˌpɜːkjuˈteɪnɪəs) *adj Med.* effected through the skin, as in the absorption of an ointment.

per diem (ˈpɜː ˈdaɪem, ˈdiːem) *adv* **1** every day or by the day. ◆ *n* **2** an allowance for daily expenses. [from L]

perdition Ⓣ (pəˈdɪʃən) *n* **1** *Christianity.* **1a** final and irrevocable spiritual ruin. **1b** this state as one that the wicked are said to be destined to endure forever. **2** another word for **hell**. **3** *Arch.* utter ruin or destruction. [C14: from LL *perditiō* ruin, from L *perdere* to lose, from PER- (away) + *dăre* to give]

perdurable (pəˈdjʊərəbᵊl) *adj Rare.* extremely durable. [C13: from LL *perdūrābilis,* from L *per-* (intensive) + *dūrābilis* long-lasting, from *dūrus* hard]

père *French.* (per; *English* peə) *n* an addition to a French surname to specify the father rather than the son of the same name: *Dumas père.*

Père David's deer *n* a large grey deer, surviving only in captivity. [C20: after Father A. *David* (died 1900), F missionary]

peregrinate (ˈperɪgrɪˌneɪt) *vb* **peregrinates, peregrinating, peregrinated. 1** (*intr*) to travel or wander about from place to place; voyage. **2** (*tr*) to travel through (a place). [C16: from L, from *peregrīnārī* to travel; see PEREGRINE]

▸ˌ**peregriˈnation** *n* ▸ˈ**peregriˌnator** *n*

peregrine (ˈperɪgrɪn) *adj Arch.* **1** coming from abroad. **2** travelling. [C14: from L *peregrīnus* foreign, from *pereger* being abroad, from *per* through + *ager* land (that is, beyond one's own land)]

peregrine falcon *n* a falcon occurring in most parts of the world, having a dark plumage on the back and wings and lighter underparts.

peremptory Ⓣ (pəˈremptərɪ) *adj* **1** urgent or commanding: *a peremptory ring on the bell.* **2** not able to be remitted or debated; decisive. **3** dogmatic. **4** *Law.* **4a** admitting of no denial or contradiction; precluding debate. **4b** obligatory rather than permissive. [C16: from Anglo-Norman *peremptorie,* from L *peremptōrius* decisive, from *perimere* to take away completely]

▸**perˈemptorily** *adv* ▸**perˈemptoriness** *n*

perennial Ⓣ (pəˈrenɪəl) *adj* **1** lasting throughout the year or through many years. **2** everlasting; perpetual. ◆ *n* **3** a woody or herbaceous plant that continues its growth for at least three years. [C17: from L *perennis* continual, from *per* through + *annus* year]

▸**perˈennially** *adv*

perestroika (ˌperəˈstrɔɪkə) *n* the policy of reconstructing the economy, etc., of the former Soviet Union under the leadership of Mikhail Gorbachov. [C20: Russian, lit.: reconstruction]

perfect Ⓣ *adj* (ˈpɜːfɪkt). **1** having all essential elements. **2** unblemished; faultless: *a perfect gemstone.* **3** correct or precise: *perfect timing.* **4** utter or absolute: *a perfect stranger.* **5** excellent in all respects: *a perfect day.* **6** *Maths.* exactly divisible into equal integral or polynomial roots: *36 is a perfect square.* **7** *Bot.* **7a** (of flowers) having functional stamens and pistils. **7b** (of plants) having all parts present. **8** *Grammar.* denoting a tense of verbs used in describing an action that has been completed. In English this is formed with *have* or *has* plus the past participle. **9** *Music.* **9a** of or relating to the intervals of the unison, fourth, fifth, and octave. **9b** (of a cadence) ending on the tonic chord, giving a feeling of conclusion. Also: **final**. ◆ *n* (ˈpɜːfɪkt). **10** *Grammar.* **10a** the perfect tense. **10b** a verb in this tense. ◆ *vb* (pəˈfekt). (*tr*) **11** to make perfect; improve to one's satisfaction: *he is in Paris to perfect his French.* **12** to make fully accomplished. [C13: from L *perfectus,* from *perficere* to perform, from *per-* through + *facere* to do]

> **USAGE NOTE** For most of its meanings, the adjective *perfect* describes an absolute state, i.e. one that cannot be qualified; thus something is either *perfect* or *not perfect,* and cannot be *more perfect.* However when *perfect* means excellent in all respects, a comparative can be used with it without absurdity: *the next day the weather was even more perfect.*

perfect gas *n* another name for **ideal gas**.

perfectible (pəˈfektəbᵊl) *adj* capable of becoming or being made perfect.

▸**perˌfectiˈbility** *n*

perfection Ⓣ (pəˈfekʃən) *n* **1** the act of perfecting or the state or quality of being perfect. **2** the highest degree of a quality, etc. **3** an embodiment of perfection. [C13: from L *perfectiō* a completing, from *perficere* to finish]

perfectionism Ⓣ (pəˈfekʃəˌnɪzəm) *n* **1** *Philosophy.* the doctrine that man can attain perfection in this life. **2** the demand for the highest standard of excellence.

▸**perˈfectionist** *n, adj*

perfective (pəˈfektɪv) *adj* **1** tending to perfect. **2** *Grammar.* denoting an aspect of verbs used to express that the action or event described by the verb is or was completed: *I lived in London for ten years* is perfective; *I have lived in London for ten years* is imperfective, since the implication is that I still live in London.

perfectly Ⓣ (ˈpɜːfɪktlɪ) *adv* **1** completely, utterly, or absolutely. **2** in a perfect way.

perfect number *n* an integer, such as 28, that is equal to the sum of all its possible factors, excluding itself.

perfect participle *n* another name for **past participle**.

perfect pitch *n* another name (not in technical usage) for **absolute pitch** (sense 1).

perfervid (pɜːˈfɜːvɪd) *adj Literary.* extremely ardent or zealous. [C19: from NL *perfervidus*]

perfidious Ⓣ (pəˈfɪdɪəs) *adj* guilty, treacherous, or faithless; deceitful. [C18: from L, from *perfidus* faithless]

▸**perˈfidiously** *adv* ▸**perˈfidiousness** *n* ▸ˈ**perfidy** *n*

perfoliate (pəˈfəʊlɪɪt, -ˌeɪt) *adj* (of a leaf) having a base that completely encloses the stem, so that the stem appears to pass through it. [C17: from NL *perfoliātus,* from L *per-* through + *folium* leaf]

▸**perˌfoliˈation** *n*

perforate Ⓣ *vb* (ˈpɜːfəˌreɪt), **perforates, perforating, perforated. 1** to make a hole or holes in (something). **2** (*tr*) to punch rows of holes between (stamps, etc.) for ease of separation. ◆ *adj* (ˈpɜːfərɪt). **3** *Biol.* pierced by small holes: *perforate shells.* **4** *Philately.* another word for **perforated**. [C16: from L *perforāre,* from *per-* through + *forāre* to pierce]

▸ˈ**perforable** *adj* ▸ˈ**perfoˌrator** *n*

perforated (ˈpɜːfəˌreɪtɪd) *adj* **1** pierced with holes. **2** (esp. of stamps) having perforations.

perforation (ˌpɜːfəˈreɪʃən) *n* **1** the act of perforating or the state of being perforated. **2** a hole or holes made in something. **3a** a method of making individual stamps, etc. easily separable by punching holes along their margins. **3b** the holes punched in this way. Abbrev.: **perf.**

perforce Ⓣ (pəˈfɔːs) *adv* by necessity; unavoidably. [C14: from OF *par force*]

perform Ⓣ (pəˈfɔːm) *vb* **1** to carry out (an action). **2** (*tr*) to fulfil: *to perform someone's request.* **3** to present or enact (a play, concert, etc.): *the group performed Hamlet.* [C14: from Anglo-Norman *perfourmer* (infl. by *forme* FORM), from OF *parfournir,* from *par-* PER- + *fournir* to provide]

▸**perˈformable** *adj* ▸**perˈformer** *n*

performance Ⓣ (pəˈfɔːməns) *n* **1** the act, process, or art of performing. **2** an artistic or dramatic production: *last night's performance was terri-*

THESAURUS

perdition *n* **1, 2** *Christianity* = **damnation**, condemnation, destruction, doom, downfall, everlasting punishment, hell, hellfire, ruin

peremptory *adj* **1, 2** = **imperative**, absolute, binding, categorical, commanding, compelling, decisive, final, incontrovertible, irrefutable, obligatory, undeniable **3** = **imperious**, arbitrary, assertive, authoritative, autocratic, bossy (*inf.*), dictatorial, dogmatic, domineering, high-handed, intolerant, overbearing

perennial *adj* **1** = **lasting**, abiding, chronic, constant, continual, continuing, enduring, incessant, inveterate, lifelong, persistent, recurrent, unchanging **2** = **eternal**, ceaseless, deathless, everlasting, immortal, imperishable, never-ending, permanent, perpetual, unceasing, undying, unfailing, uninterrupted

perfect *adj* **1, 4** = **complete**, absolute, completed, consummate, entire, finished, full, out-and-out, sheer, unadulterated, unalloyed, unmitigated, utter, whole **2** = **faultless**, blameless, clean, flawless, immaculate, impeccable, pure, spotless, unblemished, unmarred, untarnished **3** = **exact**, accurate, close, correct, faithful, on the money (*US*), precise, right, spot-on (*Brit. inf.*), strict, true, unerring **5** = **excellent**, ideal, splendid, sublime, superb, superlative, supreme ◆ *vb* **11** = **improve**, ameliorate, cultivate, develop, elaborate, hone, polish, refine **12** = **accomplish**, achieve, carry out, complete, consummate, effect, finish, fulfil, perform, realize
Antonyms *adj* ≠ **complete**: incomplete, partial, unfinished ≠ **faultless**: damaged, defective, deficient, faulty, flawed, impaired, imperfect, impure, ruined, spoiled ≠ **excellent**: bad, inferior, poor, unskilled, worthless ◆ *vb* ≠ **improve**: mar

perfection *n* **1** = **accomplishment**, achievement, achieving, completion, consummation, evolution, fulfilment, realization **1** = **completeness**, maturity **1** = **purity**, integrity, perfectness, wholeness **2** = **excellence**, exquisiteness, sublimity, superiority **3** = **ideal**, acme, crown, paragon

perfectionist *n* **2** = **stickler**, formalist, precisian, precisionist, purist

perfectly *adv* **1** = **completely**, absolutely, altogether, consummately, entirely, every inch, fully, quite, thoroughly, totally, utterly, wholly **2** = **flawlessly**, admirably, exquisitely, faultlessly, ideally, impeccably, like a dream, superbly, superlatively, supremely, to perfection, wonderfully
Antonyms *adv* ≠ **completely**: inaccurately, incompletely, mistakenly, partially ≠ **flawlessly**: badly, defectively, faultily, imperfectly, poorly

perfidious *adj* = **treacherous**, corrupt, deceitful, dishonest, disloyal, double-dealing, double-faced, faithless, false, recreant (*arch.*), traitorous, treasonous, two-faced, unfaithful, untrustworthy

perfidy *n* = **treachery**, betrayal, deceit, disloyalty, double-dealing, duplicity, faithlessness, falsity, infidelity, perfidiousness, treason

perforate *vb* **1** = **pierce**, bore, drill, hole, honeycomb, penetrate, punch, puncture

perforce *adv* = **necessarily**, by force of circumstances, by necessity, inevitably, needs must, of necessity, unavoidably, willy-nilly, without choice

perform *vb* **1, 2** = **carry out**, accomplish, achieve, act, bring about, complete, comply with, discharge, do, effect, execute, fulfil, function, observe, pull off, satisfy, transact, work **3** = **present**, act, appear as, depict, enact, play, produce, put on, render, represent, stage

performance *n* **1** = **carrying out**, accomplishment, achievement, act, completion, conduct, consummation, discharge, execution, exploit, feat, fulfilment, work **2** = **presentation**, acting, appearance, exhibition, gig, interpretation, *ble.* **3** manner or quality of functioning: *a machine's performance.* **4** *Inf.* mode of conduct or behaviour, esp. when distasteful: *what did you mean by that performance at the restaurant?* **5** *Inf.* any tiresome procedure: *the performance of preparing to go out in the snow.*

performance art *n* a theatrical presentation that incorporates various art forms, such as dance, sculpture, etc.

performative (pəˈfɔːmətɪv) *adj Linguistics, philosophy.* **1a** denoting an utterance that itself constitutes the act described by the verb. For example, the sentence *I confess that I was there* is itself a confession. **1b** (*as n*): *that sentence is a performative.* **2a** denoting a verb that may be used as the main verb in such an utterance. **2b** (*as n*): *"promise" is a performative.*

performing arts the arts, such as a music and drama, that require a public performance.

perfume ⓘ *n* (ˈpɜːfjuːm). **1** a mixture of alcohol and fragrant essential oils extracted from flowers, etc., or made synthetically. **2** a scent or odour, esp. a fragrant one. ◆ *vb* (pəˈfjuːm), **perfumes, perfuming, perfumed. 3** (*tr*) to impart a perfume to. [C16: from F *parfum,* prob. from OProvençal *perfum,* from *perfumar* to make scented, from *per* through (from L) + *fumar* to smoke, from L *fumāre* to smoke]

perfumer (pəˈfjuːmə) *or* **perfumier** (pəˈfjuːmjeɪ) *n* a person who makes or sells perfume.

perfumery (pəˈfjuːmərɪ) *n, pl* **perfumeries. 1** a place where perfumes are sold. **2** a factory where perfumes are made. **3** the process of making perfumes. **4** perfumes in general.

perfunctory ⓘ (pəˈfʌŋktərɪ) *adj* **1** done superficially, only as a matter of routine. **2** dull or indifferent. [C16: from LL *perfunctōrius* negligent, from *perfunctus* dispatched, from *perfungī* to fulfil]
▸**perˈfunctorily** *adv* ▸**perˈfunctoriness** *n*

perfuse (pəˈfjuːz) *vb* **perfuses, perfusing, perfused.** (*tr*) **1** to suffuse or permeate (a liquid, colour, etc.) through or over (something). **2** *Surgery.* to pass (a fluid) through (tissue). [C16: from L *perfūsus* wetted, from *perfundere* to pour over]
▸**perˈfused** *adj*

perfusionist (pəˈfjuːʒənɪst) *n Surgery.* the person in a surgical team who is responsible for the perfusion of blood through the patient's lung tissue to ensure adequate exchange of oxygen and carbon dioxide.

pergola (ˈpɜːgələ) *n* a horizontal trellis or framework, supported on posts, that carries climbing plants. [C17: via It. from L *pergula* projection from a roof, from *pergere* to go forward]

perhaps ⓘ (pəˈhæps; *informal* præps) *adv* **1a** possibly; maybe. **1b** (*as sentence modifier*): *he'll arrive tomorrow, perhaps.* ◆ *sentence substitute.* **2** it may happen, be so, etc.; maybe. [C16 *perhappes,* from *per* by + *happes* chance]

peri (ˈpɪərɪ) *n, pl* **peris. 1** (in Persian folklore) one of a race of beautiful supernatural beings. **2** any beautiful fairy-like creature. [C18: from Persian: fairy, from Avestan *pairikā* witch]

peri- *prefix* **1** enclosing, encircling, or around: *pericardium; pericarp.* **2** near or adjacent: *perihelion.* [from Gk *peri* around]

perianth (ˈperɪˌænθ) *n* the outer part of a flower, consisting of the calyx and corolla. [C18: from F *périanthe,* from NL, from PERI- + Gk *anthos* flower]

periapt (ˈperɪˌæpt) *n Rare.* a charm or amulet. [C16: via F from Gk *periapton,* from PERI- + *haptos* clasped, from *haptein* to fasten]

pericarditis (ˌperɪkɑːˈdaɪtɪs) *n* inflammation of the pericardium.

pericardium (ˌperɪˈkɑːdɪəm) *n, pl* **pericardia** (-dɪə). the membranous sac enclosing the heart. [C16: via NL from Gk *perikardion,* from PERI- + *kardia* heart]
▸ˌ**periˈcardial** *or* ˌ**periˈcardiˌac** *adj*

pericarp (ˈperɪˌkɑːp) *n* the part of a fruit enclosing the seeds that develops from the wall of the ovary. [C18: via F from NL *pericarpium*]
▸ˌ**periˈcarpial** *adj*

perichondrium (ˌperɪˈkɒndrɪəm) *n, pl* **perichondria** (-drɪə). the fibrous membrane that covers the cartilage. [C18: NL, from PERI- + Gk *chondros* cartilage]

periclase (ˈperɪˌkleɪs) *n* a mineral consisting of magnesium oxide. [C19: from NL *periclasia,* from Gk *peri* very + *klasis* a breaking, referring to its perfect cleavage]

pericline (ˈperɪˌklaɪn) *n* **1** a white translucent variety of albite in the form of elongated crystals. **2** Also called: **dome.** a dome-shaped formation of stratified rock with its slopes following the direction of folding. [C19: from Gk *periklinēs* sloping on all sides]
▸ˌ**periˈclinal** *adj*

pericranium (ˌperɪˈkreɪnɪəm) *n, pl* **pericrania** (-nɪə). the fibrous membrane covering the external surface of the skull. [C16: NL, from Gk *perikranion*]

peridot (ˈperɪˌdɒt) *n* a pale green transparent variety of the olivine chrysolite, used as a gemstone. [C14: from OF *peritot,* from ?]

perigee (ˈperɪˌdʒiː) *n* the point in its orbit around the earth when the moon or a satellite is nearest the earth. [C16: via F from Gk *perigeion,* from PERI- + *gea* earth]
▸ˌ**periˈgean** *adj*

periglacial (ˌperɪˈgleɪʃəl) *adj* relating to a region bordering a glacier: *periglacial climate.*

perihelion (ˌperɪˈhiːlɪən) *n, pl* **perihelia** (-lɪə). the point in its orbit when a planet or comet is nearest the sun. [C17: from NL *perihēlium,* from PERI- + Gk *hēlios* sun]

peril ⓘ (ˈperɪl) *n* exposure to risk or harm; danger or jeopardy. [C13: via OF from L *perīculum*]

perilous ⓘ (ˈperɪləs) *adj* very hazardous or dangerous: *a perilous journey.*
▸ˈ**perilously** *adv* ▸ˈ**perilousness** *n*

perilune (ˈperɪˌluːn) *n* the point in a lunar orbit when a spacecraft is nearest the moon. [C20: from PERI- + *-lune,* from L *lūna* moon]

perimeter ⓘ (pəˈrɪmɪtə) *n* **1** *Maths.* **1a** the curve or line enclosing a plane area. **1b** the length of this curve or line. **2a** any boundary around something. **2b** (*as modifier*): *a perimeter fence.* **3** a medical instrument for measuring the field of vision. [C16: from F *périmètre,* from L *perimetros*]
▸**perimetric** (ˌperɪˈmetrɪk) *adj*

perinatal (ˌperɪˈneɪtᵊl) *adj* of or occurring in the period from about three months before to one month after birth.

perineum (ˌperɪˈniːəm) *n, pl* **perinea** (-ˈniːə). **1** the region of the body between the anus and the genital organs. **2** the surface of the human trunk between the thighs. [C17: from NL, from Gk *perinaion,* from PERI- + *inein* to empty]
▸ˌ**periˈneal** *adj*

period ⓘ (ˈpɪərɪəd) *n* **1** a portion of time of indefinable length: *he spent a period away from home.* **2a** a portion of time specified in some way: *Picasso's blue period.* **2b** (*as modifier*): *period costume.* **3** a nontechnical name for an occurence of menstruation. **4** *Geol.* a unit of geological time during which a system of rocks is formed: *the Jurassic period.* **5** a division of time, esp. of the academic day. **6** *Physics, maths.* the time taken to complete one cycle of a regularly recurring phenomenon; the reciprocal of frequency. Symbol: *T* **7** *Astron.* **7a** the time required by a body to make one complete rotation on its axis. **7b** the time interval between two successive maxima or minima of light variation of a variable star. **8** *Chem.* one of the horizontal rows of elements in the periodic table. Each period starts with an alkali metal and ends with a rare gas. **9** another term (esp. US and Canad.) for **full stop. 10** a complete sentence, esp. one with several clauses. **11** a completion or end. [C14 *peryod,* from L *periodus,* from Gk *periodos* circuit, from PERI- + *hodos* way]

periodic ⓘ (ˌpɪərɪˈɒdɪk) *adj* **1** happening or recurring at intervals; intermittent. **2** of, relating to, or resembling a period. **3** having or occurring in a series of repeated periods or cycles.
▸ˌ**periˈodically** *adv* ▸**periodicity** (ˌpɪərɪəˈdɪsɪtɪ) *n*

periodical ⓘ (ˌpɪərɪˈɒdɪkᵊl) *n* **1** a publication issued at regular intervals, usually monthly or weekly. ◆ *adj* **2** of or relating to such publications. **3** published at regular intervals. **4** periodic or occasional.

periodic function *n Maths.* a function whose value is repeated at constant intervals.

periodic law *n* the principle that the chemical properties of the elements are periodic functions of their atomic weights or, more accurately, of their atomic numbers.

periodic sentence *n Rhetoric.* a sentence in which the completion of the main clause is left to the end, thus creating an effect of suspense.

periodic table *n* a table of the elements, arranged in order of increasing atomic number, based on the periodic law.

periodontal (ˌperɪəˈdɒntᵊl) *adj* of, denoting, or affecting the gums and other tissues surrounding the teeth: *periodontal disease.*

periodontics (ˌperɪəˈdɒntɪks) *n* (*functioning as sing*) the branch of dentistry concerned with diseases affecting the tissues and structures that

THESAURUS

play, portrayal, production, representation, show **3** = **functioning**, action, conduct, efficiency, operation, practice, running, working **4, 5** *Informal* = **carry-on** (*inf., chiefly Brit.*), act, behaviour, bother, business, fuss, pantomime (*inf., chiefly Brit.*), pother, rigmarole, to-do

performer *n* **3** = **artiste**, actor *or* actress, play-actor, player, Thespian, trouper

perfume *n* **1, 2** = **fragrance**, aroma, attar, balminess, bouquet, cologne, essence, incense, niff (*Brit. sl.*), odour, redolence, scent, smell, sweetness

perfunctory *adj* **1, 2** = **offhand**, automatic, careless, cursory, heedless, inattentive, indifferent, mechanical, negligent, routine, sketchy, slipshod, slovenly, stereotyped, superficial, unconcerned, unthinking, wooden

Antonyms *adj* ardent, assiduous, attentive, careful, diligent, keen, spirited, thorough, thoughtful, zealous

perhaps *adv* **1** = **maybe**, as the case may be, conceivably, feasibly, for all one knows, it may be, perchance (*arch.*), possibly

peril *n* = **danger**, exposure, hazard, insecurity, jeopardy, menace, pitfall, risk, uncertainty, vulnerability

Antonyms *n* certainty, impregnability, invulnerability, safety, security, surety

perilous *adj* = **dangerous**, chancy, exposed, fraught with danger, hairy (*sl.*), hazardous, parlous (*arch.*), precarious, risky, threatening, unsafe, unsure, vulnerable

perimeter *n* **1, 2** = **boundary**, ambit, border, borderline, bounds, circumference, confines, edge, limit, margin, periphery

Antonyms *n* central part, centre, core, heart, hub, middle, nucleus

period *n* **1** = **time**, interval, season, space, span, spell, stretch, term, while **2, 4** = **age**, aeon, course, cycle, date, days, epoch, era, generation, season, stage, term, time, years

periodic *adj* **1, 3** = **recurrent**, at fixed intervals, cyclic, cyclical, every once in a while, every so often, infrequent, intermittent, occasional, periodical, regular, repeated, seasonal, spasmodic, sporadic

periodical *n* **1** = **publication**, journal, magazine, monthly, organ, paper, quarterly, review, serial, weekly, zine (*inf.*)

surround teeth. Also called: **periodontology.** [C19: from PERI- + *-odontics*, from Gk *odōn* tooth]
▸ˌ**perio'dontical** *adj*

periosteum (ˌperɪ'ɒstɪəm) *n, pl* **periostea** (-tɪə). a thick fibrous two-layered membrane covering the surface of bones. [C16: NL, from Gk *periosteon*, from PERI- + *osteon* bone]
▸ˌ**peri'osteal** *adj*

peripatetic (ˌperɪpə'tetɪk) *adj* **1** itinerant. **2** *Brit.* employed in two or more educational establishments and travelling from one to another: *a peripatetic football coach.* ◆ *n* **3** a peripatetic person. [C16: from L *peripatēticus*, from Gk, from *peripatein* to pace to and fro]
▸ˌ**peripa'tetically** *adv*

Peripatetic (ˌperɪpə'tetɪk) *adj* **1** of or relating to the teachings of Aristotle, who used to teach philosophy while walking about the Lyceum in ancient Athens. ◆ *n* **2** a student of Aristotelianism.

peripeteia (ˌperɪpɪ'taɪə, -'tɪə) *n* (esp. in drama) an abrupt turn of events or reversal of circumstances. [C16: from Gk, from PERI- + *piptein* to fall (to change suddenly, lit.: to fall around)]

peripheral ❶ (pə'rɪfərəl) *adj* **1** not relating to the most important part of something; incidental. **2** of or relating to a periphery. **3** *Anat.* of, relating to, or situated near the surface of the body: *a peripheral nerve.*
▸**pe'ripherally** *adv*

peripheral device *or* **unit** *n Computing.* any device, such as a disk, printer, modem, or screen, concerned with input/output, storage, etc. Often shortened to **peripheral.**

periphery ❶ (pə'rɪfərɪ) *n, pl* **peripheries. 1** the outermost boundary of an area. **2** the outside surface of something. [C16: from LL *peripheria*, from Gk, from PERI- + *pherein* to bear]

periphrasis (pə'rɪfrəsɪs) *n, pl* **periphrases** (-rəˌsiːz). **1** a roundabout way of expressing something; circumlocution. **2** an expression of this kind. [C16: via L from Gk, from PERI- + *phrazein* to declare]

periphrastic (ˌperɪ'fræstɪk) *adj* **1** employing or involving periphrasis. **2** expressed in two or more words rather than by an inflected form of one: used esp. of a tense of a verb where the alternative word is an auxiliary verb, as in *He does go.*
▸ˌ**peri'phrastically** *adv*

perisarc ('perɪˌsɑːk) *n* the outer chitinous layer secreted by colonial hydrozoan coelenterates. [C19: from PERI- + *-sarc*, from Gk *sarx* flesh]

periscope ('perɪˌskəʊp) *n* any of a number of optical instruments that enable the user to view objects that are not in the direct line of vision, such as one in a submarine for looking above the surface of the water. They have a system of mirrors or prisms to reflect the light. [C19: from Gk *periskopein* to look around]
▸**periscopic** (ˌperɪ'skɒpɪk) *adj*

perish ❶ ('perɪʃ) *vb* **1** (*intr*) to be destroyed or die, esp. in an untimely way. **2** (*tr* sometimes foll. by *with* or *from*) to cause to suffer: *we were perished with cold.* **3** to rot or cause to rot: *leather perishes if exposed to bad weather.* ◆ *n* **4 do a perish.** *Austral. inf.* to die or come near to dying of thirst or starvation. [C13: from OF *périr*, from L *perīre* to pass away entirely]

perishable ❶ ('perɪʃəbᵊl) *adj* **1** liable to rot. ◆ *n* **2** (*often pl*) a perishable article, esp. food.
▸ˌ**perisha'bility** *or* '**perishableness** *n*

perishing ('perɪʃɪŋ) *adj* **1** *Inf.* (of weather, etc.) extremely cold. **2** *Sl.* (intensifier qualifying something undesirable): *it's a perishing nuisance!*
▸'**perishingly** *adv*

perisperm ('perɪˌspɜːm) *n* the nutritive tissue surrounding the embryo in certain seeds.

perissodactyl (pəˌrɪsəʊ'dæktɪl) *n* **1** any of an order of placental mammals having hooves with an odd number of toes: includes horses, tapirs, and rhinoceroses. ◆ *adj* **2** of, relating to, or belonging to this order. [C19: from NL *perissodactylus*, from Gk *perissos* uneven + *daktulos* digit]

peristalsis (ˌperɪ'stælsɪs) *n, pl* **peristalses** (-siːz). *Physiol.* the succession of waves of involuntary muscular contraction of various bodily tubes, esp. of the alimentary tract, where it effects transport of food and waste products. [C19: from NL, from PERI- + Gk *stalsis* compression, from *stellein* to press together]
▸ˌ**peri'staltic** *adj*

peristome ('perɪˌstəʊm) *n* **1** a fringe of pointed teeth surrounding the opening of a moss capsule. **2** any of various parts surrounding the mouth of invertebrates, such as echinoderms and earthworms, and of protozoans. [C18: from NL *peristoma*, from PERI- + Gk *stoma* mouth]

peristyle ('perɪˌstaɪl) *n* **1** a colonnade round a court or building. **2** an area surrounded by a colonnade. [C17: via F from L *peristȳlum*, from Gk *peristulon*, from PERI- + *stulos* column]

peritoneum (ˌperɪtə'niːəm) *n, pl* **peritonea** (-'niːə) *or* **peritoneums.** a serous sac that lines the walls of the abdominal cavity and covers the viscera. [C16: via LL from Gk *peritonaion*, from *peritonos* stretched around]
▸ˌ**perito'neal** *adj*

peritonitis (ˌperɪtə'naɪtɪs) *n* inflammation of the peritoneum.

periwig ('perɪˌwɪg) *n* a wig, such as a peruke. [C16 *perwyke*, changed from F *perruque* wig, PERUKE]

periwinkle[1] ('perɪˌwɪŋkᵊl) *n* any of various edible marine gastropods having a spirally coiled shell. Often shortened to **winkle.** [C16: from ?]

periwinkle[2] ('perɪˌwɪŋkᵊl) *n* any of several Eurasian evergreen plants having trailing stems and blue flowers. [C14 *pervenke*, from OE *perwince*, from LL *pervinca*]

perjure ❶ ('pɜːdʒə) *vb* **perjures, perjuring, perjured.** (*tr*) *Criminal law.* to render (oneself) guilty of perjury. [C15: from OF *parjurer*, from L *perjūrāre*, from PER- + *jūrāre* to make an oath, from *jūs* law]
▸'**perjurer** *n*

perjured ❶ ('pɜːdʒəd) *adj Criminal law.* **1a** having sworn falsely. **1b** having committed perjury. **2** involving or characterized by perjury: *perjured evidence.*

perjury ❶ ('pɜːdʒərɪ) *n, pl* **perjuries.** *Criminal law.* the offence committed by a witness in judicial proceedings who, having been lawfully sworn, wilfully gives false evidence. [C14: from Anglo-F *parjurie*, from L *perjūrium* a false oath; see PERJURE]
▸**perjurious** (pɜː'dʒʊərɪəs) *adj*

perk[1] (pɜːk) *adj* **1** pert; brisk; lively. ◆ *vb* **2** See **perk up.** [C16: see PERK UP]

perk[2] (pɜːk) *vb Inf.* short for **percolate** (sense 3).

perk[3] ❶ (pɜːk) *n Brit. inf.* short for **perquisite.**

perk up ❶ *vb* (*adv*) **1** to make or become more cheerful, hopeful, or lively. **2** to rise or cause to rise briskly: *the dog's ears perked up.* **3** (*tr*) to make smarter in appearance: *she perked up her outfit with a bright scarf.* [C14 *perk*, ?from Norman F *perquer*; see PERCH[1]]

perky ❶ ('pɜːkɪ) *adj* **perkier, perkiest. 1** jaunty; lively. **2** confident; spirited.
▸'**perkily** *adv* ▸'**perkiness** *n*

Perl (pɜːl) *n* a computer language that is used for text manipulation, esp. on the World Wide Web. [C20: *p(ractical) e(xtraction and) r(eport) l(anguage)*]

perlite ('pɜːlaɪt) *n* a variety of obsidian consisting of masses of globules. [C19: from F, from *perle* PEARL[1]]

perm[1] (pɜːm) *n* **1** a hairstyle produced by treatment with heat, chemicals, etc. which gives long-lasting waves or curls. Also called (esp. formerly): **permanent wave.** ◆ *vb* **2** (*tr*) to give a perm to (hair).

perm[2] (pɜːm) *vb, n Inf.* short for **permutate, permutation** (sense 4).

permafrost ('pɜːməˌfrɒst) *n* ground that is permanently frozen. [C20: from PERMA(NENT) + FROST]

permalloy (pɜːm'ælɔɪ) *n* any of various alloys containing iron and nickel and sometimes smaller amounts of chromium and molybdenum.

permanence ❶ ('pɜːmənəns) *n* the state or quality of being permanent.

permanency ('pɜːmənənsɪ) *n, pl* **permanencies. 1** a person or thing that is permanent. **2** another word for **permanence.**

permanent ❶ ('pɜːmənənt) *adj* **1** existing or intended to exist for an indefinite period: *a permanent structure.* **2** not expected to change; not temporary: *a permanent condition.* [C15: from L *permanens* continuing, from *permanēre* to stay to the end]
▸'**permanently** *adv*

THESAURUS

peripheral *adj* **1 = incidental,** beside the point, borderline, inessential, irrelevant, marginal, minor, secondary, superficial, tangential, unimportant **2 = outermost,** exterior, external, outer, outside, perimetric, surface

periphery *n* **1 = boundary,** ambit, border, brim, brink, circumference, edge, fringe, hem, outer edge, outskirts, perimeter, rim, skirt, verge

perish *vb* **1 = die,** be killed, be lost, decease, expire, lose one's life, pass away **1 = be destroyed,** collapse, decline, disappear, fall, go under, vanish **3 = rot,** break down, decay, decompose, disintegrate, moulder, waste, wither

perishable *adj* **1 = short-lived,** decaying, decomposable, destructible, easily spoilt, liable to rot, unstable
Antonyms *adj* durable, lasting, long-life, long-lived, non-perishable

perjure *vb Criminal law* **= commit perjury,** bear false witness, forswear, give false testimony, lie under oath, swear falsely

perjured *adj* **1** *Criminal law* **= lying,** deceitful, false, forsworn, mendacious, perfidious, traitorous, treacherous, untrue, untruthful

perjury *n Criminal law* **= lying under oath,** bearing false witness, false oath, false statement, false swearing, forswearing, giving false testimony, oath breaking, violation of an oath, wilful falsehood

perk[3] *n Brit. informal* **= bonus,** benefit, dividend, extra, fringe benefit, icing on the cake, perquisite, plus

perk up *vb* **1 = cheer up,** brighten, buck up, liven up, look up, pep up, rally, recover, recuperate, revive, take heart

perky *adj* **1, 2 = lively,** animated, bouncy, bright, bright-eyed and bushy-tailed, bubbly, buoyant, cheerful, cheery, chirpy (*inf.*), full of beans (*inf.*), gay, genial, in fine fettle, jaunty, spirited, sprightly, sunny, upbeat (*inf.*), vivacious

permanence *n* **= continuity,** constancy, continuance, dependability, durability, duration, endurance, finality, fixedness, fixity, immortality, indestructibility, lastingness, perdurability (*rare*), permanency, perpetuity, stability, survival

permanent *adj* **1, 2 = lasting,** abiding, constant, durable, enduring, eternal, everlasting, fixed, immovable, immutable, imperishable, indestructible, invariable, long-lasting, perennial, perpetual, persistent, stable, steadfast, unchanging, unfading
Antonyms *adj* brief, changing, ephemeral, finite, fleeting, impermanent, inconstant, momentary, mortal, passing, short-lived, temporary, transitory, variable

permanently *adv* **1, 2 = for ever,** abidingly, always, constantly, continually, enduringly, eternally, immovably, immutably, indelibly, in perpetuity, invariably, lastingly, perennially, perpetually, persistently, steadfastly, unchangingly, unfadingly, unwaveringly
Antonyms *adv* briefly, ephemerally, fleetingly, im-

permanent health insurance *n* a form of insurance that provides up to 75 per cent of a person's salary, until retirement, in case of prolonged illness or disability.

permanent magnet *n* a magnet, often of steel, that retains its magnetization after the magnetic field producing it has been removed.

permanent press *n* a chemical treatment for clothing that makes the fabric crease-resistant and sometimes provides a garment with a permanent crease or pleats.

permanent wave *n* another name (esp. formerly) for **perm**[1] (sense 1).

permanent way *n Chiefly Brit.* the track of a railway, including the sleepers, rails, etc.

permanganate (pəˈmæŋgəˌneɪt, -nɪt) *n* a salt of permanganic acid.

permanganic acid (ˌpɜːmænˈgænɪk) *n* a monobasic acid known only in solution and in the form of permanganate salts. Formula: $HMnO_4$. Systematic name: **manganic(VII) acid.**

permeability (ˌpɜːmɪəˈbɪlɪtɪ) *n* **1** the state or quality of being permeable. **2** a measure of the ability of a medium to modify a magnetic field, expressed as the ratio of the magnetic flux density in the medium to the field strength; measured in henries per metre. Symbol: μ

permeable ➊ (ˈpɜːmɪəbᵊl) *adj* capable of being permeated, esp. by liquids. [C15: from LL *permeābilis,* from L *permeāre* to pervade; see PERMEATE]
▸ˈ**permeably** *adv*

permeance (ˈpɜːmɪəns) *n* **1** the act of permeating. **2** the reciprocal of the reluctance of a magnetic circuit.
▸ˈ**permeant** *adj, n*

permeate ➊ (ˈpɜːmɪˌeɪt) *vb* **permeates, permeating, permeated. 1** to penetrate or pervade (a substance, area, etc.): *a lovely smell permeated the room.* **2** to pass through or cause to pass through by osmosis or diffusion: *to permeate a membrane.* [C17: from L *permeāre,* from *per-* through + *meāre* to pass]
▸ˌ**permeˈation** *n* ▸ˈ**permeative** *adj*

Permian (ˈpɜːmɪən) *adj* **1** of, denoting, or formed in the last period of the Palaeozoic era, between the Carboniferous and Triassic periods. ◆ *n* **2 the.** the Permian period or rock system. [C19: after *Perm,* Russian port]

permissible ➊ (pəˈmɪsəbᵊl) *adj* permitted; allowable.
▸**perˌmissiˈbility** *n* ▸**perˈmissibly** *adv*

permission ➊ (pəˈmɪʃən) *n* authorization to do something.

permissive ➊ (pəˈmɪsɪv) *adj* **1** tolerant; lenient: *permissive parents.* **2** indulgent in matters of sex: *a permissive society.* **3** granting permission.
▸**perˈmissively** *adv* ▸**perˈmissiveness** *n*

permit ➊ *vb* (pəˈmɪt), **permits, permitting, permitted. 1** (*tr*) to grant permission to do something: *you are permitted to smoke.* **2** (*tr*) to consent to or tolerate: *she will not permit him to come.* **3** (when *intr,* often foll. by *of;* when *tr,* often foll. by an infinitive) to allow the possibility (of): *the passage permits of two interpretations; his work permits him to relax nowadays.* ◆ *n* (ˈpɜːmɪt). **4** an official document granting authorization; licence. **5** permission. [C15: from L *permittere,* from *per-* through + *mittere* to send]
▸**perˈmitter** *n*

permittivity (ˌpɜːmɪˈtɪvɪtɪ) *n, pl* **permittivities.** a measure of the ability of a substance to transmit an electric field.

permutate (ˈpɜːmjuˌteɪt) *vb* **permutates, permutating, permutated.** to alter the sequence or arrangement (of): *endlessly permutating three basic designs.*

permutation ➊ (ˌpɜːmjuˈteɪʃən) *n* **1** *Maths.* **1a** an ordered arrangement of the numbers, terms, etc., of a set into specified groups: *the permutations of a, b, and c, taken two at a time, are ab, ba, ac, ca, bc, cb.* **1b** a group formed in this way. **2** a combination of items, etc., made by reordering. **3** an alteration; transformation. **4** a fixed combination for selections of results on football pools. Usually shortened to **perm.** [C14: from L *permūtātiō,* from *permūtāre* to change thoroughly]
▸ˌ**permuˈtational** *adj*

permute (pəˈmjuːt) *vb* **permutes, permuting, permuted.** (*tr*) **1** to change the sequence of. **2** *Maths.* to subject to permutation. [C14: from L *permūtāre,* from PER- + *mūtāre* to change]

pernicious ➊ (pəˈnɪʃəs) *adj* **1** wicked or malicious: *pernicious lies.* **2** causing grave harm; deadly. [C16: from L *perniciōsus,* from *perniciēs* ruin, from PER- (intensive) + *nex* death]
▸**perˈniciously** *adv* ▸**perˈniciousness** *n*

pernicious anaemia *n* a form of anaemia characterized by lesions of the spinal cord, weakness, sore tongue, diarrhoea, etc.: associated with inadequate absorption of vitamin B_{12}.

pernickety ➊ (pəˈnɪkɪtɪ) *adj Inf.* **1** excessively precise; fussy. **2** (of a task) requiring close attention. [C19: orig. Scot. from ?]

peroneal (ˌperəˈniːəl) *adj Anat.* of or relating to the fibula. [C19: from NL *peronē,* from Gk: fibula]

perorate (ˈperəˌreɪt) *vb* **perorates, perorating, perorated.** (*intr*) **1** to speak at length, esp. in a formal manner. **2** to conclude a speech or sum up.

peroration (ˌperəˈreɪʃən) *n* the conclusion of a speech or discourse, in which points made previously are summed up. [C15: from L *perōrātiō,* from PER- (thoroughly) + *orāre* to speak]

perovskite (peˈrɒvskaɪt) *n* a yellow, brown, or greyish-black mineral. [C19: after *Perovski,* Russian mineralogist]

peroxide (pəˈrɒksaɪd) *n* **1** short for **hydrogen peroxide,** esp. when used for bleaching hair. **2** any of a class of metallic oxides, such as sodium peroxide, Na_2O_2. **3** (*not in technical usage*) any of certain dioxides, such as manganese(VI) oxide, MnO_2, that resemble peroxides in their formula. **4** any of a class of organic compounds whose molecules contain two oxygen atoms bound together. **5** (*modifier*) of, relating to, bleached with, or resembling peroxide: *a peroxide blonde.* ◆ *vb* **peroxides, peroxiding, peroxided. 6** (*tr*) to bleach (the hair) with peroxide.

perpendicular ➊ (ˌpɜːpənˈdɪkjʊlə) *adj* **1** at right angles to a horizontal plane. **2** denoting, relating to, or having the style of Gothic architecture used in England during the 14th and 15th centuries, characterized by tracery having vertical lines. **3** upright; vertical. ◆ *n* **4** *Geom.* a line or plane perpendicular to another. **5** any instrument used for indicating the vertical line through a given point. [C14: from L *perpendiculāris,* from *perpendiculum* a plumb line, from *per-* through + *pendēre* to hang]
▸**perpendicularity** (ˌpɜːpənˌdɪkjuˈlærɪtɪ) *n* ▸ˌ**perpenˈdicularly** *adv*

perpetrate ➊ (ˈpɜːpɪˌtreɪt) *vb* **perpetrates, perpetrating, perpetrated.** (*tr*) to perform or be responsible for (a deception, crime, etc.). [C16: from L *perpetrāre,* from *per-* (thoroughly) + *patrāre* to perform]
▸ˌ**perpeˈtration** *n* ▸ˈ**perpeˌtrator** *n*

> **USAGE NOTE** *Perpetrate* and *perpetuate* are sometimes confused: *he must answer for the crimes he has perpetrated* (not *perpetuated*); *the book helped to perpetuate* (not *perpetrate*) *some of the myths surrounding his early life.*

perpetual ➊ (pəˈpetjʊəl) *adj* **1** (*usually prenominal*) eternal; permanent. **2** (*usually prenominal*) seemingly ceaseless because often repeated: *your perpetual complaints.* [C14: via OF from L *perpetuālis* universal, from *perpes* continuous, from *per-* (thoroughly) + *petere* to go towards]
▸**perˈpetually** *adv*

perpetual debenture *n* a bond or debenture that can either never be redeemed or cannot be redeemed on demand.

perpetual motion *n* motion of a hypothetical mechanism that continues indefinitely without any external source of energy. It is impossible in practice because of friction.

perpetuate ➊ (pəˈpetjuˌeɪt) *vb* **perpetuates, perpetuating, perpetuated.** (*tr*) to cause to continue: *to perpetuate misconceptions.* [C16: from L *perpetuāre* to continue without interruption, from *perpetuus* PERPETUAL]
▸**perˌpetuˈation** *n*

> **USAGE NOTE** See at **perpetrate.**

THESAURUS

permanently, inconstantly, momentarily, temporarily, transitorily

permeable *adj* = **penetrable**, absorbent, absorptive, pervious, porous, spongy

permeate *vb* **1, 2** = **pervade**, charge, diffuse throughout, fill, filter through, imbue, impregnate, infiltrate, pass through, penetrate, percolate, saturate, seep through, soak through, spread through

permissible *adj* = **permitted**, acceptable, admissible, allowable, all right, authorized, kosher (*inf.*), lawful, legal, legit (*sl.*), legitimate, licit, O.K. *or* okay (*inf.*), proper, sanctioned
Antonyms *adj* banned, forbidden, illegal, illicit, prohibited, unauthorized, unlawful

permission *n* = **authorization**, allowance, approval, assent, blank cheque, carte blanche, consent, dispensation, freedom, go-ahead (*inf.*), green light, leave, liberty, licence, permit, sanction, sufferance, tolerance

permissive *adj* **1, 2** = **tolerant**, acquiescent, easy-going, easy-oasy (*sl.*), forbearing, free, indulgent, latitudinarian, lax, lenient, liberal, open-minded
Antonyms *adj* authoritarian, denying, domineering, forbidding, grudging, rigid, strict

permit *vb* **1, 2** = **allow**, admit, agree, authorize, consent, empower, enable, endorse, endure, entitle, give leave *or* permission, give the green light to, grant, let, license, own, sanction, suffer, tolerate, warrant ◆ *n* **4, 5** = **licence**, authorization, liberty, pass, passport, permission, sanction, warrant

permutation *n* **3** = **transformation**, alteration, change, shift, transmutation, transposition

pernicious *adj* **1, 2** = **wicked**, bad, baleful, baneful (*arch.*), damaging, dangerous, deadly, deleterious, destructive, detrimental, evil, fatal, harmful, hurtful, injurious, maleficent, malevolent, malicious, malign, malignant, noisome, noxious, offensive, pestilent, poisonous, ruinous, venomous

pernickety *adj Informal* **1** = **fussy**, careful, carping, difficult to please, exacting, fastidious, finicky, hairsplitting, nice, nit-picking (*inf.*), overprecise, painstaking, particular, picky (*inf.*), punctilious **2** = **tricky**, detailed, exacting, fiddly, fine
Antonyms *adj* ≠ **fussy:** careless, easy to please, haphazard, heedless, inattentive, lax, slack, slapdash, slipshod, sloppy, uncritical ≠ **tricky:** easy, simple

perpendicular *adj* **1, 3** = **upright**, at right angles to, on end, plumb, straight, vertical

perpetrate *vb* = **commit**, be responsible for, bring about, carry out, do, effect, enact, execute, inflict, perform, wreak

perpetual *adj* **1** = **everlasting**, abiding, endless, enduring, eternal, immortal, infinite, lasting, never-ending, perennial, permanent, sempiternal (*literary*), unchanging, undying, unending **2** = **continual**, ceaseless, constant, continuous, endless, incessant, interminable, never-ending, perennial, persistent, recurrent, repeated, unceasing, unfailing, uninterrupted, unremitting
Antonyms *adj* brief, ephemeral, fleeting, impermanent, momentary, passing, short-lived, temporary, transitory

perpetuate *vb* = **maintain**, continue, eternalize, immortalize, keep alive, keep going, keep up, preserve, sustain

perpetuity (ˌpɜːpɪˈtjuːɪtɪ) *n, pl* **perpetuities. 1** eternity. **2** the state of being perpetual. **3** *Property law.* a limitation preventing the absolute disposal of an estate for longer than the period allowed by law. **4** an annuity that is payable indefinitely. **5 in perpetuity.** forever. [C15: from OF *perpetuite,* from L *perpetuitās* continuity; see PERPETUAL]

perplex ❶ (pəˈplɛks) *vb (tr)* **1** to puzzle; bewilder; confuse. **2** to complicate: *to perplex an issue.* [C15: from obs. *perplex* (adj) intricate, from L *perplexus* entangled, from *per-* (thoroughly) + *plectere* to entwine] ▸**perplexedly** (pəˈplɛksɪdlɪ, -ˈplɛkstlɪ) *adv* ▸**perˈplexingly** *adv*

perplexity ❶ (pəˈplɛksɪtɪ) *n, pl* **perplexities. 1** the state of being perplexed. **2** the state of being intricate or complicated. **3** something that perplexes.

per pro (ˈpɜː ˈprəʊ) *prep* by delegation to: through the agency of: used when signing documents on behalf of someone else. [L: abbrev. of *per prōcūrātiōnem*]

USAGE NOTE See at **pp.**

perquisite ❶ (ˈpɜːkwɪzɪt) *n* **1** an incidental benefit gained from a certain type of employment, such as the use of a company car. **2** a customary benefit received in addition to a regular income. **3** a customary tip. **4** something expected or regarded as an exclusive right. ◆ Often shortened (informal) to **perk.** [C15: from Med. L *perquīsītum,* from L *perquīrere* to seek earnestly for something]

Perrier water *or* **Perrier** (ˈpɛrɪeɪ) *n Trademark.* a sparkling mineral water from the south of France. [C20: after a spring, *Source Perrier,* at Vergèze, France]

perron (ˈpɛrən) *n* an external flight of steps, esp. one at the front entrance of a building. [C14: from OF, from *pierre* stone, from L *petra*]

perry (ˈpɛrɪ) *n, pl* **perries.** wine made of pears, similar in taste to cider. [C14 *pereye,* from OF *peré,* ult. from L *pirum* pear]

pers. *abbrev. for:* **1** person. **2** personal.

Pers. *abbrev. for* Persia(n).

perse (pɜːs) *n* **a** a dark greyish-blue colour. **b** *(as adj)*: *perse cloth.* [C14: from OF, from Med. L *persus,* ? changed from L *Persicus* Persian]

per se ❶ (ˈpɜː ˈseɪ) *adv* by or in itself; intrinsically. [L]

persecute ❶ (ˈpɜːsɪˌkjuːt) *vb* **persecutes, persecuting, persecuted.** *(tr)* **1** to oppress, harass, or maltreat, esp. because of race, religion, etc. **2** to bother persistently. [C15: from OF, from *persecuteur,* from LL *persecūtor* pursuer, from L *persequī* to take vengeance upon] ▸ˌ**perseˈcution** *n* ▸ˈ**perseˌcutive** *adj* ▸ˈ**perseˌcutor** *n*

persecution complex *n Psychol.* an acute irrational fear that other people are plotting one's downfall.

perseverance ❶ (ˌpɜːsɪˈvɪərəns) *n* **1** continued steady belief or efforts; persistence. **2** *Christian theol.* continuance in a state of grace.

perseveration (pɜːˌsɛvəˈreɪʃən) *n Psychol.* the tendency for an impression, idea, or feeling to dissipate only slowly and to recur during subsequent experiences.

persevere ❶ (ˌpɜːsɪˈvɪə) *vb* **perseveres, persevering, persevered.** *(intr; often foll. by in)* to show perseverance. [C14: from OF *perseverer,* from L, from *perseverus* very strict; see SEVERE]

Persian (ˈpɜːʃən) *adj* **1** of or relating to ancient Persia or modern Iran, their inhabitants, or their languages. ◆ *n* **2** a native, citizen, or inhabitant of modern Iran; an Iranian. **3** the language of Iran or Persia in any of its ancient or modern forms.

Persian carpet *or* **rug** *n* a carpet or rug made in Persia or the Near East by knotting silk or wool yarn by hand onto a woven backing in rich colours and flowing or geometric designs.

Persian cat *n* a long-haired variety of domestic cat.

Persian lamb *n* **1** a black loosely curled fur from the karakul lamb. **2** a karakul lamb.

persiennes (ˌpɜːsɪˈɛnz) *pl n* outside window shutters having louvres. [C19: from F, from *persien* Persian]

persiflage (ˈpɜːsɪˌflɑːʒ) *n* light frivolous conversation, style, or treatment; friendly teasing. [C18: via F from *persifler* to tease, from *per-* (intensive) + *siffler* to whistle, from L *sībilāre* to whistle]

persimmon (pɜːˈsɪmən) *n* **1** any of several tropical trees, typically having hard wood and large orange-red fruit. **2** Also called: **sharon fruit.** the sweet fruit of any of these trees, which is edible when completely ripe. [C17: from Amerind]

persist ❶ (pəˈsɪst) *vb (intr)* **1** (often foll. by *in*) to continue steadfastly or obstinately despite opposition. **2** to continue without interruption: *the rain persisted throughout the night.* [C16: from L *persistere,* from *per-* (intensive) + *sistere* to stand steadfast] ▸**perˈsister** *n*

persistence ❶ (pəˈsɪstəns) *or* **persistency** *n* **1** the quality of persisting; tenacity. **2** the act of persisting; continued effort or existence.

persistent ❶ (pəˈsɪstənt) *adj* **1** showing persistence. **2** incessantly repeated; unrelenting: *your persistent questioning.* **3** (of plant parts) remaining attached to the plant after the normal time of withering. **4** *Zool.* (of parts normally present only in young stages) present in the adult. **5** (of a chemical, esp. when used as a insecticide) slow to break down. ▸**perˈsistently** *adv*

persistent vegetative state *n Med.* an irreversible condition, resulting from brain damage, characterized by lack of consciousness, thought, and feeling, although reflex activities (such as breathing) continue. Abbrev.: **PVS.**

person ❶ (ˈpɜːsᵊn) *n, pl* **persons. 1** an individual human being. **2** the body of a human being: *guns hidden on his person.* **3** a grammatical category into which pronouns and forms of verbs are subdivided depending on whether they refer to the speaker, the person addressed, or some other individual, thing, etc. **4** a human being or a corporation recognized in law as having certain rights and obligations. **5 in person.** actually present: *the author will be there in person.* [C13: from OF *persone,* from L *persōna* mask, ?from Etruscan *phersu* mask]

USAGE NOTE *People* is the word usually used to refer to more than one individual: *there were a hundred people at the reception. Persons* is rarely used, except in official English: *several persons were interviewed.*

-person *n combining form.* sometimes used instead of *-man* and *-woman* or *-lady: chairperson.*

USAGE NOTE See at **-man.**

persona ❶ (pɜːˈsəʊnə) *n, pl* **personae** (-niː). **1** *(often pl)* a character in a play, novel, etc. **2** (in Jungian psychology) the mechanism that conceals a person's true thoughts and feelings, esp. in adaptation to the outside world. [L: mask]

personable ❶ (ˈpɜːsənəbᵊl) *adj* pleasant in appearance and personality. ▸ˈ**personableness** *n* ▸ˈ**personably** *adv*

personage ❶ (ˈpɜːsənɪdʒ) *n* **1** an important or distinguished person. **2** another word for **person** (sense 1). **3** *Rare.* a figure in literature, history, etc.

THESAURUS

Antonyms *vb* abolish, destroy, end, forget, ignore, put an end to, stamp out, suppress

perplex *vb* **1** = **puzzle**, baffle, befuddle, bemuse, beset, bewilder, confound, confuse, dumbfound, faze, flummox, mix up, muddle, mystify, nonplus, stump **2** = **complicate**, encumber, entangle, involve, jumble, mix up, snarl up, tangle, thicken

perplexing *adj* **1** = **puzzling**, baffling, bewildering, complex, complicated, confusing, difficult, enigmatic, hard, inexplicable, intricate, involved, knotty, labyrinthine, mysterious, mystifying, paradoxical, strange, taxing, thorny, unaccountable, weird

perplexity *n* **1** = **puzzlement**, bafflement, bewilderment, confusion, incomprehension, mystification, stupefaction **2** = **complexity**, difficulty, inextricability, intricacy, involvement, obscurity **3** = **puzzle**, difficulty, dilemma, enigma, fix (*inf.*), how-do-you-do (*inf.*), knotty problem, mystery, paradox, snarl

perquisite *n* **1, 2** = **bonus**, benefit, dividend, extra, fringe benefit, icing on the cake, perk (*Brit. inf.*), plus

per se *adv* = **in itself**, as such, by definition, by itself, by its very nature, essentially, in essence, intrinsically, of itself

persecute *vb* **1** = **victimize**, afflict, be on one's back (*sl.*), distress, dragoon, hound, hunt, ill-treat, injure, maltreat, martyr, molest, oppress, pick on, pursue, torment, torture **2** = **harass**, annoy, badger, bait, bother, hassle (*inf.*), pester, tease, vex, worry
Antonyms *vb* accommodate, back, calm, coddle, comfort, console, cosset, humour, indulge, leave alone, let alone, mollycoddle, pamper, pet, spoil, support

perseverance *n* **1** = **persistence**, constancy, dedication, determination, diligence, doggedness, endurance, indefatigability, pertinacity, purposefulness, resolution, sedulity, stamina, steadfastness, tenacity

persevere *vb* = **keep going**, be determined *or* resolved, carry on, continue, endure, go on, hang on, hold fast, hold on, keep on *or* at, keep one's hand in, maintain, persist, plug away (*inf.*), pursue, remain, stand firm, stay the course, stick at *or* to
Antonyms *vb* be irresolute, dither (*chiefly Brit.*), end, falter, give in, give up, hesitate, quit, shilly-shally (*inf.*), swither (*Scot.*), throw in the towel, vacillate, waver

persist *vb* **1** = **persevere**, be resolute, continue, hold on (*inf.*), insist, stand firm, stay the course **2** = **continue**, abide, carry on, endure, keep up, last, linger, remain

persistence *n* **1, 2** = **determination**, constancy, diligence, doggedness, endurance, grit, indefatigability, perseverance, pertinacity, pluck, resolution, stamina, steadfastness, tenacity, tirelessness

persistent *adj* **1** = **determined**, assiduous, dogged, enduring, fixed, immovable, indefatigable, obdurate, obstinate, persevering, pertinacious, resolute, steadfast, steady, stiff-necked, stubborn, tenacious, tireless, unflagging **2** = **continuous**, constant, continual, endless, incessant, interminable, lasting, never-ending, perpetual, relentless, repeated, unrelenting, unremitting
Antonyms *adj* ≠ **determined:** changeable, flexible, irresolute, tractable, yielding ≠ **continuous:** inconstant, intermittent, irregular, occasional, off-and-on, periodic

person *n* **1, 2** = **individual**, being, body, human, human being, living soul, soul **5 in person** = **personally**, bodily, in the flesh, oneself

persona *n* **1, 2** = **personality**, assumed role, character, façade, face, front, mask, part, public face, role

personable *adj* = **pleasant**, affable, agreeable, amiable, attractive, charming, good-looking, handsome, likable *or* likeable, nice, pleasing, presentable, winning
Antonyms *adj* disagreeable, sullen, surly, ugly, unattractive, unpleasant, unsightly

personage *n* **1** = **personality**, big name, big noise (*inf.*), big shot (*inf.*), celeb (*inf.*), celebrity, dignitary, luminary, megastar (*inf.*), notable,

persona grata *Latin.* (pɜːˈsəunə ˈɡrɑːtə) *n, pl* ***personae gratae*** (pɜːˈsəuniː ˈɡrɑːtiː). an acceptable person, esp. a diplomat.

personal ❶ (ˈpɜːsənᵊl) *adj* **1** of or relating to the private aspects of a person's life: *personal letters.* **2** (*prenominal*) of or relating to a person's body, its care, or its appearance: *personal hygiene.* **3** belonging to or intended for a particular person and no-one else: *for your personal use.* **4** (*prenominal*) undertaken by an individual: *a personal appearance by a celebrity.* **5** referring to or involving a person's individual personality, intimate affairs, etc., esp. in an offensive way: *personal remarks; don't be so personal.* **6** having the attributes of an individual conscious being: *a personal God.* **7** of, relating to, or denoting grammatical person. **8** *Law.* of or relating to movable property, as money, etc.

personal column *n* a newspaper column containing personal messages and advertisements.

personal computer *n* a small inexpensive computer used in word processing, computer games, etc.

personal equity plan *n* the full name for **PEP.**

personality ❶ (ˌpɜːsəˈnælɪtɪ) *n, pl* **personalities. 1** *Psychol.* the sum total of all the behavioural and mental characteristics by means of which an individual is recognized as being unique. **2** the distinctive character of a person that makes him socially attractive: *a salesman needs a lot of personality.* **3** a well-known person in a certain field, such as entertainment. **4** a remarkable person. **5** (*often pl*) a personal remark.

personalize ❶ *or* **personalise** (ˈpɜːsənəˌlaɪz) *vb* **personalizes, personalizing, personalized** *or* **personalises, personalising, personalised.** (*tr*) **1** to endow with personal or individual qualities. **2** to mark (stationery, clothing, etc.) with a person's initials, name, etc. **3** to take (a remark, etc.) personally. **4** another word for **personify.**
▸**ˌpersonaliˈzation** *or* **ˌpersonaliˈsation** *n*

personally ❶ (ˈpɜːsənəlɪ) *adv* **1** without the help or intervention of others: *I'll attend to it personally.* **2** (*sentence modifier*) in one's own opinion or as regards oneself: *personally, I hate onions.* **3** as if referring to oneself: *to take the insults personally.* **4** as a person: *we like him personally, but professionally he's incompetent.*

personal organizer *n* **1** a diary that stores personal records, appointments, notes, etc. **2** a pocket-sized electronic device that performs the same functions.

personal pronoun *n* a pronoun having a definite person or thing as an antecedent and functioning grammatically in the same way as the noun that it replaces. The personal pronouns include *I, you, he, she, it, we,* and *they.*

personal property *n Law.* movable property, such as furniture or money. Also called: **personalty.** Cf. **real property.**

personal stereo *n* a small audio cassette player worn attached to a belt and used with lightweight headphones.

persona non grata *Latin.* (pɜːˈsəunə nɒn ˈɡrɑːtə) *n, pl* ***personae non gratae*** (pɜːˈsəuniː nɒn ˈɡrɑːtiː). **1** an unacceptable or unwelcome person. **2** a diplomat who is not acceptable to the government to whom he or she is accredited.

personate ❶ (ˈpɜːsəˌneɪt) *vb* **personates, personating, personated.** (*tr*) **1** to act the part of (a character in a play); portray. **2** *Criminal law.* to assume the identity of (another person) with intent to deceive.
▸**ˌpersonˈation** *n* ▸**ˈpersonative** *adj* ▸**ˈpersonˌator** *n*

personification ❶ (pɜːˌsɒnɪfɪˈkeɪʃən) *n* **1** the attribution of human characteristics to things, abstract ideas, etc. **2** the representation of an abstract quality or idea in the form of a person, creature, etc., as in art and literature. **3** a person or thing that personifies. **4** a person or thing regarded as an embodiment of a quality: *he is the personification of optimism.*

personify ❶ (pɜːˈsɒnɪˌfaɪ) *vb* **personifies, personifying, personified.** (*tr*) **1** to attribute human characteristics to (a thing or abstraction). **2** to represent (an abstract quality) in human or animal form. **3** (of a person or thing) to represent (an abstract quality), as in art. **4** to be the embodiment of.
▸**perˈsoniˌfier** *n*

personnel ❶ (ˌpɜːsəˈnel) *n* **1** the people employed in an organization or for a service. **2a** the department that interviews, appoints, or keeps records of employees. **2b** (*as modifier*): *a personnel officer.* [C19: from F, ult. from LL *persōnālis* personal (adj); see PERSON]

perspective ❶ (pəˈspɛktɪv) *n* **1** a way of regarding situations, facts, etc., and judging their relative importance. **2** the proper or accurate point of view or the ability to see it; objectivity: *try to get some perspective on your troubles.* **3** a view over some distance in space or time; prospect. **4** the theory or art of suggesting three dimensions on a two-dimensional surface, in order to recreate the appearance and spatial relationships that objects or a scene in recession present to the eye. **5** the appearance of objects, buildings, etc., relative to each other, as determined by their distance from the viewer, or the effects of this distance on their appearance. [C14: from Med. L *perspectīva ars* the science of optics, from L *perspicere* to inspect carefully]
▸**perˈspectively** *adv*

Perspex (ˈpɜːspɛks) *n Trademark.* any of various clear acrylic resins.

perspicacious ❶ (ˌpɜːspɪˈkeɪʃəs) *adj* acutely perceptive or discerning. [C17: from L *perspicax,* from *perspicere* to look at closely]
▸**ˌperspiˈcaciously** *adv* ▸**perspicacity** (ˌpɜːspɪˈkæsɪtɪ) *or* **ˌperspiˈcaciousness** *n*

perspicuous ❶ (pəˈspɪkjuəs) *adj* (of speech or writing) easily understood; lucid. [C15: from L *perspicuus* transparent, from *perspicere* to explore thoroughly]
▸**perˈspicuously** *adv* ▸**perˈspicuousness** *or* **perspicuity** (ˌpɜːspɪˈkjuːɪtɪ) *n*

perspiration ❶ (ˌpɜːspəˈreɪʃən) *n* **1** the salty fluid secreted by the sweat glands of the skin. **2** the act of secreting this fluid.
▸**perspiratory** (pəˈspaɪərətərɪ) *adj*

perspire ❶ (pəˈspaɪə) *vb* **perspires, perspiring, perspired.** to secrete or exude (perspiration) through the pores of the skin. [C17: from L *perspīrāre* to blow, from *per-* (through) + *spīrāre* to breathe]
▸**perˈspiringly** *adv*

persuade ❶ (pəˈsweɪd) *vb* **persuades, persuading, persuaded.** (*tr; may take a clause as object or an infinitive*) **1** to induce, urge, or prevail upon successfully: *he finally persuaded them to buy it.* **2** to cause to believe; convince: *even with the evidence, the police were not persuaded.* [C16: from L *persuādēre,* from *per-* (intensive) + *suādēre* to urge, advise]
▸**perˈsuadable** *or* **perˈsuasible** *adj* ▸**perˌsuadaˈbility** *or* **perˌsuasiˈbility** *n*
▸**perˈsuader** *n*

persuasion ❶ (pəˈsweɪʒən) *n* **1** the act of persuading or of trying to persuade. **2** the power to persuade. **3** a strong belief. **4** an established creed or belief, esp. a religious one. **5** a sect, party, or faction. [C14: from L *persuāsiō*]

persuasive ❶ (pəˈsweɪsɪv) *adj* having the power or tending to persuade: *a persuasive salesman.*
▸**perˈsuasively** *adv* ▸**perˈsuasiveness** *n*

pert ❶ (pɜːt) *adj* **1** saucy, impudent, or forward. **2** jaunty: *a pert little hat.*

THESAURUS

public figure, somebody, V.I.P., well-known person, worthy

personal *adj* **1, 3 = private,** exclusive, individual, intimate, own, particular, peculiar, privy, special **2 = physical,** bodily, corporal, corporeal, exterior, material **5 = offensive,** derogatory, disparaging, insulting, nasty, pejorative, slighting

personality *n* **1 = nature,** character, disposition, identity, individuality, make-up, psyche, temper, temperament, traits **2 = character,** attraction, attractiveness, charisma, charm, dynamism, likableness *or* likeableness, magnetism, pleasantness **3 = celebrity,** big name, celeb (*inf.*), famous name, household name, megastar (*inf.*), notable, personage, star, well-known face, well-known person

personalized *adj* **2 = customized,** distinctive, individual, individualized, monogrammed, private, special, tailor-made

personally *adv* **1 = by oneself,** alone, independently, in person, in the flesh, on one's own, solely **2 = in one's opinion,** for oneself, for one's part, from one's own viewpoint, in one's books, in one's own view **4 = individually,** individualistically, privately, specially, subjectively

personate *vb* **1, 2 = impersonate,** act, depict, do (*inf.*), enact, feign, imitate, play-act, portray, represent

personification *n* **1, 2, 4 = embodiment,** epitome, image, incarnation, likeness, portrayal, recreation, representation, semblance

personify *vb* **1, 2, 4 = embody,** body forth, epitomize, exemplify, express, image (*rare*), incarnate, mirror, represent, symbolize, typify

personnel *n* **1 = employees,** helpers, human resources, liveware, members, men and women, people, staff, workers, workforce

perspective *n* **1 = outlook,** angle, attitude, broad view, context, frame of reference, overview, way of looking **2 = objectivity,** proportion, relation, relative importance, relativity **3 = view,** outlook, panorama, prospect, scene, vista

perspicacious *adj* **= perceptive,** acute, alert, astute, aware, clear-sighted, clever, discerning, keen, observant, penetrating, percipient, sagacious, sharp, sharp-witted, shrewd

perspicacity *n* **= insight,** acumen, acuteness, discernment, discrimination, keenness, penetration, perceptiveness, percipience, perspicaciousness, perspicuity, sagaciousness, sagacity, sharpness, shrewdness, smarts (*sl., chiefly US*), suss (*sl.*), wit

perspicuity *n* **= clarity,** clearness, comprehensibility, distinctness, explicitness, intelligibility, limpidity, limpidness, lucidity, plainness, precision, straightforwardness, transparency

perspicuous *adj* **= clear,** comprehensible, crystal-clear, distinct, easily understood, explicit, intelligible, limpid, lucid, obvious, plain, self-evident, straightforward, transparent, unambiguous, understandable

perspiration *n* **1 = sweat,** exudation, moisture, wetness

perspire *vb* **= sweat,** be damp, be wet, drip, exude, glow, pour with sweat, secrete, swelter

persuade *vb* **1 = talk into,** actuate, advise, allure, bring round (*inf.*), coax, counsel, entice, impel, incite, induce, influence, inveigle, prevail upon, prompt, sway, twist (someone's) arm, urge, win over **2 = convince,** cause to believe, convert, satisfy
Antonyms *vb* **≠ talk into:** deter, discourage, dissuade, forbid, prohibit

persuasion *n* **1 = urging,** blandishment, cajolery, conversion, enticement, exhortation, inducement, influencing, inveiglement, wheedling **2 = persuasiveness,** cogency, force, potency, power, pull (*inf.*) **3, 4 = creed,** belief, certitude, conviction, credo, faith, firm belief, fixed opinion, opinion, tenet, views **5 = faction,** camp, cult, denomination, party, school, school of thought, sect, side

persuasive *adj* **= convincing,** cogent, compelling, credible, effective, eloquent, forceful, impelling, impressive, inducing, influential, logical, moving, plausible, sound, telling, touching, valid, weighty, winning
Antonyms *adj* feeble, flimsy, illogical, implausible, incredible, ineffective, invalid, unconvincing, unimpressive, weak

pert *adj* **1 = impudent,** bold, brash, cheeky, flip (*inf.*), flippant, forward, fresh (*inf.*), impertinent, insolent, lippy (*US & Canad. sl.*), presump-

3 *Obs.* clever or brisk. [C13: var. of earlier *apert,* from L *apertus* open, from *aperīre* to open]
▸'**pertly** *adv* ▸'**pertness** *n*

pert. *abbrev. for* pertaining.

pertain ➊ (pə'teɪn) *vb* (*intr;* often foll. by *to*) **1** to have reference or relevance: *issues pertaining to women.* **2** to be appropriate: *the product pertains to real user needs.* **3** to belong (to) or be a part (of). [C14: from L *pertinēre,* from *per-* (intensive) + *tenēre* to hold]

pertinacious ➊ (ˌpɜːtɪ'neɪʃəs) *adj* **1** doggedly resolute in purpose or belief; unyielding. **2** stubbornly persistent. [C17: from L *pertināx,* from *per-* (intensive) + *tenāx* clinging, from *tenēre* to hold]
▸ˌ**perti'naciously** *adv* ▸**pertinacity** (ˌpɜːtɪ'næsɪtɪ) *or* ˌ**perti'naciousness** *n*

pertinent ➊ ('pɜːtɪnənt) *adj* relating to the matter at hand; relevant. [C14: from L *pertinēns,* from *pertinēre* to PERTAIN]
▸'**pertinence** *or* '**pertinency** *n* ▸'**pertinently** *adv*

perturb ➊ (pə'tɜːb) *vb* (*tr; often passive*) **1** to disturb the composure of; trouble. **2** to throw into disorder. **3** *Physics, astron.* to cause (a planet, electron, etc.) to undergo a perturbation. [C14: from OF *pertourber,* from L *perturbāre* to confuse, from *per-* (intensive) + *turbāre* to agitate]
▸**per'turbable** *adj* ▸**per'turbing** *adj*

perturbation (ˌpɜːtə'beɪʃən) *n* **1** the act of perturbing or the state of being perturbed. **2** a cause of disturbance. **3** *Physics.* a secondary influence on a system that modifies simple behaviour, such as the effect of the other electrons on one electron in an atom. **4** *Astron.* a small continuous deviation in the orbit of a planet or comet, due to the attraction of neighbouring planets.

pertussis (pə'tʌsɪs) *n* the technical name for **whooping cough**. [C18: NL, from L *per-* (intensive) + *tussis* cough]
▸**per'tussal** *adj*

Peru Current (pə'ruː) *n* a cold ocean current flowing northwards off the Pacific coast of South America. Also called: **Humboldt Current**.

peruke (pə'ruːk) *n* a wig for men in the 17th and 18th centuries. Also called: **periwig**. [C16: from F *perruque,* from It. *perrucca* wig, from ?]

peruse ➊ (pə'ruːz) *vb* **peruses, perusing, perused.** (*tr*) **1** to read or examine with care; study. **2** to browse or read in a leisurely way. [C15 (meaning: to use up): from PER- (intensive) + USE]
▸**pe'rusal** *n* ▸**pe'ruser** *n*

perv (pɜːv) *Sl.* ◆ *n* **1** a pervert. **2** *Austral.* a lascivious look. ◆ *vb also* **perve.** (*intr*) **3** *Austral.* to behave like a voyeur.

pervade ➊ (pɜː'veɪd) *vb* **pervades, pervading, pervaded.** (*tr*) to spread through or throughout, esp. subtly or gradually; permeate. [C17: from L *pervādere,* from *per-* through + *vādere* to go]
▸**pervasion** (pɜː'veɪʒən) *n* ▸**pervasive** (pɜː'veɪsɪv) *adj* ▸**per'vasively** *adv* ▸**per'vasiveness** *n*

perverse ➊ (pə'vɜːs) *adj* **1** deliberately deviating from what is regarded as normal, good, or proper. **2** persistently holding to what is wrong. **3** wayward or contrary; obstinate. [C14: from OF *pervers,* from L *perversus* turned the wrong way]
▸**per'versely** *adv* ▸**per'verseness** *or* **per'versity** *n*

perversion ➊ (pə'vɜːʃən) *n* **1** any abnormal means of obtaining sexual satisfaction. **2** the act of perverting or the state of being perverted. **3** a perverted form or usage.

pervert ➊ *vb* (pə'vɜːt). (*tr*) **1** to use wrongly or badly. **2** to interpret wrongly or badly; distort. **3** to lead into deviant or perverted beliefs or behaviour; corrupt. **4** to debase. ◆ *n* ('pɜːvɜːt). **5** a person who practises sexual perversion. [C14: from OF *pervertir,* from L *pervertere* to turn the wrong way]
▸**per'verted** *adj* ▸**per'verter** *n* ▸**per'vertible** *adj* ▸**per'versive** *adj*

pervious ('pɜːvɪəs) *adj* **1** able to be penetrated; permeable. **2** receptive to new ideas, etc.; open-minded. [C17: from L *pervius,* from *per-* (through) + *via* a way]
▸'**perviously** *adv* ▸'**perviousness** *n*

pes (peɪz, piːz) *n, pl* **pedes** ('pɛdiːz). the technical name for the human **foot**. [C19: NL: foot]

peseta (pə'seɪtə; *Spanish* pe'seta) *n* the standard monetary unit of Spain, divided into 100 céntimos. [C19: from Sp., dim. of PESO]

pesky ('pɛskɪ) *adj* **peskier, peskiest.** *US & Canad. inf.* troublesome. [C19: prob. changed from *pesty;* see PEST]
▸'**peskily** *adv* ▸'**peskiness** *n*

peso ('peɪsəʊ; *Spanish* 'peso) *n, pl* **pesos** (-səʊz; *Spanish* -sos). the standard monetary unit of Argentina, Chile, Colombia, Cuba, the Dominican Republic, Guinea-Bissau, Mexico, the Philippines, and Uruguay. [C16: from Sp.: weight, from L *pēnsum* something weighed out, from *pendere* to weigh]

pessary ('pɛsərɪ) *n, pl* **pessaries.** *Med.* **1** a device for inserting into the vagina, either as a support for the uterus or (**diaphragm pessary**) as a contraceptive. **2** a vaginal suppository. [C14: from LL *pessārium,* from L *pessum,* from Gk *pessos* plug]

pessimism ➊ ('pɛsɪˌmɪzəm) *n* **1** the tendency to expect the worst in all things. **2** the doctrine of the ultimate triumph of evil over good. **3** the doctrine that this world is corrupt and that man's sojourn in it is a preparation for some other existence. [C18: from L *pessimus* worst, sup. of *malus* bad]
▸'**pessimist** *n* ▸ˌ**pessi'mistic** *adj* ▸ˌ**pessi'mistically** *adv*

pest ➊ (pɛst) *n* **1** a person or thing that annoys, esp. by imposing itself when it is not wanted; nuisance. **2** any organism that damages crops, or injures or irritates livestock or man. **3** *Rare.* an epidemic disease. [C16: from L *pestis* plague, from ?]

pester ➊ ('pɛstə) *vb* (*tr*) to annoy or nag continually. [C16: from OF *empestrer* to hobble (a horse), from Vulgar L *impāstōriāre* (unattested) to use a hobble, ult. from L *pastor* herdsman]

pesticide ('pɛstɪˌsaɪd) *n* a chemical used for killing pests, esp. insects.
▸ˌ**pesti'cidal** *adj*

pestiferous (pɛ'stɪfərəs) *adj* **1** *Inf.* troublesome; irritating. **2** breeding, carrying, or spreading infectious disease. **3** corrupting; pernicious. [C16: from L *pestifer,* from *pestis* contagion + *ferre* to bring]

pestilence ➊ ('pɛstɪləns) *n* **1a** any epidemic of a deadly infectious disease, such as the plague. **1b** such a disease. **2** an evil influence.

pestilent ➊ ('pɛstɪlənt) *adj* **1** annoying; irritating. **2** highly destructive morally or physically; pernicious. **3** likely to cause epidemic or infec-

THESAURUS

tuous, pushy (*inf.*), sassy (*US inf.*), saucy, smart **2** = **neat**, brisk, dapper, daring, dashing, gay, jaunty, lively, nimble, perky, smart, spirited, sprightly

pertain *vb* **1-3** = **relate**, appertain, apply, be appropriate, bear on, befit, belong, be part of, be relevant, concern, refer, regard

pertinacious *adj* **1, 2** = **determined**, bull-headed, dogged, headstrong, inflexible, intractable, mulish, obdurate, obstinate, persevering, persistent, perverse, pig-headed, relentless, resolute, self-willed, stiff-necked, strong-willed, stubborn, tenacious, unyielding, wilful

pertinent *adj* = **relevant**, admissible, *ad rem,* applicable, apposite, appropriate, apropos, apt, fit, fitting, germane, material, pat, proper, suitable, to the point, to the purpose
Antonyms *adj* discordant, immaterial, inappropriate, incongruous, irrelevant, unfitting, unrelated, unsuitable

pertness *n* **1** = **impudence**, audacity, brashness, brass (*inf.*), bumptiousness, cheek (*inf.*), cheekiness, chutzpah (*US & Canad. inf.*), cockiness, effrontery, forwardness, front, impertinence, insolence, presumption, rudeness, sauciness

perturb *vb* **1** = **disturb**, agitate, alarm, bother, discompose, disconcert, discountenance, disquiet, faze, fluster, ruffle, trouble, unnerve, unsettle, upset, vex, worry **2** = **disorder**, confuse, disarrange, muddle, unsettle

perturbed *adj* **1** = **disturbed**, agitated, alarmed, anxious, disconcerted, disquieted, fearful, flurried, flustered, ill at ease, nervous, restless, shaken, troubled, uncomfortable, uneasy, upset, worried
Antonyms *adj* assured, at ease, comfortable, composed, cool, impassive, relaxed, unperturbed, unruffled

perusal *n* **1, 2** = **read**, browse, check, examination, inspection, look through, scrutiny, study

peruse *vb* **1, 2** = **read**, browse, check, examine, eyeball (*sl.*), inspect, look through, run one's eye over, scan, scrutinize, study, work over

pervade *vb* = **spread through**, affect, charge, diffuse, extend, fill, imbue, infuse, overspread, penetrate, percolate, permeate, suffuse

pervasive *adj* = **widespread**, common, extensive, general, inescapable, omnipresent, permeating, pervading, prevalent, rife, ubiquitous, universal

perverse *adj* **1** = **abnormal**, depraved, deviant, improper, incorrect, unhealthy **3** = **stubborn**, contradictory, contrary, contumacious, cross-grained, cussed (*inf.*), delinquent, disobedient, dogged, headstrong, intractable, intransigent, miscreant, mulish, obdurate, obstinate, pig-headed, rebellious, refractory, stiff-necked, troublesome, unmanageable, unreasonable, unyielding, wayward, wilful, wrong-headed
Antonyms *adj* ≠ **stubborn**: accommodating, agreeable, complaisant, cooperative, flexible, malleable, obedient, obliging

perversion *n* **1** = **deviation**, aberration, abnormality, debauchery, depravity, immorality, kink (*Brit. inf.*), kinkiness (*sl.*), unnaturalness, vice, vitiation, wickedness **2, 3** = **distortion**, corruption, falsification, misinterpretation, misrepresentation, misuse, twisting

perversity *n* **2** = **contrariness**, contradictiveness, contradictoriness, contumacy, frowardness (*arch.*), intransigence, obduracy, refractoriness, waywardness, wrong-headedness

pervert *vb* **1, 2** = **distort**, abuse, falsify, garble, misconstrue, misinterpret, misrepresent, misuse, twist, warp **3, 4** = **corrupt**, debase, debauch, degrade, deprave, desecrate, initiate, lead astray, subvert ◆ *n* **5** = **deviant**, debauchee, degenerate, weirdo *or* weirdie (*inf.*)

perverted *adj* **2-4** = **unnatural**, aberrant, abnormal, corrupt, debased, debauched, depraved, deviant, distorted, evil, immoral, impaired, kinky (*sl.*), misguided, sick, twisted, unhealthy, vicious, vitiated, warped, wicked

pessimism *n* **1** = **gloominess**, cynicism, dejection, depression, despair, despondency, distrust, gloom, gloomy outlook, glumness, hopelessness, melancholy, the hump (*Brit. inf.*)

pessimist *n* **1** = **wet blanket** (*inf.*), cynic, defeatist, doomster, gloom merchant (*inf.*), killjoy, melancholic, misanthrope, prophet of doom, worrier

pessimistic *adj* **1** = **gloomy**, bleak, cynical, dark, dejected, depressed, despairing, despondent, distrustful, downhearted, fatalistic, foreboding, glum, hopeless, melancholy, misanthropic, morose, resigned, sad
Antonyms *adj* assured, bright, buoyant, cheerful, cheery, encouraged, exhilarated, hopeful, in good heart, optimistic, sanguine

pest *n* **1** = **nuisance**, annoyance, bane, bore, bother, drag (*inf.*), gall, irritation, pain (*inf.*), pain in the neck (*inf.*), thorn in one's flesh, trial, vexation **2** = **infection**, bane, blight, bug, curse, epidemic, pestilence, plague, scourge

pester *vb* = **annoy**, aggravate (*inf.*), badger, bedevil, bother, bug (*inf.*), chivvy, disturb, fret, get at (*inf.*), harass, harry, hassle (*inf.*), irk, nag, pick on, plague, ride (*inf.*), torment, worry

pestilence *n* **1** = **plague**, Black Death, epidemic, pandemic, visitation **2** = **affliction**, bane, blight, cancer, canker, curse, scourge

pestilent *adj* **1** = **annoying**, bothersome, galling, irksome, irritating, plaguy (*inf.*), tiresome, vexing **2** = **harmful**, corrupting, deleterious, destructive, detrimental, evil, injurious, perni-

tious disease. [C15: from L *pestilens* unwholesome, from *pestis* plague]
▸'**pestilently** *adv* ▸**pestilential** (ˌpestɪˈlenʃəl) *adj* ▸ˌ**pestiˈlentially** *adv*

pestle (ˈpesᵊl) *n* **1** a club-shaped instrument for mixing or grinding substances in a mortar. **2** a tool for pounding or stamping. ◆ *vb* **pestles, pestling, pestled. 3** to pound (a substance or object) with or as if with a pestle. [C14: from OF *pestel,* from L *pistillum*]

pesto (ˈpestəʊ) *n* a sauce for pasta, consisting of basil leaves, nuts, garlic, oil, and Parmesan cheese, all crushed together. [It., shortened form of *pestato,* p.p. of *pestare* to pound, crush]

pet[1] ⓣ (pet) *n* **1** a tame animal kept for companionship, amusement, etc. **2** a person who is fondly indulged; favourite: *teacher's pet.* ◆ *adj* **3** kept as a pet: *a pet dog.* **4** of or for pet animals: *pet food.* **5** particularly cherished: *a pet hatred.* **6** familiar or affectionate: *a pet name.* ◆ *vb* **pets, petting, petted. 7** (*tr*) to treat (a person, animal, etc.) as a pet; pamper. **8** (*tr*) to pat or fondle (an animal, child, etc.). **9** (*intr*) *Inf.* (of two people) to caress each other in an erotic manner. [C16: from ?]
▸ˈ**petter** *n*

pet[2] ⓣ (pet) *n* a fit of sulkiness, esp. at what is felt to be a slight; pique. [C16: from ?]

PET (pet) *n acronym for* positron emission tomography.

Pet. *Bible. abbrev. for* Peter.

peta- *prefix* denoting 10^{15}: *petametres.* Symbol: P [C20: so named because it is the SI prefix after TERA-; on the model of PENTA-, the prefix after TETRA-]

petal (ˈpetᵊl) *n* any of the separate parts of the corolla of a flower: often brightly coloured. [C18: from NL *petalum,* from Gk *petalon* leaf]
▸ˈ**petaline** *adj* ▸ˈ**petalled** *adj* ▸ˈ**petal-ˌlike** *adj*

-petal *adj combining form.* seeking: *centripetal.* [from NL *-petus,* from L *petere* to seek]

petard (pɪˈtɑːd) *n* **1** (formerly) a device containing explosives used to breach a wall, doors, etc. **2 hoist with one's own petard.** being the victim of one's own schemes, etc. [C16: from F: firework, from *péter* to break wind, from L *pēdere*]

petaurist (pətˈɒrɪst) *n* another name for **flying phalanger.** [C19: from L, from Gk *petauristēs* performer on the springboard]

petcock (ˈpetˌkɒk) *n* a small valve for checking the water content of a steam boiler or draining waste from the cylinder of a steam engine. [C19: from PET[1] or ? F *pet,* from *péter* to break wind + COCK[1]]

petechia (pɪˈtiːkɪə) *n, pl* **petechiae** (-kɪˌiː). a minute discoloured spot on the surface of the skin. [C18: via NL from It. *petecchia* freckle, from ?]
▸**peˈtechial** *adj*

peter[1] ⓣ (ˈpiːtə) *vb* (*intr;* foll. by *out* or *away*) to fall (off) in volume, intensity, etc., and finally cease. [C19: from ?]

peter[2] (ˈpiːtə) *n Sl.* **1** a safe, till, or cashbox. **2** a prison cell. [C17 (meaning a case): from the name *Peter*]

peterman (ˈpiːtəmən) *n, pl* **petermen.** *Sl.* a burglar skilled in safe-breaking. [C19: from PETER[2]]

Peter Pan *n* a youthful, boyish, or immature man. [C20: after the main character in *Peter Pan* (1904), a play by J. M. Barrie]

Peter Principle *n* **the.** the theory, usually taken facetiously, that all members in a hierarchy rise to their own level of incompetence. [C20: from the book *The Peter Principle* (1969) by Dr Lawrence J. *Peter* and Raymond Hull]

petersham (ˈpiːtəʃəm) *n* **1** a thick corded ribbon used to stiffen belts, etc. **2** a heavy woollen fabric used for coats, etc. **3** a kind of overcoat made of such fabric. [C19: after Viscount *Petersham* (died 1851), E army officer]

Peter's pence *or* **Peter pence** *n* **1** an annual tax, originally of one penny, formerly levied for the maintenance of the Papal See: abolished by Henry VIII in 1534. **2** a voluntary contribution made by Roman Catholics in many countries for the same purpose. [C13: referring to St *Peter,* considered as the first pope]

Peters' projection *n* a form of modified Mercator's map projection that gives prominence to Third World countries. [C20: after Arno *Peters,* G historian]

pethidine (ˈpeθɪˌdiːn) *n* a white crystalline water-soluble drug used as an analgesic. [C20: ? a blend of PIPERIDINE + ETHYL]

petiole (ˈpetɪˌəʊl) *n* **1** the stalk by which a leaf is attached to the plant. **2** *Zool.* a slender stalk or stem, as between the thorax and abdomen of ants. [C18: via F from L *petiolus* little foot, from *pēs* foot]
▸**petiolate** (ˈpetɪəˌleɪt) *adj*

petit (ˈpetɪ) *adj* (*prenominal*) *Chiefly law.* of lesser importance; small. [C14: from OF: little, from ?]

petit bourgeois (ˈbʊəʒwɑː) *n, pl* **petits bourgeois** (ˈbʊəʒwɑːz). **1** Also called: **petite bourgeoisie, petty bourgeoisie.** the section of the middle class with the lowest social status, as shopkeepers, lower clerical staff, etc. **2** a member of this stratum. ◆ *adj* **3** of, relating to, or characteristic of the petit bourgeois, esp. indicating a sense of self-righteousness and conformity to established standards of behaviour.

petite ⓣ (pəˈtiːt) *adj* (of a woman) small, delicate, and dainty. [C18: from F, fem of *petit* small]

petit four (fɔː) *n, pl* **petits fours** (fɔːz). any of various very small fancy cakes and biscuits. [F, lit.: little oven]

petition ⓣ (pɪˈtɪʃən) *n* **1** a written document signed by a large number of people demanding some form of action from a government or other authority. **2** any formal request to a higher authority; entreaty. **3** *Law.* a formal application in writing made to a court asking for some specific judicial action: *a petition for divorce.* **4** the action of petitioning. ◆ *vb* **5** (*tr*) to address or present a petition to (a person in authority, government, etc.): *to petition Parliament.* **6** (*intr;* foll. by *for*) to seek by petition: *to petition for a change in the law.* [C14: from L *petītiō,* from *petere* to seek]
▸**peˈtitionary** *adj*

petitioner (pɪˈtɪʃənə) *n* **1** a person who presents a petition. **2** *Chiefly Brit.* the plaintiff in a divorce suit.

petitio principii (pɪˈtɪʃɪˌəʊ prɪnˈkɪpɪˌaɪ) *n Logic.* a form of fallacious reasoning in which the conclusion has been assumed in the premises; begging the question. [C16: L, translation of Gk *to en arkhei aiteisthai* an assumption at the beginning]

petit jury *n* a jury of 12 persons empanelled to determine the facts of a case and decide the issue pursuant to the direction of the court on points of law. Also called: **petty jury.**
▸**petit juror** *n*

petit larceny *n* (formerly, in England) the stealing of property valued at 12 pence or under. Abolished 1827. Also called: **petty larceny.**

petit mal (mæl) *n* a mild form of epilepsy characterized by periods of impairment or loss of consciousness for up to 30 seconds. Cf. **grand mal.** [C19: F: little illness]

petit point (ˈpetɪ ˈpɔɪnt; *French* pəti pwɛ̃) *n* **1** a small diagonal needlepoint stitch used for fine detail. **2** work done with such stitches. [F: small point]

Petrarchan sonnet (peˈtrɑːkən) *n* a sonnet form associated with the Italian poet Petrarch (1304–74), having an octave rhyming a b b a a b b a and a sestet rhyming either c d e c d e or c d c d c d.

petrel (ˈpetrəl) *n* any of a family of oceanic birds having a hooked bill and tubular nostrils: includes albatrosses, storm petrels, and shearwaters. [C17: var. of earlier *pitteral,* associated by folk etymology with St *Peter,* because the bird appears to walk on water]

Petri dish (ˈpetrɪ) *n* a shallow dish, often with a cover, used in laboratories, esp. for producing cultures of microorganisms. [C19: after J. R. *Petri* (1852–1921), G bacteriologist]

petrifaction (ˌpetrɪˈfækʃən) *or* **petrification** (ˌpetrɪfɪˈkeɪʃən) *n* **1** the act or process of forming petrified organic material. **2** the state of being petrified.

petrify ⓣ (ˈpetrɪˌfaɪ) *vb* **petrifies, petrifying, petrified. 1** (*tr; often passive*) to convert (organic material) into a fossilized form by impregnation with dissolved minerals so that the original appearance is preserved. **2** to make or become dull, unresponsive, etc.; deaden. **3** (*tr; often passive*) to stun or daze with horror, fear, etc. [C16: from F *pétrifier,* ult. from Gk *petra* stone]
▸ˈ**petriˌfier** *n*

petro- *or before a vowel* **petr-** *combining form.* **1** indicating stone or rock: *petrology.* **2** indicating petroleum, its products, etc.: *petrochemical.* **3** of or relating to the production, export, or sale of petroleum: *petrostate.* [from Gk *petra* rock or *petros* stone]

petrochemical (ˌpetrəʊˈkemɪkᵊl) *n* **1** any substance, such as acetone or ethanol, obtained from petroleum. ◆ *adj* **2** of, concerned with, or obtained from petrochemicals or related to petrochemistry.
▸ˌ**petroˈchemistry** *n*

petrodollar (ˈpetrəʊˌdɒlə) *n* money earned by a country by the exporting of petroleum.

petroglyph (ˈpetrəˌglɪf) *n* a drawing or carving on rock, esp. a prehistoric one. [C19: via F from Gk *petra* stone + *gluphē* carving]

petrography (peˈtrɒgrəfɪ) *n* the branch of petrology concerned with the description and classification of rocks.
▸**peˈtrographer** *n* ▸**petrographic** (ˌpetrəˈgræfɪk) *or* ˌ**petroˈgraphical** *adj*

petrol (ˈpetrəl) *n* any one of various volatile flammable liquid mixtures of hydrocarbons, obtained from petroleum and used as a solvent and

THESAURUS

cious, ruinous, vicious **3** = **contaminated**, catching, contagious, diseased, disease-ridden, infected, infectious, plague-ridden, tainted

pestilential *adj* **2** = **deadly**, dangerous, deleterious, destructive, detrimental, evil, foul, harmful, hazardous, injurious, pernicious, ruinous **3** = **contaminated**, catching, contagious, disease-ridden, infectious, malignant, noxious, pestiferous, poisonous, venomous

pet[1] *n* **2** = **favourite**, apple of one's eye, blue-eyed boy (*inf.*), darling, fave (*inf.*), idol, jewel, treasure ◆ *adj* **3** = **tame**, domesticated, house, house-broken, house-trained (*Brit.*), trained **5** = **favourite**, cherished, dearest, dear to one's heart, fave (*inf.*), favoured, particular, preferred, special ◆ *vb* **7** = **pamper**, baby, coddle, cosset, mollycoddle, spoil **8** = **fondle**, caress, pat, stroke **9** *Informal* = **cuddle**, canoodle (*sl.*), kiss, neck (*inf.*), smooch (*inf.*), snog (*Brit. sl.*)

pet[2] *n* = **sulk**, bad mood, bate (*Brit. sl.*), huff, ill temper, miff (*inf.*), paddy (*Brit. inf.*), paddywhack (*Brit. inf.*), pique, pout, sulks, tantrum, temper

peter[1] *vb, foll. by* **out** *or* **away** = **die out**, come to nothing, dwindle, ebb, evaporate, fade, fail, give out, run dry, run out, stop, taper off, wane

petite *adj* = **small**, dainty, delicate, dinky (*Brit. inf.*), elfin, little, slight

petition *n* **1, 2** = **appeal**, address, application, entreaty, invocation, memorial, plea, prayer, request, round robin, solicitation, suit, supplication ◆ *vb* **5** = **appeal**, adjure, ask, beg, beseech, call upon, crave, entreat, plead, pray, press, solicit, sue, supplicate, urge

petrified *adj* **1** = **fossilized**, ossified, rocklike **3** = **terrified**, aghast, appalled, dazed, dumbfounded, frozen, horrified, numb, scared stiff, shocked, speechless, stunned, stupefied, terror-stricken

petrify *vb* **1** = **fossilize**, calcify, harden, set, solidify, turn to stone **3** = **terrify**, amaze, appal, astonish, astound, confound, dumbfound, a fuel for internal-combustion engines. US and Canad. name: **gasoline.** [C16: via F from Med. L PETROLEUM]

petrolatum (ˌpɛtrəˈleɪtəm) *n* a translucent gelatinous substance obtained from petroleum; used as a lubricant and in medicine as an ointment base. Also called: **petroleum jelly.**

petrol bomb *n* **1** a device filled with petrol that bursts into flames on impact. ◆ *vb* **petrol-bomb.** (*tr*) **2** to attack with petrol bombs.

petrol engine *n* an internal-combustion engine that uses petrol as fuel.

petroleum (pəˈtrəʊlɪəm) *n* a dark-coloured thick flammable crude oil occurring in sedimentary rocks, consisting mainly of hydrocarbons. Fractional distillation separates the crude oil into petrol, paraffin, diesel oil, lubricating oil, etc. Fuel oil, paraffin wax, asphalt, and carbon black are extracted from the residue. [C16: from Med. L, from L *petra* stone + *oleum* oil]

petroleum jelly *n* another name for **petrolatum.**

petrology (pɛˈtrɒlədʒɪ) *n, pl* **petrologies.** the study of the composition, origin, structure, and formation of rocks.
▸**petrological** (ˌpɛtrəˈlɒdʒɪkᵊl) *adj* ▸**peˈtrologist** *n*

petrol station *n Brit.* another term for **filling station.**

petrous (ˈpɛtrəs, ˈpiː-) *adj Anat.* denoting the dense part of the temporal bone that surrounds the inner ear. [C16: from L *petrōsus* full of rocks]
▸**petrosal** (pɛˈtrəʊsᵊl) *adj*

petticoat (ˈpɛtɪˌkəʊt) *n* **1** a woman's underskirt. **2** *Inf.* **2a** a humorous or mildly disparaging name for a woman. **2b** (*as modifier*): *petticoat politics.* [C15: see PETTY, COAT]

pettifogger (ˈpɛtɪˌfɒgə) *n* **1** a lawyer who conducts unimportant cases, esp. one who resorts to trickery. **2** any person who quibbles. [C16: from PETTY + *fogger*, from ?, perhaps from *Fugger*, a family (C15–16) of G financiers]
▸ˈ**pettiˌfoggery** *n* ▸ˈ**pettiˌfog** *vb* ˈ**pettiˌfogs,** ˈ**pettiˌfogging,** ˈ**pettiˌfogged.** (*intr*) ▸ˈ**pettiˌfogging** *adj*

pettish ❶ (ˈpɛtɪʃ) *adj* peevish; petulant. [C16: from PET[2]]
▸ˈ**pettishly** *adv* ▸ˈ**pettishness** *n*

petty ❶ (ˈpɛtɪ) *adj* **pettier, pettiest. 1** trivial; trifling: *petty details.* **2** narrow-minded, mean: *petty spite.* **3** minor or subordinate in rank: *petty officialdom.* **4** *Law.* a variant of **petit.** [C14: from OF PETIT]
▸ˈ**pettily** *adv* ▸ˈ**pettiness** *n*

petty cash *n* a small cash fund for minor incidental expenses.

petty jury *n* a variant of **petit jury.**

petty larceny *n* a variant of **petit larceny.**

petty officer *n* a noncommissioned officer in a naval service comparable in rank to a sergeant in an army or marine corps.

petty sessions *n* (*functioning as sing or pl*) another term for **magistrates' court.**

petulant ❶ (ˈpɛtjʊlənt) *adj* irritable, impatient, or sullen in a peevish or capricious way. [C16: via OF from L *petulāns* bold, from *petulāre* (unattested) to attack playfully, from *petere* to assail]
▸ˈ**petulance** *or* ˈ**petulancy** *n* ▸ˈ**petulantly** *adv*

petunia (pɪˈtjuːnɪə) *n* any plant of a tropical American genus cultivated for their colourful funnel-shaped flowers. [C19: via NL from obs. F *petun* variety of tobacco, from Tupi *petyn*]

petuntse (pɪˈtʌntsɪ, -ˈtʊn-) *n* a fusible mineral used in hard-paste porcelain. [C18: from Chinese, from *pe* white + *tun* heap + *tzu* offspring]

pew (pjuː) *n* **1** (in a church) **1a** one of several long benchlike seats with backs, used by the congregation. **1b** an enclosed compartment reserved for the use of a family or other small group. **2** *Brit. inf.* a seat (esp. in **take a pew**). [C14 *pywe*, from OF, from L *podium* a balcony, from Gk *podion* supporting structure, from *pous* foot]

pewit *or* **peewit** (ˈpiːwɪt) *n* other names for **lapwing.** [C13: imit. of the bird's cry]

pewter (ˈpjuːtə) *n* **1a** any of various alloys containing tin, lead, and sometimes copper and antimony. **1b** (*as modifier*): *pewter ware; a pewter tankard.* **2** plate or kitchen utensils made from pewter. [C14: from OF *peaultre*, from ?]
▸ˈ**pewterer** *n*

peyote (peɪˈəʊtɪ, pɪ-) *n* another name for **mescal** (the plant). [Mexican Sp., from Nahuatl *peyotl*]

pF *abbrev. for* picofarad.

pf. *abbrev for:* **1** perfect. **2** Also: **pfg.** pfennig. **3** preferred.

pfennig (ˈfɛnɪg; *German* ˈpfɛnɪç) *n, pl* **pfennigs** *or* **pfennige** (*German* -nɪgə). a German monetary unit worth one hundredth of a Deutschmark. [G: PENNY]

PFI (in Britain) *abbrev. for* Private Finance Initiative.

PG *symbol for* a film certified for viewing by anyone, but which contains scenes that may be unsuitable for children, for whom parental guidance is necessary. [C20: from abbrev. of *parental guidance*]

pg. *abbrev. for* page.

Pg. *abbrev. for:* **1** Portugal. **2** Portuguese.

PGR *abbrev. for* psychogalvanic response.

pH *n* potential of hydrogen; a measure of the acidity or alkalinity of a solution. Pure water has a pH of 7, acid solutions have a pH less than 7, and alkaline solutions a pH greater than 7.

phacelia (fæˈsiːlɪə) *n* any of a genus of N American plants having clusters of blue flowers. [NL from Gk *phakelos* a cluster]

phaeton (ˈfeɪtᵊn) *n* a light four-wheeled horse-drawn carriage with or without a top. [C18: from F, from L, from Gk *Phaethon* son of Helios (the sun god), who borrowed his father's chariot]

-phage *n combining form.* indicating something that eats or consumes something specified: *bacteriophage.* [from Gk *-phagos;* see PHAGO-]
▸**-phagous** *adj combining form.*

phago- *or before a vowel* **phag-** *combining form.* eating, consuming, or destroying: *phagocyte.* [from Gk *phagein* to consume]

phagocyte (ˈfægəˌsaɪt) *n* a cell or protozoan that engulfs particles, such as microorganisms.
▸**phagocytic** (ˌfægəˈsɪtɪk) *adj*

phagocytosis (ˌfægəsaɪˈtəʊsɪs) *n* the process by which a cell, such as a white blood cell, ingests microorganisms, other cells, etc.

-phagy *or* **-phagia** *n combining form.* indicating an eating or devouring: *anthropophagy.* [from Gk *-phagia;* see PHAGO-]

phalange (ˈfælændʒ) *n, pl* **phalanges** (fæˈlændʒiːz). *Anat.* another name for **phalanx** (sense 4). [C16: via F, ult. from Gk PHALANX]

phalangeal (fəˈlændʒɪəl) *adj Anat.* of or relating to a phalanx or phalanges.

phalanger (fəˈlændʒə) *n* any of various Australasian arboreal marsupials having dense fur and a long tail. Also called (Austral. and NZ): **possum.** See also **flying phalanger.** [C18: via NL from Gk *phalaggion* spider's web, referring to its webbed hind toes]

phalanx (ˈfælæŋks) *n, pl* **phalanxes** *or* **phalanges** (fæˈlændʒiːz). **1** an ancient Greek and Macedonian battle formation of hoplites presenting long spears from behind a wall of overlapping shields. **2** any closely ranked unit or mass of people: *the police formed a phalanx to protect the embassy.* **3** a number of people united for a common purpose. **4** *Anat.* any of the bones of the fingers or toes. **5** *Bot.* a bundle of stamens. [C16: via L from Gk: infantry formation in close ranks, bone of finger or toe]

phalarope (ˈfæləˌrəʊp) *n* any of a family of aquatic shore birds of northern oceans and lakes, having a long slender bill and lobed toes. [C18: via F from NL *Phalaropus*, from Gk *phalaris* coot + *pous* foot]

phallic (ˈfælɪk) *adj* **1** of, relating to, or resembling a phallus: *a phallic symbol.* **2** *Psychoanal.* relating to a stage of psychosexual development during which a male child's interest is concentrated on the genital organs. **3** of or relating to phallicism.

phallicism (ˈfælɪˌsɪzəm) *or* **phallism** *n* the worship or veneration of the phallus.

phallus (ˈfæləs) *n, pl* **phalluses** *or* **phalli** (-laɪ). **1** another word for **penis. 2** an image of the male sexual organ, esp. as a symbol of reproductive power. [C17: via LL from Gk *phallos*]

-phane *n combining form.* indicating something resembling a specified substance: *cellophane.* [from Gk *phainein* to shine, appear]

phanerogam (ˈfænərəʊˌgæm) *n* any plant of a former major division which included all seed-bearing plants; a former name for **spermatophyte.** [C19: from NL *phanerogamus*, from Gk *phaneros* visible + *gamos* marriage]
▸ˌ**phaneroˈgamic** *or* **phanerogamous** (ˌfænəˈrɒgəməs) *adj*

phantasm ❶ (ˈfæntæzəm) *n* **1** a phantom. **2** an illusory perception of an object, person, etc. [C13: from OF *fantasme*, from L *phantasma*, from Gk]
▸**phanˈtasmal** *or* **phanˈtasmic** *adj*

phantasmagoria ❶ (ˌfæntæzməˈgɔːrɪə) *or* **phantasmagory** (fænˈtæzməgərɪ) *n* **1** *Psychol.* a shifting medley of real or imagined figures, as in a dream. **2** *Films.* a sequence of pictures made to vary in size rapidly. **3** a shifting scene composed of different elements. [C19: prob. from F, from PHANTASM + *-agorie*, ?from Gk *ageirein* to gather together]
▸**phantasmagoric** (ˌfæntæzməˈgɒrɪk) *or* ˌ**phantasmaˈgorical** *adj*

phantasy ❶ (ˈfæntəsɪ) *n, pl* **phantasies.** an archaic spelling of **fantasy.**

phantom ❶ (ˈfæntəm) *n* **1a** an apparition or spectre. **1b** (*as modifier*): *a phantom army marching through the sky.* **2** the visible representation of something abstract, esp. as in a dream or hallucination: *phantoms of*

THESAURUS

horrify, immobilize, paralyse, stun, stupefy, transfix

pettish *adj* = **peevish,** cross, fractious, fretful, grumpy, huffy, ill-humoured, irritable, liverish, petulant, querulous, sulky, tetchy, thin-skinned, touchy, waspish

petty *adj* **1** = **trivial,** contemptible, inconsiderable, inessential, inferior, insignificant, little, measly (*inf.*), negligible, paltry, piddling (*inf.*), slight, small, trifling, unimportant **2** = **small-minded,** cheap, grudging, mean, mean-minded, shabby, spiteful, stingy, ungenerous **3** = **minor,** inferior, junior, lesser, lower, secondary, subordinate

Antonyms *adj* ≠ **trivial:** consequential, considerable, essential, important, major, momentous, significant ≠ **small-minded:** broad-minded, generous, liberal, magnanimous, open-minded, tolerant

petulance *n* = **sulkiness,** bad temper, crabbiness, ill humour, irritability, peevishness, pettishness, pique, pouts, querulousness, spleen, sullenness, waspishness

petulant *adj* = **sulky,** bad-tempered, captious, cavilling, crabbed, cross, crusty, fault-finding, fretful, huffy, ill-humoured, impatient, irritable, moody, peevish, perverse, pouting, querulous, snappish, sour, sullen, ungracious, waspish

Antonyms *adj* affable, cheerful, congenial, easy-going, even-tempered, good-humoured, good-natured, happy, patient, smiling

phantasm *n* **1** = **phantom,** apparition, eidolon, ghost, revenant, shade (*literary*), spectre, spirit, spook (*inf.*), wraith **2** = **illusion,** chimera, figment, figment of the imagination, hallucination, vision

phantasmagoric *adj* **1** = **illusory,** chimerical, dreamlike, hallucinatory, Kafkaesque, kaleidoscopic, nightmarish, phantasmal, psychedelic, surreal, unreal

phantasy *see* **fantasy**

phantom *n* **1** = **spectre,** apparition, eidolon,

evil haunted his sleep. **3** something apparently unpleasant or horrific that has no material form. [C13: from OF *fantosme,* from L *phantasma*]

phantom limb *n* the illusion that a limb still exists following its amputation, sometimes with the sensation of pain (**phantom limb pain**).

phantom pregnancy *n* the occurrence of signs of pregnancy, such as enlarged abdomen and absence of menstruation, when no embryo is present, due to hormonal imbalance. Also called: **false pregnancy.**

-phany *n combining form.* indicating a manifestation: *theophany.* [from Gk *-phania,* from *phainein* to show]
▸**-phanous** *adj combining form.*

phar., Phar., pharm., *or* **Pharm.** *abbrev. for:* **1** pharmaceutical. **2** pharmacist. **3** pharmacopoeia. **4** pharmacy.

Pharaoh ('fɛərəʊ) *n* the title of the ancient Egyptian kings. [OE *Pharaon,* via L, Gk, & Heb., ult. from Egyptian *pr-'o* great house]
▸**Pharaonic** (fɛə'rɒnɪk) *adj*

Pharisaic (ˌfærɪ'seɪɪk) *or* **Pharisaical** *adj* **1** *Judaism.* of, relating to, or characteristic of the Pharisees or Pharisaism. **2** (*often not cap.*) righteously hypocritical.
▸ˌ**Phari'saically** *adv*

Pharisaism ('færɪseɪˌɪzəm) *or* **Phariseeism** ('færɪsiːˌɪzəm) *n* **1** *Judaism.* the tenets and customs of the Pharisees. **2** (*often not cap.*) observance of the external forms of religion without genuine belief; hypocrisy.

Pharisee ❶ ('færɪˌsiː) *n* **1** a member of an ancient Jewish sect teaching strict observance of Jewish traditions. **2** (*often not cap.*) a self-righteous or hypocritical person. [OE *Farīsēus,* ult. from Aramaic *perīshāiyā,* pl. of *perīsh* separated]

pharmaceutical (ˌfɑːmə'sjuːtɪkᵊl) *or* (*less commonly*) **pharmaceutic** *adj* of or relating to drugs or pharmacy. [C17: from LL *pharmaceuticus,* from Gk *pharmakeus* purveyor of drugs; see PHARMACY]
▸ˌ**pharma'ceutically** *adv*

pharmaceutics (ˌfɑːmə'sjuːtɪks) *n* **1** (*functioning as sing*) another term for **pharmacy** (sense 1). **2** pharmaceutical remedies.

pharmacist ('fɑːməsɪst) *n* a person qualified to prepare and dispense drugs.

pharmaco- *combining form.* indicating drugs: *pharmacology.* [from Gk *pharmakon* drug]

pharmacognosy (ˌfɑːmə'kɒgnəsɪ) *n* the study of crude drugs of plant and animal origin. [C19: from PHARMACO- + *gnosy,* from Gk *gnosis* knowledge]
▸ˌ**pharma'cognosist** *n*

pharmacology (ˌfɑːmə'kɒlədʒɪ) *n* the science or study of drugs, including their characteristics, action, and uses.
▸**pharmacological** (ˌfɑːməkə'lɒdʒɪkᵊl) *adj* ▸ˌ**pharmaco'logically** *adv* ▸ˌ**pharma'cologist** *n*

pharmacopoeia *or US* (*sometimes*) **pharmacopeia** (ˌfɑːməkə'piːə) *n* an authoritative book containing a list of medicinal drugs with their uses, preparation, dosages, formulas, etc. [C17: via NL from Gk *pharmakopoiia* art of preparing drugs, from PHARMACO- + *-poiia,* from *poiein* to make]
▸ˌ**pharmaco'poeial** *adj*

pharmacy ('fɑːməsɪ) *n, pl* **pharmacies. 1** Also: **pharmaceutics.** the practice or art of preparing and dispensing drugs. **2** a dispensary. [C14: from Med. L *pharmacia,* from Gk *pharmakeia* making of drugs, from *pharmakon* drug]

pharos ('fɛərɒs) *n* any marine lighthouse or beacon. [C16: after a large Hellenistic lighthouse on an island off Alexandria in Egypt]

pharyngeal (ˌfærɪn'dʒiːəl) *or* **pharyngal** (fə'rɪŋgᵊl) *adj* **1** of, relating to, or situated in or near the pharynx. **2** *Phonetics.* pronounced with an articulation in or constriction of the pharynx. [C19: from NL *pharyngeus;* see PHARYNX]

pharyngitis (ˌfærɪn'dʒaɪtɪs) *n* inflammation of the pharynx.

pharynx ('færɪŋks) *n, pl* **pharynges** (fæ'rɪndʒiːz) *or* **pharynxes.** the part of the alimentary canal between the mouth and the oesophagus. [C17: via NL from Gk *pharunx* throat]

phase ❶ (feɪz) *n* **1** any distinct or characteristic period or stage in a sequence of events: *there were two phases to the resolution.* **2** *Astron.* one of the recurring shapes of the portion of the moon or an inferior planet illuminated by the sun. **3** *Physics.* the fraction of a cycle of a periodic quantity that has been completed at a specific reference time, expressed as an angle. **4** *Physics.* a particular stage in a periodic process or phenomenon. **5 in phase.** (of two waveforms) reaching corresponding phases at the same time. **6 out of phase.** (of two waveforms) not in phase. **7** *Chem.* a distinct state of matter characterized by homogeneous composition and properties and the possession of a clearly defined boundary. **8** *Zool.* a variation in the normal form of an animal, esp. a colour variation, brought about by seasonal or geographical change. ◆ *vb* **phases, phasing, phased.** (*tr*) **9** (*often passive*) to execute, arrange, or introduce gradually or in stages: *the withdrawal was phased over several months.* **10** (sometimes foll. by *with*) to cause (a part, process, etc.) to function or coincide with (another part, etc.): *he tried to phase the intake and output of the machine; he phased the intake with the output.* **11** *Chiefly US.* to arrange (processes, goods, etc.) to be supplied or executed when required. [C19: from NL *phases,* pl. of *phasis,* from Gk: aspect]
▸**'phasic** *adj*

phase in *vb* (*tr, adv*) to introduce in a gradual or cautious manner: *the legislation was phased in over two years.*

phase modulation *n* a type of modulation in which the phase of a radio carrier wave is varied by an amount proportional to the instantaneous amplitude of the modulating signal.

phase out ❶ *vb* (*tr, adv*) **1** to discontinue or withdraw gradually. ◆ *n* **phase-out. 2** *Chiefly US.* the action or an instance of phasing out: *a phase-out of conventional forces.*

phase rule *n* the principle that in any system in equilibrium the number of degrees of freedom is equal to the number of components less the number of phases plus two.

-phasia *n combining form.* indicating speech disorder of a specified kind: *aphasia.* [from Gk, from *phanai* to speak]
▸**-phasic** *adj and n combining form.*

phatic ('fætɪk) *adj* (of speech) used to establish social contact and to express sociability rather than specific meaning. [C20: from Gk *phat(os)* spoken + -IC]

PhD *abbrev. for* Doctor of Philosophy. Also: **DPhil.**

pheasant ('fɛzᵊnt) *n* **1** any of various long-tailed gallinaceous birds, having a brightly-coloured plumage in the male: native to Asia but introduced elsewhere. **2** any of various other related birds, including the quails and partridges. **3** *US & Canad.* any of several other gallinaceous birds, esp. the ruffed grouse. [C13: from OF *fesan,* from L *phāsiānus,* from Gk *phasianos ornis* Phasian bird, after the River *Phasis,* in Colchis, an ancient country on the Black Sea]

phellem ('fɛləm) *n Bot.* the technical name for **cork** (sense 4). [C20: from Gk *phellos* cork + PHLOEM]

phenacetin (fɪ'næsɪtɪn) *n* a white crystalline solid used in medicine to relieve pain and fever. Also called: **acetophenetidin.** [C19: from PHENO- + ACETYL + -IN]

pheno- *or before a vowel* **phen-** *combining form.* **1** showing or manifesting: *phenotype.* **2** indicating that a molecule contains benzene rings: *phenobarbitone.* [from Gk *phaino-* shining, from *phainein* to show; its use in a chemical sense is exemplified in *phenol,* so called because orig. prepared from illuminating gas]

phenobarbitone (ˌfiːnəʊ'bɑːbɪˌtəʊn) *or* **phenobarbital** (ˌfiːnəʊ'bɑːbɪtᵊl) *n* a white crystalline derivative of barbituric acid used as a sedative for treating insomnia and epilepsy.

phenocryst ('fiːnəˌkrɪst, 'fɛn-) *n* any of several large crystals in igneous rocks such as porphyry. [C19: from PHENO- (shining) + CRYSTAL]

phenol ('fiːnɒl) *n* **1** Also called: **carbolic acid.** a white crystalline derivative of benzene, used as an antiseptic and disinfectant and in the manufacture of resins, explosives, and pharmaceuticals. Formula: C_6H_5OH. **2** *Chem.* any of a class of organic compounds whose molecules contain one or more hydroxyl groups bound directly to a carbon atom in an aromatic ring.
▸**phe'nolic** *adj*

phenolic resin *n* any one of a class of resins derived from phenol, used in paints, adhesives, and as thermosetting plastics.

phenology (fɪ'nɒlədʒɪ) *n* the study of recurring phenomena, such as animal migration, esp. as influenced by climatic conditions. [C19: from PHENO(MENON) + -LOGY]
▸**phenological** (ˌfiːnə'lɒdʒɪkᵊl) *adj* ▸**phe'nologist** *n*

phenolphthalein (ˌfiːnɒl'θeɪliːn, -lɪɪn, -'θæl-) *n* a colourless crystalline compound used in medicine as a laxative and in chemistry as an indicator. [from PHENO- + *phthal-,* short form of NAPHTHALENE + -IN]

phenomena (fɪ'nɒmɪnə) *n* a plural of **phenomenon.**

phenomenal ❶ (fɪ'nɒmɪnᵊl) *adj* **1** of or relating to a phenomenon. **2** extraordinary; outstanding; remarkable: *a phenomenal achievement.* **3** *Philosophy.* known or perceived by the senses rather than the mind.
▸**phe'nomenally** *adv*

phenomenalism (fɪ'nɒmɪnəˌlɪzəm) *n Philosophy.* the doctrine that statements about physical objects and the external world can be analysed in terms of possible or actual experiences, and that entities, such as physical objects, are only mental constructions out of phenomenal appearances.
▸**phe'nomenalist** *n, adj*

phenomenology (fɪˌnɒmɪ'nɒlədʒɪ) *n Philosophy.* **1** the movement that concentrates on the detailed description of conscious experience. **2** the science of phenomena as opposed to the science of being.
▸**phenomenological** (fɪˌnɒmɪnə'lɒdʒɪkᵊl) *adj*

phenomenon ❶ (fɪ'nɒmɪnən) *n, pl* **phenomena** (-ɪnə) *or* **phenomenons. 1**

THESAURUS

ghost, phantasm, revenant, shade (*literary*), spirit, spook (*inf.*), wraith **3** = **illusion,** chimera, figment, figment of the imagination, hallucination, vision

Pharisee *n* **2** *often not cap.* = **hypocrite,** canter, dissembler, dissimulator, fraud, humbug, phoney *or* phony (*inf.*), pietist, whited sepulchre

phase *n* **1** = **stage,** aspect, chapter, condition, development, juncture, period, point, position, state, step, time

phase out *vb* **1** = **wind down,** axe (*inf.*), close, deactivate, dispose of gradually, ease off, eliminate, pull, pull out, remove, replace, run down, taper off, terminate, wind up, withdraw
Antonyms *vb* activate, begin, create, establish, form, initiate, open, set up, start

phenomenal *adj* **1, 2** = **extraordinary,** exceptional, fantastic, marvellous, miraculous, notable, outstanding, prodigious, remarkable, sensational, singular, stellar (*inf.*), uncommon, unique, unparalleled, unusual, wondrous (*arch. or literary*)
Antonyms *adj* average, common, mediocre, no great shakes (*inf.*), ordinary, poor, run-of-the-mill, second-rate, unexceptional, unremarkable, usual

phenomenon *n* **1** = **occurrence,** circumstance, episode, event, fact, happening, incident **2** = **wonder,** exception, marvel, miracle, anything that can be perceived as an occurrence or fact by the senses. **2** any remarkable occurrence or person. **3** *Philosophy.* **3a** the object of perception, experience, etc. **3b** (in the writings of Kant (1724–1804), German philosopher) a thing as it appears, as distinguished from its real nature as a thing-in-itself. [C16: via LL from Gk *phainomenon,* from *phainesthai* to appear, from *phainein* to show]

> **USAGE NOTE** Although *phenomena* is often treated as if it were singular, correct usage is to employ *phenomenon* with a singular construction and *phenomena* with a plural: *that is an interesting phenomenon* (not *phenomena*); *several new phenomena were recorded in his notes.*

phenotype (ˈfiːnəʊˌtaɪp) *n* the physical constitution of an organism as determined by the interaction of its genetic constitution and the environment.
▸**phenotypic** (ˌfiːnəʊˈtɪpɪk) *or* ˌ**phenoˈtypical** *adj* ▸ˌ**phenoˈtypically** *adv*

phenyl (ˈfiːnaɪl, ˈfɛnɪl) *n* (*modifier*) of, containing, or consisting of the monovalent group C_6H_5, derived from benzene: *a phenyl group.*

phenylalanine (ˌfiːnaɪlˈæləˌniːn) *n* an essential amino acid; a component of proteins.

phenylbutazone (ˌfiːnaɪlˈbjuːtəˌzəʊn) *n* an anti-inflammatory drug used in the treatment of rheumatic diseases. [C20: from (*dioxodi*)*phenylbut*(*ylpyr*)*azo*(*lidi*)*ne*]

phenylketonuria (ˌfiːnaɪlˌkiːtəˈnjʊərɪə) *n* a congenital metabolic disorder characterized by the abnormal accumulation of phenylalanine in the body fluids, resulting in mental deficiency. [C20: NL; see PHENYL, KETONE, -URIA]

pheromone (ˈfɛrəˌməʊn) *n* a chemical substance, secreted externally by certain animals, such as insects, affecting the behaviour of other animals of the same species. [C20 *phero-,* from Gk *pherein* to bear + (HOR)MONE]

phew (fjuː) *interj* an exclamation of relief, surprise, disbelief, weariness, etc.

phi (faɪ) *n, pl* **phis.** the 21st letter in the Greek alphabet, Φ, φ.

phial (ˈfaɪəl) *n* a small bottle for liquids, etc.; vial. [C14: from OF *fiole,* from L *phiola* saucer, from Gk *phialē* wide shallow vessel]

Phi Beta Kappa (ˈfaɪ ˈbeɪtə ˈkæpə, ˈbiːtə) *n* (in the US) **1** a national honorary society, founded in 1776, membership of which is based on high academic ability. **2** a member of this society. [from the initials of the Gk motto *philosophia biou kubernētēs* philosophy the guide of life]

phil. *abbrev. for:* **1** philharmonic. **2** philosophy.

Phil. *abbrev. for:* **1** Philadelphia. **2** *Bible.* Philippians. **3** Philippines. **4** Philharmonic.

philadelphus (ˌfɪləˈdɛlfəs) *n* any of a N temperate genus of shrubs cultivated for their strongly scented showy flowers. See also **mock orange** (sense 1). [C19: NL, from Gk *philadelphon* mock orange, lit.: loving one's brother]

philander ❶ (fɪˈlændə) *vb* (*intr;* often foll. by *with*) (of a man) to flirt with women. [C17: from Gk *philandros* fond of men, used as a name for a lover in literary works]
▸**phiˈlanderer** *n*

philanthropic ❶ (ˌfɪlənˈθrɒpɪk) *or* **philanthropical** *adj* showing concern for humanity, esp. by performing charitable actions, donating money, etc.
▸ˌ**philanˈthropically** *adv*

philanthropy ❶ (fɪˈlænθrəpɪ) *n, pl* **philanthropies. 1** the practice of performing charitable or benevolent actions. **2** love of mankind in general. [C17: from LL *philanthrōpia,* from Gk: love of mankind, from *philos* loving + *anthrōpos* man]
▸**phiˈlanthropist** *or* **philanthrope** (ˈfɪlənˌθrəʊp) *n*

philately (fɪˈlætəlɪ) *n* the collection and study of postage stamps. [C19: from F *philatélie,* from PHILO- + Gk *ateleia* exemption from charges (here referring to stamps)]
▸**philatelic** (ˌfɪləˈtɛlɪk) *adj* ▸ˌ**philaˈtelically** *adv* ▸**phiˈlatelist** *n*

-phile *or* **-phil** *n combining form.* indicating a person or thing having a fondness for something specified: *bibliophile.* [from Gk *philos* loving]

Philem. *Bible. abbrev. for* Philemon.

philharmonic (ˌfɪlhɑːˈmɒnɪk, ˌfɪlə-) *adj* **1** fond of music. **2** (*cap. when part of a name*) denoting an orchestra, choir, society, etc., devoted to music. ◆ *n* **3** (*cap. when part of a name*) a specific philharmonic choir, orchestra, or society. [C18: from F *philharmonique,* from It. *filarmonico* music-loving]

philhellene (fɪlˈhɛliːn) *n* **1** a lover of Greece and Greek culture. **2** *European history.* a supporter of the cause of Greek national independence.
▸**philhellenic** (ˌfɪlhɛˈliːnɪk) *adj*

-philia *n combining form.* **1** indicating a tendency towards: *haemophilia.* **2** indicating an abnormal liking for: *necrophilia.* [from Gk *philos* loving]
▸**-philiac** *n combining form.* ▸**-philous** *or* **-philic** *adj combining form.*

philibeg (ˈfɪlɪˌbɛg) *n* a variant spelling of **filibeg.**

philippic (fɪˈlɪpɪk) *n* a bitter or impassioned speech of denunciation; invective. [C16: after the orations of Demosthenes, 4th-century orator, against Philip of Macedon (382–336 B.C.)]

Philippine (ˈfɪlɪˌpiːn) *n, adj* another word for **Filipino.**

Philistine ❶ (ˈfɪlɪˌstaɪn) *n* **1** a person who is hostile towards culture, the arts, etc.; a smug boorish person. **2** a member of the non-Semitic people who inhabited ancient Philistia, a country on the coast of SW Palestine. ◆ *adj* **3** (*sometimes not cap.*) boorishly uncultured. **4** of or relating to the ancient Philistines.
▸**Philistinism** (ˈfɪlɪstɪˌnɪzəm) *n*

phillumenist (fɪˈljuːmənɪst, -ˈluː-) *n* a person who collects matchbox labels. [C20: from PHILO- + L *lumen* light + -IST]

philo- *or before a vowel* **phil-** *combining form.* indicating a love of: *philology; philanthropic.* [from Gk *philos* loving]

philodendron (ˌfɪləˈdɛndrən) *n, pl* **philodendrons** *or* **philodendra** (-drə). an evergreen climbing plant of a tropical American genus: cultivated as a house plant. [C19: NL from Gk: lover of trees]

philogyny (fɪˈlɒdʒɪnɪ) *n Rare.* fondness for women. [C17: from Gk *philogunia,* from PHILO- + *gunē* woman]
▸**phiˈlogynist** *n*

philology (fɪˈlɒlədʒɪ) *n* **1** comparative and historical linguistics. **2** the scientific analysis of written records and literary texts. **3** (no longer in scholarly use) the study of literature. [C17: from L *philologia,* from Gk: love of language]
▸**philological** (ˌfɪləˈlɒdʒɪkᵊl) *adj* ▸ˌ**philoˈlogically** *adv* ▸**phiˈlologist** *or* (*less commonly*) **phiˈlologer** *n*

philomel (ˈfɪləˌmɛl) *or* **philomela** (ˌfɪləʊˈmiːlə) *n* poetic names for a **nightingale.** [C14 *philomene,* via Med. L from L *philomēla,* from Gk]

philoprogenitive (ˌfɪləʊprəʊˈdʒɛnɪtɪv) *adj Rare.* **1** fond of children. **2** producing many offspring.

philos. *abbrev. for:* **1** philosopher. **2** philosophical.

philosopher ❶ (fɪˈlɒsəfə) *n* **1** a student, teacher, or devotee of philosophy. **2** a person of philosophical temperament, esp. one who is patient, wise, and stoical. **3** (formerly) an alchemist or devotee of occult science.

philosopher's stone *n* a stone or substance thought by alchemists to be capable of transmuting base metals into gold.

philosophical ❶ (ˌfɪləˈsɒfɪkᵊl) *or* **philosophic** *adj* **1** of or relating to philosophy or philosophers. **2** reasonable, wise, or learned. **3** calm and stoical, esp. in the face of difficulties or disappointments.
▸ˌ**philoˈsophically** *adv*

philosophical analysis *n* a philosophical method in which language and experience are analysed in an attempt to provide new insights into various philosophical problems.

philosophize *or* **philosophise** (fɪˈlɒsəˌfaɪz) *vb* **philosophizes, philosophizing, philosophized** *or* **philosophises, philosophising, philosophised. 1** (*intr*) to make philosophical pronouncements and speculations. **2** (*tr*) to explain philosophically.
▸**phiˈlosoˌphizer** *or* **phiˈlosoˌphiser** *n*

philosophy ❶ (fɪˈlɒsəfɪ) *n, pl* **philosophies. 1** the academic discipline concerned with making explicit the nature and significance of ordinary and scientific beliefs and investigating the intelligibility of concepts by means of rational argument concerning their presuppositions, implications, and interrelationships. **2** the particular doctrines relating to these issues of a specific individual or school: *the philosophy of Descartes.* **3** the basic principles of a discipline: *the philosophy of law.* **4** any system of belief, values, or tenets. **5** a personal

THESAURUS

nonpareil, prodigy, rarity, sensation, sight, spectacle

philander *vb* = **womanize** (*inf.*), coquet, court, dally, flirt, fool around (*inf.*), toy, trifle

philanderer *n* = **womanizer** (*inf.*), Casanova, dallier, Don Juan, flirt, gallant, gay dog, ladies' man, lady-killer (*inf.*), Lothario, playboy, stud (*sl.*), trifler, wolf (*inf.*)

philanthropic *adj* **1** = **humanitarian,** almsgiving, altruistic, beneficent, benevolent, benignant, charitable, eleemosynary, generous, gracious, humane, kind, kind-hearted, munificent, public-spirited
Antonyms *adj* egoistic, mean, miserly, niggardly, penurious, selfish, self-seeking, stingy

philanthropist *n* **1** = **humanitarian,** almsgiver, altruist, benefactor, contributor, donor, giver, patron

philanthropy *n* **1, 2** = **humanitarianism,** almsgiving, altruism, beneficence, benevolence, benignity, bounty, brotherly love, charitableness, charity, generosity, generousness, kind-heartedness, largesse *or* largess, liberality, munificence, open-handedness, patronage, public-spiritedness

Philistine *n* **1** = **boor,** barbarian, bourgeois, Goth, ignoramus, lout, lowbrow, vulgarian, yahoo ◆ *adj* **3** *sometimes not cap.* = **uncultured,** anti-intellectual, boorish, bourgeois, crass, ignorant, inartistic, lowbrow, tasteless, uncultivated, uneducated, unrefined

philosopher *n* **1** = **thinker,** dialectician, logician, mahatma, metaphysician, sage, seeker after truth, theorist, wise man

philosophical *adj* **1, 2** = **rational,** abstract, erudite, learned, logical, sagacious, theoretical, thoughtful, wise **3** = **stoical,** calm, collected, composed, cool, impassive, imperturbable, patient, resigned, sedate, serene, tranquil, unruffled
Antonyms *adj* ≠ **rational:** factual, illogical, irrational, practical, pragmatic, scientific ≠ **stoical:** emotional, hot-headed, impulsive, perturbed, rash, restless, upset

philosophy *n* **1** = **thought,** aesthetics, knowledge, logic, metaphysics, rationalism, reason, reasoning, thinking, wisdom **2-5** = **outlook,** attitude to life, basic idea, beliefs, convictions, doctrine, ideology, principles, tenets, thinking, values, viewpoint, *Weltanschauung,* world view **6** = **stoicism,** calmness, composure, coolness, dispassion, equanimity, resignation, restraint, self-possession, serenity outlook or viewpoint. **6** serenity of temper. [C13: from OF *filosofie,* from L *philosophia,* from Gk, from *philosophos* lover of wisdom]

-philous *or* **-philic** *adj combining form.* indicating love of or fondness for: *heliophilous.* [from L *-philus,* from Gk *-philos*]

philtre *or US* **philter** ('fɪltə) *n* a drink supposed to arouse desire. [C16: from L *philtrum,* from Gk *philtron* love potion, from *philos* loving]

phimosis (faɪ'məʊsɪs) *n* abnormal tightness of the foreskin, preventing its being retracted. [C17: via NL from Gk: a muzzling]

phiz (fɪz) *n Sl., chiefly Brit.* the face or a facial expression. Also called: **phizog** (fɪ'zɒg). [C17: colloquial shortening of PHYSIOGNOMY]

phlebitis (flɪ'baɪtɪs) *n* inflammation of a vein. [C19: via NL from Gk]
▸**phlebitic** (flɪ'bɪtɪk) *adj*

phlebo- *or before a vowel* **phleb-** *combining form.* indicating a vein: *phlebotomy.* [from Gk *phleps, phleb-* vein]

phlebotomy (flɪ'bɒtəmɪ) *n, pl* **phlebotomies.** surgical incision into a vein. [C14: from OF *flebothomie,* from LL *phlebotomia,* from Gk]

phlegm (flem) *n* **1** the viscid mucus secreted by the walls of the respiratory tract. **2** *Arch.* one of the four bodily humours. **3** apathy; stolidity. **4** imperturbability; coolness. [C14: from OF *fleume,* from LL *phlegma,* from Gk: inflammation, from *phlegein* to burn]
▸**'phlegmy** *adj*

phlegmatic ❶ (fleg'mætɪk) *or* **phlegmatical** *adj* **1** having a stolid or unemotional disposition. **2** not easily excited.
▸**phleg'matically** *adv*

phloem ('fləʊem) *n* tissue in higher plants that conducts synthesized food substances to all parts of the plant. [C19: via G from Gk *phloos* bark]

phlogiston (flɒ'dʒɪstɒn, -tən) *n Chem.* a hypothetical substance formerly thought to be present in all combustible materials. [C18: via NL from Gk, from *phlogizein* to set alight]

phlox (flɒks) *n, pl* **phlox** *or* **phloxes.** any of a chiefly North American genus of plants cultivated for their clusters of white, red, or purple flowers. [C18: via L from Gk: a plant of glowing colour, lit.: flame]

phlyctena (flɪk'tiːnə) *n, pl* **phlyctenae** (-niː). *Pathol.* a small blister, vesicle, or pustule. [C17: via NL from Gk *phluktaina,* from *phluzein* to swell]

-phobe *n combining form.* indicating one that fears or hates: *xenophobe.* [from Gk *-phobos* fearing]
▸**-phobic** *adj combining form.*

phobia ❶ ('fəʊbɪə) *n Psychiatry.* an abnormal intense and irrational fear of a given situation, organism, or object. [C19: from Gk *phobos* fear]
▸**'phobic** *adj, n*

-phobia *n combining form.* indicating an extreme abnormal fear of or aversion to: *acrophobia; claustrophobia.* [via L from Gk, from *phobos* fear]
▸**-phobic** *adj combining form.*

phocomelia (ˌfəʊkəʊ'miːlɪə) *n* a congenital deformity characterized esp. by short stubby hands or feet attached close to the body. [C19: via NL from Gk *phōkē* a seal + *melos* a limb]

phoebe ('fiːbɪ) *n* any of several greyish-brown North American flycatchers. [C19: imit.]

Phoenician (fə'nɪʃən, -'niːʃɪən) *n* **1** a member of an ancient Semitic people of NW Syria. **2** the extinct language of this people. ◆ *adj* **3** of Phoenicia, an ancient E Mediterranean maritime country, the Phoenicians, or their language.

phoenix *or US* **phenix** ('fiːnɪks) *n* **1** a legendary Arabian bird said to set fire to itself and rise anew from the ashes every 500 years. **2** a person or thing of surpassing beauty or quality. [OE *fenix,* via L from Gk *phoinix*]

phon (fɒn) *n* a unit of loudness that measures the intensity of a sound by the number of decibels it is above a reference tone. [C20: via G from Gk *phōnē* sound]

phonate (fəʊ'neɪt) *vb* **phonates, phonating, phonated.** (*intr*) to articulate speech sounds, esp. voiced speech sounds. [C19: from Gk *phōnē* voice]
▸**pho'nation** *n*

phone[1] ❶ (fəʊn) *n, vb* **phones, phoning, phoned.** short for **telephone.**

phone[2] (fəʊn) *n Phonetics.* a single speech sound. [C19: from Gk *phōnē* sound, voice]

-phone *combining form.* **1** (*forming nouns*) indicating a device giving off sound: *telephone.* **2** (*forming nouns and adjectives*) (a person) speaking a particular language: *Francophone.* [from Gk *phōnē* voice, sound]
▸**-phonic** *adj combining form.*

phonecard ('fəʊnˌkɑːd) *n* a card used instead of coins to operate certain public telephones.

phone-in *n* **a** a radio or television programme in which listeners' or viewers' questions, comments, etc., are telephoned to the studio and broadcast live as part of a discussion. **b** (*as modifier*): *a phone-in programme.*

phoneme ('fəʊniːm) *n Linguistics.* one of the set of speech sounds in any given language that serve to distinguish one word from another. [C20: via F from Gk *phōnēma* sound, speech]
▸**phonemic** (fə'niːmɪk) *adj*

phonemics (fə'niːmɪks) *n* (*functioning as sing*) that aspect of linguistics concerned with the classification and analysis of the phonemes of a language.
▸**pho'nemicist** *n*

phonetic (fə'netɪk) *adj* **1** of or relating to phonetics. **2** denoting any perceptible distinction between one speech sound and another. **3** conforming to pronunciation: *phonetic spelling.* [C19: from NL *phōnēticus,* from Gk, from *phōnein* to make sounds, speak]
▸**pho'netically** *adv*

phonetics (fə'netɪks) *n* (*functioning as sing*) the science concerned with the study of speech processes, including the production, perception, and analysis of speech sounds.
▸**phonetician** (ˌfəʊnɪ'tɪʃən) *or* **phonetist** ('fəʊnɪtɪst) *n*

phoney ❶ *or esp. US* **phony** ('fəʊnɪ) *Inf.* ◆ *adj* **phonier, phoniest. 1** not genuine; fake. **2** (of a person) insincere or pretentious. ◆ *n, pl* **phoneys** *or esp. US* **phonies. 3** an insincere or pretentious person. **4** something that is not genuine; a fake. [C20: from ?]
▸**'phoneyness** *or esp. US* **'phoniness** *n*

phonics ('fɒnɪks) *n* (*functioning as sing*) **1** an obsolete name for **acoustics** (sense 1). **2** a method of teaching people to read by training them to associate letters with their phonetic values.
▸**'phonic** *adj* ▸**'phonically** *adv*

phono- *or before a vowel* **phon-** *combining form.* indicating a sound or voice: *phonograph; phonology.* [from Gk *phōnē* sound, voice]

phonogram ('fəʊnəˌgræm) *n* any written symbol standing for a sound, syllable, morpheme, or word.
▸**ˌphono'gramic** *or* **ˌphono'grammic** *adj*

phonograph ('fəʊnəˌgrɑːf) *n* **1** an early form of gramophone capable of recording and reproducing sound on wax cylinders. **2** another US and Canad. word for **gramophone** or **record player.**

phonography (fəʊ'nɒgrəfɪ) *n* **1** a writing system that represents sounds by individual symbols. **2** the employment of such a writing system.
▸**phonographic** (ˌfəʊnə'græfɪk) *adj*

phonology (fə'nɒlədʒɪ) *n, pl* **phonologies. 1** the study of the sound system of a language or of languages in general. **2** such a sound system.
▸**phonological** (ˌfəʊnə'lɒdʒɪkˈl, ˌfɒn-) *adj* ▸**ˌphono'logically** *adv* ▸**pho'nologist** *n*

phonon ('fəʊnɒn) *n Physics.* a quantum of vibrational energy in the acoustic vibrations of a crystal lattice. [C20: from PHONO- + -ON]

-phony *n combining form.* indicating a specified type of sound: *cacophony; euphony.* [from Gk *-phōnia,* from *phōnē* sound]
▸**-phonic** *adj combining form.*

phooey ('fuːɪ) *interj Inf.* an exclamation of scorn, contempt, etc. [C20: prob. var. of PHEW]

-phore *n combining form.* indicating one that bears or produces: *semaphore.* [from NL *-phorus,* from Gk *-phoros* bearing, from *pherein* to bear]
▸**-phorous** *adj combining form.*

-phoresis *n combining form.* indicating a transmission: *electrophoresis.* [from Gk *phorēsis* being carried, from *pherein* to bear]

phormium ('fɔːmɪəm) *n* any of a genus of plants of the lily family with tough leathery evergreen leaves. Also called: **New Zealand flax, flax lily.** [C19: NL from Gk *phormos* basket]

phosgene ('fɒzdʒiːn) *n* a colourless poisonous gas: used in chemical warfare and in the manufacture of pesticides, dyes, and polyurethane resins. [C19: from Gk *phōs* light + *-gene,* var. of -GEN]

phosphate ('fɒsfeɪt) *n* **1** any salt or ester of any phosphoric acid. **2** (*often pl*) any of several chemical fertilizers containing phosphorous compounds. [C18: from F *phosphat;* see PHOSPHORUS, -ATE[1]]
▸**phosphatic** (fɒs'fætɪk) *adj*

phosphatide ('fɒsfəˌtaɪd) *n* another name for **phospholipid.**

phosphatidylcholine (ˌfɒsfæˌtaɪdaɪl'kəʊliːn) *n* the systematic name for **lecithin.**

phosphene ('fɒsfiːn) *n* the sensation of light caused by pressure on the eyelid of a closed eye. [C19: from Gk *phōs* light + *phainein* to show]
▸**phos'phenic** *adj*

phosphide ('fɒsfaɪd) *n* any compound of phosphorus with another element, esp. a more electropositive element.

phosphine ('fɒsfiːn) *n* a colourless flammable gas that is slightly soluble in water and has a strong fishy odour: used as a pesticide. Formula: PH_3.

THESAURUS

phlegmatic *adj* **1, 2 = unemotional,** apathetic, bovine, cold, dull, frigid, heavy, impassive, indifferent, lethargic, listless, lymphatic, matter-of-fact, placid, sluggish, stoical, stolid, undemonstrative, unfeeling
Antonyms *adj* active, alert, animated, emotional, energetic, excited, hyper (*inf.*), lively, passionate

phobia *n Psychiatry* **= terror,** aversion, detestation, dislike, distaste, dread, fear, hatred, horror, irrational fear, loathing, obsession, overwhelming anxiety, repulsion, revulsion, thing (*inf.*)
Antonyms *n* bent, fancy, fondness, inclination, liking, love, partiality, passion, penchant, soft spot

phone[1] *n* **= telephone,** blower (*inf.*), dog and bone (*sl.*), **= call,** bell (*Brit. sl.*), buzz (*inf.*), ring (*inf., chiefly Brit.*), tinkle (*Brit. inf.*) ◆ *vb* **= call,** buzz (*inf.*), get on the blower (*inf.*), give someone a bell (*Brit. sl.*), give someone a buzz (*inf.*), give someone a call, give someone a ring (*inf., chiefly Brit.*), make a call, ring (up) (*inf., chiefly Brit.*), telephone

phoney *Informal adj* **1 = fake,** affected, assumed, bogus, counterfeit, ersatz, false, feigned, forged, imitation, pseudo (*inf.*), put-on, sham, spurious, trick ◆ *n* **4 = fake,** counterfeit, faker, forgery, fraud, humbug, impostor, pretender, sham
Antonyms *adj* ≠ **fake:** authentic, bona fide, genuine, original, real, sincere, unaffected, unassumed, unfeigned

phosphite ('fɒsfaɪt) *n* any salt or ester of phosphorous acid.

phospho- *or before a vowel* **phosph-** *combining form.* containing phosphorus: *phosphoric.* [from F, from *phosphore* PHOSPHORUS]

phospholipid (ˌfɒsfəˈlɪpɪd) *n* any of a group of fatty compounds: important constituents of all membranes. Also called: **phosphatide.**

phosphonic acid (fɒsˈfɒnɪk) *n* the systematic name for **phosphorous acid.**

phosphor ('fɒsfə) *n* a substance capable of emitting light when irradiated with particles of electromagnetic radiation. [C17: from F, ult. from Gk *phōsphoros* PHOSPHORUS]

phosphorate ('fɒsfəˌreɪt) *vb* **phosphorates, phosphorating, phosphorated.** to treat or combine with phosphorus.

phosphor bronze *n* any of various hard corrosion-resistant alloys containing phosphorus: used in gears, bearings, cylinder casings, etc.

phosphoresce (ˌfɒsfəˈrɛs) *vb* **phosphoresces, phosphorescing, phosphoresced.** (*intr*) to exhibit phosphorescence.

phosphorescence (ˌfɒsfəˈrɛsəns) *n* **1** *Physics.* a fluorescence that persists after the bombarding radiation producing it has stopped. **2** the light emitted in phosphorescence. **3** the emission of light in which insufficient heat is evolved to cause fluorescence. Cf. **fluorescence.**
▸ˌ**phosphoˈrescent** *adj*

phosphoric (fɒsˈfɒrɪk) *adj* of or containing phosphorus in the pentavalent state.

phosphoric acid *n* **1** a colourless solid tribasic acid used in the manufacture of fertilizers and soap. Formula: H_3PO_4. Systematic name: **phosphoric(V) acid.** Also called: **orthophosphoric acid. 2** any oxyacid of phosphorus produced by reaction between phosphorus pentoxide and water.

phosphorous ('fɒsfərəs) *adj* of or containing phosphorus in the trivalent state.

phosphorous acid *n* **1** a white or yellowish hygroscopic crystalline dibasic acid. Formula: H_3PO_3. Systematic name: **phosphonic acid.** Also called: **orthophosphorous acid. 2** any oxyacid of phosphorus containing less oxygen than the corresponding phosphoric acid.

phosphorus ('fɒsfərəs) *n* **1** an allotropic nonmetallic element occurring in phosphates and living matter. Ordinary phosphorus is a toxic flammable phosphorescent white solid; the red form is less reactive and nontoxic: used in matches, pesticides, and alloys. The radioisotope **phosphorus-32** (**radiophosphorus**), with a half-life of 14.3 days, is used in radiotherapy and as a tracer. Symbol: P; atomic no.: 15; atomic wt.: 30.974. **2** a less common name for a **phosphor.** [C17: via L from Gk *phōsphoros* light-bringing, from *phōs* light + *pherein* to bring]

Phosphorus ('fɒsfərəs) *n* a morning star, esp. Venus.

phossy jaw ('fɒsɪ) *n* a gangrenous condition of the lower jawbone caused by prolonged exposure to phosphorus fumes. [C19: *phossy,* colloquial shortening of PHOSPHORUS]

phot (fɒt, fəʊt) *n* a unit of illumination equal to one lumen per square centimetre. 1 phot is equal to 10 000 lux. [C20: from Gk *phōs* light]

phot. *abbrev. for:* **1** photograph. **2** photographic. **3** photography.

photic ('fəʊtɪk) *adj* **1** of or concerned with light. **2** designating the zone of the sea where photosynthesis takes place.

photo ('fəʊtəʊ) *n, pl* **photos.** short for **photograph.**

photo- *combining form.* **1** of, relating to, or produced by light: *photosynthesis.* **2** indicating a photographic process: *photolithography.* [from Gk *phōs, phōt-* light]

photo call *n* a time arranged for photographers, esp. press photographers, to take pictures of a celebrity.

photocell ('fəʊtəʊˌsɛl) *n* a device in which the photoelectric or photovoltaic effect or photoconductivity is used to produce a current or voltage when exposed to light or other electromagnetic radiation. They are used in exposure meters, burglar alarms, etc. Also called: **photoelectric cell, electric eye.**

photochemistry (ˌfəʊtəʊˈkɛmɪstrɪ) *n* the branch of chemistry concerned with the chemical effects of light and other electromagnetic radiations.
▸**photochemical** (ˌfəʊtəʊˈkɛmɪkᵊl) *adj*

photochromic (ˌfəʊtəʊˈkrəʊmɪk) *adj* (of glass) changing colour with the intensity of incident light, used, for example, in sunglasses that darken as the sunlight becomes brighter.

photocomposition (ˌfəʊtəʊˌkɒmpəˈzɪʃən) *n* another name (esp. US and Canad.) for **filmsetting.**

photoconductivity (ˌfəʊtəʊˌkɒndʌkˈtɪvɪtɪ) *n* the change in the electrical conductivity of certain substances, such as selenium, as a result of the absorption of electromagnetic radiation.
▸**photoconductive** (ˌfəʊtəʊkənˈdʌktɪv) *adj* ▸ˌ**photoconˈductor** *n*

photocopier ('fəʊtəʊˌkɒpɪə) *n* an instrument using light-sensitive photographic materials to reproduce written, printed, or graphic work.

photocopy ('fəʊtəʊˌkɒpɪ) *n, pl* **photocopies. 1** a photographic reproduction of written, printed, or graphic work. ◆ *vb* **photocopies, photocopying, photocopied. 2** to reproduce (written, printed, or graphic work) on photographic material.

photodegradable (ˌfəʊtəʊdɪˈgreɪdəbᵊl) *adj* (of plastic) capable of being decomposed by prolonged exposure to light.

photoelectric (ˌfəʊtəʊɪˈlɛktrɪk) *adj* of or concerned with electric or electronic effects caused by light or other electromagnetic radiation.
▸**photoelectricity** (ˌfəʊtəʊɪlɛkˈtrɪsɪtɪ) *n*

photoelectric cell *n* another name for **photocell.**

photoelectric effect *n* **1** the ejection of electrons from a solid by an incident beam of sufficiently energetic electromagnetic radiation. **2** any phenomenon involving electric current and electromagnetic radiation, such as photoemission.

photoelectron (ˌfəʊtəʊɪˈlɛktrɒn) *n* an electron ejected from an atom, molecule, or solid by an incident photon.

photoemission (ˌfəʊtəʊɪˈmɪʃən) *n* the emission of electrons due to the impact of electromagnetic radiation.

photoengraving (ˌfəʊtəʊɪnˈgreɪvɪŋ) *n* **1** a photomechanical process for producing letterpress printing plates. **2** a plate made by this process. **3** a print made from such a plate.
▸ˌ**photoenˈgrave** *vb* (*tr*)

photo finish *n* **1** a finish of a race in which contestants are so close that a photograph is needed to decide the result. **2** any race or competition in which the winners are separated by a very small margin.

Photofit ('fəʊtəʊˌfɪt) *n Trademark.* **a** a method of combining photographs of facial features, hair, etc., into a composite picture of a face: used by the police to trace suspects, criminals, etc. **b** (*as modifier*): *a Photofit picture.*

photoflash ('fəʊtəʊˌflæʃ) *n* another name for **flashbulb.**

photoflood ('fəʊtəʊˌflʌd) *n* a highly incandescent tungsten lamp used for indoor photography, television, etc.

photog. *abbrev. for:* **1** photograph. **2** photographer. **3** photographic. **4** photography.

photogenic (ˌfəʊtəˈdʒɛnɪk) *adj* **1** (esp. of a person) having a general facial appearance that looks attractive in photographs. **2** *Biol.* producing or emitting light.
▸ˌ**photoˈgenically** *adv*

photogram ('fəʊtəˌgræm) *n* **1** a picture, usually abstract, produced on a photographic material without the use of a camera. **2** *Obs.* a photograph.

photogrammetry (ˌfəʊtəʊˈgræmɪtrɪ) *n* the process of making measurements from photographs, used esp. in the construction of maps from aerial photographs.

photograph ❶ ('fəʊtəˌgrɑːf) *n* **1** an image of an object, person, scene, etc., in the form of a print or slide recorded by a camera. Often shortened to **photo.** ◆ *vb* **2** to take a photograph of (an object, person, scene, etc.).

photographic ❶ (ˌfəʊtəˈgræfɪk) *adj* **1** of or relating to photography. **2** like a photograph in accuracy or detail. **3** (of a person's memory) able to retain facts, appearances, etc., in precise detail.
▸ˌ**photoˈgraphically** *adv*

photography (fəˈtɒgrəfɪ) *n* **1** the process of recording images on sensitized material by the action of light, X-rays, etc. **2** the art, practice, or occupation of taking photographs.
▸**phoˈtographer** *n*

photogravure (ˌfəʊtəʊgrəˈvjʊə) *n* **1** any of various methods in which an intaglio plate for printing is produced by the use of photography. **2** matter printed from such a plate. [C19: from PHOTO- + F *gravure* engraving]

photojournalism (ˌfəʊtəʊˈdʒɜːnᵊˌlɪzəm) *n* journalism in which photographs are the predominant feature.
▸ˌ**photoˈjournalist** *n*

photokinesis (ˌfəʊtəʊkɪˈniːsɪs, -kaɪ-) *n Biol.* the movement of an organism in response to the stimulus of light.

photolithography (ˌfəʊtəʊlɪˈθɒgrəfɪ) *n* **1** a lithographic printing process using photographically made plates. Often shortened to **photolitho. 2** *Electronics.* a process used in the manufacture of semiconductor devices and printed circuits in which a particular pattern is transferred from a photograph onto a substrate.
▸ˌ**photoliˈthographer** *n*

photoluminescence (ˌfəʊtəʊˌluːmɪˈnɛsəns) *n* luminescence resulting from the absorption of light or infrared or ultraviolet radiation.

photolysis (fəʊˈtɒlɪsɪs) *n* chemical decomposition caused by light or other electromagnetic radiation.
▸**photolytic** (ˌfəʊtəʊˈlɪtɪk) *adj*

photomechanical (ˌfəʊtəʊmɪˈkænɪkᵊl) *adj* of or relating to any of various methods by which printing plates are made using photography.
▸ˌ**photomeˈchanically** *adv*

photometer (fəʊˈtɒmɪtə) *n* an instrument used in photometry, usually one that compares the illumination produced by a particular light source with that produced by a standard source.

photometry (fəʊˈtɒmɪtrɪ) *n* **1** the measurement of the intensity of light. **2** the branch of physics concerned with such measurements.
▸**phoˈtometrist** *n*

photomicrograph (ˌfəʊtəʊˈmaɪkrəˌgrɑːf) *n* a photograph of a microscope image.
▸**photomicrography** (ˌfəʊtəʊmaɪˈkrɒgrəfɪ) *n*

photomontage (ˌfəʊtəʊmɒnˈtɑːʒ) *n* **1** the technique of producing a

THESAURUS

photograph *n* **1** = **picture,** image, likeness, photo (*inf.*), print, shot, slide, snap (*inf.*), snapshot, transparency ◆ *vb* **2** = **take a picture of,** capture on film, film, get a shot of, record, shoot, snap (*inf.*), take, take (someone's) picture

photographic *adj* **2** = **lifelike,** graphic, natural, pictorial, realistic, visual, vivid **3** = **accurate,** detailed, exact, faithful, minute, precise, retentive composite picture by combining several photographs. **2** the composite picture so produced.

photomultiplier (ˌfəʊtəʊˈmʌltɪˌplaɪə) *n* a device sensitive to electromagnetic radiation which produces a detectable pulse of current.

photon (ˈfəʊtɒn) *n* a quantum of electromagnetic radiation with energy equal to the product of the frequency of the radiation and the Planck constant.

photo-offset *n Printing.* an offset process in which the plates are produced photomechanically.

photo opportunity *n* an opportunity, either preplanned or accidental, for the press to photograph a politician, celebrity, or event.

photoperiodism (ˌfəʊtəʊˈpɪərɪəˌdɪzəm) *n* the response of plants and animals by behaviour, growth, etc., to the period of daylight in every 24 hours (**photoperiod**).
▸ˌ**photoˌperiˈodic** *adj*

photophobia (ˌfəʊtəʊˈfəʊbɪə) *n* **1** *Pathol.* abnormal sensitivity of the eyes to light. **2** *Psychiatry.* abnormal fear of sunlight or well-lit places.
▸ˌ**photoˈphobic** *adj*

photopolymer (ˌfəʊtəʊˈpɒlɪmə) *n* a polymeric material that is sensitive to light: used in printing plates, microfilms, etc.

photoreceptor (ˌfəʊtəʊrɪˈsɛptə) *n Zool., physiol.* a light-sensitive cell or organ that conveys impulses through the sensory neuron connected to it.

photosensitive (ˌfəʊtəʊˈsɛnsɪtɪv) *adj* sensitive to electromagnetic radiation, esp. light.
▸ˌ**photoˌsensiˈtivity** *n* ▸ˌ**photoˈsensiˌtize** *or* ˌ**photoˈsensiˌtise** *vb (tr)*

photoset (ˈfəʊtəʊˌsɛt) *vb* **photosets, photosetting, photoset.** another word for **filmset.**
▸ˈ**photoˌsetter** *n*

photosphere (ˈfəʊtəʊˌsfɪə) *n* the visible surface of the sun.
▸**photospheric** (ˌfəʊtəʊˈsfɛrɪk) *adj*

photostat (ˈfəʊtəʊˌstæt) *n* **1** a machine or process used to make photographic copies of written, printed, or graphic matter. **2** any copy made by such a machine. ◆ *vb* **photostats, photostatting** *or* **photostating, photostatted** *or* **photostated. 3** to make a photostat copy (of).

photosynthesis (ˌfəʊtəʊˈsɪnθɪsɪs) *n* (in plants) the synthesis of organic compounds from carbon dioxide and water using light energy absorbed by chlorophyll.
▸ˌ**photoˈsynthesize** *or* ˌ**photoˈsynthesise** *vb* ▸**photosynthetic** (ˌfəʊtəʊsɪnˈθɛtɪk) *adj* ▸ˌ**photosynˈthetically** *adv*

phototaxis (ˌfəʊtəʊˈtæksɪs) *n* the movement of an entire organism in response to light.

phototropism (ˌfəʊtəʊˈtrəʊpɪzəm) *n* the growth response of plant parts to the stimulus of light, producing a bending towards the light source.
▸ˌ**photoˈtropic** *adj*

photovoltaic effect (ˌfəʊtəʊvɒlˈteɪɪk) *n* the effect when electromagnetic radiation falls on a thin film of one solid deposited on the surface of a dissimilar solid producing a difference in potential between the two materials.

phrasal verb *n* a phrase that consists of a verb plus an adverbial or prepositional particle, esp. one the meaning of which cannot be deduced from the constituents: *"take in" meaning "deceive" is a phrasal verb.*

phrase ➊ (freɪz) *n* **1** a group of words forming a syntactic constituent of a sentence. Cf. **clause** (sense 1). **2** an idiomatic or original expression. **3** manner or style of speech or expression. **4** *Music.* a small group of notes forming a coherent unit of melody. ◆ *vb* **phrases, phrasing, phrased.** *(tr)* **5** *Music.* to divide (a melodic line, part, etc.) into musical phrases, esp. in performance. **6** to express orally or in a phrase. [C16: from L *phrasis*, from Gk: speech, from *phrazein* to tell]
▸ˈ**phrasal** *adj*

phrase book *n* a book containing frequently used expressions and their equivalents in a foreign language.

phrase marker *n Linguistics.* a representation, esp. a tree diagram, of the constituent structure of a sentence.

phraseogram (ˈfreɪzɪəˌɡræm) *n* a symbol representing a phrase, as in shorthand.

phraseology ➊ (ˌfreɪzɪˈɒlədʒɪ) *n, pl* **phraseologies. 1** the manner in which words or phrases are used. **2** a set of phrases used by a particular group of people.
▸**phraseological** (ˌfreɪzɪəˈlɒdʒɪkᵊl) *adj*

phrasing (ˈfreɪzɪŋ) *n* **1** the way in which something is expressed, esp. in writing; wording. **2** *Music.* the division of a melodic line, part, etc., into musical phrases.

phrenetic (frɪˈnɛtɪk) *adj* an obsolete spelling of **frenetic.**
▸**phreˈnetically** *adv*

phrenic (ˈfrɛnɪk) *adj* **1a** of or relating to the diaphragm. **1b** *(as n)*: *the phrenic.* **2** *Obs.* of or relating to the mind. [C18: from NL *phrenicus*, from Gk *phrēn* mind, diaphragm]

phrenology (frɪˈnɒlədʒɪ) *n* (formerly) the branch of science concerned with determination of the strength of the faculties by the shape and size of the skull overlying the parts of the brain thought to be responsible for them.
▸**phrenological** (ˌfrɛnəˈlɒdʒɪkᵊl) *adj* ▸**phreˈnologist** *n*

phrensy (ˈfrɛnzɪ) *n, pl* **phrensies** an obsolete spelling of **frenzy.**

Phrygian (ˈfrɪdʒɪən) *adj* **1** of or relating to ancient Phrygia, a country of W central Asia Minor, its inhabitants, or their extinct language. **2** *Music.* of or relating to an authentic mode represented by the natural diatonic scale from E to E. ◆ *n* **3** a native or inhabitant of ancient Phrygia. **4** an ancient language of Phrygia.

Phrygian cap *n* a conical cap of soft material worn during ancient times, that became a symbol of liberty during the French Revolution.

phthisis (ˈθaɪsɪs, ˈfθaɪ-, ˈtaɪ-) *n* any disease that causes wasting of the body, esp. pulmonary tuberculosis. [C16: via L from Gk, from *phthinein* to waste away]

phut (fʌt) *Inf.* ◆ *n* **1** a representation of a muffled explosive sound. ◆ *adv* **2 go phut.** to break down or collapse. [C19: imit.]

phycomycete (ˌfaɪkəʊˈmaɪsiːt) *n* any of a primitive group of fungi formerly included in the class *Phycomycetes*, but now classified in different phyla: includes certain mildews and moulds. [from Gk *phukos* seaweed + -MYCETE]

phyla (ˈfaɪlə) *n* the plural of **phylum.**

phylactery (fɪˈlæktərɪ) *n, pl* **phylacteries. 1** *Judaism.* either of the pair of blackened square cases containing parchments inscribed with biblical passages, bound by leather thongs to the head and left arm, and worn by Jewish men during weekday morning prayers. **2** a reminder. **3** *Arch.* an amulet or charm. [C14: from LL *phylactērium*, from Gk *phulaktērion* outpost, from *phulax* a guard]

phyletic (faɪˈlɛtɪk) *adj* of or relating to the evolutionary development of organisms. [C19: from Gk *phuletikos* tribal]

-phyll *or* **-phyl** *n combining form.* leaf: *chlorophyll.* [from Gk *phullon*]

phyllo- *or before a vowel* **phyll-** *combining form.* leaf: *phyllopod.* [from Gk *phullon* leaf]

phyllode (ˈfɪləʊd) *n* a flattened leafstalk that resembles and functions as a leaf. [C19: from NL *phyllodium*, from Gk *phullōdēs* leaflike]

phylloquinone (ˌfɪləʊkwɪˈnəʊn) *n* a viscous fat-soluble liquid occurring in plants: essential for the production of prothrombin, required in blood clotting. Also called: **vitamin K_1.**

phyllotaxis (ˌfɪləˈtæksɪs) *or* **phyllotaxy** *n, pl* **phyllotaxes** (-ˈtæksiːz) *or* **phyllotaxies. 1** the arrangement of the leaves on a stem. **2** the study of this arrangement.
▸ˌ**phylloˈtactic** *adj*

-phyllous *adj combining form.* having leaves of a specified number or type: *monophyllous.* [from Gk *-phullos* of a leaf]

phylloxera (ˌfɪlɒkˈsɪərə, fɪˈlɒksərə) *n, pl* **phylloxerae** (-riː) *or* **phylloxeras.** any of a genus of homopterous insects, such as vine phylloxera, typically feeding on plant juices. [C19: NL, from PHYLLO- + *xēros* dry]

phylo- *or before a vowel* **phyl-** *combining form.* tribe; race; phylum: *phylogeny.* [from Gk *phulon* race]

phylogeny (faɪˈlɒdʒɪnɪ) *or* **phylogenesis** (ˌfaɪləʊˈdʒɛnɪsɪs) *n, pl* **phylogenies** *or* **phylogeneses** (-ˈdʒɛnɪˌsiːz). *Biol.* the sequence of events involved in the evolution of a species, genus, etc. Cf. **ontogeny.** [C19: from PHYLO- + -GENY]
▸**phylogenic** (ˌfaɪləʊˈdʒɛnɪk) *or* **phylogenetic** (ˌfaɪləʊdʒɪˈnɛtɪk) *adj*

phylum (ˈfaɪləm) *n, pl* **phyla. 1** a major taxonomic division of living organisms that contain one or more classes. **2** a group of related language families or linguistic stocks. [C19: NL, from Gk *phulon* race]

phys. *abbrev. for:* **1** physical. **2** physician. **3** physics. **4** physiological. **5** physiology.

physalis (faɪˈseɪlɪs) *n* any of a genus of plants producing inflated orange seed vessels. See **Chinese lantern.** [NL from Gk *physallis* bladder]

physic (ˈfɪzɪk) *n* **1** *Rare.* a medicine, esp. a cathartic. **2** *Arch.* the art or skill of healing. ◆ *vb* **physics, physicking, physicked. 3** *(tr) Arch.* to treat (a patient) with medicine. [C13: from OF *fisique*, via L, from Gk *phusikē*, from *phusis* nature]

physical ➊ (ˈfɪzɪkᵊl) *adj* **1** of or relating to the body, as distinguished from the mind or spirit. **2** of, relating to, or resembling material things or nature: *the physical universe.* **3** involving or requiring bodily contact: *rugby is a physical sport.* **4** of or concerned with matter and energy. **5** of or relating to physics. **6** perceptible to the senses; apparent: *a physical manifestation.* ◆ See also **physicals.**
▸ˈ**physically** *adv*

physical anthropology *n* the branch of anthropology dealing with the genetic aspect of human development and its physical variations.

physical chemistry *n* the branch of chemistry concerned with the way in which the physical properties of substances depend on their chemical structure, properties, and reactions.

physical education *n* training and practice in sports, gymnastics, etc. Abbrev.: **PE.**

physical geography *n* the branch of geography that deals with the natural features of the earth's surface.

physical jerks *pl n Brit. inf.* See **jerk**[1] (sense 6).

physicals (ˈfɪzɪkᵊlz) *pl n Commerce.* commodities that can be purchased and used, as opposed to those bought and sold in a futures market. Also called: **actuals.**

physical science *n* any of the sciences concerned with nonliving matter, such as physics, chemistry, astronomy, and geology.

physical therapy *n Chiefly US.* another term for **physiotherapy.**

physician ➊ (fɪˈzɪʃən) *n* **1** a person legally qualified to practise medi-

THESAURUS

phrase *n* **1-3** = **expression**, group of words, idiom, locution, motto, remark, saying, tag, utterance, way of speaking ◆ *vb* **6** = **express**, couch, formulate, frame, present, put, put into words, say, term, utter, voice, word

phraseology *n* **1** = **wording**, choice of words, diction, expression, idiom, language, parlance, phrase, phrasing, speech, style, syntax

physical *adj* **1** = **bodily**, carnal, corporal, corporeal, earthly, fleshly, incarnate, mortal, somatic, unspiritual **2** = **material**, natural, palpable, real, sensible, solid, substantial, tangible, visible

physician *n* **1** = **doctor**, doc, doctor of medicine, general practitioner, G.P., healer, M.D., cine, esp. other than surgery; doctor of medicine. **2** *Arch.* any person who treats diseases; healer. [C13: from OF *fisicien,* from *fisique* PHYSIC]

physicist ('fɪzɪsɪst) *n* a person versed in or studying physics.

physics ('fɪzɪks) *n (functioning as sing)* **1** the branch of science concerned with the properties of matter and energy and the relationships between them. It is based on mathematics and traditionally includes mechanics, optics, electricity and magnetism, acoustics, and heat. Modern physics, based on quantum theory, includes atomic, nuclear, particle, and solid-state studies. **2** physical properties of behaviour: *the physics of the electron.* **3** *Arch.* natural science. [C16: from L *physica,* translation of Gk *ta phusika* natural things, from *phusis* nature]

physio ('fɪzɪəʊ) *n Inf.* **1** short for **physiotherapy. 2** *(pl* **physios)** short for **physiotherapist.**

physio- *or before a vowel* **phys-** *combining form.* **1** of or relating to nature or natural functions: *physiology.* **2** physical: *physiotherapy.* [from Gk *phusio,* ult. from *phuein* to make grow]

physiocrat ('fɪzɪəʊˌkræt) *n* a believer in the 18th-century French economic theory that the inherent natural order governing society was based on land and its natural products as the only true form of wealth. [C18: from F *physiocrate;* see PHYSIO-, -CRAT]
▸**physiocracy** (ˌfɪzɪ'ɒkrəsɪ) *n*

physiognomy ❶ (ˌfɪzɪ'ɒnəmɪ) *n* **1** a person's features considered as an indication of personality. **2** the art or practice of judging character from facial features. **3** the outward appearance of something. [C14: from OF *phisonomie,* via Med. L, from LGk *phusiognōmia,* from *phusis* nature + *gnōmōn* judge]
▸**physiognomic** (ˌfɪzɪə'nɒmɪk) *or* ˌ**physiog'nomical** *adj* ▸ˌ**physiog'nomically** *adv* ▸ˌ**physi'ognomist** *n*

physiography (ˌfɪzɪ'ɒgrəfɪ) *n* another name for **geomorphology** or **physical geography.**
▸ˌ**physi'ographer** *n* ▸**physiographic** (ˌfɪzɪə'græfɪk) *or* ˌ**physio'graphical** *adj*

physiol. *abbrev. for:* **1** physiological. **2** physiology.

physiology (ˌfɪzɪ'ɒlədʒɪ) *n* **1** the branch of science concerned with the functioning of organisms. **2** the processes and functions of all or part of an organism. [C16: from L *physiologia,* from Gk]
▸ˌ**physi'ologist** *n* ▸**physiological** (ˌfɪzɪə'lɒdʒɪkᵊl) *adj* ▸ˌ**physio'logically** *adv*

physiotherapy (ˌfɪzɪəʊ'θerəpɪ) *n* the treatment of disease, injury, etc., by physical means, such as massage or exercises, rather than by drugs.
▸ˌ**physio'therapist** *n*

physique ❶ (fɪ'zi:k) *n* the general appearance of the body with regard to size, shape, muscular development, etc. [C19: via F from *physique* (adj) natural, from L *physicus* physical]

-phyte *n combining form.* indicating a plant of a specified type or habitat: *lithophyte.* [from Gk *phuton* plant]
▸**-phytic** *adj combining form.*

phyto- *or before a vowel* **phyt-** *combining form.* indicating a plant or vegetation: *phytogenesis.* [from Gk *phuton* plant, from *phuein* to make grow]

phytochrome ('faɪtəʊˌkrəʊm) *n Bot.* a blue-green pigment, present in most plants, that mediates many light-dependent processes, including photoperiodism and the greening of leaves.

phytogenesis (ˌfaɪtəʊ'dʒenɪsɪs) *or* **phytogeny** (faɪ'tɒdʒənɪ) *n* the branch of botany concerned with the origin and evolution of plants.

phyton ('faɪtɒn) *n* a unit of plant structure, usually considered as the smallest part of the plant that is capable of growth when detached from the parent plant. [C20: from Gk; see -PHYTE]

phytopathology (ˌfaɪtəʊpə'θɒlədʒɪ) *n* the branch of botany concerned with diseases of plants.

phytoplankton (ˌfaɪtə'plæŋktən) *n* the photosynthesizing constituent of plankton, mainly unicellular algae.

phytotoxin (ˌfaɪtə'tɒksɪn) *n* a toxin, such as strychnine, that is produced by a plant.
▸ˌ**phyto'toxic** *adj*

pi[1] (paɪ) *n, pl* **pis. 1** the 16th letter in the Greek alphabet (Π, π). **2** *Maths.* a transcendental number, fundamental to mathematics, that is the ratio of the circumference of a circle to its diameter. Approximate value: 3.141 592... ; symbol: π [C18 (mathematical use): representing the first letter of Gk *periphereia* PERIPHERY]

pi[2] *or* **pie** (paɪ) *n, pl* **pies. 1** a jumbled pile of printer's type. **2** a jumbled mixture. ◆ *vb* **pies, piing, pied** *or* **pies, pieing, pied.** *(tr)* **3** to spill and mix (set type) indiscriminately. **4** to mix up. [C17: from ?]

pi[3] (paɪ) *adj Brit. sl.* short for **pious** (sense 3).

PI *abbrev. for:* **1** Phillipine Islands. **2** private investigator.

piacevole (pi:ætʃ'ervəʊleɪ) *adv Music.* in an agreeable, pleasant manner. [It.]

piacular (paɪ'ækjʊlə) *adj* **1** making expiation. **2** requiring expiation. [C17: from L *piāculum* propitiatory sacrifice, from *piāre* to appease]

piaffe (pɪ'æf) *n Dressage.* a slow trot done on the spot. [C18: from F, from *piaffer* to strut]

pia mater ('paɪə 'meɪtə) *n* the innermost of the three membranes (see **meninges**) that cover the brain and spinal cord. [C16: from Med. L, lit.: pious mother]

pianism ('pi:əˌnɪzəm) *n* technique, skill, or artistry in playing the piano.
▸ˌ**pia'nistic** *adj*

pianissimo (pɪə'nɪsɪˌməʊ) *adj, adv Music.* to be performed very quietly. Symbol: *pp* [C18: from It., sup. of *piano* soft]

pianist ('pɪənɪst) *n* a person who plays the piano.

piano[1] (pɪ'ænəʊ) *n, pl* **pianos.** a musical stringed instrument played by depressing keys that cause hammers to strike the strings and produce audible vibrations. [C19: short for PIANOFORTE]

piano[2] ('pjɑ:nəʊ) *adj, adv Music.* to be performed softly. [C17: from It., from L *plānus* flat]

piano accordion (pɪ'ænəʊ) *n* an accordion in which the right hand plays a piano-like keyboard. See **accordion.**
▸**piano accordionist** *n*

pianoforte (pɪˌænəʊ'fɔ:tɪ) *n* the full name for **piano**[1]. [C18: from It., orig. *(gravecembalo col) piano e forte* (harpsichord with) soft & loud; see PIANO[2], FORTE[2]]

Pianola (pɪə'nəʊlə) *n Trademark.* a type of mechanical piano in which the keys are depressed by air pressure, this air flow being regulated by perforations in a paper roll.

piano roll (pɪ'ænəʊ) *n* a perforated roll of paper for a Pianola.

piastre *or* **piaster** (pɪ'æstə) *n* **1** (formerly) the standard monetary unit of South Vietnam. **2a** a fractional monetary unit of Egypt, Lebanon, and Syria worth one hundredth of a pound: also used in the Sudan but its use is being phased out. **2b** Also called: **kurus.** a Turkish monetary unit worth one hundredth of a lira. **2c** a Libyan monetary unit worth one hundredth of a dinar. [C17: from F *piastre,* from It. *piastra d'argento* silver plate]

piazza (pɪ'ætsə; *Italian* 'pjattsa) *n* **1** a large open square in an Italian town. **2** *Chiefly Brit.* a covered passageway or gallery. [C16: from It.: marketplace, from L *platēa* courtyard, from Gk *plateia;* see PLACE]

pibroch ('pi:brɒk; *Gaelic* 'pi:brɒx) *n* a form of music for Scottish bagpipes, consisting of a theme and variations. [C18: from Gaelic *piobaireachd,* from *piobair* piper]

pic (pɪk) *n, pl* **pics** *or* **pix.** *Inf.* a photograph or illustration. [C20: shortened from PICTURE]

pica[1] ('paɪkə) *n* **1** another word for **em. 2** (formerly) a size of printer's type equal to 12 point. **3** a typewriter type size having 10 characters to the inch. [C15: from Anglo-L *pīca* list of ecclesiastical regulations, apparently from L *pīca* magpie, with reference to its habit of collecting things; the connection between the orig. sense & the typography meanings is obscure]

pica[2] ('paɪkə) *n Pathol.* an abnormal craving to ingest substances such as clay, dirt, or hair. [C16: from Medical L, from L: magpie, an allusion to its omnivorous feeding habits]

picador ('pɪkəˌdɔ:) *n Bullfighting.* a horseman who pricks the bull with a lance to weaken it. [C18: from Sp., lit.: pricker, from *picar* to prick]

picaresque (ˌpɪkə'resk) *adj* of or relating to a type of fiction in which the hero, a rogue, goes through a series of episodic adventures. [C19: via F from Sp. *picaresco,* from *pícaro* a rogue]

picaroon (ˌpɪkə'ru:n) *n Arch.* an adventurer or rogue. [C17: from Sp. *picarón,* from *pícaro*]

picayune (ˌpɪkə'ju:n) *adj also* **picayunish.** *US & Canad. inf.* **1** of small value or importance. **2** mean; petty. ◆ *n* **3** any coin of little value, esp. a five-cent piece. **4** an unimportant person or thing. [C19: from F *picaillon* coin from Piedmont, from Provençal *picaioun,* from ?]

piccalilli ('pɪkəˌlɪlɪ) *n* a pickle of mixed vegetables in a mustard sauce. [C18 *piccalillo,* ? based on PICKLE]

piccanin ('pɪkəˌnɪn) *n S. African offens.* a Black African child. [var. of PICCANINNY]

piccaninny *or esp. US* **pickaninny** (ˌpɪkə'nɪnɪ) *n, pl* **piccaninnies** *or esp. US* **pickaninnies.** *Offens.* a small Black child. [C17: ?from Port. *pequenino* tiny one, from *pequeno* small]

piccolo ('pɪkəˌləʊ) *n, pl* **piccolos.** a woodwind instrument an octave higher than the flute. [C19: from It.: small]

pick[1] ❶ (pɪk) *vb* **1** to choose (something) deliberately or carefully, as from a number; select. **2** to pluck or gather (fruit, berries, or crops) from (a tree, bush, field, etc.). **3** *(tr)* to remove loose particles from (the teeth, the nose, etc.). **4** (esp. of birds) to nibble or gather (corn, etc.). **5** *(tr)* to pierce, dig, or break up (a hard surface) with a pick. **6** *(tr)* to form (a hole, etc.) in this way. **7** (when *intr,* foll. by *at)* to nibble (at) fussily or without appetite. **8** to separate (strands, fibres, etc.), as in weaving. **9** *(tr)* to provoke (an argument, fight, etc.) deliberately. **10** *(tr)* to steal (money or valuables) from (a person's pocket). **11** *(tr)* to open (a lock) with an instrument other than a key. **12** to pluck the strings of (a guitar, banjo, etc.). **13** *(tr)* to make (one's way) carefully on foot: *they picked their way through the rubble.* **14 pick and choose.** to select fastidiously, fussily, etc. **15 pick someone's brains.** to obtain information or ideas from someone. ◆ *n* **16** freedom or right of selection (esp. in **take one's pick). 17** a person, thing, etc., that is chosen first or preferred: *the pick of the bunch.* **18** the act of picking. **19** the amount of

THESAURUS

medic (*inf.*), medical practitioner, medico (*inf.*), sawbones (*sl.*), specialist

physiognomy *n* **1** = **face,** clock (*Brit. sl.*), countenance, dial (*Brit. sl.*), features, look, phiz (*sl.*), phizog (*sl.*), visage

physique *n* = **build,** body, constitution, figure, form, frame, make-up, shape, structure

pick[1] *vb* **1** = **select,** cherry-pick, choose, decide upon, elect, fix upon, hand-pick, mark out, opt for, settle upon, sift out, single out, sort out pull **2** = **gather,** collect, cull, cut, harvest, pluck, pull **7** = **nibble,** have no appetite, peck at, play *or* toy with, push the food round the plate **9** = **provoke,** foment, incite, instigate, start **11** = **open,** break into, break open, crack, force, jemmy, prise open ◆ *n* **16** = **choice,** choosing, decision, option, preference, selection **17** = **the best,** choicest, *crème de la crème,* elect, elite, flower, pride, prize, the cream, the tops (*sl.*)

Antonyms *vb* ≠ **select:** cast aside, decline, discard, dismiss, reject, spurn, turn down a crop picked at one period or from one area. ◆ See also **pick at, pick off,** etc. [C15: from earlier *piken* to pick, infl. by F *piquer* to pierce] ▸**'picker** *n*

pick[2] (pɪk) *n* **1** a tool with a handle carrying a long steel head curved and tapering to a point at one or both ends, used for loosening soil, breaking rocks, etc. **2** any of various tools used for picking, such as an ice pick or toothpick. **3** a plectrum. [C14: ? a var. of PIKE[2]]

pickaback ('pɪkəˌbæk) *n, adv* another word for **piggyback.**

pick at Ⓣ *vb (intr, prep)* to make criticisms of in a niggling or petty manner.

pickaxe *or US* **pickax** ('pɪkˌæks) *n* **1** a large pick or mattock. ◆ *vb* **pickaxes, pickaxing, pickaxed. 2** to use a pickaxe on (earth, rocks, etc.). [C15: from earlier *pikois* (but infl. also by AXE), from OF, from *pic* PICK[2]]

pickerel ('pɪkərəl, 'pɪkrəl) *n, pl* **pickerel** *or* **pickerels. 1** a small pike. **2** any of several North American freshwater game fishes of the pike family. [C14: dim. of PIKE[1]]

picket Ⓣ ('pɪkɪt) *n* **1** a pointed stake that is driven into the ground to support a fence, etc. **2** an individual or group standing outside an establishment to make a protest, to dissuade or prevent employees or clients from entering, etc. **3** a small detachment of troops positioned to give early warning of attack. ◆ *vb* **4** to post or serve as pickets at (a factory, embassy, etc.). **5** to guard (a main body or place) by using or acting as a picket. **6** *(tr)* to fasten (a horse or other animal) to a picket. **7** *(tr)* to fence (an area, etc.) with pickets. [C18: from F *piquet,* from OF *piquer* to prick; see PIKE[2]] ▸**'picketer** *n*

picket fence *n* a fence consisting of pickets driven into the ground.

picket line *n* a line of people acting as pickets.

pickings Ⓣ ('pɪkɪŋz) *pl n (sometimes sing)* money, profits, etc., acquired easily; spoils.

pickle Ⓣ ('pɪkᵊl) *n* **1** *(often pl)* vegetables, such as onions, etc., preserved in vinegar, brine, etc. **2** any food preserved in this way. **3** a liquid or marinade, such as spiced vinegar, for preserving vegetables, meat, fish, etc. **4** *Chiefly US & Canad.* a cucumber that has been preserved and flavoured in a pickling solution, as brine or vinegar. **5** *Inf.* an awkward or difficult situation: *to be in a pickle.* **6** *Brit. inf.* a mischievous child. ◆ *vb* **pickles, pickling, pickled.** *(tr)* **7** to preserve in a pickling liquid. **8** to immerse (a metallic object) in a liquid, such as an acid, to remove surface scale. [C14: ?from MDu. *pekel*] ▸**'pickler** *n*

pickled ('pɪkᵊld) *adj* **1** preserved in a pickling liquid. **2** *Inf.* intoxicated; drunk.

picklock ('pɪkˌlɒk) *n* **1** a person who picks locks. **2** an instrument for picking locks.

pick-me-up Ⓣ *n Inf.* a tonic or restorative, esp. a special drink taken as a stimulant.

pick off *vb (tr, adv)* to aim at and shoot one by one.

pick on Ⓣ *vb (intr, prep)* to select for something unpleasant, esp. in order to bully or blame.

pick out Ⓣ *vb (tr, adv)* **1** to select for use or special consideration, etc., as from a group. **2** to distinguish (an object from its surroundings), as in painting: *she picked out the woodwork in white.* **3** to recognize (a person or thing): *we picked out his face among the crowd.* **4** to distinguish (sense or meaning) as from a mass of detail or complication. **5** to play (a tune) tentatively, as by ear.

pickpocket ('pɪkˌpɒkɪt) *n* a person who steals from the pockets of others in public places.

pick-up Ⓣ *n* **1** the light balanced arm of a record player that carries the wires from the cartridge to the preamplifier. **2** an electromagnetic transducer that converts vibrations into electric signals. **3** another name for **cartridge** (sense 2). **4** Also called: **pick-up truck.** a small truck with an open body used for light deliveries. **5** *Inf., chiefly US.* an ability to accelerate rapidly: *this car has good pick-up.* **6** *Inf.* a casual acquaintance, usually one made with sexual intentions. **7** *Inf.* **7a** a stop to collect passengers, goods, etc. **7b** the people or things collected. **8** *Inf.* an improvement. **9** *Sl.* a pick-me-up. ◆ *adj* **10** *US & Canad.* organized or assembled hastily and without planning: *a pick-up game.* ◆ *vb* **pick up.** *(adv)* **11** *(tr)* to gather up in the hand or hands. **12** *(reflexive)* to raise (oneself) after a fall or setback. **13** *(tr)* to obtain casually, incidentally, etc. **14** *(intr)* to improve in health, condition, activity, etc.: *the market began to pick up.* **15** *(tr)* to learn gradually or as one goes along. **16** to resume; return to. **17** *(tr)* to accept the responsibility for paying (a bill). **18** *(tr)* to collect or give a lift to (passengers, goods, etc.). **19** *(tr) Inf.* to become acquainted with, esp. with a view to having sexual relations. **20** *(tr) Inf.* to arrest. **21** to increase (speed). **22** *(tr)* to receive (electrical signals, a radio signal, sounds, etc.).

Pickwickian (pɪk'wɪkɪən) *adj* **1** of, relating to, or resembling Mr Pickwick in Charles Dickens' *The Pickwick Papers,* esp. in being naive or benevolent. **2** (of the use or meaning of a word) odd or unusual.

picky Ⓣ ('pɪkɪ) *adj* **pickier, pickiest.** *Inf.* fussy; finicky. ▸**'pickily** *adv* ▸**'pickiness** *n*

picnic Ⓣ ('pɪknɪk) *n* **1** a trip or excursion on which people bring food to be eaten in the open air. **2a** any informal meal eaten outside. **2b** *(as modifier): a picnic lunch.* **3** *Inf.* an easy or agreeable task. ◆ *vb* **picnics, picnicking, picnicked. 4** *(intr)* to eat or take part in a picnic. [C18: from F *piquenique,* from ?] ▸**'picnicker** *n*

picnic races *pl n Austral.* horse races for amateur riders held in rural areas.

pico- *prefix* denoting 10^{-12}: *picofarad.* Symbol: p [from Sp. *pico* small quantity, odd number, peak]

picot ('piːkəʊ) *n* any of a pattern of small loops, as on lace. [C19: from F: small point, from *pic* point]

picotee (ˌpɪkə'tiː) *n* a type of carnation having pale petals edged with a darker colour. [C18: from F *picoté* marked with points, from *picot* PICOT]

picric acid ('pɪkrɪk) *n* a toxic sparingly soluble crystalline yellow acid used as a dye, antiseptic, and explosive. Formula: $C_6H_3(NO_2)_3$. Systematic name: **2,4,6-trinitrophenol.** [C19: from Gk *pikros* bitter + -IC]

Pict (pɪkt) *n* a member of any of the peoples who lived in N Britain in the first to the fourth centuries A.D. [OE *Peohtas;* later forms from LL *Picti* painted men, from *pingere* to paint] ▸**'Pictish** *adj*

pictograph ('pɪktəˌgrɑːf) *n* **1** a picture or symbol standing for a word or group of words, as in written Chinese. **2** a chart on which symbols are used to represent values. ◆ Also called: **pictogram.** [C19: from L *pictus,* from *pingere* to paint] ▸**pictographic** (ˌpɪktə'græfɪk) *adj* ▸**pictography** (pɪk'tɒgrəfɪ) *n*

pictorial Ⓣ (pɪk'tɔːrɪəl) *adj* **1** relating to, consisting of, or expressed by pictures. **2** (of language, style, etc.) suggesting a picture; vivid; graphic. ◆ *n* **3** a magazine, newspaper, etc., containing many pictures. [C17: from LL *pictōrius,* from L *pictor* painter, from *pingere* to paint] ▸**pic'torially** *adv*

picture Ⓣ ('pɪktʃə) *n* **1a** a visual representation of something, such as a person or scene, produced on a surface, as in a photograph, painting, etc. **1b** *(as modifier): picture gallery; picture postcard.* **2** a mental image: *a clear picture of events.* **3** a verbal description, esp. one that is vivid. **4** a situation considered as an observable scene: *the political picture.* **5** a person or thing resembling another: *he was the picture of his father.* **6** a person, scene, etc., typifying a particular state: *the picture of despair.* **7** the image on a television screen. **8** a motion picture; film. **9 the pictures.** *Chiefly Brit.* a cinema or film show. **10** another name for **tableau vivant. 11 in the picture.** informed about a situation. ◆ *vb* **pictures, picturing, pictured.** *(tr)* **12** to visualize or imagine. **13** to describe or depict, esp. vividly. **14** *(often passive)* to put in a picture or make a picture of: *they were pictured sitting on the rocks.* [C15: from L *pictūra* painting, from *pingere* to paint]

picture card *n* another name for **court card.**

picture hat *n* a hat with a very wide brim.

THESAURUS

pick at *vb* = **criticize,** carp, cavil, find fault, get at, nag, pick holes, pick to pieces, quibble

picket *n* **1** = **stake,** pale, paling, palisade, peg, post, stanchion, upright **2** = **protester,** demonstrator, flying picket, picketer **3** = **lookout,** guard, patrol, scout, sentinel, sentry, spotter, vedette *(Military),* watch ◆ *vb* **4** = **blockade,** boycott, demonstrate **7** = **fence,** corral, enclose, hedge in, palisade, pen in, rail in, shut in, wall in

pickings *pl n* = **profits,** booty, earnings, gravy *(sl.),* ill-gotten gains, loot, plunder, proceeds, returns, rewards, spoils, yield

pickle *n* **5** *Informal* = **predicament,** bind *(inf.),* difficulty, dilemma, fix *(inf.),* hot water *(inf.),* jam, quandary, scrape *(inf.),* spot *(inf.),* tight spot ◆ *vb* **7** = **preserve,** cure, keep, marinade, steep

pick-me-up *n Informal* = **tonic,** bracer *(inf.),* drink, pick-up, refreshment, restorative, shot in the arm *(inf.),* stimulant

pick on *vb* = **torment,** badger, bait, blame, bully, goad, hector, tease

pick out *vb* **1** = **select,** choose, cull, hand-pick, separate the sheep from the goats, single out, sort out **2, 3** = **identify,** discriminate, distinguish, make distinct, make out, notice, perceive, recognize, tell apart

pick-up *n* **5** *Informal, chiefly U.S.* = **acceleration,** response, revving *(inf.),* speed-up **8** *Informal* = **improvement,** change for the better, gain, rally, recovery, revival, rise, strengthening, upswing, upturn ◆ *vb* **pick up 11, 12** = **lift,** gather, grasp, hoist, raise, take up, uplift **13** = **obtain,** buy, come across, find, garner, happen upon, purchase, score *(sl.)* **14** = **recover,** be on the mend, gain, gain ground, get better, improve, make a comeback, mend, perk up, rally, take a turn for the better, turn the corner **15** = **learn,** acquire, get the hang of *(inf.),* master **18** = **collect,** call for, get, give someone a lift, go to get, uplift *(Scot.)* **20** *Informal* = **arrest,** apprehend, bust *(inf.),* collar *(inf.),* do *(sl.),* lift *(sl.),* nab *(inf.),* nail *(inf.),* nick *(sl., chiefly Brit.),* pinch *(inf.),* run in *(sl.),* take into custody

picky *adj Informal* = **fussy,** captious, carping, cavilling, choosy, critical, dainty, fastidious, fault-finding, finicky, nice, particular, pernickety *(inf.)*

picnic *n* **1, 2** = **excursion,** outdoor meal, outing **3** *Informal* = **walkover** *(inf.),* cakewalk, child's play *(inf.),* cinch *(sl.),* piece of cake *(Brit. inf.),* pushover *(sl.),* snap *(inf.)*

pictorial *adj* **1, 2** = **graphic,** expressive, illustrated, picturesque, representational, scenic, striking, vivid

picture *n* **1** = **representation,** delineation, drawing, effigy, engraving, illustration, image, likeness, painting, photograph, portrait, portrayal, print, similitude, sketch **3** = **description,** account, depiction, image, impression, recreation, report **5** = **double,** carbon copy, copy, dead ringer, duplicate, image, likeness, living image, lookalike, replica, ringer *(sl.),* spit *(inf., chiefly Brit.),* spit and image *(inf.),* spitting image *(inf.),* twin **6** = **personification,** archetype, embodiment, epitome, essence, living example, perfect example **8** = **film,** flick *(sl.),* motion picture, movie *(US inf.)* ◆ *vb* **12** = **imagine,** conceive of, envision, see, see in the mind's eye, visualize **13, 14** = **represent,** delineate, de-

picture moulding *n* **1** the edge around a framed picture. **2** Also called: **picture rail.** the moulding or rail near the top of a wall from which pictures are hung.
picture palace *or* **house** *n Brit., old-fashioned.* another name for **cinema.**
picturesque ⓘ (ˌpɪktʃə'rɛsk) *adj* **1** visually pleasing, esp. in being striking or quaint: *a picturesque view.* **2** (of language) graphic; vivid. [C18: from F *pittoresque* (but also infl. by PICTURE), from It., from *pittore* painter, from L *pictor*]
▸ˌ**pictur'esquely** *adv* ▸ˌ**pictur'esqueness** *n*
picture tube *n* another name for **television tube.**
picture window *n* a large window having a single pane of glass, usually facing a view.
picture writing *n* **1** any writing system that uses pictographs. **2** a system of artistic expression and communication using pictures.
PID *abbrev. for* pelvic inflammatory disease.
piddle ('pɪdᵊl) *vb* **piddles, piddling, piddled. 1** (*intr*) *Inf.* to urinate. **2** (when *tr*, often foll. by *away*) to spend (one's time) aimlessly; fritter. [C16: from ?]
▸'**piddler** *n*
piddling ⓘ ('pɪdlɪŋ) *adj Inf.* petty; trifling; trivial.
piddock ('pɪdək) *n* a marine bivalve boring into rock, clay, or wood by means of sawlike shell valves. [C19: from ?]
pidgin ('pɪdʒɪn) *n* a language made up of elements of two or more other languages and used for contacts, esp. trading contacts, between the speakers of other languages. [C19: ?from Chinese pronunciation of E *business*]
pidgin English *n* a pidgin in which one of the languages involved is English.
pie[1] (paɪ) *n* **1** a baked sweet or savoury filling in a pastry-lined dish, often covered with a pastry crust. **2 pie in the sky.** illusory hope or promise of some future good. [C14: from ?]
pie[2] (paɪ) *n* an archaic or dialect name for **magpie.** [C13: via OF from L *pīca* magpie]
pie[3] (paɪ) *n, vb* **pies, pieing, pied.** *Printing.* a variant spelling of **pi**[2].
piebald ⓘ ('paɪˌbɔːld) *adj* **1** marked in two colours, esp. black and white. ◆ *n* **2** a black-and-white horse. [C16: PIE[2] + BALD; see also PIED]
pie cart *n NZ.* a mobile van selling warmed-up food and drinks.
piece ⓘ (piːs) *n* **1** an amount or portion forming a separate mass or structure; bit: *a piece of wood.* **2** a small part, item, or amount forming part of a whole, esp. when broken off or separated: *a piece of bread.* **3** a length by which a commodity is sold, esp. cloth, wallpaper, etc. **4** an instance or occurrence: *a piece of luck.* **5** an example or specimen of a style or type: *a beautiful piece of Dresden.* **6** *Inf.* an opinion or point of view: *to state one's piece.* **7** a literary, musical, or artistic composition. **8** a coin: *a fifty-pence piece.* **9** a small object used in playing certain games: *chess pieces.* **10** a firearm or cannon. **11** any chessman other than a pawn. **12** *Brit. dialect.* a packed lunch taken to work. **13** *NZ.* fragments of fleece wool. **14 go to pieces. 14a** (of a person) to lose control of oneself; have a breakdown. **14b** (of a building, organization, etc.) to disintegrate. **15 nasty piece of work.** *Brit. inf.* a cruel or mean person. **16 of a piece.** of the same kind; alike. ◆ *vb* **pieces, piecing, pieced.** (*tr*) **17** (often foll. by *together*) to fit or assemble piece by piece. **18** (often foll. by *up*) to patch or make up (a garment, etc.) by adding pieces. [C13 *pece*, from OF, of Gaulish origin]
pièce de résistance ⓘ *French.* (pjɛs də rezistɑ̃s) *n* **1** the principal or most outstanding item in a series. **2** the main dish of a meal. [lit.: piece of resistance]
piece goods *pl n* goods, esp. fabrics, made in standard widths and lengths.
piecemeal ⓘ ('piːsˌmiːl) *adv* **1** by degrees; bit by bit; gradually. **2** in or into pieces. ◆ *adj* **3** fragmentary or unsystematic: *a piecemeal approach.* [C13 *pecemele*, from PIECE + *-mele*, from OE *mælum* quantity taken at one time]
piece of eight *n, pl* **pieces of eight.** a former Spanish coin worth eight reals; peso.
piecework ('piːsˌwɜːk) *n* work paid for according to the quantity produced.
pie chart *n* a circular graph divided into sectors proportional to the magnitudes of the quantities represented.
piecrust table ('paɪˌkrʌst) *n* a round table, edged with moulding suggestive of a pie crust.
pied ⓘ (paɪd) *adj* having markings of two or more colours. [C14: from PIE[2]; an allusion to the magpie's colouring]
pied-à-terre (ˌpjeɪtɑː'tɛə) *n, pl* **pieds-à-terre** (ˌpjeɪtɑː'tɛə). a flat or other lodging for occasional use. [from F, lit.: foot on (the) ground]
piedmont ('piːdmɒnt) *adj* (*prenominal*) (of glaciers, plains, etc.) formed or situated at the foot of a mountain. [via F from It. *piémonte*, from *pié*, var. of *piede* foot + *mont* mountain]
pied wagtail *n* a British songbird with a black throat and back, long black tail, and white underparts and face.
pie-eyed *adj Sl.* drunk.
pier ⓘ (pɪə) *n* **1** a structure with a deck that is built out over water, and used as a landing place, promenade, etc. **2** a pillar that bears heavy loads. **3** the part of a wall between two adjacent openings. **4** another name for **buttress** (sense 1). [C12 *per*, from Anglo-L *pera* pier supporting a bridge]
pierce ⓘ (pɪəs) *vb* **pierces, piercing, pierced.** (*mainly tr*) **1** to form or cut (a hole) in (something) as with a sharp instrument. **2** to thrust into sharply or violently: *the thorn pierced his heel.* **3** to force (a way, route, etc.) through (something). **4** (of light, etc.) to shine through or penetrate (darkness). **5** (*also intr*) to discover or realize (something) suddenly or (of an idea, etc.) to become suddenly apparent. **6** (of sounds or cries) to sound sharply through (the silence, etc.). **7** to move or affect deeply or sharply: *the cold pierced their bones.* **8** (*intr*) to penetrate: *piercing cold.* [C13 *percen*, from OF *percer*, ult. from L *pertundere*, from *per* through + *tundere* to strike]
▸'**piercing** *adj* ▸'**piercingly** *adv*
pier glass *n* a tall narrow mirror, designed to hang on the wall between windows.
pieris ('paɪrɪs) *n* an evergreen shrub with white flowers like lily of the valley in spring. [C19: from L, from Gk *Pīeria* the haunt of the Muses]
Pierrot ('pɪərəʊ; *French* pjɛro) *n* **1** a male character from French pantomime with a whitened face, white costume, and pointed hat. **2** (*usually not cap.*) a clown so made up.
pier table *n* a side table designed to stand against a wall between windows.
pietà (pɪe'tɑː) *n* a sculpture, painting, or drawing of the dead Christ, supported by the Virgin Mary. [It.: pity, from L *pietās* PIETY]
pietism ('paɪɪˌtɪzəm) *n* exaggerated or affected piety.
▸'**pietist** *n* ▸ˌ**pie'tistic** *or* ˌ**pie'tistical** *adj*
piet-my-vrou ('pɪtˌmeɪ'frəʊ) *n S. African.* a red-breasted cuckoo. [imit.]
piety ⓘ ('paɪɪtɪ) *n, pl* **pieties. 1** dutiful devotion to God and observance of religious principles. **2** the quality of being pious. **3** a pious action, saying, etc. **4** *Now rare.* devotion and obedience to parents or superiors. [C13 *piete*, from OF, from L *pietās* piety, dutifulness, from *pius* pious]
piezoelectric effect (paɪˌiːzəʊɪ'lɛktrɪk) *or* **piezoelectricity** (paɪˌiːzəʊɪlɛk'trɪsɪtɪ) *n Physics.* **a** the production of electricity or electric polarity by applying a mechanical stress to certain crystals. **b** the converse effect in which stress is produced in a crystal as a result of an applied potential difference. [C19: from Gk *piezein* to press]
▸**piˌezoe'lectrically** *adv*
piffle ⓘ ('pɪfᵊl) *Inf.* ◆ *n* **1** nonsense. ◆ *vb* **piffles, piffling, piffled. 2** (*intr*) to talk or behave feebly. [C19: from ?]

THESAURUS

pict, describe, draw, illustrate, paint, photograph, portray, render, show, sketch
picturesque *adj* **1 = interesting**, attractive, beautiful, charming, pretty, quaint, scenic, striking **2 = vivid**, colourful, graphic
Antonyms *adj* ≠ **interesting:** commonplace, everyday, inartistic, unattractive, uninteresting ≠ **vivid:** drab, dull
piddling *adj Informal* **= trivial**, derisory, fiddling, insignificant, little, measly (*inf.*), Mickey Mouse (*sl.*), nickel-and-dime (*US sl.*), paltry, petty, piffling, puny, trifling, unimportant, useless, worthless
Antonyms *adj* considerable, important, major, significant, sizable *or* sizeable, substantial, tidy (*inf.*), useful, valuable
piebald *adj* **1 = pied**, black and white, brindled, dappled, flecked, mottled, speckled, spotted
piece *n* **1, 2 = bit**, allotment, chunk, division, fraction, fragment, length, morsel, mouthful, part, portion, quantity, scrap, section, segment, share, shred, slice **4, 5 = instance**, case, example, occurrence, sample, specimen, stroke **7 = work**, article, bit (*inf.*), composition, creation, item, production, study, work of art **14 go to pieces = break down**, crack up (*inf.*), crumple, disintegrate, fall apart, lose control, lose one's head **16 of a piece = alike**, analogous, consistent, identical, of the same kind, similar, the same, uniform ◆ *vb* **17** *often foll. by* **together = assemble**, compose, fix, join, mend, patch, repair, restore, unite
pièce de résistance *n* **1 = masterpiece**, *chef-d'oeuvre*, jewel, masterwork, showpiece
piecemeal *adv* **1 = bit by bit**, at intervals, by degrees, by fits and starts, fitfully, gradually, intermittently, little by little, partially, slowly ◆ *adj* **3 = unsystematic**, fragmentary, intermittent, interrupted, partial, patchy, spotty
pied *adj* **= variegated**, dappled, flecked, irregular, motley, mottled, multicoloured, particoloured, piebald, spotted, streaked, varicoloured
pier *n* **1 = jetty**, landing place, promenade, quay, wharf **2 = pillar**, buttress, column, pile, piling, post, support, upright
pierce *vb* **1, 2 = penetrate**, bore, drill, enter, impale, lance, perforate, prick, probe, puncture, run through, spike, stab, stick into, transfix **7 = hurt**, affect, cut, cut to the quick, excite, move, pain, rouse, sting, stir, strike, thrill, touch, wound
piercing *adj* **2 = sharp**, acute, agonizing, excruciating, exquisite, fierce, intense, painful, powerful, racking, severe, shooting, stabbing **5 = perceptive**, alert, aware, bright (*inf.*), keen, penetrating, perspicacious, probing, quick-witted, searching, sharp, shrewd **6 = penetrating**, ear-splitting, high-pitched, loud, sharp, shattering, shrill **7 = cold**, arctic, biting, bitter, freezing, frosty, keen, nipping, nippy, numbing, raw, wintry
Antonyms *adj* ≠ **perceptive:** obtuse, slow, slow-witted, thick, unperceptive ≠ **penetrating:** inaudible, low, low-pitched, mellifluous, quiet, soundless
piety *n* **1, 2 = holiness**, devotion, devoutness, dutifulness, duty, faith, godliness, grace, piousness, religion, reverence, sanctity, veneration
piffle *n* **1** *Informal* **= nonsense**, balderdash, bilge (*inf.*), bunk (*inf.*), bunkum *or* buncombe (*chiefly US*), codswallop, drivel, eyewash (*inf.*), garbage (*inf.*), hogwash, hot air (*inf.*), moonshine, pap, poppycock (*inf.*), rot, rubbish, tommyrot, tosh (*sl., chiefly Brit.*), trash, tripe (*inf.*), twaddle

piffling ❶ ('pɪflɪŋ) *adj Inf.* worthless; trivial.

pig ❶ (pɪg) *n* **1** any artiodactyl mammal of an African and Eurasian family, esp. the domestic pig, typically having a long head with a movable snout and a thick bristle-covered skin. Related adj: **porcine.** **2** *Inf.* a dirty, greedy, or bad-mannered person. **3** the meat of swine; pork. **4** *Derog.* a slang word for **policeman.** **5a** a mass of metal cast into a simple shape. **5b** the mould used. **6** *Brit. inf.* something that is difficult or unpleasant. **7 a pig in a poke.** something bought or received without prior sight or knowledge. **8 make a pig of oneself.** *Inf.* to overindulge oneself. ◆ *vb* **pigs, pigging, pigged. 9** (*intr*) (of a sow) to give birth. **10** (*intr*) Also: **pig it.** *Inf.* to live in squalor. **11** (*tr*) *Inf.* to devour (food) greedily. [C13 *pigge,* from ?]

pigeon[1] ❶ ('pɪdʒɪn) *n* **1** any of numerous related birds having a heavy body, small head, short legs, and long pointed wings. **2** *Sl.* a victim or dupe. [C14: from OF *pijon* young dove, from LL *pīpiō* young bird, from *pīpīre* to chirp]

pigeon[2] ❶ ('pɪdʒɪn) *n Brit. inf.* concern or responsibility (often in **it's his, her,** etc., **pigeon**). [C19: altered from PIDGIN]

pigeon breast *n* a deformity of the chest characterized by an abnormal protrusion of the breastbone, caused by rickets.

pigeonhole ❶ ('pɪdʒɪn,həʊl) *n* **1** a small compartment for papers, letters, etc., as in a bureau. **2** a hole or recess in a dovecote for pigeons to nest in. ◆ *vb* **pigeonholes, pigeonholing, pigeonholed.** (*tr*) **3** to put aside or defer. **4** to classify or categorize.

pigeon-toed *adj* having the toes turned inwards.

pigface ('pɪg,feɪs) *n Austral.* a creeping succulent plant having bright-coloured flowers and red fruits and often grown for ornament.

piggery ('pɪgərɪ) *n, pl* **piggeries. 1** a place where pigs are kept. **2** great greediness.

piggish ❶ ('pɪgɪʃ) *adj* **1** like a pig, esp. in appetite or manners. **2** *Inf., chiefly Brit.* obstinate or mean.
▸**'piggishly** *adv* ▸**'piggishness** *n*

piggy ('pɪgɪ) *n, pl* **piggies. 1** a child's word for a **pig. 2** a child's word for a **toe.** ◆ *adj* **piggier, piggiest. 3** another word for **piggish.**

piggyback ('pɪgɪ,bæk) *or* **pickaback** *n* **1** a ride on the back and shoulders of another person. **2** a system whereby a vehicle, aircraft, etc., is transported for part of its journey on another vehicle. ◆ *adv* **3** on the back and shoulders of another person. **4** on or as an addition. ◆ *adj* **5** of or for a piggyback: *a piggyback ride; piggyback lorry trains.* **6** of or relating to a type of heart transplant in which the transplanted heart functions in conjunction with the patient's own heart.

piggy bank *n* a child's coin bank shaped like a pig with a slot for coins.

pig-headed ❶ *adj* stupidly stubborn.
▸**,pig-'headedly** *adv* ▸**,pig-'headedness** *n*

pig iron *n* crude iron produced in a blast furnace and poured into moulds.

piglet ('pɪglɪt) *n* a young pig.

pigmeat ('pɪg,miːt) *n* a less common name for pork, ham, or bacon.

pigment ❶ ('pɪgmənt) *n* **1** a substance occurring in plant or animal tissue and producing a characteristic colour. **2** any substance used to impart colour. **3** a powder that is mixed with a liquid to give a paint, ink, etc. [C14: from L *pigmentum,* from *pingere* to paint]
▸**'pigmentary** *adj*

pigmentation (,pɪgmən'teɪʃən) *n* **1** coloration in plants, animals, or man caused by the presence of pigments. **2** the deposition of pigment in animals, plants, or man.

Pigmy ('pɪgmɪ) *n, pl* **Pigmies.** a variant spelling of **Pygmy.**

pignut ('pɪg,nʌt) *n* **1** Also called: **hognut. 1a** the bitter nut of any of several North American hickory trees. **1b** any of the trees bearing such a nut. **2** another name for **earthnut.**

pig-root *vb* (*intr*) *Austral. & NZ sl.* (of a horse) to buck slightly.

pigs (pɪgz) *interj Austral. sl.* an expression of derision or disagreement. Also: **pig's arse, pig's bum.**

pigskin ('pɪg,skɪn) *n* **1** the skin of the domestic pig. **2** leather made of this skin. **3** *US & Canad. inf.* a football. ◆ *adj* **4** made of pigskin.

pigsticking ('pɪg,stɪkɪŋ) *n* the sport of hunting wild boar.
▸**'pig,sticker** *n*

pigsty ('pɪg,staɪ) *or US & Canad.* **pigpen** *n, pl* **pigsties** *or US & Canad.* **pigpens. 1** a pen for pigs; sty. **2** *Brit.* an untidy place.

pigswill ('pɪg,swɪl) *n* waste food or other edible matter fed to pigs. Also called: **pig's wash.**

pigtail ('pɪg,teɪl) *n* **1** a plait of hair or one of two plaits on either side of the face. **2** a twisted roll of tobacco.

pika ('paɪkə) *n* a burrowing mammal of mountainous regions of North America and Asia, having short rounded ears, a rounded body, and rudimentary tail. [C19: from E Siberian *piika*]

pikau ('piːkaʊ) *n NZ.* a pack, knapsack, or rucksack. [Maori]

pike[1] (paɪk) *n, pl* **pike** *or* **pikes. 1** any of several large predatory freshwater teleost fishes having a broad flat snout, strong teeth, and an elongated body covered with small scales. **2** any of various similar fishes. [C14: short for *pikefish,* from OE *pīc* point, with reference to the shape of its jaw]

pike[2] (paɪk) *n* **1** a medieval weapon consisting of a metal spearhead joined to a long pole. **2** a point or spike. ◆ *vb* **pikes, piking, piked. 3** (*tr*) to pierce using a pike. [OE *pīc* point, from ?]
▸**'pikeman** *n*

pike[3] (paɪk) *n* short for **turnpike** (sense 1).

pike[4] (paɪk) *n Northern English dialect.* a pointed or conical hill. [OE *pīc*]

pike[5] (paɪk) *or* **piked** (paɪkt) *adj* (of the body position of a diver) bent at the hips but with the legs straight.

pike[6] (paɪk) *vb* **pikes, piking, piked.** (*intr;* foll. by *out*) *Austral. sl.* to shirk. [from PIKER]

pikeperch ('paɪk,pɜːtʃ) *n, pl* **pikeperch** *or* **pikeperches.** any of various pike-like freshwater teleost fishes of the perch family of Europe.

piker ('paɪkə) *n US, Austral., & NZ sl.* **1** a person who will not accept a challenge; shirker. **2** a mean person. [C19: from *Pike* county, Missouri, US]

pikestaff ('paɪk,stɑːf) *n* the wooden handle of a pike.

pilaster (pɪ'læstə) *n* a shallow rectangular column attached to the face of a wall. [C16: from F *pilastre,* from L *pīla* pillar]
▸**pi'lastered** *adj*

pilau (pɪ'laʊ), **pilaf, pilaff** ('pɪlæf), *or* **pilaw** (pɪ'lɔː) *n* a dish originating from the East, consisting of rice flavoured with spices and cooked in stock, to which meat, poultry, or fish may be added. [C17: from Turkish *pilāw,* from Persian]

pilchard ('pɪltʃəd) *n* a European food fish of the herring family, with a rounded body covered with large scales. [C16 *pylcher,* from ?]

pile[1] ❶ (paɪl) *n* **1** a collection of objects laid on top of one another; heap; mound. **2** *Inf.* a large amount of money (esp. in **make a pile**). **3** (*often pl*) *Inf.* a large amount: *a pile of work.* **4** a less common word for **pyre. 5** a large building or group of buildings. **6** *Physics.* a structure of uranium and a moderator used for producing atomic energy; nuclear reactor. ◆ *vb* **piles, piling, piled. 7** (often foll. by *up*) to collect or be collected into or as if into a pile: *snow piled up in the drive.* **8** (*intr;* foll. by *in, into, off, out,* etc.) to move in a group, esp. in a hurried or disorganized manner: *to pile off the bus.* **9 pile it on.** *Inf.* to exaggerate. ◆ See also **pile up.** [C15: via OF from L *pīla* stone pier]

pile[2] ❶ (paɪl) *n* **1** a long column of timber, concrete, or steel, driven into the ground as a foundation for a structure. ◆ *vb* **piles, piling, piled.** (*tr*) **2** to drive (piles) into the ground. **3** to support (a structure) with piles. [OE *pīl,* from L *pīlum*]

pile[3] ❶ (paɪl) *n* **1** the yarns in a fabric that stand up or out from the weave, as in carpeting, velvet, etc. **2** soft fine hair, fur, wool, etc. [C15: from Anglo-Norman *pyle,* from L *pilus* hair]

pileate ('paɪlɪɪt, -,eɪt, 'pɪl-) *or* **pileated** ('paɪlɪ,eɪtɪd, 'pɪl-) *adj* **1** (of birds) having a crest. **2** *Bot.* having a pileus. [C18: from L *pileātus* wearing a felt cap, from PILEUS]

pile-driver *n* a machine that drives piles into the ground.

pileous ('paɪlɪəs, 'pɪl-) *adj Biol.* **1** hairy. **2** of or relating to hair. [C19: ult. from L *pilus* a hair]

piles ❶ (paɪlz) *pl n* a nontechnical name for **haemorrhoids.** [C15: from L *pilae* balls (referring to the external piles)]

pileum ('paɪlɪəm, 'pɪl-) *n, pl* **pilea** (-lɪə). the top of a bird's head from the base of the bill to the occiput. [C19: NL, from L PILEUS]

pile up ❶ *vb* (*adv*) **1** to gather or be gathered in a pile. **2** *Inf.* to crash or cause to crash. ◆ *n* **pile-up. 3** *Inf.* a multiple collision of vehicles.

pileus ('paɪlɪəs) *n, pl* **pilei** (-lɪ,aɪ). the upper cap-shaped part of a mushroom. [C18: (botanical use): NL, from L: felt cap]

THESAURUS

piffling *adj Informal* = **trivial**, derisory, fiddling, insignificant, little, measly (*inf.*), Mickey Mouse (*sl.*), paltry, petty, piddling (*inf.*), puny, trifling, unimportant, useless, worthless

pig *n* **1** = **hog**, boar, grunter, piggy, piglet, porker, shoat, sow, swine **2** *Informal* = **slob** (*sl.*), animal, beast, boor, brute, glutton, greedy guts (*sl.*), guzzler, hog (*inf.*), sloven, swine

pigeon[1] *n* **1** = **dove**, bird, culver (*arch.*), cushat, squab **2** *Slang* = **victim**, dupe, fall guy (*inf.*), gull (*arch.*), mug (*Brit. sl.*), sitting duck, sitting target, sucker (*sl.*)

pigeon[2] *n Brit. informal* = **responsibility**, baby (*sl.*), business, concern, lookout (*inf.*), worry

pigeonhole *n* **1** = **compartment**, cubbyhole, cubicle, locker, niche, place, section **2** = **classification**, category, class, slot (*inf.*) ◆ *vb* **3** = **put off**, defer, file, postpone, shelve **4** = **classify**, catalogue, categorize, characterize, codify, compartmentalize, ghettoize, label, slot (*inf.*), sort

piggish *adj* **1** = **greedy**, boorish, crude, gluttonous, hoggish, piggy, rude, swinish, voracious **2** *Informal* = **stubborn**, mean, obstinate, pig-headed, possessive, selfish

pig-headed *adj* = **stubborn**, bull-headed, contrary, cross-grained, dense, froward (*arch.*), inflexible, mulish, obstinate, perverse, self-willed, stiff-necked, stupid, unyielding, wilful, wrong-headed
Antonyms *adj* agreeable, amiable, complaisant, cooperative, flexible, obliging, open-minded, tractable

pigment *n* **2** = **colour**, colorant, colouring, colouring matter, dye, dyestuff, paint, stain, tincture, tint

pile[1] *n* **1** = **heap**, accumulation, assemblage, assortment, collection, hoard, mass, mound, mountain, rick, stack, stockpile **2** *Informal* = **fortune**, big money, bomb (*Brit. sl.*), mint, money, packet (*sl.*), pot, pretty penny (*inf.*), tidy sum (*inf.*), wealth **3** *often plural Informal* = **a lot**, great deal, ocean, oodles (*inf.*), quantity, stacks **5** = **building**, edifice, erection, structure ◆ *vb* **7** = **collect**, accumulate, amass, assemble, gather, heap, hoard, load up, mass, stack, store **8** = **crowd**, charge, crush, flock, flood, jam, pack, rush, stream

pile[2] *n* **1** = **foundation**, beam, column, pier, piling, pillar, post, support, upright

pile[3] *n* **1, 2** = **nap**, down, fibre, filament, fur, hair, plush, shag, surface

piles *pl n* = **haemorrhoids**

pile up *n* **pile-up 3** *Informal* = **collision**, accident, crash, multiple collision, smash, smash-up (*inf.*)

pilewort ('paɪl,wɜːt) *n* any of several plants, such as lesser celandine, thought to be effective in treating piles.

pilfer ❶ ('pɪlfə) *vb* to steal (minor items), esp. in small quantities. [C14 *pylfre* (n) from OF *pelfre* booty]
▸'**pilferage** *n* ▸'**pilferer** *n*

pilgrim ❶ ('pɪlgrɪm) *n* **1** a person who undertakes a journey to a sacred place. **2** any wayfarer. [C12: from Provençal *pelegrin*, from L *peregrīnus* foreign, from *per* through + *ager* land]

pilgrimage ❶ ('pɪlgrɪmɪdʒ) *n* **1** a journey to a shrine or other sacred place. **2** a journey or long search made for exalted or sentimental reasons. ◆ *vb* **pilgrimages, pilgrimaging, pilgrimaged. 3** (*intr*) to make a pilgrimage.

Pilgrim Fathers *or* **Pilgrims** *pl n* **the.** the English Puritans who sailed on the Mayflower to New England, where they founded Plymouth Colony in SE Massachusetts (1620).

piliferous (paɪ'lɪfərəs) *adj* (esp. of plants) bearing or ending in a hair or hairs. [C19: from L *pilus* hair + -FEROUS]
▸'**pili,form** *adj*

piling ('paɪlɪŋ) *n* **1** the act of driving piles. **2** a number of piles. **3** a structure formed of piles.

pill[1] ❶ (pɪl) *n* **1** a small spherical or ovoid mass of a medicinal substance, intended to be swallowed whole. **2 the pill.** (*sometimes cap.*) *Inf.* an oral contraceptive. **3** something unpleasant that must be endured (esp. in **bitter pill to swallow**). **4** *Sl.* a ball or disc. **5** *Sl.* an unpleasant or boring person. ◆ *vb* **6** (*tr*) to give pills to. [C15: from MFlemish *pille*, from L *pilula* a little ball, from *pila* ball]

pill[2] (pɪl) *vb* **1** *Arch. or dialect.* to peel or skin (something). **2** *Arch.* to pillage or plunder (a place, etc.). [OE *pilian*, from L *pilāre* to strip]

pillage ❶ ('pɪlɪdʒ) *vb* **pillages, pillaging, pillaged. 1** to rob (a town, village, etc.) of (booty or spoils). ◆ *n* **2** the act of pillaging. **3** something obtained by pillaging; booty. [C14: via OF from *piller* to despoil, prob. from *peille* rag, from L *pīleus* felt cap]
▸'**pillager** *n*

pillar ❶ ('pɪlə) *n* **1** an upright structure of stone, brick, metal, etc. that supports a superstructure. **2** something resembling this in shape or function: *a pillar of smoke.* **3** a prominent supporter: *a pillar of the Church.* **4 from pillar to post.** from one place to another. [C13: from OF *pilier*, from L *pīla*]

pillar box *n* (in Britain) a red pillar-shaped public letter box situated on a pavement.

pillbox ('pɪl,bɒks) *n* **1** a box for pills. **2** a small enclosed fortified emplacement, made of reinforced concrete. **3** a small round hat.

pillion ('pɪljən) *n* **1** a seat or place behind the rider of a motorcycle, scooter, horse, etc. ◆ *adv* **2** on a pillion: *to ride pillion.* [C16: from Gaelic; cf. Scot. *pillean*, Irish *pillīn* couch]

pilliwinks ('pɪlɪ,wɪŋks) *pl n* a medieval instrument of torture for the fingers. [C14: from ?]

pillock ('pɪlək) *n Brit. sl.* a stupid or annoying person. [C14: from Scand. dialect *pillicock* penis]

pillory ❶ ('pɪlərɪ) *n, pl* **pillories. 1** a wooden framework into which offenders were formerly locked by the neck and wrists and exposed to public abuse and ridicule. **2** exposure to public scorn or abuse. ◆ *vb* **pillories, pillorying, pilloried.** (*tr*) **3** to expose to public scorn or ridicule. **4** to punish by putting in a pillory. [C13: from Anglo-L *pillorium*, from OF *pilori*, from ?]

pillow ('pɪləʊ) *n* **1** a cloth case stuffed with feathers, foam rubber, etc., used to support the head, esp. during sleep. **2** Also called: **cushion.** a padded cushion or board on which pillow lace is made. **3** anything like a pillow in shape or function. ◆ *vb* (*tr*) **4** to rest (one's head) on or as if on a pillow. **5** to serve as a pillow for. [OE *pylwe*, from L *pulvīnus* cushion]

pillowcase ('pɪləʊ,keɪs) *or* **pillowslip** ('pɪləʊ,slɪp) *n* a removable washable cover of cotton, linen, nylon, etc., for a pillow.

pillow fight *n* a mock fight in which participants thump each other with pillows.

pillow lace *n* lace made by winding thread around bobbins on a padded cushion or board. Cf. **point lace.**

pillow talk *n* confidential talk between sexual partners in bed.

pilose ('paɪləʊz) *adj Biol.* covered with fine soft hairs: *pilose leaves.* [C18: from L *pilōsus*, from *pilus* hair]
▸**pilosity** (paɪ'lɒsɪtɪ) *n*

pilot ❶ ('paɪlət) *n* **1** a person who is qualified to operate an aircraft or spacecraft in flight. **2a** a person who is qualified to steer or guide a ship into or out of a port, river mouth, etc. **2b** (*as modifier*): *a pilot ship.* **3** a person who steers a ship. **4** a person who acts as a leader or guide. **5** *Machinery.* a guide used to assist in joining two mating parts together. **6** an experimental programme on radio or television. **7** (*modifier*) serving as a test or trial: *a pilot project.* **8** (*modifier*) serving as a guide: *a pilot beacon.* ◆ *vb* (*tr*) **9** to act as pilot of. **10** to control the course of. **11** to guide or lead (a project, people, etc.). [C16: from F *pilote*, from Med. L *pilotus*, ult. from Gk *pēdon* oar]

pilotage ('paɪlətɪdʒ) *n* **1** the act of piloting an aircraft or ship. **2** a pilot's fee.

pilot balloon *n* a meteorological balloon used to observe air currents.

pilot fish *n* a small fish of tropical and subtropical seas, marked with dark vertical bands: often accompanies sharks.

pilot house *n Naut.* an enclosed structure on the bridge of a vessel from which it can be navigated; a wheelhouse.

pilot lamp *n* a small light in an electric circuit or device that lights when the current is on.

pilot light *n* **1** a small auxiliary flame that ignites the main burner of a gas appliance. **2** a small electric light used as an indicator.

pilot officer *n* the most junior commissioned rank in the British Royal Air Force and in certain other air forces.

pilot study *n* a small-scale experiment undertaken to decide whether and how to launch a full-scale project.

Pils (pɪlz, pɪls) *n* a type of lager-like beer. [C20: abbrev. of PILSNER]

Pilsner ('pɪlznə) *or* **Pilsener** *n* a type of pale beer with a strong flavour of hops. [after *Pilsen*, city in the N Czech Republic, where it was orig. brewed]

pilule ('pɪljuːl) *n* a small pill. [C16: via F from L *pilula* little ball, from *pila* ball]
▸'**pilular** *adj*

pimento (pɪ'mɛntəʊ) *n, pl* **pimentos.** another name for **allspice** or **pimiento.** [C17: from Sp. *pimiento* pepper plant, from Med. L *pigmenta* spiced drink, from L *pigmentum* PIGMENT]

pi meson *n* another name for **pion.**

pimiento (pɪ'mjɛntəʊ, -'mɛn-) *n, pl* **pimientos.** a Spanish pepper with a red fruit used as a vegetable. Also called: **pimento.** [var. of PIMENTO]

pimp[1] ❶ (pɪmp) *n* **1** a man who solicits for a prostitute or brothel. **2** a man who procures sexual gratification for another; procurer; pander. ◆ *vb* **3** (*intr*) to act as a pimp. [C17: from ?]

pimp[2] (pɪmp) *Sl., chiefly Austral. & NZ.* ◆ *n* **1** a spy or informer. ◆ *vb* **2** (*intr; often foll. by on*) to inform (on). [from ?]

pimpernel ('pɪmpə,nɛl, -nəl) *n* any of several plants, such as the scarlet pimpernel, typically having small star-shaped flowers. [C15: from OF *pimpernelle*, ult. from L *piper* PEPPER]

pimple ❶ ('pɪmpəl) *n* a small round usually inflamed swelling of the skin. [C14: rel. to OE *pipilian* to break out in spots]
▸'**pimpled** *adj* ▸'**pimply** *adj* ▸'**pimpliness** *n*

pin ❶ (pɪn) *n* **1** a short stiff straight piece of wire pointed at one end and either rounded or having a flattened head at the other: used mainly for fastening pieces of cloth, paper, etc. **2** short for **cotter pin, hairpin, panel pin, rolling pin,** or **safety pin. 3** an ornamental brooch, esp. a narrow one. **4** a badge worn fastened to the clothing by a pin. **5** something of little or no importance (esp. in **not care** *or* **give a pin (for)**). **6** a peg or dowel. **7** anything resembling a pin in shape, function, etc. **8** (in various bowling games) a usually club-shaped wooden object set up in groups as a target. **9** Also called: **safety pin.** a clip on a hand grenade that prevents its detonation until removed or released. **10** *Naut.* **10a** See **belaying pin. 10b** the sliding closure for a shackle. **11** *Music.* a metal tuning peg on a piano. **12** *Surgery.* a metal rod, esp. of stainless steel, for holding together adjacent ends of fractured bones during healing. **13** *Chess.* a position in which a piece is pinned against a more valuable piece or the king. **14** *Golf.* the flagpole marking the hole on a green. **15** (*usually pl*) *Inf.* a leg. ◆ *vb* **pins, pinning, pinned.** (*tr*) **16** to attach, hold, or fasten with or as if with a pin or pins. **17** to transfix with a pin, spear, etc. **18** (foll. by *on*) *Inf.* to place (the blame for something): *he pinned the charge on his accomplice.* **19** *Chess.* to cause (an enemy piece) to be effectively immobilized since moving it would reveal a check or expose a more valuable piece to capture. ◆ See also **pin down.** [OE *pinn*]

PIN (pɪn) *n acronym for* personal identification number: a number used by a holder of a cash card or credit card used in EFTPOS.

pinaceous (paɪ'neɪʃəs) *adj* of, relating to, or belonging to a family of conifers with needle-like leaves: includes pine, spruce, fir, larch, and cedar. [C19: via NL from L *pīnus* a pine]

pinafore ('pɪnə,fɔː) *n* **1** *Chiefly Brit.* an apron, esp. one with a bib. **2** Also called: **pinafore dress.** a dress with a sleeveless bodice or bib top, worn over a jumper or blouse. [C18: from PIN + AFORE]

THESAURUS

pilfer *vb* = **steal**, appropriate, blag, embezzle, filch, lift (*inf.*), pinch (*inf.*), purloin, rifle, rob, snaffle (*Brit. inf.*), snitch (*sl.*), swipe (*sl.*), take, thieve, walk off with

pilgrim *n* **1, 2** = **traveller**, crusader, hajji, palmer, wanderer, wayfarer

pilgrimage *n* **1, 2** = **journey**, crusade, excursion, expedition, hajj, mission, tour, trip

pill[1] *n* **1** = **tablet**, bolus, capsule, pellet, pilule **2 the pill** = **oral contraceptive 5** *Slang* = **trial**, bore, drag (*inf.*), nuisance, pain (*inf.*), pain in the neck (*inf.*), pest

pillage *vb* **1** = **plunder**, depredate (*rare*), despoil, freeboot, loot, maraud, raid, ransack, ravage, reive (*dialect*), rifle, rob, sack, spoil (*arch.*), spoliate, strip ◆ *n* **2** = **plunder**, depredation, devastation, marauding, rapine, robbery, sack, spoliation **3** = **booty**, loot, plunder, spoils

pillar *n* **1** = **support**, column, obelisk, pier, pilaster, piling, post, prop, shaft, stanchion, upright **3** = **supporter**, leader, leading light (*inf.*), mainstay, rock, torchbearer, tower of strength, upholder, worthy

pillory *vb* **3** = **ridicule**, brand, cast a slur on, denounce, expose to ridicule, heap *or* pour scorn on, hold up to shame, lash, show up, stigmatize

pilot *n* **1** = **airman**, aviator, captain, flyer **2-4** = **helmsman**, conductor, coxswain, director, guide, leader, navigator, steersman ◆ *modifier* **7** = **trial**, experimental, model, test ◆ *vb* **9-11** = **fly**, conduct, control, direct, drive, guide, handle, lead, manage, navigate, operate, shepherd, steer

pimp[1] *n* **1, 2** = **procurer**, bawd (*arch.*), go-between, pander, panderer, white-slaver, whoremaster (*arch.*) ◆ *vb* **3** = **procure**, live off immoral earnings, sell, solicit, tout

pimple *n* = **spot**, boil, papule, plook (*Scot.*), pustule, swelling, zit (*sl.*)

pin *vb* **16** = **fasten**, affix, attach, fix, join, secure

pinaster (paɪˈnæstə) *n* a Mediterranean pine tree with paired needles and prickly cones. Also called: **maritime** (*or* **cluster**) **pinaster.** [C16: from L: wild pine, from *pīnus* pine]

pinball (ˈpɪnˌbɔːl) *n* **a** a game in which the player shoots a small ball through several hazards on a table, electrically operated machine, etc. **b** (*as modifier*): *a pinball machine.*

pince-nez (ˈpænsˌneɪ, ˈpɪns-; *French* pɛ̃sne) *n, pl* **pince-nez.** eyeglasses that are held in place only by means of a clip over the bridge of the nose. [C19: F, lit.: pinch-nose]

pincers (ˈpɪnsəz) *pl n* **1** Also called: **pair of pincers.** a gripping tool consisting of two hinged arms with handles at one end and, at the other, curved bevelled jaws that close on the workpiece. **2** the pair or pairs of jointed grasping appendages in lobsters and certain other arthropods. [C14: from OF *pinceour,* from OF *pincier* to pinch]

pinch ❶ (pɪntʃ) *vb* **1** to press (something, esp. flesh) tightly between two surfaces, esp. between a finger and thumb. **2** to confine, squeeze, or painfully press (toes, fingers, etc.) because of lack of space: *these shoes pinch.* **3** (*tr*) to cause stinging pain to: *the cold pinched his face.* **4** (*tr*) to make thin or drawn-looking, as from grief, lack of food, etc. **5** (usually foll. by *on*) to provide (oneself or another person) with meagre allowances, amounts, etc. **6 pinch pennies.** to live frugally because of meanness or to economize. **7** (usually foll. by *off, out,* or *back*) to remove the tips of (buds, shoots, etc.) to correct or encourage growth. **8** (*tr*) *Inf.* to steal or take without asking. **9** (*tr*) *Inf.* to arrest. ◆ *n* **10** a squeeze or sustained nip. **11** the quantity of a substance, such as salt, that can be taken between a thumb and finger. **12** a very small quantity. **13** (usually preceded by *the*) sharp, painful, or extreme stress, need, etc.: *feeling the pinch of poverty.* **14** *Sl.* a robbery. **15** *Sl.* a police raid or arrest. **16 at a pinch.** if absolutely necessary. [C16: prob. from OF *pinchier* (unattested)]

pinchbeck (ˈpɪntʃˌbɛk) *n* **1** an alloy of copper and zinc, used as imitation gold. **2** a spurious or cheap imitation. ◆ *adj* **3** made of pinchbeck. **4** sham or cheap. [C18 (the alloy), C19 (something spurious): after C. *Pinchbeck* (?1670–1732), E watchmaker who invented it]

pinchpenny (ˈpɪntʃˌpɛnɪ) *adj* **1** niggardly; miserly. ◆ *n, pl* **pinchpennies. 2** a miserly person.

pincushion (ˈpɪnˌkʊʃən) *n* a small well-padded cushion in which pins are stuck ready for use.

pin down ❶ *vb* (*tr, adv*) **1** to force (someone) to make a decision or carry out a promise. **2** to define clearly: *he had a vague suspicion that he couldn't quite pin down.* **3** to confine to a place.

pine[1] (paɪn) *n* **1** any of a genus of evergreen resinous coniferous trees of the N hemisphere, with long needle-shaped leaves (**pine needles**) and brown cones. **2** the wood of any of these trees. [OE *pīn,* from L *pīnus* pine]

pine[2] ❶ (paɪn) *vb* **pines, pining, pined. 1** (*intr;* often foll. by *for* or an infinitive) to feel great longing or desire; yearn. **2** (*intr;* often foll. by *away*) to become ill or thin through worry, longing, etc. [OE *pīnian* to torture, from *pīn* pain, from Med. L *pēna,* from L *poena* PAIN]

pineal eye (ˈpɪnɪəl) *n* an outgrowth of the pineal gland that forms an eyelike structure on the top of the head in certain cold-blooded vertebrates. [C19: from F, from L *pīnea* pine cone]

pineal gland *or* **body** *n* a pea-sized organ situated at the base of the brain that secretes a hormone, melatonin, into the bloodstream. Technical names: **epiphysis, epiphysis cerebri.**

pineapple (ˈpaɪnˌæpᵊl) *n* **1** a tropical American plant cultivated for its large fleshy edible fruit. **2** the fruit of this plant, consisting of an inflorescence clustered around a fleshy axis and surmounted by a tuft of leaves. **3** *Mil. sl.* a hand grenade. [C14 *pinappel* pine cone; C17: applied to the fruit because of its appearance]

pine cone *n* the seed-producing structure of a pine tree. See **cone** (sense 3a).

pine marten *n* a marten of N European and Asian coniferous woods, having dark brown fur with a creamy-yellow patch on the throat.

pinene (ˈpaɪniːn) *n* either of two isomeric terpenes, found in many essential oils and constituting the main part of oil of turpentine. [C20: from PINE[1] + -ENE]

pine nut *or* **kernel** *n* the edible seed of certain pine trees.

pine tar *n* a brown or black semisolid, produced by the destructive distillation of pine wood, used in roofing compositions, paints, medicines, etc.

pinfeather (ˈpɪnˌfɛðə) *n Ornithol.* a feather emerging from the skin and still enclosed in its horny sheath.

pinfold (ˈpɪnˌfəʊld) *n* **1** a pound for stray cattle. ◆ *vb* **2** (*tr*) to gather or confine in or as if in a pinfold. [OE *pundfald*]

ping (pɪŋ) *n* **1** a short high-pitched resonant sound, as of a bullet striking metal or a sonar echo. ◆ *vb* **2** (*intr*) to make such a noise. [C19: imit.]

pinger (ˈpɪŋə) *n* a device that makes a pinging sound, esp. one that can be preset to ring at a particular time.

Ping-Pong (ˈpɪŋˌpɒŋ) *n Trademark.* another name for **table tennis.** Also: **ping pong.**

pinhead (ˈpɪnˌhɛd) *n* **1** the head of a pin. **2** something very small. **3** *Inf.* a stupid person.
▸ **ˈpinˌheaded** *adj* ▸ **ˈpinˌheadedness** *n*

pinhole (ˈpɪnˌhəʊl) *n* a small hole made with or as if with a pin.

pinion[1] ❶ (ˈpɪnjən) *n* **1** *Chiefly poetic.* a bird's wing. **2** the part of a bird's wing including the flight feathers. ◆ *vb* (*tr*) **3** to hold or bind (the arms) of (a person) so as to restrain or immobilize him. **4** to confine or shackle. **5** to make (a bird) incapable of flight by removing the flight feathers. [C15: from OF *pignon* wing, from L *pinna* wing]

pinion[2] (ˈpɪnjən) *n* a cogwheel that engages with a larger wheel or rack. [C17: from F *pignon* cogwheel, from OF *peigne* comb, from L *pecten*]

pink[1] ❶ (pɪŋk) *n* **1** a pale reddish colour. **2** pink cloth or clothing: *dressed in pink.* **3** any of various Old World plants, such as the garden pink, cultivated for their fragrant flowers. See also **carnation** (sense 1). **4** the flower of any of these plants. **5** the highest or best degree, condition, etc. (esp. in **in the pink**). **6a** a huntsman's scarlet coat. **6b** a huntsman who wears a scarlet coat. ◆ *adj* **7** of the colour pink. **8** *Brit. inf.* left-wing. **9** *Inf.* of or relating to homosexuals or homosexuality: *the pink vote.* **10** (of a huntsman's coat) scarlet or red. ◆ *vb* **11** (*intr*) another word for **knock** (sense 7). [C16 (the flower), C18 (the colour): ? short for PINKEYE]
▸ **ˈpinkish** *or* **ˈpinky** *adj* ▸ **ˈpinkness** *n*

pink[2] ❶ (pɪŋk) *vb* (*tr*) **1** to prick lightly with a sword, etc. **2** to decorate (leather, etc.) with a perforated or punched pattern. **3** to cut with pinking shears. [C14: ? of Low G origin]

pink[3] (pɪŋk) *n* a sailing vessel with a narrow overhanging transom. [C15: from MDu. *pinke,* from ?]

pinkeye (ˈpɪŋkˌaɪ) *n* **1** Also called: **acute conjunctivitis.** an acute contagious inflammation of the conjunctiva of the eye, characterized by redness, discharge, etc. **2** Also called: **infectious keratitis.** a similar condition affecting the cornea of horses and cattle. [C16: partial translation of obs. Du. *pinck oogen* small eyes]

pinkie *or* **pinky** (ˈpɪŋkɪ) *n, pl* **pinkies.** *Scot., US, & Canad.* the little finger. [C19: from Du. *pinkje*]

pinking shears *pl n* scissors with a serrated edge on one or both blades, producing a wavy edge to material cut, thus preventing fraying.

pink salmon *n* **1** any salmon having pale pink flesh. **2** the flesh of such a fish.

pin money *n* **1** an allowance by a husband to his wife for personal expenditure. **2** money saved or earned for incidental expenses.

pinna (ˈpɪnə) *n, pl* **pinnae** (-niː) *or* **pinnas. 1** any leaflet of a pinnate compound leaf. **2** *Zool.* a feather, wing, fin, etc. **3** another name for **auricle** (sense 2). [C18: via NL from L: wing]

pinnace (ˈpɪnɪs, -əs) *n* any of various kinds of ship's tender. [C16: from F *pinace,* ?from OSp. *pinaza,* lit.: something made of pine, ult. from L *pīnus* pine]

pinnacle ❶ (ˈpɪnəkᵊl) *n* **1** the highest point, esp. of fame, success, etc. **2** a towering peak, as of a mountain. **3** a slender upright structure in the form of a spire on the top of a buttress, gable, or tower. ◆ *vb* **pinnacles, pinnacling, pinnacled.** (*tr*) **4** to set as on a pinnacle. **5** to furnish with a pinnacle or pinnacles. **6** to crown with a pinnacle. [C14: via OF from LL *pinnāculum* a peak, from L *pinna* wing]

pinnate (ˈpɪneɪt, ˈpɪnɪt) *adj* **1** like a feather in appearance. **2** (of compound leaves) having the leaflets growing opposite each other in pairs on either side of the stem. [C18: from L *pinnātus,* from *pinna* feather]
▸ **ˈpinnately** *adv* ▸ **pinˈnation** *n*

pinniped (ˈpɪnɪˌpɛd) *adj* **1** of, relating to, or belonging to an order of aquatic placental mammals having a streamlined body and limbs specialized as flippers: includes seals, sea lions, and the walrus. ◆ *n* **2** any pinniped animal. [C19: from NL *pinnipēs,* from L *pinna* fin + *pēs* foot]

pinnule (ˈpɪnjuːl) *n* **1** any of the lobes of a leaflet of a pinnate com-

THESAURUS

pinch *vb* **1 = squeeze,** compress, grasp, nip, press, tweak **2 = hurt,** chafe, confine, cramp, crush, pain **5 = scrimp,** afflict, be stingy, distress, economize, oppress, pinch pennies, press, skimp, spare, stint, tighten one's belt **8** *Informal* **= steal,** filch, knock off (*sl.*), lift (*inf.*), nick (*sl., chiefly Brit.*), pilfer, purloin, rob, snaffle (*Brit. inf.*), snatch, snitch (*sl.*), swipe (*sl.*) **9** *Informal* **= arrest,** apprehend, bust (*inf.*), collar (*inf.*), do (*sl.*), lift (*sl.*), nab (*inf.*), nail (*inf.*), pick up (*sl.*), pull in (*Brit. sl.*), run in (*sl.*), take into custody ◆ *n* **10 = squeeze,** nip, tweak **12 = dash,** bit, jot, mite, small quantity, *soupçon,* speck, taste **13 = hardship,** crisis, difficulty, emergency, exigency, necessity, oppression, pass, plight, predicament, pressure, strait, stress

Antonyms *vb* ≠ **scrimp:** be extravagant, blow (*sl.*), fritter away, spend like water, squander, waste ≠ **arrest:** free, let go, let out, release, set free

pinched *adj* **4 = thin,** careworn, drawn, gaunt, haggard, peaky, starved, worn

Antonyms *adj* blooming, chubby, fat, glowing, hale and hearty, healthy, plump, radiant, ruddy, well-fed

pin down *vb* **1 = force,** compel, constrain, make, press, pressurize **2 = determine,** designate, home in on, identify, locate, name, pinpoint, specify **3 = fix,** bind, confine, constrain, hold, hold down, immobilize, nail down, tie down

pine[2] *vb* **1** *often foll. by* **for = long,** ache, carry a torch for, covet, crave, desire, eat one's heart out over, hanker, hunger for, lust after, sigh, suspire (*arch. or poetic*), thirst for, wish for, yearn for **2 = waste,** decay, decline, droop, dwindle, fade, flag, languish, peak, sicken, sink, weaken, wilt, wither

pinion[1] *vb* **4 = immobilize,** bind, chain, confine, fasten, fetter, manacle, pin down, shackle, tie

pink[1] *n* **5 = best,** acme, height, peak, perfection, summit ◆ *adj* **7 = rosy,** flesh, flushed, reddish, rose, roseate, salmon

pink[2] *vb* **1, 3 = cut,** incise, notch, perforate, prick, punch, scallop, score

pinnacle *n* **1, 2 = peak,** acme, apex, apogee, crest, crown, eminence, height, meridian, summit, top, vertex, zenith **3 = spire,** belfry, cone, needle, obelisk, pyramid, steeple

pound leaf, which is itself pinnately divided. **2** *Zool.* any feather-like part, such as any of the arms of a sea lily. [C16: from L *pinnula*, dim. of *pinna* feather]
►**'pinnular** *adj*

pinny ('pɪnɪ) *n, pl* **pinnies.** a child's or informal name for **pinafore** (sense 1).

pinochle *or* **pinocle** ('piːnʌkᵊl) *n* **1** a card game for two to four players similar to bezique. **2** the combination of queen of spades and jack of diamonds in this game. [C19: from ?]

pinpoint Ⓣ ('pɪnˌpɔɪnt) *vb* (*tr*) **1** to locate or identify exactly: *to pinpoint a problem; to pinpoint a place on a map.* ◆ *n* **2** an insignificant or trifling thing. **3** the point of a pin. **4** (*modifier*) exact: *a pinpoint aim.*

pinprick ('pɪnˌprɪk) *n* **1** a slight puncture made by or as if by a pin. **2** a small irritation. ◆ *vb* **3** (*tr*) to puncture with or as if with a pin.

pins and needles *n* (*functioning as sing*) *Inf.* **1** a tingling sensation in the fingers, toes, legs, etc., caused by the return of normal blood circulation after its temporary impairment. **2 on pins and needles.** in a state of anxious suspense.

pinstripe ('pɪnˌstraɪp) *n* (in textiles) a very narrow stripe in fabric or the fabric itself.

pint Ⓣ (paɪnt) *n* **1** a unit of liquid measure of capacity equal to one eighth of a gallon. 1 Brit. pint is equal to 0.568 litre, 1 US pint to 0.473 litre. **2** a unit of dry measure of capacity equal to one half of a quart. 1 US dry pint is equal to one sixty-fourth of a US bushel or 0.5506 litre. **3** a measure having such a capacity. **4** *Brit. inf.* **4a** a pint of beer. **4b** a drink of beer: *he's gone out for a pint.* [C14: from OF *pinte*, from ?; ?from Med. L *pincta* marks used in measuring liquids, ult. from L *pingere* to paint]

pinta ('paɪntə) *n Inf.* a pint of milk. [C20: phonetic rendering of *pint of*]

pintail ('pɪnˌteɪl) *n, pl* **pintails** *or* **pintail.** a greyish-brown duck with a pointed tail.

pintle ('pɪntᵊl) *n* **1** a pin or bolt forming the pivot of a hinge. **2** the link bolt, hook, or pin on a vehicle's towing bracket. **3** the needle or plunger of the injection valve of an oil engine. [OE *pintel* penis]

pinto ('pɪntəʊ) *US & Canad.* ◆ *adj* **1** marked with patches of white; piebald. ◆ *n, pl* **pintos. 2** a pinto horse. [C19: from American Sp. (orig.: painted, spotted), ult. from L *pingere* to paint]

pint-size Ⓣ *or* **pint-sized** *adj Inf.* very small.

pin tuck *n* a narrow, ornamental fold, esp. used on shirt fronts and dress bodices.

pin-up *n* **1** *Inf.* **1a** a picture of a sexually attractive person, esp. when partially or totally undressed. **1b** (*as modifier*): *a pin-up magazine.* **2** *Sl.* a person who has appeared in such a picture. **3** a photograph of a famous personality.

pinus radiata ('paɪnəs ˌreɪdɪ'ɑːtə) *n* a pine tree grown in New Zealand and Australia to produce building timber.

pinwheel ('pɪnˌwiːl) *n* another name for a **Catherine wheel** (sense 1).

pinworm ('pɪnˌwɜːm) *n* a parasitic nematode worm, infecting the colon, rectum, and anus of humans. Also called: **threadworm.**

piny ('paɪnɪ) *adj* **pinier, piniest.** of, resembling, or covered with pine trees.

Pinyin ('pɪn'jɪn) *n* a system of spelling used to transliterate Chinese characters into the Roman alphabet.

pion ('paɪɒn) *or* **pi meson** *n Physics.* a meson having a positive or negative charge and a rest mass 273 times that of the electron, or no charge and a rest mass 264 times that of the electron. [C20: from Gk letter PI + -ON]

pioneer Ⓣ (ˌpaɪə'nɪə) *n* **1a** a colonist, explorer, or settler of a new land, region, etc. **1b** (*as modifier*): *a pioneer wagon.* **2** an innovator or developer of something new. **3** *Mil.* a member of an infantry group that digs entrenchments, makes roads, etc. ◆ *vb* **4** to be a pioneer (in or of). **5** (*tr*) to initiate, prepare, or open up: *to pioneer a medical programme.* [C16: from OF *paonier* infantryman, from *paon* PAWN²]

pious Ⓣ ('paɪəs) *adj* **1** having or expressing reverence for a god or gods; religious; devout. **2** marked by reverence. **3** marked by false reverence; sanctimonious. **4** sacred; not secular. [C17: from L *pius*]
►**'piously** *adv* ►**'piousness** *n*

pip¹ (pɪp) *n* **1** the seed of a fleshy fruit, such as an apple or pear. **2** any of the segments marking the surface of a pineapple. [C18: short for PIPPIN]

pip² (pɪp) *n* **1** a short high-pitched sound, a sequence of which can act as a time signal, esp. on radio. **2** a radar blip. **3a** a device, such as a spade, diamond, heart, or club on a playing card. **3b** any of the spots on dice or dominoes. **4** *Inf.* the emblem worn on the shoulder by junior officers in the British Army, indicating their rank. ◆ *vb* **pips, pipping, pipped. 5** (of a young bird) **5a** (*intr*) to chirp; peep. **5b** to pierce (the shell of its egg) while hatching. **6** (*intr*) to make a short high-pitched sound. [C16 (in the sense: spot); C17 (vb); C20 (in the sense: short high-pitched sound): ? imit.]

pip³ (pɪp) *n* **1** a contagious disease of poultry characterized by the secretion of thick mucus in the mouth and throat. **2** *Facetious sl.* a minor human ailment. **3** *Brit. sl.* a bad temper or depression (esp. in **give (someone) the pip**). ◆ *vb* **pips, pipping, pipped. 4** *Brit. sl.* to cause to be annoyed or depressed. [C15: from MDu. *pippe*, ult. from L *pituita* phlegm]

pip⁴ (pɪp) *vb* **pips, pipping, pipped.** (*tr*) *Brit. sl.* **1** to wound, esp. with a gun. **2** to defeat (a person), esp. when his success seems certain (often in **pip at the post**). **3** to blackball or ostracize. [C19 (orig. in the sense: to blackball): prob. from PIP²]

pipal ('piːpᵊl) *n* a variant of **peepul.**

pipe¹ Ⓣ (paɪp) *n* **1** a long tube of metal, plastic, etc., used to convey water, oil, gas, etc. **2** a long tube or case. **3** an object made in various shapes and sizes, consisting of a small bowl with an attached tubular stem, in which tobacco or other substances are smoked. **4** Also called: **pipeful.** the amount of tobacco that fills the bowl of a pipe. **5 put that in your pipe and smoke it.** *Inf.* accept that fact if you can. **6** *Zool., bot.* any of various hollow organs, such as the respiratory passage of certain animals. **7a** any musical instrument whose sound production results from the vibration of an air column in a simple tube. **7b** any of the tubular devices on an organ. **8 the pipes.** See **bagpipes. 9** a shrill voice or sound, as of a bird. **10a** a boatswain's pipe. **10b** the sound it makes. **11** (*pl*) *Inf.* the respiratory tract or vocal cords. **12** *Metallurgy.* a conical hole in the head of an ingot. **13** a cylindrical vein of rich ore. **14** Also called: **volcanic pipe.** a vertical cylindrical passage in a volcano through which molten lava is forced during eruption. ◆ *vb* **pipes, piping, piped. 15** to play (music) on a pipe. **16** (*tr*) to summon or lead by a pipe: *to pipe the dancers.* **17** to utter (something) shrilly. **18a** to signal orders to (the crew) by a boatswain's pipe. **18b** (*tr*) to signal the arrival or departure of: *to pipe the admiral aboard.* **19** (*tr*) to convey (water, gas, etc.) by a pipe or pipes. **20** (*tr*) to provide with pipes. **21** (*tr*) to trim (an article, esp. of clothing) with piping. **22** to force cream or icing, etc., through a shaped nozzle to decorate food. ◆ See also **pipe down, pipe up.** [OE *pīpe* (n), *pīpian* (vb), ult. from L *pīpāre* to chirp]

pipe² (paɪp) *n* **1** a large cask for wine, oil, etc. **2** a measure of capacity for wine equal to four barrels or 105 Brit. gallons. **3** a cask holding this quantity with its contents. [C14: via OF (in the sense: tube), ult. from L *pīpāre* to chirp]

pipe bomb *n* a small explosive device hidden in a pipe or drain, detonated by means of a timer.

pipeclay ('paɪpˌkleɪ) *n* **1** a fine white pure clay, used in the manufacture of tobacco pipes and pottery and for whitening leather and similar materials. ◆ *vb* **2** (*tr*) to whiten with pipeclay.

pipe cleaner *n* a short length of thin wires twisted so as to hold tiny tufts of yarn: used to clean the stem of a tobacco pipe.

piped music *n* light popular music prerecorded and played through amplifiers in a shop, restaurant, factory, etc., as background music.

pipe down Ⓣ *vb* (*intr, adv*) *Inf.* to stop talking, making noise, etc.

pipe dream Ⓣ *n* a fanciful or impossible plan or hope. [alluding to dreams produced by smoking an opium pipe]

pipefish ('paɪpˌfɪʃ) *n, pl* **pipefish** *or* **pipefishes.** any of various teleost fishes having a long tubelike snout and an elongated body covered with bony plates. Also called: **needlefish.**

pipefitting ('paɪpˌfɪtɪŋ) *n* **a** the act or process of bending and joining pipes. **b** the branch of plumbing involving this.
►**'pipeˌfitter** *n*

pipeline Ⓣ ('paɪpˌlaɪn) *n* **1** a long pipe used to transport oil, natural gas, etc. **2** a medium of communication, esp. a private one. **3 in the pipeline.** in the process of being completed, delivered, or produced. ◆ *vb* **pipelines, pipelining, pipelined.** (*tr*) **4** to convey by pipeline. **5** to supply with a pipeline.

pipe major *n* the noncommissioned officer responsible for the training of a pipe band.

pipe organ *n* another name for **organ** (the musical instrument).

piper ('paɪpə) *n* **1** a person who plays a pipe or bagpipes. **2 pay the piper and call the tune.** to bear the cost of an undertaking and control it.

piperidine (pɪ'perɪˌdiːn) *n* a liquid compound with a peppery ammoniacal odour: used in making rubbers and curing epoxy resins.

piperine ('pɪpəˌraɪn) *n* an alkaloid that is the active ingredient of pepper, used as a flavouring and as an insecticide. [C19: from L *piper* PEPPER]

THESAURUS

pinpoint *vb* **1** = **identify**, define, distinguish, get a fix on, home in on, locate, spot

pint *n* **4** *Brit. informal* = **beer**, ale, jar (*Brit. inf.*), jug (*Brit. inf.*)

pint-size *adj Informal* = **small**, diminutive, little, midget, miniature, pocket, pygmy *or* pigmy, teensy-weensy, teeny-weeny, tiny, wee

pioneer *n* **1** = **settler**, colonist, colonizer, explorer, frontiersman **2** = **founder**, developer, founding father, innovator, leader, trailblazer ◆ *vb* **4, 5** = **develop**, create, discover, establish, initiate, instigate, institute, invent, launch, lay the groundwork, map out, open up, originate, prepare, show the way, start, take the lead

pious *adj* **1, 2** = **religious**, dedicated, devoted, devout, God-fearing, godly, holy, reverent, righteous, saintly, spiritual **3** = **self-righteous**, goody-goody, holier-than-thou, hypocritical, pietistic, religiose, sanctimonious, unctuous
Antonyms *adj* ≠ **religious:** impious, irreligious, irreverent, ungodly, unholy ≠ **self-righteous:** humble, meek, sincere

pipe¹ *n* **1** = **tube**, conduit, conveyor, duct, hose, line, main, passage, pipeline **3** = **clay**, briar, meerschaum **7a** = **whistle**, fife, horn, tooter, wind instrument ◆ *vb* **15, 17** = **whistle**, cheep, peep, play, sing, sound, tootle, trill, tweet, twitter, warble **19** = **convey**, bring in, channel, conduct, siphon, supply, transmit

pipe down *vb Informal* = **be quiet**, belt up (*sl.*), button it (*sl.*), button one's lip (*sl.*), hold one's tongue, hush, put a sock in it (*Brit. sl.*), quieten down, shush, shut one's mouth, shut up (*inf.*)

pipe dream *n* = **daydream**, castle in the air, chimera, delusion, dream, fantasy, notion, reverie, vagary

pipeline *n* **1** = **tube**, conduit, conveyor, duct, line, passage, pipe **3 in the pipeline** = **on the way**,

piperonal (ˈpɪpərəʊˌnæl) *n* a white fragrant aldehyde used in flavourings, perfumery, and suntan lotions.

pipette (pɪˈpɛt) *n* a calibrated glass tube drawn to a fine bore at one end, filled by sucking liquid into the bulb, and used to transfer or measure known volumes of liquid. [C19: via F: little pipe]

pipe up 🅣 *vb (intr, adv)* **1** to commence singing or playing a musical instrument: *the band piped up.* **2** to speak up, esp. in a shrill voice.

pipi (ˈpɪpiː) *n, pl* **pipi** *or* **pipis. 1** an edible shellfish of New Zealand. **2** an Australian mollusc of sandy beaches, widely used as bait. [from Maori]

piping (ˈpaɪpɪŋ) *n* **1** pipes collectively, as in the plumbing of a house. **2** a cord of icing, whipped cream, etc., often used to decorate desserts and cakes. **3** a thin strip of covered cord or material, used to edge hems, etc. **4** the sound of a pipe or bagpipes. **5** the art or technique of playing a pipe or bagpipes. **6** a shrill voice or sound, esp. a whistling sound. ◆ *adj* **7** making a shrill sound. **8 piping hot.** extremely hot.

pipistrelle (ˌpɪpɪˈstrɛl) *n* any of a genus of numerous small brownish insectivorous bats, occurring in most parts of the world. [C18: via F from It. *pipistrello,* from L *vespertīliō* a bat, from *vesper* evening, because of its nocturnal habits]

pipit (ˈpɪpɪt) *n* any of various songbirds, esp. the **meadow pipit,** having brownish speckled plumage and a long tail. [C18: prob. imit.]

pipkin (ˈpɪpkɪn) *n* a small earthenware vessel. [C16: ? dim. of PIPE²; see -KIN]

pippin (ˈpɪpɪn) *n* any of several varieties of eating apple. [C13: from OF *pepin,* from ?]

pipsissewa (pɪpˈsɪsəwə) *n* any of several ericaceous plants of an Asian and American genus, having jagged evergreen leaves and white or pinkish flowers. Also called: **wintergreen.** [C19: from Algonquian *pipisisikweu,* lit.: it breaks it into pieces, so called because believed to be efficacious in treating bladder stones]

pipsqueak 🅣 (ˈpɪpˌskwiːk) *n Inf.* a person or thing that is insignificant or contemptible.

piquant 🅣 (ˈpiːkənt, -kɑːnt) *adj* **1** having an agreeably pungent or tart taste. **2** lively or stimulating to the mind. [C16: from F (lit.: prickling), from *piquer* to prick, goad]
▸ **ˈpiquancy** *n* ▸ **ˈpiquantly** *adv*

pique 🅣 (piːk) *n* **1** a feeling of resentment or irritation, as from having one's pride wounded. ◆ *vb* **piques, piquing, piqued.** *(tr)* **2** to cause to feel resentment or irritation. **3** to excite or arouse. **4** (foll. by *on* or *upon*) to pride or congratulate (oneself). [C16: from F, from *piquer* to prick]

piqué (ˈpiːkeɪ) *n* a close-textured fabric of cotton, silk, or spun rayon woven with lengthwise ribs. [C19: from F *piqué* pricked, from *piquer* to prick]

piquet (pɪˈkɛt, -ˈkeɪ) *n* a card game for two people played with a reduced pack. [C17: from F, from ?]

piracy 🅣 (ˈpaɪrəsɪ) *n, pl* **piracies. 1** *Brit.* robbery on the seas. **2** a felony, such as robbery or hijacking, committed aboard a ship or aircraft. **3** the unauthorized use or appropriation of patented or copyrighted material, ideas, etc. [C16: from Anglo-L *pirātia,* from LGk *peirāteia;* see PIRATE]

piranha *or* **piraña** (pɪˈrɑːnjə) *n* any of various small freshwater voracious fishes of tropical America, having strong jaws and sharp teeth. [C19: via Port. from Tupi: fish with teeth, from *pirá* fish + *sainha* tooth]

pirate 🅣 (ˈpaɪrɪt) *n* **1** a person who commits piracy. **2a** a vessel used by pirates. **2b** *(as modifier): a pirate ship.* **3** a person who illicitly uses or appropriates someone else's literary, artistic, or other work. **4a** a person or group of people who broadcast illegally. **4b** *(as modifier): a pirate radio station.* ◆ *vb* **pirates, pirating, pirated. 5** *(tr)* to use, appropriate, or reproduce (artistic work, ideas, etc.) illicitly. [C15: from L *pīrāta,* from Gk *peiratēs* one who attacks, from *peira* an attack]
▸ **piˈratical** *or* **piratic** (paɪˈrætɪk) *adj* ▸ **piˈratically** *adv*

pirogue (pɪˈrəʊg) *or* **piragua** (pɪˈrɑːgwə, -ˈræg-) *n* any of various kinds of dugout canoes. [C17: via F from Sp., of Amerind origin]

pirouette 🅣 (ˌpɪrʊˈɛt) *n* **1** a body spin, esp. in dancing, on the toes or the ball of the foot. ◆ *vb* **pirouettes, pirouetting, pirouetted. 2** *(intr)* to perform a pirouette. [C18: from F, from OF *pirouet* spinning top]

piscatorial (ˌpɪskəˈtɔːrɪəl) *or* **piscatory** (ˈpɪskətərɪ, -trɪ) *adj* **1** of or relating to fish, fishing, or fishermen. **2** devoted to fishing. [C19: from L *piscātōrius,* from *piscātor* fisherman]
▸ **ˌpiscaˈtorially** *adv*

Pisces (ˈpaɪsiːz, ˈpɪ-) *n, Latin genitive* **Piscium** (ˈpaɪsɪəm). **1** *Astron.* a faint extensive zodiacal constellation lying between Aquarius and Aries on the ecliptic. **2** *Astrol.* Also called: the **Fishes.** the twelfth sign of the zodiac. The sun is in this sign between about Feb. 19 and March 20. **3a** a taxonomic group that comprises all fishes. See **fish** (sense 1). **3b** a taxonomic group that comprises the bony fishes only. See **teleost.** [C14: L: the fish (pl)]

pisci- *combining form.* fish: *pisciculture.* [from L *piscis*]

pisciculture (ˈpɪsɪˌkʌltʃə) *n* the rearing and breeding of fish under controlled conditions.
▸ **ˌpisciˈcultural** *adj* ▸ **ˌpisciˈculturist** *n, adj*

piscina (pɪˈsiːnə) *n, pl* **piscinae** (-niː) *or* **piscinas.** *RC Church.* a stone basin, with a drain, in a church or sacristy where water used at Mass is poured away. [C16: from L: fish pond, from *piscis* a fish]

piscine (ˈpɪsaɪn) *adj* of, relating to, or resembling a fish.

piscivorous (pɪˈsɪvərəs) *adj* feeding on fish.

pish (pʃ, pɪʃ) *interj* **1** an exclamation of impatience or contempt. ◆ *vb* **2** to make this exclamation at (someone or something).

pisiform (ˈpɪsɪˌfɔːm) *adj* **1** *Zool., bot.* resembling a pea. ◆ *n* **2** a small pealike bone on the ulnar side of the carpus. [C18: via NL from L *pīsum* pea + *forma* shape]

pismire (ˈpɪsˌmaɪə) *n* an archaic or dialect word for an **ant.** [C14 (lit.: urinating ant, from the odour of formic acid): from PISS + obs. *mire* ant, from ON]

piss (pɪs) *Sl.* ◆ *vb* **1** *(intr) Taboo.* to urinate. **2** *(tr) Taboo.* to discharge as or in one's urine: *to piss blood.* ◆ *n* **3** *Taboo.* an act of urinating. **4** *Taboo.* urine. **5 take the piss.** to tease or make fun of someone or something. [C13: from OF *pisser,* prob. imit.]

piss artist *n Sl.* **1** a boastful or incompetent person. **2** a person who drinks heavily and gets drunk frequently.

pissed (pɪst) *adj Sl.* **1** *Brit. taboo.* drunk. **2** *US.* annoyed, irritated, or disappointed.

piss off *vb (adv) Taboo sl.* **1** *(tr; often passive)* to annoy, irritate, or disappoint. **2** *(intr) Chiefly Brit.* to go away; depart: often used to dismiss a person.

piss-up *n Sl.* a party involving a considerable amount of drinking.

pistachio (pɪˈstɑːʃɪˌəʊ) *n, pl* **pistachios. 1** a tree of the Mediterranean region and W Asia, with small hard-shelled nuts. **2** Also called: **pistachio nut.** the nut of this tree, having an edible green kernel. **3** the sweet flavour of the pistachio nut, used in ice creams, etc. ◆ *adj* **4** of a yellowish-green colour. [C16: via It. & L from Gk *pistakion* pistachio nut, from *pistakē* pistachio tree, from Persian *pistah*]

piste (piːst) *n* a slope or course for skiing. [C18: via OF from OIt. *pista,* from *pistare* to tread down]

pistil (ˈpɪstɪl) *n* the female reproductive part of a flower, consisting of one or more separate or fused carpels. [C18: from L *pistillum* pestle]

pistillate (ˈpɪstɪlɪt, -ˌleɪt) *adj* (of plants) **1** having pistils but no anthers. **2** having or producing pistils.

pistol (ˈpɪstᵊl) *n* **1** a short-barrelled handgun. **2 hold a pistol to a person's head.** to threaten a person in order to force him to do what one wants. ◆ *vb* **pistols, pistolling, pistolled** *or US* **pistols, pistoling, pistoled. 3** *(tr)* to shoot with a pistol. [C16: from F *pistole,* from G, from Czech *pišt'ala* pistol, pipe]

pistole (pɪsˈtəʊl) *n* any of various gold coins of varying value, formerly used in Europe. [C16: from OF, shortened from *pistolet,* lit.: little PISTOL]

pistol grip *n* **a** a handle shaped like the butt of a pistol. **b** *(as modifier): a pistol-grip camera.*

pistol-whip *vb* **pistol-whips, pistol-whipping, pistol-whipped.** *(tr) US.* to beat or strike with a pistol barrel.

piston (ˈpɪstən) *n* a disc or cylindrical part that slides to and fro in a hollow cylinder. In an internal-combustion engine it is attached by a pivoted connecting rod to a crankshaft or flywheel, thus converting reciprocating motion into rotation. [C18: via F from OIt. *pistone,* from *pistare* to grind, from L *pinsere* to beat]

piston ring *n* a split ring that fits into a groove on the rim of a piston to provide a spring-loaded seal against the cylinder wall.

piston rod *n* **1** the rod that connects the piston of a reciprocating steam engine to the crosshead. **2** a less common name for a **connecting rod.**

pit[1] 🅣 (pɪt) *n* **1** a large, usually deep opening in the ground. **2a** a mine or excavation, esp. for coal. **2b** the shaft in a mine. **2c** *(as modifier): pit*

THESAURUS

brewing, coming, getting ready, in preparation, in process, in production, under way

pipe up *vb* **2 = speak,** have one's say, make oneself heard, put one's oar in, raise one's voice, speak up, volunteer

pipsqueak *n Informal* = **squirt** *(inf.),* creep *(sl.),* nobody, nonentity, nothing, upstart, whippersnapper

piquancy *n* **1 = spiciness,** bite *(inf.),* edge, flavour, kick *(inf.),* pungency, relish, sharpness, spice, tang, zest **2 = interest,** colour, excitement, pep, pizzazz *or* pizazz *(inf.),* raciness, spirit, vigour, vitality, zing *(inf.),* zip *(inf.)*

piquant *adj* **1 = spicy,** biting, highly-seasoned, peppery, pungent, savoury, sharp, stinging, tangy, tart, with a kick *(inf.),* zesty **2 = interesting,** lively, provocative, racy, salty, scintillating, sparkling, spirited, stimulating
Antonyms *adj* ≠ **spicy:** bland, insipid, mild ≠ **interesting:** banal, bland, boring, dull, insipid, tame, uninteresting, vapid

pique *n* **1 = resentment,** annoyance, displeasure, huff, hurt feelings, irritation, miff *(inf.),* offence, umbrage, vexation, wounded pride ◆ *vb* **2 = displease,** affront, annoy, gall, get *(inf.),* incense, irk, irritate, miff *(inf.),* mortify, nettle, offend, peeve *(inf.),* provoke, put out, rile, sting, vex, wound **3 = arouse,** excite, galvanize, goad, kindle, provoke, rouse, spur, stimulate, stir, whet

piracy *n* **1, 2 = robbery,** buccaneering, freebooting, hijacking, infringement, rapine, stealing, theft

pirate *n* **1 = buccaneer,** corsair, filibuster, freebooter, marauder, raider, rover, sea robber, sea rover, sea wolf **3 = plagiarist,** cribber, infringer, plagiarizer ◆ *vb* **5 = copy,** appropriate, borrow, crib *(inf.),* lift *(inf.),* plagiarize, poach, reproduce, steal

piratical *adj* **1 = buccaneering,** criminal, dishonest, felonious, fraudulent, lawless, pillaging, plundering, rapacious, thieving, unprincipled, wolfish

pirouette *n, vb* **1, 2 = spin,** pivot, turn, twirl, whirl

pit[1] *n* **1, 2, 7, 8 = hole,** abyss, cavity, chasm, coal mine, crater, dent, depression, dimple, excavation, gulf, hollow, indentation, mine, pockmark, pothole, trench ◆ *vb* **13** *often with* **against = set against,** match, oppose, put in opposition pony; pit prop. **3** a concealed danger or difficulty. **4 the pit.** hell. **5** Also called: **orchestra pit.** the area that is occupied by the orchestra in a theatre, located in front of the stage. **6** an enclosure for fighting animals or birds. **7** *Anat.* **7a** a small natural depression on the surface of a body, organ, or part. **7b** the floor of any natural bodily cavity: *the pit of the stomach.* **8** *Pathol.* a small indented scar at the site of a former pustule; pockmark. **9** a working area at the side of a motor-racing track for servicing or refuelling vehicles. **10** a section on the floor of a commodity exchange devoted to a special line of trading. **11** the ground floor of the auditorium of a theatre. **12** another word for **pitfall** (sense 2). ◆ *vb* **pits, pitting, pitted. 13** (*tr;* often foll. by *against*) to match in opposition, esp. as antagonists. **14** to mark or become marked with pits. **15** (*tr*) to place or bury in a pit. [OE *pytt,* from L *puteus*]

pit[2] (pɪt) *Chiefly US & Canad.* ◆ *n* **1** the stone of a cherry, etc. ◆ *vb* **pits, pitting, pitted.** (*tr*) **2** to extract the stone from (a fruit). [C19: from Du.: kernel]

pitapat (ˈpɪtəˌpæt) *adv* **1** with quick light taps. ◆ *vb* **pitapats, pitapatting, pitapatted. 2** (*intr*) to make quick light taps. ◆ *n* **3** such taps. [C16: imit.]

pit bull terrier *n* a dog resembling the Staffordshire bull terrier but somewhat larger: originally developed for dogfighting.

pitch[1] ❶ (pɪtʃ) *vb* **1** to hurl or throw (something); cast; fling. **2** (*usually tr*) to set up (a camp, tent, etc.). **3** (*tr*) to aim or fix (something) at a particular level, position, style, etc.: *if you advertise privately you may pitch the price too low.* **4** (*tr*) to aim to sell (a product) to a specified market or on a specified basis. **5** (*intr*) to slope downwards. **6** (*intr*) to fall forwards or downwards. **7** (*intr*) (of a vessel) to dip and raise its bow and stern alternately. **8** *Cricket.* to bowl (a ball) so that it bounces on a certain part of the wicket, or (of a ball) to bounce on a certain part of the wicket. **9** (*intr*) (of a missile, aircraft, etc.) to deviate from a stable flight attitude by movement of the longitudinal axis about the lateral axis. **10** (*tr*) (in golf, etc.) to hit (a ball) steeply into the air. **11** (*tr*) *Music.* **11a** to sing or play accurately (a note, interval, etc.). **11b** (*usually passive*) (of a wind instrument) to specify or indicate its basic key or harmonic series by its size, manufacture, etc. **12** *Baseball, softball.* **12a** (*tr*) to throw (a ball) to a batter. **12b** (*intr*) to act as a pitcher in a game. ◆ *n* **13** the degree of elevation or depression. **14a** the angle of descent of a downward slope. **14b** such a slope. **15** the extreme height or depth. **16** *Mountaineering.* a section of a route between two belay points. **17** the degree of slope of a roof. **18** the distance between corresponding points on adjacent members of a body of regular form, esp. the distance between teeth on a gearwheel or between threads on a screw thread. **19** the pitching motion of a ship, missile, etc. **20** *Music.* **20a** the height or depth of a note as determined by its frequency relative to that of other notes: *high pitch; low pitch.* **20b** an absolute frequency assigned to a specific note, fixing the relative frequencies of all other notes. **21** *Cricket.* the rectangular area between the stumps, 22 yards long and 10 feet wide; the wicket. **22** the act or manner of pitching a ball, as in cricket, etc. **23** *Chiefly Brit.* a vendor's station, esp. on a pavement. **24** *Sl.* a persuasive sales talk, esp. one routinely repeated. **25** *Chiefly Brit.* (in many sports) the field of play. **26** *Golf.* Also called: **pitch shot.** an approach shot in which the ball is struck in a high arc. **27 queer someone's pitch.** *Brit. inf.* to upset someone's plans. ◆ See also **pitch in, pitch into.** [C13 *picchen*]

pitch[2] (pɪtʃ) *n* **1** any of various heavy dark viscid substances obtained as a residue from the distillation of tars. **2** any of various similar substances, such as asphalt, occurring as natural deposits. **3** crude turpentine obtained as sap from pine trees. ◆ *vb* **4** (*tr*) to apply pitch to (something). [OE *pic,* from L *pix*]

pitch-black ❶ *adj* **1** extremely dark; unlit: *the room was pitch-black.* **2** of a deep black colour.

pitchblende (ˈpɪtʃˌblɛnd) *n* a blackish mineral that occurs in veins, frequently associated with silver: the principal source of uranium and radium. [C18: partial translation of G *Pechblende,* from *Pech* PITCH[2] (from its black colour) + BLENDE]

pitch-dark ❶ *adj* extremely or completely dark.

pitched battle *n* **1** a battle ensuing from the deliberate choice of time and place. **2** any fierce encounter, esp. one with large numbers.

pitcher[1] (ˈpɪtʃə) *n* a large jug, usually rounded with a narrow neck and often of earthenware, used mainly for holding water. [C13: from OF *pichier,* from Med. L *picārium,* var. of *bicārium* BEAKER]

pitcher[2] (ˈpɪtʃə) *n Baseball.* the player on the fielding team who throws the ball to the batter.

pitcher plant *n* any of various insectivorous plants, having leaves modified to form pitcher-like organs that attract and trap insects, which are then digested.

pitchfork (ˈpɪtʃˌfɔːk) *n* **1** a long-handled fork with two or three long curved tines for tossing hay. ◆ *vb* (*tr*) **2** to use a pitchfork on (something). **3** to thrust (someone) unwillingly into a position.

pitch in ❶ *vb* (*intr, adv*) **1** to cooperate or contribute. **2** to begin energetically.

pitch into ❶ *vb* (*intr, prep*) *Inf.* **1** to assail physically or verbally. **2** to get on with doing (something).

pitch pine *n* **1** any of various coniferous trees of North America: valued as a source of turpentine and pitch. **2** the wood of any of these trees.

pitch pipe *n* a small pipe that sounds a note or notes of standard frequency. It is used for establishing the correct starting note for unaccompanied singing.

pitchy ❶ (ˈpɪtʃɪ) *adj* **pitchier, pitchiest. 1** full of or covered with pitch. **2** resembling pitch.
▸ **ˈpitchiness** *n*

piteous ❶ (ˈpɪtɪəs) *adj* exciting or deserving pity.
▸ **ˈpiteously** *adv* ▸ **ˈpiteousness** *n*

pitfall ❶ (ˈpɪtˌfɔːl) *n* **1** an unsuspected difficulty or danger. **2** a trap in the form of a concealed pit, designed to catch men or wild animals. [OE *pytt* PIT[1] + *fealle* trap]

pith ❶ (pɪθ) *n* **1** the soft fibrous tissue lining the inside of the rind in fruits such as the orange. **2** the essential or important part, point, etc. **3** weight; substance. **4** *Bot.* the central core of unspecialized cells surrounded by conducting tissue in stems. **5** the soft central part of a bone, feather, etc. ◆ *vb* (*tr*) **6** to kill (animals) by severing the spinal cord. **7** to remove the pith from (a plant). [OE *pitha*]

pithead (ˈpɪtˌhɛd) *n* the top of a mine shaft and the buildings, hoisting gear, etc., around it.

pithecanthropus (ˌpɪθɪkænˈθrəʊpəs) *n, pl* **pithecanthropi** (-ˌpaɪ). any primitive apelike man of the former genus *Pithecanthropus,* now included in the genus *Homo.* See **Java man.** [C19: NL, from Gk *pithēkos* ape + *anthrōpos* man]

pith helmet *n* a lightweight hat made of the pith of the sola, an E Indian swamp plant, that protects the wearer from the sun. Also called: **topee, topi.**

pithos (ˈpɪθɒs, ˈpaɪ-) *n, pl* **pithoi** (-θɔɪ). a large ceramic container for oil or grain. [from Gk]

pithy ❶ (ˈpɪθɪ) *adj* **pithier, pithiest. 1** terse and full of meaning or substance. **2** of, resembling, or full of pith.
▸ **ˈpithily** *adv* ▸ **ˈpithiness** *n*

pitiable ❶ (ˈpɪtɪəbˀl) *adj* exciting or deserving pity or contempt.
▸ **ˈpitiableness** *n* ▸ **ˈpitiably** *adv*

pitiful ❶ (ˈpɪtɪfʊl) *adj* **1** arousing or deserving pity. **2** arousing or deserving contempt. **3** *Arch.* full of pity or compassion.
▸ **ˈpitifully** *adv* ▸ **ˈpitifulness** *n*

pitiless ❶ (ˈpɪtɪlɪs) *adj* having or showing little or no pity or mercy.
▸ **ˈpitilessly** *adv* ▸ **ˈpitilessness** *n*

pitman (ˈpɪtmən) *n, pl* **pitmen.** *Chiefly Scot. & N English.* a person who works in a pit, esp. a coal miner.

piton (ˈpiːtɒn) *n Mountaineering.* a metal spike that may be driven into a crevice and used to secure a rope, etc. [C20: from F: ringbolt]

pits (pɪts) *pl n* **the.** *Sl.* the worst possible person, place, or thing. [C20: from ? *armpits*]

pit stop *n* **1** *Motor racing.* a brief stop made at a pit by a racing car for re-

THESAURUS

14 = **scar**, dent, dint, gouge, hole, indent, mark, nick, notch, pockmark

pitch[1] *vb* **1** = **throw**, bung (*Brit. sl.*), cast, chuck (*inf.*), fling, heave, hurl, launch, lob, sling, toss **2** = **set up**, erect, fix, locate, place, plant, put up, raise, settle, station **6** = **fall**, dive, drop, stagger, topple, tumble **7** = **toss**, flounder, lurch, make heavy weather, plunge, roll, wallow, welter ◆ *n* **13, 15** = **level**, degree, height, highest point, point, summit **14, 17** = **slope**, angle, cant, dip, gradient, incline, steepness, tilt **20** = **tone**, harmonic, modulation, sound, timbre **24** *Slang* = **sales talk**, line, patter, spiel (*inf.*) **25** *Chiefly Brit.* = **sports field**, field of play, ground, park

pitch-black *adj* **1, 2** = **jet-black**, dark, ebony, inky, jet, pitch-dark, raven, sable, unlit

pitch-dark *adj* = **black**, dark, pitch-black, pitchy, Stygian, unilluminated, unlit

pitch in *vb* **1** = **help**, chip in, contribute, cooperate, do one's bit, join in, lend a hand, lend a helping hand, participate **2** = **begin**, fall to, get busy, get cracking (*inf.*), plunge into, set about, set to, tackle

pitch into *vb* **1** *Informal* = **attack**, assail, assault, get stuck into (*inf.*), lace into, light into (*inf.*), sail into (*inf.*), tear into (*inf.*)

pitchy *adj* **2** = **black**, coal-black, dark, ebony, inky, jet, jetty, moonless, pitch-black, raven, sable, unilluminated, unlighted

piteous *adj* = **pathetic**, affecting, deplorable, dismal, distressing, doleful, grievous, gut-wrenching, harrowing, heartbreaking, heart-rending, lamentable, miserable, mournful, moving, pitiable, pitiful, plaintive, poignant, sad, sorrowful, woeful, wretched

pitfall *n* **1** = **danger**, banana skin (*inf.*), catch, difficulty, drawback, hazard, peril, snag, trap **2** = **trap**, deadfall, downfall, pit, snare

pith *n* **2** = **essence**, core, crux, gist, heart, heart of the matter, kernel, marrow, meat, nub, point, quintessence, salient point, the long and the short of it **3** = **importance**, consequence, depth, force, import, matter, moment, power, significance, strength, substance, value, weight

pithy *adj* **1** = **succinct**, brief, cogent, compact, concise, epigrammatic, expressive, finely honed, forceful, laconic, meaningful, pointed, short, terse, to the point, trenchant

Antonyms *adj* diffuse, garrulous, long, long-winded, loquacious, prolix, verbose, wordy

pitiable *adj* = **pathetic**, deplorable, dismal, distressing, doleful, grievous, gut-wrenching, harrowing, lamentable, miserable, mournful, piteous, poor, sad, sorry, woeful, wretched

pitiful *adj* **1** = **pathetic**, deplorable, distressing, grievous, gut-wrenching, harrowing, heartbreaking, heart-rending, lamentable, miserable, piteous, pitiable, sad, woeful, wretched **2** = **contemptible**, abject, base, beggarly, despicable, dismal, inadequate, insignificant, low, mean, measly, miserable, paltry, scurvy, shabby, sorry, vile, worthless

Antonyms *adj* ≠ **pathetic:** amusing, cheerful, cheering, comical, funny, happy, heartening, laughable, merry ≠ **contemptible:** adequate, admirable, honourable, laudable, praiseworthy, significant, valuable

pitiless *adj* = **merciless**, brutal, callous, cold-blooded, cold-hearted, cruel, hardhearted, harsh, heartless, implacable, inexorable, inhuman, relentless, ruthless, uncaring, unfeeling, unmerciful, unsympathetic pairs, refuelling, etc. **2** *Inf.* any stop made during a car journey for refreshment, rest, or refuelling.

pitta bread *or* **pitta** ('pɪtə) *n* a flat rounded slightly leavened bread, originally from the Middle East. [from Mod. Gk: a cake]

pittance ❶ ('pɪtᵊns) *n* a small amount or portion, esp. a meagre allowance of money. [C16: from OF *pietance* ration, ult. from L *pietās* duty]

pitter-patter ('pɪtəˌpætə) *n* **1** the sound of light rapid taps or pats, as of raindrops. ◆ *vb* **2** (*intr*) to make such a sound. ◆ *adv* **3** with such a sound.

pituitary (pɪ'tjuːɪtərɪ) *n, pl* **pituitaries. 1** See **pituitary gland.** ◆ *adj* **2** of or relating to the pituitary gland. [C17: from LL *pītuītārius* slimy, from *pītuīta* phlegm]

pituitary gland *or* **body** *n* the master endocrine gland, attached by a stalk to the base of the brain. Its two lobes secrete hormones affecting skeletal growth, development of the sex glands, and the functioning of the other endocrine glands.

pit viper *n* any venomous snake of a New World family, having a heat-sensitive organ in a pit on each side of the head: includes the rattlesnakes.

pity ❶ ('pɪtɪ) *n, pl* **pities. 1** sympathy or sorrow felt for the sufferings of another. **2 have** (*or* **take**) **pity on.** to have sympathy or show mercy for. **3** something that causes regret. **4** an unfortunate chance: *what a pity you can't come.* ◆ *vb* **pities, pitying, pitied.** (*tr*) **5** to feel pity for. [C13: from OF *pité*, from L *pietās* duty]
▸**'pitying** *adj* ▸**'pityingly** *adv*

pityriasis (ˌpɪtə'raɪəsɪs) *n* any of a group of skin diseases characterized by the shedding of dry flakes of skin. [C17: via NL from Gk *pituriasis* scurfiness, from *pituron* bran]

più (pjuː) *adv* (*in combination*) *Music.* more (quickly, etc.): *più allegro.* [It., from L *plus* more]

piupiu ('piːuːˌpiːuː) *n* a skirt made from leaves of the New Zealand flax, worn by Maoris on ceremonial occasions. [from Maori]

pivot ❶ ('pɪvət) *n* **1** a short shaft or pin supporting something that turns; fulcrum. **2** the end of a shaft or arbor that terminates in a bearing. **3** a person or thing upon which progress, success, etc., depends. **4** the person or position from which a military formation takes its reference when altering position, etc. ◆ *vb* **5** (*tr*) to mount on or provide with a pivot or pivots. **6** (*intr*) to turn on or as if on a pivot. [C17: from OF]

pivotal ❶ ('pɪvətᵊl) *adj* **1** of, involving, or acting as a pivot. **2** of crucial importance.

pix[1] (pɪks) *n* a plural of **pic.**

pix[2] (pɪks) *n* a less common spelling of **pyx.**

pixel ('pɪksel) *n* any of a number of very small picture elements that make up a picture, as on a visual display unit. [C20: from *pix* pictures + *el*(*ement*)]

pixie ❶ *or* **pixy** ('pɪksɪ) *n, pl* **pixies.** (in folklore) a fairy or elf. [C17: from ?]

pixilated *or* **pixillated** ('pɪksɪˌleɪtɪd) *adj Chiefly US.* **1** eccentric or whimsical. **2** *Sl.* drunk. [C20: from PIXIE + *-lated*, as in *stimulated, titillated*, etc.]

pizza ('piːtsə) *n* a dish of Italian origin consisting of a baked disc of dough covered with cheese and tomatoes, plus ham, mushrooms, etc. [C20: from It., ?from Vulgar L *picea* (unattested), ? rel. to Mod. Gk *pitta* cake]

pizzazz *or* **pizazz** (pə'zæz) *n Inf.* an attractive combination of energy and style; sparkle. Also: **bezazz.** [C20: ?]

pizzeria (ˌpiːtsə'riːə) *n* a place where pizzas are made, sold, or eaten.

pizzicato (ˌpɪtsɪ'kɑːtəʊ) *Music.* ◆ *adj, adv* **1** (in music for the violin family) to be plucked with the finger. ◆ *n* **2** this style or technique of playing. [C19: from It.: pinched, from *pizzicare* to twist]

pizzle ('pɪzᵊl) *n Arch. or dialect.* the penis of an animal, esp. a bull. [C16: of Gmc origin]

pk *pl* **pks** *abbrev. for:* **1** pack. **2** park. **3** peak.

pkg. *pl* **pkgs.** *abbrev. for* package.

pl *abbrev. for:* **1** place. **2** plate. **3** plural.

Pl. (in street names) *abbrev. for* Place.

PLA *abbrev. for* Port of London Authority.

plaas (plɑːs) *n S. African.* a farm. [from Afrik., from Du.]

placable ('plækəbᵊl) *adj* easily placated or appeased. [C15: via OF from L *plācābilis*, from *plācāre* to appease]
▸ˌ**placa'bility** *n*

placard ❶ ('plækɑːd) *n* **1** a notice for public display; poster. **2** a small plaque or card. ◆ *vb* (*tr*) **3** to post placards on or in. **4** to advertise by placards. **5** to display as a placard. [C15: from OF *plaquart*, from *plaquier* to plate, lay flat; see PLAQUE]

placate ❶ (plə'keɪt) *vb* **placates, placating, placated.** (*tr*) to pacify or appease. [C17: from L *plācāre*]
▸**pla'cation** *n* ▸**pla'catory** *adj*

place ❶ (pleɪs) *n* **1** a particular point or part of space or of a surface, esp. that occupied by a person or thing. **2** a geographical point, such as a town, city, etc. **3** a position or rank in a sequence or order. **4** an open square lined with houses in a city or town. **5** space or room. **6** a house or living quarters. **7** a country house with grounds. **8** any building or area set aside for a specific purpose. **9** a passage in a book, play, film, etc.: *to lose one's place.* **10** proper, right, or customary surroundings (esp. in **out of place, in place**). **11** right, prerogative, or duty: *it is your place to give a speech.* **12** appointment, position, or job: *a place at college.* **13** position, condition, or state: *if I were in your place.* **14a** a space or seat, as at a dining table. **14b** (*as modifier*): *place mat.* **15** *Maths.* the relative position of a digit in a number. **16** any of the best times in a race. **17** *Horse racing.* **17a** *Brit., Austral., & NZ.* the first, second, or third position at the finish. **17b** *US & Canad.* the first or usually the second position at the finish. **17c** (*as modifier*): *a place bet.* **18 all over the place.** in disorder or disarray. **19 give place (to).** to make room (for) or be superseded (by). **20 go places.** *Inf.* **20a** to travel. **20b** to become successful. **21 in place of. 21a** instead of; in lieu of: *go in place of my sister.* **21b** in exchange for: *he gave her it in place of her ring.* **22 know one's place.** to be aware of one's inferior position. **23 put someone in his** (*or* **her**) **place.** to humble someone who is arrogant, conceited, forward, etc. **24 take one's place.** to take up one's usual or specified position. **25 take place.** to happen or occur. **26 take the place of.** to be a substitute for. ◆ *vb* **places, placing, placed.** (*mainly tr*) **27** to put or set in a particular or appropriate place. **28** to find or indicate the place of. **29** to identify or classify by linking with an appropriate context: *to place a face.* **30** to regard or view as being: *to place prosperity above sincerity.* **31** to make (an order, bet, etc.). **32** to find a home or job for (someone). **33** to appoint to an office or position. **34** (often foll. by *with*) to put under the care (of). **35** to direct or aim carefully. **36** (*passive*) *Brit.* to cause (a racehorse, greyhound, athlete, etc.) to arrive in first, second, third, or sometimes fourth place. **37** (*intr*) *US & Canad.* (of a racehorse, greyhound, etc.) to finish among the first three in a contest, esp. in second position. **38** to invest (funds). **39** (*tr*) to insert (an advertisement) in a newspaper, journal, etc. [C13: via OF from L *platēa* courtyard, from Gk *plateia*, from *platus* broad]

placebo (plə'siːbəʊ) *n, pl* **placebos** *or* **placeboes. 1** *Med.* an inactive substance administered to a patient usually to compare its effects with those of a real drug but sometimes for the psychological benefit to the patient through his believing he is receiving treatment. **2** something said or done to please or humour another. **3** *RC Church.* a traditional name for the vespers of the office for the dead. [C13 (in the ecclesiastical sense): from L *Placebo Domino* I shall please the Lord; C19 (in the medical sense)]

placebo effect *n Med.* a positive therapeutic effect claimed by a patient after receiving a placebo believed by him to be an active drug.

place card *n* a card placed on a dinner table before a seat, indicating who is to sit there.

place kick *Football, etc.* ◆ *n* **1** a kick in which the ball is placed in position before it is kicked. ◆ *vb* **place-kick. 2** to kick (a ball) in this way.

placement ❶ ('pleɪsmənt) *n* **1** the act of placing or the state of being placed. **2** arrangement or position. **3** the process of finding employment.

placenta (plə'sentə) *n, pl* **placentas** *or* **placentae** (-tiː). **1** the vascular

THESAURUS

Antonyms *adj* caring, compassionate, kind, merciful, relenting, responsive, soft-hearted, sparing

pittance *n* = **peanuts** (*sl.*), allowance, chicken feed (*sl.*), drop, mite, modicum, portion, ration, slave wages, trifle

pity *n* **1** = **compassion**, charity, clemency, commiseration, condolence, fellow feeling, forbearance, kindness, mercy, quarter, sympathy, tenderness, understanding **2 take pity on** = **have mercy on**, feel compassion for, forgive, melt, pardon, put out of one's misery, relent, reprieve, show mercy, spare **3, 4** = **shame**, bummer (*sl.*), crime, crying shame, misfortune, regret, sad thing, sin ◆ *vb* **5** = **feel sorry for**, bleed for, commiserate with, condole with, feel for, grieve for, have compassion for, sympathize with, weep for

Antonyms *n* ≠ **compassion:** anger, apathy, brutality, cruelty, disdain, fury, hard-heartedness, indifference, inhumanity, mercilessness, pitilessness, ruthlessness, scorn, severity, unconcern, wrath

pivot *n* **1** = **axis**, axle, fulcrum, spindle, swivel **3** = **hub**, centre, focal point, heart, hinge, kingpin ◆ *vb* **6** = **turn**, revolve, rotate, spin, swivel, twirl **6** = **rely**, be contingent, depend, hang, hinge, revolve round, turn

pivotal *adj* **2** = **crucial**, central, climactic, critical, decisive, determining, focal, vital

pixie *n* = **elf**, brownie, fairy, peri, sprite

placard *n* **1** = **notice**, advertisement, *affiche*, bill, poster, public notice, sticker

placate *vb* = **calm**, appease, assuage, conciliate, humour, mollify, pacify, propitiate, satisfy, soothe, win over

placatory *adj* = **calming**, appeasing, conciliatory, designed to please, pacificatory, peacemaking, propitiative

place *n* **1** = **spot**, area, location, locus, point, position, site, situation, station, venue, whereabouts **2** = **region**, city, district, hamlet, locale, locality, neighbourhood, quarter, town, vicinity, village **3** = **position**, grade, rank, station, status **5** = **space**, accommodation, room, stead **6, 7** = **home**, abode, apartment, domicile, dwelling, flat, house, manor, mansion, pad (*sl.*), property, residence, seat **11** = **duty**, affair, charge, concern, function, prerogative, responsibility, right, role **12** = **job**, appointment, berth (*inf.*), billet, employment, position, post **21 in place of** = **instead of**, as an alternative to, as a substitute for, in exchange for, in lieu of, taking the place of **23 put (someone) in his place** = **humble**, bring down, cut down to size, humiliate, make (someone) eat humble pie, make (someone) swallow his pride, mortify, take down a peg (*inf.*) **25 take place** = **happen**, befall, betide, come about, come to pass (*arch.*), go on, occur, transpire (*inf.*) ◆ *vb* **27** = **put**, bung (*Brit. sl.*), deposit, dispose, establish, fix, install, lay, locate, plant, position, rest, set, settle, situate, stand, station, stick (*inf.*) **28** = **classify**, arrange, class, grade, group, order, rank, sort **29** = **identify**, associate, know, put one's finger on, recognize, remember, set in context **34** = **assign**, allocate, appoint, charge, commission, entrust, give

placement *n* **1, 2** = **positioning**, arrangement, deployment, disposition, distribution, emplacement, installation, locating, location, or-

organ formed in the uterus of most mammals during pregnancy, consisting of both maternal and embryonic tissues and providing oxygen and nutrients for the fetus. **2** *Bot.* the part of the ovary of flowering plants to which the ovules are attached. [C17: via L from Gk *plakoeis* flat cake, from *plax* flat]
▸**pla'cental** *adj*

placer ('plæsə) *n* **a** surface sediment containing particles of gold or some other valuable mineral. **b** (*in combination*): *placer-mining.* [C19: from American Sp.: deposit, from Sp. *plaza* PLACE]

place setting *n* the cutlery, crockery, and glassware laid for one person at a dining table.

placet ('pleɪsɛt) *n* a vote or expression of assent by saying *placet.* [C16: from L, lit.: it pleases]

placid ⓘ ('plæsɪd) *adj* having a calm appearance or nature. [C17: from L *placidus* peaceful]
▸**placidity** (plə'sɪdɪtɪ) *or* '**placidness** *n* ▸'**placidly** *adv*

placing ('pleɪsɪŋ) *n Stock Exchange.* a method of issuing securities to the public using an intermediary, such as a stockbroking firm.

placket ('plækɪt) *n Dressmaking.* **1** a piece of cloth sewn in under a closure with buttons, zips, etc. **2** the closure itself. [C16: ?from MDu. *plackaet* breastplate, from Med. L *placca* metal plate]

placoid ('plækɔɪd) *adj* **1** platelike or flattened. **2** (of the scales of sharks) toothlike; composed of dentine with an enamel tip and basal pulp cavity. [C19: from Gk *plac-, plax* flat]

plafond (plə'fɒn; *French* plafɔ̃) *n* a ceiling, esp. one having ornamentation. [C17: from F, from *plat* flat + *fond* bottom, from L *fundus*]

plagal ('pleɪgᵊl) *adj* **1** (of a cadence) progressing from the subdominant to the tonic chord, as in the *Amen* of a hymn. **2** (of a mode) commencing upon the dominant of an authentic mode, but sharing the same final as the authentic mode. ◆ Cf. **authentic** (sense 5). [C16: from Med. L *plagālis,* from *plaga,* ?from Gk *plagos* side]

plage (plɑːʒ) *n Astron.* a bright patch in the sun's chromosphere. [F, lit.: beach]

plagiarism ⓘ ('pleɪdʒəˌrɪzəm) *n* **1** the act of plagiarizing. **2** something plagiarized. [C17: from L *plagiārus* plunderer, from *plagium* kidnapping]
▸'**plagiarist** *n* ▸ˌ**plagia'ristic** *adj*

plagiarize ⓘ *or* **plagiarise** ('pleɪdʒəˌraɪz) *vb* **plagiarizes, plagiarizing, plagiarized** *or* **plagiarises, plagiarising, plagiarised.** to appropriate (ideas, passages, etc.) from (another work or author).
▸'**plagiaˌrizer** *or* '**plagiaˌriser** *n*

plagioclase ('pleɪdʒɪəʊˌkleɪz) *n* a series of feldspar minerals consisting of a mixture of sodium and calcium aluminium silicates in triclinic crystalline form. [C19: from Gk, from *plagos* side + -CLASE]
▸**plagioclastic** (ˌpleɪdʒɪəʊ'klæstɪk) *adj*

plague ⓘ (pleɪg) *n* **1** any widespread and usually highly contagious disease with a high fatality rate. **2** an infectious disease of rodents, esp. rats, transmitted to man by the bite of the rat flea. **3** See **bubonic plague. 4** something that afflicts or harasses. **5** *Inf.* an annoyance or nuisance. **6** a pestilence, affliction, or calamity on a large scale, esp. when regarded as sent by God. ◆ *vb* **plagues, plaguing, plagued.** (*tr*) **7** to afflict or harass. **8** to bring down a plague upon. **9** *Inf.* to annoy. [C14: from LL *plāga* pestilence, from L: a blow]

plaguy *or* **plaguey** ('pleɪgɪ) *Arch., inf.* ◆ *adj* **1** disagreeable or vexing. ◆ *adv* **2** disagreeably or annoyingly.
▸'**plaguily** *adv*

plaice (pleɪs) *n, pl* **plaice** *or* **plaices. 1** a European flatfish having an oval brown body marked with red or orange spots and valued as a food fish. **2** *US & Canad.* any of various other related fishes. [C13: from OF *plaïz,* from LL *platessa* flatfish, from Gk *platus* flat]

plaid (plæd, pleɪd) *n* **1** a long piece of cloth of a tartan pattern, worn over the shoulder as part of Highland costume. **2a** a crisscross weave or cloth. **2b** (*as modifier*): *a plaid scarf.* [C16: from Scot. Gaelic *plaide,* from ?]

Plaid Cymru (ˌplaɪd 'kʌmrɪ) *n* the Welsh nationalist party. [Welsh]

plain[1] ⓘ (pleɪn) *adj* **1** flat or smooth; level. **2** not complicated; clear: *the plain truth.* **3** not difficult; simple or easy: *a plain task.* **4** honest or straightforward. **5** lowly, esp. in social rank or education. **6** without adornment or show: *a plain coat.* **7** (of fabric) without pattern or of simple untwilled weave. **8** not attractive. **9** not mixed; simple: *plain vodka.* **10** (of knitting) done in plain stitch. ◆ *n* **11** a level or almost level tract of country. **12** a simple stitch in knitting made by passing the wool round the front of the needle. ◆ *adv* **13** (intensifier): *just plain tired.* [C13: from OF: simple, from L *plānus* level, clear]
▸'**plainly** *adv* ▸'**plainness** *n*

plain[2] (pleɪn) *vb* a dialect or poetic word for **complain.** [C14 *pleignen,* from OF *plaindre* to lament, from L *plangere* to beat]

plainchant ('pleɪnˌtʃɑːnt) *n* another name for **plainsong.** [C18: from F, for Med. L *cantus plānus*]

plain chocolate *n* chocolate with a slightly bitter flavour and dark colour.

plain clothes *pl n* **a** ordinary clothes, as distinguished from uniform, as worn by a police detective on duty. **b** (*as modifier*): *a plain-clothes policeman.*

plain flour *n* flour to which no raising agent has been added.

plain sailing *n* **1** *Inf.* smooth or easy progress. **2** *Naut.* sailing in a body of water that is unobstructed; clear sailing.

plainsman ('pleɪnzmən) *n, pl* **plainsmen.** a person who lives in a plains region, esp. in the Great Plains of North America.

plainsong ('pleɪnˌsɒŋ) *n* the style of unison unaccompanied vocal music used in the medieval Church, esp. in Gregorian chant. [C16: translation of Med. L *cantus plānus*]

plain-spoken ⓘ *adj* candid; frank; blunt.

plaint (pleɪnt) *n* **1** *Arch.* a complaint or lamentation. **2** *Law.* a statement in writing of grounds of complaint made to a court of law. [C13: from OF *plainte,* from L *planctus* lamentation, from *plangere* to beat]

plaintiff ('pleɪntɪf) *n* a person who brings a civil action in a court of law. [C14: from legal F *plaintif,* from OF *plaintif* (adj) complaining, from *plainte* PLAINT]

plaintive ⓘ ('pleɪntɪv) *adj* expressing melancholy; mournful. [C14: from OF *plaintif* grieving, from PLAINT]
▸'**plaintively** *adv* ▸'**plaintiveness** *n*

plait (plæt) *n* **1** a length of hair, etc., that has been plaited. **2** a rare spelling of **pleat.** ◆ *vb* **3** (*tr*) to intertwine (strands or strips) in a pattern. [C15 *pleyt,* from OF *pleit,* from L *plicāre* to fold]

plan ⓘ (plæn) *n* **1** a detailed scheme, method, etc., for attaining an objective. **2** (*sometimes pl*) a proposed, usually tentative idea for doing something. **3** a drawing to scale of a horizontal section through a building taken at a given level. **4** an outline, sketch, etc. ◆ *vb* **plans, planning, planned. 5** to form a plan (for) or make plans (for). **6** (*tr*) to make a plan of (a building). **7** (*tr; takes a clause as object or an infinitive*) to have in mind as a purpose; intend. [C18: via F from L *plānus* flat]

planar ('pleɪnə) *adj* **1** of or relating to a plane. **2** lying in one plane; flat. [C19: from LL *plānāris* on level ground, from L *plānus* flat]

planarian (plə'nɛərɪən) *n* any of various free-living mostly aquatic flatworms, having a three-branched intestine. [C19: from NL *Plānāria* type genus, from LL *plānārius* flat; see PLANE[1]]

planar process *n* a method of producing diffused junctions in semiconductor devices. A pattern of holes is etched into an oxide layer formed on a silicon substrate, into which impurities are diffused through the holes.

THESAURUS

dering, stationing **3** = **appointment**, assignment, employment, engagement

placid *adj* = **calm**, collected, composed, cool, equable, even, even-tempered, gentle, halcyon, imperturbable, mild, peaceful, quiet, self-possessed, serene, still, tranquil, undisturbed, unexcitable, unfazed (*inf.*), unmoved, unruffled, untroubled
Antonyms *adj* agitated, disturbed, emotional, excitable, impulsive, passionate, rough, temperamental, tempestuous

plagiarism *n* **1** = **copying**, appropriation, borrowing, cribbing (*inf.*), infringement, lifting (*inf.*), piracy, theft

plagiarize *vb* = **copy**, appropriate, borrow, crib (*inf.*), infringe, lift (*inf.*), pirate, steal, thieve

plague *n* **1** = **disease**, contagion, epidemic, infection, lurgy (*inf.*), pandemic, pestilence **4** = **affliction**, bane, blight, calamity, cancer, curse, evil, scourge, torment, trial **5** *Informal* = **nuisance**, aggravation, annoyance, bother, hassle (*inf.*), irritant, pain (*inf.*), pest, problem, thorn in one's flesh, vexation ◆ *vb* **7, 9** = **pester**, afflict, annoy, badger, bedevil, be on one's back (*sl.*), bother, disturb, fret, get in one's hair (*inf.*), get on one's nerves (*inf.*), harass, harry, hassle (*inf.*), haunt, molest, pain, persecute, tease, torment, torture, trouble, vex

plain[1] *adj* **1** = **flat**, even, level, plane, smooth **2** = **clear**, apparent, bold, comprehensible, distinct, evident, legible, lucid, manifest, obvious, overt, patent, transparent, unambiguous, understandable, unmistakable, visible **4** = **straightforward**, artless, blunt, candid, direct, downright, forthright, frank, guileless, honest, ingenuous, open, outspoken, round, sincere, upfront (*inf.*) **5** = **ordinary**, common, commonplace, everyday, frugal, homely, lowly, modest, simple, unaffected, unpretentious, workaday **6** = **unadorned**, austere, bare, basic, discreet, modest, muted, pure, restrained, severe, simple, Spartan, stark, unembellished, unfussy, unornamented, unpatterned, unvarnished **8** = **ugly**, ill-favoured, no oil painting (*inf.*), not beautiful, not striking, ordinary, unalluring, unattractive, unlovely, unprepossessing ◆ *n* **11** = **flatland**, grassland, llano, lowland, mesa, open country, pampas, plateau, prairie, steppe, tableland, veld
Antonyms *adj* ≠ **flat:** bumpy, not level, uneven ≠ **clear:** ambiguous, complex, concealed, deceptive, difficult, disguised, hidden, illegible, incomprehensible, inconspicuous, indiscernible, indistinct, obscure, vague, veiled ≠ **straightforward:** circuitous, indirect, meandering, rambling, roundabout ≠ **ordinary:** affected, distinguished, egotistic, ostentatious, pretentious, sophisticated, worldly ≠ **unadorned:** adorned, decorated, fancy, ornate ≠ **ugly:** attractive, beautiful, comely, good-looking, gorgeous, handsome

plain-spoken *adj* = **blunt**, candid, direct, downright, explicit, forthright, frank, open, outright, outspoken, straightforward, unequivocal, upfront (*inf.*)
Antonyms *adj* diplomatic, discreet, evasive, guarded, indirect, reticent, subtle, tactful, thoughtful

plaintive *adj* = **sorrowful**, disconsolate, doleful, grief-stricken, grievous, heart-rending, melancholy, mournful, pathetic, piteous, pitiful, rueful, sad, wistful, woebegone, woeful

plan *n* **1, 2** = **scheme**, contrivance, design, device, idea, method, plot, procedure, programme, project, proposal, proposition, scenario, strategy, suggestion, system **3, 4** = **diagram**, blueprint, chart, delineation, drawing, illustration, layout, map, representation, scale drawing, sketch ◆ *vb* **5** = **devise**, arrange, concoct, contrive, design, draft, formulate, frame, invent, organize, outline, plot, prepare, represent, scheme, think out **7** = **intend**, aim, contemplate, envisage, foresee, mean, propose, purpose

planchet ('plɑːntʃɪt) *n* a piece of metal ready to be stamped as a coin, medal, etc.; flan. [C17: from F: little board, from *planche* PLANK]

planchette (plɑːn'ʃɛt) *n* a heart-shaped board on wheels, on which messages are written under supposed spirit guidance. [C19: from F: little board, from *planche* PLANK]

Planck constant (plæŋk) *or* **Planck's constant** *n* a fundamental constant equal to the energy of any quantum of radiation divided by its frequency. [C19: after Max *Planck* (1858–1947), G physicist]

plane[1] ⓣ (pleɪn) *n* **1** *Maths.* a flat surface in which a straight line joining any two of its points lies entirely on that surface. **2** a level surface. **3** a level of existence, attainment, etc. **4a** short for **aeroplane. 4b** a wing or supporting surface of an aircraft. ◆ *adj* **5** level or flat. **6** *Maths.* lying entirely in one plane. ◆ *vb* **planes, planing, planed.** (*intr*) **7** to glide. **8** (of a boat) to rise partly and skim over the water when moving at a certain speed. [C17: from L *plānum* level surface]

plane[2] (pleɪn) *n* **1** a tool with a steel blade set obliquely in a wooden or iron body, for smoothing timber surfaces, cutting grooves, etc. **2** a flat tool, usually metal, for smoothing the surface of clay or plaster in a mould. ◆ *vb* **planes, planing, planed.** (*tr*) **3** to smooth or cut (timber, etc.) using a plane. **4** (often foll. by *off*) to remove using a plane. [C14: via OF from LL *plāna* plane, from *plānāre* to level]

plane[3] (pleɪn) *n* See **plane tree.**

plane geometry *n* the study of the properties of plane curves, figures, etc.

plane polarization *n* a type of polarization in which waves of light or other radiation are restricted to vibration in a single plane.

planet ('plænɪt) *n* **1** Also called: **major planet.** any of the nine celestial bodies, Mercury, Venus, Earth, Mars, Jupiter, Saturn, Uranus, Neptune, or Pluto, that revolve around the sun in elliptical orbits. **2** any celestial body revolving around a star. **3** *Astrol.* any of the planets of the solar system, excluding the earth but including the sun and moon, each thought to rule one or sometimes two signs of the zodiac. [C12: via OF from LL *planēta*, from Gk *planētēs* wanderer, from *planaein* to wander]

plane table *n* a surveying instrument consisting of a drawing board mounted on adjustable legs.

planetarium (ˌplænɪ'tɛərɪəm) *n, pl* **planetariums** *or* **planetaria** (-ɪə). **1** an instrument for simulating the apparent motions of the sun, moon, and planets by projecting images of these bodies onto a domed ceiling. **2** a building in which such an instrument is housed. **3** a model of the solar system.

planetary ⓣ ('plænɪtərɪ, -trɪ) *adj* **1** of a planet. **2** mundane; terrestrial. **3** wandering or erratic. **4** *Astrol.* under the influence of one of the planets. **5** (of a gear) having an axis that rotates around that of another gear.

planetesimal hypothesis (ˌplænɪ'tɛsɪməl) *n* the discredited theory that the close passage of a star to the sun caused many small bodies (**planetesimals**) to be drawn from the sun, eventually coalescing to form the planets. [C20: *planetesimal*, from PLANET + INFINITESIMAL]

planetoid ('plænɪˌtɔɪd) *n* another name for **asteroid** (sense 1).
▸ˌ**plane'toidal** *adj*

plane tree *or* **plane** *n* a tree with ball-shaped heads of fruit and leaves with pointed lobes. [C14 *plane*, from OF, from L *platanus*, from Gk, from *platos* wide, referring to the leaves]

plangent ('plændʒənt) *adj* **1** having a loud deep sound. **2** resonant and mournful. [C19: from L *plangere* to beat (esp. the breast, in grief)]

planimeter (plæ'nɪmɪtə) *n* a mechanical instrument for measuring the area of an irregular plane figure by moving a point attached to an arm.
▸**pla'nimetry** *n*

planish ('plænɪʃ) *vb* (*tr*) to give a final finish to (metal, etc.) by hammering or rolling. [C16: from OF *planir* to smooth out, from L *plānus* flat]

planisphere ('plænɪˌsfɪə) *n* a projection or representation of all or part of a sphere on a plane surface. [C14: from Med. L *plānisphaerium*, from L *plānus* flat + Gk *sphaira* globe]

plank (plæŋk) *n* **1** a stout length of sawn timber. **2** something that supports or sustains. **3** one of the policies in a political party's programme. **4 walk the plank.** to be forced by pirates, etc., to walk to one's death off the end of a plank jutting out from the side of a ship. ◆ *vb* **5** (*tr*) to cover or provide with planks. [C13: from OF *planke*, from LL *planca* board, from *plancus* flat-footed]

planking ('plæŋkɪŋ) *n* a number of planks.

plankton ('plæŋktən) *n* the organisms inhabiting the surface layer of a sea or lake, consisting of small drifting plants and animals. [C19: via G from Gk *planktos* wandering, from *plazesthai* to roam]

planned economy *n* another name for **command economy.**

planned obsolescence *n* the policy of deliberately limiting the life of a product in order to encourage the purchaser to replace it. Also called: **built-in obsolescence.**

planner ('plænə) *n* **1** a person who makes plans, esp. for the development of a town, building, etc. **2** a chart for recording future appointments, tasks, goals, etc.

planning permission *n* (in Britain) formal permission granted by a local authority for the development or changed use of land or buildings.

plano- *or sometimes before a vowel* **plan-** *combining form.* indicating flatness or planeness: *plano-concave.* [from L *plānus* flat]

plano-concave (ˌpleɪnəʊ'kɒnkeɪv) *adj* (of a lens) having one side concave and the other plane.

plano-convex (ˌpleɪnəʊ'kɒnvɛks) *adj* (of a lens) having one side convex and the other plane.

plant[1] ⓣ (plɑːnt) *n* **1** any living organism that typically synthesizes its food from inorganic substances, lacks specialized sense organs, and has no powers of locomotion. **2** such an organism that is smaller than a shrub or tree; a herb. **3** a cutting, seedling, or similar structure, esp. when ready for transplantation. **4** *Inf.* a thing positioned secretly for discovery by another, esp. in order to incriminate an innocent person. **5** *Inf.* a person, placed in an audience, whose rehearsed responses, etc., seem spontaneous to the rest of the audience. **6** *Inf.* a person placed secretly in a group or organization to obtain information, etc. ◆ *vb* (*tr*) **7** (often foll. by *out*) to set (seeds, crops, etc.) into (ground) to grow. **8** to place firmly in position. **9** to establish; found. **10** (foll. by *with*) to stock or furnish. **11** to implant in the mind. **12** *Sl.* to deliver (a blow). **13** *Inf.* to position or hide, esp. in order to deceive or observe. **14** *Inf.* to hide or secrete, esp. for some illegal purpose or in order to incriminate someone. [OE, from *planta* a shoot]
▸'**plantable** *adj*

plant[2] ⓣ (plɑːnt) *n* **1** the land, buildings, and equipment used in carrying on an industry or business. **2** a factory or workshop. **3** mobile mechanical equipment for construction, road-making, etc. [C20: special use of PLANT[1]]

plantain[1] ('plæntɪn) *n* any of various N temperate plants, esp. the great plantain, which has a rosette of broad leaves and a slender spike of small greenish flowers. See also **ribwort.** [C14 *plauntein*, from OF, from L *plantāgō*, from *planta* sole of the foot]

plantain[2] ('plæntɪn) *n* a large tropical plant with a green-skinned banana-like fruit which is eaten as a staple food in many tropical regions. [C16: Sp. *platano* plantain, PLANE TREE]

plantain lily *n* any of several Asian plants of the genus *Hosta*, having broad ribbed leaves.

plantar ('plæntə) *adj* of or on the sole of the foot. [C18: from L *plantāris*, from *planta* sole of the foot]

plantation (plæn'teɪʃən) *n* **1** an estate, esp. in tropical countries, where cash crops such as rubber, oil palm, etc., are grown on a large scale. **2** a group of cultivated trees or plants. **3** (formerly) a colony or group of settlers.

planter ('plɑːntə) *n* **1** the owner or manager of a plantation. **2** a machine designed for rapid and efficient planting of seeds. **3** a colonizer or settler. **4** a decorative pot for house plants.

plantigrade ('plæntɪˌgreɪd) *adj* **1** walking with the entire sole of the foot touching the ground, as man and bears. ◆ *n* **2** a plantigrade animal. [C19: via F from NL *plantigradus*, from L *planta* sole of the foot + *gradus* a step]

plant louse *n* another name for an **aphid.**

plaque ⓣ (plæk, plɑːk) *n* **1** an ornamental or commemorative inscribed tablet. **2** a small flat brooch or badge. **3** *Pathol.* any small abnormal patch on or within the body. **4** short for **dental plaque.** [C19: from F, from *plaquier* to plate, from MDu. *placken* to beat into a thin plate]

plash (plæʃ) *vb, n* a less common word for **splash.** [OE *plæsc*, prob. imit.]
▸'**plashy** *adj*

-plasia *or* **-plasy** *n combining form.* indicating growth, development, or change. [from NL, from Gk *plasis* a moulding, from *plassein* to mould]

plasm ('plæzəm) *n* **1** protoplasm of a specified type: *germ plasm.* **2** a variant of **plasma.**

-plasm *n combining form.* (in biology) indicating the material forming cells: *protoplasm; cytoplasm.* [from Gk *plasma* something moulded; see PLASMA]
▸**-plasmic** *adj combining form.*

plasma ('plæzmə) *or* **plasm** *n* **1** the clear yellowish fluid portion of blood or lymph in which the corpuscles and cells are suspended. **2** Also called: **blood plasma.** a sterilized preparation of such fluid, taken from the blood, for use in transfusions. **3** a former name for **protoplasm** or **cytoplasm. 4** *Physics.* a hot ionized gas containing positive ions and electrons. **5** a green variety of chalcedony. [C18: from LL: something moulded, from Gk, from *plassein* to mould]
▸**plasmatic** (plæz'mætɪk) *or* '**plasmic** *adj*

plasma torch *n* an electrical device for converting a gas into a plasma, used for melting metal, etc.

plasmid ('plæzmɪd) *n* a small circle of bacterial DNA that is independent of the main bacterial chromosome. Plasmids often contain genes for drug resistances and can be transmitted between bacteria of the

THESAURUS

plane[1] *n* **1, 2** = **flat surface**, level surface **3** = **level**, condition, degree, footing, position, stratum **4** = **aeroplane**, aircraft, jet ◆ *adj* **5** = **level**, even, flat, flush, horizontal, plain, regular, smooth, uniform ◆ *vb* **7** = **skim**, glide, sail, skate

planetary *adj* **2** = **terrestrial**, earthly, mundane, sublunary, tellurian, terrene **3** = **moving**, aberrant, erratic, journeying, travelling, vacillating, variable, wandering

plant[1] *n* **1, 2** = **vegetable**, bush, flower, herb, shrub, weed ◆ *vb* **7** = **sow**, implant, put in the ground, scatter, seed, set out, transplant **8, 9** = **place**, establish, fix, found, imbed, insert, institute, lodge, put, root, set, settle, sow the seeds

plant[2] *n* **1, 3** = **machinery**, apparatus, equipment, gear **2** = **factory**, foundry, mill, shop, works, yard

plaque *n* **1, 2** = **plate**, badge, brooch, cartouch(e), medal, medallion, panel, slab, tablet same and different species: used in genetic engineering. [C20: from PLASM + -ID[1]]

plasmodium (plæz'məʊdɪəm) *n, pl* **plasmodia** (-dɪə). **1** an amoeboid mass of protoplasm, containing many nuclei: a stage in the life cycle of certain organisms. **2** a parasitic protozoan which causes malaria. [C19: NL; see PLASMA, -ODE[1]]
▸**plas'modial** *adj*

plasmolysis (plæz'mɒlɪsɪs) *n* the shrinkage of protoplasm away from cell walls that occurs as a result of excessive water loss, esp. in plant cells.

-plast *n combining form.* indicating a living cell or particle of living matter: *protoplast.* [from Gk *plastos* formed, from *plassein* to form]

plaster ❶ ('plɑːstə) *n* **1** a mixture of lime, sand, and water that is applied to a wall or ceiling as a soft paste that hardens when dry. **2** *Brit., Austral., & NZ.* an adhesive strip of material for dressing a cut, wound, etc. **3** short for **mustard plaster** or **plaster of Paris.** ◆ *vb* **4** to coat (a wall, ceiling, etc.) with plaster. **5** (*tr*) to apply like plaster: *she plastered make-up on her face.* **6** (*tr*) to cause to lie flat or to adhere. **7** (*tr*) to apply a plaster cast to. **8** (*tr*) *Sl.* to strike or defeat with great force. [OE, from Med. L *plastrum* medicinal salve, building plaster, via L from Gk *emplastron* curative dressing]
▸**'plasterer** *n*

plasterboard ('plɑːstəˌbɔːd) *n* a thin rigid board, in the form of a layer of plaster compressed between two layers of fibreboard, used to form or cover walls, etc.

plastered ('plɑːstəd) *adj Sl.* intoxicated; drunk.

plaster of Paris *n* **1** a white powder that sets to a hard solid when mixed with water, used for making sculptures and casts, as an additive for lime plasters, and for making casts for setting broken limbs. **2** the hard plaster produced when this powder is mixed with water. [C15: from Med. L *plastrum parisiense,* orig. made from the gypsum of Paris]

plastic ❶ ('plæstɪk) *n* **1** any one of a large number of synthetic materials that have a polymeric structure and can be moulded when soft and then set. Plastics are used in the manufacture of many articles and in coatings, artificial fibres, etc. ◆ *adj* **2** made of plastic. **3** easily influenced; impressionable. **4** capable of being moulded or formed. **5a** of moulding or modelling: *the plastic arts.* **5b** produced or apparently produced by moulding: *the plastic draperies of Giotto's figures.* **6** having the power to form or influence: *the plastic forces of the imagination.* **7** *Biol.* able to change, develop, or grow: *plastic tissues.* **8** *Sl.* superficially attractive yet unoriginal or artificial: *plastic food.* [C17: from L *plasticus* relating to moulding, from Gk *plastikos,* from *plassein* to form]
▸**'plastically** *adv* ▸**plasticity** (plæ'stɪsɪtɪ) *n*

-plastic *adj combining form.* growing or forming. [from Gk *plastikos;* see PLASTIC]

plastic bomb *n* a bomb consisting of plastic explosive fitted around a detonator.

plastic bullet *n* a bullet consisting of a cylinder of plastic about four inches long, generally causing less severe injuries than an ordinary bullet, and used esp. for riot control. Also called: **baton round.**

plastic explosive *n* an adhesive jelly-like explosive substance.

Plasticine ('plæstɪˌsiːn) *n Trademark.* a soft coloured material used, esp. by children, for modelling.

plasticize *or* **plasticise** ('plæstɪˌsaɪz) *vb* **plasticizes, plasticizing, plasticized** *or* **plasticises, plasticising, plasticised.** to make or become plastic, as by the addition of a plasticizer.
▸**ˌplastici'zation** *or* **ˌplastici'sation** *n*

plasticizer *or* **plasticiser** ('plæstɪˌsaɪzə) *n* any of a number of substances added to materials. Their uses include softening and improving the flexibility of plastics and preventing dried paint coatings from becoming too brittle.

plastic money *n* credit cards as opposed to cash.

plastic surgery *n* the branch of surgery concerned with therapeutic or cosmetic repair or re-formation of missing, injured, or malformed tissues or parts.
▸**plastic surgeon** *n*

plastid ('plæstɪd) *n* any of various small particles in the cells of plants and some animals which contain starch, oil, protein, etc. [C19: via G from Gk *plastēs* sculptor, from *plassein* to form]

plastron ('plæstrən) *n* the bony plate forming the ventral part of the shell of a tortoise or turtle. [C16: via F from It. *piastrone,* from *piastra* breastplate, from L *emplastrum* PLASTER]
▸**'plastral** *adj*

-plasty *n combining form.* indicating plastic surgery: *rhinoplasty.* [from Gk *-plastia;* see -PLAST]

plat[1] (plæt) *n* a small area of ground; plot. [C16 (also in ME place names): orig. a var. of PLOT[2]]

plat[2] (plæt) *vb* **plats, platting, platted,** *n* a dialect variant spelling of **plait.** [C16]

platan ('plætᵊn) *n* another name for **plane tree.** [C14: see PLANE TREE]

plat du jour ('plɑː də 'ʒʊə; *French* pla dy zur) *n, pl* **plats du jour** ('plɑːz də 'ʒʊə; *French* pla dy zur). the specially prepared or recommended dish of the day on a restaurant's menu. [F, lit.: dish of the day]

plate ❶ (pleɪt) *n* **1a** a shallow usually circular dish made of porcelain, earthenware, glass, etc., on which food is served. **1b** (*as modifier*): *a plate rack.* **2a** Also called: **plateful.** the contents of a plate. **2b** *Austral. & NZ.* a plate of cakes, sandwiches, etc., brought by a guest to a party: *everyone was asked to bring a plate.* **3** an entire course of a meal: *a cold plate.* **4** any shallow receptacle, esp. for receiving a collection in church. **5** flat metal of uniform thickness obtained by rolling, usually having a thickness greater than about three millimetres. **6** a thin coating of metal usually on another metal, as produced by electrodeposition. **7** metal or metalware that has been coated in this way: *Sheffield plate.* **8** dishes, cutlery, etc., made of gold or silver. **9** a sheet of metal, plastic, rubber, etc., having a printing surface produced by a process such as stereotyping. **10** a print taken from such a sheet or from a woodcut. **11** a thin flat sheet of a substance, such as metal or glass. **12** a small piece of metal, plastic, etc., designed to bear an inscription and to be fixed to another surface. **13** armour made of overlapping or articulated pieces of thin metal. **14** *Photog.* a sheet of glass, or sometimes metal, coated with photographic emulsion on which an image can be formed by exposure to light. **15** a device for straightening teeth. **16** an informal word for **denture** (sense 1). **17** *Anat.* any flat platelike structure. **18a** a cup awarded to the winner of a sporting contest, esp. a horse race. **18b** a race or contest for such a prize. **19** any of the rigid layers of the earth's lithosphere. **20** *Electronics, chiefly US.* the anode in an electronic valve. **21** a horizontal timber joist that supports rafters. **22** a light horseshoe for flat racing. **23** *RC Church.* Also called: **Communion plate.** a flat plate held under the chin of a communicant in order to catch any fragments of the consecrated Host. **24 on a plate.** acquired without trouble: *he was handed the job on a plate.* **25 on one's plate.** waiting to be done or dealt with. ◆ *vb* **plates, plating, plated.** (*tr*) **26** to coat (a surface, usually metal) with a thin layer of other metal by electrolysis, etc. **27** to cover with metal plates, as for protection. **28** *Printing.* to make a stereotype or electrotype from (type or another plate). **29** to form (metal) into plate, esp. by rolling. [C13: from OF: thin metal sheet, something flat, from Vulgar L *plattus* (unattested)]

plateau ❶ ('plætəʊ) *n, pl* **plateaus** *or* **plateaux** (-əʊz). **1** a wide mainly level area of elevated land. **2** a relatively long period of stability; levelling off: *the rising prices reached a plateau.* ◆ *vb* (*intr*) **3** to remain at a stable level for a relatively long period. [C18: from F, from OF *platel* something flat, from *plat* flat]

plated ('pleɪtɪd) *adj* **a** coated with a layer of metal. **b** (*in combination*): *gold-plated.*

plate glass *n* glass formed into a sheet by rolling, used for windows, etc.

platelayer ('pleɪtˌleɪə) *n Brit.* a workman who lays and maintains railway track. US equivalent: **trackman.**

platelet ('pleɪtlɪt) *n* a minute particle occurring in the blood of vertebrates and involved in the clotting of the blood. [C19: a small PLATE]

platen ('plætᵊn) *n* **1** a flat plate in a printing press that presses the paper against the type. **2** the roller on a typewriter, against which the keys strike. [C15: from OF *platine,* from *plat* flat]

plater ('pleɪtə) *n* **1** a person or thing that plates. **2** *Horse racing.* a mediocre horse entered chiefly for minor races.

plate tectonics *n* (*functioning as sing*) *Geol.* the study of the earth's crust with reference to the theory that the lithosphere is divided into rigid blocks (plates) that float on semimolten rock and are thus able to interact with each other at their boundaries.

platform ❶ ('plætfɔːm) *n* **1** a raised floor or other horizontal surface. **2** a raised area at a railway station, from which passengers have access to the trains. **3** See **drilling platform.** **4** the declared principles, aims, etc., of a political party, etc. **5a** the thick raised sole of some shoes. **5b** (*as modifier*): *platform shoes.* **6** a vehicle or level place on which weapons are mounted and fired. **7** a specific type of computer hardware or computer operating system. [C16: from F *plateforme,* from *plat* flat + *forme* layout]

platform ticket *n* a ticket for admission to railway platforms but not for travel.

plating ('pleɪtɪŋ) *n* **1** a coating or layer of material, esp. metal. **2** a layer or covering of metal plates.

platiniridium (ˌplætɪnɪ'rɪdɪəm) *n* any alloy of platinum and iridium.

platinize *or* **platinise** ('plætɪˌnaɪz) *vb* **platinizes, platinizing, platinized** *or* **platinises, platinising, platinised.** (*tr*) to coat with platinum.
▸**ˌplatini'zation** *or* **ˌplatini'sation** *n*

platinum ('plætɪnəm) *n* a ductile malleable silvery-white metallic ele-

THESAURUS

plaster *n* **1** = **mortar**, gesso, gypsum, plaster of Paris, stucco **2** = **bandage**, adhesive plaster, dressing, Elastoplast (*Trademark*), sticking plaster ◆ *vb* **4, 5** = **cover**, bedaub, besmear, coat, daub, overlay, smear, spread

plastic *adj* **3** = **manageable**, compliant, docile, easily influenced, impressionable, malleable, pliable, receptive, responsive, tractable **4** = **pliant**, ductile, fictile, flexible, mouldable, pliable, soft, supple, tensile **8** *Slang* = **false**, artificial, meretricious, mock, phoney *or* phony (*inf.*), pseudo (*inf.*), sham, specious, spurious, superficial, synthetic
Antonyms *adj* ≠ **manageable**: intractable, rebellious, recalcitrant, refractory, unmanageable, unreceptive ≠ **pliant**: brittle, hard, inflexible, rigid, stiff, unbending, unyielding ≠ **false**: authentic, genuine, natural, real, sincere, true

plasticity *n* **3, 4** = **pliability**, flexibility, malleability, pliableness, suppleness, tractability

plate *n* **1** = **platter**, dish, trencher (*arch.*) **3** = **helping**, course, dish, portion, serving **5, 11** = **layer**, panel, sheet, slab **10** = **illustration**, lithograph, print ◆ *vb* **26** = **coat**, anodize, cover, electroplate, face, gild, laminate, nickel, overlay, platinize, silver

plateau *n* **1** = **upland**, highland, mesa, table, tableland **2** = **levelling off**, level, stability, stage

platform *n* **1** = **stage**, dais, podium, rostrum,

ment, very resistant to heat and chemicals: used in jewellery, laboratory apparatus, electrical contacts, dentistry, electroplating, and as a catalyst. Symbol: Pt; atomic no.: 78; atomic wt.: 195.08. [C19: NL, from Sp. *platina* silvery element, from *plata* silver, from Provençal: silver plate + the suffix *-um*]

platinum black *n Chem.* a black powder consisting of very finely divided platinum metal.

platinum-blond *or* (*fem*) **platinum-blonde** *adj* **1** (of hair) of a pale silver-blond colour. **2a** having hair of this colour. **2b** (*as n*): *she was a platinum blonde.*

platinum disc *n* **1** (in Britain) an LP record certified to have sold 300 000 copies or a single certified to have sold 600 000 copies. **2** (in the US) an LP record or single certified to have sold one million copies.

platinum metal *n* any of the group of precious metallic elements consisting of ruthenium, rhodium, palladium, osmium, iridium, and platinum.

platitude ❶ (ˈplætɪˌtjuːd) *n* **1** a trite, dull, or obvious remark. **2** staleness or insipidity of thought or language; triteness. [C19: from F, lit.: flatness, from *plat* flat]
▸ **ˌplatiˈtudinous** *adj*

platitudinize *or* **platitudinise** (ˌplætɪˈtjuːdɪˌnaɪz) *vb* **platitudinizes, platitudinizing, platitudinized** *or* **platitudinises, platitudinising, platitudinised.** (*intr*) to speak or write in platitudes.

Platonic ❶ (pləˈtɒnɪk) *adj* **1** of or relating to Plato or his teachings. **2** (*often not cap.*) free from physical desire: *Platonic love.*
▸ **Plaˈtonically** *adv*

Platonic solid *n* any of the five possible regular polyhedrons: cube, tetrahedron, octahedron, icosahedron, and dodecahedron.

Platonism (ˈpleɪtəˌnɪzəm) *n* the teachings of Plato (?427–?347 B.C.), Greek philosopher, and his followers; esp. the philosophical theory that the meanings of general words are real entities (Forms) and that particular objects have properties in common by virtue of their relationship with these Forms.
▸ **ˈPlatonist** *n*

platoon ❶ (pləˈtuːn) *n* **1** *Mil.* a subunit of a company, usually comprising three sections of ten to twelve men. **2** a group of people sharing a common activity, etc. [C17: from F *peloton* little ball, group of men, from *pelote* ball; see PELLET]

Plattdeutsch (*German* ˈplatdɔytʃ) *n* another name for **Low German.** [lit.: flat German]

platteland (ˈplatəˌlant) *n* **the.** (in South Africa) the country districts or rural areas. [C20: from Afrik., from Du. *plat* flat + *land* country]

platter ❶ (ˈplætə) *n* **1** a large shallow usually oval dish or plate. **2** a course of a meal, usually consisting of several different foods served on the same plate: *a seafood platter.* [C14: from Anglo-Norman *plater*, from *plat* dish, from OF *plat* flat; see PLATE]

platy- *combining form.* indicating something flat, as **platyhelminth,** the flatworm. [from Gk *platus* flat]

platypus (ˈplætɪpəs) *n, pl* **platypuses.** See **duck-billed platypus.** [C18: NL, from PLATY- + *-pus*, from Gk *pous* foot]

platyrrhine (ˈplætɪˌraɪn) *or* **platyrrhinian** (ˌplætɪˈrɪnɪən) *adj* **1** (esp. of New World monkeys) having widely separated nostrils opening to the side of the face. **2** (of a human) having an unusually short wide nose. [C19: from NL *platyrrhinus*, from PLATY- + *-rrhinus*, from Gk *rhis* nose]

plaudit ❶ (ˈplɔːdɪt) *n* (*usually pl*) **1** an expression of enthusiastic approval. **2** a round of applause. [C17: from earlier *plauditē*, from L: applaud!, from *plaudere* to APPLAUD]

plausible ❶ (ˈplɔːzɪbᵊl) *adj* **1** apparently reasonable, valid, truthful, etc.: *a plausible excuse.* **2** apparently trustworthy or believable: *a plausible speaker.* [C16: from L *plausibilis* worthy of applause, from *plaudere* to APPLAUD]
▸ **ˌplausiˈbility** *or* **ˈplausibleness** *n* ▸ **ˈplausibly** *adv*

play ❶ (pleɪ) *vb* **1** to occupy oneself in (a sport or diversion). **2** (*tr*) to contend against (an opponent) in a sport or game: *Ed played Tony at chess and lost.* **3** to fulfil or cause to fulfil (a particular role) in a team game: *he plays in the defence.* **4** (*intr;* often foll. by *about* or *around*) to behave carelessly, esp. in a way that is unconsciously cruel or hurtful: *to play about with a young girl's affections.* **5** (when *intr*, often foll. by *at*) to perform or act the part (of) in or as in a dramatic production. **6** to perform (a dramatic production). **7a** to have the ability to perform on (a musical instrument): *David plays the harp.* **7b** to perform as specified: *he plays out of tune.* **8** (*tr*) **8a** to reproduce (a piece of music, note, etc.) on an instrument. **8b** to perform works by: *to play Brahms.* **9** to discharge or cause to discharge: *he played the water from the hose onto the garden.* **10** to cause (a radio, etc.) to emit sound. **11** to move freely, quickly, or irregularly: *lights played on the scenery.* **12** (*tr*) *Stock Exchange.* to speculate or operate aggressively for gain in (a market). **13** (*tr*) *Angling.* to attempt to tire (a hooked fish) by alternately letting out and reeling in line. **14** to put (a card, counter, piece, etc.) into play. **15** to gamble. **16 play fair** (*or* **false**). (often foll. by *with*) to prove oneself fair (*or* unfair) in one's dealings. **17 play for time.** to delay the outcome of some activity so as to gain time to one's own advantage. **18 play into the hands of.** to act directly to the advantage of (an opponent). ◆ *n* **19** a dramatic composition written for performance by actors on a stage, etc.; drama. **20** the performance of a dramatic composition. **21a** games, exercise, or other activity undertaken for pleasure, esp. by children. **21b** (*in combination*): *playroom.* **22** conduct: *fair play.* **23** the playing of a game or the period during which a game is in progress: *rain stopped play.* **24** *US.* a manoeuvre in a game: *a brilliant play.* **25** the situation of a ball, etc., that is within the defined area and being played according to the rules (in **in play, out of play**). **26** gambling. **27** activity or operation: *the play of the imagination.* **28** freedom of movement: *too much play in the rope.* **29** light, free, or rapidly shifting motion: *the play of light on the water.* **30** fun, jest, or joking: *I only did it in play.* **31 call into play.** to bring into operation. **32 make a play for.** *Inf.* to make an obvious attempt to gain. ◆ See also **play along, playback,** etc. [OE *plega* (n), *plegan* (vb)]
▸ **ˈplayable** *adj*

play-act *vb* **1** (*intr*) to pretend or make believe. **2** (*intr*) to behave in an overdramatic or affected manner. **3** to act in or as in (a play).
▸ **ˈplay-ˌacting** *n* ▸ **ˈplay-ˌactor** *n*

play along *vb* (*adv*) **1** (*intr;* usually foll. by *with*) to cooperate (with), esp. as a temporary measure. **2** (*tr*) to manipulate as if in a game, esp. for one's own advantage: *he played the widow along until she gave him her money.*

playback (ˈpleɪˌbæk) *n* **1** the act or process of reproducing a recording, esp. on magnetic tape. **2** the part of a tape recorder serving to reproduce or used for reproducing recorded material. ◆ *vb* **play back.** (*adv*) **3** to reproduce (recorded material) on (a magnetic tape) by means of a tape recorder.

playbill (ˈpleɪˌbɪl) *n* **1** a poster or bill advertising a play. **2** the programme of a play.

playboy ❶ (ˈpleɪˌbɔɪ) *n* a man, esp. one of private means, who devotes himself to the pleasures of nightclubs, female company, etc.

play down ❶ *vb* (*tr, adv*) to make little or light of; minimize the importance of.

player ❶ (ˈpleɪə) *n* **1** a person who participates in or is skilled at some game or sport. **2** a person who plays a game or sport professionally. **3** a person who plays a musical instrument. **4** an actor. **5** *Inf.* a participant, esp. a powerful one, in a particular field of activity: *a leading city player.*

player piano *n* a mechanical piano; Pianola.

playful ❶ (ˈpleɪfʊl) *adj* **1** full of high spirits and fun: *a playful kitten.* **2** good-natured and humorous: *a playful remark.*
▸ **ˈplayfully** *adv*

playgoer (ˈpleɪˌɡəʊə) *n* a person who goes to theatre performances, esp. frequently.

playground (ˈpleɪˌɡraʊnd) *n* **1** an outdoor area for children's play, esp. one having swings, slides, etc., or adjoining a school. **2** a place popular as a sports or holiday resort.

THESAURUS

stand **4** = **policy**, manifesto, objective(s), party line, principle, programme, tenet(s)

platitude *n* **1** = **cliché**, banality, bromide, commonplace, hackneyed saying, inanity, stereotype, trite remark, truism **2** = **triteness**, banality, dullness, inanity, insipidity, triviality, vapidity, verbiage

platitudinous *adj* **1, 2** = **clichéd**, banal, commonplace, corny (*sl.*), hack, hackneyed, overworked, set, stale, stereotyped, stock, tired, trite, truistic, vapid, well-worn

Platonic *adj* **2** *often not cap.* = **nonphysical**, ideal, idealistic, intellectual, spiritual, transcendent

platoon *n* **1, 2** = **squad**, company, group, outfit (*inf.*), patrol, squadron, team

platter *n* **1** = **plate**, charger, dish, salver, tray, trencher (*arch.*)

plaudit *n* **1, 2** *usually plural* = **approval**, acclaim, acclamation, applause, approbation, clapping, commendation, congratulation, hand, kudos, ovation, praise, round of applause

plausible *adj* **1** = **believable**, colourable, conceivable, credible, likely, persuasive, possible, probable, reasonable, tenable, verisimilar **2** = **glib**, fair-spoken, smooth, smooth-talking, smooth-tongued, specious

Antonyms *adj* ≠ **believable**: genuine, illogical, implausible, impossible, improbable, inconceivable, incredible, real, unbelievable, unlikely

play *vb* **1** = **amuse oneself**, caper, engage in games, entertain oneself, fool, frisk, frolic, gambol, have fun, revel, romp, sport, trifle **2** = **compete**, be in a team, challenge, contend against, participate, rival, take on, take part, vie with **4** *often foll. by* **about** *or* **around** = **philander**, dally, fool around, mess around, take lightly, trifle, womanize **5, 6** = **act**, act the part of, execute, impersonate, perform, personate, portray, represent, take the part of **12** *Stock Exchange* = **gamble**, bet, chance, hazard, punt (*chiefly Brit.*), risk, speculate, take, wager ◆ *n* **19** = **drama**, comedy, dramatic piece, entertainment, farce, masque, pantomime, performance, piece, radio play, show, soap opera, stage show, television drama, tragedy **21** = **amusement**, caper, diversion, entertainment, frolic, fun, gambol, game, jest, pastime, prank, recreation, romp, sport **26** = **gambling**, gaming **27** = **action**, activity, employment, function, operation, transaction, working **28** = **space**, elbowroom, give (*inf.*), latitude, leeway, margin, motion, movement, range, room, scope, sweep, swing **30** = **fun**, foolery, humour, jest, joking, lark (*inf.*), prank, sport, teasing

playboy *n* = **womanizer**, ladies' man, lady-killer, lover boy (*sl.*), man about town, philanderer, pleasure seeker, rake, roué, socialite

play down *vb* = **minimize**, gloss over, make light of, make little of, set no store by, soft-pedal (*inf.*), underplay, underrate

player *n* **1, 2** = **sportsman** *or* **sportswoman**, competitor, contestant, participant, team member **3** = **musician**, artist, instrumentalist, music maker, performer, virtuoso **4** = **performer**, actor *or* actress, entertainer, Thespian, trouper

playful *adj* **1** = **lively**, cheerful, coltish, frisky, frolicsome, gay, impish, joyous, kittenish, larkish (*inf.*), merry, mischievous, puckish, rol-

playgroup ('pleɪˌgru:p) *n* a regular meeting of small children for supervised creative play.

playhouse ('pleɪˌhaʊs) *n* **1** a theatre. **2** *US.* a small house for children to play in.

playing card *n* one of a pack of 52 rectangular pieces of stiff card, used for playing a wide variety of games, each card having one or more symbols of the same kind on the face, but an identical design on the reverse.

playing field *n Chiefly Brit.* a field or open space used for sport.

playlet ('pleɪlɪt) *n* a short play.

playlist ('pleɪˌlɪst) *n* **1** a list of records chosen for playing, as on a radio station. ◆ *vb* **2** (*tr*) to put (a song or record) on a playlist.

playmaker ('pleɪˌmeɪkə) *n Sport.* a player whose role is to create scoring opportunities for his or her team-mates.

playmate ❶ ('pleɪˌmeɪt) *or* **playfellow** *n* a friend or partner in play or recreation.

play off *vb* (*adv*) **1** (*tr;* usually foll. by *against*) to manipulate as if in playing a game: *to play one person off against another.* **2** (*intr*) to take part in a play-off. ◆ *n* **play-off. 3** *Sport.* an extra contest to decide the winner when competitors are tied. **4** *Chiefly US & Canad.* a contest or series of games to determine a championship.

play on ❶ *vb* (*intr*) **1** (*adv*) to continue to play. **2** (*prep*) Also: **play upon.** to exploit or impose upon (the feelings or weakness of another).

play on words *n* another term for **pun**[1].

playpen ('pleɪˌpɛn) *n* a small enclosure, usually portable, in which a young child can be left to play in safety.

playschool ('pleɪˌsku:l) *n* an informal nursery group for preschool children.

plaything ❶ ('pleɪˌθɪŋ) *n* **1** a toy. **2** a person regarded or treated as a toy.

playtime ('pleɪˌtaɪm) *n* a time for play or recreation, esp. the school break.

play up ❶ *vb* (*adv*) **1** (*tr*) to highlight: *to play up one's best features.* **2** *Brit. inf.* to behave irritatingly (towards). **3** (*intr*) *Brit. inf.* (of a machine, etc.) to function erratically: *the car is playing up again.* **4** to hurt; give (one) trouble: *my back's playing up again.* **5 play up to. 5a** to support (another actor) in a performance. **5b** to try to gain favour with by flattery.

playwright ❶ ('pleɪˌraɪt) *n* a person who writes plays.

plaza ('plɑ:zə) *n* **1** an open space or square, esp. in Spain. **2** *Chiefly US & Canad.* a modern complex of shops, buildings, and parking areas. [C17: from Sp., from L *platēa* courtyard; see PLACE]

plc *or* **PLC** *abbrev. for* public limited company.

plea ❶ (pli:) *n* **1** an earnest entreaty or request. **2a** *Law.* something alleged by or on behalf of a party to legal proceedings in support of his claim or defence. **2b** *Criminal law.* the answer made by an accused to the charge: *a plea of guilty.* **2c** (in Scotland and formerly in England) a suit or action at law. **3** an excuse, justification, or pretext: *he gave the plea of a previous engagement.* [C13: from Anglo-Norman *plai,* from OF *plaid* lawsuit, from Med. L *placitum* court order (lit.: what is pleasing), from L *placēre* to please]

plea bargaining *n* an agreement between the prosecution and defence, sometimes including the judge, in which the accused agrees to plead guilty to a lesser charge in return for more serious charges being dropped.

plead ❶ (pli:d) *vb* **pleads, pleading; pleaded, plead** (plɛd), *or esp. Scot. & US.* **pled. 1** (when *intr,* often foll. by *with*) to appeal earnestly or humbly (to). **2** (*tr; may take a clause as object*) to give as an excuse: *to plead ignorance.* **3** *Law.* to declare oneself to be (guilty or not guilty) in answer to the charge. **4** *Law.* to advocate (a case) in a court of law. **5** (*intr*) *Law.* **5a** to file pleadings. **5b** to address a court as an advocate. [C13: from OF *plaidier,* from Med. L *placitāre* to have a lawsuit, from L *placēre* to please]

▸'**pleadable** *adj* ▸'**pleader** *n*

pleadings ('pli:dɪŋz) *pl n Law.* the formal written statements presented alternately by the plaintiff and defendant in a lawsuit.

pleasance ('plɛzəns) *n* **1** a secluded part of a garden laid out with trees, walks, etc. **2** *Arch.* enjoyment or pleasure. [C14 *plesaunce,* from OF *plaisance,* ult. from *plaisir* to PLEASE]

pleasant ❶ ('plɛzᵊnt) *adj* **1** giving or affording pleasure; enjoyable. **2** having pleasing or agreeable manners, appearance, habits, etc. **3** *Obs.* merry and lively. [C14: from OF *plaisant,* from *plaisir* to PLEASE]

▸'**pleasantly** *adv*

pleasantry ❶ ('plɛzᵊntrɪ) *n, pl* **pleasantries. 1** (*often pl*) an agreeable or amusing remark, etc., often one made in order to be polite: *they exchanged pleasantries.* **2** an agreeably humorous manner or style. [C17: from F *plaisanterie,* from *plaisant* PLEASANT]

please ❶ (pli:z) *vb* **pleases, pleasing, pleased. 1** to give satisfaction, pleasure, or contentment to (a person). **2** to be the will of or have the will (to): *if it pleases you; the court pleases.* **3 if you please.** if you will or wish, sometimes used in ironic exclamation. **4 pleased with.** happy because of. **5 please oneself.** to do as one likes. ◆ *adv* **6** (*sentence modifier*) used in making polite requests, pleading, etc. **7 yes please.** a polite formula for accepting an offer, invitation, etc. [C14 *plese,* from OF *plaisir,* from L *placēre*]

▸**pleased** *adj* ▸**pleasedly** ('pli:zɪdlɪ) *adv*

pleasing ❶ ('pli:zɪŋ) *adj* giving pleasure; likable or gratifying.

▸'**pleasingly** *adv*

pleasurable ❶ ('plɛʒərəbᵊl) *adj* enjoyable, agreeable, or gratifying.

▸'**pleasurably** *adv*

pleasure ❶ ('plɛʒə) *n* **1** an agreeable or enjoyable sensation or emotion: *the pleasure of hearing good music.* **2** something that gives enjoyment: *his garden was his only pleasure.* **3a** amusement, recreation, or enjoyment. **3b** (*as modifier*): *a pleasure ground.* **4** *Euphemistic.* sexual gratification: *he took his pleasure of her.* **5** a person's preference. ◆ *vb* **pleasures, pleasuring, pleasured. 6** (when *intr,* often foll. by *in*) *Arch.* to give pleasure to or take pleasure (in). [C14 *plesir,* from OF]

pleat (pli:t) *n* **1** any of various types of fold formed by doubling back fabric, etc., and pressing, stitching, or steaming into place. ◆ *vb* **2** (*tr*) to arrange (material, part of a garment, etc.) in pleats. [C16: var. of PLAIT]

pleb (plɛb) *n* **1** short for **plebeian. 2** *Brit. inf., often derog.* a common vulgar person.

plebeian ❶ (plə'bi:ən) *adj* **1** of or characteristic of the common people, esp. those of ancient Rome. **2** lacking refinement; philistine or vulgar: *plebeian tastes.* ◆ *n* **3** one of the common people, esp. one of the Roman plebs. **4** a person who is coarse, vulgar, etc. [C16: from L *plēbēius* of the people, from *plēbs* the common people of ancient Rome]

▸**ple'beian,ism** *n*

plebiscite ('plɛbɪˌsaɪt, -sɪt) *n* **1** a direct vote by the electorate of a state,

THESAURUS

licking, spirited, sportive, sprightly, vivacious **2** = **joking**, arch, coy, flirtatious, good-natured, humorous, jesting, jokey, roguish, teasing, tongue-in-cheek, waggish
Antonyms *adj* despondent, gloomy, grave, morose, sedate, serious

playmate *n* = **friend**, chum (*inf.*), companion, comrade, neighbour, pal (*inf.*), playfellow

play on *vb* **2** = **take advantage of**, abuse, capitalize on, exploit, impose on, milk, profit by, trade on, turn to account, utilize

plaything *n* **1** = **toy**, amusement, bauble, game, gewgaw, gimcrack, pastime, trifle, trinket

play up *vb* **1** = **emphasize**, accentuate, bring to the fore, call attention to, highlight, magnify, point up, stress, turn the spotlight on, underline **2** *Brit. informal* = **be awkward**, be bolshie (*Brit. inf.*), be cussed (*inf.*), be disobedient, be stroppy (*Brit. sl.*), give trouble, misbehave **3** *Brit. informal* = **malfunction**, be on the blink, be wonky (*Brit. sl.*), not work properly **4** = **hurt**, be painful, be sore, bother, give one gyp (*Brit. & NZ sl.*), give one trouble, pain, trouble **5b play up to** *Informal* = **butter up**, bootlick (*inf.*), brown-nose (*taboo sl.*), crawl to, curry favour, fawn, flatter, get in with, ingratiate oneself, keep (someone) sweet, pander to, suck up to (*inf.*), toady

playwright *n* = **dramatist**, dramaturge, dramaturgist

plea *n* **1** = **appeal**, begging, entreaty, intercession, overture, petition, prayer, request, suit, supplication **2** *Law* = **suit**, action, allegation, cause **3** = **excuse**, apology, claim, defence, explanation, extenuation, justification, pretext, vindication

plead *vb* **1** = **appeal**, ask, beg, beseech, crave, entreat, implore, importune, petition, request, solicit, supplicate **2** = **allege**, adduce, argue, assert, maintain, put forward, use as an excuse

pleasant *adj* **1** = **pleasing**, acceptable, agreeable, amusing, delectable, delightful, enjoyable, fine, gratifying, lovely, nice, pleasurable, refreshing, satisfying, welcome **2** = **friendly**, affable, agreeable, amiable, charming, cheerful, cheery, congenial, engaging, genial, good-humoured, likable *or* likeable, nice
Antonyms *adj* ≠ **pleasing:** awful, disagreeable, distasteful, horrible, horrid, miserable, offensive, repulsive, unpleasant ≠ **friendly:** cold, disagreeable, horrible, horrid, impolite, offensive, rude, unfriendly, unlikable *or* unlikeable

pleasantry *n* **1** = **joke**, badinage, banter, bon mot, good-natured remark, jest, josh (*sl., chiefly US & Canad.*), quip, sally, witticism

please *vb* **1** = **delight**, amuse, charm, cheer, content, entertain, give pleasure to, gladden, gratify, humour, indulge, rejoice, satisfy, suit, tickle, tickle pink (*inf.*) **2** = **want**, be inclined, choose, desire, like, opt, prefer, see fit, will, wish
Antonyms *vb* ≠ **delight:** anger, annoy, depress, disgust, displease, dissatisfy, grieve, incense, offend, provoke, sadden, vex

pleased *adj* **1** = **happy**, chuffed (*Brit. sl.*), contented, delighted, euphoric, glad, gratified, in high spirits, over the moon (*inf.*), pleased as punch (*inf.*), rapt, satisfied, thrilled, tickled, tickled pink (*inf.*)

pleasing *adj* = **enjoyable**, agreeable, amiable, amusing, attractive, charming, delightful, engaging, entertaining, gratifying, likable *or* likeable, pleasurable, polite, satisfying, winning
Antonyms *adj* boring, disagreeable, dull, monotonous, rude, unattractive, unlikable *or* unlikeable, unpleasant

pleasurable *adj* = **enjoyable**, agreeable, congenial, delightful, diverting, entertaining, fun, good, gratifying, lovely, nice, pleasant, welcome

pleasure *n* **1-3** = **happiness**, amusement, beer and skittles (*inf.*), bliss, comfort, contentment, delectation, delight, diversion, ease, enjoyment, gladness, gratification, jollies (*sl.*), joy, recreation, satisfaction, solace **5** = **wish**, choice, command, desire, inclination, mind, option, preference, purpose, will
Antonyms *n* ≠ **happiness:** abstinence, anger, displeasure, duty, labour, misery, necessity, obligation, pain, sadness, sorrow, suffering, unhappiness

plebeian *adj* **1, 2** = **common**, base, coarse, ignoble, low, lowborn, lower-class, mean, non-U (*Brit. inf.*), proletarian, uncultivated, unrefined, vulgar, working-class ◆ *n* **3** = **commoner**, common man, man in the street, peasant, pleb, prole (*derogatory sl., chiefly Brit.*), proletarian
Antonyms *adj* ≠ **common:** aristocratic, cultivated, highborn, high-class, patrician, polished, refined, upper-class, well-bred

region, etc., on some question, usually of national importance. **2** any expression of public opinion on some matter. ◆ See also **referendum.** [C16: from OF *plébiscite,* from L *plēbiscītum* decree of the people, from *plēbs* the populace + *scīscere* to decree, from *scīre* to know] ▸**plebiscitary** (plə'bɪsɪtərɪ, -trɪ) *adj*

plectrum ('plɛktrəm) *n, pl* **-trums** *or* **-tra** (-trə). any implement for plucking a string, such as a small piece of plastic, wood, etc., used to strum a guitar. [C17: from L, from Gk *plektron,* from *plessein* to strike]

pled (plɛd) *vb US or (esp. in legal usage) Scot.* a past tense and past participle of **plead.**

pledge ❶ (plɛdʒ) *n* **1** a formal or solemn promise or agreement. **2a** collateral for the payment of a debt or the performance of an obligation. **2b** the condition of being collateral (esp. in **in pledge**). **3** a token: *the gift is a pledge of their sincerity.* **4** an assurance of support or goodwill, conveyed by drinking a toast: *we drank a pledge to their success.* **5** a person who binds himself, as by becoming bail or surety for another. **6 take** *or* **sign the pledge.** to make a vow to abstain from alcoholic drink. ◆ *vb* **pledges, pledging, pledged. 7** to promise formally or solemnly. **8** (*tr*) to bind by or as if by a pledge: *they were pledged to secrecy.* **9** to give or offer (one's word, freedom, property, etc.) as a guarantee, as for the repayment of a loan. **10** to drink a toast to (a person, cause, etc.). [C14: from OF *plege,* from LL *plebium* security, from *plebīre* to pledge, of Gmc origin] ▸**'pledgable** *adj* ▸**'pledger** *or* **'pledgor** *n*

pledgee (plɛdʒ'iː) *n* **1** a person to whom a pledge is given. **2** a person to whom property is delivered as a pledge.

pledget ('plɛdʒɪt) *n* a small flattened pad of wool, cotton, etc., esp. for use as a pressure bandage to be applied to wounds. [C16: from ?]

-plegia *n combining form.* indicating a specified type of paralysis: *paraplegia.* [from Gk, from *plēgē* stroke, from *plēssein* to strike] ▸**-plegic** *adj and n combining form.*

pleiad ('plaɪəd) *n* a brilliant or talented group, esp. one with seven members. [C16: orig. F *Pléiade,* name given by P. de Ronsard (1524–85) to himself and six other poets, ult. after the *Pleiades,* the seven daughters of the Gk god Atlas]

Pleiocene ('plaɪəʊˌsiːn) *adj, n* a variant spelling of **Pliocene.**

Pleistocene ('plaɪstəˌsiːn) *adj* **1** of, denoting, or formed in the first epoch of the Quaternary period. It was characterized by extensive glaciations of the N hemisphere and the evolutionary development of man. ◆ *n* **2 the.** the Pleistocene epoch or rock series. [C19: from Gk *pleistos* most + *kainos* recent]

plenary ❶ ('pliːnərɪ, 'plɛn-) *adj* **1** full, unqualified, or complete: *plenary powers; plenary indulgence.* **2** (of assemblies, councils, etc.) attended by all the members. [C15: from LL *plēnārius,* from L *plēnus* full] ▸**'plenarily** *adv*

plenipotentiary ❶ (ˌplɛnɪpə'tɛnʃərɪ) *adj* **1** (esp. of a diplomatic envoy) invested with or possessing full authority. **2** conferring full authority. **3** (of power or authority) full; absolute. ◆ *n, pl* **plenipotentiaries. 4** a person invested with full authority to transact business, esp. a diplomat authorized to represent a country. See also **envoy**[1] (sense 1). [C17: from Med. L *plēnipotentiārius,* from L *plēnus* full + *potentia* POWER]

plenitude ❶ ('plɛnɪˌtjuːd) *n* **1** abundance. **2** the condition of being full or complete. [C15: via OF from L *plēnitūdō,* from *plēnus* full]

plenteous ❶ ('plɛntɪəs) *adj* **1** ample; abundant: *a plenteous supply of food.* **2** producing or yielding abundantly: *a plenteous grape harvest.* [C13 *plenteus,* from OF, from *plentif,* from *plenté* PLENTY] ▸**'plenteously** *adv* ▸**'plenteousness** *n*

plentiful ❶ ('plɛntɪful) *adj* **1** ample; abundant. **2** having or yielding an abundance: *a plentiful year.* ▸**'plentifully** *adv* ▸**'plentifulness** *n*

plenty ❶ ('plɛntɪ) *n, pl* **plenties. 1** (often foll. by *of*) a great number, amount, or quantity; lots: *plenty of time; there are plenty of cars on display here.* **2** ample supplies or resources: *the age of plenty.* **3 in plenty.** existing in abundance: *food in plenty.* ◆ *determiner* **4a** very many; ample: *plenty of people believe in ghosts.* **4b** (*as pron*): *that's plenty, thanks.* ◆ *adv* **5** *Inf.* fully or abundantly: *the coat was plenty big enough.* [C13: from OF *plenté,* from LL *plēnitās* fullness, from L *plēnus* full]

plenum ('pliːnəm) *n, pl* **plenums** *or* **plena** (-nə). **1** an enclosure containing gas at a higher pressure than the surrounding environment. **2** a fully attended meeting. **3** (esp. in the philosophy of the Stoics) space regarded as filled with matter. [C17: from L: space filled with matter, from *plēnus* full]

pleochroism (plɪ'ɒkrəʊˌɪzəm) *n* a property of certain crystals of absorbing light waves selectively and therefore of showing different colours when looked at from different directions. [C19: from Gk *pleiōn* more, from *polus* many + *-chroism* from *khrōs* skin colour] ▸**pleochroic** (ˌpliːə'krəʊɪk) *adj*

pleomorphism (ˌpliːə'mɔːfɪzəm) *or* **pleomorphy** ('pliːəˌmɔːfɪ) *n* **1** the occurrence of more than one different form in the life cycle of a plant or animal. **2** another word for **polymorphism** (sense 2). ▸ˌ**pleo'morphic** *adj*

pleonasm ('pliːəˌnæzəm) *n Rhetoric.* **1** the use of more words than necessary or an instance of this, such as *a tiny little child.* **2** a word or phrase that is superfluous. [C16: from L *pleonasmus,* from Gk *pleonasmos* excess, from *pleonazein* to be redundant] ▸ˌ**pleo'nastic** *adj*

plesiosaur ('pliːsɪəˌsɔː) *n* any of various marine reptiles of Jurassic and Cretaceous times, having a long neck, short tail, and paddle-like limbs. [C19: from NL *plēsiosaurus,* from Gk *plēsios* near + *sauros* a lizard]

plethora ❶ ('plɛθərə) *n* **1** superfluity or excess; overabundance. **2** *Pathol., obs.* a condition caused by dilation of superficial blood vessels, characterized esp. by a reddish face. [C16: via Med. L from Gk *plēthōrē* fullness, from *plēthein* to grow full] ▸**plethoric** (plɛ'θɒrɪk) *adj*

pleura ('plʊərə) *n, pl* **pleurae** ('plʊəriː). the thin transparent membrane enveloping the lungs and lining the walls of the thoracic cavity. [C17: via Med. L from Gk: side, rib] ▸**'pleural** *adj*

pleurisy ('plʊərɪsɪ) *n* inflammation of the pleura, characterized by pain that is aggravated by deep breathing or coughing. [C14: from OF *pleurisie,* from LL, from Gk *pleuritis,* from *pleura* side] ▸**pleuritic** (plʊ'rɪtɪk) *adj, n*

pleuro- *or before a vowel* **pleur-** *combining form.* **1** of or relating to the side. **2** indicating the pleura. [from Gk *pleura* side]

pleuropneumonia (ˌplʊərəʊnjuː'məʊnɪə) *n* the combined disorder of pleurisy and pneumonia.

Plexiglas ('plɛksɪˌglɑːs) *n US. trademark.* a transparent plastic, polymethylmethacrylate, used for combs, plastic sheeting, etc.

plexor ('plɛksə) *or* **plessor** *n Med.* a small hammer with a rubber head for use in percussion of the chest and testing reflexes. [C19: from Gk *plēxis* a stroke, from *plēssein* to strike]

plexus ('plɛksəs) *n, pl* **plexuses** *or* **plexus. 1** any complex network of nerves, blood vessels, or lymphatic vessels. **2** an intricate network or arrangement. [C17: NL, from L *plectere* to braid]

pliable ❶ ('plaɪəbᵊl) *adj* easily moulded, bent, influenced, or altered. ▸ˌ**plia'bility** *or* **'pliableness** *n* ▸**'pliably** *adv*

pliant ❶ ('plaɪənt) *adj* **1** easily bent; supple: *a pliant young tree.* **2** adaptable; yielding readily to influence; compliant. [C14: from OF, from *plier* to fold; see PLY[2]] ▸**'pliancy** *n* ▸**'pliantly** *adv*

plicate ('plaɪkeɪt) *or* **plicated** *adj* having or arranged in parallel folds or ridges; pleated: *a plicate leaf; plicate rock strata.* [C18: from L *plicātus* folded, from *plicāre* to fold] ▸**pli'cation** *n*

plié ('pliːeɪ) *n* a classic ballet practice posture with back erect and knees bent. [F: bent]

plier ('plaɪə) *n* a person who plies a trade.

pliers ('plaɪəz) *pl n* a gripping tool consisting of two hinged arms usually with serrated jaws. [C16: from PLY[1]]

THESAURUS

pledge *n* **1 = promise**, assurance, covenant, oath, undertaking, vow, warrant, word, word of honour **2 = guarantee**, bail, bond, collateral, deposit, earnest, gage, pawn, security, surety **4 = toast**, health ◆ *vb* **7, 8 = promise**, contract, engage, give one's oath, give one's word, give one's word of honour, swear, undertake, vouch, vow **9 = bind**, engage, gage (*arch.*), guarantee, mortgage, plight **10 = drink to**, drink the health of, toast

plenary *adj* **1 = complete**, absolute, full, sweeping, thorough, unconditional, unlimited, unqualified, unrestricted **2 = full**, complete, entire, general, open, whole

plenipotentiary *n* **4 = ambassador**, emissary, envoy, legate, minister

plenitude *n* **1 = abundance**, bounty, copiousness, cornucopia, excess, plenteousness, plenty, plethora, profusion, wealth **2 = completeness**, amplitude, fullness, repletion

plenteous *adj* **1 = plentiful**, abundant, ample, bounteous (*literary*), bountiful, copious, generous, inexhaustible, infinite, lavish, liberal, overflowing, profuse, thick on the ground **2 = productive**, bumper, fertile, fruitful, luxuriant, plentiful, prolific

plentiful *adj* **1 = abundant**, ample, bounteous (*literary*), bountiful, complete, copious, generous, inexhaustible, infinite, lavish, liberal, overflowing, plenteous, profuse, thick on the ground **2 = productive**, bumper, fertile, fruitful, luxuriant, plenteous, prolific
Antonyms *adj* ≠ **abundant**: deficient, inadequate, insufficient, scant, scarce, skimpy, small, sparing, sparse, thin on the ground

plenty *n* **1 = lots** (*inf.*), abundance, enough, fund, good deal, great deal, heap(s), mass, masses, mine, mountain(s), oodles (*inf.*), pile(s) (*inf.*), plethora, quantities, quantity, stack(s), store, sufficiency, volume **2 = abundance**, affluence, copiousness, fertility, fruitfulness, luxury, opulence, plenitude, plenteousness, plentifulness, profusion, prosperity, wealth

plethora *n* **1 = excess**, glut, overabundance, profusion, superabundance, superfluity, surfeit, surplus
Antonyms *n* dearth, deficiency, lack, scarcity, shortage, want

pliability *n* **= flexibility**, bendability, ductility, elasticity, malleability, mobility, plasticity, pliancy **= impressionableness**, adaptability, amenability, compliance, docility, susceptibility, tractableness

pliable *adj* **= flexible**, bendable, bendy, ductile, limber, lithe, malleable, plastic, pliant, supple, tensile **= compliant**, adaptable, docile, easily led, impressionable, influenceable, like putty in one's hands, manageable, persuadable, pliant, receptive, responsive, susceptible, tractable, yielding
Antonyms *adj* ≠ **flexible**: rigid, stiff ≠ **compliant**: headstrong, inflexible, intractable, obdurate, obstinate, stubborn, unadaptable, unbending, unyielding, wilful

pliant *adj* **1 = flexible**, bendable, bendy, ductile, lithe, plastic, pliable, supple, tensile **2 = impressionable**, adaptable, biddable, compliant, easily led, influenceable, manageable, persuadable, pliable, susceptible, tractable, yielding

plight[1] ⓣ (plaɪt) *n* a condition of extreme hardship, danger, etc. [C14 *plit,* from OF *pleit* fold; prob. infl. by OE *pliht* PLIGHT[2]]

plight[2] ⓣ (plaɪt) *vb* (*tr*) **1** to promise formally or pledge (allegiance, support, etc.). **2 plight one's troth.** to make a promise, esp. of marriage. ◆ *n* **3** *Arch. or dialect.* a solemn promise, esp. of engagement; pledge. [OE *pliht* peril]
▸**ˈplighter** *n*

plimsoll *or* **plimsole** (ˈplɪmsəl) *n Brit.* a light rubber-soled canvas shoe worn for various sports. Also called: **gym shoe, sandshoe.** [C20: from the resemblance of the sole to a Plimsoll line]

Plimsoll line (ˈplɪmsəl) *n* another name for **load line.** [C19: after Samuel *Plimsoll* (1824–98), Brit. politician who advocated its adoption]

plinth (plɪnθ) *n* **1** the rectangular slab or block that forms the lowest part of the base of a column, statue, pedestal, or pier. **2** Also called: **plinth course.** the lowest part of the wall of a building, esp. one that is formed of a course of stone or brick. **3** a flat block on either side of a doorframe, where the architrave meets the skirting. [C17: from L *plinthus,* from Gk *plinthos* brick]

Pliocene *or* **Pleiocene** (ˈplaɪəʊˌsiːn) *adj* **1** of, denoting, or formed in the last epoch of the Tertiary period, during which many modern mammals appeared. ◆ *n* **2 the.** the Pliocene epoch or rock series. [C19: from Gk *pleiōn* more, from *polus* many + *-cene* from *kainos* recent]

plissé (ˈpliːseɪ, ˈplɪs-) *n* **1** fabric with a wrinkled finish, achieved by treatment involving caustic soda: *cotton plissé.* **2** such a finish on a fabric. [F: pleated]

PLO *abbrev. for* Palestine Liberation Organization.

plod ⓣ (plɒd) *vb* **plods, plodding, plodded. 1** to make (one's way) or walk along (a path, etc.) with heavy usually slow steps. **2** (*intr*) to work slowly and perseveringly. ◆ *n* **3** the act of plodding. **4** *Brit.* a slang word for **policeman.** [C16: imit.]
▸**ˈplodder** *n* ▸**ˈplodding** *adj* ▸**ˈploddingly** *adv*

-ploid *adj and n combining form.* indicating a specific multiple of a single set of chromosomes: *diploid.* [from Gk *-pl(oos)* -fold + -OID]
▸**-ploidy** *n combining form.*

plonk[1] (plɒŋk) *vb* **1** (often foll. by *down*) to drop or be dropped heavily: *he plonked the money on the table.* ◆ *n* **2** the act or sound of plonking. [var. of PLUNK]

plonk[2] (plɒŋk) *n Inf.* alcoholic drink, usually wine, esp. of inferior quality. [C20: ?from F *blanc* white, as in *vin blanc* white wine]

plonker (ˈplɒŋkə) *n Sl.* a stupid person. [C20: from PLONK[1]]

plop (plɒp) *n* **1** the characteristic sound made by an object dropping into water without a splash. ◆ *vb* **plops, plopping, plopped. 2** to fall or cause to fall with the sound of a plop: *the stone plopped into the water.* ◆ *interj* **3** an exclamation imitative of this sound: *to go plop.* [C19: imit.]

plosion (ˈpləʊʒən) *n Phonetics.* the sound of an abrupt break or closure, esp. the audible release of a stop. Also called: **explosion.**

plosive (ˈpləʊsɪv) *Phonetics.* ◆ *adj* **1** accompanied by plosion. ◆ *n* **2** a plosive consonant; stop. [C20: from F, from *explosif* EXPLOSIVE]

plot[1] ⓣ (plɒt) *n* **1** a secret plan to achieve some purpose, esp. one that is illegal or underhand. **2** the story or plan of a play, novel, etc. **3** *Mil.* a graphic representation of an individual or tactical setting that pinpoints an artillery target. **4** *Chiefly US.* a diagram or plan. **5 lose the plot.** *Inf.* to lose one's ability or judgment in a given situation. ◆ *vb* **plots, plotting, plotted. 6** to plan secretly (something illegal, revolutionary, etc.); conspire. **7** (*tr*) to mark (a course, as of a ship or aircraft) on a map. **8** (*tr*) to make a plan or map of. **9a** to locate and mark (points) on a graph by means of coordinates. **9b** to draw (a curve) through these points. **10** (*tr*) to construct the plot of (a literary work, etc.). [C16: from PLOT[2], infl. by obs. *complot* conspiracy, from OF, from ?]
▸**ˈplotter** *n*

plot[2] ⓣ (plɒt) *n* a small piece of land: *a vegetable plot.* [OE]

plough ⓣ *or esp. US* **plow** (plaʊ) *n* **1** an agricultural implement with sharp blades for cutting or turning over the earth. **2** any of various similar implements, such as a device for clearing snow. **3** ploughed land. **4 put one's hand to the plough.** to begin or undertake a task. ◆ *vb* **5** to till (the soil, etc.) with a plough. **6** to make (furrows or grooves) in (something) with or as if with a plough. **7** (when *intr,* usually foll. by *through*) to move (through something) in the manner of a plough. **8** (*intr;* foll. by *through*) to work at slowly or perseveringly. **9** (*intr;* foll. by *into* or *through*) (of a vehicle) to run uncontrollably into something in its path. **10** (*intr*) *Brit. sl.* to fail an examination. [OE *plōg* plough land]
▸**ˈplougher** *or esp. US* **ˈplower** *n*

Plough (plaʊ) *n* **the.** the group of the seven brightest stars in the constellation Ursa Major. Also called: **Charles's Wain.** Usual US name: the **Big Dipper.**

plough back *vb* (*tr, adv*) to reinvest (the profits of a business) in the same business.

ploughman *or esp. US* **plowman** (ˈplaʊmən) *n, pl* **ploughmen** *or esp. US* **plowmen.** a man who ploughs, esp. using horses.

ploughman's lunch *n* a snack lunch, served esp. in a pub, consisting of bread and cheese with pickle.

ploughshare *or esp. US* **plowshare** (ˈplaʊˌʃɛə) *n* the horizontal pointed cutting blade of a mouldboard plough.

plover (ˈplʌvə) *n* **1** any of a family of shore birds, typically having a round head, straight bill, and large pointed wings. **2 green plover.** another name for **lapwing.** [C14: from OF *plovier* rainbird, from L *pluvia* rain]

plow (plaʊ) *n, vb* the usual US spelling of **plough.**

ploy ⓣ (plɔɪ) *n* **1** a manoeuvre or tactic in a game, conversation, etc. **2** any business, job, hobby, etc., with which one is occupied: *angling is his latest ploy.* **3** *Chiefly Brit.* a frolic, escapade, or practical joke. [C18: orig. Scot. & N English, obs. n sense of EMPLOY meaning an occupation]

PLP (in Britain) *abbrev. for* Parliamentary Labour Party.

PLR *abbrev. for* Public Lending Right.

pluck ⓣ (plʌk) *vb* **1** (*tr*) to pull off (feathers, fruit, etc.) from (a fowl, tree, etc.). **2** (when *intr,* foll. by *at*) to pull or tug. **3** (*tr;* foll. by *off, away,* etc.) *Arch.* to pull (something) forcibly or violently (from something or someone). **4** (*tr*) to sound (the strings) of (a musical instrument) with the fingers, a plectrum, etc. **5** (*tr*) *Sl.* to fleece or swindle. ◆ *n* **6** courage, usually in the face of difficulties or hardship. **7** a sudden pull or tug. **8** the heart, liver, and lungs, esp. of an animal used for food. [OE *pluccian, plyccan*]
▸**ˈplucker** *n*

pluck up *vb* (*tr, adv*) **1** to pull out; uproot. **2** to muster (courage, one's spirits, etc.).

plucky ⓣ (ˈplʌkɪ) *adj* **pluckier, pluckiest.** having or showing courage in the face of difficulties, danger, etc.
▸**ˈpluckily** *adv* ▸**ˈpluckiness** *n*

plug ⓣ (plʌg) *n* **1** a piece of wood, cork, or other material, used to stop up holes or waste pipes or as a wedge for taking a screw or nail. **2** a device having one or more pins to which an electric cable is attached: used to make an electrical connection when inserted into a socket. **3** Also called: **volcanic plug.** a mass of solidified magma filling the neck of an extinct volcano. **4** See **sparking plug. 5a** a cake of pressed or twisted tobacco, esp. for chewing. **5b** a small piece of such a cake. **6** *Inf.* a favourable mention of a product, show, etc., as on television. ◆ *vb* **plugs, plugging, plugged. 7** (*tr*) to stop up or secure (a hole, gap, etc.) with or as if with a plug. **8** (*tr*) to insert or use (something) as a plug: *to plug a finger into one's ear.* **9** (*tr*) *Inf.* to make favourable and often-repeated mentions of (a song, product, show, etc.), as on television. **10** (*tr*) *Sl.* to shoot: *he plugged six rabbits.* **11** (*tr*) *Sl.* to punch. **12** (*intr;* foll. by *along, away,* etc.) *Inf.* to work steadily or persistently. [C17: from MDu. *plugge*]
▸**ˈplugger** *n*

plug-and-play *adj Computing.* capable of detecting the addition of a new input or output device and automatically activating the appropriate control software.

THESAURUS

plight[1] *n* = **difficulty,** case, circumstances, condition, dilemma, extremity, hole (*sl.*), hot water (*inf.*), jam (*inf.*), perplexity, pickle (*inf.*), predicament, scrape (*inf.*), situation, spot (*inf.*), state, straits, tight spot, trouble

plight[2] *vb* **1** = **promise,** contract, covenant, engage, guarantee, pledge, propose, swear, vouch, vow

plod *vb* **1** = **trudge,** clump, drag, lumber, slog, stomp (*inf.*), tramp, tread **2** = **slog,** drudge, grind (*inf.*), grub, labour, peg away, persevere, plough through, plug away, soldier on, toil

plodder *n* **1** = **slowcoach** (*Brit. inf.*), dawdler, laggard, slowpoke (*US & Canad. inf.*), tortoise **2** = **slogger,** drudge, hack, toiler, workhorse

plot[1] *n* **1** = **plan,** cabal, conspiracy, covin, intrigue, machination, scheme, stratagem **2** = **story,** action, narrative, outline, scenario, story line, subject, theme, thread ◆ *vb* **6** = **plan,** cabal, collude, conspire, contrive, hatch, intrigue, machinate, manoeuvre, scheme **7** = **chart,** calculate, compute, draft, draw, locate, map, mark, outline **10** = **devise,** brew, conceive, concoct, contrive, cook up (*inf.*), design, frame, hatch, imagine, lay, project

plot[2] *n* = **patch,** allotment, area, ground, lot, parcel, tract

plotter *n* **6** = **conspirator,** architect, cabalist, conniver, conspirer, intriguer, Machiavellian, planner, schemer, strategist

plough *vb* **5** = **turn over,** break ground, cultivate, dig, furrow, ridge, till **7** *usually foll. by* **through** = **forge,** cut, drive, flounder, plod, plunge, press, push, stagger, surge, wade **9** *foll. by* **into** *or* **through** = **plunge into,** bulldoze into, career into, crash into, hurtle into, shove into, smash into

ploy *n* **1** = **tactic,** contrivance, device, dodge, gambit, game, manoeuvre, move, ruse, scheme, stratagem, subterfuge, trick, wile

pluck *vb* **1** = **pull out** *or* **off,** collect, draw, gather, harvest, pick **2** = **tug,** catch, clutch, jerk, pull at, snatch, tweak, yank **4** = **strum,** finger, pick, plunk, thrum, twang ◆ *n* **6** = **courage,** backbone, boldness, bottle (*Brit. sl.*), bravery, determination, grit, guts (*inf.*), hardihood, heart, intrepidity, mettle, nerve, resolution, spirit, spunk (*inf.*)

plucky *adj* = **courageous,** bold, brave, daring, doughty, feisty (*inf.*), game, gritty, gutsy (*sl.*), hardy, have-a-go (*inf.*), heroic, intrepid, mettlesome, spirited, spunky (*inf.*), undaunted, unflinching, valiant
Antonyms *adj* afraid, chicken (*sl.*), cowardly, dastardly, dispirited, scared, spineless, spiritless, timid, yellow (*inf.*)

plug *n* **1** = **stopper,** bung, cork, spigot, stopple **5** = **wad,** cake, chew, pigtail, quid, twist **6** *Informal* = **mention,** advert (*Brit. inf.*), advertisement, good word, hype, publicity, puff, push ◆ *vb* **7** = **seal,** block, bung, choke, close, cork, cover, fill, pack, stop, stopper, stopple, stop up, stuff **9** *Informal* = **mention,** advertise, build up, hype, promote, publicize, puff, push, write up **10** *Slang* = **shoot,** blow away (*sl., chiefly US*), gun down, pick off, pop, pot, put a bullet in **12** *foll. by* **along, away** *etc. Informal* = **slog,** drudge, grind (*inf.*), labour, peg away, plod, toil

plughole (ˈplʌgˌhəʊl) *n* a hole in a sink, etc., through which waste water drains and which can be closed with a plug.

plug in *vb* (*tr, adv*) to connect (an electrical appliance, etc.) with a power source by means of an electrical plug.

plug-ugly *adj* **1** *Inf.* extremely ugly. ◆ *n, pl* **plug-uglies. 2** *US sl.* a city tough; ruffian. [C19: from ?]

plum 🅣 (plʌm) *n* **1** a small rosaceous tree with an edible oval fruit that is purple, yellow, or green and contains an oval stone. **2** the fruit of this tree. **3** a raisin, as used in a cake or pudding. **4a** a dark reddish-purple colour. **4b** (*as adj*): *a plum carpet.* **5** *Inf.* **5a** something of a superior or desirable kind, such as a financial bonus. **5b** (*as modifier*): *a plum job.* [OE *plūme*]

plumage (ˈpluːmɪdʒ) *n* the layer of feathers covering the body of a bird. [C15: from OF, from *plume* feather, from L *plūma* down]

plumate (ˈpluːmeɪt, -mɪt) *or* **plumose** *adj Zool., bot.* **1** of or possessing feathers or plumes. **2** covered with small hairs: *a plumate seed.* [C19: from L *plumātus* covered with feathers; see PLUME]

plumb 🅣 (plʌm) *n* **1** a weight, usually of lead, suspended at the end of a line and used to determine water depth or verticality. **2** the perpendicular position of a freely suspended plumb line (esp. in **out of plumb, off plumb**). ◆ *adv also* **plum. 3** vertically or perpendicularly. **4** *Inf., chiefly US.* (intensifier): *plumb stupid.* **5** *Inf.* exactly; precisely. ◆ *vb* **6** (*tr;* often foll. by *up*) to test the alignment of or adjust to the vertical with a plumb line. **7** (*tr*) to experience (the worst extremes of): *to plumb the depths of despair.* **8** (*tr*) to understand or master (something obscure): *to plumb a mystery.* **9** to connect or join (a device such as a tap) to a water pipe or drainage system. [C13: from OF *plomb* (unattested) lead line, from *plon* lead, from L *plumbum*]
▸ˈ**plumbable** *adj*

plumbago (plʌmˈbeɪgəʊ) *n, pl* **plumbagos. 1** a plant of warm regions, having clusters of blue, white, or red flowers. **2** another name for **graphite.** [C17: from L: lead ore, translation of Gk *polubdaina,* from *polubdos* lead]

plumber (ˈplʌmə) *n* a person who installs and repairs pipes, fixtures, etc., for water, drainage, and gas. [C14: from OF *plommier* worker in lead, from LL *plumbārius,* from L *plumbum* lead]

plumbing (ˈplʌmɪŋ) *n* **1** the trade or work of a plumber. **2** the pipes, fixtures, etc., used in a water, drainage, or gas installation. **3** the act or procedure of using a plumb.

plumbism (ˈplʌmˌbɪzəm) *n* chronic lead poisoning. [C19: from L *plumbum* lead]

plumb line *n* a string with a metal weight, or **plumb bob,** at one end that, when suspended, points directly towards the earth's centre of gravity and so is used to determine verticality, depth, etc.

plumb rule *n* a plumb line attached to a narrow board, used by builders, surveyors, etc.

plume 🅣 (pluːm) *n* **1** a feather, esp. one that is large or ornamental. **2** a feather or cluster of feathers worn esp. formerly as a badge or ornament in a headband, hat, etc. **3** *Biol.* any feathery part. **4** something that resembles a plume: *a plume of smoke.* **5** a token or decoration of honour; prize. ◆ *vb* **plumes, pluming, plumed.** (*tr*) **6** to adorn with feathers or plumes. **7** (of a bird) to clean or preen (itself or its feathers). **8** (foll. by *on* or *upon*) to pride or congratulate (oneself). [C14: from OF, from L *plūma* downy feather]

plummet 🅣 (ˈplʌmɪt) *vb* **plummets, plummeting, plummeted. 1** (*intr*) to drop down; plunge. ◆ *n* **2** the weight on a plumb line; plumb bob. **3** a lead plumb used by anglers. [C14: from OF *plommet* ball of lead, from *plomb* lead, from L *plumbum*]

plummy 🅣 (ˈplʌmɪ) *adj* **plummier, plummiest. 1** of, full of, or resembling plums. **2** *Brit. inf.* (of speech) deep, refined, and somewhat drawling. **3** *Brit. inf.* choice; desirable.

plumose (ˈpluːməʊs, -məʊz) *adj* another word for **plumate.** [C17: from L *plūmōsus* feathery]

plump[1] 🅣 (plʌmp) *adj* **1** well filled out or rounded; chubby: *a plump turkey.* **2** bulging; full: *a plump wallet.* ◆ *vb* **3** (often foll. by *up* or *out*) to make or become plump: *to plump up a pillow.* [C15 (meaning: dull, rude), C16 (in current senses): ?from MDu. *plomp* blunt]
▸ˈ**plumply** *adv* ▸ˈ**plumpness** *n*

plump[2] 🅣 (plʌmp) *vb* **1** (often foll. by *down, into,* etc.) to drop or fall suddenly and heavily. **2** (*intr;* foll. by *for*) to give support (to) or make a choice (of) one out of a group or number. ◆ *n* **3** a heavy abrupt fall or the sound of this. ◆ *adv* **4** suddenly or heavily. **5** straight down; directly: *the helicopter landed plump in the middle of the field.* ◆ *adj, adv* **6** in a blunt, direct, or decisive manner. [C14: prob. imit.]

plum pudding *n Brit.* a boiled or steamed pudding made with flour, suet, sugar, and dried fruit.

plumule (ˈpluːmjuːl) *n* **1** the embryonic shoot of seed-bearing plants. **2** a down feather of young birds. [C18: from LL *plūmula* a little feather]

plumy (ˈpluːmɪ) *adj* **plumier, plumiest. 1** plumelike; feathery. **2** consisting of, covered with, or adorned with feathers.

plunder 🅣 (ˈplʌndə) *vb* **1** to steal (valuables, goods, sacred items, etc.) from (a town, church, etc.) by force, esp. in time of war; loot. **2** (*tr*) to rob or steal (choice or desirable things) from (a place): *to plunder an orchard.* ◆ *n* **3** anything taken by plundering; booty. **4** the act of plundering; pillage. [C17: prob. from Du. *plunderen* (orig.: to plunder household goods)]
▸ˈ**plunderer** *n*

plunge 🅣 (plʌndʒ) *vb* **plunges, plunging, plunged. 1** (usually foll. by *into*) to thrust or throw (something, oneself, etc.): *they plunged into the sea.* **2** to throw or be thrown into a certain condition: *the room was plunged into darkness.* **3** (usually foll. by *into*) to involve or become involved deeply (in). **4** (*intr*) to move or dash violently or with great speed or impetuosity. **5** (*intr*) to descend very suddenly or steeply: *the ship plunged in heavy seas; a plunging neckline.* **6** (*intr*) *Inf.* to speculate or gamble recklessly, for high stakes, etc. ◆ *n* **7** a leap or dive. **8** *Inf.* a swim; dip. **9** a pitching or tossing motion. **10 take the plunge.** *Inf.* to resolve to do something dangerous or irrevocable. [C14: from OF *plongier,* from Vulgar L *plumbicāre* (unattested) to sound with a plummet, from L *plumbum* lead]

plunger (ˈplʌndʒə) *n* **1** a rubber suction cup used to clear blocked drains, etc. **2** a device or part of a machine that has a plunging or thrusting motion; piston. **3** *Inf.* a reckless gambler.

plunk (plʌŋk) *vb* **1** to pluck (the strings) of (a banjo, etc.) or (of such an instrument) to give forth a sound when plucked. **2** (often foll. by *down*) to drop or be dropped, esp. heavily or suddenly. ◆ *n* **3** the act or sound of plunking. [C20: imit.]

pluperfect (pluːˈpɜːfɪkt) *adj, n Grammar.* another term for **past perfect.** [C16: from L *plūs quam perfectum* more than perfect]

plural (ˈplʊərəl) *adj* **1** containing, involving, or composed of more than one. **2** denoting a word indicating that more than one referent is being referred to or described. ◆ *n* **3** *Grammar.* **3a** the plural number. **3b** a plural form. [C14: from OF *plurel,* from LL *plūrālis* concerning many, from L *plūs* more]
▸ˈ**plurally** *adv*

pluralism (ˈplʊərəˌlɪzəm) *n* **1** the holding by a single person of more than one ecclesiastical benefice or office; plurality. **2** *Sociol.* a theory of society as several autonomous but interdependent groups. **3** the existence in a society of groups having distinctive ethnic origin, cultural forms, religions, etc. **4** *Philosophy.* **4a** the metaphysical doctrine that reality consists of more than two basic types of substance. Cf. **monism** (sense 1), **dualism** (sense 2). **4b** the metaphysical doctrine that reality consists of independent entities rather than one unchanging whole.
▸ˈ**pluralist** *n, adj* ▸ˌ**pluralˈistic** *adj*

plurality 🅣 (plʊəˈrælɪtɪ) *n, pl* **pluralities. 1** the state of being plural. **2** *Maths.* a number greater than one. **3** the US term for **relative majority. 4** a large number. **5** the greater number; majority. **6** another word for **pluralism** (sense 1).

pluralize *or* **pluralise** (ˈplʊərəˌlaɪz) *vb* **pluralizes, pluralizing, pluralized** *or* **pluralises, pluralising, pluralised. 1** (*intr*) to hold more than one ecclesiastical benefice or office at the same time. **2** to make or become plural.

pluri- *combining form.* denoting several. [from L *plur-, plus* more, *plures* several]

plus 🅣 (plʌs) *prep* **1** increased by the addition of: *four plus two.* **2** with or with the addition of: *a good job, plus a new car.* ◆ *adj* **3** (*prenominal*) indicating or involving addition: *a plus sign.* **4** another word for **positive** (senses 7, 8). **5** on the positive part of a scale or coordinate axis: *a value of +x.* **6** indicating the positive side of an electrical circuit. **7** involving advantage: *a plus factor.* **8** (*postpositive*) *Inf.* having a value above that which is stated: *she had charm plus.* **9** (*postpositive*) slightly above a specified standard: *he received a B+ grade for his essay.* ◆ *n* **10** short for **plus sign. 11** a positive quantity. **12** *Inf.* something positive or to the good. **13** a gain, surplus, or advantage. ◆ Mathematical symbol: + [C17: from L: more]

> **USAGE NOTE** *Plus, together with,* and *along with* do not create compound subjects in the way that *and* does: the number of the verb depends on that of the subject to which *plus, together with,* or *along with* is added: *this task, plus all the others, was* (not *were*) *undertaken by the government; the doctor, together with the nurses, was* (not *were*) *waiting for the patient.*

THESAURUS

plum *Informal* ◆ *n* **5a** = **prize**, bonus, cream, find, pick, treasure ◆ *modifier* **5b** = **choice**, best, first-class, prize

plumb *n* **1** = **weight**, lead, plumb bob, plummet ◆ *adv* **3** = **vertically**, perpendicularly, up and down **5** *Informal* = **exactly**, bang, precisely, slap, spot-on (*Brit. inf.*)

plume *n* **1, 2** = **feather**, aigrette, crest, pinion, quill ◆ *vb* **8** *foll. by* **on** *or* **upon** = **pride oneself**, congratulate oneself, pat oneself on the back, pique oneself, preen oneself

plummet *vb* **1** = **plunge**, crash, descend, dive, drop down, fall, nose-dive, stoop, swoop, tumble

plummy *adj* **2** *Brit. informal* = **deep**, fruity, posh (*inf., chiefly Brit.*), refined, resonant, upper-class

plump[1] *adj* **1** = **chubby**, beefy, burly, buxom, corpulent, dumpy, fat, fleshy, full, obese, podgy, portly, roly-poly, rotund, round, stout, tubby, well-upholstered (*inf.*)
Antonyms *adj* anorexic, bony, emaciated, lanky, lean, scrawny, skinny, slender, slim, sylphlike, thin

plump[2] *vb* **1** = **flop**, drop, dump, fall, sink, slump **2** *foll. by* **for** = **choose**, back, come down in favour of, favour, opt for, side with, support

plunder *vb* **1, 2** = **loot**, despoil, devastate, pillage, raid, ransack, ravage, rifle, rob, sack, spoil, steal, strip ◆ *n* **3** = **loot**, booty, ill-gotten gains, pillage, prey, prize, rapine, spoils, swag (*sl.*)

plunge *vb* **1** = **throw**, cast, pitch **4** = **hurtle**, career, charge, dash, jump, lurch, rush, swoop, tear **5** = **descend**, dip, dive, douse, drop, fall, go down, immerse, nose-dive, plummet, sink, submerge, tumble ◆ *n* **7, 9** = **dive**, descent, drop, fall, immersion, jump, submersion, swoop

plurality *n* **5** = **majority**, bulk, mass, most, nearly all, overwhelming number, preponderance

plus *prep* **1, 2** = **and**, added to, coupled with, with, with the addition of ◆ *adj* **3, 4** = **additional**, added, add-on, extra, positive, supple-

plus fours *pl n* men's baggy knickerbockers reaching below the knee, now only worn for golf, etc. [C20: because made with four inches of material to hang over at the knee]

plush ❶ (plʌʃ) *n* **1** a fabric with a cut pile that is longer and softer than velvet. ◆ *adj* **2** Also: **plushy.** *Inf.* lavishly appointed; rich; costly. [C16: from F *pluche,* from OF *peluchier* to pluck, ult. from L *pilus* a hair]
▸**'plushly** *adv*

plus sign *n* the symbol +, indicating addition or positive quantity.

Pluto[1] ('plu:təʊ) *n Gk myth.* the god of the underworld; Hades.
▸**Plu'tonian** *adj*

Pluto[2] ('plu:təʊ) *n* the smallest planet and the farthest known from the sun. [L, from Gk *Ploutōn,* lit.: the rich one]

plutocracy (plu:'tɒkrəsɪ) *n, pl* **plutocracies. 1** the rule of society by the wealthy. **2** a state or government characterized by the rule of the wealthy. **3** a class that exercises power by virtue of its wealth. [C17: from Gk *ploutokratia,* from *ploutos* wealth + *-kratia* rule]
▸**plutocratic** (ˌplu:tə'krætɪk) *adj* ▸**ˌpluto'cratically** *adv*

plutocrat ❶ ('plu:təˌkræt) *n* a member of a plutocracy.

pluton ('plu:tɒn) *n* any mass of igneous rock that has solidified below the surface of the earth. [C20: back formation from PLUTONIC]

plutonic (plu:'tɒnɪk) *adj* (of igneous rocks) derived from magma that has cooled and solidified below the surface of the earth. [C20: after PLUTO[1]]

plutonium (plu:'təʊnɪəm) *n* a highly toxic metallic transuranic element. It occurs in trace amounts in uranium ores and is produced in a nuclear reactor by neutron bombardment of uranium-238. The most stable isotope, **plutonium-239,** readily undergoes fission and is used as a reactor fuel. Symbol: Pu; atomic no.: 94; half-life of ^{239}Pu: 24 360 years. [C20: after PLUTO[2] because Pluto lies beyond Neptune and plutonium was discovered soon after NEPTUNIUM]

pluvial ('plu:vɪəl) *adj* **1** of, characterized by, or due to the action of rain; rainy. ◆ *n* **2** *Geol.* a period of persistent rainfall. [C17: from L *pluviālis* rainy, from *pluvia* rain]

pluviometer (ˌplu:vɪ'ɒmɪtə) *n* another name for **rain gauge.**
▸**pluviometric** (ˌplu:vɪə'metrɪk) *adj* ▸**ˌpluvio'metrically** *adv*

ply[1] ❶ (plaɪ) *vb* **plies, plying, plied.** (*mainly tr*) **1** to carry on, pursue, or work at (a job, trade, etc.). **2** to manipulate or wield (a tool, etc.). **3** to sell (goods, wares, etc.), esp. at a regular place. **4** (usually foll. by *with*) to provide (with) or subject (to) repeatedly or persistently: *he plied us with drink; he plied the speaker with questions.* **5** (*intr*) to work steadily or diligently. **6** (*also intr*) (esp. of a ship, etc.) to travel regularly along (a route) or in (an area): *to ply the trade routes.* [C14 *plye,* short for *aplye* to APPLY]

ply[2] ❶ (plaɪ) *n, pl* **plies. 1a** a layer, fold, or thickness, as of yarn. **1b** (*in combination*): *four-ply.* **2** a thin sheet of wood glued to other similar sheets to form plywood. **3** one of the strands twisted together to make rope, yarn, etc. [C15: from OF *pli* fold, from *plier* to fold, from L *plicāre*]

Plymouth Brethren ('plɪməθ) *pl n* a religious sect founded about 1827, strongly Puritanical in outlook and having no organized ministry.

plywood ('plaɪˌwʊd) *n* a structural board consisting of thin layers of wood glued together under pressure, with the grain of one layer at right angles to the grain of the adjoining layer.

pm *abbrev. for* premium.

Pm *the chemical symbol for* promethium.

PM *abbrev. for:* **1** Past Master (of a fraternity). **2** Paymaster. **3** Postmaster. **4** Prime Minister. **5** *Mil.* Provost Marshal.

p.m., P.M., pm, *or* **PM** *abbrev. for:* **1** (indicating the time from midday to midnight) post meridiem. [L: after noon] **2** postmortem (examination).

PMG *abbrev. for:* **1** Paymaster General. **2** Postmaster General.

PMS *abbrev. for* premenstrual syndrome.

PMT *abbrev. for* premenstrual tension.

PNdB *abbrev. for* perceived noise decibel.

pneumatic (nju'mætɪk) *adj* **1** of or concerned with air, gases, or wind. **2** (of a machine or device) operated by compressed air or by a vacuum. **3** containing compressed air: *a pneumatic tyre.* **4** (of the bones of birds) containing air spaces which reduce their weight as an adaptation to flying. ◆ *n* **5** a pneumatic tyre. [C17: from LL *pneumaticus* of air or wind, from Gk, from *pneuma* breath, wind]
▸**pneu'matically** *adv*

pneumatics (nju'mætɪks) *n* (*functioning as sing*) the branch of physics concerned with the mechanical properties of gases, esp. air.

pneumatology (ˌnju:mə'tɒlədʒɪ) *n* **1** the branch of theology concerned with the Holy Ghost and other spiritual beings. **2** an obsolete name for **psychology** (the science).

pneumatophore (nju:'mætəʊˌfɔ:) *n* **1** a specialized root of certain swamp plants, such as the mangrove, that branches upwards and undergoes gaseous exchange with the atmosphere. **2** a polyp such as the Portuguese man-of-war, that is specialized as a float.

pneumococcus (ˌnju:məʊ'kɒkəs) *n, pl* **pneumococci** (-'kɒksaɪ). a bacterium that causes pneumonia.

pneumoconiosis (ˌnju:məʊˌkəʊnɪ'əʊsɪs) *or* **pneumonoconiosis** (ˌnju:mənəʊˌkəʊnɪ'əʊsɪs) *n* any disease of the lungs or bronchi caused by the inhalation of metallic or mineral particles. [C19: shortened from *pneumonoconiosis,* from Gk *pneumōn* lung + *-coniosis,* from *konis* dust]

pneumoencephalogram (ˌnju:məʊenˈsɛfələˌgræm) *n* See **encephalogram.**

pneumogastric (ˌnju:məʊ'gæstrɪk) *adj Anat.* **1** of or relating to the lungs and stomach. **2** a former term for **vagus.**

pneumonectomy (ˌnju:məʊ'nɛktəmɪ) *or* **pneumectomy** *n, pl* **pneumonectomies** *or* **pneumectomies.** the surgical removal of a lung or part of a lung. [C20: from Gk *pneumōn* lung + -ECTOMY]

pneumonia (nju:'məʊnɪə) *n* inflammation of one or both lungs, in which the air sacs (alveoli) become filled with liquid. [C17: NL from Gk from *pneumōn* lung]
▸**pneumonic** (nju:'mɒnɪk) *adj*

pneumothorax (ˌnju:məʊ'θɔ:ræks) *n* the abnormal presence of air between the lung and the wall of the chest (pleural cavity), resulting in collapse of the lung.

p-n junction *n Electronics.* a boundary between a p-type and n-type semiconductor that functions as a rectifier and is used in diodes and junction transistors.

po (pəʊ) *n, pl* **pos.** *Brit.* an informal word for **chamber pot.** [C19: from POT[1]]

Po *the chemical symbol for* polonium.

PO *abbrev. for:* **1** Personnel Officer. **2** petty officer. **3** Pilot Officer. **4** Also: **p.o.** postal order. **5** Post Office.

poach[1] ❶ (pəʊtʃ) *vb* **1** to catch (game, fish, etc.) illegally by trespassing on private property. **2** to encroach on or usurp (another person's rights, duties, etc.) or steal (an idea, employee, etc.). **3** *Tennis, badminton, etc.* to take or play (shots that should belong to one's partner). **4** to break up (land) into wet muddy patches, as by riding over it. [C17: from OF *pocher,* of Gmc origin]
▸**'poacher** *n*

poach[2] (pəʊtʃ) *vb* to simmer (eggs, fish, etc.) very gently in water, milk, stock, etc. [C15: from OF *pochier* to enclose in a bag (as the yolks are enclosed by the whites)]
▸**'poacher** *n*

pochard ('pəʊtʃəd) *n, pl* **pochards** *or* **pochard.** any of various diving ducks, esp. a European variety, the male of which has a grey-and-black body and a reddish head. [C16: from ?]

pock ❶ (pɒk) *n* **1** any pustule resulting from an eruptive disease, esp. from smallpox. **2** another word for **pockmark** (sense 1). [OE *pocc*]
▸**'pocky** *adj*

pocket ❶ ('pɒkɪt) *n* **1** a small bag or pouch in a garment for carrying small articles, money, etc. **2** any bag or pouch or anything resembling this. **3** *S. African.* a bag or sack of vegetables or fruit. **4** a cavity in the earth, etc., such as one containing ore. **5** a small enclosed or isolated area: *a pocket of resistance.* **6** any of the six holes with pouches or nets let into the corners and sides of a billiard table. **7 in one's pocket.** under one's control. **8 in** *or* **out of pocket.** having made a profit or loss. **9 line one's pockets.** to make money, esp. by dishonesty when in a position of trust. **10** (*modifier*) small: *a pocket edition.* ◆ *vb* **pockets, pocketing, pocketed.** (*tr*) **11** to put into one's pocket. **12** to take surreptitiously or unlawfully; steal. **13** (*usually passive*) to confine in or as if in a pocket. **14** to conceal or keep back: *he pocketed his pride and asked for help.* **15** *Billiards, etc.* to drive (a ball) into a pocket. [C15: from Anglo-Norman *poket* a little bag, from *poque* bag, from MDu. *poke* bag]
▸**'pocketless** *adj*

pocket battleship *n* a small heavily armed battle cruiser specially built to conform with treaty limitations on tonnage and armament.

pocket billiards *n* (*functioning as sing*) *Billiards.* **1** another name for **pool**[2] (sense 5). **2** any game played on a table in which the object is to pocket the balls, esp. snooker and pool.

pocketbook ('pɒkɪtˌbʊk) *n* **1** *Chiefly US.* a small bag or case for money, papers, etc. **2** a pocket-sized notebook.

pocket borough *n* (before the Reform Act of 1832) an English borough constituency controlled by one person or family who owned the land.

pocketful ('pɒkɪtful) *n, pl* **pocketfuls.** as much as a pocket will hold.

pocketknife ('pɒkɪtˌnaɪf) *n, pl* **pocketknives.** a small knife with one or more blades that fold into the handle; penknife.

pocket money *n* **1** *Brit.* a small weekly sum of money given to children by parents as an allowance. **2** money for day-to-day spending, incidental expenses, etc.

THESAURUS

mentary ◆ *n* **12, 13** = **advantage**, asset, benefit, bonus, extra, gain, good point, icing on the cake, perk (*Brit. inf.*), surplus

plush *adj* **2** = **luxurious**, costly, de luxe, lavish, luxury, opulent, palatial, rich, ritzy (*sl.*), sumptuous
Antonyms *adj* cheap, cheap and nasty, inexpensive, ordinary, plain, spartan

plutocrat *n* = **rich man**, capitalist, Croesus, Dives, fat cat, magnate, millionaire, moneybags (*sl.*), tycoon

ply[1] *vb* **1** = **work at**, carry on, exercise, follow, practise, pursue **2** = **use**, employ, handle, manipulate, swing, utilize, wield **4** = **bombard**, assail, beset, besiege, harass, importune, press, urge

ply[2] *n* **1** = **thickness**, fold, layer, leaf, sheet

poach[1] *vb* **1** = **steal**, hunt *or* fish illegally, plunder, rob, steal game **2** = **encroach**, appropriate, infringe, intrude, trespass

pock *n* **1, 2** = **scar**, blemish, flaw, mark, pimple, pockmark, pustule, spot

pocket *n* **1, 2** = **pouch**, bag, compartment, hollow, receptacle, sack ◆ *modifier* **10** = **small**, abridged, compact, concise, little, miniature, pint-size(d) (*inf.*), portable, potted (*inf.*) ◆ *vb* **12** = **steal**, appropriate, cabbage (*Brit. sl.*), filch,

pockmark Ⓣ (ˈpɒkˌmɑːk) *n* **1** Also called: **pock.** a pitted scar left on the skin after the healing of a smallpox or similar pustule. **2** any pitting of a surface that resembles such scars. ◆ *vb* **3** (*tr*) to scar or pit with pockmarks.

poco (ˈpəʊkəʊ; *Italian* ˈpɔːko) *or* **un poco** *adj, adv* (*in combination*) *Music.* a little; to a small degree. [from It.: little, from L *paucus* few]

poco a poco *adv* (*in combination*) *Music.* little by little: *poco a poco rall.* [It.]

pod Ⓣ (pɒd) *n* **1a** the fruit of any leguminous plant, consisting of a long two-valved case that contains seeds. **1b** the seedcase as distinct from the seeds. **2** any similar fruit. **3** a streamlined structure attached to an aircraft and used to house a jet engine, fuel tank, armament, etc. ◆ *vb* **pods, podding, podded. 4** (*tr*) to remove the pod from. [C17: ? back formation from earlier *podware* bagged vegetables]

-pod *or* **-pode** *n combining form.* indicating a certain type or number of feet: *arthropod; tripod.* [from Gk *-podos* footed, from *pous* foot]

podagra (pəˈdægrə) *n* gout of the foot or big toe. [C15: via L from Gk, from *pous* foot + *agra* a trap]

poddy (ˈpɒdɪ) *n, pl* **poddies.** *Austral.* a handfed calf or lamb. [?from *poddy* (adj) fat]

podgy Ⓣ (ˈpɒdʒɪ) *adj* **podgier, podgiest. 1** short and fat; chubby. **2** (of the face, arms, etc.) unpleasantly chubby and pasty-looking. [C19: from *podge* a short plump person]
▸ˈ**podgily** *adv* ▸ˈ**podginess** *n*

podium Ⓣ (ˈpəʊdɪəm) *n, pl* **podiums** *or* **podia** (-dɪə). **1** a small raised platform used by lecturers, conductors, etc. **2** a plinth that supports a colonnade or wall. **3** a low wall surrounding the arena of an ancient amphitheatre. **4** *Zool.* any footlike organ, such as the tube foot of a starfish. [C18: from L: platform, from Gk *podion* little foot, from *pous* foot]

-podium *n combining form.* a part resembling a foot: *pseudopodium.* [from NL: footlike; see PODIUM]

podophyllin (ˌpɒdəʊˈfɪlɪn) *n* a bitter yellow resin obtained from the dried underground stems of the May apple and mandrake: used as a cathartic. [C19: from NL *Podophyllum*, genus of herbs, from *podo-*, from Gk *pous* foot + *phullon* leaf]

-podous *adj combining form.* having feet of a certain kind or number: *cephalopodous.*

podzol (ˈpɒdzɒl) *or* **podsol** (ˈpɒdsɒl) *n* a type of soil characteristic of coniferous forest regions having a greyish-white colour in its upper layers from which certain minerals have leached. [C20: from Russian: ash ground]

poem Ⓣ (ˈpəʊɪm) *n* **1** a composition in verse, usually characterized by words chosen for their sound and suggestive power as well as for their sense, and using such techniques as metre, rhyme, and alliteration. **2** a literary composition that is not in verse but exhibits the intensity of imagination and language common to it: *a prose poem.* **3** anything resembling a poem in beauty, effect, etc. [C16: from L *poēma*, from Gk, var. of *poiēma* something created, from *poiein* to make]

poesy (ˈpəʊɪzɪ) *n, pl* **poesies. 1** an archaic word for **poetry. 2** *Poetic.* the art of writing poetry. [C14: via OF from L *poēsis*, from Gk, from *poiēsis* poetic art, from *poiein* to make]

poet Ⓣ (ˈpəʊɪt) *or* (*sometimes when fem*) **poetess** *n* **1** a person who writes poetry. **2** a person with great imagination and creativity. [C13: from L *poēta*, from Gk *poiētēs* maker, poet]

poetaster (ˌpəʊɪˈtæstə, -ˈteɪ-) *n* a writer of inferior verse. [C16: from Med. L; see POET, -ASTER]

poetic Ⓣ (pəʊˈɛtɪk) *or* **poetical** *adj* **1** of poetry. **2** characteristic of poetry, as in being elevated, sublime, etc. **3** characteristic of a poet. **4** recounted in verse.
▸**poˈetically** *adv*

poeticize, poeticise (pəʊˈɛtɪˌsaɪz) *or* **poetize, poetise** (ˈpəʊɪˌtaɪz) *vb* **poeticizes, poeticizing, poeticized; poeticises, poeticising, poeticised** *or* **poetizes, poetizing, poetized; poetises, poetising, poetised. 1** (*tr*) to put into poetry or make poetic. **2** (*intr*) to speak or write poetically.

poetic justice *n* fitting retribution.

poetic licence *n* justifiable departure from conventional rules of form, fact, etc., as in poetry.

poetics (pəʊˈɛtɪks) *n* (*usually functioning as sing*) **1** the principles and forms of poetry or the study of these. **2** a treatise on poetry.

poet laureate *n, pl* **poets laureate.** *Brit.* the poet appointed as court poet of Britain who is given a lifetime post in the Royal Household.

poetry Ⓣ (ˈpəʊɪtrɪ) *n* **1** literature in metrical form; verse. **2** the art or craft of writing verse. **3** poetic qualities, spirit, or feeling in anything. **4** anything resembling poetry in rhythm, beauty, etc. [C14: from Med. L *poētria*, from L *poēta* POET]

po-faced Ⓣ *adj* **1** wearing a disapproving stern expression. **2** narrow-minded; strait-laced. [C20: from PO + POKER-FACED]

pogo stick (ˈpəʊgəʊ) *n* a stout pole with a handle at the top, steps for the feet and a spring at the bottom, so that the user can spring up, down, and along on it. [C20: from ?]

pogrom (ˈpɒgrəm) *n* an organized persecution or extermination of an ethnic group, esp. of Jews. [C20: via Yiddish from Russian: destruction, from *po-* like + *grom* thunder]

pohutukawa (pəˌhuːtuːˈkɑːwə) *n* a New Zealand tree which grows on the coast and produces red flowers in the summer. Also called: **Christmas tree.**

poi (pɔɪ) *n NZ.* a ball of woven New Zealand flax swung rhythmically by Maori women while performing poi dances.

poi dance *n NZ.* a women's formation dance that involves singing and manipulating a poi.

-poiesis *n combining form.* indicating the act of making or producing something specified. [from Gk, from *poiēsis* a making; see POESY]
▸**-poietic** *adj combining form.*

poignant Ⓣ (ˈpɔɪnjənt, -nənt) *adj* **1** sharply distressing or painful to the feelings. **2** to the point; cutting or piercing: *poignant wit.* **3** keen or pertinent in mental appeal: *a poignant subject.* **4** pungent in smell. [C14: from OF, from L *pungens* pricking, from *pungere* to sting]
▸ˈ**poignancy** *or* ˈ**poignance** *n* ▸ˈ**poignantly** *adv*

poikilothermic (ˌpɔɪkɪləʊˈθɜːmɪk) *or* **poikilothermal** (ˌpɔɪkɪləʊˈθɜːməl) *adj* (of all animals except birds and mammals) having a body temperature that varies with the temperature of the surroundings. [C19: from Gk *poikilos* various + THERMAL]
▸ˌ**poikiloˈthermy** *n*

poinciana (ˌpɔɪnsɪˈɑːnə) *n* a tree of a tropical genus having large orange or red flowers. [C17: NL, after M. de *Poinci*, 17th-cent. governor of the French Antilles]

poind (pɔɪnd) *vb* (*tr*) *Scots Law.* **1** to take (property of a debtor, etc.) in execution of distress; distrain. **2** to impound (stray cattle, etc.). [C15: from Scot., var. of OE *pyndan* to impound]

poinsettia (pɔɪnˈsɛtɪə) *n* a shrub of Mexico and Central America, widely cultivated for its showy scarlet bracts, which resemble petals. [C19: NL, after J. P. *Poinsett* (1799–1851), US Minister to Mexico]

point Ⓣ (pɔɪnt) *n* **1** a dot or tiny mark. **2** a location, spot, or position. **3** any dot used in writing or printing, such as a decimal point or a full stop. **4** the sharp tapered end of a pin, knife, etc. **5** *Maths.* **5a** a geometric element having no dimensions whose position is located by means of its coordinates. **5b** a location: *point of inflection.* **6** a small promontory. **7** a specific condition or degree. **8** a moment: *at that point he left the room.* **9** a reason, aim, etc.: *the point of this exercise is to train new teachers.* **10** an essential element in an argument: *I take your point.* **11** a suggestion or tip. **12** a detail or item. **13** a characteristic, physical attribute, etc.: *he has his good points.* **14** a distinctive characteristic or quality of an animal, esp. one used as a standard in judging livestock. **15** (*often pl*) any of the extremities, such as the tail, ears, or feet, of a domestic animal. **16** (*often pl*) *Ballet.* the tip of the toes. **17** a single unit for measuring or counting, as in the scoring of a game. **18** *Printing.* a unit of measurement equal to one twelfth of a pica. There are approximately 72 points to the inch. **19** *Finance.* a unit of value used to quote security and commodity prices and their fluctuations. **20** *Navigation.* **20a** one of the 32 marks on the compass indicating direction. **20b** the angle of 11°15′ between two adjacent marks. **21** *Cricket.* a fielding position at right angles to the batsman on the off side and relatively near the pitch. **22** either of the two electrical contacts that make or break the current flow in the distributor of an internal-combustion engine. **23** *Brit., Austral., & NZ.* (*often pl*) a junction of railway tracks in which a pair of rails can be moved so that a train can be directed onto either of two lines. US and Canad. equivalent: **switch. 24** (*often pl*) a piece of ribbon, cord, etc., with metal tags at the end: used during the 16th and 17th centuries to fasten clothing. **25** *Brit.* short for **power point. 26** the position of the body of a pointer or setter when it discovers game. **27** *Boxing.* a mark awarded for a scoring blow, knockdown, etc. **28** any diacritic used in a writing system, esp. in a phonetic transcription, to indicate modifications of vowels or consonants. **29** *Jewellery.* a unit of weight equal to 0.01 carat. **30** the act of pointing. **31 beside the point.** irrelevant. **32 case in point.** a specific

THESAURUS

help oneself to, lift (*inf.*), pilfer, purloin, snaffle (*Brit. inf.*), take

pockmark *n* **1** = **scar**, blemish, pit, pock

pod *n, vb* **1, 4** = **shell**, hull, husk, shuck

podgy *adj* **1** = **tubby**, chubby, chunky, dumpy, fat, fleshy, plump, roly-poly, rotund, short and fat, squat, stout, stubby, stumpy

podium *n* **1** = **platform**, dais, rostrum, stage

poem *n* **1** = **verse**, lyric, ode, rhyme, song, sonnet

poet *n* **1** = **bard**, lyricist, maker (*arch.*), rhymer, versifier

poetic *adj* **1, 2** = **lyrical**, elegiac, lyric, metrical, rhythmic, rhythmical, songlike

poetry *n* **1, 2** = **verse**, metrical composition, poems, poesy, rhyme, rhyming

po-faced *adj* **2** = **humourless**, disapproving, narrow-minded, prim, prudish, puritanical, solemn, stolid, strait-laced

poignancy *n* **1** = **sadness**, emotion, emotionalism, evocativeness, feeling, pathos, piteousness, plaintiveness, sentiment, tenderness **2** = **sharpness**, bitterness, intensity, keenness **4** = **pungency**, piquancy, sharpness

poignant *adj* **1** = **moving**, affecting, agonizing, bitter, distressing, gut-wrenching, harrowing, heartbreaking, heart-rending, intense, painful, pathetic, sad, touching, upsetting **2** = **cutting**, acute, biting, caustic, keen, penetrating, piercing, pointed, sarcastic, severe, sharp **4** = **pungent**, acrid, piquant, sharp, stinging, tangy

point *n* **1, 3** = **full stop**, dot, mark, period, speck, stop **2** = **place**, location, position, site, spot, stage, station **4** = **end**, apex, nib, prong, sharp end, spike, spur, summit, tine, tip, top **6** = **headland**, bill, cape, foreland, head, ness (*arch.*), promontory **7** = **stage**, circumstance, condition, degree, extent, position **8** = **moment**, instant, juncture, time, very minute **9** = **aim**, design, end, goal, intent, intention, motive, object, objective, purpose, reason, use, usefulness, utility **10** = **essence**, burden, core, crux, drift, gist, heart, import, main idea, marrow, matter, meaning, nub, pith, proposition, question, subject, text, theme, thrust **12** = **item**, aspect, detail, facet, feature, instance, nicety, particular **13** = **characteristic**, aspect, attribute, peculiarity, property, quality, respect, side, trait or relevant instance. **33 make a point of. 33a** to make (something) one's regular habit. **33b** to do (something) because one thinks it important. **34 not to put too fine a point on it.** to speak plainly and bluntly. **35 on** (*or* **at**) **the point of.** at the moment immediately before: *on the point of leaving the room.* **36 score points off.** to gain an advantage at someone else's expense. **37 to the point.** relevant. **38 up to a point.** not completely. ◆ *vb* **39** (usually foll. by *at* or *to*) to indicate the location or direction of by or as by extending (a finger or other pointed object) towards it: *he pointed to the front door; don't point that gun at me.* **40** (*intr;* usually foll. by *at* or *to*) to indicate or identify a specific person or thing among several: *all evidence pointed to Donald as the murderer.* **41** (*tr*) to direct or face in a specific direction: *point me in the right direction.* **42** (*tr*) to sharpen or taper. **43** (*intr*) (of gun dogs) to indicate the place where game is lying by standing rigidly with the muzzle turned in its direction. **44** (*tr*) to finish or repair the joints of (brickwork, masonry, etc.) with mortar or cement. **45** (*tr*) *Music.* to mark (a psalm text) with vertical lines to indicate the points at which the music changes during chanting. **46** (*tr*) *Phonetics.* to provide (a letter or letters) with diacritics. **47** (*tr*) to provide (a Hebrew or similar text) with vowel points. ◆ See also **point off, point out, point up.** [C13: from OF: spot, from L *punctum* a point, from *pungere* to pierce]

point after *n American football.* a score given for a successful kick between the goalposts and above the crossbar, following a touchdown.

point-blank ⓘ *adj* **1a** aimed or fired at a target so close that it is unnecessary to make allowance for the drop in the course of the projectile. **1b** permitting such aim or fire without loss of accuracy: *at point-blank range.* **2** aimed or fired at nearly zero range. **3** plain or blunt: *a point-blank question.* ◆ *adv* **4** directly or straight. **5** plainly or bluntly. [C16: from POINT + BLANK (in the sense: centre spot of an archery target)]

point duty *n* **1** the stationing of a policeman or traffic warden at a road junction to control and direct traffic. **2** the position at the head of a military control, regarded as being the most dangerous.

pointe (pɔɪnt) *n Ballet.* the tip of the toe (esp. in **on pointes**). [from F: point]

pointed ⓘ ('pɔɪntɪd) *adj* **1** having a point. **2** cutting or incisive: *a pointed wit.* **3** obviously directed at a particular person or aspect: *pointed criticism.* **4** emphasized or made conspicuous: *pointed ignorance.* **5** (of an arch or style of architecture) Gothic. **6** *Music.* (of a psalm text) marked to show changes in chanting. **7** (of Hebrew text) with vowel points marked.
► **'pointedly** *adv*

pointer ⓘ ('pɔɪntə) *n* **1** a person or thing that points. **2** an indicator on a measuring instrument. **3** a long rod or cane used by a lecturer to point to parts of a map, blackboard, etc. **4** one of a breed of large smooth-coated gun dogs, usually white with black, liver, or lemon markings. **5** a helpful piece of information.

pointillism ('pwæntɪˌlɪzəm) *n* the technique of painting elaborated from impressionism, in which dots of unmixed colour are juxtaposed on a white ground so that from a distance they fuse in the viewer's eye into appropriate intermediate tones. [C19: from F, from *pointiller* to mark with tiny dots, from *pointille* little point, from It., from *punto* POINT]
► **'pointillist** *n, adj*

pointing ('pɔɪntɪŋ) *n* the act or process of repairing or finishing joints in brickwork, masonry, etc., with mortar.

point lace *n* lace made by a needle with buttonhole stitch on a paper pattern. Also called: **needlepoint.** Cf. **pillow lace.**

pointless ⓘ ('pɔɪntlɪs) *adj* **1** without a point. **2** without meaning, relevance, or force. **3** *Sport.* without a point scored.
► **'pointlessly** *adv*

point off *vb* (*tr, adv*) to mark off from the right-hand side (a number of decimal places) in a whole number to create a mixed decimal: *point off three decimal places in 12345 and you get 12.345.*

point of honour *n, pl* **points of honour.** a circumstance, event, etc., that involves the defence of one's principles, social honour, etc.

point of no return *n* **1** a point at which an irreversible commitment must be made to an action, progression, etc. **2** a point in a journey at which, if one continues, supplies will be insufficient for a return to the starting place.

point of order *n, pl* **points of order.** a question raised in a meeting as to whether the rules governing procedures are being breached.

point of sale *n* (in retail distribution) **a** the place at which a sale is made. Abbrev.: **POS. b** (*as modifier*): *a point-of-sale display.*

point of view ⓘ *n, pl* **points of view. 1** a position from which someone or something is observed. **2** a mental viewpoint or attitude.

point out ⓘ *vb* (*tr, adv*) to indicate or specify.

pointsman ('pɔɪntsˌmæn, -mən) *n, pl* **pointsmen. 1** a person who operates railway points. **2** a policeman or traffic warden on point duty.

point source *n Optics.* a source of light or other radiation that can be considered to have negligible dimensions.

points system *n Brit.* a system used to assess applicants' eligibility for local authority housing, based on (points awarded for) such factors as the length of time the applicant has lived in the area, how many children are in the family, etc.

point-to-point *n Brit.* a steeplechase organized by a recognized hunt or other body, usually restricted to amateurs riding horses that have been regularly used in hunting.

point up ⓘ *vb* (*tr, adv*) to emphasize, esp. by identifying: *he pointed up the difficulties.*

poise[1] ⓘ (pɔɪz) *n* **1** composure or dignity of manner. **2** physical balance. **3** equilibrium; stability. **4** the position of hovering. ◆ *vb* **poises, poising, poised. 5** to be or cause to be balanced or suspended. **6** (*tr*) to hold, as in readiness: *to poise a lance.* [C16: from OF *pois* weight, from L *pēnsum,* from *pendere* to weigh]

poise[2] (pwɑːz, pɔɪz) *n* the cgs unit of viscosity; the viscosity of a fluid in which a tangential force of 1 dyne per square centimetre maintains a difference in velocity of 1 centimetre per second between two parallel planes 1 centimetre apart. Symbol: P [C20: after Jean Louis Marie *Poiseuille* (1799–1869), F physician]

poised ⓘ (pɔɪzd) *adj* **1** self-possessed; dignified. **2** balanced and prepared for action.

poison ⓘ ('pɔɪzᵊn) *n* **1** any substance that can impair function or otherwise injure the body. **2** something that destroys, corrupts, etc. **3** a substance that retards a chemical reaction or the activity of a catalyst. **4** a substance that absorbs neutrons in a nuclear reactor and thus slows down the reaction. ◆ *vb* (*tr*) **5** to give poison to (a person or animal), esp. with intent to kill. **6** to add poison to. **7** to taint or infect with or as if with poison. **8** (foll. by *against*) to turn (a person's mind) against: *he poisoned her mind against me.* **9** to retard or stop (a chemical or nuclear reaction) by the action of a poison. [C13: from OF *puison* potion, from L *pōtiō* a drink, esp. a poisonous one, from *pōtāre* to drink]
► **'poisoner** *n*

poison ivy *n* any of several North American shrubs or climbing plants that cause an itching rash on contact.

poisonous ⓘ ('pɔɪzənəs) *adj* **1** having the effects or qualities of a poison. **2** capable of killing or inflicting injury. **3** corruptive or malicious.
► **'poisonously** *adv* ► **'poisonousness** *n*

poison-pen letter *n* a letter written in malice, usually anonymously, and intended to abuse, frighten, or insult the recipient.

poison pill *n Finance.* a tactic used by a company fearing an unwelcome takeover bid, in which the value of the company is automatically reduced, as by the sale of an issue of shares having an option unfavourable to the bidders, if the bid is successful.

THESAURUS

17 = unit, score, tally **31 beside the point = irrelevant**, extraneous, immaterial, inapplicable, inapposite, inappropriate, incidental, inconsequential, neither here nor there, not to the purpose, off the subject, out of the way, pointless, unconnected, unimportant, without connection **37 to the point = relevant**, applicable, apposite, appropriate, apropos, apt, brief, fitting, germane, pertinent, pithy, pointed, short, suitable, terse ◆ *vb* **39, 40 = indicate**, bespeak, call attention to, denote, designate, direct, show, signify **41 = aim**, bring to bear, direct, level, train **42 = sharpen**, barb, edge, taper, whet

point-blank *adj* **3 = direct**, abrupt, blunt, categorical, downright, explicit, express, plain, straight-from-the-shoulder, unreserved ◆ *adv* **4, 5 = directly**, bluntly, brusquely, candidly, explicitly, forthrightly, frankly, openly, overtly, plainly, straight, straightforwardly

pointed *adj* **1 = sharp**, acicular, acuminate, acute, barbed, cuspidate, edged, mucronate **2 = cutting**, accurate, acute, biting, incisive, keen, penetrating, pertinent, sharp, telling, trenchant

pointer *n* **2 = indicator**, guide, hand, needle **5 = hint**, advice, caution, information, recommendation, suggestion, tip, warning

pointless *adj* **2 = senseless**, absurd, aimless, dumb-ass, fruitless, futile, inane, ineffectual, irrelevant, meaningless, nonsensical, silly, stupid, unavailing, unproductive, unprofitable, useless, vague, vain, without rhyme or reason, worthless
Antonyms *adj* appropriate, beneficial, desirable, fitting, fruitful, logical, meaningful, productive, profitable, proper, sensible, to the point, useful, worthwhile

point of view *n* **1 = perspective**, angle, orientation, outlook, position, standpoint **2 = opinion**, approach, attitude, belief, judgment, slant, view, viewpoint, way of looking at it

point out *vb* **= mention**, allude to, bring up, call attention to, identify, indicate, remind, reveal, show, specify

point up *vb* **= emphasize**, accent, accentuate, make clear, stress, underline

poise[1] *n* **1 = composure**, aplomb, assurance, calmness, cool (*sl.*), coolness, dignity, elegance, equanimity, equilibrium, grace, presence, presence of mind, sang-froid, savoir-faire, self-possession, serenity ◆ *vb* **5 = position**, balance, float, hang, hang in midair, hang suspended, hold, hover, support, suspend

poised *adj* **1 = composed**, calm, collected, debonair, dignified, graceful, nonchalant, self-confident, self-possessed, serene, suave, together (*inf.*), unfazed (*inf.*), unruffled, urbane **2 = ready**, all set, in the wings, on the brink, prepared, standing by, waiting
Antonyms *adj* ≠ **composed:** agitated, annoyed, discomposed, disturbed, excited, irritated, ruffled, worked up

poison *n* **1 = toxin**, bane, venom **2 = contamination**, bane, blight, cancer, canker, contagion, corruption, malignancy, miasma, virus ◆ *vb* **5 = murder**, give (someone) poison, kill **6, 7 = contaminate**, adulterate, envenom, infect, pollute **8 = corrupt**, defile, deprave, pervert, subvert, taint, undermine, vitiate, warp

poisonous *adj* **1, 2 = toxic**, baneful, deadly, fatal, lethal, mephitic, mortal, noxious, venomous, virulent **3 = evil**, baleful, baneful (*arch.*), corrupting, malicious, noxious, pernicious, pestiferous, pestilential, vicious

poison sumach *n* a swamp shrub of the southeastern US that causes an itching rash on contact with the skin.

Poisson distribution ('pwɑːsᵊn) *n Statistics.* a distribution that represents the number of events occurring randomly in a fixed time at an average rate λ. [C19: after S. D. *Poisson* (1781–1840), F mathematician]

poke[1] Ⓣ (pəʊk) *vb* **pokes, poking, poked. 1** (*tr*) to jab or prod, as with the elbow, a stick, etc. **2** (*tr*) to make (a hole) by or as by poking. **3** (when *intr*, often foll. by *at*) to thrust (at). **4** (*tr*) *Inf.* to hit with the fist; punch. **5** (usually foll. by *in, through,* etc.) to protrude or cause to protrude: *don't poke your arm out of the window.* **6** (*tr*) to stir (a fire, etc.) by poking. **7** (*intr*) to meddle or intrude. **8** (*intr;* often foll. by *about* or *around*) to search or pry. **9 poke one's nose into.** to interfere with or meddle in. ◆ *n* **10** a jab or prod. **11** *Inf.* a blow with one's fist; punch. [C14: from Low G & MDu. *poken* to prod]

poke[2] (pəʊk) *n* **1** *Dialect.* a pocket or bag. **2 a pig in a poke.** See **pig.** [C13: from OF *poque,* of Gmc origin]

poke[3] (pəʊk) *n* **1** Also called: **poke bonnet.** a bonnet with a brim that projects at the front, popular in the 18th and 19th centuries. **2** the brim itself. [C18: from POKE[1] (in the sense: to project)]

poker[1] ('pəʊkə) *n* a metal rod, usually with a handle, for stirring a fire.

poker[2] ('pəʊkə) *n* a card game of bluff and skill in which bets are made on the hands dealt, the highest-ranking hand winning the pool. [C19: prob. from F *poque* similar card game]

poker face *n Inf.* a face without expression, as that of a poker player attempting to conceal the value of his cards.
▸**'poker-ˌfaced** *adj*

poker machine *n Austral. & NZ.* a fruit machine.

pokerwork ('pəʊkəˌwɜːk) *n* the art of producing pictures or designs on wood by charring it with a heated tool.

pokeweed ('pəʊkˌwiːd), **pokeberry,** *or* **pokeroot** *n* a tall North American plant that has a poisonous purple root used medicinally. [C18 *poke,* from Algonquian *puccoon* plant used in dyeing, from *pak* blood]

pokie ('pəʊkɪ) *n Austral. inf.* short for **poker machine.**

poky Ⓣ *or* **pokey** ('pəʊkɪ) *adj* **pokier, pokiest. 1** (esp. of rooms) small and cramped. **2** *Inf., chiefly US.* without speed or energy; slow. [C19: from POKE[1] (in sl. sense: to confine)]
▸**'pokily** *adv* ▸**'pokiness** *n*

pol. *abbrev. for:* **1** political. **2** politics.

Pol. *abbrev. for:* **1** Poland. **2** Polish.

polar Ⓣ ('pəʊlə) *adj* **1** at, near, or relating to either of the earth's poles or the area inside the Arctic or Antarctic Circles: *polar regions.* **2** having or relating to a pole or poles. **3** pivotal or guiding in the manner of the Pole Star. **4** directly opposite, as in tendency or character. **5** *Chem.* (of a molecule) having an uneven distribution of electrons and thus a permanent dipole moment: *water has polar molecules.*

polar bear *n* a white carnivorous bear of coastal regions of the North Pole.

polar circle *n* a term for either the **Arctic Circle** or **Antarctic Circle.**

polar coordinates *pl n* a pair of coordinates for locating a point in a plane by means of the length of a radius vector, *r,* which pivots about the origin to establish the angle, θ, that the position of the point makes with a fixed line. Usually written (*r*, θ).

polar distance *n* the angular distance of a star, planet, etc., from the celestial pole; the complement of the declination.

polar front *n Meteorol.* a front dividing cold polar air from warmer temperate or tropical air.

Polari (pə'lɑːrɪ) *n* an English slang derived from the Lingua Franca of Mediterranean ports; brought to England by sailors from the 16th century onwards. [C19: from It. *parlare* to speak]

polarimeter (ˌpəʊlə'rɪmɪtə) *n* an instrument for measuring the polarization of light.
▸**polarimetric** (ˌpəʊlərɪ'mɛtrɪk) *adj*

Polaris (pə'lɑːrɪs) *n* **1** Also called: the **Pole Star,** the **North Star.** the brightest star in the constellation Ursa Minor, situated slightly less than 1° from the north celestial pole. **2** a type of US two-stage intermediate-range ballistic missile, usually fired by a submerged submarine. [from Med. L *stella polāris* polar star]

polariscope (pəʊ'lærɪˌskəʊp) *n* an instrument for detecting polarized light or for observing objects under polarized light, esp. for detecting strain in transparent materials.

polarity Ⓣ (pəʊ'lærɪtɪ) *n, pl* **polarities. 1** the condition of having poles. **2** the condition of a body or system in which it has opposing physical properties, esp. magnetic poles or electric charge. **3** the particular state of a part that has polarity: *an electrode with positive polarity.* **4** the state of having or expressing two directly opposite tendencies, opinions, etc.

polarization *or* **polarisation** (ˌpəʊləraɪ'zeɪʃən) *n* **1** the condition of having or giving polarity. **2** *Physics.* the phenomenon in which waves of light or other radiation are restricted to certain directions of vibration.

polarize *or* **polarise** ('pəʊləˌraɪz) *vb* **polarizes, polarizing, polarized** *or* **polarises, polarising, polarised. 1** to acquire or cause to acquire polarity or polarization. **2** (*tr*) to cause (people) to adopt extreme opposing positions: *to polarize opinion.*
▸**'polarˌizer** *or* **'polarˌiser** *n*

polar lights *pl n* the aurora borealis in the N hemisphere or the aurora australis in the S hemisphere.

polarography (ˌpəʊlə'rɒgrəfɪ) *n* a technique for analysing and studying ions in solution by using an electrolytic cell with a very small cathode and obtaining a graph (**polarogram**) of the current against the potential to determine the concentration and nature of the ions.

Polaroid ('pəʊləˌrɔɪd) *n Trademark.* **1** a type of plastic sheet that can polarize a transmitted beam of normal light because it is composed of long parallel molecules. It only transmits plane-polarized light if these molecules are parallel to the plane of polarization. **2 Polaroid Land Camera.** any of several types of camera yielding a finished print by means of a special developing and processing technique that occurs inside the camera and takes only a few seconds. **3** (*pl*) sunglasses with lenses made from Polaroid plastic.

polder ('pəʊldə, 'pɒl-) *n* a stretch of land reclaimed from the sea or a lake, esp. in the Netherlands. [C17: from MDu. *polre*]

pole[1] Ⓣ (pəʊl) *n* **1** a long slender usually round piece of wood, metal, or other material. **2** the piece of timber on each side of which a pair of carriage horses are hitched. **3** another name for **rod** (sense 7). **4 up the pole.** *Brit., Austral., & NZ inf.* **4a** slightly mad. **4b** mistaken; on the wrong track. ◆ *vb* **poles, poling, poled. 5** (*tr*) to strike or push with a pole. **6** (*tr*) **6a** to set out (an area of land or garden) with poles. **6b** to support (a crop, such as hops) on poles. **7** to punt (a boat). [OE *pāl,* from L *pālus* a stake]

pole[2] Ⓣ (pəʊl) *n* **1** either of the two antipodal points where the earth's axis of rotation meets the earth's surface. See also **North Pole, South Pole. 2** *Physics.* **2a** either of the two regions at the extremities of a magnet to which the lines of force converge. **2b** either of two points at which there are opposite electric charges, as at the terminals of a battery. **3** *Biol.* either end of the axis of a cell, spore, ovum, or similar body. **4** either of two mutually exclusive or opposite actions, opinions, etc. **5 poles apart** (*or* **asunder**). having widely divergent opinions, tastes, etc. [C14: from L *polus* end of an axis, from Gk *polos* pivot]

Pole (pəʊl) *n* a native, inhabitant, or citizen of Poland or a speaker of Polish.

poleaxe *or US* **poleax** ('pəʊlˌæks) *n* **1** another term for a battle-axe or a butcher's axe. ◆ *vb* **poleaxes, poleaxing, poleaxed. 2** (*tr*) to hit or fell with or as if with a poleaxe. [C14 *pollax* battle-axe, from POLL + AXE]

polecat ('pəʊlˌkæt) *n, pl* **polecats** *or* **polecat. 1** a dark brown musteline mammal of Europe, Asia, and N Africa, that is closely related to but larger than the weasel and gives off an unpleasant smell. **2** *US.* a nontechnical name for **skunk** (sense 1). [C14 *polcat,* ?from OF *pol* cock, from L *pullus,* + CAT; from its preying on poultry]

polemic Ⓣ (pə'lɛmɪk) *adj also* **polemical. 1** of or involving dispute or controversy. ◆ *n* **2** an argument or controversy, esp. over a doctrine, belief, etc. **3** a person engaged in such controversy. [C17: from Med. L *polemicus,* from Gk *polemikos* relating to war, from *polemos* war]
▸**po'lemically** *adv* ▸**polemicist** (pə'lɛmɪsɪst) *n*

polemics Ⓣ (pə'lɛmɪks) *n* (*functioning as sing*) the art or practice of dispute or argument, as in attacking or defending a doctrine or belief.

pole position *n* **1** (in motor racing) the starting position on the inside of the front row, generally considered the best one. **2** an advantageous starting position.

pole star *n* a guiding principle, rule, etc.

Pole Star *n* **the.** the star closest to the N celestial pole at any particular time. At present this is Polaris, but it will eventually be replaced owing to precession of the earth's axis.

pole vault *n* **1 the.** a field event in which competitors attempt to clear a high bar with the aid of an extremely flexible long pole. ◆ *vb* **pole-vault. 2** (*intr*) to perform a pole vault or compete in the pole vault.
▸**'pole-ˌvaulter** *n*

poley ('pəʊlɪ) *adj Austral.* (of cattle) hornless or polled.

police Ⓣ (pə'liːs) *n* **1** (often preceded by *the*) the organized civil force of a state, concerned with maintenance of law and order. **2** (*functioning as pl*) the members of such a force collectively. **3** any organized body with a similar function: *security police.* ◆ *vb* **polices, policing, policed.** (*tr*)

THESAURUS

poke[1] *vb* **1, 3, 4** = **jab,** butt, dig, elbow, hit, nudge, prod, punch, push, shove, stab, stick, thrust **7** = **interfere,** butt in, intrude, meddle, nose, peek, poke one's nose into (*inf.*), pry, put one's two cents in (*US sl.*), snoop (*inf.*), tamper ◆ *n* **10, 11** = **jab,** butt, dig, hit, nudge, prod, punch, thrust

poky *adj* **1** = **small,** confined, cramped, incommodious, narrow, tiny
Antonyms *adj* capacious, commodious, large, open, roomy, spacious, wide

polar *adj* **1** = **freezing,** Antarctic, Arctic, cold, extreme, frozen, furthest, glacial, icy, terminal **3** = **pivotal,** beacon-like, cardinal, guiding, leading **4** = **opposite,** antagonistic, antipodal, antithetical, contradictory, contrary, diametric, opposed

polarity *n* **4** = **opposition,** ambivalence, contradiction, contrariety, dichotomy, duality, paradox

pole[1] *n* **1** = **rod,** bar, mast, post, shaft, spar, staff, standard, stick

pole[2] *n* **1** = **extremity,** antipode, limit, terminus **5 poles apart** = **at opposite extremes,** at opposite ends of the earth, incompatible, irreconcilable, miles apart, widely separated, worlds apart

polemic *adj* **1** = **controversial,** argumentative, contentious, disputatious, polemical ◆ *n* **2** = **argument,** controversy, debate, dispute

polemics *n* = **dispute,** argument, argumentation, contention, controversy, debate, disputation

police *n* **1, 2** = **the law** (*inf.*), boys in blue (*inf.*), constabulary, fuzz (*sl.*), law enforcement agency, police force, the Old Bill (*sl.*) ◆ *vb* **4** = **control,** guard, keep in order, keep the peace,

4 to regulate, control, or keep in order by means of a police or similar force. **5** to observe or record the activity or enforcement of: *a committee was set up to police the new agreement on picketing.* [C16: via F from L *polītia* administration; see POLITY]

police dog *n* a dog, often an Alsatian, trained to help the police, as in tracking.

policeman (pə'liːsmən) *or (fem)* **policewoman** *n, pl* **policemen** *or* **policewomen.** a member of a police force, esp. one holding the rank of constable.

police officer *n* a member of a police force, esp. a constable; policeman.

police procedural *n* a novel, film, or television drama that deals realistically with police work.

police state *n* a state or country in which a repressive government maintains control through the police.

police station *n* the office or headquarters of the police force of a district.

policing (pə'liːsɪŋ) *n* the policies, techniques, and practice of a police force in keeping order, preventing crime, etc.

policy[1] ('pɒlɪsɪ) *n, pl* **policies. 1** a plan of action adopted or pursued by an individual, government, party, business, etc. **2** wisdom, shrewdness, or sagacity. **3** (*often pl*) *Scot.* the improved grounds surrounding a country house. [C14: from OF *policie*, from L *polītia* administration, POLITY]

policy[2] ('pɒlɪsɪ) *n, pl* **policies.** a document containing a contract of insurance. [C16: from OF *police* certificate, from OIt. from L *apodixis* proof, from Gk *apodeixis*]

▸**'policy,holder** *n*

polio ('pəʊlɪəʊ) *n* short for **poliomyelitis.**

poliomyelitis (,pəʊlɪəʊ,maɪə'laɪtɪs) *n* an acute infectious viral disease, esp. affecting children. In its paralytic form the brain and spinal cord are involved, causing paralysis and wasting of muscle. Also called: **infantile paralysis.** [C19: NL, from Gk *polios* grey + *muelos* marrow]

polish ('pɒlɪʃ) *vb* **1** to make or become smooth and shiny by rubbing, esp. with wax or an abrasive. **2** (*tr*) to make perfect or complete. **3** to make or become elegant or refined. ◆ *n* **4** a finish or gloss. **5** the act of polishing. **6** a substance used to produce a shiny, often protective surface. **7** elegance or refinement, esp. in style, manner, etc. [C13 *polis*, from OF *polir*, from L *polīre* to polish]

▸**'polisher** *n*

Polish ('pəʊlɪʃ) *adj* **1** of, relating to, or characteristic of Poland, its people, or their language. ◆ *n* **2** the official language of Poland.

polished ('pɒlɪʃt) *adj* **1** accomplished: *a polished actor.* **2** impeccably or professionally done: *a polished performance.* **3** (of rice) milled to remove the outer husk.

polish off *vb* (*tr, adv*) *Inf.* **1** to finish or process completely. **2** to dispose of or kill.

polish up *vb* (*adv*) **1** to make or become smooth and shiny by polishing. **2** (when *intr*, foll. by *on*) to study or practise until adept (at): *he's polishing up on his German.*

Politburo ('pɒlɪt,bjʊərəʊ) *n* **1** the executive and policy-making committee of a Communist Party. **2** the supreme policy-making authority in most Communist countries. [C20: from Russian: contraction of *Politicheskoe Buro* political bureau]

polite (pə'laɪt) *adj* **1** showing a great regard for others, as in manners, etc.; courteous. **2** cultivated or refined: *polite society.* **3** elegant or polished: *polite letters.* [C15: from L *polītus* polished]

▸**po'litely** *adv* ▸**po'liteness** *n*

politesse (,pɒlɪ'tɛs) *n* formal or genteel politeness. [C18: via F from It. *politezza*, ult. from L *polīre* to polish]

politic ('pɒlɪtɪk) *adj* **1** artful or shrewd; ingenious. **2** crafty or unscrupulous; cunning. **3** wise or prudent, esp. in statesmanship: *a politic choice.* **4** an archaic word for **political.** ◆ See also **body politic.** [C15: from OF *politique*, from L *polīticus* concerning civil administration, from Gk, from *politēs* citizen, from *polis* city]

▸**'politicly** *adv*

political (pə'lɪtɪkᵊl) *adj* **1** of or relating to the state, government, public administration, etc. **2a** of or relating to government policy-making as distinguished from administration or law. **2b** of or relating to the civil aspects of government as distinguished from the military. **3** of, dealing with, or relating to politics: *a political person.* **4** of or relating to the parties and the partisan aspects of politics. **5** organized with respect to government: *a political unit.*

▸**po'litically** *adv*

political economy *n* the former name for **economics** (sense 1).

politically correct *adj* demonstrating liberal ideals, esp. by using vocabulary that is intended to avoid prejudice of any kind. Often abbreviated to **PC.**

political prisoner *n* a person imprisoned for holding or expressing particular political beliefs.

political science *n* the study of the state, government, and politics: one of the social sciences.

▸**political scientist** *n*

politician (,pɒlɪ'tɪʃən) *n* **1** a person actively engaged in politics, esp. a full-time professional member of a deliberative assembly. **2** a person who is experienced or skilled in government or administration; statesman. **3** *Disparaging, chiefly US.* a person who engages in politics out of a wish for personal gain.

politicize *or* **politicise** (pə'lɪtɪ,saɪz) *vb* **politicizes, politicizing, politicized** *or* **politicises, politicising, politicised. 1** (*tr*) to render political in tone, interest, or awareness. **2** (*intr*) to participate in political discussion or activity.

▸**po,litici'zation** *or* **po,litici'sation** *n*

politicking ('pɒlɪtɪkɪŋ) *n* political activity, esp. seeking votes.

politico (pə'lɪtɪ,kəʊ) *n, pl* **politicos.** *Chiefly US.* an informal word for a **politician** (senses 1, 3). [C17: from It. or Sp.]

politics ('pɒlɪtɪks) *n* **1** (*functioning as sing*) the art and science of directing and administrating states and other political units; government. **2** (*functioning as sing*) the complex or aggregate of relationships of people in society, esp. those relationships involving authority or power. **3** (*functioning as pl*) political activities or affairs: *party politics.* **4** (*functioning as sing*) the business or profession of politics. **5** (*functioning as sing or pl*) any activity concerned with the acquisition of power, etc.: *company politics are frequently vicious.* **6** manoeuvres or factors leading up to or influencing (something): *the politics of the decision.* **7** (*functioning as pl*) opinions, sympathies, etc., with respect to politics: *his conservative politics.*

polity ('pɒlɪtɪ) *n, pl* **polities. 1** a form of government or organization of a society, etc.; constitution. **2** a politically organized society, etc. **3** the management of public affairs. **4** political organization. [C16: from L *polītia*, from Gk *politeia* citizenship, civil administration, from *politēs* citizen, from *polis* city]

polka ('pɒlkə) *n* **1** a 19th-century Bohemian dance with three steps and a hop, in fast duple time. **2** a piece of music composed for or in the rhythm of this dance. ◆ *vb* **polkas, polkaing, polkaed. 3** (*intr*) to dance a polka. [C19: via F from Czech *pulka* half-step]

polka dot *n* one of a pattern of small circular regularly spaced spots on a fabric.

poll (pəʊl) *n* **1** the casting, recording, or counting of votes in an election; a voting. **2** the result of such a voting: *a heavy poll.* **3** Also called: **opinion poll. 3a** a canvassing of a representative sample of people on some question in order to determine the general opinion. **3b** the results of such a canvassing. **4** any counting or enumeration, esp. for taxation or voting purposes. **5** the back part of the head of an animal. ◆ *vb* (*mainly tr*) **6** to receive (a vote or quantity of votes): *he polled 10 000 votes.* **7** to receive, take, or record the votes of: *he polled the whole town.* **8** to canvass (a person, group, area, etc.) as part of a survey of opinion. **9** (*sometimes intr*) to cast (a vote) in an election. **10** to clip or shear. **11** to remove or cut short the horns of (cattle). [C13 (in the sense: a human head) & C17 (in the sense: votes): from MLow G *polle* hair of the head, head, top of a tree]

pollack *or* **pollock** ('pɒlək) *n, pl* **pollacks, pollack** *or* **pollocks, pollock.** a gadoid food fish that has a projecting lower jaw and occurs in northern seas. [C17: from earlier Scot. *podlok*, from ?]

THESAURUS

patrol, protect, regulate, watch **5 = monitor,** check, observe, oversee, supervise

policeman *n* **= cop** (*sl.*), bizzy (*inf.*), bobby (*inf.*), constable, copper (*sl.*), flatfoot (*sl.*), fuzz (*sl.*), gendarme (*sl.*), officer, peeler (*obs. Brit. sl.*), plod (*Brit. sl.*), rozzer (*sl.*)

policy[1] *n* **1 = procedure,** action, approach, code, course, custom, guideline, line, plan, practice, programme, protocol, rule, scheme, stratagem, theory **2 = wisdom,** discretion, good sense, prudence, sagacity, shrewdness

polish *vb* **1 = shine,** brighten, buff, burnish, clean, furbish, rub, smooth, wax **2 = perfect,** brush up, correct, cultivate, emend, enhance, finish, improve, refine, touch up ◆ *n* **4 = sheen,** brightness, brilliance, finish, glaze, gloss, lustre, smoothness, sparkle, veneer **6 = varnish,** wax **7 = style,** breeding, class (*inf.*), elegance, finesse, finish, grace, politesse, refinement, suavity, urbanity

polished *adj* **1, 2 = accomplished,** adept, expert, faultless, fine, flawless, impeccable, masterly, outstanding, professional, skilful, superlative

Antonyms *adj* amateurish, inept, inexpert, unaccomplished, unskilled

polish off *vb* **2** *Informal* **= kill,** blow away, bump off (*inf.*), dispose of, do away with, do in (*sl.*), eliminate, get rid of, liquidate, murder, take out (*sl.*)

polite *adj* **1 = mannerly,** affable, civil, complaisant, courteous, deferential, gracious, obliging, respectful, well-behaved, well-mannered **2, 3 = refined,** civilized, courtly, cultured, elegant, genteel, polished, sophisticated, urbane, well-bred

Antonyms *adj* ≠ **mannerly:** crude, discourteous, ill-mannered, impertinent, impolite, impudent, insulting, rude ≠ **refined:** uncultured, unrefined

politeness *n* **1 = courtesy,** civility, common courtesy, complaisance, correctness, courteousness, decency, deference, etiquette, grace, graciousness, mannerliness, obligingness, respectfulness

politic *adj* **1, 2 = shrewd,** artful, astute, canny, crafty, cunning, designing, ingenious, intriguing, Machiavellian, scheming, sly, subtle, unscrupulous **3 = wise,** advisable, diplomatic, discreet, expedient, in one's best interests, judicious, prudent, sagacious, sensible, tactful

political *adj* **1, 2 = governmental,** civic, parliamentary, policy-making **4 = factional,** partisan, party

politician *n* **1 = statesman,** legislator, Member of Parliament, M.P., office bearer, politico (*inf., chiefly US*), public servant, stateswoman

politics *n* **1 = statesmanship,** affairs of state, civics, government, government policy, political science, polity, statecraft **5 = power struggle,** Machiavellianism, machination, *Realpolitik*

poll *n* **1, 3 = canvass,** ballot, census, count, Gallup Poll, (public) opinion poll, sampling, survey **2 = vote,** figures, returns, tally, voting ◆ *vb* **6 = tally,** register **8 = question,** ballot, canvass, fly a kite, interview, sample, survey

pollan ('pɒlən) *n* any of several varieties of whitefish that occur in lakes in Northern Ireland. [C18: prob. from Irish *poll* lake]

pollard ('pɒləd) *n* **1** an animal, such as a sheep or deer, that has either shed its horns or antlers or has had them removed. **2** a tree that has had its branches cut back to encourage a more bushy growth. ◆ *vb* **3** (*tr*) to convert into a pollard; poll. [C16: hornless animal; see POLL]

pollen ('pɒlən) *n* a substance produced by the anthers of seed-bearing plants, consisting of numerous fine grains containing the male gametes. [C16: from L: powder]
▸**pollinic** (pə'lɪnɪk) *adj*

pollen analysis *n* another name for **palynology.**

pollen count *n* a measure of the pollen present in the air over a 24-hour period, often published to enable sufferers from hay fever to predict the severity of their attacks.

pollex ('pɒlɛks) *n, pl* **pollices** (-lɪˌsiːz). the first digit of the forelimb of amphibians, reptiles, birds, and mammals, such as the thumb of man. [C19: from L: thumb, big toe]
▸**pollical** ('pɒlɪkᵊl) *adj*

pollinate ('pɒlɪˌneɪt) *vb* **pollinates, pollinating, pollinated.** (*tr*) to transfer pollen from the anthers to the stigma of (a flower).
▸ˌ**polli'nation** *n* ▸'**polliˌnator** *n*

polling booth *n* a semienclosed space in which a voter stands to mark a ballot paper during an election.

polling station *n* a building, such as a school, designated as the place to which voters go during an election in order to cast their votes.

polliwog *or* **pollywog** ('pɒlɪˌwɒg) *n Dialect, US, & Canad.* a tadpole. [C15 *polwygle*]

pollster ('pəʊlstə) *n* a person who conducts opinion polls.

poll tax *n* **1** a tax levied per head of adult population. **2** an informal name for **community charge.**

pollutant (pə'luːtᵊnt) *n* a substance that pollutes, esp. a chemical produced as a waste product of an industrial process.

pollute ❶ (pə'luːt) *vb* **pollutes, polluting, polluted.** (*tr*) **1** to contaminate, as with poisonous or harmful substances. **2** to make morally corrupt. **3** to desecrate. [C14 *polute,* from L *polluere* to defile]
▸**pol'luter** *n* ▸**pol'lution** *n*

Pollyanna (ˌpɒlɪ'ænə) *n* a person who is optimistic. [C20: after the chief character in *Pollyanna* (1913), a novel by Eleanor Porter (1868–1920), US writer]

polo ('pəʊləʊ) *n* **1** a game similar to hockey played on horseback using long-handled mallets (**polo sticks**) and a wooden ball. **2** short for **water polo. 3** Also called: **polo neck. 3a** a collar on a garment, worn rolled over to fit closely round the neck. **3b** a garment, esp. a sweater, with such a collar. [C19: from Balti (dialect of Kashmir): ball, from Tibetan *pulu*]

polonaise (ˌpɒlə'neɪz) *n* **1** a ceremonial marchlike dance in three-four time from Poland. **2** a piece of music composed for or in the rhythm of this dance. **3** a woman's costume with a tight bodice and an overskirt drawn back to show a decorative underskirt. [C18: from F *danse polonaise* Polish dance]

polonium (pə'ləʊnɪəm) *n* a very rare radioactive element that occurs in trace amounts in uranium ores. Symbol: Po; atomic no.: 84; half-life of most stable isotope, ^{209}Po: 103 years. [C19: NL, from Med. L *Polōnia* Poland; in honour of the nationality of its discoverer, Marie Curie]

polony (pə'ləʊnɪ) *n, pl* **polonies.** *Brit.* another name for **bologna sausage.**

polo shirt *n* a knitted cotton short-sleeved shirt with a collar and three-button opening at the neck.

poltergeist ('pɒltəˌgaɪst) *n* a spirit believed to manifest its presence by noises and acts of mischief, such as throwing furniture about. [C19: from G, from *poltern* to be noisy + *Geist* GHOST]

poltroon (pɒl'truːn) *n* an abject or contemptible coward. [C16: from OF *poultron,* from OIt. *poltrone* lazy good-for-nothing, apparently from *poltrire* to lie indolently in bed]

poly ('pɒlɪ) *n, pl* **polys.** *Inf.* short for **polytechnic.**

poly- *combining form.* **1** more than one; many or much: *polyhedron.* **2** having an excessive or abnormal number or amount: *polyphagia.* [from Gk *polus* much, many]

polyamide (ˌpɒlɪ'æmaɪd, -mɪd) *n* any of a class of synthetic polymeric materials, including nylon.

polyandry ('pɒlɪˌændrɪ) *n* **1** the practice or condition of being married to more than one husband at the same time. **2** the practice in animals of a female mating with more than one male during one breeding season. **3** the condition in flowers of having a large indefinite number of stamens. [C18: from Gk *poluandria,* from POLY- + *-andria* from *anēr* man]
▸ˌ**poly'androus** *adj*

polyanthus (ˌpɒlɪ'ænθəs) *n, pl* **polyanthuses.** any of several hybrid garden primroses with brightly coloured flowers. [C18: NL, from Gk: having many flowers]

polyatomic (ˌpɒlɪə'tɒmɪk) *adj* (of a molecule) containing more than two atoms.

poly bag ('pɒlɪ) *n Brit. inf.* a polythene bag, esp. one used to store or protect food or household articles.

polybasic (ˌpɒlɪ'beɪsɪk) *adj* (of an acid) having two or more replaceable hydrogen atoms per molecule.

polycarboxylate (ˌpɒlɪkɑː'bɒksɪˌleɪt) *n* a salt or ester of a polycarboxylic acid. Polycarboxylate esters are used in certain detergents.

polycarboxylic acid ('pɒlɪˌkɑːbɒk'sɪlɪk) *n* a type of carboxylic acid containing two or more carboxyl groups.

polycarpic (ˌpɒlɪ'kɑːpɪk) *or* **polycarpous** *adj* (of a plant) able to produce flowers and fruit several times in succession.
▸'**polyˌcarpy** *n*

polycentrism (ˌpɒlɪ'sɛntrɪzəm) *n* (formerly) the fact or advocacy of the existence of more than one predominant ideological or political centre in a political system, alliance, etc., in the Communist world.

polychaete ('pɒlɪˌkiːt) *n* **1** a marine annelid worm having a distinct head and paired fleshy appendages (parapodia) that bear bristles and are used in swimming. ◆ *adj also* **polychaetous. 2** of or denoting such a creature. [C19: from NL, from Gk *polukhaitēs* having much hair]

polychromatic (ˌpɒlɪkrəʊ'mætɪk), **polychromic** (ˌpɒlɪ'krəʊmɪk), *or* **polychromous** *adj* **1** having various or changing colours. **2** (of light or other radiation) containing radiation with more than one wavelength.
▸**polychromatism** (ˌpɒlɪ'krəʊməˌtɪzəm) *n*

polyclinic (ˌpɒlɪ'klɪnɪk) *n* a hospital or clinic able to treat a wide variety of diseases.

polycotton ('pɒlɪkɒtᵊn) *n* a fabric made from a mixture of polyester and cotton.

polycotyledon (ˌpɒlɪˌkɒtɪ'liːdᵊn) *n* any of various plants, esp. gymnosperms, that have or appear to have more than two cotyledons.
▸ˌ**polyˌcoty'ledonous** *adj*

polycyclic (ˌpɒlɪ'saɪklɪk) *adj* **1** (of a molecule or compound) having molecules that contain two or more closed rings of atoms. **2** *Biol.* having two or more rings or whorls: *polycyclic shells.* ◆ *n* **3** a polycyclic compound.

polycystic (ˌpɒlɪ'sɪstɪk) *adj Med.* containing many cysts: *a polycystic ovary.*

polydactyl (ˌpɒlɪ'dæktɪl) *adj also* **polydactylous. 1** (of man and other vertebrates) having more than the normal number of digits. ◆ *n* **2** a human or other vertebrate having more than the normal number of digits.

polyester (ˌpɒlɪ'ɛstə) *n* any of a large class of synthetic materials that are polymers containing recurring -COO- groups: used as plastics, textile fibres, and adhesives.

polyethene (ˌpɒlɪ'ɛθiːn) *n* the systematic name for **polythene.**

polyethylene (ˌpɒlɪ'ɛθɪˌliːn) *n* another name for **polythene.**

polygamy (pə'lɪgəmɪ) *n* **1** the practice of having more than one wife or husband at the same time. **2** the condition of having male, female, and hermaphrodite flowers on the same plant or on separate plants of the same species. **3** the practice in male animals of having more than one mate during one breeding season. [C16: via F from Gk *polugamia*]
▸**po'lygamist** *n* ▸**po'lygamous** *adj* ▸**po'lygamously** *adv*

polygene ('pɒlɪˌdʒiːn) *n* any of a group of genes that each produce a small quantitative effect on a particular characteristic, such as height.

polygenesis (ˌpɒlɪ'dʒɛnɪsɪs) *n* **1** *Biol.* evolution of organisms from different ancestral groups. **2** the hypothetical descent of different races from different ultimate ancestors.
▸**polygenetic** (ˌpɒlɪdʒɪ'nɛtɪk) *adj*

polyglot ('pɒlɪˌglɒt) *adj* **1** having a command of many languages. **2** written in or containing many languages. ◆ *n* **3** a person with a command of many languages. **4** a book, esp. a Bible, containing several versions of the same text written in various languages. **5** a mixture of languages. [C17: from Gk *poluglōttos,* lit.: many-tongued]

polygon ('pɒlɪˌgɒn) *n* a closed plane figure bounded by three or more straight sides that meet in pairs in the same number of vertices and do not intersect other than at these vertices. Specific polygons are named according to the number of sides, such as triangle, pentagon, etc. [C16: via L from Gk *polugōnon* figure with many angles]
▸**polygonal** (pə'lɪgənᵊl) *adj* ▸**po'lygonally** *adv*

polygonum (pə'lɪgənəm) *n* a plant having stems with knotlike joints and spikes of small white, green, or pink flowers. [C18: NL, from Gk *polugonon* knotgrass, from *polu-* POLY- + *-gonon,* from *gonu* knee]

polygraph ('pɒlɪˌgrɑːf) *n* **1** an instrument for the simultaneous recording of several involuntary physiological activities, including pulse rate and perspiration, used esp. as a lie detector. **2** a device for producing copies of written matter. [C18: from Gk *polugraphos* writing copiously]

polygyny (pə'lɪdʒɪnɪ) *n* **1** the practice or condition of being married to more than one wife at the same time. **2** the practice in animals of a male mating with more than one female during one breeding season. **3** the condition in flowers of having many styles. [C18: from POLY- + *-gyny,* from Gk *gunē* a woman]
▸**po'lygynous** *adj*

polyhedron (ˌpɒlɪ'hiːdrən) *n, pl* **polyhedrons** *or* **polyhedra** (-drə). a solid figure consisting of four or more plane faces (all polygons), pairs of which meet along an edge, three or more edges meeting at a vertex.

THESAURUS

pollute *vb* **1 = contaminate,** adulterate, befoul, dirty, foul, infect, make filthy, mar, poison, smirch, soil, spoil, stain, taint **2, 3 = defile,** besmirch, corrupt, debase, debauch, deprave, desecrate, dishonour, profane, sully, violate

Antonyms *vb* ≠ **contaminate:** clean, cleanse, decontaminate, disinfect, purge, sanitize, sterilize ≠ **defile:** esteem, honour

pollution *n* **1 = contamination,** adulteration, corruption, defilement, dirtying, foulness, impurity, taint, uncleanness, vitiation

Specific polyhedrons are named according to the number of faces, such as tetrahedron, icosahedron, etc. [C16: from Gk *poluedron*, from POLY- + *hedron* side]
▸ˌ**poly'hedral** *adj*

Polyhymnia (ˌpɒlɪ'hɪmnɪə) *n Greek myth.* the Muse of singing, mime, and sacred dance. [L, from Gk *Polumnia* full of songs]

polymath ('pɒlɪˌmæθ) *n* a person of great and varied learning. [C17: from Gk *polumathēs* having much knowledge]
▸**polymathy** (pə'lɪməθɪ) *n*

polymer ('pɒlɪmə) *n* a naturally occurring or synthetic compound, such as starch or Perspex, that has large molecules made up of many relatively simple repeated units.
▸**polymerism** (pə'lɪməˌrɪzəm, 'pɒlɪmə-) *n*

polymerase ('pɒlɪməˌreɪs, -ˌreɪz) *n* any enzyme that catalyses the synthesis of a polymer, esp. the synthesis of DNA or RNA.

polymeric (ˌpɒlɪ'mɛrɪk) *adj* of, concerned with, or being a polymer: *a polymeric compound.* [C19: from Gk *polumerēs* having many parts]

polymerization *or* **polymerisation** (pəˌlɪməraɪ'zeɪʃən, ˌpɒlɪməraɪ-) *n* the act or process of forming a polymer or copolymer.

polymerize *or* **polymerise** ('pɒlɪməˌraɪz, pə'lɪmə-) *vb* **polymerizes, polymerizing, polymerized** *or* **polymerises, polymerising, polymerised.** to react or cause to react to form a polymer.

polymerous (pə'lɪmərəs) *adj Biol.* having or being composed of many parts.

polymorph ('pɒlɪˌmɔːf) *n* a species of animal or plant, or a crystalline form of a chemical compound, that exhibits polymorphism. [C19: from Gk *polumorphos* having many forms]

polymorphic function *n Computing.* a function in a computer program that can deal with a number of different types of data.

polymorphism (ˌpɒlɪ'mɔːfɪzəm) *n* **1** the occurrence of more than one form of individual in a single species within an interbreeding population. **2** the existence or formation of different types of crystal of the same chemical compound.

polymorphous (ˌpɒlɪ'mɔːfəs) *or* **polymorphic** *adj* **1** having, taking, or passing through many different forms or stages. **2** exhibiting or undergoing polymorphism.

Polynesian (ˌpɒlɪ'niːʒən, -ʒɪən) *adj* **1** of or relating to Polynesia, a group of Pacific islands, or to its people, or any of their languages. ◆ *n* **2** a member of the people that inhabit Polynesia, generally of Caucasoid features with light skin and wavy hair. **3** a branch of the Malayo-Polynesian family of languages, including Maori and Hawaiian.

polyneuritis (ˌpɒlɪnju'raɪtɪs) *n* inflammation of many nerves at the same time.

polynomial (ˌpɒlɪ'nəumɪəl) *adj* **1** of, consisting of, or referring to two or more names or terms. ◆ *n* **2a** a mathematical expression consisting of a sum of terms each of which is the product of a constant and one or more variables raised to a positive or zero integral power. **2b** Also called: **multinomial.** any mathematical expression consisting of the sum of a number of terms. **3** *Biol.* a taxonomic name consisting of more than two terms, such as *Parus major minor* in which *minor* designates the subspecies.

polynucleotide (ˌpɒlɪ'njuːklɪəˌtaɪd) *n Biochem.* a molecular chain of nucleotides chemically bonded by a series of ester linkages between the phosphoryl group of one nucleotide and the hydroxyl group of the sugar in the adjacent nucleotide.

polynya ('pɒlənˌjɑː) *n* a stretch of open water surrounded by ice, esp. near the mouths of large rivers, in arctic seas. [C19: from Russian, from *poly* open]

polyp ('pɒlɪp) *n* **1** *Zool.* one of the two forms of individual that occur in coelenterates. It usually has a hollow cylindrical body with a ring of tentacles around the mouth. **2** Also called: **polypus.** *Pathol.* a small growth arising from the surface of a mucous membrane. [C16 *polip*, from F *polype* nasal polyp, from L *pōlypus*, from Gk *polupous* having many feet]
▸'**polypous** *or* '**polypoid** *adj*

polypeptide (ˌpɒlɪ'peptaɪd) *n* any of a group of natural or synthetic polymers made up of amino acids chemically linked together; includes the proteins.

polypetalous (ˌpɒlɪ'petələs) *adj* (of flowers) having many distinct or separate petals.

polyphagia (ˌpɒlɪ'feɪdʒə) *n* **1** an abnormal desire to consume excessive amounts of food. **2** the habit of certain animals, esp. certain insects, of feeding on many different types of food. [C17: NL, from Gk, from *poluphagos* eating much]
▸**polyphagous** (pə'lɪfəgəs) *adj*

polyphase ('pɒlɪˌfeɪz) *adj* **1** (of an electrical system, circuit, or device) having or using alternating voltages of the same frequency, the phases of which are cyclically displaced by fractions of a period. **2** having more than one phase.

polyphone ('pɒlɪˌfəun) *n* a letter or character having more than one phonetic value, such as *c* in English.

polyphonic (ˌpɒlɪ'fɒnɪk) *adj* **1** *Music.* composed of relatively independent parts; contrapuntal. **2** many-voiced. **3** *Phonetics.* denoting a polyphone.
▸ˌ**poly'phonically** *adv*

polyphony (pə'lɪfənɪ) *n, pl* **polyphonies. 1** polyphonic style of composition or a piece of music utilizing it. **2** the use of polyphones in a writing system. [C19: from Gk *poluphōnia* diversity of tones]
▸**po'lyphonous** *adj* ▸**po'lyphonously** *adv*

polyploid ('pɒlɪˌplɔɪd) *adj* (of cells, organisms, etc.) having more than twice the basic (haploid) number of chromosomes.
▸ˌ**poly'ploidal** *adj* ▸'**polyˌploidy** *n*

polypod ('pɒlɪˌpɒd) *adj* **1** (esp. of insect larvae) having many legs or similar appendages. ◆ *n* **2** an animal of this type.

polypody ('pɒlɪˌpəudɪ) *n, pl* **polypodies.** any of various ferns having deeply divided leaves and round naked sporangia. [C15: from L *polypodium*, from Gk, from POLY- + *pous* foot]

polypropylene (ˌpɒlɪ'prəupɪˌliːn) *n* any of various tough flexible synthetic thermoplastic materials made by polymerizing propylene. Systematic name: **polypropene** (ˌpɒlɪ'prəupiːn).

polypus ('pɒlɪpəs) *n, pl* **polypi** (-paɪ). *Pathol.* another word for **polyp** (sense 2). [C16: via L from Gk: POLYP]

polysaccharide (ˌpɒlɪ'sækəˌraɪd, -rɪd) *or* **polysaccharose** (ˌpɒlɪ'sækəˌrəuz, -ˌrəus) *n* any one of a class of carbohydrates whose molecules contain linked monosaccharide units: includes starch, inulin, and cellulose.

polysemy (ˌpɒlɪ'siːmɪ, pə'lɪsəmɪ) *n* the existence of several meanings in a single word. [C20: from NL *polysēmia*, from Gk *polusēmos* having many meanings]
▸ˌ**poly'semous** *adj*

polysomic (ˌpɒlɪ'səumɪk) *adj* of, relating to, or designating a basically diploid chromosome complement, in which some but not all the chromosomes are represented more than twice.

polystyrene (ˌpɒlɪ'staɪriːn) *n* a synthetic thermoplastic material obtained by polymerizing styrene; used as a white rigid foam (**expanded polystyrene**) for insulating and packing and as a glasslike material in light fittings.

polysyllable ('pɒlɪˌsɪləb[ə]l) *n* a word consisting of more than two syllables.
▸**polysyllabic** (ˌpɒlɪsɪ'læbɪk) *adj* ▸ˌ**polysyl'labically** *adv*

polysyndeton (ˌpɒlɪ'sɪndɪtən) *n Rhetoric.* the use of several conjunctions in close succession, esp. where some might be omitted, as in *he ran and jumped and laughed for joy.* [C16: POLY- + *-syndeton*, from Gk *sundetos* bound together]

polytechnic (ˌpɒlɪ'teknɪk) *n* **1** *Brit.* (formerly) a college offering advanced courses in many fields at and below degree standard. ◆ *adj* **2** of or relating to technical instruction and training. [C19: via F from Gk *polutekhnos* skilled in many arts]

polytetrafluoroethylene (ˌpɒlɪˌtetrəˌfluərəu'εθɪˌliːn) *n* a white thermoplastic material with a waxy texture, made by polymerizing tetrafluoroethylene. It is used for making gaskets, hoses, insulators, bearings, and for coating metal surfaces. Abbrev.: **PTFE.** Also called (trademark): **Teflon.**

polytheism ('pɒlɪθiːˌɪzəm, ˌpɒlɪ'θiːɪzəm) *n* the worship of or belief in more than one god.
▸ˌ**polythe'istic** *adj* ▸ˌ**polythe'istically** *adv*

polythene ('pɒlɪˌθiːn) *n* any one of various light thermoplastic materials made from ethylene with properties depending on the molecular weight of the polymer. Systematic name: **polyethene.** Also called: **polyethylene.**

polytonality (ˌpɒlɪtəu'nælɪtɪ) *or* **polytonalism** *n Music.* the simultaneous use of more than two different keys or tonalities.
▸ˌ**poly'tonal** *adj* ▸ˌ**poly'tonally** *adv*

polyunsaturated (ˌpɒlɪʌn'sætʃəˌreɪtɪd) *adj* of or relating to a class of animal and vegetable fats, the molecules of which consist of long carbon chains with many double bonds. Polyunsaturated compounds are less likely to be converted into cholesterol in the body. See also **monounsaturated.**

polyurethane (ˌpɒlɪ'juərəˌθeɪn) *n* a class of synthetic materials commonly used as a foam for insulation and packing.

polyvalent (ˌpɒlɪ'veɪlənt, pə'lɪvələnt) *adj* **1** *Chem.* having more than one valency. **2** (of a vaccine) effective against several strains of the same disease-producing microorganism, antigen, or toxin.
▸ˌ**poly'valency** *n*

polyvinyl (ˌpɒlɪ'vaɪnɪl, -'vaɪn[ə]l) *n* (*modifier*) designating a plastic or resin formed by polymerization of a vinyl derivative.

polyvinyl acetate *n* a colourless odourless tasteless resin used in emulsion paints, adhesives, sealers, a substitute for chicle in chewing gum, and for sealing porous surfaces.

polyvinyl chloride *n* the full name of **PVC.**

polyvinyl resin *n* any of a class of thermoplastic resins made by polymerizing a vinyl compound. The commonest type is PVC.

polyzoan (ˌpɒlɪ'zəuən) *n, adj* another word for **bryozoan.** [C19: from NL *Polyzoa* class name, from POLY- + *-zoan*, from Gk *zōion* an animal]

pom (pɒm) *n Austral. & NZ sl.* short for **pommy.**

POM *abbrev. for* prescription only medicine (*or* medication). Cf. **OTC.**

pomace ('pʌmɪs) *n* **1** the pulpy residue of apples or similar fruit after crushing and pressing, as in cider-making. **2** any pulpy substance left after crushing, mashing, etc. [C16: from Med. L *pōmācium* cider, from L *pōmum* apple]

pomaceous (pɒ'meɪʃəs) *adj* of, relating to, or bearing pomes, such as the apple and quince trees. [C18: from NL *pōmāceus*, from L *pōmum* apple]

pomade (pə'mɑːd) *n* **1** a perfumed oil or ointment put on the hair, as to make it smooth and shiny. ◆ *vb* **pomades, pomading, pomaded. 2** (*tr*) to put pomade on. ◆ Also: **pomatum.** [C16: from F *pommade*, from It. *pomato* (orig. made partly from apples), from L *pōmum* apple]

pomander (pəu'mændə) *n* **1** a mixture of aromatic substances in a sachet or an orange, formerly carried as scent or as a protection against disease. **2** a container for such a mixture. [C15: from OF *pome d'ambre*, from Med. L *pōmum ambrae* apple of amber]

pome (pəum) *n* the fleshy fruit of the apple and related plants, consisting of an enlarged receptacle enclosing the ovary and seeds. [C15: from OF, from LL *pōma*, pl. of L *pōmum* apple]

pomegranate ('pɒmɪˌɡrænɪt, 'pɒmˌɡrænɪt) *n* **1** an Asian shrub or small tree cultivated in semitropical regions for its edible fruit. **2** the many-chambered globular fruit of this tree, which has tough reddish rind, juicy red pulp, and many seeds. [C14: from OF *pome grenate*, from L *pōmum* apple + *grenate*, from *grānātus* full of seeds]

pomelo ('pɒmɪˌləʊ) *n, pl* **pomelos. 1** Also called: **shaddock.** the edible yellow fruit, resembling a grapefruit, of a tropical tree widely grown in oriental regions. **2** *US.* another name for **grapefruit.** [C19: from Du. *pompelmoes*]

Pomeranian (ˌpɒmə'reɪnɪən) *adj* **1** of or relating to Pomerania, a region of N central Europe now chiefly in Poland. ◆ *n* **2** a breed of toy dog of the spitz type with a long thick straight coat.

pomfret ('pʌmfrɪt, 'pɒm-) *or* **pomfret-cake** *n* a small black rounded confection of liquorice. Also called: **Pontefract cake.** [C19: from *Pomfret*, earlier form of *Pontefract*, West Yorkshire, where orig. made]

pomiculture ('pɒmɪˌkʌltʃə) *n* the cultivation of fruit. [C19: from L *pōmum* fruit + CULTURE]

pommel ('pʌməl, 'pɒm-) *n* **1** the raised part on the front of a saddle. **2** a knob at the top of a sword or similar weapon. ◆ *vb* **pommels, pommelling, pommelled** *or US* **pommels, pommeling, pommeled. 3** a less common word for **pummel.** [C14: from OF *pomel* knob, from Vulgar L *pōmellum* (unattested) little apple, from L *pōmum* apple]

pommy ('pɒmɪ) *n, pl* **pommies.** (*sometimes cap.*) *Sl.* a mildly offensive word used by Australians and New Zealanders for a British person. Sometimes shortened to **pom.** [C20: from ?, ? a blend of IMMIGRANT & POMEGRANATE (alluding to the red cheeks of British immigrants)]

pomology (pɒ'mɒlədʒɪ) *n* the branch of horticulture concerned with the study and cultivation of fruit. [C19: from NL *pōmologia*, from L *pōmum* fruit]
▸**pomological** (ˌpɒmə'lɒdʒɪkᵊl) *adj*

pomp Ⓣ (pɒmp) *n* **1** stately or magnificent display; ceremonial splendour. **2** vain display, esp. of dignity or importance. **3** *Obs.* a procession or pageant. [C14: from OF *pompe*, from L *pompa* procession, from Gk *pompē*]

pompadour ('pɒmpəˌdʊə) *n* an early 18th-century hairstyle for women, having the front hair arranged over a pad to give it greater height and bulk. [C18: after the Marquise de *Pompadour*, mistress of Louis XV of France, who originated it]

pompano ('pɒmpəˌnəʊ) *n, pl* **pompano** *or* **pompanos. 1** any of several food fishes of American coastal regions of the Atlantic. **2** a spiny-finned food fish of North American coastal regions of the Pacific. [C19: from Sp. *pámpano*, from ?]

pompom ('pɒmpɒm) *or* **pompon** *n* **1** a ball of tufted silk, wool, feathers, etc., worn on a hat for decoration. **2a** the small globelike flower head of certain varieties of dahlia and chrysanthemum. **2b** (*as modifier*): *pompom dahlia.* [C18: from F, from OF *pompe* knot of ribbons, from ?]

pom-pom ('pɒmpɒm) *n* an automatic rapid-firing small-calibre cannon, esp. a type of anti-aircraft cannon used in World War II. Also called: **pompom.** [C19: imit.]

pomposo (pɒm'pəʊsəʊ) *adv Music.* in a pompous manner. [It.]

pompous Ⓣ ('pɒmpəs) *adj* **1** exaggeratedly or ostentatiously dignified or self-important. **2** ostentatiously lofty in style: *a pompous speech.* **3** *Rare.* characterized by ceremonial pomp or splendour.
▸**pomposity** (pɒm'pɒsɪtɪ) *or* '**pompousness** *n* ▸'**pompously** *adv*

'pon (pɒn) *Poetic or arch. contraction of* upon.

ponce Ⓣ (pɒns) *Derog. sl., chiefly Brit.* ◆ *n* **1** a man given to ostentatious or effeminate display. **2** another word for **pimp**[1]. ◆ *vb* **ponces, poncing, ponced. 3** (*intr*; often foll. by *around* or *about*) to act like a ponce. [C19: from Polari, from Sp. *pu(n)to* male prostitute or F *pront* prostitute]
▸'**poncy** *or* '**poncey** *adj*

poncho ('pɒntʃəʊ) *n, pl* **ponchos.** a cloak of a kind originally worn in South America, made of a rectangular or circular piece of cloth with a hole in the middle for the head. [C18: from American Sp., of Amerind origin, from *pantho* woollen material]

pond Ⓣ (pɒnd) *n* a pool of still water, often artificially created. [C13 *ponde* enclosure]

ponder Ⓣ ('pɒndə) *vb* (when *intr*, sometimes foll. by *on* or *over*) to give thorough or deep consideration (to); meditate (upon). [C14: from OF *ponderer*, from L *ponderāre* to weigh, consider, from *pondus* weight]
▸'**ponderable** *adj*

ponderous Ⓣ ('pɒndərəs) *adj* **1** heavy; huge. **2** (esp. of movement) lacking ease or lightness; lumbering or graceless. **3** dull or laborious: *a ponderous oration.* [C14: from L *ponderōsus* of great weight, from *pondus* weight]
▸'**ponderously** *adv* ▸'**ponderousness** *or* **ponderosity** (ˌpɒndə'rɒsɪtɪ) *n*

pond lily *n* another name for **water lily.**

pondok ('pɒndɒk) *or* **pondokkie** *n* (in southern Africa) a crudely made house built of tin sheet, reeds, etc. [C20: from Malay *pondók* leaf house]

pond scum *n* a greenish layer floating on the surface of stagnant waters, consisting of algae.

pondweed ('pɒndˌwiːd) *n* **1** any of various water plants of the genus *Potamogeton*, which grow in ponds and slow streams. **2** Also called: **waterweed.** *Brit.* any of various water plants, such as mare's-tail, that have thin or much-divided leaves.

pone[1] (pəʊn, 'pəʊnɪ) *n Cards.* the player to the right of the dealer, or the nondealer in two-handed games. [C19: from L: put!, that is, play, from *ponere* to put]

pone[2] (pəʊn) *n Southern US.* bread made of maize. Also called: **pone bread, corn pone.** [C17: of Amerind origin]

pong (pɒŋ) *Brit. inf.* ◆ *n* **1** a disagreeable or offensive smell; stink. ◆ *vb* **2** (*intr*) to stink. [C20: ?from Romany *pan* to stink]
▸'**pongy** *adj*

ponga ('pɒŋə) *n* a tall New Zealand tree fern with large leathery leaves.

pongee (pɒn'dʒiː, 'pɒndʒiː) *n* **1** a thin plain-weave silk fabric from China or India, left in its natural colour. **2** a cotton or rayon fabric similar to this. [C18: from Mandarin Chinese (Peking) *pen-chī* woven at home, from *pen* own + *chi* loom]

pongid ('pɒŋɡɪd, 'pɒndʒɪd) *n* **1** any primate of the family Pongidae, which includes the gibbons and the great apes. ◆ *adj* **2** of this family. [from NL *Pongo* type genus, from Congolese *mpongo* ape]

pongo ('pɒŋɡəʊ) *n, pl* **pongos.** an anthropoid ape, esp. an orang-utan or (formerly) a gorilla. [C17: from Congolese *mpongo*]

poniard ('pɒnjəd) *n* **1** a small dagger with a slender blade. ◆ *vb* **2** (*tr*) to stab with a poniard. [C16: from OF *poignard*, from *poing* fist, from L *pugnus*]

pons Varolii (pɒnz və'rəʊlɪˌaɪ) *n, pl* **pontes Varolii** ('pɒntiːz). a broad white band of connecting nerve fibres that bridges the hemispheres of the cerebellum in mammals. Sometimes shortened to **pons.** [C16: NL, lit.: bridge of Varoli, after Costanzo *Varoli* (?1543–75), It. anatomist]

pontifex ('pɒntɪˌfɛks) *n, pl* **pontifices** (pɒn'tɪfɪˌsiːz). (in ancient Rome) any of the senior members of the Pontifical College, presided over by the **Pontifex Maximus.** [C16: from L, ?from Etruscan but infl. by folk etymology as if meaning lit.: bridge-maker]

pontiff ('pɒntɪf) *n* a former title of the pagan high priest at Rome, later used of popes and occasionally of other bishops, and now confined to the pope. [C17: from F *pontife*, from L PONTIFEX]

pontifical Ⓣ (pɒn'tɪfɪkᵊl) *adj* **1** of, relating to, or characteristic of a pontiff. **2** having an excessively authoritative manner; pompous. ◆ *n* **3** *RC Church, Church of England.* a book containing the prayers and ritual instructions for ceremonies restricted to a bishop.
▸**pon'tifically** *adv*

pontificals (pɒn'tɪfɪkᵊlz) *pl n Chiefly RC Church.* the insignia and special vestments worn by a bishop, esp. when celebrating High Mass.

pontificate Ⓣ *vb* (pɒn'tɪfɪˌkeɪt), **pontificates, pontificating, pontificated.** (*intr*) **1** to speak or behave in a pompous or dogmatic manner. **2** to serve or officiate at a Pontifical Mass. ◆ *n* (pɒn'tɪfɪkɪt). **3** the office or term of office of a pope.

pontoon[1] (pɒn'tuːn) *n* **a** a watertight float or vessel used where buoyancy is required in water, as in supporting a bridge, in salvage work, or where a temporary or mobile structure is required in military operations. **b** (*as modifier*): *a pontoon bridge.* [C17: from F *ponton*, from L *pontō* punt, from *pōns* bridge]

pontoon[2] (pɒn'tuːn) *n* a gambling game in which players try to obtain card combinations worth 21 points. Also called: **twenty-one** (esp. US), **vingt-et-un.** [C20: prob. an alteration of F *vingt-et-un*, lit.: twenty-one]

THESAURUS

pomp *n* **1** = **ceremony**, éclat, flourish, grandeur, magnificence, pageant, pageantry, parade, solemnity, splendour, state **2** = **show**, display, grandiosity, ostentation, pomposity, vainglory

pomposity *n* **1** = **self-importance**, affectation, airs, arrogance, flaunting, grandiosity, haughtiness, pompousness, portentousness, presumption, pretension, pretentiousness, vainglory, vanity **2** = **grandiloquence**, bombast, fustian, hot air (*inf.*), loftiness, magniloquence, rant, turgidity

pompous *adj* **1** = **self-important**, affected, arrogant, bloated, grandiose, imperious, magisterial, ostentatious, overbearing, pontifical, portentous, pretentious, puffed up, showy, supercilious, vainglorious **2** = **grandiloquent**, boastful, bombastic, flatulent, fustian, high-flown, inflated, magniloquent, orotund, overblown, turgid, windy
Antonyms *adj* ≠ **self-important:** humble, modest, natural, self-effacing, simple, unaffected, unpretentious ≠ **grandiloquent:** direct, plain-spoken, simple, succinct

ponce *n Derogatory slang, chiefly Brit.* **1** = **fop**, beau, coxcomb (*arch.*), dandy, popinjay, swell **2** = **pimp**, bawd (*arch.*), pander, procurer

pond *n* = **pool**, dew pond, duck pond, fish pond, lochan, millpond, small lake, tarn

ponder *vb* = **think**, brood, cerebrate, cogitate, consider, contemplate, deliberate, examine, excogitate, give thought to, meditate, mull over, muse, puzzle over, rack one's brains, reflect, ruminate, study, weigh

ponderous *adj* **1** = **unwieldy**, bulky, clunky (*inf.*), cumbersome, cumbrous, heavy, hefty, huge, massive, weighty **2** = **clumsy**, awkward, elephantine, graceless, heavy-footed, laborious, lumbering **3** = **dull**, dreary, heavy, laboured, lifeless, long-winded, pedantic, pedestrian, plodding, prolix, stilted, stodgy, tedious, tiresome, verbose
Antonyms *adj* ≠ **unwieldy:** handy, light, little, small, tiny, weightless ≠ **clumsy:** graceful, light, light-footed

pontifical *adj* **1** = **papal**, apostolic, ecclesiastical, prelatic **2** = **pompous**, bloated, condescending, dogmatic, imperious, magisterial, overbearing, portentous, pretentious, self-important

pontificate *vb* **1** = **expound**, declaim, dogmatize, hold forth, lay down the law, pontify, preach, pronounce, sound off

pony ('pəunɪ) *n, pl* **ponies. 1** any of various breeds of small horse, usually under 14.2 hands. **2** a small drinking glass, esp. for liqueurs. **3** anything small of its kind. **4** *Brit. sl.* a sum of £25, esp. in bookmaking. **5** Also called: **trot.** *US sl.* a translation used by students, often illicitly; crib. [C17: from Scot. *powney,* ?from obs. F *poulenet* a little colt, from L *pullus* young animal, foal]

ponytail ('pəunɪ,teɪl) *n* a hairstyle in which the hair is gathered together tightly by a band into a bunch at the back of the head.

pony trekking *n* the act of riding ponies cross-country, esp. as a pastime.

pooch (puːtʃ) *n Chiefly US & Canad.* a slang word for **dog.** [from ?]

poodle ('puːdᵊl) *n* **1** a breed of dog with curly hair, which is generally clipped from ribs to tail. **2** a servile person; lackey. [C19: from G *Pudel,* short for *Pudelhund,* from *pudeln* to splash + *Hund* dog; formerly trained as water dogs]

poof (pʊf, puːf), **poove** (puːv), *or* **poofter** ('puːftə) *n Brit. & Austral. derog. sl.* a male homosexual. [C20: from F *pouffe* puff]
▸ **'poofy** *adj*

pooh (puː) *interj* an exclamation of disdain, contempt, or disgust.

Pooh-Bah ('puː'bɑː) *n* a pompous self-important official holding several offices at once and fulfilling none of them. [C19: after the character, the Lord-High-Everything-Else, in *The Mikado* (1885), by Gilbert & Sullivan]

pooh-pooh Ⓣ ('puː'puː) *vb (tr)* to express disdain or scorn for; dismiss or belittle.

pool[1] Ⓣ (puːl) *n* **1** a small body of still water, usually fresh; small pond. **2** a small isolated collection of spilt liquid; puddle: *a pool of blood.* **3** a deep part of a stream or river where the water runs very slowly. **4** an underground accumulation of oil or gas. **5** See **swimming pool.** [OE *pōl*]

pool[2] Ⓣ (puːl) *n* **1** any communal combination of resources, funds, etc.: *a typing pool.* **2** the combined stakes of the betters in many gambling games; kitty. **3** *Commerce.* a group of producers who agree to establish and maintain output levels and high prices, each member of the group being allocated a maximum quota. **4** *Finance, chiefly US.* a joint fund organized by security-holders for speculative or manipulative purposes on financial markets. **5** any of various billiard games in which the object is to pot all the balls with the cue ball, esp. that played with 15 coloured and numbered balls, popular in the US. Also called: **pocket billiards.** ◆ *vb (tr)* **6** to combine (investments, money, interests, etc.) into a common fund, as for a joint enterprise. **7** *Commerce.* to organize a pool of (enterprises). [C17: from F *poule,* lit.: hen used to signify stakes in a card game, from Med. L *pulla* hen, from L *pullus* young animal]

pools (puːlz) *pl n* **the** *Brit.* an organized nationwide principally postal gambling pool betting on the result of football matches. Also called: **football pools.**

poop[1] (puːp) *Naut.* ◆ *n* **1** a raised structure at the stern of a vessel, esp. a sailing ship. **2** Also called: **poop deck.** a raised deck at the stern of a ship. ◆ *vb* **3** *(tr)* (of a wave or sea) to break over the stern of (a vessel). **4** *(intr)* (of a vessel) to ship a wave or sea over the stern, esp. repeatedly. [C15: from OF *pupe,* from L *puppis*]

poop[2] (puːp) *vb US & Canad. sl.* **1** *(tr; usually passive)* to cause to become exhausted; tire: *he was pooped after the race.* **2** *(intr;* usually foll. by *out)* to give up or fail: *he pooped out of the race.* [C14 *poupen* to blow, ? imit.]

poop[3] (puːp) *Inf.* ◆ *vb (intr)* **1** to defecate. ◆ *n* **2** faeces; excrement. [perhaps related to POOP[2]]

pooper-scooper *n* a device used to remove dogs' excrement from public areas. [C20: POOP[3] + -ER[1] + SCOOP]

poor Ⓣ (pʊə, pɔː) *adj* **1** lacking financial or other means of subsistence; needy. **2** characterized by or indicating poverty: *the country had a poor economy.* **3** scanty or inadequate: *a poor salary.* **4** (when *postpositive,* usually foll. by *in)* badly supplied (with resources, etc.): *a region poor in wild flowers.* **5** inferior. **6** contemptible or despicable. **7** disappointing or disagreeable: *a poor play.* **8** *(prenominal)* deserving of pity; unlucky: *poor John is ill again.* [C13: from OF *povre,* from L *pauper*]
▸ **'poorness** *n*

poor box *n* a box, esp. one in a church, used for the collection of alms or money for the poor.

poorhouse ('pʊə,haʊs, 'pɔː-) *n* another name for **workhouse** (sense 1).

poor law *n English history.* a law providing for the relief or support of the poor from parish funds.

poorly Ⓣ ('pʊəlɪ, 'pɔː-) *adv* **1** badly. ◆ *adj* **2** *(usually postpositive) Inf.* in poor health; rather ill.

poort (pʊət) *n* (in South Africa) a steep narrow mountain pass, usually following a river or stream. [C19: from Afrik., from Du.: gateway]

poor White *n Often offens.* **a** a poverty-stricken and underprivileged White person, esp. in the southern US and South Africa. **b** *(as modifier): poor White trash.*

pop[1] Ⓣ (pɒp) *vb* **pops, popping, popped. 1** to make or cause to make a light sharp explosive sound. **2** to burst open with such a sound. **3** *(intr;* often foll. by *in, out,* etc.) *Inf.* to come (to) or go (from) rapidly or suddenly. **4** *(intr)* (esp. of the eyes) to protrude: *her eyes popped with amazement.* **5** to shoot at (a target) with a firearm. **6** *(tr)* to place with a sudden movement: *she popped some tablets into her mouth.* **7** *(tr) Inf.* to pawn: *he popped his watch yesterday.* **8** *(tr) Sl.* to take (a drug) in pill form or as an injection. **9 pop the question.** *Inf.* to propose marriage. ◆ *n* **10** a light sharp explosive sound; crack. **11** *Inf.* a flavoured nonalcoholic carbonated beverage. ◆ *adv* **12** with a popping sound. ◆ See also **pop off.** [C14: imit.]

pop[2] (pɒp) *n* **1a** music of general appeal, esp. among young people, that originated as a distinctive genre in the 1950s. It is generally characterized by a heavy rhythmic element and the use of electrical amplification. **1b** *(as modifier): a pop group.* **2** *Inf.* a piece of popular or light classical music. ◆ *adj* **3** *Inf.* short for **popular.**

pop[3] (pɒp) *n* **1** an informal word for **father. 2** *Inf.* a name used in addressing an old man.

POP *abbrev. for* Post Office Preferred (size of envelopes, etc.).

pop. *abbrev. for:* **1** popular(ly). **2** population.

pop art *n* a movement in modern art that imitates the methods, styles, and themes of popular culture and mass media, such as comic strips, advertising, and science fiction.

popcorn ('pɒp,kɔːn) *n* **1** a variety of maize having hard pointed kernels that puff up and burst when heated. **2** the puffed edible kernels of this plant.

pope Ⓣ (pəʊp) *n* **1** *(often cap.)* the bishop of Rome as head of the Roman Catholic Church. **2** *Eastern Orthodox Churches.* a title sometimes given to a parish priest or to the Greek Orthodox patriarch of Alexandria. [OE *papa,* from Church L: bishop, esp. of Rome, from LGk *papas* father-in-God, from Gk *pappas* father]
▸ **'popedom** *n*

popery ('pəʊpərɪ) *n* a derogatory name for **Roman Catholicism.**

popeyed ('pɒp,aɪd) *adj* **1** having bulging prominent eyes. **2** staring in astonishment.

popgun ('pɒp,gʌn) *n* a toy gun that fires a pellet or cork by means of compressed air.

popinjay ('pɒpɪn,dʒeɪ) *n* **1** a conceited, foppish, or excessively talkative person. **2** an archaic word for **parrot. 3** the figure of a parrot used as a target. [C13 *papeniai,* from OF *papegay* a parrot, from Sp., from Ar. *babaghā*]

popish ('pəʊpɪʃ) *adj Derog.* belonging to or characteristic of Roman Catholicism.

poplar ('pɒplə) *n* **1** a tree of N temperate regions, having triangular leaves, flowers borne in catkins, and light soft wood. **2** *US.* the tulip tree. [C14: from OF *poplier,* from L *pōpulus*]

poplin ('pɒplɪn) *n* a strong fabric, usually of cotton, in plain weave with fine ribbing. [C18: from F *papeline,* ?from *Poperinge,* a centre of textile manufacture in Flanders]

popliteal (pɒp'lɪtɪəl, ,pɒplɪ'tiːəl) *adj* of, relating to, or near the part of the leg behind the knee. [C18: from NL *popliteus* the muscle behind the knee joint, from L *poples* the ham of the knee]

popmobility (,pɒpməʊ'bɪlɪtɪ) *n* a form of exercise that combines aerobics in a continuous dance routine, performed to pop music. [C20: POP[2] + MOBILITY]

pop off *vb (intr, adv) Inf.* **1** to depart suddenly or unexpectedly. **2** to die, esp. suddenly.

THESAURUS

pooh-pooh *vb* = **scorn,** belittle, brush aside, deride, disdain, dismiss, disregard, make little of, play down, scoff, slight, sneer, sniff at, spurn, turn up one's nose at *(inf.)*
Antonyms *vb* exalt, extol, glorify, praise

pool[1] *n* **1** = **pond,** lake, mere, puddle, splash, tarn **5** = **swimming pool,** swimming bath

pool[2] *n* **1** = **syndicate,** collective, combine, consortium, group, team, trust **2** = **kitty,** bank, funds, jackpot, pot, stakes ◆ *vb* **6** = **combine,** amalgamate, join forces, league, merge, put together, share

poor *adj* **1** = **impoverished,** badly off, broke, destitute, dirt-poor *(inf.)*, down and out, down at heel, flat broke *(inf.)*, hard up *(inf.)*, impecunious, indigent, in need, in queer street, in want, necessitous, needy, on one's uppers, on the breadline, penniless, penurious, poverty-stricken, short, skint *(Brit. sl.)*, stony-broke *(Brit. sl.)* **3, 4** = **meagre,** deficient, exiguous, inadequate, incomplete, insufficient, lacking, measly, miserable, niggardly, pathetic, pitiable, reduced, scant, scanty, skimpy, slight, sparse, straitened **5** = **inferior,** below par, faulty, feeble, low-grade, low-rent *(inf., chiefly US)*, mediocre, no great shakes *(inf.)*, not much cop *(Brit. sl.)*, rotten *(inf.)*, rubbishy, second-rate, shabby, shoddy, sorry, substandard, unsatisfactory, valueless, weak, worthless **8** = **unfortunate,** hapless, ill-fated, luckless, miserable, pathetic, pitiable, unhappy, unlucky, wretched
Antonyms *adj* ≠ **impoverished:** affluent, comfortable *(inf.)*, prosperous, rich, wealthy, well-heeled *(inf.)*, well-off ≠ **meagre:** abundant, adequate, ample, complete, dense, plentiful, satisfactory, sufficient, thick ≠ **inferior:** excellent, exceptional, first-class, first-rate, satisfactory, superior, valuable ≠ **unfortunate:** fortunate, happy, lucky, successful

poorly *adv* **1** = **badly,** crudely, inadequately, incompetently, inexpertly, inferiorly, insufficiently, meanly, shabbily, unsatisfactorily, unsuccessfully ◆ *adj* **2** *Informal* = **ill,** ailing, below par, indisposed, off colour, out of sorts, rotten *(inf.)*, seedy *(inf.)*, sick, under the weather *(inf.)*, unwell
Antonyms *adv* ≠ **badly:** acceptably, adequately, competently, expertly, satisfactorily, sufficiently, well ◆ *adj* ≠ **ill:** fit, hale and hearty, healthy, in good health, in the pink, well

pop[1] *vb* **1, 2** = **burst,** bang, crack, explode, go off, report, snap **3** *often foll. by* **in, out,** *etc. Informal* = **call,** appear, come *or* go suddenly, drop in *(inf.)*, leave quickly, nip in *or* out *(Brit. inf.)*, visit **4** = **protrude,** bulge, stick out **6** = **put,** insert, push, shove, slip, stick, thrust, tuck ◆ *n* **10** = **bang,** burst, crack, explosion, noise, report **11** *Informal* = **soft drink,** fizzy drink, ginger *(Scot.)*, lemonade, mineral water, soda water

pope *n* **1** = **Holy Father,** Bishop of Rome, pontiff, Vicar of Christ

poppadom *or* **poppadum** ('pɒpədəm) *n* a thin round crisp Indian bread, fried or roasted and served with curry, etc. [from Hindi]

popper ('pɒpə) *n* **1** a person or thing that pops. **2** *Brit.* an informal name for **press stud. 3** *Chiefly US & Canad.* a container for cooking popcorn in. **4** *Sl.* an amyl nitrite capsule, crushed and inhaled by drug users.

poppet ('pɒpɪt) *n* **1** a term of affection for a small child or sweetheart. **2** Also called: **poppet valve.** a mushroom-shaped valve that is lifted from its seating by applying an axial force to its stem. **3** *Naut.* a temporary supporting brace for a vessel hauled on land. [C14: early var. of PUPPET]

popping crease *n Cricket.* a line four feet in front of and parallel with the bowling crease, at or behind which the batsman stands. [C18: from POP[1] (in the obs. sense: to hit) + CREASE]

popple ('pɒpᵊl) *vb* **popples, poppling, poppled.** (*intr*) **1** (of boiling water or a choppy sea) to heave or toss; bubble. **2** (often foll. by *along*) (of a stream or river) to move with an irregular tumbling motion. [C14: imit.]

poppy ('pɒpɪ) *n, pl* **poppies. 1** any of numerous papaveraceous plants having red, orange, or white flowers and a milky sap. **2** any of several similar or related plants, such as the California poppy and Welsh poppy. **3** any of the drugs, such as opium, that are obtained from these plants. **4a** a strong red to reddish-orange colour. **4b** (*as adj*): *a poppy dress.* **5** an artificial red poppy flower worn to mark Remembrance Sunday. [OE *popæg,* ult. from L *papāver*]

poppycock ⓣ ('pɒpɪ,kɒk) *n Inf.* nonsense. [C19: from Du. dialect *pappekak,* lit.: soft excrement]

Poppy Day *n* an informal name for **Remembrance Sunday.**

poppyhead ('pɒpɪ,hɛd) *n* **1** the hard dry seed-containing capsule of a poppy. **2** a carved ornament, esp. one used on the top of the end of a pew or bench in Gothic church architecture.

poppy seed *n* the small grey seeds of the opium poppy, used esp. on loaves.

pop socks *pl n* knee-length nylon stockings.

popsy ('pɒpsɪ) *n, pl* **popsies.** *Old-fashioned Brit. sl.* an attractive young woman. [C19: dim. from *pop,* shortened from POPPET; orig. a nursery term]

populace ⓣ ('pɒpjʊləs) *n* (*sometimes functioning as pl*) **1** local inhabitants. **2** the common people; masses. [C16: via F from It. *popolaccio* the common herd, from *popolo* people, from L *populus*]

popular ⓣ ('pɒpjʊlə) *adj* **1** widely favoured or admired. **2** favoured by an individual or limited group: *I'm not very popular with her.* **3** prevailing among the general public; common: *popular discontent.* **4** appealing to or comprehensible to the layman: *a popular lecture on physics.* ◆ *n* **5** (*usually pl*) a cheap newspaper with a mass circulation. [C15: from L *populāris* of the people, democratic]
▸**popularity** (,pɒpjʊ'lærɪtɪ) *n* ▸**'popularly** *adv*

popular front *n* (*often cap.*) any of the left-wing groups or parties that were organized from 1935 onwards to oppose the spread of fascism.

popularize ⓣ *or* **popularise** ('pɒpjʊlə,raɪz) *vb* **popularizes, popularizing, popularized** *or* **popularises, popularising, popularised.** (*tr*) **1** to make popular. **2** to make or cause to become easily understandable or acceptable.
▸**,populari'zation** *or* **,populari'sation** *n* ▸**'popular,izer** *or* **'popular,iser** *n*

populate ⓣ ('pɒpjʊ,leɪt) *vb* **populates, populating, populated.** (*tr*) **1** (*often passive*) to live in; inhabit. **2** to provide a population for; colonize or people. [C16: from Med. L *populāre,* from L *populus* people]

population ⓣ (,pɒpjʊ'leɪʃən) *n* **1** (*sometimes functioning as pl*) all the persons inhabiting a specified place. **2** the number of such inhabitants. **3** (*sometimes functioning as pl*) all the people of a particular class in a specific area: *the Chinese population of San Francisco.* **4** the act or process of providing a place with inhabitants; colonization. **5** *Ecology.* a group of individuals of the same species inhabiting a given area. **6** *Astron.* either of two main groups of stars classified according to age and location. **7** *Statistics.* the entire aggregate of individuals or items from which samples are drawn.

population explosion *n* a rapid increase in the size of a population caused by such factors as a sudden decline in infant mortality or an increase in life expectancy.

population pyramid *n* a pyramid-shaped diagram illustrating the age distribution of a population: the youngest are represented by a rectangle at the base, the oldest by one at the apex.

populism ('pɒpjʊ,lɪzəm) *or* **popularism** *n* the practice, esp. by a politician of making a calculated appeal to the interests, tastes, or prejudices of ordinary people.

populist ('pɒpjʊ,lɪst) *adj* **1** appealing to the interests or prejudices of ordinary people. ◆ *n* **2** a person, esp. a politician, who appeals to the interests or prejudices of ordinary people.

Populist ('pɒpjʊlɪst) *n* **1** *US history.* a member of the People's Party, formed largely by agrarian interests to contest the 1892 presidential election. ◆ *adj* **2** of or relating to the People's Party or any individual or movement with similar aims. Also: **Populistic.**
▸**'Popu,lism** *n*

populous ⓣ ('pɒpjʊləs) *adj* containing many inhabitants. [C15: from LL *populōsus*]
▸**'populously** *adv* ▸**'populousness** *n*

porangi ('pɔːræŋɪ) *adj NZ inf.* crazy; mad. [from Maori]

porbeagle ('pɔː,biːgᵊl) *n* any of several voracious sharks of northern seas. Also called: **mackerel shark.** [C18: from Cornish *porgh-bugel,* from ?]

porcelain ('pɔːslɪn) *n* **1** a more or less translucent ceramic material, the principal ingredients being kaolin and petuntse (hard paste) or other clays, bone ash, etc. **2** an object made of this or such objects collectively. **3** (*modifier*) of, relating to, or made from this material: *a porcelain cup.* [C16: from F *porcelaine,* from It. *porcellana* cowrie shell, lit.: relating to a sow, from *porcella* little sow, from *porca* sow, from L; see PORK]
▸**porcellaneous** (,pɔːsə'leɪnɪəs) *adj*

porch (pɔːtʃ) *n* **1** a low structure projecting from the doorway of a house and forming a covered entrance. **2** *US & Canad.* a veranda. [C13: from F *porche,* from L *porticus* portico]

porcine ('pɔːsaɪn) *adj* of or characteristic of pigs. [C17: from L *porcinus,* from *porcus* a pig]

porcupine ('pɔːkjʊ,paɪn) *n* any of various large rodents that have a body covering of protective spines or quills. [C14 *porc despyne* pig with spines, from OF *porc espin;* see PORK, SPINE]
▸**'porcu,pinish** *adj* ▸**'porcu,piny** *adj*

porcupine fish *n* any of various fishes of temperate and tropical seas having a body that is covered with sharp spines and can be inflated into a globe. Also called: **globefish.**

porcupine grass *n Austral.* another name for **spinifex.**

porcupine provisions *pl n Finance.* provisions, such as poison pills or staggered directorships, made in the bylaws of a company to deter takeover bids. Also called: **shark repellents.**

pore[1] ⓣ (pɔː) *vb* **pores, poring, pored.** (*intr*) **1** (foll. by *over*) to make a close intent examination or study (of): *he pored over the documents for several hours.* **2** (foll. by *over, on,* or *upon*) to think deeply (about). **3** (foll. by *over, on,* or *upon*) *Rare.* to gaze fixedly (upon). [C13 *pouren*]

USAGE NOTE See at **pour.**

pore[2] ⓣ (pɔː) *n* **1** any small opening in the skin or outer surface of an animal. **2** *Bot.* any small aperture, esp. that of a stoma, through which water vapour and gases pass. **3** any other small hole, such as a space in a rock, etc. [C14: from LL *porus,* from Gk *poros* passage, pore]

porgy ('pɔːgɪ) *n, pl* **porgy** *or* **porgies.** any of various perchlike fishes, many of which occur in American Atlantic waters. [C18: from Sp. *pargo,* from L *phager,* from Gk *phagros* sea bream]

poriferan (pɔː'rɪfərən) *n* any invertebrate of the phylum *Porifera,* which comprises the sponges. [C19: from NL *porifer* bearing pores]

pork (pɔːk) *n* the flesh of pigs used as food. [C13: from OF *porc,* from L *porcus* pig]

porker ('pɔːkə) *n* a pig, esp. a young one, fattened to provide meat.

pork pie *n* **1** a pie filled with minced seasoned pork. **2** See **porky**[2].

porkpie hat ('pɔːk,paɪ) *n* a hat with a round flat crown and a brim that can be turned up or down.

porky[1] ('pɔːkɪ) *adj* **porkier, porkiest. 1** characteristic of pork. **2** *Inf.* fat; obese.

porky[2] ('pɔːkɪ) *n, pl* **porkies.** *Brit. sl.* a lie. Also called: **pork pie.** [from rhyming slang *pork pie* lie]

porn (pɔːn) *or* **porno** ('pɔːnəʊ) *n, adj Inf.* short for **pornography** or **pornographic.**

pornography ⓣ (pɔː'nɒgrəfɪ) *n* **1** writings, pictures, films, etc., de-

THESAURUS

poppycock *n Informal* = **nonsense**, babble, balderdash, baloney (*inf.*), bilge (*inf.*), bunk (*inf.*), bunkum *or* buncombe (*chiefly US*), drivel, eyewash (*inf.*), garbage (*inf.*), gibberish, gobbledegook (*inf.*), guff (*sl.*), hogwash, hokum (*sl., chiefly US & Canad.*), hot air (*inf.*), moonshine, pap, piffle (*inf.*), rot, rubbish, tommyrot, trash, tripe (*inf.*), twaddle

populace *n* **1, 2** = **people**, commonalty, crowd, general public, hoi polloi, inhabitants, Joe (and Eileen) Public (*sl.*), Joe Six-Pack (*US sl.*), masses, mob, multitude, rabble, throng

popular *adj* **1** = **well-liked**, accepted, approved, celebrated, famous, fashionable, fave (*inf.*), favoured, favourite, in, in demand, in favour, liked, sought-after **3** = **common**, conventional, current, general, prevailing, prevalent, public, standard, stock, ubiquitous, universal, widespread
Antonyms *adj* ≠ **well-liked**: despised, detested, disliked, hated, loathed, unaccepted, unpopular ≠ **common**: infrequent, rare, uncommon, unusual

popularity *n* **1** = **favour**, acceptance, acclaim, adoration, approval, celebrity, currency, esteem, fame, idolization, lionization, recognition, regard, renown, reputation, repute, vogue

popularize *vb* **1, 2** = **make popular**, disseminate, familiarize, give currency to, give mass appeal, make available to all, simplify, spread, universalize

popularly *adv* **3** = **generally**, commonly, conventionally, customarily, ordinarily, regularly, traditionally, universally, usually, widely

populate *vb* **1, 2** = **inhabit**, colonize, live in, occupy, people, settle

population *n* **1** = **inhabitants**, citizenry, community, denizens, folk, natives, people, populace, residents, society

populous *adj* = **populated**, crowded, heavily populated, overpopulated, packed, swarming, teeming, thronged

pore[1] *vb* **1, 2** *foll. by* **over** = **study**, brood, contemplate, dwell on, examine, go over, peruse, ponder, read, scrutinize, work over

pore[2] *n* **1-3** = **opening**, hole, orifice, outlet, stoma

pornographic *adj* **1** = **obscene**, blue, dirty, filthy, indecent, lewd, offensive, prurient, salacious, smutty, X-rated (*inf.*)

pornography *n* **1** = **obscenity**, dirt, erotica, filth, indecency, porn (*inf.*), porno (*inf.*), smut

signed to stimulate sexual excitement. **2** the production of such material. ◆ Sometimes (informal) shortened to **porn** or **porno.** [C19: from Gk *pornographos* writing of harlots]
▸**por'nographer** *n* ▸**pornographic** (ˌpɔːnəˈɡræfɪk) *adj* ▸ˌ**porno'graphically** *adv*

poromeric (ˌpɔːrəˈmerɪk) *adj* **1** (of a plastic) permeable to water vapour. ◆ *n* **2** a substance having this characteristic, esp. one used in place of leather in making shoe uppers. [C20: from PORO(SITY) + (POLY)MER + -IC]

porous ➊ (ˈpɔːrəs) *adj* **1** permeable to water, air, or other fluids. **2** *Biol. & geol.* having pores. [C14: from Med. L *porōsus,* from LL *porus* PORE[2]]
▸**'porously** *adv* ▸**porosity** (pɔːˈrɒsɪtɪ) *or* **'porousness** *n*

porphyria (pɔːˈfɪrɪə) *n* a hereditary disease of body metabolism, producing abdominal pain, mental confusion, etc. [C19: from NL, from *porphyrin* a purple substance excreted by patients suffering from this condition, from Gk *porphura* purple]

porphyry (ˈpɔːfɪrɪ) *n, pl* **porphyries. 1** a reddish-purple rock consisting of large crystals of feldspar in a finer groundmass of feldspar, hornblende, etc. **2** any igneous rock with large crystals embedded in a finer groundmass of minerals. [C14 *porfurie,* from LL, from Gk *porphuritēs* (*lithos*) purple (stone), from *porphuros* purple]
▸ˌ**porphy'ritic** *adj*

porpoise (ˈpɔːpəs) *n, pl* **porpoises** *or* **porpoise.** any of various small cetacean mammals having a blunt snout and many teeth. [C14: from F *pourpois,* from Med. L *porcopiscus,* from L *porcus* pig + *piscis* fish]

porridge (ˈpɒrɪdʒ) *n* **1** a dish made from oatmeal or another cereal, cooked in water or milk to a thick consistency. **2** *Sl.* a term of imprisonment. [C16: var. (infl. by ME *porray* pottage) of POTTAGE]

porringer (ˈpɒrɪndʒə) *n* a small dish, often with a handle, for soup, porridge, etc. [C16: changed from ME *potinger, poteger,* from OF, from *potage* soup; see POTTAGE]

port[1] ➊ (pɔːt) *n* **1** a town or place alongside navigable water with facilities for the loading and unloading of ships. **2** See **port of entry.** [OE, from L *portus*]

port[2] (pɔːt) *n* **1** Also called (formerly): **larboard.** the left side of an aircraft or vessel when facing the nose or bow. Cf. **starboard** (sense 1). ◆ *vb* **2** to turn or be turned towards the port. [C17: from ?]

port[3] (pɔːt) *n* a sweet fortified dessert wine. [C17: after *Oporto,* Portugal, from where it came orig.]

port[4] (pɔːt) *n* **1** *Naut.* **1a** an opening in the side of a ship, fitted with a watertight door, for access to the holds. **1b** See **porthole** (sense 1). **2** a small opening in a wall, armoured vehicle, etc., for firing through. **3** an aperture by which fluid enters or leaves the cylinder head of an engine, compressor, etc. **4** *Electronics.* a logical circuit for the input and ouput of data. **5** *Chiefly Scot.* a gate in a town or fortress. [OE, from L *porta* gate]

port[5] (pɔːt) *vb* (*tr*) *Mil.* to carry (a rifle, etc.) in a position diagonally across the body with the muzzle near the left shoulder. [C14: from OF, from *porter* to carry, from L *portāre*]

port[6] (pɔːt) *n Austral.* (esp. in Queensland) a suitcase or school case. [C20: shortened from PORTMANTEAU]

Port. *abbrev. for:* **1** Portugal. **2** Portuguese.

portable ➊ (ˈpɔːtəbᵊl) *adj* **1** able to be carried or moved easily, esp. by hand. **2** (of computer software, files, etc.) able to be transferred from one type of computer system to another. ◆ *n* **3** an article designed to be readily carried by hand, such as a television, typewriter, etc. [C14: from LL *portābilis,* from L *portāre* to carry]
▸ˌ**porta'bility** *n* ▸**'portably** *adv*

portage (ˈpɔːtɪdʒ) *n* **1** the act of carrying; transport. **2** the cost of carrying or transporting. **3** the transporting of boats, supplies, etc., overland between navigable waterways. **4** the route used for such transport. ◆ *vb* **portages, portaging, portaged. 5** to transport (boats, supplies, etc.) thus. [C15: from F, from OF *porter* to carry]

Portakabin (ˈpɔːtəˌkæbɪn) *n Trademark.* a portable building quickly set up for use as a temporary office, etc.

portal ➊ (ˈpɔːtᵊl) *n* **1** an entrance, gateway, or doorway, esp. one that is large and impressive ◆ *adj* **2** *Anat.* of or relating to a portal vein: *hepatic portal system.* [C14: via OF from Med. L *portāle,* from L *porta* gate]

portal vein *n* any vein connecting two capillary networks, esp. in the liver.

portamento (ˌpɔːtəˈmɛntəʊ) *n, pl* **portamenti** (-tɪ). *Music.* a smooth slide from one note to another in which intervening notes are not separately discernible. [C18: from It.: a carrying, from L *portāre* to carry]

portative (ˈpɔːtətɪv) *adj* **1** a less common word for **portable. 2** concerned with the act of carrying. [C14: from F, from L *portāre* to carry]

portcullis (pɔːtˈkʌlɪs) *n* an iron or wooden grating suspended vertically in grooves in the gateway of a castle or town and able to be lowered so as to bar the entrance. [C14 *port colice,* from OF *porte coleïce* sliding gate, from *porte* door + *coleïce,* from *couler* to slide, from LL *cōlāre* to filter]

Porte (pɔːt) *n* short for Sublime Porte; the court or government of the Ottoman Empire. [C17: shortened from F *Sublime Porte* High Gate, rendering the Turkish title *Babi Ali,* the imperial gate, regarded as the seat of government]

porte-cochere (ˌpɔːtkɒˈʃɛə) *n* **1** a large covered entrance for vehicles leading into a courtyard. **2** a large roof projecting over a drive to shelter travellers entering or leaving vehicles. [C17: from F: carriage entrance]

portend ➊ (pɔːˈtɛnd) *vb* (*tr*) to give warning of; foreshadow. [C15: from L *portendere* to indicate]

portent ➊ (ˈpɔːtɛnt) *n* **1** a sign of a future event; omen. **2** momentous or ominous significance: *a cry of dire portent.* **3** a marvel. [C16: from L *portentum* sign, from *portendere* to portend]

portentous ➊ (pɔːˈtɛntəs) *adj* **1** of momentous or ominous significance. **2** miraculous, amazing, or awe-inspiring. **3** self-important or pompous.

porter[1] ➊ (ˈpɔːtə) *n* **1** a person employed to carry luggage, parcels, supplies, etc., at a railway station or hotel. **2** (in hospitals) a person employed to move patients from place to place. **3** *US & Canad.* a railway employee who waits on passengers, esp. in a sleeper. [C14: from OF *portour,* from LL *portātōr,* from L *portāre* to carry]
▸**'porterage** *n*

porter[2] ➊ (ˈpɔːtə) *n* **1** *Chiefly Brit.* a person in charge of a gate or door; doorman or gatekeeper. **2** a person employed as a caretaker and doorkeeper who also answers inquiries. **3** a person in charge of the maintenance of a building, esp. a block of flats. [C13: from OF *portier,* from LL *portārius,* from L *porta* door]

porter[3] (ˈpɔːtə) *n Brit.* a dark sweet ale brewed from black malt. [C18: from *porter's ale,* apparently because it was a favourite beverage of porters]

porterhouse (ˈpɔːtəˌhaʊs) *n* **1** Also called: **porterhouse steak.** a thick choice steak of beef cut from the middle ribs or sirloin. **2** (formerly) a place in which porter, beer, etc., and sometimes chops and steaks, were served. [C19 (sense 1): said to be after a porterhouse in New York]

portfire (ˈpɔːtˌfaɪə) *n* a slow-burning fuse used for firing rockets and fireworks and, in mining, for igniting explosives. [C17: from F *porte-feu,* from *porter* to carry + *feu* fire]

portfolio (pɔːtˈfəʊlɪəʊ) *n, pl* **portfolios. 1** a flat case, esp. of leather, used for carrying maps, drawings, etc. **2** the contents of such a case, such as drawings or photographs, that demonstrate recent work. **3** such a case used for carrying ministerial or state papers. **4** the responsibilities or role of the head of a government department: *the portfolio for foreign affairs.* **5 Minister without portfolio.** a cabinet minister who is not responsible for any government department. **6** the complete investments held by an individual investor or a financial organization. [C18: from It. *portafoglio,* from *portāre* to carry + *foglio* leaf, from L *folium*]

portfolio management *n* the service provided by an investment adviser who manages a financial portfolio on behalf of the investor.

porthole (ˈpɔːtˌhəʊl) *n* **1** a small aperture in the side of a vessel to admit light and air, fitted with a watertight cover. Sometimes shortened to **port. 2** an opening in a wall or parapet through which a gun can be fired.

portico (ˈpɔːtɪkəʊ) *n, pl* **porticoes** *or* **porticos. 1** a covered entrance to a building; porch. **2** a covered walkway in the form of a roof supported by columns or pillars, esp. one built on to the exterior of a building. [C17: via It. from L *porticus*]

portière (ˌpɔːtɪˈɛə; *French* pɔrtjɛr) *n* a curtain hung in a doorway. [C19: via F from Med. L *portāria,* from L *porta* door]
▸ˌ**porti'èred** *adj*

portion ➊ (ˈpɔːʃən) *n* **1** a part of a whole. **2** a part allotted or belonging to a person or group. **3** an amount of food served to one person; helping. **4** *Law.* **4a** a share of property, esp. one coming to a child from the estate of his parents. **4b** a dowry. **5** a person's lot or destiny. ◆ *vb* (*tr*) **6** to divide up; share out. **7** to give a share to (a person). [C13: via OF from L *portiō*]
▸**'portionless** *adj*

Portland cement (ˈpɔːtlənd) *n* a cement that hardens under water and is made by heating clay and crushed chalk or limestone. [C19: after

THESAURUS

porous *adj* **1 = permeable,** absorbent, absorptive, penetrable, pervious, spongy
Antonyms *adj* impenetrable, impermeable, impervious, nonporous

port[1] *n* **1 = harbour,** anchorage, haven, roads, roadstead, seaport

portable *adj* **1 = light,** compact, convenient, easily carried, handy, lightweight, manageable, movable, portative

portal *n* **1 = doorway,** door, entrance, entrance way, entry, gateway, way in

portend *vb* **= foretell,** adumbrate, augur, bespeak, betoken, bode, foreshadow, foretoken, forewarn, harbinger, herald, indicate, omen, point to, predict, presage, prognosticate, promise, threaten, warn of

portent *n* **1 = omen,** augury, foreboding, foreshadowing, forewarning, harbinger, indication, premonition, presage, presentiment, prognostic, prognostication, sign, threat, warning

portentous *adj* **1 = significant,** alarming, crucial, fateful, forbidding, important, menacing, minatory, momentous, ominous, sinister, threatening **2 = remarkable,** amazing, astounding, awe-inspiring, extraordinary, miraculous, phenomenal, prodigious, wondrous (*arch. or literary*) **3 = pompous,** bloated, elephantine, heavy, ponderous, pontifical, self-important, solemn

porter[1] *n* **1 = baggage attendant,** bearer, carrier

porter[2] *n* **1-3 = doorman,** caretaker, concierge, gatekeeper, janitor

portion *n* **1 = part,** bit, fraction, fragment, morsel, piece, scrap, section, segment **2 = share,** allocation, allotment, allowance, division, lot, measure, parcel, quantity, quota, ration **3 = helping,** piece, serving **5 = destiny,** cup, fate, fortune, lot, luck ◆ *vb* **6 = divide,** allocate, allot, apportion, assign, deal, distribute, divvy up (*inf.*), dole out, parcel out, partition, share out the *Isle of Portland,* a peninsula in Dorset, because its colour resembles that of the stone quarried there]

portly ⓣ ('pɔ:tlɪ) *adj* **portlier, portliest. 1** stout or corpulent. **2** *Arch.* stately; impressive. [C16: from PORT[5] (in the sense: deportment)] ▸**'portliness** *n*

portmanteau (pɔ:t'mæntəʊ) *n, pl* **portmanteaus** *or* **portmanteaux** (-təʊz). **1** (formerly) a large travelling case made of stiff leather, esp. one hinged at the back so as to open out into two compartments. **2** (*modifier*) embodying several uses or qualities: *the heroine is a portmanteau figure of all the virtues.* [C16: from F: cloak carrier]

portmanteau word *n* another name for **blend** (sense 7). [C19: from the idea that two meanings are packed into one word]

port of call *n* **1** a port where a ship stops. **2** any place visited on a traveller's itinerary.

port of entry *n Law.* an airport, harbour, etc., where customs officials are stationed to supervise the entry into and exit from a country of persons and merchandise.

portrait ⓣ ('pɔ:trɪt, -treɪt) *n* **1** a painting or other likeness of an individual, esp. of the face. **2** a verbal description, esp. of a person's character. ◆ *adj* **3** *Printing.* (of an illustration in a book, magazine, etc.) of greater height than width. Cf. **landscape** (sense 5a). [C16: from F, from *portraire* to PORTRAY] ▸**'portraitist** *n*

portraiture ('pɔ:trɪtʃə) *n* **1** the practice or art of making portraits. **2a** a portrait. **2b** portraits collectively. **3** a verbal description.

portray ⓣ (pɔ:'treɪ) *vb* (*tr*) **1** to make a portrait of. **2** to depict in words. **3** to play the part of (a character) in a play or film. [C14: from OF *portraire* to depict, from L *prōtrahere* to drag forth] ▸**por'trayal** *n* ▸**por'trayer** *n*

Port-Salut ('pɔ: sə'lu:; *French* pɔrsaly) *n* a mild semihard whole-milk cheese of a round flat shape. Also called: **Port du Salut.** [C19: named after the Trappist monastery at *Port du Salut* in NW France where it was first made]

Portuguese (,pɔ:tjʊ'gi:z) *n* **1** the official language of Portugal and Brazil; it belongs to the Romance group of the Indo-European family. **2** (*pl* **Portuguese**) a native, citizen, or inhabitant of Portugal. ◆ *adj* **3** of Portugal, its inhabitants, or their language.

Portuguese man-of-war *n* any of several large hydrozoans having an aerial float and long stinging tentacles. Sometimes shortened to **man-of-war.**

portulaca (,pɔ:tjʊ'lækə, -'leɪkə) *n* any of a genus of plants of tropical and subtropical America, having yellow, pink, or purple showy flowers. [C16: from L: PURSLANE]

POS *abbrev. for* point of sale.

pose[1] ⓣ (pəʊz) *vb* **poses, posing, posed. 1** to assume or cause to assume a physical attitude, as for a photograph or painting. **2** (*intr;* often foll. by *as*) to present oneself (as something one is not). **3** (*intr*) to affect an attitude in order to impress others. **4** (*tr*) to put forward or ask: *to pose a question.* **5** (*intr*) *Sl.* to adopt a particular style of appearance and stand or strut around, esp. in bars, discotheques, etc., in order to attract attention. ◆ *n* **6** a physical attitude, esp. one deliberately adopted for an artist or photographer. **7** a mode of behaviour that is adopted for effect. [C14: from OF *poser* to set in place, from LL *pausāre* to cease, put down (infl. by L *pōnere* to place)]

pose[2] (pəʊz) *vb* **poses, posing, posed.** (*tr*) *Rare.* to puzzle or baffle. [C16: from obs. *appose,* from L *appōnere* to put to]

poser[1] ('pəʊzə) *n* **1** a person who poses. **2** *Inf.* a person who likes to be seen in trendsetting clothes in fashionable bars, discos, etc.

poser[2] ⓣ ('pəʊzə) *n* a baffling or insoluble question.

poseur ⓣ (pəʊ'zɜ:) *n* a person who strikes an attitude or assumes a pose in order to impress others. [C19: from F, from *poser* to POSE[1]]

posh ⓣ (pɒʃ) *adj Inf., chiefly Brit.* **1** smart, elegant, or fashionable. **2** upper-class or genteel. [C19: often said to be an acronym of *port out, starboard home,* the most desirable location for a cabin in British ships sailing to & from the East, being the shaded side; but more likely from obs. sl. *posh* (n) a dandy]

posit ⓣ ('pɒzɪt) *vb* (*tr*) **1** to assume or put forward as fact or the factual basis for an argument; postulate. **2** to put in position. [C17: from L *pōnere* to place]

position ⓣ (pə'zɪʃən) *n* **1** place, situation, or location: *he took up a position to the rear.* **2** the appropriate or customary location: *the telescope is in position for use.* **3** the manner in which a person or thing is placed; arrangement. **4** *Mil.* an area or point occupied for tactical reasons. **5** point of view; stand: *what's your position on this issue?* **6** social status, esp. high social standing. **7** a post of employment; job. **8** the act of positing a fact or viewpoint. **9** something posited, such as an idea. **10** *Sport.* the part of a field or playing area where a player is placed or where he generally operates. **11** *Music.* the vertical spacing or layout of the written notes in a chord. **12** (in classical prosody) the situation in which a short vowel may be regarded as long, that is, when it occurs before two or more consonants. **13** *Finance.* the market commitment of a dealer in securities, currencies, or commodities: *a short position.* **14 in a position.** (foll. by an infinitive) able (to). ◆ *vb* (*tr*) **15** to put in the proper or appropriate place; locate. **16** *Sport.* to place (oneself or another player) in a particular part of the field or playing area. [C15: from LL *positiō* a positioning, affirmation, from *pōnere* to place] ▸**po'sitional** *adj*

positional notation *n* the method of denoting numbers by the use of a finite number of digits, each digit having its value multiplied by its place value, as in 936 = (9 × 100) + (3 × 10) + 6.

position audit *n Commerce.* a systematic assessment of the current strengths and weaknesses of an organization as a prerequisite for future strategic planning.

positive ⓣ ('pɒzɪtɪv) *adj* **1** expressing certainty or affirmation: *a positive answer.* **2** possessing actual or specific qualities; real: *a positive benefit.* **3** tending to emphasize what is good or laudable; constructive: *he takes a very positive attitude when correcting pupils' mistakes.* **4** tending towards progress or improvement. **5** *Philosophy.* constructive rather than sceptical. **6** (*prenominal*) *Inf.* (intensifier): *a positive delight.* **7** *Maths.* having a value greater than zero: *a positive number.* **8** *Maths.* **8a** measured in a direction opposite to that regarded as negative. **8b** having the same magnitude as but opposite sense to an equivalent negative quantity. **9** *Grammar.* denoting the usual form of an adjective as opposed to its comparative or superlative form. **10** *Physics.* **10a** (of an electric charge) having an opposite polarity to the charge of an electron and the same polarity as the charge of a proton. **10b** (of a body, system, ion, etc.) having a positive electric charge. **11** short for **electropositive. 12** *Med.* (of the results of an examination or test) indicating the presence of a suspected disorder or organism. **13** *Economics.* of or denoting an analysis that is free of ethical, political, or value judgments. ◆ *n* **14** something that is positive. **15** *Maths.* a quantity greater than zero. **16** *Photog.* a print or slide showing a photographic image whose colours or tones correspond to those of the original subject. **17** *Grammar.* the positive degree of an adjective or adverb. **18** a positive object, such as a terminal or plate in a voltaic cell. [C13: from LL *positīvus,* from *pōnere* to place] ▸**'positiveness** *or* **,posi'tivity** *n*

positive discrimination *n* the provision of special opportunities for a disadvantaged group.

positive feedback *n* See **feedback** (sense 2).

positively ⓣ ('pɒzɪtɪvlɪ) *adv* **1** in a positive manner. **2** (intensifier): *he disliked her; in fact, he positively hated her.*

THESAURUS

portly *adj* **1** = **stout,** ample, beefy (*inf.*), bulky, burly, corpulent, fat, fleshy, heavy, large, obese, overweight, plump, rotund, tubby (*inf.*)

portrait *n* **1** = **picture,** image, likeness, painting, photograph, portraiture, representation, sketch **2** = **description,** account, characterization, depiction, portrayal, profile, thumbnail sketch, vignette

portray *vb* **1** = **represent,** delineate, depict, draw, figure, illustrate, limn, paint, picture, render, sketch **2** = **describe,** characterize, depict, paint a mental picture of, put in words **3** = **play,** act the part of, represent

portrayal *n* **1-3** = **representation,** characterization, delineation, depiction, description, impersonation, interpretation, performance, picture, rendering, take (*inf., chiefly US*)

pose[1] *vb* **1** = **position,** arrange, model, sit, sit for **2** *often foll. by* **as** = **impersonate,** feign, masquerade as, pass oneself off as, pretend to be, profess to be, sham **3** = **put on airs,** affect, attitudinize, posture, show off (*inf.*), strike an attitude **4** = **present,** advance, ask, posit, propound, put, put forward, set, state, submit ◆ *n* **6** = **posture,** attitude, bearing, mien (*literary*), position, stance **7** = **act,** affectation, air, attitudinizing, façade, front, mannerism, masquerade, posturing, pretence, role

poser[2] *n* = **puzzle,** brain-teaser, conundrum, enigma, knotty point, problem, question, riddle, teaser, tough one, vexed question

poseur *n* = **show-off** (*inf.*), attitudinizer, exhibitionist, hot dog (*chiefly US*), impostor, mannerist, masquerader, poser, posturer, self-publicist

posh *adj* **1, 2** *Informal, chiefly Brit.* = **upper-class,** classy (*sl.*), elegant, exclusive, fashionable, grand, high-class, high-toned, la-di-da (*inf.*), luxurious, luxury, ritzy (*sl.*), smart, stylish, swanky (*inf.*), swish (*inf., chiefly Brit.*), top-drawer, up-market

posit *vb* **1** = **put forward,** advance, assert, assume, postulate, predicate, presume, propound, state, submit

position *n* **1** = **place,** area, bearings, locale, locality, location, point, post, reference, site, situation, spot, station, whereabouts **3** = **posture,** arrangement, attitude, disposition, pose, stance **5** = **attitude,** angle, belief, opinion, outlook, point of view, slant, stance, stand, standpoint, view, viewpoint **6** = **status,** caste, class, consequence, eminence, importance, place, prestige, rank, reputation, standing, station, stature **7** = **job,** berth (*inf.*), billet (*inf.*), capacity, duty, employment, function, occupation, office, place, post, role, situation ◆ *vb* **15** = **place,** arrange, array, dispose, fix, lay out, locate, put, sequence, set, settle, stand, stick (*inf.*)

positive *adj* **1** = **certain,** assured, confident, convinced, sure **2** = **definite,** absolute, actual, affirmative, categorical, certain, clear, clear-cut, conclusive, concrete, decisive, direct, explicit, express, firm, incontrovertible, indisputable, real, unequivocal, unmistakable **3** = **helpful,** beneficial, constructive, effective, efficacious, forward-looking, practical, productive, progressive, useful **6** *Informal* = **absolute,** complete, consummate, downright, out-and-out, perfect, rank, thorough, thoroughgoing, unmitigated, utter

Antonyms *adj* ≠ **certain:** not confident, unassured, uncertain, unconvinced, unsure ≠ **definite:** contestable, disputable, doubtful, inconclusive, indecisive, indefinite, uncertain ≠ **helpful:** conservative, detrimental, harmful, impractical, reactionary, unhelpful, useless

positively *adv* **1, 2** = **definitely,** absolutely, assuredly, categorically, certainly, emphatically, firmly, surely, undeniably, unequivocally, unmistakably, unquestionably, with certainty, without qualification

positive vetting *n* the checking of a person's background, to assess his suitability for a position that may involve national security.

positivism (ˈpɒzɪtɪˌvɪzəm) *n* **1** a form of empiricism, esp. as established by Auguste Comte, that rejects metaphysics and theology and holds that experimental investigation and observation are the only sources of substantial knowledge. See also **logical positivism. 2** the quality of being definite, certain, etc.
▸ˈ**positivist** *n, adj*

positron (ˈpɒzɪˌtrɒn) *n Physics.* the antiparticle of the electron, having the same mass but an equal and opposite charge. [C20: from *posi(tive + elec)tron*]

positron emission tomography *n* a technique for assessing brain activity and function by recording the emission of positrons when radioactively labelled glucose, introduced into the brain, is metabolized.

positronium (ˌpɒzɪˈtrəʊnɪəm) *n Physics.* a short-lived entity consisting of a positron and an electron bound together.

posology (pəˈsɒlədʒɪ) *n* the branch of medicine concerned with the determination of appropriate doses of drugs or agents. [C19: from F *posologie,* from Gk *posos* how much]

poss. *abbrev. for:* **1** possession. **2** possessive. **3** possible. **4** possibly.

posse (ˈpɒsɪ) *n* **1** *US.* short for **posse comitatus,** the able-bodied men of a district forming a group upon whom the sheriff may call for assistance in maintaining law and order. **2** *Sl.* a Jamaican street gang in the US. **3** *Inf.* a group of friends or associates. **4** (in W Canada) a troop of trained horses and riders who perform at stampedes. **5** *Law.* possibility (esp. in **in posse**). [C16: from Med. L (n): power, from L (vb): to be able]

posse comitatus (ˌkɒmɪˈtɑːtəs) *n* the formal legal term for **posse** (sense 1). [Med. L: strength (manpower) of the county]

possess ❶ (pəˈzɛs) *vb (tr)* **1** to have as one's property; own. **2** to have as a quality, characteristic, etc.: *to possess good eyesight.* **3** to have knowledge of: *to possess a little French.* **4** to gain control over or dominate: *whatever possessed you to act so foolishly?* **5** (foll. by *of*) to cause to be the owner or possessor: *I am possessed of the necessary information.* **6** to have sexual intercourse with. **7** *Now rare.* to maintain (oneself or one's feelings) in a certain state or condition: *possess yourself in patience until I tell you the news.* [C15: from OF *possesser,* from L *possidēre*]
▸**posˈsessor** *n* ▸**posˈsessory** *adj*

possessed ❶ (pəˈzɛst) *adj* **1** (foll. by *of*) owning or having. **2** (*usually postpositive*) under the influence of a powerful force, such as a spirit or strong emotion. **3** a less common term for **self-possessed.**

possession ❶ (pəˈzɛʃən) *n* **1** the act of possessing or state of being possessed: *in possession of the crown.* **2** anything that is owned or possessed. **3** (*pl*) wealth or property. **4** the state of being controlled by or as if by evil spirits. **5** the occupancy of land, property, etc., whether or not accompanied by ownership: *to take possession of a house.* **6** a territory subject to a foreign state: *colonial possessions.* **7** *Sport.* control of the ball, puck, etc., as exercised by a player or team: *he got possession in his own half.*

possessive ❶ (pəˈzɛsɪv) *adj* **1** of or relating to possession. **2** having or showing an excessive desire to possess or dominate: *a possessive husband.* **3** *Grammar.* **3a** another word for **genitive. 3b** denoting an inflected form of a noun or pronoun used to convey the idea of possession, association, etc., as *my* or *Harry's.* ◆ *n* **4** *Grammar.* **4a** the possessive case. **4b** a word or speech element in the possessive case.
▸**posˈsessively** *adv* ▸**posˈsessiveness** *n*

posset (ˈpɒsɪt) *n* a drink of hot milk curdled with ale, beer, etc., flavoured with spices, formerly used as a remedy for colds. [C15 *poshoote,* from ?]

possibility ❶ (ˌpɒsɪˈbɪlɪtɪ) *n, pl* **possibilities. 1** the state or condition of being possible. **2** anything that is possible. **3** a competitor, candidate, etc., who has a moderately good chance of winning, being chosen, etc. **4** (*often pl*) a future prospect or potential: *my new house has great possibilities.*

possible ❶ (ˈpɒsɪbᵊl) *adj* **1** capable of existing, taking place, or proving true without contravention of any natural law. **2** capable of being achieved: *it is not possible to finish in three weeks.* **3** having potential: *the idea is a possible money-spinner.* **4** feasible but less than probable: *it is possible that man will live on Mars.* **5** *Logic.* (of a statement, formula, etc.) capable of being true under some interpretation or in some circumstances. ◆ *n* **6** another word for **possibility** (sense 3). [C14: from L *possibilis* that may be, from *posse* to be able]

> **USAGE NOTE** Although it is very common to talk about something being *very possible* or *more possible,* these uses are generally thought to be incorrect, since *possible* describes an absolute state, and therefore something can only be *possible* or *not possible: it is very likely* (not *very possible) that he will resign; it has now become easier* (not *more possible) to obtain an entry visa.*

possibly ❶ (ˈpɒsɪblɪ) *sentence substitute, adv* **1a** perhaps or maybe. **1b** (*as sentence modifier*): *possibly he'll come.* ◆ *adv* **2** by any chance; at all: *he can't possibly come.*

possum (ˈpɒsəm) *n* **1** an informal name for **opossum. 2** an Australian and New Zealand name for **phalanger. 3 play possum.** to pretend to be dead, ignorant, asleep, etc., in order to deceive an opponent. **4 stir the possum** *Austral. sl.* to cause trouble.

post[1] ❶ (pəʊst) *n* **1** a length of wood, metal, etc., fixed upright to serve as a support, marker, point of attachment, etc. **2** *Horse racing.* **2a** either of two upright poles marking the beginning (**starting post**) and end (**winning post**) of a racecourse. **2b** the finish of a horse race. ◆ *vb (tr)* **3** (sometimes foll. by *up*) to fasten or put up (a notice) in a public place. **4** to announce by or as if by means of a poster: *to post banns.* **5** to publish (a name) on a list. **6** to denounce publicly; brand. [OE, from L *postis*]

post[2] ❶ (pəʊst) *n* **1** a position to which a person is appointed or elected; appointment; job. **2** a position to which a person, such as a sentry, is assigned for duty. **3** a permanent military establishment. **4** *Brit.* either of two military bugle calls (**first post** and **last post**) giving notice of the time to retire for the night. **5** See **trading post.** ◆ *vb* **6** *(tr)* to assign to or station at a particular place or position. **7** *Chiefly Brit.* to transfer to a different unit or ship on taking up a new appointment, etc. [C16: from F *poste,* from It. *posto,* ult. from L *pōnere* to place]

post[3] ❶ (pəʊst) *n* **1** *Chiefly Brit.* letters, packages, etc., that are transported and delivered by the Post Office; mail. **2** *Chiefly Brit.* a single collection or delivery of mail. **3** *Brit.* an official system of mail delivery. **4** (formerly) any of a series of stations furnishing relays of men and horses to deliver mail over a fixed route. **5** a rider who carried mail between such stations. **6** *Brit.* a postbox or post office: *take this to the post.* **7** any of various book sizes, esp. 5¼ by 8¼ inches (**post octavo**). **8 by return of post.** *Brit.* by the next mail in the opposite direction. ◆ *vb* **9** *(tr) Chiefly Brit.* to send by post. US and Canad. word: **mail. 10** *(tr) Book-keeping.* **10a** to enter (an item) in a ledger. **10b** (often foll. by *up*) to compile or enter all paper items in (a ledger). **11** *(tr)* to inform of the latest news. **12** *(intr)* (formerly) to travel with relays of post horses. **13** *Arch.* to travel or dispatch with speed; hasten. ◆ *adv* **14** with speed; rapidly. **15** (formerly) by means of post horses. [C16: via F from It. *poste,* from L *posita* something placed, from *pōnere* to put]

post- *prefix* **1** after in time or sequence; following; subsequent: *postgraduate.* **2** behind; posterior to: *postorbital.* [from L, from *post* after, behind]

postage (ˈpəʊstɪdʒ) *n* **a** the charge for delivering a piece of mail. **b** (*as modifier*): *postage charges.*

postage meter *n Chiefly US & Canad.* a postal franking machine. Also called: **postal meter.**

postage stamp *n* **1** a printed paper label with a gummed back for attaching to mail as an official indication that the required postage has been paid. **2** a mark printed on an envelope, etc., serving the same function.

postal (ˈpəʊstᵊl) *adj* of or relating to a Post Office or to the mail-delivery service.
▸ˈ**postally** *adv*

postal note *n Austral. & NZ.* the usual name for **postal order.**

postal order *n* a written order for the payment of a sum of money, to a named payee, obtainable and payable at a post office.

postbag (ˈpəʊstˌbæg) *n* **1** *Chiefly Brit.* another name for **mailbag. 2** the mail received by a magazine, radio programme, public figure, etc.

postbox (ˈpəʊstˌbɒks) *n* another name for **letter box** (sense 2).

postcard (ˈpəʊstˌkɑːd) *n* a card, often bearing a photograph, picture, etc., on one side (**picture postcard**), for sending a message by post without an envelope. Also called (US): **postal card.**

THESAURUS

possess *vb* **1, 2** = **have,** be blessed with, be born with, be endowed with, enjoy, have to one's name, hold, own **4** = **seize,** acquire, control, dominate, hold, occupy, take over, take possession of

possessed *adj* **2** = **crazed,** bedevilled, berserk, bewitched, consumed, cursed, demented, enchanted, frenetic, frenzied, hag-ridden, haunted, maddened, obsessed, raving, under a spell

possession *n* **1** = **ownership,** control, custody, hold, occupancy, occupation, proprietorship, tenure, title **3** *plural* = **property,** assets, belongings, chattels, effects, estate, goods and chattels, things, wealth **6** = **province,** colony, dominion, protectorate, territory

possessive *adj* **2** = **jealous,** acquisitive, controlling, covetous, dominating, domineering, grasping, overprotective, selfish

possibility *n* **1** = **feasibility,** likelihood, plausibility, potentiality, practicability, workableness **2** = **likelihood,** chance, hazard, hope, liability, odds, probability, prospect, risk **4** *often plural* = **potential,** capabilities, potentiality, promise, prospects, talent

possible *adj* **1** = **conceivable,** credible, hypothetical, imaginable, likely, potential **2** = **feasible,** attainable, doable, on (*inf.*), practicable, realizable, viable, within reach, workable **3** = **likely,** hopeful, potential, probable, promising
Antonyms *adj* ≠ **conceivable:** impossible, inconceivable, incredible, unimaginable, unlikely, unthinkable ≠ **feasible:** impossible, impracticable, unfeasible, unobtainable, unreasonable ≠ **likely:** impossible, improbable

possibly *adv* **1** = **perhaps,** God willing, haply, maybe, mayhap (*arch.*), peradventure (*arch.*), perchance (*arch.*) **2** = **at all,** by any chance, by any means, in any way

post[1] *n* **1** = **support,** column, newel, pale, palisade, picket, pillar, pole, shaft, stake, standard, stock, upright ◆ *vb* **3-5** = **put up,** advertise, affix, announce, display, make known, pin up, proclaim, promulgate, publicize, publish, stick up

post[2] *n* **1** = **job,** appointment, assignment, berth (*inf.*), billet (*inf.*), employment, office, place, position, situation **2** = **station,** beat, place, position ◆ *vb* **6** = **station,** assign, establish, locate, place, position, put, situate

post[3] *n* **2, 3** = **mail,** collection, delivery, postal service ◆ *vb* **9** = **send,** dispatch, mail, transmit

post chaise *n* a closed four-wheeled horse-drawn coach used as a rapid means for transporting mail and passengers in the 18th and 19th centuries. [C18: from POST[3] + CHAISE]

postclassical (pəʊst'klæsɪkᵊl) *adj* (esp. of Greek or Roman literature) later than the classical period.

postcode ('pəʊstˌkəʊd) *n* a code of letters and digits used as part of a postal address to aid the sorting of mail. Also called: **postal code.** US name: **zip code.**

postconsonantal (pəʊstˌkɒnsə'næntᵊl) *adj* (of a speech sound) immediately following a consonant.

postdate (pəʊst'deɪt) *vb* **postdates, postdating, postdated.** (*tr*) **1** to write a future date on (a document, etc.), as on a cheque to prevent it being paid until then. **2** to assign a date to (an event, period, etc.) that is later than its previously assigned date of occurrence. **3** to be or occur at a later date than.

postdoctoral (pəʊst'dɒktərəl) *adj* of, relating to, or designating studies, research, or professional work above the level of a doctorate.

poster ❶ ('pəʊstə) *n* **1** a large printed picture, used for decoration. **2** a placard or bill posted in a public place as an advertisement. **3** a person who posts bills.

poste restante ('pəʊst rɪ'stænt) *n* **1** an address on mail indicating that it should be kept at a specified post office until collected by the addressee. **2** the mail-delivery service or post-office department that handles mail having this address. ◆ US and Canad. equivalent: **general delivery.** [F, lit.: mail remaining]

posterior ❶ (pɒ'stɪərɪə) *adj* **1** situated at the back of or behind something. **2** coming after or following another in a series. **3** coming after in time. ◆ *n* **4** the buttocks; rump. [C16: from L: latter, from *posterus* coming next, from *post* after]
▸**pos'teriorly** *adv*

posterity ❶ (pɒ'sterɪtɪ) *n* **1** future or succeeding generations. **2** all of one's descendants. [C14: from F *postérité*, from L *posteritās*, from *posterus* coming after, from *post* after]

postern ('pɒstən) *n* a back door or gate, esp. one that is for private use. [C13: from OF *posterne*, from LL *posterula* (*jānua*) a back (entrance), from *posterus* coming behind]

poster paint *or* **colour** *n* a gum-based opaque watercolour paint used for writing posters, etc.

postfeminist (pəʊst'femɪnɪst) *adj* **1** resulting from or including the beliefs and ideas of feminism. **2** differing from or showing moderation of these beliefs and ideas. ◆ *n* **3** a person who believes in or advocates any of the ideas that have developed from the feminist movement.

post-Fordism (ˌpəʊst'fɔːdɪzəm) *n* the idea that modern industrial production has moved away from mass production in huge factories, as pioneered by Henry Ford (1863–1947), US car manufacturer, towards specialized markets based on small flexible manufacturing units.
▸ˌ**post-'Fordist** *adj*

post-free *adv, adj* **1** *Brit.* with the postage prepaid; postpaid. **2** free of postal charge.

postglacial (pəʊst'gleɪsɪəl, -ʃəl) *adj* formed or occurring after a glacial period.

postgraduate (pəʊst'grædjʊɪt) *n* **1** a student who has obtained a degree from a university, etc., and is pursuing studies for a more advanced qualification. **2** (*modifier*) of or relating to such a student or his studies. ◆ Also (US and Canad.): **graduate.**

posthaste ❶ ('pəʊst'heɪst) *adv* **1** with great haste. ◆ *n* **2** *Arch.* great haste.

post horn *n* a simple valveless natural horn consisting of a long tube of brass or copper.

post horse *n* (formerly) a horse kept at an inn or post house for use by postriders or for hire to travellers.

post house *n* (formerly) a house or inn where horses were kept for postriders or for hire to travellers.

posthumous ('pɒstjʊməs) *adj* **1** happening or continuing after one's death. **2** (of a book, etc.) published after the author's death. **3** (of a child) born after the father's death. [C17: from L *postumus* the last, but modified as though from L *post* after + *humus* earth, that is, after the burial]
▸**'posthumously** *adv*

posthypnotic suggestion (ˌpəʊsthɪp'nɒtɪk) *n* a suggestion made to the subject while he is in a hypnotic trance, to be acted upon at some time after emerging from the trance.

postiche (pɒ'stiːʃ) *adj* **1** (of architectural ornament) inappropriately applied; sham. **2** false or artificial; spurious. ◆ *n* **3** another term for **hairpiece** (sense 2). **4** anything that is false; sham or pretence. [C19: from F, from It. *apposticcio* (n), from LL *appositīcius* (adj); see APPOSITE]

postilion *or* **postillion** (pɒ'stɪljən) *n* a person who rides the near horse of the leaders in order to guide a team of horses drawing a coach. [C16: from F *postillon*, from It. *postiglione*, from *posta* POST[3]]

postimpressionism (ˌpəʊstɪm'preʃəˌnɪzəm) *n* a movement in painting in France at the end of the 19th century which rejected the naturalism and momentary effects of impressionism but adapted its use of pure colour to paint subjects with greater subjective emotion.
▸ˌ**postim'pressionist** *n, adj*

post-industrial (ˌpəʊstɪn'dʌstrɪəl) *adj* denoting work or a society that is no longer based on heavy industry.

posting ('pəʊstɪŋ) *n* **1** an appointment to a position or post, usually in another town or country. **2** *Computing.* an electronic message sent to a bulletin board, website, etc., and intended for access by every user.

postliminy (pəʊst'lɪmɪnɪ) *or* **postliminium** (ˌpəʊstlɪ'mɪnɪəm) *n, pl* **postliminies** *or* **postliminia** (-ɪə). *International law.* the right by which persons and property seized in war are restored to their former status on recovery. [C17: from L *post* behind + *limen, liminis* threshold]

postlude ('pəʊstluːd) *n Music.* a final or concluding piece or movement. [C19: from POST- + *-lude*, from L *lūdus* game; cf. PRELUDE]

postman ('pəʊstmən) *or* (*fem*) **postwoman** *n, pl* **postmen** *or* **postwomen.** a person who carries and delivers mail as a profession.

postman's knock *n* a children's party game in which a kiss is exchanged for a pretend letter.

postmark ('pəʊstˌmɑːk) *n* **1** any mark stamped on mail by postal officials, usually showing the date and place of posting. ◆ *vb* **2** (*tr*) to put such a mark on (mail).

postmaster ('pəʊstˌmɑːstə) *n* **1** Also (*fem*) **postmistress.** an official in charge of a local post office. **2** the person responsible for managing the electronic mail at a site.

postmaster general *n, pl* **postmasters general.** the executive head of the postal service in certain countries.

postmeridian (ˌpəʊstmə'rɪdɪən) *adj* after noon; in the afternoon or evening. [C17: from L *postmerīdiānus* in the afternoon]

post meridiem ('pəʊst mə'rɪdɪəm) the full form of **p.m.** [C17: L: after noon]

post mill *n* a windmill built around a central post on which the whole mill can be turned so that the sails catch the wind.

postmillennialism (ˌpəʊstmɪ'lenɪəˌlɪzəm) *n Christian theol.* the doctrine or belief that the Second Coming of Christ will be preceded by the millennium.
▸ˌ**postmil'lennialist** *n*

postmodernism (pəʊst'mɒdəˌnɪzəm) *n* (in the arts, architecture, etc.) a style and school of thought that rejects the dogma and practices of any form of modernism; in architecture it contrasts with international modernism and features elements from several periods, esp. the Classical, often with ironic use of decoration.
▸**post'modernist** *n, adj*

postmortem ❶ (pəʊst'mɔːtəm) *adj* **1** (*prenominal*) occurring after death. ◆ *n* **2** analysis or study of a recent event: *a postmortem on a game of chess.* **3** See **postmortem examination.** [C18: from L, lit.: after death]

postmortem examination *n* dissection and examination of a dead body to determine the cause of death. Also called: **autopsy, necropsy.**

postnatal (pəʊst'neɪtᵊl) *adj* of or relating to the period after childbirth.

post-obit (pəʊst'əʊbɪt, -'ɒbɪt) *Chiefly law.* ◆ *n* **1** a bond given by a borrower, payable after the death of a specified person, esp. one given to a moneylender by an expectant heir promising to repay when his interest falls into possession. ◆ *adj* **2** taking effect after death. [C18: from L *post obitum* after death]

post office *n* a building or room where postage stamps are sold and other postal business is conducted.

Post Office *n* a government department or authority in many countries responsible for postal services and often telecommunications.

post office box *n* a private numbered place in a post office, in which letters received are kept until called for.

postoperative (pəʊst'ɒpərətɪv) *adj* of or occurring in the period following a surgical operation.

post-paid *adv, adj* with the postage prepaid.

postpone ❶ (pəʊst'pəʊn, pə'spəʊn) *vb* **postpones, postponing, postponed.** (*tr*) **1** to put off or delay until a future time. **2** to put behind in order of importance; defer. [C16: from L *postpōnere* to put after]
▸**post'ponement** *n*

postpositive (pəʊst'pɒzɪtɪv) *adj* **1** (of an adjective or other modifier) placed after the word modified, either immediately after, as in *two men abreast*, or as part of a complement, as in *those men are bad.* ◆ *n* **2** a postpositive modifier.

postprandial (pəʊst'prændɪəl) *adj usually humorous.* after a meal.

postrider ('pəʊstˌraɪdə) *n* (formerly) a person who delivered post on horseback.

postscript ❶ ('pəʊsˌskrɪpt, 'pəʊst-) *n* **1** a message added at the end of a letter, after the signature. **2** any supplement, as to a document or book. [C16: from LL *postscribere* to write after]

THESAURUS

poster *n* **2** = **notice**, advertisement, *affiche*, announcement, bill, placard, public notice, sticker

posterior *adj* **1** = **behind**, after, back, hind, hinder, rear **2, 3** = **later**, ensuing, following, latter, subsequent

posterity *n* **1** = **future**, future generations, succeeding generations **2** = **descendants**, children, family, heirs, issue, offspring, progeny, scions, seed (*chiefly Biblical*)

posthaste *adv* **1** = **speedily**, at once, directly, double-quick, full tilt, hastily, hotfoot, promptly, pronto (*inf.*), quickly, straightaway, swiftly

postmortem *n* **3** = **examination**, analysis, autopsy, dissection, necropsy

postpone *vb* **1, 2** = **put off**, adjourn, defer, delay, hold over, put back, put on ice (*inf.*), put on the back burner (*inf.*), shelve, suspend, table, take a rain check on (*US & Canad. inf.*)
Antonyms *vb* advance, bring forward, call to order, carry out, go ahead with

postponement *n* **1, 2** = **delay**, adjournment, deferment, deferral, moratorium, respite, stay, suspension

postscript *n* **1, 2** = **P.S.**, addition, afterthought, afterword, appendix, supplement

poststructuralism (pəʊst'strʌktʃərəˌlɪzəm) *n* an approach to literature that, proceeding from the tenets of structuralism, maintains that, as words have no absolute meaning, any text is open to an unlimited range of interpretations.
▸**post'structuralist** *n, adj*

post-traumatic stress disorder *n* a psychological condition, characterized by anxiety, withdrawal, and a proneness to physical illness, that may follow a traumatic experience.

postulant ('pɒstjʊlənt) *n* a person who makes a request or application, esp. a candidate for admission to a religious order. [C18: from L *postulāns* asking, from *postulāre* to ask]

postulate ➊ *vb* ('pɒstjʊˌleɪt), **postulates, postulating, postulated.** (*tr; may take a clause as object*) **1** to assume to be true or existent; take for granted. **2** to ask, demand, or claim. **3** to nominate (a person) to a post or office subject to approval by a higher authority. ◆ *n* ('pɒstjʊlɪt). **4** something taken as self-evident or assumed as the basis of an argument. **5** a prerequisite. **6** a fundamental principle. **7** *Logic, maths.* an unproved statement that should be taken for granted: used as an initial premise in a process of reasoning. [C16: from L *postulāre* to ask for]
▸ˌ**postu'lation** *n*

postulator ('pɒstjʊˌleɪtə) *n RC Church.* a person who presents a plea for the beatification or canonization of some deceased person.

posture ➊ ('pɒstʃə) *n* **1** a position or attitude of the limbs or body. **2** a characteristic manner of bearing the body: *good posture.* **3** the disposition of the parts of a visible object. **4** a mental attitude. **5** a state or condition. **6** a false or affected attitude; pose. ◆ *vb* **postures, posturing, postured. 7** to assume or cause to assume a bodily attitude. **8** (*intr*) to assume an affected posture; pose. [C17: via F from It. *postura,* from L *positūra,* from *pōnere* to place]
▸'**postural** *adj* ▸'**posturer** *n*

postwar (pəʊst'wɔː) *adj* happening or existing after a war.

posy ➊ ('pəʊzɪ) *n, pl* **posies. 1** a small bunch of flowers. **2** *Arch.* a brief motto or inscription, esp. one on a trinket or a ring. [C16: var. of POESY]

pot[1] ➊ (pɒt) *n* **1** a container, usually round and deep and often having a handle and lid, used for cooking and other domestic purposes. **2** the amount that a pot will hold; potful. **3** a large mug or tankard. **4** *Austral.* any of various measures used for serving beer. **5** the money or stakes in the pool in gambling games. **6** a wicker trap for catching fish, esp. crustaceans: *a lobster pot.* **7** *Billiards, etc.* a shot by which a ball is pocketed. **8** a chamber pot, esp. a small one designed for a baby or toddler. **9** (*often pl*) *Inf.* a large amount (esp. of money). **10** *Inf.* a prize or trophy. **11** *Chiefly Brit.* short for **chimneypot. 12** short for **flowerpot, teapot. 13** See **potbelly. 14 go to pot.** to go to ruin. ◆ *vb* **pots, potting, potted.** (*mainly tr*) **15** to put or preserve (meat, etc.) in a pot. **16** to plant (a cutting, seedling, etc.) in soil in a flowerpot. **17** to cause (a baby or toddler) to use or sit on a pot. **18** to shoot (game) for food rather than for sport. **19** (*also intr*) to shoot casually or without careful aim. **20** (*also intr*) to shape clay as a potter. **21** *Billiards, etc.* to pocket (a ball). **22** *Inf.* to capture or win. [LOE *pott,* from Med. L *pottus* (unattested), ?from L *pōtus* a drink]

pot[2] (pɒt) *n Sl.* cannabis used as a drug in any form. [C20: ? shortened from Mexican Indian *potiguaya*]

potable ('pəʊtəbᵊl) *adj* drinkable. [C16: from LL *pōtābilis* drinkable, from L *pōtāre* to drink]
▸ˌ**pota'bility** *n*

potae ('pɒtaɪ) *n NZ.* a hat. [Maori]

potage *French.* (pɔtaʒ; *English* pəʊ'tɑːʒ) *n* any thick soup. [C16: from OF; see POTTAGE]

potamic (pə'tæmɪk) *adj* of or relating to rivers. [C19: from Gk *potamos* river]

potash ('pɒtˌæʃ) *n* **1** another name for **potassium carbonate** or **potassium hydroxide. 2** potassium chemically combined in certain compounds: *chloride of potash.* [C17 *pot ashes,* translation of obs. Du. *potaschen;* because orig. obtained by evaporating the lye of wood ashes in pots]

potassium (pə'tæsɪəm) *n* a light silvery element of the alkali metal group that is highly reactive and rapidly oxidizes in air. Symbol: K; atomic no.: 19; atomic wt.: 39.098. [C19: NL *potassa* potash]
▸**po'tassic** *adj*

potassium-argon dating *n* a technique for determining the age of minerals based on the occurrence in natural potassium of a small fixed amount of radioisotope ^{40}K that decays to the stable argon isotope ^{40}Ar with a half-life of 1.28×10^9 years. Measurement of the ratio of these isotopes thus gives the age of the mineral.

potassium bromide *n* a white crystalline soluble substance with a bitter saline taste used in making photographic papers and plates and in medicine as a sedative. Formula: KBr.

potassium carbonate *n* a white odourless substance used in making glass and soft soap and as an alkaline cleansing agent. Formula: K_2CO_3.

potassium chlorate *n* a white crystalline soluble substance used in explosives and as a disinfectant and bleaching agent. Formula: $KClO_3$.

potassium cyanide *n* a white poisonous granular soluble solid substance used in photography. Formula: KCN.

potassium hydrogen tartrate *n* a white soluble crystalline salt used in baking powders, soldering fluxes, and laxatives. Formula: $KHC_4H_4O_6$. Also called: **cream of tartar.**

potassium hydroxide *n* a white deliquescent alkaline solid used in the manufacture of soap, liquid shampoos, and detergents. Formula: KOH.

potassium nitrate *n* a colourless or white crystalline compound used in gunpowders, pyrotechnics, fertilizers, and as a preservative for foods (**E 252**). Formula: KNO_3. Also called: **saltpetre, nitre.**

potassium permanganate *n* a dark purple poisonous odourless soluble crystalline solid, used as a bleach, disinfectant, and antiseptic. Formula: $KMnO_4$. Systematic name: **potassium manganate(VII).**

potation (pəʊ'teɪʃən) *n* **1** the act of drinking. **2** a drink or draught, esp. of alcoholic drink. [C15: from L *pōtātiō,* from *pōtāre* to drink]

potato (pə'teɪtəʊ) *n, pl* **potatoes. 1a** a plant of South America widely cultivated for its edible tubers. **1b** the starchy oval tuber of this plant, which has a brown or red skin and is cooked and eaten as a vegetable. **2** any of various similar plants, esp. the sweet potato. [C16: from Sp. *patata* white potato, from Taino *batata* sweet potato]

potato beetle *n* another name for the **Colorado beetle.**

potato chip *n* (*usually pl*) **1** another name for **chip** (sense 4). **2** the US, Canad., Austral., and NZ term for **crisp** (sense 10).

potato crisp *n* (*usually pl*) another name for **crisp** (sense 10).

potbelly ➊ ('pɒtˌbelɪ) *n, pl* **potbellies. 1** a protruding or distended belly. **2** a person having such a belly.
▸'**potˌbellied** *adj*

potboiler ('pɒtˌbɔɪlə) *n Inf.* an artistic work of little merit produced quickly to make money.

pot-bound *adj* (of a pot plant) having grown to fill all the available root space and therefore lacking room for continued growth.

potboy ('pɒtˌbɔɪ) *or* **potman** ('pɒtmən) *n, pl* **potboys** *or* **potmen.** *Chiefly Brit.* (esp. formerly) a man employed at a public house to serve beer, etc.

potch (pɒtʃ) *n Chiefly Austral., sl.* inferior quality opal. [C20: from ?]

poteen ('pɒtiːn) *or* **poitín** (pɒ'tʃiːn) *n* (in Ireland) illicit spirit, often distilled from potatoes. [C19: from Irish *poitín* little pot, from *pota* pot]

potent[1] ➊ ('pəʊtᵊnt) *adj* **1** possessing great strength; powerful. **2** (of arguments, etc.) persuasive or forceful. **3** influential or authoritative. **4** tending to produce violent physical or chemical effects: *a potent poison.* **5** (of a male) capable of having sexual intercourse. [C15: from L *potēns* able, from *posse* to be able]
▸'**potency** *or* '**potence** *n* ▸'**potently** *adv*

potent[2] ('pəʊtᵊnt) *adj Heraldry.* (of a cross) having flat bars across the ends of the arms. [C17: from obs. *potent* a crutch, from L *potentia* power]

potentate ➊ ('pəʊtᵊnˌteɪt) *n* a ruler or monarch. [C14: from LL *potentātus,* from L: rule, from *potens* powerful, from *posse* to be able]

potential ➊ (pə'tenʃəl) *adj* **1a** possible but not yet actual. **1b** (*prenominal*) capable of being or becoming; latent. **2** *Grammar.* (of a verb) expressing possibility, as English *may* and *might.* ◆ *n* **3** latent but unrealized ability: *Jones has great potential as a sales manager.* **4** *Grammar.* a potential verb or verb form. **5** short for **electric potential.** [C14: from OF *potencial,* from LL *potentiālis,* from L *potentia* power]
▸**po'tentially** *adv*

potential difference *n* the difference in electric potential between two points in an electric field; the work that has to be done in trans-

THESAURUS

postulate *vb* **1, 3** = **presuppose,** advance, assume, hypothesize, posit, predicate, propose, put forward, suppose, take for granted, theorize

posture *n* **1, 2** = **bearing,** attitude, carriage, disposition, mien (*literary*), pose, position, set, stance **4** = **attitude,** disposition, feeling, frame of mind, inclination, mood, outlook, point of view, stance, standpoint **5** = **state,** circumstance, condition, mode, phase, position, situation ◆ *vb* **8** = **show off** (*inf.*), affect, attitudinize, do for effect, hot-dog (*chiefly US*), make a show, pose, put on airs, try to attract attention

posy *n* **1** = **bouquet,** boutonniere, buttonhole, corsage, nosegay, spray

pot[1] *n* **1** = **container,** bowl, crock, jug, pan, urn, utensil, vase, vessel **5** = **pool,** bank, jackpot, kitty, stakes **10** *Informal* = **trophy,** cup **13** = **paunch,** beer belly *or* gut (*inf.*), bulge, corporation (*inf.*), gut, potbelly, spare tyre (*Brit. sl.*), spread (*inf.*) **14 go to pot** = **decline,** deteriorate, go downhill (*inf.*), go to rack and ruin, go to the dogs (*inf.*), run to seed, slump, worsen ◆ *vb* **19** = **shoot,** hit, plug (*inf.*), strike

potbellied *adj* **1** = **fat,** bloated, corpulent, distended, obese, overweight, paunchy

potbelly *n* **1** = **paunch,** beer belly (*inf.*), corporation (*inf.*), gut, middle-age spread (*inf.*), pot, spare tyre (*Brit. sl.*), spread (*inf.*)

potency *n* **1, 3** = **power,** authority, capacity, control, effectiveness, efficacy, energy, force, influence, might, muscle, potential, puissance, strength, sway, vigour

potent[1] *adj* **1** = **strong,** efficacious, forceful, mighty, powerful, puissant, vigorous **2** = **persuasive,** cogent, compelling, convincing, effective, forceful, impressive, telling **3** = **powerful,** authoritative, commanding, dominant, dynamic, influential
Antonyms *adj* ≠ **strong:** impotent, weak ≠ **persuasive:** ineffective, unconvincing

potentate *n* = **ruler,** emperor, king, mogul, monarch, overlord, prince, sovereign

potential *adj* **1** = **possible,** budding, dormant, embryonic, future, hidden, inherent, latent, likely, promising, undeveloped, unrealized ◆ *n* **3** = **ability,** aptitude, capability, capacity, possibility, potentiality, power, the makings, what it takes (*inf.*), wherewithal ferring unit positive charge from one point to the other, measured in volts. Abbrev.: **pd.**

potential energy *n* the energy of a body or system as a result of its position in an electric, magnetic, or gravitational field. Abbrev.: **PE.**

potentiality ➊ (pə,tɛnʃɪ'ælɪtɪ) *n, pl* **potentialities. 1** latent or inherent capacity for growth, fulfilment, etc. **2** a person or thing that possesses this.

potentiate (pə'tɛnʃɪ,eɪt) *vb* **potentiates, potentiating, potentiated.** *(tr)* **1** to cause to be potent. **2** *Med.* to increase (the individual action or effectiveness) of two drugs by administering them in combination.

potentilla (,pəutᵊn'tɪlə) *n* any rosaceous plant or shrub of the N temperate genus *Potentilla,* having five-petalled flowers. [C16: NL, from Med. L: garden valerian, from L *potēns* powerful]

potentiometer (pə,tɛnʃɪ'ɒmɪtə) *n* **1** an instrument for determining a potential difference of electromotive force. **2** a device used in electronic circuits, esp. as a volume control. Sometimes shortened to **pot.**
▸**po,tenti'ometry** *n*

potful ('pɒtful) *n* the amount held by a pot.

pother ('pɒðə) *n* **1** a commotion, fuss, or disturbance. **2** a choking cloud of smoke, dust, etc. ◆ *vb* **3** to make or be troubled or upset. [C16: from ?]

potherb ('pɒt,hɜːb) *n* any plant having leaves, flowers, stems, etc., that are used in cooking.

pothole ('pɒt,həul) *n* **1** *Geog.* **1a** a deep hole in limestone areas resulting from action by running water. **1b** a circular hole in the bed of a river produced by abrasion. **2** a deep hole produced in a road surface by wear or weathering.

potholing ('pɒt,həulɪŋ) *n Brit.* a sport in which participants explore underground caves.
▸**'pot,holer** *n*

pothook ('pɒt,huk) *n* **1** a curved or S-shaped hook used for suspending a pot over a fire. **2** a long hook used for lifting hot pots, lids, etc. **3** an S-shaped mark, often made by children when learning to write.

pothouse ('pɒt,haus) *n Brit.* (formerly) a small tavern or pub.

pothunter ('pɒt,hʌntə) *n* **1** a person who hunts for profit without regard to the rules of sport. **2** *Inf.* a person who enters competitions for the sole purpose of winning prizes.

potion ➊ ('pəuʃən) *n* a drink, esp. of medicine, poison, or some supposedly magic beverage. [C13: via OF from L *pōtiō* a drink, esp. a poisonous one, from *pōtāre* to drink]

potlatch ('pɒt,lætʃ) *n Anthropol.* a competitive ceremonial activity among certain North American Indians, involving a lavish distribution of gifts to emphasize the wealth and status of the chief or clan. [C19: of Amerind origin, from *patshatl* a present]

pot luck *n Inf.* **1** whatever food happens to be available without special preparation. **2** whatever is available (esp. in **take pot luck**).

pot marigold *n* a Central European and Mediterranean plant grown for its rayed orange-and-yellow showy flowers.

potometer (pə'tɒmɪtə) *n* an apparatus that measures the rate of water uptake by a plant or plant part. [from L *pōtāre* to drink + -METER]

potoroo (,pɒtə'ruː) *n* another name for **kangaroo rat.** [from Abor.]

potpourri ➊ (,pəu'puərɪ) *n, pl* **potpourris. 1** a collection of mixed flower petals dried and preserved in a pot to scent the air. **2** a collection of unrelated items; miscellany. **3** a medley of popular tunes. [C18: from F, lit.: rotten pot, translation of Sp. *olla podrida* miscellany]

pot roast *n* meat cooked slowly in a covered pot with very little water.

potsherd ('pɒt,ʃɜːd) *or* **potshard** ('pɒt,ʃɑːd) *n* a broken fragment of pottery. [C14: from POT[1] + *schoord* piece of broken crockery; see SHARD]

pot shot *n* **1** a chance shot taken casually, hastily, or without careful aim. **2** a shot fired to kill game in disregard of the rules of sport. **3** a shot fired at quarry within easy range.

pot still *n* a type of still in which heat is applied directly to the pot in which the wash is contained: used in distilling whisky.

pottage ('pɒtɪdʒ) *n* a thick soup. [C13: from OF *potage* contents of a pot, from *pot* POT[1]]

potted ('pɒtɪd) *adj* **1** placed or grown in a pot. **2** cooked or preserved in a pot: *potted shrimps.* **3** *Inf.* abridged: *a potted version of a novel.*

potter[1] ('pɒtə) *n* a person who makes pottery.

potter[2] ➊ ('pɒtə) *or esp. US & Canad.* **putter** *vb* **1** *(intr;* often foll. by *about* or *around)* to busy oneself in a desultory though agreeable manner. **2** *(intr;* often foll. by *along* or *about)* to move with little energy or direction: *to potter about town.* **3** *(tr;* usually foll. by *away)* to waste (time): *to potter the day away.* [C16 (in the sense: to poke repeatedly): from OE *potian* to thrust]
▸**'potterer** *or esp. US* **'putterer** *n*

Potteries ('pɒtərɪz) *pl n* **the.** *(sometimes functioning as sing)* a region of W central England, in Staffordshire, in which the china industries are concentrated.

potter's field *n* **1** *New Testament.* the land bought by the Sanhedrin with the money paid for the betrayal of Jesus, to be used as a burial place for strangers (Acts 1:19; Matthew 27:7). **2** *US.* a cemetery where the poor or unidentified are buried at the public's expense.

potter's wheel *n* a device with a horizontal rotating disc, on which clay is shaped by hand.

pottery ➊ ('pɒtərɪ) *n, pl* **potteries. 1** articles made from earthenware and baked in a kiln. **2** a place where such articles are made. **3** the craft or business of making such articles. [C15: from OF *poterie,* from *potier* potter, from *pot* POT[1]]

potting shed *n* a building in which plants are set in flowerpots and in which empty pots, potting compost, etc., are stored.

pottle ('pɒtᵊl) *n Arch.* a liquid measure equal to half a gallon. [C14 *potel,* from OF: a small POT[1]]

potto ('pɒtəu) *n, pl* **pottos.** a short-tailed prosimian primate having vertebral spines protruding through the skin in the neck region. Also called: **kinkajou.** [C18: of W African origin]

Pott's disease (pɒts) *n* a disease of the spine, characterized by weakening and gradual disintegration of the vertebrae. [C18: after Percivall *Pott* (1714–88), Brit. surgeon]

Pott's fracture *n* a fracture of the lower part of the fibula, usually with the dislocation of the ankle. [C18: see POTT'S DISEASE]

potty[1] ➊ ('pɒtɪ) *adj* **pottier, pottiest.** *Brit. inf.* **1** foolish or slightly crazy. **2** trivial or insignificant. **3** (foll. by *about)* very keen (on). [C19: ?from POT[1]]
▸**'pottiness** *n*

potty[2] ('pɒtɪ) *n, pl* **potties.** a child's word for **chamber pot.**

pouch ➊ (pautʃ) *n* **1** a small flexible baglike container: *a tobacco pouch.* **2** a saclike structure in any of various animals, such as the cheek fold in rodents. **3** *Anat.* any sac, pocket, or pouchlike cavity. **4** a Scot. word for **pocket.** ◆ *vb* **5** *(tr)* to place in or as if in a pouch. **6** to arrange or become arranged in a pouchlike form. **7** *(tr)* (of certain birds and fishes) to swallow. [C14: from OF *pouche,* from OF *poche* bag]
▸**'pouchy** *adj*

pouf *or* **pouffe** (puːf) *n* **1** a large solid cushion used as a seat. **2a** a woman's hairstyle, fashionable esp. in the 18th century, in which the hair is piled up in rolled puffs. **2b** a pad set in the hair to make such puffs. **3** *(also* pʊf). *Brit. derog. sl.* less common spellings of **poof.** [C19: from F]

poulard *or* **poularde** ('puːlɑːd) *n* a hen that has been spayed for fattening. Cf. **capon.** [C18: from OF *pollarde,* from *polle* hen]

poult (pəult) *n* the young of a gallinaceous bird, esp. of domestic fowl. [C15: var. of *poulet* PULLET]

poulterer ('pəultərə) *n Brit.* another word for a **poultryman.** [C17: from obs. *poulter,* from OF *pouletier,* from *poulet* PULLET]

poultice ('pəultɪs) *n Med.* a local moist and often heated application for the skin used to improve the circulation, treat inflamed areas, etc. [C16: from earlier *pultes,* from L *puls* a thick porridge]

poultry ('pəultrɪ) *n* domestic fowls collectively. [C14: from OF *pouletrie,* from *pouletier* poultry dealer]

poultryman ('pəultrɪmən) *or* **poulterer** *n, pl* **poultrymen** *or* **poulterers. 1** Also called: **chicken farmer.** a person who rears domestic fowls for their eggs or meat. **2** a dealer in poultry.

pounce[1] ➊ (pauns) *vb* **pounces, pouncing, pounced. 1** *(intr;* often foll. by *on* or *upon)* to spring or swoop, as in capturing prey. ◆ *n* **2** the act of pouncing; a spring or swoop. **3** the claw of a bird of prey. [C17: apparently from ME *punson* pointed tool]
▸**'pouncer** *n*

pounce[2] (pauns) *n* **1** a very fine resinous powder, esp. of cuttlefish bone, formerly used to dry ink. **2** a fine powder, esp. of charcoal, that is tapped through perforations in paper in order to transfer the design to another surface. ◆ *vb* **pounces, pouncing, pounced.** *(tr)* **3** to dust (paper) with pounce. **4** to transfer (a design) by means of pounce. [C18: from OF *ponce,* from L *pūmex* pumice]

pouncet box ('paunsɪt) *n* a box with a perforated top used for perfume. [C16 *pouncet,* ? alteration of *pounced* perforated]

pound[1] ➊ (paund) *vb* **1** (when *intr,* often foll. by *on* or *at)* to strike heavily and often. **2** *(tr)* to beat to a pulp; pulverize. **3** *(tr;* foll. by *out)* to produce, as by typing heavily. **4** to walk or move with heavy steps or thuds. **5** *(intr)* to throb heavily. ◆ *n* **6** the act of pounding. [OE *pūnian*]
▸**'pounder** *n*

pound[2] (paund) *n* **1** an avoirdupois unit of weight that is divided into 16 ounces and is equal to 0.453 592 kilograms. Abbrev.: **lb. 2** a troy unit of weight divided into 12 ounces equal to 0.373 242 kilograms.

THESAURUS

potentiality *n* **1** = **capacity**, ability, aptitude, capability, likelihood, potential, promise, prospect, the makings

potion *n* = **concoction**, brew, cup, dose, draught, elixir, mixture, philtre, tonic

potpourri *n* **2** = **mixture**, collection, combination, gallimaufry, hotchpotch, medley, *mélange,* miscellany, mixed bag *(inf.),* motley, pastiche, patchwork, salmagundi

potter[2] *vb* **1** = **mess about**, dabble, fiddle *(inf.),* footle *(inf.),* fribble, fritter, poke along, tinker

pottery *n* **1** = **ceramics**, earthenware, stoneware, terracotta

potty[1] *adj Brit. informal* **1** = **crazy**, barmy, crackpot *(inf.),* daft *(inf.),* dippy *(sl.),* dotty *(sl., chiefly Brit.),* eccentric, foolish, loopy *(inf.),* oddball *(inf.),* silly, soft *(inf.),* touched, up the pole *(inf.)* **2** = **trivial**, footling *(inf.),* insignificant, petty, piddling, trifling

pouch *n* **1** = **bag**, container, pocket, poke *(dialect),* purse, sack

pounce[1] *vb* **1** = **spring**, ambush, attack, bound onto, dash at, drop, fall upon, jump, leap at, snatch, strike, swoop, take by surprise, take unawares ◆ *n* **2** = **spring**, assault, attack, bound, jump, leap, swoop

pound[1] *vb* **1** = **beat**, batter, beat the living daylights out of, belabour, clobber *(sl.),* hammer, pelt, pummel, strike, thrash, thump **2** = **crush**, bray *(dialect),* bruise, comminute, powder, pulverize, triturate **3** *with* **out** = **thump**, bang, beat, hammer **4** = **stomp** *(inf.),* clomp, march, thunder, tramp **5** = **pulsate**, beat, palpitate, pitapat, pulse, throb

3a the standard monetary unit of the United Kingdom, divided into 100 pence. Official name: **pound sterling. 3b** (*as modifier*): *a pound coin.* **4** the standard monetary unit of various other countries, including Cyprus, Egypt, Israel, and Syria. **5** Also called: **pound Scots.** a former Scottish monetary unit originally worth an English pound but later declining in value to 1 shilling 8 pence. [OE *pund,* from L *pondō*]

pound[3] ❶ (paʊnd) *n* **1** an enclosure for keeping officially removed vehicles or distrained goods or animals, esp. stray dogs. **2** a place where people are confined. **3** a trap for animals. ◆ *vb* **4** (*tr*) to confine in or as if in a pound; impound, imprison, or restrain. [C14: from LOE *pund-*, as in *pundfeald* PINFOLD]

poundage (ˈpaʊndɪdʒ) *n* **1** a charge of so much per pound of weight. **2** a charge of so much per pound sterling. **3** a weight expressed in pounds.

poundal (ˈpaʊndᵊl) *n* the fps unit of force; the force that imparts an acceleration of 1 foot per second per second to a mass of 1 pound. Abbrev.: **pdl.** [C19: from POUND[2] + QUINTAL]

pound cost averaging *n Stock Exchange.* a method of accumulating capital by investing a fixed sum in a particular security at regular intervals, in order to achieve an average purchase price below the arithmetic average of the market prices on the purchase dates.

-pounder (ˈpaʊndə) *n* (*in combination*) **1** something weighing a specified number of pounds: *a 200-pounder.* **2** something worth a specified number of pounds: *a ten-pounder.* **3** a gun that discharges a shell weighing a specified number of pounds: *a two-pounder.*

pound sterling *n* See **pound**[2] (sense 3).

pour ❶ (pɔː) *vb* **1** to flow or cause to flow in a stream. **2** (*tr*) to emit in a profuse way. **3** (*intr;* often foll. by *down*) Also: **pour with rain.** to rain heavily. **4** (*intr*) to move together in large numbers; swarm. **5** (*intr*) to serve tea, coffee, etc.: *shall I pour?* **6 it never rains but it pours.** events, esp. unfortunate ones, come in rapid succession. **7 pour oil on troubled waters.** to calm a quarrel, etc. ◆ *n* **8** a pouring, downpour, etc. [C13: from ?]
▸ˈ**pourer** *n*

> **USAGE NOTE** The verbs *pour* and *pore* are sometimes confused: *she poured cream over her strudel; she pored* (not *poured*) *over the manuscript.*

pourboire *French.* (purbwar) *n* a tip; gratuity. [lit.: for drinking]

poussin (*French* pusɛ̃) *n* a young chicken reared for eating. [from F]

pout[1] ❶ (paʊt) *vb* **1** to thrust out (the lips), as when sullen or (of the lips) to be thrust out. **2** (*intr*) to swell out; protrude. **3** (*tr*) to utter with a pout. ◆ *n* **4** Also: **the pouts.** a fit of sullenness. **5** the act or state of pouting. [C14: from ?]
▸ˈ**poutingly** *adv*

pout[2] (paʊt) *n, pl* **pout** *or* **pouts. 1** short for **eelpout. 2** Also called: **horned pout.** a N American catfish with barbels round the mouth. **3** any of various gadoid food fishes. [OE *-pūte,* as in *ǣlepūte* eelpout]

pouter (ˈpaʊtə) *n* **1** a person or thing that pouts. **2** a breed of domestic pigeon with a large crop capable of being greatly puffed out.

poverty ❶ (ˈpɒvətɪ) *n* **1** the condition of being without adequate food, money, etc. **2** scarcity: *a poverty of wit.* **3** a lack of elements conducive to fertility in soil. [C12: from OF *povertė,* from L *paupertās* restricted means, from *pauper* poor]

poverty-stricken ❶ *adj* suffering from extreme poverty.

poverty trap *n* the situation of being unable to raise one's living standard because one is dependent on state benefits which are reduced or withdrawn if one gains any extra income.

pow (paʊ) *interj* an exclamation imitative of a collision, explosion, etc.

POW *abbrev. for* prisoner of war.

powan (ˈpaʊən) *n* a freshwater whitefish occurring in some Scottish lakes. [C17: Scot. var. of POLLAN]

powder ❶ (ˈpaʊdə) *n* **1** a substance in the form of tiny loose particles. **2** any of various preparations in this form, such as gunpowder, face powder, or soap powder. ◆ *vb* **3** to turn into powder; pulverize. **4** (*tr*) to cover or sprinkle with or as if with powder. [C13: from OF *poldre,* from L *pulvis* dust]
▸ˈ**powderer** *n* ▸ˈ**powdery** *adj*

powder blue *n* a dusty pale blue colour.

powder burn *n* a superficial burn of the skin caused by a momentary intense explosion.

powder flask *n* a small flask or case formerly used to carry gunpowder.

powder horn *n* a powder flask consisting of the hollow horn of an animal.

powder keg *n* **1** a small barrel to hold gunpowder. **2** a potential source of violence, disaster, etc.

powder metallurgy *n* the science and technology of producing solid metal components from metal powder by compaction and sintering.

powder monkey *n* (formerly) a boy who carried powder from the magazine to the guns on warships.

powder puff *n* a soft pad of fluffy material used for applying cosmetic powder to the skin.

powder room *n* a ladies' cloakroom.

powdery mildew *n* a plant disease characterized by a white powdery growth on stems and leaves, caused by parasitic fungi.

power ❶ (ˈpaʊə) *n* **1** ability to do something. **2** (*often pl*) a specific ability, capacity, or faculty. **3** political, financial, social, etc., force or influence. **4** control or dominion or a position of control, dominion, or authority. **5** a state or other political entity with political, industrial, or military strength. **6** a person or group that exercises control, influence, or authority: *he's a power in the state.* **7** a prerogative, privilege, or liberty. **8** legal authority to act for another. **9a** a military force. **9b** military potential. **10** *Maths.* **10a** the value of a number or quantity raised to some exponent. **10b** another name for **exponent** (sense 4). **11** *Physics, engineering.* a measure of the rate of doing work expressed as the work done per unit time. It is measured in watts, horsepower, etc. **12a** the rate at which electrical energy is fed into or taken from a device or system. It is measured in watts. **12b** (*as modifier*): *a power amplifier.* **13** the ability to perform work. **14a** mechanical energy as opposed to manual labour. **14b** (*as modifier*): *a power tool.* **15** a particular form of energy: *nuclear power.* **16a** a measure of the ability of a lens or optical system to magnify an object. **16b** another word for **magnification. 17** *Inf.* a large amount: *a power of good.* **18 in one's power.** (*often foll. by an infinitive*) able or allowed (to). **19 in (someone's) power.** under the control of (someone). **20 the powers that be.** established authority. ◆ *vb* **21** (*tr*) to give or provide power to. **22** (*tr*) to fit (a machine) with a motor or engine. **23** *Inf.* to move or cause to move by the exercise of physical power. [C13: from Anglo-Norman *poer,* from Vulgar L *potēre* (unattested), from L *posse* to be able]

power amplifier *n Electronics.* an amplifier that is usually the final amplification stage in a device and is designed to give the required power output.

powerboat (ˈpaʊəˌbəʊt) *n* a boat, esp. a fast one, propelled by an inboard or outboard motor.

powerboating (ˈpaʊəˌbəʊtɪŋ) *n* the sport of driving powerboats in racing competitions.

power cut *n* a temporary interruption or reduction in the supply of electrical power.

power dive *n* **1** a steep dive by an aircraft with its engines at high power. ◆ *vb* **power-dive, power-dives, power-diving, power-dived. 2** to cause (an aircraft) to perform a power dive or (of an aircraft) to perform a power dive.

power dressing *n* a style of dressing in severely tailored suits, adopted by some women executives to project an image of efficiency.

powerful ❶ (ˈpaʊəfʊl) *adj* **1** having great power. **2** extremely effective or efficient: *a powerful drug.* ◆ *adv* **3** *Dialect.* very: *he ran powerful fast.*
▸ˈ**powerfully** *adv* ▸ˈ**powerfulness** *n*

powerhouse (ˈpaʊəˌhaʊs) *n* **1** an electrical generating station or plant. **2** *Inf.* a forceful or powerful person or thing.

powerless ❶ (ˈpaʊəlɪs) *adj* without power or authority.
▸ˈ**powerlessly** *adv* ▸ˈ**powerlessness** *n*

power lunch *n* a high-powered business meeting conducted over lunch.

power of attorney *n* **1** legal authority to act for another person in certain specified matters. **2** the document conferring such authority.

power pack *n* a device for converting the current from a supply into

THESAURUS

pound[3] *n* **1** = **enclosure**, compound, corral (*chiefly US & Canad.*), pen, yard

pour *vb* **1, 2** = **flow**, course, emit, gush, run, rush, spew, spout, stream **3** = **rain**, bucket down (*inf.*), come down in torrents, pelt (down), rain cats and dogs (*inf.*), rain hard *or* heavily, sheet, teem **4** = **stream**, crowd, swarm, teem, throng **5** = **let flow**, decant, spill, splash

pout[1] *vb* **1** = **sulk**, glower, look petulant, look sullen, lour *or* lower, make a *moue*, mope, pull a long face, purse one's lips, turn down the corners of one's mouth ◆ *n* **5** = **sullen look**, glower, long face, *moue*

poverty *n* **1** = **pennilessness**, beggary, destitution, distress, hand-to-mouth existence, hardship, indigence, insolvency, necessitousness, necessity, need, pauperism, penury, privation, want **2** = **scarcity**, dearth, deficiency, insufficiency, lack, paucity, shortage **3** = **barrenness**, aridity, bareness, deficiency, infertility, meagreness, poorness, sterility, unfruitfulness
Antonyms *n* ≠ **pennilessness:** affluence, comfort, luxury, opulence, richness, wealth ≠ **scarcity:** abundance, plethora, sufficiency ≠ **barrenness:** fecundity, fertility, fruitfulness, productiveness

poverty-stricken *adj* = **penniless**, bankrupt, beggared, broke, destitute, dirt-poor (*inf.*), distressed, down and out, down at heel, flat broke (*inf.*), impecunious, impoverished, indigent, needy, on one's uppers, on the breadline, penurious, poor, short, skint (*Brit. sl.*)

powder *n* **1** = **dust**, fine grains, loose particles, pounce, talc ◆ *vb* **3** = **grind**, crush, granulate, pestle, pound, pulverize **4** = **dust**, cover, dredge, scatter, sprinkle, strew

powdery *adj* **1** = **fine**, chalky, crumbling, crumbly, dry, dusty, friable, grainy, granular, loose, pulverized, sandy

power *n* **1** = **ability**, capability, capacity, competence, competency, faculty, potential **3, 4** = **control**, ascendancy, authority, bottom, command, dominance, domination, dominion, influence, mastery, rule, sovereignty, supremacy, sway **7, 8** = **authority**, authorization, licence, prerogative, privilege, right, warrant
Antonyms *n* ≠ **ability:** inability, incapability, incapacity, incompetence

powerful *adj* **1** = **controlling**, authoritative, commanding, dominant, influential, prevailing, puissant, sovereign, supreme

powerless *adj* = **defenceless**, dependent, disenfranchised, disfranchised, ineffective, over a barrel (*inf.*), subject, tied, unarmed, vulnerable = **weak**, debilitated, disabled, etiolated, feeble, frail, helpless, impotent, incapable, incapacitated, ineffectual, infirm, paralysed, prostrate
Antonyms *adj* ≠ **weak:** able-bodied, fit, healthy, lusty, powerful, robust, strong, sturdy

direct or alternating current at the voltage required by a particular electrical or electronic device.

power plant *n* **1** the complex, including machinery, associated equipment, and the structure housing it, that is used in the generation of power, esp. electrical power. **2** the equipment supplying power to a particular machine.

power point *n* an electrical socket mounted on or recessed into a wall.

power-sharing *n* a political arrangement in which opposing groups in a society participate in government.

power station *n* an electrical generating station.

power steering *n* a form of steering used on vehicles, where the torque applied to the steering wheel is augmented by engine power. Also called: **power-assisted steering.**

power structure *n* the structure or distribution of power and authority in a community.

powwow ⓣ ('paʊ,waʊ) *n* **1** a talk, conference, or meeting. **2** a magical ceremony of certain North American Indians. **3** (among certain North American Indians) a medicine man. **4** a meeting of North American Indians. ◆ *vb* **5** (*intr*) to hold a powwow. [C17: of Amerind origin]

pox (pɒks) *n* **1** any disease characterized by the formation of pustules on the skin that often leave pockmarks when healed. **2** (usually preceded by *the*) an informal name for **syphilis. 3 a pox on (someone** *or* **something).** (*interj*) *Arch.* an expression of intense disgust or aversion. [C15: changed from *pocks*, pl. of POCK]

pozzuolana (,pɒtswə'lɑːnə) *or* **pozzolana** (,pɒtsə'lɑːnə) *n* **1** a type of porous volcanic ash used in making hydraulic cements. **2** any of various artificial substitutes for this ash used in cements. [C18: from It.: of *Pozzuoli*, port in SW Italy]

pp *abbrev. for:* **1** past participle. **2** (in formal correspondence) per pro. [L: *per procurationem*: by delegation to] ◆ **3** *Music. symbol for* pianissimo.

> **USAGE NOTE** In formal correspondence, when Brenda Smith is signing on behalf of Peter Jones, she should write *Peter Jones pp* (or *per pro*) *Brenda Smith*, not the other way about.

pp *or* **PP** *abbrev. for:* **1** parcel post. **2** post-paid. **3** (in prescriptions) post prandium. [L: after a meal] **4** prepaid.

PP *abbrev. for:* **1** Parish Priest. **2** past President.

pp. *abbrev. for* pages.

ppd *abbrev. for:* **1** post-paid. **2** prepaid.

PPE *abbrev. for* philosophy, politics, and economics: a university course.

ppm *Chem. abbrev. for* parts per million.

PPP *abbrev. for* purchasing power parity: a rate of exchange between two currencies that gives them equal purchasing powers in their own economies.

ppr *or* **p.pr.** *abbrev. for* present participle.

PPS *abbrev. for:* **1** parliamentary private secretary. **2** Also: **pps** post postscriptum. [L: after postscript; additional postscript]

PQ *abbrev. for:* **1** (in Canada) Parti Québecois. **2** Province of Quebec.

pr *abbrev. for:* **1** (*pl* **prs**) pair. **2** paper. **3** power.

Pr *the chemical symbol for* praseodymium.

PR *abbrev. for:* **1** proportional representation. **2** public relations. **3** Puerto Rico.

pr. *abbrev. for:* **1** price. **2** pronoun.

practicable ⓣ ('præktɪkəbᵊl) *adj* **1** capable of being done; feasible. **2** usable. [C17: from F *praticable*, from *pratiquer* to practise; see PRACTICAL] ▸**,practica'bility** *or* **'practicableness** *n* ▸**'practicably** *adv*

> **USAGE NOTE** See at **practical.**

practical ⓣ ('præktɪkᵊl) *adj* **1** of or concerned with experience or actual use; not theoretical. **2** of or concerned with ordinary affairs, work, etc. **3** adapted or adaptable for use. **4** of, involving, or trained by practice. **5** being such for all general purposes; virtual. ◆ *n* **6** an examination or lesson in a practical subject. [C17: from earlier *practic*, from F *pratique*, via LL from Gk *praktikos*, from *prassein* to experience] ▸**,practi'cality** *or* **'practicalness** *n*

> **USAGE NOTE** A distinction is usually made between *practical* and *practicable. Practical* refers to a person, idea, project, etc., as being more concerned with or relevant to practice than theory: *he is a very practical person; the idea had no practical application. Practicable* refers to a project or idea as being capable of being done or put into effect: *the plan was expensive, yet practicable.*

practical joke *n* a prank or trick usually intended to make the victim appear foolish. ▸**practical joker** *n*

practically ⓣ ('præktɪkəlɪ, -klɪ) *adv* **1** virtually; almost: *it rained practically every day.* **2** in actuality rather than in theory: *what can we do practically to help?*

practice ⓣ ('præktɪs) *n* **1** a usual or customary action: *it was his practice to rise at six.* **2** repetition of an activity in order to achieve mastery and fluency: *they had one last practice the day before the show.* **3** the condition of having mastery of a skill or activity through repetition (esp. in **in practice, out of practice**). **4** the exercise of a profession: *he set up practice as a lawyer.* **5** the act of doing something: *he put his plans into practice.* **6** the established method of conducting proceedings in a court of law. ◆ *vb* **practices, practicing, practiced. 7** the US spelling of **practise.** [C16: from Med. L *practicāre* to practise, from Gk *praktikē* practical work, from *prattein* to do]

practise ⓣ *or US* **practice** ('præktɪs) *vb* **practises, practising, practised** *or US* **practices, practicing, practiced. 1** to do or cause to do repeatedly in order to gain skill. **2** (*tr*) to do (something) habitually or frequently: *they practise ritual murder.* **3** to observe or pursue (something): *to practise Christianity.* **4** to work at (a profession, etc.): *he practises medicine.* [C15: see PRACTICE]

practised ⓣ *or US* **practiced** ('præktɪst) *adj* **1** expert; skilled; proficient. **2** acquired or perfected by practice.

practitioner (præk'tɪʃənə) *n* **1** a person who practises a profession or art. **2** *Christian Science.* a person authorized to practise spiritual healing. [C16: from *practician*, from OF, from *pratiquer* to PRACTISE]

prae- *prefix* an archaic variant of **pre-.**

praedial *or* **predial** ('priːdɪəl) *adj* **1** of or relating to land, farming, etc. **2** attached to or occupying land. [C16: from Med. L *praediālis*, from L *praedium* farm, estate]

praesidium (prɪ'sɪdɪəm) *n* a variant of **presidium.**

praetor *or esp. US* **pretor** ('priːtə, -tɔː) *n* (in ancient Rome) any of several senior magistrates ranking just below the consuls. [C15: from L: one who leads the way, prob. from *praeīre*, from *prae-* before + *īre* to go] ▸**prae'torian** *or* **pre'torian** *adj, n* ▸**'praetorship** *or* **'pretorship** *n*

pragmatic ⓣ (præg'mætɪk) *adj* **1** advocating behaviour dictated more by practical consequences than by theory. **2** *Philosophy.* of pragmatism. **3** involving everyday or practical business. **4** of or concerned with the affairs of a state or community. **5** *Rare.* meddlesome; officious. Also (for senses 3, 5): **pragmatical.** [C17: from LL *prāgmaticus*, from Gk *prāgmatikos* from *pragma* act, from *prattein* to do] ▸**prag,mati'cality** *n* ▸**prag'matically** *adv*

pragmatic sanction *n* an edict, decree, or ordinance issued with the force of fundamental law by a sovereign.

pragmatism ('prægmə,tɪzəm) *n* **1** action or policy dictated by consideration of the practical consequences rather than by theory. **2** *Philosophy.* the doctrine that the content of a concept consists only in its practical applicability. ▸**'pragmatist** *n, adj*

prairie ('prɛərɪ) *n* (*often pl*) a treeless grassy plain of the central US and S Canada. [C18: from F, from OF *praierie*, from L *prātum* meadow]

prairie chicken, fowl, grouse, *or* **hen** *n* either of two mottled brown-and-white grouse of North America.

THESAURUS

powwow *n* **1 = meeting,** chinwag (*Brit. inf.*), confab (*inf.*), confabulation, conference, congress, consultation, council, discussion, get-together (*inf.*), huddle (*inf.*), palaver, parley, seminar, talk ◆ *vb* **5 = meet,** confab (*inf.*), confer, discuss, get together, go into a huddle (*inf.*), palaver, parley, talk

practicability *n* **1 = feasibility,** advantage, operability, possibility, practicality, use, usefulness, value, viability, workability

practicable *adj* **1 = feasible,** achievable, attainable, doable, performable, possible, viable, within the realm of possibility, workable
Antonyms *adj* beyond the bounds of possibility, impossible, out of the question, unachievable, unattainable, unfeasible, unworkable

practical *adj* **1 = functional,** applied, efficient, empirical, experimental, factual, pragmatic, realistic, utilitarian **2 = sensible,** businesslike, down-to-earth, everyday, hard-headed, matter-of-fact, mundane, ordinary, realistic, workaday **3 = feasible,** doable, practicable, serviceable, sound, useful, workable **4 = skilled,** accomplished, efficient, experienced, proficient, qualified, seasoned, trained, veteran, working
Antonyms *adj* ≠ **functional:** impracticable, impractical, inefficient, speculative, theoretical, unpractical, unrealistic ≠ **sensible:** impractical, unrealistic ≠ **feasible:** impossible, impractical, unpractical, unsound, unworkable, useless ≠ **skilled:** inefficient, inexperienced, unaccomplished, unqualified, unskilled, untrained

practically *adv* **1 = almost,** all but, basically, close to, essentially, fundamentally, in effect, just about, nearly, to all intents and purposes, very nearly, virtually, well-nigh

practice *n* **1 = custom,** habit, method, mode, praxis, routine, rule, system, tradition, usage, use, usual procedure, way, wont **2 = rehearsal,** discipline, drill, exercise, preparation, repetition, study, training, work-out **4 = profession,** business, career, vocation, work **5 = use,** action, application, effect, exercise, experience, operation

practise *vb* **1 = rehearse,** discipline, drill, exercise, go over, go through, keep one's hand in, polish, prepare, repeat, study, train, warm up, work out **3 = do,** apply, carry out, follow, live up to, observe, perform, put into practice **4 = work at,** carry on, engage in, ply, pursue, specialize in, undertake

practised *adj* **1 = skilled,** able, accomplished, experienced, expert, proficient, qualified, seasoned, trained, versed
Antonyms *adj* amateurish, bungling, incompetent, inexperienced, inexpert, unqualified, unskilled, untrained

pragmatic *adj* **1, 3 = practical,** businesslike, down-to-earth, efficient, hard-headed, matter-of-fact, realistic, sensible, utilitarian
Antonyms *adj* airy-fairy, idealistic, impractical, inefficient, starry-eyed, stupid, theoretical, unprofessional, unrealistic

prairie dog *n* any of several rodents that live in large complex burrows in the prairies of North America. Also called: **prairie marmot.**
prairie oyster *n* a drink consisting of raw unbeaten egg, vinegar or Worcester sauce, salt, and pepper: a supposed cure for a hangover.
prairie schooner *n Chiefly US.* a horse-drawn covered wagon used in the 19th century to cross the prairies of North America.
prairie wolf *n* another name for **coyote.**
praise ❶ (preɪz) *n* **1** the act of expressing commendation, admiration, etc. **2** the rendering of homage and gratitude to a deity. **3 sing someone's praises.** to commend someone highly. ◆ *vb* **praises, praising, praised.** (*tr*) **4** to express commendation, admiration, etc., for. **5** to proclaim the glorious attributes of (a deity) with homage and thanksgiving. [C13: from OF *preisier,* from LL *pretiāre* to esteem highly, from L *pretium* prize]
praiseworthy ❶ ('preɪz,wɜ:ðɪ) *adj* deserving of praise; commendable. ▸**'praise,worthily** *adv* ▸**'praise,worthiness** *n*
Prakrit ('prɑ:krɪt) *n* any of the vernacular Indic languages as distinguished from Sanskrit: spoken from about 300 B.C. to the Middle Ages. [C18: from Sansk. *prākrta* original]
▸**Pra'kritic** *adj*
praline ('prɑ:li:n) *n* **1** a confection of nuts with caramelized sugar. **2** Also called: **sugared almond.** a sweet consisting of an almond encased in sugar. [C18: from F, after César de Choiseul, comte de Plessis-*Praslin* (1598–1675), F field marshal whose chef first concocted it]
pralltriller ('prɑ:l,trɪlə) *n* an ornament used in 18th-century music consisting of an inverted mordent with an added initial upper note. [G: bouncing trill]
pram[1] (præm) *n Brit.* a cotlike four-wheeled carriage for a baby. US term: **baby carriage.** [C19: shortened & altered from PERAMBULATOR]
pram[2] (prɑ:m) *n Naut.* a light tender with a flat bottom and a bow formed from the ends of the side and bottom planks meeting in a small raised transom. [C16: from MDu. *prame*]
prance ❶ (prɑ:ns) *vb* **prances, prancing, pranced. 1** (*intr*) to swagger or strut. **2** (*intr*) to caper, gambol, or dance about. **3** (*intr*) (of a horse) to move with high lively springing steps. **4** (*tr*) to cause to prance. ◆ *n* **5** the act or an instance of prancing. [C14 *prauncen,* from ?]
▸**'prancer** *n* ▸**'prancing** *adj*
prandial ('prændɪəl) *adj Facetious.* of or relating to a meal. [C19: from L *prandium* meal, luncheon]
prang (præŋ) *Chiefly Brit. sl.* ◆ *n* **1** an accident or crash in an aircraft, car, etc. **2** an aircraft bombing raid. ◆ *vb* **3** to crash or damage (an aircraft, car, etc.). **4** to damage (a town, etc.) by bombing. [C20: ? imit.]
prank[1] ❶ (præŋk) *n* a mischievous trick or joke. [C16: from ?]
▸**'prankish** *adj* ▸**'prankster** *n*
prank[2] (præŋk) *vb* **1** (*tr*) to dress or decorate showily or gaudily. **2** (*intr*) to make an ostentatious display. [C16: from MDu. *pronken*]
prase (preɪz) *n* a light green translucent variety of chalcedony. [C14: from F, from L *prasius* a leek-green stone, from Gk *prasios,* from *prason* a leek]
praseodymium (,preɪzɪəʊ'dɪmɪəm) *n* a malleable ductile silvery-white element of the lanthanide series of metals. Symbol: Pr; atomic no.: 59; atomic wt.: 140.91. [C20: NL, from Gk *prasios* of a leek-green colour + DIDYMIUM]
prate ❶ (preɪt) *vb* **prates, prating, prated. 1** (*intr*) to talk idly and at length; chatter. **2** (*tr*) to utter in an idle or empty way. ◆ *n* **3** idle or trivial talk; chatter. [C15: of Gmc origin]
▸**'prater** *n* ▸**'prating** *adj*
pratfall ('præt,fɔ:l) *n US & Canad. sl.* a fall upon one's buttocks. [C20: from C16 *prat* buttocks (from ?) + FALL]
pratincole ('prætɪŋ,kəʊl, 'preɪ-) *n* any of various swallow-like shore birds of the Old World, having long pointed wings, short legs, and a short bill. [C18: from NL *pratincola* field-dwelling, from L *prātum* meadow + *incola* inhabitant]
prattle ❶ ('præt°l) *vb* **prattles, prattling, prattled. 1** (*intr*) to talk in a foolish or childish way; babble. **2** (*tr*) to utter in a foolish or childish way. ◆ *n* **3** foolish or childish talk. [C16: from MLow G *pratelen* to chatter]
▸**'prattler** *n* ▸**'prattling** *adj*
prau (praʊ) *n* a variant of **proa.**
prawn (prɔ:n) *n* **1** any of various small edible marine decapod crustaceans having a slender flattened body with a long tail and two pairs of pincers. **2 come the raw prawn with.** *Austral. inf.* to attempt to deceive. [C15: from ?]
praxis ('præksɪs) *n, pl* **praxes** ('præksi:z) *or* **praxises. 1** the practice of a field of study, as opposed to the theory. **2** a practical exercise. **3** accepted practice or custom. [C16: via Med. L from Gk: deed, action, from *prassein* to do]
pray ❶ (preɪ) *vb* **1** (when *intr,* often foll. by *for;* when *tr, usually takes a clause as object*) to utter prayers (to God or other object of worship). **2** (when *tr, usually takes a clause as object or an infinitive*) to beg or implore: *she prayed to be allowed to go.* ◆ *sentence substitute.* **3** *Arch.* I beg you; please: *pray, leave us alone.* [C13: from OF *preier,* from L *precārī* to implore, from *prex* an entreaty]
prayer[1] ❶ (preə) *n* **1** a personal communication or petition addressed to a deity, esp. in the form of supplication, adoration, praise, contrition, or thanksgiving. **2** a similar personal communication that does not involve adoration, addressed to beings closely associated with a deity, such as saints. **3** the practice of praying: *prayer is our solution to human problems.* **4** (*often pl*) a form of devotion spent mainly or wholly praying: *morning prayers.* **5** (*cap. when part of a recognized name*) a form of words used in praying: *the Lord's Prayer.* **6** an object or benefit prayed for. **7** an earnest request or entreaty. [C13 *preiere,* from OF, from Med. L, from L *precārius* obtained by begging, from *prex* prayer]
▸**'prayerful** *adj*
prayer[2] ('preɪə) *n* a person who prays.
prayer book (preə) *n* a book containing the prayers used at church services or recommended for private devotions.
prayer rug (preə) *n* the small carpet on which a Muslim kneels and prostrates himself while saying his prayers. Also called: **prayer mat.**
prayer wheel (preə) *n Buddhism.* (esp. in Tibet) a wheel or cylinder inscribed with or containing prayers, each revolution of which is counted as an uttered prayer, so that such prayers can be repeated by turning it.
praying mantis *or* **mantid** *n* another name for **mantis.**
PRB *abbrev. for* Pre-Raphaelite Brotherhood.
pre- *prefix* before in time, position, etc.: *predate; pre-eminent.* [from L *prae* before]
preach ❶ (pri:tʃ) *vb* **1** to make known (religious truth) or give religious or moral instruction or exhortation in (sermons). **2** to advocate (a virtue, action, etc.), esp. in a moralizing way. [C13: from OF *prechier,* from Church L *praedicāre,* from L: to proclaim in public; see PREDICATE]
preacher ❶ ('pri:tʃə) *n* a person who preaches, esp. a Protestant clergyman.
preachify ('pri:tʃɪ,faɪ) *vb* **preachifies, preachifying, preachified.** (*intr*) *Inf.* to preach or moralize in a tedious manner.
▸**,preachifi'cation** *n*
preachment ('pri:tʃmənt) *n* **1** the act of preaching. **2** a tedious or pompous sermon.
preachy ❶ ('pri:tʃɪ) *adj* **preachier, preachiest.** *Inf.* inclined to or marked by preaching.
preacquisition profit (,pri:ækwɪ'zɪʃən) *n* the retained profit of a company earned before a takeover and therefore not eligible for distribution as a dividend to the shareholders of the acquiring company.
preamble ❶ (pri:'æmb°l) *n* **1** a preliminary or introductory statement, esp. attached to a statute setting forth its purpose. **2** a preliminary event, fact, etc. [C14: from OF *préambule,* from LL *praeambulum,* from L *prae-* before + *ambulāre* to walk]
preamplifier (pri:'æmplɪ,faɪə) *n* an electronic amplifier used to improve the signal-to-noise ratio of an electronic device. It boosts a low-level signal to an intermediate level before it is transmitted to the main amplifier.
prebend ('prɛbənd) *n* **1** the stipend assigned by a cathedral or collegiate church to a canon or member of the chapter. **2** the land, tithe, or other source of such a stipend. **3** a less common word for **prebendary. 4** *Church of England.* the office of a prebendary. [C15: from OF *prébende,* from Med. L *praebenda* stipend, from L *praebēre* to offer, from *prae* forth + *habēre* to have]
▸**prebendal** (prɪ'bɛnd°l) *adj*
prebendary ('prɛbəndərɪ, -drɪ) *n, pl* **prebendaries. 1** a canon or member of the chapter of a cathedral or collegiate church who holds a preb-

THESAURUS

praise *n* **1 = approval,** acclaim, acclamation, accolade, applause, approbation, cheering, commendation, compliment, congratulation, encomium, eulogy, good word, kudos, laudation, ovation, panegyric, plaudit, tribute **2 = thanks,** adoration, devotion, glory, homage, worship ◆ *vb* **4 = approve,** acclaim, admire, applaud, cheer, compliment, congratulate, crack up (*inf.*), cry up, eulogize, extol, honour, laud, pat on the back, pay tribute to, sing the praises of, take one's hat off to **5 = give thanks to,** adore, bless, exalt, glorify, magnify (*arch.*), pay homage to, worship
praiseworthy *adj* **= creditable,** admirable, commendable, estimable, excellent, exemplary, fine, honourable, laudable, meritorious, worthy
Antonyms *adj* condemnable, deplorable, despicable, discreditable, disgraceful, dishonourable, ignoble, reprehensible
prance *vb* **1 = strut,** parade, show off (*inf.*), stalk, swagger, swank (*inf.*) **2 = dance,** bound, caper, cavort, cut a rug (*inf.*), frisk, gambol, jump, leap, romp, skip, spring, trip
prank[1] *n* **= trick,** antic, caper, escapade, frolic, jape, lark, practical joke, skylarking (*inf.*)
prate *vb* **1, 2 = chatter,** babble, blather, blether, boast, brag, drivel, gab (*inf.*), gas (*inf.*), go on, jaw (*sl.*), rabbit (on) (*Brit. inf.*), waffle (*inf., chiefly Brit.*), witter (*inf.*), yak (*sl.*)
prattle *vb* **1 = chatter,** babble, blather, blether, clack, drivel, gabble, jabber, patter, rabbit (on) (*Brit. inf.*), rattle on, run on, twitter, waffle (*inf., chiefly Brit.*), witter (*inf.*)
pray *vb* **1 = say one's prayers,** offer a prayer, recite the rosary **2 = beg,** adjure, ask, beseech, call upon, crave, cry for, entreat, implore, importune, invoke, petition, plead, request, solicit, sue, supplicate, urge
prayer[1] *n* **1, 2 = orison,** communion, devotion, invocation, litany, supplication **7 = plea,** appeal, entreaty, petition, request, suit, supplication
preach *vb* **1 = deliver a sermon,** address, evangelize, exhort, orate **2 = lecture,** admonish, advocate, exhort, harangue, moralize, sermonize, urge
preacher *n* **= clergyman,** evangelist, minister, missionary, parson, revivalist
preachy *adj Informal* **= moralizing,** canting, didactic, edifying, holier-than-thou, homiletic, pharisaic, pietistic, pontifical, religiose, sanctimonious, self-righteous
preamble *n* **1 = introduction,** exordium, foreword, opening move, opening statement *or* re-

end. 2 *Church of England.* an honorary canon with the title of prebendary.

Precambrian *or* **Pre-Cambrian** (priːˈkæmbrɪən) *adj* **1** of, denoting, or formed in the earliest geological era, which lasted for about 4 000 000 000 years before the Cambrian period. ◆ *n* **2** **the.** the Precambrian era.

precancel (priːˈkænsᵊl) *vb* **precancels, precancelling, precancelled** *or US* **precancels, precanceling, precanceled.** (*tr*) to cancel (postage stamps) before placing them on mail.

precancerous *adj* (esp. of cells) displaying characteristics that may develop into cancer.

precarious ⓘ (prɪˈkɛərɪəs) *adj* **1** liable to failure or catastrophe; insecure; perilous. **2** *Arch.* dependent on another's will. [C17: from L *precārius* obtained by begging, from *prex* PRAYER[1]]
▸**preˈcariously** *adv* ▸**preˈcariousness** *n*

precast (ˈpriːˌkɑːst) *adj* (esp. of concrete when employed as a structural element in building) cast in a particular form before being used.

precaution ⓘ (prɪˈkɔːʃən) *n* **1** an action taken to avoid a dangerous or undesirable event. **2** caution practised beforehand; circumspection. [C17: from F, from LL *praecautiō*, from L, from *prae* before + *cavēre* to beware]
▸**preˈcautionary** *adj*

precede ⓘ (prɪˈsiːd) *vb* **precedes, preceding, preceded. 1** to go or be before (someone or something) in time, place, rank, etc. **2** (*tr*) to preface or introduce. [C14: via OF from L *praecēdere* to go before]

precedence ⓘ (ˈprɛsɪdəns) *or* **precedency** *n* **1** the act of preceding or the condition of being precedent. **2** the ceremonial order or priority to be observed on formal occasions: *the officers are seated according to precedence.* **3** a right to preferential treatment: *I take precedence over you.*

precedent ⓘ *n* (ˈprɛsɪdənt). **1** *Law.* a judicial decision that serves as an authority for deciding a later case. **2** an example or instance used to justify later similar occurrences. ◆ *adj* (prɪˈsiːdᵊnt, ˈprɛsɪdənt). **3** preceding.

precedented (ˈprɛsɪˌdɛntɪd) *adj* (of a decision, etc.) supported by having a precedent.

precedential (ˌprɛsɪˈdɛnʃəl) *adj* **1** of or serving as a precedent. **2** having precedence.

preceding ⓘ (prɪˈsiːdɪŋ) *adj* (*prenominal*) going or coming before; former.

precentor (prɪˈsɛntə) *n* **1** a cleric who directs the choral services in a cathedral. **2** a person who leads a congregation or choir in the sung parts of church services. [C17: from LL *praecentor*, from *prae* before + *canere* to sing]
▸**precentorial** (ˌpriːsɛnˈtɔːrɪəl) *adj* ▸**preˈcentorˌship** *n*

precept ⓘ (ˈpriːsɛpt) *n* **1** a rule or principle for action. **2** a guide or rule for morals; maxim. **3** a direction, esp. for a technical operation. **4** *Law.* **4a** a writ or warrant. **4b** (in England) an order to collect money under a rate. [C14: from L *praeceptum* injunction, from *praecipere* to admonish, from *prae* before + *capere* to take]
▸**preˈceptive** *adj*

preceptor (prɪˈsɛptə) *n Rare.* a tutor or instructor.
▸**preceptorial** (ˌpriːsɛpˈtɔːrɪəl) *or* **preˈceptoral** *adj* ▸**preˈceptress** *fem n*

precession (prɪˈsɛʃən) *n* **1** the act of preceding. **2** See **precession of the equinoxes. 3** the motion of a spinning body, such as a top, gyroscope, or planet, in which it wobbles so that the axis of rotation sweeps out a cone. [C16: from LL *praecessiō*, from L *praecādere* to precede]
▸**preˈcessional** *adj* ▸**preˈcessionally** *adv*

precession of the equinoxes *n* the slightly earlier occurrence of the equinoxes each year due to the slow continuous westward shift of the equinoctial points along the ecliptic.

precinct ⓘ (ˈpriːsɪŋkt) *n* **1a** an enclosed area or building marked by a fixed boundary such as a wall. **1b** such a boundary. **2** an area in a town, often closed to traffic, that is designed or reserved for a particular activity: *a shopping precinct.* **3** *US.* **3a** a district of a city for administrative or police purposes. **3b** a polling district. [C15: from Med. L *praecinctum* (something) surrounded, from L *praecingere* to gird around]

precincts ⓘ (ˈpriːsɪŋkts) *pl n* the surrounding region or area.

preciosity (ˌprɛʃɪˈɒsɪtɪ) *n, pl* **preciosities.** fastidiousness or affectation.

precious ⓘ (ˈprɛʃəs) *adj* **1** beloved; dear; cherished. **2** very costly or valuable. **3** very fastidious or affected, as in speech, manners, etc. **4** *Inf.* worthless: *you and your precious ideas!* ◆ *adv* **5** *Inf.* (intensifier): *there's precious little left.* [C13: from OF *precios*, from L *pretiōsus* valuable, from *pretium* price]
▸**ˈpreciously** *adv* ▸**ˈpreciousness** *n*

precious metal *n* gold, silver, or platinum.

precious stone *n* any of certain rare minerals, such as diamond, ruby, or opal, that are highly valued as gemstones.

precipice ⓘ (ˈprɛsɪpɪs) *n* **1** the steep sheer face of a cliff or crag. **2** the cliff or crag itself. [C16: from L *praecipitium* steep place, from *praeceps* headlong]
▸**ˈprecipiced** *adj*

precipitant (prɪˈsɪpɪtənt) *adj* **1** hasty or impulsive; rash. **2** rushing or falling rapidly or without heed. **3** abrupt or sudden. ◆ *n* **4** *Chem.* a substance that causes a precipitate to form.
▸**preˈcipitance** *or* **preˈcipitancy** *n*

precipitate ⓘ *vb* (prɪˈsɪpɪˌteɪt), **precipitates, precipitating, precipitated. 1** (*tr*) to cause to happen too soon; bring on. **2** to throw or fall from or as from a height. **3** to cause (moisture) to condense and fall as snow, rain, etc., or (of moisture, rain, etc.) to condense and fall thus. **4** *Chem.* to undergo or cause to undergo a process in which a dissolved substance separates from solution as a fine suspension of solid particles. ◆ *adj* (prɪˈsɪpɪtɪt). **5** rushing ahead. **6** done rashly or with undue haste. **7** sudden and brief. ◆ *n* (prɪˈsɪpɪtɪt). **8** *Chem.* a precipitated solid. [C16: from L *praecipitāre* to throw down headlong, from *praeceps* steep, from *prae* before + *caput* head]
▸**preˈcipitable** *adj* ▸**preˌcipitaˈbility** *n* ▸**preˈcipitately** *adv* ▸**preˈcipitator** *n*

precipitation (prɪˌsɪpɪˈteɪʃən) *n* **1** *Meteorol.* **1a** rain, snow, sleet, dew, etc., formed by condensation of water vapour in the atmosphere. **1b** the deposition of these on the earth's surface. **2** the formation of a chemical precipitate. **3** the act of precipitating or the state of being precipitated. **4** rash or undue haste.

precipitous ⓘ (prɪˈsɪpɪtəs) *adj* **1** resembling a precipice. **2** very steep. **3** hasty or precipitate.
▸**preˈcipitously** *adv* ▸**preˈcipitousness** *n*

USAGE NOTE The use of *precipitous* to mean *hasty* is thought by some people to be incorrect.

precis *or* **précis** ⓘ (ˈpreɪsiː) *n, pl* **precis** *or* **précis** (ˈpreɪsiːz). **1** a summary of a text; abstract. ◆ *vb* **2** (*tr*) to make a precis of. [C18: from F: PRECISE]

precise ⓘ (prɪˈsaɪs) *adj* **1** strictly correct in amount or value: *a precise sum.* **2** particular: *this precise location.* **3** using or operating with total accuracy: *precise instruments.* **4** strict in observance of rules, standards, etc.: *a precise mind.* [C16: from F *précis*, from L *praecīdere* to curtail, from *prae* before + *caedere* to cut]
▸**preˈcisely** *adv* ▸**preˈciseness** *n*

THESAURUS

marks, overture, preface, prelude, proem, prolegomenon

precarious *adj* **1** = **dangerous**, built on sand, chancy (*inf.*), dicey (*inf., chiefly Brit.*), dodgy (*Brit., Austral., & NZ inf.*), doubtful, dubious, hazardous, insecure, perilous, risky, shaky, slippery, touch and go, tricky, uncertain, unreliable, unsafe, unsettled, unstable, unsteady, unsure
Antonyms *adj* certain, dependable, reliable, safe, secure, stable, steady

precaution *n* **1** = **safeguard**, belt and braces (*inf.*), insurance, preventative measure, protection, provision, safety measure **2** = **forethought**, anticipation, care, caution, circumspection, foresight, providence, prudence, wariness

precede *vb* **1, 2** = **go before**, antecede, antedate, come first, forerun, go ahead of, head, herald, introduce, lead, pave the way, preface, take precedence, usher

precedence *n* **1, 3** = **priority**, antecedence, lead, pre-eminence, preference, primacy, rank, seniority, superiority, supremacy

precedent *n* **2** = **instance**, antecedent, authority, criterion, example, exemplar, model, paradigm, pattern, previous example, prototype, standard

preceding *adj* = **previous**, above, aforementioned, aforesaid, anterior, earlier, foregoing, former, past, prior

precept *n* **1** = **rule**, behest, canon, command, commandment, decree, dictum, direction, instruction, law, mandate, order, ordinance, principle, regulation, statute **2** = **maxim**, axiom, byword, dictum, guideline, motto, principle, rule, saying

precinct *n* **1** = **enclosure**, bound, boundary, confine, limit **2** = **area**, district, quarter, section, sector, zone

precincts *pl n* = **district**, borders, bounds, confines, environs, limits, milieu, neighbourhood, purlieus, region, surrounding area

precious *adj* **1** = **loved**, adored, beloved, cherished, darling, dear, dearest, fave (*inf.*), favourite, idolized, prized, treasured, valued **2** = **valuable**, choice, costly, dear, expensive, exquisite, fine, high-priced, inestimable, invaluable, priceless, prized, rare, recherché **3** = **affected**, alembicated, artificial, chichi, fastidious, overnice, overrefined, twee (*Brit. inf.*)

precipice *n* **1, 2** = **cliff**, bluff, brink, cliff face, crag, height, rock face, sheer drop, steep

precipitate *vb* **1** = **quicken**, accelerate, advance, bring on, dispatch, expedite, further, hasten, hurry, press, push forward, speed up, trigger **2** = **throw**, cast, discharge, fling, hurl, launch, let fly, send forth ◆ *adj* **5** = **swift**, breakneck, headlong, plunging, rapid, rushing, violent **6** = **hasty**, frantic, harum-scarum, heedless, hurried, ill-advised, impetuous, impulsive, indiscreet, madcap, precipitous, rash, reckless **7** = **sudden**, abrupt, brief, quick, unexpected, without warning

precipitous *adj* **2** = **sheer**, abrupt, dizzy, falling sharply, high, perpendicular, steep **3** = **hasty**, abrupt, careless, harum-scarum, heedless, hurried, ill-advised, precipitate, rash, reckless, sudden

precis *n* **1** = **summary**, abridgment, abstract, *aperçu*, compendium, condensation, digest, outline, résumé, rundown, sketch, synopsis ◆ *vb* **2** = **summarize**, abridge, abstract, compress, condense, outline, shorten, sum up

precise *adj* **1, 2** = **exact**, absolute, accurate, actual, clear-cut, correct, definite, explicit, express, fixed, literal, particular, specific, strict, unequivocal **4** = **strict**, careful, ceremonious, exact, fastidious, finicky, formal, inflexible, meticulous, nice, particular, prim, punctilious, puritanical, rigid, scrupulous, stiff
Antonyms *adj* ≠ **exact**: ambiguous, equivocal, incorrect, indefinite, indistinct, inexact, loose, vague ≠ **strict**: careless, flexible, haphazard, inexact, informal, relaxed, unceremonious

precisely *adv* **1, 2** = **exactly**, absolutely, accurately, bang, correctly, just, just so, literally, neither more nor less, on the button (*inf.*), plumb (*inf.*), slap (*inf.*), smack (*inf.*), square, squarely, strictly, to the letter

precision ⊙ (prɪˈsɪʒən) *n* **1** the quality of being precise; accuracy. **2** (*modifier*) characterized by a high degree of exactness: *precision grinding.* [C17: from L *praecīsiō* a cutting off; see PRECISE]
▸**preˈcisionism** *n* ▸**preˈcisionist** *n*

preclassical (priːˈklæsɪkᵊl) *adj* (of music, literature, etc.) before a period regarded as classical.

preclude ⊙ (prɪˈkluːd) *vb* **precludes, precluding, precluded.** (*tr*) **1** to exclude or debar. **2** to make impossible, esp. beforehand. [C17: from L *praeclūdere* to shut up, from *prae* before + *claudere* to close]
▸**preclusion** (prɪˈkluːʒən) *n* ▸**preclusive** (prɪˈkluːsɪv) *adj*

precocial (prɪˈkəʊʃəl) *adj* **1** denoting birds whose young, after hatching, are covered with down and capable of leaving the nest within a few days. ◆ *n* **2** a precocial bird. ◆ Cf. **altricial.**

precocious ⊙ (prɪˈkəʊʃəs) *adj* **1** ahead in development, such as the mental development of a child. **2** *Bot.* flowering or ripening early. [C17: from L *praecox,* from *prae* early + *coquere* to ripen]
▸**preˈcociously** *adv* ▸**preˈcociousness** *or* **precocity** (prɪˈkɒsɪtɪ) *n*

precognition (ˌpriːkɒgˈnɪʃən) *n Psychol.* the alleged ability to foresee future events. [C17: from LL *praecognitiō* foreknowledge, from *praecognoscere* to foresee]
▸**precognitive** (priːˈkɒgnɪtɪv) *adj*

preconceive ⊙ (ˌpriːkənˈsiːv) *vb* **preconceives, preconceiving, preconceived.** (*tr*) to form an idea of beforehand.
▸**preconception** (ˌpriːkənˈsɛpʃən) *n*

precondition ⊙ (ˌpriːkənˈdɪʃən) *n* **1** a necessary or required condition; prerequisite. ◆ *vb* **2** (*tr*) *Psychol.* to present successively two stimuli to (an organism) without reinforcement so that they become associated; if a response is then conditioned to the second stimulus on its own, the same response will be evoked by the first stimulus.

preconize *or* **preconise** (ˈpriːkəˌnaɪz) *vb* **preconizes, preconizing, preconized** *or* **preconises, preconising, preconised.** (*tr*) **1** to announce or commend publicly. **2** to summon publicly. **3** (of the pope) to approve the appointment of (a nominee) to one of the higher dignities in the Roman Catholic Church. [C15: from Med. L *praecōnīzāre* to make an announcement, from L *praecō* herald]
▸ˌ**preconiˈzation** *or* ˌ**preconiˈsation** *n*

precursor ⊙ (prɪˈkɜːsə) *n* **1** a person or thing that precedes and announces someone or something to come. **2** a predecessor. **3** a chemical substance that gives rise to another more important substance. [C16: from L *praecursor* one who runs in front, from *praecurrere,* from *prae* in front + *currere* to run]

precursory ⊙ (prɪˈkɜːsərɪ) *or* **precursive** *adj* **1** serving as a precursor. **2** preliminary.

pred. *abbrev. for* predicate.

predacious *or* **predaceous** (prɪˈdeɪʃəs) *adj* (of animals) habitually hunting and killing other animals for food. [C18: from L *praeda* plunder]
▸**preˈdaciousness, preˈdaceousness,** *or* **predacity** (prɪˈdæsɪtɪ) *n*

predate (priːˈdeɪt) *vb* **predates, predating, predated.** (*tr*) **1** to affix a date to (a document, paper, etc.) that is earlier than the actual date. **2** to assign a date to (an event, period, etc.) that is earlier than the actual or previously assigned date of occurrence. **3** to be or occur at an earlier date than; precede in time.

predation (prɪˈdeɪʃən) *n* a relationship between two species of animal in a community, in which one hunts, kills, and eats the other.

predator (ˈprɛdətə) *n* **1** any carnivorous animal. **2** a predatory person or thing.

predatory ⊙ (ˈprɛdətərɪ) *adj* **1** *Zool.* another word for **predacious. 2** of or characterized by plundering, robbing, etc. [C16: from L *praedātōrius* rapacious, from *praedārī* to pillage, from *praeda* booty]
▸ˈ**predatorily** *adv* ▸ˈ**predatoriness** *n*

predecease (ˌpriːdɪˈsiːs) *vb* **predeceases, predeceasing, predeceased.** to die before (some other person).

predecessor ⊙ (ˈpriːdɪˌsɛsə) *n* **1** a person who precedes another, as in an office. **2** something that precedes something else. **3** an ancestor. [C14: via OF from LL *praedēcessor,* from *prae* before + *dēcēdere* to go away]

predella (prɪˈdɛlə) *n, pl* **predelle** (-liː). **1** a painting or a series of small paintings in a long strip forming the lower edge of an altarpiece or the face of an altar step. **2** a platform in a church upon which the altar stands. [C19: from It.: step, prob. from OHG *bret* board]

predestinarian (ˌpriːdɛstɪˈnɛərɪən) *n* **1** a person who believes in divine predestination. ◆ *adj* **2** of or relating to predestination or those who believe in it.

predestinate *vb* (priːˈdɛstɪˌneɪt), **predestinates, predestinating, predestinated. 1** another word for **predestine.** ◆ *adj* (priːˈdɛstɪnɪt, -ˌneɪt). **2** predestined.

predestination ⊙ (priːˌdɛstɪˈneɪʃən) *n* **1** *Christian theol.* **1a** the act of God foreordaining every event from eternity. **1b** the doctrine or belief, esp. associated with Calvin, that the final salvation of some of mankind is foreordained from eternity by God. **2** the act of predestining or the state of being predestined.

predestine ⊙ (priːˈdɛstɪn) *or* **predestinate** *vb* **predestines, predestining, predestined** *or* **predestinates, predestinating, predestinated.** (*tr*) **1** to determine beforehand. **2** *Christian theol.* (of God) to decree from eternity (any event, esp. the final salvation of individuals). [C14: from L *praedestināre* to resolve beforehand]

predetermine ⊙ (ˌpriːdɪˈtɜːmɪn) *vb* **predetermines, predetermining, predetermined.** (*tr*) **1** to determine beforehand. **2** to influence or bias.
▸ˌ**predeˈterminable** *adj* ▸ˌ**predeˈterminate** *adj* ▸ˌ**predeˌtermiˈnation** *n*

predicable (ˈprɛdɪkəbᵊl) *adj* **1** capable of being predicated or asserted. ◆ *n* **2** a quality that can be predicated. **3** *Logic, obs.* any of the five Aristotelian classes of predicates, namely genus, species, difference, property, and relation. [C16: from L *praedicābilis,* from *praedicāre* to assert publicly; see PREDICATE]
▸ˌ**predicaˈbility** *n*

predicament ⊙ *n* **1** (prɪˈdɪkəmənt) a perplexing, embarrassing, or difficult situation. **2** (ˈprɛdɪkəmənt). *Logic.* a logical category. [C14: from LL *praedicāmentum* what is predicated, from *praedicāre* to announce; see PREDICATE]

predicant (ˈprɛdɪkənt) *adj* **1** of or relating to preaching. ◆ *n* **2** a member of a religious order founded for preaching, esp. a Dominican. [C17: from L *praedicāns* preaching, from *praedicāre* to say publicly; see PREDICATE]

predicate ⊙ *vb* (ˈprɛdɪˌkeɪt), **predicates, predicating, predicated.** (*mainly tr*) **1** (*also intr; when tr, may take a clause as object*) to declare or affirm. **2** to imply or connote. **3** (foll. by *on* or *upon*) *Chiefly US.* to base (a proposition, argument, etc.). **4** *Logic.* to assert (a property or condition) of the subject of a proposition. ◆ *n* (ˈprɛdɪkɪt). **5** *Grammar.* the part of a sentence in which something is asserted or denied of the subject of a sentence. **6** *Logic.* a term, property, or condition that is affirmed or denied concerning the subject of a proposition. ◆ *adj* (ˈprɛdɪkɪt). **7** of or relating to something that has been predicated. [C16: from L *praedicāre* to assert publicly, from *prae* in front + *dīcere* to say]
▸ˌ**prediˈcation** *n*

predicate calculus *n* the system of symbolic logic concerned not only with relations between propositions as wholes but also with the representation by symbols of individuals and predicates in propositions. See also **propositional calculus.**

predicative (prɪˈdɪkətɪv) *adj Grammar.* relating to or occurring within the predicate of a sentence: *a predicative adjective.* Cf. **attributive.**
▸**preˈdicatively** *adv*

predict ⊙ (prɪˈdɪkt) *vb* (*tr; may take a clause as object*) to state or make a declaration about in advance; foretell. [C17: from L *praedīcere* to mention beforehand]
▸**preˈdictable** *adj* ▸**preˌdictaˈbility** *n* ▸**preˈdictably** *adv* ▸**preˈdictive** *adj* ▸**preˈdictor** *n*

prediction ⊙ (prɪˈdɪkʃən) *n* **1** the act of predicting. **2** something predicted; a forecast.

predigest (ˌpriːdaɪˈdʒɛst, -dɪ-) *vb* (*tr*) to treat (food) artificially to aid subsequent digestion in the body.
▸ˌ**prediˈgestion** *n*

predikant (ˌprɛdɪˈkænt) *n* a minister in the Dutch Reformed Church,

THESAURUS

precision *n* **1** = **exactness,** accuracy, care, correctness, definiteness, dotting the i's and crossing the t's, exactitude, fidelity, meticulousness, nicety, particularity, preciseness, rigour

preclude *vb* **1, 2** = **prevent,** check, debar, exclude, forestall, hinder, inhibit, make impossible, make impracticable, obviate, prohibit, put a stop to, restrain, rule out, stop

precocious *adj* **1** = **advanced,** ahead, bright, developed, forward, quick, smart
Antonyms *adj* backward, dense, dull, retarded, slow, underdeveloped, unresponsive

preconceived *adj* = **presumed,** forejudged, predetermined, prejudged, premature, presupposed

preconception *n* = **preconceived idea** *or* **notion,** bias, notion, predisposition, prejudice, prepossession, presumption, presupposition

precondition *n* **1** = **necessity,** essential, must, prerequisite, requirement, *sine qua non*

precursor *n* **1** = **herald,** forerunner, harbinger, messenger, usher, vanguard **2** = **forerunner,** antecedent, forebear, originator, pioneer, predecessor

precursory *adj* **1, 2** = **preceding,** antecedent, introductory, prefatory, preliminary, preparatory, previous, prior

predatory *adj* **1** = **hunting,** carnivorous, predacious, rapacious, raptorial, ravening **2** = **rapacious,** despoiling, greedy, marauding, pillaging, plundering, ravaging, thieving, voracious, vulturine, vulturous

predecessor *n* **1** = **previous job holder,** antecedent, forerunner, former job holder, precursor, prior job holder **3** = **ancestor,** antecedent, forebear, forefather

predestination *n* **1, 2** = **fate,** destiny, doom, election (*Theology*), foreordainment, foreordination, lot, necessity, predetermination

predestined *adj* **1** = **fated,** doomed, foreordained, meant, predestinated, predetermined, pre-elected, preordained

predetermined *adj* **1** = **prearranged,** agreed, arranged in advance, cut and dried (*inf.*), decided beforehand, fixed, preplanned, set, settled, set up

predicament *n* **1** = **fix** (*inf.*), corner, dilemma, emergency, hole (*sl.*), hot water (*inf.*), how-do-you-do (*inf.*), jam (*inf.*), mess, pickle (*inf.*), pinch, plight, quandary, scrape (*inf.*), situation, spot (*inf.*), state, tight spot

predicate *vb* **1** = **declare,** affirm, assert, aver, avouch, avow, contend, maintain, proclaim, state **2** = **imply,** connote, indicate, intimate, signify, suggest **3** *Chiefly U.S. foll. by* **on** *or* **upon** = **base,** build, establish, found, ground, postulate, rest

predict *vb* = **foretell,** augur, call, divine, forebode, forecast, foresee, portend, presage, prognosticate, prophesy, soothsay, vaticinate (*rare*)

predictable *adj* = **likely,** anticipated, calculable, certain, expected, foreseeable, foreseen, on the cards, reliable, sure, sure-fire (*inf.*)
Antonyms *adj* out of the blue, surprising, unexpected, unforeseen, unlikely, unpredictable

prediction *n* **1, 2** = **prophecy,** augury, divina-

esp. in South Africa. [from Du., from OF *predicant,* from LL, from *praedicāre* to PREACH]

predilection ➊ (ˌpriːdɪˈlɛkʃən) *n* a predisposition, preference, or bias. [C18: from F *prédilection,* from Med. L *praedīligere* to prefer, from L *prae* before + *dīligere* to love]

predispose ➊ (ˌpriːdɪˈspəʊz) *vb* **predisposes, predisposing, predisposed.** (*tr*) (often foll. by *to* or *towards*) to incline or make (someone) susceptible to something beforehand.
▸ˌ**predisˈposal** *n* ▸ˌ**predispoˈsition** *n*

prednisolone (prɛdˈnɪsəˌləʊn) *n* a steroid drug derived from prednisone and having the same uses as cortisone. [C20: altered from PREDNISONE]

prednisone (ˈprɛdnɪˌsəʊn) *n* a steroid drug derived from cortisone and having the same uses. [C20: perhaps from PRE(GNANT) + -D(IE)N(E) + (CORT)ISONE]

predominant ➊ (prɪˈdɒmɪnənt) *adj* **1** superior in power, influence, etc., over others. **2** prevailing.
▸**preˈdominance** *n* ▸**preˈdominantly** *adv*

predominate ➊ *vb* (prɪˈdɒmɪˌneɪt), **predominates, predominating, predominated.** (*intr*) **1** (often foll. by *over*) to have power, influence, or control. **2** to prevail or preponderate. ◆ *adj* (prɪˈdɒmɪnɪt). **3** another word for **predominant.** [C16: from Med. L *praedominārī,* from L *prae* before + *dominārī* to bear rule]
▸**preˈdominately** *adv* ▸**preˌdomiˈnation** *n*

pre-eclampsia (ˌpriːɪˈklæmpsɪə) *n* a serious condition that can occur late in pregnancy. If not treated it can lead to eclampsia.

pre-embryo (priːˈɛmbrɪˌəʊ) *n, pl* **pre-embryos.** the structure formed after fertilization of an ovum but before differentiation of embryonic tissue.

pre-eminent ➊ (prɪˈɛmɪnənt) *adj* extremely eminent or distinguished; outstanding.
▸**pre-ˈeminence** *n* ▸**pre-ˈeminently** *adv*

pre-empt ➊ (prɪˈɛmpt) *vb* **1** (*tr*) to acquire in advance of or to the exclusion of others; appropriate. **2** (*tr*) *Chiefly US.* to occupy (public land) in order to acquire a prior right to purchase. **3** (*intr*) *Bridge.* to make a high opening bid, often on a weak hand, to shut out opposition bidding.
▸**pre-ˈemptor** *n*

pre-emption (prɪˈɛmpʃən) *n* **1** *Law.* the purchase of or right to purchase property in preference to others. **2** *International law.* the right of a government to intercept and seize property of the subjects of another state while in transit, esp. in time of war. [C16: from Med. L *praeemptiō,* from *praeemere* to buy beforehand]

pre-emptive (prɪˈɛmptɪv) *adj* **1** of, involving, or capable of pre-emption. **2** *Bridge.* (of a high bid) made to shut out opposition bidding. **3** *Mil.* designed to reduce or destroy an enemy's attacking strength before it can use it: *a pre-emptive strike.*

preen ➊ (priːn) *vb* **1** (of birds) to maintain (feathers) in a healthy condition by arrangement, cleaning, and other contact with the bill. **2** to dress or array (oneself) carefully; primp. **3** (usually foll. by *on*) to pride or congratulate (oneself). [C14 *preinen,* prob. from *prunen,* infl. by *prenen* to prick; suggestive of the pricking movement of the bird's beak]
▸**ˈpreener** *n*

pre-exist (priːɪgˈzɪst) *vb* (*intr*) to exist at an earlier time.
▸**pre-exˈistent** *adj* ▸**pre-exˈistence** *n*

pref. *abbrev. for:* **1** preface. **2** prefatory. **3** preference. **4** preferred. **5** prefix.

prefab (ˈpriːˌfæb) *n* a building that is prefabricated, esp. a small house.

prefabricate (priːˈfæbrɪˌkeɪt) *vb* **prefabricates, prefabricating, prefabricated.** (*tr*) to manufacture sections of (a building) so that they can be easily transported to and rapidly assembled on a building site.
▸**preˌfabriˈcation** *n*

preface ➊ (ˈprɛfɪs) *n* **1** a statement written as an introduction to a literary or other work, typically explaining its scope, intention, method, etc.; foreword. **2** anything introductory. ◆ *vb* **prefaces, prefacing, prefaced.** (*tr*) **3** to furnish with a preface. **4** to serve as a preface to. [C14: from Med. L *praefātia,* from L *praefātiō* a saying beforehand, from *praefārī* to utter in advance]
▸**ˈprefacer** *n*

prefatory ➊ (ˈprɛfətərɪ, -trɪ) *or* **prefatorial** (ˌprɛfəˈtɔːrɪəl) *adj* of or serving as a preface; introductory. [C17: from L *praefārī* to say in advance]

prefect (ˈpriːfɛkt) *n* **1** (in France, Italy, etc.) the chief administrative officer in a department. **2** (in France, etc.) the head of a police force. **3** *Brit., Austral., & NZ.* a schoolchild appointed to a position of limited power over his fellows. **4** (in ancient Rome) any of several magistrates or military commanders. **5** *RC Church.* one of two senior masters in a Jesuit school or college. [C14: from L *praefectus* one put in charge, from *praeficere* to place in authority over, from *prae* before + *facere* to do]
▸**prefectorial** (ˌpriːfɛkˈtɔːrɪəl) *adj*

prefecture (ˈpriːfɛkˌtjʊə) *n* **1** the office, position, or area of authority of a prefect. **2** the official residence of a prefect in France, etc.

prefer ➊ (prɪˈfɜː) *vb* **prefers, preferring, preferred. 1** (when *tr, may take a clause as object or an infinitive*) to like better or value more highly: *I prefer to stand.* **2** *Law.* (esp. of the police) to put (charges) before a court, magistrate, etc., for consideration and judgment. **3** (*tr; often passive*) to advance in rank over another or others; promote. [C14: from L *praeferre* to carry in front, prefer]

> **USAGE NOTE** Normally, *to* is used after *prefer* and *preferable,* not *than: I prefer Brahms to Tchaikovsky; a small income is preferable to no income at all.* However, *than* or *rather* should be used to link infinitives: *I prefer to walk than/rather than to catch the train.*

preferable ➊ (ˈprɛfərəbᵊl) *adj* preferred or more desirable.
▸**ˈpreferably** *adv*

> **USAGE NOTE** Since *preferable* already means *more desirable,* one should not say something is *more preferable.* See also at **prefer.**

preference ➊ (ˈprɛfərəns, ˈprɛfrəns) *n* **1** the act of preferring. **2** something or someone preferred. **3** *International trade.* the granting of favour or precedence to particular foreign countries, as by levying differential tariffs.

preference shares *pl n Brit. & Austral.* fixed-interest shares issued by a company and giving their holders a prior right over ordinary shareholders to payment of dividend and to repayment of capital if the company is liquidated. US and Canad. name: **preferred stock.** Cf. **ordinary shares, preferred ordinary shares.**

preferential ➊ (ˌprɛfəˈrɛnʃəl) *adj* **1** showing or resulting from prefer-

THESAURUS

tion, forecast, prognosis, prognostication, soothsaying, sortilege

predilection *n* = **liking,** bag (*sl.*), bias, cup of tea (*inf.*), fancy, fondness, inclination, leaning, love, partiality, penchant, predisposition, preference, proclivity, proneness, propensity, taste, tendency, weakness

predispose *vb* = **incline,** affect, bias, dispose, induce, influence, lead, make (one) of a mind to, prejudice, prepare, prime, prompt, sway

predisposed *adj* = **inclined,** agreeable, amenable, given, liable, minded, prone, ready, subject, susceptible, willing

predisposition *n* = **inclination,** bent, bias, disposition, likelihood, penchant, potentiality, predilection, proclivity, proneness, propensity, susceptibility, tendency, willingness

predominance *n* **1, 2** = **prevalence,** ascendancy, control, dominance, dominion, edge, greater number, hold, leadership, mastery, paramountcy, preponderance, supremacy, sway, upper hand, weight

predominant *adj* **1, 2** = **main,** ascendant, capital, chief, controlling, dominant, important, leading, notable, paramount, preponderant, prevailing, prevalent, primary, prime, principal, prominent, ruling, sovereign, superior, supreme, top-priority
Antonyms *adj* inferior, minor, secondary, subordinate, unimportant, uninfluential

predominantly *adv* **2** = **mainly,** chiefly, for the most part, generally, in the main, largely, mostly, on the whole, preponderantly, primarily, principally, to a great extent

predominate *vb* **1, 2** = **prevail,** be most noticeable, carry weight, get the upper hand, hold sway, outweigh, overrule, overshadow, preponderate, reign, rule, tell

pre-eminence *n* = **superiority,** distinction, excellence, paramountcy, predominance, prestige, prominence, renown, supremacy, transcendence

pre-eminent *adj* = **outstanding,** chief, consummate, distinguished, excellent, foremost, incomparable, matchless, paramount, peerless, predominant, renowned, superior, supreme, transcendent, unequalled, unrivalled, unsurpassed

pre-eminently *adv* = **particularly,** above all, by far, conspicuously, eminently, emphatically, exceptionally, far and away, incomparably, inimitably, matchlessly, notably, *par excellence,* second to none, signally, singularly, strikingly, superlatively, supremely

pre-empt *vb* **1** = **anticipate,** acquire, appropriate, arrogate, assume, seize, take over, usurp

preen *vb* **1** = **clean,** plume **2** = **smarten,** array, deck out, doll up (*sl.*), dress up, prettify, primp, prink, spruce up, titivate, trig (*arch. or dialect*), trim **3** *usually foll. by* **on** = **pride oneself,** congratulate oneself, pique oneself, plume oneself

preface *n* **1** = **introduction,** exordium, foreword, preamble, preliminary, prelude, proem, prolegomenon, prologue ◆ *vb* **4** = **introduce,** begin, launch, lead up to, open, precede, prefix

prefatory *adj* = **introductory,** antecedent, opening, precursory, prefatorial, preliminary, prelusive, prelusory, preparatory, proemial, prolegomenal

prefer *vb* **1** = **like better,** adopt, be partial to, choose, desire, elect, fancy, favour, go for, incline towards, opt for, pick, plump for, select, single out, wish, would rather, would sooner **2** *Law* = **put forward,** file, lodge, place, present, press **3** = **promote,** advance, aggrandize, elevate, move up, raise, upgrade

preferable *adj* = **better,** best, choice, chosen, favoured, more desirable, more eligible, superior, worthier
Antonyms *adj* average, fair, ineligible, inferior, mediocre, poor, second-rate, undesirable

preferably *adv* = **rather,** as a matter of choice, by choice, first, in *or* for preference, much rather, much sooner, sooner, willingly

preference *n* **1** = **priority,** advantage, favoured treatment, favouritism, first place, precedence, pride of place **2** = **first choice,** bag (*sl.*), choice, cup of tea (*inf.*), desire, election, fave (*inf.*), favourite, option, partiality, pick, predilection, selection, top of the list

preferential *adj* **1** = **privileged,** advantageous, better, favoured, partial, partisan, special, superior

ence. **2** giving, receiving, or originating from preference in international trade.
▶ **ˌprefer'entially** *adv*

preferment ❶ (prɪ'fɜːmənt) *n* **1** the act of promoting to a higher position, office, etc. **2** the state of being preferred for promotion or social advancement. **3** the act of preferring.

preferred ordinary shares *pl n Brit.* shares issued by a company that rank between preference shares and ordinary shares in the payment of dividends. Cf. **preference shares, ordinary shares.**

prefigure ❶ (priː'fɪgə) *vb* **prefigures, prefiguring, prefigured.** (*tr*) **1** to represent or suggest in advance. **2** to imagine beforehand.
▶ **ˌprefigu'ration** *n* ▶ **pre'figurement** *n*

prefix *n* ('priːfɪks). **1** *Grammar.* an affix that precedes the stem to which it is attached, as for example *un-* in *unhappy.* Cf. **suffix** (sense 1). **2** something coming or placed before. ◆ *vb* (priː'fɪks, 'priːfɪks). (*tr*) **3** to put or place before. **4** *Grammar.* to add (a morpheme) as a prefix to the beginning of a word.
▶ **prefixion** (priː'fɪkʃən) *n*

prefrontal (priː'frʌntᵊl) *adj* in or relating to the foremost part of the frontal lobe of the brain.

preglacial (priː'gleɪsɪəl, -ʃəl) *adj* formed or occurring before a glacial period, esp. before the Pleistocene epoch.

pregnable ('prɛgnəbᵊl) *adj* capable of being assailed or captured. [C15 *prenable,* from OF *prendre* to take, from L *prehendere* to catch]

pregnant ❶ ('prɛgnənt) *adj* **1** carrying a fetus or fetuses within the womb. **2** full of meaning or significance. **3** inventive or imaginative. **4** prolific or fruitful. [C16: from L *praegnāns* with child, from *prae* before + (*g*)*nascī* to be born]
▶ **'pregnancy** *n* ▶ **'pregnantly** *adv*

prehensile (prɪ'hɛnsaɪl) *adj* adapted for grasping, esp. by wrapping around a support: *a prehensile tail.* [C18: from F *préhensile,* from L *prehendere* to grasp]
▶ **prehensility** (ˌpriːhɛn'sɪlɪtɪ) *n*

prehension (prɪ'hɛnʃən) *n* **1** the act of grasping. **2** apprehension by the mind.

prehistoric ❶ (ˌpriːhɪ'stɒrɪk) *or* **prehistorical** *adj* of or relating to man's development before the appearance of the written word.
▶ **ˌprehis'torically** *adv* ▶ **pre'history** *n*

pre-ignition (ˌpriːɪg'nɪʃən) *n* ignition of all or part of the explosive charge in an internal-combustion engine before the exact instant necessary for correct operation.

prejudge ❶ (priː'dʒʌdʒ) *vb* **prejudges, prejudging, prejudged.** (*tr*) to judge beforehand, esp. without sufficient evidence.

prejudice ❶ ('prɛdʒʊdɪs) *n* **1** an opinion formed beforehand, esp. an unfavourable one based on inadequate facts. **2** the act or condition of holding such opinions. **3** intolerance of or dislike for people of a specific race, religion, etc. **4** disadvantage or injury resulting from prejudice. **5 in** (*or* **to**) **the prejudice of.** to the detriment of. **6 without prejudice.** *Law.* without dismissing or detracting from an existing right or claim. ◆ *vb* **prejudices, prejudicing, prejudiced.** (*tr*) **7** to cause to be prejudiced. **8** to disadvantage or injure by prejudice. [C13: from OF *préjudice,* from L *praejūdicium,* from *prae* before + *jūdicium* sentence, from *jūdex* a judge]

prejudicial ❶ (ˌprɛdʒʊ'dɪʃəl) *adj* causing prejudice; damaging.
▶ **ˌpreju'dicially** *adv*

prelacy ('prɛləsɪ) *n, pl* **prelacies. 1** Also called: **prelature. 1a** the office or status of a prelate. **1b** prelates collectively. **2** *Often derog.* government of the Church by prelates.

prelapsarian (ˌpriːlæp'sɛərɪən) *adj* of or relating to the human state before the Fall: *prelapsarian innocence.*

prelate ('prɛlɪt) *n* a Church dignitary of high rank, such as a cardinal, bishop, or abbot. [C13: from OF *prélat,* from Church L *praelātus,* from L *praeferre* to hold in special esteem]
▶ **prelatic** (prɪ'lætɪk) *or* **pre'latical** *adj*

preliminaries (prɪ'lɪmɪnərɪz) *pl n* the full word for **prelims.**

preliminary ❶ (prɪ'lɪmɪnərɪ) *adj* **1** (*usually prenominal*) occurring before or in preparation; introductory. ◆ *n, pl* **preliminaries. 2** a preliminary event or occurrence. **3** an eliminating contest held before the main competition. [C17: from NL *praelīminārīs,* from L *prae* before + *līmen* threshold]
▶ **pre'liminarily** *adv*

prelims ('priːlɪmz, prə'lɪmz) *pl n* **1** Also called: **front matter.** the pages of a book, such as the title page and contents, before the main text. **2** the first public examinations taken for the bachelor's degree in some universities. **3** (in Scotland) the school examinations taken before public examinations. [C19: a contraction of PRELIMINARIES]

prelude ❶ ('prɛljuːd) *n* **1a** a piece of music that precedes a fugue, or forms the first movement of a suite, or an introduction to an act in an opera, etc. **1b** (esp. for piano) a self-contained piece of music. **2** an introduction or preceding event, occurrence, etc. ◆ *vb* **preludes, preluding, preluded. 3** to serve as a prelude to (something). **4** (*tr*) to introduce by a prelude. [C16: from Med. L *praelūdium,* from *prae* before + L *lūdere* to play]
▶ **preludial** (prɪ'ljuːdɪəl) *adj*

premarital (priː'mærɪtᵊl) *adj* (esp. of sexual relations) occurring before marriage.

premature ❶ (ˌprɛmə'tjʊə, 'prɛməˌtjʊə) *adj* **1** occurring or existing before the normal or expected time. **2** impulsive or hasty: *a premature judgment.* **3** (of an infant) born before the end of the full period of gestation. [C16: from L *praemātūrus* very early, from *prae* in advance + *mātūrus* ripe]
▶ **ˌprema'turely** *adv*

premedical (priː'mɛdɪkᵊl) *adj* **1** of or relating to a course of study prerequisite for entering medical school. **2** of or relating to a person engaged in such a course of study.

premedication (ˌpriːmɛdɪ'keɪʃən) *n Surgery.* any drugs administered to sedate and otherwise prepare a patient for general anaesthesia.

premeditate ❶ (prɪ'mɛdɪˌteɪt) *vb* **premeditates, premeditating, premeditated.** to plan or consider (something, such as a violent crime) beforehand.
▶ **pre'mediˌtator** *n*

premeditation ❶ (prɪˌmɛdɪ'teɪʃən) *n* **1** *Law.* prior resolve to do some act or to commit a crime. **2** the act of premeditating.

premenstrual syndrome *or* **tension** *n* symptoms, esp. nervous tension, that may be experienced because of hormonal changes in the days before a menstrual period starts. Abbrevs.: **PMS, PMT.**

premier ❶ ('prɛmjə) *n* **1** another name for **prime minister. 2** any of the heads of government of the Canadian provinces and the Australian states. **3** *Austral.* a team that wins a premiership. ◆ *adj* (*prenominal*) **4** first in importance, rank, etc. **5** first in occurrence; earliest. [C15: from OF: first, from L *prīmārius* principal, from *prīmus* first]

premiere ❶ ('prɛmɪˌɛə, 'prɛmɪə) *n* **1** the first public performance of a film, play, opera, etc. **2** the leading lady in a theatre company. ◆ *vb* **premieres, premiering, premiered. 3** (*tr*) to give a premiere of: *the show will be premiered on Broadway.* [C19: from F, fem of *premier* first]

premiership ('prɛmjəʃɪp) *n* **1** the office of premier. **2a** a championship competition held among a number of sporting clubs. **2b** a victory in such a championship.

premillennialism (ˌpriːmɪ'lɛnɪəˌlɪzəm) *n* the doctrine or belief that the millennium will be preceded by the Second Coming of Christ.
▶ **ˌpremil'lennialist** *n* ▶ **ˌpremille'narian** *n, adj*

THESAURUS

preferment *n* **1** = **promotion,** advancement, dignity, elevation, exaltation, rise, upgrading

prefigure *vb* **1** = **foreshadow,** adumbrate, foretoken, indicate, intimate, portend, presage, shadow forth, suggest **2** = **imagine,** consider, fancy, picture, presuppose

pregnancy *n* **1** = **gestation,** gravidity

pregnant *adj* **1** = **expectant,** big *or* heavy with child, enceinte, expecting (*inf.*), gravid, in the club (*Brit. sl.*), in the family way (*inf.*), in the pudding club (*sl.*), preggers (*Brit. inf.*), with child **2** = **meaningful,** charged, eloquent, expressive, loaded, pointed, significant, suggestive, telling, weighty **3** = **imaginative,** creative, inventive, original, seminal **4** = **prolific,** abounding in, abundant, fecund, fertile, fraught, fruitful, full, productive, replete, rich in, teeming

prehistoric *adj* = **earliest,** early, primeval, primitive, primordial

prejudge *vb* = **jump to conclusions,** anticipate, forejudge, make a hasty assessment, presume, presuppose

prejudice *n* **1** = **bias,** jaundiced eye, partiality, preconceived notion, preconception, prejudgment, warp **3** = **discrimination,** bigotry, chauvinism, injustice, intolerance, narrow-mindedness, racism, sexism, unfairness **4** = **harm,** damage, detriment, disadvantage, hurt, impairment, loss, mischief ◆ *vb* **7** = **bias,** colour, distort, influence, jaundice, poison, predispose, prepossess, slant, sway, warp **8** = **harm,** damage, hinder, hurt, impair, injure, mar, spoil, undermine

prejudiced *adj* **1, 3** = **biased,** bigoted, conditioned, discriminatory, influenced, intolerant, jaundiced, narrow-minded, one-sided, opinionated, partial, partisan, prepossessed, unfair
Antonyms *adj* fair, impartial, just, neutral, not bigoted, not prejudiced, open-minded, unbiased

prejudicial *adj* = **harmful,** counterproductive, damaging, deleterious, detrimental, disadvantageous, hurtful, inimical, injurious, undermining, unfavourable

preliminary *adj* **1** = **first,** exploratory, initial, initiatory, introductory, opening, pilot, precursory, prefatory, preparatory, prior, qualifying, test, trial ◆ *n* **2** = **introduction,** beginning, foundation, groundwork, initiation, opening, overture, preamble, preface, prelims, prelude, preparation, start

prelude *n* **2** = **introduction,** beginning, commencement, curtain-raiser, exordium, foreword, intro (*inf.*), overture, preamble, preface, preliminary, preparation, proem, prolegomenon, prologue, start

premature *adj* **1** = **early,** forward, unseasonable, untimely **2** = **hasty,** ill-considered, ill-timed, impulsive, inopportune, jumping the gun, overhasty, precipitate, previous (*inf.*), rash, too soon, untimely **3** = **immature,** abortive, embryonic, incomplete, predeveloped, undeveloped, unfledged

prematurely *adv* **1** = **too early,** before one's time, too soon, untimely **2** = **overhastily,** at half-cock, half-cocked, precipitately, rashly, too hastily, too soon

premeditated *adj* = **planned,** aforethought, calculated, conscious, considered, contrived, deliberate, intended, intentional, prepense, studied, wilful
Antonyms *adj* accidental, inadvertent, unintentional, unplanned, unpremeditated, unwitting

premeditation *n* **1, 2** = **planning,** deliberation, design, determination, forethought, intention, malice aforethought, plotting, prearrangement, predetermination, purpose

premier *n* **1, 2** = **head of government,** chancellor, chief minister, P.M., prime minister ◆ *adj* **4** = **chief,** arch, first, foremost, head, highest, leading, main, primary, prime, principal, top **5** = **first,** earliest, inaugural, initial, original

premiere *n* **1** = **first night,** debut, first performance, first showing, opening

premise ⓣ *n* (ˈprɛmɪs), also **premiss. 1** *Logic.* a statement that is assumed to be true for the purpose of an argument from which a conclusion is drawn. ◆ *vb* (prɪˈmaɪz, ˈprɛmɪs), **premises, premising, premised. 2** (when *tr, may take a clause as object*) to state or assume (a proposition) as a premise in an argument, etc. [C14: from OF *prémisse,* from Med. L *praemissa* sent on before, from L *praemittere* to dispatch in advance]

premises ⓣ (ˈprɛmɪsɪz) *pl n* **1** a piece of land together with its buildings, esp. considered as a place of business. **2** *Law.* (in a deed, etc.) the matters referred to previously; the aforesaid.

premium ⓣ (ˈpriːmɪəm) *n* **1** an amount paid in addition to a standard rate, price, wage, etc.; bonus. **2** the amount paid or payable, usually in regular instalments, for an insurance policy. **3** the amount above nominal or par value at which something sells. **4** an offer of something free or at a reduced price as an inducement to buy a commodity or service. **5** a prize given to the winner of a competition. **6** *US.* an amount sometimes charged for a loan of money in addition to the interest. **7** great value or regard: *to put a premium on someone's services.* **8 at a premium. 8a** in great demand, usually because of scarcity. **8b** above par. [C17: from L *praemium* prize]

Premium Savings Bonds *pl n* (in Britain) bonds issued by the Treasury since 1956 for purchase by the public. No interest is paid but there is a monthly draw for cash prizes of various sums. Also called: **premium bonds.**

premolar (priːˈməʊlə) *adj* **1** situated before a molar tooth. ◆ *n* **2** any one of eight bicuspid teeth in the human adult, two on each side of both jaws between the first molar and the canine.

premonition ⓣ (ˌprɛməˈnɪʃən) *n* **1** an intuition of a future, usually unwelcome, occurrence; foreboding. **2** an early warning of a future event. [C16: from LL *praemonitiō,* from L *praemonēre* to admonish beforehand, from *prae* before + *monēre* to warn]
▸**premonitory** (prɪˈmɒnɪtərɪ, -trɪ) *adj*

Premonstratensian (ˌpriːmɒnstrəˈtɛnsɪən) *adj* **1** of or denoting an order of regular canons founded in 1119 at Prémontré, in France. ◆ *n* **2** a member of this order.

prenatal (priːˈneɪtᵊl) *adj* **1** occurring or present before birth; during pregnancy. ◆ *n* **2** *Inf.* a prenatal examination. ◆ Also: **antenatal.**

prenominal (priːˈnɒmɪnᵊl) *adj* placed before a noun, esp. (of an adjective or sense of an adjective) used only before a noun.

prentice (ˈprɛntɪs) *n* an archaic word for **apprentice.**

prenuptial agreement *n* a contract made between a man and woman before they marry, agreeing on the distribution of their assets in the event of divorce.

preoccupation ⓣ (priːˌɒkjʊˈpeɪʃən) *n* **1** the state of being preoccupied, esp. mentally. **2** something that preoccupies the mind.

preoccupied ⓣ (priːˈɒkjʊˌpaɪd) *adj* **1** engrossed or absorbed in something, esp. one's own thoughts. **2** already occupied or used.

preoccupy (priːˈɒkjʊˌpaɪ) *vb* **preoccupies, preoccupying, preoccupied.** (*tr*) **1** to engross the thoughts or mind of. **2** to occupy before or in advance of another. [C16: from L *praeoccupāre* to capture in advance]

preordain ⓣ (ˌpriːɔːˈdeɪn) *vb* (*tr*) to ordain, decree, or appoint beforehand.

prep (prɛp) *n Inf.* **1** short for **preparation** (sense 5) or (chiefly US) **preparatory school.** ◆ *vb* **preps, prepping, prepped. 2** (*tr*) to prepare (a patient) for a medical operation or procedure.

prep. *abbrev. for:* **1** preparation. **2** preparatory. **3** preposition.

preparation ⓣ (ˌprɛpəˈreɪʃən) *n* **1** the act or process of preparing. **2** the state of being prepared; readiness. **3** (*often pl*) a measure done in order to prepare for something; provision: *to make preparations for something.* **4** something that is prepared, esp. a medicine. **5** (esp. in a boarding school) **5a** homework. **5b** the period reserved for this. Usually shortened to **prep. 6** *Music.* **6a** the anticipation of a dissonance so that the note producing it in one chord is first heard in the preceding chord as a consonance. **6b** a note so employed.

preparative (prɪˈpærətɪv) *adj* **1** preparatory. ◆ *n* **2** something that prepares.
▸**pre'paratively** *adv*

preparatory ⓣ (prɪˈpærətərɪ, -trɪ) *adj* **1** serving to prepare. **2** introductory. **3** occupied in preparation. **4 preparatory to.** before: *a drink preparatory to eating.*
▸**pre'paratorily** *adv*

preparatory school *n* **1** (in Britain) a private school, usually single-sex and for children between the ages of 6 and 13, generally preparing pupils for public school. **2** (in the US) a private secondary school preparing pupils for college. ◆ Often shortened to **prep school.**

prepare ⓣ (prɪˈpɛə) *vb* **prepares, preparing, prepared. 1** to make ready or suitable in advance for some use, event, etc.: *to prepare a meal; to prepare to go.* **2** to put together using parts or ingredients; construct. **3** (*tr*) to equip or outfit, as for an expedition. **4** (*tr*) *Music.* to soften the impact of (a dissonant note) by the use of preparation. **5 be prepared.** (*foll. by an infinitive*) to be willing and able: *I'm not prepared to reveal these figures.* [C15: from L *praeparāre,* from *prae* before + *parāre* to make ready]
▸**pre'parer** *n*

preparedness ⓣ (prɪˈpɛərɪdnɪs) *n* the state of being prepared, esp. militarily ready for war.

prepay (priːˈpeɪ) *vb* **prepays, prepaying, prepaid.** (*tr*) to pay for in advance.
▸**pre'payable** *adj*

prepense (prɪˈpɛns) *adj* (*postpositive*) (usually in legal contexts) premeditated (esp. in **malice prepense**). [C18: from Anglo-Norman *purpensé,* from OF *purpenser* to consider in advance, from L *pēnsāre* to consider]

preponderant ⓣ (prɪˈpɒndərənt) *adj* greater in weight, force, influence, etc.
▸**pre'ponderance** *n* ▸**pre'ponderantly** *adv*

preponderate ⓣ (prɪˈpɒndəˌreɪt) *vb* **preponderates, preponderating, preponderated.** (*intr*) **1** (often foll. by *over*) to be more powerful, important, numerous, etc. (than). **2** to be of greater weight than something else. [C17: from LL *praeponderāre* to be of greater weight, from *pondus* weight]
▸**pre,ponder'ation** *n*

preposition (ˌprɛpəˈzɪʃən) *n* a word or group of words used before a noun or pronoun to relate it grammatically or semantically to some other constituent of a sentence. [C14: from L *praepositiō* a putting before, from *pōnere* to place]
▸**,prepo'sitional** *adj* ▸**,prepo'sitionally** *adv*

> **USAGE NOTE** The practice of ending a sentence with a preposition (*Venice is a place I should like to go to*) was formerly regarded as incorrect, but is now acceptable and is the preferred form in many contexts.

prepossess ⓣ (ˌpriːpəˈzɛs) *vb* (*tr*) **1** to preoccupy or engross mentally. **2** to influence in advance, esp. to make a favourable impression on beforehand.
▸**,prepos'session** *n*

prepossessing ⓣ (ˌpriːpəˈzɛsɪŋ) *adj* creating a favourable impression; attractive.

preposterous ⓣ (prɪˈpɒstərəs) *adj* contrary to nature, reason, or sense;

THESAURUS

premise *n* **1 = assumption,** argument, assertion, ground, hypothesis, postulate, postulation, presupposition, proposition, supposition, thesis ◆ *vb* **2 = assume,** hypothesize, posit, postulate, predicate, presuppose, state

premises *pl n* **1 = building,** establishment, place, property, site

premium *n* **1 = bonus,** boon, bounty, fee, percentage (*inf.*), perk (*Brit. inf.*), perquisite, prize, recompense, remuneration, reward **7 = regard,** appreciation, stock, store, value **8 at a premium = in great demand,** beyond one's means, costly, expensive, hard to come by, in short supply, like gold dust, not to be had for love or money, rare, scarce, valuable

premonition *n* **1, 2 = feeling,** apprehension, feeling in one's bones, foreboding, forewarning, funny feeling (*inf.*), hunch, idea, intuition, misgiving, omen, portent, presage, presentiment, sign, suspicion, warning

preoccupation *n* **1 = absorption,** absence of mind, absent-mindedness, abstraction, brown study, daydreaming, engrossment, immersion, inattentiveness, musing, oblivion, pensiveness, prepossession, reverie, woolgathering **2 = obsession,** bee in one's bonnet, concern, fixation, hang-up (*inf.*), hobbyhorse, *idée fixe,* pet subject

preoccupied *adj* **1 = absorbed,** absent-minded, abstracted, caught up in, distracted, distrait, engrossed, faraway, heedless, immersed, in a brown study, intent, lost in, lost in thought, oblivious, rapt, taken up, unaware, wrapped up

preordained *adj* **= predetermined,** destined, doomed, fated, mapped out in advance, predestined

preparation *n* **1 = groundwork,** development, getting ready, preparing, putting in order **2 = readiness,** alertness, anticipation, expectation, foresight, precaution, preparedness, provision, safeguard **3** *often plural* **= arrangement,** measure, plan, provision **4 = mixture,** composition, compound, concoction, medicine, tincture **5a = homework,** prep (*inf.*), revision, schoolwork, study, swotting (*Brit. inf.*)

preparatory *adj* **1, 2 = introductory,** basic, elementary, opening, prefatory, preliminary, preparative, primary **4 preparatory to = before,** in advance of, in anticipation of, in preparation for, prior to

prepare *vb* **1 = make** *or* **get ready,** adapt, adjust, anticipate, arrange, coach, dispose, form, groom, make provision, plan, practise, prime, put in order, train, warm up **2 = put together,** assemble, concoct, construct, contrive, draw up, fashion, fix up, get up (*inf.*), make, produce, turn out **3 = equip,** accoutre, fit, fit out, furnish, outfit, provide, supply

prepared *adj* **1 = ready,** all set, all systems go, arranged, fit, in order, in readiness, planned, primed, set **5 = willing,** able, disposed, inclined, minded, of a mind, predisposed

preparedness *n* **= readiness,** alertness, fitness, order, preparation

preponderance *n* **= predominance,** ascendancy, bulk, dominance, domination, dominion, extensiveness, greater numbers, greater part, lion's share, mass, power, prevalence, superiority, supremacy, sway, weight

preponderant *adj* **= prevalent,** ascendant, dominant, extensive, foremost, greater, important, larger, paramount, predominant, prevailing, significant

preponderate *vb* **1 = predominate,** dominate, hold sway, outnumber, prevail, reign supreme, rule

prepossessing *adj* **= attractive,** alluring, amiable, appealing, beautiful, bewitching, captivating, charming, engaging, fair, fascinating, fetching, glamorous, good-looking, handsome, inviting, likable *or* likeable, lovable, magnetic, pleasing, striking, taking, winning
Antonyms *adj* disagreeable, displeasing, objectionable, offensive, repulsive, ugly, unattractive, uninviting, unlikable *or* unlikeable

prepossession *n* **1 = preoccupation,** absorption, engrossment **2 = partiality,** bias, inclination, liking, predilection, predisposition, prejudice

preposterous *adj* **= ridiculous,** absurd, asi-

absurd; ridiculous. [C16: from L *praeposterus* reversed, from *prae* in front + *posterus* following]
▸**pre'posterously** *adv* ▸**pre'posterousness** *n*

prepotency (prɪ'pəʊtᵊnsɪ) *n* **1** the quality of possessing greater power or influence. **2** *Genetics.* the ability of one parent to transmit more characteristics to its offspring than the other parent. **3** *Bot.* the ability of pollen from one source to bring about fertilization more readily than that from other sources.
▸**pre'potent** *adj*

preppy ('prepɪ) *Inf.* ◆ *adj* **1** of or denoting a style of neat, understated, and often expensive clothes; young but classic. ◆ *n, pl* **preppies. 2** a person exhibiting such style. [C20: orig. US, from *preppy* a person who attends a PREPARATORY SCHOOL]

prep school *n Inf.* See **preparatory school.**

prepuce ('pri:pju:s) *n* **1** the retractable fold of skin covering the tip of the penis. Nontechnical name: **foreskin. 2** a similar fold of skin covering the tip of the clitoris. [C14: from L *praepūtium*]

prequel ('pri:kwəl) *n* a film that is made about an earlier stage of a story or character's life because the later part of it has already made a successful film. [C20: from PRE- + (*se*)*quel*]

Pre-Raphaelite (ˌpri:'ræfəlaɪt) *n* **1** a member of the **Pre-Raphaelite Brotherhood,** an association of painters and writers founded in 1848 to revive the fidelity to nature and the vivid realistic colour considered typical of Italian painting before Raphael. ◆ *adj* **2** of, in the manner of, or relating to Pre-Raphaelite painting and painters.
▸ˌ**Pre-'Raphaelitˌism** *n*

prerequisite ➊ (pri:'rekwɪzɪt) *adj* **1** required as a prior condition. ◆ *n* **2** something required as a prior condition.

prerogative ➊ (prɪ'rɒgətɪv) *n* **1** an exclusive privilege or right exercised by a person or group of people holding a particular office or hereditary rank. **2** any privilege or right. **3** a power, privilege, or immunity restricted to a sovereign or sovereign government. ◆ *adj* **4** having or able to exercise a prerogative. [C14: from L *praerogātīva* privilege, earlier: group with the right to vote first, from *prae* before + *rogāre* to ask]

pres. *abbrev. for:* **1** present (time). **2** presidential.

Pres. *abbrev. for* President.

presage ➊ *n* ('presɪdʒ). **1** an intimation or warning of something about to happen; portent; omen. **2** a sense of what is about to happen; foreboding. ◆ *vb* ('presɪdʒ, prɪ'seɪdʒ). **presages, presaging, presaged.** (*tr*) **3** to have a presentiment of. **4** to give a forewarning of; portend. [C14: from L *praesāgium,* from *praesāgīre* to perceive beforehand]
▸**pre'sageful** *adj* ▸**pre'sager** *n*

presale ('pri:ˌseɪl) *n* the practice of arranging the sale of a product before it is available.
▸**pre'sell** *vb* (*tr*)

presbyopia (ˌprezbɪ'əʊpɪə) *n* a progressively diminishing ability of the eye to focus, noticeable from middle to old age, caused by loss of elasticity of the crystalline lens. [C18: NL, from Gk *presbus* old man + *ōps* eye]
▸**presbyopic** (ˌprezbɪ'ɒpɪk) *adj*

presbyter ('prezbɪtə) *n* **1a** an elder of a congregation in the early Christian Church. **1b** (in some Churches having episcopal politics) an official who is subordinate to a bishop and has administrative and sacerdotal functions. **2** (in some hierarchical Churches) another name for **priest. 3** (in the Presbyterian Church) an elder. [C16: from LL, from Gk *presbuteros* an older man, from *presbus* old man]
▸ˌ**presby'terial** *adj*

presbyterian (ˌprezbɪ'tɪərɪən) *adj* **1** of or designating Church government by presbyters or lay elders. ◆ *n* **2** an upholder of this type of Church government.
▸ˌ**presby'terianism** *n*

Presbyterian (ˌprezbɪ'tɪərɪən) *adj* **1** of or relating to any of various Protestant Churches governed by presbyters or lay elders and adhering to various modified forms of Calvinism. ◆ *n* **2** a member of a Presbyterian Church.
▸ˌ**Presby'terianism** *n*

presbytery ('prezbɪtərɪ) *n, pl* **presbyteries. 1** *Presbyterian Church.* **1a** a local Church court. **1b** the congregations within the jurisdiction of any such court. **2** the part of a church east of the choir, in which the main altar is situated; a sanctuary. **3** presbyters or elders collectively. **4** *RC Church.* the residence of a parish priest. [C15: from OF *presbiterie,* from Church L, from Gk *presbyterion;* see PRESBYTER]

prescience ➊ ('presɪəns) *n* knowledge of events before they take place; foreknowledge. [C14: from L *praescīre* to foreknow]
▸'**prescient** *adj*

prescribe ➊ (prɪ'skraɪb) *vb* **prescribes, prescribing, prescribed. 1** (*tr*) to lay down as a rule or directive. **2** *Med.* to recommend or order the use of (a drug or other remedy). [C16: from L *praescrībere* to write previously]
▸**pre'scriber** *n*

prescript ('pri:skrɪpt) *n* something laid down or prescribed. [C16: from L *praescriptum* something written down beforehand, from *praescrībere* to PRESCRIBE]

prescription ➊ (prɪ'skrɪpʃən) *n* **1a** written instructions from a physician to a pharmacist stating the form, dosage, strength, etc., of a drug to be issued to a specific patient. **1b** the drug or remedy prescribed. **2a** written instructions for an optician specifying the lenses needed to correct defects of vision. **2b** (*as modifier*): *prescription glasses.* **3** the act of prescribing. **4** something that is prescribed. **5** a long-established custom or a claim based on one. **6** *Law.* **6a** the uninterrupted possession of property over a stated time, after which a right or title is acquired (**positive prescription**). **6b** the barring of adverse claims to property, etc., after a specified time has elapsed, allowing the possessor to acquire title (**negative prescription**). [C14: from legal L *praescriptiō* an order; see PRESCRIBE]

prescriptive ➊ (prɪ'skrɪptɪv) *adj* **1** making or giving directions, rules, or injunctions. **2** sanctioned by long-standing custom. **3** based upon legal prescription: *a prescriptive title.*
▸**pre'scriptively** *adv* ▸**pre'scriptiveness** *n*

presence ➊ ('prezəns) *n* **1** the state or fact of being present. **2** immediate proximity. **3** personal appearance or bearing, esp. of a dignified nature. **4** an imposing or dignified personality. **5** an invisible spirit felt to be nearby. **6** *Electronics.* a recording control that boosts mid-range frequencies. **7** *Obs.* assembly or company. [C14: via OF from L *praesentia* a being before, from *praeesse* to be before]

presence chamber *n* the room in which a great person, such as a monarch, receives guests, assemblies, etc.

presence of mind ➊ *n* the ability to remain calm and act constructively during times of crisis.

presenile dementia (pri:'si:naɪl) *n* a form of dementia, of unknown cause, starting before a person is old.

present[1] ➊ ('prezᵊnt) *adj* **1** (*prenominal*) in existence at the time at which something is spoken or written. **2** (*postpositive*) being in a specified place, thing, etc.: *the murderer is present in this room.* **3** (*prenominal*) now being dealt with or under discussion: *the present author.* **4** *Grammar.* denoting a tense of verbs used when the action or event described is occurring at the time of utterance or when the speaker does not wish to make any explicit temporal reference. **5** *Arch.* instant: *present help is at hand.* ◆ *n* **6** *Grammar.* **6a** the present tense. **6b** a verb in this tense. **7 at present.** now. **8 for the present.** for the time being; temporarily. **9 the present.** the time being; now. ◆ See also **presents.** [C13: from L *praesens,* from *praeesse* to be in front of]

present[2] ➊ *vb* (prɪ'zent). (*mainly tr*) **1** to introduce (a person) to another, esp. to someone of higher rank. **2** to introduce to the public: *to present a play.* **3** to introduce and compere (a radio or television show). **4** to show; exhibit: *he presented a brave face to the world.* **5** to bring or suggest to the mind: *to present a problem.* **6** to put forward; submit: *she*

THESAURUS

nine, bizarre, crazy, excessive, exorbitant, extravagant, extreme, foolish, impossible, incredible, insane, irrational, laughable, ludicrous, monstrous, nonsensical, out of the question, outrageous, risible, senseless, shocking, unreasonable, unthinkable

prerequisite *adj* **1** = **required,** called for, essential, imperative, indispensable, mandatory, necessary, needful, obligatory, of the essence, requisite, vital ◆ *n* **2** = **requirement,** condition, essential, imperative, must, necessity, precondition, qualification, requisite, *sine qua non*

prerogative *n* **1-3** = **right,** advantage, authority, birthright, choice, claim, droit, due, exemption, immunity, liberty, perquisite, privilege, sanction, title

presage *n* **1** = **omen,** augury, auspice, forecast, forewarning, harbinger, intimation, portent, prediction, prognostic, prognostication, prophecy, sign, warning **2** = **misgiving,** apprehension, boding, feeling, foreboding, forewarning, intuition, premonition, presentiment ◆ *vb* **3** = **sense,** divine, feel, foresee, have a feeling, intuit **3** = **predict,** forecast, foretell, forewarn, prognosticate, prophesy, soothsay, vaticinate (*rare*) **4** = **portend,** adumbrate, augur, betoken, bode, forebode, foreshadow, foretoken, omen, point to, signify, warn

prescience *n Formal* = **foresight,** clairvoyance, foreknowledge, precognition, prevision (*rare*), second sight

prescient *adj* = **foresighted,** clairvoyant, discerning, divinatory, divining, far-sighted, mantic, perceptive, prophetic, psychic

prescribe *vb* **1** = **order,** appoint, assign, command, decree, define, dictate, direct, enjoin, establish, fix, impose, lay down, ordain, recommend, require, rule, set, specify, stipulate

prescription *n* **1a** = **instruction,** direction, formula, recipe **1b** = **medicine,** drug, mixture, preparation, remedy

prescriptive *adj* **1** = **dictatorial,** authoritarian, didactic, dogmatic, legislating, preceptive, rigid

presence *n* **1** = **being,** attendance, companionship, company, existence, habitation, inhabitance, occupancy, residence **2** = **proximity,** closeness, immediate circle, nearness, neighbourhood, propinquity, vicinity **3** = **personality,** air, appearance, aspect, aura, bearing, carriage, comportment, demeanour, ease, mien (*literary*), poise, self-assurance **5** = **spirit,** apparition, eidolon, ghost, manifestation, revenant, shade (*literary*), spectre, supernatural being, wraith

presence of mind *n* = **level-headedness,** alertness, aplomb, calmness, composure, cool (*sl.*), coolness, imperturbability, phlegm, quickness, sang-froid, self-assurance, self-command, self-possession, wits

present[1] *adj* **1** = **current,** contemporary, existent, existing, extant, immediate, instant, present-day **2** = **here,** accounted for, at hand, available, in attendance, near, nearby, ready, there, to hand ◆ *n* **7 at present** = **just now,** at the moment, now, nowadays, right now **8 for the present** = **for now,** for a while, for the moment, for the nonce, for the time being, in the meantime, not for long, provisionally, temporarily **9 the present** = **now,** here and now, the present moment, the time being, this day and age, today

present[2] *vb* **1** = **introduce,** acquaint with, make known **4** = **put on,** demonstrate, display, exhibit, give, mount, put before the public, show, *presented a proposal for a new book.* **7** to award: *to present a prize; to present a university with a foundation scholarship.* **8** to offer formally: *to present one's compliments.* **9** to hand over for action or settlement: *to present a bill.* **10** to depict in a particular manner: *the actor presented Hamlet as a very young man.* **11** to salute someone with (one's weapon) (usually in **present arms**). **12** to aim (a weapon). **13** to nominate (a clergyman) to a bishop for institution to a benefice in his diocese. **14** to lay (a charge, etc.) before a court, magistrate, etc., for consideration or trial. **15** to bring a formal charge or accusation against (a person); indict. **16** (*intr*) *Med.* to seek treatment for a particular problem: *she presented with postnatal depression.* **17** (*intr*) *Inf.* to produce a specified impression: *she presents well in public.* **18 present oneself.** to appear, esp. at a specific time and place. ◆ *n* ('prɛzᵊnt). **19** a gift. [C13: from OF *presenter,* from L *praesentāre* to exhibit, from *praesens* PRESENT[1]]

presentable ❶ (prɪ'zɛntəbᵊl) *adj* **1** fit to be presented or introduced to other people. **2** fit to be displayed or offered.
▸**pre'sentableness** *or* **pre,senta'bility** *n* ▸**pre'sentably** *adv*

presentation ❶ (,prezən'teɪʃən) *n* **1** the act of presenting or state of being presented. **2** the manner of presenting; delivery or overall impression. **3** a verbal report, often with illustrative material: *a presentation on the company results.* **4a** an offering, as of a gift. **4b** (*as modifier*): *a presentation copy of a book.* **5** a performance or representation, as of a play. **6** the formal introduction of a person, as at court; debut. **7** the act or right of nominating a clergyman to a benefice.
▸**,presen'tational** *adj*

presentationism (,prezən'teɪʃə,nɪzəm) *n Philosophy.* the theory that objects are identical with our perceptions of them. Cf. **representationalism.**
▸**,presen'tationist** *n, adj*

presentative (prɪ'zɛntətɪv) *adj* **1** *Philosophy.* able to be known or perceived immediately. **2** conferring the right of ecclesiastical presentation.

present-day ❶ *n* (*modifier*) of the modern day; current: *I don't like present-day fashions.*

presenter (prɪ'zɛntə) *n* **1** a person who presents something or someone. **2** *Radio, television.* a person who introduces a show, links items, etc.

presentient (prɪ'senʃənt) *adj* characterized by or experiencing a presentiment. [C19: from L *praesentiens,* from *praesentire,* from *prae-* PRE- + *sentire* to feel]

presentiment ❶ (prɪ'zɛntɪmənt) *n* a sense of something about to happen; premonition. [C18: from obs. F, from *pressentir* to sense beforehand]

presently ❶ ('prezəntlɪ) *adv* **1** in a short while; soon. **2** at the moment. **3** an archaic word for **immediately.**

presentment (prɪ'zɛntmənt) *n* **1** the act of presenting or state of being presented; presentation. **2** something presented, such as a picture, play, etc. **3** *Law.* a statement on oath by a jury of something within their own knowledge or observation. **4** *Commerce.* the presenting of a bill of exchange, promissory note, etc.

present participle ('prɛzᵊnt) *n* a participial form of verbs used adjectivally when the action it describes is contemporaneous with that of the main verb of a sentence and also used in the formation of certain compound tenses. In English this form ends in *-ing.*

present perfect ('prɛzᵊnt) *adj, n Grammar.* another term for **perfect** (senses 8, 10).

presents ('prezənts) *pl n Law.* used in a deed or document to refer to itself: *know all men by these presents.*

preservative (prɪ'zɜːvətɪv) *n* **1** something that preserves, esp. a chemical added to foods. ◆ *adj* **2** tending or intended to preserve.

preserve ❶ (prɪ'zɜːv) *vb* **preserves, preserving, preserved.** (*mainly tr*) **1** to keep safe from danger or harm; protect. **2** to protect from decay or dissolution; maintain: *to preserve old buildings.* **3** to maintain possession of; keep up: *to preserve a façade of indifference.* **4** to prevent from decomposition or chemical change. **5** to prepare (food), as by salting, so that it will resist decomposition. **6** to make preserves of (fruit, etc.). **7** to rear and protect (game) in restricted places for hunting or fishing. **8** (*intr*) to maintain protection for game in preserves. ◆ *n* **9** something that preserves or is preserved. **10** a special domain: *archaeology is the preserve of specialists.* **11** (*usually pl*) fruit, etc., prepared by cooking with sugar. **12** areas where game is reared for private hunting or fishing. [C14: via OF, from LL *praeservāre,* lit.: to keep safe in advance, from L *prae* before + *servāre* to keep safe]
▸**pre'servable** *adj* ▸**preservation** (,prezə'veɪʃən) *n* ▸**pre'server** *n*

preset *vb* (priː'set), **presets, presetting, preset.** (*tr*) **1** to set (a timing device) so that something begins to operate at the time specified. ◆ *n* ('priːset). **2** *Electronics.* a control, such as a variable resistor, that is not as accessible as the main controls and is used to set initial conditions.

preshrunk (priː'ʃrʌŋk) *adj* (of fabrics) having undergone shrinking during manufacture so that further shrinkage will not occur.

preside ❶ (prɪ'zaɪd) *vb* **presides, presiding, presided.** (*intr*) **1** to sit in or hold a position of authority, as over a meeting. **2** to exercise authority; control. [C17: via F from L *praesidēre* to superintend, from *prae* before + *sedēre* to sit]

presidency ('prezɪdənsɪ) *n, pl* **presidencies. 1** the office, dignity, or term of a president. **2** (*often cap.*) the office of president of a republic, esp. of the President of the US.

president ('prezɪdənt) *n* **1** (*often cap.*) the head of state of a republic, esp. of the US **2** (in the US) the chief executive officer of a company, corporation, etc. **3** a person who presides over an assembly, meeting, etc. **4** the chief executive officer of certain establishments of higher education. [C14: via OF from LL *praesidens* ruler; see PRESIDE]
▸**presidential** (,prezɪ'denʃəl) *adj* ▸**,presi'dentially** *adv* ▸**'presidentship** *n*

presidium *or* **praesidium** (prɪ'sɪdɪəm) *n* **1** (*often cap.*) (in Communist countries) a permanent committee of a larger body, such as a legislature, that acts for it when it is in recess. **2** a collective presidency. [C20: from Russian *prezidium,* from L *praesidium,* from *praesidēre* to superintend; see PRESIDE]

press[1] ❶ (pres) *vb* **1** to apply or exert weight, force, or steady pressure (on): *he pressed the button on the camera.* **2** (*tr*) to squeeze or compress so as to alter in shape. **3** to apply heat or pressure to (clothing) so as to smooth out creases. **4** to make (objects) from soft material by pressing with a mould, etc., esp. to make gramophone records from plastic. **5** (*tr*) to clasp; embrace. **6** (*tr*) to extract or force out (juice) by pressure (from). **7** (*tr*) to force or compel. **8** to importune (a person) insistently: *they pressed for an answer.* **9** to harass or cause harassment. **10** (*tr*) to plead or put forward strongly: *to press a claim.* **11** (*intr*) to be urgent. **12** (*tr; usually passive*) to have little of: *we're hard pressed for time.* **13** (when *intr,* often foll. by *on* or *forward*) to hasten or advance or cause to hasten or advance in a forceful manner. **14** (*intr*) to crowd; push. **15** (*tr*) *Arch.* to trouble or oppress. ◆ *n* **16** any machine that exerts pressure to form, shape, or cut materials or to extract liquids, compress solids, or hold components together while an adhesive joint is formed. **17** See **printing press. 18** the art or process of printing. **19 to (the) press.** to be printed: *when is this book going to press?* **20 the press. 20a** news media collectively, esp. newspapers. **20b** (*as modifier*): *press relations.* **21** the opinions and reviews in the newspapers, etc.: *the play received a poor press.* **22** the act of pressing or state of being pressed. **23** the act of crowding or pushing together. **24** a closely packed throng; crowd. **25** a cupboard, esp. a large one used for storing clothes or linen. **26** a wood or metal clamp to prevent tennis rackets, etc., from warping when not in use. [C14 *pressen,* from OF *presser,* from L, from *premere* to press]

press[2] (prɛs) *vb* (*tr*) **1** to recruit (men) by forcible measures for military service. **2** to use for a purpose other than intended (esp. in **press into**

THESAURUS

stage **6, 8** = **put forward**, adduce, advance, declare, expound, extend, hold out, introduce, offer, pose, produce, proffer, raise, recount, relate, state, submit, suggest, tender **7** = **give**, award, bestow, confer, donate, entrust, furnish, grant, hand out, hand over, offer, proffer, put at (someone's) disposal ◆ *n* **19** = **gift**, benefaction, boon, bounty, donation, endowment, favour, grant, gratuity, hand-out, largesse *or* largess, offering, prezzie (*inf.*)

presentable *adj* **1, 2** = **decent**, acceptable, becoming, fit to be seen, good enough, not bad (*inf.*), O.K. *or* okay (*inf.*), passable, proper, respectable, satisfactory, suitable, tolerable
Antonyms *adj* below par, not good enough, not up to scratch, poor, rubbishy, unacceptable, unpresentable, unsatisfactory

presentation *n* **1** = **giving**, award, bestowal, conferral, donation, investiture, offering **3** = **performance**, demonstration, display, exhibition, production, representation, show **5** = **portrayal**, appearance, arrangement, delivery, exposition, production, rendition, staging, submission **6** = **debut**, coming out, introduction, launch, launching, reception

present-day *modifier* = **current**, contemporary, latter-day, modern, newfangled, present, recent, up-to-date

presentiment *n* = **premonition**, anticipation, apprehension, expectation, fear, feeling, foreboding, forecast, forethought, hunch, intuition, misgiving, presage

presently *adv* **1** = **soon**, anon (*arch.*), before long, by and by, erelong (*arch. or poetic*), in a minute, in a moment, in a short while, pretty soon (*inf.*), shortly

preservation *n* **1, 2** = **protection**, conservation, defence, keeping, maintenance, perpetuation, safeguarding, safekeeping, safety, salvation, security, storage, support, upholding

preserve *vb* **1** = **protect**, care for, conserve, defend, guard, keep, safeguard, save, secure, shelter, shield **2** = **maintain**, continue, keep, keep up, perpetuate, retain, sustain, uphold **3** = **keep**, conserve, put up, save, store ◆ *n* **10** = **area**, domain, field, realm, specialism, sphere **11** *usually plural* = **jam**, confection, confiture, conserve, jelly, marmalade, sweetmeat **12** = **reserve**, game reserve, reservation, sanctuary
Antonyms *vb* ≠ **protect**: assail, assault, attack, leave unprotected, turn out ≠ **maintain**: abandon, discontinue, drop, end, give up ≠ **keep**: blow (*sl.*), consume, fritter away, spend, squander, waste

preside *vb* **1, 2** = **run**, administer, be at the head of, be in authority, chair, conduct, control, direct, govern, head, lead, manage, officiate, supervise

press[1] *vb* **1, 2** = **compress**, bear down on, condense, crush, depress, force down, jam, mash, push, reduce, squeeze, stuff **3** = **smooth**, calender, finish, flatten, iron, mangle, put the creases in, steam **5** = **hug**, clasp, crush, embrace, encircle, enfold, fold in one's arms, hold close, squeeze **7** = **force**, compel, constrain, demand, enforce, enjoin, insist on **8** = **urge**, beg, entreat, exhort, implore, importune, petition, plead, pressurize, sue, supplicate **12** *usually passive* = **be hard put**, be hurried, be pushed, be rushed (*inf.*), be short of **14** = **crowd**, cluster, flock, gather, hasten, herd, hurry, mill, push, rush, seethe, surge, swarm, throng **15** *Archaic* = **trouble**, afflict, assail, beset, besiege, disquiet, harass, plague, torment, vex, worry ◆ *n* **20 the press: a** = **newspapers**, columnists, correspondents, Fleet Street, fourth estate, gentlemen of the press, journalism, journalists, journos (*sl.*), news media, newsmen, photographers, pressmen, reporters, the papers **24** = **crowd**, bunch, crush, flock, herd, horde, host, mob, multitude, pack, push (*inf.*), swarm, throng service). ◆ *n* 3 recruitment into military service by forcible measures, as by a press gang. [C16: back formation from *prest* to recruit soldiers; also infl. by PRESS[1]]

press agent *n* a person employed to obtain favourable publicity, such as notices in newspapers, for an organization, actor, etc.

press box *n* an area reserved for reporters, as in a sports stadium.

press conference *n* an interview for press reporters given by a politician, film star, etc.

press fit *n Engineering.* a type of fit for mating parts, usually tighter than a sliding fit, used when the parts do not have to move relative to each other.

press gallery *n* an area for newspaper reporters, esp. in a legislative assembly.

press gang *n* 1 (formerly) a detachment of men used to press civilians for service in the navy or army. ◆ *vb* **press-gang.** (*tr*) 2 to force (a person) to join the navy or army by a press gang. 3 to induce (a person) to perform a duty by forceful persuasion.

pressing ❶ ('prɛsɪŋ) *adj* 1 demanding immediate attention. 2 persistent or importunate. ◆ *n* 3 a large specified number of gramophone records produced at one time from a master record. 4 *Football.* the tactic of trying to stay very close to the opposition when they are in possession of the ball.
▸ **'pressingly** *adv*

pressman ('prɛsmən, -ˌmæn) *n, pl* **pressmen.** 1 a journalist. 2 a person who operates a printing press.

press of sail *n Naut.* the most sail a vessel can carry under given conditions. Also called: **press of canvas.**

press release *n* an official announcement or account of a news item circulated to the press.

pressroom ('prɛsˌruːm, -ˌrʊm) *n* the room in a printing establishment that houses the printing presses.

press stud *n* a fastening device consisting of one part with a projecting knob that snaps into a hole on another like part, used esp. on clothing. Canad. equivalent: **dome fastener.**

press-up *n* an exercise in which the body is alternately raised from and lowered to the floor by the arms only, the trunk being kept straight. Also called (US and Canad.): **push-up.**

pressure ❶ ('prɛʃə) *n* 1 the state of pressing or being pressed. 2 the exertion of force by one body on the surface of another. 3 a moral force that compels: *to bring pressure to bear.* 4 urgent claims or demands: *to work under pressure.* 5 a burdensome condition that is hard to bear: *the pressure of grief.* 6 the force applied to a unit area of a surface, usually measured in pascals, millibars, torrs, or atmospheres. 7 short for **atmospheric pressure** or **blood pressure.** ◆ *vb* **pressures, pressuring, pressured.** (*tr*) 8 to constrain or compel, as by moral force. 9 another word for **pressurize.** [C14: from LL *pressūra* a pressing, from L *premere* to press]

pressure cooker *n* a strong hermetically sealed pot in which food may be cooked quickly under pressure at a temperature above the normal boiling point of water.
▸ **'pressure-ˌcook** *vb*

pressure group *n* a group of people who seek to exert pressure on legislators, public opinion, etc., in order to promote their own ideas or welfare.

pressure point *n* any of several points on the body above an artery that, when firmly pressed, will control bleeding from the artery at a point farther away from the heart.

pressure suit *n* an inflatable suit worn by a person flying at high altitudes or in space, to provide protection from low pressure.

pressurize ❶ *or* **pressurise** ('prɛʃəˌraɪz) *vb* **pressurizes, pressurizing, pressurized** *or* **pressurises, pressurising, pressurised.** (*tr*) 1 to increase the pressure in (an enclosure, such as an aircraft cabin) in order to maintain approximately atmospheric pressure when the external pressure is low. 2 to increase pressure on (a fluid). 3 to make insistent demands of (someone); coerce.
▸ **ˌpressuri'zation** *or* **ˌpressuri'sation** *n*

pressurized-water reactor *n* a type of nuclear reactor that uses water under pressure as both coolant and moderator.

presswork ('prɛsˌwɜːk) *n* the operation of, or matter printed by, a printing press.

Prestel ('prɛstɛl) *n Trademark.* (in Britain) the viewdata service operated by British Telecom.

Prester John ('prɛstə) *n* a legendary Christian priest and king, believed in the Middle Ages to have ruled in the Far East, but identified in the 14th century with the king of Ethiopia. [C14 *Prestre Johan,* from Med. L *presbyter Iohannes* Priest John]

prestidigitation (ˌprɛstɪˌdɪdʒɪ'teɪʃən) *n* another name for **sleight of hand.** [C19: from F: quick-fingeredness, from L *praestigiae* tricks, prob. infl. by F *preste* nimble, & L *digitus* finger]
▸ **ˌpresti'digiˌtator** *n*

prestige ❶ (prɛ'stiːʒ) *n* 1 high status or reputation achieved through success, influence, wealth, etc.; renown. 2a the power to impress; glamour. 2b (*modifier*): *a prestige car.* [C17: via F from L *praestigiae* tricks]
▸ **prestigious** (prɛ'stɪdʒəs) *adj*

prestissimo (prɛ'stɪsɪˌməʊ) *Music.* ◆ *adj, adv* 1 to be played as fast as possible. ◆ *n, pl* **prestissimos.** 2 a piece to be played in this way. [C18: from It.: very quickly, from *presto* fast]

presto ('prɛstəʊ) *adj, adv* 1 *Music.* to be played very fast. ◆ *adv* 2 immediately (esp. in **hey presto**). ◆ *n, pl* **prestos.** 3 *Music.* a passage directed to be played very quickly. [C16: from It.: fast, from LL *praestus* (adj) ready to hand, L *praestō* (adv) present]

prestressed concrete (ˌpriː'strɛst) *n* concrete that contains steel wires that are stretched to counteract the stresses that will occur under load.

presumably ❶ (prɪ'zjuːməblɪ) *adv* (*sentence modifier*) one supposes that: *presumably he won't see you, if you're leaving tomorrow.*

presume ❶ (prɪ'zjuːm) *vb* **presumes, presuming, presumed.** 1 (when *tr, often takes a clause as object*) to take (something) for granted; assume. 2 (when *tr, often foll. by an infinitive*) to dare (to do something): *do you presume to copy my work?* 3 (*intr;* foll. by *on* or *upon*) to rely or depend: *don't presume on his agreement.* 4 (*intr;* foll. by *on* or *upon*) to take advantage (of): *don't presume upon his good nature too far.* 5 (*tr*) *Law.* to take as proved until contrary evidence is produced. [C14: via OF from L *praesūmere* to take in advance, from *prae* before + *sūmere* to ASSUME]
▸ **presumedly** (prɪ'zjuːmɪdlɪ) *adv* ▸ **pre'suming** *adj*

presumption ❶ (prɪ'zʌmpʃən) *n* 1 the act of presuming. 2 bold or insolent behaviour. 3 a belief or assumption based on reasonable evidence. 4 a basis on which to presume. 5 *Law.* an inference of the truth of a fact from other facts proved. [C13: via OF from L *praesumptiō* anticipation, from *praesūmere* to take beforehand; see PRESUME]

presumptive ❶ (prɪ'zʌmptɪv) *adj* 1 based on presumption or probability. 2 affording reasonable ground for belief.
▸ **pre'sumptively** *adv*

presumptuous ❶ (prɪ'zʌmptjʊəs) *adj* characterized by presumption or tending to presume; bold; forward.
▸ **pre'sumptuously** *adv* ▸ **pre'sumptuousness** *n*

presuppose ❶ (ˌpriːsə'pəʊz) *vb* **presupposes, presupposing, presupposed.** (*tr*) 1 to take for granted. 2 to require as a necessary prior condition.
▸ **presupposition** (ˌpriːsʌpə'zɪʃən) *n*

preteen (priː'tiːn) *n* a boy or girl approaching his or her teens.

pretence ❶ *or US* **pretense** (prɪ'tɛns) *n* 1 the act of pretending. 2 a false display; affectation. 3 a claim, esp. a false one, to a right, title, or distinction. 4 make-believe. 5 a pretext.

pretend ❶ (prɪ'tɛnd) *vb* 1 (when *tr, usually takes a clause as object or an in-*

THESAURUS

pressing *adj* 1, 2 = **urgent**, burning, constraining, crucial, exigent, high-priority, imperative, important, importunate, now or never, serious, vital
Antonyms *adj* dispensable, regular, routine, unimportant, unnecessary

pressure *n* 1, 2 = **force**, compressing, compression, crushing, heaviness, squeezing, weight 3 = **power**, coercion, compulsion, constraint, force, influence, obligation, sway 5 = **stress**, adversity, affliction, burden, demands, difficulty, distress, exigency, hassle (*inf.*), heat, hurry, load, press, strain, urgency

pressurize *vb* 2 = **compress**, condense, constrict, press, squash, squeeze 3 = **force**, breathe down someone's neck, browbeat, coerce, compel, dragoon, drive, intimidate, press-gang, put the screws on (*sl.*), turn on the heat (*inf.*), twist one's arm (*inf.*)

prestige *n* 1 = **status**, authority, bottom, Brownie points, cachet, celebrity, credit, distinction, eminence, esteem, fame, honour, importance, influence, kudos, regard, renown, reputation, standing, stature, weight

prestigious *adj* 1 = **celebrated**, eminent, esteemed, exalted, great, illustrious, important, imposing, impressive, influential, notable, prominent, renowned, reputable, respected
Antonyms *adj* humble, lowly, minor, obscure, unimportant, unimpressive, unknown

presumably *adv* = **it would seem**, apparently, doubtless, doubtlessly, in all likelihood, in all probability, likely, most likely, on the face of it, probably, seemingly

presume *vb* 1 = **believe**, assume, conjecture, guess (*inf., chiefly US & Canad.*), infer, posit, postulate, presuppose, suppose, surmise, take for granted, take it, think 2 = **dare**, go so far, have the audacity, make bold, make so bold, take the liberty, undertake, venture 3 = **depend**, bank on, count on, rely, trust

presumption *n* 2 = **cheek** (*inf.*), assurance, audacity, boldness, brass (*inf.*), brass neck (*Brit. inf.*), chutzpah (*US & Canad. inf.*), effrontery, forwardness, front, gall (*inf.*), impudence, insolence, neck (*inf.*), nerve (*inf.*), presumptuousness, temerity 3 = **assumption**, anticipation, belief, conjecture, guess, hypothesis, opinion, premise *or* premiss, presupposition, supposition, surmise 4 = **probability**, basis, chance, grounds, likelihood, plausibility, reason

presumptive *adj* 1 = **assumed**, believed, expected, hypothetical, inferred, supposed, understood 2 = **possible**, believable, conceivable, credible, likely, plausible, probable, reasonable, verisimilar

presumptuous *adj* = **pushy** (*inf.*), arrogant, audacious, bigheaded (*inf.*), bold, conceited, foolhardy, forward, insolent, overconfident, overfamiliar, overweening, presuming, rash
Antonyms *adj* bashful, humble, modest, retiring, shy, timid, unassuming

presuppose *vb* 1 = **presume**, accept, assume, consider, imply, posit, postulate, suppose, take as read, take for granted, take it

presupposition *n* 1 = **assumption**, belief, hypothesis, preconceived idea, preconception, premise, presumption, supposition, theory

pretence *n* 1, 4 = **deception**, acting, charade, deceit, fabrication, fakery, faking, falsehood, feigning, invention, make-believe, sham, simulation, subterfuge, trickery 2 = **show**, affectation, appearance, artifice, display, façade, hokum (*sl., chiefly US & Canad.*), posing, posturing, pretentiousness, veneer 3, 5 = **pretext**, claim, cloak, colour, cover, excuse, façade, garb, guise, mask, masquerade, ruse, semblance, show, veil, wile
Antonyms *n* ≠ **deception:** candour, frankness, honesty, ingenuousness, openness ≠ **show:** actuality, fact, reality

pretend *vb* 1 = **feign**, affect, allege, assume, counterfeit, dissemble, dissimulate, fake, falsify, impersonate, make out, pass oneself off as, pro-

finitive) to claim or allege (something untrue). **2** *(tr; may take a clause as object or an infinitive)* to make believe, as in a play: *you pretend to be Ophelia.* **3** *(intr; foll. by to)* to present a claim, esp. a dubious one: *to pretend to the throne.* **4** *(intr; foll. by to) Obs.* to aspire as a candidate or suitor (for). ◆ *adj* **5** make-believe; imaginary. [C14: from L *praetendere* to stretch forth, feign]

pretender ❶ (prɪ'tendə) *n* **1** a person who pretends or makes false allegations. **2** a person who mounts a claim, as to a throne or title.

pretension ❶ (prɪ'tenʃən) *n* **1** *(often pl)* a false claim, esp. to merit, worth, or importance. **2** a specious or unfounded allegation; pretext. **3** the quality of being pretentious.

pretentious ❶ (prɪ'tenʃəs) *adj* **1** making claim to distinction or importance, esp. undeservedly. **2** ostentatious.
▸**pre'tentiously** *adv* ▸**pre'tentiousness** *n*

preterite *or esp. US* **preterit** ('pretərɪt) *Grammar.* ◆ *n* **1** a tense of verbs used to relate past action, formed in English by inflection of the verb, as *jumped, swam.* **2** a verb in this tense. ◆ *adj* **3** denoting this tense. [C14: from LL *praeteritum (tempus)* past (time), from L *praeterīre* to go by, from *preter-* beyond + *īre* to go]

preterm (pri:'tɜ:m) *adj* **1** (of a baby) born prematurely. ◆ *adv* **2** prematurely.

pretermit (,pri:tə'mɪt) *vb* **pretermits, pretermitting, pretermitted.** *(tr) Rare.* **1** to disregard. **2** to fail to do; neglect; omit. [C16: from L *praetermittere* to let pass, from *preter-* beyond + *mittere* to send]

preternatural ❶ (,pri:tə'nætʃrəl) *adj* **1** beyond what is ordinarily found in nature; abnormal. **2** another word for **supernatural**. [C16: from Med. L *praeternātūrālis,* from L *praeter natūram* beyond the scope of nature]
▸,**preter'naturally** *adv*

pretext ❶ ('pri:tekst) *n* **1** a fictitious reason given in order to conceal the real one. **2** a pretence. [C16: from L *praetextum* disguise, from *praetexere* to weave in front, disguise]

pretor ('pri:tə, -tɔ:) *n* a variant (esp. US) spelling of **praetor**.

prettify ❶ ('prɪtɪ,faɪ) *vb* **prettifies, prettifying, prettified.** *(tr)* to make pretty, esp. in a trivial fashion; embellish.
▸,**prettifi'cation** *n* ▸**'pretti,fier** *n*

pretty ❶ ('prɪtɪ) *adj* **prettier, prettiest. 1** pleasing or appealing in a delicate or graceful way. **2** dainty, neat, or charming. **3** *Inf., often ironical.* excellent, grand, or fine: *here's a pretty mess!* **4** commendable; good of its kind: *he replied with a pretty wit.* **5** *Inf.* effeminate; foppish. **6** *Arch. or Scot.* vigorous or brave. **7 sitting pretty.** *Inf.* well placed or established financially, socially, etc. ◆ *n, pl* **pretties. 8** a pretty person or thing. ◆ *adv Inf.* **9** fairly; somewhat. **10** very. ◆ *vb* **pretties, prettying, prettied. 11** *(tr;* often foll. by *up)* to make pretty; adorn. [OE *prættig* clever]
▸**'prettily** *adv* ▸**'prettiness** *n*

pretty-pretty *adj Inf.* excessively or ostentatiously pretty.

pretzel ('pretsəl) *n* a brittle savoury biscuit, in the form of a knot or stick, eaten esp. in Germany and the US. [C19: from G, from OHG *brezitella*]

prevail ❶ (prɪ'veɪl) *vb (intr)* **1** (often foll. by *over* or *against*) to prove superior; gain mastery: *skill will prevail.* **2** to be the most important feature; be prevalent. **3** to exist widely; be in force. **4** (often foll. by *on* or *upon*) to succeed in persuading or inducing. [C14: from L *praevalēre* to be superior in strength]
▸**pre'vailer** *n*

prevailing ❶ (prɪ'veɪlɪŋ) *adj* **1** generally accepted; widespread: *the prevailing opinion.* **2** most frequent; predominant: *the prevailing wind is from the north.*
▸**pre'vailingly** *adv*

prevalent ❶ ('prevələnt) *adj* **1** widespread or current. **2** superior in force or power; predominant.
▸**'prevalence** *n* ▸**'prevalently** *adv*

prevaricate ❶ (prɪ'værɪ,keɪt) *vb* **prevaricates, prevaricating, prevaricated.** *(intr)* to speak or act falsely or evasively with intent to deceive. [C16: from L *praevāricārī* to walk crookedly, from *prae* beyond + *vāricare* to straddle the legs]
▸**pre,vari'cation** *n* ▸**pre'vari,cator** *n*

prevent ❶ (prɪ'vent) *vb* **1** *(tr)* to keep from happening, esp. by taking precautionary action. **2** *(tr;* often foll. by *from)* to keep (someone from doing something). **3** *(intr)* to interpose or act as a hindrance. **4** *(tr) Arch.* to anticipate or precede. [C15: from L *praevenīre,* from *prae* before + *venīre* to come]
▸**pre'ventable** *or* **pre'ventible** *adj* ▸**pre'ventably** *or* **pre'ventibly** *adv*

prevention ❶ (prɪ'venʃən) *n* **1** the act of preventing. **2** a hindrance or impediment.

preventive ❶ (prɪ'ventɪv) *adj* **1** tending or intended to prevent or hinder. **2** *Med.* tending to prevent disease; prophylactic. **3** (in Britain) of, relating to, or belonging to the customs and excise service or the coastguard. ◆ *n* **4** something that serves to prevent or hinder. **5** *Med.* any drug or agent that tends to prevent disease. Also (for senses 1, 2, 4, 5): **preventative.**
▸**pre'ventively** *or* **pre'ventatively** *adv*

preview ❶ ('pri:vju:) *n* **1** an advance view or sight. **2** an advance showing before public presentation of a film, art exhibition, etc., usually before an invited audience. ◆ *vb* **3** *(tr)* to view in advance.

previous ❶ ('pri:vɪəs) *adj* **1** *(prenominal)* existing or coming before something else. **2** *(postpositive) Inf.* taking place or done too soon; premature. **3 previous to.** before. [C17: from L *praevius* leading the way, from *prae* before + *via* way]
▸**'previously** *adv* ▸**'previousness** *n*

previous question *n* **1** (in the House of Commons) a motion to drop

THESAURUS

fess, put on, sham, simulate **2 = make believe**, act, imagine, make up, play, play the part of, suppose **3 = lay claim**, allege, aspire, claim, profess, purport

pretended *adj* **1, 2 = feigned**, alleged, avowed, bogus, counterfeit, fake, false, fictitious, imaginary, ostensible, phoney *or* phony *(inf.)*, pretend *(inf.)*, professed, pseudo *(inf.)*, purported, sham, so-called, spurious

pretender *n* **2 = claimant**, aspirant, claimer

pretension *n* **1 = claim**, aspiration, assertion, assumption, demand, pretence, profession **3 = affectation**, airs, conceit, hypocrisy, ostentation, pomposity, pretentiousness, self-importance, show, showiness, snobbery, snobbishness, vainglory, vanity

pretentious *adj* **1, 2 = affected**, arty-farty *(inf.)*, assuming, bombastic, conceited, exaggerated, extravagant, flaunting, grandiloquent, grandiose, highfalutin *(inf.)*, high-flown, high-sounding, hollow, inflated, magniloquent, mannered, ostentatious, overambitious, pompous, puffed up, showy, snobbish, specious, vainglorious
Antonyms *adj* modest, natural, plain, simple, unaffected, unassuming, unpretentious

preternatural *adj* **1, 2 = supernatural**, abnormal, anomalous, extraordinary, inexplicable, irregular, marvellous, miraculous, mysterious, odd, peculiar, strange, unaccountable, unearthly, unnatural, unusual

pretext *n* **1, 2 = guise**, affectation, alleged reason, appearance, cloak, cover, device, excuse, mask, ploy, pretence, red herring, ruse, semblance, show, simulation, veil

prettify *vb* **= adorn**, deck out, decorate, doll up *(sl.)*, do up, embellish, garnish, gild, ornament, pretty up, tart up *(Brit. sl.)*, titivate, trick out, trim

pretty *adj* **1 = attractive**, appealing, beautiful, bonny, charming, comely, cute, fair, good-looking, graceful, lovely, personable **2 = pleasant**, bijou, dainty, delicate, elegant, fine, neat, nice, pleasing, tasteful, trim ◆ *adv* **9** *Informal* **= fairly**, kind of *(inf.)*, moderately, quite, rather, reasonably, somewhat
Antonyms *adj* ≠ **attractive**: plain, ugly, unattractive, unshapely, unsightly

prevail *vb* **1 = win**, be victorious, carry the day, gain mastery, overcome, overrule, prove superior, succeed, triumph **2, 3 = be widespread**, abound, be current, be prevalent, exist generally, obtain, predominate, preponderate **4** *often foll. by* **on** *or* **upon = persuade**, bring round, convince, dispose, incline, induce, influence, prompt, sway, talk into, win over

prevailing *adj* **1 = widespread**, common, current, customary, established, fashionable, general, in style, in vogue, ordinary, popular, prevalent, set, usual **2 = predominating**, dominant, influential, main, operative, preponderating, principal, ruling

prevalence *n* **1 = commonness**, acceptance, common occurrence, currency, frequency, pervasiveness, popularity, profusion, regularity, ubiquity, universality **2 = predominance**, ascendancy, hold, mastery, preponderance, primacy, rule, sway

prevalent *adj* **1 = common**, accepted, commonplace, current, customary, established, everyday, extensive, frequent, general, habitual, popular, rampant, rife, ubiquitous, universal, usual, widespread **2 = predominant**, ascendant, compelling, dominant, governing, powerful, prevailing, successful, superior
Antonyms *adj* ≠ **common**: confined, infrequent, limited, localized, rare, restricted, uncommon, unusual

prevaricate *vb* **= evade**, beat about the bush, beg the question, cavil, deceive, dodge, equivocate, flannel *(Brit. inf.)*, give a false colour to, hedge, lie, palter, quibble, shift, shuffle, stretch the truth, tergiversate
Antonyms *vb* be blunt, be direct, be frank, be straightforward, come straight to the point, not beat about the bush

prevarication *n* **= evasion**, cavilling, deceit, deception, equivocation, falsehood, falsification, lie, misrepresentation, pretence, quibbling, tergiversation, untruth

prevaricator *n* **= dissembler**, deceiver, dodger, equivocator, evader, fibber, hypocrite, liar, pettifogger, quibbler, sophist

prevent *vb* **1-3 = stop**, anticipate, avert, avoid, balk, bar, block, check, counteract, defend against, foil, forestall, frustrate, hamper, head off, hinder, impede, inhibit, intercept, nip in the bud, obstruct, obviate, preclude, restrain, stave off, thwart, ward off
Antonyms *vb* allow, encourage, help, incite, permit, support, urge

prevention *n* **1 = elimination**, anticipation, avoidance, deterrence, forestalling, obviation, precaution, preclusion, prophylaxis, safeguard, thwarting

preventive *adj* **1 = hindering**, hampering, impeding, obstructive **2** *Medical* **= protective**, counteractive, deterrent, inhibitory, precautionary, prophylactic, shielding ◆ *n* **4 = hindrance**, block, impediment, obstacle, obstruction **5** *Medical* **= protection**, deterrent, neutralizer, prevention, prophylactic, protective, remedy, safeguard, shield

preview *n* **1, 2 = sample**, advance showing, foretaste, sampler, sneak preview, taster, trailer ◆ *vb* **3 = sample**, foretaste, taste

previous *adj* **1 = earlier**, antecedent, anterior, erstwhile, ex-, foregoing, former, one-time, past, preceding, prior, quondam, sometime **2** *Informal* **= premature**, ahead of oneself, precipitate, too early, too soon, untimely
Antonyms *adj* ≠ **earlier**: consequent, following, later, subsequent, succeeding

previously *adv* **1 = before**, at one time, a while ago, beforehand, earlier, formerly, heretofore, hitherto, in advance, in anticipation, in days *or* years gone by, in the past, once, then, until now the present topic under debate, put in order to prevent a vote. **2** (in the House of Lords and US legislative bodies) a motion to vote on a bill without delay.

previse (prɪˈvaɪz) *vb* **previses, previsING, prevised.** (*tr*) *Rare.* **1** to predict or foresee. **2** to notify in advance. [C16: from L *praevidēre* to foresee]
▸**prevision** (prɪˈvɪʒən) *n*

prey ❶ (preɪ) *n* **1** an animal hunted or captured by another for food. **2** a person or thing that becomes the victim of a hostile person, influence, etc. **3 bird** *or* **beast of prey.** a bird or animal that preys on others for food. **4** an archaic word for **booty.** ◆ *vb* (*intr;* often foll. by *on* or *upon*) **5** to hunt food by killing other animals. **6** to make a victim (of others), as by profiting at their expense. **7** to exert a depressing or obsessive effect (on the mind, spirits, etc.). [C13: from OF *preie,* from L *praeda* booty]
▸**ˈpreyer** *n*

priapic (praɪˈæpɪk, -ˈeɪ-) *or* **priapean** (ˌpraɪəˈpiːən) *adj* **1** (*sometimes cap.*) of or relating to Priapus, in classical antiquity the god of male procreative power and of gardens and vineyards. **2** a less common word for **phallic.**

priapism (ˈpraɪəˌpɪzəm) *n Pathol.* prolonged painful erection of the penis, caused by neurological disorders, etc. [C17: from LL *priāpismus,* ult. from Gk *Priapus;* see PRIAPIC]

price ❶ (praɪs) *n* **1** the sum in money or goods for which anything is or may be bought or sold. **2** the cost at which anything is obtained. **3** the cost of bribing a person. **4** a sum of money offered as a reward for a capture or killing. **5** value or worth, esp. high worth. **6** *Gambling.* another word for **odds. 7 at any price.** whatever the price or cost. **8 at a price.** at a high price. **9 what price (something)?** what are the chances of (something) happening now? ◆ *vb* **prices, pricing, priced.** (*tr*) **10** to fix the price of. **11** to discover the price of. **12 price out of the market.** to charge so highly for as to prevent the sale, hire, etc., of. [C13 *pris,* from OF, from L *pretium*]
▸**ˈpricer** *n*

price control *n* the establishment and maintenance of maximum price levels for basic goods and services by a government.

price-dividend ratio *n* the ratio of the price of a share on a stock exchange to the dividends per share paid in the previous year, used as a measure of a company's potential as an investment. Abbrevs.: **P-D ratio, PDR.**

price-earnings ratio *n* the ratio of the price of a share on the stock exchange to the earnings per share, used as a measure of a company's future profitability. Abbrev.: **P-E ratio.**

price-fixing *n* **1** the setting of prices by agreement among producers and distributors. **2** another name for **price control** or **resale price maintenance.**

price leadership *n Marketing.* the setting of the price of a product or service by a dominant firm at a level that competitors can match, in order to avoid a price war.

priceless ❶ (ˈpraɪslɪs) *adj* **1** of inestimable worth; invaluable. **2** *Inf.* extremely amusing or ridiculous.
▸**ˈpricelessly** *adv* ▸**ˈpricelessness** *n*

price ring *n* a group of traders formed to maintain the prices of their goods.

price-sensitive *adj* likely to affect the price of property, esp. shares and securities: *price-sensitive information.*

pricey ❶ *or* **pricy** (ˈpraɪsɪ) *adj* **pricier, priciest.** an informal word for **expensive.**

prick ❶ (prɪk) *vb* (*mainly tr*) **1a** to make (a small hole) in (something) by piercing lightly with a sharp point. **1b** to wound in this manner. **2** (*intr*) to cause or have a piercing or stinging sensation. **3** to cause to feel a sharp emotional pain: *knowledge of such poverty pricked his conscience.* **4** to puncture. **5** to outline by dots or punctures. **6** (*also intr;* usually foll. by *up*) to rise or raise erect: *the dog pricked his ears up.* **7** (usually foll. by *out* or *off*) to transplant (seedlings) into a larger container. **8** *Arch.* to urge on, esp. to spur a horse on. **9 prick up one's ears.** to start to listen attentively; become interested. ◆ *n* **10** the act of pricking or the sensation of being pricked. **11** a mark made by a sharp point; puncture. **12** a sharp emotional pain: *a prick of conscience.* **13** a taboo slang word for **penis. 14** *Sl., derog.* an obnoxious or despicable person. **15** an instrument or weapon with a sharp point. **16** the track of an animal, esp. a hare. **17 kick against the pricks.** to hurt oneself by struggling against something in vain. [OE *prica* point, puncture]
▸**ˈpricker** *n*

pricket (ˈprɪkɪt) *n* **1** a male deer in the second year of life having unbranched antlers. **2** a sharp metal spike on which to stick a candle. [C14 *priket,* from *prik* PRICK]

prickle ❶ (ˈprɪkᵊl) *n* **1** *Bot.* a pointed process arising from the outer layer of a stem, leaf, etc., and containing no woody tissue. Cf. **thorn. 2** a pricking or stinging sensation. ◆ *vb* **prickles, prickling, prickled. 3** to feel or cause to feel a stinging sensation. **4** (*tr*) to prick, as with a thorn. [OE *pricel*]

prickly ❶ (ˈprɪklɪ) *adj* **pricklier, prickliest. 1** having or covered with prickles. **2** stinging. **3** irritable. **4** full of difficulties: *a prickly problem.*
▸**ˈprickliness** *n*

prickly heat *n* a nontechnical name for **miliaria.**

prickly pear *n* **1** any of various tropical cactuses having flattened or cylindrical spiny joints and oval fruit that is edible in some species. **2** the fruit of any of these plants.

pride ❶ (praɪd) *n* **1** a feeling of honour and self-respect; a sense of personal worth. **2** excessive self-esteem; conceit. **3** a source of pride. **4** satisfaction or pleasure in one's own or another's success, achievements, etc. (esp. in **take (a) pride in**). **5** the better or superior part of something. **6** the most flourishing time. **7** a group (of lions). **8** courage; spirit. **9** *Arch.* pomp or splendour. **10 pride of place.** the most important position. ◆ *vb* **prides, priding, prided. 11** (*tr;* foll. by *on* or *upon*) to take pride in (oneself) for. [OE *prȳda*]
▸**ˈprideful** *adj* ▸**ˈpridefully** *adv*

prie-dieu (priːˈdjɜː) *n* a piece of furniture consisting of a low surface for kneeling upon and a narrow front surmounted by a rest, for use when praying. [C18: from F, from *prier* to pray + *Dieu* God]

prier *or* **pryer** (ˈpraɪə) *n* a person who pries.

priest ❶ (priːst) *n* **1** a person ordained to act as a mediator between God and man in administering the sacraments, preaching, etc. **2** (in episcopal Churches) a minister in the second grade of the hierarchy of holy orders, ranking below a bishop but above a deacon. **3** a minister of any religion. **4** an official who offers sacrifice on behalf of the people and performs other religious ceremonies. ◆ *vb* **5** (*tr*) to make a priest; ordain. [OE *prēost,* apparently from PRESBYTER]
▸**ˈpriestess** *fem n* ▸**ˈpriestˌhood** *n* ▸**ˈpriestˌlike** *adj* ▸**ˈpriestly** *adj*

priestcraft (ˈpriːstˌkrɑːft) *n* **1** the art and skills involved in the work of a priest. **2** *Derog.* the influence of priests upon politics.

priest-hole *or* **priest's hole** *n* a secret chamber in certain houses in England, built as a hiding place for Roman Catholic priests when they were proscribed in the 16th and 17th centuries.

prig[1] ❶ (prɪg) *n* a person who is smugly self-righteous and narrow-minded. [C18: from ?]
▸**ˈpriggery** *or* **ˈpriggishness** *n* ▸**ˈpriggish** *adj* ▸**ˈpriggishly** *adv*

prig[2] (prɪg) *Brit. arch. sl.* ◆ *vb* **prigs, prigging, prigged. 1** another word for **steal.** ◆ *n* **2** another word for **thief.** [C16: from ?]

prim ❶ (prɪm) *adj* **primmer, primmest. 1** affectedly proper, precise, or for-

THESAURUS

prey *n* **1 = quarry**, game, kill **2 = victim**, dupe, fall guy (*inf.*), mark, mug (*Brit. sl.*), target ◆ *vb* **5 = hunt**, devour, eat, feed upon, live off, seize **6 = victimize**, blackmail, bleed (*inf.*), bully, exploit, intimidate, take advantage of, terrorize **7 = worry**, burden, distress, hang over, haunt, oppress, trouble, weigh down, weigh heavily

price *n* **1 = cost**, amount, asking price, assessment, bill, charge, damage (*inf.*), estimate, expenditure, expense, face value, fee, figure, outlay, payment, rate, valuation, value, worth **2 = consequences**, cost, penalty, sacrifice, toll **4 = reward**, bounty, compensation, premium, recompense **7 at any price = whatever the cost**, anyhow, cost what it may, expense no object, no matter what the cost, regardless ◆ *vb* **10 = evaluate**, assess, cost, estimate, put a price on, rate, value

priceless *adj* **1 = valuable**, beyond price, cherished, costly, dear, expensive, incalculable, incomparable, inestimable, invaluable, irreplaceable, precious, prized, rare, rich, treasured, worth a king's ransom **2** *Informal* **= hilarious**, absurd, amusing, comic, droll, funny, killing (*inf.*), rib-tickling, ridiculous, riotous, side-splitting
Antonyms *adj* ≠ **valuable:** cheap, cheapo (*inf.*), common, inexpensive, worthless

pricey *adj* **= expensive**, costly, dear, exorbitant, extortionate, high-priced, over the odds (*Brit. inf.*), steep (*inf.*)

prick *vb* **1, 4 = pierce**, bore, impale, jab, lance, perforate, pink, punch, puncture, stab **2 = sting**, bite, itch, prickle, smart, tingle **3 = distress**, cut, grieve, move, pain, stab, touch, trouble, wound **6** *usually foll. by* **up = raise**, point, rise, stand erect ◆ *n* **11 = puncture**, cut, gash, hole, perforation, pinhole, wound **12 = pang**, gnawing, prickle, smart, spasm, sting, twinge

prickle *n* **1 = spike**, barb, needle, point, spine, spur, thorn **2 = tingling**, chill, formication, goose bumps, goose flesh, paraesthesia (*Medical*), pins and needles (*inf.*), smart, tickle, tingle ◆ *vb* **3 = tingle**, itch, smart, sting, twitch **4 = prick**, jab, nick, stick

prickly *adj* **1 = spiny**, barbed, brambly, briery, bristly, thorny **2 = itchy**, crawling, pricking, prickling, scratchy, sharp, smarting, stinging, tingling **3 = irritable**, bad-tempered, cantankerous, edgy, fractious, grumpy, liverish, peevish, pettish, petulant, ratty (*Brit. & NZ inf.*), shirty (*sl., chiefly Brit.*), snappish, stroppy (*Brit. sl.*), tetchy, touchy, waspish **4 = difficult**, complicated, intricate, involved, knotty, thorny, ticklish, tricky, troublesome, trying

pride *n* **1 = self-respect**, *amour-propre*, dignity, honour, self-esteem, self-worth **2 = conceit**, arrogance, bigheadedness (*inf.*), egotism, haughtiness, hauteur, hubris, loftiness, *morgue*, presumption, pretension, pretentiousness, self-importance, self-love, smugness, snobbery, superciliousness, vainglory, vanity **3 = gem**, boast, jewel, pride and joy, prize, treasure **4 = satisfaction**, delight, gratification, joy, pleasure **5 = elite**, best, choice, cream, flower, glory, pick ◆ *vb* **11** *foll. by* **on** *or* **upon = be proud of**, boast of, brag about, congratulate oneself on, crow about, exult in, flatter oneself, glory in, pique oneself, plume oneself, revel in, take pride in, vaunt
Antonyms *n* ≠ **conceit:** humility, meekness, modesty

priest *n* **1-3 = clergyman**, churchman, cleric, curate, divine, ecclesiastic, father, father confessor, holy man, man of God, man of the cloth, minister, padre (*inf.*), pastor, vicar

priestly *adj* **1-3 = ecclesiastic**, canonical, clerical, hieratic, pastoral, priestlike, sacerdotal

prig[1] *n* **= goody-goody** (*inf.*), Holy Joe (*inf.*), Holy Willie (*inf.*), Mrs Grundy, old maid (*inf.*), pedant, prude, puritan, stuffed shirt (*inf.*)

priggish *adj* **= self-righteous**, goody-goody, holier-than-thou, narrow-minded, pedantic, prim, prudish, puritanical, self-satisfied, smug, starchy (*inf.*), stiff, stuffy

prim *adj* **1 = prudish**, demure, fastidious, formal, fussy, niminy-piminy, old-maidish (*inf.*), partic-

mal. ◆ *vb* **prims, primming, primmed. 2** (*tr*) to make prim. **3** to purse (the mouth) primly or (of the mouth) to be so pursed. [C18: from ?] ▸**'primly** *adv* ▸**'primness** *n*

prima ballerina ('pri:mə) *n* a leading female ballet dancer. [from It., lit.: first ballerina]

primacy ❶ ('praɪməsɪ) *n, pl* **primacies. 1** the state of being first in rank, grade, etc. **2** *Christianity.* the office, rank, or jurisdiction of a primate, senior bishop, or pope.

prima donna ❶ ('pri:mə 'dɒnə) *n, pl* **prima donnas. 1** a leading female operatic star. **2** *Inf.* a temperamental person. [C19: from It.: first lady]

prima facie ('praɪmə 'feɪʃɪ) *adv* at first sight; as it seems at first. [C15: from L, from *prīmus* first + *faciēs* FACE]

prima-facie evidence *n Law.* evidence that is sufficient to establish a fact or to raise a presumption of the truth unless controverted.

primal ❶ ('praɪməl) *adj* **1** first or original. **2** chief or most important. [C17: from Med. L *prīmālis,* from L *prīmus* first]

primaquine ('praɪmə,kwi:n) *n* a synthetic drug used in the treatment of malaria. [C20: from *prima-,* from L *prīmus* first + QUIN(OLIN)E]

primarily ❶ ('praɪmərɪlɪ, praɪ'mærɪlɪ, -'mɛərɪlɪ) *adv* **1** principally; chiefly; mainly. **2** at first; originally.

primary ❶ ('praɪmərɪ) *adj* **1** first in importance, degree, rank, etc. **2** first in position or time, as in a series. **3** fundamental; basic. **4** being the first stage; elementary. **5** (*prenominal*) of or relating to the education of children up to the age of 11. **6** (of the flight feathers of a bird's wing) growing from the manus. **7a** being the part of an electric circuit, such as a transformer, in which a changing current induces a current in a neighbouring circuit: *a primary coil.* **7b** (of a current) flowing in such a circuit. **8a** (of a product) consisting of a natural raw material; unmanufactured. **8b** (of production or industry) involving the extraction or winning of such products. **9** (of Latin, Greek, or Sanskrit tenses) referring to present or future time. **10** *Geol., obs.* relating to the Palaeozoic or earlier eras. ◆ *n, pl* **primaries. 11** a person or thing that is first in rank, occurrence, etc. **12** (in the US) a preliminary election in which the voters of a state or region choose a party's convention delegates, nominees for office, etc. Full name: **primary election. 13** short for **primary colour** or **primary school. 14** any of the flight feathers growing from the manus of a bird's wing. **15** a primary coil, winding, inductance, or current in an electric circuit. **16** *Astron.* a celestial body around which one or more specified secondary bodies orbit: *the sun is the primary of the earth.* [C15: from L *prīmārius* principal, from *prīmus* first]

primary accent *or* **stress** *n Linguistics.* the strongest accent in a word or breath group, as that on the first syllable of *agriculture.*

primary cell *n* an electric cell that generates an electromotive force by the direct and usually irreversible conversion of chemical energy into electrical energy. Also called: **voltaic cell.**

primary colour *n* **1** any of three colours (usually red, green, and blue) that can be mixed to match any other colour, including white light but excluding black. **2** any one of the colours cyan, magenta, or yellow. An equal mixture of the three produces a black pigment. **3** any one of the colours red, yellow, green, or blue. All other colours look like a mixture of two or more of these colours.

primary school *n* **1** (in England and Wales) a school for children below the age of 11. It is usually divided into an infant and a junior section. **2** (in Scotland) a school for children below the age of 12. **3** (in the US and Canad.) a school equivalent to the first three or four grades of elementary school.

primate[1] ('praɪmeɪt) *n* **1** any placental mammal of the order *Primates,* typically having flexible hands, good eyesight, and, in the higher apes, a highly developed brain: includes lemurs, apes, and man. ◆ *adj* **2** of, relating to, or belonging to the order *Primates.* [C18: from NL *primates,* pl. of *prīmās* principal, from *prīmus* first] ▸**primatial** (praɪ'meɪʃəl) *adj*

primate[2] ('praɪmeɪt) *n* **1** another name for an **archbishop. 2 Primate of all England.** the Archbishop of Canterbury. **3 Primate of England.** the Archbishop of York. [C13: from OF, from L *prīmās* principal, from *prīmus* first]

prime ❶ (praɪm) *adj* **1** (*prenominal*) first in quality or value; first-rate. **2** (*prenominal*) fundamental; original. **3** (*prenominal*) first in importance; chief. **4** *Maths.* **4a** having no factors except itself or one: $x^2 + x + 3$ *is a prime polynomial.* **4b** (foll. by *to*) having no common factors (with): *20 is prime to 21.* **5** *Finance.* having the best credit rating: *prime investments.* ◆ *n* **6** the time when a thing is at its best. **7** a period of power, vigour, etc. (esp. in **the prime of life**). **8** *Maths.* short for **prime number. 9** *Chiefly RC Church.* the second of the seven canonical hours of the divine office, originally fixed for the first hour of the day, at sunrise. **10** the first of eight basic positions from which a parry or attack can be made in fencing. ◆ *vb* **primes, priming, primed. 11** to prepare (something). **12** (*tr*) to apply a primer, such as paint or size, to (a surface). **13** (*tr*) to fill (a pump) with its working fluid before starting, in order to expel air from it before starting. **14 prime the pump. 14a** See **pump priming. 14b** to make an initial input in order to set a process going. **15** (*tr*) to increase the quantity of fuel in the float chamber of (a carburettor) in order to facilitate the starting of an engine. **16** (*tr*) to insert a primer into (a gun, mine, etc.) preparatory to detonation or firing. **17** (*tr*) to provide with facts beforehand; brief. [(adj) C14: from L *prīmus* first; (n) C13: from L *prīma* (*hora*) the first (hour); (vb) C16: from ?] ▸**'primeness** *n*

prime cost *n* the portion of the cost of a commodity that varies directly with the amount of it produced, principally comprising materials and labour. Also called: **variable cost.**

prime meridian *n* the 0° meridian from which the other meridians are calculated, usually taken to pass through Greenwich.

prime minister *n* **1** the head of a parliamentary government. **2** the chief minister of a sovereign or a state.

prime mover *n* **1** the original force behind an idea, enterprise, etc. **2a** the source of power, such as fuel, wind, electricity, etc., for a machine. **2b** the means of extracting power from such a source, such as a steam engine.

prime number *n* an integer that cannot be factorized into other integers but is only divisible by itself or 1, such as 2, 3, 7, and 11.

primer[1] ('praɪmə) *n* an introductory text, such as a school textbook. [C14: via Anglo-Norman, from Med. L *prīmārius* (*liber*) a first (book), from L *prīmārius* PRIMARY]

primer[2] ('praɪmə) *n* **1** a person or thing that primes. **2** a device, such as a tube containing explosive, for detonating the main charge in a gun, mine, etc. **3** a substance, such as paint, applied to a surface as a base, sealer, etc. [C15: see PRIME (vb)]

prime rate *n* the lowest commercial interest rate charged by a bank at a particular time.

primers ('prɪməz) *n* (*functioning as sing*) *NZ inf.* the youngest classes in a primary school: *in the primers.*

prime time *n* the peak viewing time on television, for which advertising rates are the highest.

primeval ❶ *or* **primaeval** (praɪ'mi:vəl) *adj* of or belonging to the first ages of the world. [C17: from L *prīmaevus* youthful, from *prīmus* first + *aevum* age] ▸**pri'mevally** *or* **pri'maevally** *adv*

priming ('praɪmɪŋ) *n* **1** something used to prime. **2** a substance used to ignite an explosive charge.

primitive ❶ ('prɪmɪtɪv) *adj* **1** of or belonging to the beginning; original. **2** characteristic of an early state, esp. in being crude or uncivilized: *a primitive dwelling.* **3** *Anthropol.* denoting a preliterate and nonindustrial social system. **4** *Biol.* of, relating to, or resembling an early stage in development: *primitive amphibians.* **5** showing the characteristics of primitive painters; untrained, childlike, or naive. **6** *Geol.* of or denoting rocks formed in or before the Palaeozoic era. **7** denoting a word from which another word is derived, as for example *hope,* from which *hopeless* is derived. **8** *Protestant theol.* of or associated with a group that breaks away from a sect, denomination, or Church in order to return to what is regarded as the original simplicity of the Gospels. ◆ *n* **9** a primitive person or thing. **10a** an artist whose work does not conform to traditional standards of Western painting, such as a painter from an African civilization. **10b** a painter of the pre-Renaissance era in European painting. **10c** a painter of any era whose work appears childlike or untrained. ◆ Also called (for a, c): **naive. 11** a work by such an artist. **12** a word from which another word is derived. **13** *Maths.* a curve or other form from which another is derived. [C14: from L *prīmitīvus* earliest of its kind from *prīmus* first] ▸**'primitively** *adv* ▸**'primitiveness** *n*

THESAURUS

ular, precise, priggish, prissy (*inf.*), proper, puritanical, schoolmarmish (*Brit. inf.*), starchy (*inf.*), stiff, strait-laced

Antonyms *adj* carefree, casual, easy-going, informal, laid-back, relaxed

primacy *n* **1** = **supremacy**, ascendancy, command, dominance, dominion, leadership, pre-eminence, superiority

prima donna *n* **1** = **diva**, leading lady, star

primal *adj* **1** = **first**, earliest, initial, original, primary, prime, primitive, primordial, pristine **2** = **chief**, central, first, greatest, highest, main, major, most important, paramount, prime, principal

primarily *adv* **1** = **chiefly**, above all, basically, especially, essentially, for the most part, fundamentally, generally, largely, mainly, mostly, on the whole, principally **2** = **at first**, at *or* from the start, first and foremost, initially, in the beginning, in the first place, originally

primary *adj* **1** = **chief**, best, capital, cardinal, dominant, first, greatest, highest, leading, main, paramount, prime, principal, top **2** = **earliest**, aboriginal, initial, original, primal, primeval, primitive, primordial, pristine **3** = **basic**, beginning, bog-standard (*inf.*), elemental, essential, fundamental, radical, ultimate, underlying **4** = **elementary**, introductory, rudimentary, simple

Antonyms *adj* ≠ **chief**: inferior, lesser, lowest, subordinate, supplementary, unimportant ≠ **elementary**: ensuing, following, later, secondary, subsequent, succeeding

prime *adj* **1** = **best**, capital, choice, excellent, first-class, first-rate, grade A, highest, quality, select, selected, superior, top **2** = **fundamental**, basic, bog-standard (*inf.*), earliest, original, primary, underlying **3** = **main**, chief, leading, predominant, pre-eminent, primary, principal, ruling, senior ◆ *n* **6** = **peak**, best days, bloom, flower, full flowering, height, heyday, maturity, perfection, zenith ◆ *vb* **11** = **prepare**, break in, coach, fit, get ready, groom, make ready, train **17** = **inform**, brief, clue in (*inf.*), clue up (*inf.*), fill in (*inf.*), gen up (*Brit. inf.*), give someone the lowdown (*inf.*), notify, tell

primeval *adj* = **earliest**, ancient, early, first, old, original, prehistoric, primal, primitive, primordial, pristine

primitive *adj* **1** = **early**, earliest, elementary, first, original, primary, primeval, primordial, pristine **2** = **crude**, rough, rude, rudimentary, simple, unrefined **2** = **uncivilized**, barbarian, barbaric, savage, uncultivated, undeveloped **5** = **simple**, childlike, naive, undeveloped, unsophisticated, untrained, untutored

primitivism ('prɪmɪtɪˌvɪzəm) *n* **1** the condition of being primitive. **2** the belief that the value of primitive cultures is superior to that of the modern world.
▸**'primitivist** *n, adj*

primo ('priːməʊ) *n, pl* **primos** *or* **primi** (-miː). *Music.* **1** the upper or right-hand part of a piano duet. **2 tempo primo.** at the same speed as at the beginning of the piece. [It.: first, from L *prīmus*]

primogenitor (ˌpraɪməʊ'dʒɛnɪtə) *n* **1** a forefather; ancestor. **2** an earliest parent or ancestor, as of a race. [C17: alteration of PROGENITOR after PRIMOGENITURE]

primogeniture (ˌpraɪməʊ'dʒɛnɪtʃə) *n* **1** the state of being a first-born. **2** *Law.* the right of an eldest son to succeed to the estate of his ancestor to the exclusion of all others. [C17: from Med. L *prīmōgenitūra* birth of a first child, from L *prīmō* at first + LL *genitūra* a birth]
▸**primogenitary** (ˌpraɪməʊ'dʒɛnɪtərɪ, -trɪ) *adj*

primordial 🅣 (praɪ'mɔːdɪəl) *adj* **1** existing at or from the beginning; primeval. **2** constituting an origin; fundamental. **3** *Biol.* relating to an early stage of development. [C14: from LL *prīmōrdiālis* original, from L *prīmus* first + *ōrdīrī* to begin]
▸**priˌmordi'ality** *n* ▸**pri'mordially** *adv*

primp 🅣 (prɪmp) *vb* to dress (oneself), esp. in fine clothes; prink. [C19: prob. from PRIM]

primrose ('prɪmˌrəʊz) *n* **1** any of various temperate plants of the genus *Primula,* esp. a European variety which has pale yellow flowers. **2** short for **evening primrose. 3** Also called: **primrose yellow.** a light yellow, sometimes with a greenish tinge. ◆ *adj* **4** of or abounding in primroses. **5** of the colour primrose. [C15: from OF *primerose,* from Med. L *prīma rosa* first rose]

primrose path *n* (often preceded by *the*) a pleasurable way of life.

primula ('prɪmjʊlə) *n* any plant of the N temperate genus *Primula,* having white, yellow, pink, or purple funnel-shaped flowers with five spreading petals: includes the primrose, oxlip, cowslip, and polyanthus. [C18: NL, from Med. L *prīmula* (*vēris*) little first one (of the spring)]

primum mobile *Latin.* ('praɪməm 'məʊbɪlɪ) *n* **1** a prime mover. **2** *Astron.* the outermost empty sphere in the Ptolemaic system that was thought to revolve around the earth from east to west in 24 hours carrying with it the inner spheres of the planets, sun, moon, and fixed stars. [C15: from Med. L: first moving (thing)]

Primus ('praɪməs) *n Trademark.* a portable paraffin cooking stove, used esp. by campers. Also called: **Primus stove.**

prince 🅣 (prɪns) *n* **1** (in Britain) a son of the sovereign or of one of the sovereign's sons. **2** a nonreigning male member of a sovereign family. **3** the monarch of a small territory that was at some time subordinate to an emperor or king. **4** any monarch. **5** a nobleman in various countries, such as Italy and Germany. **6** an outstanding member of a specified group: *a merchant prince.* [C13: via OF from L *princeps* first man, ruler]
▸**'princedom** *n* ▸**'princeˌlike** *adj*

prince consort *n* the husband of a female sovereign, who is himself a prince.

princeling ('prɪnslɪŋ) *n* **1** a young prince. **2** Also called: **princelet.** the ruler of an insignificant territory.

princely 🅣 ('prɪnslɪ) *adj* **princelier, princeliest. 1** generous or lavish. **2** of or characteristic of a prince. ◆ *adv* **3** in a princely manner.
▸**'princeliness** *n*

Prince of Darkness *n* another name for **Satan.**

Prince of Peace *n Bible.* the future Messiah (Isaiah 9:6): held by Christians to be Christ.

Prince of Wales *n* the eldest son and heir apparent of the British sovereign.

prince regent *n* a prince who acts as regent during the minority, disability, or absence of the legal sovereign.

prince's-feather *n* **1** a garden plant with spikes of bristly brownish-red flowers. **2** a tall tropical plant with hanging spikes of pink flowers.

princess (prɪn'sɛs) *n* **1** (in Britain) a daughter of the sovereign or of one of the sovereign's sons. **2** a nonreigning female member of a sovereign family. **3** the wife and consort of a prince. **4** *Arch.* a female sovereign. **5** Also: **princess dress.** a style of dress having a fitted bodice and A-line skirt without a seam at the waistline.

princess royal *n* the eldest daughter of a British or (formerly) a Prussian sovereign.

principal 🅣 ('prɪnsɪp^{ə}l) *adj* (*prenominal*) **1** first in importance, rank, value, etc. **2** denoting capital or property as opposed to interest, etc. ◆ *n* **3** a person who is first in importance or directs some event, organization, etc. **4** *Law.* **4a** a person who engages another to act as his agent. **4b** an active participant in a crime. **4c** the person primarily liable to fulfil an obligation. **5** the head of a school or other educational institution. **6** (in Britain) a civil servant of an executive grade who is in charge of a section. **7** the leading performer in a play. **8** *Finance.* **8a** capital or property, as contrasted with income. **8b** the original amount of a debt on which interest is calculated. **9** a main roof truss or rafter. **10** *Music.* either of two types of open diapason organ stops. [C13: via OF from L *principālis* chief, from *princeps* chief man]
▸**'principally** *adv* ▸**'principalship** *n*

> **USAGE NOTE** See at **principle.**

principal boy *n* the leading male role in a pantomime, traditionally played by a woman.

principality (ˌprɪnsɪ'pælɪtɪ) *n, pl* **principalities. 1** a territory ruled by a prince or from which a prince draws his title. **2** the authority of a prince.

principal nursing officer *n* a grade of nurse concerned with administration in the British National Health Service.

principal parts *pl n Grammar.* the main inflected forms of a verb, from which all other inflections may be deduced.

principate ('prɪnsɪˌpeɪt) *n* **1** a state ruled by a prince. **2** a form of rule in the early Roman Empire in which some republican forms survived.

principle 🅣 ('prɪnsɪp^{ə}l) *n* **1** a standard or rule of personal conduct: *he would stoop to anything – he has no principles.* **2** a set of such moral rules: *he was a man of principle.* **3** a fundamental or general truth. **4** the essence of something. **5** a source; origin. **6** a law concerning a natural phenomenon or the behaviour of a system: *the principle of the conservation of mass.* **7** *Chem.* a constituent of a substance that gives the substance its characteristics. **8 in principle.** in theory. **9 on principle.** because of or in demonstration of a principle. [C14: from L *principium* beginning, basic tenet]

> **USAGE NOTE** *Principle* and *principal* are often confused: *the principal* (not *principle*) *reason for his departure; the plan was approved in principle* (not *principal*).

principled 🅣 ('prɪnsɪp^{ə}ld) *adj* **a** having high moral principles. **b** (*in combination*): *high-principled.*

prink 🅣 (prɪŋk) *vb* **1** to dress (oneself, etc.) finely; deck out. **2** (*intr*) to preen oneself. [C16: prob. changed from PRANK[2] (to adorn)]

print 🅣 (prɪnt) *vb* **1** to reproduce (text, pictures, etc.), esp. in large numbers, by applying ink to paper or other material. **2** to produce or reproduce (a manuscript, data, etc.) in print, as for publication. **3** to write (letters, etc.) in the style of printed matter. **4** to mark or indent (a surface) by pressing (something) onto it. **5** to produce a photographic print from (a negative). **6** (*tr*) to fix in the mind or memory. **7** (*tr*) to make (a mark) by applying pressure. ◆ *n* **8** printed matter such as newsprint. **9** a printed publication such as a book. **10 in print. 10a** in printed or published form. **10b** (of a book, etc.) offered for sale by the publisher. **11 out of print.** no longer available from a publisher. **12** a design or picture printed from an engraved plate, wood block, or other medium. **13** printed text, esp. with regard to the typeface: *small print.* **14** a positive photographic image produced from a negative image on film. **15a** a fabric with a printed design. **15b** (*as modifier*): *a print dress.* **16a** a mark made by pressing something onto a surface. **16b** a stamp, die, etc., that makes such an impression. **17** See **fingerprint.** ◆ See also

THESAURUS

Antonyms *adj* ≠ **early:** advanced, later, modern ≠ **crude:** comfortable, elaborate, refined ≠ **uncivilized:** civilized, developed ≠ **simple:** adult, developed, mature, sophisticated, trained, tutored

primordial *adj* **1** = **primeval,** earliest, first, prehistoric, primal, primitive, pristine **2** = **fundamental,** basic, elemental, original, radical

primp *vb* = **preen,** deck out, doll up (*sl.*), dress up (*sl.*), prank, prink, put on one's best bib and tucker (*inf.*), put on one's glad rags (*sl.*)

prince *n* **3, 4** = **ruler,** lord, monarch, potentate, sovereign

princely *adj* **1** = **generous,** bounteous, bountiful, gracious, lavish, liberal, magnanimous, munificent, open-handed, rich **2** = **regal,** august, dignified, grand, high-born, imperial, imposing, lofty, magnificent, majestic, noble, royal, sovereign, stately

principal *adj* **1** = **main,** arch, capital, cardinal, chief, controlling, dominant, essential, first, foremost, highest, key, leading, most important, paramount, pre-eminent, primary, prime, strongest ◆ *n* **3** = **head,** boss (*inf.*), chief, director, leader, master, ruler, superintendent **5** = **headmaster** *or* **headmistress,** dean, director, head (*inf.*), head teacher, master *or* mistress, rector **7** = **star,** lead, leader **8a** = **capital,** assets, capital funds, money
Antonyms *adj* ≠ **main:** auxiliary, inferior, minor, subordinate, subsidiary, supplementary, weakest

principally *adv* **1** = **mainly,** above all, chiefly, especially, first and foremost, for the most part, in the main, largely, mostly, particularly, predominantly, primarily

principle *n* **1, 3** = **rule,** assumption, axiom, canon, criterion, dictum, doctrine, dogma, ethic, formula, fundamental, golden rule, law, maxim, moral law, precept, proposition, standard, truth, verity **2** = **morals,** conscience, integrity, probity, rectitude, scruples, sense of duty, sense of honour, uprightness **8 in principle** = **in theory,** ideally, in essence, theoretically

principled *adj* = **moral,** conscientious, correct, decent, ethical, high-minded, honourable, just, righteous, right-minded, scrupulous, upright, virtuous

prink *vb* **1** = **dress up,** deck, dress to kill (*inf.*), dress (up) to the nines (*inf.*), fig up (*sl.*), trick out **2** = **preen,** adorn, doll up (*sl.*), groom, prank, primp, titivate

print *vb* **1, 2** = **publish,** engrave, go to press, impress, imprint, issue, mark, put to bed (*inf.*), run off, stamp ◆ *n* **8, 9** = **publication,** book, magazine, newspaper, newsprint, periodical, printed matter, typescript, zine (*inf.*) **10 in print: a** = **available,** in black and white, on paper, on the streets, out, printed **b** current, in the shops, obtainable, on the market, on the shelves **11 out of print** = **unavailable,** no longer published, o.p., unobtainable **12, 14** = **reproduction,** copy, engraving, photo, photograph, picture **13** = **typeface,** characters, face, font (*chiefly US*), fount, lettering, letters, type

print out. [C13 *priente,* from OF: something printed, from *preindre* to make an impression, from L *premere* to press]
▸'**printable** *adj*

printed circuit *n* an electronic circuit in which certain components and the connections between them are formed by etching a metallic coating or by electrodeposition on one or both sides of a thin insulating board.

printer ('prɪntə) *n* **1** a person or business engaged in printing. **2** a machine or device that prints. **3** *Computing.* an output device for printing results on paper.

printer's devil *n* an apprentice or errand boy in a printing establishment.

printing ('prɪntɪŋ) *n* **1** the business or art of producing printed matter. **2** printed text. **3** Also called: **impression.** all the copies of a book, etc., printed at one time. **4** a form of writing in which letters resemble printed letters.

printing press *n* any of various machines used for printing.

printmaker ('prɪnt,meɪkə) *n* a person who makes print or prints, esp. a craftsman or artist.

print out *vb* (*tr, adv*) **1** (of a computer output device) to produce (printed information). ◆ *n* **print-out, printout. 2** such printed information.

print shop *n* a place in which printing is carried out.

prion ('pri:ɒn) *n* a protein in the brain, an abnormal transmissible form of which is thought to be the agent responsible for certain spongiform encephalopathies, such as BSE, scrapie, Creutzfeldt-Jakob disease, and kuru. [C20: from *pro(teinaceous) in(fectious particle)*]

prior[1] ➊ ('praɪə) *adj* **1** (*prenominal*) previous. **2 prior to.** before; until. [C18: from L: previous]

prior[2] ('praɪə) *n* **1** the superior of a community in certain religious orders. **2** the deputy head of a monastery or abbey, immediately below the abbot. [C11: from LL: head, from L (adj): previous, from OL *pri* before]
▸'**priorate** *n* ▸'**prioress** *fem n*

priority ➊ (praɪ'ɒrɪtɪ) *n, pl* **priorities. 1** the condition of being prior; antecedence; precedence. **2** the right of precedence over others. **3** something given specified attention: *my first priority.*

priory ➊ ('praɪərɪ) *n, pl* **priories.** a religious house governed by a prior, sometimes being subordinate to an abbey. [C13: from Med. L *priōria*]

prise *or* **prize** (praɪz) *vb* **prises, prising, prised** *or* **prizes, prizing, prized.** (*tr*) **1** to force open by levering. **2** to extract or obtain with difficulty: *they had to prise the news out of him.* [C17: from OF *prise* a taking, from *prendre* to take, from L *prehendere;* see PRIZE[1]]

prism ('prɪzəm) *n* **1** a transparent polygonal solid, often having triangular ends and rectangular sides, for dispersing light into a spectrum or for reflecting light: used in binoculars, periscopes, etc. **2** *Maths.* a polyhedron having parallel bases and sides that are parallelograms. [C16: from Med. L *prisma,* from Gk: something shaped by sawing, from *prizein* to saw]

prismatic (prɪz'mætɪk) *adj* **1** of or produced by a prism. **2** exhibiting bright spectral colours: *prismatic light.* **3** *Crystallog.* another word for **orthorhombic.**
▸**pris'matically** *adv*

prison ➊ ('prɪz^ən) *n* **1** a public building used to house convicted criminals and accused persons awaiting trial. **2** any place of confinement. [C12: from OF *prisun,* from L *prēnsiō* a capturing, from *prehendere* to lay hold of]

prisoner ➊ ('prɪzənə) *n* **1** a person kept in custody as a punishment for a crime, while awaiting trial, or for some other reason. **2** a person confined by any of various restraints: *we are all prisoners of time.* **3 take (someone) prisoner.** to capture and hold (someone) as a prisoner.

prisoner of war *n* a person, esp. a serviceman, captured by an enemy in time of war. Abbrev.: **POW.**

prisoner's base *n* a children's game involving two teams, members of which chase and capture each other.

prissy ➊ ('prɪsɪ) *adj* **prissier, prissiest.** fussy and prim, esp. in a prudish way. [C20: prob. from PRIM + SISSY]
▸'**prissily** *adv* ▸'**prissiness** *n*

pristine ➊ ('prɪstaɪn, -ti:n) *adj* **1** of or involving the earliest period, state, etc.; original. **2** pure; uncorrupted. **3** fresh, clean, and unspoiled: *his pristine new car.* [C15: from L *pristinus* primitive]

> **USAGE NOTE** The use of *pristine* to mean *fresh, clean, and unspoiled* is considered by some people to be incorrect.

prithee ('prɪðɪ) *interj Arch.* pray thee; please. [C16: shortened from *I pray thee*]

privacy ➊ ('praɪvəsɪ, 'prɪvəsɪ) *n* **1** the condition of being private. **2** secrecy.

private ➊ ('praɪvɪt) *adj* **1** not widely or publicly known: *they had private reasons for the decision.* **2** confidential; secret: *a private conversation.* **3** not for general or public use: *a private bathroom.* **4** of or provided by a private individual or organization rather than by the state. **5** (*prenominal*) individual; special: *my own private recipe.* **6** (*prenominal*) having no public office, rank, etc.: *a private man.* **7** (*prenominal*) denoting a soldier of the lowest military rank. **8** (of a place) retired; not overlooked. ◆ *n* **9** a soldier of the lowest rank in many armies and marine corps. **10 in private.** in secret. [C14: from L *prīvātus* belonging to one individual, withdrawn from public life, from *prīvāre* to deprive]
▸'**privately** *adv*

private bill *n* a bill presented to Parliament or Congress on behalf of a private individual, corporation, etc.

private company *n* a limited company that does not issue shares for public subscription and whose owners do not enjoy an unrestricted right to transfer their shareholdings. Cf. **public company.**

private detective *n* an individual privately employed to investigate a crime or make other inquiries. Also called: **private investigator.**

private enterprise *n* economic activity undertaken by private individuals or organizations under private ownership.

privateer (,praɪvə'tɪə) *n* **1** an armed privately owned vessel commissioned for war service by a government. **2** Also called: **privateersman.** a member of the crew of a privateer. ◆ *vb* **3** (*intr*) to serve as a privateer.

private eye *n Inf.* a private detective.

Private Finance Initiative *n* (in Britain) a government scheme to encourage private investment in public projects. Abbrev.: **PFI.**

private health insurance *n* insurance against the need for medical treatment as a private patient.

private hotel *n* **1** a hotel in which the proprietor has the right to refuse to accept a person as a guest. **2** *Austral. & NZ.* a hotel not having a licence to sell alcoholic liquor.

private income *n* an income from sources other than employment, such as investment. Also called: **private means.**

private life *n* the social life or personal relationships of an individual, esp. of a celebrity.

private member *n* a member of a legislative assembly not having an appointment in the government.

private member's bill *n* a parliamentary bill sponsored by a Member of Parliament who is not a government minister.

private parts *or* **privates** *pl n* euphemistic terms for **genitals.**

private patient *n Brit.* a patient receiving medical treatment not paid for by the National Health Service.

private pay bed *n* (in Britain) a hospital bed reserved for private patients who are charged by the health service for use of hospital facilities.

private practice *n Brit.* medical practice that is not part of the National Health Service.

private school *n* a school under the financial and managerial control of a private body, accepting mostly fee-paying pupils.

private secretary *n* **1** a secretary entrusted with the personal and confidential matters of a business executive. **2** a civil servant who acts as aide to a minister or senior government official.

private sector *n* the part of a country's economy that consists of privately owned enterprises.

privation ➊ (praɪ'veɪʃən) *n* **1** loss or lack of the necessities of life, such as food and shelter. **2** hardship resulting from this. **3** the state of being deprived. [C14: from L *prīvātiō* deprivation]

privative ('prɪvətɪv) *adj* **1** causing privation. **2** expressing lack or negation, as for example the English suffix *-less* and prefix *un-*. [C16: from L *prīvātīvus* indicating loss]
▸'**privatively** *adv*

privatize *or* **privatise** ('praɪvɪ,taɪz) *vb* **privatizes, privatizing, privatized** *or*

THESAURUS

prior[1] *adj* **1 = earlier,** aforementioned, antecedent, anterior, foregoing, former, preceding, pre-existent, pre-existing, previous **2 prior to = before,** earlier than, preceding, previous to

priority *n* **1-3 = precedence,** first concern, greater importance, pre-eminence, preference, prerogative, rank, right of way, seniority, supremacy, the lead

priory *n* **= monastery,** abbey, cloister, convent, nunnery, religious house

prison *n* **1 = jail,** can (*sl.*), choky (*sl.*), clink (*sl.*), confinement, cooler (*sl.*), dungeon, lockup, nick (*Brit. sl.*), penal institution, penitentiary (*US*), poky *or* pokey (*US & Canad. sl.*), pound, quod (*sl.*), slammer (*sl.*), stir (*sl.*)

prisoner *n* **1 = convict,** con (*sl.*), jailbird, lag (*sl.*) **1 = captive,** detainee, hostage, internee

prissy *adj* **= prim,** fastidious, finicky, fussy, niminy-piminy, old-maidish (*inf.*), overnice, precious, prim and proper, prudish, schoolmarmish (*Brit. inf.*), squeamish, strait-laced

pristine *adj* **1 = original,** earliest, first, former, initial, primal, primary, primeval, primitive, primordial **2, 3 = new,** immaculate, pure, uncorrupted, undefiled, unspoiled, unsullied, untouched, virgin, virginal

privacy *n* **1 = seclusion,** isolation, privateness, retirement, retreat, separateness, sequestration, solitude **2 = secrecy,** clandestineness, concealment, confidentiality

private *adj* **2 = secret,** clandestine, closet, confidential, covert, hush-hush (*inf.*), in camera, inside, off the record, privy (*arch.*), unofficial **3, 5 = exclusive,** individual, intimate, own, particular, personal, reserved, special **4 = nonpublic,** independent **8 = secluded,** concealed, isolated, not overlooked, retired, secret, separate, sequestered ◆ *n* **9 = enlisted man** (*US*), private soldier, squaddie *or* squaddy (*Brit. sl.*), tommy (*Brit. inf.*), Tommy Atkins (*Brit. inf.*) ◆ *adj* **10 in private = in secret,** behind closed doors, confidentially, in camera, personally, privately
Antonyms *adj* ≠ **secret:** disclosed, known, official, open, public, revealed ≠ **exclusive:** common, general, open, public, unlimited, unrestricted ≠ **secluded:** bustling, busy, frequented, unsecluded

privation *n* **1, 2 = want,** destitution, distress, hardship, indigence, lack, loss, misery, necessity, need, neediness, penury, poverty, suffering

privatises, privatising, privatised. (*tr*) to take into, or return to, private ownership, a company or concern that has previously been owned by the state.
▸ ˌ**privatiˈzation** *or* ˌ**privatiˈsation** *n*

privet (ˈprɪvɪt) *n* **a** any of a genus of shrubs, esp. one having oval dark green leaves, white flowers, and purplish-black berries. **b** (*as modifier*): *a privet hedge.* [C16: from ?]

privilege ❶ (ˈprɪvɪlɪdʒ) *n* **1** a benefit, immunity, etc., granted under certain conditions. **2** the advantages and immunities enjoyed by a small usually powerful group or class, esp. to the disadvantage of others: *one of the obstacles to social harmony is privilege.* **3** *US Stock Exchange.* a speculative contract permitting its purchaser to make optional purchases or sales of securities at a specified time over a limited period. ◆ *vb* **privileges, privileging, privileged.** (*tr*) **4** to bestow a privilege or privileges upon. **5** (foll. by *from*) to free or exempt. [C12: from OF *privilège*, from L *prīvilēgium* law relevant to rights of an individual, from *prīvus* an individual + *lēx* law]

privileged ❶ (ˈprɪvɪlɪdʒd) *adj* **1** enjoying or granted as a privilege or privileges. **2** *Law.* **2a** not actionable as a libel or slander. **2b** (of a communication, document, etc.) that a witness cannot be compelled to divulge.

privity (ˈprɪvɪtɪ) *n, pl* **privities. 1** a legally recognized relationship existing between two parties, such as that between the parties to a contract: *privity of contract.* **2** secret knowledge that is shared. [C13: from OF *priveté*]

privy ❶ (ˈprɪvɪ) *adj* **privier, priviest. 1** (*postpositive;* foll. by *to*) participating in the knowledge of something secret. **2** *Arch.* secret, hidden, etc. ◆ *n, pl* **privies. 3** a lavatory, esp. an outside one. **4** *Law.* a person in privity with another. See **privity.** [C13: from OF *privé* something private, from L *prīvātus* PRIVATE]
▸ ˈ**privily** *adv*

privy council *n* **1** the council of state of a monarch, esp. formerly. **2** *Arch.* a secret council.

Privy Council *n* **1** the private council of the British sovereign, consisting of all current and former ministers of the Crown and other distinguished subjects, all of whom are appointed for life. **2** (in Canada) a ceremonial body of advisers of the governor general, the chief of them being the Federal cabinet ministers.
▸ **Privy Counsellor** *n*

privy purse *n* (*often cap.*) **1** an allowance voted by Parliament for the private expenses of the monarch. **2** an official of the royal household responsible for dealing with the monarch's private expenses. Full name: **Keeper of the Privy Purse.**

privy seal *n* (*often cap.*) (in Britain) a seal affixed to certain documents issued by royal authority: of less importance than the great seal.

Prix Goncourt (*French* pri) *n* an annual prize for a work of French fiction. [C20: after the Académie Goncourt, which awards it]

prize[1] ❶ (praɪz) *n* **1a** a reward or honour for having won a contest, competition, etc. **1b** (*as modifier*): *prize jockey; prize essay.* **2** something given to the winner of any game of chance, lottery, etc. **3** something striven for. **4** any valuable property captured in time of war, esp. a vessel. [C14: from OF *prise* a capture, from L *prehendere* to seize; infl. by ME *prise* reward]

prize[2] ❶ (praɪz) *vb* **prizes, prizing, prized.** (*tr*) to esteem greatly; value highly. [C15 *prise,* from OF *preisier* to PRAISE]

prize court *n Law.* a court having jurisdiction to determine how property captured at sea in wartime is to be distributed.

prizefight ❶ (ˈpraɪzˌfaɪt) *n* a boxing match for a prize or purse.
▸ ˈ**prizeˌfighter** *n* ▸ ˈ**prizeˌfighting** *n*

prize ring *n* **1** the enclosed area or ring used by prizefighters. **2 the prize ring.** the sport of prizefighting.

pro[1] (prəʊ) *adv* **1** in favour of a motion, issue, course of action, etc. ◆ *prep* **2** in favour of. ◆ *n, pl* **pros. 3** (*usually pl*) an argument or vote in favour of a proposal or motion. See also **pros and cons.** [from L *prō* (prep) in favour of]

pro[2] (prəʊ) *n, pl* **pros,** *adj Inf.* **1** short for **professional. 2** a prostitute. [C19]

PRO *abbrev. for:* **1** Public Records Office. **2** public relations officer.

pro-[1] *prefix* **1** in favour of; supporting: *pro-Chinese.* **2** acting as a substitute for: *proconsul; pronoun.* [from L *prō* (adv & prep). In compound words borrowed from L, *prō-* indicates: forward, out (*project*); away from (*prodigal*); onward (*proceed*); in front of (*provide, protect*); on behalf of (*procure*); substitute for (*pronominal*); and sometimes intensive force (*promiscuous*)]

pro-[2] *prefix* before in time or position; anterior; forward: *prognathous.* [from Gk *pro* (prep) before (in time, position, etc.)]

proa (ˈprəʊə) *or* **prau** *n* any of several kinds of canoe-like boats used in the South Pacific, esp. one equipped with an outrigger and sails. [C16: from Malay *parāhū* a boat]

proactive (prəʊˈæktɪv) *adj* **1** tending to initiate change rather than reacting to events. **2** *Psychol.* of or denoting a mental process that affects a subsequent process. [C20: from PRO-[2] + (RE)ACTIVE]

pro-am (ˈprəʊˈæm) *adj* (of a golf tournament, etc.) involving both professional and amateur players.

probability ❶ (ˌprɒbəˈbɪlɪtɪ) *n, pl* **probabilities. 1** the condition of being probable. **2** an event or other thing that is probable. **3** *Statistics.* a measure of the degree of confidence one may have in the occurrence of an event, measured on a scale from zero (impossibility) to one (certainty).

probable ❶ (ˈprɒbəbᵊl) *adj* **1** likely to be or to happen but not necessarily so. **2** most likely: *the probable cause of the accident.* ◆ *n* **3** a person who is probably to be chosen for a team, event, etc. [C14: via OF from L *probābilis* that may be proved, from *probāre* to prove]

probably ❶ (ˈprɒbəblɪ) *adv* **1** (*sentence modifier*) in all likelihood or probability: *I'll probably see you tomorrow.* ◆ *sentence substitute.* **2** I believe such a thing may be the case.

proband (ˈprəʊbænd) *n* another name (esp. US) for **propositus.** [C20: from L *probandus, probāre* to test]

probang (ˈprəʊbæŋ) *n Surgery.* a long flexible rod, often with a small sponge at one end, for inserting into the oesophagus, as to apply medication. [C17: var., apparently by association with PROBE, of *provang,* coined by W. Rumsey (1584–1660), Welsh judge, its inventor; from ?]

probate (ˈprəʊbɪt, -beɪt) *n* **1** the process of officially proving the validity of a will. **2** the official certificate stating a will to be genuine and conferring on the executors power to administer the estate. **3** (*modifier*) relating to probate: *a probate court.* ◆ *vb* **probates, probating, probated. 4** (*tr*) *Chiefly US.* to establish officially the validity of (a will). [C15: from L *probāre* to inspect]

probation ❶ (prəˈbeɪʃən) *n* **1** a system of dealing with offenders by placing them under the supervision of a probation officer. **2 on probation. 2a** under the supervision of a probation officer. **2b** undergoing a test period. **3** a trial period, as for a teacher.
▸ **proˈbational** *or* **proˈbationary** *adj*

probationer (prəˈbeɪʃənə) *n* a person on probation.

probation officer *n* an officer of a court who supervises offenders placed on probation and assists and befriends them.

probe ❶ (prəʊb) *vb* **probes, probing, probed. 1** (*tr*) to search into closely. **2** to examine (something) with or as if with a probe. ◆ *n* **3** something that probes or tests. **4** *Surgery.* a slender instrument for exploring a wound, sinus, etc. **5** a thorough inquiry, such as one by a newspaper into corrupt practices. **6** *Electronics.* a lead connecting to or containing a monitoring circuit used for testing. **7** anything which provides or acts as a coupling, esp. a flexible tube extended from an aircraft to link it with another so that it can refuel. **8** See **space probe.** [C16: from Med. L *proba* investigation, from L *probāre* to test]
▸ ˈ**probeable** *adj* ▸ ˈ**prober** *n*

probity ❶ (ˈprəʊbɪtɪ) *n* confirmed integrity. [C16: from L *probitās* honesty, from *probus* virtuous]

problem ❶ (ˈprɒbləm) *n* **1a** any thing, matter, person, etc., that is difficult to deal with. **1b** (*as modifier*): *a problem child.* **2** a puzzle, question, etc., set for solution. **3** *Maths.* a statement requiring a solution usually by means of several operations or constructions. **4** (*modifier*) designating a literary work that deals with difficult moral questions: *a problem play.* [C14: from LL *problēma,* from Gk: something put forward]

problematic ❶ (ˌprɒbləˈmætɪk) *or* **problematical** *adj* **1** having the na-

THESAURUS

privilege *n* **1** = **right**, advantage, benefit, birthright, claim, concession, due, entitlement, franchise, freedom, immunity, liberty, prerogative, sanction

privileged *adj* **1** = **special**, advantaged, elite, entitled, favoured, honoured, indulged, powerful, ruling **1** = **allowed**, empowered, exempt, free, granted, licensed, sanctioned, vested **2b** = **confidential**, exceptional, inside, not for publication, off the record, privy, special

privy *adj* **1** *foll. by* **to** = **informed of**, apprised of, aware of, cognizant of, hip to (*sl.*), in on, in the know about (*inf.*), in the loop, wise to (*sl.*) **2** *Archaic* = **secret**, confidential, hidden, hush-hush (*inf.*), off the record, personal, private ◆ *n* **3** = **lavatory**, bog (*sl.*), closet, earth closet, latrine, outside toilet

prize[1] *n* **1a** = **reward**, accolade, award, honour, premium, trophy ◆ *modifier* **1b** = **champion**, award-winning, best, first-rate, outstanding, top, top-notch (*inf.*), winning ◆ *n* **2** = **winnings**, haul, jackpot, purse, stakes, windfall **3** = **goal**, aim, ambition, conquest, desire, gain, Holy Grail (*inf.*), hope **4** = **booty**, capture, loot, pickings, pillage, plunder, spoil(s), trophy

prize[2] *vb* = **value**, appreciate, cherish, esteem, hold dear, regard highly, set store by, treasure

prizefighter *n* = **boxer**, bruiser (*inf.*), fighter, pug (*sl.*), pugilist

prizefighting *n* = **boxing**, fighting, pugilism, the noble art *or* science, the prize ring, the ring

probability *n* **1, 3** = **likelihood**, chance(s), expectation, liability, likeliness, odds, presumption, prospect

probable *adj* **1, 2** = **likely**, apparent, credible, feasible, most likely, odds-on, on the cards, ostensible, plausible, possible, presumable, presumed, reasonable, seeming, verisimilar
Antonyms *adj* doubtful, improbable, not likely, unlikely

probably *adv* **1** = **likely**, as likely as not, doubtless, in all likelihood, in all probability, maybe, most likely, perchance (*arch.*), perhaps, possibly, presumably

probation *n* **3** = **trial period**, apprenticeship, examination, initiation, novitiate, test, trial

probe *vb* **1** = **examine**, explore, go into, investigate, look into, query, research, scrutinize, search, sift, sound, test, verify, work over **2** = **explore**, feel around, poke, prod ◆ *n* **5** = **examination**, detection, exploration, inquest, inquiry, investigation, research, scrutiny, study

probity *n* = **integrity**, equity, fairness, fidelity, goodness, honesty, honour, justice, morality, rectitude, righteousness, sincerity, trustworthiness, truthfulness, uprightness, virtue, worth

problem *n* **1a** = **difficulty**, can of worms (*inf.*), complication, dilemma, disagreement, dispute, disputed point, doubt, Gordian knot, hard nut to crack (*inf.*), how-do-you-do (*inf.*), point at issue, predicament, quandary, trouble ◆ *modifier* **1b** = **difficult**, delinquent, intractable, uncontrollable, unmanageable, unruly ◆ *n* **2** = **puzzle**, brain-teaser (*inf.*), conundrum, enigma, poser, question, riddle, teaser

problematic *adj* **1** = **tricky**, chancy (*inf.*), de-

ture of a problem; uncertain; questionable. **2** *Logic, obs.* (of a proposition) asserting that a property may or may not hold.
▸ ˌ**problem'atically** *adv*

pro bono publico *Latin.* ('prəʊ 'bəʊnəʊ 'pʊblɪkəʊ) for the public good.

proboscidean *or* **proboscidian** (ˌprəʊbɒ'sɪdɪən) *adj* **1** of or belonging to an order of massive herbivorous placental mammals having tusks and a long trunk: contains the elephants. ◆ *n* **2** any proboscidean animal.

proboscis (prəʊ'bɒsɪs) *n, pl* **proboscises** *or* **proboscides** (-sɪˌdiːz). **1** a long flexible prehensile trunk or snout, as of an elephant. **2** the elongated mouthpart of certain insects. **3** any similar organ. **4** *Inf., facetious.* a person's nose. [C17: via L from Gk *proboskis* trunk of an elephant, from *boskein* to feed]

procaine ('prəʊkeɪn, prəʊ'keɪn) *n* a colourless or white crystalline water-soluble substance used, as **procaine hydrochloride**, as a local anaesthetic. [C20: from PRO-[1] + (CO)CAINE]

procathedral (ˌprəʊkə'θiːdrəl) *n* a church serving as a cathedral.

procedure Ⓣ (prə'siːdʒə) *n* **1** a way of acting or progressing, esp. an established method. **2** the established form of conducting the business of a legislature, the enforcement of a legal right, etc. **3** *Computing.* another name for **subroutine**.
▸ **pro'cedural** *adj* ▸ **pro'cedurally** *adv*

proceed Ⓣ (prə'siːd) *vb* (*intr*) **1** (often foll. by *to*) to advance or carry on, esp. after stopping. **2** (often foll. by *with*) to continue: *he proceeded with his reading.* **3** (often foll. by *against*) to institute or carry on a legal action. **4** to originate; arise: *evil proceeds from the heart.* [C14: from L *prōcēdere* to advance]
▸ **pro'ceeder** *n*

proceeding Ⓣ (prə'siːdɪŋ) *n* **1** an act or course of action. **2a** a legal action. **2b** any step taken in a legal action. **3** (*pl*) the minutes of the meetings of a society, etc. **4** (*pl*) legal action; litigation. **5** (*pl*) the events of an occasion.

proceeds Ⓣ ('prəʊsiːdz) *pl n* **1** the profit or return derived from a commercial transaction, investment, etc. **2** the result, esp. the total sum, accruing from some undertaking.

process[1] Ⓣ ('prəʊses) *n* **1** a series of actions which produce a change or development: *the process of digestion.* **2** a method of doing or producing something. **3** progress or course of time. **4 in the process of.** during or in the course of. **5a** a summons commanding a person to appear in court. **5b** the whole proceedings in an action at law. **6** a natural outgrowth or projection of a part or organism. **7** (*modifier*) relating to the general preparation of a printing forme or plate by the use, at some stage, of photography. ◆ *vb* (*tr*) **8** to subject to a routine procedure; handle. **9** to treat or prepare by a special method, esp. to treat (food) in order to preserve it: *to process cheese.* **10a** to institute legal proceedings against. **10b** to serve a process on. **11** *Photog.* **11a** to develop, rinse, fix, wash, and dry (exposed film, etc.). **11b** to produce final prints or slides from (undeveloped film). **12** *Computing.* to perform operations on (data) according to programmed instructions in order to obtain the required information. [C14: from OF *procès*, from L *prōcessus* an advancing, from *prōcēdere* to proceed]

process[2] (prə'ses) *vb* (*intr*) to proceed in a procession. [C19: back formation from PROCESSION]

process industry *n* a manufacturing industry, such as oil refining, which converts bulk raw materials into a workable form.

procession Ⓣ (prə'seʃən) *n* **1** the act of proceeding in a regular formation. **2** a group of people or things moving forwards in an orderly, regular, or ceremonial manner. **3** *Christianity.* the emanation of the Holy Spirit. ◆ *vb* **4** (*intr*) *Rare.* to go in procession. [C12: via OF from L *prōcessiō* a marching forwards]

processional (prə'seʃənəl) *adj* **1** of or suitable for a procession. ◆ *n* **2** *Christianity.* **2a** a book containing the prayers, hymns, etc., prescribed for processions. **2b** a hymn, etc., used in a procession.

processor ('prəʊsesə) *n* **1** *Computing.* another name for **central processing unit. 2** a person or thing that carries out a process.

process-server *n* a sheriff's officer who serves legal documents such as writs for appearance in court.

procès-verbal *French.* (prɔsevɛrbal) *n, pl* **-baux** (-bo). a written record of an official proceeding; minutes. [C17: from F: see PROCESS, VERBAL]

pro-choice *adj* (of an organization, pressure group, etc.) supporting the right of a woman to have an abortion. Cf. **pro-life.**

prochronism ('prəʊkrəˌnɪzəm) *n* an error in dating that places an event earlier than it actually occurred. [C17: from PRO-[2] + Gk *khronos* time + -ISM, by analogy with ANACHRONISM]

proclaim Ⓣ (prə'kleɪm) *vb* (*tr*) **1** (*may take a clause as object*) to announce publicly. **2** (*may take a clause as object*) to indicate plainly. **3** to praise or extol. [C14: from L *prōclāmāre* to shout aloud]
▸ **proclamation** (ˌprɒklə'meɪʃən) *n* ▸ **pro'claimer** *n* ▸ **proclamatory** (prə'klæmətərɪ, -trɪ) *adj*

proclitic (prəʊ'klɪtɪk) *adj* **1a** denoting a monosyllabic word or form having no stress and pronounced as a prefix of the following word, as in English *'t* for *it* in *'twas.* **1b** (in classical Greek) denoting a word that throws its accent onto the following word. ◆ *n* **2** a proclitic word or form. [C19: from NL *procliticus*, from Gk *proklinein* to lean forwards; on the model of ENCLITIC]

proclivity Ⓣ (prə'klɪvɪtɪ) *n, pl* **proclivities.** a tendency or inclination. [C16: from L *prōclīvitās*, from *prōclīvis* steep, from *clīvus* a slope]

proconsul (prəʊ'kɒnsᵊl) *n* **1** a governor of a colony or other dependency. **2** (in ancient Rome) the governor of a senatorial province.
▸ **proconsular** (prəʊ'kɒnsjʊlə) *adj*

procrastinate Ⓣ (prəʊ'kræstɪˌneɪt, prə-) *vb* **procrastinates, procrastinating, procrastinated.** (*usually intr*) to put off (an action) until later; delay. [C16: from L *prōcrāstināre* to postpone until tomorrow, from PRO-[1] + *crās* tomorrow]
▸ **proˌcrasti'nation** *n* ▸ **pro'crastiˌnator** *n*

procreate Ⓣ ('prəʊkrɪˌeɪt) *vb* **procreates, procreating, procreated. 1** to beget or engender (offspring). **2** (*tr*) to bring into being. [C16: from L *prōcreāre*, from PRO-[1] + *creāre* to create]
▸ **'procreant** *or* **'procreˌative** *adj* ▸ ˌ**procre'ation** *n* ▸ **'procreˌator** *n*

Procrustean (prəʊ'krʌstɪən) *adj* tending or designed to produce conformity by violent or ruthless methods. [C19: from *Procrustes*, Gk robber who fitted travellers into his bed by stretching or lopping off their limbs]

proctology (prɒk'tɒlədʒɪ) *n* the branch of medical science concerned with the rectum. [from Gk *prōktos* rectum + -OLOGY]

proctor ('prɒktə) *n* **1** a member of the staff of certain universities having duties including the enforcement of discipline. **2** (formerly) an agent, esp. one engaged to conduct another's case in a court. **3** *Church of England.* one of the elected representatives of the clergy in Convocation. [C14: syncopated var. of PROCURATOR]
▸ **proctorial** (prɒk'tɔːrɪəl) *adj*

procumbent (prəʊ'kʌmbənt) *adj* **1** (of stems) trailing loosely along the ground. **2** leaning forwards or lying on the face. [C17: from L *prōcumbere* to fall forwards]

procurator ('prɒkjʊˌreɪtə) *n* **1** (in ancient Rome) a civil official of the emperor's administration, often employed as the governor of a minor province. **2** *Rare.* a person engaged by another to manage his affairs. [C13: from L: a manager, from *prōcūrāre* to attend to]
▸ **procuracy** ('prɒkjʊrəsɪ) *or* **'procuˌratorship** *n* ▸ **procuratorial** (ˌprɒkjʊrə'tɔːrɪəl) *adj*

procurator fiscal *n* (in Scotland) a legal officer who performs the functions of public prosecutor and coroner.

procure Ⓣ (prə'kjʊə) *vb* **procures, procuring, procured. 1** (*tr*) to obtain or acquire; secure. **2** to obtain (women or girls) to act as prostitutes. [C13: from L *prōcūrāre* to look after]
▸ **pro'curable** *adj* ▸ **pro'curement, pro'cural,** *or* **procuration** (ˌprɒkjʊ'reɪʃən) *n*

procurer Ⓣ (prə'kjʊərə) *n* a person who procures, esp. one who procures women as prostitutes.

THESAURUS

batable, doubtful, dubious, enigmatic, moot, open to doubt, problematical, puzzling, questionable, uncertain, unsettled
Antonyms *adj* beyond question, certain, clear, definite, indisputable, settled, undebatable, unquestionable

procedure *n* **1 = method,** action, conduct, course, custom, form, formula, modus operandi, operation, performance, plan of action, policy, practice, process, routine, scheme, step, strategy, system, transaction

proceed *vb* **1, 2 = go on,** advance, carry on, continue, get going, get on with, get under way with, go ahead, make a start, move on, press on, progress, set in motion **4 = arise,** come, derive, emanate, ensue, flow, follow, issue, originate, result, spring, stem
Antonyms *vb* ≠ **go on:** break off, cease, discontinue, end, get behind, halt, leave off, pack in (*Brit. inf.*), retreat, stop

proceeding *n* **1 = action,** act, course of action, deed, measure, move, occurrence, procedure, process, step, undertaking, venture **3** *plural* **= business,** account, affairs, annals, archives, dealings, doings, matters, minutes, records, report, transactions

proceeds *pl n* **1 = income,** earnings, gain, produce, products, profit, receipts, returns, revenue, takings, yield

process[1] *n* **1, 2 = procedure,** action, course, course of action, manner, means, measure, method, mode, operation, performance, practice, proceeding, system, transaction **3 = development,** advance, course, evolution, formation, growth, movement, progress, progression, stage, step, unfolding **5b = action,** case, suit, trial ◆ *vb* **8 = handle,** deal with, dispose of, fulfil, take care of **9 = prepare,** alter, convert, refine, transform, treat

procession *n* **2 = parade,** cavalcade, column, cortege, file, march, motorcade, train

proclaim *vb* **1, 2 = declare,** advertise, affirm, announce, blaze (abroad), blazon (abroad), circulate, enunciate, give out, herald, indicate, make known, profess, promulgate, publish, shout from the housetops (*inf.*), show, trumpet
Antonyms *vb* conceal, hush up, keep back, keep secret, suppress, withhold

proclamation *n* **1, 2 = declaration,** announcement, decree, edict, manifesto, notice, notification, promulgation, pronouncement, pronunciamento, publication

proclivity *n* **= tendency,** bent, bias, disposition, facility, inclination, leaning, liableness, penchant, predilection, predisposition, proneness, propensity, weakness

procrastinate *vb* **= delay,** adjourn, be dilatory, dally, defer, drag one's feet (*inf.*), gain time, play a waiting game, play for time, postpone, prolong, protract, put off, retard, stall, temporize
Antonyms *vb* advance, expedite, get on with, hasten, hurry (up), proceed, speed up

procrastination *n* **= delay,** dilatoriness, hesitation, slackness, slowness, temporization *or* temporisation

procreate *vb* **1, 2 = reproduce,** beget, breed, bring into being, engender, father, generate, mother, produce, propagate, sire

procure *vb* **1 = obtain,** acquire, appropriate, buy, come by, earn, effect, find, gain, get, get hold of, land, lay hands on, manage to get, pick up, purchase, score (*sl.*), secure, win

procurer *n* **= pimp,** bawd (*arch.*), madam, pan-

prod ➊ (prɒd) *vb* **prods, prodding, prodded. 1** to poke or jab with or as if with a pointed object. **2** (*tr*) to rouse to action. ◆ *n* **3** the act or an instance of prodding. **4** a sharp object. **5** a stimulus or reminder. [C16: from ?]
▸**'prodder** *n*

prod. *abbrev. for:* **1** produce. **2** produced. **3** product.

prodigal ➊ ('prɒdɪgᵊl) *adj* **1** recklessly wasteful or extravagant, as in disposing of goods or money. **2** lavish: *prodigal of compliments.* ◆ *n* **3** a person who spends lavishly or squanders money. [C16: from Med. L *prōdigālis* wasteful, from L, from *prōdigere* to squander, from *agere* to drive]
▸**,prodi'gality** *n* ▸**'prodigally** *adv*

prodigious ➊ (prə'dɪdʒəs) *adj* **1** vast in size, extent, power, etc. **2** wonderful or amazing. [C16: from L *prōdigiōsus* marvellous, from *prōdigium;* see PRODIGY]
▸**pro'digiously** *adv* ▸**pro'digiousness** *n*

prodigy ➊ ('prɒdɪdʒɪ) *n, pl* **prodigies. 1** a person, esp. a child, of unusual or marvellous talents. **2** anything that is a cause of wonder. **3** something monstrous or abnormal. [C16: from L *prōdigium* an unnatural happening]

produce ➊ *vb* (prə'dju:s), **produces, producing, produced. 1** to bring (something) into existence; yield. **2** (*tr*) to make: *she produced a delicious dinner.* **3** (*tr*) to give birth to. **4** (*tr*) to present to view: *to produce evidence.* **5** (*tr*) to bring before the public: *he produced a film last year.* **6** (*tr*) to act as producer of. **7** (*tr*) *Geom.* to extend (a line). ◆ *n* ('prɒdju:s). **8** anything produced; a product. **9** agricultural products collectively: *farm produce.* [C15: from L *prōdūcere* to bring forward]
▸**pro'ducible** *adj* ▸**pro,duci'bility** *n*

producer ➊ (prə'dju:sə) *n* **1** a person or thing that produces. **2** *Brit.* a person responsible for the artistic direction of a play. **3** *US & Canad.* a person who organizes the stage production of a play, including the finance, management, etc. **4** the person who takes overall administrative responsibility for a film or television programme. Cf. **director** (sense 4). **5** the person who supervises the arrangement, recording, and mixing of a record. **6** *Econ.* a person or business enterprise that generates goods or services for sale. Cf. **consumer** (sense 1). **7** *Chem.* an apparatus or plant for making producer gas.

producer gas *n* a mixture of carbon monoxide and nitrogen produced by passing air over hot coke, used mainly as a fuel.

product ➊ ('prɒdʌkt) *n* **1** something produced by effort, or some mechanical or industrial process. **2** the result of some natural process. **3** a result or consequence. **4** *Maths.* the result of the multiplication of two or more numbers, quantities, etc. [C15: from L *prōductum* (something) produced, from *prōdūcere* to bring forth]

product differentiation *n Commerce.* the real or illusory distinction between competing products in a market.

production ➊ (prə'dʌkʃən) *n* **1** the act of producing. **2** anything that is produced; a product. **3** the amount produced or the rate at which it is produced. **4** *Econ.* the creation or manufacture of goods and services with exchange value. **5** any work created as a result of literary or artistic effort. **6** the presentation of a play, opera, etc. **7** *Brit.* the artistic direction of a play. **8** (*modifier*) manufactured by mass production: *a production model of a car.*
▸**pro'ductional** *adj*

production line *n* a factory system in which parts or components of the end product are transported by a conveyor through a number of different sites at each of which a manual or machine operation is performed on them.

productive ➊ (prə'dʌktɪv) *adj* **1** producing or having the power to produce; fertile. **2** yielding favourable results. **3** *Econ.* **3a** producing goods and services that have exchange value: *productive assets.* **3b** relating to such production: *the productive processes of an industry.* **4** (*postpositive;* foll. by *of*) resulting in: *productive of good results.*
▸**pro'ductively** *adv* ▸**pro'ductiveness** *n*

productivity ➊ (,prɒdʌk'tɪvɪtɪ) *n* **1** the output of an industrial concern in relation to the materials, labour, etc., it employs. **2** the state of being productive.

product liability *n* the liability to the public of a manufacturer or trader for selling a faulty product.

product life cycle *n Marketing.* the four stages (introduction, growth, maturity, and decline) into one of which the sales of a product fall during its market life.

product line *n Marketing.* a group of related products marketed by the same company.

product placement *n* the practice of a company paying for its product to be placed in a prominent position in a film or television programme as a form of advertising.

proem ('prəʊɛm) *n* an introduction or preface, such as to a work of literature. [C14: from L *prooemium* introduction, from Gk *prooimion,* from PRO-[2] + *hoimē* song]
▸**proemial** (prəʊ'i:mɪəl) *adj*

proenzyme (prəʊ'ɛnzaɪm) *n* the inactive form of an enzyme; zymogen.

Prof. *abbrev. for* Professor.

profane ➊ (prə'feɪn) *adj* **1** having or indicating contempt, irreverence, or disrespect for a divinity or something sacred. **2** not designed for religious purposes; secular. **3** not initiated into the inner mysteries or sacred rites. **4** coarse or blasphemous: *profane language.* ◆ *vb* **profanes, profaning, profaned.** (*tr*) **5** to treat (something sacred) with irreverence. **6** to put to an unworthy use. [C15: from L *profānus* outside the temple]
▸**profanation** (,prɒfə'neɪʃən) *n* ▸**pro'fanely** *adv* ▸**pro'faneness** *n* ▸**pro'faner** *n*

profanity ➊ (prə'fænɪtɪ) *n, pl* **profanities. 1** the state or quality of being profane. **2** vulgar or irreverent action, speech, etc.

profess ➊ (prə'fɛs) *vb* **1** (*tr*) to affirm or acknowledge: *to profess ignorance; to profess a belief in God.* **2** (*tr*) to claim (something), often insincerely or falsely: *to profess to be a skilled driver.* **3** to receive or be received into a religious order, as by taking vows. [C14: from L *prōfitērī* to confess openly]

professed ➊ (prə'fɛst) *adj* (*prenominal*) **1** avowed or acknowledged. **2**

THESAURUS

der, panderer, white-slaver, whoremaster (*arch.*)

prod *vb* **1** = **poke**, dig, drive, elbow, jab, nudge, prick, propel, push, shove **2** = **prompt**, egg on, goad, impel, incite, motivate, move, put a bomb under (*inf.*), rouse, spur, stimulate, stir up, urge ◆ *n* **3** = **poke**, boost, dig, elbow, jab, nudge, push, shove **4** = **goad**, poker, spur, stick **5** = **prompt**, boost, cue, reminder, signal, stimulus

prodigal *adj* **1** = **extravagant**, excessive, immoderate, improvident, intemperate, profligate, reckless, spendthrift, squandering, wanton, wasteful **2** = **lavish**, bounteous, bountiful, profuse ◆ *n* **3** = **spendthrift**, big spender, profligate, squanderer, wastrel
Antonyms *adj* ≠ **extravagant:** economical, frugal, miserly, parsimonious, sparing, stingy, thrifty, tight ≠ **lavish:** deficient, lacking, meagre, scanty, scarce, short, sparse

prodigality *n* **1** = **wastefulness**, abandon, dissipation, excess, extravagance, immoderation, intemperance, profligacy, recklessness, squandering, wantonness, waste **2** = **lavishness**, bounteousness, profusion

prodigious *adj* **1** = **huge**, colossal, enormous, giant, gigantic, immeasurable, immense, inordinate, mammoth, massive, monstrous, monumental, stellar (*inf.*), stupendous, tremendous, vast **2** = **wonderful**, abnormal, amazing, astounding, dramatic, exceptional, extraordinary, fabulous, fantastic (*inf.*), impressive, marvellous, miraculous, phenomenal, remarkable, staggering, startling, striking, stupendous, unusual
Antonyms *adj* ≠ **huge:** negligible, small, tiny ≠ **wonderful:** normal, ordinary, unexceptional, unimpressive, unremarkable, usual

prodigy *n* **1** = **genius**, brainbox, child genius, mastermind, talent, whizz (*inf.*), whizz kid (*inf.*), wizard, wonder child, wunderkind **2** = **wonder**, marvel, miracle, one in a million, phenomenon, rare bird (*inf.*), sensation **3** = **monster**, abnormality, curiosity, freak, grotesque, monstrosity, mutation, spectacle

produce *vb* **1** = **cause**, bring about, effect, generate, give rise to, make for, occasion, provoke, set off **1** = **yield**, afford, engender, furnish, give, render, supply **2** = **make**, compose, construct, create, develop, fabricate, invent, manufacture, originate, put together, turn out **3** = **bring forth**, bear, beget, breed, deliver **4** = **show**, advance, bring forward, bring to light, demonstrate, exhibit, offer, present, put forward, set forth **5** = **present**, direct, do, exhibit, mount, put before the public, put on, show, stage **7** *Geometry* = **extend**, lengthen, prolong, protract ◆ *n* **9** = **fruit and vegetables**, crop, greengrocery, harvest, product, yield

producer *n* **1** = **maker**, farmer, grower, manufacturer **2-5** = **director**, impresario, *régisseur*

product *n* **1** = **goods**, artefact, commodity, concoction, creation, invention, merchandise, produce, production, work **3** = **result**, consequence, effect, end result, fruit, issue, legacy, offshoot, outcome, returns, spin-off, upshot, yield

production *n* **1** = **producing**, assembly, construction, creation, fabrication, formation, making, manufacture, manufacturing, origination, preparation **6, 7** = **presentation**, direction, management, staging

productive *adj* **1** = **fertile**, creative, dynamic, energetic, fecund, fruitful, generative, inventive, plentiful, producing, prolific, rich, teeming, vigorous **2** = **useful**, advantageous, beneficial, constructive, effective, fruitful, gainful, gratifying, profitable, rewarding, valuable, worthwhile
Antonyms *adj* ≠ **fertile:** barren, poor, sterile, unfertile, unfruitful, unproductive ≠ **useful:** unproductive, unprofitable, useless

productivity *n* **1, 2** = **output**, abundance, mass production, production, productive capacity, productiveness, work rate, yield

profane *adj* **1** = **sacrilegious**, disrespectful, godless, heathen, idolatrous, impious, impure, irreligious, irreverent, pagan, sinful, ungodly, wicked **2** = **secular**, lay, temporal, unconsecrated, unhallowed, unholy, unsanctified, worldly **4** = **crude**, abusive, blasphemous, coarse, filthy, foul, obscene, vulgar ◆ *vb* **5, 6** = **desecrate**, abuse, commit sacrilege, contaminate, debase, defile, misuse, pervert, pollute, prostitute, violate, vitiate
Antonyms *adj* ≠ **sacrilegious:** clean, decorous, holy, proper, religious, respectful, reverent, sacred, spiritual

profanity *n* **1** = **sacrilege**, blasphemy, impiety, profaneness **2** = **swearing**, abuse, curse, cursing, execration, foul language, four-letter word, imprecation, irreverence, malediction, obscenity, swearword

profess *vb* **1** = **state**, acknowledge, admit, affirm, announce, assert, asseverate, aver, avow, certify, confess, confirm, declare, maintain, own, proclaim, vouch **2** = **claim**, act as if, allege, call oneself, dissemble, fake, feign, let on, make out, pretend, purport, sham

professed *adj* **1** = **declared**, avowed, certified, confessed, confirmed, proclaimed, self-acknowledged, self-confessed **2** = **supposed**, alleged, apparent, ostensible, pretended, pur-

alleged or pretended. **3** professing to be qualified as: *a professed philosopher.* **4** having taken vows of a religious order.
▶**professedly** (prəˈfɛsɪdlɪ) *adv*

profession ❶ (prəˈfɛʃən) *n* **1** an occupation requiring special training in the liberal arts or sciences, esp. one of the three learned professions, law, theology, or medicine. **2** the body of people in such an occupation. **3** an avowal; declaration. **4** Also called: **profession of faith.** a declaration of faith in a religion, esp. as made on entering the Church or an order belonging to it. [C13: from Med. L *professiō* the taking of vows upon entering a religious order, from L: public acknowledgment; see PROFESS]

professional ❶ (prəˈfɛʃənᵊl) *adj* **1** of, suitable for, or engaged in as a profession. **2** engaging in an activity as a means of livelihood. **3a** extremely competent in a job, etc. **3b** (of a piece of work or anything performed) produced with competence or skill. **4** undertaken or performed by people who are paid. ◆ *n* **5** a person who belongs to one of the professions. **6** a person who engages for his livelihood in some activity also pursued by amateurs. **7** a person who engages in an activity with great competence. **8** an expert player of a game who gives instruction, esp. to members of a club by whom he is hired.
▶**proˈfessionaˌlism** *n* ▶**proˈfessionally** *adv*

professional foul *n Football.* a deliberate foul committed as a last-ditch tactic to prevent an opponent from scoring.

professor ❶ (prəˈfɛsə) *n* **1** the principal teacher in a field of learning at a university or college; a holder of a university chair. **2** *Chiefly US & Canad.* any teacher in a university or college. **3** a person who professes his opinions, beliefs, etc. [C14: from Med. L: one who has made his profession in a religious order, from L: a public teacher; see PROFESS]
▶**professorial** (ˌprɒfɪˈsɔːrɪəl) *adj* ▶ˌ**profesˈsorially** *adv* ▶ˌ**profesˈsoriate** *or* **proˈfessorship** *n*

proffer ❶ (ˈprɒfə) *vb* **1** (*tr*) to offer for acceptance. ◆ *n* **2** the act of proffering. [C13: from OF *proffrir,* from PRO-[1] + *offrir* to offer]

proficient ❶ (prəˈfɪʃənt) *adj* **1** having great facility (in an art, occupation, etc.); skilled. ◆ *n* **2** an expert. [C16: from L *prōficere* to make progress]
▶**proˈficiency** *n* ▶**proˈficiently** *adv*

profile ❶ (ˈprəʊfaɪl) *n* **1** a side view or outline of an object, esp. of a human head. **2** a short biographical sketch. **3** a graph, table, etc., representing the extent to which a person, field, or object exhibits various tested characteristics: *a population profile.* **4** a vertical section of soil or rock showing the different layers. **5** the outline of the shape of a river valley either from source to mouth (**long profile**) or at right angles to the flow of the river (**cross profile**). ◆ *vb* **profiles, profiling, profiled. 6** (*tr*) to draw, write, or make a profile of. [C17: from It. *profilo,* from *profilare* to sketch lightly, from L *fīlum* thread]
▶ˈ**profiler** *or* **profilist** (ˈprəʊfɪlɪst) *n*

profile component *n Brit. education.* attainment targets in different subjects brought together for the general assessment of a pupil.

profit ❶ (ˈprɒfɪt) *n* **1** (*often pl*) excess of revenues over outlays and expenses in a business enterprise. **2** the monetary gain derived from a transaction. **3** income derived from property or an investment, as contrasted with capital gains. **4a** *Econ.* the income accruing to a successful entrepreneur and held to be the motivating factor of a capitalist economy. **4b** (*as modifier*): *the profit motive.* **5** a gain, benefit, or advantage. ◆ *vb* **6** to gain or cause to gain profit. [C14: from L *prōfectus* advance, from *prōficere* to make progress]
▶ˈ**profitless** *adj*

profitable ❶ (ˈprɒfɪtəbᵊl) *adj* affording gain or profit.
▶ˌ**profitaˈbility** *n* ▶ˈ**profitably** *adv*

profit and loss *n Book-keeping.* an account compiled at the end of a financial year showing that year's revenue and expense items and indicating gross and net profit or loss.

profit centre *n* a section of a commercial organization which is allocated financial targets in its own right.

profiteer ❶ (ˌprɒfɪˈtɪə) *n* **1** a person who makes excessive profits, esp. by charging exorbitant prices for goods in short supply. ◆ *vb* **2** (*intr*) to make excessive profits.

profiterole (ˈprɒfɪtəˌrəʊl, prəˈfɪtəˌrəʊl) *n* a small case of choux pastry with a sweet or savoury filling. [C16: from F, lit.: a small profit]

profit-sharing *n* a system in which a portion of the net profit of a business is distributed to its employees, usually in proportion to their wages or their length of service.

profit taking *n* selling commodities, securities, etc., at a profit after a rise in market values or before an expected fall in values.

profligate ❶ (ˈprɒflɪgɪt) *adj* **1** shamelessly immoral or debauched. **2** wildly extravagant or wasteful. ◆ *n* **3** a profligate person. [C16: from L *prōflīgātus* corrupt, from *prōflīgāre* to overthrow, from PRO-[1] + *flīgere* to beat]
▶**profligacy** (ˈprɒflɪgəsɪ) *n* ▶ˈ**profligately** *adv*

pro forma (ˈprəʊ ˈfɔːmə) *adj* **1** prescribing a set form or procedure. ◆ *adv* **2** performed in a set manner. [L: for form's sake]

profound ❶ (prəˈfaʊnd) *adj* **1** penetrating deeply into subjects or ideas: *a profound mind.* **2** showing or requiring great knowledge or understanding: *a profound treatise.* **3** situated at or extending to a great depth. **4** stemming from the depths of one's nature: *profound regret.* **5** intense or absolute: *profound silence.* **6** thoroughgoing; extensive: *profound changes.* ◆ *n* **7** *Arch. or literary.* a great depth; abyss. [C14: from OF *profund,* from L *profundus* deep, from *fundus* bottom]
▶**proˈfoundly** *adv* ▶**profundity** (prəˈfʌndɪtɪ) *n*

profuse ❶ (prəˈfjuːs) *adj* **1** plentiful or abundant: *profuse compliments.* **2**

THESAURUS

ported, self-styled, so-called, *soi-disant,* would-be

professedly *adv* **1** = **admittedly**, avowedly, by open declaration, confessedly **2** = **supposedly**, allegedly, apparently, by one's own account, falsely, ostensibly, purportedly, under the pretext of

profession *n* **1** = **occupation**, business, calling, career, employment, line, line of work, métier, office, position, sphere, vocation, walk of life **3** = **declaration**, acknowledgment, affirmation, assertion, attestation, avowal, claim, confession, statement, testimony, vow

professional *adj* **3** = **expert**, ace (*inf.*), adept, competent, crack (*sl.*), efficient, experienced, finished, masterly, polished, practised, proficient, qualified, skilled, slick, trained ◆ *n* **7** = **expert**, adept, authority, buff (*inf.*), dab hand (*Brit. inf.*), guru, hotshot (*inf.*), maestro, master, maven (*US*), past master, pro (*inf.*), specialist, virtuoso, whizz (*inf.*), wizard
Antonyms *adj* ≠ **expert**: amateurish, incapable, incompetent, inefficient, inept, inexperienced, unpolished, unqualified, unskilled, untrained

professor *n* **1** = **don** (*Brit.*), fellow (*Brit.*), head of faculty, prof (*inf.*)

proffer *vb* **1** = **offer**, extend, hand, hold out, present, propose, propound, submit, suggest, tender, volunteer

proficiency *n* **1** = **skill**, ability, accomplishment, aptitude, competence, craft, dexterity, expertise, expertness, facility, knack, know-how (*inf.*), mastery, skilfulness, talent

proficient *adj* **1** = **skilled**, able, accomplished, adept, apt, capable, clever, competent, conversant, efficient, experienced, expert, gifted, masterly, qualified, skilful, talented, trained, versed
Antonyms *adj* bad, incapable, incompetent, inept, unaccomplished, unskilled

profile *n* **1** = **outline**, contour, drawing, figure, form, portrait, shape, side view, silhouette, sketch **2** = **biography**, characterization, character sketch, sketch, thumbnail sketch, vignette **3** = **analysis**, chart, diagram, examination, graph, review, study, survey, table

profit *n* **1** *often plural* = **earnings**, boot, bottom line, emoluments, gain, percentage (*inf.*), proceeds, receipts, return, revenue, surplus, takings, winnings, yield **5** = **benefit**, advancement, advantage, avail, gain, good, interest, mileage (*inf.*), use, value ◆ *vb* **6** = **benefit**, aid, avail, be of advantage to, better, contribute, gain, help, improve, promote, serve, stand in good stead **6** = **capitalize on**, cash in on (*inf.*), exploit, learn from, make capital of, make good use of, make the most of, put to good use, reap the benefit of, take advantage of, turn to advantage *or* account, use, utilize

profitable *adj* = **money-making**, commercial, cost-effective, fruitful, gainful, lucrative, paying, remunerative, rewarding, worthwhile = **beneficial**, advantageous, economic, expedient, fruitful, productive, rewarding, serviceable, useful, valuable, worthwhile
Antonyms *adj* disadvantageous, fruitless, unremunerative, unrewarding, useless, vain, worthless

profiteer *n* **1** = **racketeer**, exploiter ◆ *vb* **2** = **exploit**, fleece, make a quick buck (*sl.*), make someone pay through the nose, overcharge, racketeer, skin (*sl.*), sting (*inf.*)

profitless *adj* **1, 5** = **unprofitable**, bootless, fruitless, futile, idle, ineffective, ineffectual, pointless, thankless, to no purpose, unavailing, unproductive, unremunerative, useless, vain, worthless

profligacy *n* **1** = **immorality**, abandon, corruption, debauchery, degeneracy, depravity, dissipation, dissoluteness, dolce vita, laxity, libertinism, licentiousness, promiscuity, unrestraint, wantonness **2** = **extravagance**, excess, improvidence, lavishness, prodigality, recklessness, squandering, waste, wastefulness

profligate *adj* **1** = **depraved**, abandoned, corrupt, debauched, degenerate, dissipated, dissolute, immoral, iniquitous, libertine, licentious, loose, promiscuous, shameless, sink, unprincipled, vicious, vitiated, wanton, wicked, wild **2** = **extravagant**, immoderate, improvident, prodigal, reckless, spendthrift, squandering, wasteful ◆ *n* **3** = **spendthrift**, prodigal, squanderer, waster, wastrel **3** = **degenerate**, debauchee, dissipater, libertine, rake, reprobate, roué, swinger (*sl.*)
Antonyms *adj* ≠ **depraved**: chaste, decent, moral, principled, pure, upright, virginal, virtuous

profound *adj* **1, 2** = **wise**, abstruse, deep, discerning, erudite, learned, penetrating, philosophical, recondite, sagacious, sage, serious, skilled, subtle, thoughtful, weighty **3** = **deep**, abysmal, bottomless, cavernous, fathomless, yawning **4** = **sincere**, abject, acute, deeply felt, extreme, great, heartfelt, heartrending, hearty, intense, keen **5** = **complete**, absolute, consummate, exhaustive, extensive, extreme, far-reaching, intense, out-and-out, pronounced, serious (*inf.*), thoroughgoing, total, unqualified, utter
Antonyms *adj* ≠ **wise**: imprudent, stupid, thoughtless, uneducated, uninformed, unknowledgeable, unwise ≠ **sincere**: insincere, shallow ≠ **complete**: slight, superficial

profoundly *adv* **4** = **greatly**, abjectly, acutely, deeply, extremely, from the bottom of one's heart, heartily, intensely, keenly, seriously, sincerely, thoroughly, to the core, to the nth degree, very

profundity *n* **1, 2** = **insight**, acuity, acumen, depth, erudition, intelligence, learning, penetration, perceptiveness, perspicacity, perspicuity, sagacity, wisdom **4** = **intensity**, depth, extremity, seriousness, severity, strength

profuse *adj* **1** = **plentiful**, abundant, ample, bountiful, copious, luxuriant, overflowing, prolific, teeming **2** = **extravagant**, excessive, exuberant, fulsome, generous, immoderate, lavish, liberal, open-handed, prodigal, unstinting
Antonyms *adj* ≠ **plentiful**: deficient, inadequate, meagre, scanty, scarce, skimpy, sparse ≠ **extravagant**: frugal, illiberal, moderate, provident, thrifty

(often foll. by *in*) free or generous in the giving (of): *profuse in thanks.* [C15: from L *profundere* to pour lavishly]
▸**pro'fusely** *adv* ▸**pro'fuseness** *or* **pro'fusion** *n*

progenitive (prəʊ'dʒɛnɪtɪv) *adj* capable of bearing offspring.
▸**pro'genitiveness** *n*

progenitor Ⓣ (prəʊ'dʒɛnɪtə) *n* **1** a direct ancestor. **2** an originator or founder. [C14: from L: ancestor, from *gignere* to beget]

progeny Ⓣ ('prɒdʒɪnɪ) *n, pl* **progenies. 1** the immediate descendant or descendants of a person, animal, etc. **2** a result or outcome. [C13: from L *prōgeniēs* lineage; see PROGENITOR]

progesterone (prəʊ'dʒɛstəˌrəʊn) *n* a steroid hormone, secreted mainly by the corpus luteum in the ovary, that prepares and maintains the uterus for pregnancy. [C20: from PRO-[1] + GE(STATION) + STER(OL) + -ONE]

progestogen (prəʊ'dʒɛstədʒən) *or* **progestin** (prə'dʒɛstɪn) *n* any of a group of steroid hormones with progesterone-like activity, used in oral contraceptives and in treating gynaecological disorders.

prognathous (prɒg'neɪθəs) *or* **prognathic** (prɒg'næθɪk) *adj* having a projecting lower jaw. [C19: from PRO-[2] + Gk *gnathos* jaw]

prognosis Ⓣ (prɒg'nəʊsɪs) *n, pl* **prognoses** (-'nəʊsiːz). **1** *Med.* a prediction of the course or outcome of a disease. **2** any prediction. [C17: via L from Gk: knowledge beforehand]

prognostic (prɒg'nɒstɪk) *adj* **1** of or serving as a prognosis. **2** predicting. ◆ *n* **3** *Med.* any symptom or sign used in making a prognosis. **4** a sign of some future occurrence. [C15: from OF *pronostique,* from L *prognōsticum,* from Gk, from *progignōskein* to know in advance]

prognosticate Ⓣ (prɒg'nɒstɪˌkeɪt) *vb* **prognosticates, prognosticating, prognosticated. 1** to foretell (future events); prophesy. **2** (*tr*) to foreshadow or portend. [C16: from Med. L *prognōsticāre* to predict]
▸**progˌnosti'cation** *n* ▸**prog'nosticative** *adj* ▸**prog'nostiˌcator** *n*

program *or* (*sometimes*) **programme** ('prəʊgræm) *n* **1** a sequence of coded instructions fed into a computer, enabling it to perform specified logical and arithmetical operations on data. ◆ *vb* **programs** *or* **programmes, programming, programmed. 2** (*tr*) to feed a program into (a computer). **3** (*tr*) to arrange (data) in a suitable form so that it can be processed by a computer. **4** (*intr*) to write a program.
▸**'programmer** *n*

programmable *or* **programable** (prəʊ'græməbəl) *adj* capable of being programmed for automatic operation or computer processing.

programme Ⓣ *or US* **program** ('prəʊgræm) *n* **1** a written or printed list of the events, performers, etc., in a public performance. **2** a performance presented at a scheduled time, esp. on radio or television. **3** a specially arranged selection of things to be done: *what's the programme for this afternoon?* **4** a plan, schedule, or procedure. **5** a syllabus or curriculum. ◆ *vb* **programmes, programming, programmed** *or US* **programs, programing, programed. 6** to design or schedule (something) as a programme. ◆ *n, vb* **7** *Computing.* a variant spelling of **program.** [C17: from LL *programma,* from Gk: written public notice, from PRO-[2] + *graphein* to write]
▸**ˌprogram'matic** *adj*

programmed learning *n* a teaching method in which the material to be learned is broken down into easily understandable parts on which the pupil is able to test himself.

programme music *n* music that is intended to depict or evoke a scene or idea.

programme of study *n Brit. education.* the prescribed syllabus that pupils must be taught at each key stage in the National Curriculum.

programming language *n* a simple language system designed to facilitate the writing of computer programs.

program statement *n* a single instruction in a computer program.

program trading *n* trading on international stock exchanges using a computer program to exploit differences between stock index futures and actual share prices on world equity markets.

progress Ⓣ *n* ('prəʊgrɛs). **1** movement forwards, esp. towards a place or objective. **2** satisfactory development or advance. **3** advance towards completion or perfection. **4** (*modifier*) of or relating to progress: *a progress report.* **5** (formerly) a stately royal journey. **6 in progress.** taking place. ◆ *vb* (prə'grɛs). **7** (*intr*) to move forwards or onwards. **8** (*intr*) to move towards completion or perfection. **9** (*tr*) to be responsible for the satisfactory progress of (a project, etc.) to completion. [C15: from L *prōgressus,* from *prōgredī* to advance, from *gradī* to step]

progression Ⓣ (prə'grɛʃən) *n* **1** the act of progressing; advancement. **2** the act or an instance of moving from one thing in a sequence to the next. **3** *Maths.* a sequence of numbers in which each term differs from the succeeding term by a constant relation. See also **arithmetic progression, geometric progression, harmonic progression. 4** *Music.* movement from one note or chord to the next.
▸**pro'gressional** *adj*

progressive Ⓣ (prə'grɛsɪv) *adj* **1** of or relating to progress. **2** progressing by steps or degrees. **3** (*often cap.*) favouring or promoting political or social reform: *a progressive policy.* **4** denoting an educational system that allows flexibility in learning procedures, based on activities determined by the needs and capacities of the individual child. **5** (esp. of a disease) advancing in severity, complexity, or extent. **6** (of a dance, card game, etc.) involving a regular change of partners. **7** denoting an aspect of verbs in some languages, including English, used to express continuous activity: *a progressive aspect of the verb "to walk" is "is walking".* ◆ *n* **8** a person who advocates progress, as in education, politics, etc. **9a** the progressive aspect of a verb. **9b** a verb in this aspect.
▸**pro'gressively** *adv* ▸**pro'gressiveness** *n* ▸**pro'gressivism** *n* ▸**pro'gressivist** *n*

progress payment *n* an instalment of a larger payment made to a contractor for work carried out up to a specified stage of the job.

prohibit Ⓣ (prə'hɪbɪt) *vb* (*tr*) **1** to forbid by law or other authority. **2** to hinder or prevent. [C15: from L *prohibēre* to prevent, from PRO-[1] + *habēre* to hold]
▸**pro'hibiter** *or* **pro'hibitor** *n*

prohibition Ⓣ (ˌprəʊɪ'bɪʃən) *n* **1** the act of prohibiting or state of being prohibited. **2** an order or decree that prohibits. **3** (*sometimes cap.*) (esp. in the US) a policy of legally forbidding the manufacture, sale, or consumption of alcoholic beverages. **4** *Law.* an order of a superior court forbidding an inferior court to determine a matter outside its jurisdiction.
▸**ˌprohi'bitionary** *adj* ▸**ˌprohi'bitionist** *n*

Prohibition (ˌprəʊɪ'bɪʃən) *n* the period (1920–33) when the manufacture, sale, and transportation of intoxicating liquors was banned in the US.
▸**ˌProhi'bitionist** *n*

prohibitive Ⓣ (prə'hɪbɪtɪv) *or* (*less commonly*) **prohibitory** (prə'hɪbɪtərɪ, -trɪ) *adj* **1** prohibiting or tending to prohibit. **2** (esp. of prices) tending or designed to discourage sale or purchase.
▸**pro'hibitively** *adv* ▸**pro'hibitiveness** *n*

project Ⓣ *n* ('prɒdʒɛkt). **1** a proposal, scheme, or design. **2a** a task requiring considerable or concerted effort, such as one by students. **2b** the subject of such a task. ◆ *vb* (prə'dʒɛkt). **3** (*tr*) to propose or plan. **4** (*tr*) to throw forwards. **5** to jut or cause to jut out. **6** (*tr*) to make a prediction based on known data and observations. **7** (*tr*) to transport in the imagination: *to project oneself into the future.* **8** (*tr*) to cause (an

THESAURUS

profusion *n* **1, 2 = abundance,** bounty, copiousness, cornucopia, excess, extravagance, exuberance, glut, lavishness, luxuriance, multitude, oversupply, plenitude, plethora, prodigality, quantity, riot, superabundance, superfluity, surplus, wealth

progenitor *n* **1 = ancestor,** begetter, forebear, forefather, parent, primogenitor, procreator **2 = originator,** antecedent, forerunner, instigator, precursor, predecessor, source

progeny *n* **1 = children,** breed, descendants, family, issue, lineage, offspring, posterity, race, scions, seed (*chiefly Biblical*), stock, young

prognosis *n* **1, 2 = forecast,** diagnosis, expectation, prediction, prognostication, projection, speculation, surmise

prognosticate *vb* **1 = foretell,** divine, forecast, predict, presage, prophesy, soothsay, vaticinate (*rare*) **2 = indicate,** augur, betoken, forebode, foreshadow, harbinger, herald, point to, portend, presage

prognostication *n* **1 = prediction,** expectation, forecast, prognosis, projection, prophecy, speculation, surmise

programme *n* **1, 3, 5 = schedule,** agenda, curriculum, line-up, list, listing, list of players, order of events, order of the day, plan, syllabus, timetable **2 = show,** broadcast, performance, presentation, production **4 = plan,** design, order of the day, plan of action, procedure, project, scheme ◆ *vb* **6 = schedule,** arrange, bill, book, design, engage, formulate, itemize, lay on, line up, list, map out, plan, prearrange, work out

progress *n* **1 = movement,** advance, course, onward course, passage, progression, way **2, 3 = development,** advance, advancement, amelioration, betterment, breakthrough, gain, gaining ground, growth, headway, improvement, increase, progression, promotion, step forward **6 in progress = going on,** being done, happening, occurring, proceeding, taking place, under way ◆ *vb* **7 = move on,** advance, come on, continue, cover ground, forge ahead, gain ground, gather way, get on, go forward, make headway, make inroads (into), make one's way, make strides, proceed, travel **8 = develop,** advance, ameliorate, better, blossom, gain, grow, improve, increase, mature

Antonyms *n* ≠ **movement:** regression, retrogression ≠ **development:** decline, failure, recession, regression, relapse, retrogression ◆ *vb* ≠ **move on:** get behind, recede, regress, retrogress ≠ **develop:** decrease, get behind, lose, lose ground, regress, retrogress

progression *n* **1 = progress,** advance, advancement, furtherance, gain, headway, movement forward **2 = sequence,** chain, course, cycle, order, series, string, succession

progressive *adj* **3, 4 = enlightened,** advanced, avant-garde, dynamic, enterprising, forward-looking, go-ahead, liberal, modern, radical, reformist, revolutionary, up-and-coming **5 = growing,** accelerating, advancing, continuing, continuous, developing, escalating, increasing, intensifying, ongoing

prohibit *vb* **1 = forbid,** ban, debar, disallow, interdict, outlaw, proscribe, veto **2 = prevent,** constrain, hamper, hinder, impede, make impossible, obstruct, preclude, restrict, rule out, stop

Antonyms *vb* ≠ **forbid:** allow, authorize, command, consent to, endure, further, give leave, let, license, order, permit, suffer, tolerate ≠ **prevent:** allow, let, permit

prohibited *adj* **1 = forbidden,** banned, barred, not allowed, off limits, proscribed, taboo, *verboten,* vetoed

prohibition *n* **1 = prevention,** constraint, disqualification, exclusion, forbiddance, interdiction, negation, obstruction, restriction **2 = ban,** bar, boycott, disallowance, embargo, injunction, interdict, proscription, veto

prohibitive *adj* **1 = prohibiting,** forbidding, proscriptive, repressive, restraining, restrictive, suppressive **2 = exorbitant,** beyond one's means, excessive, extortionate, high-priced, preposterous, sky-high, steep (*inf.*)

project *n* **1, 2 = scheme,** activity, assignment, design, enterprise, job, occupation, plan, image) to appear on a surface. **9** to cause (one's voice) to be heard clearly at a distance. **10** *Psychol.* **10a** (*intr*) (esp. of a child) to believe that others share one's subjective mental life. **10b** to impute to others (one's hidden desires). **11** (*tr*) *Geom.* to draw a projection of. **12** (*intr*) to communicate effectively, esp. to a large gathering. [C14: from L *prōicere* to throw down]

projectile ⓣ (prə'dʒektaɪl) *n* **1** an object thrown forwards. **2** any self-propelling missile, esp. a rocket. **3** any object that can be fired from a gun, such as a shell. ◆ *adj* **4** designed to be hurled forwards. **5** projecting forwards. **6** *Zool.* another word for **protrusile.** [C17: from NL *prōjectilis* jutting forwards]

projection ⓣ (prə'dʒekʃən) *n* **1** the act of projecting or the state of being projected. **2** a part that juts out. **3** See **map projection. 4** the representation of a line, figure, or solid on a given plane as it would be seen from a particular direction or in accordance with an accepted set of rules. **5** a scheme or plan. **6** a prediction based on known evidence and observations. **7a** the process of showing film on a screen. **7b** the images shown. **8** *Psychol.* **8a** the belief that others share one's subjective mental life. **8b** the process of projecting one's own hidden desires and impulses.
▸**pro'jectional** *adj* ▸**pro'jective** *adj*

projectionist (prə'dʒekʃənɪst) *n* a person responsible for the operation of film projection machines.

projective geometry *n* the branch of geometry concerned with the properties of solids that are invariant under projection and section.

projector (prə'dʒektə) *n* **1** an optical instrument that projects an enlarged image of individual slides. Full name: **slide projector. 2** an optical instrument in which a film is wound past a lens so that the frames can be viewed as a continuously moving sequence. Full name: **film** *or* **cine projector. 3** a device for projecting a light beam. **4** a person who devises projects.

prokaryote *or* **procaryote** (prəʊ'kærɪɒt) *n* any organism of the kingdom *Prokaryotae* having cells in which the genetic material is in a single filament of DNA, not enclosed in a nucleus. Cf. **eukaryote.** [from PRO-[2] + KARYO- + -*ote* as in *zygote*]
▸**prokaryotic** *or* **procaryotic** (prəʊˌkærɪ'ɒtɪk) *adj*

prolactin (prəʊ'læktɪn) *n* a gonadotrophic hormone secreted by the anterior lobe of the pituitary gland. In mammals it stimulates the secretion of progesterone by the corpus luteum and initiates and maintains lactation.

prolapse ('prəʊlæps, prəʊ'læps) *Pathol.* ◆ *n* **1** Also: **prolapsus** (prəʊ'læpsəs). the sinking or falling down of an organ or part, esp. the womb. ◆ *vb* **prolapses, prolapsing, prolapsed.** (*intr*) **2** (of an organ, etc.) to sink from its normal position. [C17: from L *prōlābi* to slide along]

prolate ('prəʊleɪt) *adj* having a polar diameter of greater length than the equatorial diameter. Cf. **oblate**[1]. [C17: from L *prōferre* to enlarge]
▸**'prolately** *adv*

prole (prəʊl) *n, adj Derog. sl., chiefly Brit.* short for **proletarian.**

prolegomenon (ˌprəʊle'gɒmɪnən) *n, pl* **prolegomenona** (-nə). (*often pl*) a preliminary discussion, esp. a formal critical introduction to a lengthy text. [C17: from Gk, from *prolegein,* from PRO-[2] + *legein* to say]
▸**ˌprole'gomenal** *adj*

prolepsis (prəʊ'lepsɪs) *n, pl* **prolepses** (-si:z). **1** a rhetorical device by which objections are anticipated and answered in advance. **2** use of a word after a verb in anticipation of its becoming applicable through the action of the verb, as *flat* in *hammer it flat.* [C16: via LL from Gk: anticipation, from *prolambanein* to anticipate, from PRO-[2] + *lambanein* to take]
▸**pro'leptic** *adj*

proletarian ⓣ (ˌprəʊlɪ'teərɪən) *adj* **1** of or belonging to the proletariat. ◆ *n* **2** a member of the proletariat. [C17: from L *prōlētārius* one whose only contribution to the state was his offspring, from *prōlēs* offspring]
▸**ˌprole'tarianism** *n*

proletariat ⓣ (ˌprəʊlɪ'teərɪət) *n* **1** all wage-earners collectively. **2** the lower or working class. **3** (in Marxist theory) the class of wage-earners, esp. industrial workers, in a capitalist society, whose only possession of significant material value is their labour. **4** (in ancient Rome) the lowest class of citizens, who had no property. [C19: via F from L *prōlētārius* PROLETARIAN]

pro-life *adj* (of an organization, pressure group, etc.) supporting the right to life of the unborn; against abortion, experiments on embryos, etc.
▸**ˌpro-'lifer** *n*

proliferate ⓣ (prə'lɪfəˌreɪt) *vb* **proliferates, proliferating, proliferated. 1** to grow or reproduce (new parts, cells, etc.) rapidly. **2** to grow or increase rapidly. [C19: from Med. L *prōlifer* having offspring, from L *prōlēs* offspring + *ferre* to bear]
▸**proˌlifer'ation** *n* ▸**pro'liferative** *adj*

prolific ⓣ (prə'lɪfɪk) *adj* **1** producing fruit, offspring, etc., in abundance. **2** producing constant or successful results. **3** (often foll. by *in* or *of*) rich or fruitful. [C17: from Med. L *prōlificus,* from L *prōlēs* offspring]
▸**pro'lifically** *adv* ▸**pro'lificness** *or* **pro'lificacy** *n*

prolix ('prəʊlɪks, prəʊ'lɪks) *adj* **1** (of a speech, book, etc.) so long as to be boring. **2** long-winded. [C15: from L *prōlixus* stretched out widely, from *liquī* to flow]
▸**pro'lixity** *n* ▸**pro'lixly** *adv*

prolocutor (prəʊ'lɒkjʊtə) *n* a chairman, esp. of the lower house of clergy in a convocation of the Anglican Church. [C15: from L: advocate, from *loqui* to speak]
▸**pro'locutorship** *n*

PROLOG *or* **Prolog** ('prəʊlɒg) *n* a computer programming language based on mathematical logic. [C20: from *pro(gramming in) log(ic)*]

prologue ⓣ *or US (often)* **prolog** ('prəʊlɒg) *n* **1** the prefatory lines introducing a play or speech. **2** a preliminary act or event. **3** (in early opera) **3a** an introductory scene in which a narrator summarizes the main action of the work. **3b** a brief independent play preceding the opera, esp. one in honour of a patron. ◆ *vb* **prologues, prologuing, prologued** *or US* **prologs, prologing, prologed. 4** (*tr*) to introduce with a prologue. [C13: from L *prologus,* from Gk, from PRO-[2] + *logos* discourse]

prolong ⓣ (prə'lɒŋ) *vb* (*tr*) to lengthen; extend. [C15: from LL *prōlongāre* to extend, from L PRO-[1] + *longus* long]
▸**prolongation** (ˌprəʊlɒŋ'geɪʃən) *n*

prolusion (prə'lu:ʒən) *n* **1** a preliminary written exercise. **2** an introductory essay. [C17: from L *prōlūsiō,* from *prōlūdere* to practise beforehand, from PRO-[1] + *lūdere* to play]
▸**prolusory** (prə'lu:zərɪ) *adj*

prom (prɒm) *n* **1** *Brit.* short for **promenade** (sense 1) or **promenade concert. 2** *US & Canad. inf.* a formal dance held at a high school or college.

PROM (prɒm) *n Computing. acronym for* programmable read only memory.

promenade ⓣ (ˌprɒmə'nɑ:d) *n* **1** *Chiefly Brit.* a public walk, esp. at a seaside resort. **2** a leisurely walk, esp. one in a public place for pleasure or display. **3** a marchlike step in dancing. **4** a marching sequence in a square or country dance. ◆ *vb* **promenades, promenading, promenaded. 5** to take a promenade in or through (a place). **6** (*intr*) *Dancing.* to perform a promenade. **7** (*tr*) to display or exhibit (someone or oneself) on or as if on a promenade. [C16: from F, from *promener* to lead out for a walk, from LL *prōmināre* to drive (cattle) along, from *mināre* to drive, prob. from *minārī* to threaten]
▸**ˌprome'nader** *n*

promenade concert *n* a concert at which some of the audience stand rather than sit.

promenade deck *n* an upper covered deck of a passenger ship for the use of the passengers.

promethazine (prəʊ'meθəˌzi:n) *n* an antihistamine drug used to treat allergies and to prevent vomiting. [C20: from PRO(PYL) + (*di*)*meth*(*ylamine*) + (*phenothi*)*azine*]

Promethean (prə'mi:θɪən) *adj* **1** of or relating to Prometheus, in Greek myth the Titan who stole fire from Olympus to give to mankind. He was punished by being chained to a rock and having an eagle tear out his liver. **2** creative, original, or life-enhancing.

promethium (prə'mi:θɪəm) *n* a radioactive element of the lanthanide series artificially produced by the fission of uranium. Symbol: Pm; atomic no.: 61; half-life of most stable isotope, ^{145}Pm: 17.7 years. [C20: NL from *Prometheus;* see PROMETHEAN]

prominence ⓣ ('prɒmɪnəns) *n* **1** the state of being prominent. **2** something that is prominent, such as a protuberance. **3** relative impor-

THESAURUS

programme, proposal, task, undertaking, venture, work ◆ *vb* **3** = **plan**, contemplate, contrive, design, devise, draft, frame, map out, outline, propose, purpose, scheme **4** = **throw**, cast, discharge, fling, hurl, launch, make carry, propel, shoot, transmit **5** = **stick out**, beetle, bulge, extend, jut, overhang, protrude, stand out **6** = **forecast**, calculate, call, estimate, extrapolate, gauge, predetermine, predict, reckon

projectile *n* **2, 3** = **missile**, bullet, rocket, shell

projection *n* **1** = **forecast**, calculation, computation, estimate, estimation, extrapolation, prediction, reckoning **2** = **protrusion**, bulge, eaves, jut, ledge, overhang, protuberance, ridge, shelf, sill **4** = **plan**, blueprint, diagram, map, outline, representation

proletarian *adj* **1** = **working-class**, cloth-cap (*inf.*), common, plebeian ◆ *n* **2** = **worker**, commoner, Joe Bloggs (*Brit. inf.*), man of the people, pleb, plebeian, prole (*derogatory sl., chiefly Brit.*)

proletariat *n* **1, 2** = **working class**, commonalty, commoners, hoi polloi, labouring classes, lower classes, lower orders, plebs, proles (*derogatory sl., chiefly Brit.*), the common people, the great unwashed (*inf. & derogatory*), the herd, the masses, the rabble, wage-earners
Antonyms *n* aristo (*inf.*), aristocracy, gentry, nobility, peerage, ruling class, upper class, upper crust (*inf.*)

proliferate *vb* **1, 2** = **increase**, breed, burgeon, escalate, expand, grow rapidly, multiply, mushroom, run riot, snowball

proliferation *n* **2** = **multiplication**, build-up, concentration, escalation, expansion, extension, increase, intensification, spread, step-up (*inf.*)

prolific *adj* **1, 3** = **productive**, abundant, bountiful, copious, fecund, fertile, fruitful, generative, luxuriant, profuse, rank, rich, teeming
Antonyms *adj* barren, fruitless, infertile, sterile, unfruitful, unproductive, unprolific

prologue *n* **1** = **introduction**, exordium, foreword, preamble, preface, preliminary, prelude, proem

prolong *vb* = **lengthen**, carry on, continue, delay, drag out, draw out, extend, make longer, perpetuate, protract, spin out, stretch
Antonyms *vb* abbreviate, abridge, curtail, cut, cut down, shorten, summarize

promenade *n* **1** = **walkway**, boulevard, esplanade, parade, prom, public walk **2** = **stroll**, airing, constitutional, saunter, turn, walk ◆ *vb* **5** = **stroll**, perambulate, saunter, stretch one's legs, take a walk, walk **7** = **parade**, flaunt, strut, swagger

prominence *n* **1** = **conspicuousness**, markedness, outstandingness, precedence, salience, specialness, top billing, weight **2** = **protrusion**, bulge, jutting, projection, protuberance, swelling **2** = **rising ground**, cliff, crag, crest, elevation, headland, height, high point, hummock, tance. **4** *Astron.* an eruption of incandescent gas from the sun's surface, visible during a total eclipse.

prominent ⊕ ('prɒmɪnənt) *adj* **1** jutting or projecting outwards. **2** standing out from its surroundings; noticeable. **3** widely known; eminent. [C16: from L *prōminēre* to jut out, from PRO-[1] + *ēminēre* to project]
▸**'prominently** *adv*

promiscuous ⊕ (prə'mɪskjʊəs) *adj* **1** indulging in casual and indiscriminate sexual relationships. **2** consisting of a number of dissimilar parts or elements mingled indiscriminately. **3** indiscriminate in selection. **4** casual or heedless. [C17: from L *prōmiscuus* indiscriminate, from PRO-[1] + *miscēre* to mix]
▸**pro'miscuously** *adv* ▸**promiscuity** (ˌprɒmɪ'skjuːɪtɪ) *or* **pro'miscuousness** *n*

promise ⊕ ('prɒmɪs) *vb* **promises, promising, promised.** **1** (often foll. by *to;* when *tr, may take a clause as object or an infinitive*) to give an assurance of (something to someone): *I promise that I will come.* **2** (*tr*) to undertake to give (something to someone): *he promised me a car for my birthday.* **3** (when *tr, takes an infinitive*) to cause people to expect that one is likely (to be or do something): *she promises to be a fine soprano.* **4** (*tr; usually passive*) *Obs.* to betroth: *I'm promised to Bill.* **5** (*tr*) to assure (someone) of the authenticity or inevitability of something: *there'll be trouble, I promise you.* ◆ *n* **6** an assurance given by one person to another agreeing or guaranteeing to do or not to do something. **7** indication of forthcoming excellence: *a writer showing considerable promise.* **8** the thing of which an assurance is given. [C14: from L *prōmissum* a promise, from *prōmittere* to send forth]
▸ˌ**promi'see** *n* ▸**'promiser** *or* (*Law*) **'promisor** *n*

Promised Land *n* **1** *Old Testament.* the land of Canaan, promised by God to Abraham and his descendants as their heritage (Genesis 12:7). **2** *Christianity.* heaven. **3** any longed-for place where one expects to find greater happiness.

promising ⊕ ('prɒmɪsɪŋ) *adj* showing promise of future success.
▸**'promisingly** *adv*

promissory ('prɒmɪsərɪ) *adj* **1** containing, relating to, or having the nature of a promise. **2** *Insurance.* stipulating how the provisions of an insurance contract will be fulfilled.

promissory note *n Commerce, chiefly US.* a document containing a signed promise to pay a stated sum of money to a specified person at a designated date or on demand. Also called: **note, note of hand.**

promo ('prəʊməʊ) *n, pl* **promos.** *Inf.* something used to promote a product, esp. a videotape film used to promote a pop record. [C20: shortened from *promotion*]

promontory ⊕ ('prɒməntərɪ, -trɪ) *n, pl* **promontories.** **1** a high point of land, esp. of rocky coast, that juts out into the sea. **2** *Anat.* any of various projecting structures. [C16: from L *prōmunturium* headland]

promote ⊕ (prə'məʊt) *vb* **promotes, promoting, promoted.** (*tr*) **1** to encourage the progress or existence of. **2** to raise to a higher rank, status, etc. **3** to advance (a pupil or student) to a higher course, class, etc. **4** to work for: *to promote reform.* **5** to encourage the sale of (a product) by advertising or securing financial support. [C14: from L *prōmovēre* to push onwards]
▸**pro'motion** *n* ▸**pro'motional** *adj*

promoter ⊕ (prə'məʊtə) *n* **1** a person or thing that promotes. **2** a person who helps to organize, develop, or finance an undertaking. **3** a person who organizes and finances a sporting event, esp. a boxing match.

prompt ⊕ (prɒmpt) *adj* **1** performed or executed without delay. **2** quick or ready to act or respond. ◆ *adv* **3** *Inf.* punctually. ◆ *vb* **4** (*tr*) to urge (someone to do something). **5** to remind (an actor, singer, etc.) of lines forgotten during a performance. **6** (*tr*) to refresh the memory of. **7** (*tr*) to give rise to by suggestion: *his affairs will prompt discussion.* ◆ *n* **8** *Commerce.* **8a** the time limit allowed for payment of the debt incurred by purchasing on credit. **8b** Also called: **prompt note.** a memorandum sent to a purchaser to remind him of the time limit and the sum due. **9** anything that serves to remind. [C15: from L *promptus* evident, from *prōmere* to produce, from *emere* to buy]
▸**'promptly** *adv* ▸**'promptness** *n*

prompter ⊕ ('prɒmptə) *n* **1** a person offstage who reminds the actors of forgotten lines or cues. **2** a person, thing, etc., that prompts.

promptitude ('prɒmptɪˌtjuːd) *n* the quality of being prompt; punctuality.

prompt side *n Theatre.* the side of the stage where the prompter is, usually to the actor's left in Britain and to his right in the United States.

promulgate ⊕ ('prɒməlˌgeɪt) *vb* **promulgates, promulgating, promulgated.** (*tr*) **1** to put into effect (a law, decree, etc.), esp. by formal proclamation. **2** to announce officially. **3** to make widespread. [C16: from L *prōmulgāre* to bring to public knowledge]
▸ˌ**promul'gation** *n* ▸**'promulˌgator** *n*

pron. *abbrev. for:* **1** pronominal. **2** pronoun. **3** pronounced. **4** pronunciation.

pronate (prəʊ'neɪt) *vb* **pronates, pronating, pronated.** (*tr*) to turn (the forearm or hand) so that the palmar surface is directed downwards. [C19: from LL *prōnāre* to bow]
▸**pro'nation** *n* ▸**pro'nator** *n*

prone ⊕ (prəʊn) *adj* **1** lying flat or face downwards; prostrate. **2** sloping or tending downwards. **3** having an inclination to do something. [C14: from L *prōnus* bent forward, from PRO-[1]]
▸**'pronely** *adv* ▸**'proneness** *n*

-prone *adj combining form.* liable or disposed to suffer: *accident-prone.*

THESAURUS

mound, pinnacle, projection, promontory, rise, spur **3** = **fame**, celebrity, distinction, eminence, greatness, importance, name, notability, pre-eminence, prestige, rank, reputation, standing

prominent *adj* **1** = **jutting**, bulging, hanging over, projecting, protruding, protrusive, protuberant, standing out **2** = **noticeable**, blatant, conspicuous, easily seen, eye-catching, in the foreground, obtrusive, obvious, outstanding, pronounced, remarkable, salient, striking, to the fore, unmistakable **3** = **famous**, big-time (*inf.*), celebrated, chief, distinguished, eminent, foremost, important, leading, main, major league (*inf.*), notable, noted, outstanding, popular, pre-eminent, renowned, respected, top, well-known, well-thought-of
Antonyms *adj* ≠ **jutting:** concave, indented, receding ≠ **noticeable:** inconspicuous, indistinct, insignificant, unnoticeable ≠ **famous:** insignificant, minor, secondary, undistinguished, unimportant, unknown, unnotable

promiscuity *n* **1** = **licentiousness**, abandon, amorality, debauchery, depravity, dissipation, immorality, incontinence, laxity, laxness, lechery, libertinism, looseness, permissiveness, profligacy, promiscuousness, sleeping around (*inf.*), wantonness

promiscuous *adj* **1** = **licentious**, abandoned, debauched, dissipated, dissolute, fast, immoral, lax, libertine, loose, of easy virtue, profligate, unbridled, unchaste, wanton, wild **2** = **mixed**, chaotic, confused, disordered, diverse, heterogeneous, ill-assorted, indiscriminate, intermingled, intermixed, jumbled, mingled, miscellaneous, motley **3, 4** = **indiscriminate**, careless, casual, haphazard, heedless, indifferent, irregular, irresponsible, random, slovenly, uncontrolled, uncritical, undiscriminating, unfastidious, unselective
Antonyms *adj* ≠ **licentious:** chaste, decent, innocent, modest, moral, pure, undefiled, unsullied, vestal, virginal, virtuous ≠ **mixed:** homogeneous, identical, neat, ordered, orderly, organized, shipshape, uniform, unmixed ≠ **indiscriminate:** careful, critical, discriminating, fastidious, responsible, selective

promise *vb* **1, 2** = **guarantee**, assure, contract, cross one's heart, engage, give an undertaking, give one's word, pledge, plight, stipulate, swear, take an oath, undertake, vouch, vow, warrant **3** = **seem likely**, augur, bespeak, betoken, bid fair, denote, give hope of, hint at, hold a probability, hold out hopes of, indicate, lead one to expect, look like, show signs of, suggest ◆ *n* **6** = **guarantee**, assurance, bond, commitment, compact, covenant, engagement, oath, pledge, undertaking, vow, word, word of honour **7** = **potential**, ability, aptitude, capability, capacity, flair, talent

promising *adj* = **encouraging**, auspicious, bright, favourable, full of promise, hopeful, likely, propitious, reassuring, rosy = **talented**, able, gifted, likely, rising, up-and-coming
Antonyms *adj* ≠ **encouraging:** discouraging, unauspicious, unfavourable, unpromising

promontory *n* **1** = **point**, cape, foreland, head, headland, ness, spur

promote *vb* **1** = **help**, advance, aid, assist, back, boost, contribute to, develop, encourage, forward, foster, further, gee up, nurture, stimulate, support **2** = **raise**, aggrandize, dignify, elevate, exalt, honour, kick upstairs (*inf.*), prefer, upgrade **4** = **work for**, advocate, call attention to, champion, endorse, espouse, popularize, prescribe, push for, recommend, speak for, sponsor, support, urge **5** = **advertise**, beat the drum for (*inf.*), hype, plug (*inf.*), publicize, puff, push, sell
Antonyms *vb* ≠ **help:** discourage, hinder, hold back, impede, obstruct, oppose, prevent ≠ **raise:** demote, downgrade, lower *or* reduce in rank

promoter *n* **1** = **supporter**, advocate, campaigner, champion, helper, mainstay, proponent, stalwart, upholder **2, 3** = **organizer**, arranger, entrepreneur, impresario, matchmaker

promotion *n* **1** = **encouragement**, advancement, advocacy, backing, boosting, cultivation, development, espousal, furtherance, progress, support **2** = **rise**, advancement, aggrandizement, elevation, ennoblement, exaltation, honour, move up, preferment, upgrading **5** = **publicity**, advertising, advertising campaign, ballyhoo (*inf.*), hard sell, hype, media hype, plugging (*inf.*), propaganda, puffery (*inf.*), pushing

prompt *adj* **1** = **immediate**, early, instant, instantaneous, on time, punctual, quick, rapid, speedy, swift, timely, unhesitating **2** = **quick**, alert, brisk, eager, efficient, expeditious, ready, responsive, smart, willing ◆ *adv* **3** *Informal* = **exactly**, on the dot, promptly, punctually, sharp ◆ *vb* **4** = **motivate**, cause, impel, incite, induce, inspire, instigate, move, provoke, spur, stimulate, urge **5, 6** = **remind**, assist, cue, help out, jog the memory, prod, refresh the memory **7** = **cause**, call forth, elicit, evoke, give rise to, occasion, provoke ◆ *n* **9** = **reminder**, cue, help, hint, jog, jolt, prod, spur, stimulus
Antonyms *adj* ≠ **immediate:** hesitating, late, slow ≠ **quick:** inactive, inattentive, inefficient, remiss, slack, tardy, unresponsive ◆ *vb* ≠ **motivate:** deter, discourage, prevent, restrain, talk out of

prompter *n* **2** = **autocue**, idiot board (*sl.*), Teleprompter (*Trademark*) **2** = **instigator**, agitator, catalyst, gadfly, inspirer, moving spirit, prime mover

promptly *adv* **1** = **immediately**, at once, by return, directly, hotfoot, instantly, on the dot, on time, posthaste, pronto (*inf.*), punctually, quickly, speedily, swiftly, unhesitatingly

promptness *n* **1, 2** = **swiftness**, alacrity, alertness, briskness, dispatch, eagerness, haste, promptitude, punctuality, quickness, readiness, speed, willingness

promulgate *vb* **2, 3** = **make known**, advertise, announce, broadcast, circulate, communicate, declare, decree, disseminate, issue, make public, notify, proclaim, promote, publish, spread

prone *adj* **1** = **face down**, flat, horizontal, lying down, procumbent, prostrate, recumbent **3** = **liable**, apt, bent, disposed, given, inclined,

DICTIONARY

prong Ⓣ (prɒŋ) *n* **1** a sharply pointed end of an instrument, such as on a fork. **2** any pointed projecting part. ◆ *vb* **3** (*tr*) to prick or spear with or as if with a prong. [C15]
▸**pronged** *adj*

pronghorn (ˈprɒŋˌhɔːn) *n* a ruminant mammal inhabiting rocky deserts of North America and having small branched horns. Also called: **American antelope.**

pronominal (prəʊˈnɒmɪnᵊl) *adj* relating to or playing the part of a pronoun. [C17: from LL *prōnōminālis*, from *prōnōmen* a PRONOUN]
▸**proˈnominally** *adv*

pronoun (ˈprəʊˌnaʊn) *n* one of a class of words that serves to replace a noun or noun phrase that has already been or is about to be mentioned in the sentence or context. Abbrev.: **pron.** [C16: from L *prōnōmen*, from PRO-[1] + *nōmen* noun]

pronounce Ⓣ (prəˈnaʊns) *vb* **pronounces, pronouncing, pronounced. 1** to utter or articulate (a sound or sounds). **2** (*tr*) to utter (words) in the correct way. **3** (*tr; may take a clause as object*) to proclaim officially: *I now pronounce you man and wife.* **4** (when *tr, may take a clause as object*) to declare as one's judgment: *to pronounce the death sentence upon someone.* [C14: from L *prōnuntiāre* to announce]
▸**proˈnounceable** *adj* ▸**proˈnouncer** *n*

pronounced Ⓣ (prəˈnaʊnst) *adj* **1** strongly marked or indicated. **2** (of a sound) articulated with vibration of the vocal cords; voiced.
▸**pronouncedly** (prəˈnaʊnsɪdlɪ) *adv*

pronouncement Ⓣ (prəˈnaʊnsmənt) *n* **1** an official or authoritative announcement. **2** the act of declaring or uttering formally.

pronto (ˈprɒntəʊ) *adv Inf.* at once. [C20: from Sp.: quick, from L *promptus* PROMPT]

pronunciation Ⓣ (prəˌnʌnsɪˈeɪʃən) *n* **1** the act, instance, or manner of pronouncing sounds. **2** the supposedly correct manner of pronouncing sounds in a given language. **3** a phonetic transcription of a word.

proof Ⓣ (pruːf) *n* **1** any evidence that establishes or helps to establish the truth, validity, quality, etc., of something. **2** *Law.* the whole body of evidence upon which the verdict of a court is based. **3** *Maths, logic.* a sequence of steps or statements that establishes the truth of a proposition. **4** the act of testing the truth of something (esp. in **put to the proof**). **5** *Scots Law.* trial before a judge without a jury. **6** *Printing.* a trial impression made from composed type for the correction of errors. **7** (in engraving, etc.) a print made by an artist or under his supervision for his own satisfaction before he hands the plate over to a professional printer. **8** *Photog.* a trial print from a negative. **9a** the alcoholic strength of proof spirit. **9b** the strength of a liquor as measured on a scale in which the strength of proof spirit is 100 degrees. ◆ *adj* **10** (*usually postpositive;* foll. by *against*) impervious (to): *the roof is proof against rain.* **11** having the alcoholic strength of proof spirit. **12** of proved impenetrability: *proof armour.* ◆ *vb* **13** (*tr*) to take a proof from (type matter, a plate, etc.). **14** to proofread (text) or inspect (a print, etc.), as for approval. **15** to render (something) proof, esp. to waterproof. [C13: from OF *preuve* a test, from LL *proba*, from L *probāre* to test]

-proof *adj, vb combining form.* (to make) impervious to; secure against (damage by): *waterproof.* [from PROOF (adj)]

proofread (ˈpruːfˌriːd) *vb* **proofreads, proofreading, proofread** (-ˌrɛd). to read (copy or printer's proofs) and mark errors to be corrected.
▸**ˈproofˌreader** *n*

proof spirit *n* (in Britain) a mixture of alcohol and water or an alcoholic beverage that contains 49.28 per cent of alcohol by weight, 57.1 per cent by volume at 51°F: used until 1980 as a standard of alcoholic liquids.

prop[1] Ⓣ (prɒp) *vb* **props, propping, propped.** (*tr;* often foll. by *up*) **1** to support with a rigid object, such as a stick. **2** (usually also foll. by *against*) to place or lean. **3** to sustain or support. ◆ *n* **4** something that gives rigid support, such as a stick. **5** short for **clothes prop. 6** a person or thing giving support, as of a moral nature. **7** *Rugby.* either of the forwards at either end of the front row of a scrum. [C15: rel. to M Du. *proppe* vine prop]

prop[2] (prɒp) *n* short for **property** (sense 8).

prop[3] (prɒp) *n* an informal word for **propeller.**

prop. *abbrev. for:* **1** proper(ly). **2** property. **3** proposition. **4** proprietor.

propaedeutic (ˌprəʊpɪˈdjuːtɪk) *n* **1** (*often pl*) preparatory instruction basic to further study of an art or science. ◆ *adj also* **propaedeutical. 2** of, relating to, or providing such instruction. [C19: from Gk *propaideuein* to teach in advance, from PRO-[2] + *paideuein* to rear]

propaganda Ⓣ (ˌprɒpəˈgændə) *n* **1** the organized dissemination of information, allegations, etc., to assist or damage the cause of a government, movement, etc. **2** such information, allegations, etc. [C18: from It., use of *propaganda* in the NL title *Sacra Congregatio de Propaganda Fide* Sacred Congregation for Propagating the Faith]
▸ˌ**propaˈgandism** *n* ▸ˌ**propaˈgandist** *n, adj*

Propaganda (ˌprɒpəˈgændə) *n RC Church.* a congregation responsible for directing the work of the foreign missions.

propagandize Ⓣ *or* **propagandise** (ˌprɒpəˈgænˌdaɪz) *vb* **propagandizes, propagandizing, propagandized** *or* **propagandises, propagandising, propagandised. 1** (*tr*) to spread by, or subject to, propaganda. **2** (*intr*) to spread or organize propaganda.

propagate Ⓣ (ˈprɒpəˌgeɪt) *vb* **propagates, propagating, propagated. 1** *Biol.* to reproduce or cause to reproduce; breed. **2** (*tr*) *Horticulture.* to produce (plants) by layering, grafting, cuttings, etc. **3** (*tr*) to promulgate. **4** *Physics.* to transmit, esp. in the form of a wave: *to propagate sound.* **5** (*tr*) to transmit (characteristics) from one generation to the next. [C16: from L *propāgāre* to increase (plants) by cuttings, from *propāgēs* a cutting, from *pangere* to fasten]
▸ˌ**propaˈgation** *n* ▸ˌ**propaˈgational** *adj* ▸**ˈpropagative** *adj* ▸**ˈpropaˌgator** *n*

propane (ˈprəʊpeɪn) *n* a flammable gaseous alkane found in petroleum and used as a fuel. Formula: $CH_3CH_2CH_3$. [C19: from PROPIONIC (ACID) + -ANE]

propanoic acid (ˌprəʊpəˈnəʊɪk) *n* a colourless liquid carboxylic acid used in inhibiting the growth of moulds in bread. Formula: CH_3CH_2COOH. Former name: **propionic acid.** [C20: from PROPANE + -OIC]

pro patria *Latin.* (ˈprəʊ ˈpætrɪˌɑː) for one's country.

propel Ⓣ (prəˈpɛl) *vb* **propels, propelling, propelled.** (*tr*) to impel, drive, or cause to move forwards. [C15: from L *prōpellere*]
▸**proˈpellant** *or* **proˈpellent** *n*

propeller (prəˈpɛlə) *n* **1** a device having blades radiating from a central hub that is rotated to produce thrust to propel a ship, aircraft, etc. **2** a person or thing that propels.

propelling pencil *n* a pencil consisting of a metal or plastic case containing a replaceable lead. As the point is worn away the lead can be extended, usually by turning part of the case.

propene (ˈprəʊpiːn) *n* a colourless gaseous alkene obtained by cracking petroleum. Formula: $CH_3CH{:}CH_2$. Also called: **propylene.**

propensity Ⓣ (prəˈpɛnsɪtɪ) *n, pl* **propensities. 1** a natural tendency. **2** *Obs.* partiality. [C16: from L *prōpensus* inclined to, from *prōpendēre* to hang forwards]

proper Ⓣ (ˈprɒpə) *adj* **1** (*usually prenominal*) appropriate or usual: *in its proper place.* **2** suited to a particular purpose: *use the proper knife to cut the bread.* **3** correct in behaviour. **4** vigorously or excessively moral. **5** up to a required or regular standard. **6** (*immediately postpositive*) (of an object, quality, etc.) referred to so as to exclude anything not directly connected with it: *his claim is connected with the deed proper.* **7**

THESAURUS

likely, predisposed, subject, susceptible, tending
Antonyms *adj* ≠ **face down:** erect, face up, perpendicular, supine, upright, vertical ≠ **liable:** averse, disinclined, indisposed, not likely, unlikely

proneness *n* **3** = **tendency**, bent, bias, disposition, inclination, leaning, liability, partiality, proclivity, propensity, susceptibility, weakness

prong *n* **1, 2** = **point**, projection, spike, tine, tip

pronounce *vb* **1** = **say**, accent, articulate, enunciate, sound, speak, stress, utter, vocalize, voice **3, 4** = **declare**, affirm, announce, assert, decree, deliver, judge, proclaim

pronounced *adj* **1** = **noticeable**, broad, clear, conspicuous, decided, definite, distinct, evident, marked, obvious, salient, striking, strong, unmistakable
Antonyms *adj* concealed, hidden, imperceptible, inconspicuous, unapparent, unnoticeable, vague

pronouncement *n* **1** = **announcement**, declaration, decree, dictum, edict, judgment, manifesto, notification, proclamation, promulgation, pronunciamento, statement

pronunciation *n* **1** = **intonation**, accent, accentuation, articulation, diction, elocution, enunciation, inflection, speech, stress

proof *n* **1** = **evidence**, attestation, authentication, certification, confirmation, corroboration, demonstration, substantiation, testimony, verification **4** *As in* **put to the proof** = **test**, assay, examination, experiment, ordeal, scrutiny, trial **6** *Printing* = **trial print**, galley, galley proof, page proof, pull, slip, trial impression ◆ *adj* **10** = **impervious**, impenetrable, repellent, resistant, strong, tight, treated

prop[1] *vb* **1, 3** = **support**, bolster, brace, buttress, hold up, maintain, shore, stay, sustain, truss, uphold **2** = **rest**, lean, place, set, stand ◆ *n* **4** = **support**, brace, buttress, mainstay, stanchion, stay, truss

propaganda *n* **1, 2** = **information**, advertising, agitprop, ballyhoo (*inf.*), boosterism, brainwashing, disinformation, hype, newspeak, promotion, publicity

propagandist *n* **1** = **publicist**, advocate, evangelist, indoctrinator, pamphleteer, promoter, proponent, proselytizer

propagandize *vb* **1, 2** = **persuade**, brainwash, convince, indoctrinate, instil, proselytize

propagate *vb* **1** = **reproduce**, beget, breed, engender, generate, increase, multiply, procreate, produce, proliferate **3** = **spread**, broadcast, circulate, diffuse, disseminate, make known, proclaim, promote, promulgate, publicize, publish, transmit
Antonyms *vb* ≠ **spread:** cover up, hide, hush up, keep under wraps, stifle, suppress, withhold

propagation *n* **1** = **reproduction**, breeding, generation, increase, multiplication, procreation, proliferation **3** = **spreading**, circulation, communication, diffusion, dissemination, distribution, promotion, promulgation, spread, transmission

propel *vb* = **drive**, force, impel, launch, push, send, set in motion, shoot, shove, start, thrust
Antonyms *vb* check, delay, hold back, pull, slow, stop

propensity *n* **1** = **tendency**, aptness, bent, bias, disposition, inclination, leaning, liability, penchant, predisposition, proclivity, proneness, susceptibility, weakness

proper *adj* **1** = **suitable**, appropriate, apt, becoming, befitting, fit, fitting, legitimate, meet (*arch.*), right, suited **3** = **polite**, *comme il faut*, decent, decorous, *de rigueur*, genteel, gentlemanly, ladylike, mannerly, punctilious, refined, respectable, seemly **7** = **characteristic**, individual, own, particular, peculiar, personal, respective, special, specific
Antonyms *adj* ≠ **suitable:** improper, inappropriate, unbecoming, unsuitable ≠ **polite:** coarse, common, crude, discourteous, impolite, indecent,

(*postpositive*; foll. by *to*) belonging to or characteristic of a person or thing. **8** (*prenominal*) *Brit. inf.* (intensifier): *I felt a proper fool.* **9** (*usually postpositive*) (of heraldic colours) considered correct for the natural colour of the object depicted: *three martlets proper.* **10** *Arch.* pleasant or good. **11 good and proper.** *Inf.* thoroughly. ◆ *n* **12** the parts of the Mass that vary according to the particular day or feast on which the Mass is celebrated. [C13: via OF from L *prōprius* special]
▸**'properly** *adv* ▸**'properness** *n*

proper fraction *n* a fraction in which the numerator has a lower absolute value than the denominator, as ½ or $x/(3 + x^2)$.

proper motion *n* the very small continuous change in the direction of motion of a star relative to the sun.

proper noun *or* **name** *n* the name of a person, place, or object, as for example *Iceland, Patrick,* or *Uranus.* Cf. **common noun.**

propertied ('prɒpətɪd) *adj* owning land or property.

property ⓣ ('prɒpətɪ) *n, pl* **properties. 1** something of value, either tangible, such as land, or intangible, such as copyrights. **2** *Law.* the right to possess, use, and dispose of anything. **3** possessions collectively. **4a** land or real estate. **4b** (*as modifier*): *property rights.* **5** *Chiefly Austral.* a ranch or station. **6** a quality or characteristic attribute, such as the density or strength of a material. **7** *Logic, obs.* Also called: **proprium** ('prəʊprɪəm). an attribute that is not essential to a species but is common and peculiar to it. **8** any movable object used on the set of a stage play or film. Usually shortened to **prop.** [C13: from OF *propriété*, from L *proprietās* something personal, from *proprius* one's own]

property bond *n* a bond issued by a life-assurance company, the premiums for which are invested in a property-owning fund.

property centre *n* a service for buying and selling property, including conveyancing, provided by a group of local solicitors. In full: **solicitors' property centre.**

property man *n* a member of the stage crew in charge of the stage properties. Usually shortened to **propman.**

prophecy ⓣ ('prɒfɪsɪ) *n, pl* **prophecies. 1a** a message of divine truth revealing God's will. **1b** the act of uttering such a message. **2** a prediction or guess. **3** the charismatic endowment of a prophet. [C13: ult. from Gk *prophētēs* PROPHET]

prophesy ⓣ ('prɒfɪˌsaɪ) *vb* **prophesies, prophesying, prophesied. 1** to foretell (something) by or as if by divine inspiration. **2** (*intr*) *Arch.* to give instructions in religious subjects. [C14 *prophecien*, from PROPHECY]
▸**'propheˌsiable** *adj* ▸**'propheˌsier** *n*

prophet ⓣ ('prɒfɪt) *n* **1** a person who supposedly speaks by divine inspiration, esp. one through whom a divinity expresses his will. **2** a person who predicts the future: *a prophet of doom.* **3** a spokesman for a movement, doctrine, etc. [C13: from OF *prophète*, from L, from Gk *prophētēs* one who declares the divine will, from PRO-[2] + *phanai* to speak]
▸**'prophetess** *fem n*

Prophet ('prɒfɪt) *n* **the. 1** the principal designation of Mohammed as the founder of Islam. **2** a name for Joseph Smith as the founder of the Mormon Church.

prophetic ⓣ (prə'fɛtɪk) *adj* **1** of or relating to a prophet or prophecy. **2** of the nature of a prophecy; predictive.
▸**pro'phetically** *adv*

prophylactic (ˌprɒfɪ'læktɪk) *adj* **1** protecting from or preventing disease. **2** protective or preventive. ◆ *n* **3** a prophylactic drug or device. **4** *Chiefly US.* another name for **condom.** [C16: via F from Gk *prophulaktikos*, from *prophulassein* to guard by taking advance measures, from PRO-[2] + *phulax* a guard]

prophylaxis (ˌprɒfɪ'læksɪs) *n* the prevention of disease or control of its possible spread.

propinquity (prə'pɪŋkwɪtɪ) *n* **1** nearness in place or time. **2** nearness in relationship. [C14: from L *propinquitās*, from *propinquus* near, from *prope* nearby]

propionic acid (ˌprəʊpɪ'ɒnɪk) *n* the former name for **propanoic acid.** [C19: from Gk *pro-* first + *pionic*, from *piōn* fat, because it is first in order of the fatty acids]

propitiate ⓣ (prə'pɪʃɪˌeɪt) *vb* **propitiates, propitiating, propitiated.** (*tr*) to appease or make well disposed; conciliate. [C17: from L *propitiāre*, from *propitius* gracious]
▸**pro'pitiable** *adj* ▸**proˌpiti'ation** *n* ▸**pro'pitiative** *adj* ▸**pro'pitiˌator** *n* ▸**pro'pitiatory** *adj*

propitious ⓣ (prə'pɪʃəs) *adj* **1** favourable; auguring well. **2** gracious or favourably inclined. [C15: from L *propitius* well disposed, from *prope* close to]
▸**pro'pitiously** *adv* ▸**pro'pitiousness** *n*

propjet ('prɒpˌdʒɛt) *n* another name for **turboprop.**

propolis ('prɒpəlɪs) *n* a greenish-brown resinous aromatic substance collected by bees from the buds of trees for use in the construction of hives. Also called: **bee glue, hive dross.** [C17: via L from Gk: suburb, bee glue, from *pro-* before + *polis* city]

proponent ⓣ (prə'pəʊnənt) *n* a person who argues in favour of something or puts forward a proposal, etc. [C16: from L *prōpōnere* to PROPOSE]

proportion ⓣ (prə'pɔːʃən) *n* **1** relative magnitude or extent; ratio. **2** correct or desirable relationship between parts; symmetry. **3** a part considered with respect to the whole. **4** (*pl*) dimensions or size: *a building of vast proportions.* **5** a share or quota. **6** a relationship that maintains a constant ratio between two variable quantities: *prices increase in proportion to manufacturing costs.* **7** *Maths.* a relationship between four numbers or quantities in which the ratio of the first pair equals the ratio of the second pair. ◆ *vb* (*tr*) **8** to adjust in relative amount, size, etc. **9** to cause to be harmonious in relationship of parts. [C14: from L *prōportiō*, from *prō portione*, lit.: for (its, one's) PORTION]
▸**pro'portionable** *adj* ▸**pro'portionably** *adv* ▸**pro'portionment** *n*

proportional ⓣ (prə'pɔːʃənᵊl) *adj* **1** of, involving, or being in proportion. ◆ *n* **2** *Maths.* an unknown term in a proportion: *in* $a/b = c/x$, x *is the fourth proportional.*
▸**proˌportion'ality** *n* ▸**pro'portionally** *adv*

proportional representation *n* representation of parties in an elective body in proportion to the votes they win. Abbrev.: **PR.** Cf. **first-past-the-post.** See also **Additional Member System, Alternative Vote, party list, Single Transferable Vote.**

proportionate *adj* (prə'pɔːʃənɪt). **1** being in proper proportion. ◆ *vb* (prə'pɔːʃəˌneɪt), **proportionates, proportionating, proportionated. 2** (*tr*) to make proportionate.
▸**pro'portionately** *adv*

proposal ⓣ (prə'pəʊzᵊl) *n* **1** the act of proposing. **2** something proposed, as a plan. **3** an offer, esp. of marriage.

propose ⓣ (prə'pəʊz) *vb* **proposes, proposing, proposed. 1** (when *tr, may take a clause as object*) to put forward (a plan, etc.) for consideration. **2** (*tr*) to nominate, as for a position. **3** (*tr*) to intend (to do something): *I propose to leave town now.* **4** (*tr*) to announce the drinking of (a toast). **5** (*intr*; often foll. by *to*) to make an offer of marriage. [C14: from OF *proposer*, from L *prōpōnere* to display, from PRO-[1] + *pōnere* to place]
▸**pro'posable** *adj* ▸**pro'poser** *n*

proposition ⓣ (ˌprɒpə'zɪʃən) *n* **1** a proposal for consideration. **2** *Philosophy.* the content of a sentence that affirms or denies something and is capable of being true or false. **3** *Maths.* a statement or theorem, usually containing its proof. **4** *Inf.* a person or matter to be dealt with: *he's a difficult proposition.* **5** *Inf.* an invitation to engage in sexual intercourse. ◆ *vb* **6** (*tr*) to propose a plan, deal, etc., to, esp. to engage in

THESAURUS

rude, ungentlemanly, unladylike, unrefined, unseemly

properly *adv* **1 = suitably**, appropriately, aptly, deservedly, fittingly, legitimately, rightly **3 = politely**, decently, decorously, ethically, punctiliously, respectably, respectfully
Antonyms *adv* ≠ **suitably:** improperly, inappropriately, inaptly, unfittingly, unsuitably, wrongly ≠ **politely:** badly, disrespectfully, impolitely, improperly, indecently, indecorously, unethically

property *n* **1, 3 = possessions**, assets, belongings, building(s), capital, chattels, effects, estate, goods, holdings, house(s), means, resources, riches, wealth **4 = land**, acres, estate, freehold, holding, real estate, real property, realty, title **6 = quality**, ability, attribute, characteristic, feature, hallmark, idiosyncrasy, mark, peculiarity, trait, virtue

prophecy *n* **1, 2 = prediction**, augury, divination, forecast, foretelling, prognosis, prognostication, revelation, second sight, soothsaying, sortilege, vaticination (*rare*)

prophesy *vb* **1 = predict**, augur, call, divine, forecast, foresee, foretell, forewarn, presage, prognosticate, soothsay, vaticinate (*rare*)

prophet *n* **1, 2 = soothsayer**, augur, Cassandra, clairvoyant, diviner, forecaster, oracle, prognosticator, prophesier, seer, sibyl

prophetic *adj* **1, 2 = predictive**, augural, divinatory, fatidic (*rare*), foreshadowing, mantic, oracular, presaging, prescient, prognostic, sibylline, vatic (*rare*)

propitiate *vb* **= appease**, conciliate, make peace, mollify, pacify, placate, reconcile, satisfy

propitiation *n* **= appeasement**, conciliation, mollification, peacemaking, placation, reconciliation

propitiatory *adj* **= appeasing**, assuaging, conciliatory, pacificatory, pacifying, peacemaking, placative, placatory, propitiative, reconciliatory

propitious *adj* **1 = favourable**, advantageous, auspicious, bright, encouraging, fortunate, full of promise, happy, lucky, opportune, promising, prosperous, rosy, timely **2 = well-disposed**, benevolent, benign, favourably inclined, friendly, gracious, kind

proponent *n* **= supporter**, advocate, apologist, backer, champion, defender, enthusiast, exponent, friend, partisan, patron, spokesman *or* spokeswoman, subscriber, upholder, vindicator

proportion *n* **1 = relative amount**, distribution, ratio, relationship **2 = balance**, agreement, congruity, correspondence, harmony, symmetry **3, 5 = part**, amount, cut, division, fraction, measure, percentage, quota, segment, share **4** *plural* **= dimensions**, amplitude, breadth, bulk, capacity, expanse, extent, magnitude, measurements, range, scope, size, volume

proportional *adj* **1 = balanced**, commensurate, comparable, compatible, consistent, correspondent, corresponding, equitable, equivalent, even, in proportion, just
Antonyms *adj* different, discordant, disproportionate, dissimilar, incommensurable, incompatible, inconsistent, unequal

proposal *n* **2, 3 = suggestion**, bid, design, motion, offer, overture, plan, presentation, proffer, programme, project, proposition, recommendation, scheme, tender, terms

propose *vb* **1 = put forward**, advance, come up with, present, proffer, propound, submit, suggest, tender **2 = nominate**, introduce, invite, name, present, put up, recommend **3 = intend**, aim, design, have every intention, have in mind, mean, plan, purpose, scheme **5 = offer marriage**, ask for someone's hand (in marriage), pay suit, pop the question (*inf.*)

proposition *n* **1 = proposal**, motion, plan, programme, project, recommendation, scheme, suggestion ◆ *vb* **6 = make a pass at**, accost, make an improper suggestion, make an indecent proposal, solicit

sexual intercourse. [C14 *proposicioun*, from L *prōpositiō* a setting forth; see PROPOSE]
▸ **ˌpropo'sitional** *adj*

propositional calculus *n* the system of symbolic logic concerned only with the relations between propositions as wholes, taking no account of their internal structure. Cf. **predicate calculus.**

propositus (prə'pɒzɪtəs) *or* (*fem*) **proposita** (prə'pɒzɪtə) *n, pl* **propositi** (-ˌtaɪ) *or* (*fem*) **propositae** (-tiː). *Med.* the first patient to be investigated in a family study, to whom all relationships are referred. Also called (esp. US): **proband.**

propound ❶ (prə'paʊnd) *vb* (*tr*) **1** to put forward for consideration. **2** *English law.* to produce (a will or similar instrument) to the proper court or authority for its validity to be established. [C16 *propone*, from L *prōpōnere* to set forth, from PRO-[1] + *pōnere* to place]
▸ **pro'pounder** *n*

propranolol (prəʊ'prænəˌlɒl) *n* a drug used in the treatment of heart disease.

proprietary (prə'praɪɪtərɪ, -trɪ) *adj* **1** of or belonging to property or proprietors. **2** privately owned and controlled. **3** *Med.* denoting a drug manufactured and distributed under a trade name. ◆ *n, pl* **proprietaries. 4** *Med.* a proprietary drug. **5** a proprietor or proprietors collectively. **6a** right to property. **6b** property owned. **7** (in Colonial America) an owner of a **proprietary colony,** a colony which was granted by the Crown to a particular person or group. [C15: from LL *proprietārius* an owner, from *proprius* one's own]
▸ **pro'prietarily** *adv*

proprietary name *n* a name which is restricted in use by virtue of being a trade name.

proprietor ❶ (prə'praɪətə) *n* **1** an owner of a business. **2** a person enjoying exclusive right of ownership to some property.
▸ **proprietorial** (prəˌpraɪə'tɔːrɪəl) *adj* ▸ **pro'prietress** *or* **pro'prietrix** *fem n*

propriety ❶ (prə'praɪətɪ) *n, pl* **proprieties. 1** the quality or state of being appropriate or fitting. **2** conformity to the prevailing standard of behaviour, speech, etc. **3 the proprieties.** the standards of behaviour considered correct by polite society. [C15: from OF *propriété*, from L *proprietās* a peculiarity, from *proprius* one's own]

proprioceptor (ˌprəʊprɪə'septə) *n Physiol.* any receptor, as in the gut, blood vessels, muscles, etc., that supplies information about the state of the body. [C20: from *proprio-*, from L *proprius* one's own + RECEPTOR]
▸ **ˌproprio'ceptive** *adj*

proptosis (prɒp'təʊsɪs) *n, pl* **proptoses** (-siːz). *Pathol.* the forward displacement of an organ or part, such as the eyeball. [C17: via LL from Gk, from *propiptein* to fall forwards]

propulsion ❶ (prə'pʌlʃən) *n* **1** the act of propelling or the state of being propelled. **2** a propelling force. [C15: from L *prōpellere* to propel]
▸ **propulsive** (prə'pʌlsɪv) *or* **pro'pulsory** *adj*

propyl ('prəʊpɪl) *n* (*modifier*) of or containing the monovalent group of atoms C_3H_7-. [C19: from PROP(IONIC ACID) + -YL]

propylaeum (ˌprɒpɪ'liːəm) *or* **propylon** ('prɒpɪˌlɒn) *n, pl* **propylaea** (-'liːə) *or* **propylons, propyla** (-lə). a portico, esp. one that forms the entrance to a temple. [C18: via L from Gk *propulaion* before the gate, from PRO-[2] + *pulē* gate]

propylene ('prəʊpɪˌliːn) *n* another name for **propene.** [C19]

propylene glycol *n* a colourless viscous compound used as an antifreeze and brake fluid. Formula: $CH_3CH(OH)CH_2OH$. Systematic name: **1,2-dihydroxypropane.**

pro rata ('prəʊ 'rɑːtə) in proportion. [Med. L]

prorate (prəʊ'reɪt, 'prəʊreɪt) *vb* **prorates, prorating, prorated.** *Chiefly US & Canad.* to divide, assess, or distribute proportionately. [C19: from PRO RATA]
▸ **pro'ratable** *adj* ▸ **pro'ration** *n*

prorogue (prə'rəʊg) *vb* **prorogues, proroguing, prorogued.** to discontinue the meetings of (a legislative body) without dissolving it. [C15: from L *prorogāre*, lit.: to ask publicly]
▸ **prorogation** (ˌprəʊrə'geɪʃən) *n*

prosaic ❶ (prəʊ'zeɪɪk) *adj* **1** lacking imagination. **2** having the characteristics of prose. [C16: from LL *prōsaicus*, from L *prōsa* PROSE]
▸ **pro'saically** *adv*

pros and cons *pl n* the various arguments in favour of and against a motion, course of action, etc. [C16: from L *prō* for + *con*, from *contrā* against]

proscenium (prə'siːnɪəm) *n, pl* **proscenia** (-nɪə) *or* **prosceniums. 1** the arch or opening separating the stage from the auditorium together with the area immediately in front of the arch. **2** (in ancient theatres) the stage itself. [C17: via L from Gk *proskēnion*, from *pro-* before + *skēnē* scene]

prosciutto (prəʊ'ʃuːtəʊ; *Italian* pro'ʃutto) *n* cured ham from Italy: usually served as an hors d'oeuvre. [It., lit.: dried beforehand]

proscribe ❶ (prəʊ'skraɪb) *vb* **proscribes, proscribing, proscribed.** (*tr*) **1** to condemn or prohibit. **2** to outlaw; banish; exile. [C16: from L *prōscrībere* to put up a public notice, from *prō-* in public + *scrībere* to write]
▸ **pro'scriber** *n* ▸ **proscription** (prəʊ'skrɪpʃən) *n*

prose (prəʊz) *n* **1** spoken or written language distinguished from poetry by its lack of a marked metrical structure. **2** a passage set for translation into a foreign language. **3** commonplace or dull discourse, expression, etc. **4** (*modifier*) written in prose. **5** (*modifier*) matter-of-fact. ◆ *vb* **proses, prosing, prosed. 6** to write (something) in prose. **7** (*intr*) to speak or write in a tedious style. [C14: via OF from L *prōsa ōrātiō* straightforward speech, from *prorsus* prosaic, from *prōvertere* to turn forwards]
▸ **'proseˌlike** *adj*

prosecute ❶ ('prɒsɪˌkjuːt) *vb* **prosecutes, prosecuting, prosecuted. 1** (*tr*) to bring a criminal action against (a person). **2** (*intr*) **2a** to seek redress by legal proceedings. **2b** to institute or conduct a prosecution. **3** (*tr*) to practise (a profession or trade). **4** (*tr*) to continue to do (a task, etc.). [C15: from L *prōsequī* to follow]
▸ **'proseˌcutable** *adj* ▸ **'proseˌcutor** *n*

prosecution (ˌprɒsɪ'kjuːʃən) *n* **1** the act of prosecuting or the state of being prosecuted. **2a** the institution and conduct of legal proceedings against a person. **2b** the proceedings brought in the name of the Crown to put an accused on trial. **3** the lawyers acting for the Crown to put the case against a person. **4** the following up or carrying on of something begun.

proselyte ❶ ('prɒsɪˌlaɪt) *n* **1** a person newly converted to a religious faith, esp. a Gentile converted to Judaism. ◆ *vb* **proselytes, proselyting, proselyted. 2** a less common word for **proselytize.** [C14: from Church L *prosēlytus*, from Gk *prosēlutos* recent arrival, convert, from *proserchesthai* to draw near]
▸ **proselytism** ('prɒsɪlɪˌtɪzəm) *n* ▸ **proselytic** (ˌprɒsɪ'lɪtɪk) *adj*

proselytize ❶ *or* **proselytise** ('prɒsɪlɪˌtaɪz) *vb* **proselytizes, proselytizing, proselytized** *or* **proselytises, proselytising, proselytised.** to convert (someone) from one religious faith to another.
▸ **'proselytˌizer** *or* **'proselytˌiser** *n*

prosencephalon (ˌprɒsen'sefəlɒn) *n, pl* **prosencephala** (-lə). the part of the brain that develops from the anterior portion of the neural tube. Nontechnical name: **forebrain.** [C19: from NL, from Gk *prosō* forward + *enkephalos* brain]

prosenchyma (prɒs'eŋkɪmə) *n* a plant tissue consisting of long narrow cells with pointed ends: occurs in conducting tissue. [C19: from NL, from Gk *pros-* towards + *enkhuma* infusion]

prosimian (prəʊ'sɪmɪən) *n* **1** any of a primitive suborder of primates, including lemurs, lorises, and tarsiers. ◆ *adj* **2** of or belonging to this suborder. [C19: via NL from L *sīmia* ape]

prosit *German.* ('proːzɪt) *sentence substitute.* good health! cheers! [G, from L, lit.: may it prove beneficial]

prosody ('prɒsədɪ) *n* **1** the study of poetic metre and of the art of versification. **2** a system of versification. **3** the patterns of stress and intonation in a language. [C15: from L *prosōdia* accent of a syllable, from Gk *prosōidia* song set to music, from *pros* towards + *ōidē*, from *aoidē* song; see ODE]
▸ **prosodic** (prə'sɒdɪk) *adj* ▸ **'prosodist** *n*

prosopopoeia *or* **prosopopeia** (ˌprɒsəpə'piːə) *n* **1** *Rhetoric.* another word for **personification. 2** a figure of speech that represents an imaginary, absent, or dead person speaking or acting. [C16: via L from Gk *prosōpopoiia* dramatization, from *prosōpon* face + *poiein* to make]

THESAURUS

propound *vb* **1** = **put forward**, advance, advocate, contend, lay down, postulate, present, propose, set forth, submit, suggest

proprietor *n* **1, 2** = **owner**, deed holder, freeholder, landlord *or* landlady, landowner, possessor, titleholder

propriety *n* **1** = **correctness**, appropriateness, aptness, becomingness, fitness, rightness, seemliness, suitableness **2** = **decorum**, breeding, courtesy, decency, delicacy, etiquette, good form, good manners, manners, modesty, politeness, protocol, punctilio, rectitude, refinement, respectability, seemliness **3 the proprieties** = **etiquette**, accepted conduct, amenities, civilities, niceties, rules of conduct, social code, social conventions, social graces, the done thing
Antonyms *n* ≠ **decorum:** bad form, bad manners, immodesty, impoliteness, indecency, indecorum, indelicacy, vulgarity

propulsion *n* **2** = **drive**, impetus, impulse, impulsion, momentum, motive power, power, pressure, propelling force, push, thrust

prosaic *adj* **1** = **dull**, banal, boring, commonplace, dry, everyday, flat, hackneyed, humdrum, matter-of-fact, mundane, ordinary, pedestrian, routine, stale, tame, trite, unimaginative, uninspiring, vapid, workaday
Antonyms *adj* entertaining, exciting, extraordinary, fascinating, imaginative, interesting, poetical, unusual

proscribe *vb* **1** = **prohibit**, ban, boycott, censure, condemn, damn, denounce, doom, embargo, forbid, interdict, reject **2** = **outlaw**, attaint (*arch.*), banish, blackball, deport, exclude, excommunicate, exile, expatriate, expel, ostracize
Antonyms *vb* ≠ **prohibit:** allow, authorize, endorse, give leave, give permission, license, permit, sanction, warrant

proscription *n* **1** = **prohibition**, ban, boycott, censure, condemnation, damning, denunciation, dooming, embargo, interdict, rejection **2** = **banishment**, attainder (*arch.*), deportation, ejection, eviction, exclusion, excommunication, exile, expatriation, expulsion, ostracism, outlawry

prosecute *vb* **1** *Law* = **put on trial**, arraign, bring action against, bring suit against, bring to trial, do (*sl.*), indict, litigate, prefer charges, put in the dock, seek redress, sue, summon, take to court, try **3** = **conduct**, carry on, direct, discharge, engage in, manage, perform, practise, work at **4** = **continue**, carry through, follow through, persevere, persist, pursue, see through

proselyte *n* **1** = **convert**, catechumen, initiate, neophyte, new believer, novice, tyro

proselytize *vb* = **convert**, bring into the fold, bring to God, evangelize, make converts, propagandize, spread the gospel, win over

prospect ❶ *n* ('prɒspɛkt). **1** (*sometimes pl*) a probability of future success. **2** a view or scene. **3** a mental outlook. **4** expectation, or what one expects. **5** a prospective buyer, project, etc. **6** a survey or observation. **7** *Mining.* **7a** a known or likely deposit of ore. **7b** the location of a deposit of ore. **7c** the yield of mineral obtained from a sample of ore. ◆ *vb* (prə'spɛkt). **8** (when *intr,* often foll. by *for*) to explore (a region) for gold or other valuable minerals. **9** (*tr*) to work (a mine) to discover its profitability. **10** (*intr;* often foll. by *for*) to search (for). [C15: from L *prōspectus* distant view, from *prōspicere* to look into the distance]

prospective ❶ (prə'spɛktɪv) *adj* **1** looking towards the future. **2** (*prenominal*) expected or likely.
▸**pro'spectively** *adv*

prospector (prə'spɛktə) *n* a person who searches for gold, petroleum, etc.

prospectus ❶ (prə'spɛktəs) *n, pl* **prospectuses. 1** a formal statement giving details of a forthcoming event, such as the issue of shares. **2** a brochure giving details of courses, as at a school.

prosper ❶ ('prɒspə) *vb* (*usually intr*) to thrive, succeed, etc., or cause to thrive, etc., in a healthy way. [C15: from L *prosperāre* to succeed, from *prosperus* fortunate, from PRO-[1] + *spēs* hope]

prosperity ❶ (prɒ'spɛrɪtɪ) *n* the condition of prospering; success or wealth.

prosperous ❶ ('prɒspərəs) *adj* **1** flourishing; prospering. **2** wealthy.
▸**'prosperously** *adv*

prostaglandin (ˌprɒstə'glændɪn) *n* any of a group of hormone-like compounds found in all mammalian tissues, which stimulate the muscles of the uterus and affect the blood vessels; used to induce abortion or birth. [C20: from *prosta(te) gland* + -IN; orig. believed to be secreted by the prostate gland]

prostate ('prɒsteɪt) *n* **1** Also called: **prostate gland.** a gland in male mammals that surrounds the neck of the bladder and secretes a liquid constituent of the semen. ◆ *adj* **2** Also: **prostatic** (prɒ'stætɪk). of the prostate gland. ◆ See also **PSA.** [C17: via Med. L from Gk *prostatēs* something standing in front (of the bladder), from *pro-* in front + *histanai* to cause to stand]

prosthesis ('prɒsθɪsɪs) *n, pl* **prostheses** (-ˌsiːz). **1** *Surgery.* **1a** the replacement of a missing bodily part with an artificial substitute. **1b** an artificial part such as a limb, eye, or tooth. **2** *Linguistics.* another word for **prothesis.** [C16: via LL from Gk: an addition, from *prostithenai* to add, from *pros-* towards + *tithenai* to place]
▸**prosthetic** (prɒs'θɛtɪk) *adj* ▸**pros'thetically** *adv*

prosthetics (prɒs'θɛtɪks) *n* (*functioning as sing*) the branch of surgery concerned with prosthesis.

prostitute ❶ ('prɒstɪˌtjuːt) *n* **1** a woman who engages in sexual intercourse for money. **2** a man who engages in such activity, esp. in homosexual practices. **3** a person who offers his talent for unworthy purposes. ◆ *vb* **prostitutes, prostituting, prostituted.** (*tr*) **4** to offer (oneself or another) in sexual intercourse for money. **5** to offer for unworthy purposes. [C16: from L *prōstituere* to expose to prostitution, from *prō-* in public + *statuere* to cause to stand]
▸ˌ**prosti'tution** *n* ▸**'prostiˌtutor** *n*

prostrate ❶ *adj* ('prɒstreɪt). **1** lying face downwards, as in submission. **2** exhausted physically or emotionally. **3** helpless or defenceless. **4** (of a plant) growing closely along the ground. ◆ *vb* (prɒ'streɪt), **prostrates, prostrating, prostrated.** (*tr*) **5** to cast (oneself) down, as in submission. **6** to lay or throw down flat. **7** to make helpless. **8** to make exhausted. [C14: from L *prōsternere* to throw to the ground, from *prō-* before + *sternere* to lay low]
▸**pros'tration** *n*

prostyle ('prəʊstaɪl) *adj* **1** (of a building) having a row of columns in front, esp. as in the portico of a Greek temple. ◆ *n* **2** a prostyle building, portico, etc. [C17: from L *prostȳlos,* from Gk: with pillars in front, from PRO-[2] + *stulos* pillar]

prosy ❶ ('prəʊzɪ) *adj* **prosier, prosiest. 1** of the nature of or similar to prose. **2** dull, tedious, or long-winded.
▸**'prosily** *adv* ▸**'prosiness** *n*

Prot. *abbrev. for:* **1** Protectorate. **2** Protestant.

protactinium (ˌprəʊtæk'tɪnɪəm) *n* a toxic radioactive element that occurs in uranium ores and is produced by neutron irradiation of thorium. Symbol: Pa; atomic no.: 91; half-life of most stable isotope, ^{231}Pa: 32 500 years.

protagonist ❶ (prəʊ'tægənɪst) *n* **1** the principal character in a play, story, etc. **2** a supporter, esp. when important or respected, of a cause, party, etc. [C17: from Gk *prōtagōnistēs,* from *prōtos* first + *agōnistēs* actor]
▸**pro'tagonism** *n*

protasis ('prɒtəsɪs) *n, pl* **protases** (-siːz). **1** *Logic, grammar.* the antecedent of a conditional statement, such as *it rains* in *if it rains the game will be cancelled.* **2** (in classical drama) the introductory part of a play. [C17: via L from Gk: a proposal, from *pro-* before + *teinein* to extend]

protea ('prəʊtɪə) *n* a shrub of tropical and southern Africa, having flowers with coloured bracts arranged in showy heads. [C20: from NL, from *Proteus,* a sea god who could change shape, referring to the many forms of the plant]

protean ❶ (prəʊ'tiːən, 'prəʊtɪən) *adj* readily taking on various shapes or forms; variable. [C20: from *Proteus;* see PROTEA]

protease ('prəʊtɪˌeɪs) *n* any enzyme involved in proteolysis. [C20: from PROTEIN + -ASE]

protease inhibitor *n* any one of a class of antiviral drugs that impair the growth and replication of HIV by inhibiting the action of protease produced by the virus: used in the treatment of AIDS.

protect ❶ (prə'tɛkt) *vb* (*tr*) **1** to defend from trouble, harm, etc. **2** *Econ.* to assist (domestic industries) by the imposition of protective tariffs on imports. **3** *Commerce.* to provide funds in advance to guarantee payment of (a note, etc.). [C16: from L *prōtegere* to cover before]

protectant (prə'tɛktənt) *n* a chemical substance that affords protection, as against frost, rust, insects, etc.

protection ❶ (prə'tɛkʃən) *n* **1** the act of protecting or the condition of being protected. **2** something that protects. **3a** the imposition of duties on imports, for the protection of domestic industries against overseas competition, etc. **3b** Also called: **protectionism.** the system or theory of such restrictions. **4** *Inf.* **4a** Also called: **protection money.** money demanded by gangsters for freedom from molestation. **4b** freedom from molestation purchased in this way.
▸**pro'tectionˌism** *n* ▸**pro'tectionist** *n, adj*

protective ❶ (prə'tɛktɪv) *adj* **1** giving or capable of giving protection. **2**

THESAURUS

prospect *n* **1** *sometimes plural* = **likelihood**, chance, possibility **2** = **view**, landscape, outlook, panorama, perspective, scene, sight, spectacle, vision, vista **4** = **expectation**, anticipation, calculation, contemplation, future, hope, odds, opening, outlook, plan, presumption, probability, promise, proposal, thought ◆ *vb* **10** = **look for**, explore, go after, search for, seek, survey

prospective *adj* **1, 2** = **future**, about to be, anticipated, approaching, awaited, coming, destined, eventual, expected, forthcoming, hoped-for, imminent, intended, likely, looked-for, on the cards, possible, potential, soon-to-be, -to-be, to come, upcoming

prospectus *n* **1, 2** = **catalogue**, announcement, conspectus, list, outline, plan, programme, scheme, syllabus, synopsis

prosper *vb* = **succeed**, advance, be fortunate, bloom, do well, fare well, flourish, flower, get on, grow rich, make good, make it (*inf.*), progress, thrive

prosperity *n* = **success**, affluence, boom, ease, fortune, good fortune, good times, life of luxury, life of Riley (*inf.*), luxury, plenty, prosperousness, riches, the good life, wealth, well-being
Antonyms *n* adversity, depression, destitution, failure, indigence, misfortune, poverty, shortage, want

prosperous *adj* **1** = **successful**, blooming, booming, doing well, flourishing, fortunate, lucky, on a roll, on the up and up (*Brit.*), palmy, prospering, thriving **2** = **wealthy**, affluent, in clover (*inf.*), in the money (*inf.*), moneyed, opulent, rich, well-heeled (*inf.*), well-off, well-to-do
Antonyms *adj* ≠ **successful:** defeated, failing, inauspicious, unfavourable, unfortunate, unlucky, unpromising, unsuccessful, untimely ≠ **wealthy:** impoverished, poor

prostitute *n* **1** = **whore**, bawd (*arch.*), brass (*sl.*), call girl, camp follower, cocotte, courtesan, fallen woman, *fille de joie,* harlot, hooker (*US sl.*), hustler (*US & Canad. sl.*), loose woman, moll (*sl.*), pro (*sl.*), scrubber (*Brit. & Austral. sl.*), streetwalker, strumpet, tart (*inf.*), trollop, white slave, working girl (*facetious sl.*) ◆ *vb* **5** = **cheapen**, debase, degrade, demean, devalue, misapply, pervert, profane

prostitution *n* **1** = **harlotry**, harlot's trade, Mrs. Warren's profession, streetwalking, the game (*sl.*), the oldest profession, vice, whoredom

prostrate *adj* **1** = **prone**, abject, bowed low, flat, horizontal, kowtowing, procumbent **2** = **exhausted**, at a low ebb, dejected, depressed, desolate, drained, fagged out (*inf.*), fallen, inconsolable, overcome, spent, worn out **3** = **helpless**, brought to one's knees, defenceless, disarmed, impotent, overwhelmed, paralysed, powerless, reduced ◆ *vb* **5** = **bow down to**, abase oneself, bend the knee to, bow before, cast oneself before, cringe, fall at (someone's) feet, fall on one's knees before, grovel, kneel, kowtow, submit **7** = **lay low**, bring low, crush, depress, disarm, overcome, overthrow, overturn, overwhelm, paralyse, reduce, ruin **8** = **exhaust**, drain, fag out (*inf.*), fatigue, sap, tire, wear out, weary

prostration *n* **5** = **bow**, abasement, genuflection, kneeling, kowtow, obeisance, submission **7, 8** = **exhaustion**, collapse, dejection, depression, depth of misery, desolation, despair, despondency, grief, helplessness, paralysis, weakness, weariness

prosy *adj* **2** = **dull**, boring, commonplace, flat, humdrum, long, long-drawn-out, long-winded, monotonous, overlong, pedestrian, prosaic, prosing, stale, tedious, tiresome, unimaginative, uninteresting, wordy

protagonist *n* **1** = **leading character**, central character, hero *or* heroine, lead, principal **2** = **supporter**, advocate, champion, exponent, leader, mainstay, moving spirit, prime mover, standard-bearer, torchbearer

protean *adj* = **changeable**, ever-changing, many-sided, mercurial, multiform, mutable, polymorphous, temperamental, variable, versatile, volatile

protect *vb* **1** = **keep safe**, care for, chaperon, cover, cover up for, defend, foster, give sanctuary, guard, harbour, keep, look after, mount *or* stand guard over, preserve, safeguard, save, screen, secure, shelter, shield, stick up for (*inf.*), support, take under one's wing, watch over
Antonyms *vb* assail, assault, attack, betray, endanger, expose, expose to danger, threaten

protection *n* **1** = **safety**, aegis, care, charge, custody, defence, guardianship, guarding, preservation, protecting, safeguard, safekeeping, security **2** = **safeguard**, armour, barrier, buffer, bulwark, cover, guard, refuge, screen, shelter, shield

protective *adj* **1** = **protecting**, careful, cover-

Econ. of or intended for protection of domestic industries. ◆ *n* **3** something that protects. **4** a condom.
▸**pro'tectively** *adv* ▸**pro'tectiveness** *n*

protective coloration *n* the coloration of an animal that enables it to blend with its surroundings and therefore escape the attention of predators.

protector ⓘ (prə'tɛktə) *n* **1** a person or thing that protects. **2** *History.* a person who exercised royal authority during the minority, absence, or incapacity of the monarch.
▸**pro'tectress** *fem n*

Protector (prə'tɛktə) *n* short for **Lord Protector**, the title borne by Oliver Cromwell (1653–58) and by Richard Cromwell (1658–59) as heads of state during the period known as the Protectorate.

protectorate (prə'tɛktərɪt) *n* **1a** a territory largely controlled by but not annexed to a stronger state. **1b** the relation of a protecting state to its protected territory. **2** the office or period of office of a protector.

protégé ⓘ *or (fem)* **protégée** ('prəʊtɪˌʒeɪ) *n* a person who is protected and aided by the patronage of another. [C18: from F *protéger* to PROTECT]

protein ('prəʊtiːn) *n* any of a large group of nitrogenous compounds of high molecular weight that are essential constituents of all living organisms. [C19: via G from Gk *prōteios* primary, from *protos* first + -IN]
▸ˌ**protein'aceous, pro'teinic,** *or* **pro'teinous** *adj*

pro tempore *Latin.* ('prəʊ 'tɛmpərɪ) *adv, adj* for the time being. Often shortened to **pro tem** ('prəʊ 'tɛm).

proteolysis (ˌprəʊtɪ'ɒlɪsɪs) *n* the hydrolysis of proteins into simpler compounds by the action of enzymes. [C19: from NL, from *proteo-* (from PROTEIN) + -LYSIS]
▸**proteolytic** (ˌprəʊtɪə'lɪtɪk) *adj*

protest ⓘ *n* ('prəʊtɛst). **1a** public, often organized, manifestation of dissent. **1b** *(as modifier): a protest march.* **2** a formal or solemn objection. **3** a formal notarial statement drawn up on behalf of a creditor and declaring that the debtor has dishonoured a bill of exchange, etc. **4** the act of protesting. ◆ *vb* (prə'tɛst). **5** (when *intr*, foll. by *against, at, about,* etc.; when *tr, may take a clause as object*) to make a strong objection (to something, esp. a supposed injustice or offence). **6** (when *tr, may take a clause as object*) to disagree; object: *"I'm O.K." she protested.* **7** (when *tr, may take a clause as object*) to assert in a formal or solemn manner. **8** *(tr) Chiefly US.* to object forcefully to: *leaflets protesting Dr King's murder.* **9** *(tr)* to declare formally that (a bill of exchange or promissory note) has been dishonoured. [C14: from L *prōtestārī* to make a formal declaration, from *prō-* before + *testārī* to assert]
▸**pro'testant** *adj, n* ▸**pro'tester** *or* **pro'testor** *n* ▸**pro'testingly** *adv*

Protestant ('prɒtɪstənt) *n* **a** an adherent of Protestantism. **b** *(as modifier): the Protestant Church.*

Protestantism ('prɒtɪstənˌtɪzəm) *n* the religion of any of the Churches of Western Christendom that are separated from the Roman Catholic Church and adhere substantially to principles established during the Reformation.

protestation ⓘ (ˌprəʊtɛs'teɪʃən) *n* **1** the act of protesting. **2** a strong declaration.

prothalamion (ˌprəʊθə'leɪmɪən) *or* **prothalamium** *n, pl* **prothalamia** (-mɪə). a song or poem in celebration of a marriage. [C16: from Gk *pro-* before + *thalamos* marriage]

prothallus (prəʊ'θæləs) *or* **prothallium** (prəʊ'θælɪəm) *n, pl* **prothalli** (-laɪ) *or* **prothallia** (-lɪə). *Bot.* the small flat green disc of tissue that bears the reproductive organs of ferns, horsetails, and club mosses. [C19: from NL, from *pro-* before + Gk *thallus* a young shoot]

prothesis ('prɒθɪsɪs) *n, pl* **protheses** (-siːz). **1** a development of a language by which a syllable is prefixed to a word to facilitate pronunciation: *Latin "scala" gives Spanish "escala" by prothesis.* **2** *Eastern Orthodox Church.* the solemn preparation of the Eucharistic elements before consecration. [C16: via LL from Gk: a setting out in public, from *pro-* forth + *thesis* a placing]
▸**prothetic** (prə'θɛtɪk) *adj* ▸**pro'thetically** *adv*

prothrombin (prəʊ'θrɒmbɪn) *n Biochemistry.* a zymogen found in blood that gives rise to thrombin on activation.

protist ('prəʊtɪst) *n* (in some classification systems) any organism belonging to a large group, including bacteria, protozoans, and fungi, regarded as distinct from plants and animals. The group is usually now restricted to protozoans, unicellular algae, and simple fungi. Cf. **protoctist.** [C19: from NL *Protista* most primitive organisms, from Gk *prōtistos* the very first, from *prōtos* first]

protium ('prəʊtɪəm) *n* the most common isotope of hydrogen, having a mass number of 1. [C20: NL, from PROTO- + -IUM]

proto- *or sometimes before a vowel* **prot-** *combining form.* **1** first: *protomartyr.* **2** primitive or original: *prototype.* **3** first in a series of chemical compounds: *protoxide.* [from Gk *prōtos* first, from *pro* before]

protocol ⓘ ('prəʊtəˌkɒl) *n* **1** the formal etiquette and procedure for state and diplomatic ceremonies. **2** a record of an agreement, esp. in international negotiations, etc. **3a** an amendment to a treaty or convention. **3b** an annexe appended to a treaty to deal with subsidiary matters. **4** *Chiefly US.* a record of data or observations on a particular experiment or proceeding. **5** *Computing.* the set form in which data must be presented for handling by a particular computer configuration, esp. in the transmission of information between different computer systems. [C16: from Med. L *prōtocollum,* from LGk *prōtokollon* sheet glued to the front of a manuscript, from PROTO- + *kolla* glue]

protoctist (prəʊ'tɒktɪst) *n* (in modern biological classifications) any unicellular or simple multicellular organism belonging to the kingdom that includes protozoans, algae, and slime moulds. [C19: from NL *protoctista,* ?from Gk *prototokos* first born]

protohuman (ˌprəʊtəʊ'hjuːmən) *n* **1** any of various prehistoric primates that resembled modern man. ◆ *adj* **2** of these primates.

Proto-Indo-European *n* the prehistoric unrecorded language that was the ancestor of all Indo-European languages.

protomartyr (ˌprəʊtəʊ'mɑːtə) *n* **1** St Stephen as the first Christian martyr. **2** the first martyr to lay down his life in any cause.

proton ('prəʊtɒn) *n* a stable, positively charged elementary particle, found in atomic nuclei in numbers equal to the atomic number of the element. [C20: from Gk *prōtos* first]

protoplasm ('prəʊtəˌplæzəm) *n Biol.* the living contents of a cell: a complex translucent colourless colloidal substance. [C19: from NL, from PROTO- + Gk *plasma* form]
▸ˌ**proto'plasmic,** ˌ**proto'plasmal,** *or* ˌ**protoplas'matic** *adj*

prototype ⓘ ('prəʊtəˌtaɪp) *n* **1** one of the first units manufactured of a product, which is tested so that the design can be changed if necessary before the product is manufactured commercially. **2** a person or thing that serves as an example of a type. **3** *Biol.* the ancestral or primitive form of a species.
▸ˌ**proto'typal, prototypic** (ˌprəʊtə'tɪpɪk), *or* ˌ**proto'typical** *adj*

protozoan (ˌprəʊtə'zəʊən) *n, pl* **protozoa** (-'zəʊə). **1** Also **protozoon.** any of various minute unicellular organisms formerly regarded as invertebrates of the phylum *Protozoa,* but now usually classified in certain phyla of protoctists. Protozoans include amoebas and foraminifers. ◆ *adj also* **protozoic. 2** of or belonging to protozoans. [C19: via NL from Gk PROTO- + *zoion* animal]

protract ⓘ (prə'trækt) *vb (tr)* **1** to lengthen or extend (a speech, etc.). **2** (of a muscle) to draw, thrust, or extend (a part, etc.) forwards. **3** to plot using a protractor and scale. [C16: from L *prōtrahere* to prolong, from PRO-[1] + *trahere* to drag]
▸**pro'tracted** *adj* ▸**protractedly** *adv* ▸**pro'traction** *n*

protractile (prə'træktaɪl) *adj* able to be extended: *protractile muscle.*

protractor (prə'træktə) *n* **1** an instrument for measuring or drawing angles, usually a flat semicircular transparent plastic sheet graduated in degrees. **2** *Anat.* a former term for **extensor.**

protrude ⓘ (prə'truːd) *vb* **protrudes, protruding, protruded. 1** to thrust forwards or outwards. **2** to project or cause to project. [C17: from L, from PRO-[2] + *trudere* to thrust]
▸**pro'trusion** *n* ▸**pro'trusive** *adj*

protrusile (prə'truːsaɪl) *adj Zool.* capable of being thrust forwards: *protrusile jaws.*

protuberant ⓘ (prə'tjuːbərənt) *adj* swelling out; bulging. [C17: from LL *prōtūberāre* to swell, from PRO-[1] + *tūber* swelling]
▸**pro'tuberance** *or* **pro'tuberancy** *n* ▸**pro'tuberantly** *adv*

proud ⓘ (praud) *adj* **1** (foll. by *of,* an infinitive, or a clause) pleased or

THESAURUS

ing, defensive, fatherly, insulating, jealous, maternal, motherly, paternal, possessive, safeguarding, sheltering, shielding, vigilant, warm, watchful

protector *n* **1** = **defender**, advocate, benefactor, bodyguard, champion, counsel, guard, guardian, guardian angel, knight in shining armour, patron, safeguard, tower of strength

protégé *n* = **charge**, dependant, discovery, pupil, student, ward

protest *n* **1, 2** = **objection**, complaint, declaration, demur, demurral, disapproval, dissent, formal complaint, outcry, protestation, remonstrance ◆ *vb* **5, 6** = **object**, complain, cry out, demonstrate, demur, disagree, disapprove, expostulate, express disapproval, kick (against) (*inf.*), oppose, remonstrate, say no to, take exception, take up the cudgels **7** = **assert**, affirm, argue, asseverate, attest, avow, contend, declare, insist, maintain, profess, testify, vow

protestation *n* **1** = **objection**, complaint, disagreement, dissent, expostulation, outcry, protest, remonstrance, remonstration **2** = **declaration**, affirmation, asseveration, avowal, oath, pledge, profession, vow

protester *n* **5, 6** = **demonstrator**, agitator, dissenter, dissident, protest marcher, rebel

protocol *n* **1** = **code of behaviour**, conventions, courtesies, customs, decorum, etiquette, formalities, good form, manners, politesse, propriety, p's and q's, rules of conduct **2** = **agreement**, compact, concordat, contract, convention, covenant, pact, treaty

prototype *n* **1, 2** = **original**, archetype, example, first, mock-up, model, norm, paradigm, pattern, precedent, standard, type

protract *vb* **1** = **extend**, continue, drag on *or* out, draw out, keep going, lengthen, prolong, spin out, stretch out
Antonyms *vb* abbreviate, abridge, compress, curtail, reduce, shorten, summarize

protracted *adj* **1** = **extended**, dragged out, drawn-out, interminable, lengthy, long, long-drawn-out, never-ending, overlong, prolonged, spun out, time-consuming

protrude *vb* **1, 2** = **stick out**, bulge, come through, extend, jut, obtrude, point, pop (*of eyes*), project, shoot out, stand out, start (from), stick out like a sore thumb

protrusion *n* **1, 2** = **projection**, bulge, bump, hump, jut, lump, outgrowth, protuberance, swelling

protuberance *n* = **bulge**, bump, excrescence, hump, knob, lump, outgrowth, process, projection, prominence, protrusion, swelling, tumour

protuberant *adj* = **bulging**, beetling, bulbous, gibbous, hanging over, jutting, popping (*of eyes*), prominent, protruding, protrusive, proud (*dialect*), swelling, swollen
Antonyms *adj* concave, flat, indented, receding, sunken

proud *adj* **1, 2** = **satisfied**, appreciative, con-

satisfied, as with oneself, one's possessions, achievements, etc. **2** feeling honoured or gratified by some distinction. **3** having an inordinately high opinion of oneself; haughty. **4** characterized by or proceeding from a sense of pride: *a proud moment.* **5** having a proper sense of self-respect. **6** stately or distinguished. **7** bold or fearless. **8** (of a surface, edge, etc.) projecting or protruding. **9** (of animals) restive or excited, often sexually. ◆ *adv* **10 do (someone) proud. 10a** to entertain (someone) on a grand scale: *they did us proud at the hotel.* **10b** to honour (someone): *his honesty did him proud.* [LOE *prūd,* from OF *prud, prod* brave, from LL *prōde* useful, from L *prōdesse* to be of value]
▸**'proudly** *adv* ▸**'proudness** *n*

proud flesh *n* a mass of tissue formed around a healing wound.

Prov. *abbrev. for:* **1** Provençal. **2** *Bible.* Proverbs. **3** Province. **4** Provost.

prove ❶ (pruːv) *vb* **proves, proving, proved; proved** *or* **proven.** (*mainly tr*) **1** (*may take a clause as object or an infinitive*) to demonstrate the truth or validity of, esp. by using an established sequence of procedures. **2** to establish the quality of, esp. by experiment. **3** *Law.* to establish the genuineness of (a will). **4** to show (oneself) able or courageous. **5** (*copula*) to be found (to be): *this has proved useless.* **6** (*intr*) (of dough) to rise in a warm place before baking. [C12: from OF *prover,* from L *probāre* to test, from *probus* honest]
▸**'provable** *adj* ▸**'provably** *adv* ▸**,prova'bility** *n*

proven ❶ ('pruːvᵊn, 'prəʊ-) *vb* **1** a past participle of **prove. 2** See **not proven.** ◆ *adj* **3** tried; tested: *a proven method.*

provenance ❶ ('prɒvɪnəns) *n* a place of origin, as of a work of art. [C19: from F, from *provenir,* from L *prōvenīre* to originate, from *venīre* to come]

Provençal (,prɒvɒn'sɑːl; *French* prɔvɑ̃sal) *adj* **1** denoting or characteristic of Provence, a former province of SE France, its inhabitants, their dialect of French, or their Romance language. ◆ *n* **2** a language of Provence, closely related to French and Italian, belonging to the Romance group of the Indo-European family. **3** a native or inhabitant of Provence.

provender ❶ ('prɒvɪndə) *n* **1** fodder for livestock. **2** food in general. [C14: from OF *provendre,* from LL *praebenda* grant, from L *praebēre* to proffer]

proverb ❶ ('prɒvɜːb) *n* **1** a short memorable saying embodying some commonplace fact. **2** a person or thing exemplary of a characteristic: *Antarctica is a proverb for extreme cold.* **3** *Bible.* a wise saying providing guidance. [C14: via OF from L *prōverbium,* from *verbum* word]

proverbial ❶ (prə'vɜːbɪəl) *adj* **1** (*prenominal*) commonly or traditionally referred to as an example of some peculiarity, characteristic, etc. **2** of, embodied in, or resembling a proverb.
▸**pro'verbially** *adv*

provide ❶ (prə'vaɪd) *vb* **provides, providing, provided.** (*mainly tr*) **1** to furnish or supply. **2** to afford; yield: *this meeting provides an opportunity to talk.* **3** (*intr;* often foll. by *for* or *against*) to take careful precautions: *he provided against financial ruin by wise investment.* **4** (*intr;* foll. by *for*) to supply means of support (to): *he provides for his family.* **5** (of a person, law, etc.) to state as a condition; stipulate. **6** to confer and induct into ecclesiastical offices. [C15: from L *prōvidēre* to provide for, from *prō-* beforehand + *vidēre* to see]
▸**pro'vider** *n*

providence ❶ ('prɒvɪdəns) *n* **1a** *Christianity.* God's foreseeing protection and care of his creatures. **1b** such protection and care as manifest by some other force. **2** a supposed manifestation of such care and guidance. **3** the foresight or care exercised by a person in the management of his affairs.

Providence ('prɒvɪdəns) *n Christianity.* God, esp. as showing foreseeing care of his creatures.

provident ❶ ('prɒvɪdənt) *adj* **1** providing for future needs. **2** exercising foresight in the management of one's affairs. **3** characterized by foresight. [C15: from L *prōvidens* foreseeing, from *prōvidēre* to PROVIDE]
▸**'providently** *adv*

providential ❶ (,prɒvɪ'dɛnʃəl) *adj* characteristic of or presumed to proceed from or as if from divine providence.
▸**,provi'dentially** *adv*

provident society *n* a mutual insurance society catering esp. for those on a low income, providing sickness, death, and pension benefits.

providing ❶ (prə'vaɪdɪŋ) *or* **provided** *conj* (*subordinating;* sometimes foll. by *that*) on the condition or understanding (that): *I'll play, providing you pay me.*

province ❶ ('prɒvɪns) *n* **1** a territory governed as a unit of a country or empire. **2** (*pl;* usually preceded by *the*) those parts of a country lying outside the capital and other large cities and regarded as outside the mainstream of sophisticated culture. **3** an area of learning, activity, etc. **4** the extent of a person's activities or office. **5** an ecclesiastical territory, having an archbishop or metropolitan at its head. **6** an administrative and territorial subdivision of a religious order. **7** *History.* a region of the Roman Empire outside Italy ruled by a governor from Rome. [C14: from OF, from L *prōvincia* conquered territory]

provincewide ('prɒvɪns,waɪd) *Canad.* ◆ *adj* **1** covering or available to the whole of a province: *a provincewide referendum.* ◆ *adv* **2** throughout a province: *an advertising campaign to go provincewide.*

provincial ❶ (prə'vɪnʃəl) *adj* **1** of or connected with a province. **2** characteristic of or connected with the provinces. **3** having attitudes and opinions supposedly common to people living in the provinces; unsophisticated; limited. **4** *NZ.* denoting a football team representing a province, one of the historical administrative areas of New Zealand. ◆ *n* **5** a person lacking the sophistications of city life; rustic or narrow-minded individual. **6** a person coming from or resident in a province or the provinces. **7** the head of an ecclesiastical province. **8** the head of a territorial subdivision of a religious order.
▸**provinciality** (prə,vɪnʃɪ'ælɪtɪ) *n* ▸**pro'vincially** *adv*

provincialism ❶ (prə'vɪnʃə,lɪzəm) *n* **1** narrowness of mind; lack of sophistication. **2** a word or attitude characteristic of a provincial. **3** attention to the affairs of one's local area rather than the whole nation. **4** the state or quality of being provincial.

provirus ('prəʊ,vaɪrəs) *n* the inactive form of a virus in a host cell.

provision ❶ (prə'vɪʒən) *n* **1** the act of supplying food, etc. **2** something that is supplied. **3** preparations (esp. in **make provision for**). **4** (*pl*) food and other necessities, as for an expedition. **5** a condition or stipula-

THESAURUS

tent, contented, glad, gratified, honoured, pleased, self-respecting, well-pleased **3 = conceited,** arrogant, boastful, disdainful, egotistical, haughty, high and mighty (*inf.*), imperious, lordly, narcissistic, orgulous (*arch.*), overbearing, presumptuous, self-important, self-satisfied, snobbish, snooty (*inf.*), stuck-up (*inf.*), supercilious, toffee-nosed (*sl., chiefly Brit.*), vain **4 = glorious,** exalted, gratifying, illustrious, memorable, pleasing, red-letter, rewarding, satisfying **6 = distinguished,** august, eminent, grand, great, illustrious, imposing, magnificent, majestic, noble, splendid, stately
Antonyms *adj* ≠ **satisfied:** discontented, displeased, dissatisfied ≠ **conceited:** abject, ashamed, deferential, humble, meek, modest, submissive, unobtrusive ≠ **distinguished:** base, humble, ignoble, ignominious, lowly, unassuming, undignified

provable *adj* **1, 2 = verifiable,** attestable, demonstrable, evincible, testable

prove *vb* **1 = verify,** ascertain, attest, authenticate, bear out, confirm, corroborate, demonstrate, determine, establish, evidence, evince, justify, show, show clearly, substantiate **2 = test,** analyse, assay, check, examine, experiment, put to the test, put to trial, try **5 = turn out,** be found to be, come out, end up, result
Antonyms *vb* ≠ **verify:** discredit, disprove, give the lie to, refute, rule out

proven *adj* **3 = established,** accepted, attested, authentic, certified, checked, confirmed, definite, dependable, proved, reliable, tested, tried, trustworthy, undoubted, valid, verified

provenance *n* **= origin,** birthplace, derivation, source

provender *n* **1 = fodder,** feed, forage **2 = food,** comestibles, eatables, eats (*sl.*), edibles, fare, feed, foodstuffs, groceries, grub (*sl.*), nosebag (*sl.*), nosh (*sl.*), provisions, rations, supplies, sustenance, tack (*inf.*), victuals, vittles (*obs. or dialect*)

proverb *n* **1 = saying,** adage, aphorism, apophthegm, byword, dictum, gnome, maxim, saw

proverbial *adj* **1 = conventional,** accepted, acknowledged, archetypal, axiomatic, current, customary, famed, famous, legendary, notorious, self-evident, time-honoured, traditional, typical, unquestioned, well-known

provide *vb* **1 = supply,** accommodate, cater, contribute, equip, furnish, outfit, provision, purvey, stock up **2 = give,** add, afford, bring, impart, lend, present, produce, render, serve, yield **3** *often foll. by* **for** *or* **against = take precautions,** anticipate, arrange for, forearm, get ready, make arrangements, make plans, plan ahead, plan for, prepare for, take measures **4** *foll. by* **for = support,** care for, keep, look after, maintain, sustain, take care of **5 = stipulate,** determine, lay down, require, specify, state
Antonyms *vb* ≠ **supply:** deprive, keep back, refuse, withhold ≠ **take precautions:** disregard, fail to notice, miss, neglect, overlook ≠ **support:** neglect

providence *n* **1 = fate,** destiny, divine intervention, fortune, God's will, predestination **3 = foresight,** care, caution, discretion, farsightedness, forethought, perspicacity, presence of mind, prudence

provident *adj* **1 = thrifty,** economical, frugal, prudent **2, 3 = foresighted,** canny, careful, cautious, discreet, equipped, far-seeing, farsighted, forearmed, sagacious, shrewd, vigilant, well-prepared, wise
Antonyms *adj* ≠ **thrifty:** improvident, imprudent, prodigal, profligate, spendthrift, thriftless, uneconomical, unthrifty, wasteful ≠ **foresighted:** careless, heedless, improvident, negligent, reckless, short-sighted, thoughtless

providential *adj* **= lucky,** fortuitous, fortunate, happy, heaven-sent, opportune, timely, welcome

provider *n* **1 = supplier,** benefactor, donor, giver, source **4 = breadwinner,** earner, mainstay, supporter, wage earner

providing *conj* **= on condition that,** as long as, contingent upon, given, if and only if, in case, in the event, on the assumption, subject to, upon these terms, with the proviso, with the understanding

province *n* **1 = region,** colony, county, department, dependency, district, division, domain, patch, section, territory, tract, turf (*US sl.*), zone **4 = area,** business, capacity, charge, concern, duty, employment, field, function, line, orbit, part, pigeon (*Brit. inf.*), post, responsibility, role, sphere, turf (*US sl.*)

provincial *adj* **2 = rural,** country, hick (*inf., chiefly US & Canad.*), home-grown, homespun, local, rustic **3 = parochial,** insular, inward-looking, limited, narrow, narrow-minded, parish-pump, small-minded, small-town (*chiefly US*), uninformed, unsophisticated, upcountry ◆ *n* **5 = yokel,** country cousin, hayseed (*US & Canad. inf.*), hick (*inf., chiefly US & Canad.*), rustic
Antonyms *adj* ≠ **rural:** urban ≠ **parochial:** cosmopolitan, fashionable, polished, refined, sophisticated, urbane

provincialism *n* **1 = narrow-mindedness,** insularity, lack of sophistication, parochialism, sectionalism **2 = regionalism,** dialect, idiom, localism, patois, vernacularism

provision *n* **1 = supplying,** accoutrement, ca-

tion incorporated in a document; proviso. **6** the conferring of and induction into ecclesiastical offices. ◆ *vb* **7** (*tr*) to supply with provisions. [C14: from L *prōvīsiō* a providing; see PROVIDE]
▸**pro'visioner** *n*

provisional Ⓣ (prəˈvɪʒənᵊl) *adj* subject to later alteration; temporary or conditional: *a provisional decision.*
▸**pro'visionally** *adv*

Provisional (prəˈvɪʒənᵊl) *adj* **1** designating one of the two factions of the IRA and Sinn Féin that have existed since a split in late 1969. The Provisional movement advocates terrorism to achieve Irish unity. ◆ *n* **2** Also called: **Provo.** a member of the Provisional IRA or Sinn Féin.

proviso Ⓣ (prəˈvaɪzəʊ) *n, pl* **provisos** *or* **provisoes. 1** a clause in a document or contract that embodies a condition or stipulation. **2** a condition or stipulation. [C15: from Med. L *prōvīsō quod* it being provided that, from L *prōvīsus* provided]

provisory (prəˈvaɪzərɪ) *adj* **1** containing a proviso; conditional. **2** provisional. **3** making provision.
▸**pro'visorily** *adv*

Provo (ˈprəʊvəʊ) *n, pl* **Provos.** another name for a **Provisional** (sense 2).

provocation Ⓣ (ˌprɒvəˈkeɪʃən) *n* **1** the act of provoking or inciting. **2** something that causes indignation, anger, etc.

provocative Ⓣ (prəˈvɒkətɪv) *adj* serving or intended to provoke or incite, esp. to anger or sexual desire: *a provocative look; a provocative remark.*
▸**pro'vocatively** *adv*

provoke Ⓣ (prəˈvəʊk) *vb* **provokes, provoking, provoked.** (*tr*) **1** to anger or infuriate. **2** to incite or stimulate. **3** to promote (anger, etc.) in a person. **4** to cause; bring about: *the accident provoked an inquiry.* [C15: from L *prōvocāre* to call forth]
▸**pro'voking** *adj* ▸**pro'vokingly** *adv*

provost (ˈprɒvəst) *n* **1** the head of certain university colleges or schools. **2** (in Scotland) the chairman and civic head of certain district councils or (formerly) of a burgh council. Cf. **convener** (sense 2). **3** *Church of England.* the senior dignitary of one of the more recent cathedral foundations. **4** *RC Church.* **4a** the head of a cathedral chapter. **4b** (formerly) the member of a monastic community second in authority under the abbot. **5** (in medieval times) an overseer, steward, or bailiff. [OE *profost,* from Med. L *prōpositus* placed at the head (of), from L *praepōnere* to place first]

provost marshal (prəˈvəʊ) *n* the officer in charge of military police in a camp or city.

prow Ⓣ (praʊ) *n* the bow of a vessel. [C16: from OF *proue,* from L *prora,* from Gk *prōra*]

prowess Ⓣ (ˈpraʊɪs) *n* **1** outstanding or superior skill or ability. **2** bravery or fearlessness, esp. in battle. [C13: from OF *proesce,* from *prou* good]

prowl Ⓣ (praʊl) *vb* **1** (when *intr,* often foll. by *around* or *about*) to move stealthily around (a place) as if in search of prey or plunder. ◆ *n* **2** the act of prowling. **3 on the prowl. 3a** moving around stealthily. **3b** pursuing members of the opposite sex. [C14 *prollen,* from ?]
▸**'prowler** *n*

prox. *abbrev. for* proximo (next month).

proximal (ˈprɒksɪməl) *adj Anat.* situated close to the centre, median line, or point of attachment or origin.
▸**'proximally** *adv*

proximate (ˈprɒksɪmɪt) *adj* **1** next or nearest in space or time. **2** very near; close. **3** immediately preceding or following in a series. **4** a less common word for **approximate.** [C16: from LL *proximāre* to draw near, from L *proximus* next, from *prope* near]
▸**'proximately** *adv*

proximity Ⓣ (prɒkˈsɪmɪtɪ) *n* **1** nearness in space or time. **2** nearness or closeness in a series. [C15: from L *proximitās* closeness; see PROXIMATE]

proximo (ˈprɒksɪməʊ) *adv Now rare except when abbreviated in formal correspondence.* in or during the next or coming month: *a letter of the seventh proximo.* Abbrev.: **prox.** Cf. **instant, ultimo.** [C19: from L: in or on the next]

proxy Ⓣ (ˈprɒksɪ) *n, pl* **proxies. 1** a person authorized to act on behalf of someone else; agent: *vote by proxy.* **2** authority, esp. in the form of a document, given to a person to act on behalf of someone else. [C15 *prokesye,* from *procuracy,* from L *prōcūrātiō* procuration; see PROCURE]

PRP *abbrev. for:* **1** performance-related pay. **2** profit-related pay.

PRT *abbrev. for* petroleum revenue tax.

prude Ⓣ (pruːd) *n* a person who affects or shows an excessively modest, prim, or proper attitude, esp. regarding sex. [C18: from F, from *prudefemme,* from OF *prode femme* respectable woman; see PROUD]
▸**'prudery** *n* ▸**'prudish** *adj* ▸**'prudishly** *adv*

prudence Ⓣ (ˈpruːdəns) *n* **1** caution in practical affairs; discretion. **2** care taken in the management of one's resources. **3** consideration for one's own interests. **4** the quality of being prudent.

prudent Ⓣ (ˈpruːdᵊnt) *adj* **1** discreet or cautious in managing one's activities; circumspect. **2** practical and careful in providing for the future. **3** exercising good judgment. [C14: from L *prūdēns* far-sighted, from *prōvidens* acting with foresight; see PROVIDENT]
▸**'prudently** *adv*

prudential (pruːˈdenʃəl) *adj* **1** characterized by or resulting from prudence. **2** exercising sound judgment.
▸**pru'dentially** *adv*

pruinose (ˈpruːɪˌnəʊs, -ˌnəʊz) *adj Bot.* coated with a powdery or waxy bloom. [C19: from L *pruīnōsus* frost-covered, from *pruīna* hoarfrost]

prune[1] (pruːn) *n* **1** a purplish-black partially dried fruit of any of several varieties of plum tree. **2** *Sl., chiefly Brit.* a dull or foolish person. **3 prunes and prisms.** denoting an affected and mincing way of speaking. [C14: from OF *prune,* from L *prūnum* plum, from Gk *prounon*]

prune[2] Ⓣ (pruːn) *vb* **prunes, pruning, pruned. 1** to remove (dead or superfluous twigs, branches, etc.) from (a tree, shrub, etc.), esp. by cutting off. **2** to remove (anything undesirable or superfluous) from (a book, etc.). [C15: from OF *proignier* to clip, prob. from *provigner* to prune vines, ult. from L *propāgo* a cutting]
▸**'prunable** *adj* ▸**'pruner** *n*

prunella (pruːˈnelə) *n* a strong fabric, esp. a twill-weave worsted, formerly used for academic gowns and the uppers of some shoes. [C17: ?from *prunelle,* a green French liqueur, with reference to the colour of the cloth]

pruning hook *n* a tool with a curved steel blade terminating in a hook, used for pruning.

THESAURUS

tering, equipping, fitting out, furnishing, providing, victualling **3** *As in* **make provision for** = **arrangement**, plan, prearrangement, precaution, preparation **4** *plural* = **food**, comestibles, eatables, eats (*sl.*), edibles, fare, feed, foodstuff, groceries, grub (*sl.*), nosebag (*sl.*), provender, rations, stores, supplies, sustenance, tack (*inf.*), viands, victuals, vittles (*obs. or dialect*) **5** = **condition**, agreement, clause, demand, proviso, requirement, rider, specification, stipulation, term

provisional *adj* = **temporary**, interim, pro tem, stopgap, transitional = **conditional**, contingent, limited, provisory, qualified, tentative
Antonyms *adj* ≠ **temporary:** permanent ≠ **conditional:** definite, fixed

proviso *n* **1, 2** = **condition**, clause, limitation, provision, qualification, requirement, reservation, restriction, rider, stipulation, strings

provocation *n* **2** = **cause**, *casus belli*, grounds, incitement, inducement, instigation, justification, motivation, reason, stimulus **2** = **offence**, affront, annoyance, challenge, dare, grievance, indignity, injury, insult, red rag, taunt, vexation

provocative *adj* = **offensive**, aggravating (*inf.*), annoying, challenging, disturbing, galling, goading, incensing, insulting, outrageous, provoking, stimulating = **suggestive**, alluring, arousing, erotic, exciting, inviting, seductive, sexy (*inf.*), stimulating, tantalizing, tempting

provoke *vb* **1** = **anger**, affront, aggravate (*inf.*), annoy, chafe, enrage, exasperate, gall, hassle (*inf.*), incense, infuriate, insult, irk, irritate, madden, make one's blood boil, offend, pique, put one's back up, put out, rile, try one's patience, vex **2, 4** = **rouse**, bring about, bring on *or* down, call forth, cause, draw forth, elicit, evoke, excite, fire, foment, generate, give rise to, incite, induce, inflame, inspire, instigate, kindle, lead to, motivate, move, occasion, precipitate, produce, promote, prompt, stimulate, stir
Antonyms *vb* ≠ **anger:** appease, calm, conciliate, mollify, pacify, placate, propitiate, quiet, soothe, sweeten ≠ **rouse:** abate, allay, assuage, blunt, curb, ease, lessen, lull, mitigate, moderate, modify, relieve, temper

provoking *adj* **1** = **annoying**, aggravating (*inf.*), exasperating, galling, irking, irksome, irritating, maddening, obstructive, offensive, tiresome, vexatious, vexing

prow *n* = **bow(s)**, fore, forepart, front, head, nose, sharp end (*jocular*), stem

prowess *n* **1** = **skill**, ability, accomplishment, adeptness, adroitness, aptitude, attainment, command, dexterity, excellence, expertise, expertness, facility, genius, mastery, talent **2** = **bravery**, boldness, courage, daring, dauntlessness, doughtiness, fearlessness, gallantry, hardihood, heroism, intrepidity, mettle, valiance, valour
Antonyms *n* ≠ **skill:** clumsiness, inability, incapability, incompetence, ineptitude, ineptness, inexpertise ≠ **bravery:** cowardice, faintheartedness, fear, gutlessness, timidity

prowl *vb* **1** = **move stealthily**, cruise, hunt, lurk, nose around, patrol, range, roam, rove, scavenge, skulk, slink, sneak, stalk, steal

proximity *n* **1** = **nearness**, adjacency, closeness, contiguity, juxtaposition, neighbourhood, propinquity, vicinity

proxy *n* **1** = **representative**, agent, attorney, delegate, deputy, factor, substitute, surrogate

prude *n* = **prig**, old maid (*inf.*), puritan, schoolmarm (*Brit. inf.*)

prudence *n* **1** = **common sense**, canniness, care, caution, circumspection, discretion, good sense, heedfulness, judgment, judiciousness, sagacity, vigilance, wariness, wisdom **2** = **thrift**, careful budgeting, economizing, economy, far-sightedness, foresight, forethought, frugality, good management, husbandry, planning, precaution, preparedness, providence, saving

prudent *adj* **1, 3** = **sensible**, canny, careful, cautious, circumspect, discerning, discreet, judicious, politic, sagacious, sage, shrewd, vigilant, wary, wise **2** = **thrifty**, canny, careful, economical, far-sighted, frugal, provident, sparing
Antonyms *adj* ≠ **sensible:** careless, heedless, impolitic, imprudent, inconsiderate, indiscreet, injudicious, irrational, rash, thoughtless, unwise ≠ **thrifty:** careless, extravagant, improvident, imprudent, wasteful

prudery *n* = **primness**, old-maidishness (*inf.*), overmodesty, priggishness, prudishness, puritanicalness, squeamishness, starchiness (*inf.*), strictness, stuffiness

prudish *adj* = **prim**, demure, formal, narrow-minded, niminy-piminy, old-maidish, overmodest, overnice, priggish, prissy (*inf.*), proper, puritanical, schoolmarmish (*Brit. inf.*), squeamish, starchy (*inf.*), strait-laced, stuffy, Victorian
Antonyms *adj* broad-minded, liberal, open-minded, permissive

prune[2] *vb* **1** = **cut**, clip, cut back, dock, lop, pare down, reduce, shape, shorten, snip, trim

prurient ➊ (ˈprʊərɪənt) *adj* **1** unusually or morbidly interested in sexual thoughts or practices. **2** exciting lustfulness. [C17: from L *prūrīre* to lust after, itch]
▸ˈ**prurience** *n* ▸ˈ**pruriently** *adv*

prurigo (prʊəˈraɪgəʊ) *n* a chronic inflammatory disease of the skin characterized by intense itching. [C19: from L: an itch]
▸**pruriginous** (prʊəˈrɪdʒɪnəs) *adj*

pruritus (prʊəˈraɪtəs) *n Pathol.* any intense sensation of itching. [C17: from L: an itching; see PRURIENT]
▸**pruritic** (prʊəˈrɪtɪk) *adj*

Prussian (ˈprʌʃən) *adj* **1** of Prussia, a former state in N Germany, or its people, esp. of the Junkers and their military tradition. ◆ *n* **2** a native or inhabitant of Prussia. **3 Old Prussian.** the extinct Baltic language of the non-German inhabitants of Prussia.

Prussian blue *n* **1** any of a number of blue pigments containing ferrocyanide or ferricyanide ions. **2a** the blue or deep greenish-blue colour of this. **2b** (*as adj*): *a Prussian-blue carpet.*

prussic acid (ˈprʌsɪk) *n* the extremely poisonous aqueous solution of hydrogen cyanide. [C18: from F *acide prussique* Prussian acid, because obtained from Prussian blue]

pry[1] ➊ (praɪ) *vb* **pries, prying, pried. 1** (*intr;* often foll. by *into*) to make an impertinent or uninvited inquiry (about a private matter, topic, etc.). ◆ *n, pl* **pries. 2** the act of prying. **3** a person who pries. [C14: from ?]

pry[2] (praɪ) *vb* **pries, prying, pried.** the US and Canad. word for **prise.** [C14: from ?]

pryer (ˈpraɪə) *n* a variant spelling of **prier.**

Przewalski's horse (ˌpɜːʒəˈvælskɪz) *n* a wild horse of W Mongolia, having an erect mane and no forelock: extinct in the wild, a few survive in captivity. [C19: after the Russian explorer Nikolai *Przewalski* (1839–88), who discovered it]

PS *abbrev. for:* **1** Passenger Steamer. **2** Police Sergeant. **3** Also: **ps.** postscript. **4** private secretary. **5** prompt side.

Ps. *or* **Psa.** *Bible. abbrev. for* Psalm(s).

PSA *abbrev. for* prostatic specific antigen: an enzyme secreted by the prostate gland, increased levels of which are found in the blood of patients with cancer of the prostate.

psalm ➊ (sɑːm) *n* **1** (*often cap.*) any of the sacred songs that constitute a book (Psalms) of the Old Testament. **2** a musical setting of one of these. **3** any sacred song. [OE, from LL *psalmus,* from Gk *psalmos* song accompanied on the harp, from *psallein* to play (the harp)]
▸**psalmic** (ˈsɑːmɪk, ˈsæl-) *adj*

psalmist (ˈsɑːmɪst) *n* the composer of a psalm or psalms, esp. (when *cap.* and preceded by *the*) David, traditionally regarded as the author of The Book of Psalms.

psalmody (ˈsɑːmədɪ, ˈsæl-) *n, pl* **psalmodies. 1** the act of singing psalms or hymns. **2** the art of setting psalms to music. [C14: via LL from Gk *psalmōdia* singing accompanied by a harp, from *psalmos* (see PSALM) + *ōidē* ODE]
▸ˈ**psalmodist** *n* ▸**psalmodic** (sælˈmɒdɪk) *adj*

Psalter (ˈsɔːltə) *n* **1** another name for the Book of Psalms, esp. in the version in the Book of Common Prayer. **2** a translation, musical, or metrical version of the Psalms. **3** a book containing a version of Psalms. [OE *psaltere,* from LL *psaltērium,* from Gk *psaltērion* stringed instrument, from *psallein* to play a stringed instrument]

psalterium (sɔːlˈtɪərɪəm) *n, pl* **psalteria** (-ˈtɪərɪə). the third compartment of the stomach of ruminants. Also called: **omasum.** [C19: from L *psaltērium* PSALTER; from the similarity of its folds to the pages of a book]

psaltery (ˈsɔːltərɪ) *n, pl* **psalteries.** *Music.* an ancient stringed instrument similar to the lyre, but having a trapezoidal sounding board over which the strings are stretched.

p's and q's *pl n* behaviour; manners (esp. in **mind one's p's and q's**). [altered from *p(lea)se and (than)k yous*]

PSBR (in Britain) *abbrev. for* public sector borrowing requirement; the money required by the public sector of the economy for expenditure on items that are not financed from income.

psephology (seˈfɒlədʒɪ) *n* the statistical and sociological study of elections. [C20: from Gk *psephos* pebble, vote + -LOGY, from the ancient Greeks' custom of voting with pebbles]
▸**psephological** (ˌsefəˈlɒdʒɪkˡl) *adj* ▸ˌ**psephoˈlogically** *adv* ▸**pseˈphologist** *n*

pseud ➊ (sjuːd) *n* **1** *Inf.* a false or pretentious person. ◆ *adj* **2** another word for **pseudo.**

Pseudepigrapha (ˌsjuːdɪˈpɪgrəfə) *pl n* various Jewish writings from the first century B.C. to the first century A.D. that claim to have been divinely revealed but which have been excluded from the Greek canon of the Old Testament. [C17: from Gk *pseudepigraphos* falsely entitled, from PSEUDO- + *epigraphein* to inscribe]
▸**Pseudepigraphic** (ˌsjuːdepɪˈgræfɪk) *or* ˌ**Pseudepiˈgraphical** *adj*

pseudo (ˈsjuːdəʊ) *adj Inf.* not genuine.

pseudo- ➊ *or sometimes before a vowel* **pseud-** *combining form.* **1** false, pretending, or unauthentic: *pseudo-intellectual.* **2** having a close resemblance to: *pseudopodium.* [from Gk *pseudēs* false, from *pseudein* to lie]

pseudocarp (ˈsjuːdəʊˌkɑːp) *n* a fruit, such as the apple, that includes parts other than the ripened ovary.
▸ˌ**pseudoˈcarpous** *adj*

pseudomorph (ˈsjuːdəʊˌmɔːf) *n* a mineral that has an uncharacteristic crystalline form as a result of assuming the shape of another mineral that it has replaced.
▸ˌ**pseudoˈmorphic** *or* ˌ**pseudoˈmorphous** *adj* ▸ˌ**pseudoˈmorphism** *n*

pseudonym ➊ (ˈsjuːdəˌnɪm) *n* a fictitious name adopted esp. by an author. [C19: via F from Gk *pseudōnumon*]
▸ˌ**pseudoˈnymity** *n* ▸**pseudonymous** (sjuːˈdɒnɪməs) *adj*

pseudopodium (ˌsjuːdəʊˈpəʊdɪəm) *n, pl* **pseudopodia** (-dɪə). a temporary projection from the cell of a protozoan, etc., used for feeding and locomotion.

pseudovector (ˌsjuːdəʊˈvektə) *n Maths.* a variable quantity, such as angular momentum, that has magnitude and orientation with respect to an axis.

psf *abbrev. for* pounds per square foot.

pshaw (pʃɔː) *interj Becoming rare.* an exclamation of disgust, impatience, disbelief, etc.

psi[1] (psaɪ) *n* **1** the 23rd letter of the Greek alphabet (Ψ, ψ), a composite consonant, transliterated as *ps.* **2** paranormal or psychic phenomena collectively.

psi[2] *abbrev. for* pounds per square inch.

psilocybin (ˌsɪləˈsaɪbɪn, ˌsaɪlə-) *n* a crystalline phosphate ester that is the active principle of the hallucinogenic fungus *Psilocybe mexicana.* Formula: $C_{12}H_{17}N_2O_4P$. [C20: from NL *Psilocybe* (from Gk *psilos* bare + *kubē* head) + -IN]

psi particle *n* See **J/psi particle.**

psittacine (ˈsɪtəˌsaɪn, -sɪn) *adj* of, relating to, or resembling a parrot. [C19: from LL *psittacīnus,* from L *psittacus* a parrot]

psittacosis (ˌsɪtəˈkəʊsɪs) *n* a disease of parrots that can be transmitted to man, in whom it produces pneumonia. Also called: **parrot fever.** [C19: from NL, from L *psittacus* a parrot, from Gk *psittakos;* see -OSIS]

psoas (ˈsəʊəs) *n* either of two muscles of the loins that aid in flexing and rotating the thigh. [C17: from NL, from Gk *psoai* (pl)]

psoriasis (səˈraɪəsɪs) *n* a skin disease characterized by the formation of reddish spots and patches covered with silvery scales. [C17: via NL from Gk: itching disease, from *psōra* itch]
▸**psoriatic** (ˌsɔːrɪˈætɪk) *adj*

psst (pst) *interj* an exclamation made to attract someone's attention, esp. one made surreptitiously.

PST (in the US and Canada) *abbrev. for* Pacific Standard Time.

PSV (in Britain) *abbrev. for* public service vehicle (now called passenger carrying vehicle).

psych *or* **psyche** (saɪk) *vb* **psychs** *or* **psyches, psyching, psyched.** (*tr*) *Inf.* to psychoanalyse. See also **psych out, psych up.** [C20: shortened from PSYCHOANALYSE]

psyche ➊ (ˈsaɪkɪ) *n* the human mind or soul. [C17: from L, from Gk *psukhē* breath, soul]

psychedelic ➊ (ˌsaɪkɪˈdelɪk) *adj* **1** relating to or denoting new or altered perceptions or sensory experiences, as through the use of hallucinogenic drugs. **2** denoting any of the drugs, esp. LSD, that produce these effects. **3** *Inf.* (of painting, etc.) having the vivid colours and complex patterns popularly associated with the visual effects of psychedelic states. [C20: from PSYCHE + Gk *delos* visible]
▸ˌ**psycheˈdelically** *adv*

psychiatry ➊ (saɪˈkaɪətrɪ) *n* the branch of medicine concerned with the diagnosis and treatment of mental disorders.
▸**psychiatric** (ˌsaɪkɪˈætrɪk) *or* ˌ**psychiˈatrical** *adj* ▸ˌ**psychiˈatrically** *adv* ▸**psyˈchiatrist** *n*

psychic ➊ (ˈsaɪkɪk) *adj* **1a** outside the possibilities defined by natural laws, as mental telepathy. **1b** (of a person) sensitive to forces not rec-

THESAURUS

prurient *adj* **1** = **lecherous**, concupiscent, desirous, hankering, itching, lascivious, libidinous, longing, lustful, salacious **2** = **indecent**, dirty, erotic, lewd, obscene, pornographic, salacious, smutty, steamy (*inf.*), voyeuristic, X-rated (*inf.*)

pry[1] *vb* **1** = **be inquisitive**, be a busybody, be nosy (*inf.*), ferret about, interfere, intrude, meddle, nose into, peep, peer, poke, poke one's nose in *or* into (*inf.*), snoop (*inf.*)

prying *adj* **1** = **inquisitive**, curious, eavesdropping, impertinent, interfering, intrusive, meddlesome, meddling, nosy (*inf.*), snooping (*inf.*), snoopy (*inf.*), spying

psalm *n* **1, 3** = **hymn**, carol, chant, paean, song of praise

pseud *n* **1** *Informal* = **poser** (*inf.*), fraud, humbug, phoney *or* phony, trendy (*Brit. inf.*)

pseudo- *combining form* **1** = **false**, artificial, bogus, counterfeit, ersatz, fake, imitation, mock, not genuine, phoney *or* phony (*inf.*), pretended, quasi-, sham, spurious
Antonyms *adj* actual, authentic, bona fide, genuine, heartfelt, honest, real, sincere, true, unfeigned

pseudonym *n* = **false name**, alias, assumed name, incognito, nom de guerre, nom de plume, pen name, professional name, stage name

psyche *n* = **soul**, anima, essential nature, individuality, inner man, innermost self, mind, personality, pneuma (*Philosophy*), self, spirit, subconscious, true being

psychedelic *adj* **1, 2** = **hallucinogenic**, consciousness-expanding, hallucinatory, mind-bending (*inf.*), mind-blowing (*inf.*), mind-expanding, psychoactive, psychotomimetic, psychotropic **3** *Informal* = **multicoloured**, crazy, freaky (*sl.*), kaleidoscopic, wild

psychiatrist *n* = **psychotherapist**, analyst, headshrinker (*sl.*), psychoanalyser, psychoanalyst, psychologist, shrink (*sl.*), therapist

psychic *adj* **1** = **supernatural**, clairvoyant, extrasensory, mystic, occult, preternatural, tele-

ognized by natural laws. **2** mental as opposed to physical. ◆ *n* **3** a person who is sensitive to parapsychological forces or influences.
▸**'psychical** *adj* ▸**'psychically** *adv*

psycho ('saɪkəʊ) *n, pl* **psychos,** *adj* an informal word for **psychopath** or **psychopathic.**

psycho- *or sometimes before a vowel* **psych-** *combining form.* indicating the mind or psychological or mental processes: *psychology.* [from Gk *psukhē* spirit, breath]

psychoactive (ˌsaɪkəʊ'æktɪv) *adj* (of drugs such as LSD and barbiturates) capable of affecting mental activity. Also: **psychotropic.**

psychoanalyse *or esp. US* **psychoanalyze** (ˌsaɪkəʊ'ænəˌlaɪz) *vb* **psychoanalyses, psychoanalysing, psychoanalysed** *or US* **psychoanalyzes, psychoanalyzing, psychoanalyzed.** (*tr*) to examine or treat (a person) by psychoanalysis.

psychoanalysis (ˌsaɪkəʊə'nælɪsɪs) *n* a method of studying the mind and treating mental and emotional disorders based on revealing and investigating the role of the unconscious mind.
▸**psychoanalyst** (ˌsaɪkəʊ'ænəlɪst) *n* ▸**psychoanalytic** (ˌsaɪkəʊˌænə'lɪtɪk) *or* **ˌpsychoˌana'lytical** *adj* ▸**ˌpsychoˌana'lytically** *adv*

psychobiology (ˌsaɪkəʊbaɪ'ɒlədʒɪ) *n Psychol.* the attempt to understand the psychology of organisms in terms of their biological functions and structures.
▸**psychobiological** (ˌsaɪkəʊˌbaɪə'lɒdʒɪkᵊl) *adj* ▸**ˌpsychobi'ologist** *n*

psychochemical (ˌsaɪkəʊ'kɛmɪkᵊl) *n* **1** any of various chemicals whose primary effect is the alteration of the normal state of consciousness. ◆ *adj* **2** of such compounds.

psychodrama ('saɪkəʊˌdrɑːmə) *n* **1** *Psychiatry.* a form of group therapy in which individuals act out situations from their past. **2** a film, television drama, etc., in which the psychological development of the characters is emphasized.

psychodynamics (ˌsaɪkəʊdaɪ'næmɪks) *n* (*functioning as sing*) *Psychol.* the study of interacting motives and emotions.
▸**ˌpsychody'namic** *adj*

psychogenic (ˌsaɪkəʊ'dʒɛnɪk) *adj Psychol.* (esp. of disorders or symptoms) of mental, rather than organic, origin.
▸**ˌpsycho'genically** *adv*

psychokinesis (ˌsaɪkəʊkɪ'niːsɪs, -kaɪ-) *n* (in parapsychology) alteration of the state of an object supposedly by mental influence alone. [C20: from PSYCHO- + Gk *kinēsis* motion]

psycholinguistics (ˌsaɪkəʊlɪŋ'gwɪstɪks) *n* (*functioning as sing*) the psychology of language, including language acquisition by children, language disorders, etc.
▸**ˌpsycho'linguist** *n*

psychological ❶ (ˌsaɪkə'lɒdʒɪkᵊl) *adj* **1** of or relating to psychology. **2** of or relating to the mind or mental activity. **3** having no real or objective basis; arising in the mind: *his backaches are all psychological.* **4** affecting the mind.
▸**ˌpsycho'logically** *adv*

psychological moment *n* the most appropriate time for producing a desired effect.

psychological warfare *n* the application of psychology, esp. to attempts to influence morale in time of war.

psychologize *or US* **psychologise** (saɪ'kɒləˌdʒaɪz) *vb* **psychologizes, psychologizing, psychologized** *or US* **psychologises, psychologising, psychologised.** (*intr*) **1** to make interpretations of mental processes. **2** to carry out investigation in psychology.

psychology ❶ (saɪ'kɒlədʒɪ) *n, pl* **psychologies. 1** the scientific study of all forms of human and animal behaviour. **2** *Inf.* the mental make-up of an individual that causes him to think or act in the way he does.
▸**psy'chologist** *n*

psychometrics (ˌsaɪkəʊ'mɛtrɪks) *n* (*functioning as sing*) **1** the branch of psychology concerned with the design and use of psychological tests. **2** the application of statistical techniques to psychological testing.

psychometry (saɪ'kɒmɪtrɪ) *n Psychol.* **1** measurement and testing of mental states and processes. **2** (in parapsychology) the supposed ability to deduce facts about events by touching objects related to them.
▸**psychometric** (ˌsaɪkəʊ'mɛtrɪk) *or* **ˌpsycho'metrical** *adj* ▸**ˌpsycho'metrically** *adv*

psychomotor (ˌsaɪkəʊ'məʊtə) *adj* of, relating to, or characterizing movements of the body associated with mental activity.

psychoneurosis (ˌsaɪkəʊnjʊ'rəʊsɪs) *n, pl* **psychoneuroses** (-'rəʊsiːz). another word for **neurosis.**

psychopath ❶ ('saɪkəʊˌpæθ) *n* a person with a personality disorder characterized by a tendency to commit antisocial and sometimes violent acts without feeling guilt.
▸**ˌpsycho'pathic** *adj* ▸**ˌpsycho'pathically** *adv*

psychopathology (ˌsaɪkəʊpə'θɒlədʒɪ) *n* the scientific study of mental disorders.
▸**psychopathological** (ˌsaɪkəʊˌpæθə'lɒdʒɪkᵊl) *adj*

psychopathy (saɪ'kɒpəθɪ) *n* any mental disorder or disease.

psychopharmacology (ˌsaɪkəʊˌfɑːmə'kɒlədʒɪ) *n* the study of drugs that affect the mind.

psychophysics (ˌsaɪkəʊ'fɪzɪks) *n* (*functioning as sing*) the branch of psychology concerned with the relationship between physical stimuli and their effects in the mind.
▸**ˌpsycho'physical** *adj*

psychophysiology (ˌsaɪkəʊˌfɪzɪ'ɒlədʒɪ) *n* the branch of psychology concerned with the physiological basis of mental processes.
▸**psychophysiological** (ˌsaɪkəʊˌfɪzɪə'lɒdʒɪkᵊl) *adj*

psychosexual (ˌsaɪkəʊ'sɛksjʊəl) *adj* of or relating to the mental aspects of sex, such as sexual fantasies.
▸**ˌpsycho'sexually** *adv*

psychosis (saɪ'kəʊsɪs) *n, pl* **psychoses** (-'kəʊsiːz). any form of severe mental disorder in which the individual's contact with reality becomes highly distorted. [C19: NL, from PSYCHO- + -OSIS]

psychosocial (ˌsaɪkəʊ'səʊʃəl) *adj* of or relating to processes or factors that are both social and psychological in origin.

psychosomatic (ˌsaɪkəʊsə'mætɪk) *adj* of disorders, such as stomach ulcers, thought to be caused or aggravated by psychological factors such as stress.

psychosurgery (ˌsaɪkəʊ'sɜːdʒərɪ) *n* any surgical procedure on the brain, such as a frontal lobotomy, to relieve serious mental disorders.
▸**psychosurgical** (ˌsaɪkəʊ'sɜːdʒɪkᵊl) *adj*

psychotherapy (ˌsaɪkəʊ'θɛrəpɪ) *n* the treatment of nervous disorders by psychological methods.
▸**ˌpsychoˌthera'peutic** *adj* ▸**ˌpsychoˌthera'peutically** *adv* ▸**ˌpsycho'therapist** *n*

psychotic ❶ (saɪ'kɒtɪk) *Psychiatry.* ◆ *adj* **1** of or characterized by psychosis. ◆ *n* **2** a person suffering from psychosis.
▸**psy'chotically** *adv*

psychotomimetic (saɪˌkɒtəʊmɪ'mɛtɪk) *adj* (of drugs such as LSD and mescaline) capable of inducing psychotic symptoms.

psych out *vb* (*mainly tr, adv*) *Inf.* **1** to guess correctly the intentions of (another). **2** to analyse (a problem, etc.) psychologically. **3** to intimidate or frighten.

psychrometer (saɪ'krɒmɪtə) *n* a type of hygrometer consisting of two thermometers, one of which has a dry bulb and the other a bulb that is kept moist and ventilated.

psych up *vb* (*tr, adv*) *Inf.* to get (oneself or another) into a state of psychological readiness for an action, performance, etc.

pt *abbrev. for:* **1** part. **2** patient. **3** payment. **4** point. **5** port. **6** pro tempore.

Pt *abbrev. for* (in place names): **1** Point. **2** Port. ◆ **3.** *the chemical symbol for* platinum.

PT *abbrev. for:* **1** physical therapy. **2** physical training. **3** postal telegraph.

pt. *abbrev. for:* **1** pint. **2** preterite.

PTA *abbrev. for:* **1** Parent-Teacher Association. **2** (in Britain) Passenger Transport Authority.

ptarmigan ('tɑːmɪgən) *n, pl* **ptarmigans** *or* **ptarmigan.** any of several arctic and subarctic grouse, esp. one which has a white winter plumage. [C16: changed (? infl. by Gk *pteron* wing) from Scot. Gaelic *tarmachan,* from ?]

Pte *Mil. abbrev. for* private.

pteridology (ˌtɛrɪ'dɒlədʒɪ) *n* the branch of botany concerned with the study of ferns. [C19: from *pterido-,* from Gk *pteris* fern + -LOGY]
▸**pteridological** (ˌtɛrɪdəʊ'lɒdʒɪkᵊl) *adj*

pteridophyte ('tɛrɪdəʊˌfaɪt) *n* (in traditional classification) a plant, such as a fern, horsetail, or club moss, reproducing by spores and having vascular tissue, roots, stems, and leaves. In modern classifications these plants are placed in separate phyla. [C19: from *pterido-,* from Gk *pteris* fern + -PHYTE]

ptero- *combining form.* a wing, or a part resembling a wing: *pterodactyl.* [from Gk *pteron*]

pterodactyl (ˌtɛrə'dæktɪl) *n* an extinct flying reptile having membranous wings supported on an elongated fourth digit.

pteropod ('tɛrəˌpɒd) *n* a small marine gastropod mollusc in which the foot is expanded into two winglike lobes for swimming. Also called: **sea butterfly.**

pterosaur ('tɛrəˌsɔː) *n* any of an order of extinct flying reptiles of Jurassic and Cretaceous times: included the pterodactyls.

-pterous *or* **-pteran** *adj combining form.* indicating a specified number or type of wings: *dipterous.* [from Gk *-pteros,* from *pteron* wing]

pterygoid process ('tɛrɪˌgɔɪd) *n Anat.* either of two long bony plates extending downwards from each side of the sphenoid bone within the skull. [C18 *pterygoid,* from Gk *pterugoeidēs,* from *pterux* wing; see -OID]

PTN *abbrev. for* public telephone network: the telephone network provided in Britain by British Telecom.

PTO *or* **pto** *abbrev. for* please turn over.

Ptolemaic (ˌtɒlɪ'meɪɪk) *adj* **1** of or relating to the ancient astronomer Ptolemy, 2nd-century A.D. Greek astronomer, or to his conception of the universe. **2** of or relating to the Macedonian dynasty that ruled

THESAURUS

kinetic, telepathic **2** = **mental,** psychogenic, psychological, spiritual

psychological *adj* **2** = **mental,** cerebral, cognitive, intellectual **3** = **imaginary,** all in the mind, emotional, irrational, psychosomatic, subconscious, subjective, unconscious, unreal

psychology *n* **1** = **behaviourism,** science of mind, study of personality **2** *Informal* = **way of thinking,** attitude, mental make-up, mental processes, thought processes, what makes one tick

psychopath *n* = **madman,** headbanger (*inf.*), headcase (*inf.*), insane person, lunatic, maniac, mental case (*sl.*), nutcase (*sl.*), nutter (*Brit. sl.*), psychotic, sociopath

psychotic *adj* **1** = **mad,** certifiable, demented, deranged, insane, lunatic, mental (*sl.*), *non compos mentis,* not right in the head, off one's head (*sl.*), psychopathic, round the bend (*Brit. sl.*), unbalanced

Egypt from the death of Alexander the Great (323 B.C.) to the death of Cleopatra (30 B.C.).

Ptolemaic system *n* the theory of planetary motion developed by Ptolemy from the hypotheses of earlier philosophers, stating that the earth lay at the centre of the universe with the sun, the moon, and the known planets revolving around it in complicated orbits. Beyond the largest of these orbits lay a sphere of fixed stars.

ptomaine *or* **ptomain** ('təʊmeɪn) *n* any of a group of amines formed by decaying organic matter. [C19: from It. *ptomaina,* from Gk *ptoma* corpse, from *piptein* to fall]

ptomaine poisoning *n* a popular term for **food poisoning.** Ptomaines were once erroneously thought to be a cause of food poisoning.

ptosis ('təʊsɪs) *n, pl* **ptoses** ('təʊsi:z). prolapse or drooping of a part, esp. the eyelid. [C18: from Gk: a falling]
▸**ptotic** ('tɒtɪk) *adj*

PTSD *abbrev. for* post-traumatic stress disorder.

pty *Austral., NZ, & S. African. abbrev. for* proprietary.

ptyalin ('taɪəlɪn) *n Biochemistry.* an amylase secreted in the saliva of man and other animals. [C19: from Gk *ptualon* saliva, from *ptuein* to spit]

p-type *adj* **1** (of a semiconductor) having a density of mobile holes in excess of that of conduction electrons. **2** associated with or resulting from the movement of holes in a semiconductor: *p-type conductivity.*

Pu *the chemical symbol for* plutonium.

pub ⓘ (pʌb) *n* **1** *Chiefly Brit.* a building with a bar and one or more public rooms licensed for the sale and consumption of alcoholic drink, often also providing light meals. Formal name: **public house. 2** *Austral. & NZ.* a hotel. ◆ *vb* **pubs, pubbing, pubbed. 3** (*intr*) *Inf.* to visit a pub or pubs (esp. in **go pubbing**).

pub. *abbrev. for:* **1** public. **2** publication. **3** published. **4** publisher. **5** publishing.

pub-crawl *Inf., chiefly Brit.* ◆ *n* **1** a drinking tour of a number of pubs or bars. ◆ *vb* **2** (*intr*) to make such a tour.

puberty ⓘ ('pju:bətɪ) *n* the period at the beginning of adolescence when the sex glands become functional. Also called: **pubescence.** [C14: from L *pūbertās* maturity, from *pūber* adult]
▸**'pubertal** *adj*

pubes ('pju:bi:z) *n, pl* **pubes. 1** the region above the external genital organs, covered with hair from the time of puberty. **2** pubic hair. **3** the pubic bones. **4** the plural of **pubis.** [from L]

pubescent (pju:'besᵊnt) *adj* **1** arriving or arrived at puberty. **2** (of certain plants and animals or their parts) covered with a layer of fine short hairs or down. [C17: from L *pūbēscere* to reach manhood, from *pūber* adult]
▸**pu'bescence** *n*

pubic ('pju:bɪk) *adj* of or relating to the pubes or pubis: *pubic hair.*

pubis ('pju:bɪs) *n, pl* **pubes.** one of the three sections of the hipbone that forms part of the pelvis. [C16: shortened from NL *os pūbis* bone of the PUBES]

public ⓘ ('pʌblɪk) *adj* **1** of or concerning the people as a whole. **2** open to all: *public gardens.* **3** performed or made openly: *public proclamation.* **4** (*prenominal*) well-known: *a public figure.* **5** (*usually prenominal*) maintained at the expense of, serving, or for the use of a community: *a public library.* **6** open, acknowledged, or notorious: *a public scandal.* **7 go public.** (of a private company) to issue shares for subscription by the public. ◆ *n* **8** the community or people in general. **9** a section of the community grouped because of a common interest, activity, etc.: *the racing public.* [C15: from L *pūblicus,* changed from *pōplicus* of the people, from *populus* people]
▸**'publicly** *adv*

public-address system *n* a system of microphones, amplifiers, and loudspeakers for increasing the sound level, used in auditoriums, public gatherings, etc. Sometimes shortened to **PA system.**

publican ('pʌblɪkən) *n* **1** (in Britain) a person who keeps a public house. **2** (in ancient Rome) a public contractor, esp. one who farmed the taxes of a province. [C12: from OF *publicain,* from L *pūblicānus* tax gatherer, from *pūblicum* state revenues]

publication ⓘ (ˌpʌblɪ'keɪʃən) *n* **1** the act or process of publishing a printed work. **2** any printed work offered for sale or distribution. **3** the act or an instance of making information public. [C14: via OF from L *pūblicātiō* confiscation of property, from *pūblicāre* to seize for public use]

public bar *n Brit.* a bar in a public house usually serving drinks at a cheaper price than in the lounge bar.

public company *n* a limited company whose shares may be purchased by the public and traded freely on the open market and whose share capital is not less than a statutory minimum; public limited company. Cf. **private company.**

public convenience *n* a public lavatory.

public corporation *n* (in Britain) an organization established to run a nationalized industry or state-owned enterprise. The chairman and board members are appointed by a government minister, and the government has overall control.

public domain *n* **1** the status of a published work upon which the copyright has expired or which has not been subject to copyright. **2 in the public domain.** generally known or accessible.

public enemy *n* a notorious person, such as a criminal, who is regarded as a menace to the public.

public house *n* **1** *Brit.* the formal name for a **pub. 2** *US & Canad.* an inn, tavern, or small hotel.

publicist ('pʌblɪsɪst) *n* **1** a person who publicizes something, esp. a press or publicity agent. **2** a journalist. **3** *Rare.* a person learned in public or international law.

publicity ⓘ (pʌ'blɪsɪtɪ) *n* **1a** the technique or process of attracting public attention to people, products, etc., as by the use of the mass media. **1b** (*as modifier*): *a publicity agent.* **2** public interest aroused by such a technique or process. **3** information used to draw public attention to people, products, etc. **4** the state of being public. [C18: via F from Med. L *pūblicitās;* see PUBLIC]

publicize ⓘ *or* **publicise** ('pʌblɪˌsaɪz) *vb* **publicizes, publicizing, publicized** *or* **publicises, publicising, publicised.** (*tr*) to bring to public notice; advertise.

Public Lending Right *n* the right of authors to receive payment when their books are borrowed from public libraries.

public-liability insurance *n* (in Britain) a form of insurance, compulsory for any business in contact with the public, which pays compensation to a member of the public suffering injury or damage as a result of the policyholder or his employees failing to take reasonable care.

public limited company *n* another name for **public company.** Abbrev.: **plc** *or* **PLC.**

public nuisance *n* **1** *Law.* an illegal act causing harm to members of a community rather than to any individual. **2** *Inf.* a person generally considered objectionable.

public opinion *n* the attitude of the public, esp. as a factor in determining action, policy, etc.

public prosecutor *n Law.* an official in charge of prosecuting important cases.

Public Record Office *n* an institution in which official records are stored and kept available for inspection by the public.

public relations *n* (*functioning as sing or pl*) **1a** the practice of creating, promoting, or maintaining goodwill and a favourable image among the public towards an institution, public body, etc. **1b** the professional staff employed for this purpose. Abbrev.: **PR. 1c** the techniques employed. **1d** (*as modifier*): *the public-relations industry.* **2** the relationship between an organization and the public.

public school *n* **1** (in England and Wales) a private independent fee-paying secondary school. **2** in certain Canadian provinces, a public elementary school as distinguished from a separate school. **3** (in the US) any school that is part of a free local educational system.

public sector *n* the part of an economy which consists of state-owned institutions, including nationalized industries and services provided by local authorities.

public servant *n* **1** an elected or appointed holder of a public office. **2** the Austral. and NZ equivalent of **civil servant.**

public service *n* the Austral. and NZ equivalent of the **civil service.**

public-spirited ⓘ *adj* having or showing active interest in the good of the community.

public utility *n* an enterprise concerned with the provision to the public of essentials, such as electricity or water. Also called (in the US): **public-service corporation.**

public works *pl n* engineering projects and other constructions, financed and undertaken by a government for the community.

publish ⓘ ('pʌblɪʃ) *vb* **1** to produce and issue (printed matter) for distribution and sale. **2** (*intr*) to have one's written work issued for publica-

THESAURUS

pub **1** *n* = **tavern,** alehouse (*arch.*), bar, boozer (*Brit., Austral., & NZ inf.*), hostelry, inn, local (*Brit. inf.*), roadhouse, taproom, watering hole (*facetious sl.*)

puberty *n* = **adolescence,** awkward age, juvenescence, pubescence, teenage, teens, young adulthood

public *adj* **1** = **general,** civic, civil, common, national, popular, social, state, universal, widespread **2** = **open,** accessible, communal, community, free to all, not private, open to the public, unrestricted **4** = **well-known,** important, prominent, respected **5** = **known,** acknowledged, exposed, in circulation, notorious, obvious, open, overt, patent, plain, published, recognized ◆ *n* **8** = **people,** citizens, commonalty, community, country, electorate, everyone, hoi polloi, Joe (and Eileen) Public (*sl.*), Joe Six-Pack (*US sl.*), masses, multitude, nation, populace, population, society, voters **9** = **clientele,** audience, buyers, followers, following, patrons, supporters, those interested, trade
Antonyms *adj* ≠ **open:** barred, closed, exclusive, inaccessible, personal, private, restricted, unavailable ≠ **known:** hidden, secluded, secret, unknown, unrevealed

publication *n* **1, 3** = **announcement,** advertisement, airing, appearance, broadcasting, declaration, disclosure, dissemination, notification, proclamation, promulgation, publishing, reporting **2** = **pamphlet,** book, booklet, brochure, handbill, hardback, issue, leaflet, magazine, newspaper, paperback, periodical, title, zine (*inf.*)

publicity *n* **1, 2** = **advertising,** attention, ballyhoo (*inf.*), boost, boosterism, build-up, hype, plug (*inf.*), press, promotion, public notice, puff, puffery (*inf.*)

publicize *vb* = **advertise,** beat the drum for (*inf.*), bring to public notice, broadcast, give publicity to, hype, make known, play up, plug (*inf.*), promote, puff, push, spotlight, spread about, write up
Antonyms *vb* conceal, contain, cover up, keep dark, keep secret, smother, stifle, suppress, withhold

public-spirited *adj* = **altruistic,** charitable, community-minded, generous, humanitarian, philanthropic, unselfish

publish *vb* **1** = **put out,** bring out, issue, print, produce **3** = **announce,** advertise, blow wide

tion. **3** (*tr*) to announce formally or in public. **4** (*tr*) to communicate (defamatory matter) to someone other than the person defamed: *to publish a libel.* [C14: from OF *puplier,* from L *pūblicāre* to make PUBLIC]
▸'**publishable** *adj*

publisher ('pʌblɪʃə) *n* **1** a company or person engaged in publishing periodicals, books, music, etc. **2** *US & Canad.* the proprietor of a newspaper.

puce (pju:s) *n, adj* (of) a colour varying from deep red to dark purplish brown. [C18: shortened from F *couleur puce* flea colour, from L *pūlex* flea]

puck[1] (pʌk) *n* **1** a small disc of hard rubber used in ice hockey. **2** a stroke at the ball in hurling. **3** *Irish sl.* a sharp blow. ◆ *vb* (*tr*) **4** to strike (the ball) in hurling. **5** *Irish sl.* to strike hard; punch. [C19: from ?]

puck[2] (pʌk) *n* a mischievous or evil spirit. [OE *pūca,* from ?]
▸'**puckish** *adj*

pucka ('pʌkə) *adj* a less common spelling of **pukka.**

pucker ('pʌkə) *vb* **1** to gather (a soft surface such as the skin) into wrinkles, or (of such a surface) to be so gathered. ◆ *n* **2** a wrinkle, crease, or irregular fold. [C16: ? rel. to POKE[2], from the baglike wrinkles]

pudding ('pʊdɪŋ) *n* **1** a sweetened usually cooked dessert made in many forms and of various ingredients. **2** a savoury dish, usually consisting partially of pastry or batter: *steak-and-kidney pudding.* **3** the dessert course in a meal. **4** a sausage-like mass of meat, oatmeal, etc., stuffed into a prepared skin or bag and boiled. [C13 *poding*]
▸'**puddingy** *adj*

pudding stone *n* a conglomerate rock in which there is a difference in colour and composition between the pebbles and the matrix.

puddle ('pʌdᵊl) *n* **1** a small pool of water, esp. of rain. **2** a small pool of any liquid. **3** a worked mixture of wet clay and sand that is impervious to water and is used to line a pond or canal. ◆ *vb* **puddles, puddling, puddled.** (*tr*) **4** to make (clay, etc.) into puddle. **5** to subject (iron) to puddling. [C14 *podel,* dim. of OE *pudd* ditch, from ?]
▸'**puddler** *n* ▸'**puddly** *adj*

puddling ('pʌdlɪŋ) *n* a process for converting pig iron into wrought iron by heating it with ferric oxide in a furnace and stirring it to oxidize the carbon.

pudency ('pju:dᵊnsɪ) *n* modesty or prudishness. [C17: from LL *pudentia,* from L *pudēre* to feel shame]

pudendum (pju:'dɛndəm) *n, pl* **pudenda** (-də). (*often pl*) the human external genital organs collectively, esp. of a female. [C17: from LL, from L *pudenda* the shameful (parts), from *pudēre* to be ashamed]
▸**pu'dendal** *or* **pudic** ('pju:dɪk) *adj*

pudgy ('pʌdʒɪ) *adj* **pudgier, pudgiest.** a variant spelling (esp. US) of **podgy.** [C19: from ?]
▸'**pudgily** *adv* ▸'**pudginess** *n*

pueblo ('pwɛbləʊ; *Spanish* 'pweβlo) *n, pl* **pueblos** (-ləʊz; *Spanish* -los). **1** a communal village, built by certain Indians of the southwestern US and parts of Latin America, consisting of one or more flat-roofed houses. **2** (in Spanish America) a village or town. [C19: from Sp.: people, from L *populus*]

puerile ('pjʊəraɪl) *adj* **1** exhibiting silliness; immature; trivial. **2** of or characteristic of a child. [C17: from L *puerīlis* childish, from *puer* a boy]
▸'**puerilely** *adv* ▸**puerility** (pjʊə'rɪlɪtɪ) *n*

puerperal (pju:'ɜ:pərəl) *adj* of or occurring during the period following childbirth. [C18: from NL *puerperālis,* from L *puerperium* childbirth, ult. from *puer* boy + *parere* to bear]

puerperal fever *n* a serious, formerly widespread, form of blood poisoning caused by infection contracted during childbirth.

puerperal psychosis *n* a mental disorder sometimes occurring in women after childbirth, characterized by deep depression.

puff (pʌf) *n* **1** a short quick gust or emission, as of wind, smoke, etc. **2** the amount of wind, smoke, etc., released in a puff. **3** the sound made by a puff. **4** an instance of inhaling and expelling the breath as in smoking. **5** a light aerated pastry usually filled with cream, jam, etc. **6** a powder puff. **7** exaggerated praise, as of a book, product, etc., esp. through an advertisement. **8** a piece of clothing fabric gathered up so as to bulge in the centre while being held together at the edges. **9** a cylindrical roll of hair pinned in place in a coiffure. **10** *US.* a quilted bed cover. **11** one's breath (esp. in **out of puff**). **12** *Derog. sl.* a male homosexual. ◆ *vb* **13** to blow or breathe or cause to blow or breathe in short quick draughts. **14** (*tr; often foll. by out; usually passive*) to cause to be out of breath. **15** to take draws at (a cigarette, etc.). **16** (*intr*) to move with or by the emission of puffs: *the steam train puffed up the incline.* **17** (often foll. by *up, out,* etc.) to swell, as with air, pride, etc. **18** (*tr*) to praise with exaggerated empty words, often in advertising. **19** (*tr*) to apply (powder, dust, etc.) to (something). [OE *pyffan*]
▸'**puffy** *adj*

puff adder *n* **1** a large venomous African viper that inflates its body when alarmed. **2** another name for **hognose snake.**

puffball ('pʌf,bɔ:l) *n* **1** any of various fungi having a round fruiting body that discharges a cloud of brown spores when mature. **2** short for **puffball skirt.**

puffball skirt *n* a skirt or a dress with a skirt that puffs out wide and is nipped into a narrow hem.

puffer ('pʌfə) *n* **1** a person or thing that puffs. **2** Also called: **blowfish, globefish.** a marine fish with an elongated spiny body that can be inflated to form a globe.

puffin ('pʌfɪn) *n* any of various northern diving birds, having a black-and-white plumage and a brightly coloured vertically flattened bill. [C14: ? of Cornish origin]

puff pastry *or US* **puff paste** *n* a dough used for making a rich flaky pastry.

puff-puff *n Brit.* a children's name for a steam locomotive or railway train.

pug[1] (pʌg) *n* a small compact breed of dog with a smooth coat, lightly curled tail, and a short wrinkled nose. [C16: from ?]
▸'**puggish** *adj*

pug[2] (pʌg) *vb* **pugs, pugging, pugged.** (*tr*) **1** to mix (clay) with water to form a malleable mass or paste, often in a **pug mill. 2** to fill or stop with clay or a similar substance. [C19: from ?]

pug[3] (pʌg) *n* a slang name for **boxer** (sense 1). [C20: shortened from PUGILIST]

pugging ('pʌgɪŋ) *n* material such as clay, sawdust, etc., inserted between wooden flooring and ceiling to deaden sound. Also called: **pug.**

puggree, pugree ('pʌgrɪ) *or* **puggaree, pugaree** ('pʌgərɪ) *n* **1** the usual Indian word for **turban. 2** a scarf, usually pleated, around the crown of some hats, esp. sun helmets. [C17: from Hindi *pagrī,* from Sansk. *parikara*]

pugilism ('pju:dʒɪ,lɪzəm) *n* the art, practice, or profession of fighting with the fists; boxing. [C18: from L *pugil* a boxer]
▸'**pugilist** *n* ▸,**pugi'listic** *adj* ▸,**pugi'listically** *adv*

pugnacious (pʌg'neɪʃəs) *adj* readily disposed to fight; belligerent. [C17: from L *pugnāx*]
▸**pug'naciously** *adv* ▸**pugnacity** (pʌg'næsɪtɪ) *n*

pug nose *n* a short stubby upturned nose. [C18: from PUG[1]]
▸'**pug-,nosed** *adj*

puisne ('pju:nɪ) *adj* (esp. of a subordinate judge) of lower rank. [C16: from Anglo-F, from OF *puisné* born later, from L *posteā* afterwards + *nascī* to be born]

puissance ('pju:ɪsᵊns, 'pwi:sɑ:ns) *n* **1** a competition in showjumping that tests a horse's ability to jump large obstacles. **2** *Arch. or poetic.* power. [C15: from OF; see PUISSANT]

puissant ('pju:ɪsᵊnt) *adj Arch. or poetic.* powerful. [C15: from OF, ult. from L *potēns* mighty, from *posse* to have power]
▸'**puissantly** *adv*

puke (pju:k) *Sl.* ◆ *vb* **pukes, puking, puked. 1** to vomit. ◆ *n* **2** the act of vomiting. **3** the matter vomited. [C16: prob. imit.]

pukeko ('pʊkəkəʊ) *n, pl* **pukekos.** a New Zealand wading bird with bright plumage. [from Maori]

pukka *or* **pucka** ('pʌkə) *adj Anglo-Indian.* properly or perfectly done, constructed, etc.; good; genuine. [C17: from Hindi *pakkā* firm, from Sansk. *pakva*]

pulchritude ('pʌlkrɪ,tju:d) *n Formal or literary.* physical beauty. [C15: from L *pulchritūdō,* from *pulcher* beautiful]
▸,**pulchri'tudinous** *adj*

pule (pju:l) *vb* **pules, puling, puled.** (*intr*) to cry plaintively; whimper. [C16: ? imit.]
▸'**puler** *n*

Pulitzer prize ('pʊlɪtzə) *n* one of a group of prizes awarded yearly since 1917 for excellence in American journalism, literature, and music. [after Joseph *Pulitzer* (1847–1911), Hungarian-born US newspaper publisher]

THESAURUS

open (*sl.*), broadcast, circulate, communicate, declare, disclose, distribute, divulge, impart, leak, proclaim, promulgate, publicize, reveal, shout from the rooftops (*inf.*), spread

pucker *vb* **1** = **wrinkle**, compress, contract, crease, crinkle, crumple, draw together, furrow, gather, knit, pout, purse, ruckle, ruck up, ruffle, screw up, tighten ◆ *n* **2** = **wrinkle**, crease, crinkle, crumple, fold, ruck, ruckle

puckish *adj* = **mischievous**, frolicsome, impish, naughty, playful, roguish, sly, sportive, teasing, waggish, whimsical

pudding *n* **1, 3** = **dessert**, afters (*Brit. inf.*), last course, pud (*inf.*), second course, sweet

puerile *adj* **1** = **childish**, babyish, foolish, immature, inane, infantile, irresponsible, jejune, juvenile, naive, petty, ridiculous, silly, trivial, weak

Antonyms *adj* adult, grown-up, mature, responsible, sensible

puff *n* **1** = **blast**, breath, draught, emanation, flurry, gust, whiff **4** = **smoke**, drag, pull **7** = **advertisement**, commendation, favourable mention, good word, plug (*inf.*), sales talk **8** = **bulge**, bunching, swelling ◆ *vb* **13** = **blow**, breathe, exhale, gasp, gulp, pant, wheeze **15** = **smoke**, drag, draw, inhale, pull at *or* on, suck **17** *often foll. by* **with up, out** *etc.* = **swell**, bloat, dilate, distend, expand, inflate **18** = **promote**, crack up (*inf.*), hype, overpraise, plug (*inf.*), praise, publicize, push

puffy *adj* **17** = **swollen**, bloated, distended, enlarged, inflamed, inflated, puffed up

pugilism *n* = **boxing**, fighting, prizefighting, the noble art *or* science, the prize ring, the ring

pugilist *n* = **boxer**, bruiser (*inf.*), fighter, prizefighter, pug (*sl.*)

pugnacious *adj* = **aggressive**, antagonistic, argumentative, bellicose, belligerent, choleric, combative, contentious, disputatious, hot-tempered, irascible, irritable, petulant, quarrelsome

Antonyms *adj* calm, conciliatory, gentle, irenic, pacific, peaceable, peaceful, peace-loving, placatory, placid, quiet

puke *vb* **1** *Slang* = **vomit**, barf, be nauseated, be sick, chuck (up) (*sl., chiefly US*), chunder (*sl., chiefly Austral.*), disgorge, heave, regurgitate, retch, spew, throw up (*inf.*)

pukka *adj Anglo-Indian* = **genuine**, authentic, bona fide, official, on the level (*inf.*), proper, real, the real McCoy

pull ⓣ (pʊl) *vb (mainly tr)* **1** *(also intr)* to exert force on (an object) so as to draw it towards the source of the force. **2** to remove; extract: *to pull a tooth.* **3** to strip of feathers, hair, etc.; pluck. **4** to draw the entrails from (a fowl). **5** to rend or tear. **6** to strain (a muscle or tendon). **7** (usually foll. by *off*) *Inf.* to bring about: *to pull off a million-pound deal.* **8** (often foll. by *on*) *Inf.* to draw out (a weapon) for use: *he pulled a knife on his attacker.* **9** *Inf.* to attract: *the pop group pulled a crowd.* **10** *(also intr) Sl.* to attract (a sexual partner). **11** *(intr;* usually foll. by *on* or *at)* to drink or inhale deeply: *to pull at one's pipe.* **12** to make (a grimace): *to pull a face.* **13** *(also intr;* foll. by *away, out, over,* etc.) to move (a vehicle) or (of a vehicle) to be moved in a specified manner. **14** *(intr)* to possess or exercise the power to move: *this car doesn't pull well on hills.* **15** to withdraw or remove: *the board decided to pull their support.* **16** *Printing.* to take (a proof) from type. **17** *Golf, baseball, etc.* to hit (a ball) so that it veers away from the direction in which the player intended to hit it. **18** *Cricket.* to hit (a ball pitched straight or on the off side) to the leg side. **19** *Hurling.* to strike (a fast-moving ball) in the same direction as it is already moving. **20** *(also intr)* to row (a boat) or take a stroke of (an oar) in rowing. **21** (of a rider) to restrain (a horse), esp. to prevent it from winning a race. **22 pull a fast one.** *Sl.* to play a sly trick. **23 pull apart** *or* **to pieces.** to criticize harshly. **24 pull (one's) punches. 24a** *Inf.* to restrain the force of one's criticisms or actions. **24b** *Boxing.* to restrain the force of one's blows. ◆ *n* **25** an act or an instance of pulling or being pulled. **26** the force or effort used in pulling: *the pull of the moon affects the tides.* **27** the act or an instance of taking in drink or smoke. **28** *Printing.* a proof taken from type: *the first pull was smudged.* **29** something used for pulling, such as a handle. **30** *Inf.* special advantage or influence: *his uncle is chairman of the company, so he has quite a lot of pull.* **31** *Inf.* the power to attract attention or support. **32** a period of rowing. **33** a single stroke of an oar in rowing. **34** the act of pulling the ball in golf, cricket, etc. **35** the act of reining in a horse. ◆ See also **pull down, pull in,** etc. [OE *pullian*]
▸ **'puller** *n*

pull down ⓣ *vb (tr, adv)* to destroy or demolish: *the old houses were pulled down.*

pullet ('pʊlɪt) *n* a young hen of the domestic fowl, less than one year old. [C14: from OF *poulet* chicken, from L *pullus* a young animal or bird]

pulley ('pʊlɪ) *n* **1** a wheel with a grooved rim in which a rope can run in order to change the direction of a force applied to the rope, etc. **2** a number of such wheels pivoted in parallel in a block, used to raise heavy loads. **3** a wheel with a flat, convex, or grooved rim mounted on a shaft and driven by or driving a belt passing around it. [C14 *poley,* from OF *polie,* from Vulgar L *polidium* (unattested), apparently from LGk *polidion* (unattested) a little pole, from Gk *polos* axis]

pull in ⓣ *vb (adv)* **1** *(intr;* often foll. by *to)* to reach a destination: *the train pulled in at the station.* **2** *(intr)* Also: **pull over.** (of a motor vehicle) **2a** to draw in to the side of the road. **2b** to stop (at a café, lay-by, etc.). **3** *(tr)* to attract: *his appearance will pull in the crowds.* **4** *(tr) Sl.* to arrest. **5** *(tr)* to earn or gain (money). ◆ *n* **pull-in. 6** *Brit.* a roadside café, esp. for lorry drivers.

Pullman ('pʊlmən) *n, pl* **Pullmans.** a luxurious railway coach. Also called: **Pullman car.** [C19: after G. M. *Pullman* (1831–97), its US inventor]

pull off ⓣ *vb (tr)* **1** to remove (clothing) forcefully. **2** *(adv)* to succeed in performing (a difficult feat).

pull out ⓣ *vb (adv)* **1** *(tr)* to extract. **2** *(intr)* to depart: *the train pulled out of the station.* **3** *Mil.* to withdraw or be withdrawn: *the troops were pulled out of the ruined city.* **4** *(intr)* (of a motor vehicle) **4a** to draw away from the side of the road. **4b** to draw out from behind another vehicle to overtake. **5** *(intr)* to abandon a position or situation. **6** (foll. by *of*) to level out (from a dive). ◆ *n* **pull-out. 7** an extra leaf of a book that folds out. **8** a removable section of a magazine, etc.

pullover ('pʊl,əʊvə) *n* a garment, esp. a sweater, that is pulled on over the head.

pull through ⓣ *vb* to survive or recover or cause to survive or recover, esp. after a serious illness or crisis. Also: **pull round.**

pull together *vb* **1** *(intr, adv)* to cooperate, or work harmoniously. **2 pull oneself together.** *Inf.* to regain one's self-control or composure.

pullulate ('pʌljʊ,leɪt) *vb* **pullulates, pullulating, pullulated.** *(intr)* **1** (of animals, etc.) to breed abundantly. **2** (of plants) to sprout, bud, or germinate. [C17: from L *pullulāre* to sprout, from *pullulus* a baby animal, from *pullus* young animal]
▸ **,pullu'lation** *n*

pull up ⓣ *vb (adv)* **1** *(tr)* to remove by the roots. **2** (often foll. by *with* or *on*) to move level (with) or ahead (of), esp. in a race. **3** to stop: *the car pulled up suddenly.* **4** *(tr)* to rebuke. ◆ *n* **pull-up. 5** *Brit.* a roadside café; pull-in.

pulmonary ('pʌlmənərɪ, 'pʊl-) *adj* **1** of or affecting the lungs. **2** having lungs or lunglike organs. [C18: from L *pulmōnārius,* from *pulmō* a lung]

pulmonary artery *n* either of the two arteries that convey oxygen-depleted blood from the heart to the lungs.

pulmonary vein *n* any one of the four veins that convey oxygen-rich blood from the lungs to the heart.

pulp ⓣ (pʌlp) *n* **1** soft or fleshy plant tissue, such as the succulent part of a fleshy fruit. **2** a moist mixture of cellulose fibres, as obtained from wood, from which paper is made. **3a** a magazine or book containing trite or sensational material, and usually printed on cheap rough paper. **3b** *(as modifier)*: *a pulp novel.* **4** *Dentistry.* the soft innermost part of a tooth, containing nerves and blood vessels. **5** any soft soggy mass. **6** *Mining.* pulverized ore. ◆ *vb* **7** to reduce (a material) to pulp or (of a material) to be reduced to pulp. **8** *(tr)* to remove the pulp from (fruit, etc.). [C16: from L *pulpa*]
▸ **'pulpy** *adj*

pulpit ('pʊlpɪt) *n* **1** a raised platform, usually surrounded by a barrier, set up in churches as the appointed place for preaching, etc. **2** a medium for expressing an opinion, such as a newspaper column. **3** (usually preceded by *the*) **3a** the preaching of the Christian message. **3b** the clergy or their influence. [C14: from L *pulpitum* a platform]

pulpwood ('pʌlp,wʊd) *n* pine, spruce, or any other soft wood used to make paper.

pulque ('pʊlkɪ) *n* a light alcoholic drink from Mexico made from the juice of various agave plants. [C17: from Mexican Sp., apparently from Nahuatl, from *puliuhqui* decomposed, since it will only keep for a day]

pulsar ('pʌl,sɑː) *n* any of a number of very small stars first discovered in 1967, which rotate fast, emitting regular pulses of polarized radiation. [C20: from PULS(ATING ST)AR, on the model of QUASAR]

pulsate ⓣ (pʌl'seɪt) *vb* **pulsates, pulsating, pulsated.** *(intr)* **1** to expand and contract with a rhythmic beat; throb. **2** *Physics.* to vary in intensity, magnitude, etc. **3** to quiver or vibrate. [C18: from L *pulsāre* to push]
▸ **pulsative** ('pʌlsətɪv) *adj* ▸ **pul'sation** *n* ▸ **pul'sator** *n* ▸ **pulsatory** ('pʌlsətərɪ, -trɪ) *adj*

pulsatilla (,pʌlsə'tɪlə) *n* any of a genus of plants related to the anemone, with feathery or hairy foliage. [C16: from Med. L, from *pulsāta* beaten (by the wind)]

pulsating star *n* a type of variable star, the variation in brightness resulting from expansion and subsequent contraction of the star.

pulse[1] ⓣ (pʌls) *n* **1** *Physiol.* **1a** the rhythmic contraction and expansion of an artery at each beat of the heart. **1b** a single such pulsation. **2** *Physics, electronics.* **2a** a transient sharp change in some quantity normally constant in a system. **2b** one of a series of such transient disturbances, usually recurring at regular intervals. **3a** a recurrent rhythmic series of beats, vibrations, etc. **3b** any single beat, wave, etc., in such a series. **4** an inaudible electronic "ping" to operate a slide projector. **5** bustle, vitality, or excitement: *the pulse of a city.* **6 keep one's finger on the pulse.** to be well informed about current events, opinions, etc. ◆ *vb* **pulses, pulsing, pulsed. 7** *(intr)* to beat, throb, or vibrate. **8** *(tr)* to provide an electronic pulse to operate (a slide projector). [C14 *pous,* from L *pulsus* a beating, from *pellere* to beat]
▸ **'pulseless** *adj*

pulse[2] (pʌls) *n* **1** the edible seeds of any of several leguminous plants, such as peas, beans, and lentils. **2** the plant producing any of these. [C13 *pols,* from OF, from L *puls* pottage of pulse]

pulsejet ('pʌls,dʒet) *n* a type of ramjet engine in which air is admitted through movable vanes that are closed by the pressure resulting from

THESAURUS

pull *vb* **1** = **draw**, drag, haul, jerk, tow, trail, tug, yank **2, 3** = **extract**, cull, draw out, gather, pick, pluck, remove, take out, uproot, weed **5, 6** = **strain**, dislocate, rend, rip, sprain, stretch, tear, wrench **9** *Informal* = **attract**, draw, entice, lure, magnetize **23 pull apart** *or* to pieces = **criticize**, attack, blast, find fault, flay, lambast(e), lay into *(inf.)*, pan *(inf.)*, pick holes in, put down, run down, slam *(sl.)*, slate *(inf.)*, tear into *(inf.)* ◆ *n* **25** = **tug**, jerk, twitch, yank **27** = **puff**, drag *(sl.)*, inhalation **30** *Informal* = **influence**, advantage, bottom, clout *(inf.)*, leverage, muscle, power, weight **31** *Informal* = **attraction**, drawing power, effort, exertion, force, forcefulness, influence, lure, magnetism
Antonyms *vb* ≠ **draw**: drive, nudge, push, ram, shove, thrust ≠ **extract**: implant, insert, plant ≠ **attract**: deter, discourage, put one off, repel ◆ *n* ≠ **tug**: nudge, push, shove, thrust

pull down *vb* = **demolish**, bulldoze, destroy, raze, remove
Antonyms *vb* build, construct, erect, put up, raise, set up

pull in *vb* **1, 2** = **draw in**, arrive, come in, draw up, reach, stop **3** = **attract**, bring in, draw **4** *Slang* = **arrest**, bust *(inf.)*, collar *(inf.)*, feel one's collar *(sl.)*, lift *(sl.)*, nab *(inf.)*, nail *(inf.)*, pinch *(inf.)*, run in *(sl.)*, take into custody **5** = **earn**, clear, gain, gross, make, net, pocket, take home

pull off *vb* **1** = **remove**, detach, doff, rip off, tear off, wrench off **2** = **succeed**, accomplish, bring off, carry out, crack it *(inf.)*, cut it *(inf.)*, do the trick, manage, score a success, secure one's object

pull out *vb* **2, 3** = **withdraw**, abandon, back off, depart, evacuate, leave, quit, retreat, stop participating

pull through *vb* = **survive**, come through, get better, get over, pull round, rally, recover, turn the corner, weather

pull up *vb* **1** = **uproot**, dig out, lift, raise **3** = **stop**, brake, come to a halt, halt, reach a standstill **4** = **reprimand**, admonish, bawl out *(inf.)*, carpet *(inf.)*, castigate, dress down *(inf.)*, read the riot act, rebuke, reprove, slap on the wrist, take to task, tell off *(inf.)*, tick off *(inf.)*

pulp *n* **1** = **flesh**, marrow, soft part ◆ *modifier* **3b** = **cheap**, lurid, mushy *(inf.)*, rubbishy, sensational, trashy ◆ *n* **5** = **paste**, mash, mush, pap, pomace, semiliquid, semisolid, triturate ◆ *vb* **7** = **crush**, mash, pulverize, squash, triturate

pulpy *adj* **1, 5** = **soft**, fleshy, mushy, pappy, squashy, succulent

pulsate *vb* **1, 3** = **throb**, beat, hammer, oscillate, palpitate, pound, pulse, quiver, thud, thump, tick, vibrate

pulse[1] *n* **1, 3** = **beat**, beating, oscillation, pulsa-

each intermittent explosion of the fuel in the combustion chamber, thus causing a pulsating thrust. Also called: **pulsejet engine, pulsojet.**

pulse modulation *n Electronics.* a type of modulation in which a train of pulses is used as the carrier wave, one or more of its parameters, such as amplitude, being modulated or modified in order to carry information.

pulsimeter (pʌlˈsɪmɪtə) *n Med.* an instrument for measuring the rate of the pulse.

pulverize ❶ *or* **pulverise** (ˈpʌlvəˌraɪz) *vb* **pulverizes, pulverizing, pulverized** *or* **pulverises, pulverising, pulverised. 1** to reduce (a substance) to fine particles, as by grinding, or (of a substance) to be so reduced. **2** *(tr)* to destroy completely. [C16: from LL *pulverizare,* from L *pulvis* dust]
▸ **ˈpulverˌizable** *or* **ˈpulverˌisable** *adj* ▸ **ˌpulveriˈzation** *or* **ˌpulveriˈsation** *n* ▸ **ˈpulverˌizer** *or* **ˈpulverˌiser** *n*

pulverulent (pʌlˈvɛrʊlənt) *adj* consisting of, covered with, or crumbling to dust or fine particles. [C17: from L *pulverulentus,* from *pulvis* dust]

puma (ˈpjuːmə) *n* a large American feline mammal that resembles a lion, having a plain greyish-brown coat and long tail. Also called: **cougar, mountain lion.** [C18: via Sp. from Quechua]

pumice (ˈpʌmɪs) *n* **1** Also called: **pumice stone.** a light porous volcanic rock used for scouring and, in powdered form, as an abrasive and for polishing. ◆ *vb* **pumices, pumicing, pumiced. 2** *(tr)* to rub or polish with pumice. [C15 *pomys,* from OF *pomis,* from L *pūmex*]
▸ **pumiceous** (pjuːˈmɪʃəs) *adj*

pummel ❶ (ˈpʌməl) *vb* **pummels, pummelling, pummelled** *or US* **pummels, pummeling, pummeled.** *(tr)* to strike repeatedly with or as if with the fists. Also (less commonly): **pommel.** [C16: see POMMEL]

pump[1] ❶ (pʌmp) *n* **1** any device for compressing, driving, raising, or reducing the pressure of a fluid, esp. by means of a piston or set of rotating impellers. **2** *Biol.* a mechanism for the active transport of ions, such as protons, calcium ions, and sodium ions, across cell membranes: *a sodium pump.* ◆ *vb* **3** (when *tr,* usually foll. by *from, out,* etc.) to raise or drive (air, liquid, etc., esp. into or from something) with a pump. **4** *(tr;* usually foll. by *in* or *into)* to supply in large amounts: *to pump capital into a project.* **5** *(tr)* to deliver (bullets, etc.) repeatedly. **6** to operate (something, esp. a handle) in the manner of a pump or (of something) to work in this way: *to pump the pedals of a bicycle.* **7** *(tr)* to obtain (information) from (a person) by persistent questioning. **8** *(intr;* usually foll. by *from* or *out of)* (of liquids) to flow freely in large spurts: *oil pumped from the fissure.* **9 pump iron.** *Sl.* to exercise with weights; do body-building exercises. [C15: from MDu. *pumpe* pipe, prob. from Sp. *bomba,* imit.]

pump[2] (pʌmp) *n* **1** a low-cut low-heeled shoe without fastenings, worn esp. for dancing. **2** a type of shoe with a rubber sole, used in games such as tennis; plimsoll. [C16: from ?]

pumpernickel (ˈpʌmpəˌnɪkᵊl) *n* a slightly sour black bread, originating in Germany, made of coarse rye flour. [C18: from G, from ?]

pumpkin (ˈpʌmpkɪn) *n* **1** any of several creeping plants of the genus *Cucurbita.* **2** the large round fruit of any of these plants, which has a thick orange rind, pulpy flesh, and numerous seeds. [C17: from earlier *pumpion,* from OF, from L *pepo,* from Gk, from *peptein* to ripen]

pump priming *n* **1** the process of introducing fluid into a pump to improve starting and to expel air from it. **2** government expenditure designed to stimulate economic activity in stagnant or depressed areas. **3** another term for **deficit financing.**

pun[1] ❶ (pʌn) *n* **1** the use of words to exploit ambiguities and innuendoes for humorous effect; a play on words. An example is: *"Ben Battle was a soldier bold, And used to war's alarms: But a cannonball took off his legs, So he laid down his arms."* (Thomas Hood). ◆ *vb* **puns, punning, punned. 2** *(intr)* to make puns. [C17: ?from It. *puntiglio* wordplay; see PUNCTILIO]

pun[2] (pʌn) *vb* **puns, punning, punned.** *(tr) Brit.* to pack (earth, rubble, etc.) by pounding. [C16: var. of POUND[1]]

puna *Spanish.* (ˈpuna) *n* **1** a high cold dry plateau. **2** another name for **mountain sickness.** [C17: from American Sp., of Amerind origin]

punch[1] ❶ (pʌntʃ) *vb* **1** to strike at, esp. with a clenched fist. **2** *(tr) Western US.* to herd or drive (cattle), esp. for a living. **3** *(tr)* to poke with a stick, etc. ◆ *n* **4** a blow with the fist. **5** *Inf.* point or vigour: *his arguments lacked punch.* [C15: ? var. of *pounce,* from OF *poinçonner* to stamp]
▸ **ˈpuncher** *n*

punch[2] ❶ (pʌntʃ) *n* **1** a tool or machine for piercing holes in a material. **2** a tool or machine used for stamping a design on something or shaping it by impact. **3** the solid die of a punching machine. **4** *Computing.* a device for making holes in a card or paper tape. ◆ *vb* **5** *(tr)* to pierce, cut, stamp, shape, or drive with a punch. [C14: shortened from *puncheon,* from OF *ponçon;* see PUNCHEON[2]]

punch[3] (pʌntʃ) *n* any mixed drink containing fruit juice and, usually, alcoholic liquor, generally hot and spiced. [C17: ?from Hindi *pānch,* from Sansk. *pañca* five; it orig. had five ingredients]

Punch (pʌntʃ) *n* the main character in the traditional children's puppet show **Punch and Judy.**

punchbag (ˈpʌntʃˌbæg) *n* a suspended stuffed bag that is punched for exercise, esp. boxing training. Also called (US and Canad.): **punching bag.**

punchball (ˈpʌntʃˌbɔːl) *n* **1** a stuffed or inflated ball, supported by a flexible rod, that is punched for exercise, esp. boxing training. **2** *US.* a game resembling baseball.

punchbowl (ˈpʌntʃˌbəʊl) *n* **1** a large bowl for serving punch, often having small drinking glasses hooked around the rim. **2** *Brit.* a bowl-shaped depression in the land.

punch-drunk ❶ *adj* **1** demonstrating or characteristic of the behaviour of a person who has suffered repeated blows to the head, esp. a professional boxer. **2** dazed; stupefied.

punched card *or esp. US* **punch card** *n* a card on which data can be coded in the form of punched holes, formerly used in computing.

punched tape *or US (sometimes)* **perforated tape** *n* other terms for **paper tape.**

puncheon[1] (ˈpʌntʃən) *n* a large cask of variable capacity, usually between 70 and 120 gallons. [C15 *poncion,* from OF *ponchon,* from ?]

puncheon[2] (ˈpʌntʃən) *n* **1** a short wooden post used as a vertical strut. **2** a less common name for **punch[2]** (sense 1). [C14 *ponson,* from OF *ponçon,* from L *punctiō* a puncture, from *pungere* to prick]

Punchinello (ˌpʌntʃɪˈnɛləʊ) *n, pl* **Punchinellos** *or* **Punchinelloes. 1** a clown from Italian puppet shows, the prototype of Punch. **2** *(sometimes not cap.)* any grotesque or absurd character. [C17: from earlier *Polichinello,* from It. *Polecenella,* from *pulcino* chicken, ult. from L *pullus* young animal]

punch line *n* the culminating part of a joke, funny story, etc., that gives it its point.

punch-up ❶ *n Brit. inf.* a fight or brawl.

punchy ❶ (ˈpʌntʃɪ) *adj* **punchier, punchiest. 1** an informal word for **punch-drunk. 2** *Inf.* incisive or forceful.
▸ **ˈpunchily** *adv* ▸ **ˈpunchiness** *n*

punctate (ˈpʌŋkteɪt) *adj* having or marked with minute spots or depressions. [C18: from NL *punctātus,* from L *punctum* a point]
▸ **puncˈtation** *n*

punctilio (pʌŋkˈtɪlɪˌəʊ) *n, pl* **punctilios. 1** strict attention to minute points of etiquette. **2** a petty formality or fine point of etiquette. [C16: from It. *puntiglio* small point, from L *punctum* point]

punctilious ❶ (pʌŋkˈtɪlɪəs) *adj* **1** paying scrupulous attention to correctness in etiquette. **2** attentive to detail.
▸ **puncˈtiliously** *adv* ▸ **puncˈtiliousness** *n*

punctual ❶ (ˈpʌŋktjʊəl) *adj* **1** arriving or taking place at an arranged time. **2** (of a person) having the characteristic of always keeping to arranged times. **3** *Obs.* precise; exact. **4** *Maths.* consisting of or confined to a point. [C14: from Med. L *punctuālis* concerning detail, from L *punctum* point]
▸ **ˌpunctuˈality** *n* ▸ **ˈpunctually** *adv*

punctuate ❶ (ˈpʌŋktjʊˌeɪt) *vb* **punctuates, punctuating, punctuated.** *(mainly tr)* **1** *(also intr)* to insert punctuation marks into (a written text). **2** to interrupt or insert at frequent intervals: *a meeting punctuated by heckling.* **3** to give emphasis to. [C17: from Med. L *punctuāre* to prick, from L, from *pungere* to puncture]

punctuation (ˌpʌŋktjʊˈeɪʃən) *n* **1** the use of symbols not belonging to the alphabet of a writing system to indicate aspects of the intonation and meaning not otherwise conveyed in the written language. **2** the symbols used for this purpose.

THESAURUS

tion, rhythm, stroke, throb, throbbing, vibration ◆ *vb* **7** = **beat,** pulsate, throb, tick, vibrate

pulverize *vb* **1** = **crush,** bray, comminute, granulate, grind, levigate *(Chemistry),* mill, pestle, pound, triturate **2** = **defeat,** annihilate, crush, demolish, destroy, flatten, lick *(inf.),* smash, stuff *(sl.),* tank *(sl.),* vanquish, wreck

pummel *vb* = **beat,** bang, batter, belt *(inf.),* clobber *(sl.),* hammer, knock, lambast(e), pound, punch, rain blows upon, strike, thump

pump[1] *vb* **3** *usually foll. by* **from, out** *etc.* = **drive out,** bail out, drain, draw off, empty, force out, siphon **3** *foll. by* **up** = **inflate,** blow up, dilate **4** *often with* **into** = **drive,** force, inject, pour, push, send, supply **7** = **interrogate,** cross-examine, give (someone) the third degree, grill *(inf.),* probe, question closely, quiz, worm out of

pun[1] *n* **1** = **play on words,** double entendre, equivoque, paronomasia *(Rhetoric),* quip, witticism

punch[1] *vb* **1** = **hit,** bash *(inf.),* belt *(inf.),* biff, bop *(inf.),* box, clout *(inf.),* plug *(sl.),* pummel, slam, slug, smash, sock *(sl.),* strike, swipe *(inf.),* wallop *(inf.)* ◆ *n* **4** = **blow,** bash *(inf.),* biff *(sl.),* bop *(inf.),* clout *(inf.),* hit, jab, knock, plug *(sl.),* sock *(sl.),* swipe *(inf.),* thump, wallop *(inf.)* **5** *Informal* = **effectiveness,** bite, drive, force, forcefulness, impact, point, verve, vigour

punch[2] *vb* **5** = **pierce,** bore, cut, drill, perforate, pink, prick, puncture, stamp

punch-drunk *adj* **1, 2** = **dazed,** befuddled, confused, groggy *(inf.),* in a daze, knocked silly, punchy *(inf.),* reeling, slaphappy *(inf.),* staggering, stupefied, unsteady, woozy *(inf.)*

punch-up *n Brit. informal* = **fight,** argument, battle royal, brawl, dust-up *(inf.),* free-for-all *(inf.),* row, scrap *(inf.),* set-to *(inf.),* shindig *(inf.),* shindy *(inf.),* stand-up fight *(inf.)*

punchy *adj* **2** *Informal* = **effective,** aggressive, dynamic, forceful, incisive, in-your-face *(sl.),* lively, spirited, storming *(inf.),* vigorous

punctilious *adj* **1, 2** = **particular,** careful, ceremonious, conscientious, exact, finicky, formal, fussy, meticulous, nice, precise, proper, scrupulous, strict

punctual *adj* **1** = **on time,** early, exact, in good time, on the dot, precise, prompt, seasonable, strict, timely
Antonyms *adj* behind, behindhand, belated, delayed, late, overdue, tardy, unpunctual

punctuality *n* **1** = **promptness,** promptitude, readiness, regularity

punctuate *vb* **2** = **interrupt,** break, interject, intersperse, pepper, sprinkle **3** = **emphasize,** ac-

punctuation mark *n* any of the signs used in punctuation, such as a comma.

puncture Ⓣ ('pʌŋktʃə) *n* **1** a small hole made by a sharp object. **2** a perforation and loss of pressure in a pneumatic tyre. **3** the act of puncturing or perforating. ◆ *vb* **punctures, puncturing, punctured. 4** (*tr*) to pierce a hole in (something) with a sharp object. **5** to cause (something pressurized, esp. a tyre) to lose pressure by piercing, or (of a tyre, etc.) to collapse in this way. **6** (*tr*) to depreciate (a person's self-esteem, pomposity, etc.). [C14: from L *punctūra*, from *pungere* to prick]

pundit Ⓣ ('pʌndɪt) *n* **1** an expert. **2** (formerly) a learned person. **3** Also: **pandit.** a Brahman learned in Sanskrit, Hindu religion, philosophy or law. [C17: from Hindi *pandit*, from Sansk. *pandita* learned man]

punga ('pʌŋə) *n* a variant spelling of **ponga.**

pungent Ⓣ ('pʌndʒənt) *adj* **1** having an acrid smell or sharp bitter flavour. **2** (of wit, satire, etc.) biting; caustic. **3** *Biol.* ending in a sharp point. [C16: from L *pungens* piercing, from *pungere* to prick]
▸ **'pungency** *n* ▸ **'pungently** *adv*

Punic ('pju:nɪk) *adj* **1** of or relating to ancient Carthage or the Carthaginians. **2** treacherous; faithless. ◆ *n* **3** the language of the Carthaginians; a late form of Phoenician. [C15: from L *Pūnicus*, var. of *Poenicus* Carthaginian, from Gk *Phoinix*]

punish Ⓣ ('pʌnɪʃ) *vb* **1** to force (someone) to undergo a penalty for some crime or misdemeanour. **2** (*tr*) to inflict punishment for (some crime, etc.). **3** (*tr*) to treat harshly, esp. as by overexertion: *to punish a horse.* **4** (*tr*) *Inf.* to consume in large quantities: *to punish the bottle.* [C14 *punisse*, from OF *punir*, from L *pūnīre* to punish, from *poena* penalty]
▸ **'punishable** *adj* ▸ **'punisher** *n* ▸ **'punishing** *adj*

punishment Ⓣ ('pʌnɪʃmənt) *n* **1** a penalty for a crime or offence. **2** the act of punishing or state of being punished. **3** *Inf.* rough treatment.

punitive Ⓣ ('pju:nɪtɪv) *adj* relating to, involving, or with the intention of inflicting punishment: *a punitive expedition.* [C17: from Med. L *pūnītīvus* concerning punishment, from L *pūnīre* to punish]
▸ **'punitively** *adv*

Punjabi (pʌn'dʒa:bɪ) *n* **1** (*pl* **Punjabis**) a member of the chief people of the Punjab, in NW India. **2** the language of the Punjab, belonging to the Indic branch of the Indo-European family. ◆ *adj* **3** of the Punjab, its people, or their language.

punk[1] (pʌŋk) *n* **1** a youth movement of the late 1970s, characterized by anti-Establishment slogans and outrageous clothes and hairstyles. **2** an inferior, rotten, or worthless person or thing. **3** worthless articles collectively. **4** short for **punk rock. 5** *Obs.* a young male homosexual; catamite. **6** *Obs.* a prostitute. ◆ *adj* **7** rotten or worthless. [C16: from ?]

punk[2] (pʌŋk) *n* dried decayed wood or other substance that smoulders when ignited: used as tinder. [C18: from ?]

punka *or* **punkah** ('pʌŋkə) *n* **1** a fan made of a palm leaf or leaves. **2** a large fan made of palm leaves, etc., worked mechanically to cool a room. [C17: from Hindi *pankhā*, from Sansk. *paksaka* fan, from *paksa* wing]

punk rock *n* a fast abrasive style of rock music of the late 1970s, characterized by aggressive lyrics and performance, usually expressing rage and frustration.
▸ **punk rocker** *n*

punnet ('pʌnɪt) *n* *Chiefly Brit.* a small basket for fruit. [C19: ? dim. of dialect *pun* POUND[2]]

punster ('pʌnstə) *n* a person who is fond of making puns, esp. one who makes a tedious habit of this.

punt[1] (pʌnt) *n* **1** an open flat-bottomed boat with square ends, propelled by a pole. ◆ *vb* **2** to propel (a boat, esp. a punt) by pushing with a pole on the bottom of a river, etc. [OE *punt* shallow boat, from L *pontō* punt]

punt[2] (pʌnt) *n* **1** a kick in certain sports, such as rugby, in which the ball is released and kicked before it hits the ground. **2** any long high kick. ◆ *vb* **3** to kick (a ball, etc.) using a punt. [C19: ? var. of dialect *bunt* to push]

punt[3] Ⓣ (pʌnt) *Chiefly Brit.* ◆ *vb* **1** (*intr*) to gamble; bet. ◆ *n* **2** a gamble or bet, esp. against the bank, as in roulette, or on horses. **3** Also called: **punter.** a person who bets. **4 take a punt at.** *Austral. & NZ inf.* to make an attempt at. [C18: from F *ponter* to punt, from *ponte* bet laid against the banker, from Sp. *punto* point, from L *punctum*]

punt[4] (punt) *n* the Irish pound. [Irish Gaelic: pound]

punter[1] ('pʌntə) *n* a person who punts a boat.

punter[2] ('pʌntə) *n* a person who kicks a ball.

punter[3] Ⓣ ('pʌntə) *n* **1** a person who gambles or bets. **2** *Sl.* any client or customer, esp. a prostitute's client. **3** *Sl.* a victim of a con man.

puny Ⓣ ('pju:nɪ) *adj* **punier, puniest. 1** small and weakly. **2** paltry; insignificant. [C16: from OF *puisne* PUISNE]
▸ **'puniness** *n*

pup Ⓣ (pʌp) *n* **1a** a young dog; puppy. **1b** the young of various other animals, such as the seal. **2 in pup.** (of a bitch) pregnant. **3** *Inf., chiefly Brit.* a conceited young man (esp. in **young pup**). **4 sell (someone) a pup.** to swindle (someone) by selling him something worthless. ◆ *vb* **pups, pupping, pupped. 5** (of dogs, seals, etc.) to give birth to (young). [C18: back formation from PUPPY]

pupa ('pju:pə) *n, pl* **pupae** (-pi:) *or* **pupas.** an insect at the immobile nonfeeding stage of development between larva and adult, when many internal changes occur. [C19: via NL, from L: a doll]
▸ **'pupal** *adj*

pupate (pju:'peɪt) *vb* **pupates, pupating, pupated.** (*intr*) (of an insect larva) to develop into a pupa.
▸ **pu'pation** *n*

pupil[1] Ⓣ ('pju:p^{ə}l) *n* **1** a student who is taught by a teacher. **2** *Civil & Scots Law.* a boy under 14 or a girl under 12 who is in the care of a guardian. [C14: from L *pupillus* an orphan, from *pūpus* a child]
▸ **'pupillage** *or US* **'pupilage** *n* ▸ **'pupillary** *or* **'pupilary** *adj*

pupil[2] ('pju:p^{ə}l) *n* the dark circular aperture at the centre of the iris of the eye, through which light enters. [C16: from L *pūpilla*, dim. of *pūpa* doll; from the tiny reflections in the eye]
▸ **'pupillary** *or* **'pupilary** *adj*

pupiparous (pju:'pɪpərəs) *adj* (of certain dipterous flies) producing young that have already reached the pupa stage at the time of hatching. [C19: from NL *pupiparus*, from PUPA + *parere* to bring forth]

puppet Ⓣ ('pʌpɪt) *n* **1a** a small doll or figure moved by strings attached to its limbs or by the hand inserted in its cloth body. **1b** (*as modifier*): *a puppet theatre.* **2a** a person, state, etc., that appears independent but is controlled by another. **2b** (*as modifier*): *a puppet government.* [C16 *popet*, ?from OF *poupette* little doll, ult. from L *pūpa* doll]

puppeteer (ˌpʌpɪ'tɪə) *n* a person who manipulates puppets.

puppetry ('pʌpɪtrɪ) *n* **1** the art of making and manipulating puppets and presenting puppet shows. **2** unconvincing or specious presentation.

puppy ('pʌpɪ) *n, pl* **puppies. 1** a young dog; pup. **2** *Inf., contemptuous.* a brash or conceited young man; pup. [C15 *popi*, from OF *popée* doll]
▸ **'puppyhood** *n* ▸ **'puppyish** *adj*

puppy fat *n* fatty tissue that develops in childhood or adolesence and usually disappears with maturity.

puppy love *n* another term for **calf love.**

Purana (pu'ra:nə) *n* any of a class of Sanskrit writings not included in the Vedas, characteristically recounting the birth and deeds of Hindu gods and the creation of the universe. [C17: from Sansk.: ancient, from *purā* formerly]

Purbeck marble *or* **stone** ('pɜ:bɛk) *n* a fossil-rich limestone that takes a high polish. [C15: after *Purbeck*, Dorset, where quarried]

purblind ('pɜ:ˌblaɪnd) *adj* **1** partly or nearly blind. **2** lacking in insight or understanding; obtuse. [C13: see PURE, BLIND]

purchase Ⓣ ('pɜ:tʃɪs) *vb* **purchases, purchasing, purchased.** (*tr*) **1** to obtain

THESAURUS

centuate, lay stress on, mark, point up, stress, underline

puncture *n* **1** = **hole**, break, cut, damage, leak, nick, opening, perforation, rupture, slit **2** = **flat tyre**, flat ◆ *vb* **4** = **pierce**, bore, cut, impale, nick, penetrate, perforate, prick, rupture **5** = **deflate**, go down, go flat **6** = **humble**, deflate, discourage, disillusion, flatten, take down a peg (*inf.*)

pundit *n* **1** = **expert**, buff (*inf.*), guru, maestro, one of the cognoscenti, (self-appointed) expert *or* authority

pungent *adj* **1** = **strong**, acid, acrid, aromatic, bitter, highly flavoured, hot, peppery, piquant, seasoned, sharp, sour, spicy, stinging, tangy, tart **2** = **cutting**, acrimonious, acute, barbed, biting, caustic, incisive, keen, mordacious, mordant, penetrating, piercing, poignant, pointed, sarcastic, scathing, sharp, stinging, stringent, telling, trenchant, vitriolic
Antonyms *adj* ≠ **strong:** bland, dull, mild, moderate, tasteless, unsavoury, unstimulating, weak ≠ **cutting:** dull, inane

punish *vb* **1, 2** = **discipline**, beat, bring to book, cane, castigate, chasten, chastise, correct, flog, give a lesson to, give (someone) the works (*sl.*), lash, penalize, rap someone's knuckles, scourge, sentence, slap someone's wrist, throw the book at, whip **3** = **mistreat**, abuse, batter, give (someone) a going-over (*inf.*), harm, hurt, injure, knock about, manhandle, misuse, oppress, rough up

punishable *adj* **1** = **culpable**, blameworthy, chargeable, convictable, criminal, indictable

punishing *adj* **3** = **hard**, arduous, backbreaking, burdensome, demanding, exhausting, grinding, gruelling, strenuous, taxing, tiring, uphill, wearing
Antonyms *adj* cushy (*inf.*), easy, effortless, light, simple, undemanding, unexacting, untaxing

punishment *n* **1, 2** = **penalty**, chastening, chastisement, comeuppance (*sl.*), correction, discipline, just deserts, penance, punitive measures, retribution, sanction, what for (*inf.*) **3** *Informal* = **rough treatment**, abuse, beating, hard work, maltreatment, manhandling, pain, slave labour, torture, victimization

punitive *adj* = **retaliatory**, in reprisal, in retaliation, punitory, retaliative, revengeful, vindictive

punt[3] *vb* **1** = **bet**, back, gamble, lay, stake, wager ◆ *n* **2** = **bet**, gamble, stake, wager

punter[3] *n* **1** = **gambler**, backer, better, punt (*chiefly Brit.*) **2** *Slang* = **customer**, client

puny *adj* **1** = **feeble**, diminutive, dwarfish, frail, little, pint-sized (*inf.*), pygmy *or* pigmy, sickly, stunted, tiny, underfed, undersized, undeveloped, weak, weakly **2** = **insignificant**, inconsequential, inferior, minor, paltry, petty, piddling (*inf.*), trifling, trivial, worthless
Antonyms *adj* ≠ **feeble:** brawny, burly, healthy, hefty (*inf.*), husky (*inf.*), powerful, robust, strong, sturdy, well-built, well-developed

pup *n* **3** *Informal, chiefly Brit.* = **whippersnapper**, braggart, jackanapes, popinjay, whelp

pupil[1] *n* **1** = **learner**, beginner, catechumen, disciple, neophyte, novice, scholar, schoolboy *or* schoolgirl, student, trainee, tyro
Antonyms *n* coach, guru, instructor, master *or* mistress, schoolmaster *or* schoolmistress, schoolteacher, teacher, trainer, tutor

puppet *n* **1** = **marionette**, doll **2** = **pawn**, cat's-paw, creature, dupe, figurehead, gull (*arch.*), instrument, mouthpiece, stooge, tool

purchasable *adj* **1** = **for sale**, available, in stock, obtainable, on sale, on the market, to be had

purchase *vb* **1** = **buy**, acquire, come by, gain,

(goods, etc.) by payment. **2** to obtain by effort, sacrifice, etc.: *to purchase one's freedom.* **3** to draw or lift (a load) with mechanical apparatus. ◆ *n* **4** something that is purchased. **5** the act of buying. **6** acquisition of an estate by any lawful means other than inheritance. **7** the mechanical advantage achieved by a lever. **8** a firm foothold, grasp, etc., as for climbing something. [C13: from OF *porchacier* to strive to obtain; see CHASE[1]]
▸**'purchasable** *adj* ▸**'purchaser** *n*

purchase tax *n* (in Britain, formerly) a tax levied on nonessential consumer goods and added to selling prices by retailers.

purdah ('pɜːdə) *n* **1** the custom in some Muslim and Hindu communities of keeping women in seclusion, with clothing that conceals them completely when they go out. **2** a screen in a Hindu house used to keep the women out of view. [C19: from Hindi *parda* veil, from Persian *pardah*]

pure ❶ (pjʊə) *adj* **1** not mixed with any extraneous or dissimilar materials, elements, etc. **2** free from tainting or polluting matter: *pure water.* **3** free from moral taint or defilement: *pure love.* **4** (*prenominal*) (intensifier): *a pure coincidence.* **5** (of a subject, etc.) studied in its theoretical aspects rather than for its practical applications: *pure mathematics.* **6** (of a vowel) pronounced with more or less unvarying quality without any glide. **7** (of a consonant) not accompanied by another consonant. **8** of unmixed descent. **9** *Genetics, biol.* breeding true; homozygous. [C13: from OF *pur*, from L *pūrus* unstained]
▸**'purely** *adv* ▸**'pureness** *n*

purebred ❶ *adj* ('pjʊə'brɛd). **1** denoting a pure strain obtained through many generations of controlled breeding. ◆ *n* ('pjʊəˌbrɛd). **2** a purebred animal.

purée ('pjʊəreɪ) *n* **1** a smooth thick pulp of sieved fruit, vegetables, meat, or fish. ◆ *vb* **purées, puréeing, puréed. 2** (*tr*) to make (cooked foods) into a purée. [C19: from F *purer* to PURIFY]

purfle ('pɜːfᵊl) *n also* **purfling. 1** a ruffled or curved ornamental band, as on clothing, furniture, etc. ◆ *vb* **purfles, purfling, purfled. 2** (*tr*) to decorate with such a band. [C14: from OF *purfiler* to decorate with a border, from *fil* thread, from L *filum*]

purgation (pɜːˈgeɪʃən) *n* the act of purging or state of being purged; purification.

purgative ❶ ('pɜːgətɪv) *Med.* ◆ *n* **1** a drug or agent for purging the bowels. ◆ *adj* **2** causing evacuation of the bowels.
▸**'purgatively** *adv*

purgatory ❶ ('pɜːgətərɪ, -trɪ) *n* **1** *Chiefly RC Church.* a state or place in which the souls of those who have died in a state of grace are believed to undergo a limited amount of suffering to expiate their venial sins. **2** a place or condition of suffering or torment, esp. one that is temporary. [C13: from OF *purgatoire*, from Med. L *pūrgātōrium*, lit.: place of cleansing, from L *pūrgāre* to purge]
▸ˌ**purga'torial** *adj*

purge ❶ (pɜːdʒ) *vb* **purges, purging, purged. 1** (*tr*) to rid (something) of (impure elements). **2** (*tr*) to rid (a state, political party, etc.) of (dissident people). **3** (*tr*) **3a** to empty (the bowels) by evacuation of faeces. **3b** to cause (a person) to evacuate his bowels. **4a** to clear (a person) of a charge. **4b** to free (oneself) of guilt, as by atonement. **5** (*intr*) to be purified. ◆ *n* **6** the act or process of purging. **7** the elimination of opponents or dissidents from a state, political party, etc. **8** a purgative drug or agent. [C14: from OF *purger*, from L *pūrgāre* to purify]

purificator ('pjʊərɪfɪˌkeɪtə) *n Christianity.* a small white linen cloth used to wipe the chalice and paten at the Eucharist.

purify ❶ ('pjʊərɪˌfaɪ) *vb* **purifies, purifying, purified. 1** to free (something) of contaminating or debasing matter. **2** (*tr*) to free (a person, etc.) from sin or guilt. **3** (*tr*) to make clean, as in a ritual. [C14: from OF *purifier*, from LL *pūrificāre* to cleanse, from *pūrus* pure + *facere* to make]
▸ˌ**purifi'cation** *n* ▸**purificatory** ('pjʊərɪfɪˌkeɪtərɪ, -trɪ) *adj* ▸**'puriˌfier** *n*

Purim ('pʊərɪm; *Hebrew* puːˈriːm) *n* a Jewish holiday in February or March to commemorate the deliverance of the Jews from the massacre planned by Haman (Esther 9). [Heb. *pūrīm*, pl. of *pūr* lot; from the casting of lots by Haman]

purine ('pjʊəriːn) *or* **purin** ('pjʊərɪn) *n* **1** a colourless crystalline solid that can be prepared from uric acid. Formula: $C_5H_5N_4$. **2** Also called: **purine base.** any of a number of nitrogenous bases that are derivatives of purine. [C19: from G *Purin*]

puriri (puːˈriːriː) *n* a New Zealand tree with hard timber and red berries. [from Maori]

purism ❶ ('pjʊəˌrɪzəm) *n* insistence on traditional canons of correctness of form or purity of style or content.
▸**'purist** *adj, n* ▸**pu'ristic** *adj*

puritan ❶ ('pjʊərɪtᵊn) *n* **1** a person who adheres to strict moral or religious principles, esp. one opposed to luxury and sensual enjoyment. ◆ *adj* **2** characteristic of a puritan. [C16: from LL *pūritās* purity]
▸**'puritanˌism** *n*

Puritan ('pjʊərɪtᵊn) (in the late 16th and 17th centuries) ◆ *n* **1** any of the extreme English Protestants who wished to purify the Church of England of most of its ceremony and other aspects that they deemed to be Catholic. ◆ *adj* **2** of or relating to the Puritans.
▸**'Puritanˌism** *n*

puritanical ❶ (ˌpjʊərɪˈtænɪkᵊl) *adj* **1** *Usually disparaging.* strict in moral or religious outlook, esp. in shunning sensual pleasures. **2** (*sometimes cap.*) of or relating to a puritan or the Puritans.
▸ˌ**puri'tanically** *adv*

purity ❶ ('pjʊərɪtɪ) *n* the state or quality of being pure.

purl[1] (pɜːl) *n* **1** a knitting stitch made by doing a plain stitch backwards. **2** a decorative border, as of lace. **3** gold or silver wire thread. ◆ *vb* **4** to knit in purl stitch. **5** to edge (something) with a purl. ◆ Also (for senses 2, 3, 5): **pearl.** [C16: from dialect *pirl* to twist into a cord]

purl[2] (pɜːl) *vb* **1** (*intr*) (of a stream, etc.) to flow with a gentle swirling or rippling movement and a murmuring sound. ◆ *n* **2** a swirling movement of water; eddy. **3** a murmuring sound, as of a shallow stream. [C16: rel. to Norwegian *purla* to bubble]

purler[1] ('pɜːlə) *n Inf.* a headlong or spectacular fall (esp. in **come a purler**).

purler[2] ('pɜːlə) *n Austral. sl.* something outstanding in its class. [from ?]

purlieu ❶ ('pɜːljuː) *n* **1** *English history.* land on the edge of a forest once included within the bounds of the royal forest but later separated although still subject to some of the forest laws. **2** (*usually pl*) a neighbouring area; outskirts. **3** (*often pl*) a place one frequents; haunt. [C15 *purlewe*, from Anglo-F *puralé* a going through (infl. also by OF *lieu* place), from OF *puraler*, from *pur* through + *aler* to go]

purlin *or* **purline** ('pɜːlɪn) *n* a horizontal beam that supports the common rafters of a roof and is carried by the principal rafters or trusses. [C15: from ?]

purloin ❶ (pɜːˈlɔɪn) *vb* to steal. [C15: from OF *porloigner* to put at a distance, from *por-* for + *loin* distant, from L *longus* long]
▸**pur'loiner** *n*

THESAURUS

get, get hold of, invest in, make a purchase, obtain, pay for, pick up, procure, score (*sl.*), secure, shop for **2** = **achieve**, attain, earn, gain, realize, win ◆ *n* **4** = **buy**, acquisition, asset, gain, investment, possession, property **7, 8** = **grip**, advantage, edge, foothold, footing, grasp, hold, influence, lever, leverage, support, toehold
Antonyms *vb* ≠ **buy:** hawk, market, merchandise, peddle, retail, sell, trade in, vend

purchaser *n* **1** = **buyer**, consumer, customer, vendee (*Law*)
Antonyms *n* dealer, merchant, retailer, salesman *or* saleswoman, salesperson, seller, shopkeeper, tradesman, vendor

pure *adj* **1** = **unmixed**, authentic, clear, flawless, genuine, natural, neat, perfect, real, simple, straight, true, unalloyed **2** = **clean**, disinfected, germ-free, immaculate, pasteurized, sanitary, spotless, squeaky-clean, sterile, sterilized, unadulterated, unblemished, uncontaminated, unpolluted, untainted, wholesome **3** = **innocent**, blameless, chaste, guileless, honest, immaculate, impeccable, maidenly, modest, squeaky-clean, true, uncorrupted, undefiled, unspotted, unstained, unsullied, upright, virgin, virginal, virtuous **4** = **complete**, absolute, mere, outright, sheer, thorough, unmitigated, unqualified, utter **5** = **theoretical**, abstract, academic, philosophical, speculative
Antonyms *adj* ≠ **unmixed:** adulterated, alloyed, flawed, imperfect, mixed ≠ **clean:** contaminated, dirty, filthy, impure, infected, polluted, tainted ≠ **innocent:** contaminated, corrupt, defiled, guilty, immodest, immoral, impure, indecent, obscene, sinful, spoiled, unchaste, unclean, untrue ≠ **complete:** qualified ≠ **theoretical:** applied, practical

purebred *adj* **1** = **thoroughbred**, blood, full-blooded, pedigree

purely *adv* **4** = **absolutely**, completely, entirely, exclusively, just, merely, only, plainly, simply, solely, totally, wholly

purgative *n* **1** = **purge**, aperient, cathartic, depurative, emetic, enema, evacuant, laxative, physic (*rare*) ◆ *adj* **2** = **purging**, aperient (*Medical*), cleansing, depurative, evacuant, laxative

purgatory *n* **2** = **torment**, agony, hell (*inf.*), hell on earth, misery, murder (*inf.*), the rack, torture

purge *vb* **1** = **cleanse**, clean out, clear, expiate, purify, wash **2** = **get rid of**, dismiss, do away with, eject, eradicate, expel, exterminate, kill, liquidate, oust, remove, rid of, rout out, sweep out, wipe out **4** = **absolve**, exonerate, forgive, pardon ◆ *n* **7** = **removal**, cleanup, crushing, ejection, elimination, eradication, expulsion, liquidation, reign of terror, suppression, witch hunt **8** = **purgative** (*Medical*), aperient (*Medical*), cathartic, dose of salts, emetic, enema, laxative, physic (*rare*)

purify *vb* **1** = **clean**, clarify, cleanse, decontaminate, disinfect, filter, fumigate, refine, sanitize, wash **2** = **absolve**, cleanse, exculpate, exonerate, lustrate, redeem, sanctify, shrive
Antonyms *vb* ≠ **clean:** adulterate, befoul, contaminate, corrupt, defile, foul, infect, pollute, soil, taint ≠ **absolve:** stain, sully, taint, vitiate

purist *n* = **stickler**, classicist, formalist, pedant, precisian

puritan *n* **1** = **moralist**, fanatic, pietist, prude, rigorist, zealot ◆ *adj* **2** = **strict**, ascetic, austere, hidebound, intolerant, moralistic, narrow, narrow-minded, prudish, puritanical, severe, strait-laced

puritanical *adj* **1** = **strict**, ascetic, austere, bigoted, disapproving, fanatical, forbidding, narrow, narrow-minded, prim, proper, prudish, puritan, rigid, severe, stiff, strait-laced, stuffy
Antonyms *adj* broad-minded, hedonistic, indulgent, latitudinarian, liberal, permissive, tolerant

puritanism *n* **2** = **strictness**, asceticism, austerity, fanaticism, moralism, narrowness, piety, piousness, prudishness, rigidity, rigorism, severity, zeal

purity *n* = **cleanness**, brilliance, clarity, cleanliness, clearness, faultlessness, fineness, genuineness, immaculateness, pureness, untaintedness, wholesomeness = **innocence**, blamelessness, chasteness, chastity, decency, guilelessness, honesty, integrity, piety, rectitude, sincerity, virginity, virtue, virtuousness
Antonyms *n* ≠ **cleanness:** cloudiness, contamination, impurity ≠ **innocence:** immodesty, immorality, impurity, unchasteness, vice, wickedness

purlieu *n* **2** *usually plural* = **outskirts**, borders, confines, environs, fringes, limits, neighbourhood, periphery, precincts, suburbs, vicinity **3** *often plural* = **stamping ground**, hang-out (*inf.*), haunt, patch, resort, territory

purloin *vb* = **steal**, appropriate, blag (*sl.*), filch,

purple ('pɜːpəl) *n* **1** a colour between red and blue. **2** a dye or pigment producing such a colour. **3** cloth of this colour, often used to symbolize royalty or nobility. **4** (usually preceded by *the*) high rank; nobility. **5a** the official robe of a cardinal. **5b** the rank of a cardinal as signified by this. ◆ *adj* **6** of the colour purple. **7** (of writing) excessively elaborate or full of imagery: *purple prose.* [OE, from L *purpura* purple dye, from Gk *porphura* the purple fish (murex)]
▸**'purpleness** *n* ▸**'purplish** *or* **'purply** *adj*

purple heart *n* **1** any of several tropical American trees. **2** *Inf., chiefly Brit.* a heart-shaped purple tablet consisting mainly of amphetamine.

Purple Heart *n* a decoration awarded to members of the US Armed Forces for a wound received in action.

purple patch *n* **1** Also called: **purple passage.** a section in a piece of writing characterized by fanciful or ornate language. **2** *Sl.* a period of good fortune.

purport Ⓣ *vb* (pɜː'pɔːt). (*tr*) **1** to claim to be (true, official, etc.) by manner or appearance, esp. falsely. **2** (esp. of speech or writing) to signify or imply. ◆ *n* ('pɜːpɔːt). **3** meaning; significance. **4** object; intention. [C15: from Anglo-F: contents, from OF *porporter* to convey, from L *portāre*]

purpose Ⓣ ('pɜːpəs) *n* **1** the reason for which anything is done, created, or exists. **2** a fixed design or idea that is the object of an action or other effort. **3** determination: *a man of purpose.* **4** practical advantage or use: *to work to good purpose.* **5** that which is relevant (esp. in **to** *or* **from the purpose**). **6** *Arch.* purport. **7 on purpose.** intentionally. ◆ *vb* **purposes, purposing, purposed. 8** (*tr*) to intend or determine to do (something). [C13: from OF *porpos*, from *porposer* to plan, from L *prōpōnere* to PROPOSE]
▸**'purposeless** *adj*

purpose-built *adj* made to serve a specific purpose.

purposeful Ⓣ ('pɜːpəsful) *adj* **1** having a definite purpose in view. **2** determined.
▸**'purposefully** *adv* ▸**'purposefulness** *n*

> **USAGE NOTE** *Purposefully* is sometimes wrongly used where *purposely* is meant: *he had purposely* (not *purposefully*) *left the door unlocked.*

purposely Ⓣ ('pɜːpəslɪ) *adv* on purpose.

> **USAGE NOTE** See at **purposeful.**

purposive ('pɜːpəsɪv) *adj* **1** having or indicating conscious intention. **2** serving a purpose; useful.
▸**'purposively** *adv* ▸**'purposiveness** *n*

purpura ('pɜːpjurə) *n Pathol.* any of several blood diseases causing purplish spots on the skin due to subcutaneous bleeding. [C18: via L from Gk *porphura* a shellfish yielding purple dye]

purr (pɜː) *vb* **1** (*intr*) (esp. of cats) to make a low vibrant sound, usually considered as expressing pleasure, etc. **2** (*tr*) to express (pleasure, etc.) by this sound or by a sound suggestive of purring. ◆ *n* **3** a purring sound. [C17: imit.]

purse Ⓣ (pɜːs) *n* **1** a small bag or pouch for carrying money, esp. coins. **2** *US & Canad.* a woman's handbag. **3** anything resembling a small bag or pouch in form or function. **4** wealth; funds; resources. **5** a sum of money that is offered, esp. as a prize. ◆ *vb* **purses, pursing, pursed. 6** (*tr*) to contract (the mouth, lips, etc.) into a small rounded shape. [OE *purs*, prob. from LL *bursa* bag, ult. from Gk: leather]

purser ('pɜːsə) *n* an officer aboard a ship or aircraft who keeps the accounts and attends to the welfare of the passengers.

purse seine *n* a large net that encloses fish and is then closed at the bottom by means of a line resembling the string formerly used to draw shut the neck of a money pouch.

purse strings *pl n* control of expenditure (esp. in **hold** *or* **control the purse strings**).

purslane ('pɜːslɪn) *n* a plant with fleshy leaves used (esp. formerly) in salads and as a potherb. [C14 *purcelane*, from OF *porcelaine*, from LL, from L *porcillāca*, var. of *portulāca*]

pursuance Ⓣ (pə'sjuːəns) *n* the carrying out or pursuing of an action, plan, etc.

pursuant (pə'sjuːənt) *adj* **1** (*usually postpositive;* often foll. by *to*) *Chiefly law.* in agreement or conformity. **2** *Arch.* pursuing. [C17: rel. to ME *poursuivant* following after, from OF; see PURSUE]
▸**pur'suantly** *adv*

pursue Ⓣ (pə'sjuː) *vb* **pursues, pursuing, pursued.** (*mainly tr*) **1** (*also intr*) to follow (a fugitive, etc.) in order to capture or overtake. **2** to follow closely or accompany: *ill health pursued her.* **3** to seek or strive to attain (some desire, etc.). **4** to follow the precepts of (a plan, policy, etc.). **5** to apply oneself to (studies, interests, etc.). **6** to follow persistently or seek to become acquainted with. **7** to continue to discuss or argue (a point, subject, etc.). [C13: from Anglo-Norman *pursiwer*, from OF *poursivre*, from L *prōsequī* to follow after]
▸**pur'suer** *n*

pursuit Ⓣ (pə'sjuːt) *n* **1a** the act of pursuing. **1b** (*as modifier*): *a pursuit plane.* **2** an occupation or pastime. **3** (in cycling) a race in which the riders set off at intervals along the track and attempt to overtake each other. [C14: from OF *poursieute*, from *poursivre* to PURSUE]

pursuivant ('pɜːsɪvənt) *n* **1** the lowest rank of heraldic officer. **2** *History.* a state or royal messenger. **3** *History.* a follower or attendant. [C14: from OF, from *poursivre* to PURSUE]

purulent ('pjuərulənt) *adj* of, relating to, or containing pus. [C16: from L *pūrulentus*, from *pūs*]
▸**'purulence** *n* ▸**'purulently** *adv*

purvey Ⓣ (pə'veɪ) *vb* (*tr*) **1** to sell or provide (commodities, esp. foodstuffs) on a large scale. **2** to publish (lies, scandal, etc.). [C13: from OF *porveeir*, from L *prōvidēre* to PROVIDE]
▸**pur'veyor** *n*

purveyance (pə'veɪəns) *n* **1** *History.* the collection or requisition of provisions for a sovereign. **2** *Rare.* the act of purveying.

purview Ⓣ ('pɜːvjuː) *n* **1** scope of operation. **2** breadth or range of outlook. **3** *Law.* the body of a statute, containing the enacting clauses. [C15: from Anglo-Norman *purveu*, from *porveeir* to furnish; see PURVEY]

pus (pʌs) *n* the yellow or greenish fluid product of inflammation. [C16: from L *pūs*]

push Ⓣ (puʃ) *vb* **1** (when *tr*, often foll. by *off, away,* etc.) to apply steady force to in order to move. **2** to thrust (one's way) through something, such as a crowd. **3** (*tr*) to encourage or urge (a person) to some action, decision, etc. **4** (when *intr*, often foll. by *for*) to be an advocate or promoter (of): *to push for acceptance of one's theories.* **5** (*tr*) to use one's influence to help (a person): *to push one's own candidate.* **6** to bear upon (oneself or another person) in order to achieve better results, etc. **7** *Cricket, etc.* to hit (a ball) with a stiff pushing stroke. **8** (*tr*) *Inf.* to sell (narcotic drugs) illegally. **9** (*intr;* foll. by *out, into,* etc.) to extend: *the*

THESAURUS

knock off (*sl.*), lift (*inf.*), nick (*sl., chiefly Brit.*), pilfer, pinch (*inf.*), rob, snaffle (*Brit. inf.*), snitch (*sl.*), swipe (*sl.*), thieve, walk off with

purport *vb* **1 = claim,** allege, assert, declare, maintain, pose as, pretend, proclaim, profess **2 = signify,** betoken, convey, denote, express, imply, import, indicate, intend, mean, point to, suggest ◆ *n* **3 = significance,** bearing, drift, gist, idea, implication, import, meaning, sense, spirit, tendency, tenor **4 = intention,** aim, design, intent, object, objective, plan, purpose

purpose *n* **1 = reason,** aim, design, function, idea, intention, object, point, principle, the why and wherefore **2 = aim,** ambition, aspiration, design, desire, end, goal, Holy Grail (*inf.*), hope, intention, object, objective, plan, project, scheme, target, view, wish **3 = determination,** constancy, firmness, persistence, resolution, resolve, single-mindedness, steadfastness, tenacity, will **4 = use,** advantage, avail, benefit, effect, gain, good, mileage (*inf.*), outcome, profit, result, return, utility **7 on purpose = deliberately,** by design, designedly, intentionally, knowingly, purposely, wilfully, wittingly ◆ *vb* **8 = intend,** aim, aspire, commit oneself, contemplate, decide, design, determine, have a mind to, make up one's mind, mean, meditate, plan, propose, resolve, set one's sights on, think to, work towards

purposeful *adj* **2 = determined,** decided, deliberate, firm, fixed, immovable, positive, resolute, resolved, settled, single-minded, steadfast, strong-willed, tenacious, unfaltering
Antonyms *adj* aimless, faltering, irresolute, otiose, purposeless, undecided, undetermined, vacillating, wavering

purposeless *adj* **1 = pointless,** aimless, empty, goalless, motiveless, needless, otiose, senseless, uncalled-for, unnecessary, useless, vacuous, wanton, without rhyme or reason

purposely *adv* **= deliberately,** by design, calculatedly, consciously, designedly, expressly, intentionally, knowingly, on purpose, wilfully, with intent
Antonyms *adv* accidentally, by accident, by chance, by mistake, inadvertently, unconsciously, unintentionally, unknowingly, unwittingly

purse *n* **1 = pouch,** money-bag, wallet **4 = money,** coffers, exchequer, funds, means, resources, treasury, wealth, wherewithal **5 = prize,** award, gift, reward ◆ *vb* **6 = pucker,** close, contract, knit, pout, press together, tighten, wrinkle

pursuance *n* **= carrying out,** bringing about, discharge, doing, effecting, execution, following, performance, prosecution, pursuing

pursue *vb* **1, 2 = follow,** accompany, attend, chase, dog, give chase to, go after, harass, harry, haunt, hound, hunt, hunt down, plague, run after, shadow, stalk, tail (*inf.*), track **3 = try for,** aim for, aspire to, desire, have as one's goal, purpose, seek, strive for, work towards **4 = continue,** adhere to, carry on, cultivate, hold to, keep on, maintain, persevere in, persist in, proceed, see through **5 = engage in,** apply oneself, carry on, conduct, perform, ply, practise, prosecute, tackle, wage, work at **6 = court,** chase after, make up to (*inf.*), pay attention to, pay court to, set one's cap at, woo
Antonyms *vb* ≠ **follow:** avoid, flee, give (someone *or* something) a wide berth, keep away from, run away from, shun, steer clear of ≠ **try for:** eschew, fight shy of

pursuit *n* **1 = pursuing,** chase, hunt, hunting, inquiry, quest, search, seeking, tracking, trail, trailing **2 = occupation,** activity, hobby, interest, line, pastime, pleasure, vocation

purvey *vb* **1 = supply,** cater, deal in, furnish, provide, provision, retail, sell, trade in, victual **2 = communicate,** make available, pass on, publish, retail, spread, transmit

purview *n* **1 = scope,** ambit, compass, confine(s), extent, field, limit, orbit, province, range, reach, sphere **2 = understanding,** comprehension, ken, overview, perspective, range of view

push *vb* **1 = shove,** depress, drive, poke, press, propel, ram, thrust **2 = make** *or* **force one's way,** elbow, jostle, move, shoulder, shove, squeeze, thrust **3 = urge,** egg on, encourage, expedite, gee up, hurry, impel, incite, persuade, press, prod, speed (up), spur **4 = promote,** advertise, boost, cry up, hype, make known, plug (*inf.*), propagandize, publicize, puff ◆ *n* **11 = shove,**

cliffs pushed out to the sea. **10 push one's luck** *or* **push it. 10a** to take undue risks, esp. through overconfidence. **10b** (*intr*) to act overconfidently. ◆ *n* **11** the act of pushing; thrust. **12** a part or device that is pressed to operate some mechanism. **13** *Inf.* drive, energy, etc. **14** *Inf.* a special effort or attempt to advance, as of an army: *to make a push.* **15** *Austral. sl.* a group, gang, or clique. **16** *Cricket, etc.* a stiff pushing stroke. **17 at a push.** *Inf.* with difficulty; only just. **18 the push.** *Inf., chiefly Brit.* dismissal, esp. from employment. ◆ See also **push off, push in,** etc. [C13: from OF *pousser,* from L *pulsāre,* from *pellere* to drive]

push-bike *n Brit.* an informal name for **bicycle.**

push button *n* **1** an electrical switch operated by pressing a button, which closes or opens a circuit. ◆ *modifier.* **push-button. 2a** operated by a push button: *a push-button radio.* **2b** initiated as simply as by pressing a button: *push-button warfare.*

pushcart ('pʊʃˌkɑːt) *n* another name (esp. US and Canad.) for **barrow**[1] (sense 3).

pushchair ('pʊʃˌtʃɛə) *n* a usually collapsible chair-shaped carriage for a small child. Also called: **baby buggy, buggy.** US and Canad. word: **stroller.** Austral. words: **pusher, stroller.**

pushed Ⓣ (pʊʃt) *adj* (often foll. by *for*) *Inf.* short (of) or in need (of time, money, etc.).

pusher ('pʊʃə) *n* **1** *Inf.* a person who sells illegal drugs, esp. narcotics such as heroin. **2** *Inf.* an aggressively ambitious person. **3** a person or thing that pushes. **4** *Austral.* the usual name for **pushchair.**

push in *vb* (*intr, adv*) to force one's way into a group of people, queue, etc.

pushing Ⓣ ('pʊʃɪŋ) *adj* **1** enterprising or aggressively ambitious. **2** impertinently self-assertive. ◆ *adv* **3** almost or nearly (a certain age, speed, etc.): *pushing fifty.*
▸ **'pushingly** *adv*

push money *n* a cash inducement provided by a manufacturer or distributor for a retailer or his staff, to reward successful selling.

push off Ⓣ *vb* (*adv*) **1** Also: **push out.** to move into open water, as by being cast off from a mooring. **2** (*intr*) *Inf.* to go away; leave.

pushover Ⓣ ('pʊʃˌəʊvə) *n Inf.* **1** something that is easily achieved. **2** a person, team, etc., that is easily taken advantage of or defeated.

push-pull *n* (*modifier*) using two similar electronic devices made to operate out of phase with each other to produce a signal that replicates the input waveform: *a push-pull amplifier.*

push-start *vb* (*tr*) **1** to start (a motor vehicle) by pushing it while it is in gear, thus turning the engine. ◆ *n* **2** this process.

push through *vb* (*tr*) to compel to accept: *the bill was pushed through Parliament.*

Pushto ('pʌʃtəʊ) *or* **Pushtu** ('pʌʃtuː) *n, adj* variant spellings of **Pashto.**

push-up *n* the US and Canad. term for **press-up.**

pushy Ⓣ ('pʊʃɪ) *adj* **pushier, pushiest.** *Inf.* **1** offensively assertive. **2** aggressively or ruthlessly ambitious.
▸ **'pushily** *adv* ▸ **'pushiness** *n*

pusillanimous Ⓣ (ˌpjuːsɪ'lænɪməs) *adj* characterized by a lack of courage or determination. [C16: from LL *pusillanimis* from L *pusillus* weak + *animus* courage]
▸ **pusillanimity** (ˌpjuːsɪlə'nɪmɪtɪ) *n* ▸ **ˌpusil'lanimously** *adv*

puss (pʊs) *n* **1** an informal name for a **cat. 2** *Sl.* a girl or woman. **3** an informal name for a **hare.** [C16: rel. to MLow G *pūs*]

pussy[1] ('pʊsɪ) *n, pl* **pussies. 1** Also called: **puss, pussycat.** an informal name for a **cat. 2** a furry catkin. **3** *Taboo sl.* the female pudenda. [C18: from PUSS]

pussy[2] ('pʌsɪ) *adj* **pussier, pussiest.** containing or full of pus.

pussycat ('pʊsɪˌkæt) *n* **1** an informal or child's name for **cat**[1]. **2** *Brit. inf.* an endearing or gentle person.

pussyfoot Ⓣ ('pʊsɪˌfʊt) *vb* (*intr*) *Inf.* **1** to move about stealthily or warily like a cat. **2** to avoid committing oneself.

pussy willow ('pʊsɪ) *n* a willow tree with silvery silky catkins.

pustulant ('pʌstjʊlənt) *adj* **1** causing the formation of pustules. ◆ *n* **2** an agent causing such formation.

pustulate *vb* ('pʌstjʊˌleɪt), **pustulates, pustulating, pustulated. 1** to form or cause to form into pustules. ◆ *adj* ('pʌstjʊlɪt). **2** covered with pustules.
▸ **ˌpustu'lation** *n*

pustule Ⓣ ('pʌstjuːl) *n* **1** a small inflamed elevated area of skin containing pus. **2** any spot resembling a pimple. [C14: from L *pustula* a blister, var. of *pūsula*]
▸ **pustular** ('pʌstjʊlə) *adj*

put Ⓣ (pʊt) *vb* **puts, putting, put.** (*mainly tr*) **1** to cause to be (in a position or place): *to put a book on the table.* **2** to cause to be (in a state, relation, etc.): *to put one's things in order.* **3** (foll. by *to*) to cause (a person) to experience or suffer: *to put to death.* **4** to set or commit (to an action, task, or duty), esp. by force: *he put him to work.* **5** to render or translate: *to put into English.* **6** to set (words) in a musical form (esp. in **put to music**). **7** (foll. by *at*) to estimate: *he put the distance at fifty miles.* **8** (foll. by *to*) to utilize: *he put his knowledge to use.* **9** (foll. by *to*) to couple (a female animal) with a male for breeding: *the farmer put his heifer to the bull.* **10** to express: *to put it bluntly.* **11** to make (an end or limit): *he put an end to the proceedings.* **12** to present for consideration; propose: *he put the question to the committee.* **13** to invest (money) in or expend (time, energy, etc.) on: *he put five thousand pounds into the project.* **14** to impart: *to put zest into a party.* **15** to throw or cast. **16 not know where to put oneself.** to feel embarrassed. **17 stay put.** to remain in one place; keep one's position. ◆ *n* **18** a throw, esp. in putting the shot. **19** Also called: **put option.** *Stock Exchange.* an option to sell a stated number of securities at a specified price during a limited period. ◆ See also **put about, put across,** etc. [C12 *puten* to push]

put about *vb* (*adv*) **1** *Naut.* to change course. **2** (*tr*) to make widely known: *he put about the news of the air disaster.* **3** (*tr; usually passive*) to disconcert or disturb.

put across Ⓣ *vb* (*tr*) **1** (*adv*) to communicate in a comprehensible way: *he couldn't put things across very well.* **2 put one across.** *Inf.* to get (someone) to believe a claim, excuse, etc., by deception: *they put one across their teacher.*

put aside Ⓣ *vb* (*tr, adv*) **1** to move (an object, etc.) to one side, esp. in rejection. **2** to save: *to put money aside for a rainy day.* **3** to disregard: *let us put aside our differences.*

putative Ⓣ ('pjuːtətɪv) *adj* (*prenominal*) **1** commonly regarded as being: *the putative father.* **2** considered to exist or have existed; inferred. [C15: from LL *putātīvus* supposed, from L *putāre* to consider]
▸ **'putatively** *adv*

put away Ⓣ *vb* (*tr, adv*) **1** to return (something) to the proper place. **2** to save: *to put away money for the future.* **3** to lock up in a prison, mental institution, etc.: *they put him away for twenty years.* **4** to eat or drink, esp. in large amounts.

put back *vb* (*tr, adv*) **1** to return to its former place. **2** to move to a later time: *the wedding was put back a fortnight.* **3** to impede the progress of: *the strike put back production.*

put by *vb* (*tr, adv*) to set aside for the future; save.

put down Ⓣ *vb* (*tr, adv*) **1** to make a written record of. **2** to repress: *to put down a rebellion.* **3** to consider: *they put him down for an ignoramus.* **4** to attribute: *I put the mistake down to inexperience.* **5** to put (an animal) to

THESAURUS

butt, jolt, nudge, poke, prod, thrust **13** *Informal* = **drive**, ambition, determination, dynamism, energy, enterprise, get-up-and-go (*inf.*), go (*inf.*), gumption (*inf.*), initiative, pep, vigour, vitality **14** *Informal* = **effort**, advance, assault, attack, campaign, charge, offensive, onset, thrust **18 the push** *Informal, chiefly Brit.* = **dismissal**, discharge, marching orders (*inf.*), one's books (*inf.*), one's cards (*inf.*), the boot (*sl.*), the (old) heave-ho (*inf.*), the sack (*inf.*)
Antonyms *vb* ≠ **shove**: drag, draw, haul, jerk, pull, tow, trail, tug, yank ≠ **urge**: deter, discourage, dissuade, put off ◆ *n* ≠ **shove**: jerk, pull, tug, yank

pushed *adj Informal often foll. by* **for** = **short of**, hurried, in difficulty, pressed, rushed, tight, under pressure, up against it (*inf.*)

pushing *adj* **1** = **ambitious**, determined, driving, dynamic, enterprising, go-ahead, on the go, purposeful, resourceful **2** = **self-assertive**, assertive, bold, brash, bumptious, forward, impertinent, intrusive, presumptuous, pushy (*inf.*)

push off *vb* **2** *Informal* = **go away**, beat it (*sl.*), depart, get lost (*inf.*), launch, leave, light out (*inf.*), make oneself scarce (*inf.*), make tracks, pack one's bags (*inf.*), shove off (*inf.*), slope off, take off (*inf.*)

pushover *Informal n* **1** = **piece of cake** (*Brit. inf.*), breeze (*US & Canad. inf.*), cakewalk (*inf.*), child's play (*inf.*), cinch (*sl.*), doddle (*Brit. sl.*), duck soup (*US sl.*), picnic (*inf.*), plain sailing, walkover (*inf.*) **2** = **sucker** (*sl.*), chump (*inf.*), easy game (*inf.*), easy *or* soft mark (*inf.*), mug (*Brit. sl.*), soft touch (*sl.*), stooge (*sl.*), walkover (*inf.*)
Antonyms *n* ≠ **piece of cake**: challenge, hassle (*inf.*), ordeal, test, trial, undertaking

pushy *adj* **1, 2** = **forceful**, aggressive, ambitious, assertive, bold, brash, bumptious, loud, obnoxious, obtrusive, offensive, officious, presumptuous, pushing, self-assertive
Antonyms *adj* diffident, inoffensive, meek, mousy, quiet, reserved, retiring, self-effacing, shy, timid, unassertive, unassuming, unobtrusive

pusillanimous *adj* = **cowardly**, abject, chicken-hearted, craven, faint-hearted, fearful, feeble, gutless (*inf.*), lily-livered, recreant (*arch.*), spineless, timid, timorous, weak, yellow (*inf.*)
Antonyms *adj* bold, brave, courageous, daring, dauntless, fearless, gallant, heroic, intrepid, plucky, valiant, valorous

pussyfoot *vb* **1** = **creep**, prowl, slink, steal, tiptoe, tread warily **2** = **hedge**, beat about the bush, be noncommittal, equivocate, flannel (*Brit. inf.*), hum and haw, prevaricate, sit on the fence, tergiversate

pustule *n* **1** = **boil**, abscess, blister, fester, gathering, pimple, ulcer, zit (*sl.*)

put *vb* **1** = **place**, bring, deposit, establish, fix, lay, position, rest, set, settle, situate **3** = **impose**, commit, condemn, consign, doom, enjoin, inflict, levy, subject **4** = **make**, assign, constrain, employ, force, induce, oblige, require, set, subject to **10** = **express**, phrase, pose, set, state, utter, word **12** = **present**, advance, bring forward, forward, offer, posit, propose, set before, submit, tender **15** = **throw**, cast, fling, heave, hurl, lob, pitch, toss

put across *vb* **1** = **communicate**, convey, explain, get across, get through, make clear, make oneself understood, spell out

put aside *vb* **2** = **save**, cache, deposit, keep in reserve, lay by, salt away, squirrel away, stockpile, store, stow away **3** = **disregard**, bury, discount, forget, ignore

putative *adj* **1** = **supposed**, alleged, assumed, commonly believed, imputed, presumed, presumptive, reported, reputed

put away *vb* **1** = **put back**, replace, return to (its) place, tidy away **2** = **save**, deposit, keep, lay in, put by, set aside, store away **3** = **commit**, certify, confine, institutionalize, lock up **4** = **consume**, devour, eat up, gobble, gulp down, wolf down

put down *vb* **1** = **record**, enter, inscribe, log, set down, take down, transcribe, write down **2** = **repress**, crush, quash, quell, silence, stamp out, suppress **4** = **attribute**, ascribe, impute, set down **5** = **put to sleep**, destroy, do away with, put away, put out of its misery **7** *Slang* = **humiliate**, condemn, crush, deflate, dismiss, dispar-

death, because of old age or illness. **6** to table on the agenda: *the MPs put down a motion on the increase in crime.* **7** *Sl.* to reject or humiliate. ◆ *n* **put-down. 8** a cruelly crushing remark.

put forth *vb* (*tr, adv*) *Formal.* **1** to propose. **2** (of a plant) to produce or bear (leaves, etc.).

put forward Ⓣ *vb* (*tr, adv*) **1** to propose; suggest. **2** to offer the name of; nominate.

put in *vb* (*adv*) **1** (*intr*) *Naut.* to bring a vessel into port. **2** (often foll. by *for*) to apply (for a job, etc.). **3** (*tr*) to submit: *he put in his claims form.* **4** to intervene with (a remark) during a conversation. **5** (*tr*) to devote (time, effort, etc.): *he put in three hours overtime last night.* **6** (*tr*) to establish or appoint: *he put in a manager.* **7** (*tr*) *Cricket.* to cause to bat: *England won the toss and put the visitors in to bat.*

put off Ⓣ *vb* (*tr*) **1** (*adv*) to postpone: *they have put off the dance until tomorrow.* **2** (*adv*) to evade (a person) by postponement or delay: *they tried to put him off, but he came anyway.* **3** (*adv*) to cause aversion: *he was put off by her appearance.* **4** (*prep*) to cause to lose interest in: *the accident put him off driving.*

put on Ⓣ *vb* (*tr, mainly adv*) **1** to clothe oneself in. **2** (*usually passive*) to adopt (an attitude or feeling) insincerely: *his misery was just put on.* **3** to present (a play, show, etc.). **4** to add: *she put on weight.* **5** to cause (an electrical device) to function. **6** (*also prep*) to wager (money) on a horse race, game, etc. **7** (*also prep*) to impose: *to put a tax on cars.* **8** *Cricket.* to cause (a bowler) to bowl.

put out Ⓣ *vb* (*tr, adv*) **1** (*often passive*) **1a** to annoy; anger. **1b** to disturb; confuse. **2** to extinguish (a fire, light, etc.). **3** to poke forward: *to put out one's tongue.* **4** to be a source of inconvenience to: *I hope I'm not putting you out.* **5** to publish; broadcast: *the authorities put out a leaflet.* **6** to render unconscious. **7** to dislocate: *he put out his shoulder in the accident.* **8** to give out (work to be done) at different premises. **9** to lend (money) at interest. **10** *Cricket, etc.* to dismiss (a player or team).

put over *vb* (*tr, adv*) **1** *Inf.* to communicate (facts, information, etc.). **2** *Chiefly US.* to postpone. **3 put (a fast) one over on.** *Inf.* to get (someone) to believe a claim, excuse, etc., by deception: *he put one over on his boss.*

put-put (ˈpʌtˌpʌt) *Inf.* ◆ *n* **1** a light chugging or popping sound, as made by a petrol engine. ◆ *vb* **put-puts, put-putting, put-putted. 2** (*intr*) to make such a sound.

putrefy Ⓣ (ˈpjuːtrɪˌfaɪ) *vb* **putrefies, putrefying, putrefied.** (of organic matter) to decompose or rot with an offensive smell. [C15: from OF *putrefier* + L *putrefacere,* from *puter* rotten + *facere* to make]
▸**putrefaction** (ˌpjuːtrɪˈfækʃən) *n* ▸ˌ**putreˈfactive** *or* **putrefacient** (ˌpjuːtrɪˈfeɪʃənt) *adj*

putrescent Ⓣ (pjuːˈtrɛsᵊnt) *adj* **1** becoming putrid; rotting. **2** characterized by or undergoing putrefaction. [C18: from L *putrescere* to become rotten]
▸**puˈtrescence** *n*

putrid Ⓣ (ˈpjuːtrɪd) *adj* **1** (of organic matter) in a state of decomposition: *putrid meat.* **2** morally corrupt. **3** sickening; foul: *a putrid smell.* **4** *Inf.* deficient in quality or value: *a putrid film.* [C16: from L *putridus,* from *putrēre* to be rotten]
▸**puˈtridity** *or* ˈ**putridness** *n* ▸ˈ**putridly** *adv*

putsch (pʊtʃ) *n* a violent and sudden uprising; political revolt. [C20: from G, from Swiss G: a push, imit.]

putt (pʌt) *Golf.* ◆ *n* **1** a stroke on the green with a putter to roll the ball into or near the hole. ◆ *vb* **2** to strike (the ball) in this way. [C16: of Scot. origin]

puttee *or* **putty** (ˈpʌtɪ) *n, pl* **puttees** *or* **putties.** (*usually pl*) a strip of cloth worn wound around the leg from the ankle to the knee, esp. as part of a military uniform in World War I. [C19: from Hindi *paṭṭī,* from Sansk. *paṭṭikā,* from *patta* cloth]

putter[1] (ˈpʌtə) *n Golf.* **1** a club for putting, usually having a solid metal head. **2** a golfer who putts: *he is a good putter.*

putter[2] (ˈpʌtə) *vb* the usual US and Canad. word for **potter**[2].
▸ˈ**putterer** *n*

putter[3] (ˈpʊtə) *n* **1** a person who puts: *the putter of a question.* **2** a person who puts the shot.

put through Ⓣ *vb* (*tr, mainly adv*) **1** to carry out to a conclusion: *he put through his plan.* **2** (*also prep*) to organize the processing of: *she put through his application to join the organization.* **3** to connect by telephone. **4** to make (a telephone call).

putting green (ˈpʌtɪŋ) *n* **1** (on a golf course) the area of closely mown grass at the end of a fairway where the hole is. **2** an area of smooth grass with several holes for putting games.

putto (ˈpʊtəʊ) *n, pl* **putti** (-tiː). a representation of a small boy, a cherub or cupid, esp. in baroque painting or sculpture. [from It., from L *putus* boy]

putty (ˈpʌtɪ) *n, pl* **putties. 1** a stiff paste made of whiting and linseed oil that is used to fix glass into frames and to fill cracks in woodwork, etc. **2** any substance with a similar function or appearance. **3** a mixture of lime and water with sand or plaster of Paris used on plaster as a finishing coat. **4** (*as modifier*): *a putty knife.* **5** a person who is easily influenced: *he's putty in her hands.* **6a** a colour varying from greyish yellow to greyish brown. **6b** (*as adj*): *putty wool.* ◆ *vb* **putties, puttying, puttied. 7** (*tr*) to fix, fill, or coat with putty. [C17: from F *potée* a potful]

put up Ⓣ *vb* (*adv, mainly tr*) **1** to build; erect: *to put up a statue.* **2** to accommodate or be accommodated at: *can you put me up for tonight?* **3** to increase (prices). **4** to submit (a plan, case, etc.). **5** to offer: *to put a house up for sale.* **6** to give: *to put up a good fight.* **7** to provide (money) for: *they put up five thousand for the new project.* **8** to preserve or can (jam, etc.). **9** to pile up (long hair) on the head in any of several styles. **10** (*also intr*) to nominate or be nominated as a candidate: *he put up for president.* **11** *Arch.* to return (a weapon) to its holder: *put up your sword!* **12 put up to. 12a** to inform or instruct (a person) about (tasks, duties, etc.). **12b** to incite to. **13 put up with.** *Inf.* to endure; tolerate. ◆ *adj* **put-up. 14** dishonestly or craftily prearranged (esp. in **put-up job**).

put upon Ⓣ *vb* (*intr, prep; usually passive*) **1** to presume on (a person's generosity, good nature, etc.): *he's always being put upon.* **2** to impose hardship on: *he was sorely put upon.*

putz (pʌts) *n US sl.* a despicable or stupid person. [from Yiddish *puts* ornament]

puzzle Ⓣ (ˈpʌzᵊl) *vb* **puzzles, puzzling, puzzled. 1** to perplex or be perplexed. **2** (*intr;* foll. by *over*) to ponder about the cause of: *he puzzled over her absence.* **3** (*tr;* usually foll. by *out*) to solve by mental effort: *he puzzled out the meaning.* ◆ *n* **4** a person or thing that puzzles. **5** a problem that cannot be easily solved. **6** the state of being puzzled. **7** a toy, game, or question presenting a problem that requires skill or ingenuity for its solution. [C16: from ?]
▸ˈ**puzzlement** *n* ▸ˈ**puzzler** *n* ▸ˈ**puzzling** *adj* ▸ˈ**puzzlingly** *adv*

PVC *abbrev. for* polyvinyl chloride; a synthetic thermoplastic material

THESAURUS

age, mortify, reject, shame, slight, snub ◆ *n* **put-down 8** = **humiliation**, barb, dig, disparagement, gibe, rebuff, sarcasm, slight, sneer, snub

put forward *vb* **1, 2** = **recommend**, advance, introduce, move, nominate, prescribe, present, press, proffer, propose, submit, suggest, tender

put off *vb* **1** = **postpone**, defer, delay, hold over, put back, put on ice, put on the back burner (*inf.*), reschedule **3** = **disconcert**, abash, confuse, discomfit, dismay, distress, faze, nonplus, perturb, rattle (*inf.*), throw (*inf.*), unsettle **4** = **discourage**, dishearten, dissuade
Antonyms *vb* ≠ **discourage:** egg on, encourage, gee up, incite, persuade, prompt, push, spur, urge

put on *vb* **1** = **don**, change into, dress, get dressed in, slip into **2** = **fake**, affect, assume, feign, make believe, play-act, pretend, sham, simulate **3** = **present**, do, mount, produce, show, stage **4** = **add**, gain, increase by **6** = **bet**, back, lay, place, wager
Antonyms *vb* ≠ **don:** cast off, doff, remove, shed, slip off, slip out of, take off, throw off, undress

put out *vb* **1a** = **annoy**, anger, confound, disturb, exasperate, harass, irk, irritate, nettle, perturb, provoke, vex **1b** = **disconcert**, discompose, discountenance, disturb, embarrass, put on the spot, take the wind out of someone's sails **2** = **extinguish**, blow out, douse, quench, smother, snuff out, stamp out **4** = **inconvenience**, bother, discomfit, discommode, disturb, impose upon, incommode, trouble, upset **5** = **issue**, bring out, broadcast, circulate, make known, make public, publish, release

putrefy *vb* = **rot**, break down, corrupt, decay, decompose, deteriorate, go bad, spoil, stink, taint

putrescent *adj* **1, 2** = **rotting**, decaying, decomposing, going bad, stinking

putrid *adj* **1, 3** = **rotten**, bad, contaminated, corrupt, decayed, decomposed, fetid, foul, off, olid, putrefied, rancid, rank, reeking, rotting, spoiled, stinking, tainted
Antonyms *adj* clean, fresh, pure, sweet, uncontaminated, untainted, wholesome

put through *vb* **1** = **carry out**, accomplish, achieve, bring off, conclude, do, effect, execute, manage, pull off, realize

put up *vb* **1** = **build**, construct, erect, fabricate, raise **2** = **accommodate**, board, entertain, give one lodging, house, lodge, take in **4** = **submit**, float, nominate, offer, present, propose, put forward, recommend **7** = **provide**, advance, give, invest, pay, pledge, supply **12b put up to** = **encourage**, egg on, goad, incite, instigate, prompt, put the idea into one's head, urge **13 put up with** *Informal* = **stand**, abide, bear, brook, endure, hack (*sl.*), lump (*inf.*), stand for, stomach, suffer, swallow, take, tolerate
Antonyms *vb* ≠ **build:** demolish, destroy, flatten, knock down, level, pull down, raze, tear down ≠ **stand:** not stand for, object to, oppose, protest against, reject, take exception to

put upon *vb* **1, 2** = **take advantage of**, abuse, beset, exploit, harry, impose upon, inconvenience, overwork, put out, saddle, take for a fool, take for granted, trouble

puzzle *vb* **1** = **perplex**, baffle, beat (*sl.*), bewilder, confound, confuse, flummox, mystify, nonplus, stump **2** *usually foll. by* **over** = **think about**, ask oneself, brood, cudgel *or* rack one's brains, mull over, muse, ponder, study, think hard, wonder **3** *usually foll. by* **out** = **solve**, clear up, crack, crack the code, decipher, figure out, find the key, get it, get the answer, resolve, see, sort out, suss (out) (*sl.*), think through, unravel, work out ◆ *n* **4, 5, 7** = **problem**, brain-teaser (*inf.*), conundrum, enigma, labyrinth, maze, mystery, paradox, poser, question, question mark, riddle, teaser **6** = **perplexity**, bafflement, bewilderment, confusion, difficulty, dilemma, quandary, uncertainty

puzzled *adj* **1** = **perplexed**, at a loss, at sea, baffled, beaten, bewildered, clueless, confused, doubtful, flummoxed, in a fog, lost, mixed up, mystified, nonplussed, stuck, stumped, without a clue

puzzlement *n* **1** = **perplexity**, bafflement, bewilderment, confusion, disorientation, doubt, doubtfulness, mystification, questioning, surprise, uncertainty, wonder

puzzling *adj* **1** = **perplexing**, abstruse, ambiguous, baffling, bewildering, beyond one, enigmatic, full of surprises, hard, incomprehensible, inexplicable, involved, knotty, labyrinthine, misleading, mystifying, oracular, unaccountable, unclear, unfathomable
Antonyms *adj* clear, comprehensible, easy, evident, intelligible, lucid, manifest, obvious, patent, plain, simple, unambiguous, unequivocal, unmistakable

made by polymerizing vinyl chloride. The flexible forms are used in insulation, shoes, etc. Rigid PVC is used for moulded articles.

PVS *abbrev. for:* **1** persistent vegetative state. **2** postviral syndrome.

Pvt. *Mil. abbrev. for* private.

PW *abbrev. for* policewoman.

PWA *abbrev. for* person with AIDS.

PWR *abbrev. for* pressurized-water reactor.

pyaemia *or* **pyemia** (paɪ'iːmɪə) *n* blood poisoning characterized by pus-forming microorganisms in the blood. [C19: from NL, from Gk *puon* pus + *haima* blood]
▸**py'aemic** *or* **py'emic** *adj*

pye-dog, pie-dog, *or* **pi-dog** ('paɪˌdɒg) *n* an ownerless half-wild Asian dog. [C19: Anglo-Indian, from Hindi *pāhī* outsider]

pyelitis (ˌpaɪə'laɪtɪs) *n* inflammation of the pelvis of the kidney. [C19: NL, from Gk *puelos* trough]
▸**pyelitic** (ˌpaɪə'lɪtɪk) *adj*

pygmy ❶ *or* **pigmy** ('pɪgmɪ) *n, pl* **pygmies** *or* **pigmies. 1** an abnormally undersized person. **2** something that is a very small example of its type. **3** a person of little importance or significance. **4** (*modifier*) very small. [C14 *pigmeis* the Pygmies, from L *Pygmaeus* a Pygmy, from Gk *pugmaios* undersized, from *pugmē* fist]
▸**pygmaean** *or* **pygmean** (pɪg'miːən) *adj*

Pygmy *or* **Pigmy** ('pɪgmɪ) *n, pl* **Pygmies** *or* **Pigmies.** a member of one of the dwarf peoples of Equatorial Africa, noted for their hunting and forest culture.

pyinkado (pjɪŋ'kɑːdəʊ) *n, pl* **pyinkados. 1** a leguminous tree, native to India and Myanmar. **2** the heavy durable timber of this tree, used for construction. [C19: from Burmese]

pyjamas *or US* **pajamas** (pə'dʒɑːməz) *pl n* **1** loose-fitting nightclothes comprising a jacket or top and trousers. **2** full loose-fitting ankle-length trousers worn by either sex in various Eastern countries. [C19: from Hindi, from Persian *pai* leg + *jāma* garment]

pyknic ('pɪknɪk) *adj* characterized by a broad squat fleshy physique with a large chest and abdomen. [C20: from Gk *puknos* thick]

pylon ('paɪlən) *n* **1** a large vertical steel tower-like structure supporting high-tension electrical cables. **2** a post or tower for guiding pilots or marking a turning point in a race. **3** a streamlined aircraft structure for attaching an engine pod, etc., to the main body of the aircraft. **4** a monumental gateway, such as one at the entrance to an ancient Egyptian temple. [C19: from Gk *pulōn* a gateway]

pylorus (paɪ'lɔːrəs) *n, pl* **pylori** (-raɪ). the small circular opening at the base of the stomach through which partially digested food passes to the duodenum. [C17: via LL from Gk *pulōrus* gatekeeper, from *pulē* gate + *ouros* guardian]

pyo- *or before a vowel* **py-** *combining form.* denoting pus: *pyosis.* [from Gk *puon*]

pyorrhoea *or esp. US* **pyorrhea** (ˌpaɪə'rɪə) *n* inflammation of the gums characterized by the discharge of pus and loosening of the teeth; periodontal disease.
▸ˌ**pyor'rhoeal,** ˌ**pyor'rhoeic** *or esp. US* ˌ**pyor'rheal,** ˌ**pyor'rheic** *adj*

pyracantha (ˌpaɪrə'kænθə) *n* any of a genus of shrubs with yellow, orange, or scarlet berries, widely cultivated for ornament. [C17: from Gk *purakantha,* from PYRO- + *akantha* thorn]

pyramid ('pɪrəmɪd) *n* **1** a huge masonry construction that has a square base and, as in the case of the ancient Egyptian royal tombs, four sloping triangular sides. **2** an object or structure resembling such a construction. **3** *Maths.* a solid having a polygonal base and triangular sides that meet in a common vertex. **4** *Crystallography.* a crystal form in which three planes intersect all three axes of the crystal. **5** *Finance.* a group of enterprises containing a series of holding companies structured so that the top holding company controls the entire group with a relatively small proportion of the total capital invested. **6** (*pl*) a game similar to billiards. ◆ *vb* **pyramids, pyramiding, pyramided. 7** to build up or be arranged in the form of a pyramid. **8** *Finance.* to form (companies) into a pyramid. [C16 (earlier *pyramis*): from L *pyramis,* from Gk *puramis,* prob. from Egyptian]
▸**pyramidal** (pɪ'ræmɪdᵊl), ˌ**pyra'midical,** *or* ˌ**pyra'midic** *adj* ▸**py'ramidally** *or* ˌ**pyra'midically** *adv*

pyramid selling *n* a practice adopted by some manufacturers of advertising for distributors and selling them batches of goods. The first distributors then advertise for more distributors who are sold subdivisions of the original batches at an increased price. This process continues until the final distributors are left with a stock that is unsaleable except at a loss.

pyre ('paɪə) *n* a pile of wood or other combustible material, esp. one for cremating a corpse. [C17: from L *pyra,* from Gk *pura* hearth, from *pur* fire]

pyrethrin (paɪ'riːθrɪn) *n* either of two oily compounds found in pyrethrum and used as insecticides. [C19: from PYRETHRUM + -IN]

pyrethrum (paɪ'riːθrəm) *n* **1** any of several cultivated Eurasian chrysanthemums with white, pink, red, or purple flowers. **2** any insecticide prepared from the dried flowers of any of these plants. [C16: via L from Gk *purethron* feverfew, prob. from *puretos* fever; see PYRETIC]

pyretic (paɪ'rɛtɪk) *adj Pathology.* of, relating to, or characterized by fever. [C18: from NL *pyreticus,* from Gk *puretos* fever, from *pur* fire]

Pyrex ('paɪrɛks) *n Trademark.* **a** any of a variety of glasses that have low coefficients of expansion, making them suitable for heat-resistant glassware used in cookery and chemical apparatus. **b** (*as modifier*): *a Pyrex dish.*

pyrexia (paɪ'rɛksɪə) *n* a technical name for **fever.** [C18: from NL, from Gk *purexis,* from *puressein* to be feverish, from *pur* fire]
▸**py'rexial** *or* **py'rexic** *adj*

pyridine ('pɪrɪˌdiːn) *n* a colourless hygroscopic liquid heterocyclic compound with a characteristic odour: used as a solvent and in preparing other organic chemicals. Formula: C_5H_5N. [C19: from PYRO- + -ID[2] + -INE[2]]

pyridoxine (ˌpɪrɪ'dɒksiːn) *n Biochemistry.* a derivative of pyridine that is a precursor of the compounds pyridoxal and pyridoxamine. Also called: **vitamin B_6.**

pyrimidine (paɪ'rɪmɪˌdiːn) *n* **1** a liquid or crystalline organic compound with a penetrating odour. Formula: $C_4H_4N_2$. **2** Also called: **pyrimidine base.** any of a number of similar compounds having a basic structure that is derived from pyrimidine, and which are constituents of nucleic acids. [C20: var. of PYRIDINE]

pyrite ('paɪraɪt) *n* a yellow mineral consisting of iron sulphide in cubic crystalline form. It occurs in igneous and metamorphic rocks and in veins, associated with various metals, and is used mainly in the manufacture of sulphuric acid and paper. Formula: FeS_2. Also called: **iron pyrites, pyrites.** [C16: from L *pyrites* flint, from Gk *puritēs* (*lithos*) fire(stone), from *pur* fire]
▸**pyritic** (paɪ'rɪtɪk) *or* **py'ritous** *adj*

pyrites (paɪ'raɪtiːz; *in combination* 'paɪraɪts) *n, pl* **pyrites. 1** another name for **pyrite. 2** any of a number of other disulphides of metals, esp. of copper and tin.

pyro- *or before a vowel* **pyr-** *combining form.* **1** denoting fire or heat: *pyromania; pyrometer.* **2** *Chem.* denoting a new substance obtained by heating another: *pyroboric acid is obtained by heating boric acid.* **3** *Mineralogy.* **3a** having a property that changes upon the application of heat. **3b** having a flame-coloured appearance: *pyroxylin.* [from Gk *pur* fire]

pyroelectricity (ˌpaɪrəʊɪlɛk'trɪsɪtɪ) *n* the development of opposite charges at the ends of the axis of certain crystals as a result of a change in temperature.

pyrogallol (ˌpaɪrəʊ'gælɒl) *n* a crystalline soluble phenol with weakly acidic properties: used as a photographic developer and for absorbing oxygen in gas analysis. Formula: $C_6H_3(OH)_3$. [C20: from PYRO- + GALL(IC ACID) + -OL[1]]

pyrogenic (ˌpaɪrəʊ'dʒɛnɪk) *or* **pyrogenous** (paɪ'rɒdʒɪnəs) *adj* **1** produced by or producing heat. **2** *Pathology.* causing or resulting from fever. **3** *Geol.* less common words for **igneous.**

pyrography (paɪ'rɒgrəfɪ) *n* another name for **pokerwork.**

pyroligneous (ˌpaɪrəʊ'lɪgnɪəs) *or* **pyrolignic** *adj* (of a substance) produced by the action of heat on wood, esp. by destructive distillation.

pyrolysis (paɪ'rɒlɪsɪs) *n* **1** the application of heat to chemical compounds in order to cause decomposition. **2** such chemical decomposition.
▸**pyrolytic** (ˌpaɪrəʊ'lɪtɪk) *adj*

pyromania (ˌpaɪrəʊ'meɪnɪə) *n Psychiatry.* the uncontrollable impulse and practice of setting things on fire.
▸ˌ**pyro'maniˌac** *n*

pyrometer (paɪ'rɒmɪtə) *n* an instrument for measuring high temperatures, esp. by measuring the brightness or total quantity of the radiation produced.
▸**pyrometric** (ˌpaɪrəʊ'metrɪk) *or* ˌ**pyro'metrical** *adj* ▸ˌ**pyro'metrically** *adv* ▸**py'rometry** *n*

pyrope ('paɪrəʊp) *n* a deep yellowish-red garnet that consists of magnesium aluminium silicate and is used as a gemstone. [C14 (used loosely of a red gem; modern sense C19): from OF *pirope,* from L *pyrōpus* bronze, from Gk *purōpus* fiery-eyed]

pyrophoric (ˌpaɪrəʊ'fɒrɪk) *adj* **1** (of a chemical) igniting spontaneously on contact with air. **2** (of an alloy) producing sparks when struck or scraped: *lighter flints are made of pyrophoric alloy.* [C19: from NL *pyrophorus,* from Gk *purophoros* fire-bearing, from *pur* fire + *pherein* to bear]

pyrosis (paɪ'rəʊsɪs) *n Pathology.* a technical name for **heartburn.** [C18: from NL, from Gk: a burning, from *puroun* to burn, from *pur* fire]

pyrostat ('paɪrəʊˌstæt) *n* **1** a device that activates an alarm or extinguisher in the event of a fire. **2** a thermostat for use at high temperatures.
▸ˌ**pyro'static** *adj*

pyrotechnics (ˌpaɪrəʊ'tɛknɪks) *n* **1** (*functioning as sing*) the art of making fireworks. **2** (*functioning as sing or pl*) a firework display. **3** (*functioning as sing or pl*) brilliance of display, as in the performance of music.
▸ˌ**pyro'technic** *or* ˌ**pyro'technical** *adj*

pyroxene (paɪ'rɒksiːn) *n* any of a large group of minerals consisting of the silicates of magnesium, iron, and calcium. They occur in basic igneous rocks. [C19: PYRO- + *-xene* from Gk *xenos* foreign, because mistakenly thought to have originated elsewhere when found in igneous rocks]

THESAURUS

pygmy *n* **1** = **midget,** dwarf, homunculus, Lilliputian, manikin, shrimp (*inf.*), Tom Thumb **3** = **nonentity,** cipher, lightweight (*inf.*), mediocrity, nobody, pipsqueak (*inf.*), small fry ◆ *modifier* **4** = **small,** baby, diminutive, dwarf, dwarfish, elfin, Lilliputian, midget, miniature, minuscule, pocket, pygmean, stunted, teensy-weensy, teeny-weeny, tiny, undersized, wee

pyromaniac *n* = **arsonist,** firebug (*inf.*), fire raiser, incendiary

pyroxylin (paɪˈrɒksɪlɪn) *n* a yellow substance obtained by nitrating cellulose with a mixture of nitric and sulphuric acids; guncotton: used to make collodion, plastics, lacquers, and adhesives.

pyrrhic (ˈpɪrɪk) *Prosody.* ◆ *n* **1** a metrical foot of two short or unstressed syllables. ◆ *adj* **2** of or composed in pyrrhics. [C16: via L, from Gk *purrhikhē*, said to be after its inventor *Purrhikhos*]

Pyrrhic victory *n* a victory in which the victor's losses are as great as those of the defeated. Also called: **Cadmean victory.** [after *Pyrrhus* (319–272 B.C.), who defeated the Romans at Asculum in 279 B.C. but suffered heavy losses]

Pyrrhonism (ˈpɪrəˌnɪzəm) *n* the doctrine of Pyrrho (?365–?275 B.C.), Greek sceptic philosopher, that certain knowledge is impossible to obtain.

pyruvic acid (paɪˈruːvɪk) *n* a liquid formed during the metabolism of proteins and carbohydrates, helping to release energy to the body. [C19: from PYRO- + L *ūva* grape]

Pythagoras' theorem *n* (paɪˈθæɡərəs) the theorem that in a right-angled triangle the square of the length of the hypotenuse equals the sum of the squares of the other two sides. [after *Pythagoras* (?580–?500 B.C.) Gk philosopher and mathematician]

Pythagorean (paɪˌθæɡəˈriːən) *adj* **1** of or relating to Pythagoras. ◆ *n* **2** a follower of Pythagoras.

Pythian (ˈpɪθɪən) *adj also* **Pythic. 1** of or relating to Delphi or its oracle. ◆ *n* **2** the priestess of Apollo at the oracle of Delphi. [C16: via L *Pȳthius* from Gk *Puthios* of Delphi]

python (ˈpaɪθən) *n* any of a family of large nonvenomous snakes of Africa, S Asia, and Australia. They can reach a length of more than 20 feet and kill their prey by constriction. [C16: NL, after *Python*, a dragon killed by Apollo]
▸**pythonic** (paɪˈθɒnɪk) *adj*

pythoness (ˈpaɪθənes) *n* a woman, such as Apollo's priestess at Delphi, believed to be possessed by an oracular spirit. [C14: *phitonesse*, ult. from Gk *Puthōn* Python; see PYTHON]

pyuria (paɪˈjʊərɪə) *n Pathol.* any condition characterized by the presence of pus in the urine. [C19: from NL, from Gk *puon* pus + *ouron* urine]

pyx (pɪks) *n* **1** Also called: **pyx chest.** the chest in which coins from the British mint are placed to be tested for weight, etc. **2** *Christianity.* any receptacle in which the Eucharistic Host is kept. [C14: from L *pyxis* small box, from Gk, from *puxos* box tree]

pyxidium (pɪkˈsɪdɪəm) *or* **pyxis** (ˈpɪksɪs) *n, pl* **pyxidia** (-ɪə) *or* **pyxides** (ˈpɪksɪˌdiːz). the dry fruit of such plants as the plantain: a capsule whose upper part falls off when mature so that the seeds are released. [C19: via NL from Gk *puxidion* a little box, from *puxis* box]

pyxis (ˈpɪksɪs) *n, pl* **pyxides** (ˈpɪksɪˌdiːz). **1** a small box used by the ancient Greeks and Romans to hold medicines, etc. **2** another name for **pyxidium.** [C14: via L from Gk: box]

Qq

q *or* **Q** (kjuː) *n, pl* **q's, Q's,** *or* **Qs. 1** the 17th letter of the English alphabet. **2** a speech sound represented by this letter.
q *symbol for* quintal.
Q *symbol for:* **1** *Physics.* heat. **2** *Chess.* queen. **3** question.
q. *abbrev. for:* **1** quart. **2** quarter. **3** quarterly. **4** query. **5** question. **6** quire.
Q. *abbrev. for:* **1** quartermaster. **2** (*pl* **Qq., qq.**) Also: **q.** quarto. **3** Quebec. **4** Queen. **5** question. **6** *Electronics.* Q factor.
qadi ('kɑːdɪ, 'keɪdɪ) *n, pl* **qadis.** a variant spelling of **cadi.**
QANTAS ('kwɒntəs) *n* the national airline of Australia. [C20: from *Q(ueensland) a(nd) N(orthern) T(erritory) A(erial) S(ervices Ltd.)*]
QARANC *abbrev. for* Queen Alexandra's Royal Army Nursing Corps.
qawwali (kə'vɑːlɪ) *n* an Islamic religious song, esp. in Asia.
QB *abbrev. for* Queen's Bench.
QC *abbrev. for* Queen's Counsel.
QED *abbrev. for:* **1** quantum electrodynamics. **2** quod erat demonstrandum. [L: which was to be shown or proved]
Q factor *n* **1** a measure of the relationship between stored energy and rate of energy dissipation in certain electrical components, devices, etc. **2** Also called: **Q value.** the heat released in a nuclear reaction. ◆ Symbol: Q [C20: short for *quality factor*]
Q fever *n* an acute disease characterized by fever and pneumonia, transmitted to man by a rickettsia. [C20: from *q(uery) fever* (the cause being orig. unknown)]
qi (tʃiː) *n* a variant spelling of **chi**[2].
Qld *or* **QLD** *abbrev. for* Queensland.
QM *abbrev. for* Quartermaster.
QMG *abbrev. for* Quartermaster General.
QMV *abbrev. for* Qualified Majority Voting.
qr. *pl* **qrs.** *abbrev. for:* **1** quarter. **2** quarterly. **3** quire.
Q-ship *n* a merchant ship with concealed guns, used to decoy enemy ships. [C20: from Q short for QUERY]
QSM (in New Zealand) *abbrev. for* Queen's Service Medal.
QSO *abbrev. for:* **1** quasi-stellar object. **2** (in New Zealand) Queen's Service Order.
qt *pl* **qt** *or* **qts** *abbrev. for* quart.
q.t. *Inf.* **1** *abbrev. for* quiet. **2 on the q.t.** secretly.
qua (kweɪ, kwɑː) *prep* in the capacity of; by virtue of being. [C17: from L, ablative sing (fem) of *qui* who]
quack[1] (kwæk) *vb* (*intr*) **1** (of a duck) to utter a harsh guttural sound. **2** to make a noise like a duck. ◆ *n* **3** the sound made by a duck. [C17: imit.]
quack[2] ❶ (kwæk) *n* **1a** an unqualified person who claims medical knowledge or other skills. **1b** (*as modifier*): *a quack doctor.* **2** *Brit., Austral., & NZ inf.* a doctor; physician or surgeon. ◆ *vb* **3** (*intr*) to act in the manner of a quack. [C17: short for QUACKSALVER]
▸**'quackish** *adj*
quackery ('kwækərɪ) *n, pl* **quackeries.** the activities or methods of a quack.
quack grass *n* another name for **couch grass.**
quacksalver ('kwæk,sælvə) *n* an archaic word for **quack**[2]. [C16: from Du., from *quack,* apparently: to hawk + *salf* SALVE]
quad[1] (kwɒd) *n* short for **quadrangle.**
quad[2] (kwɒd) *n Printing.* a block of type metal used for spacing. [C19: shortened from QUADRAT]
quad[3] (kwɒd) *n* short for **quadruplet.**
quad[4] (kwɒd) *n, adj Inf.* short for **quadraphonics** *or* **quadraphonic.**
quad bike *or* **quad** *n* a vehicle like a motorcycle, with four large wheels, designed for agricultural, sporting, and other off-road uses.
Quadragesima (,kwɒdrə'dʒesɪmə) *n* the first Sunday in Lent. Also called: **Quadragesima Sunday.** [C16: from Med. L *quadrāgēsima dies* the fortieth day]
Quadragesimal (,kwɒdrə'dʒesɪməl) *adj* of, relating to, or characteristic of Lent.
quadrangle ('kwɒd,ræŋgᵊl) *n* **1** *Geom.* a plane figure consisting of four points connected by four lines. **2** a rectangular courtyard, esp. one having buildings on all four sides. **3** the building surrounding such a courtyard. [C15: from LL *quadrangulum* figure having four corners]
▸**quadrangular** (kwɒ'dræŋgjʊlə) *adj*
quadrant ('kwɒdrənt) *n* **1** *Geom.* **1a** a quarter of the circumference of a circle. **1b** the area enclosed by two perpendicular radii of a circle. **1c** any of the four sections into which a plane is divided by two coordinate axes. **2** a piece of a mechanism in the form of a quarter circle. **3** an instrument formerly used in astronomy and navigation for measuring the altitudes of stars. [C14: from L *quadrāns* a quarter]
▸**quadrantal** (kwɒ'dræntᵊl) *adj*
quadraphonics *or* **quadrophonics** (,kwɒdrə'fɒnɪks) *n* (*functioning as sing*) a system of sound recording and reproduction that uses four independent loudspeakers to give directional sources of sound.
▸**,quadra'phonic** *or* **,quadro'phonic** *adj*
quadrat ('kwɒdrət) *n* **1** *Ecology.* an area of vegetation selected at random for study. **2** *Printing.* an archaic name for **quad**[2]. [C14 (meaning "a square"): var. of QUADRATE]
quadrate *n* ('kwɒdrɪt, -,dreɪt). **1** a cube, square, or a square or cubelike object. **2** one of a pair of bones of the upper jaw of fishes, amphibians, reptiles, and birds. ◆ *adj* ('kwɒdrɪt, -,dreɪt). **3** of or relating to this bone. **4** square or rectangular. ◆ *vb* (kwɒ'dreɪt), **quadrates, quadrating, quadrated. 5** (*tr*) to make square or rectangular. **6** (often foll. by *with*) to conform or cause to conform. [C14: from L *quadrāre* to make square]
quadratic (kwɒ'drætɪk) *Maths.* ◆ *n* **1** Also called: **quadratic equation.** an equation containing one or more terms in which the variable is raised to the power of two, but to no higher power. ◆ *adj* **2** of or relating to the second power.
quadrature ('kwɒdrətʃə) *n* **1** *Maths.* the process of determining a square having an area equal to that of a given figure or surface. **2** the process of making square or dividing into squares. **3** *Astron.* a configuration in which two celestial bodies form an angle of 90° with a third body. **4** *Electronics.* the relationship between two waves that are 90° out of phase.
quadrella (kwɒ'drelə) *n Austral.* a form of betting in which the punter must select the winner of four specified races.
quadrennial (kwɒ'drenɪəl) *adj* **1** occurring every four years. **2** lasting four years. ◆ *n* **3** a period of four years.
▸**quad'rennially** *adv*
quadrennium (kwɒ'drenɪəm) *n, pl* **quadrenniums** *or* **quadrennia** (-nɪə). a period of four years. [C17: from L *quadriennium,* from QUADRI- + *annus* year]
quadri- *or before a vowel* **quadr-** *combining form.* four: *quadrilateral.* [from L; cf. *quattuor* four]
quadric ('kwɒdrɪk) *Maths.* ◆ *adj* **1** having or characterized by an equation of the second degree. **2** of the second degree. ◆ *n* **3** a quadric curve, surface, or function.
quadriceps ('kwɒdrɪ,seps) *n, pl* **quadricepses** (-,sepsɪz) *or* **quadriceps.** *Anat.* a large four-part muscle of the front of the thigh, which extends the leg. [C19: NL, from QUADRI- + *-ceps* as in BICEPS]
quadrifid ('kwɒdrɪfɪd) *adj Bot.* divided into four lobes or other parts: *quadrifid leaves.*
quadrilateral (,kwɒdrɪ'lætərəl) *adj* **1** having or formed by four sides. ◆ *n* **2** Also called: **tetragon.** a polygon having four sides.
quadrille[1] (kwɒ'drɪl) *n* **1** a square dance for four couples. **2** a piece of music for such a dance. [C18: via F from Sp. *cuadrilla,* dim. of *cuadro* square, from L *quadra*]
quadrille[2] (kwɒ'drɪl, kwə-) *n* an old card game for four players. [C18: from F, from Sp. *cuartillo,* from *cuarto* fourth, from L *quartus,* infl. by QUADRILLE[1]]
quadrillion (kwɒ'drɪljən) *n, pl* **quadrillions** *or* **quadrillion. 1** (in Britain, France, and Germany) the number represented as one followed by 24 zeros (10^{24}). US and Canad. word: **septillion. 2** (in the US and Canada) the number represented as one followed by 15 zeros (10^{15}). ◆ *determiner* **3** amounting to this number: *a quadrillion atoms.* [C17: from F *quadrillon,* from QUADRI- + *-illion,* on the model of *million*]
▸**quad'rillionth** *adj*
quadrinomial (,kwɒdrɪ'nəʊmɪəl) *n* an algebraic expression containing four terms.
quadriplegia (,kwɒdrɪ'pliːdʒɪə) *n* paralysis of all four limbs. Also called: **tetraplegia.** [C20: from QUADRI- + Gk *plēssein* to strike]
▸**quadriplegic** (,kwɒdrɪ'pliːdʒɪk) *adj*
quadrivalent (,kwɒdrɪ'veɪlənt) *adj Chem.* another word for **tetravalent.**
▸**,quadri'valency** *or* **,quadri'valence** *n*
quadrivium (kwɒ'drɪvɪəm) *n, pl* **quadrivia** (ɪə). (in medieval learning) a course consisting of arithmetic, geometry, astronomy, and music. [from Med. L, from L: crossroads, from QUADRI- + *via* way]
quadroon (kwɒ'druːn) *n* a person who is one-quarter Black. [C18: from Sp. *cuarterón,* from *cuarto* quarter, from L *quartus*]
quadrumanous (kwɒ'druːmənəs) *adj* (of monkeys and apes) having all four feet specialized for use as hands. [C18: from NL *quadrumanus,* from QUADRI- + L *manus* hand]
quadruped ('kwɒdrʊ,ped) *n* **1** an animal, esp. a mammal, that has all four limbs specialized for walking. ◆ *adj* **2** having four feet. [C17: from L *quadrupēs,* from *quadru-* (see QUADRI-) + *pēs* foot]
▸**quadrupedal** (kwɒ'druːpɪdᵊl) *adj*
quadruple ('kwɒdrʊpᵊl, kwɒ'druːpᵊl) *vb* **quadruples, quadrupling, quadrupled. 1** to multiply by four or increase fourfold. ◆ *adj* **2** four times as much or as many; fourfold. **3** consisting of four parts. **4** *Music.* having four beats in each bar. ◆ *n* **5** a quantity or number four times as great as another. [C16: via OF from L *quadruplus,* from *quadru-* (see QUADRI-) + *-plus* -fold]
▸**'quadruply** *adv*

THESAURUS

quack[2] *n* **1a** = **charlatan,** fake, fraud, humbug, impostor, mountebank, phoney *or* phony (*inf.*), pretender, quacksalver (*arch.*) ◆ *modifier* **1b** = **fake,** counterfeit, fraudulent, phoney *or* phony (*inf.*), pretended, sham

quadruplet ('kwɒdruplɪt, kwɒ'dru:plɪt) *n* **1** one of four offspring born at one birth. **2** a group of four similar things. **3** *Music.* a group of four notes to be played in a time value of three.

quadruplicate *adj* (kwɒ'dru:plɪkɪt). **1** fourfold or quadruple. ◆ *vb* (kwɒ'dru:plɪ,keɪt), **quadruplicates, quadruplicating, quadruplicated. 2** to multiply or be multiplied by four. ◆ *n* (kwɒ'dru:plɪkɪt). **3** a group or set of four things. [C17: from L *quadruplicāre* to increase fourfold]

quaestor ('kwi:stə) *or US* (*sometimes*) **questor** ('kwɛstə) *n* any of several magistrates of ancient Rome, usually a financial administrator. [C14: from L, from *quaerere* to inquire]
▸**quaestorial** (kwɛ'stɔ:rɪəl) *adj*

quaff ❶ (kwɒf) *vb* to drink heartily or in one draught. [C16: ? imit.; cf. MLow G *quassen* to eat or drink excessively]
▸**'quaffer** *n*

quag (kwæg) *n* a quagmire. [C16: ? rel. to QUAKE]

quagga ('kwægə) *n, pl* **quaggas** *or* **quagga.** a recently extinct member of the horse family of southern Africa: it had zebra-like stripes on the head and shoulders. [C18: from obs. Afrik., from Khoikhoi *qŭagga*]

quaggy ❶ ('kwægɪ) *adj* **quaggier, quaggiest. 1** resembling a quagmire; boggy. **2** soft or flabby.

quagmire ❶ ('kwæg,maɪə) *n* **1** a soft wet area of land that gives way under the feet; bog. **2** an awkward, complex, or embarrassing situation. [C16: from QUAG + MIRE]

quahog ('kwɑ:,hɒg) *n* an edible clam native to the Atlantic coast of North America, having a large heavy rounded shell. [C18: from Amerind, short for *poquauhock*, from *pohkeni* dark + *hogki* shell]

quaich *or* **quaigh** (kweɪx) *n Scot.* a small shallow drinking cup, usually with two handles. [from Gaelic *cuach* cup]

Quai d'Orsay (*French* ke dɔrsɛ) *n* the quay along the S bank of the Seine, Paris, where the French foreign office is situated.

quail[1] (kweɪl) *n, pl* **quails** *or* **quail.** any of various small Old World game birds having rounded bodies and small tails. [C14: from OF *quaille*, from Med. L *quaccula*, prob. imit.]

quail[2] ❶ (kweɪl) *vb* (*intr*) to shrink back with fear; cower. [C15: ?from OF *quailler*, from L *coāgulāre* to curdle]

quaint ❶ (kweɪnt) *adj* **1** attractively unusual, esp. in an old-fashioned style. **2** odd or inappropriate. [C13 (in the sense: clever): from OF *cointe*, from L *cognitus* known, from *cognoscere* to ascertain]
▸**'quaintly** *adv* ▸**'quaintness** *n*

quair (kwɛə) *n Scot.* a book. [var. of QUIRE[1]]

quake ❶ (kweɪk) *vb* **quakes, quaking, quaked.** (*intr*) **1** to shake or tremble with or as with fear. **2** to convulse or quiver, as from instability. ◆ *n* **3** a quaking. **4** *Inf.* an earthquake. [OE *cwacian*]

Quaker ('kweɪkə) *n* **1** a member of the Religious Society of Friends, a Christian sect founded by George Fox about 1650. Quakers reject sacraments, ritual, and formal ministry, and have promoted many causes for social reform. ◆ *adj* **2** of the Religious Society of Friends or its beliefs or practices. [C17: orig. a derog. nickname]
▸**'Quakeress** *fem n* ▸**'Quakerish** *adj* ▸**'Quakerism** *n*

quaking ('kweɪkɪŋ) *adj* unstable or unsafe to walk on, as a bog or quicksand.

quaking grass *n* any of various grasses having delicate branches that shake in the wind.

quaky ('kweɪkɪ) *adj* **quakier, quakiest.** inclined to quake; shaky.
▸**'quakiness** *n*

qualification ❶ (,kwɒlɪfɪ'keɪʃən) *n* **1** an official record of achievement awarded on the successful completion of a course of training or passing of an examination. **2** an ability, quality, or attribute, esp. one that fits a person to perform a particular job or task. **3** a condition that modifies or limits; restriction. **4** a qualifying or being qualified.

qualified ❶ ('kwɒlɪ,faɪd) *adj* **1** having the abilities, qualities, attributes, etc., necessary to perform a particular job or task. **2** limited, modified, or restricted; not absolute.

Qualified Majority Voting *n* a voting system, used by the EU Council of Ministers, by which resolutions concerning certain areas of policy may be passed without unanimity. Abbrev.: **QMV.**

qualify ❶ ('kwɒlɪ,faɪ) *vb* **qualifies, qualifying, qualified. 1** to provide or be provided with the abilities or attributes necessary for a task, office, duty, etc.: *his degree qualifies him for the job.* **2** (*tr*) to make less strong, harsh, or violent; moderate or restrict. **3** (*tr*) to modify or change the strength or flavour of. **4** (*tr*) *Grammar.* another word for **modify. 5** (*tr*) to attribute a quality to; characterize. **6** (*intr*) to progress to the final stages of a competition, as by winning preliminary contests. [C16: from OF *qualifier*, from Med. L *quālificāre* to characterize, from L *quālis* of what kind + *facere* to make]
▸**'quali,fiable** *adj* ▸**'quali,fier** *n*

qualitative ('kwɒlɪtətɪv) *adj* involving or relating to distinctions based on quality or qualities.
▸**'qualitatively** *adv*

qualitative analysis *n* See **analysis** (sense 4).

quality ❶ ('kwɒlɪtɪ) *n, pl* **qualities. 1** a distinguishing characteristic or attribute. **2** the basic character or nature of something. **3** a feature of personality. **4** degree or standard of excellence, esp. a high standard. **5** (formerly) high social status or the distinction associated with it. **6** musical tone colour; timbre. **7** *Logic.* the characteristic of a proposition that makes it affirmative or negative. **8** *Phonetics.* the distinctive character of a vowel, determined by the configuration of the mouth, tongue, etc. **9** (*modifier*) having or showing excellence or superiority: *a quality product.* [C13: from OF *qualité*, from L *quālitās* state, from *quālis* of what sort]

quality control *n* control of the quality of a manufactured product, usually by statistical sampling techniques.

quality time *n* a short period during the day in which a person gives the whole of his or her attention to some matter other than work, esp. family relationships.

qualm ❶ (kwɑ:m) *n* **1** a sudden feeling of sickness or nausea. **2** a pang of doubt, esp. concerning moral conduct; scruple. **3** a sudden sensation of misgiving. [OE *cwealm* death or plague]
▸**'qualmish** *adj*

quandary ❶ ('kwɒndrɪ) *n, pl* **quandaries.** a difficult situation; predicament. [C16: from ?; ? rel. to L *quandō* when]

quandong, quandang ('kwɒn,dɒŋ), *or* **quantong** ('kwɒn,tɒŋ) *n* **1** Also called: **native peach. 1a** a small Australian tree. **1b** the edible fruit or nut of this tree. **2** *Austral. sl.* a sponger or parasite. **3 silver quandong. 3a** an Australian tree. **3b** its timber. [from Abor.]

quango ('kwæŋgəʊ) *n, pl* **quangos.** a semipublic government-financed administrative body whose members are appointed by the government. [C20: *qu(asi-)a(utonomous) n(on) g(overnmental) o(rganization)*]

quant[1] (kwɒnt) *n* **1** a long pole for propelling a boat, esp. a punt. ◆ *vb* **2** to propel (a boat) with a quant. [C15: prob. from L *contus* pole, from Gk *kontos*]

quant[2] (kwɒnt) *n Inf.* a highly paid analyst with a degree in a quantitative science, employed by a financial house to predict price movements of securities, commodities, etc. [C20: from QUANTITATIVE]

quanta ('kwɒntə) *n* the plural of **quantum.**

quantic ('kwɒntɪk) *n* a homogeneous function of two or more variables in a rational and integral form. [C19: from L *quantus* how great]

quantifier ('kwɒntɪ,faɪə) *n* **1** *Logic.* a symbol indicating the quantity of a term: *the existential quantifier corresponds to the words "there is something, such that".* **2** *Grammar.* a word or phrase, such as *some, all,* or *no,* expressing quantity.

quantify ('kwɒntɪ,faɪ) *vb* **quantifies, quantifying, quantified.** (*tr*) **1** to discover or express the quantity of. **2** *Logic.* to specify the quantity of (a term) by using a quantifier, such as *all, some,* or *no.* [C19: from Med. L *quantificāre*, from L *quantus* how much + *facere* to make]
▸**'quantifiable** *adj* ▸**,quantifi'cation** *n*

THESAURUS

quaff *vb* = **drink**, bend the elbow (*inf.*), bevvy (*dialect*), carouse, down, gulp, guzzle, imbibe, swallow, swig (*inf.*), tope

quaggy *adj* **1** = **boggy**, fenny, marshy, miry, muddy, mushy, paludal, soft, soggy, squelchy, swampy, yielding

quagmire *n* **1** = **bog**, fen, marsh, mire, morass, quicksand, slough, swamp **2** = **entanglement**, difficulty, dilemma, fix (*inf.*), imbroglio, impasse, jam (*inf.*), muddle, pass, pickle (*inf.*), pinch, plight, predicament, quandary, scrape (*inf.*)

quail[2] *vb* = **shrink**, blanch, blench, cower, cringe, faint, falter, flinch, recoil, shudder, tremble

quaint *adj* **1** = **old-fashioned**, antiquated, antique, artful, charming, gothic, ingenious, old-world, picturesque **2** = **unusual**, bizarre, curious, droll, eccentric, fanciful, fantastic, odd, original, peculiar, queer, rum (*Brit. sl.*), singular, strange, whimsical
Antonyms ≠ **old-fashioned:** fashionable, modern, new, up-to-date *adj* ≠ **unusual:** normal, ordinary

quake *vb* **1, 2** = **shake**, convulse, quiver, rock, shiver, shudder, totter, tremble, vibrate, wobble

qualification *n* **2** = **attribute**, ability, accomplishment, aptitude, capability, capacity, eligibility, endowment(s), fitness, quality, skill, suitability, suitableness **3** = **condition**, allowance, caveat, criterion, exception, exemption, limitation, modification, objection, prerequisite, proviso, requirement, reservation, restriction, rider, stipulation

qualified *adj* **1** = **capable**, able, accomplished, adept, certificated, competent, efficient, eligible, equipped, experienced, expert, fit, knowledgeable, licensed, practised, proficient, skilful, talented, trained **2** = **restricted**, bounded, circumscribed, conditional, confined, contingent, equivocal, guarded, limited, modified, provisional, reserved
Antonyms *adj* ≠ **capable:** amateur, apprentice, self-styled, self-taught, trainee, uncertificated, unqualified, untrained ≠ **restricted:** categorical, outright, unconditional, unequivocal, wholehearted

qualify *vb* **1** = **certify**, capacitate, commission, condition, empower, endow, equip, fit, ground, permit, prepare, ready, sanction, train **2, 3** = **moderate**, abate, adapt, assuage, circumscribe, diminish, ease, lessen, limit, mitigate, modify, modulate, reduce, regulate, restrain, restrict, soften, temper, vary **5** = **be described**, be characterized, be designated, be distinguished, be named
Antonyms *vb* ≠ **certify:** ban, debar, disqualify, forbid, preclude, prevent

quality *n* **1** = **characteristic**, aspect, attribute, condition, feature, mark, peculiarity, property, trait **2** = **nature**, character, constitution, description, essence, kind, make, sort, worth **4** = **excellence**, calibre, distinction, grade, merit, position, pre-eminence, rank, standing, status, superiority, value **5** = **nobility**, aristocracy, gentry, ruling class, upper class

qualm *n* **1** = **nausea**, agony, attack, pang, queasiness, sickness, spasm, throe (*rare*), twinge **2** = **misgiving**, anxiety, apprehension, compunction, disquiet, doubt, hesitation, regret, reluctance, remorse, scruple, twinge *or* pang of conscience, uncertainty, uneasiness

quandary *n* = **difficulty**, bewilderment, cleft stick, delicate situation, dilemma, doubt, embarrassment, impasse, perplexity, plight, predicament, puzzle, strait, uncertainty

quantity *n* **1** = **amount**, aggregate, allotment, lot, number, part, portion, quota, sum, total

quantitative ('kwɒntɪtətɪv) *or* **quantitive** *adj* **1** involving or relating to considerations of amount or size. **2** capable of being measured. **3** *Prosody.* of a metrical system that is based on the length of syllables. ▸ **'quantitatively** *or* **'quantitively** *adv*
quantitative analysis *n* See **analysis** (sense 4).
quantity ➊ ('kwɒntɪtɪ) *n, pl* **quantities. 1a** a specified or definite amount, number, etc. **1b** (*as modifier*): *a quantity estimate.* **2** the aspect of anything that can be measured, weighed, counted, etc. **3 unknown quantity.** a person or thing whose action, effort, etc., is unknown or unpredictable. **4** a large amount. **5** *Maths.* an entity having a magnitude that may be denoted by a numerical expression. **6** *Physics.* a specified magnitude or amount. **7** *Logic.* the characteristic of a proposition that makes it universal or particular. **8** *Prosody.* the relative duration of a syllable or the vowel in it. [C14: from OF *quantité,* from L *quantitās* amount, from *quantus* how much]

> **USAGE NOTE** The use of a plural noun after *quantity of* as in *a large quantity of bananas* was formerly considered incorrect, but is now acceptable.

quantity surveyor *n* a person who estimates the cost of the materials and labour necessary for a construction job.
quantize *or* **quantise** ('kwɒntaɪz) *vb* **quantizes, quantizing, quantized** *or* **quantises, quantising, quantised.** (*tr*) **1** *Physics.* to restrict (a physical quantity) to one of a set of fixed values. **2** *Maths.* to limit to values that are multiples of a basic unit. ▸ **,quanti'zation** *or* **,quanti'sation** *n*
quantum ('kwɒntəm) *n, pl* **quanta. 1** *Physics.* **1a** the smallest quantity of some physical property that a system can possess according to the quantum theory. **1b** a particle with such a unit of energy. **2** amount or quantity, esp. a specific amount. ◆ *adj* **3** of or designating a major breakthrough or sudden advance: *a quantum leap forward.* [C17: from L *quantus* (adj) how much]
quantum electrodynamics *n Physics.* the study of electromagnetic radiation and its interaction with charged particles in terms of quantum theory. Abbrev.: **QED.**
quantum mechanics *n* (*functioning as sing*) the branch of mechanics, based on the quantum theory, used for interpreting the behaviour of elementary particles and atoms, which do not obey Newtonian mechanics.
quantum meruit *Latin.* ('mɛruːɪt) as much as he has earned.
quantum number *n Physics.* one of a set of integers or half-integers characterizing the energy states of a particle or system of particles.
quantum theory *n* a theory concerning the behaviour of physical systems based on the idea that they can only possess certain properties, such as energy and angular momentum, in discrete amounts (quanta).
quaquaversal (,kwɑːkwə'vɜːsəl) *adj Geol.* directed outwards in all directions from a common centre. [C18: from L *quāquā* in every direction + *versus* towards]
quarantine ('kwɒrən,tiːn) *n* **1** a period of isolation or detention, esp. of persons or animals arriving from abroad, to prevent the spread of disease. **2** the place where such detention is enforced. **3** any period or state of enforced isolation. ◆ *vb* **quarantines, quarantining, quarantined. 4** (*tr*) to isolate in or as if in quarantine. [C17: from It. *quarantina* period of forty days, from *quaranta* forty, from L *quadrāgintā*]
quarantine flag *n Naut.* the yellow signal flag for the letter Q, flown alone from a vessel to indicate that there is no disease aboard or, with a second signal flag, to indicate that there is disease aboard. Also called: **yellow jack.**
quark[1] (kwɑːk) *n Physics.* any of a set of six elementary particles that, together with their antiparticles, are thought to be fundamental units of all baryons and mesons but unable to exist in isolation. [C20: coined by James Joyce in the novel *Finnegans Wake* (1939) & given special application in physics]
quark[2] (kwɑːk) *n* a type of low-fat soft cheese. [from G]
quarrel[1] ➊ ('kwɒrəl) *n* **1** an angry disagreement; argument. **2** a cause of dispute; grievance. ◆ *vb* **quarrels, quarrelling, quarrelled** *or US* **quarrels, quarreling, quarreled.** (*intr;* often foll. by *with*) **3** to engage in a disagreement or dispute; argue. **4** to find fault; complain. [C14: from OF *querele,* from L *querēlla* complaint, from *querī* to complain] ▸ **'quarreller** *or US* **'quarreler** *n*
quarrel[2] ('kwɒrəl) *n* **1** an arrow having a four-edged head, fired from a crossbow. **2** a small square or diamond-shaped pane of glass. [C13: from OF *quarrel* pane, from Med. L *quadrellus,* dim. of L *quadrus* square]
quarrelsome ➊ ('kwɒrəlsəm) *adj* inclined to quarrel or disagree; belligerent.
quarrian *or* **quarrion** ('kwɒrɪən) *n* a cockatiel of inland Australia that feeds on seeds and grasses. [C20: prob. from Abor.]
quarry[1] ('kwɒrɪ) *n, pl* **quarries. 1** an open surface excavation for the extraction of building stone, slate, marble, etc. **2** a copious source, esp. of information. ◆ *vb* **quarries, quarrying, quarried. 3** to extract (stone, slate, etc.) from or as if from a quarry. **4** (*tr*) to excavate a quarry in. **5** to obtain (something) diligently and laboriously. [C15: from OF *quarriere,* from *quarre* (unattested) square-shaped stone, from L *quadrāre* to make square]
quarry[2] ➊ ('kwɒrɪ) *n, pl* **quarries. 1** an animal, etc., that is hunted, esp. by other animals; prey. **2** anything pursued. [C14 *quirre* entrails offered to the hounds, from OF *cuirée* what is placed on the hide, from *cuir* hide, from L *corium* leather; prob. also infl. by OF *coree* entrails, from L *cor* heart]
quarryman ('kwɒrɪmən) *n, pl* **quarrymen.** a man who works in or manages a quarry.
quarry tile *n* an unglazed floor tile.
quart (kwɔːt) *n* **1** a unit of liquid measure equal to a quarter of a gallon or two pints. 1 US quart (0.946 litre) is equal to 0.8326 UK quart. 1 UK quart (1.136 litres) is equal to 1.2009 US quarts. **2** a unit of dry measure equal to 2 pints or one eighth of a peck. [C14: from OF *quarte,* from L *quartus* fourth]
quartan ('kwɔːtᵊn) *adj* (of a fever) occurring every third day. [C13: from L *febris quartāna* fever occurring every fourth day, reckoned inclusively]
quarte (kɑːt) *n* the fourth of eight basic positions from which a parry or attack can be made in fencing. [C18: F from OF *quarte,* from L *quartus* fourth]
quarter ➊ ('kwɔːtə) *n* **1** one of four equal parts of an object, quantity, etc. **2** the fraction equal to one divided by four (¼). **3** *US, Canad., etc.* a 25-cent piece. **4** a unit of weight equal to a quarter of a hundredweight. 1 US quarter is equal to 25 pounds; 1 Brit. quarter is equal to 28 pounds. **5** short for **quarter-hour. 6** a fourth part of a year; three months. **7** *Astron.* **7a** one fourth of the moon's period of revolution around the earth. **7b** either of two phases of the moon when half of the lighted surface is visible. **8** *Inf.* a unit of weight equal to a quarter of a pound or 4 ounces. **9** *Brit.* a unit of capacity for grain, etc., usually equal to 8 UK bushels. **10** *Sport.* one of the four periods into which certain games are divided. **11** *Naut.* the part of a vessel's side towards the stern. **12** a region or district of a town or city: *the Spanish quarter.* **13** a region, direction, or point of the compass. **14** (*sometimes pl*) an unspecified person or group of people: *to get word from the highest quarter.* **15** mercy or pity, as shown to a defeated opponent (esp. in **ask for** *or* **give quarter**). **16** any of the four limbs, including the adjacent parts, of a quadruped or bird. **17** *Heraldry.* one of four quadrants into which a shield may be divided. ◆ *vb* **18** (*tr*) to divide into four equal parts. **19** (*tr*) to divide into any number of parts. **20** (*tr*) (esp. formerly) to dismember (a human body). **21** to billet or be billeted in lodgings, esp. (of military personnel) in civilian lodgings. **22** (*intr*) (of hounds) to range over an area of ground in search of game or the scent of quarry. **23** (*intr*) *Naut.* (of the wind) to blow onto a vessel's quarter. **24** (*tr*) *Heraldry.* **24a** to divide (a shield) into four separate bearings. **24b** to place (one set of arms) in diagonally opposite quarters to another. ◆ *adj* **25** being or consisting of one of four equal parts. ◆ See also **quarters.** [C13: from OF *quartier,* from L *quartārius* a fourth part, from *quartus* fourth]
quarterback ('kwɔːtə,bæk) *n* a player in American football who directs attacking play.
quarter-bound *adj* (of a book) having a binding consisting of two types of material, the better type being used on the spine.
quarter day *n* any of four days in the year when certain payments become due. In England, Wales, and Northern Ireland these are Lady Day, Midsummer's Day, Michaelmas, and Christmas. In Scotland they are Candlemas, Whit Sunday, Lammas, and Martinmas.
quarterdeck ('kwɔːtə,dɛk) *n Naut.* the after part of the upper deck of a ship, traditionally the deck for official or ceremonial use.
quartered ('kwɔːtəd) *adj* **1** *Heraldry.* (of a shield) divided into four sections, each having contrasting arms or having two sets of arms, each repeated in diagonally opposite corners. **2** (of a log) sawn into four equal parts along two diameters at right angles to each other.
quarterfinal (,kwɔːtə'faɪnᵊl) *n* the round before the semifinal in a competition.
quarter-hour *n* **1** a period of 15 minutes. **2** either of the points on a timepiece that mark 15 minutes before or after the hour.
quartering ('kwɔːtərɪŋ) *n* **1** *Mil.* the allocation of accommodation to

THESAURUS

4 = size, bulk, capacity, expanse, extent, greatness, length, magnitude, mass, measure, volume
quarrel[1] *n* **1 = disagreement,** affray, altercation, argument, brawl, breach, commotion, contention, controversy, difference (of opinion), discord, disputation, dispute, dissension, dissidence, disturbance, feud, fight, fracas, fray, row, scrap (*inf.*), shindig (*inf.*), shindy (*inf.*), skirmish, spat, squabble, strife, tiff, vendetta, wrangle ◆ *vb* **3 = disagree,** altercate, argue, bicker, brawl, clash, differ, dispute, fall out (*inf.*), fight, fight like cat and dog, go at it hammer and tongs, row, spar, squabble, wrangle **4 = object to,** carp, cavil, complain, decry, disapprove, find fault, take exception to
Antonyms *n* ≠ **disagreement:** accord, agreement, concord ◆ *vb* ≠ **disagree:** agree, get on *or* along (with)
quarrelsome *adj* **= argumentative,** belligerent, cantankerous, cat-and-dog (*inf.*), choleric, combative, contentious, cross, disputatious, fractious, ill-tempered, irascible, irritable, litigious, peevish, petulant, pugnacious, querulous
Antonyms *adj* easy-going, equable, even-tempered, placid
quarry[2] *n* **1 = prey,** game, victim **2 = goal,** aim, objective, prize
quarter *n* **12 = district,** area, direction, locality, location, neighbourhood, part, place, point, position, province, region, side, spot, station, territory, zone **15 = mercy,** clemency, compassion, favour, forgiveness, leniency, pity ◆ *vb* **21 = accommodate,** billet, board, house, install, lodge, place, post, put up, station

service personnel. **2** *Heraldry.* **2a** the marshalling of several coats of arms on one shield, usually representing intermarriages. **2b** any coat of arms marshalled in this way.

quarterlight ('kwɔːtəˌlaɪt) *n Brit.* a small pivoted window in the door of a car for ventilation.

quarterly ('kwɔːtəlɪ) *adj* **1** occurring, done, paid, etc., at intervals of three months. **2** of, relating to, or consisting of a quarter. ◆ *n, pl* **quarterlies. 3** a periodical issued every three months. ◆ *adv* **4** once every three months.

quartermaster ('kwɔːtəˌmɑːstə) *n* **1** an officer responsible for accommodation, food, and equipment in a military unit. **2** a rating in the navy, usually a petty officer, with particular responsibility for navigational duties.

quarter-miler *n* an athlete who specializes in running the quarter mile.

quartern ('kwɔːtən) *n* **1** a fourth part of certain weights or measures. **2** Also called: **quartern loaf.** *Brit.* **2a** a type of loaf 4 inches square. **2b** any loaf weighing 1600 g. [C13: from OF *quarteron,* from *quart* a quarter]

quarter note *n* the usual US and Canad. name for **crotchet** (sense 1).

quarter plate *n* a photographic plate measuring 3¼ × 4¼ inches (8.3 × 10.8 cm).

quarters ⓘ ('kwɔːtəz) *pl n* **1** accommodation, esp. as provided for military personnel. **2** the stations assigned to crew members of a warship: *general quarters.*

quarter sessions *n (functioning as sing or pl)* (formerly) any of various courts held four times a year before justices of the peace or a recorder.

quarterstaff ('kwɔːtəˌstɑːf) *n, pl* **quarterstaves** (-ˌsteɪvz). a stout iron-tipped wooden staff about 6ft long, formerly used as a weapon. [C16: from ?]

quarter tone *n Music.* a quarter of a whole tone.

quartet *or* **quartette** (kwɔː'tɛt) *n* **1** a group of four singers or instrumentalists or a piece of music composed for such a group. **2** any group of four. [C18: from It. *quartetto,* dim. of *quarto* fourth]

quartic ('kwɔːtɪk) *adj, n* another word for **biquadratic.** [C19: from L *quartus* fourth]

quartile ('kwɔːtaɪl) *n* **1** *Statistics.* one of three values of a variable dividing its distribution into four groups with equal frequencies. ◆ *adj* **2** *Statistics.* of a quartile. **3** *Astrol.* denoting an aspect of two heavenly bodies when their longitudes differ by 90°. [C16: from Med. L *quartīlis,* from L *quartus* fourth]

quarto ('kwɔːtəʊ) *n, pl* **quartos.** a book size resulting from folding a sheet of paper into four leaves or eight pages. [C16: from NL *in quartō* in quarter]

quartz (kwɔːts) *n* a hard glossy mineral consisting of silicon dioxide in crystalline form. It occurs as colourless rock crystal and as several impure coloured varieties including agate, chalcedony, flint, and amethyst. Formula: SiO_2. [C18: from G *Quarz,* of Slavic origin]

quartz clock *or* **watch** *n* a clock or watch that is operated by a vibrating quartz crystal.

quartz crystal *n* a thin plate or rod cut from a piece of piezoelectric quartz and ground so that it vibrates at a particular frequency.

quartz glass *n* a colourless glass composed of almost pure silica, resistant to very high temperatures.

quartz-iodine lamp *or* **quartz lamp** *n* a type of tungsten-halogen lamp containing small amounts of iodine and having a quartz envelope, operating at high temperature and producing an intense light for use in car headlamps, etc.

quartzite ('kwɔːtsaɪt) *n* **1** a sandstone composed of quartz. **2** a very hard rock consisting of intergrown quartz crystals.

quasar ('kweɪzɑː, -sɑː) *n* any of a class of quasi-stellar objects that emit an immense amount of energy in the form of light, infrared radiation, etc., from a compact source. They are extremely distant and hence the youngest objects observed in the universe, and their energy generation is thought to involve a black hole located in a galaxy. [C20: *quasi(i-stell)ar (object)*]

quash ⓘ (kwɒʃ) *vb (tr)* **1** to subdue forcefully and completely. **2** to annul or make void (a law, etc.). **3** to reject (an indictment, etc.) as invalid. [C14: from OF *quasser,* from L *quassāre* to shake]

quasi- ⓘ *combining form.* **1** almost but not really; seemingly: *a quasi-religious cult.* **2** resembling but not actually being; so-called: *a quasi-scholar.* [from L, lit.: as if]

quasi-stellar object ('kwɑːzɪ, 'kweɪsaɪ) *n* a member of any of several classes of astronomical bodies, including **quasars** and **quasi-stellar galaxies,** both of which have exceptionally large red shifts. Abbrev.: **QSO.**

quassia ('kwɒʃə) *n* **1** any of a genus of tropical American trees having bitter bark and wood. **2** the wood of this tree or a bitter compound extracted from it, formerly used as a tonic and vermifuge, now used in insecticides. [C18: from NL, after Graman *Quassi,* a slave who discovered (1730) the medicinal value of the root]

quatercentenary (ˌkwætəsɛn'tiːnərɪ) *n, pl* **quatercentenaries.** a 400th anniversary. [C19: from L *quater* four times + CENTENARY]
▸ˌ**quatercen'tennial** (ˌkwætəsɛn'tɛnɪəl) *adj, n*

quaternary (kwə'tɜːnərɪ) *adj* **1** consisting of fours or by fours. **2** fourth in a series. **3** *Chem.* containing or being an atom bound to four other atoms or groups. ◆ *n, pl* **quaternaries. 4** the number four or a set of four. [C15: from L *quaternārius* each containing four, from *quaternī* by fours, from *quattuor* four]

Quaternary (kwə'tɜːnərɪ) *adj* **1** of or denoting the most recent period of geological time, which succeeded the Tertiary period one million years ago. ◆ *n* **2 the.** the Quaternary period or rock system.

quaternion (kwə'tɜːnɪən) *n* **1** *Maths.* a generalized complex number consisting of four components, $x = x_0 + x_1i + x_2j + x_3k$, where $x, x_0 \ldots x_3$ are real numbers and $i^2 = j^2 = k^2 = -1$, $ij = -ji = k$, etc. **2** a set of four. [C14: from LL, from L *quaternī* four at a time]

quatrain ('kwɒtreɪn) *n* a stanza or poem of four lines. [C16: from F, from *quatre* four, from L *quattuor*]

quatrefoil ('kætrəˌfɔɪl) *n* **1** a leaf composed of four leaflets. **2** *Archit.* a carved ornament having four foils arranged about a common centre. [C15: from OF, from *quatre* four + *-foil* leaflet]

quattrocento (ˌkwætrəʊ'tʃɛntəʊ) *n* the 15th century, esp. in reference to Renaissance Italian art and literature. [It., lit.: four hundred (short for fourteen hundred)]

quaver ⓘ ('kweɪvə) *vb* **1** to say or sing (something) with a trembling voice. **2** *(intr)* (esp. of the voice) to quiver or tremble. **3** *(intr) Rare.* to sing or play trills. ◆ *n* **4** *Music.* a note having the time value of an eighth of a semibreve. Usual US and Canad. name: **eighth note. 5** a tremulous sound or note. [C15 (in the sense: to vibrate): from *quaven* to tremble, of Gmc origin]
▸'**quavering** *adj* ▸'**quaveringly** *adv*

quay (kiː) *n* a wharf, typically one built parallel to the shoreline. [C14 *keye,* from OF *kai,* of Celtic origin]

quayage ('kiːɪdʒ) *n* **1** a system of quays. **2** a charge for the use of a quay.

quayside ('kiːˌsaɪd) *n* the edge of a quay along the water.

Que. *abbrev. for* Quebec.

quean (kwiːn) *n* **1** *Arch.* **1a** a boisterous impudent woman. **1b** a prostitute. **2** *Scot.* an unmarried girl. [OE *cwene*]

queasy ⓘ ('kwiːzɪ) *adj* **queasier, queasiest. 1** having the feeling that one is about to vomit; nauseous. **2** feeling or causing uneasiness. [C15: from ?]
▸'**queasily** *adv* ▸'**queasiness** *n*

Quebecker *or* **Quebecer** (kwɪ'bɛkə, kə'bɛkə) *n* a native or inhabitant of Quebec.

Québecois *(French* kebɛkwa) *n, pl* **Québecois** (-kwa). a native or inhabitant of the province of Quebec, esp. a French-speaking one.

quebracho (keɪ'brɑːtʃəʊ) *n, pl* **quebrachos** (-tʃəʊz). **1** either of two South American trees having a tannin-rich hard wood used in tanning and dyeing. **2** a South American tree, whose bark yields alkaloids used in medicine and tanning. **3** the wood or bark of any of these trees. [C19: from American Sp., from *quiebracha,* from *quebrar* to break (from L *crepāre* to rattle) + *hacha* axe (from F)]

Quechua ('kɛtʃwə) *n* **1** *(pl* **Quechuas** *or* **Quechua)** a member of any of a group of South American Indian peoples of the Andes, including the Incas. **2** the language or family of languages spoken by these peoples.
▸'**Quechuan** *adj, n*

queen ⓘ (kwiːn) *n* **1** a female sovereign who is the official ruler or head of state. **2** the wife of a king. **3** a woman or a thing personified as a woman considered the best or most important of her kind: *the queen of ocean liners.* **4** *Sl.* an effeminate male homosexual. **5** the only fertile female in a colony of bees, ants, etc. **6** an adult female cat. **7** a playing card bearing the picture of a queen. **8** the most powerful chess piece, able to move in a straight line in any direction or diagonally. ◆ *vb* **9** *Chess.* to promote (a pawn) to a queen when it reaches the eighth rank. **10** *(tr)* to crown as queen. **11** *(intr)* to reign as queen. **12 queen it.** (often foll. by *over) Inf.* to behave in an overbearing manner. [OE *cwēn*]

Queen-Anne *n* **1** a style of furniture popular in England about 1700–20 and in America about 1720–70, characterized by walnut veneer and cabriole legs. ◆ *adj* **2** in or of this style. **3** of a style of architecture popular in early 18th-century England, characterized by red-brick construction with classical ornamentation.

Queen Anne's lace *n* another name for the **wild carrot.**

queen bee *n* **1** the fertile female bee in a hive. **2** *Inf.* a woman in a position of dominance over her associates.

queen consort *n* the wife of a reigning king.

queen dowager *n* the widow of a king.

queenly ⓘ ('kwiːnlɪ) *adj* **queenlier, queenliest. 1** resembling or appropriate to a queen. ◆ *adv* **2** in a manner appropriate to a queen.

THESAURUS

quarters *pl n* **1** = **lodgings**, abode, accommodation, barracks, billet, cantonment *(Military)*, digs *(Brit. inf.)*, domicile, dwelling, habitation, lodging, post, residence, rooms, shelter, station

quash *vb* **1** = **suppress**, beat, crush, destroy, extinguish, extirpate, overthrow, put down, quell, quench, repress, squash, subdue **2, 3** = **annul**, cancel, declare null and void, invalidate, nullify, overrule, overthrow, rescind, reverse, revoke, set aside, void

quasi- *combining form* **1** = **almost**, apparently, partly, seemingly, supposedly **2** = **pseudo-**, apparent, fake, mock, near, nominal, pretended, seeming, semi-, sham, so-called, synthetic, virtual, would-be

quaver *vb* **2** = **tremble**, quake, quiver, shake, shudder, thrill, trill, twitter, vibrate, waver ◆ *n* **5** = **trembling**, break, quiver, shake, sob, throb, tremble, tremor, trill, vibration, warble

queasy *adj* **1** = **sick**, bilious, giddy, green around the gills *(inf.)*, groggy *(inf.)*, ill, indisposed, nauseated, off colour, queer, sickish, squeamish, uncomfortable, unwell, upset **2** = **uneasy**, anxious, concerned, fidgety, ill at ease, restless, troubled, uncertain, worried

queen *n* **1, 2** = **sovereign**, consort, monarch, ruler **3** = **ideal**, diva, doyenne, idol, mistress, model, perfection, prima donna, star

queenly *adj* **1** = **majestic**, grand, imperial, noble, regal, royal, stately

queen mother *n* the widow of a former king who is also the mother of the reigning sovereign.

queen olive *n* a variety of olive having large fleshy fruit suitable for pickling.

queen post *n* one of a pair of vertical posts that connect the tie beam of a truss to the principal rafters. Cf. **king post.**

Queen's Award *n* either of two awards instituted by royal warrant (1976) for increased export earnings by a British firm (**Queen's Award for Export Achievement**) or for an advance in technology (**Queen's Award for Technological Achievement**).

Queen's Bench *n* (in England when the sovereign is female) one of the divisions of the High Court of Justice.

Queensberry rules ('kwi:nzbərɪ) *pl n* **1** the code of rules followed in modern boxing. **2** *Inf.* gentlemanly conduct, esp. in a dispute. [C19: after the ninth Marquess of *Queensberry*, who originated the rules in 1869]

Queen's Counsel *n* (when the sovereign is female) **1** a barrister (in England and Wales) or an advocate (in Scotland) appointed Counsel to the Crown by the sovereign on the recommendation of the Lord Chancellor (in England and Wales) or the Lord President (in Scotland). **2** (in Australia) a similar appointment, usually made on the recommendation of the Chief Justice of each state, through the state governor. **3** (in Canada) an honorary title which may be bestowed by the government on lawyers with long experience.

Queen's English *n* (when the British sovereign is female) standard Southern British English.

queen's evidence *n English law.* (when the sovereign is female) evidence given for the Crown against his former associates in crime by an accomplice (esp. in **turn queen's evidence**). US equivalent: **state's evidence.**

Queen's Guide *n* (in Britain and the Commonwealth when the sovereign is female) a Guide who has passed the highest tests of proficiency.

queen's highway *n* **1** (in Britain when the sovereign is female) any public road or right of way. **2** (in Canada) a main road maintained by the provincial government.

queen-size *or* **queen-sized** *adj* (of a bed, etc.) larger or longer than normal size but smaller or shorter than king-size.

Queensland nut ('kwi:nz,lænd) *n* another name for **macadamia.**

Queen's Scout *n* (in Britain and the Commonwealth when the sovereign is female) a Scout who has passed the highest tests of proficiency. US equivalent: **Eagle Scout.**

queer ❶ (kwɪə) *adj* **1** differing from the normal or usual; odd or strange. **2** dubious; shady. **3** faint, giddy, or queasy. **4** *Inf., derog.* homosexual. **5** *Inf.* eccentric or slightly mad. **6** *Sl.* worthless or counterfeit. ◆ *n* **7** *Inf., derog.* a homosexual. ◆ *vb* (*tr*) *Inf.* **8** to spoil or thwart (esp. in **queer someone's pitch**). **9** to put in a difficult position. [C16: ? from G *quer* oblique, ult. from OHG *twërh*]
▸'**queerly** *adv* ▸'**queerness** *n*

> **USAGE NOTE** Although the term *queer* meaning homosexual is still considered derogatory when used by nonhomosexuals, it is now used by homosexuals of themselves as a positive term, as in *queer politics, queer cinema.*

queer fish *n Brit. inf.* an odd person.

queer street *n* (*sometimes cap.*) *Inf.* a difficult situation, such as debt or bankruptcy (in **in queer street**).

quell ❶ (kwɛl) *vb* (*tr*) **1** to suppress (rebellion, etc.); subdue. **2** to overcome or allay. [OE *cwellan* to kill]
▸'**queller** *n*

quench ❶ (kwɛntʃ) *vb* (*tr*) **1** to satisfy (one's thirst, desires, etc.); slake. **2** to put out (a fire, etc.); extinguish. **3** to put down; suppress; subdue. **4** to cool (hot metal) by plunging it into cold water. [OE *ācwencan* to extinguish]
▸'**quenchable** *adj* ▸'**quencher** *n*

quenelle (kə'nɛl) *n* a ball of sieved meat or fish. [C19: from F, from G *Knödel* dumpling, from OHG *knodo* knot]

querist ('kwɪərɪst) *n* a person who makes inquiries or queries; questioner.

quern (kwɜ:n) *n* a stone hand mill for grinding corn. [OE *cweorn*]

quernstone ('kwɜ:n,stəun) *n* **1** another name for **millstone** (sense 1). **2** one of the two stones used in a quern.

querulous ❶ ('kwɛruləs, 'kwɛrju-) *adj* **1** inclined to make whining or peevish complaints. **2** characterized by or proceeding from a complaining fretful attitude or disposition. [C15: from L *querulus*, from *querī* to complain]
▸'**querulously** *adv* ▸'**querulousness** *n*

query ❶ ('kwɪərɪ) *n, pl* **queries. 1** a question, esp. one expressing doubt. **2** a question mark. ◆ *vb* **queries, querying, queried.** (*tr*) **3** to express uncertainty, doubt, or an objection concerning (something). **4** to express as a query. **5** *US.* to put a question to (a person); ask. [C17: from earlier *quere*, from L *quaerē* ask!, from *quaerere* to seek]

query language *n Computing.* the instructions and procedures used to retrieve information from a database.

quest ❶ (kwɛst) *n* **1** a looking for or seeking; search. **2** (in medieval romance) an expedition by a knight or knights to accomplish a task, such as finding the Holy Grail. **3** the object of a search; a goal or target. ◆ *vb* (*mainly intr*) **4** (foll. by *for* or *after*) to go in search (of). **5** (of dogs, etc.) to search for game. **6** (*also tr*) *Arch.* to seek. [C14: from OF *queste*, from L *quaesita* sought, from *quaerere* to seek]
▸'**quester** *n* ▸'**questing** *adj* ▸'**questingly** *adv*

question ❶ ('kwɛstʃən) *n* **1** a form of words addressed to a person in order to elicit information or evoke a response; interrogative sentence. **2** a point at issue: *it's only a question of time until she dies.* **3** a difficulty or uncertainty. **4a** an act of asking. **4b** an investigation into some problem. **5** a motion presented for debate. **6 put the question.** to require members of a deliberative assembly to vote on a motion presented. **7** *Law.* a matter submitted to a court or other tribunal. **8 beyond (all) question.** beyond (any) dispute or doubt. **9 call in** *or* **into question. 9a** to make (something) the subject of disagreement. **9b** to cast doubt upon the truth, etc., of (something). **10 in question.** under discussion: *this is the man in question.* **11 out of the question.** beyond consideration; unthinkable or impossible. **12 put to the question.** (formerly) to interrogate by torture. ◆ *vb* (*mainly tr*) **13** to put a question or questions to (a person); interrogate. **14** to make (something) the subject of dispute. **15** to express uncertainty about the truth of (something); doubt. [C13: via OF from L *quaestiō*, from *quaerere* to seek]
▸'**questioner** *n*

> **USAGE NOTE** *The question whether* should be used rather than *the question of whether* or *the question as to whether: this leaves open the question whether he acted correctly.*

questionable ❶ ('kwɛstʃənəb°l) *adj* **1** (esp. of a person's morality or honesty) admitting of some doubt; dubious. **2** of disputable value or authority.
▸'**questionableness** *n* ▸'**questionably** *adv*

questioning ('kwɛstʃənɪŋ) *adj* **1** proceeding from or characterized by a feeling of doubt or uncertainty. **2** intellectually inquisitive: *a questioning mind.*
▸'**questioningly** *adv*

questionless ('kwɛstʃənlɪs) *adj* **1** blindly adhering; unquestioning. **2** a less common word for **unquestionable.**
▸'**questionlessly** *adv*

question mark *n* **1** the punctuation mark ?, used at the end of ques-

THESAURUS

queer *adj* **1** = **strange**, abnormal, anomalous, atypical, curious, disquieting, droll, eerie, erratic, extraordinary, funny, left-field (*inf.*), odd, outlandish, outré, peculiar, remarkable, rum (*Brit. sl.*), singular, uncanny, uncommon, unconventional, unnatural, unorthodox, unusual, weird **2** = **dubious**, doubtful, fishy (*inf.*), irregular, mysterious, puzzling, questionable, shady (*inf.*), suspicious **3** = **faint**, dizzy, giddy, lightheaded, queasy, reeling, uneasy **5** *Informal* = **eccentric**, crazy, demented, idiosyncratic, irrational, mad, odd, touched, unbalanced, unhinged ◆ *vb Informal* **8** = **spoil**, bodge (*inf.*), botch, endanger, harm, impair, imperil, injure, jeopardize, mar, ruin, thwart, wreck
Antonyms *adj* ≠ **strange:** believable, common, conventional, customary, natural, normal, ordinary, orthodox, rational, regular, straight, unexceptional, unoriginal ◆ *vb* ≠ **spoil:** aid, boost, enhance, help

quell *vb* **1** = **suppress**, conquer, crush, defeat, extinguish, overcome, overpower, put down, quash, squelch, stamp out, stifle, subdue, vanquish **2** = **assuage**, allay, alleviate, appease, calm, compose, deaden, dull, mitigate, moderate, mollify, pacify, quiet, silence, soothe

quench *vb* **1** = **satisfy**, allay, appease, cool, sate, satiate, slake **2** = **put out**, douse, extinguish, smother, snuff out **3** = **suppress**, check, crush, destroy, end, squelch, stifle

querulous *adj* **1, 2** = **complaining**, cantankerous, captious, carping, censorious, critical, cross, discontented, dissatisfied, fault-finding, fretful, grouchy (*inf.*), grumbling, hard to please, irascible, irritable, peevish, petulant, plaintive, ratty (*Brit. & NZ inf.*), sour, testy, tetchy, touchy, whining
Antonyms *adj* contented, easy to please, equable, placid, uncomplaining, uncritical, undemanding

query *n* **1** = **question**, demand, doubt, hesitation, inquiry, objection, problem, reservation, scepticism, suspicion ◆ *vb* **3** = **doubt**, challenge, disbelieve, dispute, distrust, mistrust, suspect **4, 5** = **ask**, inquire *or* enquire, question

quest *n* **1** = **search**, hunt, pursuit **2** = **expedition**, adventure, crusade, enterprise, exploration, journey, mission, pilgrimage, voyage

question *n* **3** = **difficulty**, argument, can of worms (*inf.*), confusion, contention, controversy, debate, dispute, doubt, dubiety, misgiving, problem, query, uncertainty **4b** = **inquiry**, examination, interrogation, investigation **5** = **motion**, issue, point, proposal, proposition, subject, theme, topic **9 call into question** = **dispute**, cast doubt upon, challenge, controvert, disbelieve, distrust, doubt, impugn, mistrust, oppose, query, suspect **10 in question** = **under discussion**, at issue, in doubt, open to debate **11 out of the question** = **impossible**, inconceivable, not to be thought of, unthinkable ◆ *vb* **13** = **ask**, catechize, cross-examine, examine, grill (*inf.*), inquire, interrogate, interview, investigate, probe, pump (*inf.*), quiz, sound out
Antonyms *n* ≠ **inquiry:** answer, reply ◆ *vb* ≠ **ask:** answer, reply

questionable *adj* **1** = **dubious**, dodgy, doubtful, fishy (*inf.*), iffy (*inf.*), shady (*inf.*), suspect, suspicious **2** = **disputable**, arguable, controversial, controvertible, debatable, dubitable, equivocal, moot, paradoxical, problematical, uncertain, unproven, unreliable
Antonyms *adj* ≠ **disputable:** authoritative, certain, incontrovertible, indisputable, straightforward, unequivocal

tions and in other contexts where doubt or ignorance is implied. **2** this mark used for any other purpose, as to draw attention to a possible mistake.

question master *n Brit.* the chairman of a quiz or panel game.

questionnaire (ˌkwɛstʃəˈnɛə, ˌkɛs-) *n* a set of questions on a form, submitted to a number of people in order to collect statistical information.

question time *n* (in parliamentary bodies of the British type) the time set aside each day for questions to government ministers.

quetzal (ˈkɛtsəl) *n, pl* **quetzals** *or* **quetzales** (-ˈsɑːlɛs). **1** a crested bird of Central and N South America, which has a brilliant green, red, and white plumage and, in the male, long tail feathers. **2** the standard monetary unit of Guatemala. [via American Sp. from Nahuatl *quetzalli* brightly coloured tail feather]

queue ➊ (kjuː) *Chiefly Brit.* ◆ *n* **1** a line of people, vehicles, etc., waiting for something. **2** *Computing.* a list in which entries are deleted from one end and inserted at the other. **3** a pigtail. ◆ *vb* **queues, queuing** *or* **queueing, queued.** **4** (*intr*, often foll. by *up*) to form or remain in a line while waiting. **5** *Computing.* to arrange (a number of programs) in a predetermined order for accessing by a computer. ◆ Usual US word (senses 1, 4): **line.** [C16 (in the sense: tail); C18 (in the sense: pigtail): via F from L *cauda* tail]

queue-jump *vb* (*intr*) **1** to take a place in a queue ahead of those already queuing; push in. **2** to obtain some advantage out of turn or unfairly.
▸**ˈqueue-ˌjumper** *n*

quibble ➊ (ˈkwɪbᵊl) *vb* **quibbles, quibbling, quibbled.** (*intr*) **1** to make trivial objections. **2** *Arch.* to play on words; pun. ◆ *n* **3** a trivial objection or equivocation, esp. one used to avoid an issue. **4** *Arch.* a pun. [C17: prob. from obs. *quib*, ?from L *quibus* (from *quī* who, which), as used in legal documents, with reference to their obscure phraseology]
▸**ˈquibbler** *n* ▸**ˈquibbling** *adj*

quiche (kiːʃ) *n* an open savoury tart with an egg custard filling to which bacon, onion, cheese, etc., are added. [F, from G *Kuchen* cake]

quick ➊ (kwɪk) *adj* **1** performed or occurring during a comparatively short time: *a quick move.* **2** lasting a short time; brief. **3** accomplishing something in a time that is shorter than normal: *a quick worker.* **4** characterized by rapidity of movement; fast. **5** immediate or prompt. **6** (*postpositive*) eager or ready to perform (an action): *quick to criticize.* **7** responsive to stimulation; alert; lively. **8** eager or enthusiastic for learning. **9** easily excited or aroused. **10** nimble in one's movements or actions; deft: *quick fingers.* **11** *Arch.* **11a** alive; living. **11b** (*as n*) living people (esp. in **the quick and the dead**). **12 quick with child.** *Arch.* pregnant. ◆ *n* **13** any area of sensitive flesh, esp. that under a toenail or fingernail. **14** the most important part (of a thing). **15 cut (someone) to the quick.** to hurt (someone's) feelings deeply. ◆ *adv Inf.* **16** in a rapid manner; swiftly. **17** soon: *I hope he comes quick.* ◆ *sentence substitute.* **18** a command to perform an action immediately. [OE *cwicu* living]
▸**ˈquickly** *adv* ▸**ˈquickness** *n*

quick-change artist *n* an actor or entertainer who undertakes several rapid changes of costume during his performance.

quicken ➊ (ˈkwɪkən) *vb* **1** to make or become faster; accelerate. **2** to impart to or receive vigour, enthusiasm, etc.: *science quickens man's imagination.* **3** to make or become alive; revive. **4a** (of an unborn fetus) to begin to show signs of life. **4b** (of a pregnant woman) to reach the stage of pregnancy at which movements of the fetus can be felt.

quick-freeze *vb* **quick-freezes, quick-freezing, quick-froze, quick-frozen.** (*tr*) to preserve (food) by subjecting it to rapid refrigeration at temperatures of 0°C or lower.

quickie (ˈkwɪkɪ) *n Inf.* **1** Also called (esp. Brit.): **quick one.** a speedily consumed alcoholic drink. **2a** anything made or done rapidly. **2b** (*as modifier*): *a quickie divorce.*

quicklime (ˈkwɪkˌlaɪm) *n* another name for **calcium oxide.**

quick march *n* **1** a march at quick time or the order to proceed at such a pace. ◆ *interj* **2** a command to commence such a march.

quicksand (ˈkwɪkˌsænd) *n* a deep mass of loose wet sand that sucks anything on top of it inextricably into it.

quickset (ˈkwɪkˌsɛt) *Chiefly Brit.* ◆ *n* **1a** a plant or cutting, esp. of hawthorn, set so as to form a hedge. **1b** such plants or cuttings collectively. **2** a hedge composed of such plants. ◆ *adj* **3** composed of such plants.

quicksilver (ˈkwɪkˌsɪlvə) *n* **1** another name for **mercury** (sense 1). ◆ *adj* **2** rapid or unpredictable in movement or change.

quickstep (ˈkwɪkˌstɛp) *n* **1** a modern ballroom dance in rapid quadruple time. **2** a piece of music composed for or in the rhythm of this dance. ◆ *vb* **quicksteps, quickstepping, quickstepped.** **3** (*intr*) to perform this dance.

quick-tempered ➊ *adj* readily roused to anger; irascible.

quickthorn (ˈkwɪkˌθɔːn) *n* hawthorn, esp. when planted as a hedge. [C17: prob. from *quick* in the sense "fast-growing": cf. QUICKSET]

quick time *n Mil.* the normal marching rate of 120 paces to the minute.

quick-witted ➊ *adj* having a keenly alert mind, esp. as used to avert danger, make effective reply, etc.
▸**ˌquick-ˈwittedly** *adv* ▸**ˌquick-ˈwittedness** *n*

quid[1] (kwɪd) *n* a piece of tobacco, suitable for chewing. [OE *cwidu* chewing resin]

quid[2] (kwɪd) *n, pl* **quid.** *Brit. sl.* **1** a pound (sterling). **2 (be) quids in.** (to be) in a very favourable or advantageous position. [C17: from ?]

quiddity (ˈkwɪdɪtɪ) *n, pl* **quiddities.** **1** the essential nature of something. **2** a petty or trifling distinction; quibble. [C16: from Med. L *quidditās*, from L *quid* what]

quidnunc (ˈkwɪdˌnʌŋk) *n* a person eager to learn news and scandal; gossipmonger. [C18: from L, lit.: what now]

quid pro quo ➊ (ˈkwɪd prəʊ ˈkwəʊ) *n, pl* **quid pro quos.** **1** a reciprocal exchange. **2** something given in compensation, esp. an advantage or object given in exchange for another. [C16: from L: something for something]

quiescent ➊ (kwɪˈɛsᵊnt) *adj* quiet, inactive, or dormant. [C17: from L *quiescere* to rest]
▸**quiˈescence** *or* **quiˈescency** *n* ▸**quiˈescently** *adv*

quiet ➊ (ˈkwaɪət) *adj* **1** characterized by an absence of noise. **2** calm or tranquil: *the sea is quiet tonight.* **3** free from activities, distractions, etc.; untroubled: *a quiet life.* **4** short of work, orders, etc.; not busy: *business is quiet today.* **5** private; not public; secret: *a quiet word with someone.* **6** free from anger, impatience, or other extreme emotion. **7** free from pretentiousness; modest or reserved: *quiet humour.* **8** *Astron.* (of the sun) exhibiting a very low number of sunspots, solar flares, etc.; inactive. ◆ *n* **9** the state of being silent, peaceful, or untroubled. **10 on the quiet.** without other people knowing. ◆ *vb* **11** a less common word for **quieten.** [C14: from L *quiētus*, p.p. of *quiēscere* to rest, from *quiēs* repose]
▸**ˈquietness** *n*

quieten ➊ (ˈkwaɪətᵊn) *vb Chiefly Brit.* **1** (often foll. by *down*) to make or become calm, silent, etc. **2** (*tr*) to allay (fear, doubts, etc.).

quietism (ˈkwaɪəˌtɪzəm) *n* **1** a form of religious mysticism originating

THESAURUS

queue *n* **1 = line**, chain, concatenation, file, order, progression, sequence, series, string, succession, train

quibble *vb* **1 = split hairs**, carp, cavil, equivocate, evade, pretend, prevaricate, shift ◆ *n* **3 = objection**, cavil, complaint, criticism, nicety, niggle, prevarication, protest, sophism, subtlety

quibbling *adj* **1 = hair-splitting**, carping, caviling, critical, jesuitical, niggling, nit-picking (*inf.*), overnice, sophistical

quick *adj* **1, 4 = fast**, active, brisk, express, fleet, hasty, rapid, speedy, swift **2 = brief**, cursory, hasty, hurried, perfunctory **5 = prompt**, expeditious, sudden **7, 8 = intelligent**, acute, alert, all there (*inf.*), astute, bright (*inf.*), clever, discerning, nimble-witted, perceptive, quick on the uptake (*inf.*), quick-witted, receptive, sharp, shrewd, smart **9 = excitable**, passionate **10 = nimble**, able, adept, adroit, agile, deft, dexterous, skilful **11a** *Archaic* **= alive**, animate, existing, live, living, viable
Antonyms *adj* ≠ **fast:** dull, heavy, inactive, lazy, lethargic ≠ **fast:** slow, sluggish, unresponsive ≠ **brief:** gradual, long ≠ **intelligent:** stupid, unintelligent ≠ **excitable:** calm, deliberate, patient, restrained ≠ **deft:** inexpert, maladroit, unskilful

quicken *vb* **1 = speed**, accelerate, dispatch, expedite, hasten, hurry, impel, precipitate **2, 3 = invigorate**, activate, animate, arouse, energize, excite, galvanize, incite, inspire, kindle, refresh, reinvigorate, resuscitate, revitalize, revive, rouse, stimulate, strengthen, vitalize, vivify

quickly *adv* **1, 4 = swiftly**, abruptly, apace, at a rate of knots (*inf.*), at *or* on the double, at speed, briskly, expeditiously, fast, hastily, hell for leather (*inf.*), hotfoot, hurriedly, immediately, instantly, like greased lightning (*inf.*), like lightning, like the clappers (*Brit. inf.*), posthaste, promptly, pronto (*inf.*), quick, rapidly, soon, speedily, with all speed
Antonyms *adv* carefully, eventually, slowly, sluggishly, unhurriedly

quick-tempered *adj* **= hot-tempered**, cantankerous, choleric, excitable, fiery, impatient, impulsive, irascible, irritable, petulant, quarrelsome, ratty (*Brit. & NZ inf.*), shrewish, splenetic, testy, tetchy, waspish
Antonyms *adj* cool, dispassionate, phlegmatic, placid, slow to anger, tolerant

quick-witted *adj* **= clever**, alert, astute, bright (*inf.*), keen, perceptive, sharp, shrewd, smart
Antonyms *adj* dull, obtuse, slow, slow-witted, stupid, thick (*inf.*), unperceptive

quid pro quo *n* **1, 2 = exchange**, compensation, equivalent, interchange, reprisal, retaliation, substitution, tit for tat

quiescent *adj* **= quiet**, calm, dormant, in abeyance, inactive, latent, motionless, peaceful, placid, resting, serene, silent, smooth, still, tranquil, unagitated, undisturbed, unmoving, unruffled

quiet *adj* **1 = silent**, dumb, hushed, inaudible, low, low-pitched, noiseless, peaceful, soft, soundless **2 = calm**, contented, gentle, mild, motionless, pacific, peaceful, placid, restful, serene, smooth, still, tranquil, untroubled **5 = undisturbed**, isolated, private, retired, secluded, secret, sequestered, unfrequented **6 = reserved**, collected, docile, even-tempered, gentle, imperturbable, meek, mild, phlegmatic, retiring, sedate, shy, unexcitable **7 = unobtrusive**, conservative, modest, plain, reserved, restrained, simple, sober, subdued, unassuming, unpretentious ◆ *n* **9 = peace**, calmness, ease, quietness, repose, rest, serenity, silence, stillness, tranquillity
Antonyms *adj* ≠ **silent:** deafening, ear-splitting, high-decibel, high-volume, loud, noisy, stentorian ≠ **calm:** agitated, alert, excitable, exciting, frenetic, troubled, turbulent, violent ≠ **undisturbed:** bustling, busy, crowded, exciting, fashionable, lively, popular, vibrant ≠ **reserved:** excitable, excited, high-spirited, impatient, loquacious, passionate, restless, talkative, verbose, violent ◆ *n* ≠ **peace:** activity, bustle, commotion, din, disturbance, noise, racket

quieten *vb* **1 = silence**, compose, hush, muffle, mute, quell, quiet, shush (*inf.*), stifle, still, stop, subdue **2 = soothe**, allay, alleviate, appease, as-

in Spain in the late 17th century, requiring complete passivity to God's will. 2 passivity and calmness of mind towards external events.
▸'quietist *n, adj*

quietly ('kwaɪətlɪ) *adv* 1 in a quiet manner. 2 **just quietly.** *Austral.* confidentially.

quietude ('kwaɪə,tju:d) *n* the state or condition of being quiet, peaceful, calm, or tranquil.

quietus ➊ (kwaɪ'i:təs, -'eɪtəs) *n, pl* **quietuses.** 1 anything that serves to quash, eliminate, or kill. 2 a release from life; death. 3 the discharge or settlement of debts, duties, etc. [C16: from L *quiētus est,* lit.: he is at rest]

quiff (kwɪf) *n Brit.* a tuft of hair brushed up above the forehead. [C19: from ?]

quill (kwɪl) *n* 1a any of the large stiff feathers of the wing or tail of a bird. 1b the long hollow part of a feather; calamus. 2 Also called: **quill pen.** a feather made into a pen for writing. 3 any of the stiff hollow spines of a porcupine or hedgehog. 4 a device, formerly made from a crow quill, for plucking a harpsichord string. 5 a small roll of bark, esp. one of dried cinnamon. 6 a bobbin or spindle. 7 a fluted fold, as in a ruff. ◆ *vb (tr)* 8 to wind (thread, etc.) onto a spool or bobbin. 9 to make or press fluted folds in (a ruff, etc.). [C15 (in the sense: hollow reed or pipe): from ?; cf. MLow G *quiele* quill]

quilt ➊ (kwɪlt) *n* 1 a cover for a bed, consisting of a soft filling sewn between two layers of material, usually with crisscross seams. 2 short for **continental quilt.** 3 a bedspread. 4 anything resembling a quilt. ◆ *vb (tr)* 5 to stitch together (two pieces of fabric) with (a thick padding or lining) between them. 6 to create (a garment, etc.) in this way. 7 to pad with material. [C13: from OF *coilte* mattress, from L *culcita* stuffed item of bedding]
▸'quilted *adj* ▸'quilter *n*

quilting ('kwɪltɪŋ) *n* 1 material for quilts. 2 the act of making a quilt. 3 quilted work.

quin (kwɪn) *n Brit.* short for **quintuplet** (sense 1). US and Canad. word: **quint.**

quinary ('kwaɪnərɪ) *adj* 1 of or by fives. 2 fifth in a series. 3 (of a number system) having a base of five. [C17: from L *quīnārius* containing five, from *quīnī* five each]

quince (kwɪns) *n* 1 a small widely cultivated Asian tree with edible pear-shaped fruits. 2 the fruit of this tree, much used in preserves. [C14 *qwince* pl. of *quyn,* from OF *coin,* from L *cotōneum,* from Gk *kudōnion* quince]

quincentenary (,kwɪnsɛn'ti:nərɪ) *n, pl* **quincentenaries.** a 500th anniversary. [C19: irregularly from L *quinque* five + CENTENARY]
▸**quincentennial** (,kwɪnsɛn'tɛnɪəl) *adj, n*

quincunx ('kwɪnkʌŋks) *n* a group of five objects arranged in the shape of a rectangle with one at each of the four corners and the fifth in the centre. [C17: from L: five twelfths, from *quinque* five + *uncia* twelfth; in ancient Rome, this was a coin worth five twelfths of an AS[2] and marked with five spots]
▸**quincuncial** (kwɪn'kʌnʃəl) *adj*

quinella (kwɪ'nɛlə) *n Austral.* a form of betting in which the punter must select the first and second place winners, in any order. [from American Sp. *quiniela*]

quinidine ('kwɪnɪ,di:n) *n* a crystalline alkaloid drug used to treat heart arrhythmias.

quinine (kwɪ'ni:n; *US* 'kwaɪnaɪn) *n* a bitter crystalline alkaloid extracted from cinchona bark, the salts of which are used as a tonic, analgesic, etc., and in malaria therapy. [C19: from Sp. *quina* cinchona bark, from Quechua *kina* bark]

quinol ('kwɪnɒl) *n* another name for **hydroquinone.**

quinoline ('kwɪnə,li:n, -lɪn) *n* an oily colourless insoluble compound synthesized by heating aniline, nitrobenzene, glycerol, and sulphuric acid: used as a food preservative and in the manufacture of dyes and antiseptics. Formula: C_9H_7N.

quinquagenarian (,kwɪŋkwədʒɪ'nɛərɪən) *n* 1 a person between 50 and 59 years old. ◆ *adj* 2 being between 50 and 59 years old. 3 of a quinquagenarian. [C16: from L *quinquāgēnārius* containing fifty, from *quinquāgēnī* fifty each]

Quinquagesima (,kwɪŋkwə'dʒɛsɪmə) *n* the Sunday preceding Lent. Also called: **Quinquagesima Sunday.** [C14: via Med. L from L *quinquāgēsima diēs* fiftieth day]

quinquecentenary (,kwɪŋkwɪsɛn'ti:nərɪ) *n, pl* **quinquecentenaries.** another name for **quincentenary.**

quinquennial (kwɪn'kwɛnɪəl) *adj* 1 occurring once every five years or over a period of five years. ◆ *n* 2 a fifth anniversary.
▸**quin'quennially** *adv*

quinquennium (kwɪn'kwɛnɪəm) *n, pl* **quinquennia** (-nɪə). a period or cycle of five years. [C17: from L *quinque* five + *annus* year]

quinquereme ('kwɪŋkwɪ'ri:m) *n* an ancient Roman galley with five banks of oars. [C16: from L *quinquerēmis,* from *quinque-* five + *rēmus* oar]

quinquevalent (,kwɪŋkwɪ'veɪlənt) *adj Chem.* another word for **pentavalent.**
▸,**quinque'valency** *or* ,**quinque'valence** *n*

quinsy ('kwɪnzɪ) *n* inflammation of the tonsils and surrounding tissues with the formation of abscesses. [C14: via OF & Med. L from Gk *kunankhē,* from *kuōn* dog + *ankhein* to strangle]

quint[1] *n* 1 (kwɪnt). an organ stop sounding a note a fifth higher. 2 (kɪnt). *Piquet.* a sequence of five cards in the same suit. [C17: from F. *quinte,* from L *quintus* fifth]

quint[2] (kwɪnt) *n* the US and Canad. word for **quin.**

quintain ('kwɪntɪn) *n* (esp. in medieval Europe) a post or target set up for tilting exercises for mounted knights or foot soldiers. [C14: from OF *quintaine,* from L: street in a Roman camp between the fifth & sixth maniples (the maniple was a unit of 120–200 soldiers in ancient Rome), from *quintus* fifth]

quintal ('kwɪntᵊl) *n* 1 a unit of weight equal to (esp. in Britain) 112 pounds or (esp. in US) 100 pounds. 2 a unit of weight equal to 100 kilograms. [C15: via OF from Ar. *qinṭār,* possibly from L *centēnārius* consisting of a hundred]

quintan ('kwɪntən) *adj* (of a fever) occurring every fourth day. [C17: from L *febris quintāna* fever occurring every fifth day, reckoned inclusively]

quinte (kænt) *n* the fifth of eight basic positions from which a parry or attack can be made in fencing. [C18: F from L *quintus* fifth]

quintessence ➊ (kwɪn'tɛsəns) *n* 1 the most typical representation of a quality, state, etc. 2 an extract of a substance containing its principle in its most concentrated form. 3 (in ancient philosophy) ether, the fifth essence or element, which was thought to be the constituent matter of the heavenly bodies and latent in all things. [C15: via F from Med. L *quinta essentia* the fifth essence, translation of Gk]
▸**quintessential** (,kwɪntɪ'sɛnʃəl) *adj* ▸,**quintes'sentially** *adv*

quintet *or* **quintette** (kwɪn'tɛt) *n* 1 a group of five singers or instrumentalists or a piece of music composed for such a group. 2 any group of five. [C19: from It. *quintetto,* from *quinto* fifth]

quintillion (kwɪn'tɪljən) *n, pl* **quintillions** *or* **quintillion.** 1 (in Britain, France, and Germany) the number represented as one followed by 30 zeros (10^{30}). US and Canad. word: **nonillion.** 2 (in the US and Canada) the number represented as one followed by 18 zeros (10^{18}). Brit. word: **trillion.** [C17: from L *quintus* fifth + *-illion,* as in MILLION]
▸**quin'tillionth** *adj*

quintuple ('kwɪntjupᵊl, kwɪn'tju:pᵊl) *vb* **quintuples, quintupling, quintupled.** 1 to multiply by five. ◆ *adj* 2 five times as much or as many; fivefold. 3 consisting of five parts. ◆ *n* 4 a quantity or number five times as great as another. [C16: from F, from L *quintus,* on the model of QUADRUPLE]

quintuplet ('kwɪntjuplɪt, kwɪn'tju:plɪt) *n* 1 one of five offspring born at one birth. 2 a group of five similar things. 3 *Music.* a group of five notes to be played in a time value of three or four.

quintuplicate *adj* (kwɪn'tju:plɪkɪt). 1 fivefold or quintuple. ◆ *vb* (kwɪn'tju:plɪ,keɪt), **quintuplicates, quintuplicating, quintuplicated.** 2 to multiply or be multiplied by five. ◆ *n* (kwɪn'tju:plɪkɪt). 3 a group or set of five things.

quip ➊ (kwɪp) *n* 1 a sarcastic remark. 2 a witty saying. 3 *Arch.* another word for **quibble.** ◆ *vb* **quips, quipping, quipped.** 4 *(intr)* to make a quip. [C16: from earlier *quippy,* prob. from L *quippe* indeed, to be sure]
▸'**quipster** *n*

quire[1] ('kwaɪə) *n* 1 a set of 24 or 25 sheets of paper. 2 four sheets of paper folded to form 16 pages. 3 a set of all the sheets in a book. [C15 *quayer,* from OF *quaier,* from L *quaternī* four at a time, from *quater* four times]

quire[2] ('kwaɪə) *n* an obsolete spelling of **choir.**

quirk ➊ (kw3:k) *n* 1 a peculiarity of character; mannerism or foible. 2 an unexpected twist or turn: *a quirk of fate.* 3 a continuous groove in an architectural moulding. 4 a flourish, as in handwriting. [C16: from ?]
▸'**quirky** *adj* ▸'**quirkiness** *n*

quirt (kw3:t) *US & S. African.* ◆ *n* 1 a whip with a leather thong at one end. ◆ *vb (tr)* 2 to strike with a quirt. [C19: from Sp. *cuerda* CORD]

quisling ➊ ('kwɪzlɪŋ) *n* a traitor who aids an occupying enemy force; collaborator. [C20: after Major Vidkun *Quisling* (1887–1945), Norwegian collaborator with the Nazis]

quit ➊ (kwɪt) *vb* **quits, quitting, quitted** *or* **quit.** 1 *(tr)* to depart from; leave. 2

THESAURUS

suage, blunt, calm, deaden, dull, lull, mitigate, mollify, palliate, tranquillize
Antonyms *vb* ≠ **soothe:** aggravate, exacerbate, intensify, provoke, upset, worsen

quietness *n* 1 = **peace,** hush, quiet, silence 2 = **calmness,** calm, placidity, quiescence, quietude, repose, rest, serenity, still, stillness, tranquillity

quietus *n* 1 = **death,** clincher *(inf.), coup de grâce,* deathblow, demise, end, final blow, finish

quilt *n* 1-3 = **bedspread,** comforter *(US),* continental quilt, counterpane, coverlet, doona *(Austral.),* duvet, eiderdown

quintessence *n* 1 = **essence,** gist, heart, kernel, lifeblood, marrow, pith, soul, spirit 2 = **extract,** core, distillation, essence

quintessential *adj* 1 = **ultimate,** archetypal, definitive, essential, fundamental, prototypical, typical

quip *n* 2 = **joke,** badinage, bon mot, jest, pleasantry, repartee, retort, riposte, sally, wisecrack *(inf.),* witticism

quirk *n* 1 = **peculiarity,** aberration, bee in one's bonnet, caprice, characteristic, eccentricity, fancy, fetish, foible, habit, *idée fixe,* idiosyncrasy, kink, mannerism, oddity, singularity, trait, vagary, whim

quirky *adj* 1 = **odd,** capricious, curious, eccentric, fanciful, idiosyncratic, offbeat, peculiar, rum *(Brit. sl.),* singular, unpredictable, unusual, whimsical

quisling *n* = **traitor,** betrayer, collaborator, fifth columnist, Judas, renegade, turncoat

quit *vb* 1 = **depart,** abandon, decamp, desert, exit, forsake, go, leave, pack one's bags *(inf.),* pull out, take off *(inf.),* withdraw 2 = **resign,** abdicate, go, leave, pull out, relinquish, to resign; give up (a job). **3** (*intr*) (of a tenant) to give up occupancy of premises and leave them. **4** to desist or cease from (something or doing something). **5** (*tr*) to pay off (a debt). **6** (*tr*) *Arch.* to conduct or acquit (oneself); comport (oneself). ◆ *adj* **7** (*usually predicative;* foll. by *of*) free (from); released (from). [C13: from OF *quitter,* from L *quiētus* QUIET]

quitch grass (kwɪtʃ) *n* another name for **couch grass.** Sometimes shortened to **quitch.** [OE *cwice;* ? rel. to *cwicu* living, QUICK (with the implication that the grass cannot be killed)]

quitclaim ('kwɪtˌkleɪm) *Law.* ◆ *n* **1** a renunciation of a claim or right. ◆ *vb* **2** (*tr*) to renounce (a claim). [C14: from Anglo-F *quiteclame,* from *quite* QUIT + *clamer* to declare (from L *clamāre* to shout)]

quite ❶ (kwaɪt) *adv* **1** completely or absolutely: *you're quite right.* **2** (*not used with a negative*) somewhat: *she's quite pretty.* **3** in actuality; truly. **4** **quite a** *or* **an.** (*not used with a negative*) of an exceptional, considerable, or noticeable kind: *quite a girl.* **5** **quite something.** a remarkable or noteworthy thing or person. ◆ *sentence substitute.* **6** Also: **quite so.** an expression used to indicate agreement. [C14: adverbial use of *quite* (adj) QUIT]

USAGE NOTE See at **very.**

quitrent ('kwɪtˌrɛnt) *n* (formerly) a rent payable by a freeholder or copyholder to his lord in lieu of services.

quits (kwɪts) *adj* (*postpositive*) *Inf.* **1** on an equal footing; even. **2** **call it quits.** to agree to end a dispute, contest, etc., agreeing that honours are even.

quittance ('kwɪtᵊns) *n* **1** release from debt or other obligation. **2** a receipt or other document certifying this. [C13: from OF, from *quitter* to release from obligation; see QUIT]

quitter ('kwɪtə) *n* a person who gives up easily.

quiver[1] ❶ ('kwɪvə) *vb* **1** (*intr*) to shake with a tremulous movement; tremble. ◆ *n* **2** the state, process, or noise of shaking or trembling. [C15: from obs. *cwiver* quick, nimble]
▸'**quivering** *adj* ▸'**quivery** *adj*

quiver[2] ('kwɪvə) *n* a case for arrows. [C13: from OF *cuivre*]

qui vive (ˌkiː 'viːv) *n* **on the qui vive.** on the alert; attentive. [C18: from F, lit.: long live who?, sentry's challenge (equivalent to "Whose side are you on?")]

Quixote ('kwɪksət; *Spanish* ki'xote) *n* See **Don Quixote.**

quixotic ❶ (kwɪk'sɒtɪk) *adj* preoccupied with an unrealistically optimistic or chivalrous approach to life; impractically idealistic. [C18: after DON QUIXOTE]
▸**quix'otically** *adv*

quiz ❶ (kwɪz) *n, pl* **quizzes. 1a** an entertainment in which the knowledge of the players is tested by a series of questions. **1b** (*as modifier*): *a quiz programme.* **2** any set of quick questions designed to test knowledge. **3** an investigation by close questioning. **4** *Obs.* a practical joke. **5** *Obs.* a puzzling individual. **6** *Obs.* a person who habitually looks quizzically at others. ◆ *vb* **quizzes, quizzing, quizzed.** (*tr*) **7** to investigate by close questioning; interrogate. **8** *US & Canad. inf.* to test the knowledge of (a student or class). **9** (*tr*) *Obs.* to look quizzically at, esp. through a small monocle. [C18: from ?]
▸'**quizzer** *n*

quizzical ❶ ('kwɪzɪkᵊl) *adj* questioning and mocking or supercilious.
▸'**quizzically** *adv*

quod (kwɒd) *n Chiefly Brit.* a slang word for **jail.** [C18: from ?]

quod erat demonstrandum *Latin.* ('kwɒd 'ɛræt ˌdɛmən'strændʊm) (at the conclusion of a proof, esp. of a theorem in Euclidean geometry) which was to be proved. Abbrev.: **QED.**

quodlibet ('kwɒdlɪˌbɛt) *n* **1** a light piece of music. **2** a subtle argument, esp. one prepared as an exercise on a theological topic. [C14: from L, from *quod* what + *libet* pleases, that is, whatever you like]

quoin (kwɔɪn, kɔɪn) *n* **1** an external corner of a wall. **2** a stone forming the external corner of a wall. **3** another name for **keystone** (sense 1). **4** *Printing.* a wedge or an expanding device used to lock type up in a chase. **5** a wedge used for any of various other purposes. [C16: var. of *coin* (in former sense of corner)]

quoit (kɔɪt) *n* a ring of iron, plastic, etc., used in the game of quoits. [C15: from ?]

quoits (kɔɪts) *pl n* (*usually functioning as sing*) a game in which quoits are tossed at a stake in the ground in attempts to encircle it.

quokka ('kwɒkə) *n* a small wallaby of Western Australia, now rare. [of Abor. origin]

quondam ❶ ('kwɒndæm) *adj* (*prenominal*) of an earlier time; former. [C16: from L]

quorate ('kwɔːˌreɪt) *adj Brit.* consisting of or being a quorum: *the meeting was quorate.*

Quorn (kwɔːn) *n Trademark.* a vegetable protein developed from a type of fungus and used as a meat substitute.

quorum ('kwɔːrəm) *n* a minimum number of members in an assembly, etc., required to be present before any business can be transacted. [C15: from L, lit.: of whom, occurring in L commissions in the formula *quorum vos...duos* (etc.) *volumus* of whom we wish that you be...two (etc.)]

quota ❶ ('kwəʊtə) *n* **1** the proportional share or part that is due from, due to, or allocated to a person or group. **2** a prescribed number or quantity, as of items to be imported or students admitted to a college, etc. [C17: from L *quota pars* how big a share?, from *quotus* of what number]

quotable ('kwəʊtəbᵊl) *adj* apt or suitable for quotation.
▸ˌ**quota'bility** *n*

quotation ❶ (kwəʊ'teɪʃən) *n* **1** a phrase or passage from a book, speech, etc., remembered and repeated, usually with an acknowledgment of its source. **2** the act or habit of quoting. **3a** a cost estimate for goods or services given to a prospective client. **3b** the current market price of a commodity, security, etc. **4** *Printing.* a quad used to fill up spaces.

quotation mark *n* either of the punctuation marks used to begin or end a quotation, respectively " and " or ' and '. Also called: **inverted comma.**

quote ❶ (kwəʊt) *vb* **quotes, quoting, quoted. 1** to recite a quotation. **2** (*tr*) to put quotation marks round (a phrase, etc.). **3a** to give (a cost estimate for specified goods or services) to a prospective client. **3b** to state (the current market price) of (a security or commodity). ◆ *n* **4** an informal word for **quotation. 5** (*often pl*) an informal word for **quotation mark.** ◆ *interj* **6** an expression used to indicate that the words that follow it form a quotation. [C14: from Med. L *quotāre* to assign reference numbers to passages, from L *quot* how many]

quoted company *n* a company whose shares are quoted on a stock exchange.

quote-driven *adj* denoting an electronic market system, esp. for stock exchanges, in which prices are determined by quotations made by market makers or dealers. Cf. **order-driven.**

quote-unquote *interj* an expression used before or part before and part after a quotation to identify it as such, and sometimes to dissociate the writer or speaker from it.

quoth (kwəʊθ) *vb Arch.* (used with all pronouns except *thou* and *you,* and with nouns) said. [OE *cwæth,* third person sing of *cwethan* to say]

quotha ('kwəʊθə) *interj Arch.* an expression of mild sarcasm, used in picking up a word or phrase used by someone else. [C16: from *quoth a* quoth he]

quotidian (kwəʊ'tɪdɪən) *adj* **1** (esp. of fever) recurring daily. **2** commonplace. ◆ *n* **3** a fever characterized by attacks that recur daily. [C14: from L *quotīdiānus,* var. of *cottīdiānus* daily]

quotient ('kwəʊʃənt) *n* **1a** the result of the division of one number or quantity by another. **1b** the integral part of the result of division. **2** a ratio of two numbers or quantities to be divided. [C15: from L *quotiens* how often]

quo vadis ('kwəʊ 'vɑːdɪs) whither goest thou? [L from the Vulgate version of John 16:5]

quo warranto ('kwəʊ wɒ'ræntəʊ) *n Law.* a proceeding initiated to determine or (formerly) a writ demanding by what authority a person claims an office, franchise, or privilege. [from Med. L: by what warrant]

Qur'an (kʊ'rɑːn, -'ræn) *n* a variant spelling of **Koran.**

q.v. (denoting a cross-reference) *abbrev. for* quod vide. [NL: which (word, item, etc.) see]

qwerty *or* **QWERTY keyboard** ('kwɜːtɪ) *n* the standard English language typewriter keyboard layout with the characters q, w, e, r, t, and y at the top left of the keyboard.

THESAURUS

renounce, retire, step down (*inf.*), surrender **4** = **stop**, abandon, belay (*Nautical*), cease, conclude, discontinue, drop, end, give up, halt, suspend, throw in the towel
Antonyms *vb* ≠ **stop:** complete, continue, finish, go on with, see through

quite *adv* **1** = **absolutely**, completely, considerably, entirely, fully, in all respects, largely, perfectly, precisely, totally, wholly, without reservation **2** = **somewhat**, fairly, moderately, rather, reasonably, relatively, to a certain extent, to some degree **3** = **truly**, in fact, in reality, in truth, really

quiver[1] *vb* **1** = **shake**, agitate, convulse, oscillate, palpitate, pulsate, quake, quaver, shiver, shudder, tremble, vibrate ◆ *n* **2** = **shake**, convulsion, oscillation, palpitation, pulsation, shiver, shudder, spasm, throb, tic, tremble, tremor, vibration

quixotic *adj* = **unrealistic**, absurd, dreamy, fanciful, fantastical, idealistic, imaginary, impracticable, impractical, romantic, unworldly, Utopian, visionary

quiz *n* **3** = **examination**, investigation, questioning, test ◆ *vb* **7** = **question**, ask, catechize, examine, grill (*inf.*), interrogate, investigate, pump (*inf.*)

quizzical *adj* = **mocking**, arch, curious, derisive, inquiring, questioning, sardonic, supercilious, teasing

quondam *adj* = **former**, bygone, earlier, ex-, foregoing, late, one-time, past, previous, retired, sometime

quota *n* **1** = **share**, allocation, allowance, assignment, cut (*inf.*), part, portion, proportion, ration, slice, whack (*inf.*)

quotation *n* **1** = **passage**, citation, cutting, excerpt, extract, quote (*inf.*), reference, selection **3** = **estimate**, bid price, charge, cost, figure, price, quote (*inf.*), rate, tender

quote *vb* **1** = **repeat**, cite, detail, extract, instance, name, paraphrase, recite, refer to, retell

Rr

r *or* **R** (ɑː) *n, pl* **r's, R's,** *or* **Rs. 1** the 18th letter of the English alphabet. **2** a speech sound represented by this letter. **3** See **three Rs.**

R *symbol for:* **1** *Chem.* gas constant. **2** *Chem.* radical. **3** *Currency.* **3a** rand. **3b** rupee. **4** Réaumur (scale). **5** *Physics, electronics.* resistance. **6** roentgen *or* röntgen. **7** *Chess.* rook. **8** Royal. **9** (in the US and Australia) **9a** restricted exhibition (used to describe a category of film certified as unsuitable for viewing by anyone under the age of 18). **9b** (*as modifier*): *an R film.*

r. *abbrev. for:* **1** rare. **2** recto. **3** Also: **r** rod (unit of length). **4** ruled. **5** *Cricket.* run(s).

R. *abbrev. for:* **1** rabbi. **2** rector. **3** Regiment. **4** Regina. [L: Queen] **5** Republican. **6** Rex. [L: King] **7** River. **8** Royal.

R. *or* **r.** *abbrev. for:* **1** radius. **2** railway. **3** registered (trademark). **4** right. **5** river. **6** road. **7** rouble.

Ra *the chemical symbol for* radium.

RA *abbrev. for:* **1** rear admiral. **2** *Astron.* right ascension. **3** (in Britain) Royal Academician *or* Academy. **4** (in Britain) Royal Artillery.

RAAF *abbrev. for* Royal Australian Air Force.

rabbet (ˈræbɪt) *or* **rebate** *n* **1** a recess, groove, or step, usually of rectangular section, cut into a piece of timber to receive a mating piece. ◆ *vb* **rabbets, rabbeting, rabbeted** *or* **rebates, rebating, rebated.** (*tr*) **2** to cut a rabbet in (timber). **3** to join (pieces of timber) using a rabbet. [C15: from OF *rabattre* to beat down]

rabbi (ˈræbaɪ) *n, pl* **rabbis. 1** the spiritual leader of a Jewish congregation; the chief religious minister of a synagogue. **2** a scholar learned in Jewish Law, esp. one authorized to teach it. [Heb., from *rabh* master + -*ī* my]

rabbinate (ˈræbɪnɪt) *n* **1** the position, function, or tenure of office of a rabbi. **2** rabbis collectively.

rabbinic (rəˈbɪnɪk) *or* **rabbinical** (rəˈbɪnɪkᵊl) *adj* of or relating to the rabbis, their teachings, writings, views, language, etc.
▸**rabˈbinically** *adv*

Rabbinic (rəˈbɪnɪk) *n* the form of the Hebrew language used by the rabbis of the Middle Ages.

rabbit (ˈræbɪt) *n, pl* **rabbits** *or* **rabbit. 1** any of various common gregarious burrowing mammals of Europe and North Africa. They are closely related and similar to hares but are smaller and have shorter ears. **2** the fur of such an animal. **3** *Brit. inf.* a poor performer at a game or sport. ◆ *vb* **4** (*intr*) to hunt or shoot rabbits. **5** (*intr*) (often foll. by *on* or *away*) *Brit. inf.* to talk inconsequentially; chatter. [C14: ?from Walloon *robett,* dim. of Flemish *robbe* rabbit, from ?]

rabbit fever *n Pathol.* another name for **tularaemia.**

rabbit punch *n* a short sharp blow to the back of the neck that can cause loss of consciousness or even death. Austral. name: **rabbit killer.**

rabble Ⓣ (ˈræbᵊl) *n* **1** a disorderly crowd; mob. **2 the rabble.** *Contemptuous.* the common people. [C14 (in the sense: a pack of animals): from ?]

rabble-rouser Ⓣ *n* a person who manipulates the passions of the mob; demagogue.
▸**ˈrabble-ˌrousing** *adj, n*

Rabelaisian Ⓣ (ˌræbəˈleɪzɪən, -ʒən) *adj* **1** of, relating to, or resembling the work of François Rabelais (?1494–1553), French writer, esp. by broad, often bawdy, humour and sharp satire. ◆ *n* **2** a student or admirer of Rabelais.
▸**ˌRabeˈlaisianism** *n*

rabid Ⓣ (ˈræbɪd, ˈreɪ-) *adj* **1** relating to or having rabies. **2** zealous; fanatical; violent; raging. [C17: from L *rabidus* frenzied, from *rabere* to be mad]
▸**rabidity** (rəˈbɪdɪtɪ) *or* **ˈrabidness** *n* ▸**ˈrabidly** *adv*

rabies (ˈreɪbiːz) *n Pathol.* an acute infectious viral disease of the nervous system transmitted by the saliva of infected animals, esp. dogs. [C17: from L: madness, from *rabere* to rave]
▸**rabic** (ˈræbɪk) *or* **rabietic** (ˌreɪbɪˈɛtɪk) *adj*

RAC *abbrev. for:* **1** Royal Armoured Corps. **2** Royal Automobile Club.

raccoon *or* **racoon** (rəˈkuːn) *n, pl* **raccoons, raccoon** *or* **racoons, racoon. 1** an omnivorous mammal, esp. the **North American raccoon,** inhabiting forests of North and Central America. Raccoons have a pointed muzzle, long tail, and greyish-black fur with black bands around the tail and across the face. **2** the fur of the raccoon. [C17: from Algonquian *ärähkun,* from *ärähkuněm* he scratches with his hands]

race[1] Ⓣ (reɪs) *n* **1** a contest of speed, as in running, etc. **2** any competition or rivalry. **3** rapid or constant onward movement: *the race of time.* **4** a rapid current of water, esp. one through a narrow channel that has a tidal range greater at one end than the other. **5** a channel of a stream, esp. one for conducting water to or from a water wheel for energy: *a mill race.* **6a** a channel or groove that contains ball bearings or roller bearings. **6b** the inner or outer cylindrical ring in a ball bearing or roller bearing. **7** *Austral. & NZ.* a narrow passage or enclosure in a sheep yard through which sheep pass individually, as to a sheep dip. **8** *Austral.* a wire tunnel through which footballers pass from the changing room onto a football field. **9** *Arch.* the span or course of life. ◆ *vb* **races, racing, raced. 10** to engage in a contest of speed with (another). **11** to cause (animals, etc.) to engage in a race: *to race pigeons.* **12** to move or go as fast as possible. **13** to run (an engine, propeller, etc.) or (of an engine, propeller, etc.) to run at high speed, esp. after reduction of the load. ◆ See also **races.** [C13: from ON *rās* running]

race[2] Ⓣ (reɪs) *n* **1** a group of people of common ancestry, distinguished from others by physical characteristics, such as hair type, colour of skin, stature, etc. **2 the human race.** human beings collectively. **3** a group of animals or plants having common characteristics that distinguish them from other members of the same species, usually forming a geographically isolated group; subspecies. **4** a group of people sharing the same interests, characteristics, etc.: *race of authors.* [C16: from F, from It. *razza,* from ?]

racecard (ˈreɪsˌkɑːd) *n* a card at a race meeting with the races and runners, etc., printed on it.

racecourse (ˈreɪsˌkɔːs) *n* a long broad track, over which horses are raced. Also called (esp. US and Canad.): **racetrack.**

racehorse (ˈreɪsˌhɔːs) *n* a horse specially bred for racing.

raceme (rəˈsiːm) *n* an inflorescence in which the flowers are borne along the main stem. [C18: from L *racēmus* bunch of grapes]
▸**racemose** (ˈræsɪˌməʊs, -məʊz) *adj*

race meeting *n* a prearranged fixture for racing horses (or greyhounds) over a set course.

racemic (rəˈsiːmɪk, -ˈsɛm-) *adj Chem.* of, or being a mixture of dextrorotatory and laevorotatory isomers in such proportions that the mixture has no optical activity. [C19: from RACEME + -IC]
▸**racemism** (ˈræsɪˌmɪzəm) *n*

racer (ˈreɪsə) *n* **1** a person, animal, or machine that races. **2** a turntable used to traverse a heavy gun. **3** any of several slender nonvenomous North American snakes, such as the **striped racer.**

race relations *n* **1** (*functioning as pl*) the relations between members of two or more human races, esp. within a single community. **2** (*functioning as sing*) the branch of sociology concerned with such relations.

race riot *n* a riot among members of different races in the same community.

races (ˈreɪsɪz) *pl n* **the races.** a series of contests of speed between horses (or greyhounds) over a set course.

racetrack (ˈreɪsˌtræk) *n* **1** a circuit or course, esp. an oval one, used for motor racing, etc. **2** the usual US and Canad. word for **racecourse.**

raceway (ˈreɪsˌweɪ) *n* **1** another word for **race**[1] (senses 5, 6). **2** *Chiefly US.* a racetrack.

rachis *or* **rhachis** (ˈreɪkɪs) *n, pl* **rachises, rhachises** *or* **rachides, rhachides** (ˈrækɪˌdiːz, ˈreɪ-). **1** *Bot.* the main axis or stem of an inflorescence or compound leaf. **2** *Ornithol.* the shaft of a feather, esp. the part that carries the barbs. **3** another name for **spinal column.** [C17: via NL from Gk *rhakhis* ridge]
▸**rachial, rhachial** (ˈreɪkɪəl) *or* **rachidial, rhachidial** (rəˈkɪdɪəl) *adj*

rachitis (rəˈkaɪtɪs) *n Pathol.* another name for **rickets.**
▸**rachitic** (rəˈkɪtɪk) *adj*

Rachmanism (ˈrækməˌnɪzəm) *n* extortion or exploitation by a landlord of tenants of slum property. [C20: after Perec *Rachman* (1920–62), Brit. property-owner]

racial Ⓣ (ˈreɪʃəl) *adj* **1** denoting or relating to the division of the human species into races on grounds of physical characteristics. **2** characteristic of any such group.
▸**ˈracially** *adv*

racism (ˈreɪsɪzəm) *or* **racialism** (ˈreɪʃəˌlɪzəm) *n* **1** the belief that races have distinctive cultural characteristics determined by hereditary factors and that this endows some races with an intrinsic superiority. **2**

THESAURUS

rabble *n* **1 = mob,** crowd, herd, horde, swarm, throng **2 the rabble** *Contemptuous* **= commoners,** canaille, commonalty, common people, crowd, dregs, hoi polloi, lower classes, lumpenproletariat, masses, peasantry, populace, proletariat, riffraff, scum, the great unwashed (*inf. & derogatory*), trash (*chiefly US & Canad.*)
Antonyms *n* ≠ **commoners:** aristocracy, bourgeoisie, elite, gentry, high society, nobility, upper classes

rabble-rouser *n* **= agitator,** demagogue, firebrand, incendiary, stirrer (*inf.*), troublemaker

Rabelaisian *adj* **1 = bawdy,** broad, coarse, earthy, extravagant, exuberant, gross, lusty, raunchy (*sl.*), robust, satirical, uninhibited, unrestrained

rabid *adj* **1 = mad,** hydrophobic **2 = fanatical,** bigoted, extreme, fervent, intemperate, intolerant, irrational, narrow-minded, zealous
Antonyms *adj* ≠ **fanatical:** half-hearted, moderate, wishy-washy (*inf.*)

race[1] *n* **1, 2 = contest,** chase, competition, contention, dash, pursuit, rivalry ◆ *vb* **10 = compete,** contest, run **13 = run,** barrel (along), burn rubber (*inf.*), career, dart, dash, fly, gallop, go like a bomb (*Brit. & NZ inf.*), hare (*Brit. inf.*), hasten, hurry, run like mad (*inf.*), speed, tear, zoom

race[2] *n* **1 = people,** blood, breed, clan, ethnic group, family, folk, house, issue, kin, kindred, line, lineage, nation, offspring, progeny, seed (*chiefly Biblical*), stock, tribe, type

racial *adj* **1, 2 = ethnic,** ethnological, folk, genealogical, genetic, national, tribal

abusive or aggressive behaviour towards members of another race on the basis of such a belief.
▸'**racist** *or* '**racialist** *n, adj*

rack[1] ❶ (ræk) *n* **1** a framework for holding, carrying, or displaying a specific load or object. **2** a toothed bar designed to engage a pinion to form a mechanism that will adjust the position of something. **3** (preceded by *the*) an instrument of torture that stretched the body of the victim. **4** a cause or state of mental or bodily stress, suffering, etc. (esp. in **on the rack**). **5** *US & Canad.* (in pool, snooker, etc.) **5a** the triangular frame used to arrange the balls for the opening shot. **5b** the balls so grouped. Brit. equivalent: **frame.** ◆ *vb (tr)* **6** to torture on the rack. **7** to cause great suffering to: *guilt racked his conscience.* **8** to strain or shake (something) violently: *the storm racked the town.* **9** to place or arrange in or on a rack. **10** to move (parts of machinery or a mechanism) using a toothed rack. **11** to raise (rents) exorbitantly. **12 rack one's brains.** to strain in mental effort. [C14 *rekke,* prob. from MDu. *rec* framework]
▸'**racker** *n*

USAGE NOTE See at **wrack**[1].

rack[2] (ræk) *n* destruction; wreck (obs. except in **go to rack and ruin**). [C16: var. of WRACK[1]]

rack[3] (ræk) *n* another word for **single-foot.** [C16: ? based on ROCK[2]]

rack[4] (ræk) *n* **1** a group of broken clouds moving in the wind. ◆ *vb* **2** *(intr)* (of clouds) to be blown along by the wind. [OE *wræc* what is driven]

rack[5] (ræk) *vb (tr)* to clear (wine, beer, etc.) as by siphoning it off from the dregs. [C15: from OProvençal *arraca,* from *raca* dregs of grapes after pressing]

rack-and-pinion *n* **1** a device for converting rotary into linear motion and vice versa, in which a gearwheel (the pinion) engages with a flat toothed bar (the rack). ◆ *adj* **2** (of a type of steering gear in motor vehicles) having a track rod with a rack along part of its length that engages with a pinion attached to the steering column.

racket[1] ❶ ('rækɪt) *n* **1** a noisy disturbance or loud commotion; clamour; din. **2** an illegal enterprise carried on for profit, such as extortion, fraud, etc. **3** *Sl.* a business or occupation: *what's your racket?* **4** *Music.* a medieval woodwind instrument of deep bass pitch. ◆ *vb* **5** *(intr;* often foll. by *about) Now rare.* to go about gaily or noisily, in search of pleasure, etc. [C16: prob. imit.]
▸'**rackety** *adj*

racket[2] *or* **racquet** ('rækɪt) *n* **1** a bat consisting of an open network of strings stretched in an oval frame with a handle, used to strike a tennis ball, etc. **2** a snowshoe shaped like a tennis racket. ◆ *vb* **3** *(tr)* to strike (a ball, etc.) with a racket. ◆ See also **rackets.** [C16: from F *raquette,* from Ar. *rāhat* palm of the hand]

racketeer (ˌrækɪ'tɪə) *n* **1** a person engaged in illegal enterprises for profit. ◆ *vb* **2** *(intr)* to operate an illegal enterprise.
▸ˌ**racket'eering** *n*

racket press *n* a device consisting of a frame closed by a spring mechanism, for keeping taut the strings of a tennis racket, squash racket, etc.

rackets ('rækɪts) *n (functioning as sing)* **a** a game similar to squash played in a four-walled court by two or four players using rackets and a small hard ball. **b** *(as modifier): a rackets court.*

rack railway *n* a steep mountain railway having a middle rail fitted with a rack that engages a pinion on the locomotive to provide traction. Also called: **cog railway.**

rack-rent *n* **1** a high rent that annually equals the value of the property upon which it is charged. **2** any extortionate rent. ◆ *vb* **3** to charge an extortionate rent for.
▸'**rack-**ˌ**renter** *n*

rack saw *n Building trades.* a wide-toothed saw.

racon ('reɪkɒn) *n* another name for **radar beacon.** [C20: from RA(DAR) + (BEA)CON]

raconteur (ˌrækɒn'tɜː) *n* a person skilled in telling stories. [C19: F, from *raconter* to tell]

racoon (rə'kuːn) *n, pl* **racoons** *or* **racoon.** a variant spelling of **raccoon.**

racquet ('rækɪt) *n* a variant spelling of **racket**[2].

racy ❶ ('reɪsɪ) *adj* **racier, raciest. 1** (of a person's manner, literary style, etc.) having a distinctively lively and spirited quality. **2** having a characteristic or distinctive flavour: *a racy wine.* **3** suggestive; slightly indecent; risqué.
▸'**racily** *adv* ▸'**raciness** *n*

rad[1] (ræd) *n* a former unit of absorbed ionizing radiation dose equivalent to an energy absorption per unit mass of 0.01 joule per kilogram of irradiated material. [C20: from RADIATION]

rad[2] *symbol for* radian.

rad. *abbrev. for:* **1** radical. **2** radius.

RADA ('rɑːdə) *n* (in Britain) *acronym for* Royal Academy of Dramatic Art.

radar ('reɪdɑː) *n* **1** a method for detecting the position and velocity of a distant object. A narrow beam of extremely high-frequency radio pulses is transmitted and reflected by the object back to the transmitter. The direction of the reflected beam and the time between transmission and reception of a pulse determine the position of the object. **2** the equipment used in such detection. [C20: *ra(dio) d(etecting) a(nd) r(anging)*]

radar astronomy *n* the use of radar to map the surfaces of the planets, their satellites, and other bodies.

radar beacon *n* a device for transmitting a coded radar signal in response to a signal from an aircraft or ship. The coded signal is then used by the navigator to determine his position. Also called: **racon.**

radarscope ('reɪdɑːˌskəʊp) *n* a cathode-ray oscilloscope on which radar signals can be viewed.

radar trap *n* a device using radar to detect motorists who exceed the speed limit.

raddle ('ræd[ə]l) *vb* **raddles, raddling, raddled. 1** *(tr) Chiefly Brit.* to paint (the face) with rouge. ◆ *n, vb* **2** another word for **ruddle.** [C16: var. of RUDDLE]

raddled ❶ ('ræd[ə]ld) *adj* (esp. of a person) unkempt or run-down in appearance.

radial ('reɪdɪəl) *adj* **1** (of lines, etc.) emanating from a common central point; arranged like the radii of a circle. **2** of, like, or relating to a radius or ray. **3** short for **radial-ply. 4** *Anat.* of or relating to the radius or forearm. **5** *Astron.* (of velocity) in a direction along the line of sight of a celestial object and measured by means of the red shift (or blue shift) of the spectral lines of the object. ◆ *n* **6** a radial part or section. [C16: from Med. L *radiālis,* from RADIUS]
▸'**radially** *adv*

radial engine *n* an internal-combustion engine having a number of cylinders arranged about a central crankcase.

radial-ply *adj* (of a motor tyre) having the fabric cords in the outer casing running radially to enable the sidewalls to be flexible.

radial symmetry *n* a type of structure of an organism in which a vertical cut through the axis in any of two or more planes produces two halves that are mirror images of each other. Cf. **bilateral symmetry.**

radian ('reɪdɪən) *n* an SI unit of plane angle; the angle between two radii of a circle that cut off on the circumference an arc equal in length to the radius. 1 radian is equivalent to 57.296 degrees. Symbol: rad. [C19: from RADIUS]

radiance ❶ ('reɪdɪəns) *or* **radiancy** *n, pl* **radiances** *or* **radiancies. 1** the quality or state of being radiant. **2** a measure of the amount of electromagnetic radiation leaving or arriving at a point on a surface.

radiant ❶ ('reɪdɪənt) *adj* **1** sending out rays of light; bright; shining. **2** characterized by health, happiness, etc.: *a radiant smile.* **3** emitted or propagated by or as radiation; radiated: *radiant heat.* **4** sending out heat by radiation: *a radiant heater.* **5** *Physics.* (of a physical quantity in photometry) evaluated by absolute energy measurements: *radiant flux.* ◆ *n* **6** a point or object that emits radiation, esp. the part of a heater that gives out heat. **7** *Astron.* the point in the sky from which a meteor shower appears to emanate. [C15: from L *radiāre* to shine, from *radius* ray of light]
▸'**radiancy** *n* ▸'**radiantly** *adv*

radiant energy *n* energy that is emitted or propagated in the form of particles or electromagnetic radiation.

radiant heat *n* heat transferred in the form of electromagnetic radiation rather than by conduction or convection; infrared radiation.

radiata pine (ˌreɪdɪ'ɑːtə) *n* a pine tree grown in Australia and New Zealand to produce building timber. Often shortened to **radiata.** [from NL]

radiate ❶ *vb* ('reɪdɪˌeɪt), **radiates, radiating, radiated. 1** Also: **eradiate.** to emit (heat, light, or other forms of radiation) or (of heat, light, etc.) to be emitted as radiation. **2** *(intr)* (of lines, beams, etc.) to spread out from a centre or be arranged in a radial pattern. **3** *(tr)* (of a person) to show (happiness, etc.) to a great degree. ◆ *adj* ('reɪdɪɪt, -ˌeɪt). **4** having rays; radiating. **5** (of a capitulum) consisting of ray flowers. **6** (of animals) showing radial symmetry. [C17: from L *radiāre* to emit rays]
▸'**radiative** *adj*

THESAURUS

rack[1] *n* **1** = **frame,** framework, stand, structure **4** = **torture,** affliction, agony, anguish, misery, pain, pang, persecution, suffering, torment ◆ *vb* **7** = **torture,** afflict, agonize, crucify, distress, excruciate, harass, harrow, oppress, pain, torment **8** = **strain,** force, pull, shake, stress, stretch, tear, wrench

racket[1] *n* **1** = **noise,** babel, ballyhoo *(inf.),* clamour, commotion, din, disturbance, fuss, hubbub, hullabaloo, outcry, pandemonium, row, rumpus, shouting, tumult, uproar **2** = **fraud,** criminal activity, illegal enterprise, scheme **3** *Slang* = **business,** game *(inf.),* line, occupation

rackety *adj* **1** = **noisy,** blaring, boisterous, clamorous, disorderly, rowdy, uproarious

racy *adj* **1** = **lively,** animated, buoyant, dramatic, energetic, entertaining, exciting, exhilarating, heady, sexy *(inf.),* sparkling, spirited, stimulating, vigorous, zestful **3** = **risqué,** bawdy, blue, broad, immodest, indecent, indelicate, naughty, near the knuckle *(inf.),* off colour, smutty, spicy *(inf.),* suggestive

raddled *adj* = **run-down,** broken-down, coarsened, dilapidated, dishevelled, haggard, tattered, the worse for wear, unkempt

radiance *n* **1** = **brightness,** brilliance, effulgence, glare, gleam, glitter, glow, incandescence, light, luminosity, lustre, resplendence, shine **1** = **happiness,** delight, gaiety, joy, pleasure, rapture, warmth

radiant *adj* **1** = **bright,** beaming, brilliant, effulgent, gleaming, glittering, glorious, glowing, incandescent, luminous, lustrous, resplendent, shining, sparkling, sunny **2** = **happy,** beaming, beatific, blissful, delighted, ecstatic, floating on air, gay, glowing, joyful, joyous, on cloud nine *(inf.),* rapt, rapturous, sent
Antonyms *adj* ≠ **bright:** black, dark, dull, gloomy, sombre ≠ **happy:** disconsolate, down in the dumps *(inf.),* gloomy, joyless, low, miserable, sad, sombre, sorrowful

radiate *vb* **1** = **emit,** diffuse, disseminate, emanate, give off *or* out, gleam, glitter, pour, scatter, send out, shed, shine, spread **2** = **spread out,** branch out, diverge, issue

radiation Ⓣ (ˌreɪdɪˈeɪʃən) *n* **1** *Physics.* **1a** the emission or transfer of radiant energy as particles, electromagnetic waves, sound, etc. **1b** the particles, etc., emitted, esp. the particles and gamma rays emitted in nuclear decay. **2** Also called: **radiation therapy.** *Med.* treatment using a radioactive substance. **3** the act, state, or process of radiating or being radiated.
▸ˌ**radiˈational** *adj*

radiation sickness *n Pathol.* illness caused by overexposure of the body to ionizing radiations from radioactive material or X-rays.

radiator (ˈreɪdɪˌeɪtə) *n* **1** a device for heating a room, building, etc., consisting of a series of pipes through which hot water or steam passes. **2** a device for cooling an internal-combustion engine, consisting of thin-walled tubes through which water passes. **3** *Electronics.* the part of an aerial or transmission line that radiates electromagnetic waves.

radical Ⓣ (ˈrædɪkᵊl) *adj* **1** of, relating to, or characteristic of the basic or inherent constitution of a person or thing; fundamental: *a radical fault.* **2** concerned with or tending to concentrate on fundamental aspects of a matter; searching or thoroughgoing: *radical thought.* **3** favouring or tending to produce extreme or fundamental changes in political, economic, or social conditions, institutions, etc.: *a radical party.* **4** *Med.* (of treatment) aimed at removing the source of a disease: *radical surgery.* **5** *Sl., chiefly US.* very good; excellent. **6** of or arising from the root or the base of the stem of a plant: *radical leaves.* **7** *Maths.* of, relating to, or containing roots of numbers or quantities. **8** *Linguistics.* of or relating to the root of a word. ◆ *n* **9** a person who favours extreme or fundamental change in existing institutions or in political, social, or economic conditions. **10** *Maths.* a root of a number or quantity, such as $\sqrt[3]{5}$, $\sqrt{x}$. **11** *Chem.* **11a** short for **free radical. 11b** another name for **group** (sense 9). **12** *Linguistics.* another word for **root**[1] (sense 8). [C14: from LL *rādīcālis* having roots, from L *rādix* a root]
▸ˈ**radicalness** *n*

radicalism (ˈrædɪkəˌlɪzəm) *n* **1** the principles, desires, or practices of political radicals. **2** a radical movement, esp. in politics.
▸ˌ**radicalˈistic** *adj* ▸ˌ**radicalˈistically** *adv*

radically (ˈrædɪkəlɪ) *adv* thoroughly; completely; fundamentally: *to alter radically.*

radical sign *n* the symbol √ placed before a number or quantity to indicate the extraction of a root, esp. a square root. The value of a higher root is indicated by a raised digit in front of the symbol, as in $\sqrt[3]{}$.

radicand (ˈrædɪˌkænd, ˌrædɪˈkænd) *n* a number or quantity from which a root is to be extracted, usually preceded by a radical sign: 3 *is the radicand of* $\sqrt{3}$. [C20: from L *rādīcandum,* lit.: that which is to be rooted, from *rādīcāre,* from *rādīx* root]

radicchio (ræˈdiːkɪəʊ) *n, pl* **radicchios.** an Italian variety of chicory, having purple leaves streaked with white that are eaten raw in salads.

radices (ˈreɪdɪˌsiːz) *n* a plural of **radix.**

radicle (ˈrædɪkᵊl) *n* **1** *Bot.* **1a** the part of the embryo of seed-bearing plants that develops into the main root. **1b** a very small root or rootlike part. **2** *Anat.* any bodily structure resembling a rootlet, esp. one of the smallest branches of a vein or nerve. **3** *Chem.* a variant spelling of **radical** (sense 11). [C18: from L *rādīcula,* from *rādīx* root]

radii (ˈreɪdɪˌaɪ) *n* a plural of **radius.**

radio (ˈreɪdɪəʊ) *n, pl* **radios. 1** the use of electromagnetic waves, lying in the radio-frequency range, for broadcasting, two-way communications, etc. **2** an electronic device designed to receive, demodulate, and amplify radio signals from sound broadcasting stations, etc. **3** the broadcasting, content, etc., of radio programmes: *he thinks radio is poor these days.* **4** the occupation or profession concerned with any aspect of the broadcasting of radio programmes. **5** short for **radiotelegraph, radiotelegraphy,** or **radiotelephone. 6** *(modifier)* **6a** of, relating to, or sent by radio signals: *a radio station.* **6b** of, concerned with, using, or operated by radio frequencies: *radio spectrum.* **6c** relating to or produced for radio: *radio drama.* ◆ *vb* **radios, radioing, radioed. 7** to transmit (a message, etc.) to (a person, etc.) by means of radio waves. ◆ Also called (esp. Brit.): **wireless.** [C20: short for *radiotelegraphy*]

radio- *combining form.* **1** denoting radio, broadcasting, or radio frequency: *radiogram.* **2** indicating radioactivity or radiation: *radiocarbon; radiochemistry.* [from F, from L *radius* ray]

radioactive (ˌreɪdɪəʊˈæktɪv) *adj* exhibiting, using, or concerned with radioactivity.
▸ˌ**radioˈactively** *adv*

radioactive dating *n* another term for **radiometric dating.**

radioactive decay *n* disintegration of a nucleus that occurs spontaneously or as a result of electron capture. Also called: **disintegration.**

radioactive series *n Physics.* a series of nuclides each of which undergoes radioactive decay into the next member of the series, ending with a stable element, usually lead.

radioactive tracer *n Med.* See **tracer** (sense 3).

radioactive waste *n* any waste material containing radionuclides. Also called: **nuclear waste.**

radioactivity (ˌreɪdɪəʊækˈtɪvɪtɪ) *n* the spontaneous emission of radiation from atomic nuclei. The radiation can consist of alpha, beta, or gamma radiation.

radio astronomy *n* a branch of astronomy in which a radio telescope is used to detect and analyse radio signals received on earth from radio sources in space.

radio beacon *n* a fixed radio transmitting station that broadcasts a characteristic signal by means of which a vessel or aircraft can determine its bearing or position.

radiobiology (ˌreɪdɪəʊbaɪˈɒlədʒɪ) *n* the branch of biology concerned with the effects of radiation on living organisms and the study of biological processes using radioactive substances as tracers.
▸**radiobiological** (ˌreɪdɪəʊˌbaɪəˈlɒdʒɪkᵊl) *adj* ▸ˌ**radioˌbioˈlogically** *adv* ▸ˌ**radiobiˈologist** *n*

radiocarbon (ˌreɪdɪəʊˈkɑːbᵊn) *n* a radioactive isotope of carbon, esp. carbon-14. See **carbon** (sense 1).

radiocarbon dating *n* See **carbon dating.**

radiochemistry (ˌreɪdɪəʊˈkɛmɪstrɪ) *n* the chemistry of radioactive elements and their compounds.
▸ˌ**radioˈchemical** *adj* ▸ˌ**radioˈchemist** *n*

radio compass *n* any navigational device that gives a bearing by determining the direction of incoming radio waves transmitted from a particular radio station or beacon. See also **goniometer** (sense 2).

radio control *n* remote control by means of radio signals from a transmitter.
▸ˈ**radio-conˈtrolled** *adj*

radioelement (ˌreɪdɪəʊˈɛlɪmənt) *n* an element that is naturally radioactive.

radio frequency *n* **1a** any frequency that lies in the range 10 kilohertz to 300 000 megahertz and can be used for broadcasting. Abbrevs.: **rf, RF. 1b** *(as modifier): a radio-frequency amplifier.* **2** the frequency transmitted by a particular radio station.

radio galaxy *n* a galaxy that is a strong emitter of radio waves.

radiogram (ˈreɪdɪəʊˌɡræm) *n* **1** *Brit.* a unit comprising a radio and record player. **2** a message transmitted by radiotelegraphy. **3** another name for **radiograph.**

radiograph (ˈreɪdɪəʊˌɡrɑːf) *n* an image produced on a specially sensitized photographic film or plate by radiation, usually by X-rays or gamma rays.

radiography (ˌreɪdɪˈɒɡrəfɪ) *n* the production of radiographs of opaque objects for use in medicine, surgery, industry, etc.
▸ˌ**radiˈographer** *n* ▸**radiographic** (ˌreɪdɪəʊˈɡræfɪk) *adj* ▸ˌ**radioˈgraphically** *adv*

radio-immuno-assay (ˈreɪdɪəʊˌɪmjʊnəʊˈæseɪ) *n* a sensitive immunological assay, making use of radioactive labelling, of such things as hormone levels in the blood.

radioisotope (ˌreɪdɪəʊˈaɪsətəʊp) *n* a radioactive isotope.
▸**radioisotopic** (ˌreɪdɪəʊˌaɪsəˈtɒpɪk) *adj*

radiolarian (ˌreɪdɪəʊˈlɛərɪən) *n* any of various marine protozoans typically having a siliceous shell and stiff radiating cytoplasmic projections. [C19: from NL *Radiolaria,* from LL *radiolus* little sunbeam, from L *radius* ray]

radiology (ˌreɪdɪˈɒlədʒɪ) *n* the use of X-rays and radioactive substances in the diagnosis and treatment of disease.
▸ˌ**radiˈologist** *n*

radiometer (ˌreɪdɪˈɒmɪtə) *n* any instrument for the detection or measurement of radiant energy.
▸**radiometric** (ˌreɪdɪəʊˈmɛtrɪk) *adj* ▸ˌ**radiˈometry** *n*

radiometric dating *n* any method of dating material based on the decay of its constituent radioactive atoms, such as potassium-argon dating or rubidium-strontium dating. Also called: **radioactive dating.**

radiopager (ˈreɪdɪəʊˌpeɪdʒə) *n* a small radio receiver fitted with a buzzer to alert a person to telephone their home, office, etc., to receive a message.
▸ˈ**radioˌpaging** *n*

radiopaque (ˌreɪdɪəʊˈpeɪk) *or* **radio-opaque** *adj* not permitting X-rays or other radiation to pass through.
▸**radiopacity** (ˌreɪdɪəʊˈpæsɪtɪ) *or* ˌ**radio-oˈpacity** *n*

radio receiver *n* an apparatus that receives incoming modulated radio waves and converts them into sound.

radioscopy (ˌreɪdɪˈɒskəpɪ) *n* another word for **fluoroscopy.**
▸**radioscopic** (ˌreɪdɪəʊˈskɒpɪk) *adj* ▸ˌ**radioˈscopically** *adv*

radiosonde (ˈreɪdɪəʊˌsɒnd) *n* an airborne instrument to send meteorological information back to earth by radio. [C20: RADIO- + F *sonde* sounding line]

radio source *n* a celestial object, such as a supernova remnant or quasar, that is a source of radio waves.

radio spectrum *n* the range of electromagnetic frequencies used in radio transmission, between 10 kilohertz and 300 000 megahertz.

radio star *n* a former name for **radio source.**

radiotelegraphy (ˌreɪdɪəʊtɪˈlɛɡrəfɪ) *n* a type of telegraphy in which messages (formerly in Morse code) are transmitted by radio waves.
▸ˌ**radioˈteleˌgraph** *vb, n* ▸**radiotelegraphic** (ˌreɪdɪəʊˌtɛlɪˈɡræfɪk) *adj*

radiotelephone (ˌreɪdɪəʊˈtɛlɪˌfəʊn) *n* **1** a device for communications by means of radio waves rather than by transmitting along wires or cables. ◆ *vb* **radiotelephones, radiotelephoning, radiotelephoned. 2** to telephone (a person) by radiotelephone.

THESAURUS

radiation *n* **1** = **emission,** emanation, rays

radical *adj* **1** = **fundamental,** basic, constitutional, deep-seated, essential, innate, natural, organic **2** = **thoroughgoing,** profound **3** = **extreme,** drastic, excessive, extremist, fanatical, revolutionary, sweeping ◆ *n* **9** = **extremist,** fanatic, militant, revolutionary

Antonyms *adj* ≠ **fundamental:** insignificant, minor, superficial, token, trivial ◆ *n* ≠ **extremist:** conservative, moderate, reactionary

▶**radiotelephonic** (ˌreɪdɪəʊˌtɛlɪˈfɒnɪk) *adj* ▶**radiotelephony** (ˌreɪdɪəʊtɪˈlɛfənɪ) *n*

radio telescope *n* an instrument consisting of an antenna or system of antennas connected to one or more radio receivers, used in radio astronomy to detect and analyse radio waves from space.

radioteletype (ˌreɪdɪəʊˈtɛlɪˌtaɪp) *n* **1** a teleprinter that transmits or receives information by means of radio waves. **2** a network of such devices widely used for communicating news, messages, etc. Abbrevs.: **RTT, RTTY.**

radiotherapy (ˌreɪdɪəʊˈθɛrəpɪ) *n* the treatment of disease by means of alpha or beta particles emitted from an implanted or ingested radioisotope, or by means of a beam of high-energy radiation. Cf. **chemotherapy.**
▶**radiotherapeutic** (ˌreɪdɪəʊˌθɛrəˈpjuːtɪk) *adj* ▶ˌ**radioˈtherapist** *n*

radio wave *n* an electromagnetic wave of radio frequency.

radish (ˈrædɪʃ) *n* **1** any of a genus of plants of Europe and Asia, with petals arranged like a cross, cultivated for their edible roots. **2** the root of this plant, which has a pungent taste and is eaten raw in salads. [OE *rǣdīc*, from L *rādīx* root]

radium (ˈreɪdɪəm) *n* **a** a highly radioactive luminescent white element of the alkaline earth group of metals. It occurs in pitchblende and other uranium ores. Symbol: Ra; atomic no.: 88; half-life of most stable isotope, ^{226}Ra: 1620 years. **b** (*as modifier*): *radium needle.* [C20: from L *radius* ray]

radium therapy *n* treatment of disease, esp. cancer, by exposing affected tissues to radiation from radium.

radius (ˈreɪdɪəs) *n, pl* **radii** *or* **radiuses. 1** a straight line joining the centre of a circle or sphere to any point on the circumference or surface. **2** the length of this line, usually denoted by the symbol *r.* **3** *Anat.* the outer, slightly shorter of the two bones of the human forearm, extending from the elbow to the wrist. **4** a corresponding bone in other vertebrates. **5** any of the veins of an insect's wing. **6** a group of ray flowers, occurring in such plants as the daisy. **7a** any radial or radiating part, such as a spoke. **7b** (*as modifier*): *a radius arm.* **8** a circular area of a size indicated by the length of its radius: *the police stopped every lorry within a radius of four miles.* **9** the operational limit of a ship, aircraft, etc. [C16: from L: rod, ray, spoke]

radix (ˈreɪdɪks) *n, pl* **radices** *or* **radixes. 1** *Maths.* any number that is the base of a number system or of a system of logarithms: *10 is the radix of the decimal system.* **2** *Biol.* the root or point of origin of a part or organ. **3** *Linguistics.* a less common word for **root**[1] (sense 8). [C16: from L *rādīx* root]

radix point *n* a point, such as the decimal point in the decimal system, separating the integral part of a number from the fractional part.

radome (ˈreɪdəʊm) *n* a protective housing for a radar antenna made from a material that is transparent to radio waves. [C20: RA(DAR) + DOME]

radon (ˈreɪdɒn) *n* a colourless radioactive element of the rare gas group, the most stable isotope of which, radon-222, is a decay product of radium. Symbol: Rn; atomic no.: 86; half-life of ^{222}Rn: 3.82 days. [C20: from RADIUM + -ON]

radula (ˈrædjʊlə) *n, pl* **radulae** (-ˌliː). a horny tooth-bearing strip on the tongue of molluscs that is used for rasping food. [C19: from LL: a scraping iron, from L *rādere* to scrape]
▶ˈ**radular** *adj*

RAF (*Not standard* ræf) *abbrev. for* Royal Air Force.

Rafferty (ˈræfətɪ) *or* **Rafferty's rules** *pl n Austral. & NZ sl.* no rules at all. [C20: from ?]

raffia *or* **raphia** (ˈræfɪə) *n* **1** a palm tree, native to Madagascar, that has large plumelike leaves, the stalks of which yield a useful fibre. **2** the fibre obtained from this plant, used for weaving, etc. **3** any of several related palms or the fibre obtained from them. [C19: from Malagasy]

raffish **T** (ˈræfɪʃ) *adj* **1** careless or unconventional in dress, manners, etc.; rakish. **2** tawdry; flashy; vulgar. [C19: from *raff* rubbish, rabble]
▶ˈ**raffishly** *adv* ▶ˈ**raffishness** *n*

raffle **T** (ˈræfᵊl) *n* **1a** a lottery in which the prizes are goods rather than money. **1b** (*as modifier*): *a raffle ticket.* ◆ *vb* **raffles, raffling, raffled. 2** (*tr; often foll. by off*) to dispose of (goods) in a raffle. [C14 (a dice game): from OF, from ?]
▶ˈ**raffler** *n*

rafflesia (ræˈfliːzɪə) *n* any of various tropical Asian parasitic leafless plants, the flowers of which grow up to 45 cm (18 inches) across, smell of putrid meat, and are pollinated by carrion flies. [C19: NL, after Sir Stamford *Raffles* (1781–1826), Brit. colonial administrator, who discovered it]

raft[1] (rɑːft) *n* **1** a buoyant platform of logs, planks, etc., used as a vessel or moored platform. **2** a thick slab of reinforced concrete laid over soft ground to provide a foundation for a building. ◆ *vb* **3** to convey on or travel by raft, or make a raft from. [C15: from ON *raptr* RAFTER]

raft[2] (rɑːft) *n Inf.* a large collection or amount: *a raft of old notebooks discovered in a cupboard.*

rafter (ˈrɑːftə) *n* any one of a set of parallel sloping beams that form the framework of a roof. [OE *ræfter*]

RAFVR *abbrev. for* Royal Air Force Volunteer Reserve.

rag[1] (ræg) *n* **1a** a small piece of cloth, such as one torn from a discarded garment, or such pieces of cloth collectively. **1b** (*as modifier*): *a rag doll.* **2** a fragmentary piece of any material; scrap; shred. **3** *Inf.* a newspaper, esp. one considered as worthless, sensational, etc. **4** *Inf.* an item of clothing. **5** *Inf.* a handkerchief. **6** *Brit. sl., esp. naval.* a flag or ensign. **7** **from rags to riches.** *Inf.* **7a** from poverty to great wealth. **7b** (*as modifier*): *a rags-to-riches tale.* [C14: prob. back formation from RAGGED from OE *raggig*]

rag[2] (ræg) *vb* **rags, ragging, ragged.** (*tr*) **1** to draw attention facetiously and persistently to the shortcomings of (a person). **2** *Brit.* to play rough practical jokes on. ◆ *n* **3** *Brit.* a boisterous practical joke. **4** (in British universities, etc.) **4a** a period in which various events are organized to raise money for charity. **4b** (*as modifier*): *rag day.* [C18: from ?]

rag[3] (ræg) *Jazz.* ◆ *n* **1** a piece of ragtime music. ◆ *vb* **rags, ragging, ragged. 2** (*tr*) to compose or perform in ragtime. [C20: from RAGTIME]

raga (ˈrɑːgə) *n* (in Indian music) **1** any of several conventional patterns of melody and rhythm that form the basis for freely interpreted compositions. **2** a composition based on one of these patterns. [C18: from Sansk. *rāga* tone, colour]

ragamuffin **T** (ˈrægəˌmʌfɪn) *n* **1** a ragged unkempt person, esp. a child. **2** another name for **ragga.** [C14 *Ragamoffyn,* a demon in the poem *Piers Plowman* (1393); prob. based on RAG[1]]

rag-and-bone man *n Brit.* a man who buys and sells discarded clothing, etc. US equivalent: **junkman.**

ragbag **T** (ˈrægˌbæg) *n* **1** a bag for storing odd rags. **2** a confused assortment; jumble.

ragbolt (ˈrægˌbəʊlt) *n* a bolt that has angled projections on it to prevent it working loose.

rage **T** (reɪdʒ) *n* **1** intense anger; fury. **2** violent movement or action, esp. of the sea, wind, etc. **3** great intensity of hunger or other feelings. **4** a fashion or craze (esp. in **all the rage**). **5** *Austral. & NZ inf.* a dance or party. ◆ *vb* **rages, raging, raged.** (*intr*) **6** to feel or exhibit intense anger. **7** (esp. of storms, fires, etc.) to move or surge with great violence. **8** (esp. of a disease) to spread rapidly and uncontrollably. **9** *Austral. & NZ inf.* to have a good time. [C13: via OF from L *rabiēs* madness]

ragga (ˈrægə) *n* a dance-oriented style of reggae. Also called: **ragamuffin.** [C20: shortened from RAGAMUFFIN]

ragged **T** (ˈrægɪd) *adj* **1** (of clothes) worn to rags; tattered. **2** (of a person) dressed in tattered clothes. **3** having a neglected or unkempt appearance: *ragged weeds.* **4** having a rough or uneven surface or edge; jagged. **5** uneven or irregular: *a ragged beat; a ragged shout.* [C13: prob. from *ragge* RAG[1]]
▶ˈ**raggedly** *adv* ▶ˈ**raggedness** *n*

ragged robin *n* a plant related to the carnation family and native to Europe and Asia, that has pink or white flowers with ragged petals. See also **catchfly.**

raggedy (ˈrægɪdɪ) *adj Inf., chiefly US & Canad.* somewhat ragged; tattered: *a raggedy doll.*

ragi, raggee, *or* **raggy** (ˈrægɪ) *n* a cereal grass, cultivated in Africa and Asia for its edible grain. [C18: from Hindi]

raglan (ˈræglən) *n* **1** a coat, jumper, etc., with sleeves that continue to the collar instead of having armhole seams. ◆ *adj* **2** cut in this design: *a raglan sleeve.* [C19: after Lord *Raglan* (1788–1855), Brit. field marshal]

ragout (ræˈguː) *n* **1** a richly seasoned stew of meat and vegetables. ◆ *vb* **ragouts** (-ˈguːz), **ragouting** (-ˈguːɪŋ), **ragouted** (-ˈguːd). **2** (*tr*) to make into a ragout. [C17: from F, from *ragoûter* to stimulate the appetite again, from *ra-* RE- + *goûter* from L *gustāre* to taste]

rag-rolling *n* a decorating technique in which paint is applied with a roughly folded cloth in order to create a marbled effect.

ragtag (ˈrægˌtæg) *n Derog.* the common people; rabble (esp. in **ragtag and bobtail**). [C19: from RAG[1] + TAG[1]]

ragtime (ˈrægˌtaɪm) *n* a style of jazz piano music, developed by Scott Joplin around 1900, having a two-four rhythm base and a syncopated melody. [C20: prob. from RAGGED + TIME]

rag trade *n Inf.* the clothing business.

THESAURUS

raffish *adj* **1** = **dashing,** bohemian, careless, casual, devil-may-care, disreputable, jaunty, rakish, sporty, unconventional **2** = **vulgar,** coarse, flashy, garish, gaudy, gross, loud, meretricious, showy, tasteless, tawdry, trashy, uncouth

raffle *n* **1** = **draw,** lottery, sweep, sweepstake

ragamuffin *n* **1** = **urchin,** gamin, guttersnipe, scarecrow (*inf.*), street arab (*offens.*), tatterdemalion (*rare*)

ragbag *n* **2** = **mixture,** confusion, hotchpotch, jumble, medley, miscellany, mixed bag (*inf.*), omnium-gatherum, potpourri

rage *n* **1** = **fury,** agitation, anger, high dudgeon, ire, madness, passion, rampage, raving, wrath **3** = **frenzy,** fury, mania, obsession, passion, vehemence, violence **4** = **craze,** enthusiasm, fad (*inf.*), fashion, latest thing, vogue ◆ *vb* **6** = **be furious,** be beside oneself, be incandescent, blow a fuse (*sl., chiefly US*), blow one's top, blow up (*inf.*), crack up (*inf.*), fly off the handle (*inf.*), foam at the mouth, fret, fume, go ballistic (*sl., chiefly US*), go off the deep end (*inf.*), go up the wall (*sl.*), lose it (*inf.*), lose one's rag (*sl.*), lose one's temper, lose the plot (*inf.*), see red (*inf.*), seethe, storm, throw a fit (*inf.*) **7** = **be at its height,** be uncontrollable, rampage, storm, surge
Antonyms *n* ≠ **fury:** acceptance, calmness, equanimity, gladness, good humour, joy, pleasure, resignation ◆ *vb* ≠ **be furious:** accept, keep one's cool, remain unruffled, resign oneself to, stay calm

ragged *adj* **1** = **shabby,** down at heel, frayed, in holes, in rags, in tatters, mean, poor, tattered, tatty, threadbare, torn, worn-out **4** = **rough,** crude, jagged, notched, rugged, serrated, uneven, unfinished **5** = **irregular,** broken, desultory, disorganized, fragmented, uneven
Antonyms *adj* ≠ **shabby:** fashionable, smart

raging *adj* **6** = **furious,** beside oneself, boiling mad (*inf.*), doing one's nut (*Brit. sl.*), enraged, fit to be tied (*sl.*), fizzing (*Scot.*), foaming at the

ragweed ('ræg,wi:d) *n* a North American plant of the composite family such as the **common ragweed.** Its green tassel-like flowers produce large amounts of pollen, which causes hay fever. Also called: **ambrosia.**

ragworm ('ræg,wɜ:m) *n* any polychaete worm living chiefly in burrows in sand and having a flattened body with a row of fleshy lateral appendages along each side. US name: **clamworm.**

ragwort ('ræg,wɜ:t) *n* any of several European plants of the composite family that have yellow daisy-like flowers. See also **groundsel.**

rah (rɑ:) *interj Inf., chiefly US.* short for **hurrah.**

rai (raɪ) *n* a type of Algerian popular music based on traditional Algerian music influenced by modern Western pop. [C20: Ar., lit.: opinion]

raid ❶ (reɪd) *n* **1** a sudden surprise attack. **2** a surprise visit by police searching for criminals or illicit goods: *a fraud-squad raid.* See also **bear raid, dawn raid, ram raid.** ◆ *vb* **3** to make a raid against (a person, thing, etc.). **4** to sneak into (a place) in order to take something, steal, etc.: *raiding the larder.* [C15: Scot. dialect, from OE *rād* military expedition]
▸**'raider** *n*

rail[1] (reɪl) *n* **1** a horizontal bar of wood, etc., supported by vertical posts, functioning as a fence, barrier, etc. **2** a horizontal bar fixed to a wall on which to hang things: *a picture rail.* **3** a horizontal framing member in a door. Cf. **stile**[2]. **4** short for **railing. 5** one of a pair of parallel bars laid on a track, roadway, etc., that serve as a guide and running surface for the wheels of a train, tramcar, etc. **6a** short for **railway. 6b** (*as modifier*): *rail transport.* **7** *Naut.* a trim for finishing the top of a bulwark. **8 off the rails. 8a** into or in a state of disorder. **8b** eccentric or mad. ◆ *vb* (*tr*) **9** to provide with a rail or railings. **10** (usually foll. by *in* or *off*) to fence (an area) with rails. [C13: from OF *raille* rod, from L *rēgula* ruler]

rail[2] ❶ (reɪl) *vb* (*intr;* foll. by *at* or *against*) to complain bitterly or vehemently. [C15: from OF *railler* to mock, from OProvençal *ralhar* to chatter, from LL *ragere* to yell]
▸**'railer** *n*

rail[3] (reɪl) *n* any of various small cranelike wading marsh birds with short wings and neck, long legs, and dark plumage. [C15: from OF *raale,* ?from L *rādere* to scrape]

railcar ('reɪl,kɑ:) *n* a passenger-carrying railway vehicle consisting of a single coach with its own power unit.

railcard ('reɪl,kɑ:d) *n Brit.* a card issued to students or senior citizens to entitle them to cheap rail fares.

railhead ('reɪl,hɛd) *n* **1** a terminal of a railway. **2** the farthest point reached by completed track on an unfinished railway.

railing ❶ ('reɪlɪŋ) *n* **1** (*often pl*) a fence, balustrade, or barrier that consists of rails supported by posts. **2** rails collectively or material for making rails.

raillery ❶ ('reɪlərɪ) *n, pl* **railleries. 1** light-hearted satire or ridicule; banter. **2** a bantering remark. [C17: from F, from *railler* to tease; see RAIL[2]]

railroad ('reɪl,rəʊd) *n* **1** the usual US word for **railway.** ◆ *vb* **2** (*tr*) *Inf.* to force (a person) into (an action) with haste or by unfair means.

railway ('reɪl,weɪ) *or US* **railroad** *n* **1** a permanent track composed of a line of parallel metal rails fixed to sleepers, for transport of passengers and goods in trains. **2** any track for the wheels of a vehicle to run on: *a cable railway.* **3** the entire equipment, rolling stock, buildings, property, and system of tracks used in such a transport system. **4** the organization responsible for operating a railway network. **5** (*modifier*) of, relating to, or used on a railway: *a railway engine.*

raiment ('reɪmənt) *n Arch. or poetic.* attire; clothing. [C15: from *arrayment,* from OF *areement;* see ARRAY]

rain ❶ (reɪn) *n* **1a** precipitation from clouds in the form of drops of water, formed by the condensation of water vapour in the atmosphere. **1b** a fall of rain; shower. **1c** (*in combination*): *a raindrop.* **2** a large quantity of anything falling rapidly or in quick succession: *a rain of abuse.* **3** (**come**) **rain or** (**come**) **shine.** regardless of the weather or circumstances. **4 right as rain.** *Brit. inf.* perfectly all right. ◆ *vb* **5** (*intr;* with *it* as subject) to be the case that rain is falling. **6** (often with *it* as subject) to fall or cause to fall like rain. **7** (*tr*) to bestow in large measure: *to rain abuse on someone.* **8 rained off.** cancelled or postponed on account of rain. US and Canad. term: **rained out.** ◆ See also **rains.** [OE *regn*]
▸**'rainless** *adj*

rainbow ('reɪn,bəʊ) *n* **1a** a bow-shaped display in the sky of the colours of the spectrum, caused by the refraction and reflection of the sun's rays through rain. **1b** (*as modifier*): *a rainbow pattern.* **2** an illusory hope: *to chase rainbows.* **3** (*modifier*) of or relating to a political grouping together by several minorities, esp. of different races: *the rainbow coalition.*

rainbow nation *n S. African.* an epithet, alluding to its multiracial population, of South Africa. [C20: coined by Nelson Mandela (born 1918), South African statesman, following the end of apartheid]

rainbow trout *n* a freshwater trout of North American origin, marked with many black spots and two longitudinal red stripes.

rain check *n US & Canad.* **1** a ticket stub for a baseball game that allows readmission on a future date if the event is cancelled because of rain. **2** the deferral of acceptance of an offer. **3 take a rain check.** *Inf.* to accept or request the postponement of an offer.

raincoat ('reɪn,kəʊt) *n* a coat made of a waterproof material.

rainfall ('reɪn,fɔ:l) *n* **1** precipitation in the form of raindrops. **2** *Meteorol.* the amount of precipitation in a specified place and time.

rainforest ('reɪn,fɒrɪst) *n* dense forest found in tropical areas of heavy rainfall.

rain gauge *n* an instrument for measuring rainfall or snowfall, consisting of a cylinder covered by a funnel-like lid.

rainproof ('reɪn,pru:f) *adj* **1** Also: **'rain,tight.** (of garments, materials, etc.) impermeable to rainwater. ◆ *vb* **2** (*tr*) to make rainproof.

rains (reɪnz) *pl n* **the rains.** the season of heavy rainfall, esp. in the tropics.

rain shadow *n* the relatively dry area on the leeward side of high ground in the path of rain-bearing winds.

rainstorm ('reɪn,stɔ:m) *n* a storm with heavy rain.

rainwater ('reɪn,wɔ:tə) *n* pure water from rain (as distinguished from spring water, tap water, etc., which may contain minerals and impurities).

rainy ❶ ('reɪnɪ) *adj* **rainier, rainiest. 1** characterized by a large rainfall: *a rainy climate.* **2** wet or showery; bearing rain.
▸**'rainily** *adv* ▸**'raininess** *n*

rainy day *n* a future time of need, esp. financial.

raise ❶ (reɪz) *vb* **raises, raising, raised.** (*mainly tr*) **1** to move or elevate to a higher position or level; lift. **2** to set or place in an upright position. **3** to construct, build, or erect: *to raise a barn.* **4** to increase in amount, size, value, etc.: *to raise prices.* **5** to increase in degree, strength, intensity, etc.: *to raise one's voice.* **6** to advance in rank or status; promote. **7** to arouse or awaken from sleep or death. **8** to stir up or incite; activate: *to raise a mutiny.* **9 raise Cain** (*or* **the devil, hell, the roof,** etc.). **9a** to create a disturbance, esp. by making a great noise. **9b** to protest vehemently. **10** to give rise to; cause or provoke: *to raise a smile.* **11** to put forward for consideration: *to raise a question.* **12** to cause to assemble or gather together: *to raise an army.* **13** to grow or cause to grow: *to raise a crop.* **14** to bring up; rear: *to raise a family.* **15** to cause to be heard or known; utter or express: *to raise a shout.* **16** to bring to an end; remove: *to raise a siege.* **17** to cause (bread, etc.) to rise, as by the addition of yeast. **18** *Poker.* to bet more than (the previous player). **19** *Bridge.* to bid (one's partner's suit) at a higher level. **20** *Naut.* to cause (something) to seem to rise above the horizon by approaching: *we raised land after 20 days.* **21** to establish radio communications with: *we raised Moscow last night.* **22** to obtain (money, funds, etc.). **23** to bring (a surface, a design, etc.) into relief; cause to project. **24** to cause (a blister, etc.) to form on the skin. **25** *Maths.* to multiply (a number) by itself a specified number of times: *8 is 2 raised to the power 3.* **26 raise one's glass** (**to**). to drink a toast (to). **27 raise one's hat.** *Old-fashioned.* to take one's hat briefly off one's head as a greeting or mark of respect. ◆ *n* **28** the act or an instance of raising. **29** *Chiefly US & Canad.* an increase, esp. in salary, wages, etc.; rise. [C12: from ON *reisa*]
▸**'raisable** *or* **'raiseable** *adj*

raised beach *n* a wave-cut platform raised above the shoreline by a relative fall in the water level.

raisin ('reɪz°n) *n* a dried grape. [C13: from OF: grape, ult. from L *racēmus* cluster of grapes]
▸**'raisiny** *adj*

THESAURUS

mouth, frenzied, fuming, incandescent, incensed, infuriated, mad, raving, seething

raid *n* **1** = **attack**, break-in, descent, foray, hit-and-run attack, incursion, inroad, invasion, irruption, onset, sally, seizure, sortie, surprise attack ◆ *vb* **3** = **attack**, assault, break into, descend on, fall upon, forage (*Military*), foray, invade, pillage, plunder, reive (*dialect*), rifle, sack, sally forth, swoop down upon

raider *n* **1** = **attacker**, forager (*Military*), invader, marauder, plunderer, reiver (*dialect*), robber, thief

rail[2] *vb* = **complain**, abuse, attack, blast, censure, criticize, fulminate, inveigh, lambast(e), put down, revile, scold, tear into (*inf.*), upbraid, vituperate, vociferate

railing *n* **1** = **fence**, balustrade, barrier, paling, rails

raillery *n* **1** = **teasing**, badinage, banter, chaff, irony, jesting, joke, joking, josh (*sl., chiefly US & Canad.*), kidding (*inf.*), mockery, persiflage, pleasantry, repartee, ridicule, satire, sport

rain *n* **1** = **rainfall**, cloudburst, deluge, downpour, drizzle, fall, precipitation, raindrops, showers **2** = **shower**, deluge, flood, hail, spate, stream, torrent, volley ◆ *vb* **5** = **pour**, bucket down (*inf.*), come down in buckets (*inf.*), drizzle, fall, pelt (down), rain cats and dogs (*inf.*), shower, teem **6** = **fall**, deposit, drop, shower, sprinkle **7** = **bestow**, lavish, pour, shower

rainy *adj* **1, 2** = **wet**, damp, drizzly, showery
Antonyms *adj* arid, dry, fine, sunny

raise *vb* **1** = **lift**, elevate, exalt, heave, hoist, move up, rear, uplift **3** = **build**, construct, erect, put up **4, 5** = **increase**, advance, aggravate, amplify, augment, boost, enhance, enlarge, escalate, exaggerate, heighten, hike (up) (*inf.*), inflate, intensify, jack up, magnify, put up, reinforce, strengthen **6** = **promote**, advance, aggrandize, elevate, exalt, prefer, upgrade **8** = **stir up**, activate, arouse, awaken, cause, evoke, excite, foment, foster, incite, instigate, kindle, motivate, provoke, rouse, set on foot, summon up, whip up **10** = **cause**, bring about, create, engender, give rise to, occasion, originate, produce, provoke, start **11** = **put forward**, advance, bring up, broach, introduce, moot, suggest **12** = **collect**, assemble, form, gather, get, levy, mass, mobilize, muster, obtain, rally, recruit **13** = **grow**, breed, cultivate, produce, propagate, rear **14** = **bring up**, develop, nurture, rear **16** = **end**, abandon, give up, lift, relieve, relinquish, remove, terminate
Antonyms *vb* ≠ **build:** demolish, destroy, level, ruin, wreck ≠ **increase:** cut, decrease, diminish, drop, lessen, lower, reduce, sink ≠ **promote:** demote, downgrade, reduce ≠ **stir up:** calm, depress, lessen, lower, quash, quell, reduce, sink, soothe, suppress ≠ **end:** begin, establish, start

raison d'être *French.* (rɛzɔ̃ dɛtrə) *n, pl* ***raisons d'être*** (rɛzɔ̃ dɛtrə). reason or justification for existence.

raita ('raɪtə) *n* an Indian dish of finely chopped cucumber, peppers, mint, etc., in yogurt, served with curries. [C20: from Hindi]

raj (rɑːdʒ) *n* **1** (in India) government; rule. **2** (cap. and preceded by *the*) the British government in India before 1947. [C19: from Hindi, from Sansk., from *rājati* he rules]

rajah *or* **raja** ('rɑːdʒə) *n* **1** (in India, formerly) a ruler: sometimes used as a title preceding a name. **2** a Malayan or Javanese prince or chieftain. [C16: from Hindi, from Sansk. *rājan* king]

Rajput *or* **Rajpoot** ('rɑːdʒput) *n Hinduism.* one of a Hindu military caste claiming descent from the Kshatriya, the original warrior caste. [C16: from Hindi, from Sansk. *rājan* king]

rake[1] ❶ (reɪk) *n* **1** a hand implement consisting of a row of teeth set in a headpiece attached to a long shaft and used for gathering hay, straw, etc., or for smoothing loose earth. **2** any of several mechanical farm implements equipped with rows of teeth or rotating wheels mounted with tines and used to gather hay, straw, etc. **3** any of various implements similar in shape or function. **4** the act of raking. ◆ *vb* **rakes, raking, raked. 5** to scrape, gather, or remove (leaves, refuse, etc.) with a rake. **6** to level or prepare (a surface) with a rake. **7** (*tr;* sometimes foll. by *out*) to clear (ashes, etc.) from (a fire). **8** (*tr;* foll. by *up* or *together*) to gather (items or people) with difficulty, as from a scattered area or limited supply. **9** (*tr;* often foll. by *through, over,* etc.) to search or examine carefully. **10** (when *intr,* foll. by *against, along,* etc.) to scrape or graze: *the ship raked the side of the quay.* **11** (*tr*) to direct (gunfire) along the length of (a target): *machine-guns raked the column.* **12** (*tr*) to sweep (one's eyes) along the length of (something); scan. ◆ See also **rake in, rake-off,** etc. [OE *raca*]
▸'**raker** *n*

rake[2] ❶ (reɪk) *n* a dissolute man, esp. one in fashionable society; roué. [C17: short for *rakehell* a dissolute man]

rake[3] (reɪk) *vb* **rakes, raking, raked.** (*mainly intr*) **1** to incline from the vertical by a perceptible degree, esp. (of a ship's mast) towards the stern. **2** (*tr*) to construct with a backward slope. ◆ *n* **3** the degree to which an object, such as a ship's mast, inclines from the perpendicular, esp. towards the stern. **4** *Theatre.* the slope of a stage from the back towards the footlights. **5** the angle between the working face of a cutting tool and a plane perpendicular to the surface of the workpiece. [C17: from ?; ? rel. to G *ragen* to project, Swedish *raka*]

rake in *vb* (*tr, adv*) *Inf.* to acquire (money) in large amounts.

rake-off *Sl.* ◆ *n* **1** a share of profits, esp. one that is illegal or given as a bribe. ◆ *vb* **rake off. 2** (*tr, adv*) to take or receive (such a share of profits).

rake up *vb* (*tr, adv*) to revive, discover, or bring to light (something forgotten): *to rake up an old quarrel.*

raki *or* **rakee** (rɑː'kiː, 'rækɪ) *n* a strong spirit distilled in Turkey from grain, usually flavoured with aniseed or other aromatics. [C17: from Turkish *rāqī*]

rakish[1] ❶ ('reɪkɪʃ) *adj* dissolute; profligate. [C18: from RAKE[2]]
▸'**rakishly** *adv* ▸'**rakishness** *n*

rakish[2] ❶ ('reɪkɪʃ) *adj* **1** dashing; jaunty: *a hat set at a rakish angle.* **2** *Naut.* (of a ship or boat) having lines suggestive of speed. [C19: prob. from RAKE[3]]

rale *or* **râle** (rɑːl) *n Med.* an abnormal crackling sound heard on auscultation of the chest, usually caused by the accumulation of fluid in the lungs. [C19: from F, from *râler* to breathe with a rattling sound]

rallentando (ˌrælɛn'tændəʊ) *adj, adv Music.* becoming slower. Also: **ritardando.** [C19: It., from *rallentare* to slow down]

rally[1] ❶ ('rælɪ) *vb* **rallies, rallying, rallied. 1** to bring (a group, unit, etc.) into order, as after dispersal, or (of such a group) to reform and come to order. **2** (when *intr,* foll. by *to*) to organize (supporters, etc.) for a common cause or (of such people) to come together for a purpose. **3** to summon up (one's strength, spirits, etc.) or (of a person's health, strength, or spirits) to revive or recover. **4** (*intr*) *Stock Exchange.* to increase sharply after a decline. **5** (*intr*) *Tennis, squash, etc.* to engage in a rally. ◆ *n, pl* **rallies. 6** a large gathering of people for a common purpose. **7** a marked recovery of strength or spirits, as during illness. **8** a return to order after dispersal or rout, as of troops, etc. **9** *Stock Exchange.* a sharp increase in price or trading activity after a decline. **10** *Tennis, squash, etc.* an exchange of several shots before one player wins the point. **11** a type of motoring competition over public roads. [C16: from OF *rallier,* from RE- + *alier* to unite]
▸'**rallier** *n*

rally[2] ❶ ('rælɪ) *vb* **rallies, rallying, rallied.** to mock or ridicule (someone) in a good-natured way; chaff; tease. [C17: from OF *railler* to tease; see RAIL[2]]

rallycross ('rælɪˌkrɒs) *n* a form of motor sport in which cars race over a one-mile circuit of rough grass with some hard-surfaced sections.

rally round *vb* (*intr*) to come to the aid of (someone); offer moral or practical support.

ram ❶ (ræm) *n* **1** an uncastrated adult male sheep. **2** a piston or moving plate, esp. one driven hydraulically or pneumatically. **3** the falling weight of a pile driver. **4** short for **battering ram. 5** a pointed projection in the stem of an ancient warship for puncturing the hull of enemy ships. **6** a warship equipped with a ram. ◆ *vb* **rams, ramming, rammed. 7** (*tr;* usually foll. by *into*) to force or drive, as by heavy blows: *to ram a post into the ground.* **8** (of a moving object) to crash with force (against another object) or (of two moving objects) to collide in this way. **9** (*tr;* often foll. by *in* or *down*) to stuff or cram (something into a hole, etc.). **10** (*tr;* foll. by *onto, against,* etc.) to thrust violently: *he rammed the books onto the desk.* **11** (*tr*) to present (an idea, argument, etc.) forcefully or aggressively (esp. in **ram (something) down someone's throat**). **12** (*tr*) to drive (a charge) into a firearm. [OE *ramm*]
▸'**rammer** *n*

Ram (ræm) *n* **the.** the constellation Aries, the first sign of the zodiac.

RAM[1] (ræm) *n Computing. acronym for* random access memory: semiconductor memory in which all storage locations can be rapidly accessed in the same amount of time. It forms the main memory of a computer, used by applications to perform tasks while the device is operating.

RAM[2] *abbrev. for* Royal Academy of Music.

Ramadan *or* **Rhamadhan** (ˌræmə'dɑːn) *n* **1** the ninth month of the Muslim year, lasting 30 days, during which strict fasting is observed from sunrise to sunset. **2** the fast itself. [C16: from Ar., lit.: the hot month, from *ramad* dryness]

Raman effect ('rɑːmən) *n* the change in wavelength of light that is scattered by electrons within a material: used in **Raman spectroscopy** for studying molecules. [C20: after Sir Chandasekhara *Raman* (1888–1970), Indian physicist]

ramble ❶ ('ræmb°l) *vb* **rambles, rambling, rambled.** (*intr*) **1** to stroll about freely, as for relaxation, with no particular direction. **2** (of paths, streams, etc.) to follow a winding course; meander. **3** to grow or develop in a random fashion. **4** (of speech, writing, etc.) to lack organization. ◆ *n* **5** a leisurely stroll, esp. in the countryside. [C17: prob. rel. to MDu. *rammelen* to ROAM (of animals)]

rambler ❶ ('ræmblə) *n* **1** a weak-stemmed plant that straggles over other vegetation. **2** a person who rambles, esp. one who takes country walks. **3** a person who lacks organization in his speech or writing.

rambling ❶ ('ræmblɪŋ) *adj* **1** straggling or sprawling haphazardly: *a rambling old house.* **2** (of speech or writing) diffuse and disconnected. **3** (of a plant, esp. a rose) climbing and straggling. **4** nomadic; wandering.

Ramboesque (ˌræmbəʊ'ɛsk) *adj* looking or behaving like or characteristic of Rambo, a mindlessly brutal fictional film character.
▸'**Ramboˌism** *n*

rambunctious (ræm'bʌŋkʃəs) *adj Inf.* boisterous; unruly. [C19: prob. from Icelandic *ram* (intensifying prefix) + *-bunctious,* from BUMPTIOUS]
▸**ram'bunctiousness** *n*

rambutan (ræm'buːt°n) *n* **1** a tree related to the soapberry, native to SE Asia, that has bright red edible fruit covered with hairs. **2** the fruit of this tree. [C18: from Malay, from *rambut* hair]

RAMC *abbrev. for* Royal Army Medical Corps.

ramekin *or* **ramequin** ('ræmɪkɪn) *n* **1** a savoury dish made from a

THESAURUS

rake[1] *vb* **5** = **gather**, collect, remove, scrape up **6** = **scrape**, break up, harrow, hoe, scour, scratch **8** *with* **together** *or* **up** = **collect**, assemble, dig up, dredge up, gather, scrape together **9** = **search**, comb, examine, forage, hunt, ransack, scan, scour, scrutinize **10** = **graze**, scrape, scratch **11** = **sweep**, enfilade, pepper

rake[2] *n* = **libertine**, debauchee, dissolute man, lech *or* letch, lecher, playboy, profligate, roué, sensualist, swinger (*sl.*), voluptuary
Antonyms *n* ascetic, celibate, monk, puritan

rakish[1] *adj* = **immoral**, abandoned, debauched, depraved, dissipated, dissolute, lecherous, licentious, loose, prodigal, profligate, sinful, wanton

rakish[2] *adj* **1** = **dashing**, breezy, dapper, debonair, devil-may-care, flashy, jaunty, natty (*inf.*), raffish, smart, snazzy (*inf.*), sporty

rally[1] *vb* **1** = **reassemble**, bring *or* come to order, re-form, regroup, reorganize, unite **2** = **gather**, assemble, bond together, bring *or* come together, collect, convene, get together, marshal, mobilize, muster, organize, round up, summon, unite **3** = **recover**, be on the mend, come round, get better, get one's second wind, improve, perk up, pick up, pull through, recuperate, regain one's strength, revive, take a turn for the better, turn the corner ◆ *n* **6** = **gathering**, assembly, conference, congregation, congress, convention, convocation, mass meeting, meeting, muster **7** = **recovery**, comeback (*inf.*), improvement, recuperation, renewal, resurgence, revival, turn for the better **8** = **regrouping**, reorganization, reunion, stand
Antonyms *vb* ≠ **gather**: disband, disperse, separate, split up ≠ **recover**: deteriorate, fail, get worse, relapse, take a turn for the worse, worsen ◆ *n* ≠ **recovery**: collapse, deterioration, relapse, turn for the worse

rally[2] *vb* = **tease**, chaff, make fun of, mock, poke fun at, ridicule, send up (*Brit. inf.*), take the mickey out of (*inf.*), taunt, twit

ram *vb* **7, 9** = **cram**, beat, crowd, drum, force, hammer, jam, pack, pound, stuff, tamp, thrust **8** = **hit**, butt, collide with, crash, dash, drive, force, impact, run into, slam, smash, strike

ramble *vb* **1** = **walk**, amble, drift, perambulate, peregrinate, range, roam, rove, saunter, straggle, stravaig (*Scot. & N English dialect*), stray, stroll, traipse (*inf.*), wander **2** = **meander**, snake, twist and turn, wind, zigzag **4** = **babble**, chatter, digress, expatiate, maunder, rabbit (on) (*Brit. inf.*), rattle on, run off at the mouth (*sl.*), waffle (*inf., chiefly Brit.*), wander, witter on (*inf.*) ◆ *n* **5** = **walk**, excursion, hike, perambulation, peregrination, roaming, roving, saunter, stroll, tour, traipse (*inf.*), trip

rambler *n* **2** = **walker**, drifter, hiker, roamer, rover, stroller, wanderer, wayfarer

rambling *adj* **1** = **sprawling**, irregular, spreading, straggling, trailing **2** = **long-winded**, circuitous, desultory, diffuse, digressive, disconnected, discursive, disjointed, incoherent, irregular, periphrastic, prolix, wordy cheese mixture baked in a fireproof container. **2** the container itself. [C18: F *ramequin,* of Gmc origin]

ramification ❶ (ˌræmɪfɪˈkeɪʃən) *n* **1** the act or process of ramifying or branching out. **2** an offshoot or subdivision. **3** a structure of branching parts.

ramify ❶ (ˈræmɪˌfaɪ) *vb* **ramifies, ramifying, ramified. 1** to divide into branches or branchlike parts. **2** (*intr*) to develop complicating consequences. [C16: from F *ramifier,* from L *rāmus* branch + *facere* to make]

ramjet *or* **ramjet engine** (ˈræmˌdʒɛt) *n* **a** a type of jet engine in which fuel is burned in a duct using air compressed by the forward speed of the aircraft. **b** an aircraft powered by such an engine.

ramose (ˈreɪməʊs, ræˈməʊs) *or* **ramous** (ˈreɪməs) *adj* having branches. [C17: from L *rāmōsus,* from *rāmus* branch]
▸ **ˈramosely** *or* **ˈramously** *adv* ▸ **ramosity** (ræˈmɒsɪtɪ) *n*

ramp ❶ (ræmp) *n* **1** a sloping floor, path, etc., that joins two surfaces at different levels. **2** a place where the level of a road surface changes because of roadworks. **3** a movable stairway by which passengers enter and leave an aircraft. **4** the act of ramping. **5** *Brit. sl.* a swindle, esp. one involving exorbitant prices. ◆ *vb* **6** (*intr*) (often foll. by *about* or *around*) (esp. of animals) to rush around in a wild excited manner. **7** (*intr*) to act in a violent or threatening manner (esp. in **ramp and rage**). **8** (*tr*) *Finance.* to buy (a security) in the market with the object of raising its price and enhancing the image of the company behind it for financial gain. [C18 (n): from C13 *rampe,* from OF *ramper* to crawl or rear, prob. of Gmc origin]

rampage ❶ *vb* (ræmˈpeɪdʒ), **rampages, rampaging, rampaged. 1** (*intr*) to rush about in a violent or agitated fashion. ◆ *n* (ˈræmpeɪdʒ, ræmˈpeɪdʒ). **2** angry or destructive behaviour. **3 on the rampage.** behaving violently or destructively. [C18: from Scot., from ?; ? based on RAMP]
▸ **ramˈpageous** *adj* ▸ **ramˈpageously** *adv* ▸ **ˈrampager** *n*

rampant ❶ (ˈræmpənt) *adj* **1** unrestrained or violent in behaviour, etc. **2** growing or developing unchecked. **3** (*postpositive*) *Heraldry.* (of a beast) standing on the hind legs, the right foreleg raised above the left. **4** (of an arch) having one abutment higher than the other. [C14: from OF *ramper* to crawl, rear; see RAMP]
▸ **ˈrampancy** *n* ▸ **ˈrampantly** *adv*

rampart ❶ (ˈræmpɑːt) *n* **1** the surrounding embankment of a fort, often including any walls, parapets, etc., that are built on the bank. **2** any defence or bulwark. ◆ *vb* **3** (*tr*) to provide with a rampart; fortify. [C16: from OF, from RE- + *emparer* to take possession of, from OProvençal *antparar,* from L *ante* before + *parāre* to prepare]

rampike (ˈræmˌpaɪk) *n Canad.* a tall tree that has been burned or is bare of branches.

rampion (ˈræmpɪən) *n* a plant, native to Europe and Asia, that has clusters of bell-shaped bluish flowers and an edible white tuberous root used in salads. [C16: prob. from OF *raiponce,* from OIt. *raponzo,* from *rapa* turnip, from L *rāpum*]

ram raid *n Inf.* a raid in which a stolen car is driven through a shop window in order to steal goods from the shop.
▸ **ram raiding** *n* ▸ **ram raider** *n*

ramrod (ˈræmˌrɒd) *n* **1** a rod for cleaning the barrel of a rifle, etc. **2** a rod for ramming in the charge of a muzzle-loading firearm.

ramshackle ❶ (ˈræmˌʃækᵊl) *adj* (esp. of buildings) rickety, shaky, or derelict. [C17 *ramshackled,* from obs. *ransackle* to RANSACK]

ramsons (ˈræmzənz, -sənz) *pl n* (*usually functioning as sing*) **1** a broad-leaved garlic native to Europe and Asia. **2** the bulbous root of this plant, eaten as a relish. [OE *hramesa*]

ran (ræn) *vb* the past tense of **run.**

RAN *abbrev. for* Royal Australian Navy.

ranch (rɑːntʃ) *n* **1** a large tract of land, esp. one in North America, together with the necessary personnel, buildings, and equipment, for rearing livestock, esp. cattle. **2a** any large farm for the rearing of a particular kind of livestock or crop: *a mink ranch.* **2b** the buildings, land, etc., connected with it. ◆ *vb* **3** (*intr*) to run a ranch. **4** (*tr*) to raise (animals) on or as if on a ranch. [C19: from Mexican Sp. *rancho* small farm]
▸ **ˈrancher** *n*

rancherie (ˈrɑːntʃərɪ) *n* (in British Columbia, Canada) a settlement of North American Indians, esp. on a reserve. [from Sp. *ranchería*]

rancid ❶ (ˈrænsɪd) *adj* **1** (of food) having an unpleasant stale taste or smell as the result of decomposition. **2** (of a taste or smell) rank or sour; stale. [C17: from L *rancidus,* from *rancēre* to stink]
▸ **rancidity** (rænˈsɪdɪtɪ) *or* **ˈrancidness** *n*

rancour ❶ *or US* **rancor** (ˈræŋkə) *n* malicious resentfulness or hostility; spite. [C14: from OF, from LL *rancor* rankness]
▸ **ˈrancorous** *adj* ▸ **ˈrancorously** *adv*

rand[1] (rænd, rɒnt) *n* the standard monetary unit of South Africa, divided into 100 cents. [C20: from Afrik., from *Witwatersrand,* S Transvaal, referring to the gold-mining there; rel. to RAND[2]]

rand[2] (rænd) *n* **1** *Shoemaking.* a leather strip put in the heel of a shoe before the lifts are put on. **2** *Dialect.* **2a** a strip or margin; border. **2b** a strip of cloth; selvage. [OE; rel. to OHG *rant* border, rim of a shield, ON *rönd* shield, rim]

Rand (rænd) *n* **the.** short for Witwatersrand, an area in South Africa rich in mineral deposits, esp. gold.

R & B *abbrev. for* rhythm and blues.

R & D *abbrev. for* research and development.

random ❶ (ˈrændəm) *adj* **1** lacking any definite plan or prearranged order; haphazard: *a random selection.* **2** *Statistics.* **2a** having a value which cannot be determined but only described in terms of probability: *a random variable.* **2b** chosen without regard to any characteristics of the individual members of the population so that each has an equal chance of being selected: *random sampling.* ◆ *n* **3 at random.** not following any prearranged order. [C14: from OF *randon,* from *randir* to gallop, of Gmc origin]
▸ **ˈrandomly** *adv* ▸ **ˈrandomness** *n*

random access *n* another name for **direct access.**

randomize *or* **randomise** (ˈrændəˌmaɪz) *vb* **randomizes, randomizing, randomized** *or* **randomises, randomising, randomised.** (*tr*) to set up (a selection process, sample, etc.) in a deliberately random way in order to enhance the statistical validity of any results obtained.
▸ **ˌrandomiˈzation** *or* **ˌrandomiˈsation** *n* ▸ **ˈrandomˌizer** *or* **ˈrandomˌiser** *n*

random walk theory *n Stock Exchange.* the theory that the future movement of share prices does not reflect past movements and therefore will not follow a discernible pattern.

R and R *US mil. abbrev. for* rest and recreation.

randy ❶ (ˈrændɪ) *adj* **randier, randiest. 1** *Inf., chiefly Brit.* sexually eager or lustful. **2** *Chiefly Scot.* lacking any sense of propriety; reckless. ◆ *n, pl* **randies. 3** *Chiefly Scot.* a rude or reckless person. [C17: prob. from obs. *rand* to RANT]
▸ **ˈrandily** *adv* ▸ **ˈrandiness** *n*

ranee (ˈrɑːnɪ) *n* a variant spelling of **rani.**

rang (ræŋ) *vb* the past tense of **ring**[2].

USAGE NOTE See at **ring**[2].

rangatira (ˌrʌŋgəˈtɪərə) *n NZ.* a Maori chief of either sex. [from Maori]

range ❶ (reɪndʒ) *n* **1** the limits within which a person or thing can function effectively: *the violin has a range of five octaves.* **2** the limits within which any fluctuation takes place: *a range of values.* **3** the total products of a manufacturer, designer, or stockist: *the new spring range.* **4a** the maximum effective distance of a projectile fired from a weapon. **4b** the distance between a target and a weapon. **5** an area set aside for shooting practice or rocket testing. **6** the total distance which a ship, aircraft, or land vehicle is capable of covering without taking on fresh fuel: *the range of this car is about 160 miles.* **7** *Maths.* (of a function or variable) the set of values that a function or variable can

THESAURUS

Antonyms *adj ≠* **long-winded:** coherent, concise, direct, to the point

ramification *n* **1** = **consequences**, complications, developments, results, sequel, upshot **2** = **outgrowth**, branch, development, divarication, division, excrescence, extension, forking, offshoot, subdivision

ramify *vb* **1** = **divide**, branch, divaricate, fork, separate, split up **2** = **become complicated**, multiply, thicken

ramp *n* **1** = **slope**, grade, gradient, incline, inclined plane, rise

rampage *vb* **1** = **go berserk**, go ape (*sl.*), go ballistic (*sl., chiefly US*), rage, run amok, run riot, run wild, storm, tear ◆ *n* **2** = **frenzy**, destruction, fury, rage, storm, tempest, tumult, uproar, violence **3 on the rampage** = **berserk**, amok, destructive, out of control, raging, rampant, riotous, violent, wild

rampant *adj* **1** = **unrestrained**, aggressive, dominant, excessive, flagrant, on the rampage, out of control, out of hand, outrageous, raging, rampaging, riotous, unbridled, uncontrollable, ungovernable, vehement, violent, wanton, wild **2** = **widespread**, epidemic, exuberant, luxuriant, prevalent, profuse, rank, rife, spreading like wildfire, unchecked, uncontrolled, unrestrained **3** *Heraldry* = **upright**, erect, rearing, standing

rampart *n* **1, 2** = **defence**, barricade, bastion, breastwork, bulwark, earthwork, embankment, fence, fort, fortification, guard, parapet, security, stronghold, wall

ramshackle *adj* = **rickety**, broken-down, crumbling, decrepit, derelict, dilapidated, flimsy, jerry-built, shaky, tottering, tumbledown, unsafe, unsteady
Antonyms *adj* solid, stable, steady, well-built

rancid *adj* **1, 2** = **rotten**, bad, fetid, foul, frowsty, fusty, musty, off, putrid, rank, sour, stale, strong-smelling, tainted
Antonyms *adj* fresh, pure, undecayed

rancorous *adj* = **bitter**, acrimonious, hostile, implacable, malevolent, malicious, malign, malignant, resentful, spiteful, splenetic, venomous, vindictive, virulent

rancour *n* = **hatred**, animosity, animus, antipathy, bad blood, bitterness, chip on one's shoulder (*inf.*), enmity, grudge, hate, hostility, ill feeling, ill will, malevolence, malice, malignity, resentfulness, resentment, spite, spleen, venom

random *adj* **1** = **chance**, accidental, adventitious, aimless, arbitrary, casual, desultory, fortuitous, haphazard, hit or miss, incidental, indiscriminate, purposeless, spot, stray, unplanned, unpremeditated ◆ *n* **3 at random** = **haphazardly**, accidentally, adventitiously, aimlessly, arbitrarily, by chance, casually, indiscriminately, irregularly, purposelessly, randomly, unsystematically, willy-nilly
Antonyms *adj ≠* **chance:** definite, deliberate, intended, planned, premeditated, specific

randy *adj* **1** *Informal* = **lustful**, amorous, aroused, concupiscent, horny (*sl.*), hot, lascivious, lecherous, raunchy (*sl.*), satyric, sexually excited, sexy (*inf.*), turned-on (*sl.*)

range *n* **1, 2** = **limits**, ambit, amplitude, area, bounds, compass, confines, distance, domain, extent, field, latitude, orbit, pale, parameters (*inf.*), province, purview, radius, reach, scope, span, sphere, sweep **3** = **series**, assortment, class, collection, gamut, kind, lot, order, selection, sort, variety **10** = **sequence**, chain, file, line, rank, row, series, string, tier ◆ *vb* **14** = **ar-**

take. **8** *US & Canad.* **8a** an extensive tract of open land on which livestock can graze. **8b** (*as modifier*): *range cattle.* **9** the geographical region in which a species of plant or animal normally grows or lives. **10** a rank, row, or series of items. **11** a series or chain of mountains. **12** a large stove with burners and one or more ovens, usually heated by solid fuel. **13** the act or process of ranging. ◆ *vb* **ranges, ranging, ranged. 14** to establish or be situated in a line, row, or series. **15** (*tr; often reflexive,* foll. by *with*) to put into a specific category; classify: *she ranges herself with the angels.* **16** (foll. by *on*) to aim or point (a telescope, gun, etc.) or (of a gun, telescope, etc.) to be pointed or aimed. **17** to establish the distance of (a target) from (a weapon). **18** (*intr*) (of a gun or missile) to have a specified range. **19** (when *intr,* foll. by *over*) to wander about (in) an area; roam (over). **20** (*intr;* foll. by *over*) (of an animal or plant) to live or grow in its normal habitat. **21** (*tr*) to put (cattle) to graze on a range. **22** (*intr*) to fluctuate within specific limits. **23** (*intr*) to extend or run in a specific direction. **24** (*intr*) *Naut.* (of a vessel) to swing back and forth while at anchor. **25** (*tr*) to make (lines of printers' type) level or even at the margin. [C13: from OF: row, from *ranger* to position, from *renc* line]

rangefinder (ˈreɪndʒˌfaɪndə) *n* an instrument for determining the distance of an object from the observer, esp. in order to sight a gun or focus a camera.

ranger (ˈreɪndʒə) *n* **1** (*sometimes cap.*) an official in charge of a forest, park, nature reserve, etc. **2** *Orig. US.* a person employed to patrol a State or national park. Brit. equivalent: **warden. 3** *US.* one of a body of armed troops employed to police a State or district: *a Texas ranger.* **4** (in the US) a commando specially trained in making raids. **5** a person who wanders about; a rover.

Ranger *or* **Ranger Guide** (ˈreɪndʒə) *n Brit.* a member of the senior branch of the Guides.

rangiora (ˌræŋɡɪˈɔːrə) *n* a broad-leaved shrub of New Zealand. [from Maori]

rangy Ⓣ (ˈreɪndʒɪ) *adj* **rangier, rangiest. 1** having long slender limbs. **2** adapted to wandering or roaming. **3** allowing considerable freedom of movement; spacious.
▸ **ˈrangily** *adv* ▸ **ˈranginess** *n*

rani *or* **ranee** (ˈrɑːnɪ) *n* an Indian queen or princess; the wife of a rajah. [C17: from Hindi: queen, from Sansk. *rājñī*]

rank[1] Ⓣ (ræŋk) *n* **1** a position, esp. an official one, within a social organization: *the rank of captain.* **2** high social or other standing; status. **3** a line or row of people or things. **4** the position of an item in any ordering or sequence. **5** *Brit.* a place where taxis wait to be hired. **6** a line of soldiers drawn up abreast of each other. **7** any of the eight horizontal rows of squares on a chessboard. **8 close ranks.** to maintain discipline or solidarity. **9 pull rank.** to get one's own way by virtue of one's superior position or rank. **10 rank and file. 10a** the ordinary soldiers, excluding the officers. **10b** the great mass or majority of any group, as opposed to the leadership. **10c** (*modifier*): *rank-and-file support.* ◆ *vb* **11** (*tr*) to arrange (people or things) in rows or lines; range. **12** to accord or be accorded a specific position in an organization or group. **13** (*tr*) to array a set of objects as a sequence: *to rank students by their test scores.* **14** (*intr*) to be important; rate: *money ranks low in her order of priorities.* **15** *Chiefly US.* to take precedence or surpass in rank. [C16: from OF *ranc* row, rank, of Gmc origin]

rank[2] Ⓣ (ræŋk) *adj* **1** showing vigorous and profuse growth: *rank weeds.* **2** highly offensive or disagreeable, esp. in smell or taste. **3** (*prenominal*) complete or absolute; utter: *a rank outsider.* **4** coarse or vulgar; gross: *his language was rank.* [OE *ranc* straight, noble]
▸ **ˈrankly** *adv* ▸ **ˈrankness** *n*

ranker (ˈræŋkə) *n* **1** a soldier in the ranks. **2** a commissioned officer who entered service as a noncommissioned recruit.

ranking (ˈræŋkɪŋ) *adj* **1** *Chiefly US & Canad.* prominent; high ranking. **2** *Caribbean sl.* possessed of style; exciting. ◆ *n* **3** a position on a scale; rating: *a ranking in a tennis tournament.*

rankle Ⓣ (ˈræŋkᵊl) *vb* **rankles, rankling, rankled.** (*intr*) to cause severe and continuous irritation, anger, or bitterness; fester. [C14 *ranclen,* from OF *draoncle* ulcer, from L *dracunculus* dim. of *dracō* serpent]

ransack Ⓣ (ˈrænsæk) *vb* (*tr*) **1** to search through every part of (a house, box, etc.); examine thoroughly. **2** to plunder; pillage. [C13: from ON *rann* house + *saka* to search]
▸ **ˈransacker** *n*

ransom Ⓣ (ˈrænsəm) *n* **1** the release of captured prisoners, property, etc., on payment of a stipulated price. **2** the price demanded or stipulated for such a release. **3 hold to ransom. 3a** to keep (prisoners, etc.) in confinement until payment for their release is received. **3b** to attempt to force (a person) to comply with one's demands. **4 a king's ransom.** a very large amount of money or valuables. ◆ *vb* (*tr*) **5** to pay a stipulated price and so obtain the release of (prisoners, property, etc.). **6** to set free (prisoners, property, etc.) upon receiving the payment demanded. **7** to redeem; rescue: *Christ ransomed men from sin.* [C14: from OF *ransoun,* from L *redemptiō* a buying back]
▸ **ˈransomer** *n*

rant Ⓣ (rænt) *vb* **1** to utter (something) in loud, violent, or bombastic tones. ◆ *n* **2** loud, declamatory, or extravagant speech; bombast. [C16: from Du. *ranten* to rave]
▸ **ˈranter** *n* ▸ **ˈranting** *adj, n* ▸ **ˈrantingly** *adv*

ranunculaceous (rəˌnʌŋkjʊˈleɪʃəs) *adj* of, relating to, or belonging to a N temperate family of flowering plants typically having flowers with five petals and numerous anthers and styles. The family includes the buttercup, clematis, and columbine.

ranunculus (rəˈnʌŋkjʊləs) *n, pl* **ranunculuses** *or* **ranunculi** (-ˌlaɪ). any of a genus of ranunculaceous plants having finely divided leaves and typically yellow five-petalled flowers. The genus includes buttercup, crowfoot, and spearwort. [C16: from L: tadpole, from *rāna* frog]

RAOC *abbrev. for* Royal Army Ordnance Corps.

rap[1] Ⓣ (ræp) *vb* **raps, rapping, rapped. 1** to strike (a fist, stick, etc.) against (something) with a sharp quick blow; knock. **2** (*intr*) to make a sharp loud sound, esp. by knocking. **3** (*tr*) to rebuke or criticize sharply. **4** (*tr;* foll. by *out*) to put (forth) in sharp rapid speech; utter in an abrupt fashion: *to rap out orders.* **5** (*intr*) *Sl.* to talk, esp. volubly. **6** (*intr*) to perform a rhythmic monologue with musical backing. **7 rap over the knuckles.** to reprimand. ◆ *n* **8** a sharp quick blow or the sound produced by such a blow. **9** a sharp rebuke or criticism. **10** *Sl.* voluble talk; chatter. **11a** a fast, rhythmic monologue over a musical backing. **11b** (*as modifier*): *rap music.* **12 beat the rap.** *US & Canad. sl.* to escape punishment or be acquitted of a crime. **13 take the rap.** *Sl.* to suffer the punishment for a crime, whether guilty or not. [C14: prob. from ON; cf. Swedish *rappa* to beat]

rap[2] (ræp) *n* (*used with a negative*) the least amount (esp. in **not care a rap**). [C18: prob. from *ropaire* counterfeit coin formerly current in Ireland]

rap[3] (ræp) *vb* **raps, rapping, rapped,** *n Austral. inf.* a variant spelling of **wrap** (senses 8, 14).

rapacious Ⓣ (rəˈpeɪʃəs) *adj* **1** practising pillage or rapine. **2** greedy or grasping. **3** (of animals, esp. birds) subsisting by catching living prey. [C17: from L *rapāx,* from *rapere* to seize]
▸ **raˈpaciously** *adv* ▸ **rapacity** (rəˈpæsɪtɪ) *or* **raˈpaciousness** *n*

rape[1] Ⓣ (reɪp) *n* **1** the offence of forcing a person, esp. a woman, to submit to sexual intercourse against that person's will. **2** the act of despoiling a country in warfare. **3** any violation or abuse: *the rape of justice.* **4** *Arch.* abduction: *the rape of the Sabine women.* ◆ *vb* **rapes, raping, raped.** (*mainly tr*) **5** to commit rape upon (a person). **6** *Arch.* to carry off by force; abduct. [C14: from L *rapere* to seize]
▸ **ˈrapist** *n*

THESAURUS

range, align, array, dispose, draw up, line up, order, sequence **15** = **group**, arrange, bracket, catalogue, categorize, class, classify, file, grade, pigeonhole, rank **16** = **point**, aim, align, direct, level, train **19** = **roam**, cruise, explore, ramble, rove, straggle, stray, stroll, sweep, traverse, wander **22** = **vary**, extend, fluctuate, go, reach, run, stretch

rangy *adj* **1** = **long-limbed**, gangling, lanky, leggy, long-legged

rank[1] *n* **1, 2** = **status**, caste, class, classification, degree, dignity, division, echelon, grade, level, nobility, order, position, quality, sort, standing, station, stratum, type **3** = **row**, column, file, formation, group, line, range, series, tier **10 rank and file: a** = **lower ranks**, men, other ranks, private soldiers, soldiers, troops **b** = **general public**, body, Joe (and Eileen) Public (*sl.*), Joe Six-Pack (*US sl.*), majority, mass, masses ◆ *vb* **11, 13** = **arrange**, align, array, class, classify, dispose, grade, line up, locate, marshal, order, position, range, sequence, sort

rank[2] *adj* **1** = **abundant**, dense, exuberant, flourishing, lush, luxuriant, productive, profuse, strong-growing, vigorous **2** = **foul**, bad, disagreeable, disgusting, fetid, fusty, gamey, mephitic, musty, noisome, noxious, off, offensive, olid, pungent, putrid, rancid, revolting, stale, stinking, strong-smelling, yucky *or* yukky (*sl.*) **3** = **absolute**, arrant, blatant, complete, downright, egregious, excessive, extravagant, flagrant, glaring, gross, rampant, sheer, thorough, total, undisguised, unmitigated, utter **4** = **vulgar**, abusive, atrocious, coarse, crass, filthy, foul, gross, indecent, nasty, obscene, outrageous, scurrilous, shocking

rankle *vb* = **annoy**, anger, chafe, embitter, fester, gall, get one's goat (*sl.*), get on one's nerves (*inf.*), irk, irritate, rile

ransack *vb* **1** = **search**, comb, explore, forage, go through, rake, rummage, scour, turn inside out **2** = **plunder**, despoil, gut, loot, pillage, raid, ravage, rifle, sack, strip

ransom *n* **1** = **release**, deliverance, liberation, redemption, rescue **2** = **payment**, money, payoff, price ◆ *vb* **5** = **buy the freedom of**, buy (someone) out (*inf.*), deliver, liberate, obtain *or* pay for the release of, redeem, release, rescue, set free

rant *vb* **1** = **shout**, bellow, bluster, cry, declaim, rave, roar, spout (*inf.*), vociferate, yell ◆ *n* **2** = **tirade**, bluster, bombast, diatribe, fanfaronade (*rare*), harangue, philippic, rhetoric, vociferation

rap[1] *vb* **1, 2** = **hit**, crack, knock, strike, tap **3** = **reprimand**, blast, carpet, castigate, censure, chew out (*US & Canad. inf.*), criticize, give a rocket (*Brit. & NZ inf.*), knock (*inf.*), lambast(e), pan (*inf.*), read the riot act, scold, tick off (*inf.*) **4** = **bark**, speak abruptly, spit **5** *Slang* = **talk**, chat, confabulate, converse, discourse, shoot the breeze (*sl., chiefly US*) ◆ *n* **8** = **blow**, clout (*inf.*), crack, knock, tap **9** *Slang* = **rebuke**, blame, censure, chiding, punishment, responsibility, sentence **10** *Slang, chiefly U.S.* = **talk**, chat, colloquy, confabulation, conversation, dialogue, discourse, discussion

rapacious *adj* **1** = **marauding**, plundering **2** = **greedy**, avaricious, extortionate, grasping, insatiable, ravenous, voracious, wolfish **3** = **predatory**, preying

rapacity *n* **2** = **greed**, avarice, avidity, cupidity, graspingness, greediness, insatiableness, rapaciousness, ravenousness, voraciousness, voracity, wolfishness **3** = **predatoriness**

rape[1] *n* **1** = **sexual assault**, outrage, ravishment, violation **2** = **desecration**, abuse, defilement, maltreatment, perversion, violation **3** = **plundering**, depredation, despoilment, despoliation, pillage, rapine, sack, spoliation ◆ *vb* **5** = **sexually assault**, abuse, force, outrage, ravish, violate

rape[2] (reɪp) *n* a Eurasian plant that is cultivated for its seeds, **rapeseed,** which yield a useful oil, **rape oil,** and as a fodder plant. Also called: **colza, cole.** [C14: from L *rāpum* turnip]

rape[3] (reɪp) *n* (*often pl*) the skins and stalks of grapes left after wine-making: used in making vinegar. [C17: from F *râpe,* of Gmc origin]

raphia ('ræfɪə) *n* a variant spelling of **raffia.**

raphide ('reɪfaɪd) *or* **raphis** ('reɪfɪs) *n, pl* **raphides** ('ræfɪˌdiːz). needle-shaped crystals, usually of calcium oxalate, that occur in many plant cells. [C18: from F, from Gk *rhaphis* needle]

rapid ❶ ('ræpɪd) *adj* **1** (of an action) performed or occurring during a short interval of time; quick. **2** acting or moving quickly; fast: *a rapid worker.* ◆ See also **rapids.** [C17: from L *rapidus* tearing away, from *rapere* to seize]
▸ **'rapidly** *adv* ▸ **rapidity** (rə'pɪdɪtɪ) *or* **'rapidness** *n*

rapid eye movement *n* movement of the eyeballs during paradoxical sleep, while the sleeper is dreaming. Abbrev.: **REM.**

rapid fire *n* **1** a fast rate of gunfire. ◆ *adj* **rapid-fire. 2** firing shots rapidly. **3** done, delivered, or occurring in rapid succession.

rapids ('ræpɪdz) *pl n* part of a river where the water is very fast and turbulent.

rapier ('reɪpɪə) *n* **1** a long narrow two-edged sword with a guarded hilt, used as a thrusting weapon, popular in the 16th and 17th centuries. **2** a smaller single-edged 18th-century sword, used principally in France. [C16: from OF *espee rapiere,* lit.: rasping sword]

rapine ❶ ('ræpaɪn) *n* the seizure of property by force; pillage. [C15: from L *rapīna* plundering, from *rapere* to snatch]

rappee (ræ'piː) *n* a moist English snuff. [C18: from F *tabac râpé,* lit.: scraped tobacco]

rappel (ræ'pɛl) *vb* **rappels, rappelling, rappelled,** *n* **1** another word for **abseil.** ◆ *n* **2** (formerly) a drumbeat to call soldiers to arms. [C19: from F, from *rappeler* to call back, from L *appellāre* to summon]

rapport ❶ (ræ'pɔː) *n* (often foll. by *with*) a sympathetic relationship or understanding. See also **en rapport.** [C15: from F, from *rapporter* to bring back, from RE- + *aporter,* from L *apportāre,* from *ad-* to + *portāre* to carry]

rapprochement ❶ *French.* (raprɔʃmɑ̃) *n* a resumption of friendly relations, esp. between two countries. [C19: lit.: bringing closer]

rapscallion (ræp'skæljən) *n* a disreputable person; rascal or rogue. [C17: from earlier *rascallion;* see RASCAL]

rapt[1] ❶ (ræpt) *adj* **1** totally absorbed; engrossed; spellbound, esp. through or as if through emotion: *rapt with wonder.* **2** characterized by or proceeding from rapture: *a rapt smile.* [C14: from L *raptus* carried away, from *rapere* to seize]
▸ **'raptly** *adv*

rapt[2] (ræpt) *adj Austral. inf.* Also: **wrapped.** very pleased; delighted.

raptor ('ræptə) *n* another name for **bird of prey.** [C17: from L: plunderer, from *rapere* to take by force]

raptorial (ræp'tɔːrɪəl) *adj Zool.* **1** (of the feet of birds) adapted for seizing prey. **2** of or relating to birds of prey. [C19: from L *raptor* robber, from *rapere* to snatch]

rapture ❶ ('ræptʃə) *n* **1** the state of mind resulting from feelings of high emotion; joyous ecstasy. **2** (*often pl*) an expression of ecstatic joy. **3** the act of transporting a person from one sphere of existence to another. ◆ *vb* **raptures, rapturing, raptured. 4** (*tr*) *Arch. or literary.* to enrapture. [C17: from Med. L *raptūra,* from L *raptus* RAPT[1]]
▸ **'rapturous** *adj*

RAR *abbrev. for* Royal Australian Regiment.

rara avis ('rɛərə 'eɪvɪs) *n, pl* **rarae aves** ('rɛəriː 'eɪviːz). an unusual, uncommon, or exceptional person or thing. [L: rare bird]

rare[1] ❶ (rɛə) *adj* **1** not widely known; not frequently used or experienced; uncommon or unusual: *a rare word.* **2** not widely distributed; not generally occurring: *a rare herb.* **3** (of a gas, esp. the atmosphere at high altitudes) having a low density; thin; rarefied. **4** uncommonly great; extreme: *kind to a rare degree.* **5** exhibiting uncommon excellence: *rare skill.* [C14: from L *rārus* sparse]
▸ **'rareness** *n*

rare[2] ❶ (rɛə) *adj* (of meat, esp. beef) very lightly cooked. [OE *hrēr;* rel. to *hreaw* RAW]

rarebit ('rɛəbɪt) *n* another term for **Welsh rabbit.** [C18: by folk etymology from (WELSH) RABBIT; see RARE[2], BIT[1]]

rare earth *n* **1** any oxide of a lanthanide. **2** Also called: **rare-earth element.** any element of the lanthanide series.

raree show ('rɛəriː) *n* **1** a street show or carnival. **2** another name for **peepshow.** [C17: *raree* from RARE[1]]

rarefaction (ˌrɛərɪ'fækʃən) *or* **rarefication** (ˌrɛərɪfɪ'keɪʃən) *n* the act or process of making less dense or the state of being less dense.
▸ ˌ**rare'factive** *adj*

rarefied ❶ ('rɛərɪˌfaɪd) *adj* **1** exalted in nature or character; lofty: *a rarefied spiritual existence.* **2** current within only a small group. **3** thin: *air rarefied at altitude.*

rarefy ❶ ('rɛərɪˌfaɪ) *vb* **rarefies, rarefying, rarefied.** to make or become rarer or less dense; thin out. [C14: from OF *raréfier,* from L *rārēfacere,* from *rārus* RARE[1] + *facere* to make]
▸ **'rareˌfiable** *adj* ▸ **'rareˌfier** *n*

rare gas *n* another name for **inert gas.**

rarely ❶ ('rɛəlɪ) *adv* **1** hardly ever; seldom. **2** to an unusual degree; exceptionally. **3** *Dialect.* uncommonly well; excellently: *he did rarely at market yesterday.*

> **USAGE NOTE** Since *rarely* means *hardly ever,* one should not say something *rarely ever* happens.

raring ❶ ('rɛərɪŋ) *adj* ready; willing; enthusiastic (esp. in **raring to go**). [C20: from *rare,* var. of REAR[2]]

rarity ❶ ('rɛərɪtɪ) *n, pl* **rarities. 1** a rare person or thing, esp. something valued because it is uncommon. **2** the state of being rare.

rasbora (ræz'bɔːrə) *n* any of the small cyprinid fishes of tropical Asia and East Africa. Many species are brightly coloured and are popular aquarium fishes. [from NL, from an East Indian language]

rascal ❶ ('rɑːskᵊl) *n* **1** a disreputable person; villain. **2** a mischievous or impish rogue. **3** an affectionate or mildly reproving term, esp. for a child: *you little rascal.* **4** *Obs.* a person of lowly birth. ◆ *adj* **5** (*prenominal*) *Obs.* **5a** belonging to the rabble. **5b** dishonest; knavish. [C14: from OF *rascaille* rabble, ?from OF *rasque* mud]

rascality (rɑː'skælɪtɪ) *n, pl* **rascalities.** mischievous or disreputable character or action.

rascally ❶ ('rɑːskəlɪ) *adj* **1** dishonest or mean; base. ◆ *adv* **2** in a dishonest or mean fashion.

rase (reɪz) *vb* **rases, rasing, rased.** a variant spelling of **raze.**

rash[1] ❶ (ræʃ) *adj* **1** acting without due thought; impetuous. **2** resulting from excessive haste or impetuosity: *a rash word.* [C14: from OHG *rasc* hurried, clever]
▸ **'rashly** *adv* ▸ **'rashness** *n*

THESAURUS

rapid *adj* **1 = quick,** brisk, expeditious, express, fast, fleet, flying, hasty, hurried, precipitate, prompt, quickie (*inf.*), speedy, swift
Antonyms *adj* deliberate, gradual, leisurely, slow, tardy, unhurried

rapidity *n* **1 = speed,** alacrity, briskness, celerity, dispatch, expedition, fleetness, haste, hurry, precipitateness, promptitude, promptness, quickness, rush, speediness, swiftness, velocity

rapidly *adv* **1 = quickly,** apace, at speed, briskly, expeditiously, fast, hastily, hell for leather, hotfoot, hurriedly, in a hurry, in a rush, in haste, like a shot, like greased lightning, like lightning, like the clappers (*Brit. inf.*), posthaste, precipitately, promptly, pronto (*inf.*), speedily, swiftly, with dispatch

rapine *n* **= pillage,** depredation, despoilment, despoliation, looting, marauding, plundering, ransacking, rape, robbery, sack, seizure, spoliation, theft

rapport *n* **= bond,** affinity, empathy, harmony, interrelationship, link, relationship, sympathy, tie, understanding

rapprochement *French n* **= reconciliation,** détente, reconcilement, restoration of harmony, reunion, softening
Antonyms *n* antagonism, dissension, exacerbation, falling-out, quarrel, resumption of hostilities, schism

rapt[1] *adj* **1 = spellbound,** absorbed, carried away, engrossed, enthralled, entranced, fascinated, gripped, held, intent, preoccupied **2 = blissful,** bewitched, blissed out, captivated, charmed, delighted, ecstatic, enchanted, enraptured, rapturous, ravished, sent, transported
Antonyms *adj* ≠ **spellbound:** bored, detached, left cold, unaffected, uninterested, uninvolved, unmoved

rapture *n* **1 = ecstasy,** beatitude, bliss, cloud nine, delectation, delight, enthusiasm, euphoria, exaltation, felicity, happiness, joy, ravishment, rhapsody, seventh heaven, spell, transport

rapturous *adj* **1 = ecstatic,** blissed out, blissful, delighted, enthusiastic, euphoric, exalted, floating on air, happy, in seventh heaven, joyful, joyous, on cloud nine (*inf.*), overjoyed, over the moon (*inf.*), rapt, ravished, rhapsodic, sent, transported

rare[1] *adj* **1 = uncommon,** exceptional, few, infrequent, out of the ordinary, recherché, scarce, singular, sparse, sporadic, strange, thin on the ground, unusual **5 = superb,** admirable, choice, excellent, exquisite, extreme, fine, great, incomparable, peerless, superlative
Antonyms *adj* ≠ **uncommon:** abundant, bountiful, common, frequent, habitual, manifold, many, plentiful, profuse, regular

rare[2] *adj* **= underdone,** bloody, half-cooked, half-raw, undercooked

rarefied *adj* **1 = exalted,** elevated, high, lofty, noble, spiritual, sublime **2 = exclusive,** clannish, cliquish, esoteric, occult, private, select

rarefy *vb* **= thin out,** attenuate, clarify, purify, refine, sublimate

rarely *adv* **1 = seldom,** almost never, hardly, hardly ever, infrequently, little, once in a blue moon, once in a while, only now and then, on rare occasions, scarcely ever **2 = exceptionally,** extraordinarily, finely, notably, remarkably, singularly, uncommonly, unusually
Antonyms *adv* ≠ **seldom:** commonly, frequently, often, regularly, usually

raring *adj* **= eager,** athirst, avid, champing at the bit (*inf.*), desperate, enthusiastic, impatient, keen, keen as mustard, longing, ready, willing, yearning

rarity *n* **1 = curio,** collector's item, curiosity, find, gem, one-off, pearl, treasure **2 = uncommonness,** infrequency, scarcity, shortage, singularity, sparseness, strangeness, unusualness

rascal *n* **1 = rogue,** bad egg (*old-fashioned inf.*), blackguard, caitiff (*arch.*), devil, disgrace, good-for-nothing, knave (*arch.*), miscreant, ne'er-do-well, rake, rapscallion, reprobate, scally (*Northwest English dialect*), scoundrel, varmint (*inf.*), villain, wastrel, wretch **2, 3 = scamp,** imp, pickle (*Brit. inf.*), scallywag (*inf.*)

rascally *adj* **1 = villainous,** bad, base, crooked, dishonest, disreputable, evil, good-for-nothing, low, mean, reprobate, scoundrelly, unscrupulous, vicious, wicked

rash[1] *adj* **1 = reckless,** audacious, brash, care-

rash[2] ❶ (ræʃ) *n* **1** *Pathol.* any skin eruption. **2** a series of unpleasant and unexpected occurrences: *a rash of forest fires.* [C18: from OF *rasche,* from *raschier* to scratch, from L *rādere* to scrape]

rasher ('ræʃə) *n* a thin slice of bacon or ham. [C16: from ?]

rasp ❶ (rɑːsp) *n* **1** a harsh grating noise. **2** a coarse file with rows of raised teeth. ◆ *vb* **3** (*tr*) to scrape or rub (something) roughly, esp. with a rasp; abrade. **4** to utter with or make a harsh grating noise. **5** to irritate (one's nerves); grate (upon). [C16: from OF *raspe,* of Gmc origin; cf. OHG *raspōn* to scrape]
▸ **'rasper** *n* ▸ **'rasping** *adj* ▸ **'raspish** *adj*

raspberry ('rɑːzbərɪ, -brɪ) *n, pl* **raspberries. 1** a prickly rosaceous shrub of North America and Europe that has pinkish-white flowers and typically red berry-like fruits (drupelets). See also **bramble. 2a** the fruit of any such plant. **2b** (*as modifier*): *raspberry jelly.* **3a** a dark purplish-red colour. **3b** (*as adj*): *a raspberry dress.* **4** a spluttering noise made with the tongue and lips to express contempt (esp. in **blow a raspberry**). [C17: from earlier *raspis* raspberry, from ? + BERRY]

Rastafarian (ˌræstə'fɛərɪən) *n* **1** a member of an originally Jamaican religion that regards Ras Tafari, the former emperor of Ethiopia, Haile Selassie, as God. ◆ *adj* **2** of, characteristic of, or relating to the Rastafarians. ◆ Often shortened to **Rasta.**

raster ('ræstə) *n* a pattern of horizontal scanning lines, esp. those traced by an electron beam on a television screen or those in a digitized bitmap image. [C20: via G from L: rake, from *rādere* to scrape]

rat ❶ (ræt) *n* **1** any of numerous long-tailed Old World rodents, that are similar to but larger than mice and are now distributed all over the world. **2** *Inf.* a person who deserts his friends or associates, esp. in time of trouble. **3** *Inf.* a worker who works during a strike; blackleg; scab. **4** *Inf.* a despicable person. **5 have** *or* **be rats.** *Austral. sl.* to be mad or eccentric. **6 smell a rat.** to detect something suspicious. ◆ *vb* **rats, ratting, ratted. 7** (*intr;* usually foll. by *on*) **7a** to divulge secret information (about); betray the trust (of). **7b** to default (on); abandon. **8** to hunt and kill rats. [OE *rætt*]

rata ('rɑːtə) *n* a New Zealand tree with red flowers. [from Maori]

ratable *or* **rateable** ('reɪtəb°l) *adj* **1** able to be rated or evaluated. **2** *Brit.* (of property) liable to payment of rates.
▸ **ˌrata'bility** *or* **ˌratea'bility** *n* ▸ **'ratably** *or* **'rateably** *adv*

ratable value *n Brit.* (formerly) a fixed value assigned to a property by a local authority, on the basis of which variable annual rates are charged.

ratafia (ˌrætə'fɪə) *or* **ratafee** (ˌrætə'fiː) *n* **1** any liqueur made from fruit or from brandy with added fruit. **2** a flavouring essence made from almonds. **3** *Chiefly Brit.* Also called: **ratafia biscuit.** a small macaroon flavoured with almonds. [C17: from West Indian Creole F]

ratan (ræ'tæn) *n* a variant spelling of **rattan.**

rat-arsed *adj Brit. sl.* drunk.

rat-a-tat-tat ('rætəˌtæt'tæt) *or* **rat-a-tat** ('rætə'tæt) *n* the sound of knocking on a door.

ratatouille (ˌrætə'twiː) *n* a vegetable casserole made of tomatoes, aubergines, peppers, etc., fried in oil and stewed slowly. [C19: from F, from *touiller* to stir, from L, from *tudes* hammer]

ratbag ('rætˌbæg) *n Sl.* an eccentric, stupid, or unreliable person.

rat-catcher *n* a person whose job is to destroy or drive away vermin, esp. rats.

ratchet ('rætʃɪt) *n* **1** a device in which a toothed rack or wheel is engaged by a pawl to permit motion in one direction only. **2** the toothed rack or wheel forming part of such a device. [C17: from F *rochet,* from OF *rocquet* blunt head of a lance, of Gmc origin]

ratchet effect *n Econ.* an effect that occurs when a price or wage increases as a result of temporary pressure but fails to fall back when the pressure is removed.

rate[1] ❶ (reɪt) *n* **1** a quantity or amount considered in relation to or measured against another quantity or amount: *a rate of 70 miles an hour.* **2a** a price or charge with reference to a standard or scale: *rate of interest.* **2b** (*as modifier*): *a rate card.* **3** a charge made per unit for a commodity, service, etc. **4** See **rates. 5** the relative speed of progress or change of something variable; pace: *the rate of production has doubled.* **6a** relative quality; class or grade. **6b** (*in combination*): *first-rate ideas.* **7 at any rate.** in any case; at all events; anyway. ◆ *vb* **rates, rating, rated.** (*mainly tr*) **8** (*also intr*) to assign or receive a position on a scale of relative values; rank: *he is rated fifth in the world.* **9** to estimate the value of; evaluate: *we rate your services highly.* **10** to be worthy of; deserve: *this hotel does not rate four stars.* **11** to consider; regard: *I rate him among my friends.* **12** *Brit.* to assess the value of (property) for the purpose of local taxation. [C15: from OF, from Med. L *rata,* from L *prō ratā parte* according to a fixed proportion, from *ratus* fixed, from *rērī* to think, decide]

rate[2] ❶ (reɪt) *vb* **rates, rating, rated.** (*tr*) to scold or criticize severely; rebuke harshly. [C14: ? rel. to Swedish *rata* to chide]

rateable ('reɪtəb°l) *adj* a variant spelling of **ratable.**

rate-cap ('reɪtˌkæp) *vb* **rate-caps, rate-capping, rate-capped.** (*tr*) (formerly in Britain) to impose on (a local authority) an upper limit on the rate it may levy.
▸ **'rate-ˌcapping** *n*

ratel ('reɪt°l) *n* **1** a carnivorous mammal related to the badger family, inhabiting wooded regions of Africa and S Asia. It has a massive body, strong claws, and a thick coat that is paler on the back. It feeds on honey and small animals. **2** *S. African.* a six-wheeled armoured vehicle. [C18: from Afrik.]

rate of exchange *n* See **exchange rate.**

rate of return *n Finance.* the ratio of the annual income from an investment to the original investment, often expressed as a percentage.

ratepayer ('reɪtˌpeɪə) *n Brit.* (formerly) a person who paid local rates, esp. a householder.

rates (reɪts) *pl n Brit.* a tax formerly levied on property by a local authority.

rather ❶ ('rɑːðə) *adv* (*in senses 1-4, not used with a negative*) **1** relatively or fairly; somewhat: *it's rather dull.* **2** to a significant or noticeable extent; quite: *she's rather pretty.* **3** to a limited extent or degree: *I rather thought that was the case.* **4** with better or more just cause: *this text is rather to be deleted than rewritten.* **5** more readily or willingly; sooner: *I would rather not see you tomorrow.* ◆ *sentence connector.* **6** on the contrary: *it's not cold. Rather, it's very hot.* ◆ *sentence substitute.* ('rɑː'ðɜː). **7** an expression of strong affirmation: *Is it worth seeing? Rather!* [OE *hrathor* comp. of *hræth* READY, quick]

> **USAGE NOTE** Both *would* and *had* are used with *rather* in sentences such as *I would rather* (or *had rather*) *go to the film than to the play. Had rather* is less common and now widely regarded as slightly old-fashioned.

ratify ❶ ('rætɪˌfaɪ) *vb* **ratifies, ratifying, ratified.** (*tr*) to give formal approval or consent to. [C14: via OF from L *ratus* fixed (see RATE[1]) + *facere* to make]
▸ **'ratiˌfiable** *adj* ▸ **ˌratifi'cation** *n* ▸ **'ratiˌfier** *n*

rating[1] ❶ ('reɪtɪŋ) *n* **1** a classification according to order or grade; ranking. **2** an ordinary seaman. **3** *Sailing.* a handicap assigned to a racing boat based on its dimensions, draught, etc. **4** the estimated financial or credit standing of a business enterprise or individual. **5** *Radio, television, etc.* a figure based on statistical sampling indicating what proportion of the total audience tune in to a specific programme.

rating[2] ❶ ('reɪtɪŋ) *n* a sharp scolding or rebuke.

ratio ❶ ('reɪʃɪəʊ) *n, pl* **ratios. 1** a measure of the relative size of two classes expressible as a proportion: *the ratio of boys to girls is 2 to 1.* **2** *Maths.* a quotient of two numbers or quantities. See also **proportion** (sense 6). [C17: from L: a reckoning, from *rērī* to think]

THESAURUS

less, foolhardy, harebrained, harum-scarum, hasty, headlong, headstrong, heedless, helter-skelter, hot-headed, ill-advised, impetuous, imprudent, impulsive, incautious, indiscreet, injudicious, madcap, precipitate, premature, thoughtless, unguarded, unthinking, unwary
Antonyms *adj* canny, careful, cautious, considered, premeditated, prudent

rash[2] *n* **1 = outbreak,** eruption **2 = spate,** epidemic, flood, outbreak, plague, series, succession, wave

rashness *n* **1 = recklessness,** adventurousness, audacity, brashness, carelessness, foolhardiness, hastiness, heedlessness, indiscretion, precipitation, temerity, thoughtlessness

rasp *n* **1 = grating,** grinding, scrape, scratch ◆ *vb* **3 = scrape,** abrade, excoriate, file, grind, rub, sand, scour **5 = irritate,** grate (upon), irk, jar (upon), rub (someone) up the wrong way, set one's teeth on edge, wear upon

rasping *adj* **4 = harsh,** creaking, croaking, croaky, grating, gravelly, gruff, hoarse, husky, jarring, rough

rat *n* **2** *Informal* **= traitor,** betrayer, deceiver, defector, deserter, double-crosser, grass (*Brit. inf.*), informer, nark (*sl.*), quisling, snake in the grass, stool pigeon, two-timer (*inf.*) **4** *Informal* **= rogue,** bad lot, bastard (*offens.*), bounder (*old-fashioned Brit. sl.*), cad (*old-fashioned Brit. inf.*), heel (*sl.*), ratfink (*sl., chiefly US and Canad.*), rotter (*sl., chiefly Brit.*), scoundrel, shyster (*inf., chiefly US*) ◆ *vb* **7** *usually foll. by* **on = betray,** abandon, defect, desert, do the dirty on (*Brit. inf.*), leave high and dry, leave (someone) in the lurch, run out on (*inf.*), sell down the river (*inf.*)

rate[1] *n* **1 = degree,** percentage, proportion, ratio, relation, scale, standard **3 = charge,** cost, dues, duty, fee, figure, hire, price, tariff, tax, toll **5 = speed,** gait, measure, pace, tempo, time, velocity **6a = grade,** class, classification, degree, position, quality, rank, rating, status, value, worth **7 at any rate = in any case,** anyhow, anyway, at all events, nevertheless ◆ *vb* **8 = rank,** class, classify, grade **9 = evaluate,** adjudge, appraise, assess, estimate, measure, value, weigh **10 = deserve,** be entitled to, be worthy of, merit **11 = consider,** count, reckon, regard

rate[2] *vb* **= rebuke,** bawl out, berate, blame, carpet (*inf.*), castigate, censure, chew out (*US & Canad. inf.*), chide, criticize severely, give a rocket (*Brit. & NZ inf.*), haul over the coals (*inf.*), read the riot act, reprimand, reprove, scold, take to task, tear into (*inf.*), tear (someone) off a strip (*inf.*), tell off (*inf.*), tongue-lash, upbraid

rather *adv* **1 = to some extent,** a bit, a little, fairly, kind of (*inf.*), moderately, pretty (*inf.*), quite, relatively, slightly, somewhat, sort of (*inf.*), to some degree **2 = significantly,** a good bit, noticeably, very **5 = preferably,** instead, more readily, more willingly, sooner

ratify *vb* **= approve,** affirm, authenticate, authorize, bear out, certify, confirm, consent to, corroborate, endorse, establish, sanction, sign, uphold, validate
Antonyms *vb* abrogate, annul, cancel, reject, repeal, repudiate, revoke

rating[1] *n* **1 = position,** class, classification, degree, designation, estimate, evaluation, grade, order, placing, rank, rate, standing, status

rating[2] *n* **= rebuke,** chiding, dressing down (*inf.*), lecture, piece of one's mind, reprimand, reproof, roasting (*inf.*), row (*inf.*), scolding, telling-off (*inf.*), ticking-off (*inf.*), tongue-lashing

ratio *n* **1 = proportion,** arrangement, correlation, correspondence, equation, fraction, percentage, rate, relation, relationship

ratiocinate (ˌrætɪˈɒsɪˌneɪt) *vb* **ratiocinates, ratiocinating, ratiocinated.** (*intr*) to think or argue logically and methodically; reason. [C17: from L *ratiōcinārī* to calculate, from *ratiō* REASON]
▸**ˌratiˌociˈnation** *n* ▸**ˌratiˈociˌnative** *adj* ▸**ˌratiˈociˌnator** *n*

ration 🅣 (ˈræʃən) *n* **1a** a fixed allowance of food, provisions, etc., esp. a statutory one for civilians in time of scarcity or soldiers in time of war. **1b** (*as modifier*): *a ration book.* **2** a sufficient or adequate amount: *you've had your ration of television for today.* ◆ *vb* (*tr*) **3** (often foll. by *out*) to distribute (provisions), esp. to an army. **4** to restrict the distribution or consumption of (a commodity) by (people): *the government has rationed sugar.* ◆ See also **rations.** [C18: via F from L *ratiō* REASON]

rational 🅣 (ˈræʃən^{ə}l) *adj* **1** using reason or logic in thinking out a problem. **2** in accordance with the principles of logic or reason; reasonable. **3** of sound mind; sane: *the patient seemed rational.* **4** endowed with the capacity to reason: *rational beings.* **5** *Maths.* **5a** expressible as a ratio of two integers. **5b** (of an expression, equation, etc.) containing no variable either in irreducible radical form or raised to a fractional power. ◆ *n* **6** a rational number. [C14: from L *ratiōnālis,* from *ratiō* REASON]
▸**ˌratioˈnality** *n* ▸**ˈrationally** *adv* ▸**ˈrationalness** *n*

rationale 🅣 (ˌræʃəˈnɑːl) *n* a reasoned exposition, esp. one defining the fundamental reasons for an action, etc. [C17: from NL, from L *ratiōnālis*]

rationalism (ˈræʃənəˌlɪzəm) *n* **1** reliance on reason rather than intuition to justify one's beliefs or actions. **2** *Philosophy.* the doctrine that knowledge is acquired by reason without regard to experience. **3** the belief that knowledge and truth are ascertained by rational thought and not by divine or supernatural revelation.
▸**ˈrationalist** *n* ▸**ˌrationalˈistic** *adj* ▸**ˌrationalˈistically** *adv*

rationalize 🅣 *or* **rationalise** (ˈræʃənəˌlaɪz) *vb* **rationalizes, rationalizing, rationalized** *or* **rationalises, rationalising, rationalised. 1** to justify (one's actions) with plausible reasons, esp. after the event. **2** to apply logic or reason to (something). **3** (*tr*) to eliminate unnecessary equipment, etc., from (a group of businesses, factory, etc.), in order to make it more efficient. **4** (*tr*) *Maths.* to eliminate radicals without changing the value of (an expression) or the roots of (an equation).
▸**ˌrationaliˈzation** *or* **ˌrationaliˈsation** *n* ▸**ˈrationalˌizer** *or* **ˈrationalˌiser** *n*

rational number *n* any real number of the form *a*/*b*, where *a* and *b* are integers and *b* is not zero, as 7 or 7/3.

rations (ˈræʃənz) *pl n* (*sometimes sing*) a fixed daily allowance of food, esp. to military personnel or when supplies are limited.

ratite (ˈrætaɪt) *adj* **1** (of flightless birds) having a breastbone that lacks a keel for the attachment of flight muscles. **2** of or denoting the flightless birds, that have a flat breastbone, feathers lacking vanes, and reduced wings. ◆ *n* **3** a bird, such as an ostrich that belongs to this group; a flightless bird. [C19: from L *ratis* raft]

rat kangaroo *n* any of several ratlike kangaroos that occur in Australia and Tasmania.

ratline *or* **ratlin** (ˈrætlɪn) *n Naut.* any of a series of light lines tied across the shrouds of a sailing vessel for climbing aloft. [C15: from ?]

ratoon *or* **rattoon** (ræˈtuːn) *n* **1** a new shoot that grows from near the root of crop plants, esp. the sugar cane, after the old growth has been cut back. ◆ *vb* **2** to propagate by such a growth. [C18: from Sp. *retoño,* from RE- + *otoñar* to sprout in autumn, from *otoño* AUTUMN]

ratpack (ˈrætˌpæk) *n Derog. sl.* those members of the press who pursue celebrities and give wide, often intrusive, coverage of their private lives: *the royal ratpack.*

rat race *n* a continual routine of hectic competitive activity: *working in the City is a real rat race.*

rat-running *n* the practice of driving through residential side streets to avoid congested main roads.
▸**rat-run** *n* ▸**rat-runner** *n*

ratsbane (ˈrætsˌbeɪn) *n* rat poison, esp. arsenic oxide.

rat-tail *n* **1a** a horse's tail that has no hairs. **1b** a horse having such a tail. **2** a style of spoon in which the line of the handle is prolonged in a tapering moulding along the back of the bowl.

rattan *or* **ratan** (ræˈtæn) *n* **1** a climbing palm having tough stems used for wickerwork and canes. **2** the stems of such a plant collectively. **3** a stick made from one of these stems. [C17: from Malay *rōtan*]

ratter (ˈrætə) *n* **1** a dog or cat that catches and kills rats. **2** another word for **rat** (sense 3).

rattle 🅣 (ˈræt^{ə}l) *vb* **rattles, rattling, rattled. 1** to make a rapid succession of short sharp sounds, as of loose pellets colliding when shaken in a container. **2** to shake with such a sound. **3** to send, move, drive, etc., with such a sound: *the car rattled along the country road.* **4** (*intr;* foll. by *on*) to chatter idly: *he rattled on about his work.* **5** (*tr;* foll. by *off, out,* etc.) to recite perfunctorily or rapidly. **6** (*tr*) *Inf.* to disconcert; make frightened or anxious. ◆ *n* **7** a rapid succession of short sharp sounds. **8** a baby's toy filled with small pellets that rattle when shaken. **9** a series of loosely connected horny segments on the tail of a rattlesnake, vibrated to produce a rattling sound. **10** any of various European scrophulariaceous plants having a capsule in which the seeds rattle, such as the **red rattle** and the **yellow rattle. 11** idle chatter. **12** *Med.* another name for **rale.** [C14: from MDu. *ratelen,* imit.]
▸**ˈrattly** *adj*

rattler (ˈrætlə) *n* **1** a person or thing that rattles. **2** *Inf.* a rattlesnake.

rattlesnake (ˈræt^{ə}lˌsneɪk) *n* any of the venomous New World snakes such as the **black** or **timber rattlesnake** belonging to the family of pit vipers. They have a series of loose horny segments on the tail that are vibrated to produce a buzzing or whirring sound.

rattletrap (ˈræt^{ə}lˌtræp) *n Inf.* a broken-down old vehicle, esp. an old car.

rattling (ˈrætlɪŋ) *adv Inf.* (intensifier qualifying something good, fine, etc.): *a rattling good lunch.*

ratty 🅣 (ˈrætɪ) *adj* **rattier, rattiest. 1** *Brit. & NZ inf.* irritable; annoyed. **2** *Inf.* (of the hair) straggly, unkempt, or greasy. **3** *US & Canad. sl.* shabby; dilapidated. **4** *Austral. sl.* mad, eccentric, or odd. **5** of, like, or full of rats.
▸**ˈrattily** *adv* ▸**ˈrattiness** *n*

raucous 🅣 (ˈrɔːkəs) *adj* (of voices, cries, etc.) harshly or hoarsely loud. [C18: from L *raucus* hoarse]
▸**ˈraucously** *adv* ▸**ˈraucousness** *n*

raunchy 🅣 (ˈrɔːntʃɪ) *adj* **raunchier, raunchiest.** *Sl.* **1** openly sexual; lusty; earthy. **2** *Chiefly US.* slovenly; dirty. [C20: from ?]
▸**ˈraunchily** *adv* ▸**ˈraunchiness** *n*

raupo (ˈraupəu) *n, pl* **raupos.** a marsh reed common in New Zealand. [from Maori]

rauwolfia (rɔːˈwʊlfɪə, rau-) *n* **1** a tropical flowering tree or shrub of SE Asia with latex in its stem. **2** the powdered root of this plant: a source of various drugs, esp. reserpine. [C19: NL, after Leonhard *Rauwolf* (died 1596), G botanist]

ravage 🅣 (ˈrævɪdʒ) *vb* **ravages, ravaging, ravaged. 1** to cause extensive damage to. ◆ *n* **2** (*often pl*) destructive action: *the ravages of time.* [C17: from F, from OF *ravir* to snatch away, RAVISH]
▸**ˈravager** *n*

rave 🅣 (reɪv) *vb* **raves, raving, raved. 1** to utter (something) in a wild or incoherent manner, as when delirious. **2** (*intr*) to speak in an angry uncontrolled manner. **3** (*intr*) (of the sea, wind, etc.) to rage or roar. **4** (*intr;* foll. by *over* or *about*) *Inf.* to write or speak (about) with great enthusiasm. **5** (*intr*) *Brit. sl.* to enjoy oneself wildly or uninhibitedly. ◆ *n* **6** *Inf.* **6a** enthusiastic or extravagant praise. **6b** (*as modifier*): *a rave review.* **7** *Brit. sl.* **7a** Also called: **rave-up.** a party. **7b** a professionally organized party for young people, with electronic dance music, sometimes held in a field or disused building. **8** a name given to various types of dance music, such as techno, that feature fast electronic rhythm. [C14 *raven,* apparently from OF *resver* to wander]

ravel (ˈræv^{ə}l) *vb* **ravels, ravelling, ravelled** *or US* **ravels, raveling, raveled. 1** to tangle (threads, fibres, etc.) or (of threads, etc.) to become entangled. **2** (often foll. by *out*) to tease or draw out (the fibres of a fabric) or (of a fabric) to fray out in loose ends; unravel. **3** (*tr;* usually foll. by *out*) to disentangle or resolve: *to ravel out a complicated story.* ◆ *n* **4** a tangle or complication. [C16: from MDu. *ravelen*]
▸**ˈraveller** *n* ▸**ˈravelly** *adj*

raven[1] (ˈreɪv^{ə}n) *n* **1** a large passerine bird of the crow family, having a

THESAURUS

ration *n* **1a** = **allowance**, allotment, dole, helping, measure, part, portion, provision, quota, share ◆ *vb* **3** = **distribute**, allocate, allot, apportion, deal, dole, give out, issue, measure out, mete, parcel out **4** = **limit**, budget, conserve, control, restrict, save

rational *adj* **1, 4** = **reasoning**, cerebral, cognitive, ratiocinative, thinking **2** = **sensible**, enlightened, intelligent, judicious, logical, lucid, realistic, reasonable, sagacious, sane, sound, wise **3** = **sane**, all there (*inf.*), balanced, *compos mentis,* in one's right mind, lucid, normal, of sound mind
Antonyms *adj* insane, irrational, unreasonable, unsound

rationale *n* = **reason**, exposition, grounds, logic, motivation, philosophy, principle, *raison d'être,* theory

rationalize *vb* **1** = **justify**, account for, excuse, explain away, extenuate, make allowance for, make excuses for, vindicate **2** = **reason out**, apply logic to, elucidate, resolve, think through **3** = **streamline**, make cuts, make more efficient, trim

rattle *vb* **1** = **clatter**, bang, jangle **2, 3** = **shake**, bounce, jar, jiggle, jolt, jounce, vibrate **4** *with* **on** *or* **away** = **prattle**, blether, cackle, chatter, gabble, gibber, jabber, prate, rabbit (on) (*Brit. inf.*), run on, witter (*inf.*), yak (away) (*sl.*) **5** *with* **off** *or* **out** = **recite**, list, reel off, rehearse, run through, spiel off (*inf.*) **6** *Informal* = **fluster**, discomfit, discompose, disconcert, discountenance, disturb, faze, frighten, perturb, put (someone) off his stride, put (someone) out of countenance, scare, shake, upset

ratty *adj* **1** *Brit. & N.Z. informal* = **irritable**, angry, annoyed, crabbed, cross, impatient, short-tempered, snappy, testy, tetchy, touchy

raucous *adj* = **harsh**, grating, hoarse, husky, loud, noisy, rasping, rough, strident
Antonyms *adj* dulcet, mellifluous, quiet, smooth, sweet

raunchy *adj* **1** *Slang* = **sexy**, bawdy, coarse, earthy, lecherous, lewd, lustful, lusty, ribald, salacious, sexual, smutty, steamy (*inf.*), suggestive

ravage *vb* **1** = **destroy**, demolish, desolate, despoil, devastate, gut, lay waste, leave in ruins, loot, pillage, plunder, ransack, raze, ruin, sack, shatter, spoil, wreak havoc on, wreck ◆ *n* **2** *often plural* = **damage**, demolition, depredation, desolation, destruction, devastation, havoc, pillage, plunder, rapine, ruin, ruination, spoliation, waste

rave *vb* **1, 2** = **rant**, babble, be delirious, fume, go mad (*inf.*), rage, roar, splutter, storm, talk wildly, thunder **4** *Informal* = **enthuse**, be delighted by, be mad about (*inf.*), be wild about (*inf.*), cry up, gush, praise, rhapsodize ◆ *n* **6a** *Informal* = **praise**, acclaim, applause, encomium ◆ *modifier* **6b** *Informal* = **enthusiastic**, ecstatic, excellent, favourable, laudatory ◆ *n* **7a** = **party**, affair, bash, beano (*Brit. sl.*), blow-out (*sl.*), celebration, do (*inf.*), hooley or hoolie (*chiefly Irish & NZ*) large straight bill, long wedge-shaped tail, and black plumage. **2a** a shiny black colour. **2b** (*as adj*): *raven hair.* [OE *hræfn*]

raven[2] ('ræv^{ə}n) *vb* **1** to seize or seek (plunder, prey, etc.). **2** to eat (something) voraciously or greedily. [C15: from OF *raviner* to attack impetuously; see RAVENOUS]

ravening ('rævənɪŋ) *adj* (of animals) voracious; predatory.
▸'**raveningly** *adv*

ravenous ❶ ('rævənəs) *adj* **1** famished; starving. **2** rapacious; voracious. [C16: from OF *ravineux*, from L *rapīna* plunder, from *rapere* to seize]
▸'**ravenously** *adv* ▸'**ravenousness** *n*

raver ('reɪvə) *n* **1** *Brit. sl.* a person who leads a wild or uninhibited social life. **2** *Sl.* a person who enjoys rave music, esp. one who frequents raves.

ravine ❶ (rə'viːn) *n* a deep narrow steep-sided valley. [C15: from OF: torrent, from L *rapīna* robbery, infl. by L *rapidus* RAPID, both from *rapere* to snatch]

raving ❶ ('reɪvɪŋ) *adj* **1a** delirious; frenzied. **1b** (*as adv*): *raving mad.* **2** *Inf.* (intensifier): *a raving beauty.* ◆ *n* **3** (*usually pl*) frenzied or wildly extravagant talk or utterances.
▸'**ravingly** *adv*

ravioli (ˌrævɪ'əʊlɪ) *n* small squares of pasta containing a savoury mixture of meat, cheese, etc. [C19: It. dialect, lit.: little turnips, from It. *rava* turnip, from L *rāpa*]

ravish ❶ ('rævɪʃ) *vb* (*tr*) **1** (*often passive*) to enrapture. **2** to rape. **3** *Arch.* to carry off by force. [C13: from OF *ravir*, from L *rapere* to seize]
▸'**ravisher** *n* ▸'**ravishment** *n*

ravishing ❶ ('rævɪʃɪŋ) *adj* delightful; lovely; entrancing.
▸'**ravishingly** *adv*

raw ❶ (rɔː) *adj* **1** (of food) not cooked. **2** (*prenominal*) in an unfinished, natural, or unrefined state; not treated by manufacturing or other processes: *raw materials.* **3** (of the skin, a wound, etc.) having the surface exposed or abraded, esp. painfully. **4** (of an edge of material) unhemmed; liable to fray. **5** ignorant, inexperienced, or immature: *a raw recruit.* **6** (*prenominal*) not selected or modified: *raw statistics.* **7** frank or realistic: *a raw picture of a marriage.* **8** (of spirits) undiluted. **9** *Chiefly US.* coarse, vulgar, or obscene. **10** (of the weather) harshly cold and damp. **11** *Inf.* unfair; unjust (esp. in **a raw deal**). ◆ *n* **12 in the raw. 12a** *Inf.* without clothes; naked. **12b** in a natural or unmodified state. **13 the raw.** *Brit. inf.* a sensitive point: *his criticism touched me on the raw.* [OE *hreaw*]
▸'**rawish** *adj* ▸'**rawly** *adv* ▸'**rawness** *n*

rawboned ('rɔː'bəʊnd) *adj* having a lean bony physique.

rawhide ('rɔːˌhaɪd) *n* **1** untanned hide. **2** a whip or rope made of strips cut from such a hide.

rawhide hammer *n* a hammer, used to avoid damaging a surface, having a head consisting of a metal tube from each end of which a tight roll of hide protrudes.

rawinsonde ('reɪwɪnˌsɒnd) *n* a hydrogen balloon carrying meteorological instruments and a radar target, enabling the velocity of winds in the atmosphere to be measured. [C20: blend of *radar* + *wind* + *radiosonde*]

Rawlplug ('rɔːlplʌg) *n Trademark.* a short fibre or plastic tube used to provide a fixing in a wall for a screw.

raw material *n* **1** material on which a particular manufacturing process is carried out. **2** a person or thing regarded as suitable for some particular purpose: *raw material for the army.*

raw silk *n* **1** untreated silk fibres reeled from the cocoon. **2** fabric woven from such fibres.

ray[1] ❶ (reɪ) *n* **1** a narrow beam of light; gleam. **2** a slight indication: *a ray of solace.* **3** *Maths.* a straight line extending from a point. **4** a thin beam of electromagnetic radiation or particles. **5** any of the bony or cartilaginous spines of the fin of a fish that form the support for the soft part of the fin. **6** any of the arms or branches of a starfish. **7** *Bot.* any strand of tissue that runs radially through the vascular tissue of some higher plants. ◆ *vb* **8** (of an object) to emit (light) in rays or (of light) to issue in the form of rays. **9** (*intr*) (of lines, etc.) to extend in rays or on radiating paths. **10** (*tr*) to adorn (an ornament, etc.) with rays or radiating lines. [C14: from OF *rai*, from L *radius* spoke]

ray[2] (reɪ) *n* any of various marine selachian fishes typically having a flattened body, greatly enlarged winglike pectoral fins, gills on the undersurface of the fins, and a long whiplike tail. [C14: from OF *raie*, from L *raia*]

ray[3] (reɪ) *n Music.* (in tonic sol-fa) the second degree of any major scale; supertonic. [C18: later variant of *re*; see GAMUT]

Raybans ('reɪˌbænz) *pl n Trademark.* a brand of sunglasses.

ray flower *or* **floret** *n* any of the small strap-shaped flowers in the flower head of certain composite plants, such as the daisy.

ray gun *n* (in science fiction) a gun that emits rays to paralyse, stun, or destroy.

rayless ('reɪlɪs) *adj* **1** dark; gloomy. **2** lacking rays: *a rayless flower.*

raylet ('reɪlɪt) *n* a small ray.

rayon ('reɪɒn) *n* **1** any of a number of textile fibres made from wood pulp or other forms of cellulose. **2** any fabric made from such a fibre. **3** (*as modifier*): *a rayon shirt.* [C20: from F, from OF *rai* RAY[1]]

raze ❶ *or* **rase** (reɪz) *vb* **razes, razing, razed** *or* **rases, rasing, rased.** (*tr*) **1** to demolish (buildings, etc.) completely (esp. in **raze to the ground**). **2** to delete; erase. **3** *Arch.* to graze. [C16: from OF *raser*, from L *rādere* to scrape]
▸'**razer** *or* '**raser** *n*

razoo (rɑː'zuː) *n, pl* **razoos.** *Austral. & NZ inf.* an imaginary coin: *not a brass razoo; they took every last razoo.* [C20: from ?]

razor ('reɪzə) *n* **1** a sharp implement used esp. for shaving the face. **2 on a razor's edge** *or* **razor-edge.** in an acute dilemma. ◆ *vb* **3** (*tr*) to cut or shave with a razor. [C13: from OF *raseor*, from *raser* to shave; see RAZE]

razorback ('reɪzəˌbæk) *n* **1** Also called: **finback.** another name for the **common rorqual** (see **rorqual**). **2** a wild pig of the US, having a narrow body, long legs, and a ridged back.

razorbill ('reɪzəˌbɪl) *or* **razor-billed auk** *n* a common auk of the North Atlantic, having a thick laterally compressed bill with white markings.

razor blade *n* a small rectangular piece of metal sharpened on one or both long edges for use in a razor for shaving.

razor-shell *n* any of various sand-burrowing bivalve molluscs which have a long tubular shell. US name: **razor clam.**

razor wire *n* strong wire with pieces of sharp metal set across it at close intervals.

razz (ræz) *US & Canad. sl.* ◆ *vb* **1** (*tr*) to make fun of; deride. ◆ *n* **2** short for **raspberry** (sense 4).

razzle-dazzle ❶ ('ræz^{ə}l'dæz^{ə}l) *or* **razzmatazz** ('ræzmə'tæz) *n Sl.* **1** noisy or showy fuss or activity. **2** a spree or frolic. [C19: rhyming compound from DAZZLE]

Rb *the chemical symbol for* rubidium.

RBT *abbrev. for* random breath testing.

RC *abbrev. for:* **1** Red Cross. **2** Roman Catholic.

RCA *abbrev. for:* **1** (formerly) Radio Corporation of America. **2** Royal College of Art.

RCAF *abbrev. for* Royal Canadian Air Force.

RC CH *abbrev. for* Roman Catholic Church.

RCM *abbrev. for* Royal College of Music.

RCMP *abbrev. for* Royal Canadian Mounted Police.

RCN *abbrev. for:* **1** Royal Canadian Navy. **2** Royal College of Nursing.

RCP *abbrev. for* Royal College of Physicians.

RCS *abbrev. for:* **1** Royal College of Science. **2** Royal College of Surgeons. **3** Royal Corps of Signals.

rd *abbrev. for:* **1** road. **2** rod (unit of length). **3** round. **4** *Physics.* rutherford.

Rd *abbrev. for* Road.

RDC (in Britain, formerly) *abbrev. for* Rural District Council.

re[1] (reɪ, riː) *n Music.* the syllable used in the fixed system of solmization for the note D. [C14: see GAMUT]

re[2] ❶ (riː) *prep* with reference to. [C18: from L *rē*, ablative case of *rēs* thing]

> **USAGE NOTE** *Re*, in contexts such as *re your letter, your remarks have been noted* or *he spoke to me re your complaint*, is common in business or official correspondence. In general English *with reference to* is preferable in the former case and *about* or *concerning* in the latter. Even in business correspondence, the use of *re* is often restricted to the letter heading.

THESAURUS

ravenous *adj* **1** = **starving**, esurient, famished, starved, very hungry **2** = **voracious**, devouring, edacious, gluttonous, insatiable, predatory, rapacious, ravening
Antonyms *adj* ≠ **starving:** full, glutted, sated, satiated

ravine *n* = **canyon**, clough (*dialect*), defile, flume, gap (*US*), gorge, gulch (*US*), gully, linn (*Scot.*), pass

raving *adj* **1a** = **mad**, berserk, crazed, crazy, delirious, frantic, frenzied, furious, hysterical, insane, irrational, out of one's mind, rabid, raging, wild

ravish *vb* **1** = **enchant**, captivate, charm, delight, enrapture, entrance, fascinate, overjoy, spellbind, transport **2** = **rape**, abuse, force, outrage, sexually assault, violate

ravishing *adj* = **enchanting**, beautiful, bewitching, charming, dazzling, delightful, drop-dead (*sl.*), entrancing, gorgeous, lovely, radiant, stunning (*inf.*)

raw *adj* **1** = **uncooked**, bloody (*of meat*), fresh, natural, undressed, unprepared **2** = **unrefined**, basic, coarse, crude, green, natural, organic, rough, unfinished, unprocessed, unripe, untreated **3** = **sore**, abraded, chafed, grazed, open, scratched, sensitive, skinned, tender **5** = **inexperienced**, callow, green, ignorant, immature, new, undisciplined, unpractised, unseasoned, unskilled, untrained, untried **7** = **frank**, bare, blunt, brutal, candid, naked, plain, realistic, unembellished, unvarnished **10** = **chilly**, biting, bitter, bleak, chill, cold, damp, freezing, harsh, parky (*Brit. inf.*), piercing, unpleasant, wet
Antonyms *adj* ≠ **uncooked:** baked, cooked, done ≠ **unrefined:** finished, prepared, refined ≠ **inexperienced:** experienced, practised, professional, skilled, trained ≠ **frank:** embellished, gilded

ray[1] *n* **1** = **beam**, bar, flash, gleam, shaft **2** = **trace**, flicker, glimmer, hint, indication, scintilla, spark

raze *vb* **1** = **destroy**, bulldoze, demolish, flatten, knock down, level, pull down, remove, ruin, tear down, throw down **2** = **erase**, delete, efface, excise, expunge, extinguish, extirpate, obliterate, rub out, scratch out, strike out, wipe from the face of the earth, wipe out

razzle-dazzle *n* **1** *Slang* = **fuss**, carry-on (*inf., chiefly Brit.*), commotion, hullabaloo, performance (*inf.*), rigmarole, song and dance (*inf.*), to-do

re[2] *prep* = **concerning**, about, anent (*Scot.*), apropos, in respect of, on the subject of, regarding, respecting, with reference to, with regard to

Re *the chemical symbol for* rhenium.
RE *abbrev. for:* **1** Religious Education. **2** Royal Engineers.
re- *prefix* **1** indicating return to a previous condition, withdrawal, etc.: *rebuild; renew.* **2** indicating repetition of an action: *remarry.* [L]

> **USAGE NOTE** Verbs beginning with *re-* indicate repetition or restoration. It is unnecessary to add an adverb such as *back* or *again: This must not occur again* (not *recur again*); *we recounted the votes* (not *recounted the votes again,* which implies that the votes were counted three times, not twice).

reach ❶ (ri:tʃ) *vb* **1** (*tr*) to arrive at or get to (a place, person, etc.) in the course of movement or action: *to reach the office.* **2** to extend as far as (a point or place): *to reach the ceiling; can you reach?* **3** (*tr*) to come to (a certain condition or situation): *to reach the point of starvation.* **4** (*intr*) to extend in influence or operation: *the Roman conquest reached throughout England.* **5** (*tr*) *Inf.* to pass or give (something to a person) with the outstretched hand. **6** (*intr;* foll. by *out, for,* or *after*) to make a movement (towards), as if to grasp or touch. **7** (*tr*) to make contact or communication with (someone): *we tried to reach him all day.* **8** (*tr*) to strike, esp. in fencing or boxing. **9** (*tr*) to amount to (a certain sum): *to reach five million.* **10** (*intr*) *Naut.* to sail on a tack with the wind on or near abeam. ◆ *n* **11** the act of reaching. **12** the extent or distance of reaching: *within reach.* **13** the range of influence, power, etc. **14** an open stretch of water, esp. on a river. **15** *Naut.* the direction or distance sailed by a vessel on one tack. **16** *Advertising.* the proportion of a market that an advertiser hopes to reach at least once in a campaign. [OE *rǣcan*]
▸**'reachable** *adj* ▸**'reacher** *n*
reach-me-down *n* **1a** (*often pl*) a cheaply ready-made or second-hand garment. **1b** (*as modifier*): *reach-me-down finery.* **2** (*modifier*) not original; derivative: *reach-me-down ideas.*
react ❶ (rɪ'ækt) *vb* **1** (*intr;* foll. by *to, upon,* etc.) (of a person or thing) to act in response to another person, a stimulus, etc. **2** (*intr;* foll. by *against*) to act in an opposing or contrary manner. **3** (*intr*) *Physics.* to exert an equal force in the opposite direction to an acting force. **4** *Chem.* to undergo or cause to undergo a chemical reaction. [C17: from LL *reagere,* from RE- + L *agere* to do]
re-act (ri:'ækt) *vb* (*tr*) to act or perform again.
reactance (rɪ'æktəns) *n* the opposition to the flow of alternating current by the capacitance or inductance of an electrical circuit.
reactant (rɪ'æktənt) *n* a substance that participates in a chemical reaction.
reaction ❶ (rɪ'ækʃən) *n* **1** a response to some foregoing action or stimulus. **2** the reciprocal action of two things acting together. **3** opposition to change, esp. political change, or a desire to return to a former system. **4** a response indicating a person's feelings or emotional attitude. **5** *Med.* **5a** any effect produced by the action of a drug. **5b** any effect produced by a substance (allergen) to which a person is allergic. **6** *Chem.* a process that involves changes in the structure and energy content of atoms, molecules, or ions. **7** the equal and opposite force that acts on a body whenever it exerts a force on another body.
▸**re'actional** *adj*

> **USAGE NOTE** *Reaction* is used to refer both to an instant response (*her reaction was one of amazement*) and to a considered response in the form of a statement (*the Minister gave his reaction to the court's decision*). Some people think this second use is incorrect.

reactionary ❶ (rɪ'ækʃənərɪ, -ʃənrɪ) *or* **reactionist** *adj* **1** of, relating to, or characterized by reaction, esp. against radical political or social change. ◆ *n, pl* **reactionaries** *or* **reactionists. 2** a person opposed to radical change.
▸**re'actionism** *n*
reaction engine *or* **motor** *n* an engine, such as a jet engine, that ejects gas at high velocity and develops its thrust from the ensuing reaction.
reaction turbine *n* a turbine in which the working fluid is accelerated by expansion in both the static nozzles and the rotor blades.
reactivate (rɪ'æktɪˌveɪt) *vb* **reactivates, reactivating, reactivated.** (*tr*) to make (something) active again.
▸**reˌacti'vation** *n*
reactive (rɪ'æktɪv) *adj* **1** readily partaking in chemical reactions: *sodium is a reactive metal.* **2** of, concerned with, or having a reactance. **3** responsive to stimulus. **4** (of mental illnesses) precipitated by an external cause.
▸**reactivity** (ˌri:æk'tɪvɪtɪ) *or* **re'activeness** *n*
reactor (rɪ'æktə) *n* **1** short for **nuclear reactor. 2** a vessel in which a chemical reaction takes occurs. **3** a coil of low resistance and high inductance that introduces reactance into a circuit. **4** *Med.* a person sensitive to a particular drug or agent. **5** *Chem.* a substance that takes part in a reaction.
read[1] ❶ (ri:d) *vb* **reads, reading, read** (rɛd). **1** to comprehend the meaning of (something written or printed) by looking at and interpreting the written or printed characters. **2** (when *tr,* often foll. by *out*) to look at, interpret, and speak aloud (something written or printed). **3** (*tr*) to interpret the significance or meaning of through scrutiny and recognition: *to read a map.* **4** (*tr*) to interpret or understand the meaning of (signs, characters, etc.) other than by visual means: *to read Braille.* **5** (*tr*) to have sufficient knowledge of (a language) to understand the written or printed word. **6** (*tr*) to discover or make out the true nature or mood of: *to read someone's mind.* **7** to interpret or understand (something read) in a specified way: *I read this speech as satire.* **8** (*tr*) to adopt as a reading in a particular passage: *for "boon" read "bone".* **9** (*intr*) to have or contain a certain form or wording: *the sentence reads as follows.* **10** to undertake a course of study in (a subject): *to read history.* **11** to gain knowledge by reading: *he read about the war.* **12** (*tr*) to register, indicate, or show: *the meter reads 100.* **13** (*tr*) to put into a specified condition by reading: *to read a child to sleep.* **14** (*tr*) to hear and understand, esp. when using a two-way radio: *we are reading you loud and clear.* **15** *Computing.* to obtain (data) from a storage device, such as magnetic tape. **16 read a lesson** (*or* **lecture**). *Inf.* to censure or reprimand. ◆ *n* **17** matter suitable for reading: *this book is a very good read.* **18** the act or a spell of reading. ◆ See also **read into, read out,** etc. [OE *rǣdan* to advise, explain]
read[2] (rɛd) *vb* **1** the past tense and past participle of **read**[1]. ◆ *adj* **2** having knowledge gained from books (esp. in **widely read** and **well-read**). **3 take (something) as read.** to take (something) for granted as a fact; understand or presume.
readable ❶ ('ri:dəbᵊl) *adj* **1** (of handwriting, etc.) able to be read or deciphered; legible. **2** (of style of writing) interesting, easy, or pleasant to read.
▸**ˌreada'bility** *or* **'readableness** *n* ▸**'readably** *adv*
reader ('ri:də) *n* **1** a person who reads. **2** *Chiefly Brit.* a member of staff below a professor but above a senior lecturer at a university. **3a** a book that is part of a planned series for those learning to read. **3b** a standard textbook, esp. for foreign-language learning. **4** a person who reads aloud in public. **5** a person who reads and assesses the merit of manuscripts submitted to a publisher. **6** a proofreader. **7** short for **lay reader.**
readership ('ri:dəʃɪp) *n* all the readers collectively of a publication or author: *a readership of five million.*
reading ❶ ('ri:dɪŋ) *n* **1a** the act of a person who reads. **1b** (*as modifier*): *a reading room.* **2a** ability to read. **2b** (*as modifier*): *a child of reading age.* **3** any matter that can be read; written or printed text. **4** a public recital or rendering of a literary work. **5** the form of a particular word or passage in a given text, esp. where more than one version exists. **6** an interpretation, as of a piece of music, a situation, or something said or written. **7** knowledge gained from books: *a person of little reading.* **8** a measurement indicated by a gauge, dial, scientific instrument, etc. **9** *Parliamentary procedure.* **9a** the formal recital of the body or title of a bill in a legislative assembly in order to begin one of the stages of its

THESAURUS

reach *vb* **1** = **arrive at,** attain, get as far as, get to, land at, make **2** = **touch,** contact, extend to, get (a) hold of, go as far as, grasp, stretch to **5** *Informal* = **pass,** hand, hold out, stretch **7** = **contact,** communicate with, establish contact with, find, get, get hold of, get in touch with, get through to, make contact with **9** = **come to,** amount to, arrive at, attain, climb to, drop to, fall to, move to, rise to, sink to ◆ *n* **12** = **range,** distance, extension, extent, grasp, stretch, sweep **13** = **power,** ambit, capacity, command, compass, influence, jurisdiction, mastery, scope, spread
react *vb* **1** = **respond,** behave, conduct oneself, function, operate, proceed, work
reaction *n* **1, 2** = **counteraction,** backlash, compensation, counterbalance, counterpoise, recoil **3** = **conservatism,** counter-revolution, obscurantism, the right **4** = **response,** acknowledgment, answer, feedback, reply
reactionary *adj* **1** = **conservative,** blimpish, counter-revolutionary, obscurantist, right-wing ◆ *n* **2** = **conservative,** Colonel Blimp, counter-revolutionary, die-hard, obscurantist, rightist, right-winger
Antonyms *adj, n* ≠ **conservative:** leftist, progressive, radical, reformist, revolutionary, socialist
read[1] *vb* **1** = **look at,** glance at, peruse, pore over, refer to, run one's eye over, scan, study **2** = **recite,** announce, declaim, deliver, speak, utter **3** = **understand,** comprehend, construe, decipher, discover, interpret, perceive the meaning of, see **12** = **register,** display, indicate, record, show
readable *adj* **1** = **legible,** clear, comprehensible, decipherable, intelligible, plain, understandable **2** = **enjoyable,** easy to read, entertaining, enthralling, gripping, interesting, pleasant, worth reading
Antonyms *adj* ≠ **legible:** illegible, incomprehensible, indecipherable, unintelligible, unreadable ≠ **enjoyable:** as dry as dust, badly-written, boring, dull, heavy, heavy going, pretentious, turgid, unreadable
readily *adv* **2** = **willingly,** cheerfully, eagerly, freely, gladly, lief (*rare*), quickly, voluntarily, with good grace, with pleasure **3** = **promptly,** at once, easily, effortlessly, hotfoot, in no time, quickly, right away, smoothly, speedily, straight away, unhesitatingly, without delay, without demur, without difficulty, without hesitation
Antonyms *adv* ≠ **willingly:** reluctantly, unwillingly ≠ **promptly:** hesitatingly, slowly, with difficulty
readiness *n* **1** = **preparedness,** fitness, maturity, preparation, ripeness **2** = **willingness,** aptness, eagerness, gameness (*inf.*), inclination, keenness **3** = **promptness,** promptitude, quickness, rapidity
reading *n* **1a** = **perusal,** examination, inspection, review, scrutiny, study **4** = **recital,** homily, lecture, lesson, performance, rendering, rendition, sermon **6** = **interpretation,** conception, construction, grasp, impression, take (*inf., chiefly US*), treatment, understanding, version **7** = **learning,** book-learning, edification, education, erudition, knowledge, scholarship

passage. **9b** one of the three stages in the passage of a bill through a legislative assembly. See **first reading, second reading, third reading. 10** the formal recital of something written, esp. a will.

read into (riːd) *vb (tr, prep)* to discern in or infer from a statement (meanings not intended by the speaker or writer).

read out (riːd) *vb (adv)* **1** *(tr)* to read (something) aloud. **2** to retrieve (information) from a computer memory or storage device. **3** *(tr) US & Canad.* to expel (someone) from a political party or other society. ◆ *n* **read-out. 4a** the act of retrieving information from a computer memory or storage device. **4b** the information retrieved.

read up (riːd) *vb (adv; when intr,* often foll. by *on)* to acquire information about (a subject) by reading intensively.

read-write head (ˈriːdˈraɪt) *n Computing.* an electromagnet that can both read and write information on a magnetic tape or disk.

ready ❶ (ˈrɛdɪ) *adj* **readier, readiest. 1** in a state of completion or preparedness, as for use or action. **2** willing or eager: *ready helpers.* **3** prompt or rapid: *a ready response.* **4** *(prenominal)* quick in perceiving; intelligent: *a ready mind.* **5** *(postpositive)* (foll. by *to)* on the point (of) or liable (to): *ready to collapse.* **6** *(postpositive)* conveniently near (esp. in **ready to hand**). **7 make** *or* **get ready.** to prepare (oneself or something) for use or action. ◆ *n* **8** *Inf. (often preceded by* the) short for **ready money. 9 at** *or* **to the ready. 9a** (of a rifle) in the position adopted prior to aiming and firing. **9b** poised for use or action: *with pen at the ready.* ◆ *vb* **readies, readying, readied. 10** *(tr)* to put in a state of readiness; prepare. [OE *(ge)rǣde*]

▸ˈ**readily** *adv* ▸ˈ**readiness** *n*

ready-made *adj* **1** made for purchase and immediate use by any customer. **2** extremely convenient or ideally suited: *a ready-made solution.* **3** unoriginal or conventional: *ready-made phrases.* ◆ *n* **4** a ready-made article, esp. a garment.

ready-mix *n* **1** *(modifier)* consisting of ingredients blended in advance, esp. of food that is ready to cook or eat after addition of milk or water: *a ready-mix cake.* **2** concrete that is mixed before or during delivery to a building site.

ready money *or* **cash** *n* funds for immediate use; cash. Also: **the ready, the readies.**

ready reckoner *n* a table of numbers for facilitating simple calculations, esp. for working out interest, etc.

ready-to-wear *adj* (**ready to wear** *when postpositive*). **1** (of clothes) not tailored for the wearer; of a standard size. ◆ *n* **2** an article or suit of such clothes.

reafforest (ˌriːəˈfɒrɪst) *or* **reforest** *vb (tr)* to replant (an area that was formerly forested).

▸ˌ**reafˌforestˈation** *or* ˌ**reforestˈation** *n*

reagent (riːˈeɪdʒənt) *n* a substance for use in a chemical reaction, esp. for use in chemical synthesis and analysis.

real[1] ❶ (rɪəl) *adj* **1** existing or occurring in the physical world; not imaginary, fictitious, or theoretical; actual. **2** *(prenominal)* true; actual; not false: *the real reason.* **3** *(prenominal)* deserving the name; rightly so called: *a real friend.* **4** not artificial or simulated; genuine: *real fur.* **5** (of food, etc.) traditionally made and having a distinct flavour: *real ale; real cheese.* **6** *Philosophy.* existent or relating to actual existence (as opposed to nonexistent, potential, contingent, or apparent). **7** *(prenominal) Econ.* (of prices, incomes, etc.) considered in terms of purchasing power rather than nominal currency value. **8** *(prenominal)* denoting or relating to immovable property such as land and tenements: *real estate.* **9** *Maths.* involving or containing real numbers alone; having no imaginary part. **10** *Inf.* (intensifier): *a real genius.* **11 the real thing.** the genuine article, not a substitute. ◆ *n* **12 for real.** *Sl.* not as a test or trial; in earnest. **13 the real.** that which exists in fact; reality. [C15: from OF *réel,* from LL *reālis,* from L *rēs* thing]

▸ˈ**realness** *n*

real[2] (reɪˈɑːl) *n, pl* **reals** *or* **reales** *(Spanish* reˈales). a former small Spanish or Spanish-American silver coin. [C17: from Sp., lit.: royal, from L *rēgālis;* see REGAL]

real ale *n* any beer which is allowed to ferment in the barrel and which is pumped up from the keg without using carbon dioxide.

real estate *n* another term, chiefly US and Canad., for **real property.**

realgar (rɪˈælgə) *n* a rare orange-red soft mineral consisting of arsenic sulphide in monoclinic crystalline form. [C14: via Med. L from Ar. *rahj al-ghar* powder of the mine]

realism (ˈrɪəˌlɪzəm) *n* **1** awareness or acceptance of the physical universe, events, etc., as they are, as opposed to the abstract or ideal. **2** a style of painting and sculpture that seeks to represent the familiar or typical in real life. **3** any similar style in other arts, esp. literature. **4** *Philosophy.* the thesis that general terms refer to entities that have a real existence separate from the individuals which fall under them. **5** *Philosophy.* the theory that physical objects continue to exist whether they are perceived or not.

▸ˈ**realist** *n*

realistic ❶ (ˌrɪəˈlɪstɪk) *adj* **1** showing awareness and acceptance of reality. **2** practical or pragmatic rather than ideal or moral. **3** (of a book, etc.) depicting what is real and actual. **4** of or relating to philosophical realism.

▸ˌ**realˈistically** *adv*

reality ❶ (rɪˈælɪtɪ) *n, pl* **realities. 1** the state of things as they are or appear to be, rather than as one might wish them to be. **2** something that is real. **3** the state of being real. **4** *Philosophy.* **4a** that which exists, independent of human awareness. **4b** the totality of facts. **5 in reality.** actually; in fact.

reality principle *n Psychoanal.* control of behaviour by the ego to meet the conditions imposed by the external world.

realize ❶ *or* **realise** (ˈrɪəˌlaɪz) *vb* **realizes, realizing, realized** *or* **realises, realising, realised. 1** (when *tr, may take a clause as object)* to become conscious or aware of (something). **2** *(tr, often passive)* to bring (a plan, ambition, etc.) to fruition. **3** *(tr)* to give (a drama or film) the appearance of reality. **4** *(tr)* (of goods, property, etc.) to sell for or make (a certain sum): *this table realized £800.* **5** *(tr)* to convert (property or goods) into cash. **6** *(tr)* (of a musicologist or performer) to reconstruct (a composition) from an incomplete set of parts.

▸ˈ**realˌizable** *or* ˈ**realˌisable** *adj* ▸ˈ**realˌizably** *or* ˈ**realˌisably** *adv* ▸ˌ**realiˈzation** *or* ˌ**realiˈsation** *n* ▸ˈ**realˌizer** *or* ˈ**realˌiser** *n*

real life *n* actual human life, as lived by real people, esp. contrasted with the lives of fictional characters: *miracles don't happen in real life.*

really ❶ (ˈrɪəlɪ) *adv* **1** in reality; in actuality; assuredly: *it's really quite harmless.* **2** truly; genuinely: *really beautiful.* ◆ *interj* **3** an exclamation of dismay, disapproval, doubt, surprise, etc. **4 not really?** an exclamation of surprise or polite doubt.

USAGE NOTE See at **very.**

realm ❶ (rɛlm) *n* **1** a royal domain; kingdom: *peer of the realm.* **2** a field of interest, study, etc.: *the realm of the occult.* [C13: from OF *reialme,* from L *regimen* rule, infl. by OF *reial,* from L *rēgālis* REGAL]

real number *n* any rational or irrational number. See **number.**

real presence *n* the doctrine that the body of Christ is actually present in the Eucharist.

real property *n Property law.* immovable property, esp. freehold land. Cf. **personal property.**

real tennis *n* an ancient form of tennis played in a four-walled indoor court.

real-time *adj* denoting or relating to a data-processing system in which a computer is on-line to a source of data and processes the data as it is generated.

realtor (ˈrɪəltə, -ˌtɔː) *n* a US word for an **estate agent,** esp. an accredited one. [C20: from REALTY + -OR[1]]

realty (ˈrɪəltɪ) *n* another term for **real property.**

ream[1] (riːm) *n* **1** a number of sheets of paper, formerly 480 sheets (**short ream**), now 500 sheets (**long ream**) or 516 sheets (**printer's ream** or **perfect**

THESAURUS

ready *adj* **1** = **prepared,** all set, arranged, completed, fit, in readiness, organized, primed, ripe, set **2** = **willing,** agreeable, apt, disposed, eager, game *(inf.),* glad, happy, have-a-go *(inf.),* inclined, keen, minded, predisposed, prone **3** = **prompt,** quick, rapid, smart **4** = **intelligent,** acute, alert, astute, bright, clever, keen, perceptive, quick-witted, sharp, smart **5** *foll. by* **to** = **on the point of,** about to, close to, in danger of, liable to, likely to, on the brink of, on the verge of **6** = **available,** accessible, at *or* on hand, at one's fingertips, at the ready, close to hand, convenient, handy, near, on call, on tap *(inf.),* present ◆ *n* **9b at** *or* **to the ready** = **poised,** all systems go, in readiness, prepared, ready for action, waiting ◆ *vb* **10** = **prepare,** arrange, equip, fit out, get ready, make ready, order, organize, set

Antonyms *adj* ≠ **prepared:** immature, unequipped, unfit, unprepared ≠ **willing:** disinclined, hesitant, loath, reluctant, unprepared, unwilling ≠ **prompt:** slow ≠ **available:** distant, inaccessible, late, unavailable

real[1] *adj* **1** = **actual,** existent, factual, veritable **2** = **true,** genuine **4** = **genuine,** authentic, bona fide, heartfelt, honest, sincere, unaffected, unfeigned

Antonyms *adj* ≠ **genuine:** affected, counterfeit, fake, faked, false, feigned, imitation, insincere

realistic *adj* **1, 2** = **practical,** businesslike, common-sense, down-to-earth, hard-headed, level-headed, matter-of-fact, pragmatic, rational, real, sensible, sober, unromantic, unsentimental **3** = **lifelike,** authentic, faithful, genuine, graphic, natural, naturalistic, representational, true, true to life, truthful, vérité

Antonyms *adj* ≠ **practical:** fanciful, idealistic, impractical, unrealistic

reality *n* **1** = **realism,** truth **2** = **truth,** certainty, fact, verity **3** = **genuineness,** actuality, authenticity, corporeality, materiality, validity, verisimilitude **5 in reality** = **in fact,** actually, as a matter of fact, in actuality, in point of fact, in truth, really

realization *n* **1** = **awareness,** appreciation, apprehension, cognizance, comprehension, conception, consciousness, grasp, imagination, perception, recognition, understanding **2** = **achievement,** accomplishment, carrying-out, completion, consummation, effectuation, fulfilment

realize *vb* **1** = **become aware of,** appreciate, apprehend, be cognizant of, become conscious of, catch on *(inf.),* comprehend, conceive, get the message, grasp, imagine, recognize, take in, twig *(Brit. inf.),* understand **2** = **achieve,** accomplish, actualize, bring about, bring off, bring to fruition, carry out *or* through, complete, consummate, do, effect, effectuate, fulfil, incarnate, make concrete, make happen, perform, reify **4** = **sell for,** acquire, bring *or* take in, clear, earn, gain, get, go for, make, net, obtain, produce

really *adv* **1, 2** = **truly,** absolutely, actually, assuredly, categorically, certainly, genuinely, in actuality, indeed, in fact, in reality, positively, surely, undoubtedly, verily, without a doubt

realm *n* **1** = **kingdom,** country, domain, dominion, empire, land, monarchy, principality, province, state **2** = **field,** area, branch, department, orbit, patch, province, region, sphere, territory, turf *(US sl.),* world, zone

ream). One ream is equal to 20 quires. **2** (*often pl*) *Inf.* a large quantity, esp. of written matter: *he wrote reams.* [C14: from OF, from Sp., from Ar. *rizmah* bale]

ream[2] (riːm) *vb* (*tr*) **1** to enlarge (a hole) by use of a reamer. **2** *US.* to extract (juice) from (a citrus fruit) using a reamer. [C19: ?from C14 *remen* to open up, from OE *rȳman* to widen]

reamer (ˈriːmə) *n* **1** a steel tool with a cylindrical or tapered shank around which longitudinal teeth are ground, used for smoothing the bores of holes accurately to size. **2** *US.* a utensil with a conical projection used for extracting juice from citrus fruits.

reap ❶ (riːp) *vb* **1** to cut or harvest (a crop) from (a field). **2** (*tr*) to gain or get (something) as a reward for or result of some action or enterprise. [OE *riopan*]
▸**ˈreapable** *adj*

reaper (ˈriːpə) *n* **1** a person who reaps or a machine for reaping. **2 the grim reaper.** death.

rear[1] ❶ (rɪə) *n* **1** the back or hind part. **2** the area or position that lies at the back: *a garden at the rear of the house.* **3** the section of a military force farthest from the front. **4** an informal word for **buttocks** (see **buttock**). **5 bring up the rear.** to be at the back in a procession, race, etc. **6 in the rear.** at the back. **7** (*modifier*) of or in the rear: *the rear side.* [C17: prob. from REARWARD or REARGUARD]

rear[2] ❶ (rɪə) *vb* **1** (*tr*) to care for and educate (children) until maturity; raise. **2** (*tr*) to breed (animals) or grow (plants). **3** (*tr*) to place or lift (a ladder, etc.) upright. **4** (*tr*) to erect (a monument, building, etc.). **5** (*intr; often foll. by up*) (esp. of horses) to lift the front legs in the air and stand nearly upright. **6** (*intr; often foll. by up or over*) (esp. of tall buildings) to rise high; tower. **7** (*intr*) to start with anger, resentment, etc. [OE *rǣran*]
▸**ˈrearer** *n*

rear admiral *n* an officer holding flag rank in any of certain navies, junior to a vice admiral.

rearguard (ˈrɪəˌgɑːd) *n* **1** a detachment detailed to protect the rear of a military formation, esp. in retreat. **2** an entrenched or conservative element, as in a political party. **3** (*modifier*) of, relating to, or characteristic of a rearguard: *a rearguard action.* [C15: from OF *rereguarde*, from *rer*, from L *retro* back + *guarde* GUARD]

rear light *or* **lamp** *n* a red light, usually one of a pair, attached to the rear of a motor vehicle. Also called: **tail-light, tail lamp.**

rearm (riːˈɑːm) *vb* **1** to arm again. **2** (*tr*) to equip (an army, etc.) with better weapons.
▸**reˈarmament** *n*

rearmost (ˈrɪəˌməʊst) *adj* nearest the rear; coming last.

rear-view mirror *n* a mirror on a motor vehicle enabling the driver to see traffic behind him.

rearward (ˈrɪəwəd) *adj, adv* **1** Also (for adv only): **rearwards.** towards or in the rear. ◆ *n* **2** a position in the rear, esp. the rear division of a military formation. [C14 (*as n:* the part of an army behind the main body of troops): from Anglo-F *rerewarde*, var. of *reregarde;* see REARGUARD]

reason ❶ (ˈriːzᵊn) *n* **1** the faculty of rational argument, deduction, judgment, etc. **2** sound mind; sanity. **3** a cause or motive, as for a belief, action, etc. **4** an argument in favour or a justification for something. **5** *Philosophy.* the intellect regarded as a source of knowledge, as contrasted with experience. **6** *Logic.* a premise of an argument in favour of the given conclusion. **7 by reason of.** because of. **8 in** *or* **within reason.** within moderate or justifiable bounds. **9 it stands to reason.** it is logical or obvious. **10 listen to reason.** to be persuaded peaceably. **11 reasons of State.** political justifications for an immoral act. ◆ *vb* **12** (*when tr, takes a clause as object*) to think logically or draw (logical conclusions) from facts or premises. **13** (*intr; usually foll. by with*) to seek to persuade by reasoning. **14** (*tr; often foll. by out*) to work out or resolve (a problem) by reasoning. [C13: from OF *reisun*, from L *ratiō* reckoning, from *rērī* to think]
▸**ˈreasoner** *n*

> **USAGE NOTE** The expression *the reason is because...* should be avoided. Instead one should say either *this is because...* or *the reason is that...*

reasonable ❶ (ˈriːzənəbᵊl) *adj* **1** showing reason or sound judgment. **2** having the ability to reason. **3** having modest or moderate expectations. **4** moderate in price. **5** fair; average: *reasonable weather.*
▸**ˈreasonably** *adv* ▸**ˈreasonableness** *n*

reasoned ❶ (ˈriːzᵊnd) *adj* well thought-out or well presented: *a reasoned explanation.*

reasoning ❶ (ˈriːzənɪŋ) *n* **1** the act or process of drawing conclusions from facts, evidence, etc. **2** the arguments, proofs, etc., so adduced.

reassure ❶ (ˌriːəˈʃʊə) *vb* **reassures, reassuring, reassured.** (*tr*) **1** to relieve (someone) of anxieties; restore confidence to. **2** to insure again.
▸ˌ**reasˈsurance** *n* ▸ˌ**reasˈsurer** *n* ▸ˌ**reasˈsuringly** *adv*

Réaumur (ˈreɪəˌmjʊə) *adj* indicating measurement on the Réaumur scale.

Réaumur scale *n* a scale of temperature in which the freezing point of water is taken as 0° and the boiling point as 80°. [C18: after René de *Réaumur* (1683–1757), F physicist, who introduced it]

reave (riːv) *vb* **reaves, reaving, reaved** *or* **reft.** *Arch.* **1** to carry off (property, prisoners, etc.) by force. **2** (*tr; foll. by of*) to deprive; strip. See **reive.** [OE *reāfian*]

rebarbative (rɪˈbɑːbətɪv) *adj* fearsome; forbidding. [C19: from F *rébarbatif*, from OF *rebarber* to repel (an enemy)]

rebate[1] ❶ *n* (ˈriːbeɪt). **1** a refund of a fraction of the amount payable; discount. ◆ *vb* (rɪˈbeɪt), **rebates, rebating, rebated.** (*tr*) **2** to deduct (a part) of a payment from (the total). **3** *Arch.* to reduce. [C15: from OF *rabattre* to beat down, hence reduce, from RE- + *abatre* to put down]
▸**reˈbatable** *or* **reˈbateable** *adj* ▸**ˈrebater** *n*

rebate[2] (ˈriːbeɪt, ˈræbɪt) *n, vb* **rebates, rebating, rebated.** another word for **rabbet.**

rebec *or* **rebeck** (ˈriːbɛk) *n* a medieval stringed instrument resembling the violin but having a lute-shaped body. [C16: from OF *rebebe*, from Ar. *rebāb;* ? infl. by OF *bec* beak]

rebel ❶ *vb* (rɪˈbɛl), **rebels, rebelling, rebelled.** (*intr; often foll. by against*) **1** to resist or rise up against a government or authority, esp. by force of arms. **2** to dissent from an accepted moral code or convention of behaviour, etc. **3** to show repugnance (towards). ◆ *n* (ˈrɛbᵊl). **4a** a person who rebels. **4b** (*as modifier*): *a rebel soldier.* **5** a person who dissents from some accepted moral code or convention of behaviour, etc. [C13: from OF *rebelle*, from L *rebellis* insurgent, from RE- + *bellum* war]

rebellion ❶ (rɪˈbɛljən) *n* **1** organized opposition to a government or other authority. **2** dissent from an accepted moral code or convention of behaviour, etc. [C14: via OF from L *rebelliō* revolt (of those conquered); see REBEL]

rebellious ❶ (rɪˈbɛljəs) *adj* **1** showing a tendency towards rebellion. **2** (of a problem, etc.) difficult to overcome; refractory.
▸**reˈbelliously** *adv* ▸**reˈbelliousness** *n*

rebirth ❶ (riːˈbɜːθ) *n* **1** a revival or renaissance: *the rebirth of learning.* **2** a second or new birth.

THESAURUS

reap *vb* **1** = **collect**, bring in, cut, garner, gather, harvest **2** = **get**, acquire, derive, gain, obtain, win

rear[1] *n* **1** = **back**, back end, end, rearguard, stern, tail, tail end ◆ *modifier* **7** = **back**, aft, after (*Nautical*), following, hind, hindmost, last, trailing
Antonyms *n* ≠ **back:** bow, forward end, front, nose, stem, vanguard ◆ *modifier* ≠ **back:** foremost, forward, front, leading

rear[2] *vb* **1** = **bring up**, care for, educate, foster, nurse, nurture, raise, train **2** = **breed**, cultivate, grow **3** = **raise**, elevate, hoist, hold up, lift, set upright **4** = **build**, construct, erect, fabricate, put up **6** = **rise**, loom, soar, tower

reason *n* **1** = **logic**, apprehension, brains, comprehension, intellect, judgment, ratiocination, reasoning, sense, understanding **2** = **sanity**, mentality, mind, rationality, sense, sound mind, soundness **3** = **cause**, aim, basis, design, end, goal, grounds, impetus, incentive, inducement, intention, motive, object, occasion, purpose, target, warrant, why and wherefore (*inf.*) **4** = **justification**, apologia, apology, argument, case, defence, excuse, explanation, exposition, ground, rationale, vindication **8 in** *or* **within reason** = **in moderation**, proper, reasonable, sensible, warrantable, within bounds, within limits ◆ *vb* **12** = **deduce**, conclude, draw conclusions, infer, make out, ratiocinate, resolve, solve, syllogize, think, work out **13** *usually foll. by* **with** = **persuade**, argue with, bring round, debate with, dispute with, dissuade, expostulate with, move, prevail upon, remonstrate with, show (someone) the error of his ways, talk into *or* out of, urge, win over
Antonyms *n* ≠ **logic:** emotion, feeling, instinct, sentiment

reasonable *adj* **1** = **sensible**, advisable, arguable, believable, credible, intelligent, judicious, justifiable, logical, plausible, practical, reasoned, tenable, well-advised, well-thought-out, wise **2** = **sane**, rational, sober, sound **3, 4** = **fair**, acceptable, equitable, fit, just, moderate, proper, right, within reason **5** = **average**, fair, moderate, modest, O.K. *or* okay (*inf.*), tolerable
Antonyms *adj* ≠ **sensible:** impossible, irrational, unintelligent, unreasonable, unsound ≠ **fair:** unfair, unreasonable

reasoned *adj* = **sensible**, clear, judicious, logical, systematic, well-expressed, well-presented, well-thought-out

reasoning *n* **1** = **thinking**, analysis, cogitation, deduction, logic, ratiocination, reason, thought **2** = **case**, argument, exposition, hypothesis, interpretation, proof, train of thought

reassure *vb* **1** = **encourage**, bolster, buoy up, cheer up, comfort, gee up, hearten, inspirit, put *or* set one's mind at rest, relieve (someone) of anxiety, restore confidence to

rebate[1] *n* **1** = **refund**, allowance, bonus, deduction, discount, reduction

rebel *vb* **1** = **revolt**, man the barricades, mutiny, resist, rise up, take to the streets, take up arms **2** = **defy**, come out against, dig one's heels in (*inf.*), disobey, dissent, refuse to obey **3** = **recoil**, flinch, show repugnance, shrink, shy away ◆ *n* **4a** = **revolutionary**, insurgent, insurrectionary, mutineer, resistance fighter, revolutionist, secessionist ◆ *modifier* **4b** = **rebellious**, insubordinate, insurgent, insurrectionary, mutinous, revolutionary ◆ *n* **5** = **nonconformist**, apostate, dissenter, heretic, schismatic

rebellion *n* **1** = **resistance**, insurgence, insurgency, insurrection, mutiny, revolt, revolution, rising, uprising **2** = **nonconformity**, apostasy, defiance, disobedience, dissent, heresy, insubordination, schism

rebellious *adj* **1** = **revolutionary**, disaffected, disloyal, disobedient, disorderly, insubordinate, insurgent, insurrectionary, mutinous, rebel, recalcitrant, seditious, turbulent, ungovernable, unruly **2** = **defiant**, contumacious, difficult, incorrigible, intractable, obstinate, recalcitrant, refractory, resistant, unmanageable
Antonyms *adj* ≠ **revolutionary:** dutiful, loyal, obedient, patriotic, subordinate ≠ **defiant:** dutiful, obedient, subservient

rebirth *n* **1** = **revival**, new beginning, regeneration, reincarnation, renaissance, renascence, renewal, restoration, resurgence, resurrection, revitalization

reboot (riːˈbuːt) *vb* to shut down and then restart (a computer system) or (of a computer system) to shut down and restart.

rebore *n* (ˈriːˌbɔː). **1** the process of boring out the cylinders of a worn reciprocating engine and fitting oversize pistons. ◆ *vb* (riːˈbɔː), **rebores, reboring, rebored. 2** (*tr*) to carry out this process.

rebound ❶ *vb* (rɪˈbaʊnd). (*intr*) **1** to spring back, as from a sudden impact. **2** to misfire, esp. so as to hurt the perpetrator. ◆ *n* (ˈriːbaʊnd). **3** the act or an instance of rebounding. **4 on the rebound. 4a** in the act of springing back. **4b** *Inf.* in a state of recovering from rejection, etc.: *he married her on the rebound from an unhappy love affair.* [C14: from OF *rebondir,* from RE- + *bondir* to BOUND[2]]

rebounder (rɪˈbaʊndə) *n* a type of small trampoline used for aerobic exercising.

rebozo (rɪˈbəʊzəʊ) *n, pl* **rebozos.** a long wool or linen scarf covering the shoulders and head, worn by Latin American women. [C19: from Sp., from *rebozar* to muffle]

rebrand (ˌriːˈbrænd) *vb* (*tr*) to change or update the image of (an organization or product).

rebuff ❶ (rɪˈbʌf) *vb* (*tr*) **1** to snub, reject, or refuse (help, sympathy, etc.). **2** to beat back (an attack); repel. ◆ *n* **3** a blunt refusal or rejection; snub. [C16: from OF *rebuffer,* from It., from *ribuffo* a reprimand, from *ri-* RE- + *buffo* puff, gust, apparently imit.]

rebuke ❶ (rɪˈbjuːk) *vb* **rebukes, rebuking, rebuked. 1** (*tr*) to scold or reprimand (someone). ◆ *n* **2** a reprimand or scolding. [C14: from OF *rebuker,* from RE- + *buchier* to hack down, from *busche* log, of Gmc origin]
►**reˈbukable** *adj* ►**reˈbuker** *n* ►**reˈbukingly** *adv*

rebus (ˈriːbəs) *n, pl* **rebuses. 1** a puzzle consisting of pictures, symbols, etc., representing syllables and words; the word *hear* might be represented by H and a picture of an ear. **2** a heraldic device that is a pictorial representation of the name of the bearer. [C17: from F *rébus,* from L *rēbus* by things, from RES]

rebut ❶ (rɪˈbʌt) *vb* **rebuts, rebutting, rebutted.** (*tr*) to refute or disprove, esp. by offering a contrary contention or argument. [C13: from OF *reboter,* from RE- + *boter* to thrust, BUTT[3]]
►**reˈbuttable** *adj* ►**reˈbuttal** *n*

rebutter (rɪˈbʌtə) *n* **1** *Law.* a defendant's pleading in reply to a plaintiff's surrejoinder. **2** a person who rebuts.

rec. *abbrev. for:* **1** receipt. **2** recipe. **3** record.

recalcitrant ❶ (rɪˈkælsɪtrənt) *adj* **1** not susceptible to control; refractory. ◆ *n* **2** a recalcitrant person. [C19: via F from L, from RE- + *calcitrāre* to kick, from *calx* heel]
►**reˈcalcitrance** *n*

recalescence (ˌriːkəˈlɛsəns) *n* a sudden spontaneous increase in the temperature of cooling iron. [C19: from L *recalēscere* to grow warm again, from RE- + *calēscere,* from *calēre* to be hot]
►ˌ**recalˈesce** *vb* (*intr*) ►ˌ**recaˈlescent** *adj*

recall ❶ (rɪˈkɔːl) *vb* (*tr*) **1** (*may take a clause as object*) to bring back to mind; recollect; remember. **2** to order to return. **3** to revoke or take back. **4** to cause (one's thoughts, attention, etc.) to return from a reverie or digression. ◆ *n* **5** the act of recalling or state of being recalled. **6** revocation or cancellation. **7** the ability to remember things; recollection. **8** *Mil.* (formerly) a signal to call back troops, etc. **9** *US.* the process by which elected officials may be deprived of office by popular vote.
►**reˈcallable** *adj*

recant ❶ (rɪˈkænt) *vb* to repudiate or withdraw (a former belief or statement), esp. formally in public. [C16: from L *recantāre,* from RE- + *cantāre* to sing]
►**recantation** (ˌriːkænˈteɪʃən) *n* ►**reˈcanter** *n*

recap *vb* (ˈriːˌkæp, riːˈkæp), **recaps, recapping, recapped,** *n* (ˈriːˌkæp). *Inf.* short for **recapitulate** *or* **recapitulation.**
►**reˈcappable** *adj*

recapitulate ❶ (ˌriːkəˈpɪtjʊˌleɪt) *vb* **recapitulates, recapitulating, recapitulated. 1** to restate the main points of (an argument, speech, etc.). **2** (*tr*) (of an animal) to repeat (stages of its evolutionary development) during the embryonic stages of its life. [C16: from LL *recapitulāre,* lit.: to put back under headings; see CAPITULATE]
►ˌ**recaˈpitulative** *or* ˌ**recaˈpitulatory** *adj*

recapitulation (ˌriːkəˌpɪtjʊˈleɪʃən) *n* **1** the act of recapitulating, esp. summing up, as at the end of a speech. **2** Also called: **palingenesis.** *Biol.* the apparent repetition in the embryonic development of an animal of the changes that occurred during its evolutionary history. **3** *Music.* the repeating of earlier themes, esp. in the final section of a movement in sonata form.

recapture (riːˈkæptʃə) *vb* **recaptures, recapturing, recaptured.** (*tr*) **1** to capture or take again. **2** to recover, renew, or repeat (a lost or former ability, sensation, etc.). ◆ *n* **3** the act of recapturing or fact of being recaptured.

recce (ˈrɛkɪ) *n, vb* **recces, recceing, recced** *or* **recceed.** a slang word for **reconnaissance** or **reconnoitre.**

recd *or* **rec'd** *abbrev. for* received.

recede ❶ (rɪˈsiːd) *vb* **recedes, receding, receded.** (*intr*) **1** to withdraw from a point or limit; go back: *the tide receded.* **2** to become more distant: *hopes of rescue receded.* **3** to slope backwards: *apes have receding foreheads.* **4a** (of a man's hair) to cease to grow at the temples and above the forehead. **4b** (of a man) to start to go bald in this way. **5** to decline in value. **6** (usually foll. by *from*) to draw back or retreat, as from a promise. [C15: from L *recēdere* to go back, from RE- + *cēdere* to yield]

re-cede (riːˈsiːd) *vb* **re-cedes, re-ceding, re-ceded.** (*tr*) to restore to a former owner.

receipt ❶ (rɪˈsiːt) *n* **1** a written acknowledgment by a receiver of money, goods, etc., that payment or delivery has been made. **2** the act of receiving or fact of being received. **3** (*usually pl*) an amount or article received. **4** *Obs.* another word for **recipe.** ◆ *vb* **5** (*tr*) to acknowledge payment of (a bill), as by marking it. [C14: from OF *receite,* from Med. L *recepta,* from L *recipere* to RECEIVE]

receivable (rɪˈsiːvəbᵊl) *adj* **1** suitable for or capable of being received, esp. as payment or legal tender. **2** (of a bill, etc.) awaiting payment: *accounts receivable.* ◆ *n* **3** (*usually pl*) the part of the assets of a business represented by accounts due for payment.

receive ❶ (rɪˈsiːv) *vb* **receives, receiving, received.** (*mainly tr*) **1** to take (something offered) into one's hand or possession. **2** to have (an honour, blessing, etc.) bestowed. **3** to accept delivery or transmission of (a letter, etc.). **4** to be informed of (news). **5** to hear and consent to or acknowledge (a confession, etc.). **6** (of a container) to take or hold (a substance, commodity, or certain amount). **7** to support or sustain (the weight of something); bear. **8** to apprehend or perceive (ideas, etc.). **9** to experience, undergo, or meet with: *to receive a crack on the skull.* **10** (*also intr*) to be at home to (visitors). **11** to greet or welcome (guests), esp. in formal style. **12** to admit (a person) to a place, society, condition, etc.: *he was received into the priesthood.* **13** to accept or acknowledge (a precept or principle) as true or valid. **14** to convert (incoming radio signals) into sounds, pictures, etc., by means of a receiver. **15** (*also intr*) *Tennis, etc.* to play at the other end from the server. **16** (*also intr*) to partake of (the Christian Eucharist). **17** (*intr*) *Chiefly Brit.* to buy and sell stolen goods. [C13: from OF *receivre,* from L *recipere,* from RE- + *capere* to take]

received (rɪˈsiːvd) *adj* generally accepted or believed: *received wisdom.*

Received Pronunciation *n* the accent of standard Southern British English. Abbrev.: **RP.**

receiver (rɪˈsiːvə) *n* **1** a person who receives something; recipient. **2** a person appointed by a court to manage property pending the outcome of litigation, during the infancy of the owner, or after the owner has been declared bankrupt or insane. **3** *Chiefly Brit.* a person

THESAURUS

rebound *vb* **1 = bounce,** recoil, resound, return, ricochet, spring back **2 = misfire,** backfire, boomerang, recoil ◆ *n* **3 = bounce,** comeback, kickback, repercussion, return, ricochet

rebuff *vb* **1 = reject,** brush off, check, cold-shoulder, cut, decline, deny, discourage, knock back (*sl.*), put off, refuse, repulse, resist, slight, snub, spurn, turn down ◆ *n* **3 = rejection,** brush-off (*sl.*), check, cold shoulder, defeat, denial, discouragement, kick in the teeth (*sl.*), knock-back (*sl.*), opposition, refusal, repulse, slap in the face (*inf.*), slight, snub, thumbs down
Antonyms *vb* ≠ **reject:** encourage, lead on (*inf.*), submit to, welcome ◆ *n* ≠ **rejection:** come-on (*inf.*), encouragement, thumbs up, welcome

rebuke *vb* **1 = scold,** admonish, bawl out (*inf.*), berate, blame, carpet (*inf.*), castigate, censure, chew out (*US & Canad. inf.*), chide, dress down (*inf.*), give a rocket (*Brit. & NZ inf.*), haul (someone) over the coals (*inf.*), lecture, read the riot act, reprehend, reprimand, reproach, reprove, take to task, tear into (*inf.*), tear (someone) off a strip (*inf.*), tell off (*inf.*), tick off (*inf.*), upbraid ◆ *n* **2 = scolding,** admonition, blame, castigation, censure, dressing down (*inf.*), lecture, reprimand, reproach, reproof, reproval, row, telling-off (*inf.*), ticking-off (*inf.*), tongue-lashing
Antonyms *vb* ≠ **scold:** applaud, approve, commend, compliment, congratulate, laud, praise ◆ *n* ≠ **scolding:** commendation, compliment, laudation, praise

rebut *vb* **= disprove,** confute, defeat, invalidate, negate, overturn, prove wrong, quash, refute

rebuttal *n* **= disproof,** confutation, defeat, invalidation, negation, refutation

recalcitrant *adj* **1 = disobedient,** contrary, contumacious, defiant, insubordinate, intractable, obstinate, refractory, stubborn, uncontrollable, ungovernable, unmanageable, unruly, unwilling, wayward, wilful
Antonyms *adj* amenable, compliant, docile, obedient, submissive

recall *vb* **1 = recollect,** bring *or* call to mind, call *or* summon up, evoke, look *or* think back to, mind (*dialect*), remember, reminisce about **3 = annul,** abjure, call back, call in, cancel, countermand, nullify, repeal, rescind, retract, revoke, take back, withdraw ◆ *n* **6 = annulment,** cancellation, nullification, recision, repeal, rescindment, rescission, retraction, revocation, withdrawal **7 = recollection,** memory, remembrance

recant *vb* **= withdraw,** abjure, apostatize, deny, disavow, disclaim, disown, forswear, recall, renege, renounce, repudiate, retract, revoke, take back, unsay
Antonyms *vb* insist, maintain, profess, reaffirm, reiterate, repeat, restate, uphold

recapitulate *vb* **1 = restate,** epitomize, go over again, outline, recap (*inf.*), recount, reiterate, repeat, review, run over, run through again, summarize, sum up

recede *vb* **1 = fall back,** abate, back off, draw back, ebb, go back, regress, retire, retreat, retrocede, retrogress, return, subside, withdraw **5 = lessen,** decline, diminish, dwindle, fade, shrink, sink, wane

receipt *n* **1 = sales slip,** acknowledgment, counterfoil, proof of purchase, stub, voucher **2 = receiving,** acceptance, delivery, reception, recipience **3** *usually plural* **= takings,** gains, gate, income, proceeds, profits, return

receive *vb* **1 = get,** accept, accept delivery of, acquire, be given, be in receipt of, collect, derive, obtain, pick up, take **4 = be informed of,** be told, gather, hear **8 = perceive,** apprehend **9 = experience,** bear, be subjected to, encounter, who receives stolen goods knowing that they have been stolen. **4** the equipment in a telephone, radio, or television that receives incoming electrical signals or modulated radio waves and converts them into the original audio or video signals. **5** the detachable part of a telephone that is held to the ear. **6** *Chem.* a vessel in which the distillate is collected during distillation. **7** *US sport.* a player whose function is to receive the ball.

receivership (rɪ'siːvəʃɪp) *n Law.* **1** the office or function of a receiver. **2** the condition of being administered by a receiver.

receiving order *n Brit.* a court order appointing a receiver to manage the property of a debtor or bankrupt.

recension (rɪ'sɛnʃən) *n* **1** a critical revision of a literary work. **2** a text revised in this way. [C17: from L *recēnsiō*, from *recēnsēre*, from RE- + *cēnsēre* to assess]

recent Ⓣ ('riːsᵊnt) *adj* having appeared, happened, or been made not long ago; modern, fresh, or new. [C16: from L *recens* fresh; rel. to Gk *kainos* new]
▸**'recently** *adv* ▸**'recentness** *or* **'recency** *n*

Recent ('riːsᵊnt) *adj, n Geol.* another word for **Holocene.**

receptacle Ⓣ (rɪ'sɛptəkᵊl) *n* **1** an object that holds something; container. **2** *Bot.* **2a** the enlarged or modified tip of the flower stalk that bears the parts of the flower. **2b** the part of lower plants that bears the reproductive organs or spores. [C15: from L *receptāculum* store-place, from *receptāre*, from *recipere* to RECEIVE]

reception Ⓣ (rɪ'sɛpʃən) *n* **1** the act of receiving or state of being received. **2** the manner in which something, such as a guest or a new idea, is received: *a cold reception.* **3** a formal party for guests, such as after a wedding. **4** an area in an office, hotel, etc., where visitors or guests are received and appointments or reservations dealt with. **5** short for **reception room. 6** the quality or fidelity of a received radio or television broadcast: *the reception was poor.* [C14: from L *receptiō*, from *recipere* to RECEIVE]

reception centre *n* a place to which distressed people, such as vagrants, addicts, victims of a disaster, refugees, etc., go pending more permanent arrangements.

receptionist (rɪ'sɛpʃənɪst) *n* a person employed in an office, surgery, etc., to receive clients or guests, arrange appointments, etc.

reception room *n* **1** a room in a private house suitable for entertaining guests. **2** a room in a hotel suitable for receptions, etc.

receptive Ⓣ (rɪ'sɛptɪv) *adj* **1** able to apprehend quickly. **2** tending to receive new ideas or suggestions favourably. **3** able to hold or receive.
▸**re'ceptively** *adv* ▸**receptivity** (ˌriːsɛp'tɪvɪtɪ) *or* **re'ceptiveness** *n*

receptor (rɪ'sɛptə) *n* **1** *Physiol.* a sensory nerve ending that changes specific stimuli into nerve impulses. **2** any of various devices that receive information, signals, etc.

recess Ⓣ *n* (rɪ'sɛs, 'riːsɛs). **1** a space, such as a niche or alcove, set back or indented. **2** (*often pl*) a secluded or secret place: *recesses of the mind.* **3** a cessation of business, such as the closure of Parliament during a vacation. **4** *Anat.* a small cavity or depression in a bodily organ. **5** *US & Canad.* a break between classes at a school. ◆ *vb* (rɪ'sɛs). **6** (*tr*) to place or set (something) in a recess. **7** (*tr*) to build a recess in (a wall, etc.). [C16: from L *recessus* a retreat, from *recēdere* to RECEDE]

recession[1] Ⓣ (rɪ'sɛʃən) *n* **1** a temporary depression in economic activity or prosperity. **2** the withdrawal of the clergy and choir in procession after a church service. **3** the act of receding. **4** a part of a building, wall, etc., that recedes. [C17: from L *recessio*; see RECESS]

recession[2] (riː'sɛʃən) *n* the act of restoring possession to a former owner. [C19: from RE- + CESSION]

recessional (rɪ'sɛʃənᵊl) *adj* **1** of or relating to recession. ◆ *n* **2** a hymn sung as the clergy and choir withdraw after a church service.

recessive (rɪ'sɛsɪv) *adj* **1** tending to recede or go back. **2** *Genetics.* **2a** (of a gene) capable of producing its characteristic phenotype in the organism only when its allele is identical. **2b** (of a character) controlled by such a gene. Cf. **dominant** (sense 4). **3** *Linguistics.* (of stress) tending to be placed on or near the initial syllable of a polysyllabic word. ◆ *n* **4** *Genetics.* a recessive gene or character.
▸**re'cessively** *adv* ▸**re'cessiveness** *n*

recharge (ˌriː'tʃɑːdʒ) *vb* **recharges, recharging, recharged.** (*tr*) **1** to cause (an accumulator, capacitor, etc.) to take up and store electricity again. **2** to revive or renew (one's energies) (esp. in **recharge one's batteries**).
▸**re'chargeable** *adj*

recherché Ⓣ (rə'ʃɛəʃeɪ) *adj* **1** known only to connoisseurs; choice or rare. **2** studiedly refined or elegant. [C18: from F: p.p. of *rechercher* to make a thorough search for]

recidivism (rɪ'sɪdɪˌvɪzəm) *n* habitual relapse into crime. [C19: from L *recidīvus* falling back, from RE- + *cadere* to fall]
▸**re'cidivist** *n, adj* ▸**reˌcidi'vistic** *or* **re'cidivous** *adj*

recipe Ⓣ ('rɛsɪpɪ) *n* **1** a list of ingredients and directions for making something, esp. when preparing food. **2** *Med.* (formerly) a medical prescription. **3** a method for achieving some desired objective: *a recipe for success.* [C14: from L, lit.: take (it)! from *recipere* to take]

recipient (rɪ'sɪpɪənt) *n* **1** a person who or thing that receives. ◆ *adj* **2** receptive. [C16: via F from L, from *recipere* to RECEIVE]
▸**re'cipience** *or* **re'cipiency** *n*

reciprocal Ⓣ (rɪ'sɪprəkᵊl) *adj* **1** of, relating to, or designating something given by each of two people, countries, etc., to the other; mutual: *reciprocal trade.* **2** given or done in return: *a reciprocal favour.* **3** (of a pronoun) indicating that action is given and received by each subject; for example, *each other* in *they started to shout at each other.* **4** *Maths.* of or relating to a number or quantity divided into one. ◆ *n* **5** something that is reciprocal. **6** Also called: **inverse.** *Maths.* a number or quantity that when multiplied by a given number or quantity gives a product of one: *the reciprocal of 2 is 0.5.* [C16: from L *reciprocus* alternating]
▸**reˌcipro'cality** *n* ▸**re'ciprocally** *adv*

reciprocate Ⓣ (rɪ'sɪprəˌkeɪt) *vb* **reciprocates, reciprocating, reciprocated. 1** to give or feel in return. **2** to move or cause to move backwards and forwards. **3** (*intr*) to be correspondent or equivalent. [C17: from L *reciprocāre*, from *reciprocus* RECIPROCAL]
▸**reˌcipro'cation** *n* ▸**re'ciprocative** *or* **re'ciproˌcatory** *adj* ▸**re'ciproˌcator** *n*

reciprocating engine *n* an engine in which one or more pistons move backwards and forwards inside a cylinder or cylinders.

reciprocity (ˌrɛsɪ'prɒsɪtɪ) *n* **1** reciprocal action or relation. **2** a mutual exchange of commercial or other privileges. [C18: via F from L *reciprocus* RECIPROCAL]

recision (rɪ'sɪʒən) *n* the act of cancelling or rescinding; annulment: *the recision of a treaty.* [C17: from L *recīsiō*, from *recīdere* to cut back]

recital Ⓣ (rɪ'saɪtᵊl) *n* **1** a musical performance by a soloist or soloists. **2** the act of reciting or repeating something learned or prepared. **3** an account, narration, or description. **4** (*often pl*) *Law.* the preliminary statement in a deed showing the reason for its existence and explaining the operative part.
▸**re'citalist** *n*

recitation Ⓣ (ˌrɛsɪ'teɪʃən) *n* **1a** the act of reciting from memory. **1b** a formal reading of verse before an audience. **2** something recited.

recitative[1] (ˌrɛsɪtə'tiːv) *n* a passage in a musical composition, esp. the narrative parts in an oratorio, reflecting the natural rhythms of speech. [C17: from It. *recitativo*; see RECITE]

recitative[2] (rɪ'saɪtətɪv) *adj* of or relating to recital.

recite Ⓣ (rɪ'saɪt) *vb* **recites, reciting, recited. 1** to repeat (a poem, etc.) aloud from memory before an audience. **2** (*tr*) to give a detailed account of. **3** (*tr*) to enumerate (examples, etc.). [C15: from L *recitāre* to cite again, from RE- + *citāre* to summon]
▸**re'citable** *adj* ▸**re'citer** *n*

reck (rɛk) *vb Arch.* (*used mainly with a negative*) **1** to mind or care about (something): *to reck nought.* **2** (*usually impersonal*) to concern or interest (someone). [OE *reccan*]

reckless Ⓣ ('rɛklɪs) *adj* having or showing no regard for danger or consequences; heedless; rash: *a reckless driver.* [OE *recceleās*; see RECK, -LESS]
▸**'recklessly** *adv* ▸**'recklessness** *n*

THESAURUS

go through, meet with, suffer, sustain, undergo **10, 11** = **greet**, accommodate, admit, be at home to, entertain, meet, take in, welcome

recent *adj* = **new**, contemporary, current, fresh, happening (*inf.*), late, latter, latter-day, modern, novel, present-day, up-to-date, young
Antonyms *adj* ancient, antique, earlier, early, former, historical, old

recently *adv* = **newly**, currently, freshly, lately, latterly, not long ago, of late

receptacle *n* **1** = **container**, holder, repository

reception *n* **1** = **receiving**, acceptance, admission, receipt, recipience **2** = **response**, acknowledgment, greeting, reaction, recognition, treatment, welcome **3** = **party**, do (*inf.*), entertainment, function, levee, soirée

receptive *adj* **1** = **perceptive**, alert, bright, quick on the uptake (*inf.*), responsive, sensitive **2** = **open**, accessible, amenable, approachable, favourable, friendly, hospitable, interested, open-minded, open to suggestions, susceptible, sympathetic, welcoming
Antonyms *adj* ≠ **perceptive**: unreceptive, unresponsive ≠ **open**: biased, narrow-minded, prejudiced, unreceptive, unresponsive

recess *n* **1** = **alcove**, bay, cavity, corner, depression, hollow, indentation, niche, nook, oriel **2** *often plural* = **depths**, bowels, heart, innards (*inf.*), innermost parts, reaches, retreats, secret places **3** = **break**, cessation of business, closure, holiday, intermission, interval, respite, rest, vacation

recession[1] *n* **1** = **depression**, decline, downturn, drop, slump
Antonyms *n* boom, upturn

recherché *adj* **1** = **rare**, arcane, choice, esoteric, exotic

recipe *n* **1** = **directions**, ingredients, instructions, receipt (*obs.*) **3** = **method**, formula, modus operandi, prescription, procedure, process, programme, technique

reciprocal *adj* **1, 2** = **mutual**, alternate, complementary, correlative, corresponding, equivalent, exchanged, give-and-take, interchangeable, interdependent, reciprocative, reciprocatory
Antonyms *adj* one-way, unilateral, unreciprocated

reciprocate *vb* **1** = **return**, barter, exchange, feel in return, interchange, reply, requite, respond, return the compliment, swap, trade **3** = **be equivalent**, correspond, equal, match

recital *n* **1** = **performance**, rehearsal, rendering **2** = **recitation**, repetition **3** = **account**, description, detailing, narration, narrative, recapitulation, relation, statement, story, tale, telling

recitation *n* **1** = **recital**, lecture, narration, performance, reading, rendering, telling **2** = **piece**, passage

recite *vb* **1** = **repeat**, declaim, deliver, do one's party piece (*inf.*), narrate, perform, rehearse, speak **2** = **recount**, describe, detail, recapitulate, relate, tell **3** = **enumerate**, itemize

reckless *adj* = **careless**, daredevil, devil-may-care, foolhardy, harebrained, harum-scarum, hasty, headlong, heedless, ill-advised, imprudent, inattentive, incautious, indiscreet, irresponsible, madcap, mindless, negligent, precipitate, rash, regardless, thoughtless, wild

reckon ❶ (ˈrɛkən) *vb* **1** to calculate or ascertain by calculating; compute. **2** (*tr*) to include; count as part of a set or class. **3** (*usually passive*) to consider or regard: *he is reckoned clever.* **4** (when *tr, takes a clause as object*) to think or suppose; be of the opinion: *I reckon you don't know.* **5** (*intr;* foll. by *with*) to settle accounts (with). **6** (*intr;* foll. by *with* or *without*) to take into account or fail to take into account: *they reckoned without John.* **7** (*intr;* foll. by *on* or *upon*) to rely or depend: *I reckon on your support.* **8** (*tr*) *Inf.* to have a high opinion of. **9 to be reckoned with.** of considerable importance or influence. [OE *(ge)recenian* recount]

reckoner (ˈrɛkənə) *n* any of various devices or tables used to facilitate reckoning, esp. a ready reckoner.

reckoning ❶ (ˈrɛkənɪŋ) *n* **1** the act of counting or calculating. **2** settlement of an account or bill. **3** a bill or account. **4** retribution for one's actions (esp. in **day of reckoning**). **5** *Navigation.* short for **dead reckoning.**

reclaim ❶ (rɪˈkleɪm) *vb* (*tr*) **1** to claim back: *reclaim baggage.* **2** to convert (desert, marsh, etc.) into land suitable for growing crops. **3** to recover (useful substances) from waste products. **4** to convert (someone) from sin, folly, vice, etc. ◆ *n* **5** the act of reclaiming or state of being reclaimed. [C13: from OF *réclamer,* from L *reclāmāre* to cry out, from RE- + *clāmāre* to shout]
▸**reˈclaimable** *adj* ▸**reˈclaimant** *or* **reˈclaimer** *n*

reclamation (ˌrɛkləˈmeɪʃən) *n* **1** the conversion of desert, marsh, etc., into land suitable for cultivation. **2** the recovery of useful substances from waste products. **3** the act of reclaiming or state of being reclaimed.

réclame *French.* (reklam) *n* **1** public acclaim or attention; publicity. **2** the capacity for attracting publicity.

reclinate (ˈrɛklɪˌneɪt) *adj Bot.* naturally curved or bent backwards so that the upper part rests on the ground. [C18: from L *reclīnātus* bent back]

recline ❶ (rɪˈklaɪn) *vb* **reclines, reclining, reclined.** to rest in a leaning position. [C15: from OF *recliner,* from L *reclīnāre,* from RE- + *clīnāre* to LEAN[1]]
▸**reˈclinable** *adj* ▸**reclination** (ˌrɛklɪˈneɪʃən) *n*

recliner (rɪˈklaɪnə) *n* a person or thing that reclines, esp. a type of armchair having a back that can be adjusted to slope at various angles.

recluse ❶ (rɪˈkluːs) *n* **1** a person who lives in seclusion, esp. to devote himself to prayer and religious meditation; a hermit. ◆ *adj* **2** solitary; retiring. [C13: from OF *reclus,* from LL *reclūdere* to shut away, from L RE- + *claudere* to close]
▸**reclusion** (rɪˈkluːʒən) *n* ▸**reˈclusive** *adj*

recognition ❶ (ˌrɛkəgˈnɪʃən) *n* **1** the act of recognizing or fact of being recognized. **2** acceptance or acknowledgment of a claim, duty, etc. **3** a token of thanks. **4** formal acknowledgment of a government or of the independence of a country. [C15: from L *recognitiō,* from *recognoscere,* from RE- + *cognoscere* to know]
▸**recognitive** (rɪˈkɒgnɪtɪv) *or* **reˈcognitory** *adj*

recognizance *or* **recognisance** (rɪˈkɒgnɪzəns) *n Law.* **a** a bond entered into before a court or magistrate by which a person binds himself to do a specified act, as to appear in court on a stated day, keep the peace, or pay a debt. **b** a monetary sum pledged to the performance of such an act. [C14: from OF *reconoissance,* from *reconoistre* to RECOGNIZE]
▸**reˈcognizant** *or* **reˈcognisant** *adj*

recognize ❶ *or* **recognise** (ˈrɛkəgˌnaɪz) *vb* **recognizes, recognizing, recognized** *or* **recognises, recognising, recognised.** (*tr*) **1** to perceive (a person or thing) to be the same as or belong to the same class as something previously seen or known; know again. **2** to accept or be aware of (a fact, problem, etc.): *to recognize necessity.* **3** to give formal acknowledgment of the status or legality of (a government, a representative, etc.). **4** *Chiefly US & Canad.* to grant (a person) the right to speak in a deliberative body. **5** to give a token of thanks for (a service rendered, etc.). **6** to make formal acknowledgment of (a claim, etc.). **7** to show approval or appreciation of (something good). **8** to acknowledge or greet (a person). [C15: from L *recognoscere,* from RE- + *cognoscere* to know]
▸**ˈrecogˌnizable** *or* **ˈrecogˌnisable** *adj* ▸**ˌrecogˌnizaˈbility** *or* **ˌrecogˌnisaˈbility** *n* ▸**ˈrecogˌnizably** *or* **ˈrecogˌnisably** *adv* ▸**ˈrecogˌnizer** *or* **ˈrecogˌniser** *n*

recoil ❶ *vb* (rɪˈkɔɪl). (*intr*) **1** to jerk back, as from an impact or violent thrust. **2** (often foll. by *from*) to draw back in fear, horror, or disgust. **3** (foll. by *on* or *upon*) to go wrong, esp. so as to hurt the perpetrator. **4** (of an atom, etc.) to change momentum as a result of the emission of a particle. ◆ *n* (rɪˈkɔɪl, ˈriːkɔɪl). **5a** the backward movement of a gun when fired. **5b** the distance moved. **6** the motion acquired by an atom, etc., as a result of its emission of a particle. **7** the act of recoiling. [C13: from OF *reculer,* from RE- + *cul* rump, from L *cūlus*]
▸**reˈcoiler** *n*

recollect ❶ (ˌrɛkəˈlɛkt) *vb* (when *tr, often takes a clause as object*) to recall from memory; remember. [C16: from L *recolligere,* from RE- + *colligere* to COLLECT]
▸**ˌrecolˈlection** *n* ▸**ˌrecolˈlective** *adj* ▸**ˌrecolˈlectively** *adv*

recombinant (riːˈkɒmbɪnənt) *Genetics.* ◆ *adj* **1** produced by the combining of genetic material from more than one origin. ◆ *n* **2** a chromosome, cell, organism, etc., the genetic makeup of which results from recombination.

recombinant DNA *n* DNA molecules that are extracted from different sources and chemically joined together.

recombination (ˌriːkɒmbɪˈneɪʃən) *n Genetics.* any of several processes by which genetic material of different origins becomes combined.

recommend ❶ (ˌrɛkəˈmɛnd) *vb* (*tr*) **1** (*may take a clause as object or an infinitive*) to advise as the best course or choice; counsel. **2** to praise or commend: *to recommend a new book.* **3** to make attractive or advisable: *the trip has little to recommend it.* **4** *Arch.* to entrust (a person or thing) to someone else's care; commend. [C14: via Med. L from L RE- + *commendāre* to COMMEND]
▸**ˌrecomˈmendable** *adj* ▸**ˌrecomˈmendatory** *adj* ▸**ˌrecomˈmender** *n*

recommendation ❶ (ˌrɛkəmɛnˈdeɪʃən) *n* **1** the act of recommending. **2** something that recommends, esp. a letter. **3** something that is recommended, such as a course of action.

recommit (ˌriːkəˈmɪt) *vb* **recommits, recommitting, recommitted.** (*tr*) **1** to send (a bill) back to a committee for further consideration. **2** to commit again.
▸**ˌrecomˈmitment** *or* **ˌrecomˈmittal** *n*

recompense ❶ (ˈrɛkəmˌpɛns) *vb* **recompenses, recompensing, recompensed.** (*tr*) **1** to pay or reward for service, work, etc. **2** to compensate for loss, injury, etc. ◆ *n* **3** compensation for loss, injury, etc. **4** reward, remuneration, or repayment. [C15: from OF *recompenser,* from L RE- + *compensāre* to balance in weighing]
▸**ˈrecomˌpensable** *adj* ▸**ˈrecomˌpenser** *n*

reconcile ❶ (ˈrɛkənˌsaɪl) *vb* **reconciles, reconciling, reconciled.** (*tr*) **1** (*often passive;* usually foll. by *to*) to make (oneself or another) no longer opposed; cause to acquiesce in something unpleasant: *she reconciled herself to poverty.* **2** to become friendly with (someone) after estrangement or to re-establish friendly relations between (two or

THESAURUS

Antonyms *adj* careful, cautious, heedful, mindful, observant, responsible, thoughtful, wary

reckon *vb* **1 = count**, add up, calculate, compute, enumerate, figure, number, tally, total **3 = consider**, account, appraise, count, deem, esteem, estimate, evaluate, gauge, hold, judge, look upon, rate, regard, think of **4 = think**, assume, believe, be of the opinion, conjecture, expect, fancy, guess (*inf., chiefly US & Canad.*), imagine, suppose, surmise **5** *foll. by* **with = deal**, cope, face, handle, settle accounts, treat **6 = take into account**, anticipate, bargain for, bear in mind, be prepared for, expect, foresee, plan for, take cognizance of **7** *with* **on** *or* **upon = rely on**, bank on, calculate, count on, depend on, hope for, take for granted, trust in **9 to be reckoned with = powerful**, consequential, considerable, important, influential, significant, strong, weighty

reckoning *n* **1 = count**, adding, addition, calculation, computation, counting, estimate, summation, working **3 = bill**, account, charge, due, score **4 = retribution**, doom, judgment, last judgment

reclaim *vb* **1 = regain**, get *or* take back, recover, retrieve **3 = salvage**

recline *vb* **= lean**, be recumbent, lay (something) down, lie (down), loll, lounge, repose, rest, sprawl, stretch out
Antonyms *vb* get up, rise, sit up, stand, stand up, stand upright

recluse *n* **1 = hermit**, anchoress, anchorite, ascetic, eremite, monk, solitary

reclusive *adj* **1, 2 = solitary**, ascetic, cloistered, eremitic, hermitic, hermit-like, isolated, monastic, recluse, retiring, secluded, sequestered, withdrawn
Antonyms *adj* gregarious, sociable

recognition *n* **1 = identification**, detection, discovery, recall, recollection, remembrance **2 = acceptance**, admission, allowance, avowal, awareness, concession, confession, perception, realization, understanding **3 = approval**, acknowledgment, appreciation, gratitude, greeting, honour, respect, salute

recognize *vb* **1 = identify**, know, know again, make out, notice, place, put one's finger on, recall, recollect, remember, spot **2 = acknowledge**, accept, admit, allow, avow, be aware of, concede, confess, grant, own, perceive, realize, see, take on board, understand **7 = approve**, acknowledge, appreciate, honour, respect **8 = greet**, acknowledge, salute
Antonyms *vb* ≠ **acknowledge:** be unaware of, forget, ignore, overlook

recoil *vb* **1 = jerk back**, kick, react, rebound, resile, spring back **2 = draw back**, balk at, falter, flinch, quail, shrink, shy away **3 = backfire**, boomerang, go pear-shaped (*inf.*), go wrong, misfire, rebound ◆ *n* **5a = reaction**, backlash, kick

recollect *vb* **= remember**, call to mind, mind (*dialect*), place, recall, reminisce, summon up

recollection *n* **= memory**, impression, mental image, recall, remembrance, reminiscence

recommend *vb* **1 = advise**, advance, advocate, counsel, enjoin, exhort, prescribe, propose, put forward, suggest, urge **2 = commend**, approve, endorse, praise, put in a good word for, speak well of, vouch for **3 = make attractive**, make acceptable, make appealing, make interesting
Antonyms *vb* ≠ **advise, commend:** argue against, disapprove of, reject, veto

recommendation *n* **1, 3 = advice**, counsel, proposal, suggestion, urging **2 = commendation**, advocacy, approbation, approval, blessing, endorsement, favourable mention, good word, plug (*inf.*), praise, reference, sanction, testimonial

recompense *vb* **1 = reward**, pay, remunerate **2 = compensate**, indemnify, make amends for, make good, make restitution for, make up for, pay for, redress, reimburse, repay, requite, satisfy ◆ *n* **3 = compensation**, amends, damages, emolument, indemnification, indemnity, payment, reparation, repayment, requital, restitution, satisfaction **4 = reward**, meed (*arch.*), pay, payment, remuneration, repayment, return, wages

reconcile *vb* **1 = accept**, accommodate, get used, make the best of, put up with (*inf.*), resign oneself, submit, yield **2 = make peace between**, appease, bring to terms, conciliate, pacify, placate, propitiate, re-establish friendly relations

more people). **3** to settle (a quarrel). **4** to make (two apparently conflicting things) compatible or consistent with each other. **5** to reconsecrate (a desecrated church, etc.). [C14: from L *reconciliāre*, from RE- + *conciliāre* to make friendly, CONCILIATE]
▸**'recon,cilement** *n* ▸**'recon,ciler** *n* ▸**reconciliation** (,rɛkən,sɪlɪ'eɪʃən) *n*
▸**reconciliatory** (,rɛkən'sɪlɪətərɪ, -trɪ) *adj*

recondite ❶ (rɪ'kɒndaɪt, 'rɛkən,daɪt) *adj* **1** requiring special knowledge; abstruse. **2** dealing with abstruse or profound subjects. [C17: from L *reconditus* hidden away, from RE- + *condere* to conceal]
▸**re'conditely** *adv* ▸**re'conditeness** *n*

recondition ❶ (,riːkən'dɪʃən) *vb* (*tr*) to restore to good condition or working order: *to recondition an engine*.
▸**,recon'ditioned** *adj*

reconnaissance ❶ (rɪ'kɒnɪsəns) *n* **1** the act of reconnoitring. **2** the process of obtaining information about the position, etc., of an enemy. **3** a preliminary inspection of an area of land. [C18: from F, from OF *reconoistre* to explore, RECOGNIZE]

reconnoitre ❶ *or US* **reconnoiter** (,rɛkə'nɔɪtə) *vb* **reconnoitres, reconnoitring, reconnoitred** *or US* **reconnoiters, reconnoitering, reconnoitered. 1** to survey or inspect (an enemy's position, region of land, etc.). ◆ *n* **2** the act or process of reconnoitring; a reconnaissance. [C18: from obs. F *reconnoître* to inspect, explore; see RECOGNIZE]
▸**,recon'noitrer** *or US* **,recon'noiterer** *n*

reconsider ❶ (,riːkən'sɪdə) *vb* to consider (something) again, with a view to changing one's policy or course of action.
▸**,recon,sider'ation** *n*

reconstitute (riː'kɒnstɪ,tjuːt) *vb* **reconstitutes, reconstituting, reconstituted.** (*tr*) **1** to restore (food, etc.) to its former or natural state, as by the addition of water to a concentrate. **2** to reconstruct; form again.
▸**reconstituent** (,riːkən'stɪtjuənt) *adj, n* ▸**,reconsti'tution** *n*

reconstruct ❶ (,riːkən'strʌkt) *vb* (*tr*) **1** to construct or form again; rebuild. **2** to form a picture of (a crime, past event, etc.) by piecing together evidence.
▸**,recon'structible** *adj* ▸**,recon'struction** *n* ▸**,recon'structive** *or* **,recon'structional** *adj* ▸**,recon'structor** *n*

reconvert (,riːkən'vɜːt) *vb* (*tr*) **1** to change (something) back to a previous state or form. **2** to bring (someone) back to his former religion.
▸**reconversion** (,riːkən'vɜːʃən) *n*

record ❶ *n* ('rɛkɔːd). **1** an account in permanent form, esp. in writing, preserving knowledge or information. **2** a written account of some transaction that serves as legal evidence of the transaction. **3** a written official report of the proceedings of a court of justice or legislative body. **4** anything serving as evidence or as a memorial: *the First World War is a record of human folly*. **5** (*often pl*) information or data on a specific subject collected methodically over a long period: *weather records*. **6a** the best or most outstanding amount, rate, height, etc., ever attained, as in some field of sport: *a world record*. **6b** (*as modifier*): *a record time*. **7** the sum of one's recognized achievements, career, or performance. **8** a list of crimes of which an accused person has previously been convicted. **9 have a record.** to be a known criminal. **10** Also called: **gramophone record, disc.** a thin disc of a plastic material upon which sound has been recorded. Each side has a spiral groove, which undulates in accordance with the frequency and amplitude of the sound. **11** the markings made by a recording instrument such as a seismograph. **12** *Computing.* a group of data or piece of information preserved as a unit in machine-readable form. **13 for the record.** for the sake of strict factual accuracy. **14 go on record.** to state one's views publicly. **15 off the record.** confidential or confidentially. **16 on record. 16a** stated in a public document. **16b** publicly known. **17 set** *or* **put the record straight.** to correct an error. ◆ *vb* (rɪ'kɔːd). (*mainly tr*) **18** to set down in some permanent form so as to preserve the true facts of: *to record the minutes of a meeting*. **19** to contain or serve to relate (facts, information, etc.). **20** to indicate, show, or register: *his face recorded his disappointment*. **21** to remain as or afford evidence of: *these ruins record the life of the Romans in Britain*. **22** (*also intr*) to make a recording of (music, speech, etc.) for reproduction, esp. on a record player or tape recorder, or for later broadcasting. **23** (*also intr*) (of an instrument) to register or indicate (information) on a scale: *the barometer recorded a low pressure*. [C13: from OF *recorder*, from L *recordārī* to remember, from RE- + *cor* heart]
▸**re'cordable** *adj*

recorded delivery *n* a Post Office service by which an official record of posting and delivery is obtained for a letter or package.

recorder ❶ (rɪ'kɔːdə) *n* **1** a person who records, such as an official or historian. **2** something that records, esp. an apparatus that provides a permanent record of experiments, etc. **3** short for **tape recorder. 4** *Music.* a wind instrument of the flute family, blown through a fipple in the mouth end, having a reedlike quality of tone. **5** (in England) a barrister or solicitor of at least ten years' standing appointed to sit as a part-time judge in the crown court.
▸**re'cordership** *n*

recording ❶ (rɪ'kɔːdɪŋ) *n* **1a** the act or process of making a record, esp. of sound on a gramophone record or magnetic tape. **1b** (*as modifier*): *recording studio*. **2** the record or tape so produced. **3** something that has been recorded, esp. a radio or television programme.

Recording Angel *n* an angel who supposedly keeps a record of every person's good and bad acts.

record of achievement *n Brit.* a statement of the personal and educational development of each pupil.

record player *n* a device for reproducing the sounds stored on a record. A stylus vibrates in accordance with the undulations of the walls of the groove in the record as it rotates.

recount ❶ (rɪ'kaʊnt) *vb* (*tr*) to tell the story or details of; narrate. [C15: from OF *reconter*, from RE- + *conter* to tell; see COUNT[1]]
▸**re'countal** *n*

re-count *vb* (riː'kaʊnt). **1** to count (votes, etc.) again. ◆ *n* ('riː,kaʊnt). **2** a second or further count, esp. of votes in an election.

recoup ❶ (rɪ'kuːp) *vb* **1** to regain or make good (a financial or other loss). **2** (*tr*) to reimburse or compensate (someone), as for a loss. **3** *Law.* to keep back (something due), having rightful claim to do so. ◆ *n* **4** *Rare.* the act of recouping; recoupment. [C15: from OF *recouper* to cut back, from RE- + *couper*, from *coper* to behead]
▸**re'coupable** *adj* ▸**re'coupment** *n*

recourse ❶ (rɪ'kɔːs) *n* **1** the act of resorting to a person, course of action, etc., in difficulty (esp. in **have recourse to**). **2** a person, organization, or course of action that is turned to for help, etc. **3** the right to demand payment, esp. from the drawer or endorser of a bill of exchange or other negotiable instrument when the person accepting it fails to pay. **4 without recourse.** a qualified endorsement on such a negotiable instrument, by which the endorser protects himself from liability to subsequent holders. [C14: from OF *recours*, from LL *recursus* a running back, from RE- + L *currere* to run]

recover ❶ (rɪ'kʌvə) *vb* **1** (*tr*) to find again or obtain the return of (something lost). **2** to regain (loss of money, time, etc.). **3** (of a person) to regain (health, spirits, composure, etc.). **4** to regain (a former and better condition): *industry recovered after the war*. **5** *Law.* **5a** (*tr*) to gain (something) by the judgment of a court of law: *to recover damages*. **5b** (*intr*) to succeed in a lawsuit. **6** (*tr*) to obtain (useful substances) from waste. **7** (*intr*) (in fencing, rowing, etc.) to make a recovery. [C14: from OF *recoverer*, from L *recuperāre* RECUPERATE]
▸**re'coverable** *adj* ▸**re,covera'bility** *n* ▸**re'coverer** *n*

THESAURUS

between, restore harmony between, reunite **3** = **resolve**, adjust, compose, harmonize, patch up, put to rights, rectify, settle, square

reconciliation *n* **1** = **accommodation**, adjustment, compromise, settlement **2** = **pacification**, appeasement, conciliation, détente, propitiation, *rapprochement*, reconcilement, reunion, understanding
Antonyms *n* ≠ **pacification:** alienation, antagonism, break-up, estrangement, falling-out, separation

recondite *adj* **1, 2** = **obscure**, abstruse, arcane, cabbalistic, concealed, dark, deep, difficult, esoteric, hidden, involved, mysterious, mystical, occult, profound, secret
Antonyms *adj* exoteric, simple, straightforward

recondition *vb* = **restore**, do up (*inf.*), fix up (*inf., chiefly US & Canad.*), overhaul, remodel, renew, renovate, repair, revamp

reconnaissance *n* **1-3** = **inspection**, exploration, investigation, observation, patrol, recce (*sl.*), reconnoitring, scan, scouting, scrutiny, survey

reconnoitre *vb* **1** = **inspect**, case (*sl.*), explore, get the lie of the land, investigate, make a reconnaissance (of), observe, patrol, recce (*sl.*), scan, scout, scrutinize, see how the land lies, spy out, survey

reconsider *vb* = **rethink**, change one's mind, have second thoughts, reassess, re-evaluate, reexamine, review, revise, take another look at, think again, think better of, think over, think twice

reconstruct *vb* **1** = **rebuild**, reassemble, recreate, re-establish, reform, regenerate, remake, remodel, renovate, reorganize, restore **2** = **deduce**, build up, build up a picture of, piece together

record *n* **1** = **document**, account, annals, archives, chronicle, diary, entry, file, journal, log, memoir, memorandum, memorial, minute, register, report **2, 3** = **documentation**, evidence **4** = **evidence**, memorial, remembrance, testimony, witness **7** = **background**, career, curriculum vitae, history, performance, track record (*inf.*) **10** = **disc**, album, black disc, EP, forty-five, gramophone record, LP, platter (*US sl.*), recording, release, seventy-eight, single, vinyl, waxing (*inf.*) **15 off the record** = **not for publication**, confidential, confidentially, in confidence, in private, private, sub rosa, under the rose, unofficial, unofficially ◆ *vb* **18** = **set down**, chalk up (*inf.*), chronicle, document, enrol, enter, inscribe, log, minute, note, preserve, put down, put on file, put on record, register, report, take down, transcribe, write down **22** = **make a recording of**, cut, lay down (*sl.*), put on wax (*inf.*), tape, tape-record, video, video-tape, wax (*inf.*) **23** = **register**, contain, give evidence of, indicate, read, say, show

recorder *n* **1** = **chronicler**, annalist, archivist, clerk, diarist, historian, registrar, scorekeeper, scorer, scribe

recording *n* **2** = **record**, cut (*inf.*), disc, gramophone record, tape, video

recount *vb* = **tell**, delineate, depict, describe, detail, enumerate, give an account of, narrate, portray, recite, rehearse, relate, repeat, report, tell the story of

recoup *vb* **1** = **regain**, make good, recover, redeem, retrieve, win back **2** = **compensate**, make redress for, make up for, refund, reimburse, remunerate, repay, requite, satisfy

recourse *n* **2** = **option**, alternative, appeal, choice, expedient, refuge, remedy, resort, resource, way out

recover *vb* **1, 2** = **regain**, find again, get back, make good, recapture, reclaim, recoup, redeem, repair, repossess, restore, retake, retrieve, take back, win back **3** = **get better**, be on the mend, bounce back, come round, convalesce, feel oneself again, get back on one's feet, get well, heal, improve, mend, pick up, pull through, rally, recuperate, regain one's health *or* strength, revive, take a turn for the better, turn the corner
Antonyms *vb* ≠ **regain:** abandon, forfeit, lose ≠ **get**

re-cover (riːˈkʌvə) *vb* (*tr*) **1** to cover again. **2** to provide (furniture, etc.) with a new cover.

recovery ❶ (rɪˈkʌvərɪ) *n, pl* **recoveries. 1** the act or process of recovering, esp. from sickness, a shock, or a setback. **2** restoration to a former or better condition. **3** the regaining of something lost. **4** the extraction of useful substances from waste. **5** the retrieval of a space capsule after a spaceflight. **6** *Law.* the obtaining of a right, etc., by the judgment of a court. **7** *Fencing.* a return to the position of guard after making an attack. **8** *Swimming, rowing, etc.* the action of bringing the arm, an oar, etc., forward for another stroke. **9** *Golf.* a stroke played from the rough or a bunker to the fairway or green.

recovery stock *n Stock Exchange.* a security that has fallen in price but is believed to have the ability to recover.

recreant (ˈrɛkrɪənt) *Arch.* ◆ *adj* **1** cowardly; faint-hearted. **2** disloyal. ◆ *n* **3** a disloyal or cowardly person. [C14: from OF, from *recroire* to surrender, from RE- + L *crēdere* to believe]
▸**ˈrecreance** *or* **ˈrecreancy** *n* ▸**ˈrecreantly** *adv*

recreate (ˈrɛkrɪˌeɪt) *vb* **recreates, recreating, recreated.** *Rare.* to amuse (oneself or someone else). [C15: from L *recreāre* to invigorate, renew, from RE- + *creāre* to CREATE]
▸**ˈrecreative** *adj* ▸**ˈrecreatively** *adv* ▸**ˈrecreˌator** *n*

re-create (ˌriːkrɪˈeɪt) *vb* **re-creates, re-creating, re-created.** to create anew; reproduce.
▸**ˌre-creˈation** *n* ▸**ˌre-creˈator** *n*

recreation ❶ (ˌrɛkrɪˈeɪʃən) *n* **1** refreshment of health or spirits by relaxation and enjoyment. **2** an activity that promotes this. **3a** an interval of free time between school lessons. **3b** (*as modifier*): *recreation period.*

recreational (ˌrɛkrɪˈeɪʃənᵊl) *adj* **1** of, relating to, or used for recreation: *recreational facilities.* **2** (of a drug) taken for pleasure rather than for medical reasons or because of an addiction.

recreational vehicle *n Chiefly US.* a large vanlike vehicle equipped to be lived in. Abbrev.: **RV.**

recriminate ❶ (rɪˈkrɪmɪˌneɪt) *vb* **recriminates, recriminating, recriminated.** (*intr*) to return an accusation against someone or engage in mutual accusations. [C17: via Med. L, from L *crīminārī* to accuse, from *crīmen* accusation]
▸**reˌcrimiˈnation** *n* ▸**reˈcriminative** *or* **reˈcriminatory** *adj* ▸**reˈcrimiˌnator** *n*

recrudesce (ˌriːkruːˈdɛs) *vb* **recrudesces, recrudescing, recrudesced.** (*intr*) (of a disease, trouble, etc.) to break out or appear again after a period of dormancy. [C19: from L *recrūdēscere,* from RE- + *crūdēscere* to grow worse, from *crūdus* bloody, raw]
▸**ˌrecruˈdescence** *n*

recruit ❶ (rɪˈkruːt) *vb* **1a** to enlist (men) for military service. **1b** to raise or strengthen (an army, etc.) by enlistment. **2** (*tr*) to enrol or obtain (members, support, etc.). **3** to furnish or be furnished with a fresh supply; renew. **4** *Arch.* to recover (health, spirits, etc.). ◆ *n* **5** a newly joined member of a military service. **6** any new member or supporter. [C17: from F *recrute* lit.: new growth, from *recroître,* from L, from RE- + *crēscere* to grow]
▸**reˈcruitable** *adj* ▸**reˈcruiter** *n* ▸**reˈcruitment** *n*

recta (ˈrɛktə) *n* a plural of **rectum.**

rectal (ˈrɛktəl) *adj* of or relating to the rectum.
▸**ˈrectally** *adv*

rectangle (ˈrɛkˌtæŋgᵊl) *n* a parallelogram having four right angles. [C16: from Med. L *rectangulum,* from L *rectus* straight + *angulus* angle]

rectangular (rɛkˈtæŋgjʊlə) *adj* **1** shaped like a rectangle. **2** having or relating to right angles. **3** mutually perpendicular: *rectangular coordinates.* **4** having a base or section shaped like a rectangle.
▸**recˌtanguˈlarity** *n* ▸**recˈtangularly** *adv*

rectangular coordinates *pl n* the Cartesian coordinates in a system of mutually perpendicular axes.

rectangular hyperbola *n* a hyperbola with perpendicular asymptotes.

recti (ˈrɛktaɪ) *n* the plural of **rectus.**

recti- *or before a vowel* **rect-** *combining form.* straight or right: *rectangle.* [from L *rectus*]

rectifier (ˈrɛktɪˌfaɪə) *n* **1** an electronic device that converts an alternating current to a direct current. **2** *Chem.* an apparatus for condensing a hot vapour to a liquid in distillation; condenser. **3** a thing or person that rectifies.

rectify ❶ (ˈrɛktɪˌfaɪ) *vb* **rectifies, rectifying, rectified.** (*tr*) **1** to put right; correct; remedy. **2** to separate (a substance) from a mixture or refine (a substance) by fractional distillation. **3** to convert (alternating current) into direct current. **4** *Maths.* to determine the length of (a curve). [C14: via OF from Med. L *rectificāre,* from L *rectus* straight + *facere* to make]
▸**ˈrectiˌfiable** *adj* ▸**ˌrectifiˈcation** *n*

rectilinear (ˌrɛktɪˈlɪnɪə) *or* **rectilineal** *adj* **1** in, moving in, or characterized by a straight line. **2** consisting of, bounded by, or formed by a straight line.
▸**ˌrectiˈlinearly** *or* **ˌrectiˈlineally** *adv*

rectitude ❶ (ˈrɛktɪˌtjuːd) *n* **1** moral or religious correctness. **2** correctness of judgment. [C15: from LL *rectitūdō,* from L *rectus* right, from *regere* to rule]

recto (ˈrɛktəʊ) *n, pl* **rectos. 1** the front of a sheet of printed paper. **2** the right-hand pages of a book. Cf. **verso** (sense 1b). [C19: from L *rectō foliō* on the right-hand page]

rectocele (ˈrɛktəʊˌsiːl) *n Pathol.* a protrusion or herniation of the rectum into the vagina.

rector (ˈrɛktə) *n* **1** *Church of England.* a clergyman in charge of a parish in which, as its incumbent, he would formerly have been entitled to the whole of the tithes. **2** *RC Church.* a cleric in charge of a college, religious house, or congregation. **3** *Protestant Episcopal Church.* a clergyman in charge of a parish. **4** *Chiefly Brit.* the head of certain schools, colleges, or universities. **5** (in Scotland) a high-ranking official in a university. **6** (in South Africa) a principal of an Afrikaans university. [C14: from L: director, ruler, from *regere* to rule]
▸**ˈrectorate** *n* ▸**rectorial** (rɛkˈtɔːrɪəl) *adj* ▸**ˈrectorship** *n*

rectory (ˈrɛktərɪ) *n, pl* **rectories. 1** the official house of a rector. **2** *Church of England.* the office and benefice of a rector.

rectrix (ˈrɛktrɪks) *n, pl* **rectrices** (ˈrɛktrɪˌsiːz, rɛkˈtraɪsiːz). any of the large stiff feathers of a bird's tail, used in controlling the direction of flight. [C17: from LL, fem of L *rector* RECTOR]
▸**rectricial** (rɛkˈtrɪʃəl) *adj*

rectum (ˈrɛktəm) *n, pl* **rectums** *or* **recta.** the lower part of the alimentary canal, between the sigmoid flexure of the colon and the anus. [C16: from NL *rectum intestinum* the straight intestine]

rectus (ˈrɛktəs) *n, pl* **recti.** *Anat.* a straight muscle. [C18: from NL *rectus musculus*]

recumbent ❶ (rɪˈkʌmbənt) *adj* **1** lying down; reclining. **2** (of an organ) leaning or resting against another organ. [C17: from L *recumbere* to lie back, from RE- + *cumbere* to lie]
▸**reˈcumbence** *or* **reˈcumbency** *n* ▸**reˈcumbently** *adv*

recuperate ❶ (rɪˈkuːpəˌreɪt, -ˈkjuː-) *vb* **recuperates, recuperating, recuperated. 1** (*intr*) to recover from illness or exhaustion. **2** to recover (financial losses, etc.). [C16: from L *recuperāre* to recover, from RE- + *capere* to gain]
▸**reˌcuperˈation** *n* ▸**reˈcuperative** *adj*

recur ❶ (rɪˈkɜː) *vb* **recurs, recurring, recurred.** (*intr*) **1** to happen again. **2** (of a thought, etc.) to come back to the mind. **3** (of a problem, etc.) to come up again. **4** *Maths.* (of a digit or group of digits) to be repeated an infinite number of times at the end of a decimal fraction. [C15: from L *recurrere,* from RE- + *currere* to run]
▸**reˈcurring** *adj*

recurrent ❶ (rɪˈkʌrənt) *adj* **1** tending to happen again or repeatedly. **2** *Anat.* (of certain nerves, etc.) turning back, so as to run in the opposite direction.
▸**reˈcurrence** *n* ▸**reˈcurrently** *adv*

recurrent fever *n* another name for **relapsing fever.**

recurring decimal *n* a rational number that contains a pattern of digits repeated indefinitely after the decimal point.

recursion (rɪˈkɜːʃən) *n* **1** the act or process of returning or running back. **2** *Maths, logic.* the application of a function to its own values to generate an infinite sequence of values. [C17: from L *recursio,* from *recurrere* RECUR]
▸**reˈcursive** *adj*

recurve (rɪˈkɜːv) *vb* **recurves, recurving, recurved.** to curve or bend (some-

THESAURUS

better: deteriorate, go downhill, relapse, take a turn for the worse, weaken, worsen

recovery *n* **1 = improvement,** convalescence, healing, mending, rally, recuperation, return to health, revival, turn for the better **2 = revival,** amelioration, betterment, improvement, rally, rehabilitation, restoration, upturn **3 = retrieval,** recapture, reclamation, redemption, repair, repossession, restoration

recreation *n* **1, 2 = pastime,** amusement, beer and skittles (*inf.*), distraction, diversion, enjoyment, entertainment, exercise, fun, hobby, leisure activity, play, pleasure, refreshment, relaxation, relief, sport

recrimination *n* **= bickering,** counterattack, countercharge, mutual accusation, name-calling, quarrel, retaliation, retort, squabbling

recruit *vb* **1 = enlist,** draft, enrol, impress, levy, mobilize, muster, raise **2 = win (over),** engage, enrol, gather, obtain, procure, proselytize, round up, take on ◆ *n* **5 = beginner,** apprentice, convert, greenhorn (*inf.*), helper, initiate, learner, neophyte, novice, proselyte, rookie (*inf.*), trainee, tyro
Antonyms *vb* ≠ **enlist:** dismiss, fire, lay off, make redundant, sack (*inf.*)

rectify *vb* **1 = correct,** adjust, amend, emend, fix, improve, make good, mend, put right, redress, reform, remedy, repair, right, set the record straight, square **2 = separate,** distil, purify, refine

rectitude *n* **1 = morality,** correctness, decency, equity, goodness, honesty, honour, incorruptibility, integrity, justice, principle, probity, righteousness, scrupulousness, uprightness, virtue **2 = correctness,** accuracy, exactness, justice, precision, rightness, soundness, verity
Antonyms *n* ≠ **morality:** baseness, corruption, dishonesty, dishonour, immorality, scandalousness

recumbent *adj* **1 = lying down,** flat, flat on one's back, horizontal, leaning, lying, prone, prostrate, reclining, resting, stretched out, supine

recuperate *vb* **1 = recover,** be on the mend, convalesce, get back on one's feet, get better, improve, mend, pick up, regain one's health, turn the corner

recur *vb* **1, 3 = happen again,** come again, come and go, come back, persist, reappear, repeat, return, revert **2 = return to mind,** be remembered, come back, haunt one's thoughts, run through one's mind

recurrent *adj* **1 = periodic,** continued, cyclical, frequent, habitual, recurring, regular, repeated, repetitive
Antonyms *adj* isolated, one-off

thing) back or down or (of something) to be so curved or bent. [C16: from L *recurvāre*, from RE- + *curvāre* to CURVE]

recusant ('rɛkjuzənt) *n* **1** (in 16th to 18th century England) a Roman Catholic who did not attend the services of the Church of England. **2** any person who refuses to submit to authority. ◆ *adj* **3** (formerly, of Catholics) refusing to attend services of the Church of England. **4** refusing to submit to authority. [C16: from L *recūsāns* refusing, from *recūsāre*, from RE- + *causārī* to dispute, from *causa* a CAUSE]
▸**'recusance** *or* **'recusancy** *n*

recycle ❶ (riː'saɪkəl) *vb* **recycles, recycling, recycled.** (*tr*) **1** to pass (a substance) through a system again for further treatment or use. **2** to reclaim (packaging or products with a limited useful life) for further use: *to recycle water.* ◆ *n* **3** the repetition of a fixed sequence of events.
▸**re'cyclable** *or* **re'cycleable** *adj*

red[1] ❶ (rɛd) *n* **1** any of a group of colours, such as that of a ripe tomato or fresh blood. **2** a pigment or dye of or producing these colours. **3** red cloth or clothing: *dressed in red.* **4** a red ball in snooker, etc. **5** (in roulette) one of two colours on which players may place even bets. **6** *Inf.* red wine: *a bottle of red.* **7 in the red.** *Inf.* in debt. **8 see red.** *Inf.* to become very angry. ◆ *adj* **redder, reddest. 9** of the colour red. **10** reddish in colour or having parts or marks that are reddish: *red deer.* **11** having the face temporarily suffused with blood, being a sign of anger, shame, etc. **12** (of the complexion) rosy; florid. **13** (of the eyes) bloodshot. **14** (of the hands) stained with blood. **15** bloody or violent: *red revolution.* **16** denoting the highest degree of urgency in an emergency; used by the police and the army and informally (esp. in the phrase **red alert**). **17** (of wine) made from black grapes and coloured by their skins. ◆ *vb* **reds, redding, redded. 18** another word for **redden.** [OE *rēad*]
▸**'reddish** *adj* ▸**'redness** *n*

red[2] (rɛd) *vb* **reds, redding, red** *or* **redded.** (*tr*) a variant spelling of **redd.**

Red (rɛd) *Inf.* ◆ *adj* **1** Communist, Socialist, or Soviet. **2** radical, leftist, or revolutionary. ◆ *n* **3** a member or supporter of a Communist or Socialist Party or a national of the Soviet Union. **4** a radical, leftist, or revolutionary. [C19: from the colour chosen to symbolize revolutionary socialism]

redact (rɪ'dækt) *vb* (*tr*) **1** to compose or draft (an edict, proclamation, etc.). **2** to put (a literary work, etc.) into appropriate form for publication; edit. [C15: from L *redigere* to bring back, from *red*- RE- + *agere* to drive]
▸**re'daction** *n* ▸**re'dactional** *adj* ▸**re'dactor** *n*

red admiral *n* a butterfly of temperate Europe and Asia, having black wings with red and white markings. See also **white admiral.**

red algae *pl n* the numerous algae which contain a red pigment in addition to chlorophyll. The group includes carrageen and dulse.

redback ('rɛd,bæk) *n Austral.* a small, venomous spider, the female of which has a red stripe on its back. Also called: **redback spider.**

red bark *n* a kind of cinchona containing a high proportion of alkaloids.

red biddy *n Inf.* cheap red wine fortified with methylated spirits.

red blood cell *n* another name for **erythrocyte.**

red-blooded ❶ *adj Inf.* vigorous; virile.
▸**,red-'bloodedness** *n*

red book *n Brit.* (sometimes caps.) a government publication bound in red, esp. the Treasury's annual forecast of revenue, expenditure, growth, and inflation.

redbreast ('rɛd,brɛst) *n* any of various birds having a red breast, esp. the Old World robin.

redbrick ('rɛd,brɪk) *n* (*modifier*) denoting, relating to, or characteristic of a provincial British university of relatively recent foundation.

redcap ('rɛd,kæp) *n* **1** *Brit. inf.* a military policeman. **2** *US & Canad.* a porter at an airport or station.

red card *Soccer, etc.* ◆ *n* **1** a card of a red colour displayed by a referee to indicate that a player has been sent off. ◆ *vb* **red-card. 2** (*tr*) to send off (a player).

red carpet *n* **1** a strip of red carpeting laid for important dignitaries to walk on. **2a** deferential treatment accorded to a person of importance. **2b** (*as modifier*): *a red-carpet reception.*

red cedar *n* **1** any of several North American coniferous trees, esp. a juniper that has fragrant reddish wood. **2** the wood of any of these trees. **3** any of several Australian timber trees.

red cent *n* (*used with a negative*) *Inf., chiefly US.* a cent considered as a trivial amount of money (esp. in **not have a red cent,** etc.).

redcoat ('rɛd,kəut) *n* **1** (formerly) a British soldier. **2** *Canad. inf.* another name for **Mountie.**

red coral *n* any of several corals, the skeletons of which are pinkish red in colour and used to make ornaments, etc.

red corpuscle *n* another name for **erythrocyte.**

Red Crescent *n* the emblem of the Red Cross Society in a Muslim country.

Red Cross *n* **1** an international humanitarian organization (**Red Cross Society**) formally established by the Geneva Convention of 1864. **2** the emblem of this organization, consisting of a red cross on a white background.

redcurrant (,rɛd'kʌrənt) *n* **1** a N temperate shrub having greenish flowers and small edible rounded red berries. **2a** the fruit of this shrub. **2b** (*as modifier*): *redcurrant jelly.*

redd *or* **red** (rɛd) *Scot. & N English dialect.* ◆ *vb* **redds, redding, redd** *or* **redded. 1** (*tr*; often foll. by *up*) to bring order to; tidy (up). ◆ *n* **2** the act or an instance of redding. [C15: *redden* to clear, ? a variant of RID]
▸**'redder** *n*

red deer *n* a large deer formerly widely distributed in the woodlands of Europe and Asia. The coat is reddish brown in summer and the short tail is surrounded by a patch of light-coloured hair.

redden ❶ ('rɛdən) *vb* **1** to make or become red. **2** (*intr*) to flush with embarrassment, anger, etc.

reddle ('rɛdəl) *n, vb* **reddles, reddling, reddled.** a variant spelling of **ruddle.**

red duster *n Brit.* an informal name for the **Red Ensign.**

red dwarf *n* one of a class of stars of relatively small mass and low luminosity.

rede (riːd) *Arch.* ◆ *n* **1** advice or counsel. **2** an explanation. ◆ *vb* **redes, reding, reded.** (*tr*) **3** to advise; counsel. **4** to explain. [OE *rǣdan* to rule]

red earth *n* a clayey zonal soil of tropical savanna lands, formed by extensive chemical weathering and coloured by iron compounds.

redeem ❶ (rɪ'diːm) *vb* (*tr*) **1** to recover possession or ownership of by payment of a price or service; regain. **2** to convert (bonds, shares, etc.) into cash. **3** to pay off (a loan, etc.). **4** to recover (something pledged, mortgaged, or pawned). **5** to convert (paper money) into bullion or specie. **6** to fulfil (a promise, pledge, etc.). **7** to exchange (coupons, etc.) for goods. **8** to reinstate in someone's estimation or good opinion: *he redeemed himself by his altruistic action.* **9** to make amends for. **10** to recover from captivity, esp. by a money payment. **11** *Christianity.* (of Christ as Saviour) to free (humanity) from sin by death on the Cross. [C15: from OF *redimer*, from L *redimere*, from *red*- RE- + *emere* to buy]
▸**re'deemable** *or* **re'demptible** *adj* ▸**re'deemer** *n*

Redeemer (rɪ'diːmə) *n* **the.** Jesus Christ as having brought redemption to mankind.

redeeming (rɪ'diːmɪŋ) *adj* serving to compensate for faults or deficiencies.

redemption ❶ (rɪ'dɛmpʃən) *n* **1** the act or process of redeeming. **2** the state of being redeemed. **3** *Christianity.* **3a** deliverance from sin through the incarnation, sufferings, and death of Christ. **3b** atonement for guilt. [C14: via OF from L *redemptiō* a buying back; see REDEEM]
▸**re'demptional, re'demptive,** *or* **re'demptory** *adj* ▸**re'demptively** *adv*

redemption yield *n Stock Exchange.* the yield produced by a redeemable gilt-edged security taking into account the annual interest it pays and an annualized amount to account for any profit or loss when it is redeemed.

Red Ensign *n* the ensign of the British Merchant Navy, having the Union Jack on a red background at the upper corner of the vertical edge alongside the hoist. It was also the national flag of Canada until 1965.

redeploy (,riːdɪ'plɔɪ) *vb* to assign new positions or tasks to (labour, troops, etc.).
▸**,rede'ployment** *n*

redevelopment area (,riːdɪ'vɛləpmənt) *n* an urban area in which all or most of the buildings are demolished and rebuilt.

redeye ('rɛd,aɪ) *n* **1** *US sl.* inferior whisky. **2** *Sl., chiefly US.* a flight that departs late at night and arrives early next morning. **3** another name for **rudd.**

red-faced *adj* **1** flushed with embarrassment or anger. **2** having a florid complexion.
▸**red-facedly** (,rɛd'feɪsɪdlɪ, -'feɪstlɪ) *adv*

redfin ('rɛd,fɪn) *n* any of various small cyprinid fishes with reddish fins.

THESAURUS

recycle *vb* **1** = **reprocess**, reuse **2** = **reclaim**, reuse, salvage, save

red[1] *n, adj* **1, 9** = **crimson**, cardinal, carmine, cherry, claret, coral, gules (*Heraldry*), maroon, pink, rose, ruby, scarlet, vermeil, vermilion, wine ◆ *n* **7 in the red** *Informal* = **in debt**, bankrupt, in arrears, in debit, in deficit, insolvent, on the rocks, overdrawn, owing money, showing a loss **8 see red** *Informal* = **lose one's temper**, be beside oneself with rage (*inf.*), become enraged, blow a fuse, blow one's top, boil, crack up (*inf.*), fly off the handle (*inf.*), go ballistic (*sl., chiefly US*), go mad (*inf.*), go off one's head (*sl.*), go off the deep end (*inf.*), go up the wall (*sl.*), lose it (*inf.*), lose one's rag (*sl.*), lose the plot (*inf.*), seethe ◆ *adj* **10** = **chestnut**, bay, carroty, flame-coloured, flaming, foxy, reddish, sandy, titian **11** = **flushed**, blushing, embarrassed, florid, rubicund, shamefaced, suffused **12** = **rosy**, blooming, glowing, healthy, roseate, ruddy **13** = **bloodshot**, inflamed, red-rimmed **14** = **bloody**, bloodstained, ensanguined (*literary*), gory, sanguine

red-blooded *adj Informal* = **vigorous**, hearty, lusty, manly, robust, strong, virile, vital

redden *vb* **2** = **flush**, blush, colour (up), crimson, go red, suffuse

redeem *vb* **1** = **buy back**, reclaim, recover, recover possession of, regain, repossess, repurchase, retrieve, win back **2, 7** = **trade in**, cash (in), change, exchange **6** = **fulfil**, abide by, acquit, adhere to, be faithful to, carry out, discharge, hold to, keep, keep faith with, make good, meet, perform, satisfy **8** = **reinstate**, absolve, rehabilitate, restore to favour **9** = **make up for**, atone for, compensate for, defray, make amends for, make good, offset, outweigh, redress, save **10** = **save**, buy the freedom of, deliver, emancipate, extricate, free, liberate, pay the ransom of, ransom, rescue, set free

redemption *n* **1** = **recovery**, reclamation, repossession, repurchase, retrieval **2** = **salvation**, deliverance, emancipation, liberation, ransom, release, rescue **3b** = **compensation**, amends, atonement, expiation, reparation

redfish ('rɛd,fɪʃ) *n, pl* **redfish** *or* **redfishes. 1** a male salmon that has recently spawned. Cf. **blackfish** (sense 2). **2** *Canad.* another name for **kokanee.**

red flag *n* **1** a symbol of socialism, communism, or revolution. **2** a warning of danger or a signal to stop.

red fox *n* the common European fox which has a reddish-brown coat.

red giant *n* a giant star that emits red light.

red grouse *n* a reddish-brown grouse of upland moors of Great Britain.

Red Guard *n* a member of a Communist Chinese youth movement that attempted to effect the Cultural Revolution (1966–69).

red-handed ❶ *adj (postpositive)* in the act of committing a crime or doing something wrong or shameful (esp. in **catch red-handed**). [C19 (earlier, C15 *red hand*)]
▸,**red-'handedly** *adv* ▸,**red-'handedness** *n*

red hat *n* the broad-brimmed crimson hat given to cardinals as the symbol of their rank.

redhead ('rɛd,hɛd) *n* a person with red hair.
▸**'red,headed** *adj*

red heat *n* **1** the temperature at which a substance is red-hot. **2** the state or condition of being red-hot.

red herring *n* **1** anything that diverts attention from a topic or line of inquiry. **2** a herring cured by salting and smoking.

red-hot *adj* **1** (esp. of metal) heated to the temperature at which it glows red. **2** extremely hot. **3** keen, excited, or eager. **4** furious; violent: *red-hot anger.* **5** very recent or topical: *red-hot information.* **6** *Austral. sl.* extreme, unreasonable, or unfair.

red-hot poker *n* a liliaceous plant: widely cultivated for its showy spikes of red or yellow flowers.

Red Indian *n, adj* another name, now considered offensive, for **American Indian.** [see REDSKIN]

redingote ('rɛdɪŋ,gəʊt) *n* **1** a man's full-skirted outer coat of the 18th and 19th centuries. **2** a woman's coat of the 18th century, with an open-fronted skirt, revealing a decorative underskirt. **3** a woman's coat with a close-fitting top and a full skirt. [C19: from F, from E *riding coat*]

redintegrate (rɛ'dɪntɪ,greɪt) *vb* **redintegrates, redintegrating, redintegrated.** (*tr*) to make whole or complete again; restore to a perfect state; renew. [C15: from L *redintegrāre* to renew, from *red-* RE- + *integer* complete]
▸**re,dinte'gration** *n* ▸**red'integrative** *adj*

redistribution (,riːdɪstrɪ'bjuːʃən) *n* **1** the act or an instance of distributing again. **2** a revision of the number of seats in the Canadian House of Commons allocated to each province, made every ten years on the basis of a new census.

redivivus (,rɛdɪ'vaɪvəs) *adj Rare.* returned to life; revived. [C17: from LL, from L *red-* RE- + *vīvus* alive]

red lead (lɛd) *n* a bright-red poisonous insoluble oxide of lead.

red-letter day *n* a memorably important or happy occasion. [C18: from the red letters used in ecclesiastical calendars to indicate saints' days and feasts]

red light *n* **1** a signal to stop, esp. a red traffic signal. **2** a danger signal. **3a** a red lamp indicating that a house is a brothel. **3b** (*as modifier*): *a red-light district.*

redline ('rɛd,laɪn) *vb* **redlines, redlining, redlined.** (*tr*) (esp. of a bank or group of banks) to refuse to consider giving a loan to (a person or country) because of the presumed risks involved.

red meat *n* any meat that is dark in colour, esp. beef and lamb. Cf. **white meat.**

red mullet *n* a food fish of European waters with a pair of long barbels beneath the chin and a reddish coloration. US name: **goatfish.**

redneck ('rɛd,nɛk) *n Disparaging.* **1** (in the southwestern US) a poor uneducated White farm worker. **2** a person or institution that is extremely reactionary. ◆ *adj* **3** reactionary and bigoted: *redneck laws.*

redo (riː'duː) *vb* **redoes, redoing, redid, redone.** (*tr*) **1** to do over again. **2** *Inf.* to redecorate, esp. thoroughly: *we redid the house last summer.*

red ochre *n* any of various natural red earths containing ferric oxide: used as pigments.

redolent ❶ ('rɛdəʊlənt) *adj* **1** having a pleasant smell; fragrant. **2** (*postpositive;* foll. by *of* or *with*) having the odour or smell (of): *a room redolent of flowers.* **3** (*postpositive;* foll. by *of* or *with*) reminiscent or suggestive (of): *a picture redolent of the 18th century.* [C14: from L *redolens* smelling (of), from *redolēre* to give off an odour, from *red-* RE- + *olēre* to smell]
▸**'redolence** *or* **'redolency** *n* ▸**'redolently** *adv*

redouble (rɪ'dʌbᵊl) *vb* **redoubles, redoubling, redoubled. 1** to make or become much greater in intensity, number, etc.: *to redouble one's efforts.* **2** to send back (sounds) or (of sounds) to be sent back. **3** *Bridge.* to double (an opponent's double). ◆ *n* **4** the act of redoubling.

redoubt (rɪ'daʊt) *n* **1** an outwork or fieldwork defending a hilltop, pass, etc. **2** a temporary defence work built inside a fortification as a last defensive position. [C17: via F from obs. It. *ridotta,* from Med. L *reductus* shelter, from L *redūcere,* from RE- + *dūcere* to lead]

redoubtable ❶ (rɪ'daʊtəbᵊl) *adj* **1** to be feared; formidable. **2** worthy of respect. [C14: from OF, from *redouter* to dread, from RE- + *douter* to be afraid, DOUBT]
▸**re'doubtableness** *n* ▸**re'doubtably** *adv*

redound ❶ (rɪ'daʊnd) *vb* **1** (*intr;* foll. by *to*) to have an advantageous or disadvantageous effect (on): *brave deeds redound to your credit.* **2** (*intr;* foll. by *on* or *upon*) to recoil or rebound. **3** (*tr*) *Arch.* to reflect; bring: *his actions redound dishonour upon him.* [C14: from OF *redonder,* from L *redundāre* to stream over, from *red-* RE- + *undāre* to rise in waves]

redox ('riːdɒks) *n* (*modifier*) another term for **oxidation-reduction.** [C20: from RED(UCTION) + OX(IDATION)]

red pepper *n* **1** any of several varieties of the pepper plant cultivated for their hot pungent red podlike fruits. **2** the fruit of any of these plants. **3** the ripe red fruit of the sweet pepper. **4** another name for **cayenne pepper.**

Red Planet *n* **the.** an informal name for **Mars**[2].

redpoll ('rɛd,pɒl) *n* either of two widely distributed types of finches, having a greyish-brown plumage with a red crown and pink breast.

red rag *n* a provocation; something that infuriates. [so called because red objects supposedly infuriate bulls]

redress ❶ (rɪ'drɛs) *vb* (*tr*) **1** to put right (a wrong), esp. by compensation; make reparation for. **2** to correct or adjust (esp. in **redress the balance**). **3** to make compensation to (a person) for a wrong. ◆ *n* **4** the act or an instance of setting right a wrong; remedy or cure. **5** compensation, amends, or reparation for a wrong, injury, etc. [C14: from OF *redrecier* to set up again, from RE- + *drecier* to straighten; see DRESS]
▸**re'dressable** *or* **re'dressible** *adj* ▸**re'dresser** *or* **re'dressor** *n*

re-dress (riː'drɛs) *vb* (*tr*) to dress (something) again.

Red River cart *n Canad. history.* a strongly-built, two-wheeled, ox- or horse-drawn cart used in W Canada.

red rose *n English history.* the emblem of the House of Lancaster.

red salmon *n* any salmon having reddish flesh, esp. the sockeye salmon.

redshank ('rɛd,ʃæŋk) *n* any of various large common European sandpipers, esp. the **spotted redshank,** having red legs.

red shift *n* a shift in the lines of the spectrum of an astronomical object towards a longer wavelength (the red end of an optical spectrum), relative to the wavelength of these lines in the terrestrial spectrum, usually as a result of the Doppler effect caused by the recession of the object.

redskin ('rɛd,skɪn) *n* an informal name, now considered offensive, for an **American Indian.** [so called because one now extinct tribe painted themselves with red ochre]

red snapper *n* any of various marine percoid food fishes of the snapper family, having a reddish coloration, common in American coastal regions of the Atlantic.

red spider *n* short for **red spider mite** (see **spider mite**).

red squirrel *n* a reddish-brown squirrel, inhabiting woodlands of Europe and parts of Asia.

redstart ('rɛd,stɑːt) *n* **1** a European songbird of the thrush family: the male has a black throat, orange-brown tail and breast, and grey back. **2** a North American warbler. [OE *rēad* red + *steort* tail]

red tape *n* obstructive official routine or procedure; time-consuming bureaucracy. [C18: from the red tape used to bind official government documents]

reduce ❶ (rɪ'djuːs) *vb* **reduces, reducing, reduced.** (*mainly tr*) **1** (*also intr*) to make or become smaller in size, number, etc. **2** to bring into a certain state, condition, etc.: *to reduce a forest to ashes; he was reduced to tears.* **3** (*also intr*) to make or become slimmer; lose or cause to lose excess weight. **4** to impoverish (esp. in **in reduced circumstances**). **5** to bring into a state of submission to one's authority; subjugate: *the whole country was reduced after three months.* **6** to bring down the price of (a commodity). **7** to lower the rank or status of; demote: *reduced to the ranks.* **8** to set out systematically as an aid to understanding; simplify: *his theories have been reduced in a treatise.* **9** *Maths.* to modify or simplify the form of (an expression or equation), esp. by substitution of one term by another. **10** *Cookery.* to make (a sauce, stock, etc.) more con-

THESAURUS

red-handed *adj* = **in the act**, bang to rights (*sl.*), (in) flagrante delicto, with one's fingers *or* hand in the till (*inf.*), with one's pants down (*US sl.*)

redolent *adj* **1** = **scented**, aromatic, fragrant, odorous, perfumed, sweet-smelling **2** = **reminiscent**, evocative, remindful, suggestive

redoubtable *adj* **1** = **formidable**, awful, doughty, dreadful, fearful, fearsome, mighty, powerful, resolute, strong, terrible, valiant

redound *vb* **1** *foll. by* **to** = **contribute to**, conduce, effect, lead to, militate for, tend towards **2** *foll. by* **on** *or* **upon** = **rebound**, accrue, come back, ensue, recoil, reflect, result

redress *vb* **1** = **make amends for**, compensate for, make reparation for, make restitution for, make up for, pay for, put right, recompense for **2** = **put right**, adjust, amend, balance, correct, ease, even up, mend, rectify, reform, regulate, relieve, remedy, repair, restore the balance, square ◆ *n* **4** = **rectification**, aid, assistance, correction, cure, ease, help, justice, relief, remedy, satisfaction **5** = **amends**, atonement, compensation, payment, quittance, recompense, reparation, requital, restitution

reduce *vb* **1** = **lessen**, abate, abridge, contract, curtail, cut, cut down, debase, decrease, depress, dilute, diminish, downsize, impair, lower, moderate, shorten, slow down, tone down, truncate, turn down, weaken, wind down **3** = **slim**, be *or* go on a diet, diet, lose weight, shed weight, slenderize (*chiefly US*), trim **4** = **impoverish**, bankrupt, break, pauperize, ruin **5** = **drive**, bring, bring to the point of, conquer, force, master, overpower, subdue, vanquish **6** = **cheapen**, bring down the price of, cut, discount, lower, mark down, slash **7** = **degrade**, break, bring low, demote, downgrade,

centrated by boiling away some of the water in it. **11** to thin out (paint) by adding oil, turpentine, etc. **12** (*also intr*) *Chem.* **12a** to undergo or cause to undergo a chemical reaction with hydrogen. **12b** to lose or cause to lose oxygen atoms. **12c** to undergo or cause to undergo an increase in the number of electrons. **13** *Photog.* to lessen the density of (a negative or print). **14** *Surgery.* to manipulate or reposition (a broken or displaced bone, organ, or part) back to its normal site. [C14: from L *redūcere* to bring back, from RE- + *dūcere* to lead]
▸**re'ducible** *adj* ▸**re,duci'bility** *n* ▸**re'ducibly** *adv*

reducer (rɪ'dju:sə) *n* **1** *Photog.* a chemical solution used to lessen the density of a negative or print by oxidizing some of the blackened silver to soluble silver compounds. **2** a pipe fitting connecting two pipes of different diameters. **3** a person or thing that reduces.

reducing agent *n Chem.* a substance that reduces another substance in a chemical reaction, being itself oxidized in the process.

reducing glass *n* a lens or curved mirror that produces an image smaller than the object observed.

reductase (rɪ'dʌkteɪz) *n* any enzyme that catalyses a biochemical reduction reaction. [C20: from REDUCTION + -ASE]

reductio ad absurdum (rɪ'dʌktɪəʊ æd æb'sɜ:dəm) *n* **1** a method of disproving a proposition by showing that its inevitable consequences would be absurd. **2** a method of indirectly proving a proposition by assuming its negation to be true and showing that this leads to an absurdity. **3** application of a principle or proposed principle to an instance in which it is absurd. [L, lit.: reduction to the absurd]

reduction (rɪ'dʌkʃən) *n* **1** the act or process or an instance of reducing. **2** the state or condition of being reduced. **3** the amount by which something is reduced. **4** a form of an original resulting from a reducing process, such as a copy on a smaller scale. **5** *Maths.* **5a** the process of converting a fraction into its decimal form. **5b** the process of dividing out the common factors in the numerator and denominator of a fraction.
▸**re'ductive** *adj*

reduction formula *n Maths.* a formula expressing the values of a trigonometric function of any angle greater than 90° in terms of a function of an acute angle.

reductionism (rɪ'dʌkʃə,nɪzəm) *n* **1** the analysis of complex things, data, etc., into less complex constituents. **2** *Often disparaging.* any theory or method that holds that a complex idea, system, etc., can be completely understood in terms of its simpler parts or components.
▸**re'ductionist** *n, adj* ▸**re,duction'istic** *adj*

redundancy ❶ (rɪ'dʌndənsɪ) *n, pl* **redundancies. 1a** the state or condition of being redundant or superfluous, esp. superfluous in one's job. **1b** (*as modifier*): *a redundancy payment.* **2** excessive proliferation or profusion, esp. of superfluity.

redundant ❶ (rɪ'dʌndənt) *adj* **1** surplus to requirements; unnecessary or superfluous. **2** verbose or tautological. **3** deprived of one's job because it is no longer necessary. [C17: from L *redundans* overflowing, from *redundāre* to stream over; see REDOUND]
▸**re'dundantly** *adv*

red underwing *n* a large noctuid moth having hind wings coloured red and black.

reduplicate *vb* (rɪ'dju:plɪ,keɪt), **reduplicates, reduplicating, reduplicated. 1** to make or become double; repeat. **2** to repeat (a sound or syllable) in a word or (of a sound or syllable) to be repeated. ◆ *adj* (rɪ'dju:plɪkɪt). **3** doubled or repeated. **4** (of petals or sepals) having the margins curving outwards.
▸**re,dupli'cation** *n* ▸**re'duplicative** *adj*

red-water *n* a disease of cattle which destroys the red blood cells, characterized by the passage of red or blackish urine.

redwing ('rɛd,wɪŋ) *n* a small European thrush having a speckled breast, reddish flanks, and brown back.

redwood ('rɛd,wʊd) *n* a giant coniferous tree of coastal regions of California, having reddish fibrous bark and durable timber.

reebok ('ri:bʌk, -bɒk) *n, pl* **reeboks** *or* **reebok.** a variant spelling of **rhebuck** *or* **rhebok.**

re-echo (ri:'ɛkəʊ) *vb* **re-echoes, re-echoing, re-echoed. 1** to echo (a sound that is already an echo); resound. **2** (*tr*) to repeat like an echo.

reed (ri:d) *n* **1** any of various widely distributed tall grasses that grow in swamps and shallow water and have jointed hollow stalks. **2** the stalk, or stalks collectively, of any of these plants, esp. as used for thatching. **3** *Music.* **3a** a thin piece of cane or metal inserted into the tubes of certain wind instruments, which sets in vibration the air column inside the tube. **3b** a wind instrument or organ pipe that sounds by means of a reed. **4** one of the several vertical parallel wires on a loom that may be moved upwards to separate the warp threads. **5** a small semicircular architectural moulding. **6** an archaic word for **arrow. 7 broken reed.** a weak, unreliable, or ineffectual person. ◆ *vb* (*tr*) **8** to fashion into or supply with reeds or reeding. **9** to thatch using reeds. [OE *hreod*]

reedbuck ('ri:d,bʌk) *n, pl* **reedbucks** *or* **reedbuck.** an antelope of Africa south of the Sahara, having a buff-coloured coat and inward-curving horns.

reed bunting *n* a common European bunting that has a brown streaked plumage with, in the male, a black head.

reed grass *n* a tall perennial grass of rivers and ponds of Europe, Asia, and Canada.

reeding ('ri:dɪŋ) *n* **1** a set of small semicircular architectural mouldings. **2** the milling on the edges of a coin.

reedling ('ri:dlɪŋ) *n* a titlike Eurasian songbird, common in reed beds, which belongs to the family of Old World flycatchers and has a tawny back and tail and, in the male, a grey-and-black head. Also called: **bearded tit.**

reed mace *n* a tall reedlike marsh plant, with straplike leaves and flowers in long brown spikes. Also called: (popularly) **bulrush, cat's-tail.**

reed organ *n* **1** a wind instrument, such as the harmonium, accordion, or harmonica, in which the sound is produced by reeds, each reed producing one note only. **2** a type of pipe organ in which all the pipes are fitted with reeds.

reed pipe *n* an organ pipe sounded by a vibrating reed.

reed stop *n* an organ stop controlling a rank of reed pipes.

reed warbler *n* any of various common Old World warblers that inhabit marshy regions and have a brown plumage.

reedy ('ri:dɪ) *adj* **reedier, reediest. 1** (of a place) abounding in reeds. **2** of or like a reed. **3** having a tone like a reed instrument; shrill or piping.
▸**'reedily** *adv* ▸**'reediness** *n*

reef[1] (ri:f) *n* **1** a ridge of rock, sand, coral, etc., the top of which lies close to the surface of the sea. **2** a vein of ore, esp. one of gold-bearing quartz. **3** (*cap.*) **the. 3a** the Great Barrier Reef in Australia. **3b** the Witwatersrand in South Africa, a gold-bearing ridge. [C16: from MDu. *ref,* from ON *rif* RIB[1], REEF[2]]

reef[2] (ri:f) *Naut.* ◆ *n* **1** the part gathered in when sail area is reduced, as in a high wind. ◆ *vb* **2** to reduce the area of (sail) by taking in a reef. **3** (*tr*) to shorten or bring inboard (a spar). [C14: from MDu. *rif;* rel. to ON *rif* reef, RIB[1]]

reefer ('ri:fə) *n* **1** *Naut.* a person who reefs, such as a midshipman. **2** another name for **reefing jacket. 3** *Sl.* a hand-rolled cigarette containing cannabis. [C19: from REEF[2]; applied to the cigarette from its resemblance to the rolled reef of a sail]

reefing jacket *n* a man's short double-breasted jacket of sturdy wool.

reef knot *n* a knot consisting of two overhand knots turned opposite ways. Also called: **square knot.**

reef point *n Naut.* one of several short lengths of line stitched through a sail for tying a reef.

reek ❶ (ri:k) *vb* **1** (*intr*) to give off or emit a strong unpleasant odour; smell or stink. **2** (*intr;* often foll. by *of*) to be permeated (by): *the letter reeks of subservience.* **3** (*tr*) to treat with smoke; fumigate. **4** (*tr*) *Chiefly dialect.* to give off or emit (smoke, fumes, etc.). ◆ *n* **5** a strong offensive smell; stink. **6** *Chiefly dialect.* smoke or steam; vapour. [OE *rēocan*]
▸**'reeky** *adj*

reel[1] (ri:l, rɪəl) *n* **1** any of various cylindrical objects or frames that turn on an axis and onto which film, tape, wire, etc., may be wound. US equivalent: **spool. 2** *Angling.* a device for winding, casting, etc., consisting of a revolving spool with a handle, attached to a fishing rod. ◆ *vb* (*tr*) **3** to wind (cotton, thread, etc.) onto a reel. **4** (foll. by *in, out,* etc.) to wind or draw with a reel: *to reel in a fish.* [OE *hrēol*]
▸**'reelable** *adj* ▸**'reeler** *n*

reel[2] ❶ (ri:l, rɪəl) *vb* (*mainly intr*) **1** to sway, esp. under the shock of a blow or through dizziness or drunkenness. **2** to whirl about or have the feeling of whirling about: *his brain reeled.* ◆ *n* **3** a staggering or swaying motion or sensation. [C14 *relen,* prob. from REEL[1]]

reel[3] (ri:l, rɪəl) *n* **1** any of various lively Scottish dances for a fixed number of couples who combine in square and circular formations. **2** a piece of music composed for or in the rhythm of this dance. [C18: from REEL[2]]

reel-fed *adj Printing.* involving or printing on a web of paper: *a reel-fed press.*

reelman ('ri:lmən, 'rɪəl-) *n, pl* **reelmen.** *Austral. & NZ.* (formerly) the member of a beach life-saving team who controlled the reel on which the line was wound.

reel off *vb* (*tr, adv*) to recite or write fluently and without apparent effort.

reel-to-reel *adj* **1** (of magnetic tape) wound from one reel to another in use. **2** (of a tape recorder) using magnetic tape wound from one reel to another, as opposed to cassettes.

re-entrant (ri:'ɛntrənt) *adj* **1** (of an angle) pointing inwards. ◆ *n* **2** an angle or part that points inwards.

re-entry (ri:'ɛntrɪ) *n, pl* **re-entries. 1** the act of retaking possession of land, etc. **2** the return of a spacecraft into the earth's atmosphere.

re-entry vehicle *n* the portion of a ballistic missile that carries a nuclear warhead and re-enters the earth's atmosphere.

THESAURUS

humble, humiliate, lower in rank, lower the status of, take down a peg (*inf.*)
Antonyms *vb* ≠ **lessen:** augment, enhance, enlarge, extend, heighten, increase ≠ **degrade:** elevate, enhance, exalt, promote

redundancy *n* **1a** = **unemployment**, joblessness, layoff, the axe, the sack (*inf.*) **2** = **superfluity**, superabundance, surfeit, surplus

redundant *adj* **1** = **superfluous**, *de trop*, excessive, extra, inessential, inordinate, supererogatory, supernumerary, surplus, unnecessary, unwanted **2** = **tautological**, diffuse, iterative, padded, periphrastic, pleonastic, prolix, repetitious, verbose, wordy
Antonyms *adj* ≠ **superfluous:** essential, necessary, needed, vital

reek *vb* **1** = **stink**, hum (*sl.*), pong (*Brit. inf.*), smell, smell to high heaven **2** *often foll. by* **of** = **be redolent of**, be characterized by, be permeated by **4** *Chiefly dialect* = **be redolent of**, fume, give off smoke *or* fumes, smoke, steam ◆ *n* **5** = **stink**, effluvium, fetor, malodour, mephitis, niff (*Brit. sl.*), odour, pong (*Brit. inf.*), smell, stench **6** *Chiefly dialect* = **smoke**, exhalation, fumes, steam, vapour

reel[2] *vb* **1** = **stagger**, falter, lurch, pitch, rock, roll, stumble, sway, totter, waver, wobble **2** = **whirl**,

reeve[1] (riːv) *n* **1** *English history.* the local representative of the king in a shire until the early 11th century. **2** (in medieval England) a manorial steward who supervised the daily affairs of the manor. **3** *Canad. government.* (in some provinces) a president of a local council, esp. in a rural area. **4** (formerly) a minor local official in England and the US. [OE *gerēva*]

reeve[2] (riːv) *vb* **reeves, reeving, reeved** *or* **rove.** (*tr*) *Naut.* **1** to pass (a rope or cable) through an eye or other narrow opening. **2** to fasten by passing through or around something. [C17: ?from Du. *rēven* REEF[2]]

reeve[3] (riːv) *n* the female of the ruff (the bird). [C17: from ?]

re-export *vb* (ˌriːɪk'spɔːt, ˌriː'ɛkspɔːt). **1** to export (imported goods, esp. after processing). ◆ *n* (riː'ɛkspɔːt). **2** the act of re-exporting. **3** a re-exported commodity.
▸**ˌre-expor'tation** *n* ▸**ˌre-ex'porter** *n*

ref (rɛf) *n Inf.* short for **referee.**

ref. *abbrev. for:* **1** referee. **2** reference. **3** reformed.

refection (rɪ'fɛkʃən) *n* refreshment with food and drink. [C14: from L *refectiō* a restoring, from *reficere,* from RE- + *facere* to make]

refectory (rɪ'fɛktərɪ, -trɪ) *n, pl* **refectories.** a dining hall in a religious or academic institution. [C15: from LL *refectōrium,* from L *refectus* refreshed]

refectory table *n* a long narrow dining table.

refer ❶ (rɪ'fɜː) *vb* **refers, referring, referred.** (often foll. by *to*). **1** (*intr*) to make mention (of). **2** (*tr*) to direct the attention of (someone) for information, facts, etc.: *the reader is referred to Chomsky, 1965.* **3** (*intr*) to seek information (from): *he referred to his notes.* **4** (*intr*) to be relevant (to); pertain or relate (to). **5** (*tr*) to assign or attribute: *Cromwell referred his victories to God.* **6** (*tr*) to hand over for consideration, reconsideration, or decision: *to refer a complaint to another department.* **7** (*tr*) to hand back to the originator as unacceptable or unusable. **8** (*tr*) *Brit.* to fail (a student) in an examination. **9 refer to drawer.** a request by a bank that the payee consult the drawer concerning a cheque payable by that bank. **10** (*tr*) to direct (a patient, client, etc.) to another doctor, agency, etc. [C14: from L *referre,* from RE- + *ferre* to BEAR[1]]
▸**referable** ('rɛfərəbᵊl) *or* **referrable** (rɪ'fɜːrəbᵊl) *adj* ▸**re'ferral** *n* ▸**re'ferrer** *n*

USAGE NOTE The common practice of adding *back* to *refer* is tautologous, since this meaning is already contained in the *re-* of *refer: this refers to* (not *back to*) *what has already been said.* However, when *refer* is used in the sense of passing a document or question for further consideration to the person from whom it was received, it may be appropriate to say *he referred the matter back.*

referee ❶ (ˌrɛfə'riː) *n* **1** a person to whom reference is made, esp. for an opinion, information, or a decision. **2** the umpire or judge in any of various sports, esp. football and boxing. **3** a person who is willing to testify to the character or capabilities of someone. **4** *Law.* a person appointed by a court to report on a matter. ◆ *vb* **referees, refereeing, refereed. 5** to act as a referee (in); preside (over).

reference ❶ ('rɛfərəns, 'rɛfrəns) *n* **1** the act or an instance of referring. **2** something referred, esp. proceedings submitted to a referee in law. **3** a direction of the attention to a passage elsewhere or to another book, etc. **4** a book or passage referred to. **5** a mention or allusion: *this book contains several references to the Civil War.* **6** the relation between a word or phrase and the object or idea to which it refers. **7a** a source of information or facts. **7b** (*as modifier*): *a reference book; a reference library.* **8** a written testimonial regarding one's character or capabilities. **9** a person referred to for such a testimonial. **10a** (foll. by *to*) relation or delimitation, esp. to or by membership of a specific group: *without reference to sex or age.* **10b** (*as modifier*): *a reference group.* **11 terms of reference.** the specific limits of responsibility that determine the activities of an investigating body, etc. ◆ *vb* **references, referencing, referenced.** (*tr*) **12** to furnish or compile a list of references for (a publication, etc.). **13** to make a reference to; refer to. ◆ *prep* **14** *Business jargon.* with reference to: *reference your letter of the 9th inst.* Abbrev.: **re.**
▸**referential** (ˌrɛfə'rɛnʃəl) *adj*

referendum ❶ (ˌrɛfə'rɛndəm) *n, pl* **referendums** *or* **referenda** (-də). **1** submission of an issue of public importance to the direct vote of the electorate. **2** a vote on such a measure. ◆ See also **plebiscite.** [C19: from L: something to be carried back, from *referre* to REFER]

referent ('rɛfərənt) *n* the object or idea to which a word or phrase refers. [C19: from L *referens* from *referre* to REFER]

referred pain *n Psychol.* pain felt at some place other than its actual place of origin.

refill *vb* (riː'fɪl). **1** to fill (something) again. ◆ *n* ('riːfɪl). **2** a replacement for a consumable substance in a permanent container. **3** a second or subsequent filling.
▸**re'fillable** *adj*

refine ❶ (rɪ'faɪn) *vb* **refines, refining, refined. 1** to make or become free from impurities or foreign matter; purify. **2** (*tr*) to separate (a mixture) into pure constituents, as in an oil refinery. **3** to make or become elegant or polished. **4** (*intr;* often foll. by *on* or *upon*) to enlarge or improve (upon) by making subtle or fine distinctions. **5** (*tr*) to make (language) more subtle or polished. [C16: from RE- + FINE[1]]
▸**re'finable** *adj* ▸**re'finer** *n*

refined ❶ (rɪ'faɪnd) *adj* **1** not coarse or vulgar; genteel, elegant, or polite. **2** subtle; discriminating. **3** freed from impurities; purified.

refinement ❶ (rɪ'faɪnmənt) *n* **1** the act of refining or the state of being refined. **2** a fine or delicate point or distinction; a subtlety. **3** fineness or precision of thought, expression, manners, etc. **4** an improvement to a piece of equipment, etc.

refinery (rɪ'faɪnərɪ) *n, pl* **refineries.** a factory for the purification of some crude material, such as sugar, oil, etc.

refit *vb* (riː'fɪt), **refits, refitting, refitted. 1** to make or be made ready for use again by repairing, re-equipping, or resupplying. ◆ *n* ('riːˌfɪt). **2** a repair or re-equipping, as of a ship, for further use.
▸**re'fitment** *n*

refl. *abbrev. for:* **1** reflection. **2** reflective. **3** reflex(ive).

reflate (riː'fleɪt) *vb* **reflates, reflating, reflated.** to inflate or be inflated again. [C20: back formation from REFLATION]

reflation (riː'fleɪʃən) *n* **1** an increase in economic activity. **2** an increase in the supply of money and credit designed to cause such economic activity. ◆ Cf. **inflation** (sense 2). [C20: from RE- + *-flation,* as in INFLATION]

reflect ❶ (rɪ'flɛkt) *vb* **1** to undergo or cause to undergo a process in which light, other electromagnetic radiation, sound, particles, etc., are thrown back after impinging on a surface. **2** (of a mirror, etc.) to form an image of (something) by reflection. **3** (*tr*) to show or express: *his tactics reflect his desire for power.* **4** (*tr*) to bring as a consequence: *their success reflected great credit on them.* **5** (*intr;* foll. by *on* or *upon*) to cause to be regarded in a specified way: *her behaviour reflects well on her.* **6** (*intr;* often foll. by *on* or *upon*) to cast dishonour or honour, credit or discredit, etc. (on). **7** (*intr;* usually foll. by *on*) to think, meditate, or ponder. [C15: from L *reflectere,* from RE- + *flectere* to bend]
▸**re'flectingly** *adv*

reflectance (rɪ'flɛktəns) *or* **reflection factor** *n* a measure of the ability of a surface to reflect light or other electromagnetic radiation, equal to the ratio of the reflected flux to the incident flux.

reflecting telescope *n* a type of telescope in which the initial image is formed by a concave mirror. Also called: **reflector.** Cf. **refracting telescope.**

reflection ❶ *or* **reflexion** (rɪ'flɛkʃən) *n* **1** the act of reflecting or the state of being reflected. **2** something reflected or the image so produced, as by a mirror. **3** careful or long consideration or thought. **4** attribution of discredit or blame. **5** *Maths.* a transformation in which the direction of one axis is reversed or changes the polarity of one of the variables. **6** *Anat.* the bending back of a structure or part upon itself.
▸**re'flectional** *or* **re'flexional** *adj*

reflection density *n Physics.* a measure of the extent to which a surface reflects light or other electromagnetic radiation. Symbol: *D*

reflective ❶ (rɪ'flɛktɪv) *adj* **1** characterized by quiet thought or con-

THESAURUS

go round and round, revolve, spin, swim, swirl, twirl

refer *vb* **1** = **allude**, advert, bring up, cite, hint, invoke, make mention of, make reference, mention, speak of, touch on **2** = **direct**, guide, point, recommend, send **3** = **consult**, apply, go, have recourse to, look up, seek information from, turn to **4** = **relate**, apply, be directed to, belong, be relevant to, concern, pertain **5** = **attribute**, accredit, ascribe, assign, credit, impute, put down to **6** = **pass on**, commit, consign, deliver, hand over, submit, transfer, turn over

referee *n* **2** = **umpire**, adjudicator, arbiter, arbitrator, judge, ref ◆ *vb* **5** = **umpire**, adjudicate, arbitrate, judge, mediate

reference *n* **5** = **citation**, allusion, mention, note, quotation, remark **8** = **testimonial**, certification, character, credentials, endorsement, good word, recommendation **10a** *foll. by* **to** = **relevance**, applicability, bearing, concern, connection, consideration, regard, relation, respect

referendum *n* **1, 2** = **public vote**, plebiscite, popular vote

refine *vb* **1, 2** = **purify**, clarify, cleanse, distil, filter, process, rarefy **5** = **improve**, hone, perfect, polish

refined *adj* **1** = **cultured**, civil, civilized, courtly, cultivated, elegant, genteel, gentlemanly, gracious, ladylike, polished, polite, sophisticated, urbane, well-bred, well-mannered **2** = **discerning**, delicate, discriminating, exact, fastidious, fine, nice, precise, punctilious, sensitive, sublime, subtle **2** = **purified**, clarified, clean, distilled, filtered, processed, pure

Antonyms *adj* ≠ **cultured:** boorish, coarse, common, ill-bred, inelegant, uncultured, ungentlemanly, unladylike, unmannerly, unrefined ≠ **purified:** coarse, impure, unrefined

refinement *n* **1** = **purification**, clarification, cleansing, distillation, filtering, processing, rarefaction, rectification **2** = **subtlety**, fine point, fine tuning, nicety, nuance **3** = **sophistication**, breeding, civility, civilization, courtesy, courtliness, cultivation, culture, delicacy, discrimination, elegance, fastidiousness, fineness, finesse, finish, gentility, good breeding, good manners, grace, graciousness, polish, politeness, politesse, precision, style, taste, urbanity

reflect *vb* **1, 2** = **throw back**, echo, give back, imitate, mirror, reproduce, return **3** = **show**, bear out, bespeak, communicate, demonstrate, display, evince, exhibit, express, indicate, manifest, reveal **7** = **consider**, cogitate, contemplate, deliberate, meditate, mull over, muse, ponder, ruminate, think, wonder

reflection *n* **2** = **image**, counterpart, echo, mirror image **3** = **consideration**, cerebration, cogitation, contemplation, deliberation, idea, impression, meditation, musing, observation, opinion, perusal, pondering, rumination, study, thinking, thought, view **4** = **criticism**, aspersion, censure, derogation, imputation, reproach, slur

reflective *adj* **1** = **thoughtful**, cogitating, con-

templation. **2** capable of reflecting: *a reflective surface.* **3** produced by reflection.
▸**re'flectively** *adv*
reflectivity (ˌriːflɛk'tɪvɪtɪ) *n* **1** *Physics.* a measure of the ability of a surface to reflect radiation, equal to the reflectance of a layer of material sufficiently thick for the reflectance not to depend on the thickness. **2** Also: **reflectiveness.** the quality or capability of being reflective.
reflector (rɪ'flɛktə) *n* **1** a person or thing that reflects. **2** a surface or object that reflects light, sound, heat, etc. **3** another name for **reflecting telescope.**
reflet (rə'fleɪ) *n* an iridescent glow or lustre, as on ceramic ware. [C19: from F: a reflection, from It. *riflesso,* from L *reflexus,* from *reflectere* to reflect]
reflex *n* ('riːflɛks). **1a** an immediate involuntary response, such as coughing, evoked by a given stimulus. **1b** (*as modifier*): *a reflex action.* See also **reflex arc. 2a** a mechanical response to a particular situation, involving no conscious decision. **2b** (*as modifier*): *a reflex response.* **3** a reflection; an image produced by or as if by reflection. ◆ *adj* ('riːflɛks). **4** *Maths.* (of an angle) between 180° and 360°. **5** (*prenominal*) turned, reflected, or bent backwards. ◆ *vb* (rɪ'flɛks). **6** (*tr*) to bend, turn, or reflect backwards. [C16: from L *reflexus* bent back, from *reflectere* to reflect]
▸**re'flexible** *adj* ▸**reˌflexi'bility** *n*
reflex arc *n Physiol.* the neural pathway over which impulses travel to produce a reflex action.
reflex camera *n* a camera in which the image is composed and focused on a ground-glass viewfinder screen.
reflexion (rɪ'flɛkʃən) *n Brit.* a less common spelling of **reflection.**
▸**re'flexional** *adj*
reflexive (rɪ'flɛksɪv) *adj* **1** denoting a class of pronouns that refer back to the subject of a sentence or clause. Thus, in *that man thinks a great deal of himself,* the pronoun *himself* is reflexive. **2** denoting a verb used transitively with the reflexive pronoun as its direct object, as in *to dress oneself.* **3** *Physiol.* of or relating to a reflex. ◆ *n* **4** a reflexive pronoun or verb.
▸**re'flexively** *adv* ▸**re'flexiveness** *or* **reflexivity** (ˌriːflɛk'sɪvɪtɪ) *n*
reflexology (ˌriːflɛk'sɒlədʒɪ) *n* a form of therapy in alternative medicine in which the soles of the feet are massaged: designed to stimulate the blood supply and nerves and thus relieve tension.
▸ˌ**reflex'ologist** *n*
reflux ('riːflʌks) *vb* **1** *Chem.* to boil or be boiled in a vessel attached to a condenser, so that the vapour condenses and flows back into the vessel. ◆ *n* **2** *Chem.* **2a** an act of refluxing. **2b** (*as modifier*): *a reflux condenser.* **3** the act or an instance of flowing back; ebb. [C15: from Med. L *refluxus,* from L *refluere* to flow back]
reflux oesophagitis (iːˌsɒfə'dʒaɪtɪs) *n* inflammation of the gullet caused by regurgitation of stomach acids, producing heartburn: may be associated with a hiatus hernia.
reform ❶ (rɪ'fɔːm) *vb* **1** (*tr*) to improve (an existing institution, law, etc.) by alteration or correction of abuses. **2** to give up or cause to give up a reprehensible habit or immoral way of life. ◆ *n* **3** an improvement or change for the better, esp. as a result of correction of legal or political abuses or malpractices. **4** a principle, campaign, or measure aimed at achieving such change. **5** improvement of morals or behaviour. [C14: via OF from L *reformāre* to form again]
▸**re'formable** *adj* ▸**re'formative** *adj* ▸**re'former** *n*
re-form (riː'fɔːm) *vb* to form anew.
▸ˌ**re-for'mation** *n*
reformation (ˌrɛfə'meɪʃən) *n* **1** the act or an instance of reforming or the state of being reformed. **2** (*usually cap.*) a religious and political movement of 16th-century Europe that began as an attempt to reform the Roman Catholic Church and resulted in the establishment of the Protestant Churches.
▸ˌ**refor'mational** *adj*
reformatory (rɪ'fɔːmətərɪ, -trɪ) *n, pl* **reformatories. 1** Also called: **reform school.** (formerly) a place of instruction where young offenders were sent for corrective training. ◆ *adj* **2** having the purpose or function of reforming.
Reformed (rɪ'fɔːmd) *adj* **1** of or designating a Protestant Church, esp. the Calvinist. **2** of or designating Reform Judaism.
reformism (rɪ'fɔːmɪzəm) *n* a doctrine advocating reform, esp. political or religious reform rather than abolition.
▸**re'formist** *n, adj*
Reform Judaism *n* a movement in Judaism that does not require strict observance of the law, but adapts to the contemporary world.
refract (rɪ'frækt) *vb* **1** to cause to undergo refraction. **2** (*tr*) to measure the amount of refraction of (the eye, a lens, etc.). [C17: from L *refractus* broken up, from *refringere,* from RE- + *frangere* to break]
▸**re'fractable** *adj* ▸**re'fractive** *adj*
refracting telescope *n* a type of telescope in which the image is formed by a set of lenses. Also called: **refractor.** Cf. **reflecting telescope.**
refraction (rɪ'frækʃən) *n* **1** *Physics.* the change in direction of a propagating wave, such as light or sound, in passing from one medium to another in which it has a different velocity. **2** the amount by which a wave is refracted. **3** the ability of the eye to refract light.
▸**re'fractional** *adj*
refractive index *n Physics.* a measure of the extent to which a medium refracts light; the ratio of the speed of light in free space to that in the medium.
refractometer (ˌriːfræk'tɒmɪtə) *n* any instrument for measuring the refractive index.
▸**refractometric** (rɪˌfræktə'mɛtrɪk) *adj* ▸ˌ**refrac'tometry** *n*
refractor (rɪ'fræktə) *n* **1** an object or material that refracts. **2** another name for **refracting telescope.**
refractory ❶ (rɪ'fræktərɪ) *adj* **1** unmanageable or obstinate. **2** *Med.* not responding to treatment. **3** *Physiol.* (of a nerve or muscle) incapable of responding to stimulation. **4** (of a material) able to withstand high temperatures without fusion or decomposition. ◆ *n, pl* **refractories. 5** a material, such as fire clay, that is able to withstand high temperatures.
▸**re'fractorily** *adv* ▸**re'fractoriness** *n*
refrain[1] ❶ (rɪ'freɪn) *vb* (*intr; usually foll. by from*) to abstain (from action); forbear. [C14: from L *refrēnāre* to check with a bridle, from RE- + *frēnum* a bridle]
▸**re'frainer** *n* ▸**re'frainment** *n*
refrain[2] ❶ (rɪ'freɪn) *n* **1** a regularly recurring melody, such as the chorus of a song. **2** a much repeated saying or idea. [C14: via OF, ult. from L *refringere* to break into pieces]
refrangible (rɪ'frændʒɪbᵊl) *adj* capable of being refracted. [C17: from L *refringere* to break up, from RE- + *frangere* to break]
▸**reˌfrangi'bility** *or* **re'frangibleness** *n*
refresh ❶ (rɪ'frɛʃ) *vb* **1** (*usually tr or reflexive*) to make or become fresh or vigorous, as through rest, drink, or food; revive or reinvigorate. **2** (*tr*) to enliven (something worn or faded), as by adding new decorations. **3** to pour cold water over previously blanched and drained food. **4** (*tr*) to stimulate (the memory, etc.). **5** (*tr*) to replenish, as with new equipment or stores. [C14: from OF *refreschir;* see RE-, FRESH]
▸**re'fresher** *n* ▸**re'freshing** *adj*
refresher course *n* a short educational course for people to review their subject and developments in it.
refreshment ❶ (rɪ'frɛʃmənt) *n* **1** the act of refreshing or the state of being refreshed. **2** (*pl*) snacks and drinks served as a light meal.
refrigerant (rɪ'frɪdʒərənt) *n* **1** a fluid capable of changes of phase at low temperatures: used as the working fluid of a refrigerator. **2** a cooling substance, such as ice or solid carbon dioxide. **3** *Med.* an agent that provides a sensation of coolness or reduces fever. ◆ *adj* **4** causing cooling or freezing.
refrigerate ❶ (rɪ'frɪdʒəˌreɪt) *vb* **refrigerates, refrigerating, refrigerated.** to make or become frozen or cold, esp. for preservative purposes; chill or freeze. [C16: from L *refrīgerāre* to make cold, from RE- + *frīgus* cold]
▸**reˌfriger'ation** *n* ▸**re'frigerative** *adj* ▸**re'frigeratory** *adj, n*
refrigerator (rɪ'frɪdʒəˌreɪtə) *n* a chamber in which food, drink, etc., are kept cool. Informal name: **fridge.**
refringent (rɪ'frɪndʒənt) *adj Physics.* of, concerned with, or causing refraction; refractive. [C18: from L *refringere;* see REFRACT]
▸**re'fringency** *or* **re'fringence** *n*
reft (rɛft) *vb* a past tense and past participle of **reave.**
refuel (riː'fjuːəl) *vb* **refuels, refuelling, refuelled** *or US* **refuels, refueling, refueled.** to supply or be supplied with fresh fuel.
refuge ❶ ('rɛfjuːdʒ) *n* **1** shelter or protection, as from the weather or danger. **2** any place, person, action, or thing that offers protection, help, or relief. [C14: via OF from L *refugium,* from *refugere,* from RE- + *fugere* to escape]
refugee ❶ (ˌrɛfju'dʒiː) *n* **a** a person who has fled from some danger or problem, esp. political persecution. **b** (*as modifier*): *a refugee camp.*
▸ˌ**refu'geeism** *n*

THESAURUS

templative, deliberative, meditative, pensive, pondering, reasoning, ruminative
reform *vb* **1 = improve,** ameliorate, amend, better, correct, emend, mend, rebuild, reclaim, reconstitute, reconstruct, rectify, regenerate, rehabilitate, remodel, renovate, reorganize, repair, restore, revolutionize **2 = mend one's ways,** clean up one's act (*inf.*), get back on the straight and narrow (*inf.*), get it together (*inf.*), get one's act together (*inf.*), go straight (*inf.*), pull one's socks up (*Brit. inf.*), shape up (*inf.*), turn over a new leaf ◆ *n* **3 = improvement,** amelioration, amendment, betterment, correction, rectification, rehabilitation, renovation
refractory *adj* **1 = unmanageable,** cantankerous, contentious, contumacious, difficult, disobedient, disputatious, headstrong, intractable, mulish, obstinate, perverse, recalcitrant, stiff-necked, stubborn, uncontrollable, uncooperative, unruly, wilful
refrain[1] *vb* **= stop,** abstain, avoid, cease, desist, do without, eschew, forbear, give up, kick (*inf.*), leave off, renounce
refrain[2] *n* **1 = chorus,** burden, melody, song, tune
refresh *vb* **1 = revive,** brace, breathe new life into, cheer, cool, enliven, freshen, inspirit, invigorate, kick-start (*inf.*), reanimate, rejuvenate, revitalize, revivify, stimulate **2 = renovate,** renew, repair, restore **4 = stimulate,** brush up (*inf.*), jog, prod, prompt, renew **5 = replenish,** top up
refreshing *adj* **1 = stimulating,** bracing, cooling, fresh, inspiriting, invigorating, revivifying, thirst-quenching **2 = new,** different, novel, original
Antonyms *adj* ≠ **stimulating:** enervating, exhausting, soporific, tiring, wearisome
refreshment *n* **1 = revival,** enlivenment, freshening, reanimation, renewal, renovation, repair, restoration, stimulation **2** *plural* **= food and drink,** drinks, snacks, titbits
refrigerate *vb* **= cool,** chill, freeze, keep cold
refuge *n* **1, 2 = shelter,** asylum, bolt hole, harbour, haven, hide-out, protection, resort, retreat, sanctuary, security
refugee *n* **a = exile,** displaced person, émigré, escapee, fugitive, runaway

refugee capital *n Finance.* money from abroad invested, esp. for a short term, in the country offering the highest interest rate.

refugium (rɪˈfjuːdʒɪəm) *n, pl* **refugia** (-dʒɪə). a geographical region that has remained unaltered by a climatic change affecting surrounding regions and that therefore forms a haven for relict fauna and flora. [C20: L: REFUGE]

refulgent (rɪˈfʌldʒənt) *adj Literary.* shining, brilliant, or radiant. [C16: from L *refulgēre,* from RE- + *fulgēre* to shine]
▸**reˈfulgence** *or* **reˈfulgency** *n* ▸**reˈfulgently** *adv*

refund ❶ *vb* (rɪˈfʌnd). *(tr)* **1** to give back (money, etc.), as when an article purchased is unsatisfactory. **2** to reimburse (a person). ◆ *n* (ˈriːˌfʌnd). **3** return of money to a purchaser or the amount so returned. [C14: from L *refundere,* from RE- + *fundere* to pour]
▸**reˈfundable** *adj* ▸**reˈfunder** *n*

re-fund (riːˈfʌnd) *vb (tr) Finance.* to discharge (an old or matured debt) by new borrowing, as by a new bond issue. [C20: from RE- + FUND]

refurbish ❶ (riːˈfɜːbɪʃ) *vb (tr)* to renovate, re-equip, or restore.
▸**reˈfurbishment** *n*

refusal ❶ (rɪˈfjuːzᵊl) *n* **1** the act or an instance of refusing. **2** the opportunity to reject or accept; option.

refuse[1] ❶ (rɪˈfjuːz) *vb* **refuses, refusing, refused. 1** *(tr)* to decline to accept (something offered): *to refuse promotion.* **2** to decline to give or grant (something) to (a person, etc.). **3** (when *tr, takes an infinitive*) to express determination not (to do something); decline: *he refuses to talk about it.* **4** (of a horse) to be unwilling to take (a jump). [C14: from OF *refuser,* from L *refundere* to pour back]
▸**reˈfusable** *adj* ▸**reˈfuser** *n*

refuse[2] ❶ (ˈrɛfjuːs) *n* **a** anything thrown away; waste; rubbish. **b** *(as modifier): a refuse collection.* [C15: from OF *refuser* to REFUSE[1]]

refusenik *or* **refusnik** (rɪˈfjuːznɪk) *n* **1** (formerly) a Jew in the Soviet Union who had been refused permission to emigrate. **2** a person who refuses to cooperate with a system or comply with a law because of a moral conviction. [C20: from REFUSE[1] + -NIK]

refute ❶ (rɪˈfjuːt) *vb* **refutes, refuting, refuted.** *(tr)* to prove (a statement, theory, charge, etc.) of (a person) to be false or incorrect; disprove. [C16: from L *refūtāre* to rebut]
▸**refutable** (ˈrɛfjutəbᵊl, rɪˈfjuː-) *adj* ▸**ˈrefutably** *adv* ▸**ˌrefuˈtation** *n* ▸**reˈfuter** *n*

> **USAGE NOTE** The use of *refute* to mean *deny* is thought by many people to be incorrect.

reg. *abbrev. for:* **1** regiment. **2** register(ed). **3** registrar. **4** regular(ly). **5** regulation.

regain ❶ (rɪˈgeɪn) *vb (tr)* **1** to take or get back; recover. **2** to reach again.
▸**reˈgainer** *n*

regal ❶ (ˈriːgᵊl) *adj* of, relating to, or befitting a king or queen; royal. [C14: from L *rēgālis,* from *rēx* king]
▸**reˈgality** *n* ▸**ˈregally** *adv*

regale ❶ (rɪˈgeɪl) *vb* **regales, regaling, regaled.** *(tr;* usually foll. by *with)* **1** to give delight or amusement to: *he regaled them with stories.* **2** to provide with choice or abundant food or drink. ◆ *n* **3** *Arch.* **3a** a feast. **3b** a delicacy of food or drink. [C17: from F *régaler,* from *gale* pleasure]
▸**reˈgalement** *n*

regalia ❶ (rɪˈgeɪlɪə) *n (pl, sometimes functioning as sing)* **1** the ceremonial emblems or robes of royalty, high office, an order, etc. **2** any splendid or special clothes; finery. [C16: from Med. L: royal privileges, from L *rēgālis* REGAL]

regard ❶ (rɪˈgɑːd) *vb* **1** to look closely or attentively at (something or someone); observe steadily. **2** *(tr)* to hold (a person or thing) in respect, admiration, or affection: *we regard your work very highly.* **3** *(tr)* to look upon or consider in a specified way: *she regarded her brother as her responsibility.* **4** *(tr)* to relate to; concern; have a bearing on. **5** to take notice of or pay attention to (something); heed: *he has never regarded the conventions.* **6 as regards.** *(prep)* in respect of; concerning. ◆ *n* **7** a gaze; look. **8** attention; heed: *he spends without regard to his bank balance.* **9** esteem, affection, or respect. **10** reference, relation, or connection (esp. in **with regard to** or **in regard to**). **11** *(pl)* good wishes or greetings (esp. in **with kind regards,** used at the close of a letter). **12 in this regard.** on this point. [C14: from OF *regarder* to look at, care about, from RE- + *garder* to GUARD]

regardant (rɪˈgɑːdᵊnt) *adj (usually postpositive) Heraldry.* (of a beast) shown looking backwards over its shoulder. [C15: from OF; see REGARD]

regardful ❶ (rɪˈgɑːdfʊl) *adj* **1** (often foll. by *of)* showing regard (for); heedful (of). **2** showing regard, respect, or consideration.
▸**reˈgardfully** *adv*

regarding ❶ (rɪˈgɑːdɪŋ) *prep* in respect of; on the subject of.

regardless ❶ (rɪˈgɑːdlɪs) *adj* **1** (usually foll. by *of)* taking no regard or heed; heedless. ◆ *adv* **2** in spite of everything; disregarding drawbacks.
▸**reˈgardlessly** *adv* ▸**reˈgardlessness** *n*

regatta (rɪˈgætə) *n* an organized series of races of yachts, rowing boats, etc. [C17: from obs. It. *rigatta* contest, from ?]

regd *abbrev. for* registered.

regelation (ˌriːdʒɪˈleɪʃən) *n* the rejoining together of two pieces of ice as a result of melting under pressure at the interface between them and subsequent refreezing.
▸**ˈregeˌlate** *vb*

regency (ˈriːdʒənsɪ) *n, pl* **regencies. 1** government by a regent. **2** the office of a regent. **3** a territory under the jurisdiction of a regent. [C15: from Med. L *regentia,* from L *regere* to rule]

Regency (ˈriːdʒənsɪ) *n* (preceded by *the)* **1** (in Britain) the period (1811–20) of the regency of the Prince of Wales (later George IV). **2** (in France) the period (1715-23) of the regency of Philip, Duke of Orleans. ◆ *adj* **3** characteristic of or relating to the Regency periods or to the styles of architecture, art, etc., produced in them.

regenerate ❶ *vb* (rɪˈdʒɛnəˌreɪt), **regenerates, regenerating, regenerated. 1** to undergo or cause to undergo moral, spiritual, or physical renewal or invigoration. **2** to form or be formed again; come or bring into existence once again. **3** to replace (lost or damaged tissues or organs) by new growth, or to cause (such tissues) to be replaced. **4** *(tr) Electronics.* to use positive feedback to improve the demodulation and amplification of a signal. ◆ *adj* (rɪˈdʒɛnərɪt). **5** morally, spiritually, or physically renewed or reborn.
▸**reˈgeneracy** *n* ▸**reˌgenerˈation** *n* ▸**reˈgenerative** *adj* ▸**reˈgeneratively** *adv* ▸**reˈgenerˌator** *n*

regent (ˈriːdʒənt) *n* **1** the ruler or administrator of a country during the minority, absence, or incapacity of its monarch. **2** *US & Canad.* a member of the governing board of certain schools and colleges. ◆ *adj* **3** *(usually postpositive)* acting or functioning as a regent: *a queen regent.* [C14: from L *regēns,* from *regere* to rule]
▸**ˈregental** *adj* ▸**ˈregentship** *n*

regent-bird *n Austral.* a bowerbird, the male of which has showy yellow and velvety-black plumage. [after the Prince *Regent*]

reggae (ˈrɛgeɪ) *n* a type of West Indian popular music having four beats to the bar, the upbeat being strongly accented. [C20: of West Indian origin]

regicide (ˈrɛdʒɪˌsaɪd) *n* **1** the killing of a king. **2** a person who kills a king. [C16: from L *rēx* king + -CIDE]
▸**ˌregiˈcidal** *adj*

regime ❶ *or* **régime** (reɪˈʒiːm) *n* **1** a system of government or a particu-

THESAURUS

refund *vb* **1 = give back**, make good, pay back, reimburse, repay, restore, return **2 = reimburse**, pay back, repay ◆ *n* **3 = repayment**, reimbursement, return

refurbish *vb* **= renovate**, clean up, do up, fix up *(inf., chiefly US & Canad.)*, mend, overhaul, re-equip, refit, remodel, repair, restore, revamp, set to rights, spruce up

refusal *n* **1 = rejection**, defiance, denial, kick in the teeth *(sl.)*, knock-back *(sl.)*, negation, no, rebuff, repudiation, thumbs down **2 = option**, choice, consideration, opportunity

refuse[1] *vb* **1 = turn down**, decline, reject, repudiate, say no, spurn **2 = withhold**, deny **3 = abstain**, decline
Antonyms *vb* ≠ **turn down:** accept, agree, consent ≠ **withhold:** allow, approve, give, permit

refuse[2] *n* **= rubbish**, dregs, dross, garbage, junk *(inf.)*, leavings, lees, litter, offscourings, scum, sediment, sweepings, trash, waste

refute *vb* **= disprove**, blow out of the water *(sl.)*, confute, counter, discredit, give the lie to, negate, overthrow, prove false, rebut, silence
Antonyms *vb* confirm, prove, substantiate

regain *vb* **1 = recover**, get back, recapture, recoup, redeem, repossess, retake, retrieve, take back, win back **2 = get back to**, reach again, reattain, return to

regal *adj* **= royal**, fit for a king *or* queen, kingly *or* queenly, magnificent, majestic, noble, princely, proud, sovereign

regale *vb* **1 = entertain**, amuse, delight, divert, gratify **2 = serve**, feast, ply, refresh

regalia *pl n* **1, 2 = trappings**, accoutrements, finery, garb, gear, paraphernalia, rigout *(inf.)*

regard *vb* **1 = look at**, behold, check, check out *(inf.)*, clock *(Brit. sl.)*, eye, eyeball, gaze at, get a load of *(inf.)*, mark, notice, observe, remark, scrutinize, take a dekko at *(Brit. sl.)*, view, watch **3 = consider**, account, adjudge, believe, deem, esteem, estimate, hold, imagine, judge, look upon, rate, see, suppose, think, treat, value, view **5 = heed**, attend, listen to, mind, note, pay attention to, respect, take into consideration, take notice of **6 as regards = concerning**, pertaining to, regarding, relating to ◆ *n* **7 = look**, gaze, glance, scrutiny, stare **8 = heed**, attention, interest, mind, notice **9 = respect**, account, affection, attachment, care, concern, consideration, deference, esteem, honour, love, note, reputation, repute, store, sympathy, thought **10 = relation**, bearing, concern, connection, reference, relevance **11** *plural* **= good wishes**, best wishes, compliments, devoirs, greetings, respects, salutations **12** *As in* **in this regard = point**, aspect, detail, feature, item, matter, particular, respect

regardful *adj* **1, 2 = mindful**, attentive, aware, careful, considerate, dutiful, heedful, observant, respectful, thoughtful, watchful

regarding *prep* **= concerning**, about, apropos, as regards, as to, in *or* with regard to, in re, in respect of, in the matter of, on the subject of, re, respecting, with reference to

regardless *adj* **1 = heedless**, disregarding, inattentive, inconsiderate, indifferent, neglectful, negligent, rash, reckless, remiss, unconcerned, unmindful ◆ *adv* **2 = in spite of everything**, anyway, come what may, despite everything, for all that, in any case, nevertheless, no matter what, nonetheless, rain or shine
Antonyms *adj* ≠ **heedless:** heedful, mindful, regardful

regenerate *vb* **1 = renew**, breathe new life into, change, give a shot in the arm, inspirit, invigorate, kick-start, reawaken, reconstruct, re-establish, reinvigorate, rejuvenate, renovate, reproduce, restore, revive, revivify, uplift
Antonyms *vb* become moribund, decline, degenerate, stagnate, stultify

regime *n* **1, 2 = government**, administration, establishment, leadership, management, reign, rule, system lar administration: *a fascist regime.* **2** a social system or order. **3** another word for **regimen** (sense 1). [C18: from F, from L *regimen* guidance, from *regere* to rule]

regimen ('rɛdʒɪˌmɛn) *n* **1** Also called: **regime.** a systematic course of therapy, often including a recommended diet. **2** administration or rule. [C14: from L: guidance]

regiment *n* ('rɛdʒɪmənt). **1** a military formation varying in size from a battalion to a number of battalions. **2** a large number in regular or organized groups. ◆ *vb* ('rɛdʒɪˌmɛnt). (*tr*) **3** to force discipline or order on, esp. in a domineering manner. **4** to organize into a regiment. **5** to form into organized groups. [C14: via OF from LL *regimentum* government, from L *regere* to rule]
▸**ˌregi'mental** *adj* ▸**ˌregi'mentally** *adv* ▸**ˌregimen'tation** *n*

regimentals (ˌrɛdʒɪ'mɛntᵊlz) *pl n* **1** the uniform and insignia of a regiment. **2** military dress.

Regina (rɪ'dʒaɪnə) *n* queen: now used chiefly in documents, inscriptions, etc. Cf. **Rex.** [L]

region ❶ ('riːdʒən) *n* **1** any large, indefinite, and continuous part of a surface or space. **2** an area considered as a unit for geographical, functional, social, or cultural reasons. **3** an administrative division of a country, or a Canadian province. **4** a realm or sphere of activity or interest. **5** range, area, or scope: *in what region is the price likely to be?* **6** a division or part of the body: *the lumbar region.* [C14: from L *regiō*, from *regere* to govern]

regional ❶ ('riːdʒənᵊl) *adj* of, characteristic of, or limited to a region.
▸**'regionally** *adv*

regionalism ('riːdʒənəˌlɪzəm) *n* **1** division of a country into administrative regions having partial autonomy. **2** loyalty to one's home region; regional patriotism.
▸**'regionalist** *n, adj*

régisseur *French.* (reʒisœr) *n* an official in a dance company with varying duties, usually including directing productions. [F, from *régir* to manage]

register ❶ ('rɛdʒɪstə) *n* **1** an official or formal list recording names, events, or transactions. **2** the book in which such a list is written. **3** an entry in such a list. **4** a recording device that accumulates data, totals sums of money, etc.: *a cash register.* **5** a movable plate that controls the flow of air into a furnace, chimney, room, etc. **6** *Music.* **6a** the timbre characteristic of a certain manner of voice production. **6b** any of the stops on an organ as classified in respect of its tonal quality: *the flute register.* **7** *Printing.* the exact correspondence of lines of type, etc., on the two sides of a printed sheet of paper. **8** a form of a language associated with a particular social situation or subject matter. **9** the act or an instance of registering. ◆ *vb* **10** (*tr*) to enter or cause someone to enter (an event, person's name, ownership, etc.) on a register. **11** to show or be shown on a scale or other measuring instrument: *the current didn't register on the meter.* **12** to show or be shown in a person's face, bearing, etc.: *his face registered surprise.* **13** (*intr*) *Inf.* to have an effect; make an impression: *the news of her uncle's death just did not register.* **14** to send (a letter, package, etc.) by registered post. **15** (*tr*) *Printing.* to adjust (a printing press, forme, etc.) to ensure that the printed matter is in register. [C14: from Med. L *registrum*, from L *regerere* to transcribe, from RE- + *gerere* to bear]
▸**'registrable** *adj*

Registered General Nurse *n* (in Britain) a nurse who has completed a three-year training course and has been registered with the United Kingdom Central Council for Nursing, Midwifery, and Health Visiting. Abbrev.: **RGN.**

registered post *n* **1** a Post Office service by which compensation is paid for loss or damage to mail for which a registration fee has been paid. **2** mail sent by this service.

Registered Trademark *n* See **trademark** (sense 1).

register office *n Brit.* a government office where civil marriages are performed and births, marriages, and deaths are recorded. Often called: **registry office.**

register ton *n* the full name for **ton**[1] (sense 6).

registrar (ˌrɛdʒɪ'strɑː, 'rɛdʒɪˌstrɑː) *n* **1** a person who keeps official records. **2** an administrative official responsible for student records, enrolment procedure, etc., in a school, college, or university. **3** *Brit.* & *NZ.* a hospital doctor senior to a houseman but junior to a consultant. **4** *Austral.* the chief medical administrator of a large hospital. **5** *Chiefly US.* a person employed by a company to maintain a register of its security issues.
▸**'regisˌtrarship** *n*

registration (ˌrɛdʒɪ'streɪʃən) *n* **1a** the act of registering or state of being registered. **1b** (*as modifier*): *a registration number.* **2** an entry in a register. **3** a group of people, such as students, who register at a particular time. **4** *Austral.* **4a** a tax payable by the owner of a motor vehicle. **4b** the period paid for.

registration document *n Brit.* a document giving identification details of a motor vehicle, including its manufacturer, date of registration, and owner's name.

registration number *n* a sequence of letters and numbers assigned to a motor vehicle when it is registered, usually indicating the year and place of registration, displayed on numberplates at the front and rear of the vehicle.

registration plate *n Austral.* & *NZ.* the numberplate of a vehicle.

registry ('rɛdʒɪstrɪ) *n, pl* **registries. 1** a place where registers are kept. **2** the registration of a ship's country of origin: *a ship of Liberian registry.* **3** another word for **registration.**

registry office *n Brit.* another term for **register office.**

Regius professor ('riːdʒɪəs) *n Brit.* a person appointed by the Crown to a university chair founded by a royal patron. [C17: *regius*, from L: royal, from *rex* king]

reglet ('rɛglɪt) *n* **1** a flat narrow architectural moulding. **2** *Printing.* a strip of oiled wood used for spacing between lines. [C16: from OF, lit.: a little rule, from *régle* rule, from L *rēgula*]

regmaker ('rɛxˌmɑːkə) *n S. African.* a drink to relieve the symptoms of a hangover. [from Afrik., right maker]

regnal ('rɛgnəl) *adj* **1** of a sovereign or reign. **2** designating a year of a sovereign's reign calculated from the date of accession. [C17: from Med. L *rēgnālis*, from L *rēgnum* sovereignty; see REIGN]

regnant ('rɛgnənt) *adj* **1** (*postpositive*) reigning. **2** prevalent; current. [C17: from L *regnāre* to REIGN]
▸**'regnancy** *n*

regorge (rɪ'gɔːdʒ) *vb* **regorges, regorging, regorged. 1** (*tr*) to vomit up; disgorge. **2** (*intr*) (esp. of water) to flow or run back. [C17: from F *regorger*; see GORGE]

regress ❶ *vb* (rɪ'grɛs). **1** (*intr*) to return or revert, as to a former place, condition, or mode of behaviour. **2** (*tr*) *Statistics.* to measure the extent to which (a dependent variable) is associated with one or more independent variables. ◆ *n* ('riːgrɛs). **3** movement in a backward direction; retrogression. [C14: from L *regressus*, from *regredī* to go back, from RE- + *gradī* to go]
▸**re'gressive** *adj* ▸**re'gressor** *n*

regression (rɪ'grɛʃən) *n* **1** *Psychol.* the adoption by an adult of behaviour more appropriate to a child. **2** *Statistics.* **2a** the measure of the association between one variable (the dependent variable) and other variables (the independent variables). **2b** (*as modifier*): *regression curve.* **3** *Geol.* the retreat of the sea from the land. **4** the act of regressing.

regret ❶ (rɪ'grɛt) *vb* **regrets, regretting, regretted.** (*tr*) **1** (*may take a clause as object or an infinitive*) to feel sorry, repentant, or upset about. **2** to bemoan or grieve the death or loss of. ◆ *n* **3** a sense of repentance, guilt, or sorrow. **4** a sense of loss or grief. **5** (*pl*) a polite expression of sadness, esp. in a formal refusal of an invitation. [C14: from OF *regreter*, from ON]
▸**re'gretful** *adj* ▸**re'gretfully** *adv* ▸**re'gretfulness** *n* ▸**re'grettable** *adj* ▸**re'grettably** *adv*

> **USAGE NOTE** *Regretful* and *regretfully* are sometimes wrongly used where *regrettable* and *regrettably* are meant: *he gave a regretful smile; he smiled regretfully; this is a regrettable* (not *a regretful*) *mistake; regrettably* (not *regretfully*), *I shall be unable to attend.*

regroup (riː'gruːp) *vb* **1** to reorganize (military forces), esp. after an attack or a defeat. **2** (*tr*) to rearrange into a new grouping.

Regt *abbrev. for:* **1** Regent. **2** Regiment.

regulable ('rɛgjʊləbᵊl) *adj* able to be regulated.

regular ❶ ('rɛgjʊlə) *adj* **1** normal, customary, or usual. **2** according to a uniform principle, arrangement, or order. **3** occurring at fixed or prearranged intervals: *a regular call on a customer.* **4** following a set rule or nor-

THESAURUS

region *n* **1, 2 = area**, country, district, division, expanse, land, locality, part, patch, place, province, quarter, section, sector, territory, tract, turf (*US sl.*), zone **4 = sphere**, domain, field, province, realm, world **5 = vicinity**, area, neighbourhood, range, scope, sphere

regional *adj* **= local**, district, parochial, provincial, sectional, zonal

register *n* **1, 2 = list**, annals, archives, catalogue, chronicle, diary, file, ledger, log, memorandum, record, roll, roster, schedule ◆ *vb* **10 = record**, catalogue, check in, chronicle, enlist, enrol, enter, inscribe, list, note, set down, sign on *or* up, take down **12 = show**, be shown, bespeak, betray, display, exhibit, express, indicate, manifest, record, reflect, reveal, say **13** *Informal* **= have an effect**, come home, dawn on, get through, impress, make an impression, sink in, tell

regress *vb* **1 = revert**, backslide, degenerate, deteriorate, ebb, fall away *or* off, fall back, go back, lapse, lose ground, recede, relapse, retreat, retrocede, retrogress, return, turn the clock back, wane
Antonyms *vb* advance, improve, progress, wax

regret *vb* **1 = feel sorry about**, be upset, bewail, cry over spilt milk, deplore, feel remorse about, lament, repent, rue, weep over **2 = grieve**, bemoan, miss, mourn ◆ *n* **3 = sorrow**, bitterness, compunction, contrition, lamentation, pang of conscience, penitence, remorse, repentance, ruefulness, self-reproach **4 = grief**
Antonyms *vb* **≠ feel sorry about:** be happy, be satisfied, feel satisfaction, have not looked back, rejoice ◆ *n* **≠ sorrow:** callousness, contentment, impenitence, lack of compassion, pleasure, satisfaction

regretful *adj* **1 = sorry**, apologetic, ashamed, contrite, disappointed, mournful, penitent, remorseful, repentant, rueful, sad, sorrowful

regrettable *adj* **1 = unfortunate**, deplorable, disappointing, distressing, ill-advised, lamentable, pitiable, sad, shameful, unhappy, woeful, wrong

regular *adj* **1 = normal**, common, commonplace, customary, daily, everyday, habitual, ordinary, routine, typical, unvarying, usual **2 = systematic**, consistent, constant, established, even, ordered, set, stated, steady, uniform **3 = periodic**, fixed, rhythmic, set, systematic **4 = methodical**, dependable, efficient, formal, orderly, standardized, steady, systematic **5 = even**, balanced, flat, level, smooth, straight,

mal practice; methodical or orderly. **5** symmetrical in appearance or form; even: *regular features.* **6** (*prenominal*) organized, elected, conducted, etc., in a proper or officially prescribed manner. **7** (*prenominal*) officially qualified or recognized: *he's not a regular doctor.* **8** (*prenominal*) (intensifier): *a regular fool.* **9** *US & Canad. inf.* likable, dependable, or nice: *a regular guy.* **10** denoting or relating to the personnel or units of the permanent military services: *a regular soldier.* **11** (of flowers) having any of their parts, esp. petals, alike in size, etc.; symmetrical. **12** *Grammar.* following the usual pattern of formation in a language. **13** *Maths.* **13a** (of a polygon) equilateral and equiangular. **13b** (of a polyhedron) having identical regular polygons as faces. **13c** (of a prism) having regular polygons as bases. **13d** (of a pyramid) having a regular polygon as a base and the altitude passing through the centre of the base. **14** *Bot.* (of a flower) having radial symmetry. **15** (*postpositive*) subject to the rule of an established religious order or community: *canons regular.* ◆ *n* **16** a professional long-term serviceman in a military unit. **17** *Inf.* a person who does something regularly, such as attending a theatre. **18** a member of a religious order or congregation, as contrasted with a secular. [C14: from OF *reguler,* from L *rēgulāris* of a bar of wood or metal, from *rēgula* ruler, model]
▸ **ˌreguˈlarity** *n* ▸ **ˈregularˌize** *or* **ˈregularˌise** *vb* ▸ **ˈregularly** *adv*

regulate ❶ (ˈrɛgjʊˌleɪt) *vb* **regulates, regulating, regulated.** (*tr*) **1** to adjust (the amount of heat, sound, etc.) as required; control. **2** to adjust (an instrument or appliance) so that it operates correctly. **3** to bring into conformity with a rule, principle, or usage. [C17: from LL *rēgulāre* to control, from L *rēgula* ruler]
▸ **ˈregulative** *or* **ˈregulatory** *adj* ▸ **ˈregulatively** *adv*

regulation ❶ (ˌrɛgjʊˈleɪʃən) *n* **1** the act or process of regulating. **2** a rule, principle, or condition that governs procedure or behaviour. **3** (*modifier*) as required by official rules: *regulation uniform.* **4** (*modifier*) normal; usual; conforming to accepted standards: *a regulation haircut.*

regulator (ˈrɛgjʊˌleɪtə) *n* **1** a person or thing that regulates. **2** the mechanism by which the speed of a timepiece is regulated. **3** any of various mechanisms or devices, such as a governor valve, for controlling fluid flow, pressure, temperature, etc.

regulo (ˈrɛgjʊləʊ) *n* any of a number of temperatures to which a gas oven may be set: *cook at regulo 4.* [C20: from *Regulo,* trademark for a type of thermostatic control on gas ovens]

regulus (ˈrɛgjʊləs) *n, pl* **reguluses** *or* **reguli** (-ˌlaɪ). impure metal forming beneath the slag during the smelting of ores. [C16: from L: a petty king, from *rēx* king; formerly used for *antimony,* because it combines readily with gold, the king of metals]
▸ **ˈreguline** *adj*

regurgitate ❶ (rɪˈgɜːdʒɪˌteɪt) *vb* **regurgitates, regurgitating, regurgitated. 1** to vomit forth (partially digested food). **2** (of some birds and animals) to bring back to the mouth (undigested or partly digested food to feed the young). **3** (*intr*) to be cast up or out, esp. from the mouth. **4** (*intr*) *Med.* (of blood) to flow in a direction opposite to the normal one, esp. through a defective heart valve. [C17: from Med. L *regurgitāre,* from RE- + *gurgitāre* to flood, from L *gurges* whirlpool]
▸ **reˈgurgitant** *n, adj* ▸ **reˌgurgiˈtation** *n*

rehabilitate ❶ (ˌriːəˈbɪlɪˌteɪt) *vb* **rehabilitates, rehabilitating, rehabilitated.** (*tr*) **1** to help (a physically or mentally disabled person or an ex-prisoner) to readapt to society or a new job, as by vocational guidance, retraining, or therapy. **2** to restore to a former position or rank. **3** to restore the good reputation of. [C16: from Med. L *rehabilitāre* to restore, from RE- + L *habilitās* skill]
▸ **ˌrehaˌbiliˈtation** *n* ▸ **ˌrehaˈbilitative** *adj*

Rehabilitation Department *n NZ.* a government department set up after World War II to assist ex-servicemen. Often shortened to **rehab.**

rehash ❶ *vb* (riːˈhæʃ). **1** (*tr*) to rework, reuse, or make over (old or already used material). ◆ *n* (ˈriːˌhæʃ). **2** something consisting of old, reworked, or reused material. [C19: from RE- + HASH[1] (to chop into pieces)]

rehearsal ❶ (rɪˈhɜːsᵊl) *n* **1** a session of practising a play, concert, etc., in preparation for public performance. **2 in rehearsal.** being prepared for public performance.

rehearse ❶ (rɪˈhɜːs) *vb* **rehearses, rehearsing, rehearsed. 1** to practise (a play, concert, etc.), in preparation for public performance. **2** (*tr*) to run through; recount; recite: *he rehearsed the grievances of the committee.* **3** (*tr*) to train or drill (a person) for public performance. [C16: from Anglo-Norman *rehearser,* from OF *rehercier* to harrow a second time, from RE- + *herce* harrow]
▸ **reˈhearser** *n*

reheat *vb* (riːˈhiːt). **1** to heat or be heated again: *to reheat yesterday's soup.* **2** (*tr*) to add fuel to (the exhaust gases of an aircraft jet engine) to produce additional heat and thrust. ◆ *n* (ˈriːˌhiːt), *also* **reheating. 3** a process in which additional fuel is ignited in the exhaust gases of a jet engine to produce additional thrust.
▸ **reˈheater** *n*

rehoboam (ˌriːəˈbəʊəm) *n* a wine bottle holding the equivalent of six normal bottles. [after *Rehoboam,* a son of King Solomon, from Heb., lit.: the nation is enlarged]

Reich (raɪk) *n* **1** the Holy Roman Empire (962–1806) (**First Reich**). **2** the Hohenzollern empire in Germany from 1871 to 1918 (**Second Reich**). **3** the Nazi dictatorship (1933–45) in Germany (**Third Reich**). [G: kingdom]

Reichsmark (ˈraɪksˌmɑːk) *n, pl* **Reichsmarks** *or* **Reichsmark.** the standard monetary unit of Germany between 1924 and 1948.

Reichstag (ˈraɪksˌtɑːg) *n* **1** the legislative assembly of Germany (1867–1933). **2** the building in Berlin in which this assembly met.

reify (ˈriːɪˌfaɪ) *vb* **reifies, reifying, reified.** (*tr*) to consider or make (an abstract idea or concept) real or concrete. [C19: from L *rēs* thing]
▸ **ˌreifiˈcation** *n* ▸ **ˌreifiˈcatory** *adj* ▸ **ˈreiˌfier** *n*

reign ❶ (reɪn) *n* **1** the period during which a monarch is the official ruler of a country. **2** a period during which a person or thing is dominant or powerful: *the reign of violence.* ◆ *vb* (*intr*) **3** to exercise the power and authority of a sovereign. **4** to be accorded the rank and title of a sovereign without having ruling authority. **5** to predominate; prevail: *darkness reigns.* **6** (*usually present participle*) to be the most recent winner of a contest, etc.: *the reigning champion.* [C13: from OF *reigne,* from L *rēgnum* kingdom, from *rēx* king]

> **USAGE NOTE** *Reign* is sometimes wrongly written for *rein* in certain phrases: *he gave full rein* (not *reign*) *to his feelings; it will be necessary to rein in* (not *reign in*) *public spending.*

reiki (ˈreɪkɪ) *n* a form of therapy in which the practitioner is believed to channel energy into the patient in order to encourage healing or restore well-being. [Japanese, from *rei* universal + *ki* life force]

reimburse ❶ (ˌriːɪmˈbɜːs) *vb* **reimburses, reimbursing, reimbursed.** (*tr*) to repay or compensate (someone) for (money already spent, losses, damages, etc.). [C17: from RE- + *imburse,* from Med. L *imbursāre* to put in a moneybag, from *bursa* PURSE]
▸ **ˌreimˈbursable** *adj* ▸ **ˌreimˈbursement** *n* ▸ **ˌreimˈburser** *n*

reimport *vb* (ˌriːɪmˈpɔːt, riːˈɪmpɔːt). **1** (*tr*) to import (goods manufactured from exported raw materials). ◆ *n* (riːˈɪmpɔːt). **2** the act of reimporting. **3** a reimported commodity.
▸ **ˌreimporˈtation** *n*

rein ❶ (reɪn) *n* **1** (*often pl*) one of a pair of long straps, usually connected together and made of leather, used to control a horse. **2** a similar device used to control a very young child. **3** any form or means of control: *to take up the reins of government.* **4** the direction in which a rider turns (in **on a left rein**). **5** something that restrains, controls, or guides. **6 give (a) free rein.** to allow considerable freedom; remove restraints. **7 keep a tight rein on.** to control carefully; limit: *we have to keep a tight rein on expenditure.* ◆ *vb* **8** (*tr*) to check, restrain, hold back, or halt with or as if with reins. **9** to control or guide (a horse) with a rein or reins: *they reined left.* ◆ See also **rein in.** [C13: from OF *resne,* from L *retinēre* to hold back, from RE- + *tenēre* to hold]

> **USAGE NOTE** See at **reign.**

THESAURUS

symmetrical, uniform **7** = **official**, approved, bona fide, classic, correct, established, formal, orthodox, prevailing, proper, sanctioned, standard, time-honoured, traditional
Antonyms *adj* ≠ **normal**: abnormal, exceptional, infrequent, irregular, occasional, rare, uncommon, unconventional, unusual ≠ **systematic**: erratic, inconsistent, inconstant, irregular, varied ≠ **methodical**: disorderly, unmethodical ≠ **even**: erratic, irregular, uneven

regulate *vb* **1, 2** = **adjust**, balance, fit, moderate, modulate, tune **3** = **control**, administer, arrange, conduct, direct, govern, guide, handle, manage, monitor, order, organize, oversee, rule, run, settle, superintend, supervise, systematize

regulation *n* **1** = **adjustment**, modulation, tuning **1** = **control**, administration, arrangement, direction, governance, government, management, supervision **2** = **rule**, canon, commandment, decree, dictate, direction, edict, law, order, ordinance, precept, procedure, requirement, standing order, statute ◆ *adj* **3** = **official**, mandatory, prescribed, required **4** = **usual**, conventional, customary, normal, standard

regurgitate *vb* **1** = **vomit**, barf (*US sl.*), chuck (up) (*sl., chiefly US*), chunder, disgorge, puke (*sl.*), sick up (*inf.*), spew (out *or* up), throw up (*inf.*)

rehabilitate *vb* **1** = **reintegrate**, adjust **2** = **restore**, re-establish, reinstate **3** = **redeem**, clear, reform, restore, save

rehash *vb* **1** = **rework**, alter, change, make over, rearrange, refashion, rejig (*inf.*), reshuffle, reuse, rewrite ◆ *n* **2** = **reworking**, new version, rearrangement, rewrite

rehearsal *n* **1** = **practice**, drill, going-over (*inf.*), practice session, preparation, reading, rehearsing, run-through

rehearse *vb* **1** = **practise**, act, drill, go over, prepare, ready, recite, repeat, run through, study, train, try out **2** = **recite**, delineate, depict, describe, detail, enumerate, go over, list, narrate, recount, relate, review, run through, spell out, tell, trot out (*inf.*)

reign *n* **1, 2** = **rule**, ascendancy, command, control, dominion, empire, hegemony, influence, monarchy, power, sovereignty, supremacy, sway ◆ *vb* **3** = **rule**, administer, be in power, command, govern, hold sway, influence, occupy *or* sit on the throne, wear the crown, wield the sceptre **5** = **be supreme**, be rampant, be rife, hold sway, obtain, predominate, prevail

reimburse *vb* = **pay back**, compensate, indemnify, recompense, refund, remunerate, repay, restore, return, square up

rein *n* **1, 3** = **control**, brake, bridle, check, curb, harness, hold, restraint, restriction **6 give (a) free rein** = **give a free hand**, free, give a blank cheque, give carte blanche, give (someone) his *or* her head, give way to, indulge, let go, remove restraints ◆ *vb* **8** = **control**, bridle, check, curb, halt, hold, hold back, limit, restrain, restrict, slow down

reincarnate *vb* (ˌriːɪnˈkɑːˌneɪt), **reincarnates, reincarnating, reincarnated.** (*tr; often passive*) **1** to cause to undergo reincarnation; be born again. ◆ *adj* (ˌriːɪnˈkɑːnɪt). **2** born again in a new body.

reincarnation ⓣ (ˌriːɪnkɑːˈneɪʃən) *n* **1** the belief that on the death of the body the soul transmigrates to or is born again in another body. **2** the incarnation or embodiment of a soul in a new body after it has left the old one at physical death. **3** embodiment again in a new form, as of a principle or idea.
▸ **ˌreincarˈnationist** *n, adj*

reindeer (ˈreɪnˌdɪə) *n, pl* **reindeer** *or* **reindeers.** a large deer, having large branched antlers in the male and female and inhabiting the arctic regions. It also occurs in North America, where it is known as a caribou. [C14: from ON *hreindýri*, from *hreinn* reindeer + *dyr* animal]

reindeer moss *n* any of various lichens which occur in arctic and subarctic regions, providing food for reindeer.

reinforce ⓣ (ˌriːɪnˈfɔːs) *vb* **reinforces, reinforcing, reinforced.** (*tr*) **1** to give added strength or support to. **2** to give added emphasis to; stress or increase: *his rudeness reinforced my determination.* **3** to give added support to (a military force) by providing more men, supplies, etc. [C17: from F *renforcer*]
▸ **ˌreinˈforcement** *n*

reinforced concrete *n* concrete with steel bars, mesh, etc., embedded in it to enable it to withstand tensile and shear stresses.

reinforced plastic *n* plastic with fibrous matter, such as carbon fibre, embedded in it to strengthen it.

rein in *vb* (*adv*) to stop (a horse) by pulling on the reins.

reins (reɪnz) *pl n Arch.* the kidneys or loins. [C14: from OF, from L *rēnēs* the kidneys]

reinstate ⓣ (ˌriːɪnˈsteɪt) *vb* **reinstates, reinstating, reinstated.** (*tr*) to restore to a former rank or condition.
▸ **ˌreinˈstatement** *n* ▸ **ˌreinˈstator** *n*

reinsurer (ˌriːɪnˈʃʊərə) *n* an insurance company which will accept business from other insurance companies, thus enabling the risks to be spread.
▸ **ˌreinˈsurance** *n*

reinvent (ˌriːɪnˈvent) *vb* (*tr*) **1** to replace (a product, etc.) with an entirely new version. **2** to duplicate (something that already exists) in what is therefore a wasted effort (esp. in **reinvent the wheel**).

reissue (ˌriːˈɪʃjuː) *n* **1** a book, record, etc., that is published or released again after being unavailable for a time. ◆ *vb* **2** (*tr*) to publish or release (a book, record, etc.) again after a period of unavailability.

reiterate ⓣ (riːˈɪtəˌreɪt) *vb* **reiterates, reiterating, reiterated.** (*tr; may take a clause as object*) to say or do again or repeatedly. [C16: from L *reiterāre*, from RE- + *iterāre* to do again, from *iterum* again]
▸ **reˌiterˈation** *n* ▸ **reˈiterative** *adj* ▸ **reˈiteratively** *adv*

reive (riːv) *vb* **reives, reiving, reived.** (*intr*) *Scot. & N English dialect.* to go on a plundering raid. [var. of REAVE]
▸ **ˈreiver** *n*

reject ⓣ *vb* (rɪˈdʒɛkt). (*tr*) **1** to refuse to accept, use, believe, etc. **2** to throw out as useless or worthless; discard. **3** to rebuff (a person). **4** (of an organism) to fail to accept (a foreign tissue graft or organ transplant). ◆ *n* (ˈriːdʒɛkt). **5** something rejected as imperfect, unsatisfactory, or useless. [C15: from L *rēicere* to throw back, from RE- + *jacere* to hurl]
▸ **reˈjecter** *or* **reˈjector** *n* ▸ **reˈjection** *n* ▸ **reˈjective** *adj*

rejig ⓣ (riːˈdʒɪg) *vb* **rejigs, rejigging, rejigged.** (*tr*) **1** to re-equip (a factory or plant). **2** *Inf.* to rearrange, manipulate, etc., sometimes in an unscrupulous way. ◆ *n* **3** the act or process of rejigging.
▸ **reˈjigger** *n*

rejoice ⓣ (rɪˈdʒɔɪs) *vb* **rejoices, rejoicing, rejoiced.** (when *tr, takes a clause as object or an infinitive;* when *intr*, often foll. by *in*) to feel or express great joy or happiness. [C14: from OF *resjoir*, from RE- + *joir* to be glad, from L *gaudēre* to rejoice]
▸ **reˈjoicer** *n*

rejoin[1] (riːˈdʒɔɪn) *vb* **1** to come again into company with (someone or something). **2** (*tr*) to put or join together again; reunite.

rejoin[2] ⓣ (rɪˈdʒɔɪn) *vb* (*tr*) **1** to answer or reply. **2** *Law.* to answer (a plaintiff's reply). [C15: from OF *rejoign-*, stem of *rejoindre;* see RE-, JOIN]

rejoinder ⓣ (rɪˈdʒɔɪndə) *n* **1** a reply or response to a question or remark. **2** *Law.* (in pleading) the answer made by a defendant to the plaintiff's reply. [C15: from OF *rejoindre* to REJOIN[2]]

rejuvenate ⓣ (rɪˈdʒuːvɪˌneɪt) *vb* **rejuvenates, rejuvenating, rejuvenated.** (*tr*) **1** to give new youth, restored vitality, or youthful appearance to. **2** (*usually passive*) *Geog.* to cause (a river) to begin eroding more vigorously to a new lower base level. [C19: from RE- + L *juvenis* young]
▸ **reˌjuveˈnation** *n* ▸ **reˈjuveˌnator** *n*

rejuvenesce (rɪˌdʒuːvəˈnɛs) *vb* **rejuvenesces, rejuvenescing, rejuvenesced.** **1** to make or become youthful or restored to vitality. **2** *Biol.* to convert (cells) or (of cells) to be converted into a more active form.
▸ **reˌjuveˈnescence** *n* ▸ **reˌjuveˈnescent** *adj*

rel. *abbrev. for:* **1** relating. **2** relative(ly). **3** released. **4** religion. **5** religious.

relapse ⓣ (rɪˈlæps) *vb* **relapses, relapsing, relapsed.** (*intr*) **1** to lapse back into a former state or condition, esp. one involving bad habits. **2** to become ill again after apparent recovery. ◆ *n* **3** the act or an instance of relapsing. **4** the return of ill health after an apparent or partial recovery. [C16: from L *relabī*, from RE- + *labī* to slip, slide]
▸ **reˈlapser** *n*

relapsing fever *n* any of various infectious diseases characterized by recurring fever, caused by the bite of body lice or ticks. Also called: **recurrent fever.**

relate ⓣ (rɪˈleɪt) *vb* **relates, relating, related.** **1** (*tr*) to tell or narrate (a story, etc.). **2** (often foll. by *to*) to establish association (between two or more things) or (of something) to have relation or reference (to something else). **3** (*intr;* often foll. by *to*) to form a sympathetic or significant relationship (with other people, things, etc.). [C16: from L *relātus* brought back, from *referre*, from RE- + *ferre* to bear]
▸ **reˈlatable** *adj* ▸ **reˈlater** *n*

related ⓣ (rɪˈleɪtɪd) *adj* **1** connected; associated. **2** connected by kinship or marriage. **3** (in diatonic music) denoting or relating to a key that has notes in common with another key or keys.
▸ **reˈlatedness** *n*

relation ⓣ (rɪˈleɪʃən) *n* **1** the state or condition of being related or the manner in which things are related. **2** connection by blood or marriage; kinship. **3** a person who is connected by blood or marriage; relative. **4** reference or regard (esp. in **in** *or* **with relation to**). **5** the position, association, connection, or status of one person or thing with regard to another. **6** the act of relating or narrating. **7** an account or narrative. **8** *Law.* the statement of grounds of complaint made by a relator. **9** *Logic, maths.* **9a** an association between ordered pairs of objects, numbers, etc., such as ... is greater than .... **9b** the set of ordered pairs whose members have such an association. ◆ See also **relations.** [C14: from L *relātiō* a narration, a relation (between philosophical concepts)]

relational (rɪˈleɪʃənᵊl) *adj* **1** *Grammar.* indicating or expressing syntactic relation, as for example the case endings in Latin. **2** having relation or

THESAURUS

reincarnation *n* **1** = **rebirth**, metempsychosis, transmigration of souls

reinforce *vb* **1** = **strengthen**, augment, bolster, buttress, fortify, harden, prop, shore up, stiffen, supplement, support, toughen **2** = **stress**, emphasize, increase, underline
Antonyms *vb* undermine, weaken

reinforcement *n* **1** = **support**, brace, buttress, prop, shore, stay **2** = **strengthening**, addition, amplification, augmentation, enlargement, fortification, increase, supplement **3** *plural* = **reserves**, additional *or* fresh troops, auxiliaries, support

reinstate *vb* = **restore**, bring back, recall, re-establish, rehabilitate, replace, return

reiterate *vb Formal* = **repeat**, do again, iterate, recapitulate, restate, retell, say again

reject *vb* **1** = **deny**, decline, disallow, exclude, renounce, repudiate, veto **2** = **discard**, bin, cast aside, eliminate, jettison, scrap, throw away *or* out **3** = **rebuff**, jilt, refuse, repulse, say no to, spurn, turn down ◆ *n* **5** = **castoff**, discard, failure, flotsam, second
Antonyms *vb* ≠ **deny:** accept, agree, allow, approve, permit ≠ **rebuff:** accept ≠ **discard:** accept, receive, select ◆ *n* ≠ **castoff:** prize, treasure

rejection *n* **1** = **denial**, dismissal, exclusion, renunciation, repudiation, thumbs down, veto **3** = **rebuff**, brushoff, bum's rush (*sl.*), kick in the teeth (*sl.*), knock-back (*sl.*), refusal, the (old) heave-ho (*inf.*)
Antonyms *n* ≠ **denial:** acceptance, affirmation, approval ≠ **rebuff:** acceptance, selection

rejig *vb* **2** *Informal* = **rearrange**, alter, juggle, manipulate, massage, reorganize, reshuffle, tweak

rejoice *vb* = **be glad**, be happy, be overjoyed, celebrate, delight, exult, glory, joy, jump for joy, make merry, revel, triumph
Antonyms *vb* be sad, be unhappy, be upset, grieve, lament, mourn

rejoicing *n* = **happiness**, celebration, cheer, delight, elation, exultation, festivity, gaiety, gladness, joy, jubilation, merrymaking, revelry, triumph

rejoin[2] *vb* **1** = **reply**, answer, come back with, respond, retort, return, riposte

rejoinder *n* **1** = **reply**, answer, comeback (*inf.*), counter, counterattack, response, retort, riposte

rejuvenate *vb* **1** = **revitalize**, breathe new life into, give new life to, make young again, reanimate, refresh, regenerate, reinvigorate, renew, restore, restore vitality to, revivify

relapse *vb* **1** = **lapse**, backslide, degenerate, fail, fall back, regress, retrogress, revert, slip back, weaken **2** = **worsen**, deteriorate, fade, fail, sicken, sink, weaken ◆ *n* **3** = **lapse**, backsliding, fall from grace, recidivism, regression, retrogression, reversion **4** = **worsening**, deterioration, recurrence, setback, turn for the worse, weakening
Antonyms *vb* ≠ **worsen:** get better, improve, rally, recover ◆ *n* ≠ **worsening:** improvement, rally, recovery, turn for the better

relate *vb* **1** = **tell**, chronicle, describe, detail, give an account of, impart, narrate, present, recite, recount, rehearse, report, set forth **2** = **connect**, ally, associate, coordinate, correlate, couple, join, link **2** = **concern**, appertain, apply, bear upon, be relevant to, have reference to, have to do with, pertain, refer
Antonyms *vb* ≠ **connect:** detach, disconnect, dissociate, divorce ≠ **concern:** be irrelevant to, be unconnected, have nothing to do with

related *adj* **1** = **associated**, accompanying, affiliated, agnate, akin, allied, cognate, concomitant, connected, correlated, interconnected, joint, linked **2** = **akin**, agnate, cognate, consanguineous, kin, kindred
Antonyms *adj* ≠ **associated:** separate, unconnected, unrelated ≠ **akin:** unrelated

relation *n* **1** = **connection**, application, bearing, bond, comparison, correlation, interdependence, link, pertinence, similarity, tie-in **2** = **kinship**, affiliation, affinity, consanguinity, kindred, propinquity, relationship **3** = **relative**, kin, kinsman *or* kinswoman **4** = **regard**, reference **6** = **narration**, description, recital, recountal **7** = **account**, description, narrative, report, story, tale being related. **3** *Computing.* based on data that is interconnected, often in tabular form.

relations ➊ (rɪˈleɪʃənz) *pl n* **1** social, political, or personal connections or dealings between or among individuals, groups, nations, etc. **2** family or relatives. **3** *Euphemistic.* sexual intercourse.

relationship ➊ (rɪˈleɪʃənʃɪp) *n* **1** the state of being connected or related. **2** association by blood or marriage; kinship. **3** the mutual dealings, connections, or feelings that exist between two countries, people, etc. **4** an emotional or sexual affair or liaison.

relative ➊ (ˈrɛlətɪv) *adj* **1** having meaning or significance only in relation to something else; not absolute. **2** (*prenominal*) (of a scientific quantity) being measured or stated relative to some other substance or measurement: *relative density.* **3** (*prenominal*) comparative or respective: *the relative qualities of speed and accuracy.* **4** (*postpositive;* foll. by *to*) in proportion (to); corresponding (to): *earnings relative to production.* **5** having reference (to); pertinent (to). **6** *Grammar.* denoting or belonging to a class of words that function as subordinating conjunctions in introducing relative clauses such as *who, which,* and *that.* Cf. **demonstrative. 7** *Grammar.* denoting or relating to a clause (**relative clause**) that modifies a noun or pronoun occurring earlier in the sentence. **8** (of a musical key or scale) having the same key signature as another key or scale. ◆ *n* **9** a person who is related by blood or marriage; relation. **10** a relative pronoun, clause, or grammatical construction. [C16: from LL *relātīvus* referring]
▸ **ˈrelatively** *adv* ▸ **ˈrelativeness** *n*

relative aperture *n Photog.* the ratio of the equivalent focal length of a lens to the effective aperture of the lens.

relative atomic mass *n* the ratio of the average mass per atom of the naturally occurring form of an element to one-twelfth of the mass of an atom of carbon-12. Symbol: A_r Abbrev.: **r.a.m.** Former name: **atomic weight.**

relative density *n* the ratio of the density of a substance to the density of a standard substance under specified conditions. For liquids and solids the standard is usually water at 4°C. For gases the standard is air or hydrogen at the same temperature and pressure as the substance. See also **specific gravity, vapour density.**

relative frequency *n Statistics.* the ratio of the actual number of favourable events to the total possible number of events.

relative humidity *n* the mass of water vapour present in the air expressed as a percentage of the mass present in an equal volume of saturated air at the same temperature.

relative majority *n Brit.* the excess of votes or seats won by the winner of an election over the runner-up when no candidate or party has more than 50 per cent. Cf. **absolute majority.**

relative molecular mass *n* the sum of all the relative atomic masses of the atoms in a molecule; the ratio of the average mass per molecule of a specified isotopic composition of a substance to one-twelfth the mass of an atom of carbon-12. Symbol: M_r Abbrev.: **r.m.m.** Former name: **molecular weight.**

relative permeability *n* the ratio of the permeability of a medium to that of free space.

relative permittivity *n* the ratio of the permittivity of a substance to that of free space.

relativism (ˈrɛlətɪˌvɪzəm) *n* any theory holding that truth or moral or aesthetic value, etc., is not universal or absolute but may differ between individuals or cultures.
▸ **ˈrelativist** *n, adj* ▸ **ˌrelativˈistic** *adj*

relativity (ˌrɛləˈtɪvɪtɪ) *n* **1** either of two theories developed by Albert Einstein, the **special theory of relativity**, which requires that the laws of physics shall be the same as seen by any two different observers in uniform relative motion, and the **general theory of relativity**, which considers observers with relative acceleration and leads to a theory of gravitation. **2** the state or quality of being relative.

relator (rɪˈleɪtə) *n* **1** a person who relates a story; narrator. **2** *English law.* a person who gives information upon which the attorney general brings an action.

relatum (rɪˈleɪtəm) *n, pl* **relata** (-tə). *Logic.* one of the objects between which a relation is said to hold.

relax ➊ (rɪˈlæks) *vb* **1** to make (muscles, a grip, etc.) less tense or rigid or (of muscles, a grip, etc.) to become looser or less rigid. **2** (*intr*) to take rest, as from work or effort. **3** to lessen the force of (effort, concentration) or (of effort) to become diminished. **4** to make (rules or discipline) less rigid or strict or (of rules, etc.) to diminish in severity. **5** (*intr*) (of a person) to become less formal; unbend. [C15: from L *relaxāre* to loosen, from RE- + *laxāre,* from *laxus* loose]
▸ **reˈlaxed** *adj* ▸ **relaxedly** (rɪˈlæksɪdlɪ) *adv* ▸ **reˈlaxer** *n*

relaxant (rɪˈlæksᵊnt) *n* **1** *Med.* a drug or agent that relaxes, esp. one that relaxes tense muscles. ◆ *adj* **2** of or tending to produce relaxation.

relaxation ➊ (ˌriːlækˈseɪʃən) *n* **1** rest or refreshment, as after work or effort; recreation. **2** a form of rest or recreation: *his relaxation is cricket.* **3** a partial lessening of a punishment, duty, etc. **4** the act of relaxing or state of being relaxed. **5** *Physics.* the return of a system to equilibrium after a displacement from this state.

relaxin (rɪˈlæksɪn) *n* **1** a mammalian polypeptide hormone secreted during pregnancy, which relaxes the pelvic ligaments. **2** a preparation of this hormone, used to facilitate childbirth. [C20: from RELAX + -IN]

relay ➊ *n* (ˈriːleɪ). **1** a person or team of people relieving others, as on a shift. **2** a fresh team of horses, etc., posted along a route to relieve others. **3** the act of relaying or process of being relayed. **4** short for **relay race. 5** an automatic device that controls a valve, switch, etc., by means of an electric motor, solenoid, or pneumatic mechanism. **6** *Electronics.* an electrical device in which a small change in current or voltage controls the switching on or off of circuits. **7** *Radio.* **7a** a combination of a receiver and transmitter designed to receive radio signals and retransmit them. **7b** (*as modifier*): *a relay station.* ◆ *vb* (rɪˈleɪ). (*tr*) **8** to carry or spread (news or information) by relays. **9** to supply or replace with relays. **10** to retransmit (a signal) by means of a relay. **11** *Brit.* to broadcast (a performance) by sending out signals through a transmitting station. [C15 *relaien,* from OF *relaier* to leave behind, from RE- + *laier* to leave, ult. from L *laxāre* to loosen]

relay race *n* a race between two or more teams of contestants in which each contestant covers a specified portion of the distance.

release ➊ (rɪˈliːs) *vb* **releases, releasing, released.** (*tr*) **1** to free (a person or animal) from captivity or imprisonment. **2** to free (someone) from obligation or duty. **3** to free (something) from (one's grip); let fall. **4** to issue (a record, film, or book) for sale or circulation. **5** to make (news or information) known or allow (news, etc.) to be made known. **6** *Law.* to relinquish (a right, claim, or title) in favour of someone else. ◆ *n* **7** the act of freeing or state of being freed. **8** the act of issuing for sale or publication. **9** something issued for sale or public showing, esp. a film or a record: *a new release from Bob Dylan.* **10** a news item, etc., made available for publication, broadcasting, etc. **11** *Law.* the surrender of a claim, right, title, etc., in favour of someone else. **12** a control mechanism for starting or stopping an engine. **13** the control mechanism for the shutter in a camera. [C13: from OF *relesser,* from L *relaxāre* to slacken]
▸ **reˈleaser** *n*

relegate ➊ (ˈrɛlɪˌgeɪt) *vb* **relegates, relegating, relegated.** (*tr*) **1** to move to a position of less authority, importance, etc.; demote. **2** (*usually passive*) *Chiefly Brit.* to demote (a football team, etc.) to a lower division. **3** to assign or refer (a matter) to another. **4** (foll. by *to*) to banish or exile. **5** to assign (something) to a particular group or category. [C16: from L *relēgāre,* from RE- + *lēgāre* to send]
▸ **ˈreleˌgatable** *adj* ▸ **ˌreleˈgation** *n*

relent ➊ (rɪˈlɛnt) *vb* (*intr*) **1** to change one's mind about some decision, esp. a harsh one; become more mild or amenable. **2** (of the pace or in-

THESAURUS

relations *pl n* **1 = dealings**, affairs, associations, communications, connections, contact, interaction, intercourse, liaison, meetings, rapport, relationship, terms **2 = family**, clan, kin, kindred, kinsfolk, kinsmen, relatives, tribe

relationship *n* **1 = connection**, correlation, link, parallel, proportion, ratio, similarity, tie-up **3 = association**, affinity, bond, communications, conjunction, connection, exchange, kinship, rapport **4 = affair**, liaison

relative *adj* **1, 3 = dependent**, allied, associated, comparative, connected, contingent, corresponding, proportionate, reciprocal, related, respective **4** *foll. by* **to = in proportion to**, corresponding to, proportional to **5 = relevant**, applicable, apposite, appropriate, appurtenant, apropos, germane, pertinent ◆ *n* **9 = relation**, connection, kinsman *or* kinswoman, member of one's *or* the family

relatively *adv* **3 = comparatively**, in *or* by comparison, rather, somewhat, to some extent

relax *vb* **2 = rest**, laze, put one's feet up, take it easy, take one's ease **3 = lessen**, abate, diminish, ease, ebb, let up, loosen, lower, mitigate, moderate, reduce, relieve, slacken, weaken **5 = be** *or* **feel at ease**, chill out (*sl., chiefly US*), hang loose (*sl.*), let oneself go (*inf.*), let one's hair down (*inf.*), lighten up (*sl.*), loosen up, make oneself at home, mellow out (*inf.*), take it easy, unbend, unwind
Antonyms *vb* ≠ **lessen:** heighten, increase, intensify, tense, tighten, work ≠ **be** *or* feel at ease: be alarmed, be alert

relaxation *n* **1, 2 = leisure**, amusement, beer and skittles (*inf.*), enjoyment, entertainment, fun, pleasure, recreation, refreshment, rest **3 = lessening**, abatement, diminution, easing, let-up (*inf.*), moderation, reduction, slackening, weakening

relaxed *adj* **5 = easy-going**, casual, comfortable, downbeat (*inf.*), easy, free and easy, informal, insouciant, laid-back (*inf.*), leisurely, mellow, mild, nonchalant, unhurried, untaxing

relay *n* **1 = shift**, relief, turn ◆ *vb* **8 = pass on**, broadcast, carry, communicate, hand on, send, spread, transmit

release *vb* **1 = set free**, deliver, discharge, disengage, drop, emancipate, extricate, free, let go, let out, liberate, loose, manumit, turn loose, unbridle, unchain, undo, unfasten, unfetter, unloose, unshackle, untie **2 = acquit**, absolve, dispense, excuse, exempt, exonerate, let go, let off **4 = issue**, circulate, disseminate, distribute, launch, present, publish, put out **5 = make known**, break, make public, unveil ◆ *n* **7 = liberation**, deliverance, delivery, discharge, emancipation, freedom, liberty, manumission, relief **8, 9 = publication**, issue **10 = announcement**, proclamation
Antonyms *vb* ≠ **set free:** detain, engage, fasten, hold, imprison, incarcerate, keep ≠ **issue:** suppress, withhold ◆ *n* ≠ **liberation:** detention, imprisonment, incarceration, internment

relegate *vb* **1 = demote**, downgrade **3 = pass on**, assign, consign, delegate, entrust, refer, transfer **4 = banish**, deport, eject, exile, expatriate, expel, oust, throw out

relent *vb* **1 = be merciful**, acquiesce, capitulate, change one's mind, come round, forbear, give in, give quarter, give way, have pity, melt, show mercy, soften, unbend, yield **2 = ease**, die down, drop, fall, let up, relax, slacken, slow, weaken
Antonyms *vb* ≠ **be merciful:** be unyielding, give no

tensity of something) to slacken. **3** (of the weather) to become more mild. [C14: from RE- + L *lentāre* to bend, from *lentus* flexible]
relentless Ⓣ (rɪ'lɛntlɪs) *adj* **1** (of an enemy, etc.) implacable; inflexible; inexorable. **2** (of pace or intensity) sustained; unremitting.
▸**re'lentlessly** *adv* ▸**re'lentlessness** *n*
relevant Ⓣ ('rɛlɪvənt) *adj* having direct bearing on the matter in hand; pertinent. [C16: from Med. L *relevans,* from L *relevāre,* from RE- + *levāre* to raise, RELIEVE]
▸**'relevance** *or* **'relevancy** *n* ▸**'relevantly** *adv*
reliable Ⓣ (rɪ'laɪəbᵊl) *adj* able to be trusted; dependable.
▸**re,lia'bility** *or* **re'liableness** *n* ▸**re'liably** *adv*
reliance Ⓣ (rɪ'laɪəns) *n* **1** dependence, confidence, or trust. **2** something or someone upon which one relies.
▸**re'liant** *adj* ▸**re'liantly** *adv*
relic Ⓣ ('rɛlɪk) *n* **1** something that has survived from the past, such as an object or custom. **2** something treasured for its past associations; keepsake. **3** (*usually pl*) a remaining part or fragment. **4** *RC Church, Eastern Church.* part of the body of a saint or his belongings, venerated as holy. **5** *Inf.* an old or old-fashioned person or thing. **6** (*pl*) *Arch.* the remains of a dead person; corpse. [C13: from OF *relique,* from L *reliquiae* remains, from *relinquere* to leave behind]
relict ('rɛlɪkt) *n* **1** *Ecology.* **1a** a group of animals or plants that exists as a remnant of a formerly widely distributed group. **1b** (*as modifier*): *a relict fauna.* **2** *Geol.* a mountain, lake, glacier, etc., that is a remnant of a pre-existing formation after a destructive process has occurred. **3** an archaic word for **widow.** **4** an archaic word for **relic.** [C16: from L *relictus* left behind, from *relinquere* to RELINQUISH]
relief Ⓣ (rɪ'li:f) *n* **1** a feeling of cheerfulness or optimism that follows the removal of anxiety, pain, or distress. **2** deliverance from or alleviation of anxiety, pain, etc. **3a** help or assistance, as to the poor or needy. **3b** (*as modifier*): *relief work.* **4** a diversion from monotony. **5** a person who replaces another at some task or duty. **6** a bus, plane, etc., that carries additional passengers when a scheduled service is full. **7** a road (**relief road**) carrying traffic round an urban area; bypass. **8a** the act of freeing a beleaguered town, fortress, etc.: *the relief of Mafeking.* **8b** (*as modifier*): *a relief column.* **9** Also called: **relievo, rilievo.** *Sculpture, archit.* **9a** the projection of forms or figures from a flat ground, so that they are partly or wholly free of it. **9b** a piece of work of this kind. **10** a printing process that employs raised surfaces from which ink is transferred to the paper. **11** any vivid effect resulting from contrast: *comic relief.* **12** variation in altitude in an area; difference between highest and lowest level. **13** *Law.* redress of a grievance or hardship: *to seek relief through the courts.* **14 on relief.** *US & Canad.* (of people) in receipt of government aid because of personal need. [C14: from OF, from *relever;* see RELIEVE]
relief map *n* a map that shows the configuration and height of the land surface, usually by means of contours.
relieve Ⓣ (rɪ'li:v) *vb* **relieves, relieving, relieved.** (*tr*) **1** to bring alleviation of (pain, distress, etc.) to (someone). **2** to bring aid or assistance to (someone in need, etc.). **3** to take over the duties or watch of (someone). **4** to bring aid or a relieving force to (a besieged town, etc.). **5** to free (someone) from an obligation. **6** to make (something) less unpleasant, arduous, or monotonous. **7** to bring into relief or prominence, as by contrast. **8** (foll. by *of*) *Inf.* to take from: *the thief relieved him of his watch.* **9 relieve oneself.** to urinate or defecate. [C14: from OF *relever,* from L *relevāre* to lift up, relieve, from RE- + *levāre* to lighten]
▸**re'lievable** *adj* ▸**re'liever** *n*
relieved (rɪ'li:vd) *adj* (*postpositive;* often foll. by *at, about,* etc.) experiencing relief, esp. from worry or anxiety.
religieuse *French.* (rəliʒjøz) *n* a nun. [C18: fem of RELIGIEUX]
religieux *French.* (rəliʒjø) *n, pl* ***religieux*** (-ʒjø). a member of a monastic order or clerical body. [C17: from L *religiōsus* religious]
religion (rɪ'lɪdʒən) *n* **1** belief in, worship of, or obedience to a supernatural power or powers considered to be divine or to have control of human destiny. **2** any formal or institutionalized expression of such belief: *the Christian religion.* **3** the attitude and feeling of one who believes in a transcendent controlling power or powers. **4** *Chiefly RC Church.* the way of life entered upon by monks and nuns: *to enter religion.* **5** something of overwhelming importance to a person: *football is his religion.* [C12: via OF from L *religiō* fear of the supernatural, piety, prob. from *religāre,* from RE- + *ligāre* to bind]
religionism (rɪ'lɪdʒə,nɪzəm) *n* extreme religious fervour.
▸**re'ligionist** *n, adj*
religiose (rɪ'lɪdʒɪ,əʊs) *adj* affectedly or extremely pious; sanctimoniously religious.
▸**re'ligi,osely** *adv* ▸**religiosity** (rɪ,lɪdʒɪ'ɒsɪtɪ) *n*
religious Ⓣ (rɪ'lɪdʒəs) *adj* **1** of, relating to, or concerned with religion. **2a** pious; devout; godly. **2b** (*as collective n;* preceded by *the*): *the religious.* **3** appropriate to or in accordance with the principles of a religion. **4** scrupulous, exact, or conscientious. **5** *Christianity.* of or relating to a way of life dedicated to religion and defined by a monastic rule. ◆ *n* **6** *Christianity.* a monk or nun.
▸**re'ligiously** *adv* ▸**re'ligiousness** *n*
Religious Society of Friends *n* the official name for the **Quakers.**
relinquish Ⓣ (rɪ'lɪŋkwɪʃ) *vb* (*tr*) **1** to give up (a task, struggle, etc.); abandon. **2** to surrender or renounce (a claim, right, etc.). **3** to release; let go. [C15: from F *relinquir,* from L *relinquere,* from RE- + *linquere* to leave]
▸**re'linquisher** *n* ▸**re'linquishment** *n*
reliquary ('rɛlɪkwərɪ) *n, pl* **reliquaries.** a receptacle or repository for relics, esp. relics of saints. [C17: from OF *reliquaire,* from *relique* RELIC]
relique (rə'li:k, 'rɛlɪk) *n* an archaic spelling of **relic.**
reliquiae (rɪ'lɪkwɪ,i:) *pl n* fossil remains of animals or plants. [C19: from L: remains]
relish Ⓣ ('rɛlɪʃ) *vb* (*tr*) **1** to savour or enjoy (an experience) to the full. **2** to anticipate eagerly; look forward to. **3** to enjoy the taste or flavour of (food, etc.); savour. ◆ *n* **4** liking or enjoyment, as of something eaten or experienced (esp. in **with relish**). **5** pleasurable anticipation: *he didn't have much relish for the idea.* **6** an appetizing or spicy food added to a main dish to enhance its flavour. **7** an appetizing taste or flavour. **8** a zestful trace or touch: *there was a certain relish in all his writing.* [C16: from earlier *reles* aftertaste, from OF, from *relaisser* to leave behind; see RELEASE]
▸**'relishable** *adj*
relive (ri:'lɪv) *vb* **relives, reliving, relived.** (*tr*) to experience (a sensation, event, etc.) again, esp. in the imagination.
▸**re'livable** *adj*
relocate (,ri:ləʊ'keɪt) *vb* **relocates, relocating, relocated.** to move or be moved to a new place, esp. (of an employee, a business, etc.) to a new area or place of employment.
▸**,relo'cation** *n*
reluctance Ⓣ (rɪ'lʌktəns) *or* **reluctancy** *n* **1** lack of eagerness or willingness; disinclination. **2** *Physics.* a measure of the resistance of a closed magnetic circuit to a magnetic flux. [C16: from L *reluctārī* to resist, from RE- + *luctārī* to struggle]
reluctant Ⓣ (rɪ'lʌktənt) *adj* not eager; unwilling; disinclined. [C17: from L *reluctārī* to resist]
▸**re'luctantly** *adv*
reluctivity (,rɛlʌk'tɪvɪtɪ) *n, pl* **reluctivities.** *Physics.* a specific or relative

THESAURUS

quarter, remain firm, show no mercy ≠ **ease:** increase, intensify, strengthen
relentless *adj* **1** = **merciless,** cruel, fierce, grim, hard, harsh, implacable, inexorable, inflexible, pitiless, remorseless, ruthless, uncompromising, undeviating, unforgiving, unrelenting, unstoppable, unyielding **2** = **unremitting,** incessant, nonstop, persistent, punishing, sustained, unabated, unbroken, unfaltering, unflagging, unrelenting, unrelieved, unstoppable
Antonyms *adj* ≠ **merciless:** compassionate, forgiving, merciful, submissive, yielding
relevant *adj* = **significant,** admissible, *ad rem,* applicable, apposite, appropriate, appurtenant, apt, fitting, germane, material, pertinent, proper, related, relative, suited, to the point, to the purpose
Antonyms *adj* beside the point, extraneous, extrinsic, immaterial, inapplicable, inappropriate, irrelevant, unconnected, unrelated
reliable *adj* = **dependable,** certain, faithful, honest, predictable, regular, reputable, responsible, safe, sound, stable, staunch, sure, tried and true, true, trustworthy, trusty, unfailing, upright
Antonyms *adj* irresponsible, undependable, unreliable, untrustworthy
reliance *n* **1** = **trust,** assurance, belief, confidence, credence, credit, dependence, faith
relic *n* **1** = **remnant,** fragment, scrap, survival, token, trace, vestige **2** = **keepsake,** memento, remembrance, souvenir
relief *n* **2** = **ease,** abatement, alleviation, assuagement, balm, comfort, cure, deliverance, easement, mitigation, palliation, release, remedy, solace **3a** = **aid,** assistance, help, succour, support, sustenance **4** = **rest,** break, breather (*inf.*), diversion, let-up (*inf.*), refreshment, relaxation, remission, respite
relieve *vb* **1** = **ease,** abate, allay, alleviate, appease, assuage, calm, comfort, console, cure, diminish, dull, mitigate, mollify, palliate, relax, salve, soften, solace, soothe **2** = **help,** aid, assist, bring aid to, succour, support, sustain **3** = **take over from,** give (someone) a break *or* rest, stand in for, substitute for, take the place of **5** = **free,** deliver, discharge, disembarrass, disencumber, exempt, release, unburden **6** = **interrupt,** break, brighten, let up on (*inf.*), lighten, slacken, vary
Antonyms *vb* ≠ **ease:** aggravate, exacerbate, heighten, intensify, worsen
religious *adj* **1-3** = **devout,** churchgoing, devotional, divine, doctrinal, faithful, god-fearing, godly, holy, pious, pure, reverent, righteous, sacred, scriptural, sectarian, spiritual, theological **4** = **conscientious,** exact, faithful, fastidious, meticulous, punctilious, rigid, rigorous, scrupulous, unerring, unswerving
Antonyms *adj* ≠ **devout:** godless, infidel, irreligious, rational, secular, unbelieving
relinquish *vb* **1** = **give up,** abandon, drop **2** = **renounce,** abandon, abdicate, cede, drop, forgo, forsake, give up, hand over, lay aside, quit, repudiate, resign, retire from, surrender, vacate, waive, yield **3** = **release,** let go
relish *vb* **1** = **enjoy,** appreciate, delight in, fancy, lick one's lips, like, look forward to, luxuriate in, prefer, revel in, savour, taste ◆ *n* **5** = **enjoyment,** appetite, appreciation, fancy, fondness, gusto, liking, love, partiality, penchant, predilection, stomach, taste, zest, zing (*inf.*) **6** = **condiment,** appetizer, sauce, seasoning **7** = **flavour,** piquancy, savour, smack, spice, tang, taste, trace
Antonyms *vb* ≠ **enjoy:** be unenthusiastic about, dislike, loathe ◆ *n* ≠ **enjoyment:** dislike, distaste, loathing
reluctance *n* **1** = **unwillingness,** aversion, backwardness, disinclination, dislike, disrelish, distaste, hesitancy, indisposition, loathing, repugnance
reluctant *adj* = **unwilling,** averse, backward, disinclined, grudging, hesitant, indisposed, loath, recalcitrant, slow, unenthusiastic
Antonyms *adj* eager, enthusiastic, inclined, keen, willing

reluctance of a magnetic material. [C19: from obs. *reluct* to struggle + *-ivity*]

rely ⊕ (rɪˈlaɪ) *vb* **relies, relying, relied.** (*intr;* foll. by *on* or *upon*) **1** to be dependent (on): *he relies on his charm.* **2** to have trust or confidence (in): *you can rely on us.* [C14: from OF *relier* to fasten together, from L *religāre,* from RE- + *ligāre* to tie]

REM *abbrev. for* rapid eye movement.

remain ⊕ (rɪˈmeɪn) *vb* (*mainly intr*) **1** to stay behind or in the same place: *to remain at home.* **2** (*copula*) to continue to be: *to remain cheerful.* **3** to be left, as after use, the passage of time, etc. **4** to be left to be done, said, etc.: *it remains to be pointed out.* [C14: from OF *remanoir,* from L *remanēre,* from RE- + *manēre* to stay]

remainder ⊕ (rɪˈmeɪndə) *n* **1** a part or portion that is left, as after use, subtraction, expenditure, the passage of time, etc.: *the remainder of the milk.* **2** *Maths.* **2a** the amount left over when one quantity cannot be exactly divided by another: *for 10 ÷ 3, the remainder is 1.* **2b** another name for **difference** (sense 7). **3** *Property law.* a future interest in property; an interest in a particular estate that will pass to one at some future date, as on the death of the current possessor. **4** a number of copies of a book left unsold when demand ceases, which are sold at a reduced price. ◆ *vb* **5** (*tr*) to sell (copies of a book) as a remainder.

remains ⊕ (rɪˈmeɪnz) *pl n* **1** any pieces, fragments, etc., that are left unused or still extant, as after use, consumption, the passage of time: *archaeological remains.* **2** the body of a dead person; corpse. **3** Also called: **literary remains.** the unpublished writings of an author at the time of his death.

remake *n* (ˈriːˌmeɪk). **1** something that is made again, esp. a new version of an old film. **2** the act of making again. ◆ *vb* (riːˈmeɪk), **remakes, remaking, remade. 3** (*tr*) to make again or anew.

remand (rɪˈmɑːnd) *vb* (*tr*) **1** *Law.* (of a court or magistrate) to send (a prisoner or accused person) back into custody. **2** to send back. ◆ *n* **3** the sending of a prisoner or accused person back into custody to await trial. **4** the act of remanding or state of being remanded. **5 on remand.** in custody or on bail awaiting trial. [C15: from Med. L *remandāre* to send back word, from L RE- + *mandāre* to command]

remand centre *n* (in Britain) an institution to which accused persons are sent for detention while awaiting appearance before a court.

remanence (ˈrɛmənəns) *n Physics.* the ability of a material to retain magnetization after the removal of the magnetizing field. [C17: from L *remanēre* to stay behind]

remark ⊕ (rɪˈmɑːk) *vb* **1** (when *intr,* often foll. by *on* or *upon;* when *tr, may take a clause as object*) to pass a casual comment (about); reflect in informal speech or writing. **2** (*tr; may take a clause as object*) to perceive; observe; notice. ◆ *n* **3** a brief casually expressed thought or opinion. **4** notice, comment, or observation: *the event passed without remark.* **5** a variant of **remarque.** [C17: from OF *remarquer* to observe, from RE- + *marquer* to note, MARK[1]]
▸**reˈmarker** *n*

remarkable ⊕ (rɪˈmɑːkəbᵊl) *adj* **1** worthy of note or attention: *a remarkable achievement.* **2** unusual, striking, or extraordinary: *a remarkable sight.*
▸**reˈmarkableness** *n* ▸**reˈmarkably** *adv*

remarque (rɪˈmɑːk) *n* a mark in the margin of an engraved plate to indicate the stage of production. [C19: from F; see REMARK]

remaster (riːˈmɑːstə) *vb* (*tr*) to make a new master audio recording, now usually digital, from (an earlier original recording), in order to produce compact discs or stereo records with improved sound reproduction.

REME (ˈriːmɪ) *n acronym for* Royal Electrical and Mechanical Engineers.

remedial (rɪˈmiːdɪəl) *adj* **1** affording a remedy; curative. **2** denoting or relating to special teaching for backward and slow learners: *remedial education.*
▸**reˈmedially** *adv*

remedy ⊕ (ˈrɛmɪdɪ) *n, pl* **remedies. 1** (usually foll. by *for* or *against*) any drug or agent that cures a disease or controls its symptoms. **2** (usually foll. by *for* or *against*) anything that serves to cure defects, improve conditions, etc.: *a remedy for industrial disputes.* **3** the legally permitted variation from the standard weight or quality of coins. ◆ *vb* (*tr*) **4** to relieve or cure (a disease, etc.) by a remedy. **5** to put to rights (a fault, error, etc.); correct. [C13: from Anglo-Norman *remedie,* from L *remedium* a cure, from *remedērī,* from RE- + *medērī* to heal]
▸**remediable** (rɪˈmiːdɪəbᵊl) *adj* ▸**reˈmediably** *adv* ▸**ˈremediless** *adj*

remember ⊕ (rɪˈmɛmbə) *vb* **1** to become aware of (something forgotten) again; bring back to one's consciousness. **2** to retain (an idea, intention, etc.) in one's conscious mind: *remember to do one's shopping.* **3** (*tr*) to give money, etc., to (someone), as in a will or in tipping. **4** (*tr;* foll. by *to*) to mention (a person's name) to another person, as by way of greeting: *remember me to your mother.* **5** (*tr*) to mention (a person) favourably, as in prayer. **6** (*tr*) to commemorate (a person, event, etc.): *to remember the dead of the wars.* **7 remember oneself.** to recover one's good manners after a lapse. [C14: from OF *remembrer,* from LL *rememorārī* to recall to mind, from L RE- + *memor* mindful]
▸**reˈmemberer** *n*

remembrance ⊕ (rɪˈmɛmbrəns) *n* **1** the act of remembering or state of being remembered. **2** something that is remembered; reminiscence. **3** a memento or keepsake. **4** the extent in time of one's power of recollection. **5** the act of honouring some past event, person, etc.

Remembrance Day *n* **1** (in Britain) another name for **Remembrance Sunday. 2** (in Canada) a statutory holiday observed on November 11 in memory of the dead of both World Wars.

remembrancer (rɪˈmɛmbrənsə) *n* **1** *Arch.* a reminder, memento, or keepsake. **2** (*usually cap.*) (in Britain) any of several officials of the Exchequer, esp. one (**Queen's** *or* **King's Remembrancer**) whose duties include collecting debts due to the Crown. **3** (*usually cap.*) an official (**City Remembrancer**) appointed by the Corporation of the City of London to represent its interests to Parliament.

Remembrance Sunday *n* (in Britain) the Sunday closest to November 11, on which the dead of both World Wars are commemorated. Also called: **Remembrance Day.**

remex (ˈriːmɛks) *n, pl* **remiges** (ˈrɛmɪˌdʒiːz). any of the large flight feathers of a bird's wing. [C18: from L: rower, from *rēmus* oar]
▸**remigial** (rɪˈmɪdʒɪəl) *adj*

remind ⊕ (rɪˈmaɪnd) *vb* (*tr;* usually foll. by *of; may take a clause as object or an infinitive*) to cause (a person) to remember (something or to do something); put (a person) in mind (of something): *remind me to phone home; flowers remind me of holidays.*
▸**reˈminder** *n*

remindful (rɪˈmaɪndful) *adj* **1** serving to remind. **2** (*postpositive*) mindful.

reminisce ⊕ (ˌrɛmɪˈnɪs) *vb* **reminisces, reminiscing, reminisced.** (*intr*) to talk or write about old times, past experiences, etc.

reminiscence ⊕ (ˌrɛmɪˈnɪsəns) *n* **1** the act of recalling or narrating past experiences. **2** (*often pl*) some past experience, event, etc., that is recalled. **3** an event, phenomenon, or experience that reminds one of something else. **4** *Philosophy.* the doctrine that the mind has seen the universal forms of all things in a previous disembodied existence.

reminiscent ⊕ (ˌrɛmɪˈnɪsᵊnt) *adj* **1** (*postpositive;* foll. by *of*) stimulating memories (of) or comparisons (with). **2** characterized by reminiscence. **3** (of a person) given to reminiscing. [C18: from L *reminiscī* to call to mind, from RE- + *mēns* mind]
▸**ˌremiˈniscently** *adv*

remise (rɪˈmaɪz) *vb* **remises, remising, remised. 1** (*tr*) *Law.* to give up or relinquish (a right, claim, etc.). **2** (*intr*) *Fencing.* to make a remise. ◆ *n* **3** *Fencing.* a second thrust made on the same lunge after the first has missed. **4** *Obs.* a coach house. [C17: from F *remettre* to put back, from L *remittere,* from RE- + *mittere* to send]

THESAURUS

rely *vb* **2** = **depend,** bank, be confident of, be sure of, bet, count, have confidence in, lean, reckon, repose trust in, swear by, trust

remain *vb* **1** = **continue,** abide, bide, dwell, endure, go on, last, persist, prevail, stand, stay, survive **3** = **stay behind,** be left, delay, hang in the air, linger, stay put (*inf.*), tarry, wait
Antonyms *vb* ≠ **stay behind:** depart, go, leave

remainder *n* **1** = **rest,** balance, butt, dregs, excess, leavings, oddment, relic, remains, remnant, residue, residuum, stub, surplus, tail end, trace, vestige(s)

remaining *adj* **3** = **left-over,** abiding, lasting, lingering, outstanding, residual, surviving, unfinished

remains *pl n* **1** = **remnants,** balance, crumbs, debris, detritus, dregs, fragments, leavings, leftovers, oddments, odds and ends, pieces, relics, remainder, residue, rest, scraps, traces, vestiges **2** = **corpse,** body, cadaver, carcass

remark *vb* **1** = **comment,** animadvert, declare, mention, observe, pass comment, reflect, say, state **2** = **notice,** espy, heed, make out, mark, note, observe, perceive, regard, see, take note *or* notice of ◆ *n* **3** = **comment,** assertion, declaration, observation, opinion, reflection, statement, thought, utterance, word **4** = **notice,** acknowledgment, attention, comment, consideration, heed, mention, observation, recognition, regard, thought

remarkable *adj* **1** = **noteworthy,** distinguished, famous, impressive, notable, outstanding, pre-eminent, prominent **2** = **extraordinary,** conspicuous, miraculous, odd, phenomenal, rare, signal, singular, strange, striking, surprising, uncommon, unusual, wonderful
Antonyms *adj* banal, common, commonplace, everyday, insignificant, mundane, ordinary, unexceptional, unimpressive, unsurprising, usual

remediable *adj* **4** = **curable,** medicable, repairable, soluble, solvable, treatable

remedy *n* **1** = **cure,** antidote, counteractive, medicament, medicine, nostrum, panacea, physic (*rare*), relief, restorative, specific, therapy, treatment **2** = **solution,** antidote, corrective, countermeasure, panacea, redress, relief ◆ *vb* **3** = **cure,** alleviate, assuage, control, ease, heal, help, mitigate, palliate, relieve, restore, soothe, treat **4** = **put right,** ameliorate, correct, fix, rectify, redress, reform, relieve, repair, set to rights, solve

remember *vb* **1** = **recall,** call to mind, call up, commemorate, look back (on), put one's finger on, recognize, recollect, reminisce, retain, summon up, think back **2** = **bear in mind,** keep in mind
Antonyms *vb* disregard, forget, ignore, neglect, overlook

remembrance *n* **1, 2** = **memory,** mind, recall, recognition, recollection, regard, reminiscence, retrospect, thought **3** = **souvenir,** commemoration, keepsake, memento, memorial, monument, relic, remembrancer (*arch.*), reminder, testimonial, token

remind *vb* = **call to mind,** awaken memories of, bring back to, bring to mind, call up, jog one's memory, make (someone) remember, prompt, put in mind, refresh one's memory

reminisce *vb* = **recall,** go over in the memory, hark back, live in the past, look back, recollect, remember, review, think back

reminiscence *n* **1, 2** = **recollection,** anecdote, memoir, memory, recall, reflection, remembrance, retrospection, review

reminiscent *adj* **1** = **suggestive,** evocative, redolent, remindful, similar

remiss ❶ (rɪˈmɪs) *adj* (*postpositive*) **1** lacking in care or attention to duty; negligent. **2** lacking in energy. [C15: from L *remissus*, from *remittere*, from RE- + *mittere* to send]
▸**reˈmissly** *adv* ▸**reˈmissness** *n*

remissible (rɪˈmɪsɪbᵊl) *adj* able to be remitted. [C16: from L *remissibilis*; see REMIT]
▸**re,missiˈbility** *n*

remission ❶ (rɪˈmɪʃən) *or* (*less commonly*) **remittal** (rɪˈmɪtᵊl) *n* **1** the act of remitting or state of being remitted. **2** a reduction of the term of a sentence of imprisonment, as for good conduct. **3** forgiveness for sin. **4** discharge or release from penalty, obligation, etc. **5** lessening of intensity; abatement, as in the symptoms of a disease. **6** *Rare.* the act of sending a remittance.
▸**reˈmissive** *adj* ▸**reˈmissively** *adv*

remit ❶ *vb* (rɪˈmɪt), **remits, remitting, remitted.** (*mainly tr*) **1** (*also intr*) to send (payment, etc.), as for goods or service, esp. by post. **2** *Law.* (esp. of an appeal court) to send back (a case) to an inferior court for further consideration. **3** to cancel or refrain from exacting (a penalty or punishment). **4** (*also intr*) to relax (pace, intensity, etc.) or (of pace) to slacken or abate. **5** to postpone; defer. **6** *Arch.* to pardon or forgive (crime, sins, etc.). ◆ *n* (ˈriːmɪt, rɪˈmɪt). **7** area of authority (of a committee, etc.). **8** *Law.* the transfer of a case from one court or jurisdiction to another. **9** the act of remitting. [C14: from L *remittere*, from RE- + *mittere* to send]
▸**reˈmittable** *adj* ▸**reˈmitter** *n*

remittance ❶ (rɪˈmɪtəns) *n* **1** payment for goods or services received or as an allowance, esp. when sent by post. **2** the act of remitting.

remittance man *n* a man living abroad on money sent from home, esp. in the days of the British Empire.

remittent (rɪˈmɪtᵊnt) *adj* (of the symptoms of a disease) characterized by periods of diminished severity.
▸**reˈmittence** *n* ▸**reˈmittently** *adv*

remix *vb* (riːˈmɪks). **1** to change the balance and separation of (a recording). ◆ *n* (ˈriː,mɪks). **2** a remixed version of a recording.

remnant ❶ (ˈrɛmnənt) *n* **1** (*often pl*) a part left over after use, processing, etc. **2** a surviving trace or vestige: *a remnant of imperialism.* **3** a piece of material from the end of a roll. ◆ *adj* **4** remaining; left over. [C14: from OF *remenant* remaining, from *remanoir* to REMAIN]

remonetize *or* **remonetise** (riːˈmʌnɪ,taɪz) *vb* **remonetizes, remonetizing, remonetized** *or* **remonetises, remonetising, remonetised.** (*tr*) to reinstate as legal tender: *to remonetize silver.*
▸**re,monetiˈzation** *or* **re,monetiˈsation** *n*

remonstrance ❶ (rɪˈmɒnstrəns) *n* **1** the act of remonstrating. **2** a protest or reproof, esp. a petition protesting against something.

remonstrant (rɪˈmɒnstrənt) *n* **1** a person who remonstrates, esp. one who signs a remonstrance. ◆ *adj* **2** *Rare.* remonstrating.

remonstrate ❶ (ˈrɛmən,streɪt) *vb* **remonstrates, remonstrating, remonstrated.** (*intr*) (usually foll. by *with, against*, etc.) to argue in protest or objection: *to remonstrate with the government.* [C16: from Med. L *remonstrāre* to point out (errors, etc.), from L RE- + *monstrāre* to show]
▸**,remonˈstration** *n* ▸**remonstrative** (rɪˈmɒnstrətɪv) *adj* ▸**ˈremon,strator** *n*

remontant (rɪˈmɒntənt) *adj* **1** (esp. of roses) flowering more than once in a single season. ◆ *n* **2** a rose having such a growth. [C19: from F: coming up again, from *remonter*]

remora (ˈrɛmərə) *n* a marine spiny-finned fish which has a flattened elongated body and attaches itself to larger fish, rocks, etc., by a sucking disc on the top of the head. [C16: from L, from RE- + *mora* delay; from its alleged habit of delaying ships]

remorse ❶ (rɪˈmɔːs) *n* **1** a sense of deep regret and guilt for some misdeed. **2** compunction; pity; compassion. [C14: from Med. L *remorsus* a gnawing, from L *remordēre*, from RE- + *mordēre* to bite]
▸**reˈmorseful** *adj* ▸**reˈmorsefully** *adv* ▸**reˈmorsefulness** *n* ▸**reˈmorseless** *adj*

remote ❶ (rɪˈməʊt) *adj* **1** located far away; distant. **2** far from society or civilization; out-of-the-way. **3** distant in time. **4** distantly related or connected: *a remote cousin.* **5** slight or faint (esp. in **not the remotest idea**). **6** (of a person's manner) aloof or abstracted. **7** operated from a distance; remote-controlled: *a remote monitor.* [C15: from L *remōtus* far removed, from *removēre*, from RE- + *movēre* to move]
▸**reˈmotely** *adv* ▸**reˈmoteness** *n*

remote access *n Computing.* access to a computer from a physically separate terminal.

remote control *n* control of a system or activity from a distance, usually by radio, ultrasonic, or electrical signals.
▸**re,mote-conˈtrolled** *adj*

remote sensor *n* any instrument, such as a radar device or camera, that scans the earth or another planet from space in order to collect data about some aspect of it.
▸**remote sensing** *adj, n*

rémoulade (,rɛməˈleɪd) *n* a mayonnaise sauce flavoured with herbs, mustard, and capers, served with salads, cold meat, etc. [C19: from F, from dialect *ramolas* horseradish, from L *armoracea*]

remould *vb* (,riːˈməʊld). (*tr*) **1** to mould again. **2** to bond a new tread onto the casing of (a worn pneumatic tyre). ◆ *n* (ˈriː,məʊld). **3** a tyre made by this process.

remount *vb* (riːˈmaʊnt). **1** to get on (a horse, bicycle, etc.) again. **2** (*tr*) to mount (a picture, jewel, exhibit, etc.) again. ◆ *n* (ˈriː,maʊnt). **3** a fresh horse.

removal ❶ (rɪˈmuːvᵊl) *n* **1** the act of removing or state of being removed. **2a** a change of residence. **2b** (*as modifier*): *a removal company.* **3** dismissal from office.

removalist (rɪˈmuːvəlɪst) *n Austral.* a person or company that transports household effects to a new home.

remove ❶ (rɪˈmuːv) *vb* **removes, removing, removed.** (*mainly tr*) **1** to take away and place elsewhere. **2** to dismiss (someone) from office. **3** to do away with; abolish; get rid of. **4** *Euphemistic.* to assassinate; kill. **5** (*intr*) *Formal.* to change the location of one's home or place of business. ◆ *n* **6** the act of removing, esp. (formal) a removal of one's residence or place of work. **7** the degree of difference: *only one remove from madness.* **8** *Brit.* (in certain schools) a class or form. [C14: from OF *removoir*, from L *removēre*; see MOVE]
▸**reˈmovable** *adj* ▸**re,movaˈbility** *n* ▸**reˈmover** *n*

removed (rɪˈmuːvd) *adj* **1** separated by distance or abstract distinction. **2** (*postpositive*) separated by a degree of descent or kinship: *the child of a person's first cousin is his first cousin once removed.*

remunerate ❶ (rɪˈmjuːnə,reɪt) *vb* **remunerates, remunerating, remunerated.** (*tr*) to reward or pay for work, service, etc. [C16: from L *remūnerārī* to reward, from RE- + *mūnerāre* to give, from *mūnus* a gift]

THESAURUS

remiss *adj* **1 = negligent**, careless, culpable, delinquent, derelict, dilatory, forgetful, heedless, inattentive, indifferent, lax, neglectful, regardless, slack, slapdash, slipshod, sloppy (*inf.*), tardy, thoughtless, unmindful **2 = lackadaisical**, slothful, slow
Antonyms *adj* ≠ **negligent:** attentive, careful, diligent, painstaking, scrupulous

remission *n* **2 = reduction**, decrease, diminution, lessening, suspension **3, 4 = pardon**, absolution, acquittal, amnesty, discharge, excuse, exemption, exoneration, forgiveness, indulgence, release, reprieve **5 = lessening**, abatement, abeyance, alleviation, amelioration, ebb, let-up (*inf.*), lull, moderation, relaxation, respite

remit *vb* **1 = send**, dispatch, forward, mail, post, transmit **3 = cancel**, desist, forbear, halt, repeal, rescind, stop **4 = lessen**, abate, alleviate, decrease, diminish, dwindle, ease up, fall away, mitigate, moderate, reduce, relax, sink, slacken, soften, wane, weaken **5 = postpone**, defer, delay, put off, put on the back burner (*inf.*), shelve, suspend, take a rain check on (*US & Canad. inf.*) ◆ *n* **7 = instructions**, authorization, brief, guidelines, orders, terms of reference

remittance *n* **1 = payment**, allowance, consideration, fee

remnant *n* **1 = remainder**, balance, bit, butt, end, fragment, leftovers, oddment, piece, remains, residue, residuum, rest, rump, scrap, shred, stub, tail end **2 = vestige**, hangover, survival, trace

remonstrance *n* **2 = protest**, complaint, expostulation, grievance, objection, petition, protestation, reprimand, reproof

remonstrate *vb* **= protest**, argue, challenge, complain, dispute, dissent, expostulate, object, take exception, take issue

remorse *n* **1 = regret**, anguish, bad *or* guilty conscience, contrition, grief, guilt, pangs of conscience, penitence, repentance, ruefulness, self-reproach, shame, sorrow **2 = pity**, compassion, compunction

remorseful *adj* **1 = regretful**, apologetic, ashamed, chastened, conscience-stricken, contrite, guilt-ridden, guilty, penitent, repentant, rueful, sad, self-reproachful, sorrowful, sorry

remorseless *adj* **1 = pitiless**, callous, cruel, hard, hardhearted, harsh, implacable, inhumane, merciless, ruthless, savage, uncompassionate, unforgiving, unmerciful

remote *adj* **2 = out-of-the-way**, backwoods, distant, far, faraway, far-off, godforsaken, inaccessible, in the middle of nowhere, isolated, lonely, off the beaten track, outlying, secluded **5 = slight**, doubtful, dubious, faint, implausible, inconsiderable, meagre, negligible, outside, poor, slender, slim, small, unlikely **6 = aloof**, abstracted, cold, detached, distant, faraway, indifferent, introspective, introverted, removed, reserved, standoffish, unapproachable, uncommunicative, uninterested, uninvolved, withdrawn
Antonyms *adj* ≠ **out-of-the-way:** adjacent, central, close, just round the corner, near, nearby, neighbouring ≠ **slight:** considerable, good, likely, strong ≠ **aloof:** alert, attentive, aware, gregarious, interested, involved, outgoing, sociable

removal *n* **1 = taking away** *or* **off** *or* **out**, abstraction, dislodgment, displacement, dispossession, ejection, elimination, eradication, erasure, expunction, extraction, purging, stripping, subtraction, uprooting, withdrawal **2 = move**, departure, flitting (*Scot. & N English dialect*), relocation, transfer **33 = dismissal**, expulsion

remove *vb* **1 = take away** *or* **off** *or* **out**, abstract, amputate, carry off *or* away, cart off (*sl.*), delete, detach, dislodge, displace, doff, extract, move, pull, purge, shed, transfer, withdraw **2 = dismiss**, depose, dethrone, discharge, expel, give the bum's rush (*sl.*), oust, relegate, show one the door, throw out, throw out on one's ear (*inf.*), transport, unseat **3 = do away with**, abolish, eject, eliminate, erase, excise, expunge, get rid of, see the back of, strike out, wipe from the face of the earth, wipe out **4** *Euphemistic* **= kill**, assassinate, bump off, dispose of, do away with, do in (*sl.*), eliminate, execute, get rid of, liquidate, murder, take out (*sl.*), wipe from the face of the earth **5** *Formal* **= move**, depart, flit (*Scot. & N English dialect*), move away, quit, relocate, shift, transfer, transport, vacate
Antonyms *vb* ≠ **take away** *or* **off** *or* **out:** don, insert, join, link, place, put, put back, put in, put on, replace, set ≠ **dismiss:** appoint, install

remunerate *vb* **= pay**, compensate, indemnify, recompense, redress, reimburse, repay, requite, reward

remuneration *n* **= payment**, compensation, earnings, emolument, fee, income, indemnity, meed (*arch.*), pay, profit, recompense, reim-

▸re,muner'ation *n* ▸re'munerable *adj* ▸re'munerative *adj* ▸re'muneratively *adv* ▸re'muner,ator *n*

renaissance ⓘ (rəˈneɪsəns, ˈrɛnəˌsɑːns) *or* **renascence** *n* a revival or rebirth, esp. of culture and learning. [C19: from F, from L RE- + *nascī* to be born]

Renaissance (rəˈneɪsəns, ˈrɛnəˌsɑːns) *n* **1 the.** the great revival of art, literature, and learning in Europe in the 14th, 15th, and 16th centuries. **2** the spirit, culture, art, science, and thought of this period. ◆ *adj* **3** of, characteristic of, or relating to the Renaissance, its culture, etc.

renal (ˈriːnᵊl) *adj* of, relating to, resembling, or situated near the kidney. [C17: from F, from LL *rēnālis,* from L *rēnēs* kidneys, from ?]

renal pelvis *n* a small funnel-shaped cavity of the kidney into which urine is discharged before passing into the ureter.

renascent (rɪˈnæsᵊnt, -ˈneɪ-) *adj* becoming active or vigorous again; reviving: *renascent nationalism.* [C18: from L *renascī* to be born again]

rencounter (rɛnˈkaʊntə) *Arch.* ◆ *n also* **rencontre** (rɛnˈkɒntə). **1** an unexpected meeting. **2** a hostile clash, as of two armies, adversaries, etc.; skirmish. ◆ *vb* **3** to meet (someone) unexpectedly. [C16: from F *rencontre,* from *rencontrer;* as ENCOUNTER]

rend ⓘ (rɛnd) *vb* **rends, rending, rent. 1** to tear with violent force or to be torn in this way; rip. **2** (*tr*) to tear or pull (one's clothes, etc.), esp. as a manifestation of rage or grief. **3** (*tr*) (of a noise or cry) to disturb (the silence) with a shrill or piercing tone. [OE *rendan*]
▸'rendible *adj*

render ⓘ (ˈrɛndə) *vb* (*tr*) **1** to present or submit (accounts, etc.) for payment, etc. **2** to give or provide (aid, charity, a service, etc.). **3** to show (obedience), as expected. **4** to give or exchange, as by way of return or requital: *to render blow for blow.* **5** to cause to become: *grief had rendered him simple-minded.* **6** to deliver (a verdict or opinion) formally. **7** to portray or depict (something), as in painting, music, or acting. **8** to translate (something). **9** (sometimes foll. by *up*) to yield or give: *the tomb rendered up its secret.* **10** (often foll. by *back*) to return (something); give back. **11** to cover the surface of (brickwork, etc.) with a coat of plaster. **12** (often foll. by *down*) to extract (fat) from (meat) by melting. ◆ *n* **13** a first thin coat of plaster applied to a surface. **14** one who or that which rends. [C14: from OF *rendre,* from L *reddere* to give back (infl. by L *prendere* to grasp), from RE- + *dare* to give]
▸'renderable *adj* ▸'renderer *n* ▸'rendering *n*

rendezvous ⓘ (ˈrɒndɪˌvuː) *n, pl* **rendezvous** (-ˌvuːz). **1** a meeting or appointment to meet at a specified time and place. **2** a place where people meet. ◆ *vb* (*intr*) **3** to meet at a specified time or place. [C16: from F, from *rendez-vous!* present yourselves! from *se rendre* to present oneself; see RENDER]

rendition ⓘ (rɛnˈdɪʃən) *n* **1** a performance of a musical composition, dramatic role, etc. **2** a translation. **3** the act of rendering. [C17: from obs. F, from LL *redditiō;* see RENDER]

renegade ⓘ (ˈrɛnɪˌgeɪd) *n* **1a** a person who deserts his cause or faith for another; traitor. **1b** (*as modifier*): *a renegade priest.* **2** any outlaw or rebel. [C16: from Sp. *renegado,* ult. from L RE- + *negāre* to deny]

renege ⓘ *or* **renegue** (rɪˈniːg, -ˈneɪg) *vb* **reneges, reneging, reneged** *or* **renegues, reneguing, renegued. 1** (*intr;* often foll. by *on*) to go back (on one's promise, etc.). ◆ *vb, n* **2** *Cards.* other words for **revoke.** [C16 (in the sense: to deny, renounce): from Med. L *renegāre* to renounce]
▸re'neger *or* re'neguer *n*

renew ⓘ (rɪˈnjuː) *vb* (*mainly tr*) **1** to take up again. **2** (*also intr*) to begin (an activity) again; recommence. **3** to restate or reaffirm (a promise, etc.). **4** (*also intr*) to make (a lease, etc.) valid for a further period. **5** to regain or recover (vigour, strength, activity, etc.). **6** to restore to a new or fresh condition. **7** to replace (an old or worn-out part or piece). **8** to replenish (a supply, etc.).
▸re'newable *adj* ▸re'newal *n* ▸re'newer *n*

renewable energy *n* another name for **alternative energy.**

renewables *pl n* sources of alternative energy, such as wind and wave power.

reni- *combining form.* kidney or kidneys: *reniform.* [from L *rēnēs*]

reniform (ˈrɛnɪˌfɔːm) *adj* having the shape or profile of a kidney: *a reniform leaf.*

renin (ˈriːnɪn) *n* a proteolytic enzyme secreted by the kidneys, which plays an important part in the maintenance of blood pressure. [C20: from RENI- + -IN]

rennet (ˈrɛnɪt) *n* **1** the membrane lining the fourth stomach of a young calf. **2** a substance prepared esp. from the stomachs of calves and used for curdling milk in making cheese. [C15: rel. to OE *gerinnan* to curdle, RUN]

rennin (ˈrɛnɪn) *n* an enzyme that occurs in gastric juice and is an active constituent of rennet. It coagulates milk. [C20: from RENNET + -IN]

renounce ⓘ (rɪˈnaʊns) *vb* **renounces, renouncing, renounced. 1** (*tr*) to give up formally (a claim or right): *to renounce a title.* **2** (*tr*) to repudiate: *to renounce Christianity.* **3** (*tr*) to give up (some habit, etc.) voluntarily: *to renounce one's old ways.* **4** (*intr*) *Cards.* to fail to follow suit because one has no more cards of the suit led. ◆ *n* **5** *Cards.* a failure to follow suit. [C14: from OF *renoncer,* from L *renuntiāre,* from RE- + *nuntiāre* to announce, from *nuntius* messenger]
▸re'nouncement *n* ▸re'nouncer *n*

renovate ⓘ (ˈrɛnəˌveɪt) *vb* **renovates, renovating, renovated.** (*tr*) **1** to restore (something) to good condition. **2** to revive or refresh (one's spirits, health, etc.). [C16: from L *renovāre,* from RE- + *novāre* to make new]
▸,reno'vation *n* ▸'reno,vative *adj* ▸'reno,vator *n*

renown ⓘ (rɪˈnaʊn) *n* widespread reputation, esp. of a good kind; fame. [C14: from Anglo-Norman *renoun,* from OF *renom,* from *renomer* to celebrate, from RE- + *nomer* to name, from L *nōmināre*]
▸re'nowned *adj*

rent[1] ⓘ (rɛnt) *n* **1** a payment made periodically by a tenant to a landlord or owner for the occupation or use of land, buildings, etc. **2** *Econ.* the return derived from the cultivation of land in excess of production costs. **3 for rent.** *Chiefly US & Canad.* available for use and occupation subject to the payment of rent. ◆ *vb* **4** (*tr*) to grant (a person) the right to use one's property in return for periodic payments. **5** (*tr*) to occupy or use (property) in return for periodic payments. **6** (*intr;* often foll. by *at*) to be let or rented (for a specified rental). [C12: from OF *rente* revenue, from Vulgar L *rendere* (unattested) to yield; see RENDER]
▸'rentable *adj* ▸'renter *n*

rent[2] ⓘ (rɛnt) *n* **1** a slit or opening made by tearing or rending. **2** a breach or division. ◆ *vb* **3** the past tense and past participle of **rend.**

rent-a- *prefix* **1** denoting a rental service. **2** *Derog. or facetious.* denoting a person or group that performs a function as if hired from a rental service: *rent-a-mob.*

rental (ˈrɛntᵊl) *n* **1a** the amount paid by a tenant as rent. **1b** an income derived from rents received. **2** property available for renting. ◆ *adj* **3** of or relating to rent.

rent boy *n* a young male prostitute.

rent control *n* regulation by law of the rent a landlord can charge for domestic accommodation and of his right to evict tenants.

rent-free *adj, adv* without payment of rent.

rentier *French.* (rɑ̃tje) *n* a person whose income consists primarily of fixed unearned amounts, such as rent or interest. [from *rente;* see RENT[1]]

rent-roll *n* **1** a register of lands and buildings owned by a person, company, etc., showing the rent due from each tenant. **2** the total income arising from rented property.

renunciation ⓘ (rɪˌnʌnsɪˈeɪʃən) *n* **1** the act or an instance of renouncing. **2** a formal declaration renouncing something. **3** *Stock Exchange.*

THESAURUS

bursement, reparation, repayment, retainer, return, reward, salary, stipend, wages

remunerative *adj* = **profitable,** economic, gainful, lucrative, moneymaking, paying, recompensing, rewarding, rich, worthwhile

renaissance *n* = **rebirth,** awakening, new birth, new dawn, reappearance, reawakening, re-emergence, regeneration, renewal, restoration, resurgence, resurrection, revival

rend *vb* **1** = **tear,** break, burst, cleave, crack, divide, fracture, lacerate, pierce, pull, rip, rupture, separate, sever, shatter, smash, splinter, split, sunder (*literary*), tear to pieces, wrench

render *vb* **2** = **provide,** contribute, deliver, furnish, give, hand out, make available, pay, present, show, submit, supply, tender, turn over, yield **5** = **make,** cause to become, leave **7** = **represent,** act, depict, do, give, interpret, perform, play, portray, present **8** = **translate,** construe, explain, interpret, put, reproduce, restate, transcribe **9** = **give up,** cede, deliver, give, hand over, relinquish, surrender, turn over, yield

rendezvous *n* **1** = **appointment,** assignation, date, engagement, meeting, tryst (*arch.*) **2** = **meeting place,** gathering point, place of assignation, trysting-place (*arch.*), venue ◆ *vb* **3** = **meet,** assemble, be reunited, collect, come together, converge, gather, get together, join up, muster, rally

rendition *n* **1** = **performance,** arrangement, delivery, depiction, execution, interpretation, portrayal, presentation, reading, rendering, take (*inf., chiefly US*), version **2** = **translation,** construction, explanation, interpretation, reading, transcription, version

renegade *n* **1a** = **deserter,** apostate, backslider, betrayer, defector, dissident, recreant (*arch.*), runaway, traitor, turncoat ◆ *modifier* **1b** = **traitorous,** apostate, backsliding, disloyal, dissident, recreant, runaway, unfaithful

renege *vb* **1** = **break one's word,** back out, break a promise, default, go back, repudiate, welsh (*sl.*)

renew *vb* **1, 2** = **recommence,** begin again, breathe new life into, bring up to date, continue, extend, prolong, recreate, re-establish, regenerate, rejuvenate, reopen, resume, revitalize **3** = **reaffirm,** repeat, restate **6** = **restore,** fix up, mend, modernize, overhaul, refit, refurbish, renovate, repair, transform **8** = **replace,** refresh, replenish, restock

renounce *vb* **1** = **give up,** abandon, abdicate, abjure, abnegate, abstain from, cast off, decline, discard, disown, eschew, forgo, forsake, forswear, leave off, quit, relinquish, renege, resign, retract, swear off, throw off, waive, wash one's hands of **2** = **deny,** disclaim, recant, reject, repudiate, spurn
Antonyms *vb* assert, avow, claim, maintain, reassert

renovate *vb* **1** = **restore,** do up, fix up (*inf., chiefly US & Canad.*), modernize, overhaul, recondition, reconstitute, recreate, refit, reform, refurbish, rehabilitate, remodel, renew, repair, revamp

renown *n* = **fame,** acclaim, celebrity, distinction, eminence, glory, honour, illustriousness, lustre, mark, note, reputation, repute, stardom

renowned *adj* = **famous,** acclaimed, celebrated, distinguished, eminent, esteemed, famed, illustrious, notable, noted, well-known
Antonyms *adj* forgotten, little-known, neglected, obscure, unknown

rent[1] *n* **1** = **hire,** fee, lease, payment, rental, tariff ◆ *vb* **4** = **let,** charter, hire, lease **5** = **hire,** charter, lease

rent[2] *n* **1** = **tear,** breach, break, chink, crack, flaw, gash, hole, opening, perforation, rip, slash, slit, split **2** = **division,** breach, break, cleavage, discord, dissension, disunity, faction, rift, rupture, schism, split

renunciation *n* **1, 2** = **giving up,** abandonment, abdication, abjuration, abnegation,

the surrender to another of the rights to buy new shares in a rights issue. [C14: from L *renunciātiō* a declaration, from *renuntiāre* to report]
▸**re'nunciative** *or* **re'nunciatory** *adj*

rep[1] *or* **repp** (rɛp) *n* a silk, wool, rayon, or cotton fabric with a transversely corded surface. [C19: from F *reps*, ?from E *ribs*]
▸**repped** *adj*

rep[2] (rɛp) *n Theatre.* short for **repertory company.**

rep[3] (rɛp) *n* **1** short for **representative** (sense 2). **2** *NZ inf.* a rugby player selected to represent his district.

rep[4] (rɛp) *n US inf.* short for **reputation.**

rep. *abbrev. for:* **1** report. **2** reporter. **3** reprint.

Rep. *abbrev. for:* **1** *US.* Representative. **2** Republic. **3** *US.* Republican.

repair[1] ❶ (rɪ'pɛə) *vb* (*tr*) **1** to restore (something damaged or broken) to good condition or working order. **2** to heal (a breach or division) in (something): *to repair a broken marriage.* **3** to make amends for (a mistake, injury, etc.). ◆ *n* **4** the act, task, or process of repairing. **5** a part that has been repaired. **6** state or condition: *in good repair.* [C14: from OF *reparer*, from L *reparāre*, from RE- + *parāre* to make ready]
▸**re'pairable** *adj* ▸**re'pairer** *n*

repair[2] ❶ (rɪ'pɛə) *vb* (*intr*) **1** (usually foll. by *to*) to go (to a place). **2** (usually foll. by *to*) to have recourse (to) for help, etc.: *to repair to one's lawyer.* ◆ *n* **3** a haunt or resort. [C14: from OF *repairier*, from LL *repatriāre* to return to one's native land, from L RE- + *patria* fatherland]

repairman (rɪ'pɛə,mæn) *n, pl* **repairmen.** a man whose job it is to repair machines, etc.

repand (rɪ'pænd) *adj Bot.* having a wavy margin: *a repand leaf.* [C18: from L *repandus* bent backwards, from RE- + *pandus* curved]
▸**re'pandly** *adv*

reparable ❶ ('rɛpərəbᵊl, 'rɛprə-) *adj* able to be repaired, recovered, or remedied. [C16: from L *reparābilis*, from *reparāre* to REPAIR[1]]
▸**'reparably** *adv*

reparation ❶ (,rɛpə'reɪʃən) *n* **1** the act or process of making amends. **2** (*usually pl*) compensation exacted as an indemnity from a defeated nation by the victors. **3** the act or process of repairing or state of having been repaired. [C14 *reparacioun*, ult. from L *reparāre* to REPAIR[1]]
▸**reparative** (rɪ'pærətɪv) *or* **re'paratory** *adj*

repartee ❶ (,rɛpɑː'tiː) *n* **1** a sharp, witty, or aphoristic remark made as a reply. **2** skill in making sharp witty replies. [C17: from F *repartie*, from *repartir* to retort, from RE- + *partir* to go away]

repast ❶ (rɪ'pɑːst) *n* a meal or the food provided at a meal: *a light repast.* [C14: from OF, from *repaistre* to feed, from LL *repāscere*, from L RE- + *pāscere* to feed, pasture (of animals)]

repatriate *vb* (riː'pætrɪ,eɪt), **repatriates, repatriating, repatriated.** (*tr*) **1** to send back (a refugee, prisoner of war, etc.) to the country of his birth or citizenship. **2** to send back (a sum of money previously invested abroad) to its country of origin. ◆ *n* (riː'pætrɪɪt). **3** a person who has been repatriated. [C17: from LL *repatriāre*, from L RE- + *patria* fatherland]
▸**re,patri'ation** *n*

repay ❶ (rɪ'peɪ) *vb* **repays, repaying, repaid. 1** to pay back (money, etc.) to (a person); refund or reimburse. **2** to make a return for (something): *to repay kindness.*
▸**re'payable** *adj* ▸**re'payment** *n*

repeal ❶ (rɪ'piːl) *vb* (*tr*) **1** to annul or rescind officially; revoke: *these laws were repealed.* ◆ *n* **2** an instance or the process of repealing; annulment. [C14: from OF *repeler*, from RE- + *apeler* to call, APPEAL]
▸**re'pealable** *adj* ▸**re'pealer** *n*

repeat ❶ (rɪ'piːt) *vb* **1** (when *tr, may take a clause as object*) to do or experience (something) again once or several times, esp. to say or write (something) again. **2** (*intr*) to occur more than once: *the last figure repeats.* **3** (*tr; may take a clause as object*) to reproduce (the words, sounds, etc.) uttered by someone else; echo. **4** (*tr*) to utter (a poem, etc.) from memory; recite. **5** (*intr*) (of food) to be tasted again after ingestion as the result of belching. **6** (*tr; may take a clause as object*) to tell to another person (the secrets imparted to one by someone else). **7** (*intr*) (of a clock) to strike the hour or quarter-hour just past. **8** (*intr*) *US.* to vote (illegally) more than once in a single election. **9 repeat oneself.** to say or do the same thing more than once, esp. so as to be tedious. ◆ *n* **10a** the act or an instance of repeating. **10b** (*as modifier*): *a repeat performance.* **11** a word, action, etc., that is repeated. **12** an order made out for goods, etc., that duplicates a previous order. **13** *Radio, television.* a broadcast of a programme which has been broadcast before. **14** *Music.* a passage that is an exact restatement of the passage preceding it. [C14: from OF *repeter*, from L *repetere*, from RE- + *petere* to seek]
▸**re'peatable** *adj*

USAGE NOTE Since *again* is part of the meaning of *repeat*, one should not say something is *repeated again.*

repeated (rɪ'piːtɪd) *adj* done, made, or said again and again; continual.
▸**re'peatedly** *adv*

repeater (rɪ'piːtə) *n* **1** a person or thing that repeats. **2** Also called: **repeating firearm.** a firearm capable of discharging several shots without reloading. **3** a timepiece that strikes the hour or quarter-hour just past, when a spring is pressed. **4** a device that amplifies incoming electrical signals and retransmits them.

repeating decimal *n* another name for **recurring decimal.**

repechage (,rɛpɪ'ʃɑːʒ) *n* a heat of a competition, esp. in rowing or fencing, in which eliminated contestants have another chance to qualify for the next round or the final. [C19: from F *repêchage*, lit.: fishing out again, from RE- + *pêcher* to fish + -AGE]

repel ❶ (rɪ'pɛl) *vb* **repels, repelling, repelled.** (*mainly tr*) **1** to force or drive back (something or somebody). **2** (*also intr*) to produce a feeling of aversion or distaste in (someone or something); be disgusting (to). **3** to be effective in keeping away, controlling, or resisting: *a spray that repels flies.* **4** to have no affinity for; fail to mix with or absorb: *water and oil repel each other.* **5** to disdain to accept (something); turn away from or spurn: *she repelled his advances.* [C15: from L *repellere*, from RE- + *pellere* to push]
▸**re'peller** *n* ▸**re'pellingly** *adv*

USAGE NOTE See at **repulse.**

repellent ❶ (rɪ'pɛlənt) *adj* **1** distasteful or repulsive. **2** driving or forcing away or back; repelling. ◆ *n also* **repellant. 3** something, esp. a chemical substance, that repels: *insect repellent.* **4** a substance with which fabrics are treated to increase their resistance to water.
▸**re'pellence** *or* **re'pellency** *n* ▸**re'pellently** *adv*

repent[1] ❶ (rɪ'pɛnt) *vb* to feel remorse (for); be contrite (about); show penitence (for). [C13: from OF *repentir*, from RE- + *pentir*, from L *paenitēre* to repent]
▸**re'penter** *n*

repent[2] ('riːpᵊnt) *adj Bot.* lying or creeping along the ground: *repent stems.* [C17: from L *rēpere* to creep]

repentance ❶ (rɪ'pɛntəns) *n* **1** remorse or contrition for one's past actions. **2** an act or the process of being repentant; penitence.
▸**re'pentant** *adj*

repercussion ❶ (,riːpə'kʌʃən) *n* **1** (*often pl*) a result or consequence of

THESAURUS

abstention, denial, disavowal, disclaimer, eschewal, forswearing, rejection, relinquishment, repudiation, resignation, spurning, surrender, waiver

repair[1] *vb* **1 = mend**, fix, heal, make good, patch, patch up, put back together, recover, renew, renovate, restore, restore to working order **3 = put right**, compensate for, make up for, rectify, redress, retrieve, square ◆ *n* **5 = mend**, adjustment, darn, overhaul, patch, restoration **6 = condition**, fettle, form, nick (*inf.*), shape (*inf.*), state
Antonyms *vb* ≠ **mend**: damage, destroy, harm, ruin, wreck

repair[2] *vb* **1 = go**, betake oneself, head for, leave for, move, remove, retire, set off for, withdraw **2 = have recourse**, resort, turn

reparable *adj* **= curable**, recoverable, rectifiable, remediable, restorable, retrievable, salvageable

reparation *n* **1 = compensation**, amends, atonement, damages, indemnity, propitiation, recompense, redress, renewal, repair, requital, restitution, satisfaction

repartee *n* **1 = witticism**, badinage, banter, bon mot, persiflage, pleasantry, raillery, riposte, sally, wit, wittiness, wordplay

repast *n* **= meal**, collation, food, nourishment, refection, spread (*inf.*), victuals

repay *vb* **1 = pay back**, compensate, make restitution, recompense, refund, reimburse, remunerate, requite, restore, return, reward, settle up with, square **2 = reciprocate**, avenge, even *or* settle the score with, get back at, get even with (*inf.*), get one's own back on (*inf.*), hit back, make reprisal, pay (someone) back in his *or* her own coin, retaliate, return the compliment, revenge

repeal *vb* **1 = abolish**, abrogate, annul, cancel, countermand, declare null and void, invalidate, nullify, obviate, recall, rescind, reverse, revoke, set aside, withdraw ◆ *n* **2 = abolition**, abrogation, annulment, cancellation, invalidation, nullification, rescinding, rescindment, rescission, revocation, withdrawal
Antonyms *vb* ≠ **abolish**: confirm, enact, introduce, pass, ratify, reaffirm, validate ◆ *n* ≠ **abolition**: confirmation, enactment, introduction, passing, ratification, reaffirmation, validation

repeat *vb* **1 = redo**, duplicate, recapitulate, renew, replay, reproduce, rerun, reshow **3 = reiterate**, echo, iterate, quote, relate, restate, retell **4 = recite** ◆ *n* **10a = repetition**, duplicate, echo, recapitulation, reiteration, replay, reproduction, rerun, reshowing

repeatedly *adv* **1 = over and over**, again and again, frequently, many a time and oft (*arch.* or *poetic*), many times, often, time after time, time and (time) again

repel *vb* **1 = drive off**, beat off, check, confront, decline, fight, hold off, keep at arm's length, oppose, parry, put to flight, rebuff, refuse, reject, repulse, resist, ward off **2 = disgust**, give one the creeps (*inf.*), gross out (*US sl.*), make one shudder, make one sick, nauseate, offend, put one off, revolt, sicken, turn one off (*inf.*), turn one's stomach
Antonyms *vb* ≠ **disgust**: attract, delight, draw, entrance, fascinate, invite, please

repellent *adj* **1 = disgusting**, abhorrent, abominable, cringe-making (*Brit. inf.*), discouraging, distasteful, hateful, horrid, loathsome, nauseating, noxious, obnoxious, obscene, odious, offensive, off-putting (*Brit. inf.*), repugnant, repulsive, revolting, sickening, yucky *or* yukky (*sl.*)

repent[1] *vb* **= regret**, atone, be ashamed, be contrite, be sorry, deplore, feel remorse, lament, relent, reproach oneself, rue, see the error of one's ways, show penitence, sorrow

repentance *n* **1, 2 = regret**, compunction, contrition, grief, guilt, penitence, remorse, sackcloth and ashes, self-reproach, sorriness, sorrow

repentant *adj* **1, 2 = regretful**, apologetic, ashamed, chastened, contrite, penitent, remorseful, rueful, self-reproachful, sorry

an action or event: *the repercussions of the war are still felt.* **2** a recoil after impact; a rebound. **3** a reflection, esp. of sound; echo or reverberation. [C16: from L *repercussiō*, from *repercutere* to strike back]
▸ˌ**reper'cussive** *adj*

repertoire ➊ ('rɛpəˌtwɑː) *n* **1** all the works collectively that a company, actor, etc., is competent to perform. **2** the entire stock of things available in a field or of a kind. **3 in repertoire.** denoting the performance of two or more plays, etc., by the same company in the same venue on different evenings over a period of time: *"Tosca" returns to Leeds next month in repertoire with "Wozzeck".* [C19: from F, from LL *repertōrium* inventory; see REPERTORY]

repertory ➊ ('rɛpətərɪ, -trɪ) *n, pl* **repertories. 1** the entire stock of things available in a field or of a kind; repertoire. **2** a place where a stock of things is kept; repository. **3** short for **repertory company.** [C16: from LL *repertōrium* storehouse, from L *reperire* to obtain, from RE- + *parere* to bring forth]
▸**repertorial** (ˌrɛpə'tɔːrɪəl) *adj*

repertory company *n* a theatrical company that performs plays from a repertoire. US name: **stock company.**

repetend ('rɛpɪˌtɛnd) *n* **1** *Maths.* the digit in a recurring decimal that repeats itself. **2** anything repeated. [C18: from L *repetendum* what is to be repeated, from *repetere* to REPEAT]

répétiteur *French.* (repetitœr) *n* a member of an opera company who coaches the singers.

repetition ➊ (ˌrɛpɪ'tɪʃən) *n* **1** the act or an instance of repeating; reiteration. **2** a thing, word, action, etc., that is repeated. **3** a replica or copy.
▸**repetitive** (rɪ'pɛtɪtɪv) *adj*

repetitious ➊ (ˌrɛpɪ'tɪʃəs) *adj* characterized by unnecessary repetition.
▸ˌ**repe'titiously** *adv* ▸ˌ**repe'titiousness** *n*

repetitive strain *or* **stress injury** *n* a condition, characterized by arm or wrist pains, that can affect musicians, computer operators, etc., who habitually perform awkward hand movements. Abbrev.: **RSI.**

repine ➊ (rɪ'paɪn) *vb* **repines, repining, repined.** (*intr*) to be fretful or low-spirited through discontent. [C16: from RE- + PINE[2]]

replace ➊ (rɪ'pleɪs) *vb* **replaces, replacing, replaced.** (*tr*) **1** to take the place of; supersede. **2** to substitute a person or thing for (another); put in place of: *to replace an old pair of shoes.* **3** to restore to its rightful place.
▸**re'placeable** *adj* ▸**re'placer** *n*

replacement ➊ (rɪ'pleɪsmənt) *n* **1** the act or process of replacing. **2** a person or thing that replaces another.

replay *n* ('riːˌpleɪ). **1** Also called: **action replay.** a showing again of a sequence of action in slow motion immediately after it happens. **2** a second match between a pair or group of contestants. ◆ *vb* (riː'pleɪ). **3** to play again (a record, sporting contest, etc.).

replenish ➊ (rɪ'plɛnɪʃ) *vb* (*tr*) **1** to make full or complete again by supplying what has been used up. **2** to put fresh fuel on (a fire). [C14: from OF *replenir*, from RE- + *plenir*, from L *plēnus* full]
▸**re'plenisher** *n* ▸**re'plenishment** *n*

replete ➊ (rɪ'pliːt) *adj* (*usually postpositive*) **1** (often foll. by *with*) copiously supplied (with); abounding (in). **2** having one's appetite completely or excessively satisfied; gorged; satiated. [C14: from L *replētus*, from *replēre*, from RE- + *plēre* to fill]
▸**re'pletely** *adv* ▸**re'pleteness** *n* ▸**re'pletion** *n*

replevin (rɪ'plɛvɪn) *Law.* ◆ *n* **1** the recovery of goods unlawfully taken, made subject to establishing the validity of the recovery in a legal action and returning the goods if the decision is adverse. **2** (formerly) a writ of replevin. ◆ *vb* **3** another word for **replevy.** [C15: from Anglo-F, from OF *replevir* to give security for, from RE- + *plevir* to PLEDGE]

replevy (rɪ'plɛvɪ) *Law.* ◆ *vb* **replevies, replevying, replevied.** (*tr*) **1** to recover possession of (goods) by replevin. ◆ *n, pl* **replevies. 2** another word for **replevin.** [C15: from OF *replevir*; see REPLEVIN]
▸**re'pleviable** *or* **re'plevisable** *adj*

replica ➊ ('rɛplɪkə) *n* an exact copy or reproduction, esp. on a smaller scale. [C19: from It., lit.: a reply, from *replicare*, from L: to bend back, repeat]

replicate ➊ *vb* ('rɛplɪˌkeɪt), **replicates, replicating, replicated.** (*mainly tr*) **1** (*also intr*) to make or be a copy (of); reproduce. **2** to fold (something) over on itself; bend back. ◆ *adj* ('rɛplɪkɪt). **3** folded back on itself: *a replicate leaf.* [C19: from L *replicātus* bent back; see REPLICA]
▸ˌ**repli'cation** *n* ▸'**replicative** *adj*

reply ➊ (rɪ'plaɪ) *vb* **replies, replying, replied.** (*mainly intr*) **1** to make answer (to) in words or writing or by an action; respond. **2** (*tr; takes a clause as object*) to say (something) in answer: *he replied that he didn't want to come.* **3** *Law.* to answer a defendant's plea. **4** to return (a sound); echo. ◆ *n, pl* **replies. 5** an answer; response. **6** the answer made by a plaintiff or petitioner to a defendant's case. [C14: from OF *replier* to fold again, reply, from L *replicāre*, from RE- + *plicāre* to fold]
▸**re'plier** *n*

repo ('riːpəʊ) *n Inf.* short for: **1** repurchase agreement. **2a** repossession of property. **2b** (*as modifier*): *a repo car.*

repoint (ˌriː'pɔɪnt) *vb* (*tr*) to repair the joints of (brickwork, masonry, etc.) with mortar or cement.

report ➊ (rɪ'pɔːt) *n* **1** an account prepared after investigation and published or broadcast. **2** a statement made widely known; rumour: *according to report, he is not dead.* **3** an account of the deliberations of a committee, body, etc.: *a report of parliamentary proceedings.* **4** *Brit.* a statement on the progress of each schoolchild. **5** a written account of a case decided at law. **6** comment on a person's character or actions; reputation: *he is of good report here.* **7** a sharp loud noise, esp. one made by a gun. ◆ *vb* (when *tr, may take a clause as object;* when *intr,* often foll. by *on*) **8** to give an account (of); describe. **9** to give an account of the results of an investigation (into): *to report on housing conditions.* **10** (of a committee, legislative body, etc.) to make a formal report on (a bill). **11** (*tr*) to complain about (a person), esp. to a superior. **12** to present (oneself) or be present at an appointed place or for a specific purpose: *report to the manager's office.* **13** (*intr*) to say or show that one is (in a certain state): *to report fit.* **14** (*intr;* foll. by *to*) to be responsible (to) and under the authority (of). **15** (*intr*) to act as a reporter. **16** *Law.* to take down in writing details of (the proceedings of a court of law, etc.) as a record or for publication. [C14: from OF, from *reporter*, from L *reportāre*, from RE- + *portāre* to carry]
▸**re'portable** *adj* ▸**re'portedly** *adv*

reportage (rɪ'pɔːtɪdʒ, ˌrɛpɔː'tɑːʒ) *n* **1** the act or process of reporting news or other events of general interest. **2** a journalist's style of reporting.

reported speech *n* another term for **indirect speech.**

reporter ➊ (rɪ'pɔːtə) *n* **1** a person who reports, esp. one employed to gather news for a newspaper or broadcasting organization. **2** a person authorized to report the proceedings of a legislature.

report stage *n* the stage preceding the third reading in the passage of a bill through Parliament.

repose[1] ➊ (rɪ'pəʊz) *n* **1** a state of quiet restfulness; peace or tranquillity. **2** dignified calmness of manner; composure. ◆ *vb* **reposes, reposing, reposed. 3** to lie or lay down at rest. **4** (*intr*) to lie when dead, as in the grave. **5** (*intr;* foll. by *on, in,* etc.) *Formal.* to be based (on): *your plan re-*

THESAURUS

repercussion *n* **1** *often plural* = **consequences**, backlash, result, sequel, side effects **3** = **reverberation**, echo, rebound, recoil

repertoire *n* **2** = **range**, collection, list, repertory, repository, stock, store, supply

repertory *n* **1** = **repertoire**, collection, list, range, stock, store, supply **2** = **repository**

repetition *n* **1** = **repeating**, duplication, echo, iteration, reappearance, recapitulation, recital, recurrence, redundancy, rehearsal, reiteration, relation, renewal, repetitiousness, replication, restatement, return, tautology

repetitious *adj* = **long-winded**, iterative, pleonastic, prolix, redundant, tautological, tedious, verbose, windy, wordy

repetitive *adj* **1** = **monotonous**, boring, dull, mechanical, recurrent, samey (*inf.*), tedious, unchanging, unvaried

repine *vb* = **complain**, brood, eat one's heart out, fret, grieve, grumble, lament, languish, moan, mope, murmur, sulk

replace *vb* **1** = **take the place of**, fill (someone's) shoes *or* boots, follow, oust, stand in lieu of, step into (someone's) shoes *or* boots, substitute, succeed, supersede, supplant, supply, take over from **3** = **put back**, re-establish, reinstate, restore

replacement *n* **2** = **successor**, double, fill-in, proxy, stand-in, substitute, surrogate, understudy

replenish *vb* **1** = **refill**, fill, furnish, make up, provide, reload, renew, replace, restock, restore, stock, supply, top up
Antonyms *vb* consume, drain, empty, exhaust, use up

replete *adj* **1** = **filled**, abounding, brimful, brimming, charged, chock-full, crammed, full to bursting, glutted, jammed, jam-packed, stuffed, teeming, well-provided, well-stocked **2** = **sated**, full, full up, gorged, satiated
Antonyms *adj* ≠ **filled**: bare, barren, empty, lacking, wanting ≠ **sated**: empty, esurient, famished, hungry, starving

repletion *n* **1** = **surfeit**, completeness, glut, plethora, superfluity **2** = **fullness**, overfullness, satiation, satiety

replica *n* = **duplicate**, carbon copy, copy, facsimile, imitation, model, reproduction
Antonyms *n* master, original, prototype

replicate *vb* **1** = **copy**, ape, duplicate, follow, mimic, recreate, reduplicate, repeat, reproduce

reply *vb* **1, 2** = **answer**, acknowledge, come back, counter, make answer, react, reciprocate, rejoin, respond, retaliate, retort, return, riposte, write back ◆ *n* **5** = **answer**, acknowledgment, comeback (*inf.*), counter, counterattack, echo, reaction, reciprocation, rejoinder, response, retaliation, retort, return, riposte

report *n* **1** = **account**, announcement, communication, declaration, description, detail, information, narrative, news, note, recital, record, relation, statement, summary, tale, tidings, version, word **2** = **rumour**, buzz, gossip, hearsay, scuttlebutt (*US sl.*), talk **3** = **article**, communiqué, dispatch, message, paper, piece, story, write-up **6** = **repute**, character, eminence, esteem, fame, regard, reputation **7** = **bang**, blast, boom, crack, crash, detonation, discharge, explosion, noise, reverberation, sound ◆ *vb* **8** = **communicate**, air, announce, bring word, broadcast, circulate, cover, declare, describe, detail, document, give an account of, inform of, mention, narrate, note, notify, pass on, proclaim, publish, recite, record, recount, relate, relay, state, tell, write up **12** = **present oneself**, appear, arrive, be present, clock in *or* on, come, show up (*inf.*), turn up

reporter *n* **1** = **journalist**, announcer, correspondent, hack (*derogatory*), journo (*sl.*), newscaster, newshound (*inf.*), newspaperman *or* newspaperwoman, pressman, writer

repose[1] *n* **1** = **peace**, ease, inactivity, quiet, quietness, quietude, relaxation, respite, rest, restfulness, stillness, tranquillity **2** = **composure**, aplomb, calmness, dignity, equanimity, peace

poses on a fallacy. [C15: from OF *reposer,* from LL *repausāre,* from RE- + *pausāre* to stop]
▸**re'posal** *n* ▸**re'poser** *n* ▸**re'poseful** *adj* ▸**re'posefully** *adv*

repose[2] ❶ (rɪˈpəuz) *vb* **reposes, reposing, reposed.** *(tr)* **1** to put (trust) in a person or thing. **2** to place or put (an object) somewhere. [C15: from L *repōnere* to store up, from RE- + *pōnere* to put]
▸**re'posal** *n*

reposition (ˌriːpəˈzɪʃən) *n* **1** the act or process of depositing or storing. ◆ *vb (tr)* **2** to place in a new position. **3** to target (a product or brand) at a new market by changing its image.

repository ❶ (rɪˈpɒzɪtərɪ, -trɪ) *n, pl* **repositories. 1** a place or container in which things can be stored for safety. **2** a place where things are kept for exhibition; museum. **3** a place of burial; sepulchre. **4** a person to whom a secret is entrusted; confidant. [C15: from L *repositōrium,* from *repōnere* to place]

repossess (ˌriːpəˈzɛs) *vb (tr)* to take back possession of (property), esp. for nonpayment of money due under a hire-purchase agreement.
▸**repossession** (ˌriːpəˈzɛʃən) *n* ▸ˌ**repos'sessor** *n*

repoussé (rəˈpuːseɪ) *adj* **1** raised in relief, as a design on a thin piece of metal hammered through from the underside. ◆ *n* **2** a design or surface made in this way. [C19: from F, from *repousser,* from RE- + *pousser* to PUSH]

repp (rɛp) *n* a variant spelling of **rep**[1].

reprehend (ˌrɛprɪˈhɛnd) *vb (tr)* to find fault with; criticize. [C14: from L *reprehendere* to hold fast, rebuke, from RE- + *prendere* to grasp]
▸ˌ**repre'hender** *n* ▸ˌ**repre'hension** *n*

reprehensible ❶ (ˌrɛprɪˈhɛnsɪbᵊl) *adj* open to criticism or rebuke; blameworthy. [C14: from LL *reprehensibilis,* from L *reprehendere;* see REPREHEND]
▸ˌ**repreˌhensi'bility** *n* ▸ˌ**repre'hensibly** *adv*

represent ❶ (ˌrɛprɪˈzɛnt) *vb (tr)* **1** to stand as an equivalent of; correspond to. **2** to act as a substitute or proxy (for). **3** to act as or be the authorized delegate or agent for (a person, country, etc.): *an MP represents his constituency.* **4** to serve or use as a means of expressing: *letters represent the sounds of speech.* **5** to exhibit the characteristics of; exemplify; typify: *romanticism in music is represented by Beethoven.* **6** to present an image of through the medium of a picture or sculpture; portray. **7** to bring clearly before the mind. **8** to set forth in words; state or explain. **9** to describe as having a specified character or quality: *he represented her as a saint.* **10** to act out the part of on stage; portray. [C14: from L *repraesentāre* to exhibit, from RE- + *praesentāre* to PRESENT[2]]
▸ˌ**repre'sentable** *adj* ▸ˌ**repreˌsenta'bility** *n*

re-present (ˌriːprɪˈzɛnt) *vb (tr)* to present again.
▸**re-presentation** (ˌriːˌprɛzənˈteɪʃən) *n*

representation ❶ (ˌrɛprɪzɛnˈteɪʃən) *n* **1** the act or an instance of representing or the state of being represented. **2** anything that represents, such as a verbal or pictorial portrait. **3** anything that is represented, such as an image brought clearly to mind. **4** the principle by which delegates act for a constituency. **5** a body of representatives. **6** an instance of acting for another in a particular capacity, such as executor. **7** a dramatic production or performance. **8** *(often pl)* a statement of facts, true or alleged, esp. one set forth by way of remonstrance or expostulation.

representational (ˌrɛprɪzɛnˈteɪʃənᵊl) *adj* **1** *Art.* depicting objects, scenes, etc., directly as seen; naturalistic. **2** of or relating to representation.

representationalism (ˌrɛprɪzɛnˈteɪʃənəˌlɪzəm) *or* **representationism** *n* **1** *Philosophy.* the doctrine that in perceptions of objects what is before the mind is not the object but a representation of it. Cf. **presentationism. 2** *Art.* the practice of depicting objects, scenes, etc., directly as seen.
▸ˌ**representˌtational'istic** *adj* ▸ˌ**represen'tationist** *n, adj*

representative ❶ (ˌrɛprɪˈzɛntətɪv) *n* **1** a person or thing that represents another. **2** a person who represents and tries to sell the products or services of a firm. **3** a typical example. **4** a person representing a constituency in a deliberative, legislative, or executive body, esp. *(cap.)* a member of the **House of Representatives** (the lower house of Congress). ◆ *adj* **5** serving to represent; symbolic. **6a** exemplifying a class or kind; typical. **6b** containing or including examples of all the interests, types, etc., in a group. **7** acting as deputy or proxy for another. **8** representing a constituency or the whole people in the process of government: *a representative council.* **9** of or relating to the political representation of the people: *representative government.* **10** of or relating to a mental picture or representation.
▸ˌ**repre'sentatively** *adv* ▸ˌ**repre'sentativeness** *n*

repress ❶ (rɪˈprɛs) *vb (tr)* **1** to keep (feelings, etc.) under control; suppress or restrain. **2** to put into a state of subjugation: *to repress a people.* **3** *Psychol.* to banish (unpleasant thoughts) from one's conscious mind. [C14: from L *reprimere* to press back, from RE- + *premere* to PRESS[1]]
▸**re'pressed** *adj* ▸**re'presser** *or* **re'pressor** *n* ▸**re'pressible** *adj* ▸**re'pression** *n* ▸**re'pressive** *adj*

reprieve ❶ (rɪˈpriːv) *vb* **reprieves, reprieving, reprieved.** *(tr)* **1** to postpone or remit the punishment of (a person, esp. one condemned to death). **2** to give temporary relief to (a person or thing), esp. from otherwise irrevocable harm. ◆ *n* **3** a postponement or remission of punishment. **4** a warrant granting a postponement. **5** a temporary relief from pain or harm; respite. [C16: from OF *repris* (something) taken back, from *reprendre,* from L *reprehendere;* ? also infl. by obs. E *repreve* to reprove]
▸**re'prievable** *adj* ▸**re'priever** *n*

reprimand ❶ (ˈrɛprɪˌmɑːnd) *n* **1** a reproof or formal admonition; rebuke. ◆ *vb* **2** *(tr)* to admonish or rebuke, esp. formally. [C17: from F *réprimande,* from L *reprimenda* (things) to be repressed; see REPRESS]
▸ˌ**repri'manding** *adj*

reprint *n* (ˈriːˌprɪnt). **1** a reproduction in print of any matter already published. **2** a reissue of a printed work using the same type, plates, etc., as the original. ◆ *vb* (riːˈprɪnt). **3** *(tr)* to print again.
▸**re'printer** *n*

reprisal ❶ (rɪˈpraɪzᵊl) *n* **1** the act or an instance of retaliation in any form. **2** *(often pl)* retaliatory action against an enemy in wartime. **3** (formerly) the forcible seizure of the property or subjects of one nation by another. [C15: from OF *reprisaille,* from OIt., from *riprendere* to recapture, from L *reprehendere;* see REPREHEND]

reprise (rɪˈpriːz) *Music.* ◆ *n* **1** the repeating of an earlier theme. ◆ *vb* **reprises, reprising, reprised. 2** to repeat (an earlier theme). [C14: from OF, from *reprendre* to take back, from L *reprehendere;* see REPREHEND]

repro (ˈriːprəu) *n, pl* **repros. 1** short for **reproduction** (sense 2): *repro furniture.* **2** short for **reproduction proof.**

reproach ❶ (rɪˈprəutʃ) *vb (tr)* **1** to impute blame to (a person) for an ac-

THESAURUS

of mind, poise, self-possession, serenity, tranquillity ◆ *vb* **3** = **rest**, drowse, lay down, lie, lie down, lie upon, recline, relax, rest upon, sleep, slumber, take it easy, take one's ease

repose[2] *vb* **1** = **entrust**, confide **2** = **place**, deposit, lodge, put, store

repository *n* **1** = **store**, archive, depository, depot, emporium, magazine, receptacle, storehouse, treasury, vault, warehouse

reprehensible *adj* = **blameworthy**, bad, censurable, condemnable, culpable, delinquent, discreditable, disgraceful, errant, erring, ignoble, objectionable, opprobrious, remiss, shameful, unworthy
Antonyms *adj* acceptable, admirable, forgivable, laudable, pardonable, praiseworthy, unobjectionable

represent *vb* **1, 2** = **stand for**, act for, be, betoken, correspond to, equal, equate with, express, mean, serve as, speak for, substitute for, symbolize **5** = **exemplify**, embody, epitomize, personify, symbolize, typify **6** = **depict**, delineate, denote, describe, designate, evoke, express, illustrate, outline, picture, portray, render, reproduce, show, sketch **9** = **make out to be**, describe as, pass off as, pose as, pretend to be **10** = **portray**, act, appear as, assume the role of, enact, exhibit, perform, play the part of, produce, put on, show, stage

representation *n* **1** = **portrayal**, account, delineation, depiction, description, narration, narrative, relation, resemblance **2** = **picture**, illustration, image, likeness, model, portrait, sketch **5** = **body of representatives**, committee, delegates, delegation, embassy **7** = **performance**, exhibition, play, production, show, sight, spectacle **8** *often plural* = **statement**, account, argument, explanation, exposition, expostulation, remonstrance

representative *n* **1** = **delegate**, agent, commissioner, councillor, depute (*Scot.*), deputy, member, member of parliament, M.P., proxy, spokesman *or* spokeswoman **2** = **salesman**, agent, commercial traveller, rep, traveller **3** = **typical example**, archetype, embodiment, epitome, exemplar, personification, type ◆ *adj* **5** = **typical**, archetypal, characteristic, emblematic, evocative, exemplary, illustrative, symbolic **8** = **chosen**, delegated, elected, elective
Antonyms *adj* ≠ **typical:** atypical, extraordinary, uncharacteristic

repress *vb* **1** = **control**, bottle up, check, curb, hold back, hold in, inhibit, keep in check, master, muffle, overcome, overpower, restrain, silence, smother, stifle, suppress, swallow **2** = **subdue**, crush, quash, quell, subjugate
Antonyms *vb* ≠ **control:** encourage, express, give free rein to, let out, release ≠ **subdue:** free, liberate

repression *n* **2** = **subjugation**, authoritarianism, censorship, coercion, constraint, control, despotism, domination, restraint, suppression, tyranny

repressive *adj* **2** = **oppressive**, absolute, authoritarian, coercive, despotic, dictatorial, harsh, severe, tough, tyrannical
Antonyms *adj* democratic, liberal, libertarian

reprieve *vb* **1** = **grant a stay of execution to**, let off the hook (*sl.*), pardon, postpone *or* remit the punishment of **2** = **relieve**, abate, allay, alleviate, mitigate, palliate, respite ◆ *n* **3, 4** = **stay of execution**, abeyance, amnesty, deferment, pardon, postponement, remission, suspension **5** = **relief**, abatement, alleviation, let-up (*inf.*), mitigation, palliation, respite

reprimand *n* **1** = **blame**, admonition, castigation, censure, dressing-down (*inf.*), flea in one's ear (*inf.*), lecture, rebuke, reprehension, reproach, reproof, row, talking-to (*inf.*), telling-off (*inf.*), ticking-off (*inf.*), tongue-lashing ◆ *vb* **2** = **blame**, admonish, bawl out, carpet (*inf.*), castigate, censure, check, chew out (*US & Canad. inf.*), chide, dress down (*inf.*), give a rocket (*Brit. & NZ inf.*), give (someone) a row (*inf.*), haul over the coals (*inf.*), lecture, rap over the knuckles, read the riot act, rebuke, reprehend, reproach, reprove, scold, slap on the wrist (*inf.*), take to task, tear into (*inf.*), tear (someone) off a strip (*Brit. inf.*), tell off (*inf.*), tick off (*inf.*), upbraid
Antonyms *n* ≠ **blame:** commendation, compliment, congratulations, praise ◆ *vb* ≠ **blame:** applaud, commend, compliment, congratulate, praise

reprisal *n* **1** = **retaliation**, an eye for an eye, counterstroke, requital, retribution, revenge, vengeance

reproach *vb* **1** = **blame**, abuse, bawl out (*inf.*), blast, carpet (*inf.*), censure, chew out (*US & Canad. inf.*), chide, condemn, criticize, defame, discredit, disparage, find fault with, give a rocket (*Brit. & NZ inf.*), have a go at (*inf.*), lambast(e), read the riot act, rebuke, reprehend, reprimand, reprove, scold, take to task, tear

tion or fault; rebuke. ◆ *n* **2** the act of reproaching. **3** rebuke or censure; reproof. **4** disgrace or shame: *to bring reproach upon one's family.* **5** **above** *or* **beyond reproach.** perfect; beyond criticism. [C15: from OF *reprochier,* from L RE- + *prope* near]
▸**re'proachable** *adj* ▸**re'proacher** *n* ▸**re'proachingly** *adv*

reproachful ❶ (rɪ'prəʊtʃfʊl) *adj* full of or expressing reproach.
▸**re'proachfully** *adv* ▸**re'proachfulness** *n*

reprobate ❶ ('rɛprəʊ,beɪt) *adj* **1** morally unprincipled; depraved. **2** *Christianity.* condemned to eternal punishment in hell. ◆ *n* **3** an unprincipled, depraved, or damned person. **4** a disreputable or roguish person. ◆ *vb* **reprobates, reprobating, reprobated.** (*tr*) **5** to disapprove of; condemn. **6** (of God) to condemn to eternal punishment in hell. [C16: from LL *reprobātus* held in disfavour, from L RE- + *probāre* to test, APPROVE]
▸**reprobacy** ('rɛprəbəsɪ) *n* ▸**'repro,bater** *n* ▸**,repro'bation** *n*

reprocess (riː'prəʊsɛs) *vb* (*tr*) to treat again (something already made and used) in order to make it reusable in some form.
▸**re'processing** *n, adj*

reproduce ❶ (,riːprə'djuːs) *vb* **reproduces, reproducing, reproduced.** (*mainly tr*) **1** to make a copy, representation, or imitation of; duplicate. **2** (*also intr*) *Biol.* to undergo or cause to undergo a process of reproduction. **3** to produce again; bring back into existence again; re-create. **4** (*intr*) to come out (well, badly, etc.) when copied.
▸**,repro'ducer** *n* ▸**,repro'ducible** *adj* ▸**,repro'ducibly** *adv* ▸**,repro,duci'bility** *n*

reproduction ❶ (,riːprə'dʌkʃən) *n* **1** *Biol.* any of various processes, either sexual or asexual, by which an animal or plant produces one or more individuals similar to itself. **2a** an imitation or facsimile of a work of art. **2b** (*as modifier*): *a reproduction portrait.* **3** the quality of sound from an audio system. **4** the act or process of reproducing.

reproduction proof *n Printing.* a proof of very good quality used for photographic reproduction to make a printing plate.

reproductive (,riːprə'dʌktɪv) *adj* of, relating to, characteristic of, or taking part in reproduction.
▸**,repro'ductively** *adv* ▸**,repro'ductiveness** *n*

reprography (rɪ'prɒgrəfɪ) *n* the art or process of copying, reprinting, or reproducing printed material.
▸**reprographic** (,rɛprə'græfɪk) *adj* ▸**,repro'graphically** *adv*

reproof ❶ (rɪ'pruːf) *n* an act or expression of rebuke or censure. Also: **reproval** (rɪ'pruːvᵊl). [C14 *reproffe,* from OF *reprove,* from LL *reprobāre* to disapprove of; see REPROBATE]

re-proof (riː'pruːf) *vb* (*tr*) **1** to treat (a coat, jacket, etc.) so as to renew its texture, waterproof qualities, etc. **2** to provide a new proof of (a book, galley, etc.).

reprove ❶ (rɪ'pruːv) *vb* **reproves, reproving, reproved.** (*tr*) to rebuke or scold. [C14: from OF *reprover,* from LL *reprobāre,* from L RE- + *probāre* to examine]
▸**re'provable** *adj* ▸**re'prover** *n* ▸**re'provingly** *adv*

reptant ('rɛptənt) *adj Biol.* creeping, crawling, or lying along the ground. [C17: from L *reptāre* to creep]

reptile ('rɛptaɪl) *n* **1** any of the cold-blooded vertebrates characterized by lungs, an outer covering of horny scales or plates, and young produced in eggs, such as the tortoises, turtles, snakes, lizards, and crocodiles. **2** a grovelling insignificant person: *you miserable little reptile!* ◆ *adj* **3** creeping, crawling, or squirming. [C14: from LL *reptilis* creeping, from L *rēpere* to crawl]
▸**reptilian** (rɛp'tɪlɪən) *n, adj*

republic (rɪ'pʌblɪk) *n* **1** a form of government in which the people or their elected representatives possess the supreme power. **2** a political or national unit possessing such a form of government. **3** a constitutional form in which the head of state is an elected or nominated president. [C17: from F *république,* from L *rēspublica,* lit.: the public thing, from *rēs* thing + *publica* PUBLIC]

republican (rɪ'pʌblɪkən) *adj* **1** of, resembling, or relating to a republic. **2** supporting or advocating a republic. ◆ *n* **3** a supporter or advocate of a republic.

Republican (rɪ'pʌblɪkən) *adj* **1** of, belonging to, or relating to a Republican Party. **2** of, belonging to, or relating to the Irish Republican Army. ◆ *n* **3** a member or supporter of a Republican Party. **4** a member or supporter of the Irish Republican Army.

republicanism (rɪ'pʌblɪkə,nɪzəm) *n* **1** the principles or theory of republican government. **2** support for a republic. **3** (*often cap.*) support for a Republican Party.

Republican Party *n* **1** one of the two major political parties in the US: established around 1854. **2** any of a number of political parties in other countries, usually so named to indicate their opposition to monarchy.

repudiate ❶ (rɪ'pjuːdɪ,eɪt) *vb* **repudiates, repudiating, repudiated.** (*tr*) **1** to reject the authority or validity of; refuse to accept or ratify. **2** to refuse to acknowledge or pay (a debt). **3** to cast off or disown (a son, lover, etc.). [C16: from L *repudiāre* to put away, from *repudium* separation, divorce, from RE- + *pudēre* to be ashamed]
▸**re'pudiable** *adj* ▸**re,pudi'ation** *n* ▸**re'pudiative** *adj* ▸**re'pudi,ator** *n*

repugnant ❶ (rɪ'pʌgnənt) *adj* **1** repellent to the senses; causing aversion. **2** distasteful; offensive; disgusting. **3** contradictory; inconsistent or incompatible. [C14: from L *repugnāns* resisting, from *repugnāre,* from RE- + *pugnāre* to fight]
▸**re'pugnance** *n* ▸**re'pugnantly** *adv*

repulse ❶ (rɪ'pʌls) *vb* **repulses, repulsing, repulsed.** (*tr*) **1** to drive back or ward off (an attacking force); repel; rebuff. **2** to reject with coldness or discourtesy: *she repulsed his advances.* ◆ *n* **3** the act or an instance of driving back or warding off; rebuff. **4** a cold discourteous rejection or refusal. [C16: from L *repellere* to drive back]
▸**re'pulser** *n*

> **USAGE NOTE** Some people think that the use of *repulse* in sentences such as *he was repulsed by what he saw* is incorrect and that the correct word is *repel.*

repulsion ❶ (rɪ'pʌlʃən) *n* **1** a feeling of disgust or aversion. **2** *Physics.* a force separating two objects, such as the force between two like electric charges.

repulsive ❶ (rɪ'pʌlsɪv) *adj* **1** causing or occasioning repugnance; loathsome; disgusting or distasteful. **2** tending to repel, esp. by coldness and discourtesy. **3** *Physics.* concerned with, producing, or being a repulsion.
▸**re'pulsively** *adv* ▸**re'pulsiveness** *n*

repurchase (riː'pɜːtʃɪs) *vb* **1** (*tr*) to buy back or buy again (goods, securities, assets, etc.). ◆ *n* **2** an act or instance of repurchasing.

reputable ❶ ('rɛpjʊtəbᵊl) *adj* **1** having a good reputation; honoured, trustworthy, or respectable. **2** (of words) acceptable as good usage; standard.
▸**'reputably** *adv*

reputation ❶ (,rɛpjʊ'teɪʃən) *n* **1** the estimation in which a person or

THESAURUS

into (*inf.*), tear (someone) off a strip (*Brit. inf.*), upbraid ◆ *n* **3** = **blame**, abuse, blemish, censure, condemnation, contempt, disapproval, discredit, disgrace, dishonour, disrepute, ignominy, indignity, obloquy, odium, opprobrium, rebuke, scorn, shame, slight, slur, stain, stigma

reproachful *adj* = **critical**, abusive, admonitory, castigatory, censorious, condemnatory, contemptuous, disappointed, disapproving, fault-finding, reproving, scolding, upbraiding

reprobate *adj* **1** = **unprincipled**, abandoned, bad, base, corrupt, degenerate, depraved, dissolute, hardened, immoral, incorrigible, profligate, shameless, sinful, vile, wicked ◆ *n* **3, 4** = **scoundrel**, bastard (*offens.*), blackguard, degenerate, evildoer, miscreant, ne'er-do-well, outcast, rake, rascal, roué, scumbag (*sl.*), shit (*taboo sl.*), sinner, son-of-a-bitch (*sl., chiefly US & Canad.*), villain, wretch, wrongdoer ◆ *vb* **5** = **condemn**, damn, denounce, disapprove of, frown upon, reprehend, vilify

reproduce *vb* **1** = **copy**, duplicate, echo, emulate, imitate, match, mirror, parallel, print, recreate, repeat, replicate, represent, transcribe **2** *Biology* = **breed**, generate, multiply, procreate, produce young, proliferate, propagate, spawn

reproduction *n* **1** *Biology* = **breeding**, generation, increase, multiplication, procreation, proliferation, propagation **2** = **copy**, duplicate, facsimile, imitation, picture, print, replica
Antonyms *n* ≠ **copy:** master, original, prototype

reproof *n* = **rebuke**, admonition, blame, castigation, censure, chiding, condemnation, criticism, dressing-down (*inf.*), reprehension, reprimand, reproach, reproval, scolding, ticking-off (*inf.*), tongue-lashing, upbraiding
Antonyms *n* commendation, compliment, encouragement, praise

reprove *vb* = **rebuke**, abuse, admonish, bawl out (*inf.*), berate, blame, carpet (*inf.*), censure, check, chew out (*US & Canad. inf.*), chide, condemn, give a rocket (*Brit. & NZ inf.*), read the riot act, reprehend, reprimand, scold, take to task, tear into (*inf.*), tear (someone) off a strip (*Brit. inf.*), tell off (*inf.*), tick off (*inf.*), upbraid
Antonyms *vb* applaud, commend, compliment, encourage, praise

repudiate *vb* **1** = **deny**, abjure, disavow, disclaim, reject, renounce, rescind, retract, reverse, revoke **3** = **disown**, abandon, cast off, desert, discard, forsake, reject, turn one's back on, wash one's hands of
Antonyms *vb* ≠ **deny:** accept, acknowledge, admit, assert, avow, defend, proclaim, ratify

repugnance *n* **1, 2** = **distaste**, abhorrence, antipathy, aversion, disgust, dislike, disrelish, hatred, loathing, odium, reluctance, repulsion, revulsion

repugnant *adj* **1, 2** = **distasteful**, abhorrent, abominable, disgusting, foul, hateful, horrid, loathsome, nauseating, objectionable, obnoxious, odious, offensive, repellent, revolting, sickening, vile, yucky *or* yukky (*sl.*) **3** = **incompatible**, adverse, antagonistic, antipathetic, averse, contradictory, hostile, inconsistent, inimical, opposed
Antonyms *adj* ≠ **distasteful:** agreeable, attractive, pleasant, unobjectionable ≠ **incompatible:** compatible

repulse *vb* **1** = **drive back**, beat off, check, defeat, fight off, rebuff, repel, throw back, ward off **2** = **reject**, disdain, disregard, give the cold shoulder to, rebuff, refuse, snub, spurn, turn down ◆ *n* **3** = **defeat**, check, disappointment, failure, reverse **4** = **rejection**, cold shoulder, kick in the teeth, knock-back (*sl.*), rebuff, refusal, snub, spurning, the (old) heave-ho (*inf.*)

repulsion *n* **1** = **disgust**, abhorrence, aversion, detestation, disrelish, distaste, hatred, loathing, odium, repugnance, revulsion

repulsive *adj* **1** = **disgusting**, abhorrent, abominable, disagreeable, distasteful, forbidding, foul, hateful, hideous, horrid, loathsome, nauseating, objectionable, obnoxious, obscene, odious, offensive, repellent, revolting, sickening, ugly, unpleasant, vile
Antonyms *adj* appealing, attractive, delightful, enticing, lovely, pleasant

reputable *adj* **1** = **respectable**, creditable, estimable, excellent, good, honourable, honoured, legitimate, of good repute, reliable, trustworthy, upright, well-thought-of, worthy
Antonyms *adj* cowboy (*inf.*), disreputable, fly-by-night, shady (*inf.*), unreliable, untrustworthy

reputation *n* **1** = **name**, character, estimation, opinion, renown, repute, standing, stature **2** =

thing is generally held; opinion. **2** a high opinion generally held about a person or thing; esteem. **3** notoriety or fame, esp. for some specified characteristic. [C14: from L *reputātiō*, from *reputāre* to calculate; see REPUTE]

repute ❶ (rɪˈpjuːt) *vb* **repute*s*, reputing, reputed. 1** (*tr; usually passive*) to consider (a person or thing) to be as specified: *he is reputed to be rich.* ◆ *n* **2** public estimation; reputation: *a writer of little repute.* [C15: from OF *reputer*, from L *reputāre*, from RE- + *putāre* to think]

reputed ❶ (rɪˈpjuːtɪd) *adj* (*prenominal*) generally reckoned or considered; supposed: *the reputed writer of two epic poems.*
▸**reˈputedly** *adv*

request ❶ (rɪˈkwɛst) *vb* (*tr*) **1** to express a desire for, esp. politely; ask for or demand: *to request a bottle of wine.* ◆ *n* **2** the act or an instance of requesting, esp. in the form of a written statement, etc.; petition or solicitation. **3 by request.** in accordance with someone's desire. **4 in request.** in demand; popular: *he is in request all over the world.* **5 on request.** on the occasion of a demand or request: *application forms are available on request.* [C14: from OF *requeste*, from Vulgar L *requaerere*; see REQUIRE, QUEST]
▸**reˈquester** *n*

request stop *n* a point on a route at which a bus, etc., will stop only if signalled to do so. US equivalent: **flag stop.**

Requiem (ˈrɛkwɪəm) *n* **1** *RC Church.* a Mass celebrated for the dead. **2** a musical setting of this Mass. **3** any piece of music composed or performed as a memorial to a dead person. [C14: from L *requiēs* rest, from the introit, *Requiem aeternam dona eis* Rest eternal grant unto them]

requiem shark *n* any of a family of sharks occurring mostly in tropical seas and characterized by a nictitating membrane.

requiescat (ˌrɛkwɪˈɛskæt) *n* a prayer for the repose of the souls of the dead. [L, from *requiescat in pace* may he rest in peace]

require ❶ (rɪˈkwaɪə) *vb* **requires, requiring, required.** (*mainly tr; may take a clause as object or an infinitive*) **1** to have need of; depend upon; want. **2** to impose as a necessity; make necessary: *this work requires precision.* **3** (*also intr*) to make formal request (for); insist upon. **4** to call upon or oblige (a person) authoritatively; order or command: *to require someone to account for his actions.* [C14: from OF *requerre*, via Vulgar L from L *requīrere* to seek to know; also infl. by *quaerere* to seek]
▸**reˈquirer** *n*

> **USAGE NOTE** The use of *require to* as in *I require to see the manager* or *you require to complete a special form* is thought by many people to be incorrect: *I need to see the manager; you are required to complete a special form.*

requirement ❶ (rɪˈkwaɪəmənt) *n* **1** something demanded or imposed as an obligation. **2** a thing desired or needed. **3** the act or an instance of requiring.

requisite ❶ (ˈrɛkwɪzɪt) *adj* **1** absolutely essential; indispensable. ◆ *n* **2** something indispensable; necessity. [C15: from L *requisītus* sought after, from *requīrere* to seek for]
▸**ˈrequisitely** *adv*

requisition ❶ (ˌrɛkwɪˈzɪʃən) *n* **1** a request or demand, esp. an authoritative or formal one. **2** an official form on which such a demand is made. **3** the act of taking something over, esp. temporarily for military or public use. ◆ *vb* (*tr*) **4** to demand and take for use, esp. by military or public authority. **5** (*may take an infinitive*) to require (someone) formally to do (something): *to requisition a soldier to drive an officer's car.*
▸ˌ**requiˈsitionary** *adj* ▸ˌ**requiˈsitionist** *n*

requite ❶ (rɪˈkwaɪt) *vb* **requites, requiting, requited.** (*tr*) to make return to (a person for a kindness or injury); repay with a similar action. [C16: RE- + obs. *quite* to discharge, repay; see QUIT]
▸**reˈquitable** *adj* ▸**reˈquital** *n* ▸**reˈquitement** *n* ▸**reˈquiter** *n*

reredos (ˈrɪədɒs) *n* **1** a screen or wall decoration at the back of an altar. **2** another word for **fireback.** [C14: from OF *areredos*, from *arere* behind + *dos* back, from L *dorsum*]

rerun *vb* (riːˈrʌn), **reruns, rerunning, reran, rerun.** (*tr*) **1** to broadcast or put on (a film, etc.) again. **2** to run (a race, etc.) again. ◆ *n* (ˈriːˌrʌn). **3** a film, etc., that is broadcast again; repeat. **4** a race that is run again. **5** *Computing.* the repeat of a part of a computer program.

res (reɪs) *n, pl* **res.** *Latin.* a thing, matter, or object.

res. *abbrev. for:* **1** research. **2** reserve. **3** residence. **4** resides. **5** resigned. **6** resolution.

resale price maintenance (ˈriːseɪl) *n* the practice by which a manufacturer establishes a fixed or minimum price for the resale of a brand product by retailers or other distributors. US equivalent: **fair trade.** Abbrev.: **rpm.**

reschedule (riːˈʃɛdjuːl; *also, esp. US* -ˈskɛdʒuəl) *vb* (*tr*) **1** to change the time, date, or schedule of. **2** to arrange a revised schedule for repayment of (a debt).

rescind ❶ (rɪˈsɪnd) *vb* (*tr*) to annul or repeal. [C17: from L *rēscindere* to cut off, from *re-* (intensive) + *scindere* to cut]
▸**reˈscindable** *adj* ▸**reˈscinder** *n* ▸**reˈscindment** *n*

rescission (rɪˈsɪʒən) *n* **1** the act of rescinding. **2** *Law.* the right to have a contract set aside if it has been entered into mistakenly, as a result of misrepresentation, undue influence, etc.

rescript (ˈriːˌskrɪpt) *n* **1** (in ancient Rome) a reply by the emperor to a question on a point of law. **2** any official announcement or edict; a decree. **3** something rewritten. [C16: from L *rēscriptum* reply, from *rēscribere* to write back]

rescue ❶ (ˈrɛskjuː) *vb* **rescues, rescuing, rescued.** (*tr*) **1** to bring (someone or something) out of danger, etc.; deliver or save. **2** to free (a person) from legal custody by force. **3** *Law.* to seize (goods) by force. ◆ *n* **4a** the act or an instance of rescuing. **4b** (*as modifier*): *a rescue party.* **5** the forcible removal of a person from legal custody. **6** *Law.* the forcible seizure of goods or property. [C14: *rescowen*, from OF *rescourre*, from RE- + *escourre* to pull away, from L *excutere* to shake off, from *quatere* to shake]
▸**ˈrescuer** *n*

research ❶ (rɪˈsɜːtʃ) *n* **1** systematic investigation to establish facts or collect information on a subject. ◆ *vb* **2** to carry out investigations into (a subject, etc.). [C16: from OF *recercher* to seek, search again, from RE- + *cercher* to SEARCH]
▸**reˈsearchable** *adj* ▸**reˈsearcher** *n*

research and development *n* a commercial company's application of scientific research to develop new products. Abbrev.: **R & D.**

reseat (riːˈsiːt) *vb* (*tr*) **1** to show (a person) to a new seat. **2** to put a new seat on (a chair, etc.). **3** to provide new seats for (a theatre, etc.). **4** to re-form the seating of (a valve).

resect (rɪˈsɛkt) *vb* (*tr*) *Surgery.* to cut out part of (a bone, organ, or other structure or part). [C17: from L *resecāre*, from RE- + *secāre* to cut]

resection (rɪˈsɛkʃən) *n* **1** *Surgery.* excision of part of a bone, organ, or other part. **2** *Surveying.* a method of fixing the position of a point by making angular observations to three fixed points.
▸**reˈsectional** *adj*

resemblance ❶ (rɪˈzɛmbləns) *n* **1** the state or quality of resembling; likeness or similarity. **2** the degree or extent to which a likeness exists. **3** semblance; likeness.
▸**reˈsemblant** *adj*

THESAURUS

esteem, credit, honour **3** = **fame**, distinction, eminence

repute *n* **2** = **reputation**, celebrity, distinction, eminence, esteem, estimation, fame, name, renown, standing, stature

reputed *adj* = **supposed**, accounted, alleged, believed, considered, deemed, estimated, held, ostensible, putative, reckoned, regarded, rumoured, said, seeming, thought

reputedly *adv* = **supposedly**, allegedly, apparently, ostensibly, seemingly

request *vb* **1** = **ask (for)**, appeal for, apply for, beg, beseech, call for, demand, desire, entreat, invite, petition, pray, put in for, requisition, seek, solicit, sue for, supplicate ◆ *n* **2** = **asking**, appeal, application, begging, call, demand, desire, entreaty, petition, prayer, requisition, solicitation, suit, supplication
Antonyms *vb* ≠ **ask (for)**: command, order ◆ *n* ≠ **asking**: command, order

require *vb* **1** = **need**, crave, depend upon, desire, have need of, lack, miss, stand in need of, want, wish **2** = **demand**, call for, entail, involve, necessitate, take **3, 4** = **order**, ask, bid, call upon, command, compel, constrain, demand, direct, enjoin, exact, insist upon, instruct, oblige

required *adj* **2** = **necessary**, called for, compulsory, demanded, *de rigueur*, essential, mandatory, needed, obligatory, prescribed, recommended, requisite, set, unavoidable, vital
Antonyms *adj* elective, noncompulsory, not necessary, not vital, optional, unimportant, voluntary

requirement *n* **1** = **necessity**, demand, desideratum, essential, must, precondition, prerequisite, qualification, requisite, *sine qua non*, specification, stipulation **2** = **need**, lack, want

requisite *adj* **1** = **necessary**, called for, essential, indispensable, mandatory, needed, needful, obligatory, prerequisite, required, vital ◆ *n* **2** = **necessity**, condition, desideratum, essential, must, need, precondition, prerequisite, requirement, *sine qua non*

requisition *n* **1** = **demand**, application, call, request, summons **3** = **takeover**, appropriation, commandeering, occupation, seizure ◆ *vb* **4** = **take over**, appropriate, commandeer, occupy, seize, take possession of **5** = **demand**, apply for, call for, put in for, request

requital *n* = **return**, amends, compensation, payment, recompense, redress, reimbursement, remuneration, repayment, restitution, reward

requite *vb* = **return**, compensate, get even, give in return, give tit for tat, make amends, make good, make restitution, pay, pay (someone) back in his *or* her own coin, reciprocate, recompense, redress, reimburse, remunerate, repay, respond, retaliate, return like for like, reward, satisfy

rescind *vb* = **annul**, abrogate, cancel, countermand, declare null and void, invalidate, obviate, overturn, quash, recall, repeal, retract, reverse, revoke, set aside, void
Antonyms *vb* confirm, enact, implement, reaffirm, support, uphold, validate

rescue *vb* **1** = **save**, deliver, extricate, free, get out, liberate, recover, redeem, release, salvage, save (someone's) bacon (*Brit. inf.*), save the life of, set free ◆ *n* **4a** = **liberation**, deliverance, extrication, recovery, redemption, release, relief, salvage, salvation, saving
Antonyms *vb* ≠ **save**: abandon, desert, leave, leave behind, lose, strand

research *n* **1** = **investigation**, analysis, delving, examination, experimentation, exploration, fact-finding, groundwork, inquiry, probe, scrutiny, study ◆ *vb* **2** = **investigate**, analyse, consult the archives, do tests, examine, experiment, explore, look into, make inquiries, probe, scrutinize, study, work over

resemblance *n* **1, 2** = **similarity**, affinity, analogy, closeness, comparability, comparison, conformity, correspondence, counterpart, kin-

resemble ➊ (rɪˈzɛmbᵊl) *vb* **resembles, resembling, resembled.** (*tr*) to possess some similarity to; be like. [C14: from OF *resembler*, from RE- + *sembler* to look like, from L *similis* like]
▸**reˈsembler** *n*

resent ➊ (rɪˈzɛnt) *vb* (*tr*) to feel bitter, indignant, or aggrieved at. [C17: from F *ressentir*, from RE- + *sentir* to feel, from L *sentīre* to perceive; see SENSE]
▸**reˈsentful** *adj* ▸**reˈsentment** *n*

reserpine (ˈrɛsəpɪn) *n* an insoluble alkaloid, extracted from the roots of a rauwolfia, used medicinally to lower blood pressure and as a sedative and tranquillizer. [C20: from G *Reserpin*, prob. from the NL name of the plant]

reservation ➊ (ˌrɛzəˈveɪʃən) *n* **1** the act or an instance of reserving. **2** something reserved, esp. accommodation or a seat. **3** (*often pl*) a stated or unstated qualification of opinion that prevents one's wholehearted acceptance of a proposal, etc. **4** an area of land set aside, esp. (in the US) for American Indian peoples. **5** *Brit.* the strip of land between the two carriageways of a dual carriageway. **6** the act or process of keeping back, esp. for oneself; withholding. **7** *Law.* a right or interest retained by the grantor in property dealings.

reserve ➊ (rɪˈzɜːv) *vb* **reserves, reserving, reserved.** (*tr*) **1** to keep back or set aside, esp. for future use or contingency; withhold. **2** to keep for oneself; retain: *I reserve the right to question these men later.* **3** to obtain or secure by advance arrangement: *I have reserved two tickets for tonight's show.* **4** to delay delivery of (a judgment). ◆ *n* **5a** something kept back or set aside, esp. for future use or contingency. **5b** (*as modifier*): *a reserve stock.* **6** the state or condition of being reserved: *I have plenty in reserve.* **7** a tract of land set aside for a special purpose: *a nature reserve.* **8** *Austral. & NZ.* a public park. **9** the usual Canadian name for **reservation** (sense 4). **10** *Sport.* a substitute. **11** (*often pl*) **11a** a part of an army not committed to immediate action in a military engagement. **11b** that part of a nation's armed services not in active service. **12** coolness or formality of manner; restraint, silence, or reticence. **13** (*often pl*) *Finance.* liquid assets or a portion of capital not invested or a portion of profits not distributed by a bank or business enterprise and held to meet future liabilities or contingencies. **14 without reserve.** without reservations; fully. [C14: from OF *reserver*, from L *reservāre*, from RE- + *servāre* to keep]
▸**reˈservable** *adj* ▸**reˈserver** *n*

re-serve (riːˈsɜːv) *vb* **re-serves, re-serving, re-served.** (*tr*) to serve again.

reserve bank *n* one of the twelve banks forming part of the US Federal Reserve System.

reserve currency *n* foreign currency that is acceptable as a medium of international payments and is held in reserve by many countries.

reserved ➊ (rɪˈzɜːvd) *adj* **1** set aside for use by a particular person. **2** cool or formal in manner; restrained or reticent. **3** destined; fated: *a man reserved for greatness.*
▸**reservedly** (rɪˈzɜːvɪdlɪ) *adv* ▸**reˈservedness** *n*

reserved list *n Brit.* a list of retired naval, army, or air-force officers available for recall to active service in an emergency.

reserved occupation *n Brit.* an occupation from which one will not be called up for military service in time of war.

reserve-grade *adj Austral.* denoting a sporting team of the second rank in a club.

reserve price *n Brit.* the minimum price acceptable to the owner of property being auctioned or sold. Also called (esp. Scot. and US): **upset price.**

reserve tranche *n* the quota of 25 per cent to which a member of the IMF has unconditional access. Prior to 1978 it was paid in gold and known as the **gold tranche.**

reservist (rɪˈzɜːvɪst) *n* one who serves in the reserve formations of a nation's armed forces.

reservoir ➊ (ˈrɛzəˌvwɑː) *n* **1** a natural or artificial lake or large tank used for collecting and storing water for community use. **2** *Biol.* a cavity in an organism containing fluid. **3** a place where a great stock of anything is accumulated. **4** a large supply of something: *a reservoir of talent.* [C17: from F *réservoir*, from *réserver* to RESERVE]

reservoir rock *n* porous and permeable rock containing producible oil or gas in its pore spaces.

reset[1] *vb* (riːˈsɛt), **resets, resetting, reset.** (*tr*) **1** to set again (a broken bone, matter in type, a gemstone, etc.). **2** to restore (a gauge, etc.) to zero. ◆ *n* (ˈriːˌsɛt). **3** the act or an instance of setting again. **4** a thing that is set again.
▸**reˈsetter** *n*

reset[2] *Scot.* ◆ *vb* (riːˈsɛt), **resets, resetting, reset. 1** to receive or handle goods knowing they have been stolen. ◆ *n* (ˈriːsɛt). **2** the receiving of stolen goods. [C14: from OF *receter*, from L *receptāre*, from *recipere* to receive]
▸**reˈsetter** *n*

res gestae (ˈdʒɛstiː) *pl n* **1** things done or accomplished; achievements. **2** *Law.* incidental facts and circumstances that are admissible in evidence because they explain the matter at issue. [L]

reside ➊ (rɪˈzaɪd) *vb* **resides, residing, resided.** (*intr*) *Formal.* **1** to live permanently (in a place); have one's home (in): *he resides in London.* **2** (of things, qualities, etc.) to be inherently present (in); be vested (in): *political power resides in military strength.* [C15: from L *residēre* to sit back, from RE- + *sedēre* to sit]
▸**reˈsider** *n*

residence ➊ (ˈrɛzɪdəns) *n* **1** the place in which one resides; abode or home. **2** a large imposing house; mansion. **3** the fact of residing in a place or a period of residing. **4 in residence. 4a** actually resident: *the Queen is in residence.* **4b** designating a creative artist resident and active for a set period at a college, gallery, etc.: *writer in residence.*

residency (ˈrɛzɪdənsɪ) *n, pl* **residencies. 1** a variant of **residence. 2** a regular series of concerts by a band or singer at one venue. **3** *US & Canad.* the period, following internship, during which a physician undergoes specialized training. **4** (in India, formerly) the official house of the governor general at the court of a native prince.

resident ➊ (ˈrɛzɪdənt) *n* **1** a person who resides in a place. **2** (esp. formerly) a representative of the British government in a British protectorate. **3** (in India, formerly) a representative of the British governor general at the court of a native prince. **4** a bird or animal that does not migrate. **5** *Brit. & NZ.* a junior doctor who lives in the hospital where he works. **6** *US & Canad.* a physician who lives in the hospital while undergoing specialist training after completing his internship. ◆ *adj* **7** living in a place; residing. **8** living or staying at a place in order to discharge a duty, etc. **9** (of qualities, etc.) existing or inherent (in). **10** (of birds and animals) not in the habit of migrating.
▸**ˈresidentship** *n*

residential (ˌrɛzɪˈdɛnʃəl) *adj* **1** suitable for or allocated for residence: *a residential area.* **2** relating to residence.
▸**ˌresiˈdentially** *adv*

residentiary (ˌrɛzɪˈdɛnʃərɪ) *adj* **1** residing in a place, esp. officially. **2** obliged to reside in an official residence: *a residentiary benefice.* ◆ *n, pl* **residentiaries. 3** a clergyman obliged to reside in the place of his official appointment.

residual ➊ (rɪˈzɪdjuəl) *adj* **1** of, relating to, or designating a residue or remainder; remaining; leftover. **2** *US.* of or relating to the payment of residuals. ◆ *n* **3** something left over as a residue; remainder. **4** *Statistics.* **4a** the difference between the mean of a set of observations and one particular observation. **4b** the difference between the numerical

THESAURUS

ship, likeness, parallel, parity, sameness, similitude **3** = **semblance**, facsimile, image, likeness
Antonyms *n* ≠ **similarity:** difference, disparity, dissimilarity, heterogeneity, unlikeness, variation

resemble *vb* = **be like**, bear a resemblance to, be similar to, duplicate, echo, favour (*inf.*), look like, mirror, parallel, put one in mind of, remind one of, take after

resent *vb* = **be bitter about**, be angry about, bear a grudge about, begrudge, be in a huff about, be offended by, dislike, grudge, harbour a grudge against, have hard feelings about, object to, take amiss, take as an insult, take exception to, take offence at, take umbrage at
Antonyms *vb* accept, approve, be content with, be pleased by, feel flattered by, like, welcome

resentful *adj* = **bitter**, aggrieved, angry, choked, embittered, exasperated, grudging, huffish, huffy, hurt, in a huff, incensed, indignant, in high dudgeon, irate, jealous, miffed (*inf.*), offended, peeved (*inf.*), piqued, put out, revengeful, unforgiving, wounded
Antonyms *adj* content, flattered, gratified, pleased, satisfied

resentment *n* = **bitterness**, anger, animosity, bad blood, chip on one's shoulder (*inf.*), displeasure, fury, grudge, huff, hurt, ill feeling, ill will, indignation, ire, irritation, malice, pique, rage, rancour, umbrage, vexation, wrath

reservation *n* **3** = **doubt**, demur, hesitancy, scepticism, scruple **3** = **condition**, proviso, qualification, rider, stipulation **4** = **reserve**, enclave, homeland, preserve, sanctuary, territory, tract

reserve *vb* **1, 2** = **keep**, conserve, hang on to, hoard, hold, husband, keep back, lay up, preserve, put by, retain, save, set aside, stockpile, store, withhold **3** = **book**, bespeak, engage, prearrange, pre-engage, retain, secure **4** = **delay**, defer, keep back, postpone, put off, withhold ◆ *n* **5a** = **store**, backlog, cache, capital, fall-back, fund, hoard, reservoir, savings, stock, stockpile, supply ◆ *modifier* **5b** = **substitute**, alternate, auxiliary, extra, fall-back, secondary, spare ◆ *n* **7** = **reservation**, park, preserve, sanctuary, tract **12** = **shyness**, aloofness, constraint, coolness, formality, modesty, reluctance, reservation, restraint, reticence, secretiveness, silence, taciturnity

reserved *adj* **1** = **set aside**, booked, engaged, held, kept, restricted, retained, spoken for, taken **2** = **uncommunicative**, aloof, cautious, close-mouthed, cold, cool, demure, formal, modest, prim, restrained, reticent, retiring, secretive, shy, silent, standoffish, taciturn, unapproachable, undemonstrative, unforthcoming, unresponsive, unsociable
Antonyms *adj* ≠ **uncommunicative:** ardent, demonstrative, forward, open, sociable, uninhibited, unreserved, warm

reservoir *n* **1** = **lake**, basin, pond, tank **3** = **repository**, container, holder, receptacle, store, tank **4** = **store**, accumulation, fund, pool, reserves, source, stock, stockpile, supply

reside *vb Formal* **1** = **live**, abide, dwell, hang out (*inf.*), have one's home, inhabit, lodge, remain, settle, sojourn, stay **2** = **be present**, abide, be intrinsic to, be vested, consist, dwell, exist, inhere, lie, rest with
Antonyms *vb* ≠ **live:** holiday in, visit

residence *n* **1** = **home**, abode, domicile, dwelling, flat, habitation, house, household, lodging, pad (*sl.*), place, quarters **2** = **mansion**, hall, manor, palace, seat, villa **3** = **stay**, occupancy, occupation, sojourn, tenancy

resident *n* **1** = **inhabitant**, citizen, denizen, indweller, local, lodger, occupant, tenant ◆ *adj* **7** = **inhabiting**, dwelling, living, local, neighbourhood, settled
Antonyms *n* ≠ **inhabitant:** nonresident, visitor ◆ *adj* ≠ **inhabiting:** nonresident, visiting

residual *adj* **1** = **remaining**, leftover, net, nett, unconsumed, unused, vestigial

value of one particular observation and the theoretical result. **5** (*often pl*) payment made to an actor, musician, etc., for subsequent use of film in which the person appears.
▸**re'sidually** *adv*

residual unemployment *n* the unemployment that remains in periods of full employment, as a result of those mentally, physically, or emotionally unfit to work.

residuary (rɪ'zɪdjʊərɪ) *adj* **1** of, relating to, or constituting a residue; residual. **2** *Law.* entitled to the residue of an estate after payment of debts and distribution of specific gifts.

residue ❶ ('rɛzɪˌdjuː) *n* **1** matter remaining after something has been removed. **2** *Law.* what is left of an estate after the discharge of debts and distribution of specific gifts. [C14: from OF *residu,* from L *residuus* remaining over, from *residēre* to stay behind]

residuum (rɪ'zɪdjʊəm) *n, pl* **residua** (-jʊə). a more formal word for **residue.**

resign ❶ (rɪ'zaɪn) *vb* **1** (when *intr,* often foll. by *from*) to give up tenure of (a job, office, etc.). **2** (*tr*) to reconcile (oneself) to; yield: *to resign oneself to death.* **3** (*tr*) to give up (a right, claim, etc.); relinquish. [C14: from OF *resigner,* from L *resignāre* to unseal, destroy, from RE- + *signāre* to seal]
▸**re'signer** *n*

re-sign (riː'saɪn) *vb* to sign again.

resignation ❶ (ˌrɛzɪg'neɪʃən) *n* **1** the act of resigning. **2** a formal document stating one's intention to resign. **3** a submissive unresisting attitude; passive acquiescence.

resigned ❶ (rɪ'zaɪnd) *adj* characteristic of or proceeding from an attitude of resignation; acquiescent or submissive.
▸**resignedly** (rɪ'zaɪnɪdlɪ) *adv* ▸**re'signedness** *n*

resile (rɪ'zaɪl) *vb* **resiles, resiling, resiled.** (*intr*) to spring or shrink back; recoil or resume original shape. [C16: from OF *resilir,* from L *resilīre* to jump back, from RE- + *salīre* to jump]
▸**re'silement** *n*

resilient ❶ (rɪ'zɪlɪənt) *adj* **1** (of an object) capable of regaining its original shape or position after bending, stretching, or other deformation; elastic. **2** (of a person) recovering easily and quickly from illness, hardship, etc.
▸**re'silience** *or* **re'siliency** *n* ▸**re'siliently** *adv*

resin ('rɛzɪn) *n* **1** any of a group of solid or semisolid amorphous compounds that are obtained directly from certain plants as exudations. **2** any of a large number of synthetic, usually organic, materials that have a polymeric structure, esp. such a substance in a raw state before it is moulded or treated with plasticizer, etc. ◆ *vb* **3** (*tr*) to treat or coat with resin. [C14: from OF *resine,* from L *rēsīna,* from Gk *rhētinē* resin from a pine]
▸**'resinous** *adj* ▸**'resinously** *adv* ▸**'resinousness** *n*

resinate ('rɛzɪˌneɪt) *vb* **resinates, resinating, resinated.** (*tr*) to impregnate with resin.

resipiscence (ˌrɛsɪ'pɪsəns) *n Literary.* acknowledgment that one has been mistaken. [C16: from LL *resipiscentia,* from *resipiscere* to recover one's senses, from L *sapere* to know]
▸ˌ**resi'piscent** *adj*

resist ❶ (rɪ'zɪst) *vb* **1** to stand firm (against); not yield (to); fight (against). **2** (*tr*) to withstand the deleterious action of; be proof against: *to resist corrosion.* **3** (*tr*) to oppose; refuse to accept or comply with: *to resist arrest.* **4** (*tr*) to refrain from, esp. in spite of temptation (esp. in **cannot resist (something)**). ◆ *n* **5** a substance used to protect something, esp. a coating that prevents corrosion. [C14: from L *resistere,* from RE- + *sistere* to stand firm]
▸**re'sister** *n* ▸**re'sistible** *adj* ▸**reˌsisti'bility** *n* ▸**re'sistibly** *adv* ▸**re'sistless** *adj*

resistance ❶ (rɪ'zɪstəns) *n* **1** the act or an instance of resisting. **2** the capacity to withstand something, esp. the body's natural capacity to withstand disease. **3a** the opposition to a flow of electric current through a circuit component, medium, or substance. It is measured in ohms. Symbol: R **3b** (*as modifier*): *a resistance thermometer.* **4** any force that tends to retard or oppose motion: *air resistance; wind resistance.* **5 line of least resistance.** the easiest, but not necessarily the best or most honourable, course of action. **6** See **passive resistance.**
▸**re'sistant** *adj, n*

Resistance ❶ (rɪ'zɪstəns) *n* **the.** an illegal organization fighting for national liberty in a country under enemy occupation.

resistance thermometer *n* an accurate type of thermometer in which temperature is calculated from the resistance of a coil of wire or of a semiconductor placed at the point at which the temperature is to be measured.

resistivity (ˌriːzɪs'tɪvɪtɪ) *n* **1** the electrical property of a material that determines the resistance of a piece of given dimensions. It is measured in ohms. Former name: **specific resistance. 2** the power or capacity to resist; resistance.

resistor (rɪ'zɪstə) *n* an electrical component designed to introduce a known value of resistance into a circuit.

resit *vb* (riː'sɪt), **resits, resitting, resat.** (*tr*) **1** to sit (an examination) again. ◆ *n* ('riːsɪt). **2** an examination which one must sit again.

res judicata (ˌdʒuːdɪ'kɑːtə) *or* **res adjudicata** *n Law.* a matter already adjudicated upon that cannot be raised again. [L]

resoluble (rɪ'zɒljʊb^əl, 'rɛzəl-) *adj* another word for **resolvable.**

re-soluble (riː'sɒljʊb^əl) *adj* capable of being dissolved again.
▸**re-'solubleness** *or* **re-ˌsolu'bility** *n* ▸**re-'solubly** *adv*

resolute ❶ ('rɛzəˌluːt) *adj* **1** firm in purpose or belief; steadfast. **2** characterized by resolution; determined: *a resolute answer.* [C16: from L *resolutus,* from *resolvere* to RESOLVE]
▸**'resoˌlutely** *adv* ▸**'resoˌluteness** *n*

resolution ❶ (ˌrɛzə'luːʃən) *n* **1** the act or an instance of resolving. **2** firmness or determination. **3** something resolved or determined; decision. **4** a formal expression of opinion by a meeting. **5** a judicial decision on some matter; verdict; judgment. **6** the act of separating something into its constituent parts or elements. **7** *Med.* subsidence of the symptoms of a disease, esp. the disappearance of inflammation without pus. **8** *Music.* the process in harmony whereby a dissonant note or chord is followed by a consonant one. **9** the ability of a television or film image to reproduce fine detail. **10** *Physics.* another word for **resolving power.**
▸ˌ**reso'lutioner** *or* ˌ**reso'lutionist** *n*

resolvable (rɪ'zɒlvəb^əl) *or* **resoluble** *adj* able to be resolved or analysed.
▸**reˌsolva'bility, reˌsolu'bility** *or* **re'solvableness, re'solubleness** *n*

resolve ❶ (rɪ'zɒlv) *vb* **resolves, resolving, resolved.** (*mainly tr*) **1** (*takes a clause as object or an infinitive*) to decide or determine firmly. **2** to express (an opinion) formally, esp. by a vote. **3** (*also intr;* usually foll. by *into*) to separate or cause to separate (into) (constituent parts). **4** (*usually reflexive*) to change; alter: *the ghost resolved itself into a tree.* **5** to make up the mind of; cause to decide: *the tempest resolved him to stay at home.* **6** to find the answer or solution to. **7** to explain away or dispel: *to resolve a doubt.* **8** to bring to an end; conclude: *to resolve an argument.* **9** *Med.* to cause (an inflammation) to subside, esp. without the formation of pus. **10** *Music.* (*also intr*) to follow (a dissonant note or chord) by one producing a consonance. **11** *Physics.* to distinguish between (separate parts) of (an image) as in a microscope, telescope, or other optical instrument. ◆ *n* **12** something determined or decided; resolution: *he had made a resolve to work all day.* **13** firmness of purpose; determination: *nothing can break his resolve.* [C14: from L *resolvere* to unfasten, reveal, from RE- + *solvere* to loosen]
▸**re'solvable** *adj* ▸**reˌsolva'bility** *n* ▸**re'solver** *n*

resolved (rɪ'zɒlvd) *adj* fixed in purpose or intention; determined.
▸**resolvedly** (rɪ'zɒlvɪdlɪ) *adv* ▸**re'solvedness** *n*

THESAURUS

residue *n* **1** = **remainder**, balance, dregs, excess, extra, leftovers, remains, remnant, residuum, rest, surplus

resign *vb* **1** = **quit**, abdicate, call it a day *or* night, give in one's notice, leave, step down (*inf.*), vacate **2** = **accept**, acquiesce, bow, give in, give up, reconcile, submit, succumb, yield **3** = **give up**, abandon, cede, forgo, forsake, hand over, relinquish, renounce, surrender, turn over, yield

resignation *n* **1** = **leaving**, abandonment, abdication, departure, notice, relinquishment, renunciation, retirement, surrender **3** = **acceptance**, acquiescence, compliance, endurance, forbearing, fortitude, nonresistance, passivity, patience, submission, sufferance
Antonyms *n* ≠ **acceptance:** defiance, dissent, kicking up a fuss, protest, resistance

resigned *adj* = **stoical**, acquiescent, compliant, long-suffering, patient, subdued, submissive, unprotesting, unresisting

resilient *adj* **1** = **flexible**, bouncy, elastic, plastic, pliable, rubbery, springy, supple **2** = **tough**, bouncy, buoyant, feisty, hardy, irrepressible, quick to recover, strong
Antonyms *adj* ≠ **flexible:** flaccid, inflexible, limp, rigid, stiff ≠ **tough:** delicate, effete, sensitive, sickly, weak

resist *vb* **1, 3** = **oppose**, battle, check, combat, confront, contend with, counteract, countervail, curb, defy, dispute, fight, hinder, hold out against, put up a fight (against), refuse, stand up to, struggle against, thwart, weather **2** = **withstand**, be proof against, repel **4** = **refrain from**, abstain from, avoid, forbear, forgo, keep from, leave alone, prevent oneself from, refuse, turn down
Antonyms *vb* ≠ **oppose:** accept, acquiesce, cave in (*inf.*), give in, submit, succumb, surrender, welcome, yield ≠ **refrain from:** enjoy, give in to, indulge in, surrender to

resistance *n* **1** = **fighting**, battle, combat, contention, counteraction, defiance, fight, hindrance, impediment, intransigence, obstruction, opposition, refusal, struggle

Resistance *n* = **freedom fighters**, guerrillas, irregulars, maquis, partisans, underground

resistant *adj* **1** = **opposed**, antagonistic, combative, defiant, dissident, hostile, intractable, intransigent, recalcitrant, unwilling **2** = **impervious**, hard, insusceptible, proof against, strong, tough, unaffected by, unyielding

resolute *adj* **1, 2** = **determined**, bold, constant, dogged, firm, fixed, immovable, inflexible, obstinate, persevering, purposeful, relentless, set, stalwart, staunch, steadfast, strong-willed, stubborn, tenacious, unbending, undaunted, unflinching, unshakable, unshaken, unwavering
Antonyms *adj* doubtful, irresolute, undecided, undetermined, unresolved, unsteady, weak

resolution *n* **1** = **solution**, answer, end, finding, outcome, settlement, solving, sorting out, unravelling, upshot, working out **2** = **determination**, boldness, constancy, courage, dedication, doggedness, earnestness, energy, firmness, fortitude, obstinacy, perseverance, purpose, relentlessness, resoluteness, resolve, sincerity, staunchness, staying power, steadfastness, stubbornness, tenacity, willpower **3, 5** = **decision**, declaration, determination, intent, intention, judgment, motion, purpose, resolve, verdict

resolve *vb* **1** = **decide**, agree, conclude, design, determine, fix, intend, make up one's mind, purpose, settle, undertake **3** = **break down**, analyse, anatomize, clear, disentangle, disintegrate, dissect, dissolve, liquefy, melt, reduce,

resolvent (rɪˈzɒlvənt) *adj* **1** serving to dissolve or separate something into its elements; resolving. ◆ *n* **2** a drug or agent able to reduce swelling or inflammation.

resolving power *n* **1** Also called: **resolution.** *Physics.* the ability of a microscope or telescope to produce separate images of closely placed objects. **2** *Photog.* the ability of an emulsion to show up fine detail in an image.

resonance (ˈrezənəns) *n* **1** the condition or quality of being resonant. **2** sound produced by a body vibrating in sympathy with a neighbouring source of sound. **3** the condition of a body or system when it is subjected to a periodic disturbance of the same frequency as the natural frequency of the body or system. **4** amplification of speech sounds by sympathetic vibration in the bone structure of the head and chest, resounding in the cavities of the nose, mouth, and pharynx. **5** *Electronics.* the condition of an electrical circuit when the frequency is such that the capacitive and inductive reactances are equal in magnitude. **6** *Med.* the sound heard when tapping a hollow bodily structure, esp. the chest or abdomen. **7** *Chem.* the phenomenon in which the electronic structure of a molecule can be represented by two or more hypothetical structures involving single, double, and triple chemical bonds. **8** *Physics.* the condition of a system in which there is a sharp maximum probability for the absorption of electromagnetic radiation or capture of particles. [C16: from L *resonāre* to RESOUND]

resonant 🅣 (ˈrɛzənənt) *adj* **1** resounding or re-echoing. **2** producing resonance: *resonant walls.* **3** full of, or intensified by, resonance: *a resonant voice.*
▸**ˈresonantly** *adv*

resonate (ˈrɛzəˌneɪt) *vb* **resonates, resonating, resonated. 1** to resound or cause to resound; reverberate. **2** *Chem., electronics.* to exhibit or cause to exhibit resonance. [C19: from L *resonāre*]
▸**ˌresoˈnation** *n*

resonator (ˈrɛzəˌneɪtə) *n* any body or system that displays resonance, esp. a tuned electrical circuit or a conducting cavity in which microwaves are generated by a resonant current.

resorb (rɪˈsɔːb) *vb* (*tr*) to absorb again. [C17: from L *resorbēre,* from RE- + *sorbēre* to suck in]
▸**reˈsorbent** *adj* ▸**reˈsorptive** *adj*

resorcinol (rɪˈzɔːsɪˌnɒl) *n* a colourless crystalline phenol, used in making dyes, drugs, resins, and adhesives. Formula: $C_6H_4(OH)_2$. [C19: NL, from RESIN + *orcinol,* a crystalline solid]
▸**reˈsorcinal** *adj*

resorption (rɪˈsɔːpʃən) *n* **1** the process of resorbing or the state of being resorbed. **2** *Geol.* the remelting of a mineral by magma, resulting in a new crystal form being produced.

resort 🅣 (rɪˈzɔːt) *vb* (*intr*) **1** (usually foll. by *to*) to have recourse (to) for help, use, etc.: *to resort to violence.* **2** to go, esp. often or habitually: *to resort to the beach.* ◆ *n* **3** a place to which many people go for recreation, etc.: *a holiday resort.* **4** the use of something as a means, help, or recourse. **5 last resort.** the last possible course of action open to one. [C14: from OF *resortir,* from RE- + *sortir* to emerge]
▸**reˈsorter** *n*

re-sort (riːˈsɔːt) *vb* (*tr*) to sort again.

resound 🅣 (rɪˈzaʊnd) *vb* (*intr*) **1** to ring or echo with sound; reverberate. **2** to make a prolonged echoing noise: *the trumpet resounded.* **3** (of sounds) to echo or ring. **4** to be widely famous: *his fame resounded throughout India.* [C14: from OF *resoner,* from L *resonāre* to sound again]

re-sound (riːˈsaʊnd) *vb* to sound or cause to sound again.

resounding 🅣 (rɪˈzaʊndɪŋ) *adj* **1** clear and emphatic: *a resounding vote of confidence.* **2** resonant; reverberating: *a resounding slap.*
▸**reˈsoundingly** *adv*

resource 🅣 (rɪˈzɔːs, -ˈsɔːs) *n* **1** capability, ingenuity, and initiative; quick-wittedness: *a man of resource.* **2** (*often pl*) a source of economic wealth, esp. of a country or business enterprise. **3** a supply or source of aid or support; something resorted to in time of need. **4** a means of doing something; expedient. [C17: from OF *ressourse* relief, from *resourdre,* from L *resurgere,* from RE- + *surgere* to rise]
▸**reˈsourceless** *adj*

resourceful 🅣 (rɪˈzɔːsful, -ˈsɔːs-) *adj* ingenious, capable, and full of initiative.
▸**reˈsourcefully** *adv* ▸**reˈsourcefulness** *n*

respect 🅣 (rɪˈspɛkt) *n* **1** an attitude of deference, admiration, or esteem; regard. **2** the state of being honoured or esteemed. **3** a detail, point, or characteristic: *they differ in some respects.* **4** reference or relation (esp. in **in respect of, with respect to**). **5** polite or kind regard; consideration: *respect for people's feelings.* **6** (*often pl*) an expression of esteem or regard (esp. in **pay one's respects**). ◆ *vb* (*tr*) **7** to have an attitude of esteem towards: *to respect one's elders.* **8** to pay proper attention to; not violate: *to respect Swiss neutrality.* **9** *Arch.* to concern or refer to. [C14: from L *rēspicere* to look back, pay attention to, from RE- + *specere* to look]
▸**reˈspecter** *n*

respectable 🅣 (rɪˈspɛktəbᵊl) *adj* **1** having or deserving the respect of other people; estimable; worthy. **2** having good social standing or reputation. **3** having socially or conventionally acceptable morals, etc.: *a respectable woman.* **4** relatively or fairly good; considerable: *a respectable salary.* **5** fit to be seen by other people; presentable.
▸**reˌspectaˈbility** *n* ▸**reˈspectably** *adv*

respectful 🅣 (rɪˈspɛktful) *adj* full of, showing, or giving respect.
▸**reˈspectfully** *adv* ▸**reˈspectfulness** *n*

respecting (rɪˈspɛktɪŋ) *prep* concerning; regarding.

respective 🅣 (rɪˈspɛktɪv) *adj* belonging or relating separately to each of several people or things; several: *we took our respective ways home.*
▸**reˈspectiveness** *n*

respectively (rɪˈspɛktɪvlɪ) *adv* (in listing a number of items or attributes that refer to another list) separately in the order given: *he gave Janet and John a cake and a chocolate respectively.*

respirable (ˈrɛspɪrəbᵊl) *adj* **1** able to be breathed. **2** suitable or fit for breathing.
▸**ˌrespiraˈbility** *n*

respiration (ˌrɛspɪˈreɪʃən) *n* **1** the process in living organisms of taking in oxygen from the surroundings and giving out carbon dioxide. **2** the chemical breakdown of complex organic substances that takes place in the cells and tissues of animals and plants, during which energy is released and carbon dioxide produced.
▸**respiratory** (ˈrɛspɪrətərɪ, -trɪ) *or* **ˌrespiˈrational** *adj*

respirator (ˈrɛspɪˌreɪtə) *n* **1** an apparatus for providing long-term artificial respiration. **2** a device worn over the mouth and nose to prevent inhalation of noxious fumes or to warm cold air before it is breathed.

respiratory failure *n* a condition in which the respiratory system is unable to provide an adequate supply of oxygen or to remove carbon dioxide efficiently.

respiratory quotient *n Biol.* the ratio of the volume of carbon dioxide expired to the volume of oxygen consumed by an organism, tissue, or cell in a given time.

respiratory system *n* the specialized organs, collectively, concerned with external respiration: in humans and other mammals it includes the trachea, bronchi, bronchioles, lungs, and diaphragm.

respire (rɪˈspaɪə) *vb* **respires, respiring, respired. 1** to inhale and exhale (air); breathe. **2** (*intr*) to undergo the process of respiration. [C14: from L *rēspīrāre* to exhale, from RE- + *spīrāre* to breathe]

respite 🅣 (ˈrɛspɪt, -paɪt) *n* **1** a pause from exertion; interval of rest. **2** a temporary delay. **3** a temporary stay of execution; reprieve. ◆ *vb* **re-**

THESAURUS

separate, solve, split up, unravel **4** = **change,** alter, convert, metamorphose, transform, transmute **6** = **work out,** answer, clear up, crack, elucidate, fathom, find the solution to, suss (out) (*sl.*) **7** = **dispel,** banish, clear up, explain, remove ◆ *n* **12** = **decision,** conclusion, design, intention, objective, project, purpose, resolution, undertaking **13** = **determination,** boldness, courage, earnestness, firmness, resoluteness, resolution, steadfastness, willpower
Antonyms *n* ≠ **determination:** cowardice, half-heartedness, indecision, vacillation, wavering

resonant *adj* **1, 3** = **echoing,** booming, full, resounding, reverberant, reverberating, rich, ringing, sonorous, vibrant

resort *vb* **1** *usually foll. by* **to** = **have recourse to,** avail oneself of, bring into play, employ, exercise, fall back on, look to, make use of, turn to, use, utilize **2** = **go,** frequent, haunt, head for, repair, visit ◆ *n* **3** = **holiday centre,** haunt, refuge, retreat, spot, tourist centre, watering place (*Brit.*) **4** = **recourse,** reference

resound *vb* = **echo,** fill the air, re-echo, resonate, reverberate, ring

resounding *adj* **2** = **echoing,** booming, full, powerful, resonant, reverberating, rich, ringing, sonorous, sounding, vibrant

resource *n* **1** = **ingenuity,** ability, capability, cleverness, initiative, inventiveness, quick-wittedness, resourcefulness, talent **2** *often plural* = **funds,** assets, capital, holdings, materials, means, money, property, reserves, riches, supplies, wealth, wherewithal **3** = **supply,** hoard, reserve, source, stockpile **4** = **means,** appliance, contrivance, course, device, expedient, resort

resourceful *adj* = **ingenious,** able, bright, capable, clever, creative, imaginative, inventive, quick-witted, sharp, talented
Antonyms *adj* gormless (*Brit. inf.*), unimaginative, uninventive

respect *n* **1, 2** = **regard,** admiration, appreciation, approbation, consideration, deference, esteem, estimation, honour, recognition, reverence, veneration **3** = **particular,** aspect, characteristic, detail, facet, feature, matter, point, sense, way **4** *As in* **in respect of** *or* **with respect to** = **relation,** bearing, connection, reference, regard **6** *often plural* = **greetings,** compliments, devoirs, good wishes, regards, salutations ◆ *vb* **7** = **think highly of,** admire, adore, appreciate, defer to, esteem, have a good *or* high opinion of, honour, look up to, recognize, regard, revere, reverence, set store by, value, venerate **8** = **abide by,** adhere to, attend, comply with, follow, heed, honour, notice, obey, observe, pay attention to, regard, show consideration for
Antonyms *n* ≠ **regard:** contempt, disdain, disregard, disrespect, irreverence, scorn ◆ *vb* ≠ **abide by:** abuse, disregard, disrespect, ignore, neglect, scorn

respectable *adj* **1-3** = **honourable,** admirable, decent, decorous, dignified, estimable, good, honest, proper, reputable, respected, upright, venerable, worthy **4** = **reasonable,** ample, appreciable, considerable, decent, fair, fairly good, goodly, presentable, sizable *or* sizeable, substantial, tidy (*inf.*), tolerable
Antonyms *adj* ≠ **honourable:** dishonourable, disreputable, ignoble, impolite, improper, indecent, unrefined, unworthy ≠ **reasonable:** paltry, poor, small

respectful *adj* = **polite,** civil, courteous, courtly, deferential, dutiful, gracious, humble, mannerly, obedient, regardful, reverent, reverential, self-effacing, solicitous, submissive, well-mannered

respective *adj* = **specific,** corresponding, individual, own, particular, personal, relevant, separate, several, various

respite *n* **1** = **pause,** break, breather (*inf.*), breathing space, cessation, halt, hiatus, inter-

spites, respiting, respited. 4 (*tr*) to grant a respite to; reprieve. [C13: from OF *respit*, from L *respectus* a looking back; see RESPECT]

resplendent ➊ (rɪ'splɛndənt) *adj* having a brilliant or splendid appearance. [C15: from L *resplendēre*, from RE- + *splendēre* to shine] ▸**re'splendence** *or* **re'splendency** *n* ▸**re'splendently** *adv*

respond ➊ (rɪ'spɒnd) *vb* **1** to state or utter (something) in reply. **2** (*intr*) to act in reply; react: *to respond by issuing an invitation.* **3** (*intr;* foll. by *to*) to react favourably: *this patient will respond to treatment.* **4** an archaic word for **correspond.** ◆ *n* **5** *Archit.* a pilaster or an engaged column that supports an arch or a lintel. **6** *Christianity.* a choral anthem chanted in response to a lesson read. [C14: from OF *respondre*, from L *rēspondēre* to return like for like, from RE- + *spondēre* to pledge] ▸**re'spondence** *or* **re'spondency** *n* ▸**re'sponder** *n*

respondent (rɪ'spɒndənt) *n* **1** *Law.* a person against whom a petition is brought. ◆ *adj* **2** a less common word for **responsive.**

response ➊ (rɪ'spɒns) *n* **1** the act of responding; reply or reaction. **2** *Bridge.* a bid replying to a partner's bid or double. **3** (*usually pl*) *Christianity.* a short sentence or phrase recited or sung in reply to the officiant at a church service. **4** *Electronics.* the ratio of the output to the input level of an electrical device. **5** a glandular, muscular, or electrical reaction that arises from stimulation of the nervous system. [C14: from L *rēsponsum* answer, from *rēspondēre* to RESPOND] ▸**re'sponseless** *adj*

responser *or* **responsor** (rɪ'spɒnsə) *n* a radio or radar receiver used to receive and display signals from a transponder.

responsibility ➊ (rɪˌspɒnsɪ'bɪlɪtɪ) *n, pl* **responsibilities.** **1** the state or position of being responsible. **2** a person or thing for which one is responsible.

responsible ➊ (rɪ'spɒnsɪbᵊl) *adj* **1** (*postpositive;* usually foll. by *for*) having control or authority (over). **2** (*postpositive;* foll. by *to*) being accountable for one's actions and decisions (to): *responsible to one's commanding officer.* **3** (of a position, duty, etc.) involving decision and accountability. **4** (often foll. by *for*) being the agent or cause (of some action): *responsible for a mistake.* **5** able to take rational decisions without supervision; accountable for one's own actions. **6** able to meet financial obligations; of sound credit. [C16: from L *rēsponsus*, from *rēspondēre* to RESPOND] ▸**re'sponsibleness** *n* ▸**re'sponsibly** *adv*

responsive ➊ (rɪ'spɒnsɪv) *adj* **1** reacting or replying quickly or favourably, as to a suggestion, initiative, etc. **2** (of an organism) reacting to a stimulus. ▸**re'sponsively** *adv* ▸**re'sponsiveness** *n*

responsory (rɪ'spɒnsərɪ) *n, pl* **responsories.** an anthem or chant recited or sung after a lesson in a church service. [C15: from LL *rēsponsōrium*, from L *rēspondēre* to answer]

rest[1] ➊ (rɛst) *n* **1a** relaxation from exertion or labour. **1b** (*as modifier*): *a rest period.* **2** repose; sleep. **3** any relief or refreshment, as from worry. **4** calm; tranquillity. **5** death regarded as repose: *eternal rest.* **6** cessation from motion. **7 at rest. 7a** not moving. **7b** calm. **7c** dead. **7d** asleep. **8** a pause or interval. **9** a mark in a musical score indicating a pause of specific duration. **10** *Prosody.* a pause at the end of a line; caesura. **11** a shelter or lodging: *a seaman's rest.* **12** a thing or place on which to put something for support or to steady it. **13** *Billiards, snooker.* any of various special poles sometimes used as supports for the cue. **14 come to rest.** to slow down and stop. **15 lay to rest.** to bury (a dead person). **16 set (someone's mind) at rest.** to reassure (someone) or settle (someone's mind). ◆ *vb* **17** to take or give rest, as by sleeping, lying down, etc. **18** to place or position (oneself, etc.) for rest or relaxation. **19** (*tr*) to place or position for support or steadying: *to rest one's elbows on the table.* **20** (*intr*) to be at ease; be calm. **21** to cease or cause to cease from motion or exertion. **22** (*intr*) to remain without further attention or action: *let the matter rest.* **23** to direct (one's eyes) or (of one's eyes) to be directed: *her eyes rested on the child.* **24** to depend or cause to depend; base; rely: *the whole argument rests on one crucial fact.* **25** (*intr;* foll. by *with, on, upon,* etc.) to be a responsibility (of): *it rests with us to apportion blame.* **26** *Law.* to finish the introduction of evidence in (a case). **27** to put pastry in a cool place to allow the gluten to contract. **28 rest on one's oars.** to stop doing anything for a time. [OE *ræst, reste*, of Gmc origin] ▸**'rester** *n*

rest[2] ➊ (rɛst) *n* (usually preceded by *the*) **1** something left or remaining; remainder. **2** the others: *the rest of the world.* ◆ *vb* **3** (*copula*) to continue to be (as specified); remain: *rest assured.* [C15: from OF *rester* to remain, from L *rēstāre*, from RE- + *stāre* to stand]

rest area *n Austral. & NZ.* a motorists' stopping place, usually off a highway, equipped with tables, seats, etc.

restaurant ➊ ('rɛstəˌrɒŋ, 'rɛstrɒŋ) *n* a commercial establishment where meals are prepared and served to customers. [C19: from F, from *restaurer* to RESTORE]

restaurant car *n Brit.* a railway coach in which meals are served. Also called: **dining car.**

restaurateur (ˌrɛstərə'tɜː) *n* a person who owns or runs a restaurant. [C18: via F from LL *restaurātor*, from L *restaurāre* to RESTORE]

rest-cure *n* **1** a rest taken as part of a course of medical treatment, so as to relieve stress, anxiety, etc. **2** an easy time or assignment: usually used with a negative: *it's no rest-cure, I assure you.*

restful ➊ ('rɛstfʊl) *adj* **1** giving or conducive to rest. **2** being at rest; tranquil; calm. ▸**'restfully** *adv* ▸**'restfulness** *n*

restharrow ('rɛstˌhærəʊ) *n* any of a genus of Eurasian papilionaceous plants with tough woody stems and roots. [C16: from *rest*, var. of ARREST (to hinder, stop) + HARROW]

resting ('rɛstɪŋ) *adj* **1** not moving or working; at rest. **2** *Euphemistic.* (of an actor) out of work. **3** (esp. of plant spores) undergoing a period of dormancy before germination.

restitution ➊ (ˌrɛstɪ'tjuːʃən) *n* **1** the act of giving back something that has been lost or stolen. **2** *Law.* compensating for loss or injury by reverting as far as possible to the original position. **3** the return of an object or system to its original state, esp. after elastic deformation. [C13: from L *rēstitūtiō*, from *rēstituere* to rebuild, from RE- + *statuere* to set up] ▸**'restiˌtutive** *or* **ˌresti'tutory** *adj*

restive ➊ ('rɛstɪv) *adj* **1** restless, nervous, or uneasy. **2** impatient of control or authority. [C16: from OF *restif* balky, from *rester* to remain] ▸**'restively** *adv* ▸**'restiveness** *n*

restless ➊ ('rɛstlɪs) *adj* **1** unable to stay still or quiet. **2** ceaselessly active or moving: *the restless wind.* **3** worried; anxious; uneasy. **4** not restful; without repose: *a restless night.* ▸**'restlessly** *adv* ▸**'restlessness** *n*

THESAURUS

mission, interruption, interval, let-up (*inf.*), lull, recess, relaxation, relief, rest **2** = **delay**, adjournment, moratorium, postponement, suspension **3** = **reprieve**, stay

resplendent *adj* = **brilliant**, beaming, bright, dazzling, effulgent, gleaming, glittering, glorious, irradiant, luminous, lustrous, radiant, refulgent (*literary*), shining, splendid

respond *vb* **1, 2** = **answer**, acknowledge, act in response, come back, counter, react, reciprocate, rejoin, reply, retort, return, rise to the bait, take the bait
Antonyms *vb* ignore, remain silent, turn a blind eye

response *n* **1** = **answer**, acknowledgment, comeback (*inf.*), counterattack, counterblast, feedback, reaction, rejoinder, reply, retort, return, riposte

responsibility *n* **1** = **authority**, importance, power **1** = **accountability**, amenability, answerability, liability **1** = **fault**, blame, burden, culpability, guilt, liability **1** = **level-headedness**, conscientiousness, dependability, maturity, rationality, reliability, sensibleness, soberness, stability, trustworthiness **2** = **duty**, care, charge, liability, obligation, onus, pigeon (*inf.*), trust

responsible *adj* **1** = **in charge**, at the helm, carrying the can (*inf.*), in authority, in control **2** = **accountable**, amenable, answerable, bound, chargeable, duty-bound, liable, subject, under obligation **3** = **authoritative**, decision-making, executive, high, important **4** = **to blame**, at fault, culpable, guilty **5** = **sensible**, adult, conscientious, dependable, level-headed, mature, rational, reliable, sober, sound, stable, trustworthy
Antonyms *adj* ≠ **accountable**: unaccountable ≠ **sensible**: irresponsible, unconscientious, undependable, unreliable, untrustworthy

responsive *adj* **1** = **sensitive**, alive, awake, aware, forthcoming, impressionable, open, perceptive, quick to react, reactive, receptive, sharp, susceptible, sympathetic
Antonyms *adj* apathetic, impassive, insensitive, silent, unresponsive, unsympathetic

rest[1] *n* **1** = **relaxation**, idleness, leisure **2** = **repose**, doze, forty winks (*inf.*), kip (*Brit. sl.*), lie-down, nap, siesta, sleep, slumber, snooze (*inf.*) **3** = **refreshment**, relief **4** = **calm**, somnolence, stillness, tranquillity **6** = **inactivity**, motionlessness, standstill **7 at rest: a** = **asleep**, at a standstill, still, stopped, unmoving **b** = **peaceful**, tranquil **c** = **at peace d** = **resting**, sleeping **8** = **pause**, break, breather (*inf.*), breathing space, cessation, halt, holiday, interlude, intermission, interval, lull, respite, stop, time off, vacation **12** = **support**, base, holder, prop, shelf, stand, trestle ◆ *vb* **17** = **relax**, doze, drowse, have a snooze (*inf.*), have forty winks (*inf.*), idle, kip (*Brit. sl.*), laze, lie down, lie still, nap, put one's feet up, refresh oneself, sit down, sleep, slumber, snooze (*inf.*), take a nap, take it easy, take one's ease **19** = **place**, be supported, lay, lean, lie, prop, recline, repose, sit, stand, stretch out **20** = **be calm**, be at ease, take it easy **21** = **stop**, break off, cease, come to a standstill, desist, discontinue, halt, have a break, knock off (*inf.*), stay, take a breather (*inf.*) **24** = **depend**, base, be based, be founded, found, hang, hinge, lie, rely, reside, turn
Antonyms *n* ≠ **relaxation, pause:** activity, bustle, work ◆ *vb* ≠ **relax, stop:** keep going, slog away (*inf.*), work

rest[2] *n* **1** = **remainder**, balance, excess, leftovers, remains, remnants, residue, residuum, rump, surplus **2** = **others** ◆ *vb* **3** = **continue being**, be left, go on being, keep, remain, stay

restaurant *n* = **café**, bistro, cafeteria, diner (*chiefly US & Canad.*), eatery *or* eaterie, tearoom, trattoria

restful *adj* **1, 2** = **relaxing**, calm, calming, comfortable, pacific, peaceful, placid, quiet, relaxed, serene, sleepy, soothing, tranquil, tranquillizing, undisturbed, unhurried
Antonyms *adj* agitated, busy, disturbing, restless, uncomfortable, unrelaxed

restitution *n* **1** = **return**, restoration **2** *Law* = **compensation**, amends, indemnification, indemnity, recompense, redress, refund, reimbursement, remuneration, reparation, repayment, requital, satisfaction

restive *adj* **1** = **restless**, agitated, edgy, fidgety, ill at ease, impatient, jittery (*inf.*), jumpy, nervous, on edge, uneasy, unquiet **2** = **unruly**, fractious, recalcitrant, refractory
Antonyms *adj* ≠ **restless:** at ease, calm, content, peaceful, relaxed, satisfied, serene, tranquil

restless *adj* **1, 2** = **moving**, active, bustling, changeable, footloose, having itchy feet, hurried, inconstant, irresolute, nomadic, roving, transient, turbulent, unsettled, unstable, unsteady, wandering **3** = **uneasy**, agitated, anxious, disturbed, edgy, fidgeting, fidgety, fitful,

rest mass *n* the mass of an object that is at rest relative to an observer. It is the mass used in Newtonian mechanics.

restoration ❶ (ˌrestəˈreɪʃən) *n* **1** the act of restoring to a former or original condition, place, etc. **2** the giving back of something lost, stolen, etc. **3** something restored, replaced, or reconstructed. **4** a model or representation of an extinct animal, etc. **5** (*usually cap.*) *Brit. history.* the re-establishment of the monarchy in 1660 or the reign of Charles II (1660–85).

restorative (rɪˈstɒrətɪv) *adj* **1** tending to revive or renew health, spirits, etc. ◆ *n* **2** anything that restores or revives, esp. a drug.

restore ❶ (rɪˈstɔː) *vb* **restores, restoring, restored.** (*tr*) **1** to return (something) to its original or former condition. **2** to bring back to health, good spirits, etc. **3** to return (something lost, stolen, etc.) to its owner. **4** to reintroduce or re-enforce: *to restore discipline.* **5** to reconstruct (an extinct animal, etc.). [C13: from OF, from L *restaurāre* to rebuild, from RE- + -*staurāre*, as in *instaurāre* to renew]
▸**reˈstorable** *adj* ▸**reˈstorer** *n*

restrain ❶ (rɪˈstreɪn) *vb* (*tr*) **1** to hold (someone) back from some action, esp. by force. **2** to deprive (someone) of liberty, as by imprisonment. **3** to limit or restrict. [C14 *restreyne*, from OF *restreindre*, from L *restringere*, from RE- + *stringere* to draw, bind]
▸**reˈstrainable** *adj* ▸**restrainedly** (rɪˈstreɪnɪdlɪ) *adv* ▸**reˈstrainer** *n*

restraint ❶ (rɪˈstreɪnt) *n* **1** the ability to control or moderate one's impulses, passions, etc. **2** the act of restraining or the state of being restrained. **3** something that restrains; restriction. [C15: from OF *restreinte*, from *restreindre* to RESTRAIN]

restraint of trade *n* action interfering with the freedom to compete in business.

restrict ❶ (rɪˈstrɪkt) *vb* (often foll. by *to*) to confine or keep within certain, often specified, limits or selected bounds. [C16: from L *restrictus* bound up, from *restringere*; see RESTRAIN]

restricted (rɪˈstrɪktɪd) *adj* **1** limited or confined. **2** not accessible to the general public or (*esp. US*) out of bounds to military personnel. **3** *Brit.* denoting a zone in which a speed limit or waiting restrictions for vehicles apply.
▸**reˈstrictedly** *adv* ▸**reˈstrictedness** *n*

restriction ❶ (rɪˈstrɪkʃən) *n* **1** something that restricts; a restrictive measure, law, etc. **2** the act of restricting or the state of being restricted.
▸**reˈstrictionist** *n, adj*

restrictive (rɪˈstrɪktɪv) *adj* **1** restricting or tending to restrict. **2** *Grammar.* denoting a relative clause or phrase that restricts the number of possible referents of its antecedent. The relative clause in *Americans who live in New York* is restrictive; the relative clause in *Americans, who are generally extrovert,* is nonrestrictive.
▸**reˈstrictively** *adv* ▸**reˈstrictiveness** *n*

restrictive practice *n Brit.* **1** a trading agreement against the public interest. **2** a practice of a union or other group tending to limit the freedom of other workers or employers.

rest room *n* a room in a public building with toilets, washbasins, and, sometimes, couches.

restructure (riːˈstrʌktʃə) *vb* (*tr*) to organize (a system, business, society, etc.) in a different way: *radical attempts to restructure the economy.*
▸**reˈstructuring** *n*

result ❶ (rɪˈzʌlt) *n* **1** something that ensues from an action, policy, etc.; outcome; consequence. **2** a number, quantity, or value obtained by solving a mathematical problem. **3** *US.* a decision of a legislative body. **4** (*often pl*) the final score or outcome of a sporting contest. **5** a favourable result, esp. a victory or success. ◆ *vb* (*intr*) **6** (often foll. by *from*) to be the outcome or consequence (of). **7** (foll. by *in*) to issue or terminate (in a specified way, etc.); end: *to result in tragedy.* [C15: from L *resultāre* to rebound, spring from, from RE- + *saltāre* to leap]

resultant (rɪˈzʌltənt) *adj* **1** that results; resulting. ◆ *n* **2** *Maths, physics.* a single vector that is the vector sum of two or more other vectors.

resume ❶ (rɪˈzjuːm) *vb* **resumes, resuming, resumed. 1** to begin again or go on with (something interrupted). **2** (*tr*) to occupy again, take back, or recover: *to resume one's seat; resume the presidency.* **3** *Arch.* to summarize; make a résumé of. [C15: from L *resūmere*, from RE- + *sūmere* to take up]
▸**reˈsumable** *adj* ▸**reˈsumer** *n*

résumé ❶ (ˈrezjuˌmeɪ) *n* **1** a short descriptive summary, as of events, etc. **2** *US & Canad.* another name for **curriculum vitae.** [C19: from F, from *résumer* to RESUME]

resumption ❶ (rɪˈzʌmpʃən) *n* the act of resuming or beginning again. [C15: via OF from LL *resumptiō*, from L *resūmere* to RESUME]
▸**reˈsumptive** *adj* ▸**reˈsumptively** *adv*

resupinate (rɪˈsjuːpɪnɪt) *adj Bot.* (of plant parts) reversed or inverted in position, so as to appear to be upside down. [C18: from L *resupīnātus* bent back, from *resupīnāre*, from RE- + *supīnāre* to place on the back]
▸**reˌsupiˈnation** *n*

resurge (rɪˈsɜːdʒ) *vb* **resurges, resurging, resurged.** (*intr*) *Rare.* to rise again as if from the dead. [C16: from L *resurgere* to rise again, reappear, from RE- + *surgere* to lift, arise]

resurgent ❶ (rɪˈsɜːdʒənt) *adj* rising again, as to new life, vigour, etc.: *resurgent nationalism.*
▸**reˈsurgence** *n*

resurrect ❶ (ˌrezəˈrekt) *vb* **1** to rise or raise from the dead; bring or be brought back to life. **2** (*tr*) to bring back into use or activity; revive. **3** (*tr*) *Facetious.* (formerly) to exhume and steal (a body) from its grave.

resurrection ❶ (ˌrezəˈrekʃən) *n* **1** a supposed act or instance of a dead person coming back to life. **2** belief in the possibility of this as part of a religious or mystical system. **3** the condition of those who have risen from the dead: *we shall all live in the resurrection.* **4** (*usually cap.*) *Christian theol.* the rising again of Christ from the tomb three days after his death. **5** (*usually cap.*) the rising again from the dead of all men at the Last Judgment. [C13: via OF from LL *resurrectiō*, from L *resurgere* to rise again]
▸**ˌresurˈrectional** *or* **ˌresurˈrectionary** *adj*

resurrectionism (ˌrezəˈrekʃəˌnɪzəm) *n* belief that men will rise again from the dead, esp. according to Christian doctrine.

resurrectionist (ˌrezəˈrekʃənɪst) *n* **1** *Facetious.* (formerly) a body snatcher. **2** a person who believes in the Resurrection.

resurrection plant *n* any of several unrelated desert plants that form a tight ball when dry and unfold and bloom when moistened.

resuscitate ❶ (rɪˈsʌsɪˌteɪt) *vb* **resuscitates, resuscitating, resuscitated.** (*tr*) to restore to consciousness; revive. [C16: from L *resuscitāre*, from RE- +

THESAURUS

fretful, ill at ease, jumpy, nervous, on edge, restive, troubled, unquiet, unruly, unsettled, worried **4** = **sleepless**, tossing and turning, unsettled
Antonyms *adj* ≠ **moving:** settled, stable, steady ≠ **uneasy:** comfortable, composed, easy, quiet, relaxed ≠ **sleepless:** restful, undisturbed

restlessness *n* **1, 2** = **movement**, activity, bustle, hurry, hurry-scurry, inconstancy, instability, transience, turbulence, turmoil, unrest, unsettledness **3** = **restiveness**, agitation, ants in one's pants (*sl.*), anxiety, disquiet, disturbance, edginess, fitfulness, fretfulness, heebie-jeebies (*sl.*), inquietude, insomnia, jitters (*inf.*), jumpiness, nervousness, uneasiness, worriedness

restoration *n* **1** = **repair**, reconstruction, recovery, refreshment, refurbishing, rehabilitation, rejuvenation, renewal, renovation, revitalization, revival **2** = **reinstatement**, re-establishment, reinstallation, replacement, restitution, return
Antonyms *n* ≠ **repair:** demolition, scrapping, wrecking ≠ **reinstatement:** abolition, overthrow

restore *vb* **1** = **repair**, fix, mend, rebuild, recondition, reconstruct, recover, refurbish, rehabilitate, renew, renovate, retouch, set to rights, touch up **2** = **revive**, bring back to health, build up, reanimate, refresh, rejuvenate, revitalize, revivify, strengthen **3** = **return**, bring back, give back, hand back, recover, re-establish, reinstate, replace, retrocede, send back **4** = **reinstate**, reconstitute, re-enforce, re-establish, reimpose, reintroduce
Antonyms *vb* ≠ **repair:** demolish, scrap, wreck ≠ **revive:** make worse, sicken, weaken ≠ **reinstate:** abolish, abrogate, repeal, rescind

restrain *vb* **2** = **imprison**, arrest, bind, chain, confine, detain, fetter, hold, jail, lock up, manacle, pinion, tie up **3** = **hold back**, bridle, check, confine, constrain, contain, control, curb, curtail, debar, govern, hamper, handicap, harness, have on a tight leash, hinder, hold, inhibit, keep, keep under control, limit, muzzle, prevent, rein, repress, restrict, straiten, subdue, suppress
Antonyms *vb* ≠ **imprison:** free, liberate, release ≠ **hold back:** assist, encourage, gee up, help, incite, urge on

restraint *n* **1** = **self-control**, coercion, command, compulsion, constraint, control, curtailment, hindrance, hold, inhibition, limitation, moderation, prevention, pulling one's punches, restriction, self-discipline, self-possession, self-restraint, suppression **2** = **confinement**, arrest, bondage, captivity, detention, fetters, imprisonment **3** = **limitation**, ban, boycott, bridle, check, curb, disqualification, embargo, interdict, limit, rein, restriction, taboo **3** = **bonds**, chains, manacles, pinions, straitjacket
Antonyms *n* ≠ **self-control:** excess, immoderation, intemperance, licence, self-indulgence ≠ **limitation:** freedom, liberty

restrict *vb* = **limit**, bound, circumscribe, clip someone's wings, confine, contain, cramp, demarcate, hamper, handicap, hem in, impede, inhibit, keep within bounds *or* limits, regulate, restrain, straiten
Antonyms *vb* allow, broaden, encourage, foster, free, permit, promote, widen

restriction *n* **1** = **limitation**, check, condition, confinement, constraint, containment, control, curb, demarcation, handicap, inhibition, regulation, restraint, rule, stipulation

result *n* **1** = **consequence**, conclusion, development, effect, end, end result, event, fruit, issue, outcome, product, reaction, sequel, termination, upshot ◆ *vb* **6** = **arise**, appear, derive, develop, emanate, ensue, eventuate, flow, follow, happen, issue, spring, stem, turn out **7 result in** = **end in**, culminate in, finish with, pan out (*inf.*), terminate in, wind up
Antonyms *n* ≠ **consequence:** beginning, cause, germ, origin, outset, root, source

resume *vb* **1** = **begin again**, carry on, continue, go on, proceed, recommence, reinstitute, reopen, restart, take up *or* pick up where one left off **2** = **occupy again**, assume again, reoccupy, take back, take up again
Antonyms *vb* ≠ **begin again:** cease, discontinue, stop

résumé *n* **1** = **summary**, abstract, digest, epitome, précis, recapitulation, review, rundown, synopsis

resumption *n* = **continuation**, carrying on, fresh outbreak, new beginning, re-establishment, renewal, reopening, restart, resurgence

resurgence *n* = **revival**, rebirth, recrudescence, re-emergence, renaissance, renascence, resumption, resurrection, return

resurrect *vb* **1** = **restore to life**, raise from the dead **2** = **revive**, breathe new life into, bring back, kick-start (*inf.*), reintroduce, renew

resurrection *n* **1** = **raising** *or* **rising from the dead**, return from the dead
Antonyms *n* ≠ **raising** *or* **rising from the dead:** burial, demise

resuscitate *vb* = **revive**, breathe new life into,

suscitāre to raise, from *sub-* up from below + *citāre* to rouse, from *citus* quick]
▸**re͵susci'tation** *n* ▸**re'suscitative** *adj* ▸**re'susci͵tator** *n*

ret (rɛt) *vb* **rets, retting, retted.** *(tr)* to moisten or soak (flax, hemp, etc.) in order to separate the fibres from the woody tissue by beating. [C15: of Gmc origin]

ret. *abbrev. for:* **1** retain. **2** retired. **3** return(ed).

retable (rɪ'teɪbᵊl) *n* an ornamental screenlike structure above and behind an altar. [C19: from F, from Sp. *retablo,* from L *retrō* behind + *tabula* board]

retail ('ri:teɪl) *n* **1** the sale of goods individually or in small quantities to consumers. Cf. **wholesale.** ◆ *adj* **2** of, relating to, or engaged in such selling: *retail prices.* ◆ *adv* **3** in small amounts or at a retail price. ◆ *vb* **4** to sell or be sold in small quantities to consumers. **5** (rɪ'teɪl). *(tr)* to relate (gossip, scandal, etc.) in detail. [C14: from OF *retaillier,* from RE- + *taillier* to cut; see TAILOR]
▸**'retailer** *n*

retail price index *n* a measure of the changes in the average level of retail prices of selected goods, usually on a monthly basis. Abbrev.: **RPI.**

retain ❶ (rɪ'teɪn) *vb (tr)* **1** to keep in one's possession. **2** to be able to hold or contain: *soil that retains water.* **3** (of a person) to be able to remember (information, etc.) without difficulty. **4** to hold in position. **5** to keep for one's future use, as by paying a retainer or nominal charge. **6** *Law.* to engage the services of (a barrister) by payment of a preliminary fee. [C14: from OF *retenir,* from L *retinēre* to hold back, from RE- + *tenēre* to hold]
▸**re'tainable** *adj* ▸**re'tainment** *n*

retained object *n Grammar.* a direct or indirect object of a passive verb. The phrase *the drawings* in *she was given the drawings* is a retained object.

retainer ❶ (rɪ'teɪnə) *n* **1** *History.* a supporter or dependant of a person of rank. **2** a servant, esp. one who has been with a family for a long time. **3** a clip, frame, or similar device that prevents a part of a machine, etc., from moving. **4** a fee paid in advance to secure first option on the services of a barrister, jockey, etc. **5** a reduced rent paid for a flat, etc., to reserve it for future use.

retaining wall *n* a wall constructed to hold back earth, loose rock, etc. Also called: **revetment.**

retake *vb* (ri:'teɪk), **retakes, retaking, retook, retaken.** *(tr)* **1** to take back or capture again: *to retake a fortress.* **2** *Films.* to shoot (a scene) again. **3** to tape (a recording) again. ◆ *n* ('ri:͵teɪk). **4** *Films.* a rephotographed scene. **5** a retaped recording.
▸**re'taker** *n*

retaliate ❶ (rɪ'tælɪ͵eɪt) *vb* **retaliates, retaliating, retaliated.** *(intr)* **1** to take retributory action, esp. by returning some injury or wrong in kind. **2** to cast (accusations) back upon a person. [C17: from LL *retāliāre,* from L RE- + *tālis* of such kind]
▸**re͵tali'ation** *n* ▸**re'taliative** *or* **re'taliatory** *adj*

retard ❶ (rɪ'tɑ:d) *vb (tr)* to delay or slow down (the progress or speed) of (something). [C15: from OF *retarder,* from L *retardāre,* from RE- + *tardāre* to make slow, from *tardus* sluggish]

retardant (rɪ'tɑ:dᵊnt) *n* **1** a substance that reduces the rate of a chemical reaction. ◆ *adj* **2** having a slowing effect.

retardation (͵ri:tɑ:'deɪʃən) *or* **retardment** (rɪ'tɑ:dmənt) *n* **1** the act of retarding or the state of being retarded. **2** something that retards.
▸**re'tardative** *or* **re'tardatory** *adj*

retarded (rɪ'tɑ:dɪd) *adj* underdeveloped, usually mentally and esp. having an IQ of 70 to 85.

retarder (rɪ'tɑ:də) *n* **1** a person or thing that retards. **2** a substance added to slow down the rate of a chemical change, such as one added to cement to delay its setting.

retch ❶ (rɛtʃ, ri:tʃ) *vb* **1** *(intr)* to undergo an involuntary spasm of ineffectual vomiting. ◆ *n* **2** an involuntary spasm of ineffectual vomiting. [OE *hrǣcan;* rel. to ON *hrǣkja* to spit]

retd *abbrev. for:* **1** retired. **2** retained. **3** returned.

rete ('ri:tɪ) *n, pl* **retia** ('ri:ʃɪə, -tɪə). *Anat.* any network of nerves or blood vessels; plexus. [C14 (referring to a metal network used with an astrolabe): from L *rēte* net]
▸**retial** ('ri:ʃɪəl) *adj*

retention (rɪ'tɛnʃən) *n* **1** the act of retaining or state of being retained. **2** the capacity to hold or retain liquid, etc. **3** the capacity to remember. **4** *Pathol.* the abnormal holding within the body of urine, faeces, etc. **5** *Commerce.* a sum of money owed to a contractor but not paid for an agreed period as a safeguard against the appearance of any faults. **6** *(pl) Account.* profits earned by a company but not distributed as dividends; retained earnings. [C14: from L *retentiō,* from *retinēre* to RETAIN]

retentive (rɪ'tɛntɪv) *adj* having the capacity to retain or remember.
▸**re'tentively** *adv* ▸**re'tentiveness** *n*

retiarius (͵ri:tɪ'ɛərɪəs, ͵ri:ʃɪ-) *n, pl* **retiarii** (-'ɛərɪ͵aɪ). (in ancient Rome) a gladiator armed with a net and trident. [L, from *rēte* net]

reticent ❶ ('rɛtɪsənt) *adj* not communicative; not saying all that one knows; taciturn; reserved. [C19: from L *reticēre* to keep silent, from RE- + *tacēre* to be silent]
▸**'reticence** *n* ▸**'reticently** *adv*

reticle ('rɛtɪkᵊl) *or (less commonly)* **reticule** *n* a network of fine lines, wires, etc., placed in the focal plane of an optical instrument. [C17: from L *rēticulum* a little net, from *rēte* net]

reticulate *adj* (rɪ'tɪkjʊlɪt) *also* **reticular.** **1** in the form of a network or having a network of parts: *a reticulate leaf.* ◆ *vb* (rɪ'tɪkjʊ͵leɪt), **reticulates, reticulating, reticulated.** **2** to form or be formed into a net. [C17: from LL *rēticulātus* made like a net]
▸**re'ticulately** *adv* ▸**re͵ticu'lation** *n*

reticule ('rɛtɪ͵kju:l) *n* **1** (formerly) a woman's small bag or purse, usually with a drawstring and made of net, beading, brocade, etc. **2** a less common variant of **reticle.** [C18: from F *réticule,* from L *rēticulum* RETICLE]

reticulum (rɪ'tɪkjʊləm) *n, pl* **reticula** (-lə). **1** any fine network, esp. one in the body composed of cells, fibres, etc. **2** the second compartment of the stomach of ruminants. [C17: from L: little net, from *rēte* net]

retiform ('ri:tɪ͵fɔ:m, 'rɛt-) *adj Rare.* netlike; reticulate. [C17: from L *rēte* net + *forma* shape]

retina ('rɛtɪnə) *n, pl* **retinas** *or* **retinae** (-͵ni:). the light-sensitive membrane forming the inner lining of the posterior wall of the eyeball. [C14: from Med. L, ?from L *rēte* net]
▸**'retinal** *adj*

retinene ('rɛtɪ͵ni:n) *n* a yellow pigment, the aldehyde of vitamin A, that is involved in the formation of rhodopsin. [C20: from RETINA + -ENE]

retinitis (͵rɛtɪ'naɪtɪs) *n* inflammation of the retina. [C20: from NL, from RETINA + -ITIS]

retinoscopy (͵rɛtɪ'nɒskəpɪ) *n Ophthalmol.* a procedure for detecting errors of refraction in the eye by means of an instrument (**retinoscope**) that reflects a beam of light from a mirror into the eye.
▸**retinoscopic** (͵rɛtɪnə'skɒpɪk) *adj* ▸͵**retino'scopically** *adv* ▸͵**reti'noscopist** *n*

retinue ❶ ('rɛtɪ͵nju:) *n* a body of aides and retainers attending an important person. [C14: from OF *retenue,* from *retenir* to RETAIN]

retiral (rɪ'taɪərᵊl) *n esp. Scot.* the act of retiring; retirement.

retire ❶ (rɪ'taɪə) *vb* **retires, retiring, retired.** *(mainly intr)* **1** *(also tr)* to give up or to cause (a person) to give up his work, esp. on reaching pensionable age. **2** to go away, as into seclusion, for recuperation, etc. **3** to go to bed. **4** to recede or disappear: *the sun retired behind the clouds.* **5** to withdraw from a sporting contest, esp. because of injury. **6** *(also tr)* to pull back (troops, etc.) from battle or (of troops, etc.) to fall back. **7** *(tr)* to remove (money, bonds, shares, etc.) from circulation. [C16: from F *retirer,* from OF RE- + *tirer* to pull, draw]
▸**re'tired** *adj* ▸**re'tirement** *n* ▸**re'tirer** *n*

retirement pension *n Brit.* a weekly payment made by the government to a retired man over 65 or a woman over 60.

retirement relief *n* (in Britain) relief from capital-gains tax given to persons over 60 when disposing of business assets.

retiring ❶ (rɪ'taɪərɪŋ) *adj* shunning contact with others; shy; reserved.
▸**re'tiringly** *adv*

THESAURUS

bring round, bring to life, give artificial respiration to, give the kiss of life, quicken, reanimate, renew, rescue, restore, resurrect, revitalize, revivify, save

retain *vb* **1 = keep**, contain, detain, grasp, grip, hang *or* hold onto, hold, hold back, hold fast, keep possession of, maintain, preserve, reserve, restrain, save **3 = remember**, bear in mind, impress on the memory, keep in mind, memorize, recall, recollect **5 = hire**, commission, employ, engage, pay, reserve
Antonyms *vb* ≠ **keep:** let go, lose, release, use up ≠ **remember:** forget

retainer *n* **2 = servant**, attendant, dependant, domestic, flunky, footman, henchman, lackey, supporter, valet **4 = fee**, advance, deposit

retaliate *vb* **1 = pay (someone) back**, even the score, exact retribution, get back at, get even with (*inf.*), get one's own back (*inf.*), give as good as one gets (*inf.*), give (someone) a taste of his *or* her own medicine, give tit for tat, hit back, make reprisal, reciprocate, return like for like, strike back, take an eye for an eye, take revenge, wreak vengeance
Antonyms *vb* accept, submit, turn the other cheek

retaliation *n* **1 = revenge**, an eye for an eye, a taste of one's own medicine, counterblow, counterstroke, reciprocation, repayment, reprisal, requital, retribution, tit for tat, vengeance

retard *vb* **= slow down**, arrest, brake, check, clog, decelerate, defer, delay, detain, encumber, handicap, hinder, hold back *or* up, impede, obstruct, set back, stall
Antonyms *vb* accelerate, advance, expedite, hasten, speed, speed up, stimulate

retch *vb* **1 = gag**, barf (*US sl.*), be sick, chuck (up) (*sl., chiefly US*), chunder (*sl., chiefly Austral.*), disgorge, heave, puke (*sl.*), regurgitate, spew, throw up (*inf.*), toss one's cookies (*US sl.*), vomit

reticence *n* **= silence**, quietness, reserve, restraint, secretiveness, taciturnity, uncommunicativeness, unforthcomingness

reticent *adj* **= uncommunicative**, close-lipped, mum, quiet, reserved, restrained, secretive, silent, taciturn, tight-lipped, unforthcoming, unspeaking
Antonyms *adj* candid, communicative, expansive, frank, open, talkative, voluble

retinue *n* **= attendants**, aides, cortege, entourage, escort, followers, following, servants, suite, train

retire *vb* **1 = stop working**, be pensioned off, (be) put out to grass, give up work **2 = withdraw**, absent oneself, betake oneself, depart, exit, go away, leave, remove **3 = go to bed**, go to one's room, go to sleep, hit the hay (*sl.*), hit the sack (*sl.*), kip down (*Brit. sl.*), turn in (*inf.*) **6 = fall back**, back off, decamp, give ground, give way, pull back, pull out, recede, retreat, withdraw

retirement *n* **2 = withdrawal**, loneliness, obscurity, privacy, retreat, seclusion, solitude

retiring *adj* **= shy**, bashful, coy, demure, diffident, humble, meek, modest, quiet, reclusive, reserved, reticent, self-effacing, shrinking, timid, timorous, unassertive, unassuming

retool (riːˈtuːl) *vb* **1** to replace, re-equip, or rearrange the tools in (a factory, etc.). **2** (*tr*) *Chiefly US & Canad.* to revise or reorganize.

retort[1] Ⓣ (rɪˈtɔːt) *vb* **1** (when *tr, takes a clause as object*) to utter (something) quickly, wittily, or angrily, in response. **2** to use (an argument) against its originator. ◆ *n* **3** a sharp, angry, or witty reply. **4** an argument used against its originator. [C16: from L *retorquēre,* from RE- + *torquēre* to twist, wrench]
▸**reˈtorter** *n*

retort[2] (rɪˈtɔːt) *n* **1** a glass vessel with a long tapering neck that is bent down, used for distillation. **2** a vessel used for heating ores in the production of metals or heating coal to produce gas. ◆ *vb* **3** (*tr*) to heat in a retort. [C17: from F *retorte,* from Med. L *retorta,* from L *retorquēre* to twist back; see RETORT[1]]

retouch Ⓣ (riːˈtʌtʃ) *vb* (*tr*) **1** to restore, correct, or improve (a painting, make-up, etc.) with new touches. **2** *Photog.* to alter (a negative or print) by painting over blemishes or adding details. ◆ *n* **3** the art or practice of retouching. **4** a detail that is the result of retouching. **5** a photograph, painting, etc., that has been retouched.
▸**reˈtoucher** *n*

retrace (rɪˈtreɪs) *vb* **retraces, retracing, retraced.** (*tr*) **1** to go back over (one's steps, a route, etc.) again. **2** to go over (a past event) in the mind; recall. **3** to go over (a story, account, etc.) from the beginning.

re-trace (riːˈtreɪs) *vb* **re-traces, re-tracing, re-traced.** (*tr*) to trace (a map, etc.) again.

retract Ⓣ (rɪˈtrækt) *vb* **1** (*tr*) to draw in (a part or appendage): *a snail can retract its horns; to retract the landing gear of an aircraft.* **2** to withdraw (a statement, opinion, charge, etc.) as invalid or unjustified. **3** to go back on (a promise or agreement). [C16: from L *retractāre* to withdraw, from *tractāre,* from *trahere* to drag]
▸**reˈtractable** *or* **reˈtractible** *adj* ▸**reˈtraction** *n* ▸**reˈtractive** *adj*

retractile (rɪˈtræktaɪl) *adj* capable of being drawn in: *the retractile claws of a cat.*
▸**retractility** (ˌriːtrækˈtɪlɪtɪ) *n*

retractor (rɪˈtræktə) *n* **1** *Anat.* any of various muscles that retract an organ or part. **2** *Surgery.* an instrument for holding back an organ or part. **3** a person or thing that retracts.

retral (ˈriːtrəl, ˈrɛtrəl) *adj Rare.* at, near, or towards the back. [C19: from L *retrō* backwards]
▸**ˈretrally** *adv*

retread *vb* (riːˈtrɛd), **retreads, retreading, retreaded. 1** (*tr*) another word for **remould** (sense 2). ◆ *n* (ˈriːˌtrɛd). **2** another word for **remould** (sense 3). **3** *NZ sl.* a pensioner who has resumed employment, esp. in the same profession as formerly.

re-tread (riːˈtrɛd) *vb* **re-treads, re-treading, re-trod, re-trodden** *or* **re-trod.** (*tr*) to tread (one's steps, etc.) again.

retreat Ⓣ (rɪˈtriːt) *vb* (*mainly intr*) **1** *Mil.* to withdraw or retire in the face of or from action with an enemy. **2** to retire or withdraw, as to seclusion or shelter. **3** (of a person's features) to slope back; recede. **4** (*tr*) *Chess.* to move (a piece) back. ◆ *n* **5** the act of retreating or withdrawing. **6** *Mil.* **6a** a withdrawal or retirement in the face of the enemy. **6b** a bugle call signifying withdrawal or retirement. **7** retirement or seclusion. **8** a place to which one may retire for religious contemplation. **9** a period of seclusion, esp. for religious contemplation. **10** an institution for the care and treatment of the mentally ill, infirm, elderly, etc. [C14: from OF *retret,* from *retraire* to withdraw, from L *retrahere* to pull back]

retrench Ⓣ (rɪˈtrɛntʃ) *vb* **1** to reduce (costs); economize. **2** (*tr*) to shorten, delete, or abridge. [C17: from OF *retrenchier,* from RE- + *trenchier* to cut, from L *truncāre* to lop]
▸**reˈtrenchment** *n*

retribution Ⓣ (ˌrɛtrɪˈbjuːʃən) *n* **1** the act of punishing or taking vengeance for wrongdoing, sin, or injury. **2** punishment or vengeance. [C14: via OF from Church L *retribūtiō,* from L *retribuere,* from RE- + *tribuere* to pay]
▸**retributive** (rɪˈtrɪbjʊtɪv) *adj* ▸**reˈtributively** *adv*

retrieval (rɪˈtriːvᵊl) *n* **1** the act or process of retrieving. **2** the possibility of recovery, restoration, or rectification. **3** a computer operation that recalls data from a file.

retrieve Ⓣ (rɪˈtriːv) *vb* **retrieves, retrieving, retrieved.** (*mainly tr*) **1** to get or fetch back again; recover. **2** to bring back to a more satisfactory state; revive. **3** to rescue or save. **4** to recover or make newly available (stored information) from a computer system. **5** (*also intr*) (of dogs) to find and fetch (shot game, etc.). **6** *Tennis, etc.* to return successfully (a shot difficult to reach). **7** to recall; remember. ◆ *n* **8** the act of retrieving. **9** the chance of being retrieved. [C15: from OF *retrover,* from RE- + *trouver* to find, ?from Vulgar L *tropāre* (unattested) to compose]
▸**reˈtrievable** *adj*

retriever (rɪˈtriːvə) *n* **1** one of a breed of large dogs that can be trained to retrieve game. **2** any dog used to retrieve shot game. **3** a person or thing that retrieves.

retro Ⓣ (ˈrɛtrəʊ) *n, pl* **retros. 1** short for **retrorocket.** ◆ *adj* **2** denoting something associated with or revived from the past: *retro fashion.*

retro- *prefix* **1** back or backwards: *retroactive.* **2** located behind: *retrochoir.* [from L *retrō* behind, backwards]

retroact (ˈrɛtrəʊˌækt) *vb* (*intr*) **1** to act in opposition. **2** to influence or have reference to past events.
▸ˌ**retroˈaction** *n*

retroactive (ˌrɛtrəʊˈæktɪv) *adj* **1** applying or referring to the past: *retroactive legislation.* **2** effective from a date or for a period in the past.
▸ˌ**retroˈactively** *adv* ▸ˌ**retroacˈtivity** *n*

retrocede (ˌrɛtrəʊˈsiːd) *vb* **retrocedes, retroceding, retroceded. 1** (*tr*) to give back; return. **2** (*intr*) to go back; recede.
▸**retrocession** (ˌrɛtrəʊˈsɛʃən) *or* ˌ**retroˈcedence** *n* ▸ˌ**retroˈcessive** *or* ˌ**retroˈcedent** *adj*

retrochoir (ˈrɛtrəʊˌkwaɪə) *n* the space in a large church or cathedral behind the high altar.

retrofire (ˈrɛtrəʊˌfaɪə) *n* **1** the act of firing a retrorocket. **2** the moment at which it is fired.

retrofit (ˈrɛtrəʊˌfɪt) *vb* **retrofits, retrofitting, retrofitted.** (*tr*) to equip (a vehicle, piece of equipment, etc.) with new parts, safety devices, etc., after manufacture.

retroflex (ˈrɛtrəʊˌflɛks) *or* **retroflexed** *adj* **1** bent or curved backwards. **2** *Phonetics.* of or involving retroflexion. [C18: from L *retrōflexus,* from *retrōflectere,* from RETRO- + *flectere* to bend]

retroflexion *or* **retroflection** (ˌrɛtrəʊˈflɛkʃən) *n* **1** the act or condition of bending or being bent backwards. **2** the act of turning the tip of the tongue upwards and backwards in the articulation of a vowel or a consonant.

retrograde Ⓣ (ˈrɛtrəʊˌgreɪd) *adj* **1** moving or bending backwards. **2** (esp. of order) reverse or inverse. **3** tending towards an earlier worse condition; declining or deteriorating. **4** *Astron.* **4a** occurring or orbiting in a direction opposite to that of the earth's motion around the sun. Cf. **direct** (sense 18). **4b** occurring or orbiting in a direction around a planet opposite to the planet's rotational direction. **4c** appearing to move in a clockwise direction due to the rotational period exceeding the period of revolution around the sun: *Venus has retrograde rotation.* ◆ *vb* **retrogrades, retrograding, retrograded.** (*intr*) **5** to move in a retrograde direction; retrogress. [C14: from L *retrōgradī,* from *gradi* to walk, go]
▸ˌ**retrograˈdation** *n* ▸ˈ**retroˌgradely** *adv*

retrogress Ⓣ (ˌrɛtrəʊˈgrɛs) *vb* (*intr*) **1** to go back to an earlier, esp. worse, condition; degenerate or deteriorate. **2** to move backwards; recede. [C19: from L *retrōgressus* having moved backwards; see RETROGRADE]
▸ˌ**retroˈgression** *n* ▸ˌ**retroˈgressive** *adj* ▸ˌ**retroˈgressively** *adv*

retrorocket (ˈrɛtrəʊˌrɒkɪt) *n* a small auxiliary rocket engine on a larger rocket, missile, or spacecraft, that produces thrust in the opposite direction to the direction of flight in order to decelerate. Often shortened to **retro.**

retrorse (rɪˈtrɔːs) *adj* (esp. of plant parts) pointing backwards. [C19: from L *retrōrsus,* from *retrōversus* turned back, from RETRO- + *vertere* to turn]
▸**reˈtrorsely** *adv*

retrospect Ⓣ (ˈrɛtrəʊˌspɛkt) *n* the act of surveying things past (often in **in retrospect**). [C17: from L *retrōspicere* to look back, from RETRO- + *specere* to look]
▸ˌ**retroˈspection** *n*

THESAURUS

Antonyms *adj* audacious, bold, brassy, forward, gregarious, outgoing, sociable

retort[1] *vb* **1 = reply,** answer, answer back, come back with, counter, rejoin, respond, retaliate, return, riposte ◆ *n* **3 = reply,** answer, comeback (*inf.*), rejoinder, response, riposte

retouch *vb* **1 = touch up,** brush up, correct, finish, improve, recondition, renovate, restore

retract *vb* **1 = draw in,** pull back, pull in, reel in, sheathe **2 = withdraw,** abjure, cancel, deny, disavow, disclaim, disown, eat one's words, recall, recant, renege, renounce, repeal, repudiate, rescind, reverse, revoke, take back, unsay **3 = go back on,** back out of, renege on

retreat *vb* **1, 2 = withdraw,** back away, back off, depart, draw back, fall back, give ground, go back, leave, pull back, recede, recoil, retire, shrink, turn tail ◆ *n* **5, 6a = withdrawal,** departure, evacuation, flight, retirement **7, 9 = seclusion,** privacy, retirement **8 = refuge,** asylum, den, haunt, haven, hideaway, resort, sanctuary, shelter
Antonyms *vb* ≠ **withdraw:** advance, engage, move forward ◆ *n* ≠ **withdrawal:** advance, charge, entrance

retrench *vb* **1 = economize,** cut back, husband, make economies, save, tighten one's belt **2 = reduce,** curtail, cut, cut back, decrease, diminish, lessen, limit, pare, prune, trim

retrenchment *n* **1 = cutback,** cost-cutting, economy, tightening one's belt **2 = reduction,** contraction, curtailment, cut, cutback, pruning, rundown
Antonyms *n* ≠ **cutback:** expansion, investment

retribution *n* **1, 2 = punishment,** an eye for an eye, compensation, justice, Nemesis, reckoning, recompense, redress, repayment, reprisal, requital, retaliation, revenge, reward, satisfaction, vengeance

retrieve *vb* **1, 3 = get back,** fetch back, recall, recapture, recoup, recover, redeem, regain, repair, repossess, rescue, restore, salvage, save, win back

retro *adj* **2 = old-time,** antique, bygone, former, nostalgia, of yesteryear, old, old-fashioned, old-world, past, period

retrograde *adj* **3 = deteriorating,** backward, declining, degenerative, downward, inverse, negative, regressive, relapsing, retreating, retrogressive, reverse, waning, worsening ◆ *vb* **5 = deteriorate,** backslide, decline, degenerate, go downhill (*inf.*), regress, relapse, retreat, retrogress, revert, wane, worsen

retrogress *vb* **1 = deteriorate,** backslide, decline, go back, go downhill (*inf.*), regress, relapse, retrocede, retrograde, return, revert, worsen **2 = recede,** drop, ebb, fall, go back, lose ground, retire, retreat, sink, wane, withdraw

retrospect *n* **= hindsight,** afterthought, recollection, re-examination, remembrance, reminiscence, review, survey
Antonyms *n* anticipation, foresight

retrospective (ˌretrəʊˈspɛktɪv) *adj* **1** looking or directed backwards, esp. in time; characterized by retrospection. **2** applying to the past; retroactive. ♦ *n* **3** an exhibition of an artist's life's work.
▸ˌ**retro'spectively** *adv*

retroussé (rəˈtruːseɪ) *adj* (of a nose) turned up. [C19: from F *retrousser* to tuck up]

retroversion (ˌrɛtrəʊˈvɜːʃən) *n* **1** the act of turning or condition of being turned backwards. **2** the condition of a part or organ, esp. the uterus, that is turned backwards.
▸'**retro,verted** *adj*

Retrovir (ˈrɛtrəʊˌvɪə) *n Trademark.* the brand name for AZT.

retrovirus (ˈrɛtrəʊˌvaɪrəs) *n* any of several viruses that are able to reverse the normal flow of genetic information from DNA to RNA by transcribing RNA into DNA: many retroviruses are known to cause cancer in animals.
▸'**retro,viral** *adj*

retsina (rɛtˈsiːnə) *n* a Greek wine flavoured with resin. [Mod. Gk, from It. *resina* RESIN]

retune (riːˈtjuːn) *vb* **retunes, retuning, retuned.** (*tr*) **1** to tune (a musical instrument) differently or again. **2** to tune (a radio, television, etc.) to another frequency.

return ➊ (rɪˈtɜːn) *vb* **1** (*intr*) to come back to a former place or state. **2** (*tr*) to give, take, or carry back; replace or restore. **3** (*tr*) to repay or recompense, esp. with something of equivalent value: *return the compliment.* **4** (*tr*) to earn or yield (profit or interest) as an income from an investment or venture. **5** (*intr*) to come back or revert in thought or speech: *I'll return to that later.* **6** (*intr*) to recur or reappear: *the symptoms have returned.* **7** to answer or reply. **8** (*tr*) to vote into office; elect. **9** (*tr*) *Law.* (of a jury) to deliver or render (a verdict). **10** (*tr*) to submit (a report, etc.) about (someone or something) to someone in authority. **11** (*tr*) *Cards.* to lead back (the suit led by one's partner). **12** (*tr*) *Ball games.* to hit, throw, or play (a ball) back. **13 return thanks.** (of Christians) to say grace before a meal. ♦ *n* **14** the act or an instance of coming back. **15** something that is given or sent back, esp. unsatisfactory merchandise or a theatre ticket for resale. **16** the act or an instance of putting, sending, or carrying back; replacement or restoration. **17** (*often pl*) the yield or profit from an investment or venture. **18** the act or an instance of reciprocation or repayment (esp. in **in return for**). **19** a recurrence or reappearance. **20** an official report, esp. of the financial condition of a company. **21a** a form (a **tax return**) on which a statement of one's taxable income is made. **21b** the statement itself. **22** (*often pl*) a statement of the votes counted at an election. **23** an answer or reply. **24** *Brit.* short for **return ticket. 25** *Archit.* a part of a building that forms an angle with the façade. **26** *Law.* a report by a bailiff or other officer on the outcome of a formal document such as a writ, summons, etc. **27** *Cards.* a lead of a card in the suit that one's partner has previously led. **28** *Ball games.* the act of playing or throwing a ball, etc., back. **29 by return (of post).** *Brit.* by the next post back to the sender. **30 many happy returns (of the day).** a conventional birthday greeting. ♦ *adj* **31** of, relating to, or characterized by a return: *a return visit.* **32** denoting a second, reciprocal occasion: *a return match.* [C14: from OF *retorner;* see RE-, TURN]
▸**re'turnable** *adj*

return crease *n Cricket.* one of two lines marked at right-angles to each bowling crease, from inside which a bowler must deliver the ball.

returned soldier *n Austral. & NZ.* a soldier who has served abroad. Also (Austral. and Canad.): **returned man.**

returner (rɪˈtɜːnə) *n* **1** a person or thing that returns. **2** a person who goes back to work after a break, esp. a woman who has had children.

returning officer *n* (in Britain, Canada, Australia, etc.) an official in charge of conducting an election in a constituency, etc.

return ticket *n Brit., Austral., & NZ.* a ticket entitling a passenger to travel to his destination and back.

retuse (rɪˈtjuːs) *adj Bot.* having a rounded apex and a central depression. [C18: from L *retundere* to make blunt, from RE- + *tundere* to pound]

reunify (riːˈjuːnɪˌfaɪ) *vb* **reunifies, reunifying, reunified.** (*tr*) to bring together again (something, esp. a country previously divided).
▸ˌ**reunifi'cation** *n*

reunion (riːˈjuːnjən) *n* **1** the act of coming together again. **2** the state or condition of having been brought together again. **3** a gathering of relatives, friends, or former associates.

reunite (ˌriːjuːˈnaɪt) *vb* **reunites, reuniting, reunited.** to bring or come together again.
▸ˌ**reu'nitable** *adj*

Reuters (ˈrɔɪtəz) *n* a private news agency in London that distributes news to member newspapers. It was founded by Baron Paul Julius von Reuter (1816–99), German telegrapher.

rev (rɛv) *Inf.* ♦ *n* **1** revolution per minute. ♦ *vb* **revs, revving, revved. 2** (often foll. by *up*) to increase the speed of revolution of (an engine).

rev. *abbrev. for:* **1** revenue. **2** reverse(d). **3** review. **4** revise(d). **5** revision. **6** revolution. **7** revolving.

Rev. *abbrev. for:* **1** *Bible.* Revelation (of Saint John the Divine). **2** Reverend.

revalue (riːˈvæljuː) *or US* **revaluate** *vb* **revalues, revaluing, revalued** *or US* **revaluates, revaluating, revaluated. 1** to adjust the exchange value of (a currency), esp. upwards. Cf. **devalue. 2** (*tr*) to make a fresh valuation of.
▸ˌ**re,valu'ation** *n*

revamp ➊ (riːˈvæmp) *vb* (*tr*) **1** to patch up or renovate; repair or restore. ♦ *n* **2** something that has been renovated or revamped. **3** the act or process of revamping. [C19: from RE- + VAMP²]

revanchism (rɪˈvæntʃɪzəm) *n* **1** a foreign policy aimed at revenge or the regaining of lost territories. **2** support for such a policy. [C20: from F *revanche* REVENGE]
▸**re'vanchist** *n, adj*

rev counter *n Brit.* an informal name for **tachometer.**

Revd *abbrev. for* Reverend.

reveal ➊ (rɪˈviːl) *vb* (*tr*) **1** (*may take a clause as object or an infinitive*) to disclose (a secret); divulge. **2** to expose to view or show (something concealed). **3** (of God) to disclose (divine truths). ♦ *n* **4** *Archit.* the vertical side of an opening in a wall, esp. the side of a window or door between the frame and the front of the wall. [C14: from OF *reveler,* from L *revēlāre* to unveil, from RE- + *vēlum* a VEIL]
▸**re'vealable** *adj* ▸**re'vealer** *n* ▸**re'vealment** *n*

revealed religion *n* **1** religion based on the revelation by God to man of ideas that he would not have arrived at by reason alone. **2** religion in which the existence of God depends on revelation.

revealing (rɪˈviːlɪŋ) *adj* **1** of significance or import: *a very revealing experience.* **2** showing more of the body than is usual: *a revealing costume.*
▸**re'vealingly** *adv*

reveille (rɪˈvælɪ) *n* **1** a signal, given by a bugle, drum, etc., to awaken soldiers or sailors in the morning. **2** the hour at which this takes place. [C17: from F *réveillez!* awake! from RE- + OF *esveillier* to be wakeful, ult. from L *vigilāre* to keep watch]

revel ➊ (ˈrevᵊl) *vb* **revels, revelling, revelled** *or US* **revels, reveling, reveled.** (*intr*) **1** (foll. by *in*) to take pleasure or wallow: *to revel in success.* **2** to take part in noisy festivities; make merry. ♦ *n* **3** (*often pl*) an occasion of noisy merrymaking. [C14: from OF *reveler* to be merry, noisy, from L *rebellāre* to revolt]
▸'**reveller** *n*

revelation ➊ (ˌrɛvəˈleɪʃən) *n* **1** the act or process of disclosing something previously secret or obscure, esp. something true. **2** a fact disclosed or revealed, esp. in a dramatic or surprising way. **3** *Christianity.* God's disclosure of his own nature and his purpose for mankind. [C14: from Church L *revēlātiō,* from L *revēlāre* to REVEAL]
▸ˌ**reve'lational** *or* ˌ**reve'latory** *adj*

Revelation (ˌrɛvəˈleɪʃən) *n* (*popularly, often pl*) the last book of the New Testament, containing visionary descriptions of heaven, and of the end of the world. Also called: the **Apocalypse,** the **Revelation of Saint John the Divine.**

revelationist (ˌrɛvəˈleɪʃənɪst) *n* a person who believes that God has revealed certain truths to man.

revelry ➊ (ˈrevᵊlrɪ) *n, pl* **revelries.** noisy or unrestrained merrymaking.

THESAURUS

return *vb* **1** = **come back**, come round again, go back, reappear, rebound, recoil, recur, repair, retreat, revert, turn back **2** = **put back**, carry back, convey, give back, re-establish, reinstate, remit, render, replace, restore, retrocede, send, send back, take back, transmit **3** = **give back**, pay back, reciprocate, recompense, refund, reimburse, repay, requite **4** = **earn**, bring in, make, net, repay, yield **7** = **reply**, answer, come back (with), communicate, rejoin, respond, retort **8** = **elect**, choose, pick, vote in **9** *Law* = **announce**, arrive at, bring in, come to, deliver, render, report, submit ♦ *n* **16** = **restoration**, re-establishment, reinstatement, replacement **17** = **profit**, advantage, benefit, boot (*dialect*), gain, income, interest, proceeds, revenue, takings, yield **18** = **repayment**, compensation, meed (*arch.*), reciprocation, recompense, reimbursement, reparation, requital, retaliation, reward **19** = **reappearance**, recurrence **20, 21** = **statement**, account, form, list, report, summary **23** = **reply**, answer, comeback (*inf.*), rejoinder, response, retort, riposte
Antonyms *vb* ≠ **come back**: depart, disappear, go away, leave ≠ **put back**, **give back**: hold, keep, leave, remove, retain ≠ **earn**: lose ♦ *n* ≠ **restoration**: removal

revamp *vb* **1** = **renovate**, do up (*inf.*), fix up (*inf.*, *chiefly US & Canad.*), give a face-lift to, overhaul, patch up, recondition, refit, refurbish, rehabilitate, repair, restore

reveal *vb* **1** = **make known**, announce, betray, blow wide open (*sl.*), broadcast, communicate, disclose, divulge, get off one's chest (*inf.*), give away, give out, impart, leak, let on, let out, let slip, make public, proclaim, publish, take the wraps off (*inf.*), tell **2** = **show**, bare, bring to light, display, exhibit, expose to view, lay bare, manifest, open, uncover, unearth, unmask, unveil
Antonyms *vb* ≠ **make known**: conceal, cover up, hide, keep quiet about, sweep under the carpet (*inf.*) ≠ **show**: conceal, cover up, hide

revel *vb* **1** *foll. by* **in** = **enjoy**, bask in, crow about, delight in, drool over, gloat about, indulge in, lap up, luxuriate in, rejoice over, relish, rub one's hands, savour, take pleasure in, thrive on, wallow in **2** = **celebrate**, carouse, go on a spree, live it up (*inf.*), make merry, paint the town red (*inf.*), push the boat out (*Brit. inf.*), rave (*Brit. sl.*), roister, whoop it up (*inf.*) ♦ *n* **3** *often plural* = **merrymaking**, bacchanal, beano, carousal, carouse, celebration, debauch, festivity, gala, hooley *or* hoolie (*chiefly Irish & NZ*), jollification, party, rave (*Brit. sl.*), rave-up (*Brit. sl.*), saturnalia, spree
Antonyms *vb* ≠ **enjoy**: abhor, be uninterested in, dislike, hate, have no taste for

revelation *n* **1** = **disclosure**, announcement, betrayal, broadcasting, communication, discovery, display, exhibition, exposé, exposition, exposure, giveaway, leak, manifestation, news, proclamation, publication, telling, uncovering, unearthing, unveiling

reveller *n* **2** = **merrymaker**, carouser, celebrator, partygoer, pleasure-seeker, roisterer

revelry *n* = **merrymaking**, beano (*Brit. sl.*), carousal, carouse, celebration, debauch, debauchery, festivity, fun, hooley *or* hoolie (*chiefly*

revenant ('rɛvɪnənt) *n* something, esp. a ghost, that returns. [C19: from F: ghost, from *revenir*, from L *revenīre*, from RE- + *venīre* to come]

revenge ❶ (rɪ'vɛndʒ) *n* **1** the act of retaliating for wrongs or injury received; vengeance. **2** something done as a means of vengeance. **3** the desire to take vengeance. **4** a return match, regarded as a loser's opportunity to even the score. ◆ *vb* **revenges, revenging, revenged.** (*tr*) **5** to inflict equivalent injury or damage for (injury received). **6** to take vengeance for (oneself or another); avenge. [C14: from OF *revenger*, from LL *revindicāre*, from RE- + *vindicāre* to VINDICATE]
▸**re'venger** *n* ▸**re'venging** *adj* ▸**re'vengingly** *adv*

revengeful ❶ (rɪ'vɛndʒfʊl) *adj* full of or characterized by desire for vengeance; vindictive.
▸**re'vengefully** *adv* ▸**re'vengefulness** *n*

revenue ❶ ('rɛvɪˌnjuː) *n* **1** the income accruing from taxation to a government. **2a** a government department responsible for the collection of government revenue. **2b** (*as modifier*): *revenue men.* **3** the gross income from a business enterprise, investment, etc. **4** a particular item of income. **5** a source of income. [C16: from OF, from *revenir* to return, from L *revenīre*; see REVENANT]

revenue cutter *n* a small lightly armed boat used to enforce customs regulations and catch smugglers.

reverb (rɪ'vɜːb) *n* an electronic device that creates artificial acoustics.

reverberate ❶ (rɪ'vɜːbəˌreɪt) *vb* **reverberates, reverberating, reverberated. 1** (*intr*) to resound or re-echo. **2** to reflect or be reflected many times. **3** (*intr*) to rebound or recoil. **4** (*intr*) (of the flame or heat in a reverberatory furnace) to be deflected onto the metal or ore on the hearth. **5** (*tr*) to heat, melt, or refine (a metal or ore) in a reverberatory furnace. [C16: from L *reverberāre*, from RE- + *verberāre* to beat, from *verber* a lash]
▸**re'verberantly** *adv* ▸**reˌverber'ation** *n* ▸**re'verberative** *adj* ▸**re'verbeˌrator** *n* ▸**re'verberatory** *adj*

reverberation time *n* a measure of the acoustic properties of a room, equal to the time taken for a sound to fall in intensity by 60 decibels. It is usually measured in seconds.

reverberatory furnace *n* a metallurgical furnace having a curved roof that deflects heat onto the charge so that the fuel is not in direct contact with the ore.

revere ❶ (rɪ'vɪə) *vb* **reveres, revering, revered.** (*tr*) to be in awe of and respect deeply; venerate. [C17: from L *reverērī*, from RE- + *verērī* to fear, be in awe of]

reverence ❶ ('rɛvərəns) *n* **1** a feeling or attitude of profound respect, usually reserved for the sacred or divine. **2** an outward manifestation of this feeling, esp. a bow or act of obeisance. **3** the state of being revered or commanding profound respect. ◆ *vb* **reverences, reverencing, reverenced. 4** (*tr*) to revere or venerate.

Reverence ('rɛvərəns) *n* (preceded by *Your* or *His*) a title sometimes used to address or refer to a Roman Catholic priest.

reverend ('rɛvərənd) *adj* **1** worthy of reverence. **2** relating to or designating a clergyman. ◆ *n* **3** *Inf.* a clergyman. [C15: from L *reverendus* fit to be revered]

Reverend ('rɛvərənd) *adj* a title of respect for a clergyman. Abbrev.: **Rev., Revd.**

> **USAGE NOTE** *Reverend* with a surname alone (*Reverend Smith*), as a term of address (*"Yes, Reverend"*), or in the salutation of a letter (*Dear Rev. Mr Smith*) are all generally considered to be wrong usage. Preferred are (*the*) *Reverend John Smith* or *Reverend Mr Smith* and *Dear Mr Smith.*

reverent ❶ ('rɛvərənt, 'rɛvrənt) *adj* feeling, expressing, or characterized by reverence. [C14: from L *reverēns* respectful]
▸**'reverently** *adv*

reverential (ˌrɛvə'rɛnʃəl) *adj* resulting from or showing reverence.
▸**ˌrever'entially** *adv*

reverie ❶ ('rɛvərɪ) *n* **1** an act or state of absent-minded daydreaming: *to fall into a reverie.* **2** a piece of instrumental music suggestive of a daydream. **3** *Arch.* a fanciful or visionary notion; daydream. [C14: from OF *resverie* wildness, from *resver* to behave wildly, from ?]

revers (rɪ'vɪə) *n, pl* **revers** (-'vɪəz). (*usually pl*) the turned-back lining of part of a garment, esp. of a lapel or cuff. [C19: from F, lit.: REVERSE]

reversal (rɪ'vɜːsᵊl) *n* **1** the act or an instance of reversing. **2** a change for the worse; reverse. **3** the state of being reversed. **4** the annulment of a judicial decision, esp. by an appeal court.

reverse ❶ (rɪ'vɜːs) *vb* **reverses, reversing, reversed.** (*mainly tr*) **1** to turn or set in an opposite direction, order, or position. **2** to change into something different or contrary; alter completely: *reverse one's policy.* **3** (*also intr*) to move or cause to move backwards or in an opposite direction: *to reverse a car.* **4** to run (machinery, etc.) in the opposite direction to normal. **5** to turn inside out. **6** *Law.* to revoke or set aside (a judgment, decree, etc.); annul. **7 reverse the charge(s).** to make a telephone call at the recipient's expense. ◆ *n* **8** the opposite or contrary of something. **9** the back or rear side of something. **10** a change to an opposite position, state, or direction. **11** a change for the worse; setback or defeat. **12a** the mechanism or gears by which machinery, a vehicle, etc., can be made to reverse its direction. **12b** (*as modifier*): *reverse gear.* **13** the side of a coin bearing a secondary design. **14a** printed matter in which normally black or coloured areas, esp. lettering, appear white, and vice versa. **14b** (*as modifier*): *reverse plates.* **15 in reverse.** in an opposite or backward direction. **16 the reverse of.** emphatically not; not at all: *he was the reverse of polite when I called.* ◆ *adj* **17** opposite or contrary in direction, position, order, nature, etc.; turned backwards. **18** back to front; inverted. **19** operating or moving in a manner contrary to that which is usual. **20** denoting or relating to a mirror image. [C14: from OF, from L *reversus*, from *revertere* to turn back]
▸**re'versely** *adv* ▸**re'verser** *n*

reverse-charge *adj* (*prenominal*) (of a telephone call) made at the recipient's expense.

reverse takeover *n Finance.* the purchase of a larger company by a smaller company, esp. of a public company by a private company.

reverse transcriptase (træn'skrɪpteɪz) *n* an enzyme present in retroviruses that copies RNA into DNA, thus reversing the usual flow of genetic information in which DNA is copied into RNA.

reverse video *n Computing.* highlighting by reversing the colours of normal characters and background on a visual display unit.

reversible (rɪ'vɜːsɪbᵊl) *adj* **1** capable of being reversed: *a reversible decision.* **2** capable of returning to an original condition. **3** *Chem., physics.* capable of assuming or producing either of two possible states and changing from one to the other: *a reversible reaction.* **4** (of a fabric or garment) woven, printed, or finished so that either side may be used as the outer side. ◆ *n* **5** a reversible garment, esp. a coat.
▸**reˌversi'bility** *n* ▸**re'versibly** *adv*

reversing lights *pl n* lights on the rear of a motor vehicle that go on when the vehicle is being reversed.

reversion (rɪ'vɜːʃən) *n* **1** a return to an earlier condition, practice, or belief; act of reverting. **2** *Biol.* the return of individuals, organs, etc., to a more primitive condition or type. **3** *Property law.* **3a** an interest in an estate that reverts to the grantor or his heirs at the end of a period, esp. at the end of the life of a grantee. **3b** an estate so reverting. **3c** the right to succeed to such an estate. **4** the benefit payable on the death of a life-insurance policyholder.
▸**re'versionary** *or* **re'versional** *adj*

reversionary bonus *n Insurance.* a bonus added to the sum payable on death or at the maturity of a with-profits assurance policy.

revert ❶ (rɪ'vɜːt) *vb* (*intr*; foll. by *to*). **1** to go back to a former practice, condition, belief, etc.: *he reverted to his old wicked ways.* **2** to take up again or come back to a former topic. **3** *Biol.* (of individuals, organs, etc.) to return to a more primitive, earlier, or simpler condition or type. **4** *Property law.* (of an estate or interest in land) to return to its former owner or his heirs. **5 revert to type.** to resume characteristics that were

THESAURUS

Irish & NZ), jollification, jollity, party, rave (*Brit. sl.*), rave-up (*Brit. sl.*), roistering, saturnalia, spree

revenge *n* **1, 2** = **retaliation**, an eye for an eye, reprisal, requital, retribution, satisfaction, vengeance ◆ *vb* **5, 6** = **avenge**, even the score for, get even, get one's own back for (*inf.*), hit back, make reprisal for, pay (someone) back, repay, requite, retaliate, take an eye for an eye for, take revenge for, vindicate

revengeful *adj* = **vengeful**, bitter, malevolent, malicious, malignant, merciless, pitiless, resentful, spiteful, unforgiving, unmerciful, vindictive

revenue *n* **1, 3** = **income**, gain, interest, proceeds, profits, receipts, returns, rewards, takings, yield
Antonyms *n* expenditure, expenses, outgoings

reverberate *vb* **1** = **echo**, rebound, recoil, re-echo, resound, ring, vibrate

reverberation *n* **1** = **echo**, rebound, recoil, re-echoing, resonance, resounding, ringing, vibration

revere *vb* = **be in awe of**, adore, defer to, exalt, have a high opinion of, honour, look up to, put on a pedestal, respect, reverence, think highly of, venerate, worship
Antonyms *vb* deride, despise, hold in contempt, scorn, sneer at

reverence *n* **1** = **respect**, admiration, adoration, awe, deference, devotion, high esteem, homage, honour, veneration, worship ◆ *vb* **4** = **revere**, admire, adore, be in awe of, hold in awe, honour, pay homage to, respect, venerate, worship
Antonyms *n* ≠ **respect**: contempt, contumely, derision, disdain, scorn

reverent *adj* = **respectful**, adoring, awed, deferential, devout, humble, loving, meek, pious, reverential, solemn, submissive
Antonyms *adj* cheeky, disrespectful, flippant, impious, irreverent, mocking, sacrilegious

reverie *n* **1** = **daydream**, absent-mindedness, abstraction, brown study, castles in the air *or* Spain, daydreaming, inattention, musing, preoccupation, trance, woolgathering

reverse *vb* **1** = **turn round**, invert, transpose, turn back, turn over, turn upside down, upend **3** = **go backwards**, back, backtrack, back up, move backwards, retreat **6** *Law* = **change**, alter, annul, cancel, countermand, declare null and void, invalidate, negate, obviate, overrule, overset, overthrow, overturn, quash, repeal, rescind, retract, revoke, set aside, undo, upset ◆ *n* **8** = **opposite**, antithesis, contradiction, contrary, converse, inverse **9** = **back**, flip side, other side, rear, underside, verso, wrong side **11** = **misfortune**, adversity, affliction, blow, check, defeat, disappointment, failure, hardship, misadventure, mishap, repulse, reversal, setback, trial, vicissitude ◆ *adj* **18** = **opposite**, back to front, backward, contrary, converse, inverse, inverted
Antonyms *vb* ≠ **go backwards**: advance, go forward, move forward ≠ **change**: carry out, enforce, implement, validate ◆ *n* ≠ **back**: forward side, front, obverse, recto, right side

revert *vb* **1** = **return**, backslide, come back, go back, lapse, recur, regress, relapse, resume

thought to have disappeared. [C13: from L *revertere*, from RE- + *vertere* to turn]
▸**re'verter** *n* ▸**re'vertible** *adj*

> **USAGE NOTE** Since *back* is part of the meaning of *revert*, one should not say that someone *reverts back* to a certain type of behaviour.

revet (rɪ'vɛt) *vb* **revets, revetting, revetted.** to face (a wall or embankment) with stones. [C19: from F *revêt*, from OF *revestir* to reclothe; see REVETMENT]

revetment (rɪ'vɛtmənt) *n* **1** a facing of stones, sandbags, etc., to protect a wall, embankment, or earthworks. **2** another name for **retaining wall.** [C18: from F *revêtement*, lit.: a reclothing, from *revêtir;* ult. from L RE- + *vestīre* to clothe]

review ➊ (rɪ'vju:) *vb* (*mainly tr*) **1** to look at or examine again: *to review a situation.* **2** to look back upon (a period of time, sequence of events, etc.); remember: *he reviewed his achievements with pride.* **3** to inspect, esp. formally or officially: *the general reviewed his troops.* **4** *Law.* to re-examine (a decision) judicially. **5** to write a critical assessment of (a book, film, play, concert, etc.), esp. as a profession. ◆ *n* **6** Also called: **reviewal.** the act or an instance of reviewing. **7** a general survey or report: *a review of the political situation.* **8** a critical assessment of a book, film, play, concert, etc., esp. one printed in a newspaper or periodical. **9** a publication containing such articles. **10** a second consideration; re-examination. **11** a retrospective survey. **12** a formal or official inspection. **13** a US and Canad. word for **revision** (sense 2). **14** *Law.* judicial re-examination of a case, esp. by a superior court. **15** a less common spelling of **revue.** [C16: from F, from *revoir* to see again, from L RE- + *vidēre* to see]
▸**re'viewer** *n*

revile ➊ (rɪ'vaɪl) *vb* **reviles, reviling, reviled.** to use abusive or scornful language against (someone or something). [C14: from OF *reviler*, from RE- + *vil* VILE]
▸**re'vilement** *n* ▸**re'viler** *n*

revise ➊ (rɪ'vaɪz) *vb* **revises, revising, revised. 1** (*tr*) to change or amend: *to revise one's opinion.* **2** *Brit.* to reread (a subject or notes on it) so as to memorize it, esp. for an examination. **3** (*tr*) to prepare a new version or edition of (a previously printed work). ◆ *n* **4** the act, process, or result of revising; revision. [C16: from L *revīsere*, from RE- + *vīsere* to inspect, from *vidēre* to see]
▸**re'visal** *n* ▸**re'viser** *n*

Revised Standard Version *n* a revision by American scholars of the American Standard Version of the Bible. The New Testament was published in 1946 and the entire Bible in 1953.

Revised Version *n* a revision of the Authorized Version of the Bible by two committees of British scholars, the New Testament being published in 1881 and the Old in 1885.

revision ➊ (rɪ'vɪʒən) *n* **1** the act or process of revising. **2** *Brit.* the process of rereading a subject or notes on it, esp. for an examination. **3** a corrected or new version of a book, article, etc.
▸**re'visionary** *adj*

revisionism (rɪ'vɪʒə,nɪzəm) *n* **1** (*sometimes cap.*) **1a** a moderate, nonrevolutionary version of Marxism developed in Germany around 1900. **1b** (in Marxist-Leninist ideology) any dangerous departure from the true interpretation of Marx's teachings. **2** the advocacy of revision of some political theory, etc.
▸**re'visionist** *n, adj*

revisory (rɪ'vaɪzərɪ) *adj* of, relating to, or having the power of revision.

revitalize ➊ *or* **revitalise** (ri:'vaɪtᵊ,laɪz) *vb* **revitalizes, revitalizing, revitalized** *or* **revitalises, revitalising, revitalised.** (*tr*) to restore vitality or animation to.

revival ➊ (rɪ'vaɪvᵊl) *n* **1** the act or an instance of reviving or the state of being revived. **2** an instance of returning to life or consciousness; restoration of vigour or vitality. **3** a renewed use, acceptance of, or interest in (past customs, styles, etc.): *the Gothic revival.* **4** a new production of a play that has not been recently performed. **5** a reawakening of faith. **6** an evangelistic meeting or meetings intended to effect such a reawakening in those present.

revivalism (rɪ'vaɪvə,lɪzəm) *n* **1** a movement that seeks to reawaken faith. **2** the tendency or desire to revive former customs, styles, etc.
▸**re'vivalist** *n* ▸**re,vival'istic** *adj*

revive ➊ (rɪ'vaɪv) *vb* **revives, reviving, revived. 1** to bring or be brought back to life, consciousness, or strength: *revived by a drop of whisky.* **2** to give or assume new vitality; flourish again or cause to flourish again. **3** to make or become operative or active again: *the youth movement was revived.* **4** to bring or come back to mind. **5** (*tr*) *Theatre.* to mount a new production of (an old play). [C15: from OF *revivre* to live again, from L *revīvere*, from RE- + *vīvere* to live]
▸**re'vivable** *adj* ▸**re,viva'bility** *n* ▸**re'viver** *n* ▸**re'viving** *adj*

revivify ➊ (rɪ'vɪvɪ,faɪ) *vb* **revivifies, revivifying, revivified.** (*tr*) to give new life or spirit to.
▸**re,vivifi'cation** *n*

revocable ('rɛvəkəbᵊl) *or* **revokable** (rɪ'vəukəbᵊl) *adj* capable of being revoked.
▸**,revoca'bility** *or* **re,voka'bility** *n* ▸**'revocably** *or* **re'vokably** *adv*

revocation (,rɛvə'keɪʃən) *n* **1** the act of revoking or state of being revoked. **2a** the cancellation or annulment of a legal instrument. **2b** the withdrawal of an offer, power of attorney, etc.
▸**revocatory** ('rɛvəkətərɪ, -trɪ) *adj*

revoice (ri:'vɔɪs) *vb* **revoices, revoicing, revoiced.** (*tr*) **1** to utter again; echo. **2** to adjust the design of (an organ pipe or wind instrument) as after disuse or to conform with modern pitch.

revoke ➊ (rɪ'vəuk) *vb* **revokes, revoking, revoked. 1** (*tr*) to take back or withdraw; cancel; rescind. **2** (*intr*) *Cards.* to break a rule by failing to follow suit when able to do so. ◆ *n* **3** *Cards.* the act of revoking. [C14: from L *revocāre* to call back, withdraw, from RE- + *vocāre* to call]
▸**re'voker** *n*

revolt ➊ (rɪ'vəult) *n* **1** a rebellion or uprising against authority. **2 in revolt.** in the process or state of rebelling. ◆ *vb* **3** (*intr*) to rise up in rebellion against authority. **4** (*usually passive*) to feel or cause to feel revulsion, disgust, or abhorrence. [C16: from F *révolter*, from OIt. *rivoltare* to overturn, ult. from L *revolvere* to roll back]

revolting ➊ (rɪ'vəultɪŋ) *adj* **1** causing revulsion; nauseating, disgusting, or repulsive. **2** *Inf.* unpleasant or nasty.
▸**re'voltingly** *adv*

revolute ('rɛvə,lu:t) *adj* (esp. of the margins of a leaf) rolled backwards and downwards. [C18: from L *revolūtus* rolled back; see REVOLVE]

revolution ➊ (,rɛvə'lu:ʃən) *n* **1** the overthrow or repudiation of a regime or political system by the governed. **2** (in Marxist theory) the inevitable, violent transition from one system of production in a society to the next. **3** a far-reaching and drastic change, esp. in ideas, methods, etc. **4a** movement in or as if in a circle. **4b** one complete turn in such a circle: *33 revolutions per minute.* **5a** the orbital motion of one body, such as a planet, around another. **5b** one complete turn in such motion. **6** a cycle of successive events or changes. [C14: via OF from LL *revolūtiō*, from L *revolvere* to REVOLVE]

THESAURUS

review *vb* **1** = **reconsider**, go over again, look at again, reassess, recapitulate, re-evaluate, re-examine, rethink, revise, run over, take another look at, think over **2** = **look back on**, call to mind, recall, recollect, reflect on, remember, summon up **3** = **inspect**, examine, scrutinize **5** = **assess**, criticize, discuss, evaluate, give one's opinion of, judge, read through, study, weigh, write a critique of ◆ *n* **7** = **report**, analysis, examination, perusal, scrutiny, study, survey **8** = **critique**, commentary, critical assessment, criticism, evaluation, judgment, notice, study **9** = **magazine**, journal, periodical, zine (*inf.*) **10** = **re-examination**, another look, fresh look, reassessment, recapitulation, reconsideration, re-evaluation, rethink, retrospect, revision, second look **12** = **inspection**, display, march past, parade, procession

reviewer *n* **5** = **critic**, arbiter, commentator, connoisseur, essayist, judge

revile *vb* = **malign**, abuse, asperse, bad-mouth (*sl., chiefly US & Canad.*), calumniate, defame, denigrate, knock (*inf.*), libel, reproach, rubbish (*inf.*), run down, scorn, slag (off) (*sl.*), slander, smear, traduce, vilify, vituperate

revise *vb* **1** = **change**, alter, amend, correct, edit, emend, modify, reconsider, redo, re-examine, revamp, review, rework, rewrite, update **2** = **study**, cram (*inf.*), go over, memorize, reread, run through, swot up (*Brit. inf.*)

revision *n* **1** = **change**, alteration, amendment, correction, editing, emendation, modification, re-examination, review, rewriting, updating **2** = **studying**, cramming (*inf.*), homework, memorizing, rereading, swotting (*Brit. inf.*)

revitalize *vb* = **reanimate**, breathe new life into, bring back to life, refresh, rejuvenate, renew, restore, resurrect, revivify

revival *n* **1, 2** = **renewal**, awakening, quickening, reanimation, reawakening, rebirth, recrudescence, refreshment, renaissance, renascence, restoration, resurgence, resurrection, resuscitation, revitalization, revivification
Antonyms *n* disappearance, extinction, falling off, suppression

revive *vb* **1-3** = **revitalize**, animate, awaken, breathe new life into, bring back to life, bring round, cheer, come round, comfort, invigorate, kick-start, quicken, rally, reanimate, recover, refresh, rekindle, renew, renovate, restore, resuscitate, rouse, spring up again
Antonyms *vb* die out, disappear, enervate, exhaust, tire out, weary

revivify *vb* = **revive**, breathe new life into, give new life to, inspirit, invigorate, kick-start (*inf.*), reanimate, refresh, renew, restore, resuscitate

revoke *vb* **1** = **cancel**, abolish, abrogate, annul, call back, countermand, declare null and void, disclaim, invalidate, negate, nullify, obviate, quash, recall, recant, renege, renounce, repeal, repudiate, rescind, retract, reverse, set aside, take back, withdraw
Antonyms *vb* confirm, endorse, implement, maintain, put into effect, uphold

revolt *n* **1** = **uprising**, defection, insurgency, insurrection, mutiny, putsch, rebellion, revolution, rising, sedition ◆ *vb* **3** = **rebel**, defect, mutiny, resist, rise, take to the streets, take up arms (against) **4** = **disgust**, give one the creeps (*inf.*), gross out (*US sl.*), make one's flesh creep, nauseate, offend, repel, repulse, shock, sicken, turn off (*inf.*), turn one's stomach

revolting *adj* **1, 2** = **disgusting**, abhorrent, abominable, appalling, cringe-making (*Brit. inf.*), distasteful, foul, horrible, horrid, loathsome, nasty, nauseating, nauseous, noisome, obnoxious, obscene, offensive, repellent, repugnant, repulsive, shocking, sickening, yucky *or* yukky (*sl.*)
Antonyms *adj* agreeable, attractive, delightful, fragrant, palatable, pleasant

revolution *n* **1** = **revolt**, coup, coup d'état, insurgency, mutiny, putsch, rebellion, rising, uprising **3** = **transformation**, drastic *or* radical change, innovation, metamorphosis, reformation, sea change, shift, upheaval **4** = **rotation**, circle, circuit, cycle, gyration, lap, round, spin, turn, wheel, whirl **5** = **orbit**, circuit

revolutionary ❶ (ˌrɛvəˈluːʃənərɪ) *n, pl* **revolutionaries. 1** a person who advocates or engages in revolution. ◆ *adj* **2** relating to or characteristic of a revolution. **3** advocating or engaged in revolution. **4** radically new or different: *a revolutionary method of making plastics.*

Revolutionary (ˌrɛvəˈluːʃənərɪ) *adj* **1** *Chiefly US.* of or relating to the War of American Independence (1775–83). **2** of or relating to any of various other Revolutions, esp. the **Russian Revolution** (1917) or the **French Revolution** (1789).

revolutionist (ˌrɛvəˈluːʃənɪst) *n* **1** a less common word for a **revolutionary.** ◆ *adj* **2** of or relating to revolution or revolutionaries.

revolutionize ❶ *or* **revolutionise** (ˌrɛvəˈluːʃəˌnaɪz) *vb* **revolutionizes, revolutionizing, revolutionized** *or* **revolutionises, revolutionising, revolutionised.** (*tr*) **1** to bring about a radical change in: *science has revolutionized civilization.* **2** to inspire or infect with revolutionary ideas: *they revolutionized the common soldiers.* **3** to cause a revolution in (a country, etc.).
▸ **ˌrevoˈlutionˌizer** *or* **ˌrevoˈlutionˌiser** *n*

revolve ❶ (rɪˈvɒlv) *vb* **revolves, revolving, revolved. 1** to move or cause to move around a centre or axis; rotate. **2** (*intr*) to occur periodically or in cycles. **3** to consider or be considered. **4** (*intr; foll. by around* or *about*) to be centred or focused (upon): *Juliet's thoughts revolved around Romeo.* ◆ *n* **5** *Theatre.* a circular section of a stage that can be rotated by electric power to provide a scene change. [C14: from L *revolvere,* from RE- + *volvere* to roll, wind]
▸ **reˈvolvable** *adj*

revolver (rɪˈvɒlvə) *n* a pistol having a revolving multichambered cylinder that allows several shots to be discharged without reloading.

revolving (rɪˈvɒlvɪŋ) *adj* **1** moving round a central axis: *revolving door.* **2** (of a fund) constantly added to from income from its investments to offset outgoing payments. **3** (of a letter of credit, loan, etc.) available to be repeatedly drawn on by the beneficiary provided that a specified amount is never exceeded.

revue (rɪˈvjuː) *n* a light entertainment consisting of topical sketches, songs, dancing, etc. [C20: from F; see REVIEW]

revulsion ❶ (rɪˈvʌlʃən) *n* **1** a sudden violent reaction in feeling, esp. one of extreme loathing. **2** the act or an instance of drawing back or recoiling from something. **3** the diversion of disease from one part of the body to another by cupping, counterirritants, etc. [C16: from L *revulsiō* a pulling away, from *revellere,* from RE- + *vellere* to pull, tear]

revulsive (rɪˈvʌlsɪv) *adj* **1** of or causing revulsion. ◆ *n* **2** *Med.* a counterirritant.
▸ **reˈvulsively** *adv*

reward ❶ (rɪˈwɔːd) *n* **1** something given in return for a deed or service rendered. **2** a sum of money offered, esp. for help in finding a criminal or for the return of lost or stolen property. **3** profit or return. **4** something received in return for good or evil; deserts. ◆ *vb* **5** (*tr*) to give something to (someone), esp. in gratitude for (a service rendered); recompense. [C14: from OF *rewarder,* from RE- + *warder* to care for, guard, of Gmc origin]
▸ **reˈwardless** *adj*

reward claim *n Austral. history.* a claim granted to a miner who discovered gold in a new area.

rewarding ❶ (rɪˈwɔːdɪŋ) *adj* giving personal satisfaction; gratifying.

rewa-rewa (ˈreɪwəˈreɪwə) *n* a tall tree of New Zealand, yielding reddish timber. [C19: from Maori]

rewind *vb* (riːˈwaɪnd), **rewinds, rewinding, rewound. 1** (*tr*) to wind back, esp. a film or tape onto the original reel. ◆ *n* (ˈriːˌwaɪnd, riːˈwaɪnd). **2** something rewound. **3** the act of rewinding.
▸ **reˈwinder** *n*

rewire (riːˈwaɪə) *vb* **rewires, rewiring, rewired.** (*tr*) to provide (a house, engine, etc.) with new wiring.
▸ **reˈwirable** *adj*

reword ❶ (riːˈwɜːd) *vb* (*tr*) to alter the wording of; express differently.

rework (riːˈwɜːk) *vb* (*tr*) **1** to use again in altered form. **2** to rewrite or revise. **3** to reprocess for use again.

rewrite ❶ *vb* (riːˈraɪt), **rewrites, rewriting, rewrote, rewritten.** (*tr*) **1** to write (material) again, esp. changing the words or form. ◆ *n* (ˈriːˌraɪt). **2** *Computing.* to return (data) to a store when it has been erased during reading. **3** something rewritten.

Rex (rɛks) *n* king: part of the official title of a king, now used chiefly in documents, legal proceedings, on coins, etc. Cf. **Regina.** [L]

Rexine (ˈrɛksiːn) *n Trademark.* a form of artificial leather.

Reye's syndrome (raɪz, reɪz) *n* a rare metabolic disease in children that can be fatal, involving damage to the brain, liver, and kidneys. [C20: after R.D.K. *Reye* (1912–78), Austral. paediatrician]

Reynard *or* **Renard** (ˈrɛnəd, ˈrɛnɑːd) *n* a name for a fox, used in fables, etc.

RF *abbrev. for* radio frequency.

RFC *abbrev. for:* **1** Royal Flying Corps. **2** Rugby Football Club.

RGN (in Britain) *abbrev. for* Registered General Nurse.

RGS *abbrev. for* Royal Geographical Society.

rh *or* **RH** *abbrev. for* right hand.

Rh 1 *the chemical symbol for* rhodium. ◆ **2** *abbrev. for* rhesus (esp. in **Rh factor**).

RHA *abbrev. for:* **1** Regional Health Authority. **2** Royal Horse Artillery.

rhabdomancy (ˈræbdəˌmænsɪ) *n* divination for water or mineral ore by means of a rod or wand. [C17: via LL from LGk *rhabdomanteia,* from Gk *rhabdos* rod + *manteia* divination]
▸ **ˈrhabdoˌmantist** *or* **ˈrhabdoˌmancer** *n*

rhachis (ˈreɪkɪs) *n, pl* **rhachises** *or* **rhachides** (ˈrækɪˌdiːz, ˈreɪ-). a variant spelling of **rachis.**

Rhadamanthine (ˌrædəˈmænθaɪn) *adj* impartial; judicially strict. [C19: after *Rhadamanthus,* in Gk myth one of the judges of the dead in the underworld]

rhapsodic (ræpˈsɒdɪk) *adj* **1** of or like a rhapsody. **2** lyrical or romantic.

rhapsodize ❶ *or* **rhapsodise** (ˈræpsəˌdaɪz) *vb* **rhapsodizes, rhapsodizing, rhapsodized** *or* **rhapsodises, rhapsodising, rhapsodised. 1** to speak or write (something) with extravagant enthusiasm. **2** (*intr*) to recite or write rhapsodies.
▸ **ˈrhapsodist** *n*

rhapsody (ˈræpsədɪ) *n, pl* **rhapsodies. 1** *Music.* a composition free in structure and highly emotional in character. **2** an expression of ecstatic enthusiasm. **3** (in ancient Greece) an epic poem or part of an epic recited by a rhapsodist. **4** a literary work composed in an intense or exalted style. **5** rapturous delight or ecstasy. [C16: via L from Gk *rhapsōidia,* from *rhaptein* to sew together + *ōidē* song]

rhatany (ˈrætənɪ) *n, pl* **rhatanies. 1** either of two South American leguminous shrubs that have thick fleshy roots. **2** the dried roots used as an astringent. ◆ Also called: **krameria.** [C19: from NL *rhatānia,* ult. from Quechua *ratánya*]

rhea (rɪə) *n* either of two large fast-running flightless birds inhabiting the open plains of S South America. They are similar to but smaller than the ostrich. [C19: NL; arbitrarily after *Rhea,* in Gk myth., mother of Zeus]

rhebuck *or* **rhebok** (ˈriːbʌk) *n, pl* **rhebucks, rhebuck** *or* **rheboks, rhebok.** an antelope of southern Africa, having woolly brownish-grey hair. [C18: Afrik., from Du. *reebok* ROEBUCK]

Rhenish (ˈrɛnɪʃ, ˈriː-) *adj* **1** of or relating to the River Rhine or the lands adjacent to it. ◆ *n* **2** another word for **hock**[2].

rhenium (ˈriːnɪəm) *n* a dense silvery-white metallic element that has a high melting point. Symbol: Re; atomic no.: 75; atomic wt.: 186.2. [C19: NL, from *Rhēnus* the Rhine]

rheo- *combining form.* indicating stream, flow, or current: *rheostat.* [from Gk *rheos* stream, anything flowing, from *rhein* to flow]

rheology (rɪˈɒlədʒɪ) *n* the branch of physics concerned with the flow and change of matter, esp. the viscosity of liquids.
▸ **rheological** (ˌriːəˈlɒdʒɪkˡl) *adj* ▸ **rheˈologist** *n*

rheostat (ˈrɪəˌstæt) *n* a variable resistance, usually a coil of wire with a terminal at one end and a sliding contact that moves along the coil to tap off the current.
▸ **ˌrheoˈstatic** *adj*

rhesus baby (ˈriːsəs) *n* a baby suffering from haemolytic disease at birth as its red blood cells (which are Rh positive) have been attacked in the womb by antibodies from its Rh negative mother. [C20: see RH FACTOR]

rhesus factor *n* See **Rh factor.**

rhesus monkey *n* a macaque monkey of S Asia. [C19: NL, arbitrarily from Gk *Rhesos,* mythical Thracian king]

rhetoric ❶ (ˈrɛtərɪk) *n* **1** the study of the technique of using language effectively. **2** the art of using speech to persuade, influence, or please; oratory. **3** excessive ornamentation and contrivance in spoken or written discourse; bombast. **4** speech or discourse that pretends to

THESAURUS

revolutionary *n* **1** = **rebel,** insurgent, insurrectionary, insurrectionist, mutineer, revolutionist ◆ *adj* **3** = **rebel,** extremist, insurgent, insurrectionary, mutinous, radical, seditious, subversive **4** = **innovative,** avant-garde, different, drastic, experimental, fundamental, ground-breaking, new, novel, progressive, radical, thoroughgoing
Antonyms *adj, n* ≠ **rebel:** counter-revolutionary, loyalist, reactionary ◆ *adj* ≠ **innovative:** conservative, conventional, mainstream, minor, traditional, trivial

revolutionize *vb* **1** = **transform,** break with the past, metamorphose, modernize, reform, revamp

revolve *vb* **1** = **go round,** circle, gyrate, orbit, rotate, spin, turn, twist, wheel, whirl **3** = **consider,** deliberate, meditate, mull over, ponder, reflect, ruminate, study, think about, think over, turn over (in one's mind)

revulsion *n* **1** = **disgust,** abhorrence, abomination, aversion, detestation, distaste, loathing, odium, recoil, repugnance, repulsion
Antonyms *n* attraction, desire, fascination, liking, pleasure

reward *n* **1, 2** = **payment,** benefit, bounty, compensation, honour, meed, merit, prize, recompense, remuneration, repayment, requital **3** = **profit,** bonus, gain, premium, return, wages **4** = **punishment,** comeuppance (*sl.*), desert, just deserts, requital, retribution ◆ *vb* **5** = **compensate,** honour, make it worth one's while, pay, recompense, remunerate, repay, requite
Antonyms *n* ≠ **payment:** fine, penalty, punishment ◆ *vb* ≠ **compensate:** fine, penalize, punish

rewarding *adj* = **satisfying,** advantageous, beneficial, economic, edifying, enriching, fruitful, fulfilling, gainful, gratifying, pleasing, productive, profitable, remunerative, valuable, worthwhile
Antonyms *adj* barren, boring, fruitless, unproductive, unprofitable, unrewarding, vain

reword *vb* = **put in other words,** express differently, paraphrase, put another way, recast, rephrase

rewrite *vb* **1** = **revise,** correct, edit, emend, recast, redraft, touch up

rhapsodize *vb* **1** = **enthuse,** drool, go into ecstasies, gush, rave (*inf.*), wax lyrical

rhetoric *n* **2** = **oratory,** eloquence **3, 4** = **hyperbole,** bombast, fustian, grandiloquence, hot air (*inf.*), magniloquence, pomposity, rant, verbosity, wordiness significance but lacks true meaning: *mere rhetoric.* [C14: via L from Gk *rhētorikē* (*tekhnē*) (the art of) rhetoric, from *rhētōr* teacher of rhetoric, orator]

rhetorical ⓣ (rɪˈtɒrɪkᵊl) *adj* **1** concerned with effect or style rather than content or meaning; bombastic. **2** of or relating to rhetoric or oratory.
▸**rheˈtorically** *adv*

rhetorical question *n* a question to which no answer is required: used esp. for dramatic effect. An example is *Who knows?* (with the implication *Nobody knows*).

rhetorician (ˌretəˈrɪʃən) *n* **1** a teacher of rhetoric. **2** a stylish or eloquent writer or speaker. **3** a pompous or extravagant speaker.

rheum (ruːm) *n* a watery discharge from the eyes or nose. [C14: from OF *reume*, ult. from Gk *rheuma* bodily humour, stream, from *rhein* to flow]
▸ˈ**rheumy** *adj*

rheumatic (ruːˈmætɪk) *adj* **1** of, relating to, or afflicted with rheumatism. ◆ *n* **2** a person afflicted with rheumatism. [C14: ult. from Gk *rheumatikos*, from *rheuma* a flow; see RHEUM]
▸**rheuˈmatically** *adv*

rheumatic fever *n* a disease characterized by inflammation and pain in the joints.

rheumatics (ruːˈmætɪks) *n* (*functioning as sing*) *Inf.* rheumatism.

rheumatism (ˈruːməˌtɪzəm) *n* any painful disorder of joints, muscles, or connective tissue. [C17: from L *rheumatismus* catarrh, from Gk *rheumatismos;* see RHEUM]

rheumatoid (ˈruːməˌtɔɪd) *adj* (of symptoms) resembling rheumatism.

rheumatoid arthritis *n* a chronic disease characterized by inflammation and swelling of joints (esp. in the hands, wrists, knees, and feet), muscle weakness, and fatigue.

rheumatology (ˌruːməˈtɒlədʒɪ) *n* the study of rheumatic diseases.
▸**rheumatological** (ˌruːmətəˈlɒdʒɪkᵊl) *adj*

Rh factor *n* an antigen commonly found in human blood: the terms **Rh positive** and **Rh negative** are used to indicate its presence or absence. It may cause a haemolytic reaction, esp. during pregnancy or following transfusion of blood that does not contain this antigen. Full name: **rhesus factor.** [after the rhesus monkey, in which it was first discovered]

rhinal (ˈraɪnᵊl) *adj* of or relating to the nose.

rhinestone (ˈraɪnˌstəʊn) *n* an imitation gem made of paste. [C19: translation of F *caillou du Rhin,* referring to Strasbourg, where such gems were made]

Rhine wine (raɪn) *n* any wine produced along the Rhine, characteristically a white table wine.

rhinitis (raɪˈnaɪtɪs) *n* inflammation of the mucous membrane that lines the nose.
▸**rhinitic** (raɪˈnɪtɪk) *adj*

rhino[1] (ˈraɪnəʊ) *n, pl* **rhinos** *or* **rhino.** short for **rhinoceros.**

rhino[2] (ˈraɪnəʊ) *n Brit.* a slang word for **money.** [C17: from ?]

rhino- *or before a vowel* **rhin-** *combining form.* the nose: *rhinology.* [from Gk *rhis, rhin*]

rhinoceros (raɪˈnɒsərəs, -ˈnɒsrəs) *n, pl* **rhinoceroses** *or* **rhinoceros.** any of several mammals constituting a family of SE Asia and Africa and having either one horn on the nose, like the **Indian rhinoceros,** or two horns, like the African **white rhinoceros.** They have a very thick skin and a massive body. [C13: via L from Gk *rhinokerōs,* from *rhis* nose + *keras* horn]
▸**rhinocerotic** (ˌraɪnəʊsɪˈrɒtɪk) *adj*

rhinology (raɪˈnɒlədʒɪ) *n* the branch of medical science concerned with the nose.
▸**rhinological** (ˌraɪnᵊˈlɒdʒɪkᵊl) *adj* ▸**rhiˈnologist** *n*

rhinoplasty (ˈraɪnəʊˌplæstɪ) *n* plastic surgery of the nose.
▸ˌ**rhinoˈplastic** *adj*

rhinoscopy (raɪˈnɒskəpɪ) *n Med.* examination of the nasal passages, esp. with a special instrument called a **rhinoscope** (ˈraɪnəʊˌskəʊp).

rhizo- *or before a vowel* **rhiz-** *combining form.* root: *rhizocarpous.* [from Gk *rhiza*]

rhizocarpous (ˌraɪzəʊˈkɑːpəs) *adj* **1** (of plants) producing subterranean flowers and fruit. **2** (of plants) having perennial roots but stems and leaves that wither.

rhizoid (ˈraɪzɔɪd) *n* any of various hairlike structures that function as roots in mosses, ferns, and fungi.
▸**rhiˈzoidal** *adj*

rhizome (ˈraɪzəʊm) *n* a thick horizontal underground stem whose buds develop into new plants. Also called: **rootstock, rootstalk.** [C19: from NL *rhizoma,* from Gk, from *rhiza* a root]
▸**rhizomatous** (raɪˈzɒmətəs, -ˈzəʊ-) *adj*

rhizopod (ˈraɪzəʊˌpɒd) *n* **1** any of various protozoans characterized by naked protoplasmic processes (pseudopodia). ◆ *adj* **2** of, relating to, or belonging to rhizopods.

rho (rəʊ) *n, pl* **rhos.** the 17th letter in the Greek alphabet (Ρ, ρ).

rhodamine (ˈrəʊdəˌmiːn, -mɪn) *n* any one of a group of synthetic red or pink basic dyestuffs used for wool and silk. [C20: from RHODO- + AMINE]

Rhode Island Red *n* a breed of domestic fowl, originating in America, characterized by a dark reddish-brown plumage and the production of brown eggs.

Rhodesian man *n* a type of early man, occurring in Africa in late Pleistocene times and resembling Neanderthal man.

Rhodes scholarship (rəʊdz) *n* one of 72 scholarships founded by Cecil Rhodes (1853–1902), South African statesman and financier, awarded annually to Commonwealth and US students to study at Oxford University.
▸**Rhodes scholar** *n*

rhodium (ˈrəʊdɪəm) *n* a hard silvery-white element of the platinum metal group. Used as an alloying agent to harden platinum and palladium. Symbol: Rh; atomic no.: 45; atomic wt.: 102.90. [C19: NL, from Gk *rhodon* rose, from the pink colour of its compounds]

rhodo- *or before a vowel* **rhod-** *combining form.* rose or rose-coloured: *rhododendron; rhodolite.* [from Gk *rhodon* rose]

rhodochrosite (ˌrəʊdəʊˈkrəʊsaɪt) *n* a pink, grey, or brown mineral that consists of manganese carbonate in hexagonal crystalline form. Formula: $MnCO_3$. [C19: from Gk *rhodokhrōs,* from *rhodon* rose + *khrōs* colour]

rhododendron (ˌrəʊdəˈdendrən) *n* any of various shrubs native to S Asia but widely cultivated in N temperate regions. They are mostly evergreen and have clusters of showy red, purple, pink, or white flowers. [C17: from L: oleander, from Gk, from *rhodon* rose + *dendron* tree]

rhodolite (ˈrɒdəˌlaɪt) *n* a pale violet or red variety of garnet, used as a gemstone.

rhodonite (ˈrɒdəˌnaɪt) *n* a brownish translucent mineral consisting of manganese silicate in crystalline form with calcium, iron, or magnesium sometimes replacing the manganese. It is used as an ornamental stone, glaze, and pigment. [C19: from G *Rhodonit,* from Gk *rhodon* rose + -ITE[1]]

rhodopsin (rəʊˈdɒpsɪn) *n* a red pigment in the rods of the retina in vertebrates. Also called: **visual purple.** See also **iodopsin.** [C20: from RHODO- + Gk *opsis* sight + -IN]

rhomb (rɒm) *n* another name for **rhombus.**

rhombencephalon (ˌrɒmbenˈsefəˌlɒn) *n* the part of the brain that develops from the posterior portion of the embryonic neural tube. Nontechnical name: **hindbrain.** [C20: from RHOMBUS + ENCEPHALON]

rhombic aerial *n* a directional travelling-wave aerial, usually horizontal, consisting of two conductors forming a rhombus.

rhombohedral (ˌrɒmbəʊˈhiːdrəl) *adj* **1** of or relating to a rhombohedron. **2** *Crystallog.* another term for **trigonal** (sense 2).

rhombohedron (ˌrɒmbəʊˈhiːdrən) *n, pl* **rhombohedrons** *or* **rhombohedra** (-drə). a six-sided prism whose sides are parallelograms. [C19: from RHOMBUS + -HEDRON]

rhomboid (ˈrɒmbɔɪd) *n* **1** a parallelogram having adjacent sides of unequal length. ◆ *adj also* **rhomˈboidal. 2** having such a shape. [C16: from LL, from Gk *rhomboeidēs* shaped like a RHOMBUS]

rhombus (ˈrɒmbəs) *n, pl* **rhombuses** *or* **rhombi** (-baɪ). an oblique-angled parallelogram having four equal sides. Also called: **rhomb.** [C16: from Gk *rhombos* something that spins; rel. to *rhembein* to whirl]
▸ˈ**rhombic** *adj*

rhonchus (ˈrɒŋkəs) *n, pl* **rhonchi** (-kaɪ). a rattling or whistling respiratory sound resembling snoring, caused by secretions in the trachea or bronchi. [C19: from L, from Gk *rhenkhos* snoring]

RHS *abbrev. for:* **1** Royal Historical Society. **2** Royal Horticultural Society. **3** Royal Humane Society.

rhubarb (ˈruːbɑːb) *n* **1** any of several temperate and subtropical plants, esp. **common garden rhubarb,** which has long green and red acid-tasting edible leafstalks, usually eaten sweetened and cooked. **2** the leafstalks of this plant. **3** a related plant of central Asia, having a bitter-tasting underground stem that can be dried and used as a laxative or astringent. **4** *US & Canad. sl.* a heated discussion or quarrel. ◆ *interj, n, vb* **5** the noise made by actors to simulate conversation, esp. by repeating the word *rhubarb.* [C14: from OF *reubarbe,* from Med. L *reubarbum,* prob. var. of *rha barbarum,* from *rha* rhubarb (from Gk, ?from *Rha,* ancient name of the Volga) + L *barbarus* barbarian]

rhumb (rʌm) *n* short for **rhumb line.**

rhumba (ˈrʌmbə, ˈrʊm-) *n, pl* **rhumbas.** a variant spelling of **rumba.**

rhumb line *n* **1** an imaginary line on the surface of a sphere that intersects all meridians at the same angle. **2** the course navigated by a vessel or aircraft that maintains a uniform compass heading. [C16: from OSp. *rumbo,* apparently from MDu. *ruum* space, ship's hold, infl. by RHOMBUS]

rhyme ⓣ *or* (*arch.*) **rime** (raɪm) *n* **1** identity of the terminal sounds in lines of verse or in words. **2** a word that is identical to another in its terminal sound: *"while" is a rhyme for "mile".* **3** a piece of poetry, esp. having corresponding sounds at the ends of the lines. **4 rhyme or reason.** sense, logic, or meaning. ◆ *vb* **rhymes, rhyming, rhymed** *or* **rimes, riming, rimed. 5** to use (a word) or (of a word) to be used so as to form a rhyme. **6** to render (a subject) into rhyme. **7** to compose (verse) in a metrical structure. ◆ See also **eye rhyme.** [C12: from OF *rime,* ult. from OHG *rīm* a number; spelling infl. by RHYTHM]

rhymester, rimester (ˈraɪmstə), **rhymer,** *or* **rimer** *n* a poet, esp. one considered to be mediocre; poetaster or versifier.

THESAURUS

rhetorical *adj* **1** = **high-flown,** arty-farty (*inf.*), bombastic, declamatory, flamboyant, flashy, florid, flowery, grandiloquent, high-sounding, hyperbolic, magniloquent, oratorical, pompous, pretentious, showy, silver-tongued, verbose, windy **2** = **oratorical,** linguistic, stylistic, verbal

rhyme *n* **3** = **poetry,** ode, poem, song, verse **4 rhyme or reason** = **sense,** logic, meaning, method, plan ◆ *vb* **5** = **sound like,** chime, harmonize

rhyming slang *n* slang in which a word is replaced by another word or phrase that rhymes with it; e.g. *apples and pears* meaning *stairs*.

rhyolite ('raɪəˌlaɪt) *n* a fine-grained igneous rock consisting of quartz, feldspars, and mica or amphibole. [C19: *rhyo-* from Gk *rhuax* a stream of lava + -LITE]
▸**rhyolitic** (ˌraɪə'lɪtɪk) *adj*

rhythm ❶ ('rɪðəm) *n* **1a** the arrangement of the durations of and accents on the notes of a melody, usually laid out into regular groups (**bars**) of beats. **1b** any specific arrangement of such groupings; time: *quadruple rhythm.* **2** (in poetry) **2a** the arrangement of words into a sequence of stressed and unstressed or long and short syllables. **2b** any specific such arrangement; metre. **3** (in painting, sculpture, etc.) a harmonious sequence or pattern of masses alternating with voids, of light alternating with shade, of alternating colours, etc. **4** any sequence of regularly recurring functions or events, such as certain physiological functions of the body. [C16: from L *rhythmus,* from Gk *rhuthmos;* rel. to *rhein* to flow]

rhythm and blues *n (functioning as sing)* any of various kinds of popular music derived from or influenced by the blues. Abbrev.: **R & B.**

rhythmic ❶ ('rɪðmɪk) *or* **rhythmical** ('rɪðmɪkᵊl) *adj* of, relating to, or characterized by rhythm, as in movement or sound; metrical, periodic, or regularly recurring.
▸**'rhythmically** *adv* ▸**rhythmicity** (rɪð'mɪsɪtɪ) *n*

rhythm method *n* a method of contraception by restricting sexual intercourse to those days in a woman's menstrual cycle on which conception is considered least likely to occur.

rhythm section *n* those instruments in a band or group (usually piano, double bass, and drums) whose prime function is to supply the rhythm.

RI *abbrev. for:* **1** Regina et Imperatrix. [L: Queen and Empress] **2** Rex et Imperator. [L: King and Emperor] **3** Royal Institution. **4** religious instruction.

ria (rɪə) *n* a long narrow inlet of the seacoast, being a former valley that was submerged by the sea. [C19: from Sp., from *rio* river]

riata *or* **reata** (rɪ'ɑːtə) *n South & West US.* a lariat or lasso. [C19: from American Sp., from Sp. *reatar* to tie together again, from RE- + *atar* to tie, from L *aptāre* to fit]

rib[1] (rɪb) *n* **1** any of the 24 elastic arches of bone that together form the chest wall in man. All are attached behind to the thoracic part of the spinal column. **2** the corresponding bone in other vertebrates. **3** a cut of meat including one or more ribs. **4** a part or element similar in function or appearance to a rib, esp. a structural member or a ridge. **5** a structural member in a wing that extends from the leading edge to the trailing edge. **6** a projecting moulding or band on the underside of a vault or ceiling. **7** one of a series of raised rows in knitted fabric. **8** a raised ornamental line on the spine of a book where the stitching runs across it. **9** any of the transverse stiffening timbers or joists forming the frame of a ship's hull. **10** any of the larger veins of a leaf. **11** a vein of ore in rock. **12** a projecting ridge of a mountain; spur. ◆ *vb* **ribs, ribbing, ribbed.** *(tr)* **13** to furnish or support with a rib or ribs. **14** to mark with or form into ribs or ridges. **15** to knit plain and purl stitches alternately in order to make raised rows in (knitting). [OE *ribb;* rel. to OHG *rippi,* ON *rif* REEF[1]]
▸**'ribless** *adj*

rib[2] (rɪb) *vb* **ribs, ribbing, ribbed.** *(tr) Inf.* to tease or ridicule. [C20: short for *rib-tickle* (vb)]

RIBA *abbrev. for* Royal Institute of British Architects.

ribald ❶ ('rɪbᵊld) *adj* **1** coarse, obscene, or licentious, usually in a humorous or mocking way. ◆ *n* **2** a ribald person. [C13: from OF *ribauld,* from *riber* to live licentiously, of Gmc origin]

ribaldry ❶ ('rɪbᵊldrɪ) *n* ribald language or behaviour.

riband *or* **ribband** ('rɪbənd) *n* a ribbon, esp. one awarded for some achievement. [C14: var. of RIBBON]

ribbing ('rɪbɪŋ) *n* **1** a framework or structure of ribs. **2** a pattern of ribs in woven or knitted material. **3** *Inf.* teasing.

ribbon ('rɪbᵊn) *n* **1** a narrow strip of fine material, esp. silk, used for trimming, tying, etc. **2** something resembling a ribbon; a long strip. **3** a long thin flexible band of metal used as a graduated measure, spring, etc. **4** a long narrow strip of ink-impregnated cloth for making the impression of type characters on paper in a typewriter, etc. **5** *(pl)* ragged strips or shreds (esp. in **torn to ribbons**). **6** a small strip of coloured cloth signifying membership of an order or award of military decoration, prize, etc. **7** a small, usually looped, strip of coloured cloth worn to signify support for a charity or cause: *a red AIDS ribbon.* ◆ *vb (tr)* **8** to adorn with a ribbon or ribbons. **9** to mark with narrow ribbon-like marks. [C14 *ryban,* from OF *riban,* apparently of Gmc origin]

ribbon development *n Brit.* the building of houses in a continuous row along a main road.

ribbonfish ('rɪbᵊnˌfɪʃ) *n, pl* **ribbonfish** *or* **ribbonfishes.** any of various soft-finned deep-sea fishes that have an elongated compressed body.

ribbonwood ('rɪbᵊnˌwʊd) *n* a small evergreen malvaceous tree of New Zealand. Its wood is used in furniture making. Also: **lacebark.**

ribcage ('rɪbˌkeɪdʒ) *n* the bony structure of the ribs and their connective tissue that encloses the lungs, heart, etc.

riboflavin *or* **riboflavine** (ˌraɪbəʊ'fleɪvɪn) *n* a vitamin of the B complex that occurs in green vegetables, milk, fish, egg yolk, liver, and kidney: used as a yellow or orange food colouring (**E 101**). Also called: **vitamin B_2.** [C20: from RIBOSE + FLAVIN]

ribonuclease (ˌraɪbəʊ'njuːklɪˌeɪz) *n* any of a group of enzymes that catalyse the hydrolysis of RNA. [C20: from RIBONUCLE(IC ACID) + -ASE]

ribonucleic acid (ˌraɪbəʊnjuː'kliːɪk, -'kleɪ-) *n* the full name of **RNA.** [C20: from RIBO(SE) + NUCLEIC ACID]

ribose ('raɪbəʊz, -bəʊs) *n* a sugar that occurs in RNA and riboflavin. [C20: changed from *arabinose,* from (GUM) ARAB(IC) + -IN+ -OSE[2]]

ribosomal RNA (ˌraɪbə'səʊməl) *n* a type of RNA thought to form the component of ribosomes on which the translation of messenger RNA into protein chains is accomplished.

ribosome ('raɪbəˌsəʊm) *n* any of numerous minute particles in the cytoplasm of cells that contain RNA and protein and are the site of protein synthesis. [C20: from RIBO(NUCLEIC ACID) + -SOME[3]]
▸**ˌribo'somal** *adj*

rib-tickler *n* a very amusing joke or story.
▸**'rib-ˌtickling** *adj*

ribwort ('rɪbˌwɜːt) *n* a Eurasian plant that has lancelike ribbed leaves. Also called: **ribgrass.** See also **plantain**[1].

rice (raɪs) *n* **1** an erect grass that grows in warm climates on wet ground and has yellow oblong edible grains that become white when polished. **2** the grain of this plant. ◆ *vb* **rices, ricing, riced. 3** *(tr) US & Canad.* to sieve (potatoes or other vegetables) to a coarse mashed consistency. [C13 *rys,* via F, It., & L from Gk *orūza,* of Oriental origin]

rice bowl *n* **1** a small bowl used for eating rice. **2** a fertile rice-producing region.

rice paper *n* **1** a thin edible paper made from the straw of rice, on which macaroons and similar cakes are baked. **2** a thin delicate Chinese paper made from the **rice-paper plant**, the pith of which is pared and flattened into sheets.

ricercare (ˌriːtʃə'kɑːreɪ) *or* **ricercar** ('riːtʃəˌkɑː) *n, pl* **ricercari** (-'kɑːriː) *or* **ricercars.** (in music of the 16th and 17th centuries) **1** an elaborate polyphonic composition making extensive use of contrapuntal imitation and usually very slow in tempo. **2** an instructive composition to illustrate instrumental technique; étude. [It., lit.: to seek again]

rich ❶ (rɪtʃ) *adj* **1a** well supplied with wealth, property, etc.; owning much. **1b** *(as collective n; preceded by the): the rich.* **2** (when *postpositive,* usually foll. by *in*) having an abundance of natural resources, minerals, etc.: *a land rich in metals.* **3** producing abundantly; fertile: *rich soil.* **4** (when *postpositive,* foll. by *in* or *with*) well supplied (with desirable qualities); abundant (in): *a country rich with cultural interest.* **5** of great worth or quality: *a rich collection of antiques.* **6** luxuriant or prolific: *a rich growth of weeds.* **7** expensively elegant, elaborate, or fine; costly: *a rich display.* **8** (of food) having a large proportion of flavoursome or fatty ingredients. **9** having a full-bodied flavour: *a rich ruby port.* **10** (of a smell) pungent or fragrant. **11** (of colour) intense or vivid; deep: *a rich red.* **12** (of sound or a voice) full, mellow, or resonant. **13** (of a fuel-air mixture) containing a relatively high proportion of fuel. **14** very amusing or ridiculous: *a rich joke.* ◆ *n* **15** See **riches.** [OE *rīce* (orig. of persons: great, mighty), of Gmc origin, ult. from Celtic]

riches ❶ ('rɪtʃɪz) *pl n* wealth; an abundance of money, valuable possessions, or property.

richly ❶ ('rɪtʃlɪ) *adv* **1** in a rich or elaborate manner: *a richly decorated carving.* **2** fully and appropriately: *he was richly rewarded.*

THESAURUS

rhythm *n* **1, 2** = **beat**, accent, cadence, flow, lilt, measure (*Prosody*), metre, movement, pattern, periodicity, pulse, swing, tempo, time

rhythmic *adj* = **cadenced**, flowing, harmonious, lilting, melodious, metrical, musical, periodic, pulsating, throbbing

ribald *adj* **1** = **coarse**, bawdy, blue, broad, earthy, filthy, gross, indecent, licentious, naughty, near the knuckle (*inf.*), obscene, off colour, Rabelaisian, racy, raunchy (*sl.*), risqué, rude, scurrilous, smutty, vulgar, X-rated (*inf.*)
Antonyms *adj* chaste, decent, decorous, genteel, inoffensive, polite, proper, refined, tasteful

ribaldry *n* = **coarseness**, bawdiness, billingsgate, earthiness, filth, grossness, indecency, licentiousness, naughtiness, obscenity, raciness, rudeness, scurrility, smut, smuttiness, vulgarity

rich *adj* **1** = **wealthy**, affluent, filthy rich, flush, loaded (*sl.*), made of money (*inf.*), moneyed, opulent, propertied, prosperous, rolling (*sl.*), stinking rich (*inf.*), well-heeled (*inf.*), well-off, well-to-do **2** = **well-stocked**, abounding, full, productive, well-endowed, well-provided, well-supplied **3, 6** = **fruitful**, abounding, abundant, ample, copious, exuberant, fecund, fertile, full, lush, luxurious, plenteous, plentiful, productive, prolific **5, 7** = **costly**, beyond price, elaborate, elegant, expensive, exquisite, fine, gorgeous, lavish, palatial, precious, priceless, splendid, sumptuous, superb, valuable **8, 9** = **full-bodied**, creamy, delicious, fatty, flavoursome, heavy, highly-flavoured, juicy, luscious, savoury, spicy, succulent, sweet, tasty **11** = **vivid**, bright, deep, gay, intense, strong, vibrant, warm **12** = **resonant**, deep, dulcet, full, mellifluous, mellow **14** = **funny**, amusing, comical, hilarious, humorous, laughable, ludicrous, ridiculous, risible, side-splitting
Antonyms *adj* ≠ **wealthy:** destitute, impoverished, needy, penniless, poor ≠ **well-stocked:** lacking, poor, scarce, wanting ≠ **fruitful:** barren, poor, unfertile, unfruitful, unproductive ≠ **costly:** cheap, cheapo (*inf.*), inexpensive, valueless, worthless ≠ **full-bodied:** bland, dull ≠ **vivid:** dull, insipid, weak ≠ **resonant:** high-pitched

riches *pl n* = **wealth**, abundance, affluence, assets, fortune, gold, money, opulence, plenty, property, resources, richness, substance, treasure
Antonyms *pl n* dearth, indigence, lack, need, paucity, poverty, scantiness, scarcity, want

richly *adv* **1** = **elaborately**, elegantly, expensively, exquisitely, gorgeously, lavishly, luxuriously, opulently, palatially, splendidly,

richness (ˈrɪtʃnɪs) *n* **1** the state or quality of being rich. **2** *Ecology.* the number of individuals of a species in a given area.

Richter scale (ˈrɪxtə) *n* a scale for expressing the magnitude of an earthquake, ranging from 0 to over 8. [C20: after Charles *Richter* (1900–85), US seismologist]

rick[1] (rɪk) *n* **1** a large stack of hay, corn, etc., built in a regular-shaped pile, esp. with a thatched top. ◆ *vb* **2** (*tr*) to stack into ricks. [OE *hrēac*]

rick[2] (rɪk) *n* **1** a wrench or sprain, as of the back. ◆ *vb* **2** (*tr*) to wrench or sprain (a joint, a limb, the back, etc.). [C18: var. of *wrick*]

rickets (ˈrɪkɪts) *n* (*functioning as sing or pl*) a disease mainly of children, characterized by softening of developing bone, and hence bow legs, caused by a deficiency of vitamin D. [C17: from ?]

rickettsia (rɪˈkɛtsɪə) *n, pl* **rickettsiae** (-sɪˌiː) *or* **rickettsias.** any of a group of parasitic microorganisms, that live in the tissues of ticks, mites, etc., and cause disease when transmitted to man. [C20: after Howard T. *Ricketts* (1871–1910), US pathologist]
▸**rickˈettsial** *adj*

rickettsial disease *n* any of several acute infectious diseases, such as typhus, caused by ticks, mites, or body lice infected with rickettsiae.

rickety Ⓣ (ˈrɪkɪtɪ) *adj* **1** (of a structure, piece of furniture, etc.) likely to collapse or break. **2** feeble. **3** resembling or afflicted with rickets. [C17: from RICKETS]
▸**ˈricketiness** *n*

rickrack *or* **ricrac** (ˈrɪkˌræk) *n* a zigzag braid used for trimming. [C20: reduplication of RACK[1]]

rickshaw (ˈrɪkʃɔː) *or* **ricksha** (ˈrɪkʃə) *n* **1** Also called: **jinrikisha.** a small two-wheeled passenger vehicle drawn by one or two men, used in parts of Asia. **2** Also called: **trishaw.** a similar vehicle with three wheels, propelled by a man pedalling as on a tricycle. [C19: shortened from JINRIKISHA]

ricochet (ˈrɪkəˌʃeɪ, ˈrɪkəˌʃɛt) *vb* **ricochets** (-ˌʃeɪz), **ricocheting** (-ˌʃeɪɪŋ), **ricocheted** (-ˌʃeɪd) *or* **ricochets** (-ˌʃɛtz), **ricochetting** (-ˌʃɛtɪŋ), **ricochetted** (-ˌʃɛtɪd). **1** (*intr*) (esp. of a bullet) to rebound from a surface, usually with a whining or zipping sound. ◆ *n* **2** the motion or sound of a rebounding object, esp. a bullet. **3** an object that ricochets. [C18: from F]

ricotta (rɪˈkɒtə) *n* a soft white unsalted cheese made from sheep's milk. [It., from L *recocta* recooked, from *recoquere*, from RE- + *coquere* to COOK]

RICS *abbrev. for* Royal Institution of Chartered Surveyors.

rictus (ˈrɪktəs) *n, pl* **rictus** *or* **rictuses. 1.** the gap or cleft of an open mouth or beak. **2** a fixed or unnatural grin or grimace as in horror or death. [C18: from L, from *ringī* to gape]
▸**ˈrictal** *adj*

rid Ⓣ (rɪd) *vb* **rids, ridding, rid** *or* **ridded.** (*tr*) **1** (foll. by *of*) to relieve from something disagreeable or undesirable; make free (of). **2 get rid of.** to relieve or free oneself of (something unpleasant or undesirable). [C13 (meaning: to clear land): from ON *rythja*]

riddance (ˈrɪdᵊns) *n* the act of getting rid of something; removal (esp. in **good riddance**).

ridden (ˈrɪdᵊn) *vb* **1** the past participle of **ride.** ◆ *adj* **2** (*in combination*) afflicted or dominated by something specified: *disease-ridden.*

riddle[1] Ⓣ (ˈrɪdᵊl) *n* **1** a question, puzzle, or verse so phrased that ingenuity is required for elucidation of the answer or meaning. **2** a person or thing that puzzles, perplexes, or confuses. ◆ *vb* **riddles, riddling, riddled. 3** to solve, explain, or interpret (a riddle). **4** (*intr*) to speak in riddles. [OE *rǣdelle, rǣdelse*, from *rǣd* counsel]
▸**ˈriddler** *n*

riddle[2] Ⓣ (ˈrɪdᵊl) *vb* **riddles, riddling, riddled.** (*tr*) **1** (usually foll. by *with*) to pierce or perforate with numerous holes: *riddled with bullets.* **2** to put through a sieve; sift. ◆ *n* **3** a sieve, esp. a coarse one used for sand, grain, etc. [OE *hriddel* a sieve]
▸**ˈriddler** *n*

ride Ⓣ (raɪd) *vb* **rides, riding, rode, ridden. 1** to sit on and control the movements of (a horse or other animal). **2** (*tr*) to sit on and propel (a bicycle or similar vehicle). **3** (*intr; often foll. by on* or *in*) to be carried along or travel on or in a vehicle: *she rides to work on the bus.* **4** (*tr*) to travel over or traverse: *they rode the countryside in search of shelter.* **5** (*tr*) to take part in by riding: *to ride a race.* **6** to travel through or be carried across (sea, sky, etc.): *the small boat rode the waves; the moon was riding high.* **7** (*tr*) *US & Canad.* to cause to be carried: *to ride someone out of town.* **8** (*intr*) to be supported as if floating: *the candidate rode to victory on his new policies.* **9** (*intr*) (of a vessel) to lie at anchor. **10** (*tr*) (of a vessel) to be attached to (an anchor). **11** (*tr*) **11a** *Sl.* to have sexual intercourse with (someone). **11b** (of a male animal) to copulate with; mount. **12** (*tr; usually passive*) to tyrannize over or dominate: *ridden by fear.* **13** (*tr*) *Inf.* to persecute, esp. by constant or petty criticism: *don't ride me so hard.* **14** (*intr*) *Inf.* to continue undisturbed: *let it ride.* **15** (*tr*) to endure successfully; ride out. **16** (*tr*) to yield slightly to (a punch, etc.) to lessen its impact. **17** (*intr; often foll. by on*) (of a bet) to remain placed: *let your winnings ride on the same number.* **18 ride again.** *Inf.* to return to a former activity or scene. **19 ride for a fall.** to act in such a way as to invite disaster. **20 riding high.** confident, popular, and successful. ◆ *n* **21** a journey or outing on horseback or in a vehicle. **22** a path specially made for riding on horseback. **23** transport in a vehicle; lift: *can you give me a ride to the station?* **24** a device or structure, such as a roller coaster at a fairground, in which people ride for pleasure or entertainment. **25** *Sl.* an act of sexual intercourse. **26** *Sl.* a partner in sexual intercourse. **27 take for a ride.** *Inf.* **27a** to cheat, swindle, or deceive. **27b** to take (someone) away in a car and murder him. [OE *rīdan*]
▸**ˈridable** *or* **ˈrideable** *adj*

ride out *vb* (*tr, adv*) to endure successfully; survive (esp. in **ride out the storm**).

rider (ˈraɪdə) *n* **1** a person or thing that rides. **2** an additional clause, amendment, or stipulation added to a document, esp. (in Britain) a legislative bill at its third reading. **3** *Brit.* a statement made by a jury in addition to its verdict, such as a recommendation for mercy. **4** any of various objects or devices resting on or strengthening something else.
▸**ˈriderless** *adj*

ride up *vb* (*intr, adv*) to work away from the proper position: *her new skirt rode up.*

ridge (rɪdʒ) *n* **1** a long narrow raised land formation with sloping sides. **2** any long narrow raised strip or elevation, as on a fabric or in ploughed land. **3** *Anat.* any elongated raised margin or border on a bone, tissue, etc. **4a** the top of a roof at the junction of two sloping sides. **4b** (*as modifier*): *a ridge tile.* **5** *Meteorol.* an elongated area of high pressure, esp. an extension of an anticyclone. Cf. **trough** (sense 4). ◆ *vb* **ridges, ridging, ridged. 6** to form into a ridge or ridges. [OE *hrycg*]
▸**ˈridgeˌlike** *adj* ▸**ˈridgy** *adj*

ridgepole (ˈrɪdʒˌpəʊl) *n* **1** a timber along the ridge of a roof, to which the rafters are attached. **2** the horizontal pole at the apex of a tent.

ridgeway (ˈrɪdʒˌweɪ) *n Brit.* a road or track along a ridge, esp. one of great antiquity.

ridicule Ⓣ (ˈrɪdɪˌkjuːl) *n* **1** language or behaviour intended to humiliate or mock. ◆ *vb* **ridicules, ridiculing, ridiculed. 2** (*tr*) to make fun of or mock. [C17: from F, from L *rīdiculus*, from *rīdēre* to laugh]

ridiculous Ⓣ (rɪˈdɪkjʊləs) *adj* worthy of or exciting ridicule; absurd, preposterous, laughable, or contemptible. [C16: from L *rīdiculōsus*, from *rīdēre* to laugh]
▸**riˈdiculousness** *n*

riding[1] (ˈraɪdɪŋ) *n* **1a** the art or practice of horsemanship. **1b** (*as modifier*): *a riding school.* **2** a track for riding.

riding[2] (ˈraɪdɪŋ) *n* (*cap. when part of a name*) any of the three former administrative divisions of Yorkshire: **North Riding, East Riding,** and **West Riding.** [from OE *thriding*, from ON *thrithjungr* a third]

riding crop *n* a short whip with a handle at one end for opening gates.

riding lamp *or* **light** *n* a light on a boat or ship showing that it is at anchor.

riempie (ˈrɪmpɪ) *n S. African.* a leather thong or lace used mainly to make chair seats. [C19: Afrik., dim. of *riem*, from Du.: RIM]

riesling (ˈriːzlɪŋ, ˈraɪz-) *n* **1** a white wine from the Rhine valley in Germany and from certain districts in other countries. **2** the grape used to make this wine. [C19: from G, from earlier *Rüssling*, from ?]

rife Ⓣ (raɪf) *adj* (*postpositive*) **1** of widespread occurrence; current. **2** very plentiful; abundant. **3** (foll. by *with*) abounding (in): *a garden rife with weeds.* [OE *rīfe*]
▸**ˈrifely** *adv* ▸**ˈrifeness** *n*

riff (rɪf) *Jazz, rock.* ◆ *n* **1** an ostinato played over changing harmonies. ◆ *vb* **2** (*intr*) to play riffs. [C20: prob. altered from REFRAIN[2]]

riffle (ˈrɪfᵊl) *vb* **riffles, riffling, riffled. 1** (when *intr*, often foll. by *through*) to flick rapidly through (pages of a book, etc.). **2** to shuffle (cards) by

THESAURUS

sumptuously **2** = **fully**, amply, appropriately, in full measure, properly, suitably, thoroughly, well

rickety *adj* **1** = **shaky**, broken, broken-down, decrepit, derelict, dilapidated, imperfect, infirm, insecure, jerry-built, precarious, ramshackle, tottering, unsound, unsteady, wobbly **2** = **feeble**, flimsy, frail, weak

rid *vb* **1** = **free**, clear, deliver, disabuse, disburden, disembarrass, disencumber, lighten, make free, purge, relieve, unburden **2 get rid of** = **dispose of**, dispense with, do away with, dump, eject, eliminate, expel, give the bum's rush (*sl.*), jettison, remove, see the back of, shake off, throw away *or* out, unload, weed out, wipe from the face of the earth

riddle[1] *n* **1** = **puzzle**, brain-teaser (*inf.*), Chinese puzzle, conundrum, enigma, mystery, poser, problem, rebus, teaser

riddle[2] *vb* **1** = **pierce**, honeycomb, pepper, perforate, puncture **2** = **sieve**, bolt, filter, screen, sift, strain, winnow ◆ *n* **3** = **sieve**, filter, screen, strainer

riddled *adj* **1** = **filled**, corrupted, damaged, impaired, infested, marred, permeated, pervaded, spoilt

ride *vb* **1, 2** = **control**, handle, manage, sit on **3** = **travel**, be borne, be carried, be supported, float, go, journey, move, progress, sit **12** = **dominate**, enslave, grip, haunt, oppress, tyrannize over ◆ *n* **21** = **journey**, drive, jaunt, lift, outing, spin (*inf.*), trip, whirl (*inf.*)

ridicule *n* **1** = **mockery**, banter, chaff, derision, gibe, irony, jeer, laughter, raillery, rib, sarcasm, satire, scorn, sneer, taunting ◆ *vb* **2** = **laugh at**, banter, caricature, chaff, deride, humiliate, jeer, lampoon, laugh out of court, laugh to scorn, make a fool of, make a monkey out of, make fun of, make one a laughing stock, mock, parody, poke fun at, pooh-pooh, satirize, scoff, send up (*Brit. inf.*), sneer, take the mickey out of (*inf.*), taunt

ridiculous *adj* = **laughable**, absurd, comical, contemptible, derisory, farcical, foolish, funny, hilarious, inane, incredible, ludicrous, nonsensical, outrageous, preposterous, risible, silly, stupid, unbelievable, zany
Antonyms *adj* bright, clever, intelligent, logical, prudent, rational, reasonable, sagacious, sane, sensible, serious, smart, solemn, well-thought-out, wise

rife *adj* **1** = **widespread**, common, current, epidemic, frequent, general, prevailing, prevalent, raging, ubiquitous, universal **2** = **abundant**, plentiful, rampant, teeming halving the pack and flicking the corners together. **3** to cause or form a ripple on water. ◆ *n* **4** *US & Canad.* **4a** a rapid in a stream. **4b** a rocky shoal causing a rapid. **4c** a ripple on water. **5** *Mining.* a contrivance on the bottom of a sluice, containing grooves for trapping particles of gold. **6** the act or an instance of riffling. [C18: prob. from RUFFLE[1], infl. by RIPPLE[1]]

riffraff Ⓣ ('rɪfˌræf) *n* (*sometimes functioning as pl*) worthless people, esp. collectively; rabble. [C15 *rif and raf*, from OF *rif et raf*; rel. to *rifler* to plunder, and *rafle* a sweeping up]

rifle[1] ('raɪfəl) *n* **1a** a firearm having a long barrel with a spirally grooved interior, which imparts to the bullet spinning motion and thus greater accuracy over a longer range. **1b** (*as modifier*): *rifle fire.* **2** (formerly) a large cannon with a rifled bore. **3** one of the grooves in a rifled bore. **4** (*pl*) **4a** a unit of soldiers equipped with rifles. **4b** (*cap. when part of a name*): *the King's Own Rifles.* ◆ *vb* **rifles, rifling, rifled.** (*tr*) **5** to make spiral grooves inside the barrel of (a gun). [C18: from OF *rifler* to scratch; rel. to Low G *rifeln* from *riefe* groove]

rifle[2] Ⓣ ('raɪfəl) *vb* **rifles, rifling, rifled.** (*tr*) **1** to search (a house, safe, etc.) and steal from it; ransack. **2** to steal and carry off: *to rifle goods.* [C14: from OF *rifler* to plunder, scratch, of Gmc origin]
►'**rifler** *n*

riflebird ('raɪfəlˌbɜːd) *n* any of various Australian birds of paradise whose plumage has a metallic sheen.

rifleman ('raɪfəlmən) *n, pl* **riflemen. 1** a person skilled in the use of a rifle, esp. a soldier. **2** a wren of New Zealand.

rifle range *n* an area used for target practice with rifles.

rifling ('raɪflɪŋ) *n* **1** the cutting of spiral grooves on the inside of a firearm's barrel. **2** the series of grooves so cut.

rift Ⓣ (rɪft) *n* **1** a gap or space made by cleaving or splitting. **2** *Geol.* a fault produced by tension on either side of the fault plane. **3** a gap between two cloud masses; break or chink. **4** a break in friendly relations between people, nations, etc. ◆ *vb* **5** to burst or cause to burst open; split. [C13: from ON]

rift valley *n* a long narrow valley resulting from the subsidence of land between two faults.

rig Ⓣ (rɪg) *vb* **rigs, rigging, rigged.** (*tr*) **1** *Naut.* to equip (a vessel, mast, etc.) with (sails, rigging, etc.). **2** *Naut.* to set up or prepare ready for use. **3** to put the components of (an aircraft, etc.) into their correct positions. **4** to manipulate in a fraudulent manner, esp. for profit: *to rig prices.* ◆ *n* **5** *Naut.* the distinctive arrangement of the sails, masts, etc., of a vessel. **6** the installation used in drilling for and exploiting natural gas and oil deposits: *an oil rig.* **7** apparatus or equipment. **8** *US & Canad.* an articulated lorry. ◆ See also **rig out, rig up.** [C15: of Scand. origin; rel. to Norwegian *rigga* to wrap]

rigadoon (ˌrɪgəˈduːn) *n* **1** an old Provençal couple dance, light and graceful, in lively duple time. **2** a piece of music composed for or in the rhythm of this dance. [C17: from F, allegedly after *Rigaud*, a dancing master at Marseilles]

rigamarole ('rɪgəməˌrəʊl) *n* a variant of **rigmarole.**

-rigged *adj* (*in combination*) (of a sailing vessel) having a rig of a certain kind: *ketch-rigged; schooner-rigged.*

rigger ('rɪgə) *n* **1** a workman who rigs vessels, etc. **2** *Rowing.* a bracket on a boat to support a projecting rowlock. **3** a person skilled in the use of pulleys, cranes, etc.

rigging ('rɪgɪŋ) *n* **1** the shrouds, stays, etc., of a vessel. **2** the bracing wires, struts, and lines of a biplane, etc. **3** any form of lifting gear.

right Ⓣ (raɪt) *adj* **1** in accordance with accepted standards of moral or legal behaviour, justice, etc.: *right conduct.* **2** correct or true: *the right answer.* **3** appropriate, suitable, or proper: *the right man for the job.* **4** most favourable or convenient: *the right time to act.* **5** in a satisfactory condition: *things are right again now.* **6** indicating or designating the correct time: *the clock is right.* **7** correct in opinion or judgment. **8** sound in mind or body. **9** (*usually prenominal*) of, designating, or located near the side of something or someone that faces east when the front is turned towards the north. **10** (*usually prenominal*) worn on a right hand, foot, etc. **11** (*sometimes cap.*) of, designating, belonging to, or relating to the political or intellectual right (see sense 36). **12** (*sometimes cap.*) conservative: *the right wing of the party.* **13** *Geom.* **13a** formed by or containing a line or plane perpendicular to another line or plane. **13b** having the axis perpendicular to the base: *a right circular cone.* **13c** straight: *a right line.* **14** relating to or designating the side of cloth worn or facing outwards. **15 in one's right mind.** sane. **16 she'll be right.** *Austral. & NZ inf.* that's all right; not to worry. **17 the right side of. 17a** in favour with: *you'd better stay on the right side of him.* **17b** younger than: *she's still on the right side of fifty.* **18 too right.** *Austral. & NZ inf.* an exclamation of agreement. ◆ *adv* **19** in accordance with correctness or truth: *to guess right.* **20** in the appropriate manner: *do it right next time!* **21** in a straight line: *right to the top.* **22** in the direction of the east from the point of view of a person or thing facing north. **23** absolutely or completely: *he went right through the floor.* **24** all the way: *the bus goes right into town.* **25** without delay: *I'll be right over.* **26** exactly or precisely: *right here.* **27** in a manner consistent with a legal or moral code: *do right by me.* **28** in accordance with propriety; fittingly: *it serves you right.* **29** to good or favourable advantage: *it all came out right in the end.* **30** (esp. in religious titles) most or very: *right reverend.* **31 right, left, and centre.** on all sides. ◆ *n* **32** any claim, title, etc., that is morally just or legally granted as allowable or due to a person: *I know my rights.* **33** anything that accords with the principles of legal or moral justice. **34** the fact or state of being in accordance with reason, truth, or accepted standards (esp. in **in the right**) **35** the right side, direction, position, area, or part: *the right of the army.* **36** (*often cap.* and preceded by *the*) the supporters or advocates of social, political, or economic conservatism or reaction. **37** *Boxing.* **37a** a punch with the right hand. **37b** the right hand. **38** (*often pl*) *Finance.* the privilege of a company's shareholders to subscribe for new issues of the company's shares on advantageous terms. **39 by right** (*or* **rights**). properly: *by rights you should be in bed.* **40 in one's own right.** having a claim or title oneself rather than through marriage or other connection. **41 to rights.** consistent with justice or orderly arrangement: *he put the matter to rights.* ◆ *vb* (*mainly tr*) **42** (*also intr*) to restore to or attain a normal, esp. an upright, position: *the raft righted in a few seconds.* **43** to make (something) accord with truth or facts. **44** to restore to an orderly state or condition. **45** to compensate for or redress (esp. in **right a wrong**). ◆ *interj* **46** an expression of agreement or compliance. [OE *riht, reoht*]
►'**rightable** *adj* ►'**righter** *n* ►'**rightness** *n*

right about *n* **1** a turn executed through 180°. ◆ *adj, adv* **2** in the opposite direction.

right angle *n* **1** the angle between radii of a circle that cut off on the circumference an arc equal in length to one quarter of the circumference; an angle of 90° or $\pi/2$ radians. **2 at right angles.** perpendicular or perpendicularly.
►'**right-ˌangled** *adj*

right-angled triangle *n* a triangle one angle of which is a right angle. US and Canad. name: **right triangle.**

right ascension *n Astron.* the angular distance measured eastwards along the celestial equator from the vernal equinox to the point at which the celestial equator intersects a great circle passing through the celestial pole and the heavenly object in question.

right away Ⓣ *adv* without delay.

righteous Ⓣ ('raɪtʃəs) *adj* **1a** characterized by, proceeding from, or in accordance with accepted standards of morality or uprightness: *a righteous man.* **1b** (*as collective n;* preceded by *the*): *the righteous.* **2** mor-

THESAURUS

riffraff *n* = **rabble**, *canaille*, dregs of society, hoi polloi, ragtag and bobtail, scum, undesirables

rifle[2] *vb* **1** = **ransack**, burgle, despoil, go through, gut, loot, pillage, plunder, rob, rummage, sack, strip

rift *n* **1** = **split**, breach, break, chink, cleavage, cleft, crack, cranny, crevice, fault, fissure, flaw, fracture, gap, opening, space **4** = **breach**, alienation, difference, disagreement, division, estrangement, falling out (*inf.*), quarrel, schism, separation, split

rig *vb* **1** *Nautical* = **equip**, accoutre, fit out, furnish, kit out, outfit, provision, supply, turn out **4** = **fix** (*inf.*), arrange, doctor, engineer, fake, falsify, fiddle with (*inf.*), gerrymander, juggle, manipulate, tamper with, trump up ◆ *n* **7** = **apparatus**, accoutrements, equipage, equipment, fitments, fittings, fixtures, gear, machinery, outfit, tackle

right *adj* **1** = **just**, equitable, ethical, fair, good, honest, honourable, lawful, moral, proper, righteous, true, upright, virtuous **2** = **correct**, accurate, admissible, authentic, exact, factual, genuine, on the money (*US*), precise, satisfactory, sound, spot-on (*Brit. inf.*), true, unerring, valid, veracious **3** = **proper**, appropriate, becoming, *comme il faut*, desirable, done, fit, fitting, seemly, suitable **4** = **favourable**, advantageous, convenient, deserved, due, ideal, opportune, propitious, rightful **8** = **healthy**, all there (*inf.*), balanced, *compos mentis*, fine, fit, in good health, in the pink, lucid, normal, rational, reasonable, sane, sound, unimpaired, up to par, well **11, 12** = **conservative**, reactionary, Tory ◆ *adv* **19** = **correctly**, accurately, aright, exactly, factually, genuinely, precisely, truly **20** = **suitably**, appropriately, aptly, befittingly, fittingly, properly, satisfactorily **23** = **completely**, absolutely, altogether, entirely, perfectly, quite, thoroughly, totally, utterly, wholly **25** = **straight**, directly, immediately, instantly, promptly, quickly, straightaway, without delay **26** = **exactly**, bang, precisely, slap-bang (*inf.*), squarely **27** = **fairly**, ethically, honestly, honourably, justly, morally, righteously, virtuously **28** = **properly**, fittingly **29** = **favourably**, advantageously, beneficially, for the better, fortunately, to advantage, well ◆ *n* **32** = **prerogative**, authority, business, claim, due, freedom, interest, liberty, licence, permission, power, privilege, title **33, 34** = **justice**, equity, fairness, good, goodness, honour, integrity, lawfulness, legality, morality, propriety, reason, rectitude, righteousness, truth, uprightness, virtue **39 by right** *or* **rights** = **in fairness**, equitably, justly, properly **41 to rights** = **in order**, arranged, straight, tidy ◆ *vb* **45** = **rectify**, compensate for, correct, fix, put right, redress, repair, settle, sort out, straighten, vindicate
Antonyms *adj* ≠ **just**: bad, dishonest, immoral, improper, indecent, unethical, unfair, unjust, wrong ≠ **correct**: counterfeit, erroneous, fake, false, fraudulent, illegal, illicit, inaccurate, incorrect, inexact, invalid, mistaken, questionable, uncertain, unlawful, untruthful, wrong ≠ **proper**: inappropriate, undesirable, unfitting, unseemly, unsuitable, wrong ≠ **favourable**: disadvantageous, inconvenient, unfavourable ≠ **healthy**: abnormal, unsound ≠ **conservative**: left, leftist, left-wing, liberal, radical, right-on (*inf.*), socialist ◆ *adv* ≠ **correctly**: inaccurately, incorrectly ≠ **completely**: improperly, incompletely ≠ **straight**: indirectly, slowly ≠ **favourably**: badly, poorly, unfavourably ◆ *n* ≠ **justice**: badness, dishonour, evil, immorality, impropriety

right away *adv* = **immediately**, at once, directly, forthwith, instantly, now, posthaste, promptly, pronto (*inf.*), right off, straightaway, straight off (*inf.*), this instant, without delay, without hesitation

righteous *adj* **1** = **virtuous**, blameless, equitable, ethical, fair, good, honest, honourable,

ally justifiable or right: *righteous indignation.* [OE *rihtwīs,* from RIGHT + WISE²]
▸'**righteously** *adv* ▸'**righteousness** *n*

rightful ⓣ ('raɪtful) *adj* **1** in accordance with what is right. **2** (*prenominal*) having a legally or morally just claim: *the rightful owner.* **3** (*prenominal*) held by virtue of a legal or just claim: *my rightful property.*
▸'**rightfully** *adv*

right-hand *adj* (*prenominal*) **1** of, located on, or moving towards the right: *a right-hand bend.* **2** for use by the right hand. **3 right-hand man.** one's most valuable assistant.

right-handed *adj* **1** using the right hand with greater skill or ease than the left. **2** performed with the right hand. **3** made for use by the right hand. **4** turning from left to right.
▸ˌ**right-'handedness** *n*

rightist ('raɪtɪst) *adj* **1** of, tending towards, or relating to the political right or its principles. ◆ *n* **2** a person who supports or belongs to the political right.
▸'**rightism** *n*

rightly ('raɪtlɪ) *adv* **1** in accordance with the true facts. **2** in accordance with principles of justice or morality. **3** with good reason: *he was rightly annoyed with her.* **4** properly or suitably. **5** (*used with a negative*) *Inf.* with certainty (usually in **I don't rightly know**).

right-minded *adj* holding opinions or principles that accord with what is right or with the opinions of the speaker.

righto *or* **right oh** ('raɪt'əʊ) *sentence substitute. Brit. inf.* an expression of agreement or compliance.

right off *adv* immediately; right away.

right of way *n, pl* **rights of way. 1** the right of one vehicle or vessel to take precedence over another, as laid down by law or custom. **2a** the legal right of someone to pass over another's land, acquired by grant or by long usage. **2b** the path used by this right. **3** *US.* the strip of land over which a power line, road, etc., extends.

right-on *adj Inf.* modern, trendy, and socially aware or relevant: *right-on green politics.*

Right Reverend *adj* (in Britain) a title of respect for an Anglican or Roman Catholic bishop.

rights issue *n Stock Exchange.* an issue of new shares offered by a company to its existing shareholders on favourable terms.

rightsize ('raɪtˌsaɪz) *vb* to restructure (an organization) to cut costs and improve effectiveness without ruthlessly downsizing.

right-thinking ('raɪtˌθɪŋkɪŋ) *adj* possessing reasonable and generally acceptable opinions.

rightward ('raɪtwəd) *adj* **1** situated on or directed towards the right. ◆ *adv* **2** a variant of **rightwards.**

rightwards ('raɪtwədz) *or* **rightward** *adv* towards or on the right.

right whale *n* a large whalebone whale which is grey or black, has a large head and no dorsal fin, and is hunted as a source of whalebone and oil. See also **bowhead.** [C19: ? because it was *right* for hunting]

right wing *n* **1** (*often cap.*) the conservative faction of an assembly, party, etc. **2** the part of an army or field of battle on the right from the point of view of one facing the enemy. **3a** the right-hand side of the field of play from the point of view of a team facing its opponent's goal. **3b** a player positioned in this area in any of various games. ◆ *adj* **right-wing. 4** of, belonging to, or relating to the right wing.
▸'**right-'winger** *n*

rigid ⓣ ('rɪdʒɪd) *adj* **1** physically inflexible or stiff: *a rigid piece of plastic.* **2** rigorously strict: *rigid rules.* [C16: from L *rigidus,* from *rigēre* to be stiff]
▸**ri'gidity** *n* ▸'**rigidly** *adv*

rigidify (rɪ'dʒɪdɪˌfaɪ) *vb* **rigidifies, rigidifying, rigidified.** to make or become rigid.

rigmarole ⓣ ('rɪgməˌrəʊl) *or* **rigamarole** *n* **1** any long complicated procedure. **2** a set of incoherent or pointless statements. [C18: from earlier *ragman roll* a list, prob. a roll used in a medieval game, wherein characters were described in verse, beginning with *Ragemon le bon* Ragman the good]

rigor ('raɪgɔː, 'rɪgə) *n* **1** *Med.* a sudden feeling of chilliness, often accompanied by shivering: it sometimes precedes a fever. **2** ('rɪgə). *Pathol.* rigidity of a muscle. **3** a state of rigidity assumed in reaction to shock. [see RIGOUR]

rigor mortis ('rɪgə 'mɔːtɪs) *n Pathol.* the stiffness of joints and muscular rigidity of a dead body. [C19: L, lit.: rigidity of death]

rigorous ⓣ ('rɪgərəs) *adj* **1** harsh, strict, or severe: *rigorous discipline.* **2** severely accurate: *rigorous book-keeping.* **3** (esp. of weather) extreme or harsh. **4** *Maths, logic.* (of a proof) making the validity of each step explicit.
▸'**rigorously** *adv*

rigour ⓣ *or US* **rigor** ('rɪgə) *n* **1** harsh but just treatment or action. **2** a severe or cruel circumstance: *the rigours of famine.* **3** strictness, harshness, or severity of character. **4** strictness in judgment or conduct. [C14: from L *rigor*]

rig out ⓣ *vb* **1** (*tr, adv;* often foll. by *with*) to equip or fit out (with): *his car is rigged out with gadgets.* **2** to dress or be dressed: *rigged out smartly.* ◆ *n* **rigout. 3** *Inf.* a person's clothing or costume, esp. a bizarre outfit.

rig up ⓣ *vb* (*tr, adv*) to erect or construct, esp. as a temporary measure: *cameras were rigged up.*

Rig-Veda (rɪg'veɪdə) *n* a compilation of Hindu poems dating from 2000 B.C. or earlier. [C18: from Sansk. *rigveda,* from *ric* song of praise + VEDA]

rile ⓣ (raɪl) *vb* **riles, riling, riled.** (*tr*) **1** to annoy or anger. **2** *US & Canad.* to agitate (water, etc.). [C19: var. of ROIL]

rill (rɪl) *n* **1** a brook or stream. **2** a channel or gulley, such as one formed during soil erosion. **3** Also: **rille.** one of many winding cracks on the moon. [C15: from Low G *rille*]

rim ⓣ (rɪm) *n* **1** the raised edge of an object, esp. of something more or less circular such as a cup or crater. **2** the peripheral part of a wheel, to which the tyre is attached. **3** *Basketball.* the hoop from which the net is suspended. ◆ *vb* **rims, rimming, rimmed.** (*tr*) **4** to put a rim on (a pot, cup, wheel, etc.). **5** *Sl.* to lick, kiss, or suck the anus of (one's sexual partner). [OE *rima*]

rime¹ (raɪm) *n* **1** frost formed by the freezing of water droplets in fog onto solid objects. ◆ *vb* **rimes, riming, rimed. 2** (*tr*) to cover with rime or something resembling rime. [OE *hrīm*]

rime² (raɪm) *n, vb* **rimes, riming, rimed.** an archaic spelling of **rhyme.**

rim-fire *adj* **1** (of a cartridge) having the primer in the rim of the base. **2** (of a firearm) adapted for such cartridges.

rimose (raɪ'məʊs, -'məʊz) *adj* (esp. of plant parts) having the surface marked by a network of cracks. [C18: from L *rīmōsus,* from *rīma* a split]

rimu ('riːmuː) *n* a New Zealand tree. Also called: **red pine.** [from Maori]

rimy ('raɪmɪ) *adj* **rimier, rimiest.** coated with rime.

rind ⓣ (raɪnd) *n* **1** a hard outer layer or skin on bacon, cheese, etc. **2** the outer layer of a fruit or of the spore-producing body of certain fungi. **3** the outer layer of the bark of a tree. [OE *rinde*]

rinderpest ('rɪndəˌpest) *n* an acute contagious viral disease of cattle, characterized by severe inflammation of the intestinal tract and diarrhoea. [C19: from G *Rinderpest* cattle pest]

ring¹ ⓣ (rɪŋ) *n* **1** a circular band of a precious metal often set with gems and worn upon the finger as an adornment or as a token of engage-

THESAURUS

just, law-abiding, moral, pure, squeaky-clean, upright
Antonyms *adj* bad, corrupt, dishonest, dishonourable, evil, false, guilty, immoral, improper, indecent, insincere, sinful, unethical, unfair, unjust, unprincipled, unrighteous, unscrupulous, unseemly, wicked

righteousness *n* **1 = virtue,** blamelessness, equity, ethicalness, faithfulness, goodness, honesty, honour, integrity, justice, morality, probity, purity, rectitude, uprightness

rightful *adj* **1 = just,** due, proper, suitable **2, 3 = lawful,** authorized, bona fide, de jure, legal, legitimate, real, true, valid

rigid *adj* **1 = stiff,** inelastic, inflexible, unyielding **2 = strict,** adamant, austere, exact, fixed, harsh, inflexible, intransigent, invariable, rigorous, set, severe, stern, stringent, unalterable, unbending, uncompromising, undeviating, unrelenting, unyielding
Antonyms *adj* ≠ **stiff:** bending, elastic, flexible, limber, lissom(e), mobile, pliable, pliant, soft, supple, yielding ≠ **strict:** flexible, indulgent, lax, lenient, merciful, soft, tolerant

rigmarole *n* **1 = procedure,** bother, carry-on (*inf., chiefly Brit.*), fuss, hassle (*inf.*), nonsense, palaver, pantomime (*inf.*), performance (*inf.*), red tape, to-do **2 = twaddle,** balderdash, gibberish, jargon, trash

rigorous *adj* **1 = strict,** austere, challenging, demanding, exacting, firm, hard, harsh, inflexible, rigid, severe, stern, stringent, tough **2 = thorough,** accurate, conscientious, exact, meticulous, nice, painstaking, precise, punctilious, scrupulous
Antonyms *adj* ≠ **strict:** easy, flexible, friendly, genial, gentle, humane, indulgent, kind, lax, lenient, loose, mild, permissive, relaxed, soft, sympathetic, tolerant, weak ≠ **thorough:** careless, half-hearted, haphazard, imperfect, inaccurate, incorrect, inexact, loose, negligent, slapdash, sloppy, slovenly, unscrupulous

rigour *n* **2 = hardship,** ordeal, privation, suffering, trial **3 = strictness,** asperity, austerity, firmness, hardness, harshness, inflexibility, rigidity, sternness, stringency **4 = thoroughness,** accuracy, conscientiousness, exactitude, exactness, meticulousness, preciseness, precision, punctiliousness

rig out *vb* **1 = dress,** array, attire, clothe, costume, kit out **2 = equip,** accoutre, fit, furnish, kit out, outfit, set up ◆ *n* **rigout 3** *Informal* **= outfit,** apparel, clobber, clothing, costume, dress, garb, gear (*inf.*), get-up (*inf.*), habit, raiment (*arch. or poetic*), togs

rig up *vb* **= set up,** arrange, assemble, build, cobble together, construct, erect, fix up, improvise, put together, put up, throw together

rile *vb* **1 = anger,** aggravate (*inf.*), annoy, bug (*inf.*), gall, get *or* put one's back up, get one's goat (*sl.*), get on one's nerves (*inf.*), get under one's skin (*inf.*), irk, irritate, nark (*Brit., Austral., & NZ sl.*), nettle, peeve (*inf.*), pique, provoke, rub one up the wrong way, try one's patience, upset, vex

rim *n* **1 = edge,** border, brim, brink, circumference, flange, lip, margin, verge

rind *n* **1 = skin,** crust, outer layer, peel **2 = skin,** epicarp, husk, integument

ring¹ *n* **1, 2 = circle,** band, circuit, halo, hoop, loop, round **5 = arena,** circus, enclosure, rink **9 = gang,** association, band, cabal, cartel, cell, circle, clique, combine, coterie, crew (*inf.*), group, junta, knot, mob, organization, syndicate ◆ *vb* **20 = encircle,** circumscribe, enclose, encompass, gird, girdle, hem in, seal off, surround

ment or marriage. **2** any object or mark that is circular in shape. **3** a circular path or course: *to run around in a ring.* **4** a group of people or things standing or arranged so as to form a circle: *a ring of spectators.* **5** an enclosed space, usually circular in shape, where circus acts are performed. **6** a square raised platform, marked off by ropes, in which contestants box or wrestle. **7 the ring.** the sport of boxing. **8 throw one's hat in the ring.** to announce one's intention to be a candidate or contestant. **9** a group of people usually operating illegally and covertly: *a drug ring; a paedophile ring.* **10** (esp. at country fairs) an enclosure where horses, cattle, and other livestock are paraded and auctioned. **11** an area reserved for betting at a racecourse. **12** a circular strip of bark cut from a tree or branch. **13** a single turn in a spiral. **14** *Geom.* the area of space lying between two concentric circles. **15** *Maths.* a set that is subject to two binary operations, addition and multiplication, such that the set is a commutative group under addition and is closed under multiplication, this latter operation being associative. **16** *Bot.* short for **annual ring. 17** *Chem.* a closed loop of atoms in a molecule. **18** *Astron.* any of the thin circular bands of small bodies orbiting a giant planet, esp. Saturn. **19 run rings round.** *Inf.* to outclass completely. ◆ *vb* **rings, ringing, ringed.** (*tr*) **20** to surround with, or as if with, or form a ring. **21** to mark a bird with a ring or clip for subsequent identification. **22** to fit a ring in the nose of (a bull, etc.) so that it can be led easily. **23** to ringbark. [OE *hring*]
▸**ringed** *adj*

ring[2] ❶ (rɪŋ) *vb* **rings, ringing, rang, rung. 1** to emit or cause to emit a resonant sound, characteristic of certain metals when struck. **2** to cause (a bell, etc.) to emit a ringing sound by striking it once or repeatedly or (of a bell) to emit such a sound. **3a** (*tr*) to cause (a large bell) to emit a ringing sound by pulling on a rope attached to a wheel on which the bell swings back and forth, being sounded by a clapper inside it. **3b** (*intr*) (of a bell) to sound by being swung in this way. **4** (*intr*) (of a building, place, etc.) to be filled with sound: *the church rang with singing.* **5** (*intr;* foll. by *for*) to call by means of a bell, etc.: *to ring for the butler.* **6** Also: **ring up.** *Chiefly Brit.* to call (a person) by telephone. **7** (*tr*) to strike or tap (a coin) in order to assess its genuineness by the sound produced. **8** *Sl.* to change the identity of (a stolen vehicle) by using the licence plate, serial number, etc., of another, usually disused, vehicle. **9** (*intr*) (of the ears) to have or give the sensation of humming or ringing. **10 ring a bell.** to bring something to the mind or memory: *that rings a bell.* **11 ring down the curtain. 11a** to lower the curtain at the end of a theatrical performance. **11b** (foll. by *on*) to put an end (to). **12 ring false.** to give the impression of being false. **13 ring true.** to give the impression of being true. ◆ *n* **14** the act of or a sound made by ringing. **15** a sound produced by or suggestive of a bell. **16** any resonant or metallic sound: *the ring of trumpets.* **17** *Inf., chiefly Brit.* a telephone call. **18** the complete set of bells in a tower or belfry: *a ring of eight bells.* **19** an inherent quality or characteristic: his words had the ring of sincerity. ◆ See also **ring in, ring off,** etc. [OE *hringan*]

> **USAGE NOTE** *Rang* and *sang* are the correct forms of the past tenses of *ring* and *sing,* although *rung* and *sung* are still heard informally and dialectally: *he rung (rang) the bell.*

ringbark (ˈrɪŋˌbɑːk) *vb* (*tr*) to kill (a tree) by cutting away a strip of bark from around the trunk.

ring binder *n* a loose-leaf binder with metal rings that can be opened to insert perforated paper.

ringbolt (ˈrɪŋˌbəʊlt) *n* a bolt with a ring fitted through an eye attached to the bolt head.

ringdove (ˈrɪŋˌdʌv) *n* **1** another name for **wood pigeon. 2** an Old World turtledove, having a black neck band.

ringed plover *n* a European shorebird with a greyish-brown back, white underparts, a black throat band, and orange legs.

ringer (ˈrɪŋə) *n* **1** a person or thing that rings a bell, etc. **2** Also called: **dead ringer.** *Sl.* a person or thing that is almost identical to another. **3** *Sl.* a stolen vehicle the identity of which has been changed by the use of the licence plate, serial number, etc., of another, usually disused, vehicle. **4** *Chiefly US.* a contestant, esp. a horse, entered in a competition under false representations of identity, record, or ability. **5** *Austral.* a stockman; station hand. **6** *Austral.* the fastest shearer in a shed. **7** *Austral. inf.* the fastest or best at anything. **8** a quoit thrown so as to encircle a peg. **9** such a throw.

ring-fence *vb* **1** to assign (money, a grant, fund, etc.) to one particular purpose, so as to restrict its use: *to ring-fence a financial allowance.* **2** to oblige (a person or organization) to use money for a particular purpose: *to ring-fence a local authority.* ◆ *n* **ring fence. 3** an agreement, contract, etc., in which the use of money is restricted to a particular purpose.

ring finger *n* the third finger, esp. of the left hand, on which a wedding ring is worn.

ring in *vb* (*adv*) **1** (*intr*) *Chiefly Brit.* to report to someone by telephone. **2** (*tr*) to accompany the arrival of with bells (esp. in **ring in the new year**). ◆ *n* **ring-in. 3** *Austral. & NZ inf.* a person or thing that is not normally a member of a particular group; outsider.

ringing tone *n Brit.* a sequence of pairs of tones heard by the dialler on a telephone when the number dialled is ringing. Cf. **engaged tone, dialling tone.**

ringleader (ˈrɪŋˌliːdə) *n* a person who leads others in unlawful or mischievous activity.

ringlet (ˈrɪŋlɪt) *n* **1** a lock of hair hanging down in a spiral curl. **2** a butterfly that occurs in S Europe and has dark brown wings marked with small black-and-white eyespots.
▸ˈ**ringleted** *adj*

ring main *n* a domestic electrical supply in which outlet sockets are connected to the mains supply through a continuous closed circuit (**ring circuit**).

ringmaster (ˈrɪŋˌmɑːstə) *n* the master of ceremonies in a circus.

ring-necked *adj* (of animals, esp. birds and snakes) having a band of distinctive colour around the neck.

ring-necked pheasant *n* a common pheasant originating in Asia. The male has a bright plumage with a band of white around the neck and the female is mottled brown.

ring off *vb* (*intr, adv*) *Chiefly Brit.* to terminate a telephone conversation by replacing the receiver; hang up.

ring out *vb* (*adv*) **1** (*tr*) to accompany the departure of with bells (esp. in **ring out the old year**). **2** (*intr*) to send forth a loud resounding noise.

ring ouzel *n* a European thrush common in rocky areas. The male has a blackish plumage and the female is brown.

ring road *n* a main road that bypasses a town or town centre. US names: **belt, beltway.**

ringside (ˈrɪŋˌsaɪd) *n* **1** the row of seats nearest a boxing or wrestling ring. **2a** any place affording a close uninterrupted view. **2b** (*as modifier*): *a ringside seat.*

ringtail (ˈrɪŋˌteɪl) *n Austral.* any of several tree-living phalangers having curling prehensile tails used to grasp branches while climbing.

ring up *vb* (*adv*) **1** *Chiefly Brit.* to make a telephone call (to). **2** (*tr*) to record on a cash register. **3 ring up the curtain. 3a** to begin a theatrical performance. **3b** (often foll. by *on*) to make a start (on).

ringworm (ˈrɪŋˌwɜːm) *n* any of various fungal infections of the skin or nails, often appearing as itching circular patches. Also called: **tinea.**

rink (rɪŋk) *n* **1** an expanse of ice for skating on, esp. one that is artificially prepared and under cover. **2** an area for roller-skating on. **3** a building or enclosure for ice-skating or roller-skating. **4** *Bowls.* a strip of the green on which a game is played. **5** *Curling.* the strip of ice on which the game is played. **6** (in bowls and curling) the players on one side in a game. [C14 (Scots): from OF *renc* row]

rinkhals (ˈrɪŋkˌhæls) *or* **ringhals** (ˈrɪŋgˌhæls) *n, pl* **rinkhals, rinkhalses, ringhals** *or* **ringhalses.** a venomous snake of southern Africa, which can spit venom over 2 m (7 ft). [Afrik., lit.: ring neck]

rink rat *n Canad. sl.* a youth who helps with odd chores around an ice-hockey rink in return for free admission to games, etc.

rinse ❶ (rɪns) *vb* **rinses, rinsing, rinsed.** (*tr*) **1** to remove soap from (clothes, etc.) by applying clean water in the final stage in washing. **2** to wash lightly, esp. without using soap. **3** to give a light tint to (hair). ◆ *n* **4** the act or an instance of rinsing. **5** *Hairdressing.* a liquid preparation put on the hair when wet to give a tint to it: *a blue rinse.* [C14: from OF *rincer,* from L *recens* fresh]
▸ˈ**rinser** *n*

rioja (rɪˈəʊxə) *n* a red or white wine, with a distinctive vanilla bouquet and flavour, produced around the Ebro river in central N Spain. [C20: from *La Rioja,* the area where it is produced]

riot ❶ (ˈraɪət) *n* **1a** a disturbance made by an unruly mob or (in law) three or more persons. **1b** (*as modifier*): *a riot shield.* **2** unrestrained revelry. **3** an occasion of boisterous merriment. **4** *Sl.* a person who occasions boisterous merriment. **5** a dazzling display: *a riot of colour.* **6** *Hunting.* the indiscriminate following of any scent by hounds. **7** *Arch.* wanton lasciviousness. **8 run riot. 8a** to behave without restraint. **8b** (of plants) to grow profusely. ◆ *vb* **9** (*intr*) to take part in a riot. **10** (*intr*) to indulge in unrestrained revelry. **11** (*tr;* foll. by *away*) to spend (time or money) in wanton or loose living. [C13: from OF *riote* dispute, from *ruihoter* to quarrel, prob. from *ruir* to make a commotion, from L *rugīre* to roar]
▸ˈ**rioter** *n*

Riot Act *n* **1** *Criminal law.* (formerly, in England) a statute of 1715 by which persons committing a riot had to disperse within an hour of the reading of the act by a magistrate. **2 read the riot act to.** to warn or reprimand severely.

riotous ❶ (ˈraɪətəs) *adj* **1** proceeding from or of the nature of riots or ri-

THESAURUS

ring[2] *vb* **1-3** = **chime,** clang, peal, resonate, resound, reverberate, sound, toll **6** = **phone,** buzz, call, telephone ◆ *n* **14, 15** = **chime,** knell, peal **17** = **call,** buzz, phone call

rinse *vb* **2** = **wash,** bathe, clean, cleanse, dip, splash, wash out, wet ◆ *n* **4** = **wash,** bath, dip, splash, wetting

riot *n* **1a** = **disturbance,** anarchy, commotion, confusion, disorder, donnybrook, fray, lawlessness, mob violence, quarrel, row, street fighting, strife, tumult, turbulence, turmoil, upheaval, uproar **2, 3** = **merrymaking,** blast (*US sl.*), boisterousness, carousal, excess, festivity, frolic, high jinks, jollification, revelry, romp **5** = **display,** extravaganza, flourish, profusion, show, splash **8 run riot: a** = **grow profusely,** be out of control, break *or* cut loose, go wild, let oneself go, raise hell, throw off all restraint **b** grow like weeds, luxuriate, spread like wildfire ◆ *vb* **9** = **rampage,** fight in the streets, go on the rampage, raise an uproar, run riot, take to the streets **10** = **make merry,** carouse, cut loose, frolic, go on a binge, go on a spree, paint the town red (*inf.*), revel, roister, romp

riotous *adj* **1** = **unruly,** anarchic, disorderly, insubordinate, lawless, mutinous, rampageous, rebellious, refractory, rowdy, tumultuous, ungovernable, violent **2** = **unrestrained,** boister-

oting. **2** characterized by wanton revelry: *riotous living*. **3** characterized by unrestrained merriment: *riotous laughter*.
▸**'riotously** *adv* ▸**'riotousness** *n*

riot shield *n* (in Britain) a shield used by police controlling crowds.

rip[1] (rɪp) *vb* **rips, ripping, ripped. 1** to tear or be torn violently or roughly. **2** (*tr;* foll. by *off* or *out*) to remove hastily or roughly. **3** (*intr*) *Inf.* to move violently or precipitously. **4** (*intr;* foll. by *into*) *Inf.* to pour violent abuse (on). **5** (*tr*) to saw or split (wood) in the direction of the grain. **6 let rip.** to act or speak without restraint. ◆ *n* **7** a tear or split. **8** short for **ripsaw.** ◆ See also **rip off.** [C15: ?from Flemish *rippen*]

rip[2] (rɪp) *n* short for **riptide.** [C18: ?from RIP[1]]

rip[3] (rɪp) *n Inf., arch.* **1** a debauched person. **2** an old worn-out horse. [C18: ?from *rep,* shortened from REPROBATE]

RIP *abbrev. for* requiescat *or* requiescant in pace. [L: may he, she, *or* they rest in peace]

riparian (raɪ'pɛərɪən) *adj* **1** of, inhabiting, or situated on the bank of a river. **2** denoting or relating to the legal rights of the owner of land on a river bank, such as fishing. ◆ *n* **3** *Property law.* a person who owns land on a river bank. [C19: from L, from *ripa* river bank]

ripcord ('rɪp,kɔːd) *n* **1** a cord that when pulled opens a parachute from its pack. **2** a cord on the gas bag of a balloon that when pulled enables gas to escape and the balloon to descend.

ripe (raɪp) *adj* **1** (of fruit, grain, etc.) mature and ready to be eaten or used. **2** mature enough to be eaten or used: *ripe cheese*. **3** fully developed in mind or body. **4** resembling ripe fruit, esp. in redness or fullness: *a ripe complexion*. **5** (*postpositive;* foll. by *for*) ready or eager (to undertake or undergo an action). **6** (*postpositive;* foll. by *for*) suitable: *the time is not yet ripe*. **7** mature in judgment or knowledge. **8** advanced but healthy (esp. in **a ripe old age**). **9** *Sl.* **9a** complete; thorough. **9b** excessive; exorbitant. **10** *Sl.* slightly indecent; risqué. [OE *rīpe*]
▸**'ripely** *adv* ▸**'ripeness** *n*

ripen ('raɪpᵊn) *vb* to make or become ripe.

ripieno (,rɪpɪ'eɪnəʊ) *n, pl* **ripieni** (-niː) *or* **ripienos.** *Music.* a supplementary instrument or player. [It.]

rip off *vb* (*tr*) **1** to tear roughly (from). **2** (*adv*) *Sl.* to steal from or cheat (someone). ◆ *n* **rip-off. 3** *Sl.* a grossly overpriced article. **4** *Sl.* the act of stealing or cheating.

riposte (rɪ'pɒst, rɪ'pəʊst) *n* **1** a swift sharp reply in speech or action. **2** *Fencing.* a counterattack made immediately after a successful parry. ◆ *vb* **ripostes, riposting, riposted. 3** (*intr*) to make a riposte. [C18: from F, from It., from *rispondere* to reply]

ripper ('rɪpə) *n* **1** a person or thing that rips. **2** a murderer who dissects or mutilates his victim's body. **3** *Inf., chiefly Austral. & NZ.* a fine or excellent person or thing.

ripping ('rɪpɪŋ) *adj Arch. Brit. sl.* excellent; splendid.
▸**'rippingly** *adv*

ripple[1] ('rɪpᵊl) *n* **1** a slight wave or undulation on the surface of water. **2** a small wave or undulation in fabric, hair, etc. **3** a sound reminiscent of water flowing quietly in ripples: *a ripple of laughter*. **4** *Electronics.* an oscillation of small amplitude superimposed on a steady value. **5** *US & Canad.* another word for **riffle** (sense 4). ◆ *vb* **ripples, rippling, rippled. 6** (*intr*) to form ripples or flow with an undulating motion. **7** (*tr*) to stir up (water) so as to form ripples. **8** (*tr*) to make ripple marks. **9** (*intr*) (of sounds) to rise and fall gently. [C17: ?from RIP[1]]
▸**'rippler** *n* ▸**'rippling** *or* **'ripply** *adj*

ripple[2] ('rɪpᵊl) *n* **1** a special kind of comb designed to separate the seed from the stalks in flax or hemp. ◆ *vb* **ripples, rippling, rippled. 2** (*tr*) to comb with this tool. [C14: of Gmc origin]
▸**'rippler** *n*

ripple effect *n* the repercussions of an event or situation experienced far beyond its immediate location.

ripple mark *n* one of a series of small wavy ridges of sand formed by waves on a beach, by a current in a sandy riverbed, or by wind on land: sometimes found fossilized on bedding planes of sedimentary rock.

rip-roaring *adj Inf.* characterized by excitement, intensity, or boisterous behaviour.

ripsaw ('rɪp,sɔː) *n* a handsaw for cutting along the grain of timber.

ripsnorter ('rɪp,snɔːtə) *n Sl.* a person or thing noted for intensity or excellence.
▸**'rip,snorting** *adj*

riptide ('rɪp,taɪd) *n* **1** Also called: **rip.** a stretch of turbulent water in the sea, caused by the meeting of currents. **2** Also called: **rip current.** a strong current, esp. one flowing outwards from the shore.

rise (raɪz) *vb* **rises, rising, rose, risen** ('rɪzᵊn). (*mainly intr*) **1** to get up from a lying, sitting, kneeling, or prone position. **2** to get out of bed, esp. to begin one's day: *he always rises early*. **3** to move from a lower to a higher position or place. **4** to ascend or appear above the horizon: *the sun is rising*. **5** to increase in height or level: *the water rose above the normal level*. **6** to attain higher rank, status, or reputation: *he will rise in the world*. **7** to be built or erected: *those blocks of flats are rising fast*. **8** to appear: *new troubles rose to afflict her*. **9** to increase in strength, degree, etc.: *the wind is rising*. **10** to increase in amount or value: *house prices are always rising*. **11** to swell up: *dough rises*. **12** to become erect, stiff, or rigid: *the hairs on his neck rose in fear*. **13** (of one's stomach or gorge) to manifest nausea. **14** to revolt: *the people rose against their oppressors*. **15** to slope upwards: *the ground rises beyond the lake*. **16** to be resurrected. **17** to originate: *that river rises in the mountains*. **18** (of a session of a court, legislative assembly, etc.) to come to an end. **19** *Angling.* (of fish) to come to the surface of the water. **20** (often foll. by *to*) *Inf.* to respond (to teasing, etc.). ◆ *n* **21** the act or an instance of rising. **22** an increase in height. **23** an increase in rank, status, or position. **24** an increase in amount, cost, or value. **25** an increase in degree or intensity. **26** *Brit.* an increase in salary or wages. US and Canad. word: **raise. 27** the vertical height of a step or of a flight of stairs. **28** the vertical height of a roof above the walls or columns. **29** *Angling.* the act or instance of fish coming to the surface of the water to take flies, etc. **30** the beginning, origin, or source. **31** a piece of rising ground; incline. **32 get** *or* **take a rise out of.** *Sl.* to provoke an angry or petulant reaction from. **33 give rise to.** to cause the development of. [OE *rīsan*]

riser ('raɪzə) *n* **1** a person who rises, esp. from bed: *an early riser*. **2** the vertical part of a stair. **3** a vertical pipe, esp. one within a building.

rise to *vb* (*intr, prep*) to respond adequately to (the demands of something, esp. a testing challenge).

risibility (,rɪzɪ'bɪlɪtɪ) *n, pl* **risibilities. 1** a tendency to laugh. **2** hilarity; laughter.

risible ('rɪzɪbᵊl) *adj* **1** having a tendency to laugh. **2** causing laughter; ridiculous. [C16: from LL *risibilis,* from L *rīdēre* to laugh]
▸**'risibly** *adv*

rising ('raɪzɪŋ) *n* **1** a rebellion; revolt. **2** the leaven used to make dough rise in baking. ◆ *adj* (*prenominal*) **3** increasing in rank, status, or reputation: *a rising young politician*. **4** growing up to adulthood: *the rising generation*. ◆ *adv* **5** *Inf.* approaching: *he's rising 50*.

rising damp *n* capillary movement of moisture from the ground into the walls of buildings, resulting in damage up to a level of 3 feet.

rising trot *n* a horse's trot in which the rider rises from the saddle every second beat.

risk (rɪsk) *n* **1** the possibility of incurring misfortune or loss. **2** *Insurance.* **2a** chance of a loss or other event on which a claim may be filed. **2b** the type of such an event, such as fire or theft. **2c** the amount of the claim should such an event occur. **2d** a person or thing considered with respect to the characteristics that may cause an insured event to occur. **3 at risk.** vulnerable. **4 take** *or* **run a risk.** to proceed in an action without regard to the possibility of danger involved. ◆ *vb* (*tr*) **5** to expose to danger or loss. **6** to act in spite of the possibility of (in-

THESAURUS

ous, loud, luxurious, noisy, orgiastic, rambunctious (*inf.*), roisterous, rollicking, saturnalian, uproarious, wanton, wild **3** = **uproarious**, side-splitting
Antonyms *adj* ≠ **unruly, unrestrained:** calm, civilized, disciplined, gentle, lawful, mild, obedient, orderly, peaceful, quiet, restrained, well-behaved

rip[1] *vb* **1** = **tear**, be rent, burst, claw, cut, gash, hack, lacerate, rend, score, slash, slit, split ◆ *n* **7** = **tear**, cleavage, cut, gash, hole, laceration, rent, slash, slit, split

ripe *adj* **1, 2** = **mature**, fully developed, fully grown, mellow, ready, ripened, seasoned **5** *foll. by* **for** = **ready for**, eager for, in readiness for, prepared for **6** = **suitable**, auspicious, favourable, ideal, opportune, right, timely
Antonyms *adj* ≠ **mature:** green, immature, undeveloped, unripe ≠ **suitable:** disadvantageous, inappropriate, inconvenient, inopportune, unfavourable, unfitting, unseemly, unsuitable, untimely

ripen *vb* = **mature**, burgeon, come of age, come to fruition, develop, get ready, grow ripe, make ripe, prepare, season

rip off *vb Slang* **2** = **steal**, cabbage (*Brit. sl.*), filch, knock off (*sl.*), lift (*inf.*), pilfer, pinch (*inf.*), swipe (*sl.*), thieve *Slang* **2** = **cheat**, con (*inf.*), cozen, defraud, diddle (*inf.*), do the dirty on (*Brit. inf.*), dupe, fleece, gyp (*sl.*), rob, skin (*sl.*), steal from, stiff (*sl.*), swindle, trick ◆ *n* **rip-off 4** *Slang* = **cheat**, con (*inf.*), con trick (*inf.*), exploitation, fraud, robbery, scam (*sl.*), sting (*inf.*), swindle, theft

riposte *n* **1** = **retort**, answer, comeback (*inf.*), counterattack, rejoinder, repartee, reply, response, return, sally ◆ *vb* **3** = **retort**, answer, come back, reciprocate, rejoin, reply, respond, return

ripple[1] *n* **1, 2** = **wave**, undulation

rise *vb* **2** = **get up**, arise, get out of bed, get to one's feet, rise and shine, stand up, surface **3** = **go up**, ascend, climb, levitate, move up **6** = **advance**, be promoted, climb the ladder, get on, get somewhere, go places (*inf.*), progress, prosper, work one's way up **8** = **originate**, appear, become apparent, crop up, emanate, emerge, eventuate, flow, happen, issue, occur, spring, turn up **9** = **increase**, enlarge, go up, grow, intensify, lift, mount, soar, swell, wax **14** = **rebel**, mount the barricades, mutiny, resist, revolt, take up arms **15** = **get steeper**, ascend, climb, go uphill, mount, slope upwards ◆ *n* **22** = **upward slope**, acclivity, ascent, elevation, hillock, incline, rising ground **23** = **promotion**, advance, aggrandizement, climb, progress **25** = **increase**, advance, ascent, climb, improvement, upsurge, upswing, upturn, upward turn **26** = **pay increase**, increment, raise (*US*) **33 give rise to** = **cause**, bring about, bring on, effect, produce, provoke, result in
Antonyms *vb* ≠ **go up, get steeper:** descend, drop, fall, plunge, sink ≠ **increase:** abate, abbreviate, abridge, condense, curtail, decline, decrease, descend, diminish, drop, dwindle, fall, lessen, plunge, reduce, shrink, sink, wane ◆ *n* ≠ **increase:** blip, decline, decrease, downswing, downturn, drop, fall

risible *adj* **2** = **ridiculous**, absurd, amusing, comical, droll, farcical, funny, hilarious, humorous, laughable, ludicrous, rib-tickling (*inf.*), side-splitting

risk *n* **1** = **danger**, chance, gamble, hazard, jeopardy, peril, pitfall, possibility, speculation, uncertainty, venture ◆ *vb* **5, 6** = **dare**, chance, endanger, expose to danger, gamble, hazard, imperil, jeopardize, put in jeopardy, skate on jury or loss): *to risk a fall in climbing.* [C17: from F, from It., from *rischiare* to be in peril, from Gk *rhiza* cliff (from the hazards of sailing along rocky coasts)]

risk capital *n Chiefly Brit.* capital invested in an issue of ordinary shares, esp. of a speculative enterprise. Also called: **venture capital.**

risk factor *n Med.* a factor, such as a habit or an environmental condition, that predisposes an individual to develop a particular disease.

risky ❶ ('rɪskɪ) *adj* **riskier, riskiest.** involving danger.
▸**'riskily** *adv* ▸**'riskiness** *n*

risotto (rɪ'zɒtəʊ) *n, pl* **risottos.** a dish of rice cooked in stock and served variously with tomatoes, cheese, chicken, etc. [C19: from It., from *riso* RICE]

risqué ❶ ('rɪskeɪ) *adj* bordering on impropriety or indecency: *a risqué joke.* [C19: from F *risquer* to hazard, RISK]

rissole ('rɪsəʊl) *n* a mixture of minced cooked meat coated in egg and breadcrumbs and fried. [C18: from F, prob. ult. from L *russus* red]

risus sardonicus ('riːsəs sɑː'dɒnɪkəs) *n Pathol.* fixed contraction of the facial muscles resulting in a peculiar distorted grin, caused esp. by tetanus. Also called: **trismus cynicus** ('trɪzməs 'sɪnɪkəs). [C17: NL, lit.: sardonic laugh]

rit. *Music. abbrev. for:* **1** ritardando. **2** ritenuto.

ritardando (ˌrɪtɑː'dændəʊ) *adj, adv* another term for **rallentando.** Abbrev.: **rit.** [C19: from It., from *ritardare* to slow down]

rite ❶ (raɪt) *n* **1** a formal act prescribed or customary in religious ceremonies: *the rite of baptism.* **2** a particular body of such acts, esp. of a particular Christian Church: *the Latin rite.* **3** a Christian Church: *the Greek rite.* [C14: from L *rītus* religious ceremony]

ritenuto (ˌrɪtə'nuːtəʊ) *adj, adv Music.* **1** held back momentarily. **2** Abbrev.: **rit.** another term for **rallentando.** [C19: from It., from L *retinēre* to hold back]

rite of passage *n* a ceremony performed in some cultures at times when an individual changes his status, as at puberty and marriage.

ritornello (ˌrɪtə'neləʊ) *n, pl* **ritornellos** *or* **ritornelli** (-liː). *Music.* a short piece of instrumental music interpolated in a song. [It., lit.: a little return]

ritual ❶ ('rɪtjʊəl) *n* **1** the prescribed or established form of a religious or other ceremony. **2** such prescribed forms in general or collectively. **3** stereotyped activity or behaviour. **4** any formal act, institution, or procedure that is followed consistently: *the ritual of the law.* ◆ *adj* **5** of or characteristic of religious, social, or other rituals. [C16: from L *rītuālis,* from *rītus* RITE]
▸**'ritually** *adv*

ritualism ('rɪtjʊəˌlɪzəm) *n* **1** exaggerated emphasis on the importance of rites and ceremonies. **2** the study of rites and ceremonies, esp. magical or religious ones.
▸**'ritualist** *n* ▸**ˌritual'istic** *adj* ▸**ˌritual'istically** *adv*

ritualize *or* **ritualise** ('rɪtjʊəˌlaɪz) *vb* **ritualizes, ritualizing, ritualized** *or* **ritualises, ritualising, ritualised. 1** (*intr*) to engage in ritualism or devise rituals. **2** (*tr*) to make (something) into a ritual.

ritzy ❶ ('rɪtsɪ) *adj* **ritzier, ritziest.** *Sl.* luxurious or elegant. [C20: after the hotels established by César *Ritz* (1850–1918), Swiss hotelier]
▸**'ritzily** *adv* ▸**'ritziness** *n*

rival ❶ ('raɪvᵊl) *n* **1a** a person, organization, team, etc., that competes with another for the same object or in the same field. **1b** (*as modifier*): *rival suitors.* **2** a person or thing that is considered the equal of another: *she is without rival in the field of physics.* ◆ *vb* **rivals, rivalling, rivalled** *or US* **rivals, rivaling, rivaled.** (*tr*) **3** to be the equal or near equal of: *an empire that rivalled Rome.* **4** to try to equal or surpass. [C16: from L *rīvalis,* lit.: one who shares the same brook, from *rīvus* a brook]

rivalry ❶ ('raɪvəlrɪ) *n, pl* **rivalries. 1** the act of rivalling. **2** the state of being a rival or rivals.

rive (raɪv) *vb* **rives, riving, rived; rived** *or* **riven** ('rɪvᵊn). (*usually passive*) **1** to split asunder: *a tree riven by lightning.* **2** to tear apart: *riven to shreds.* [C13: from ON *rīfa*]

river ❶ ('rɪvə) *n* **1a** a large natural stream of fresh water flowing along a definite course, usually into the sea, being fed by tributary streams. **1b** (*as modifier*): *river traffic.* **1c** (*in combination*): *riverside; riverbed.* Related adjs.: **fluvial, potamic. 2** any abundant stream or flow: *a river of blood.* [C13: from OF, from L *rīpārius* of a river bank, from *rīpa* bank]
▸**'riverless** *adj*

riverine ('rɪvəˌraɪn) *adj* **1** of, like, relating to, or produced by a river. **2** located or dwelling near a river; riparian.

rivet ❶ ('rɪvɪt) *n* **1** a short metal pin for fastening two or more pieces together, having a head at one end, the other end being hammered flat after being passed through holes in the pieces. ◆ *vb* **rivets, riveting, riveted.** (*tr*) **2** to join by riveting. **3** to hammer in order to form into a head. **4** (*often passive*) to cause to be fixed, as in fascinated attention, horror, etc.: *to be riveted to the spot.* [C14: from OF, from *river* to fasten, from ?]
▸**'riveter** *n* ▸**'riveting** *adj*

riviera (ˌrɪvɪ'ɛərə) *n* a coastal region reminiscent of the mediterranean coast of France and N Italy. [C20: from *Riviera,* from It., lit.: shore, ult. from L *ripa* shore]

rivière (ˌrɪvɪ'ɛə) *n* a necklace the diamonds or other precious stones of which gradually increase in size up to a large centre stone. [C19: from F: brook, RIVER]

rivulet ('rɪvjʊlɪt) *n* a small stream. [C16: from It. *rivoletto,* from L *rīvulus,* from *rīvus* stream]

riyal (rɪ'jɑːl) *n* the standard monetary and currency unit of Saudi Arabia or Yemen. [from Ar. *riyāl,* from Sp. *real*]

RL *abbrev. for* Rugby League.

rly *abbrev. for* railway.

rm *abbrev. for:* **1** ream. **2** room.

RM *abbrev. for:* **1** Royal Mail. **2** Royal Marines. **3** (in Canada) Rural Municipality.

RMA *abbrev. for* Royal Military Academy (Sandhurst).

rms *abbrev. for* root mean square.

Rn *the chemical symbol for* radon.

RN *abbrev. for:* **1** (in Canada) Registered Nurse. **2** Royal Navy.

RNA *n Biochem.* ribonucleic acid; any of a group of nucleic acids, present in all living cells, that play an essential role in the synthesis of proteins.

RNAS *abbrev. for:* **1** Royal Naval Air Service(s). **2** Royal Naval Air Station.

RNIB (in Britain) *abbrev. for* Royal National Institute for the Blind.

RNID (in Britain) *abbrev. for* Royal National Institute for Deaf People.

RNLI *abbrev. for* Royal National Lifeboat Institution.

RNZAF *abbrev. for* Royal New Zealand Air Force.

RNZN *abbrev. for* Royal New Zealand Navy.

roach[1] (rəʊtʃ) *n, pl* **roaches** *or* **roach.** a European freshwater food fish having a deep compressed body and reddish ventral and tail fins. [C14: from OF *roche,* from ?]

roach[2] (rəʊtʃ) *n* **1** short for **cockroach. 2** *Sl.* the butt of a cannabis cigarette.

roach[3] (rəʊtʃ) *n Naut.* the curve at the foot of a square sail. [C18: from ?]

roach clip *n Sl.* a small clip resembling tweezers, used to hold the butt of a cannabis cigarette, in order to avoid burning one's fingers.

road ❶ (rəʊd) *n* **1a** an open way, usually surfaced with tarmac or concrete, providing passage from one place to another. **1b** (*as modifier*): *road traffic; a road sign.* **1c** (*in combination*): *the roadside.* **2a** a street. **2b** (*cap. when part of a name*): *London Road.* **3** *Brit.* one of the tracks of a railway. **4** a way, path, or course: *the road to fame.* **5** (*often pl*) *Naut.* Also called: **roadstead.** a partly sheltered anchorage. **6** a drift or tunnel in a mine, esp. a level one. **7 hit the road.** *Sl.* to start or resume travelling. **8 one for the road.** *Inf.* a last alcoholic drink before leaving. **9 on the road. 9a** travelling about; on tour. **9b** leading a wandering life. **10 take (to) the road.** to begin a journey or tour. [OE *rād;* rel. to *rīdan* to RIDE]
▸**'roadless** *adj*

road allowance *n Canad.* land reserved by the government to be used for public roads.

roadblock ('rəʊdˌblɒk) *n* a barrier set up across a road by the police or military, in order to stop a fugitive, inspect traffic, etc.

road-fund licence *n Brit.* a paper disc showing that the tax in respect of a motor vehicle has been paid. [C20: from the former *road fund* for the maintenance of public highways]

road hog *n Inf.* a selfish or aggressive driver.

roadholding ('rəʊdˌhəʊldɪŋ) *n* the extent to which a motor vehicle is stable and does not skid, esp. on sharp bends or wet roads.

THESAURUS

thin ice, take a chance on, take the plunge, venture

risky *adj* = **dangerous**, chancy (*inf.*), dicey (*inf., chiefly Brit.*), dodgy (*Brit., Austral., & NZ inf.*), fraught with danger, hazardous, perilous, precarious, touch-and-go, tricky, uncertain, unsafe
Antonyms *adj* certain, reliable, safe, secure, stable, sure

risqué *adj* = **suggestive**, bawdy, blue, daring, immodest, improper, indelicate, naughty, near the knuckle (*inf.*), off colour, Rabelaisian, racy, ribald

rite *n* **1** = **ceremony**, act, ceremonial, communion, custom, form, formality, liturgy, mystery, observance, ordinance, practice, procedure, ritual, sacrament, service, solemnity, usage

ritual *n* **1** = **ceremony**, ceremonial, communion, liturgy, mystery, observance, rite, sacrament, service, solemnity **4** = **custom**, convention, form, formality, habit, ordinance, practice, prescription, procedure, protocol, red tape, routine, tradition, usage ◆ *adj* **5** = **ceremonial**, ceremonious, conventional, customary, formal, habitual, prescribed, procedural, routine, stereotyped

ritzy *adj Slang* = **luxurious**, de luxe, elegant, glamorous, glittering, grand, high-class, luxury, opulent, plush (*inf.*), posh (*inf., chiefly Brit.*), stylish, sumptuous, swanky (*inf.*)

rival *n* **1a** = **opponent**, adversary, antagonist, challenger, competitor, contender, contestant, emulator ◆ *modifier* **1b** = **competing**, competitive, conflicting, emulating, opposed, opposing ◆ *n* **2** = **equal**, compeer, equivalent, fellow, match, peer ◆ *vb* **3** = **equal**, be a match for, bear comparison with, come up to, compare with, match, measure up to **4** = **compete**, contend, emulate, oppose, seek to displace, vie with
Antonyms *n* ≠ **opponent:** ally, friend, helper, supporter ◆ *vb* ≠ **compete:** aid, back, help, support

rivalry *n* **1, 2** = **competition**, antagonism, competitiveness, conflict, contention, contest, duel, emulation, opposition, struggle, vying

river *n* **1a** = **stream**, beck, brook, burn (*Scot.*), creek, rivulet, tributary, watercourse, waterway **2** = **flow**, flood, rush, spate, torrent

riveting *adj* **4** = **enthralling**, absorbing, arresting, captivating, engrossing, fascinating, gripping, hypnotic, spellbinding

road *n* **1** = **way**, avenue, course, direction, highway, lane, motorway, path, pathway, roadway, route, thoroughfare, track **2** = **street 5** *Nautical* = **roadstead**, anchorage

roadhouse (ˈrəʊdˌhaʊs) *n* a pub, restaurant, etc., that is situated at the side of a road.
road hump *n* the official name for **sleeping policeman.**
roadie (ˈrəʊdɪ) *n Inf.* a person who transports and sets up equipment for a band or group. [C20: shortened from *road manager*]
road metal *n* crushed rock, broken stone, etc., used to construct a road.
road movie *n* a genre of film in which the chief character takes to the road, esp. to escape the law, his own past, etc.
road pricing *n* the practice of charging motorists for using certain stretches of road, in order to reduce congestion.
road rage *n* aggressive behaviour by a motorist in response to the actions of another road user.
roadroller (ˈrəʊdˌrəʊlə) *n* a motor vehicle with heavy rollers for compressing road surfaces during road-making.
road show *n* **1** *Radio.* **1a** a live programme, usually with some audience participation, transmitted from a radio van taking a particular show on the road. **1b** the personnel and equipment needed for such a show. **2** a group of entertainers on tour. **3** any occasion when an organization attracts publicity while touring or visiting: *the royal road show.*
roadstead (ˈrəʊdˌstɛd) *n Naut.* another word for **road** (sense 5).
roadster (ˈrəʊdstə) *n* **1** an open car, esp. one seating only two. **2** a kind of bicycle.
road tax *n* a tax paid, usually annually, on motor vehicles in use on the roads.
road test *n* **1** a test to ensure that a vehicle is roadworthy, esp. after repair or servicing, by driving it on roads. **2** a test of something in actual use. ◆ *vb* **road-test.** (*tr*) **3** to test (a vehicle, etc.) in this way.
road train *n Austral.* a truck pulling one or more large trailers, esp. on western roads.
roadway (ˈrəʊdˌweɪ) *n* **1** the surface of a road. **2** the part of a road that is used by vehicles.
roadwork (ˈrəʊdˌwɜːk) *n* sports training by running along roads.
roadworks (ˈrəʊdˌwɜːks) *pl n* repairs to a road or cable under a road, esp. when forming a hazard or obstruction to traffic.
roadworthy (ˈrəʊdˌwɜːðɪ) *adj* (of a motor vehicle) mechanically sound; fit for use on the roads.
▸**ˈroadˌworthiness** *n*
roam ❶ (rəʊm) *vb* **1** to travel or walk about with no fixed purpose or direction. ◆ *n* **2** the act of roaming. [C13: from ?]
▸**ˈroamer** *n*
roan (rəʊn) *adj* **1** (of a horse) having a bay (**red roan**), chestnut (**strawberry roan**), or black (**blue roan**) coat sprinkled with white hairs. ◆ *n* **2** a horse having such a coat. **3** a soft sheepskin leather used in bookbinding, etc. [C16: from OF, from Sp. *roano,* prob. from Gothic *rauths* red]
roar ❶ (rɔː) *vb* (*mainly intr*) **1** (of lions and other animals) to utter characteristic loud growling cries. **2** (*also tr*) (of people) to utter (something) with a loud deep cry, as in anger or triumph. **3** to laugh in a loud hearty unrestrained manner. **4** (of horses) to breathe with laboured rasping sounds. **5** (of the wind, waves, etc.) to blow or break loudly and violently, as during a storm. **6** (of a fire) to burn fiercely with a roaring sound. **7** (*tr*) to bring (oneself) into a certain condition by roaring: *to roar oneself hoarse.* ◆ *n* **8** a loud deep cry, uttered by a person or crowd, esp. in anger or triumph. **9** a prolonged loud cry of certain animals, esp. lions. **10** any similar noise made by a fire, the wind, waves, an engine, etc. [OE *rārian*]
▸**ˈroarer** *n*
roaring (ˈrɔːrɪŋ) *adj* **1** *Inf.* very brisk and profitable (esp. in **a roaring trade**). ◆ *adv* **2** noisily or boisterously (esp. in **roaring drunk**). ◆ *n* **3** a loud prolonged cry.
▸**ˈroaringly** *adv*
roast (rəʊst) *vb* (*mainly tr*) **1** to cook (meat or other food) by dry heat, usually with added fat and esp. in an oven. **2** to brown or dry (coffee, etc.) by exposure to heat. **3** *Metallurgy.* to heat (an ore) in order to produce a concentrate that is easier to smelt. **4** to heat (oneself or something) to an extreme degree, as when sunbathing, etc. **5** (*intr*) to be excessively and uncomfortably hot. **6** (*tr*) *Inf.* to criticize severely. ◆ *n* **7** something that has been roasted, esp. meat. [C13: from OF *rostir,* of Gmc origin]
▸**ˈroaster** *n*
roasting (ˈrəʊstɪŋ) *Inf.* ◆ *adj* **1** extremely hot. ◆ *n* **2** severe criticism.
rob ❶ (rɒb) *vb* **robs, robbing, robbed. 1** to take something from (someone) illegally, as by force. **2** (*tr*) to plunder (a house, etc.). **3** (*tr*) to deprive unjustly: *to be robbed of an opportunity.* [C13: from OF *rober,* of Gmc origin]
▸**ˈrobber** *n*
robbery ❶ (ˈrɒbərɪ) *n, pl* **robberies. 1** *Criminal law.* the stealing of property from a person by using or threatening to use force. **2** the act or an instance of robbing.
robe ❶ (rəʊb) *n* **1** any loose flowing garment, esp. the official vestment of a peer, judge, or academic. **2** a dressing gown or bathrobe. ◆ *vb* **robes, robing, robed. 3** to put a robe, etc., on (oneself or someone else). [C13: from OF; of Gmc origin]
robin (ˈrɒbɪn) *n* **1** Also called: **robin redbreast.** a small Old World songbird related to the thrushes. The adult has a brown back, orange-red breast and face, and grey underparts. **2** a North American thrush similar to but larger than the Old World robin. [C16: arbitrary use of name *Robin*]
Robin Hood *n* a legendary English outlaw, who lived in Sherwood Forest (in the reign of Richard I) and robbed the rich to give to the poor.
robinia (rəˈbɪnɪə) *n* any tree of the leguminous genus *Robinia,* esp. the locust tree.
roborant (ˈrəʊbərənt, ˈrɒb-) *adj* **1** tending to fortify or increase strength. ◆ *n* **2** a drug or agent that increases strength. [C17: from L *roborāre* to strengthen, from *rōbur* an oak]
robot ❶ (ˈrəʊbɒt) *n* **1** any automated machine programmed to perform specific mechanical functions in the manner of a human. **2** (*modifier*) automatic: *a robot pilot.* **3** a person who works or behaves like a machine. **4** *S. African.* a set of traffic lights. [C20: (used in *R.U.R.,* a play by Karel *Čapek* (1890–1938), Czech writer) from Czech *robota* work]
▸**roˈbotic** *adj* ▸**ˈrobot-ˌlike** *adj*
robot bomb *n* another name for the **V-1.**
robot dancing *or* **robotic dancing** (rəʊˈbɒtɪk) *n* a dance of the 1980s, characterized by jerky, mechanical movements. Also called: **robotics.**
robotics (rəʊˈbɒtɪks) *n* (*functioning as sing*) **1** the science or technology of designing, building, and using robots. **2** another name for **robot dancing.**
robust ❶ (rəʊˈbʌst, ˈrəʊbʌst) *adj* **1** strong in constitution. **2** sturdily built: *a robust shelter.* **3** requiring or suited to physical strength: *a robust sport.* **4** (esp. of wines) having a full-bodied flavour. **5** rough or boisterous. **6** (of thought, intellect, etc.) straightforward. [C16: from L *rōbustus,* from *rōbur* an oak, strength]
▸**roˈbustly** *adv*
robusta (rəʊˈbʌstə) *n* **1** a species of coffee tree, *Coffea canephora.* **2** coffee or coffee beans obtained from this plant. [from L *rōbustus* robust]
robustious (rəʊˈbʌstʃəs) *adj Arch.* **1** rough; boisterous. **2** strong, robust, or stout.
▸**roˈbustiously** *adv* ▸**roˈbustiousness** *n*
robustness (rəʊˈbʌstnɪs) *n* **1** the quality of being robust. **2** *Computing.* the ability of a computer system to cope with errors during execution.
roc (rɒk) *n* (in Arabian legend) a bird of enormous size and power. [C16: from Ar., from Persian *rukh*]
ROC *abbrev. for* Royal Observer Corps.
rocaille (rɒˈkaɪ) *n* decorative rock or shell work, esp. as ornamentation in a rococo fountain, grotto, or interior. [from F, from *roc* ROCK[1]]
rocambole (ˈrɒkəmˌbəʊl) *n* a variety of alliaceous plant whose garlic-like bulb is used for seasoning. [C17: from F, from G *Rockenbolle,* lit.: distaff bulb (with reference to its shape)]
Rochelle salt (rɒˈʃɛl) *n* a white crystalline double salt used in Seidlitz powder. Formula: $KNaC_4H_4O_6.4H_2O$. [C18: after *La Rochelle,* port in W France]
roche moutonnée (rəʊʃ ˌmuːtəˈneɪ) *n, pl* **roches moutonnées** (rəʊʃ ˌmuːtəˈneɪz). a rounded mass of rock smoothed and striated by ice that has flowed over it. [C19: F, lit.: fleecy rock, from *mouton* sheep]
rochet (ˈrɒtʃɪt) *n* a white surplice with tight sleeves, worn by bishops, abbots, and certain other Church dignitaries. [C14: from OF, from *roc* coat, of Gmc origin]
rock[1] ❶ (rɒk) *n* **1** *Geol.* any aggregate of minerals that makes up part of the earth's crust. It may be unconsolidated, such as a sand, clay, or mud, or consolidated, such as granite, limestone, or coal. **2** any hard mass of consolidated mineral matter, such as a boulder. **3** *US, Canad., & Austral.* a stone. **4** a person or thing suggesting a rock, esp. in being dependable, unchanging, or providing firm foundation. **5** *Brit.* a hard sweet, typically a long brightly coloured peppermint-flavoured stick,

THESAURUS

roam *vb* **1** = **wander,** drift, meander, peregrinate, prowl, ramble, range, rove, stravaig (*Scot. & N English dialect*), stray, stroll, travel, walk
roar *vb* **1, 2** = **cry,** bawl, bay, bell, bellow, clamour, howl, rumble, shout, thunder, vociferate, yell **3** = **guffaw,** bust a gut (*inf.*), crack up (*inf.*), hoot, laugh heartily, split one's sides (*inf.*) ◆ *n* **8, 9** = **cry,** bellow, clamour, howl, outcry, rumble, shout, thunder, yell
rob *vb* **1** = **steal from,** bereave, cheat, con, defraud, deprive, despoil, dispossess, do out of (*inf.*), gyp (*sl.*), hold up, mug (*inf.*), rip off (*sl.*), skin (*sl.*), stiff (*sl.*), swindle **2** = **plunder,** burgle, loot, pillage, raid, ransack, rifle, sack, strip
robber *n* **1** = **thief,** bandit, brigand, cheat, con man, footpad (*arch.*), fraud, fraudster, highwayman, mugger (*inf.*), pirate, stealer, swindler **2** = **plunderer,** burglar, looter, raider
robbery *n* **1, 2** = **theft,** burglary, depredation, embezzlement, filching, fraud, hold-up, larceny, mugging (*inf.*), pillage, plunder, raid, rip-off (*sl.*), spoliation, stealing, steaming (*inf.*), stick-up (*sl., chiefly US*), swindle, thievery
robe *n* **1** = **gown,** costume, habit, vestment **2** = **dressing gown,** bathrobe, housecoat, negligee, peignoir, wrapper ◆ *vb* **3** = **clothe,** apparel (*arch.*), attire, drape, dress, garb
robot *n* **1** = **machine,** android, automaton, mechanical man
robust *adj* **1** = **strong,** able-bodied, alive and kicking, athletic, brawny, fighting fit, fit, fit as a fiddle (*inf.*), hale, hardy, healthy, hearty, husky (*inf.*), in fine fettle, in good health, lusty, muscular, powerful, rude, rugged, sinewy, sound, staunch, stout, strapping, sturdy, thickset, tough, vigorous, well **5** = **rough,** boisterous, coarse, earthy, indecorous, raunchy (*sl.*), raw, roisterous, rollicking, rude, unsubtle **6** = **straightforward,** common-sensical, down-to-earth, hard-headed, practical, pragmatic, realistic, sensible
Antonyms *adj* ≠ **strong:** delicate, feeble, frail, hothouse (*inf., often disparaging*), infirm, sickly, slender, unfit, unhealthy, unsound, weak, weedy (*inf.*), wimpish *or* wimpy (*inf.*) ≠ **rough:** refined
rock[1] *n* **2** = **stone,** boulder **4** = **tower of strength,** anchor, bulwark, cornerstone, foundation, mainstay, protection, support

sold esp. in holiday resorts. **6** *Sl.* a jewel, esp. a diamond. **7** *Sl.* another name for **crack** (sense 28). **8 on the rocks. 8a** in a state of ruin or destitution. **8b** (of drinks, esp. whisky) served with ice. [C14: from OF *roche,* from ?]

rock[2] Ⓣ (rɒk) *vb* **1** to move or cause to move from side to side or backwards and forwards. **2** to reel or sway or cause (someone) to reel or sway, as with a violent shock or emotion. **3** (*tr*) to shake or move (something) violently. **4** (*intr*) to dance in the rock-and-roll style. ◆ *n* **5** a rocking motion. **6** short for **rock and roll. 7** Also called: **rock music.** any of various styles of pop music having a heavy beat, derived from rock and roll. [OE *roccian*]

rockabilly (ˈrɒkəˌbɪlɪ) *n* a fast, spare style of White rock music which originated in the mid-1950s in the US South. [C20: from ROCK (AND ROLL) + (HILL)BILLY]

rock and roll *or* **rock'n'roll** *n* **1a** a type of pop music originating in the 1950s as a blend of rhythm and blues and country and western. **1b** (*as modifier*): *the rock-and-roll era.* **2** dancing performed to such music, with exaggerated body movements stressing the beat. ◆ *vb* **3** (*intr*) to perform this dance.
▸**rock and roller** *or* **rock'n'roller** *n*

rock bass (bæs) *n* an eastern North American freshwater food fish, related to the sunfish family.

rock bottom *n* **a** the lowest possible level. **b** (*as modifier*): *rock-bottom prices.*

rock-bound *adj* hemmed in or encircled by rocks. Also (poetic): **rock-girt.**

rock cake *n* a small cake containing dried fruit and spice, with a rough surface supposed to resemble a rock.

rock crystal *n* a pure transparent colourless quartz, used in electronic and optical equipment.

rock dove *or* **pigeon** *n* a common dove from which domestic and feral pigeons are descended.

rocker (ˈrɒkə) *n* **1** any of various devices that transmit or operate with a rocking motion. See also **rocker arm. 2** another word for **rocking chair. 3** either of two curved supports on the legs of a chair on which it may rock. **4a** an ice skate with a curved blade. **4b** the curve itself. **5** a rock-music performer, fan, or song. **6** *Brit.* an adherent of a youth movement rooted in the 1950s, characterized by motorcycle trappings. **7 off one's rocker.** *Sl.* crazy.

rocker arm *n* a lever that rocks about a pivot, esp. a lever in an internal-combustion engine that transmits the motion of a pushrod or cam to a valve.

rockery (ˈrɒkərɪ) *n, pl* **rockeries.** a garden constructed with rocks, esp. one where alpine plants are grown.

rocket[1] (ˈrɒkɪt) *n* **1** a self-propelling device, esp. a cylinder containing a mixture of solid explosives, used as a firework, distress signal, etc. **2a** any vehicle that carries its own fuel and oxidant to burn in a rocket engine, esp. one used to carry a spacecraft, etc. **2b** (*as modifier*): *rocket launcher.* **3** *Brit. & NZ inf.* a severe reprimand (esp. in **get a rocket**). ◆ *vb* **rockets, rocketing, rocketed. 4** (*tr*) to propel (a missile, spacecraft, etc.) by means of a rocket. **5** (*intr*; foll. by *off, away,* etc.) to move off at high speed. **6** (*intr*) to rise rapidly: *he rocketed to the top.* [C17: from OF, from It. *rochetto,* dim. of *rocca* distaff, of Gmc origin]

rocket[2] (ˈrɒkɪt) *n* any of several plants of the mustard family, typically having yellowish flowers, such as **London rocket** and **yellow rocket.** See also **arugula, wall rocket.** [C16: from F *roquette,* from It. *rochetta,* from L *ērūca* hairy plant]

rocket engine *n* a reaction engine in which a fuel and oxidizer are burnt in a combustion chamber, the products of combustion expanding through a nozzle and producing thrust.

rocketry (ˈrɒkɪtrɪ) *n* the science and technology of the design, operation, maintenance, and launching of rockets.

rockfish (ˈrɒkˌfɪʃ) *n, pl* **rockfish** *or* **rockfishes. 1** any of various fishes that live among rocks, such as the goby, bass, etc. **2** *Brit.* any of several coarse fishes when used as food, esp. the dogfish or wolffish.

rock garden *n* a garden featuring rocks or rockeries.

rocking chair *n* a chair set on curving supports so that the sitter may rock backwards and forwards.

rocking horse *n* a toy horse mounted on a pair of rockers on which a child can rock to and fro in a seesaw movement.

rocking stone *n* a boulder so delicately poised that it can be rocked.

rockling (ˈrɒklɪŋ) *n, pl* **rocklings** *or* **rockling.** a small gadoid fish which has an elongated body with barbels around the mouth and occurs mainly in the North Atlantic Ocean. [C17: from ROCK[1] + -LING[1]]

rock lobster *n* another name for the **spiny lobster.**

rock melon *n US, Austral., & NZ.* another name for **cantaloupe.**

rock pigeon *n* another name for **rock dove.**

rock plant *n* any plant that grows on rocks or in rocky ground.

rock rabbit *n S. African.* another name for **dassie.** See **hyrax.**

rockrose (ˈrɒkˌrəʊz) *n* any of various shrubs or herbaceous plants cultivated for their yellow-white or reddish roselike flowers.

rock salmon *n Brit.* a former term for **rockfish** (sense 2).

rock salt *n* another name for **halite.**

rock snake *or* **python** *n* any large Australasian python of the genus *Liasis.*

rock tripe *n Canad.* any of various edible lichens that grow on rocks and are used in the North as a survival food.

rock wool *n* another name for **mineral wool.**

rocky[1] Ⓣ (ˈrɒkɪ) *adj* **rockier, rockiest. 1** consisting of or abounding in rocks: *a rocky shore.* **2** unyielding: *rocky determination.* **3** hard like rock: *rocky muscles.*
▸ˈ**rockiness** *n*

rocky[2] Ⓣ (ˈrɒkɪ) *adj* **rockier, rockiest. 1** weak or unstable. **2** *Inf.* (of a person) dizzy; nauseated.
▸ˈ**rockily** *adv* ▸ˈ**rockiness** *n*

Rocky Mountain spotted fever *n* an acute rickettsial disease characterized by high fever, chills, pain in muscles and joints, etc. It is caused by the bite of an infected tick.

rococo (rəˈkəʊkəʊ) *n* (*often cap.*) **1** a style of architecture and decoration that originated in France in the early 18th century, characterized by elaborate but graceful ornamentation. **2** an 18th-century style of music characterized by prettiness and extreme use of ornamentation. **3** any florid or excessively ornamental style. ◆ *adj* **4** denoting, being in, or relating to the rococo. **5** florid or excessively elaborate. [C19: from F, from ROCAILLE, from *roc* ROCK[1]]

rod Ⓣ (rɒd) *n* **1** a slim cylinder of metal, wood, etc. **2** a switch or bundle of switches used to administer corporal punishment. **3** any of various staffs of insignia or office. **4** power, esp. of a tyrannical kind: *a dictator's iron rod.* **5** a straight slender shoot, stem, or cane of a woody plant. **6** See **fishing rod. 7** Also called: **pole, perch. 7a** a unit of length equal to 5½ yards. **7b** a unit of square measure equal to 30¼ square yards. **8** *Surveying.* another name (esp. US) for **staff**[1] (sense 8). **9** Also called: **retinal rod.** any of the elongated cylindrical cells in the retina of the eye, which are sensitive to dim light but not to colour. **10** any rod-shaped bacterium. **11** *US.* a slang name for **pistol. 12** short for **hot rod.** [OE *rodd*]
▸ˈ**rodˌlike** *adj*

rode (rəʊd) *vb* the past tense of **ride.**

rodent (ˈrəʊdᵊnt) *n* **a** any of the relatively small placental mammals having constantly growing incisor teeth specialized for gnawing. The group includes rats, mice, squirrels, etc. **b** (*as modifier*): *rodent characteristics.* [C19: from L *rōdere* to gnaw]
▸ˈ**rodent-ˌlike** *adj*

rodent ulcer *n* a slow-growing malignant tumour on the face, usually occurring at the edge of the eyelids, lips, or nostrils.

rodeo (ˈrəʊdɪˌəʊ) *n, pl* **rodeos.** *Chiefly US & Canad.* **1** a display of the skills of cowboys, including bareback riding. **2** the rounding up of cattle for branding, etc. **3** an enclosure for cattle that have been rounded up. [C19: from Sp., from *rodear* to go around, from *rueda* a wheel, from L *rota*]

rodomontade (ˌrɒdəmɒnˈteɪd, -ˈtɑːd) *Literary.* ◆ *n* **1a** boastful words or behaviour. **1b** (*as modifier*): *rodomontade behaviour.* ◆ *vb* **rodomontades, rodomontading, rodomontaded. 2** (*intr*) to boast or rant. [C17: from F, from It. *rodomonte* a boaster, from *Rodomonte,* the name of a braggart king of Algiers in epic poems]

roe[1] (rəʊ) *n* **1** Also called: **hard roe.** the ovary of a female fish filled with mature eggs. **2** Also called: **soft roe.** the testis of a male fish filled with mature sperm. [C15: from MDu. *roge,* from OHG *roga*]

roe[2] (rəʊ) *n, pl* **roes** *or* **roe.** short for **roe deer.** [OE *rā(ha)*]

Roe (rəʊ) *n* **Richard.** *Law.* (formerly) the defendant in a fictitious action, Doe versus Roe, to test a point of law. See also **Doe.**

roebuck (ˈrəʊˌbʌk) *n, pl* **roebucks** *or* **roebuck.** the male of the roe deer.

roe deer *n* a small graceful deer of woodlands of Europe and Asia. The antlers are small and the summer coat is reddish-brown.

roentgen *or* **röntgen** (ˈrɒntgən, -tjən, ˈrent-) *n* a unit of dose of electromagnetic radiation equal to the dose that will produce in air a charge of 0.258×10^{-3} coulomb on all ions of one sign. [C19: after Wilhelm Konrad *Roentgen* (1845–1923), G physicist who discovered x-rays]

roentgen ray *n* a former name for **X-ray.**

rogation (rəʊˈgeɪʃən) *n* (*usually pl*) *Christianity.* a solemn supplication, esp. in a form of ceremony prescribed by the Church. [C14: from L *rogātiō,* from *rogāre* to ask, make supplication]

Rogation Days *pl n* April 25 (the **Major Rogation**) and the Monday, Tuesday, and Wednesday before Ascension Day, observed by Christians as days of solemn supplication and marked by processions and special prayers.

roger (ˈrɒdʒə) *interj* **1** (used in signalling, telecommunications, etc.) message received and understood. **2** an expression of agreement. ◆ *vb* **3** *Taboo sl.* (of a man) to copulate (with). [C20: from the name *Roger,* representing *R* for *received*]

rogue Ⓣ (rəʊg) *n* **1** a dishonest or unprincipled person, esp. a man. **2** *Often jocular.* a mischievous or wayward person, often a child. **3** a crop plant which is inferior, diseased, or of a different, unwanted variety. **4a** any inferior or defective specimen. **4b** (*as modifier*): *rogue heroin.* **5** *Arch.* a vagrant. **6a** an animal of vicious character that leads a solitary

THESAURUS

rock[2] *vb* **1** = **sway,** lurch, pitch, reel, roll, swing, toss, wobble **2** = **shock,** astonish, astound, daze, dumbfound, jar, set one back on one's heels (*inf.*), shake, stagger, stun, surprise

rocky[1] *adj* **1** = **rough,** boulder-strewn, craggy, pebbly, rugged, stony

rocky[2] *adj* **1** = **unstable,** doubtful, rickety, shaky, uncertain, undependable, unreliable, unsteady, weak, wobbly

rod *n* **2** = **cane,** birch, switch **3** = **stick,** bar, baton, crook, dowel, mace, pole, sceptre, shaft, staff, wand

rogue *n* **1** = **scoundrel,** blackguard, charlatan, cheat, con man (*inf.*), crook (*inf.*), deceiver, devil, fraud, fraudster, knave (*arch.*), mountebank, ne'er-do-well, rapscallion, rascal, reprobate, scally (*Northwest English dialect*), scumbag (*sl.*), sharper, swindler, villain **2** = **scamp,** rascal life. **6b** (*as modifier*): *a rogue elephant.* ◆ *vb* **rogues, roguing, rogued. 7** (*tr*) to rid (a field or crop) of plants that are inferior, diseased, etc. [C16: from ?]

roguery ('rəʊgərɪ) *n, pl* **rogueries. 1** behaviour characteristic of a rogue. **2** a roguish or mischievous act.

rogues' gallery *n* **1** a collection of photographs of known criminals kept by the police for identification purposes. **2** a group of undesirable people.

roguish Ⓣ ('rəʊgɪʃ) *adj* **1** dishonest or unprincipled. **2** mischievous.
▸**'roguishly** *adv*

roil (rɔɪl) *vb* **1** (*tr*) to make (a liquid) cloudy or turbid by stirring up dregs or sediment. **2** (*intr*) (esp. of a liquid) to be agitated. **3** (*intr*) *Dialect.* to be noisy. **4** (*tr*) *Now rare.* another word for **rile** (sense 1). [C16: from ?]

roister Ⓣ ('rɔɪstə) *vb* (*intr*) **1** to engage in noisy or unrestrained merrymaking. **2** to brag, bluster, or swagger. [C16: from OF *rustre* lout, from *ruste* uncouth, from L *rusticus* rural]
▸**'roisterer** *n* ▸**'roisterous** *adj* ▸**'roisterously** *adv*

Roland ('rəʊlənd) *n* **1** the greatest of the legendary 12 peers or paladins (of whom Oliver was another) in attendance on Charlemagne. **2 a Roland for an Oliver.** an effective retort or retaliation.

role Ⓣ *or* **rôle** (rəʊl) *n* **1** a part or character in a play, film, etc., to be played by an actor or actress. **2** *Psychol.* the part played by a person in a particular social setting, influenced by his expectation of what is appropriate. **3** usual function: *what is his role in the organization?* [C17: from F *rôle* ROLL, an actor's script]

role model *n* a person regarded by others, esp. younger people, as a good example to follow.

role-playing *n Psychol.* activity in which a person imitates, consciously or unconsciously, a role uncharacteristic of himself. See also **psychodrama.**

roll Ⓣ (rəʊl) *vb* **1** to move or cause to move along by turning over and over. **2** to move or cause to move along on wheels or rollers. **3** to flow or cause to flow onwards in an undulating movement. **4** (*intr*) (of animals, etc.) to turn onto the back and kick. **5** (*intr*) to extend in undulations: *the hills roll down to the sea.* **6** (*intr;* usually foll. by *around*) to move or occur in cycles. **7** (*intr*) (of a planet, the moon, etc.) to revolve in an orbit. **8** (*intr;* foll. by *on, by,* etc.) to pass or elapse: *the years roll by.* **9** to rotate or cause to rotate wholly or partially: *to roll one's eyes.* **10** to curl, cause to curl, or admit of being curled, so as to form a ball, tube, or cylinder. **11** to make or form by shaping into a ball, tube, or cylinder: *to roll a cigarette.* **12** (often foll. by *out*) to spread or cause to spread out flat or smooth under or as if under a roller: *to roll pastry.* **13** to emit or utter with a deep prolonged reverberating sound: *the thunder rolled continuously.* **14** to trill or cause to be trilled: *to roll one's r's.* **15** (*intr*) (of a vessel, aircraft, rocket, etc.) to turn from side to side around the longitudinal axis. **16** to cause (an aircraft) to execute a roll or (of an aircraft) to execute a roll (sense 34). **17** (*intr*) to walk with a swaying gait, as when drunk. **18** *Chiefly US.* to throw (dice). **19** (*intr*) to operate or begin to operate: *the presses rolled.* **20** (*intr*) *Inf.* to make progress: *let the good times roll.* **21** (*tr*) *Inf., chiefly US & NZ.* to rob (a helpless person). ◆ *n* **22** the act or an instance of rolling. **23** anything rolled up in a cylindrical form: *a roll of newspaper.* **24** an official list or register, esp. of names: *an electoral roll.* **25** a rounded mass: *rolls of flesh.* **26** a cylinder used to flatten something; roller. **27** a small cake of bread for one person. **28** a flat pastry or cake rolled up with a meat (**sausage roll**), jam (**jam roll**), or other filling. **29** a swell or undulation on a surface: *the roll of the hills.* **30** a swaying, rolling, or unsteady movement or gait. **31** a deep prolonged reverberating sound: *the roll of thunder.* **32** a trilling sound; trill. **33** a very rapid beating of the sticks on a drum. **34** a flight manoeuvre in which an aircraft makes one complete rotation about its longitudinal axis without loss of height or change in direction. **35** *Sl.* an act of sexual intercourse or petting (esp. in **a roll in the hay**). **36** *US sl.* an amount of money, esp. a wad of paper money. **37 on a roll.** *Sl.* experiencing continued good luck or success. **38 strike off the roll(s). 38a** to expel from membership. **38b** to debar (a solicitor) from practising, usually because of dishonesty. ◆ See also **roll in, roll on,** etc. [C14 *rollen,* from OF *roler,* from L *rotulus,* dim. of *rota* a wheel]

rollbar ('rəʊl,bɑː) *n* a bar that reinforces the frame of a car used for racing, rallying, etc., to protect the driver if the car should turn over.

roll call *n* the reading aloud of an official list of names, those present responding when their names are read out.

rolled gold *n* a metal, such as brass, coated with a thin layer of gold. Also (US): **filled gold.**

rolled-steel joist *n* a steel beam, esp. one with a cross section in the form of a letter *H* or *I.* Abbrev.: **RSJ.**

roller ('rəʊlə) *n* **1** a cylinder having an absorbent surface and a handle, used for spreading paint. **2** Also called: **garden roller.** a heavy cast-iron cylinder on an axle to which a handle is attached; used for flattening lawns. **3** a long heavy wave of the sea, advancing towards the shore. **4** a hardened cylinder of precision-ground steel that forms one of the rolling components of a roller bearing or of a linked driving chain. **5** a cylinder fitted on pivots, used to enable heavy objects to be easily moved. **6** *Printing.* a cylinder, usually of hard rubber, used to ink a plate before impression. **7** any of various other cylindrical devices that rotate about a cylinder, used for any of various purposes. **8** a small cylinder onto which a woman's hair may be rolled to make it curl. **9** *Med.* a bandage consisting of a long strip of muslin rolled tightly into a cylindrical form before application. **10** any of various Old World birds, such as the **European roller,** that have a blue, green, and brown plumage, a slightly hooked bill, and an erratic flight. **11** (*often cap.*) a variety of tumbler pigeon. **12** a person or thing that rolls. **13** short for **steamroller.**

rollerball ('rəʊlə,bɔːl) *n* a pen having a small moving nylon, plastic, or metal ball as a writing point.

roller bearing *n* a bearing in which a shaft runs on a number of hardened-steel rollers held within a cage.

roller chain *n Engineering.* a chain for transmitting power in which each link consists of two free-moving rollers held in position by pins connected to sideplates.

roller coaster *n* another term for **big dipper.**

roller derby *n* a race on roller skates, esp. one involving aggressive tactics.

roller skate *n* **1** a device having straps for fastening to a shoe and four small wheels that enable the wearer to glide swiftly over a floor. ◆ *vb* **roller-skate, roller-skates, roller-skating, roller-skated. 2** (*intr*) to move on roller skates.
▸**roller skater** *n*

roller towel *n* **1** a towel with the two ends sewn together, hung on a roller. **2** a towel wound inside a roller enabling a clean section to be pulled out when needed.

rollick Ⓣ ('rɒlɪk) *vb* **1** (*intr*) to behave in a carefree or boisterous manner. ◆ *n* **2** a boisterous or carefree escapade. [C19: Scot. dialect, prob. from ROMP + FROLIC]

rollicking[1] Ⓣ ('rɒlɪkɪŋ) *adj* boisterously carefree. [C19: from ROLLICK]

rollicking[2] Ⓣ ('rɒlɪkɪŋ) *n Brit. inf.* a very severe telling-off. [C20: from ROLLICK (vb) (in former sense: to be angry, make a fuss); ? infl. by BOLLOCKING]

roll in *vb* (*mainly intr*) **1** (*adv*) to arrive in abundance or in large numbers. **2** (*adv*) *Inf.* to arrive at one's destination. **3 be rolling in.** (*prep*) *Sl.* to abound or luxuriate in (wealth, money, etc.).

rolling ('rəʊlɪŋ) *adj* **1** having gentle rising and falling slopes: *rolling country.* **2** progressing by stages or by occurrences in different places in succession: *a rolling strike.* **3** subject to regular review and updating: *a rolling plan for overseas development.* **4** reverberating: *rolling thunder.* **5** *Sl.* extremely rich. **6** that may be turned up or down: *a rolling hat brim.* ◆ *adv* **7** *Sl.* swaying or staggering (in **rolling drunk**).

rolling launch *n Marketing.* the process of introducing a product onto a market gradually. Cf. **roll out** (sense 3).

rolling mill *n* **1** a mill or factory where ingots of heated metal are passed between rollers to produce sheets or bars of a required cross section and form. **2** a machine having rollers that may be used for this purpose.

rolling pin *n* a cylinder with handles at both ends used for rolling dough, pastry, etc., out flat.

rolling stock *n* the wheeled vehicles collectively used on a railway, including the locomotives, coaches, etc.

rolling stone *n* a restless or wandering person.

rollmop ('rəʊl,mɒp) *n* a herring fillet rolled, usually around onion slices, and pickled in spiced vinegar. [C20: from G *Rollmops,* from *rollen* to ROLL + *Mops* pug dog]

rollneck ('rəʊl,nɛk) *adj* **1** (of a garment) having a high neck that may be rolled over. ◆ *n* **2** a rollneck sweater or other garment.

roll of honour *n* a list of those who have died in war for their country.

roll on *vb* **1** *Brit.* used to express the wish that an eagerly anticipated event or date will come quickly: *roll on Saturday.* ◆ *adj* **roll-on. 2** (of a deodorant, etc.) dispensed by means of a revolving ball fitted into the

THESAURUS

roguish *adj* **1** = **unprincipled,** criminal, crooked, deceitful, deceiving, dishonest, fraudulent, knavish, raffish, rascally, shady (*inf.*), swindling, unscrupulous, villainous **2** = **mischievous,** arch, cheeky, coquettish, frolicsome, impish, playful, puckish, sportive, waggish

roister *vb* **1** = **make merry,** carouse, celebrate, frolic, go on a spree, live it up (*inf.*), paint the town red (*inf.*), push the boat out (*Brit. inf.*), revel, rollick, romp, whoop it up (*inf.*) **2** = **swagger,** bluster, boast, brag, show off (*inf.*), strut

role *n* **1** = **part,** character, impersonation, portrayal, representation **3** = **job,** capacity, duty, function, part, position, post, task

roll *vb* **1, 2** = **turn,** go round, gyrate, pivot, reel, revolve, rotate, spin, swivel, trundle, twirl, wheel, whirl **3** = **flow,** run, undulate **10** = **wind,** bind, coil, curl, enfold, entwine, envelop, furl, swathe, twist, wrap **12** = **level,** even, flatten, press, smooth, spread **13** = **rumble,** boom, drum, echo, grumble, resound, reverberate, roar, thunder **15** = **toss,** billow, lurch, reel, rock, sway, swing, tumble, wallow, welter **17** = **sway,** lumber, lurch, reel, stagger, swagger, waddle ◆ *n* **22** = **turn,** cycle, gyration, reel, revolution, rotation, run, spin, twirl, undulation, wheel, whirl **23** = **spool,** ball, bobbin, cylinder, reel, scroll **24** = **register,** annals, catalogue, census, chronicle, directory, index, inventory, list, record, roster, schedule, scroll, table **29** = **undulation,** billowing, swell, waves **30** = **tossing,** lurching, pitching, rocking, rolling, wallowing **31** = **rumble,** boom, drumming, growl, grumble, resonance, reverberation, roar, thunder

rollick *vb* **1** = **romp,** caper, cavort, frisk, galumph (*inf.*), gambol, make merry, revel

rollicking[1] *adj* = **boisterous,** carefree, cavorting, devil-may-care, exuberant, frisky, frolicsome, full of beans (*inf.*), hearty, jaunty, jovial, joyous, lively, merry, playful, rip-roaring (*inf.*), romping, spirited, sportive, sprightly, swashbuckling
Antonyms *adj* cheerless, despondent, dull, gloomy, lifeless, melancholy, morose, sad, sedate, serious, unhappy

rollicking[2] *n Brit. informal* = **scolding,** dressing-down, lecture, reprimand, roasting (*inf.*), neck of the container. ◆ *n* **roll-on.** **3** a woman's foundation garment, made of elasticized material and having no fastenings.

roll-on/roll-off *adj* denoting a cargo ship or ferry designed so that vehicles can be driven on and off.

roll out *vb* (*tr, adv*) **1** to cause (pastry) to become flatter and thinner by pressure with a rolling pin. **2** to show (a new type of aircraft) to the public for the first time. **3** to launch (a new film, product, etc.) in a series of successive waves, as over the whole country. ◆ *n* **roll-out.** **4** a presentation to the public of a new aircraft, product, etc.; a launch.

roll over *vb* (*adv*) **1** (*intr*) to overturn. **2** (*intr*) (of an animal, esp. a dog) to lie on its back while kicking its legs in the air. **3** (*intr*) to capitulate. **4** (*tr*) to allow (a loan, prize, etc.) to continue in force for a further period. ◆ *n* **rollover.** **5** an instance of such continuance of a loan, prize, etc.

roll-top desk *n* a desk having a slatted wooden panel that can be pulled down over the writing surface when not in use.

roll up *vb* (*adv*) **1** to form or cause to form a cylindrical shape. **2** (*tr*) to wrap (an object) round on itself or on an axis: *to roll up a map.* **3** (*intr*) *Inf.* to arrive, esp. in a vehicle. **4** (*intr*) *Austral.* to assemble; congregate. ◆ *n* **roll-up.** **5** *Brit. inf.* a cigarette made by hand from loose tobacco and cigarette papers. **6** *Austral.* the number attending a meeting, etc.

Rolodex ('rəulə,dɛks) *n Trademark, chiefly US.* a small file for holding names, addresses, and telephone numbers, consisting of cards attached horizontally to a rotatable central cylinder.

roly-poly 🅣 ('rəulɪ'pəulɪ) *adj* **1** plump, buxom, or rotund. ◆ *n, pl* **roly-polies.** **2** *Brit.* a strip of suet pastry spread with jam, fruit, or a savoury mixture, rolled up, and baked or steamed. [C17: apparently by reduplication from *roly,* from ROLL]

ROM (rɒm) *n Computing. acronym for* read only memory: a storage device that holds data permanently and cannot be altered by the programmer.

rom. *Printing. abbrev. for* roman (type).

Rom. *abbrev. for:* **1** Roman. **2** Romance (languages). **3** Romania(n). **4** *Bible.* Romans.

Romaic (rəu'meɪɪk) *Obs.* ◆ *n* **1** the modern Greek vernacular. ◆ *adj* **2** of or relating to Greek. [C19: from Gk *Rhōmaikos* Roman, with reference to the Eastern Roman Empire]

roman ('rəumən) *adj* **1** of, relating to, or denoting a vertical style of printing type: the usual form of type for most printed matter. Cf. **italic.** ◆ *n* **2** roman type. [C16: so called because the style of letters is that used in ancient Roman inscriptions]

Roman ('rəumən) *adj* **1** of or relating to Rome or its inhabitants in ancient or modern times. **2** of or relating to Roman Catholicism or the Roman Catholic Church. ◆ *n* **3** a citizen or inhabitant of ancient or modern Rome.

roman à clef *French.* (rɔmɑ̃ a kle) *n, pl* ***romans à clef*** (rɔmɑ̃ a kle). a novel in which real people are depicted under fictitious names. [lit.: novel with a key]

Roman alphabet *n* the alphabet evolved by the ancient Romans for the writing of Latin, derived ultimately from the Phoenicians. The alphabet serves for writing most of the languages of W Europe.

Roman blind *n* a window blind consisting of a length of material which, when drawn up, gathers into horizontal folds from the bottom.

Roman candle *n* a firework that produces a continuous shower of sparks punctuated by coloured balls of fire. [C19: it originated in Italy]

Roman Catholic *adj* **1** of or relating to the Roman Catholic Church. ◆ *n* **2** a member of this Church. ◆ Often shortened to **Catholic.**
▸**Roman Catholicism** *n*

Roman Catholic Church *n* the Christian Church over which the pope presides, with administrative headquarters in the Vatican. Also called: **Catholic Church, Church of Rome.**

romance 🅣 *n* (rə'mæns, 'rəumæns). **1** a love affair. **2** love, esp. romantic love idealized for its purity or beauty. **3** a spirit of or inclination for adventure or mystery. **4** a mysterious, exciting, sentimental, or nostalgic quality, esp. one associated with a place. **5** a narrative in verse or prose, written in a vernacular language in the Middle Ages, dealing with adventures of chivalrous heroes. **6** any similar narrative work dealing with events and characters remote from ordinary life. **7** a story, novel, film, etc., dealing with love, usually in an idealized or sentimental way. **8** an extravagant, absurd, or fantastic account. **9** a lyrical song or short instrumental composition having a simple melody. ◆ *vb* (rə'mæns), **romances, romancing, romanced.** **10** (*intr*) to tell, invent, or write extravagant or romantic fictions. **11** (*intr*) to tell extravagant or improbable lies. **12** (*intr*) to have romantic thoughts. **13** (*intr*) (of a couple) to indulge in romantic behaviour. **14** (*tr*) to be romantically involved with. [C13: *romauns,* from OF *romans,* ult. from L *Rōmānicus* Roman]
▸**ro'mancer** *n*

Romance (rə'mæns, 'rəumæns) *adj* **1** denoting, relating to, or belonging to the languages derived from Latin, including Italian, Spanish, Portuguese, French, and Romanian. **2** denoting a word borrowed from a Romance language. ◆ *n* **3** this group of languages.

Roman Empire *n* **1** the territories ruled by ancient Rome. At its height the Roman Empire included W and S Europe, N Africa, and SW Asia. In 395 A.D. it was divided into the **Eastern Roman Empire,** whose capital was Byzantium, and the **Western Roman Empire,** whose capital was Rome. **2** the government of Rome and its dominions by the emperors from 27 B.C. **3** the Byzantine Empire. **4** the Holy Roman Empire.

Romanesque (,rəumə'nɛsk) *adj* **1** denoting or having the style of architecture used in W and S Europe from the 9th to the 12th century, characterized by the rounded arch and massive-masonry wall construction. **2** denoting a corresponding style in painting, sculpture, etc. [C18: see ROMAN, -ESQUE]

Roman holiday *n* entertainment or pleasure that depends on the suffering of others. [C19: from Byron's poem *Childe Harold* (IV, 141)]

Romanian (rəu'meɪnɪən), **Rumanian,** *or* **Roumanian** *n* **1** the official language of Romania in SE Europe. **2** a native, citizen, or inhabitant of Romania. ◆ *adj* **3** relating to, denoting, or characteristic of Romania, its people, or their language.

Romanic (rəu'mænɪk) *adj* another word for **Roman** or **Romance.**

Romanism ('rəumə,nɪzəm) *n* Roman Catholicism, esp. when regarded as excessively or superstitiously ritualistic.
▸**'Romanist** *n*

Romanize *or* **Romanise** ('rəumə,naɪz) *vb* **Romanizes, Romanizing, Romanized** *or* **Romanises, Romanising, Romanised.** **1** (*tr*) to impart a Roman Catholic character to (a ceremony, etc.). **2** (*intr*) to be converted to Roman Catholicism. **3** (*tr*) to transcribe (a language) into the Roman alphabet.
▸**,Romani'zation** *or* **,Romani'sation** *n*

Roman law *n* the system of jurisprudence of ancient Rome, codified under Justinian and forming the basis of many modern legal systems.

Roman nose *n* a nose having a high prominent bridge.

Roman numerals *pl n* the letters used by the Romans for the representation of cardinal numbers, still used occasionally today. The integers are represented by the following letters: I (= 1), V (= 5), X (= 10), L (= 50), C (= 100), D (= 500), and M (= 1000). VI = 6 (V + I) but IV = 4 (V – I).

Romansch *or* **Romansh** (rəu'mænʃ) *n* a group of Romance dialects spoken in the Swiss canton of Grisons; an official language of Switzerland since 1938. [C17: from Romansch, lit.: Romance language]

romantic 🅣 (rəu'mæntɪk) *adj* **1** of, relating to, imbued with, or characterized by romance. **2** evoking or given to thoughts and feelings of love, esp. idealized or sentimental love: *a romantic setting.* **3** impractical, visionary, or idealistic: *a romantic scheme.* **4** *Often euphemistic.* imaginary or fictitious: *a romantic account of one's war service.* **5** (*often cap.*) of or relating to a movement in European art, music, and literature in the late 18th and early 19th centuries, characterized by an emphasis on feeling and content rather than order and form. ◆ *n* **6** a person who is romantic, as in being idealistic, amorous, or soulful. **7** a person whose tastes in art, literature, etc., lie mainly in romanticism. **8** (*often cap.*) a poet, composer, etc., of the romantic period or whose main inspiration is romanticism. [C17: from F, from obs. *romant* story, romance, from OF *romans* ROMANCE]
▸**ro'mantically** *adv*

romanticism (rəu'mæntɪ,sɪzəm) *n* **1** (*often cap.*) the theory, practice, and style of the romantic art, music, and literature of the late 18th and early 19th centuries, usually opposed to classicism. **2** romantic attitudes, ideals, or qualities.
▸**ro'manticist** *n*

romanticize *or* **romanticise** (rəu'mæntɪ,saɪz) *vb* **romanticizes, romanticizing, romanticized** *or* **romanticises, romanticising, romanticised.** **1** (*intr*) to think or act in a romantic way. **2** (*tr*) to interpret according to romantic precepts. **3** to make or become romantic, as in style.
▸**ro,mantici'zation** *or* **ro,mantici'sation** *n*

Romany *or* **Romani** ('rɒmənɪ, 'rəu-) *n* **1a** (*pl* **Romanies** *or* **Romanis**) another name for a **Gypsy.** **1b** (*as modifier*): *Romany customs.* **2** the language of the Gypsies, belonging to the Indic branch of the Indo-European family. [C19: from Romany *romani* (adj) Gypsy, ult. from Sansk. *domba* man of a low caste of musicians, of Dravidian origin]

THESAURUS

telling-off (*inf.*), ticking off (*inf.*), tongue-lashing

roly-poly *adj* **1** = **plump**, buxom, chubby, fat, overweight, podgy, pudgy, rotund, rounded, tubby

romance *n* **1** = **love affair**, affair, *affaire (du coeur)*, affair of the heart, amour, attachment, intrigue, liaison, passion, relationship **3** = **excitement**, adventure, charm, colour, exoticness, fascination, glamour, mystery, nostalgia, sentiment **7** = **story**, fairy tale, fantasy, fiction, idyll, legend, love story, melodrama, novel, tale, tear-jerker (*inf.*) **8** = **tall story** (*inf.*), absurdity, exaggeration, fabrication, fairy tale, falsehood, fiction, flight of fancy, invention, lie, trumped-up story, urban legend, urban myth ◆ *vb* **10** = **exaggerate**, be economical with the truth, fantasize, let one's imagination run away with one, lie, make up stories, stretch the truth, tell stories

romantic *adj* **1** = **exciting**, charming, colourful, exotic, fascinating, glamorous, mysterious, nostalgic, picturesque **2** = **loving**, amorous, fond, lovey-dovey, mushy (*inf.*), passionate, sentimental, sloppy (*inf.*), soppy (*Brit. inf.*), tender **3** = **idealistic**, dreamy, high-flown, impractical, quixotic, starry-eyed, unrealistic, utopian, visionary, whimsical **4** = **fictitious**, chimerical, exaggerated, extravagant, fabulous, fairy-tale, fanciful, fantastic, idyllic, imaginary, imaginative, improbable, legendary, made-up, unrealistic, wild ◆ *n* **6** = **idealist**, Don Quixote, dreamer, romancer, sentimentalist, utopian, visionary

Antonyms *adj* ≠ **exciting:** uninspiring ≠ **loving:** cold-hearted, insensitive, unaffectionate, unimpassioned, unloving, unromantic, unsentimental ≠ **idealistic:** practical, realistic ≠ **fictitious:** realistic

romanza (rəʊˈmænzə) *n* a short instrumental piece of songlike character. [It.]
romaunt (rəˈmɔːnt) *n Arch.* a verse romance. [C16: from OF; see ROMANTIC]
Romeo (ˈrəʊmɪəʊ) *n, pl* **Romeos.** an ardent male lover. [after the hero of Shakespeare's *Romeo and Juliet* (1594)]
Romish (ˈrəʊmɪʃ) *adj Usually derog.* of or resembling Roman Catholic beliefs or practices.
romp ❶ (rɒmp) *vb* (*intr*) **1** to play or run about wildly, boisterously, or joyfully. **2 romp home** (*or* **in**). to win a race, etc., easily. ◆ *n* **3** a noisy or boisterous game or prank. **4** an instance of sexual activity between two or more people that is entered into light-heartedly and without emotional commitment: *naked sex romps.* **5** *Arch.* a playful or boisterous child, esp. a girl. **6** an easy victory. [C18: prob. var. of RAMP, from OF *ramper* to crawl, climb]
rompers (ˈrɒmpəz) *pl n* **1** a one-piece baby garment consisting of trousers and a bib with straps. **2** *NZ.* a type of costume worn by schoolgirls for games and gymnastics.
rondavel (ˌrɒnˈdɑːvəl) *n S. African.* a circular, often thatched, building with a conical roof. [from ?]
rondeau (ˈrɒndəʊ) *n, pl* **rondeaux** (-dəʊ, -dəʊz). a poem consisting of 13 or 10 lines with two rhymes and having the opening words of the first line used as an unrhymed refrain. [C16: from OF, from *rondel* a little round, from *rond* ROUND]
rondel (ˈrɒndᵊl) *n* a rondeau consisting of three stanzas of 13 or 14 lines with a two-line refrain appearing twice or three times. [C14: from OF, lit.: a little circle, from *rond* ROUND]
rondo (ˈrɒndəʊ) *n, pl* **rondos.** a piece of music in which a refrain is repeated between episodes: often constitutes the form of the last movement of a sonata or concerto. [C18: from It., from F RONDEAU]
rone (rəʊn) *or* **ronepipe** *n Scot.* a drainpipe for carrying rainwater from a roof. [C19: from ?]
röntgen (ˈrɒntgən, -tjən, ˈrɛnt-) *n* a variant spelling of **roentgen.**
roo (ruː) *n Austral. inf.* a kangaroo.
rood (ruːd) *n* **1a** a crucifix, esp. one set on a beam or screen at the entrance to the chancel of a church. **1b** (*as modifier*): *rood screen.* **2** the Cross on which Christ was crucified. **3** a unit of area equal to one quarter of an acre or 0.10117 hectare. **4** a unit of area equal to 40 square rods. [OE *rōd*]
roof (ruːf) *n, pl* **roofs** (ruːfs, ruːvz). **1a** a structure that covers or forms the top of a building. **1b** (*in combination*): *the rooftop.* **1c** (*as modifier*): *a roof garden.* **2** the top covering of a vehicle, oven, or other structure: *the roof of a car.* **3** *Anat.* any structure that covers an organ or part: *the roof of the mouth.* **4** a highest or topmost point or part: *Mount Everest is the roof of the world.* **5** a house or other shelter: *a poor man's roof.* **6 hit** (*or* **raise** *or* **go through**) **the roof.** *Inf.* to get extremely angry. ◆ *vb* **7** (*tr*) to provide or cover with a roof or rooflike part. [OE *hrōf*]
▸ˈ**roofer** *n* ▸ˈ**roofless** *adj*
roof garden *n* a garden on a flat roof of a building.
roofing (ˈruːfɪŋ) *n* **1** material used to construct a roof. **2** the act of constructing a roof.
roof rack *n* a rack attached to the roof of a motor vehicle for carrying luggage, skis, etc.
rooftree (ˈruːfˌtriː) *n* another name for **ridgepole.**
rooibos (ˈrɔɪˌbɒs, ˈrʊɪˌbɒs) *n* any of various South African trees with red leaves. [from Afrik. *rooi* red + *bos* bush]
rooibos tea *n S. African.* a tealike drink made from the leaves of the rooibos.
rooikat (ˈrɔɪˌkæt, ˈrʊɪˌkæt) *n* a South African lynx. [from Afrik. *rooi* red + *kat* cat]
rooinek (ˈrɔɪˌnɛk, ˈrʊɪˌnɛk) *n S. African.* a contemptuous name for an **Englishman.** [C19: Afrik., lit.: red neck]
rook[1] ❶ (rʊk) *n* **1** a large Eurasian passerine bird, with a black plumage and a whitish base to its bill. **2** *Sl.* a swindler or cheat, esp. one who cheats at cards. ◆ *vb* **3** (*tr*) *Sl.* to overcharge, swindle, or cheat. [OE *hrōc*]
rook[2] (rʊk) *n* a chesspiece that may move any number of unoccupied squares in a straight line, horizontally or vertically. Also called: **castle.** [C14: from OF *rok*, ult. from Ar. *rukhkh*]
rookery (ˈrʊkərɪ) *n, pl* **rookeries. 1** a group of nesting rooks. **2** a clump of trees containing rooks' nests. **3a** a breeding ground or communal living area of certain other birds or mammals, esp. penguins or seals. **3b** a colony of any such creatures. **4** *Arch.* an overcrowded slum.
rookie (ˈrʊkɪ) *n Inf.* a newcomer, esp. a raw recruit in the army. [C20: changed from RECRUIT]
room ❶ (ruːm, rʊm) *n* **1** space or extent, esp. unoccupied or unobstructed space for a particular purpose: *is there room to pass?* **2** an area within a building enclosed by a floor, a ceiling, and walls or partitions. **3** (*functioning as sing or pl*) the people present in a room: *the whole room was laughing.* **4** (foll. by *for*) opportunity or scope: *room for manoeuvre.* **5** (*pl*) a part of a house, hotel, etc., that is rented out as separate accommodation: *living in dingy rooms in Dalry.* ◆ *vb* **6** (*intr*) to occupy or share a room or lodging: *where does he room?* [OE *rūm*]
▸ˈ**roomer** *n*
roomful (ˈruːmˌfʊl, ˈrʊm-) *n, pl* **roomfuls.** a number or quantity sufficient to fill a room: *a roomful of furniture.*
rooming house *n US & Canad.* a house having self-contained furnished rooms or flats for renting.
roommate (ˈruːmˌmeɪt, ˈrʊm-) *n* a person with whom one shares a room or lodging.
room service *n* service in a hotel providing meals, drinks, etc., in guests' rooms.
roomy ❶ (ˈruːmɪ, ˈrʊmɪ) *adj* **roomier, roomiest.** spacious.
▸ˈ**roomily** *adv* ▸ˈ**roominess** *n*
roost (ruːst) *n* **1** a place, perch, branch, etc., where birds, esp. domestic fowl, rest or sleep. **2** a temporary place to rest or stay. ◆ *vb* **3** (*intr*) to rest or sleep on a roost. **4** (*intr*) to settle down or stay. **5 come home to roost.** to have unfavourable repercussions. [OE *hrōst*]
Roost (ruːst) *n* **the.** a powerful current caused by conflicting tides around the Shetland and Orkney Islands. [C16: from ON *röst*]
rooster (ˈruːstə) *n Chiefly US & Canad.* the male of the domestic fowl; a cock.
root[1] ❶ (ruːt) *n* **1a** the organ of a higher plant that anchors the rest of the plant in the ground and absorbs water and mineral salts from the soil. **1b** (loosely) any of the branches of such an organ. **2** any plant part, such as a tuber, that is similar to a root in function or appearance. **3a** the essential part or nature of something: *your analysis strikes at the root of the problem.* **3b** (*as modifier*): *the root cause of the problem.* **4** *Anat.* the embedded portion of a tooth, nail, hair, etc. **5** origin or derivation. **6** (*pl*) a person's sense of belonging in a community, place, etc., esp. the one in which he was born or brought up. **7** *Bible.* a descendant. **8** *Linguistics.* the form of a word that remains after removal of all affixes. **9** *Maths.* a quantity that when multiplied by itself a certain number of times equals a given quantity: *3 is a cube root of 27.* **10** Also called: **solution.** *Maths.* a number that when substituted for the variable satisfies a given equation. **11** *Music.* (in harmony) the note forming the foundation of a chord. **12** *Austral. & NZ sl.* sexual intercourse. **13 root and branch.** (*adv*) entirely; utterly. ◆ Related adj: **radical.** ◆ *vb* **14** (*intr*) Also: **take root.** to establish a root and begin to grow. **15** (*intr*) Also: **take root.** to become established, embedded, or effective. **16** (*tr*) to embed with or as if with a root or roots. **17** *Austral. & NZ sl.* to have sexual intercourse (with). ◆ See also **root out, roots.** [OE *rōt*, from ON]
▸ˈ**rooter** *n* ▸ˈ**root,like** *adj* ▸ˈ**rooty** *adj* ▸ˈ**rootiness** *n*
root[2] ❶ (ruːt) *vb* (*intr*) **1** (of a pig) to burrow in or dig up the earth in search of food, using the snout. **2** (foll. by *about, around, in,* etc.) *Inf.* to search vigorously but unsystematically. [C16: changed (through infl. of ROOT[1]) from earlier *wroot*, from OE *wrōtan*; rel. to OE *wrōt* snout]
▸ˈ**rooter** *n*
root[3] (ruːt) *vb* (*intr*; usually foll. by *for*) *Inf.* to give support to (a contestant, team, etc.), as by cheering. [C19: ? var. of Scot. *rout* to make a loud noise, from ON *rauta* to roar]
root beer *n US & Canad.* an effervescent drink made from extracts of various roots and herbs.
root canal *n* the passage in the root of a tooth through which its nerves and blood vessels enter the pulp cavity.
root-canal therapy *n* another name for **root treatment.**
root climber *n* any of various climbing plants, such as the ivy, that adhere to a supporting structure by means of small roots growing from the side of the stem.
root crop *n* a crop, as of turnips or beets, cultivated for the food value of its roots.
rooted ❶ (ˈruːtɪd) *adj* **1** having roots. **2** deeply felt: *rooted objections.*
root ginger *n* the raw underground stem of the ginger plant used finely chopped or grated, esp. in Chinese dishes.
root hair *n* any of the hollow hairlike outgrowths of the outer cells of a root, just behind the tip, that absorb water and salts from the soil.
rooting compound *n Horticulture.* a substance, usually a powder, containing auxins in which plant cuttings are dipped in order to promote root growth.
rootle (ˈruːtᵊl) *vb* **rootles, rootling, rootled.** (*intr*) *Brit.* another word for **root**[2].

THESAURUS

romp *vb* **1** = **frolic**, caper, cavort, cut capers, frisk, gambol, have fun, make merry, revel, roister, rollick, skip, sport **2 romp home** *or* **in** = **win easily**, run away with it, walk it (*inf.*), win by a mile (*inf.*), win hands down ◆ *n* **3** = **frolic**, caper, lark (*inf.*)
rook[1] *vb* **3** *Slang* = **cheat**, bilk, clip (*sl.*), cozen, defraud, diddle (*inf.*), do (*sl.*), fleece, gyp (*sl.*), overcharge, rip off (*sl.*), skin (*sl.*), stiff (*sl.*), sting (*inf.*), swindle
room *n* **1** = **space**, allowance, area, capacity, compass, elbowroom, expanse, extent, latitude, leeway, margin, play, range, scope, territory, volume **2** = **chamber**, apartment, office **4** = **opportunity**, chance, occasion, scope
roomy *adj* = **spacious**, ample, broad, capacious, commodious, extensive, generous, large, sizable *or* sizeable, wide
Antonyms *adj* bounded, confined, cramped, narrow, small, tiny
root[1] *n* **1, 2** = **stem**, radicle, radix, rhizome, tuber **3** = **heart**, core, crux, essence, fundamental, nub, nucleus **5** = **source**, base, beginnings, bottom, cause, derivation, foundation, fountainhead, germ, mainspring, origin, seat, seed, starting point **6** *plural* = **sense of belonging**, birthplace, cradle, family, heritage, home, origins **13 root and branch** = **completely**, entirely, finally, radically, thoroughly, totally, to the last man, utterly, wholly, without exception ◆ *vb* **15** = **become established**, anchor, become settled, embed, entrench, establish, fasten, fix, ground, implant, moor, set, stick, take root
root[2] *vb* **1, 2** = **dig**, burrow, delve, ferret, forage, hunt, nose, poke, pry, rootle, rummage
rooted *adj* **2** = **deep-seated**, confirmed, deep, deeply felt, entrenched, established, firm, fixed, ingrained, radical, rigid

rootless ❶ (ˈruːtlɪs) *adj* having no roots, esp. (of a person) having no ties with a particular place.
rootlet (ˈruːtlɪt) *n* a small root.
root mean square *n* the square root of the average of the squares of a set of numbers or quantities: *the root mean square of* 1, 2, *and* 4 *is* $\sqrt{[(1^2 + 2^2 + 4^2)/3]} = \sqrt{7}$. Abbrev.: **rms.**
root nodule *n* a swelling on the root of a leguminous plant, such as clover, that contains bacteria capable of nitrogen fixation.
root out ❶ *vb* (*tr, adv*) to remove or eliminate completely: *we must root out inefficiency*.
roots (ruːts) *adj* (of popular music) going back to the origins of a style, esp. in being genuine and unpretentious: *roots rock*.
roots music *n* **1** another name for **world music. 2** reggae, esp. when regarded as authentic and uncommercialized.
rootstock (ˈruːtˌstɒk) *n* **1** another name for **rhizome. 2** another name for **stock** (sense 7). **3** *Biol.* a basic structure from which offshoots have developed.
root treatment *n Dentistry.* a procedure, used for treating an abscess at the tip of the root of a tooth, in which the pulp is removed and a filling (**root filling**) inserted in the root canal. Also called: **root-canal therapy.**
ropable *or* **ropeable** (ˈrəʊpəbᵊl) *adj* **1** capable of being roped. **2** *Austral. & NZ inf.* **2a** angry. **2b** wild or intractable: *a ropable beast*.
rope ❶ (rəʊp) *n* **1a** a fairly thick cord made of intertwined hemp or other fibres or of wire or other strong material. **1b** (*as modifier*): *a rope ladder*. **2** a row of objects fastened to form a line: *a rope of pearls*. **3** a quantity of material wound in the form of a cord. **4** a filament or strand, esp. of something viscous or glutinous: *a rope of slime*. **5 give (someone) enough (*or* plenty of) rope to hang himself.** to allow (someone) to accomplish his own downfall by his own foolish acts. **6 know the ropes.** to have a thorough understanding of a particular sphere of activity. **7 on the ropes. 7a** *Boxing.* driven against the ropes enclosing the ring by an opponent's attack. **7b** in a hopeless position. **8 the rope. 8a** a rope halter used for hanging. **8b** death by hanging. ◆ *vb* **ropes, roping, roped. 9** (*tr*) to bind or fasten with or as if with a rope. **10** (*tr*; usually foll. by *off*) to enclose or divide by means of a rope. **11** (when *intr*, foll. by *up*) *Mountaineering.* to tie (climbers) together with a rope. [OE *rāp*]
rope in ❶ *vb* (*tr, adv*) **1** *Brit.* to persuade to take part in some activity. **2** *US & Canad.* to trick or entice into some activity.
rope's end *n* a short piece of rope, esp. as formerly used for flogging sailors.
ropewalk (ˈrəʊpˌwɔːk) *n* a long narrow usually covered path or shed where ropes are made.
ropey ❶ *or* **ropy** (ˈrəʊpɪ) *adj* **ropier, ropiest. 1** *Brit. inf.* **1a** inferior. **1b** slightly unwell. **2** (of a viscous or sticky substance) forming strands. **3** resembling a rope.
▸ˈ**ropily** *adv* ▸ˈ**ropiness** *n*
Roquefort (ˈrɒkfɔː) *n* a blue-veined cheese with a strong flavour, made from ewe's and goat's milk. [C19: after *Roquefort*, village in S France]
roquet (ˈrəʊkɪ) *Croquet.* ◆ *vb* **roquets** (-kɪz), **roqueting** (-kɪɪŋ), **roqueted** (-kɪd). **1** to drive one's ball against (another person's ball) in order to be allowed to croquet. ◆ *n* **2** the act of roqueting. [C19: var. of CROQUET]
ro-ro (ˈrəʊrəʊ) *adj acronym for* roll-on/roll-off.
rorqual (ˈrɔːkwəl) *n* any of several whalebone whales that have a dorsal fin and a series of grooves along the throat and chest. Also called: **finback.** [C19: from F, from Norwegian *rörhval*, from ON *reytharhvalr*, from *reythr* (from *rauthr* red) + *hvalr* whale]
Rorschach test (ˈrɔːʃɑːk) *n Psychol.* a personality test consisting of a number of unstructured inkblots presented for interpretation. [C20: after Hermann *Rorschach* (1884–1922), Swiss psychiatrist]
rort (rɔːt) *Austral. inf.* ◆ *n* **1** a rowdy party or celebration. **2** a fraud; deception. ◆ *vb* (*tr*) **3** to take unfair advantage of (something): *our voting system can be rorted*. [C20: back formation from E dialect *rorty* (in the sense: good, splendid)]
▸ˈ**rorty** *adj*
rosace (ˈrəʊzeɪs) *n* **1** another name for **rose window. 2** another name for **rosette.** [C19: from F, from L *rosāceus* ROSACEOUS]
rosaceous (rəʊˈzeɪʃəs) *adj* **1** of or belonging to the Rosaceae, a family of plants typically having white, yellow, pink, or red five-petalled flowers. The family includes the rose, strawberry, blackberry, and many fruit trees. **2** like a rose, esp., rose-coloured. [C18: from L *rosāceus* composed of roses, from *rosa* ROSE[1]]
rosarian (rəʊˈzɛərɪən) *n* a person who cultivates roses, esp. professionally.
rosarium (rəʊˈzɛərɪəm) *n, pl* **rosariums** *or* **rosaria** (-ˈzɛərɪə). a rose garden. [C19: NL]
rosary (ˈrəʊzərɪ) *n, pl* **rosaries. 1** *RC Church.* **1a** a series of prayers counted on a string of beads, usually five or 15 decades of Aves, each decade beginning with a Paternoster and ending with a Gloria. **1b** a string of 55 or 165 beads used to count these prayers as they are recited. **2** (in other religions) a similar string of beads used in praying. **3** an archaic word for a **garland** (of flowers, etc.). [C14: from L *rosārium* rose garden, from *rosārius* of roses, from *rosa* ROSE[1]]
rose[1] (rəʊz) *n* **1a** a shrub or climbing plant having prickly stems, compound leaves, and fragrant flowers. **1b** (*in combination*): *rosebush*. **2** the flower of any of these plants. **3** any of various similar plants, such as the Christmas rose. **4a** a purplish-pink colour. **4b** (*as adj*): *rose paint*. **5** a rose, or a representation of one, as the national emblem of England. **6a** a cut for a gemstone, having a hemispherical faceted crown and a flat base. **6b** a gem so cut. **7** a perforated cap fitted to a watering can or hose, causing the water to issue in a spray. **8** a design or decoration shaped like a rose; rosette. **9** Also called: **ceiling rose.** *Electrical engineering.* a circular boss attached to a ceiling through which the flexible lead of an electric-light fitting passes. **10** *History.* See **red rose, white rose. 11 bed of roses.** a situation of comfort or ease. **12 under the rose.** in secret; privately; sub rosa. ◆ *vb* **roses, rosing, rosed. 13** (*tr*) to make rose-coloured; cause to blush or redden. [OE, from L *rosa*, prob. from Gk *rhodon* rose]
▸ˈ**roseˌlike** *adj*
rose[2] (rəʊz) *vb* the past tense of **rise.**
rosé (ˈrəʊzeɪ) *n* any pink wine, made either by removing the skins of red grapes after only a little colour has been extracted or by mixing red and white wines. [C19: from F, lit.: pink, from L *rosa* ROSE[1]]
roseate ❶ (ˈrəʊzɪˌeɪt) *adj* **1** of the colour rose or pink. **2** excessively or idealistically optimistic.
rosebay (ˈrəʊzˌbeɪ) *n* **1** any of several rhododendrons. **2 rosebay willowherb.** a perennial plant that has spikes of deep pink flowers and is widespread in N temperate regions. **3** another name for **oleander.**
rosebud (ˈrəʊzˌbʌd) *n* **1** the bud of a rose. **2** *Literary.* a pretty young woman.
rose campion *n* a European plant widely cultivated for its pink flowers. Its stems and leaves are covered with white woolly down. Also called: **dusty miller.**
rose chafer *or* **beetle** *n* a British beetle that has a greenish-golden body with a metallic lustre and feeds on plants.
rose-coloured *adj* **1** of the colour rose; rosy. **2** Also: **rose-tinted.** excessively optimistic. **3 see through rose-coloured** *or* **rose-tinted glasses** (*or* **spectacles**). to view in an excessively optimistic light.
rose-cut *adj* (of a gemstone) cut with a hemispherical faceted crown and a flat base.
rosehip (ˈrəʊzˌhɪp) *n* the berry-like fruit of a rose plant.
rosella (rəʊˈzɛlə) *n* any of various Australian parrots. [C19: prob. alteration of *Rose-hiller*, after *Rose Hill*, Parramatta, near Sydney]
rosemary (ˈrəʊzmərɪ) *n, pl* **rosemaries.** an aromatic European shrub widely cultivated for its grey-green evergreen leaves, which are used in cookery and in the manufacture of perfumes. It is the traditional flower of remembrance. [C15: earlier *rosmarine*, from L *rōs* dew + *marīnus* marine; modern form infl. by folk etymology, as if ROSE[1] + *Mary*]
rose of Sharon (ˈʃærən) *n* a creeping shrub native to SE Europe but widely cultivated, having large yellow flowers. Also called: **Aaron's beard.**
roseola (rəʊˈziːələ) *n Pathol.* **1** any red skin rash. **2** another name for **rubeola.** [C19: from NL, dim. of L *roseus* rosy]
▸**roˈseolar** *adj*
rosery (ˈrəʊzərɪ) *n, pl* **roseries.** a bed or garden of roses.
Rosetta stone *n* a basalt slab discovered in 1799 at Rosetta, N Egypt, dating to the reign of Ptolemy V (196 B.C.) and carved with parallel inscriptions in hieroglyphics, Egyptian demotic, and Greek, which provided the key to the decipherment of ancient Egyptian texts.
rosette (rəʊˈzɛt) *n* **1** a decoration resembling a rose, esp. an arrangement of ribbons in a rose-shaped design worn as a badge or presented as a prize. **2** another name for **rose window. 3** *Bot.* a circular cluster of leaves growing from the base of a stem. [C18: from OF: a little ROSE[1]]
rose-water *n* **1** scented water made by the distillation of rose petals or by impregnation with oil of roses. **2** (*modifier*) elegant or delicate, esp. excessively so.
rose window *n* a circular window, esp. one that has ornamental tracery radiating from the centre to form a symmetrical roselike pattern. Also called: **wheel window, rosette.**
rosewood (ˈrəʊzˌwʊd) *n* the hard dark wood of any of various tropical trees. It has a roselike scent and is used in cabinetwork.
Rosh Hashanah *or* **Rosh Hashana** (ˈrɒʃ həˈʃɑːnə; *Hebrew* ˈrɔʃ haʃaˈna) *n* the Jewish New Year festival, celebrated on the first and second of Tishri. [from Heb., lit.: beginning of the year, from *rōsh* head + *hash-shānāh* year]
Rosicrucian (ˌrəʊzɪˈkruːʃən) *n* **1** a member of a society professing esoteric religious doctrines, venerating the rose and Cross as symbols of Christ's Resurrection and Redemption, and claiming various occult powers. ◆ *adj* **2** of or designating the Rosicrucians or Rosicrucianism.

THESAURUS

rootless *adj* = **footloose**, homeless, itinerant, roving, transient, vagabond
root out *vb* = **get rid of**, abolish, cut out, destroy, dig up by the roots, do away with, efface, eliminate, eradicate, erase, exterminate, extirpate, remove, tear out by the roots, uproot, weed out, wipe from the face of the earth
rope *n* **1** = **cord**, cable, hawser, line, strand **6 know the ropes** = **be experienced**, be an old hand, be knowledgeable, know all the ins and outs, know one's way around, know the score (*inf.*), know what's what, know where it's at (*sl.*) **8 the rope** = **hanging**, capital punishment, halter, lynching, noose ◆ *vb* **9** = **tie**, bind, fasten, hitch, lash, lasso, moor, pinion, tether
rope in *vb* **1** *Brit.* = **persuade**, drag in, engage, enlist, inveigle, involve, talk into
ropey *adj Brit. informal* **1a** = **inferior**, deficient, inadequate, indifferent, mediocre, no great shakes (*inf.*), of poor quality, poor, sketchy, substandard **1b** = **unwell**, below par, off colour, poorly (*inf.*), rough (*inf.*), sickish, under the weather (*inf.*)
roseate *adj* **1** = **pink**, blooming, blushing, pinkish, red, rose-coloured, rosy, rubicund, ruddy **2**

[C17: from L *Rosae Crucis* Rose of the Cross, translation of the G name Christian *Rosenkreuz,* supposed founder of the society]

rosin (ˈrɒzɪn) *n* **1** Also called: **colophony.** a translucent brittle amber substance produced in the distillation of crude turpentine oleoresin and used esp. in making varnishes, printing inks, and sealing waxes and for treating the bows of stringed instruments. **2** (not in technical usage) another name for **resin** (sense 1). ◆ *vb* **3** (*tr*) to treat or coat with rosin. [C14: var. of RESIN]
▸**ˈrosiny** *adj*

ROSPA (ˈrɒspə) *n* (in Britain) *acronym for* Royal Society for the Prevention of Accidents.

roster Ⓣ (ˈrɒstə) *n* **1** a list or register, esp. one showing the order of people enrolled for duty. ◆ *vb* **2** (*tr*) to place on a roster. [C18: from Du. *rooster* grating or list (the lined paper looking like a grid)]

rostrum Ⓣ (ˈrɒstrəm) *n, pl* **rostrums** *or* **rostra** (-trə). **1** any platform on which public speakers stand to address an audience. **2** a platform in front of an orchestra on which the conductor stands. **3** another word for **ram** (sense 5). **4** the prow of an ancient Roman ship. **5** *Biol., zool.* a beak or beaklike part. [C16: from L *rōstrum* beak, ship's prow, from *rōdere* to nibble, gnaw; in pl, *rōstra* orator's platform, because this platform in the Roman forum was adorned with the prows of captured ships]
▸**ˈrostral** *adj*

rosy Ⓣ (ˈrəʊzɪ) *adj* **rosier, rosiest. 1** of the colour rose or pink. **2** having a healthy pink complexion: *rosy cheeks.* **3** optimistic, esp. excessively so: *a rosy view of social improvements.* **4** resembling or abounding in roses.
▸**ˈrosily** *adv* ▸**ˈrosiness** *n*

rot Ⓣ (rɒt) *vb* **rots, rotting, rotted. 1** to decay or cause to decay as a result of bacterial or fungal action. **2** (*intr;* usually foll. by *off* or *away*) to crumble (off) or break (away), as from decay or long use. **3** (*intr*) to become weak or depressed through inertia, confinement, etc.; languish: *rotting in prison.* **4** to become or cause to become morally degenerate. ◆ *n* **5** the process of rotting or the state of being rotten. **6** something decomposed. Related adj: **putrid. 7** short for **dry rot. 8** *Pathol.* any putrefactive decomposition of tissues. **9** a condition in plants characterized by decay of tissues, caused by bacteria, fungi, etc. **10** *Vet. science.* a contagious fungal disease of sheep. **11** (*also interj*) nonsense; rubbish. [OE *rotian* (vb); rel. to ON, *rotna;* C13 (n), from ON]

rota (ˈrəʊtə) *n Chiefly Brit.* a register of names showing the order in which people take their turn to perform certain duties. [C17: from L: a wheel]

Rota (ˈrəʊtə) *n RC Church.* the supreme ecclesiastical tribunal.

rotachute (ˈrəʊtə,ʃuːt) *n* a device serving the same purpose as a parachute, in which the canopy is replaced by freely revolving rotor blades, used for the delivery of stores or recovery of missiles.

rotaplane (ˈrəʊtə,pleɪn) *n* an aircraft that derives its lift from freely revolving rotor blades.

rotary Ⓣ (ˈrəʊtərɪ) *adj* **1** operating by rotation. **2** turning; revolving. ◆ *n, pl* **rotaries. 3** a part of a machine that rotates about an axis. **4** *US & Canad.* another term for **roundabout** (sense 2). [C18: from Med. L *rotārius,* from L *rota* wheel]

Rotary Club *n* any of the local clubs that form **Rotary International,** an international association of professional and businessmen founded in the US in 1905 to promote community service.
▸**Rotarian** (rəʊˈtɛərɪən) *n, adj*

rotary engine *n* **1** an internal-combustion engine having radial cylinders that rotate about a fixed crankshaft. **2** an engine, such as a turbine or wankel engine, in which power is transmitted directly to rotating components.

rotary plough *or* **tiller** *n* an implement with a series of blades mounted on a power-driven shaft which rotates so as to break up soil.

rotary press *n* a machine for printing from a revolving cylindrical forme, usually onto a continuous strip of paper.

rotary table *n* a chain or gear-driven unit, mounted in the derrick floor which rotates the drill pipe and bit.

rotate Ⓣ *vb* (rəʊˈteɪt), **rotates, rotating, rotated. 1** to turn or cause to turn around an axis; revolve or spin. **2** to follow or cause to follow a set sequence. **3** to replace (one set of personnel) with another. ◆ *adj* (ˈrəʊteɪt). **4** *Bot.* designating a corolla the petals of which radiate like the spokes of a wheel.
▸**roˈtatable** *adj*

rotation Ⓣ (rəʊˈteɪʃən) *n* **1** the act of rotating; rotary motion. **2** a regular cycle of events in a set order or sequence. **3** a planned sequence of cropping according to which the crops grown in successive seasons on the same land are varied so as to make a balanced demand on its resources of fertility. **4** the spinning motion of a body, such as a planet, about an internal axis. **5** *Maths.* **5a** a circular motion of a configuration about a given point, without a change in shape. **5b** a transformation in which the coordinate axes are rotated by a fixed angle about the origin.
▸**roˈtational** *adj*

rotator (rəʊˈteɪtə) *n* **1** a person, device, or part that rotates or causes rotation. **2** *Anat.* any of various muscles that revolve a part on its axis.

rotatory (ˈrəʊtətərɪ, -trɪ) *or* (*less commonly*) **rotative** *adj* of, possessing, or causing rotation.
▸**ˈrotatorily** *adv*

Rotavator (ˈrəʊtə,veɪtə) *n Trademark.* a mechanical cultivator with rotary blades. [C20: from ROTA(RY) + (CULTI)VATOR]
▸**ˈRota,vate** *vb* (*tr*)

rote (rəʊt) *n* **1** a habitual or mechanical routine or procedure. **2 by rote.** by repetition; by heart (often in **learn by rote**). [C14: from ?]

rotenone (ˈrəʊtɪ,nəʊn) *n* a white odourless crystalline substance extracted from the roots of derris: a powerful insecticide. [C20: from Japanese *rōten* derris + -ONE]

rotgut (ˈrɒt,gʌt) *n Facetious sl.* alcoholic drink, esp. spirits, of inferior quality.

rotifer (ˈrəʊtɪfə) *n* a minute aquatic multicellular invertebrate having a ciliated wheel-like organ used in feeding and locomotion: common constituents of freshwater plankton. Also called: **wheel animalcule.** [C18: from NL *Rotifera,* from L *rota* wheel + *ferre* to bear]
▸**rotiferal** (rəʊˈtɪfərəl) *or* **roˈtiferous** *adj*

rotisserie (rəʊˈtɪsərɪ) *n* **1** a rotating spit on which meat, poultry, etc., can be cooked. **2** a shop or restaurant where meat is roasted to order. [C19: from F, from OF *rostir* to ROAST]

rotogravure (,rəʊtəʊgrəˈvjʊə) *n* **1** a printing process using cylinders with many small holes, from which ink is transferred to a moving web of paper, etc., in a rotary press. **2** printed material produced in this way, esp. magazines. [C20: from L *rota* wheel + GRAVURE]

rotor (ˈrəʊtə) *n* **1** the rotating member of a machine or device, such as the revolving arm of the distributor of an internal-combustion engine. **2** a rotating device having radiating blades projecting from a hub which produces thrust to lift and propel a helicopter. [C20: shortened form of ROTATOR]

rotten Ⓣ (ˈrɒtᵊn) *adj* **1** decomposing, decaying, or putrid. **2** breaking up, esp. through age or hard use: *rotten ironwork.* **3** morally corrupt. **4** disloyal or treacherous. **5** *Inf.* unpleasant: *rotten weather.* **6** *Inf.* unsatisfactory or poor: *rotten workmanship.* **7** *Inf.* miserably unwell. **8** *Inf.* distressed and embarrassed: *I felt rotten breaking the bad news to him.* ◆ *adv Inf.* **9** extremely; very much: *men fancy her rotten.* [C13: from ON *rottin;* rel. to OE *rotian* to ROT]
▸**ˈrottenly** *adv* ▸**ˈrottenness** *n*

rotten borough *n* (before the Reform Act of 1832) any of certain English parliamentary constituencies with few or no electors.

rottenstone (ˈrɒtᵊn,stəʊn) *n* a much-weathered limestone, rich in silica: used in powdered form for polishing metal.

rotter Ⓣ (ˈrɒtə) *n Sl., chiefly Brit.* a worthless, unpleasant, or despicable person.

Rottweiler (ˈrɒt,waɪlə, -,vaɪlə) *n* **1** a breed of large dog with a smooth black and tan coat, noted for strength and aggression. **2** (*often not cap.*) **2a** an aggressive and unscrupulous person. **2b** (*as modifier*): *rottweiler*

THESAURUS

= **overoptimistic**, idealistic, rose-coloured, unrealistic, utopian

roster *n* **1** = **rota**, agenda, catalogue, inventory, list, listing, register, roll, schedule, scroll, table

rostrum *n* **1, 2** = **stage**, dais, platform, podium, stand

rosy *adj* **1** = **pink**, red, roseate, rose-coloured **2** = **glowing**, blooming, blushing, flushed, fresh, healthy-looking, radiant, reddish, roseate, rubicund, ruddy **3** = **promising**, auspicious, bright, cheerful, encouraging, favourable, hopeful, optimistic, reassuring, roseate, rose-coloured, sunny
Antonyms *adj* ≠ **glowing:** ashen, colourless, grey, pale, pallid, sickly, wan, white ≠ **promising:** cheerless, depressing, discouraging, dismal, down in the dumps (*inf.*), dull, gloomy, hopeless, miserable, pessimistic, unhappy, unpromising

rot *vb* **1** = **decay**, break down, corrode, corrupt, decompose, degenerate, deteriorate, disintegrate, fester, go bad, moulder, perish, putrefy, spoil, taint **3** = **deteriorate**, decline, degenerate, languish, waste away, wither away ◆ *n* **5** = **decay**, blight, canker, corrosion, corruption, decomposition, deterioration, disintegration, mould, putrefaction, putrescence **11** *Informal* = **nonsense**, balderdash, bilge (*inf.*), bosh (*inf.*), bunk (*inf.*), bunkum *or* buncombe (*chiefly US*), claptrap (*inf.*), cobblers (*Brit. taboo sl.*), codswallop (*Brit. sl.*), crap (*sl.*), drivel, garbage (*chiefly US*), hogwash, hokum (*sl., chiefly US & Canad.*), hot air (*inf.*), moonshine, piffle (*inf.*), poppycock (*inf.*), rubbish, shit (*taboo sl.*), stuff and nonsense, tommyrot, tosh (*sl., chiefly Brit.*), trash, tripe (*inf.*), twaddle

rotary *adj* **2** = **revolving**, gyratory, rotating, rotational, rotatory, spinning, turning

rotate *vb* **1** = **revolve**, go round, gyrate, pirouette, pivot, reel, spin, swivel, turn, wheel **2** = **follow in sequence**, alternate, interchange, switch, take turns

rotation *n* **1** = **revolution**, gyration, orbit, pirouette, reel, spin, spinning, turn, turning, wheel **2** = **sequence**, alternation, cycle, interchanging, succession, switching

rotten *adj* **1** = **decaying**, bad, corroded, corrupt, decayed, decomposed, decomposing, festering, fetid, foul, mouldering, mouldy, perished, putrescent, putrid, rank, sour, stinking, tainted, unsound **2** = **disintegrating**, crumbling **3** *Informal* = **corrupt**, base, bent, contemptible, crooked (*inf.*), degenerate, despicable, dirty, disagreeable, dishonest, dishonourable, filthy, immoral, mean, nasty, scurrilous, unpleasant, venal, vicious, vile, wicked **4** = **treacherous**, deceitful, disloyal, faithless, mercenary, perfidious, untrustworthy **5** *Informal* = **bad**, deplorable, disappointing, regrettable, unfortunate, unlucky **6** *Informal* = **inferior**, crummy, duff (*Brit. inf.*), ill-considered, ill-thought-out, inadequate, lousy (*sl.*), low-grade, of a sort *or* of sorts, poor, poxy (*sl.*), ropey *or* ropy (*Brit. inf.*), sorry, substandard, unacceptable, unsatisfactory **7** *Informal* = **unwell**, bad, below par, ill, off colour, poorly (*inf.*), ropey *or* ropy (*Brit. inf.*), rough (*inf.*), sick, under the weather (*inf.*)
Antonyms *adj* ≠ **decaying:** fresh, good, pure, sweet, wholesome ≠ **corrupt:** decent, honest, honourable, moral, scrupulous, trustworthy

rotter *n Slang, chiefly Brit.* = **scoundrel**, bad lot, blackguard, blighter (*Brit. inf.*), bounder (*old-fashioned Brit. sl.*), cad (*Brit. inf.*), cur, louse (*sl.*), rat (*inf.*), scumbag (*sl.*), stinker (*sl.*), swine politics. [G, from *Rottweil*, town in Swabia, Germany, where the breed originated]

rotund ➊ (rəʊ'tʌnd) *adj* **1** rounded or spherical in shape. **2** plump. **3** sonorous or grandiloquent. [C18: from L *rotundus* round, from *rota* wheel]
▸**ro'tundity** *n* ▸**ro'tundly** *adv*

rotunda (rəʊ'tʌndə) *n* a circular building or room, esp. one that has a dome. [C17: from It. *rotonda*, from L *rotundus* round, from *rota* a wheel]

rouble *or* **ruble** ('ru:bᵊl) *n* the standard monetary unit of Belarus, Russia, and Tajikistan. [C16: from Russian *rubl* silver bar, from ORussian *rublĭ* bar, block of wood, from *rubiti* to cut up]

roué ➊ ('ru:eɪ) *n* a debauched or lecherous man; rake. [C19: from F, lit.: one broken on the wheel; with reference to the fate deserved by a debauchee]

rouge (ru:ʒ) *n* **1** a red powder or cream, used as a cosmetic for adding redness to the cheeks. **2** short for **jeweller's rouge.** ◆ *vb* **rouges, rouging, rouged. 3** (*tr*) to apply rouge to. [C18: F: red, from L *rubeus*]

rouge et noir ('ru:ʒ eɪ 'nwɑ:) *n* a card game in which the players put their stakes on any of two red and two black diamond-shaped spots marked on the table. [F, lit.: red and black]

rough ➊ (rʌf) *adj* **1** (of a surface) not smooth; uneven or irregular. **2** (of ground) covered with scrub, boulders, etc. **3** denoting or taking place on uncultivated ground: *rough grazing.* **4** shaggy or hairy. **5** turbulent: *a rough sea.* **6** (of performance or motion) uneven; irregular: *a rough engine.* **7** (of behaviour or character) rude, coarse, or violent. **8** harsh or sharp: *rough words.* **9** *Inf.* severe or unpleasant: *a rough lesson.* **10** (of work, etc.) requiring physical rather than mental effort. **11** *Inf.* ill: *he felt rough after an evening of heavy drinking.* **12** unfair: *rough luck.* **13** harsh or grating to the ear. **14** without refinement, luxury, etc. **15** not perfected in any detail; rudimentary: *rough workmanship; rough justice.* **16** not prepared or dressed: *rough gemstones.* **17** (of a guess, etc.) approximate. **18** having the sound of *h*; aspirated. **19 rough on.** *Inf., chiefly Brit.* **19a** severe towards. **19b** unfortunate for (a person). **20 the rough side of one's tongue.** harsh words; a rebuke. ◆ *n* **21** rough ground. **22** a sketch or preliminary piece of artwork. **23** unfinished or crude state (esp. in **in the rough**). **24 the rough.** *Golf.* the part of the course bordering the fairways where the grass is untrimmed. **25** *Inf.* a violent person; thug. **26** the unpleasant side of something (esp. in **take the rough with the smooth**). ◆ *adv* **27** roughly. **28 sleep rough.** to spend the night in the open; be without shelter. ◆ *vb* (*tr*) **29** to make rough; roughen. **30** (foll. by *out, in,* etc.) to prepare (a sketch, report, etc.) in preliminary form. **31 rough it.** *Inf.* to live without the usual comforts of life. ◆ See also **rough up.** [OE *rūh*]
▸**'roughly** *adv* ▸**'roughness** *n*

roughage ('rʌfɪdʒ) *n* **1** the coarse indigestible constituents of food, which provide bulk to the diet and aid digestion. **2** any rough material.

rough-and-ready ➊ *adj* **1** crude, unpolished, or hastily prepared, but sufficient for the purpose. **2** (of a person) without formality or refinement.

rough-and-tumble ➊ *n* **1** a fight or scuffle without rules. ◆ *adj* **2** characterized by disorderliness and disregard for rules.

rough breathing *n* (in Greek) the sign (ʽ) placed over an initial letter, indicating that (in ancient Greek) it was pronounced with an *h.*

roughcast ('rʌf,kɑ:st) *n* **1** a mixture of plaster and small stones used to cover the surface of an external wall. **2** any rough or preliminary form, model, etc. ◆ *adj* **3** covered with roughcast. ◆ *vb* **roughcasts, roughcasting, roughcast. 4** to apply roughcast to (a wall, etc.). **5** to prepare in rough.
▸**'rough,caster** *n*

rough-cut *n* a first basic edited version of a film with the scenes in sequence and the soundtrack synchronized.

rough diamond *n* **1** an unpolished diamond. **2** an intrinsically trustworthy or good person with uncouth manners or dress.

rough-dry *adj* **1** (of clothes or linen) dried ready for pressing. ◆ *vb* **rough-dries, rough-drying, rough-dried. 2** (*tr*) to dry (clothes, etc.) without ironing them.

roughen ('rʌfᵊn) *vb* to make or become rough.

rough-hew *vb* **rough-hews, rough-hewing, rough-hewed; rough-hewed** *or* **rough-hewn.** (*tr*) to cut or shape roughly without finishing the surface.

roughhouse ➊ ('rʌf,haʊs) *n Sl.* rough, disorderly, or noisy behaviour.

roughish ('rʌfɪʃ) *adj* somewhat rough.

rough music *n* (formerly) a loud cacophony created with tin pans, drums, etc., esp. as a protest or demonstration of indignation outside someone's house.

roughneck ➊ ('rʌf,nɛk) *n Sl.* **1** a rough or violent person; thug. **2** a worker in an oil-drilling operation.

rough puff pastry *n* a rich flaky pastry.

roughrider ('rʌf,raɪdə) *n* a rider of wild or unbroken horses.

roughshod ('rʌf,ʃɒd) *adj* **1** (of a horse) shod with rough-bottomed shoes to prevent sliding. ◆ *adv* **2 ride roughshod over.** to domineer over or act with complete disregard for.

rough stuff *n Inf.* violence.

rough trade *n Sl.* (in homosexual use) a tough or violent sexual partner, esp. one casually picked up.

rough up ➊ *vb* (*tr, adv*) **1** *Inf.* to treat violently; beat up. **2** to cause (feathers, hair, etc.) to stand up by rubbing against the grain.

roulade (ru:'lɑ:d) *n* **1** something cooked in the shape of a roll, esp. a slice of meat. **2** an elaborate run in vocal music. [C18: from F, lit.: a rolling, from *rouler* to ROLL]

roulette (ru:'lɛt) *n* **1** a gambling game in which a ball is dropped onto a spinning horizontal wheel divided into numbered slots, with players betting on the slot into which the ball will fall. **2** a toothed wheel for making a line of perforations. **3** a curve generated by a point on one curve rolling on another. ◆ *vb* **roulettes, rouletting, rouletted.** (*tr*) **4** to use a roulette on (something), as in engraving, making stationery, etc. [C18: from F, from *rouelle*, dim. of *roue* a wheel, from L *rota*]

round ➊ (raʊnd) *adj* **1** having a flat circular shape, as a hoop. **2** having the shape of a ball. **3** curved; not angular. **4** involving or using circular motion. **5** (*prenominal*) complete: *a round dozen.* **6** *Maths.* **6a** forming or expressed by a whole number, with no fraction. **6b** expressed to the nearest ten, hundred, or thousand: *in round figures.* **7** (of a sum of money) considerable. **8** fully depicted or developed, as a character in a book. **9** full and plump: *round cheeks.* **10** (of sound) full and sonorous. **11** (of pace) brisk; lively. **12** (*prenominal*) (of speech) candid; unmodified: *a round assertion.* **13** (of a vowel) pronounced with rounded lips. ◆ *n* **14** a round shape or object. **15 in the round. 15a** in full detail. **15b** *Theatre.* with the audience all round the stage. **16** a session, as of a negotiation: *a round of talks.* **17** a series: *a giddy round of parties.* **18 the daily round.** the usual activities of one's day. **19** a stage of a competi-

THESAURUS

rotund *adj* **1 = round,** bulbous, globular, orbicular, rounded, spherical **2 = plump,** chubby, corpulent, fat, fleshy, heavy, obese, podgy, portly, roly-poly, rounded, stout, tubby **3 = sonorous,** full, grandiloquent, magniloquent, orotund, pompous, resonant, rich, round
Antonyms *adj* ≠ **plump:** angular, gaunt, lank, lanky, lean, scrawny, skinny, slender, slight, slim, thin

roué *n* **= libertine,** debauchee, dirty old man (*sl.*), lech *or* letch (*inf.*), lecher, profligate, rake, sensualist, wanton

rough *adj* **1, 2 = uneven,** broken, bumpy, craggy, irregular, jagged, rocky, rugged, stony **4 = coarse,** bristly, bushy, dishevelled, disordered, fuzzy, hairy, shaggy, tangled, tousled, uncut, unshaven, unshorn **5 = stormy,** agitated, boisterous, choppy, inclement, squally, tempestuous, turbulent, wild **7 = rude,** bearish, bluff, blunt, brusque, churlish, coarse, curt, discourteous, ill-bred, ill-mannered, impolite, inconsiderate, indelicate, loutish, unceremonious, uncivil, uncouth, uncultured, ungracious, unmannerly, unpolished, unrefined, untutored **10 = arduous,** tough **11** *Informal* **= unwell,** below par, ill, not a hundred per cent (*inf.*), off colour, poorly (*inf.*), ropey *or* ropy (*Brit. inf.*), rotten (*inf.*), sick, under the weather (*inf.*), upset **13 = grating,** cacophonous, discordant, gruff, harsh, husky, inharmonious, jarring, rasping, raucous, unmusical **14 = uncomfortable,** austere, hard, rugged, spartan, unpleasant **15 = basic,** crude, cursory, formless, hasty, imperfect, incomplete, quick, raw, rough-and-ready, rough-hewn, rudimentary, shapeless, sketchy, unfinished, unpolished, unrefined **16 = unprocessed,** crude, raw, rough-hewn, uncut, undressed, unhewn, unpolished, unwrought **17 = approximate,** estimated, foggy, general, hazy, imprecise, inexact, sketchy, vague **19a = harsh,** cruel, curt, drastic, extreme, hard, nasty, severe, sharp, tough, unfeeling, unjust, unpleasant, violent ◆ *n* **22 = outline,** draft, mock-up, preliminary sketch, suggestion **25** *Informal* **= thug,** bruiser, bully boy, casual, lager lout, roughneck (*sl.*), rowdy, ruffian, tough ◆ *vb* **30** *foll. by* **out = outline,** adumbrate, block out, delineate, draft, plan, sketch, suggest
Antonyms *adj* ≠ **uneven:** even, level, regular, smooth, unbroken ≠ **coarse:** smooth, soft ≠ **stormy:** calm, gentle, quiet, smooth, tranquil ≠ **rude:** civil, considerate, courteous, courtly, delicate, elegant, graceful, gracious, pleasant, polite, refined, smooth, sophisticated, urbane, well-bred, well-mannered ≠ **arduous:** comfortable, cushy (*inf.*), easy, pleasant, soft ≠ **grating:** harmonious, smooth ≠ **basic:** complete, detailed, finished, perfected, polished, refined, specific ≠ **approximate:** exact, perfected, specific ≠ **harsh:** gentle, just, kind, mild, pleasant, quiet, soft

rough-and-ready *adj* **1 = makeshift,** adequate, cobbled together, crude, improvised, provisional, sketchy, stopgap, thrown together, unpolished, unrefined

rough-and-tumble *n* **1 = fight,** affray (*Law*), brawl, donnybrook, dust-up, fracas, melee *or* mêlée, punch-up (*Brit. inf.*), roughhouse (*sl.*), scrap (*inf.*), scrimmage, scuffle, shindig (*inf.*), shindy (*inf.*), struggle ◆ *adj* **2 = disorderly,** boisterous, haphazard, indisciplined, irregular, rough, rowdy, scrambled, scrambling

roughhouse *n Slang* **= rough behaviour,** boisterousness, brawl, brawling, disorderliness, disturbance, horseplay, row, rowdiness, rowdyism, skylarking (*inf.*)

roughneck *n Slang* **1 = thug,** bruiser (*inf.*), bully boy, heavy (*sl.*), rough (*inf.*), rowdy, ruffian, tough

rough up *vb* **1** *Informal* **= beat up,** bash up (*inf.*), batter, beat the living daylights out of (*inf.*), do over (*Brit., Austral., & NZ sl.*), knock about *or* around, maltreat, manhandle, mistreat, thrash, work over (*sl.*)

round *adj* **1-3 = spherical,** ball-shaped, bowed, bulbous, circular, curved, curvilinear, cylindrical, discoid, disc-shaped, globular, orbicular, ring-shaped, rotund, rounded **5 = complete,** entire, full, solid, unbroken, undivided, whole **7 = considerable,** ample, bounteous, bountiful, generous, great, large, liberal, substantial **9 = plump,** ample, fleshy, full, full-fleshed, roly-poly, rotund, rounded **10 = sonorous,** full, mellifluous, orotund, resonant, rich, rotund **12 = candid,** blunt, direct, downright, frank, outspoken, plain, straightforward, unmodified ◆ *n* **14 = sphere,** ball, band, circle, disc, globe, orb, ring **17 = series,** bout, cycle, sequence, session, succession **19 = stage,** division, lap, level, period, session, turn **20 = course,** ambit, beat, circuit, compass, routine, schedule, series, tour, turn **24, 25 = bullet,** cartridge, discharge, shell, shot ◆ *vb* **48 = encircle,** circle, flank, surround

tion: *he was eliminated in the first round.* **20** (*often pl*) a series of calls: *a milkman's round.* **21** a playing of all the holes on a golf course. **22** a single turn of play by each player, as in a card game. **23** one of a number of periods in a boxing, wrestling, or other match. **24** a single discharge by a gun. **25** a bullet or other charge of ammunition. **26** a number of drinks bought at one time for a group of people. **27a** a single slice of bread. **27b** a sandwich made from two slices of bread. **28** a general outburst of applause, etc. **29** movement in a circle. **30** *Music.* a part song in which the voices follow each other at equal intervals at the same pitch. **31** a sequence of bells rung in order of treble to tenor. **32** a cut of beef from the thigh. **33 go** *or* **make the rounds. 33a** to go from place to place, as in making social calls. **33b** (of information, rumour, etc.) to be passed around, so as to be generally known. ◆ *prep* **34** surrounding, encircling, or enclosing: *a band round her head.* **35** on all or most sides of: *to look round one.* **36** on or outside the circumference or perimeter of. **37** from place to place in: *driving round Ireland.* **38** reached by making a partial circuit about: *the shop round the corner.* **39** revolving round (a centre or axis): *the earth's motion round its axis.* ◆ *adv* **40** on all or most sides. **41** on or outside the circumference or perimeter: *the racing track is two miles round.* **42** to all members of a group: *pass the food round.* **43** in rotation or revolution: *the wheels turn round.* **44** by a circuitous route: *the road to the farm goes round by the pond.* **45** to a specific place: *she came round to see me.* **46 all year round.** throughout the year. ◆ *vb* **47** to make or become round. **48** (*tr*) to encircle; surround. **49** to move or cause to move with turning motion: *to round a bend.* **50** (*tr*) **50a** to pronounce (a speech sound) with rounded lips. **50b** to purse (the lips). ◆ See also **round down, round off,** etc. [C13: from OF *ront,* from L *rotundus* round, from *rota* a wheel]
▸'**roundish** *adj* ▸'**roundness** *n*

USAGE NOTE See at **around.**

roundabout ❶ ('raʊndəˌbaʊt) *n* **1** *Brit.* a revolving circular platform provided with wooden animals, seats, etc., on which people ride for amusement; merry-go-round. **2** a road junction in which traffic streams circulate around a central island. US and Canad. name: **traffic circle.** ◆ *adj* **3** indirect; devious. ◆ *adv, prep* **round about. 4** on all sides: *spectators standing round about.* **5** approximately: *at round about 5 o'clock.*

round dance *n* **1** a dance in which the dancers form a circle. **2** a ballroom dance, such as the waltz, in which couples revolve.

round down *vb* (*tr, adv*) to lower (a number) to the nearest whole number or ten, hundred, or thousand below it.

rounded ('raʊndɪd) *adj* **1** round or curved. **2** mature or complete. **3** (of the lips) pursed. **4** (of a speech sound) articulated with rounded lips.

roundel ('raʊndᵊl) *n* **1** a form of rondeau consisting of three stanzas each of three lines with a refrain after the first and the third. **2** a circular identifying mark in national colours on military aircraft. **3** a small circular window, medallion, etc. **4** a round plate of armour used to protect the armpit. **5** another word for **roundelay.** [C13: from OF *rondel;* see RONDEL]

roundelay ('raʊndɪˌleɪ) *n* **1** Also called: **roundel.** a slow medieval dance performed in a circle. **2** a song in which a line or phrase is repeated as a refrain. [C16: from OF *rondelet* a little rondel, from *rondel;* also infl. by LAY[4]]

rounders ('raʊndəz) *n* (*functioning as sing*) *Brit.* a ball game in which players run between posts after hitting the ball, scoring a **rounder** if they run round all four before the ball is retrieved.

Roundhead ('raʊndˌhɛd) *n English history.* a supporter of Parliament against Charles I during the Civil War. [referring to their short-cut hair]

roundhouse ('raʊndˌhaʊs) *n* **1** *US & Canad.* a building in which railway locomotives are serviced, radial tracks being fed by a central turntable. **2** *US boxing sl.* a swinging punch or style of punching. **3** an obsolete word for **jail. 4** *Obs.* a cabin on the quarterdeck of a sailing ship.

rounding ('raʊndɪŋ) *n Computing.* a process in which a number is approximated as the closest number that can be expressed using the number of bits or digits available.

roundly ❶ ('raʊndlɪ) *adv* **1** frankly, bluntly, or thoroughly: *to be roundly criticized.* **2** in a round manner or so as to be round.

round off ❶ *vb* (*tr, adv*) **1** (often foll. by *with*) to complete, esp. agreeably: *we rounded off the evening with a brandy.* **2** to make less jagged.

round on ❶ *vb* (*intr, prep*) to attack or reply to (someone) with sudden irritation or anger.

round robin *n* **1** a petition or protest having the signatures in a circle to disguise the order of signing. **2** a tournament in which each player plays against every other player.

round-shouldered *adj* denoting a faulty posture characterized by drooping shoulders and a slight forward bending of the back.

roundsman ('raʊndzmən) *n, pl* **roundsmen. 1** *Brit.* a person who makes rounds, as for inspection or to deliver goods. **2** *Austral. & NZ.* a reporter covering a particular district or topic.

round table *n* **a** a meeting of parties or people on equal terms for discussion. **b** (*as modifier*): *a round-table conference.*

Round Table *n* **the. 1** (in Arthurian legend) the circular table of King Arthur, enabling his knights to sit around it without any having precedence. **2** Arthur and his knights collectively. **3** one of an organization of clubs of young business and professional men who meet in order to further charitable work.

round-the-clock *adj* (*or as adv* **round the clock**) throughout the day and night.

round tower *n* a freestanding circular stone belfry built in Ireland from the 10th century beside a monastery and used as a place of refuge.

round trip *n* a trip to a place and back again, esp. returning by a different route.

roundtripping ('raʊndˌtrɪpɪŋ) *n Finance.* a form of trading in which a company borrows a sum of money from one source and takes advantage of a short-term rise in interest rates to make a profit by lending it to another.

round up ❶ *vb* (*tr, adv*) **1** to gather together: *to round ponies up.* **2** to raise (a number) to the nearest whole number or ten, hundred, or thousand above it. ◆ *n* **roundup. 3** the act of gathering together livestock, esp. cattle, so that they may be branded, counted, or sold. **4** any similar act of bringing together: *a roundup of today's news.*

roundworm ('raʊndˌwɜːm) *n* a nematode worm that is a common intestinal parasite of man and pigs.

roup (raʊp) *Scot. & N English dialect.* ◆ *vb* (*tr*) **1** to sell by auction. ◆ *n* **2** an auction. [C16 (orig.: to shout): of Scand. origin]

rouse ❶ (raʊz) *vb* **rouses, rousing, roused. 1** to bring (oneself or another person) out of sleep, etc., or (of a person) to come to consciousness in this way. **2** (*tr*) to provoke: *to rouse someone's anger.* **3 rouse oneself.** to become energetic. **4** to start or cause to start from cover: *to rouse game birds.* **5** (*intr;* foll. by *on*) *Austral.* to scold or rebuke. [C15 (in sense of hawks ruffling their feathers): from ?]
▸'**rouser** *n*

rouseabout ('raʊzəˌbaʊt) *n* **1** *Austral. & NZ.* an unskilled labourer in a shearing shed. **2** a variant of **roustabout** (sense 1).

rousing ❶ ('raʊzɪŋ) *adj* tending to excite; lively or vigorous: *a rousing chorus.*
▸'**rousingly** *adv*

roust (raʊst) *vb* (*tr;* often foll. by *out*) to rout or stir, as out of bed. [C17: ?from ROUSE]

roustabout ('raʊstəˌbaʊt) *n* **1** an unskilled labourer, esp. on an oil rig. **2** *Austral. & NZ.* a variant of **rouseabout** (sense 1).

rout[1] ❶ (raʊt) *n* **1** an overwhelming defeat. **2** a disorderly retreat. **3** a noisy rabble. **4** *Law.* a group of three or more people proceeding to commit an illegal act. **5** *Arch.* a large party or social gathering. ◆ *vb* **6** (*tr*) to defeat and cause to flee in confusion. [C13: from Anglo-Norman *rute,* from OF: disorderly band, from L *ruptus,* from *rumpere* to burst]

rout[2] (raʊt) *vb* **1** to dig over or turn up (something), esp. (of an animal) with the snout; root. **2** (*tr;* usually foll. by *out* or *up*) to find by searching. **3** (*tr;* usually foll. by *out*) to drive out: *they routed him out of bed at midnight.* **4** (*tr;* often foll. by *out*) to hollow or gouge out. **5** (*intr*) to search, poke, or rummage. [C16: var. of ROOT[2]]

route ❶ (ruːt) *n* **1** the choice of roads taken to get to a place. **2** a regular journey travelled. **3** (*cap.*) *US.* a main road between cities: *Route 66.* ◆ *vb* **routes, routeing, routed.** (*tr*) **4** to plan the route of; send by a particular route. [C13: from OF *rute,* from Vulgar L *rupta via* (unattested), lit.: a broken (established) way, from L *ruptus,* from *rumpere* to break]

USAGE NOTE When forming the present participle or verbal noun from the verb *to route* it is preferable to retain the *e* in order to distinguish the word from *routing,* the present participle or verbal noun from *rout*[1], to defeat or *rout*[2], to dig, rummage: *the routeing of buses from the city centre to the suburbs.* The spelling *routing* in this sense is, however, sometimes encountered, esp. in American English.

THESAURUS

49 = **go round,** bypass, circumnavigate, skirt, turn

roundabout *adj* **3** = **indirect,** circuitous, circumlocutory, devious, discursive, evasive, meandering, oblique, periphrastic, tortuous
Antonyms *adj* direct, straight, straightforward

roundly *adv* **1** = **thoroughly,** bitterly, bluntly, fiercely, frankly, intensely, outspokenly, rigorously, severely, sharply, vehemently, violently

round off *vb* **1** = **complete,** bring to a close, cap, close, conclude, crown, finish off, put the finishing touch to, settle
Antonyms *vb* begin, commence, initiate, open, start

round on *vb* = **attack,** abuse, bite (someone's) head off (*inf.*), have a go at (*Brit. sl.*), lose one's temper with, retaliate, snap at, turn on, wade into

round up *vb* **1** = **gather,** assemble, bring together, collect, drive, group, herd, marshal, muster, rally ◆ *n* **roundup 3** = **gathering,** assembly, collection, herding, marshalling, muster, rally **4** = **summary,** collation, survey

rouse *vb* **1** = **wake up,** arouse, awaken, call, get up, rise, wake **2** = **provoke,** agitate, anger, arouse, galvanize, get going, incite, inflame, instigate, move, prod, stimulate, stir, whip up

rousing *adj* = **lively,** brisk, electrifying, exciting, exhilarating, inflammatory, inspiring, moving, spirited, stimulating, stirring, vigorous
Antonyms *adj* boring, dreary, dull, lifeless, sluggish, spiritless, unenergetic, wearisome, wishy-washy (*inf.*)

rout[1] *n* **1** = **defeat,** beating, debacle, disorderly retreat, drubbing, headlong flight, hiding (*inf.*), licking (*inf.*), overthrow, overwhelming defeat, pasting (*sl.*), ruin, shambles, thrashing ◆ *vb* **6** = **defeat,** beat, chase, clobber, conquer, crush, cut to pieces, destroy, dispel, drive off, drub, lick (*inf.*), overpower, overthrow, put to flight, put to rout, scatter, stuff (*sl.*), tank (*sl.*), thrash, throw back in confusion, wipe the floor with (*inf.*), worst

route *n* **1** = **way,** beat, circuit, course, direction, itinerary, journey, passage, path, road, round,

routemarch ('ruːtˌmɑːtʃ) *n* **1** *Mil.* a long training march. **2** *Inf.* any long exhausting walk.

router ('rautə) *n* any of various tools or machines for hollowing out, cutting grooves, etc.

routine ❶ (ruː'tiːn) *n* **1** a usual or regular method of procedure, esp. one that is unvarying. **2** *Computing.* a program or part of a program performing a specific function: *an input routine.* **3** a set sequence of dance steps. **4** *Inf.* a hackneyed or insincere speech. ◆ *adj* **5** relating to or characteristic of routine. [C17: from OF, from *route* a customary way, ROUTE]

▸**rou'tinely** *adv*

roux (ruː) *n* a mixture of equal amounts of fat and flour, heated, blended, and used as a basis for sauces. [F: brownish, from L *russus* RUSSET]

rove[1] ❶ (rəuv) *vb* **roves, roving, roved. 1** to wander about (a place) with no fixed direction; roam. **2** (*intr*) (of the eyes) to look around; wander. ◆ *n* **3** the act of roving. [C15 *roven* (in archery) to shoot at a target chosen at random (C16: to wander, stray), from ON]

rove[2] (rəuv) *vb* **roves, roving, roved. 1** (*tr*) to pull out and twist (fibres of wool, cotton, etc.) lightly, as before spinning. ◆ *n* **2** wool, cotton, etc., thus prepared. [C18: from ?]

rove[3] (rəuv) *vb* a past tense and past participle of **reeve**[2].

rover[1] ❶ ('rəuvə) *n* **1** a person who roves. **2** *Archery.* a mark selected at random for use as a target. **3** *Australian Rules football.* a player without a fixed position who, with the ruckmen, forms the ruck. [C15: from ROVE[1]]

rover[2] ('rəuvə) *n* a pirate or pirate ship. [C14: prob. from MDu. or MLow G, from *roven* to rob]

Rover *or* **Rover Scout** ('rəuvə) *n Brit.* the former name for **Venture Scout.**

roving commission *n* authority or power given in a general area, without precisely defined terms of reference.

row[1] ❶ (rəu) *n* **1** an arrangement of persons or things in a line: *a row of chairs.* **2** *Chiefly Brit.* a street, esp. a narrow one lined with identical houses. **3** a line of seats, as in a cinema, theatre, etc. **4** *Maths.* a horizontal linear arrangement of numbers, quantities, or terms. **5** a horizontal rank of squares on a chessboard or draughtboard. **6 a hard row to hoe.** a difficult task or assignment. **7 in a row.** in succession; one after the other: *he won two gold medals in a row.* [OE *rāw, rǣw*]

row[2] (rəu) *vb* **1** to propel (a boat) by using oars. **2** (*tr*) to carry (people, goods, etc.) in a rowing boat. **3** to be propelled by means of (oars or oarsmen). **4** (*intr*) to take part in the racing of rowing boats as a sport. **5** (*tr*) to race against in a boat propelled by oars: *Oxford row Cambridge every year.* ◆ *n* **6** an act, instance, period, or distance of rowing. **7** an excursion in a rowing boat. [OE *rōwan*]

▸**'rower** *n*

row[3] ❶ (rau) *n* **1** a noisy quarrel. **2** a noisy disturbance: *we couldn't hear the music for the row next door.* **3** a reprimand. ◆ *vb* **4** (*intr; often foll. by with*) to quarrel noisily. **5** (*tr*) *Arch.* to reprimand. [C18: from ?]

rowan ('rəuən, 'rau-) *n* another name for the (European) **mountain ash.** [C16: of Scand. origin]

rowdy ❶ ('raudɪ) *adj* **rowdier, rowdiest. 1** tending to create noisy disturbances; rough, loud, or disorderly: *a rowdy gang of football supporters.* ◆ *n, pl* **rowdies. 2** a person who behaves in such a fashion. [C19: orig. US sl., ? rel. to ROW[3]]

▸**'rowdily** *adv* ▸**'rowdiness** *or* **'rowdyism** *n*

rowel ('rauəl) *n* **1** a small spiked wheel attached to a spur. **2** *Vet. science.* a piece of leather inserted under the skin of a horse to cause a discharge. ◆ *vb* **rowels, rowelling, rowelled** *or US* **rowels, roweling, roweled.** (*tr*) **3** to goad (a horse) using a rowel. **4** *Vet. science.* to insert a rowel in (the skin of a horse) to cause a discharge. [C14: from OF *roel* a little wheel, from *roe* a wheel, from L *rota*]

rowing boat ('rəuɪŋ) *n Chiefly Brit.* a small pleasure boat propelled by one or more pairs of oars. Usual US and Canad. word: **rowboat.**

rowing machine ('rəuɪŋ) *n* a device with oars and a sliding seat, resembling a sculling boat, used to provide exercise.

rowlock ('rɒlək) *n* a swivelling device attached to the gunwale of a boat that holds an oar in place. Usual US and Canad. word: **oarlock.**

royal ❶ ('rɔɪəl) *adj* **1** of, relating to, or befitting a king, queen, or other monarch; regal. **2** (*prenominal; often cap.*) established by, chartered by, under the patronage of, or in the service of royalty: *the Royal Society of St George.* **3** being a member of a royal family. **4** above the usual or normal in standing, size, quality, etc. **5** *Inf.* unusually good or impressive; first-rate. **6** *Naut.* just above the topgallant (in **royal mast**). ◆ *n* **7** (*sometimes cap.*) a member of a royal family. **8** Also: **royal stag.** a stag with antlers having 12 or more branches. **9** *Naut.* a sail set next above the topgallant, on a royal mast. **10** a size of printing paper, 20 by 25 inches. [C14: from OF *roial,* from L *rēgālis* fit for a king, from *rēx* king; cf. REGAL]

▸**'royally** *adv*

Royal Academy *n* a society founded by George III in 1768 to foster a national school of painting, sculpture, and design in England. Full name: **Royal Academy of Arts.**

Royal Air Force *n* the air force of Great Britain. Abbrev.: **RAF.**

Royal and Ancient Club *n* **the.** a golf club, headquarters of the sport's ruling body, based in St Andrews, Scotland. Abbrev.: **R&A.**

royal assent *n Brit.* the formal signing of an act of Parliament by the sovereign, by which it becomes law.

royal blue *n* **a** a deep blue colour. **b** (*as adj*): *a royal-blue carpet.*

Royal Commission *n* (in Britain) a body set up by the monarch on the recommendation of the prime minister to gather information about the operation of existing laws or to investigate any social, educational, or other matter.

royal fern *n* a fern of damp regions, having large fronds up to 2 metres (7 feet) in height.

royal flush *n Poker.* a hand made up of the five top honours of a suit.

royalist ('rɔɪəlɪst) *n* **1** a supporter of a monarch or monarchy, esp. during the English Civil War. **2** *Inf.* an extreme reactionary: *an economic royalist.* ◆ *adj* **3** of or relating to royalists.

▸**'royalism** *n*

royal jelly *n* a substance secreted by the pharyngeal glands of worker bees and fed to all larvae when very young and to larvae destined to become queens throughout their development.

Royal Marines *pl n Brit.* a corps of soldiers specially trained in amphibious warfare. Abbrev.: **RM.**

Royal Mint *n* a British organization having the sole right to manufacture coins since the 16th century. In 1968 it moved from London to Llantrisant in Wales.

Royal Navy *n* the navy of Great Britain. Abbrev.: **RN.**

royal palm *n* any of several palm trees of tropical America, having a tall trunk with a tuft of feathery pinnate leaves.

royal standard *n* a flag bearing the arms of the British sovereign, flown only when she or he is present.

royal tennis *n* another name for **real tennis.**

royalty ('rɔɪəltɪ) *n, pl* **royalties. 1** the rank, power, or position of a king or queen. **2a** royal persons collectively. **2b** a person who belongs to a royal family. **3** any quality characteristic of a monarch. **4** a percentage of the revenue from the sale of a book, performance of a theatrical work, use of a patented invention or of land, etc., paid to the author, inventor, or proprietor.

royal warrant *n* an authorization to a tradesman to supply goods to a royal household.

rozzer ('rɒzə) *n Sl.* a policeman. [C19: from ?]

RPG *abbrev. for* report program generator: a business-oriented computer programming language.

RPI (in Britain) *abbrev. for* retail price index.

rpm *abbrev. for:* **1** resale price maintenance. **2** revolutions per minute.

RPV *abbrev. for* remotely piloted vehicle.

RR *abbrev. for:* **1** Right Reverend. **2** *Canad. & US.* rural route.

-rrhagia *n combining form.* (in pathology) an abnormal discharge: *menorrhagia.* [from Gk *-rrhagia* a bursting forth, from *rhēgnunai* to burst]

-rrhoea *or esp. US* **-rrhea** *n combining form.* (in pathology) a flow: *diarrhoea.* [from NL, from Gk *-rrhoia,* from *rhein* to flow]

r-RNA *abbrev. for* ribosomal RNA.

RRP *abbrev. for* recommended retail price.

Rs *symbol for* rupees.

RS (in Britain) *abbrev. for* Royal Society.

RSA *abbrev. for:* **1** Republic of South Africa. **2** (in New Zealand) Returned Services Association. **3** Royal Scottish Academician. **4** Royal Scottish Academy. **5** Royal Society of Arts.

RSFSR (formerly) *abbrev. for* Russian Soviet Federative Socialist Republic.

RSI *abbrev. for* repetitive strain injury.

RSL (in Australia) *abbrev. for* Returned Services League.

THESAURUS

run ◆ *vb* **4** = **send**, convey, direct, dispatch, forward, steer

routine *n* **1** = **procedure**, custom, formula, grind (*inf.*), groove, method, order, pattern, practice, programme, usage, way, wont **4** *Informal* = **performance**, act, bit (*inf.*), line, piece, spiel (*inf.*) ◆ *adj* **5** = **usual**, conventional, customary, everyday, familiar, habitual, normal, ordinary, standard, typical, wonted, workaday
Antonyms *adj* ≠ **usual:** abnormal, different, exceptional, irregular, special, unusual

rove[1] *vb* **1** = **wander**, cruise, drift, gad about, gallivant, meander, ramble, range, roam, stravaig (*Scot. & N English dialect*), stray, stroll, traipse (*inf.*)

rover[1] *n* **1** = **wanderer**, bird of passage, drifter, gadabout (*inf.*), gypsy, itinerant, nomad, rambler, ranger, rolling stone, stroller, transient, traveller, vagrant

row[1] *n* **1** = **line**, bank, column, file, queue, range, rank, sequence, series, string, tier **7 in a row** = **consecutively**, one after the other, successively

row[3] *n* **1** = **quarrel**, altercation, brawl, controversy, dispute, falling-out (*inf.*), fracas, fray, fuss, ruckus (*inf.*), ruction (*inf.*), scrap (*inf.*), shindig (*inf.*), shindy (*inf.*), shouting match (*inf.*), slanging match (*Brit.*), squabble, tiff, trouble **2** = **disturbance**, commotion, noise, racket, rumpus, tumult, uproar **3** = **telling-off** (*inf.*), castigation, dressing-down, flea in one's ear (*inf.*), lecture, reprimand, reproof, rollicking (*Brit. inf.*), talking-to (*inf.*), ticking-off (*inf.*), tongue-lashing ◆ *vb* **4** = **quarrel**, argue, brawl, dispute, fight, go at it hammer and tongs, scrap (*inf.*), spar, squabble, wrangle

rowdy *adj* **1** = **disorderly**, boisterous, loud, loutish, noisy, obstreperous, rough, unruly, uproarious, wild ◆ *n* **2** = **hooligan**, brawler, casual, lager lout, lout, rough (*inf.*), ruffian, tearaway (*Brit.*), tough, troublemaker, yahoo, yob *or* yobbo (*Brit. sl.*)
Antonyms *adj* ≠ **disorderly:** decorous, gentle, law-abiding, mannerly, orderly, peaceful, refined

royal *adj* **1** = **regal**, imperial, kinglike, kingly, monarchical, princely, queenly, sovereign **5** *Informal* = **splendid**, august, grand, impressive, magnificent, majestic, stately, superb, superior

RSM *abbrev. for:* **1** regimental sergeant major. **2** Royal School of Music. **3** Royal Society of Medicine.
RSNZ *abbrev. for* Royal Society of New Zealand.
RSPB (in Britain) *abbrev. for* Royal Society for the Protection of Birds.
RSPCA (in Britain and Australia) *abbrev. for* Royal Society for the Prevention of Cruelty to Animals.
RSV *abbrev. for* Revised Standard Version (of the Bible).
RSVP *abbrev. for* répondez s'il vous plaît. [F: please reply]
rt *abbrev. for* right.
RTE *abbrev. for* Radio Telefis Éireann. [Irish Gaelic: Irish Radio and Television]
Rt Hon. *abbrev. for* Right Honourable.
Ru *the chemical symbol for* ruthenium.
RU *abbrev. for* Rugby Union.
RU486 *n Trademark.* a brand name for the **abortion pill.**
rub ❶ (rʌb) *vb* **rubs, rubbing, rubbed. 1** to apply pressure and friction to (something) with a backward and forward motion. **2** to move (something) with pressure along, over, or against (a surface). **3** to chafe or fray. **4** (*tr*) to bring into a certain condition by rubbing: *rub it clean.* **5** (*tr*) to spread with pressure, esp. in order to cause to be absorbed: *she rubbed ointment into his back.* **6** (*tr*) to mix (fat) into flour with the fingertips, as in making pastry. **7** (foll. by *off, out, away,* etc.) to remove or be removed by rubbing: *the mark would not rub off the chair.* **8** (*intr*) *Bowls.* (of a bowl) to be slowed or deflected by an uneven patch on the green. **9** (*tr;* often foll. by *together*) to move against each other with pressure and friction (esp. in **rub one's hands,** often a sign of glee, keen anticipation, or satisfaction, and **rub noses,** a greeting among Eskimos). **10 rub (up) the wrong way.** to arouse anger in; annoy. ◆ *n* **11** the act of rubbing. **12** (preceded by *the*) an obstacle or difficulty (esp. in **there's the rub**). **13** something that hurts the feelings or annoys; cut; rebuke. **14** *Bowls.* an uneven patch in the green. ◆ See also **rub along, rub down,** etc. [C15: ?from Low G *rubben,* from ?]
rub along *vb (intr, adv) Brit.* **1** to continue in spite of difficulties. **2** to maintain an amicable relationship; not quarrel.
rubato (ru:'bɑ:təʊ) *Music.* ◆ *n, pl* **rubatos. 1** flexibility of tempo in performance. ◆ *adj, adv* **2** to be played with a flexible tempo. [C19: from It. *tempo rubato,* lit.: stolen time, from *rubare* to ROB]
rubber[1] ('rʌbə) *n* **1** Also called: **India rubber, gum elastic, caoutchouc.** a cream to dark brown elastic material obtained by coagulating and drying the latex from certain plants, esp. the rubber tree. **2** any of a large variety of elastomers produced from natural rubber or by synthetic means. **3** *Chiefly Brit.* a piece of rubber used for erasing something written; eraser. **4** a cloth, pad, etc., used for polishing. **5** a person who rubs something in order to smooth, polish, or massage. **6** (*often pl*) *Chiefly US & Canad.* a rubberized waterproof overshoe. **7** *Sl.* a condom. **8** (*modifier*) made of or producing rubber: *a rubber ball; a rubber factory.* [C17: from RUB + -ER[1]; the tree was so named because its product was used for rubbing out writing]
▸ **'rubbery** *adj*
rubber[2] ('rʌbə) *n* **1** *Bridge, whist, etc.* **1a** a match of three games. **1b** the deal that wins such a match. **2** a series of matches or games in any of various sports. [C16: from ?]
rubber band *n* a continuous loop of thin rubber, used to hold papers, etc., together. Also called: **elastic band.**
rubber cement *n* any of a number of adhesives made by dissolving rubber in a solvent such as benzene.
rubberize *or* **rubberise** ('rʌbəˌraɪz) *vb* **rubberizes, rubberizing, rubberized** *or* **rubberises, rubberising, rubberised.** (*tr*) to coat or impregnate with rubber.
rubberneck ('rʌbəˌnɛk) *Sl.* ◆ *n* **1** a person who stares or gapes inquisitively. **2** a sightseer or tourist. ◆ *vb* **3** (*intr*) to stare in a naive or foolish manner.
rubber plant *n* **1** a plant with glossy leathery leaves that grows as a tall tree in India and Malaya but is cultivated as a house plant in Europe and North America. **2** any of several tropical trees, the sap of which yields crude rubber.
rubber stamp *n* **1** a device used for imprinting dates, etc., on forms, invoices, etc. **2** automatic authorization of a payment, proposal, etc. **3** a person who makes such automatic authorizations; a cipher or person of little account. ◆ *vb* **rubber-stamp.** (*tr*) **4** to imprint (forms, invoices, etc.) with a rubber stamp. **5** *Inf.* to approve automatically.
rubber tree *n* a tropical American tree cultivated throughout the tropics, esp. in Malaya, for the latex of its stem, which is the major source of commercial rubber.
rubbing ('rʌbɪŋ) *n* an impression taken of an incised or raised surface by laying paper over it and rubbing with wax, graphite, etc.
rubbish ❶ ('rʌbɪʃ) *n* **1** worthless, useless, or unwanted matter. **2** discarded or waste matter; refuse. **3** foolish words or speech; nonsense. ◆ *vb* **4** (*tr*) *Inf.* to criticize; attack verbally. [C14 *robys,* from ?]
▸ **'rubbishy** *adj*
rubble ('rʌbᵊl) *n* **1** fragments of broken stones, bricks, etc. **2** debris from ruined buildings. **3** Also called: **rubblework.** masonry constructed of broken pieces of rock, stone, etc. [C14 *robyl;* ? rel. to RUBBISH, or to ME *rubben* to rub]
▸ **'rubbly** *adj*
rub down *vb (adv)* **1** to dry or clean (a horse, athlete, oneself, etc.) vigorously, esp. after exercise. **2** to make or become smooth by rubbing. **3** (*tr*) to prepare (a surface) for painting by rubbing it with sandpaper. ◆ *n* **rubdown. 4** the act of rubbing down.
rube (ru:b) *n US sl.* an unsophisticated countryman. [C20: prob. from the name *Reuben*]
rubella (ru:'bɛlə) *n* a mild contagious viral disease, somewhat similar to measles, characterized by cough, sore throat, and skin rash. Also called: **German measles.** [C19: from NL, from L *rubellus* reddish, from *rubeus* red]
rubellite ('ru:bɪˌlaɪt, ru:'bɛl-) *n* a red transparent variety of tourmaline, used as a gemstone. [C18: from L *rubellus* reddish]
rubeola (ru:'bi:ələ) *n* the technical name for **measles.** [C17: from NL, from L *rubeus* reddish]
Rubicon ('ru:bɪkən) *n* **1** a stream in N Italy: in ancient times the boundary between Italy and Cisalpine Gaul. By leading his army across it and marching on Rome in 49 B.C., Julius Caesar committed himself to civil war with the senatorial party. **2** (*sometimes not cap.*) a point of no return. **3** a penalty in piquet by which the score of a player who fails to reach 100 points in six hands is added to his opponent's. **4 cross** (*or* **pass**) **the Rubicon.** to commit oneself irrevocably to some course of action.
rubicund ❶ ('ru:bɪkənd) *adj* of a reddish colour; ruddy; rosy. [C16: from L *rubicundus,* from *rubēre* to be ruddy, from *ruber* red]
▸ **rubicundity** (ˌru:bɪ'kʌndɪtɪ) *n*
rubidium (ru:'bɪdɪəm) *n* a soft highly reactive radioactive element of the alkali metal group. It is used in electronic valves, photocells, and special glass. Symbol: Rb; atomic no.: 37; atomic wt.: 85.47; half-life of ^{87}Rb: 5×10^{11} years. [C19: from NL, from L *rubidus* dark red, with reference to the two red lines in its spectrum]
▸ **ru'bidic** *adj*
rubidium-strontium dating *n* a technique for determining the age of minerals based on the occurrence in natural rubidium of a fixed amount of the radioisotope ^{87}Rb which decays to the stable strontium isotope ^{87}Sr with a half-life of 5×10^{11} years.
rubiginous (ru:'bɪdʒɪnəs) *adj* rust-coloured. [C17: from L *rūbīginōsus,* from *rūbīgō* rust, from *ruber* red]
rub in *vb (tr, adv)* **1** to spread with pressure, esp. in order to cause to be absorbed. **2 rub it in.** *Inf.* to harp on something distasteful to a person.
ruble ('ru:bᵊl) *n* a variant spelling of **rouble.**
rub off *vb* **1** to remove or be removed by rubbing. **2** (*intr;* often foll. by *on* or *onto*) to have an effect through close association or contact: *her crude manners have rubbed off on you.*
rub out ❶ *vb (tr, adv)* **1** to remove or be removed with a rubber. **2** *US sl.* to murder.
rubric ('ru:brɪk) *n* **1** a title, heading, or initial letter in a book, manuscript, or section of a legal code, esp. one printed or painted in red ink or in some similarly distinguishing manner. **2** a set of rules of conduct or procedure. **3** a set of directions for the conduct of Christian church services, often printed in red in a prayer book or missal. [C15 *rubrike* red ochre, red lettering, from L *rubrīca* (*terra*) red (earth), ruddle, from *ruber* red]
▸ **'rubrical** *adj* ▸ **'rubrically** *adv*
ruby ('ru:bɪ) *n, pl* **rubies. 1** a deep red transparent precious variety of corundum: used as a gemstone, in lasers, and for bearings and rollers in watchmaking. **2a** the deep-red colour of a ruby. **2b** (*as adj*): *ruby lips.* **3a** something resembling, made of, or containing a ruby. **3b** (*as modifier*): *a ruby necklace.* **4** (*modifier*) denoting a fortieth anniversary: *our ruby wedding.* [C14: from OF *rubi,* from L *rubeus,* from *ruber* red]
RUC *abbrev. for* Royal Ulster Constabulary.
ruche (ru:ʃ) *n* a strip of pleated or frilled lawn, lace, etc., used to decorate blouses, dresses, etc. [C19: from F, lit.: beehive, from Med. L *rūsca* bark of a tree, of Celtic origin]
ruching ('ru:ʃɪŋ) *n* **1** material used for a ruche. **2** a ruche or ruches collectively.
ruck[1] (rʌk) *n* **1** a large number or quantity; mass, esp. of undistinguished people or things. **2** (in a race) a group of competitors who are well behind the leaders. **3** *Rugby.* a loose scrum that forms around the ball when it is on the ground. **4** *Australian Rules football.* the three players who do not have fixed positions but follow the ball closely.

THESAURUS

rub *vb* **1** = **stroke**, caress, knead, massage, smooth **3** = **chafe**, abrade, fray, grate, scrape **5** = **spread**, apply, put, smear **10 rub up the wrong way** = **annoy**, aggravate (*inf.*), anger, bug (*inf.*), get in one's hair (*inf.*), get one's goat (*sl.*), get on one's nerves (*inf.*), get under one's skin (*inf.*), irk, irritate, nark (*Brit., Austral., & NZ sl.*), peeve (*inf.*), vex ◆ *n* **11** = **massage**, caress, kneading **12** *As in* **the rub** = **difficulty**, catch, drawback, hazard, hindrance, hitch, impediment, obstacle, problem, snag, trouble

rubbish *n* **1, 2** = **waste**, crap (*sl.*), debris, dreck (*sl., chiefly US*), dregs, dross, flotsam and jetsam, garbage (*chiefly US*), grot (*sl.*), junk (*inf.*), litter, lumber, offal, offscourings, refuse, scrap, trash **3** = **nonsense**, balderdash, bilge (*inf.*), bosh (*inf.*), bunkum *or* buncombe (*chiefly US*), claptrap (*inf.*), codswallop (*Brit. sl.*), crap (*sl.*), drivel, garbage (*chiefly US*), gibberish, hogwash, hokum (*sl., chiefly US & Canad.*), hot air (*inf.*), moonshine, piffle (*inf.*), poppycock (*inf.*), rot, stuff and nonsense, tommyrot, tosh (*sl., chiefly Brit.*), trash, tripe (*inf.*), twaddle

rubbishy *adj* **1** = **trashy**, cheap, paltry, shoddy, tatty, tawdry, throwaway, twopenny, twopenny-halfpenny, valueless, worthless

rubicund *adj Old-fashioned* = **reddish**, blushing, florid, flushed, pink, roseate, rosy, ruddy

rub out *vb* **1** = **erase**, cancel, delete, efface, excise, expunge, obliterate, remove, wipe out **2** *U.S. slang* = **murder**, assassinate, blow away (*sl., chiefly US*), bump off, butcher, dispatch, do in

◆ *vb* **5** (*intr*) *Rugby.* to try to win the ball by mauling and scrummaging. [C13 (meaning "heap of firewood"): ?from ON]

ruck[2] (rʌk) *n* **1** a wrinkle, crease, or fold. ◆ *vb* **2** (usually foll. by *up*) to become or make wrinkled, creased, or puckered. [C18: of Scand. origin; rel. to ON *hrukka*]

ruckman ('rʌkmən) *n, pl* **ruckmen.** *Australian Rules football.* either of two players who, with the rover, form the ruck.

ruck-rover *n Australian Rules football.* a player playing a role midway between that of the rover and the ruckmen.

rucksack ('rʌk,sæk) *n* a large bag, usually having two straps, carried on the back and often used by climbers, campers, etc. Also called: **backpack.** [C19: from G, lit.: back sack]

ruction ❶ ('rʌkʃən) *n Inf.* **1** an uproar; noisy or quarrelsome disturbance. **2** (*pl*) an unpleasant row; trouble. [C19: ? changed from INSURRECTION]

rudaceous (ru:'deɪʃəs) *adj* (of conglomerate, breccia, and similar rocks) composed of coarse-grained material. [C20: from L *rudis* coarse, rough + -ACEOUS]

rudbeckia (rʌd'bɛkɪə) *n* any of a genus of North American plants of the composite family, cultivated for their showy flowers, which have golden-yellow rays and green or black conical centres. See also **black-eyed Susan.** [C18: NL, after Olaus *Rudbeck* (1630–1702), Swedish botanist]

rudd (rʌd) *n* a European freshwater fish, having a compressed dark greenish body and reddish ventral and tail fins. [C17: prob. from dialect *rud* red colour, from OE *rudu* redness]

rudder ('rʌdə) *n* **1** *Naut.* a pivoted vertical vane that projects into the water at the stern and can be used to steer a vessel. **2** a vertical control surface attached to the rear of the fin used to steer an aircraft. **3** anything that guides or directs. [OE *rōther*]
▸ **'rudderless** *adj*

rudderpost ('rʌdə,pəʊst) *n Naut.* **1** a postlike member at the forward edge of a rudder. **2** the part of the stern frame of a vessel to which a rudder is fitted.

ruddle ('rʌdᵊl), **raddle,** *or* **reddle** *n* **1** a red ochre, used esp. to mark sheep. ◆ *vb* **ruddles, ruddling, ruddled. 2** (*tr*) to mark (sheep) with ruddle. [C16: dim. formed from OE *rudu* redness; see RUDD]

ruddy ❶ ('rʌdɪ) *adj* **ruddier, ruddiest. 1** (of the complexion) having a healthy reddish colour. **2** coloured red or pink: *a ruddy sky.* ◆ *adv, adj Inf., chiefly Brit.* **3** (intensifier) bloody; damned: *a ruddy fool.* [OE *rudig,* from *rudu* redness]
▸ **'ruddily** *adv* ▸ **'ruddiness** *n*

rude ❶ (ru:d) *adj* **1** insulting or uncivil; discourteous; impolite. **2** lacking refinement; coarse or uncouth. **3** vulgar or obscene: *a rude joke.* **4** unexpected and unpleasant: *a rude awakening.* **5** roughly or crudely made: *we made a rude shelter on the island.* **6** rough or harsh in sound, appearance, or behaviour. **7** humble or lowly. **8** (*prenominal*) robust or sturdy: *in rude health.* **9** (*prenominal*) approximate or imprecise: *a rude estimate.* [C14: via OF from L *rudis* coarse, unformed]
▸ **'rudely** *adv* ▸ **'rudeness** *or* (*inf.*) **'rudery** *n*

ruderal ('ru:dərəl) *n* **1** a plant that grows on waste ground. ◆ *adj* **2** growing in waste places. [C19: from NL *rūderālis,* from L *rūdus* rubble]

rudiment ❶ ('ru:dɪmənt) *n* **1** (*often pl*) the first principles or elementary stages of a subject. **2** (*often pl*) a partially developed version of something. **3** *Biol.* an organ or part in an embryonic or vestigial state. [C16: from L *rudīmentum* a beginning, from *rudis* unformed]

rudimentary ❶ (,ru:dɪ'mɛntərɪ, -trɪ) *or* **rudimental** *adj* **1** basic; fundamental. **2** incompletely developed; vestigial: *rudimentary leaves.*
▸ **,rudi'mentarily** *or* (*less commonly*) **,rudi'mentally** *adv*

rudish ('ru:dɪʃ) *adj* somewhat rude.

rue[1] ❶ (ru:) *vb* **rues, ruing, rued. 1** to feel sorrow, remorse, or regret for (one's own wrongdoing, past events, etc.). ◆ *n* **2** *Arch.* sorrow, pity, or regret. [OE *hrēowan*]
▸ **'ruer** *n*

rue[2] (ru:) *n* an aromatic Eurasian shrub with small yellow flowers and evergreen leaves which yield an acrid volatile oil, formerly used medicinally as a narcotic and stimulant. Archaic name: **herb of grace.** [C14: from OF, from L *rūta,* from Gk *rhutē*]

rueful ❶ ('ru:fʊl) *adj* **1** feeling or expressing sorrow or regret: *a rueful face.* **2** inspiring sorrow or pity.
▸ **'ruefully** *adv* ▸ **'ruefulness** *n*

ruff[1] (rʌf) *n* **1** a circular pleated or fluted collar of lawn, muslin, etc., worn by both men and women in the 16th and 17th centuries. **2** a natural growth of long or coloured hair or feathers around the necks of certain animals or birds. **3** an Old World shore bird of the sandpiper family, the male of which has a large erectile ruff of feathers in the breeding season. [C16: back formation from RUFFLE[1]]
▸ **'ruff,like** *adj*

ruff[2] (rʌf) *Cards.* ◆ *n, vb* **1** another word for **trump**[1] (senses 1, 4). ◆ *n* **2** an old card game similar to whist. [C16: from OF *roffle;* ? changed from It. *trionfa* TRUMP[1]]

ruffe *or* **ruff** (rʌf) *n* a European freshwater teleost fish of the perch family, having a single spiny dorsal fin. [C15: ? alteration of ROUGH (referring to its scales)]

ruffian ❶ ('rʌfɪən) *n* a violent or lawless person; hoodlum. [C16: from OF *rufien,* from It. *ruffiano* pander]
▸ **'ruffianism** *n* ▸ **'ruffianly** *adj*

ruffle[1] ❶ ('rʌfᵊl) *vb* **ruffles, ruffling, ruffled. 1** to make, be, or become irregular or rumpled: *a breeze ruffling the water.* **2** to annoy, irritate, or be annoyed or irritated. **3** (*tr*) to make into a ruffle; pleat. **4** (of a bird) to erect (its feathers) in anger, display, etc. **5** (*tr*) to flick (cards, pages, etc.) rapidly. ◆ *n* **6** an irregular or disturbed surface. **7** a strip of pleated material used as a trim. **8** *Zool.* another name for **ruff**[1] (sense 2). **9** annoyance or irritation. [C13: of Gmc origin; cf. MLow G *ruffelen* to crumple, ON *hrufla* to scratch]

ruffle[2] ('rʌfᵊl) *n* **1** a low continuous drumbeat. ◆ *vb* **ruffles, ruffling, ruffled. 2** (*tr*) to beat (a drum) with a low repetitive beat. [C18: from earlier *ruff,* imit.]

rufous ('ru:fəs) *adj* reddish-brown. [C18: from L *rūfus*]

rufty-tufty (,rʌftɪ 'tʌftɪ) *adj Sl.* rugged in appearance or manner.

rug (rʌg) *n* **1** a floor covering, smaller than a carpet and made of thick wool or of other material, such as an animal skin. **2** *Chiefly Brit.* a blanket, esp. one used for travellers. **3** *Sl.* a wig. **4 pull the rug out from under.** to betray, expose, or leave defenceless. [C16: of Scand. origin]

ruga ('ru:gə) *n, pl* **rugae** (-dʒi:). (*usually pl*) *Anat.* a fold, wrinkle, or crease. [C18: L]

rugby *or* **rugby football** ('rʌgbɪ) *n* **1** a form of football played with an oval ball in which the handling and carrying of the ball is permitted. Also called: **rugger. 2** *Canad.* another name for **Canadian football.** See also **rugby league, rugby union.** [after the public school at *Rugby,* where it was first played]

rugby league *n* a form of rugby football played between teams of 13 players.

rugby union *n* a form of rugby football played between teams of 15 players.

rugged ❶ ('rʌgɪd) *adj* **1** having an uneven or jagged surface. **2** rocky or steep: *rugged scenery.* **3** (of the face) strong-featured or furrowed. **4** rough, severe, or stern in character. **5** without refinement or culture; rude: *rugged manners.* **6** involving hardship; harsh: *he leads a rugged life in the mountains.* **7** difficult or hard: *a rugged test.* **8** (of equipment, machines, etc.) designed to withstand rough treatment or use in rough conditions. **9** *Chiefly US & Canad.* sturdy or strong; robust. [C14: from ON]
▸ **'ruggedly** *adv* ▸ **'ruggedness** *n*

rugger ('rʌgə) *n Chiefly Brit.* an informal name for **rugby.**

rugose ('ru:gəʊs, -gəʊz) *adj* wrinkled: *rugose leaves.* [C18: from L *rūgōsus,* from *rūga* wrinkle]
▸ **'rugosely** *adv* ▸ **rugosity** (ru:'gɒsɪtɪ) *n*

THESAURUS

(*inf.*), eliminate (*sl.*), hit (*sl.*), kill, knock off (*sl.*), slaughter, slay, take out (*sl.*), waste (*inf.*)

ruction *n* **2** *Informal, plural* = **row,** altercation, brawl, commotion, dispute, disturbance, fracas, fuss, hue and cry, quarrel, racket, rumpus, scrap (*inf.*), scrimmage, shindig (*inf.*), shindy (*inf.*), storm, to-do, trouble, uproar

ruddy *adj* **1** = **rosy,** blooming, blushing, florid, flushed, fresh, glowing, healthy, radiant, red, reddish, rosy-cheeked, rubicund, sanguine, sunburnt **2** = **red,** crimson, pink, reddish, roseate, ruby, scarlet
Antonyms *adj* ≠ **rosy:** anaemic, ashen, colourless, grey, pale, pallid, sickly, wan, white

rude *adj* **1** = **impolite,** abrupt, abusive, blunt, brusque, cheeky, churlish, curt, discourteous, disrespectful, ill-mannered, impertinent, impudent, inconsiderate, insolent, insulting, offhand, peremptory, short, uncivil, unmannerly **2** = **coarse,** barbarous, boorish, brutish, crude, graceless, gross, ignorant, illiterate, loutish, low, oafish, rough, savage, scurrilous, uncivilized, uncouth, uncultured, uneducated, ungracious, unpolished, unrefined, untutored, vulgar **4** = **unpleasant,** abrupt, harsh, sharp, startling, sudden, violent **5** = **roughly-made,** artless, crude, inartistic, inelegant, makeshift, primitive, raw, rough, rough-hewn, simple
Antonyms *adj* ≠ **impolite:** civil, considerate, cordial, courteous, courtly, decent, gentlemanly, gracious, ladylike, mannerly, polite, respectful, sociable, urbane, well-bred ≠ **coarse:** civilized, cultured, educated, elegant, learned, polished, refined, sophisticated, urbane ≠ **roughly-made:** artful, even, finished, shapely, smooth, well-made

rudiment *n* **1** *often plural* = **basics,** beginnings, elements, essentials, first principles, foundation, fundamentals, nuts and bolts

rudimentary *adj* **1** = **basic,** early, elementary, fundamental, initial, introductory, primary, primitive **2** = **undeveloped,** embryonic, immature, vestigial
Antonyms *adj* ≠ **basic:** advanced, complete, higher, later, mature, refined, secondary, sophisticated, supplementary

rue[1] *vb* **1** = **regret,** bemoan, be sorry for, bewail, deplore, grieve, kick oneself for, lament, mourn, repent, reproach oneself for, sorrow for, weep over

rueful *adj* **1** = **regretful,** conscience-stricken, contrite, dismal, doleful, grievous, lugubrious, melancholy, mournful, penitent, plaintive, remorseful, repentant, sad, self-reproachful, sorrowful, sorry, woebegone, woeful
Antonyms *adj* cheerful, delighted, glad, happy, joyful, pleased, unrepentant

ruffian *n* = **thug,** bruiser (*inf.*), brute, bully, bully boy, heavy (*sl.*), hoodlum, hooligan, lager lout, miscreant, ned (*Scot. sl.*), rascal, rogue, rough (*inf.*), roughneck (*sl.*), rowdy, scoundrel, tough, villain, wretch, yardie

ruffle[1] *vb* **1** = **disarrange,** derange, discompose, dishevel, disorder, mess up, rumple, tousle, wrinkle **2** = **annoy,** agitate, confuse, disconcert, disquiet, disturb, faze, fluster, harass, hassle (*inf.*), irritate, nettle, peeve (*inf.*), perturb, put out, rattle (*inf.*), shake up (*inf.*), stir, trouble, unnerve, unsettle, upset, vex, worry
Antonyms *vb* ≠ **annoy:** appease, calm, comfort, compose, console, ease, mollify, solace, soothe

rugged *adj* **1, 2** = **rocky,** broken, bumpy, craggy, difficult, irregular, jagged, ragged, rough, stark, uneven **3** = **strong-featured,** furrowed, leathery, lined, rough-hewn, weather-

rug rat *n US & Canad. inf.* a young child not yet walking.

ruin Ⓣ (ˈruːɪn) *n* **1** a destroyed or decayed building or town. **2** the state of being destroyed or decayed. **3** loss of wealth, position, etc., or something that causes such loss; downfall. **4** something that is severely damaged: *his life was a ruin.* **5** a person who has suffered a downfall, bankruptcy, etc. **6** *Arch.* loss of her virginity by a woman outside marriage. ◆ *vb* **7** (*tr*) to bring to ruin; destroy. **8** (*tr*) to injure or spoil: *the town has been ruined with tower blocks.* **9** (*intr*) *Arch. or poetic.* to fall into ruins; collapse. **10** (*tr*) *Arch.* to seduce and abandon (a woman). [C14: from OF *ruine,* from L *ruīna* a falling down, from *ruere* to fall violently]

ruination (ˌruːɪˈneɪʃən) *n* **1** the act of ruining or the state of being ruined. **2** something that causes ruin.

ruinous Ⓣ (ˈruːɪnəs) *adj* causing, tending to cause, or characterized by ruin or destruction.
▸ **ˈruinously** *adv* ▸ **ˈruinousness** *n*

rule Ⓣ (ruːl) *n* **1** an authoritative regulation or direction concerning method or procedure, as for a court of law, legislative body, game, or other activity: *judges' rules; play according to the rules.* **2** the exercise of governmental authority or control: *the rule of Caesar.* **3** the period of time in which a monarch or government has power: *his rule lasted 100 days.* **4** a customary form or procedure: *he made a morning swim his rule.* **5** (usually preceded by *the*) the common order of things: *violence was the rule rather than the exception.* **6** a prescribed method or procedure for solving a mathematical problem. **7** any of various devices with a straight edge for guiding or measuring; ruler: *a carpenter's rule.* **8** *Printing.* **8a** a printed or drawn character in the form of a long thin line. **8b** another name for **dash**[1] (sense 12): *en rule; em rule.* **8c** a strip of metal used to print such a line. **9** *Christianity.* a systematic body of prescriptions followed by members of a religious order. **10** *Law.* an order by a court or judge. **11 as a rule.** normally or ordinarily. ◆ *vb* **rules, ruling, ruled. 12** to exercise governing or controlling authority over (a people, political unit, individual, etc.). **13** (when *tr, often takes a clause as object*) to decide authoritatively; decree: *the chairman ruled against the proposal.* **14** (*tr*) to mark with straight parallel lines or one straight line. **15** (*tr*) to restrain or control. **16** (*intr*) to be customary or prevalent: *chaos rules in this school.* **17** (*intr*) to be pre-eminent or superior: *football rules in the field of sport.* **18 rule the roost** (*or* **roast**). to be pre-eminent; be in charge. [C13: from OF *riule,* from L *rēgula* a straight edge]
▸ **ˈrulable** *adj*

rule of three *n* a mathematical rule asserting that the value of one unknown quantity in a proportion is found by multiplying the denominator of each ratio by the numerator of the other.

rule of thumb *n* **a** a rough and practical approach, based on experience, rather than theory. **b** (*as modifier*): *a rule-of-thumb decision.*

rule out Ⓣ *vb* (*tr, adv*) **1** to dismiss from consideration. **2** to make impossible; preclude.

ruler Ⓣ (ˈruːlə) *n* **1** a person who rules or commands. **2** Also called: **rule.** a strip of wood, metal, or other material, having straight edges, used for measuring and drawing straight lines.

Rules (ruːlz) *pl n* **1** short for **Australian Rules** (football). **2 the Rules.** *English history.* the neighbourhood around certain prisons in which trusted prisoners were allowed to live under specified restrictions.

ruling Ⓣ (ˈruːlɪŋ) *n* **1** a decision of someone in authority, such as a judge. **2** one or more parallel ruled lines. ◆ *adj* **3** controlling or exercising authority. **4** predominant.

rum[1] (rʌm) *n* spirit made from sugar cane. [C17: ? shortened from C16 *rumbullion,* from ?]

rum[2] Ⓣ (rʌm) *adj* **rummer, rummest.** *Brit. sl.* strange; peculiar; odd. [C19: ?from Romany *rom* man]
▸ **ˈrumly** *adv* ▸ **ˈrumness** *n*

Rumanian (ruːˈmeɪnɪən) *n, adj* a variant of **Romanian.**

rumba *or* **rhumba** (ˈrʌmbə, ˈrum-) *n* **1** a rhythmic and syncopated Cuban dance in duple time. **2** a ballroom dance derived from this. **3** a piece of music composed for or in the rhythm of this dance. [C20: from Sp.: lavish display, from ?]

rumble (ˈrʌmbᵊl) *vb* **rumbles, rumbling, rumbled. 1** to make or cause to make a deep resonant sound: *thunder rumbled in the sky.* **2** (*intr*) to move with such a sound: *the train rumbled along.* **3** (*tr*) to utter with a rumbling sound: *he rumbled an order.* **4** (*tr*) *Brit. sl.* to find out about (someone or something): *the police rumbled their plans.* **5** (*intr*) *US sl.* to be involved in a gang fight. ◆ *n* **6** a deep resonant sound. **7** a widespread murmur of discontent. **8** *US, Canad., & NZ sl.* a gang fight. [C14: ?from MDu. *rummelen*]
▸ **ˈrumbler** *n* ▸ **ˈrumbling** *adj*

rumble seat *n* a folding outside seat at the rear of some early cars; dicky.

rumbustious Ⓣ (rʌmˈbʌstʃəs) *adj* boisterous or unruly. [C18: prob. var. of ROBUSTIOUS]
▸ **rumˈbustiously** *adv* ▸ **rumˈbustiousness** *n*

rumen (ˈruːmɛn) *n, pl* **rumens** *or* **rumina** (-mɪnə). the first compartment of the stomach of ruminants, in which food is partly digested before being regurgitated as cud. [C18: from L: gullet]

ruminant (ˈruːmɪnənt) *n* **1** any of a suborder of artiodactyl mammals which chew the cud and have a stomach of four compartments. The suborder includes deer, antelopes, cattle, sheep, and goats. **2** any other animal that chews the cud, such as a camel. ◆ *adj* **3** of, relating to, or belonging to this suborder. **4** (of members of this suborder and related animals, such as camels) chewing the cud; ruminating. **5** meditating or contemplating in a slow quiet way.

ruminate Ⓣ (ˈruːmɪˌneɪt) *vb* **ruminates, ruminating, ruminated. 1** (of ruminants) to chew (the cud). **2** (when *intr,* often foll. by *upon, on,* etc.) to meditate or ponder (upon). [C16: from L *rūmināre* to chew the cud, from RUMEN]
▸ **ˌrumiˈnation** *n* ▸ **ˈruminative** *adj* ▸ **ˈruminatively** *adv* ▸ **ˈrumiˌnator** *n*

rummage Ⓣ (ˈrʌmɪdʒ) *vb* **rummages, rummaging, rummaged. 1** (when *intr,* often foll. by *through*) to search (through) while looking for something, often causing disorder. ◆ *n* **2** an act of rummaging. **3** a jumble of articles. [C14 (in the sense: to pack a cargo): from OF *arrumage,* from *arrumer* to stow in a ship's hold, prob. of Gmc origin]
▸ **ˈrummager** *n*

rummage sale *n* **1** the US and Canad. term for **jumble sale. 2** *US.* a sale of unclaimed property.

rummer (ˈrʌmə) *n* a drinking glass having an ovoid bowl on a short stem. [C17: from Du. *roemer* a glass for drinking toasts, from *roemen* to praise]

rummy (ˈrʌmɪ) *or* **rum** *n* a card game based on collecting sets and sequences. [C20: ?from RUM[2]]

rumour Ⓣ *or US* **rumor** (ˈruːmə) *n* **1a** information, often a mixture of

THESAURUS

beaten, weathered, worn, wrinkled **4** = **stern,** austere, crabbed, dour, gruff, hard, harsh, rough, rude, severe, sour, surly **5** = **rude,** barbarous, blunt, churlish, crude, graceless, uncouth, uncultured, unpolished, unrefined **7** = **difficult,** arduous, demanding, exacting, hard, harsh, laborious, rigorous, stern, strenuous, taxing, tough, trying, uncompromising **8, 9** = **sturdy,** robust, strong, tough, well-built

Antonyms *adj* ≠ **rocky:** even, gentle, level, regular, smooth, unbroken ≠ **strong-featured:** delicate, pretty, refined, smooth, unmarked, youthful ≠ **rude:** civil, courteous, cultivated, cultured, elegant, polished, polite, refined, sophisticated, subtle, urbane, well-bred ≠ **difficult:** agreeable, easy, gentle, mild, pleasant, simple, soft, tender, uncomplicated, unexacting ≠ **sturdy:** delicate, fragile

ruin *n* **2** = **destruction,** breakdown, collapse, crackup, crash, damage, decay, defeat, devastation, disintegration, disrepair, dissolution, downfall, failure, fall, havoc, overthrow, ruination, subversion, the end, undoing, wreck **3** = **bankruptcy,** destitution, insolvency ◆ *vb* **7** = **destroy,** break, bring down, bring to nothing, bring to ruin, crush, defeat, demolish, devastate, lay in ruins, lay waste, overthrow, overturn, overwhelm, raze, shatter, smash, total (*sl.*), trash (*sl.*), wreak havoc upon, wreck **8** = **spoil,** blow (*sl.*), bodge (*inf.*), botch, damage, disfigure, injure, make a mess of, mangle, mar, mess up, screw up (*inf.*), undo

Antonyms *n* ≠ **destruction:** creation, preservation, success, triumph, victory ◆ *vb* ≠ **destroy:** build, construct, create, keep, preserve, save ≠ **spoil:** enhance, enrich, improve, mend, repair, restore, strengthen, support

ruinous *adj* = **destructive,** baleful, baneful (*arch.*), calamitous, catastrophic, deadly, deleterious, devastating, dire, disastrous, fatal, injurious, murderous, noxious, pernicious, shattering, withering

rule *n* **1** = **regulation,** axiom, canon, criterion, decree, dictum, direction, guide, guideline, law, maxim, order, ordinance, precept, principle, ruling, standard, tenet **2, 3** = **government,** administration, ascendancy, authority, command, control, direction, domination, dominion, empire, influence, jurisdiction, leadership, mastery, power, regime, reign, supremacy, sway **4** = **procedure,** course, formula, method, policy, way **5** = **custom,** condition, convention, form, habit, order *or* way of things, practice, procedure, routine, tradition, wont **11 as a rule** = **usually,** customarily, for the most part, generally, mainly, normally, on the whole, ordinarily ◆ *vb* **12** = **govern,** administer, be in authority, be in power, be number one (*inf.*), command, control, direct, guide, hold sway, lead, manage, preside over, regulate, reign, wear the crown **13** = **decree,** adjudge, adjudicate, decide, determine, establish, find, judge, lay down, pronounce, resolve, settle **16** = **be prevalent,** be customary, hold sway, obtain, predominate, preponderate, prevail **17** = **be pre-eminent,** be superior, dominate

rule out *vb* **1** = **dismiss,** leave out, reject **2** = **exclude,** ban, debar, disqualify, eliminate, forbid, obviate, preclude, prevent, prohibit, proscribe

Antonyms *vb* ≠ **exclude:** allow, approve, authorize, let, license, order, permit, sanction

ruler *n* **1** = **governor,** commander, controller, crowned head, emperor *or* empress, head of state, king *or* queen, leader, lord, monarch, potentate, prince *or* princess, sovereign **2** = **measure,** rule, straight edge, yardstick

ruling *n* **1** = **decision,** adjudication, decree, finding, judgment, pronouncement, resolution, verdict ◆ *adj* **3** = **governing,** commanding, controlling, dominant, leading, regnant, reigning, upper **4** = **predominant,** chief, current, dominant, main, pre-eminent, preponderant, prevailing, prevalent, principal, supreme

Antonyms *adj* ≠ **predominant:** auxiliary, inferior, least, minor, secondary, subordinate, subsidiary, unimportant

rum[2] *adj Brit. slang* = **strange,** curious, dodgy (*Brit., Austral., & NZ inf.*), funny, odd, peculiar, queer, singular, suspect, suspicious, unusual, weird

rumbustious *adj* = **unruly,** boisterous, clamorous, disorderly, exuberant, loud, noisy, obstreperous, refractory, robust, rough, rowdy, unmanageable, uproarious, wayward, wild, wilful

ruminate *vb* **2** = **ponder,** brood, chew over, cogitate, consider, contemplate, deliberate, meditate, mull over, muse, rack one's brains, reflect, revolve, think, turn over in one's mind, weigh

rummage *vb* **1** = **search,** delve, examine, explore, forage, hunt, ransack, root, rootle

rumour *n* **1, 2** = **story,** bruit (*arch.*), bush tele-

truth and untruth, passed around verbally. **1b** (*in combination*): *a rumourmonger.* **2** gossip or hearsay. ◆ *vb* **3** (*tr; usually passive*) to pass around or circulate in the form of a rumour: *it is rumoured that the Queen is coming.* [C14: via OF from L *rūmor* common talk]

rump ⓣ (rʌmp) *n* **1** the hindquarters of a mammal, not including the legs. **2** the rear part of a bird's back, nearest to the tail. **3** a person's buttocks. **4** Also called: **rump steak.** a cut of beef from behind the loin. **5** an inferior remnant. [C15: from ON]
▸ **'rumpless** *adj*

rumple ⓣ ('rʌmpᵊl) *vb* **rumples, rumpling, rumpled. 1** to make or become crumpled or dishevelled. ◆ *n* **2** a wrinkle, fold, or crease. [C17: from MDu. *rompelen*; rel. to OE *gerumpen* wrinkled]
▸ **'rumply** *adj*

Rump Parliament *or* **the Rump** *n English history.* the remainder of the Long Parliament after Pride's Purge (the expulsion by Thomas Pride in 1648 of those members hostile to the army). It sat from 1648–53.

rumpus ⓣ ('rʌmpəs) *n, pl* **rumpuses.** a noisy, confused, or disruptive commotion. [C18: from ?]

rumpus room *n* a room used for noisy activities, such as parties or children's games.

rumpy-pumpy ('rʌmpɪ'pʌmpɪ) *n Inf.* sexual intercourse.

run ⓣ (rʌn) *vb* **runs, running, ran, run. 1** (*intr*) **1a** (of a two-legged creature) to move on foot at a rapid pace so that both feet are off the ground for part of each stride. **1b** (of a four-legged creature) to move at a rapid gait. **2** (*tr*) to pass over (a distance, route, etc.) in running: *to run a mile.* **3** (*intr*) to run in or finish a race as specified, esp. in a particular position: *John is running third.* **4** (*tr*) to perform as by running: *to run an errand.* **5** (*intr*) to flee; run away. **6** (*tr*) to bring into a specified state by running: *to run oneself to a standstill.* **7** (*tr*) to track down or hunt (an animal): *to run a fox to earth.* **8** (*tr*) to set (animals) loose on (a field or tract of land) so as to graze freely: *he ran stock on that pasture last year.* **9** (*intr; often foll. by over, round, or up*) to make a short trip or brief visit: *I'll run over this afternoon.* **10** (*intr*) to move quickly and easily on wheels by rolling, or in any of certain other ways: *a sledge running over snow.* **11** to move or cause to move with a specified result: *to run a ship aground; run into a tree.* **12** (often foll. by *over*) to move or pass or cause to move or pass quickly: *to run one's eyes over a page.* **13** (*tr*; foll. by *into, out of, through,* etc.) to force, thrust, or drive: *she ran a needle into her finger.* **14** (*tr*) to drive or maintain and operate (a vehicle). **15** (*tr*) to give a lift to (someone) in a vehicle: *he ran her to the station.* **16** to ply or cause to ply between places on a route: *the bus runs from Piccadilly to Golders Green.* **17** to function or cause to function: *the engine is running smoothly.* **18** (*tr*) to manage: *to run a company.* **19** to extend or continue or cause to extend or continue in a particular direction, for a particular duration or distance, etc.: *the road runs north; the play ran for two years.* **20** (*intr*) *Law.* to have legal force or effect: *the house lease runs for two more years.* **21** (*tr*) to be subjected to, be affected by, or incur: *to run a risk; run a temperature.* **22** (*intr*; often foll. by *to*) to be characterized (by); tend or incline: *to run to fat.* **23** (*intr*) to recur persistently or be inherent: *red hair runs in my family.* **24** to cause or allow (liquids) to flow or (of liquids) to flow: *the well has run dry.* **25** (*intr*) to melt and flow: *the wax grew hot and began to run.* **26** *Metallurgy.* **26a** to melt or fuse. **26b** (*tr*) to cast (molten metal): *to run lead into ingots.* **27** (*intr*) (of waves, tides, rivers, etc.) to rise high, surge, or be at a specified height: *a high sea was running that night.* **28** (*intr*) to be diffused: *the colours in my dress ran when I washed it.* **29** (*intr*) (of stitches) to unravel or come undone or (of a garment) to have stitches unravel or come undone. **30** (*intr*) (of growing creepers, etc.) to trail, spread, or climb: *ivy running over a cottage wall.* **31** (*intr*) to spread or circulate quickly: *a rumour ran through the town.* **32** (*intr*) to be stated or reported: *his story runs as follows.* **33** to publish or print or be published or printed in a newspaper, magazine, etc.: *they ran his story in the next issue.* **34** (often foll. by *for*) *Chiefly US & Canad.* to be a candidate or present as a candidate for political or other office: *Jones is running for president.* **35** (*tr*) to get past or through: *to run a blockade.* **36** (*tr*) to deal in (arms, etc.), esp. by importing illegally: *he runs guns for the rebels.* **37** *Naut.* to sail (a vessel, esp. a sailing vessel) or (of such a vessel) to be sailed with the wind coming from astern. **38** (*intr*) (of fish) to migrate upstream from the sea, esp. in order to spawn. **39** (*tr*) *Cricket.* to score (a run or number of runs) by hitting the ball and running between the wickets. **40** (*tr*) *Billiards, etc.* to make (a number of successful shots) in sequence. **41** (*tr*) *Golf.* to hit (the ball) so that it rolls along the ground. **42** (*tr*) *Bridge.* to cash (all one's winning cards in a long suit) successively. ◆ *n* **43** an act, instance, or period of running. **44** a gait, pace, or motion faster than a walk: *she went off at a run.* **45** a distance covered by running or a period of running: *a run of ten miles.* **46** an instance or period of travelling in a vehicle, esp. for pleasure: *to go for a run in the car.* **47** free and unrestricted access: *we had the run of the house.* **48a** a period of time during which a machine, computer, etc., operates. **48b** the amount of work performed in such a period. **49** a continuous or sustained period: *a run of good luck.* **50** a continuous sequence of performances: *the play had a good run.* **51** *Cards.* a sequence of winning cards in one suit: *a run of spades.* **52** tendency or trend: *the run of the market.* **53** type, class, or category: *the usual run of graduates.* **54** (usually foll. by *on*) a continuous and urgent demand: *a run on the dollar.* **55** a series of unravelled stitches, esp. in tights; ladder. **56** the characteristic pattern or direction of something: *the run of the grain on wood.* **57a** a period during which water or other liquid flows. **57b** the amount of such a flow. **58** a pipe, channel, etc., through which water or other liquid flows. **59** *US.* a small stream. **60** a steeply inclined course, esp. a snow-covered one used for skiing. **61** an enclosure for domestic fowls or other animals: *a chicken run.* **62** (esp. in Australia and New Zealand) a tract of land for grazing livestock. **63** the migration of fish upstream in order to spawn. **64** *Mil.* **64a** a mission in a warplane. **64b** Also called: **bombing run.** an approach by a bomber to a target. **65** the movement of an aircraft along the ground during takeoff or landing. **66** *Music.* a rapid scalelike passage of notes. **67** *Cricket.* a score of one, normally achieved by both batsmen running from one end of the wicket to the other after one of them has hit the ball. **68** *Baseball.* an instance of a batter touching all four bases safely, thereby scoring. **69** *Golf.* the distance that a ball rolls after hitting the ground. **70 a run for (one's) money.** *Inf.* **70a** a close competition. **70b** pleasure derived from an activity. **71 in the long run.** as the eventual outcome of a series of events, etc. **72 in the short run.** as the immediate outcome of a series of events, etc. **73 on the run. 73a** escaping from arrest; fugitive. **73b** in rapid flight; retreating: *the enemy is on the run.* **73c** hurrying from place to place. **74 the runs.** *Sl.* diarrhoea. ◆ See also **runabout, run across,** etc. [OE *runnen*, p.p. of (*ge*)*rinnan*]

runabout ('rʌnə,baut) *n* **1** a small light vehicle or aeroplane. ◆ *vb* **run about. 2** (*intr, adv*) to move busily from place to place.

run across ⓣ *vb* (*intr, prep*) to meet unexpectedly; encounter by chance.

run along *vb* (*intr, adv*) (often said patronizingly) to go away; leave.

run around *Inf.* ◆ *vb* (*intr, adv*) **1** (often foll. by *with*) to associate habitually (with). **2** to behave in a fickle or promiscuous manner. ◆ *n* **run-around. 3** deceitful or evasive treatment of a person (esp. in **give** *or* **get the run-around**).

run away ⓣ *vb* (*intr, adv*) **1** to take flight; escape. **2** to go away; depart. **3** (of a horse) to gallop away uncontrollably. **4 run away with. 4a** to abscond or elope with: *he ran away with his boss's daughter.* **4b** to make off with; steal. **4c** to escape from the control of: *his enthusiasm ran away with him.* **4d** to win easily or be assured of victory in (a competition): *he ran away with the race.* ◆ *n* **runaway. 5a** a person or animal that runs away. **5b** (*as modifier*): *a runaway horse.* **6** the act or an instance of running away. **7** (*modifier*) rising rapidly, as prices: *runaway inflation.* **8** (*modifier*) (of a race, victory, etc.) easily won.

THESAURUS

graph, buzz, canard, dirt (*US sl.*), gossip, hearsay, news, report, scuttlebutt (*US sl.*), talk, tidings, whisper, word ◆ *vb* **3** *usually passive* = **be said**, be circulated, be noised abroad, be passed around, be published, be put about, be reported, be told, be whispered

rump *n* **1** = **hindquarters**, haunch, rear, tail **3** = **buttocks**, arse (*taboo sl.*), ass (*US & Canad. taboo sl.*), backside (*inf.*), bottom, bum (*Brit. sl.*), buns (*US sl.*), butt (*US & Canad. inf.*), derrière (*euphemistic*), jacksy (*Brit. sl.*), posterior, rear, rear end, seat, tail (*inf.*)

rumple *vb* **1** = **ruffle**, crease, crinkle, crumple, crush, derange, dishevel, disorder, mess up, pucker, screw up, scrunch, tousle, wrinkle

rumpus *n* = **commotion**, brouhaha, confusion, disruption, disturbance, furore, fuss, hue and cry, kerfuffle (*inf.*), noise, row, shindig (*inf.*), shindy (*inf.*), tumult, uproar

run *vb* **1** = **race**, barrel (along) (*inf., chiefly US & Canad.*), bolt, career, dart, dash, gallop, hare (*Brit. inf.*), hasten, hie, hotfoot, hurry, jog, leg it (*inf.*), lope, rush, scamper, scramble, scud, scurry, speed, sprint, stampede **5** = **flee**, abscond, beat a retreat, beat it (*sl.*), bolt, clear out, cut and run (*inf.*), decamp, depart, do a runner (*sl.*), escape, fly the coop (*US & Canad. inf.*), leg it (*inf.*), make a run for it, make off, scarper (*Brit. sl.*), show a clean pair of heels, skedaddle (*inf.*), slope off, take flight, take off (*inf.*), take to one's heels **10** = **move**, course, glide, go, pass, roll, skim, slide **14** = **operate 15** = **give a lift to**, bear, carry, convey, drive, manoeuvre, operate, propel, transport **17** = **work**, function, go, operate, perform, tick **18** = **manage**, administer, be in charge of, boss (*inf.*), carry on, conduct, control, coordinate, direct, handle, head, lead, look after, mastermind, operate, oversee, own, regulate, superintend, supervise, take care of **19** = **continue**, extend, go, last, lie, proceed, range, reach, stretch **24** = **flow**, cascade, discharge, go, gush, issue, leak, move, pour, proceed, spill, spout, stream **25** = **melt**, dissolve, fuse, go soft, liquefy, turn to liquid **28** = **spread**, be diffused, bleed, lose colour, mix **29** = **unravel**, come apart, come undone, ladder, tear **31** = **circulate**, be current, climb, creep, go round, spread, trail **33** = **publish**, display, feature, print **34** *chiefly U.S. & Canad.* = **compete**, be a candidate, challenge, contend, put oneself up for, stand, take part **36** = **smuggle**, bootleg, deal in, ship, sneak, traffic in ◆ *n* **43, 44** = **race**, dash, gallop, jog, rush, sprint, spurt **46** = **ride**, drive, excursion, jaunt, journey, joy ride (*inf.*), lift, outing, round, spin (*inf.*), trip **49** = **sequence**, chain, course, cycle, passage, period, round, season, series, spell, streak, stretch, string **52** = **tendency**, course, current, direction, drift, flow, motion, movement, passage, path, progress, stream, tenor, tide, trend, way **53** = **type**, category, class, kind, order, sort, variety **54** = **demand**, pressure, rush **55** = **tear**, ladder, rip, snag **61** = **enclosure**, coop, pen **71 in the long run** = **in the end**, at the end of the day, eventually, in the final analysis, in the fullness of time, in time, ultimately, when all is said and done **73 on the run: a** = **escaping**, at liberty, fugitive, in flight, on the lam (*US sl.*), on the loose **b** = **in retreat**, defeated, falling back, fleeing, in flight, retreating, running away **c** = **hurrying**, at speed, hastily, hurriedly, in a hurry, in a rush, in haste
Antonyms *vb* ≠ **race:** crawl, creep, dawdle, walk ≠ **flee:** remain, stay ≠ **continue:** cease, stop

run across *vb* = **meet**, bump into, chance upon, come across, come upon, encounter, meet with, run into

run away *vb* **1** = **flee**, abscond, beat it (*sl.*), bolt, clear out, cut and run, decamp, do a bunk

runcible spoon ('rʌnsɪbəl) *n* a forklike utensil with two broad prongs and one sharp curved prong. [*runcible* coined by Edward Lear, E humorist, in a nonsense poem (1871)]

run down ❶ *vb* (*mainly adv*) **1** to allow (an engine, etc.) to lose power gradually and cease to function or (of an engine, etc.) to do this. **2** to decline or reduce in number or size: *the firm ran down its sales force.* **3** (*tr; usually passive*) to tire, sap the strength of, or exhaust: *he was thoroughly run down.* **4** (*tr*) to criticize adversely; decry. **5** (*tr*) to hit and knock to the ground with a moving vehicle. **6** (*tr*) *Naut.* to collide with and cause to sink. **7** (*tr*) to pursue and find or capture: *to run down a fugitive.* **8** (*tr*) to read swiftly or perfunctorily: *he ran down their list of complaints.* ◆ *adj* **run-down. 9** tired; exhausted. **10** worn-out, shabby, or dilapidated. ◆ *n* **rundown. 11** a brief review, résumé, or summary. **12** the process of a mechanism coming gradually to a standstill after the power is removed. **13** a reduction in number or size.

rune (ruːn) *n* **1** any of the characters of an ancient Germanic alphabet, in use, esp. in Scandinavia, from the 3rd century A.D. to the end of the Middle Ages. **2** any obscure piece of writing using mysterious symbols. **3** a kind of Finnish poem or a stanza in such a poem. [OE *rūn*, from ON *rūn* secret]
▸ **'runic** *adj*

rung[1] (rʌŋ) *n* **1** one of the bars or rods that form the steps of a ladder. **2** a crosspiece between the legs of a chair, etc. **3** *Naut.* a spoke on a ship's wheel or a handle projecting from the periphery. [OE *hrung*]
▸ **'rungless** *adj*

rung[2] (rʌŋ) *vb* the past participle of **ring**[2].

> **USAGE NOTE** See at **ring**[2].

run in ❶ *vb* (*adv*) **1** to run (an engine) gently, usually when it is new. **2** (*tr*) to insert or include. **3** (*intr*) (of an aircraft) to approach a point or target. **4** (*tr*) *Inf.* to take into custody; arrest. ◆ *n* **run-in. 5** *Inf.* an argument or quarrel. **6** an approach to the end of an event, etc.: *the run-in for the championship.* **7** *Printing.* matter inserted in an existing paragraph.

run into ❶ *vb* (*prep, mainly intr*) **1** (*also tr*) to collide with or cause to collide with: *her car ran into a tree.* **2** to encounter unexpectedly. **3** (*also tr*) to be beset by: *the project ran into financial difficulties.* **4** to extend to; be of the order of: *debts running into thousands.*

runnel ('rʌnəl) *n Literary.* a small stream. [C16: from OE *rynele;* rel. to RUN]

runner ❶ ('rʌnə) *n* **1** a person who runs, esp. an athlete. **2** a messenger for a bank, etc. **3** a person engaged in the solicitation of business. **4** a person on the run; fugitive. **5a** a person or vessel engaged in smuggling. **5b** (*in combination*): *a gunrunner.* **6** a person who operates, manages, or controls something. **7a** either of the strips of metal or wood on which a sledge runs. **7b** the blade of an ice skate. **8** a roller or guide for a sliding component. **9** *Bot.* **9a** Also called: **stolon.** a slender horizontal stem, as of the strawberry, that grows along the surface of the soil and propagates by producing roots and shoots at the nodes or tip. **9b** a plant that propagates in this way. **10** a strip of lace, linen, etc., placed across a table or dressing table for protection and decoration. **11** another word for **rocker** (on a rocking chair). **12 do a runner.** *Sl.* to run away in order to escape trouble or to avoid paying for something.

runner bean *n* another name for **scarlet runner.**

runner-up *n, pl* **runners-up.** a contestant finishing a race or competition in second place.

running ❶ ('rʌnɪŋ) *adj* **1** maintained continuously; incessant: *running commentary.* **2** (*postpositive*) without interruption; consecutive: *he lectured for two hours running.* **3** denoting or relating to the scheduled operation of a public vehicle: *the running time of a train.* **4** accomplished at a run: *a running jump.* **5** moving or slipping easily, as a rope or a knot. **6** (of a wound, etc.) discharging pus. **7** prevalent; current: *running prices.* **8** repeated or continuous: *a running design.* **9** (of plants, plant stems, etc.) creeping along the ground. **10** flowing: *running water.* **11** (of handwriting) having the letters run together. ◆ *n* **12** management or organization: *the running of a company.* **13** operation or maintenance: *the running of a machine.* **14** competition or competitive situation (in **in the running, out of the running**). **15 make the running.** to set the pace in a competition or race.

running board *n* a footboard along the side of a vehicle, esp. an early motorcar.

running head *or* **title** *n Printing.* a heading printed at the top of every page of a book.

running light *n Naut.* one of several lights displayed by vessels operating at night.

running mate *n* **1** *US.* a candidate for the subordinate of two linked positions, esp. a candidate for the vice-presidency. **2** a horse that pairs another in a team.

running repairs *pl n* repairs that do not, or do not greatly, interrupt operations.

runny ❶ ('rʌnɪ) *adj* **runnier, runniest. 1** tending to flow; liquid. **2** (of the nose) exuding mucus.

run off ❶ *vb* (*adv*) **1** (*intr*) to depart in haste. **2** (*tr*) to produce quickly, as copies on a duplicating machine. **3** to drain (liquid) or (of liquid) to be drained. **4** (*tr*) to decide (a race) by a run-off. **5 run off with. 5a** to steal; purloin. **5b** to elope with. ◆ *n* **run-off. 6** an extra race, contest, election, etc., to decide the winner after a tie. **7** *NZ.* grazing land for store cattle. **8** that portion of rainfall that runs into streams as surface water rather than being absorbed by the soil. **9** the overflow of a liquid from a container.

run-of-the-mill ❶ *adj* ordinary, average, or undistinguished in quality, character, or nature.

run on *vb* (*adv*) **1** (*intr*) to continue without interruption. **2** to write with linked-up characters. **3** *Printing.* to compose text matter without indentation or paragraphing. ◆ *n* **run-on. 4** *Printing.* **4a** text matter composed without indenting. **4b** an additional quantity required in excess of the originally stated amount, whilst the job is being produced. **5a** a word added at the end of a dictionary entry whose meaning can be easily inferred from the definition of the headword. **5b** (*as modifier*): *a run-on entry.*

run out ❶ *vb* (*adv*) **1** (*intr;* often foll. by *of*) to exhaust (a supply of something) or (of a supply) to become exhausted. **2 run out on.** *Inf.* to desert or abandon. **3** (*tr*) *Cricket.* to dismiss (a running batsman) by breaking the wicket with the ball, or with the ball in the hand, while he is out of his ground. ◆ *n* **run-out. 4** *Cricket.* dismissal of a batsman by running him out.

run over ❶ *vb* **1** (*tr, adv*) to knock down (a person) with a moving vehicle. **2** (*intr*) to overflow the capacity of (a container). **3** (*intr, prep*) to examine hastily or make a rapid survey of. **4** (*intr, prep*) to exceed (a limit): *we've run over our time.*

runt (rʌnt) *n* **1** the smallest and weakest young animal in a litter, esp. the smallest piglet in a litter. **2** *Derog.* an undersized or inferior person. **3** a large pigeon, originally bred for eating. [C16: from ?]
▸ **'runtish** *or* **'runty** *adj* ▸ **'runtiness** *n*

THESAURUS

(*Brit. sl.*), do a runner (*sl.*), escape, fly the coop (*US & Canad. inf.*), make a run for it, run off, scarper (*Brit. sl.*), scram (*inf.*), show a clean pair of heels, skedaddle (*inf.*), take flight, take off, take to one's heels, turn tail **4 run away with: a** = **abscond**, abduct, elope **b** = **steal**, abscond, make off, pinch (*inf.*), run off, snatch **d** = **win easily**, romp home, walk it (*inf.*), win by a mile (*inf.*), win hands down ◆ *n* **runaway 5a** = **fugitive**, absconder, deserter, escapee, escaper, refugee, truant ◆ *modifier* **5b** = **escaped**, fleeing, fugitive, loose, out of control, uncontrolled, wild **8** = **easily won**, easy, effortless

run down *vb* **2** = **reduce**, curtail, cut, cut back, decrease, downsize, drop, pare down, trim **3** = **weaken**, debilitate, exhaust, sap the strength of, tire, undermine the health of **4** = **criticize**, asperse, bad-mouth (*sl., chiefly US & Canad.*), belittle, decry, defame, denigrate, disparage, knock (*inf.*), put down, revile, rubbish (*inf.*), slag (off) (*sl.*), speak ill of, vilify **5** = **knock down**, hit, knock over, run into, run over, strike ◆ *adj* **run-down 9** = **exhausted**, below par, debilitated, drained, enervated, fatigued, out of condition, peaky, tired, under the weather (*inf.*), unhealthy, weak, weary, worn-out **10** = **dilapidated**, broken-down, decrepit, dingy, ramshackle, seedy, shabby, tumbledown, worn-out ◆ *n* **rundown 11** = **summary**, briefing, outline, précis, recap (*inf.*), résumé, review, run-through, sketch, synopsis

Antonyms *adj* ≠ **exhausted:** fighting fit, fine, fit, fit as a fiddle, full of beans (*inf.*), healthy, well

run in *vb* **1** = **break in gently**, run gently **4** *Informal* = **arrest**, apprehend, bust (*inf.*), collar (*inf.*), feel one's collar (*sl.*), jail, lift (*sl.*), nab (*inf.*), nail (*inf.*), pick up, pinch (*inf.*), pull in (*Brit. sl.*), take into custody, take to jail, throw in jail ◆ *n* **run-in 5** *Informal* = **fight**, altercation, argument, brush, confrontation, contretemps, dispute, dust-up (*inf.*), encounter, face-off (*sl.*), quarrel, row, set-to (*inf.*), skirmish, tussle

run into *vb* **1** = **collide with**, bump into, crash into, dash against, hit, ram, strike **2** = **meet**, bump into, chance upon, come across *or* upon, encounter, meet with, run across **3** = **be beset by**, be confronted by

runner *n* **1** = **athlete**, harrier, jogger, miler, sprinter **2** = **messenger**, courier, dispatch bearer, errand boy **9a** *Botany* = **stem**, offshoot, shoot, sprig, sprout, stolon (*Botany*), tendril

running *adj* **1, 2** = **continuous**, constant, incessant, in succession, on the trot (*inf.*), perpetual, together, unbroken, unceasing, uninterrupted **10** = **flowing**, moving, streaming ◆ *n* **12** = **management**, administration, charge, conduct, control, coordination, direction, leadership, organization, regulation, superintendency, supervision **13** = **working**, functioning, maintenance, operation, performance

runny *adj* **1** = **flowing**, diluted, fluid, liquefied, liquid, melted, streaming, watery

run off *vb* **1** = **flee**, bolt, clear out, cut and run (*inf.*), decamp, do a runner (*sl.*), escape, fly the coop (*US & Canad. inf.*), hook it (*sl.*), make off, run away, scarper (*Brit. sl.*), show a clean pair of heels, skedaddle (*inf.*), take flight, take to one's heels, turn tail **2** = **produce**, churn out (*inf.*), duplicate, print **3** = **drain**, bleed, flow away, siphon, tap **5 run off with: a** = **steal**, lift (*inf.*), make off with, pinch (*inf.*), purloin, run away with, swipe (*sl.*) **b** = **run away with**, abscond with, elope with

run-of-the-mill *adj* = **ordinary**, average, banal, bog-standard (*Brit. & Irish sl.*), common, commonplace, dime-a-dozen (*inf.*), fair, mediocre, middling, modest, no great shakes (*inf.*), passable, tolerable, undistinguished, unexceptional, unexciting, unimpressive, vanilla (*inf.*)

Antonyms *adj* excellent, exceptional, extraordinary, marvellous, out of the ordinary, splendid, unusual

run out *vb* **1** *often foll. by* **of** = **finish**, be cleaned out, be exhausted, be out of, be used up, cease, dry up, exhaust one's supply of, fail, give out, have no more of, have none left, have no remaining, peter out, use up **2 run out on** *Informal* = **desert**, abandon, forsake, leave high and dry, leave holding the baby, leave in the lurch, rat on (*inf.*), run away from, strand

run over *vb* **1** = **knock down**, hit, knock over, run down, strike **2** = **overflow**, brim over, spill, spill over **3** = **review**, check, examine, go over,

run through ⓘ *vb* **1** (*tr, adv*) to transfix with a sword or other weapon. **2** (*intr, prep*) to exhaust (money) by wasteful spending. **3** (*intr, prep*) to practise or rehearse: *let's run through the plan.* **4** (*intr, prep*) to examine hastily. ◆ *n* **run-through. 5** a practice or rehearsal. **6** a brief survey.

run time *n Computing.* the time during which a computer program is executed.

run to *vb* (*intr, prep*) to be sufficient for: *my income doesn't run to luxuries.*

run up ⓘ *vb* (*tr, adv*) **1** to amass; incur: *to run up debts.* **2** to make by sewing together quickly. **3** to hoist: *to run up a flag.* ◆ *n* **run-up. 4** an approach run by an athlete for the long jump, pole vault, etc. **5** a preliminary or preparatory period: *the run-up to the election.*

runway (ˈrʌnˌweɪ) *n* **1** a hard level roadway from which aircraft take off and on which they land. **2** *Forestry, North American.* a chute for sliding logs down. **3** *Chiefly US.* a narrow ramp extending from the stage into the audience in a theatre, etc. esp. as used by models in a fashion show.

rupee (ruːˈpiː) *n* the standard monetary unit of India, Mauritius, Nepal, Pakistan, the Seychelles, and Sri Lanka. **[C17:** from Hindi *rupaīyā,* from Sansk. *rūpya* coined silver, from *rūpa* shape, beauty**]**

rupiah (ruːˈpiːə) *n, pl* **rupiah** *or* **rupiahs.** the standard monetary unit of Indonesia. **[**from Hindi: RUPEE**]**

rupture ⓘ (ˈrʌptʃə) *n* **1** the act of breaking or bursting or the state of being broken or burst. **2** a breach of peaceful or friendly relations. **3** *Pathol.* **3a** the breaking or tearing of a bodily structure or part. **3b** another word for **hernia.** ◆ *vb* **ruptures, rupturing, ruptured. 4** to break or burst. **5** to affect or be affected with a rupture or hernia. **6** to undergo or cause to undergo a breach in relations or friendship. **[C15:** from L *ruptūra,* from *rumpere* to burst forth**]**
▸ **ˈrupturable** *adj*

rural ⓘ (ˈrʊərəl) *adj* **1** of, relating to, or characteristic of the country or country life. **2** living in the country. **3** of, relating to, or associated with farming. ◆ Cf. **urban. [C15:** via OF from L *rūrālis,* from *rūs* the country**]**
▸ **ˈruralism** *n* ▸ **ˈruralist** *n* ▸ **ruˈrality** *n* ▸ **ˈrurally** *adv*

rural dean *n Chiefly Brit.* a clergyman having authority over a group of parishes.

rural district *n* (formerly) a rural division of a county.

ruralize *or* **ruralise** (ˈrʊərəˌlaɪz) *vb* **ruralizes, ruralizing, ruralized** *or* **ruralises, ruralising, ruralised. 1** (*tr*) to make rural in character, appearance, etc. **2** (*intr*) to go into the country to live.
▸ **ˌruraliˈzation** *or* **ˌruraliˈsation** *n*

rural route *n US & Canad.* a mail service or route in a rural area, the mail being delivered by car or van.

Ruritanian (ˌrʊərɪˈteɪnɪən) *adj* of or characteristic of a romantic and idealistic setting in which adventure and intrigue occur. **[C19:** after the imaginary kingdom created by Anthony Hope (1863–1933), in *The Prisoner of Zenda***]**

ruse ⓘ (ruːz) *n* an action intended to mislead, deceive, or trick; stratagem. **[C15:** from OF: trick, esp. to evade capture, from *ruser* to retreat, from L *recūsāre* to refuse**]**

rush[1] ⓘ (rʌʃ) *vb* **1** to hurry or cause to hurry; hasten. **2** (*tr*) to make a sudden attack upon (a fortress, position, person, etc.). **3** (when *intr,* often foll. by *at, in,* or *into*) to proceed or approach in a reckless manner. **4 rush one's fences.** to proceed with precipitate haste. **5** (*intr*) to come, flow, swell, etc., quickly or suddenly: *tears rushed to her eyes.* **6** (*tr*) *Sl.* to cheat, esp. by grossly overcharging. **7** (*tr*) *US & Canad.* to make a concerted effort to secure the agreement, participation, etc., of (a person). **8** (*intr*) *American football.* to gain ground by running forwards with the ball. ◆ *n* **9** the act or condition of rushing. **10** a sudden surge towards someone or something: *a gold rush.* **11** a sudden surge of sensation, esp. from a drug. **12** a sudden demand. ◆ *adj* (*prenominal*) **13** requiring speed or urgency: *a rush job.* **14** characterized by much movement, business, etc.: *a rush period.* **[C14** *ruschen,* from OF *ruser* to put to flight, from L *recūsāre* to refuse**]**
▸ **ˈrusher** *n*

rush[2] (rʌʃ) *n* **1** an annual or perennial plant growing in wet places and typically having grasslike cylindrical leaves and small green or brown flowers. **2** something valueless; a trifle; straw: *not worth a rush.* **3** short for **rush light. [**OE *risce, rysce***]**
▸ **ˈrushˌlike** *adj* ▸ **ˈrushy** *adj*

rushes (ˈrʌʃɪz) *pl n* (*sometimes sing*) (in film-making) the initial prints of a scene or scenes before editing, usually prepared daily.

rush hour *n* a period at the beginning and end of the working day when large numbers of people are travelling to or from work.

rush light *or* **candle** *n* a narrow candle, formerly in use, made of the pith of various types of rush dipped in tallow.

rusk (rʌsk) *n* a light bread dough, sweet or plain, baked twice until it is brown, hard, and crisp: often given to babies. **[C16:** from Sp. or Port. *rosca* screw, bread shaped in a twist, from ?**]**

Russ. *abbrev. for* Russia(n).

russet (ˈrʌsɪt) *n* **1** brown with a yellowish or reddish tinge. **2** a rough homespun fabric, reddish-brown in colour, formerly in use for clothing. **3** any of various apples with rough brownish-red skins. ◆ *adj* **4** *Arch.* simple; homely; rustic: *a russet life.* **5** of the colour russet: *russet hair.* **[C13:** from Anglo-Norman, from OF *rosset,* from *rous,* from L *russus;* rel. to L *ruber* red**]**
▸ **ˈrussety** *adj*

Russia leather *n* a smooth dyed leather made from calfskin and scented with birch tar oil, originally produced in Russia.

Russian (ˈrʌʃən) *n* **1** the official language of Russia, and of the former Soviet Union: an Indo-European language belonging to the East Slavonic branch. **2** a native or inhabitant of Russia. ◆ *adj* **3** of, relating to, or characteristic of Russia, its people, or their language.

Russian doll *n* a hollow wooden figure, usually representing a Russian peasant woman, that comes apart to reveal a similar smaller figure, which itself contains another, and so on.

Russianize *or* **Russianise** (ˈrʌʃəˌnaɪz) *vb* **Russianizes, Russianizing, Russianized** *or* **Russianises, Russianising, Russianised.** to make or become Russian in style, etc.
▸ **ˌRussianiˈzation** *or* **ˌRussianiˈsation** *n*

Russian roulette *n* **1** an act of bravado in which each person in turn spins the cylinder of a revolver loaded with only one cartridge and presses the trigger with the barrel against his own head. **2** any foolish or potentially suicidal undertaking.

Russian salad *n* a salad of cold diced cooked vegetables mixed with mayonnaise and pickles.

Russo- (ˈrʌsəʊ) *combining form.* Russia or Russian: *Russo-Japanese.*

rust ⓘ (rʌst) *n* **1** a reddish-brown oxide coating formed on iron or steel by the action of oxygen and moisture. **2** Also called: **rust fungus.** *Plant pathol.* **2a** any of a group of fungi which are parasitic on cereal plants, conifers, etc. **2b** any of various plant diseases characterized by reddish-brown discoloration of the leaves and stem, esp. that caused by the rust fungi. **3a** a strong brown colour, sometimes with a reddish or yellowish tinge. **3b** (*as adj*): *a rust carpet.* **4** any corrosive or debilitating influence, esp. lack of use. ◆ *vb* **5** to become or cause to become coated with a layer of rust. **6** to deteriorate or cause to deteriorate through some debilitating influence or lack of use: *he allowed his talent to rust over the years.* **[**OE *rūst***]**
▸ **ˈrustless** *adj*

rust belt *n* an area where heavy industry is in decline, esp. in the Midwest of the US.

rustic ⓘ (ˈrʌstɪk) *adj* **1** of, characteristic of, or living in the country; rural. **2** having qualities ascribed to country life or people; simple; unsophisticated: *rustic pleasures.* **3** crude, awkward, or uncouth. **4** made of untrimmed branches: *a rustic seat.* **5** (of masonry, etc.) having a rusticated finish. ◆ *n* **6** a person who comes from or lives in the country. **7** an unsophisticated, simple, or clownish person from the country. **8** Also called: **rusticwork.** brick or stone having a rough finish. **[C16:** from OF *rustique,* from L *rūsticus,* from *rūs* the country**]**
▸ **ˈrustically** *adv* ▸ **rusticity** (rʌˈstɪsɪtɪ) *n*

rusticate (ˈrʌstɪˌkeɪt) *vb* **rusticates, rusticating, rusticated. 1** to banish or retire to the country. **2** to make or become rustic in style, etc. **3** (*tr*) *Architect.* to finish (an exterior wall) with large blocks of masonry sepa-

THESAURUS

go through, rehearse, reiterate, run through, survey

run through *vb* **1 = pierce**, impale, spit, stab, stick, transfix **2 = squander**, blow (*sl.*), dissipate, exhaust, fritter away, spend like water, throw away, waste **3 = rehearse**, go over, practise, read, run over **4 = review**, check, examine, go through, look over, run over, survey

run up *n* **run-up 5 = build-up**, approach, preliminaries

rupture *n* **1 = break**, breach, burst, cleavage, cleft, crack, fissure, fracture, rent, split, tear **2 = breach**, altercation, break, bust-up (*inf.*), contention, disagreement, disruption, dissolution, estrangement, falling-out (*inf.*), feud, hostility, quarrel, rift, schism, split **3b** *Medical* **= hernia** ◆ *vb* **4 = break**, burst, cleave, crack, fracture, puncture, rend, separate, sever, split, tear **6 = cause a breach**, break off, come between, disrupt, dissever, divide, split

rural *adj* **1, 2 = rustic**, Arcadian, bucolic, countrified, country, hick (*inf., chiefly US & Canad.*), pastoral, sylvan, upcountry **3 = agricultural**, agrarian, agrestic
Antonyms *adj* ≠ **rustic:** city, cosmopolitan, town, urban

ruse *n* **= trick**, artifice, blind, deception, device, dodge, hoax, imposture, manoeuvre, ploy, sham, stratagem, subterfuge, wile

rush[1] *vb* **1 = push**, accelerate, dispatch, expedite, hurry, hustle, press, quicken, speed up **2 = attack**, capture, charge, overcome, storm, take by storm **3 = hurry**, barrel (along), bolt, burn rubber (*inf.*), career, dart, dash, fly, hasten, hotfoot, lose no time, make haste, race, run, scramble, scurry, shoot, speed, sprint, stampede, tear ◆ *n* **9 = attack**, assault, charge, onslaught, push, storm, surge **10 = hurry**, charge, dash, dispatch, expedition, haste, race, scramble, speed, stampede, surge, swiftness, urgency ◆ *adj* **13 = hasty**, brisk, cursory, emergency, expeditious, fast, hurried, prompt, quick, rapid, swift, urgent
Antonyms *vb* ≠ **hurry:** dally, dawdle, delay, procrastinate, slow down, tarry, wait ◆ *adj* ≠ **hasty:** careful, detailed, leisurely, not urgent, slow, thorough, unhurried

rust *n* **1 = corrosion**, oxidation **2 = mildew**, blight, mould, must, rot ◆ *vb* **5 = corrode**, oxidize **6 = deteriorate**, atrophy, decay, decline, go stale, stagnate, tarnish

rustic *adj* **1 = rural**, agrestic, Arcadian, bucolic, countrified, country, pastoral, sylvan, upcountry **2 = simple**, artless, homely, homespun, plain, unaffected, unpolished, unrefined, unsophisticated **3 = uncouth**, awkward, boorish, churlish, cloddish, clodhopping, clownish, coarse, crude, graceless, hick (*inf., chiefly US & Canad.*), loutish, lumpish, maladroit, rough, uncultured, unmannerly ◆ *n* **7 = yokel**, boor, bumpkin, clod, clodhopper (*inf.*), clown, country boy, country cousin, countryman *or* countrywoman, hayseed (*US & Canad. inf.*), hick (*inf., chiefly US & Canad.*), hillbilly, Hodge, peasant, son of the soil, swain (*arch.*)
Antonyms *adj* ≠ **rural:** cosmopolitan, urban ≠ **simple:** elegant, grand, polished, refined, sophisticated ≠ **uncouth:** courtly, polished, refined,

rated by deep joints. **4** (*tr*) *Brit.* to send down from university for a specified time as a punishment. [C17: from L *rūsticārī*, from *rūs* the country]
▸ˌrustiˈcation *n* ▸ˈrustiˌcator *n*

rusticated (ˈrʌstɪˌkeɪtɪd) *or* **rusticating** (ˈrʌstɪˌkeɪtɪŋ) *n* (in New Zealand) a wide type of weatherboarding used in older houses.

rustle[1] ❶ (ˈrʌsᵊl) *vb* **rustles, rustling, rustled. 1** to make or cause to make a low crisp whispering or rubbing sound, as of dry leaves or paper. **2** to move with such a sound. ◆ *n* **3** such a sound or sounds. [OE *hrūxlian*]

rustle[2] (ˈrʌsᵊl) *vb* **rustles, rustling, rustled. 1** *Chiefly US & Canad.* to steal (cattle, horses, etc.). **2** *Inf., US & Canad.* to move swiftly and energetically. [C19: prob. special use of RUSTLE[1] (in the sense: to move with a quiet sound)]
▸ˈ**rustler** *n*

rustle up *vb* (*tr, adv*) *Inf.* **1** to prepare (a meal, etc.) rapidly, esp. at short notice. **2** to forage for and obtain.

rustproof (ˈrʌstˌpruːf) *adj* treated against rusting.

rusty ❶ (ˈrʌstɪ) *adj* **rustier, rustiest. 1** covered with, affected by, or consisting of rust: *a rusty machine.* **2** of the colour rust. **3** discoloured by age: *a rusty coat.* **4** (of the voice) tending to croak. **5** old-fashioned in appearance: *a rusty old gentleman.* **6** impaired in skill or knowledge by inaction or neglect. **7** (of plants) affected by the rust fungus.
▸ˈ**rustily** *adv* ▸ˈ**rustiness** *n*

rut[1] ❶ (rʌt) *n* **1** a groove or furrow in a soft road, caused by wheels. **2** a narrow or predictable way of life; dreary or undeviating routine (esp. in **in a rut**). ◆ *vb* **ruts, rutting, rutted. 3** (*tr*) to make a rut in. [C16: prob. from F *route* road]

rut[2] (rʌt) *n* **1** a recurrent period of sexual excitement and reproductive activity in certain male ruminants. ◆ *vb* **ruts, rutting, rutted. 2** (*intr*) (of male ruminants) to be in a period of sexual excitement and activity. [C15: from OF *rut* noise, roar, from L *rugītus*, from *rugīre* to roar]

rutabaga (ˌruːtəˈbeɪɡə) *n* the US and Canad. name for **swede.** [C18: from Swedish dialect *rotabagge*, lit.: root bag]

rutaceous (ruːˈteɪʃəs) *adj* of, relating to, or belonging to a family of tropical and temperate flowering plants many of which have aromatic leaves. The family includes rue, citrus trees, and dittany. [C19: from NL *Rutaceae*, from L *rūta* RUE[2]]

ruth (ruːθ) *n Arch.* **1** pity; compassion. **2** repentance; remorse. [C12: from *rewen* to RUE[1]]

ruthenium (ruːˈθiːnɪəm) *n* a hard brittle white element of the platinum metal group. It is used to harden platinum and palladium. Symbol: Ru; atomic no.: 44; atomic wt.: 101.07. [C19: from Med. L *Ruthenia* Russia, where it was discovered]

rutherford (ˈrʌðəfəd) *n* a former unit of activity equal to the quantity of a radioactive nuclide required to produce one million disintegrations per second. Abbrev.: **rd.** [C20: after Ernest *Rutherford* (1871–1937), Brit. physicist who discovered the atomic nucleus]

rutherfordium (ˌrʌðəˈfɔːdɪəm) *n* the US name for the element with the atomic no. 104.Symbol: Rf [C20: after E. *Rutherford*; see RUTHERFORD]

ruthful (ˈruːθfʊl) *adj Arch.* full of or causing sorrow or pity.
▸ˈ**ruthfully** *adv* ▸ˈ**ruthfulness** *n*

ruthless ❶ (ˈruːθlɪs) *adj* feeling or showing no mercy; hardhearted.
▸ˈ**ruthlessly** *adv* ▸ˈ**ruthlessness** *n*

rutile (ˈruːtaɪl) *n* a mineral consisting of titanium(IV) oxide (TiO_2) in tetragonal crystalline form. It is an important source of titanium. [C19: via F from G *Rutil*, from L *rutilus* red, glowing]

ruttish (ˈrʌtɪʃ) *adj* **1** (of an animal) in a condition of rut. **2** lascivious or salacious.
▸ˈ**ruttishly** *adv* ▸ˈ**ruttishness** *n*

rutty (ˈrʌtɪ) *adj* **ruttier, ruttiest.** full of ruts or holes: *a rutty track.*
▸ˈ**ruttily** *adv* ▸ˈ**ruttiness** *n*

RV *abbrev. for:* **1** *Chiefly US.* recreational vehicle. **2** Revised Version (of the Bible).

-ry *suffix forming nouns.* a variant of **-ery:** *dentistry.*

Ryder Cup *n* **the.** the trophy awarded in a professional golfing competition between teams representing Europe and the US. [C20: after Samuel *Ryder* (1859–1936), Brit. businessman and golf patron]

rye (raɪ) *n* **1** a tall hardy widely cultivated annual grass having bristly flower spikes and light brown grain. **2** the grain of this grass, used in making flour and whisky, and as a livestock food. **3** Also called: (esp. US): **rye whiskey.** whisky distilled from rye. **4** *US.* short for **rye bread.** [OE *ryge*]

rye bread *n* any of various breads made entirely or partly from rye flour, often with caraway seeds.

rye-grass *n* any of various grasses native to Europe, N Africa, and Asia, and widely cultivated as forage crops. They have flattened flower spikes and hairless leaves.

THESAURUS

sophisticated, urbane ◆ *n* ≠ **yokel:** city slicker, cosmopolitan, courtier, sophisticate, townie, townsman

rustle[1] *vb* **1** = **crackle**, crepitate, crinkle, susurrate (*literary*), swish, whish, whisper, whoosh ◆ *n* **3** = **crackle**, crepitation, crinkling, rustling, susurration *or* susurrus (*literary*), whisper

rusty *adj* **1** = **corroded**, oxidized, rust-covered, rusted **2** = **reddish-brown**, chestnut, coppery, reddish, russet, rust-coloured **4** = **croaking**, cracked, creaking, croaky, hoarse **5** = **old-fashioned**, ancient, antiquated, antique, dated, outmoded, out of date, passé **6** = **out of practice**, deficient, impaired, not what it was, sluggish, stale, unpractised, weak

rut[1] *n* **1** = **groove**, furrow, gouge, indentation, pothole, score, track, trough, wheel mark **2** = **habit**, dead end, groove, humdrum existence, pattern, routine, system

ruthless *adj* = **merciless**, adamant, barbarous, brutal, callous, cruel, ferocious, fierce, hard, hard-hearted, harsh, heartless, inexorable, inhuman, pitiless, relentless, remorseless, savage, severe, stern, unfeeling, unmerciful, unpitying, unrelenting, without pity
Antonyms *adj* compassionate, forgiving, gentle, humane, kind, lenient, merciful, pitying, sparing

rutted *adj* **1** = **grooved**, cut, furrowed, gouged, holed, indented, marked, scored

Ss

s *or* **S** (es) *n, pl* **s's, S's,** *or* **Ss. 1** the 19th letter of the English alphabet. **2** a speech sound represented by this letter, either voiceless, as in *sit,* or voiced, as in *dogs.* **3a** something shaped like an S. **3b** (*in combination*): *an S-bend in a road.*

s *symbol for* second (of time).

S *symbol for:* **1** small. **2** Society. **3** South. **4** *Chem.* sulphur. **5** *Physics.* **5a** entropy. **5b** siemens. **5c** strangeness. **6** *Currency.* Schilling.

s. *abbrev. for:* **1** shilling. **2** singular. **3** son. **4** succeeded.

s. *or* **S.** *Music. abbrev. for* soprano.

S. *abbrev. for:* **1** sabbath. **2** (*pl* **SS**) Saint. **3** Saturday. **4** Saxon. **5** school. **6** September. **7** Signor. **8** Sunday.

-s[1] *or* **-es** *suffix.* forming the plural of most nouns: *boys; boxes.* [from OE *-as,* pl. nominative and accusative ending of some masc nouns]

-s[2] *or* **-es** *suffix.* forming the third person singular present indicative tense of verbs: *he runs.* [from OE (northern dialect) *-es, -s,* orig. the ending of the second person singular]

-'s *suffix.* **1** forming the possessive singular of nouns and some pronouns: *man's; one's.* **2** forming the possessive plural of nouns whose plurals do not end in *-s: children's.* (The possessive plural of nouns ending in *s* and of some singular nouns is formed by the addition of an apostrophe after the final *s: girls'; for goodness' sake.*) **3** forming the plural of numbers, letters, or symbols: *20's.* **4** *Inf.* contraction of *is* or *has: it's gone.* **5** *Inf.* contraction of *us* with *let: let's.* **6** *Inf.* contraction of *does* in some questions: *what's he do?* [senses 1, 2: assimilated contraction from ME *-es,* from OE, masc and neuter genitive sing; sense 3, equivalent to *-s*[1]]

SA *abbrev. for:* **1** Salvation Army. **2** South Africa. **3** South America. **4** South Australia. **5** *Sturmabteilung:* the Nazi terrorist militia.

sabadilla (ˌsæbə'dɪlə) *n* **1** a tropical American liliaceous plant. **2** the bitter brown seeds of this plant, which contain the alkaloid veratrine used in insecticides. [C19: from Sp. *cebadilla,* dim. of *cebada* barley, from L *cibāre* to feed, from *cibus* food]

Sabaean *or* **Sabean** (sə'biːən) *n* **1** an inhabitant or native of ancient Saba. **2** the ancient Semitic language of Saba. ◆ *adj* **3** of or relating to ancient Saba, its inhabitants, or their language. [C16: from L *Sabaeus,* from Gk *Sabaios* belonging to Saba (Sheba)]

sabbat ('sæbæt, -ət) *n* another word for **Sabbath** (sense 4).

Sabbatarian (ˌsæbə'tɛərɪən) *n* **1** a person advocating the strict religious observance of Sunday. **2** a person who observes Saturday as the Sabbath. ◆ *adj* **3** of the Sabbath or its observance. [C17: from LL *sabbatārius* a Sabbath-keeper]
▸ˌ**Sabba'tarianism** *n*

Sabbath ('sæbəθ) *n* **1** the seventh day of the week, Saturday, devoted to worship and rest from work in Judaism and in certain Christian Churches. **2** Sunday, observed by Christians as the day of worship and rest. **3** (*not cap.*) a period of rest. **4** Also called: **sabbat, witches' Sabbath.** a midnight meeting for practitioners of witchcraft or devil worship. [OE *sabbat,* from L, from Gk *sabbaton,* from Heb., from *shābath* to rest]

sabbatical (sə'bætɪkəl) *adj* **1** denoting a period of leave granted to university staff, teachers, etc., esp. originally every seventh year: *a sabbatical year.* ◆ *n* **2** any sabbatical period. [C16: from Gk *sabbatikos;* see SABBATH]

Sabbatical (sə'bætɪkəl) *adj* of, relating to, or appropriate to the Sabbath as a day of rest and religious observance.

SABC *abbrev. for* South African Broadcasting Corporation.

saber ('seɪbə) *n, vb* the US spelling of **sabre.**

sabin ('sæbɪn, 'seɪ-) *n Physics.* a unit of acoustic absorption. [C20: introduced by Wallace C. *Sabine* (1868–1919), US physicist]

Sabine ('sæbaɪn) *n* **1** a member of an ancient people who lived in central Italy. ◆ *adj* **2** of or relating to this people or their language.

sabkha ('sæbxə, -kə) *n* a flat coastal plain with a salt crust, common in Arabia. [C19: from Ar.]

sable ❶ ('seɪbəl) *n, pl* **sables** *or* **sable. 1** a marten of N Asian forests, with dark brown luxuriant fur. **2a** the highly valued fur of this animal. **2b** (*as modifier*): *a sable coat.* **3 American sable.** the brown, slightly less valuable fur of the American marten. **4** a dark brown to yellowish-brown colour. ◆ *adj* **5** of the colour of sable fur. **6** black; dark. **7** (*usually postpositive*) *Heraldry.* of the colour black. [C15: from OF, from OHG *zobel,* of Slavic origin]

sable antelope *n* a large black E African antelope with long backward-curving horns.

sabot ('sæbəʊ) *n* **1** a shoe made from a single block of wood. **2** a shoe with a wooden sole and a leather or cloth upper. **3** *Austral.* a small sailing boat with a shortened bow. [C17: from F, prob. from OF *savate* an old shoe, also infl. by *bot* BOOT[1]]

sabotage ❶ ('sæbəˌtɑːʒ) *n* **1** the deliberate destruction, disruption, or damage of equipment, a public service, etc., as by enemy agents, dissatisfied employees, etc. **2** any similar action. ◆ *vb* **sabotages, sabotaging, sabotaged. 3** (*tr*) to destroy or disrupt, esp. by secret means. [C20: from F, from *saboter* to spoil through clumsiness (lit.: to clatter in sabots)]

saboteur (ˌsæbə'tɜː) *n* a person who commits sabotage. [C20: from F]

sabra ('sɑːbrə) *n* a native-born Israeli Jew. [from Heb. *Sabēr* prickly pear, common plant in the coastal areas of the country]

sabre *or US* **saber** ('seɪbə) *n* **1** a stout single-edged cavalry sword, having a curved blade. **2** a sword used in fencing, having a narrow V-shaped blade. ◆ *vb* **sabres, sabring, sabred** *or US* **sabers, sabering, sabered. 3** (*tr*) to injure or kill with a sabre. [C17: via F from G (dialect) *Sabel,* from MHG *sebel,* ?from Magyar *száblya*]

sabre-rattling *n, adj Inf.* seeking to intimidate by an aggressive display of military power.

sabre-toothed tiger *or* **cat** *n* any of various extinct felines with long curved upper canine teeth.

sac ❶ (sæk) *n* a pouch, bag, or pouchlike part in an animal or plant. [C18: from F, from L *saccus;* see SACK[1]]
▸**saccate** ('sækɪt, -eɪt) *adj* ▸'**sac**ˌ**like** *adj*

saccharide ('sækəˌraɪd) *n* any sugar or other carbohydrate, esp. a simple sugar.

saccharimeter (ˌsækə'rɪmɪtə) *n* any instrument for measuring the strength of sugar solutions.
▸ˌ**saccha'rimetry** *n*

saccharin ('sækərɪn) *n* a very sweet white crystalline slightly soluble powder used as a nonfattening sweetener. [C19: from SACCHARO- + -IN]

saccharine ❶ ('sækəˌriːn) *adj* **1** excessively sweet; sugary: *a saccharine smile.* **2** of the nature of or containing sugar or saccharin.

saccharo- *or before a vowel* **sacchar-** *combining form.* sugar. [via L from Gk *sakkharon,* ult. from Sansk. *śarkarā* sugar]

saccharose ('sækəˌrəʊz, -ˌrəʊs) *n* a technical name for **sugar** (sense 1).

saccule ('sækjuːl) *or* **sacculus** ('sækjʊləs) *n* **1** a small sac. **2** the smaller of the two parts of the membranous labyrinth of the internal ear. Cf. **utricle.** [C19: from L *sacculus* dim. of *saccus* SACK[1]]

sacerdotal (ˌsæsə'dəʊtəl) *adj* of, relating to, or characteristic of priests. [C14: from L *sacerdōtālis,* from *sacerdōs* priest, from *sacer* sacred]
▸ˌ**sacer'dota**ˌ**lism** *n* ▸ˌ**sacer'dotally** *adv*

sachem ('seɪtʃəm) *n* **1** *US.* a leader of a political party or organization. **2** another name for **sagamore.** [C17: from Amerind *săchim* chief]

sachet ('sæʃeɪ) *n* **1** a small sealed envelope, usually made of plastic, for containing shampoo, etc. **2a** a small soft bag containing perfumed powder, placed in drawers to scent clothing. **2b** the powder contained in such a bag. [C19: from OF: a little bag, from *sac* bag; see SACK[1]]

sack[1] ❶ (sæk) *n* **1** a large bag made of coarse cloth, thick paper, etc., used as a container. **2** Also called: **sackful.** the amount contained in a sack. **3a** a woman's loose tube-shaped dress. **3b** Also called: **sacque** (sæk). a woman's full loose hip-length jacket. **4 the sack.** *Inf.* dismissal from employment. **5** a slang word for **bed. 6 hit the sack.** *Sl.* to go to bed. ◆ *vb* (*tr*) **7** *Inf.* to dismiss from employment. **8** to put into a sack or sacks. [OE *sacc,* from L *saccus* bag, from Gk *sakkos*]
▸'**sack**ˌ**like** *adj*

sack[2] ❶ (sæk) *n* **1** the plundering of a place by an army or mob. **2** *American football.* a tackle on a quarterback that brings him down before he has passed the ball. ◆ *vb* (*tr*) **3** to plunder and partially destroy (a place). **4** *American football.* to tackle and bring down (a quarterback) before he has passed the ball. [C16: from F *mettre à sac,* lit.: to put (loot) in a sack, from L *saccus* SACK[1]]
▸'**sacker** *n*

sack[3] (sæk) *n Arch. except in trademarks.* any dry white wine from SW Europe. [C16 *wyne seck,* from F *vin sec* dry wine, from L *siccus* dry]

THESAURUS

sable *adj* **6** = **black,** dark, dusty, ebon (*poetic*), ebony, jet, jetty, raven, sombre

sabotage *n* **1** = **damage,** destruction, disruption, subversion, treachery, treason, wrecking ◆ *vb* **3** = **damage,** cripple, destroy, disable, disrupt, incapacitate, sap the foundations of, subvert, throw a spanner in the works (*Brit. inf.*), undermine, vandalize, wreck

sac *n* = **pouch,** bag, bladder, bursa, cyst, pocket, pod, vesicle

saccharine *adj* **1** = **oversweet,** cloying, honeyed, maudlin, mawkish, nauseating, sentimental, sickly, soppy (*Brit. inf.*), sugary, syrupy (*inf.*), treacly

sack[1] *n* **4 the sack** = **dismissal,** discharge, termination of employment, the axe (*inf.*), the boot (*sl.*), the chop (*Brit. sl.*), the (old) heave-ho (*inf.*), the push (*sl.*) **6 hit the sack** *Slang* = **go to bed,** bed down, hit the hay (*sl.*), retire, turn in (*inf.*) ◆ *vb* **7** *Informal* = **dismiss,** axe (*inf.*), discharge, fire (*inf.*), give (someone) his cards, give (someone) his marching orders, give (someone) the boot (*sl.*), kick out (*inf.*)

sack[2] *n* **1** = **plundering,** depredation, despoliation, destruction, devastation, looting, pillage, plunder, rape, rapine, ravage, ruin, waste ◆ *vb* **3** = **plunder,** demolish, despoil, destroy, devastate, lay waste, loot, maraud, pillage, raid, ravage, rifle, rob, ruin, spoil, strip

sackbut ('sæk,bʌt) *n* a medieval form of trombone. [C16: from F *saqueboute,* from OF *saquer* to pull + *bouter* to push]

sackcloth ❶ ('sæk,klɒθ) *n* **1** coarse cloth such as sacking. **2** garments made of such cloth, worn formerly to indicate mourning. **3 sackcloth and ashes.** a public display of extreme grief.

sacking ('sækɪŋ) *n* coarse cloth used for making sacks, woven from flax, hemp, jute, etc.

sack race *n* a race in which the competitors' legs and often bodies are enclosed in sacks.

sacral[1] ('seɪkrəl) *adj* of or associated with sacred rites. [C19: from L *sacrum* sacred object]

sacral[2] ('seɪkrəl) *adj* of or relating to the sacrum. [C18: from NL *sacrālis* of the SACRUM]

sacrament ('sækrəmənt) *n* **1** an outward sign combined with a prescribed form of words and regarded as conferring grace upon those who receive it. The Protestant sacraments are baptism and the Lord's Supper. In the Roman Catholic and Eastern Churches they are baptism, penance, confirmation, the Eucharist, holy orders, matrimony, and the anointing of the sick (formerly extreme unction). **2** (*often cap.*) the Eucharist. **3** the consecrated elements of the Eucharist, esp. the bread. **4** something regarded as possessing a sacred significance. **5** a pledge. [C12: from Church L *sacrāmentum* vow, from L *sacrāre* to consecrate]

sacramental (,sækrə'mentᵊl) *adj* **1** of or having the nature of a sacrament. ◆ *n* **2** *RC Church.* a sacrament-like ritual action, such as the sign of the cross or the use of holy water.
▸,**sacra'menta,lism** *n* ▸**sacramentality** (,sækrəmen'tælɪtɪ) *n*

sacrarium (sæ'krɛərɪəm) *n, pl* **sacraria** (-'krɛərɪə). **1** the sanctuary of a church. **2** *RC Church.* a place near the altar of a church where materials used in the sacred rites are deposited or poured away. [C18: from L, from *sacer* sacred]

sacred ❶ ('seɪkrɪd) *adj* **1** exclusively devoted to a deity or to some religious ceremony or use. **2** worthy of or regarded with reverence and awe. **3** connected with or intended for religious use: *sacred music.* **4 sacred to.** dedicated to. [C14: from L *sacrāre* to set apart as holy, from *sacer* holy]
▸'**sacredly** *adv* ▸'**sacredness** *n*

sacred cow *n Inf.* a person, custom, etc., held to be beyond criticism. [alluding to the Hindu belief that cattle are sacred]

sacred mushroom *n* **1** any of various hallucinogenic mushrooms that have been eaten in rituals in various parts of the world. **2** a mescal button, used in a similar way.

sacrifice ❶ ('sækrɪ,faɪs) *n* **1** a surrender of something of value as a means of gaining something more desirable or of preventing some evil. **2** a ritual killing of a person or animal with the intention of propitiating or pleasing a deity. **3** a symbolic offering of something to a deity. **4** the person, animal, or object killed or offered. **5** loss entailed by giving up or selling something at less than its value. **6** *Chess.* the act or an instance of sacrificing a piece. ◆ *vb* **sacrifices, sacrificing, sacrificed. 7** to make a sacrifice (of). **8** *Chess.* to permit or force one's opponent to capture a piece freely, as in playing a gambit: *he sacrificed his queen and checkmated his opponent on the next move.* [C13: via OF from L *sacrificium,* from *sacer* holy + *facere* to make]
▸'**sacri,ficer** *n*

sacrifice paddock *n NZ.* a grassed field which is allowed to be grazed completely, so that it can be cultivated and resown later.

sacrificial ❶ (,sækrɪ'fɪʃəl) *adj* used in or connected with a sacrifice.
▸,**sacri'ficially** *adv*

sacrilege ❶ ('sækrɪlɪdʒ) *n* **1** the misuse or desecration of anything regarded as sacred or as worthy of extreme respect. **2** the act or an instance of taking anything sacred for secular use. [C13: from OF, from L, from *sacrilegus* temple-robber, from *sacra* sacred things + *legere* to take]
▸**sacrilegist** (,sækrɪ'li:dʒɪst) *n*

sacrilegious ❶ (,sækrɪ'lɪdʒəs) *adj* **1** of, relating to, or involving sacrilege. **2** guilty of sacrilege.
▸,**sacri'legiously** *adv*

sacring bell ('seɪkrɪŋ) *n Chiefly RC Church.* a small bell rung at the elevation of the Host and chalice during Mass.

sacristan ('sækrɪstən) *or* **sacrist** ('sækrɪst, 'seɪ-) *n* **1** a person who has charge of the contents of a church. **2** a less common word for **sexton.** [C14: from Med. L *sacristānus,* ult. from L *sacer* holy]

sacristy ('sækrɪstɪ) *n, pl* **sacristies.** a room attached to a church or chapel where the sacred vessels, vestments, etc., are kept. [C17: from Med. L *sacristia;* see SACRISTAN]

sacroiliac (,seɪkrəʊ'ɪlɪ,æk) *Anat.* ◆ *adj* **1** of or relating to the sacrum and ilium or their articulation. ◆ *n* **2** the joint where these bones meet.

sacrosanct ❶ ('sækrəʊ,sæŋkt) *adj* very sacred or holy. [C17: from L *sacrōsanctus* made holy by sacred rite, from *sacer* holy + *sanctus,* from *sancīre* to hallow]
▸,**sacro'sanctity** *n*

sacrum ('seɪkrəm) *n, pl* **sacra** (-krə). the large wedge-shaped bone, consisting of five fused vertebrae, in the lower part of the back. [C18: from L *os sacrum* holy bone, because it was used in sacrifices, from *sacer* holy]

sad ❶ (sæd) *adj* **sadder, saddest. 1** feeling sorrow; unhappy. **2** causing, suggestive, or expressive of such feelings: *a sad story.* **3** unfortunate; shabby: *her clothes were in a sad state.* **4** *Brit. inf.* ludicrously contemptible; pathetic: *a sad, boring little wimp.* [OE *sæd* weary]
▸'**sadly** *adv* ▸'**sadness** *n*

SAD *abbrev. for* seasonal affective disorder.

sadden ❶ ('sædᵊn) *vb* to make or become sad.

saddle ❶ ('sædᵊl) *n* **1** a seat for a rider, usually made of leather, placed on a horse's back and secured with a girth under the belly. **2** a similar seat on a bicycle, tractor, etc. **3** a back pad forming part of the harness of a packhorse. **4** anything that resembles a saddle in shape, position, or function. **5** a cut of meat, esp. mutton, consisting of both loins. **6** the part of a horse or similar animal on which a saddle is placed. **7** the part of the back of a domestic chicken that is nearest to the tail. **8** another word for **col** (sense 1). **9 in the saddle.** in a position of control. ◆ *vb* **saddles, saddling, saddled. 10** (sometimes foll. by *up*) to put a saddle on (a horse). **11** (*intr*) to mount into the saddle. **12** (*tr*) to burden: *I didn't ask to be saddled with this job.* [OE *sadol, sædel*]
▸'**saddle-,like** *adj*

saddleback ('sædᵊl,bæk) *n* a marking resembling a saddle on the backs of various animals.
▸'**saddle-,backed** *adj*

saddlebag ('sædᵊl,bæg) *n* a pouch or small bag attached to the saddle of a horse, bicycle, etc.

saddlebill ('sædᵊl,bɪl) *n* a large black-and-white stork of tropical Africa, having a heavy red bill with a black band around the middle. Also called: **jabiru.**

saddlebow ('sædᵊl,bəʊ) *n* the pommel of a saddle.

saddlecloth ('sædᵊl,klɒθ) *n* a light cloth put under a horse's saddle, so as to prevent rubbing.

saddle horse *n* a lightweight horse kept for riding only.

saddler ('sædlə) *n* a person who makes, deals in, or repairs saddles and other leather equipment for horses.

saddle roof *n* a roof that has a ridge and two gables.

saddlery ('sædlərɪ) *n, pl* **saddleries. 1** saddles, harness, and other leather equipment for horses collectively. **2** the business, work, or place of work of a saddler.

saddle soap *n* a soft soap containing neat's-foot oil used to preserve and clean leather.

saddletree ('sædᵊl,tri:) *n* the frame of a saddle.

Sadducee ('sædjʊ,si:) *n Judaism.* a member of an ancient Jewish sect that was opposed to the Pharisees, denying the resurrection of the dead and the validity of oral tradition. [OE *saddūcēas,* via L & Gk from LHeb. *ṣāddūqī,* prob. from *Sadoq* Zadok, high priest and supposed founder of the sect]
▸,**Saddu'cean** *adj*

sadhu *or* **saddhu** ('sɑ:du:) *n* a Hindu wandering holy man. [Sansk., from *sādhu* good]

sadiron ('sæd,aɪən) *n* a heavy iron, pointed at both ends for pressing clothes. [C19: from SAD (in the obs. sense: heavy) + IRON]

sadism ❶ ('seɪdɪzəm) *n* the gaining of pleasure or sexual gratification from the infliction of pain and mental suffering on another person. Cf. **masochism.** [C19: from F, after the Marquis de *Sade* (1740–1814), F soldier & writer]
▸'**sadist** *n* ▸**sadistic** (sə'dɪstɪk) *adj* ▸**sa'distically** *adv*

THESAURUS

sackcloth *n* **3 sackcloth and ashes** = **penitence**, compunction, contrition, grief, hair shirt, mortification, mourning, penance, remorse, repentance

sacred *adj* **1, 2** = **holy**, blessed, consecrated, divine, hallowed, revered, sanctified, venerable **3** = **religious**, ecclesiastical, holy, solemn
Antonyms *adj* ≠ **holy, religious:** lay, nonspiritual, profane, secular, temporal, unconsecrated, worldly

sacrifice *n* **1** = **surrender**, destruction, holocaust (*rare*), loss, renunciation **2** = **offering**, hecatomb, immolation, oblation ◆ *vb* **7** = **give up**, forego, forfeit, immolate, let go, lose, offer, offer up, say goodbye to, surrender

sacrificial *adj* = **propitiatory**, atoning, expiatory, oblatory, reparative

sacrilege *n* **1** = **desecration**, blasphemy, heresy, impiety, irreverence, mockery, profanation, profaneness, profanity, violation
Antonyms *n* piety, respect, reverence

sacrilegious *adj* **1** = **profane**, blasphemous, desecrating, godless, impious, irreligious, irreverent, ungodly, unholy

sacrosanct *adj* = **inviolable**, hallowed, inviolate, sacred, sanctified, set apart, untouchable

sad *adj* **1** = **unhappy**, blue, cheerless, dejected, depressed, disconsolate, dismal, doleful, down, downcast, down in the dumps (*inf.*), down in the mouth (*inf.*), gloomy, glum, grief-stricken, grieved, heavy-hearted, low, low-spirited, lugubrious, melancholy, mournful, pensive, sick at heart, sombre, wistful, woebegone **2** = **tragic**, calamitous, dark, depressing, disastrous, dismal, grievous, harrowing, heart-rending, lachrymose, moving, pathetic, pitiable, pitiful, poignant, sorry, tearful, upsetting **3** = **deplorable**, bad, dismal, lamentable, miserable, shabby, sorry, to be deplored, wretched
Antonyms *adj* ≠ **unhappy:** blithe, cheerful, cheery, chirpy (*inf.*), glad, happy, in good spirits, jolly, joyful, joyous, light-hearted, merry, pleased ≠ **deplorable:** good

sadden *vb* = **upset**, aggrieve, bring tears to one's eyes, cast a gloom upon, cast down, dash, deject, depress, desolate, dispirit, distress, grieve, make one's heart bleed, make sad

saddle *vb* **12** = **burden**, charge, encumber, load, lumber (*Brit. inf.*), task, tax

sadistic *adj* = **cruel**, barbarous, beastly, brutal, fiendish, inhuman, perverse, perverted, ruthless, savage, vicious

sadness *n* **1** = **unhappiness**, bleakness, cheerlessness, dejection, depression, despondency,

sadomasochism (ˌseɪdəʊ'mæsəˌkɪzəm) *n* **1** the combination of sadistic and masochistic elements in one person. **2** sexual practice in which one partner adopts a sadistic role and the other a masochistic one.
▸ˌ**sadomaso'chistic** *adj*

s.a.e. *abbrev. for* stamped addressed envelope.

safari (sə'fɑːrɪ) *n, pl* **safaris. 1** an overland journey or hunting expedition, esp. in Africa. **2** the people, animals, etc., that go on the expedition. [C19: from Swahili: journey, from Ar., from *safara* to travel]

safari park *n* an enclosed park in which lions and other wild animals are kept uncaged in the open and can be viewed by the public from cars, etc.

safari suit *n* an outfit made of tough cotton, denim, etc., consisting of a bush jacket with matching trousers, shorts, or skirt.

safe 🅣 (seɪf) *adj* **1** affording security or protection from harm: *a safe place.* **2** (*postpositive*) free from danger: *you'll be safe here.* **3** secure from risk: *a safe investment.* **4** worthy of trust: *a safe companion.* **5** tending to avoid controversy or risk: *a safe player.* **6** not dangerous: *water safe to drink.* **7 on the safe side.** as a precaution. ◆ *adv* **8** in a safe condition: *the children are safe in bed now.* **9 play safe.** to act in a way least likely to cause danger, controversy, or defeat. ◆ *n* **10** a strong container, usually of metal and provided with a secure lock, for storing money or valuables. **11** a small cupboard-like container for storing food. [C13: from OF *salf,* from L *salvus*]
▸'**safely** *adv* ▸'**safeness** *n*

safe-breaker *n* a person who breaks open and robs safes. Also called: **safe-cracker.**

safe-conduct 🅣 *n* **1** a document giving official permission to travel through a region, esp. in time of war. **2** the protection afforded by such a document.

safe-deposit *or* **safety-deposit** *n* **a** a place with facilities for the safe storage of money. **b** (*as modifier*): *a safe-deposit box.*

safeguard 🅣 ('seɪfˌgɑːd) *n* **1** a person or thing that ensures protection against danger, injury, etc. **2** a safe-conduct. ◆ *vb* **3** (*tr*) to protect.

safe house *n* a place used secretly by undercover agents, terrorists, etc., as a refuge.

safekeeping 🅣 ('seɪf'kiːpɪŋ) *n* the act of keeping or state of being kept in safety.

safe period *n Inf.* the period during the menstrual cycle when conception is considered least likely to occur.

safe seat *n* a Parliamentary seat that at an election is sure to be held by the same party as held it before.

safe sex *n* sexual intercourse using physical protection, such as a condom, or nonpenetrative methods to prevent the spread of such diseases as AIDS.

safety 🅣 ('seɪftɪ) *n, pl* **safeties. 1** the quality of being safe. **2** freedom from danger or risk of injury. **3** a contrivance designed to prevent injury. **4** *American football.* Also called: **safetyman.** either of two players who defend the area furthest back in the field.

safety belt *n* **1** another name for **seat belt** (sense 1). **2** a belt or strap worn by a person working at a great height to prevent him from falling.

safety curtain *n* a curtain made of fireproof material that can be lowered to separate the auditorium and stage in a theatre to prevent the spread of a fire.

safety factor *n* the ratio of the breaking stress of a material to the calculated maximum stress in use. Also called: **factor of safety.**

safety glass *n* glass that if broken will not shatter.

safety lamp *n* an oil-burning miner's lamp in which the flame is surrounded by a metal gauze to prevent it from igniting combustible gas.

safety match *n* a match that will light only when struck against a specially prepared surface.

safety net *n* **1** a net used in a circus to catch high-wire and trapeze artistes if they fall. **2** any means of protection from hardship or loss.

safety pin *n* a spring wire clasp with a covering catch, made so as to shield the point when closed.

safety razor *n* a razor with a guard over the blade or blades to prevent deep cuts.

safety valve *n* **1** a valve in a pressure vessel that allows fluid to escape at excess pressure. **2** a harmless outlet for emotion, etc.

saffian ('sæfɪən) *n* leather tanned with sumach and usually dyed a bright colour. [C16: via Russian & Turkish from Persian *sakhtiyān* goatskin, from *sakht* hard]

safflower ('sæflaʊə) *n* **1** a thistle-like Eurasian annual plant having large heads of orange-yellow flowers and yielding a dye and an oil used in paints, medicines, etc. **2** a red dye used for cotton and for colouring foods and cosmetics. [C16: via Du. *saffloer* or G *safflor* from OF *saffleur*]

saffron ('sæfrən) *n* **1** an Old World crocus having purple or white flowers with orange stigmas. **2** the dried stigmas of this plant, used to flavour or colour food. **3 meadow saffron.** another name for **autumn crocus. 4a** an orange to orange-yellow colour. **4b** (*as adj*): *a saffron dress.* [C13: from OF *safran,* from Med. L *safranum,* from Ar. *za'farān*]

S.Afr. *abbrev. for* South Africa(n).

safranine *or* **safranin** ('sæfrənɪn) *n* any of a class of azine dyes used for textiles. [C19: from F *safran* SAFFRON + -INE[2]]

sag 🅣 (sæg) *vb* **sags, sagging, sagged.** (*mainly intr*) **1** (*also tr*) to sink or cause to sink in parts, as under weight or pressure: *the bed sags in the middle.* **2** to fall in value: *prices sagged to a new low.* **3** to hang unevenly. **4** (of courage, etc.) to weaken. ◆ *n* **5** the act or an instance of sagging: *a sag in profits.* **6** *Naut.* the extent to which a vessel's keel sags at the centre. [C15: from ON]
▸'**saggy** *adj*

saga 🅣 ('sɑːgə) *n* **1** any of several medieval prose narratives written in Iceland and recounting the exploits of a hero or a family. **2** any similar heroic narrative. **3** a series of novels about several generations or members of a family. **4** *Inf.* a series of events or a story stretching over a long period. [C18: from ON: a narrative]

sagacious 🅣 (sə'geɪʃəs) *adj* having or showing sagacity; wise. [C17: from L *sagāx,* from *sāgīre* to be astute]
▸**sa'gaciously** *adv*

sagacity 🅣 (sə'gæsɪtɪ) *n* foresight, discernment, or keen perception; ability to make good judgments.

sagamore ('sægəˌmɔː) *n* (among some North American Indians) a chief or eminent man. [C17: from Amerind *sāgimau,* lit.: he overcomes]

sage[1] 🅣 (seɪdʒ) *n* **1** a man revered for his profound wisdom. ◆ *adj* **2** profoundly wise or prudent. [C13: from OF, from L *sapere* to be sensible]
▸'**sagely** *adv* ▸'**sageness** *n*

sage[2] (seɪdʒ) *n* **1** a perennial Mediterranean plant having grey-green leaves and purple, blue, or white flowers. **2** the leaves of this plant, used in cooking for flavouring. **3** short for **sagebrush.** [C14: from OF *saulge,* from L *salvia,* from *salvus* in good health (from its curative properties)]

sagebrush ('seɪdʒˌbrʌʃ) *n* any of a genus of aromatic plants of W North America, having silver-green leaves and large clusters of small white flowers.

saggar *or* **sagger** ('sægə) *n* a clay box in which ceramic wares are placed during firing. [C17: ? alteration of SAFEGUARD]

sagittal suture ('sædʒɪt°l) *n* a serrated line on the top of the skull that marks the junction of the two parietal bones.

Sagittarius (ˌsædʒɪ'teərɪəs) *n, Latin genitive* **Sagittarii** (ˌsædʒɪ'teərɪˌaɪ). **1** *Astron.* a S constellation. **2** Also called: the **Archer.** *Astrol.* the ninth sign of the zodiac. The sun is in this sign between Nov. 22 and Dec. 21. [C14: from L: an archer, from *sagitta* an arrow]
▸**Sagittarian** (ˌsædʒɪ'teərɪən) *adj*

sagittate ('sædʒɪˌteɪt) *adj* (esp. of leaves) shaped like the head of an arrow. [C18: from NL *sagittātus,* from L *sagitta* arrow]

sago ('seɪgəʊ) *n* a starchy cereal obtained from the powdered pith of a palm (**sago palm**), used for puddings and as a thickening agent. [C16: from Malay *sāgū*]

saguaro (sə'gwɑːrəʊ) *n, pl* **saguaros.** a giant cactus of desert regions of Arizona, S California, and Mexico. [Mexican Sp., var. of *sahuaro,* an Indian name]

sahib ('sɑːhɪb) *n* (in India) a form of address placed after a man's name,

THESAURUS

dolefulness, dolour (*poetic*), gloominess, grief, heavy heart, melancholy, misery, mournfulness, poignancy, sorrow, sorrowfulness, the blues, the dumps (*inf.*), tragedy, wretchedness

safe *adj* **1** = **secure**, free from harm, impregnable, in safe hands, in safety, out of danger, out of harm's way, out of the woods, protected, safe and sound **2** = **unharmed**, all right, intact, O.K. *or* okay (*inf.*), undamaged, unhurt, unscathed **3** = **risk-free**, certain, impregnable, riskless, secure, sound **5** = **cautious**, circumspect, conservative, dependable, discreet, on the safe side, prudent, realistic, reliable, sure, tried and true, trustworthy, unadventurous **6** = **harmless**, innocuous, nonpoisonous, nontoxic, pure, tame, unpolluted, wholesome ◆ *n* **10** = **strongbox**, coffer, deposit box, repository, safe-deposit box, vault
Antonyms *adj* ≠ **secure:** at risk, damaged, endangered, imperilled, insecure, jeopardized, put at risk, put in danger, threatened ≠ **cautious:** imprudent, incautious, reckless, risky, unsafe ≠ **harmless:** baneful, dangerous, harmful, hazardous, hurtful, injurious, noxious, pernicious, unsafe

safe-conduct *n* **1** = **permit**, authorization, licence, pass, passport, safeguard, warrant

safeguard *n* **1** = **protection**, aegis, armour, bulwark, convoy, defence, escort, guard, security, shield, surety ◆ *vb* **3** = **protect**, defend, guard, look after, preserve, screen, shield, watch over

safekeeping *n* = **protection**, care, charge, custody, guardianship, keeping, supervision, surveillance, trust, tutelage, ward

safely *adv* **1-3** = **in safety**, in one piece, safe and sound, securely, with impunity, without risk, with safety

safety *n* **1** = **security**, assurance, immunity, impregnability, protection

sag *vb* **1** = **sink**, bag, bulge, cave in, dip, droop, drop, fall, fall unevenly, give way, hang loosely, seat (*of skirts, etc.*), settle, slump, swag **4** = **tire**, decline, droop, fall, flag, slide, slip, slump, wane, weaken, wilt ◆ *n* **5** = **drop**, decline, depression, dip, downturn, fall, lapse, slip, slump

saga *n* **2** = **tale**, adventure, chronicle, epic, narrative, *roman-fleuve*, soap opera, story, yarn

sagacious *adj* = **wise**, able, acute, apt, astute, canny, clear-sighted, discerning, far-sighted, fly (*sl.*), insightful, intelligent, judicious, knowing, long-headed, perceptive, perspicacious, sage, sharp, sharp-witted, shrewd, smart

sagacity *n* = **wisdom**, acuteness, astuteness, canniness, discernment, foresight, insight, judiciousness, knowingness, penetration, perspicacity, prudence, sapience, sense, sharpness, shrewdness, understanding

sage[1] *n* **1** = **wise man**, authority, elder, expert, guru, mahatma, man of learning, master, Nestor, philosopher, pundit, savant, Solomon, Solon ◆ *adj* **2** = **wise**, acute, canny, discerning, intelligent, judicious, learned, perspicacious, politic, prudent, sagacious, sapient, sensible used as a mark of respect. [C17: from Urdu, from Ar. *çāhib*, lit.: friend]

said[1] (sɛd) *adj* **1** (*prenominal*) (in contracts, etc.) aforesaid. ◆ *vb* **2** the past tense and past participle of **say.**

said[2] ('sɑːɪd) *n* a variant of **sayyid.**

saiga ('saɪgə) *n* either of two antelopes of the plains of central Asia, having a slightly elongated nose. [C19: from Russian]

sail ❶ (seɪl) *n* **1** an area of fabric, usually Terylene or nylon (formerly canvas), with fittings for holding it in any suitable position to catch the wind, used for propelling certain kinds of vessels, esp. over water. **2** a voyage on such a vessel: *a sail down the river.* **3** a vessel with sails or such vessels collectively: *to travel by sail.* **4** a ship's sails collectively. **5** something resembling a sail in shape, position, or function, such as the part of a windmill that is turned by the wind. **6 in sail.** having the sail set. **7 make sail. 7a** to run up the sail or to run up more sail. **7b** to begin a voyage. **8 set sail. 8a** to embark on a voyage by ship. **8b** to hoist sail. **9 under sail. 9a** with sail hoisted. **9b** under way. ◆ *vb* (*mainly intr*) **10** to travel in a boat or ship: *we sailed to Le Havre.* **11** to begin a voyage: *we sail at 5 o'clock.* **12** (of a vessel) to move over the water. **13** (*tr*) to manoeuvre or navigate a vessel: *he sailed the schooner up the channel.* **14** (*tr*) to sail over: *she sailed the Atlantic single-handed.* **15** (often foll. by *over, through,* etc.) to move fast or effortlessly: *we sailed through customs.* **16** to move along smoothly; glide. **17** (often foll. by *in* or *into*) *Inf.* **17a** to begin (something) with vigour. **17b** to make an attack (on) violently. [OE *segl*]

▸**'sailable** *adj* ▸**'sailless** *adj*

sailboard ('seɪl,bɔːd) *n* the craft used for windsurfing, consisting of a moulded board to which a mast bearing a single sail is attached.

sailboarding ('seɪl,bɔːdɪŋ) *n* another name for **windsurfing.**

sailcloth ('seɪl,klɒθ) *n* **1** any of various fabrics from which sails are made. **2** a canvas-like cloth used for clothing, etc.

sailer ('seɪlə) *n* a vessel, with specified sailing characteristics: *a good sailer.*

sailfish ('seɪl,fɪʃ) *n, pl* **sailfish** *or* **sailfishes. 1** any of several large game fishes of warm and tropical seas. They have an elongated upper jaw and a long sail-like dorsal fin. **2** another name for **basking shark.**

sailing ship *n* a large sailing vessel.

sailor ❶ ('seɪlə) *n* **1** any member of a ship's crew, esp. one below the rank of officer. **2** a person who sails, esp. with reference to the likelihood of his becoming seasick: *a good sailor.*

sailplane ('seɪl,pleɪn) *n* a high-performance glider.

sainfoin ('sænfɔɪn) *n* a Eurasian perennial plant, widely grown as a forage crop, having pale pink flowers and curved pods. [C17: from F, from Med. L *sānum faenum* wholesome hay, referring to its former use as a medicine]

saint (seɪnt; *unstressed* sənt) *n* **1** a person who after death is formally recognized by a Christian Church as having attained a specially exalted place in heaven and the right to veneration. **2** a person of exceptional holiness. **3** (*pl*) *Bible.* the collective body of those who are righteous in God's sight. ◆ *vb* **4** (*tr*) to recognize formally as a saint. [C12: from OF, from L *sanctus* holy, from *sancīre* to hallow]

▸**'sainthood** *n* ▸**'saintlike** *adj*

Saint Agnes' Eve ('ægnəs) *n, usually abbreviated to* **St Agnes' Eve.** the night of Jan. 20, when according to tradition a woman can discover the identity of her future husband by performing certain rites.

Saint Andrew's Cross ('ændruːz) *n, usually abbreviated to* **St Andrew's Cross. 1** a diagonal cross with equal arms. **2** a white diagonal cross on a blue ground.

Saint Anthony's fire ('æntənɪz) *n, usually abbreviated to* **St Anthony's fire.** *Pathol.* another name for **ergotism** or **erysipelas.**

Saint Bernard ('bɜːnəd) *n, usually abbreviated to* **St Bernard.** a large breed of dog with a dense red-and-white coat, formerly used as a rescue dog in mountainous areas.

sainted ('seɪntɪd) *adj* **1** canonized. **2** like a saint in character or nature. **3** hallowed or holy.

Saint Elmo's fire ('ɛlməʊz) *n, usually abbreviated to* **St Elmo's fire.** (not in technical usage) a luminous region that sometimes appears around church spires, the masts of ships, etc.

Saint John's wort ('dʒɒnz) *n, usually abbreviated to* **St John's wort.** any of a genus of shrubs or herbaceous plants, having yellow flowers.

Saint Leger ('lɛdʒə) *n, usually abbreviated to* **St Leger. the.** an annual horse race run at Doncaster, England, since 1776.

saintly ❶ ('seɪntlɪ) *adj* like, relating to, or suitable for a saint.

▸**'saintlily** *adv* ▸**'saintliness** *n*

saintpaulia (sənt'pɔːlɪə) *n* another name for **African violet.** [C20: NL, after Baron W. von *Saint Paul,* G soldier (died 1910), who discovered it]

saint's day *n Christianity.* a day in the church calendar commemorating a saint.

Saint Vitus's dance ('vaɪtəsɪz) *n, usually abbreviated to* **St Vitus's dance.** *Pathol.* a nontechnical name for **Sydenham's chorea.**

saith (sɛθ) *vb* (used with *he, she,* or *it*) *Arch.* a form of the present tense of **say.**

saithe (seɪθ) *n Brit.* another name for **coalfish.** [C19: from ON]

sake[1] ❶ (seɪk) *n* **1** benefit or interest (esp. in **for (someone's** *or* **one's own) sake). 2** the purpose of obtaining or achieving (esp. in **for the sake of (something)). 3** used in various exclamations of impatience, urgency, etc.: *for heaven's sake.* [C13 (in the phrase *for the sake of,* prob. from legal usage): from OE *sacu* lawsuit (hence, a cause)]

sake[2], **saké,** *or* **saki** ('sækɪ) *n* a Japanese alcoholic drink made from fermented rice. [C17: from Japanese]

saker ('seɪkə) *n* a large falcon of E Europe and Asia. [C14 *sagre,* from OF *sacre,* from Ar. *saqr*]

saki ('sɑːkɪ) *n* **1** any of several small mostly arboreal New World monkeys having a long bushy tail. **2** another name for **sake**[2]. [sense 1: C20: F, from Tupi *saqi*]

sal (sæl) *n* a pharmacological term for **salt** (sense 3). [L]

salaam (sə'lɑːm) *n* **1** a Muslim salutation consisting of a deep bow with the right palm on the forehead. **2** a salutation signifying peace. ◆ *vb* **3** to make a salaam (to). [C17: from Ar. *salām* peace, from *assalām 'alaikum* peace be to you]

salable ('seɪləbᵊl) *adj* the US spelling of **saleable.**

salacious ❶ (sə'leɪʃəs) *adj* **1** having an excessive interest in sex. **2** (of books, etc.) erotic, bawdy, or lewd. [C17: from L *salax* fond of leaping, from *salīre* to leap]

▸**sa'laciously** *adv* ▸**sa'laciousness** *or* **salacity** (sə'læsɪtɪ) *n*

salad ('sæləd) *n* **1** a dish of raw vegetables, such as lettuce, tomatoes, etc., served as a separate course with cold meat, eggs, etc., or as part of a main course. **2** any dish of cold vegetables or fruit served with a dressing: *potato salad.* **3** any green vegetable or herb used in such a dish. [C15: from OF *salade,* from OProvençal *salada,* from *salar* to season with salt, from L *sal* salt]

salad days *pl n* a period of youth and inexperience.

salad dressing *n* a sauce for salad, such as oil and vinegar or mayonnaise.

salade niçoise (sæ'lɑːd niː'swɑːz) *n* a cold dish consisting of a variety of ingredients, usually including hard-boiled eggs, anchovy fillets, olives, tomatoes, and sometimes tuna fish. [C20: from F, lit.: salad of or from *Nice,* S France]

salamander ('sælə,mændə) *n* **1** any of various amphibians of central and S Europe. They have an elongated body, and only return to water to breed. **2** *Chiefly US & Canad.* any amphibian with a tail, as the newt. **3** a mythical reptilian creature supposed to live in fire. **4** an elemental fire-inhabiting being. [C14: from OF *salamandre,* from L *salamandra,* from Gk]

salami (sə'lɑːmɪ) *n* a highly seasoned type of sausage, usually flavoured with garlic. [C19: from It., pl of *salame,* from Vulgar L *salāre* (unattested) to salt, from L *sal* salt]

sal ammoniac *n* another name for **ammonium chloride.**

salaried ('sælərɪd) *adj* earning or yielding a salary: *a salaried worker; salaried employment.*

salary ❶ ('sælərɪ) *n, pl* **salaries. 1** a fixed payment made by an employer, often monthly, for professional or office work. Cf. **wage.** ◆ *vb* **salaries, salarying, salaried. 2** (*tr*) to pay a salary to. [C14: from Anglo-Norman *salarie,* from L *salārium* the sum given to Roman soldiers to buy salt, from *sal* salt]

salchow ('sælkəʊ) *n Figure skating.* a jump from the inner backward edge of one foot with one, two, or three full turns in the air, returning to the outer backward edge of the opposite foot. [C20: after Ulrich *Salchow* (1877–1949), Swedish figure skater, who originated it]

sale ❶ (seɪl) *n* **1** the exchange of goods, property, or services for an agreed sum of money or credit. **2** the amount sold. **3** the opportunity to sell: *there was no sale for luxuries.* **4a** an event at which goods are sold at reduced prices, usually to clear old stocks. **4b** (*as modifier*): *sale bargains.* **5** an auction. [OE *sala,* from ON *sala*]

saleable *or US* **salable** ('seɪləbᵊl) *adj* fit for selling or capable of being sold.

▸**,salea'bility** *or US* **,sala'bility** *n*

sale of work *n* a sale of articles, often handmade, the proceeds of which benefit a charity or charities.

sale or return *n* an arrangement by which a retailer pays only for goods sold, returning those that are unsold.

saleroom ('seɪl,ruːm, -,rʊm) *n Chiefly Brit.* a room where objects are displayed for sale, esp. by auction.

THESAURUS

sail *vb* **10 = go by water,** cruise, ride the waves, voyage **11 = embark,** cast *or* weigh anchor, get under way, hoist the blue peter, put to sea, set sail **13 = pilot,** captain, navigate, skipper, steer **16 = glide,** drift, float, fly, scud, shoot, skim, skirr, soar, sweep, wing **17** *with* **into** *Informal* **= attack,** assault, begin, belabour, fall upon, get going, get to work on, lambast(e), set about, tear into (*inf.*)

sailor *n* **1 = mariner,** hearty (*inf.*), Jack Tar, lascar, leatherneck (*sl.*), marine, matelot (*sl., chiefly Brit.*), navigator, salt, sea dog, seafarer, seafaring man, seaman, tar (*inf.*)

saintly *adj* **= virtuous,** angelic, beatific, blameless, blessed, devout, full of good works, god-fearing, godly, holy, pious, religious, righteous, sainted, saintlike, sinless, worthy

sake[1] *n* **1** *As in* **for someone's** *or* **one's own sake = benefit,** account, advantage, behalf, consideration, gain, good, interest, profit, regard, respect, welfare, wellbeing **2** *As in* **for the sake of = purpose,** aim, cause, end, motive, objective, principle, reason

salacious *adj* **2 = lascivious,** bawdy, blue, carnal, concupiscent, erotic, indecent, lecherous, lewd, libidinous, lustful, obscene, pornographic, prurient, ribald, ruttish, smutty, steamy (*inf.*), wanton, X-rated (*inf.*)

salary *n* **1 = pay,** earnings, emolument, income, remuneration, stipend, wage, wages

sale *n* **1 = selling,** auction, deal, disposal, marketing, transaction, vending

salesclerk ('seɪlz,klɜːk) *n US & Canad.* a shop assistant.

salesman ('seɪlzmən) *n, pl* **salesmen. 1** Also called: **saleswoman** *(fem),* **salesgirl** *(fem), or* **salesperson.** a person who sells merchandise or services in a shop. **2** short for **travelling salesman.**

salesmanship ('seɪlzmənʃɪp) *n* **1** the technique of, skill, or ability in selling. **2** the work of a salesman.

sales pitch *or* **talk** *n* an argument or other persuasion used in selling.

sales resistance *n* opposition of potential customers to selling, esp. aggressive selling.

sales tax *n* a tax levied on retail sales receipts and added to selling prices by retailers.

sales trader *n Stock Exchange.* a person employed by a market maker, or his firm, to find clients.

Salian ('seɪlɪən) *adj* **1** denoting or relating to a group of Franks (the **Salii**) who settled in the Netherlands in the 4th century A.D. ◆ *n* **2** a member of this group.

salicin ('sælɪsɪn) *n* a crystalline water-soluble glucoside obtained from the bark of poplar trees and used as a medical analgesic. [C19: from F, from L *salix* willow]

Salic law ('sælɪk) *n History.* **1** the code of laws of the Salian Franks and other Germanic tribes. **2** a law excluding women from succession to the throne in certain countries, such as France.

salicylate (sə'lɪsɪ,leɪt) *n* any salt or ester of salicylic acid.

salicylic acid (,sælɪ'sɪlɪk) *n* a white crystalline substance with a sweet taste and bitter aftertaste, used in the manufacture of aspirin, and as a fungicide. [C19: *salicyl* (from F, from L *salix* a willow + -YL) + -IC]

salient ❶ ('seɪlɪənt) *adj* **1** conspicuous or striking: *a salient feature.* **2** projecting outwards at an angle of less than 180°. **3** (esp. of animals) leaping. ◆ *n* **4** *Mil.* a projection of the forward line into enemy-held territory. **5** a salient angle. [C16: from L *salīre* to leap]
▸**'salience** *or* **'saliency** *n* ▸**'saliently** *adv*

salientian (,seɪlɪ'ɛnʃɪən) *n* **1** any of an order of vertebrates with no tail and long hind legs adapted for hopping, as the frog or the toad. ◆ *adj* **2** of or belonging to this order. [C19: from NL *Salientia,* lit.: leapers, from L *salīre* to leap]

salina (sə'laɪnə) *n* a salt marsh or lake. [C17: from Sp., from Med. L: salt pit, from LL *salīnus* SALINE]

saline ('seɪlaɪn) *adj* **1** of, consisting of, or containing common salt: *a saline taste.* **2** *Med.* of or relating to a saline. **3** of, consisting of, or containing any chemical salt, esp. sodium chloride. ◆ *n* **4** *Med.* a solution of sodium chloride and water. [C15: from LL *salīnus,* from L *sal* salt]
▸**salinity** (sə'lɪnɪtɪ) *n*

salinometer (,sælɪ'nɒmɪtə) *n* a hydrometer for determining the amount of salt in a solution.
▸**,sali'nometry** *n*

saliva (sə'laɪvə) *n* the secretion of salivary glands, consisting of a clear usually slightly acid aqueous fluid of variable composition. [C17: from L, from ?]
▸**salivary** (sə'laɪvərɪ) *adj*

salivary gland *n* any of the glands in mammals that secrete saliva.

salivate ('sælɪ,veɪt) *vb* **salivates, salivating, salivated. 1** *(intr)* to secrete saliva, esp. an excessive amount. **2** *(tr)* to cause (an animal, etc.) to produce saliva, as by the administration of mercury.
▸**,sali'vation** *n*

Salk vaccine (sɔːlk) *n* a vaccine against poliomyelitis. [C20: after Jonas *Salk* (1914–95), US virologist, who developed it]

sallee *or* **sally** ('sælɪ) *n Austral.* **1** a SE Australian eucalyptus tree with pale grey bark. **2** any of various acacia trees. [prob. from Abor.]

sallow[1] ❶ ('sæləʊ) *adj* **1** (esp. of human skin) of an unhealthy pale or yellowish colour. ◆ *vb* **2** *(tr)* to make sallow. [OE *salu*]
▸**'sallowish** *adj* ▸**'sallowness** *n*

sallow[2] ('sæləʊ) *n* **1** any of several small willow trees, esp. the common sallow, which has large catkins that appear before the leaves. **2** a twig or the wood of any of these trees. [OE *sealh*]
▸**'sallowy** *adj*

sally ❶ ('sælɪ) *n, pl* **sallies. 1** a sudden sortie, esp. by troops. **2** a sudden outburst or emergence into action or expression. **3** an excursion. **4** a jocular retort. ◆ *vb* **sallies, sallying, sallied.** *(intr)* **5** to make a sudden violent sortie. **6** (often foll. by *forth*) to go out on an expedition, etc. **7** to come or set out in an energetic manner. **8** to rush out suddenly. [C16: from OF *saillie,* from *saillir* to dash forwards, from L *salīre* to leap]

Sally Lunn (lʌn) *n* a flat round cake made from a sweet yeast dough. [C19: said to be after an 18th-century E baker who invented it]

salmagundi (,sælmə'gʌndɪ) *n* **1** a mixed salad dish of cooked meats, eggs, beetroot, etc., popular in 18th-century England. **2** a miscellany. [C17: from F *salmigondis,* ?from It. *salami conditi* pickled salami]

salmon ('sæmən) *n, pl* **salmons** *or* **salmon. 1** a soft-finned fish of the Atlantic and the Pacific, which is an important food fish. Salmon occur in cold and temperate waters and many species migrate to fresh water to spawn. **2** *Austral.* any of several unrelated fish. [C13: from OF *saumon,* from L *salmō*]
▸**'salmo,noid** *adj*

salmonella (,sælmə'nɛlə) *n, pl* **salmonellae** (-,liː). any of a genus of rod-shaped aerobic bacteria including many species which cause food poisoning. [C19: NL, after Daniel E. *Salmon* (1850–1914), US veterinary surgeon]

salmon ladder *n* a series of steps designed to enable salmon to move upstream to their breeding grounds.

salon ('sælɒn) *n* **1** a room in a large house in which guests are received. **2** an assembly of guests in a fashionable household, esp. a gathering of major literary, artistic, and political figures. **3** a commercial establishment in which hairdressers, etc., carry on their businesses. **4a** a hall for exhibiting works of art. **4b** such an exhibition, esp. one showing the work of living artists. [C18: from F, from It. *salone,* augmented form of *sala* hall, of Gmc origin]

saloon (sə'luːn) *n* **1** Also called: **saloon bar.** *Brit.* another word for **lounge** (sense 5). **2** a large public room on a passenger ship. **3** any large public room used for a purpose: *a dancing saloon.* **4** *Chiefly US & Canad.* a place where alcoholic drink is sold and consumed. **5** a closed two-door or four-door car with four to six seats. US, Canad., and NZ name: **sedan.** [C18: from F SALON]

salopettes (,sælə'pɛts) *pl n* a garment worn for skiing, consisting of quilted trousers held up by shoulder straps. [C20: from F]

salpiglossis (,sælpɪ'glɒsɪs) *n* any of a genus of plants, some species of which are cultivated for their bright funnel-shaped flowers. [C19: NL, from Gk *salpinx* trumpet + *glōssa* tongue]

salpinx ('sælpɪŋks) *n, pl* **salpinges** (sæl'pɪndʒiːz). *Anat.* another name for **Fallopian tube** or **Eustachian tube.** [C19: from Gk: trumpet]
▸**salpingectomy** (,sælpɪn'dʒɛktəmɪ) *n* ▸**salpingitis** (,sælpɪn'dʒaɪtɪs) *n*

salsa ('sælsə) *n* **1** a type of Latin American big-band dance music. **2** a dance performed to this. **3** *Cookery.* a spicy Mexican tomato-based sauce. [C20: from Sp.: sauce]

salsify ('sælsɪfɪ) *n, pl* **salsifies. 1** Also called: **oyster plant, vegetable oyster.** a Mediterranean plant having grasslike leaves, purple flower heads, and a long white edible taproot. **2** the root of this plant, which tastes of oysters and is eaten as a vegetable. [C17: from F, from It. *sassefrica,* from LL, from L *saxum* rock + *fricāre* to rub]

sal soda *n* the crystalline decahydrate of sodium carbonate, $Na_2CO_3.10H_2O$.

salt ❶ (sɔːlt) *n* **1** a white powder or colourless crystalline solid, consisting mainly of sodium chloride and used for seasoning and preserving food. **2** *(modifier)* preserved in, flooded with, containing, or growing in salt or salty water: *salt pork.* **3** *Chem.* any of a class of crystalline solid compounds that are formed from, or can be regarded as formed from, an acid and a base. **4** liveliness or pungency: *his wit added salt to the discussion.* **5** dry or laconic wit. **6** an experienced sailor. **7** short for **saltcellar. 8 rub salt into someone's wounds.** to make someone's pain, shame, etc., even worse. **9 salt of the earth.** a person or group of people regarded as the finest of their kind. **10 with a grain** (*or* **pinch**) **of salt.** with reservations. **11 worth one's salt.** worthy of one's pay. ◆ *vb (tr)* **12** to season or preserve with salt. **13** to scatter salt over (an iced road, etc.) to melt the ice. **14** to add zest to. **15** (often foll. by *down* or *away*) to preserve or cure with salt. **16** *Chem.* to treat with salt. **17** to give a false appearance of value to, esp. to introduce valuable ore fraudulently into (a mine, sample, etc.). ◆ *adj* **18** not sour, sweet, or bitter; salty. ◆ See also **salt away, salts.** [OE *sealt*]
▸**'salt,like** *adj* ▸**'saltness** *n*

SALT (sɔːlt) *n acronym for* Strategic Arms Limitation Talks *or* Treaty.

saltation (sæl'teɪʃən) *n* **1** *Biol.* an abrupt variation in the appearance of an organism, species, etc. **2** *Geol.* the leaping movement of sand or soil particles carried in water or by the wind. **3** a sudden abrupt movement. [C17: from L *saltātiō* a dance, from *saltāre* to leap about]
▸**saltatorial** (,sæltə'tɔːrɪəl) *or* **'saltatory** *adj*

salt away ❶ *or (less commonly)* **down** *vb (tr, adv)* to hoard or save (money, valuables, etc.).

saltbush ('sɔːlt,bʊʃ) *n* any of certain shrubs that grow in alkaline desert regions.

salt cake *n* an impure form of sodium sulphate used in the manufacture of detergents, glass, and ceramic glazes.

saltcellar ('sɔːlt,sɛlə) *n* **1** a small container for salt used at the table. **2** *Brit. inf.* either of the two hollows formed above the collarbones. [changed (through infl. of cellar) from C15 *salt saler; saler* from OF *saliere* container for salt, from L *salārius* belonging to salt, from *sal* salt]

salt dome *or* **plug** *n* a domelike structure of stratified rocks containing a central core of salt.

salted ('sɔːltɪd) *adj* seasoned, preserved, or treated with salt.

THESAURUS

salient *adj* **1** = **prominent**, arresting, conspicuous, important, marked, noticeable, outstanding, pronounced, remarkable, signal, striking **2** = **projecting**, jutting, protruding

sallow[1] *adj* **1** = **wan**, anaemic, bilious, jaundiced-looking, pale, pallid, pasty, peely-wally (*Scot.*), sickly, unhealthy, yellowish
Antonyms *adj* glowing, healthy-looking, radiant, rosy, ruddy

sally *n* **1** = **attack**, campaign, foray, incursion, offensive, raid, sortie, thrust **3** = **excursion**, escapade, frolic, jaunt, trip **4** = **witticism**, bon mot, crack, jest, joke, quip, retort, riposte, smart remark, wisecrack (*inf.*) ◆ *vb* **5-8** = **go forth**, erupt, issue, rush, set out, surge

salt *n* **2** *modifier* = **salty**, brackish, briny, saline, salted **4** = **seasoning**, flavour, relish, savour, taste **5** = **wit**, Attic wit, bite, dry humour, liveliness, piquancy, punch, pungency, sarcasm, sharpness, zest, zip (*inf.*) **6** = **sailor**, mariner, sea dog, seaman, tar (*inf.*) **10 with a grain** *or* **pinch of salt** = **sceptically**, cynically, disbelievingly, doubtfully, suspiciously, with reservations

salt away *vb* = **save**, accumulate, amass, bank, cache, hide, hoard up, lay by, lay in, lay up, put by, save for a rainy day, stash away (*inf.*), stockpile

salt flat *n* a flat expanse of salt left by the total evaporation of a body of water.

saltigrade ('sæltɪˌgreɪd) *adj* (of animals) adapted for moving in a series of jumps. [C19: from NL *Saltigradae*, name formerly applied to jumping spiders, from L *saltus* a leap + *gradī* to move]

saltings ('sɔːltɪŋz) *pl n* meadow land or marsh that is periodically flooded by sea water.

saltire *or* **saltier** ('sɔːlˌtaɪə) *n Heraldry.* an ordinary consisting of a diagonal cross on a shield. [C14 *sawturoure*, from OF *sauteour* cross-shaped barricade, from *saulter* to jump, from L *saltāre*]

salt lick *n* **1** a place where wild animals go to lick salt deposits. **2** a block of salt given to domestic animals to lick. **3** *Austral. & NZ.* a soluble cake of minerals used to supplement the diet of farm animals.

saltpan ('sɔːltˌpæn) *n* a shallow basin, usually in a desert region, containing salt, gypsum, etc., that was deposited from an evaporated salt lake.

saltpetre *or US* **saltpeter** (ˌsɔːlt'piːtə) *n* **1** another name for **potassium nitrate. 2** short for **Chile saltpetre.** [C16: from OF *salpetre*, from L *sal petrae* salt of rock]

salt pork *n* pork, esp. taken from the back and belly, that has been cured with salt.

salts (sɔːlts) *pl n* **1** *Med.* any of various mineral salts, such as magnesium sulphate, for use as a cathartic. **2** short for **smelling salts. 3 like a dose of salts.** *Inf.* very quickly.

saltus ('sæltəs) *n, pl* **saltuses.** a break in the continuity of a sequence. [L: a leap]

saltwater ('sɔːltˌwɔːtə) *adj* of or inhabiting salt water, esp. the sea: *saltwater fishes.*

saltworks ('sɔːltˌwɜːks) *n* (*functioning as sing*) a building or factory where salt is produced.

saltwort ('sɔːltˌwɜːt) *n* any of various plants, of beaches and salt marshes, having prickly leaves, striped stems, and small green flowers. Also called: **glasswort, kali.**

salty ❶ ('sɔːltɪ) *adj* **saltier, saltiest. 1** of, tasting of, or containing salt. **2** (esp. of humour) sharp. **3** relating to life at sea.
▸**'saltiness** *n*

salubrious ❶ (sə'luːbrɪəs) *adj* conducive or favourable to health. [C16: from L, from *salūs* health]
▸**sa'lubriously** *adv* ▸**sa'lubrity** *n*

Saluki (sə'luːkɪ) *n* a tall breed of hound with a smooth coat and long fringes on the ears and tail. [C19: from Ar. *salūqīy* of Saluq, an ancient Arabian city]

salutary ❶ ('sæljʊtərɪ) *adj* **1** promoting or intended to promote an improvement: *a salutary warning.* **2** promoting or intended to promote health. [C15: from L *salūtāris* wholesome, from *salūs* safety]
▸**'salutarily** *adv*

salutation ❶ (ˌsælju'teɪʃən) *n* **1** an act, phrase, gesture, etc., that serves as a greeting. **2** a form of words used as an opening to a speech or letter, such as *Dear Sir.* [C14: from L *salūtātiō*, from *salūtāre* to greet; see SALUTE]

salutatory (sə'luːtətərɪ) *adj* of, relating to, or resembling a salutation.
▸**sa'lutatorily** *adv*

salute ❶ (sə'luːt) *vb* **salutes, saluting, saluted. 1** (*tr*) to address or welcome with friendly words or gestures of respect, such as bowing. **2** (*tr*) to acknowledge with praise: *we salute your gallantry.* **3** *Mil.* to pay formal respect, as by raising the right arm. ◆ *n* **4** the act of saluting. **5** a formal military gesture of respect. [C14: from L *salūtāre* to greet, from *salūs* wellbeing]
▸**sa'luter** *n*

salvable ('sælvəbᵊl) *adj* capable of or suitable for being saved or salvaged. [C17: from LL *salvāre* to save, from *salvus* safe]

salvage ❶ ('sælvɪdʒ) *n* **1** the act, process, or business of rescuing vessels or their cargoes from loss at sea. **2a** the act of saving any goods or property in danger of damage or destruction. **2b** (*as modifier*): *a salvage operation.* **3** the goods or property so saved. **4** compensation paid for the salvage of a vessel or its cargo. **5** the proceeds from the sale of salvaged goods. ◆ *vb* **salvages, salvaging, salvaged.** (*tr*) **6** to save or rescue (goods or property) from fire, shipwreck, etc. **7** to gain (something beneficial) from a failure. [C17: from OF, from Med. L *salvāgium*, from *salvāre* to SAVE[1]]
▸**'salvageable** *adj* ▸**'salvager** *n*

salvation ❶ (sæl'veɪʃən) *n* **1** the act of preserving or the state of being preserved from harm. **2** a person or thing that is the means of preserving from harm. **3** *Christianity.* deliverance by redemption from the power of sin. [C13: from OF, from LL *salvātiō*, from L *salvātus* saved, from *salvāre* to SAVE[1]]

Salvation Army *n* a Christian body founded in 1865 by William Booth and organized on quasi-military lines for evangelism and social work among the poor.

salvationist (sæl'veɪʃənɪst) *n* **1** a member of an evangelical sect emphasizing the doctrine of salvation. **2** (*often cap.*) a member of the Salvation Army.

salve ❶ (sælv, sɑːv) *n* **1** an ointment for wounds, etc. **2** anything that heals or soothes. ◆ *vb* **salves, salving, salved.** (*tr*) **3** to apply salve to (a wound, etc.). **4** to soothe, comfort, or appease. [OE *sealf*]

salver ('sælvə) *n* a tray, esp. one of silver, on which food, letters, visiting cards, etc., are presented. [C17: from F *salve*, from Sp. *salva* tray from which the king's taster sampled food, from L *salvāre* to SAVE[1]]

salvia ('sælvɪə) *n* any of a genus of herbaceous plants or small shrubs, such as the sage, grown for their medicinal or culinary properties or for ornament. [C19: from L: SAGE[2]]

salvo ('sælvəʊ) *n, pl* **salvos** *or* **salvoes. 1** a discharge of fire from weapons in unison, esp. on a ceremonial occasion. **2** concentrated fire from many weapons, as in a naval battle. **3** an outburst, as of applause. [C17: from It. *salva*, from OF *salve*, from L *salvē!* greetings!, ult. from *salvus* safe]

Salvo ('sælvəʊ) *n, pl* **Salvos.** *Austral. sl.* a member of the Salvation Army.

sal volatile (vɒ'lætɪlɪ) *n* a solution of ammonium carbonate in alcohol and aqueous ammonia, used as smelling salts. Also called: **spirits of ammonia.** [C17: from NL: volatile salt]

SAM (sæm) *n acronym for* surface-to-air missile.

Sam. *Bible. abbrev. for* Samuel.

samara (sə'mɑːrə, 'sæmərə) *n* a dry winged one-seeded fruit: occurs in the ash, maple, etc. Also called: **key fruit.** [C16: from NL, from L: seed of an elm]

Samaritan (sə'mærɪtᵊn) *n* **1** a native or inhabitant of Samaria, a kingdom in ancient Palestine. **2** short for **Good Samaritan. 3** (in the UK) a member of a voluntary organization (**the Samaritans**) that offers counselling to people in despair, esp. by telephone.

samarium (sə'mɛərɪəm) *n* a silvery metallic element of the lanthanide series used in carbon-arc lighting, as a doping agent in laser crystals, and as a neutron-absorber. Symbol: Sm; atomic no.: 62; atomic wt.: 150.35. [C19: from NL, from mineral, *samarskite*, after Col. von *Samarski*, 19th-century Russian inspector of mines + -IUM]

samba ('sæmbə) *n, pl* **sambas. 1** a modern ballroom dance from Brazil in bouncy duple time. **2** a piece of music composed for or in the rhythm of this dance. ◆ *vb* **sambas, sambaing, sambaed. 3** (*intr*) to perform such a dance. [Port., of African origin]

sambar *or* **sambur** ('sæmbə) *n, pl* **sambars, sambar** *or* **samburs, sambur.** a S Asian deer with three-tined antlers. [C17: from Hindi, from Sansk. *śambarra*, from ?]

Sam Browne belt (ˌsæm 'braʊn) *n* a military officer's wide belt supported by a strap passing from the left side of the belt over the right shoulder. [C20: after Sir *Samuel J. Browne* (1824–1901), British general, who devised it]

same ❶ (seɪm) *adj* (usually preceded by *the*) **1** being the very one: *she is wearing the same hat.* **2a** being the one previously referred to. **2b** (*as n*): *a note received about same.* **3a** identical in kind, quantity, etc.: *two girls of the same age.* **3b** (*as n*): *we'd like the same.* **4** unchanged in character or nature: *his attitude is the same as ever.* **5 all the same. 5a** Also: **just the same.** nevertheless; yet. **5b** immaterial: *it's all the same to me.* ◆ *adv* **6** in an identical manner. [C12: from ON *samr*]
▸**'sameness** *n*

> **USAGE NOTE** The use of *same* exemplified in *if you send us your order for the materials, we will deliver same tomorrow* is common in business and official English. In general English, however, this use of the word is avoided: *may I borrow your book? I will return it* (not *same*) *tomorrow.*

samfoo ('sæmfuː) *n* a style of dress worn by Chinese women, consisting of a waisted blouse and trousers. [from Chinese *sam* dress + *foo* trousers]

Samian ('seɪmɪən) *adj* **1** of or relating to Samos, an island in the Aegean, or its inhabitants. ◆ *n* **2** a native or inhabitant of Samos.

THESAURUS

salty *adj* **1** = **salt**, brackish, briny, over-salted, saline, salted **2** = **witty**, colourful, humorous, lively, piquant, pungent, racy, sharp, snappy (*inf.*), spicy, tangy, tart, zestful

salubrious *adj* = **health-giving**, beneficial, good for one, healthful, healthy, invigorating, salutary, wholesome

salutary *adj* **1** = **beneficial**, advantageous, good, good for one, helpful, practical, profitable, timely, useful, valuable **2** = **healthy**, healthful, salubrious

salutation *n* **1** = **greeting**, address, obeisance, salute, welcome

salute *vb* **1** = **greet**, accost, acknowledge, address, doff one's cap to, hail, kiss, pay one's respects to, salaam, welcome **2** = **honour**, acknowledge, pay tribute *or* homage to, present arms, recognize, take one's hat off to (*inf.*) ◆ *n* **4** = **greeting**, address, kiss, obeisance, recognition, salaam, salutation, tribute

salvage *vb* **6, 7** = **save**, glean, recover, redeem, rescue, restore, retrieve

salvation *n* **1** = **saving**, deliverance, escape, lifeline, preservation, redemption, rescue, restoration
Antonyms *n* condemnation, damnation, doom, downfall, hell, loss, perdition, ruin

salve *n* **1, 2** = **ointment**, balm, cream, dressing, emollient, liniment, lotion, lubricant, medication, unguent

same *adj* **1, 2** = **aforementioned**, aforesaid, selfsame, very **3** = **identical**, alike, corresponding, duplicate, equal, equivalent, indistinguishable, interchangeable, synonymous, twin **4** = **unchanged**, changeless, consistent, constant, invariable, unaltered, unfailing, uniform, unvarying **5 all the same: a** = **unimportant**, after all, anyhow, be that as it may, in any event, just the same, nonetheless, still **b** = **immaterial**, not worth mentioning, of no consequence
Antonyms *adj* ≠ **identical:** different, dissimilar, diverse, miscellaneous, other ≠ **unchanged:** altered, inconsistent, variable

sameness *n* **3** = **similarity**, identicalness, identity, indistinguishability, likeness, oneness, resemblance, standardization, uniformity **4** = **lack of variety**, consistency, monotony, predictability, repetition, tedium

Samian ware *n* a fine earthenware pottery, reddish-brown or black in colour, found in large quantities on Roman sites. [C19: after the island of *Samos*, source of a reddish earth similar to that from which the pottery was made]

samisen ('sæmɪˌsɛn) *n* a Japanese plucked stringed instrument with a long neck and a rectangular soundbox. [Japanese, from Chinese *san-hsien*, from *san* three + *hsien* string]

samite ('sæmaɪt) *n* a heavy fabric of silk, often woven with gold or silver threads, used in the Middle Ages. [C13: from OF *samit*, from Med. L *examitum*, from Gk *hexamitos* having six threads]

samizdat (*Russian* səmiz'dat) *n* (formerly, in the Soviet Union) **a** a system of clandestine printing and distribution of banned literature. **b** (*as modifier*): *a samizdat publication*. [from Russian]

samosa (sə'məʊsə) *n, pl* **samosas** *or* **samosa.** (in Indian cookery) a small, fried, triangular spiced meat or vegetable pasty. [C20: from Hindi]

samovar ('sæməˌvɑː) *n* (esp. in Russia) a metal urn for making tea, in which the water is usually heated by an inner container. [C19: from Russian, from *samo-* self + *varit'* to boil]

Samoyed (ˌsæmə'jɛd) *n* **1** (*pl* **Samoyed** *or* **Samoyeds**) a member of a group of peoples who live chiefly in the area of the N Urals: related to the Finns. **2** the languages of these peoples. **3** (sə'mɔɪɛd) a white or cream breed of dog having a dense coat and a tightly curled tail. [C17: from Russian *Samoed*]

samp (sæmp) *n S. African*. crushed maize used for porridge. [from Amerind *nasaump* softened by water]

sampan ('sæmpæn) *n* a small skiff, widely used in the Orient, that is propelled by oars. [C17: from Chinese, from *san* three + *pan* board]

samphire ('sæmˌfaɪə) *n* **1** an umbelliferous plant of Eurasian coasts, having fleshy divided leaves and clusters of small white flowers. **2** **golden samphire.** a Eurasian coastal plant with fleshy leaves and yellow flower heads. **3** **marsh samphire.** another name for **glasswort** (sense 1). **4** any of several other plants of coastal areas. [C16 *sampiere*, from F *herbe de Saint Pierre* Saint Peter's herb]

sample ❶ ('sɑːmpᵊl) *n* **1a** a small part of anything, intended as representative of the whole. **1b** (*as modifier*): *a sample bottle*. **2** Also called: **sampling.** *Statistics*. a set of individuals or items selected from a population and analysed to test hypotheses about or yield estimates of the population. ◆ *vb* **samples, sampling, sampled. 3** (*tr*) to take a sample or samples of. **4** *Music*. **4a** to take a short extract from (one record) and mix it into a different backing track. **4b** to record (a sound) and feed it into a computerized synthesizer so that it can be reproduced at any pitch. [C13: from OF *essample*, from L *exemplum* EXAMPLE]

sampler ('sɑːmplə) *n* **1** a person who takes samples. **2** a piece of embroidery done to show the embroiderer's skill in using many different stitches. **3** *Music*. a piece of electronic equipment used for sampling. **4** a recording comprising a collection of tracks from other albums, to stimulate interest in the featured products.

sampling ('sɑːmplɪŋ) *n* **1** the process of selecting a random sample. **2** a variant of **sample** (sense 2). **3** *Music*. the process of taking a short extract from a record and mixing it into a different backing track.

sampling distribution *n Statistics*. the distribution of a random, experimentally obtained sample.

Samson ('sæmsən) *n* **1** a judge of Israel, who performed feats of strength until he was betrayed by his mistress Delilah (Judges 13–16). **2** any man of outstanding physical strength.

samurai ('sæmʊˌraɪ) *n, pl* **samurai. 1** the Japanese warrior caste from the 11th to the 19th centuries. **2** a member of this aristocratic caste. [C19: from Japanese]

samurai bond *n Finance*. a bond issued in Japan and denominated in yen, available for purchase by nonresidents of Japan. Cf. **shogun bond.**

sanative ('sænətɪv) *adj, n* a less common word for **curative.** [C15: from Med. L *sānātīvus*, from L *sānāre* to heal, from *sānus* healthy]

sanatorium (ˌsænə'tɔːrɪəm) *or US* **sanitarium** *n, pl* **sanatoriums** *or* **sanatoria** (-rɪə). **1** an institution for the medical care and recuperation of persons who are chronically ill. **2** *Brit*. a room as in a boarding school where sick pupils may receive treatment. [C19: from NL, from L *sānāre* to heal]

sanctified ('sæŋktɪˌfaɪd) *adj* **1** consecrated or made holy. **2** sanctimonious.

sanctify ❶ ('sæŋktɪˌfaɪ) *vb* **sanctifies, sanctifying, sanctified.** (*tr*) **1** to make holy. **2** to free from sin. **3** to sanction (an action or practice) as religiously binding: *to sanctify a marriage*. **4** to declare or render (something) productive of or conductive to holiness or grace. [C14: from LL *sanctificāre*, from L *sanctus* holy + *facere* to make]
▸ˌ**sanctifi'cation** *n* ▸'**sanctiˌfier** *n*

sanctimonious ❶ (ˌsæŋktɪ'məʊnɪəs) *adj* affecting piety or making a display of holiness. [C17: from L *sanctimonia* sanctity, from *sanctus* holy]
▸ˌ**sancti'moniously** *adv* ▸ˌ**sancti'moniousness** *or* '**sanctimony** *n*

sanction ❶ ('sæŋkʃən) *n* **1** authorization. **2** aid or encouragement. **3** something, such as an ethical principle, that imparts binding force to a rule, oath, etc. **4** the penalty laid down in a law for contravention of its provisions. **5** (*often pl*) a coercive measure, esp. one taken by one or more states against another guilty of violating international law. ◆ *vb* (*tr*) **6** to give authority to. **7** to confirm. [C16: from L *sanctiō* the establishment of an inviolable decree, from *sancīre* to decree]

sanctitude ('sæŋktɪˌtjuːd) *n* saintliness; holiness.

sanctity ❶ ('sæŋktɪtɪ) *n, pl* **sanctities. 1** the condition of being sanctified; holiness. **2** anything regarded as sanctified or holy. **3** the condition of being inviolable: *the sanctity of marriage*. [C14: from OF *saincteté*, from L *sanctitās*, from *sanctus* holy]

sanctuary ❶ ('sæŋktjʊərɪ) *n, pl* **sanctuaries. 1** a holy place. **2** a consecrated building or shrine. **3** *Old Testament*. **3a** the Israelite temple at Jerusalem. **3b** the tabernacle in which the Ark was enshrined. **4** the chancel, or that part of a sacred building surrounding the main altar. **5a** a sacred building where fugitives were formerly entitled to immunity from arrest or execution. **5b** the immunity so afforded. **6** a place of refuge. **7** a place, protected by law, where animals can live and breed without interference. [C14: from OF *sainctuarie*, from LL *sanctuārium* repository for holy things, from L *sanctus* holy]

sanctuary lamp *n Christianity*. a lamp, usually red, placed in a prominent position in the sanctuary of a church, which, when lit, indicates the presence of the Blessed Sacrament.

sanctum ❶ ('sæŋktəm) *n, pl* **sanctums** *or* **sancta** (-tə). **1** a sacred or holy place. **2** a room or place of total privacy. [C16: from L, from *sanctus* holy]

sanctum sanctorum (sæŋk'tɔːrəm) *n* **1** *Bible*. another term for the **holy of holies. 2** *Often facetious*. an especially private place. [C14: from L, lit.: holy of holies, rendering Heb. *qōdesh haqqodāshīm*]

Sanctus ('sæŋktəs) *n* **1** *Liturgy*. the hymn that occurs immediately after the preface in the celebration of the Eucharist. **2** a musical setting of this. [C14: from the hymn, *Sanctus sanctus sanctus* Holy, holy, holy, from L *sancīre* to consecrate]

Sanctus bell *n Chiefly RC Church*. a bell rung as the opening words of the Sanctus are pronounced.

sand (sænd) *n* **1** loose material consisting of rock or mineral grains, esp. rounded grains of quartz. **2** (*often pl*) a sandy area, esp. on the seashore or in a desert. **3a** a greyish-yellow colour. **3b** (*as adj*): *sand upholstery*. **4** the grains of sandlike material in an hourglass. **5** *US inf*. courage. **6** **the sands are running out.** there is not much time left before the end. ◆ *vb* **7** (*tr*) to smooth or polish the surface of with sandpaper or sand. **8** (*tr*) to sprinkle or cover with or as if with sand. **9** to fill or cause to fill with sand: *the channel sanded up*. [OE]
▸'**sandˌlike** *adj*

sandal ('sændᵊl) *n* **1** a light shoe consisting of a sole held on the foot by thongs, straps, etc. **2** a strap passing over the instep or around the ankle to keep a low shoe on the foot. **3** another name for **sandalwood.** [C14: from L *sandalium*, from Gk, from *sandalon* sandal]
▸'**sandalled** *adj*

sandalwood ('sændᵊlˌwʊd) *or* **sandal** *n* **1** any of a genus of evergreen trees, esp. the **white sandalwood,** of S Asia and Australia, having hard light-coloured heartwood. **2** the wood of any of these trees, which is used for carving, is burned as incense, and yields an aromatic oil used in perfumery. **3** any of various similar trees or their wood, esp. a leguminous tree of SE Asia having dark red wood used as a dye. [C14 *sandal*, from Med. L, from LGk *sandanon*, from Sansk. *candana* sandalwood]

sandarac *or* **sandarach** ('sændəˌræk) *n* **1** a pinaceous tree of NW Africa, having hard fragrant dark wood. **2** a brittle pale yellow transparent resin obtained from the bark of this tree and used in making varnish and incense. [C16 *sandaracha*, from L *sandaraca* red pigment, from Gk *sandarakē*]

sandbag ('sændˌbæg) *n* **1** a sack filled with sand used for protection against gunfire, floodwater, etc., or as ballast in a balloon, etc. **2** a bag filled with sand and used as a weapon. ◆ *vb* **sandbags, sandbagging, sandbagged.** (*tr*) **3** to protect or strengthen with sandbags. **4** to hit with or as if with a sandbag. **5** *Finance*. to obstruct (an unwelcome takeover bid) by having prolonged talks in the hope that a more acceptable bidder will come forward.
▸'**sandˌbagger** *n*

THESAURUS

sample *n* **1a** = **specimen**, cross section, exemplification, illustration, indication, instance, model, pattern, representative, sign ◆ *modifier* **1b** = **test**, illustrative, pilot, representative, specimen, trial ◆ *vb* **3** = **test**, experience, inspect, partake of, taste, try

sanctify *vb* **1, 2** = **consecrate**, absolve, anoint, bless, cleanse, hallow, purify, set apart

sanctimonious *adj* = **holier-than-thou**, canting, false, goody-goody (*inf.*), hypocritical, pharisaical, pi (*Brit. sl.*), pietistic, pious, priggish, self-righteous, self-satisfied, smug, Tartuffian *or* Tartufian, too good to be true, unctuous

sanction *n* **1** = **permission**, allowance, approbation, approval, authority, authorization, backing, confirmation, countenance, endorsement, O.K. or okay (*inf.*), ratification, stamp *or* seal of approval, support **5** *often plural* = **ban**, boycott, coercive measures, embargo, penalty ◆ *vb* **6** = **permit**, allow, approve, authorize, back, countenance, endorse, entitle, lend one's name to, support, vouch for **7** = **confirm**, ratify, warrant
Antonyms *n* ≠ **permission:** ban, disapproval, embargo, prohibition, proscription, refusal, veto ≠ **ban:** approbation, approval, authority, authorization, dispensation, licence, permission ◆ *vb* ≠ **permit:** ban, boycott, disallow, forbid, refuse, reject, veto

sanctity *n* **1** = **holiness**, devotion, godliness, goodness, grace, piety, purity, religiousness, righteousness, sanctitude, spirituality **3** = **sacredness**, inviolability, solemnity

sanctuary *n* **1** = **shrine**, altar, church, Holy of Holies, sanctum, temple **6** = **protection**, asylum, haven, refuge, retreat, shelter **7** = **reserve**, conservation area, national park, nature reserve

sanctum *n* **1** = **sanctuary**, Holy of Holies, shrine **2** = **refuge**, den, private room, retreat, study

sandbank ('sænd,bæŋk) *n* a bank of sand in a sea or river, that may be exposed at low tide.
sand bar *n* a ridge of sand in a river or sea, built up by the action of tides, currents, etc., and often exposed at low tide.
sandblast ('sænd,blɑ:st) *n* **1** a jet of sand blown from a nozzle under air or steam pressure. ◆ *vb* **2** (*tr*) to clean or decorate (a surface) with a sandblast.
▸'**sand,blaster** *n*
sand-blind *adj* not completely blind. Cf. **stone-blind.** [C15: changed (through infl. of SAND) from OE *samblind* (unattested), from *sam-* half, + BLIND]
▸'**sand-,blindness** *n*
sandbox ('sænd,bɒks) *n* **1** a container on a railway locomotive from which sand is released onto the rails to assist the traction. **2** a container of sand for small children to play in.
sandboy ('sænd,bɔɪ) *n* **happy** (*or* **jolly**) **as a sandboy.** very happy; high-spirited.
sand castle *n* a mass of sand moulded into a castle-like shape, esp. by a child on the beach.
sand eel *or* **lance** *n* a silvery eel-like marine spiny-finned fish found burrowing in sand or shingle. Popular name: **launce.**
sander ('sændə) *n* **1** a power-driven tool for smoothing surfaces by rubbing with an abrasive disc. **2** a person who uses such a device.
sanderling ('sændəlɪŋ) *n* a small sandpiper that frequents sandy shores. [C17: ?from SAND + OE *erthling, eorthling* inhabitant of earth]
sand flea *n* another name for the **chigoe** or **sand hopper.**
sandfly ('sænd,flaɪ) *n, pl* **sandflies. 1** any of various small mothlike dipterous flies: the bloodsucking females transmit diseases including leishmaniasis. **2** any of various similar flies.
sandgrouse ('sænd,graʊs) *n* a bird of dry regions of the Old World, having very short feet, a short bill, and long pointed wings and tail.
sand hopper *n* any of various small hopping crustaceans, common in intertidal regions of seashores. Also called: **beach flea, sand flea.**
sandman ('sænd,mæn) *n, pl* **sandmen.** (in folklore) a magical person supposed to put children to sleep by sprinkling sand in their eyes.
sand martin *n* a small brown European songbird with white underparts: it nests in tunnels bored in sand, river banks, etc.
sandpaper ('sænd,peɪpə) *n* **1** a strong paper coated with sand or other abrasive material for smoothing and polishing. ◆ *vb* **2** (*tr*) to polish or grind (a surface) with or as if with sandpaper.
sandpiper ('sænd,paɪpə) *n* **1** any of numerous N hemisphere shore birds having a long slender bill and legs and cryptic plumage. **2** any other bird of the family which includes snipes and woodcocks.
sandpit ('sænd,pɪt) *n* **1** a shallow pit or container holding sand for children to play in. **2** a pit from which sand is extracted.
sandshoe ('sænd,ʃu:) *n* a light canvas shoe with a rubber sole.
sandstone ('sænd,stəʊn) *n* any of a group of common sedimentary rocks consisting of sand grains consolidated with such materials as quartz, haematite, and clay minerals.
sandstorm ('sænd,stɔ:m) *n* a strong wind that whips up clouds of sand, esp. in a desert.
sand trap *n* another name (esp. US) for **bunker** (sense 2).
sand viper *n* a S European viper having a yellowish-brown coloration with a zigzag pattern along the back.
sandwich ('sænwɪdʒ, -wɪtʃ) *n* **1** two or more slices of bread, usually buttered, with a filling of meat, cheese, etc. **2** anything that resembles a sandwich in arrangement. ◆ *vb* (*tr*) **3** to insert tightly between two other things. **4** to put into a sandwich. **5** to place between two dissimilar things. [C18: after 4th Earl of *Sandwich* (1718–92), who ate sandwiches rather than leave the gambling table for meals]
sandwich board *n* one of two connected boards that are hung over the shoulders in front of and behind a person to display advertisements.
sandwich course *n* any of several courses consisting of alternate periods of study and industrial work.
sandwich man *n* a man who carries sandwich boards.
sandwort ('sænd,wɜ:t) *n* **1** any of various plants which grow in dense tufts on sandy soil and have white or pink solitary flowers. **2** any of various related plants.
sandy ('sændɪ) *adj* **sandier, sandiest. 1** consisting of, containing, or covered with sand. **2** (esp. of hair) reddish-yellow. **3** resembling sand in texture.
▸'**sandiness** *n*
sand yacht *n* a wheeled boat with sails, built to be propelled over sand by the wind.
sandy blight *n Austral. inf.* any inflammation and irritation of the eye.
sane ⓣ (seɪn) *adj* **1** free from mental disturbance. **2** having or showing reason or sound sense. [C17: from L *sānus* healthy]
▸'**sanely** *adv* ▸'**saneness** *n*
Sanforized *or* **Sanforised** ('sænfə,raɪzd) *adj Trademark.* (of a fabric) preshrunk using a patented process.
sang (sæŋ) *vb* the past tense of **sing.**

> **USAGE NOTE** See at **ring**[2].

sang-froid ⓣ (*French* sɑ̃frwa) *n* composure; self-possession. [C18: from F, lit.: cold blood]
sangoma (sæŋ'gəʊmə) *n, pl* **sangomas.** *S. African.* a witch doctor. [from Bantu]
Sangraal (sæŋ'greɪl), **Sangrail,** *or* **Sangreal** ('sæŋgrɪəl) *n* another name for the **Holy Grail.**
sangria (sæŋ'gri:ə) *n* a Spanish drink of red wine, sugar, and orange or lemon juice, sometimes laced with brandy. [Sp.: a bleeding]
sanguinary ⓣ ('sæŋgwɪnərɪ) *adj* **1** accompanied by much bloodshed. **2** bloodthirsty. **3** consisting of or stained with blood. [C17: from L *sanguinārius*]
▸'**sanguinarily** *adv* ▸'**sanguinariness** *n*
sanguine ⓣ ('sæŋgwɪn) *adj* **1** cheerful and confident; optimistic. **2** (esp. of the complexion) ruddy in appearance. **3** blood-red. ◆ *n* **4** a red pencil containing ferric oxide, used in drawing. [C14: from L *sanguineus* bloody, from *sanguis* blood]
▸'**sanguinely** *adv* ▸'**sanguineness** *n*
sanguineous (sæŋ'gwɪnɪəs) *adj* **1** of, containing, or associated with blood. **2** a less common word for **sanguine.**
▸**san'guineousness** *n*
Sanhedrin ('sænɪdrɪn) *n Judaism.* the supreme judicial, ecclesiastical, and administrative council of the Jews in New Testament times. [C16: from LHeb., from Gk *sunedrion* council, from *sun-* SYN- + *hedra* seat]
sanies ('seɪnɪ,i:z) *n Pathol.* a thin greenish foul-smelling discharge from a wound, ulcer, etc., containing pus and blood. [C16: from L, from ?]
sanitarium (,sænɪ'teərɪəm) *n, pl* **sanitariums** *or* **sanitaria** (-rɪə). the US word for **sanatorium.** [C19: from L *sānitās* health]
sanitary ⓣ ('sænɪtərɪ) *adj* **1** of or relating to health and measures for the protection of health. **2** free from dirt, germs, etc.; hygienic. [C19: from F *sanitaire*, from L *sānitās* health]
▸**sanitarian** (,sænɪ'teərɪən) *n* ▸'**sanitariness** *n*
sanitary engineering *n* the branch of civil engineering associated with the supply of water, disposal of sewage, and other public health services.
▸**sanitary engineer** *n*
sanitary towel *or esp. US* **napkin** *n* an absorbent pad worn externally by women during menstruation to absorb the menstrual flow.
sanitation (,sænɪ'teɪʃən) *n* the study and use of practical measures for the preservation of public health.
sanitize ⓣ *or* **sanitise** ('sænɪ,taɪz) *vb* **sanitizes, sanitizing, sanitized** *or* **sanitises, sanitising, sanitised.** (*tr*) **1** *Chiefly US & Canad.* to make hygienic, as by sterilizing. **2** to omit unpleasant details from (a news report, document, etc.) to make it more palatable to the recipients.
▸,**saniti'zation** *or* ,**saniti'sation** *n*
sanity ⓣ ('sænɪtɪ) *n* **1** the state of being sane. **2** good sense or soundness of judgment. [C15: from L *sānitās* health, from *sānus* healthy]
sank (sæŋk) *vb* the past tense of **sink.**
sans (sænz) *prep* an archaic word for **without.** [C13: from OF *sanz*, from L *sine* without, but prob. also infl. by L *absentiā* in the absence of]
Sans. *or* **Sansk.** *abbrev. for* Sanskrit.
sans-culotte (,sænzkju'lɒt) *n* **1** (during the French Revolution) **1a** (originally) a revolutionary of the poorer class. **1b** (later) any revolutionary. **2** any revolutionary extremist. [C18: from F, lit.: without knee breeches, because the revolutionaries wore pantaloons or trousers rather than knee breeches]
sansevieria (,sænsɪ'vɪərɪə) *n* any of a genus of herbaceous perennial plants of Old World tropical regions: some are cultivated as house plants for their bayonet-like leaves; others yield a useful fibre. [NL, after Raimondo di Sangro (1710–71), It. scholar and prince of *San Severo*]
Sanskrit ('sænskrɪt) *n* an ancient language of India. It is the oldest recorded member of the Indic branch of the Indo-European family of languages. Although it is used only for religious purposes, it is one of

THESAURUS

sane *adj* **1** = **rational**, all there (*inf.*), *compos mentis*, in one's right mind, in possession of all one's faculties, lucid, mentally sound, of sound mind **2** = **sensible**, balanced, judicious, level-headed, moderate, reasonable, sober, sound
Antonyms *adj* ≠ **rational:** crazy, daft (*inf.*), doolally (*sl.*), insane, loony (*sl.*), mad, mentally ill, *non compos mentis*, nuts (*sl.*), off one's head (*sl.*), round the bend *or* twist (*sl.*) ≠ **sensible:** foolish, stupid, unreasonable, unsound, up the pole (*inf.*)
sang-froid *n* = **composure**, aplomb, calmness, cool (*sl.*), cool-headedness, coolness, equanimity, imperturbability, indifference, nonchalance, phlegm, poise, self-possession, unflappability (*inf.*)
sanguinary *adj* **2** = **savage**, bloodthirsty, cruel, fell, grim, merciless, murderous, pitiless, ruthless **3** = **bloody**, bloodied, flowing with blood, gory
sanguine *adj* **1** = **cheerful**, animated, assured, buoyant, confident, hopeful, in good heart, lively, optimistic, spirited **2** = **ruddy**, florid, red, rubicund
Antonyms *adj* ≠ **cheerful:** despondent, dispirited, down, gloomy, heavy-hearted, melancholy, pessimistic ≠ **ruddy:** anaemic, ashen, pale, pallid, peely-wally (*Scot.*)
sanitary *adj* **2** = **hygienic**, clean, germ-free, healthy, salubrious, unpolluted, wholesome
sanitize *vb* **1** = **sterilize**, cleanse, decontaminate, disinfect, fumigate, pasteurize, purge, purify
sanity *n* **1** = **mental health**, normality, rationality, reason, right mind (*inf.*), saneness, stability **2** = **good sense**, common sense, judiciousness, level-headedness, rationality, sense, soundness of judgment
Antonyms *n* ≠ **mental health:** craziness, dementia, insanity, lunacy, madness, mental derangement, mental illness ≠ **good sense:** folly, senselessness, stupidity

the official languages of India. [C17: from Sansk. *samskrta* perfected, lit.: put together]
▸**San'skritic** *adj*

sans serif *or* **sanserif** (sæn'serɪf) *n* a style of printer's typeface in which the characters have no serifs.

Santa ('sæntə) *n Inf.* short for **Santa Claus.**

Santa Claus ('sæntə ˌklɔːz) *n* the legendary patron saint of children, commonly identified with Saint Nicholas. Often shortened to **Santa.** Also called: **Father Christmas.**

Santa Gertrudis ('sæntə gə'truːdɪs) *n* one of a breed of red beef cattle developed in Texas.

santonica (sæn'tɒnɪkə) *n* **1** an oriental wormwood plant. **2** the dried flower heads of this plant, formerly used as a vermifuge. ◆ Also called: **wormseed.** [C17: NL, from LL *herba santonica* herb of the *Santones* (prob. wormwood), from L *Santonī* a people of Aquitania]

santonin ('sæntənɪn) *n* a white crystalline soluble substance extracted from the dried flower heads of santonica and used in medicine as an anthelmintic. [C19: from SANTONICA + -IN]

sap[1] ❶ (sæp) *n* **1** a solution of mineral salts, sugars, etc., that circulates in a plant. **2** any vital body fluid. **3** energy; vigour. **4** *Sl.* a gullible person. **5** another name for **sapwood.** ◆ *vb* **saps, sapping, sapped.** (*tr*) **6** to drain of sap. [OE *sæp*]

sap[2] ❶ (sæp) *n* **1** a deep and narrow trench used to approach or undermine an enemy position. ◆ *vb* **saps, sapping, sapped. 2** to undermine (a fortification, etc.) by digging saps. **3** (*tr*) to weaken. [C16 *zappe*, from It. *zappa* spade, from ?]

sapele (sə'piːlɪ) *n* **1** any of various W African trees yielding a hard timber resembling mahogany. **2** the timber of such a tree, used to make furniture. [C20: West African name]

sapid ('sæpɪd) *adj* **1** having a pleasant taste. **2** agreeable or engaging. [C17: from L *sapidus*, from *sapere* to taste]
▸**sapidity** (sə'pɪdɪtɪ) *n*

sapient ❶ ('seɪpɪənt) *adj Often used ironically.* wise or sagacious. [C15: from L *sapere* to taste]
▸**'sapience** *n* ▸**'sapiently** *adv*

sapiential (ˌseɪpɪ'ɛnʃəl) *adj* showing, having, or providing wisdom.

sapling ('sæplɪŋ) *n* **1** a young tree. **2** *Literary.* a youth.

sapodilla (ˌsæpə'dɪlə) *n* **1** a large tropical American evergreen tree, the latex of which yields chicle. **2** Also called: **sapodilla plum.** the edible brown rough-skinned fruit of this tree. [C17: from Sp. *zapotillo*, dim. of *zapote* sapodilla fruit, from Nahuatl *tsapotl*]

saponaceous (ˌsæpəʊ'neɪʃəs) *adj* resembling soap. [C18: from NL, from L *sāpō* soap]

saponify (sə'pɒnɪˌfaɪ) *vb* **saponifies, saponifying, saponified.** *Chem.* **1** to undergo or cause to undergo a process in which a fat is converted into a soap by treatment with alkali. **2** to undergo or cause to undergo a reaction in which an ester is hydrolysed to an acid and an alcohol as a result of treatment with an alkali. [C19: from F *saponifier*, from L *sāpō* soap]
▸**saˌponifi'cation** *n*

saponin ('sæpənɪn) *n* any of a group of plant glycosides with a steroid structure that foam when shaken and are used in detergents. [C19: from F *saponine*, from L *sāpō* soap]

sappanwood *or* **sapanwood** ('sæpənˌwʊd) *n* **1** a small tree of S Asia producing wood that yields a red dye. **2** the wood of this tree. [C16: *sapan*, via Du. from Malay *sapang*]

sapper ('sæpə) *n* **1** a soldier who digs trenches, etc. **2** (in the British Army) a private of the Royal Engineers.

Sapphic ('sæfɪk) *adj* **1** *Prosody.* denoting a metre associated with Sappho, 6th-century B.C. Greek poetess of Lesbos. **2** of or relating to Sappho or her poetry. **3** lesbian. ◆ *n* **4** *Prosody.* a verse, line, or stanza written in the Sapphic form of classical lyric poetry.

sapphire ('sæfaɪə) *n* **1a** any precious corundum gemstone that is not red, esp. the highly valued transparent blue variety. **1b** (*as modifier*): *a sapphire ring.* **2a** the blue colour of sapphire. **2b** (*as adj*): *sapphire eyes.* **3** (*modifier*) denoting a forty-fifth anniversary: *our sapphire wedding.* [C13 *safir*, from OF, from L *sapphīrus*, from Gk *sappheiros*, ?from Sansk. *śanipriya*, lit.: beloved of the planet Saturn]

sappy ('sæpɪ) *adj* **sappier, sappiest. 1** (of plants) full of sap. **2** full of energy or vitality.

sapro- *or before a vowel* **sapr-** *combining form.* indicating dead or decaying matter: *saprogenic.* [from Gk *sapros* rotten]

saprogenic (ˌsæprəʊ'dʒɛnɪk) *or* **saprogenous** (sæ'prɒdʒɪnəs) *adj* **1** producing or resulting from decay. **2** growing on decaying matter.

saprophyte ('sæprəʊˌfaɪt) *n* any plant that lives and feeds on dead organic matter.
▸**saprophytic** (ˌsæprəʊ'fɪtɪk) *adj*

saprotroph ('sæprəʊtrəʊf) *n* any organism, esp. a fungus or bacterium, that lives and feeds on dead organic matter. Also called: **saprobe, saprobiont.**
▸**saprotrophic** (ˌsæprəʊ'trəʊfɪk) *adj* ▸ˌ**sapro'trophically** *adv*

saprozoic (ˌsæprəʊ'zəʊɪk) *adj* (of animals or plants) feeding on dead organic matter.

sapsucker ('sæpˌsʌkə) *n* either of two North American woodpeckers that have white wing patches and feed on the sap from trees.

sapwood ('sæpˌwʊd) *n* the soft wood, just beneath the bark in tree trunks, that consists of living tissue.

sarabande *or* **saraband** ('særəˌbænd) *n* **1** a decorous 17th-century courtly dance. **2** a piece of music composed for or in the rhythm of this dance, in slow triple time. [C17: from F *sarabande*, from Sp. *zarabanda*, from ?]

Saracen ('særəsᵊn) *n* **1** *History.* a member of one of the nomadic Arabic tribes, esp. of the Syrian desert. **2a** a Muslim, esp. one who opposed the crusades. **2b** (in later use) any Arab. ◆ *adj* **3** of or relating to Arabs of either of these periods, regions, or types. [C13: from OF *Sarrazin*, from LL *Saracēnus*, from LGk *Sarakēnos*, ?from Ar. *sharq* sunrise]
▸**Saracenic** (ˌsærə'sɛnɪk) *adj*

sarcasm ❶ ('sɑːkæzəm) *n* **1** mocking or ironic language intended to convey scorn or insult. **2** the use or tone of such language. [C16: from LL *sarcasmus*, from Gk, from *sarkazein* to rend the flesh, from *sarx* flesh]

sarcastic ❶ (sɑː'kæstɪk) *adj* **1** characterized by sarcasm. **2** given to the use of sarcasm.
▸**sar'castically** *adv*

sarcenet *or* **sarsenet** ('sɑːsnɪt) *n* a fine soft silk fabric used for clothing, ribbons, etc. [C15: from OF *sarzinet*, from *Sarrazin* SARACEN]

sarco- *or before a vowel* **sarc-** *combining form.* indicating flesh: *sarcoma.* [from Gk *sark-*, *sarx* flesh]

sarcocarp ('sɑːkəʊˌkɑːp) *n Bot.* the fleshy mesocarp of such fruits as the peach or plum.

sarcoma (sɑː'kəʊmə) *n, pl* **sarcomata** (-mətə) *or* **sarcomas.** *Pathol.* a usually malignant tumour arising from connective tissue. [C17: via NL from Gk *sarkōma* fleshy growth]
▸**sar'comatous** *adj*

sarcomatosis (sɑːˌkəʊmə'təʊsɪs) *n Pathol.* a condition characterized by the development of several sarcomas at various bodily sites. [C19: see SARCOMA, -OSIS]

sarcophagus (sɑː'kɒfəgəs) *n, pl* **sarcophagi** (-ˌgaɪ) *or* **sarcophaguses.** a stone or marble coffin or tomb, esp. one bearing sculpture or inscriptions. [C17: via L from Gk *sarkophagos* flesh-devouring; from the type of stone used, which was believed to destroy the flesh of corpses]

sarcoplasm ('sɑːkəʊˌplæzəm) *n* the cytoplasm of a muscle fibre.
▸ˌ**sarco'plasmic** *adj*

sarcous ('sɑːkəs) *adj* (of tissue) muscular or fleshy. [C19: from Gk *sarx* flesh]

sard (sɑːd) *or* **sardius** ('sɑːdɪəs) *n* an orange, red, or brown variety of chalcedony, used as a gemstone. Also called: **sardine.** [C14: from L *sarda*, from Gk *sardios* stone from Sardis]

sardar *or* **sirdar** (sə'dɑː) *n* (in India) **1** a title used before the name of Sikh men. **2** a leader. [Hindi, from Persian]

sardine[1] (sɑː'diːn) *n, pl* **sardines** *or* **sardine. 1** any of various small food fishes of the herring family, esp. a young pilchard. **2 like sardines.** very closely crowded together. [C15: via OF from L *sardīna*, dim. of *sarda* a fish suitable for pickling]

sardine[2] ('sɑːdiːn) *n* another name for **sard.** [C14: from LL *sardinus*, from Gk *sardinos lithos* Sardian stone, from *Sardeis* Sardis]

Sardinian (sɑː'dɪnɪən) *adj* **1.** of or relating to Sardinia, Italian island in the Mediterranean, its inhabitants, or their language. ◆ *n* **2** a native or inhabitant of Sardinia. **3** the spoken language of Sardinia, sometimes regarded as a dialect of Italian but containing many loan words from Spanish.

sardonic ❶ (sɑː'dɒnɪk) *adj* characterized by irony, mockery, or derision. [C17: from F, from L, from Gk *sardonios* derisive, lit.: of Sardinia, alteration of Homeric *sardanios* scornful (laughter or smile)]
▸**sar'donically** *adv* ▸**sar'donicism** *n*

sardonyx ('sɑːdənɪks) *n* a variety of chalcedony with alternating reddish-brown and white parallel bands. [C14: via L from Gk *sardonux*, ?from *sardion* SARD + *onux* nail]

sargassum (sɑː'gæsəm) *n* a floating brown seaweed having ribbon-like fronds containing air sacs, esp. abundant in the **Sargasso Sea** in the N Atlantic. [C16: from Port. *sargaço* from ?]

sarge (sɑːdʒ) *n Inf.* sergeant.

sari *or* **saree** ('sɑːrɪ) *n, pl* **saris** *or* **sarees.** the traditional dress of women of India, Pakistan, etc., consisting of a very long piece of cloth swathed around the body. [C18: from Hindi *sārī*, from Sansk. *śāṭī*]

THESAURUS

sap[1] *n* **2** = **vital fluid**, animating force, essence, lifeblood **4** *Slang* = **fool**, chump (*inf.*), drip (*inf.*), idiot, jerk (*sl., chiefly US & Canad.*), muggins (*Brit. sl.*), nincompoop, numskull *or* numbskull, oaf, prat (*sl.*), simpleton, twit (*inf.*), wally (*sl.*), weakling

sap[2] *vb* **3** = **weaken**, bleed, deplete, devitalize, drain, enervate, erode, exhaust, rob, undermine, wear down

sapience *n Often used ironically* = **wisdom**, acuity, acuteness, discernment, insight, mother wit, nous (*Brit. sl.*), perspicacity, sagacity, sense, shrewdness, suss (*sl.*), understanding

sapient *adj Often used ironically* = **wise**, acute, canny, discerning, discriminating, intelligent, judicious, knowing, long-headed, perspicacious, sagacious, sage, shrewd, would-be-wise

sarcasm *n* **1** = **irony**, bitterness, causticness, contempt, cynicism, derision, mockery, mordancy, ridicule, satire, scorn, sneering, venom, vitriol

sarcastic *adj* **1, 2** = **ironical**, acerbic, acid, acrimonious, backhanded, bitchy (*inf.*), biting, caustic, contemptuous, cutting, cynical, derisive, disparaging, mocking, mordacious, mordant, sardonic, sarky (*Brit. inf.*), satirical, sharp, sneering, taunting, vitriolic

sardonic *adj* = **mocking**, bitter, cynical, derisive, dry, ironical, jeering, malevolent, malicious, malignant, mordacious, mordant, sarcastic, sneering, wry

sarking ('sɑːkɪŋ) *n Scot., northern English, & NZ.* flat planking supporting the roof cladding of a building. [C15 in England: from Scot. *sark* shirt]
sarky ('sɑːkɪ) *adj* **sarkier, sarkiest.** *Brit. inf.* sarcastic.
sarmentose (sɑː'mɛntəus) *or* **sarmentous** (sɑː'mɛntəs) *adj* (of plants such as the strawberry) having stems in the form of runners. [C18: from L *sarmentōsus* full of twigs, from *sarmentum* brushwood, from *sarpere* to prune]
sarnie ('sɑːnɪ) *n Brit. inf.* a sandwich. [C20: prob. from N or dialect pronunciation of first syllable of *sandwich*]
sarod (sæ'rəud) *n* an Indian stringed musical instrument that may be played with a bow or plucked. [C19: from Hindi]
sarong (sə'rɒŋ) *n* **1** a garment worn by men and women in the Malay Archipelago, Sri Lanka, etc., consisting of a long piece of cloth tucked around the waist or under the armpits. **2** a western adaptation of this garment, worn by women as beachwear. [C19: from Malay, lit.: sheath]
saros ('seɪrɒs) *n* a cycle of about 18 years 11 days (6585.32 days) in which eclipses of the sun and moon occur in the same sequence. [C19: from Gk, from Babylonian *šāru* 3600 (years); modern use apparently based on mistaken interpretation of *šāru* as a period of 18½ years]
sarrusophone (sə'ruːzə,fəun) *n* a wind instrument resembling the oboe but made of brass. [C19: after *Sarrus*, F bandmaster, who invented it (1856)]
sarsaparilla (,sɑːsəpə'rɪlə) *n* **1** any of a genus of tropical American prickly climbing plants having large aromatic roots and heart-shaped leaves. **2** the dried roots of any of these plants, formerly used as a medicine. **3** a nonalcoholic drink prepared from these roots. [C16: from Sp. *sarzaparrilla*, from *zarza* a bramble + *-parrilla*, from *parra* a climbing plant]
sarsen ('sɑːsᵊn) *n* **1** *Geol.* a boulder of silicified sandstone, probably of Tertiary age. **2** such a stone used in a megalithic monument. ◆ Also called: **greywether.** [C17: prob. a var. of SARACEN]
sarsenet ('sɑːsnɪt) *n* a variant spelling of **sarcenet.**
sartorial (sɑː'tɔːrɪəl) *adj* **1** of or relating to a tailor or to tailoring. **2** *Anat.* of the sartorius. [C19: from LL *sartōrius* from L *sartor* a patcher, from *sarcīre* to patch]
▸**sar'torially** *adv*
sartorius (sɑː'tɔːrɪəs) *n, pl* **sartorii** (-'tɔːrɪ,aɪ). *Anat.* a long ribbon-shaped muscle that aids in flexing the knee. [C18: NL, from *sartorius musculus*, lit.: tailor's muscle, because it is used when one sits in the cross-legged position in which tailors traditionally sat while sewing]
Sarum use *n* the distinctive local rite or system of rites used at Salisbury cathedral in late medieval times. [from *Sarum*, ancient name of Salisbury]
SAS *abbrev. for* Special Air Service.
sash¹ (sæʃ) *n* a long piece of ribbon, etc., worn around the waist or over one shoulder, as a symbol of rank. [C16: from Ar. *shāsh* muslin]
sash² (sæʃ) *n* **1** a frame that contains the panes of a window or door. **2** a complete frame together with panes of glass. ◆ *vb* **3** *(tr)* to furnish with a sash, sashes, or sash windows. [C17: orig. pl *sashes*, var. of *shashes*, from CHASSIS]
sashay (sæ'ʃeɪ) *vb (intr) Inf., chiefly US & Canad.* **1** to move, walk, or glide along casually. **2** to move or walk in a showy way; parade. [C19: from an alteration of *chassé*, a gliding dance step]
sash cord *n* a strong cord connecting a sash weight to a sliding sash.
sashimi ('sæʃɪmɪ) *n* a Japanese dish of thin fillets of raw fish. [C19: from Japanese *sashi* pierce + *mi* flesh]
sash saw *n* a small tenon saw used for cutting sashes.
sash weight *n* a weight used to counterbalance the weight of a sliding sash in a sash window and thus hold it in position at any height.
sash window *n* a window consisting of two sashes placed one above the other so that they can be slid past each other.
sasquatch ('sæs,kwætʃ) *n* (in Canadian folklore) in British Columbia, a hairy beast or manlike monster said to leave huge footprints. [from Amerind]
sass (sæs) *US & Canad. inf.* ◆ *n* **1** impudent talk or behaviour. ◆ *vb (intr)* **2** to talk or answer back in such a way. [C20: back formation from SASSY]
sassaby ('sæsəbɪ) *n, pl* **sassabies.** an African antelope of grasslands and semideserts, having angular curved horns. [C19: from Bantu *tshêsêbê*]
sassafras ('sæsə,fræs) *n* **1** an aromatic deciduous tree of North America, having three-lobed leaves and dark blue fruits. **2** the aromatic dried root bark of this tree, used as a flavouring, and yielding **sassafras oil. 3** *Austral.* any of several unrelated trees having a similar fragrant bark. [C16: from Sp. *sasafras*, from ?]
Sassenach ('sæsə,næx) *n Scot. & occasionally Irish.* an English person or a Lowland Scot. [C18: from Gaelic *Sassunach*, from LL *saxonēs* Saxons]
sassy ('sæsɪ) *adj* **sassier, sassiest.** *US & Canad. inf.* insolent; impertinent. [C19: var. of SAUCY]
▸'**sassily** *adv* ▸'**sassiness** *n*
sat (sæt) *vb* the past tense and past participle of **sit.**
Sat. *abbrev. for:* **1** Saturday. **2** Saturn.
Satan ❶ ('seɪtᵊn) *n* the devil, adversary of God, and tempter of mankind: sometimes identified with Lucifer (Luke 4:5–8). [OE, from LL, from Gk, from Heb.: plotter, from *sātan* to plot against]
satanic ❶ (sə'tænɪk) *adj* **1** of or relating to Satan. **2** supremely evil or wicked.
▸**sa'tanically** *adv*
Satanism ('seɪtᵊ,nɪzəm) *n* **1** the worship of Satan. **2** a form of such worship which includes blasphemous parodies of Christian prayers, etc. **3** a satanic disposition.
▸'**Satanist** *n, adj*
SATB *abbrev. for* soprano, alto, tenor, bass: a combination of voices in choral music.
satchel ('sætʃəl) *n* a rectangular bag, usually made of leather or cloth and provided with a shoulder strap, used for carrying school books. [C14: from OF *sachel*, from LL *saccellus*, from L *saccus* SACK¹]
▸'**satchelled** *adj*
sate¹ ❶ (seɪt) *vb* **sates, sating, sated.** *(tr)* **1** to satisfy (a desire or appetite) fully. **2** to supply beyond capacity or desire. [OE *sadian*]
sate² (sæt, seɪt) *vb Arch.* a past tense and past participle of **sit.**
sateen (sæ'tiːn) *n* a glossy linen or cotton fabric that resembles satin. [C19: changed from SATIN, on the model of VELVETEEN]
satellite ❶ ('sætᵊ,laɪt) *n* **1** a celestial body orbiting around a planet or star: *the earth is a satellite of the sun.* **2** a man-made device orbiting around the earth, moon, or another planet transmitting to earth scientific information or used for communication. **3** a country or political unit under the domination of a foreign power. **4** a subordinate area that is dependent upon a larger adjacent town. **5** *(modifier)* subordinate to or dependent upon another: *a satellite nation.* **6** *(modifier)* of, used in, or relating to the transmission of television signals from a satellite to the house: *a satellite dish aerial.* [C16: from L *satelles* an attendant, prob. of Etruscan origin]
satiable ('seɪʃɪəbᵊl) *adj* capable of being satiated.
▸,**satia'bility** *n* ▸'**satiably** *adv*
satiate ❶ ('seɪʃɪ,eɪt) *vb* **satiates, satiating, satiated.** *(tr)* **1** to fill or supply beyond capacity or desire. **2** to supply to capacity. [C16: from L *satiāre* to satisfy, from *satis* enough]
▸,**sati'ation** *n*
satiety ❶ (sə'taɪɪtɪ) *n* the state of being satiated. [C16: from L *satietās*, from *satis* enough]
satin ('sætɪn) *n* **1** a fabric of silk, rayon, etc., closely woven to show much of the warp, giving a smooth glossy appearance. **2** *(modifier)* like satin in texture: *a satin finish.* [C14: via OF from Ar. *zaitūnī*, Ar. rendering of Chinese *Tseutung* (now *Tsinkiang*), port from which the cloth was prob. first exported]
▸'**satiny** *adj*
satinet *or* **satinette** (,sætɪ'nɛt) *n* a thin satin or satin-like fabric. [C18: from F: small satin]
satinflower ('sætɪn,flauə) *n* another name for **greater stitchwort** (see **stitchwort**).
satinwood ('sætɪn,wud) *n* **1** a tree that occurs in the East Indies and has hard wood with a satiny texture. **2** the wood of this tree, used in veneering, marquetry, etc.
satire ❶ ('sætaɪə) *n* **1** a novel, play, etc., in which topical issues, folly, or evil are held up to scorn by means of ridicule. **2** the genre constituted by such works. **3** the use of ridicule, irony, etc., to create such an effect. [C16: from L *satira* a mixture, from *satur* sated, from *satis* enough]
satirical ❶ (sə'tɪrɪkᵊl) *or* **satiric** *adj* **1** of, relating to, or containing satire. **2** given to the use of satire.
▸**sa'tirically** *adv*
satirist ('sætərɪst) *n* **1** a person who writes satire. **2** a person given to the use of satire.
satirize ❶ *or* **satirise** ('sætə,raɪz) *vb* **satirizes, satirizing, satirized** *or* **satirises, satirising, satirised.** to deride (a person or thing) by means of satire.
▸,**satiri'zation** *or* ,**satiri'sation** *n*
satisfaction ❶ (,sætɪs'fækʃən) *n* **1** the act of satisfying or state of being

THESAURUS

Satan *n* = **The Devil**, Apollyon, Beelzebub, Lord of the Flies, Lucifer, Mephistopheles, Old Nick (*inf.*), Old Scratch (*inf.*), Prince of Darkness, The Evil One
satanic *adj* **2** = **evil**, accursed, black, demoniac, demoniacal, demonic, devilish, diabolic, fiendish, hellish, infernal, inhuman, iniquitous, malevolent, malignant, wicked
Antonyms *adj* benevolent, benign, divine, godly, holy
sate¹ *vb* **1** = **satisfy**, indulge to the full, satiate, slake **2** = **overfill**, cloy, glut, gorge, saturate, sicken, surfeit, weary
satellite *n* **1** = **moon 2** = **sputnik**, communications satellite ◆ *adj* **5** = **dependent**, client, puppet, subordinate, tributary, vassal
satiate *vb* **1** = **glut**, cloy, gorge, jade, nauseate, overfill, stuff, surfeit **2** = **satisfy**, sate, slake
satiety *n* = **fullness**, gratification, repletion, satiation, satisfaction, saturation, surfeit
satire *n* **1** = **mockery**, burlesque, caricature, irony, lampoon, parody, pasquinade, raillery, ridicule, sarcasm, send-up (*Brit. inf.*), skit, spoof (*inf.*), takeoff (*inf.*), travesty, wit
satirical *adj* **1** = **mocking**, biting, bitter, burlesque, caustic, censorious, cutting, cynical, incisive, ironical, mordacious, mordant, pungent, Rabelaisian, sarcastic, sardonic, taunting, vitriolic
satirize *vb* = **ridicule**, abuse, burlesque, censure, criticize, deride, hold up to ridicule, lampoon, lash, parody, pillory, send up (*Brit. inf.*), take off (*inf.*), travesty
satisfaction *n* **1** = **contentment**, comfort,

satisfied. **2** the fulfilment of a desire. **3** the pleasure obtained from such fulfilment. **4** a source of fulfilment. **5** compensation for a wrong done or received. **6** *RC Church, Church of England.* the performance of a penance. **7** *Christianity.* the atonement for sin by the death of Christ.

satisfactory Ⓣ (ˌsætɪs'fæktərɪ) *adj* **1** adequate or suitable; acceptable. **2** giving satisfaction. **3** constituting or involving atonement or expiation for sin.
▸ˌ**satis'factorily** *adv*

satisfice ('sætɪsˌfaɪs) *vb* **satisfices, satisficing, satisficed. 1** (*intr*) to act in such a way as to satisfy the minimum requirements for achieving a particular result. **2** (*tr*) *Obs.* to satisfy. [C16: altered from SATISFY]
▸'**satisˌficer** *n*

satisficing behaviour *n Econ.* the form of behaviour demonstrated by firms who seek satisfactory profits and satisfactory growth rather than maximum profits.

satisfy Ⓣ ('sætɪsˌfaɪ) *vb* **satisfies, satisfying, satisfied.** (*mainly tr*) **1** (*also intr*) to fulfil the desires or needs of (a person). **2** to provide amply for (a need or desire). **3** to convince. **4** to dispel (a doubt). **5** to make reparation to or for. **6** to discharge or pay off (a debt) to (a creditor). **7** to fulfil the requirements of; comply with: *you must satisfy the terms of your lease.* **8** *Maths, logic.* to fulfil the conditions of (a theorem, assumption, etc.); to yield a truth by substitution of the given value. [C15: from OF *satisfier,* from L *satisfacere,* from *satis* enough + *facere* to make]
▸'**satisˌfiable** *adj* ▸'**satisˌfying** *adj* ▸'**satisˌfyingly** *adv*

satori (sə'tɔːrɪ) *n Zen Buddhism.* a state of sudden intuitive enlightenment. [from Japanese]

satrap ('sætræp) *n* **1** (in ancient Persia) a provincial governor. **2** a subordinate ruler. [C14: from L *satrapa,* from Gk *satrapēs,* from OPersian *khshathrapāvan,* lit.: protector of the land]

satrapy ('sætrəpɪ) *n, pl* **satrapies.** the province, office, or period of rule of a satrap.

SATs (sæts) *pl n Brit. education. acronym for* standard assessment tasks: see **assessment tests.**

satsuma (sæt'suːmə) *n* **1** a small citrus tree cultivated, esp. in Japan, for its edible fruit. **2** the fruit of this tree, which has easily separable segments. [from name of former province of Japan]

saturable ('sætʃərəbəl) *adj Chem.* capable of being saturated.
▸ˌ**satura'bility** *n*

saturate Ⓣ *vb* ('sætʃəˌreɪt), **saturates, saturating, saturated. 1** to fill, soak, or imbue totally. **2** to make (a chemical compound, solution, etc.) saturated or (of a compound, etc.) to become saturated. **3** (*tr*) *Mil.* to bomb or shell heavily. ◆ *adj* ('sætʃərɪt, -ˌreɪt). **4** saturated. [C16: from L *saturāre,* from *satur* sated, from *satis* enough]

saturated ('sætʃəˌreɪtɪd) *adj* **1** (of a solution or solvent) containing the maximum amount of solute that can normally be dissolved at a given temperature and pressure. **2** (of a chemical compound) containing no multiple bonds: *a saturated hydrocarbon.* **3** (of a fat) containing a high proportion of fatty acids having single bonds. **4** (of a vapour) containing the maximum amount of gaseous material at a given temperature and pressure.

saturation (ˌsætʃə'reɪʃən) *n* **1** the act of saturating or the state of being saturated. **2** *Chem.* the state of a chemical compound, solution, or vapour when it is saturated. **3** *Meteorol.* the state of the atmosphere when it can hold no more water vapour at its particular temperature and pressure. **4** the attribute of a colour that enables an observer to judge its proportion of pure chromatic colour. **5** the level beyond which demand for a product or service is not expected to rise. ◆ *modifier.* **6** denoting the maximum possible intensity of coverage of an area: *saturation bombing.*

saturation point *n* the point at which no more can be absorbed, accommodated, used, etc.

Saturday ('sætədɪ) *n* the seventh and last day of the week: the Jewish Sabbath. [OE *sæternes dæg,* translation of L *Sāturnī diēs* day of Saturn]

Saturn[1] ('sætɜːn) *n* the Roman god of agriculture and vegetation. Greek counterpart: **Cronus.**

Saturn[2] ('sætɜːn) *n* **1** the sixth planet from the sun, around which revolve planar concentric rings (**Saturn's rings**) consisting of small frozen particles. **2** the alchemical name for **lead**[2].
▸**Saturnian** (sæ'tɜːnɪən) *adj*

Saturnalia (ˌsætə'neɪlɪə) *n, pl* **Saturnalia** *or* **Saturnalias. 1** an ancient Roman festival celebrated in December: renowned for its general merrymaking. **2** (*sometimes not cap.*) a period or occasion of wild revelry. [C16: from L *Sāturnālis* relating to SATURN[1]]
▸ˌ**Satur'nalian** *adj*

saturnine Ⓣ ('sætəˌnaɪn) *adj* **1** having a gloomy temperament. **2** *Arch.* **2a** of or relating to lead. **2b** having lead poisoning. [C15: from F *saturnin,* from Med. L *sāturnīnus* (unattested), from L *Sāturnus* Saturn, from the gloomy influence attributed to the planet Saturn]
▸'**saturˌninely** *adv*

satyagraha ('sʌtjɑːgrʌhɑː) *n* the policy of nonviolent resistance adopted by Mahatma Gandhi to oppose British rule in India. [via Hindi from Sansk., lit.: insistence on truth, from *satya* truth + *agraha* fervour]

satyr ('sætə) *n* **1** *Greek myth.* one of a class of sylvan deities, represented as goatlike men who drank and danced in the train of Dionysus and chased the nymphs. **2** a man who has strong sexual desires. **3** any of various butterflies, having dark wings often marked with eyespots. [C14: from L *satyrus,* from Gk *saturos*]
▸**satyric** (sə'tɪrɪk) *adj*

satyriasis (ˌsætɪ'raɪəsɪs) *n* a neurotic compulsion in men to have sexual intercourse with many women without being able to have lasting relationships with them. [C17: via NL from Gk *saturiasis*]

sauce Ⓣ (sɔːs) *n* **1** any liquid or semiliquid preparation eaten with food to enhance its flavour. **2** anything that adds piquancy. **3** *US & Canad.* stewed fruit. **4** *Inf.* impudent language or behaviour. ◆ *vb* **sauces, saucing, sauced.** (*tr*) **5** to prepare (food) with sauce. **6** to add zest to. **7** *Inf.* to be saucy to. [C14: via OF from L *salsus* salted, from *sal* salt]

saucepan ('sɔːspən) *n* a metal or enamel pan with a long handle and often a lid, used for cooking food.

saucer ('sɔːsə) *n* **1** a small round dish on which a cup is set. **2** any similar dish. [C14: from OF *saussier* container for SAUCE]
▸'**saucerful** *n*

saucy Ⓣ ('sɔːsɪ) *adj* **saucier, sauciest. 1** impertinent. **2** pert; jaunty: *a saucy hat.*
▸'**saucily** *adv* ▸'**sauciness** *n*

sauerkraut ('saʊəˌkraʊt) *n* finely shredded cabbage which has been fermented in brine. [G, from *sauer* sour + *Kraut* cabbage]

sauger ('sɔːgə) *n* a small North American pikeperch with a spotted dorsal fin: valued as a food and game fish. [C19: from ?]

sault (suː) *n Canad.* a waterfall or rapids. [C17: from Canad. F, from F *saut* a leap]

sauna ('sɔːnə) *n* **1** an invigorating bath originating in Finland in which the bather is subjected to hot steam, usually followed by a cold plunge. **2** the place in which such a bath is taken. [C20: from Finnish]

saunter Ⓣ ('sɔːntə) *vb* **1** (*intr*) to walk in a casual manner; stroll. ◆ *n* **2** a leisurely pace or stroll. [C17 (meaning: to wander aimlessly), C15 (to muse): from ?]
▸'**saunterer** *n*

-saur *or* **-saurus** *n combining form.* lizard: *dinosaur.* [from NL *saurus*]

saurian ('sɔːrɪən) *adj* **1** of or resembling a lizard. ◆ *n* **2** a former name for **lizard.** [C15: from NL *Sauria,* from Gk *sauros*]

saury ('sɔːrɪ) *n, pl* **sauries.** a fish of tropical and temperate seas, having an elongated body and long toothed jaws. Also called: **skipper.** [C18: ? from LL *saurus,* from ?]

sausage ('sɒsɪdʒ) *n* **1** finely minced meat, esp. pork or beef, mixed with fat, cereal, and seasonings (**sausage meat**), and packed into a tube-

THESAURUS

complacency, content, contentedness, ease, enjoyment, gratification, happiness, peace of mind, pleasure, pride, repletion, satiety, well-being **2** = **fulfilment**, achievement, appeasing, assuaging, gratification, resolution, settlement **5** = **compensation**, amends, atonement, damages, indemnification, justice, recompense, redress, reimbursement, remuneration, reparation, requital, restitution, settlement, vindication
Antonyms *n* ≠ **contentment:** annoyance, discontent, displeasure, dissatisfaction, frustration, grief, misgivings, pain, shame, unhappiness ≠ **compensation:** injury

satisfactory *adj* **1** = **adequate**, acceptable, all right, average, competent, fair, good enough, passable, sufficient, suitable, up to scratch, up to standard, up to the mark
Antonyms *adj* bad, below par, inadequate, insufficient, leaving a lot to be desired, mediocre, no great shakes (*inf.*), not up to scratch (*inf.*), poor, sub-standard, unacceptable, unsatisfactory, unsuitable

satisfied *adj* **1** = **contented**, at ease, complacent, content, convinced, easy in one's mind, happy, like the cat that swallowed the canary (*inf.*), pacified, positive, smug, sure

satisfy *vb* **1** = **be sufficient**, answer, be adequate, be enough, come up to expectations, cut the mustard, do, fill the bill (*inf.*), fulfil, meet, qualify, serve, serve the purpose, suffice **2** = **content**, appease, assuage, feed, fill, gratify, indulge, mollify, pacify, pander to, please, quench, sate, satiate, slake, surfeit **3, 4** = **convince**, assure, dispel (someone's) doubts, persuade, put (someone's) mind at rest, quiet, reassure **5** = **compensate**, atone, indemnify, make good, make reparation for, recompense, remunerate, requite, reward **6** = **pay (off)**, settle, square up **7** = **fulfil**, answer, comply with, discharge, meet
Antonyms *vb* ≠ **be sufficient:** fail to meet ≠ **content:** annoy, displease, dissatisfy, exasperate, frustrate, give cause for complaint ≠ **convince:** dissuade, fail to persuade

satisfying *adj* **1** = **satisfactory**, cheering, convincing, filling, gratifying, pleasing, pleasurable

saturate *vb* **1** = **soak**, douse, drench, imbue, impregnate, seep, souse, steep, suffuse, waterlog, wet through

saturnine *adj* **1** = **gloomy**, dour, dull, glum, grave, heavy, morose, phlegmatic, sedate, sluggish, sombre, taciturn, uncommunicative

sauce *n* **4** *Informal* = **impudence**, audacity, backchat (*inf.*), brass (*inf.*), brass neck (*Brit. inf.*), cheek (*inf.*), cheekiness, disrespectfulness, face (*inf.*), front, impertinence, insolence, lip (*sl.*), neck (*inf.*), nerve (*inf.*), rudeness

sauciness *n* **1** = **impudence**, backchat (*inf.*), brass (*inf.*), brazenness, cheek (*inf.*), flippancy, impertinence, insolence, lip (*sl.*), pertness, rudeness, sauce (*inf.*)

saucy *adj* **1** = **impudent**, cheeky (*inf.*), disrespectful, flip (*inf.*), flippant, forward, fresh (*inf.*), impertinent, insolent, lippy (*US & Canad. sl.*), pert, presumptuous, rude, sassy (*US inf.*), smart-alecky (*inf.*) **2** = **jaunty**, dashing, gay, natty (*inf.*), perky, rakish, sporty

saunter *vb* **1** = **stroll**, amble, dally, linger, loiter, meander, mosey (*inf.*), ramble, roam, rove, stravaig (*Scot. & N English dialect*), take a stroll, tarry, wander ◆ *n* **2** = **stroll**, airing, amble, breather, constitutional, perambulation, promenade, ramble, turn, walk shaped edible casing. **2** *Scot.* sausage meat. **3** an object shaped like a sausage. **4 not a sausage.** nothing at all. [C15: from OF *saussiche,* from LL *salsīcia,* from L *salsus* salted; see SAUCE]

sausage dog *n* an informal name for **dachshund.**

sausage roll *n Brit.* a roll of sausage meat in pastry.

sauté ('səuteɪ) *vb* **sautés, sautéing** *or* **sautéeing, sautéed. 1** to fry (food) quickly in a little fat. ◆ *n* **2** a dish of sautéed food, esp. meat that is browned and then cooked in a sauce. ◆ *adj* **3** sautéed until lightly brown: *sauté potatoes.* [C19: from F: tossed, from *sauter* to jump, from L, from *salīre* to spring]

savage ⓘ ('sævɪdʒ) *adj* **1** wild; untamed: *savage beasts.* **2** ferocious in temper: *a savage dog.* **3** uncivilized; crude: *savage behaviour.* **4** (of peoples) nonliterate or primitive: *a savage tribe.* **5** (of terrain) rugged and uncultivated. ◆ *n* **6** a member of a nonliterate society, esp. one regarded as primitive. **7** a fierce or vicious person or animal. ◆ *vb* **savages, savaging, savaged.** (*tr*) **8** to criticize violently. **9** to attack ferociously and wound. [C13: from OF *sauvage,* from L *silvāticus* belonging to a wood, from *silva* a wood]
▸**'savagely** *adv* ▸**'savageness** *n*

savagery ⓘ ('sævɪdʒrɪ) *n, pl* **savageries. 1** an uncivilized condition. **2** a savage act or nature. **3** savages collectively.

savanna *or* **savannah** (sə'vænə) *n* open grasslands, usually with scattered bushes or trees, characteristic of much of tropical Africa. [C16: from Sp. *zavana,* from Amerind *zabana*]

savant ⓘ ('sævənt) *n* a man of great learning; sage. [C18: from F, from *savoir* to know, from L *sapere* to be wise]
▸**'savante** *fem n*

savate (sə'væt) *n* a form of boxing in which blows may be delivered with the feet as well as the hands. [C19: from F, lit.: old worn-out shoe]

save[1] ⓘ (seɪv) *vb* **saves, saving, saved. 1** (*tr*) to rescue, preserve, or guard (a person or thing) from danger or harm. **2** to avoid the spending, waste, or loss of (money, possessions, etc.). **3** (*tr*) to deliver from sin; redeem. **4** (often foll. by *up*) to set aside or reserve (money, goods, etc.) for future use. **5** (*tr*) to treat with care so as to avoid or lessen wear or degeneration. **6** (*tr*) to prevent the necessity for; obviate the trouble of. **7** (*tr*) *Soccer, hockey, etc.* to prevent (a goal) by stopping (a struck ball or puck). ◆ *n* **8** *Soccer, hockey, etc.* the act of saving a goal. **9** *Computing.* an instruction to write information from the memory onto a tape or disk. [C13: from OF *salver,* via LL from L *salvus* safe]
▸**'savable** *or* **'saveable** *adj* ▸**'saver** *n*

save[2] (seɪv) *Arch.* ◆ *prep* **1** (often foll. by *for*) Also: **saving.** with the exception of. ◆ *conj* **2** but. [C13 *sauf,* from OF, from L *salvō,* from *salvus* safe]

save as you earn *n* (in Britain) a savings scheme operated by the government, in which monthly contributions earn tax-free interest. Abbrev.: **SAYE.**

saveloy ('sævɪˌlɔɪ) *n* a smoked sausage made from salted pork, coloured red with saltpetre. [C19: prob. via F from It. *cervellato,* from *cervello* brain, from L, from *cerebrum* brain]

savin *or* **savine** ('sævɪn) *n* **1** a small spreading juniper bush of Europe, N Asia, and North America. **2** the oil derived from the shoots and leaves of this plant, formerly used in medicine to treat rheumatism, etc. [C14: from OF *savine,* from L *herba Sabīna* the Sabine plant]

saving ⓘ ('seɪvɪŋ) *adj* **1** tending to save or preserve. **2** redeeming or compensating (esp. in **saving grace**). **3** thrifty or economical. **4** *Law.* denoting or relating to an exception or reservation: *a saving clause in an agreement.* ◆ *n* **5** preservation or redemption. **6** economy or avoidance of waste. **7** reduction in cost or expenditure. **8** anything saved. **9** (*pl*) money saved for future use. ◆ *prep* **10** with the exception of. ◆ *conj* **11** except.
▸**'savingly** *adv*

savings bank *n* a bank that accepts the savings of depositors and pays interest on them.

savings ratio *n Econ.* the ratio of personal savings to disposable income, esp. using the difference between national figures for disposable income and consumer spending as a measure of savings.

saviour ⓘ *or US* **savior** ('seɪvjə) *n* a person who rescues another person or a thing from danger or harm. [C13 *saveour,* from OF, from Church L *Salvātor* the Saviour]

Saviour ⓘ *or US* **Savior** ('seɪvjə) *n Christianity.* Jesus Christ regarded as the saviour of men from sin.

savoir-faire ⓘ ('sævwɑː'fɛə) *n* the ability to do the right thing in any situation. [F, lit.: a knowing how to do]

savory ('seɪvərɪ) *n, pl* **savories. 1** any of numerous aromatic plants, including the **winter savory** and **summer savory,** of the Mediterranean region, having narrow leaves and white, pink, or purple flowers. **2** the leaves of any of these plants, used as a potherb. [C14: prob. from OE *sætherie,* from L *saturēia,* from ?]

savour ⓘ *or US* **savor** ('seɪvə) *n* **1** the quality in a substance that is perceived by the sense of taste or smell. **2** a specific taste or smell: *the savour of lime.* **3** a slight but distinctive quality or trace. **4** the power to excite interest: *the savour of wit has been lost.* ◆ *vb* **5** (*intr;* often foll. by *of*) to possess the taste or smell (of). **6** (*intr;* often foll. by *of*) to have a suggestion (of). **7** (*tr*) to season. **8** (*tr*) to taste or smell, esp. appreciatively. **9** (*tr*) to relish or enjoy. [C13: from OF *savour,* from L *sapor* taste, from *sapere* to taste]
▸**'savourless** *or US* **'savorless** *adj*

savoury ⓘ *or US* **savory** ('seɪvərɪ) *adj* **1** attractive to the sense of taste or smell. **2** salty or spicy: *a savoury dish.* **3** pleasant. **4** respectable. ◆ *n, pl* **savouries** *or US* **savories. 5** *Chiefly Brit.* a savoury dish served as an hors d'oeuvre or dessert. [C13 *savure,* from OF, from *savourer* to SAVOUR]
▸**'savouriness** *or US* **'savoriness** *n*

savoy (sə'vɔɪ) *n* a cultivated variety of cabbage having a compact head and wrinkled leaves. [C16: after the *Savoy* region in France]

Savoyard (sə'vɔɪɑːd; *French* savwajar) *n* **1.** a native of Savoy, region in SE France. **2** the dialect of French spoken in Savoy. ◆ *adj* **3** of or relating to Savoy, its inhabitants, or their dialect.

savvy ⓘ ('sævɪ) *Sl.* ◆ *vb* **savvies, savvying, savvied. 1** to understand or get the sense of (an idea, etc.). ◆ *n* **2** comprehension. ◆ *adj* **savvier, savviest. 3** *Chiefly US.* shrewd. [C18: corruption of Sp. *sabe* (*usted*) (you) know, from *saber* to know, from L *sapere* to be wise]

saw[1] (sɔː) *n* **1** any of various hand tools for cutting wood, metal, etc., having a blade with teeth along one edge. **2** any of various machines or devices for cutting by use of a toothed blade, such as a power-driven toothed band of metal. ◆ *vb* **saws, sawing, sawed; sawed** *or* **sawn. 3** to cut with a saw. **4** to form by sawing. **5** to cut as if wielding a saw: *to saw the air.* **6** to move (an object) from side to side as if moving a saw. [OE *sagu:* rel. to L *secare* to cut]
▸**'sawer** *n* ▸**'saw,like** *adj*

saw[2] (sɔː) *vb* the past tense of **see**[1].

saw[3] ⓘ (sɔː) *n* a wise saying, maxim, or proverb. [OE *sagu* a saying]

sawbones ('sɔːˌbəʊnz) *n, pl* **sawbones** *or* **sawboneses.** *Sl.* a surgeon or doctor.

sawdust ('sɔːˌdʌst) *n* particles of wood formed by sawing.

sawfish ('sɔːˌfɪʃ) *n, pl* **sawfish** *or* **sawfishes.** a sharklike ray of subtropical coastal waters, having a serrated bladelike mouth.

sawfly ('sɔːˌflaɪ) *n, pl* **sawflies.** any of various hymenopterous insects, the females of which have a sawlike ovipositor.

sawhorse ('sɔːˌhɔːs) *n* a stand for timber during sawing.

sawmill ('sɔːˌmɪl) *n* an industrial establishment where timber is sawn into planks, etc.

sawn (sɔːn) *vb* a past participle of **saw**[1].

THESAURUS

savage *adj* **1 = wild,** feral, undomesticated, untamed **2 = cruel,** barbarous, beastly, bestial, bloodthirsty, bloody, brutal, brutish, devilish, diabolical, ferocious, fierce, harsh, inhuman, merciless, murderous, pitiless, ravening, ruthless, sadistic, vicious **3 = uncultivated,** rough, rugged, uncivilized **4 = primitive,** in a state of nature, nonliterate, rude, unspoilt ◆ *n* **6 = primitive,** autochthon, barbarian, heathen, indigene, native **7 = brute,** beast, fiend, monster ◆ *vb* **8 = criticise,** attack, tear into (*inf.*) **9 = attack,** lacerate, mangle, maul
Antonyms *adj* ≠ **wild:** domesticated, tame ≠ **cruel:** gentle, humane, kind, merciful, mild, restrained ≠ **uncultivated:** civilized, cultivated, refined ◆ *vb* ≠ **criticise:** acclaim, celebrate, praise, rave about (*inf.*)

savagery *n* **1, 2 = cruelty,** barbarity, bestiality, bloodthirstiness, brutality, ferocity, fierceness, inhumanity, ruthlessness, sadism, viciousness

savant *n* **= sage,** authority, intellectual, mahatma, master, mastermind, philosopher, scholar

save[1] *vb* **1 = rescue,** bail (someone) out, come to (someone's) rescue, deliver, free, liberate, recover, redeem, salvage, save (someone's) bacon (*Brit. inf.*), set free **2 = protect,** conserve, guard, keep safe, look after, preserve, safeguard, screen, shield, take care of **4 = keep,** be frugal, be thrifty, collect, economize, gather, hide away, hoard, hold, husband, keep up one's sleeve (*inf.*), lay by, put aside for a rainy day, put by, reserve, retrench, salt away, set aside, store, tighten one's belt (*inf.*), treasure up **6 = prevent,** obviate, rule out, spare
Antonyms *vb* ≠ **rescue, protect:** abandon, endanger, expose, imperil, risk, threaten ≠ **keep:** be extravagant (with), blow (*sl.*), consume, discard, fritter away, spend, splurge, squander, use, use up, waste

saving *adj* **2** *As in* **saving grace = redeeming,** compensatory, extenuating, qualifying ◆ *n* **7 = economy,** bargain, discount, reduction **9** *plural* **= nest egg,** fall-back, fund, provision for a rainy day, reserves, resources, store

saviour *n* **= rescuer,** defender, deliverer, friend in need, Good Samaritan, guardian, knight in shining armour, liberator, preserver, protector, redeemer, salvation

Saviour *n* **= Christ,** Jesus, Messiah, Redeemer

savoir-faire *n* **= social know-how** (*inf.*), accomplishment, address, diplomacy, discretion, finesse, poise, social graces, tact, urbanity

savour *n* **1 = flavour,** piquancy, relish, smack, smell, tang, taste, zest, zing (*inf.*) **3 = trace,** distinctive quality **4 = zest,** excitement, flavour, interest, salt, spice ◆ *vb* **6** *with* **of = suggest,** bear the hallmarks of, be indicative of, be suggestive of, partake of, show signs of, smack of, verge on **9 = enjoy,** appreciate, delight in, drool, enjoy to the full, gloat over, like, luxuriate in, partake, relish, revel in, smack one's lips over

savoury *adj* **1 = tasty,** agreeable, appetizing, dainty, delectable, delicious, full-flavoured, good, luscious, mouthwatering, palatable, piquant, rich, scrumptious (*inf.*), spicy, tangy, toothsome **4 = wholesome,** apple-pie (*inf.*), decent, edifying, honest, reputable, respectable
Antonyms *adj* ≠ **tasty:** insipid, tasteless, unappetizing, unpalatable, unpleasant, wersh (*Scot.*) ≠ **wholesome:** disreputable, distasteful, nasty, unpleasant, unsavoury

savvy *Slang vb* **1 = understand,** apprehend, catch on, catch the drift, comprehend, get the gist, grasp, perceive, take in ◆ *n* **2 = understanding,** apprehension, comprehension, grasp, ken, perception

saw[3] *n* **= saying,** adage, aphorism, apophthegm, axiom, byword, dictum, gnome, maxim, proverb

sawn-off *or esp. US* **sawed-off** *adj (prenominal)* (of a shotgun) having the barrel cut short, mainly to facilitate concealment of the weapon.

saw set *n* a tool used for setting the teeth of a saw, consisting of a clamp used to bend each tooth at a slight angle to the plane of the saw, alternate teeth being bent in the same direction.

sawyer ('sɔːjə) *n* a person who saws timber for a living. [C14 *sawier*, from SAW[1] + *-ier*, var. of -ER[1]]

sax (sæks) *n Inf.* short for **saxophone.**

saxe blue (sæks) *n* **a** a light greyish-blue colour. **b** *(as adj): a saxe-blue dress.* [C19: from F *Saxe* Saxony, source of a dye of this colour]

saxhorn ('sæks,hɔːn) *n* a valved brass instrument used chiefly in brass and military bands, having a tube of conical bore. It resembles the tuba. [C19: after Adolphe *Sax* (see SAXOPHONE), who invented it (1845)]

saxicolous (sæk'sɪkələs) *adj* living on or among rocks: *saxicolous plants.* Also: **saxicole** ('sæksɪ,kəʊl), **saxatile** ('sæksə,taɪl). [C19: from NL *saxicolus*, from L *saxum* rock + *colere* to dwell]

saxifrage ('sæksɪ,freɪdʒ) *n* a plant having small white, yellow, purple, or pink flowers. [C15: from LL *saxifraga*, lit.: rock-breaker, from L *saxum* rock + *frangere* to break]

Saxon ('sæksən) *n* **1** a member of a West Germanic people who raided and settled parts of S Britain in the fifth and sixth centuries A.D. **2** a native or inhabitant of Saxony, in SE Germany. **3a** the Low German dialect of Saxony. **3b** any of the West Germanic dialects spoken by the ancient Saxons. ◆ *adj* **4** of or characteristic of the ancient Saxons, the Anglo-Saxons, or their descendants. **5** of or characteristic of Saxony, its inhabitants, or their Low German dialect. [C13 (replacing OE *Seaxe*): via OF from LL *Saxon-, Saxo*, from Gk; of Gmc origin]

saxophone ('sæksə,fəʊn) *n* a keyed single-reed wind instrument of mellow tone colour, used mainly in jazz and dance music. Often shortened to **sax.** [C19: after Adolphe *Sax* (1814–94), Belgian musical-instrument maker, who invented it (1846)]
▸**saxophonic** (,sæksə'fɒnɪk) *adj* ▸**saxophonist** (sæk'sɒfənɪst) *n*

say ❶ (seɪ) *vb* **says, saying, said.** *(mainly tr)* **1** to speak, pronounce, or utter. **2** *(also intr)* to express (an idea, etc.) in words; tell. **3** *(also intr; may take a clause as object)* to state (an opinion, fact, etc.) positively. **4** to recite: *to say grace.* **5** *(may take a clause as object)* to report or allege: *they say we shall have rain today.* **6** *(may take a clause as object)* to suppose: *let us say that he is lying.* **7** *(may take a clause as object)* to convey by means of artistic expression. **8** to make a case for: *there is much to be said for it.* **9 go without saying.** to be so obvious as to need no explanation. **10 I say!** *Inf., chiefly Brit.* an exclamation of surprise. **11 not to say.** even. **12 that is to say.** in other words. **13 to say the least.** at the very least. ◆ *adv* **14** approximately: *there were, say, 20 people present.* **15** for example: *choose a number, say, four.* ◆ *n* **16** the right or chance to speak: *let him have his say.* **17** authority, esp. to influence a decision: *he has a lot of say.* **18** a statement of opinion: *you've had your say.* ◆ *interj* **19** *US & Canad. inf.* an exclamation to attract attention or express surprise. [OE *secgan*]
▸'**sayer** *n*

SAYE (in Britain) *abbrev. for* save as you earn.

saying ❶ ('seɪɪŋ) *n* a maxim, adage, or proverb.

say-so ❶ *n Inf.* **1** an arbitrary assertion. **2** an authoritative decision. **3** the authority to make a final decision.

sayyid ('saɪɪd) *or* **said** *n* **1** a Muslim claiming descent from Mohammed's grandson Husain. **2** a Muslim honorary title. [C17: from Ar.: lord]

Sb *the chemical symbol for* antimony. [from NL *stibium*]

SBU *abbrev. for* strategic business unit: a division within an organization responsible for marketing its own range of products.

sc *Printing. abbrev. for* small capitals.

Sc *the chemical symbol for* scandium.

SC *abbrev. for:* **1** *NZ.* School Certificate. **2** Signal Corps. **3** *Canad.* Social Credit.

sc. *abbrev. for:* **1** scale. **2** scene. **3** science. **4** scilicet. **5** screw. **6** scruple (unit of weight).

scab (skæb) *n* **1** the dried crusty surface of a healing skin wound or sore. **2** a contagious disease of sheep resembling mange, caused by a mite. **3** a fungal disease of plants characterized by crusty spots on the fruits, leaves, etc. **4** *Derog.* **4a** Also called: **blackleg.** a person who refuses to support a trade union's actions, esp. strikes. **4b** *(as modifier): scab labour.* **5** a despicable person. ◆ *vb* **scabs, scabbing, scabbed.** *(intr)* **6** to become covered with a scab. **7** to replace a striking worker. [OE *sceabb*]

scabbard ('skæbəd) *n* a holder for a bladed weapon such as a sword or bayonet. [C13 *scauberc*, from Norman F *escaubers*, (pl) of Gmc origin]

scabby ('skæbɪ) *adj* **scabbier, scabbiest. 1** *Pathol.* having an area of the skin covered with scabs. **2** *Pathol.* having scabies. **3** *Inf.* despicable.
▸'**scabbily** *adv* ▸'**scabbiness** *n*

scabies ('skeɪbiːz) *n* a contagious skin infection caused by a mite, characterized by intense itching and inflammation. [C15: from L: scurf, from *scabere* to scratch]

scabious[1] ('skeɪbɪəs) *adj* **1** having or covered with scabs. **2** of, relating to, or resembling scabies. [C17: from L *scabiōsus*, from SCABIES]

scabious[2] ('skeɪbɪəs) *n* any of a genus of plants of the Mediterranean region, having blue, red, or whitish dome-shaped flower heads. [C14: from Med. L *scabiōsa herba* the scabies plant, referring to its use in treating scabies]

scabrous ('skeɪbrəs) *adj* **1** roughened because of small projections. **2** indecent or salacious: *scabrous humour.* **3** difficult to deal with. [C17: from L *scaber* rough]
▸'**scabrously** *adv*

scad (skæd) *n, pl* **scad** *or* **scads.** any of various marine fishes having a deeply forked tail, such as the large mackerel. [C17: from ?]

scads (skædz) *pl n Inf.* a large amount or number. [C19: from ?]

scaffold ('skæfəld) *n* **1** a temporary framework that is used to support workmen and materials during the erection, repair, etc., of a building. **2** a raised wooden platform on which plays are performed, tobacco, etc., is dried, or (esp. formerly) criminals are executed. ◆ *vb (tr)* **3** to provide with a scaffold. **4** to support by means of a scaffold. [C14: from OF *eschaffaut*, from Vulgar L *catafalicum* (unattested)]
▸'**scaffolder** *n*

scaffolding ('skæfəldɪŋ) *n* **1** a scaffold or system of scaffolds. **2** the building materials used to make scaffolds.

scalable ('skeɪləbᵊl) *adj* capable of being climbed.
▸'**scalableness** *n* ▸'**scalably** *adv*

scalar ('skeɪlə) *n* **1** a quantity, such as time or temperature, that has magnitude but not direction. **2** *Maths.* an element of a field associated with a vector space. ◆ *adj* **3** having magnitude but not direction. [C17 (meaning: resembling a ladder): from L *scālāris*, from *scāla* ladder]

scalar product *n* the product of two vectors to form a scalar, whose value is the product of the magnitudes of the vectors and the cosine of the angle between them. Also called: **dot product.**

scalawag ('skælə,wæg) *n* a variant of **scallywag.**

scald[1] (skɔːld) *vb* **1** to burn or be burnt with or as if with hot liquid or steam. **2** *(tr)* to subject to the action of boiling water, esp. so as to sterilize. **3** *(tr)* to heat (a liquid) almost to boiling point. **4** to plunge (tomatoes, etc.) into boiling water in order to skin them more easily. ◆ *n* **5** the act or result of scalding. **6** an abnormal condition in plants, caused by exposure to excessive sunlight, gases, etc. [C13: via OF from LL *excaldāre* to wash in warm water, from *calida (aqua)* warm (water), from *calēre* to be warm]
▸'**scalder** *n*

scald[2] (skɔːld) *n* a variant spelling of **skald.**

scaldfish ('skɔːld,fɪʃ, 'skɑːld-) *n, pl* **scaldfish** *or* **scaldfishes.** a small European flatfish, covered with large fragile scales.

scale[1] ❶ (skeɪl) *n* **1** any of the numerous plates, made of various substances, covering the bodies of fishes. **2a** any of the horny or chitinous plates covering a part or the entire body of certain reptiles and mammals. **2b** any of the numerous minute structures covering the wings of lepidoptera. **3** a thin flat piece or flake. **4** a thin flake of dead epidermis shed from the skin. **5** a specialized leaf or bract, esp. the protective covering of a bud or the dry membranous bract of a catkin. **6** See **scale insect. 7** any oxide formed on a metal when heated. **8** tartar formed on the teeth. ◆ *vb* **scales, scaling, scaled. 9** *(tr)* to remove the scales or coating from. **10** to peel off or cause to peel off in flakes or scales. **11** *(intr)* to shed scales. **12** to cover or become covered with scales, incrustation, etc. [C14: from OF *escale*, of Gmc origin]

scale[2] (skeɪl) *n* **1** *(often pl)* a machine or device for weighing. **2** one of the pans of a balance. **3 tip the scales. 3a** to exercise a decisive influence. **3b** (foll. by *at*) to amount in weight (to). ◆ *vb* **scales, scaling, scaled.** *(tr)* **4** to weigh with or as if with scales. [C13: from ON *skāl* bowl]

scale[3] ❶ (skeɪl) *n* **1** a sequence of marks either at regular intervals, or representing equal steps, used as a reference in making measurements. **2** a measuring instrument having such a scale. **3a** the ratio between the size of something real and that of a representation of it. **3b** *(as modifier): a scale model.* **4** a line, numerical ratio, etc., for showing

THESAURUS

say *vb* **1 = speak,** add, affirm, announce, assert, asseverate, come out with *(inf.)*, declare, express, give voice *or* utterance to, maintain, mention, pronounce, put into words, remark, state, utter, voice **3 = tell,** answer, disclose, divulge, give as one's opinion, make known, reply, respond, reveal **4 = recite,** deliver, do, orate, perform, read, rehearse, render, repeat **5 = report,** allege, bruit, claim, noise abroad, put about, rumour, suggest **6 = suppose,** assume, conjecture, dare say, estimate, guess, hazard a guess, imagine, judge, presume, surmise **7 = express,** communicate, convey, give the impression that, imply **9 go without saying = be obvious,** be accepted, be a matter of course, be self-evident, be taken as read, be taken for granted, be understood **13 to say the least = at the very least,** to put it mildly, without any exaggeration ◆ *n* **16 = chance to speak,** crack *(inf.)*, opportunity to speak, turn to speak, voice, vote **17 = influence,** authority, clout *(inf.)*, power, sway, weight

saying *n* **= proverb,** adage, aphorism, apophthegm, axiom, byword, dictum, gnome, maxim, saw, slogan

say-so *n Informal* **1 = assertion,** asseveration, assurance, dictum, guarantee, word **2 = authorization,** agreement, assent, authority, consent, O.K. *or* okay *(inf.)*, permission, sanction

scale[1] *n* **3 = flake,** lamina, layer, plate, squama *(Biology)*

scale[3] *n* **1 = graduation,** calibration, degrees, gamut, gradation, graduated system, hierarchy, ladder, pecking order *(inf.)*, progression, ranking, register, seniority system, sequence, series, spectrum, spread, steps **3 = ratio,** proportion **7 = degree,** extent, range, reach, scope, way ◆ *vb* **10 = climb,** ascend, clamber, escalade, mount, surmount **12 = adjust,** proportion, prorate *(chiefly US)*, regulate

DICTIONARY

this ratio. **5** a progressive or graduated table of things, wages, etc.: *a wage scale for carpenters.* **6** an established standard. **7** a relative degree or extent: *he entertained on a grand scale.* **8** *Music.* a group of notes taken in ascending or descending order, esp. within the compass of one octave. **9** *Maths.* the notation of a given number system: *the decimal scale.* ◆ *vb* **scales, scaling, scaled. 10** to climb to the top of (a height) by or as if by a ladder. **11** (*tr*) to make or draw (a model, etc.) according to a particular ratio of proportionate reduction. **12** (*tr*; usually foll. by *up* or *down*) to increase or reduce proportionately in size, etc. **13** (*intr*) *Austral. inf.* to ride on public transport without paying a fare. [C15: via It. from L *scāla* ladder]

scaleboard ('skeɪl,bɔːd) *n* a very thin piece of board, used for backing a picture, etc.

scale insect *n* a small insect which typically lives and feeds on plants and secretes a protective scale around itself. Many species are pests.

scalene ('skeɪliːn) *adj* **1** *Maths.* (of a triangle) having all sides of unequal length. **2** *Anat.* of or relating to any of the scalenus muscles. [C17: from LL *scalēnus* with unequal sides, from Gk *skalēnos*]

scalenus (skə'liːnəs) *n, pl* **scaleni** (-naɪ). *Anat.* any one of the three muscles situated on each side of the neck extending from the cervical vertebrae to the first or second pair of ribs. [C18: from NL; see SCALENE]

scaling ladder *n* a ladder used to climb high walls, esp. one used formerly to enter a besieged town, fortress, etc.

scallion ('skæljən) *n* any of various onions, such as the spring onion, that have a small bulb and long leaves and are eaten in salads. [C14: from Anglo-F *scalun*, from L *Ascalōnia* (*caepa*) Ascalonian (onion), from *Ascalo* Ascalon, a Palestinian port]

scallop ('skɒləp, 'skæl-) *n* **1** any of various marine bivalves having a fluted fan-shaped shell. **2** the edible adductor muscle of certain of these molluscs. **3** either of the shell valves of any of these molluscs. **4** a scallop shell in which fish, esp. shellfish, is cooked and served. **5** one of a series of curves along an edge. **6** the shape of a scallop shell used as the badge of a pilgrim, esp. in the Middle Ages. **7** *Chiefly Austral.* a potato cake fried in batter. ◆ *vb* **8** (*tr*) to decorate (an edge) with scallops. **9** to bake (food) in a scallop shell or similar dish. [C14: from OF *escalope* shell, of Gmc origin]
▸**'scalloper** *n* ▸**'scalloping** *n*

scally ('skælɪ) *n, pl* **scallies.** *Northwest English dialect.* a rascal; rogue. [C20: from SCALLYWAG]

scallywag ('skælɪ,wæg) *n Inf.* a scamp; rascal. ◆ Also: **scalawag, scallawag.** [C19: (orig. undersized animal): from ?]

scalp (skælp) *n* **1** *Anat.* the skin and subcutaneous tissue covering the top of the head. **2** (among North American Indians) a part of this removed as a trophy from a slain enemy. **3** a trophy or token signifying conquest. **4** *Scot. dialect.* a projection of bare rock from vegetation. ◆ *vb* (*tr*) **5** to cut the scalp from. **6** *Inf., chiefly US.* to purchase and resell (securities) quickly so as to make several small profits. **7** *Inf.* to buy (tickets) cheaply and resell at an inflated price. [C13: prob. from ON]
▸**'scalper** *n*

scalpel ('skælpəl) *n* a surgical knife with a short thin blade. [C18: from L *scalpellum*, from *scalper* a knife, from *scalpere* to scrape]

scaly Ⓣ ('skeɪlɪ) *adj* **scalier, scaliest. 1** resembling or covered in scales. **2** peeling off in scales.
▸**'scaliness** *n*

scaly anteater *n* another name for **pangolin.**

scamp^1 Ⓣ (skæmp) *n* **1** an idle mischievous person. **2** a mischievous child. [C18: from *scamp* (vb) to be a highway robber, prob. from MDu. *schampen* to decamp, from OF *escamper*, from L *campus* field]
▸**'scampish** *adj*

scamp^2 (skæmp) *vb* a less common word for **skimp.**
▸**'scamper** *n*

scamper Ⓣ ('skæmpə) *vb* **1** (*intr*) to run about playfully. **2** (often foll. by *through*) to hurry through (a place, task, etc.) ◆ *n* **3** the act of scampering. [C17: prob. from *scamp* (vb); see SCAMP^1]

scampi ('skæmpɪ) *n* (*usually functioning as sing*) large prawns, usually eaten fried in breadcrumbs. [It.: pl of *scampo* shrimp, from ?]

scan Ⓣ (skæn) *vb* **scans, scanning, scanned. 1** (*tr*) to scrutinize minutely. **2** (*tr*) to glance at quickly. **3** (*tr*) *Prosody.* to read or analyse (verse) according to the rules of metre and versification. **4** (*intr*) *Prosody.* to conform to the rules of metre and versification. **5** (*tr*) *Electronics.* to move a beam of light, electrons, etc., in a predetermined pattern over (a surface or region) to obtain information, esp. to reproduce a television image. **6** (*tr*) to examine data stored on (magnetic tape, etc.), usually in order to retrieve information. **7** to examine or search (a prescribed region) by systematically varying the direction of a radar or sonar beam. **8** *Med.* to obtain an image of (a part of the body) by means of a scanner. ◆ *n* **9** the act or an instance of scanning. **10** *Med.* **10a** the examination of a part of the body by means of a scanner: *a brain scan; an ultrasound scan.* **10b** the image produced by a scanner. [C14: from LL *scandere* to scan (verse), from L: to climb]
▸**'scannable** *adj*

Scand. *or* **Scan.** *abbrev. for* Scandinavia(n).

scandal Ⓣ ('skændəl) *n* **1** a disgraceful action or event: *his negligence was a scandal.* **2** censure or outrage arising from an action or event. **3** a person whose conduct causes reproach or disgrace. **4** malicious talk, esp. gossip. **5** *Law.* a libellous action or statement. [C16: from LL *scandalum* stumbling block, from Gk *skandalon* a trap]
▸**'scandalous** *adj* ▸**'scandalously** *adv*

scandalize Ⓣ *or* **scandalise** ('skændə,laɪz) *vb* **scandalizes, scandalizing, scandalized** *or* **scandalises, scandalising, scandalised.** (*tr*) to shock, as by improper behaviour.
▸**,scandali'zation** *or* **,scandali'sation** *n*

scandalmonger Ⓣ ('skændəl,mʌŋgə) *n* a person who spreads or enjoys scandal, gossip, etc.

Scandinavian (,skændɪ'neɪvɪən) *adj* **1** of or characteristic of Scandinavia (Norway, Sweden, Denmark, and Iceland), its inhabitants, or their languages. ◆ *n* **2** a native or inhabitant of Scandinavia. **3** the group of Germanic languages, consisting of Swedish, Danish, Norwegian, Icelandic, and Faeroese.

scandium ('skændɪəm) *n* a rare silvery-white metallic element occurring in minute quantities in numerous minerals. Symbol: Sc; atomic no.: 21; atomic wt.: 44.96. [C19: from NL, from L *Scandia* Scandinavia, where discovered]

scanner ('skænə) *n* **1** a person or thing that scans. **2** a device, usually electronic, used to measure or sample the distribution of some quantity or condition in a particular system, region, or area. **3** an aerial or similar device designed to transmit or receive signals, esp. radar signals, inside a given solid angle of space. **4** any device used in medical diagnosis to obtain an image of an internal organ or part. **5** short for **optical scanner.**

scanning electron microscope *n* a type of electron microscope that produces a three-dimensional image.

scansion ('skænʃən) *n* the analysis of the metrical structure of verse. [C17: from L: climbing up, from *scandere* to climb]

scant Ⓣ (skænt) *adj* **1** scarcely sufficient: *he paid her scant attention.* **2** (*prenominal*) bare: *a scant ten inches.* **3** (*postpositive;* foll. by *of*) having a short supply (of). ◆ *vb* (*tr*) **4** to limit in size or quantity. **5** to provide with a limited supply of. **6** to treat in an inadequate manner. ◆ *adv* **7** scarcely; barely. [C14: from ON *skamt*, from *skammr* short]
▸**'scantly** *adv*

scantling ('skæntlɪŋ) *n* **1** a piece of sawn timber, such as a rafter, that has a small cross section. **2** the dimensions of a piece of building material or the structural parts of a ship or aircraft. **3** a building stone. **4** a small quantity or amount. [C16: changed (through infl. of SCANT & -LING^1) from earlier *scantillon* a carpenter's gauge, from OF *escantillon*, ult. from L *scandere* to climb]

scanty Ⓣ ('skæntɪ) *adj* **scantier, scantiest. 1** limited; barely enough. **2** inadequate. **3** lacking fullness.
▸**'scantily** *adv* ▸**'scantiness** *n*

scape *or* **'scape** (skeɪp) *vb* **scapes, scaping, scaped,** *n* an archaic word for **escape.**

-scape *suffix forming nouns.* indicating a scene or view of something: *seascape.* [from LANDSCAPE]

scapegoat Ⓣ ('skeɪp,gəʊt) *n* **1** a person made to bear the blame for others. **2** *Bible.* a goat symbolically laden with the sins of the Israelites and sent into the wilderness. ◆ *vb* **3** (*tr*) to make a scapegoat of. [C16: from ESCAPE + GOAT, coined by William Tyndale to translate Biblical Heb. *azāzēl* (prob.) goat for Azazel, mistakenly thought to mean "goat that escapes"]

scapegrace Ⓣ ('skeɪp,greɪs) *n* a mischievous person. [C19: from SCAPE + GRACE, alluding to a person who lacks God's grace]

scaphoid ('skæfɔɪd) *adj Anat.* an obsolete word for **navicular.** [C18: via NL from Gk *skaphoeidēs*, from *skaphē* boat]

scapula ('skæpjʊlə) *n, pl* **scapulae** (-liː) *or* **scapulas.** either of two large flat

THESAURUS

scaly *adj* **1 = flaky,** furfuraceous (*Medical*), scabrous, scurfy, squamous *or* squamose (*Biology*), squamulose

scamp^1 *n* **1 = rascal,** devil, imp, knave (*arch.*), mischief-maker, monkey, pickle (*Brit. inf.*), prankster, rogue, scallywag (*inf.*), scapegrace, toerag (*sl.*), tyke (*inf.*), whippersnapper, wretch

scamper *vb* **2 = run,** beetle, dart, dash, fly, hasten, hie (*arch.*), hurry, romp, scoot, scurry, scuttle, sprint

scan *vb* **1 = scrutinize,** con (*arch.*), investigate, recce (*sl.*), scour, search, survey, sweep, take stock of **2 = glance over,** check, check out (*inf.*), clock (*Brit. sl.*), examine, eye, eyeball (*sl.*), get a load of (*inf.*), look one up and down, look through, run one's eye over, run over, size up (*inf.*), skim, take a dekko at (*Brit. sl.*)

scandal *n* **1 = crime,** crying shame (*inf.*), disgrace, embarrassment, offence, sin, skeleton in the cupboard, wrongdoing **2 = shame,** calumny, defamation, detraction, discredit, disgrace, dishonour, ignominy, infamy, obloquy, offence, opprobrium, reproach, stigma **4 = gossip,** abuse, aspersion, backbiting, dirt, dirty linen (*inf.*), rumours, slander, talk, tattle

scandalize *vb* **= shock,** affront, appal, cause a few raised eyebrows (*inf.*), disgust, horrify, offend, outrage, raise eyebrows

scandalmonger *n* **= gossip,** calumniator, defamer, destroyer of reputations, muckraker, tattle, tattler, traducer

scandalous *adj* **1 = shocking,** atrocious, disgraceful, disreputable, highly improper, infamous, monstrous, odious, opprobrious, outrageous, shameful, unseemly **4 = slanderous,** defamatory, gossiping, libellous, scurrilous, untrue
Antonyms *adj* ≠ **shocking:** decent, proper, reputable, respectable, seemly, upright ≠ **slanderous:** laudatory, unimpeachable

scant *adj* **1 = meagre,** bare, barely sufficient, deficient, inadequate, insufficient, limited, little, minimal, sparse
Antonyms *adj* abundant, adequate, ample, full, generous, plentiful, satisfactory, sufficient

scanty *adj* **1-3 = meagre,** bare, deficient, exiguous, inadequate, insufficient, narrow, pathetic, poor, restricted, scant, short, skimpy, slender, sparing, sparse, thin

scapegoat *n* **1 = whipping boy,** fall guy (*inf.*)

scapegrace *n* **= scamp,** bad lot (*inf.*), good-for-nothing, limb of Satan, ne'er-do-well, rascal, rogue, scallywag (*inf.*)

triangular bones, one on each side of the back part of the shoulder in man. Nontechnical name: **shoulder blade.** [C16: from LL: shoulder]

scapular ('skæpjʊlə) *adj* **1** *Anat.* of or relating to the scapula. ◆ *n* **2** part of the monastic habit worn by members of many Christian religious orders, consisting of a piece of woollen cloth worn over the shoulders, and hanging down to the ankles. **3** two small rectangular pieces of cloth joined by tapes passing over the shoulders and worn in token of affiliation to a religious order. **4** any of the small feathers of a bird that lie along the shoulder. ◆ Also called (for senses 2 and 3): **scapulary.**

scar[1] Ⓣ (skɑː) *n* **1** any mark left on the skin or other tissue following the healing of a wound, etc. **2** a permanent change in a person's character resulting from emotional distress. **3** the mark on a plant indicating the former point of attachment of a part. **4** a mark of damage. ◆ *vb* **scars, scarring, scarred. 5** to mark or become marked with a scar. **6** (*intr*) to heal leaving a scar. [C14: via LL from Gk *eskhara* scab]

scar[2] (skɑː) *n* a bare craggy rock formation. [C14: from ON *sker* low reef]

scarab ('skærəb) *n* **1** any scarabaeid beetle, esp. the **sacred scarab,** regarded by the ancient Egyptians as divine. **2** the scarab as represented on amulets, etc. [C16: from L *scarabaeus*]

scarabaeid (ˌskærə'biːɪd) *n* **1** any of a family of beetles including the sacred scarab and other dung beetles, the chafers, and rhinoceros beetles. ◆ *adj* **2** of or belonging to this family. [C19: from NL]

Scaramouch ('skærəˌmuːʃ) *n* a stock character who appears as a boastful coward in commedia dell'arte. [C17: via F from It. *Scaramuccia*, from *scaramuccia* a SKIRMISH]

scarce Ⓣ (skɛəs) *adj* **1** rarely encountered. **2** insufficient to meet the demand. **3 make oneself scarce.** *Inf.* to go away. ◆ *adv* **4** *Arch. or literary.* scarcely. [C13: from OF *scars*, from Vulgar L *excarpsus* (unattested) plucked out, from L *excerpere* to select]
▸ **'scarceness** *n*

scarcely Ⓣ ('skɛəslɪ) *adv* **1** hardly at all. **2** *Often used ironically.* probably or definitely not: *that is scarcely justification for your actions.*

USAGE NOTE See at **hardly.**

scarcity Ⓣ ('skɛəsɪtɪ) *n, pl* **scarcities. 1** inadequate supply. **2** rarity or infrequent occurrence.

scare Ⓣ (skɛə) *vb* **scares, scaring, scared. 1** to fill or be filled with fear or alarm. **2** (*tr*; often foll. by *away* or *off*) to drive (away) by frightening. ◆ *n* **3** a sudden attack of fear or alarm. **4** a period of general fear or alarm. ◆ *adj* **5** causing (needless) fear or alarm: *a scare story.* [C12: from ON *skirra*]
▸ **'scarer** *n*

scarecrow ('skɛəˌkrəʊ) *n* **1** an object, usually in the shape of a man, made out of sticks and old clothes to scare birds away from crops. **2** a person or thing that appears frightening. **3** *Inf.* an untidy-looking person.

scaremonger Ⓣ ('skɛəˌmʌŋgə) *n* a person who delights in spreading rumours of disaster.
▸ **'scareˌmongering** *n*

scarf[1] (skɑːf) *n, pl* **scarves** *or* **scarfs.** a rectangular, triangular, or long narrow piece of cloth worn around the head, neck, or shoulders for warmth or decoration. [C16: from ?]

scarf[2] (skɑːf) *n, pl* **scarfs. 1** Also called: **scarf joint, scarfed joint.** a lapped joint between two pieces of timber made by notching the ends and strapping or gluing the two pieces together. **2** the end of a piece of timber shaped to form such a joint. **3** *Whaling.* an incision made along a whale before stripping off the blubber. ◆ *vb* (*tr*) **4** to join (two pieces of timber) by means of a scarf. **5** to make a scarf on (a piece of timber). **6** to cut a scarf in (a whale). [C14: prob. from ON]

scarfskin ('skɑːfˌskɪn) *n* the outermost layer of the skin; epidermis or cuticle. [C17: from SCARF[1] (in the sense: an outer covering)]

scarify ('skɛərɪˌfaɪ, 'skærɪ-) *vb* **scarifies, scarifying, scarified.** (*tr*) **1** *Surgery.* to make tiny punctures or superficial incisions in (the skin or other tissue), as for inoculating. **2** *Agriculture.* to break up and loosen (soil) to a shallow depth. **3** to wound with harsh criticism. [C15: via OF from L *scarīfāre* to scratch open, from Gk *skariphasthai* to draw, from *skariphos* a pencil]
▸ **ˌscarifi'cation** *n* ▸ **'scariˌfier** *n*

USAGE NOTE *Scarify* is sometimes wrongly thought to mean the same as *scare*: *a frightening* (not *scarifying*) *film.*

scarlatina (ˌskɑːlə'tiːnə) *n* the technical name for **scarlet fever.** [C19: from NL, from It. *scarlattina*, dim. of *scarlatto* scarlet]

scarlet ('skɑːlɪt) *n* **1** a vivid orange-red colour. **2** cloth or clothing of this colour. ◆ *adj* **3** of the colour scarlet. **4** sinful or immoral. [C13: from OF *escarlate* fine cloth, from ?]

scarlet fever *n* an acute communicable disease characterized by fever, strawberry-coloured tongue, and a rash starting on the neck and chest and spreading to the abdomen and limbs. Technical name: **scarlatina.**

scarlet letter *n* (esp. among US Puritans) a scarlet letter *A* formerly worn by a person convicted of adultery.

scarlet pimpernel *n* a plant, related to the primrose, having small red, purple, or white star-shaped flowers that close in bad weather. Also called: **shepherd's** (or **poor man's**) **weatherglass.**

scarlet runner *n* a climbing perennial bean plant of South America, having scarlet flowers: widely cultivated for its long green edible pods containing edible seeds. Also: **runner bean.**

scarlet woman *n* **1** a sinful woman described in the Bible (Rev. 17), interpreted as a symbol of pagan Rome or of the Roman Catholic Church. **2** any sexually promiscuous woman.

scarp (skɑːp) *n* **1** a steep slope, esp. one formed by erosion or faulting. **2** *Fortifications.* the side of a ditch cut nearest to a rampart. ◆ *vb* **3** (*tr*; *often passive*) to wear or cut so as to form a steep slope. [C16: from It. *scarpa*]

scarper Ⓣ ('skɑːpə) *Brit. sl.* ◆ *vb* **1** (*intr*) to depart in haste. ◆ *n* **2** a hasty departure. [from ?]

Scart *or* **SCART** (skɑːt) *n Electronics.* **a** a 21-pin plug-and-socket system which carries picture, sound, and other signals, used especially in home entertainment systems. **b** (*as modifier*): *a Scart cable.* [C20: after *Syndicat des Constructeurs des Appareils Radiorécepteurs et Téléviseurs*, the company that designed it]

scarves (skɑːvz) *n* a plural of **scarf**[1].

scary Ⓣ ('skɛərɪ) *adj* **scarier, scariest.** *Inf.* **1** causing fear or alarm. **2** timid.

scat[1] (skæt) *vb* **scats, scatting, scatted.** (*intr*; *usually imperative*) *Inf.* to go away in haste. [C19: ?from a hiss + *cat*, used to frighten away cats]

scat[2] (skæt) *n* **1** a type of jazz singing characterized by improvised vocal sounds instead of words. ◆ *vb* **scats, scatting, scatted. 2** (*intr*) to sing jazz in this way. [C20: ? imit.]

scathe (skeɪð) *vb* **scathes, scathing, scathed.** (*tr*) **1** *Rare.* to attack with severe criticism. **2** *Arch. or dialect.* to injure. ◆ *n* **3** *Arch. or dialect.* harm. [OE *sceatha*]

scathing Ⓣ ('skeɪðɪŋ) *adj* **1** harshly critical; scornful. **2** damaging.
▸ **'scathingly** *adv*

scatology (skæ'tɒlədʒɪ) *n* **1** the scientific study of excrement, esp. in medicine and in palaeontology. **2** obscenity or preoccupation with obscenity, esp. in the form of references to excrement. [C19: from Gk *skat-* excrement + -LOGY]
▸ **scatological** (ˌskætə'lɒdʒɪkᵊl) *adj*

scatter Ⓣ ('skætə) *vb* **1** (*tr*) to throw about in various directions. **2** to separate and move or cause to separate and move in various directions. **3** to deviate or cause to deviate in many directions, as in the refraction of light. ◆ *n* **4** the act of scattering. **5** a substance or a number of objects scattered about. [C13: prob. a var. of SHATTER]
▸ **'scatterer** *n*

scatterbrain Ⓣ ('skætəˌbreɪn) *n* a person who is incapable of serious thought or concentration.
▸ **'scatterˌbrained** *adj*

scatter diagram *n Statistics.* a representation by a Cartesian graph of the correlation between two quantities, such as height and weight.

THESAURUS

scar[1] *n* **1** = **mark**, blemish, cicatrix, injury, trauma (*Pathology*), wound ◆ *vb* **5** = **mark**, brand, damage, disfigure, traumatize

scarce *adj* **1** = **rare**, at a premium, deficient, few, few and far between, infrequent, in short supply, insufficient, seldom met with, thin on the ground, uncommon, unusual, wanting
Antonyms *adj* abundant, ample, common, commonplace, frequent, numerous, plenteous, plentiful, sufficient

scarcely *adv* **1** = **hardly**, barely, only just, scarce (*arch.*) **2** *Often used ironically* = **definitely not**, by no means, hardly, not at all, on no account, under no circumstances

scarcity *n* **1** = **shortage**, dearth, deficiency, infrequency, insufficiency, lack, paucity, poverty, rareness, undersupply, want
Antonyms *n* abundance, excess, glut, superfluity, surfeit, surplus

scare *vb* **1** = **frighten**, affright (*arch.*), alarm, daunt, dismay, give (someone) a fright, give (someone) a turn (*inf.*), intimidate, panic, put the wind up (someone) (*inf.*), shock, startle, terrify, terrorize ◆ *n* **3** = **fright**, alarm, alert, panic, shock, start, terror

scared *adj* **1** = **frightened**, fearful, panicky, panic-stricken, petrified, shaken, startled, terrified

scaremonger *n* = **alarmist**, Calamity Jane, doom merchant (*inf.*), prophet of doom, spreader of despair and despondency

scarper *vb* **1** = **run away**, abscond, beat a hasty retreat, beat it (*sl.*), clear off (*inf.*), cut and run (*inf.*), decamp, depart, disappear, do a bunk (*Brit. sl.*), flee, go, make off, make oneself scarce (*inf.*), run for it, scram (*inf.*), skedaddle (*inf.*), slope off, take flight, take oneself off, take to one's heels, vamoose (*sl., chiefly US*)

scary *adj* **1** *Informal* = **frightening**, alarming, bloodcurdling, chilling, creepy (*inf.*), hair-raising, hairy (*sl.*), horrendous, horrifying, intimidating, shocking, spine-chilling, spooky (*inf.*), terrifying, unnerving

scathing *adj* **1** = **critical**, belittling, biting, brutal, caustic, cutting, harsh, mordacious, mordant, sarcastic, savage, scornful, searing, trenchant, vitriolic, withering

scatter *vb* **1** = **throw about**, broadcast, diffuse, disseminate, fling, litter, shower, sow, spread, sprinkle, strew **2** = **disperse**, disband, dispel, dissipate, disunite, put to flight, separate
Antonyms *vb* ≠ **throw about:** cluster, collect ≠ **disperse:** assemble, congregate, converge, rally, unite

scatterbrain *n* = **featherbrain**, bird-brain (*inf.*), butterfly, flibbertigibbet, grasshopper mind, madcap

scatterbrained *adj* = **empty-headed**, bird-brained (*inf.*), careless, featherbrained, forgetful, frivolous, giddy, goofy (*inf.*), inattentive, irresponsible, madcap, scatty (*Brit. inf.*), silly, slaphappy (*inf.*), thoughtless

scattering Ⓣ ('skætərɪŋ) *n* **1** a small amount. **2** *Physics.* the process in which particles, atoms, etc., are deflected as a result of collision.

scatty ('skætɪ) *adj* **scattier, scattiest.** *Brit. inf.* **1** empty-headed or thoughtless. **2** distracted (esp. in **drive someone scatty**). [C20: from SCATTERBRAINED]
▸'**scattily** *adv* ▸'**scattiness** *n*

scaup *or* **scaup duck** (skɔːp) *n* either of two diving ducks, the **greater scaup** or the **lesser scaup**, of Europe and America, having a black-and-white plumage in the male. [C16: Scot. var. of SCALP]

scavenge ('skævɪndʒ) *vb* **scavenges, scavenging, scavenged.** **1** to search for (anything usable) among discarded material. **2** (*tr*) to purify (a molten metal) by bubbling a suitable gas through it. **3** to clean up filth from (streets, etc.).

scavenger ('skævɪndʒə) *n* **1** a person who collects things discarded by others. **2** any animal that feeds on decaying organic matter. **3** a person employed to clean the streets. [C16: from Anglo-Norman *scawager*, from OF *escauwage* examination, from *escauwer* to scrutinize, of Gmc origin]
▸'**scavengery** *n*

ScD *abbrev. for* Doctor of Science.

SCE (in Scotland) *abbrev. for* Scottish Certificate of Education: either of two public examinations in specific subjects taken as school-leaving qualifications or as qualifying examinations for entry into a university, college, etc.

scena ('ʃeɪnə) *n, pl* **scene** (-ˌneɪ). a solo vocal piece of dramatic style and large scope, esp. in opera. [C19: It., from L *scēna* scene]

scenario Ⓣ (sɪ'nɑːrɪˌəʊ) *n, pl* **scenarios.** **1** a summary of the plot of a play, etc., including information about its characters, scenes, etc. **2** a predicted sequence of events. [C19: via It. from L *scēnārium*, from *scēna*; see SCENE]

scene Ⓣ (siːn) *n* **1** the place where an action or event, real or imaginary, occurs. **2** the setting for the action of a play, novel, etc. **3** an incident or situation, real or imaginary, esp. as described or represented. **4a** a subdivision of an act of a play, in which the setting is fixed. **4b** a single event, esp. a significant one, in a play. **5** *Films.* a shot or series of shots that constitutes a unit of the action. **6** the backcloths, etc., for a play or film set. **7** the prospect of a place, landscape, etc. **8** a display of emotion. **9** *Inf.* the environment for a specific activity: *the fashion scene.* **10** *Inf.* interest or chosen occupation: *classical music is not my scene.* **11** *Rare.* the stage. **12 behind the scenes.** out of public view. [C16: from L *scēna* theatrical stage, from Gk *skēnē* tent, stage]

scene dock *or* **bay** *n* a place in a theatre where scenery is stored, usually near the stage.

scenery Ⓣ ('siːnərɪ) *n, pl* **sceneries.** **1** the natural features of a landscape. **2** *Theatre.* the painted backcloths, etc., used to represent a location in a theatre or studio. [C18: from It. SCENARIO]

scenic Ⓣ ('siːnɪk) *adj* **1** of or relating to natural scenery. **2** having beautiful natural scenery: *a scenic drive.* **3** of or relating to the stage or stage scenery. **4** (in painting, etc.) representing a scene.
▸'**scenically** *adv*

scenic railway *n* a miniature railway used for amusement in a park, zoo, etc.

scenic reserve *n NZ.* an area of natural beauty, set aside for public recreation.

scent Ⓣ (sɛnt) *n* **1** a distinctive smell, esp. a pleasant one. **2** a smell left in passing, by which a person or animal may be traced. **3** a trail, clue, or guide. **4** an instinctive ability for detecting. **5** another word (esp. Brit.) for **perfume.** ◆ *vb* **6** (*tr*) to recognize by or as if by the smell. **7** (*tr*) to have a suspicion of: *I scent foul play.* **8** (*tr*) to fill with odour or fragrance. **9** (*intr*) (of hounds, etc.) to hunt by the sense of smell. **10** to smell (at): *the dog scented the air.* [C14: from OF *sentir* to sense, from L *sentīre* to feel]
▸'**scented** *adj*

sceptic Ⓣ *or arch. & US* **skeptic** ('skɛptɪk) *n* **1** a person who habitually doubts the authenticity of accepted beliefs. **2** a person who mistrusts people, ideas, etc., in general. **3** a person who doubts the truth of religion. [C16: from L *scepticus*, from Gk *skeptikos* one who reflects upon, from *skeptesthai* to consider]
▸'**sceptical** *or arch. & US* '**skeptical** *adj* ▸'**sceptically** *or arch. & US* '**skeptically** *adv* ▸'**scepticism** *or arch. & US* '**skepticism** *n*

Sceptic *or arch. & US* **Skeptic** ('skɛptɪk) *n* **1** a member of one of the ancient Greek schools of philosophy, esp. that of Pyrrho ?365–?275 B.C., who believed that real knowledge of things is impossible. ◆ *adj* **2** of or relating to the Sceptics.
▸'**Scepticism** *or arch. & US* '**Skepticism** *n*

sceptre *or US* **scepter** ('sɛptə) *n* **1** a ceremonial staff held by a monarch as the symbol of authority. **2** imperial authority; sovereignty. [C13: from OF *sceptre*, from L, from Gk *skeptron* staff]
▸'**sceptred** *or US* '**sceptered** *adj*

schedule Ⓣ ('ʃɛdjuːl; *also, esp. US* 'skɛdʒʊəl) *n* **1** a plan of procedure for a project. **2** a list of items: *a schedule of fixed prices.* **3** a list of times; timetable. **4** a list of tasks to be performed, esp. within a set period. **5** *Law.* a list or inventory. ◆ *vb* **schedules, scheduling, scheduled.** (*tr*) **6** to make a schedule of or place in a schedule. **7** to plan to occur at a certain time. [C14: earlier *cedule*, *sedule* via OF from LL *schedula* small piece of paper, from L *scheda* sheet of paper]

scheduled castes *pl n* certain classes in Indian society officially granted special concessions. See **Harijan.**

scheduled territories *pl n* **the.** another name for **sterling area.**

scheelite ('ʃiːlaɪt) *n* a white, brownish, or greenish mineral, usually fluorescent, consisting of calcium tungstate with some tungsten often replaced by molybdenum. It is an important source of tungsten. [C19: from G *Scheelit*, after K. W. *Scheele* (1742–86), Swedish chemist]

schema ('skiːmə) *n, pl* **schemata** (-mətə). **1** a plan, diagram, or scheme. **2** (in the philosophy of Kant) a rule or principle that enables the understanding to unify experience. **3** *Logic.* **3a** a syllogistic figure. **3b** a representation of the form of an inference. [C19: from Gk: form]

schematic Ⓣ (skɪ'mætɪk) *adj* **1** of or relating to the nature of a diagram, plan, or schema. ◆ *n* **2** a schematic diagram, esp. of an electrical circuit, etc.
▸**sche'matically** *adv*

schematize Ⓣ *or* **schematise** ('skiːməˌtaɪz) *vb* **schematizes, schematizing, schematized** *or* **schematises, schematising, schematised.** (*tr*) to form into or arrange in a scheme.
▸'**schemaˌtism** *n* ▸ˌ**schemati'zation** *or* ˌ**schemati'sation** *n*

scheme Ⓣ (skiːm) *n* **1** a systematic plan for a course of action. **2** a systematic arrangement of parts. **3** a secret plot. **4** a chart, diagram, or outline. **5** an astrological diagram giving the aspects of celestial bodies. **6** *Chiefly Brit.* a plan formally adopted by a commercial enterprise or governmental body, as for pensions, etc. **7** Short for **housing scheme.** ◆ *vb* **schemes, scheming, schemed.** **8** (*tr*) to devise a system for. **9** to form intrigues (for) in an underhand manner. [C16: from L *schema*, from Gk *skhēma* form]
▸'**schemer** *n*

scheming Ⓣ ('skiːmɪŋ) *adj* **1** given to making plots; cunning. ◆ *n* **2** intrigues.

Schengen Convention *or* **Agreement** ('ʃɛŋən) *n* an agreement, signed in 1985, but not implemented until 1995, to abolish border controls within Europe: thirteen countries had acceded by 1995; the UK is not a signatory.

scherzando (skɛə'tsændəʊ) *Music.* ◆ *adj, adv* **1** to be performed in a light-hearted manner. ◆ *n, pl* **scherzandi** (-diː) *or* **scherzandos.** **2** a movement, passage, etc., directed to be performed in this way. [It., lit.: joking; see SCHERZO]

scherzo ('skɛətsəʊ) *n, pl* **scherzos** *or* **scherzi** (-tsiː). a brisk lively move-

THESAURUS

scattering *n* **1** = **sprinkling**, few, handful, scatter, smatter, smattering

scenario *n* **1** = **story line**, outline, résumé, rundown, sketch, summary, synopsis **2** = **sequence of events**, master plan, scheme

scene *n* **1** = **site**, area, locality, place, position, setting, situation, spot, stage, whereabouts **2** = **setting**, backdrop, background, location, *mise en scène*, set **4** = **act**, division, episode, part **7** = **view**, landscape, panorama, prospect, vista **8** = **fuss**, carry-on (*inf., chiefly Brit.*), commotion, confrontation, display of emotion, drama, exhibition, hue and cry, performance, row, tantrum, to-do, upset **9** *Informal* = **world**, arena, business, environment, field of interest, milieu

scenery *n* **1** = **landscape**, surroundings, terrain, view, vista **2** *Theatre* = **set**, backdrop, décor, flats, *mise en scène*, setting, stage set

scenic *adj* **2** = **picturesque**, beautiful, breathtaking, grand, impressive, panoramic, spectacular, striking

scent *n* **1** = **fragrance**, aroma, bouquet, niff (*Brit. sl.*), odour, perfume, redolence, smell **2** = **trail**, spoor, track ◆ *vb* **6** = **detect**, be on the track *or* trail of, discern, get wind of (*inf.*), nose out, recognize, sense, smell, sniff, sniff out

scented *adj* **5** = **fragrant**, ambrosial, aromatic, odoriferous, perfumed, redolent, sweet-smelling

sceptic *n* **1-3** = **doubter**, agnostic, cynic, disbeliever, doubting Thomas, Pyrrhonist, scoffer, unbeliever

sceptical *adj* **1-3** = **doubtful**, cynical, disbelieving, doubting, dubious, hesitating, incredulous, mistrustful, questioning, quizzical, scoffing, unbelieving, unconvinced
Antonyms *adj* believing, certain, convinced, credulous, dogmatic, free from doubt, of fixed mind, sure, trusting, undoubting, unquestioning

scepticism *n* **1-3** = **doubt**, agnosticism, cynicism, disbelief, incredulity, Pyrrhonism, suspicion, unbelief

schedule *n* **1-4** = **plan**, agenda, calendar, catalogue, inventory, itinerary, list, list of appointments, programme, timetable ◆ *vb* **6** = **plan**, appoint, arrange, book, organize, programme, slot (*inf.*), time

schematic *adj* **1** = **diagrammatic**, diagrammatical, graphic, illustrative, representational

schematize *vb* = **systematize**, arrange, catalogue, categorize, classify, file, grade, methodize, order, pigeonhole, put into order, regulate, sort, standardize, systemize, tabulate

scheme *n* **1** = **plan**, contrivance, course of action, design, device, programme, project, proposal, strategy, system, tactics, theory **2** = **system**, arrangement, codification, disposition, layout, pattern, schedule, schema **3** = **plot**, conspiracy, dodge, game (*inf.*), intrigue, machinations, manoeuvre, ploy, ruse, shift, stratagem, subterfuge **4** = **diagram**, blueprint, chart, draft, outline ◆ *vb* **8** = **plan**, contrive, design, devise, frame, imagine, lay plans, project, work out **9** = **plot**, collude, conspire, intrigue, machinate, manoeuvre, wheel and deal (*inf.*)

schemer *n* **9** = **plotter**, conniver, deceiver, intriguer, Machiavelli, slyboots (*inf.*), wangler (*inf.*), wheeler-dealer (*inf.*)

scheming *adj* **1** = **calculating**, artful, conniving, cunning, deceitful, designing, duplicitous, foxy, Machiavellian, slippery, sly, tricky, underhand, wily
Antonyms *adj* above-board, artless, guileless, honest, ingenuous, naive, straightforward, trustworthy, undesigning

ment, developed from the minuet, with a contrastive middle section (a trio). [It.: joke, of Gmc origin]

Schick test (ʃɪk) *n Med.* a skin test to determine immunity to diphtheria. [C20: after Bela *Schick* (1877–1967), US paediatrician]

schilling ('ʃɪlɪŋ) *n* the standard monetary unit of Austria. [C18: from G: SHILLING]

schism ❶ ('sɪzəm, 'skɪz-) *n* **1** the division of a group into opposing factions. **2** the factions so formed. **3** division within or separation from an established Church, not necessarily involving differences in doctrine. [C14: from Church L *schisma*, from Gk *skhisma* a cleft, from *skhizein* to split]

schismatic ❶ (sɪz'mætɪk, skɪz-) *or* **schismatical** *adj* **1** of or promoting schism. ◆ *n* **2** a person who causes schism or belongs to a schismatic faction.
▸**schis'matically** *adv*

schist (ʃɪst) *n* any metamorphic rock that can be split into thin layers. [C18: from F *schiste*, from L *lapis schistos* stone that may be split, from Gk *skhizein* to split]
▸'**schistose** *adj*

schistosome ('ʃɪstəˌsəum) *n* any of a genus of blood flukes which cause disease in man and domestic animals. Also called: **bilharzia**. [C19: from NL *Schistosoma*; see SCHIST, -SOME[3]]

schistosomiasis (ˌʃɪstəsəu'maɪəsɪs) *n* a disease caused by infestation of the body with schistosomes. Also called: **bilharziasis**.

schizanthus (skɪz'ænθəs) *n* a flowering annual plant, native to Chile, that has finely divided leaves. [C19: NL from Gk *skhizein* to cut + *anthos* flower]

schizo ('skɪtsəu) *Offens.* ◆ *adj* **1** schizophrenic. ◆ *n, pl* **schizos**. **2** a schizophrenic person.

schizo- *or before a vowel* **schiz-** *combining form.* indicating a cleavage, split, or division: *schizophrenia*. [from Gk *skhizein* to split]

schizocarp ('skɪzəˌkɑːp) *n Bot.* a dry fruit that splits into two or more one-seeded portions at maturity.
▸ˌ**schizo'carpous** *adj*

schizoid ('skɪtsɔɪd) *adj* **1** *Psychol.* denoting a personality disorder characterized by extreme shyness and oversensitivity. **2** *Inf.* characterized by conflicting or contradictory ideas, attitudes, etc. ◆ *n* **3** a person who has a schizoid personality.

schizomycete (ˌskɪtsəumaɪ'siːt) *n* any microscopic organism of the class *Schizomycetes*, which includes the bacteria.

schizophrenia (ˌskɪtsəu'friːnɪə) *n* **1** any of a group of psychotic disorders characterized by progressive deterioration of the personality, withdrawal from reality, hallucinations, emotional instability, etc. **2** *Inf.* behaviour that seems to be motivated by contradictory or conflicting principles. [C20: from SCHIZO- + Gk *phrēn* mind]
▸ˌ**schizo'phrenic** *adj, n*

schizothymia (ˌskɪtsəu'θaɪmɪə) *n Psychiatry.* the condition of being schizoid or introverted. It encompasses elements of schizophrenia. [C20: NL, from SCHIZO- + *-thymia*, from Gk *thumos* spirit]
▸ˌ**schizo'thymic** *adj*

schlieren ('ʃlɪərən) *n* **1** *Physics.* visible streaks produced in a transparent fluid as a result of variations in the fluid's density. **2** streaks or platelike masses of mineral in a rock mass. [G, pl of *Schliere* streak]

schmaltz ❶ *or* **schmalz** (ʃmælts, ʃmɔːlts) *n* excessive sentimentality. [C20: from G (*Schmalz*) & Yiddish: melted fat, from OHG *smalz*]
▸'**schmaltzy** *or* '**schmalzy** *adj*

Schmidt telescope *or* **camera** (ʃmɪt) *n* a catadioptric telescope designed to produce a very sharp image of a large area of sky in one photographic exposure. [C20: after B. V. *Schmidt* (1879–1935), Estonian-born G inventor]

schnapper ('ʃnæpə) *n* a variant spelling of **snapper** (senses 1, 2).

schnapps *or* **schnaps** (ʃnæps) *n* **1** a Dutch spirit distilled from potatoes. **2** (in Germany) any strong spirit. [C19: from G *Schnaps*, from *schnappen* to SNAP]

schnauzer ('ʃnautsə) *n* a wire-haired breed of dog of the terrier type, originally from Germany, with a greyish coat. [C19: from G *Schnauze* snout]

schnitzel ('ʃnɪtsəl) *n* a thin slice of meat, esp. veal. [G: cutlet, from *schnitzen* to carve, *schnitzeln* to whittle]

schnorkel ('ʃnɔːkᵊl) *n, vb* **schnorkels, schnorkelling, schnorkelled.** a less common variant of **snorkel**.

schnozzle ('ʃnɒzᵊl) *n Chiefly US.* a slang word for **nose**. [alteration of Yiddish *shnoitsl*, from G *Schnauze* snout]

scholar ❶ ('skɒlə) *n* **1** a learned person, esp. in the humanities. **2** a person, esp. a child, who studies; pupil. **3** a student receiving a scholarship. **4** *S. African.* a school pupil. [C14: from OF *escoler*, via LL from L *schola* SCHOOL[1]]
▸'**scholarly** *adj* ▸'**scholarliness** *n*

scholarship ❶ ('skɒləʃɪp) *n* **1** academic achievement; learning. **2a** financial aid provided for a scholar because of academic merit. **2b** the position of a student who gains this financial aid. **2c** (*as modifier*): *a scholarship student.* **3** the qualities of a scholar.

scholastic ❶ (skə'læstɪk) *adj* **1** of or befitting schools, scholars, or education. **2** pedantic or precise. **3** (*often cap.*) characteristic of or relating to the medieval Schoolmen. ◆ *n* **4** a student or pupil. **5** a person who is given to logical subtleties. **6** (*often cap.*) a disciple or adherent of scholasticism; Schoolman. **7** a Jesuit student who is undergoing a period of probation prior to commencing his theological studies. [C16: via L from Gk *skholastikos* devoted to learning, ult. from *skholē* SCHOOL[1]]
▸**scho'lastically** *adv*

scholasticism (skə'læstɪˌsɪzəm) *n* (*sometimes cap.*) the system of philosophy, theology, and teaching that dominated medieval western Europe and was based on the writings of the Church Fathers and Aristotle.

scholiast ('skəulɪˌæst) *n* a medieval annotator, esp. of classical texts. [C16: from LGk, ult. from Gk *skholē* school]
▸ˌ**scholi'astic** *adj*

school[1] ❶ (skuːl) *n* **1a** an institution or building at which children and young people receive education. **1b** (*as modifier*): *school day.* **1c** (*in combination*): *schoolwork.* **2** any educational institution or building. **3** a faculty or department specializing in a particular subject: *a law school.* **4** the staff and pupils of a school. **5** the period of instruction in a school or one session of this: *he stayed after school to do extra work.* **6** a place or sphere of activity that instructs: *the school of hard knocks.* **7** a body of people or pupils adhering to a certain set of principles, doctrines, or methods. **8** a group of artists, writers, etc., linked by the same style, teachers, or aims. **9** a style of life: *a gentleman of the old school.* **10** *Inf.* a group assembled for a common purpose, esp. gambling or drinking. ◆ *vb* (*tr*) **11** to train or educate in or as in a school. **12** to discipline or control. [OE *scōl*, from L *schola* school, from Gk *skholē* leisure spent in the pursuit of knowledge]

school[2] (skuːl) *n* **1** a group of fish or other aquatic animals that swim together. ◆ *vb* **2** (*intr*) to form such a group. [OE *scolu* SHOAL[2]]

school board *n* **1** *English History.* an elected board of ratepayers who provided elementary schools (**board schools**). **2** (in the US and Canada) a local board of education.

schoolboy ('skuːlˌbɔɪ) *or* (*fem*) **schoolgirl** *n* a child attending school.

schoolhouse ('skuːlˌhaus) *n* **1** a building used as a school. **2** a house attached to a school.

schoolie ('skuːlɪ) *n Austral. sl.* **1** a schoolteacher. **2** a high school student.

schooling ❶ ('skuːlɪŋ) *n* **1** education, esp. when received at school. **2** the process of teaching or being taught in a school. **3** the training of an animal, esp. of a horse for dressage.

schoolman ('skuːlmən) *n, pl* **schoolmen**. (*sometimes cap.*) a scholar versed in the learning of the **Schoolmen**, the masters in the universities of the Middle Ages who were versed in scholasticism.

schoolmarm ('skuːlˌmɑːm) *n Inf.* **1** a woman schoolteacher. **2** any woman considered to be prim or old-fashioned.
▸'**school,marmish** *adj*

schoolmaster ('skuːlˌmɑːstə) *or* (*fem*) **schoolmistress** *n* **1** a person who teaches in or runs a school. **2** a person or thing that acts as an instructor.

schoolmate ('skuːlˌmeɪt) *or* **schoolfellow** *n* a companion at school; fellow pupil.

school of arts *n Austral.* a public building in a small town: orig. one used for adult education.

Schools (skuːlz) *pl n* **1 the Schools.** the medieval Schoolmen collectively. **2** (at Oxford University) **2a** the University building in which examinations are held. **2b** *Inf.* the Second Public Examination for the degree of Bachelor of Arts.

schoolteacher ❶ ('skuːlˌtiːtʃə) *n* a person who teaches in a school.
▸'**school,teaching** *n*

school year *n* **1** a twelve-month period, usually of three terms, during which pupils remain in the same class. **2** the time during this period when the school is open.

schooner ('skuːnə) *n* **1** a sailing vessel with at least two masts, with all lower sails rigged fore-and-aft, and with the main mast stepped aft. **2**

THESAURUS

schism *n* **1** = **division**, breach, break, discord, disunion, rift, rupture, separation, splintering, split

schismatic *adj* **1** = **separatist**, discordant, dissentient, dissenting, dissident, heretical, heterodox, seceding, splinter

schmaltzy *adj* = **sentimental**, bathetic, cloying, corny (*sl.*), maudlin, mawkish, mushy (*inf.*), overemotional, sloppy (*inf.*), slushy (*inf.*), soppy (*inf.*), tear-jerking

scholar *n* **1** = **intellectual**, academic, bluestocking (*usually disparaging*), bookworm, egghead (*inf.*), man of letters, savant **2** = **student**, disciple, learner, pupil, schoolboy *or* schoolgirl

scholarly *adj* **1** = **learned**, academic, bookish, erudite, intellectual, lettered, scholastic, studious, well-read
Antonyms *adj* lowbrow, middlebrow, philistine, unacademic, uneducated, unintellectual, unlettered

scholarship *n* **1** = **learning**, accomplishments, attainments, book-learning, education, erudition, knowledge, lore **2** = **bursary**, exhibition, fellowship

scholastic *adj* **1** = **learned**, academic, bookish, lettered, literary, scholarly **2** = **pedantic**, pedagogic, precise

school[1] *n* **1-3** = **academy**, alma mater, college, department, discipline, faculty, institute, institution, seminary **7** = **group**, adherents, circle, class, clique, denomination, devotees, disciples, faction, followers, following, schism, sect, set **9** = **way of life**, creed, faith, outlook, persuasion, school of thought, stamp ◆ *vb* **11** = **train**, coach, discipline, drill, educate, indoctrinate, instruct, prepare, prime, tutor, verse

schooling *n* **1** = **teaching**, book-learning, education, formal education, grounding, guidance, instruction, training, tuition

schoolteacher *n* = **schoolmaster** *or* **schoolmistress**, dominie (*Scot.*), instructor, pedagogue, schoolmarm (*inf.*)

Brit. a large glass for sherry. **3** *US, Canad., Austral., & NZ.* a large glass for beer. [C18: from ?]

schottische (ʃɒ'tiːʃ) *n* **1** a 19th-century German dance resembling a slow polka. **2** a piece of music composed for or in the manner of this dance. [C19: from G *der schottische Tanz* the Scottish dance]

Schottky effect ('ʃɒtkɪ) *n Physics.* a reduction in the energy required to remove an electron from a solid surface in a vacuum when an electric field is applied to the surface. [C20: after W. *Schottky* (1886–1976), G physicist]

schuss (ʃʊs) *Skiing.* ◆ *n* **1** a straight high-speed downhill run. ◆ *vb* **2** (*intr*) to perform a schuss. [G: SHOT[1]]

schwa *or* **shwa** (ʃwɑː) *n* **1** a central vowel represented in the International Phonetic Alphabet by (ə). The sound occurs in unstressed syllables in English, as in *around* and *sofa.* **2** the symbol (ə) used to represent this sound. [C19: via G from Heb. *shewā*, a diacritic indicating lack of a vowel sound]

sci. *abbrev. for:* **1** science. **2** scientific.

sciatic (saɪ'ætɪk) *adj* **1** *Anat.* of or relating to the hip or the hipbone. **2** of or afflicted with sciatica. [C16: from F, from LL, from L *ischiadicus* relating to pain in the hip, from Gk, from *iskhia* hip-joint]

sciatica (saɪ'ætɪkə) *n* a form of neuralgia characterized by intense pain along the body's longest nerve (**sciatic nerve**), extending from the back of the thigh down to the calf of the leg. [C15: from LL *sciatica;* see SCIATIC]

science Ⓣ ('saɪəns) *n* **1** the systematic study of the nature and behaviour of the material and physical universe, based on observation, experiment, and measurement. **2** the knowledge so obtained or the practice of obtaining it. **3** any particular branch of this knowledge: *the applied sciences.* **4** any body of knowledge organized in a systematic manner. **5** skill or technique. **6** *Arch.* knowledge. [C14: via OF from L *scientia* knowledge, from *scīre* to know]

science fiction *n* **a** a literary genre that makes imaginative use of scientific knowledge. **b** (*as modifier*): *a science-fiction writer.*

Science Museum *n* a museum in London, originating from 1852 and given its present name and site in 1899: contains collections relating to the history of science, technology, and industry.

science park *n* an area where scientific research and commercial development are carried on in cooperation.

scienter (saɪ'ɛntə) *adv Law.* knowingly; wilfully. [from L]

sciential (saɪ'ɛnʃəl) *adj* **1** of or relating to science. **2** skilful or knowledgeable.

scientific Ⓣ (ˌsaɪən'tɪfɪk) *adj* **1** (*prenominal*) of, derived from, or used in science: *scientific equipment.* **2** (*prenominal*) occupied in science: *scientific manpower.* **3** conforming with the methods used in science.
▸ˌ**scien'tifically** *adv*

scientism ('saɪənˌtɪzəm) *n* **1** the application of the scientific method. **2** the uncritical application of scientific methods to inappropriate fields of study.
▸ˌ**scien'tistic** *adj*

scientist Ⓣ ('saɪəntɪst) *n* a person who studies or practises any of the sciences or who uses scientific methods.

Scientology (ˌsaɪən'tɒlədʒɪ) *n Trademark.* the philosophy of the Church of Scientology, a nondenominational movement founded in the US in the 1950s, which emphasizes self-knowledge as a means of realizing full spiritual potential. [C20: from L *scient(ia)* SCIENCE + -LOGY]
▸ˌ**Scien'tologist** *n*

sci-fi ('saɪ'faɪ) *n* short for **science fiction.**

scilicet ('sɪlɪˌsɛt) *adv* namely: used esp. in explaining an obscure text or supplying a missing word. [L: from *scīre licet* it is permitted to know]

scilla ('sɪlə) *n* any of a genus of liliaceous plants having small bell-shaped flowers. See also **squill** (sense 3). [C19: via L from Gk *skilla*]

scimitar ('sɪmɪtə) *n* an oriental sword with a curved blade broadening towards the point. [C16: from OIt., prob. from Persian *shimshīr,* from ?]

scintigraphy (ˌsɪn'tɪgrəfɪ) *n Med.* a diagnostic technique using a radioactive tracer and scintillation counter for producing pictures (**scintigrams**) of internal parts of the body. [C20: from SCINTI(LLATION) + -GRAPHY]

scintilla (sɪn'tɪlə) *n* a minute amount; hint, trace, or particle. [C17: from L: a spark]

scintillate Ⓣ ('sɪntɪˌleɪt) *vb* **scintillates, scintillating, scintillated.** (*mainly intr*) **1** (*also tr*) to give off (sparks); sparkle. **2** to be animated or brilliant. **3** *Physics.* to give off flashes of light as a result of the impact of photons. [C17: from L *scintillāre,* from *scintilla* a spark]
▸**'scintillant** *adj* ▸**'scintilˌlating** *adj*

scintillation (ˌsɪntɪ'leɪʃən) *n* **1** the act of scintillating. **2** a spark or flash. **3** the twinkling of stars. **4** *Physics.* a flash of light produced when a material scintillates.

scintillation counter *n* an instrument for detecting and measuring the intensity of high-energy radiation. It consists of a phosphor with which particles collide producing flashes of light that are converted into pulses of electric current that are counted by electronic equipment.

sciolism ('saɪəˌlɪzəm) *n Rare.* the practice of opinionating on subjects of which one has only superficial knowledge. [C19: from LL *sciolus* someone with a smattering of knowledge, from L *scīre* to know]
▸**'sciolist** *n* ▸ˌ**scio'listic** *adj*

scion Ⓣ ('saɪən) *n* **1** a descendant or young member of a family. **2** a shoot of a plant used to form a graft. [C14: from OF *cion,* of Gmc origin]

scirrhus ('sɪrəs) *n, pl* **scirrhi** (-raɪ) *or* **scirrhuses.** *Pathol.* a firm cancerous growth composed of fibrous tissues. [C17: from NL, from L *scirros,* from Gk, from *skiros* hard]
▸**scirrhoid** ('sɪrɔɪd) *adj*

scission ('sɪʃən) *n* the act or an instance of cutting, splitting, or dividing. [C15: from LL *scissiō,* from *scindere* to split]

scissor ('sɪzə) *vb* to cut (an object) with scissors.

scissors ('sɪzəz) *pl n* **1** Also called: **pair of scissors.** a cutting instrument used for cloth, hair, etc., having two crossed pivoted blades that cut by a shearing action. **2** a wrestling hold in which a wrestler wraps his legs round his opponent's body or head and squeezes. **3** any gymnastic feat in which the legs cross and uncross in a scissor-like movement. [C14 *sisoures,* from OF *cisoires,* from Vulgar L *cīsōria* (unattested), ult. from L *caedere* to cut]

scissors kick *n* a type of swimming kick in which one leg is moved forward and the other bent back and they are then brought together again in a scissor-like action.

sciurine ('sarjurɪn, -ˌraɪn) *adj* of or belonging to a family of rodents inhabiting most parts of the world except Australia and southern South America: includes squirrels, marmots, and chipmunks. [C19: from L *sciūrus,* from Gk *skiouros* squirrel, from *skia* a shadow + *oura* a tail]

sclera ('sklɪərə) *n* the firm white fibrous membrane that forms the outer covering of the eyeball. Also called: **sclerotic.** [C19: from NL, from Gk *sklēros* hard]
▸**scle'ritis** *n*

sclerenchyma (sklɪə'rɛŋkɪmə) *n* a supporting tissue in plants consisting of dead cells with very thick lignified walls. [C19: from SCLERO- + PARENCHYMA]

sclero- *or before a vowel* **scler-** *combining form.* **1** indicating hardness: *sclerosis.* **2** of the sclera: *sclerotomy.* [from Gk *sklēros* hard]

scleroderma (ˌsklɪərəʊ'dɜːmə) *or* **sclerodermia** (ˌsklɪərəʊ'dɜːmɪə) *n* a chronic disease common among women, characterized by thickening and hardening of the skin.

scleroma (sklɪə'rəʊmə) *n, pl* **scleromata** (-mətə). *Pathol.* any small area of abnormally hard tissue, esp. in a mucous membrane. [C17: from NL, from Gk, from *sklēroun* to harden, from *sklēros* hard]

scleroprotein (ˌsklɪərəʊ'prəʊtiːn) *n* any of a group of insoluble stable proteins such as keratin that occur in skeletal and connective tissues. Also called: **albuminoid.**

sclerosis (sklɪə'rəʊsɪs) *n, pl* **scleroses** (-siːz). **1** *Pathol.* a hardening or thickening of organs, tissues, or vessels from inflammation, degeneration, or (esp. on the inner walls of arteries) deposition of fatty plaques. **2** the hardening of a plant cell wall or tissue. [C14: via Med. L from Gk *sklērōsis* a hardening]

sclerotic (sklɪə'rɒtɪk) *adj* **1** of or relating to the sclera. **2** of, relating to, or having sclerosis. ◆ *n* **3** another name for **sclera.** [C16: from Med. L *sclērōticus,* from Gk; see SCLEROMA]

sclerous ('sklɪərəs) *adj Anat., pathol.* hard; bony; indurated. [C19: from Gk *sklēros* hard]

SCM (in Britain) *abbrev. for:* **1** State Certified Midwife. **2** Student Christian Movement.

scoff[1] Ⓣ (skɒf) *vb* **1** (*intr;* often foll. by *at*) to speak contemptuously (about); mock. **2** (*tr*) *Obs.* to regard with derision. ◆ *n* **3** an expression of derision. **4** an object of derision. [C14: prob. from ON]
▸**'scoffer** *n* ▸**'scoffing** *adj, n*

scoff[2] Ⓣ (skɒf) *Inf., chiefly Brit.* ◆ *vb* **1** to eat (food) fast and greedily. ◆ *n* **2** food or rations. [C19: var. of *scaff* food]

scold Ⓣ (skəʊld) *vb* **1** to find fault with or reprimand (a person) harshly. **2** (*intr*) to use harsh or abusive language. ◆ *n* **3** a person, esp. a woman, who constantly finds fault. [C13: from ON SKALD]
▸**'scolder** *n* ▸**'scolding** *n*

THESAURUS

science *n* **3, 4 = discipline,** body of knowledge, branch of knowledge **5 = skill,** art, technique

scientific *adj* **3 = systematic,** accurate, controlled, exact, mathematical, precise

scientist *n* **= inventor,** boffin (*inf.*), technophile

scintillate *vb* **1 = sparkle,** blaze, coruscate, flash, give off sparks, gleam, glint, glisten, glitter, twinkle

scintillating *adj* **2 = brilliant,** animated, bright, dazzling, ebullient, exciting, glittering, lively, sparkling, stimulating, witty

scion *n* **1 = descendant,** child, heir, offspring, successor **2 = offshoot,** branch, graft, shoot, slip, sprout, twig

scoff[1] *vb* **1 = scorn,** belittle, deride, despise, flout, gibe, jeer, knock (*inf.*), laugh at, make light of, make sport of, mock, poke fun at, pooh-pooh, revile, ridicule, sneer, taunt, twit

scoff[2] *vb* **1 = gobble (up),** bolt, cram, cram oneself on, devour, gollop, gorge oneself on, gulp down, guzzle, make a pig of oneself on (*inf.*), put away, stuff oneself with, wolf ◆ *n* **2 = food,** chow (*inf.*), eats (*sl.*), fare, feed, grub (*sl.*), meal, nosh (*sl.*), nosh-up (*Brit. sl.*), rations

scold *vb* **1 = reprimand,** bawl out (*inf.*), berate, blame, bring (someone) to book, carpet (*inf.*), castigate, censure, chide, find fault with, give a rocket (*Brit. & NZ inf.*), haul (someone) over the coals (*inf.*), have (someone) on the carpet (*inf.*), lecture, nag, rate, read the riot act, rebuke, remonstrate with, reproach, reprove, slate (*inf., chiefly Brit.*), take (someone) to task, tear into (*inf.*), tear (someone) off a strip (*Brit. inf.*), tell off (*inf.*), tick off (*inf.*), upbraid, vituperate ◆ *n* **3 = nag,** shrew, termagant (*rare*), Xanthippe

Antonyms *vb* ≠ **reprimand:** acclaim, applaud, approve, commend, compliment, extol, laud, praise

scoliosis (ˌskɒlɪˈəʊsɪs) *n Pathol.* an abnormal lateral curvature of the spine. [C18: from NL, from Gk: a curving, from *skolios* bent]
▸**scoliotic** (ˌskɒlɪˈɒtɪk) *adj*

scollop (ˈskɒləp) *n, vb* a variant spelling of **scallop.**

scombroid (ˈskɒmbrɔɪd) *adj* **1** of, relating to, or belonging to the *Scombroidea,* a suborder of marine spiny-finned fishes having a forked powerful tail: includes the mackerels, tunnies, and sailfish. ◆ *n* **2** any fish belonging to the suborder *Scombroidea.* [C19: from Gk *skombros* a mackerel; see -OID]

sconce[1] (skɒns) *n* **1** a bracket fixed to a wall for holding candles or lights. **2** a flat candlestick with a handle. [C14: from OF *esconse* hiding place, lantern, or from LL *sconsa,* from *absconsa* dark lantern]

sconce[2] (skɒns) *n* a small protective fortification, such as an earthwork. [C16: from Du. *schans,* from MHG *schanze* bundle of brushwood]

scone (skɒn, skəʊn) *n* a light plain doughy cake made from flour with very little fat, cooked in an oven or (esp. originally) on a griddle. [C16: Scot., ?from MDu. *schoonbrot* fine bread]

scoop ⓣ (skuːp) *n* **1** a utensil used as a shovel or ladle, esp. a small shovel with deep sides and a short handle, used for taking up flour, etc. **2** a utensil with a long handle and round bowl used for dispensing liquids, etc. **3** anything that resembles a scoop in action, such as the bucket on a dredge. **4** a utensil used for serving mashed potatoes, ice cream, etc. **5** a spoonlike surgical instrument for extracting foreign matter, etc., from the body. **6** the quantity taken up by a scoop. **7** the act of scooping, dredging, etc. **8** a hollow cavity. **9** *Sl.* a large quick gain, as of money. **10** a news story reported in one newspaper before all the others. ◆ *vb (mainly tr)* **11** (often foll. by *up*) to take up and remove (an object or substance) with or as if with a scoop. **12** (often foll. by *out*) to hollow out with or as if with a scoop. **13** to make (a large sudden profit). **14** to beat (rival newspapers) in uncovering a news item. [C14: via MDu. *schōpe* from Gmc]
▸**ˈscooper** *n* ▸**ˈscoopˌful** *n*

scoot ⓣ (skuːt) *vb* **1** to go or cause to go quickly or hastily; dart or cause to dart off or away. ◆ *n* **2** the act of scooting. [C19 (US): from ?]

scooter (ˈskuːtə) *n* **1** a child's vehicle consisting of a low footboard on wheels, steered by handlebars. **2** See **motor scooter.**

scope ⓣ (skəʊp) *n* **1** opportunity for exercising the faculties or abilities. **2** range of view or grasp. **3** the area covered by an activity, topic, etc.: *the scope of his thesis was vast.* **4** *Naut.* slack left in an anchor cable. **5** *Logic.* the part of a formula that follows a quantifier or an operator. **6** *Inf.* short for **telescope, microscope, oscilloscope,** etc. **7** *Arch.* purpose. [C16: from It. *scopo* goal, from L *scopus,* from Gk *skopos* target]

-scope *n combining form.* indicating an instrument for observing or detecting: *microscope.* [from NL *-scopium,* from Gk *-skopion,* from *skopein* to look at]
▸**-scopic** *adj combining form.*

scopolamine (skəˈpɒləˌmiːn) *n* a colourless viscous liquid alkaloid extracted from certain plants, such as henbane: used in preventing travel sickness and as a sedative and truth serum. Also called: **hyoscine.** [C20: *scopol-* from NL *scopolia Japonica* Japanese belladonna (from which the alkaloid is extracted), after G. A. *Scopoli* (1723–88), It. naturalist, + AMINE]

-scopy *n combining form.* indicating a viewing or observation: *microscopy.* [from Gk *-skopia,* from *skopein* to look at]

scorbutic (skɔːˈbjuːtɪk) *adj* of or having scurvy. [C17: from NL *scorbūticus,* from Med. L *scorbūtus,* prob. of Gmc origin]
▸**scorˈbutically** *adv*

scorch ⓣ (skɔːtʃ) *vb* **1** to burn or become burnt, esp. so as to affect the colour, taste, etc. **2** to wither or parch or cause to wither from exposure to heat. **3** *(intr) Inf.* to be very hot: *it is scorching outside.* **4** *(tr) Inf.* to criticize harshly. ◆ *n* **5** a slight burn. **6** a mark caused by the application of too great heat. **7** *Horticulture.* a mark on fruit, etc., caused by pests or insecticides. [C15: prob. from ON *skorpna* to shrivel up]
▸**ˈscorching** *adj*

scorched earth policy *n* **1** the policy in warfare of removing or destroying everything that might be useful to an invading enemy. **2** *Business.* a manoeuvre by a company expecting an unwelcome takeover bid in which apparent profitability is greatly reduced by a reversible operation, such as borrowing at an exorbitant interest rate.

scorcher (ˈskɔːtʃə) *n* **1** a person or thing that scorches. **2** something caustic. **3** *Inf.* a very hot day. **4** *Brit. inf.* something remarkable.

score ⓣ (skɔː) *n* **1** a numerical record of a competitive game or match. **2** the total number of points made by a side or individual in a game. **3** the act of scoring, esp. a point or points. **4 the score.** *Inf.* the actual situation. **5** a group or set of twenty: *three score years and ten.* **6** *(usually pl;* foll. by *of)* lots: *I have scores of things to do.* **7** *Music.* **7a** the printed form of a composition in which the instrumental or vocal parts appear on separate staves vertically arranged on large pages (**full score**) or in a condensed version, usually for piano (**short score**) or voices and piano (**vocal score**). **7b** the incidental music for a film or play. **7c** the songs, music, etc., for a stage or film musical. **8** a mark or notch, esp. one made in keeping a tally. **9** an account of amounts due. **10** an amount recorded as due. **11** a reason: *the book was rejected on the score of length.* **12** a grievance. **13a** a line marking a division or boundary. **13b** *(as modifier): score line.* **14 over the score.** *Inf.* excessive; unfair. **15 settle** *or* **pay off a score. 15a** to avenge a wrong. **15b** to repay a debt. ◆ *vb* **scores, scoring, scored. 16** to gain (a point or points) in a game or contest. **17** *(tr)* to make a total score of. **18** to keep a record of the score (of). **19** *(tr)* to be worth (a certain amount) in a game. **20** *(tr)* to record by making notches in. **21** to make (cuts, lines, etc.) in or on. **22** *(intr) Sl.* to obtain something desired, esp. to purchase an illegal drug. **23** *(intr) Sl.* (of men) to be successful in seducing a person. **24** *(tr)* **24a** to arrange (a piece of music) for specific instruments or voices. **24b** to write the music for (a film, play, etc.). **25** to achieve (success or an advantage): *your idea scored with the boss.* [OE *scora*]
▸**ˈscorer** *n*

scoreboard (ˈskɔːˌbɔːd) *n Sport, etc.* a board for displaying the score of a game or match.

scorecard (ˈskɔːˌkɑːd) *n* **1** a card on which scores are recorded, as in golf. **2** a card identifying the players in a sports match, esp. cricket.

score off ⓣ *vb (intr, prep)* to gain an advantage at someone else's expense.

scoria (ˈskɔːrɪə) *n, pl* **scoriae** (-rɪˌiː). **1** a mass of solidified lava containing many cavities. **2** refuse obtained from smelted ore. [C17: from L: dross, from Gk *skōria,* from *skōr* excrement]

scorify (ˈskɔːrɪˌfaɪ) *vb* **scorifies, scorifying, scorified.** to remove (impurities) from metals by forming scoria.
▸**ˌscorifiˈcation** *n* ▸**ˈscoriˌfier** *n*

scoring (ˈskɔːrɪŋ) *n* another name for **orchestration** (see **orchestrate**).

scorn ⓣ (skɔːn) *n* **1** open contempt for a person or thing. **2** an object of contempt or derision. ◆ *vb* **3** to treat with contempt or derision. **4** *(tr)* to reject with contempt. [C12 *schornen,* from OF *escharnir,* of Gmc origin]
▸**ˈscorner** *n* ▸**ˈscornful** *adj* ▸**ˈscornfully** *adv*

Scorpio (ˈskɔːpɪˌəʊ) *n* **1** Also called: **Scorpius.** *Astron.* a large S constellation. **2** Also called: the **Scorpion.** *Astrol.* the eighth sign of the zodiac. The sun is in this sign between about Oct. 23 and Nov. 21. [L: SCORPION]

scorpion (ˈskɔːpɪən) *n* **1** an arachnid of warm dry regions, having a segmented body with a long tail terminating in a venomous sting. **2 false scorpion.** a small nonvenomous arachnid that superficially resembles the scorpion but lacks the long tail. **3** *Bible.* a barbed scourge (I Kings 12:11). [C13: via OF from L *scorpiō,* from Gk *skorpios,* from ?]

THESAURUS

scolding *n* = **rebuke,** dressing-down, (good) talking-to *(inf.),* lecture, piece of one's mind, telling-off *(inf.),* ticking-off *(inf.),* tongue-lashing, wigging *(Brit. sl.)*

scoop *n* **1-4** = **ladle,** dipper, spoon **10** = **exclusive,** coup, exposé, inside story, revelation, sensation ◆ *vb* **11** *often with* **up** = **lift,** clear away, gather up, pick up, remove, sweep up *or* away, take up **12** *with* **out** = **hollow,** bail, dig, dip, empty, excavate, gouge, ladle, scrape, shovel

scoot *vb* **1** = **dash,** bolt, dart, run, scamper, scurry, scuttle, skedaddle *(inf.),* skitter, sprint, zip

scope *n* **1** = **opportunity,** elbowroom, freedom, latitude, liberty, room, space **2** = **range,** ambit, area, capacity, field of reference, orbit, outlook, purview, reach, span, sphere **3** = **extent,** compass, confines, range

scorch *vb* **1, 2** = **burn,** blacken, blister, char, parch, roast, sear, shrivel, singe, wither

scorching *adj* **3** = **burning,** baking, boiling, broiling, fiery, flaming, red-hot, roasting, searing, sizzling, sweltering, torrid, tropical, unbearably hot

score *n* **1** = **points,** grade, mark, outcome, record, result, total **4 the score** *Informal* = **the situation,** the equation, the facts, the lie of the land, the reality, the setup *(inf.),* the truth **6** *plural* = **lots,** a flock, a great number, an army, a throng, crowds, droves, hosts, hundreds, legions, masses, millions, multitudes, myriads, swarms, very many **9** = **amount due,** account, bill, charge, debt, obligation, reckoning, tab *(US inf.),* tally, total **11** = **grounds,** account, basis, cause, ground, reason **12** = **grievance,** a bone to pick, grudge, injury, injustice, wrong **15a settle** *or* **pay off a score** = **get one's own back** *(inf.),* avenge, get even with, give an eye for an eye, give like for like *or* tit for tat, give (someone) a taste of his own medicine, hit back, pay (someone) back (in his own coin), repay, requite, retaliate ◆ *vb* **16** = **gain,** achieve, amass, chalk up *(inf.),* make, notch up *(inf.),* win **18** = **keep count,** count, keep a tally of, record, register, tally **21** = **cut,** crosshatch, deface, gouge, graze, indent, mar, mark, nick, notch, scrape, scratch, slash **24** *Music* = **arrange,** adapt, orchestrate, set **25** = **go down well with (someone),** gain an advantage, impress, make a hit *(inf.),* make an impact *or* impression, make a point, put oneself across, triumph

score off *vb* = **get the better of,** be one up on *(inf.),* have the laugh on, humiliate, make a fool of, make (someone) look silly, worst

scorn *n* **1** = **contempt,** contemptuousness, contumely, derision, despite, disdain, disparagement, mockery, sarcasm, scornfulness, slight, sneer ◆ *vb* **3, 4** = **despise,** be above, consider beneath one, contemn, curl one's lip at, deride, disdain, flout, hold in contempt, look down on, make fun of, reject, scoff at, scout *(arch.),* slight, sneer at, spurn, turn up one's nose at *(inf.)*

Antonyms *n* ≠ **contempt:** acceptance, admiration, affection, esteem, high regard, respect, tolerance, toleration, veneration, worship ◆ *vb* ≠ **despise:** accept, admire, esteem, look favourably on, respect, revere, tolerate, venerate, worship

scornful *adj* **1** = **contemptuous,** contumelious, defiant, derisive, disdainful, haughty, insolent, insulting, jeering, mocking, sarcastic, sardonic, scathing, scoffing, slighting, sneering, supercilious, withering

scornfully *adv* **1** = **contemptuously,** disdainfully, dismissively, scathingly, slightingly, with a sneer, with contempt, with disdain, witheringly, with lip curled

Scorpion ('skɔːprən) *n* **the.** the constellation Scorpio, the eighth sign of the zodiac.
scorpion fish *n* any of a genus of fish of temperate and tropical seas, having venomous spines on the dorsal and anal fins.
Scot (skɒt) *n* **1** a native or inhabitant of Scotland. **2** a member of a tribe of Celtic raiders from the north of Ireland who eventually settled in N Britain during the 5th and 6th centuries.
Scot. *abbrev. for:* **1** Scotch (whisky). **2** Scotland. **3** Scottish.
scot and lot *n Brit. history.* a municipal tax paid by burgesses that came to be regarded as a qualification for the borough franchise in parliamentary elections. [C13 *scot* tax, from Gmc]
scotch[1] (skɒtʃ) *vb (tr)* **1** to put an end to; crush: *bad weather scotched our plans.* **2** *Obs.* to cut or score. ◆ *n* **3** *Arch.* a gash. **4** a line marked down, as for hopscotch. [C15: from ?]
scotch[2] (skɒtʃ) *vb* **1** *(tr)* to block, prop, or prevent from moving with or as if with a wedge. ◆ *n* **2** a block or wedge to prevent motion. [C17: from ?]
Scotch[1] (skɒtʃ) *adj* **1** another word for **Scottish.** ◆ *n* **2** the Scots or their language.

> **USAGE NOTE** In the north of England and in Scotland, *Scotch* is not used outside fixed expressions such as *Scotch whisky*. The use of *Scotch* for *Scots* or *Scottish* is otherwise felt to be incorrect, esp. when applied to people.

Scotch[2] (skɒtʃ) *n* whisky distilled from fermented malted barley and made in Scotland. Also called: **Scotch whisky.**
Scotch broth *n Brit.* a thick soup made from mutton or beef stock, vegetables, and pearl barley.
Scotch egg *n Brit.* a hard-boiled egg enclosed in a layer of sausage meat, covered in egg and crumbs, and fried.
Scotchman ('skɒtʃmən) *or (fem)* **Scotchwoman** *n, pl* **Scotchmen** *or* **Scotchwomen.** *(regarded as bad usage by the Scots)* another word for **Scotsman** or **Scotswoman.**
Scotch mist *n* **1** a heavy wet mist. **2** drizzle.
Scotch snap *n Music.* a rhythmic pattern consisting of a short note followed by a long one. Also called: **Scotch catch.**
Scotch terrier *n* another name for **Scottish terrier.**
scoter ('skəʊtə) *n, pl* **scoters** *or* **scoter.** a sea duck of northern regions. The male plumage is black with white patches around the head and eyes. [C17: from ?]
scot-free ❶ *adv, adj (predicative)* without harm, loss, or penalty. [C16: see SCOT AND LOT]
Scotland Yard *n* the headquarters of the police force of metropolitan London. Official name: **New Scotland Yard.**
scotoma (skɒ'təʊmə) *n, pl* **scotomas** *or* **scotomata** (-mətə). **1** *Pathol.* a blind spot. **2** *Psychol.* a mental blind spot. [C16: via Med. L from Gk *skotōma* giddiness, from *skotoun* to make dark, from *skotos* darkness]
Scots ❶ (skɒts) *adj* **1** of or characteristic of Scotland, its people, their English dialects, or their Gaelic language. ◆ *n* **2** any of the English dialects spoken or written in Scotland.
Scotsman ('skɒtsmən) *or (fem)* **Scotswoman** *n, pl* **Scotsmen** *or* **Scotswomen.** a native or inhabitant of Scotland.
Scots pine *or* **Scotch pine** *n* **1** a coniferous tree of Europe and W and N Asia, having blue-green needle-like leaves and brown cones with a small prickle on each scale. **2** the wood of this tree.
Scotticism ('skɒtɪ,sɪzəm) *n* a Scottish idiom, word, etc.
Scottie *or* **Scotty** ('skɒtɪ) *n, pl* **Scotties.** **1** See **Scottish terrier.** **2** *Inf.* a Scotsman.
Scottish ('skɒtɪʃ) *adj* of, relating to, or characteristic of Scotland, its people, their Gaelic language, or their English dialects.
Scottish Certificate of Education *n* See **SCE.**
Scottish Gaelic *n* the Goidelic language of the Celts of Scotland, used esp. in the Highlands and Western Isles.
Scottish National Party *n* a political party advocating the independence of Scotland. Abbrev.: **SNP.**
Scottish terrier *n* a small but sturdy long-haired breed of terrier, usually with a black coat.
scoundrel ❶ ('skaʊndrəl) *n* a worthless or villainous person. [C16: from ?]
scour[1] ❶ ('skaʊə) *vb* **1** to clean or polish (a surface) by washing and rubbing. **2** to remove dirt from or have the dirt removed from. **3** *(tr)* to clear (a channel) by the force of water. **4** *(tr)* to remove by or as if by rubbing. **5** *(tr)* to cause (livestock) to purge their bowels. ◆ *n* **6** the act of scouring. **7** the place scoured, esp. by running water. **8** something that scours, such as a cleansing agent. **9** *(often pl)* prolonged diarrhoea in livestock, esp. cattle. [C13: via MLow G *schūren*, from OF *escurer*, from LL *excūrāre* to cleanse, from *cūrāre*; see CURE]
▸ **'scourer** *n*
scour[2] ❶ ('skaʊə) *vb* **1** to range over (territory), as in making a search. **2** to move swiftly or energetically over (territory). [C14: from ON *skūr*]
scourge ❶ (skɜːdʒ) *n* **1** a person who harasses or causes destruction. **2** a means of inflicting punishment or suffering. **3** a whip used for inflicting punishment or torture. ◆ *vb* **scourges, scourging, scourged.** *(tr)* **4** to whip. **5** to punish severely. [C13: from Anglo-F, from OF *escorgier* (unattested) to lash, from *es-* EX-[1] + L *corrigia* whip]
▸ **'scourger** *n*
scourings ('skaʊərɪŋz) *pl n* **1** the residue left after cleaning grain. **2** residue that remains after scouring.
scouse (skaʊs) *n Liverpool dialect.* a stew made from left-over meat. [C19: shortened from LOBSCOUSE]
Scouse (skaʊs) *Brit. inf.* ◆ *n* **1** Also: **Scouser.** a person who comes from Liverpool. **2** the dialect spoken by such a person. ◆ *adj* **3** of or from Liverpool. [C20: from SCOUSE]
scout[1] ❶ (skaʊt) *n* **1** a person, ship, or aircraft sent out to gain information. **2** *Mil.* a person or unit despatched to reconnoitre the position of the enemy, etc. **3** the act or an instance of scouting. **4** (esp. at Oxford University) a college servant. **5** *Inf.* a fellow. ◆ *vb* **6** to examine or observe (anything) in order to obtain information. **7** *(tr; sometimes foll. by out or up)* to seek. **8** *(intr; foll. by about or around)* to go in search (for). [C14: from OF *ascouter* to listen to, from L *auscultāre* to AUSCULTATE]
▸ **'scouter** *n*
scout[2] (skaʊt) *vb* to reject (a person, etc.) with contempt. [C17: from ON *skūta* derision]
Scout (skaʊt) *n (sometimes not cap.)* a boy or (in some countries) a girl who is a member of a worldwide movement (the **Scout Association**) founded as the Boy Scouts in England in 1908 by Lord Baden-Powell.
▸ **'Scouting** *n*
Scouter ('skaʊtə) *n* the leader of a troop of Scouts. Also called (esp. formerly): **Scoutmaster.**
scow (skaʊ) *n* an unpowered barge used for freight, etc.; lighter. [C18: via Du. *schouw* from Low G *schalde*]
scowl ❶ (skaʊl) *vb* **1** *(intr)* to contract the brows in a threatening or angry manner. ◆ *n* **2** a gloomy or threatening expression. [C14: prob. from ON]
▸ **'scowler** *n*
SCPS (in Britain) *abbrev. for* Society of Civil and Public Servants.
scrabble ❶ ('skræbᵊl) *vb* **scrabbles, scrabbling, scrabbled.** **1** *(intr; often foll. by about or at)* to scrape (at) or grope (for), as with hands or claws. **2** to struggle (with). **3** *(intr; often foll. by for)* to struggle to gain possession. **4** to scribble. ◆ *n* **5** the act or an instance of scrabbling. **6** a scribble. **7** a disorderly struggle. [C16: from MDu. *shrabbelen*, frequentative of *shrabben* to scrape]
▸ **'scrabbler** *n*
Scrabble ('skræbᵊl) *n Trademark.* a game in which words are formed by placing lettered tiles in a pattern similar to a crossword puzzle.
scrag (skræg) *n* **1** a thin or scrawny person or animal. **2** the lean end of a neck of veal or mutton. **3** *Inf.* the neck of a human being. ◆ *vb* **scrags, scragging, scragged.** **4** *(tr) Inf.* to wring the neck of. [C16: ? var. of CRAG]
scraggly ('skræglɪ) *adj* **scragglier, scraggliest.** *Chiefly US.* untidy or irregular.
scraggy ❶ ('skrægɪ) *adj* **scraggier, scraggiest.** **1** lean or scrawny. **2** rough; unkempt.
▸ **'scraggily** *adv* ▸ **'scragginess** *n*
scram[1] ❶ (skræm) *vb* **scrams, scramming, scrammed.** *(intr; often imperative) Inf.* to go away hastily. [C20: from SCRAMBLE]
scram[2] (skræm) *n* **1** an emergency shutdown of a nuclear reactor. ◆ *vb* **scrams, scramming, scrammed.** **2** (of a nuclear reactor) to shut down or be shut down in an emergency. [C20: ?from SCRAM[1]]

THESAURUS

scot-free *adj* = **unharmed**, clear, safe, scatheless (*arch.*), undamaged, unhurt, uninjured, unpunished, unscathed, without a scratch
Scots *adj* **1** = **Scottish**, Caledonian
scoundrel *n* = **rogue**, bad egg (*old-fashioned inf.*), bastard (*offens.*), blackguard, caitiff (*arch.*), cheat, good-for-nothing, heel (*sl.*), knave (*arch.*), miscreant, ne'er-do-well, rascal, reprobate, rotter (*sl., chiefly Brit.*), scally (*Northwest English dialect*), scamp, scapegrace, swine, vagabond, villain, wretch
scour[1] *vb* **1** = **rub**, abrade, buff, burnish, clean, cleanse, furbish, polish, scrub, whiten **2** = **wash**, cleanse, flush, purge
scour[2] *vb* **1** = **search**, beat, comb, forage, go over with a fine-tooth comb, hunt, look high and low, rake, ransack
scourge *n* **2** = **affliction**, bane, curse, infliction, misfortune, penalty, pest, plague, punishment, terror, torment, visitation **3** = **whip**, cat, cat-o'-nine-tails, lash, strap, switch, thong ◆ *vb* **4** = **whip**, beat, belt (*inf.*), cane, castigate, chastise, discipline, flog, horsewhip, lash, lather (*inf.*), leather, punish, take a strap to, tan (someone's) hide (*sl.*), thrash, trounce, wallop (*inf.*), whale **5** = **afflict**, curse, excoriate, harass, plague, terrorize, torment
Antonyms *n* ≠ **affliction:** benefit, blessing, boon, favour, gift, godsend
scout[1] *n* **2** = **vanguard**, advance guard, escort, lookout, outrider, precursor, reconnoitrer ◆ *vb* **6** = **reconnoitre**, case (*sl.*), check out, investigate, make a reconnaissance, observe, probe, recce (*sl.*), see how the land lies, spy, spy out, survey, watch **8** *with* **about** *or* **around** = **search for**, cast around for, ferret out, hunt for, look for, rustle up, search out, seek, track down
scowl *vb* **1** = **glower**, frown, grimace, look daggers at, lour *or* lower ◆ *n* **2** = **glower**, black look, dirty look, frown, grimace
scrabble *vb* **1** = **scrape**, clamber, claw, dig, grope, paw, scramble, scratch
scraggy *adj* **1** = **scrawny**, angular, bony, emaciated, gangling, gaunt, lanky, lean, rawboned, skinny, undernourished **2** = **unkempt**, draggle-tailed (*arch.*), grotty (*sl.*), lank, meagre, rough, scanty, scruffy, tousled
scram[1] *vb Informal* = **go away**, abscond, beat it (*sl.*), clear off (*inf.*), depart, disappear, get lost (*inf.*), get on one's bike (*Brit. sl.*), go to hell (*inf.*), leave, make oneself scarce (*inf.*), make tracks, quit, scarper (*Brit. sl.*), scoot, skedaddle (*inf.*),

scramble ➊ ('skræmbᵊl) *vb* **scrambles, scrambling, scrambled. 1** (*intr*) to climb or crawl, esp. by using the hands to aid movement. **2** to proceed hurriedly or in a disorderly fashion. **3** (*intr; often foll. by for*) to compete with others, esp. in a disordered manner. **4** (*intr;* foll. by *through*) to deal with hurriedly. **5** (*tr*) to throw together in a haphazard manner. **6** (*tr*) to collect in a hurried or disorganized manner. **7** (*tr*) to cook (eggs that have been whisked up with milk) in a pan containing a little melted butter. **8** *Mil.* to order (a crew or aircraft) to take off immediately or (of a crew or aircraft) to take off immediately. **9** (*tr*) to render (speech) unintelligible during transmission by means of an electronic scrambler. ◆ *n* **10** the act of scrambling. **11** a climb or trek over difficult ground. **12** a disorderly struggle, esp. to gain possession. **13** *Mil.* an immediate preparation for action, as of crew, aircraft, etc. **14** *Brit.* a motorcycle rally in which competitors race across rough open ground. [C16: blend of SCRABBLE & RAMP]

scrambler ('skræmblə) *n* an electronic device that renders speech unintelligible during transmission, by altering frequencies.

scrap[1] ➊ (skræp) *n* **1** a small piece of something larger; fragment. **2** an extract from something written. **3a** waste material or used articles, esp. metal, often collected and reprocessed. **3b** (*as modifier*): *scrap iron.* **4** (*pl*) pieces of discarded food. ◆ *vb* **scraps, scrapping, scrapped.** (*tr*) **5** to discard as useless. [C14: from ON *skrap*]

scrap[2] ➊ (skræp) *Inf.* ◆ *n* **1** a fight or argument. ◆ *vb* **scraps, scrapping, scrapped. 2** (*intr*) to quarrel or fight. [C17: ?from SCRAPE]

scrapbook ('skræpˌbʊk) *n* a book or album of blank pages in which to mount newspaper cuttings, pictures, etc.

scrape ➊ (skreɪp) *vb* **scrapes, scraping, scraped. 1** to move (a rough or sharp object) across (a surface), esp. to smooth or clean. **2** (*tr;* often foll. by *away* or *off*) to remove (a layer) by rubbing. **3** to produce a harsh or grating sound by rubbing against (a surface, etc.). **4** (*tr*) to injure or damage by rough contact: *to scrape one's knee.* **5** (*intr*) to be very economical (esp. in **scrimp and scrape**). **6** (*intr*) to draw the foot backwards in making a bow. **7 scrape acquaintance with.** to contrive an acquaintance with. ◆ *n* **8** the act of scraping. **9** a scraped place. **10** a harsh or grating sound. **11** *Inf.* an awkward or embarrassing predicament. **12** *Inf.* a conflict or struggle. [OE *scrapian*]
▸'**scraper** *n*

scraperboard ('skreɪpəˌbɔːd) *n* thin card covered with a layer of china clay and a top layer of Indian ink, which can be scraped away with a special tool to leave a white line.

scrape through ➊ *vb* (*adv*) **1** (*intr*) to manage or survive with difficulty. **2** to succeed in with difficulty or by a narrow margin.

scrape together ➊ *or* **up** *vb* (*tr, adv*) to collect with difficulty: *to scrape together money for a new car.*

scrapheap ➊ ('skræpˌhiːp) *n* **1** a pile of discarded material. **2 on the scrapheap.** (of people or things) having outlived their usefulness.

scrappy ➊ ('skræpɪ) *adj* **scrappier, scrappiest.** fragmentary; disjointed.
▸'**scrappily** *adv*

scratch ➊ (skrætʃ) *vb* **1** to mark or cut (the surface of something) with a rough or sharp instrument. **2** (often foll. by *at, out, off,* etc.) to scrape (the surface of something), as with claws, nails, etc. **3** to scrape (the surface of the skin) with the nails, as to relieve itching. **4** to chafe or irritate (a surface, esp. the skin). **5** to make or cause to make a grating sound. **6** (*tr;* sometimes foll. by *out*) to erase by or as if by scraping. **7** (*tr*) to write or draw awkwardly. **8** (*intr;* sometimes foll. by *along*) to earn a living, manage, etc., with difficulty. **9** to withdraw (an entry) from a race, (US) election, etc. ◆ *n* **10** the act of scratching. **11** a slight injury. **12** a mark made by scratching. **13** a slight grating sound. **14** (in a handicap sport) a competitor or the status of a competitor who has no allowance. **15a** the line from which competitors start in a race. **15b** (formerly) a line drawn on the floor of a prize ring at which the contestants stood to begin fighting. **16** *Billiards, etc.* a lucky shot. **17 from scratch.** *Inf.* from the very beginning. **18 up to scratch.** (*usually used with a negative*) *Inf.* up to standard. ◆ *adj* **19** *Sport.* (of a team) assembled hastily. **20** (in a handicap sport) with no allowance or penalty. **21** *Inf.* rough or haphazard. [C15: via OF *escrater* from Gmc]
▸'**scratcher** *n* ▸'**scratchy** *adj*

scratchcard ('skrætʒˌkɑːd) *n* a ticket that reveals whether or not the holder is eligible for a prize when the surface is removed by scratching.

scratch file *n Computing.* a temporary store for use during the execution of a program.

scratching ('skrætʃɪŋ) *n* a percussive effect obtained by rotating a gramophone record manually: a disc-jockey and dub technique.

scratch pad *n* **1** *Chiefly US & Canad.* a notebook, esp. one with detachable leaves. **2** *Computing.* a small semiconductor memory for temporary storage.

scratch video *n* the recycling of images from films or television to make collages.

scrawl ➊ (skrɔːl) *vb* **1** to write or draw (words, etc.) carelessly or hastily. ◆ *n* **2** careless or scribbled writing or drawing. [C17: ? a blend of SPRAWL & CRAWL[1]]
▸'**scrawly** *adj*

scrawny ➊ ('skrɔːnɪ) *adj* **scrawnier, scrawniest. 1** very thin and bony. **2** meagre or stunted. [C19: var. of dialect *scranny*]
▸'**scrawnily** *adv* ▸'**scrawniness** *n*

scream ➊ (skriːm) *vb* **1** to utter or emit (a sharp piercing cry or similar sound), esp. as of fear, pain, etc. **2** (*intr*) to laugh wildly. **3** (*intr*) to speak, shout, or behave in a wild manner. **4** (*tr*) to bring (oneself) into a specified state by screaming: *she screamed herself hoarse.* **5** (*intr*) to be extremely conspicuous: *these orange curtains scream; you need something more restful.* ◆ *n* **6** a sharp piercing cry or sound, esp. one denoting fear or pain. **7** *Inf.* a person or thing that causes great amusement. [C13: from Gmc]

screamer ('skriːmə) *n* **1** a person or thing that screams. **2** a goose-like aquatic bird, such as the **crested screamer** of tropical and subtropical South America. **3** *Inf.* (in printing) an exclamation mark. **4** someone or something that raises screams of laughter or astonishment. **5** *US & Canad. sl.* a sensational headline. **6** *Austral. sl.* a person or thing that is excellent of its kind.

scree (skriː) *n* an accumulation of rock fragments at the foot of a cliff or hillside, often forming a sloping heap. [OE *scrīthan* to slip; rel. to ON *skrītha* to slide]

screech[1] ➊ (skriːtʃ) *n* **1** a shrill or high-pitched sound or cry. ◆ *vb* **2** to utter with or produce a screech. [C16: var. of earlier *scritch*, imit.]
▸'**screecher** *n* ▸'**screechy** *adj*

screech[2] (skriːtʃ) *n Canad. sl.* (esp. in Newfoundland) a dark rum. [?from SCREECH[1]]

screech owl *n* **1** *Brit.* another name for **barn owl. 2** a small North American owl having a reddish-brown or grey plumage.

screed ➊ (skriːd) *n* **1** a long or prolonged speech or piece of writing. **2** a strip of wood, plaster, or metal placed on a surface to act as a guide to the thickness of the cement or plaster coat to be applied. **3** a mixture of cement, sand, and water applied to a concrete slab, etc., to give a smooth surface finish. [C14: prob. var. of OE *scrēade* shred]

screen ➊ (skriːn) *n* **1** a light movable frame, panel, or partition serving to shelter, divide, hide, etc. **2** anything that serves to shelter, protect, or conceal. **3** a frame containing a mesh that is placed over a window to keep out insects. **4** a decorated partition, esp. in a church around the choir. **5** a sieve. **6** the wide end of a cathode-ray tube, esp. in a television set, on which a visible image is formed. **7** a white or silvered surface, placed in front of a projector to receive the enlarged image of

THESAURUS

sling one's hook (*Brit. sl.*), slope off, take oneself off, vamoose (*sl., chiefly US*)

scramble *vb* **1** = **struggle**, clamber, climb, crawl, move with difficulty, push, scrabble, swarm **3** = **strive**, contend, hasten, jockey for position, jostle, make haste, push, run, rush, vie ◆ *n* **11** = **climb**, trek **12** = **struggle**, commotion, competition, confusion, free-for-all (*inf.*), hassle (*inf.*), hustle, melee *or* mêlée, muddle, race, rat race, rush, tussle

scrap[1] *n* **1** = **piece**, atom, bit, bite, crumb, fragment, grain, iota, mite, modicum, morsel, mouthful, part, particle, portion, remnant, sliver, snatch, snippet, trace **3** = **waste**, junk, off cuts **4** *plural* = **leftovers**, bits, leavings, remains, scrapings ◆ *vb* **5** = **get rid of**, abandon, break up, chuck, demolish, discard, dispense with, ditch (*sl.*), drop, jettison, junk (*inf.*), shed, throw away *or* out, throw on the scrapheap, toss out, trash (*sl.*), write off
Antonyms *vb* ≠ **get rid of:** bring back, recall, re-establish, reinstall, reinstate, restore, return

scrap[2] *Informal n* **1** = **fight**, argument, battle, brawl, disagreement, dispute, dust-up (*inf.*), quarrel, row, scrimmage, scuffle, set-to (*inf.*), shindig (*inf.*), squabble, tiff, wrangle ◆ *vb* **2** = **fight**, argue, barney (*inf.*), bicker, come to blows, fall out (*inf.*), have a shouting match (*inf.*), have words, row, spar, squabble, wrangle

scrape *vb* **1** = **rub**, abrade, bark, graze, scratch, scuff, skin **2** = **scour**, clean, erase, file, remove, rub **3** = **grate**, grind, rasp, scratch, screech, set one's teeth on edge, squeak **5** = **scrimp**, live from hand to mouth, pinch, save, skimp, stint, tighten one's belt ◆ *n* **11** *Informal* = **predicament**, awkward situation, difficulty, dilemma, distress, fix (*inf.*), mess, plight, pretty pickle (*inf.*), spot (*inf.*), tight spot, trouble

scrape through *vb* **2** = **get by** (*inf.*), cut it fine (*inf.*), have a close shave (*inf.*), just make it, struggle

scrape together *vb* = **collect**, amass, dredge up, get hold of, glean, hoard, muster, rake up *or* together, save

scrapheap *n* **2 on the scrapheap** = **discarded**, ditched (*sl.*), jettisoned, put out to grass (*inf.*), redundant, written off

scrappy *adj* = **incomplete**, bitty, disjointed, fragmentary, perfunctory, piecemeal, sketchy, thrown together

scratch *vb* **1, 2** = **mark**, claw, cut, damage, etch, grate, graze, incise, lacerate, make a mark on, rub, score, scrape **6** = **erase**, annul, cancel, cross out, delete, eliminate, strike off **9** = **withdraw**, pull out, stand down ◆ *n* **12** = **mark**, blemish, claw mark, gash, graze, laceration, scrape **18 up to scratch** *Informal* = **adequate**, acceptable, capable, competent, satisfactory, sufficient, up to snuff (*inf.*), up to standard ◆ *adj* **19** = **improvised**, haphazard, hastily prepared, impromptu, rough, rough-and-ready

scrawl *vb* **1** = **scribble**, doodle, scratch, squiggle ◆ *n* **2** = **scribble**, doodle, squiggle

scrawny *adj* **1** = **thin**, angular, bony, gaunt, lanky, lean, rawboned, scraggy, skeletal, skin-and-bones (*inf.*), skinny, undernourished

scream *vb* **1** = **cry**, bawl, holler (*inf.*), screech, shriek, shrill, sing out, squeal, yell **5** = **be conspicuous**, clash, jar, shriek ◆ *n* **6** = **cry**, howl, outcry, screech, shriek, wail, yell, yelp **7** *Informal* = **laugh**, card, caution (*inf.*), character (*inf.*), comedian, comic, entertainer, hoot (*inf.*), joker, riot (*sl.*), sensation, wag, wit

screech[1] *n* **1** = **cry**, scream, shriek, squawk, squeal, yelp ◆ *vb* **2** = **cry**, scream, shriek, squawk, squeal, yelp

screed *n* **1** = **passage**, speech

screen *n* **1, 2** = **cover**, awning, canopy, cloak, concealment, guard, hedge, mantle, partition, room divider, shade, shelter, shield, shroud **3** = **mesh**, net ◆ *vb* **12** = **cover**, cloak, conceal, defend, guard, hide, mask, protect, safeguard, shade, shelter, shield, shroud, shut out, veil **14**

a film or of slides. **8 the screen.** the film industry or films collectively. **9** *Photog.* a plate of ground glass in some types of camera on which the image of a subject is focused. **10** men or ships deployed around and ahead of a larger military formation to warn of attack. **11** *Electronics.* See **screen grid.** ◆ *vb (tr)* **12** (sometimes foll. by *off*) to shelter, protect, or conceal. **13** to sieve or sort. **14** to test or check (an individual or group) so as to determine suitability for a task, etc. **15** to examine for the presence of a disease, weapons, etc. **16** to provide with a screen or screens. **17** to project (a film) onto a screen, esp. for public viewing. [C15: from OF *escren* (F *écran*)]
▸ **'screenable** *adj* ▸ **'screener** *n* ▸ **'screenful** *n*

screen grid *n Electronics.* an electrode placed between the control grid and anode of a valve which acts as an electrostatic shield, thus increasing the stability of the device. Sometimes shortened to **screen.**

screenings ('skri:nɪŋz) *pl n* refuse separated by sifting.

screening test *n* a simple test performed on a large number of people to identify those who have or are likely to develop a specified disease.

screenplay ('skri:nˌpleɪ) *n* the script for a film, including instructions for sets and camera work.

screen process *n* a method of printing using a fine mesh of silk, nylon, etc., treated with an impermeable coating except in the areas through which ink is subsequently forced onto the paper behind. Also called: **silk-screen printing.**

screensaver ('skri:nseɪvə) *n Computing.* a computer program that reduces screen damage resulting from an unchanging display, when the computer is switched on but not in use, by blanking the screen or generating moving patterns, pictures, etc.

screenwriter ('skri:nˌraɪtə) *n* a person who writes screenplays.

screw ❶ (skru:) *n* **1** a device used for fastening materials together, consisting of a threaded shank that has a slotted head by which it may be rotated so as to cut its own thread. **2** Also called: **screw-bolt.** a threaded cylindrical rod that engages with a similarly threaded cylindrical hole. **3** a thread in a cylindrical hole corresponding with that on the screw with which it is designed to engage. **4** anything resembling a screw in shape or spiral form. **5** a twisting movement of or resembling that of a screw. **6** Also called: **screw-back.** *Billiards, etc.* a stroke in which the cue ball moves backward after striking the object ball. **7** another name for **propeller** (sense 1). **8** *Sl.* a prison guard. **9** *Brit. sl.* salary, wages, or earnings. **10** *Brit.* a small amount of salt, tobacco, etc., in a twist of paper. **11** *Sl.* a person who is mean with money. **12** *Sl.* an old or worthless horse. **13** (*often pl*) *Sl.* force or compulsion (esp. in **put the screws on**). **14** *Taboo sl.* sexual intercourse. **15 have a screw loose.** *Inf.* to be insane. ◆ *vb* **16** (*tr*) to rotate (a screw or bolt) so as to drive it into or draw it out of a material. **17** (*tr*) to cut a screw thread in (a rod or hole) with a tap or die or on a lathe. **18** to turn or cause to turn in the manner of a screw. **19** (*tr*) to attach or fasten with a screw or screws. **20** (*tr*) *Inf.* to take advantage of; cheat. **21** (*tr;* often foll. by *up*) *Inf.* to distort or contort: *he screwed his face into a scowl.* **22** (*tr;* often foll. by *from* or *out of*) *Inf.* to coerce or force out of; extort. **23** *Taboo sl.* to have sexual intercourse (with). **24** (*tr*) *Sl.* to burgle. **25 have one's head screwed on the right way.** *Inf.* to be sensible. ◆ See also **screw up.** [C15: from F *escroe,* from Med. L *scrōfa* screw, from L: sow, presumably because the thread of the screw is like the spiral of the sow's tail]
▸ **'screwer** *n*

screwball ('skru:ˌbɔ:l) *Sl., chiefly US & Canad.* ◆ *n* **1** an odd or eccentric person. ◆ *adj* **2** odd; eccentric.

screwdriver ('skru:ˌdraɪvə) *n* **1** a tool used for turning screws, usually having a steel shank with a flattened square-cut tip that fits into a slot in the head of the screw. **2** an alcoholic beverage consisting of orange juice and vodka.

screwed (skru:d) *adj* **1** fastened by a screw or screws. **2** having spiral grooves like a screw. **3** twisted or distorted. **4** *Brit. sl.* drunk.

screw eye *n* a wood screw with its shank bent into a ring.

screw pine *n* any of various tropical Old World plants having a spiral mass of pineapple-like leaves and conelike fruits.

screw propeller *n* an early form of ship's propeller in which an Archimedes' screw is used to produce thrust by accelerating a flow of water.

screw top *n* **1** a bottle top that screws onto the bottle, allowing the bottle to be resealed after use. **2** a bottle with such a top.
▸ **'screw-ˌtop** *adj*

screw up ❶ *vb (tr, adv)* **1** to twist out of shape or distort. **2** to summon up: *to screw up one's courage.* **3** (*also intr*) *Inf.* to mishandle or bungle.

screwy ❶ ('skru:ɪ) *adj* **screwier, screwiest.** *Inf.* odd, crazy, or eccentric.

scribble ❶ ('skrɪbᵊl) *vb* **scribbles, scribbling, scribbled. 1** to write or draw in a hasty or illegible manner. **2** to make meaningless or illegible marks (on). **3** *Derog. or facetious.* to write poetry, novels, etc. ◆ *n* **4** hasty careless writing or drawing. **5** meaningless or illegible marks. [C15: from Med. L *scrībillāre* to write hastily, from L *scrībere* to write]
▸ **'scribbler** *n* ▸ **'scribbly** *adj*

scribbly gum *n Austral.* a eucalypt with smooth white bark, marked with random patterns made by wood-boring insects.

scribe ❶ (skraɪb) *n* **1** a person who copies documents, esp. a person who made handwritten copies before the invention of printing. **2** a clerk or public copyist. **3** *Bible.* a recognized scholar and teacher of the Jewish Law. ◆ *vb* **scribes, scribing, scribed. 4** to score a line on (a surface) with a pointed instrument, as in metalworking. [(in the senses: writer, etc.) C14: from L *scrība* clerk, from *scrībere* to write; C17 (vb): ?from INSCRIBE]
▸ **'scribal** *adj*

scriber ('skraɪbə) *n* a pointed steel tool used to score materials as a guide to cutting, etc. Also called: **scribe.**

scrim (skrɪm) *n* a fine open-weave fabric, used in upholstery, lining, building, and in the theatre to create the illusion of a solid wall. [C18: from ?]

scrimmage ❶ ('skrɪmɪdʒ) *n* **1** a rough or disorderly struggle. **2** *American football.* the clash of opposing linemen at every down. ◆ *vb* **scrimmages, scrimmaging, scrimmaged. 3** (*intr*) to engage in a scrimmage. **4** (*tr*) to put (the ball) into a scrimmage. [C15: from earlier *scrimish,* var. of SKIRMISH]
▸ **'scrimmager** *n*

scrimp ❶ (skrɪmp) *vb* **1** (when *intr,* sometimes foll. by *on*) to be very sparing in the use (of) (esp. in **scrimp and save**). **2** (*tr*) to treat meanly: *he is scrimping his children.* [C18: Scot., from ?]
▸ **'scrimpy** *adj* ▸ **'scrimpiness** *n*

scrimshank ('skrɪmˌʃæŋk) *vb (intr) Brit. mil. sl.* to shirk work. [C19: from ?]

scrimshaw ('skrɪmˌʃɔ:) *n* **1** the art of decorating or carving shells, bone, ivory, etc., done by sailors as a leisure activity. **2** an article or articles made in this manner. [C19: from ?]

scrip[1] (skrɪp) *n* **1** a written certificate, list, etc. **2** a small scrap, esp. of paper with writing on it. **3** *Finance.* **3a** a certificate representing a claim to part of a share of stock. **3b** the shares issued by a company (**scrip** or **bonus issue**) without charge and distributed among existing shareholders. [C18: in some senses, prob. from SCRIPT; otherwise, short for *subscription receipt*]

scrip[2] (skrɪp) *or* **script** *n Inf.* a medical prescription. [C20: from PRESCRIPTION]

script ❶ (skrɪpt) *n* **1** handwriting as distinguished from print. **2** the letters, characters, or figures used in writing by hand. **3** any system or style of writing. **4** written copy for the use of performers in films and plays. **5** *Law.* an original or principal document. **6** an answer paper in an examination. **7** another word for **scrip**[2]. ◆ *vb* **8** (*tr*) to write a script for. [C14: from L *scriptum* something written, from *scrībere* to write]

Script. *abbrev. for* Scripture(s).

scriptorium (skrɪp'tɔ:rɪəm) *n, pl* **scriptoriums** *or* **scriptoria** (-rɪə). a room, esp. in a monastery, set apart for the copying of manuscripts. [from Med. L]

scripture ('skrɪptʃə) *n* a sacred, solemn, or authoritative book or piece of writing. [C13: from L *scriptūra* written material, from *scrībere* to write]
▸ **'scriptural** *adj*

Scripture ❶ ('skrɪptʃə) *n* **1** Also called: **Holy Scripture, Holy Writ, the Scriptures.** *Christianity.* the Old and New Testaments. **2** any book or body of writings, esp. when regarded as sacred by a particular religious group.

scriptwriter ('skrɪptˌraɪtə) *n* a person who prepares scripts, esp. for a film.
▸ **'scriptˌwriting** *n*

scrivener ('skrɪvnə) *n Arch.* **1** a person who writes out deeds, etc. **2** a notary. [C14: from *scrivein* clerk, from OF *escrivain,* ult. from L *scrība* SCRIBE]

scrod (skrɒd) *n US.* a young cod or haddock. [C19: ? from obs. Du. *schrood,* from MDu. *schrode* SHRED (n); the name perhaps refers to the method of preparing the fish for cooking]

scrofula ('skrɒfjʊlə) *n Pathol.* (*no longer in technical use*) tuberculosis of the lymphatic glands. Also called (formerly): (the) **king's evil.** [C14: from Med. L, from LL *scrōfulae* swollen glands in the neck, lit.: little sows (sows were thought to be particularly prone to the disease), from L *scrōfa* sow]
▸ **'scrofulous** *adj*

THESAURUS

= **vet**, cull, evaluate, examine, filter, gauge, grade, process, riddle, scan, sieve, sift, sort **17** = **broadcast**, present, put on, show

screw *vb* **16, 18** = **turn**, tighten, twist, work in **21** *Informal* = **contort**, contract, crumple, distort, pucker, wrinkle **22** *Informal often with* **from** *or* **out of** = **extort**, bleed, coerce, extract, force, pressurize, squeeze, wrest, wring

screw up *vb* **1** = **contort**, contract, crumple, distort, knit, knot, pucker, wrinkle **3** *Informal* = **bungle**, bitch (up), bodge (*inf.*), botch, cock up (*Brit. sl.*), louse up (*sl.*), make a hash of (*inf.*), make a mess of (*sl.*), make a nonsense of, mess up, mishandle, mismanage, queer (*inf.*), spoil

screwy *adj Informal* = **crazy**, batty (*sl.*), crackers (*Brit. sl.*), crackpot (*inf.*), dotty (*sl., chiefly Brit.*), eccentric, nutty (*sl.*), odd, off-the-wall (*sl.*), outré, out to lunch (*inf.*), queer (*inf.*), round the bend (*Brit. sl.*), rum (*Brit. sl.*), weird

scribble *vb* **1, 2** = **scrawl**, dash off, doodle, jot, pen, scratch, write

scribe *n* **1, 2** = **copyist**, amanuensis, clerk, notary (*arch.*), penman (*rare*), scrivener (*arch.*), secretary, writer

scrimmage *n* **1** = **fight**, affray (*Law*), brawl, disturbance, dust-up (*inf.*), fray, free-for-all (*inf.*), melee or mêlée, riot, row, scrap (*inf.*), scuffle, set-to (*inf.*), shindig (*inf.*), skirmish, squabble, struggle

scrimp *vb* **1** = **economize**, be frugal, curtail, limit, pinch, pinch pennies, reduce, save, scrape, shorten, skimp, stint, straiten, tighten one's belt

script *n* **1** = **handwriting**, calligraphy, hand, letters, longhand, penmanship, writing **4** = **text**, book, copy, dialogue, libretto, lines, manuscript, words

Scripture *n* **1** = **The Bible**, Holy Bible, Holy Scripture, Holy Writ, The Book of Books, The Good Book, The Gospels, The Scriptures, The Word, The Word of God

scroll Ⓣ (skrəul) *n* **1** a roll of parchment, etc., usually inscribed with writing. **2** an ancient book in the form of a roll of parchment, papyrus, etc. **3** a decorative carving or moulding resembling a scroll. ◆ *vb* **4** (*tr*) to saw into scrolls. **5** to roll up like a scroll. **6** *Computing.* to move (text) on a screen in order to view a section that cannot be fitted into a single display. [C15 *scrowle,* from *scrowe,* from OF *escroe* scrap of parchment, but also infl. by ROLL]

scroll saw *n* a saw with a narrow blade for cutting intricate ornamental curves in wood.

scrollwork ('skrəul,wɜːk) *n* ornamental work in scroll-like patterns.

Scrooge Ⓣ (skruːdʒ) *n* a mean or miserly person. [C19: after a character in Dickens' story *A Christmas Carol* (1843)]

scrophulariaceous (,skrɒfjʊ,leərɪ'eɪʃəs) *adj* of or belonging to the *Scrophulariaceae,* a family of plants including figwort, snapdragon, foxglove, and mullein. [C19: from NL (*herba*) *scrophularia* scrofula (plant), from the use of such plants in treating scrofula]

scrotum ('skrəutəm) *n, pl* **scrota** (-tə) *or* **scrotums.** the pouch of skin containing the testes in most mammals. [C16: from L]
▸**'scrotal** *adj*

scrounge Ⓣ (skraundʒ) *vb* **scrounges, scrounging, scrounged.** *Inf.* **1** (when *intr,* sometimes foll. by *around*) to search in order to acquire (something) without cost. **2** to obtain or seek to obtain (something) by begging. [C20: var. of dialect *scrunge* to steal, from ?]
▸**'scrounger** *n*

scrub[1] Ⓣ (skrʌb) *vb* **scrubs, scrubbing, scrubbed. 1** to rub (a surface, etc.) hard, with or as if with a brush, soap, and water, in order to clean it. **2** to remove (dirt) by rubbing, esp. with a brush and water. **3** (*intr;* foll. by *up*) (of a surgeon) to wash the hands and arms thoroughly before operating. **4** (*tr*) to purify (a gas) by removing impurities. **5** (*tr*) *Inf.* to delete or cancel. ◆ *n* **6** the act of or an instance of scrubbing. [C14: from MLow G *schrubben,* or MDu. *schrobben*]

scrub[2] (skrʌb) *n* **1a** vegetation consisting of stunted trees, bushes, and other plants growing in an arid area. **1b** (*as modifier*): *scrub vegetation.* **2** an area of arid land covered with such vegetation. **3a** an animal of inferior breeding or condition. **3b** (*as modifier*): *a scrub bull.* **4** a small person. **5** anything stunted or inferior. **6** *Sport, US & Canad.* a player not in the first team. **7 the scrub.** *Austral. inf.* a remote or uncivilized place. ◆ *adj* (*prenominal*) **8** small or inferior. **9** *Sport, US.* **9a** (of a player) not in the first team. **9b** (of a team) composed of such players. [C16: var. of SHRUB[1]]

scrubber ('skrʌbə) *n* **1** a person or thing that scrubs. **2** an apparatus for purifying a gas. **3** *Derog. sl.* a promiscuous woman.

scrubby Ⓣ ('skrʌbɪ) *adj* **scrubbier, scrubbiest. 1** covered with or consisting of scrub. **2** (of trees, etc.) stunted in growth. **3** *Brit. inf.* messy.

scrubland ('skrʌb,lænd) *n* an area of scrub vegetation.

scrub turkey *n* another term for **megapode.**

scrub typhus *n* a disease characterized by severe headache, skin rash, chills, and swelling of the lymph nodes, caused by the bite of mites infected with a microorganism: occurs mainly in Asia and Australia.

scruff[1] Ⓣ (skrʌf) *n* the nape of the neck (esp. in **by the scruff of the neck**). [C18: var. of *scuft,* ?from ON *skoft* hair]

scruff[2] Ⓣ (skrʌf) *n Inf.* **1** an untidy scruffy person. **2** a disreputable person; ruffian.

scruffy Ⓣ ('skrʌfɪ) *adj* **scruffier, scruffiest.** unkempt or shabby.

scrum (skrʌm) *n* **1** *Rugby.* the act or method of restarting play when the two opposing packs of forwards group together with heads down and arms interlocked and push to gain ground while the scrum half throws the ball in and the hookers attempt to scoop it out to their own team. **2** *Inf.* a disorderly struggle. ◆ *vb* **scrums, scrumming, scrummed. 3** (*intr;* usually foll. by *down*) *Rugby.* to form a scrum. [C19: from SCRUMMAGE]

scrum half *n Rugby.* **1** a player who puts in the ball at scrums and tries to get it away to his three-quarter backs. **2** this position in a team.

scrummage ('skrʌmɪdʒ) *n, vb* **scrummages, scrummaging, scrummaged. 1** *Rugby.* another word for **scrum. 2** a variant of **scrimmage.** [C19: var. of SCRIMMAGE]

scrump (skrʌmp) *vb Dialect.* to steal (apples) from an orchard or garden. [var. of SCRIMP]

scrumptious Ⓣ ('skrʌmpʃəs) *adj Inf.* very pleasing; delicious. [C19: prob. changed from SUMPTUOUS]
▸**'scrumptiously** *adv*

scrumpy ('skrʌmpɪ) *n* a rough dry cider, brewed esp. in the West Country of England. [from *scrump,* var. of SCRIMP (in obs. sense: withered), referring to the apples used]

scrunch Ⓣ (skrʌntʃ) *vb* **1** to crumple or crunch or to be crumpled or crunched. ◆ *n* **2** the act or sound of scrunching. [C19: var. of CRUNCH]

scrunchie ('skrʌntʃɪ) *n* a loop of elastic covered loosely with fabric, used to hold the hair in a ponytail.

scruple Ⓣ ('skruːpᵊl) *n* **1** (*often pl*) a doubt or hesitation as to what is morally right in a certain situation. **2** *Arch.* a very small amount. **3** a unit of weight equal to 20 grains (1.296 grams). ◆ *vb* **scruples, scrupling, scrupled. 4** (*obs. when tr*) to have doubts (about), esp. from a moral compunction. [C16: from L *scrūpulus* a small weight, from *scrūpus* rough stone]

scrupulous Ⓣ ('skruːpjuləs) *adj* **1** characterized by careful observation of what is morally right. **2** very careful or precise. [C15: from L *scrūpulōsus* punctilious]
▸**'scrupulously** *adv* ▸**'scrupulousness** *n*

scrutineer (,skruːtɪ'nɪə) *n* a person who examines, esp. one who scrutinizes the conduct of an election poll.

scrutinize Ⓣ *or* **scrutinise** ('skruːtɪ,naɪz) *vb* **scrutinizes, scrutinizing, scrutinized** *or* **scrutinises, scrutinising, scrutinised.** (*tr*) to examine carefully or in minute detail.
▸**'scruti,nizer** *or* **'scruti,niser** *n*

scrutiny Ⓣ ('skruːtɪnɪ) *n, pl* **scrutinies. 1** close or minute examination. **2** a searching look. **3** (in the early Christian Church) a formal testing that catechumens had to undergo before being baptized. [C15: from LL *scrūtinium* an investigation, from *scrūtārī* to search (orig. referring to rag-and-bone men), from *scrūta* rubbish]

scry (skraɪ) *vb* **scries, scrying, scried.** (*intr*) to divine, esp. by crystal gazing. [C16: from DESCRY]

scuba ('skjuːbə) *n* an apparatus used in skin diving, consisting of a cylinder or cylinders containing compressed air attached to a breathing apparatus. [C20: from the initials of *self-contained underwater breathing apparatus*]

scud Ⓣ (skʌd) *vb* **scuds, scudding, scudded.** (*intr*) **1** (esp. of clouds) to move along swiftly and smoothly. **2** *Naut.* to run before a gale. ◆ *n* **3** the act of scudding. **4a** a formation of low ragged clouds driven by a strong wind beneath rain-bearing clouds. **4b** a sudden shower or gust of wind. [C16: prob. of Scand. origin]

scuff (skʌf) *vb* **1** to drag (the feet) while walking. **2** to scratch (a surface) or (of a surface) to become scratched. **3** (*tr*) *US.* to poke at (something) with the foot. ◆ *n* **4** the act or sound of scuffing. **5** a rubbed place caused by scuffing. **6** a backless slipper. [C19: prob. imit.]

scuffle Ⓣ ('skʌfᵊl) *vb* **scuffles, scuffling, scuffled.** (*intr*) **1** to fight in a disorderly manner. **2** to move by shuffling. ◆ *n* **3** a disorderly struggle. **4** the sound made by scuffling. [C16: of Scand. origin; cf. Swedish *skuff, skuffa* to push]

scull (skʌl) *n* **1** a single oar moved from side to side over the stern of a boat to propel it. **2** one of a pair of short-handled oars, both of which are pulled by one oarsman. **3** a racing shell propelled by an oarsman or oarsmen pulling two oars. **4** an act, instance, period, or distance of sculling. ◆ *vb* **5** to propel (a boat) with a scull. [C14: from ?]
▸**'sculler** *n*

scullery ('skʌlərɪ) *n, pl* **sculleries.** *Chiefly Brit.* a small room or part of a kitchen where washing-up, vegetable preparation, etc., is done. [C15: from Anglo-Norman *squillerie,* from OF, from *escuele* a bowl, from L *scutella,* from *scutra* a flat tray]

THESAURUS

scroll *n* **1, 2 = roll,** parchment

Scrooge *n* **= miser,** cheapskate (*inf.*), meanie *or* meany (*inf., chiefly Brit.*), money-grubber (*inf.*), niggard, penny-pincher (*inf.*), skinflint, tightwad (*US & Canad. sl.*)

scrounge *vb* **1** *Informal* **= cadge,** beg, blag (*sl.*), bum (*inf.*), forage for, freeload (*sl.*), hunt around (for), mooch (*sl.*), sponge (*inf.*), touch (someone) for (*sl.*), wheedle

scrounger *adj* **1 = cadger,** bum (*inf.*), freeloader (*sl.*), parasite, sponger (*inf.*)

scrub[1] *vb* **1, 2 = scour,** clean, cleanse, rub **5** *Informal* **= cancel,** abandon, abolish, call off, delete, discontinue, do away with, drop, forget about, give up

scrubby *adj* **2 = stunted,** meagre, scrawny, spindly, underdeveloped, undersized

scruff[1] *n* **= nape,** scrag (*inf.*)

scruff[2] *n* **1** *Informal* **= ragamuffin,** ragbag (*inf.*), scarecrow, sloven, tramp

scruffy *adj* **= tatty,** disreputable, draggletailed (*arch.*), frowzy, grungy, ill-groomed, mangy, messy, ragged, run-down, scrubby (*Brit. inf.*), seedy, shabby, slatternly, sloppy (*inf.*), slovenly, sluttish, squalid, tattered, ungroomed, unkempt, untidy
Antonyms *adj* chic, dapper, natty, neat, soigné *or* soignée, spruce, tidy, well-dressed, well-groomed, well-turned-out

scrumptious *adj Informal* **= delicious,** appetizing, delectable, exquisite, inviting, luscious, magnificent, moreish (*inf.*), mouthwatering, succulent, yummy (*sl.*)

scrunch *vb* **1 = crumple,** champ, chew, crunch, crush, mash, ruck up, squash

scruple *n* **1 = misgiving,** caution, compunction, difficulty, doubt, hesitation, perplexity, qualm, reluctance, second thoughts, squeamishness, twinge of conscience, uneasiness ◆ *vb* **4 = have misgivings about,** balk at, be loath, be reluctant, demur, doubt, falter, have qualms about, hesitate, stick at, think twice about, vacillate, waver

scrupulous *adj* **1 = moral,** conscientious, honourable, principled, upright **2 = careful,** exact, fastidious, meticulous, minute, nice, painstaking, precise, punctilious, rigorous, strict
Antonyms *adj* ≠ **moral:** amoral, dishonest, uncaring, unconscientious, unprincipled, unscrupulous, without scruples ≠ **careful:** careless, inexact, reckless, slapdash, superficial

scrutinize *vb* **= examine,** analyse, dissect, explore, go over with a fine-tooth comb, inquire into, inspect, investigate, peruse, pore over, probe, research, scan, search, sift, study, work over

scrutiny *n* **1 = examination,** analysis, close study, exploration, inquiry, inspection, investigation, once-over (*inf.*), perusal, search, sifting, study

scud *vb* **1 = fly,** blow, haste, hasten, race, sail, shoot, skim, speed

scuffle *vb* **1 = fight,** clash, come to blows, contend, exchange blows, grapple, jostle, struggle, tussle ◆ *n* **3 = fight,** affray (*Law*), barney (*inf.*), brawl, commotion, disturbance, fray, ruckus (*inf.*), ruction (*inf.*), rumpus, scrap (*inf.*), scrimmage, set-to (*inf.*), shindig (*inf.*), skirmish, tussle

sculIion (ˈskʌljən) *n* **1** a mean or despicable person. **2** *Arch.* a servant employed to work in a kitchen. [C15: from OF *escouillon* cleaning cloth, from *escouve* a broom, from L *scōpa* a broom, twig]

sculpt (skʌlpt) *vb* **1** a variant of **sculpture. 2** (*intr*) to practise sculpture. ◆ Also: **sculp.** [C19: from F *sculpter,* from L *sculpere* to carve]

sculptor (ˈskʌlptə) *or* (*fem*) **sculptress** *n* a person who practises sculpture.

sculpture ❶ (ˈskʌlptʃə) *n* **1** the art of making figures or designs in relief or the round by carving wood, moulding plaster, etc., or casting metals, etc. **2** works or a work made in this way. **3** ridges or indentations as on a shell, formed by natural processes. ◆ *vb* **sculptures, sculpturing, sculptured.** (*mainly tr*) **4** (*also intr*) to carve, cast, or fashion (stone, bronze, etc.) three-dimensionally. **5** to portray (a person, etc.) by means of sculpture. **6** to form in the manner of sculpture. **7** to decorate with sculpture. [C14: from L *sculptūra* a carving]
▸ **ˈsculptural** *adj*

sculpturesque (ˌskʌlptʃəˈrɛsk) *adj* resembling sculpture.
▸ **ˌsculpturˈesquely** *adv*

scum ❶ (skʌm) *n* **1** a layer of impure matter that forms on the surface of a liquid, often as the result of boiling or fermentation. **2** the greenish film of algae and similar vegetation surface of a stagnant pond. **3** the skin of oxides or impurities on the surface of a molten metal. **4** waste matter. **5** a worthless person or group of people. ◆ *vb* **scums, scumming, scummed. 6** (*tr*) to remove scum from. **7** (*intr*) *Rare.* to form a layer of or become covered with scum. [C13: of Gmc origin]
▸ **ˈscummy** *adj*

scumbag (ˈskʌmˌbæg) *n Sl* an offensive or despicable person. [C20: ?from earlier US sense: condom, from US slang *scum* semen + bag]

scumble (ˈskʌmbᵊl) *vb* **scumbles, scumbling, scumbled. 1** (in painting and drawing) to soften or blend (an outline or colour) with an upper coat of opaque colour, applied very thinly. **2** to produce an effect of broken colour on doors, panelling, etc., by exposing coats of paint below the top coat. ◆ *n* **3** the upper layer of colour applied in this way. [C18: prob. from SCUM]

scuncheon (ˈskʌntʃən) *n* the inner part of a door jamb or window frame. [C15: from OF *escoinson,* from *coin* angle]

scungy (ˈskʌndʒɪ) *adj* **scungier, scungiest.** *Austral.* & *NZ sl.* miserable; sordid; dirty. [C20: from ?]

scunner (ˈskʌnə) *Dialect, chiefly Scot.* ◆ *vb* **1** (*intr*) to feel aversion. **2** (*tr*) to produce a feeling of aversion in. ◆ *n* **3** a strong aversion (often in **take a scunner**). **4** an object of dislike; nuisance. [C14: from Scot. *skunner,* from ?]

scup (skʌp) *n* a common fish of American coastal regions of the Atlantic. [C19: from Amerind *mishcup,* from *mishe* big + *kuppe* close together; from the form of the scales]

scupper^{1} (ˈskʌpə) *n Naut.* a drain or spout allowing water on the deck of a vessel to flow overboard. [C15 *skopper,* from ?]

scupper^{2} ❶ (ˈskʌpə) *vb* (*tr*) *Brit. sl.* **1** to overwhelm, ruin, or disable. **2** to sink (one's ship) deliberately. [C19: from ?]

scurf (skɜːf) *n* **1** another name for **dandruff. 2** flaky or scaly matter adhering to or peeling off a surface. [OE *scurf*]
▸ **ˈscurfy** *adj*

scurrilous ❶ (ˈskʌrɪləs) *adj* **1** grossly or obscenely abusive or defamatory. **2** characterized by gross or obscene humour. [C16: from L *scurrīlis* derisive, from *scurra* buffoon]
▸ **scurrility** (skəˈrɪlɪtɪ) *n* ▸ **ˈscurrilously** *adv*

scurry ❶ (ˈskʌrɪ) *vb* **scurries, scurrying, scurried. 1** to move about hurriedly. **2** (*intr*) to whirl about. ◆ *n, pl* **scurries. 3** the act or sound of scurrying. **4** a brisk light whirling movement, as of snow. [C19: prob. from *hurry-scurry,* from HURRY]

scurvy ❶ (ˈskɜːvɪ) *n* **1** a disease caused by a lack of vitamin C, characterized by anaemia, spongy gums, and bleeding beneath the skin. ◆ *adj* **scurvier, scurviest. 2** mean or despicable. [C16: see SCURF]
▸ **ˈscurvily** *adv* ▸ **ˈscurviness** *n*

scurvy grass *n* any of various plants of Europe and North America, formerly used to treat scurvy.

scut (skʌt) *n* the short tail of animals such as the deer and rabbit. [C15: prob. from ON]

scutage (ˈskjuːtɪdʒ) *n* (in feudal society) a payment sometimes exacted by a lord from his vassal in lieu of military service. [C15: from Med. L *scūtāgium,* lit.: shield dues, from L *scūtum* a shield]

scutate (ˈskjuːteɪt) *adj* **1** (of animals) covered with large bony or horny plates. **2** *Bot.* shaped like a round shield. [C19: from L *scūtātus* armed with a shield, from *scūtum* a shield]

scutcheon (ˈskʌtʃən) *n* **1** a variant of **escutcheon. 2** any rounded or shield-shaped structure.

scutch grass (skʌtʃ) *n* another name for **couch grass.** [var. of COUCH GRASS]

scute (skjuːt) *n Zool.* a horny plate that makes up part of the exoskeleton in armadillos, turtles, etc. [C14 (the name of a F coin; C19 in zoological sense): from L *scūtum* shield]

scutellum (skjuːˈtɛləm) *n, pl* **scutella** (-lə). *Biol.* **1** the last of three plates into which an insect's thorax is divided. **2** one of the scales on the tarsus of a bird's leg. **3** the cotyledon of a developing grass seed. [C18: from NL: a little shield, from L *scūtum* a shield]
▸ **scutellate** (ˈskjuːtɪˌleɪt, -lɪt) *adj*

scutter (ˈskʌtə) *vb, n Brit. inf.* scurry. [C18: prob. from SCUTTLE^{2}, with -ER^{1} as in SCATTER]

scuttle^{1} ❶ (ˈskʌtᵊl) *n* **1** See **coal scuttle. 2** *Dialect, chiefly Brit.* a shallow basket, esp. for carrying vegetables. **3** the part of a motorcar body lying immediately behind the bonnet. [OE *scutel* trencher, from L *scutella* bowl, dim. of *scutra* platter]

scuttle^{2} (ˈskʌtᵊl) *vb* **scuttles, scuttling, scuttled. 1** (*intr*) to run or move about with short hasty steps. ◆ *n* **2** a hurried pace or run. [C15: ?from SCUD, infl. by SHUTTLE]

scuttle^{3} (ˈskʌtᵊl) *vb* **scuttles, scuttling, scuttled.** (*tr*) **1** *Naut.* to cause (a vessel) to sink by opening the seacocks or making holes in the bottom. **2** to give up (hopes, plans, etc.). ◆ *n* **3** *Naut.* a small hatch or its cover. [C15 (n): via OF from Sp. *escotilla* a small opening, from *escote* opening in a piece of cloth, from *escotar* to cut out]

scuttlebutt (ˈskʌtᵊlˌbʌt) *n Naut.* **1** a drinking fountain. **2** (formerly) a cask of drinking water aboard a ship. **3** *Chiefly US sl.* gossip.

scutum (ˈskjuːtəm) *n, pl* **scuta** (-tə). **1** the middle of three plates into which an insect's thorax is divided. **2** another word for **scute.** [L: shield]

scuzzy (ˈskʌzɪ) *adj* **scuzzier, scuzziest.** *Sl., chiefly US.* unkempt, dirty, or squalid. [C20: ?from *disgusting* or ?from blend of *scum* & *fuzz*]

Scylla (ˈsɪlə) *n* **1** *Greek myth.* a sea nymph transformed into a sea monster believed to drown sailors navigating the Strait of Messina. Cf. **Charybdis. 2 between Scylla and Charybdis.** in a predicament in which avoidance of either of two dangers means exposure to the other.

scythe (saɪð) *n* **1** a long-handled implement for cutting grass, etc., having a curved sharpened blade that moves in a plane parallel to the ground. ◆ *vb* **scythes, scything, scythed. 2** (*tr*) to cut (grass, etc.) with a scythe. [OE *sigthe*]

Scythian (ˈsɪðɪən) *adj* **1** of or relating to ancient Scythia, in SE Europe, its inhabitants, or their language. ◆ *n* **2** a member of an ancient nomadic people of Scythia.

SDI *abbrev. for* Strategic Defense Initiative. See **Star Wars.**

SDLP *abbrev. for* Social Democratic and Labour Party (in Northern Ireland).

SDP *abbrev. for* Social Democratic Party.

SDRs *Finance. abbrev. for* special drawing rights.

Se *the chemical symbol for* selenium.

SE *symbol for* southeast(ern).

sea ❶ (siː) *n* **1a** (usually preceded by *the*) the mass of salt water on the earth's surface as differentiated from the land. Related adjs.: **marine, maritime. 1b** (*as modifier*): *sea air.* **2** (*cap. when part of place name*) **2a** one of the smaller areas of ocean: *the Irish Sea.* **2b** a large inland area of water: *the Caspian Sea.* **3** turbulence or swell: *heavy seas.* **4** (*cap. when part of a name*) *Astron.* any of many huge dry plains on the surface of the moon: *Sea of Serenity.* See also **mare**^{2}. **5** anything resembling the sea in size or apparent limitlessness. **6 at sea. 6a** on the ocean. **6b** in a state of confusion. **7 go to sea.** to become a sailor. **8 put (out) to sea.** to embark on a sea voyage. [OE *sǣ*]

sea anchor *n Naut.* any device, such as a bucket, dragged in the water to keep a vessel heading into the wind or reduce drifting.

sea anemone *n* any of various coelenterates having a polypoid body with oral rings of tentacles.

sea bag *n* a canvas bag used by a seaman for his belongings.

sea bass (bæs) *n* any of various American coastal fishes having an elongated body with a long spiny dorsal fin almost divided into two.

sea bird *n* a bird such as a gull, that lives on the sea.

seaboard (ˈsiːˌbɔːd) *n* land bordering on the sea.

seaborgium (ˈsiːbɔːgɪəm) *n* a synthetic transuranic element, synthesized and identified in 1974. Symbol: Sg; atomic no.: 106. [C20: after Glenn *Seaborg* (1912–99), US scientist]

THESAURUS

sculpture *vb* **4** = **sculpt**, carve, chisel, cut, fashion, form, hew, model, mould, sculp, shape

scum *n* **1-4** = **impurities**, algae, crust, dross, film, froth, offscourings, scruff **5** = **rabble**, *canaille*, dregs of society, dross, lowest of the low, ragtag and bobtail, riffraff, rubbish, trash (*chiefly US & Canad.*)

scupper^{2} *vb* **1** *Brit. slang* = **destroy**, defeat, demolish, disable, discomfit, overthrow, overwhelm, put paid to, ruin, torpedo, undo, wreck

scurrility *n* **1, 2** = **slanderousness**, abusiveness, billingsgate, coarseness, grossness, indecency, infamousness, invective, obloquy, obscenity, offensiveness, scurrilousness, vituperation

scurrilous *adj* **1, 2** = **slanderous**, abusive, coarse, defamatory, foul, foul-mouthed, gross, indecent, infamous, insulting, low, obscene, offensive, Rabelaisian, ribald, salacious, scabrous, scandalous, vituperative, vulgar
Antonyms *adj* civilized, decent, polite, proper, refined, respectful

scurry *vb* **1** = **hurry**, beetle, dart, dash, fly, race, scamper, scoot, scud, scuttle, skim, sprint, whisk ◆ *n* **3** = **flurry**, bustle, scampering, whirl
Antonyms *vb* ≠ **hurry**: amble, mooch (*sl.*), mosey (*inf.*), saunter, stroll, toddle, wander

scurvy *adj* **2** = **contemptible**, abject, bad, base, despicable, dishonourable, ignoble, low, low-down (*inf.*), mean, pitiful, rotten, scabby (*inf.*), shabby, sorry, vile, worthless

scuttle^{1} *vb* **1** = **run**, beetle, bustle, hare (*Brit. inf.*), hasten, hurry, rush, scamper, scoot, scramble, scud, scurry, scutter (*Brit. inf.*)

sea *n* **1a** = **ocean**, main, the briny (*inf.*), the deep, the drink (*inf.*), the waves **1b** *as modifier* = **marine**, aquatic, briny, maritime, ocean, ocean-going, oceanic, pelagic, salt, saltwater, sea-going **5** = **expanse**, abundance, mass, multitude, plethora, profusion, sheet, vast number **6b at sea** = **bewildered**, adrift, astray, at a loss, at sixes and sevens, baffled, confused, disoriented, lost, mystified, puzzled, upset

seaborne ('siː,bɔːn) *adj* **1** carried on or by the sea. **2** transported by ship.
sea bream *n* a fish of European seas, valued as a food fish.
sea breeze *n* a wind blowing from the sea to the land, esp. during the day when the land surface is warmer.
SEAC ('siːæk) *n* (in Britain) *acronym for* School Examination and Assessment Council.
sea change *n* a seemingly magical change. [from Ariel's song "Full Fathom Five" in *The Tempest* (1611)]
seacoast ('siː,kəʊst) *n* land bordering on the sea; a coast.
seacock ('siː,kɒk) *n Naut.* a valve in the hull of a vessel below the water line for admitting sea water or for pumping out bilge water.
sea cow *n* **1** a dugong or manatee. **2** an archaic name for the **walrus.**
sea cucumber *n* an echinoderm having an elongated body covered with a leathery skin and a cluster of tentacles at the oral end.
sea dog *n* an experienced or old sailor.
sea eagle *n* any of various fish-eating eagles of coastal areas, esp. the **European sea eagle,** having a brown plumage and white tail.
seafarer ('siː,fɛərə) *n* **1** a traveller who goes by sea. **2** a sailor.
seafaring ❶ ('siː,fɛərɪŋ) *adj (prenominal)* **1** travelling by sea. **2** working as a sailor. ◆ *n* **3** the act of travelling by sea. **4** the work of a sailor.
seafood ('siː,fuːd) *n* edible saltwater fish or shellfish.
seafront ('siː,frʌnt) *n* a built-up area facing the sea.
sea-girt *adj Literary.* surrounded by the sea.
seagoing ('siː,gəʊɪŋ) *adj* intended for or used at sea.
sea green *n* **a** a moderate green colour, sometimes with a bluish or yellowish tinge. **b** (*as adj*): *a sea-green carpet.*
sea gull *n* **1** a popular name for the **gull** (the bird). **2** *NZ inf.* a casual dock worker.
sea holly *n* a European plant of sandy shores, having bluish-green stems and blue flowers.
sea horse *n* **1** a marine teleost fish of temperate and tropical waters, having a bony-plated body, a prehensile tail, and a horselike head and swimming in an upright position. **2** an archaic name for the **walrus.** **3** a fabled sea creature with the tail of a fish and the front parts of a horse.
sea-island cotton *n* **1** a cotton plant of the Sea Islands, off the Florida coast, widely cultivated for its fine long fibres. **2** the fibre of this plant or the material woven from it.
sea kale *n* a European coastal plant with broad fleshy leaves and white flowers: cultivated for its edible asparagus-like shoots. Cf. **kale.**
seal[1] ❶ (siːl) *n* **1** a device impressed on a piece of wax, etc., fixed to a letter, etc., as a mark of authentication. **2** a stamp, ring, etc., engraved with a device to form such an impression. **3** a substance, esp. wax, so placed over an envelope, etc., that it must be broken before the object can be opened or used. **4** any substance or device used to close or fasten tightly. **5** a small amount of water contained in the trap of a drain to prevent the passage of foul smells. **6** anything that gives a pledge or confirmation. **7** a token; sign: *seal of death.* **8** a decorative stamp sold in aid of charity. **9** *RC Church.* Also called: **seal of confession.** the obligation never to reveal anything said in confession. **10 set one's seal on** (*or* **to**). **10a** to mark with one's sign or seal. **10b** to endorse. ◆ *vb (tr)* **11** to affix a seal to, as proof of authenticity, etc. **12** to stamp with or as if with a seal. **13** to approve or authorize. **14** (sometimes foll. by *up*) to close or secure with or as if with a seal: *to seal one's lips.* **15** (foll. by *off*) to enclose (a place) with a fence, etc. **16** to decide irrevocably. **17** to close tightly so as to render airtight or watertight. **18** to subject (the outside of meat, etc.) to fierce heat so as to retain the juices during cooking. **19** to paint (a porous material) with a nonporous coating. **20** *Austral.* to cover (a road) with bitumen, asphalt, tarmac, etc. [C13 *seel,* from OF, from L *sigillum* little figure, from *signum* a sign]
▸**'sealable** *adj*
seal[2] (siːl) *n* **1** a fish-eating mammal with four flippers which is aquatic but comes on shore to breed. **2** sealskin. ◆ *vb* **3** *(intr)* to hunt for seals. [OE *seolh*]
▸**'sealer** *n* ▸**'seal-,like** *adj*
sea lane *n* an established route for ships.
sealant ('siːlənt) *n* **1** any substance, such as wax, used for sealing documents, bottles, etc. **2** any of a number of substances used for stopping leaks, waterproofing wood, etc.
sea lavender *n* any of various plants found on temperate salt marshes, having spikes of white, pink, or mauve flowers.
sealed-beam *adj* (esp. of a car headlight) having a lens and prefocused reflector sealed in the lamp vacuum.
sealed road *n Austral. & NZ.* a road surfaced with bitumen or some other hard material.
sea legs *pl n Inf.* **1** the ability to maintain one's balance on board ship. **2** the ability to resist seasickness.
sea level *n* the level of the surface of the sea with respect to the land, taken to be the mean level between high and low tide.
sea lily *n* any of various echinoderms in which the body consists of a long stalk bearing a central disc with delicate radiating arms.
sealing wax *n* a hard material made of shellac, turpentine, and pigment that softens when heated.
sea lion *n* any of various large eared seals, such as the **Californian sea lion,** of the N Pacific, often used as a performing animal.
Sea Lord *n* (in Britain) either of the two serving naval officers (**First** and **Second Sea Lords**) who sit on the admiralty board of the Ministry of Defence.
seal ring *n* another term for **signet ring.**
sealskin ('siːl,skɪn) *n* **a** the skin or pelt of a fur seal, esp. when dressed with the outer hair removed and the underfur dyed dark brown. **b** (*as modifier*): *a sealskin coat.*
Sealyham terrier ('siːlɪəm) *n* a short-legged wire-haired breed of terrier with a medium-length white coat. [C19: after *Sealyham,* village in S Wales]
seam ❶ (siːm) *n* **1** the line along which pieces of fabric, etc., are joined, esp. by stitching. **2** a ridge or line made by joining two edges. **3** a stratum of coal, ore, etc. **4** a linear indentation, such as a wrinkle or scar. **5** (*modifier*) *Cricket.* of or relating to a style of bowling in which the bowler utilizes the stitched seam round the ball in order to make it swing in flight and after touching the ground: *a seam bowler.* **6 bursting at the seams.** full to overflowing. ◆ *vb* **7** *(tr)* to join or sew together by or as if by a seam. **8** to mark or become marked with or as if with a seam or wrinkle. [OE]
seaman ('siːmən) *n, pl* **seamen. 1** a naval rating trained in seamanship. **2** a man who serves as a sailor. **3** a person skilled in seamanship.
▸**'seamanly** *adj, adv* ▸**'seaman-,like** *adj*
seamanship ('siːmənʃɪp) *n* skill in and knowledge of the work of navigating, maintaining, and operating a vessel.
sea mile *n* a unit of distance used in navigation, defined as the length of one minute of arc, measured along the meridian, in the latitude of the position. Its actual length varies slightly with latitude, but is about 1853 metres (6080 feet). See also **nautical mile.**
seamless ('siːmlɪs) *adj* **1** (of a garment) having no seams. **2** continuous or flowing: *seamless output; a seamless performance.*
sea mouse *n* any of various large worms having a broad flattened body covered dorsally with a dense mat of iridescent hairlike setae.
seamstress ('sɛmstrɪs) *or (rarely)* **sempstress** ('sɛmpstrɪs) *n* a woman who sews and makes clothes, esp. professionally.
seamy ❶ ('siːmɪ) *adj* **seamier, seamiest.** showing the least pleasant aspect; sordid.
▸**'seaminess** *n*
Seanad Éireann ('ʃænəð 'eːrən) *n* (in the Republic of Ireland) the upper chamber of parliament. [from Irish, lit.: senate of Ireland]
seance *or* **séance** ('seɪɑ̃ns) *n* a meeting at which spiritualists attempt to receive messages from the spirits of the dead. [C19: from F, lit.: a sitting, from OF *seoir* to sit, from L *sedēre*]
sea otter *n* a large marine otter of N Pacific coasts, formerly hunted for its thick brown fur.
sea pink *n* another name for **thrift** (the plant).
seaplane ('siː,pleɪn) *n* any aircraft that lands on and takes off from water.
seaport ('siː,pɔːt) *n* **1** a port or harbour accessible to seagoing vessels. **2** a town or city located at such a place.
SEAQ ('siː,æk) *n acronym for* Stock Exchange Automated Quotations: an electronic system that collects and displays information needed to trade in equities.
sear ❶ (sɪə) *vb (tr)* **1** to scorch or burn the surface of. **2** to brand with a hot iron. **3** to cause to wither. **4** *Rare.* to make unfeeling. ◆ *adj* **5** *Poetic.* dried up. [OE *sēarian* to become withered, from *sēar* withered]
search ❶ (sɜːtʃ) *vb* **1** to look through (a place, etc.) thoroughly in order to find someone or something. **2** *(tr)* to examine (a person) for concealed objects. **3** to look at or examine (something) closely: *to search one's conscience.* **4** (*tr;* foll. by *out*) to discover by investigation. **5** *Surgery.* to probe (a wound, etc.). **6** *Computing.* to review (a file) to locate specific information. **7** *Arch.* to penetrate. **8 search me.** *Inf.* I don't know. ◆ *n* **9** the act or an instance of searching. **10** the examination of a vessel by the right of search. **11 right of search.** *International law.* the right possessed by the warships of a belligerent state to search merchant vessels to ascertain whether ship or cargo is liable to seizure. [C14: from OF *cerchier,* from LL *circāre* to go around, from L *circus* circle]
▸**'searchable** *adj* ▸**'searcher** *n*

THESAURUS

seafaring *adj* **1** = **nautical,** marine, maritime, naval, oceanic

seal[1] *n* **6** = **authentication,** assurance, attestation, confirmation, imprimatur, insignia, notification, ratification, stamp ◆ *vb* **13** = **authenticate,** assure, attest, confirm, establish, ratify, stamp, validate **15** *with* **off** = **isolate,** board up, fence off, put out of bounds, quarantine, segregate **16** = **settle,** clinch, conclude, consummate, finalize, shake hands on (*inf.*) **17** = **close,** bung, cork, enclose, fasten, make airtight, plug, secure, shut, stop, stopper, stop up, waterproof

seam *n* **1** = **joint,** closure, suture (*Surgery*) **3** = **layer,** lode, stratum, vein **4** = **ridge,** furrow, line, scar, wrinkle

seamy *adj* = **sordid,** corrupt, dark, degraded, disagreeable, disreputable, low, nasty, rough, squalid, unpleasant, unwholesome

sear *vb* **1, 2** = **scorch,** brand, burn, cauterize, desiccate, dry up *or* out, sizzle **3** = **wither,** blight, shrivel, wilt

search *vb* **1-3** = **look,** cast around, check, comb, examine, explore, ferret, forage, frisk (*inf.*), go over with a fine-tooth comb, hunt, inquire, inspect, investigate, leave no stone unturned, look high and low, probe, pry, ransack, rifle through, rummage through, scour, scrutinize, seek, sift, turn inside out, turn upside down ◆ *n* **9** = **look,** examination, exploration, going-over (*inf.*), hunt, inquiry, inspection, investigation, pursuit, quest, researches, rummage, scrutiny

search engine *n Computing.* a service provided on the Internet that carries out searches and locates information on the Internet.

searching ❶ ('sɜːtʃɪŋ) *adj* keenly penetrating: *a searching look.*
▸**'searchingly** *adv*

searchlight ('sɜːtʃˌlaɪt) *n* **1** a device that projects a powerful beam of light in a particular direction. **2** the beam of light produced by such a device.

search party *n* a group of people taking part in an organized search, as for a lost, missing, or wanted person.

search warrant *n* a written order issued by a justice of the peace authorizing a constable to enter and search premises for stolen goods, etc.

seascape ('siːˌskeɪp) *n* a sketch, etc., of the sea.

sea scorpion *n* any of various northern marine fishes having a tapering body and a large head covered with bony plates and spines.

Sea Scout *n* a Scout belonging to any of a number of Scout troops whose main activities are canoeing, sailing, etc.

sea serpent *n* a huge legendary creature of the sea resembling a snake or dragon.

sea shanty *n* another name for **shanty**².

seashell ('siːˌʃɛl) *n* the empty shell of a marine mollusc.

seashore ('siːˌʃɔː) *n* **1** land bordering on the sea. **2** *Law.* the land between the marks of high and low water.

seasick ❶ ('siːˌsɪk) *adj* suffering from nausea and dizziness caused by the motion of a ship at sea.
▸**'seaˌsickness** *n*

seaside ('siːˌsaɪd) *n* **a** any area bordering on the sea, esp. one regarded as a resort. **b** (*as modifier*): *a seaside hotel.*

sea snail *n* a small spiny-finned fish of cold seas, having a soft scaleless tadpole-shaped body with the pelvic fins fused into a sucker.

sea snake *n* a venomous snake of tropical seas that swims by means of a laterally compressed oarlike tail.

season ❶ ('siːzᵊn) *n* **1** one of the four equal periods into which the year is divided by the equinoxes and solstices. These periods (spring, summer, autumn, and winter) have characteristic weather conditions, and occur at opposite times of the year in the N and S hemispheres. **2** a period of the year characterized by particular conditions or activities: *the rainy season.* **3** the period during which any particular species of animal, bird, or fish is legally permitted to be caught or killed: *open season on red deer.* **4** a period during which a particular entertainment, sport, etc., takes place: *the football season.* **5** any definite or indefinite period. **6** any of the major periods into which the ecclesiastical calendar is divided, such as Lent or Easter. **7** fitting or proper time. **8 in good season.** early enough. **9 in season. 9a** (of game) permitted to be killed. **9b** (of fresh food) readily available. **9c** Also: **in** *or* **on heat.** (of some female mammals) sexually receptive. **9d** appropriate. ◆ *vb* **10** (*tr*) to add herbs, salt, pepper, or spice to (food). **11** (*tr*) to add zest to. **12** (in the preparation of timber) to undergo or cause to undergo drying. **13** (*tr; usually passive*) to make or become experienced: *seasoned troops.* **14** (*tr*) to mitigate or temper. [C13: from OF *seson*, from L *satiō* a sowing, from *serere* to sow]
▸**'seasoned** *adj* ▸**'seasoner** *n*

seasonable ❶ ('siːzənəbᵊl) *adj* **1** suitable for the season: *a seasonable Christmas snow scene.* **2** taking place at the appropriate time.
▸**'seasonableness** *n* ▸**'seasonably** *adv*

seasonal ('siːzənᵊl) *adj* of, relating to, or occurring at a certain season or seasons of the year: *seasonal labour.*
▸**'seasonally** *adv*

seasonal affective disorder *n* a state of depression sometimes experienced by people in winter, thought to be related to lack of sunlight. Abbrev.: **SAD.**

seasoning ❶ ('siːzənɪŋ) *n* **1** something that enhances the flavour of food, such as salt or herbs. **2** another term (not now in technical usage) for **drying.**

season ticket *n* a ticket for a series of events, number of journeys, etc., within a limited time, usually obtained at a reduced rate.

sea squirt *n* a minute primitive marine animal, most of which are sedentary, having a saclike body with openings through which water enters and leaves.

sea swallow *n* a popular name for **tern.**

seat ❶ (siːt) *n* **1** a piece of furniture designed for sitting on, such as a chair or sofa. **2** the part of a chair, bench, etc., on which one sits. **3** a place to sit, esp. one that requires a ticket: *I have two seats for the film tonight.* **4** the buttocks. **5** the part of a garment covering the buttocks. **6** the part or area serving as the base of an object. **7** the part or surface on which the base of an object rests. **8** the place or centre in which something is located: *a seat of government.* **9** a place of abode, esp. a country mansion. **10** a membership or the right to membership in a legislative or similar body. **11** *Chiefly Brit.* a parliamentary constituency. **12** the manner in which a rider sits on a horse. ◆ *vb* **13** (*tr*) to bring to or place on a seat. **14** (*tr*) to provide with seats. **15** (*tr; often passive*) to place or centre: *the ministry is seated in the capital.* **16** (*tr*) to set firmly in place. **17** (*tr*) to fix or install in a position of power. **18** (*intr*) (of garments) to sag in the area covering the buttocks: *your skirt has seated badly.* [OE *gesete*]

seat belt *n* **1** Also called: **safety belt.** a belt or strap worn in a vehicle to restrain forward motion in the event of a collision. **2** a similar belt or strap worn in an aircraft at takeoff and landing.

seating ❶ ('siːtɪŋ) *n* **1** the act of providing with a seat or seats. **2a** the provision of seats, as in a theatre, etc. **2b** (*as modifier*): *seating arrangements.* **3** material used for covering seats. **4** a surface on which a part, such as a valve, is supported.

sea trout *n* a silvery marine variety of the brown trout that migrates to fresh water to spawn.

sea urchin *n* any echinoderm such as the **edible sea urchin,** having a globular body enclosed in a rigid spiny test and occurring in shallow marine waters.

sea vegetables *pl n* edible seaweed.

sea wall *n* a wall or embankment built to prevent encroachment or erosion by the sea.

seaward ('siːwəd) *adv* **1** Also called: **seawards.** towards the sea. ◆ *adj* **2** directed or moving towards the sea. **3** (esp. of a wind) coming from the sea.

seaway ('siːˌweɪ) *n* **1** a waterway giving access to an inland port. **2** a vessel's progress. **3** a route across the sea.

seaweed ('siːˌwiːd) *n* any of numerous multicellular marine algae that grow on the seashore, in salt marshes, in brackish water, or submerged in the ocean.

seaworthy ('siːˌwɜːðɪ) *adj* in a fit condition or ready for a sea voyage.
▸**'seaˌworthiness** *n*

sebaceous (sɪ'beɪʃəs) *adj* **1** of or resembling sebum, fat, or tallow. **2** secreting fat. [C18: from LL *sēbāceus*, from SEBUM]

sebaceous glands *pl n* the small glands in the skin that secrete sebum into hair follicles and onto most of the body surface except the soles of the feet and the palms of the hands.

seborrhoea *or esp. US* **seborrhea** (ˌsɛbə'rɪə) *n* a disease of the sebaceous glands characterized by excessive secretion of sebum.

sebum ('siːbəm) *n* the oily secretion of the sebaceous glands that acts as a lubricant for the hair and skin and provides some protection against bacteria. [C19: from NL, from L: tallow]

sec¹ (sɛk) *adj* **1** (of wines) dry. **2** (of champagne) of medium sweetness. [C19: from F, from L *siccus*]

sec² (sɛk) *n Inf.* short for **second**²: *wait a sec.*

sec³ (sɛk) *abbrev. for* secant.

SEC *abbrev. for* Securities and Exchange Commission.

sec. *abbrev. for:* **1** second (of time). **2** secondary. **3** secretary. **4** section. **5** sector.

secant ('siːkənt) *n* **1** (of an angle) a trigonometric function that in a right-angled triangle is the ratio of the length of the hypotenuse to that of the adjacent side; the reciprocal of cosine. Abbrev.: **sec. 2** a line that intersects a curve. [C16: from L *secāre* to cut]

secateurs ('sɛkətəz) *pl n Chiefly Brit.* a small pair of shears for pruning, having a pair of pivoted handles and usually a single cutting blade that closes against a flat surface. [C19: pl of F *sécateur*, from L *secāre* to cut]

secede ❶ (sɪ'siːd) *vb* **secedes, seceding, seceded.** (*intr*; often foll. by *from*) (of a person, section, etc.) to make a formal withdrawal of membership, as from a political alliance, etc. [C18: from L *sēcēdere* to withdraw, from *sē-* apart + *cēdere* to go]
▸**se'ceder** *n*

secession ❶ (sɪ'sɛʃən) *n* **1** the act of seceding. **2** (*often cap.*) *Chiefly US.* the withdrawal in 1860–61 of 11 Southern states from the Union to form the Confederacy, precipitating the American Civil War. [C17: from L *sēcessiō* a withdrawing, from *sēcēdere* to SECEDE]
▸**se'cessionˌism** *n* ▸**se'cessionist** *n, adj*

sech (ʃɛk, sɛtʃ, 'sɛk'eɪtʃ) *n* hyperbolic secant.

seclude (sɪ'kluːd) *vb* **secludes, secluding, secluded.** (*tr*) **1** to remove from contact with others. **2** to shut off or screen from view. [C15: from L *sēclūdere* to shut off, from *sē-* + *claudere* to imprison]

THESAURUS

searching *adj* = **keen,** close, intent, minute, penetrating, piercing, probing, quizzical, severe, sharp, thorough
Antonyms *adj* cursory, perfunctory, peripheral, sketchy, superficial

seasickness *n* = **mal de mer**

season *n* **1-7** = **period,** division, interval, juncture, occasion, opportunity, spell, term, time, time of year ◆ *vb* **10, 11** = **flavour,** colour, enliven, lace, leaven, pep up, salt, salt and pepper, spice **13** = **make experienced,** acclimatize, accustom, anneal, discipline, habituate, harden, inure, mature, prepare, toughen, train **14** = **mitigate,** moderate, qualify, temper

seasonable *adj* **1, 2** = **appropriate,** convenient, fit, opportune, providential, suitable, timely, welcome, well-timed

seasoned *adj* **13** = **experienced,** battle-scarred, hardened, long-serving, mature, old, practised, time-served, veteran, weathered, well-versed
Antonyms *adj* callow, green, inexperienced, new, novice, unpractised, unseasoned, unskilled

seasoning *n* **1** = **flavouring,** condiment, dressing, relish, salt and pepper, sauce, spice

seat *n* **1** = **chair,** bench, pew, settle, stall, stool, throne **6** = **base,** bed, bottom, cause, footing, foundation, ground, groundwork **8** = **centre,** axis, capital, cradle, headquarters, heart, hub, location, place, site, situation, source, station **9** = **mansion,** abode, ancestral hall, house, residence **10** = **membership,** chair, constituency, incumbency, place ◆ *vb* **13** = **sit,** deposit, fix, install, locate, place, set, settle

seating *n* **2** = **accommodation,** chairs, places, room, seats

secede *vb* = **withdraw,** apostatize, break with, disaffiliate, leave, pull out, quit, resign, retire, separate, split from

secession *n* **1** = **withdrawal,** apostasy, break, defection, disaffiliation, seceding, split

secluded ❶ (sɪ'klu:dɪd) *adj* **1** kept apart from the company of others: *a secluded life.* **2** private.
▸**se'cludedly** *adv* ▸**se'cludedness** *n*

seclusion ❶ (sɪ'klu:ʒən) *n* **1** the act of secluding or the state of being secluded. **2** a secluded place. [C17: from Med. L *sēclūsiō*; see SECLUDE]

second[1] ❶ ('sɛkənd) *adj* (*usually prenominal*) **1a** coming directly after the first in numbering or counting order, position, time, etc.; being the ordinal number of *two:* often written 2nd. **1b** (*as n*): *the second in line.* **2** graded or ranked between the first and third levels. **3** alternate: *every second Thursday.* **4** extra: *a second opportunity.* **5** resembling a person or event from an earlier period of history: *a second Wagner.* **6** of lower quality; inferior. **7** denoting the lowest but one forward ratio of a gearbox in a motor vehicle. **8** *Music.* denoting a musical part, voice, or instrument subordinate to or lower in pitch than another (the first): *the second tenors.* **9 at second hand.** by hearsay. ◆ *n* **10** *Brit. education.* an honours degree of the second class, usually further divided into an upper and lower designation. Full term: **second-class honours degree. 11** the lowest but one forward ratio of a gearbox in a motor vehicle. **12** (in boxing, duelling, etc.) an attendant who looks after a competitor. **13** a speech seconding a motion or the person making it. **14** *Music.* the interval between one note and another lying next above or below it in the diatonic scale. **15** (*pl*) goods of inferior quality. **16** (*pl*) *Inf.* a second helping of food. **17** (*pl*) the second course of a meal. ◆ *vb* (*tr*) **18** to give aid or backing to. **19** (in boxing, etc.) to act as second to (a competitor). **20** to express formal support for (a motion already proposed). ◆ *adv* **21** Also: **secondly.** in the second place. ◆ *sentence connector.* **22** Also: **secondly.** as the second point. [C13: via OF from L *secundus* coming next in order, from *sequī* to follow]
▸**'seconder** *n*

second[2] ❶ ('sɛkənd) *n* **1a** 1/60 of a minute of time. **1b** the basic SI unit of time: the duration of 9 192 631 770 periods of radiation corresponding to the transition between two hyperfine levels of the ground state of caesium-133. Symbol: s **2** 1/60 of a minute of angle. Symbol: ″ **3** a very short period of time. [C14: from OF, from Med. L *pars minūta secunda* the second small part (a minute being the first small part of an hour); see SECOND[1]]

second[3] (sɪ'kɒnd) *vb* (*tr*) *Brit.* **1** to transfer (an employee) temporarily to another branch, etc. **2** *Mil.* to transfer (an officer) to another post. [C19: from F *en second* in second rank (or position)]
▸**se'condment** *n*

secondary ❶ ('sɛkəndərɪ) *adj* **1** one grade or step after the first. **2** derived from or depending on what is primary or first: *a secondary source.* **3** below the first in rank, importance, etc. **4** (*prenominal*) of or relating to the education of young people between the ages of 11 and 18: *secondary education.* **5** (of the flight feathers of a bird's wing) growing from the ulna. **6a** being the part of an electric circuit, such as a transformer or induction coil, in which a current is induced by a changing current in a neighbouring coil: *a secondary coil.* **6b** (of a current) flowing in such a circuit. **7** *Chem.* **7a** (of an amine) containing the group NH. **7b** (of a salt) derived from a tribasic acid by replacement of two acidic hydrogen atoms with metal atoms. ◆ *n, pl* **secondaries. 8** a person or thing that is secondary. **9** a subordinate, deputy, or inferior. **10** a secondary coil, winding, inductance, or current in an electric circuit. **11** *Ornithol.* any of the flight feathers that grow from the ulna of a bird's wing. **12** *Astron.* a celestial body that orbits around a specified primary body: *the moon is the secondary of the earth.* **13** *American football.* **13a** (usually preceded by *the*) cornerbacks and safeties collectively. **13b** their area in the field. **14** short for **secondary colour.**
▸**'secondarily** *adv* ▸**'secondariness** *n*

secondary cell *n* an electric cell that can be recharged and can therefore be used to store electrical energy in the form of chemical energy.

secondary colour *n* a colour formed by mixing two primary colours.

secondary emission *n Physics.* the emission of electrons (**secondary electrons**) from a solid as a result of bombardment with a beam of electrons, ions, or metastable atoms.

secondary picketing *n* the picketing by striking workers of a factory, distribution outlet, etc., that supplies goods to or distributes goods from their employer.

secondary sexual characteristic *n* any of various features distinguishing individuals of different sex but not directly concerned in reproduction. Examples are the antlers of a stag and the beard of a man.

second ballot *n* an electoral procedure in which, after a first ballot, candidates at the bottom of the poll are eliminated and another ballot is held among the remaining candidates.

second-best *adj* **1** next to the best. **2 come off second best.** *Inf.* to be worsted by someone. ◆ *n* **3 second best.** an inferior alternative.

second chamber *n* the upper house of a bicameral legislative assembly.

second childhood ❶ *n* dotage; senility (esp. in **in his, her,** etc., **second childhood**).

second class ❶ *n* **1** the class or grade next in value, quality, etc., to the first. ◆ *adj* (**second-class** *when prenominal*). **2** of the class or grade next to the best in quality, etc. **3** shoddy or inferior. **4** of or denoting the class of accommodation in a hotel or on a train, etc., lower in quality and price than first class. **5** (in Britain) of mail that is processed more slowly than first-class mail. **6** *Education.* See **second**[1] (sense 10). ◆ *adv* **7** by second-class mail, transport, etc.

second-class citizen *n* a person whose rights and opportunities are treated as less important than those of other people in the same society.

Second Coming *n* the prophesied return of Christ to earth at the Last Judgment.

second cousin *n* the child of a first cousin of either of one's parents.

second-degree burn *n Pathol.* a burn in which blisters appear on the skin.

seconde (sɪ'kɒnd) *n* the second of eight positions from which a parry or attack can be made in fencing. [C18: from F *seconde parade* the second parry]

Second Empire *n* the style of furniture and decoration of the Second Empire in France (1852–70), reviving the Empire style, but with fussier ornamentation.

second fiddle *n Inf.* **1a** the second violin in a string quartet or an orchestra. **1b** the musical part assigned to such an instrument. **2** a person who has a secondary status.

second floor *n Brit.* the storey of a building immediately above the first and two floors up from the ground. US and Canad. term: **third floor.**

second generation *n* **1** offspring of parents born in a given country. **2** (*modifier*) of a refined stage of development in manufacture: *a second-generation robot.*

second growth *n* natural regrowth of a forest after fire, cutting, etc.

second hand *n* a pointer on the face of a timepiece that indicates the seconds.

second-hand ❶ *adj* **1** previously owned or used. **2** not from an original source or experience. **3** dealing in or selling goods that are not new: *a second-hand car dealer.* ◆ *adv* **4** from a source of previously owned or used goods: *he prefers to buy second-hand.* **5** not directly: *he got the news second-hand.*

second language *n* **1** a language other than the mother tongue used for business transactions, teaching, debate, etc. **2** a language that is officially recognized in a country, other than the main national language.

second lieutenant *n* an officer holding the lowest commissioned rank in the armed forces of certain nations.

secondly ❶ ('sɛkəndlɪ) *adv* another word for **second**[1], usually used to precede the second item in a list of topics.

second nature *n* a habit, characteristic, etc., long practised or acquired so as to seem innate.

second person *n* a grammatical category of pronouns and verbs used when referring to or describing the individual or individuals being addressed.

second-rate ❶ *adj* **1** not of the highest quality; mediocre. **2** second in importance, etc.

second reading *n* the second presentation of a bill in a legislative assembly, as to approve its general principles (in Britain), or to discuss a committee's report on it (in the US).

second sight *n* the alleged ability to foresee the future, see actions taking place elsewhere, etc.
▸**'second-'sighted** *adj*

THESAURUS

secluded *adj* **1, 2** = **private,** cloistered, cut off, isolated, lonely, off the beaten track, out-of-the-way, reclusive, remote, retired, sequestered, sheltered, solitary, tucked away, unfrequented
Antonyms *adj* accessible, busy, frequented, open, public

seclusion *n* **1** = **privacy,** concealment, hiding, isolation, ivory tower, purdah, remoteness, retirement, retreat, shelter, solitude

second[1] *adj* **1** = **next,** following, subsequent, succeeding **4** = **additional,** alternative, extra, further, other, repeated **5** = **duplicate,** double, reproduction, twin **6** = **inferior,** lesser, lower, secondary, subordinate, supporting ◆ *n* **12** = **supporter,** assistant, backer, helper ◆ *vb* **18** = **support,** advance, aid, approve, assist, back, commend, encourage, endorse, forward, further, give moral support to, go along with, help, promote

second[2] *n* **1** = **moment,** bat of an eye (*inf.*), flash, instant, jiffy (*inf.*), minute, sec (*inf.*), split second, tick (*Brit. inf.*), trice, twinkling, twinkling of an eye, two shakes of a lamb's tail (*inf.*)

secondary *adj* **1** = **backup,** alternate, auxiliary, extra, fall-back, relief, reserve, second, subsidiary, supporting **2** = **resultant,** consequential, contingent, derivative, derived, indirect, resulting, second-hand **3** = **subordinate,** inferior, lesser, lower, minor, second-rate, unimportant
Antonyms *adj* ≠ **backup:** only, primary ≠ **resultant:** original, preceding ≠ **subordinate:** cardinal, chief, head, larger, main, major, more important, prime, principal, superior

second childhood *n* = **senility,** caducity, dotage

second class *adj* **second-class 3** = **inferior,** déclassé, indifferent, mediocre, no great shakes (*inf.*), outclassed, second-best, second-rate, undistinguished, uninspiring

second-hand *adj* **1** = **used,** handed down, hand-me-down (*inf.*), nearly new, reach-me-down (*inf.*) ◆ *adv* **5** = **indirectly,** at second-hand, on the grapevine (*inf.*)

secondly *adv* = **next,** in the second place, second

second-rate *adj* **1** = **inferior,** bush-league (*Austral. & NZ inf.*), cheap, cheap and nasty (*inf.*), commonplace, dime-a-dozen (*inf.*), end-of-the-pier (*Brit. inf.*), for the birds (*inf.*), low-grade, low-quality, mediocre, no great shakes (*inf.*), not much cop (*Brit. sl.*), poor, rubbishy, shoddy, strictly for the birds (*inf.*), substandard, tacky (*inf.*), tawdry, tinhorn (*US sl.*), two-bit (*US & Canad. sl.*)
Antonyms *adj* a cut above (*inf.*), choice, de luxe,

second string *n* **1** *Chiefly Brit.* an alternative course of action, etc., intended to come into use should the first fail (esp. in **a second string to one's bow**). **2** *Chiefly US & Canad.* a substitute or reserve player or team.

second thought *n* (*usually pl*) a revised opinion or idea on a matter already considered.

second wind (wɪnd) *n* **1** the return of the ability to breathe at a comfortable rate, esp. following a period of exertion. **2** renewed ability to continue in an effort.

secrecy Ⓣ ('siːkrɪsɪ) *n, pl* **secrecies. 1** the state or quality of being secret. **2** the state of keeping something secret. **3** the ability or tendency to keep things secret.

secret Ⓣ ('siːkrɪt) *adj* **1** kept hidden or separate from the knowledge of others. Related adj: **cryptic. 2** known only to initiates: *a secret password.* **3** hidden from general view or use: *a secret garden.* **4** able or tending to keep things private or to oneself. **5** operating without the knowledge of outsiders: *a secret society.* ◆ *n* **6** something kept or to be kept hidden. **7** something unrevealed; a mystery. **8** an underlying explanation, reason, etc.: *the secret of success.* **9** a method, plan, etc., known only to initiates. **10** *Liturgy.* a prayer said by the celebrant of the Mass after the offertory and before the preface. [C14: via OF from L *sēcrētus* concealed, from *sēcernere* to sift]
▸**'secretly** *adv*

secret agent Ⓣ *n* a person employed in espionage.

secretaire (ˌsɛkrɪ'tɛə) *n* an enclosed writing desk, usually having an upper cabinet section. [C19: from F; see SECRETARY]

secretariat (ˌsɛkrɪ'tɛərɪət) *n* **1a** an office responsible for the secretarial, clerical, and administrative affairs of a legislative body or international organization. **1b** the staff of such an office. **2** a body of secretaries. **3** a secretary's place of work; office. **4** the position of a secretary. [C19: via F from Med. L *sēcrētāriātus,* from *sēcrētārius* SECRETARY]

secretary ('sɛkrətrɪ) *n, pl* **secretaries. 1** a person who handles correspondence, keeps records, and does general clerical work for an individual, organization, etc. **2** the official manager of the day-to-day business of a society or board. **3** (in Britain) a senior civil servant who assists a government minister. **4** (in the US) the head of a government administrative department. **5** (in Britain) See **secretary of state. 6** Another name for **secretaire.** [C14: from Med. L *sēcrētārius,* from L *sēcrētum* something hidden; see SECRET]
▸**secretarial** (ˌsɛkrɪ'tɛərɪəl) *adj* ▸**'secretaryship** *n*

secretary bird *n* a large African long-legged bird of prey having a crest and tail of long feathers and feeding chiefly on snakes.

secretary-general *n, pl* **secretaries-general.** a chief administrative official, as of the United Nations.

secretary of state *n* **1** (in Britain) the head of any of several government departments. **2** (in the US) the head of the government department in charge of foreign affairs (**State Department**).

secrete[1] Ⓣ (sɪ'kriːt) *vb* **secretes, secreting, secreted.** (of a cell, organ, etc.) to synthesize and release (a secretion). [C18: back formation from SECRETION]
▸**se'cretor** *n* ▸**se'cretory** *adj*

secrete[2] Ⓣ (sɪ'kriːt) *vb* **secretes, secreting, secreted.** (*tr*) to put in a hiding place. [C18: var. of obs. *secret* to hide away]

secretion Ⓣ (sɪ'kriːʃən) *n* **1** a substance that is released from a cell, esp. a glandular cell. **2** the process involved in producing and releasing such a substance from the cell. [C17: from Med. L *sēcrētiō,* from L: a separation]

secretive Ⓣ ('siːkrɪtɪv) *adj* inclined to secrecy.
▸**'secretively** *adv* ▸**'secretiveness** *n*

secretory (sɪ'kriːtərɪ) *adj* of, relating to, or producing a secretion: *secretory function.*

secret police *n* a police force that operates relatively secretly to check subversion or political dissent.

secret service *n* a government agency or department that conducts intelligence or counterintelligence operations.

sect Ⓣ (sɛkt) *n* **1** a subdivision of a larger religious group (esp. the Christian Church as a whole) the members of which have to some extent diverged from the rest by developing deviating beliefs, practices, etc. **2** *Often disparaging.* **2a** a schismatic religious body. **2b** a religious group regarded as extreme or heretical. **3** a group of people with a common interest, doctrine, etc. [C14: from L *secta* faction, from *sequī* to follow]

-sect *vb combining form.* to cut or divide, esp. into a specified number of parts: *trisect.* [from L *sectus* cut, from *secāre* to cut]

sectarian Ⓣ (sɛk'tɛərɪən) *adj* **1** of, relating to, or characteristic of sects or sectaries. **2** adhering to a particular sect, faction, or doctrine. **3** narrow-minded, esp. as a result of adherence to a particular sect. ◆ *n* **4** a member of a sect or faction, esp. one who is intolerant towards other sects, etc.
▸**sec'tarian,ism** *n*

sectary ('sɛktərɪ) *n, pl* **sectaries. 1** a member of a sect, esp. a religous sect. **2** a member of a Nonconformist denomination, esp. one that is small. [C16: from Med. L *sectārius,* from L *secta* SECT]

section Ⓣ ('sɛkʃən) *n* **1** a part cut off or separated from the main body of something. **2** a part or subdivision of a piece of writing, book, etc.: *the sports section of the newspaper.* **3** one of several component parts. **4** a distinct part of a country, community, etc. **5** *US & Canad.* an area one mile square. **6** *NZ.* a plot of land for building, esp. in a suburban area. **7** the section of a railway track that is controlled by a particular signal box. **8** the act or process of cutting or separating by cutting. **9** a representation of an object cut by an imaginary vertical plane so as to show its construction and interior. **10** *Geom.* a plane surface formed by cutting through a solid. **11** a thin slice of biological tissue, etc., prepared for examination by microscope. **12** a segment of an orange or other citrus fruit. **13** a small military formation. **14** *Austral. & NZ.* a fare stage on a bus, tram, etc. **15** *Music.* **15a** an extended division of a composition or movement: *the development section.* **15b** a division in an orchestra, band, etc., containing instruments belonging to the same class: *the brass section.* **16** Also called: **signature, gathering.** a folded printing sheet or sheets ready for gathering and binding. ◆ *vb* (*tr*) **17** to cut or divide into sections. **18** to cut through so as to reveal a section. **19** (in drawing, esp. mechanical drawing) to shade so as to indicate sections. [C16: from L *sectiō,* from *secāre* to cut]

sectional Ⓣ ('sɛkʃənᵊl) *adj* **1** composed of several sections. **2** of or relating to a section. **3** of or concerned with a particular group within a community, esp. to the exclusion of others.
▸**'sectiona,lize** *or* **'sectiona,lise** *vb* (*tr*) ▸**'sectionally** *adv*

sectionalism ('sɛkʃənəˌlɪzəm) *n* excessive or narrow-minded concern for local or regional interests.
▸**'sectionalist** *n, adj*

sector Ⓣ ('sɛktə) *n* **1** a part or subdivision, esp. of a society or an economy: *the private sector.* **2** *Geom.* either portion of a circle included between two radii and an arc. **3** a measuring instrument consisting of two graduated arms hinged at one end. **4** a part or subdivision of an area of military operations. **5** *Computing.* the smallest addressable portion of the track on a magnetic tape, disk, or drum store. [C16: from LL: sector, from L: a cutter, from *secāre* to cut]
▸**'sectoral** *adj*

sectorial (sɛk'tɔːrɪəl) *adj* **1** of or relating to a sector. **2** *Zool.* adapted for cutting: *the sectorial teeth of carnivores.*

secular Ⓣ ('sɛkjʊlə) *adj* **1** of or relating to worldly as opposed to sacred things. **2** not concerned with or related to religion. **3** not within the control of the Church. **4** (of an education, etc.) having no particular religious affinities. **5** (of clerics) not bound by religious vows to a monastic or other order. **6** occurring or appearing once in an age or cen-

THESAURUS

excellent, fine, first-class, first-rate, good quality, high-class, quality, superior

secrecy *n* **1 = mystery,** cloak and dagger, concealment, confidentiality, huggermugger (*rare*), privacy, retirement, seclusion, silence, solitude, surreptitiousness **2 = secretiveness,** clandestineness, covertness, furtiveness, stealth

secret *adj* **1 = concealed,** backstairs, behind someone's back, camouflaged, cloak-and-dagger, close, closet (*inf.*), confidential, conspiratorial, covered, covert, disguised, furtive, hidden, hole-and-corner (*inf.*), hush-hush (*inf.*), reticent, shrouded, undercover, underground, under wraps, undisclosed, unknown, unpublished, unrevealed, unseen **2 = mysterious,** abstruse, arcane, cabbalistic, clandestine, classified, cryptic, esoteric, occult, recondite **4 = stealthy,** close, deep, discreet, reticent, secretive, sly, underhand ◆ *n* **6-9 = mystery,** code, confidence, enigma, formula, key, recipe, skeleton in the cupboard
Antonyms *adj* ≠ **concealed, stealthy:** apparent, candid, disclosed, frank, manifest, obvious, open, overt, public, unconcealed, visible ≠ **mysterious:** exoteric, straightforward, well-known

secret agent *n* **= spy,** cloak-and-dagger man, nark (*Brit., Austral., & NZ sl.*), spook (*US & Canad. inf.*), undercover agent

secrete[1] *vb* **= give off,** emanate, emit, extravasate (*Medical*), extrude, exude

secrete[2] *vb* **= hide,** bury, cache, conceal, cover, disguise, harbour, screen, secure, shroud, stash (*inf.*), stash away (*inf.*), stow, veil
Antonyms *vb* bare, display, exhibit, expose to view, leave in the open, reveal, show, uncover, unmask, unveil

secretion *n* **2 = discharge,** emission, excretion, extravasation (*Medical*), exudation

secretive *adj* **= reticent,** cagey, clamlike, close, cryptic, deep, enigmatic, playing one's cards close to one's chest, reserved, tight-lipped, uncommunicative, unforthcoming, withdrawn
Antonyms *adj* candid, communicative, expansive, forthcoming, frank, open, unreserved

secretly *adv* **1-5 = in secret,** behind closed doors, behind (someone's) back, clandestinely, confidentially, covertly, furtively, in camera, in confidence, in one's heart, in one's heart of hearts, in one's innermost thoughts, on the fly (*sl., chiefly Brit.*), on the q.t. (*inf.*), on the sly, privately, quietly, stealthily, surreptitiously, under the counter, unobserved

sect *n* **1-3 = group,** camp, denomination, division, faction, party, schism, school, school of thought, splinter group, wing

sectarian *adj* **3 = narrow-minded,** bigoted, clannish, cliquish, doctrinaire, dogmatic, exclusive, factional, fanatic, fanatical, hidebound, insular, limited, parochial, partisan, rigid ◆ *n* **4 = bigot,** adherent, disciple, dogmatist, extremist, fanatic, partisan, true believer, zealot
Antonyms *adj* ≠ **narrow-minded:** broad-minded, catholic, free-thinking, liberal, non-sectarian, open-minded, tolerant, unbigoted, unprejudiced

section *n* **1 = part,** component, cross section, division, fraction, fragment, instalment, passage, piece, portion, sample, segment, slice, subdivision **4 = district,** area, department, region, sector, zone

sectional *adj* **3 = regional,** divided, exclusive, factional, local, localized, partial, separate, separatist

sector *n* **1 = part,** area, category, district, division, quarter, region, stratum, subdivision, zone

secular *adj* **1-3 = worldly,** civil, earthly, laic, laical, lay, nonspiritual, profane, state, temporal

tury. 7 lasting for a long time. 8 *Astron.* occurring slowly over a long period of time. ◆ *n* 9 a member of the secular clergy. [C13: from OF *seculer,* from LL *saecularis* temporal, from L: concerning an age, from *saeculum* an age]
▸**secularity** (ˌsɛkjʊˈlærɪtɪ) *n* ▸**ˈsecularly** *adv*

secularism (ˈsɛkjʊləˌrɪzəm) *n* 1 *Philosophy.* a doctrine that rejects religion, esp. in ethics. 2 the attitude that religion should have no place in civil affairs.
▸**ˈsecularist** *n, adj*

secularize *or* **secularise** (ˈsɛkjʊləˌraɪz) *vb* **secularizes, secularizing, secularized** *or* **secularises, secularising, secularised.** (*tr*) 1 to change from religious or sacred to secular functions, etc. 2 to dispense from allegiance to a religious order. 3 *Law.* to transfer (property) from ecclesiastical to civil possession or use.
▸**ˌseculariˈzation** *or* **ˌseculariˈsation** *n*

secund (sɪˈkʌnd) *adj Bot.* having parts arranged on or turned to one side of the axis. [C18: from L *secundus* following, from *sequī* to follow]

secure ❶ (sɪˈkjʊə) *adj* 1 free from danger, damage, etc. 2 free from fear, care, etc. 3 in safe custody. 4 not likely to fail, become loose, etc. 5 able to be relied on: *a secure investment.* 6 *Arch.* overconfident. ◆ *vb* **secures, securing, secured.** 7 (*tr*) to obtain: *I will secure some good seats.* 8 (when *intr,* often foll. by *against*) to make or become free from danger, fear, etc. 9 (*tr*) to make fast or firm. 10 (when *intr,* often foll. by *against*) to make or become certain: *this plan will secure your happiness.* 11 (*tr*) to assure (a creditor) of payment, as by giving security. 12 (*tr*) to make (a military position) safe from attack. 13 *Naut.* to make (a vessel or its contents) safe or ready by battening down hatches, etc. [C16: from L *sēcūrus* free from care]
▸**seˈcurable** *adj* ▸**seˈcurely** *adv* ▸**seˈcurement** *n* ▸**seˈcurer** *n*

Securities and Investment Board *n* a British regulatory body set up in 1986 to oversee London's financial markets, each of which has its own self-regulatory organization. Abbrev.: **SIB.**

securitization *or* **securitisation** (sɪˌkjʊərɪtaɪˈzeɪʃən) *n Finance.* the use of such securities as eurobonds to enable investors to lend directly to borrowers with a minimum of risk but without using banks as intermediaries.

security ❶ (sɪˈkjʊərɪtɪ) *n, pl* **securities.** 1 the state of being secure. 2 assured freedom from poverty or want: *he needs the security of a permanent job.* 3 a person or thing that secures, guarantees, etc. 4 precautions taken to ensure against theft, espionage, etc. 5 (*often pl*) 5a a certificate of creditorship or property carrying the right to receive interest or dividend, such as shares or bonds. 5b the financial asset represented by such a certificate. 6 the specific asset that a creditor can claim in the event of default on an obligation. 7 something given or pledged to secure the fulfilment of a promise or obligation. 8 the protection of data to ensure that only authorised personnel have access to computer files.

security blanket *n* 1 a policy of temporary secrecy by police or those in charge of security, in order to protect a person, place, etc., threatened with danger, from further risk. 2 a baby's blanket, soft toy, etc., to which a baby or young child becomes very attached, using it as a comforter. 3 *Inf.* anything used or thought of as providing reassurance.

Security Council *n* an organ of the United Nations established to maintain world peace.

security guard *n* someone employed to protect buildings, people, etc., and to collect and deliver large sums of money.

security risk *n* a person deemed to be a threat to state security in that he could be open to pressure, have subversive political beliefs, etc.

secy. *or* **sec'y.** *abbrev. for* secretary.

sedan (sɪˈdæn) *n* 1 *US, Canad., & NZ.* a saloon car. 2 short for **sedan chair.** [C17: from ?]

sedan chair *n* a closed chair for one passenger, carried on poles by two bearers, commonly used in the 17th and 18th centuries.

sedate[1] ❶ (sɪˈdeɪt) *adj* 1 habitually calm and composed in manner. 2 sober or decorous. [C17: from L *sēdāre* to soothe]
▸**seˈdately** *adv* ▸**seˈdateness** *n*

sedate[2] (sɪˈdeɪt) *vb* **sedates, sedating, sedated.** (*tr*) to administer a sedative to. [C20: back formation from SEDATIVE]

sedation (sɪˈdeɪʃən) *n* 1 a state of calm or reduced nervous activity. 2 the administration of a sedative.

sedative ❶ (ˈsɛdətɪv) *adj* 1 having a soothing or calming effect. 2 of or relating to sedation. ◆ *n* 3 *Med.* a sedative drug or agent. [C15: from Med. L *sēdātīvus,* from L *sēdātus* assuaged; see SEDATE[1]]

sedentary ❶ (ˈsɛdᵊntərɪ) *adj* 1 characterized by or requiring a sitting position: *sedentary work.* 2 tending to sit about without taking much exercise. 3 (of animals) moving about very little. 4 (of birds) not migratory. [C16: from L *sedentārius,* from *sedēre* to sit]
▸**ˈsedentarily** *adv* ▸**ˈsedentariness** *n*

Seder (ˈseɪdə) *n Judaism.* a ceremonial meal on the first night or first two nights of Passover. [from Heb. *sēdher* order]

sedge (sɛdʒ) *n* a grasslike plant growing on wet ground and having rhizomes, triangular stems, and minute flowers in spikelets. [OE *secg*]
▸**ˈsedgy** *adj*

sedge warbler *n* a European songbird of reed beds and swampy areas, having a streaked brownish plumage with white eye stripes.

sedilia (sɛˈdaɪlɪə) *n* (*functioning as sing*) the group of three seats, each called a **sedile** (sɛˈdaɪlɪ) on the south side of a sanctuary where the celebrant and ministers sit during High Mass. [C18: from L, from *sedīle* a chair, from *sedēre* to sit]

sediment ❶ (ˈsɛdɪmənt) *n* 1 matter that settles to the bottom of a liquid. 2 material that has been deposited from water, ice, or wind. [C16: from L *sedimentum* a settling, from *sedēre* to sit]
▸**ˌsedimenˈtation** *n*

sedimentary (ˌsɛdɪˈmɛntərɪ) *adj* 1 characteristic of, resembling, or containing sediment. 2 (of rocks) formed by the accumulation of mineral and organic fragments that have been deposited by water, ice, or wind.
▸**ˌsediˈmentarily** *adv*

sedimentation tank *n* a tank into which sewage is passed to allow suspended solid matter to separate out.

sedition ❶ (sɪˈdɪʃən) *n* 1 speech or behaviour directed against the peace of a state. 2 an offence that tends to undermine the authority of a state. 3 an incitement to public disorder. [C14: from L *sēditiō* discord, from *sēd-* apart + *itiō* a going, from *īre* to go]
▸**seˈditionary** *n, adj*

seditious ❶ (sɪˈdɪʃəs) *adj* 1 of, like, or causing sedition. 2 inclined to or taking part in sedition.

seduce ❶ (sɪˈdjuːs) *vb* **seduces, seducing, seduced.** (*tr*) 1 to persuade to engage in sexual intercourse. 2 to lead astray, as from the right action. 3 to win over, attract, or lure. [C15: from L *sēdūcere* to lead apart]
▸**seˈducible** *adj*

seducer ❶ (sɪˈdjuːsə) *or* (*fem*) **seductress** (sɪˈdʌktrɪs) *n* a person who entices, allures, or seduces, esp. one who entices another to engage in sexual intercourse.

seduction ❶ (sɪˈdʌkʃən) *n* 1 the act of seducing or the state of being seduced. 2 a means of seduction.

seductive ❶ (sɪˈdʌktɪv) *adj* tending to seduce or capable of seducing; enticing; alluring.
▸**seˈductively** *adv* ▸**seˈductiveness** *n*

sedulous ❶ (ˈsɛdjʊləs) *adj* assiduous; diligent. [C16: from L *sēdulus,* from ?]
▸**sedulity** (sɪˈdjuːlɪtɪ) *or* **ˈsedulousness** *n* ▸**ˈsedulously** *adv*

THESAURUS

Antonyms *adj* divine, holy, religious, sacred, spiritual, theological

secure *adj* 1 = **safe**, immune, impregnable, in safe hands, out of harm's way, protected, sheltered, shielded, unassailable, undamaged, unharmed 2 = **sure**, assured, certain, confident, easy, reassured 4 = **fixed**, dependable, fast, fastened, firm, fortified, immovable, stable, steady, tight 5 = **reliable**, absolute, conclusive, definite, in the bag (*inf.*), solid, steadfast, tried and true, well-founded ◆ *vb* 7 = **obtain**, acquire, come by, gain, get, get hold of, land, make sure of, pick up, procure, score (*sl.*), win possession of 9 = **fasten**, attach, batten down, bolt, chain, fix, lash, lock, lock up, make fast, moor, padlock, rivet, tie up 10 = **guarantee**, assure, ensure, insure
Antonyms *adj* ≠ **safe:** endangered, unprotected, unsafe ≠ **sure:** ill-at-ease, insecure, unassured, uncertain, uneasy, unsure ≠ **fixed:** insecure, loose, not fastened, precarious, unfixed, unsafe, unsound ◆ *vb* ≠ **obtain:** give up, let (something) slip through (one's) fingers, lose ≠ **fasten:** loose, unloose, untie ≠ **guarantee:** endanger, imperil, leave unguaranteed

security *n* 1 = **safety**, asylum, care, cover, custody, immunity, preservation, protection, refuge, retreat, safekeeping, sanctuary 3 = **assurance**, certainty, confidence, conviction, ease of mind, freedom from doubt, positiveness, reliance, sureness 4 = **precautions**, defence, guards, protection, safeguards, safety measures, surveillance 6 = **pledge**, collateral, gage, guarantee, hostage, insurance, pawn, surety
Antonyms *n* ≠ **safety:** exposure, jeopardy, vulnerability ≠ **assurance:** insecurity, uncertainty

sedate[1] *adj* 1-2 = **calm**, collected, composed, cool, decorous, demure, dignified, earnest, grave, imperturbable, placid, proper, quiet, seemly, serene, serious, sober, solemn, staid, tranquil, unflappable (*inf.*), unhurried, unruffled
Antonyms *adj* ≠ **calm:** agitated, excitable, excited, flighty, impassioned, jumpy, nervous, undignified, unsteady, wild

sedative *adj* 1 = **calming**, allaying, anodyne, calmative, lenitive, relaxing, sleep-inducing, soothing, soporific, tranquillizing ◆ *n* 3 = **tranquillizer**, anodyne, calmative, downer *or* down (*sl.*), narcotic, opiate, sleeping pill

sedentary *adj* 1, 2 = **inactive**, desk, desk-bound, motionless, seated, sitting, torpid
Antonyms *adj* active, mobile, motile, moving, on the go (*inf.*)

sediment *n* 1 = **dregs**, deposit, grounds, lees, precipitate, residue, settlings

sedition *n* 1-3 = **rabble-rousing**, agitation, disloyalty, incitement to riot, subversion, treason

seditious *adj* 1, 2 = **revolutionary**, disloyal, dissident, insubordinate, mutinous, rebellious, refractory, subversive, treasonable

seduce *vb* 1 = **corrupt**, betray, debauch, deflower, deprave, dishonour, ruin (*arch.*) 2, 3 = **tempt**, allure, attract, beguile, deceive, decoy, ensnare, entice, inveigle, lead astray, lure, mislead

seduction *n* 1 = **corruption**, defloration, ruin (*arch.*) 2 = **temptation**, allure, enticement, lure, snare

seductive *adj* = **alluring**, attractive, beguiling, bewitching, captivating, come-hither (*inf.*), come-to-bed (*inf.*), enticing, flirtatious, inviting, irresistible, provocative, ravishing, sexy (*inf.*), siren, specious, tempting

seductress *n* = **temptress**, Circe, enchantress, *femme fatale*, Lorelei, siren, vamp (*inf.*)

sedulous *adj* = **diligent**, assiduous, busy, conscientious, constant, industrious, laborious, painstaking, persevering, persistent, tireless, unflagging, unremitting

sedum (ˈsiːdəm) *n* a rock plant having thick fleshy leaves and clusters of white, yellow, or pink flowers. [C15: from L: houseleek]

see[1] (siː) *vb* **sees, seeing, saw, seen. 1** to perceive with the eyes. **2** (when *tr, may take a clause as object*) to understand: *I explained the problem but he could not see it.* **3** (*tr*) to perceive with any or all of the senses: *I hate to see you so unhappy.* **4** (*tr; may take a clause as object*) to foresee: *I can see what will happen if you don't help.* **5** (when *tr, may take a clause as object*) to ascertain or find out (a fact): *see who is at the door.* **6** (when *tr, takes a clause as object;* when *intr,* foll. by *to*) to make sure (of something) or take care (of something): *see that he gets to bed early.* **7** (when *tr, may take a clause as object*) to consider, deliberate, or decide: *see if you can come next week.* **8** (*tr*) to have experience of: *he had seen much unhappiness in his life.* **9** (*tr*) to allow to be in a specified condition: *I cannot stand by and see a child in pain.* **10** (*tr*) to be characterized by: *this period of history has seen much unrest.* **11** (*tr*) to meet or pay a visit to: *to see one's solicitor.* **12** (*tr*) to receive: *the Prime Minister will see the deputation now.* **13** (*tr*) to frequent the company of: *she is seeing a married man.* **14** (*tr*) to accompany: *I saw her to the door.* **15** (*tr*) to refer to or look up: *for further information see the appendix.* **16** (in gambling, esp. in poker) to match (another player's bet) or match the bet of (another player) by staking an equal sum. **17 as far as I can see.** to the best of my judgment. **18 see fit.** (*takes an infinitive*) to consider proper, etc.: *I don't see fit to allow her to come here.* **19 see (someone) hanged** *or* **damned first.** *Inf.* to refuse absolutely to do what one has been asked. **20 see you, see you later,** *or* **be seeing you.** an expression of farewell. ◆ See also **see about, see into,** etc. [OE *sēon*]

see[2] (siː) *n* the diocese of a bishop, or the place within it where his cathedral is situated. [C13: from OF *sed,* from L *sēdēs* a seat]

see about *vb* (*intr, prep*) **1** to take care of: *he couldn't see about the matter because he was ill.* **2** to investigate: *to see about a new car.*

Seebeck effect (ˈsiːbɛk) *n* the phenomenon in which a current is produced in a circuit containing two or more different metals when the junctions between the metals are maintained at different temperatures. Also called: **thermoelectric effect.** [C19: after Thomas *Seebeck* (1770–1831), G physicist]

seed (siːd) *n* **1** *Bot.* a mature fertilized plant ovule, consisting of an embryo and its food store surrounded by a protective seed coat (testa). Related adj: **seminal. 2** the small hard seedlike fruit of plants such as wheat. **3** any propagative part of a plant, such as a tuber, spore, or bulb. **4** the source, beginning, or germ of anything: *the seeds of revolt.* **5** *Chiefly Bible.* descendants: *the seed of Abraham.* **6** an archaic term for **sperm** or **semen. 7** *Sport.* a seeded player. **8** *Chem.* a small crystal added to a supersaturated solution to induce crystallization. **9 go** *or* **run to seed. 9a** (of plants) to produce and shed seeds. **9b** to lose vigour, usefulness, etc. ◆ *vb* **10** to plant (seeds, grain, etc.) in (soil): *we seeded this field with oats.* **11** (*intr*) (of plants) to form or shed seeds. **12** (*tr*) to remove the seeds from (fruit, etc.). **13** (*tr*) *Chem.* to add a small crystal to (a supersaturated solution) in order to cause crystallization. **14** (*tr*) to scatter certain substances, such as silver iodide, in (clouds) in order to cause rain. **15** (*tr*) to arrange (the draw of a tournament) so that outstanding teams or players will not meet in the early rounds. [OE *sǣd*]

▸ˈ**seeder** *n* ▸ˈ**seedless** *adj*

seedbed (ˈsiːdˌbɛd) *n* **1** a plot of land in which seedlings are grown before being transplanted. **2** the place where something develops.

seedcake (ˈsiːdˌkeɪk) *n* a sweet cake flavoured with caraway seeds and lemon rind or essence.

seed capital *n Finance.* a small amount of capital required to finance the research necessary to produce a business plan for a new company.

seed coral *n* small pieces of coral used in jewellery, etc.

seed corn *n* **1** the good quality ears or kernels of corn that are used as seed. **2** assets that are expected to provide future benefits.

seed leaf *n* the nontechnical name for **cotyledon.**

seedling (ˈsiːdlɪŋ) *n* a plant produced from a seed, esp. a very young plant.

seed money *n* money used for the establishment of an enterprise.

seed oyster *n* a young oyster, esp. a cultivated oyster, ready for transplantation.

seed pearl *n* a tiny pearl weighing less than a quarter of a grain.

seed pod *n* a carpel or pistil enclosing the seeds of a plant, esp. a flowering plant.

seed potato *n* a potato tuber used for planting.

seed vessel *n Bot.* a dry fruit, such as a capsule.

seedy (ˈsiːdɪ) *adj* **seedier, seediest. 1** shabby in appearance: *seedy clothes.* **2** (of a plant) at the stage of producing seeds. **3** *Inf.* not physically fit.

▸ˈ**seedily** *adv* ▸ˈ**seediness** *n*

seeing (ˈsiːɪŋ) *n* **1** the sense or faculty of sight. **2** *Astron.* the condition of the atmosphere with respect to observation of stars, planets, etc. ◆ *conj* **3** (*subordinating;* often foll. by *that*) in light of the fact (that).

> **USAGE NOTE** The use of *seeing as how* as in *seeing as (how) the bus is always late, I don't need to hurry* is generally thought to be incorrect or nonstandard.

see into *vb* (*intr, prep*) to discover the true nature of: *I can't see into your thoughts.*

seek (siːk) *vb* **seeks, seeking, sought.** (*mainly tr*) **1** (when *intr,* often foll. by *for* or *after*) to try to find by searching: *to seek a solution.* **2** (*also intr*) to try to obtain or acquire: *to seek happiness.* **3** to attempt (to do something): *I'm only seeking to help.* **4** (*also intr*) to inquire about or request (something). **5** to resort to: *to seek the garden for peace.* [OE *sēcan*]

▸ˈ**seeker** *n*

seek out *vb* (*tr, adv*) to search hard for and find a specific person or thing: *she sought out her friend from amongst the crowd.*

seem (siːm) *vb* (*may take an infinitive*) **1** (*copula*) to appear to the mind or eye; look: *the car seems to be running well.* **2** to appear to be: *there seems no need for all this nonsense.* **3** used to diminish the force of a following infinitive to be polite, more noncommittal, etc.: *I can't seem to get through to you.* [C12: ?from ON *soma* to beseem, from *sœmr* befitting]

> **USAGE NOTE** See at **like.**

seeming (ˈsiːmɪŋ) *adj* **1** (*prenominal*) apparent but not actual or genuine. ◆ *n* **2** outward or false appearance.

▸ˈ**seemingly** *adv*

seemly (ˈsiːmlɪ) *adj* **seemlier, seemliest. 1** proper or fitting. **2** *Obs.* pleasing in appearance. ◆ *adv* **3** *Arch.* decorously. [C13: from ON *sœmiligr,* from *sœmr* befitting]

seen (siːn) *vb* the past participle of **see**[1].

see off *vb* (*tr, adv*) **1** to be present at the departure of (a person making a journey). **2** *Inf.* to cause to leave or depart, esp. by force.

seep (siːp) *vb* **1** (*intr*) to pass gradually or leak as if through small openings. ◆ *n* **2** a small spring or place where water, oil, etc., has oozed through the ground. [OE *sīpian*]

▸ˈ**seepage** *n*

seer[1] (sɪə) *n* **1** a person who can supposedly see into the future. **2** a person who professes supernatural powers. **3** a person who sees.

seer[2] (sɪə) *n* a varying unit of weight used in India, usually about two pounds or one kilogram. [from Hindi]

seersucker (ˈsɪəˌsʌkə) *n* a light cotton, linen, or other fabric with a

THESAURUS

see[1] *vb* **1 = perceive,** behold, catch a glimpse of, catch sight of, check, check out, clock (*Brit. sl.*), descry, discern, distinguish, espy, eye, eyeball (*sl.*), get a load of (*sl.*), glimpse, heed, identify, lay *or* clap eyes on (*inf.*), look, make out, mark, note, notice, observe, recognize, regard, sight, spot, take a dekko at (*Brit. sl.*), view, witness **2 = understand,** appreciate, catch on (*inf.*), comprehend, fathom, feel, follow, get, get the drift of, get the hang of (*inf.*), grasp, know, make out, realize, take in **4 = foresee,** anticipate, divine, envisage, foretell, imagine, picture, visualize **5 = find out,** ascertain, determine, discover, investigate, learn, make inquiries, refer to **6 = make sure,** ensure, guarantee, make certain, mind, see to it, take care **7 = consider,** decide, deliberate, give some thought to, judge, make up one's mind, mull over, reflect, think over **11 = visit,** confer with, consult, encounter, interview, meet, receive, run into, speak to **13 = go out with,** consort *or* associate with, court, date (*inf., chiefly US*), go steady with (*inf.*), keep company with, walk out with (*obs.*) **14 = accompany,** attend, escort, lead, show, usher, walk

see[2] *n* **= diocese,** bishopric

see about *vb* **1 = take care of,** attend to, consider, deal with, give some thought to, look after, see to **2 = investigate,** look into, make inquiries, research

seed *n* **1 = grain,** egg, egg cell, embryo, germ, kernel, ovule, ovum, pip, spore **4 = origin,** beginning, germ, inkling, nucleus, source, start, suspicion **5** *Chiefly Bible* **= offspring,** children, descendants, heirs, issue, progeny, race, scions, spawn, successors **9 go** *or* run to seed **= decline,** decay, degenerate, deteriorate, go downhill (*inf.*), go to pieces, go to pot, go to rack and ruin, go to waste, let oneself go, retrogress

seedy *adj* **1 = shabby,** crummy (*sl.*), decaying, dilapidated, down at heel, faded, grotty (*sl.*), grubby, mangy, manky (*Scot. dialect*), old, rundown, scruffy, sleazy, slovenly, squalid, tatty, unkempt, worn **3** *Informal* **= unwell,** ailing, ill, off colour, out of sorts, peely-wally (*Scot.*), poorly (*inf.*), sickly, under the weather (*inf.*)

Antonyms *adj* ≠ **shabby:** classy, elegant, fashionable, high-toned, posh (*inf., chiefly Brit.*), ritzy (*sl.*), smart, swanky (*inf.*), swish (*inf., chiefly Brit.*), top-drawer, up-market

seeing *conj* **3 = since,** as, inasmuch as, in view of the fact that

seek *vb* **1, 2 = look for,** be after, follow, go gunning for, go in pursuit of, go in quest of, go in search of, hunt, inquire, pursue, search for **3 = try,** aim, aspire to, attempt, endeavour, essay, have a go (*inf.*), strive **4 = request,** ask, beg, entreat, inquire, invite, petition, solicit

seem *vb* **1 = appear,** assume, give the impression, have the *or* every appearance of, look, look as if, look like, look to be, pretend, sound like, strike one as being

seeming *adj* **1 = apparent,** appearing, illusory, ostensible, outward, quasi-, specious, surface

seemingly *adv* **1 = apparently,** as far as anyone could tell, on the face of it, on the surface, ostensibly, outwardly, to all appearances, to all intents and purposes

seemly *adj* **1 = fitting,** appropriate, becoming, befitting, *comme il faut,* decent, decorous, fit, in good taste, meet (*arch.*), nice, proper, suitable, suited, the done thing

Antonyms *adj* improper, inappropriate, indecorous, in poor taste, out of keeping, out of place, unbecoming, unbefitting, unseemly, unsuitable

seep *vb* **1 = ooze,** bleed, exude, leach, leak, percolate, permeate, soak, trickle, weep, well

seepage *n* **1 = leakage,** exudation, leak, oozing, percolation

seer[1] *n* **1 = prophet,** augur, predictor, sibyl, soothsayer crinkled surface and often striped. [C18: from Hindi *śīrśakar,* from Persian *shīr o shakkar,* lit.: milk and sugar]

seesaw 🅣 (ˈsiːˌsɔː) *n* **1** a plank balanced in the middle so that two people seated on the ends can ride up and down by pushing on the ground with their feet. **2** the pastime of riding up and down on a seesaw. **3** an up-and-down or back-and-forth movement. ◆ *vb* **4** (*intr*) to move up and down or back and forth in such a manner. [C17: reduplication of SAW[1], alluding to the movement from side to side, as in sawing]

seethe 🅣 (siːð) *vb* **seethes, seething, seethed. 1** (*intr*) to boil or to foam as if boiling. **2** (*intr*) to be in a state of extreme agitation, esp. through anger. **3** (*tr*) to soak in liquid. **4** (*tr*) *Arch.* to cook by boiling. [OE *sēothan*]
▸ˈ**seething** *adj* ▸ˈ**seethingly** *adv*

see through 🅣 *vb* **1** (*tr*) to help out in time of need or trouble. **2** (*tr, adv*) to remain with until the end or completion: *let's see the job through.* **3** (*intr, prep*) to perceive the true nature of: *I can see through your evasion.* ◆ *adj* **see-through. 4** partly or wholly transparent or translucent, esp. (of clothes) in a titillating way.

segment 🅣 *n* (ˈsɛɡmənt). **1** *Maths.* **1a** a part of a line or curve between two points. **1b** a part of a plane or solid figure cut off by an intersecting line, plane, or planes. **2** one of several parts or sections into which an object is divided. **3** *Zool.* any of the parts into which the body or appendages of an annelid or arthropod are divided. **4** *Linguistics.* a speech sound considered in isolation. ◆ *vb* (sɛɡˈmɛnt). **5** to cut or divide (a whole object) into segments. [C16: from L *segmentum,* from *secāre* to cut]
▸**segˈmental** *adj* ▸ˈ**segmentary** *adj*

segmentation (ˌsɛɡmɛnˈteɪʃən) *n* **1** the act or an instance of dividing into segments. **2** *Embryol.* another name for **cleavage** (sense 4).

segregate 🅣 (ˈsɛɡrɪˌɡeɪt) *vb* **segregates, segregating, segregated. 1** to set or be set apart from others or from the main group. **2** (*tr*) to impose segregation on (a racial or minority group). **3** *Genetics.* to undergo or cause to undergo segregation. [C16: from L *sēgregāre,* from *sē-* apart + *grex* a flock]
▸ˈ**segreˌgative** *adj* ▸ˈ**segreˌgator** *n*

segregation 🅣 (ˌsɛɡrɪˈɡeɪʃən) *n* **1** the act of segregating or state of being segregated. **2** *Sociol.* the practice or policy of creating separate facilities within the same society for the use of a particular group. **3** *Genetics.* the separation at meiosis of the two members of any pair of alleles into separate gametes.
▸ˌ**segreˈgational** *adj* ▸ˌ**segreˈgationist** *n*

segue (ˈseɪɡwɪ) *vb* **segues, segueing, segued.** (*intr*) **1** (often foll. by *into*) to proceed from one piece of music to another without a break. ◆ *n* **2** the practice or an instance of segueing. [from It: follows, from *seguire* to follow, from L *sequī*]

seguidilla (ˌsɛɡɪˈdiːljə) *n* **1** a Spanish dance in a fast triple rhythm. **2** a piece of music composed for or in the rhythm of this dance. [Sp.: a little dance, from *seguida* a dance, from *seguir* to follow, from L *sequī*]

seiche (seɪʃ) *n* a tide-like movement of a body of water caused by barometric pressure, earth tremors, etc. [C19: from Swiss F, from ?]

Seidlitz powder *or* **powders** (ˈsɛdlɪts) *n* a laxative consisting of two powders, tartaric acid and a mixture of sodium bicarbonate and Rochelle salt. [C19: after *Seidlitz,* a village in Bohemia with mineral springs having similar laxative effects]

seif dune (seɪf) *n* (in deserts, esp. the Sahara) a long ridge of blown sand, often several miles long. [*seif,* from Ar.: sword, from the shape of the dune]

seigneur (seˈnjɜː; *French* sɛɲœr) *n* a feudal lord, esp. in France. [C16: from OF, from Vulgar L *senior,* from L: an elderly man; see SENIOR]
▸**seiˈgneurial** *adj*

seigneury (ˈseɪnjərɪ) *n, pl* **seigneuries.** the estate of a seigneur.

seignior (ˈseɪnjə) *n* **1** a less common name for a **seigneur. 2** (in England) the lord of a seigniory. [C14: from Anglo-F *segnour*]
▸**seigniorial** (seɪˈnjɔːrɪəl) *adj*

seigniory (ˈseɪnjərɪ) *or* **signory** (ˈsiːnjərɪ) *n, pl* **seigniories** *or* **seignories. 1** less common names for a **seigneury. 2** (in England) the fee or manor of a seignior; a feudal domain. **3** the authority of a seignior.

seine (seɪn) *n* **1** a large fishing net that hangs vertically in the water by means of floats at the top and weights at the bottom. ◆ *vb* **seines, seining, seined. 2** to catch (fish) using this net. [OE *segne,* from L *sagēna,* from Gk *sagēnē*]

seise *or US* **seize** (siːz) *vb* **seises, seising, seised** *or US* **seizes, seizing, seized.** to put into legal possession of (property, etc.).
▸ˈ**seiser** *n*

seisin *or US* **seizin** (ˈsiːzɪn) *n Property law.* feudal possession of an estate in land. [C13: from OF *seisine,* from *seisir* to SEIZE]

seismic (ˈsaɪzmɪk) *adj* relating to or caused by earthquakes or artificially produced earth tremors.

seismo- *or before a vowel* **seism-** *combining form.* earthquake: *seismology.* [from Gk *seismos*]

seismograph (ˈsaɪzməˌɡrɑːf) *n* an instrument that registers and records earthquakes. A **seismogram** is the record from such an instrument.
▸**seismographic** (ˌsaɪzməˈɡræfɪk) *adj* ▸**seismographer** (saɪzˈmɒɡrəfə) *n* ▸**seisˈmography** *n*

seismology (saɪzˈmɒlədʒɪ) *n* the branch of geology concerned with the study of earthquakes.
▸**seismologic** (ˌsaɪzməˈlɒdʒɪk) *or* ˌ**seismoˈlogical** *adj* ▸ˌ**seismoˈlogically** *adv* ▸**seisˈmologist** *n*

seize[1] 🅣 (siːz) *vb* **seizes, seizing, seized.** (*mainly tr*) **1** (also *intr,* foll. by *on*) to take hold of quickly; grab. **2** (sometimes foll. by *on* or *upon*) to grasp mentally, esp. rapidly: *she immediately seized his idea.* **3** to take mental possession of: *alarm seized the crowd.* **4** to take possession of rapidly and forcibly: *the thief seized the woman's purse.* **5** to take legal possession of. **6** to take by force or capture: *the army seized the undefended town.* **7** to take immediate advantage of: *to seize an opportunity.* **8** *Naut.* to bind (two ropes together). **9** (*intr;* often foll. by *up*) (of mechanical parts) to become jammed, esp. because of excessive heat. [C13 *saisen,* from OF *saisir,* from Med. L *sacīre* to position, of Gmc origin]
▸ˈ**seizable** *adj*

seize[2] (siːz) *vb* **seizes, seizing, seized.** the US spelling of **seise.**

seizure 🅣 (ˈsiːʒə) *n* **1** the act or an instance of seizing or the state of being seized. **2** *Pathol.* a sudden manifestation or recurrence of a disease, such as an epileptic convulsion.

selachian (sɪˈleɪkɪən) *adj* of or belonging to a large subclass of cartilaginous fishes including the sharks, rays, dogfish, and skates. [C19: from NL *Selachiī,* from Gk *selakhē* a shark]

seldom 🅣 (ˈsɛldəm) *adv* rarely. [OE *seldon*]

select 🅣 (sɪˈlɛkt) *vb* **1** to choose (someone or something) in preference to another or others. ◆ *adj also* **selected. 2** chosen in preference to others. **3** of particular quality. **4** limited as to membership or entry: *a select gathering.* ◆ *n Austral. history.* **5** a piece of land acquired by a free-selector. **6** the process of free-selection. [C16: from L *sēligere* to sort, from *sē-* apart + *legere* to choose]
▸**seˈlectness** *n* ▸**seˈlector** *n*

select committee *n* (in Britain) a small committee of members of parliament, set up to investigate and report on a specified matter.

selection 🅣 (sɪˈlɛkʃən) *n* **1** the act or an instance of selecting or the state of being selected. **2** a thing or number of things that have been selected. **3** a range from which something may be selected: *a good selection of clothes.* **4** *Biol.* the process by which certain organisms or characters are reproduced and perpetuated in the species in preference to others.

selective 🅣 (sɪˈlɛktɪv) *adj* **1** of or characterized by selection. **2** tending to choose carefully or characterized by careful choice. **3** *Electronics.* occurring at or operating at a particular frequency or band of frequencies.
▸**seˈlectively** *adv*

selectivity (sɪˌlɛkˈtɪvɪtɪ) *n* **1** the state or quality of being selective. **2** the degree to which a radio receiver, etc., can respond to the frequency of a desired signal.

selenite (ˈsɛlɪˌnaɪt) *n* a colourless glassy variety of gypsum.

THESAURUS

seesaw *vb* **4** = **alternate,** fluctuate, go from one extreme to the other, oscillate, pitch, swing, teeter

seethe *vb* **1** = **boil,** bubble, churn, ferment, fizz, foam, froth **2** = **be furious,** be in a state (*inf.*), be incandescent, be incensed, be livid, foam at the mouth, fume, get hot under the collar (*inf.*), go ballistic (*sl., chiefly US*), rage, see red (*inf.*), simmer, storm

see through *vb* **1** = **help out,** stick by, support **2** = **persevere (with),** keep at, persist, see out, stay to the bitter end, stick out (*inf.*) **3** = **be undeceived by,** be wise to (*inf.*), fathom, get to the bottom of, have (someone's) number (*inf.*), not fall for, penetrate, read (someone) like a book ◆ *adj* **see-through 4** = **transparent,** diaphanous, filmy, fine, flimsy, gauzy, gossamer, sheer, thin, translucent

segment *n* **2** = **section,** bit, compartment, division, part, piece, portion, slice, wedge

segregate *vb* **1, 2** = **set apart,** discriminate against, dissociate, isolate, separate, single out
Antonyms *vb* amalgamate, desegregate, join together, mix, unify, unite

segregation *n* **1, 2** = **separation,** apartheid, discrimination, isolation

seize[1] *vb* **1** = **grab,** catch up, clutch, fasten, grasp, grip, lay hands on, snatch, take **5** = **confiscate,** appropriate, commandeer, impound, take possession of **6** = **capture,** abduct, annex, apprehend, arrest, catch, collar (*inf.*), get, grasp, nab (*inf.*), nail (*inf.*), take by storm, take captive
Antonyms *vb* ≠ **grab:** let go, loose ≠ **confiscate:** hand back, relinquish ≠ **capture:** free, release, set free, turn loose

seizure *n* **1** = **capture,** abduction, annexation, apprehension, arrest, commandeering, confiscation, grabbing, taking **2** = **attack,** convulsion, fit, paroxysm, spasm

seldom *adv* = **rarely,** hardly ever, infrequently, not often, occasionally, once in a blue moon (*inf.*), scarcely ever
Antonyms *adv* again and again, frequently, many a time, much, often, over and over again, time after time, time and again

select *vb* **1** = **choose,** cherry-pick, opt for, pick, prefer, single out, sort out ◆ *adj* **2, 3** = **choice,** excellent, first-class, first-rate, hand-picked, picked, posh (*inf., chiefly Brit.*), preferable, prime, rare, recherché, selected, special, superior, top-notch (*inf.*) **4** = **exclusive,** cliquish, elite, limited, privileged
Antonyms *vb* ≠ **choose:** eliminate, reject, turn down ◆ *adj* ≠ **choice:** cheap, indifferent, inferior, ordinary, random, run-of-the-mill, second-rate, shoddy, substandard, unremarkable ≠ **exclusive:** indiscriminate

selection *n* **1** = **choice,** choosing, option, pick, preference **2, 3** = **range,** anthology, assortment, choice, collection, line-up, medley, miscellany, mixed bag (*inf.*), pick 'n' mix, potpourri, variety

selective *adj* **2** = **particular,** careful, discerning, discriminating, discriminatory, eclectic
Antonyms *adj* all-embracing, careless, desultory, indiscriminate, unselective

selenium (sɪˈliːnɪəm) *n* a nonmetallic element that exists in several allotropic forms. The common form is a grey crystalline solid that is photoconductive, photovoltaic, and semiconducting: used in photocells, solar cells, and in xerography. Symbol: Se; atomic no.: 34; atomic wt.: 78.96. [C19: from NL, from Gk *selēnē* moon; by analogy to TELLURIUM (from L *tellus* earth)]

seleno- *or before a vowel* **selen-** *combining form.* denoting the moon: *selenography.* [from Gk *selēnē* moon]

selenography (ˌsiːlɪˈnɒgrəfɪ) *n* the branch of astronomy concerned with the description and mapping of the surface features of the moon.
▸ˌ**seleˈnographer** *n* ▸**selenographic** (sɪˌliːnəʊˈgræfɪk) *adj*

self (sɛlf) *n, pl* **selves. 1** the distinct individuality or identity of a person or thing. **2** a person's typical bodily make-up or personal characteristics: *she's looking her old self again.* **3** one's own welfare or interests: *he only thinks of self.* **4** an individual's consciousness of his own identity or being. **5** a bird, animal, etc., that is a single colour throughout. ◆ *pron* **6** *Not standard.* myself, yourself, etc.: *seats for self and wife.* ◆ *adj* **7** of the same colour or material. **8** *Obs.* the same. [OE *seolf*]

self- *combining form.* **1** of oneself or itself: *self-defence.* **2** by, to, in, due to, for, or from the self: *self-employed; self-respect.* **3** automatic or automatically: *self-propelled.*

self-abnegation *n* the denial of one's own interests in favour of the interests of others.

self-absorption *n* **1** preoccupation with oneself to the exclusion of others. **2** *Physics.* the process in which some of the radiation emitted by a material is absorbed by the material itself.

self-abuse *n* **1** disparagement or misuse of one's own abilities, etc. **2** a censorious term for **masturbation.**

self-acting *adj* not requiring an external influence or control to function; automatic.

self-addressed *adj* **1** addressed for return to the sender. **2** directed to oneself: *a self-addressed remark.*

self-aggrandizement *n* the act of increasing one's own power, importance, etc.
▸ˌ**self-agˈgranˌdizing** *adj*

self-appointed *adj* having assumed authority without the agreement of others: *a self-appointed critic.*

self-assertion *n* the act or an instance of putting forward one's own opinions, etc., esp. in an aggressive or conceited manner.
▸ˌ**self-asˈserting** *adj* ▸ˌ**self-asˈsertive** *adj*

self-assurance **T** *n* confidence in the validity, value, etc., of one's own ideas, opinions, etc.
▸ˌ**self-asˈsured** *adj* ▸ˌ**self-asˈsuredly** *adv*

self-centred **T** *adj* totally preoccupied with one's own concerns.
▸ˌ**self-ˈcentredness** *n*

self-certification *n* (in Britain) a formal assertion by a worker to his employer that absence from work for up to seven days was due to sickness.

self-coloured *adj* **1** having only a single and uniform colour: *a self-coloured dress.* **2** (of cloth, etc.) having the natural or original colour.

self-command *n* another term for **self-control.**

self-confessed *adj* according to one's own testimony or admission: *a self-confessed liar.*

self-confidence **T** *n* confidence in one's own powers, judgment, etc.
▸ˌ**self-ˈconfident** *adj* ▸ˌ**self-ˈconfidently** *adv*

self-conscious **T** *adj* **1** unduly aware of oneself as the object of the attention of others. **2** conscious of one's existence.
▸ˌ**self-ˈconsciously** *adv* ▸ˌ**self-ˈconsciousness** *n*

self-contained *adj* **1** containing within itself all parts necessary for completeness. **2** (of a flat) having its own kitchen, bathroom, and lavatory not shared by others. **3** able or tending to keep one's feelings, thoughts, etc., to oneself.
▸ˌ**self-conˈtainedness** *n*

self-contradictory *adj Logic.* (of a proposition) both asserting and denying a given proposition.

self-control **T** *n* the ability to exercise restraint or control over one's feelings, emotions, reactions, etc.
▸ˌ**self-conˈtrolled** *adj*

self-deception *or* **self-deceit** *n* the act or an instance of deceiving oneself.
▸ˌ**self-deˈceptive** *adj*

self-defence *n* **1** the act of defending oneself, one's actions, ideas, etc. **2** boxing as a means of defending the person (esp. in **noble art of self-defence**). **3** *Law.* the right to defend one's person, family, or property against attack or threat of attack.
▸ˌ**self-deˈfensive** *adj*

self-denial **T** *n* the denial or sacrifice of one's own desires.
▸ˌ**self-deˈnying** *adj*

self-deprecating *or* **self-depreciating** *adj* having a tendency to disparage oneself.

self-determination *n* **1** the ability to make a decision for oneself without influence from outside. **2** the right of a nation or people to determine its own form of government.
▸ˌ**self-deˈtermined** *adj* ▸ˌ**self-deˈtermining** *adj*

self-discipline *n* the act of disciplining or power to discipline one's own feelings, desires, etc.
▸ˌ**self-ˈdisciplined** *adj*

self-drive *adj* denoting or relating to a hired car that is driven by the hirer.

self-educated *adj* **1** educated through one's own efforts without formal instruction. **2** educated at one's own expense.

self-effacement *n* the act of making oneself, one's actions, etc., inconspicuous, esp. because of timidity.
▸ˌ**self-efˈfacing** *adj*

self-employed *adj* earning one's living in one's own business or through freelance work, rather than as the employee of another.
▸ˌ**self-emˈployment** *n*

self-esteem **T** *n* **1** respect for or a favourable opinion of oneself. **2** an unduly high opinion of oneself.

self-evident **T** *adj* containing its own evidence or proof without need of further demonstration.
▸ˌ**self-ˈevidence** *n* ▸ˌ**self-ˈevidently** *adv*

self-existent *adj Philosophy.* existing independently of any other being or cause.

self-explanatory *adj* understandable without explanation; self-evident.

self-expression *n* the expression of one's own personality, feelings, etc., as in painting or poetry.
▸ˌ**self-exˈpressive** *adj*

self-government **T** *n* **1** the government of a country, nation, etc., by its own people. **2** the state of being self-controlled.
▸ˌ**self-ˈgoverned** *adj* ▸ˌ**self-ˈgoverning** *adj*

selfheal (ˈsɛlfˌhiːl) *n* **1** a low-growing European herbaceous plant with tightly clustered violet-blue flowers and reputedly having healing powers. **2** any of several other plants thought to have healing powers.

self-help *n* **1** the act or state of providing the means to help oneself without relying on the assistance of others. **2a** the practice of solving one's problems by joining or forming a group designed to help those suffering from a particular problem. **2b** *(as modifier): a self-help group.*

self-image *n* one's own idea of oneself or sense of one's worth.

self-important **T** *adj* having or showing an unduly high opinion of one's own abilities, importance, etc.
▸ˌ**self-imˈportantly** *adv* ▸ˌ**self-imˈportance** *n*

self-improvement *n* the improvement of one's status, position, education, etc., by one's own efforts.

self-induced *adj* **1** induced or brought on by oneself or itself. **2** *Electronics.* produced by self-induction.

self-induction *n* the production of an electromotive force in a circuit when the magnetic flux linked with the circuit changes as a result of a change in current in the same circuit.

self-indulgent *adj* tending to indulge one's own desires, etc.
▸ˌ**self-inˈdulgence** *n*

self-interest *n* **1** one's personal interest or advantage. **2** the act or an instance of pursuing one's own interest.
▸ˌ**self-ˈinterested** *adj*

selfish **T** (ˈsɛlfɪʃ) *adj* **1** chiefly concerned with one's own interest, advantage, etc., esp. to the exclusion of the interests of others. **2** relating to or characterized by self-interest.
▸ˈ**selfishly** *adv* ▸ˈ**selfishness** *n*

self-justification *n* the act or an instance of justifying or providing excuses for one's own behaviour, etc.

selfless **T** (ˈsɛlflɪs) *adj* having little concern for one's own interests.
▸ˈ**selflessly** *adv* ▸ˈ**selflessness** *n*

THESAURUS

self-assurance *n* = **confidence**, assertiveness, nerve, poise, positiveness, self-confidence, self-possession

self-centred *adj* = **selfish**, egotistic, inward looking, narcissistic, self-absorbed, self-seeking, wrapped up in oneself

self-confidence *n* = **self-assurance**, aplomb, confidence, high morale, nerve, poise, self-reliance, self-respect

self-confident *adj* = **self-assured**, assured, confident, fearless, poised, secure, self-reliant, sure of oneself

self-conscious *adj* **1** = **embarrassed**, affected, awkward, bashful, diffident, ill at ease, insecure, like a fish out of water, nervous, out of countenance, shamefaced, sheepish, uncomfortable

self-control *n* = **willpower**, calmness, cool, coolness, restraint, self-discipline, self-mastery, self-restraint, strength of mind *or* will

self-denial *n* = **abstemiousness**, asceticism, renunciation, self-abnegation, selflessness, self-sacrifice, unselfishness

self-esteem *n* **1, 2** = **self-respect**, *amour-propre*, confidence, faith in oneself, pride, self-assurance, self-regard, vanity

self-evident *adj* = **obvious**, axiomatic, clear, cut-and-dried (*inf.*), incontrovertible, inescapable, manifestly *or* patently true, undeniable, written all over (something)

self-government *n* **1** = **autonomy**, democracy, devolution, home rule, independence, self-determination, self-rule, sovereignty

self-important *adj* = **conceited**, arrogant, bigheaded, bumptious, cocky, full of oneself, overbearing, pompous, presumptuous, pushy (*inf.*), strutting, swaggering, swollen-headed

self-indulgence *n* = **intemperance**, dissipation, excess, extravagance, incontinence, self-gratification, sensualism

selfish *adj* **1** = **self-centred**, egoistic, egoistical, egotistic, egotistical, greedy, looking out for number one (*inf.*), mean, mercenary, narrow, self-interested, self-seeking, ungenerous
Antonyms *adj* altruistic, benevolent, considerate, generous, magnanimous, philanthropic, self-denying, selfless, self-sacrificing, ungrudging, unselfish

selfless *adj* = **unselfish**, altruistic, generous, magnanimous, self-denying, self-sacrificing, ungrudging

self-loading *adj* (of a firearm) utilizing some of the force of the explosion to eject the empty shell and replace it with a new one. ▸ˌ**self-ˈloader** *n*
self-love *n* the instinct to seek one's own well-being or to further one's own interest.
self-made *adj* **1** having achieved wealth, status, etc., by one's own efforts. **2** made by oneself.
self-opinionated *adj* **1** having an unduly high regard for oneself or one's own opinions. **2** clinging stubbornly to one's own opinions.
self-pity *n* the act or state of pitying oneself, esp. in an exaggerated or self-indulgent manner. ▸ˌ**self-ˈpitying** *adj* ▸ˌ**self-ˈpityingly** *adv*
self-pollination *n* the transfer of pollen from the anthers to the stigma of the same flower. ▸ˌ**self-ˈpolliˌnated** *adj*
self-possessed ❶ *adj* having control of one's emotions, etc. ▸ˌ**self-posˈsession** *n*
self-preservation *n* the preservation of oneself from danger or injury.
self-pronouncing *adj* (in a phonetic transcription) of or denoting a word that, except for marks of stress, keeps the letters of its ordinary orthography to represent its pronunciation.
self-propelled *adj* (of a vehicle) provided with its own source of tractive power rather than requiring an external means of propulsion. ▸ˌ**self-proˈpelling** *adj*
self-raising *adj* (of flour) having a raising agent, such as baking powder, already added.
self-realization *n* the realization or fulfilment of one's own potential or abilities.
self-regard *n* **1** concern for one's own interest. **2** proper esteem for oneself.
self-regulating organization *n* one of several British organizations set up in 1986 under the auspices of the Securities and Investment Board to regulate the activities of London investment markets. Abbrev.: **SRO**.
self-reliance ❶ *n* reliance on one's own abilities, decisions, etc. ▸ˌ**self-reˈliant** *adj*
self-reproach *n* the act of finding fault with or blaming oneself. ▸ˌ**self-reˈproachful** *adj*
self-respect ❶ *n* a proper sense of one's own dignity and integrity. ▸ˌ**self-reˈspecting** *adj*
self-restraint ❶ *n* restraint imposed by oneself on one's own feelings, desires, etc.
self-righteous ❶ *adj* having an exaggerated awareness of one's own virtuousness. ▸ˌ**self-ˈrighteously** *adv* ▸ˌ**self-ˈrighteousness** *n*
self-rule *n* another term for **self-government** (sense 1).
self-sacrifice ❶ *n* the sacrifice of one's own desires, etc., for the sake of duty or for the well-being of others. ▸ˌ**self-ˈsacriˌficing** *adj*
selfsame (ˈsɛlfˌseɪm) *adj* (*prenominal*) the very same.
self-satisfied ❶ *adj* having or showing a complacent satisfaction with oneself, one's own actions, behaviour, etc. ▸ˌ**self-ˌsatisˈfaction** *n*
self-sealing *adj* (esp. of an envelope) designed to become sealed with the application of pressure only.
self-seeking ❶ *n* **1** the act or an instance of seeking one's own profit or interest. ◆ *adj* **2** having or showing an exclusive preoccupation with one's own profit or interest: *a self-seeking attitude.* ▸ˌ**self-ˈseeker** *n*
self-service *adj* **1** of or denoting a shop, restaurant, petrol station, etc., where the customer serves himself. ◆ *n* **2** the practice of serving oneself, as in a shop, etc.
self-serving *adj* habitually seeking one's own advantage, esp. at the expense of others.
self-sown *adj* (of plants) growing from seed dispersed by any means other than by the agency of man or animals. Also: **self-seeded.**
self-starter *n* **1** an electric motor used to start an internal-combustion engine. **2** the switch that operates this motor. **3** a person who is strongly motivated and shows initiative, esp. at work.
self-styled ❶ *adj* (*prenominal*) claiming to be of a specified nature, quality, profession, etc.: *a self-styled expert.*
self-sufficient *or* **self-sufficing** *adj* **1** able to provide for or support oneself without the help of others. **2** *Rare.* having undue confidence in oneself. ▸ˌ**self-sufˈficiency** *n* ▸ˌ**self-sufˈficiently** *adv*
self-supporting *adj* **1** able to support or maintain oneself without the help of others. **2** able to stand up or hold firm without support, props, attachments, etc.
self-tender *n* an offer by a company to buy back some or all of its shares from its shareholders, esp. as a protection against an unwelcome takeover bid.
self-will ❶ *n* stubborn adherence to one's own will, desires, etc., esp. at the expense of others. ▸ˌ**self-ˈwilled** *adj*
self-winding *adj* (of a wrist watch) having a mechanism in which a rotating or oscillating weight rewinds the mainspring.
Seljuk (sɛlˈdʒuːk) *n* **1** a member of any of the pre-Ottoman Turkish dynasties ruling over large parts of Asia in the 11th, 12th, and 13th centuries A.D. ◆ *adj* **2** of or relating to these dynasties. [C19: from Turkish]
sell ❶ (sɛl) *vb* **sells, selling, sold. 1** to dispose of or transfer or be disposed of or transferred to a purchaser in exchange for money or other consideration. **2** to deal in (objects, property, etc.): *he sells used cars.* **3** (*tr*) to give up or surrender for a price or reward: *to sell one's honour.* **4** to promote or facilitate the sale of (objects, property, etc.): *publicity sells many products.* **5** to gain acceptance of: *to sell an idea.* **6** (*intr*) to be in demand on the market: *these dresses sell well.* **7** (*tr*) *Inf.* to deceive. **8 sell down the river.** *Inf.* to betray. **9 sell oneself. 9a** to convince someone else of one's potential or worth. **9b** to give up one's moral standards, etc. **10 sell short. 10a** *Inf.* to belittle. **10b** *Finance.* to sell securities or goods without owning them in anticipation of buying them before delivery at a lower price. ◆ *n* **11** the act or an instance of selling: *a soft sell.* **12** *Inf.* a hoax or deception. ◆ See also **sell off, sell out,** etc. [OE *sellan* to lend, deliver] ▸ˈ**sellable** *adj* ▸ˈ**seller** *n*
sell-by date *n* **1** a date printed on the packaging of perishable goods, indicating the date after which the goods should not be offered for sale. **2 past one's sell-by date.** *Inf.* beyond one's prime.
selling race *or* **plate** *n* a horse race in which the winner must be offered for sale at auction.
sell off *vb* (*tr, adv*) to sell (remaining or unprofitable items), esp. at low prices.
Sellotape (ˈsɛləˌteɪp) *n* **1** *Trademark.* a type of transparent adhesive tape. ◆ *vb* **Sellotapes, Sellotaping, Sellotaped.** (*tr*) **2** to seal or stick using adhesive tape.
sell out ❶ *vb* (*adv*) **1** Also (*chiefly Brit.*): **sell up.** to dispose of (something) completely by selling. **2** (*tr*) *Inf.* to betray. **3** (*intr*) *Inf.* to abandon one's principles, standards, etc. ◆ *n* **sellout. 4** *Inf.* a performance for which all tickets are sold. **5** a commercial success. **6** *Inf.* a betrayal.
sell-through *adj* **1** (of prerecorded video cassettes) sold without first being available for hire only. ◆ *n* **2** the sale of prerecorded video cassettes in this way.
sell up *vb* (*adv*) *Chiefly Brit.* **1** (*tr*) to sell all (the possessions) of (a bankrupt debtor) in order to discharge his debts. **2** (*intr*) to sell a business.
selsyn (ˈsɛlsɪn) *n* another name for **synchro.** [from SEL(F-) + SYN(CHRONOUS)]
Seltzer (ˈsɛltsə) *n* **1** a natural effervescent water with a high content of minerals. **2** a similar synthetic water, used as a beverage. [C18: changed from G *Selterser Wasser* water from (*Nieder*) *Selters,* district where mineral springs are located, near Wiesbaden, Germany]
selva (ˈsɛlvə) *n* **1** dense equatorial forest, esp. in the Amazon basin,

THESAURUS

self-possessed *adj* = **self-assured,** collected, confident, cool, cool as a cucumber (*inf.*), poised, sure of oneself, together (*sl.*), unruffled
self-possession *n* = **self-assurance,** aplomb, composure, confidence, cool (*sl.*), poise, sang-froid, self-command, unflappability (*inf.*)
self-reliant *adj* = **independent,** able to stand on one's own two feet (*inf.*), capable, self-sufficient, self-supporting
Antonyms *adj* dependent, helpless, reliant, relying on
self-respect *n* = **pride,** *amour-propre,* dignity, faith in oneself, morale, one's own image, self-esteem
self-restraint *n* = **self-control,** abstemiousness, forbearance, patience, self-command, self-discipline, willpower
self-righteous *adj* = **sanctimonious,** complacent, goody-goody (*inf.*), holier-than-thou, hypocritical, pharisaic, pi (*Brit. sl.*), pietistic, pious, priggish, self-satisfied, smug, superior, too good to be true
self-sacrifice *n* = **selflessness,** altruism, generosity, self-abnegation, self-denial
self-satisfaction *n* = **smugness,** complacency, contentment, ease of mind, flush of success, glow of achievement, pride, self-approbation, self-approval
self-satisfied *adj* = **smug,** complacent, flushed with success, like a cat that has swallowed the canary, pleased with oneself, proud of oneself, puffed up, self-congratulatory, too big for one's boots *or* breeches, well-pleased
self-seeking *adj* **1** = **selfish,** acquisitive, calculating, careerist, fortune-hunting, gold-digging, looking out for number one (*inf.*), mercenary, on the make (*sl.*), opportunistic, out for what one can get, self-interested, self-serving
self-styled *adj* = **so-called,** professed, quasi-, self-appointed, *soi-disant,* would-be
self-willed *adj* = **stubborn,** cussed (*inf.*), headstrong, intractable, obstinate, opinionated, pig-headed, refractory, stiff-necked, stubborn as a mule, ungovernable, wilful
sell *vb* **1** = **trade,** barter, dispose of, exchange, put up for sale **2** = **deal in,** be in the business of, handle, hawk, market, merchandise, peddle, retail, stock, trade in, traffic in, vend **3** = **give up,** betray, deliver up, sell down the river (*inf.*), sell out (*inf.*), surrender **4, 5** = **promote,** gain acceptance for, put across
Antonyms *vb* ≠ **trade, deal in:** acquire, buy, get, invest in, obtain, pay for, procure, purchase, shop for
seller *n* **2** = **dealer,** agent, merchant, purveyor, rep, representative, retailer, salesman *or* saleswoman, shopkeeper, supplier, tradesman, traveller, vendor
sell out *vb* **1** = **dispose of,** be out of stock of, get rid of, run out of, sell up **2** *Informal* = **betray,** break faith with, double-cross (*inf.*), fail, give away, play false, rat on (*inf.*), sell down the river (*inf.*), stab in the back

characterized by tall broad-leaved evergreen trees. 2 a tract of such forest. [C19: from Sp. & Port., from L *silva* forest]

selvage *or* **selvedge** ('sɛlvɪdʒ) *n* 1 the finished nonfraying edge of a length of woven fabric. 2 a similar strip of material allowed in fabricating a metal or plastic article. [C15: from SELF + EDGE]
▸ **'selvaged** *adj*

selves (sɛlvz) *n* **a** the plural of **self. b** (*in combination*): *ourselves, yourselves, themselves.*

Sem. *abbrev. for:* 1 Seminary. 2 Semitic.

semantic (sɪ'mæntɪk) *adj* 1 of or relating to the meanings of different words or symbols. 2 of or relating to semantics. [C19: from Gk *sēmantikos* having significance, from *sēmainein* to signify, from *sēma* a sign]
▸ **se'mantically** *adv*

semantics (sɪ'mæntɪks) *n* (*functioning as sing*) 1 the branch of linguistics that deals with the study of meaning. 2 the study of the relationships between signs and symbols and what they represent. 3 *Logic.* the principles that determine the truth-values of the formulas in a logical system.
▸ **se'manticist** *n*

semaphore ('sɛmə,fɔː) *n* 1 an apparatus for conveying information by means of visual signals, as with flags, etc. 2 a system of signalling by holding a flag in each hand and moving the arms to designated positions for each letter of the alphabet. ◆ *vb* **semaphores, semaphoring, semaphored.** 3 to signal (information) by means of semaphore. [C19: via F, from Gk *sēma* a signal + -PHORE]
▸ **semaphoric** (,sɛmə'fɒrɪk) *adj*

semasiology (sɪ,meɪsɪ'ɒlədʒɪ) *n* another name for **semantics.** [C19: from Gk *sēmasia* meaning, from *sēmainein* to signify + -LOGY]

sematic (sɪ'mætɪk) *adj* (of the conspicuous coloration of certain animals) acting as a warning. [C19: from Gk *sēma* a sign]

semblance 🅣 ('sɛmbləns) *n* 1 outward appearance, esp. without any inner substance. 2 a resemblance. [C13: from OF, from *sembler* to seem, from L *simulāre* to imitate, from *similis* like]

sememe ('siːmiːm) *n Linguistics.* the meaning of a morpheme. [C20 (coined in 1933 by L. Bloomfield, US linguist): from Gk *sēma* a sign + -EME]

semen 🅣 ('siːmɛn) *n* 1 the thick whitish fluid containing spermatozoa that is ejaculated from the male genital tract. 2 another name for **sperm**[1]. [C14: from L: seed]

semester (sɪ'mɛstə) *n* 1 *Chiefly US & Canad.* either of two divisions of the academic year. 2 (in German universities) a session of six months. [C19: via G from L *sēmestris* half-yearly, from *sex* six + *mensis* a month]

semi ('sɛmɪ) *n, pl* **semis.** *Inf.* 1 *Brit.* short for **semidetached (house).** 2 short for **semifinal.**

semi- *prefix* 1 half: *semicircle.* 2 partially, partly, or almost: *semiprofessional.* 3 occurring twice in a specified period of time: *semiweekly.* [from L]

semiannual (,sɛmɪ'ænjʊəl) *adj* 1 occurring every half-year. 2 lasting for half a year.
▸ **,semi'annually** *adv*

semiarid (,sɛmɪ'ærɪd) *adj* characterized by scanty rainfall and scrubby vegetation, often occurring in continental interiors.

semiautomatic (,sɛmɪ,ɔːtə'mætɪk) *adj* 1 partly automatic. 2 (of a firearm) self-loading but firing only one shot at each pull of the trigger. ◆ *n* 3 a semiautomatic firearm.
▸ **,semi,auto'matically** *adv*

semibreve ('sɛmɪ,briːv) *n Music.* a note, now the longest in common use, having a time value that may be divided by any power of 2 to give all other notes. Usual US and Canad. name: **whole note.**

semicircle ('sɛmɪ,sɜːkᵊl) *n* 1a one half of a circle. 1b half the circumference of a circle. 2 anything having the shape or form of half a circle.
▸ **semicircular** (,sɛmɪ'sɜːkjʊlə) *adj*

semicircular canal *n Anat.* any of the three looped fluid-filled membranous tubes, at right angles to one another, that comprise the labyrinth of the ear.

semicolon (,sɛmɪ'kəʊlən) *n* the punctuation mark ; used to indicate a pause intermediate in value or length between that of a comma and that of a full stop.

semiconductor (,sɛmɪkən'dʌktə) *n* 1 a substance, such as germanium or silicon, that has an electrical conductivity that increases with temperature. 2a a device, such as a transistor or integrated circuit, that depends on the properties of such a substance. 2b (*as modifier*): *a semiconductor diode.*

semiconscious (,sɛmɪ'kɒnʃəs) *adj* not fully conscious.
▸ **,semi'consciously** *adv* ▸ **,semi'consciousness** *n*

semidetached (,sɛmɪdɪ'tætʃt) *adj* **a** (of a building) joined to another building on one side by a common wall. **b** (*as n*): *they live in a semidetached.*

semifinal (,sɛmɪ'faɪnᵊl) *n* **a** the round before the final in a competition. **b** (*as modifier*): *the semifinal draw.*
▸ **,semi'finalist** *n*

semifluid (,sɛmɪ'fluːɪd) *adj* 1 having properties between those of a liquid and those of a solid. ◆ *n* 2 a substance that has such properties because of high viscosity: *tar is a semifluid.* ◆ Also: **semiliquid.**

semiliterate (,sɛmɪ'lɪtərɪt) *adj* 1 hardly able to read or write. 2 able to read but not to write.

semilunar (,sɛmɪ'luːnə) *adj* shaped like a crescent or half-moon.

semilunar valve *n Anat.* either of two crescent-shaped valves, one in the aorta and one in the pulmonary artery, that prevent regurgitation of blood into the heart.

seminal 🅣 ('sɛmɪnəl) *adj* 1 potentially capable of development. 2 highly original and important. 3 rudimentary or unformed. 4 of or relating to semen: *seminal fluid.* 5 *Biol.* of or relating to seed. [C14: from LL *sēminālis* belonging to seed, from L *sēmen* seed]
▸ **'seminally** *adv*

seminar ('sɛmɪ,nɑː) *n* 1 a small group of students meeting regularly under the guidance of a tutor, professor, etc. 2 one such meeting or the place in which it is held. 3 a higher course for postgraduates. 4 any group or meeting for holding discussions or exchanging information. [C19: via G from L *sēminārium* SEMINARY]

seminary 🅣 ('sɛmɪnərɪ) *n, pl* **seminaries.** 1 an academy for the training of priests, etc. 2 *Arch.* a private secondary school, esp. for girls. [C15: from L *sēminārium* a nursery garden, from *sēmen* seed]
▸ **,semi'narial** *adj* ▸ **seminarian** (,sɛmɪ'nɛərɪən) *n*

seminiferous (,sɛmɪ'nɪfərəs) *adj* 1 containing, conveying, or producing semen. 2 (of plants) bearing or producing seeds.

semiotics (,sɛmɪ'ɒtɪks) *n* (*functioning as sing*) 1 the study of signs and symbols, esp. the relations between written or spoken signs and their referents in the physical world or the world of ideas. 2 the scientific study of the symptoms of disease. ◆ Also called: **semiology.** [from Gk *sēmeiōtikos,* from *sēmeion* a sign]
▸ **,semi'otic** *adj*

semipermeable (,sɛmɪ'pɜːmɪəbᵊl) *adj* (esp. of a cell membrane) selectively permeable.
▸ **,semi,permea'bility** *n*

semiprecious (,sɛmɪ'prɛʃəs) *adj* (of certain stones) having less value than a precious stone.

semiprofessional (,sɛmɪprə'fɛʃənᵊl) *adj* 1 (of a person) engaged in an activity or sport part-time but for pay. 2 (of an activity or sport) engaged in by semiprofessional people. 3 of or relating to a person whose activities are professional in some respects. ◆ *n* 4 a semiprofessional person.
▸ **,semipro'fessionally** *adv*

semiquaver ('sɛmɪ,kweɪvə) *n Music.* a note having the time value of one-sixteenth of a semibreve. Usual US and Canad. name: **sixteenth note.**

semirigid (,sɛmɪ'rɪdʒɪd) *adj* 1 partly but not wholly rigid. 2 (of an airship) maintaining shape by means of a main supporting keel and internal gas pressure.

semiskilled (,sɛmɪ'skɪld) *adj* partly skilled or trained but not sufficiently so to perform specialized work.

semisolid (,sɛmɪ'sɒlɪd) *adj* having a viscosity and rigidity intermediate between that of a solid and a liquid.

semisolus (,sɛmɪ'səʊləs) *n* an advertisement that appears on the same page as another advertisement but not adjacent to it.

semisweet ('sɛmɪ,swiːt) *adj* (of biscuits, etc.) slightly sweetened.

Semite ('siːmaɪt) *n* a member of the group of peoples who speak a Semitic language, including the Jews and Arabs as well as the ancient Babylonians, Assyrians, and Phoenicians. [C19: from NL *sēmīta* descendant of Shem, eldest of Noah's sons (Genesis 10:21)]

Semitic (sɪ'mɪtɪk) *n* 1 a branch or subfamily of the Afro-Asiatic family of languages that includes Arabic, Hebrew, Aramaic, and such ancient languages as Phoenician. ◆ *adj* 2 denoting or belonging to this group of languages. 3 denoting or characteristic of any of the peoples speaking a Semitic language, esp. the Jews or the Arabs. 4 another word for **Jewish.**

semitone ('sɛmɪ,təʊn) *n* an interval denoting the pitch difference between certain adjacent degrees of the diatonic scale (**diatonic semitone**) or between one note and its sharpened or flattened equivalent (**chromatic semitone**); minor second. Also called (US and Canad.): **half step.** Cf. **whole tone.**
▸ **semitonic** (,sɛmɪ'tɒnɪk) *adj*

semitrailer (,sɛmɪ'treɪlə) *n* a type of trailer or articulated lorry that has wheels only at the rear, the front end being supported by the towing vehicle.

semitropical (,sɛmɪ'trɒpɪkᵊl) *adj* partly tropical.
▸ **,semi'tropics** *pl n*

semivowel ('sɛmɪ,vaʊəl) *n Phonetics.* a vowel-like sound that acts like a consonant. In English and many other languages the chief semivowels are (w) in *well* and (j), represented as *y,* in *yell.* Also called: **glide.**

semiyearly (,sɛmɪ'jɪəlɪ) *adj* another word for **semiannual.**

semolina (,sɛmə'liːnə) *n* the large hard grains of wheat left after flour has been bolted, used for puddings, soups, etc. [C18: from It. *semolino,* dim. of *semola* bran, from L *simila* very fine wheat flour]

THESAURUS

semblance *n* 1 = **appearance,** air, aspect, bearing, façade, figure, form, front, guise, image, likeness, mask, mien, pretence, resemblance, show, similarity, veneer

semen *n* 1 = **sperm,** seed (*arch. or dialect*), seminal fluid, spermatic fluid, spunk (*taboo*)

seminal *adj* 2 = **influential,** creative, formative, ground-breaking, imaginative, important, innovative, original, productive

seminary *n* 1, 2 = **college,** academy, high school, institute, institution, school

sempervivum (ˌsɛmpəˈvaɪvəm) *n* any of a genus of hardy perennials including the houseleek. [C16 (used of the houseleek, adopted C18 by Linnaeus (1707-78), Swedish botanist, for the genus): L, from *sempervivus* ever-living]

sempiternal (ˌsɛmpɪˈtɜːnᵊl) *adj Literary.* everlasting; eternal. [C15: from OF, from LL *sempiternālis*, from L, from *semper* always + *aeternus* ETERNAL]
▸**ˌsempiˈternally** *adv*

semplice (ˈsɛmplɪtʃɪ) *adj, adv Music.* to be performed in a simple manner. [It.: simple, from L *simplex*]

sempre (ˈsɛmprɪ) *adv Music.* (preceding a tempo or dynamic marking) always; consistently. It is used to indicate that a specified volume, tempo, etc., is to be sustained throughout a piece or passage. [It.: always, from L *semper*]

sempstress (ˈsɛmpstrɪs) *n* a rare word for **seamstress.**

Semtex (ˈsɛmtɛks) *n* a pliable plastic explosive. [orig. a trade name]

SEN (in Britain) *abbrev. for:* **1** (formerly) State Enrolled Nurse. **2** special educational needs: needs arising from any of a wide range of problems that affect a pupil's normal educational development and for which special provisions are made.

Sen. *or* **sen.** *abbrev. for:* **1** senate. **2** senator. **3** senior.

senate (ˈsɛnɪt) *n* **1** any legislative body considered to resemble a Senate. **2** the main governing body at some universities. [C13: from L *senātus* council of the elders, from *senex* an old man]

Senate (ˈsɛnɪt) *n* (*sometimes not cap.*) **1** the upper chamber of the legislatures of the US, Canada, Australia, and many other countries. **2** the legislative council of ancient Rome.

senator (ˈsɛnətə) *n* **1** (*often cap.*) a member of a Senate or senate. **2** any legislator.
▸**senatorial** (ˌsɛnəˈtɔːrɪəl) *adj*

send ❶ (sɛnd) *vb* **sends, sending, sent. 1** (*tr*) to cause or order (a person or thing) to be taken, directed, or transmitted to another place: *to send a letter.* **2** (when *intr*, foll. by *for;* when *tr, takes an infinitive*) to dispatch a request or command (for something or to do something): *he sent for a bottle of wine.* **3** (*tr*) to direct or cause to go to a place or point: *his blow sent the champion to the floor.* **4** (*tr*) to bring to a state or condition: *this noise will send me mad.* **5** (*tr;* often foll. by *forth, out,* etc.) to cause to issue: *his cooking sent forth a lovely smell.* **6** (*tr*) to cause to happen or come: *misery sent by fate.* **7** to transmit (a message) by radio. **8** (*tr*) *Sl.* to move to excitement or rapture: *this music really sends me.* ◆ *n* **9** another word for **swash** (sense 4). [OE *sendan*]
▸**ˈsendable** *adj* ▸**ˈsender** *n*

send down *vb* (*tr, adv*) **1** *Brit.* to expel from a university. **2** *Inf.* to send to prison.

sendoff ❶ (ˈsɛndˌɒf) *n Inf.* **1** a demonstration of good wishes to a person about to set off on a journey, etc. ◆ *vb* **send off.** (*tr, adv*) **2** to cause to depart. **3** *Soccer, rugby, etc.* (of the referee) to dismiss (a player) from the field of play for some offence. **4** *Inf.* to give a sendoff to.

send up ❶ *vb* (*tr, adv*) **1** *Sl.* to send to prison. **2** *Brit. inf.* to make fun of, esp. by doing an imitation or parody of. ◆ *n* **send-up. 3** *Brit. inf.* a parody or imitation.

senescent (sɪˈnɛsᵊnt) *adj* **1** growing old. **2** characteristic of old age. [C17: from L *senēscere* to grow old, from *senex* old]
▸**seˈnescence** *n*

seneschal (ˈsɛnɪʃəl) *n* **1** a steward of the household of a medieval prince or nobleman. **2** *Brit.* a cathedral official. [C14: from OF, from Med. L *siniscalcus,* of Gmc origin]

senile ❶ (ˈsiːnaɪl) *adj* **1** of or characteristic of old age. **2** mentally or physically weak or infirm on account of old age. [C17: from L *senīlis,* from *senex* an old man]
▸**senility** (sɪˈnɪlɪtɪ) *n*

senile dementia *n* dementia starting in old age with no clear physical cause.

senior ❶ (ˈsiːnjə) *adj* **1** higher in rank or length of service. **2** older in years: *senior citizens.* **3** of or relating to maturity or old age: *senior privileges.* **4** *Education.* **4a** of or designating more advanced or older pupils. **4b** of or relating to a secondary school. **4c** *US.* denoting a student in the last year of school or university. ◆ *n* **5** a senior person. **6** a senior pupil, student, etc. [C14: from L: older, from *senex* old]

Senior (ˈsiːnjə) *adj Chiefly US.* being the older: used to distinguish the father from the son: *Charles Parker, Senior.* Abbrevs.: **Sr., Sen.**

senior aircraftman *n* a rank in the Royal Air Force comparable to that of a private in the army, though not the lowest rank in the Royal Air Force.

senior citizen ❶ *n* an old age pensioner.

senior common room *n* (in British universities, colleges, etc.) a common room for the use of academic staff.

seniority ❶ (ˌsiːnɪˈɒrɪtɪ) *n, pl* **seniorities. 1** the state of being senior. **2** precedence in rank, etc., due to senior status.

senior service *n Brit.* the Royal Navy.

senna (ˈsɛnə) *n* **1** any of a genus of tropical plants having typically yellow flowers and long pods. **2 senna leaf.** the dried leaflets of any of these plants, used as a cathartic and laxative. **3 senna pods.** the dried fruits of any of these plants, used as a cathartic and laxative. [C16: via NL from Ar. *sanā*]

sennight *or* **se'nnight** (ˈsɛnaɪt) *n* an archaic word for **week.** [OE *seofan nihte;* see SEVEN, NIGHT]

señor (sɛˈnjɔː; *Spanish* seˈɲor) *n, pl* **señors** *or* **señores** (*Spanish* -ˈɲores). a Spaniard: a title of address equivalent to *Mr* when placed before a name or *sir* when used alone. [Sp., from L *senior* an older man, SENIOR]

señora (sɛˈnjɔːrə; *Spanish* seˈɲora) *n, pl* **señoras** (-rəz; *Spanish* -ras). a married Spanish woman: a title of address equivalent to *Mrs* when placed before a name or *madam* when used alone.

señorita (ˌsɛnjɔːˈriːtə; *Spanish* ˌseɲoˈrita) *n, pl* **señoritas** (-təz; *Spanish* -tas). an unmarried Spanish woman: title of address equivalent to *Miss* when placed before a name or *madam* or *miss* when used alone.

sensation ❶ (sɛnˈseɪʃən) *n* **1** the power of perceiving through the senses. **2** a physical experience resulting from the stimulation of one of the sense organs. **3** a general feeling or awareness: *a sensation of fear.* **4** a state of widespread public excitement: *his announcement caused a sensation.* **5** anything that causes such a state: *your speech was a sensation.* [C17: from Med. L, from LL *sensātus* endowed with SENSE]

sensational ❶ (sɛnˈseɪʃənᵊl) *adj* **1** causing or intended to cause intense feelings, esp. of curiosity, horror, etc.: *sensational disclosures in the press.* **2** *Inf.* extremely good: *a sensational skater.* **3** of or relating to the faculty of sensation.
▸**senˈsationally** *adv*

sensationalism (sɛnˈseɪʃənᵊˌlɪzəm) *n* **1** the use of sensational language, etc., to arouse an intense emotional response. **2** such sensational matter itself. **3** *Philosophy.* the doctrine that knowledge cannot go beyond the analysis of experience.
▸**senˈsationalist** *n* ▸**senˌsationalˈistic** *adj*

sensationalize *or* **sensationalise** (sɛnˈseɪʃənᵊˌlaɪz) *vb* **sensationalizes, sensationalizing, sensationalized** *or* **sensationalises, sensationalising, sensationalised.** (*tr*) to cause (events, esp. in newspaper reports) to seem more vivid, shocking, etc., than they really are.

sense ❶ (sɛns) *n* **1** any of the faculties by which the mind receives information about the external world or the state of the body. The five traditional senses are sight, hearing, touch, taste, and smell. **2** the ability to perceive. **3** a feeling perceived through one of the senses: *a sense of warmth.* **4** a mental perception or awareness: *a sense of happiness.* **5** moral discernment: *a sense of right and wrong.* **6** (*sometimes pl*)

THESAURUS

send *vb* **1 = dispatch**, communicate, consign, convey, direct, forward, remit, transmit **2** *with* **for = summon**, call for, demand, order, request **5** *with* **forth, out,** *etc.* **= emit**, broadcast, discharge, exude, give off, radiate **8** *Slang* **= enrapture**, charm, delight, electrify, enthrall, excite, intoxicate, move, please, ravish, stir, thrill, titillate, turn (someone) on (*sl.*)

sendoff *n* **1 = farewell**, departure, going-away party, leave-taking, start, valediction

send up *vb* **2 = imitate**, burlesque, lampoon, make fun of, mimic, mock, parody, satirize, spoof (*inf.*), take off (*inf.*), take the mickey out of (*inf.*) ◆ *n* **send-up 3 = imitation**, mickey-take (*inf.*), mockery, parody, satire, skit, spoof (*inf.*), take-off (*inf.*)

senile *adj* **2 = doddering**, decrepit, doting, failing, gaga (*inf.*), imbecile, in one's dotage, in one's second childhood

senility *n* **2 = dotage**, caducity, decrepitude, infirmity, loss of one's faculties, second childhood, senescence, senile dementia

senior *adj* **1 = higher ranking**, superior **2 = older**, elder, major (*Brit.*)
Antonyms *adj* ≠ **higher ranking:** inferior, junior, lesser, lower, minor, subordinate ≠ **older:** junior, younger

senior citizen *n* **= pensioner**, elder, O.A.P., old age pensioner, old *or* elderly person, retired person

seniority *n* **1, 2 = superiority**, eldership, longer service, precedence, priority, rank

sensation *n* **1-3 = feeling**, awareness, consciousness, impression, perception, sense, tingle **4 = excitement**, agitation, commotion, furore, scandal, stir, surprise, thrill, vibes (*sl.*) **5 = hit** (*inf.*), crowd puller (*inf.*), wow (*sl., chiefly US*)

sensational *adj* **1 = exciting**, amazing, astounding, breathtaking, dramatic, electrifying, hair-raising, horrifying, lurid, melodramatic, revealing, scandalous, sensationalistic, shock- horror (*facetious*), shocking, spectacular, staggering, startling, thrilling, yellow (*of the press*) **2** *Informal* **= excellent**, awesome (*sl.*), brilliant, cracking (*Brit. inf.*), crucial, exceptional, fabulous (*inf.*), first class, impressive, jim-dandy (*sl.*), marvellous, mean (*sl.*), mind-blowing (*inf.*), out of this world (*inf.*), smashing (*inf.*), sovereign, superb
Antonyms *adj* ≠ **exciting:** boring, dull, humdrum, understated, undramatic, unexaggerated, unexciting ≠ **excellent:** commonplace, mediocre, no great shakes (*inf.*), ordinary, prosaic, run-of-the-mill, vanilla (*inf.*)

sense *n* **1 = faculty**, feeling, sensation, sensibility **3, 4 = feeling**, appreciation, atmosphere, aura, awareness, consciousness, impression, intuition, perception, premonition, presentiment, sentiment **6** *sometimes plural* **= intelligence**, brains (*inf.*), clear-headedness, cleverness, common sense, discernment, discrimination, gumption (*Brit. inf.*), judgment, mother wit, nous (*Brit. sl.*), quickness, reason, sagacity, sanity, sharpness, smarts (*sl., chiefly US*), tact, understanding, wisdom, wit(s) **7 = point**, advantage, good, logic, purpose, reason, use, value, worth **8 = meaning**, definition, denotation, drift, gist, implication, import, interpretation, message, nuance, purport, significance, signification, substance ◆ *vb* **15, 16 = perceive**, appreciate, apprehend, be aware of, discern, divine, feel, get the impression, grasp, have a (funny) feeling (*inf.*), have a hunch, just know, notice, observe, pick up, realize, suspect, understand
Antonyms *n* ≠ **intelligence:** folly, foolishness, idiocy, nonsense, silliness, stupidity ◆ *vb* ≠ **perceive:** be unaware of, fail to grasp *or* notice, miss, misunderstand, overlook

sound practical judgment or intelligence. **7** reason or purpose: *what is the sense of going out?* **8** meaning: *what is the sense of this proverb?* **9** specific meaning; definition: *in what sense are you using the word?* **10** an opinion or consensus. **11** *Maths.* one of two opposite directions in which a vector can operate. **12** **make sense.** to be understandable. **13** **take leave of one's senses.** *Inf.* to go mad. ◆ *vb* **senses, sensing, sensed.** (*tr*) **14** to perceive through one or more of the senses. **15** to apprehend or detect without or in advance of the evidence of the senses. **16** to understand. **17** *Computing.* **17a** to test or locate the position of (a part of computer hardware). **17b** to read (data). [C14: from L *sēnsus,* from *sentīre* to feel]

sense datum *n* a unit of sensation, such as a sharp pain, detached both from any information it may convey and from its putative source in the external world.

senseless 🅣 ('sɛnslɪs) *adj* **1** foolish: *a senseless plan.* **2** lacking in feeling; unconscious. **3** lacking in perception.
▸**'senselessly** *adv* ▸**'senselessness** *n*

sense organ *n* a structure in animals that is specialized for receiving external or internal stimuli and transmitting them in the form of nervous impulses to the brain.

sensibility 🅣 (ˌsɛnsɪ'bɪlɪtɪ) *n, pl* **sensibilities. 1** the ability to perceive or feel. **2** (*often pl*) the capacity for responding to emotion, etc. **3** (*often pl*) the capacity for responding to aesthetic stimuli. **4** discernment; awareness. **5** (*usually pl*) emotional or moral feelings: *cruelty offends most people's sensibilities.*

sensible 🅣 ('sɛnsɪbᵊl) *adj* **1** having or showing good sense or judgment. **2** (of clothing) serviceable; practical. **3** having the capacity for sensation; sensitive. **4** capable of being apprehended by the senses. **5** perceptible to the mind. **6** (sometimes foll. by *of*) having perception; aware: *sensible of your kindness.* **7** readily perceived: *a sensible difference.* [C14: from OF, from LL *sēnsibilis,* from L *sentīre* to sense]
▸**'sensibleness** *n* ▸**'sensibly** *adv*

sensitive 🅣 ('sɛnsɪtɪv) *adj* **1** having the power of sensation. **2** responsive to or aware of feelings, moods, etc. **3** easily irritated; delicate. **4** affected by external conditions or stimuli. **5** easily offended. **6** of or relating to the senses or the power of sensation. **7** capable of registering small differences or changes in amounts, etc.: *a sensitive instrument.* **8** *Photog.* responding readily to light: *a sensitive emulsion.* **9** *Chiefly US.* connected with matters affecting national security. **10** (of a stock market or prices) quickly responsive to external influences. [C14: from Med. L *sēnsitīvus,* from L *sentīre* to feel]
▸**'sensitively** *adv* ▸**ˌsensi'tivity** *n*

sensitive plant *n* a tropical American mimosa plant, the leaflets and stems of which fold if touched.

sensitize *or* **sensitise** ('sɛnsɪˌtaɪz) *vb* **sensitizes, sensitizing, sensitized** *or* **sensitises, sensitising, sensitised. 1** to make or become sensitive. **2** (*tr*) to render (an individual) sensitive to a drug, etc. **3** (*tr*) *Photog.* to make (a material) sensitive to light by coating it with a photographic emulsion often containing special chemicals, such as dyes.
▸**ˌsensiti'zation** *or* **ˌsensiti'sation** *n* ▸**'sensiˌtizer** *or* **'sensiˌtiser** *n*

sensitometer (ˌsɛnsɪ'tɒmɪtə) *n* an instrument for measuring the sensitivity to light of a photographic material over a range of exposures.

sensor ('sɛnsə) *n* anything, such as a photoelectric cell, that receives a signal or stimulus and responds to it. [C19: from L *sēnsus* perceived, from *sentīre* to observe]

sensorimotor (ˌsɛnsərɪ'məʊtə) *or* **sensomotor** (ˌsɛnsə'məʊtə) *adj* of or relating to both the sensory and motor functions of an organism or to the nerves controlling them.

sensorium (sɛn'sɔːrɪəm) *n, pl* **sensoriums** *or* **sensoria** (-rɪə). **1** the area of the brain considered responsible for receiving and integrating sensations from the outside world. **2** *Physiol.* the entire sensory and intellectual apparatus of the body. [C17: from LL, from L *sēnsus* felt, from *sentīre* to perceive]

sensory ('sɛnsərɪ) *adj* of or relating to the senses or the power of sensation. [C18: from L *sensōrius,* from *sentīre* to feel]

sensual 🅣 ('sɛnsjʊəl) *adj* **1** of or relating to any of the senses or sense organs; bodily. **2** strongly or unduly inclined to gratification of the senses. **3** tending to arouse the bodily appetites, esp. the sexual appetite. [C15: from LL *sensuālis,* from L *sēnsus* SENSE]
▸**'sensually** *adv*

sensualism ('sɛnsjʊəˌlɪzəm) *n* **1** the quality or state of being sensual. **2** the doctrine that the ability to gratify the senses is the only criterion of goodness.

sensuality 🅣 (ˌsɛnsjʊ'ælɪtɪ) *n, pl* **sensualities. 1** the quality or state of being sensual. **2** excessive indulgence in sensual pleasures.
▸**sensualist** ('sɛnsjʊəlɪst) *n*

sensuous 🅣 ('sɛnsjʊəs) *adj* **1** aesthetically pleasing to the senses. **2** appreciative of qualities perceived by the senses. **3** of or derived from the senses. [C17, but not common until C19: apparently coined by Milton to avoid the sexual overtones of SENSUAL]
▸**'sensuously** *adv* ▸**'sensuousness** *n*

sent (sɛnt) *vb* the past tense and past participle of **send.**

sentence 🅣 ('sɛntəns) *n* **1** a sequence of words capable of standing alone to make an assertion, ask a question, or give a command, usually consisting of a subject and a predicate. **2** the judgment formally pronounced upon a person convicted in criminal proceedings, esp. the decision as to what punishment is to be imposed. **3** *Music.* a passage or division of a piece of music, usually consisting of two or more contrasting musical phrases and ending in a cadence. **4** *Arch.* a proverb, maxim, or aphorism. ◆ *vb* **sentences, sentencing, sentenced. 5** (*tr*) to pronounce sentence on (a convicted person) in a court of law. [C13: via OF from L *sententia* a way of thinking, from *sentīre* to feel]
▸**sentential** (sɛn'tɛnʃəl) *adj*

sentence connector *n* a word or phrase that introduces a clause or sentence and serves as a transition between it and a previous clause or sentence, as for example *also* in *I'm buying eggs and also I'm looking for a dessert for tonight.*

sentence substitute *n* a word or phrase, esp. one traditionally classified as an adverb, that is used in place of a finite sentence, such as *yes, no, certainly,* and *never.*

sententious 🅣 (sɛn'tɛnʃəs) *adj* **1** characterized by or full of aphorisms or axioms. **2** constantly using aphorisms, etc. **3** tending to indulge in pompous moralizing. [C15: from L *sententiōsus* full of meaning, from *sententia;* see SENTENCE]
▸**sen'tentiously** *adv* ▸**sen'tentiousness** *n*

sentient 🅣 ('sɛnʃənt, 'sɛntɪənt) *adj* **1** having the power of sense perception or sensation; conscious. ◆ *n* **2** *Rare.* a sentient person or thing. [C17: from L *sentiēns* feeling, from *sentīre* to perceive]
▸**sentience** ('sɛnʃəns) *n*

sentiment 🅣 ('sɛntɪmənt) *n* **1** susceptibility to tender or romantic emotion: *she has too much sentiment to be successful.* **2** (*often pl*) a thought, opinion, or attitude. **3** exaggerated or mawkish feeling or emotion. **4** an expression of response to deep feeling, esp. in art. **5** a feeling or awareness: *a sentiment of pity.* **6** a mental attitude determined by feeling: *there is a strong revolutionary sentiment in his country.* **7**

THESAURUS

senseless *adj* **1** = **stupid**, absurd, asinine, crazy, daft (*inf.*), fatuous, foolish, halfwitted, idiotic, illogical, imbecilic, inane, incongruous, inconsistent, irrational, ludicrous, mad, meaningless, mindless, moronic, nonsensical, pointless, ridiculous, silly, simple, unintelligent, unreasonable, unwise, without rhyme or reason **2** = **unconscious**, anaesthetized, cold, deadened, insensate, insensible, numb, numbed, out, out cold, stunned, unfeeling
Antonyms *adj* ≠ **stupid:** intelligent, meaningful, rational, reasonable, sensible, useful, valid, wise, worthwhile ≠ **unconscious:** conscious, feeling, sensible

sensibility *n* **1** = **sensitivity**, responsiveness, sensitiveness, susceptibility **2** *often plural* = **feelings**, emotions, moral sense, sentiments, susceptibilities **4** = **awareness**, appreciation, delicacy, discernment, insight, intuition, perceptiveness, taste
Antonyms *n* ≠ **sensitivity:** deadness, insensibility, insensitivity, numbness, unresponsiveness ≠ **awareness:** insensibility, lack of awareness, unconsciousness, unperceptiveness

sensible *adj* **1** = **wise**, canny, discreet, discriminating, down-to-earth, far-sighted, intelligent, judicious, matter-of-fact, practical, prudent, rational, realistic, reasonable, sagacious, sage, sane, shrewd, sober, sound, well-reasoned, well-thought-out **5** = **perceptible**, appreciable, considerable, discernable, noticeable, palpable, significant, tangible, visible **6** *usually with* **of** = **aware**, acquainted with, alive to, conscious, convinced, mindful, observant, sensitive to, understanding
Antonyms *adj* ≠ **wise:** daft (*inf.*), dumb-ass (*sl.*), foolish, idiotic, ignorant, injudicious, irrational, senseless, silly, stupid, unreasonable, unwise ≠ **aware:** blind, ignorant, insensible, insensitive, unaware, unmindful

sensitive *adj* **2** = **susceptible**, delicate, easily affected, impressionable, reactive, responsive, sentient, touchy-feely (*inf.*) **3** = **easily hurt**, delicate, tender **5** = **touchy**, easily offended, easily upset, irritable, temperamental, thin-skinned **7** = **precise**, acute, fine, keen, perceptive, responsive
Antonyms *adj* ≠ **susceptible, touchy:** callous, hard, hardened, insensitive, thick-skinned, tough, uncaring, unfeeling ≠ **easily hurt:** insensitive, tough ≠ **precise:** approximate, imprecise, inexact, unperceptive

sensitivity *n* **2** = **sensitiveness**, delicacy, reactiveness, reactivity, receptiveness, responsiveness, susceptibility

sensual *adj* **1, 2** = **physical**, animal, bodily, carnal, epicurean, fleshly, luxurious, unspiritual, voluptuous **3** = **erotic**, lascivious, lecherous, lewd, libidinous, licentious, lustful, randy (*inf., chiefly Brit.*), raunchy (*sl.*), sexual, sexy (*inf.*), steamy (*inf.*), unchaste

sensualist *n* **2** = **pleasure-lover**, *bon vivant,* bon viveur, epicure, epicurean, hedonist, sybarite, voluptuary

sensuality *n* **1** = **eroticism**, animalism, carnality, lasciviousness, lecherousness, lewdness, libidinousness, licentiousness, prurience, salaciousness, sexiness (*inf.*), voluptuousness

sensuous *adj* **1, 2** = **pleasurable**, bacchanalian, epicurean, gratifying, hedonistic, lush, rich, sensory, sumptuous, sybaritic
Antonyms *adj* abstemious, ascetic, celibate, plain, self-denying, Spartan

sentence *n* **2** = **punishment**, condemnation, decision, decree, doom, judgment, order, pronouncement, ruling, verdict ◆ *vb* **5** = **condemn**, doom, mete out justice to, pass judgment on, penalize

sententious *adj* **1** = **gnomic**, aphoristic, axiomatic, brief, compact, concise, epigrammatic, laconic, pithy, pointed, short, succinct, terse **3** = **pompous**, canting, judgmental, moralistic, ponderous, preachifying (*inf.*), sanctimonious

sentient *adj* **1** = **feeling**, conscious, live, living, reactive, sensitive

sentiment *n* **1** = **emotion**, sensibility, soft-heartedness, tender feeling, tenderness **2** *often plural* = **feeling**, attitude, belief, idea, judgment, opinion, persuasion, saying, thought, view, way of thinking **3** = **sentimentality**, emotionalism, mawkishness, overemotionalism, romanticism, slush (*inf.*)

a feeling conveyed, or intended to be conveyed, in words. [C17: from Med. L *sentīmentum,* from L *sentīre* to feel]

sentimental ❶ (ˌsɛntɪˈmɛntᵊl) *adj* **1** tending to indulge the emotions excessively. **2** making a direct appeal to the emotions, esp. to romantic feelings. **3** relating to or characterized by sentiment.
▸ˌ**sentiˈmentaˌlism** *n* ▸ˌ**sentiˈmentalist** *n* ▸ˌ**sentiˈmentally** *adv*

sentimentality ❶ (ˌsɛntɪmɛnˈtælɪtɪ) *n, pl* **sentimentalities. 1** the state, quality, or an instance of being sentimental. **2** an act, statement, etc., that is sentimental.

sentimentalize *or* **sentimentalise** (ˌsɛntɪˈmɛntᵊˌlaɪz) *vb* **sentimentalizes, sentimentalizing, sentimentalized** *or* **sentimentalises, sentimentalising, sentimentalised.** to make sentimental or behave sentimentally.
▸ˌ**sentiˌmentaliˈzation** *or* ˌ**sentiˌmentaliˈsation** *n*

sentimental value *n* the value of an article in terms of its sentimental associations for a particular person.

sentinel ❶ (ˈsɛntɪnᵊl) *n* **1** a person, such as a sentry, assigned to keep guard. ◆ *vb* **sentinels, sentinelling, sentinelled** *or US* **sentinels, sentineling, sentineled.** (*tr*) **2** to guard as a sentinel. **3** to post as a sentinel. [C16: from OF *sentinelle,* from OIt., from *sentina* watchfulness, from *sentire* to notice, from L]

sentry (ˈsɛntrɪ) *n, pl* **sentries.** a soldier who guards or prevents unauthorized access to a place, etc. [C17: ? shortened from obs. *centrinel,* C16 var. of SENTINEL]

sentry box *n* a small shelter with an open front in which a sentry may stand to be sheltered from the weather.

senza (ˈsɛntsɑː) *prep Music.* omitting. [It.]

Sep. *abbrev. for:* **1** September. **2** Septuagint.

sepal (ˈsɛpᵊl) *n* any of the separate parts of the calyx of a flower. [C19: from NL *sepalum: sep-* from Gk *skepē* a covering + *-alum,* from NL *petalum* PETAL]

-sepalous *adj combining form.* having sepals of a specified type or number: *polysepalous.*
▸**-sepaly** *n combining form.*

separable ❶ (ˈsɛpərəbᵊl) *adj* able to be separated, divided, or parted.
▸ˌ**separaˈbility** *or* ˈ**separableness** *n* ▸ˈ**separably** *adv*

separate ❶ *vb* (ˈsɛpəˌreɪt), **separates, separating, separated. 1** (*tr*) to act as a barrier between: *a range of mountains separates the two countries.* **2** to part or be parted from a mass or group. **3** (*tr*) to discriminate between: *to separate the men from the boys.* **4** to divide or be divided into component parts. **5** to sever or be severed. **6** (*intr*) (of a married couple) to cease living together. ◆ *adj* (ˈsɛprɪt, ˈsɛpərɪt). **7** existing or considered independently: *a separate problem.* **8** disunited or apart. **9** set apart from the main body or mass. **10** distinct, individual, or particular. **11** solitary or withdrawn. [C15: from L *sēparāre,* from *sē-* apart + *parāre* to obtain]
▸ˈ**separately** *adv* ▸ˈ**separateness** *n* ▸ˈ**separative** *adj* ▸ˈ**sepaˌrator** *n*

separates (ˈsɛprɪts, ˈsɛpərɪts) *pl n* women's outer garments that only cover part of the body; skirts, blouses, jackets, trousers, etc.

separate school *n* **1** (in certain Canadian provinces) a school for a large religious minority financed by provincial grants in addition to the education tax. **2** a Roman Catholic school.

separation ❶ (ˌsɛpəˈreɪʃən) *n* **1** the act of separating or state of being separated. **2** the place or line where a separation is made. **3** a gap that separates. **4** *Family law.* the cessation of cohabitation between a man and wife, either by mutual agreement or under a decree of a court.

separatist (ˈsɛpərətɪst) *n* **a** a person who advocates secession from an organization, federation, union, etc. **b** (*as modifier*): *a separatist movement.*
▸ˈ**separaˌtism** *n*

Sephardi (sɪˈfɑːdiː) *n, pl* **Sephardim** (-dɪm). *Judaism.* **1** a Jew of Spanish, Portuguese, or North African descent. **2** the pronunciation of Hebrew used by these Jews, and of Modern Hebrew as spoken in Israel. ◆ Cf. **Ashkenazi.** [C19: from LHeb., from Heb. *sepharad* a region mentioned in Obadiah 20, thought to have been Spain]
▸**Seˈphardic** *adj*

sepia (ˈsiːpɪə) *n* **1** a dark reddish-brown pigment obtained from the inky secretion of the cuttlefish. **2** a brownish tone imparted to a photograph, esp. an early one. **3** a brownish-grey to dark yellowish-brown colour. **4** a drawing or photograph in sepia. ◆ *adj* **5** of the colour sepia or done in sepia: *a sepia print.* [C16: from L: a cuttlefish, from Gk]

sepoy (ˈsiːpɔɪ) *n* (formerly) an Indian soldier in the service of the British. [C18: from Port. *sipaio,* from Urdu *sipāhī,* from Persian: horseman, from *sipāh* army]

seppuku (sɛˈpuːkuː) *n* another word for **hara-kiri.** [from Japanese, from Chinese *ch'ieh* to cut + *fu* bowels]

sepsis (ˈsɛpsɪs) *n* the presence of pus-forming bacteria in the body. [C19: via NL from Gk *sēpsis* a rotting]

sept (sɛpt) *n* **1** *Anthropol.* a clan that believes itself to be descended from a common ancestor. **2** a branch of a tribe, esp. in Ireland or Scotland. [C16: ? a var. of SECT]

Sept. *abbrev. for:* **1** September. **2** Septuagint.

septa (ˈsɛptə) *n* the plural of **septum.**

septal (ˈsɛptəl) *adj* of or relating to a septum.

September (sɛpˈtɛmbə) *n* the ninth month of the year, consisting of 30 days. [OE, from L: the seventh (month) according to the original calendar of ancient Rome, from *septem* seven]

septenary (ˈsɛptɪnərɪ) *adj* **1** of or relating to the number seven. **2** forming a group of seven. ◆ *n, pl* **septenaries. 3** the number seven. **4** a group of seven things. **5** a period of seven years. [C16: from L *septēnārius,* from *septēnī* seven each, from *septem* seven]

septennial (sɛpˈtɛnɪəl) *adj* **1** occurring every seven years. **2** relating to or lasting seven years. [C17: from L, from *septem* seven + *annus* a year]

septet (sɛpˈtɛt) *n* **1** *Music.* a group of seven singers or instrumentalists or a piece of music composed for such a group. **2** a group of seven people or things. [C19: from G, from L *septem* seven]

septic ❶ (ˈsɛptɪk) *adj* **1** of or caused by sepsis. **2** of or caused by putrefaction. ◆ *n* **3** *Austral. & NZ inf.* short for **septic tank.** [C17: from L *sēpticus,* from Gk, from *sēptos* decayed, from *sēpein* to make rotten]
▸ˈ**septically** *adv* ▸**septicity** (sɛpˈtɪsɪtɪ) *n*

septicaemia *or US* **septicemia** (ˌsɛptɪˈsiːmɪə) *n* any of various diseases caused by microorganisms in the blood. Nontechnical name: **blood poisoning.** [C19: from NL, from Gk *sēptik(os)* SEPTIC + -AEMIA]
▸ˌ**septiˈcaemic** *or US* ˌ**septiˈcemic** *adj*

septic tank *n* a tank, usually below ground, for containing sewage to be decomposed by anaerobic bacteria. Also called (Austral.): **septic system.**

septillion (sɛpˈtɪljən) *n, pl* **septillions** *or* **septillion. 1** (in Britain, France, and Germany) the number represented as one followed by 42 zeros (10^{42}). **2** (in the US and Canada) the number represented as one followed by 24 zeros (10^{24}). Brit. word: **quadrillion.** [C17: from F, from *sept* seven + *-illion,* on the model of *million*]
▸**sepˈtillionth** *adj, n*

septime (ˈsɛptiːm) *n* the seventh of eight basic positions from which a parry or attack can be made in fencing. [C19: from L *septimus* seventh, from *septem* seven]

septuagenarian (ˌsɛptjʊədʒɪˈnɛərɪən) *n* **1** a person who is from 70 to 79 years old. ◆ *adj* **2** being between 70 and 79 years old. **3** of or relating to a septuagenarian. [C18: from L, from *septuāgintā* seventy]

Septuagesima (ˌsɛptjʊəˈdʒɛsɪmə) *n* the third Sunday before Lent. [C14: from Church L *septuāgēsima (dīes)* the seventieth (day)]

Septuagint (ˈsɛptjʊəˌdʒɪnt) *n* the principal Greek version of the Old Testament, including the Apocrypha, believed to have been translated by 70 or 72 scholars. [C16: from L *septuāgintā* seventy]

septum (ˈsɛptəm) *n, pl* **septa.** *Biol., anat.* a dividing partition between two tissues or cavities. [C18: from L *saeptum* wall, from *saepīre* to enclose]

septuple (ˈsɛptjʊpᵊl) *adj* **1** seven times as much or as many. **2** consisting of seven parts or members. ◆ *vb* **septuples, septupling, septupled. 3** (*tr*) to multiply by seven. [C17: from LL *septuplus,* from *septem* seven]
▸**septuplicate** (sɛpˈtjuːplɪkɪt) *n, adj*

sepulchral ❶ (sɪˈpʌlkrəl) *adj* **1** suggestive of a tomb; gloomy. **2** of or relating to a sepulchre.
▸**seˈpulchrally** *adv*

sepulchre ❶ *or US* **sepulcher** (ˈsɛpəlkə) *n* **1** a burial vault, tomb, or grave. **2** Also called: **Easter sepulchre.** an alcove in some churches in

THESAURUS

sentimental *adj* **1** = **romantic**, corny (*sl.*), dewy-eyed, emotional, gushy, impressionable, maudlin, mawkish, mushy (*inf.*), nostalgic, overemotional, pathetic, schmaltzy (*sl.*), simpering, sloppy (*inf.*), slushy (*inf.*), soft-hearted, tearful, tear-jerking (*inf.*), tender, touching, weepy (*inf.*)
Antonyms *adj* commonsensical, dispassionate, down-to-earth, earthy, hard-headed, practical, realistic, undemonstrative, unemotional, unfeeling, unromantic, unsentimental

sentimentality *n* **1** = **romanticism**, bathos, corniness (*sl.*), emotionalism, gush (*inf.*), mawkishness, mush (*inf.*), nostalgia, pathos, play on the emotions, schmaltz (*sl.*), sloppiness (*inf.*), slush (*inf.*), tenderness

sentinel *n* **1** = **guard**, lookout, picket, sentry, watch, watchman

separable *adj* = **distinguishable**, detachable, divisible, scissile, severable

separate *vb* **1** = **divide**, come between, keep apart, split **2** = **divide**, break off, cleave, come apart, come away, disentangle, disjoin **3** = **isolate**, discriminate between, put on one side, segregate, single out, sort out **4, 5** = **disunite**, bifurcate, detach, disconnect, diverge, divide, remove, sever, sunder, uncouple **6** = **part**, break up, divorce, estrange, go different ways, part company, split up ◆ *adj* **7** = **unconnected**, detached, disconnected, discrete, disjointed, divided, divorced, isolated, unattached **10** = **individual**, alone, apart, autonomous, distinct, independent, particular, single, solitary
Antonyms *vb* ≠ **divide, part, isolate**: amalgamate, combine, connect, join, link, merge, mix, unite ◆ *adj* ≠ **unconnected, individual**: affiliated, alike, connected, interdependent, joined, similar, unified, united

separated *adj* **2, 4-6** = **disconnected**, apart, broken up, disassociated, disunited, divided, living apart, parted, put asunder, separate, split up, sundered

separately *adv* **7** = **individually**, alone, apart, independently, one at a time, one by one, personally, severally, singly
Antonyms *adv* as a group, as one, collectively, in a body, in concert, in unison, jointly, together

separation *n* **1** = **division**, break, detachment, disconnection, disengagement, disjunction, dissociation, disunion, gap, segregation, severance **4** = **split-up**, break-up, divorce, estrangement, farewell, leave-taking, parting, rift, split

septic *adj* **1, 2** = **infected**, festering, poisoned, pussy, putrefactive, putrefying, putrid, suppurating, toxic

sepulchral *adj* **1** = **gloomy**, cheerless, dismal, funereal, grave, lugubrious, melancholy, morbid, mournful, sad, sombre, Stygian, woeful

sepulchre *n* **1** = **tomb**, burial place, grave, mausoleum, sarcophagus, vault which the Eucharistic elements were kept from Good Friday until Easter. ◆ *vb* **sepulchres, sepulchring, sepulchred** *or US* **sepulchers, sepulchering, sepulchered. 3** *(tr)* to bury in a sepulchre. [C12: from OF *sépulcre,* from L *sepulcrum,* from *sepelīre* to bury]

sepulture ('sepəltʃə) *n* the act of placing in a sepulchre. [C13: via OF from L *sepultūra,* from *sepultus* buried, from *sepelīre* to bury]

seq. *abbrev. for:* **1** sequel. **2** sequens. [L: the following (one)]

sequel **T** ('si:kwəl) *n* **1** anything that follows from something else. **2** a consequence. **3** a novel, play, etc., that continues a previously related story. [C15: from LL *sequēla,* from L *sequī* to follow]

sequela (sɪ'kwi:lə) *n, pl* **sequelae** (-li:). *(often pl) Med.* **1** any abnormal bodily condition or disease arising from a pre-existing disease. **2** any complication of a disease. [C18: from L: SEQUEL]

sequence **T** ('si:kwəns) *n* **1** an arrangement of two or more things in a successive order. **2** the successive order of two or more things: *chronological sequence.* **3** an action or event that follows another or others. **4a** *Cards.* a set of three or more consecutive cards, usually of the same suit. **4b** *Bridge.* a set of two or more consecutive cards. **5** *Music.* an arrangement of notes or chords repeated several times at different pitches. **6** *Maths.* an ordered set of numbers or other mathematical entities in one-to-one correspondence with the integers 1 to *n* **7** a section of a film constituting a single continuous uninterrupted episode. **8** *Biochem.* the unique order of amino acids in a protein or of nucleotides in DNA or RNA. ◆ *vb (tr)* **9** to arrange in a sequence. [C14: from Med. L *sequentia* that which follows, from L *sequī* to follow]

sequence of tenses *n Grammar.* the sequence according to which the tense of a subordinate verb in a sentence is determined by the tense of the principal verb, as in *I believe he is lying, I believed he was lying,* etc.

sequencing ('si:kwənsɪŋ) *n Biochem.* the procedure of determining the order of amino acids in the polypeptide chain of a protein (**protein sequencing**) or of nucleotides in a DNA section comprising a gene (**gene sequencing**).

sequent ('si:kwənt) *adj* **1** following in order or succession. **2** following as a result. ◆ *n* **3** something that follows. [C16: from L *sequēns,* from *sequī* to follow]
▸**'sequently** *adv*

sequential (sɪ'kwenʃəl) *adj* **1** characterized by or having a regular sequence. **2** another word for **sequent.**
▸**sequentiality** (sɪˌkwenʃɪ'ælɪtɪ) *n* ▸**se'quentially** *adv*

sequential access *n* a method of reading data from a computer file by reading through the file from the beginning.

sequester (sɪ'kwestə) *vb (tr)* **1** to remove or separate. **2** *(usually passive)* to retire into seclusion. **3** *Law.* to take (property) temporarily out of the possession of its owner, esp. until creditors are satisfied or a court order is complied with. **4** *International law.* to appropriate (enemy property). [C14: from LL *sequestrāre* to surrender for safekeeping, from L *sequester* a trustee]

sequestrate (sɪ'kwestreɪt) *vb* **sequestrates, sequestrating, sequestrated.** *(tr) Law.* a variant of **sequester** (sense 3). [C16: from LL *sequestrāre* to SEQUESTER]
▸**sequestrator** ('si:kwesˌtreɪtə) *n*

sequestration (ˌsi:kwe'streɪʃən) *n* **1** the act of sequestering or state of being sequestered. **2** *Law.* the sequestering of property. **3** *Chem.* the effective removal of ions from a solution by coordination with another type of ion or molecule to form complexes.

sequestrum (sɪ'kwestrəm) *n, pl* **sequestra** (-trə). *Pathol.* a detached piece of dead bone that often migrates to a wound, etc. [C19: from NL, from L: something deposited]
▸**se'questral** *adj*

sequin ('si:kwɪn) *n* **1** a small piece of shiny often coloured metal foil, usually round, used to decorate garments, etc. **2** a gold coin formerly minted in Italy. [C17: via F from It. *zecchino,* from *zecca* mint, from Ar. *sikkah* die for striking coins]
▸**'sequined** *adj*

sequoia (sɪ'kwɔɪə) *n* either of two giant Californian coniferous trees, the **redwood,** or the **big tree** or **giant sequoia.** [C19: NL, after *Sequoya,* known also as George Guess, (?1770–1843), American Indian scholar and leader]

sérac ('seræk) *n* a pinnacle of ice among crevasses on a glacier, usually on a steep slope. [C19: from Swiss F: a variety of white cheese (hence the ice that resembles it), from Med. L *serācium,* from L *serum* whey]

seraglio (se'rɑ:lɪˌəʊ) *or* **serail** (sə'raɪ) *n, pl* **seraglios** *or* **serails. 1** the harem of a Muslim house or palace. **2** a sultan's palace, esp. in the former Turkish empire. [C16: from It. *serraglio* animal cage, from Med. L *serrāculum* bolt, from L *sera* a door bar; associated also with Turkish *seray* palace]

serape (sə'rɑ:pɪ) *n* **1** a blanket-like shawl, often of brightly coloured wool, worn by men in Latin America. **2** a large shawl worn around the shoulders by women as a fashion garment. [C19: Mexican Sp.]

seraph **T** ('serəf) *n, pl* **seraphs** *or* **seraphim** (-əfɪm). *Theol.* a member of the highest order of angels in the celestial hierarchies, often depicted as the winged head of a child. [C17: back formation from pl *seraphim,* via LL from Heb.]
▸**seraphic** (sɪ'ræfɪk) *adj*

Serb (sɜ:b) *n, adj* another word for **Serbian.** [C19: from Serbian *Srb*]

Serbian ('sɜ:bɪən) *adj* **1** of, relating to, or characteristic of Serbia, in Yugoslavia, its people, or their dialect of Serbo-Croatian. ◆ *n* **2** the dialect of Serbo-Croat spoken in Serbia. **3** a native or inhabitant of Serbia.

Serbo-Croat *or* **Serbo-Croatian** ('sɜ:bəʊ-) *n* **1** the language of the Serbs and the Croats. The Serbian dialect is usually written in the Cyrillic alphabet, the Croatian in Roman. ◆ *adj* **2** of or relating to this language.

SERC (in Britain) *abbrev. for* Science and Engineering Research Council.

sere[1] (sɪə) *adj* **1** *Arch.* dried up. ◆ *vb* **seres, sering, sered,** *n* **2** a rare spelling of **sear.** [OE *sēar*]

sere[2] (sɪə) *n* the series of changes occurring in the ecological succession of a community. [C20: from SERIES]

serenade (ˌserɪ'neɪd) *n* **1** a piece of music characteristically played outside the house of a woman. **2** a piece of music suggestive of this. **3** an extended composition in several movements similar to the modern suite. ◆ *vb* **serenades, serenading, serenaded. 4** *(tr)* to play a serenade for (someone). **5** *(intr)* to play a serenade. [C17: from F *sérénade,* from It. *serenata,* from *sereno* peaceful, from L *serēnus;* also infl. in meaning by It. *sera* evening, from L *sērus* late]
▸**ˌsere'nader** *n*

serendipity (ˌserən'dɪpɪtɪ) *n* the faculty of making fortunate discoveries by accident. [C18: coined by Horace Walpole, from the Persian fairytale *The Three Princes of Serendip,* in which the heroes possess this gift]
▸**ˌseren'dipitous** *adj*

serene **T** (sɪ'ri:n) *adj* **1** peaceful or tranquil; calm. **2** clear or bright: *a serene sky.* **3** *(often cap.)* honoured: *His Serene Highness.* [C16: from L *serēnus*]
▸**se'renely** *adv* ▸**serenity** (sɪ'renɪtɪ) *n*

serf **T** (sɜ:f) *n* (esp. in medieval Europe) an unfree person, esp. one bound to the land. [C15: from OF, from L *servus* a slave]
▸**'serfdom** *or* **'serfhood** *n*

serge (sɜ:dʒ) *n* **1** a twill-weave woollen or worsted fabric used for clothing. **2** a similar twilled cotton, silk, or rayon fabric. [C14: from OF *sarge,* from Vulgar L *sārica* (unattested), from L *sēricum,* from Gk *sērikon* silk, ult. from *sēr* silkworm]

sergeant ('sɑ:dʒənt) *n* **1** a noncommissioned officer in certain armies, air forces, and marine corps, usually ranking immediately above a corporal. **2a** (in Britain) a police officer ranking between constable and inspector. **2b** (in the US) a police officer ranking below a captain. **3** a court or municipal officer who has ceremonial duties. ◆ Also: **serjeant.** [C12: from OF *sergent,* from L *serviēns,* lit.: serving, from *servīre* to SERVE]

sergeant at arms *n* an officer of a legislative or fraternal body responsible for maintaining internal order. Also: **sergeant, serjeant at arms.**

Sergeant Baker ('beɪkə) *n* a large brightly coloured Australian sea fish.

sergeant major *n* the chief administrative noncommissioned officer of a military headquarters. See also **warrant officer.**

Sergt *abbrev. for* Sergeant.

serial ('sɪərɪəl) *n* **1** a novel, film, etc., presented in instalments at regular intervals. **2** a publication, regularly issued and consecutively numbered. ◆ *adj* **3** of or resembling a series. **4** published or presented as a serial. **5** of or relating to such publication or presentation. **6** *Computing.* of or operating on items of information, etc., in the order in which they occur. **7** of or using the techniques of serialism. [C19: from NL *seriālis,* from L *seriēs* SERIES]
▸**'serially** *adv*

serialism ('sɪərɪəˌlɪzəm) *n* (in 20th-century music) the use of a sequence of notes in a definite order as a thematic basis for a composition. See also **twelve-tone.**

serialize *or* **serialise** ('sɪərɪəˌlaɪz) *vb* **serializes, serializing, serialized** *or* **serialises, serialising, serialised.** *(tr)* to publish or present in the form of a serial.
▸**ˌseriali'zation** *or* **ˌseriali'sation** *n*

serial killer *n* a person who carries out a series of murders, selecting victims at random or according to a perverse pattern.

serial monogamy *n* the practice of having a number of long-term monogamous romantic or sexual relationships or marriages in succession.

serial number *n* any of the consecutive numbers assigned to machines, tools, books, etc.

seriate ('sɪərɪɪt) *adj* forming a series.

seriatim (ˌsɪərɪ'ætɪm) *adv* one after another in order. [C17: from Med. L, from L *seriēs* SERIES]

THESAURUS

sequel *n* **1** = **follow-up**, continuation, development **2** = **consequence**, conclusion, end, issue, outcome, payoff (*inf.*), result, upshot

sequence *n* **1, 2** = **succession**, arrangement, chain, course, cycle, order, procession, progression, series

seraphic *adj* = **angelic**, beatific, blissful, celestial, divine, heavenly, holy, pure, sublime

serene *adj* **1** = **calm**, composed, imperturbable, peaceful, placid, sedate, tranquil, undisturbed, unruffled, untroubled **2** = **clear**, bright, cloudless, fair, halcyon, unclouded
Antonyms *adj* ≠ **calm:** agitated, anxious, disturbed, excitable, flustered, perturbed, troubled, uptight (*inf.*)

serenity *n* **1** = **calmness**, calm, composure, peace, peacefulness, peace of mind, placidity, quietness, quietude, stillness, tranquillity **2** = **clearness**, brightness, fairness

serf *n* = **vassal**, bondsman, helot, liegeman, servant, slave, thrall, varlet (*arch.*), villein

sericeous (sɪˈrɪʃəs) *adj Bot.* **1** covered with a layer of small silky hairs: *a sericeous leaf.* **2** silky. [C18: from LL *sēriceus* silken, from L *sēricus;* see SERGE]

sericulture (ˈsɛrɪˌkʌltʃə) *n* the rearing of silkworms for the production of raw silk. [C19: via F; *seri-* from L *sēricum* silk, ult. from Gk *sēr* a silkworm]
▸ **ˌseriˈcultural** *adj* ▸ **ˌseriˈculturist** *n*

series ❶ (ˈsɪəriːz) *n, pl* **series. 1** a group or succession of related things, usually arranged in order. **2** a set of radio or television programmes having the same characters but different stories. **3** a set of books having the same format, related content, etc., published by one firm. **4** a set of stamps, coins, etc., issued at a particular time. **5** *Maths.* the sum of a finite or infinite sequence of numbers or quantities. **6** *Electronics.* an arrangement of two or more components connected in a circuit so that the same current flows in turn through each of them (esp. in **in series**). Cf. **parallel** (sense 10). **7** *Geol.* a stratigraphical unit that represents the rocks formed during an epoch. [C17: from L: a row, from *serere* to link]

series-wound (ˈsɪəriːzˌwaʊnd) *adj* (of a motor or generator) having the field and armature circuits connected in series.

serif (ˈsɛrɪf) *n Printing.* a small line at the extremities of a main stroke in a type character. [C19: ?from Du. *schreef* dash, prob. of Gmc origin]

serigraph (ˈsɛrɪˌgrɑːf) *n* a colour print made by an adaptation of the silk-screen process. [C19: from *seri-*, from L *sēricum* silk + -GRAPH]
▸ **serigraphy** (səˈrɪgrəfɪ) *n*

serin (ˈsɛrɪn) *n* any of various small yellow-and-brown finches of parts of Europe. [C16: from F, ?from OProvençal *sirena* a bee-eater, from L *sīrēn,* a kind of bird, from SIREN]

seringa (səˈrɪŋgə) *n* **1** any of a Brazilian genus of trees that yield rubber. **2** a deciduous tree of southern Africa with a graceful shape. [C18: from Port., var. of SYRINGA]

seriocomic (ˌsɪərɪəʊˈkɒmɪk) *adj* mixing serious and comic elements.
▸ **ˌserioˈcomically** *adv*

serious ❶ (ˈsɪərɪəs) *adj* **1** grave in nature or disposition: *a serious person.* **2** marked by deep feeling; sincere: *is he serious or joking?* **3** concerned with important matters: *a serious conversation.* **4** requiring effort or concentration: *a serious book.* **5** giving rise to fear or anxiety: *a serious illness.* **6** *Inf.* worthy of regard because of substantial quantity or quality: *serious money; serious wine.* **7** *Inf.* extreme or remarkable: *a serious haircut.* [C15: from LL *sēriōsus,* from L *sērius*]
▸ **ˈseriousness** *n*

serjeant (ˈsɑːdʒənt) *n* a variant spelling of **sergeant.**

serjeant at law *n* (formerly, in England) a barrister of a special rank. Also: **serjeant, sergeant at law, sergeant.**

sermon ❶ (ˈsɜːmən) *n* **1a** an address of religious instruction or exhortation, often based on a passage from the Bible, esp. one delivered during a church service. **1b** a written version of such an address. **2** a serious speech, esp. one administering reproof. [C12: via OF from L *sermō* discourse, prob. from *serere* to join together]

sermonize *or* **sermonise** (ˈsɜːməˌnaɪz) *vb* **sermonizes, sermonizing, sermonized** *or* **sermonises, sermonising, sermonised.** to address (a person or audience) as if delivering a sermon.
▸ **ˈsermonˌizer** *or* **ˈsermonˌiser** *n*

Sermon on the Mount *n Bible.* a major discourse delivered by Christ, including the Beatitudes and the Lord's Prayer (Matthew 5–7).

sero- *combining form.* indicating a serum: *serology.*

seroconvert (ˌsɪərəʊkənˈvɜːt) *vb* (*intr*) (of an individual) to produce antibodies specific to, and in response to the presence in the blood of, a particular antigen, such as a virus or vaccine.
▸ **ˌseroconˈversion** *n*

serology (sɪˈrɒlədʒɪ) *n* the branch of science concerned with serums.
▸ **serologic** (ˌsɪərəˈlɒdʒɪk) *or* **ˌseroˈlogical** *adj*

seropositive (ˌsɪərəʊˈpɒzɪtɪv) *adj* (of a person whose blood has been tested for a specific disease, such as AIDS) showing a serological reaction indicating the presence of the disease.

serotine (ˈsɛrəˌtaɪn) *adj* **1** *Biol.* produced, flowering, or developing late in the season. ◆ *n* **2** a reddish-coloured European insectivorous bat. [C16: from L *sērōtinus* late, from *sērus* late; applied to the bat because it flies late in the evening]

serotonin (ˌsɛrəˈtəʊnɪn) *n* a compound that occurs in the brain, intestines, and blood platelets and induces vasoconstriction.

serous (ˈsɪərəs) *adj* of, producing, or containing serum. [C16: from L *serōsus*]
▸ **serosity** (sɪˈrɒsɪtɪ) *n*

serous fluid *n* a thin watery fluid found in many body cavities.

serous membrane *n* any of the smooth moist delicate membranes, such as the pleura, that line the closed cavities of the body.

serow (ˈsɛrəʊ) *n* either of two antelopes of mountainous regions of S and SE Asia, having a dark coat and conical backward-pointing horns. [C19: from native name *să-ro* Tibetan goat]

serpent (ˈsɜːpənt) *n* **1** a literary word for **snake. 2** *Bible.* a manifestation of Satan as a guileful tempter (Genesis 3:1–5). **3** a sly or unscrupulous person. **4** an obsolete wind instrument resembling a snake in shape. [C14: via OF from L *serpēns* a creeping thing, from *serpere* to creep]

serpentine[1] ❶ (ˈsɜːpənˌtaɪn) *adj* **1** of, relating to, or resembling a serpent. **2** twisting; winding. [C14: from LL *serpentīnus,* from *serpēns* SERPENT]

serpentine[2] (ˈsɜːpənˌtaɪn) *n* any of several secondary minerals, consisting of hydrated magnesium silicate, that are green to brown in colour and greasy to the touch. [C15 *serpentyn,* from Med. L *serpentīnum* SERPENTINE[1]; referring to the snakelike patterns of these minerals]

serpigo (sɜːˈpaɪgəʊ) *n Pathol.* any progressive skin eruption, such as ringworm or herpes. [C14: from Med. L, from L *serpere* to creep]

SERPS *or* **Serps** (sɜːps) *n* (in Britain) *acronym for* state earnings-related pension scheme.

serrate ❶ *adj* (ˈsɛrɪt, -eɪt). **1** (of leaves) having a margin of forward pointing teeth. **2** having a notched or sawlike edge. ◆ *vb* (sɛˈreɪt), **serrates, serrating, serrated. 3** (*tr*) to make serrate. [C17: from L *serrātus* saw-shaped, from *serra* a saw]
▸ **serˈrated** *adj*

serration (sɛˈreɪʃən) *n* **1** the state or condition of being serrated. **2** a row of toothlike projections on an edge. **3** a single notch.

serried ❶ (ˈsɛrɪd) *adj* in close or compact formation: *serried ranks of troops.* [C17: from OF *serré* close-packed, from *serrer* to shut up]

serriform (ˈsɛrɪˌfɔːm) *adj Biol.* resembling a notched or sawlike edge. [*serri-*, from L *serra* saw]

serrulate (ˈsɛrʊˌleɪt, -lɪt) *adj* (esp. of leaves) minutely serrate. [C18: from NL *serrulātus,* from L *serrula* dim. of *serra* a saw]
▸ **ˌserruˈlation** *n*

serum (ˈsɪərəm) *n, pl* **serums** *or* **sera** (-rə). **1** Also called: **blood serum.** blood plasma from which the clotting factors have been removed. **2** antitoxin obtained from the blood serum of immunized animals. **3** *Physiol., zool.* clear watery fluid, esp. that exuded by serous membranes. **4** a less common word for **whey.** [C17: from L: whey]

serum albumin *n* a form of albumin that is the most abundant protein constituent of blood plasma.

serum hepatitis *n* a former name for **hepatitis B.**

serum sickness *n* an allergic reaction, such as vomiting, skin rash, etc., that sometimes follows injection of a foreign serum.

serval (ˈsɜːvəl) *n, pl* **servals** *or* **serval.** a slender feline mammal of the African bush, having an orange-brown coat with black spots. [C18: via F from LL *cervālis* staglike, from L *cervus* a stag]

servant ❶ (ˈsɜːvənt) *n* **1** a person employed to work for another, esp. one who performs household duties. **2** See **public servant.** [C13: via OF from *servant* serving, from *servir* to SERVE]

serve ❶ (sɜːv) *vb* **serves, serving, served. 1** to be in the service of (a person). **2** to render or be of service to (a person, cause, etc.); help. **3** to attend to (customers) in a shop, etc. **4** (*tr*) to provide (guests, etc.) with food, drink, etc.: *she served her guests with cocktails.* **5** to distribute or provide (food, etc.) for guests, etc.: *do you serve coffee?* **6** (*tr;* sometimes foll. by *up*) to present (food, etc.) in a specified manner: *peaches served with cream.* **7** (*tr*) to provide with a regular supply of. **8** (*tr*) to work actively for: *to serve the government.* **9** (*tr*) to pay homage to: *to serve God.* **10** to suit: *this will serve my purpose.* **11** (*intr; may take an infinitive*) to function: *this wood will serve to build a fire.* **12** to go through (a period of service, enlistment, etc.). **13** (*intr*) (of weather, conditions, etc.) to be suitable. **14** (*tr*) Also: **service.** (of a male animal) to copulate with (a female animal). **15** *Tennis, squash, etc.* to put (the ball) into play. **16** (*tr*) to deliver (a legal document) to (a person). **17** (*tr*) *Naut.* to bind (a rope, etc.) with fine cord to protect it from chafing, etc. **18 serve (a person) right.** *Inf.* to pay (a person) back, esp. for wrongful or foolish treatment or behaviour. ◆ *n* **19** *Tennis, squash, etc.* short for **service. 20**

THESAURUS

series *n* **1** = **sequence,** arrangement, chain, course, line, order, progression, run, set, string, succession, train

serious *adj* **1** = **solemn,** grave, humourless, long-faced, pensive, sedate, sober, stern, thoughtful, unsmiling **2** = **sincere,** deliberate, determined, earnest, genuine, honest, in earnest, resolute, resolved **3** = **important,** crucial, deep, difficult, far-reaching, fateful, grim, momentous, no laughing matter, of moment *or* consequence, pressing, significant, urgent, weighty, worrying **5** = **grave,** acute, alarming, critical, dangerous, severe
Antonyms *adj* ≠ **solemn:** carefree, flippant, frivolous, jolly, joyful, light-hearted, smiling ≠ **sincere:** capricious, flighty, flippant, frivolous, insincere, uncommitted, undecided ≠ **important:** insignificant, minor, slight, trivial, unimportant

seriously *adv* **1** = **sincerely,** acutely, badly, critically, dangerously, distressingly, earnestly, grievously, in earnest, severely, solemnly, sorely, thoughtfully, with a straight face

seriousness *n* **1** = **solemnity,** earnestness, gravitas, gravity, humourlessness, sedateness, sobriety, staidness, sternness **3** = **importance,** danger, gravity, moment, significance, urgency, weight

sermon *n* **1** = **homily,** address, exhortation **2** = **lecture,** dressing-down (*inf.*), harangue, talking-to (*inf.*)

serpentine[1] *adj* **2** = **twisting,** coiling, crooked, meandering, sinuous, snaking, snaky, tortuous, twisty, winding

serrated *adj* **3** = **notched,** sawlike, sawtoothed, serrate, serriform (*Biology*), serrulate, toothed

serried *adj Literary* = **massed,** assembled, close, compact, dense, phalanxed

servant *n* **1** = **attendant,** domestic, drudge, help, helper, lackey, liegeman, maid, menial, retainer, servitor (*arch.*), skivvy (*chiefly Brit.*), slave, vassal

serve *vb* **1-3** = **work for,** aid, assist, attend to, be in the service of, be of assistance, be of use, help, minister to, oblige, succour, wait on **5** = **provide,** arrange, deal, deliver, dish up, distribute, handle, present, purvey, set out, supply **10, 11** = **be adequate,** answer, answer the purpose, be acceptable, be good enough, content, do, do duty as, do the work of, fill the bill (*inf.*), function as, satisfy, suffice, suit **12** = **perform,** act, attend, complete, discharge, do, fulfil, go through, observe, officiate, pass

Austral. inf. hostile or critical remarks. [C13: from OF *servir,* from L *servīre,* from *servus* a slave]
▸**'servable** *or* **'serveable** *adj*

server ('sɜːvə) *n* **1** a person who serves. **2** *RC Church.* a person who assists the priest at Mass. **3** something that is used in serving food and drink. **4** the player who serves in racket games. **5** *Computing.* a computer or program that supplies data or resources to other machines on a network.

service ➊ ('sɜːvɪs) *n* **1** an act of help or assistance. **2** an organized system of labour and material aids used to supply the needs of the public: *telephone service.* **3** the supply, installation, or maintenance of goods carried out by a dealer. **4** the state of availability for use by the public (esp. in **into** *or* **out of service**). **5** a periodic overhaul made on a car, etc. **6** the act or manner of serving guests, customers, etc., in a shop, hotel, etc. **7** a department of public employment and its employees: *civil service.* **8** employment in or performance of work for another: *in the service of his firm.* **9a** one of the branches of the armed forces. **9b** (*as modifier*): *service life.* **10** the state or duties of a domestic servant (esp. in **in service**). **11** the act or manner of serving food. **12** a set of dishes, cups, etc., for use at table. **13** public worship carried out according to certain prescribed forms: *divine service.* **14** the prescribed form according to which a specific kind of religious ceremony is to be carried out: *the burial service.* **15** *Tennis, squash, etc.* **15a** the act, manner, or right of serving a ball. **15b** the game in which a particular player serves: *he has lost his service.* **16** the serving of a writ, summons, etc., upon a person. **17** (of male animals) the act of mating. **18** (*modifier*) of or for the use of servants or employees. **19** (*modifier*) serving the public rather than producing goods: *service industry.* ◆ *vb* **services, servicing, serviced.** (*tr*) **20** to provide service or services to. **21** to make fit for use. **22** to supply with assistance. **23** to overhaul (a car, machine, etc.). **24** (of a male animal) to mate with (a female). **25** *Brit.* to meet interest on (debt). ◆ See also **services.** [C12 *servise,* from OF, from L *servitium* condition of a slave, from *servus* a slave]

serviceable ➊ ('sɜːvɪsəbᵊl) *adj* **1** capable of or ready for service. **2** capable of giving good service.
▸ˌ**servicea'bility** *n* ▸**'serviceably** *adv*

service area *n* a place on a motorway providing garage services, restaurants, toilet facilities, etc.

service car *n NZ.* a bus operating on a long-distance route.

service charge *n* a percentage of a bill, as at a hotel, added to the total to pay for service.

service contract *n* a contract between an employer and a senior employee, esp. a director, executive, etc.

service flat *n Brit.* a flat in which domestic services are provided by the management. Also called (esp. Austral.): **serviced flat.**

serviceman ('sɜːvɪsmən) *n, pl* **servicemen. 1** a person who serves in the armed services of a country. **2** a man employed to service and maintain equipment.
▸**'serviceˌwoman** *fem n*

service road *n Brit.* a narrow road running parallel to a main road and providing access to houses, shops, etc., situated along its length.

services ('sɜːvɪsɪz) *pl n* **1** work performed for remuneration. **2** (usually preceded by *the*) the armed forces. **3** (*sometimes sing*) *Econ.* commodities, such as banking, that are mainly intangible and usually consumed concurrently with their production. **4** a system of providing the public with gas, water, etc.

service station *n* a place that supplies fuel, oil, etc., for motor vehicles and often carries out repairs, servicing, etc.

service tree *n* **1** Also called: **sorb.** a Eurasian rosaceous tree, cultivated for its white flowers and brown edible apple-like fruits. **2 wild service tree.** a similar and related Eurasian tree. [*service* from OE *syrfe,* from Vulgar L *sorbea* (unattested), from L *sorbus* sorb]

serviette (ˌsɜːvɪ'ɛt) *n Chiefly Brit.* a small square of cloth or paper used while eating to protect the clothes, etc. [C15: from OF, from *servir* to SERVE; on the model of OUBLIETTE]

servile ➊ ('sɜːvaɪl) *adj* **1** obsequious or fawning in attitude or behaviour. **2** of or suitable for a slave. **3** existing in or relating to a state of slavery. **4** (when *postpositive,* foll. by *to*) submitting or obedient. [C14: from L *servīlis,* from *servus* slave]
▸**servility** (sɜː'vɪlɪtɪ) *n*

serving ➊ ('sɜːvɪŋ) *n* a portion or helping of food or drink.

servitor ('sɜːvɪtə) *n Arch.* a person who serves another. [C14: from OF, from LL, from L *servīre* to SERVE]

servitude ➊ ('sɜːvɪˌtjuːd) *n* **1** the state or condition of a slave. **2** the state or condition of being subjected to or dominated by a person or thing. **3** *Law.* a burden attaching to an estate for the benefit of an adjoining estate or of some definite person. See also **easement.** [C15: via OF from L *servitūdō,* from *servus* a slave]

servo ('sɜːvəʊ) *adj* **1** (*prenominal*) of or activated by a servomechanism: *servo brakes.* ◆ *n, pl* **servos. 2** *Inf.* short for **servomechanism.** [from *servomotor* from F, from L *servus* slave + F *moteur* motor]

servomechanism ('sɜːvəʊˌmɛkəˌnɪzəm) *n* a mechanical or electromechanical system for control of the position or speed of an output transducer.

servomotor ('sɜːvəʊˌməʊtə) *n* any motor that supplies power to a servomechanism.

servqual ('sɜːvˌkwɒl) *n Marketing.* the provision of high-quality products by an organization backed by a high level of service for consumers. [C20: from SERV(ICE) + QUAL(ITY)]

sesame ('sɛsəmɪ) *n* **1** a tropical herbaceous plant of the East Indies, cultivated, esp. in India, for its small oval seeds. **2** the seeds of this plant, used in flavouring bread and yielding an edible oil (**benne oil** or **gingili**). [C15: from L *sēsamum,* from Gk *sēsamon, sēsamē,* of Semitic origin]

sesamoid ('sɛsəˌmɔɪd) *adj Anat.* **1** of or relating to various small bones formed in tendons, such as the patella. **2** of or relating to any of various small cartilages, esp. those of the nose. [C17: from L *sēsamoīdēs* like sesame (seed), from Gk]

sesqui- *prefix* **1** indicating one and a half: *sesquicentennial.* **2** (in a chemical compound) indicating a ratio of two to three. [from L, contraction of SEMI- + *as* AS[2] + *-que* and]

sesquicentennial (ˌsɛskwɪsɛn'tɛnɪəl) *adj* **1** of a period of 150 years. ◆ *n* **2** a period of 150 years. **3** a 150th anniversary or its celebration.
▸ˌ**sesquicen'tennially** *adv*

sessile ('sɛsaɪl) *adj* **1** (of flowers or leaves) having no stalk. **2** (of animals such as the barnacle) permanently attached. [C18: from L *sēssilis* concerning sitting, from *sedēre* to sit]
▸**sessility** (sɛ'sɪlɪtɪ) *n*

sessile oak *n* another name for the **durmast.**

session ➊ ('sɛʃən) *n* **1** the meeting of a court, legislature, judicial body, etc., for the execution of its function or the transaction of business. **2** a single continuous meeting of such a body. **3** a series or period of such meetings. **4** *Education.* **4a** the time during which classes are held. **4b** a school or university year. **5** *Presbyterian Church.* the body presiding over a local congregation and consisting of the minister and elders. **6** a meeting of a group of musicians to record in a studio. **7** any period devoted to an activity. [C14: from L *sessiō* a sitting, from *sedēre* to sit]
▸**'sessional** *adj*

sesterce ('sɛstɜːs) *or* **sestertius** (sɛ'stɜːtɪəs) *n* a silver or, later, bronze coin of ancient Rome worth a quarter of a denarius. [C16: from L *sēstertius* a coin worth two and a half asses, from *sēmis* half + *tertius* a third]

sestet (sɛ'stɛt) *n* **1** *Prosody.* the last six lines of a sonnet. **2** another word for **sextet** (sense 1). [C19: from It., from *sesto* sixth, from L, from *sex* six]

sestina (sɛ'stiːnə) *n* an elaborate verse form of Italian origin in which the six final words of the lines in the first stanza are repeated in a different order in each of the remaining five stanzas. [C19: from It., from *sesto* sixth, from L *sextus*]

set[1] ➊ (sɛt) *vb* **sets, setting, set.** (*mainly tr*) **1** to put or place in position or into a specified state or condition: *to set someone free.* **2** (*also intr;* foll. by *to* or *on*) to put or be put (to); apply or be applied: *he set fire to the house.* **3** to put into order or readiness for use: *to set the table for dinner.* **4** (*also intr*) to put, form, or be formed into a jelled, firm, or rigid state: *the jelly set in three hours.* **5** (*also intr*) to put or be put into a position that will restore a normal state: *to set a broken bone.* **6** to adjust (a clock

THESAURUS

service *n* **1, 4 = help,** advantage, assistance, avail, benefit, ministrations, supply, use, usefulness, utility **5 = overhaul,** check, maintenance, servicing **8 = work,** business, duty, employ, employment, labour, office **13 = ceremony,** function, observance, rite, worship ◆ *vb* **23 = overhaul,** check, fine tune, go over, maintain, recondition, repair, tune (up)

serviceable *adj* **1 = useful,** advantageous, beneficial, convenient, dependable, durable, efficient, functional, hard-wearing, helpful, operative, practical, profitable, usable, utilitarian
Antonyms *adj* impractical, inefficient, unserviceable, unusable, useless, worn-out

servile *adj* **1 = subservient,** abject, base, bootlicking (*inf.*), craven, cringing, fawning, grovelling, humble, low, mean, menial, obsequious, slavish, submissive, sycophantic, toadying, toadyish, unctuous

servility *n* **1 = subservience,** abjection, baseness, bootlicking (*inf.*), fawning, grovelling, meanness, obsequiousness, self-abasement, slavishness, submissiveness, sycophancy, toadyism, unctuousness

serving *n* **= portion,** helping, plateful

servitude *n* **1 = slavery,** bondage, bonds, chains, enslavement, obedience, serfdom, subjugation, thraldom, thrall, vassalage

session *n* **1 = meeting,** assembly, conference, congress, discussion, get-together (*inf.*), hearing, period, seminar, sitting, term

set[1] *vb* **1 = put,** aim, apply, deposit, direct, embed, fasten, fix, install, lay, locate, lodge, mount, park (*inf.*), place, plant, plonk, plump, position, rest, seat, situate, station, stick, turn **3 = prepare,** arrange, lay, make ready, spread **4 = harden,** cake, condense, congeal, crystallize, gelatinize, jell, solidify, stiffen, thicken **6 = adjust,** coordinate, rectify, regulate, synchronize **7 = arrange,** agree upon, allocate, appoint, conclude, decide (upon), designate, determine, establish, fix, fix up, name, ordain, regulate, resolve, schedule, settle, specify **8 = assign,** allot, decree, impose, lay down, ordain, prescribe, specify **18 = go down,** decline, dip, disappear, sink, subside, vanish ◆ *n* **30 = position,** attitude, bearing, carriage, fit, hang, posture, turn **31 = scenery,** *mise-en-scène,* scene, setting, stage set, stage setting ◆ *adj* **36 = fixed,** agreed, appointed, arranged, customary, decided, definite, established, firm, prearranged, predetermined, prescribed, regular, scheduled, settled, usual **37 = inflexible,** entrenched, firm, hard and fast, hardened, hidebound, immovable, rigid, strict, stubborn **39 = conventional,** artificial, formal, hackneyed, rehearsed, routine, standard, stereotyped, stock, traditional, unspontaneous **40** *with* **on** *or* **upon = determined,** bent, intent, resolute or other instrument) to a position. **7** to establish: *we have set the date for our wedding.* **8** to prescribe (an undertaking, course of study, etc.): *the examiners have set "Paradise Lost".* **9** to arrange in a particular fashion, esp. an attractive one: *she set her hair.* **10** Also: **set to music.** to provide music for (a poem or other text to be sung). **11** Also: **set up.** *Printing.* to arrange or produce (type, film, etc.) from (text or copy). **12** to arrange (a stage, television studio, etc.) with scenery and props. **13** to describe (a scene or the background to a literary work, etc.) in words: *his novel is set in Russia.* **14** to present as a model of good or bad behaviour (esp. in **set an example**). **15** (foll. by *on* or *by*) to value (something) at a specified price or estimation of worth: *he set a high price on his services.* **16** (*also intr*) to give or be given a particular direction: *his course was set to the East.* **17** (*also intr*) to rig (a sail) or (of a sail) to be rigged so as to catch the wind. **18** (*intr*) (of the sun, moon, etc.) to disappear beneath the horizon. **19** to leave (dough, etc.) in one place so that it may prove. **20** to sink (the head of a nail) below the surface surrounding it by using a nail set. **21** *Computing.* to give (a binary circuit) the value 1. **22** (of plants) to produce (fruits, seeds, etc.) after pollination or (of fruits or seeds) to develop after pollination. **23** to plant (seeds, seedlings, etc.). **24** to place (a hen) on (eggs) for the purpose of incubation. **25** (*intr*) (of a gun dog) to turn in the direction of game. **26** *Bridge.* to defeat (one's opponents) in their attempt to make a contract. **27** a dialect word for **sit.** ◆ *n* **28** the act of setting or the state of being set. **29** a condition of firmness or hardness. **30** bearing, carriage, or posture: *the set of a gun dog when pointing.* **31** the scenery and other props used in a dramatic production, film, etc. **32** Also called: **set width.** *Printing.* **32a** the width of the body of a piece of type. **32b** the width of the lines of type in a page or column. **33** *Psychol.* a temporary bias disposing an organism to react to a stimulus in one way rather than in others. **34** a seedling, cutting, or similar part that is ready for planting: *onion sets.* **35** a variant spelling of **sett.** ◆ *adj* **36** fixed or established by authority or agreement: *set hours of work.* **37** (*usually postpositive*) rigid or inflexible: *she is set in her ways.* **38** unmoving; fixed: *a set expression on his face.* **39** conventional, artificial, or stereotyped: *she made her apology in set phrases.* **40** (*postpositive;* foll. by *on* or *upon*) resolute in intention: *he is set upon marrying.* **41** (of a book, etc.) prescribed for students' preparation for an examination. ◆ See also **set about, set against,** etc. [OE *settan,* causative of *sittan* to SIT]

set^{2} Ⓣ (sɛt) *n* **1** a number of objects or people grouped or belonging together, often having certain features or characteristics in common: *a set of coins.* **2** a group of people who associate together, etc.: *he's part of the jet set.* **3** *Maths.* a collection of numbers, objects, etc., that are treated as an entity: {3, the moon} is the set the two members of which are the number 3 and the moon. **4** any apparatus that receives or transmits television or radio signals. **5** *Tennis, squash, etc.* one of the units of a match, in tennis, one in which one player or pair of players must win at least six games: *Hingis lost the first set.* **6a** the number of couples required for a formation dance. **6b** a series of figures that make up a formation dance. **7a** a band's or performer's concert repertoire on a given occasion: *the set included no new songs.* **7b** a continuous performance: *the Who played two sets.* **8 make a dead set at. 8a** to attack by arguing or ridiculing. **8b** (of a woman) to try to gain the affections of (a man). ◆ *vb* **sets, setting, set. 9** (*intr*) (in square and country dancing) to perform a sequence of steps while facing towards another dancer. **10** (*usually tr*) to divide into sets: *in this school we set our older pupils for English.* [C14 (in the obs. sense: a religious sect): from OF *sette,* from L *secta* SECT; later sense infl. by the verb SET^{1}]

seta (ˈsiːtə) *n, pl* **setae** (-tiː). (in invertebrates and plants) any bristle or bristle-like appendage. [C18: from L]
➤**setaceous** (sɪˈteɪʃəs) *adj*

set about Ⓣ *vb* (*intr, prep*) **1** to start or begin. **2** to attack physically or verbally.

set against Ⓣ *vb* (*tr, prep*) **1** to balance or compare. **2** to cause to be unfriendly to.

set aside Ⓣ *vb* (*tr, adv*) **1** to reserve for a special purpose. **2** to discard or quash. ◆ *n* **set-aside. 3a** (in the European Union) a scheme in which a proportion of farmland is taken out of production in order to reduce surpluses or maintain or increase prices of a specific crop. **3b** (*as modifier*): *set-aside land.*

set back Ⓣ *vb* (*tr, adv*) **1** to hinder; impede. **2** *Inf.* to cost (a person) a specified amount. ◆ *n* **setback. 3** anything that serves to hinder or impede. **4** a recession in the upper part of a high building. **5** a steplike shelf where a wall is reduced in thickness.

set down *vb* (*tr, adv*) **1** to record. **2** to judge or regard: *he set him down as an idiot.* **3** (foll. by *to*) to attribute: *his attitude was set down to his illness.* **4** to rebuke. **5** to snub. **6** *Brit.* to allow (passengers) to alight from a bus, etc.

set forth *vb* (*adv*) *Formal or arch.* **1** (*tr*) to state, express, or utter. **2** (*intr*) to start out on a journey.

SETI (ˈsɛtɪ) *n acronym for* Search for Extraterrestrial Intelligence; a scientific programme attempting, by radio transmissions, to make contact with beings from other planets.

setiferous (sɪˈtɪfərəs) *or* **setigerous** (sɪˈtɪdʒərəs) *adj Biol.* bearing bristles. [C19: see SETA, -FEROUS, -GEROUS]

set in *vb* (*intr, adv*) **1** to become established: *the winter has set in.* **2** (of wind) to blow or (of current) to move towards shore. ◆ *adj* **set-in. 3** (of a part) made separately and then added to a larger whole: *a set-in sleeve.*

setline (ˈsɛtˌlaɪn) *n* any of various types of fishing line that consist of a long suspended line having shorter hooked and baited lines attached.

set off Ⓣ *vb* (*adv*) **1** (*intr*) to embark on a journey. **2** (*tr*) to cause (a person) to act or do something, such as laugh. **3** (*tr*) to cause to explode. **4** (*tr*) to act as a foil or contrast to: *that brooch sets your dress off well.* **5** (*tr*) *Accounting.* to cancel a credit on (one account) against a debit on another. ◆ *n* **setoff. 6** anything that serves as a counterbalance. **7** anything that serves to contrast with or enhance something else; foil. **8** a cross claim brought by a debtor that partly offsets the creditor's claim.

set-off *n Printing.* a fault in which ink is transferred from a heavily inked or undried printed sheet to the sheet next to it in a pile.

set on Ⓣ *vb* **1** (*prep*) Also: **set upon.** to attack or cause to attack: *they set the dogs on him.* **2** (*tr, adv*) to instigate or incite; urge.

setose (ˈsiːtəʊs) *adj Biol.* covered with setae; bristly. [C17: from L *saetōsus,* from *saeta* a bristle]

set out Ⓣ *vb* (*adv, mainly tr*) **1** to present, arrange, or display. **2** to give a full account of: *he set out the matter in full.* **3** to plan or lay out (a garden, etc.). **4** (*intr*) to begin or embark on an undertaking, esp. a journey.

set piece *n* **1** a work of literature, music, etc., often having a conventional or prescribed theme, intended to create an impressive effect. **2** a display of fireworks. **3** *Sport.* a rehearsed team manoeuvre usually attempted at a restart of play.

setscrew (ˈsɛtˌskruː) *n* a screw that fits into the boss or hub of a wheel, coupling, cam, etc., and prevents motion of the part relative to the shaft on which it is mounted.

set square *n* a thin flat piece of plastic, metal, etc., in the shape of a right-angled triangle, used in technical drawing.

sett *or* **set** (sɛt) *n* **1** a small rectangular paving block made of stone. **2** the burrow of a badger. **3a** a square in a pattern of tartan. **3b** the pattern itself. [C19: var. of SET^{1} (n)]

settee (sɛˈtiː) *n* a seat, for two or more people, with a back and usually with arms. [C18: changed from SETTLE^{2}]

setter (ˈsɛtə) *n* any of various breeds of large long-haired gun dog trained to point out game by standing rigid.

set theory *n Maths.* the branch of mathematics concerned with the properties and interrelationships of sets.

setting Ⓣ (ˈsɛtɪŋ) *n* **1** the surroundings in which something is set. **2** the scenery, properties, or background used to create the location for a stage play, film, etc. **3** *Music.* a composition consisting of a certain text and music arranged for it. **4** the metal mounting and surround of a gem. **5** the tableware, cutlery, etc., for a single place at table. **6** any of a set of points on a scale or dial that can be selected to control the speed, temperature, etc., at which a machine operates.

settle^{1} Ⓣ (ˈsɛt^{ə}l) *vb* **settles, settling, settled. 1** (*tr*) to put in order: *he settled his affairs before he died.* **2** to arrange or be arranged in a fixed or comfortable position: *he settled himself by the fire.* **3** (*intr*) to come to rest or a halt: *a bird settled on the hedge.* **4** to take up or cause to take up resi-

THESAURUS

Antonyms *adj* ≠ **inflexible:** flexible, free, open, open-minded, undecided

set^{2} *n* **1** = **series,** assemblage, assortment, batch, collection, compendium, coordinated group, kit, outfit **2** = **group,** band, circle, class, clique, company, coterie, crew (*inf.*), crowd, faction, gang, outfit, posse (*inf.*), schism, sect

set about *vb* **1** = **begin,** address oneself to, attack, get cracking (*inf.*), get down to, get to work, make a start on, put one's shoulder to the wheel (*inf.*), roll up one's sleeves, sail into (*inf.*), set to, start, tackle, take the first step, wade into **2** = **assault,** assail, attack, belabour, lambast(e), mug (*inf.*), sail into (*inf.*)

set against *vb* **1** = **balance,** compare, contrast, juxtapose, weigh **2** = **alienate,** disunite, divide, drive a wedge between, estrange, make bad blood, make mischief, oppose, set at cross purposes, set at odds, sow dissension

set aside *vb* **1** = **reserve,** earmark, keep, keep back, put on one side, save, select, separate, set apart, single out **2** = **reject,** abrogate, annul, cancel, discard, dismiss, nullify, overrule, overturn, quash, render null and void, repudiate, reverse

set back *vb* **1** = **hold up,** delay, hinder, impede, retard, slow ◆ *n* **setback 3** = **hold-up,** bit of trouble, blow, bummer, check, defeat, disappointment, hitch, misfortune, rebuff, reverse, upset, whammy (*inf., chiefly US*)

set off *vb* **1** = **leave,** depart, embark, sally forth, set out, start out **3** = **detonate,** explode, ignite, kick-start, light, set in motion, touch off, trigger (off) **4** = **enhance,** bring out the highlights in, show off, throw into relief

set on *vb* **1** = **attack,** ambush, assail, assault, beat up, fall upon, fly at, go for, lay into (*inf.*), let fly at, mug (*inf.*), pitch into (*inf.*), pounce on, put the boot in (*sl.*), sail into (*inf.*), set about, sic, turn on, work over (*sl.*)

set out *vb* **1** = **arrange,** array, display, dispose, exhibit, expose to view, lay out, present, set forth **2** = **explain,** describe, detail, elaborate, elucidate **4** = **embark,** begin, get under way, hit the road (*sl.*), sally forth, set off, start out, take to the road

setting *n* **1, 2** = **surroundings,** backdrop, background, context, frame, locale, location, *mise en scène,* perspective, scene, scenery, set, site, surround

settle^{1} *vb* **1** = **put in order,** adjust, dispose, order, regulate, set to rights, straighten out, work out **2** = **make oneself comfortable,** bed down **3** = **land,** alight, come to rest, descend, light **4** = **move to,** dwell, inhabit, live, make one's home, put down roots, reside, set up home, take up residence **6** = **colonize,** found, people, pioneer, plant, populate **7** = **calm,** allay, compose, lull, pacify, quell, quiet, quieten, reassure, relax, relieve, sedate, soothe, tranquillize **9** = **subside,** decline, fall, sink **10** = **pay,** acquit oneself of,

dence: *the family settled in the country.* **5** to establish or become established in a way of life, job, etc. **6** (*tr*) to migrate to and form a community; colonize. **7** to make or become quiet, calm, or stable. **8** to cause (sediment) to sink to the bottom, as in a liquid, or (of sediment) to sink thus. **9** to subside or cause to subside: *the dust settled.* **10** (sometimes foll. by *up*) to pay off or account for (a bill, debt, etc.). **11** (*tr*) to decide or dispose of: *to settle an argument.* **12** (*intr;* often foll. by *on* or *upon*) to agree or fix: *to settle upon a plan.* **13** (*tr;* usually foll. by *on* or *upon*) to secure (title, property, etc.) to a person: *he settled his property on his wife.* **14** to determine (a legal dispute, etc.) by agreement of the parties without resort to court action (esp. in **settle out of court**). [OE *setlan*]
▸**'settleable** *adj*

settle[2] ('setəl) *n* a seat, for two or more people, usually made of wood with a high back and arms, and sometimes having a storage space in the boxlike seat. [OE *setl*]

settle down *vb* (*adv, mainly intr*) **1** (*also tr*) to make or become quiet and orderly. **2** (often foll. by *to*) to apply oneself diligently: *please settle down to work.* **3** to adopt an orderly and routine way of life, esp. after marriage.

settle for *vb* (*intr, prep*) to accept or agree to in spite of dispute or dissatisfaction.

settlement ❶ ('setəlmənt) *n* **1** the act or state of settling or being settled. **2** the establishment of a new region; colonization. **3** a place newly settled; colony. **4** a community formed by members of a group, esp. of a religious sect. **5** a public building used to provide educational and general welfare facilities for persons living in deprived areas. **6** a subsidence of all or part of a structure. **7a** the payment of an outstanding account, invoice, charge, etc. **7b** (*as modifier*): *settlement day.* **8** an agreement reached in matters of finance, business, etc. **9** *Law.* **9a** a conveyance, usually to trustees, of property to be enjoyed by several persons in succession. **9b** the deed conveying such property.

settler ❶ ('setlə) *n* a person who settles in a new country or a colony.

settlings ('setlɪŋz) *pl n* any matter that has settled at the bottom of a liquid.

set to *vb* (*intr, adv*) **1** to begin working. **2** to start fighting. ◆ *n* **set-to. 3** *Inf.* a brief disagreement or fight.

set-top box *n* a device which converts the signals from a digital television broadcast into a form which can be viewed on a standard analogue television set.

set up ❶ *vb* (*adv, mainly tr*) **1** (*also intr*) to put into a position of power, etc. **2** (*also intr*) to begin or enable (someone) to begin (a new venture), as by acquiring or providing means, etc. **3** to build or construct: *to set up a shed.* **4** to raise or produce: *to set up a wail.* **5** to advance or propose: *to set up a theory.* **6** to restore the health of: *the sea air will set you up again.* **7** to establish (a record). **8** *Inf.* to cause (a person) to be blamed, accused, etc. ◆ *n* **setup. 9** *Inf.* the way in which anything is organized or arranged. **10** *Sl.* an event the result of which is prearranged: *it's a setup.* **11** a prepared arrangement of materials, machines, etc., for a job or undertaking. ◆ *adj* **set-up. 12** physically well-built.

seven ('sevən) *n* **1** the cardinal number that is the sum of six and one and is a prime number. **2** a numeral, 7, VII, etc., representing this number. **3** the amount or quantity that is one greater than six. **4** anything representing, represented by, or consisting of seven units, such as a playing card with seven symbols on it. **5** Also called: **seven o'clock.** seven hours after noon or midnight. ◆ *determiner* **6a** amounting to seven: *seven swans a-swimming.* **6b** (*as pron*): *you've eaten seven already.* ◆ See also **sevens.** [OE *seofon*]

seven deadly sins *pl n* a fuller name for the **deadly sins.**

sevenfold ('sevən,fəʊld) *adj* **1** equal to or having seven times as many or as much. **2** composed of seven parts. ◆ *adv* **3** by or up to seven times as many or as much.

sevens ('sevənz) *n* (*functioning as sing*) a rugby union match or competition played with seven players on each side.

seven seas *pl n* the oceans of the world considered as the N and S Pacific, the N and S Atlantic, and the Arctic, Antarctic, and Indian Oceans.

seven-segment display *n* an arrangement of seven bars forming a square figure of eight, used in electronic displays of alphanumeric characters: any letter or figure can be represented by illuminating selected bars.

seventeen ('sevən'ti:n) *n* **1** the cardinal number that is the sum of ten and seven and is a prime number. **2** a numeral, 17, XVII, etc., representing this number. **3** the amount or quantity that is seven more than ten. **4** something represented by, representing, or consisting of 17 units. ◆ *determiner* **5a** amounting to seventeen: *seventeen attempts.* **5b** (*as pron*): *seventeen were sold.* [OE *seofontīene*]
▸**'seven'teenth** *adj, n*

seventh ('sevənθ) *adj* **1** (*usually prenominal*) **1a** coming after the sixth and before the eighth in numbering, position, etc.; being the ordinal number of *seven:* often written 7th. **1b** (*as n*): *she left on the seventh.* ◆ *n* **2a** one of seven equal parts of an object, quantity, measurement, etc. **2b** (*as modifier*): *a seventh part.* **3** the fraction equal to one divided by seven (1/7). **4** *Music.* **4a** the interval between one note and another seven notes away from it in a diatonic scale. **4b** one of two notes constituting such an interval in relation to the other. ◆ *adv* **5** Also: **seventhly.** after the sixth person, event, etc.

Seventh-Day Adventist *n* a member of that branch of the Adventists which constituted itself as a separate body after the expected Second Coming of Christ failed to be realized in 1844. They believe that Christ's coming is imminent and observe Saturday instead of Sunday as their Sabbath.

seventh heaven *n* **1** the final state of eternal bliss. **2** a state of supreme happiness.

seventy ('sevəntɪ) *n, pl* **seventies. 1** the cardinal number that is the product of ten and seven. **2** a numeral, 70, LXX, etc., representing this number. **3** (*pl*) the numbers 70–79, esp. the 70th to the 79th year of a person's life or of a particular century. **4** the amount or quantity that is seven times as big as ten. **5** something represented by, representing, or consisting of 70 units. ◆ *determiner* **6a** amounting to seventy: *the seventy varieties of fabric.* **6b** (*as pron*): *to invite seventy to the wedding.* [OE *seofontig*]
▸**'seventieth** *adj, n*

Seven Wonders of the World *pl n* the seven structures considered by ancient and medieval scholars to be the most wondrous of the ancient world. The list varies, but generally consists of the Pyramids of Egypt, the Hanging Gardens of Babylon, Phidias' statue of Zeus at Olympia, the temple of Artemis at Ephesus, the mausoleum of Halicarnassus, the Colossus of Rhodes, and the Pharos (or lighthouse) of Alexandria.

Seven Years' War *n* the war (1756–63) of Britain and Prussia, who emerged in the ascendant, against France and Austria, resulting from commercial and colonial rivalry between Britain and France and from the conflict in Germany between Prussia and Austria.

sever ❶ ('sevə) *vb* **1** to put or be put apart. **2** to divide or be divided into parts. **3** (*tr*) to break off or dissolve (a tie, relationship, etc.). [C14 *severen,* from OF, from L *sēparāre* to SEPARATE]
▸**'severable** *adj*

several ❶ ('sevrəl) *determiner* **1a** more than a few: *several people objected.* **1b** (*as pronoun; functioning as pl*): *several of them know.* ◆ *adj* **2** (*prenominal*) various; separate: *the members with their several occupations.* **3** (*prenominal*) distinct; different: *three several times.* **4** *Law.* capable of being dealt with separately. [C15: via Anglo-F from Med. L *sēparālis,* from L *sēpār,* from *sēparāre* to SEPARATE]

severally ('sevrəlɪ) *adv* **1** separately or distinctly. **2** each in turn.

severalty ('sevrəltɪ) *n, pl* **severalties. 1** the state of being several or separate. **2** (usually preceded by *in*) *Property law.* the tenure of property, esp. land, in a person's own right.

severance ('sevərəns) *n* **1** the act of severing or state of being severed. **2** a separation. **3** *Law.* the division into separate parts of a joint estate, contract, etc.

severance pay *n* compensation paid by a firm to employees for loss of employment.

severe ❶ (sɪ'vɪə) *adj* **1** rigorous or harsh in the treatment of others: *a severe parent.* **2** serious in appearance or manner. **3** critical or dangerous: *a severe illness.* **4** causing discomfort by its harshness: *severe weather.* **5**

THESAURUS

clear, discharge, liquidate, quit, square (up) **11** = **resolve**, clear up, complete, conclude, decide, dispose of, put an end to, reconcile **12** *often with* **on** *or* **upon** = **decide**, agree, appoint, arrange, choose, come to an agreement, confirm, determine, establish, fix
Antonyms *vb* ≠ **calm:** agitate, bother, discompose, disquieten, disturb, rattle, trouble, unsettle, upset

settlement *n* **1** = **agreement**, adjustment, arrangement, completion, conclusion, confirmation, disposition, establishment, resolution, termination, working out **2** = **agreement**, colonization, peopling **3** = **colony**, community, encampment, hamlet, outpost **7** = **payment**, clearance, clearing, defrayal, discharge, liquidation, satisfaction

settler *n* = **colonist**, colonizer, frontiersman, immigrant, pioneer, planter

set up *vb* **2** = **establish**, arrange, begin, compose, found, initiate, install, institute, make provision for, organize, prearrange, prepare **3** = **build**, assemble, construct, elevate, erect, put together, put up, raise ◆ *n* **setup 9** = **arrangement**, circumstances, conditions, organization, regime, structure, system

sever *vb* **1, 2** = **cut**, bisect, cleave, cut in two, detach, disconnect, disjoin, disunite, divide, part, rend, separate, split, sunder **3** = **discontinue**, abandon, break off, dissociate, dissolve, put an end to, terminate
Antonyms *vb* ≠ **cut:** attach, connect, fix together, join, link, unite ≠ **discontinue:** continue, maintain, uphold

several *adj* **2** = **various**, assorted, different, disparate, divers (*arch.*), diverse, indefinite, manifold, many, sundry **3** = **different**, distinct, individual, particular, respective, single

severe *adj* **1** = **strict**, austere, cruel, Draconian, drastic, hard, harsh, inexorable, iron-handed, oppressive, pitiless, relentless, rigid, unbending, unrelenting **2** = **grim**, cold, disapproving, dour, flinty, forbidding, grave, serious, sober, stern, strait-laced, tight-lipped, unsmiling **3** = **critical**, acute, dangerous, distressing **4** = **intense**, bitter, extreme, fierce, grinding, inclement, violent **5** = **plain**, ascetic, austere, chaste, classic, functional, restrained, simple, Spartan, unadorned, unembellished, unfussy **6** = **tough**, arduous, demanding, difficult, exacting, fierce, hard, punishing, rigorous, stringent, taxing, unrelenting
Antonyms *adj* ≠ **strict:** easy, lax, lenient, relaxed, tractable ≠ **grim:** affable, genial ≠ **intense:** gentle, mild, minor, moderate, temperate ≠ **plain:** embellished, fancy, ornamental, ornate ≠ **tough:** easy, manageable

strictly restrained in appearance: *a severe way of dressing.* **6** hard to perform or accomplish: *a severe test.* [C16: from L *sevērus*]
▸**se'verely** *adv* ▸**severity** (sɪ'verɪtɪ) *n*

Seville orange *n* **1** an orange tree of tropical and semitropical regions: grown for its bitter fruit, which is used to make marmalade. **2** the fruit of this tree. [C16: after *Seville* in Spain]

Sèvres (*French* sɛvrə) *n* porcelain ware manufactured at Sèvres, near Paris, from 1756, characterized by the use of clear colours and elaborate decorative detail.

sew (səʊ) *vb* **sews, sewing, sewed; sewn** *or* **sewed. 1** to join or decorate (pieces of fabric, etc.) by means of a thread repeatedly passed through with a needle. **2** (*tr; often foll. by on or up*) to attach, fasten, or close by sewing. **3** (*tr*) to make (a garment, etc.) by sewing. ◆ See also **sew up.** [OE *sēowan*]

sewage ('suːɪdʒ) *n* waste matter from domestic or industrial establishments that is carried away in sewers or drains. [C19: back formation from SEWER[1]]

sewage farm *n* a place where sewage is treated, esp. for use as manure.

sewer[1] (sʊə) *n* **1** a drain or pipe, esp. one that is underground, used to carry away surface water or sewage. ◆ *vb* **2** (*tr*) to provide with sewers. [C15: from OF, from *essever* to drain, from Vulgar L *exaquāre* (unattested), from L EX-[1] + *aqua* water]

sewer[2] ('səʊə) *n* a person or thing that sews.

sewerage ('sʊərɪdʒ) *n* **1** an arrangement of sewers. **2** the removal of surface water or sewage by means of sewers. **3** another word for **sewage.**

sewing ('səʊɪŋ) *n* **a** a piece of cloth, etc., that is sewn or to be sewn. **b** (*as modifier*): *sewing basket.*

sewing machine *n* any machine designed to sew material. It is now usually driven by electric motor but is sometimes operated by a foot treadle or by hand.

sewn (səʊn) *vb* a past participle of **sew.**

sew up *vb* (*tr, adv*) **1** to fasten or mend completely by sewing. **2** *US.* to acquire sole use or control of. **3** *Inf.* to complete or negotiate successfully: *to sew up a deal.*

sex ❶ (sɛks) *n* **1** the sum of the characteristics that distinguish organisms on the basis of their reproductive function. **2** either of the two categories, male or female, into which organisms are placed on this basis. **3** short for **sexual intercourse. 4** feelings or behaviour resulting from the urge to gratify the sexual instinct. **5** sexual matters in general. ◆ *modifier.* **6** of or concerning sexual matters: *sex education.* **7** based on or arising from the difference between the sexes: *sex discrimination.* ◆ *vb* **8** (*tr*) to ascertain the sex of. [C14: from L *sexus*]

sex- *combining form.* six: *sexcentenary.* [from L]

sexagenarian (ˌsɛksədʒɪ'nɛərɪən) *n* **1** a person from 60 to 69 years old. ◆ *adj* **2** being from 60 to 69 years old. **3** of or relating to a sexagenarian. [C18: from L, from *sexāgēnī* sixty each, from *sexāgintā* sixty]

Sexagesima (ˌsɛksə'dʒɛsɪmə) *n* the second Sunday before Lent. [C16: from L: sixtieth, from *sexāgintā* sixty]

sexagesimal (ˌsɛksə'dʒɛsɪməl) *adj* **1** relating to or based on the number 60: *sexagesimal measurement of angles.* ◆ *n* **2** a fraction in which the denominator is some power of 60.

sex-and-shopping *adj* (*prenominal*) (of a novel) belonging to a genre of novel in which the central character, a woman, has a number of sexual encounters, and the author mentions the name of many upmarket products.

sex appeal ❶ *n* the quality or power of attracting the opposite sex.

sexcentenary (ˌsɛksɛn'tiːnərɪ) *adj* **1** of or relating to 600 or a period of 600 years. **2** of or celebrating a 600th anniversary. ◆ *n, pl* **sexcentenaries. 3** a 600th anniversary or its celebration. [C18: from L *sexcentēnī* six hundred each]

sex chromosome *n* either of the chromosomes determining the sex of animals.

sexed (sɛkst) *adj* **1** (*in combination*) having a specified degree of sexuality: *undersexed.* **2** of, relating to, or having sexual differentiation.

sex hormone *n* an animal hormone affecting development and growth of reproductive organs and related parts.

sexism ('sɛksɪzəm) *n* discrimination on the basis of sex, esp. the oppression of women by men.
▸**'sexist** *n, adj*

sexless ❶ ('sɛkslɪs) *adj* **1** having or showing no sexual differentiation. **2** having no sexual desires. **3** sexually unattractive.

sex linkage *n Genetics.* the condition in which a gene is located on a sex chromosome so that the character controlled by the gene is associated with either of the sexes.
▸**'sex-ˌlinked** *adj*

sex object *n* someone, esp. a woman, regarded only from the point of view of someone else's sexual desires.

sexology (sɛk'sɒlədʒɪ) *n* the study of sexual behaviour in human beings.
▸**sex'ologist** *n* ▸**sexological** (ˌsɛksə'lɒdʒɪkᵊl) *adj*

sexpartite (sɛks'pɑːtaɪt) *adj* **1** (esp. of vaults, arches, etc.) divided into or composed of six parts. **2** involving six participants.

sex shop *n* a shop selling aids to sexual activity, pornographic material, etc.

sext (sɛkst) *n Chiefly RC Church.* the fourth of the seven canonical hours of the divine office or the prayers prescribed for it. [C15: from Church L *sexta hōra* the sixth hour]

sextan ('sɛkstən) *adj* (of a fever) marked by paroxysms that recur every fifth day. [C17: from Med. L *sextana* (*febris*) (fever) of the sixth (day)]

sextant ('sɛkstənt) *n* **1** an instrument used in navigation and consisting of a telescope through which a sighting of a heavenly body is taken, with protractors for determining its angular distance above the horizon. **2** a sixth part of a circle. [C17: from L *sextāns* one sixth of a unit]

sextet *or* **sextette** (sɛks'tɛt) *n* **1** *Music.* a group of six singers or instrumentalists or a piece of music composed for such a group. **2** a group of six people or things. [C19: var. of SESTET]

sextillion (sɛks'tɪljən) *n, pl* **sextillions** *or* **sextillion. 1** (in Britain, France, and Germany) the number represented as one followed by 36 zeros (10^{36}). **2** (in the US and Canada) the number represented as one followed by 21 zeros (10^{21}). [C17: from F, from SEX- + *-illion,* on the model of SEPTILLION]

sexton ('sɛkstən) *n* a person employed to act as caretaker of a church and often also as a bell-ringer, grave-digger, etc. [C14: from OF, from Med. L *sacristānus* SACRISTAN]

sextuple ('sɛkstjʊpᵊl) *n* **1** a quantity or number six times as great as another. ◆ *adj* **2** six times as much or as many. **3** consisting of six parts or members. [C17: L *sextus* sixth + *-uple,* as in QUADRUPLE]

sextuplet ('sɛkstjʊplɪt) *n* **1** one of six offspring at one birth. **2** a group of six. **3** *Music.* a group of six notes played in a time value of four.

sexual ❶ ('sɛksjʊəl) *adj* **1** of or characterized by sex. **2** (of reproduction) characterized by the union of male and female gametes. Cf. **asexual** (sense 2). [C17: from LL *sexuālis*]
▸**sexuality** (ˌsɛksjʊ'ælɪtɪ) *n* ▸**'sexually** *adv*

sexual harassment *n* the persistent unwelcome directing of sexual remarks and looks, and unnecessary physical contact, at a person, usually a woman, esp. in the work place.

sexual intercourse ❶ *n* the sexual act in which the male's erect penis is inserted into the female's vagina; copulation; coitus.

sexually transmitted disease *n* any of various diseases, such as syphilis or gonorrhoea, transmitted by sexual intercourse. Also called: **venereal disease.**

sexual selection *n* an evolutionary process in animals, in which selection by females of males with certain characters results in the preservation of these characters in the species.

sexy ❶ ('sɛksɪ) *adj* **sexier, sexiest.** *Inf.* **1** provoking or intended to provoke sexual interest: *a sexy dress.* **2** feeling sexual interest; aroused. **3** interesting, exciting, or trendy: *a sexy project; a sexy new car.*
▸**'sexily** *adv* ▸**'sexiness** *n*

sf *or* **sfz** *Music. abbrev. for* sforzando.

SF *or* **sf** *abbrev. for* science fiction.

SFA *abbrev. for:* **1** Scottish Football Association. **2** sweet Fanny Adams. See **fanny adams.**

SFO *abbrev. for* Serious Fraud Office: the department of the British government which investigates cases of serious financial fraud.

sforzando (sfɔː'tsɑːndəʊ) *or* **sforzato** (sfɔː'tsɑːtəʊ) *Music.* ◆ *adj, adv* **1** to be played with strong initial attack. Abbrevs.: **sf, sfz.** ◆ *n* **2** a symbol, mark, etc., indicating this. [C19: from It., from *sforzare* to force, from Vulgar L *fortiāre* (unattested) to FORCE]

SG *abbrev. for* solicitor general.

sgd *abbrev. for* signed.

S. Glam *abbrev. for* South Glamorgan.

SGML *abbrev. for* standard generalized mark-up language: an international standard used in publishing for defining the structure and formatting of documents.

sgraffito (sgræ'fiːtəʊ) *n, pl* **sgraffiti** (-tɪ). **1** a technique in mural or ceramic decoration in which the top layer of glaze, plaster, etc., is incised with a design to reveal parts of the ground. **2** such a decoration. [C18: from It., from *sgraffire* to scratch]

Sgt *abbrev. for* Sergeant.

sh (*spelling pron* ʃʃʃ) *interj* an exclamation to request silence or quiet.

THESAURUS

severely *adv* **1** = **strictly,** harshly, like a ton of bricks (*inf.*), rigorously, sharply, sternly, with an iron hand, with a rod of iron **3** = **seriously,** acutely, badly, critically, dangerously, extremely, gravely, hard, sorely

severity *n* **1, 2** = **strictness,** austerity, hardness, harshness, rigour, seriousness, severeness, sternness, stringency, toughness

sex *n* **2** = **gender 3** = **(sexual) intercourse,** coition, coitus, copulation, fornication, going to bed (with someone), intimacy, lovemaking, nookie (*sl.*), rumpy-pumpy (*sl.*), sexual relations, the other (*inf.*) **4, 5** = **facts of life,** desire, libido, reproduction, sexuality, the birds and the bees (*inf.*)

sex appeal *n* = **desirability,** allure, attractiveness, glamour, it (*inf.*), magnetism, oomph (*inf.*), seductiveness, sensuality, sexiness (*inf.*), voluptuousness

sexless *adj* **1** = **asexual,** androgynous, epicene, hermaphrodite, neuter, nonsexual, parthenogenetic

sexual *adj* **1** = **carnal,** coital, erotic, intimate, of the flesh, sensual, sexy **2** = **reproductive,** genital, procreative, sex, venereal

sexual intercourse *n* = **copulation,** bonking (*inf.*), carnal knowledge, coition, coitus, commerce (*arch.*), congress, consummation, coupling, intimacy, mating, nookie (*sl.*), penetration, rumpy-pumpy (*sl.*), sex (*inf.*), the other (*inf.*), union

sexuality *n* **1** = **desire,** bodily appetites, carnality, eroticism, lust, sensuality, sexiness (*inf.*), virility, voluptuousness

sexy *adj* **1** = **erotic,** arousing, beddable, bedroom, come-hither (*inf.*), cuddly, flirtatious, inviting, kissable, naughty, provocative, provoking, seductive, sensual, sensuous, slinky, suggestive, titillating, voluptuous

sh. *abbrev. for:* **1** *Stock Exchange.* share. **2** sheep. **3** *Bookbinding.* sheet.

shabby 🅣 (ˈʃæbɪ) *adj* **shabbier, shabbiest. 1** threadbare or dilapidated in appearance. **2** wearing worn and dirty clothes. **3** mean or unworthy: *shabby treatment.* **4** dirty or squalid. [C17: from OE *sceabb* scab]
▸ **ˈshabbily** *adv* ▸ **ˈshabbiness** *n*

shack 🅣 (ʃæk) *n* **1** a roughly built hut. ◆ *vb* **2** See **shack up.** [C19: ?from dialect *shackly* ramshackle, from dialect *shack* to shake]

shackle 🅣 (ˈʃæk^{ə}l) *n* **1** (*often pl*) a metal ring or fastening, usually part of a pair used to secure a person's wrists or ankles. **2** (*often pl*) anything that confines or restricts freedom. **3** a U-shaped bracket, the open end of which is closed by a bolt (**shackle pin**), used for securing ropes, chains, etc. ◆ *vb* **shackles, shackling, shackled.** (*tr*) **4** to confine with or as if with shackles. **5** to fasten or connect with a shackle. [OE *sceacel*]
▸ **ˈshackler** *n*

shack up *vb* (*intr, adv;* usually foll. by *with*) *Sl.* to live, esp. with a lover.

shad (ʃæd) *n, pl* **shad** *or* **shads.** any of various herring-like food fishes that migrate from the sea to fresh water to spawn. [OE *sceadd*]

shaddock (ˈʃædək) *n* another name for **pomelo** (sense 1). [C17: after Captain *Shaddock,* who brought its seed from the East Indies to Jamaica in 1696]

shade 🅣 (ʃeɪd) *n* **1** relative darkness produced by the blocking out of light. **2** a place made relatively darker or cooler than other areas by the blocking of light, esp. sunlight. **3** a position of relative obscurity. **4** something used to provide a shield or protection from a direct source of light, such as a lampshade. **5** a darker area indicated in a painting, drawing, etc., by shading. **6** a colour that varies slightly from a standard colour: *a darker shade of green.* **7** a slight amount: *a shade of difference.* **8** *Literary.* a ghost. ◆ *vb* **shades, shading, shaded.** (*mainly tr*) **9** to screen or protect from heat, light, view, etc. **10** to make darker or dimmer. **11** to represent (a darker area) in (a painting, etc.), by means of hatching, etc. **12** (*also intr*) to change or cause to change slightly. **13** to lower (a price) slightly. [OE *sceadu*]
▸ **ˈshadeless** *adj*

shades (ʃeɪdz) *pl n* **1** gathering darkness at nightfall. **2** *Sl.* sunglasses. **3** (*often cap.;* preceded by *the*) a literary term for **Hades. 4** (foll. by *of*) undertones: *shades of my father!*

shading (ˈʃeɪdɪŋ) *n* the graded areas of tone, lines, dots, etc., indicating light and dark in a painting or drawing.

shadoof (ʃəˈduːf) *n* a mechanism for raising water, consisting of a pivoted pole with a bucket at one end and a counterweight at the other, esp. as used in Egypt. [C19: from Egyptian Ar.]

shadow 🅣 (ˈʃædəʊ) *n* **1** a dark image or shape cast on a surface by the interception of light rays by an opaque body. **2** an area of relative darkness. **3** the dark portions of a picture. **4** a hint or faint semblance: *beyond a shadow of a doubt.* **5** a remnant or vestige: *a shadow of one's past self.* **6** a reflection. **7** a threatening influence: *a shadow over one's happiness.* **8** a spectre. **9** an inseparable companion. **10** a person who trails another in secret, such as a detective. **11** *Med.* a dark area on an X-ray film representing an opaque structure or part. **12** (in Jungian psychology) the archetype that represents man's animal ancestors. **13** *Arch.* shelter. **14** (*modifier*) *Brit.* designating a member or members of the main opposition party in Parliament who would hold ministerial office if their party were in power: *shadow cabinet.* ◆ *vb* (*tr*) **15** to cast a shadow over. **16** to make dark or gloomy. **17** to shade from light. **18** to follow or trail secretly. **19** (often foll. by *forth*) to represent vaguely. [OE *sceadwe,* oblique case of *sceadu* shade]
▸ **ˈshadower** *n*

shadow-box *vb* (*intr*) *Boxing.* to practise blows and footwork against an imaginary opponent.
▸ **ˈshadow-ˌboxing** *n*

shadowgraph (ˈʃædəʊˌgrɑːf) *n* **1** a silhouette made by casting a shadow on a lighted surface. **2** another name for **radiograph.**

shadow play *n* a theatrical entertainment using shadows thrown by puppets or actors onto a lighted screen.

shadow price *n Econ.* the calculated price of a good or service for which no market price exists.

shadowy 🅣 (ˈʃædəʊɪ) *adj* **1** dark; shady. **2** resembling a shadow in faintness. **3** illusory or imaginary. **4** mysterious or secretive: *a shadowy underworld figure.*
▸ **ˈshadowiness** *n*

shady 🅣 (ˈʃeɪdɪ) *adj* **shadier, shadiest. 1** shaded. **2** affording or casting a shade. **3** quiet or concealed. **4** *Inf.* questionable as to honesty or legality.
▸ **ˈshadily** *adv* ▸ **ˈshadiness** *n*

SHAEF (ʃeɪf) (in WWII) *n acronym for* Supreme Headquarters Allied Expeditionary Forces.

shaft 🅣 (ʃɑːft) *n* **1** the long narrow pole that forms the body of a spear, arrow, etc. **2** something directed at a person in the manner of a missile. **3** a ray or streak, esp. of light. **4** a rod or pole forming the handle of a hammer, golf club, etc. **5** a revolving rod that transmits motion or power. **6** one of the two wooden poles by which an animal is harnessed to a vehicle. **7** *Anat.* the middle part of a long bone. **8** the middle part of a column or pier, between the base and the capital. **9** *Archit.* a column that supports a vaulting rib, sometimes one of a set. **10** a vertical passageway through a building, as for a lift. **11** a vertical passageway into a mine. **12** *Ornithol.* the central rib of a feather. **13** an archaic or literary word for **arrow.** ◆ *vb* **14** *US & Canad. sl.* to trick or cheat. [OE *sceaft*]

shag[1] (ʃæg) *n* **1** a matted tangle, esp. of hair, etc. **2** a napped fabric, usually a rough wool. **3** shredded coarse tobacco. [OE *sceacga*]

shag[2] (ʃæg) *n* another name for **green cormorant** (*Phalacrocorax aristotelis*). [C16: special use of SHAG[1], with reference to its crest]

shag[3] (ʃæg) *Brit. sl.* ◆ *vb* **shags, shagging, shagged. 1** *Taboo.* to have sexual intercourse with (a person). **2** (*tr;* often foll. by *out; usually passive*) to exhaust. ◆ *n* **3** *Taboo.* an act of sexual intercourse. [C20: from ?]

shaggy 🅣 (ˈʃægɪ) *adj* **shaggier, shaggiest. 1** having or covered with rough unkempt fur, hair, wool, etc.: *a shaggy dog.* **2** rough or unkempt.
▸ **ˈshaggily** *adv* ▸ **ˈshagginess** *n*

shaggy dog story *n Inf.* a long rambling joke ending in a deliberate anticlimax, such as a pointless punch line.

shagreen (ʃæˈgriːn) *n* **1** the rough skin of certain sharks and rays, used as an abrasive. **2** a rough grainy leather made from certain animal hides. [C17: from F *chagrin,* from Turkish *çagri* rump]

shah (ʃɑː) *n* a ruler of certain Middle Eastern countries, esp. (formerly) Iran. [C16: from Persian: king]
▸ **ˈshahdom** *n*

shake 🅣 (ʃeɪk) *vb* **shakes, shaking, shook, shaken. 1** to move or cause to move up and down or back and forth with short quick movements. **2** to sway or totter or cause to sway or totter. **3** to clasp or grasp (the hand) of (a person) in greeting, agreement, etc.: *he shook John's hand.* **4 shake hands.** to clasp hands in greeting, agreement, etc. **5 shake on it.** *Inf.* to shake hands in agreement, reconciliation, etc. **6** to bring or come to a specified condition by or as if by shaking: *he shook free and ran.* **7** (*tr*) to wave or brandish: *he shook his sword.* **8** (*tr;* often foll. by *up*) to rouse or agitate. **9** (*tr*) to shock, disturb, or upset: *he was shaken by the news.* **10** (*tr*) to undermine or weaken: *the crisis shook his faith.* **11** to mix (dice) by rattling in a cup or the hand before throwing. **12** *Austral. old-fashioned sl.* to steal. **13** (*tr*) *US & Canad. inf.* to get rid of. **14** *Music.* to perform a trill on (a note). **15 shake in one's shoes.** to tremble with fear or apprehension. **16 shake one's head.** to indicate disagreement or disapproval by moving the head from side to side. ◆ *n* **17** the act or

THESAURUS

shabby *adj* **1** = **tatty,** dilapidated, down at heel, faded, frayed, having seen better days, mean, neglected, poor, ragged, run-down, scruffy, seedy, tattered, the worse for wear, threadbare, worn, worn-out **3** = **mean,** cheap, contemptible, despicable, dirty, dishonourable, ignoble, low, low-down (*inf.*), rotten (*inf.*), scurvy, shameful, shoddy, ungentlemanly, unworthy
Antonyms *adj* ≠ **tatty:** handsome, in mint condition, neat, new, smart, well-dressed, well-kempt, well-kept, well-to-do ≠ **mean:** fair, generous, honourable, praiseworthy, worthy

shack *n* **1** = **hut,** cabin, dump (*inf.*), hovel, lean-to, shanty, shiel (*Scot.*), shieling (*Scot.*)

shackle *n* **1** *often plural* = **fetter,** bond, chain, handcuff, hobble, iron, leg-iron, manacle, rope, tether ◆ *vb* **4** = **fetter,** bind, chain, constrain, handcuff, hobble, manacle, pinion, put in irons, restrain, restrict, secure, tether, tie, trammel

shade *n* **1** = **dimness,** coolness, dusk, gloom, gloominess, obscurity, screen, semidarkness, shadiness, shadow, shadows **3 put into the shade** = **outshine,** eclipse, make pale by comparison, outclass, overshadow **4** = **screen,** blind, canopy, cover, covering, curtain, shield, veil **6** = **hue,** colour, stain, tinge, tint, tone **7** = **dash,** amount, degree, difference, gradation, graduation, hint, nuance, semblance, suggestion, suspicion, trace **8** *Literary* = **ghost,** apparition, eidolon, manes, phantom, shadow, spectre, spirit ◆ *vb* **9** = **cover,** conceal, hide, mute, obscure, protect, screen, shield, veil **10** = **darken,** cast a shadow over, cloud, dim, shadow, shut out the light

shadow *n* **1, 2** = **dimness,** cover, darkness, dusk, gathering darkness, gloaming (*Scot. or poetic*), gloom, obscurity, protection, shade, shelter **4** = **trace,** hint, suggestion, suspicion **7** = **cloud,** blight, gloom, sadness **8** = **ghost,** eidolon, image, phantom, remnant, representation, spectre, vestige ◆ *vb* **15-17** = **shade,** cast a shadow over, darken, overhang, screen, shield **18** = **follow,** dog, spy on, stalk, tail (*inf.*), trail

shadowy *adj* **1** = **dark,** crepuscular, dim, dusky, funereal, gloomy, indistinct, murky, obscure, shaded, shady, tenebrious, tenebrous **3, 4** = **vague,** dim, dreamlike, faint, ghostly, illusory, imaginary, impalpable, intangible, nebulous, obscure, phantom, spectral, undefined, unreal, unsubstantial, wraithlike

shady *adj* **1** = **shaded,** bosky (*literary*), bowery, cool, dim, leafy, shadowy, umbrageous **4** *Informal* = **crooked,** disreputable, dodgy (*Brit., Austral., & NZ inf.*), dubious, fishy (*inf.*), questionable, shifty, slippery, suspect, suspicious, unethical, unscrupulous, untrustworthy
Antonyms *adj* ≠ **shaded:** bright, exposed, open, out in the open, sunlit, sunny, unshaded ≠ **crooked:** above-board, ethical, honest, honourable, reputable, respectable, straight, trustworthy, upright

shaft *n* **1** = **handle,** pole, rod, shank, stem, upright **2** *As in* **shaft of wit** *or* **humour** = **gibe,** barb, cut, dart, sting, thrust **3** = **ray,** beam, gleam, streak

shaggy *adj* **1, 2** = **unkempt,** hairy, hirsute, long-haired, rough, tousled, unshorn
Antonyms *adj* close-cropped, crew-cut, cropped, flat-woven, neatly-trimmed, shorn, short-haired, short-piled, smooth

shake *vb* **1, 2** = **vibrate,** bump, fluctuate, jar, joggle, jolt, jounce, oscillate, quake, quiver, rock, shiver, shudder, sway, totter, tremble, waver, wobble **7** = **wave,** brandish, flourish **8** *often with* **up** = **agitate,** churn, convulse, rouse, stir **9** = **upset,** discompose, distress, disturb, frighten, intimidate, move, rattle (*inf.*), shock, unnerve **10** = **undermine,** impair, pull the rug out from under (*inf.*), weaken ◆ *n* **17, 18** = **vibration,** agitation, convulsion, disturbance, jar, jerk, jolt, jounce, pulsation, quaking, shiver, shock, shudder, trembling, tremor **20** *Informal* = **moment,** instant, jiffy (*inf.*), second, tick (*Brit. inf.*), trice

an instance of shaking. **18** a tremor or vibration. **19 the shakes.** *Inf.* a state of uncontrollable trembling or a condition that causes it, such as a fever. **20** *Inf.* a very short period of time: *in half a shake.* **21** a fissure or crack in timber or rock. **22** an instance of shaking dice before casting. **23** *Music.* another word for **trill** (sense 1). **24** an informal name for **earthquake. 25** short for **milk shake. 26 no great shakes.** *Inf.* of no great merit or value. ◆ See also **shake down, shake off, shake up.** [OE *sceacan*]
▸**'shakable** *or* **'shakeable** *adj*

shake down *vb (adv)* **1** to fall or settle or cause to fall or settle by shaking. **2** *(tr) US sl.* to extort money from, esp. by blackmail. **3** *(tr) Inf., chiefly US.* to submit (a vessel, etc.) to a shakedown test. **4** *(intr)* to go to bed, esp. to a makeshift bed. ◆ *n* **shakedown. 5** *US sl.* a swindle or act of extortion. **6** a makeshift bed, esp. of straw, blankets, etc. **7** *Inf., chiefly US.* **7a** a voyage to test the performance of a ship or aircraft or to familiarize the crew with their duties. **7b** *(as modifier): a shakedown run.*

shake off ❶ *vb (adv)* **1** to remove or be removed with or as if with a quick movement: *she shook off her depression.* **2** *(tr)* to escape from; elude: *they shook off the police.*

shaker ('ʃeɪkə) *n* **1** a person or thing that shakes. **2** a container from which a condiment is shaken. **3** a container in which the ingredients of alcoholic drinks are shaken together.

Shakers ('ʃeɪkəz) *pl n* **the.** an American millenarian sect, founded in 1747 as an offshoot of the Quakers, given to ecstatic shaking and practising common ownership of property.

Shakespearean *or* **Shakespearian** (ʃeɪk'spɪərɪən) *adj* **1** of, relating to, or characteristic of William Shakespeare (1564–1616), English dramatist and poet, or his works. ◆ *n* **2** a student of or specialist in Shakespeare's works.

Shakespearean sonnet *n* a sonnet form developed in 16th-century England and employed by Shakespeare, having the rhyme scheme a b a b c d c d e f e f g g.

shake up ❶ *vb (tr, adv)* **1** to shake in order to mix. **2** to reorganize drastically. **3** to stir. **4** to restore the shape of (a pillow, etc.). **5** *Inf.* to shock mentally or physically. ◆ *n* **shake-up. 6** *Inf.* a radical reorganization.

shako ('ʃækəʊ) *n, pl* **shakos** *or* **shakoes.** a tall usually cylindrical military headdress, having a plume and often a peak. [C19: via F from Hungarian *csákó,* from MHG *zacke* a sharp point]

shaky ❶ ('ʃeɪkɪ) *adj* **shakier, shakiest. 1** tending to shake or tremble. **2** liable to prove defective. **3** uncertain or questionable: *your arguments are very shaky.*
▸**'shakily** *adv* ▸**'shakiness** *n*

shale (ʃeɪl) *n* a dark fine-grained sedimentary rock formed by compression of successive layers of clay. [OE *scealu* shell]
▸**'shaly** *adj*

shale oil *n* an oil distilled from shales and used as fuel.

shall (ʃæl; *unstressed* ʃəl) *vb past* **should.** (takes an infinitive without *to* or an implied infinitive) used as an auxiliary: **1** (esp. with *I* or *we* as subject) to make the future tense: *we shall see you tomorrow.* Cf. **will**[1] (sense 1). **2** (with *you, he, she, it, they,* or a noun as subject) **2a** to indicate determination on the part of the speaker, as in issuing a threat: *you shall pay for this!* **2b** to indicate compulsion, now esp. in official documents. **2c** to indicate certainty or inevitability: *our day shall come.* **3** *(with any noun or pronoun as subject, esp. in conditional clauses or clauses expressing doubt)* to indicate nonspecific futurity: *I don't think I shall ever see her again.* [OE *sceal*]

> **USAGE NOTE** The usual rule given for the use of *shall* and *will* is that where the meaning is one of simple futurity, *shall* is used for the first person of the verb and *will* for the second and third: *I shall go tomorrow; they will be there now.* Where the meaning involves command, obligation, or determination, the positions are reversed: *it shall be done; I will definitely go.* However, *shall* has come to be largely neglected in favour of *will,* which has become the commonest form of the future in all three persons.

shallop ('ʃæləp) *n* a light boat used for rowing in shallow water. [C16: from F *chaloupe,* from Du. *sloep* sloop]

shallot (ʃə'lɒt) *n* **1** an alliaceous plant cultivated for its edible bulb. **2** the bulb of this plant, which divides into small sections and is used in cooking for flavouring. [C17: from OF, from *eschaloigne,* from L *Ascalōnia caepa* Ascalonian onion, from *Ascalon,* a Palestinian town]

shallow ❶ ('ʃæləʊ) *adj* **1** having little depth. **2** lacking intellectual or mental depth or subtlety. ◆ *n* **3** *(often pl)* a shallow place in a body of water. ◆ *vb* **4** to make or become shallow. [C15: rel. to OE *sceald* shallow]
▸**'shallowly** *adv* ▸**'shallowness** *n*

shalom aleichem *Hebrew.* (ʃa'lɒm a'lexɛm) *sentence substitute.* peace be to you: used by Jews as a greeting or farewell. Often shortened to **shalom.**

shalt (ʃælt) *vb Arch. or dialect.* (used with the pronoun *thou*) a singular form of the present tense (indicative mood) of **shall.**

sham ❶ (ʃæm) *n* **1** anything that is not what it appears to be. **2** something false or fictitious that purports to be genuine. **3** a person who pretends to be something other than he is. ◆ *adj* **4** counterfeit or false. ◆ *vb* **shams, shamming, shammed. 5** to assume the appearance of (something); counterfeit: *to sham illness.* [C17: ? a N English dialect var. of SHAME]

shaman ('ʃæmən) *n* **1** a priest of shamanism. **2** a medicine man of a similar religion, esp. among certain tribes of North American Indians. [C17: from Russian *shaman,* ult. from Sansk. *śrama* religious exercise]

shamanism ('ʃæmə,nɪzəm) *n* **1** the religion of certain peoples of northern Asia, based on the belief that the world is pervaded by good and evil spirits who can be influenced or controlled only by the shamans. **2** any similar religion involving forms of spiritualism.
▸**'shamanist** *n, adj*

shamateur ('ʃæmətə) *n* a sportsperson who is officially an amateur but accepts payment. [C20: from SHAM + AMATEUR]

shamble ❶ ('ʃæmbᵊl) *vb* **shambles, shambling, shambled. 1** *(intr)* to walk or move along in an awkward or unsteady way. ◆ *n* **2** an awkward or unsteady walk. [C17: from *shamble* (adj) ungainly, ?from *shamble legs* legs resembling those of a meat vendor's table; see SHAMBLES]
▸**'shambling** *adj, n*

shambles ❶ ('ʃæmbᵊlz) *n (functioning as sing or pl)* **1** a place of great disorder: *the room was a shambles after the party.* **2** a place where animals are brought to be slaughtered. **3** any place of slaughter or carnage. [C14 *shamble* table used by meat vendors, from OE *sceamel* stool, from LL *scamellum* a small bench, from L *scamnum* stool]

shambolic ❶ (ʃæm'bɒlɪk) *adj Inf.* completely disorganized; chaotic. [C20: from SHAMBLES]

shame ❶ (ʃeɪm) *n* **1** a painful emotion resulting from an awareness of having done something dishonourable, unworthy, etc. **2** capacity to feel such an emotion. **3** ignominy or disgrace. **4** a person or thing that causes this. **5** an occasion for regret, disappointment, etc.: *it's a shame you can't come with us.* **6 put to shame. 6a** to disgrace. **6b** to surpass totally. ◆ *vb* **shames, shaming, shamed.** *(tr)* **7** to cause to feel shame. **8** to bring shame on. **9** (often foll. by *into*) to compel through a sense of shame. ◆ *interj* **10** *S. African inf.* **10a** an expression of sympathy. **10b** an expression of pleasure or endearment. [OE *scamu*]
▸**'shamable** *or* **'shameable** *adj*

shamefaced ❶ ('ʃeɪm,feɪst) *adj* **1** bashful or modest. **2** showing a sense of shame. [C16: alteration of earlier *shamefast,* from OE *sceamfaest*]
▸**shamefacedly** (,ʃeɪm'feɪsɪdlɪ) *adv*

shameful ❶ ('ʃeɪmfʊl) *adj* causing or deserving shame.
▸**'shamefully** *adv* ▸**'shamefulness** *n*

THESAURUS

shake off *vb* **1, 2** = **get rid of,** dislodge, elude, get away from, get shot of *(sl.),* give the slip, leave behind, lose, rid oneself of, throw off

shake up *vb* **1** = **stir (up),** agitate, churn (up), mix **2** = **reorganize,** overturn, turn upside down **5** *Informal* = **upset,** disturb, shock, unsettle

shaky *adj* **1** = **unsteady,** all of a quiver *(inf.),* faltering, insecure, precarious, quivery, rickety, tottering, trembling, tremulous, unstable, weak, wobbly **2, 3** = **uncertain,** dubious, iffy *(inf.),* questionable, suspect, undependable, unreliable, unsound, unsupported
Antonyms *adj* ≠ **unsteady:** firm, secure, stable, steady, strong ≠ **uncertain:** dependable

shallow *adj* **2** = **superficial,** empty, flimsy, foolish, frivolous, idle, meaningless, simple, skin-deep, slight, surface, trivial ◆ *n* **3** *often plural* = **bank,** flat, sandbank, sand bar, shelf, shoal
Antonyms *adj* ≠ **superficial:** analytical, comprehensive, deep, in-depth, meaningful, penetrating, perceptive, profound, searching, serious, weighty

sham *n* **1-3** = **phoney** *or* **phony** *(inf.),* counterfeit, feint, forgery, fraud, hoax, humbug, imitation, impostor, imposture, pretence, pretender, pseud *(inf.),* wolf in sheep's clothing ◆ *adj* **4** = **false,** artificial, bogus, counterfeit, ersatz, feigned, imitation, mock, phoney *or* phony *(inf.),* pretended, pseudo *(inf.),* simulated, spurious, synthetic ◆ *vb* **5** = **fake,** affect, assume, counterfeit, feign, imitate, play possum, pretend, put on, simulate
Antonyms *n* ≠ **phoney** *or* **phony:** master, original, the genuine article, the real McCoy (*or* McKay), the real thing ◆ *adj* ≠ **false:** authentic, bona fide, genuine, legitimate, natural, real, sound, true, unfeigned, veritable

shambles *n* **1** = **chaos,** anarchy, confusion, disarray, disorder, disorganization, havoc, madhouse, mess, muddle

shambling *adj* **1** = **clumsy,** awkward, lumbering, lurching, shuffling, ungainly, unsteady

shambolic *adj Informal* = **disorganized,** anarchic, at sixes and sevens, chaotic, confused, disordered, inefficient, in total disarray, muddled, topsy-turvy, unsystematic

shame *n* **1** = **embarrassment,** abashment, chagrin, compunction, humiliation, ignominy, loss of face, mortification, shamefacedness **3** = **disgrace,** blot, contempt, degradation, derision, discredit, dishonour, disrepute, ill repute, infamy, obloquy, odium, opprobrium, reproach, scandal, skeleton in the cupboard, smear **6 put to shame** = **outdo,** disgrace, eclipse, outclass, outstrip, show up, surpass ◆ *vb* **7** = **embarrass,** abash, confound, disconcert, disgrace, humble, humiliate, mortify, reproach, ridicule, take (someone) down a peg *(inf.)* **8** = **dishonour,** blot, debase, defile, degrade, discredit, smear, stain
Antonyms *n* ≠ **embarrassment:** brass neck *(Brit. inf.),* brazenness, cheek, shamelessness, unabashedness ≠ **disgrace:** credit, distinction, esteem, glory, honour, pride, renown, self-respect ◆ *vb* ≠ **embarrass:** do credit to, make proud ≠ **dishonour:** acclaim, credit, enhance the reputation of, honour

shamefaced *adj* **1** = **shy,** bashful, blushing, diffident, hesitant, modest, shrinking, timid **2** = **embarrassed,** abashed, ashamed, chagrined, conscience-stricken, contrite, discomfited, humiliated, mortified, red-faced, remorseful, sheepish

shameful *adj* = **disgraceful,** atrocious, base, dastardly, degrading, dishonourable, ig-

shameless ❶ (ˈʃeɪmlɪs) *adj* **1** having no sense of shame. **2** without decency or modesty.
▸ **ˈshamelessly** *adv* ▸ **ˈshamelessness** *n*

shammy (ˈʃæmɪ) *n, pl* **shammies.** *Inf.* another word for **chamois** (sense 3). Also called: **shammy leather.** [C18: variant of CHAMOIS]

shampoo (ʃæmˈpuː) *n* **1** a preparation of soap or detergent to wash the hair. **2** a similar preparation for washing carpets, etc. **3** the process of shampooing. ◆ *vb* **shampoos, shampooing, shampooed.** (*tr*) **4** to wash (the hair, etc.) with such a preparation. [C18: from Hindi, from *chāmpnā* to knead]

shamrock (ˈʃæmˌrɒk) *n* a plant having leaves divided into three leaflets: the national emblem of Ireland. [C16: from Irish Gaelic *seamróg*, dim. of *seamar* clover]

shamus (ˈʃɑːməs, ˈʃeɪ-) *n, pl* **shamuses.** *US sl.* a police or private detective. [prob. from *shammes* caretaker of a synagogue, infl. by Irish *Séamas* James]

shandy (ˈʃændɪ) *n, pl* **shandies.** an alcoholic drink made of beer and ginger beer or lemonade. [C19: from ?]

shanghai (ˈʃæŋhaɪ, ʃæŋˈhaɪ) *Sl.* ◆ *vb* **shanghais, shanghaiing, shanghaied.** (*tr*) **1** to kidnap (a man or seaman) for enforced service at sea. **2** to force or trick (someone) into doing something, etc. **3** *Austral. & NZ.* to shoot with a catapult. ◆ *n* **4** *Austral. & NZ.* a catapult. [C19: from the port of *Shanghai*, in E China, from the forceful methods formerly used to collect crews for voyages to the Orient]

Shangri-la (ˌʃæŋgrɪˈlɑː) *n* a remote or imaginary utopia. [C20: from the name of an imaginary valley in the Himalayas, from *Lost Horizon* (1933), a novel by James Hilton]

shank (ʃæŋk) *n* **1** *Anat.* the shin. **2** the corresponding part of the leg in vertebrates other than man. **3** a cut of meat from the top part of an animal's shank. **4** the main part of a tool, between the working part and the handle. **5** the part of a bolt between the thread and the head. **6** the ring or stem on the back of some buttons. **7** the stem or long narrow part of a key, hook, spoon handle, nail, etc. **8** the band of a ring as distinguished from the setting. **9** the part of a shoe connecting the wide part of the sole with the heel. **10** *Printing.* the body of a piece of type. ◆ *vb* **11** (*intr*) (of fruits, roots, etc.) to show disease symptoms, esp. discoloration. **12** (*tr*) *Golf.* to mishit (the ball) with the foot of the shaft. [OE *scanca*]

shanks's pony *or US* **shanks's mare** (ˈʃæŋksɪz) *n Inf.* one's own legs as a means of transportation.

shanny (ˈʃænɪ) *n, pl* **shannies.** a European blenny of rocky coastal waters. [C19: from ?]

shan't (ʃɑːnt) *contraction of* shall not.

shantung (ˌʃænˈtʌŋ) *n* **1** a heavy silk fabric with a knobbly surface. **2** a cotton or rayon imitation of this. [C19: after province of NE China]

shanty[1] ❶ (ˈʃæntɪ) *n, pl* **shanties. 1** a ramshackle hut; crude dwelling. **2** *Austral. & NZ.* a public house, esp. an unlicensed one. [C19: from Canad. F *chantier* cabin built in a lumber camp, from OF *gantier* GANTRY]

shanty[2] (ˈʃæntɪ) *or* **chanty** *n, pl* **shanties** *or* **chanties.** a song originally sung by sailors, esp. a rhythmic one forming an accompaniment to work. [C19: from F *chanter* to sing; see CHANT]

shantytown (ˈʃæntɪˌtaʊn) *n* a town or section of a town or city inhabited by very poor people living in shanties.

shape ❶ (ʃeɪp) *n* **1** the outward form of an object defined by outline. **2** the figure or outline of the body of a person. **3** a phantom. **4** organized or definite form: *my plans are taking shape.* **5** the form that anything assumes. **6** pattern; mould. **7** condition or state of efficiency: *to be in good shape.* **8 out of shape. 8a** in bad physical condition. **8b** bent, twisted, or deformed. **9 take shape.** to assume a definite form. ◆ *vb* **shapes, shaping, shaped. 10** (when *intr*, often foll. by *into* or *up*) to receive or cause to receive shape or form. **11** (*tr*) to mould into a particular pattern or form. **12** (*tr*) to plan, devise, or prepare: *to shape a plan of action.* ◆ See also **shape up.** [OE *gesceap*, lit.: that which is created, from *scieppan* to create]
▸ **ˈshapable** *or* **ˈshapeable** *adj* ▸ **ˈshaper** *n*

SHAPE (ʃeɪp) *n acronym for* Supreme Headquarters Allied Powers Europe.

-shaped (ʃeɪpt) *adj combining form.* having the shape of: *an L-shaped room; a pear-shaped figure.*

shapeless ❶ (ˈʃeɪplɪs) *adj* **1** having no definite shape or form: *a shapeless mass.* **2** lacking a symmetrical or aesthetically pleasing shape: *a shapeless figure.*
▸ **ˈshapelessness** *n*

shapely ❶ (ˈʃeɪplɪ) *adj* **shapelier, shapeliest.** (esp. of a woman's body or legs) pleasing or attractive in shape.
▸ **ˈshapeliness** *n*

shape up ❶ *vb* (*intr, adv*) *Inf.* **1** to proceed or develop satisfactorily. **2** to develop a definite or proper form.

shard (ʃɑːd) *or* **sherd** *n* **1** a broken piece or fragment of a brittle substance, esp. of pottery. **2** *Zool.* a tough sheath, scale, or shell, esp. the elytra of a beetle. [OE *sceard*]

share[1] ❶ (ʃɛə) *n* **1** a part or portion of something owned or contributed by a person or group. **2** (*often pl*) any of the equal parts, usually of low par value, into which the capital stock of a company is divided. **3 go shares.** *Inf.* to share (something) with another or others. ◆ *vb* **shares, sharing, shared. 4** (*tr;* often foll. by *out*) to divide or apportion, esp. equally. **5** (when *intr*, often foll. by *in*) to receive or contribute a portion of: *we can share the cost of the petrol.* **6** to join with another or others in the use of (something): *can I share your umbrella?* [OE *scearu*]
▸ **ˈsharable** *or* **ˈshareable** *adj* ▸ **ˈsharer** *n*

share[2] (ʃɛə) *n* short for **ploughshare.** [OE *scear*]

sharecrop (ˈʃɛəˌkrɒp) *vb* **sharecrops, sharecropping, sharecropped.** *Chiefly US.* to cultivate (farmland) as a sharecropper.

sharecropper (ˈʃɛəˌkrɒpə) *n Chiefly US.* a farmer, esp. a tenant farmer, who pays over a proportion of a crop or crops as rent.

shared ownership *n* (in Britain) a form of house purchase whereby the purchaser buys a proportion of the dwelling, usually from a local authority or housing association, and rents the rest.

share-farmer *n Chiefly Austral.* a farmer who pays a fee to another in return for use of land to raise crops, etc.

shareholder (ˈʃɛəˌhəʊldə) *n* the owner of one or more shares in a company.

share index *n* an index showing the movement of share prices. See **FT Index.**

share-milker *n* (in New Zealand) a person who lives on a dairy farm and milks the farmer's herd in return for an agreed share of the profits.

share option *n* a scheme giving employees an option to buy shares in the company for which they work at a favourable price or discount.

share premium *n Brit.* the excess of the amount actually subscribed for an issue of corporate capital over its par value.

share shop *n* a stockbroker, bank, or other financial intermediary that handles the buying and selling of shares for members of the public, esp. during a privatization issue.

shareware (ˈʃɛəˌwɛə) *n Computing.* software available to all users without the need for a licence and for which a token fee is requested.

sharia *or* **sheria** (ʃəˈriːə) *n* the body of doctrines that regulate the lives of those who profess Islam. [Ar.]

sharif (ʃæˈriːf) *n* a variant transliteration of **sherif.**

shark[1] (ʃɑːk) *n* any of various usually ferocious fishes, with a long body, two dorsal fins, and rows of sharp teeth. [C16: from ?]
▸ **ˈsharkˌlike** *adj*

shark[2] (ʃɑːk) *n* a person who preys on or victimizes others, esp. by swindling or extortion. [C18: prob. from G *Schurke* rogue]

shark repellent *pl n* **1** any of various substances used by divers to deter shark attack. **2** (*pl*) *Finance.* another name for **porcupine provisions.**

sharkskin (ˈʃɑːkˌskɪn) *n* a smooth glossy fabric of acetate rayon, used for sportswear, etc.

shark watcher *n Inf.* a business consultant who assists companies in identifying and preventing unwelcome takeover bids.

sharon fruit (ˈʃærən) *n* another name for **persimmon** (sense 2).

sharp ❶ (ʃɑːp) *adj* **1** having a keen edge suitable for cutting. **2** having an edge or point. **3** involving a sudden change, esp. in direction: *a sharp bend.* **4** moving, acting, or reacting quickly, etc.: *sharp reflexes.* **5** clearly defined. **6** mentally acute; keen-witted; attentive. **7** sly or artful: *sharp practice.* **8** bitter or harsh: *sharp words.* **9** shrill or penetrating:

THESAURUS

nominious, indecent, infamous, low, mean, outrageous, reprehensible, scandalous, unbecoming, unworthy, vile, wicked
Antonyms *adj* admirable, creditable, estimable, exemplary, honourable, laudable, right, worthy

shameless *adj* **2** = **brazen**, abandoned, audacious, barefaced, brash, corrupt, depraved, dissolute, flagrant, hardened, immodest, improper, impudent, incorrigible, indecent, insolent, profligate, reprobate, unabashed, unashamed, unblushing, unprincipled, wanton

shanty[1] *n* **1** = **shack**, bothy (*Scot.*), cabin, hovel, hut, lean-to, shed, shiel (*Scot.*), shieling (*Scot.*)

shape *n* **1** = **form**, build, configuration, contours, cut, figure, lines, make, outline, profile, silhouette **2** = **appearance**, aspect, form, guise, likeness, semblance **6** = **pattern**, frame, model, mould **7** = **condition**, fettle, health, kilter, state, trim ◆ *vb* **11** = **form**, create, fashion, make, model, mould, produce **12** = **develop**, accommodate, adapt, convert, define, devise, frame, guide, modify, plan, prepare, regulate, remodel

shapeless *adj* **1, 2** = **formless**, amorphous, asymmetrical, irregular, misshapen, unstructured
Antonyms *adj* well-formed, well-proportioned, well-turned

shapely *adj* = **well-formed**, comely, curvaceous, elegant, graceful, neat, sightly, trim, well-proportioned, well-turned

shape up *vb* **1** *Informal* = **progress**, be promising, come on, develop, look good, proceed, turn out

share[1] *n* **1** = **part**, allotment, allowance, contribution, cut (*inf.*), division, due, lot, portion, proportion, quota, ration, whack (*inf.*) ◆ *vb* **4** = **divide**, apportion, assign, distribute, divvy up (*inf.*), parcel out, split **5** = **go halves**, go Dutch (*inf.*), go fifty-fifty (*inf.*) **6** = **partake**, participate, receive, use in common

sharp *adj* **1** = **keen**, acute, cutting, honed, jagged, knife-edged, knifelike, pointed, razor-sharp, serrated, sharpened, spiky **3** = **sudden**, abrupt, distinct, extreme, marked **5** = **clear**, clear-cut, crisp, distinct, well-defined **6** = **quick-witted**, alert, apt, astute, bright, clever, discerning, knowing, long-headed, observant, on the ball (*inf.*), penetrating, perceptive, quick, ready, subtle **7** = **cunning**, artful, crafty, dishonest, fly (*sl.*), shrewd, sly, smart, unscrupulous, wily **8** = **cutting**, acerb, acrimonious, barbed, biting, bitter, caustic, harsh, hurtful, mordacious, mordant, sarcastic, sardonic, scathing, severe, trenchant, vitriolic **10** = **sour**, acerb, acerbic, acetic, acid, acrid, burning, hot, piquant, pungent, tart, vinegary **13** *Informal* = **stylish**, chic, classy (*sl.*), dressy, fashionable, natty (*inf.*), smart, snappy, trendy (*inf.*) ◆ *adv*

a sharp cry. **10** having an acrid taste. **11** keen; biting: *a sharp wind.* **12** *Music.* **12a** (*immediately postpositive*) denoting a note that has been raised in pitch by one chromatic semitone: *F sharp.* **12b** (of an instrument, voice, etc.) out of tune by being too high in pitch. Cf. **flat**[1] (sense 20). **13** *Inf.* **13a** stylish. **13b** too smart. **14 at the sharp end.** involved in the most competitive or difficult aspect of any activity. ◆ *adv* **15** in a sharp manner. **16** exactly: *six o'clock sharp.* **17** *Music.* **17a** higher than a standard pitch. **17b** out of tune by being too high in pitch: *she sings sharp.* Cf. **flat**[1] (sense 25). ◆ *n* **18** *Music.* **18a** an accidental that raises the pitch of a note by one chromatic semitone. Usual symbol: ♯ **18b** a note affected by this accidental. Cf. **flat**[1] (sense 31). **19** a thin needle with a sharp point. **20** *Inf.* a sharper. ◆ *vb* **21** (*tr*) *Music.* the usual US and Canad. word for **sharpen.** [OE *scearp*]
▸ **'sharply** *adv* ▸ **'sharpness** *n*

sharpbender ('ʃɑːpˌbɛndə) *n Inf.* an organization that has been underperforming its competitors but suddenly becomes more successful, often as a result of new management or changes in its business strategy. [C20: from the sharp upward bend in its sales or profits]

sharpen ❶ ('ʃɑːpᵊn) *vb* **1** to make or become sharp or sharper. **2** *Music.* to raise the pitch of (a note), esp. by one semitone.
▸ **'sharpener** *n*

sharper ('ʃɑːpə) *n* a person who cheats or swindles; fraud.

sharpish ('ʃɑːpɪʃ) *adj* **1** rather sharp. ◆ *adv* **2** *Inf.* quickly; fairly sharply: *quick sharpish.*

sharp-set *adj* **1** set to give an acute cutting angle. **2** keenly hungry. **3** keen or eager.

sharpshooter ('ʃɑːpˌʃuːtə) *n* an expert marksman.
▸ **'sharpˌshooting** *n*

sharp-tongued *adj* bitter or critical in speech; sarcastic.

sharp-witted *adj* having or showing a keen intelligence; perceptive.
▸ **ˌsharp-'wittedly** *adv* ▸ **ˌsharp-'wittedness** *n*

Shasta daisy ('ʃæstə) *n* a plant widely cultivated for its large white daisy-like flowers.

shastra ('ʃɑːstrə), **shaster** ('ʃɑːstə), *or* **sastra** ('ʃɑːstrə) *n* any of the sacred writings of Hinduism. [C17: from Sansk. *śāstra*, from *śās* to teach]

shat (ʃæt) *vb Taboo.* a past tense and past participle of **shit.**

shatter ❶ ('ʃætə) *vb* **1** to break or be broken into many small pieces. **2** (*tr*) to impair or destroy: *his nerves were shattered by the torture.* **3** (*tr*) to dumbfound or thoroughly upset: *she was shattered by the news.* **4** (*tr*) *Inf.* to cause to be tired out or exhausted. [C12: ? obscurely rel. to SCATTER]
▸ **'shattered** *adj* ▸ **'shattering** *adj* ▸ **'shatteringly** *adv*

shatterproof ('ʃætəˌpruːf) *adj* designed to resist shattering.

shave ❶ (ʃeɪv) *vb* **shaves, shaving, shaved; shaved** *or* **shaven.** (*mainly tr*) **1** (*also intr*) to remove (the beard, hair, etc.) from (the face, head, or body) by scraping the skin with a razor. **2** to cut or trim very closely. **3** to reduce to shavings. **4** to remove thin slices from (wood, etc.) with a sharp cutting tool. **5** to touch or graze in passing. **6** *Inf.* to reduce (a price) by a slight amount. ◆ *n* **7** the act or an instance of shaving. **8** any tool for scraping. **9** a thin slice or shaving. [OE *sceafan*]
▸ **'shavable** *or* **'shaveable** *adj*

shaveling ('ʃeɪvlɪŋ) *n Arch.* **1** *Derog.* a priest or clergyman with a shaven head. **2** a young fellow; youth.

shaven ('ʃeɪvᵊn) *adj* **a** closely shaved or tonsured. **b** (*in combination*): *clean-shaven.*

shaver ('ʃeɪvə) *n* **1** a person or thing that shaves. **2** Also called: **electric razor, electric shaver.** an electrically powered implement for shaving, having rotating blades behind a fine metal comb. **3** *Inf.* a youngster, esp. a young boy.

Shavian ('ʃeɪvɪən) *adj* **1** of or like George Bernard Shaw (1856–1950), Irish dramatist, his works, ideas, etc. ◆ *n* **2** an admirer of Shaw or his works.

shaving ('ʃeɪvɪŋ) *n* **1** a thin paring or slice, esp. of wood, that has been shaved from something. ◆ *modifier.* **2** used when shaving the face, etc.: *shaving cream.*

Shavuot *or* **Shabuoth** (ʃə'vuːəs, -əʊs; *Hebrew* ʃavuː'ɔt) *n* the Hebrew name for **Pentecost** (sense 2). [from Heb. *shābhū'ōth*, pl of *shābhūā'* week]

shawl (ʃɔːl) *n* a piece of fabric or knitted or crocheted material worn around the shoulders by women or wrapped around a baby. [C17: from Persian *shāl*]

shawm (ʃɔːm) *n Music.* a medieval form of the oboe with a conical bore and flaring bell. [C14 *shalmye*, from OF *chalemie*, ult. from L *calamus* a reed, from Gk *kalamos*]

shay (ʃeɪ) *n* a dialect word for **chaise.** [C18: back formation from CHAISE, mistaken for pl]

she (ʃiː) *pron* (*subjective*) **1** refers to a female person or animal: *she is a doctor.* **2** refers to things personified as feminine, such as cars, ships, and nations. **3** *Austral. & NZ.* a pronoun often used instead of *it*, as in **she'll be right** (it will be all right). ◆ *n* **4a** a female person or animal. **4b** (*in combination*): *she-cat.* [OE *sīe*, accusative of *sēo*, fem. demonstrative pron]

shea (ʃɪə) *n* **1** a tropical African tree with oily seeds. **2 shea butter.** the white butter-like fat obtained from the seeds of this plant and used as food, etc. [C18: from W African *si*]

sheading ('ʃiːdɪŋ) *n* any of the six subdivisions of the Isle of Man. [var. of *shedding*]

sheaf (ʃiːf) *n, pl* **sheaves. 1** a bundle of reaped but unthreshed corn tied with one or two bonds. **2** a bundle of objects tied together. **3** the arrows contained in a quiver. ◆ *vb* **4** (*tr*) to bind or tie into a sheaf. [OE *sceaf*]

shear (ʃɪə) *vb* **shears, shearing, sheared** *or* (*arch., Austral., & NZ*) *sometimes* **shore; sheared** *or* **shorn. 1** (*tr*) to remove (the fleece or hair) of (sheep, etc.) by cutting or clipping. **2** to cut or cut through (something) with shears or a sharp instrument. **3** *Engineering.* to cause (a part, member, etc.) to deform or fracture or (of a part, etc.) to deform or fracture as a result of excess torsion. **4** (*tr; often foll. by of*) to strip or divest: *to shear someone of his power.* **5** (when *intr*, foll. by *through*) to move through (something) by or as if by cutting. ◆ *n* **6** the act, process, or an instance of shearing. **7** a shearing of a sheep or flock of sheep: *a sheep of two shears.* **8** a form of deformation or fracture in which parallel planes in a body slide over one another. **9** *Physics.* the deformation of a body, part, etc., expressed as the lateral displacement between two points in parallel planes divided by the distance between the planes. **10** either one of the blades of a pair of shears, scissors, etc. ◆ See also **shears.** [OE *sceran*]
▸ **'shearer** *n*

shearling ('ʃɪəlɪŋ) *n* **1** a young sheep after its first shearing. **2** the skin of such an animal.

shear pin *n* an easily replaceable pin in a machine designed to break and stop the machine if the stress becomes too great.

shears (ʃɪəz) *pl n* **1a** large scissors, as for cutting cloth, jointing poultry, etc. **1b** a large scissor-like and usually hand-held cutting tool with flat blades, as for cutting hedges. **2** any of various analogous cutting implements.

shearwater ('ʃɪəˌwɔːtə) *n* any of several oceanic birds specialized for an aerial or aquatic existence.

sheatfish ('ʃiːtˌfɪʃ) *n, pl* **sheatfish** *or* **sheatfishes.** another name for **European catfish** (see **silurid** (sense 1)). [C16: var. of *sheathfish*; ? infl. by G *Schaid* sheatfish]

sheath (ʃiːθ) *n, pl* **sheaths** (ʃiːðz). **1** a case or covering for the blade of a knife, sword, etc. **2** any similar close-fitting case. **3** *Biol.* an enclosing or protective structure. **4** the protective covering on an electric cable. **5** a figure-hugging dress with a narrow tapering skirt. **6** another name for **condom.** [OE *scēath*]

sheathe (ʃiːð) *vb* **sheathes, sheathing, sheathed.** (*tr*) **1** to insert (a knife, sword, etc.) into a sheath. **2** (esp. of cats) to retract (the claws). **3** to surface with or encase in a sheath or sheathing.

sheathing ('ʃiːðɪŋ) *n* **1** any material used as an outer layer, as on a ship's hull. **2** boarding, etc., used to cover a timber frame.

sheath knife *n* a knife carried in or protected by a sheath.

sheave[1] (ʃiːv) *vb* **sheaves, sheaving, sheaved.** (*tr*) to gather or bind into sheaves.

sheave[2] (ʃiːv) *n* a wheel with a grooved rim, esp. one used as a pulley. [C14: of Gmc origin]

sheaves (ʃiːvz) *n* the plural of **sheaf.**

shebang (ʃɪ'bæŋ) *n Sl., chiefly US & Canad.* a situation or affair (esp. in **the whole shebang**). [C19: from ?]

shebeen *or* **shebean** (ʃə'biːn) *n* **1** *Irish, Scot., & S. African.* a place where alcoholic drink is sold illegally. **2** (in Ireland) alcohol, esp. home-distilled whiskey, sold without a licence. **3** (in South Africa) a place where Black African men engage in social drinking. [C18: from Irish Gaelic *sībīn* beer of poor quality]

shebeen king *or* (*fem*) **shebeen queen** *n* (in South Africa) the proprietor of a shebeen.

shed[1] ❶ (ʃɛd) *n* **1** a small building or lean-to of light construction, used for storage, shelter, etc. **2** a large roofed structure, esp. one with open sides, used for storage, repairing locomotives, etc. **3** *Austral. & NZ.* the building in which sheep are shorn. [OE *sced*; prob. var. of *scead* shelter]

shed[2] ❶ (ʃɛd) *vb* **sheds, shedding, shed.** (*mainly tr*) **1** to pour forth or cause to pour forth: *to shed tears.* **2 shed light on** *or* **upon.** to clarify (a problem,

THESAURUS

16 = promptly, exactly, on the dot, on time, precisely, punctually
Antonyms *adj* ≠ **keen:** blunt, dull, edgeless, rounded, unsharpened ≠ **sudden:** even, gentle, gradual, moderate, progressive ≠ **clear:** blurred, fuzzy, ill-defined, indistinct, unclear ≠ **quick-witted:** dim, dull-witted, dumb (*inf.*), slow, slow on the uptake, stupid ≠ **cunning:** artless, guileless, ingenuous, innocent, naive, simple, undesigning ≠ **cutting:** amicable, courteous, friendly, gentle, kindly, mild ≠ **sour:** bland, mild, tasteless ◆ *adv* ≠ **promptly:** approximately, more or less, roughly, round about, vaguely

sharpen *vb* **1 = whet,** edge, grind, hone, put an edge on, strop

shatter *vb* **1 = smash,** break, burst, crack, crush, crush to smithereens, demolish, explode, implode, pulverize, shiver, split **2 = destroy,** blast, blight, bring to nought, demolish, disable, exhaust, impair, overturn, ruin, torpedo, wreck **3 = upset,** break (someone's) heart, crush, devastate, dumbfound, knock the stuffing out of (someone)

shattered *adj* **3 = devastated,** crushed, gutted (*sl.*) **4** *Informal* **= exhausted,** all in (*sl.*), clapped out (*Austral. & NZ inf.*), dead beat (*inf.*), dead tired (*inf.*), dog-tired (*inf.*), done in (*inf.*), drained, jiggered (*inf.*), knackered (*sl.*), ready to drop, spent, tired out, weary, wiped out (*inf.*), worn out

shattering *adj* **3 = devastating,** crushing, overwhelming, paralysing, severe, stunning

shave *vb* **2 = trim,** crop, pare, plane, shear **5 = brush,** graze, touch

shed[1] *n* **1 = hut,** bothy, lean-to, lockup, outhouse, shack

shed[2] *vb* **1 = give out,** afford, cast, diffuse, drop, emit, give, pour forth, radiate, scatter, shower, spill, throw **2 shed light on** *or* **upon = explain,**

etc.). **3** to cast off or lose: *the snake shed its skin.* **4** (of a lorry) to drop (its load) on the road by accident. **5** to repel: *this coat sheds water.* **6** to separate or divide a group of sheep: *a good dog can shed his sheep in minutes.* **7** *Dialect.* to make a parting in (the hair). ◆ *n* **8** short for **watershed.** **9** the action of separating or dividing a group of sheep: *the old dog was better at the shed than the young one.* [OE *sceadan*]
▸ˈ**shedable** *or* ˈ**sheddable** *adj*

she'd (ʃiːd) *contraction of* she had *or* she would.

shedder[1] (ˈʃɛdə) *n* **1** a person or thing that sheds. **2** an animal, such as a llama, snake, or lobster, that moults.

shedder[2] (ˈʃɛdə) *n NZ.* a person who milks cows in a cow shed.

shed hand *n Chiefly Austral.* an unskilled worker in a sheepshearing shed.

shed out *vb* (*tr, adv*) *NZ.* to separate off (sheep that have lambed) and move them to better pasture.

sheen 🅣 (ʃiːn) *n* **1** a gleaming or glistening brightness; lustre. **2** *Poetic.* splendid clothing. ◆ *adj* **3** *Rare.* beautiful. [OE *sciene*]
▸ˈ**sheeny** *adj*

sheep (ʃiːp) *n, pl* **sheep.** **1** any of a genus of ruminant mammals having transversely ribbed horns and a narrow face. **2 Barbary sheep.** another name for **aoudad.** **3** a meek or timid person. **4 separate the sheep from the goats.** to pick out the members of a group who are superior in some respects. [OE *sceap*]
▸ˈ**sheep,like** *adj*

sheepcote (ˈʃiːpˌkəʊt) *n Chiefly Brit.* another word for **sheepfold.**

sheep-dip *n* **1** any of several liquid disinfectants and insecticides in which sheep are immersed. **2** a deep trough containing such a liquid.

sheepdog (ˈʃiːpˌdɒg) *n* **1** a dog used for herding sheep. **2** any of various breeds of dog reared originally for herding sheep. See **Old English sheepdog, Shetland sheepdog.**

sheepdog trial *n* (*often pl*) a competition in which sheepdogs are tested in their tasks.

sheepfold (ˈʃiːpˌfəʊld) *n* a pen or enclosure for sheep.

sheepish 🅣 (ˈʃiːpɪʃ) *adj* **1** abashed or embarrassed, esp. through looking foolish. **2** resembling a sheep in timidity.
▸ˈ**sheepishly** *adv* ▸ˈ**sheepishness** *n*

sheepo (ˈʃiːpəʊ) *n, pl* **sheepos.** *NZ.* a person employed to bring sheep to the catching pen in a shearing shed.

sheep's eyes *pl n Old-fashioned.* amorous or inviting glances.

sheepshank (ˈʃiːpˌʃæŋk) *n* a knot made in a rope to shorten it temporarily.

sheepskin (ˈʃiːpˌskɪn) *n* **a** the skin of a sheep, esp. when used for clothing, etc. **b** (*as modifier*): *a sheepskin coat.*

sheepwalk (ˈʃiːpˌwɔːk) *n Chiefly Brit.* a tract of land for grazing sheep.

sheer[1] 🅣 (ʃɪə) *adj* **1** perpendicular; very steep: *a sheer cliff.* **2** (of textiles) so fine as to be transparent. **3** (*prenominal*) absolute: *sheer folly.* **4** *Obs.* bright. ◆ *adv* **5** steeply. **6** completely or absolutely. [OE *scīr*]
▸ˈ**sheerly** *adv* ▸ˈ**sheerness** *n*

sheer[2] (ʃɪə) *vb* (foll. by *off* or *away* (*from*)). **1** to deviate or cause to deviate from a course. **2** (*intr*) to avoid an unpleasant person, thing, topic, etc. ◆ *n* **3** *Naut.* the position of a vessel relative to its mooring. [C17: ? var. of SHEAR]

sheerlegs *or* **shearlegs** (ˈʃɪəˌlɛgz) *n* (*functioning as sing*) a device for lifting weights consisting of two spars lashed together at the upper ends from which a lifting tackle is suspended. Also called: **shears.** [C19: var. of *shear legs*]

sheet[1] 🅣 (ʃiːt) *n* **1** a large rectangular piece of cloth, generally one of a pair used as inner bedclothes. **2a** a thin piece of a substance such as paper or glass, usually rectangular in form. **2b** (*as modifier*): *sheet iron.* **3** a broad continuous surface: *a sheet of water.* **4** a newspaper, esp. a tabloid. **5** a piece of printed paper to be folded into a section for a book. ◆ *vb* **6** (*tr*) to provide with, cover, or wrap in a sheet. [OE *sciete*]

sheet[2] (ʃiːt) *n Naut.* a line or rope for controlling the position of a sail relative to the wind. [OE *scēata* corner of a sail]

sheet anchor *n* **1** *Naut.* a large strong anchor for use in emergency. **2** a person or thing to be relied on in an emergency. [C17: from earlier *shute anker,* from *shoot* (obs.) the sheet of a sail]

sheet bend *n* a knot used esp. for joining ropes of different sizes.

sheeting (ˈʃiːtɪŋ) *n* fabric from which sheets are made.

sheet lightning *n* lightning that appears as a broad sheet, caused by the reflection of more distant lightning.

sheet metal *n* metal in the form of a sheet, the thickness being intermediate between that of plate and that of foil.

sheet music *n* **1** the printed or written copy of a short composition or piece. **2** music in its written or printed form.

sheikh *or* **sheik** (ʃeɪk) *n* (in Muslim countries) **a** the head of an Arab tribe, village, etc. **b** a religious leader. [C16: from Ar. *shaykh* old man]
▸ˈ**sheikhdom** *or* ˈ**sheikdom** *n*

sheila (ˈʃiːlə) *n Austral. & NZ old-fashioned.* an informal word for **girl** or **woman.** [C19: from the girl's name *Sheila*]

shekel (ˈʃɛkᵊl) *n* **1** the standard monetary unit of modern Israel, divided into 100 agorot. **2** any of several former coins and units of weight of the Near East. **3** (*often pl*) *Inf.* any coin or money. [C16: from Heb. *sheqel*]

shelduck (ˈʃɛlˌdʌk) *or* (*masc*) **sheldrake** (ˈʃɛlˌdreɪk) *n, pl* **shelducks, shelduck** *or* **sheldrakes, sheldrake.** any of various large usually brightly coloured gooselike ducks of the Old World. [C14: *shel,* prob. from dialect *sheld* pied]

shelf (ʃɛlf) *n, pl* **shelves.** **1** a thin flat plank of wood, metal, etc., fixed horizontally against a wall, etc., for the purpose of supporting objects. **2** something resembling this in shape or function. **3** the objects placed on a shelf: *a shelf of books.* **4** a projecting layer of ice, rock, etc., on land or in the sea. **5** See **off the shelf.** **6 on the shelf.** put aside or abandoned; used esp. of unmarried women considered to be past the age of marriage. [OE *scylfe* ship's deck]
▸ˈ**shelf,like** *adj*

shelf life *n* the length of time a packaged food, etc., will last without deteriorating.

shell 🅣 (ʃɛl) *n* **1** the protective outer layer of an egg, esp. a bird's egg. **2** the hard outer covering of many molluscs. **3** any other hard outer layer, such as the exoskeleton of many arthropods. **4** the hard outer layer of some fruits, esp. of nuts. **5** any hard outer case. **6** a hollow artillery projectile filled with explosive primed to explode either during flight or on impact. **7** a small-arms cartridge. **8** a pyrotechnic cartridge designed to explode in the air. **9** *Rowing.* a very light narrow racing boat. **10** the external structure of a building, esp. one that is unfinished. **11** *Physics.* **11a** a class of electron orbits in an atom in which the electrons have the same principal quantum number and little difference in their energy levels. **11b** an analogous energy state of nucleons in certain theories (**shell models**) of the structure of the atomic nucleus. **12 come** (*or* **bring**) **out of one's shell.** to become (or help to become) less shy and reserved. ◆ *vb* **13** to divest or be divested of a shell, husk, etc. **14** to separate or be separated from an ear, husk, etc. **15** (*tr*) to bombard with artillery shells. ◆ See also **shell out.** [OE *sciell*]
▸ˈ**shell-less** *adj* ▸ˈ**shell-ˌlike** *adj* ▸ˈ**shelly** *adj*

she'll (ʃiːl; *unstressed* ʃɪl) *contraction of* she will *or* she shall.

shellac (ʃəˈlæk, ˈʃɛlæk) *n* **1** a yellowish resin secreted by the lac insect, esp. a commercial preparation of this used in varnishes, polishes, etc. **2** Also called: **shellac varnish.** a varnish made by dissolving shellac in ethanol or a similar solvent. ◆ *vb* **shellacs, shellacking, shellacked.** (*tr*) **3** to coat (an article) with a shellac varnish. [C18: SHELL + LAC[1], translation of F *laque en écailles,* lit.: lac in scales, that is, in thin plates]

shellback (ˈʃɛlˌbæk) *n* an experienced or old sailor.

shell company *n Business.* **1** a near-defunct company, esp. one with a stock-exchange listing, used as a vehicle for a thriving company. **2** a company that has ceased to trade but retains its registration and is sold for a small sum to enable its new owners to avoid the cost and trouble of registering a new company.

shellfire (ˈʃɛlˌfaɪə) *n* the firing of artillery shells.

shellfish (ˈʃɛlˌfɪʃ) *n, pl* **shellfish** *or* **shellfishes.** any aquatic invertebrate having a shell or shell-like carapace, esp. such an animal used as human food. Examples are crustaceans such as crabs and lobsters and molluscs such as oysters.

shell out 🅣 *vb* (*adv*) *Inf.* to pay out or hand over (money).

shell program *n Computing.* a basic low-cost computer program that provides a framework within which the user can develop the program to suit his personal requirements.

shellproof (ˈʃɛlˌpruːf) *adj* designed, intended, or able to resist shellfire.

shell shock *n* loss of sight, etc., resulting from psychological strain during prolonged engagement in warfare.
▸ˈ**shell-ˌshocked** *adj*

shell suit *n* a lightweight tracksuit consisting of an inner cotton layer covered by a waterproof nylon layer.

Shelta (ˈʃɛltə) *n* a secret language used by some itinerant tinkers in Ireland and parts of Britain, based on Gaelic. [C19: from earlier *sheldrū,* ? an arbitrary alteration of OIrish *bēlre* speech]

shelter 🅣 (ˈʃɛltə) *n* **1** something that provides cover or protection, as from weather or danger. **2** the protection afforded by such a cover. **3** the state of being sheltered. ◆ *vb* **4** (*tr*) to provide with or protect by a

THESAURUS

clarify, clear up, elucidate, simplify **3** = **cast off**, discard, exuviate, moult, slough

sheen *n* **1** = **shine**, brightness, burnish, gleam, gloss, lustre, patina, polish, shininess

sheepish *adj* **1** = **embarrassed**, abashed, ashamed, chagrined, foolish, mortified, self-conscious, shamefaced, silly, uncomfortable
Antonyms *adj* assertive, audacious, bold, brash, brass-necked (*Brit. inf.*), brazen, confident, unabashed, unapologetic, unblushing, unembarrassed

sheer[1] *adj* **1** = **steep**, abrupt, headlong (*arch.*), perpendicular, precipitous **2** = **fine**, diaphanous, gauzy, gossamer, see-through, thin, transparent **3** = **total**, absolute, arrant, complete, downright, out-and-out, pure, rank, thoroughgoing, unadulterated, unalloyed, unmitigated, unqualified, utter
Antonyms *adj* ≠ **steep:** gentle, gradual, horizontal, slanting, sloping ≠ **fine:** coarse, heavy, impenetrable, opaque, thick ≠ **total:** moderate

sheet[1] *n* **2** = **piece**, folio, pane, panel, plate, slab **3** = **expanse**, area, blanket, covering, stretch, sweep

shell *n* **5** = **case**, carapace, husk, pod, shuck **10** = **frame**, chassis, framework, hull, skeleton, structure ◆ *vb* **13, 14** = **husk**, shuck **15** = **bomb**, attack, barrage, blitz, bombard, strafe, strike

shell out *vb* = **pay out**, ante up (*inf., chiefly US*), disburse, expend, fork out (*sl.*), give, hand over, lay out (*inf.*)

shelter *n* **1** = **protection**, awning, cover, covert, defence, guard, roof over one's head, screen, shiel (*Scot.*), umbrella **2, 3** = **safety**, asylum, haven, refuge, retreat, sanctuary, security ◆ *vb* **4** = **protect**, cover, defend, guard, harbour, hide, safeguard, shield, take in **5** = **take shelter**, hide, seek refuge

shelter. **5** (*intr*) to take cover, as from rain. **6** (*tr*) to act as a shelter for. [C16: from ?]
▸**'shelterer** *n*

sheltered ➊ ('ʃɛltəd) *adj* **1** protected from wind or weather. **2** protected from outside influences: *a sheltered upbringing.* **3** specially designed to provide a safe environment for the elderly, handicapped, or disabled: *sheltered housing.*

sheltie *or* **shelty** ('ʃɛltɪ) *n, pl* **shelties.** another name for **Shetland pony** or **Shetland sheepdog.** [C17: prob. from Orkney dialect *sjalti,* from ON *Hjalti* Shetlander, from *Hjaltland* Shetland]

shelve[1] ➊ (ʃɛlv) *vb* **shelves, shelving, shelved.** (*tr*) **1** to place on a shelf. **2** to provide with shelves. **3** to put aside or postpone from consideration. **4** to dismiss or cause to retire. [C16: from *shelves,* pl of SHELF]
▸**'shelver** *n*

shelve[2] (ʃɛlv) *vb* **shelves, shelving, shelved.** (*intr*) to slope away gradually. [C16: from ?]

shelves (ʃɛlvz) *n* the plural of **shelf.**

shelving ('ʃɛlvɪŋ) *n* **1** material for making shelves. **2** a set of shelves; shelves collectively.

shemozzle (ʃɪ'mɒzᵊl) *n Inf.* a noisy confusion or dispute; uproar. [C19: ?from Yiddish *shlimazl* misfortune]

shenanigan (ʃɪ'nænɪgən) *n Inf.* **1** (*usually pl*) roguishness; mischief. **2** an act of treachery; deception. [C19: from ?]

she-oak *n* any of various Australian trees of the genus *Casuarina.* See **casuarina.** [C18: *she* (in the sense: inferior) + OAK]

Sheol ('ʃiːəʊl, -ɒl) *n Bible.* **1** the abode of the dead. **2** (*often not cap.*) hell. [C16: from Heb. *shĕʼōl*]

shepherd ➊ ('ʃɛpəd) *n* **1** a person employed to tend sheep. Fem. equivalent: **shepherdess. 2** a person, such as a clergyman, who watches over a group of people. ◆ *vb* (*tr*) **3** to guide or watch over in the manner of a shepherd. **4** *Australian Rules, rugby, etc.* to prevent opponents from tackling (a member of one's own team) by blocking their path: illegal in rugby.

shepherd dog *n* another term for **sheepdog** (sense 1).

shepherd's pie *n Chiefly Brit.* a baked dish of minced meat covered with mashed potato.

shepherd's-purse *n* a plant having small white flowers and flattened triangular seed pods.

shepherd's weatherglass *n Brit.* another name for the **scarlet pimpernel.**

Sheraton ('ʃɛrətən) *adj* denoting furniture made by or in the style of Thomas Sheraton (1751–1806), British furniture maker, characterized by lightness and elegance.

sherbet ('ʃɜːbət) *n* **1** a fruit-flavoured slightly effervescent powder, eaten as a sweet or used to make a drink. **2** another word (esp. US and Canad.) for **sorbet** (sense 1). **3** *Austral. sl.* beer. **4** a cooling Oriental drink of sweetened fruit juice. [C17: from Turkish, from Persian, from Ar. *sharbah* drink, from *shariba* to drink]

sherd (ʃɜːd) *n* a variant of **shard.**

sherif *or* **shereef** (ʃɛ'riːf) *or* **sharif** *n Islam.* **1** a descendant of Mohammed through his daughter Fatima. **2** an honorific title accorded to any Muslim ruler. [C16: from Ar. *sharīf* noble]

sheriff ('ʃɛrɪf) *n* **1** (in the US) the chief elected law-enforcement officer in a county. **2** (in Canada) a municipal official who enforces court orders, escorts convicted criminals to prison, etc. **3** (in England and Wales) the chief executive officer of the Crown in a county, having chiefly ceremonial duties. **4** (in Scotland) a judge in any of the sheriff courts. **5** (in New Zealand) an officer of the High Court. [OE *scīrgerēfa,* from *scīr* SHIRE + *gerēfa* REEVE[1]]
▸**'sheriffdom** *n*

sheriff court *n* (in Scotland) a court having jurisdiction to try all but the most serious crimes and to deal with most civil actions.

Sherpa ('ʃɜːpə) *n, pl* **Sherpas** *or* **Sherpa.** a member of a people of Mongolian origin living on the southern slopes of the Himalayas in Nepal, noted as mountaineers.

sherry ('ʃɛrɪ) *n, pl* **sherries.** a fortified wine, originally only from the Jerez region of southern Spain. [C16: from earlier *sherris* (assumed to be pl), from Sp. *Xeres,* now *Jerez*]

sherwani (ʃɛə'wɑːnɪ) *n* a long coat closed up to the neck, worn by men in India. [Hindi]

she's (ʃiːz) *contraction of* she is *or* she has.

Shetland pony ('ʃɛtlənd) *n* a very small sturdy breed of pony with a long shaggy mane and tail. Also called: **sheltie.**

Shetland sheepdog *n* a small dog similar in appearance to a collie. Also called: **sheltie.**

shew (ʃəʊ) *vb* **shews, shewing, shewed; shewn** *or* **shewed.** an archaic spelling of **show.**

shewbread *or* **showbread** ('ʃəʊˌbrɛd) *n Bible.* the loaves of bread placed every Sabbath on the table beside the altar of incense in the tabernacle or temple of ancient Israel.

SHF *or* **shf** *Radio. abbrev. for* superhigh frequency.

Shiah *or* **Shia** ('ʃiːə) *n* **1** one of the two main branches of Islam (the other being the Sunni), now mainly in Iran, which regards Mohammed's cousin Ali and his successors as the true imams. ◆ *adj* **2** designating or characteristic of this sect or its beliefs and practices. [C17: from Ar. *shīʻah* sect, from *shāʻa* to follow]

shiatsu (ʃiː'ætsuː) *n* a type of massage in which pressure is applied to the same points of the body as in acupuncture. Also called: **acupressure.** [Japanese from Chinese *chǐ* finger + *yā* pressure]

shibboleth ('ʃɪbəˌlɛθ) *n* **1** a slogan or catch phrase, usually considered outworn, characteristic of a particular party or sect. **2** a custom, phrase, or use of language that acts as a test of belonging to, or as a stumbling block to joining a particular social class, profession, etc. [C14: from Heb., lit.: ear of grain; the word is used in the Old Testament by the Gileadites as a test word for the Ephraimites, who could not pronounce the sound *sh*]

shickered ('ʃɪkəd) *adj Austral. & NZ sl.* drunk; intoxicated. [via Yiddish from Heb.]

shied (ʃaɪd) *vb* the past tense and past participle of **shy**[1] and **shy**[2].

shield ➊ (ʃiːld) *n* **1** any protection used to intercept blows, missiles, etc., such as a tough piece of armour carried on the arm. **2** any similar protective device. **3** *Heraldry.* a pointed stylized shield used for displaying armorial bearings. **4** anything that resembles a shield in shape, such as a prize in a sports competition. **5** *Physics.* a structure of concrete, lead, etc., placed around a nuclear reactor. **6** a broad stable plateau of ancient Precambrian rocks forming the rigid nucleus of a particular continent. **7 the shield.** *NZ.* the Bledisloe Shield, a trophy competed for by provincial rugby teams. ◆ *vb* **8** (*tr*) to protect, hide, or conceal (something) from danger or harm. [OE *sceld*]
▸**'shieldˌlike** *adj*

Shield (ʃiːld) *n* **the.** *Canad.* another term for the **Canadian Shield.**

shield match *n* **1** *Austral.* a cricket match for the Sheffield Shield. **2** *NZ.* a rugby match for the Ranfurly Shield.

shield volcano *n* a broad volcano built up from the repeated nonexplosive eruption of basalt to form a low dome or shield, usually having a large caldera at the summit.

shieling ('ʃiːlɪŋ) *or* **shiel** (ʃiːl) *n Chiefly Scot.* **1** a temporary shelter used by people tending cattle on high or remote ground. **2** pasture land for the grazing of cattle in summer. [C16: from earlier *shiel,* from ME *shale* hut, from ?]

shier ('ʃaɪə) *adj* a comparative of **shy**[1].

shiest ('ʃaɪɪst) *adj* a superlative of **shy**[1].

shift ➊ (ʃɪft) *vb* **1** to move or cause to move from one place or position to another. **2** (*tr*) to change for another or others. **3** to change (gear) in a motor vehicle. **4** (*intr*) (of a sound or set of sounds) to alter in a systematic way. **5** (*intr*) to provide for one's needs (esp. in **shift for oneself**). **6** to remove or be removed, esp. with difficulty: *no detergent can shift these stains.* **7** (*intr*) *Sl.* to move quickly. **8** (*tr*) *Computing.* to move (bits held in a store location) to the left or right. ◆ *n* **9** the act or an instance of shifting. **10** a group of workers who work for a specific period. **11** the period of time worked by such a group. **12** an expedient, contrivance, or artifice. **13** an underskirt or dress with little shaping. [OE *sciftan*]
▸**'shifter** *n*

shiftless ➊ ('ʃɪftlɪs) *adj* lacking in ambition or initiative.
▸**'shiftlessness** *n*

shifty ➊ ('ʃɪftɪ) *adj* **shiftier, shiftiest. 1** given to evasions. **2** furtive in character or appearance.
▸**'shiftily** *adv* ▸**'shiftiness** *n*

shigella (ʃɪ'gɛlə) *n* any of a genus of rod-shaped bacteria, some species of which cause dysentery. [C20: after K. *Shiga* (1870–1957), Japanese bacteriologist, who discovered them]

THESAURUS

Antonyms *vb* ≠ **protect:** endanger, expose, hazard, imperil, lay open, leave open, make vulnerable, risk, subject

sheltered *adj* **2** = **protected,** cloistered, conventual, ensconced, hermitic, isolated, quiet, reclusive, retired, screened, secluded, shaded, shielded, withdrawn
Antonyms *adj* exposed, laid bare, made public, open, public, unconcealed, unprotected, unsheltered

shelve[1] *vb* **3** = **postpone,** defer, dismiss, freeze, hold in abeyance, hold over, lay aside, mothball, pigeonhole, put aside, put off, put on ice, put on the back burner (*inf.*), suspend, table (*US*), take a rain check on (*US & Canad. inf.*)

shepherd *n* **1** = **herdsman,** drover, grazier, stockman ◆ *vb* **3** = **guide,** conduct, convoy, herd, marshal, steer, usher

shield *n* **1** = **buckler,** escutcheon (*Heraldry*), targe (*arch.*) **2** = **protection,** aegis, bulwark, cover, defence, guard, rampart, safeguard, screen, shelter, ward (*arch.*) ◆ *vb* **8** = **protect,** cover, defend, guard, safeguard, screen, shelter, ward off

shift *vb* **1** = **move,** alter, budge, change, displace, fluctuate, move around, rearrange, relocate, remove, reposition, swerve, switch, transfer, transpose, vary, veer **5** *As in* **shift for oneself** = **manage,** assume responsibility, contrive, devise, fend, get along, look after, make do, plan, scheme, take care of ◆ *n* **9** = **move,** about-turn, alteration, change, displacement, fluctuation, modification, permutation, rearrangement, removal, shifting, switch, transfer, veering **12** = **scheme,** artifice, contrivance, craft, device, dodge, equivocation, evasion, expedient, move, resource, ruse, stratagem, subterfuge, trick, wile

shiftless *adj* = **lazy,** aimless, good-for-nothing, idle, incompetent, indolent, inefficient, inept, irresponsible, lackadaisical, slothful, unambitious, unenterprising

shifty *adj* **1, 2** = **untrustworthy,** contriving, crafty, deceitful, devious, duplicitous, evasive, fly-by-night (*inf.*), furtive, scheming, slippery, sly, tricky, underhand, unprincipled, wily
Antonyms *adj* dependable, guileless, honest, honourable, open, reliable, trustworthy, upright

Shiite ('ʃiːaɪt) *or* **Shiah** *Islam.* ◆ *n* **1** an adherent of Shiah. ◆ *adj* **2** of or relating to Shiah.
▸**Shiism** ('ʃiːɪzəm) *n* ▸**Shiitic** (ʃiː'ɪtɪk) *adj*

shillelagh *or* **shillala** (ʃə'leɪlə, -lɪ) *n* (in Ireland) a stout club or cudgel. [C18: from Irish Gaelic *sail* cudgel + *éille* leash, thong]

shilling ('ʃɪlɪŋ) *n* **1** a former British or Australian silver or cupronickel coin worth one twentieth of a pound, not minted in Britain since 1970. Abbrevs.: **s., sh. 2** the standard monetary unit of Kenya, Somalia, Tanzania, and Uganda. [OE *scilling*]

shillyshally ('ʃɪlɪˌʃælɪ) *Inf.* ◆ *vb* **shillyshallies, shillyshallying, shillyshallied. 1** (*intr*) to be indecisive, esp. over unimportant matters. ◆ *adv* **2** in an indecisive manner. ◆ *adj* **3** indecisive or hesitant. ◆ *n, pl* **shillyshallies. 4** vacillation. [C18: from *shill I shall I,* by reduplication of *shall I*]
▸'**shillyˌshallier** *n*

shily ('ʃaɪlɪ) *adv* a less common spelling of **shyly.** See **shy**[1].

shim (ʃɪm) *n* **1** a thin washer or strip often used with a number of similar washers or strips to adjust a clearance for gears, etc. ◆ *vb* **shims, shimming, shimmed. 2** (*tr*) to modify clearance on (a gear, etc.) by use of shims. [C18: from ?]

shimmer ('ʃɪmə) *vb* **1** (*intr*) to shine with a glistening or tremulous light. ◆ *n* **2** a faint, glistening, or tremulous light. [OE *scimerian*]
▸'**shimmering** *or* '**shimmery** *adj*

shimmy ('ʃɪmɪ) *n, pl* **shimmies. 1** an American ragtime dance with much shaking of the hips and shoulders. **2** abnormal wobbling motion in a motor vehicle, esp. in the front wheels or steering. ◆ *vb* **shimmies, shimmying, shimmied.** (*intr*) **3** to dance the shimmy. **4** to vibrate or wobble. [C19: changed from CHEMISE, mistaken for pl]

shin (ʃɪn) *n* **1** the front part of the lower leg. **2** the front edge of the tibia. **3** *Chiefly Brit.* a cut of beef, the lower foreleg. ◆ *vb* **shins, shinning, shinned. 4** (when *intr,* often foll. by *up*) to climb (a pole, tree, etc.) by gripping with the hands or arms and the legs and hauling oneself up. **5** (*tr*) to kick (a person) in the shins. [OE *scinu*]

shinbone ('ʃɪnˌbəʊn) *n* the nontechnical name for **tibia** (sense 1).

shindig ('ʃɪnˌdɪg) *or* **shindy** ('ʃɪndɪ) *n, pl* **shindigs** *or* **shindies.** *Sl.* **1** a noisy party, dance, etc. **2** a quarrel or commotion. [C19: var. of SHINTY]

shine (ʃaɪn) *vb* **shines, shining, shone. 1** (*intr*) to emit light. **2** (*intr*) to glow or be bright with reflected light. **3** (*tr*) to direct the light of (a lamp, etc.): *he shone the torch in my eyes.* **4** (*tr; p.t. & p.p.* **shined**) to cause to gleam by polishing: *to shine shoes.* **5** (*intr*) to excel: *she shines at tennis.* **6** (*intr*) to appear clearly. ◆ *n* **7** the state or quality of shining; sheen; lustre. **8** *Inf.* a liking or fancy (esp. in **take a shine to**). [OE *scīnan*]

shiner ('ʃaɪnə) *n* **1** something that shines, such as a polishing device. **2** any of numerous small North American freshwater cyprinid fishes. **3** *Inf.* a black eye. **4** *NZ. old-fashioned inf.* a tramp.

shingle[1] ('ʃɪŋgᵊl) *n* **1** a thin rectangular tile, esp. one made of wood, that is laid with others in overlapping rows to cover a roof or a wall. **2** a woman's short-cropped hairstyle. **3** *US & Canad.* a small signboard fixed outside the office of a doctor, lawyer, etc. ◆ *vb* **shingles, shingling, shingled.** (*tr*) **4** to cover (a roof or a wall) with shingles. **5** to cut (the hair) in a short-cropped style. [C12 *scingle,* from LL *scindula* a split piece of wood, from L *scindere* to split]
▸'**shingler** *n*

shingle[2] ('ʃɪŋgᵊl) *n* **1** coarse gravel, esp. the pebbles found on beaches. **2** a place or area strewn with shingle. [C16: of Scand. origin]
▸'**shingly** *adj*

shingles ('ʃɪŋgᵊlz) *n* (*functioning as sing*) an acute viral disease characterized by inflammation, pain, and skin eruptions along the course of affected nerves. Technical names: **herpes zoster, zoster.** [C14: from Med. L *cingulum* girdle, rendering Gk *zōnē* zone]

Shinto ('ʃɪntəʊ) *n* the indigenous religion of Japan, incorporating the worship of a number of ethnic divinities. [C18: from Japanese: the way of the gods, from Chinese *shên* gods + *tao* way]
▸'**Shintoism** *n* ▸'**Shintoist** *n, adj*

shinty ('ʃɪntɪ) *n* **1** a game resembling hockey played with a ball and sticks curved at the lower end. **2** (*pl* **shinties**) the stick used in this game. [C17: ? from Scot. Gaelic *sinteag* a pace, bound]

shiny ('ʃaɪnɪ) *adj* **shinier, shiniest. 1** glossy or polished; bright. **2** (of clothes or material) worn to a smooth and glossy state, as by continual rubbing.
▸'**shininess** *n*

ship (ʃɪp) *n* **1** a vessel propelled by engines or sails for navigating on the water, esp. a large vessel. **2** *Naut.* a large sailing vessel with three or more square-rigged masts. **3** the crew of a ship. **4** short for **airship** or **spaceship. 5 when one's ship comes in** (*or* **home**). when one has become successful. ◆ *vb* **ships, shipping, shipped. 6** to place, transport, or travel on any conveyance, esp. aboard a ship. **7** (*tr*) *Naut.* to take (water) over the side. **8** to bring or go aboard a vessel: *to ship oars.* **9** (*tr;* often foll. by *off*) *Inf.* to send away: *they shipped the children off to boarding school.* **10** (*intr*) to engage to serve aboard a ship: *I shipped aboard a Liverpool liner.* [OE *scip*]
▸'**shippable** *adj*

-ship *suffix forming nouns.* **1** indicating state or condition: *fellowship.* **2** indicating rank, office, or position: *lordship.* **3** indicating craft or skill: *scholarship.* [OE *-scipe*]

shipboard ('ʃɪpˌbɔːd) *n* (*modifier*) taking place, used, or intended for use aboard a ship: *a shipboard encounter.*

shipbuilder ('ʃɪpˌbɪldə) *n* a person or business engaged in building ships.
▸'**shipˌbuilding** *n*

ship chandler *n* a person or business dealing in supplies for ships.
▸**ship chandlery** *n*

shipload ('ʃɪpˌləʊd) *n* the quantity carried by a ship.

shipmaster ('ʃɪpˌmɑːstə) *n* the master or captain of a ship.

shipmate ('ʃɪpˌmeɪt) *n* a sailor who serves on the same ship as another.

shipment ('ʃɪpmənt) *n* **1a** goods shipped together as part of the same lot: *a shipment of grain.* **1b** (*as modifier*): *a shipment schedule.* **2** the act of shipping cargo.

ship money *n English history.* a tax levied to finance the fitting out of warships: abolished 1640.

ship of the line *n Naut.* (formerly) a warship large enough to fight in the first line of battle.

shipowner ('ʃɪpˌəʊnə) *n* a person who owns or has shares in a ship or ships.

shipper ('ʃɪpə) *n* a person or company in the business of shipping freight.

shipping ('ʃɪpɪŋ) *n* **1a** the business of transporting freight, esp. by ship. **1b** (*as modifier*): *a shipping magnate; shipping line.* **2** ships collectively: *there is a lot of shipping in the Channel.*

ship's biscuit *n* another name for **hardtack.**

shipshape ('ʃɪpˌʃeɪp) *adj* **1** neat; orderly. ◆ *adv* **2** in a neat and orderly manner.

shipworm ('ʃɪpˌwɜːm) *n* any of a genus of wormlike marine bivalve molluscs that bore into wooden piers, ships, etc., by means of drill-like shell valves.

shipwreck ('ʃɪpˌrɛk) *n* **1** the partial or total destruction of a ship at sea. **2** a wrecked ship or part of such a ship. **3** ruin or destruction: *the shipwreck of all my hopes.* ◆ *vb* (*tr*) **4** to wreck or destroy (a ship). **5** to bring to ruin or destruction. [OE *scipwræc,* from SHIP + *wræc* something driven by the sea]

shipwright ('ʃɪpˌraɪt) *n* an artisan skilled in one or more of the tasks required to build vessels.

shipyard ('ʃɪpˌjɑːd) *n* a place or facility for the building, maintenance, and repair of ships.

shiralee (ˌʃɪrə'liː) *n Austral. sl.* a swagman's bundle. [from ?]

shire ('ʃaɪə) *n* **1a** one of the British counties. **1b** (*in combination*): *Yorkshire.* **2** (in Australia) a rural district having its own local council. **3** See **shire horse. 4 the Shires.** the Midland counties of England, famous for hunting, etc. [OE *scīr* office]

shire horse *n* a large heavy breed of carthorse with long hair on the fetlocks.

shirk (ʃɜːk) *vb* **1** to avoid discharging (work, a duty, etc.); evade. ◆ *n also* **shirker. 2** a person who shirks. [C17: prob. from G *Schurke* rogue]

shirr (ʃɜː) *vb* **1** to gather (fabric) into two or more parallel rows to decorate a dress, blouse, etc., often using elastic thread. **2** (*tr*) to bake (eggs) out of their shells. ◆ *n also* **shirring. 3** a series of gathered rows decorating a dress, blouse, etc. [C19: from ?]

shirt (ʃɜːt) *n* **1** a garment worn on the upper part of the body, esp. by men, usually having a collar and sleeves and buttoning up the front. **2** short for **nightshirt. 3 keep your shirt on.** *Inf.* refrain from losing your temper. **4 put** *or* **lose one's shirt on.** *Inf.* to bet or lose all one has on (a horse, etc.). [OE *scyrte*]

shirting ('ʃɜːtɪŋ) *n* fabric used in making men's shirts.

shirt-lifter *n Derog. sl.* a male homosexual.

shirtsleeve ('ʃɜːtˌsliːv) *n* **1** the sleeve of a shirt. **2 in one's shirtsleeves.** not wearing a jacket.

shirt-tail *n* the part of a shirt that extends below the waist.

THESAURUS

shillyshally *vb* **1** *Informal* = **be irresolute** *or* **indecisive**, dilly-dally (*inf.*), dither (*chiefly Brit.*), falter, fluctuate, haver (*Brit.*), hem and haw *or* hum and haw, hesitate, seesaw, swither (*Scot.*), vacillate, waver, yo-yo (*inf.*)

shimmer *vb* **1** = **gleam**, dance, glimmer, glisten, phosphoresce, scintillate, twinkle ◆ *n* **2** = **gleam**, diffused light, glimmer, glow, incandescence, iridescence, lustre, phosphorescence, unsteady light

shin *vb* **4** *with* **up** = **climb**, ascend, clamber, scale, scramble, swarm

shine *vb* **1, 2** = **gleam**, beam, emit light, flash, give off light, glare, glimmer, glisten, glitter, glow, radiate, scintillate, shimmer, sparkle, twinkle **4** = **polish**, brush, buff, burnish, rub up **5** = **be outstanding**, be conspicuous, be distinguished, be pre-eminent, excel, stand out, stand out in a crowd, star, steal the show ◆ *n* **7** = **brightness**, glaze, gloss, light, luminosity, lustre, patina, radiance, sheen, shimmer, sparkle

shining *adj* **2** = **bright**, aglow, beaming, brilliant, effulgent, gleaming, glistening, glittering, luminous, radiant, resplendent, shimmering, sparkling **5** = **outstanding**, brilliant, celebrated, conspicuous, distinguished, eminent, glorious, illustrious, leading, splendid

shiny *adj* **1** = **bright**, agleam, burnished, gleaming, glistening, glossy, lustrous, nitid (*poetic*), polished, satiny, sheeny

ship *n* **1** = **vessel**, boat, craft

shipshape *adj* **1** = **tidy**, Bristol fashion, businesslike, neat, orderly, spick-and-span, trig (*arch. or dialect*), trim, uncluttered, well-ordered, well-organized, well-regulated

shirk *vb* **1** = **dodge**, avoid, body-swerve (*Scot.*), duck (out of) (*inf.*), evade, get out of, scrimshank (*Brit. military sl.*), shun, sidestep, skive (*Brit. sl.*), slack

shirker *n* **2** = **slacker**, clock-watcher, dodger, gold brick (*US sl.*), idler, malingerer, quitter, scrimshanker (*Brit. military sl.*), shirk, skiver (*Brit. sl.*)

shirtwaister ('ʃɜːtˌweɪstə) *or US* **shirtwaist** *n* a woman's dress with a tailored bodice resembling a shirt.

shirty ('ʃɜːtɪ) *adj* **shirtier, shirtiest.** *Sl., chiefly Brit.* bad-tempered or annoyed. [C19: ? based on such phrases as *to get someone's shirt out* to annoy someone]
▸**'shirtily** *adv*

shish kebab ('ʃiːʃ kə'bæb) *n* a dish consisting of small pieces of meat and vegetables threaded onto skewers and grilled. [from Turkish *şiş kebab*, from *şiş* skewer; see KEBAB]

shit (ʃɪt) *Taboo.* ◆ *vb* **shits, shitting; shitted, shit,** *or* **shat. 1** to defecate. **2** (usually foll. by *on*) *Sl.* to give the worst possible treatment (to). ◆ *n* **3** faeces; excrement. **4** an act of defecation. **5** *Sl.* rubbish; nonsense. **6** *Sl.* an obnoxious or worthless person. ◆ *interj* **7** *Sl.* an exclamation expressing anger, disgust, etc. [OE *scite* (unattested) dung, *scītan* to defecate, of Gmc origin]
▸**'shitty** *adj*

shiv (ʃɪv) *n* a variant of **chiv.**

Shiva ('ʃiːvə, 'ʃɪvə) *n* a variant spelling of **Siva.**

shivaree (ˌʃɪvə'riː) *n* a variant spelling (esp. US and Canad.) of **charivari.**

shiver[1] **T** ('ʃɪvə) *vb* (*intr*) **1** to shake or tremble, as from cold or fear. ◆ *n* **2** the act of shivering; a tremulous motion. **3 the shivers.** an attack of shivering, esp. through fear or illness. [C13 *chiveren*, ? var. of *chevelen* to chatter (used of teeth), from OE *ceafl* jowl]
▸**'shiverer** *n* ▸**'shivering** *n, adj* ▸**'shivery** *adj*

shiver[2] **T** ('ʃɪvə) *vb* **1** to break or cause to break into fragments. ◆ *n* **2** a splintered piece. [C13: of Gmc origin]

shoal[1] **T** (ʃəʊl) *n* **1** a stretch of shallow water. **2** a sandbank or rocky area, esp. one that is visible at low water. ◆ *vb* **3** to make or become shallow. **4** (*intr*) *Naut.* to sail into shallower water. ◆ *adj also* **shoaly. 5** a less common word for **shallow.** [OE *sceald* shallow]

shoal[2] (ʃəʊl) *n* **1** a large group of fish. **2** a large group of people or things. ◆ *vb* **3** (*intr*) to collect together in such a group. [OE *scolu*]

shock[1] **T** (ʃɒk) *vb* **1** to experience or cause to experience extreme horror, disgust, surprise, etc.: *the atrocities shocked us.* **2** to cause a state of shock in (a person). **3** to come or cause to come into violent contact. ◆ *n* **4** a sudden and violent jarring blow or impact. **5** something that causes a sudden and violent disturbance in the emotions. **6** *Pathol.* a state of bodily collapse, as from severe bleeding, burns, fright, etc. **7** Also: **electric shock.** pain and muscular spasm as the physical reaction to an electric current passing through the body. [C16: from OF *choc*, from *choquier* to make violent contact with, of Gmc origin]
▸**'shockable** *adj* ▸ˌ**shocka'bility** *n*

shock[2] (ʃɒk) *n* **1** a number of sheaves set on end in a field to dry. **2** a pile or stack of unthreshed corn. ◆ *vb* **3** (*tr*) to set up (sheaves) in shocks. [C14: prob. of Gmc origin]

shock[3] (ʃɒk) *n* a thick bushy mass, esp. of hair. [C19: ?from SHOCK[2]]

shock absorber *n* any device designed to absorb mechanical shock, esp. one fitted to a motor vehicle to damp the recoil of the road springs.

shocker ('ʃɒkə) *n Inf.* **1** a person or thing that shocks. **2** a sensational novel, film, or play.

shockheaded ('ʃɒkˌhedɪd) *adj* having a head of bushy or tousled hair.

shock-horror *adj Facetious.* (esp. of newspaper headlines) sensationalistic: *shock-horror stories about the British diet.*

shocking **T** ('ʃɒkɪŋ) *adj* **1** causing shock, horror, or disgust. **2 shocking pink. 2a** of a garish shade of pink. **2b** (*as n*): *dressed in shocking pink.* **3** *Inf.* very bad or terrible: *shocking weather.*
▸**'shockingly** *adv*

shockproof ('ʃɒkˌpruːf) *adj* capable of absorbing shock without damage.

shock therapy *or* **treatment** *n* the treatment of certain psychotic conditions by injecting drugs or by passing an electric current through the brain (**electroconvulsive therapy**) to produce convulsions or coma.

shock troops *pl n* soldiers specially trained and equipped to carry out an assault.

shock wave *n* a region across which there is a rapid pressure, temperature, and density rise caused by a body moving supersonically in a gas or by a detonation. See also **sonic boom.**

shod (ʃɒd) *vb* the past participle of **shoe.**

shoddy **T** ('ʃɒdɪ) *adj* **shoddier, shoddiest. 1** imitating something of better quality. **2** of poor quality. ◆ *n, pl* **shoddies. 3** a yarn or fabric made from wool waste or clippings. **4** anything of inferior quality that is designed to simulate superior quality. [C19: from ?]
▸**'shoddily** *adv* ▸**'shoddiness** *n*

shoe (ʃuː) *n* **1a** one of a matching pair of coverings shaped to fit the foot, esp. one ending below the ankle, having an upper of leather, plastic, etc., on a sole and heel of heavier material. **1b** (*as modifier*): *shoe cleaner.* **2** anything resembling a shoe in shape, function, position, etc., such as a horseshoe. **3** a band of metal or wood on the bottom of the runner of a sledge. **4** *Engineering.* a lining to protect from wear: see **brake shoe. 5 be in (a person's) shoes.** *Inf.* to be in (another person's) situation. ◆ *vb* **shoes, shoeing, shod.** (*tr*) **6** to furnish with shoes. **7** to fit (a horse) with horseshoes. **8** to furnish with a hard cover, such as a metal plate, for protection against friction or bruising. [OE *scōh*]

shoeblack ('ʃuːˌblæk) *n* (esp. formerly) a person who shines boots and shoes.

shoehorn ('ʃuːˌhɔːn) *n* **1** a smooth curved implement of horn, metal, plastic, etc., inserted at the heel of a shoe to ease the foot into it. ◆ *vb* (*tr*) **2** to cram (people or things) into a small space.

shoelace ('ʃuːˌleɪs) *n* a cord for fastening shoes.

shoe leather *n* **1** leather used to make shoes. **2 save shoe leather.** to avoid wearing out shoes, as by taking a bus rather than walking.

shoemaker **T** ('ʃuːˌmeɪkə) *n* a person who makes or repairs shoes or boots.
▸**'shoeˌmaking** *n*

shoer ('ʃuːə) *n Rare.* a person who shoes horses; farrier.

shoeshine ('ʃuːˌʃaɪn) *n* the act or an instance of polishing a pair of shoes.

shoestring ('ʃuːˌstrɪŋ) *n* **1** another word for **shoelace. 2** *Inf.* a very small or petty amount of money (esp. in **on a shoestring**).

shoetree ('ʃuːˌtriː) *n* a wooden or metal form inserted into a shoe or boot to stretch it or preserve its shape.

shofar *or* **shophar** (*Hebrew* ʃɔ'far) *n, pl* **shofars, shophars** *or* **shofroth, shophroth** (*Hebrew* -'frɔt). *Judaism.* a ram's horn sounded on certain religious occasions. [from Heb. *shōphār* ram's horn]

shogun ('ʃəʊˌguːn) *n Japanese history.* (from about 1192 to 1867) any of a line of hereditary military dictators who relegated the emperors to a position of purely theoretical supremacy. [C17: from Japanese, from Chinese *chiang chün* general, from *chiang* to lead + *chün* army]
▸**'shogunate** *n*

shogun bond *n* a bond sold on the Japanese market by a foreign institution and denominated in a foreign currency. Cf. **samurai bond.**

shone (ʃɒn; *US* ʃəʊn) *vb* a past tense and past participle of **shine.**

shoo (ʃuː) *sentence substitute.* **1** go away!: used to drive away unwanted or annoying people, animals, etc. ◆ *vb* **shoos, shooing, shooed. 2** (*tr*) to drive away by or as if by crying "shoo". **3** (*intr*) to cry "shoo". [C15: imit.]

shoo-in *n US & Canad.* **1** a person or thing that is certain to win or succeed. **2** a match or contest that is easy to win.

shook[1] (ʃʊk) *n* **1** a set of parts ready for assembly, esp. of a barrel. **2** a group of sheaves piled together on end; shock. [C18: from ?]

shook[2] (ʃʊk) *vb* the past tense of **shake.**

shoon (ʃuːn) *n Dialect, chiefly Scot.* a plural of **shoe.**

shoot **T** (ʃuːt) *vb* **shoots, shooting, shot. 1** (*tr*) to hit, wound, damage, or kill with a missile discharged from a weapon. **2** to discharge (a missile or missiles) from a weapon. **3** to fire (a weapon) or (of a weapon) to be fired. **4** to send out or be sent out as if from a weapon: *he shot questions at her.* **5** (*intr*) to move very rapidly. **6** (*tr*) to slide or push into or out of a fastening: *to shoot a bolt.* **7** to emit (a ray of light) or (of a ray of light) to be emitted. **8** (*tr*) to go or pass quickly over or through: *to shoot rapids.* **9** (*intr*) to hunt game with a gun for sport. **10** (*tr*) to pass over (an area) in hunting game. **11** (*intr*) (of a plant) to produce (buds, branches, etc.). **12** to photograph or record (a sequence, etc.). **13** (*tr; usually passive*) to variegate or streak, as with colour. **14** *Soccer, hockey, etc.* to hit or propel (the ball, etc.) towards the goal. **15** (*tr*) *Sport, chiefly US & Canad.* to score (strokes, etc.): *he shot 72 on the first round.* **16** (*tr*) to measure the altitude of (a celestial body). **17** (often foll. by *up*) *Sl.* to inject (someone, esp. oneself) with (a drug, esp. heroin). **18 shoot a line.** *Sl.* **18a** to boast. **18b** to tell a lie. **19 shoot oneself in the foot.** *Inf.* to

THESAURUS

shiver[1] *vb* **1** = **tremble,** palpitate, quake, quiver, shake, shudder ◆ *n* **2** = **trembling,** flutter, *frisson,* quiver, shudder, thrill, tremble, tremor **3 the shivers** = **the shakes** (*inf.*), chattering teeth, chill, goose flesh, goose pimples

shiver[2] *vb* **1** = **splinter,** break, crack, fragment, shatter, smash, smash to smithereens

shivery *adj* **2** = **shaking,** chilled, chilly, cold, quaking, quivery, shuddery, trembly

shoal[1] *n* **1** = **shallow 2** = **sandbank,** sand bar, shelf

shock[1] *vb* **1** = **horrify,** agitate, appal, disgust, disquiet, give (someone) a turn (*inf.*), gross out (*US sl.*), nauseate, offend, outrage, raise eyebrows, revolt, scandalize, sicken, traumatize, unsettle **2** = **astound,** jar, jolt, numb, paralyse, shake, shake out of one's complacency, shake up (*inf.*), stagger, stun, stupefy ◆ *n* **4** = **impact,** blow, clash, collision, encounter, jarring, jolt **5** = **upset,** blow, bolt from the blue, bombshell, breakdown, collapse, consternation, distress, disturbance, prostration, rude awakening, state of shock, stupefaction, stupor, trauma, turn (*inf.*), whammy (*inf., chiefly US*)

shocking *adj* **1** = **dreadful,** abominable, appalling, atrocious, detestable, disgraceful, disgusting, disquieting, distressing, foul, frightful, from hell (*inf.*), ghastly, hideous, horrible, horrifying, loathsome, monstrous, nauseating, obscene, odious, offensive, outrageous, repulsive, revolting, scandalous, sickening, stupefying, unspeakable, X-rated (*inf.*)
Antonyms *adj* admirable, decent, delightful, excellent, fine, first-rate, gratifying, honourable, laudable, marvellous, pleasant, praiseworthy, satisfying, wonderful

shoddy *adj* **1, 2** = **inferior,** cheap, cheap-jack (*inf.*), cheapo (*inf.*), junky (*inf.*), low-rent (*inf., chiefly US*), poor, rubbishy, second-rate, slipshod, tacky (*inf.*), tatty, tawdry, trashy
Antonyms *adj* accurate, careful, considerate, craftsman-like, excellent, fine, first-rate, meticulous, quality, superlative, well-made

shoemaker *n* = **cobbler,** bootmaker, souter (*Scot.*)

shoot *vb* **1** = **hit,** bag, blast, blow away (*sl., chiefly US*), bring down, kill, open fire, pick off, plug (*sl.*), pump full of lead (*sl.*), zap (*sl.*) **2, 3** = **fire,** discharge, emit, fling, hurl, launch, let fly, project, propel **5** = **speed,** barrel (along) (*inf., chiefly US & Canad.*), bolt, burn rubber (*inf.*), charge, dart, dash, flash, fly, hurtle, race, rush, scoot, spring, streak, tear, whisk, whizz (*inf.*) **11** = **sprout,** bud, burgeon, germinate, put forth new growth ◆ *n* **22, 23** = **sprout,** branch, bud, offshoot, scion, slip, sprig, twig damage one's own cause inadvertently. ◆ *n* **20** the act of shooting. **21** the action or motion of something that is shot. **22** the first aerial part of a plant to develop from a germinating seed. **23** any new growth of a plant, such as a bud, etc. **24** *Chiefly Brit.* a meeting or party organized for hunting game with guns. **25** an area where game can be hunted with guns. **26** a steep descent in a stream; rapid. **27** *Inf.* a photographic assignment **28 the whole shoot.** *Sl.* everything. ◆ *interj* **29** *US & Canad.* an exclamation expressing disbelief, scepticism, disappointment, etc. ◆ See also **shoot down, shoot through.** [OE *sceōtan*]

shoot down *vb (tr, adv)* **1** to shoot callously. **2** to defeat or disprove: *he shot down her argument.*

shoot-'em-up *or* **shoot-em-up** *n Inf.* **1** a type of computer game, the object of which is to shoot as many enemies, targets, etc. as possible. **2** a fast-moving film involving many gunfights, battles, etc.

shooter ('ʃuːtə) *n* **1** a person or thing that shoots. **2** *Sl.* a gun.

shooting box *n* a small country house providing accommodation for a shooting party. Also called: **shooting lodge.**

shooting brake *n Brit.* another name for **estate car.**

shooting star *n Inf.* a meteor.

shooting stick *n* a device that resembles a walking stick, having a spike at one end and a folding seat at the other.

shoot through *vb (intr, adv) Austral. inf.* to leave; go away.

shop ❶ (ʃɒp) *n* **1** a place, esp. a small building, for the retail sale of goods and services. **2** an act or instance of shopping. **3** a place for the performance of a specified type of work; workshop. **4 all over the shop.** *Inf.* **4a** in disarray: *his papers were all over the shop.* **4b** in every direction: *I've searched for it all over the shop.* **5 shut up shop.** to close business at the end of the day or permanently. **6 talk shop.** *Inf.* to discuss one's business, profession, etc., esp. on a social occasion. ◆ *vb* **shops, shopping, shopped.** **7** *(intr; often foll. by for)* to visit a shop or shops in search of (goods) with the intention of buying them. **8** *(tr) Sl., chiefly Brit.* to inform on (someone), esp. to the police. [OE *sceoppa* stall]
▸'**shopping** *n*

shop around *vb (intr, adv) Inf.* **1** to visit a number of shops or stores to compare goods and prices. **2** to consider a number of possibilities before making a choice.

shop assistant *n* a person who serves in a shop.

shop floor *n* **1** the part of a factory housing the machines and men directly involved in production. **2** workers, esp. factory workers organized in a union.

shopkeeper ('ʃɒpˌkiːpə) *n* a person who owns or manages a shop or small store.
▸'**shopˌkeeping** *n*

shoplifter ('ʃɒpˌlɪftə) *n* a customer who steals goods from a shop.
▸'**shopˌlifting** *n*

shopper ('ʃɒpə) *n* **1** a person who buys goods in a shop. **2** a bag for shopping.

shopping centre *n* **1** a purpose-built complex of stores, restaurants, etc. **2** the area of a town where most of the shops are situated.

shopping mall *n* a large enclosed shopping centre.

shopping plaza *n Chiefly US & Canad.* a shopping centre, esp. a small group of stores built as a strip.

shopsoiled ('ʃɒpˌsɔɪld) *adj* worn, faded, etc., from being displayed in a shop or store.

shop steward *n* an elected representative of the union workers in a shop, factory, etc.

shoptalk ('ʃɒpˌtɔːk) *n* conversation concerning one's work, esp. when carried on outside business hours.

shopwalker ('ʃɒpˌwɔːkə) *n Brit.* a person employed by a departmental store to supervise sales personnel, assist customers, etc.

shoran ('ʃɔːræn) *n* a short-range radar system by which an aircraft, ship, etc., can accurately determine its position. [C20: *sho(rt-)ra(nge) n(avigation)*]

shore[1] ❶ (ʃɔː) *n* **1** the land along the edge of a sea, lake, or wide river. Related adj: **littoral. 2a** land, as opposed to water. **2b** *(as modifier): shore duty.* **3** *Law.* the tract of coastland lying between the ordinary marks of high and low water. **4** *(often pl)* a country: *his native shores.* [C14: prob. from MLow G, MDu. *schōre*]

shore[2] ❶ (ʃɔː) *n* **1** a prop or beam used to support a wall, building, etc. ◆ *vb* **shores, shoring, shored. 2** *(tr; often foll. by up)* to make safe with or as if with a shore. [C15: from MDu. *schōre*]
▸'**shoring** *n*

shore[3] (ʃɔː) *vb Arch., Austral., & NZ.* a past tense of **shear.**

shore bird *n* any of various birds that live close to water, esp. plovers, sandpipers, etc. Also called (Brit.): **wader.**

shore leave *n Naval.* **1** permission to go ashore. **2** time spent ashore during leave.

shoreless ('ʃɔːlɪs) *adj* **1** without a shore suitable for landing. **2** *Poetic.* boundless; vast.

shoreline ('ʃɔːˌlaɪn) *n* the edge of a body of water.

shoreward ('ʃɔːwəd) *adj* **1** near or facing the shore. ◆ *adv also* **shorewards. 2** towards the shore.

shorn (ʃɔːn) *vb* a past participle of **shear.**

short ❶ (ʃɔːt) *adj* **1** of little length; not long. **2** of little height; not tall. **3** of limited duration. **4** deficient: *the number of places laid at the table was short by four.* **5** *(postpositive; often foll. by of or on)* lacking (in) or needful (of): *I'm always short of money.* **6** concise; succinct. **7** (of drinks) consisting chiefly of a spirit, such as whisky. **8** *Cricket.* (of a fielding position) near the batsman: *short leg.* **9** lacking in the power of retentiveness: *a short memory.* **10** abrupt to the point of rudeness: *the salesgirl was very short with him.* **11** (of betting odds) almost even. **12** *Finance.* **12a** not possessing the securities or commodities that have been sold under contract and therefore obliged to make a purchase before the delivery date. **12b** of or relating to such sales, which depend on falling prices for profit. **13** *Phonetics.* **13a** denoting a vowel of relatively brief temporal duration. **13b** (in popular usage) denoting the qualities of the five English vowels represented orthographically in the words *pat, pet, pit, pot, put,* and *putt.* **14** *Prosody.* **14a** denoting a vowel that is phonetically short or a syllable containing such a vowel. **14b** (of a vowel or syllable in verse) not carrying emphasis or accent. **15** (of pastry) crumbly in texture. **16 in short supply.** scarce. **17 short and sweet.** unexpectedly brief. **18 short for.** an abbreviation for. ◆ *adv* **19** abruptly: *to stop short.* **20** briefly or concisely. **21** rudely or curtly. **22** *Finance.* without possessing the securities or commodities at the time of their contractual sale: *to sell short.* **23 caught** *or* **taken short.** having a sudden need to urinate or defecate. **24 go short.** not to have a sufficient amount, etc. **25 short of.** except: *nothing short of a miracle can save him now.* ◆ *n* **26** anything that is short. **27** a drink of spirits. **28** *Phonetics, prosody.* a short vowel or syllable. **29** *Finance.* **29a** a short contract or sale. **29b** a short seller. **30** a short film, usually of a factual nature. **31** See **short circuit. 32 for short.** *Inf.* as a shortened form: *he is called J.R. for short.* **33 in short. 33a** as a summary. **33b** in a few words. ◆ *vb* **34** See **short circuit** (sense 2). ◆ See also **shorts.** [OE *scort*]
▸'**shortness** *n*

short-acting *adj* (of a drug) quickly effective, but requiring regularly repeated doses for long-term treatment. Cf. **intermediate-acting, long-acting.**

shortage ❶ ('ʃɔːtɪdʒ) *n* a deficiency or lack in the amount needed, expected, or due; deficit.

shortbread ('ʃɔːtˌbrɛd) *n* a rich crumbly biscuit made with a large proportion of butter.

shortcake ('ʃɔːtˌkeɪk) *n* **1** shortbread. **2** a dessert made of layers of biscuit or cake filled with fruit and cream.

short-change *vb* **short-changes, short-changing, short-changed.** *(tr)* **1** to give less than correct change to. **2** *Sl.* to treat unfairly or dishonestly, esp. by giving less than is expected or deserved.

short circuit *n* **1** a faulty or accidental connection between two points of different potential in an electric circuit, establishing a path of low resistance through which an excessive current can flow. ◆ *vb* **short-circuit. 2** to develop or cause to develop a short circuit. **3** *(tr)* to bypass (a procedure, etc.). **4** *(tr)* to hinder or frustrate (plans, etc.). ◆ Sometimes (for senses 1, 2) shortened to **short.**

shortcoming ❶ ('ʃɔːtˌkʌmɪŋ) *n* a failing, defect, or deficiency.

short corner *n Hockey.* another name for **penalty corner.**

short covering *n* the purchase of securities or commodities by a short seller to meet delivery requirements.

shortcrust pastry ('ʃɔːtˌkrʌst) *n* a basic type of pastry that has a crisp but crumbly texture. Also: **short pastry.**

short cut *n* **1** a route that is shorter than the usual one. **2** a means of saving time or effort. ◆ *vb* **short-cut, short-cuts, short-cutting, short-cut. 3** *(intr)* to use a short cut.

short-dated *adj* (of a gilt-edged security) having less than five years to run before redemption. Cf. **medium-dated, long-dated.**

short-day *adj* (of plants) able to flower only if exposed to short periods of daylight, each followed by a long dark period. Cf. **long-day.**

THESAURUS

shop *n* **1 = store,** boutique, emporium, hypermarket, market, mart, supermarket

shore[1] *n* **1 = beach,** coast, foreshore, lakeside, sands, seaboard *(chiefly US),* seashore, strand *(poetic),* waterside

shore[2] *vb* **2** *with* **up = support,** augment, brace, buttress, hold, prop, reinforce, strengthen, underpin

short *adj* **1 = concise,** abridged, brief, clipped, compendious, compressed, curtailed, laconic, pithy, sententious, succinct, summary, terse **2 = small,** diminutive, dumpy, fubsy *(arch. or dialect),* knee high to a gnat, knee high to a grasshopper, little, low, petite, squat, wee **3 = brief,** fleeting, momentary, short-lived, short-term **5** *often with* **of** *or* **on = lacking,** deficient, inadequate, in need of, insufficient, limited, low (on), meagre, missing, poor, scant, scanty, scarce, short-handed, slender, slim, sparse, strapped (for) *(sl.),* tight, wanting **10 = abrupt,** blunt, brusque, crusty, curt, discourteous, gruff, impolite, offhand, sharp, terse, testy, uncivil **15 = crumbly,** brittle, crisp, friable ◆ *adv* **19 = abruptly,** by surprise, suddenly, unaware, without warning **25 short of = except,** apart from, other than, unless ◆ *n* **33 in short = briefly,** in a nutshell, in a word, in essence, to come to the point, to cut a long story short, to put it briefly
Antonyms *adj* ≠ **concise:** diffuse, lengthy, long, long-drawn-out, long-winded, prolonged, rambling, unabridged, verbose, wordy ≠ **small:** big, high, lanky, lofty, tall ≠ **brief:** extended, long, long-term ≠ **lacking:** abundant, adequate, ample, bountiful, copious, inexhaustible, plentiful, sufficient, well-stocked ≠ **abrupt:** civil, courteous, polite ◆ *adv* ≠ **abruptly:** bit by bit, gently, gradually, little by little, slowly

shortage *n* **= deficiency,** dearth, deficit, failure, inadequacy, insufficiency, lack, leanness, paucity, poverty, scarcity, shortfall, want
Antonyms *n* abundance, adequate amount, excess, overabundance, plethora, profusion, sufficiency, surfeit, surplus

shortcoming *n* **= failing,** defect, drawback, fault, flaw, foible, frailty, imperfection, weakness, weak point

shorten Ⓣ ('ʃɔːtən) *vb* **1** to make or become short or shorter. **2** (*tr*) *Naut.* to reduce the area of (sail). **3** (*tr*) to make (pastry, etc.) short, by adding fat. **4** *Gambling.* to cause (the odds) to lessen or (of odds) to become less.

shortening ('ʃɔːtənɪŋ) *n* butter or other fat, used in a dough, etc., to make the mixture short.

Shorter Catechism *n Chiefly Presbyterian Church.* the more widely used of two catechisms of religious instruction drawn up in 1647.

shortfall ('ʃɔːtˌfɔːl) *n* **1** failure to meet a goal or a requirement. **2** the amount of such a failure.

shorthand ('ʃɔːtˌhænd) *n* **a** a system of rapid handwriting employing simple strokes and other symbols to represent words or phrases. **b** (*as modifier*): *a shorthand typist.*

short-handed *adj* **1** lacking the usual or necessary number of assistants, workers, etc. **2** *Sport, US & Canad.* with less than the full complement of players.

shorthand typist *n Brit.* a person skilled in the use of shorthand and in typing. US and Canad. name: **stenographer.**

short head *n Horse racing.* a distance shorter than the length of a horse's head.

shorthorn ('ʃɔːtˌhɔːn) *n* a short-horned breed of cattle with several regional varieties.

shortie *or* **shorty** ('ʃɔːtɪ) *n, pl* **shorties.** *Inf.* **a** a person or thing that is extremely short. **b** (*as modifier*): *a shortie nightdress.*

short list *Chiefly Brit.* ◆ *n* **1** Also called (Scot.): **short leet.** a list of suitable applicants for a job, post, etc., from which the successful candidate will be selected. ◆ *vb* **short-list.** (*tr*) **2** to put (someone) on a short list.

short-lived Ⓣ *adj* living or lasting only for a short time.

shortly Ⓣ ('ʃɔːtlɪ) *adv* **1** in a short time; soon. **2** briefly. **3** in a curt or rude manner.

short-order *adj Chiefly US.* of or connected with food that is easily and quickly prepared.

short-range *adj* of small or limited extent in time or distance: *a short-range forecast.*

shorts (ʃɔːts) *pl n* **1** trousers reaching the top of the thigh or partway to the knee, worn by both sexes for sport, etc. **2** *Chiefly US & Canad.* men's underpants that usually reach mid-thigh. **3** short-dated gilt-edged securities. **4** short-term bonds. **5** securities or commodities that have been sold short. **6** a livestock feed containing a large proportion of bran and wheat germ.

short shrift *n* **1** brief and unsympathetic treatment. **2** (formerly) a brief period allowed to a condemned prisoner to make confession. **3** **make short shrift of.** to dispose of quickly.

short-sighted Ⓣ *adj* **1** relating to or suffering from myopia. **2** lacking foresight: *a short-sighted plan.*
▸ˌ**short-'sightedly** *adv* ▸ˌ**short-'sightedness** *n*

short-spoken *adj* tending to be abrupt in speech.

short story *n* a prose narrative of shorter length than the novel.

short-tempered Ⓣ *adj* easily moved to anger.

short-term *adj* **1** of, for, or extending over a limited period. **2** *Finance.* extending over, maturing within, or required within a short period of time, usually twelve months: *short-term credit; short-term capital.*

short-termism (-'tɜːmɪzəm) *n* the tendency to focus attention on short-term gains, often at the expense of long-term success or stability.

short time *n* the state or condition of working less than the normal working week, esp. because of a business recession.

short ton *n* the full name for **ton**[1] (sense 2).

short-waisted *adj* unusually short from the shoulders to the waist.

short wave *n* **a** a radio wave with a wavelength in the range 10–100 metres. **b** (*as modifier*): *a short-wave broadcast.*

short-winded *adj* **1** tending to run out of breath, esp. after exertion. **2** (of speech or writing) terse or abrupt.

shot[1] Ⓣ (ʃɒt) *n* **1** the act or an instance of discharging a projectile. **2** (*pl* **shot**) a solid missile, such as an iron ball or a lead pellet, discharged from a firearm. **3a** small round pellets of lead collectively, as used in cartridges. **3b** metal in the form of coarse powder or small pellets. **4** the distance that a discharged projectile travels or is capable of travelling. **5** a person who shoots, esp. with regard to his ability: *he is a good shot.* **6** *Inf.* an attempt. **7** *Inf.* a guess. **8** any act of throwing or hitting something, as in certain sports. **9** the launching of a rocket, etc., esp. to a specified destination: *a moon shot.* **10a** a single photograph. **10b** a length of film taken by a single camera without breaks. **11** *Inf.* an injection, as of a vaccine or narcotic drug. **12** *Inf.* a glass of alcoholic drink, esp. spirits. **13** *Sport.* a heavy metal ball used in the shot put. **14** **call the shots.** *Sl.* to have control over an organization, etc. **15** **have a shot at.** *Inf.* to attempt. **16** **like a shot.** very quickly, esp. willingly. **17** **shot in the arm.** *Inf.* anything that regenerates, increases confidence or efficiency, etc. **18** **shot in the dark.** a wild guess. [OE *scot*]

shot[2] Ⓣ (ʃɒt) *vb* **1** the past tense and past participle of **shoot.** ◆ *adj* **2** (of textiles) woven to give a changing colour effect: *shot silk.* **3** streaked with colour.

shotgun ('ʃɒtˌgʌn) *n* **1** a shoulder firearm with unrifled bore used mainly for hunting small game. **2** *American football.* an offensive formation in which the quarterback lines up for a snap unusually far behind the line of scrimmage. ◆ *adj* **3** *Chiefly US.* involving coercion or duress: *a shotgun merger.*

shotgun wedding *n Inf.* a wedding into which one or both partners are coerced, usually because the woman is pregnant.

shot put *n* an athletic event in which contestants hurl or put a heavy metal ball or shot as far as possible.
▸**'shot-ˌputter** *n*

shotten ('ʃɒtən) *adj* **1** (of fish, esp. herring) having recently spawned. **2** *Arch.* worthless. [C15: from obs. p.p. of SHOOT]

shot tower *n* a building formerly used in the production of shot, in which molten lead was graded and dropped from a great height into water, thus cooling it and forming the shot.

should (ʃʊd) *vb* the past tense of **shall:** used as an auxiliary verb to indicate that an action is considered by the speaker to be obligatory (*you should go*) or to form the subjunctive mood with *I* or *we* (*I should like to see you*). [OE *sceold*]

> **USAGE NOTE** *Should* has, as its most common meaning in modern English, the sense *ought* as in *I should go to the graduation, but I don't see how I can.* However, the older sense of the subjunctive of *shall* is often used with *I* or *we* to indicate a more polite form than *would: I should like to go, but I can't.* In much speech and writing, *should* has been replaced by *would* in contexts of this kind, but it remains in formal English when a conditional subjunctive is used: *should he choose to remain, he would be granted asylum.*

shoulder Ⓣ ('ʃəʊldə) *n* **1** the part of the vertebrate body where the arm or a corresponding forelimb joins the trunk. **2** the joint at the junction of the forelimb with the pectoral girdle. **3** a cut of meat including the upper part of the foreleg. **4** *Printing.* the flat surface of a piece of type from which the face rises. **5** the part of a garment that covers the shoulder. **6** anything that resembles a shoulder in shape or position. **7** the strip of unpaved land that borders a road. **8** **a shoulder to cry on.** a person one turns to for sympathy with one's troubles. **9** **give (someone) the cold shoulder.** *Inf.* **9a** to treat in a cold manner; snub. **9b** to ignore or shun. **10** **put one's shoulder to the wheel.** *Inf.* to work very hard. **11** **rub shoulders with.** *Inf.* to mix with socially or associate with. **12** **shoulder to shoulder.** **12a** side by side. **12b** in a corporate effort. ◆ *vb* **13** (*tr*) to bear or carry (a burden, etc.) as if on one's shoulders. **14** to push (something) with or as if with the shoulder. **15** (*tr*) to lift or carry on the shoulders. **16** **shoulder arms.** *Mil.* to bring the rifle vertically close to the right side with the muzzle uppermost. [OE *sculdor*]

shoulder blade Ⓣ *n* the nontechnical name for **scapula.**

shoulder strap *n* a strap over the shoulders, as to hold up a garment or to support a bag, etc.

shouldn't ('ʃʊdənt) *contraction of* should not.

shouldst (ʃʊdst) *or* **shouldest** ('ʃʊdɪst) *vb Arch. or dialect.* (used with the pronoun *thou*) a form of the past tense of **shall.**

shout Ⓣ (ʃaʊt) *n* **1** a loud cry, esp. to convey emotion or a command. **2** *Inf.* **2a** a round, esp. of drinks. **2b** one's turn to buy a round of drinks. ◆ *vb* **3** to utter (something) in a loud cry. **4** (*intr*) to make a loud noise.

THESAURUS

shorten *vb* **1** = **cut**, abbreviate, abridge, curtail, cut back, cut down, decrease, diminish, dock, downsize, lessen, prune, reduce, trim, truncate, turn up
Antonyms *vb* draw out, elongate, expand, extend, increase, lengthen, make longer, prolong, protract, spin out, stretch

short-lived *adj* = **brief**, ephemeral, fleeting, impermanent, passing, short, temporary, transient, transitory

shortly *adv* **1** = **soon**, anon, any minute now, before long, erelong (*arch. or poetic*), in a little while, presently **2** = **briefly**, concisely, in a few words, succinctly **3** = **curtly**, abruptly, sharply, tartly, tersely

short-sighted *adj* **1** = **near-sighted**, blind as a bat, myopic **2** = **unthinking**, careless, ill-advised, ill-considered, impolitic, impractical, improvident, imprudent, injudicious, seeing no further than (the end of) one's nose

short-tempered *adj* = **quick-tempered**, choleric, fiery, hot-tempered, impatient, irascible, peppery, ratty (*Brit. & NZ inf.*), testy, touchy

shot[1] *n* **1** = **throw**, discharge, lob, pot shot **2** = **pellet**, ball, bullet, lead, projectile, slug **5** = **marksman**, shooter **6** *Informal* = **attempt**, chance, crack (*inf.*), effort, endeavour, essay, go (*inf.*), opportunity, stab (*inf.*), try, turn **7** *Informal* = **guess**, conjecture, surmise **15** **have a shot at** *Informal* = **attempt**, have a bash (*inf.*), have a crack (*inf.*), have a go, have a stab (*inf.*), tackle, try, try one's luck **16** **like a shot** = **at once**, eagerly, immediately, like a bat out of hell (*sl.*), like a flash, quickly, unhesitatingly **17** **shot in the arm** *Informal* = **boost**, encouragement, fillip, geeing-up, impetus, lift, stimulus

shot[2] *adj* **2, 3** = **iridescent**, moiré, opalescent, watered

shoulder *n* **9** **give (someone) the cold shoulder** *Informal* = **snub**, blank, cut (*inf.*), ignore, kick in the teeth (*sl.*), ostracize, put down, rebuff, send (someone) to Coventry, shun **10** **put one's shoulder to the wheel** *Informal* = **work hard**, apply oneself, buckle down to (*inf.*), exert oneself, get down to, make every effort, set to work, strive **11** **rub shoulders with** *Informal* = **mix with**, associate with, consort with, fraternize with, hobnob with, socialize with **12** **shoulder to shoulder: a** = **side by side b** = **together** as one, in cooperation, in partnership, in unity, jointly, united ◆ *vb* **13** = **bear**, accept, assume, be responsible for, carry, take on, take upon oneself **14** = **push**, elbow, jostle, press, shove, thrust

shoulder blade *n* = **scapula**

shout *n* **1** = **cry**, bellow, call, roar, scream, yell ◆ *vb* **3, 4** = **cry (out)**, bawl, bay, bellow, call (out), holler (*inf.*), hollo, raise one's voice, roar, scream, yell

5 (*tr*) *Austral. & NZ inf.* to treat (someone) to (something, esp. a round of drinks). [C14: prob. from ON *skūta* taunt]
►'**shouter** *n*

shout down ❶ *vb* (*tr, adv*) to drown, overwhelm, or silence by talking loudly.

shove ❶ (ʃʌv) *vb* **shoves, shoving, shoved. 1** to give a thrust or push to (a person or thing). **2** (*tr*) to give a violent push to. **3** (*intr*) to push one's way roughly. **4** (*tr*) *Inf.* to put (something) somewhere: *shove it in the bin.* ◆ *n* **5** the act or an instance of shoving. ◆ See also **shove off.** [OE *scūfan*]
►'**shover** *n*

shove-halfpenny *n Brit.* a game in which players try to propel coins, originally old halfpennies, with the hand into lined sections of a wooden board.

shovel ❶ ('ʃʌvᵊl) *n* **1** an instrument for lifting or scooping loose material, such as earth, coal, etc., consisting of a curved blade or a scoop attached to a handle. **2** any machine or part resembling a shovel in action. **3** Also called: **shovelful.** the amount that can be contained in a shovel. ◆ *vb* **shovels, shovelling, shovelled** *or US* **shovels, shoveling, shoveled. 4** to lift (earth, etc.) with a shovel. **5** (*tr*) to clear or dig (a path) with or as if with a shovel. **6** (*tr*) to gather, load, or unload in a hurried or careless way. [OE *scofl*]
►'**shoveller** *or US* '**shoveler** *n*

shoveler ('ʃʌvələ) *n* a duck of ponds and marshes, having a spoon-shaped bill, a blue patch on each wing, and in the male a green head, white breast, and reddish-brown body.

shovelhead ('ʃʌvᵊlˌhɛd) *n* a common shark of the Atlantic and Pacific Oceans, having a shovel-shaped head.

shove off ❶ *vb* (*intr, adv; often imperative*) **1** to move from the shore in a boat. **2** *Inf.* to go away; depart.

show ❶ (ʃəʊ) *vb* **shows, showing, showed; shown** *or* **showed. 1** to make, be, or become visible or noticeable: *to show one's dislike.* **2** (*tr*) to exhibit: *he showed me a picture.* **3** (*tr*) to indicate or explain; prove: *to show that the earth moves round the sun.* **4** (*tr*) to present (oneself or itself) in a specific character: *to show oneself to be trustworthy.* **5** (*tr*; foll. by *how* and an infinitive) to instruct by demonstration: *show me how to swim.* **6** (*tr*) to indicate: *a barometer shows changes in the weather.* **7** (*tr*) to grant or bestow: *to show favour to someone.* **8** (*intr*) to appear: *to show to advantage.* **9** to exhibit, display, or offer (goods, etc.) for sale: *three artists were showing at the gallery.* **10** (*tr*) to allege, as in a legal document: *to show cause.* **11** to present (a film, etc.) or (of a play, etc.) to be presented, as at a theatre or cinema. **12** (*tr*) to guide or escort: *please show me to my room.* **13 show in** *or* **out.** to conduct a person into or out of a room or building by opening the door for him. **14** (*intr*) *Inf.* to arrive. ◆ *n* **15** a display or exhibition. **16** a public spectacle. **17** an ostentatious display. **18** a theatrical or other entertainment. **19** a trace or indication. **20** *Obstetrics.* a discharge of blood at the onset of labour. **21** *US, Austral., & NZ inf.* a chance (esp. in **give someone a show**). **22** *Sl., chiefly Brit.* a thing or affair (esp. in **good show, bad show,** etc.). **23 for show.** in order to attract attention. **24 run the show.** *Inf.* to take charge of or manage an affair, business, etc. **25 steal the show.** *Inf.* to be looked upon as the most interesting, popular, etc., esp. unexpectedly. ◆ See also **show off, show up.** [OE *scēawian*]

showboat ('ʃəʊˌbəʊt) *n* **1** a paddle-wheel river steamer with a theatre and a repertory company. ◆ *vb* **2** (*intr*) to perform or behave in a showy flamboyant way.

showbread ('ʃəʊˌbrɛd) *n* a variant spelling of **shewbread.**

show business *n* the entertainment industry, including theatre, films, television, and radio. Informal term: **show biz.**

show card *n Commerce.* a card containing a tradesman's advertisement; poster.

showcase ('ʃəʊˌkeɪs) *n* **1** a glass case used to display objects in a museum or shop. **2** a setting in which anything may be displayed to best advantage. ◆ *vb* **showcases, showcasing, showcased. 3** (*tr*) to display or exhibit.

show day *n* (in Australia) a public holiday in a state on the date of its annual agricultural and industrial show.

showdown ❶ ('ʃəʊˌdaʊn) *n* **1** *Inf.* an action that brings matters to a head or acts as a conclusion. **2** *Poker.* the exposing of the cards in the players' hands at the end of the game.

shower[1] ❶ ('ʃaʊə) *n* **1** a brief period of rain, hail, sleet, or snow. **2** a sudden abundant fall or downpour, as of tears, sparks, or light. **3** a rush: *a shower of praise.* **4a** a kind of bath in which a person stands upright and is sprayed with water from a nozzle. **4b** the room, booth, etc., containing such a bath. Full name: **shower bath. 5** *Brit. sl.* a derogatory term applied to a person or group. **6** *US, Canad., Austral., & NZ.* a party held to honour and present gifts to a person, as to a prospective bride. **7** a large number of particles formed by the collision of a cosmic-ray particle with a particle in the atmosphere. **8** *NZ.* a light fabric put over a tea table to protect the food from flies, etc. ◆ *vb* **9** (*tr*) to sprinkle or spray with or as if with a shower. **10** (often with *it* as subject) to fall or cause to fall in the form of a shower. **11** (*tr*) to give (gifts, etc.) in abundance or present (a person) with (gifts, etc.): *they showered gifts on him.* **12** (*intr*) to take a shower. [OE *scūr*]
►'**showery** *adj*

shower[2] ('ʃəʊə) *n* a person or thing that shows.

showgirl ('ʃəʊˌgɜːl) *n* a girl who appears in variety shows, nightclub acts, etc.

show house *n* a house on a newly built estate that is decorated and furnished for prospective buyers to view.

showing ❶ ('ʃəʊɪŋ) *n* **1** a presentation, exhibition, or display. **2** manner of presentation.

showjumping ('ʃəʊˌdʒʌmpɪŋ) *n* the riding of horses in competitions to demonstrate skill in jumping over or between various obstacles.
►'**show-ˌjumper** *n*

showman ❶ ('ʃəʊmən) *n, pl* **showmen. 1** a person who presents or produces a theatrical show, etc. **2** a person skilled at presenting anything in an effective manner.
►'**showmanship** *n*

shown (ʃəʊn) *vb* a past participle of **show.**

show off ❶ *vb* (*adv*) **1** (*tr*) to exhibit or display so as to invite admiration. **2** (*intr*) *Inf.* to behave in such a manner as to make an impression. ◆ *n* **show-off. 3** *Inf.* a person who makes a vain display of himself.

showpiece ('ʃəʊˌpiːs) *n* **1** anything displayed or exhibited. **2** anything prized as a very fine example of its type.

showplace ('ʃəʊˌpleɪs) *n* a place exhibited or visited for its beauty, historic interest, etc.

showroom ('ʃəʊˌruːm, -ˌrʊm) *n* a room in which goods for sale, such as cars, are on display.

show up ❶ *vb* (*adv*) **1** to reveal or be revealed clearly. **2** (*tr*) to expose or reveal the faults or defects of by comparison. **3** (*tr*) *Inf.* to put to shame; embarrass. **4** (*intr*) *Inf.* to appear or arrive.

showy ❶ ('ʃəʊɪ) *adj* **showier, showiest. 1** gaudy or ostentatious. **2** making an imposing display.
►'**showily** *adv* ►'**showiness** *n*

shrank (ʃræŋk) *vb* a past tense of **shrink.**

shrapnel ('ʃræpnᵊl) *n* **1** a projectile containing a number of small pellets or bullets exploded before impact. **2** fragments from this type of shell. [C19: after H. *Shrapnel* (1761–1842), E army officer, who invented it]

shred ❶ (ʃrɛd) *n* **1** a long narrow strip or fragment torn or cut off. **2** a very small piece or amount. ◆ *vb* **shreds, shredding, shredded** *or* **shred. 3** (*tr*) to tear or cut into shreds. [OE *scread*]
►'**shredder** *n*

shrew ❶ (ʃruː) *n* **1** Also called: **shrewmouse.** a small mouselike long-

THESAURUS

shout down *vb* = **silence**, drown, drown out, overwhelm

shove *vb* **1-3** = **push**, crowd, drive, elbow, impel, jostle, press, propel, shoulder, thrust

shovel *vb* **4** = **move**, convey, dredge, heap, ladle, load, scoop, shift, spoon, toss

shove off *vb* **2** *Informal* = **go away**, bugger off (*taboo sl.*), clear off (*inf.*), depart, get on one's bike, go to hell (*inf.*), leave, pack one's bags (*inf.*), push off (*inf.*), scram (*inf.*), sling one's hook (*Brit. sl.*), slope off, take oneself off, vamoose (*sl., chiefly US*)

show *vb* **1, 2** = **present**, display, exhibit **3** = **prove**, assert, clarify, demonstrate, elucidate, evince, point out **5** = **instruct**, demonstrate, explain, teach **6** = **indicate**, demonstrate, disclose, display, divulge, evidence, evince, make known, manifest, register, reveal, testify to **7** = **act with**, accord, bestow, confer, grant **8** = **be visible**, appear **12** = **guide**, accompany, attend, conduct, escort, lead ◆ *n* **15** = **exhibition**, array, demonstration, display, expo (*inf.*), exposition, fair, manifestation, pageant, pageantry, parade, representation, sight, spectacle, view **17** = **pretence**, affectation, air, appearance, display, illusion, likeness, ostentation, parade, pose, pretext, profession, semblance **18** = **entertainment**, presentation, production
Antonyms *vb* ≠ **present, indicate:** conceal, hide, keep secret, mask, obscure, suppress, veil, withhold ≠ **prove:** deny, disprove, gainsay (*arch. or literary*), refute ≠ **be visible:** be invisible

showdown *n* **1** *Informal* = **confrontation**, breaking point, clash, climax, crisis, culmination, denouement, exposé, face-off (*sl.*), moment of truth

shower[1] *n* **2** = **deluge**, barrage, downpour, fusillade, plethora, rain, stream, torrent, volley **5** *Brit. slang* = **rabble**, bunch of layabouts, crew ◆ *vb* **9** = **spray**, pour, rain, sprinkle **11** = **inundate**, deluge, heap, lavish, load

showing *n* **1** = **display**, demonstration, exhibition, presentation, staging

showman *n* **1** = **impresario**, publicist, stage manager **2** = **performer**, entertainer

show off *vb* **1** = **exhibit**, advertise, demonstrate, display, flaunt, parade, spread out **2** *Informal* = **boast**, blow one's own trumpet, brag, hot-dog (*chiefly US*), make a spectacle of oneself, shoot a line (*inf.*), strut one's stuff (*chiefly US*), swagger ◆ *n* **show-off 3** *Informal* = **exhibitionist**, boaster, braggadocio, braggart, egotist, hot dog (*chiefly US*), peacock, poseur, swaggerer

show up *vb* **1** = **stand out**, appear, be conspicuous, be visible, catch the eye, leap to the eye **2** = **reveal**, expose, highlight, lay bare, pinpoint, put the spotlight on, unmask **3** *Informal* = **embarrass**, let down, mortify, put to shame, shame, show in a bad light **4** *Informal* = **arrive**, appear, come, make an appearance, put in an appearance, show one's face, turn up

showy *adj* **1** = **ostentatious**, brash, flamboyant, flash (*inf.*), flashy, garish, gaudy, over the top (*inf.*), pompous, pretentious, splashy (*inf.*), tawdry, tinselly
Antonyms *adj* discreet, low-key, muted, quiet, restrained, subdued, tasteful, unobtrusive

shred *n* **1** = **strip**, bit, fragment, piece, rag, ribbon, scrap, sliver, snippet, tatter **2** = **particle**, atom, grain, iota, jot, scrap, trace, whit

shrew *n* **2** = **nag**, ballbreaker (*sl.*), dragon (*inf.*), fury, harpy, harridan, scold, spitfire, termagant (*rare*), virago, vixen, Xanthippe snouted insectivorous mammal. **2** a bad-tempered or mean-spirited woman. [OE *scrēawa*]

shrewd ◐ (ʃruːd) *adj* **1** astute and penetrating, often with regard to business. **2** artful: *a shrewd politician.* **3** *Obs.* piercing: *a shrewd wind.* [C14: from *shrew* (obs. vb) to curse, from SHREW]
▸ **'shrewdly** *adv* ▸ **'shrewdness** *n*

shrewish ◐ ('ʃruːɪʃ) *adj* (esp. of a woman) bad-tempered and nagging.

shriek ◐ (ʃriːk) *n* **1** a shrill and piercing cry. ◆ *vb* **2** to produce or utter (words, sounds, etc.) in a shrill piercing tone. [C16: prob. from ON *skrækja* to screech]
▸ **'shrieker** *n*

shrieval ('ʃriːvᵊl) *adj* of or relating to a sheriff.

shrievalty ('ʃriːvəltɪ) *n, pl* **shrievalties. 1** the office or term of office of a sheriff. **2** the jurisdiction of a sheriff. [C16: from arch. *shrieve* sheriff, on the model of *mayoralty*]

shrift (ʃrɪft) *n Arch.* the act or an instance of shriving or being shriven. See also **short shrift.** [OE *scrift,* from L *scriptum* SCRIPT]

shrike (ʃraɪk) *n* an Old World songbird having a heavy hooked bill and feeding on smaller animals which it sometimes impales on thorns, etc. Also called: **butcherbird.** [OE *scrīc* thrush]

shrill ◐ (ʃrɪl) *adj* **1** sharp and high-pitched in quality. **2** emitting a sharp high-pitched sound. ◆ *vb* **3** to utter (words, sounds, etc.) in a shrill tone. [C14: prob. from OE *scralletan*]
▸ **'shrillness** *n* ▸ **'shrilly** *adv*

shrimp (ʃrɪmp) *n* **1** any of a genus of chiefly marine decapod crustaceans having a slender flattened body with a long tail and a single pair of pincers. **2** *Inf.* a diminutive person, esp. a child. ◆ *vb* **3** (*intr*) to fish for shrimps. [C14: prob. of Gmc origin]
▸ **'shrimper** *n*

shrine (ʃraɪn) *n* **1** a place of worship hallowed by association with a sacred person or object. **2** a container for sacred relics. **3** the tomb of a saint or other holy person. **4** a place or site venerated for its association with a famous person or event. **5** *RC Church.* a building, alcove, or shelf arranged as a setting for a statue, picture, etc., of Christ, the Virgin Mary, or a saint. ◆ *vb* **shrines, shrining, shrined. 6** short for **enshrine.** [OE *scrīn,* from L *scrīnium* bookcase]
▸ **'shrine,like** *adj*

shrink ◐ (ʃrɪŋk) *vb* **shrinks, shrinking; shrank** *or* **shrunk; shrunk** *or* **shrunken. 1** to contract or cause to contract as from wetness, heat, cold, etc. **2** to become or cause to become smaller in size. **3** (*intr;* often foll. by *from*) **3a** to recoil or withdraw: *to shrink from the sight of blood.* **3b** to feel great reluctance (at). ◆ *n* **4** the act or an instance of shrinking. **5** a slang word for **psychiatrist.** [OE *scrincan*]
▸ **'shrinkable** *adj* ▸ **'shrinker** *n* ▸ **'shrinking** *adj*

shrinkage ('ʃrɪŋkɪdʒ) *n* **1** the act or fact of shrinking. **2** the amount by which anything decreases in size, value, weight, etc. **3** *Commerce.* the loss of merchandise through shoplifting or damage.

shrinking violet *n Inf.* a shy person.

shrink-wrap *vb* **shrink-wraps, shrink-wrapping, shrink-wrapped.** (*tr*) to package a product in a flexible plastic wrapping designed to shrink about its contours to protect and seal it.

shrive (ʃraɪv) *vb* **shrives, shriving; shrove** *or* **shrived; shriven** ('ʃrɪvᵊn) *or* **shrived.** *Chiefly RC Church.* **1** to hear the confession of (a penitent). **2** (*tr*) to impose a penance upon (a penitent) and grant him absolution. **3** (*intr*) to confess one's sins to a priest in order to obtain forgiveness. [OE *scrīfan,* from L *scrībere* to write]
▸ **'shriver** *n*

shrivel ◐ ('ʃrɪvᵊl) *vb* **shrivels, shrivelling, shrivelled** *or US* **shrivels, shriveling, shriveled. 1** to make or become shrunken and withered. **2** to lose or cause to lose vitality. [C16: prob. of Scand. origin]

shroud ◐ (ʃraʊd) *n* **1** a garment or piece of cloth used to wrap a dead body. **2** anything that envelops like a garment: *a shroud of mist.* **3** a protective covering for a piece of equipment. **4** *Astronautics.* a streamlined protective covering used to protect the payload during a rocket-powered launch. **5** *Naut.* one of a pattern of ropes or cables used to stay a mast. ◆ *vb* (*tr*) **6** to wrap in a shroud. **7** to cover, envelop, or hide. [OE *scrūd* garment]
▸ **'shroudless** *adj*

shrove (ʃrəʊv) *vb* a past tense of **shrive.**

Shrovetide ('ʃrəʊv,taɪd) *n* the Sunday, Monday, and Tuesday before Ash Wednesday, formerly a time when confessions were made for Lent.

shrub[1] (ʃrʌb) *n* a woody perennial plant, smaller than a tree, with several major branches arising from near the base of the main stem. [OE *scrybb*]
▸ **'shrub,like** *adj*

shrub[2] (ʃrʌb) *n* a mixed drink of rum, fruit juice, sugar, and spice. [C18: from Ar. *sharāb,* var. of *shurb* drink; see SHERBET]

shrubbery ('ʃrʌbərɪ) *n, pl* **shrubberies. 1** a place where a number of shrubs are planted. **2** shrubs collectively.

shrubby ('ʃrʌbɪ) *adj* **shrubbier, shrubbiest. 1** consisting of, planted with, or abounding in shrubs. **2** resembling a shrub.
▸ **'shrubbiness** *n*

shrug (ʃrʌg) *vb* **shrugs, shrugging, shrugged. 1** to draw up and drop (the shoulders) abruptly in a gesture expressing indifference, ignorance, etc. ◆ *n* **2** the gesture so made. [C14: from ?]

shrug off *vb* (*tr, adv*) **1** to minimize the importance of; dismiss. **2** to get rid of.

shrunk (ʃrʌŋk) *vb* a past participle and past tense of **shrink.**

shrunken ('ʃrʌŋkᵊn) *vb* **1** a past participle of **shrink.** ◆ *adj* **2** (*usually prenominal*) reduced in size.

shtoom (ʃtʊm) *adj Sl.* silent, dumb (esp. in **keep shtoom**). [from Yiddish, from G *stumm* silent]

shuck (ʃʌk) *n* **1** the outer covering of something, such as the husk of a grain of maize, a pea pod, or an oyster shell. ◆ *vb* (*tr*) **2** to remove the shucks from. [C17: US dialect, from ?]
▸ **'shucker** *n*

shucks (ʃʌks) *interj US & Canad. inf.* an exclamation of disappointment, annoyance, etc.

shudder ◐ ('ʃʌdə) *vb* **1** (*intr*) to shake or tremble suddenly and violently, as from horror, fear, aversion, etc. ◆ *n* **2** a convulsive shiver. [C18: from MLow G *schōderen*]
▸ **'shuddering** *adj* ▸ **'shudderingly** *adv* ▸ **'shuddery** *adj*

shuffle ◐ ('ʃʌfᵊl) *vb* **shuffles, shuffling, shuffled. 1** to walk or move (the feet) with a slow dragging motion. **2** to change the position of (something), esp. in order to deceive others. **3** (*tr*) to mix together in a careless manner: *he shuffled the papers nervously.* **4** to mix up (cards in a pack) to change their order. **5** (*intr*) to behave in an evasive or underhand manner. **6** (when *intr,* often foll. by *into* or *out of*) to move or cause to move clumsily: *he shuffled out of the door.* ◆ *n* **7** the act or an instance of shuffling. **8** a rearrangement: *a Cabinet shuffle.* **9** a dance or dance step with short dragging movements of the feet. [C16: prob. from Low G *schüffeln*]
▸ **'shuffler** *n*

shuffleboard ('ʃʌfᵊl,bɔːd) *n* a game in which players push wooden or plastic discs with a long cue towards numbered scoring sections marked on a floor, esp. a ship's deck.

shuffle off *vb* (*tr, adv*) to thrust off or put aside: *shuffle off responsibility.*

shuffle play *n* a facility on a compact disc player that selects tracks at random from a number of compact discs.

shufty *or* **shufti** ('ʃʊftɪ, 'ʃʌftɪ) *n, pl* **shufties.** *Brit. sl.* a look; peep. [C20: from Ar.]

shun ◐ (ʃʌn) *vb* **shuns, shunning, shunned.** (*tr*) to avoid deliberately. [OE *scunian,* from ?]

shunt (ʃʌnt) *vb* **1** to turn or cause to turn to one side. **2** *Railways.* to transfer (rolling stock) from track to track. **3** *Electronics.* to divert or be diverted through a shunt. **4** (*tr*) to evade by putting off onto someone else. ◆ *n* **5** the act or an instance of shunting. **6** a railway point. **7** *Electronics.* a low-resistance conductor connected in parallel across a part of a circuit to provide an alternative path for a known fraction of the

THESAURUS

shrewd *adj* **1, 2** = **clever**, acute, artful, astute, calculated, calculating, canny, crafty, cunning, discerning, discriminating, far-seeing, far-sighted, fly (*sl.*), intelligent, keen, knowing, long-headed, perceptive, perspicacious, sagacious, sharp, sly, smart, wily
Antonyms *adj* artless, dull, gullible, imprudent, ingenuous, innocent, naive, obtuse, slow-witted, stupid, trusting, undiscerning, unsophisticated, unworldly

shrewdly *adv* **1, 2** = **cleverly**, artfully, astutely, cannily, far-sightedly, knowingly, perceptively, perspicaciously, sagaciously, with all one's wits about one, with consummate skill

shrewdness *n* **1, 2** = **cleverness**, acumen, acuteness, astuteness, canniness, discernment, grasp, judgment, penetration, perspicacity, quick wits, sagacity, sharpness, smartness, suss (*sl.*)

shrewish *adj* = **bad-tempered**, cantankerous, complaining, discontented, fault-finding, ill-humoured, ill-natured, ill-tempered, litigious, nagging, peevish, petulant, quarrelsome, scolding, sharp-tongued, vixenish

shriek *n* **1** = **cry**, holler, howl, scream, screech, squeal, wail, whoop, yell ◆ *vb* **2** = **cry**, holler, howl, scream, screech, squeal, wail, whoop, yell

shrill *adj* **1** = **piercing**, acute, ear-piercing, ear-splitting, high, high-pitched, penetrating, piping, screeching, sharp
Antonyms *adj* deep, dulcet, mellifluous, silver-toned, soft, soothing, sweet-sounding, velvety, well-modulated

shrink *vb* **1, 2** = **decrease**, contract, deflate, diminish, downsize, drop off, dwindle, fall off, grow smaller, lessen, narrow, shorten, shrivel, wither, wrinkle **3** = **recoil**, cower, cringe, draw back, flinch, hang back, quail, retire, shy away, wince, withdraw
Antonyms *vb* ≠ **decrease:** balloon, dilate, distend, enlarge, expand, increase, inflate, mushroom, stretch, swell ≠ **recoil:** attack, challenge, confront, embrace, face, receive, welcome

shrivel *vb* **1** = **wither**, dehydrate, desiccate, dry up, dwindle, shrink, wilt, wizen, wrinkle

shrivelled *adj* **1** = **withered**, desiccated, dried up, dry, sere (*arch.*), shrunken, wizened, wrinkled

shroud *n* **1** = **winding sheet**, cerecloth, cerement, covering, grave clothes **2** = **covering**, cloud, mantle, pall, screen, veil ◆ *vb* **7** = **conceal**, blanket, cloak, cover, envelop, hide, screen, swathe, veil

shudder *vb* **1** = **shiver**, convulse, quake, quiver, shake, tremble ◆ *n* **2** = **shiver**, convulsion, quiver, spasm, trembling, tremor

shuffle *vb* **1** = **scuffle**, drag, scrape, scuff, shamble **2, 3** = **rearrange**, confuse, disarrange, disorder, intermix, jumble, mix, shift **5** = **be evasive**, beat about the bush, beg the question, cavil, dodge, equivocate, evade, flannel (*Brit. inf.*), gloss over, hedge, prevaricate, pussyfoot (*inf.*), quibble

shun *vb* = **avoid**, body-swerve (*Scot.*), cold-shoulder, elude, eschew, evade, fight shy of, give (someone *or* something) a wide berth, have no part in, keep away from, shy away from, steer clear of current. **8** *Med.* a channel that bypasses the normal circulation of the blood. **9** *Brit. inf.* a collision that occurs when a vehicle runs into the back of the vehicle in front. [C13: ?from *shunen* to SHUN]

shunt-wound ('ʃʌnt,waʊnd) *adj Electrical engineering.* (of a motor or generator) having the field and armature circuits connected in parallel.

shush (ʃʊʃ) *interj* **1** be quiet! hush! ◆ *vb* **2** to silence or calm (someone) by or as if by saying "shush". [C20: reduplication of SH, infl. by HUSH]

shut ❶ (ʃʌt) *vb* **shuts, shutting, shut. 1** to move (something) so as to cover an aperture: *to shut a door.* **2** to close (something) by bringing together the parts: *to shut a book.* **3** (*tr;* often foll. by *up*) to close or lock the doors of: *to shut up a house.* **4** (*tr;* foll. by *in, out,* etc.) to confine, enclose, or exclude. **5** (*tr*) to prevent (a business, etc.) from operating. **6 shut the door on. 6a** to refuse to think about. **6b** to render impossible. ◆ *adj* **7** closed or fastened. ◆ *n* **8** the act or time of shutting. ◆ See also **shutdown, shut-off,** etc. [OE *scyttan*]

shutdown ❶ ('ʃʌt,daʊn) *n* **1a** the closing of a factory, shop, etc. **1b** (*as modifier*): *shutdown costs.* ◆ *vb* **shut down.** (*adv*) **2** to cease or cause to cease operation. **3** (*tr*) to close by lowering.

shuteye ('ʃʌt,aɪ) *n* a slang term for **sleep.**

shut-in *n Chiefly US.* **a** a person confined indoors by illness. **b** (*as modifier*): *a shut-in patient.*

shut-off *n* **1** a device that shuts something off, esp. a machine control. **2** a stoppage or cessation. ◆ *vb* **shut off.** (*tr, adv*) **3** to stem the flow of. **4** to block off the passage through. **5** to isolate or separate.

shutout ❶ ('ʃʌt,aʊt) *n* **1** a less common word for a **lockout. 2** *Sport.* a match in which the opposition does not score. ◆ *vb* **shut out.** (*tr, adv*) **3** to keep out or exclude. **4** to conceal from sight: *we planted trees to shut out the view of the road.*

shutter ('ʃʌtə) *n* **1** a hinged doorlike cover, often louvred and usually one of a pair, for closing off a window. **2 put up the shutters.** to close business at the end of the day or permanently. **3** *Photog.* an opaque shield in a camera that, when tripped, admits light to expose the film or plate for a predetermined period, usually a fraction of a second. **4** *Music.* one of the louvred covers over the mouths of organ pipes, operated by the swell pedal. **5** a person or thing that shuts. ◆ *vb* (*tr*) **6** to close with a shutter or shutters. **7** to equip with a shutter or shutters.

shuttering ('ʃʌtərɪŋ) *n* another word (esp. Brit.) for **formwork.**

shuttle ❶ ('ʃʌtᵊl) *n* **1** a bobbin-like device used in weaving for passing the weft thread between the warp threads. **2** a small bobbin-like device used to hold the thread in a sewing machine, etc. **3a** a bus, train, aircraft, etc., that plies between two points. **3b** short for **space shuttle. 4a** the movement between various countries of a diplomat in order to negotiate with rulers who refuse to meet each other. **4b** (*as modifier*): *shuttle diplomacy.* **5** *Badminton, etc.* short for **shuttlecock.** ◆ *vb* **shuttles, shuttling, shuttled. 6** to move or cause to move by or as if by a shuttle. [OE *scytel* bolt]

shuttlecock ('ʃʌtᵊl,kɒk) *n* **1** a light cone consisting of a cork stub with feathered flights, struck to and fro in badminton and battledore. **2** anything moved to and fro, as in an argument.

shut up ❶ *vb* (*adv*) **1** (*tr*) to prevent all access to. **2** (*tr*) to confine or imprison. **3** *Inf.* to cease to talk or make a noise or cause to cease to talk or make a noise: often used in commands.

shwa (ʃwɑː) *n* a variant spelling of **schwa.**

shy[1] ❶ (ʃaɪ) *adj* **shyer, shyest** *or* **shier, shiest. 1** not at ease in the company of others. **2** easily frightened; timid. **3** (often foll. by *of*) watchful or wary. **4** (foll. by *of*) *Inf., chiefly US & Canad.* short (of). **5** (*in combination*) showing reluctance or disinclination: *workshy.* ◆ *vb* **shies, shying, shied.** (*intr*) **6** to move suddenly, as from fear: *the horse shied at the snake in the road.* **7** (usually foll. by *off* or *away*) to draw back. ◆ *n, pl* **shies. 8** a sudden movement, as from fear. [OE *sceoh*]
▸**'shyer** *n* ▸**'shyly** *adv* ▸**'shyness** *n*

shy[2] ❶ (ʃaɪ) *vb* **shies, shying, shied. 1** to throw (something) with a sideways motion. ◆ *n, pl* **shies. 2** a quick throw. **3** *Inf.* a gibe. **4** *Inf.* an attempt. [C18: of Gmc origin]
▸**'shyer** *n*

Shylock ('ʃaɪ,lɒk) *n* a heartless or demanding creditor. [C19: after *Shylock,* the heartless usurer in Shakespeare's *The Merchant of Venice* (1596)]

shyster ('ʃaɪstə) *n Sl., chiefly US.* a person, esp. a lawyer or politician, who uses discreditable methods. [C19: prob. based on *Scheuster,* a disreputable 19th-cent. New York lawyer]

si (siː) *n Music.* the syllable used in the fixed system of solmization for the note B. [C14: see GAMUT]

Si *the chemical symbol for* silicon.

SI 1 *symbol for* Système International (d'Unités). See **SI unit. 2** *NZ abbrev. for* South Island.

sial ('saɪəl) *n* the silicon-rich and aluminium-rich rocks of the earth's continental upper crust. [C20: *si(licon)* + *al(uminium)*]
▸**sialic** (saɪ'ælɪk) *adj*

siamang ('saɪə,mæŋ) *n* a large black gibbon of Sumatra and the Malay Peninsula, having the second and third toes united. [C19: from Malay]

Siamese (,saɪə'miːz) *n, pl* **Siamese. 1** See **Siamese cat.** ◆ *adj* **2** characteristic of, relating to, or being a Siamese twin. ◆ *adj, n, pl* **Siamese. 3** another word for **Thai.**

Siamese cat *n* a short-haired breed of cat with a tapering tail, blue eyes, and dark ears, mask, tail, and paws.

Siamese fighting fish *n* a brightly coloured labyrinth fish of Thailand and Malaysia: the males are very pugnacious.

Siamese twins *pl n* twin babies born joined together at some point, such as at the hips.

sib (sɪb) *n* **1** a blood relative. **2** kinsmen collectively; kindred. [OE *sibb*]

SIB (in Britain) *abbrev. for* Securities and Investments Board: a body that regulates financial dealings in the City of London.

Siberian (saɪ'bɪərɪən) *adj* **1** of or relating to Siberia or to its peoples. ◆ *n* **2** a native or inhabitant of Siberia.

sibilant ('sɪbɪlənt) *adj* **1** *Phonetics.* relating to or denoting the consonants (s, z, ʃ, ʒ), all pronounced with a characteristic hissing sound. **2** having a hissing sound. ◆ *n* **3** a sibilant consonant. [C17: from L *sībilāre* to hiss, imit.]
▸**'sibilance** *or* **'sibilancy** *n* ▸**'sibilantly** *adv*

sibilate ('sɪbɪ,leɪt) *vb* **sibilates, sibilating, sibilated.** to pronounce or utter (words or speech) with a hissing sound.
▸**,sibi'lation** *n*

sibling ('sɪblɪŋ) *n* **a** a person's brother or sister. **b** (*as modifier*): *sibling rivalry.* [C19: specialized modern use of OE *sibling* relative, from SIB]

sibyl ❶ ('sɪbɪl) *n* **1** (in ancient Greece and Rome) any of a number of women believed to be oracles or prophetesses. **2** a witch, fortuneteller, or sorceress. [C13: ult. from Gk *Sibulla,* from ?]
▸**sibylline** ('sɪbɪ,laɪn) *adj*

sic[1] (sɪk) *adv* so or thus: inserted in brackets in a text to indicate that an odd or questionable reading is what was actually written or printed. [L]

sic[2] (sɪk) *vb* **sics, sicking, sicked.** (*tr*) **1** to attack: used only in commands, as to a dog. **2** to urge (a dog) to attack. [C19: dialect var. of SEEK]

siccative ('sɪkətɪv) *n* a substance added to a liquid to promote drying: used in paints and some medicines. [C16: from LL *siccātīvus,* from L *siccāre* to dry up, from *siccus* dry]

Sicilian (sɪ'sɪlɪən) *adj* **1** of or relating to the island of Sicily, in the Mediterranean. ◆ *n* **2** a native or inhabitant of Sicily.

siciliano (,siːtʃiː'ljɑːnəʊ) *n, pl* **sicilianos. 1** an old dance in six-beat or twelve-beat time. **2** a piece of music composed for or in the rhythm of this dance. [It.]

sick[1] ❶ (sɪk) *adj* **1** inclined or likely to vomit. **2a** suffering from ill health. **2b** (*as collective n;* preceded by *the*): *the sick.* **3a** of or used by people who are unwell: *sick benefits.* **3b** (*in combination*): *a sickroom.* **4** deeply affected with a mental or spiritual feeling akin to physical sickness: *sick at heart.* **5** mentally or spiritually disturbed. **6** *Inf.* delighting in or catering for the macabre: *sick humour.* **7** Also: **sick and tired.** (often foll. by *of*) *Inf.* disgusted or weary: *I am sick of his everlasting laughter.* **8** (often foll. by *for*) weary with longing: *I am sick for my own country.* **9** pallid or sickly. **10** not in working order. ◆ *n, vb* **11** an informal word for **vomit.** [OE *sēoc*]
▸**'sickish** *adj*

sick[2] (sɪk) *vb* a variant spelling of **sic**[2].

sickbay ('sɪk,beɪ) *n* a room for the treatment of the sick or injured, as on board a ship or at a boarding school.

sick building syndrome *n* a group of symptoms, such as headaches, eye irritation, and lethargy, that may be experienced by workers in offices that are totally air-conditioned.

THESAURUS

shut *vb* **1** = **close**, bar, draw to, fasten, push to, seal, secure, slam **4** = **confine**, cage, enclose, exclude, impound, imprison, keep, pound, wall off *or* up
Antonyms *vb* ≠ **close**: open, throw wide, unbar, unclose, undo, unfasten, unlock

shutdown *vb* **shut down 2** = **stop**, cease, cease operating, discontinue, halt, switch off **3** = **close**, shut up

shutout *vb* **shut out 3** = **exclude**, bar, black, blackball, debar, keep out, lock out, ostracize **4** = **conceal**, block out, cover, hide, mask, screen, veil

shuttle *vb* **6** = **go back and forth**, alternate, commute, go to and fro, ply, seesaw, shunt

shut up *vb* **2** = **confine**, bottle up, box in, cage, coop up, immure, imprison, incarcerate, intern, keep in **3** *Informal* = **be quiet**, button one's lip (*sl.*), fall silent, gag, hold one's tongue, hush, keep one's trap shut (*sl.*), muzzle, pipe down (*sl.*), put a sock in it (*Brit. sl.*), silence

shy[1] *adj* **1, 2** = **timid**, backward, bashful, coy, diffident, modest, mousy, nervous, reserved, reticent, retiring, self-conscious, self-effacing, shrinking **3 shy of** = **cautious of**, chary of, distrustful of, hesitant about, suspicious of, wary of ◆ *vb* **7** *usually with* **off** *or* **away** = **recoil**, balk, buck, draw back, flinch, quail, rear, start, swerve, take fright, wince
Antonyms *adj* ≠ **timid**: assured, bold, brash, cheeky, confident, fearless, forward, pushy (*inf.*), self-assured, self-confident ≠ **cautious of**: rash, reckless, unsuspecting, unwary

shy[2] *vb* **1** = **throw**, cast, chuck (*inf.*), fling, hurl, lob (*inf.*), pitch, propel, send, sling, toss

shyness *n* **1, 2** = **timidness**, bashfulness, diffidence, lack of confidence, modesty, mousiness, nervousness, reticence, self-consciousness, timidity, timorousness

sibyl *n* **1, 2** = **prophetess**, Cassandra, oracle, Pythia, pythoness, seer

sick[1] *adj* **1** = **nauseous**, green about the gills (*inf.*), ill, nauseated, puking (*sl.*), qualmish, queasy **2** = **unwell**, ailing, diseased, feeble, indisposed, laid up, on the sick list (*inf.*), poorly (*inf.*), under par (*inf.*), under the weather, weak **6** *Informal* = **morbid**, black, ghoulish, macabre, sadistic **7** *with* **of** = **tired**, blasé, bored, disgusted, displeased, fed up, jaded, revolted, satiated, weary
Antonyms *adj* ≠ **unwell**: able-bodied, fine, fit, fit and well, fit as a fiddle, hale and hearty, healthy, robust, up to par, well

sicken ➊ ('sɪkən) *vb* **1** to make or become nauseated or disgusted. **2** (*intr;* often foll. by *for*) to show symptoms (of an illness).
▸**'sickener** *n*

sickening ➊ ('sɪkənɪŋ) *adj* **1** causing sickness or revulsion. **2** *Inf.* extremely annoying.
▸**'sickeningly** *adv*

sick headache *n* **1** a headache accompanied by nausea. **2** a nontechnical name for **migraine.**

sickie ('sɪkɪ) *n Inf.* a day of sick leave from work. [C20: from SICK[1] + -IE]

sickle ('sɪkᵊl) *n* an implement for cutting grass, corn, etc., having a curved blade and a short handle. [OE *sicol,* from L *sēcula*]

sick leave *n* leave of absence from work through illness.

sicklebill ('sɪkᵊl,bɪl) *n* any of various birds having a markedly curved bill, such as certain hummingbirds and birds of paradise.

sickle-cell anaemia *n* a hereditary form of anaemia occurring mainly in Black populations, in which a large number of red blood cells become sickle-shaped.

sick list *n* **1** a list of the sick, esp. in the army or navy. **2 on the sick list.** ill.

sickly ➊ ('sɪklɪ) *adj* **sicklier, sickliest. 1** disposed to frequent ailments; not healthy; weak. **2** of or caused by sickness. **3** (of a smell, taste, etc.) causing revulsion or nausea. **4** (of light or colour) faint or feeble. **5** mawkish; insipid. ◆ *adv* **6** in a sick or sickly manner.
▸**'sickliness** *n*

sick-making *adj Inf.* galling; sickening.

sickness ➊ ('sɪknɪs) *n* **1** an illness or disease. **2** nausea or queasiness. **3** the state or an instance of being sick.

sick pay *n* wages paid to an employee while he is on sick leave.

sic transit gloria mundi *Latin.* ('sɪk 'trænsɪt 'glɔːrɪ,ɑː 'mundiː) thus passes the glory of the world.

sidalcea (sɪ'dælsɪə) *n* any of a genus of hardy perennial plants with pink flowers. Also called **Greek mallow.** [from NL]

side ➊ (saɪd) *n* **1** a line or surface that borders anything. **2** *Geom.* **2a** any line segment forming part of the perimeter of a plane geometric figure. **2b** another name for **face** (sense 13). **3** either of two parts into which an object, surface, area, etc., can be divided: *the right side and the left side.* **4** either of the two surfaces of a flat object: *the right and wrong side of the cloth.* **5** a surface or part of an object that extends vertically: *the side of a cliff.* **6** either half of a human or animal body, esp. the area around the waist: *I have a pain in my side.* **7** the area immediately next to a person or thing: *he stood at her side.* **8** a district, point, or direction within an area identified by reference to a central point: *the south side of the city.* **9** the area at the edge of a room, road, etc. **10** aspect or part: *look on the bright side.* **11** one of two or more contesting factions, teams, etc. **12** a page in an essay, etc. **13** a position, opinion, etc., held in opposition to another in a dispute. **14** line of descent: *he gets his brains from his mother's side.* **15** *Inf.* a television channel. **16** *Billiards, etc.* spin imparted to a ball by striking it off-centre with the cue. **17** *Brit. sl.* insolence or pretentiousness: *to put on side.* **18 on one side.** set apart from the rest, as provision for emergencies, etc. **19 on the side. 19a** apart from or in addition to the main object. **19b** as a sideline. **19c** *US.* as a side dish. **20 take sides.** to support one group, opinion, etc., as against another. ◆ *adj* **21** being on one side; lateral. **22** from or viewed as if from one side. **23** directed towards one side. **24** subordinate or incidental: *side road.* ◆ *vb* **sides, siding, sided. 25** (*intr;* usually foll. by *with*) to support or associate oneself (with a faction, interest, etc.). [OE *sīde*]

side arms *pl n* weapons carried on the person, by belt or holster, such as a sword, pistol, etc.

sideband ('saɪd,bænd) *n* the frequency band either above (**upper sideband**) or below (**lower sideband**) the carrier frequency, within which fall the components produced by modulation of a carrier wave.

sideboard ('saɪd,bɔːd) *n* a piece of furniture intended to stand at the side of a dining room, with drawers, cupboards, and shelves to hold silver, china, linen, etc.

sideboards ('saɪd,bɔːdz) *pl n* another term for **sideburns.**

sideburns ('saɪd,bɜːnz) *pl n* a man's whiskers grown down either side of the face in front of the ears. Also called: **sideboards, side whiskers,** (*Austral.*) **sidelevers.**

sidecar ('saɪd,kɑː) *n* a small car attached on one side to a motorcycle, the other side being supported by a single wheel.

side chain *n Chem.* a group of atoms bound to an atom, usually a carbon atom, that forms part of a larger chain or ring in a molecule.

-sided *adj* (*in combination*) having a side or sides as specified: *three-sided; many-sided.*

side deal *n* a transaction between two people for their private benefit, which is subsidiary to a contract negotiated by them on behalf of the organizations they represent.

side dish *n* a portion of food served in addition to the main dish.

side drum *n* a small double-headed drum carried at the side with snares that produce a rattling effect.

side effect *n* **1** any unwanted nontherapeutic effect caused by a drug. **2** any secondary effect, esp. an undesirable one.

side-foot *Soccer.* ◆ *n* **1** a shot or pass played with the side of the foot. ◆ *vb* **2** (*tr*) to strike (a ball) with the side of the foot.

sidekick ('saɪd,kɪk) *n Inf.* a close friend or follower who accompanies another on adventures, etc.

sidelight ('saɪd,laɪt) *n* **1** light coming from the side. **2** a side window. **3** either of the two navigational running lights used by vessels at night, a red light on the port and a green on the starboard. **4** *Brit.* either of two small lights on the front of a motor vehicle. **5** additional or incidental information.

sideline ➊ ('saɪd,laɪn) *n* **1** *Sport.* a line that marks the side boundary of a playing area. **2** a subsidiary interest or source of income. **3** an auxiliary business activity or line of merchandise. ◆ *vb* **sidelines, sidelining, sidelined. 4** (*tr*) *Chiefly US & Canad.* to prevent (a player) from taking part in a game.

sidelines ➊ ('saɪd,laɪnz) *pl n* **1** *Sport.* the area immediately outside the playing area, where substitute players sit. **2** the peripheral areas of any region, organization, etc.

sidelong ➊ ('saɪd,lɒŋ) *adj* (*prenominal*) **1** directed or inclining to one side. **2** indirect or oblique. ◆ *adv* **3** from the side; obliquely.

sidereal (saɪ'dɪərɪəl) *adj* **1** of or involving the stars. **2** determined with reference to one or more stars: *the sidereal day.* [C17: from L *sīdereus,* from *sīdus* a star]
▸**si'dereally** *adv*

sidereal day *n* See **day** (sense 5).

sidereal period *n Astron.* the period of revolution of a body about another with respect to one or more stars.

sidereal time *n* time based upon the rotation of the earth with respect to a particular star, the **sidereal day** being the unit of measurement.

sidereal year *n* See **year** (sense 5).

siderite ('saɪdə,raɪt) *n* **1** a pale yellow to brownish-black mineral consisting chiefly of iron(II) carbonate. It occurs mainly in ore veins and sedimentary rocks and is an important source of iron. Formula: $FeCO_3$. **2** a meteorite consisting principally of metallic iron.

sidero- *or before a vowel* **sider-** *combining form.* indicating iron: *siderolite.* [from Gk *sidēros*]

siderolite ('saɪdərə,laɪt) *n* a meteorite consisting of a mixture of iron, nickel, and such ferromagnesian minerals as olivine.

siderosis (,saɪdə'rəʊsɪs) *n* a lung disease caused by breathing in fine particles of iron or other metallic dust.

siderostat ('saɪdərəʊ,stæt) *n* an astronomical instrument consisting of a plane mirror rotated by a clock mechanism about two axes so that light from a celestial body, esp. the sun, is reflected along a constant direction for a long period of time. [C19: from *sidero-,* from L *sidus* a star + -STAT]

side-saddle *n* **1** a riding saddle originally designed for women riders in skirts who sit with both legs on the near side of the horse. ◆ *adv* **2** on or as if on a side-saddle.

sideshow ('saɪd,ʃəʊ) *n* **1** a small show or entertainment offered in conjunction with a larger attraction, as at a circus or fair. **2** a subordinate event or incident.

sideslip ('saɪd,slɪp) *n* **1** a sideways skid, as of a motor vehicle. ◆ *vb* **sideslips, sideslipping, sideslipped. 2** another name for **slip**[1] (sense 11).

sidesman ('saɪdzmən) *n, pl* **sidesmen.** *Church of England.* a man elected to help the parish church-warden.

side-splitting ➊ *adj* **1** producing great mirth. **2** (of laughter) uproarious or very hearty.

sidestep ➊ ('saɪd,stɛp) *vb* **sidesteps, sidestepping, sidestepped. 1** to step aside from or out of the way of (something). **2** (*tr*) to dodge or circum-

THESAURUS

sicken *vb* **1 = disgust,** gross out (*US sl.*), make one's gorge rise, nauseate, repel, revolt, turn one's stomach **2 = fall ill,** ail, be stricken by, contract, go down with, show symptoms of, take sick

sickening *adj* **1 = disgusting,** cringe-making (*Brit. inf.*), distasteful, foul, gut-wrenching, loathsome, nauseating, nauseous, noisome, offensive, putrid, repulsive, revolting, stomach-turning (*inf.*), vile, yucky *or* yukky (*sl.*)
Antonyms *adj* beneficial, curative, delightful, health-giving, heartening, inviting, marvellous, mouth-watering, pleasant, salutary, tempting, therapeutic, wholesome, wonderful

sickly *adj* **1 = unhealthy,** ailing, bilious, bloodless, delicate, faint, feeble, indisposed, infirm, in poor health, lacklustre, languid, pallid, peaky, pining, wan, weak **3 = nauseating,** bilious (*inf.*), cloying, mawkish, revolting (*inf.*), syrupy (*inf.*)

sickness *n* **1 = illness,** affliction, ailment, bug (*inf.*), complaint, disease, disorder, indisposition, infirmity, lurgy (*inf.*), malady **2 = nausea,** barfing (*US sl.*), (the) collywobbles (*sl.*), puking (*sl.*), queasiness, vomiting

side *n* **1 = border,** boundary, division, edge, limit, margin, part, perimeter, periphery, rim, sector, verge **3, 4 = part,** aspect, face, facet, flank, hand, surface, view **11 = party,** camp, cause, faction, sect, team **13 = point of view,** angle, light, opinion, position, slant, stand, standpoint, viewpoint **17** *Brit. slang* **= conceit,** airs, arrogance, insolence, pretentiousness ◆ *adj* **21 = lateral,** flanking **24 = subordinate,** ancillary, incidental, indirect, lesser, marginal, minor, oblique, roundabout, secondary, subsidiary ◆ *vb* **25** *usually with* **with = support,** ally with, associate oneself with, befriend, favour, go along with, join with, second, take the part of, team up with (*inf.*)
Antonyms *n* ≠ **border:** centre, core, heart, middle ◆ *adj* ≠ **subordinate:** central, essential, focal, fundamental, key, main, middle, primary, principal ◆ *vb* ≠ **support:** counter, oppose, stand against, withstand

sideline *n* **2 = supplement,** subsidiary

sidelines *pl n* **2 = periphery,** border, boundary, edge, fringe, margin

sidelong *adj* **2 = sideways,** covert, indirect, oblique

side-splitting *adj* **1 = hilarious,** farcical, hysterical, rollicking, uproarious

sidestep *vb* **1, 2 = avoid,** body-swerve (*Scot.*), bypass, circumvent, dodge, duck (*inf.*), elude, evade, find a way round, skip, skirt

vent. ◆ *n* **side step. 3** a movement to one side, as in dancing, boxing, etc.
▸**'side,stepper** *n*

sidestroke ('saɪd,strəʊk) *n* a type of swimming stroke in which the swimmer lies sideways in the water making a scissors kick with his legs.

sideswipe ('saɪd,swaɪp) *n* **1** a glancing blow or hit along or from the side. **2** an unexpected criticism of someone or something while discussing another subject. ◆ *vb* **sideswipes, sideswiping, sideswiped. 3** to strike (someone) with a glancing blow from the side.
▸**'side,swiper** *n*

sidetrack ❶ ('saɪd,træk) *vb* **1** to distract or be distracted from a main subject or topic. ◆ *n* **2** *US & Canad.* a railway siding. **3** a digression.

side-valve engine *n* a type of internal-combustion engine in which the inlet and exhaust valves are in the cylinder block at the side of the pistons.

sidewalk ('saɪd,wɔːk) *n* the US and Canad. word for **pavement.**

sidewall ('saɪd,wɔːl) *n* either of the sides of a pneumatic tyre between the tread and the rim.

sideward ('saɪdwəd) *adj* **1** directed or moving towards one side. ◆ *adv also* **sidewards. 2** towards one side.

sideways ❶ ('saɪd,weɪz) *adv* **1** moving, facing, or inclining towards one side. **2** from one side; obliquely. **3** with one side forward. ◆ *adj* (*prenominal*) **4** moving or directed to or from one side. **5** towards or from one side.

side whiskers *pl n* another name for **sideburns.**

sidewinder ('saɪd,waɪndə) *n* **1** a North American rattlesnake that moves forwards by a sideways looping motion. **2** *Boxing, US.* a heavy swinging blow from the side.

siding ('saɪdɪŋ) *n* **1** a short stretch of railway track connected to a main line, used for storing rolling stock. **2** a short railway line giving access to the main line for freight from a factory, etc. **3** *US & Canad.* material attached to the outside of a building to make it weatherproof.

sidle ❶ ('saɪdᵊl) *vb* **sidles, sidling, sidled.** (*intr*) **1** to move in a furtive or stealthy manner. **2** to move along sideways. [C17: back formation from obs. *sideling* sideways]

SIDS *abbrev. for* sudden infant death syndrome. See **cot death.**

siege (siːdʒ) *n* **1a** the offensive operations carried out to capture a fortified place by surrounding it and deploying weapons against it. **1b** (*as modifier*): *siege warfare.* **2** a persistent attempt to gain something. **3** *Obs.* a seat or throne. **4 lay siege to. 4a** to besiege. **4b** to importune. [C13: from OF *sege* a seat, from Vulgar L *sēdicāre* (unattested) to sit down, from L *sedēre*]

siege mentality *n* a state of mind in which a person believes that he or she is being constantly oppressed or attacked.

siemens ('siːmənz) *n, pl* **siemens.** the derived SI unit of electrical conductance equal to 1 reciprocal ohm. Symbol: S Formerly called: **mho.** [C20: after Ernst Werner von *Siemens* (1816–92) G engineer]

sienna (sɪ'ɛnə) *n* **1** a natural earth containing ferric oxide used as a yellowish-brown pigment when untreated (**raw sienna**) or a reddish-brown pigment when roasted (**burnt sienna**). **2** the colour of this pigment. [C18: from It. *terra di Siena* earth of Siena]

sierra (sɪ'ɛərə) *n* a range of mountains with jagged peaks, esp. in Spain or America. [C17: from Sp., lit.: saw, from L *serra*]
▸**si'erran** *adj*

siesta ❶ (sɪ'ɛstə) *n* a rest or nap, usually taken in the early afternoon, as in hot countries. [C17: from Sp., from L *sexta hōra* the sixth hour, i.e. noon]

sieve ❶ (sɪv) *n* **1** a device for separating lumps from powdered material, straining liquids, etc., consisting of a container with a mesh or perforated bottom through which the material is shaken or poured. ◆ *vb* **sieves, sieving, sieved. 2** to pass or cause to pass through a sieve. **3** (*tr;* often foll. by *out*) to separate or remove (lumps, materials, etc.) by use of a sieve. [OE *sife*]
▸**'sieve,like** *adj*

sift ❶ (sɪft) *vb* **1** (*tr*) to sieve (sand, flour, etc.) in order to remove the coarser particles. **2** to scatter (something) over a surface through a sieve. **3** (*tr*) to separate with or as if with a sieve. **4** (*tr*) to examine minutely: *to sift evidence.* **5** (*intr*) to move as if through a sieve. [OE *siftan*]
▸**'sifter** *n*

siftings ('sɪftɪŋz) *pl n* material or particles separated out by or as if by a sieve.

sigh ❶ (saɪ) *vb* **1** (*intr*) to draw in and exhale audibly a deep breath as an expression of weariness, relief, etc. **2** (*intr*) to make a sound resembling this. **3** (*intr;* often foll. by *for*) to yearn, long, or pine. **4** (*tr*) to utter or express with sighing. ◆ *n* **5** the act or sound of sighing. [OE *sīcan,* from ?]
▸**'sigher** *n*

sight ❶ (saɪt) *n* **1** the power or faculty of seeing; vision. Related adj: **visual. 2** the act or an instance of seeing. **3** the range of vision: *within sight of land.* **4** point of view; judgment: *in his sight she could do no wrong.* **5** a glimpse or view (esp. in **catch** *or* **lose sight of**). **6** anything that is seen. **7** (*often pl*) anything worth seeing: *the sights of London.* **8** *Inf.* anything unpleasant or undesirable to see: *his room was a sight!* **9** any of various devices or instruments used to assist the eye in making alignments or directional observations, esp. such a device used in aiming a gun. **10** an observation or alignment made with such a device. **11 a sight.** *Inf.* a great deal: *she's a sight too good for him.* **12 a sight for sore eyes.** a person or thing that one is pleased or relieved to see. **13 at** *or* **on sight. 13a** as soon as seen. **13b** on presentation: *a bill payable at sight.* **14 know by sight.** to be familiar with the appearance of without having personal acquaintance. **15 not by a long sight.** *Inf.* on no account. **16 set one's sights on.** to have (a specified goal) in mind. **17 sight unseen.** without having seen the object at issue: *to buy a car sight unseen.* ◆ *vb* **18** (*tr*) to see, view, or glimpse. **19** (*tr*) **19a** to furnish with a sight or sights. **19b** to adjust the sight of. **20** to aim (a firearm) using the sight. [OE *sihth*]
▸**'sightable** *adj*

sighted ('saɪtɪd) *adj* **1** not blind. **2** (*in combination*) having sight of a specified kind: *short-sighted.*

sighting ('saɪtɪŋ) *n* **1** an occasion on which something is seen, esp. something rare or unusual. **2** another name for **sight** (sense 10).

sighting shot *n* an experimental shot made to assist gunmen in setting their sights.

sightless ('saɪtlɪs) *adj* **1** blind. **2** invisible.
▸**'sightlessly** *adv* ▸**'sightlessness** *n*

sightly ('saɪtlɪ) *adj* **sightlier, sightliest.** pleasing or attractive to see.
▸**'sightliness** *n*

sight-read ('saɪt,riːd) *vb* **sight-reads, sight-reading, sight-read** (-,rɛd). to sing or play (music in a printed or written form) without previous preparation.
▸**'sight-,reader** *n* ▸**'sight-,reading** *n*

sightscreen ('saɪt,skriːn) *n Cricket.* a large white screen placed near the boundary behind the bowler to help the batsman see the ball.

sightsee ('saɪt,siː) *vb* **sightsees, sightseeing, sightsaw, sightseen.** to visit the famous or interesting sights of (a place).
▸**'sight,seeing** *n* ▸**'sight,seer** *n*

sigla ('sɪglə) *n* the list of symbols used in a book, usually collected together as part of the preliminaries. [L: pl of *siglum,* dim. of *signum* sign]

sigma ('sɪgmə) *n* **1** the 18th letter in the Greek alphabet (Σ, σ, or, when final, ς), a consonant, transliterated as *S.* **2** *Maths.* the symbol Σ, indicating summation of the numbers of quantities indicated. [C17: from Gk]

sigma notation *n* an algebraic notation in which a capital Greek sigma (Σ) is used to indicate that all values of the expression following the sigma are to be added together (usually for values of a variable between specified limits).

sigmoid ('sɪgmɔɪd) *or* **sigmoidal** *adj* **1** shaped like the letter S. **2** of or relating to the sigmoid flexure of the large intestine. [C17: from Gk *sigmoeidēs* sigma-shaped]

sigmoid flexure *n* the S-shaped bend in the final portion of the large intestine.

sign ❶ (saɪn) *n* **1** something that indicates a fact, condition, etc., that is not immediately or outwardly observable. **2** an action or gesture intended to convey information, a command, etc. **3a** a board, placard, etc., displayed in public and intended to inform, warn, etc. **3b** (*as modifier*): *a sign painter.* **4** an arbitrary mark or device that stands for a word, phrase, etc. **5** *Maths, logic.* **5a** any symbol used to indicate an operation: *a plus sign.* **5b** the positivity or negativity of a number, expression, etc. **6** an indication or vestige: *the house showed no signs of being occupied.* **7** a portentous or significant event. **8** the scent or spoor of an animal. **9** *Med.* any objective evidence of the presence of a disease or disorder. **10** *Astrol.* See **sign of the zodiac.** ◆ *vb* **11** to write (one's name) as a signature to (a document, etc.) in attestation, confirmation, etc. **12** (*intr;* often foll. by *to*) to make a sign. **13** to engage or be engaged by written agreement, as a player for a team, etc. **14** (*tr*) to outline in gestures a sign over, esp. the sign of the cross. **15** (*tr*) to indicate by or as if

THESAURUS

sidetrack *vb* **1** = **distract,** deflect, divert, lead off the subject

sideways *adv* **1, 2** = **obliquely,** crabwise, edgeways, laterally, sidelong, sidewards, to the side ◆ *adj* **4, 5** = **oblique,** side, sidelong, slanted

sidle *vb* **1** = **edge,** creep, inch, slink, sneak, steal

siesta *n* = **nap,** catnap, doze, forty winks (*inf.*), kip (*Brit. sl.*), rest, sleep, snooze (*inf.*)

sieve *n* **1** = **strainer,** colander, riddle, screen, sifter, tammy cloth ◆ *vb* **2, 3** = **sift,** bolt, remove, riddle, separate, strain

sift *vb* **1** = **sieve,** bolt, filter, pan, part, riddle, separate **4** = **examine,** analyse, fathom, go through, investigate, pore over, probe, research, screen, scrutinize, work over

sigh *vb* **1** = **breathe,** complain, grieve, lament, moan, sorrow, sough, suspire (*arch.*) **3 sigh for** = **long for,** eat one's heart out over, languish over, mourn for, pine for, yearn for

sight *n* **1** = **vision,** eye, eyes, eyesight, seeing **3** = **view,** appearance, apprehension, eyeshot, field of vision, ken, perception, range of vision, viewing, visibility **7** = **spectacle,** display, exhibition, pageant, scene, show, vista **8** *Informal* = **eyesore,** blot on the landscape (*inf.*), fright (*inf.*), mess, monstrosity, spectacle ◆ *vb* **18** = **spot,** behold, discern, distinguish, make out, observe, perceive, see

sign *n* **1** = **indication,** clue, evidence, giveaway, hint, manifestation, mark, note, proof, signal, suggestion, symptom, token, trace, vestige **3** = **notice,** board, placard, warning **4** = **symbol,** badge, character, cipher, device, emblem, ensign, figure, logo, mark, representation **7** = **omen,** augury, auspice, foreboding, forewarning, portent, presage, warning, writing on the wall ◆ *vb* **11** = **autograph,** endorse, initial, inscribe, set one's hand to, subscribe **12** = **gesture,** beckon, gesticulate, indicate, signal, use sign language, wave

by a sign; betoken. ◆ See also **sign away, sign in,** etc. [C13: from OF, from L *signum* a sign]
▸ **'signable** *adj* ▸ **'signer** *n*

signal ❶ ('sɪgnᵊl) *n* **1** any sign, gesture, etc., that serves to communicate information. **2** anything that acts as an incitement to action: *the rise in prices was a signal for rebellion.* **3a** a variable parameter, such as a current or electromagnetic wave, by which information is conveyed through an electronic circuit, etc. **3b** the information so conveyed. **3c** (*as modifier*): *a signal generator.* ◆ *adj* **4** distinguished or conspicuous. **5** used to give or act as a signal. ◆ *vb* **signals, signalling, signalled** *or US* **signals, signaling, signaled. 6** to communicate (a message, etc.) to (a person). [C16: from OF *seignal,* from Med. L *signāle,* from L *signum* sign]
▸ **'signaller** *or US* **'signaler** *n*

signal box *n* **1** a building containing signal levers for all the railway lines in its section. **2** a control point for a large area of a railway system.

signalize *or* **signalise** ('sɪgnəˌlaɪz) *vb* **signalizes, signalizing, signalized** *or* **signalises, signalising, signalised.** (*tr*) **1** to make noteworthy. **2** to point out carefully.

signally ('sɪgnəlɪ) *adv* conspicuously or especially.

signalman ('sɪgnᵊlmən) *n, pl* **signalmen.** a railway employee in charge of the signals and points within a section.

signal-to-noise ratio *n* the ratio of one parameter, such as power of a wanted signal, to the same parameter of the noise at a specified point in an electronic circuit, etc.

signatory ('sɪgnətərɪ, -trɪ) *n, pl* **signatories. 1** a person who has signed a document such as a treaty or an organization, state, etc., on whose behalf such a document has been signed. ◆ *adj* **2** having signed a document, treaty, etc. [C17: from L *signātōrius* concerning sealing, from *signāre* to seal, from *signum* a mark]

signature ('sɪgnɪtʃə) *n* **1** the name of a person or a mark or sign representing his name. **2** the act of signing one's name. **3** a distinctive mark, characteristic, etc., that identifies a person or thing. **4** *Music.* See **key signature, time signature. 5** *Printing.* **5a** a sheet of paper printed with several pages that upon folding will become a section or sections of a book. **5b** such a sheet so folded. **5c** a mark, esp. a letter, printed on the first page of a signature. [C16: from OF, from Med. L *signātura,* from L *signāre* to sign]

signature tune *n Brit.* a melody used to introduce or identify a television or radio programme, a performer, etc.

sign away ❶ *vb* (*tr, adv*) to dispose of by or as if by signing a document.

signboard ('saɪnˌbɔːd) *n* a board carrying a sign or notice, esp. one used to advertise a product, event, etc.

signet ('sɪgnɪt) *n* **1** a small seal, esp. one as part of a finger ring. **2** a seal used to stamp or authenticate documents. **3** the impression made by such a seal. [C14: from Med. L *signētum* a little seal, from L *signum* a sign]

signet ring *n* a finger ring bearing a signet.

significance ❶ (sɪg'nɪfɪkəns) *n* **1** consequence or importance. **2** something expressed or intended. **3** the state or quality of being significant. **4** *Statistics.* a measure of the confidence that can be placed in a result as not being merely a matter of chance.

significant ❶ (sɪg'nɪfɪkənt) *adj* **1** having or expressing a meaning. **2** having a covert or implied meaning. **3** important or momentous. **4** *Statistics.* of or relating to a difference between a result derived from a hypothesis and its observed value that is too large to be attributed to chance. [C16: from L *significāre* to SIGNIFY]
▸ **sig'nificantly** *adv*

significant figures *pl n* **1** the figures of a number that express a magnitude to a specified degree of accuracy: *3.141 59 to four significant figures is 3.142.* **2** the number of such figures: *3.142 has four significant figures.*

significant other *n US inf.* a spouse or lover.

signification (ˌsɪgnɪfɪ'keɪʃən) *n* **1** meaning or sense. **2** the act of signifying.

signify ❶ ('sɪgnɪˌfaɪ) *vb* **signifies, signifying, signified.** (when *tr, may take a clause as object*) **1** (*tr*) to indicate or suggest. **2** (*tr*) to imply or portend: *the clouds signified the coming storm.* **3** (*tr*) to stand as a symbol, sign, etc. (for). **4** (*intr*) to be important. [C13: from OF, from L *significāre,* from *signum* a mark + *facere* to make]
▸ **sig'nificative** *adj* ▸ **'signiˌfier** *n*

sign in *vb* (*adv*) **1** to sign or cause to sign a register, as at a hotel, club, etc. **2** to make or become a member, as of a club.

signing ('saɪnɪŋ) *n* a specific set of manual signs used to communicate with deaf people.

sign language *n* any system of communication by manual signs or gestures, such as one used by deaf people.

sign off *vb* (*adv*) **1** (*intr*) to announce the end of a radio or television programme, esp. at the end of a day. **2** (*tr*) (of a doctor) to declare (someone) unfit for work, because of illness. **3** (*intr*) *Brit.* to terminate one's claim to social security benefits.

sign of the zodiac *n* any of the 12 equal areas into which the zodiac can be divided, named after the 12 zodiacal constellations. In astrology, it is thought that a person's attitudes to life can be correlated with the sign in which the sun lay at the moment of their birth. Also called: **sign, star sign, sun sign.**

sign on *vb* (*adv*) **1** (*tr*) to hire or employ. **2** (*intr*) to commit oneself to a job, activity, etc. **3** (*intr*) *Brit.* to claim social security benefits.

signor *or* **signior** ('siːnjɔː; *Italian* siɲ'ɲor) *n, pl* **signors** *or* **signori** (*Italian* -'ɲori). an Italian man: usually used before a name as a title equivalent to *Mr.*

signora (siːn'jɔːrə; *Italian* siɲ'ɲora) *n, pl* **signoras** *or* **signore** (*Italian* -re). a married Italian woman: a title of address equivalent to *Mrs* when placed before a name or *madam* when used alone. [It., fem of SIGNORE]

signore (siːn'jɔːreɪ; *Italian* siɲ'ɲore) *n, pl* **signori** (-rɪ; *Italian* -ri). an Italian man: a title of respect equivalent to *sir* when used alone. [It., ult. from L *senior* an elder, from *senex* an old man]

signorina (ˌsiːnjɔː'riːnə; *Italian* siɲɲo'rina) *n, pl* **signorinas** *or* **signorine** (*Italian* -ne). an unmarried Italian woman: a title of address equivalent to *Miss* when placed before a name or *madam* or *miss* when used alone. [It., dim. of SIGNORA]

signory ('siːnjərɪ) *n, pl* **signories.** a variant spelling of **seigniory.**

sign out *vb* (*adv*) to sign (one's name) to indicate that one is leaving a place: *he signed out for the evening.*

signpost ('saɪnˌpəʊst) *n* **1** a post bearing a sign that shows the way, as at a roadside. **2** something that serves as a clue or indication. ◆ *vb* (*tr; usually passive*) **3** to mark with signposts. **4** to indicate direction towards.

sign up ❶ *vb* (*adv*) to enlist or cause to enlist, as for military service.

sika ('siːkə) *n* a Japanese forest-dwelling deer, now introduced into Britain, having a brown coat and a large white patch on the rump. [from Japanese *shika*]

Sikh (siːk) *n* **1** a member of an Indian religion that separated from Hinduism and was founded in the 16th century, that teaches monotheism and rejects the authority of the Vedas. ◆ *adj* **2** of or relating to the Sikhs or their religious beliefs. [C18: from Hindi, lit.: disciple, from Sansk. *śiksati* he studies]
▸ **'Sikhˌism** *n*

silage ('saɪlɪdʒ) *n* any crop harvested while green for fodder and kept succulent by partial fermentation in a silo. Also called: **ensilage.** [C19: alteration (infl. by SILO) of ENSILAGE]

sild (sɪld) *n* any of various small young herrings, esp. when prepared and canned in Norway. [Norwegian]

silence ❶ ('saɪləns) *n* **1** the state or quality of being silent. **2** the absence of sound or noise. **3** refusal or failure to speak, etc., when expected: *his silence on their promotion was alarming.* **4** a period of time without noise. **5** oblivion or obscurity. ◆ *vb* **silences, silencing, silenced.** (*tr*) **6** to bring to silence. **7** to put a stop to: *to silence all complaint.*

silencer ('saɪlənsə) *n* **1** any device designed to reduce noise, esp. the device in the exhaust system of a motor vehicle. US and Canad. name: **muffler. 2** a device fitted to the muzzle of a firearm to deaden the report. **3** a person or thing that silences.

silene (saɪ'liːnɪ) *n* any of a genus of plants with pink or white flowers and slender leaves. [C18: NL, from L]

silent ❶ ('saɪlənt) *adj* **1** characterized by an absence or near absence of noise or sound: *a silent house.* **2** tending to speak very little or not at all. **3** unable to speak. **4** failing to speak, communicate, etc., when expected: *the witness chose to remain silent.* **5** not spoken or expressed. **6** (of a letter) used in the orthography of a word but no longer pronounced in that word: *the "k" in "know" is silent.* **7** denoting a film that

THESAURUS

signal *n* **1** = **sign**, beacon, cue, flare, gesture, go-ahead (*inf.*), green light, indication, indicator, mark, token ◆ *adj* **4** = **significant**, conspicuous, distinguished, eminent, exceptional, extraordinary, famous, memorable, momentous, notable, noteworthy, outstanding, remarkable, serious (*inf.*), striking ◆ *vb* **6** = **gesture**, beckon, communicate, gesticulate, give a sign to, indicate, motion, nod, sign, wave

sign away *vb* = **give up**, abandon, dispose of, forgo, lose, relinquish, renounce, surrender, transfer, waive

significance *n* **1** = **importance**, consequence, consideration, impressiveness, matter, moment, relevance, weight **2** = **meaning**, force, implication(s), import, message, point, purport, sense, signification

significant *adj* **1, 2** = **meaningful**, denoting, eloquent, expressing, expressive, indicative, knowing, meaning, pregnant, suggestive **3** = **important**, critical, material, momentous, noteworthy, serious, vital, weighty

Antonyms *adj* ≠ **meaningful:** meaningless ≠ **important:** immaterial, inconsequential, insignificant, irrelevant, nit-picking, nugatory, of no consequence, paltry, petty, trivial, unimportant, worthless

signify *vb* **1-3** = **indicate**, announce, be a sign of, betoken, communicate, connote, convey, denote, evidence, exhibit, express, imply, intimate, matter, mean, portend, proclaim, represent, show, stand for, suggest, symbolize **4** *Informal* = **matter**, be important, carry weight, count

sign up *vb* = **enlist**, contract with, enrol, join, join up, register, volunteer

silence *n* **1** = **quiet**, calm, hush, lull, noiselessness, peace, quiescence, stillness **3** = **muteness**, dumbness, reticence, speechlessness, taciturnity, uncommunicativeness ◆ *vb* **6** = **quieten**, cut off, cut short, deaden, extinguish, gag, muffle, quell, quiet, stifle, still, strike dumb, subdue, suppress

Antonyms *n* ≠ **quiet:** cacophony, din, noise, racket, sound, tumult, uproar ≠ **muteness:** babble, bawling, chatter, clamour, garrulousness, hubbub, loquaciousness, murmuring, prattle, shouting, speech, talk, talking, verbosity, whispering, yelling ◆ *vb* ≠ **quieten:** amplify, broadcast, disseminate, encourage, foster, make louder, promote, promulgate, publicize, rouse, spread, support, ungag

silent *adj* **1** = **quiet**, hushed, muted, noiseless, soundless, still, stilly (*poetic*) **2-4** = **mute**, dumb, mum, nonvocal, not talkative, speechless, struck dumb, taciturn, tongue-tied, uncommunicative, unspeaking, voiceless, wordless **5** = **unspoken**, aphonic (*Phonetics*), implicit, im-

has no accompanying soundtrack. [C16: from L *silēns*, from *silēre* to be quiet]
▸ **'silently** *adv* ▸ **'silentness** *n*

silent cop *n Austral. sl.* a small raised hemispherical marker in the middle of a crossroads.

silent majority *n* a presumed moderate majority of the citizens who are too passive to make their views known.

Silenus (saɪ'liːnəs; 'silenəs) *n Greek myth.* **1** chief of the satyrs and foster father to Dionysus. **2** (*pl* **Sileni** (saɪ'liːnaɪ; 'silenɪː). (*often not cap.*) one of a class of woodland deities, closely similar to the satyrs.

silex ('saɪlɛks) *n* a type of heat-resistant glass made from fused quartz. [C16: from L: hard stone]

silhouette ❶ (ˌsɪluː'ɛt) *n* **1** the outline of a solid figure as cast by its shadow. **2** an outline drawing filled in with black, often a profile portrait cut out of black paper and mounted on a light ground. ◆ *vb* **silhouettes, silhouetting, silhouetted. 3** (*tr*) to cause to appear in silhouette. [C18: after Étienne de *Silhouette* (1709–67), F politician]

silica ('sɪlɪkə) *n* the dioxide of silicon (SiO_2), occurring naturally as quartz. It is a refractory insoluble material used in the manufacture of glass, ceramics, and abrasives. [C19: NL, from L *silex* hard stone]

silica gel *n* an amorphous form of silica capable of absorbing large quantities of water: used esp. in drying gases and oils.

silicate ('sɪlɪkɪt, -ˌkeɪt) *n* a salt or ester that can be regarded as derived from silicic acid. Silicates constitute a large proportion of the earth's minerals and are present in cement and glass.

siliceous *or* **silicious** (sɪ'lɪʃəs) *adj* **1** of, relating to, or containing silica: *a siliceous clay*. **2** (of plants) growing in soil rich in silica.

silicic (sɪ'lɪsɪk) *adj* of or containing silicon or an acid obtained from silicon.

silicic acid *n* a white gelatinous substance obtained by adding an acid to a solution of sodium silicate. It is best regarded as hydrated silica.

silicify (sɪ'lɪsɪˌfaɪ) *vb* **silicifies, silicifying, silicified.** to convert or be converted into silica: *silicified wood*.
▸ **siˌlicifi'cation** *n*

silicon ('sɪlɪkən) *n* **a** a brittle metalloid element that exists in two allotropic forms; occurs principally in sand, quartz, granite, feldspar, and clay. It is usually a grey crystalline solid but is also found as a brown amorphous powder. It is used in transistors, solar cells, and alloys. Its compounds are widely used in glass manufacture and the building industry. Symbol: Si; atomic no.: 14; atomic wt.: 28.09. **b** (*modifier; sometimes cap.*) denoting an area of a country that contains much high-technology industry. [C19: from SILICA, on the model of *boron, carbon*]

silicon carbide *n* an extremely hard bluish-black insoluble crystalline substance produced by heating carbon with sand at a high temperature and used as an abrasive and refractory material. Very pure crystals are used as semiconductors. Formula: SiC.

silicon chip *n* another term for **chip** (sense 7).

silicon-controlled rectifier *n* a semiconductor rectifier whose forward current between two electrodes, the anode and cathode, is initiated by means of a signal applied to a third electrode, the gate. The current subsequently becomes independent of the signal. Also called: **thyristor.**

silicone ('sɪlɪˌkəʊn) *n Chem.* **a** any of a large class of polymeric synthetic materials that usually have resistance to temperature, water, and chemicals, and good insulating and lubricating properties, making them suitable for wide use as oils, water repellents, resins, etc. **b** (*as modifier*): *silicone rubber*.

Silicon Valley *n* any area in which industries associated with information technology are concentrated.

silicosis (ˌsɪlɪ'kəʊsɪs) *n Pathol.* a form of pneumoconiosis caused by breathing in tiny particles of silica, quartz, or slate, and characterized by shortness of breath.

siliqua (sɪ'liːkwə, 'sɪlɪkwə) *or* **silique** (sɪ'liːk, 'sɪlɪk) *n, pl* **siliquae** (-'liːkwiː), **siliquas,** *or* **siliques.** the long dry dehiscent fruit of cruciferous plants, such as the wallflower. [C18: via F from L *siliqua* a pod]
▸ **siliquose** ('sɪlɪˌkwəʊs) *or* **siliquous** ('sɪlɪkwəs) *adj*

silk (sɪlk) *n* **1** the very fine soft lustrous fibre produced by a silkworm to make its cocoon. **2a** thread or fabric made from this fibre. **2b** (*as modifier*): *a silk dress*. **3** a garment made of this. **4** a very fine fibre produced by a spider to build its web, nest, or cocoon. **5** the tuft of long fine styles on an ear of maize. **6** *Brit.* **6a** the gown worn by a Queen's (or King's) Counsel. **6b** *Inf.* a Queen's (or King's) Counsel. **6c take silk.** to become a Queen's (or King's) Counsel. [OE *sioluc*; ult. from Chinese *ssŭ* silk]
▸ **'silkˌlike** *adj*

silk cotton *n* another name for **kapok.**

silk-cotton tree *n* any of a genus of tropical trees having seeds covered with silky hairs from which kapok is obtained. Also called: **kapok tree.**

silken ('sɪlkən) *adj* **1** made of silk. **2** resembling silk in smoothness or gloss. **3** dressed in silk. **4** soft and delicate.

silk hat *n* a man's top hat covered with silk.

silkworm ('sɪlkˌwɜːm) *n* **1** the larva of the Chinese moth that feeds on the leaves of the mulberry tree: widely cultivated as a source of silk. **2** any of various similar or related larvae.

silky ❶ ('sɪlkɪ) *adj* **silkier, silkiest. 1** resembling silk in texture; glossy. **2** made of silk. **3** (of a voice, manner, etc.) suave; smooth. **4** *Bot.* covered with long fine soft hairs: *silky leaves*.
▸ **'silkily** *adv* ▸ **'silkiness** *n*

silky oak *n* any of an Australian genus of trees having divided leaves and showy clusters of orange, red, or white flowers: cultivated in the tropics as shade trees.

sill (sɪl) *n* **1** a shelf at the bottom of a window inside a room. **2** a horizontal piece along the outside lower member of a window, that throws water clear of the wall below. **3** the lower horizontal member of a window or door frame. **4** a horizontal member placed on top of a foundation wall in order to carry a timber framework. **5** a mass of igneous rock, situated between two layers of older sedimentary rock. [OE *syll*]

sillabub ('sɪləˌbʌb) *n* a variant spelling of **syllabub.**

silly ❶ ('sɪlɪ) *adj* **sillier, silliest. 1** lacking in good sense; absurd. **2** frivolous, trivial, or superficial. **3** feeble-minded. **4** dazed, as from a blow. ◆ *n* **5** (*modifier*) *Cricket.* (of a fielding position) near the batsman's wicket: *silly mid-on*. **6** (*pl* **sillies**) Also called: **silly-billy.** *Inf.* a foolish person. [C15 (in the sense: pitiable, hence the later senses: foolish): from OE *sǣlig* (unattested) happy, from *sǣl* happiness]
▸ **'silliness** *n*

silly season *n Brit.* a period, usually during the summer months, when journalists fill space reporting on frivolous events and activities.

silo ('saɪləʊ) *n, pl* **silos. 1** a pit, trench, or tower, often cylindrical in shape, in which silage is made and stored. **2** an underground position in which missile systems are sited for protection. [C19: from Sp., ? of Celtic origin]

silt ❶ (sɪlt) *n* **1** a fine deposit of mud, clay, etc., esp. one in a river or lake. ◆ *vb* **2** (usually foll. by *up*) to fill or become filled with silt; choke. [C15: from ON]
▸ **sil'tation** *n* ▸ **'silty** *adj*

Silurian (saɪ'lʊərɪən) *adj* **1** of or formed in the third period of the Palaeozoic era, during which fishes first appeared. ◆ *n* **2 the.** the Silurian period or rock system. [C19: from *Silures*, a Welsh tribe who opposed the Romans]

silurid (saɪ'lʊərɪd) *n* **1** any freshwater teleost fish of the family Siluridae, such as the **European catfish,** which has an elongated body, naked skin, and a long anal fin. ◆ *adj* **2** of, relating to, or belonging to the family Siluridae. [C19: from L *silūrus*, from Gk *silouros* a river fish]

silva ('sɪlvə) *n* a variant spelling of **sylva.**

silvan ('sɪlvən) *adj, n* a variant spelling of **sylvan.**

silver ❶ ('sɪlvə) *n* **1a** a ductile malleable brilliant greyish-white element having the highest electrical and thermal conductivity of any metal. It occurs free and in argentite and other ores: used in jewellery, tableware, coinage, electrical contacts, and electroplating. Symbol: Ag; atomic no.: 47; atomic wt.: 107.870. **1b** (*as modifier*): *a silver coin*. Related adj: **argent. 2** coin made of, or having the appearance of, this metal. **3** cutlery, whether made of silver or not. **4** any household articles made of silver. **5** short for **silver medal. 6a** a brilliant or light greyish-white colour. **6b** (*as adj*): *silver hair*. ◆ *adj* **7** well-articulated: *silver speech*. **8** (*prenominal*) denoting the 25th in a series: *a silver wedding anniversary*. ◆ *vb* **9** (*tr*) to coat with silver or a silvery substance: *to silver a spoon*. **10** to become or cause to become silvery in colour. [OE *siolfor*]
▸ **'silvering** *n*

silver age *n* **1** (in Greek and Roman mythology) the second of the world's major epochs, inferior to the preceding golden age. **2** the postclassical period of Latin literature, occupying the early part of the Roman imperial era.

silver beet *n* an Australian and New Zealand variety of beet, cultivated for its edible leaves with white stems.

silver bell *n* any of various deciduous trees of North America and China, having white bell-shaped flowers. Also called: **snowdrop tree.**

silver birch *n* a tree of N temperate regions of the Old World, having silvery-white peeling bark.

silver bromide *n* a yellowish powder that darkens when exposed to light: used in making photographic emulsions. Formula: AgBr.

silver chloride *n* a white powder that darkens on exposure to

THESAURUS

plied, tacit, understood, unexpressed, unpronounced

silently *adv* **1 = quietly,** as quietly as a mouse (*inf.*), dumbly, inaudibly, in silence, mutely, noiselessly, soundlessly, speechlessly, without a sound, wordlessly

silhouette *n* **1 = outline,** delineation, form, profile, shape ◆ *vb* **3 = outline,** delineate, etch, stand out

silky *adj* **1 = smooth,** silken, sleek, velvety

silly *adj* **1 = foolish,** absurd, asinine, brainless, childish, daft, fatuous, foolhardy, frivolous, giddy, idiotic, immature, imprudent, inane, inappropriate, irresponsible, meaningless, pointless, preposterous, puerile, ridiculous, senseless, stupid, unwise, witless **4 = dazed,** benumbed, groggy (*inf.*), in a daze, muzzy, stunned, stupefied ◆ *n* **6** *Informal* **= fool,** clot (*Brit. inf.*), duffer (*inf.*), goose (*inf.*), ignoramus, ninny, nitwit (*inf.*), silly-billy (*inf.*), simpleton, twit (*inf.*), wally (*sl.*)

Antonyms *adj* ≠ **foolish:** acute, aware, bright, clever, intelligent, mature, perceptive, profound, prudent, reasonable, sane, sensible, serious, smart, thoughtful, well-thought-out, wise

silt *n* **1 = sediment,** alluvium, deposit, ooze, residue, sludge ◆ *vb* **2** *with* **up = clog,** choke, congest, dam

silver *modifier* **1b = silvery,** argent (*poetic*), pearly, silvered ◆ *n* **4 = silverware,** silver plate light: used in making photographic emulsions and papers. Formula: AgCl.

silver disc *n* (in Britain) an album certified to have sold 60 000 copies or a single certified to have sold 200 000 copies.

silver-eye *n Austral. & NZ.* another name for **waxeye** or **white-eye.**

silver fern *n NZ.* **1** another name for **ponga. 2** a formalized spray of fern leaf, silver on a black background: the symbol of New Zealand sporting teams.

silver fir *n* any of various fir trees the leaves of which have a silvery undersurface.

silverfish ('sɪlvə,fɪʃ) *n, pl* **silverfish** *or* **silverfishes. 1** a silver variety of the goldfish. **2** any of various other silvery fishes, such as the moonfish. **3** any of various small primitive wingless insects that have long antennae and tail appendages and occur in buildings, feeding on food scraps, book-bindings, etc.

silver fox *n* **1** an American red fox in a colour phase in which the fur is black with long silver-tipped hairs. **2** the valuable fur or pelt of this animal.

silver-gilt *n* silver covered with a thin film of gold.

silver iodide *n* a yellow powder that darkens on exposure to light: used in photography and artificial rainmaking. Formula: AgI.

silver lining *n* a hopeful aspect of an otherwise desperate or unhappy situation (esp. in the phrase **every cloud has a silver lining**).

silver medal *n* a medal of silver awarded to a competitor who comes second in a contest or race.

silver nitrate *n* a white crystalline soluble poisonous substance used in making photographic emulsions and as a medical antiseptic and astringent. Formula: $AgNO_3$.

silver plate *n* **1** a thin layer of silver deposited on a base metal. **2** articles, esp. tableware, made of silver plate. ◆ *vb* **silver-plate, silver-plates, silver-plating, silver-plated. 3** (*tr*) to coat (a metal, object, etc.) with silver, as by electroplating.

silver screen *n* **the.** *Inf.* **1** films collectively or the film industry. **2** the screen onto which films are projected.

silver service *n* (in restaurants) a style of serving food using a spoon and fork in one hand like a pair of tongs.

silverside ('sɪlvə,saɪd) *n* **1** *Brit. & NZ.* a cut of beef below the aitchbone and above the leg. **2** a small marine or freshwater teleost fish related to the grey mullets.

silversmith ('sɪlvə,smɪθ) *n* a craftsman who makes or repairs articles of silver.
▸**'silver,smithing** *n*

silverware ('sɪlvə,wɛə) *n* articles, esp. tableware, made of or plated with silver.

silverweed ('sɪlvə,wiːd) *n* **1** a rosaceous perennial creeping plant with silvery pinnate leaves and yellow flowers. **2** any of various twining shrubs of SE Asia and Australia, having silvery leaves and showy purple flowers.

silvery ('sɪlvərɪ) *adj* **1** of or having the appearance of silver: *the silvery moon.* **2** containing or covered with silver. **3** having a clear ringing sound.
▸**'silveriness** *n*

silviculture ('sɪlvɪ,kʌltʃə) *n* the branch of forestry that is concerned with the cultivation of trees. [C20: *silvi-*, from L *silva* woodland + CULTURE]
▸**,silvi'cultural** *adj* ▸**,silvi'culturist** *n*

sima ('saɪmə) *n* **1** the silicon-rich and magnesium-rich rocks of the earth's oceanic crust. **2** the earth's continental lower crust. [C20: from SI(LICA) + MA(GNESIA)]

simian ('sɪmɪən) *adj* **1** of or resembling a monkey or ape. ◆ *n* **2** a monkey or ape. [C17: from L *sīmia* an ape, prob. from Gk *sīmos* flat-nosed]

similar ❶ ('sɪmɪlə) *adj* **1** showing resemblance in qualities, characteristics, or appearance. **2** *Geom.* (of two or more figures) having corresponding angles equal and all corresponding sides in the same ratio. [C17: from OF, from L *similis*]
▸**similarity** (,sɪmɪ'lærɪtɪ) *n* ▸**'similarly** *adv*

> **USAGE NOTE** *As should not be used after similar: Wilson held a similar position to Jones (not a similar position as Jones); the system is similar to the one in France (not similar as in France).*

simile ('sɪmɪlɪ) *n* a figure of speech that expresses the resemblance of one thing to another of a different category, usually introduced by *as* or *like*. Cf. **metaphor.** [C14: from L *simile* something similar, from *similis* like]

similitude (sɪ'mɪlɪ,tjuːd) *n* **1** likeness. **2** a thing or sometimes a person that is like or the counterpart of another. **3** *Arch.* a simile or parable. [C14: from L *similitūdō*, from *similis* like]

simmer ❶ ('sɪmə) *vb* **1** to cook (food) gently at or just below the boiling point. **2** (*intr*) to be about to break out in rage or excitement. ◆ *n* **3** the act, sound, or state of simmering. [C17: ? imit.]

simmer down ❶ *vb* (*adv*) **1** (*intr*) *Inf.* to grow calmer, as after intense rage. **2** (*tr*) to reduce the volume of (a liquid) by boiling slowly.

simnel cake ('sɪmnᵊl) *n Brit.* a fruit cake covered with a layer of marzipan, traditionally eaten during Lent or at Easter. [C13 *simenel*, from OF, from L *simila* fine flour, prob. of Semitic origin]

simon-pure ('saɪmən-) *adj Rare.* real; authentic. [C19: from *the real Simon Pure*, a character in the play *A Bold Stroke for a Wife* (1717) by Susannah Centlivre (1669–1723), who is impersonated by another character in some scenes]

simony ('saɪmənɪ) *n Christianity.* the practice, now usually regarded as a sin, of buying or selling spiritual or Church benefits such as pardons, relics, etc. [C13: from OF *simonie*, from LL *simōnia*, from *Simon Magus*, a biblical sorcerer who tried to buy magical powers]
▸**'simonist** *n*

simoom (sɪ'muːm) *or* **simoon** (sɪ'muːn) *n* a strong suffocating sand-laden wind of the deserts of Arabia and North Africa. [from Ar. *samūm* poisonous, from Aramaic *sammā* poison]

simpatico (sɪm'pɑːtɪ,kəʊ) *adj Inf.* **1** pleasant or congenial. **2** of similar mind or temperament. [It.: from *simpatia* SYMPATHY]

simper ❶ ('sɪmpə) *vb* **1** (*intr*) to smile coyly, affectedly, or in a silly self-conscious way. **2** (*tr*) to utter (something) in such a manner. ◆ *n* **3** a simpering smile; smirk. [C16: prob. from Du. *simper* affected]
▸**'simpering** *adj* ▸**'simperingly** *adv*

simple ❶ ('sɪmpᵊl) *adj* **1** easy to understand or do: *a simple problem.* **2** plain; unadorned: *a simple dress.* **3** not combined or complex: *a simple mechanism.* **4** unaffected or unpretentious: *despite his fame, he remained a simple man.* **5** sincere; frank: *her simple explanation was readily accepted.* **6** of humble condition or rank: *the peasant was of simple birth.* **7** feeble-minded. **8** (*prenominal*) without additions or modifications: *the witness told the simple truth.* **9** (*prenominal*) straightforward: *a simple case of mumps.* **10** *Chem.* (of a substance) consisting of only one chemical compound. **11** *Maths.* (of an equation) containing variables to the first power only. **12** *Biol.* **12a** not divided into parts: *a simple leaf.* **12b** formed from only one ovary: *simple fruit.* **13** *Music.* relating to or denoting a time where the number of beats per bar may be two, three, or four. ◆ *n Arch.* **14** a simpleton. **15** a plant having medicinal properties. [C13: via OF from L *simplex* plain]
▸**simplicity** (sɪm'plɪsɪtɪ) *n*

simple fraction *n* a fraction in which the numerator and denominator are both integers. Also called: **common fraction, vulgar fraction.**

simple fracture *n* a fracture in which the broken bone does not pierce the skin.

simple harmonic motion *n* a form of periodic motion of a particle, etc., in which the acceleration is always directed towards some equilibrium point and is proportional to the displacement from this point. Abbrev.: **SHM.**

simple-hearted *adj* free from deceit; frank.

simple interest *n* interest paid on the principal alone. Cf. **compound interest.**

simple machine *n* a simple device for altering the magnitude or direction of a force. The six basic types are the lever, wheel and axle, pulley, screw, wedge, and inclined plane.

THESAURUS

similar *adj* **1 = alike,** analogous, close, comparable, congruous, corresponding, cut from the same cloth, homogeneous, homogenous, in agreement, like, much the same, of a piece, resembling, uniform
Antonyms *adj* antithetical, clashing, contradictory, contrary, different, disparate, dissimilar, diverse, heterogeneous, irreconcilable, opposite, unalike, unrelated, various, varying

similarity *n* **1 = resemblance,** affinity, agreement, analogy, closeness, comparability, concordance, congruence, correspondence, likeness, point of comparison, relation, sameness, similitude
Antonyms *n* antithesis, contradictoriness, difference, disagreement, discordance, discrepancy, disparity, dissimilarity, diversity, heterogeneity, incomparability, irreconcilability, unalikeness, variation, variety

similarly *adv* **1 = in the same way,** by the same token, correspondingly, in like manner, likewise

simmer *vb* **2 = fume,** be agitated, be angry, be tense, be uptight, boil, burn, rage, see red (*inf.*), seethe, smart, smoulder

simmer down *vb* **1** *Informal* **= calm down,** collect oneself, contain oneself, control oneself, cool off *or* down, get down off one's high horse (*inf.*), grow quieter, unwind (*inf.*)

simper *vb* **1 = smile coyly,** grimace, smile affectedly, smile self-consciously, smirk

simpering *adj* **1 = coy,** affected, self-conscious

simple *adj* **1 = uncomplicated,** clear, easy, easy-peasy (*sl.*), elementary, intelligible, lucid, manageable, plain, straightforward, understandable, uninvolved **2 = plain,** classic, clean, natural, severe, Spartan, unadorned, uncluttered, unembellished, unfussy **3 = pure,** elementary, single, unalloyed, unblended, uncombined, undivided, unmixed **4 = artless,** childlike, frank, green, guileless, ingenuous, innocent, naive, natural, simplistic, sincere, unaffected, unpretentious, unsophisticated **5 = honest,** bald, basic, direct, frank, naked, plain, sincere, stark, undeniable, unvarnished **6 = unpretentious,** homely, humble, lowly, modest, rustic **7** *Informal* **= feeble-minded,** brainless, credulous, dense, dumb (*inf.*), feeble, foolish, half-witted, moronic, obtuse, shallow, silly, slow, stupid, thick
Antonyms *adj* ≠ **uncomplicated:** advanced, complex, complicated, convoluted, difficult, elaborate, highly developed, intricate, involved, refined, sophisticated ≠ **plain:** contrived, elaborate, fussy, intricate, ornate ≠ **artless:** artful, smart, sophisticated, worldly, worldly-wise ≠ **unpretentious:** extravagant, fancy, flashy ≠ **feeble-minded:** astute, bright, clever, intelligent, knowing, on the ball, quick, quick on the uptake, quick-witted, sharp, smart, wise

simple-minded ⓣ *adj* **1** stupid; foolish; feeble-minded. **2** unsophisticated; artless.
▸ˌ**simple-'mindedly** *adv* ▸ˌ**simple-'mindedness** *n*

simple sentence *n* a sentence consisting of a single main clause.

simpleton ⓣ ('sɪmpᵊltən) *n* a foolish or ignorant person.

simplify ⓣ ('sɪmplɪˌfaɪ) *vb* **simplifies, simplifying, simplified.** *(tr)* **1** to make less complicated or easier. **2** *Maths.* to reduce (an equation, fraction, etc.) to its simplest form. [C17: via F from Med. L *simplificāre,* from L *simplus* simple + *facere* to make]
▸ˌ**simplifi'cation** *n*

simplistic ⓣ (sɪm'plɪstɪk) *adj* **1** characterized by extreme simplicity. **2** making unrealistically simple judgments or analyses.
▸**'simplism** *n* ▸**sim'plistically** *adv*

> **USAGE NOTE** Since *simplistic* already has *too* as part of its meaning, it is tautologous to talk about something being *too simplistic* or *over-simplistic.*

simply ⓣ ('sɪmplɪ) *adv* **1** in a simple manner. **2** merely. **3** absolutely; altogether: *a simply wonderful holiday.* **4** *(sentence modifier)* frankly.

simulacrum (ˌsɪmjʊ'leɪkrəm) *n, pl* **simulacra** (-krə). *Arch.* **1** any image or representation of something. **2** a superficial likeness. [C16: from L: likeness, from *simulāre* to imitate, from *similis* like]

simulate ⓣ *vb* ('sɪmjʊˌleɪt), **simulates, simulating, simulated.** *(tr)* **1** to make a pretence of: *to simulate anxiety.* **2** to reproduce the conditions of (a situation, etc.), as in carrying out an experiment: *to simulate weightlessness.* **3** to have the appearance of. ◆ *adj* ('sɪmjʊlɪt, -ˌleɪt). **4** *Arch.* assumed. [C17: from L *simulāre* to copy, from *similis* like]
▸ˌ**simu'lation** *n* ▸**'simulative** *adj*

simulated ⓣ ('sɪmjʊˌleɪtɪd) *adj* **1** (of fur, leather, pearls, etc.) being an imitation of the genuine article, usually made from cheaper material. **2** (of actions, emotions, etc.) imitated; feigned.

simulator ('sɪmjʊˌleɪtə) *n* **1** any device that simulates specific conditions for the purposes of research or operator training: *space simulator.* **2** a person who simulates.

simulcast ('sɪməlˌkɑːst) *vb* **1** *(tr)* to broadcast (a programme, etc.) simultaneously on radio and television. ◆ *n* **2** a programme, etc., so broadcast. [C20: from SIMUL(TANEOUS) + (BROAD)CAST]

simultaneous ⓣ (ˌsɪməl'teɪnɪəs) *adj* occurring, existing, or operating at the same time. [C17: on the model of INSTANTANEOUS from L *simul* at the same time]
▸ˌ**simul'taneously** *adv* ▸ˌ**simul'taneousness** *or* **simultaneity** (ˌsɪməltə'niːɪtɪ) *n*

> **USAGE NOTE** See at **unique.**

simultaneous equations *pl n* a set of equations that are all satisfied by the same values of the variables, the number of variables being equal to the number of equations.

sin[1] ⓣ (sɪn) *n* **1a** transgression of God's known will or any principle or law regarded as embodying this. **1b** the condition of estrangement from God arising from such transgression. **2** any serious offence, as against a religious or moral principle. **3** any offence against a principle or standard. **4 live in sin.** *Inf.* (of an unmarried couple) to live together. ◆ *vb* **sins, sinning, sinned.** *(intr)* **5** to commit a sin. **6** (usually foll. by *against*) to commit an offence (against a person, etc.). [OE *synn*]
▸**'sinner** *n*

sin[2] (saɪn) *Maths. abbrev. for* sine.

SIN (in Canada) *abbrev. for* Social Insurance Number.

sinanthropus (sɪn'ænθrəpəs) *n* a primitive apelike man of the genus *Sinanthropus,* now considered a subspecies of *Homo erectus.* [C20: from NL, from LL *Sīnae* the Chinese + *-anthropus,* from Gk *anthrōpos* man]

sin bin *n* **1** *Sl.* (in ice hockey, etc.) an area off the field of play where a player who has committed a foul can be sent to sit for a specified period. **2** *Inf.* a separate unit for disruptive schoolchildren.

since (sɪns) *prep* **1** during or throughout the period of time after: *since May it has only rained once.* ◆ *conj* *(subordinating)* **2** (sometimes preceded by *ever*) continuously from or starting from the time when. **3** seeing that; because. ◆ *adv* **4** since that time: *I haven't seen him since.* [OE *sīththan,* lit.: after that]

> **USAGE NOTE** See at **ago.**

sincere ⓣ (sɪn'sɪə) *adj* **1** not hypocritical or deceitful; genuine: *sincere regret.* **2** *Arch.* pure; unmixed. [C16: from L *sincērus*]
▸**sin'cerely** *adv* ▸**sincerity** (sɪn'serɪtɪ) *or* **sin'cereness** *n*

sinciput ('sɪnsɪˌpʌt) *n, pl* **sinciputs** *or* **sincipita** (sɪn'sɪpɪtə). *Anat.* the forward upper part of the skull. [C16: from L: half a head, from SEMI- + *caput* head]
▸**sin'cipital** *adj*

sine[1] (saɪn) *n* (of an angle) a trigonometric function that in a right-angled triangle is the ratio of the length of the opposite side to that of the hypotenuse. [C16: from L *sinus* a bend; in NL, *sinus* was mistaken as a translation of Ar. *jiba* sine (from Sansk. *jīva,* lit.: bowstring) because of confusion with Ar. *jaib* curve]

sine[2] ('saɪnɪ) *prep* (esp. in Latin phrases or legal terms) lacking; without.

sinecure ⓣ ('saɪnɪˌkjʊə) *n* **1** a paid office or post involving minimal duties. **2** a Church benefice to which no spiritual charge is attached. [C17: from Med. L *(beneficium) sine cūrā* (benefice) without cure (of souls), from L *sine* without + *cūra* cure]
▸**'sineˌcurism** *n* ▸**'sineˌcurist** *n*

sine curve (saɪn) *n* a curve of the equation $y = \sin x$. Also called: **sinusoid.**

sine die *Latin.* ('saɪnɪ 'daɪɪ) *adv, adj* without a day fixed. [lit.: without a day]

sine qua non *Latin.* ('saɪnɪ kweɪ 'nɒn) *n* an essential requirement. [lit.: without which not]

sinew ('sɪnjuː) *n* **1** *Anat.* another name for **tendon. 2** *(often pl)* **2a** a source of strength or power. **2b** a literary word for **muscle.** [OE *sionu*]
▸**'sinewless** *adj*

sine wave (saɪn) *n* any oscillation, such as an alternating current, whose waveform is that of a sine curve.

sinewy ⓣ ('sɪnjʊɪ) *adj* **1** consisting of or resembling a tendon or tendons. **2** muscular. **3** (esp. of language, style, etc.) forceful. **4** (of meat, etc.) tough.
▸**'sinewiness** *n*

sinfonia (ˌsɪnfə'nɪə) *n, pl* **sinfonie** (-'niːeɪ) *or* **sinfonias. 1** another word for **symphony** (senses 2, 3). **2** *(cap. when part of a name)* a symphony orchestra. [It.]

sinfonietta (ˌsɪnfən'jetə) *n* **1** a short or light symphony. **2** *(cap. when part of a name)* a small symphony orchestra. [It.: a little symphony]

sinful ⓣ ('sɪnfʊl) *adj* **1** having committed or tending to commit sin: *a sinful person.* **2** characterized by or being a sin: *a sinful act.*
▸**'sinfully** *adv* ▸**'sinfulness** *n*

THESAURUS

simple-minded *adj* **1** = **feeble-minded**, a bit lacking *(inf.)*, addle-brained, backward, brainless, dead from the neck up *(inf.)*, dim-witted, foolish, idiot, idiotic, moronic, retarded, simple, stupid **2** = **unsophisticated**, artless, natural

simpleton *n* = **halfwit**, blockhead, booby, chump, coot, dolt, dope *(inf.)*, dullard, dunce, fool, idiot, imbecile *(inf.)*, jackass, moron, nincompoop, ninny, nitwit *(inf.)*, numbskull *or* numbskull, oaf, schmuck *(US sl.)*, Simple Simon, stupid *(inf.)*, twerp *or* twirp *(inf.)*, twit *(inf., chiefly Brit.)*

simplicity *n* **1** = **ease**, absence of complications, clarity, clearness, easiness, elementariness, obviousness, straightforwardness **2** = **plainness**, clean lines, lack of adornment, modesty, naturalness, purity, restraint **4** = **artlessness**, candour, directness, guilelessness, innocence, lack of sophistication, naivety, openness
Antonyms *n* ≠ **ease:** complexity, complicatedness, difficulty, intricacy, lack of clarity ≠ **plainness:** decoration, elaborateness, embellishment, fanciness, fussiness, ornateness, ostentation ≠ **artlessness:** brains, craftiness, cunning, deviousness, guile, insincerity, knowingness, sharpness, slyness, smartness, sophistication, wariness, wisdom, worldliness

simplify *vb* **1** = **make simpler**, abridge, decipher, disentangle, dumb down, facilitate, make intelligible, reduce to essentials, streamline

simplistic *adj* **2** = **oversimplified**, naive

simply *adv* **1** = **plainly**, clearly, directly, easily, intelligibly, modestly, naturally, straightforwardly, unaffectedly, unpretentiously, without any elaboration **2** = **just**, merely, only, purely, solely **3** = **totally**, absolutely, altogether, completely, really, unreservedly, utterly, wholly

simulate *vb* **1** = **pretend**, act, affect, assume, counterfeit, fabricate, feign, imitate, make believe, put on, reproduce, sham

simulated *adj* **1** = **synthetic**, artificial, fake, imitation, man-made, mock, pseudo *(inf.)*, sham, substitute **2** = **pretended**, artificial, assumed, feigned, insincere, make-believe, phoney *or* phony *(inf.)*, put-on

simultaneous *adj* = **coinciding**, at the same time, coincident, concurrent, contemporaneous, synchronous

simultaneously *adv* = **at the same time**, all together, concurrently, in chorus, in concert, in the same breath, in unison, together

sin[1] *n* **1-3** = **wrongdoing**, crime, damnation, error, evil, guilt, iniquity, misdeed, offence, sinfulness, transgression, trespass, ungodliness, unrighteousness, wickedness, wrong ◆ *vb* **5** = **transgress**, err, fall, fall from grace, go astray, lapse, offend, trespass *(arch.)*

sincere *adj* **1** = **honest**, artless, bona fide, candid, earnest, frank, genuine, guileless, heartfelt, natural, no-nonsense, open, real, serious, straightforward, true, unaffected, unfeigned, upfront *(inf.)*, wholehearted
Antonyms *adj* affected, artful, artificial, deceitful, deceptive, dishonest, false, feigned, hollow, insincere, phoney *or* phony *(inf.)*, pretended, put on, synthetic, token, two-faced

sincerely *adv* **1** = **honestly**, earnestly, from the bottom of one's heart, genuinely, in all sincerity, in earnest, in good faith, really, seriously, truly, wholeheartedly

sincerity *n* **1** = **honesty**, artlessness, bona fides, candour, frankness, genuineness, good faith, guilelessness, probity, seriousness, straightforwardness, truth, wholeheartedness

sinecure *n* **1** = **cushy number** *(inf.)*, gravy train *(sl.)*, money for jam *or* old rope *(inf.)*, soft job *(inf.)*, soft option

sinewy *adj* **2** = **muscular**, athletic, brawny, lusty, powerful, robust, strong, sturdy, vigorous, wiry

sinful *adj* **1, 2** = **wicked**, bad, corrupt, criminal, depraved, erring, guilty, immoral, iniquitous, irreligious, morally wrong, ungodly, unholy, unrighteous
Antonyms *adj* beatified, blessed, chaste, decent, free from sin, godly, holy, honest, honourable, immaculate, moral, pure, righteous, sinless, spotless, squeaky-clean, unblemished, upright, virtuous, without sin

sing ⓣ (sɪŋ) *vb* **sings, singing, sang, sung. 1** to produce or articulate (sounds, words, a song, etc.) with musical intonation. **2** (when *intr*, often foll. by *to*) to perform (a song) to the accompaniment (of): *to sing to a guitar*. **3** (*intr*; foll. by *of*) to tell a story in song (about): *I sing of a maiden*. **4** (*intr*) to perform songs for a living. **5** (*intr*) (esp. of certain birds and insects) to utter calls or sounds reminiscent of music. **6** (when *intr*, usually foll. by *of*) to tell (something), esp. in verse: *the poet who sings of the war*. **7** (*intr*) to make a whining, ringing, or whistling sound: *the arrow sang past his ear*. **8** (*intr*) (of the ears) to experience a continuous ringing. **9** (*tr*) to bring to a given state by singing: *to sing a child to sleep*. **10** (*intr*) *Sl., chiefly US.* to confess or act as an informer. ◆ *n* **11** *Inf.* an act or performance of singing. ◆ See also **sing out**. [OE *singan*]
▸ˈ**singable** *adj* ▸ˈ**singer** *n* ▸ˈ**singing** *adj, n*

USAGE NOTE See at **ring**².

sing. *abbrev. for* singular.
singe ⓣ (sɪndʒ) *vb* **singes, singeing, singed. 1** to burn or be burnt superficially; scorch: *to singe one's clothes*. **2** (*tr*) to burn the ends of (hair, etc.). **3** (*tr*) to expose (a carcass) to flame to remove bristles or hair. ◆ *n* **4** a superficial burn. [OE *sengan*]
Singh (sɪŋ) *n* a title assumed by a Sikh when he becomes a full member of the community. [from Hindi, from Sansk. *sinhá* a lion]
Singhalese (ˌsɪŋəˈliːz) *n, pl* **Singhaleses** *or* **Singhalese**, *adj* a variant spelling of **Sinhalese**.
singing telegram *n* **a** a service by which a person is employed to present greetings or congratulations by singing. **b** the greetings or congratulations presented thus.
single ⓣ (ˈsɪŋgᵊl) *adj* (*usually prenominal*) **1** existing alone; solitary: *upon the hill stood a single tower*. **2** distinct from other things. **3** composed of one part. **4** designed or sufficient for one user: *a single bed*. **5** (*also postpositive*) unmarried. **6** connected with the condition of being unmarried: *he led a single life*. **7** (esp. of combat) involving two individuals. **8** even one: *there wasn't a single person on the beach*. **9** (of a flower) having only one set or whorl of petals. **10** single-minded: *a single devotion to duty*. **11** *Rare.* honest or sincere. ◆ *n* **12** something forming one individual unit. **13** (*often pl*) **13a** an unmarried person. **13b** (*as modifier*): *singles bar*. **14** a gramophone record, CD, or cassette with a short recording, usually of pop music, on it. **15** *Cricket.* a hit from which one run is scored. **16a** *Brit.* a pound note. **16b** *US & Canad.* a dollar note. **17** See **single ticket**. ◆ *vb* **singles, singling, singled. 18** (*tr*; usually foll. by *out*) to select from a group of people or things: *he singled him out for special mention*. ◆ See also **singles**. [C14: from OF *sengle*, from L *singulus* individual]
▸ˈ**singleness** *n*
single-acting *adj* (of a reciprocating engine or pump) having a piston or pistons pressurized on one side only.
single-breasted *adj* (of a garment) having the fronts overlapping only slightly and with one row of fastenings.
single cream *n* cream having a low fat content that does not thicken with beating.
single-decker *n Brit. inf.* a bus with only one passenger deck.
single-end *n Scot.* a dwelling consisting of a single room.
single entry *n* **a** a book-keeping system in which transactions are entered in one account only. **b** (*as modifier*): *a single-entry account*.
single file *n* a line of persons, animals, or things ranged one behind the other.
single-foot *n* **1** a rapid showy gait of a horse in which each foot strikes the ground separately. ◆ *vb* **2** to move or cause to move at this gait.
single-handed ⓣ *adj, adv* **1** unaided or working alone: *a single-handed crossing of the Atlantic*. **2** having or operated by one hand or one person only.
▸ˌ**single-ˈhandedly** *adv* ▸ˌ**single-ˈhandedness** *n*
single-lens reflex *n* See **reflex camera**.
single-minded ⓣ *adj* having but one aim or purpose; dedicated.
▸ˌ**single-ˈmindedly** *adv* ▸ˌ**single-ˈmindedness** *n*
single-parent family *n* a household consisting of at least one dependent child and the mother or father, the other parent being dead or permanently absent. Also called: **one-parent family**.
singles (ˈsɪŋgᵊlz) *pl n Tennis, etc.* a match played with one person on each side.
singles bar *n* a bar or club that is a social meeting place for single people.
single-sex *adj* (of schools, etc.) admitting members of one sex only.
single sideband transmission *n* a method of transmitting radio waves in which either the upper or the lower sideband is transmitted, the carrier being either wholly or partially suppressed.
singlestick (ˈsɪŋgᵊlˌstɪk) *n* **1** a wooden stick used instead of a sword for fencing. **2** fencing with such a stick. **3** any short heavy stick.
singlet (ˈsɪŋglɪt) *n* **1** a sleeveless undergarment covering the body from the shoulders to the hips. **2** a garment worn with shorts by athletes, boxers, etc. [C18: from SINGLE, on the model of *doublet*]
single ticket *n Brit.* a ticket entitling a passenger to travel only to his destination, without returning.
singleton (ˈsɪŋgᵊltən) *n* **1** *Bridge, etc.* an original holding of one card only in a suit. **2** a single object, etc., distinguished from a pair or group. **3** *Maths.* a set containing only one member. [C19: from SINGLE, on the model of SIMPLETON]
single-track *adj* **1** (of a railway) having only a single pair of lines, so that trains can travel in only one direction at a time. **2** (of a road) only wide enough for one vehicle.
Single Transferable Vote *n* (*modifier*) of or relating to a system of voting in which voters list the candidates in order of preference. Abbrev.: **STV**. See **proportional representation**.
singletree (ˈsɪŋgᵊlˌtriː) *n US & Austral.* another word for **swingletree**.
singly ⓣ (ˈsɪŋglɪ) *adv* **1** one at a time; one by one. **2** apart from others; separately; alone.
sing out ⓣ *vb* (*tr, adv*) to call out in a loud voice; shout.
singsong (ˈsɪŋˌsɒŋ) *n* **1** an accent or intonation that is characterized by an alternately rising and falling rhythm, such as in a person's voice. **2** *Brit.* an informal session of singing, esp. of popular songs. ◆ *adj* **3** having a monotonous rhythm: *a singsong accent*.
singular ⓣ (ˈsɪŋgjʊlə) *adj* **1** remarkable; extraordinary: *a singular feat*. **2** unusual; odd: *a singular character*. **3** unique. **4** denoting a word or an inflected form of a word indicating that one referent is being referred to or described. **5** *Logic.* (of a proposition) referring to a specific thing or person. ◆ *n* **6** *Grammar.* **6a** the singular number. **6b** a singular form of a word. [C14: from L *singulāris* single]
▸ˈ**singularly** *adv*
singularity ⓣ (ˌsɪŋgjʊˈlærɪtɪ) *n, pl* **singularities. 1** the state or quality of being singular. **2** something distinguishing a person or thing from others. **3** something unusual. **4** *Maths.* a point at which a function is not differentiable although it is differentiable in a neighbourhood of that point. **5** *Astron.* a hypothetical point in space-time at which matter is infinitely compressed to infinitesimal volume.
singularize *or* **singularise** (ˈsɪŋgjʊləˌraɪz) *vb* **singularizes, singularizing, singularized** *or* **singularises, singularising, singularised.** (*tr*) **1** to make (a word, etc.) singular. **2** to make conspicuous.
▸ˌ**singulariˈzation** *or* ˌ**singulariˈsation** *n*
singultus (sɪŋˈgʌltəs) *n, pl* **singultuses.** a technical name for **hiccup**. [C18: from L, lit.: a sob]
sinh (ʃaɪn, sɪnʃ) *n* hyperbolic sine. [C20: from SIN(E)¹ + H(YPERBOLIC)]
Sinhalese (ˌsɪnhəˈliːz) *or* **Singhalese** *n* **1** (*pl* **Sinhaleses** *or* **Sinhalese**) a member of a people living chiefly in Sri Lanka, where they constitute the majority of the population. **2** the language of this people: the official language of Sri Lanka. ◆ *adj* **3** of or relating to this people or their language.
sinister ⓣ (ˈsɪnɪstə) *adj* **1** threatening or suggesting evil or harm: *a sinister glance*. **2** evil or treacherous. **3** (*usually postpositive*) *Heraldry.* of, on, or starting from the left side from the bearer's point of view. **4** *Arch.* located on the left side. [C15: from L *sinister* on the left-hand side, considered by Roman augurs to be the unlucky one]
▸ˈ**sinisterly** *adv* ▸ˈ**sinisterness** *n*

THESAURUS

sing *vb* **1, 5** = **warble**, carol, chant, chirp, croon, make melody, pipe, trill, vocalize, yodel **7, 8** = **hum**, buzz, purr, whine, whistle **10** *Slang, chiefly U.S.* = **inform (on)**, betray, blow the whistle (on), fink (on) (*sl., chiefly US*), grass (*Brit. sl.*), peach (*sl.*), rat (on) (*inf.*), shop (*sl., chiefly Brit.*), spill one's guts (*sl.*), spill the beans (*inf.*), squeal (*sl.*), tell all, turn in (*inf.*)

singe *vb* **1** = **burn**, char, scorch, sear

singer *n* **2, 4** = **vocalist**, balladeer, cantor, chanteuse (*fem.*), chorister, crooner, minstrel, soloist, songster *or* songstress, troubadour

single *adj* **1** = **one**, distinct, individual, lone, only, particular, separate, singular, sole, solitary, unique **2** = **individual**, exclusive, separate, undivided, unshared **3** = **simple**, unblended, uncompounded, unmixed **5** = **unmarried**, free, unattached, unwed ◆ *vb* **18** *with* **out** = **pick**, choose, cull, distinguish, fix on, pick on *or* out, put on one side, select, separate, set apart, winnow

single-handed *adv* **1** = **unaided**, alone, by oneself, independently, on one's own, solo, unassisted, under one's own steam, without help

single-minded *adj* = **determined**, dedicated, dogged, fixed, hellbent (*inf.*), monomaniacal, steadfast, stubborn, tireless, undeviating, unswerving, unwavering

singly *adv* **1, 2** = **one by one**, individually, one at a time, separately

sing out *vb* = **call (out)**, cooee, cry (out), halloo, holler (*inf.*), make oneself heard, shout, shout ahoy, yell

singular *adj* **1** = **remarkable**, conspicuous, eminent, exceptional, extraordinary, notable, noteworthy, outstanding, prodigious, rare, uncommon, unique, unparalleled **2** = **unusual**, atypical, curious, eccentric, extraordinary, odd, oddball (*inf.*), out-of-the-way, outré, peculiar, puzzling, queer, strange **3** = **single**, individual, separate, sole

Antonyms *adj* ≠ **remarkable, unusual:** common, common or garden, commonplace, conventional, everyday, familiar, normal, routine, run-of-the-mill, unexceptional, unremarkable, usual

singularity *n* **1** = **oddness**, abnormality, curiousness, extraordinariness, irregularity, peculiarity, queerness, strangeness **2, 3** = **idiosyncrasy**, eccentricity, oddity, particularity, peculiarity, quirk, twist

singularly *adv* **1** = **remarkably**, conspicuously, especially, exceptionally, extraordinarily, notably, outstandingly, particularly, prodigiously, seriously (*inf.*), surprisingly, uncommonly, unusually

sinister *adj* **1** = **threatening**, baleful, dire, disquieting, evil, forbidding, injurious, malevolent, malign, malignant, menacing, ominous
Antonyms *adj* auspicious, benevolent, benign, calming, encouraging, good, heartening, heroic, honourable, just, noble, promising, propitious, reassuring, righteous, upright, worthy

sinistral ('sɪnɪstrəl) *adj* **1** of or located on the left side, esp. the left side of the body. **2** a technical term for **left-handed. 3** (of the shells of certain molluscs) coiling in a clockwise direction from the apex.
▸**'sinistrally** *adv*

sinistrorse ('sɪnɪˌstrɔːs, ˌsɪnɪ'strɔːs) *adj* (of some climbing plants) growing upwards in a spiral from right to left. [C19: from L *sinistrōrsus* turned towards the left, from *sinister* on the left + *vertere* to turn]
▸**ˌsinis'trorsal** *adj*

Sinitic (sɪ'nɪtɪk) *n* **1** a branch of the Sino-Tibetan family of languages, consisting of the various dialects of Chinese. ◆ *adj* **2** belonging to this group of languages.

sink ⓣ (sɪŋk) *vb* **sinks, sinking, sank; sunk** *or* **sunken. 1** to descend or cause to descend, esp. beneath the surface of a liquid. **2** (*intr*) to appear to move down towards or descend below the horizon. **3** (*intr*) to slope downwards. **4** (*intr; often foll. by in or into*) to pass into a specified lower state or condition: *to sink into apathy*. **5** to make or become lower in volume, pitch, etc. **6** to make or become lower in value, price, etc. **7** (*intr*) to become weaker in health, strength, etc. **8** (*intr*) to seep or penetrate. **9** (*tr*) to dig, cut, drill, bore, or excavate (a hole, shaft, etc.). **10** (*tr*) to drive into the ground: *to sink a stake*. **11** (*tr*; usually foll. by *in* or *into*) **11a** to invest (money). **11b** to lose (money) in an unwise investment. **12** (*tr*) to pay (a debt). **13** (*intr*) to become hollow: *his cheeks had sunk during his illness*. **14** (*tr*) to hit or propel (a ball) into a hole, pocket, etc.: *he sank a 15-foot putt*. **15** (*tr*) *Brit. inf.* to drink, esp. quickly: *he sank three pints in half an hour*. **16 sink or swim.** to take risks where the alternatives are loss or success. ◆ *n* **17** a fixed basin, esp. in a kitchen, made of stone, metal, etc., used for washing. **18** a place of vice or corruption. **19** an area of ground below that of the surrounding land, where water collects. **20** *Physics.* a device by which energy is removed from a system: *a heat sink*. ◆ *adj* **21** *Inf.* (of a housing estate or school) deprived or having low standards of achievement. [OE *sincan*]
▸**'sinkable** *adj*

sinker ('sɪŋkə) *n* **1** a weight attached to a fishing line, net, etc., to cause it to sink in water. **2** a person who sinks shafts, etc.

sinkhole ('sɪŋkˌhəʊl) *n* **1** Also called (esp. in Britain): **swallow hole.** a depression in the ground surface, esp. in limestone, where a surface stream disappears underground. **2** a place into which foul matter runs.

sink in ⓣ *vb* (*intr, adv*) to enter or penetrate the mind: *eventually the news sank in*.

sinking ('sɪŋkɪŋ) *n* **a** a feeling in the stomach caused by hunger or uneasiness. **b** (*as modifier*): *a sinking feeling*.

sinking fund *n* a fund accumulated out of a business enterprise's earnings or a government's revenue and invested to repay a long-term debt.

sinless ⓣ ('sɪnlɪs) *adj* free from sin or guilt; pure.
▸**'sinlessly** *adv* ▸**'sinlessness** *n*

Sinn Féin (ʃɪn 'feːn) *n* an Irish republican political movement founded about 1905 and linked to the revolutionary Irish Republican Army. [C20: from Irish Gaelic: we ourselves]
▸**'Sinn 'Féiner** *n* ▸**'Sinn 'Féinism** *n*

Sino- *combining form.* Chinese: *Sino-Tibetan; Sinology*. [from F, from LL *Sīnae* the Chinese, from LGk, from Ar. *Sīn* China, prob. from Chinese *Ch'in*]

Sinology (saɪ'nɒlədʒɪ) *n* the study of Chinese history, language, culture, etc.
▸**Sinological** (ˌsaɪnə'lɒdʒɪkᵊl) *adj* ▸**Si'nologist** *n* ▸**Sinologue** ('saɪnəˌlɒg) *n*

Sino-Tibetan ('saɪnəʊ-) *n* **1** a family of languages that includes most of the languages of China, as well as Tibetan, Burmese, and possibly Thai. ◆ *adj* **2** belonging or relating to this family of languages.

sinsemilla (ˌsɪnsə'miːljə) *n* **1** a type of marijuana with a very high narcotic content. **2** the plant from which it is obtained, a strain of *Cannabis sativa*. [C20: from American Sp., lit.: without seed]

sinter ('sɪntə) *n* **1** a whitish porous incrustation, usually consisting of silica, that is deposited from hot springs. **2** the product of a sintering process. ◆ *vb* **3** (*tr*) to form large particles, lumps, or masses from (metal powders) by heating or pressure or both. [C18: from G *Sinter* CINDER]

sinuate ('sɪnjʊɪt, -ˌeɪt) *adj* **1** Also: **sinuous.** (of leaves) having a strongly waved margin. **2** another word for **sinuous.** [C17: from L *sinuātus* curved]
▸**'sinuately** *adv*

sinuous ⓣ ('sɪnjʊəs) *adj* **1** full of turns or curves. **2** devious; not straightforward. **3** supple. [C16: from L *sinuōsus* winding, from *sinus* a curve]
▸**'sinuously** *adv* ▸**sinuosity** (ˌsɪnju'ɒsɪtɪ) *n*

sinus ('saɪnəs) *n, pl* **sinuses. 1** *Anat.* **1a** any bodily cavity or hollow space. **1b** a large channel for venous blood, esp. between the brain and the skull. **1c** any of the air cavities in the cranial bones. **2** *Pathol.* a passage leading to a cavity containing pus. [C16: from L: a curve]

sinusitis (ˌsaɪnə'saɪtɪs) *n* inflammation of the membrane lining a sinus, esp. a nasal sinus.

sinusoid ('saɪnəˌsɔɪd) *n* **1** any of the irregular terminal blood vessels that replace capillaries in certain organs, such as the liver, heart, spleen, and pancreas. **2** another name for **sine curve.** ◆ *adj* **3** resembling a sinus. [C19: from F *sinusoïde*. See SINUS, -OID]

sinusoidal projection *n* an equal-area map projection on which all parallels are straight lines and all except the prime meridian are sine curves, often used to show tropical latitudes.

Siouan ('suːən) *n* a family of North American Indian languages, including Sioux.

Sioux (suː) *n* **1** (*pl* **Sioux** (suː, suːz)). a member of a group of North American Indian peoples. **2** any of the languages of the Sioux. [from F, shortened from *Nadowessioux*]

sip ⓣ (sɪp) *vb* **sips, sipping, sipped. 1** to drink (a liquid) by taking small mouthfuls. ◆ *n* **2** a small quantity of a liquid taken into the mouth and swallowed. **3** an act of sipping. [C14: prob. from Low G *sippen*]
▸**'sipper** *n*

siphon *or* **syphon** ('saɪfᵊn) *n* **1** a tube placed with one end at a certain level in a vessel of liquid and the other end outside the vessel below this level, so that atmospheric pressure forces the liquid through the tube and out of the vessel. **2** See **soda siphon. 3** *Zool.* any of various tubular organs in different aquatic animals, such as molluscs, through which water passes. ◆ *vb* **4** (often foll. by *off*) to draw off through or as if through a siphon. [C17: from L *sīphō*, from Gk *siphōn*]
▸**'siphonal** *or* **siphonic** (saɪ'fɒnɪk) *adj*

siphon bottle *n* another name (esp. US) for **soda siphon.**

siphonophore ('saɪfənəˌfɔː) *n* any of an order of marine colonial hydrozoans, including the Portuguese man-of-war. [C19: from NL, from Gk *siphōnophoros* tube-bearing]

sippet ('sɪpɪt) *n* a small piece of something, esp. a piece of toast or fried bread eaten with soup or gravy. [C16: used as dim. of SOP]

sir (sɜː) *n* **1** a formal or polite term of address for a man. **2** *Arch.* a gentleman of high social status. [C13: var. of SIRE]

Sir (sɜː) *n* **1** a title of honour placed before the name of a knight or baronet: *Sir Walter Raleigh*. **2** *Arch.* a title placed before the name of a figure from ancient history.

sirdar ('sɜːdɑː) *n* **1** a general or military leader in Pakistan and India. **2** (formerly) the title of the British commander in chief of the Egyptian Army. **3** a variant of **sardar.** [from Hindi *sardār*, from Persian, from *sar* head + *dār* possession]

sire ('saɪə) *n* **1** a male parent, esp. of a horse or other domestic animal. **2** a respectful term of address, now used only in addressing a male monarch. ◆ *vb* **sires, siring, sired. 3** (*tr*) (esp. of a domestic animal) to father. [C13: from OF, from L *senior* an elder, from *senex* an old man]

siren ⓣ ('saɪərən) *n* **1** a device for emitting a loud wailing sound, esp. as a warning or signal, consisting of a rotating perforated metal drum through which air or steam is passed under pressure. **2** (*sometimes cap.*) *Greek myth.* one of several sea nymphs whose singing was believed to lure sailors to destruction on the rocks the nymphs inhabited. **3** a woman considered to be dangerously alluring or seductive. **4** an aquatic eel-like salamander of North America, having external gills, no hind limbs, and reduced forelimbs. [C14: from OF *sereine*, from L *sīrēn*, from Gk *seirēn*]

sirenian (saɪ'riːnɪən) *adj* **1** of or belonging to the *Sirenia*, an order of aquatic herbivorous placental mammals having forelimbs modified as paddles and a horizontally flattened tail: contains only the dugong and manatees. ◆ *n* **2** an animal belonging to this order; sea cow.

Sirius ('sɪrɪəs) *n* the brightest star in the sky, lying in the constellation Canis Major. Also called: the **Dog Star.** [C14: via L from Gk *Seirios*, from ?]

sirloin ('sɜːˌlɔɪn) *n* a prime cut of beef from the loin, esp. the upper part. [C16 *surloyn*, from OF *surlonge*, from *sur* above + *longe*, from *loigne* LOIN]

sirocco (sɪ'rɒkəʊ) *n, pl* **siroccos.** a hot oppressive and often dusty wind usually occurring in spring, beginning in N Africa and reaching S Europe. [C17: from It., from Ar. *sharq* east wind]

sironize *or* **sironise** ('saɪrəˌnaɪz) *vb* **sironizes, sironizing, sironized** *or* **sironises, sironising, sironised.** (*tr*) *Austral.* to treat (a woollen fabric) chemically to prevent it wrinkling after being washed. [C20: from (C)SIRO + -*n*- + -IZE]

siroset ('saɪrəʊˌsɛt) *adj Austral.* of or relating to the chemical treatment of woollen fabrics to give a permanent-press effect, or a garment so treated.

THESAURUS

sink *vb* **1** = **descend**, cave in, decline, dip, disappear, droop, drop, drown, ebb, engulf, fall, founder, go down, go under, lower, merge, plummet, plunge, sag, slope, submerge, subside **4** = **fall**, abate, collapse, drop, lapse, relapse, retrogress, slip, slump, subside **7** = **decline**, decay, decrease, degenerate, depreciate, deteriorate, die, diminish, dwindle, fade, fail, flag, go downhill (*inf.*), lessen, weaken, worsen **9** = **dig**, bore, drill, drive, excavate, lay, put down

Antonyms *vb* ≠ **descend**: arise, ascend, climb, go up, move up, rise, rise up ≠ **decline**: enlarge, go up, grow, improve, increase, intensify, rise, rise up, swell, wax

sink in *vb* = **be understood**, get through to, make an impression, penetrate, register (*inf.*), take hold of

sinless *adj* = **innocent**, faultless, guiltless, immaculate, pure, squeaky-clean, unblemished, uncorrupted, undefiled, unsullied, virtuous, without fault, without sin

sinner *n* **5** = **wrongdoer**, evildoer, malefactor, miscreant, offender, reprobate, transgressor, trespasser (*arch.*)

sinuous *adj* **1** = **curving**, coiling, crooked, curvy, lithe, mazy, meandering, serpentine, tortuous, twisty, undulating, winding

sip *vb* **1** = **drink**, sample, sup, taste ◆ *n* **2** = **swallow**, drop, taste, thimbleful

siren *n* **3** = **seductress**, charmer, Circe, *femme fatale*, Lorelei, temptress, vamp (*inf.*), witch

sirrah ('sɪrə) *n Arch.* a contemptuous term used in addressing a man or boy. [C16: prob. var. of SIRE]
sirree (sə'riː) *interj (sometimes cap.) US inf.* an exclamation used with *yes* or *no*.
sirup ('sɪrəp) *n US.* a less common spelling of **syrup.**
sis (sɪs) *n Inf.* short for **sister.**
SIS (in Britain) *abbrev. for* Secret Intelligence Service. Also called: **MI6.**
sisal ('saɪsᵊl) *n* **1** a Mexican agave plant cultivated for its large fleshy leaves, which yield a stiff fibre used for making rope. **2** the fibre of this plant. ◆ Also called: **sisal hemp.** [C19: from Mexican Sp., after *Sisal*, a port in Yucatán, Mexico]
siskin ('sɪskɪn) *n* **1** a yellow-and-black Eurasian finch. **2 pine siskin.** a North American finch, having a streaked yellowish-brown plumage. [C16: from MDu. *sīseken*, from MLow G *sīsek*]
sissy ➊ *or* **cissy** ('sɪsɪ) *n, pl* **sissies. 1** an effeminate, weak, or cowardly boy or man. ◆ *adj* **2** effeminate, weak, or cowardly.
sister ('sɪstə) *n* **1** a female person having the same parents as another person. **2** a female person who belongs to the same group, trade union, etc., as another or others. **3** a senior nurse. **4** *Chiefly RC Church.* a nun or a title given to a nun. **5** a woman fellow member of a religious body. **6** (*modifier*) belonging to the same class, fleet, etc., as another or others: *a sister ship.* **7** (*modifier*) *Biol.* denoting any of the cells or cell components formed by division of a parent cell or cell component: *sister nuclei.* [OE *sweostor*]
sisterhood ('sɪstəˌhʊd) *n* **1** the state of being related as a sister or sisters. **2** a religious body or society of sisters.
sister-in-law *n, pl* **sisters-in-law. 1** the sister of one's husband or wife. **2** the wife of one's brother.
sisterly ('sɪstəlɪ) *adj* of or suitable to a sister, esp. in showing kindness.
▸ **'sisterliness** *n*
sistrum ('sɪstrəm) *n, pl* **sistra** (-trə). a musical instrument of ancient Egypt consisting of a metal rattle. [C14: via L from Gk *seistron*, from *seiein* to shake]
Sisyphean (ˌsɪsɪ'fiːən) *adj* **1** relating to Sisyphus, in Greek myth doomed to roll a stone uphill eternally. **2** actually or seemingly endless and futile.
sit ➊ (sɪt) *vb* **sits, sitting, sat.** (*mainly intr*) **1** (*also tr;* when *intr*, often foll. by *down, in,* or *on*) to adopt a posture in which the body is supported on the buttocks and the torso is more or less upright: *to sit on a chair.* **2** (*tr*) to cause to adopt such a posture. **3** (of an animal) to adopt or rest in a posture with the hindquarters lowered to the ground. **4** (of a bird) to perch or roost. **5** (of a hen or other bird) to cover eggs to hatch them. **6** to be situated or located. **7** (of the wind) to blow from the direction specified. **8** to adopt and maintain a posture for one's portrait to be painted, etc. **9** to occupy or be entitled to a seat in some official capacity, as a judge, etc. **10** (of a deliberative body) to be in session. **11** to remain inactive or unused: *his car sat in the garage.* **12** (of a garment) to fit or hang as specified: *that dress sits well on you.* **13** to weigh, rest, or lie as specified: *greatness sits easily on him.* **14** (*tr*) *Chiefly Brit.* to take (an examination): *he's sitting his bar finals.* **15** (usually foll. by *for*) *Chiefly Brit.* to be a candidate (for a qualification): *he's sitting for a BA.* **16** (*intr; in combination*) to look after a specified person or thing for someone else: *granny-sit.* **17** (*tr*) to have seating capacity for. **18 sit tight.** *Inf.* **18a** to wait patiently. **18b** to maintain one's stand, opinion, etc., firmly. ◆ See also **sit back, sit down,** etc. [OE *sittan*]
sitar (sɪ'tɑː) *n* a stringed musical instrument, esp. of India, having a long neck, a rounded body, and movable frets. [from Hindi *sitār*, lit.: three-stringed]
▸ **si'tarist** *n*
sit back *vb* (*intr, adv*) to relax, as when action should be taken: *many people just sit back and ignore the problems of today.*
sitcom ('sɪtˌkɒm) *n* an informal term for **situation comedy.**
sit down *vb* (*adv*) **1** to adopt or cause (oneself or another) to adopt a sitting posture. **2** (*intr;* foll. by *under*) to suffer (insults, etc.) without protests or resistance. ◆ *n* **sit-down. 3** a form of civil disobedience in which demonstrators sit down in a public place. **4** See **sit-down strike.** ◆ *adj* **sit-down. 5** (of a meal, etc.) eaten while sitting down at a table.
sit-down strike *n* a strike in which workers refuse to leave their place of employment until a settlement is reached.
site ➊ (saɪt) *n* **1a** the piece of land where something was, is, or is intended to be located: *a building site.* **1b** (*as modifier*): *site office.* **2** *Computing.* an Internet location where information relating to a specific subject or group of subjects can be accessed. ◆ *vb* **sites, siting, sited. 3** (*tr*) to locate or install (something) in a specific place. [C14: from L *situs* situation, from *sinere* to be placed]
sith (sɪθ) *adv, conj, prep* an archaic word for **since.** [OE *siththa*]
sit-in *n* **1** a form of civil disobedience in which demonstrators occupy seats in a public place and refuse to move. **2** another term for **sit-down strike.** ◆ *vb* **sit in.** (*intr, adv*) **3** (often foll. by *for*) to deputize (for). **4** (foll. by *on*) to take part (in) as a visitor or guest. **5** to organize or take part in a sit-in.
sitkamer ('sɪtˌkɑːmə) *n S. African.* a sitting room. [from Afrik.]
sitka spruce ('sɪtkə) *n* a tall North American spruce tree having yellowish-green needle-like leaves. [from *Sitka*, a town in SE Alaska]
sit on *vb* (*intr, prep*) **1** to be a member of (a committee, etc.). **2** *Inf.* to suppress. **3** *Inf.* to check or rebuke.
sit out *vb* (*tr, adv*) **1** to endure to the end: *I sat out the play although it was terrible.* **2** to remain seated throughout (a dance, etc.).
sitter ('sɪtə) *n* **1** a person or animal that sits. **2** a person who is posing for his or her portrait to be painted, etc. **3** a broody hen that is sitting on its eggs to hatch them. **4** (*in combination*) a person who looks after a specified person or thing for someone else: *flat-sitter.* **5** *US.* short for **baby-sitter. 6** anyone, other than the medium, taking part in a seance. **7** anything that is extremely easy, such as an easy catch in cricket.
sitting ➊ ('sɪtɪŋ) *n* **1** a continuous period of being seated: *I read his novel at one sitting.* **2** such a period in a restaurant, canteen, etc.: *dinner will be served in two sittings.* **3** the act or period of posing for one's portrait to be painted, etc. **4** a meeting, esp. of an official body, to conduct business. **5** the incubation period of a bird's eggs during which the mother sits on them. ◆ *adj* **6** in office: *a sitting councillor.* **7** seated: *in a sitting position.*
sitting duck *n Inf.* a person or thing in a defenceless or vulnerable position. Also called: **sitting target.**
sitting room *n* a room in a private house or flat used for relaxation and entertainment of guests.
sitting tenant *n* a tenant occupying a house, flat, etc.
situate ('sɪtjʊˌeɪt) *vb* **situates, situating, situated. 1** (*tr; often passive*) to place. ◆ *adj* **2** (now used esp. in legal contexts) situated. [C16: from LL *situāre* to position, from L *situs* a SITE]
situation ➊ (ˌsɪtjʊ'eɪʃən) *n* **1** physical placement, esp. with regard to the surroundings. **2a** state of affairs. **2b** a complex or critical state of affairs in a novel, play, etc. **3** social or financial status, position, or circumstances. **4** a position of employment.
▸ **ˌsitu'ational** *adj*

> **USAGE NOTE** *Situation* is often used in contexts in which it is redundant or imprecise. Typical examples are: *the company is in a crisis situation* or *people in a job situation.* In the first example, *situation* does not add to the meaning and should be omitted. In the second example, it would be clearer and more concise to substitute a phrase such as *people at work.*

situation comedy *n* (on television or radio) a comedy series involving the same characters in various day-to-day situations which are developed as separate stories for each episode. Also called: **sitcom.**
sit up *vb* (*adv*) **1** to raise (oneself or another) from a recumbent to an upright posture. **2** (*intr*) to remain out of bed and awake, esp. until a late hour. **3** (*intr*) *Inf.* to become suddenly interested: *devaluation of the dollar made the money market sit up.* ◆ *n* **sit-up. 4** a physical exercise in which the body is brought into a sitting position from one of lying on the back. Also called: **trunk curl.**
sitz bath (sɪts, zɪts) *n* a bath in which the buttocks and hips are immersed in hot water. [half translation of G *Sitzbad*, from *Sitz* seat + *Bad* bath]
SI unit *n* any of the units adopted for international use under the Système International d'Unités, now employed for all scientific and most technical purposes. There are seven fundamental units: the metre, kilogram, second, ampere, kelvin, candela, and mole; and two supplementary units: the radian and the steradian. All other units are derived by multiplication or division of these units.
Siva ('siːvə) *n Hinduism.* the destroyer, one of the three chief divinities of the later Hindu pantheon. [from Sansk. *Śiva*, lit.: the auspicious (one)]
▸ **'Sivaˌism** *n*
six (sɪks) *n* **1** the cardinal number that is the sum of five and one. **2** a numeral, 6, VI, etc., representing this number. **3** something representing, represented by, or consisting of six units, such as a playing card with six symbols on it. **4** Also: **six o'clock.** six hours after noon or midnight. **5** *Cricket.* **5a** a stroke from which the ball crosses the boundary without bouncing. **5b** the six runs scored for such a stroke. **6** a division of a Brownie Guide or Cub Scout pack. **7 at sixes and sevens. 7a** in disagreement. **7b** in a state of confusion. **8 knock (someone) for six.** *Inf.* to upset or overwhelm (someone) completely. **9 six of one and half a dozen of the other.** a situation in which the alternatives are considered equivalent. ◆ *determiner* **10a** amounting to six: *six nations.* **10b** (*as pron*): *set the table for six.* [OE *siex*]
Six Counties *pl n* the counties of Northern Ireland.
sixer ('sɪksə) *n* the leader of a group of six Cub Scouts or Brownie Guides.
sixfold ('sɪksˌfəʊld) *adj* **1** equal to or having six times as many or as

THESAURUS

sissy *n* **1 = wimp** (*inf.*), baby, coward, jessie (*Scot. sl.*), milksop, milquetoast (*US*), mollycoddle, mummy's boy, namby-pamby, pansy, softie (*inf.*), weakling, wet (*Brit. inf.*) ◆ *adj* **2 = wimpish** *or* **wimpy** (*inf.*), cowardly, effeminate, feeble, namby-pamby, sissified (*inf.*), soft (*inf.*), unmanly, weak, wet (*Brit. inf.*)
sit *vb* **1 = rest**, be seated, perch, settle, take a seat, take the weight off one's feet **9 = preside**, officiate **10 = convene**, assemble, be in session, deliberate, meet **17 = hold**, accommodate, contain, have space for, seat
site *n* **1 = location**, ground, place, plot, position, setting, spot ◆ *vb* **3 = locate**, install, place, position, set, situate
sitting *n* **4 = meeting**, congress, consultation, get-together (*inf.*), hearing, period, session
situation *n* **1 = location**, locale, locality, place, position, seat, setting, site, spot **2 = state of affairs**, ball game (*inf.*), case, circumstances, condition, equation, kettle of fish (*inf.*), lie of the land, plight, scenario, state, status quo, the picture (*inf.*) **3 = status**, rank, sphere, station **4 = job**, berth (*inf.*), employment, office, place, position, post

much. **2** composed of six parts. ◆ *adv* **3** by or up to six times as many or as much.

sixmo ('sɪksməʊ) *n, pl* **sixmos.** a book size resulting from folding a sheet of paper into six leaves or twelve pages, each one sixth the size of the sheet. Often written: **6mo, 6°.** Also called: **sexto.**

sixpence ('sɪkspəns) *n* (formerly) a small British cupronickel coin with a face value of six old pennies, worth 2½ pence.

six-shooter *n US inf.* a revolver with six chambers. Also called: **six-gun.**

sixte (sɪkst) *n* the sixth of eight basic positions from which a parry or attack can be made in fencing. [from F: (the) sixth (parrying position), from L *sextus* sixth]

sixteen ('sɪks'tiːn) *n* **1** the cardinal number that is the sum of ten and six. **2** a numeral, 16, XVI, etc., representing this number. **3** something represented by, representing, or consisting of 16 units. ◆ *determiner* **4a** amounting to sixteen: *sixteen tons.* **4b** (*as pron*): *sixteen are known to the police.* [OE *sextyne*]
▸'**six'teenth** *adj, n*

sixteenmo ('sɪks'tiːnməʊ) *n, pl* **sixteenmos.** a book size resulting from folding a sheet of paper into 16 leaves or 32 pages. Often written: **16mo, 16°.** Also called: **sextodecimo.**

sixteenth note *n* the usual US and Canad. name for **semiquaver.**

sixth (sɪksθ) *adj* **1** (*usually prenominal*) **1a** coming after the fifth and before the seventh in numbering, position, time, etc.; being the ordinal number of *six:* often written 6th. **1b** (*as n*): *the sixth to go.* ◆ *n* **2a** one of six parts of an object, quantity, measurement, etc. **2b** (*as modifier*): *a sixth part.* **3** the fraction equal to one divided by six (1/6). **4** *Music.* **4a** the interval between one note and another six notes away from it in the diatonic scale. **4b** one of two notes constituting such an interval in relation to the other. ◆ *adv* **5** Also: **sixthly.** after the fifth person, position, etc. ◆ *sentence connector.* **6** Also: **sixthly.** as the sixth point.

sixth form *n* (in England and Wales) **a** the most senior level in a secondary school to which pupils, usually above the legal leaving age, may proceed to take A levels, retake GCSEs, etc. **b** (*as modifier*): *a sixth-form college.*
▸'**sixth-ˌformer** *n*

sixth sense ❶ *n* any supposed means of perception, such as intuition, other than the five senses of sight, hearing, touch, taste, and smell.

sixty ('sɪkstɪ) *n, pl* **sixties. 1** the cardinal number that is the product of ten and six. **2** a numeral, 60, LX, etc., representing sixty. **3** something represented by, representing, or consisting of 60 units. ◆ *determiner* **4a** amounting to sixty: *sixty soldiers.* **4b** (*as pron*): *sixty are dead.* [OE *sixtig*]
▸'**sixtieth** *adj, n*

sixty-fourmo (ˌsɪkstɪ'fɔːməʊ) *n, pl* **sixty-fourmos.** a book size resulting from folding a sheet of paper into 64 leaves or 128 pages, each one sixty-fourth the size of the sheet. Often written **64mo, 64°.**

sixty-fourth note *n* the usual US and Canad. name for **hemidemisemiquaver.**

sixty-nine *n* another term for **soixante-neuf.**

sizable ❶ *or* **sizeable** ('saɪzəbᵊl) *adj* quite large.
▸'**sizably** *or* '**sizeably** *adv*

size[1] ❶ (saɪz) *n* **1** the dimensions, amount, or extent of something. **2** large dimensions, etc. **3** one of a series of graduated measurements, as of clothing: *she takes size 4 shoes.* **4** *Inf.* state of affairs as summarized: *he's bankrupt, that's the size of it.* ◆ *vb* **sizes, sizing, sized. 5** to sort according to size. **6** (*tr*) to cut to a particular size or sizes. [C13: from OF *sise,* shortened from *assise* ASSIZE]
▸'**sizer** *n*

> **USAGE NOTE** The use of *-size* and *-sized* after *large* or *small* is redundant, except when describing something which is made in specific sizes: *a large* (not *large-size*) *organization.* Similarly, *in size* is redundant in the expressions *large in size* and *small in size.*

size[2] (saɪz) *n* **1** Also called: **sizing.** a thin gelatinous mixture, made from glue, clay, or wax, that is used as a sealer on paper or plaster surfaces. ◆ *vb* **sizes, sizing, sized. 2** (*tr*) to treat or coat (a surface) with size. [C15: ?from OF *sise;* see SIZE[1]]

sized (saɪzd) *adj* of a specified size: *medium-sized.*

> **USAGE NOTE** See at **size**[1].

size up ❶ *vb* (*adv*) **1** (*tr*) *Inf.* to make an assessment of (a person, problem, etc.). **2** to conform to or make so as to conform to certain specifications of dimension.

sizzle ❶ ('sɪzᵊl) *vb* **sizzles, sizzling, sizzled.** (*intr*) **1** to make the hissing sound characteristic of frying fat. **2** *Inf.* to be very hot. **3** *Inf.* to be very angry. ◆ *n* **4** a hissing sound. [C17: imit.]
▸'**sizzler** *n* ▸'**sizzling** *adj*

SJ *abbrev. for* Society of Jesus.

SJA *abbrev. for* Saint John's Ambulance (Brigade *or* Association).

sjambok ('ʃæmbʌk) *n* (in South Africa) a heavy whip of rhinoceros or hippopotamus hide. [C19: from Afrik., ult. from Urdu *chābuk* horsewhip]

ska (skɑː) *n* a type of West Indian pop music: a precursor of reggae. [C20: from ?]

skaapsteker ('skɑːpˌstɪəkə) *n* any of several back-fanged venomous South African snakes. [from Afrik. *skaap* sheep + *steek* to pierce]

skald *or* **scald** (skɔːld) *n* (in ancient Scandinavia) a bard or minstrel. [from ON, from ?]
▸'**skaldic** *or* '**scaldic** *adj*

skat (skæt) *n* a three-handed card game using 32 cards, popular in German-speaking communities. [C19: from G, from It. *scarto* played cards, from *scartare* to discard, from L *charta* CARD[1]]

skate[1] (skeɪt) *n* **1** See **roller skate, ice skate. 2** the steel blade or runner of an ice skate. **3** such a blade fitted with straps for fastening to a shoe. **4 get one's skates on.** to hurry. ◆ *vb* **skates, skating, skated.** (*intr*) **5** to glide swiftly on skates. **6** to slide smoothly over a surface. **7 skate on thin ice.** to place oneself in a dangerous situation. [C17: via Du. from OF *éschasse* stilt, prob. of Gmc origin]
▸'**skater** *n*

skate[2] (skeɪt) *n, pl* **skate** *or* **skates.** any of a family of large rays of temperate and tropical seas, having two dorsal fins, a short spineless tail, and a long snout. [C14: from ON *skata*]

skateboard ('skeɪtˌbɔːd) *n* **1** a board mounted on roller-skate wheels, usually ridden while standing up. ◆ *vb* **2** (*intr*) to ride on a skateboard.
▸'**skateˌboarder** *n* ▸'**skateˌboarding** *n*

skate over *vb* (*intr, prep*) **1** to cross on or as if on skates. **2** to avoid dealing with (a matter) fully.

skean-dhu (ˌskiːən'duː) *n* a dirk worn in the stocking as part of Highland dress. [C19: from Gaelic *sgian dubh* black knife]

skedaddle ❶ (skɪ'dædᵊl) *Inf.* ◆ *vb* **skedaddles, skedaddling, skedaddled. 1** (*intr*) to run off hastily. ◆ *n* **2** a hasty retreat. [C19: from ?]

skeet (skiːt) *n* a form of clay-pigeon shooting in which targets are hurled from two traps at varying speeds and angles. [C20: changed from ON *skeyti* a thrown object, from *skjōta* to shoot]

skein (skeɪn) *n* **1** a length of yarn, etc., wound in a long coil. **2** something resembling this, such as a lock of hair. **3** a flock of geese flying. [C15: from OF *escaigne,* from ?]

skeleton ❶ ('skelɪtən) *n* **1** a hard framework consisting of inorganic material that supports and protects the soft parts of an animal's body: may be internal, as in vertebrates, or external, as in arthropods. **2** *Inf.* a very thin emaciated person or animal. **3** the essential framework of any structure, such as a building or leaf. **4** an outline consisting of bare essentials: *the skeleton of a novel.* **5** (*modifier*) reduced to a minimum: *a skeleton staff.* **6 skeleton in the cupboard** *or US & Canad.* **closet.** a scandalous fact or event in the past that is kept secret. [C16: via NL from Gk: something desiccated, from *skellein* to dry up]
▸'**skeletal** *or* '**skeleton-ˌlike** *adj*

skeletonize *or* **skeletonise** ('skelɪtəˌnaɪz) *vb* **skeletonizes, skeletonizing, skeletonized** *or* **skeletonises, skeletonising, skeletonised.** (*tr*) **1** to reduce to a minimum framework or outline. **2** to create the essential framework of.

skeleton key *n* a key with the serrated edge filed down so that it can open numerous locks. Also called: **passkey.**

skep (skep) *n* **1** a beehive, esp. one constructed of straw. **2** *Now chiefly dialect.* a large basket of wickerwork or straw. [OE *sceppe*]

skeptic ('skeptɪk) *n, adj* an archaic and the usual US spelling of **sceptic.**

skerrick ('skerɪk) *n US, Austral., & NZ.* a small fragment or amount (esp. in **not a skerrick**). [C20: N English dialect, prob. of Scand. origin]

skerry ('skerɪ) *n, pl* **skerries.** *Chiefly Scot.* **1** a small rocky island. **2** a reef. [C17: Orkney dialect, from ON *sker* scar (rock formation)]

sketch ❶ (sketʃ) *n* **1** a rapid drawing or painting. **2** a brief usually descriptive essay or other literary composition. **3** a short play, often comic, forming part of a revue. **4** a short evocative piece of instrumental music. **5** any brief outline. ◆ *vb* **6** to make a rough drawing (of). **7** (*tr; often foll. by out*) to make a brief description of. [C17: from Du. *schets,* via It. from L *schedius* hastily made, from Gk *skhedios* unprepared]
▸'**sketcher** *n*

sketchbook ('sketʃˌbʊk) *n* **1** a book of plain paper containing sketches or for making sketches in. **2** a book of literary sketches.

THESAURUS

sixth sense *n* = **intuition**, clairvoyance, feyness, second sight

sizable *adj* = **large**, considerable, decent, decent-sized, goodly, largish, respectable, substantial, tidy (*inf.*)

size[1] *n* **1, 2** = **dimensions**, amount, bigness, bulk, extent, greatness, hugeness, immensity, largeness, magnitude, mass, measurement(s), proportions, range, vastness, volume

size up *vb* **1** *Informal* = **assess**, appraise, evaluate, eye up, get (something) taped (*Brit. inf.*), get the measure of, take stock of

sizzle *vb* **1** = **hiss**, crackle, frizzle, fry, spit, sputter

skedaddle *vb* **1** *Informal* = **run away**, abscond, beat a hasty retreat, bolt, decamp, disappear, do a bunk (*Brit. sl.*), flee, scarper (*Brit. sl.*), scoot, scram (*inf.*), scurry away, scuttle away, vamoose (*sl., chiefly US*)

skeletal *adj* **2** = **emaciated**, cadaverous, fleshless, gaunt, hollow-cheeked, lantern-jawed, skin-and-bone (*inf.*), wasted, worn to a shadow

skeleton *n* **3** = **framework**, bare bones, bones, draft, frame, outline, sketch, structure

sketch *n* **1** = **drawing**, delineation, design, draft, outline, plan, skeleton ◆ *vb* **6** = **draw**, block out, delineate, depict, draft, outline, paint, plot, portray, represent, rough out

sketchy ❶ (ˈsketʃɪ) *adj* **sketchier, sketchiest. 1** existing only in outline. **2** superficial or slight.
▸ˈ**sketchily** *adv* ▸ˈ**sketchiness** *n*

skew (skjuː) *adj* **1** placed in or turning into an oblique position or course. **2** *Machinery.* having a component that is at an angle to the main axis of an assembly: *a skew bevel gear.* **3** *Maths.* composed of or being elements that are neither parallel nor intersecting. **4** (of a statistical distribution) not having equal probabilities above and below the mean. **5** distorted or biased. ◆ *n* **6** an oblique, slanting, or indirect course or position. ◆ *vb* **7** to take or cause to take an oblique course or direction. **8** (*intr*) to look sideways. **9** (*tr*) to distort. [C14: from OF *escuer* to shun, of Gmc origin]
▸ˈ**skewness** *n*

skewback (ˈskjuːˌbæk) *n Archit.* the sloping surface on both sides of a segmental arch that takes the thrust.

skewbald (ˈskjuːˌbɔːld) *adj* **1** marked or spotted in white and any colour except black. ◆ *n* **2** a horse with this marking. [C17: see SKEW, PIEBALD]

skewer (skjʊə) *n* **1** a long pin for holding meat in position while being cooked, etc. **2** a similar pin having some other function. ◆ *vb* **3** (*tr*) to drive a skewer through or fasten with a skewer. [C17: prob. from dialect *skiver*]

skewwhiff ❶ (ˈskjuːˈwɪf) *adj* (*postpositive*) *Brit. inf.* not straight. [C18: prob. infl. by ASKEW]

ski (skiː) *n, pl* **skis** *or* **ski. 1a** one of a pair of wood, metal, or plastic runners that are used for gliding over snow. **1b** (*as modifier*): *a ski boot.* **2** a water-ski. ◆ *vb* **skis, skiing; skied** *or* **ski'd. 3** (*intr*) to travel on skis. [C19: from Norwegian, from ON *skith* snowshoes]
▸ˈ**skier** *n* ▸ˈ**skiing** *n*

skibob (ˈskiːbɒb) *n* a vehicle made of two short skis, the forward one having a steering handle and the rear one supporting a low seat, for gliding down snow slopes.
▸ˈ**skibobber** *n*

skid (skɪd) *vb* **skids, skidding, skidded. 1** to cause (a vehicle) to slide sideways or (of a vehicle) to slide sideways while in motion, esp. out of control. **2** (*intr*) to slide without revolving, as the wheel of a moving vehicle after sudden braking. ◆ *n* **3** an instance of sliding, esp. sideways. **4** a support on which heavy objects may be stored and moved short distances by sliding. **5** a shoe or drag used to apply pressure to the metal rim of a wheel to act as a brake. [C17: ? of Scand. origin]

Skidoo (ˈskɪduː) *n Canad., trademark.* another name for **snowmobile.**

skid row (rəʊ) *or* **skid road** *n Sl., chiefly US & Canad.* a dilapidated section of a city inhabited by vagrants, etc.

skied[1] (skaɪd) *vb* the past tense and past participle of **sky.**

skied[2] (skiːd) *vb* a past tense and past participle of **ski.**

skiff (skɪf) *n* a small narrow boat. [C18: from F *esquif,* from OIt. *schifo* a boat, of Gmc origin]

skiffle (ˈskɪfᵊl) *n* a style of popular music of the 1950s, played chiefly on guitars and improvised percussion instruments. [C20: from ?]

skijoring (skiːˈdʒɔːrɪŋ, -ˈjɔːrɪŋ) *n* a sport in which a skier is pulled over snow or ice, usually by a horse. [Norwegian *skikjöring,* lit.: ski-driving]
▸**skiˈjorer** *n*

ski jump *n* **1** a high ramp overhanging a slope from which skiers compete to make the longest jump. ◆ *vb* **ski-jump. 2** (*intr*) to perform a ski jump.
▸**ski jumper** *n*

skilful ❶ *or US* **skillful** (ˈskɪlfʊl) *adj* **1** possessing or displaying accomplishment or skill. **2** involving or requiring accomplishment or skill.
▸ˈ**skilfully** *or US* ˈ**skillfully** *adv*

ski lift *n* any device for carrying skiers up a slope, such as a chairlift.

skill ❶ (skɪl) *n* **1** special ability in a sport, etc., esp. ability acquired by training. **2** something, esp. a trade or technique, requiring special training or manual proficiency. [C12: from ON *skil* distinction]
▸ˈ**skill-less** *or* ˈ**skilless** *adj*

skilled ❶ (skɪld) *adj* **1** demonstrating accomplishment or special training. **2** (*prenominal*) involving skill or special training: *a skilled job.*

skillet (ˈskɪlɪt) *n* **1** a small frying pan. **2** *Chiefly Brit.* a saucepan. [C15: prob. from *skele* bucket, from ON]

skilly (ˈskɪlɪ) *n Chiefly Brit.* a thin soup or gruel. [C19: from *skilligallee,* from ?]

skim ❶ (skɪm) *vb* **skims, skimming, skimmed. 1** (*tr*) to remove floating material from the surface of (a liquid), as with a spoon: *to skim milk.* **2** to glide smoothly or lightly over (a surface). **3** (*tr*) to throw (something) in a path over a surface, so as to bounce or ricochet: *to skim stones over water.* **4** (when *intr,* usually foll. by *through*) to read (a book) in a superficial manner. ◆ *n* **5** the act or process of skimming. **6** material skimmed off a liquid, esp. off milk. **7** any thin layer covering a surface. [C15 *skimmen,* prob. from *scumen* to skim]

skimmed milk *n* milk from which the cream has been removed. Also called: **skim milk.**

skimmer (ˈskɪmə) *n* **1** a person or thing that skims. **2** any of several mainly tropical coastal aquatic birds having a bill with an elongated lower mandible for skimming food from the surface of the water. **3** a flat perforated spoon used for skimming fat from liquids.

skimmia (ˈskɪmɪə) *n* any of a genus of rutaceous shrubs grown for their ornamental red berries and evergreen foliage. [C18: NL from Japanese (*mijama-*) *shikimi,* a native name of the plant]

skimp ❶ (skɪmp) *vb* **1** to be extremely sparing or supply (someone) sparingly. **2** to perform (work, etc.) carelessly or with inadequate materials. [C17: ? a combination of SCANT & SCRIMP]

skimpy ❶ (ˈskɪmpɪ) *adj* **skimpier, skimpiest. 1** made of too little material. **2** excessively thrifty; mean.
▸ˈ**skimpily** *adv* ▸ˈ**skimpiness** *n*

skin ❶ (skɪn) *n* **1** the tissue forming the outer covering of the vertebrate body: it consists of two layers, the outermost of which may be covered with hair, scales, feathers, etc. **2** a person's complexion: *a fair skin.* **3** any similar covering in a plant or lower animal. **4** any coating or film, such as one that forms on the surface of a liquid. **5** the outer covering of a fur-bearing animal, dressed and finished with the hair on. **6** a container made from animal skin. **7** the outer covering surface of a vessel, rocket, etc. **8** a person's skin regarded as his life: *to save one's skin.* **9** (*often pl*) *Inf.* (in jazz or pop use) a drum. **10** *Inf.* short for **skinhead. 11 by the skin of one's teeth.** only just. **12 get under one's skin.** *Inf.* to irritate. **13 no skin off one's nose.** *Inf.* not a matter that affects one adversely. **14 skin and bone.** extremely thin. **15 thick** (*or* **thin**) **skin.** an insensitive (*or* sensitive) nature. ◆ *vb* **skins, skinning, skinned. 16** (*tr*) to remove the outer covering from (fruit, etc.). **17** (*tr*) to scrape a small piece of skin from (a part of oneself) in falling, etc.: *he skinned his knee.* **18** (often foll. by *over*) to cover (something) with skin or a skinlike substance or (of something) to become covered in this way. **19** (*tr*) *Sl.* to swindle. ◆ *adj* **20** of or for the skin: *skin cream.* [OE *scinn*]
▸ˈ**skinless** *adj* ▸ˈ**skinˌlike** *adj*

skin-deep ❶ *adj* **1** superficial; shallow. ◆ *adv* **2** superficially.

skin diving *n* the sport or activity of diving and underwater swimming without wearing a diver's costume.
▸ˈ**skin-ˌdiver** *n*

skin flick *n Sl.* a film containing much nudity and explicit sex for sensational purposes.

skinflint ❶ (ˈskɪnˌflɪnt) *n* an ungenerous or niggardly person. [C18: referring to a person so avaricious that he would skin (swindle) a flint]

skinful (ˈskɪnˌfʊl) *n, pl* **skinfuls.** *Sl.* sufficient alcoholic drink to make one drunk.

skin graft *n* a piece of skin removed from one part of the body and surgically grafted at the site of a severe burn or similar injury.

skinhead (ˈskɪnˌhɛd) *n* **1** a member of a group of White youths, noted for their closely cropped hair, aggressive behaviour, and overt racism. **2** a closely cropped hairstyle.

skink (skɪŋk) *n* any of a family of lizards commonest in tropical Africa

THESAURUS

sketchily *adv* **2** = **incompletely,** cursorily, hastily, imperfectly, patchily, perfunctorily, roughly

sketchy *adj* **2** = **incomplete,** bitty, cobbled together, crude, cursory, inadequate, outline, perfunctory, rough, scrappy, skimpy, slight, superficial, unfinished, vague
Antonyms *adj* complete, detailed, full, thorough

skewwhiff *adj Brit. informal* = **crooked,** askew, aslant, cockeyed (*inf.*), out of true, squint (*inf.*), tilted

skilful *adj* **1** = **expert,** able, accomplished, adept, adroit, apt, clever, competent, dexterous, experienced, handy, masterly, practised, professional, proficient, quick, ready, skilled, trained
Antonyms *adj* amateurish, awkward, bungling, cack-handed, clumsy, cowboy (*inf.*), ham-fisted, incompetent, inept, inexperienced, inexpert, maladroit, slapdash, unaccomplished, unqualified, unskilful, unskilled

skill *n* **1** = **expertise,** ability, accomplishment, adroitness, aptitude, art, cleverness, competence, craft, dexterity, experience, expertness, facility, finesse, handiness, ingenuity, intelligence, knack, proficiency, quickness, readiness, skilfulness, talent, technique
Antonyms *n* awkwardness, brute force, cack-handedness, clumsiness, gaucheness, ham-fistedness, inability, incompetence, ineptitude, inexperience, lack of finesse, maladroitness, unhandiness

skilled *adj* **1** = **expert,** able, accomplished, a dab hand at (*Brit. inf.*), experienced, masterly, practised, professional, proficient, skilful, trained
Antonyms *adj* amateurish, cowboy (*inf.*), inexperienced, inexpert, uneducated, unprofessional, unqualified, unskilled, untalented, untrained

skim *vb* **1** = **separate,** cream **2** = **glide,** brush, coast, dart, float, fly, sail, soar **4** *usually with* **through** = **scan,** glance, run one's eye over, skip (*inf.*), thumb *or* leaf through

skimp *vb* **1** = **stint,** be mean with, be niggardly, be sparing with, cut corners, pinch, scamp, scant, scrimp, tighten one's belt, withhold
Antonyms *vb* act as if one had money to burn, be extravagant, be generous with, be prodigal, blow (*sl.*), fritter away, lavish, overspend, pour on, splurge, squander, throw money away

skimpy *adj* **1** = **inadequate,** exiguous, insufficient, meagre, miserly, niggardly, scant, scanty, short, sparse, thin, tight

skin *n* **3** = **hide,** fell, integument, pelt, tegument **4** = **coating,** casing, crust, film, husk, membrane, outside, peel, rind **11 by the skin of one's teeth** = **narrowly,** by a hair's-breadth, by a narrow margin, by a whisker (*inf.*), only just **12 get under one's skin** *Informal* = **annoy,** aggravate (*inf.*), get in one's hair (*inf.*), get on one's nerves (*inf.*), grate on, irk, irritate, needle (*inf.*), nettle, piss one off (*taboo sl.*), rub up the wrong way ◆ *vb* **16** = **peel,** abrade, bark, excoriate, flay **17** = **graze,** scrape

skin-deep *adj* **1** = **superficial,** artificial, external, meaningless, on the surface, shallow, surface

skinflint *n* = **miser,** meanie *or* meany (*inf., chiefly Brit.*), niggard, penny-pincher (*inf.*), Scrooge, tightwad (*US & Canad. sl.*)

and Asia, having an elongated body covered with smooth scales. [C16: from L *scincus* a lizard, from Gk *skinkos*]

skinned (skɪnd) *adj* **1** stripped of the skin. **2a** having a skin as specified. **2b** (*in combination*): *thick-skinned*.

skinny ❶ ('skɪnɪ) *adj* **skinnier, skinniest. 1** lacking in flesh; thin. **2** consisting of or resembling skin.

skint (skɪnt) *adj* (*usually postpositive*) *Brit. sl.* without money. [var. of *skinned*, p.p. of SKIN]

skin test *n Med.* any test to determine immunity to a disease or hypersensitivity by introducing a small amount of the test substance beneath the skin.

skintight ('skɪn'taɪt) *adj* (of garments) fitting tightly over the body; clinging.

skip[1] ❶ (skɪp) *vb* **skips, skipping, skipped. 1** (when *intr*, often foll. by *over*, *into*, etc.) to spring or move lightly, esp. to move by hopping from one foot to the other. **2** (*intr*) to jump over a skipping-rope. **3** to cause (a stone, etc.) to skim over a surface or (of a stone) to move in this way. **4** to omit (intervening matter): *he skipped a chapter of the book.* **5** (*intr*; foll. by *through*) *Inf.* to read or deal with quickly or superficially. **6 skip it!** *Inf.* it doesn't matter! **7** (*tr*) *Inf.* to miss deliberately: *to skip school.* **8** (*tr*) *Inf., chiefly US & Canad.* to leave (a place) in haste: *to skip town.* ◆ *n* **9** a skipping movement or gait. **10** the act of passing over or omitting. [C13: prob. from ON]

skip[2] (skɪp) *n, vb* **skips, skipping, skipped.** *Inf.* short for **skipper**[1].

skip[3] (skɪp) *n* **1** a large open container for transporting building materials, etc. **2** a cage used as a lift in mines, etc. [C19: var. of SKEP]

ski pants *pl n* stretch trousers, worn for skiing or as a fashion garment, kept taut by a strap under the foot.

skip distance *n* the shortest distance between a transmitter and a receiver that will permit reception of radio waves of a specified frequency by one reflection from the ionosphere.

skipjack ('skɪp,dʒæk) *n, pl* **skipjack** *or* **skipjacks. 1** Also called: **skipjack tuna.** an important food fish that has a striped abdomen and occurs in all tropical seas. **2 black skipjack.** a small spotted tuna of Indo-Pacific seas.

skiplane ('skiː,pleɪn) *n* an aircraft fitted with skis to enable it to land on and take off from snow.

skipper[1] ('skɪpə) *n* **1** the captain of any vessel. **2** the captain of an aircraft. **3** a leader, as of a sporting team. ◆ *vb* **4** to act as skipper (of). [C14: from MLow G, MDu. *schipper* shipper]

skipper[2] ('skɪpə) *n* **1** a person or thing that skips. **2** a small butterfly having a hairy mothlike body and erratic darting flight.

skipping ('skɪpɪŋ) *n* the act of jumping over a rope that is held either by the person jumping or by two other people, as a game or for exercise.

skipping-rope *n Brit.* a cord, usually having handles at each end, that is held in the hands and swung round and down so that the holder or others can jump over it.

skip-tooth saw *n* a saw with alternate teeth absent.

skip zone *n* a region surrounding a broadcasting station that cannot receive transmissions either directly or by reflection off the ionosphere.

skirl (skɜːl) *Scot. & N English dialect.* ◆ *vb* **1** (*intr*) (esp. of bagpipes) to emit a shrill sound. ◆ *n* **2** the sound of bagpipes. [C14: prob. from ON]

skirmish ❶ ('skɜːmɪʃ) *n* **1** a minor short-lived military engagement. **2** any brisk clash or encounter. ◆ *vb* **3** (*intr*; often foll. by *with*) to engage in a skirmish. [C14: from OF *eskirmir*, of Gmc origin]
▸ **'skirmisher** *n*

skirt ❶ (skɜːt) *n* **1** a garment hanging from the waist, worn chiefly by women and girls. **2** the part of a dress below the waist. **3** Also called: **apron.** a circular flap, as round the base of a hovercraft. **4** the flaps on a saddle. **5** *Brit.* a cut of beef from the flank. **6** (*often pl*) an outlying area. **7 bit of skirt.** *Sl.* a girl or woman. ◆ *vb* **8** (*tr*) to form the edge of. **9** (*tr*) to provide with a border. **10** (when *intr*, foll. by *around, along*, etc.) to pass (by) or be situated (near) the outer edge of (an area, etc.). **11** (*tr*) to avoid (a difficulty, etc.): *he skirted the issue.* **12** *Chiefly Austral. & NZ.* to trim the ragged edges from (a fleece). [C13: from ON *skyrta* shirt]
▸ **'skirted** *adj*

skirting ('skɜːtɪŋ) *n* **1** a border, esp. of wood or tiles, fixed round the base of an interior wall to protect it. **2** material used for skirts.

skirting board *n* a skirting made of wood.

skirtings ('skɜːtɪŋz) *pl n* ragged edges trimmed from the fleece of a sheep.

ski stick *or* **pole** *n* a stick, usually with a metal point, used by skiers to gain momentum and maintain balance.

skit ❶ (skɪt) *n* **1** a brief satirical theatrical sketch. **2** a short satirical piece of writing. [C18: rel. to earlier verb *skit* to move rapidly, hence to score a satirical hit, prob. of Scand. origin]

skite[1] (skaɪt) *Scot. dialect.* ◆ *vb* **skites, skiting, skited. 1** (*intr*) to slide or slip, as on ice. **2** (*tr*) to strike with a sharp blow. ◆ *n* **3** an instance of slipping or sliding. **4** a sharp blow. [C18: from ?]

skite[2] (skaɪt) *Austral. & NZ inf.* ◆ *vb* **skites, skiting, skited.** (*intr*) **1** to boast. ◆ *n* **2** boastful talk. **3** a person who boasts. [C19: from Scot. & N English dialect]

ski tow *n* a device for pulling skiers uphill, usually a motor-driven rope grasped by the skier while riding on his skis.

skitter ('skɪtə) *vb* **1** (*intr*; often foll. by *off*) to move or run rapidly or lightly. **2** to skim or cause to skim lightly and rapidly. **3** (*intr*) *Angling.* to draw a bait lightly over the surface of water. [C19: prob. from dialect *skite* to dash about]

skittish ❶ ('skɪtɪʃ) *adj* **1** playful, lively, or frivolous. **2** difficult to handle or predict. [C15: prob. from ON]
▸ **'skittishly** *adv* ▸ **'skittishness** *n*

skittle ('skɪtᵊl) *n* **1** a wooden or plastic pin, typically widest just above the base. **2** (*pl*; *functioning as sing*) Also called (esp. US): **ninepins.** a bowling game in which players knock over as many skittles as possible by rolling a wooden ball at them. [C17: from ?]

skive[1] (skaɪv) *vb* **skives, skiving, skived.** (*tr*) to shave or remove the surface of (leather). [C19: of Scand. origin, from *skifa*]
▸ **'skiver** *n*

skive[2] ❶ (skaɪv) *vb* **skives, skiving, skived.** (when *intr*, often foll. by *off*) *Brit. inf.* to evade (work or responsibility). [C20: from ?]
▸ **'skiver** *n*

skivvy[1] ('skɪvɪ) *n, pl* **skivvies. 1** *Chiefly Brit., often contemptuous.* a servant, esp. a female; drudge. ◆ *vb* **skivvies, skivvying, skivvied. 2** (*intr*) *Brit.* to work as a skivvy. [C20: from ?]

skivvy[2] ('skɪvɪ) *n, pl* **skivvies.** *Austral. & NZ.* a lightweight sweater-like garment with long sleeves and a polo neck. [from ?]

skol (skɒl) *or* **skoal** (skəʊl) *sentence substitute* good health! (a drinking toast). [C16: from Danish *skaal* bowl, of Scand. origin, from *skal*]

skookum ('skuːkəm) *adj W Canad.* large or big. [from Chinook Jargon]

Skt, Skt., Skr, *or* **Skr.** *abbrev. for* Sanskrit.

skua ('skjuːə) *n* any of various predatory aquatic gull-like birds having a dark plumage and long tail. [C17: from NL, from Faeroese *skūgvur*, of Scand. origin, from *skūfr*]

skulduggery ❶ *or US* **skullduggery** (skʌl'dʌgərɪ) *n Inf.* underhand dealing; trickery. [C18: from earlier Scot. *skulduddery*, from ?]

skulk ❶ (skʌlk) *vb* (*intr*) **1** to move stealthily so as to avoid notice. **2** to lie in hiding; lurk. **3** to shirk duty or evade responsibilities. ◆ *n* **4** a person who skulks. **5** *Obs.* a pack of foxes. [C13: from ON]
▸ **'skulker** *n*

skull (skʌl) *n* **1** the bony skeleton of the head of vertebrates. **2** *Often derog.* the head regarded as the mind or intelligence: *to have a dense skull.* **3** a picture of a skull used to represent death or danger. [C13: from ON]

skull and crossbones *n* a picture of the human skull above two crossed thighbones, formerly on the pirate flag, now used as a warning of danger or death.

skullcap ('skʌl,kæp) *n* **1** a rounded brimless hat fitting the crown of the head. **2** the top part of the skull. **3** any of a genus of perennial plants, that have helmet-shaped flowers.

skunk (skʌŋk) *n, pl* **skunks** *or* **skunk. 1** any of various American mammals having a black-and-white coat and bushy tail: they eject an unpleasant-smelling fluid from the anal gland when attacked. **2** *Inf.* a despicable person. [C17: of Amerind origin]

skunk cabbage *n* a low-growing fetid aroid swamp plant of E North America, having broad leaves and minute flowers enclosed in a greenish spathe.

sky ❶ (skaɪ) *n, pl* **skies. 1** (*sometimes pl*) the apparently dome-shaped expanse extending upwards from the horizon that is blue or grey during the day and black at night. **2** outer space, as seen from the earth. **3** (*often pl*) weather, as described by the appearance of the upper air:

THESAURUS

skinny *adj* **1 = thin**, emaciated, lean, scraggy, scrawny, skeletal, skin-and-bone (*inf.*), twiggy, undernourished
Antonyms *adj* beefy (*inf.*), broad in the beam (*inf.*), fat, fleshy, heavy, obese, plump, podgy, portly, stout, tubby

skip[1] *vb* **1 = hop**, bob, bounce, caper, cavort, dance, flit, frisk, gambol, prance, trip **4 = pass over**, eschew, give (something) a miss, leave out, miss out, omit, skim over **7** *Informal* **= miss**, bunk off (*sl.*), cut (*inf.*), dog it *or* dog off (*dialect*), play truant from, wag (*dialect*)

skirmish *n* **1, 2 = fight**, affair, affray (*Law*), battle, brush, clash, combat, conflict, contest, dust-up (*inf.*), encounter, engagement, fracas, incident, scrap (*inf.*), scrimmage, set-to (*inf.*), spat, tussle ◆ *vb* **3 = fight**, clash, collide, come to blows, scrap (*inf.*), tussle

skirt *n* **6** *often plural* **= outskirts**, edge, fringe, hem, margin, periphery, purlieus, rim ◆ *vb* **8 = border**, edge, flank, lie alongside **11 = avoid**, body-swerve (*Scot.*), bypass, circumvent, detour, evade, steer clear of

skit *n* **1, 2 = parody**, burlesque, sketch, spoof (*inf.*), takeoff (*inf.*), travesty, turn

skittish *adj* **1 = lively**, excitable, fickle, fidgety, frivolous, highly strung, jumpy, nervous, playful, restive
Antonyms *adj* calm, composed, demure, laid-back, placid, relaxed, sober, staid, steady, unexcitable, unfazed (*inf.*), unflappable, unruffled

skive[2] *vb Brit. informal* **= slack**, bob off (*Brit. sl.*), dodge, gold-brick (*US sl.*), idle, malinger, scrimshank (*Brit. military sl.*), shirk, skulk, swing the lead

skiver *n Brit. informal* **= slacker**, dodger, do-nothing, gold brick (*US sl.*), idler, loafer, scrimshanker (*Brit. military sl.*), shirker

skulduggery *n Informal* **= trickery**, double-dealing, duplicity, fraudulence, machinations, shenanigan(s) (*inf.*), swindling, underhandedness, unscrupulousness

skulk *vb* **1 = sneak**, creep, pad, prowl, slink **2 = lurk**, lie in wait, loiter

sky *n* **1 = heavens**, azure (*poetic*), empyrean, firmament, upper atmosphere, vault of heaven, welkin (*arch.*) **6 to the skies = fulsomely**, excessively, extravagantly, highly, immoderately, inordinately, profusely *sunny skies.* **4** heaven. **5** *Inf.* the highest level of attainment: *the sky's the limit.* **6 to the skies.** extravagantly. ◆ *vb* **skies, skying, skied. 7** *Rowing.* to lift (the blade of an oar) too high before a stroke. **8** (*tr*) *Inf.* to hit (a ball) high in the air. [C13: from ON *ský*]

sky blue *n, adj* (of) a light or pale blue colour.

skydiving ('skaɪˌdaɪvɪŋ) *n* the sport of parachute jumping, in which participants perform manoeuvres before opening the parachute.
▸**'skyˌdive** *vb* **'skyˌdives, 'skyˌdiving, 'skyˌdived** *or US* **'skyˌdove; 'skyˌdived** ▸**'skyˌdiver** *n*

Skye terrier *n* a short-legged long-bodied breed of terrier with long wiry hair and erect ears. [C19: after *Skye,* Scot. island]

sky-high *adj, adv* **1** at or to an unprecedented level: *prices rocketed sky-high.* ◆ *adv* **2** high into the air. **3 blow sky-high.** to destroy.

skyjack ('skaɪˌdʒæk) *vb* (*tr*) to hijack (an aircraft). [C20: from SKY + HIJACK]

skylark ('skaɪˌlɑːk) *n* **1** an Old World lark, noted for singing while hovering at a great height. ◆ *vb* **2** (*intr*) *Inf.* to romp or play jokes.

skylight ('skaɪˌlaɪt) *n* a window placed in a roof or ceiling to admit daylight. Also called: **fanlight.**

skyline ('skaɪˌlaɪn) *n* **1** the line at which the earth and sky appear to meet. **2** the outline of buildings, trees, etc., seen against the sky.

sky pilot *n Sl.* a clergyman, esp. a chaplain.

skyrocket ('skaɪˌrɒkɪt) *n* **1** another word for **rocket**[1] (sense 1). ◆ *vb* **2** (*intr*) *Inf.* to rise rapidly, as in price.

skysail ('skaɪˌseɪl) *n Naut.* a square sail set above the royal on a square-rigger.

skyscraper ('skaɪˌskreɪpə) *n* a tall multistorey building.

skyward ('skaɪwəd) *adj* **1** directed or moving towards the sky. ◆ *adv* **2** Also: **skywards.** towards the sky.

skywriting ('skaɪˌraɪtɪŋ) *n* **1** the forming of words in the sky by the release of smoke or vapour from an aircraft. **2** the words so formed.
▸**'skyˌwriter** *n*

slab ❶ (slæb) *n* **1** a broad flat thick piece of wood, stone, or other material. **2** a thick slice of cake, etc. **3** any of the outside parts of a log that are sawn off while the log is being made into planks. **4** *Austral.* & *NZ.* **4a** a rough-hewn wooden plank. **4b** (*as modifier*): *a slab hut.* **5** *Inf., chiefly Brit.* an operating or mortuary table. ◆ *vb* **slabs, slabbing, slabbed.** (*tr*) **6** to cut or make into a slab or slabs. **7** to saw slabs from (a log). [C13: from ?]

slack[1] ❶ (slæk) *adj* **1** not tight, tense, or taut. **2** negligent or careless. **3** (esp. of water, etc.) moving slowly. **4** (of trade, etc.) not busy. **5** *Phonetics.* another term for **lax** (sense 4). ◆ *adv* **6** in a slack manner. ◆ *n* **7** a part of a rope, etc., that is slack: *take in the slack.* **8** a period of decreased activity. ◆ *vb* **9** to neglect (one's duty, etc.). **10** (often foll. by *off*) to loosen. ◆ See also **slacks.** [OE *slæc, sleac*]
▸**'slackly** *adv* ▸**'slackness** *n*

slack[2] (slæk) *n* small pieces of coal with a high ash content. [C15: prob. from MLow G *slecke*]

slacken ❶ ('slækən) *vb* (often foll. by *off*) **1** to make or become looser. **2** to make or become slower, less intense, etc.

slacker ❶ ('slækə) *n* a person who evades work or duty; shirker.

slacks (slæks) *pl n* informal trousers worn by both sexes.

slack water *n* the period of still water around the turn of the tide, esp. at low tide.

slag ❶ (slæg) *n* **1** Also called: **cinder.** the fused material formed during the smelting or refining of metals. It usually consists of a mixture of silicates with calcium, phosphorus, sulphur, etc. **2** the mass of rough fragments of rock derived from volcanic lava. **3** a mixture of shale, clay, coal dust, etc., produced during coal mining. **4** *Brit. sl.* a coarse or dissipated woman or girl. ◆ *vb* **slags, slagging, slagged. 5** to convert into or become slag. **6** (*tr;* sometimes foll. by *off*) *Sl.* to make disparaging comments about; slander. [C16: from MLow G *slagge,* ?from *slagen* to slay]
▸**'slagging** *n* ▸**'slaggy** *adj*

slag heap *n* a hillock of waste matter from coal mining, etc.

slain (sleɪn) *vb* the past participle of **slay.**

slake ❶ (sleɪk) *vb* **slakes, slaking, slaked. 1** (*tr*) *Literary.* to satisfy (thirst, desire, etc.). **2** (*tr*) *Poetic.* to cool or refresh. **3** to undergo or cause to undergo the process in which lime reacts with water to produce calcium hydroxide. [OE *slacian,* from *slæc* SLACK[1]]
▸**'slakable** *or* **'slakeable** *adj*

slaked lime *n* another name for **calcium hydroxide.**

slalom ('slɑːləm) *n Skiing, canoeing, etc.* a race over a winding course marked by artificial obstacles. [Norwegian, from *slad* sloping + *lom* path]

slam[1] ❶ (slæm) *vb* **slams, slamming, slammed. 1** to cause (a door or window) to close noisily or (of a door, etc.) to close in this way. **2** (*tr*) to throw (something) down violently. **3** (*tr*) *Sl.* to criticize harshly. **4** (*intr;* usually foll. by *into* or *out of*) *Inf.* to go (into or out of a room, etc.) in violent haste or anger. **5** (*tr*) to strike with violent force. **6** (*tr*) *Inf.* to defeat easily. ◆ *n* **7** the act or noise of slamming. [C17: of Scand. origin]

slam[2] (slæm) *n* **a** the winning of all (**grand slam**) or all but one (**little** *or* **small slam**) of the 13 tricks at bridge or whist. **b** the bid to do so in bridge. [C17: from ?]

slam-dance *vb* **slam-dances, slam-dancing, slam-danced.** (*intr*) to hurl oneself repeatedly into or through a crowd at a rock-music concert.

slammer ('slæmə) *n* **the.** *Sl.* prison.

slander ❶ ('slɑːndə) *n* **1** *Law.* **1a** defamation in some transient form, as by spoken words, gestures, etc. **1b** a slanderous statement, etc. **2** any defamatory words spoken about a person. ◆ *vb* **3** to utter or circulate slander (about). [C13: via Anglo-F from OF *escandle,* from LL *scandalum* a cause of offence; see SCANDAL]
▸**'slanderer** *n* ▸**'slanderous** *adj*

slang ❶ (slæŋ) *n* **1a** vocabulary, idiom, etc., that is not appropriate to the standard form of a language or to formal contexts and may be restricted as to social status or distribution. **1b** (*as modifier*): *a slang word.* ◆ *vb* **2** to abuse (someone) with vituperative language. [C18: from ?]
▸**'slangy** *adj* ▸**'slangily** *adv* ▸**'slanginess** *n*

slant ❶ (slɑːnt) *vb* **1** to incline or be inclined at an oblique or sloping angle. **2** (*tr*) to write or present (news, etc.) with a bias. **3** (*intr;* foll. by *towards*) (of a person's opinions) to be biased. ◆ *n* **4** an inclined or oblique line or direction. **5** a way of looking at something. **6** a bias or opinion, as in an article. **7 on a** (*or* **the**) **slant.** sloping. ◆ *adj* **8** oblique; sloping. [C17: short for ASLANT, prob. of Scand. origin]
▸**'slanting** *adj*

slantwise ('slɑːntˌwaɪz) *or* **slantways** *adv, adj* (*prenominal*) in a slanting or oblique direction.

slap ❶ (slæp) *n* **1** a sharp blow or smack, as with the open hand, something flat, etc. **2** the sound made by or as if by such a blow. **3** (**a bit of**) **slap and tickle.** *Brit. inf.* sexual play. **4 a slap in the face.** an insult or rebuff. **5 a slap on the back.** congratulation. ◆ *vb* **slaps, slapping, slapped. 6** (*tr*) to strike (a person or thing) sharply, as with the open hand or something flat. **7** (*tr*) to bring down (the hand, etc.) sharply. **8** (when *intr,* usually foll. by *against*) to strike (something) with or as if with a slap. **9** (*tr*) *Inf., chiefly Brit.* to apply in large quantities, haphazardly, etc.: *she slapped butter on the bread.* **10 slap on the back.** to congratulate. ◆ *adv Inf.* **11** exactly: *slap on time.* **12** forcibly or abruptly: *to fall slap on the floor.* [C17: from Low G *slapp,* G *Schlappe,* imit.]

slapdash ❶ ('slæpˌdæʃ) *adv* **1** in a careless, hasty, or haphazard manner. ◆ *adj* **2** careless, hasty, or haphazard. ◆ *n* **3** slapdash activity or work.

slaphappy ❶ ('slæpˌhæpɪ) *adj* **slaphappier, slaphappiest.** *Inf.* **1** cheerfully

THESAURUS

slab *n* **1, 2 = piece,** chunk, hunk, lump, nugget, portion, slice, wedge, wodge (*Brit. inf.*)

slack[1] *adj* **1 = loose,** baggy, easy, flaccid, flexible, lax, limp, not taut, relaxed **2 = negligent,** asleep on the job (*inf.*), easy-going, idle, inactive, inattentive, lax, lazy, neglectful, remiss, slapdash, slipshod, tardy **3, 4 = slow,** dull, inactive, quiet, slow-moving, sluggish ◆ *n* **7 = room,** excess, give (*inf.*), leeway, looseness, play ◆ *vb* **9 = shirk,** bob off (*Brit. sl.*), dodge, flag, idle, neglect, relax, skive (*Brit. sl.*), slacken
Antonyms *adj* ≠ **loose:** inflexible, rigid, stiff, strained, stretched, taut, tight ≠ **negligent:** concerned, diligent, exacting, hard, hard-working, meticulous, stern, strict ≠ **slow:** active, bustling, busy, fast-moving, hectic

slacken *vb, often with* **off 2 = lessen,** abate, decrease, diminish, drop off, ease (off), let up, loosen, moderate, reduce, relax, release, slack off, slow down, tire

slacker *n* **= layabout,** dodger, do-nothing, gold brick (*US sl.*), good-for-nothing, idler, loafer, passenger, scrimshanker (*Brit. military sl.*), shirker, skiver (*Brit. sl.*)

slag *vb* **6** *sometimes with* **off** *Slang* **= criticize,** abuse, berate, deride, insult, lambast(e), malign, mock, slam, slander, slang, slate

slake *vb* **1 = satisfy,** assuage, gratify, quench, sate, satiate

slam[1] *vb* **1 = bang,** crash, smash, thump **2 = throw,** dash, fling, hurl **3** *Slang* **= criticize,** attack, blast, castigate, damn, excoriate, lambast(e), pan (*inf.*), pillory, shoot down (*inf.*), slate (*inf.*), tear into (*inf.*), vilify

slander *n* **2 = defamation,** aspersion, backbiting, calumny, detraction, libel, misrepresentation, muckraking, obloquy, scandal, smear ◆ *vb* **3 = defame,** backbite, blacken (someone's) name, calumniate, decry, detract, disparage, libel, malign, muckrake, slur, smear, traduce, vilify
Antonyms *n* ≠ **defamation:** acclaim, acclamation, approval, laudation, praise, tribute ◆ *vb* ≠ **defame:** acclaim, applaud, approve, compliment, eulogize, laud, praise, sing the praises of

slanderous *adj* **2 = defamatory,** abusive, calumnious, damaging, libellous, malicious

slang *vb* **2 = insult,** abuse, berate, call names, hurl insults at, inveigh against, malign, rail against, revile, vilify, vituperate

slant *vb* **1 = slope,** angle off, bend, bevel, cant, heel, incline, lean, list, shelve, skew, tilt **2 = bias,** angle, colour, distort, twist, weight ◆ *n* **4 = slope,** camber, declination, diagonal, gradient, incline, pitch, rake, ramp, tilt **5, 6 = bias,** angle, attitude, emphasis, leaning, one-sidedness, point of view, prejudice, viewpoint

slanting *adj* **1 = sloping,** angled, aslant, asymmetrical, at an angle, atilt, bent, canted, cater-cornered (*US inf.*), diagonal, inclined, oblique, on the bias, sideways, slanted, slantwise, tilted, tilting

slap *n* **1 = smack,** bang, blow, chin (*sl.*), clout (*inf.*), cuff, deck (*sl.*), spank, swipe, wallop (*inf.*), whack **4 a slap in the face = insult,** affront, blow, humiliation, put-down, rebuff, rebuke, rejection, repulse, snub ◆ *vb* **6 = smack,** bang, clap, clout (*inf.*), cuff, hit, spank, strike, swipe, whack **9** *Informal, chiefly Brit.* **= plaster,** daub, plonk, spread ◆ *adv* **11** *Informal* **= exactly,** bang, directly, plumb (*inf.*), precisely, slap-bang (*inf.*), smack (*inf.*)

slapdash *adj* **2 = careless,** clumsy, disorderly, haphazard, hasty, hurried, last-minute, messy, negligent, perfunctory, slipshod, sloppy (*inf.*), slovenly, thoughtless, thrown-together, untidy
Antonyms *adj* careful, conscientious, fastidious, meticulous, ordered, orderly, painstaking, precise, punctilious, thoughtful, tidy

slaphappy *adj* **1 = happy-go-lucky,** casual, haphazard, hit-or-miss (*inf.*), irresponsible,

irresponsible or careless. **2** dazed or giddy from or as if from repeated blows.

slapstick ⓘ (ˈslæpˌstɪk) *n* **1a** comedy characterized by horseplay and physical action. **1b** (*as modifier*): *slapstick humour.* **2** a pair of paddles formerly used in pantomime to strike a blow with a loud sound but without injury.

slap-up ⓘ *adj* (*prenominal*) *Brit. inf.* (esp. of meals) lavish; excellent; first-class.

slash ⓘ (slæʃ) *vb* (*tr*) **1** to cut or lay about (a person or thing) with sharp sweeping strokes, as with a sword, etc. **2** to lash with a whip. **3** to make large gashes in: *to slash tyres.* **4** to reduce (prices, etc.) drastically. **5** to criticize harshly. **6** to slit (the outer fabric of a garment) so that the lining material is revealed. **7** to clear (scrub or undergrowth) by cutting. ◆ *n* **8** a sharp sweeping stroke, as with a sword or whip. **9** a cut or rent made by such a stroke. **10** a decorative slit in a garment revealing the lining material. **11** *US & Canad.* littered wood chips that remain after trees have been cut down. **12** another name for **solidus.** **13** *Brit. sl.* the act of urinating. [C14 *slaschen,* ?from OF *esclachier* to break]

slasher (ˈslæʃə) *n* **1** a person or thing that slashes. **2** *Austral. & NZ.* a tool or machine used for cutting scrub or undergrowth in the bush.

slasher movie *n Sl.* a film in which victims, usually women, are slashed with knives, razors, etc. Also called: **stalk-and-slash movie.**

slashing ⓘ (ˈslæʃɪŋ) *adj* aggressively or harshly critical (esp. in **slashing attack**).

slat (slæt) *n* **1** a narrow thin strip of wood or metal, as used in a Venetian blind, etc. **2** a movable or fixed aerofoil attached to the leading edge of an aircraft wing to increase lift. [C14: from OF *esclat* splinter, from *esclater* to shatter]

slate[1] (sleɪt) *n* **1a** a compact fine-grained metamorphic rock that can be split into thin layers and is used as a roofing and paving material. **1b** (*as modifier*): *a slate tile.* **2** a roofing tile of slate. **3** (formerly) a writing tablet of slate. **4** a dark grey colour. **5** *Chiefly US & Canad.* a list of candidates in an election. **6 clean slate.** a record without dishonour. **7 have a slate loose.** *Brit. & Irish inf.* to be eccentric or crazy. **8 on the slate.** *Brit. inf.* on credit. ◆ *vb* **slates, slating, slated.** (*tr*) **9** to cover (a roof) with slates. **10** *Chiefly US.* to enter (a person's name) on a list, esp. on a political slate. ◆ *adj* **11** of the colour slate. [C14: from OF *esclate,* from *esclat* a fragment]
▸ˈ**slaty** *adj*

slate[2] ⓘ (sleɪt) *vb* **slates, slating, slated.** (*tr*) *Inf., chiefly Brit.* to criticize harshly. [C19: prob. from SLATE[1]]
▸ˈ**slating** *n*

slater (ˈsleɪtə) *n* **1** a person trained in laying roof slates. **2** another name for **woodlouse.**

slather (ˈslɑːðə) *n* **1** (*usually pl*) *Inf., chiefly US & Canad.* a large quantity. **2 open slather.** *Austral. & NZ sl.* a free-for-all. [C19: from ?]

slattern ⓘ (ˈslætən) *n* a slovenly woman or girl. [C17: prob. from *slattering,* from dialect *slatter* to slop]
▸ˈ**slatternly** *adj* ▸ˈ**slatternliness** *n*

slaughter ⓘ (ˈslɔːtə) *n* **1** the killing of animals, esp. for food. **2** the savage killing of a person. **3** the indiscriminate or brutal killing of large numbers of people, as in war. ◆ *vb* (*tr*) **4** to kill (animals), esp. for food. **5** to kill in a brutal manner. **6** to kill indiscriminately or in large numbers. [OE *sleaht*]
▸ˈ**slaughterer** *n* ▸ˈ**slaughterous** *adj*

slaughterhouse ⓘ (ˈslɔːtəˌhaʊs) *n* a place where animals are butchered for food; abattoir.

Slav (slɑːv) *n* a member of any of the peoples of E Europe or NW Asia who speak a Slavonic language. [C14: from Med. L *Sclāvus* a captive Slav; see SLAVE]

slave ⓘ (sleɪv) *n* **1** a person legally owned by another and having no freedom of action or right to property. **2** a person who is forced to work for another against his will. **3** a person under the domination of another person or some habit or influence. **4** a drudge. **5** a device that is controlled by or that duplicates the action of another similar device. ◆ *vb* **slaves, slaving, slaved.** **6** (*intr;* often foll. by *away*) to work like a slave. [C13: via OF from Med. L *Sclāvus* a Slav, one held in bondage (the Slavonic races were frequently conquered in the Middle Ages), from LGk *Sklabos* a Slav]

slave cylinder *n* a small cylinder containing a piston that operates the brake shoes or pads in hydraulic brakes or the working part in any other hydraulically operated system.

slave-driver *n* **1** (esp. formerly) a person forcing slaves to work. **2** an employer who demands excessively hard work from his employees.

slaveholder (ˈsleɪvˌhəʊldə) *n* a person who owns slaves.
▸ˈ**slaveˌholding** *n*

slaver[1] (ˈsleɪvə) *n* **1** an owner of or dealer in slaves. **2** another name for **slave ship.**

slaver[2] ⓘ (ˈslævə) *vb* (*intr*) **1** to dribble saliva. **2** (often foll. by *over*) **2a** to fawn or drool (over someone). **2b** to show great desire (for). ◆ *n* **3** saliva dribbling from the mouth. **4** *Inf.* drivel. [C14: prob. from Low Du.]
▸ˈ**slaverer** *n*

slavery ⓘ (ˈsleɪvərɪ) *n* **1** the state or condition of being a slave. **2** the subjection of a person to another person, esp. in being forced into work. **3** the condition of being subject to some influence or habit. **4** work done in harsh conditions for low pay.

slave ship *n* a ship used to transport slaves, esp. formerly from Africa to the New World.

Slave State *n US history.* any of the 15 Southern states in which slavery was legal until the Civil War.

slave trade *n* the business of trading in slaves, esp. the transportation of Black Africans to America from the 16th to 19th centuries.
▸ˈ**slave-ˌtrader** *n* ▸ˈ**slave-ˌtrading** *n*

slavey (ˈsleɪvɪ) *n Brit. inf.* a female general servant.

Slavic (ˈslɑːvɪk) *n, adj* another word (esp. US) another word (esp. US) for **Slavonic.**

slavish ⓘ (ˈsleɪvɪʃ) *adj* **1** of or befitting a slave. **2** being or resembling a slave. **3** unoriginal; imitative.
▸ˈ**slavishly** *adv*

Slavonic (sləˈvɒnɪk) *or esp. US* **Slavic** *n* **1** a branch of the Indo-European family of languages, usually divided into three subbranches: **South Slavonic** (including Bulgarian), **East Slavonic** (including Russian), and **West Slavonic** (including Polish and Czech). ◆ *adj* **2** of or relating to this group of languages. **3** of or relating to the people who speak these languages.

slaw (slɔː) *n Chiefly US & Canad.* short for **coleslaw.** [C19: from Danish *sla,* short for *salade* SALAD]

slay ⓘ (sleɪ) *vb* **slays, slaying, slew, slain.** (*tr*) **1** *Arch. or literary.* to kill, esp. violently. **2** *Sl.* to impress (someone of the opposite sex). [OE *slēan*]
▸ˈ**slayer** *n*

SLCM *abbrev. for* sea-launched cruise missile: a type of cruise missile that can be launched from either a submarine or a surface ship.

SLD *abbrev. for* Social and Liberal Democrats.

sleaze ⓘ (sliːz) *n Inf.* **1** sleaziness. **2** dishonest, disreputable, or immoral behaviour, esp. of public officials or employees: *political sleaze.*

sleazy ⓘ (ˈsliːzɪ) *adj* **sleazier, sleaziest.** **1** disreputable: *a sleazy nightclub.* **2** flimsy, as cloth. [C17: from ?]
▸ˈ**sleazily** *adv* ▸ˈ**sleaziness** *n*

sledge[1] (slɛdʒ) *or esp. US & Canad.* **sled** (slɛd) *n* **1** Also called: **sleigh.** a vehicle mounted on runners, drawn by horses or dogs, for transporting people or goods, esp. over snow. **2** a light wooden frame used, esp. by children, for sliding over snow. ◆ *vb* **sledges, sledging, sledged.** **3** to convey, travel, or go by sledge. [C17: from MDu. *sleedse;* C14 *sled,* from MLow G, from ON *slethi*]
▸ˈ**sledger** *n*

sledge[2] (slɛdʒ) *n* short for **sledgehammer.**

sledge[3] (slɛdʒ) *vb* **sledges, sledging, sledged.** (*tr*) *Austral.* to bait (an opponent, esp. a batsman in cricket) in order to upset his concentration. [from ?]

sledgehammer (ˈslɛdʒˌhæmə) *n* **1** a large heavy hammer with a long

THESAURUS

nonchalant **2** = **dazed**, giddy, punch-drunk, reeling, woozy (*inf.*)

slapstick *n* **1** = **knockabout comedy**, buffoonery, farce, horseplay

slap-up *adj Brit. informal* = **luxurious**, elaborate, excellent, first-rate, fit for a king, lavish, magnificent, no-expense-spared, princely, splendid, sumptuous, superb

slash *vb* **1** = **cut**, gash, hack, lacerate, rend, rip, score, slit **4** = **reduce**, cut, drop, lower ◆ *n* **9** = **cut**, gash, incision, laceration, rent, rip, slit

slashing *adj* = **savage**, aggressive, biting, brutal, ferocious, harsh, searing, vicious

slate[2] *vb Informal, chiefly Brit.* = **criticize**, berate, blame, blast, castigate, censure, excoriate, haul over the coals (*inf.*), lambast(e), pan (*inf.*), pitch into (*inf.*), rail against, rap (someone's) knuckles, rebuke, roast (*inf.*), scold, slam (*sl.*), slang, take to task, tear into (*inf.*), tear (someone) off a strip (*inf.*)

slattern *n* = **sloven**, drab (*arch.*), slut, trollop

slatternly *adj* = **slovenly**, bedraggled, dirty, draggletailed, frowzy, slipshod, sloppy (*inf.*), sluttish, unclean, unkempt, untidy

slaughter *n* **3** = **slaying**, blood bath, bloodshed, butchery, carnage, extermination, holocaust, killing, liquidation, massacre, murder ◆ *vb* **4-6** = **slay**, butcher, destroy, do to death, exterminate, kill, liquidate, massacre, murder, put to the sword, take out (*sl.*)

slaughterhouse *n* = **abattoir**, butchery, shambles

slave *n* **1-4** = **servant**, bondservant, bondsman, drudge, scullion (*arch.*), serf, skivvy (*chiefly Brit.*), slavey (*Brit. inf.*), varlet (*arch.*), vassal, villein ◆ *vb* **6** = **toil**, drudge, grind (*inf.*), skivvy (*Brit.*), slog, sweat, work one's fingers to the bone

slaver[2] *vb* **1** = **drool**, dribble, salivate, slobber

slavery *n* **1, 2** = **enslavement**, bondage, captivity, serfdom, servitude, subjugation, thraldom, thrall, vassalage
Antonyms *n* emancipation, freedom, liberty, manumission, release

slavish *adj* **1** = **servile**, abject, base, cringing, despicable, fawning, grovelling, low, mean, menial, obsequious, submissive, sycophantic **3** = **imitative**, conventional, second-hand, unimaginative, uninspired, unoriginal
Antonyms *adj* ≠ **servile:** assertive, domineering, masterful, rebellious, self-willed, wilful ≠ **imitative:** creative, imaginative, independent, inventive, original, radical, revolutionary

slay *vb* **1** *Archaic* = **kill**, annihilate, assassinate, butcher, destroy, dispatch, do away with, do in (*sl.*), eliminate, exterminate, massacre, mow down, murder, rub out (*US sl.*), slaughter **2** *Slang* = **impress**, amuse, be the death of (*inf.*), make a hit with (*inf.*), wow (*sl., chiefly US*)

sleaze *n* **2** *Informal* = **corruption**, bribery, crookedness (*inf.*), dishonesty, extortion, fiddling (*inf.*), fraud, shady dealings (*inf.*), unscrupulousness, venality

sleazy *adj* **1** = **sordid**, crummy, disreputable, low, run-down, seedy, squalid, tacky (*inf.*)

handle used with both hands for heavy work such as breaking rocks, etc. 2 (*modifier*) resembling the action of a sledgehammer in power, etc.: *a sledgehammer blow.* [C15: *sledge,* from OE *slecg* a large hammer]

sleek ⓣ (sliːk) *adj* 1 smooth and shiny. 2 polished in speech or behaviour. 3 (of an animal or bird) having a shiny healthy coat or feathers. 4 (of a person) having a prosperous appearance. ◆ *vb (tr)* 5 to make smooth and glossy, as by grooming, etc. 6 (usually foll. by *over*) to gloss (over). [C16: var. of SLICK]
▸**'sleekly** *adv* ▸**'sleekness** *n* ▸**'sleeky** *adj*

sleep ⓣ (sliːp) *n* 1 a periodic state of physiological rest during which consciousness is suspended. 2 *Bot.* the nontechnical name for **nyctitropism.** 3 a period spent sleeping. 4 a state of quiescence or dormancy. 5 a poetic word for **death.** ◆ *vb* **sleeps, sleeping, slept.** 6 *(intr)* to be in or as in the state of sleep. 7 *(intr)* (of plants) to show nyctitropism. 8 *(intr)* to be inactive or quiescent. 9 *(tr)* to have sleeping accommodation for (a certain number): *the boat could sleep six.* 10 *(tr;* foll. by *away)* to pass (time) sleeping. 11 *(intr) Poetic.* to be dead. 12 **sleep on it.** to give (something) extended consideration, esp. overnight. ◆ See also **sleep around, sleep in,** etc. [OE *slǣpan*]

sleep around *vb (intr, adv) Inf.* to be sexually promiscuous.

sleeper ('sliːpə) *n* 1 a person, animal, or thing that sleeps. 2 a railway sleeping car or compartment. 3 *Brit.* one of the blocks supporting the rails on a railway track. 4 a heavy timber beam, esp. one that is laid horizontally on the ground. 5 *Chiefly Brit.* a small plain gold circle worn in a pierced ear lobe to prevent the hole from closing up. 6 *Inf.* a person or thing that achieves unexpected success after an initial period of obscurity. 7 a spy planted in advance for future use.

sleep in *vb (intr, adv)* 1 *Brit.* to sleep longer than usual. 2 to sleep at the place of one's employment.

sleeping bag *n* a large well-padded bag designed for sleeping in, esp. outdoors.

sleeping car *n* a railway carriage fitted with compartments containing bunks for people to sleep in.

sleeping partner *n* a partner in a business who does not play an active role. Also called: **silent partner.**

sleeping pill *n* a pill or tablet containing a sedative drug, such as a barbiturate, used to induce sleep.

sleeping policeman *n* a bump built across a road to deter motorists from speeding. Official name: **road hump.**

sleeping sickness *n* 1 Also called: **African sleeping sickness.** an African disease transmitted by the bite of the tsetse fly, characterized by fever and sluggishness. 2 Also called: **sleepy sickness.** an epidemic viral form of encephalitis characterized by extreme drowsiness. Technical name: **encephalitis lethargica.**

sleepless ⓣ ('sliːplɪs) *adj* 1 without sleep or rest: *a sleepless journey.* 2 unable to sleep. 3 always alert. 4 *Chiefly poetic.* always active or moving.
▸**'sleeplessly** *adv* ▸**'sleeplessness** *n*

sleep off *vb (tr, adv) Inf.* to lose by sleeping: *to sleep off a hangover.*

sleep out *vb (intr, adv)* 1 (esp. of a tramp) to sleep in the open air. 2 to sleep away from the place of one's employment. ◆ *n* **sleep-out.** 3 *Austral. & NZ.* an area of a veranda partitioned off so that it may be used as a bedroom.

sleepwalk ⓣ ('sliːpˌwɔːk) *vb (intr)* to walk while asleep.
▸**'sleepˌwalker** *n* ▸**'sleepˌwalking** *n, adj*

sleep with *vb (intr, prep)* to have sexual intercourse and (usually) spend the night with. Also: **sleep together.**

sleepy ⓣ ('sliːpɪ) *adj* **sleepier, sleepiest.** 1 inclined to or needing sleep. 2 characterized by or exhibiting drowsiness, etc. 3 conducive to sleep. 4 without activity or bustle: *a sleepy town.*
▸**'sleepily** *adv* ▸**'sleepiness** *n*

sleet (sliːt) *n* 1 partly melted falling snow or hail or (esp. US) partly frozen rain. 2 *Chiefly US.* the thin coat of ice that forms when sleet or rain freezes on cold surfaces. ◆ *vb* 3 *(intr)* to fall as sleet. [C13: of Gmc origin]
▸**'sleety** *adj*

sleeve (sliːv) *n* 1 the part of a garment covering the arm. 2 a tubular piece that is shrunk into a cylindrical bore to reduce its bore or to line it with a different material. 3 a tube fitted externally over two cylindrical parts in order to join them. 4 a flat cardboard container to protect a gramophone record. US name: **jacket.** 5 **(have a few tricks) up one's sleeve.** (to have options, etc.) secretly ready. 6 **roll up one's sleeves.** to prepare oneself for work, a fight, etc. ◆ *vb* **sleeves, sleeving, sleeved.** 7 *(tr)* to provide with a sleeve or sleeves. [OE *slīf, slēf*]
▸**'sleeveless** *adj* ▸**'sleeveˌlike** *adj*

sleeve board *n* a small ironing board for pressing sleeves, fitted onto an ironing board or table.

sleeving ('sliːvɪŋ) *n Electronics, chiefly Brit.* tubular flexible insulation into which bare wire can be inserted.

sleigh (sleɪ) *n* 1 another name for **sledge**[1] (sense 1). ◆ *vb* 2 *(intr)* to travel by sleigh. [C18: from Du. *slee,* var. of *slede* SLEDGE[1]]

sleight (slaɪt) *n Arch.* 1 skill; dexterity. 2 a trick or stratagem. 3 cunning. [C14: from ON *slægth,* from *slægr* SLY]

sleight of hand ⓣ *n* 1 manual dexterity used in performing conjuring tricks. 2 the performance of such tricks.

slender ⓣ ('slɛndə) *adj* 1 of small width relative to length or height. 2 (esp. of a person's figure) slim and well-formed. 3 small or inadequate in amount, size, etc.: *slender resources.* 4 (of hopes, etc.) feeble. 5 very small: *a slender margin.* [C14 *slendre,* from ?]
▸**'slenderly** *adv* ▸**'slenderness** *n*

slenderize *or* **slenderise** ('slɛndəˌraɪz) *vb* **slenderizes, slenderizing, slenderized** *or* **slenderises, slenderising, slenderised.** *Chiefly US & Canad.* to make or become slender.

slept (slɛpt) *vb* the past tense and past participle of **sleep.**

sleuth ⓣ (sluːθ) *n* 1 an informal word for **detective.** 2 short for **sleuthhound** (sense 1). ◆ *vb* 3 *(tr)* to track or follow. [C19: short for *sleuthhound,* from C12 *sleuth* trail, from ON *sloth*]

sleuthhound ('sluːθˌhaʊnd) *n* 1 a dog trained to track people, esp. a bloodhound. 2 an informal word for **detective.**

S level *n Brit.* the Special level of a subject taken for the General Certificate of Education: usually taken at the same time as A levels as an additional qualification.

slew[1] (sluː) *vb* the past tense of **slay.**

slew[2] *or esp. US* **slue** (sluː) *vb* 1 to twist or be twisted sideways, esp. awkwardly. 2 *Naut.* to cause (a mast) to rotate in its step or (of a mast) to rotate in its step. ◆ *n* 3 the act of slewing. [C18: from ?]

slew[3] (sluː) *n* a variant spelling (esp. US) of **slough**[1] (sense 2).

slew[4] *or* **slue** (sluː) *n Inf., chiefly US & Canad.* a great number. [C20: from Irish Gaelic *sluagh*]

slice ⓣ (slaɪs) *n* 1 a thin flat piece cut from something having bulk: *a slice of pork.* 2 a share or portion: *a slice of the company's revenue.* 3 any of various utensils having a broad flat blade and resembling a spatula. 4 (in golf, tennis, etc.) 4a the flight of a ball that travels obliquely. 4b the action of hitting such a shot. 4c the shot so hit. ◆ *vb* **slices, slicing, sliced.** 5 to divide or cut (something) into parts or slices. 6 (when *intr,* usually foll. by *through)* to cut in a clean and effortless manner. 7 (when *intr,* foll. by *into* or *through)* to move or go (through something) like a knife. 8 (usually foll. by *off, from, away,* etc.) to cut or be cut (from) a larger piece. 9 *(tr)* to remove by use of a slicing implement. 10 to hit (a ball) with a slice. [C14: from OF *esclice* a piece split off, from *esclicier* to splinter]
▸**'sliceable** *adj* ▸**'slicer** *n*

slick ⓣ (slɪk) *adj* 1 flattering and glib: *a slick salesman.* 2 adroitly devised or executed: *a slick show.* 3 *Inf., chiefly US & Canad.* shrewd; sly. 4 *Inf.* superficially attractive: *a slick publication.* 5 *Chiefly US & Canad.* slippery. ◆ *n* 6 a slippery area, esp. a patch of oil floating on water. ◆ *vb (tr)* 7 *Chiefly US & Canad.* to make smooth or sleek. [C14: prob. from ON]
▸**'slickly** *adv* ▸**'slickness** *n*

slicker ('slɪkə) *n* 1 *Inf.* a sly or untrustworthy person (esp. in **city slicker**). 2 *US & Canad.* a shiny raincoat, esp. an oilskin.

slide ⓣ (slaɪd) *vb* **slides, sliding, slid** (slɪd); **slid** *or* **slidden** ('slɪdᵊn). 1 to move or cause to move smoothly along a surface in continual contact

THESAURUS

sleek *adj* 1 = **glossy,** lustrous, shiny, smooth 4 = **well-groomed,** well-fed
Antonyms *adj* ≠ **glossy:** rough, shaggy ≠ **well-groomed:** badly groomed, bedraggled, dishevelled, frowzy, ill-nourished, in poor condition, ratty (*Brit. & NZ inf.*), sloppy, slovenly, unkempt

sleep *n* 1, 3 = **slumber(s),** beauty sleep (*inf.*), dormancy, doze, forty winks (*inf.*), hibernation, kip (*Brit. sl.*), nap, repose, rest, shuteye (*sl.*), siesta, snooze (*inf.*), zizz (*Brit. inf.*) ◆ *vb* 6 = **slumber,** be in the land of Nod, catnap, doze, drop off (*inf.*), drowse, go out like a light, hibernate, kip (*Brit. sl.*), nod off (*inf.*), rest in the arms of Morpheus, snooze (*inf.*), snore, take a nap, take forty winks (*inf.*), zizz (*Brit. inf.*)

sleepiness *n* 2 = **drowsiness,** doziness, heaviness, lethargy, somnolence, torpor

sleepless *adj* 2 = **wakeful,** disturbed, insomniac, restless, unsleeping 3 = **alert,** unsleeping, vigilant, watchful, wide awake

sleeplessness *n* 2 = **insomnia,** wakefulness

sleepwalker *n* = **somnambulist,** noctambulist

sleepwalking *n* = **somnambulism,** noctambulation, noctambulism, somnambulation

sleepy *adj* 2 = **drowsy,** dull, heavy, inactive, lethargic, sluggish, slumbersome, somnolent, torpid 3 = **quiet,** dull, hypnotic, inactive, sleep-inducing, slow, slumberous, somnolent, soporific
Antonyms *adj* ≠ **drowsy:** active, alert, alive and kicking, animated, attentive, awake, boisterous, energetic, full of beans (*inf.*), lively, restless, wakeful, wide-awake ≠ **quiet:** active, bustling, busy, lively, thriving

sleight of hand *n* 1 = **dexterity,** adroitness, artifice, legerdemain, manipulation, prestidigitation, skill

slender *adj* 1, 2 = **slim,** lean, narrow, slight, svelte, sylphlike, willowy 3 = **meagre,** inadequate, inconsiderable, insufficient, little, scant, scanty, small, spare 4 = **faint,** feeble, flimsy, fragile, poor, remote, slight, slim, tenuous, thin, weak
Antonyms *adj* ≠ **slim:** bulky, chubby, fat, heavy, large, podgy, stout, tubby, well-built ≠ **meagre:** ample, appreciable, considerable, generous, large, substantial ≠ **faint:** good, solid, strong

sleuth *n* 1 *Informal* = **detective,** dick (*sl., chiefly US*), gumshoe (*US sl.*), private eye (*inf.*), (private) investigator, sleuthhound (*inf.*), tail (*inf.*)

slice *n* 1, 2 = **piece,** cut, helping, portion, segment, share, sliver, wedge ◆ *vb* 5, 6 = **cut,** carve, divide, sever

slick *adj* 1 = **glib,** meretricious, plausible, polished, smooth, sophistical, specious 2 = **skilful,** adroit, deft, dexterous, dextrous, polished, professional, sharp ◆ *vb* 7 = **smooth,** make glossy, plaster down, sleek, smarm down (*Brit. inf.*)
Antonyms *adj* ≠ **skilful:** amateur, amateurish, clumsy, crude, inexpert, unaccomplished, unpolished, unprofessional, unskilful

slide *vb* 1 = **slip,** coast, glide, glissade, skim, slither, toboggan, veer 6 **let slide** = **neglect,** forget, gloss over, ignore, let ride, pass over, push to the back of one's mind, turn a blind eye to

with it: *doors that slide open.* **2** (*intr*) to lose grip or balance: *he slid on his back.* **3** (*intr;* usually foll. by *into, out of, away from,* etc.) to pass or move unobtrusively: *she slid into the room.* **4** (*intr;* usually foll. by *into*) to go (into a specified condition) by degrees, etc.: *he slid into loose living.* **5** (foll. by *in, into,* etc.) to move (an object) unobtrusively or (of an object) to move in this way: *he slid the gun into his pocket.* **6 let slide.** to allow to deteriorate: *to let things slide.* ◆ *n* **7** the act or an instance of sliding. **8** a smooth surface, as of ice or mud, for sliding on. **9** a construction incorporating an inclined smooth slope for sliding down in playgrounds, etc. **10** a small glass plate on which specimens are mounted for microscopical study. **11** Also called: **diapositive, transparency.** a positive photograph on a transparent base, mounted in a frame, that can be viewed by means of a slide projector. **12** Also called: **hair slide.** *Chiefly Brit.* an ornamental clip to hold hair in place. **13** *Machinery.* a sliding part or member. **14** *Music.* a portamento. **15** *Music.* the sliding curved tube of a trombone that is moved in or out. **16** *Music.* **16a** a tube placed over a finger held against the frets of a guitar to produce a portamento. **16b** the style of guitar playing using a slide. **17** *Geol.* **17a** the downward movement of a large mass of earth, rocks, etc. **17b** the mass of material involved in this descent. See also **landslide.** [OE *slīdan*]
▸ **'slidable** *adj* ▸ **'slider** *n*

slide over *vb* (*intr, prep*) **1** to cross as if by sliding. **2** to avoid dealing with (a matter) fully.

slide rule *n* a mechanical calculating device consisting of two strips, one sliding along a central groove in the other, each strip graduated in two or more logarithmic scales of numbers, trigonometric functions, etc.

sliding scale *n* a variable scale according to which specified wages, prices, etc., fluctuate in response to changes in some other factor.

slier ('slaɪə) *adj* a comparative of **sly.**

sliest ('slaɪɪst) *adj* a superlative of **sly.**

slight ⓣ (slaɪt) *adj* **1** small in quantity or extent. **2** of small importance. **3** slim and delicate. **4** lacking in strength or substance. ◆ *vb* (*tr*) **5** to show disregard for (someone); snub. **6** to treat as unimportant or trifling. **7** *US.* to devote inadequate attention to (work, duties, etc.). ◆ *n* **8** an act or omission indicating supercilious neglect. [C13: from ON *slēttr* smooth]
▸ **'slightingly** *adv* ▸ **'slightly** *adv* ▸ **'slightness** *n*

slily ('slaɪlɪ) *adv* a variant spelling of **slyly.**

slim ⓣ (slɪm) *adj* **slimmer, slimmest. 1** small in width relative to height or length. **2** poor; meagre: *slim chances of success.* ◆ *vb* **3** to make or become slim, esp. by diets and exercise. **4** (*tr*) to reduce in size: *the workforce was slimmed.* [C17: from Du.: crafty, from MDu. *slimp* slanting]
▸ **'slimmer** *n* ▸ **'slimming** *n* ▸ **'slimness** *n*

Slim (slɪm) *n* the E African name for **AIDS.** [from its wasting effects]

slim down *vb* (*adv*) **1** to make or become slim, esp. intentionally. **2** to make (an organization) more efficient or (of an organization) to become more efficient, esp. by cutting staff. ◆ *n* **slimdown. 3** an instance of an organization slimming down.

slime (slaɪm) *n* **1** soft thin runny mud or filth. **2** any moist viscous fluid, esp. when noxious or unpleasant. **3** a mucous substance produced by various organisms, such as fish, slugs, and fungi. ◆ *vb* **slimes, sliming, slimed.** (*tr*) **4** to cover with slime. [OE *slīm*]

slimline ('slɪm,laɪn) *adj* slim or conducive to slimness.

slimy ⓣ ('slaɪmɪ) *adj* **slimier, slimiest. 1** characterized by, covered with, secreting, or resembling slime. **2** offensive or repulsive. **3** *Chiefly Brit.* characterized by servility.

sling[1] ⓣ (slɪŋ) *n* **1** a simple weapon consisting of a loop of leather, etc., in which a stone is whirled and then let fly. **2** a rope or strap by which something may be secured or lifted. **3** *Med.* a wide piece of cloth suspended from the neck for supporting an injured hand or arm. **4** a loop or band attached to an object for carrying. **5** the act of slinging. ◆ *vb* **slings, slinging, slung. 6** (*tr*) to hurl with or as if with a sling. **7** to attach a sling or slings to (a load, etc.). **8** (*tr*) to carry or hang loosely from or as if from a sling: *to sling washing from the line.* **9** (*tr*) *Inf.* to throw. [C13: ?from ON]
▸ **'slinger** *n*

sling[2] (slɪŋ) *n* a mixed drink with a spirit base, usually sweetened. [C19: from ?]

slingback ('slɪŋ,bæk) *n* a shoe with a strap instead of a full covering for the heel.

sling off *vb* (*intr, adv;* often foll. by *at*) *Austral. & NZ inf.* to mock; deride; jeer (at).

slingshot ('slɪŋ,ʃɒt) *n* **1** the US and Canad. name for **catapult** (sense 1). **2** another name for **sling**[1] (sense 1).

slink ⓣ (slɪŋk) *vb* **slinks, slinking, slunk. 1** (*intr*) to move or act in a furtive manner from or as if from fear, guilt, etc. **2** (*intr*) to move in a sinuous alluring manner. **3** (*tr*) (of animals, esp. cows) to give birth to prematurely. ◆ *n* **4** an animal, esp. a calf, born prematurely. [OE *slincan*]

slinky ⓣ ('slɪŋkɪ) *adj* **slinkier, slinkiest.** *Inf.* **1** moving in a sinuously graceful or provocative way. **2** (of clothes) figure-hugging.
▸ **'slinkily** *adv* ▸ **'slinkiness** *n*

slip[1] ⓣ (slɪp) *vb* **slips, slipping, slipped. 1** to move or cause to move smoothly and easily. **2** (*tr*) to place, insert, or convey quickly or stealthily. **3** (*tr*) to put on or take off easily or quickly: *to slip on a sweater.* **4** (*intr*) to lose balance and slide unexpectedly: *he slipped on the ice.* **5** to let loose or be let loose. **6** to be released from (something). **7** (*tr*) to let go (mooring or anchor lines) over the side. **8** (when *intr,* often foll. by *from* or *out of*) to pass out of (the mind or memory). **9** (*intr*) to move or pass swiftly or unperceived: *to slip quietly out of the room.* **10** (*intr;* sometimes foll. by *up*) to make a mistake. **11** Also: **sideslip.** to cause (an aircraft) to slide sideways or (of an aircraft) to slide sideways. **12** (*intr*) to decline in health, mental ability, etc. **13** (*intr*) (of an intervertebral disc) to become displaced from the normal position. **14** (*tr*) to dislocate (a bone). **15** (of animals) to give birth to (offspring) prematurely. **16** (*tr*) to pass (a stitch) from one needle to another without knitting it. **17a** (*tr*) to operate (the clutch of a motor vehicle) so that it partially disengages. **17b** (*intr*) (of the clutch of a motor vehicle) to fail to engage, esp. as a result of wear. **18 let slip. 18a** to allow to escape. **18b** to say unintentionally. ◆ *n* **19** the act or an instance of slipping. **20** a mistake or oversight: *a slip of the pen.* **21** a moral lapse or failing. **22** a woman's sleeveless undergarment, worn as a lining for a dress. **23** a pillowcase. **24** See **slipway. 25** *Cricket.* **25a** the position of the fielder who stands a little way behind and to the offside of the wicketkeeper. **25b** the fielder himself. **26** the relative movement of rocks along a fault plane. **27** *Metallurgy, crystallog.* the deformation of a metallic crystal caused when one part glides over another part along a plane. **28** a landslide. **29** the deviation of a propeller from its helical path through a fluid. **30** another name for **sideslip** (sense 1). **31 give someone the slip.** to elude or escape from someone. ◆ See also **slip up.** [C13: from MLow G or Du. *slippen*]
▸ **'slipless** *adj*

slip[2] ⓣ (slɪp) *n* **1** a narrow piece; strip. **2** a small piece of paper: *a receipt slip.* **3** a part of a plant that, when detached from the parent, will grow into a new plant; cutting. **4** a young slender person: *a slip of a child.* **5** *Printing.* **5a** a long galley. **5b** a galley proof. ◆ *vb* **slips, slipping, slipped. 6** (*tr*) to detach (portions of stem, etc.) from (a plant) for propagation. [C15: prob. from MLow G, MDu. *slippe* to cut, strip]

slip[3] (slɪp) *n* clay mixed with water to a creamy consistency, used for decorating or patching a ceramic piece. [OE *slyppe* slime]

slipcase ('slɪp,keɪs) *n* a protective case for a book or set of books that is open at one end so that only the spines of the books are visible.

slipcover ('slɪp,kʌvə) *n US & Canad.* **1** a loose cover. **2** a book jacket; dust cover.

slipe (slaɪp) *n NZ.* **a** wool removed from the pelt of a slaughtered sheep by immersion in a chemical bath. **b** (*as modifier*): *slipe wool.* [C14 in England: from *slype* to strip, skin]

slipknot ('slɪp,nɒt) *n* **1** Also called: **running knot.** a nooselike knot tied so that it will slip along the rope round which it is made. **2** a knot that can be easily untied by pulling one free end.

slip-on *adj* **1** (of a garment or shoe) made so as to be easily and quickly put on or taken off. ◆ *n* **2** a slip-on garment or shoe.

slipover ('slɪp,əʊvə) *adj* **1** of or denoting a garment that can be put on easily over the head. ◆ *n* **2** such a garment, esp. a sleeveless pullover.

slippage ('slɪpɪdʒ) *n* **1** the act or an instance of slipping. **2** the amount

THESAURUS

slight *adj* **1, 2, 4** = **small**, feeble, inconsiderable, insignificant, insubstantial, meagre, measly, minor, modest, negligible, paltry, scanty, superficial, trifling, trivial, unimportant, weak **3** = **slim**, delicate, feeble, fragile, lightly-built, small, spare ◆ *vb* **5** = **snub**, affront, cold-shoulder, despise, disdain, disparage, give offence *or* umbrage to, ignore, insult, neglect, put down, scorn, show disrespect for, treat with contempt ◆ *n* **8** = **insult**, affront, contempt, discourtesy, disdain, disregard, disrespect, inattention, indifference, neglect, rebuff, slap in the face (*inf.*), snub, (the) cold shoulder
Antonyms *adj* ≠ **small**: appreciable, considerable, great, heavy, important, large, noticeable, obvious, significant, substantial ≠ **slim**: muscular, solid, strong, sturdy, well-built ◆ *vb* ≠ **snub**: compliment, flatter, praise, speak well of, treat considerately ◆ *n* ≠ **insult**: compliment, flattery, praise

slightly *adv* **1** = **a little**, marginally, on a small scale, somewhat, to some extent *or* degree

slim *adj* **1** = **slender**, lean, narrow, slight, svelte, sylphlike, thin, trim **2** = **slight**, faint, poor, remote, slender ◆ *vb* **3** = **lose weight**, diet, reduce, slenderize (*chiefly US*)
Antonyms *adj* ≠ **slender**: broad, bulky, chubby, fat, heavy, muscular, obese, overweight, sturdy, tubby, well-built, wide ≠ **slight**: good, strong ◆ *vb* ≠ **lose weight**: build oneself up, put on weight

slimy *adj* **1** = **viscous**, clammy, gloopy, glutinous, miry, mucous, muddy, oozy **3** *Chiefly Brit.* = **obsequious**, creeping, grovelling, oily, servile, smarmy (*Brit. inf.*), soapy (*sl.*), sycophantic, toadying, unctuous

sling[1] *vb* **8** = **hang**, dangle, suspend, swing **9** *Informal* = **throw**, cast, chuck, fling, heave, hurl, lob (*inf.*), shy, toss

slink *vb* **1** = **creep**, prowl, pussyfoot (*inf.*), skulk, slip, sneak, steal

slinky *adj* **1** = **sinuous**, feline **2** = **figure-hugging**, clinging, close-fitting, skintight, sleek

slip[1] *vb* **1** = **slide**, glide, skate, slither **4** = **fall**, lose one's balance, miss *or* lose one's footing, skid, trip (over) **10** *sometimes with* **up** = **make a mistake**, blunder, boob (*Brit. sl.*), drop a brick *or* clanger (*inf.*), err, go wrong, miscalculate, misjudge, mistake **18b let slip** = **give away**, blurt out, come out with (*inf.*), disclose, divulge, leak, let out (*inf.*), let the cat out of the bag, reveal ◆ *n* **20** = **mistake**, bloomer (*Brit. inf.*), blunder, boob (*Brit. sl.*), error, failure, fault, faux pas, imprudence, indiscretion, lapse, omission, oversight, slip of the tongue, slip-up (*inf.*) **31 give (someone) the slip** = **escape from**, dodge, elude, evade, get away from, lose (someone), outwit, shake (someone) off

slip[2] *n* **1** = **strip**, piece, sliver **3** = **cutting**, offshoot, runner, scion, shoot, sprig, sprout of slipping or the extent to which slipping occurs. **3a** an instance of not reaching a target, etc. **3b** the extent of this.

slipped disc *n Pathol.* a herniated intervertebral disc, often resulting in pain because of pressure on the spinal nerves.

slipper ('slɪpə) *n* **1** a light shoe of some soft material, for wearing around the house. **2** a woman's evening shoe. ◆ *vb* **3** (*tr*) *Inf.* to hit or beat with a slipper.
▸ **'slippered** *adj*

slipper bath *n* a bath in the shape of a slipper, with a covered end.

slipperwort ('slɪpəˌwɜːt) *n* another name for **calceolaria.**

slippery ⓣ ('slɪpərɪ, -prɪ) *adj* **1** causing or tending to cause objects to slip: *a slippery road.* **2** liable to slip from the grasp, etc. **3** not to be relied upon: *a slippery character.* **4** (esp. of a situation) unstable. [C16: prob. coined by Coverdale to translate G *schlipfferig* in Luther's Bible (Psalm 35:6)]
▸ **'slipperiness** *n*

slippery elm *n* **1** a North American tree, having notched winged fruits and a mucilaginous inner bark. **2** the bark of this tree, used medicinally as a demulcent. ◆ Also called: **red elm.**

slippy ('slɪpɪ) *adj* **slippier, slippiest. 1** *Inf. or dialect.* another word for **slippery** (senses 1, 2). **2** *Brit. inf.* alert; quick.
▸ **'slippiness** *n*

slip rail *n Austral. & NZ.* a rail in a fence that can be slipped out of place to make an opening.

slip road *n Brit.* a short road connecting a motorway to another road.

slipshod ⓣ ('slɪpˌʃɒd) *adj* **1** (of an action) negligent; careless. **2** (of a person's appearance) slovenly; down-at-heel. [C16: from SLIP[1] + SHOD]

slip-slop *n S. African.* the usual name for **flip-flop** (sense 5).

slipstream ('slɪpˌstriːm) *n* Also called: **airstream. a** the stream of air forced backwards by an aircraft propeller. **b** a stream of air behind any moving object.

slip up *Inf.* ◆ *vb* (*intr, adv*) **1** to make a blunder or mistake. ◆ *n* **slip-up. 2** a mistake or mishap.

slipware ('slɪpˌwɛə) *n* pottery that has been decorated with slip and glazed.

slipway ('slɪpˌweɪ) *n* **1** the sloping area in a shipyard, containing the ways. **2** the ways on which a vessel is launched.

slit ⓣ (slɪt) *vb* **slits, slitting, slit.** (*tr*) **1** to make a straight long incision in. **2** to cut into strips lengthwise. ◆ *n* **3** a long narrow cut. **4** a long narrow opening. [OE *slītan* to slice]
▸ **'slitter** *n*

slither ⓣ ('slɪðə) *vb* **1** to move or slide or cause to move or slide unsteadily, as on a slippery surface. **2** (*intr*) to travel with a sliding motion. ◆ *n* **3** a slithering motion. [OE *slidrian*, from *slīdan* to slide]
▸ **'slithery** *adj*

slit trench *n Mil.* a narrow trench dug for the protection of a small number of people.

sliver ⓣ ('slɪvə) *n* **1** a thin piece that is cut or broken off lengthwise. **2** a loose fibre obtained by carding. ◆ *vb* **3** to divide or be divided into splinters. **4** (*tr*) to form (wool, etc.) into slivers. [C14: from *sliven* to split]

Sloane Ranger (sləʊn) *n* (in Britain) *Inf.* a young upper-class person having a home in London and in the country, characterized as wearing expensive informal clothes. Also called: **Sloane.** [C20: pun on *Sloane* Square, London, and *Lone Ranger*, television cowboy character]

slob ⓣ (slɒb) *n* **1** *Inf.* a slovenly, unattractive, and lazy person. **2** *Irish.* mire. [C19: from Irish Gaelic *slab* mud]
▸ **'slobbish** *adj*

slobber ⓣ ('slɒbə) *or* **slabber** *vb* **1** to dribble (saliva, food, etc.) from the mouth. **2** (*intr*) to speak or write mawkishly. **3** (*tr*) to smear with matter dribbling from the mouth. ◆ *n* **4** liquid or saliva spilt from the mouth. **5** maudlin language or behaviour. [C15: from MLow G, MDu. *slubberen*]
▸ **'slobberer** *or* **'slabberer** *n* ▸ **'slobbery** *or* **'slabbery** *adj*

sloe (sləʊ) *n* **1** the small sour blue-black fruit of the blackthorn. **2** another name for **blackthorn.** [OE *slāh*]

sloe-eyed *adj* having dark slanted or almond-shaped eyes.

sloe gin *n* gin flavoured with sloe juice.

slog ⓣ (slɒg) *vb* **slogs, slogging, slogged. 1** to hit with heavy blows, as in boxing. **2** (*intr*) to work hard; toil. **3** (*intr;* foll. by *down, up, along,* etc.) to move with difficulty. **4** *Cricket.* to take large swipes at the ball. ◆ *n* **5** a tiring walk. **6** long exhausting work. **7** a heavy blow or swipe. [C19: from ?]
▸ **'slogger** *n*

slogan ⓣ ('sləʊgən) *n* **1** a distinctive or topical phrase used in politics, advertising, etc. **2** *Scot. history.* a Highland battle cry. [C16: from Gaelic *sluagh-ghairm* war cry]

sloop (sluːp) *n* a single-masted sailing vessel, rigged fore-and-aft. [C17: from Du. *sloep*]

sloot (sluːt) *n S. African.* a ditch for irrigation or drainage. [from Afrik., from Du. *sluit, sluis* SLUICE]

slop[1] ⓣ (slɒp) *vb* **slops, slopping, slopped. 1** (when *intr*, often foll. by *about*) to cause (liquid) to splash or spill or (of liquid) to splash or spill. **2** (*intr;* foll. by *along, through,* etc.) to tramp (through) mud or slush. **3** (*tr*) to feed slop or swill to: *to slop the pigs.* **4** (*tr*) to ladle or serve, esp. clumsily. **5** (*intr;* foll. by *over*) *Inf., chiefly US & Canad.* to be unpleasantly effusive. ◆ *n* **6** a puddle of spilt liquid. **7** (*pl*) wet feed, esp. for pigs, made from kitchen waste, etc. **8** (*pl*) waste food or liquid refuse. **9** (*often pl*) *Inf.* liquid or semiliquid food of low quality. **10** soft mud, snow, etc. [C14: prob. from OE *-sloppe* in *cūsloppe* COWSLIP]

slop[2] (slɒp) *n* **1** (*pl*) sailors' clothing and bedding issued from a ship's stores. **2** any loose article of clothing, esp. a smock. **3** (*pl*) shoddy manufactured clothing. [OE *oferslop* surplice]

slop basin *n* a bowl or basin into which the dregs from teacups are emptied at the table.

slope ⓣ (sləʊp) *vb* **slopes, sloping, sloped. 1** to lie or cause to lie at a slanting or oblique angle. **2** (*intr*) (esp. of natural features) to follow an inclined course: *many paths sloped down the hillside.* **3** (*intr;* foll. by *off, away,* etc.) to go furtively. **4** (*tr*) *Mil.* (formerly) to hold (a rifle) in the slope position. ◆ *n* **5** an inclined portion of ground. **6** (*pl*) hills or foothills. **7** any inclined surface or line. **8** the degree or amount of such inclination. **9** *Maths.* (of a line) the tangent of the angle between the line and another line parallel to the *x*-axis. **10** (formerly) the position adopted for military drill when the rifle is rested on the shoulder. [C15: short for *aslope*, ?from the p.p. of OE *āslūpan* to slip away]
▸ **'sloper** *n* ▸ **'sloping** *adj*

slop out *vb* (*intr, adv*) (of prisoners) to empty chamber pots and collect water for washing.

sloppy ⓣ ('slɒpɪ) *adj* **sloppier, sloppiest. 1** (esp. of the ground, etc.) wet; slushy. **2** *Inf.* careless; untidy. **3** *Inf.* mawkishly sentimental. **4** (of food or drink) watery and unappetizing. **5** splashed with slops. **6** (of clothes) loose; baggy.
▸ **'sloppily** *adv* ▸ **'sloppiness** *n*

slosh ⓣ (slɒʃ) *n* **1** watery mud, snow, etc. **2** *Brit. sl.* a heavy blow. **3** the sound of splashing liquid. ◆ *vb* **4** (*tr;* foll. by *around, on, in,* etc.) *Inf.* to throw or pour (liquid). **5** (when *intr*, often foll. by *about* or *around*) *Inf.* **5a** to shake or stir (something) in a liquid. **5b** (of a person) to splash (around) in water, etc. **6** (*tr*) *Brit. sl.* to deal a heavy blow to. **7** (usually foll. by *about* or *around*) *Inf.* to shake (a container of liquid) or (of liquid within a container) to be shaken. [C19: var. of SLUSH, infl. by SLOP[1]]
▸ **'sloshy** *adj*

sloshed (slɒʃt) *adj Chiefly Brit. sl.* drunk.

slot[1] ⓣ (slɒt) *n* **1** an elongated aperture or groove, such as one in a vending machine for inserting a coin. **2** *Inf.* a place in a series or scheme. ◆ *vb* **slots, slotting, slotted. 3** (*tr*) to furnish with a slot or slots. **4** (usually foll. by *in* or *into*) to fit or adjust in a slot. **5** *Inf.* to situate or be situated in a series. [C13: from OF *esclot* the depression of the breastbone, from ?]
▸ **'slotter** *n*

slot[2] (slɒt) *n* the trail of an animal, esp. a deer. [C16: from OF *esclot* horse's hoofprint, prob. of Scand. origin]

sloth ⓣ (sləʊθ) *n* **1** any of a family of shaggy-coated arboreal edentate mammals, such as the three-toed sloth or ai or the two-toed sloth or

THESAURUS

slippery *adj* **1** = **smooth**, glassy, greasy, icy, lubricious (*rare*), perilous, skiddy (*inf.*), slippy (*inf. or dialect*), unsafe, unstable, unsteady **3** = **untrustworthy**, crafty, cunning, devious, dishonest, duplicitous, evasive, false, foxy, shifty, sneaky, treacherous, tricky, two-faced, unpredictable, unreliable

slipshod *adj* **1** = **careless**, casual, loose, slapdash, sloppy (*inf.*), slovenly, unsystematic, untidy

slit *vb* **1** = **cut (open)**, gash, impale, knife, lance, pierce, rip, slash, split open ◆ *n* **3, 4** = **cut**, fissure, gash, incision, opening, rent, split, tear

slither *vb* **1, 2** = **slide**, glide, skitter, slink, slip, snake, undulate

sliver *n* **1** = **shred**, flake, fragment, paring, shaving, slip, splinter

slob *n* **1** *Informal* = **layabout**, couch potato (*sl.*), good-for-nothing, idler, loafer, lounger

slobber *vb* **1** = **drool**, dribble, drivel, salivate, slabber (*dialect*), slaver, water at the mouth

slobbish *adj* **1** = **messy**, slatternly, sloppy (*inf.*), slovenly, unclean, unkempt, untidy

slog *vb* **1** = **hit**, hit for six, punch, slosh (*Brit. sl.*), slug, sock (*sl.*), strike, thump, wallop (*inf.*) **2** = **work**, apply oneself to, keep one's nose to the grindstone, labour, peg away at, persevere, plod, plough through, slave, sweat blood (*inf.*), toil, work one's fingers to the bone **3** = **trudge**, tramp, trek ◆ *n* **5** = **trudge**, hike, tramp, trek **6** = **labour**, blood, sweat, and tears (*inf.*), effort, exertion, struggle

slogan *n* **1** = **catch phrase**, catchword, jingle, motto, rallying cry, tag-line

slop[1] *vb* **1** = **spill**, overflow, slosh (*inf.*), spatter, splash, splatter

slope *vb* **1** = **slant**, drop away, fall, incline, lean, pitch, rise, tilt **3** *with* **off** *or* **away** = **slink away**, creep away, make oneself scarce, skulk, slip away, steal ◆ *n* **5** = **inclination**, brae (*Scot.*), declination, declivity, descent, downgrade (*chiefly US*), gradient, incline, ramp, rise, scarp, slant, tilt

sloping *adj* **1** = **slanting**, atilt, bevelled, cant, inclined, inclining, leaning, oblique

sloppy *adj* **1** = **wet**, sludgy, slushy, splashy, watery **2** *Informal* = **careless**, amateurish, clumsy, hit-or-miss (*inf.*), inattentive, messy, slipshod, slovenly, unkempt, untidy, weak **3** *Informal* = **sentimental**, banal, gushing, mawkish, mushy (*inf.*), overemotional, slushy (*inf.*), soppy (*Brit. inf.*), three-hankie (*inf.*), trite, wet (*Brit. inf.*)

slosh *vb Informal* **4** = **pour**, shower, slap, spray **5** = **splash**, flounder, plash, slop, swash, wade **6** *Brit. slang* = **hit**, bash (*inf.*), belt (*inf.*), biff (*sl.*), punch, slog, slug, sock (*sl.*), strike, swipe (*inf.*), thwack, wallop (*inf.*)

slot[1] *n* **1** = **opening**, aperture, channel, groove, hole, slit, vent **2** *Informal* = **place**, niche, opening, position, space, time, vacancy ◆ *vb* **4** = **fit in**, adjust, assign, fit, insert, pigeonhole

sloth *n* **2** = **laziness**, idleness, inactivity, indolence, inertia, slackness, slothfulness, sluggishness, torpor unau, of Central and South America. They are slow-moving, hanging upside down by their long arms and feeding on vegetation. **2** reluctance to exert oneself. [OE *slǣwth*, from *slǣw*, var. of *slāw* slow]

sloth bear *n* a bear of forests of S India and Sri Lanka, having an elongated snout specialized for feeding on termites.

slothful ❶ ('sləʊθfʊl) *adj* lazy; indolent.
▸**'slothfully** *adv* ▸**'slothfulness** *n*

slot machine *n* a machine, esp. one for gambling, activated by placing a coin in a slot.

slouch ❶ (slaʊtʃ) *vb* **1** (*intr*) to sit or stand with a drooping bearing. **2** (*intr*) to walk or move with an awkward slovenly gait. **3** (*tr*) to cause (the shoulders) to droop. ◆ *n* **4** a drooping carriage. **5** (*usually used in negative constructions*) *Inf.* an incompetent or slovenly person: *he's no slouch at football.* [C16: from ?]
▸**'slouching** *adj*

slouch hat *n* any soft hat with a brim that can be pulled down over the ears, esp. an Australian army hat with the left side of the brim turned up.

slough[1] (slaʊ) *n* **1** a hollow filled with mud; bog. **2** (sluː) Also: **slew** (esp. US), **slue.** *North American.* a large hole where water collects or a marshy inlet. **3** despair or degradation. [OE *slōh*]
▸**'sloughy** *adj*

slough[2] (slʌf) *n* **1** any outer covering that is shed, such as the dead outer layer of the skin of a snake, the cellular debris in a wound, etc. ◆ *vb* **2** (often foll. by *off*) to shed (a skin, etc.) or (of a skin, etc.) to be shed. [C13: of Gmc origin]
▸**'sloughy** *adj*

slough off (slʌf) *vb* (*tr, adv*) to cast off (cares, etc.).

Slovak ('sləʊvæk) *adj* **1** of or characteristic of Slovakia in E Europe, its people, or their language. ◆ *n* **2** the official language of Slovakia. Slovak is closely related to Czech; they are mutually intelligible. **3** a native or inhabitant of Slovakia.

sloven ('slʌvᵊn) *n* a person who is habitually negligent in appearance, hygiene, or work. [C15: prob. rel. to Flemish *sloef* dirty, Du. *slof* negligent]

Slovene (sləʊ'viːn) *adj* **1** of or characteristic of Slovenia, in SE Europe, its people or their language. ◆ *n* **2** Also **Slovenian.** the official language of Slovenia. **3** a native or inhabitant of Slovenia.

slovenly ❶ ('slʌvənlɪ) *adj* **1** frequently or habitually unclean or untidy. **2** negligent and careless: *slovenly manners.* ◆ *adv* **3** in a negligent or slovenly manner.
▸**'slovenliness** *n*

slow ❶ (sləʊ) *adj* **1** performed or occurring during a comparatively long interval of time. **2** lasting a comparatively long time: *a slow journey.* **3** characterized by lack of speed: *a slow walker.* **4** (*prenominal*) adapted to or productive of slow movement: *the slow lane of a motorway.* **5** (of a clock, etc.) indicating a time earlier than the correct time. **6** not readily responsive to stimulation: *a slow mind.* **7** dull or uninteresting: *the play was very slow.* **8** not easily aroused: *a slow temperament.* **9** lacking promptness or immediacy: *a slow answer.* **10** unwilling to perform an action or enter into a state: *slow to anger.* **11** behind the times. **12** (of trade, etc.) unproductive; slack. **13** (of a fire) burning weakly. **14** (of an oven) cool. **15** *Photog.* requiring a relatively long time of exposure to produce a given density: *a slow lens.* **16** *Sport.* (of a court, track, etc.) tending to reduce the speed of the ball or the competitors. **17** *Cricket.* (of a bowler, etc.) delivering the ball slowly, usually with spin. ◆ *adv* **18** in a manner characterized by lack of speed; slowly. ◆ *vb* **19** (often foll. by *up, down,* etc.) to decrease or cause to decrease in speed, efficiency, etc. [OE *slāw* sluggish]
▸**'slowly** *adv* ▸**'slowness** *n*

slowcoach ('sləʊˌkəʊtʃ) *n Brit. inf.* a person who moves or works slowly. US and Canad. equivalent: **slowpoke.**

slow handclap *n Brit.* slow rhythmic clapping, esp. used by an audience to indicate dissatisfaction or impatience.

slow march *n Mil.* a march in **slow time,** usually 65 or 75 paces to the minute.

slow match *or* **fuse** *n* a match or fuse that burns slowly without flame.

slow-mo *or* **slo-mo** ('sləʊˌməʊ) *n, adj Inf.* short for **slow motion** *or* **slow-motion.**

slow motion *n* **1** *Films, television, etc.* action that is made to appear slower than normal by passing the film through the camera at a faster rate or by replaying a video recording more slowly. ◆ *adj* **slow-motion. 2** of or relating to such action. **3** moving or functioning at considerably less than usual speed.

slow virus *n* a type of virus that is present in the body for a long time before it becomes active or infectious.

slowworm ('sləʊˌwɜːm) *n* a Eurasian legless lizard with a brownish-grey snakelike body. Also called: **blindworm.**

SLR *abbrev. for* single-lens reflex: see **reflex camera.**

SLSC *Austral. abbrev. for* Surf Life Saving Club.

slub (slʌb) *n* **1** a lump in yarn or fabric, often made intentionally to give a knobbly effect. **2** a loosely twisted roll of fibre prepared for spinning. ◆ *vb* **slubs, slubbing, slubbed. 3** (*tr*) to draw out and twist (a sliver of fibre). ◆ *adj* **4** (of material) having an irregular appearance. [C18: from ?]

sludge ❶ (slʌdʒ) *n* **1** soft mud, snow, etc. **2** any deposit or sediment. **3** a surface layer of ice that is not frozen solid but has a slushy appearance. **4** (in sewage disposal) the solid constituents of sewage that are removed for purification. [C17: prob. rel. to SLUSH]
▸**'sludgy** *adj*

slue[1] (sluː) *n, vb* **slues, sluing, slued.** a variant spelling (esp. US) of **slew**[2].

slue[2] (sluː) *n* a variant spelling of **slough**[1] (sense 2).

slug[1] (slʌg) *n* **1** any of various terrestrial gastropod molluscs in which the body is elongated and the shell is absent or very much reduced. **2** any of various other invertebrates having a soft slimy body, esp. the larvae of certain sawflies. [C15 (in the sense: a slow person or animal): prob. from ON]

slug[2] (slʌg) *n* **1** an fps unit of mass; the mass that will acquire an acceleration of 1 foot per second per second when acted upon by a force of 1 pound. **2** *Metallurgy.* a metal blank from which small forgings are worked. **3** a bullet. **4** *Chiefly US & Canad.* a metal token for use in slot machines, etc. **5** *Printing.* **5a** a thick strip of type metal that is used for spacing. **5b** a metal strip containing a line of characters as produced by a Linotype machine. **6** a draught of a drink, esp. an alcoholic one. [C17 (bullet), C19 (printing): ?from SLUG[1], with allusion to the shape of the animal]

slug[3] (slʌg) *vb* **slugs, slugging, slugged. 1** *Chiefly US & Canad.* to hit very hard and solidly. **2** (*tr*) *Austral. & NZ inf.* to charge (someone) an exorbitant price. ◆ *n* **3** *US & Canad.* a heavy blow. **4** *Austral. & NZ inf.* an exorbitant price. [C19: ?from SLUG[2] (bullet)]

sluggard ('slʌgəd) *n* **1** a person who is habitually indolent. ◆ *adj* **2** lazy. [C14 *slogarde*]
▸**'sluggardly** *adj*

sluggish ❶ ('slʌgɪʃ) *adj* **1** lacking energy; inactive. **2** functioning at below normal rate or level. **3** exhibiting poor response to stimulation.
▸**'sluggishly** *adv* ▸**'sluggishness** *n*

sluice ❶ (sluːs) *n* **1** Also called: **sluiceway.** a channel that carries a rapid current of water, esp. one that has a sluicegate to control the flow. **2** the body of water controlled by a sluicegate. **3** See **sluicegate. 4** *Mining.* an inclined trough for washing ore. **5** an artificial channel through which logs can be floated. ◆ *vb* **sluices, sluicing, sluiced. 6** (*tr*) to draw out or drain (water, etc.) from (a pond, etc.) by means of a sluice. **7** (*tr*) to wash or irrigate with a stream of water. **8** (*tr*) *Mining.* to wash in a sluice. **9** (*tr*) to send (logs, etc.) down a sluice. **10** (*intr;* often foll. by *away* or *out*) (of water, etc.) to run or flow from or as if from a sluice. **11** (*tr*) to provide with a sluice. [C14: from OF *escluse,* from LL *exclūsa aqua* water shut out, from L *exclūdere* to shut out]
▸**'sluiceˌlike** *adj*

sluicegate ('sluːsˌgeɪt) *n* a valve or gate fitted to a sluice to control the rate of flow of water. See also **floodgate** (sense 1).

slum ❶ (slʌm) *n* **1** a squalid overcrowded house, etc. **2** (*often pl*) a

THESAURUS

slothful *adj* = **lazy,** do-nothing (*inf.*), good-for-nothing, idle, inactive, indolent, inert, skiving (*Brit. sl.*), slack, sluggish, torpid, workshy

slouch *vb* **1** = **slump,** droop, loll, stoop

slouching *adj* **2** = **shambling,** awkward, loutish, lumbering, uncouth, ungainly

slovenly *adj* **1** = **untidy,** disorderly, slatternly, unkempt **2** = **careless,** heedless, loose, negligent, slack, slapdash, slipshod, sloppy (*inf.*)
Antonyms *adj* ≠ **untidy:** clean, meticulous, neat, orderly, shipshape, smart, soigné *or* soignée, tidy, trim, well-groomed ≠ **careless:** careful, conscientious, disciplined, methodical, meticulous, well-ordered

slow *adj* **1, 2** = **prolonged,** gradual, lingering, long-drawn-out, protracted, time-consuming **3** = **unhurried,** creeping, dawdling, deliberate, easy, lackadaisical, laggard, lagging, lazy, leaden, leisurely, loitering, measured, plodding, ponderous, slow-moving, sluggardly, sluggish, tortoise-like **6** = **stupid,** blockish, bovine, braindead (*inf.*), dense, dim, dozy (*Brit. inf.*), dull, dull-witted, dumb (*inf.*), obtuse, retarded, slow on the uptake (*inf.*), slow-witted, thick, unresponsive **7** = **dull,** boring, conservative, dead, dead-and-alive (*Brit.*), inactive, one-horse (*inf.*), quiet, slack, sleepy, sluggish, stagnant, tame, tedious, uneventful, uninteresting, unproductive, unprogressive, wearisome **9** = **late,** backward, behind, behindhand, delayed, dilatory, long-delayed, tardy, unpunctual **10** = **unwilling,** averse, disinclined, hesitant, indisposed, loath, reluctant ◆ *vb* **19** *often with* **up** *or* **down** = **reduce speed,** brake, check, curb, decelerate, delay, detain, handicap, hold up, lag, rein in, relax, restrict, retard, slacken (off), spin out
Antonyms *adj* ≠ **unhurried:** brisk, eager, fast, hectic, hurried, precipitate, prompt, quick, quickie (*inf.*), quick-moving, sharp, speedy, swift ≠ **stupid:** bright, clever, intelligent, perceptive, quick, quick-witted, sharp, smart ≠ **dull:** action-packed, animated, exciting, interesting, lively, stimulating ◆ *vb* ≠ **reduce speed:** accelerate, advance, aid, boost, help, pick up speed, quicken, speed up

slowly *adv* **1-3** = **gradually,** at a snail's pace, at one's leisure, by degrees, inchmeal, in one's own (good) time, leisurely, ploddingly, steadily, taking one's time, unhurriedly, with leaden steps

sludge *n* **2** = **sediment,** dregs, gloop (*inf.*), mire, muck, mud, ooze, residue, silt, slime, slob (*Irish*), slop, slush

sluggish *adj* **1-3** = **inactive,** dull, heavy, indolent, inert, lethargic, lifeless, listless, phlegmatic, slothful, slow, slow-moving, torpid, unresponsive
Antonyms *adj* alive and kicking, animated, brisk, dynamic, energetic, enthusiastic, fast, free-flowing, full of beans (*inf.*), full of life, industrious, lively, swift, vigorous

sluggishness *n* **1-3** = **inactivity,** apathy, drowsiness, dullness, heaviness, indolence, inertia, languor, lassitude, lethargy, listlessness, slothfulness, somnolence, stagnation, torpor

sluice *vb* **6** = **drain,** flush **7** = **wash out,** cleanse, drench, irrigate, wash down

slum *n* **1, 2** = **hovel,** ghetto, rookery (*arch.*), warren

squalid section of a city, characterized by inferior living conditions. **3** (*modifier*) of or characteristic of slums: *slum conditions.* ◆ *vb* **slums, slumming, slummed.** (*intr*) **4** to visit slums, esp. for curiosity. **5** Also: **slum it.** to suffer conditions below those to which one is accustomed. [C19: orig. sl., from ?]
▸ **'slummy** *adj*

slumber ⓣ ('slʌmbə) *vb* **1** (*intr*) to sleep, esp. peacefully. **2** (*intr*) to be quiescent or dormant. **3** (*tr*; foll. by *away*) to spend (time) sleeping. ◆ *n* **4** (*sometimes pl*) sleep. **5** a dormant or quiescent state. [OE *slūma* sleep (n)]
▸ **'slumberer** *n* ▸ **'slumbering** *adj*

slumberous ('slʌmbərəs) *or* **slumbrous** *adj Chiefly poetic.* **1** sleepy; drowsy. **2** inducing sleep.
▸ **'slumberously** *adv* ▸ **'slumberousness** *n*

slump ⓣ (slʌmp) *vb* (*intr*) **1** to sink or fall heavily and suddenly. **2** to relax ungracefully. **3** (of business activity, etc.) to decline suddenly. **4** (of health, interest, etc.) to deteriorate or decline suddenly. ◆ *n* **5** a sudden or marked decline or failure, as in progress or achievement. **6** a decline in commercial activity, prices, etc.; depression. **7** the act of slumping. [C17: prob. of Scand. origin]

slung (slʌŋ) *vb* the past tense and past participle of **sling**[1].

slunk (slʌŋk) *vb* the past tense and past participle of **slink.**

slur ⓣ (slɜː) *vb* **slurs, slurring, slurred.** (*mainly tr*) **1** (often foll. by *over*) to treat superficially, hastily, or without due deliberation. **2** (*also intr*) to pronounce or utter (words, etc.) indistinctly. **3** to speak disparagingly of. **4** *Music.* to execute (a melodic interval of two or more notes) smoothly, as in legato performance. ◆ *n* **5** an indistinct sound or utterance. **6** a slighting remark. **7** a stain or disgrace, as upon one's reputation. **8** *Music.* **8a** a performance or execution of a melodic interval of two or more notes in a part. **8b** the curved line (⌒ or ‿) indicating this. [C15: prob. from MLow G]

slurp (slɜːp) *Inf.* ◆ *vb* **1** to eat or drink (something) noisily. ◆ *n* **2** a sound produced in this way. [C17: from MDu. *slorpen* to sip]

slurry ('slʌrɪ) *n, pl* **slurries.** a suspension of solid particles in a liquid, as in a mixture of cement, coal dust, manure, meat, etc. with water. [C15 *slory*]

slush (slʌʃ) *n* **1** any watery muddy substance, esp. melting snow. **2** *Inf.* sloppily sentimental language. ◆ *vb* **3** (*intr*; often foll. by *along*) to make one's way through or as if through slush. [C17: rel. to Danish *slus* sleet, Norwegian *slusk* slops]
▸ **'slushy** *adj* ▸ **'slushiness** *n*

slush fund *n* a fund for financing political or commercial corruption.

slushy ('slʌʃɪ) *adj* **slushier, slushiest.** of, resembling, or consisting of slush.
▸ **'slushiness** *n*

slut ⓣ (slʌt) *n* **1** a dirty slatternly woman. **2** an immoral woman. [C14: from ?]
▸ **'sluttish** *adj* ▸ **'sluttishness** *n*

sly ⓣ (slaɪ) *adj* **slyer, slyest** *or* **slier, sliest.** **1** crafty; artful: *a sly dodge.* **2** insidious; furtive: *a sly manner.* **3** roguish: *sly humour.* ◆ *n* **4** **on the sly.** in a secretive manner. [C12: from ON *slǣgr* clever, lit.: able to strike, from *slā* to slay]
▸ **'slyly** *or* **'slily** *adv* ▸ **'slyness** *n*

slype (slaɪp) *n* a covered passage in a church that connects the transept to the chapterhouse. [C19: prob. from MFlemish *slijpen* to slip]

Sm *the chemical symbol for* samarium.

SM *abbrev. for* **1** sergeant major. **2** sadomasochism.

smack[1] ⓣ (smæk) *n* **1** a smell or flavour that is distinctive though faint. **2** a distinctive trace: *the smack of corruption.* **3** a small quantity, esp. a taste. **4** a slang word for **heroin.** ◆ *vb* (*intr*; foll. by *of*) **5** to have the characteristic smell or flavour (of something): *to smack of the sea.* **6** to have an element suggestive (of something): *his speeches smacked of bigotry.* [OE *smæc*]

smack[2] ⓣ (smæk) *vb* **1** (*tr*) to strike or slap smartly, with or as if with the open hand. **2** to strike or send forcibly or loudly or to be struck or sent forcibly or loudly. **3** to open and close (the lips) loudly, esp. to show pleasure. ◆ *n* **4** a sharp resounding slap or blow with something flat, or the sound of such a blow. **5** a loud kiss. **6** a sharp sound made by the lips, as in enjoyment. **7** **have a smack at.** *Inf., chiefly Brit.* to attempt. **8** **smack in the eye.** *Inf., chiefly Brit.* a snub or setback. ◆ *adv Inf.* **9** directly; squarely. **10** sharply and unexpectedly. [C16: from MLow G or MDu. *smacken,* prob. imit.]

smack[3] (smæk) *n* a sailing vessel, usually sloop-rigged, used in coasting and fishing along the British coast. [C17: from Low G *smack* or Du. *smak,* from ?]

smacker ('smækə) *n Sl.* **1** a loud kiss; smack. **2** a pound note or dollar bill.

small ⓣ (smɔːl) *adj* **1** limited in size, number, importance, etc. **2** of little importance or on a minor scale: *a small business.* **3** lacking in moral or mental breadth or depth: *a small mind.* **4** modest or humble: *small beginnings.* **5** of low or inferior status, esp. socially. **6** **feel small.** to be humiliated. **7** (of a child or animal) young; not mature. **8** unimportant; trivial: *a small matter.* **9** of or designating the ordinary modern minuscule letter used in printing and cursive writing. **10** lacking great strength or force: *a small effort.* **11** in fine particles: *small gravel.* ◆ *adv* **12** into small pieces: *cut it small.* **13** in a small or soft manner. ◆ *n* **14** (often preceded by *the*) an object, person, or group considered to be small: *the small or the large?* **15** a small slender part, esp. of the back. **16** (*pl*) *Inf., chiefly Brit.* items of personal laundry, such as underwear. [OE *smæl*]
▸ **'smallish** *adj* ▸ **'smallness** *n*

small arms *pl n* portable firearms of relatively small calibre.

small beer *n Inf., chiefly Brit.* people or things of no importance.

small change *n* **1** coins, esp. those of low value. **2** a person or thing that is not outstanding or important.

small circle *n* a circular section of a sphere that does not contain the centre of the sphere.

small claims court *n Brit. & Canad.* a local court with jurisdiction to try civil actions involving small claims.

small fry *pl n* **1** people or things regarded as unimportant. **2** young children. **3** young or small fishes.

small goods *pl n Austral. & NZ.* meats bought from a delicatessen, such as sausages.

smallholding ('smɔːl,həʊldɪŋ) *n* a holding of agricultural land smaller than a small farm.
▸ **'small,holder** *n*

small hours *pl n* **the.** the early hours of the morning, after midnight and before dawn.

small intestine *n* the longest part of the alimentary canal, in which digestion is completed. Cf. **large intestine.**

small-minded ⓣ *adj* narrow-minded; intolerant.
▸ **,small-'mindedly** *adv* ▸ **,small-'mindedness** *n*

smallpox ('smɔːl,pɒks) *n* a highly contagious viral disease characterized by high fever and a rash changing to pustules, which dry up and form scabs that are cast off, leaving pitted depressions. Technical name: **variola.**

small print *n* matter in a contract, etc., printed in small type, esp. when considered to be a trap for the unwary.

small-scale *adj* **1** of limited size or scope. **2** (of a map, model, etc.) giving a relatively small representation of something.

small screen *n* an informal name for **television.**

small slam *n Bridge.* another name for **little slam.**

small talk *n* light conversation for social occasions.

THESAURUS

slumber *vb* **1** = **sleep**, be inactive, doze, drowse, kip (*Brit. sl.*), lie dormant, nap, repose, snooze (*inf.*), zizz (*Brit. inf.*)

slummy *adj* **1, 2** = **squalid**, decayed, overcrowded, run-down, seedy, sleazy, sordid, wretched

slump *vb* **1, 3** = **fall**, collapse, crash, decline, deteriorate, fall off, go downhill (*inf.*), plummet, plunge, reach a new low, sink, slip **2** = **sag**, bend, droop, hunch, loll, slouch ◆ *n* **5** = **fall**, collapse, crash, decline, depreciation, downturn, drop, failure, falling-off, lapse, low, meltdown (*inf.*), reverse, stagnation, trough **6** = **recession**, depression
Antonyms *vb* ≠ **fall:** advance, boom, develop, expand, flourish, grow, increase, prosper, thrive ◆ *n* ≠ **fall:** advance, boom, boost, development, expansion, gain, growth, improvement, increase, upsurge, upswing, upturn

slur *n* **6, 7** = **insult**, affront, aspersion, blot, blot on one's escutcheon, brand, calumny, discredit, disgrace, innuendo, insinuation, reproach, smear, stain, stigma

slut *n* **2** = **tart**, drab (*arch.*), scrubber (*Brit. & Austral. sl.*), slag (*Brit. sl.*), slapper (*Brit. sl.*), slattern, sloven, trollop

sluttish *adj* **1** = **slovenly**, dirty, slatternly **2** = **promiscuous**, coarse, dissipated, immoral, tarty (*inf.*), trollopy, whorish

sly *adj* **1, 2** = **cunning**, artful, astute, clever, conniving, covert, crafty, devious, foxy, furtive, guileful, insidious, scheming, secret, shifty, stealthy, subtle, underhand, wily **3** = **roguish**, arch, impish, knowing, mischievous ◆ *n* **4** **on the sly** = **secretly**, behind (someone's) back, covertly, like a thief in the night, on the q.t. (*inf.*), on the quiet, privately, surreptitiously, underhandedly, under the counter (*inf.*)
Antonyms *adj* ≠ **cunning:** above-board, artless, direct, frank, guileless, honest, ingenuous, open, straightforward, trustworthy

smack[1] *vb, with* **of 5** = **smell of**, be redolent of, reek of **6** = **be suggestive** *or* **indicative of**, bear the stamp of, betoken, have all the hallmarks of, suggest, testify to

smack[2] *vb* **1, 2** = **slap**, box, clap, cuff, hit, pat, sock (*sl.*), spank, strike, swipe, tap ◆ *n* **4** = **slap**, blow, crack, swipe **8** **smack in the eye** *Informal, chiefly Brit.* = **snub**, blow, rebuff, repulse, setback, slap in the face ◆ *adv* **9** *Informal* = **directly**, exactly, plumb, point-blank, precisely, right, slap (*inf.*), squarely, straight

small *adj* **1** = **little**, diminutive, immature, Lilliputian, mini, miniature, minute, petite, pint-sized (*inf.*), pocket-sized, puny, pygmy *or* pigmy, slight, teeny, tiny, undersized, wee, young **2** = **minor**, lesser **3** = **petty**, base, grudging, illiberal, mean, narrow, selfish **4** = **modest**, humble, small-scale, unpretentious **6** **make (someone) feel small** = **humiliate**, chagrin, disconcert, humble, make (someone) look foolish, mortify, put down (*sl.*), show up (*inf.*), take down a peg or two (*inf.*) **8** = **unimportant**, insignificant, negligible, paltry, petty, trifling, trivial **10** = **meagre**, inadequate, inconsiderable, insufficient, limited, measly, scant, scanty
Antonyms *adj* ≠ **little:** big, colossal, enormous, great, huge, immense, massive, mega (*sl.*), sizable *or* sizeable, stellar (*inf.*), vast ≠ **modest:** grand, large-scale ≠ **unimportant:** appreciable, important, major, powerful, serious, significant, urgent, vital, weighty ≠ **meagre:** ample, considerable, generous, substantial

small-minded *adj* = **petty**, bigoted, envious, grudging, hidebound, intolerant, mean, narrow-minded, rigid, ungenerous
Antonyms *adj* broad-minded, far-sighted, generous, liberal, open, open-minded, tolerant, unbigoted

small-time Ⓣ *adj Inf.* insignificant; minor: *a small-time criminal.*
▸**'small-'timer** *n*

smalt (smɔːlt) *n* **1** a type of silica glass coloured deep blue with cobalt oxide. **2** a pigment made by crushing this glass, used in colouring enamels. [C16: via F from It. *smalto* coloured glass, of Gmc origin]

smarm (smɑːm) *vb Brit. inf.* **1** (*tr;* often foll. by *down*) to flatten (the hair, etc.) with grease. **2** (when *intr,* foll. by *up to*) to ingratiate oneself (with). [C19: from ?]

smarmy Ⓣ ('smɑːmɪ) *adj* **smarmier, smarmiest.** *Brit. inf.* obsequiously flattering or unpleasantly suave.
▸**'smarmily** *adv* ▸**'smarminess** *n*

smart Ⓣ (smɑːt) *adj* **1** astute, as in business. **2** quick, witty, and often impertinent in speech: *a smart talker.* **3** fashionable; chic: *a smart hotel.* **4** well-kept; neat. **5** causing a sharp stinging pain. **6** vigorous or brisk. **7** (of systems) operating as if by human intelligence by using automatic computer control. **8** (of a weapon, etc.) containing a device which enables it to be guided to its target: *smart bombs.* ◆ *vb* (*mainly intr*) **9** to feel, cause, or be the source of a sharp stinging physical pain or keen mental distress: *he smarted under their abuse.* **10** (often foll. by *for*) to suffer a harsh penalty. ◆ *n* **11** a stinging pain or feeling. ◆ *adv* **12** in a smart manner. ◆ See also **smarts.** [OE *smeortan*]
▸**'smartly** *adv* ▸**'smartness** *n*

smart aleck Ⓣ ('ælɪk) *n Inf.* **a** an irritatingly oversmart person. **b** (*as modifier*): *a smart-aleck remark.* [C19: from *Aleck, Alec,* short for *Alexander*]
▸**'smart-ˌalecky** *adj*

smart card *n* a plastic card with integrated circuits used for storing and processing computer data. Also called: **laser card, intelligent card.**

smart drug *n* any of various drugs that are claimed to improve the intelligence or memory of the person taking them.

smarten Ⓣ ('smɑːtᵊn) *vb* (usually foll. by *up*) **1** (*intr*) to make oneself neater. **2** (*tr*) to make quicker or livelier.

smart money *n* **1** money bet or invested by experienced gamblers or investors. **2** money paid in order to extricate oneself from an unpleasant situation or agreement, esp. from military service. **3** *Law.* damages awarded to a plaintiff where the wrong was aggravated by fraud, malice, etc.

smarts (smɑːts) *pl n Sl., chiefly US.* know-how, intelligence, or wits: *street smarts.*

smart set *n* (*functioning as sing or pl*) fashionable people considered as a group.

smash Ⓣ (smæʃ) *vb* **1** to break into pieces violently and usually noisily. **2** (when *intr,* foll. by *against, through, into,* etc.) to throw or crash (against) vigorously, causing shattering: *he smashed the equipment.* **3** (*tr*) to hit forcefully and suddenly. **4** (*tr*) *Tennis, etc.* to hit (the ball) fast and powerfully, esp. with an overhead stroke. **5** (*tr*) to defeat (persons, theories, etc.). **6** to make or become bankrupt. **7** (*intr*) to collide violently; crash. ◆ *n* **8** an act, instance, or sound of smashing or the state of being smashed. **9** a violent collision, esp. of vehicles. **10** a total failure or collapse, as of a business. **11** *Tennis, etc.* a fast and powerful overhead stroke. **12** *Inf.* **12a** something having popular success. **12b** (*in combination*): *smash-hit.* ◆ *adv* **13** with a smash. ◆ See also **smash-up.** [C18: prob. from SM(ACK² + M)ASH]
▸**'smashable** *adj*

smash-and-grab *adj Inf.* of or relating to a robbery in which a shop window is broken and the contents removed.

smashed (smæʃt) *adj Sl.* drunk or under the influence of a drug.

smasher ('smæʃə) *n Inf., chiefly Brit.* a person or thing that is very attractive or outstanding.

smashing Ⓣ ('smæʃɪŋ) *adj Inf., chiefly Brit.* excellent or first-rate: *we had a smashing time.*

smash-up *Inf.* ◆ *n* **1** a bad collision, esp of cars. ◆ *vb* **smash up. 2** (*tr, adv*) to damage to the point of complete destruction: *they smashed the place up.*

smatter ('smætə) *n* **1** a smattering. ◆ *vb* **2** (*tr*) *Arch.* to dabble in. [C14 (in the sense: to prattle): from ?]
▸**'smatterer** *n*

smattering Ⓣ ('smætərɪŋ) *n* **1** a slight or superficial knowledge. **2** a small amount.

smear Ⓣ (smɪə) *vb* (*mainly tr*) **1** to bedaub or cover with oil, grease, etc. **2** to rub over or apply thickly. **3** to rub so as to produce a smudge. **4** to slander. **5** (*intr*) to be or become smeared or dirtied. ◆ *n* **6** a dirty mark or smudge. **7a** a slanderous attack. **7b** (*as modifier*): *smear tactics.* **8** a preparation of blood, secretions, etc., smeared onto a glass slide for examination under a microscope. [OE *smeoru* (n)]
▸**'smeary** *adj* ▸**'smearily** *adv* ▸**'smeariness** *n*

smear test *n Med.* another name for **Pap test.**

smectic ('smɛktɪk) *adj Chem.* (of a substance) existing in or having a mesomorphic state in which the molecules are oriented in layers. [C17: via L from Gk *smēktikos,* from *smēkhein* to wash; from the soaplike consistency of a smectic substance]

smegma ('smɛgmə) *n Physiol.* a whitish sebaceous secretion that accumulates beneath the prepuce. [C19: via L from Gk *smēgma* detergent, from *smekhein* to wash]

smell Ⓣ (smɛl) *vb* **smells, smelling, smelt** *or* **smelled. 1** (*tr*) to perceive the scent of (a substance) by means of the olfactory nerves. **2** (*copula*) to have a specified smell: *the curry smells very spicy.* **3** (*intr;* often foll. by *of*) to emit an odour (of): *the park smells of flowers.* **4** (*intr*) to emit an unpleasant odour. **5** (*tr;* often foll. by *out*) to detect through shrewdness or instinct. **6** (*intr*) to have or use the sense of smell; sniff. **7** (*intr;* foll. by *of*) to give indications (of): *he smells of money.* **8** (*intr;* foll. by *around, about,* etc.) to search, investigate, or pry. **9** (*copula*) to be or seem to be untrustworthy. ◆ *n* **10** that sense (olfaction) by which scents or odours are perceived. Related adj: **olfactory. 11** anything detected by the sense of smell. **12** a trace or indication. **13** the act or an instance of smelling. [C12: from ?]
▸**'smeller** *n*

smelling salts *pl n* a pungent preparation containing crystals of ammonium carbonate that has a stimulant action when sniffed in cases of faintness, headache, etc.

smelly Ⓣ ('smɛlɪ) *adj* **smellier, smelliest.** having a strong or nasty smell.
▸**'smelliness** *n*

smelt[1] (smɛlt) *vb* (*tr*) to extract (a metal) from (an ore) by heating. [C15: from MLow G, MDu. *smelten*]

smelt[2] (smɛlt) *n, pl* **smelt** *or* **smelts.** a marine or freshwater salmonoid food fish having a long silvery body and occurring in temperate and cold northern waters. [OE *smylt*]

smelt[3] (smɛlt) *vb* a past tense and past participle of **smell.**

smelter ('smɛltə) *n* **1** a person engaged in smelting. **2** Also called: **smeltery.** an industrial plant in which smelting is carried out.

smew (smjuː) *n* a merganser of N Europe and Asia, having a male plumage of white with black markings. [C17: from ?]

smidgen *or* **smidgin** ('smɪdʒən) *n Inf., chiefly US.* a very small amount. [C20: from ?]

smilax ('smaɪlæks) *n* **1** any of a genus of climbing shrubs having slightly lobed leaves, small greenish or yellow flowers, and berry-like fruits: includes the sarsaparilla plant and greenbrier. **2** a fragile, much branched vine of southern Africa: cultivated for its glossy green foliage. [C17: via L from Gk: bindweed]

smile Ⓣ (smaɪl) *n* **1** a facial expression characterized by an upturning of the corners of the mouth, usually showing amusement, friendliness, etc. **2** favour or blessing: *the smile of fortune.* ◆ *vb* **smiles, smiling,**

THESAURUS

small-time *adj* = **minor,** insignificant, no-account (*US inf.*), of no account, of no consequence, petty, piddling (*inf.*), unimportant

smarmy *adj Brit. informal* = **obsequious,** bootlicking (*inf.*), bowing and scraping, crawling, fawning, fulsome, greasy, ingratiating, oily, servile, slimy, smooth, soapy (*sl.*), suave, sycophantic, toadying, unctuous

smart *adj* **1** = **clever,** acute, adept, agile, apt, astute, bright, brisk, canny, ingenious, intelligent, keen, nimble, quick, quick-witted, ready, sharp, shrewd **2** = **impertinent,** nimble-witted, pointed, ready, saucy, smart-alecky (*inf.*), witty **3** = **chic,** as fresh as a daisy, elegant, fashionable, fine, modish, natty (*inf.*), neat, snappy, spruce, stylish, trendy (*Brit. inf.*), trim, well turned-out **5** = **stinging,** hard, keen, painful, piercing, resounding, sharp **6** = **brisk,** cracking (*inf.*), jaunty, lively, quick, spanking, spirited, vigorous ◆ *vb* **9** = **sting,** burn, hurt, pain, throb, tingle ◆ *n* **11** = **sting,** burning sensation, pain, pang, smarting, soreness
Antonyms *adj* ≠ **clever:** daft (*inf.*), dense, dim-witted (*inf.*), dull, dumb (*inf.*), dumb-ass (*sl.*), foolish, idiotic, moronic, slow, stupid, thick, unintelligent ≠ **chic:** dowdy, dull, fogeyish, naff (*Brit. sl.*), old-fashioned, outmoded, out-of-date, passé, scruffy, sloppy, uncool, unfashionable, untrendy (*Brit. inf.*)

smart aleck *n Informal* = **know-all** (*inf.*), clever-clogs (*inf.*), clever Dick (*inf.*), smartarse (*sl.*), smarty boots (*inf.*), smarty pants (*inf.*), wise guy (*inf.*)

smarten *vb* **1** = **tidy,** beautify, groom, put in order, put to rights, spruce up

smash *vb* **1, 2** = **break,** crush, demolish, disintegrate, pulverize, shatter, shiver **5** = **destroy,** defeat, lay waste, overthrow, ruin, total (*sl.*), trash (*sl.*), wreck **7** = **collide,** crash ◆ *n* **9** = **collision,** accident, crash, pile-up (*inf.*), smash-up (*inf.*) **10** = **destruction,** collapse, defeat, disaster, downfall, failure, ruin, shattering

smashing *adj Informal, chiefly Brit.* = **excellent,** brilliant (*inf.*), cracking, exhilarating, fabulous (*inf.*), fantastic (*inf.*), first-class, first-rate, great (*inf.*), jim-dandy (*sl.*), magnificent, marvellous, out of this world (*inf.*), sensational (*inf.*), sovereign, stupendous, super (*inf.*), superb, superlative, terrific (*inf.*), wonderful, world-class
Antonyms *adj* abysmal, appalling, average, awful, bad, boring, disappointing, disgraceful, disgusting, dreadful, dreary, dull, hideous, horrible, mediocre, no great shakes (*inf.*), ordinary, rotten, run-of-the-mill, sickening, terrible, unexciting, uninspired, vile

smattering *n* **1, 2** = **modicum,** bit, dash, elements, nodding acquaintance, passing acquaintance, rudiments, smatter, sprinkling

smear *vb* **1** = **spread over,** bedaub, coat, cover, daub, plaster, rub on **3** = **dirty,** bedim, besmirch, blur, smirch, smudge, soil, stain, sully **4** = **slander,** asperse, besmirch, blacken, calumniate, drag (someone's) name through the mud, malign, sully, tarnish, traduce, vilify ◆ *n* **6** = **smudge,** blot, blotch, daub, smirch, splotch, streak **7** = **slander,** calumny, defamation, libel, mudslinging, vilification, whispering campaign

smell *vb* **1** = **sniff,** get a whiff of, nose, scent **4** = **stink,** be malodorous, hum (*sl.*), niff, pong (*Brit. inf.*), reek, stink to high heaven (*inf.*), whiff (*Brit. sl.*) ◆ *n* **11** = **odour,** aroma, bouquet, fragrance, niff (*Brit. sl.*), perfume, redolence, scent, stench, stink, whiff

smelly *adj* = **stinking,** evil-smelling, fetid, foul, foul-smelling, high, malodorous, mephitic, niffy (*Brit. sl.*), noisome, olid, pongy (*Brit. inf.*), putrid, reeking, stinky (*inf.*), strong, strong-smelling, whiffy (*Brit. sl.*)

smile *n* **1** = **grin,** beam ◆ *vb* **3** = **grin,** beam

smiled. 3 (*intr*) to wear or assume a smile. **4** (*intr;* foll. by *at*) **4a** to look (at) with a kindly expression. **4b** to look derisively (at). **4c** to bear (troubles, etc.) patiently. **5** (*intr;* foll. by *on* or *upon*) to show approval. **6** (*tr*) to express by means of a smile: *she smiled a welcome.* **7** (*tr;* often foll. by *away*) to drive away or change by smiling. **8 come up smiling.** to recover cheerfully from misfortune. [C13: prob. from ON]
▸**'smiler** *n* ▸**'smiling** *adj* ▸**'smilingly** *adv*

smiley ('smaɪlɪ) *adj* **1** given to smiling; cheerful. **2** depicting a smile: *a smiley badge.* ◆ *n* **3** any of a group of symbols depicting a smile, or other facial expression, used in electronic mail.

smirch (smɜːtʃ) *vb* (*tr*) **1** to dirty; soil. ◆ *n* **2** the act of smirching or state of being smirched. **3** a smear or stain. [C15 *smorchen,* from ?]

smirk ⓣ (smɜːk) *n* **1** a smile expressing scorn, smugness, etc., rather than pleasure. ◆ *vb* **2** (*intr*) to give such a smile. **3** (*tr*) to express with such a smile. [OE *smearcian*]
▸**'smirker** *n* ▸**'smirking** *adj* ▸**'smirkingly** *adv*

smite (smaɪt) *vb* **smites, smiting, smote; smitten** *or* **smit** (smɪt). (*mainly tr*) *Now arch. in most senses.* **1** to strike with a heavy blow. **2** to damage with or as if with blows. **3** to affect severely: *smitten with flu.* **4** to afflict in order to punish. **5** (*intr;* foll. by *on*) to strike forcibly or abruptly: *the sun smote down on him.* [OE *smītan*]
▸**'smiter** *n*

smith (smɪθ) *n* **1a** a person who works in metal. **1b** (*in combination*): *a silversmith.* **2** See **blacksmith.** [OE]

smithereens (ˌsmɪðə'riːnz) *pl n* little shattered pieces or fragments. [C19: from Irish Gaelic *smidirīn,* from *smiodar*]

smithery ('smɪθərɪ) *n, pl* **smitheries. 1** the trade or craft of a blacksmith. **2** a rare word for **smithy.**

smithy ('smɪðɪ) *n, pl* **smithies.** a place in which metal, usually iron or steel, is worked by heating and hammering; forge. [OE *smiththe*]

smitten ⓣ ('smɪtᵊn) *vb* **1** a past participle of **smite.** ◆ *adj* **2** (*postpositive*) affected by love (for).

smock (smɒk) *n* **1** any loose protective garment, worn by artists, laboratory technicians, etc. **2** a woman's loose blouselike garment, reaching to below the waist, worn over slacks, etc. **3** Also called: **smock frock.** a loose protective overgarment decorated with smocking, worn formerly esp. by farm workers. **4** *Arch.* a woman's loose undergarment. ◆ *vb* **5** to ornament (a garment) with smocking. [OE *smocc*]
▸**'smockˌlike** *adj*

smocking ('smɒkɪŋ) *n* ornamental needlework used to gather and stitch material in a honeycomb pattern so that the part below the gathers hangs in even folds.

smog (smɒg) *n* a mixture of smoke, fog, and chemical fumes. [C20: from SM(OKE + F)OG[1]]
▸**'smoggy** *adj*

smoke (sməʊk) *n* **1** the product of combustion, consisting of fine particles of carbon carried by hot gases and air. **2** any cloud of fine particles suspended in a gas. **3a** the act of smoking tobacco, esp. as a cigarette. **3b** the duration of smoking such substances. **4** *Inf.* a cigarette or cigar. **5** something with no concrete or lasting substance: *everything turned to smoke.* **6** a thing or condition that obscures. **7 go** *or* **end up in smoke. 7a** to come to nothing. **7b** to burn up vigorously. **7c** to flare up in anger. ◆ *vb* **smokes, smoking, smoked. 8** (*intr*) to emit smoke or the like, sometimes excessively or in the wrong place. **9** to draw in on (a burning cigarette, etc.) and exhale the smoke. **10** (*tr*) to bring (oneself) into a specified state by smoking. **11** (*tr*) to subject or expose to smoke. **12** (*tr*) to cure (meat, fish, etc.) by treating with smoke. **13** (*tr*) to fumigate or purify the air of (rooms, etc.). **14** (*tr*) to darken (glass, etc.) by exposure to smoke. ◆ See also **smoke out.** [OE *smoca* (n)]
▸**'smokable** *or* **'smokeable** *adj*

Smoke (sməʊk) *n* **the.** short for the **Big Smoke.**

smoke-dried *adj* (of fish, etc.) cured in smoke.

smoked rubber *n* a type of crude natural rubber in the form of brown sheets obtained by coagulating latex with an acid, rolling it into sheets, and drying over open wood fires. It is the main raw material for natural rubber products.

smokeho ('sməʊkəʊ) *n* a variant spelling of **smoko.**

smokehouse ('sməʊkˌhaʊs) *n* a building or special construction for curing meat, fish, etc., by smoking.

smokeless ('sməʊklɪs) *adj* having or producing little or no smoke: *smokeless fuel.*

smokeless zone *n* an area where only smokeless fuels are permitted to be used.

smoke out *vb* (*tr, adv*) **1** to subject to smoke in order to drive out of hiding. **2** to bring into the open: *they smoked out the plot.*

smoker ('sməʊkə) *n* **1** a person who habitually smokes tobacco. **2** Also called: **smoking compartment.** a compartment of a train where smoking is permitted. **3** an informal social gathering, as at a club.

smoke screen *n* **1** *Mil.* a cloud of smoke produced to obscure movements. **2** something said or done in order to hide the truth.

smokestack ('sməʊkˌstæk) *n* a tall chimney that conveys smoke into the air.

smokestack industry *n Inf.* any of the traditional British industries, esp. heavy engineering or manufacturing, as opposed to such modern industries as electronics.

smoking jacket *n* (formerly) a man's comfortable jacket of velvet, etc., closed by a tie belt or fastenings, worn at home.

smoko *or* **smokeho** ('sməʊkəʊ) *n, pl* **smokos** *or* **smokehos.** *Austral. & NZ inf.* **1** a short break from work for tea, a cigarette, etc. **2** refreshment taken during this break.

smoky ⓣ ('sməʊkɪ) *adj* **smokier, smokiest. 1** emitting or resembling smoke. **2** emitting smoke excessively or in the wrong place: *a smoky fireplace.* **3** having the flavour of having been cured by smoking. **4** made dirty or hazy by smoke: *a smoky atmosphere.*
▸**'smokily** *adv* ▸**'smokiness** *n*

smolder ('sməʊldə) *vb, n* the US spelling of **smoulder.**

smolt (sməʊlt) *n* a young salmon at the stage when it migrates from fresh water to the sea. [C14: Scot., from ?]

smooch (smuːtʃ) *Sl.* ◆ *vb* (*intr*) **1** Also (Austral. and NZ): **smoodge, smooge.** (of two people) to kiss and cuddle. **2** *Brit.* to dance very slowly and amorously with one's arms around another person or (of two people) to dance together in such a way. ◆ *n* **3** the act of smooching. [C20: var. of dialect *smouch,* imit.]

smoodge *or* **smooge** (smuːdʒ) *vb* **smoodges, smoodging, smoodged** *or* **smooges, smooging, smooged.** (*intr*) *Austral. & NZ.* **1** another word for **smooch** (sense 1). **2** to seek to ingratiate oneself.

smooth ⓣ (smuːð) *adj* **1** without bends or irregularities. **2** silky to the touch: *smooth velvet.* **3** lacking roughness of surface; flat. **4** tranquil or unruffled: *smooth temper.* **5** lacking obstructions or difficulties. **6a** suave or persuasive, esp. as suggestive of insincerity. **6b** (*in combination*): *smooth-tongued.* **7** (of the skin) free from hair. **8** of uniform consistency: *smooth batter.* **9** free from jolts: *smooth driving.* **10** not harsh or astringent: *a smooth wine.* **11** having all projections worn away: *smooth tyres.* **12** *Phonetics.* without preliminary aspiration. **13** *Physics.* (of a plane, etc.) regarded as being frictionless. ◆ *adv* **14** in a calm or even manner. ◆ *vb* (*mainly tr*) **15** (*also intr;* often foll. by *down*) to make or become flattened or without roughness. **16** (often foll. by *out* or *away*) to take or rub (away) in order to make smooth: *she smoothed out the creases in her dress.* **17** to make calm; soothe. **18** to make easier: *smooth his path.* ◆ *n* **19** the smooth part of something. **20** the act of smoothing. **21** *Tennis, etc.* the side of a racket on which the binding strings form a continuous line. ◆ See also **smooth over.** [OE *smōth*]
▸**'smoother** *n* ▸**'smoothly** *adv* ▸**'smoothness** *n*

smoothbore ('smuːðˌbɔː) *n* (*modifier*) (of a firearm) having an unrifled bore: *a smoothbore shotgun.*
▸**'smoothˌbored** *adj*

smooth breathing *n* (in Greek) the sign (') placed over an initial vowel, indicating that (in ancient Greek) it was not pronounced with an *h.*

smoothen ('smuːðən) *vb* to make or become smooth.

smooth hound *n* any of several small sharks of North Atlantic coastal regions.

smoothie *or* **smoothy** ('smuːðɪ) *n, pl* **smoothies.** *Sl., usually derog.* a person, esp. a man, who is suave or slick, esp. in speech, dress, or manner.

smoothing iron *n* a former name for **iron** (sense 3).

smooth muscle *n* muscle that is capable of slow rhythmic involuntary contractions: occurs in the walls of the blood vessels, etc.

smooth over *vb* (*tr*) to ease or gloss over: *to smooth over a difficulty.*

smooth snake *n* any of several slender nonvenomous European snakes having very smooth scales and a reddish-brown coloration.

smooth-spoken *adj* speaking or spoken in a gently persuasive or competent manner.

smooth-tongued *adj* suave or persuasive in speech.

smorgasbord ('smɔːgəsˌbɔːd) *n* a variety of cold or hot savoury dishes served in Scandinavia as hors d'oeuvres or as a buffet meal. [Swedish, from *smörgås* sandwich + *bord* table]

smote (sməʊt) *vb* the past tense of **smite.**

smother ⓣ ('smʌðə) *vb* **1** to suffocate or stifle by cutting off or being cut off from the air. **2** (*tr*) to surround (with) or envelop (in): *he smothered her with love.* **3** (*tr*) to extinguish (a fire) by covering so as to cut it

THESAURUS

smirk *n* **1** = **smug look,** grin, leer, simper, sneer

smitten *adj* **1** = **afflicted,** beset, laid low, plagued, struck **2** = **infatuated,** beguiled, bewitched, bowled over (*inf.*), captivated, charmed, enamoured, swept off one's feet

smoky *adj* **4** = **black,** begrimed, caliginous (*arch.*), grey, grimy, hazy, murky, reeky, smoke-darkened, sooty, thick

smooth *adj* **2** = **sleek,** glassy, glossy, mirror-like, polished, shiny, silky, soft, velvety **3** = **even,** flat, flush, horizontal, level, plain, plane, unwrinkled **4** = **calm,** equable, peaceful, serene, tranquil, undisturbed, unruffled **5** = **easy,** effortless, untroubled, well-ordered **6** = **suave,** debonair, facile, glib, ingratiating, persuasive, silky, slick, smarmy (*Brit. inf.*), unctuous, urbane **9** = **flowing,** fluent, regular, rhythmic, steady, uniform **10** = **mellow,** agreeable, bland, mild, pleasant, soothing ◆ *vb* **15, 16** = **flatten,** iron, level, plane, polish, press **17** = **ease,** allay, alleviate, appease, assuage, calm, extenuate, mitigate, mollify, palliate, soften, soothe **18** = **facilitate,** ease, iron out the difficulties of, pave the way
Antonyms *adj* ≠ **sleek:** abrasive, coarse, jagged, rough, sharp ≠ **even:** bumpy, irregular, lumpy, rough, uneven ≠ **calm:** agitated, edgy, excitable, nervous, ruffled, troubled, troublesome, turbulent, uneasy ◆ *vb* ≠ **ease:** aggravate, exacerbate, hamper, hinder, intensify, make worse, roughen

smoothness *n* **2** = **sleekness,** silkiness, smooth texture, softness, velvetiness **3** = **evenness,** flushness, levelness, regularity, unbrokenness **4** = **calmness,** placidity, serenity, stillness **5** = **fluency,** ease, efficiency, effortlessness, felicity, finish, flow, polish, rhythm, slickness, smooth running **6** = **suavity,** glibness, oiliness, smarminess (*Brit. inf.*), urbanity

smother *vb* **1** = **suffocate,** choke, stifle, stran-

off from the air. **4** to be or cause to be suppressed or stifled: *smother a giggle.* **5** (*tr*) to cook or serve (food) thickly covered with sauce, etc. ◆ *n* **6** anything, such as a cloud of smoke, that stifles. **7** a profusion or turmoil. [OE *smorian* to suffocate]
▸**ˈsmothery** *adj*

smothered mate *n Chess.* checkmate given by a knight when the king is prevented from moving by surrounding men.

smoulder Ⓣ *or US* **smolder** (ˈsməʊldə) *vb* (*intr*) **1** to burn slowly without flame, usually emitting smoke. **2** (esp. of anger, etc.) to exist in a suppressed state. **3** to have strong repressed feelings, esp. anger. ◆ *n* **4** a smouldering fire. [C14: from *smolder* (n), from ?]

SMP *abbrev. for* statutory maternity pay.

smudge Ⓣ (smʌdʒ) *vb* **smudges, smudging, smudged. 1** to smear or soil or cause to do so. **2** (*tr*) *Chiefly US & Canad.* to fill (an area) with smoke in order to drive insects away. ◆ *n* **3** a smear or dirty mark. **4** a blurred form or area: *that smudge in the distance is a quarry.* **5** *Chiefly US & Canad.* a smoky fire for driving insects away or protecting plants from frost. [C15: from ?]
▸**ˈsmudgy** *adj* ▸**ˈsmudgily** *adv* ▸**ˈsmudginess** *n*

smug Ⓣ (smʌg) *adj* **smugger, smuggest.** excessively self-satisfied or complacent. [C16: of Gmc origin]
▸**ˈsmugly** *adv* ▸**ˈsmugness** *n*

smuggle Ⓣ (ˈsmʌgᵊl) *vb* **smuggles, smuggling, smuggled. 1** to import or export (prohibited or dutiable goods) secretly. **2** (*tr; often foll. by into or out of*) to bring or take secretly, as against the law or rules. [C17: from Low G *smukkelen* & Du. *smokkelen,* ?from OE *smūgen* to creep]
▸**ˈsmuggler** *n* ▸**ˈsmuggling** *n*

smut Ⓣ (smʌt) *n* **1** a small dark smudge or stain, esp. one caused by soot. **2** a speck of soot or dirt. **3** something obscene or indecent. **4a** any of various fungal diseases of flowering plants, esp. cereals, in which black sooty masses of spores cover the affected parts. **4b** any parasitic fungus that causes such a disease. ◆ *vb* **smuts, smutting, smutted. 5** to mark or become marked or smudged, as with soot. **6** to affect (grain, etc.) or (of grain) to be affected with smut. [OE *smitte;* associated with SMUDGE, SMUTCH]
▸**ˈsmutty** *adj* ▸**ˈsmuttily** *adv* ▸**ˈsmuttiness** *n*

smutch (smʌtʃ) *vb* **1** (*tr*) to smudge; mark. ◆ *n* **2** a mark; smudge. **3** soot; dirt. [C16: prob. from MHG *smutzen* to soil]
▸**ˈsmutchy** *adj*

Sn *the chemical symbol for* tin. [from NL *stannum*]

snack Ⓣ (snæk) *n* **1** a light quick meal eaten between or in place of main meals. **2** a sip or bite. ◆ *vb* **3** (*intr*) to eat a snack. [C15: prob. from MDu. *snacken,* var. of *snappen* to snap]

snack bar *n* a place where light meals or snacks can be obtained, often with a self-service system.

snaffle (ˈsnæfᵊl) *n* **1** Also called: **snaffle bit.** a simple jointed bit for a horse. ◆ *vb* **snaffles, snaffling, snaffled.** (*tr*) **2** *Brit. inf.* to steal or take for oneself. **3** to equip or control with a snaffle. [C16: from ?]

snafu (snæˈfu:) *Sl., chiefly mil.* ◆ *n* **1** confusion or chaos regarded as the normal state. ◆ *adj* **2** (*postpositive*) confused or muddled up, as usual. ◆ *vb* **snafus, snafuing, snafued. 3** (*tr*) *US & Canad.* to throw into chaos. [C20: from *s(ituation) n(ormal): a(ll) f(ucked) u(p)*]

snag[1] Ⓣ (snæg) *n* **1** a difficulty or disadvantage: *the snag is that I have nothing suitable to wear.* **2** a sharp protuberance, such as a tree stump. **3** a small loop or hole in a fabric caused by a sharp object. **4** *Chiefly US & Canad.* a tree stump in a riverbed that is dangerous to navigation. **5** *US & Canad.* a standing dead tree, esp. one used as a perch by an eagle. ◆ *vb* **snags, snagging, snagged. 6** (*tr*) to hinder or impede. **7** (*tr*) to tear or catch (fabric). **8** (*intr*) to develop a snag. **9** (*intr*) *Chiefly US & Canad.* (of a boat) to strike a snag. **10** (*tr*) *Chiefly US & Canad.* to clear (a stretch of water) of snags. **11** (*tr*) *US.* to seize (an opportunity, etc.). [C16: of Scand. origin]
▸**ˈsnaggy** *adj*

snag[2] (snæg) *n* (*usually pl*) *Austral. sl.* a sausage. [from ?]

snaggletooth (ˈsnægᵊl,tu:θ) *n, pl* **snaggleteeth.** a tooth that is broken or projecting.

snail (sneɪl) *n* **1** any of numerous terrestrial or freshwater gastropod molluscs with a spirally coiled shell, esp. the **garden snail. 2** any other gastropod with a spirally coiled shell, such as a whelk. **3** a slow-moving person or animal. [OE *snægl*]
▸**ˈsnail-,like** *adj*

snail mail *Inf. n* **1** the conventional postal system, as opposed to electronic mail. ◆ *vb* **snail-mail. 2** (*tr*) to send by the conventional postal system, rather than by electronic mail. [C20: so named because of the relative slowness of the conventional postal system]

snail's pace *n* a very slow speed or rate.

snake (sneɪk) *n* **1** a reptile having a scaly cylindrical limbless body, fused eyelids, and a jaw modified for swallowing large prey: includes venomous forms such as cobras and rattlesnakes, large nonvenomous constrictors (boas and pythons), and small harmless types such as the grass snake. **2** Also: **snake in the grass.** a deceitful or treacherous person. **3** anything resembling a snake in appearance or action. **4** (in the European Union) a group of currencies, any one of which can only fluctuate within narrow limits, but each can fluctuate more against other currencies. **5** a tool in the form of a long flexible wire for unblocking drains. ◆ *vb* **snakes, snaking, snaked. 6** (*intr*) to glide or move like a snake. **7** (*tr*) to move in or follow (a sinuous course). [OE *snaca*]
▸**ˈsnake,like** *adj*

snakebird (ˈsneɪk,bɜ:d) *n* another name for **darter** (the bird).

snakebite (ˈsneɪk,baɪt) *n* **1** a bite inflicted by a snake, esp. a venomous one. **2** a drink of cider and lager.

snake charmer *n* an entertainer, esp. in Asia, who charms or appears to charm snakes by playing music.

snakeroot (ˈsneɪk,ru:t) *n* **1** any of various North American plants the roots or rhizomes of which have been used as a remedy for snakebite. **2** the rhizome or root of any such plant.

snakes and ladders *n* (*functioning as sing*) a board game in which players move counters along a series of squares according to throws of a dice. A ladder provides a short cut to a square nearer the finish and a snake obliges a player to return to a square nearer the start.

snake's head *n* a European fritillary plant of damp meadows, having purple-and-white flowers.

snakeskin (ˈsneɪk,skɪn) *n* the skin of a snake, esp. when made into a leather valued for handbags, shoes, etc.

snaky Ⓣ (ˈsneɪkɪ) *adj* **snakier, snakiest. 1** of or like a snake. **2** treacherous or insidious. **3** infested with snakes. **4** *Austral. & NZ sl.* angry or bad-tempered.
▸**ˈsnakily** *adv* ▸**ˈsnakiness** *n*

snap Ⓣ (snæp) *vb* **snaps, snapping, snapped. 1** to break or cause to break suddenly, esp. with a sharp sound. **2** to make or cause to make a sudden sharp cracking sound. **3** (*intr*) to give way or collapse suddenly, esp. from strain. **4** to move, close, etc., or cause to move, close, etc., with a sudden sharp sound. **5** to move or cause to move in a sudden or abrupt way. **6** (*intr; often foll. by at or up*) to seize something suddenly or quickly. **7** (when *intr,* often foll. by *at*) to bite at (something) bringing the jaws rapidly together. **8** to speak (words) sharply or abruptly. **9** to take a snapshot of (something). **10** (*tr*) *American football.* to put (the ball) into play by sending it back from the line of scrimmage. **11 snap one's fingers at.** *Inf.* **11a** to dismiss with contempt. **11b** to defy. **12 snap out of it.** *Inf.* to recover quickly, esp. from depression or anger. ◆ *n* **13** the act of breaking suddenly or the sound produced by a sudden breakage. **14** a sudden sharp sound, esp. of bursting, popping, or cracking. **15** a catch, clasp, or fastener that operates with a snapping sound. **16** a sudden grab or bite. **17** a thin crisp biscuit: *ginger snaps.* **18** *Inf.* See **snapshot. 19** *Inf.* vigour, liveliness, or energy. **20** *Inf.* a task or job that is easy or profitable to do. **21** a short spell or period, esp. of cold weather. **22** *Brit.* a card game in which the word *snap* is called when two cards of equal value are turned up on the separate piles dealt by each player. **23** *American football.* the start of each play when the centre passes the ball back from the line of scrimmage to a teammate. **24** (*modifier*) done on the spur of the moment: *a snap decision.* **25** (*modifier*) closed or fastened with a snap. ◆ *adv* **26** with a snap. ◆ *interj* **27a** *Cards.* the word called while playing snap. **27b** an exclamation used to draw attention to the similarity of two things. ◆ See also **snap up.** [C15: from MLow G or MDu. *snappen* to seize]
▸**ˈsnapless** *adj* ▸**ˈsnappingly** *adv*

snapdragon (ˈsnæp,drægən) *n* any of several plants of the genus *Antirrhinum* having spikes of showy white, yellow, pink, red, or purplish flowers. Also called: **antirrhinum.**

snap fastener *n* another name for **press stud.**

snapper (ˈsnæpə) *n, pl* **snapper** *or* **snappers. 1** any large sharp-toothed percoid food fish of warm and tropical coastal regions. See also **red snapper. 2** a food fish of Australia and New Zealand that has a pinkish body covered with blue spots. **3** another name for the **snapping turtle. 4** a person or thing that snaps. ◆ Also (for sense 1, 2): **schnapper.**

THESAURUS

gle **2** = **overwhelm**, cocoon, cover, envelop, heap, inundate, shower, shroud, surround **3** = **extinguish**, snuff **4** = **suppress**, conceal, hide, keep back, muffle, repress, stifle

smoulder *vb* **3** = **seethe**, be resentful, boil, burn, fester, fume, rage, simmer, smart under

smudge *vb* **1** = **smear**, blacken, blur, daub, dirty, mark, smirch, soil ◆ *n* **3** = **smear**, blemish, blot, blur, smut, smutch

smug *adj* = **self-satisfied**, complacent, conceited, holier-than-thou, priggish, self-opinionated, self-righteous, superior

smuggler *n* **1** = **trafficker**, bootlegger, contrabandist, gentleman, moonshiner (*US*), rum-runner, runner, wrecker

smutty *adj* **3** = **obscene**, bawdy, blue, coarse, crude, dirty, filthy, improper, indecent, indelicate, lewd, off colour, pornographic, prurient, racy, raunchy (*US sl.*), risqué, salacious, suggestive, vulgar, X-rated (*inf.*)

snack *n* **1** = **light meal**, bite, bite to eat, break, elevenses (*Brit. inf.*), nibble, refreshment(s), titbit

snag[1] *n* **1** = **difficulty**, catch, complication, disadvantage, downside, drawback, hazard, hitch, inconvenience, obstacle, problem, stumbling block, the rub ◆ *vb* **7** = **catch**, hole, rip, tear

snaky *adj* **1** = **twisting**, convoluted, serpentine, sinuous, tortuous, twisty, writhing **2** = **treacherous**, crafty, insidious, perfidious, sly, venomous

snap *vb* **1** = **break**, come apart, crack, give way, separate **2** = **crackle**, click, pop **7** = **bite at**, bite, catch, grip, nip, seize, snatch **8** = **speak sharply**, bark, flash, fly off the handle at (*inf.*), growl, jump down (someone's) throat (*inf.*), lash out at, retort, snarl **11 snap one's fingers at** *Informal* = **defy**, cock a snook at (*Brit.*), flout, pay no attention to, scorn, set at naught, wave two fingers at (*sl.*) **12 snap out of it** *Informal* = **get over**, cheer up, get a grip on oneself, liven up, perk up, pull oneself together (*inf.*), recover ◆ *n* **14** = **crackle**, pop **16** = **bite**, grab, nip **19** *Informal* = **liveliness**, energy, get-up-and-go (*inf.*), go (*inf.*), pep, pizzazz *or* pizazz (*inf.*), vigour, zip (*inf.*) **24** *modifier* = **instant**, abrupt, immediate, spur-of-the-moment, sudden, unpremeditated

snapping turtle *n* any large aggressive North American river turtle having powerful hooked jaws and a rough shell. Also called: **snapper.**

snappy ❶ ('snæpɪ) *adj* **snappier, snappiest. 1** Also: **snappish.** apt to speak sharply or irritably. **2** Also: **snappish.** apt to snap or bite. **3** crackling in sound: *a snappy fire.* **4** brisk, sharp, or chilly: *a snappy pace.* **5** smart and fashionable: *a snappy dresser.* **6 make it snappy.** *Sl.* hurry up!
▸**'snappily** *adv* ▸**'snappiness** *n*

snap ring *n Mountaineering.* another name for **karabiner.**

snapshot ('snæp,ʃɒt) *n* an informal photograph taken with a simple camera. Often shortened to **snap.**

snap shot *n Sport.* a sudden, fast shot at goal.

snap up ❶ *vb* (*tr, adv*) **1** to avail oneself of eagerly and quickly: *she snapped up the bargains.* **2** to interrupt abruptly.

snare[1] ❶ (snɛə) *n* **1** a device for trapping birds or small animals, esp. a flexible loop that is drawn tight around the prey. **2** a surgical instrument for removing certain tumours, consisting of a wire loop that may be drawn tight around their base to sever them. **3** anything that traps or entangles someone or something unawares. ◆ *vb* **snares, snaring, snared.** (*tr*) **4** to catch (birds or small animals) with a snare. **5** to catch or trap in or as if in a snare. [OE *sneare*]
▸**'snarer** *n*

snare[2] (snɛə) *n Music.* a set of gut strings wound with wire fitted against the lower drumhead of a snare drum. They produce a rattling sound when the drum is beaten. [C17: from MDu. *snaer* or MLow G *snare* string]

snare drum *n Music.* a cylindrical drum with two drumheads, the upper of which is struck and the lower fitted with a snare. See **snare**[2].

snarl[1] ❶ (snɑːl) *vb* **1** (*intr*) (of an animal) to growl viciously, baring the teeth. **2** to speak or express (something) viciously. ◆ *n* **3** a vicious growl or facial expression. **4** the act of snarling. [C16: of Gmc origin]
▸**'snarler** *n* ▸**'snarling** *adj* ▸**'snarly** *adj*

snarl[2] ❶ (snɑːl) *n* **1** a tangled mass of thread, hair, etc. **2** a complicated or confused state or situation. **3** a knot in wood. ◆ *vb* **4** (often foll. by *up*) to be, become, or make tangled or complicated. **5** (*tr;* often foll. by *up*) to confuse mentally. **6** (*tr*) to emboss (metal) by hammering on a tool held against the under surface. [C14: from ON]
▸**'snarler** *n* ▸**'snarly** *adj*

snarl-up ❶ *n Inf., chiefly Brit.* a confusion, obstruction, or tangle, esp. a traffic jam.

snatch ❶ (snætʃ) *vb* **1** (*tr*) to seize or grasp (something) suddenly or peremptorily: *he snatched the chocolate.* **2** (*intr;* usually foll. by *at*) to seize or attempt to seize suddenly. **3** (*tr*) to take hurriedly: *to snatch some sleep.* **4** (*tr*) to remove suddenly: *she snatched her hand away.* **5** (*tr*) to gain, win, or rescue, esp. narrowly: *they snatched victory in the closing seconds.* ◆ *n* **6** an act of snatching. **7** a fragment or incomplete part: *snatches of conversation.* **8** a brief spell: *snatches of time off.* **9** *Weightlifting.* a lift in which the weight is raised in one quick motion from the floor to an overhead position. **10** *Sl., chiefly US.* an act of kidnapping. **11** *Brit. sl.* a robbery: *a diamond snatch.* [C13 *snacchen*]
▸**'snatcher** *n*

snatchy ('snætʃɪ) *adj* **snatchier, snatchiest.** disconnected or spasmodic.
▸**'snatchily** *adv*

snazzy ❶ ('snæzɪ) *adj* **snazzier, snazziest.** *Inf.* (esp. of clothes) stylishly and often flashily attractive. [C20: ?from SN(APPY + J)AZZY]
▸**'snazzily** *adv* ▸**'snazziness** *n*

sneak ❶ (sniːk) *vb* **1** (*intr;* often foll. by *along, off, in,* etc.) to move furtively. **2** (*intr*) to behave in a cowardly or underhand manner. **3** (*tr*) to bring, take, or put stealthily. **4** (*intr*) *Inf., chiefly Brit.* to tell tales (esp. in schools). **5** (*tr*) *Inf.* to steal. **6** (*intr;* foll. by *off, out, away,* etc.) *Inf.* to leave unobtrusively. ◆ *n* **7** a person who acts in an underhand or cowardly manner, esp. as an informer. **8a** a stealthy act. **8b** (*as modifier*): *a sneak attack.* [OE *snīcan* to creep]
▸**'sneaky** *adj* ▸**'sneakily** *adv* ▸**'sneakiness** *n*

sneakers ('sniːkəz) *pl n Chiefly US & Canad.* canvas shoes with rubber soles worn informally.

sneaking ❶ ('sniːkɪŋ) *adj* **1** acting in a furtive or cowardly way. **2** secret: *a sneaking desire to marry a millionaire.* **3** slight but nagging (esp. in **a sneaking suspicion**).
▸**'sneakingly** *adv*

sneak thief *n* a person who steals paltry articles from premises, which he enters through open doors, windows, etc.

sneer ❶ (snɪə) *n* **1** a facial expression of scorn or contempt, typically with the upper lip curled. **2** a scornful or contemptuous remark or utterance. ◆ *vb* **3** (*intr*) to assume a facial expression of scorn or contempt. **4** to say or utter (something) in a scornful manner. [C16: ?from Low Du.]
▸**'sneerer** *n* ▸**'sneering** *adj, n*

sneeze ❶ (sniːz) *vb* **sneezes, sneezing, sneezed. 1** (*intr*) to expel air from the nose involuntarily, esp. as the result of irritation of the nasal mucous membrane. ◆ *n* **2** the act or sound of sneezing. [OE *fnēosan* (unattested)]
▸**'sneezer** *n* ▸**'sneezy** *adj*

sneeze at *vb* (*intr, prep;* usually with a negative) *Inf.* to dismiss lightly: *his offer is not to be sneezed at.*

sneezewood ('sniːz,wʊd) *n* **1** a South African tree. **2** its exceptionally hard wood, used for furniture, gateposts and railway sleepers.

sneezewort ('sniːz,wɜːt) *n* a Eurasian plant having daisy-like flowers and long grey-green leaves, which cause sneezing when powdered.

snick (snɪk) *n* **1** a small cut; notch. **2** *Cricket.* **2a** a glancing blow off the edge of the bat. **2b** the ball so hit. ◆ *vb* (*tr*) **3** to cut a small corner or notch in (material, etc.). **4** *Cricket.* to hit (the ball) with a snick. [C18: prob. of Scand. origin]

snicker ('snɪkə) *n, vb* **1** another word (esp. US and Canad.) for **snigger.** ◆ *vb* **2** (*intr*) (of a horse) to whinny. [C17: prob. imit.]

snide ❶ (snaɪd) *adj* **1** Also: **snidey** ('snaɪdɪ). (of a remark, etc.) maliciously derogatory. **2** counterfeit. ◆ *n* **3** *Sl.* sham jewellery. [C19: from ?]
▸**'snidely** *adv* ▸**'snideness** *n*

sniff ❶ (snɪf) *vb* **1** to inhale through the nose, usually in short rapid audible inspirations, as for clearing a congested nasal passage or for taking a drug. **2** (when *intr,* often foll. by *at*) to perceive or attempt to perceive (a smell) by inhaling through the nose. ◆ *n* **3** the act or sound of sniffing. **4** a smell perceived by sniffing, esp. a faint scent. ◆ See also **sniff at, sniff out.** [C14: prob. rel. to *snivelen* to snivel]
▸**'sniffer** *n* ▸**'sniffing** *n, adj*

sniff at *vb* (*intr, prep*) to express contempt or dislike for.

sniffer dog *n* a police dog trained to detect drugs or explosives by smell.

sniffle ('snɪfᵊl) *vb* **sniffles, sniffling, sniffled. 1** (*intr*) to breathe audibly through the nose, as when the nasal passages are congested. ◆ *n* **2** the act, sound, or an instance of sniffling.
▸**'sniffler** *n* ▸**'sniffly** *adj*

sniffles ('snɪfᵊlz) *or* **snuffles** *pl n Inf.* **the.** a cold in the head.

sniff out *vb* (*tr, adv*) to detect through shrewdness or instinct.

sniffy ❶ ('snɪfɪ) *adj* **sniffier, sniffiest.** *Inf.* contemptuous or disdainful.
▸**'sniffily** *adv* ▸**'sniffiness** *n*

snifter ('snɪftə) *n* **1** a pear-shaped glass with a bowl that narrows towards the top so that the aroma of brandy or a liqueur is retained. **2** *Inf.* a small quantity of alcoholic drink. [C19: ?from dialect *snifter* to sniff, ? of Scand. origin]

snig (snɪg) *vb* **snigs, snigging, snigged.** (*tr*) *NZ.* to drag (a felled log) by a chain or cable. [from E dialect]

snigger ❶ ('snɪgə) *n* **1** a sly or disrespectful laugh, esp. one partly stifled. ◆ *vb* (*intr*) **2** to utter such a laugh. [C18: var. of SNICKER]
▸**'sniggering** *n, adj*

snigging chain *n Austral. & NZ.* a chain attached to a log when being hauled out of the bush.

snip ❶ (snɪp) *vb* **snips, snipping, snipped. 1** to cut or clip with a small quick stroke or a succession of small quick strokes, esp. with scissors or shears. ◆ *n* **2** the act of snipping. **3** the sound of scissors or shears closing. **4** Also called: **snipping.** a small piece of anything. **5** a small cut made by snipping. **6** *Chiefly Brit.* an informal word for **bargain. 7** *Inf.*

THESAURUS

snappy *adj* **1 = irritable,** cross, edgy, hasty, impatient, like a bear with a sore head (*inf.*), quick-tempered, ratty (*Brit. & NZ inf.*), snappish, tart, testy, tetchy, touchy, waspish **5 = smart,** chic, dapper, fashionable, modish, natty, stylish, trendy (*Brit. inf.*), up-to-the-minute, voguish **6 make it snappy = hurry (up),** be quick, buck up (*inf.*), get a move on (*inf.*), get one's skates on, look lively, make haste

snap up *vb* **1 = take advantage of,** avail oneself of, grab, grasp, nab (*inf.*), pounce upon, seize, swoop down on

snare[1] *n* **1 = trap,** catch, gin, net, noose, pitfall, springe, wire ◆ *vb* **4 = trap,** catch, entrap, net, seize, springe, trepan (*arch.*), wire

snarl[1] *vb* **1 = growl,** show one's teeth (*of an animal*)

snarl[2] *vb* **4, 5** *often with* **up = tangle,** complicate, confuse, embroil, enmesh, entangle, entwine, muddle, ravel

snarl-up *n* **= tangle,** confusion, entanglement, muddle, (traffic) jam

snatch *vb* **1 = seize,** catch up, clutch, gain, grab, grasp, grip, make off with, pluck, pull, rescue, take, win, wrench, wrest ◆ *n* **7, 8 = bit,** fragment, part, piece, smattering, snippet, spell

snazzy *adj Informal* **= stylish,** attractive, dashing, flamboyant, flashy, jazzy (*inf.*), raffish, ritzy (*sl.*), showy, smart, sophisticated, sporty, swinging (*sl.*), with it (*inf.*)

sneak *vb* **1 = slink,** cower, lurk, pad, sidle, skulk, slip, steal **3 = slip,** smuggle, spirit **4** *Informal, chiefly Brit.* **= inform on,** grass on, peach (*sl.*), shop (*sl., chiefly Brit.*), sing (*sl., chiefly US*), spill one's guts (*sl.*), tell on (*inf.*), tell tales ◆ *n* **7 = informer,** snake in the grass, telltale ◆ *modifier* **8b = surprise,** clandestine, furtive, quick, secret, stealthy

sneaking *adj* **1 = underhand,** contemptible, furtive, mean, sly, sneaky, surreptitious, two-faced **2 = secret,** hidden, private, suppressed, unavowed, unconfessed, undivulged, unexpressed, unvoiced **3 = nagging,** intuitive, niggling, persistent, uncomfortable, worrying

sneaky *adj* **7 = sly,** base, contemptible, cowardly, deceitful, devious, dishonest, disingenuous, double-dealing, furtive, low, malicious, mean, nasty, shifty, slippery, snide, unreliable, unscrupulous, untrustworthy

sneer *n* **2 = scorn,** derision, disdain, gibe, jeer, mockery, ridicule, snigger ◆ *vb* **3 = scorn,** curl one's lip, deride, disdain, gibe, hold in contempt, hold up to ridicule, jeer, laugh, look down on, mock, ridicule, scoff, sniff at, snigger, turn up one's nose (*inf.*)

sneeze *n* **2 = sternutation**

snide *adj* **1 = nasty,** cynical, disparaging, hurtful, ill-natured, insinuating, malicious, mean, sarcastic, scornful, shrewish, sneering, spiteful, unkind

sniff *vb* **1 = inhale,** breathe, smell, snuff, snuffle

sniffy *adj Informal* **= contemptuous,** condescending, disdainful, haughty, scornful, supercilious, superior

snigger *n* **1 = laugh,** giggle, smirk, sneer, snicker, titter ◆ *vb* **2 = laugh,** giggle, smirk, sneer, snicker, titter

snip *vb* **1 = cut,** clip, crop, dock, nick, nip off,

something easily done; cinch. ◆ See also **snips.** [C16: from Low G, Du. *snippen*]

snipe ➊ (snaɪp) *n, pl* **snipe** *or* **snipes. 1** any of a genus of birds, such as the common snipe, of marshes and river banks, having a long straight bill. **2** a shot, esp. a gunshot, fired from a place of concealment. ◆ *vb* **snipes, sniping, sniped. 3** (when *intr*, often foll. by *at*) to attack (a person or persons) with a rifle from a place of concealment. **4** (*intr;* often foll. by *at*) to criticize a person or persons from a position of security. **5** (*intr*) to hunt or shoot snipe. [C14: from ON *snīpa*]
▸ **'sniper** *n*

snipefish ('snaɪp,fɪʃ) *n, pl* **snipefish** *or* **snipefishes.** a teleost fish of tropical and temperate seas, having a deep body, long snout, and a single long dorsal fin. Also called: **bellows fish.**

snippet ➊ ('snɪpɪt) *n* a small scrap or fragment of fabric, news, etc.
▸ **'snippetiness** *n* ▸ **'snippety** *adj*

snips (snɪps) *pl n* a small pair of shears used for cutting sheet metal.

snitch (snɪtʃ) *Sl.* ◆ *vb* **1** (*tr*) to steal; take, esp. in an underhand way. **2** (*intr*) to act as an informer. ◆ *n* **3** an informer. **4** the nose. [C17: from ?]

snitchy ('snɪtʃɪ) *adj* **snitchier, snitchiest.** *NZ inf.* bad-tempered or irritable.

snivel ➊ ('snɪvᵊl) *vb* **snivels, snivelling, snivelled** *or US* **snivels, sniveling, sniveled. 1** (*intr*) to sniffle as a sign of distress. **2** to utter (something) tearfully; whine. **3** (*intr*) to have a runny nose. ◆ *n* **4** an instance of snivelling. [C14 *snivelen*]
▸ **'sniveller** *n* ▸ **'snivelling** *adj, n*

snob ➊ (snɒb) *n* **1a** a person who strives to associate with those of higher social status and who behaves condescendingly to others. **1b** (*as modifier*): *snob appeal.* **2** a person having similar pretensions with regard to his tastes, etc.: *an intellectual snob.* [C18 (in the sense: shoemaker; hence, C19: a person who flatters those of higher station, etc.): from ?]
▸ **'snobbery** *n* ▸ **'snobbish** *adj* ▸ **'snobbishly** *adv*

SNOBOL ('snəʊbɒl) *n* String Oriented Symbolic Language: a computer-programming language for handling strings of symbols.

Sno-Cat ('snəʊ,kæt) *n Trademark.* a type of snowmobile.

snoek (snʊk) *n* a South African edible marine fish. [Afrik., from Du. *snoek* pike]

snog (snɒg) *Brit. sl.* ◆ *vb* **snogs, snogging, snogged. 1** to kiss and cuddle (someone). ◆ *n* **2** the act of kissing and cuddling. [from ?]

snood (snu:d) *n* **1** a pouchlike hat, often of net, loosely holding a woman's hair at the back. **2** a headband, esp. one formerly worn by young unmarried women in Scotland. [OE *snōd;* from ?]

snook[1] (snu:k) *n, pl* **snook** *or* **snooks. 1** any of a genus of large game fishes of tropical American marine and fresh waters. **2** *Austral.* the sea pike. [C17: from Du. *snoek* pike]

snook[2] (snu:k) *n Brit.* a rude gesture, made by putting one thumb to the nose with the fingers of the hand outstretched (esp. in **cock a snook**). [C19: from ?]

snooker ('snu:kə) *n* **1** a game played on a billiard table with 15 red balls, six balls of other colours, and a white cue ball. The object is to pot the balls in a certain order. **2** a shot in which the cue ball is left in a position such that another ball blocks the target ball. ◆ *vb* (*tr*) **3** to leave (an opponent) in an unfavourable position by playing a snooker. **4** to place (someone) in a difficult situation. **5** (*often passive*) to thwart; defeat. [C19: from ?]

snoop ➊ (snu:p) *Inf.* ◆ *vb* **1** (*intr;* often foll. by *about* or *around*) to pry into the private business of others. ◆ *n* **2** a person who pries into the business of others. **3** an act or instance of snooping. [C19: from Du. *snoepen* to eat furtively]
▸ **'snooper** *n* ▸ **'snoopy** *adj*

snooperscope ('snu:pə,skəʊp) *n Mil., US.* an instrument that enables the user to see objects in the dark by illuminating the object with infrared radiation.

snoot (snu:t) *n Sl.* the nose. [C20: var. of SNOUT]

snooty ➊ ('snu:tɪ) *adj* **snootier, snootiest.** *Inf.* **1** aloof or supercilious. **2** snobbish: *a snooty restaurant.*
▸ **'snootily** *adv* ▸ **'snootiness** *n*

snooze ➊ (snu:z) *Inf.* ◆ *vb* **snoozes, snoozing, snoozed. 1** (*intr*) to take a brief light sleep. ◆ *n* **2** a nap. [C18: from ?]
▸ **'snoozer** *n* ▸ **'snoozy** *adj*

snore (snɔ:) *vb* **snores, snoring, snored. 1** (*intr*) to breathe through the mouth and nose while asleep with snorting sounds caused by the soft palate vibrating. ◆ *n* **2** the act or sound of snoring. [C14: imit.]
▸ **'snorer** *n*

snorkel ('snɔ:kᵊl) *n* **1** a device allowing a swimmer to breathe while face down on the surface of the water, consisting of a bent tube fitting into the mouth and projecting above the surface. **2** (on a submarine) a retractable vertical device containing air-intake and exhaust pipes for the engines and general ventilation. ◆ *vb* **snorkels, snorkelling, snorkelled** *or US* **snorkels, snorkeling, snorkeled. 3** (*intr*) to swim with a snorkel. [C20: from G *Schnorchel*]

snort (snɔ:t) *vb* **1** (*intr*) to exhale forcibly through the nostrils, making a characteristic noise. **2** (*intr*) (of a person) to express contempt or annoyance by such an exhalation. **3** (*tr*) to utter in a contemptuous or annoyed manner. **4** *Sl.* to inhale (a powdered drug) through the nostrils. ◆ *n* **5** a forcible exhalation of air through the nostrils, esp. (of persons) as a noise of contempt. **6** *Sl.* an instance of snorting a drug. [C14 *snorten*]
▸ **'snorting** *n, adj* ▸ **'snortingly** *adv*

snorter ('snɔ:tə) *n* **1** a person or animal that snorts. **2** *Brit. sl.* something outstandingly impressive or difficult.

snot (snɒt) *n* (*usually considered vulgar*) **1** nasal mucus or discharge. **2** *Sl.* a contemptible person. [OE *gesnot*]

snotty ('snɒtɪ) *adj* **snottier, snottiest.** (*considered vulgar*) **1** dirty with nasal discharge. **2** *Sl.* contemptible; nasty. **3** snobbish; conceited.
▸ **'snottily** *adv* ▸ **'snottiness** *n*

snout (snaʊt) *n* **1** the part of the head of a vertebrate, esp. a mammal, consisting of the nose, jaws, and surrounding region. **2** the corresponding part of the head of such insects as weevils. **3** anything projecting like a snout, such as a nozzle. **4** *Sl.* a person's nose. **5** *Brit. sl.* a cigarette or tobacco. **6** *Sl.* an informer. [C13: of Gmc origin]
▸ **'snouted** *adj* ▸ **'snoutless** *adj* ▸ **'snout,like** *adj*

snout beetle *n* another name for **weevil.**

snow (snəʊ) *n* **1** precipitation from clouds in the form of flakes of ice crystals formed in the upper atmosphere. **2** a layer of snowflakes on the ground. **3** a fall of such precipitation. **4** anything resembling snow in whiteness, softness, etc. **5** the random pattern of white spots on a television or radar screen, occurring when the signal is weak. **6** *Sl.* cocaine. ◆ *vb* **7** (*intr,* with *it* as subject) to be the case that snow is falling. **8** (*tr;* usually passive, foll. by *over, under, in,* or *up*) to cover or confine with a heavy fall of snow. **9** (often with *it* as subject) to fall or cause to fall as or like snow. **10** (*tr*) *US & Canad. sl.* to overwhelm with elaborate often insincere talk. **11 be snowed under.** to be overwhelmed, esp. with paperwork. [OE *snāw*]
▸ **'snowless** *adj* ▸ **'snow,like** *adj*

snowball ('snəʊ,bɔ:l) *n* **1** snow pressed into a ball for throwing, as in play. **2** a drink made of advocaat and lemonade. ◆ *vb* **3** (*intr*) to increase rapidly in size, importance, etc. **4** (*tr*) to throw snowballs at.

snowball tree *n* any of several shrubs of the genus *Viburnum,* with spherical clusters of white or pinkish flowers.

snowberry ('snəʊbərɪ) *n, pl* **snowberries. 1** a shrub cultivated for its small pink flowers and white berries. **2** Also called: **waxberry.** any of the berries of such a plant.

snow-blind *adj* having temporarily impaired vision because of the intense reflection of sunlight from snow.
▸ **snow blindness** *n*

snowblower ('snəʊ,bləʊə) *n* a snow-clearing machine that draws the snow in and blows it away.

snowboard ('snəʊ,bɔ:d) *n* a shaped board, resembling a skateboard without wheels, on which a person can stand to slide across snow. [C20: on the model of SURFBOARD]
▸ **'snow,boarding** *n*

snowbound ('snəʊ,baʊnd) *adj* confined to one place by heavy falls or drifts of snow; snowed in.

snow bunting *n* a bunting of northern and arctic regions, having a white plumage with dark markings on the wings, back, and tail.

snowcap ('snəʊ,kæp) *n* a cap of snow, as on top of a mountain.
▸ **'snow,capped** *adj*

snowdrift ('snəʊ,drɪft) *n* a bank of deep snow driven together by the wind.

snowdrop ('snəʊ,drɒp) *n* a Eurasian plant having drooping white bell-shaped flowers that bloom in early spring.

snowfall ('snəʊ,fɔ:l) *n* **1** a fall of snow. **2** *Meteorol.* the amount of snow received in a specified place and time.

snow fence *n* a lath-and-wire fence put up in winter beside windy roads to prevent snowdrifts.

snowfield ('snəʊ,fi:ld) *n* a large area of permanent snow.

snowflake ('snəʊ,fleɪk) *n* **1** one of the mass of small thin delicate ar-

THESAURUS

notch, shave, trim ◆ *n* **4** = **bit,** clipping, fragment, piece, scrap, shred, snippet **6** *Informal, chiefly Brit.* = **bargain,** giveaway, good buy, steal (*inf.*)

snipe *vb* **4** = **criticize,** bitch, carp, denigrate, disparage, have a go (at) (*inf.*), jeer, knock (*inf.*), put down

snippet *n* = **piece,** fragment, part, particle, scrap, shred, snatch

snivel *vb* **1, 2** = **whine,** blubber, cry, gripe (*inf.*), grizzle (*inf., chiefly Brit.*), mewl, moan, sniffle, snuffle, weep, whimper, whinge (*inf.*)

snob *n* **1, 2** = **elitist,** highbrow, prig, social climber

snobbery *n* **1, 2** = **arrogance,** airs, condescension, pretension, pride, side (*Brit. sl.*), snobbishness, snootiness (*inf.*), uppishness (*Brit. inf.*)

snobbish *adj* **1, 2** = **superior,** arrogant, condescending, high and mighty (*inf.*), high-hat (*inf., chiefly US*), hoity-toity (*inf.*), patronizing, pretentious, snooty (*inf.*), stuck-up (*inf.*), toffee-nosed (*sl., chiefly Brit.*), uppish (*Brit. inf.*), uppity
Antonyms *adj* down to earth, humble, modest, natural, unassuming, unostentatious, unpretentious, without airs

snoop *vb* **1** = **pry,** interfere, poke one's nose in (*inf.*), spy

snooper *n* **1** = **nosy parker** (*inf.*), busybody, meddler, Paul Pry, pry, snoop (*inf.*), stickybeak (*Austral. inf.*)

snooty *adj* **1, 2** = **snobbish,** aloof, condescending, disdainful, haughty, high and mighty (*inf.*), high-hat (*inf., chiefly US*), hoity-toity (*inf.*), pretentious, proud, snotty, stuck-up (*inf.*), supercilious, superior, toffee-nosed (*sl., chiefly Brit*), toplofty (*inf.*), uppish (*Brit. inf.*), uppity
Antonyms *adj* down to earth, humble, modest, natural, unassuming, unpretentious, without airs

snooze *Informal vb* **1** = **doze,** catnap, drop off (*inf.*), drowse, kip (*Brit. sl.*), nap, nod off (*inf.*), take forty winks (*inf.*) ◆ *n* **2** = **doze,** catnap, forty winks (*inf.*), kip (*Brit. sl.*), nap, siesta rangements of ice crystals that fall as snow. **2** any of various European plants that have white nodding bell-shaped flowers.

snow goose *n* a North American goose having a white plumage with black wing tips.

snow gum *n* any of several eucalypts of mountainous regions of SE Australia.

snow-in-summer *n* a plant of SE Europe and Asia having white flowers and downy stems and leaves: cultivated as a rock plant.

snow leopard *n* a large feline mammal of mountainous regions of central Asia, closely related to the leopard but having a long pale brown coat marked with black rosettes.

snow lily *n Canad.* another name for **dogtooth violet.**

snow line *n* the altitudinal or latitudinal limit of permanent snow.

snowman ('snəʊˌmæn) *n, pl* **snowmen.** a figure resembling a man, made of packed snow.

snowmobile ('snəʊməˌbiːl) *n* a motor vehicle for travelling on snow, esp. one with caterpillar tracks and front skis.

snowplough *or esp. US* **snowplow** ('snəʊˌplaʊ) *n* an implement or vehicle for clearing away snow.

snowshoe ('snəʊˌʃuː) *n* **1** a device to facilitate walking on snow, esp. a racket-shaped frame with a network of thongs stretched across it. ◆ *vb* **snowshoes, snowshoeing, snowshoed. 2** (*intr*) to walk or go using snowshoes.
▸ **'snowˌshoer** *n*

snowstorm ('snəʊˌstɔːm) *n* a storm with heavy snow.

snow tyre *n* a motor-vehicle tyre with deep treads to give improved grip on snow and ice.

snow-white *adj* **1** white as snow. **2** pure as white snow.

snowy ('snəʊɪ) *adj* **snowier, snowiest. 1** covered with or abounding in snow: *snowy hills.* **2** characterized by snow: *snowy weather.* **3** resembling snow in whiteness, purity, etc.
▸ **'snowily** *adv* ▸ **'snowiness** *n*

snowy owl *n* a large owl of tundra regions, having a white plumage flecked with brown.

SNP *abbrev. for* Scottish National Party.

Snr *or* **snr** *abbrev. for* senior.

snub ❶ (snʌb) *vb* **snubs, snubbing, snubbed.** (*tr*) **1** to insult (someone) deliberately. **2** to stop or check the motion of (a boat, horse, etc.) by taking turns of a rope around a post. ◆ *n* **3** a deliberately insulting act or remark. **4** *Naut.* an elastic shock absorber attached to a mooring line. ◆ *adj* **5** short and blunt. See also **snub-nosed.** [C14: from ON *snubba* to scold]
▸ **'snubber** *n* ▸ **'snubby** *adj*

snub-nosed *adj* **1** having a short turned-up nose. **2** (of a pistol) having an extremely short barrel.

snuff[1] (snʌf) *vb* **1** (*tr*) to inhale through the nose. **2** (when *intr*, often foll. by *at*) (esp. of an animal) to examine by sniffing. ◆ *n* **3** an act or the sound of snuffing. [C16: prob. from MDu. *snuffen* to snuffle, ult. imit.]
▸ **'snuffer** *n*

snuff[2] (snʌf) *n* **1** finely powdered tobacco, esp. for sniffing up the nostrils. **2** a small amount of this. **3 up to snuff.** *Inf.* **3a** in good health or in good condition. **3b** *Chiefly Brit.* not easily deceived. ◆ *vb* **4** (*intr*) to use or inhale snuff. [C17: from Du. *snuf*, shortened from *snuftabale*, lit.: tobacco for snuffing]

snuff[3] (snʌf) *vb* (*tr*) **1** (often foll. by *out*) to extinguish (a light from a candle). **2** to cut off the charred part of (the wick of a candle, etc.). **3** (usually foll. by *out*) *Inf.* to put an end to. **4 snuff it.** *Brit. inf.* to die. ◆ *n* **5** the burned portion of the wick of a candle. [C14 *snoffe*, from ?]

snuffbox ('snʌfˌbɒks) *n* a container, often of elaborate ornamental design, for holding small quantities of snuff.

snuff-dipping *n* the practice of absorbing nicotine by holding in one's mouth, between the cheek and the gum, a small amount of tobacco.

snuffer ('snʌfə) *n* **1** a cone-shaped implement for extinguishing candles. **2** (*pl*) an instrument resembling a pair of scissors for trimming the wick or extinguishing the flame of a candle.

snuffle ('snʌfᵊl) *vb* **snuffles, snuffling, snuffled. 1** (*intr*) to breathe noisily or with difficulty. **2** to say or speak in a nasal tone. **3** (*intr*) to snivel. ◆ *n* **4** an act or the sound of snuffling. **5** a nasal voice. **6 the snuffles.** a condition characterized by snuffling. [C16: from Low G or Du. *snuffelen*]
▸ **'snuffly** *adj*

snuff movie *or* **film** *n Sl.* a pornographic film in which an unsuspecting actress or actor is murdered as the climax of the film.

snuffy ('snʌfɪ) *adj* **snuffier, snuffiest. 1** of or resembling snuff. **2** covered with or smelling of snuff. **3** disagreeable.
▸ **'snuffiness** *n*

snug ❶ (snʌg) *adj* **snugger, snuggest. 1** comfortably warm and well protected; cosy: *the children were snug in bed.* **2** small but comfortable: *a snug cottage.* **3** well ordered; compact: *a snug boat.* **4** sheltered and secure: *a snug anchorage.* **5** fitting closely and comfortably. **6** offering safe concealment. ◆ *n* **7** (in Britain and Ireland) one of the bars in certain pubs, offering intimate seating for only a few persons. ◆ *vb* **snugs, snugging, snugged. 8** to make or become comfortable and warm. [C16 (in the sense: prepared for storms (used of a ship)) from O Icelandic *snǒggr* short-haired, from Swedish *snygg* tidy]
▸ **'snugly** *adv* ▸ **'snugness** *n*

snuggery ('snʌgərɪ) *n, pl* **snuggeries. 1** a cosy and comfortable place or room. **2** another name for **snug** (sense 7).

snuggle ❶ ('snʌgᵊl) *vb* **snuggles, snuggling, snuggled. 1** (usually *intr;* usually foll. by *down, up,* or *together*) to nestle into or draw close to (somebody or something) for warmth or from affection. ◆ *n* **2** the act of snuggling. [C17: frequentative of SNUG (vb)]

so[1] (səʊ) *adv* **1** (foll. by an adjective or adverb and a correlative clause often introduced by *that*) to such an extent: *the river is so dirty that it smells.* **2** (*used with a negative;* it replaces the first *as* in an equative comparison) to the same extent as: *she is not so old as you.* **3** (intensifier): *it's so lovely.* **4** in the state or manner expressed or implied: *they're happy and will remain so.* **5** (*not used with a negative;* foll. by an auxiliary verb or *do, have,* or *be* used as main verbs) also: *I can speak Spanish and so can you.* **6** *Dialect.* indeed: used to contradict a negative statement: *"you didn't phone her." "I did so!"* **7** *Arch.* provided that. **8 and so on** *or* **forth.** and continuing similarly. **9 or so.** approximately: *fifty or so people came to see me.* **10 so be it.** used to express agreement or resignation. **11 so much. 11a** a certain degree or amount (of). **11b** a lot (of): *it's just so much nonsense.* **12 so much for. 12a** no more can or need be said about. **12b** used to express contempt for something that has failed. ◆ *conj* (*subordinating;* often foll. by *that*) **13** in order (that): *to die so that you might live.* **14** with the consequence (that): *he was late home, so that there was trouble.* **15 so as.** (*takes an infinitive*) in order (to): *to diet so as to lose weight.* ◆ *sentence connector.* **16** in consequence: *she wasn't needed, so she left.* **17** thereupon: *and so we ended up in France.* **18 so what!** *Inf.* what importance does that have? ◆ *pron* **19** used to substitute for a clause or sentence, which may be understood: *you'll stop because I said so.* ◆ *adj* **20** (used with *is, was,* etc.) factual: *it can't be so.* ◆ *interj* **21** an exclamation of surprise, etc. [OE *swā*]

so[2] (səʊ) *n Music.* a variant spelling of **soh.**

> **USAGE NOTE** In formal English, *so* is not used as a conjunction, to indicate either purpose (*he left by a back door so he could avoid photographers*) or result (*the project was abandoned so his services were no longer needed*). In the former case *to* or *in order to* should be used instead, and in the latter case *and so* or *and therefore.*

So. *abbrev. for* south(ern).

soak ❶ (səʊk) *vb* **1** to make, become, or be thoroughly wet or saturated, esp. by immersion in a liquid. **2** (when *intr*, usually foll. by *in* or *into*) (of a liquid) to penetrate or permeate. **3** (*tr;* usually foll. by *in* or *up*) (of a permeable solid) to take in (a liquid) by absorption: *the earth soaks up rainwater.* **4** (*tr;* foll. by *out* or *out of*) to remove by immersion in a liquid: *she soaked the stains out of the dress.* **5** *Inf.* to drink excessively or make or become drunk. **6** (*tr*) *Sl.* to overcharge. ◆ *n* **7** the act of immersing in a liquid or the period of immersion. **8** the liquid in which something may be soaked. **9** *Austral.* a natural depression holding rainwater, esp. just beneath the surface of the ground. **10** *Sl.* a person who drinks to excess. [OE *sōcian* to cook]
▸ **'soaker** *n* ▸ **'soaking** *n, adj* ▸ **'soakingly** *adv*

soakaway ('səʊkəˌweɪ) *n* a pit filled with rubble, etc., into which waste water drains.

so-and-so *n, pl* **so-and-sos.** *Inf.* **1** a person whose name is forgotten or ignored. **2** *Euphemistic.* a person or thing regarded as unpleasant: *which so-and-so broke my razor?*

soap (səʊp) *n* **1** a cleaning agent made by reacting animal or vegetable fats or oils with potassium or sodium hydroxide. Soaps act by emulsifying grease and lowering the surface tension of water, so that it more readily penetrates open materials such as textiles. **2** any metallic salt of a fatty acid, such as palmitic or stearic acid. **3** *Sl.* flattery or persuasive talk (esp. in **soft soap**). **4** *Inf.* short for **soap opera. 5 no soap.** *Sl.* not possible. ◆ *vb* (*tr*) **6** to apply soap to. **7** (often foll. by *up*) *Sl.* to flatter. [OE *sāpe*]
▸ **'soapless** *adj* ▸ **'soapˌlike** *adj*

soapberry ('səʊpˌberɪ) *n, pl* **soapberries. 1** any of various chiefly tropical American trees having pulpy fruit containing saponin. **2** the fruit of any of these trees.

soapbox ('səʊpˌbɒks) *n* **1** a box or crate for packing soap. **2** a crate used as a platform for speech-making. **3** a child's home-made racing cart.

soap opera *n* a serialized drama, usually dealing with domestic themes, broadcast on radio or television. Often shortened to **soap.** [C20: so called because manufacturers of soap were typical sponsors]

soapstone ('səʊpˌstəʊn) *n* a massive compact soft variety of talc, used for making table tops, hearths, ornaments, etc. Also called: **steatite.**

THESAURUS

snub *vb* **1** = **insult**, cold-shoulder, cut, cut dead (*inf.*), give (someone) the brush-off (*sl.*), give (someone) the cold shoulder, humble, humiliate, kick in the teeth (*sl.*), mortify, put down, rebuff, shame, slight ◆ *n* **3** = **insult**, affront, brush-off (*sl.*), bum's rush (*sl.*), humiliation, put-down, slap in the face

snug *adj* **1** = **cosy**, comfortable, comfy (*inf.*), homely, intimate, sheltered, warm **5** = **close**, compact, neat, trim

snuggle *vb* **1** = **nestle**, cuddle, nuzzle

soak *vb* **1** = **wet**, bathe, damp, drench, immerse, infuse, marinate (*Cookery*), moisten, saturate, steep **2** = **penetrate**, permeate, seep **3** *with* **up** = **absorb**, assimilate, drink in, take in *or* up

soaking *adj* **1** = **soaked**, drenched, dripping, droukit *or* drookit (*Scot.*), like a drowned rat, saturated, soaked to the skin, sodden, sopping, streaming, waterlogged, wet through, wringing wet

soapsuds ('səʊpˌsʌdz) *pl n* foam or lather made from soap.
▸**'soapˌsudsy** *adj*

soapwort ('səʊpˌwɜːt) *n* a Eurasian plant having rounded clusters of fragrant pink or white flowers and leaves that were formerly used as a soap substitute. Also called: **bouncing Bet.**

soapy ('səʊpɪ) *adj* **soapier, soapiest. 1** containing or covered with soap: *soapy water.* **2** resembling or characteristic of soap. **3** *Sl.* flattering.
▸**'soapily** *adv* ▸**'soapiness** *n*

soar ❶ (sɔː) *vb (intr)* **1** to rise or fly upwards into the air. **2** (of a bird, aircraft, etc.) to glide while maintaining altitude by the use of ascending air currents. **3** to rise or increase in volume, size, etc.: *soaring prices.* [C14: from OF *essorer,* from Vulgar L *exaurāre* (unattested) to expose to the breezes, from L EX-[1] + *aura* breeze]
▸**'soarer** *n* ▸**'soaring** *n, adj* ▸**'soaringly** *adv*

sob ❶ (sɒb) *vb* **sobs, sobbing, sobbed. 1** *(intr)* to weep with convulsive gasps. **2** *(tr)* to utter with sobs. **3** to cause (oneself) to be in a specified state by sobbing: *to sob oneself to sleep.* ◆ *n* **4** a convulsive gasp made in weeping. [C12: prob. from Low G]
▸**'sobbing** *n, adj*

sober ❶ ('səʊbə) *adj* **1** not drunk. **2** not given to excessive indulgence in drink or any other activity. **3** sedate and rational: *a sober attitude to a problem.* **4** (of colours) plain and dull or subdued. **5** free from exaggeration or speculation: *he told us the sober truth.* ◆ *vb* **6** (usually foll. by *up*) to make or become less intoxicated. [C14 *sobre,* from OF, from L *sōbrius*]
▸**'sobering** *n, adj* ▸**'soberly** *adv*

sobriety ❶ (səʊ'braɪətɪ) *n* **1** the state or quality of being sober. **2** the quality of refraining from excess. **3** the quality of being serious or sedate.

sobriquet *or* **soubriquet** ('səʊbrɪˌkeɪ) *n* a humorous epithet, assumed name, or nickname. [C17: from F *soubriquet,* from ?]

sob story *n* a tale of personal distress intended to arouse sympathy.

Soc. *or* **soc.** *abbrev. for:* **1** socialist. **2** society.

soca ('səʊkə) *n* a mixture of soul and calypso music typical of the E Caribbean. [C20: a blend of *soul* + *calypso*]

socage ('sɒkɪdʒ) *n English legal history.* the tenure of land by certain services, esp. of an agricultural nature. [C14: from Anglo-F, from *soc* SOKE]

so-called ❶ *adj* **a** *(prenominal)* designated or styled by the name or word mentioned, esp. (in the speaker's opinion) incorrectly: *a so-called genius.* **b** (also used parenthetically after a noun): *these experts, so-called, are no help.*

soccer ('sɒkə) *n* **a** a game in which two teams of eleven players try to kick or head a ball into their opponents' goal, only the goalkeeper on either side being allowed to touch the ball with his hands and arms, except in the case of throw-ins. **b** *(as modifier): a soccer player.* ◆ Also called: **Association Football.** [C19: from *Assoc(iation Football)* + -ER[1]]

socceroo (ˌsɒkə'ruː) *n, pl* **socceroos.** *Austral. sl.* a member of the Australian national soccer team. [C20: from SOCCER + (KANGAR)OO]

sociable ❶ ('səʊʃəbᵊl) *adj* **1** friendly or companionable. **2** (of an occasion) providing the opportunity for friendliness and conviviality. ◆ *n* **3** *Chiefly US.* a social. **4** a type of open carriage with two seats facing each other. [C16: via F from L, from *sociāre* to unite, from *socius* an associate]
▸**ˌsocia'bility** *n* ▸**'sociably** *adv*

social ❶ ('səʊʃəl) *adj* **1** living or preferring to live in a community rather than alone. **2** denoting or relating to human society or any of its subdivisions. **3** of or characteristic of the behaviour and interaction of persons forming groups. **4** relating to or having the purpose of promoting companionship, communal activities, etc.: *a social club.* **5** relating to or engaged in social services: *a social worker.* **6** relating to or considered appropriate to a certain class of society. **7** (esp. of certain species of insects) living together in organized colonies: *social bees.* **8** (of plant species) growing in clumps. ◆ *n* **9** an informal gathering, esp. of an organized group. [C16: from L *sociālis* companionable, from *socius* a comrade]
▸**'socially** *adv*

Social and Liberal Democrats *pl n* (in Britain) a political party formed in 1988 by the merging of the Liberal Party and part of the Social Democratic Party; in 1989 it changed its name to the Liberal Democrats.

social anthropology *n* the branch of anthropology that deals with cultural and social phenomena such as kinship systems or beliefs.

Social Chapter *n* the section of the **Maastricht Treaty** concerning working conditions, consultation of workers, employment rights, and social security.

Social Charter *n* a declaration of the rights, minimum wages, maximum hours, etc., of workers in the European Union, codified in the Maastricht Treaty (1992).

social climber *n* a person who seeks advancement to a higher social class, esp. by obsequious behaviour.
▸**social climbing** *n*

social contract *or* **compact** *n* (in the theories of Locke, Hobbes, Rousseau, and others) an agreement, entered into by individuals, that results in the formation of the state, the prime motive being the desire for protection, which entails the surrender of some personal liberties.

Social Credit *n* **1** (esp. in Canada) a right-wing Populist political party, movement, or doctrine. **2 Social Credit League.** (in New Zealand) a middle-of-the-road political party, in favour of free enterprise. **3 Social Credit Rally.** (in Canada) a political party formed in 1963 from a splinter group of the Social Credit Party.

social democrat *n* **1** any socialist who believes in the gradual transformation of capitalism into democratic socialism. **2** *(usually cap.)* a member of a Social Democratic Party.
▸**social democracy** *n*

Social Democratic and Labour Party *n* a Northern Irish political party, which advocates peaceful union with the Republic of Ireland. Abbrev.: **SDLP.**

Social Democratic Party *n* **1** (in Britain, 1981–90) a political party founded by ex-members of the Labour Party. It formed an alliance with the Liberal Party and continued in a reduced form after many members left to join the Social and Liberal Democrats in 1988. **2** one of the two major political parties in Germany, favouring gradual reform. **3** any of the parties in many other countries similar to that of Germany.

social engineering *n* the manipulation of the social position and function of individuals in order to manage change in a society.

social fund *n* (in Britain) a social security fund from which loans or payments may be made to people in cases of extreme need.

social insurance *n* government insurance providing coverage for the unemployed, the injured, the old, etc.: usually financed by contributions from employers and employees.

Social Insurance Number *n Canad.* an identification number issued to individuals by the government in connection with income tax and social insurance.

socialism ('səʊʃəˌlɪzəm) *n* **1** an economic theory or system in which the means of production, distribution, and exchange are owned by the community collectively, usually through the state. Cf. **capitalism. 2** any of various social or political theories or movements in which the common welfare is to be achieved through the establishment of a socialist economic system. **3** (in Leninist theory) a transitional stage in the development of a society from capitalism to communism: characterized by the distribution of income according to work rather than need.

socialist ('səʊʃəlɪst) *n* **1** a supporter or advocate of socialism or any party promoting socialism (**socialist party**). ◆ *adj* **2** of, implementing, or relating to socialism. **3** *(sometimes cap.)* of or relating to socialists or a socialist party.
▸**ˌsocia'listic** *adj*

Socialist International *n* an international association of largely anti-Communist Social Democratic Parties founded in Frankfurt in 1951.

socialist realism *n* (in Communist countries, esp. formerly) the doctrine that art, literature, etc., should present an idealized portrayal of reality, which glorifies the achievements of the Communist Party.

socialite ('səʊʃəˌlaɪt) *n* a person who is or seeks to be prominent in fashionable society.

sociality (ˌsəʊʃɪ'ælɪtɪ) *n, pl* **socialities. 1** the tendency of groups and persons to develop social links and live in communities. **2** the quality or state of being social.

socialize ❶ *or* **socialise** ('səʊʃəˌlaɪz) *vb* **socializes, socializing, socialized** *or* **socialises, socialising, socialised. 1** *(intr)* to behave in a friendly or socia-

THESAURUS

soar *vb* **1** = **ascend**, fly, mount, rise, tower, wing **3** = **rise**, climb, escalate, rocket, shoot up
Antonyms *vb* descend, dive, drop, fall, nose-dive, plummet, plunge, swoop

sob *vb* **1** = **cry**, bawl, blubber, boohoo, greet (*Scot. or arch.*), howl, shed tears, snivel, weep

sober *adj* **2** = **abstinent**, abstemious, moderate, on the wagon (*inf.*), temperate **3** = **serious**, calm, clear-headed, composed, cool, dispassionate, grave, level-headed, lucid, practical, rational, realistic, reasonable, sedate, solemn, sound, staid, steady, unexcited, unruffled **4** = **plain**, dark, drab, quiet, severe, sombre, subdued ◆ *vb* **6** *usually with* **up** = **clear one's head**, come *or* bring to one's senses
Antonyms *adj* ≠ **abstinent**: drunk, inebriated, intoxicated, merry (*Brit. inf.*), paralytic (*inf.*), pie-eyed (*sl.*), pissed (*taboo sl.*), plastered, smashed (*sl.*), tiddly (*sl., chiefly Brit.*), tight (*inf.*), tipsy, tired and emotional (*euphemistic*) ≠ **serious**: excessive, frivolous, happy, immoderate, imprudent, injudicious, irrational, light-hearted, sensational, unrealistic ≠ **plain**: bright, flamboyant, flashy, garish, gaudy, light ◆ *vb* ≠ **clear one's head**: become intoxicated, get drunk

sobriety *n* **2** = **abstinence**, abstemiousness, moderation, nonindulgence, self-restraint, soberness, temperance **3** = **seriousness**, calmness, composure, coolness, gravity, level-headedness, reasonableness, restraint, sedateness, solemnity, staidness, steadiness

so-called *adj* = **alleged**, ostensible, pretended, professed, self-styled, *soi-disant*, supposed

sociability *n* **1** = **friendliness**, affability, companionability, congeniality, conviviality, cordiality, gregariousness, neighbourliness

sociable *adj* **1** = **friendly**, accessible, affable, approachable, companionable, conversable, convivial, cordial, familiar, genial, gregarious, neighbourly, outgoing, social, warm
Antonyms *adj* antisocial, businesslike, cold, distant, formal, introverted, reclusive, standoffish, stiff, tense, uncommunicative, unfriendly, unsociable, uptight (*inf.*), withdrawn

social *adj* **1** = **sociable**, companionable, friendly, gregarious, neighbourly **2** = **communal**, collective, common, community, general, group, organized, public, societal ◆ *n* **9** = **get-together** (*inf.*), do (*inf.*), gathering, party

socialize *vb* **1** = **mix**, be a good mixer, break the ice, entertain, fraternize, get about *or* around, get together, go out ble manner. **2** (*tr*) to prepare for life in society. **3** (*tr*) *Chiefly US.* to alter or create so as to be in accordance with socialist principles.

social market *n* **a** an economic system in which industry and commerce are run by private enterprise within limits set by the government to ensure equality of opportunity and social and environmental responsibility. **b** (*as modifier*): *a social-market economy.*

social realism *n* **1** the use of realist art, literature, etc., as a medium for social or political comment. **2** another name for **socialist realism.**

social science *n* **1** the study of society and of the relationship of individual members within society, including economics, history, political science, psychology, anthropology, and sociology. **2** any of these subjects studied individually.
▸**social scientist** *n*

social secretary *n* **1** a member of an organization who arranges its social events. **2** a personal secretary who deals with private correspondence, etc.

social security *n* **1** public provision for the economic welfare of the aged, unemployed, etc., esp. through pensions and other monetary assistance. **2** (*often cap.*) a government programme designed to provide such assistance.

social services *pl n* welfare activities organized by the state or a local authority and carried out by trained personnel.

social studies *n* (*functioning as sing*) the study of how people live and organize themselves in society, embracing geography, history, economics, and other subjects.

social welfare *n* **1** social services provided by a state for the benefit of its citizens. **2** (*caps.*) (in New Zealand) a government department concerned with pensions and benefits for the elderly, the sick, etc.

social work *n* any of various social services designed to alleviate the conditions of the poor and aged and to increase the welfare of children.
▸**social worker** *n*

societal (səˈsaɪətᵊl) *adj* of or relating to society, esp. human society.
▸**soˈcietally** *adv*

societal marketing *n* **1** marketing that takes into account society's long-term welfare. **2** the marketing of a social or charitable cause, such as an anti-apartheid campaign.

society ❶ (səˈsaɪətɪ) *n, pl* **societies. 1** the totality of social relationships among organized groups of human beings or animals. **2** a system of human organizations generating distinctive cultural patterns and institutions. **3** such a system with reference to its mode of social and economic organization or its dominant class: *middle-class society.* **4** those with whom one has companionship. **5** an organized group of people associated for some specific purpose or on account of some common interest: *a learned society.* **6a** the privileged class of people in a community, esp. as considered superior or fashionable. **6b** (*as modifier*): *a society woman.* **7** the social life and intercourse of such people: *to enter society.* **8** companionship: *I enjoy her society.* **9** *Ecology.* a small community of plants within a larger association. [C16: via OF *societé* from L *societās,* from *socius* a comrade]

Society of Jesus *n* the religious order of the Jesuits, founded by Ignatius Loyola.

socio- *combining form.* denoting social or society: *socioeconomic; sociopolitical; sociology.*

sociobiology (ˌsəʊsɪəʊbaɪˈɒlədʒɪ) *n* the study of social behaviour in animals and humans.
▸ˌ**sociobiˈologist** *n*

socioeconomic (ˌsəʊsɪəʊˌiːkəˈnɒmɪk, -ˌɛkə-) *adj* of, relating to, or involving both economic and social factors.
▸ˌ**socioˌecoˈnomically** *adv*

sociolinguistics (ˌsəʊsɪəʊlɪŋˈgwɪstɪks) *n* (*functioning as sing*) the study of language in relation to its social context.
▸ˌ**socioˈlinguist** *n*

sociology (ˌsəʊsɪˈɒlədʒɪ) *n* the study of the development, organization, functioning, and classification of human societies.
▸**sociological** (ˌsəʊsɪəˈlɒdʒɪkᵊl) *adj* ▸ˌ**sociˈologist** *n*

sociometry (ˌsəʊsɪˈɒmɪtrɪ) *n* the study of sociological relationships within groups.
▸**sociometric** (ˌsəʊsɪəˈmɛtrɪk) *adj* ▸ˌ**sociˈometrist** *n*

sociopath (ˈsəʊsɪəˌpæθ) *n Psychiatry.* another term for **psychopath.**
▸ˌ**socioˈpathic** *adj* ▸**sociopathy** (ˌsəʊsɪˈɒpəθɪ) *n*

sociopolitical (ˌsəʊsɪəʊpəˈlɪtɪkᵊl) *adj* of or involving both political and social factors.

sock[1] (sɒk) *n* **1** a cloth covering for the foot, reaching to between the ankle and knee and worn inside a shoe. **2** an insole put in a shoe, as to make it fit better. **3** a light shoe worn by actors in ancient Greek and Roman comedy. **4 pull one's socks up.** *Brit. inf.* to make a determined effort, esp. to improve one's behaviour or performance. **5 put a sock in it.** *Brit. sl.* be quiet! [OE *socc* a light shoe, from L *soccus,* from Gk *sukkhos*]

sock[2] (sɒk) *Sl.* ◆ *vb* **1** (*usually tr*) to hit with force. **2 sock it to.** *Sl.* to make a forceful impression on. ◆ *n* **3** a forceful blow. [C17: from ?]

socket (ˈsɒkɪt) *n* **1** a device into which an electric plug can be inserted in order to make a connection in a circuit. **2** *Chiefly Brit.* such a device mounted on a wall and connected to the electricity supply; power point. **3** a part with an opening or hollow into which some other part can be fitted. **4** *Anat.* **4a** a bony hollow into which a part or structure fits: *an eye socket.* **4b** the receptacle of a ball-and-socket joint. ◆ *vb* **5** (*tr*) to furnish with or place into a socket. [C13: from Anglo-Norman *soket* a little ploughshare, from *soc,* of Celtic origin]

socket set *n* a set of tools consisting of a handle into which various interchangeable heads can be fitted.

sockeye (ˈsɒkˌaɪ) *n* a Pacific salmon having red flesh and valued as a food fish. Also called: **red salmon.** [by folk etymology from *sukkegh,* of Amerind origin]

socle (ˈsəʊkᵊl) *n* another name for **plinth** (sense 1). [C18: via F from It. *zoccolo,* from L *socculus* a little shoe, from *soccus* a SOCK[1]]

Socratic (sɒˈkrætɪk) *adj* **1** of Socrates (?470–399 B.C.), the Greek philosopher, his methods, etc. ◆ *n* **2** a person who follows the teachings of Socrates.
▸**Soˈcratically** *adv* ▸**Soˈcratiˌcism** *n* ▸**Socratist** (ˈsɒkrətɪst) *n*

Socratic irony *n Philosophy.* a means by which the feigned ignorance of a questioner leads the person answering to expose his own ignorance.

Socratic method *n Philosophy.* the method of instruction by question and answer used by Socrates in order to elicit from his pupils truths he considered to be implicitly known by all rational beings.

sod[1] (sɒd) *n* **1** a piece of grass-covered surface soil held together by the roots of the grass; turf. **2** *Poetic.* the ground. ◆ *vb* **sods, sodding, sodded. 3** (*tr*) to cover with sods. [C15: from Low G]

sod[2] (sɒd) *Sl., chiefly Brit.* ◆ *n* **1** a person considered to be obnoxious. **2** a jocular word for a **person. 3 sod all.** *Sl.* nothing. ◆ *interj* **4 sod it.** a strong exclamation of annoyance. See also **sod off.** [C19: shortened from SODOMITE]
▸ˈ**sodding** *adj*

soda (ˈsəʊdə) *n* **1** any of a number of simple inorganic compounds of sodium, such as sodium carbonate (**washing soda**), sodium bicarbonate (**baking soda**), and sodium hydroxide (**caustic soda**). **2** See **soda water. 3** *US & Canad.* a fizzy drink. [C16: from Med. L, from *sodanum* barilla, a plant that was burned to obtain a type of sodium carbonate, ?from Ar.]

soda ash *n* the anhydrous commercial form of sodium carbonate.

soda bread *n* a type of bread leavened with sodium bicarbonate combined with milk and cream of tartar.

soda fountain *n US & Canad.* **1** a counter that serves drinks, snacks, etc. **2** an apparatus dispensing soda water.

sodality (səʊˈdælɪtɪ) *n, pl* **sodalities. 1** *RC Church.* a religious society. **2** fellowship. [C16: from L *sodālitās* fellowship, from *sodālis* a comrade]

sodamide (ˈsəʊdəˌmaɪd) *n* a white crystalline compound used as a dehydrating agent and in making sodium cyanide. Formula: $NaNH_2$.

soda siphon *n* a sealed bottle containing and dispensing soda water. The water is forced up a tube reaching to the bottom of the bottle by the pressure of gas above the water.

soda water *n* an effervescent beverage made by charging water with carbon dioxide under pressure. Sometimes shortened to **soda.**

sodden ❶ (ˈsɒdᵊn) *adj* **1** completely saturated. **2a** dulled, esp. by excessive drinking. **2b** (*in combination*): *a drink-sodden mind.* **3** doughy, as bread is when improperly cooked. ◆ *vb* **4** to make or become sodden. [C13 *soden,* p.p. of SEETHE]
▸ˈ**soddenness** *n*

sodium (ˈsəʊdɪəm) *n* **a** a very reactive soft silvery-white element of the alkali metal group occurring principally in common salt, Chile saltpetre, and cryolite. It is used in the production of chemicals, in metallurgy, and, alloyed with potassium, as a cooling medium in nuclear reactors. Symbol: Na; atomic no.: 11; atomic wt.: 22.99. **b** (*as modifier*): *sodium light.* [C19: NL, from SODA + -IUM]

sodium amytal *n* another name for **Amytal.**

sodium benzoate *n* a white crystalline soluble compound used in preserving food (**E 211**), as an antiseptic, and in making dyes.

sodium bicarbonate *n* a white crystalline soluble compound used in effervescent drinks, baking powders, fire-extinguishers, and in medicine as an antacid; sodium hydrogen carbonate. Formula: $NaHCO_3$. Systematic name: **sodium hydrogencarbonate.** Also called: **bicarbonate of soda, baking soda.**

sodium carbonate *n* a colourless or white odourless soluble crystalline compound used in the manufacture of glass, ceramics, soap, and paper, and as a cleansing agent. Formula: Na_2CO_3.

sodium chlorate *n* a colourless crystalline soluble compound used as a bleaching agent, antiseptic, and weedkiller. Formula: $NaClO_3$.

sodium chloride *n* common table salt; a soluble colourless crystalline compound widely used as a seasoning and preservative for food and in the manufacture of chemicals, glass, and soap. Formula: NaCl. Also called: **salt.**

sodium cyanide *n* a white odourless crystalline soluble poisonous

THESAURUS

society *n* **1** = **civilization**, culture, humanity, mankind, people, population, social order, the community, the general public, the public, the world at large **5** = **organization**, association, brotherhood *or* sisterhood, circle, club, corporation, fellowship, fraternity, group, guild, institute, league, order, union **6** = **upper classes**, beau monde, elite, gentry, *haut monde,* high society, polite society, the country set, the nobs (*sl.*), the smart set, the swells (*inf.*), the toffs, the top drawer, upper crust (*inf.*) **8** = **companionship**, camaraderie, company, fellowship, friendship

sodden *adj* **1** = **soaked**, boggy, drenched, droukit *or* drookit (*Scot.*), marshy, miry, saturated, soggy, sopping, waterlogged compound used for extracting gold and silver from their ores and for case-hardening steel. Formula: NaCN.

sodium glutamate ('glu:tə,meɪt) *n* another name for **monosodium glutamate.**

sodium hydrogencarbonate *n* the systematic name for **sodium bicarbonate.**

sodium hydroxide *n* a white strongly alkaline solid used in the manufacture of rayon, paper, aluminium, soap, and sodium compounds. Formula: NaOH. Also called: **caustic soda.**

sodium hyposulphite *n* another name (not in technical usage) for **sodium thiosulphate.**

sodium lamp *n* another name for **sodium-vapour lamp.**

sodium nitrate *n* a white crystalline soluble solid compound used in matches, explosives, and rocket propellants, as a fertilizer, and as a curing salt for preserving food (**E 251**). Formula: $NaNO_3$.

Sodium Pentothal *n Trademark.* another name for **thiopentone sodium.**

sodium silicate *n* **1** Also called: **soluble glass.** See **water glass. 2** any sodium salt of a silicic acid.

sodium sulphate *n* a solid white substance used in making glass, detergents, and pulp. Formula: Na_2SO_4. See **salt cake** and **Glauber's salt.**

sodium thiosulphate *n* a white soluble substance used in photography as a fixer to dissolve unchanged silver halides and also to remove excess chlorine from chlorinated water. Formula: $Na_2S_2O_3$. Also called (not in technical usage): **sodium hyposulphite, hypo.**

sodium-vapour lamp *n* a type of electric lamp consisting of a glass tube containing neon and sodium vapour at low pressure through which an electric current is passed to give an orange light: used in street lighting.

sod off *Brit. taboo sl.* ◆ *interj* **1** a forceful expression of dismissal. ◆ *vb* **sods, sodding, sodded. 2** (*intr, adv*) to go away.

Sodom ('sɒdəm) *n* **1** *Old Testament.* a city destroyed by God for its wickedness that, with Gomorrah, traditionally typifies depravity (Genesis 19:24). **2** this city as representing homosexuality. **3** any place notorious for depravity.

sodomite ('sɒdə,maɪt) *n* a person who practises sodomy.

sodomize *or* **sodomise** ('sɒdə,maɪz) *vb* **sodomizes, sodomizing, sodomized** *or* **sodomises, sodomising, sodomised.** (*tr*) to have anal intercourse with (a person).

sodomy ❶ ('sɒdəmɪ) *n* anal intercourse committed by a man with another man or a woman. [C13: via OF *sodomie* from L (Vulgate) *Sodoma* Sodom]

Sod's law (sɒdz) *n Inf.* a facetious precept stating that if something can go wrong or turn out inconveniently it will.

soever (səʊ'ɛvə) *adv* in any way at all: used to emphasize or make less precise a word or phrase, usually in combination with *what, where, when, how,* etc., or else separated by intervening words. Cf. **whatsoever.**

sofa ❶ ('səʊfə) *n* an upholstered seat with back and arms for two or more people. [C17 (in the sense: dais upholstered as a seat): from Ar. *suffah*]

soffit ('sɒfɪt) *n* the underside of a part of a building or a structural component, such as an arch, beam, stair, etc. [C17: via F from It. *soffitto,* from L *suffixus* something fixed underneath, from *suffigere,* from *sub-* under + *figere* to fasten]

S. of Sol. *Bible. abbrev. for* Song of Solomon.

soft ❶ (sɒft) *adj* **1** easy to dent, work, or cut without shattering; malleable. **2** not hard; giving little or no resistance to pressure or weight. **3** fine, light, smooth, or fluffy to the touch. **4** gentle; tranquil. **5** (of music, sounds, etc.) low and pleasing. **6** (of light, colour, etc.) not excessively bright or harsh. **7** (of a breeze, climate, etc.) temperate, mild, or pleasant. **8** slightly blurred; not sharply outlined: *soft focus.* **9** (of a diet) consisting of easily digestible foods. **10** kind or lenient, often excessively so. **11** easy to influence or impose upon. **12** prepared to compromise; not doctrinaire: *the soft left.* **13** *Inf.* feeble or silly; simple (often in **soft in the head**). **14** unable to endure hardship, esp. through pampering. **15** physically out of condition; flabby: *soft muscles.* **16** loving; tender: *soft words.* **17** *Inf.* requiring little exertion; easy: *a soft job.* **18** *Chem.* (of water) relatively free of mineral salts and therefore easily able to make soap lather. **19** (of a drug such as cannabis) nonaddictive. **20** *Phonetics.* (not in technical usage) denoting the consonants *c* and *g* in English when they are pronounced as palatal or alveolar fricatives or affricates (s, dʒ, ʃ, ð, tʃ) before *e* and *i,* rather than as velar stops (k, g). **21** *Finance, chiefly US.* (of prices, a market, etc.) unstable and tending to decline. **22** (of currency) in relatively little demand, esp. because of a weak balance of payments situation. **23** (of radiation, such as X-rays and ultraviolet radiation) having low energy and not capable of deep penetration of materials. **24 soft on** *or* **about. 24a** gentle, sympathetic, or lenient towards. **24b** feeling affection or infatuation for. ◆ *adv* **25** in a soft manner: *to speak soft.* ◆ *n* **26** a soft object, part, or piece. **27** *Inf.* See **softie.** ◆ *sentence substitute. Arch.* **28** quiet! **29** wait! [OE *sōfte*]

▸**'softly** *adv* ▸**'softness** *n*

softa ('sɒftə) *n* a Muslim student of divinity and jurisprudence, esp. in Turkey. [C17: from Turkish, from Persian *sōkhtah* aflame (with love of learning)]

softball ('sɒft,bɔ:l) *n* a variation of baseball using a larger softer ball, pitched underhand.

soft ball *n Cookery.* a term used for sugar syrup boiled to a consistency at which it may be rubbed into balls after dipping in cold water.

soft-boiled *adj* (of an egg) boiled for a short time so that the yolk is still soft.

soft coal *n* another name for **bituminous coal.**

soft commodities *pl n* nonmetal commodities, such as cocoa, sugar, and grains, bought and sold on a futures market. Also called: **softs.**

soft-core *adj* (of pornography) suggestive and titillating through not being totally explicit.

soft-cover *adj* a less common word for **paperback.**

soft drink *n* a nonalcoholic drink.

soften ❶ ('sɒfᵊn) *vb* **1** to make or become soft or softer. **2** to make or become more gentle.

▸**'softener** *n*

softening of the brain *n* an abnormal softening of the tissues of the cerebrum characterized by mental impairment.

soft-focus lens *n Photog.* a lens designed to produce an image that is slightly out of focus: typically used for portrait work.

soft furnishings *pl n Brit.* curtains, hangings, rugs, etc.

soft goods *pl n* textile fabrics and related merchandise. Also called (US and Canad.): **dry goods.**

soft-headed *adj* **1** *Inf.* feeble-minded; stupid; simple. **2** (of a stick or hammer for playing a percussion instrument) having a soft head.

▸**,soft-'headedness** *n*

softhearted ❶ (,sɒft'hɑ:tɪd) *adj* easily moved to pity.

▸**,soft'heartedly** *adv* ▸**,soft'heartedness** *n*

softie *or* **softy** ('sɒftɪ) *n, pl* **softies.** *Inf.* a person who is sentimental, weakly foolish, or lacking in physical endurance.

soft landing *n* **1** a landing by a spacecraft on the moon or a planet at a sufficiently low velocity for the equipment or occupants to remain unharmed. **2** a painless resolution of a problem, esp. an economic problem. Cf. **hard landing.**

soft option *n* in a number of choices, the one involving the least difficulty or exertion.

soft palate *n* the posterior fleshy portion of the roof of the mouth.

soft paste *n* **a** artificial porcelain made from clay, bone ash, etc. **b** (*as modifier*): *softpaste porcelain.*

soft-pedal ❶ *vb* **soft-pedals, soft-pedalling, soft-pedalled** *or US* **soft-pedals, soft-pedaling, soft-pedaled.** (*tr*) **1** to mute the tone of (a piano) by depressing the soft pedal. **2** *Inf.* to make (something, esp. something unpleasant) less obvious by deliberately failing to emphasize or allude to it. ◆ *n* **soft pedal. 3** a foot-operated lever on a piano, the left one of two, that either moves the whole action closer to the strings so that the hammers strike with less force or causes fewer of the strings to sound.

soft porn *n Inf.* soft-core pornography.

softs (sɒfts) *pl n* another name for **soft commodities.**

soft sell *n* a method of selling based on indirect suggestion or inducement.

soft shoulder *or* **verge** *n* a soft edge along the side of a road that is unsuitable for vehicles to drive on.

soft soap *n* **1** *Med.* Also called: **green soap.** a soft or liquid alkaline soap used in treating certain skin disorders. **2** *Inf.* flattering, persuasive, or cajoling talk. ◆ *vb* **soft-soap. 3** *Inf.* to use such talk on (a person).

soft-spoken *adj* **1** speaking or said with a soft gentle voice. **2** able to persuade or impress by glibness of tongue.

THESAURUS

sodomy *n* = **anal intercourse,** anal sex, buggery

sofa *n* = **couch,** chaise longue, chesterfield, divan, ottoman, settee

soft *adj* **1** = **pliable,** bendable, ductile (*of metals*), elastic, flexible, impressible, malleable, mouldable, plastic, supple, tensile **2** = **yielding,** cushioned, cushiony, doughy, elastic, gelatinous, pulpy, quaggy, spongy, squashy, swampy **3** = **velvety,** downy, feathery, fleecy, flowing, fluid, furry, like a baby's bottom (*inf.*), rounded, silky, smooth **5** = **quiet,** dulcet, gentle, low, mellifluous, mellow, melodious, murmured, muted, soft-toned, soothing, subdued, sweet, understated, whispered **6** = **pale,** bland, light, mellow, pastel, pleasing, subdued **7** = **mild,** balmy, caressing, delicate, shaded, temperate **8** = **dim,** diffuse, dimmed, faint, restful, twilight **10** = **lenient,** boneless, easy-going, indulgent, lax, liberal, overindulgent, permissive, spineless, weak **13** *Informal* = **feeble-minded,** a bit lacking (*inf.*), daft (*inf.*), foolish, silly, simple, soft in the head (*inf.*), soppy (*Brit. inf.*) **14, 15** = **out of condition,** effeminate, flabby, flaccid, limp, namby-pamby, out of training, overindulged, pampered, podgy, weak **16** = **kind,** compassionate, gentle, pitying, sensitive, sentimental, sympathetic, tender, tenderhearted, touchy-feely (*inf.*) **17** *Informal* = **easy,** comfortable, cushy (*inf.*), easy-peasy (*sl.*), undemanding

Antonyms *adj* ≠ **pliable, yielding:** firm, hard, inflexible, rigid, solid, stiff, tough, unyielding ≠ **velvety:** abrasive, coarse, grating, hard, rough ≠ **quiet:** harsh, loud, noisy, strident ≠ **pale:** bright, garish, gaudy, glaring, harsh ≠ **dim:** bright, glaring, harsh ≠ **lenient:** austere, harsh, no-nonsense, stern, strict

soften *vb* **2** = **lessen,** abate, allay, alleviate, appease, assuage, calm, cushion, diminish, ease, lighten, lower, melt, mitigate, moderate, modify, mollify, muffle, palliate, quell, relax, soothe, still, subdue, temper, tone down, turn down

softhearted *adj* = **kind,** charitable, compassionate, generous, indulgent, sentimental, sympathetic, tender, tenderhearted, warm-hearted

Antonyms *adj* callous, cold, cruel, hard, hard-hearted, heartless, insensitive, uncaring, unkind, unsympathetic

soft-pedal *vb* **2** = **play down,** de-emphasize, go easy (*inf.*), moderate, tone down

soft spot ❶ *n* a sentimental fondness (esp. in **have a soft spot for**).

soft touch *n Inf.* a person easily persuaded or imposed on, esp. to lend money.

software ('sɒftˌwɛə) *n Computing.* the programs that can be used with a particular computer system. Cf. **hardware** (sense 2).

softwood ('sɒftˌwʊd) *n* **1** the open-grained wood of any of numerous coniferous trees, such as pine and cedar. **2** any tree yielding this wood.

SOGAT ('səʊɡæt) *n* (formerly, in Britain) *acronym for* Society of Graphical and Allied Trades.

soggy ❶ ('sɒɡɪ) *adj* **soggier, soggiest. 1** soaked with liquid. **2** (of bread, pastry, etc.) moist and heavy. **3** *Inf.* lacking in spirit or positiveness. [C18: prob. from dialect *sog* marsh, from ?]
▸'**soggily** *adv* ▸'**sogginess** *n*

soh *or* **so** (səʊ) *n Music.* (in tonic sol-fa) the name used for the fifth note or dominant of any scale. [C14: later variant of *sol*; see GAMUT]

soi-disant *French.* (swadizɑ̃) *adj* so-called; self-styled. [lit.: calling oneself]

soigné *or (fem)* **soignée** ('swɑːnjeɪ) *adj* well-groomed; elegant. [F, from *soigner* to take good care of, of Gmc origin]

soil[1] ❶ (sɔɪl) *n* **1** the top layer of the land surface of the earth that is composed of disintegrated rock particles, humus, water, and air. **2** a type of this material having specific characteristics: *loamy soil.* **3** land, country, or region: *one's native soil.* **4 the soil.** life and work on a farm; land: *he belonged to the soil.* **5** any place or thing encouraging growth or development. [C14: from Anglo-Norman, from L *solium* a seat, but confused with L *solum* the ground]

soil[2] ❶ (sɔɪl) *vb* **1** to make or become dirty or stained. **2** *(tr)* to pollute with sin or disgrace; sully; defile. ◆ *n* **3** the state or result of soiling. **4** refuse, manure, or excrement. [C13: from OF *soillier* to defile, from *soil* pigsty, prob. from L *sūs* a swine]

soil[3] (sɔɪl) *vb (tr)* to feed (livestock) green fodder to fatten or purge them. [C17: ?from obs. vb (C16) *soil* to manure, from SOIL[2] (n)]

soil pipe *n* a pipe that conveys sewage or waste water from a toilet, etc., to a soil drain or sewer.

soiree ('swɑːreɪ) *n* an evening party or gathering, usually at a private house, esp. where guests listen to, play, or dance to music. [C19: from F, from OF *soir* evening, from L *sērum* a late time, from *sērus* late]

soixante-neuf *French.* (swasɑ̃tnœf) *n* a sexual activity in which two people simultaneously stimulate each other's genitalia with their mouths. Also called: **sixty-nine.** [lit.: sixty-nine, from the position adopted by the participants]

sojourn ❶ ('sɒdʒɜːn, 'sʌdʒ-) *n* **1** a temporary stay. ◆ *vb* **2** *(intr)* to stay or reside temporarily. [C13: from OF *sojorner*, from Vulgar L *subdiurnāre* (unattested) to spend a day, from L *sub-* during + LL *diurnum* day]
▸'**sojourner** *n*

soke (səʊk) *n English legal history.* **1** the right to hold a local court. **2** the territory under the jurisdiction of a particular court. [C14: from Med. L *sōca*, from OE *sōcn* a seeking]

sol[1] (sɒl) *n Music.* the syllable used in the fixed system of solmization for the note G. [C14: see GAMUT]

sol[2] (sɒl) *n* a colloid that has a continuous liquid phase, esp. one in which a solid is suspended in a liquid. [C20: shortened from SOLUTION]

Sol (sɒl) *n* **1** the Roman god personifying the sun. **2** a poetic word for **the sun.**

sol. *abbrev. for:* **1** soluble. **2** solution.

Sol. *abbrev. for:* **1** Also: **Solr.** solicitor. **2** *Bible.* Solomon.

sola *Latin.* ('səʊlə) *adj* the feminine form of ***solus.***

solace ❶ ('sɒlɪs) *n* **1** comfort in misery, disappointment, etc. **2** something that gives comfort or consolation. ◆ *vb* **solaces, solacing, solaced.** *(tr)* **3** to give comfort or cheer to (a person) in time of sorrow, distress, etc. **4** to alleviate (sorrow, misery, etc.). [C13: from OF *solas*, from L *sōlātium* comfort, from *sōlārī* to console]
▸'**solacer** *n*

solan *or* **solan goose** ('səʊlən) *n* an archaic name for the **gannet.** [C15 *soland*, from ON]

solanaceous (ˌsɒlə'neɪʃəs) *adj* of or relating to the Solanaceae, a family of plants having typically tubular flowers, protruding anthers, and often poisonous or narcotic properties: includes the potato, tobacco, and several nightshades. [C19: from NL *Sōlānāceae*, from L *sōlānum* nightshade]

solanum (səʊ'leɪnəm) *n* any tree, shrub, or herbaceous plant of the mainly tropical solanaceous genus *Solanum:* includes the potato and certain nightshades. [C16: from L: nightshade]

solar ('səʊlə) *adj* **1** of or relating to the sun. **2** operating by or utilizing the energy of the sun: *solar cell.* **3** *Astron.* determined from the motion of the earth relative to the sun: *solar year.* **4** *Astrol.* subject to the influence of the sun. [C15: from L *sōlāris*, from *sōl* the sun]

solar cell *n* a cell that produces electricity from the sun's rays, used esp. in spacecraft.

solar constant *n* the rate at which the sun's energy is received per unit area at the top of the earth's atmosphere when the sun is at its mean distance from the earth and atmospheric absorption has been corrected for.

solar day *n* See under **day** (sense 6).

solar energy *n* energy obtained from solar power.

solar flare *n* a brief powerful eruption of intense high-energy radiation from the sun's surface, associated with sunspots and causing radio and magnetic disturbances on earth.

solarium (səʊ'lɛərɪəm) *n, pl* **solariums** *or* **solaria** (-'lɛərɪə) **1** a room built largely of glass to afford exposure to the sun. **2** a bed equipped with ultraviolet lights used for acquiring an artificial suntan. **3** an establishment offering such facilities. [C19: from L: a terrace, from *sōl* sun]

solar month *n* See under **month** (sense 4).

solar plexus *n* **1** *Anat.* the network of nerves situated behind the stomach that supply the abdominal organs. **2** (not in technical usage) the part of the stomach beneath the diaphragm; pit of the stomach. [C18: referring to resemblance between the radial network of nerves & ganglia & the rays of the sun]

solar power *n* radiation from the sun used to heat a fluid or to generate electricity using solar cells.

solar system *n* the system containing the sun and the bodies held in its gravitational field, including the planets (Mercury, Venus, earth, Mars, Jupiter, Saturn, Uranus, Neptune, Pluto), the asteroids, and comets.

solar wind (wɪnd) *n* the stream of charged particles, such as protons, emitted by the sun at high velocities, its intensity increasing during periods of solar activity.

solar year *n* See under **year** (sense 4).

solatium (səʊ'leɪʃɪəm) *n, pl* **solatia** (-ʃɪə). *Law, chiefly US & Scot.* compensation awarded for injury to the feelings as distinct from physical suffering and pecuniary loss. [C19: from L: see SOLACE]

sold ❶ (səʊld) *vb* **1** the past tense and past participle of **sell.** ◆ *adj* **2 sold on.** *Sl.* uncritically attached to or enthusiastic about.

solder ('sɒldə; *US* 'sɒdər) *n* **1** an alloy used for joining two metal surfaces by melting the alloy so that it forms a thin layer between the surfaces. **2** something that joins things together firmly; a bond. ◆ *vb* **3** to join or mend or be joined or mended with or as if with solder. [C14: via OF from L *solidāre* to strengthen, from *solidus* solid]
▸'**solderable** *adj* ▸'**solderer** *n*

soldering iron *n* a hand tool consisting of a handle fixed to a copper tip that is heated and used to melt and apply solder.

soldier ❶ ('səʊldʒə) *n* **1a** a person who serves or has served in an army. **1b** Also called: **common soldier.** a noncommissioned member of an army as opposed to a commissioned officer. **2** a person who works diligently for a cause. **3** *Zool.* an individual in a colony of social insects, esp. ants, that has powerful jaws adapted for defending the colony, crushing food, etc. ◆ *vb* **4** *(intr)* to serve as a soldier. [C13: from OF *soudier*, from *soude* (army) pay, from LL *solidus* a gold coin, from L: firm]
▸'**soldierly** *adj*

soldier of fortune *n* a man who seeks money or adventure as a soldier; mercenary.

soldier on *vb (intr, adv)* to persist in one's efforts in spite of difficulties, pressure, etc.

soldiery ('səʊldʒərɪ) *n, pl* **soldieries. 1** soldiers collectively. **2** a group of soldiers. **3** the profession of being a soldier.

sole[1] ❶ (səʊl) *adj* **1** *(prenominal)* being the only one; only. **2** *(prenominal)* of or relating to one individual or group and no other: *sole rights.* **3** *Law.* having no wife or husband. **4** an archaic word for **solitary.** [C14: from OF *soule*, from L *sōlus* alone]
▸'**soleness** *n*

sole[2] (səʊl) *n* **1** the underside of the foot. **2** the underside of a shoe. **3a** the bottom of a furrow. **3b** the bottom of a plough. **4** the underside of a golf-club head. ◆ *vb* **soles, soling, soled.** *(tr)* **5** to provide (a shoe) with a sole. [C14: via OF from L *solea* sandal]

sole[3] (səʊl) *n, pl* **sole** *or* **soles.** any of various tongue-shaped flatfishes, esp. the **European sole:** most common in warm seas and highly valued as food fishes. [C14: via OF from Vulgar L *sola* (unattested), from L *solea* a sandal (from the fish's shape)]

solecism ('sɒlɪˌsɪzəm) *n* **1a** the nonstandard use of a grammatical construction. **1b** any mistake, incongruity, or absurdity. **2** a violation of good manners. [C16: from L *soloecismus*, from Gk, from *soloikos* speaking incorrectly, from *Soloi* an Athenian colony of Cilicia where the inhabitants spoke a corrupt form of Greek]
▸'**solecist** *n* ▸ˌ**sole'cistic** *adj* ▸ˌ**sole'cistically** *adv*

THESAURUS

soft spot *n* = **fondness,** liking, partiality, weakness

soggy *adj* **1** = **sodden,** dripping, heavy, moist, mushy, pulpy, saturated, soaked, sopping, spongy, waterlogged

soil[1] *n* **1** = **earth,** clay, dirt, dust, ground, loam **3** = **land,** country, region

soil[2] *vb* **1, 2** = **dirty,** bedraggle, befoul, begrime, besmirch, defile, foul, maculate *(literary)*, muddy, pollute, smear, smirch, spatter, spot, stain, sully, tarnish

sojourn *n* **1** = **stay,** rest, stop, stopover, visit ◆ *vb* **2** = **stay,** abide, dwell, lodge, reside, rest, stop, tarry

solace *n* **1** = **comfort,** alleviation, assuagement, consolation, relief ◆ *vb* **3, 4** = **comfort,** allay, alleviate, console, mitigate, soften, soothe

sold *adj* **2 sold on** *Slang* = **convinced of,** converted to, hooked on, persuaded of, talked into, won over to

soldier *n* **1** = **fighter,** enlisted man *(US)*, GI *(US inf.)*, man-at-arms, military man, redcoat, serviceman, squaddie *or* squaddy *(Brit. sl.)*, Tommy *(Brit. inf.)*, trooper, warrior

sole[1] *adj* **1, 2** = **only,** alone, exclusive, individual, one, one and only, single, singular, solitary

solely ⓣ ('səʊllɪ) *adv* **1** only; completely. **2** without others; singly. **3** for one thing only.

solemn ⓣ ('sɒləm) *adj* **1** characterized or marked by seriousness or sincerity: *a solemn vow.* **2** characterized by pomp, ceremony, or formality. **3** serious, glum, or pompous. **4** inspiring awe: *a solemn occasion.* **5** performed with religious ceremony. **6** gloomy or sombre: *solemn colours.* [C14: from OF *solempne,* from L *sōllemnis* appointed, ?from *sollus* whole]
▸**'solemnly** *adv* ▸**'solemnness** *or* **'solemness** *n*

solemnify (sə'lɛmnɪˌfaɪ) *vb* **solemnifies, solemnifying, solemnified.** (*tr*) to make serious or grave.
▸**soˌlemnifi'cation** *n*

solemnity ⓣ (sə'lɛmnɪtɪ) *n, pl* **solemnities. 1** the state or quality of being solemn. **2** (*often pl*) solemn ceremony, observance, etc. **3** *Law.* a formality necessary to validate a deed, contract, etc.

solemnize ⓣ *or* **solemnise** ('sɒləmˌnaɪz) *vb* **solemnizes, solemnizing, solemnized** *or* **solemnises, solemnising, solemnised.** (*tr*) **1** to celebrate or observe with rites or formal ceremonies, as a religious occasion. **2** to celebrate or perform the ceremony of (marriage). **3** to make solemn or serious. **4** to perform or hold (ceremonies, etc.) in due manner.
▸**ˌsolemni'zation** *or* **ˌsolemni'sation** *n* ▸**'solemˌnizer** *or* **'solemˌniser** *n*

solenodon (sə'lɛnədən) *n* either of two rare shrewlike nocturnal mammals of the Caribbean having a long hairless tail and an elongated snout. [C19: from NL, from L *sōlēn* sea mussel (from Gk: pipe) + Gk *odōn* tooth]

solenoid ('səʊlɪˌnɔɪd) *n* **1** a coil of wire, usually cylindrical, in which a magnetic field is set up by passing a current through it. **2** a coil of wire, partially surrounding an iron core, that is made to move inside the coil by the magnetic field set up by a current: used to convert electrical to mechanical energy, as in the operation of a switch. [C19: from F *solénoïde,* from Gk *sōlēn* a tube]
▸**ˌsole'noidal** *adj*

sol-fa ('sɒl'fɑː) *n* **1** short for **tonic sol-fa.** ◆ *vb* **sol-fas, sol-faing, sol-faed. 2** *US.* to use tonic sol-fa syllables in singing (a tune). [C16: see GAMUT]

solfatara (ˌsɒlfə'tɑːrə) *n* a volcanic vent emitting only sulphurous gases and water vapour or sometimes hot mud. [C18: from It.: a sulphurous volcano near Naples, from *solfo* sulphur]

solfeggio (sɒl'fɛdʒɪəʊ) *or* **solfège** (sɒl'fɛʒ) *n, pl* **solfeggi** (-'fɛdʒiː), **solfeggios,** *or* **solfèges.** *Music.* **1** a voice exercise in which runs, scales, etc., are sung to the same syllable or syllables. **2** solmization, esp. the French or Italian system, in which the names correspond to the notes of the scale of C major. [C18: from It. *solfeggiare* to use the syllables sol-fa; see GAMUT]

soli ('səʊlɪ) *adj, adv Music.* (of a piece or passage) (to be performed) by or with soloists.

solicit ⓣ (sə'lɪsɪt) *vb* **solicits, soliciting, solicited. 1** (when *intr,* foll. by *for*) to make a request, application, etc., to (a person for business, support, etc.). **2** to accost (a person) with an offer of sexual relations in return for money. **3** to provoke or incite (a person) to do something wrong or illegal. [C15: from OF *solliciter* to disturb, from L *sollicitāre* to harass, from *sollus* whole + *ciēre* to excite]
▸**soˌlici'tation** *n*

solicitor (sə'lɪsɪtə) *n* **1** (in Britain) a lawyer who advises clients on matters of law, draws up legal documents, prepares cases for barristers, etc. **2** (in the US) an officer responsible for the legal affairs of a town, city, etc. **3** a person who solicits.
▸**so'licitorˌship** *n*

Solicitor General *n, pl* **Solicitors General. 1** (in Britain) the law officer of the Crown ranking next to the Attorney General (in Scotland to the Lord Advocate) and acting as his assistant. **2** (in New Zealand) the government's chief lawyer.

solicitous ⓣ (sə'lɪsɪtəs) *adj* **1** showing consideration, concern, attention, etc. **2** keenly anxious or willing; eager. [C16: from L *sollicitus* anxious; see SOLICIT]
▸**so'licitousness** *n*

solicitude ⓣ (sə'lɪsɪˌtjuːd) *n* **1** the state or quality of being solicitous. **2** (*often pl*) something that causes anxiety or concern. **3** anxiety or concern.

solid ⓣ ('sɒlɪd) *adj* **1** of, concerned with, or being a substance in a physical state in which it resists changes in size and shape. Cf. **gas** (sense 1), **liquid** (sense 1). **2** consisting of matter all through. **3** of the same substance all through: *solid rock.* **4** sound; proved or provable: *solid facts.* **5** reliable or sensible; upstanding: *a solid citizen.* **6** firm, strong, compact, or substantial: *a solid table; solid ground.* **7** (of a meal or food) substantial. **8** (*often postpositive*) without interruption or respite: *solid bombardment.* **9** financially sound or solvent: *a solid institution.* **10** strongly linked or consolidated: *a solid relationship.* **11 solid for.** unanimously in favour of. **12** *Geom.* having or relating to three dimensions. **13** (of a word composed of two or more elements) written or printed as a single word without a hyphen. **14** *Printing.* with no space or leads between lines of type. **15** (of a writer, work, etc.) adequate; sensible. **16** of or having a single uniform colour or tone. **17** *Austral. & NZ inf.* excessively severe or unreasonable. ◆ *n* **18** *Geom.* **18a** a closed surface in three-dimensional space. **18b** such a surface together with the volume enclosed by it. **19** a solid substance, such as wood, iron, or diamond. [C14: from OF *solide,* from L *solidus* firm]
▸**solidity** (sə'lɪdɪtɪ) *n* ▸**'solidly** *adv* ▸**'solidness** *n*

solidago (ˌsɒlɪ'deɪgəʊ) *n, pl* **solidagos.** any plant of a chiefly American genus, which includes the goldenrods. [C18: via NL from Med. L *soldago* a plant reputed to have healing properties, from *soldāre* to strengthen, from L *solidāre,* from *solidus* solid]

solid angle *n* an area subtended in three dimensions by lines intersecting at a point on a sphere whose radius is the distance to the point. See also **steradian.**

solidarity ⓣ (ˌsɒlɪ'dærɪtɪ) *n, pl* **solidarities.** unity of interests, sympathies, etc., as among members of the same class.

solid fuel *n* **1** a fuel, such as coal or coke, that is a solid rather than an oil or gas. **2** Also called: **solid propellant.** a rocket fuel that is a solid rather than a liquid or a gas.

solid geometry *n* the branch of geometry concerned with three-dimensional geometric figures.

solidify ⓣ (sə'lɪdɪˌfaɪ) *vb* **solidifies, solidifying, solidified. 1** to make or become solid or hard. **2** to make or become strong, united, determined, etc.
▸**soˌlidifi'cation** *n* ▸**so'lidiˌfier** *n*

solid-state *n* (*modifier*) **1** (of an electronic device) activated by a semiconductor component in which current flow is through solid material rather than in a vacuum. **2** of, concerned with, characteristic of, or consisting of solid matter.

solid-state physics *n* (*functioning as sing*) the branch of physics concerned with the properties of solids, such as superconductivity, photoconductivity, and ferromagnetism.

solidus ('sɒlɪdəs) *n, pl* **solidi** (-ˌdaɪ). **1** Also called: **diagonal, oblique, separatrix, shilling mark, slash, stroke, virgule.** a short oblique stroke used in text to separate items of information, such as days, months, and years in dates (*18/7/80*), alternative words (*and/or*), numerator from denominator in fractions (*55/103*), etc. **2** a gold coin of the Byzantine empire. [C14: from LL *solidus* (*nummus*) a gold coin (from *solidus* solid); in Med. L, *solidus* referred to a shilling and was indicated by a long *s,* which ult. became the virgule]

solifluction *or* **solifluxion** ('sɒlɪˌflʌkʃən, 'səʊlɪ-) *n* slow downhill movement of soil, saturated with meltwater, over a permanently frozen subsoil in tundra regions. [C20: from L *solum* soil + *fluctio* act of flowing]

soliloquize *or* **soliloquise** (sə'lɪləˌkwaɪz) *vb* **soliloquizes, soliloquizing, soliloquized** *or* **soliloquises, soliloquising, soliloquised.** (*intr*) to utter a soliloquy.
▸**so'liloquist** *n* ▸**so'liloˌquizer** *or* **so'liloˌquiser** *n*

soliloquy (sə'lɪləkwɪ) *n, pl* **soliloquies. 1** the act of speaking alone or to oneself, esp. as a theatrical device. **2** a speech in a play that is spoken in soliloquy. [C17: via LL *sōliloquium,* from L *sōlus* sole + *loquī* to speak]

> **USAGE NOTE** *Soliloquy* is sometimes wrongly used where *monologue* is meant. Both words refer to a long speech by one person, but a *monologue* can be addressed to other people, whereas in a *soliloquy* the speaker is always talking to himself or herself.

solipsism ('sɒlɪpˌsɪzəm) *n Philosophy.* the extreme form of scepticism

THESAURUS

solely *adv* **1-3** = **only,** alone, completely, entirely, exclusively, merely, single-handedly, singly

solemn *adj* **1, 2** = **formal,** august, awe-inspiring, ceremonial, ceremonious, dignified, grand, grave, imposing, impressive, majestic, momentous, stately **3** = **serious,** earnest, glum, grave, portentous, sedate, sober, staid, thoughtful **5** = **sacred,** devotional, hallowed, holy, religious, reverential, ritual, sanctified, venerable
Antonyms *adj* ≠ **formal:** informal, relaxed, unceremonious ≠ **serious:** bright, cheerful, chirpy (*inf.*), comical, frivolous, genial, happy, jovial, light-hearted, merry ≠ **sacred:** irreligious, irreverent, unholy

solemnity *n* **1** = **formality,** earnestness, grandeur, gravitas, gravity, impressiveness, momentousness, portentousness, seriousness **2** *often plural* = **ritual,** celebration, ceremonial, ceremony, formalities, observance, proceedings, rite

solemnize *vb* **1, 2** = **celebrate,** commemorate, honour, keep, observe, perform

solicit *vb* **1** = **request,** ask, beg, beseech, canvass, crave, entreat, implore, importune, petition, plead for, pray, seek, supplicate

solicitous *adj* **1** = **concerned,** anxious, apprehensive, attentive, careful, caring, earnest, troubled, uneasy, worried **2** = **eager,** zealous

solicitude *n* **1** = **concern,** anxiety, attentiveness, care, considerateness, consideration, regard, worry

solid *adj* **1, 2** = **firm,** compact, concrete, dense, hard, massed **3** = **continuous,** complete, unalloyed, unanimous, unbroken, undivided, uninterrupted, united, unmixed **4** = **sound,** genuine, good, pure, real, reliable **5** = **reliable,** constant, decent, dependable, estimable, law-abiding, level-headed, sensible, serious, sober, trusty, upright, upstanding, worthy **6, 10** = **strong,** stable, sturdy, substantial, unshakable
Antonyms *adj* ≠ **firm:** gaseous, hollow, liquid, permeable, unsubstantial ≠ **sound:** impure, unreliable, unsound ≠ **reliable:** flighty, irresponsible, unreliable, unsound, unstable, unsteady ≠ **strong:** crumbling, decaying, flimsy, precarious, shaky, unstable, unsteady

solidarity *n* = **unity,** accord, camaraderie, cohesion, community of interest, concordance, esprit de corps, harmony, like-mindedness, singleness of purpose, soundness, stability, team spirit, unanimity, unification

solidify *vb* **1** = **harden,** cake, coagulate, cohere, congeal, jell, set

which denies the possibility of any knowledge other than of one's own existence. [C19: from L *sōlus* alone + *ipse* self]
►ˈ**solipsist** *n, adj* ►ˌ**solipˈsistic** *adj*

solitaire (ˈsɒlɪˌtɛə, ˌsɒlɪˈtɛə) *n* **1** Also called: **pegboard.** a game played by one person, esp. one involving moving and taking pegs in a pegboard with the object of being left with only one. **2** the US name for **patience** (the card game). **3** a gem, esp. a diamond, set alone in a ring. **4** any of several extinct birds related to the dodo. **5** any of several dull grey North American songbirds. [C18: from OF: SOLITARY]

solitary (ˈsɒlɪtərɪ, -trɪ) *adj* **1** following or enjoying a life of solitude: *a solitary disposition.* **2** experienced or performed alone: *a solitary walk.* **3** (of a place) unfrequented. **4** (*prenominal*) single; sole: *a solitary cloud.* **5** having few companions; lonely. **6** (of animals) not living in organized colonies or large groups: *solitary bees.* **7** (of flowers) growing singly. ◆ *n, pl* **solitaries. 8** a person who lives in seclusion; hermit. **9** *Inf.* short for **solitary confinement.** [C14: from L *sōlitārius,* from *sōlus* SOLE[1]]
►ˈ**solitarily** *adv* ►ˈ**solitariness** *n*

solitary confinement *n* isolation imposed on a prisoner, as by confinement in a special cell.

solitude (ˈsɒlɪˌtjuːd) *n* **1** the state of being solitary or secluded. **2** *Poetic.* a solitary place. [C14: from L *sōlitūdō,* from *sōlus* alone, SOLE[1]]
►ˌ**soliˈtudinous** *adj*

solmization *or* **solmisation** (ˌsɒlmɪˈzeɪʃən) *n Music.* a system of naming the notes of a scale by syllables instead of letters, which assigns the names *ut* (or *do*), *re, mi, fa, sol, la, si* (or *ti*) to the degrees of the major scale of C (**fixed system**) or (excluding the syllables *ut* and *si*) to the major scale in any key (**movable system**). See also **tonic sol-fa.** [C18: from F *solmisation,* from *solmiser* to use the sol-fa syllables, from SOL[1] + MI]

solo (ˈsəʊləʊ) *n, pl* **solos. 1** (*pl* **solos** *or* **soli** (-liː)). a musical composition for one performer with or without accompaniment. **2** any of various card games in which each person plays on his own, such as solo whist. **3** a flight in which an aircraft pilot is unaccompanied. **4a** any performance carried out by an individual without assistance. **4b** (*as modifier*)*: a solo attempt.* ◆ *adj* **5** *Music.* unaccompanied: *a sonata for cello solo.* ◆ *adv* **6** by oneself; alone: *to fly solo.* ◆ *vb* **7** (*intr*) to operate an aircraft alone. [C17: via It. from L *sōlus* alone]
►**soloist** (ˈsəʊləʊɪst) *n*

Solomon (ˈsɒləmən) *n* any person credited with great wisdom. [after 10th-cent. B.C. king of Israel]
►**Solomonic** (ˌsɒləˈmɒnɪk) *adj*

Solomon's seal *n* **1** another name for **Star of David. 2** any of several plants of N temperate regions, having greenish or yellow paired flowers, long narrow waxy leaves, and prominent leaf scars. [C16: translation of Med. L *sigillum Solomonis,* ?from resemblance of the leaf scars to seals]

Solon (ˈsəʊlən) *n* a wise lawmaker. [after Athenian statesman (?638–?559 B.C.), who introduced economic, political, and legal reforms]

so long *sentence substitute.* **1** *Inf.* farewell; goodbye. ◆ *adv* **2** *S. African sl.* for the time being; meanwhile.

solo whist *n* a version of whist for four players acting independently, each of whom may bid to win or lose a fixed number of tricks.

solstice (ˈsɒlstɪs) *n* **1** either the shortest day of the year (**winter solstice**) or the longest day of the year (**summer solstice**). **2** either of the two points on the ecliptic at which the sun is overhead at the tropic of Cancer or Capricorn at the summer and winter solstices. [C13: via OF from L *sōlstitium,* lit.: the (apparent) standing still of the sun, from *sōl* sun + *sistere* to stand still]
►**solstitial** (sɒlˈstɪʃəl) *adj*

soluble (ˈsɒljubᵊl) *adj* **1** (of a substance) capable of being dissolved, esp. easily dissolved. **2** capable of being solved or answered. [C14: from LL *solūbilis,* from L *solvere* to dissolve]
►ˌ**soluˈbility** *n* ►ˈ**solubly** *adv*

solus (ˈsəʊləs) *adj* **1** alone; separate. **2** of or denoting the position of an advertising poster or press advertisement that is separated from competing advertisements: *a solus position.* **3** of or denoting a retail outlet, such as a petrol station, that sells the products of one company exclusively: *a solus site.* **4** (*fem* **sola**) alone; by oneself (formerly used in stage directions). [C17: from L *sōlus* alone]

solute (ˈsɒljuːt) *n* **1** the substance in a solution that is dissolved. ◆ *adj* **2** *Bot.* loose or unattached; free. [C16: from L *solūtus* free, from *solvere* to release]

solution (səˈluːʃən) *n* **1** a homogeneous mixture of two or more substances in which the molecules or atoms of the substances are completely dispersed. **2** the act or process of forming a solution. **3** the state of being dissolved (esp. in **in solution**). **4** a mixture of substances in which one or more components are present as small particles with colloidal dimension: *a colloidal solution.* **5** a specific answer to or way of answering a problem. **6** the act or process of solving a problem. **7** *Maths.* **7a** the unique set of values that yield a true statement when substituted for the variables in an equation. **7b** a member of a set of assignments of values to variables under which a given statement is satisfied; a member of a solution set. [C14: from L *solūtiō* an unloosing, from *solūtus;* see SOLUTE]

solution set *n* another name for **truth set.**

Solutrean (səˈluːtrɪən) *adj* of or relating to an Upper Palaeolithic culture of Europe. [C19: after *Solutré,* village in central France where traces of this culture were orig. found]

solvation (sɒlˈveɪʃən) *n* the process in which there is some chemical association between the molecules of a solute and those of the solvent.

Solvay process (ˈsɒlveɪ) *n* an industrial process for manufacturing sodium carbonate. Carbon dioxide is passed into a solution of sodium chloride saturated with ammonia. Sodium bicarbonate is precipitated and heated to form the carbonate. [C19: after Ernest *Solvay* (1838–1922), Belgian chemist who invented it]

solve (sɒlv) *vb* **solves, solving, solved.** (*tr*) **1** to find the explanation for or solution to (a mystery, problem, etc.). **2** *Maths.* **2a** to work out the answer to (a problem). **2b** to obtain the roots of (an equation). [C15: from L *solvere* to loosen]
►ˈ**solvable** *adj*

solvent (ˈsɒlvənt) *adj* **1** capable of meeting financial obligations. **2** (of a substance, esp. a liquid) capable of dissolving another substance. ◆ *n* **3** a liquid capable of dissolving another substance. **4** something that solves. [C17: from L *solvēns* releasing, from *solvere* to free]
►ˈ**solvency** *n*

solvent abuse *n* the deliberate inhaling of intoxicating fumes given off by certain solvents.

Som. *abbrev. for* Somerset.

soma[1] (ˈsəʊmə) *n, pl* **somata** (-mətə) *or* **somas.** the body of an organism, as distinct from the germ cells. [C19: via NL from Gk *sōma* the body]

soma[2] (ˈsəʊmə) *n* an intoxicating plant juice drink used in Vedic rituals. [from Sansk.]

Somali (səʊˈmɑːlɪ) *n* **1** (*pl* **Somalis** *or* **Somali**) a member of a tall dark-skinned people inhabiting Somalia in NE Africa. **2** the Cushitic language of this people. ◆ *adj* **3** of, relating to, or characteristic of Somalia, the Somalis, or their language.

somatic (səʊˈmætɪk) *adj* **1** of or relating to the soma: *somatic cells.* **2** of or relating to an animal body or body wall as distinct from the viscera, limbs, and head. **3** of or relating to the human body as distinct from the mind: *a somatic disease.* [C18: from Gk *sōmatikos* concerning the body, from *sōma* the body]
►**soˈmatically** *adv*

somato- *or before a vowel* **somat-** *combining form.* body: *somatotype.* [from Gk *sōma, sōmat-* body]

somatogenic (səˌmætəʊˈdʒɛnɪk) *adj Med.* originating in the cells of the body: of organic, rather than mental, origin: *a somatogenic disorder.*

somatotype (ˈsəʊmətəˌtaɪp) *n* a type or classification of physique or body build. See **endomorph, mesomorph, ectomorph.**

sombre *or US* **somber** (ˈsɒmbə) *adj* **1** dismal; melancholy: *a sombre mood.* **2** dim, gloomy, or shadowy. **3** (of colour, clothes, etc.) sober, dull, or dark. [C18: from F, from Vulgar L *subumbrāre* (unattested) to shade, from L *sub* beneath + *umbra* shade]
►ˈ**sombrely** *or US* ˈ**somberly** *adv* ►ˈ**sombreness** *or US* ˈ**somberness** *n*
►**sombrous** (ˈsɒmbrəs) *adj*

sombrero (sɒmˈbrɛərəʊ) *n, pl* **sombreros.** a hat with a wide brim, as worn in Mexico. [C16: from Sp., from *sombrero de sol* shade from the sun]

some (sʌm; *unstressed* səm) *determiner* **1a** (a) certain unknown or unspecified: *some people never learn.* **1b** (*as pron; functioning as sing or pl*)*: some can teach and others can't.* **2a** an unknown or unspecified quantity or amount of: *there's some rice on the table; he owns some horses.* **2b** (*as pron; functioning as sing or pl*)*: we'll buy some.* **3a** a considerable number or amount of: *he lived some years afterwards.* **3b** a little: *show him some respect.* **4** (*usually stressed*) *Inf.* an impressive or remarkable: *that was some game!* ◆ *adv* **5** about; approximately: *some thirty pounds.* **6** a certain amount (more) (in **some more** and (*inf.*) **and then some**). **7** *US, not standard.* to a certain degree or extent: *I like him some.* [OE *sum*]

-some[1] *suffix forming adjectives.* characterized by; tending to: *awesome; tiresome.* [OE *-sum*]

-some[2] *suffix forming nouns.* indicating a group of a specified number of members: *threesome.* [OE *sum,* special use of SOME (determiner)]

-some[3] (-səʊm) *n combining form.* a body: *chromosome.* [from Gk *sōma* body]

THESAURUS

solitary *adj* **1** = **unsociable,** cloistered, hermitical, isolated, reclusive, retired, unsocial **3** = **isolated,** desolate, hidden, out-of-the-way, remote, sequestered, unfrequented, unvisited **4** = **single,** alone, lone, sole **5** = **lonely,** companionless, friendless, lonesome ◆ *n* **8** = **hermit,** introvert, loner (*inf.*), lone wolf, recluse
Antonyms *adj* ≠ **unsociable:** companionable, convivial, cordial, gregarious, outgoing, sociable, social ≠ **isolated:** bustling, busy, frequented, public, well-frequented ◆ *n* ≠ **hermit:** extrovert, mixer, socialite

solitude *n* **1** = **isolation,** ivory tower, loneliness, privacy, reclusiveness, retirement, seclusion **2** *Poetic* = **wilderness,** desert, emptiness, waste, wasteland

solution *n* **1** = **mixture,** blend, compound, emulsion, mix, solvent, suspension **2** = **dissolving,** disconnection, dissolution, liquefaction, melting **5, 6** = **answer,** clarification, elucidation, explanation, explication, key, resolution, result, solving, unfolding, unravelling

solve *vb* **1** = **answer,** clarify, clear up, crack, decipher, disentangle, elucidate, explain, expound, get to the bottom of, interpret, resolve, suss (out) (*sl.*), unfold, unravel, work out

solvent *adj* **1** = **financially sound,** in the black, solid, unindebted **2** = **resolvent,** dissolvent

sombre *adj* **1** = **gloomy,** dismal, doleful, funereal, grave, joyless, lugubrious, melancholy, mournful, sad, sepulchral, sober **2** = **dark,** dim, drab, dull, dusky, gloomy, obscure, shadowy, shady, sober
Antonyms *adj* ≠ **gloomy:** bright, cheerful, chirpy (*inf.*), effusive, full of beans, genial, happy, lively, sunny, upbeat (*inf.*) ≠ **dark:** bright, colourful, dazzling, garish, gaudy

somebody ⓣ ('sʌmbədɪ) *pron* **1** some person; someone. ◆ *n, pl* **somebodies. 2** a person of great importance: *he is somebody in this town.*

> **USAGE NOTE** See at **everyone.**

someday ⓣ ('sʌmˌdeɪ) *adv* at some unspecified time in the (distant) future.

somehow ⓣ ('sʌmˌhaʊ) *adv* **1** in some unspecified way. **2** Also: **somehow or other.** by any means that are necessary.

someone ('sʌmˌwʌn, -wən) *pron* some person; somebody.

> **USAGE NOTE** See at **everyone.**

someplace ('sʌmˌpleɪs) *adv US & Canad. inf.* in, at, or to some unspecified place or region.

somersault *or* **summersault** ('sʌməˌsɔːlt) *n* **1a** a forward roll in which the head is placed on the ground and the trunk and legs are turned over it. **1b** a similar roll in a backward direction. **2** an acrobatic feat in which either of these rolls is performed in midair, as in diving or gymnastics. **3** a complete reversal of opinion, policy, etc. ◆ *vb* **4** (*intr*) to perform a somersault. [C16: from OF *soubresault,* prob. from OProvençal *sobresaut,* from *sobre* over (from L *super*) + *saut* a jump, leap (from L *saltus*)]

something ('sʌmθɪŋ) *pron* **1** an unspecified or unknown thing; some thing: *take something warm with you.* **2 something or other.** one unspecified thing or an alternative thing. **3** an unspecified or unknown amount: *something less than a hundred.* **4** an impressive or important person, thing, or event: *isn't that something?* ◆ *adv* **5** to some degree; a little; somewhat: *to look something like me.* **6** (foll. by an *adj*) *Inf.* (intensifier): *it hurts something awful.* **7 something else.** *Sl., chiefly US.* a remarkable person or thing.

-something *n combining form.* **a** a person whose age can be approximately expressed by a specified decade. **b** (*as modifier*): *the thirty-something market.* [C20: from the US television series *thirtysomething*]

sometime ('sʌmˌtaɪm) *adv* **1** at some unspecified point of time. ◆ *adj* **2** (*prenominal*) having been at one time; former: *the sometime President.*

> **USAGE NOTE** The form *sometime* should not be used to refer to a fairly long period of time: *he has been away for some time* (not *for sometime*).

sometimes ⓣ ('sʌmˌtaɪmz) *adv* **1** now and then; from time to time. **2** *Obs.* formerly; sometime.

someway ('sʌmˌweɪ) *adv* in some unspecified manner.

somewhat ('sʌmˌwɒt) *adv* (*not used with a negative*) rather; a bit: *she found it somewhat odd.*

somewhere ('sʌmˌwɛə) *adv* **1** in, to, or at some unknown or unspecified place or point: *somewhere in England; somewhere between 3 and 4 o'clock.* **2 get somewhere.** *Inf.* to make progress.

sommelier ('sʌməlˌjeɪ) *n* a wine waiter. [F: butler, via OF from OProvençal *saumalier* pack-animal driver, from LL *sagma* a pack-saddle, from Gk]

somnambulate (sɒm'næmbjʊˌleɪt) *vb* **somnambulates, somnambulating, somnambulated.** (*intr*) to walk while asleep. [C19: from L *somnus* sleep + *ambulāre* to walk]

▸**som'nambulance** *n* ▸**som'nambulant** *adj, n* ▸**somˌnambu'lation** *n* ▸**som'nambuˌlator** *n*

somnambulism (sɒm'næmbjʊˌlɪzəm) *n* a condition characterized by walking while asleep or in a hypnotic trance. Also called: **noctambulism.**

▸**som'nambulist** *n*

somniferous (sɒm'nɪfərəs) *or* **somnific** *adj Rare.* tending to induce sleep.

somnolent ⓣ ('sɒmnələnt) *adj* **1** drowsy; sleepy. **2** causing drowsiness. [C15: from L *somnus* sleep]

▸**'somnolence** *or* **'somnolency** *n* ▸**'somnolently** *adv*

son (sʌn) *n* **1** a male offspring; a boy or man in relation to his parents. **2** a male descendant. **3** (*often cap.*) a familiar term of address for a boy or man. **4** a male from a certain country, environment, etc.: *a son of the circus.* ◆ Related adj: **filial.** [OE *sunu*]

▸**'sonless** *adj*

Son (sʌn) *n Christianity.* the second person of the Trinity, Jesus Christ.

sonant ('səʊnənt) *adj* **1** *Phonetics.* denoting a voiced sound capable of forming a syllable or syllable nucleus. **2** inherently possessing, exhibiting, or producing a sound. **3** *Rare.* resonant; sounding. ◆ *n* **4** *Phonetics.* a voiced sound belonging to the class of frictionless continuants or nasals (l, r, m, n, ŋ) considered from the point of view of being a vowel and, in this capacity, able to form a syllable or syllable nucleus. [C19: from L *sonāns* sounding, from *sonāre* to make a noise, resound]

▸**'sonance** *n*

sonar ('səʊnɑː) *n* a communication and position-finding device used in underwater navigation and target detection using echolocation. [C20: from *so(und) na(vigation and) r(anging)*]

sonata (sə'nɑːtə) *n* **1** an instrumental composition, usually in three or more movements, for piano alone (**piano sonata**) or for any other instrument with or without piano accompaniment (**violin sonata, cello sonata,** etc.). See also **sonata form. 2** a one-movement keyboard composition of the baroque period. [C17: from It., from *sonare* to sound, from L]

sonata form *n* a musical structure consisting of an expanded ternary form whose three sections (exposition, development, and recapitulation), followed by a coda, are characteristic of the first movement in a sonata, symphony, string quartet, concerto, etc.

sondage (sɒn'dɑːʒ) *n, pl* **sondages** (-'dɑːʒɪz, -'dɑːʒ). *Archaeol.* a deep trial trench for inspecting stratigraphy. [C20: from F: a sounding, from *sonder* to sound]

sonde (sɒnd) *n* a rocket, balloon, or probe used for observing in the upper atmosphere. [C20: from F: plummet, plumb line; see SOUND[3]]

sone (səʊn) *n* a unit of loudness equal to 40 phons. [C20: from L *sonus* a sound]

son et lumière ('sɒn eɪ 'luːmɪˌɛə) *n* an entertainment staged at night at a famous building, historical site, etc., whereby the history of the location is presented by means of lighting effects, sound effects, and narration. [F, lit.: sound and light]

song ⓣ (sɒŋ) *n* **1a** a piece of music, usually employing a verbal text, composed for the voice, esp. one intended for performance by a soloist. **1b** the whole repertory of such pieces. **1c** (*as modifier*): *a song book.* **2** poetical composition; poetry. **3** the characteristic tuneful call or sound made by certain birds or insects. **4** the act or process of singing: *they raised their voices in song.* **5 for a song.** at a bargain price. **6 on song.** *Brit. inf.* performing at peak efficiency or ability. [OE *sang*]

song and dance ⓣ *n Inf.* **1** *Brit.* a fuss, esp. one that is unnecessary. **2** *US & Canad.* a long or elaborate story or explanation.

songbird ('sɒŋˌbɜːd) *n* **1** any of a suborder of passerine birds having highly developed vocal organs and, in most, a musical call. **2** any bird having a musical call.

song cycle *n* any of several groups of songs written during and after the Romantic period, each series relating a story or grouped around a central motif.

songololo (ˌsɒŋgɒ'lɒlɒ) *n, pl* **songololos.** *S. African.* a millipede. [from Nguni, from *ukusonga* to roll up]

songster ('sɒŋstə) *n* **1** a singer or poet. **2** a singing bird; songbird.

▸**'songstress** *fem n*

song thrush *n* a common Old World thrush with a spotted breast, noted for its song.

songwriter ('sɒŋˌraɪtə) *n* a person who composes songs in a popular idiom.

sonic ('sɒnɪk) *adj* **1** of, involving, or producing sound. **2** having a speed about equal to that of sound in air. [C20: from L *sonus* sound]

sonic barrier *n* another name for **sound barrier.**

sonic boom *n* a loud explosive sound caused by the shock wave of an aircraft, etc., travelling at supersonic speed.

sonic depth finder *n* an instrument for detecting the depth of water or of a submerged object by means of sound waves; Fathometer.

sonics ('sɒnɪks) *n* (*functioning as sing*) *Physics.* the study of mechanical vibrations in matter.

son-in-law *n, pl* **sons-in-law.** the husband of one's daughter.

sonnet ('sɒnɪt) *Prosody.* ◆ *n* **1** a verse form consisting of 14 lines in iambic pentameter with a fixed rhyme scheme, usually divided into octave and sestet or, in the English form, into three quatrains and a couplet. ◆ *vb* **2** (*intr*) to compose sonnets. **3** (*tr*) to celebrate in a sonnet. [C16: via It. from OProvençal *sonet* a little poem, from *son* song, from L *sonus* a sound]

sonneteer (ˌsɒnɪ'tɪə) *n* a writer of sonnets.

sonny ('sʌnɪ) *n, pl* **sonnies.** *Often patronizing.* a familiar term of address to a boy or man.

sonobuoy ('səʊnəˌbɔɪ) *n* a buoy equipped to detect underwater noises and transmit them by radio. [SONIC + BUOY]

sonorant ('sɒnərənt) *n Phonetics.* **1** one of the frictionless continuants or nasals (l, r, m, n, ŋ) having consonantal or vocalic functions depending on its situation within the syllable. **2** either of the two con-

THESAURUS

somebody *n* **2** = **celebrity,** big hitter, big name, big noise (*inf.*), big shot (*inf.*), bigwig (*inf.*), dignitary, heavyweight (*inf.*), household name, luminary, megastar (*inf.*), name, notable, personage, public figure, star, superstar, V.I.P.
Antonyms *n* also-ran, cipher, lightweight (*inf.*), menial, nobody, nonentity, nothing (*inf.*)

someday *adv* = **eventually,** in the fullness of time, one day, one of these (fine) days, sooner or later, ultimately

somehow *adv* **2** = **one way or another,** by fair means or foul, by hook or (by) crook, by some means or other, come hell or high water (*inf.*), come what may

sometimes *adv* **1** = **occasionally,** at times, every now and then, every so often, from time to time, now and again, now and then, off and on, once in a while, on occasion
Antonyms *adv* always, consistently, constantly, continually, eternally, ever, everlastingly, evermore, forever, invariably, perpetually, unceasingly, without exception

somnolent *adj* **1** = **sleepy,** comatose, dozy, drowsy, half-awake, heavy-eyed, nodding off (*inf.*), soporific, torpid

song *n* **1** = **ballad,** air, anthem, canticle, canzonet, carol, chant, chorus, ditty, hymn, lay, lyric, melody, number, pop song, psalm, shanty, strain, tune

song and dance *n* **1** *Brit. informal* = **fuss,** ado, commotion, flap, hoo-ha, kerfuffle (*inf.*), pantomime (*inf.*), performance (*inf.*), pother, shindig (*inf.*), stir, to-do sonants represented in English orthography by *w* or *y* and regarded as either consonantal or vocalic articulations of the vowels (iː) and (uː).

sonorous (səˈnɔːrəs, ˈsɒnərəs) *adj* **1** producing or capable of producing sound. **2** (of language, sound, etc.) deep or resonant. **3** (esp. of speech) high-flown; grandiloquent. [C17: from L *sonōrus* loud, from *sonor* a noise]
▸**sonority** (səˈnɒrɪtɪ) *n* ▸**soˈnorously** *adv* ▸**soˈnorousness** *n*

sonsy *or* **sonsie** (ˈsɒnsɪ) *adj* **sonsier, sonsiest.** *Scot., Irish, & English dialect.* **1** plump; buxom. **2** cheerful; good-natured. **3** lucky. [C16: from Gaelic *sonas* good fortune]

sook (sʊk) *n* **1** *SW English dialect.* a baby. **2** *Derog.* a coward. [?from OE *sūcan* to suck, infl. by Welsh *swci swead* tame]

sool (suːl) *vb (tr) Austral. & NZ sl.* **1** to incite (esp. a dog) to attack. **2** to attack.
▸ˈ**sooler** *n*

soon (suːn) *adv* **1** in or after a short time; in a little while; before long. **2 as soon as.** at the very moment that: *as soon as she saw him.* **3 as soon ... as.** used to indicate that the second alternative is not preferable to the first: *I'd just as soon go by train as drive.* [OE *sōna*]

sooner (ˈsuːnə) *adv* **1** the comparative of **soon:** *he came sooner than I thought.* **2** rather; in preference: *I'd sooner die than give up.* **3 no sooner ... than.** immediately after or when: *no sooner had he got home than the rain stopped.* **4 sooner or later.** eventually; inevitably.

> **USAGE NOTE** *When* is sometimes used instead of *than* after *no sooner*, but this use is generally regarded as incorrect: *no sooner had he arrived than* (not *when*) *the telephone rang.*

soot (sʊt) *n* **1** finely divided carbon deposited from flames during the incomplete combustion of organic substances such as coal. ◆ *vb* **2** *(tr)* to cover with soot. [OE *sōt*]

sooth (suːθ) *Arch. or poetic.* ◆ *n* **1** truth or reality (esp. in **in sooth**). ◆ *adj* **2** true or real. [OE *sōth*]

soothe (suːð) *vb* **soothes, soothing, soothed. 1** *(tr)* to make calm or tranquil. **2** *(tr)* to relieve or assuage (pain, longing, etc.). **3** *(intr)* to bring tranquillity or relief. [C16 (in the sense: to mollify): from OE *sōthian* to prove]
▸ˈ**soother** *n* ▸ˈ**soothing** *adj* ▸ˈ**soothingly** *adv* ▸ˈ**soothingness** *n*

soothsayer (ˈsuːθˌseɪə) *n* a seer or prophet.

sooty (ˈsʊtɪ) *adj* **sootier, sootiest. 1** covered with soot. **2** resembling or consisting of soot.
▸ˈ**sootily** *adv* ▸ˈ**sootiness** *n*

sop (sɒp) *n* **1** *(often pl)* food soaked in a liquid before being eaten. **2** a concession, bribe, etc., given to placate or mollify: *a sop to one's feelings.* **3** *Inf.* a stupid or weak person. ◆ *vb* **sops, sopping, sopped. 4** *(tr)* to dip or soak (food) in liquid. **5** (when *intr*, often foll. by *in*) to soak or be soaked. **6** *(tr;* often foll. by *up)* to mop or absorb (liquid) as with a sponge. [OE *sopp*]

SOP *abbrev. for* standard operating procedure.

sop. *abbrev. for* soprano.

sophism (ˈsɒfɪzəm) *n* an instance of sophistry. Cf. **paralogism.** [C14: from L *sophisma*, from Gk: ingenious trick, from *sophizesthai* to use clever deceit, from *sophos* wise]

sophist (ˈsɒfɪst) *n* **1** a person who uses clever or quibbling but unsound arguments. **2** one of the pre-Socratic philosophers who were prepared to enter into debate on any subject however specious. [C16: from L *sophista*, from Gk *sophistēs* a wise man, from *sophizesthai* to act craftily]

sophistic (səˈfɪstɪk) *or* **sophistical** *adj* **1** of or relating to sophists or sophistry. **2** consisting of sophisms or sophistry; specious.
▸**soˈphistically** *adv*

sophisticate *vb* (səˈfɪstɪˌkeɪt), **sophisticates, sophisticating, sophisticated. 1** *(tr)* to make (someone) less natural or innocent, as by education. **2** to pervert or corrupt (an argument, etc.) by sophistry. **3** *(tr)* to make more complex or refined. **4** *Rare.* to falsify (a text, etc.) by alterations. ◆ *n* (səˈfɪstɪˌkeɪt, -kɪt). **5** a sophisticated person. [C14: from Med. L *sophisticāre*, from L *sophisticus* sophistic]
▸**soˌphistiˈcation** *n* ▸**soˈphistiˌcator** *n*

sophisticated (səˈfɪstɪˌkeɪtɪd) *adj* **1** having refined or cultured tastes and habits. **2** appealing to sophisticates: *a sophisticated restaurant.* **3** unduly refined or cultured. **4** pretentiously or superficially wise. **5** (of machines, methods, etc.) complex and refined.

sophistry (ˈsɒfɪstrɪ) *n, pl* **sophistries. 1a** a method of argument that is seemingly plausible though actually invalid and misleading. **1b** the art of using such arguments. **2** subtle but unsound or fallacious reasoning. **3** an instance of this.

sophomore (ˈsɒfəˌmɔː) *n Chiefly US & Canad.* a second-year student at a secondary (high) school or college. [C17: ?from earlier *sophumer*, from *sophum*, var. of SOPHISM, + -ER[1]]

Sophy *or* **Sophi** (ˈsəʊfɪ) *n, pl* **Sophies.** (formerly) a title of the Persian monarchs. [C16: from L *sophī* wise men, from Gk *sophos* wise]

-sophy *n combining form.* indicating knowledge or an intellectual system: *philosophy.* [from Gk, from *sophia* wisdom, from *sophos* wise]
▸**-sophic** *or* **-sophical** *adj combining form.*

soporific (ˌsɒpəˈrɪfɪk) *adj also (arch.)* ˌ**soporˈiferous. 1** inducing sleep. **2** drowsy; sleepy. ◆ *n* **3** a drug or other agent that induces sleep. [C17: from F, from L *sopor* sleep + -FIC]

sopping (ˈsɒpɪŋ) *adj* completely soaked; wet through. Also: **sopping wet.**

soppy (ˈsɒpɪ) *adj* **soppier, soppiest. 1** wet or soggy. **2** *Brit. inf.* silly or sentimental. **3 soppy on.** *Brit. inf.* foolishly charmed or affected by.
▸ˈ**soppily** *adv* ▸ˈ**soppiness** *n*

sopranino (ˌsɒprəˈniːnəʊ) *n, pl* **sopraninos. a** the instrument with the highest possible pitch in a family of instruments. **b** *(as modifier)*: *a sopranino recorder.* [It., dim. of SOPRANO]

soprano (səˈprɑːnəʊ) *n, pl* **sopranos** *or* **soprani** (-ˈprɑːniː). **1** the highest adult female voice. **2** the voice of a young boy before puberty. **3** a singer with such a voice. **4** the highest part of a piece of harmony. **5a** the highest or second highest instrument in a family of instruments. **5b** *(as modifier)*: *a soprano saxophone.* ◆ See also **treble.** [C18: from It., from *sopra* above, from L *suprā*]

soprano clef *n* the clef that establishes middle C as being on the bottom line of the staff.

sorb (sɔːb) *n* **1** another name for **service tree. 2** any of various related trees, esp. the mountain ash. **3** Also called: **sorb apple.** the fruit of any of these trees. [C16: from L *sorbus*]

sorbefacient (ˌsɔːbɪˈfeɪʃənt) *adj* **1** inducing absorption. ◆ *n* **2** a sorbefacient drug. [C19: from L *sorbē(re)* to absorb + -FACIENT]

sorbet (ˈsɔːbeɪ, -bɪt) *n* **1** a water ice made from fruit juice, egg whites, etc. **2** a US word for **sherbet** (sense 1). [C16: from F, from OIt. *sorbetto*, from Turkish *şerbet*, from Ar. *sharbah* a drink]

sorbic acid (ˈsɔːbɪk) *n* a white crystalline carboxylic acid found in berries of the mountain ash and used to inhibit the growth of moulds and as an additive (**E 200**) for certain synthetic coatings. [C19: from SORB (the tree), from its discovery in berries of the mountain ash]

sorbitol (ˈsɔːbɪˌtɒl) *n* a white crystalline alcohol, found in certain fruits and berries and manufactured by the catalytic hydrogenation of sucrose: used as a sweetener (**E 420**) and in the manufacture of ascorbic acid and synthetic resins. [C19: from SORB + -ITOL]

sorbo rubber (ˈsɔːbəʊ) *n Brit.* a spongy form of rubber. [C20: from ABSORB]

sorcerer (ˈsɔːsərə) *or (fem)* **sorceress** (ˈsɔːsərɪs) *n* a person who seeks to control and use magic powers; a wizard or magician. [C16: from OF *sorcier*, from Vulgar L *sortiārius* (unattested) caster of lots, from L *sors* lot]

sorcery (ˈsɔːsərɪ) *n, pl* **sorceries.** the art, practices, or spells of magic, esp. black magic. [C13: from OF *sorcerie*, from *sorcier* SORCERER]

sordid (ˈsɔːdɪd) *adj* **1** dirty, foul, or squalid. **2** degraded; vile; base. **3** selfish and grasping: *sordid avarice.* [C16: from L *sordidus*, from *sordēre* to be dirty]
▸ˈ**sordidly** *adv* ▸ˈ**sordidness** *n*

sordino (sɔːˈdiːnəʊ) *n, pl* **sordini** (-niː). **1** a mute for a stringed or brass musical instrument. **2** any of the dampers in a piano. **3 con sordino** *or* **sordini.** a musical direction to play with a mute. **4 senza sordino** *or* **sordini.** a musical direction to remove or play without the mute or (on the piano) with the sustaining pedal pressed down. [It.: from *sordo* deaf, from L *surdus*]

THESAURUS

sonorous *adj* **2** = **rich**, deep, full, loud, plangent, resonant, resounding, ringing, rounded, sounding **3** = **grandiloquent**, high-flown, high-sounding, orotund

soon *adv* **1** = **before long**, anon, any minute now, betimes (*arch.*), erelong (*arch. or poetic*), in a couple of shakes, in a little while, in a minute, in a short time, in the near future, in two shakes of a lamb's tail, shortly

soothe *vb* **1** = **calm**, allay, appease, calm down, compose, hush, lull, mitigate, mollify, pacify, quiet, settle, smooth down, soften, still, tranquillize **2** = **relieve**, alleviate, assuage, ease
Antonyms *vb* ≠ **calm:** aggravate (*inf.*), agitate, annoy, disquiet, disturb, excite, get on one's nerves (*inf.*), hassle (*inf.*), inflame, irritate, rouse, upset, vex, worry ≠ **relieve:** exacerbate, increase, inflame, irritate, stimulate

soothing *adj* **1** = **calming**, relaxing, restful **2** = **emollient**, balsamic, demulcent, easeful, lenitive, palliative

soothsayer *n* = **prophet**, augur, diviner, fortune-teller, seer, sibyl

sophisticated *adj* **1-3** = **cultured**, citified, cosmopolitan, cultivated, jet-set, refined, seasoned, urbane, worldly, worldly-wise, world-weary **5** = **complex**, advanced, complicated, delicate, elaborate, highly-developed, intricate, multifaceted, refined, subtle
Antonyms *adj* ≠ **cultured:** naive, unrefined, unsophisticated, unworldly, wet behind the ears (*inf.*) ≠ **complex:** basic, old-fashioned, plain, primitive, simple, uncomplicated, unrefined, unsophisticated, unsubtle

sophistication *n* **1** = **savoir-faire**, finesse, poise, *savoir-vivre*, urbanity, worldliness, worldly wisdom

sophistry *n* **1-3** = **fallacy**, casuistry, quibble, sophism

soporific *adj* **1** = **sleep-inducing**, hypnotic, sedative, sleepy, somniferous (*rare*), somnolent, tranquillizing ◆ *n* **3** = **sedative**, anaesthetic, hypnotic, narcotic, opiate, tranquillizer

soppy *adj* **2** *Brit. informal* = **sentimental**, corny (*sl.*), daft (*inf.*), drippy, gushy (*inf.*), lovey-dovey, mawkish, overemotional, schmaltzy (*sl.*), silly, slushy (*inf.*), soft (*inf.*), weepy (*inf.*)

sorcerer *n* = **magician**, enchanter, mage (*arch.*), magus, necromancer, warlock, witch, wizard

sorcery *n* = **black magic**, black art, charm, divination, enchantment, incantation, magic, necromancy, spell, witchcraft, witchery, wizardry

sordid *adj* **1** = **dirty**, filthy, foul, mean, seamy, seedy, sleazy, slovenly, slummy, squalid, unclean, wretched **2** = **base**, debauched, degenerate, degraded, despicable, disreputable, low, shabby, shameful, vicious, vile **3** = **mercenary**, avaricious, corrupt, covetous, grasping, miserly, niggardly, selfish, self-seeking, ungenerous, venal

sore ❶ (sɔː) *adj* **1** (esp. of a wound, injury, etc.) painfully sensitive; tender. **2** causing annoyance: *a sore point.* **3** resentful; irked. **4** urgent; pressing: *in sore need.* **5** (*postpositive*) grieved; distressed. **6** causing grief or sorrow. ◆ *n* **7** a painful or sensitive wound, injury, etc. **8** any cause of distress or vexation. ◆ *adv* **9** *Arch.* direly; sorely (now only in such phrases as **sore afraid**). [OE *sār*]
▸'**soreness** *n*

sorehead ('sɔːˌhɛd) *n Inf., chiefly US & Canad.* a peevish or disgruntled person.

sorely ('sɔːlɪ) *adv* **1** painfully or grievously: *sorely wounded.* **2** pressingly or greatly: *to be sorely taxed.*

sorghum ('sɔːgəm) *n* any grass of the Old World genus *Sorghum,* having glossy seeds: cultivated for grain, hay, and as a source of syrup. [C16: from NL, from It. *sorgo,* prob. from Vulgar L *Syricum grānum* (unattested) Syrian grain]

soroptimist (sə'rɒptɪmɪst) *n* a member of Soroptimist International, an organization of clubs for professional and executive businesswomen.

sorority (sə'rɒrɪtɪ) *n, pl* **sororities.** *Chiefly US.* a social club or society for university women. [C16: from Med. L *sorōritās,* from L *soror* sister]

sorption ('sɔːpʃən) *n* the process in which one substance takes up or holds another; adsorption or absorption. [C20: back formation from ABSORPTION, ADSORPTION]

sorrel[1] ('sɒrəl) *n* **1a** a light brown to brownish-orange colour. **1b** (*as adj*): *a sorrel carpet.* **2** a horse of this colour. [C15: from OF *sorel,* from *sor* a reddish brown, of Gmc origin]

sorrel[2] ('sɒrəl) *n* **1** any of several plants of Eurasia and North America, having acid-tasting leaves used in salads and sauces. **2** short for **wood sorrel.** [C14: from OF *surele,* from *sur* sour, of Gmc origin]

sorrow ❶ ('sɒrəʊ) *n* **1** the feeling of sadness, grief, or regret associated with loss, bereavement, sympathy for another's suffering, etc. **2** a particular cause or source of this. **3** Also called: **sorrowing.** the outward expression of grief or sadness. ◆ *vb* **4** (*intr*) to mourn or grieve. [OE *sorg*]
▸'**sorrowful** *adj* ▸'**sorrowfully** *adv* ▸'**sorrowfulness** *n*

sorry ❶ ('sɒrɪ) *adj* **sorrier, sorriest. 1** (*usually postpositive;* often foll. by *for*) feeling or expressing pity, sympathy, grief, or regret: *I feel sorry for him.* **2** pitiful, wretched, or deplorable: *a sorry sight.* **3** poor; paltry: *a sorry excuse.* **4** affected by sorrow; sad. **5** causing sorrow or sadness. ◆ *interj* **6** an exclamation expressing apology. [OE *sārig*]
▸'**sorrily** *adv* ▸'**sorriness** *n*

sort ❶ (sɔːt) *n* **1** a class, group, kind, etc., as distinguished by some common quality or characteristic. **2** *Inf.* a type of character, nature, etc.: *he's a good sort.* **3** *Austral. sl.* a person, esp. a girl. **4** a more or less definable or adequate example: *it's a sort of review.* **5** (*often pl*) *Printing.* any of the individual characters making up a fount of type. **6** *Arch.* manner; way: *in this sort we struggled home.* **7 after a sort.** to some extent. **8 of sorts** *or* **of a sort. 8a** of an inferior kind. **8b** of an indefinite kind. **9 out of sorts.** not in normal good health, temper, etc. **10 sort of.** in some way or other; as it were; rather. ◆ *vb* **11** (*tr*) to arrange according to class, type, etc. **12** (*tr*) to put (something) into working order. **13** to arrange (computer information) by machine in an order convenient to the user. **14** (*intr*) *Arch.* to agree; accord. [C14: from OF, from Med. L *sors* kind, from L: fate]
▸'**sortable** *adj* ▸'**sorter** *n*

USAGE NOTE See at **kind**[2].

sortie ('sɔːtɪ) *n* **1a** (of troops, etc.) the act of attacking from a contained or besieged position. **1b** the troops doing this. **2** an operational flight made by one aircraft. **3** a short or relatively short return trip. ◆ *vb* **sorties, sortieing, sortied. 4** (*intr*) to make a sortie. [C17: from F: a going out, from *sortir* to go out]

sortilege ('sɔːtɪlɪdʒ) *n* the act or practice of divination by drawing lots. [C14: via OF from Med. L *sortilegium,* from L *sortilegus* a soothsayer, from *sors* fate + *legere* to select]

sort out ❶ *vb* (*tr, adv*) **1** to find a solution to (a problem, etc.), esp. to make clear or tidy: *to sort out the mess.* **2** to take or separate, as from a larger group: *to sort out the likely ones.* **3** to organize into an orderly and disciplined group. **4** *Inf.* to beat or punish.

SOS *n* **1** an internationally recognized distress signal in which the letters SOS are repeatedly spelt out, as by radiotelegraphy: used esp. by ships and aircraft. **2** a message broadcast in an emergency for people otherwise unobtainable. **3** *Inf.* a call for help.

sosatie (sə'sɑːtɪ) *n S. African.* curried meat on skewers. [from Afrik., from Du.]

so-so ❶ *Inf.* ◆ *adj* **1** (*postpositive*) neither good nor bad. ◆ *adv* **2** in an average or indifferent manner.

sostenuto (ˌsɒstə'nuːtəʊ) *adj, adv Music.* to be performed in a smooth sustained manner. [C18: from It., from *sostenere* to sustain, from L *sustinēre*]

sot (sɒt) *n* **1** a habitual or chronic drunkard. **2** a person stupefied by or as if by drink. [OE, from Med. L *sottus*]
▸'**sottish** *adj*

soteriology (sɒˌtɪərɪ'ɒlədʒɪ) *n Christian theol.* the doctrine of salvation. [C19: from Gk *sōtēria* deliverance (from *sōtēr* a saviour) + -LOGY]

sotto voce ('sɒtəʊ 'vəʊtʃɪ) *adv* in an undertone. [C18: from It.: under (one's) voice]

sou (suː) *n* **1** a former French coin of low denomination. **2** a very small amount of money: *I haven't a sou.* [C19: from F, from OF *sol,* from L: SOLIDUS]

soubrette (suː'brɛt) *n* **1** a minor female role in comedy, often that of a pert lady's maid. **2** any pert or flirtatious girl. [C18: from F: maidservant, from Provençal, from *soubret* conceited, from *soubra* to exceed, from L *superāre* to surmount]

soubriquet ('səʊbrɪˌkeɪ) *n* a variant spelling of **sobriquet.**

soufflé ('suːfleɪ) *n* **1** a light fluffy dish made with beaten egg whites combined with cheese, fish, etc. **2** a similar sweet or savoury cold dish, set with gelatine. ◆ *adj also* **souffléed. 3** made light and puffy, as by beating and cooking. [C19: from F, from *souffler* to blow, from L *sufflāre*]

sough (saʊ) *vb* **1** (*intr*) (esp. of the wind) to make a sighing sound. ◆ *n* **2** a soft continuous murmuring sound. [OE *swōgan* to resound]

sought (sɔːt) *vb* the past tense and past participle of **seek.**

souk (suːk) *n* an open-air marketplace in Muslim countries, esp. North Africa and the Middle East. [from Ar.]

soukous ('suːkʊs) *n* a style of African popular music that originated in Zaïre (now the Democratic Republic of the Congo), characterized by syncopated rhythms and intricate contrasting guitar melodies. [C20: ? from F *secouer* to shake]

soul ❶ (səʊl) *n* **1** the spirit or immaterial part of man, the seat of human personality, intellect, will, and emotions: regarded as an entity that survives the body after death. **2** *Christianity.* the spiritual part of a person, capable of redemption from sin through divine grace. **3** the essential part or fundamental nature of anything. **4** a person's feelings or moral nature. **5a** Also called: **soul music.** a type of Black music resulting from the addition of jazz, gospel, and pop elements to the urban blues style. **5b** (*as modifier*): *a soul singer.* **6** (*modifier*) of or relating to Black Americans and their culture: *soul food.* **7** nobility of spirit or temperament: *a man of great soul.* **8** an inspiring or leading figure, as of a movement. **9** a person regarded as typifying some characteristic or quality: *the soul of discretion.* **10** a person; individual: *an honest soul.* **11 upon my soul!** an exclamation of surprise. [OE *sāwol*]

THESAURUS

Antonyms *adj* ≠ **dirty:** clean, fresh, pure, spotless, squeaky-clean, unblemished, undefiled, unsullied ≠ **base:** blameless, decent, honourable, noble, pure, upright

sore *adj* **1 = painful,** angry, burning, chafed, inflamed, irritated, raw, reddened, sensitive, smarting, tender **2 = annoying,** distressing, grievous, harrowing, severe, sharp, troublesome **3 = annoyed,** afflicted, aggrieved, angry, cross, grieved, hurt, irked, irritated, pained, peeved (*inf.*), resentful, stung, upset, vexed **4 = urgent,** acute, critical, desperate, dire, extreme, pressing ◆ *n* **7 = abscess,** boil, chafe, gathering, inflammation, ulcer

sorrow *n* **1 = grief,** affliction, anguish, distress, heartache, heartbreak, misery, mourning, regret, sadness, unhappiness, woe **2 = affliction,** blow, bummer (*sl.*), hardship, misfortune, trial, tribulation, trouble, woe, worry ◆ *vb* **4 = grieve,** agonize, bemoan, be sad, bewail, eat one's heart out, lament, moan, mourn, weep
Antonyms *n* ≠ **grief:** bliss, delight, elation, exaltation, exultation, gladness, happiness, joy, pleasure ≠ **affliction:** good fortune, lucky break ◆ *vb* ≠ **grieve:** celebrate, delight, exult, jump for joy, rejoice, revel

sorrowful *adj* **1 = sad,** affecting, afflicted, dejected, depressed, disconsolate, dismal, distressing, doleful, down in the dumps (*inf.*), grieving, harrowing, heartbroken, heart-rending, heavy-hearted, lamentable, lugubrious, melancholy, miserable, mournful, painful, piteous, rueful, sick at heart, sorry, tearful, unhappy, woebegone, woeful, wretched

sorry *adj* **1 = regretful,** apologetic, commiserative, compassionate, conscience-stricken, contrite, guilt-ridden, in sackcloth and ashes, penitent, pitying, remorseful, repentant, self-reproachful, shamefaced, sympathetic **2, 3 = wretched,** abject, base, deplorable, dismal, distressing, mean, miserable, paltry, pathetic, piteous, pitiable, pitiful, poor, sad, shabby, vile **4 = sad,** disconsolate, distressed, grieved, melancholy, mournful, sorrowful, unhappy
Antonyms *adj* ≠ **regretful:** heartless, impenitent, indifferent, not contrite, shameless, unapologetic, unashamed, uncompassionate, unconcerned, unmoved, unpitying, unremorseful, unrepentant, unsympathetic ≠ **sad:** cheerful, delighted, elated, happy, joyful

sort *n* **1 = kind,** brand, breed, category, character, class, denomination, description, family, genus, group, ilk, make, nature, order, quality, race, species, stamp, style, type, variety **9 out of sorts = in low spirits,** crotchety, down in the dumps (*inf.*), down in the mouth (*inf.*), grouchy (*inf.*), mopy, not up to par, not up to snuff (*inf.*), off colour, poorly (*inf.*), under the weather (*inf.*) **10 sort of = rather,** as it were, in part, moderately, reasonably, slightly, somewhat, to some extent ◆ *vb* **11 = arrange,** assort, catalogue, categorize, choose, class, classify, distribute, divide, file, grade, group, order, put in order, rank, select, separate, sequence, systematize, tabulate

sort out *vb* **1 = resolve,** clarify, clear up, put *or* get straight **2 = separate,** pick out, put on one side, segregate, select, sift **3 = organize,** tidy up

so-so *adj* **1** *Informal* **= average,** adequate, fair, fair to middling (*inf.*), indifferent, middling, moderate, not bad (*inf.*), O.K. *or* okay (*inf.*), ordinary, passable, respectable, run-of-the-mill, tolerable, undistinguished

soul *n* **1 = spirit,** animating principle, essence, intellect, life, mind, psyche, reason, vital force **7 = feeling,** animation, ardour, courage, energy, fervour, force, inspiration, vitality, vivacity **9 = embodiment,** epitome, incarnation, personification, quintessence **10 = person,** being, body, creature, individual, man *or* woman, mortal

DICTIONARY

soul-destroying Ⓣ *adj* (of an occupation, situation, etc.) unremittingly monotonous.

soul food *n Inf.* food, such as chitterlings, yams, etc., traditionally eaten by African-Americans.

soulful Ⓣ ('səʊlfʊl) *adj* expressing profound thoughts or feelings.
▸**'soulfully** *adv* ▸**'soulfulness** *n*

soulless Ⓣ ('səʊllɪs) *adj* **1** lacking humanizing qualities or influences; mechanical: *soulless work.* **2** (of a person) lacking in sensitivity or nobility.
▸**'soullessness** *n*

soul mate *n* a person for whom one has a deep affinity, esp. a lover, wife, husband, etc.

soul-searching *n* **1** deep or critical examination of one's motives, actions, beliefs, etc. ◆ *adj* **2** displaying the characteristics of this.

sound[1] Ⓣ (saʊnd) *n* **1a** a periodic disturbance in the pressure or density of a fluid or in the elastic strain of a solid, produced by a vibrating object. It travels as longitudinal waves. **1b** (*as modifier*): *a sound wave.* **2** the sensation produced by such a periodic disturbance in the organs of hearing. **3** anything that can be heard. **4** (*modifier*) of or relating to radio as distinguished from television: *sound broadcasting.* **5** a particular instance or type of sound: *the sound of running water.* **6** volume or quality of sound: *a radio with poor sound.* **7** the area or distance over which something can be heard: *within the sound of Big Ben.* **8** impression or implication: *I don't like the sound of that.* **9** (*often pl*) *Sl.* music, esp. rock, jazz, or pop. ◆ *vb* **10** to cause (an instrument, etc.) to make a sound or (of an instrument, etc.) to emit a sound. **11** to announce or be announced by a sound: *to sound the alarm.* **12** (*intr*) (of a sound) to be heard. **13** (*intr*) to resonate with a certain quality or intensity: *to sound loud.* **14** (*copula*) to give the impression of being as specified: *to sound reasonable.* **15** (*tr*) to pronounce distinctly or audibly: *to sound one's consonants.* [C13: from OF *soner* to make a sound, from L *sonāre*, from *sonus* a sound]
▸**'soundable** *adj*

sound[2] Ⓣ (saʊnd) *adj* **1** free from damage, injury, decay, etc. **2** firm; substantial: *a sound basis.* **3** financially safe or stable: *a sound investment.* **4** showing good judgment or reasoning; wise: *sound advice.* **5** valid, logical, or justifiable: *a sound argument.* **6** holding approved beliefs; ethically correct; honest. **7** (of sleep) deep; peaceful; unbroken. **8** thorough: *a sound examination.* ◆ *adv* **9** soundly; deeply: now archaic except when applied to sleep. [OE *sund*]
▸**'soundly** *adv* ▸**'soundness** *n*

sound[3] Ⓣ (saʊnd) *vb* **1** to measure the depth of (a well, the sea, etc.) by plumb line, sonar, etc. **2** to seek to discover (someone's views, etc.), as by questioning. **3** (*intr*) (of a whale, etc.) to dive downwards swiftly and deeply. **4** *Med.* **4a** to probe or explore (a bodily cavity or passage) by means of a sound. **4b** to examine (a patient) by means of percussion and auscultation. ◆ *n* **5** *Med.* an instrument for insertion into a bodily cavity or passage to dilate strictures, dislodge foreign material, etc. ◆ See also **sound out.** [C14: from OF *sonder*, from *sonde* sounding line, prob. of Gmc origin]
▸**'sounder** *n*

sound[4] Ⓣ (saʊnd) *n* **1** a relatively narrow channel between two larger areas of sea or between an island and the mainland. **2** an inlet or deep bay of the sea. **3** the air bladder of a fish. [OE *sund* swimming, narrow sea]

soundalike ('saʊndəˌlaɪk) *n* **a** a person or thing that sounds like another, often well-known, person or thing. **b** (*as modifier*): *a soundalike band.*

sound barrier *n* (not in technical usage) a hypothetical barrier to flight at or above the speed of sound, when a sudden large increase in drag occurs. Also called: **sonic barrier.**

sound bite *n* a short pithy sentence or phrase extracted from a longer speech for use on radio or television.

soundbox ('saʊndˌbɒks) *n* the resonating chamber of the hollow body of a violin, guitar, etc.

sound effect *n* any sound artificially produced, reproduced from a recording, etc., to create a theatrical effect, as in plays, films, etc.

sounding[1] ('saʊndɪŋ) *adj* **1** resounding; resonant. **2** having an imposing sound and little content; pompous: *sounding phrases.*

sounding[2] ('saʊndɪŋ) *n* **1** (*sometimes pl*) the act or process of measuring depth of water or examining the bottom of a river, lake, etc., as with a sounding line. **2** an observation or measurement of atmospheric conditions, as made using a sonde. **3** (*often pl*) measurements taken by sounding. **4** (*pl*) a place where a sounding line will reach the bottom, esp. less than 100 fathoms in depth.

sounding board *n* **1** Also called: **soundboard.** a thin wooden board in a violin, piano, etc., serving to amplify the vibrations produced by the strings passing across it. **2** Also called: **soundboard.** a thin screen suspended over a pulpit, stage, etc., to reflect sound towards an audience. **3** a person, group, experiment, etc., used to test a new idea, policy, etc.

sounding line *n* a line marked off to indicate its length and having a **sounding lead** at one end. It is dropped over the side of a vessel to determine the depth of the water.

soundless ('saʊndlɪs) *adj* extremely still or silent.
▸**'soundlessness** *n*

sound out Ⓣ *vb* (*tr, adv*) to question (someone) in order to discover (opinions, facts, etc.).

soundpost ('saʊndˌpəʊst) *n Music.* a small wooden post in guitars, violins, etc., that joins the front to the back and helps support the bridge.

soundproof ('saʊndˌpruːf) *adj* **1** not penetrable by sound. ◆ *vb* **2** (*tr*) to render soundproof.

sound spectrograph *n* an electronic instrument that produces a record (**sound spectrogram**) of the frequencies and intensities of the components of a sound.

sound system *n* **1** any system of sounds, as in the speech of a language. **2** integrated equipment for producing amplified sound, as in a hi-fi or mobile disco, or as a public-address system on stage.

soundtrack ('saʊndˌtræk) *n* **1** the recorded sound accompaniment to a film. **2** a narrow strip along the side of a spool of film, which carries the sound accompaniment.

sound wave *n* a wave that propagates sound.

soup (suːp) *n* **1** a liquid food made by boiling or simmering meat, fish, vegetables, etc. **2** *Inf.* a photographic developer. **3** *Inf.* anything resembling soup, esp. thick fog. **4** a slang name for **nitroglycerine. 5 in the soup.** *Sl.* in trouble or difficulties. [C17: from OF *soupe*, from LL *suppa*, of Gmc origin]
▸**'soupy** *adj*

soupçon *French.* (supsɔ̃) *n* a slight amount; dash. [C18: from F, ult. from L *suspicio* SUSPICION]

soup kitchen *n* **1** a place or mobile stall where food and drink, esp. soup, is served to destitute people. **2** *Mil.* a mobile kitchen.

soup plate *n* a deep plate with a wide rim, used esp. for drinking soup.

soup up *vb* (*tr, adv*) *Sl.* to modify the engine of (a car or motorcycle) in order to increase its power. Also: **hot up,** (esp. US and Canad.) **hop up.**

sour Ⓣ ('saʊə) *adj* **1** having or denoting a sharp biting taste like that of lemon juice or vinegar. **2** made acid or bad, as in the case of milk, by the action of microorganisms. **3** having a rancid or unwholesome smell. **4** (of a person's temperament) sullen, morose, or disagreeable. **5** (esp. of the weather) harsh and unpleasant. **6** disagreeable; distasteful: *a sour experience.* **7** (of land, etc.) lacking in fertility, esp. due to excessive acidity. **8** (of petrol, gas, etc.) containing a relatively large amount of sulphur compounds. **9 go** *or* **turn sour.** to become unfavourable or inharmonious: *his marriage went sour.* ◆ *n* **10** something sour. **11** *Chiefly US.* an iced drink usually made with spirits, lemon juice, and ice: *a whiskey sour.* **12** an acid used in bleaching clothes or in curing skins. ◆ *vb* **13** to make or become sour. [OE *sūr*]
▸**'sourish** *adj* ▸**'sourly** *adv* ▸**'sourness** *n*

source Ⓣ (sɔːs) *n* **1** the point or place from which something originates. **2a** a spring that forms the starting point of a stream. **2b** the area where the headwaters of a river rise. **3** a person, group, etc., that creates, issues, or originates something: *the source of a complaint.* **4a** any person, book, organization, etc., from which information, evidence,

THESAURUS

soul-destroying *adj* = **mind-numbing**, dreary, dull, humdrum, monotonous, tedious, tiresome, treadmill, unvarying, wearisome

soulful *adj* = **expressive**, eloquent, heartfelt, meaningful, mournful, moving, profound, sensitive

soulless *adj* **1** = **spiritless**, dead, lifeless, mechanical, soul-destroying, uninteresting **2** = **unfeeling**, callous, cold, cruel, harsh, inhuman, unkind, unsympathetic

sound[1] *n* **2, 3, 5** = **noise**, din, report, resonance, reverberation, tone, voice **7** = **range**, earshot, hearing **8** = **impression**, drift, idea, implication(s), look, tenor ◆ *vb* **10, 12, 13** = **resound**, echo, resonate, reverberate **11** = **pronounce**, announce, articulate, declare, enunciate, express, signal, utter **14** = **seem**, appear, give the impression of, look, strike one as being

sound[2] *adj* **1, 2** = **perfect**, complete, entire, firm, fit, hale, hale and hearty, healthy, intact, robust, solid, sturdy, substantial, undamaged, unhurt, unimpaired, uninjured, vigorous, well-constructed, whole **3** = **safe**, established, proven, recognized, reliable, reputable, secure, solid, solvent, stable, tried-and-true **4-6** = **sensible**, correct, fair, just, level-headed, logical, orthodox, proper, prudent, rational, reasonable, reliable, responsible, right, right-thinking, true, trustworthy, valid, well-founded, well-grounded, wise **7** = **deep**, peaceful, unbroken, undisturbed, untroubled
Antonyms *adj* ≠ **perfect:** ailing, damaged, flimsy, frail, light, shaky, sketchy, superficial, unbalanced, unstable, weak ≠ **safe:** unreliable, unsound, unstable ≠ **sensible:** fallacious, faulty, flawed, irrational, irresponsible, specious ≠ **deep:** broken, fitful, shallow, troubled

sound[3] *vb* **1** = **fathom**, plumb, probe **2** = **examine**, inspect, investigate, test

sound[4] *n* **1** = **channel**, passage, strait **2** = **inlet**, arm of the sea, fjord, voe

sound out *vb* = **probe**, canvass, examine, pump, put out feelers to, question, see how the land lies, test the water

sour *adj* **1** = **sharp**, acetic, acid, acidulated, bitter, pungent, tart, unpleasant **2** = **gone off**, curdled, fermented, gone bad, rancid, turned, unsavoury, unwholesome **4** = **ill-natured**, acrid, acrimonious, churlish, crabbed, cynical, disagreeable, discontented, embittered, grouchy (*inf.*), grudging, ill-tempered, jaundiced, peevish, tart, ungenerous, waspish ◆ *vb* **13** = **embitter**, alienate, disenchant, envenom, exacerbate, exasperate, turn off (*inf.*)
Antonyms *adj* ≠ **sharp:** agreeable, bland, mild, pleasant, savoury, sugary, sweet ≠ **gone off:** fresh, unimpaired, unspoiled ≠ **ill-natured:** affable, amiable, congenial, friendly, genial, good-humoured, good-natured, good-tempered, pleasant, warm-hearted ◆ *vb* ≠ **embitter:** enhance, improve, strengthen

source *n* **1, 3** = **origin**, author, begetter, beginning, cause, commencement, derivation, fount, fountainhead, originator, rise, spring, wellspring **4** = **informant**, authority etc., is obtained. **4b** (*as modifier*): *source material*. **5** anything, such as a story or work of art, that provides a model or inspiration for a later work. **6 at source.** at the point of origin. ◆ *vb* **sources, sourcing, sourced.** (*tr*) **7** to establish an originator or source of (a product, etc.). **8** (foll. by *from*) to originate from. [C14: from OF *sors*, from *sourdre* to spring forth, from L *surgere* to rise]

source program *n* an original computer program written by a programmer that is converted into the equivalent object program, written in machine language.

sour cherry *n* **1** a Eurasian tree with white flowers: cultivated for its tart red fruits. **2** the fruit.

sour cream *n* cream soured by lactic acid bacteria, used in making salads, dips, etc.

sourdough ('saʊə,dəʊ) *Dialect.* ◆ *adj* **1** (of bread) made with fermented dough used as leaven. ◆ *n* **2** (in the Western US, Canada, and Alaska) an old-time prospector or pioneer.

sour gourd *n* **1** a large tree of N Australia, having gourdlike fruit. **2** the acid-tasting fruit. **3** the fruit of the baobab tree.

sour grapes *n* (*functioning as sing*) the attitude of affecting to despise something because one cannot have it oneself.

sourpuss ❶ ('saʊə,pʊs) *n Inf.* a person who is habitually gloomy or sullen.

sourveld ('saʊə,fɛlt) *n* (in South Africa) a type of grazing characterized by long coarse grass. [from Afrik. *suur* sour + *veld* grassland]

sousaphone ('suːzə,fəʊn) *n* a large tuba that encircles the player's body and has a bell facing forwards. [C20: after J. P. *Sousa* (1854–1932), US composer & bandmaster]

▸ **'sousa,phonist** *n*

souse ❶ (saʊs) *vb* **souses, sousing, soused. 1** to plunge (something) into water or other liquid. **2** to drench or be drenched. **3** (*tr*) to pour or dash (liquid) over (a person or thing). **4** to steep or cook (food) in a marinade. **5** (*tr*) *Sl.* to make drunk. ◆ *n* **6** the liquid used in pickling. **7** the act or process of sousing. **8** *Sl.* a drunkard. [C14: from OF *sous*, of Gmc origin]

soutane (suː'tæn) *n RC Church.* a priest's cassock. [C19: from F, from OIt. *sottana*, from Med. L *subtanus* (adj) (worn) beneath, from L *subtus* below]

souterrain ('suːtə,reɪn) *n Archaeol.* an underground chamber or passage. [C18: from F]

south (saʊθ) *n* **1** one of the four cardinal points of the compass, at 180° from north and 90° clockwise from east and anticlockwise from west. **2** the direction along a meridian towards the South Pole. **3 the south.** (*often cap.*) any area lying in or towards the south. **4** (*usually cap.*) *Cards.* the player or position corresponding to south on the compass. ◆ *adj* **5** in, towards, or facing the south. **6** (esp. of the wind) from the south. ◆ *adv* **7** in, to, or towards the south. [OE *sūth*]

South (saʊθ) *n* **the. 1** the southern part of England, generally regarded as lying to the south of an imaginary line between the Wash and the Severn. **2** (in the US) **2a** the states south of the Mason-Dixon Line that formed the Confederacy during the Civil War. **2b** the Confederacy itself. **3** the countries of the world that are not economically and technically advanced. ◆ *adj* **4** of or denoting the southern part of a specified country, area, etc.

southbound ('saʊθ,baʊnd) *adj* going or leading towards the south.

south by east *n* **1** one point on the compass east of south. ◆ *adj, adv* **2** in, from, or towards this direction.

south by west *n* **1** one point on the compass west of south. ◆ *adj, adv* **2** in, from, or towards this direction.

Southdown ('saʊθ,daʊn) *n* an English breed of sheep with short wool and a greyish-brown face and legs. [C18: so called because it was originally bred on the *South Downs* in SE England]

southeast (,saʊθ'iːst; *Naut.* ,saʊ'iːst) *n* **1** the point of the compass or the direction midway between south and east. **2** (*often cap.*; usually preceded by *the*) any area lying in or towards this direction. ◆ *adj also* **southeastern. 3** (*sometimes cap.*) of or denoting the southeastern part of a specified country, area, etc. **4** in, towards, or facing the southeast. **5** (esp. of the wind) from the southeast. ◆ *adv* **6** in, to, or towards the southeast.

▸ **,south'easternmost** *adj*

Southeast (,saʊθ'iːst) *n* (usually preceded by *the*) the southeastern part of Britain, esp. the London area.

southeast by east *n* **1** one point on the compass north of southeast. ◆ *adj, adv* **2** in, from, or towards this direction.

southeast by south *n* **1** one point on the compass south of southeast. ◆ *adj, adv* **2** in, from, or towards this direction.

southeaster (,saʊθ'iːstə; *Naut.* ,saʊ'iːstə) *n* a strong wind or storm from the southeast.

southeasterly (,saʊθ'iːstəlɪ; *Naut.* ,saʊ'iːstəlɪ) *adj, adv* **1** in, towards, or (esp. of the wind) from the southeast. ◆ *n, pl* **southeasterlies. 2** a strong wind or storm from the southeast.

southeastward (,saʊθ'iːstwəd; *Naut.* ,saʊ'iːstwəd) *adj* **1** towards or (esp. of a wind) from the southeast. ◆ *n* **2** a direction towards or area in the southeast. ◆ *adv* **3** Also: **southeastwards.** towards the southeast.

souther ('saʊðə) *n* a strong wind or storm from the south.

southerly ('sʌðəlɪ) *adj* **1** of or situated in the south. ◆ *adv, adj* **2** towards the south. **3** from the south. ◆ *n, pl* **southerlies. 4** a wind from the south.

▸ **'southerliness** *n*

southern ('sʌðən) *adj* **1** in or towards the south. **2** (of a wind, etc.) coming from the south. **3** native to or inhabiting the south.

▸ **'southern,most** *adj*

Southern ('sʌðən) *adj* of, relating to, or characteristic of the south of a particular region or country.

Southern Cross *n* a small constellation in the S hemisphere whose four brightest stars form a cross. It is represented on the national flags of Australia and New Zealand.

Southerner ('sʌðənə) *n* (*sometimes not cap.*) a native or inhabitant of the south of any specified region, esp. the South of England or the Southern states of the US.

southern hemisphere *n* (*often caps.*) that half of the earth lying south of the equator.

southern lights *pl n* another name for **aurora australis.**

South Gloucestershire *n* a unitary authority of SW England, in Gloucestershire. Pop.: 220 000 (1996 est.). Area: 510 sq. km (197 sq. miles).

southing ('saʊðɪŋ) *n* **1** *Navigation.* movement, deviation, or distance covered in a southerly direction. **2** *Astron.* a south or negative declination.

southpaw ('saʊθ,pɔː) *Inf.* ◆ *n* **1** a left-handed boxer. **2** any left-handed person. ◆ *adj* **3** of or relating to a southpaw.

South Pole *n* **1** the southernmost point on the earth's axis, at the latitude of 90°S. **2** *Astron.* the point of intersection of the earth's extended axis and the southern half of the celestial sphere. **3** (*usually not caps.*) the south-seeking pole of a freely suspended magnet.

South Sea Bubble *n Brit. history.* the financial crash that occurred in 1720 after the **South Sea Company** had taken over the national debt in return for a monopoly of trade with the South Seas, causing feverish speculation in their stocks.

South Seas *pl n* the seas south of the equator.

south-southeast *n* **1** the point on the compass or the direction midway between southeast and south. ◆ *adj, adv* **2** in, from, or towards this direction.

south-southwest *n* **1** the point on the compass or the direction midway between south and southwest. ◆ *adj, adv* **2** in, from, or towards this direction.

southward ('saʊθwəd; *Naut.* 'sʌðəd) *adj* **1** situated, directed, or moving towards the south. ◆ *n* **2** the southward part, direction, etc. ◆ *adv* **3** Also: **southwards.** towards the south.

southwest (,saʊθ'west; *Naut.* ,saʊ'west) *n* **1** the point of the compass or the direction midway between west and south. **2** (*often cap.*; usually preceded by *the*) any area lying in or towards this direction. ◆ *adj also* **southwestern. 3** (*sometimes cap.*) of or denoting the southwestern part of a specified country, area, etc.: *southwest Italy*. **4** in or towards the southwest. **5** (esp. of the wind) from the southwest. ◆ *adv* **6** in, to, or towards the southwest.

▸ **,south'westernmost** *adj*

Southwest (,saʊθ'west) *n* (usually preceded by *the*) the southwestern part of Britain, esp. Cornwall, Devon, and Somerset.

southwest by south *n* **1** one point on the compass south of southwest. ◆ *adj, adv* **2** in, from, or towards this direction.

southwest by west *n* **1** one point on the compass north of southwest. ◆ *adj, adv* **2** in, from, or towards this direction.

southwester (,saʊθ'westə; *Naut.* ,saʊ'westə) *n* a strong wind or storm from the southwest.

southwesterly (,saʊθ'westəlɪ; *Naut.* ,saʊ'westəlɪ) *adj, adv* **1** in, towards, or (esp. of a wind) from the southwest. ◆ *n, pl* **southwesterlies. 2** a wind or storm from the southwest.

southwestward (,saʊθ'westwəd; *Naut.* ,saʊ'westwəd) *adj* **1** from or towards the southwest. ◆ *adv* **2** Also: **southwestwards.** towards the southwest. ◆ *n* **3** a direction towards or area in the southwest.

souvenir ❶ (,suːvə'nɪə, 'suːvə,nɪə) *n* **1** an object that recalls a certain place, occasion, or person; memento. **2** *Rare.* a thing recalled. ◆ *vb* **3** (*tr*) *Austral. & NZ. sl.* to steal or keep for one's own use; purloin. [C18: from F, from (*se*) *souvenir* to remember, from L *subvenīre* to come to mind]

sou'wester (saʊ'westə) *n* a waterproof hat having a very broad rim behind, worn esp. by seamen. [C19: a contraction of SOUTHWESTER]

sovereign ❶ ('sɒvrɪn) *n* **1** a person exercising supreme authority, esp. a monarch. **2** a former British gold coin worth one pound sterling. ◆ *adj* **3** supreme in rank or authority: *a sovereign lord*. **4** excellent or outstanding: *a sovereign remedy*. **5** of or relating to a sovereign. **6** independent of outside authority: *a sovereign state*. [C13: from OF *soverain*,

THESAURUS

sourpuss *n Informal* = **killjoy**, crosspatch (*inf.*), grouser, grump (*inf.*), misery (*Brit. inf.*), prophet of doom, shrew, wowser (*Austral. & NZ sl.*)

souse *vb* **1-4** = **steep**, drench, dunk, immerse, marinate (*Cookery*), pickle, soak

souvenir *n* **1** = **keepsake**, memento, relic, remembrancer (*arch.*), reminder, token

sovereign *n* **1** = **monarch**, chief, emperor *or* empress, king *or* queen, potentate, prince *or* princess, ruler, shah, supreme ruler, tsar *or* tsarina ◆ *adj* **3** = **supreme**, absolute, chief, dominant, imperial, kingly *or* queenly, monarchal, paramount, predominant, principal, regal, royal, ruling, unlimited **4** = **excellent**, effectual, efficacious, efficient

from Vulgar L *superānus* (unattested), from L *super* above; also infl. by REIGN]
▸ **'sovereignly** *adv*
sovereignty ❶ ('sɒvrəntɪ) *n, pl* **sovereignties. 1** supreme and unrestricted power, as of a state. **2** the position, dominion, or authority of a sovereign. **3** an independent state.
soviet ('səʊvɪət, 'sɒv-) *n* **1** (in the former Soviet Union) an elected government council at the local, regional, and national levels, culminating in the Supreme Soviet. ◆ *adj* **2** of or relating to a soviet. [C20: from Russian *sovyet* council, from ORussian *sŭvětŭ*]
▸ **'sovie,tism** *n*
Soviet ('səʊvɪət, 'sɒv-) *adj* of or relating to the former Soviet Union, its people, or its government.
sovietize *or* **sovietise** ('səʊvɪɪ,taɪz, 'sɒv-) *vb* **sovietizes, sovietizing, sovietized** *or* **sovietises, sovietising, sovietised.** (*tr*) (*often cap.*) **1** to bring (a country, person, etc.) under Soviet control or influence. **2** to cause (a country) to conform to the Soviet model in its social, political, and economic structure.
▸ **,sovieti'zation** *or* **,sovieti'sation** *n*
Soviets ('səʊvɪəts, 'sɒv-) *pl n* the people or government of the former Soviet Union.
sow[1] ❶ (səʊ) *vb* **sows, sowing, sowed; sown** *or* **sowed. 1** to scatter or place (seed, a crop, etc.) in or on (a piece of ground, field, etc.) so that it may grow: *to sow wheat; to sow a strip of land.* **2** (*tr*) to implant or introduce: *to sow a doubt in someone's mind.* [OE *sāwan*]
▸ **'sower** *n*
sow[2] (saʊ) *n* **1** a female adult pig. **2** the female of certain other animals, such as the mink. **3** *Metallurgy.* **3a** the channels for leading molten metal to the moulds in casting pig iron. **3b** iron that has solidified in these channels. [OE *sugu*]
sown (səʊn) *vb* a past participle of **sow**[1].
sow thistle (saʊ) *n* any of various plants of an Old World genus, having milky juice, prickly leaves, and heads of yellow flowers.
soya bean ('sɔɪə) *or US & Canad.* **soybean** ('sɔɪ,biːn) *n* **1** an Asian bean plant cultivated for its nutritious seeds, for forage, and to improve the soil. **2** the seed, used as food, forage, and as the source of an oil. [C17 *soya,* via Du. from Japanese *shōyu,* from Chinese *chiang yu,* from *chiang* paste + *yu* sauce]
soy sauce (sɔɪ) *n* a salty dark brown sauce made from fermented soya beans, used esp. in Chinese cookery. Also called: **soya sauce.**
sozzled ('sɒzəld) *adj* an informal word for **drunk.** [C19: ?from obs. *sozzle* stupor]
SP *abbrev. for* starting price.
sp. *abbrev. for:* **1** special. **2** (*pl* **spp.**) species. **3** specific. **4** specimen. **5** spelling.
Sp. *abbrev. for:* **1** Spain. **2** Spaniard. **3** Spanish.
spa (spɑː) *n* a mineral spring or a place or resort where such a spring is found. [C17: after *Spa,* a watering place in Belgium]
space ❶ (speɪs) *n* **1** the unlimited three-dimensional expanse in which all material objects are located. Related adj: **spatial. 2** an interval of distance or time between two points, objects, or events. **3** a blank portion or area. **4a** unoccupied area or room: *there is no space for a table.* **4b** (*in combination*): *space-saving.* Related adj: **spacious. 5a** the region beyond the earth's atmosphere containing other planets, stars, galaxies, etc.; universe. **5b** (*as modifier*): *a space probe.* **6** a seat or place, as on a train, aircraft, etc. **7** *Printing.* a piece of metal, less than type-high, used to separate letters or words. **8** *Music.* any of the gaps between the lines that make up the staff. **9** Also called: **spacing.** *Telegraphy.* the period of time that separates characters in Morse code. ◆ *vb* **spaces, spacing, spaced.** (*tr*) **10** to place or arrange at intervals or with spaces between. **11** to divide into or by spaces: *to space one's time evenly.* **12** *Printing.* to separate (letters, words, or lines) by the insertion of spaces. [C13: from OF *espace,* from L *spatium*]
▸ **'spacer** *n*
space age *n* **1** the period in which the exploration of space has become possible. ◆ *adj* **space-age. 2** (*usually prenominal*) futuristic or ultramodern.
space-bar *n* a horizontal bar on a typewriter that is depressed in order to leave a space between words, letters, etc.
space capsule *n* a vehicle, sometimes carrying people or animals, designed to obtain scientific information from space, planets, etc., and be recovered on returning to earth.
spacecraft ('speɪs,krɑːft) *n* a manned or unmanned vehicle designed to orbit the earth or travel to celestial objects.
spaced out *adj Sl.* intoxicated through or as if through taking a drug. Often shortened to **spaced.**
space heater *n* a heater used to warm the air in an enclosed area, such as a room.
Space Invaders *n Trademark.* a video or computer game, the object of which is to destroy attacking alien spacecraft.
spaceman ❶ ('speɪs,mæn) *or* (*fem*) **spacewoman** *n, pl* **spacemen** *or* (*fem*) **spacewomen.** a person who travels in outer space.
space platform *n* another name for **space station.**
spaceport ('speɪs,pɔːt) *n* a base equipped to launch, maintain, and test spacecraft.
space probe *n* a vehicle, such as a satellite, equipped to obtain scientific information, normally transmitted back to earth by radio, about a planet, conditions in space, etc.
spaceship ('speɪs,ʃɪp) *n* a manned spacecraft.
space shuttle *n* any of a series of reusable US space vehicles (*Columbia, Challenger* (exploded 1986), *Discovery, Atlantis, Endeavor*) that can be launched into earth orbit transporting astronauts and equipment for a period of observation, research, etc., before re-entry and an unpowered landing on a runway; the first operational flight was in 1982.
space station *n* any large manned artificial satellite designed to orbit the earth during a long period of time thus providing a base for scientific research in space and a construction site, launch pad, and docking arrangements for spacecraft.
spacesuit ('speɪs,suːt, -,sjuːt) *n* a sealed and pressurized suit worn by astronauts providing an artificial atmosphere, acceptable temperature, radiocommunication link, and protection from radiation.
space-time *or* **space-time continuum** *n Physics.* the four-dimensional continuum having three spatial coordinates and one time coordinate that together completely specify the location of a particle or an event.
spacewalk ('speɪs,wɔːk) *n* **1** the act or an instance of floating and manoeuvring in space, outside but attached by a lifeline to a spacecraft. Technical name: **extravehicular activity.** ◆ *vb* **2** (*intr*) to engage in this activity.
spacey ('speɪsɪ) *adj* **spacier, spaciest.** *Sl.* vague and dreamy, as if under the influence of drugs. [C20: SPACE + -EY]
spacial ('speɪʃəl) *adj* a variant spelling of **spatial.**
spacing ('speɪsɪŋ) *n* **1** the arrangement of letters, words, spaces, etc., on a page. **2** the arrangement of objects in a space.
spacious ❶ ('speɪʃəs) *adj* having a large capacity or area.
▸ **'spaciously** *adv* ▸ **'spaciousness** *n*
spade[1] (speɪd) *n* **1** a tool for digging, typically consisting of a flat rectangular steel blade attached to a long wooden handle. **2** something resembling a spade. **3** a cutting tool for stripping the blubber from a whale or skin from a carcass. **4 call a spade a spade.** to speak plainly and frankly. ◆ *vb* **spades, spading, spaded. 5** (*tr*) to use a spade on. [OE *spadu*]
▸ **'spader** *n*
spade[2] (speɪd) *n* **1a** the black symbol on a playing card resembling a heart-shaped leaf with a stem. **1b** a card with one or more of these symbols or (*when pl*) the suit of cards so marked, usually the highest ranking of the four. **2** a derogatory word for a **Black**[1]. **3 in spades.** *Inf.* in an extreme or emphatic way. [C16: from It. *spada* sword, used as an emblem on playing cards, from L *spatha,* from Gk *spathē* blade]
spadework ❶ ('speɪd,wɜːk) *n* dull or routine preparatory work.
spadix ('speɪdɪks) *n, pl* **spadices** (speɪ'daɪsiːz). a spike of small flowers on a fleshy stem, the whole being enclosed in a spathe. [C18: from L: pulled-off branch of a palm, with its fruit, from Gk: torn-off frond]
spaghetti (spə'ɡetɪ) *n* pasta in the form of long strings. [C19: from It.: little cords, from *spago* a cord]
spaghetti junction *n* a junction, usually between motorways, in which there are a large number of intersecting roads used by a large volume of high-speed traffic. [C20: from the nickname given to the Gravelly Hill Interchange, Birmingham, where the M6, A38M, A38, and A5127 intersect]
spaghetti western *n* a cowboy film made in Europe, esp. by an Italian director.
spahi *or* **spahee** ('spɑːhiː, 'spɑːiː) *n, pl* **spahis** *or* **spahees. 1** (formerly) an irregular cavalryman in the Turkish army. **2** (formerly) a member of a body of native Algerian cavalry in the French army. [C16: from OF, from Turkish *sipahi,* from Persian *sipāhī* soldier]
spake (speɪk) *vb Arch.* a past tense of **speak.**
spam (spæm) *vb* **spams, spamming, spammed.** *Computing sl.* to send unsolicited electronic mail simultaneously to a number of newsgroups on the Internet. [C20: from the repeated use of the word *Spam* in a popular sketch from the Brit. television show *Monty Python's Flying Circus,* first broadcast in 1969]
Spam (spæm) *n Trademark.* a kind of tinned luncheon meat, made largely from pork.
span[1] ❶ (spæn) *n* **1** the interval, space, or distance between two points, such as the ends of a bridge or arch. **2** the complete duration or extent: *the span of his life.* **3** *Psychol.* the amount of material that can be processed in a single mental act: *span of attention.* **4** short for **wingspan. 5** a unit of length based on the width of an expanded hand, usually

THESAURUS

sovereignty *n* **1 = supreme power,** ascendancy, domination, kingship, primacy, supremacy, suzerainty, sway
sow[1] *vb* **1 = scatter,** broadcast, disseminate, implant, inseminate, lodge, plant, seed
space *n* **1 = expanse,** amplitude, extension, extent, volume **2 = interval,** capacity, duration, elbowroom, leeway, margin, period, play, room, scope, spaciousness, span, time, while **3 = gap,** blank, distance, interval, lacuna, omission **6 = place,** accommodation, berth, seat
spaceman *n* **= astronaut,** cosmonaut
spacious *adj* **= roomy,** ample, broad, capacious, comfortable, commodious, expansive, extensive, huge, large, sizable *or* sizeable, uncrowded, vast
Antonyms *adj* close, confined, cramped, crowded, limited, narrow, poky, restricted, small
spadework *n* **= preparation,** donkey-work, groundwork, labour
span[1] *n* **1 = extent,** amount, distance, length, reach, spread, stretch **2 = period,** duration, spell, term ◆ *vb* **6 = extend across,** arch across, bridge, cover, cross, link, range over, traverse, vault

taken as nine inches. ◆ *vb* **spans, spanning, spanned.** (*tr*) **6** to stretch or extend across, over, or around. **7** to provide with something that spans: *to span a river with a bridge.* **8** to measure or cover, esp. with the extended hand. [OE *spann*]

span[2] (spæn) *n* a team of horses or oxen, esp. two matched animals. [C16 (in the sense: yoke): from MDu.: something stretched, from *spannen* to stretch]

span[3] (spæn) *vb Arch. or dialect.* a past tense of **spin.**

Span. *abbrev. for* Spanish.

spandrel *or* **spandril** ('spændrəl) *n Archit.* **1** an approximately triangular surface bounded by the outer curve of an arch and the adjacent wall. **2** the surface area between two adjacent arches and the horizontal cornice above them. [C15 *spaundrell,* from Anglo-F *spaundre,* from OF *spandre* to spread]

spangle ('spæŋgᵊl) *n* **1** a small thin piece of metal or other shiny material used as a decoration, esp. on clothes; sequin. **2** any glittering or shiny spot or object. ◆ *vb* **spangles, spangling, spangled. 3** (*intr*) to glitter or shine with or like spangles. **4** (*tr*) to cover with spangles. [C15: dim. of *spange,* ?from MDu.: clasp]

▸**'spangly** *adj*

Spaniard ('spænjəd) *n* a native or inhabitant of Spain.

spaniel ('spænjəl) *n* **1** any of several breeds of gundog with long drooping ears and a silky coat. **2** an obsequiously devoted person. [C14: from OF *espaigneul* Spanish (dog), from OProvençal *espanhol,* ult. from L *Hispānĭolus* Spanish]

Spanish ('spænɪʃ) *n* **1** the official language of Spain, Mexico, and most countries of South and Central America except Brazil. Spanish is an Indo-European language belonging to the Romance group. **2 the Spanish.** (*functioning as pl*) the natives, citizens, or inhabitants of Spain. ◆ *adj* **3** of or relating to the Spanish language or its speakers. **4** of or relating to Spain or Spaniards.

Spanish America *n* the parts of America colonized by Spaniards and now chiefly Spanish-speaking: includes most of South and Central America, Mexico, and much of the Caribbean.

Spanish-American *adj* **1** of or relating to any of the Spanish-speaking countries or peoples of the Americas. ◆ *n* **2** a native or inhabitant of Spanish America. **3** a Spanish-speaking person in the US.

Spanish customs *or* **practices** *pl n Inf.* irregular practices among a group of workers to gain increased financial allowances, reduced working hours, etc.

Spanish fly *n* **1** a European blister beetle, the dried body of which yields cantharides. **2** another name for **cantharides.**

Spanish guitar *n* the classic form of the guitar; a six-stringed instrument with a waisted body and a central sound hole.

Spanish Main *n* **1** the mainland of Spanish America, esp. the N coast of South America. **2** the Caribbean Sea, the S part of which in colonial times was the haunt of pirates.

Spanish moss *n* **1** an epiphytic plant growing in tropical and subtropical regions as long bluish-grey strands suspended from the branches of trees. **2** a tropical lichen growing as long trailing green threads from the branches of trees.

Spanish omelette *n* an omelette containing green peppers, onions, tomato, etc.

Spanish rice *n* rice cooked with tomatoes, onions, green peppers, etc.

spank[1] ❶ (spæŋk) *vb* **1** (*tr*) to slap with the open hand, esp. on the buttocks. ◆ *n* **2** one or a series of these slaps. [C18: prob. imit.]

spank[2] (spæŋk) *vb* (*intr*) to go at a quick and lively pace. [C19: back formation from SPANKING[2]]

spanker ('spæŋkə) *n* **1** a person or thing that spanks. **2** *Naut.* a fore-and-aft sail or a mast that is aftermost in a sailing vessel. **3** *Inf.* something outstandingly fine or large.

spanking[1] ('spæŋkɪŋ) *n* a series of spanks, usually as a punishment for children.

spanking[2] ❶ ('spæŋkɪŋ) *adj* (*prenominal*) **1** *Inf.* outstandingly fine, smart, large, etc. **2** quick and energetic. **3** (esp. of a breeze) fresh and brisk.

spanner ('spænə) *n* **1** a steel hand tool with jaws or a hole, designed to grip a nut or bolt head. **2 spanner in the works.** *Brit. inf.* an impediment or annoyance. [C17: from G, from *spannen* to stretch]

span roof *n* a roof consisting of two equal sloping sides.

spanspek ('spæn,spɛk) *n S. African.* the sweet melon. [C19: possibly from Afrik.: literally, Spanish bacon]

spar[1] (spɑː) *n* **1** any piece of nautical gear resembling a pole and used as a mast, boom, gaff, etc. **2** a principal supporting structural member of an aerofoil that runs from tip to tip or root to tip. [C13: from ON *sperra* beam]

spar[2] ❶ (spɑː) *vb* **spars, sparring, sparred.** (*intr*) **1** *Boxing & martial arts.* to box using light blows, as in training. **2** to dispute or argue. **3** (of gamecocks, etc.) to fight with the feet or spurs. ◆ *n* **4** an unaggressive fight. **5** an argument or wrangle. [OE, ? from SPUR]

spar[3] (spɑː) *n* any of various minerals, such as feldspar, that are light-coloured, crystalline, and easily cleavable. [C16: from MLow G *spar*]

sparaxis (spə'ræksɪs) *n* a South African plant of the iris family, having lacerated spathes and showy flowers. [C19: NL, from Gk, from *sparassō* to tear]

spare ❶ (spɛə) *vb* **spares, sparing, spared. 1** (*tr*) to refrain from killing, punishing, or injuring. **2** (*tr*) to release or relieve, as from pain, suffering, etc. **3** (*tr*) to refrain from using: *spare the rod, spoil the child.* **4** (*tr*) to be able to afford or give: *I can't spare the time.* **5** (*usually passive*) (esp. of Providence) to allow to survive: *I'll see you next year if we are spared.* **6** (*intr*) *Now rare.* to act or live frugally. **7 not spare oneself.** to exert oneself to the full. **8 to spare.** more than is required: *two minutes to spare.* ◆ *adj* **9** (*often immediately postpositive*) in excess of what is needed; additional. **10** able to be used when needed: *a spare part.* **11** (of a person) thin and lean. **12** scanty or meagre. **13** (*postpositive*) *Brit. sl.* upset, angry, or distracted (esp. in **go spare**). ◆ *n* **14** a duplicate kept as a replacement in case of damage or loss. **15** a spare tyre. **16** *Tenpin bowling.* **16a** the act of knocking down all the pins with the two bowls of a single frame. **16b** the score thus made. [OE *sparian* to refrain from injuring]

▸**'sparely** *adv* ▸**'spareness** *n* ▸**'sparer** *n*

spare-part surgery *n* surgical replacement of defective or damaged organs by transplant or insertion of artficial devices.

sparerib (,spɛə'rɪb) *n* a cut of pork ribs with most of the meat trimmed off.

spare tyre *n* **1** an additional tyre carried by a motor vehicle in case of puncture. **2** *Brit. sl.* a deposit of fat just above the waist.

sparing ❶ ('spɛərɪŋ) *adj* **1** (sometimes foll. by *of*) economical or frugal (with). **2** scanty; meagre. **3** merciful or lenient.

▸**'sparingly** *adv* ▸**'sparingness** *n*

spark[1] ❶ (spɑːk) *n* **1** a fiery particle thrown out or left by burning material or caused by the friction of two hard surfaces. **2a** a momentary flash of light accompanied by a sharp crackling noise, produced by a sudden electrical discharge through the air or some other insulating medium between two points. **2b** the electrical discharge itself. **2c** (*as modifier*): *a spark gap.* **3** anything that serves to animate or kindle. **4** a trace or hint: *a spark of interest.* **5** vivacity, enthusiasm, or humour. **6** a small piece of diamond, as used in cutting glass. ◆ *vb* **7** (*intr*) to give off sparks. **8** (*intr*) (of the sparking plug or ignition system of an internal-combustion engine) to produce a spark. **9** (*tr;* often foll. by *off*) to kindle or animate. ◆ See also **sparks.** [OE *spearca*]

spark[2] (spɑːk) *n* **1** *Rare.* a fashionable or gallant young man. **2 bright spark.** *Brit., usually ironic.* a person who appears clever or witty. [C16 (in the sense: beautiful or witty woman): ? of Scand. origin]

▸**'sparkish** *adj*

spark gap *n* the space between two electrodes across which a spark can jump.

sparking plug *n* a device screwed into the cylinder head of an internal-combustion engine to ignite the explosive mixture by means of an electric spark. Also called: **spark plug.**

sparkle ❶ ('spɑːkᵊl) *vb* **sparkles, sparkling, sparkled. 1** to issue or reflect or cause to issue or reflect bright points of light. **2** (*intr*) (of wine, mineral water, etc.) to effervesce. **3** (*intr*) to be vivacious or witty. ◆ *n* **4** a point of light, spark, or gleam. **5** vivacity or wit. [C12 *sparklen,* frequentative of *sparken* to SPARK[1]]

sparkler ('spɑːklə) *n* **1** a type of firework that throws out sparks. **2** *Inf.* a sparkling gem.

sparkling wine *n* a wine made effervescent by carbon dioxide gas added artificially or produced naturally by secondary fermentation.

THESAURUS

spank[1] *vb* **1 = smack,** belt (*inf.*), cuff, give (someone) a hiding (*inf.*), put (someone) over one's knee, slap, slipper (*inf.*), tan (*sl.*), wallop (*inf.*), whack

spanking[2] *adj* **1** *Informal* **= smart,** brand-new, fine, gleaming **2 = fast,** brisk, energetic, invigorating, lively, quick, smart, snappy, vigorous

spar[2] *vb* **2 = argue,** bicker, dispute, fall out (*inf.*), have a tiff, row, scrap (*inf.*), skirmish, spat (*US*), squabble, wrangle

spare *vb* **1, 2 = have mercy on,** be merciful to, deal leniently with, go easy on (*inf.*), leave, let off (*inf.*), pardon, refrain from, release, relieve from, save from **4 = afford,** allow, bestow, dispense with, do without, give, grant, let (someone) have, manage without, part with, relinquish ◆ *adj* **9, 10 = extra,** additional, emergency, free, going begging, in excess, in reserve, leftover, odd, over, superfluous, supernumerary, surplus, unoccupied, unused, unwanted **11 = thin,** gaunt, lank, lean, meagre, slender, slight, slim, wiry **12 = meagre,** economical, frugal, modest, scanty, sparing **13 go spare** *Brit. slang* **= become enraged,** become angry, become distracted, become distraught, become mad (*inf.*), become upset, blow one's top (*inf.*), do one's nut (*Brit. sl.*), go mental (*sl.*), go up the wall (*sl.*), have *or* throw a fit (*inf.*)

Antonyms *vb* ≠ **have mercy on:** afflict, condemn, damn, destroy, hurt, punish, show no mercy to ◆ *adj* ≠ **extra:** allocated, designated, earmarked, in use, necessary, needed, set aside, spoken for ≠ **thin:** corpulent, fat, flabby, fleshy, generous, heavy, large, plump

sparing *adj* **1 = economical,** careful, chary, cost-conscious, frugal, money-conscious, prudent, saving, thrifty

Antonyms *adj* extravagant, lavish, liberal, openhanded, prodigal, spendthrift

spark[1] *n* **1 = flicker,** flare, flash, gleam, glint, scintillation, spit **4 = trace,** atom, hint, jot, scintilla, scrap, vestige ◆ *vb* **9** *often with* **off = start,** animate, excite, inspire, kick-start, kindle, precipitate, prod, provoke, rouse, set in motion, set off, stimulate, stir, touch off, trigger (off)

sparkle *vb* **1 = glitter,** beam, coruscate, dance, flash, gleam, glint, glisten, glister (*arch.*), glow, scintillate, shimmer, shine, spark, twinkle, wink **2 = fizz,** bubble, effervesce, fizzle ◆ *n* **4 = glitter,** brilliance, coruscation, dazzle, flash, flicker, gleam, glint, radiance, spark, twinkle **5 = vivacity,** animation, brio, dash, élan, gaiety, life, liveliness, panache, spirit, vim (*sl.*), vitality, zip (*inf.*)

spark plug *n* another name for **sparking plug.**

sparks (spɑːks) *n* (*functioning as sing*) *Inf.* **1** an electrician. **2** a radio officer, esp. on a ship.

sparky (ˈspɑːkɪ) *adj* **sparkier, sparkiest.** lively, vivacious, spirited.

sparring partner (ˈspɑːrɪŋ) *n* **1** a person who practises with a boxer during training. **2** a person with whom one has friendly arguments.

sparrow (ˈspærəʊ) *n* **1** any of various weaverbirds, esp. the house sparrow, having a brown or grey plumage and feeding on seeds or insects. **2** *US & Canad.* any of various North American finches, such as the chipping sparrow, that have a dullish streaked plumage. ◆ See also **hedge sparrow, tree sparrow.** [OE *spearwa*]

sparrowgrass (ˈspærəʊˌgrɑːs) *n* a dialect or popular name for **asparagus.**

sparrowhawk (ˈspærəʊˌhɔːk) *n* any of several small hawks of Eurasia and N Africa that prey on smaller birds.

sparrow hawk *n* a very small North American falcon, closely related to the kestrels.

sparse ➊ (spɑːs) *adj* scattered or scanty; not dense. [C18: from L *sparsus,* from *spargere* to scatter]
▸ˈ**sparsely** *adv* ▸ˈ**sparseness** *or* ˈ**sparsity** *n*

Spartan ➊ (ˈspɑːtᵊn) *adj* **1** of or relating to the ancient Greek city of Sparta or its citizens. **2** (*sometimes not cap.*) very strict or austere: *a Spartan upbringing.* **3** (*sometimes not cap.*) possessing courage and resolve. ◆ *n* **4** a citizen of Sparta. **5** (*sometimes not cap.*) a disciplined or brave person.

spasm ➊ (ˈspæzəm) *n* **1** an involuntary muscular contraction, esp. one resulting in cramp or convulsion. **2** a sudden burst of activity, emotion, etc. [C14: from L *spasmus,* from Gk *spasmos* a cramp, from *span* to tear]

spasmodic ➊ (spæzˈmɒdɪk) *or* (*rarely*) **spasmodical** *adj* **1** taking place in sudden brief spells. **2** of or characterized by spasms. [C17: NL, from Gk *spasmos* SPASM]
▸**spasˈmodically** *adv*

spastic (ˈspæstɪk) *n* **1** a person who is affected by spasms or convulsions, esp. one who has cerebral palsy. **2** *Offens. sl.* a clumsy, incapable, or incompetent person. ◆ *adj* **3** affected by or resembling spasms. **4** *Offens. sl.* clumsy, incapable, or incompetent. [C18: from L *spasticus,* from Gk, from *spasmos* SPASM]
▸ˈ**spastically** *adv* ▸**spasˈticity** (spæsˈtɪsɪtɪ) *n*

spat[1] ➊ (spæt) *n* **1** *Now rare.* a slap or smack. **2** a slight quarrel. ◆ *vb* **spats, spatting, spatted. 3** *Rare.* to slap (someone). **4** (*intr*) *US, Canad.,* & *NZ.* to have a slight quarrel. [C19: prob. imit.]

spat[2] (spæt) *vb* a past tense and past participle of **spit**[1].

spat[3] (spæt) *n* another name for **gaiter** (sense 2). [C19: short for SPATTERDASH]

spat[4] (spæt) *n* **1** a larval oyster or similar bivalve mollusc. **2** such oysters or other molluscs collectively. [C17: from Anglo-Norman *spat*]

spatchcock (ˈspætʃˌkɒk) *n* **1** a chicken or game bird split down the back and grilled. ◆ *vb* (*tr*) **2** to interpolate (words, a story, etc.) into a sentence, narrative, etc., esp. inappropriately. [C18: ? var. of *spitchcock* eel when prepared & cooked]

spate ➊ (speɪt) *n* **1** a fast flow, rush, or outpouring: *a spate of words.* **2** *Chiefly Brit.* a sudden flood: *the rivers were in spate.* **3** *Chiefly Brit.* a sudden heavy downpour. [C15 (Scot. & N English): from ?]

spathe (speɪð) *n* a large bract that encloses the inflorescence of several members of the lily family. [C18: from L *spatha,* from Gk *spathē* a blade]
▸**spathaceous** (spəˈθeɪʃəs) *adj*

spathic (ˈspæθɪk) *or* **spathose** (ˈspæθəʊs) *adj* (of minerals) resembling spar, esp. in having good cleavage. [C18: from G *Spat* SPAR[3]]

spatial *or* **spacial** (ˈspeɪʃəl) *adj* **1** of or relating to space. **2** existing or happening in space.
▸**spatiality** (ˌspeɪʃɪˈælɪtɪ) *n* ▸ˈ**spatially** *adv*

spatiotemporal (ˌspeɪʃɪəʊˈtɛmpərəl) *adj* **1** of or existing in both space and time. **2** of or concerned with space-time.
▸ˌ**spatioˈtemporally** *adv*

spatter ➊ (ˈspætə) *vb* **1** to scatter or splash (a substance, esp. a liquid) or (of a substance) to splash (something) in scattered drops: *to spatter mud on the car; mud spattered in her face.* **2** (*tr*) to sprinkle, cover, or spot (with a liquid). **3** (*tr*) to slander or defame. **4** (*intr*) to shower or rain down: *bullets spattered around them.* ◆ *n* **5** the sound of spattering. **6** something spattered, such as a spot or splash. **7** the act or an instance of spattering. [C16: imit.]

spatterdash (ˈspætəˌdæʃ) *n* **1** *US.* another name for **roughcast. 2** (*pl*) long leather leggings worn in the 18th century, as to protect from mud when riding. [C17: see SPATTER, DASH[1]]

spatula (ˈspætjʊlə) *n* a utensil with a broad flat blade, used for lifting, spreading, or stirring foods, etc. [C16: from L: a broad piece, from *spatha* a flat wooden implement; see SPATHE]
▸ˈ**spatular** *adj*

spatulate (ˈspætjʊlɪt) *adj* **1** shaped like a spatula; having thickened rounded ends: *spatulate fingers.* **2** Also: **spathulate.** *Bot.* having a narrow base and a broad rounded apex.

spavin (ˈspævɪn) *n* enlargement of the hock of a horse by a bony growth (**bony spavin**) or distension of the ligament (**bog spavin**), often resulting in lameness. [C15: from OF *espavin,* from ?]
▸ˈ**spavined** *adj*

spawn ➊ (spɔːn) *n* **1** the mass of eggs deposited by fish, amphibians, or molluscs. **2** *Often derog.* offspring, product, or yield. **3** *Bot.* the nontechnical name for **mycelium.** ◆ *vb* **4** (of fish, amphibians, etc.) to produce or deposit (eggs). **5** *Often derog.* (of people) to produce (offspring). **6** (*tr*) to produce or engender. [C14: from Anglo-Norman *espaundre,* from OF *spandre* to spread out]
▸ˈ**spawner** *n*

spay (speɪ) *vb* (*tr*) to remove the ovaries from (a female animal). [C15: from OF *espeer* to cut with the sword, from *espee* sword, from L *spatha*]

SPCK (in Britain) *abbrev. for* Society for Promoting Christian Knowledge.

speak ➊ (spiːk) *vb* **speaks, speaking, spoke, spoken. 1** to make (verbal utterances); utter (words). **2** to communicate or express (something) in or as if in words. **3** (*intr*) to deliver a speech, discourse, etc. **4** (*tr*) to know how to talk in (a language or dialect): *he does not speak German.* **5** (*intr*) to make a characteristic sound: *the clock spoke.* **6** (*intr*) (of hounds used in hunting) to give tongue; bark. **7** (*tr*) *Naut.* to hail and communicate with (another vessel) at sea. **8** (*intr*) (of a musical instrument) to produce a sound. **9 on speaking terms.** on good terms; friendly. **10 so to speak.** in a manner of speaking; as it were. **11 speak one's mind.** to express one's opinions frankly and plainly. **12 to speak of.** of a significant or worthwhile nature: *no support to speak of.* ◆ See also **speak for, speak out, speak to.** [OE *specan*]
▸ˈ**speakable** *adj*

speakeasy (ˈspiːkˌiːzɪ) *n, pl* **speakeasies.** *US.* a place where alcoholic drink was sold illicitly during Prohibition.

speaker ➊ (ˈspiːkə) *n* **1** a person who speaks, esp. at a formal occasion. **2** See **loudspeaker.**
▸ˈ**speakership** *n*

Speaker (ˈspiːkə) *n* the presiding officer in any of numerous legislative bodies.

speak for ➊ *vb* (*intr, prep*) **1** to speak as a representative of (other people). **2 speak for itself.** to be so evident that no further comment is necessary. **3 speak for yourself.** *Inf.* (used as an imperative) do not presume that other people agree with you.

speaking ➊ (ˈspiːkɪŋ) *adj* **1** (*prenominal*) eloquent, impressive, or striking. **2a** able to speak. **2b** (*in combination*) able to speak a particular language: *French-speaking.*

speaking clock *n Brit.* a telephone service that gives a verbal statement of the time.

speaking in tongues *n* another term for **gift of tongues.**

speaking tube *n* a tube for conveying a person's voice from one room or building to another.

speak out ➊ *or* **up** *vb* (*intr, adv*) **1** to state one's beliefs, objections, etc., bravely and firmly. **2** to speak more loudly and clearly.

speak to ➊ *vb* (*intr, prep*) **1** to address (a person). **2** to reprimand. **3** *Formal.* to give evidence of or comments on (a subject).

spear[1] (spɪə) *n* **1** a weapon consisting of a long shaft with a sharp pointed end of metal, stone, or wood that may be thrown or thrust. **2** a similar implement used to catch fish. **3** another name for **spearman.** ◆ *vb* **4** to pierce (something) with or as if with a spear. [OE *spere*]

spear[2] (spɪə) *n* a shoot, stalk, or blade, as of grass. [C16: prob. var. of SPIRE[1], infl. by SPEAR[1]]

spear grass *n* **1** Also called: **wild Spaniard.** a New Zealand grass with sharp leaves that grows on mountains. **2** any of various other grasses with sharp stiff blades or seeds.

spear gun *n* a device for shooting spears underwater.

spearhead ➊ (ˈspɪəˌhɛd) *n* **1** the pointed head of a spear. **2** the leading force in a military attack. **3** any person or thing that leads or initiates

THESAURUS

sparse *adj* = **scattered,** few and far between, meagre, scanty, scarce, sporadic
Antonyms *adj* crowded, dense, lavish, lush, luxuriant, numerous, plentiful, thick

Spartan *adj* **2** *sometimes not cap.* = **austere,** abstemious, ascetic, bleak, disciplined, extreme, frugal, plain, rigorous, self-denying, severe, stern, strict, stringent

spasm *n* **1** = **convulsion,** contraction, paroxysm, throe (*rare*), twitch **2** = **burst,** access, eruption, fit, frenzy, outburst, seizure

spasmodic *adj* **1** = **sporadic,** erratic, fitful, intermittent, irregular **2** = **convulsive,** jerky

spat[1] *n* **2** = **quarrel,** altercation, bicker, contention, controversy, dispute, squabble, tiff

spate *n* **1** = **flood,** deluge, flow, outpouring, rush, torrent

spatter *vb* **1** = **splash,** bespatter, bestrew, daub, dirty, scatter, soil, speckle, splodge, spray, sprinkle

spawn *n* **2** *Often derogatory* = **offspring,** issue, product, progeny, seed (*chiefly Biblical*), yield

speak *vb* **1, 2** = **talk,** articulate, communicate, converse, discourse, enunciate, express, make known, pronounce, say, state, tell, utter, voice **3** = **lecture,** address, argue, declaim, deliver an address, descant, discourse, harangue, hold forth, plead, speechify, spiel (*inf.*), spout

speaker *n* **1** = **orator,** lecturer, mouthpiece, public speaker, spokesman *or* spokeswoman, spokesperson, word-spinner

speak for *vb* **1** = **represent,** act for *or* on behalf of, appear for, hold a brief for, hold a mandate for

speaking *adj* **1** = **expressive,** eloquent, moving, noticeable, striking

speak out *vb* **1** = **speak one's mind,** have one's say, make one's position plain, sound off, stand up and be counted **2** = **speak loudly,** make oneself heard, say it loud and clear

speak to *vb* **1** = **address,** accost, apostrophize, direct one's words at, talk to **2** = **reprimand,** admonish, bring to book, dress down (*inf.*), lecture, rebuke, scold, tell off (*inf.*), tick off (*inf.*), warn

spearhead *vb* **4** = **lead,** be in the van, blaze the an attack, campaign, etc. ◆ *vb* **4** (*tr*) to lead or initiate (an attack, campaign, etc.).

spearman ('spɪəmən) *n, pl* **spearmen.** a soldier armed with a spear.

spearmint ('spɪəmɪnt) *n* a purple-flowered mint plant of Europe, having leaves that yield an oil used for flavouring.

spec (spɛk) *n* **1 on spec.** *Inf.* as a speculation or gamble: *all the tickets were sold so I went to the theatre on spec.* ◆ *adj* **2** (*prenominal*) *Austral. & NZ inf.* speculative: *a spec developer.*

spec. *abbrev. for:* **1** special. **2** specification. **3** speculation.

special Ⓣ ('spɛʃəl) *adj* **1** distinguished from, set apart from, or excelling others of its kind. **2** (*prenominal*) designed or reserved for a particular purpose. **3** not usual or commonplace. **4** (*prenominal*) particular or primary: *his special interest was music.* **5** of or relating to the education of handicapped children: *a special school.* ◆ *n* **6** a special person or thing, such as an extra edition of a newspaper or a train reserved for a particular purpose. **7** a dish or meal given prominence, esp. at a low price, in a café, etc. **8** short for **special constable. 9** *US, Canad., Austral., & NZ inf.* an item in a store advertised at a reduce price. ◆ *vb* **specials, specialling, specialled.** (*tr*) **10** (of a nurse) to give (a gravely ill patient) constant individual care. **11** *NZ inf.* to advertise and sell (an item) at a reduced price. [C13: from OF *especial,* from L *speciālis* individual, special, from *speciēs* appearance]
▸ **'specially** *adv* ▸ **'specialness** *n*

USAGE NOTE See at **especial.**

Special Branch *n* (in Britain) the department of the police force that is concerned with political security.

special clearing *n Banking.* (in Britain) the clearing of a cheque through a bank in less than the usual three days, for an additional charge.

special constable *n* a person recruited for temporary or occasional police duties, esp. in time of emergency.

special delivery *n* the delivery of a piece of mail outside the time of a scheduled delivery.

special drawing rights *pl n* (*sometimes caps.*) the reserve assets of the International Monetary Fund on which member nations may draw.

special effects *pl n Films.* techniques used in the production of scenes that cannot be achieved by normal techniques.

specialist Ⓣ ('spɛʃəlɪst) *n* a person who specializes in a particular activity, field of research, etc.
▸ **'special,ism** *n* ▸ **,special'istic** *adj*

speciality Ⓣ (,spɛʃɪ'ælɪtɪ) *or esp. US & Canad.* **specialty** *n, pl* **specialities** *or esp. US & Canad.* **specialties. 1** a special interest or skill. **2a** a service or product specialized in, as at a restaurant. **2b** (*as modifier*): *a speciality dish.* **3** a special feature or characteristic.

specialize *or* **specialise** ('spɛʃə,laɪz) *vb* **specializes, specializing, specialized** *or* **specialises, specialising, specialised. 1** (*intr*) to train in or devote oneself to a particular area of study, occupation, or activity. **2** (*usually passive*) to cause (organisms or parts) to develop in a way most suited to a particular environment or way of life or (of organisms, etc.) to develop in this way. **3** (*tr*) to modify for a special use or purpose.
▸ **,speciali'zation** *or* **,speciali'sation** *n*

special licence *n Brit.* a licence permitting a marriage to take place by dispensing with the usual legal conditions.

special pleading *n Law.* **1** a pleading that alleges new facts that offset those put forward by the other side rather than directly admitting or denying those facts. **2** a pleading that emphasizes the favourable aspects of a case while omitting the unfavourable.

special school *n Brit.* a school for children who are unable to benefit from ordinary schooling because they have learning difficulties, physical or mental handicaps, etc.

special team *n American football.* any of several predetermined permutations of the players within a team that play in situations, such as kickoffs and attempts at field goals, where the standard offensive and defensive formations are not appropriate.

specialty ('spɛʃəltɪ) *n, pl* **specialties. 1** *Law.* a formal contract or obligation expressed in a deed. **2** a variant (esp. US and Canad.) of **speciality.**

speciation (,spiːʃɪ'eɪʃən) *n* the evolutionary development of a biological species.

specie ('spiːʃiː) *n* **1** coin money, as distinguished from bullion or paper money. **2 in specie. 2a** (of money) in coin. **2b** in kind. [C16: from L *in speciē* in kind]

species Ⓣ ('spiːʃiːz; *Latin* 'spiːʃɪ,iːz) *n, pl* **species. 1** *Biol.* **1a** any of the taxonomic groups into which a genus is divided, the members of which are capable of interbreeding. Abbrev.: **sp. 1b** the animals of such a group. **1c** any group of related animals or plants not necessarily of this taxonomic rank. **2** (*modifier*) denoting a plant that is a natural member of a species rather than a hybrid or cultivar: *a species clematis.* **3** *Logic.* a group of objects or individuals, all sharing common attributes, that forms a subdivision of a genus. **4** a kind, sort, or variety: *a species of treachery.* **5** *Chiefly RC Church.* the outward form of the bread and wine in the Eucharist. **6** *Obs.* an outward appearance or form. [C16: from L: appearance, from *specere* to look]

specif. *abbrev. for* specifically.

specific Ⓣ (spɪ'sɪfɪk) *adj* **1** explicit, particular, or definite. **2** relating to a specified or particular thing: *a specific treatment for arthritis.* **3** of or relating to a biological species. **4** (of a disease) caused by a particular pathogenic agent. **5** *Physics.* **5a** characteristic of a property of a substance, esp. in relation to the same property of a standard reference substance: *specific gravity.* **5b** characteristic of a property of a substance per unit mass, length, area, etc.: *specific heat.* **5c** (of an extensive physical quantity) divided by mass: *specific volume.* **6** denoting a tariff levied at a fixed sum per unit of weight, quantity, volume, etc., irrespective of value. ◆ *n* **7** (*sometimes pl*) a designated quality, thing, etc. **8** *Med.* any drug used to treat a particular disease. [C17: from Med. L *specificus,* from L SPECIES]
▸ **spe'cifically** *adv* ▸ **specificity** (,spɛsɪ'fɪsɪtɪ) *n*

specification Ⓣ (,spɛsɪfɪ'keɪʃən) *n* **1** the act or an instance of specifying. **2** (in patent law) a written statement accompanying an application for a patent that describes the nature of an invention. **3** a detailed description of the criteria for the constituents, construction, appearance, performance, etc., of a material, apparatus, etc., or of the standard of workmanship required in its manufacture. **4** an item, detail, etc., specified.

specific charge *n Physics.* the charge-to-mass ratio of an elementary particle.

specific gravity *n* the ratio of the density of a substance to that of water.

specific heat capacity *n* the heat required to raise unit mass of a substance by unit temperature interval under specified conditions, such as constant pressure. Also called: **specific heat.**

specific humidity *n* the mass of water vapour in a sample of moist air divided by the mass of the sample.

specific volume *n Physics.* the volume of matter per unit mass.

specify Ⓣ ('spɛsɪ,faɪ) *vb* **specifies, specifying, specified.** (*tr; may take a clause as object*) **1** to refer to or state specifically. **2** to state as a condition. **3** to state or include in the specification of. [C13: from Med. L *specificāre* to describe]
▸ **'speci,fiable** *adj* ▸ **specificative** ('spɛsɪfɪ,keɪtɪv) *adj*

specimen Ⓣ ('spɛsɪmɪn) *n* **1a** an individual, object, or part regarded as typical of its group or class. **1b** (*as modifier*): *a specimen page.* **2** *Med.* a sample of tissue, blood, urine, etc., taken for diagnostic examination or evaluation. **3** the whole or a part of an organism, plant, rock, etc., collected and preserved as an example of its class, species, etc. **4** *Inf., often derog.* a person. [C17: from L: mark, proof, from *specere* to look at]

specious Ⓣ ('spiːʃəs) *adj* **1** apparently correct or true, but actually wrong or false. **2** deceptively attractive in appearance. [C14 (orig.: fair): from L *speciōsus* plausible, from *speciēs* outward appearance, from *specere* to look at]
▸ **'speciously** *adv* ▸ **speciosity** (,spiːʃɪ'ɒsɪtɪ) *or* **'speciousness** *n*

speck Ⓣ (spɛk) *n* **1** a very small mark or spot. **2** a small or tiny piece of something. ◆ *vb* **3** (*tr*) to mark with specks or spots. [OE *specca*]

speckle Ⓣ ('spɛkəl) *n* **1** a small mark usually of a contrasting colour, as on the skin, eggs, etc. ◆ *vb* **speckles, speckling, speckled. 2** (*tr*) to mark with or as if with speckles. [C15: from MDu. *spekkel*]
▸ **'speckled** *adj*

specs (spɛks) *pl n Inf.* short for **spectacles.**

spectacle Ⓣ ('spɛktəkəl) *n* **1** a public display or performance, esp. a showy or ceremonial one. **2** a thing or person seen, esp. an unusual or

THESAURUS

trail, head, initiate, launch, lay the first stone, lead the way, pioneer, set in motion, set off

special *adj* **1, 3 = exceptional**, distinguished, especial, extraordinary, festive, gala, important, memorable, momentous, one in a million, out of the ordinary, red-letter, significant, uncommon, unique, unusual **2 = specific**, appropriate, certain, characteristic, distinctive, especial, individual, particular, peculiar, precise, specialized **4 = particular**, chief, main, major, primary
Antonyms *adj* ≠ **exceptional:** common, everyday, humdrum, mediocre, no great shakes (*inf.*), normal, ordinary, routine, run-of-the-mill, undistinguished, unexceptional, usual ≠ **specific:** general, multi-purpose, undistinctive, unspecialized

specialist *n* = **expert**, authority, buff (*inf.*), connoisseur, consultant, guru, hotshot (*inf.*), master, maven (*US*), professional, whizz (*inf.*)

speciality *n* **1 = forte**, bag (*sl.*), claim to fame, distinctive *or* distinguishing feature, métier, *pièce de résistance*, special, specialty

species *n* **4 = kind**, breed, category, class, collection, description, genus, group, sort, type, variety

specific *adj* **1 = precise**, clear-cut, definite, exact, explicit, express, limited, unambiguous, unequivocal **2 = particular**, characteristic, definite, distinguishing, especial, peculiar, special
Antonyms *adj* ≠ **precise:** approximate, general, hazy, imprecise, non-specific, uncertain, unclear, vague, woolly ≠ **particular:** common, general

specification *n* **4 = requirement**, condition, detail, item, particular, qualification, stipulation

specify *vb* **1, 2 = state**, be specific about, cite, define, designate, detail, enumerate, indicate, individualize, itemize, mention, name, particularize, spell out, stipulate

specimen *n* **1 = sample**, copy, embodiment, example, exemplar, exemplification, exhibit, individual, instance, model, pattern, proof, representative, type

specious *adj* **1 = fallacious**, casuistic, deceptive, misleading, plausible, sophistic, sophistical, unsound

speck *n* **1 = mark**, blemish, blot, defect, dot, fault, flaw, fleck, mote, speckle, spot, stain **2 = particle**, atom, bit, dot, grain, iota, jot, mite, modicum, shred, tittle, whit

speckled *adj* **2 = flecked**, brindled, dappled, dotted, freckled, mottled, speckledy, spotted, spotty, sprinkled, stippled

spectacle *n* **1 = show**, display, event, exhibition, extravaganza, pageant, parade, perfor-

ridiculous one: *he makes a spectacle of himself.* **3** a strange or interesting object or phenomenon. [C14: via OF from L *spectaculum* a show, from *spectāre* to watch, from *specere* to look at]

spectacles ('spɛktəkᵊlz) *pl n* a pair of glasses for correcting defective vision. Often (informal) shortened to **specs**.
▸**'spectacled** *adj*

spectacular ❶ (spɛk'tækjulə) *adj* **1** of or resembling a spectacle; impressive, grand, or dramatic. **2** unusually marked or great: *a spectacular increase.* ◆ *n* **3** a lavishly produced performance.
▸**spec'tacularly** *adv*

spectate (spɛk'teɪt) *vb* **spectates, spectating, spectated.** (*intr*) to be a spectator; watch. [C20: back formation from SPECTATOR]

spectator ❶ (spɛk'teɪtə) *n* a person viewing anything; onlooker; observer. [C16: from L, from *spectāre* to watch; see SPECTACLE]

spectator sport *n* a sport that attracts more people as spectators than as participants.

spectra ('spɛktrə) *n* the plural of **spectrum.**

spectral ❶ ('spɛktrəl) *adj* **1** of or like a spectre. **2** of or relating to a spectrum.
▸**spectrality** (spɛk'trælɪtɪ) *n* ▸**'spectrally** *adv*

spectral type *or* **class** *n* any of various groups into which stars are classified according to characteristic spectral lines and bands.

spectre ❶ *or US* **specter** ('spɛktə) *n* **1** a ghost; phantom; apparition. **2** an unpleasant or menacing mental image: *the spectre of redundancy.* [C17: from L *spectrum*, from *specere* to look at]

spectro- *combining form.* indicating a spectrum: *spectrogram.*

spectrograph ('spɛktrəʊˌgrɑːf) *n* a spectroscope or spectrometer that produces a photographic record (**spectrogram**) of a spectrum. See also **sound spectrograph.**
▸ˌ**spectro'graphic** *adj* ▸ˌ**spectro'graphically** *adv* ▸**spectrography** (spɛk'trɒgrəfɪ) *n*

spectroheliograph (ˌspɛktrəʊ'hiːlɪəˌgrɑːf) *n* an instrument used to take a photograph (**spectroheliogram**) of the sun in light of a particular wavelength, usually that of calcium or hydrogen, to show the distribution of the element over the surface and in the atmosphere.
▸ˌ**spectroˌhelio'graphic** *adj*

spectrometer (spɛk'trɒmɪtə) *n* any instrument for producing a spectrum, esp. one in which wavelength, energy, intensity, etc., can be measured. See also **mass spectrometer.**
▸**spectrometric** (ˌspɛktrəʊ'mɛtrɪk) *adj* ▸**spec'trometry** *n*

spectrophotometer (ˌspɛktrəʊfəʊ'tɒmɪtə) *n* an instrument for producing or recording a spectrum and measuring the photometric intensity of each wavelength present.
▸**spectrophotometric** (ˌspɛktrəʊˌfəʊtə'mɛtrɪk) *adj* ▸ˌ**spectropho'tometry** *n*

spectroscope ('spɛktrəˌskəʊp) *n* any of a number of instruments for dispersing electromagnetic radiation and thus forming or recording a spectrum.
▸**spectroscopic** (ˌspɛktrə'skɒpɪk) *or* ˌ**spectro'scopical** *adj*

spectroscopy (spɛk'trɒskəpɪ) *n* the science and practice of using spectrometers and spectroscopes and of analysing spectra.
▸**spec'troscopist** *n*

spectrum ('spɛktrəm) *n, pl* **spectra. 1** the distribution of colours produced when white light is dispersed by a prism or diffraction grating. There is a continuous change in wavelength from red, the longest wavelength, to violet, the shortest. Seven colours are usually distinguished: violet, indigo, blue, green, yellow, orange, and red. **2** the whole range of electromagnetic radiation with respect to its wavelength or frequency. **3** any particular distribution of electromagnetic radiation often showing lines or bands characteristic of the substance emitting the radiation or absorbing it. **4** any similar distribution or record of the energies, velocities, masses, etc., of atoms, ions, electrons, etc.: *a mass spectrum.* **5** any range or scale, as of capabilities, emotions, or moods. **6** another name for an **afterimage.** [C17: from L: image, from *spectāre* to observe, from *specere* to look at]

spectrum analysis *n* the analysis of a spectrum to determine the properties of its source.

specular ('spɛkjulə) *adj* **1** of, relating to, or having the properties of a mirror. **2** of or relating to a speculum. [C16: from L *speculāris*, from *speculum* a mirror, from *specere* to look at]

speculate ❶ ('spɛkjuˌleɪt) *vb* **speculates, speculating, speculated. 1** (when *tr, takes a clause as object*) to conjecture without knowing the complete facts. **2** (*intr*) to buy or sell securities, property, etc., in the hope of deriving capital gains. **3** (*intr*) to risk loss for the possibility of considerable gain. **4** (*intr*) *NZ.* in rugby football, to make an emergency undirected forward kick at the ball. [C16: from L *speculārī* to spy out, from *specula* a watchtower, from *specere* to look at]

speculation ❶ (ˌspɛkju'leɪʃən) *n* **1** the act or an instance of speculating. **2** a supposition, theory, or opinion arrived at through speculating. **3** investment involving high risk but also possible high profits.
▸**'speculative** *adj*

speculator ('spɛkjuˌleɪtə) *n* **1** a person who speculates. **2** *NZ rugby.* an undirected kick of the ball.

speculum ('spɛkjuləm) *n, pl* **specula** (-lə) *or* **speculums. 1** a mirror, esp. one made of polished metal for use in a telescope, etc. **2** *Med.* an instrument for dilating a bodily cavity or passage to permit examination of its interior. **3** a patch of distinctive colour on the wing of a bird. [C16: from L: mirror, from *specere* to look at]

sped (spɛd) *vb* a past tense and past participle of **speed.**

speech ❶ (spiːtʃ) *n* **1a** the act or faculty of speaking. **1b** (*as modifier*): *speech therapy.* **2** that which is spoken; utterance. **3** a talk or address delivered to an audience. **4** a person's characteristic manner of speaking. **5** a national or regional language or dialect. **6** *Linguistics.* another word for **parole.** [OE *spēc*]

speech day *n Brit.* (in schools) an annual day on which prizes are presented, speeches are made by guest speakers, etc.

speechify ('spiːtʃɪˌfaɪ) *vb* **speechifies, speechifying, speechified.** (*intr*) **1** to make a speech or speeches. **2** to talk pompously and boringly.
▸**'speechiˌfier** *n*

speechless ❶ ('spiːtʃlɪs) *adj* **1** not able to speak. **2** temporarily deprived of speech. **3** not expressed or able to be expressed in words: *speechless fear.*
▸**'speechlessly** *adv* ▸**'speechlessness** *n*

speed ❶ (spiːd) *n* **1** the act or quality of acting or moving fast; rapidity. **2** the rate at which something moves, is done, or acts. **3** *Physics.* **3a** a scalar measure of the rate of movement of a body expressed either as the distance travelled divided by the time taken (**average speed**) or the rate of change of position with respect to time at a particular point (**instantaneous speed**). **3b** another word for **velocity** (sense 2). **4** a rate of rotation, usually expressed in revolutions per unit time. **5a** a gear ratio in a motor vehicle, bicycle, etc. **5b** (*in combination*): *a three-speed gear.* **6** *Photog.* a numerical expression of the sensitivity to light of a particular type of film, paper, or plate. See also **ISO rating. 7** *Photog.* a measure of the ability of a lens to pass light from an object to the image position. **8** a slang word for **amphetamine. 9** *Arch.* prosperity or success. **10 at speed.** quickly. ◆ *vb* **speeds, speeding; sped** *or* **speeded. 11** to move or go or cause to move or go quickly. **12** (*intr*) to drive (a motor vehicle) at a high speed, esp. above legal limits. **13** (*tr*) to help further the success or completion of. **14** (*intr*) *Sl.* to take or be under the influence of amphetamines. **15** (*intr*) to operate or run at a high speed. **16** *Arch.* **16a** (*intr*) to prosper or succeed. **16b** (*tr*) to wish success to. ◆ See also **speed up.** [OE *spēd* (orig. in the sense: success)]
▸**'speeder** *n*

speedball ('spiːdˌbɔːl) *n Sl.* a mixture of heroin with amphetamine or cocaine.

speedboat ('spiːdˌbəʊt) *n* a high-speed motorboat.

speed chess *n* a form of chess in which each player's game is limited to a total stipulated time, usually half an hour; the first player to exceed the time limit loses.

speed limit *n* the maximum permitted speed at which a vehicle may travel on certain roads.

THESAURUS

mance, sight **3** = **sight**, curiosity, marvel, phenomenon, scene, wonder

spectacular *adj* **1** = **impressive**, breathtaking, daring, dazzling, dramatic, eye-catching, fantastic (*inf.*), grand, magnificent, marked, remarkable, sensational, splendid, staggering, striking, stunning (*inf.*) ◆ *n* **3** = **show**, display, extravaganza, spectacle
Antonyms *adj* ≠ **impressive:** everyday, modest, ordinary, plain, run-of-the-mill, simple, unimpressive, unostentatious, unspectacular

spectator *n* = **onlooker**, beholder, bystander, eyewitness, looker-on, observer, viewer, watcher, witness
Antonyms *n* contestant, contributor, partaker, participant, participator, party, player

spectral *adj* **1** = **ghostly**, eerie, incorporeal, insubstantial, phantom, shadowy, spooky (*inf.*), supernatural, uncanny, unearthly, weird, wraithlike

spectre *n* **1** = **ghost**, apparition, eidolon, phantom, presence, shade (*literary*), shadow, spirit, vision, wraith

speculate *vb* **1** = **conjecture**, cogitate, consider, contemplate, deliberate, guess, hypothesize, meditate, muse, scheme, suppose, surmise, theorize, wonder **2, 3** = **gamble**, have a flutter (*inf.*), hazard, play the market, risk, take a chance with, venture

speculation *n* **2** = **conjecture**, consideration, contemplation, deliberation, guess, guesswork, hypothesis, opinion, supposition, surmise, theory

speculative *adj* **1** = **risky**, chancy, dicey (*inf., chiefly Brit.*), hazardous, uncertain, unpredictable **2** = **hypothetical**, abstract, academic, conjectural, notional, suppositional, tentative, theoretical

speech *n* **1** = **communication**, conversation, dialogue, discussion, intercourse, talk **2, 4, 5** = **language**, articulation, dialect, diction, enunciation, idiom, jargon, lingo (*inf.*), parlance, tongue, utterance, voice **3** = **talk**, address, discourse, disquisition, harangue, homily, lecture, oration, spiel (*inf.*)

speechless *adj* **1** = **mute**, dumb, inarticulate, lost for words, mum, silent, tongue-tied, unable to get a word out (*inf.*), wordless **2** = **astounded**, aghast, amazed, dazed, dumbfounded, dumbstruck, shocked, thunderstruck

speed *n* **1, 2** = **swiftness**, acceleration, celerity, expedition, fleetness, haste, hurry, momentum, pace, precipitation, quickness, rapidity, rush, velocity ◆ *vb* **11** = **race**, bomb (along), bowl along, burn rubber (*inf.*), career, dispatch, flash, gallop, get a move on (*inf.*), go hell for leather (*inf.*), go like the wind, hasten, hurry, lose no time, make haste, press on, put one's foot down (*inf.*), quicken, rush, sprint, step on it (*inf.*), tear, urge, zoom **13** = **help**, advance, aid, assist, boost, expedite, facilitate, further, impel, promote
Antonyms *n* ≠ **swiftness:** delay, slowness, sluggishness, tardiness ◆ *vb* ≠ **race:** crawl, creep, dawdle, delay, take one's time, tarry ≠ **help:** delay, hamper, hinder, hold up, retard, slow

speedo ('spi:dəʊ) *n, pl* **speedos.** an informal name for **speedometer.**

speed of light *n* the speed at which electromagnetic radiation travels in a vacuum; 2.997 924 58 × 10^8 metres per second exactly. Symbol: *c* Also called (not in technical usage): **velocity of light.**

speedometer (spɪ'dɒmɪtə) *n* a device fitted to a vehicle to measure and display the speed of travel. See also **mileometer.**

speed up ⓘ *vb (adv)* **1** to increase or cause to increase in speed or rate; accelerate. ◆ *n* **speed-up. 2** an instance of this; acceleration.

> **USAGE NOTE** The past tense and past participle of *speed up* is *speeded up*, not *sped up*.

speedway ('spi:dˌweɪ) *n* **1** the sport of racing on light powerful motorcycles round cinder tracks. **2** the track or stadium where such races are held. **3** *US & Canad.* **3a** a racetrack for cars. **3b** a road on which fast driving is allowed.

speedwell ('spi:dˌwɛl) *n* any of various temperate plants, such as the **common speedwell** and the **germander speedwell,** having small blue or pinkish-white flowers.

speedy ⓘ ('spi:dɪ) *adj* **speedier, speediest. 1** characterized by speed. **2** done or decided without delay.
▸**'speedily** *adv* ▸**'speediness** *n*

spek (spɛk) *n S. African.* bacon. [from Afrik., from Du.]

speleology *or* **spelaeology** (ˌspi:lɪ'ɒlədʒɪ) *n* **1** the scientific study of caves. **2** the sport or pastime of exploring caves. [C19: from L *spēlaeum* cave]
▸**speleological** *or* **spelaeological** (ˌspi:lɪə'lɒdʒɪkᵊl) *adj* ▸ˌ**spele'ologist** *or* ˌ**spelae'ologist** *n*

spell[1] ⓘ (spɛl) *vb* **spells, spelling; spelt** *or* **spelled. 1** to write or name in correct order the letters that comprise the conventionally accepted form of (a word). **2** *(tr)* (of letters) to go to make up the conventionally established form of (a word) when arranged correctly: *d-o-g spells dog.* **3** *(tr)* to indicate or signify: *such actions spell disaster.* ◆ See also **spell out.** [C13: from OF *espeller*, of Gmc origin]
▸**'spellable** *adj*

spell[2] ⓘ (spɛl) *n* **1** a verbal formula considered as having magical force. **2** any influence that can control the mind or character; fascination. **3** a state induced as by the pronouncing of a spell; trance: *to break the spell.* **4 under a spell.** held in or as if in a spell. [OE *spell* speech]

spell[3] ⓘ (spɛl) *n* **1** an indeterminate, usually short, period of time: *a spell of cold weather.* **2** a period or tour of duty after which one person or group relieves another. **3** *Scot., Austral., & NZ.* a period or interval of rest. ◆ *vb* **4** *(tr)* to take over from (a person) for an interval of time; relieve temporarily. [OE *spelian* to take the place of, from ?]

spellbind ('spɛlˌbaɪnd) *vb* **spellbinds, spellbinding, spellbound.** *(tr)* to cause to be spellbound; entrance or enthral.
▸**'spellˌbinder** *n*

spellbound ⓘ ('spɛlˌbaʊnd) *adj* having one's attention held as though one is bound by a spell.

spellchecker ('spɛlˌtʃɛkə) *n Computing.* a program that highlights any word in a word-processed document that is not recognized as being correctly spelt.

speller ('spɛlə) *n* **1** a person who spells words in the manner specified: *a bad speller.* **2** a book designed to teach or improve spelling.

spelling ⓘ ('spɛlɪŋ) *n* **1** the act or process of writing words by using the letters conventionally accepted for their formation; orthography. **2** the art or study of orthography. **3** the way in which a word is spelt. **4** the ability of a person to spell.

spelling bee *n* a contest in which players are required to spell words.

spell out ⓘ *vb (tr, adv)* **1** to make clear, distinct, or explicit; clarify in detail: *let me spell out the implications.* **2** to read laboriously or with difficulty, working out each word letter by letter. **3** to discern by study; puzzle out.

spelt[1] (spɛlt) *vb* a past tense and past participle of **spell**[1].

spelt[2] (spɛlt) *n* a species of wheat that was formerly much cultivated and was used to develop present-day cultivated wheats. [OE]

spelter ('spɛltə) *n* impure zinc. [C17: prob. from MDu. *speauter*, from ?]

spelunker (spɪ'lʌŋkə) *n* a person whose hobby is the exploration of caves. [C20: from L *spēlunca*, from Gk *spēlunx* a cave]
▸**spe'lunking** *n*

spencer[1] ('spɛnsə) *n* **1** a short fitted coat or jacket. **2** a woman's knitted vest. [C18: after Earl *Spencer* (1758–1834)]

spencer[2] ('spɛnsə) *n Naut.* a large loose-footed gaffsail on a square-rigger or barque. [C19: ?from a proper name]

spend ⓘ (spɛnd) *vb* **spends, spending, spent. 1** to pay out (money, wealth, etc.). **2** *(tr)* to concentrate (time, effort, etc.) upon an object, activity, etc. **3** *(tr)* to pass (time) in a specific way, place, etc. **4** *(tr)* to use up completely: *the hurricane spent its force.* **5** *(tr)* to give up (one's blood, life, etc.) in a cause. [OE *spendan*, from L *expendere;* infl. also by OF *despendre* to spend; see EXPEND, DISPENSE]
▸**'spendable** *adj* ▸**'spender** *n*

spendthrift ⓘ ('spɛndˌθrɪft) *n* **1** a person who spends money in an extravagant manner. ◆ *adj* **2** *(usually prenominal)* of or like a spendthrift.

Spenserian (spɛn'sɪərɪən) *adj* **1** relating to or characteristic of the 16th-century English poet Edmund Spenser or his poetry. ◆ *n* **2** a student or imitator of Edmund Spenser.

Spenserian stanza *n Prosody.* the stanza form used by the poet Spenser in his poem *The Faerie Queene*, consisting of eight lines in iambic pentameter and a concluding Alexandrine, rhyming a b a b b c b c c.

spent ⓘ (spɛnt) *vb* **1** the past tense and past participle of **spend.** ◆ *adj* **2** used up or exhausted; consumed. **3** (of a fish) exhausted by spawning.

sperm[1] ⓘ (spɜ:m) *n, pl* **sperms** *or* **sperm. 1** another name for **semen. 2** a male reproductive cell; male gamete. [C14: from LL *sperma*, from Gk]

sperm[2] (spɜ:m) *n* short for **sperm whale, spermaceti,** or **sperm oil.**

-sperm *n combining form.* (in botany) a seed: *gymnosperm.*
▸**-spermous** *or* **-spermal** *adj combining form.*

spermaceti (ˌspɜ:mə'sɛtɪ, -'si:tɪ) *n* a white waxy substance obtained from oil from the head of the sperm whale. [C15: from Med. L *sperma cētī* whale's sperm, from *sperma* SPERM[1] + L *cētus* whale, from Gk *kētos*]

spermatic (spɜ:'mætɪk), **spermic** ('spɜ:mɪk), *or* **spermous** ('spɜ:məs) *adj* **1** of or relating to spermatozoa: *spermatic fluid.* **2** of or relating to the testis: *the spermatic artery.* [C16: from LL *spermaticus*, from Gk *spermatikos* concerning seed, from *sperma* seed]
▸**sper'matically** *adv*

spermatid ('spɜ:mətɪd) *n Zool.* any of four immature male gametes that are formed from a spermatocyte, each of which develops into a spermatozoon.

spermato-, spermo- *or before a vowel* **spermat-, sperm-** *combining form.* **1** indicating sperm: *spermatozoon.* **2** indicating seed: *spermatophyte.* [from Gk *sperma, spermat-* seed]

spermatocyte ('spɜ:mətəʊˌsaɪt) *n* an immature male germ cell.

spermatogenesis (ˌspɜ:mətəʊ'dʒɛnɪsɪs) *n* the formation and maturation of spermatozoa in the testis.
▸**spermatogenetic** (ˌspɜ:mətəʊdʒɪ'nɛtɪk) *adj*

spermatogonium (ˌspɜ:mətə'gəʊnɪəm) *n, pl* **spermatogonia** (-nɪə). *Zool.* an immature male germ cell that divides to form many spermatocytes.

spermatophyte ('spɜ:mətəʊˌfaɪt) *or* **spermophyte** *n* (in traditional classifications) any seed-bearing plant. Former name: **phanerogam.**
▸**spermatophytic** (ˌspɜ:mətəʊ'fɪtɪk) *adj*

spermatozoon (ˌspɜ:mətəʊ'zəʊɒn) *n, pl* **spermatozoa** (-zəʊə). any of the male reproductive cells released in the semen during ejaculation. Also called: **sperm, zoosperm.**
▸ˌ**spermato'zoal,** ˌ**spermato'zoan,** *or* ˌ**spermato'zoic** *adj*

spermicide ('spɜ:mɪˌsaɪd) *n* any agent that kills spermatozoa.
▸ˌ**spermi'cidal** *adj*

sperm oil *n* an oil obtained from the head of the sperm whale, used as a lubricant.

spermous ('spɜ:məs) *adj* **1** of or relating to the sperm whale or its products. **2** another word for **spermatic.**

sperm whale *n* a large toothed whale, having a square-shaped head

THESAURUS

speed up *vb* **1** = **accelerate**, gather momentum, get moving, get under way, increase, increase the tempo, open up the throttle, put one's foot down (*inf.*), put on speed
Antonyms *vb* brake, decelerate, reduce speed, rein in, slacken (off), slow down

speedy *adj* **1, 2** = **quick**, expeditious, express, fast, fleet, fleet of foot, hasty, headlong, hurried, immediate, nimble, precipitate, prompt, rapid, summary, swift, winged
Antonyms *adj* dead slow and stop, delayed, dilatory, late, leisurely, lingering, long-drawn-out, plodding, slow, sluggish, tardy, unhurried, unrushed

spell[1] *vb* **3** = **indicate**, amount to, augur, herald, imply, mean, point to, portend, presage, promise, signify, suggest

spell[2] *n* **1** = **incantation**, abracadabra, charm, conjuration, exorcism, sorcery, witchery **2, 3** = **enchantment**, allure, bewitchment, fascination, glamour, magic, trance

spell[3] *n* **1, 2** = **period**, bout, course, interval, patch, season, stint, stretch, term, time, turn

spellbound *adj* = **entranced**, bemused, bewitched, captivated, charmed, enthralled, fascinated, gripped, hooked, mesmerized, possessed, rapt, transfixed, transported, under a spell

spelling *n* **1-4** = **orthography**

spell out *vb* **1** = **make clear** *or* **plain**, clarify, elucidate, explicate, make explicit, specify **3** = **puzzle out**, discern, make out

spend *vb* **1** = **pay out**, disburse, expend, fork out, lay out, shell out (*inf.*), splash out (*Brit. inf.*) **2** = **apply**, bestow, concentrate, devote, employ, exert, invest, lavish, put in, use **3** = **pass**, fill, occupy, while away **4** = **use up**, blow (*sl.*), consume, deplete, dissipate, drain, empty, exhaust, fritter away, run through, squander, waste
Antonyms *vb* ≠ **pay out, use up:** hoard, invest, keep, put aside, put by, save, store

spendthrift *n* **1** = **squanderer**, big spender, prodigal, profligate, spender, waster, wastrel ◆ *adj* **2** = **wasteful**, extravagant, improvident, prodigal, profligate
Antonyms *n* ≠ **squanderer:** meanie *or* meany (*inf., chiefly Brit.*), miser, penny-pincher (*inf.*), Scrooge, skinflint, tightwad (*US & Canad. sl.*) ◆ *adj* ≠ **wasteful:** careful, economical, frugal, parsimonious, provident, prudent, sparing, thrifty

spent *adj* **2** = **used up**, consumed, expended, finished, gone **2** = **exhausted**, all in (*sl.*), burnt out, bushed (*inf.*), clapped out (*Austral. & NZ inf.*), dead beat (*inf.*), debilitated, dog-tired (*inf.*), done in *or* up (*inf.*), drained, effete, knackered (*sl.*), played out (*inf.*), prostrate, ready to drop (*inf.*), shattered (*inf.*), tired out, weakened, wearied, weary, whacked (*Brit. inf.*), wiped out (*inf.*), worn out

sperm[1] *n* **1** = **semen**, scum (*US sl.*), seed (*arch. or dialect*), spermatozoa **2** = **spermatozoon**, male gamete, reproductive cell and hunted for sperm oil, spermaceti, and ambergris. Also called: **cachalot.** [C19: short for SPERMACETI *whale*]

spew ❶ (spjuː) *vb* **1** to eject (the contents of the stomach) involuntarily through the mouth; vomit. **2** to spit (spittle, phlegm, etc.) out of the mouth. **3** (usually foll. by *out*) to send or be sent out in a stream: *flames spewed out.* ◆ *n* **4** something ejected from the mouth. ◆ Also (archaic): **spue.** [OE *spīwan*]
▸**'spewer** *n*

sp. gr. *abbrev. for* specific gravity.

sphagnum ('sfægnəm) *n* any moss of the genus *Sphagnum,* of temperate bogs: layers of these mosses decay to form peat. Also called: **peat moss, bog moss.** [C18: from NL, from Gk *sphagnos* a variety of moss]
▸**'sphagnous** *adj*

sphairee (sfaɪriː) *n Austral.* a game resembling tennis played with wooden bats and a perforated plastic ball. [from Gk *sphaira* a ball]

sphalerite ('sfæləˌraɪt, 'sfeɪlə-) *n* a yellow to brownish-black mineral consisting mainly of zinc sulphide in cubic crystalline form: the chief source of zinc. Formula: ZnS. Also called: **zinc blende.** [C19: from Gk *sphaleros* deceitful, from *sphallein* to cause to stumble]

sphene (sfiːn) *n* a brown, yellow, green, or grey lustrous mineral consisting of calcium titanium silicate in monoclinic crystalline form. Also called: **titanite.** [C19: from F *sphène,* from Gk *sphēn* a wedge, alluding to its crystals]

sphenoid ('sfiːnɔɪd) *adj also* **sphenoidal. 1** wedge-shaped. **2** of or relating to the sphenoid bone. ◆ *n* **3** See **sphenoid bone.**

sphenoid bone *n* the large butterfly-shaped compound bone at the base of the skull.

sphere ❶ (sfɪə) *n* **1** *Maths.* **1a** a three-dimensional closed surface such that every point on the surface is equidistant from a given point, the centre. **1b** the solid figure bounded by this surface or the space enclosed by it. **2** any object having approximately this shape; a globe. **3** the night sky considered as a vaulted roof; firmament. **4** any heavenly object such as a planet, natural satellite, or star. **5** (in the Ptolemaic or Copernican systems of astronomy) one of a series of revolving hollow globes, arranged concentrically, on whose transparent surfaces the sun, the moon, the planets, and fixed stars were thought to be set. **6** a particular field of activity; environment. **7** a social class or stratum of society. ◆ *vb* **spheres, sphering, sphered.** (*tr*) *Chiefly poetic.* **8** to surround or encircle. **9** to place aloft or in the heavens. [C14: from LL *sphēra,* from L *sphaera* globe, from Gk *sphaira*]
▸**'spheral** *adj*

-sphere *n combining form.* **1** having the shape or form of a sphere: *bathysphere.* **2** indicating a spherelike enveloping mass: *atmosphere.*
▸**-spheric** *adj combining form.*

spherical ❶ ('sfɛrɪkᵊl) *or* **spheric** *adj* **1** shaped like a sphere. **2** of or relating to a sphere: *spherical geometry.* **3** *Geom.* formed on the surface of or inside a sphere: *a spherical triangle.* **4a** of or relating to heavenly bodies. **4b** of or relating to the spheres of the Ptolemaic or the Copernican system.
▸**'spherically** *adv* ▸**'sphericalness** *n*

spherical aberration *n Physics.* a defect of optical systems that arises when light striking a mirror or lens near its edge is focused at different points on the axis to the light striking near the centre. The effect occurs when the mirror or lens has spherical surfaces.

spherical angle *n* an angle formed at the intersection of two great circles of a sphere.

spherical coordinates *pl n* three coordinates that define the location of a point in space in terms of its radius vector, *r,* the angle, θ, which this vector makes with one axis, and the angle, ϕ, which the plane of this vector makes with a mutually perpendicular axis.

spherical trigonometry *n* the branch of trigonometry concerned with the measurement of the angles and sides of spherical triangles.

spheroid ('sfɪərɔɪd) *n* **1** another name for **ellipsoid of revolution.** ◆ *adj* **2** shaped like but not exactly a sphere.
▸**spher'oidal** *adj* ▸ˌ**spheroid'icity** *n*

spherometer (sfɪə'rɒmɪtə) *n* an instrument for measuring the curvature of a surface.

spherule ('sfɛruːl) *n* a very small sphere. [C17: from LL *sphaerula*]
▸**'spherular** *adj*

spherulite ('sfɛrʊˌlaɪt) *n* any of several spherical masses of radiating needle-like crystals of one or more minerals occurring in rocks such as obsidian.
▸**spherulitic** (ˌsfɛrʊ'lɪtɪk) *adj*

sphincter ('sfɪŋktə) *n Anat.* a ring of muscle surrounding the opening of a hollow organ or body and contracting to close it. [C16: from LL, from Gk *sphinktēr,* from *sphingein* to grip tightly]
▸**'sphincteral** *adj*

sphinx (sfɪŋks) *n, pl* **sphinxes** *or* **sphinges** ('sfɪndʒiːz). **1** any of a number of huge stone statues built by the ancient Egyptians, having the body of a lion and the head of a man. **2** an inscrutable person.

Sphinx (sfɪŋks) *n* **the. 1** *Greek myth.* a monster with a woman's head and a lion's body. She lay outside Thebes, asking travellers a riddle and killing them when they failed to answer it. Oedipus answered the riddle and the Sphinx then killed herself. **2** the huge statue of a sphinx near the pyramids at El Gîza in Egypt. [C16: via L from Gk, apparently from *sphingein* to hold fast]

sphragistics (sfrə'dʒɪstɪks) *n* (*functioning as sing*) the study of seals and signet rings. [C19: from Gk *sphragistikos,* from *sphragizein* to seal, from *sphragis* a seal]
▸**sphra'gistic** *adj*

sphygmo- *or before a vowel* **sphygm-** *combining form.* indicating the pulse: *sphygmograph.* [from Gk *sphugmos* pulsation, from *sphuzein* to throb]

sphygmograph ('sfɪgməʊˌgrɑːf) *n Med.* an instrument for making a recording (**sphygmogram**) of variations in blood pressure and pulse.
▸**sphygmographic** (ˌsfɪgməʊ'græfɪk) *adj* ▸**sphygmography** (sfɪg'mɒgrəfɪ) *n*

sphygmomanometer (ˌsfɪgməʊmə'nɒmɪtə) *n Med.* an instrument for measuring arterial blood pressure.

spicate ('spaɪkeɪt) *adj Bot.* having, arranged in, or relating to spikes: *a spicate inflorescence.* [C17: from L *spīcātus* having spikes, from *spīca* a point]

spiccato (spɪ'kɑːtəʊ) *Music.* ◆ *n* **1** a style of playing a bowed stringed instrument in which the bow bounces lightly off the strings. ◆ *adj, adv* **2** (to be played) in this manner. [It.: detached]

spice ❶ (spaɪs) *n* **1a** any of a variety of aromatic vegetable substances, such as ginger, cinnamon, or nutmeg, used as flavourings. **1b** these substances collectively. **2** something that represents or introduces zest, charm, or gusto. **3** *Rare.* a small amount. ◆ *vb* **spices, spicing, spiced.** (*tr*) **4** to prepare or flavour (food) with spices. **5** to introduce charm or zest into. [C13: from OF *espice,* from LL *speciēs* (pl) spices, from L *speciēs* (sing) kind; also associated with LL *spīcea* (unattested) fragrant herb, from L *spīceus* having spikes of foliage]

spicebush ('spaɪsˌbʊʃ) *n* a North American shrub having aromatic leaves and bark.

spick-and-span ❶ *or* **spic-and-span** ('spɪkən'spæn) *adj* **1** extremely neat and clean. **2** new and fresh. [C17: shortened from *spick-and-span-new,* from obs. *spick* spike + *span-new,* from ON *spānnÿr* absolutely new]

spicule ('spɪkjuːl) *n* **1** Also called: **spiculum.** a small slender pointed structure or crystal, esp. any of the calcareous or siliceous elements of the skeleton of sponges, corals, etc. **2** *Astron.* a spiked ejection of hot gas above the sun's surface. [C18: from L *spiculum* small, sharp point]
▸**spiculate** ('spɪkjʊˌleɪt, -lɪt) *adj*

spicy ❶ ('spaɪsɪ) *adj* **spicier, spiciest. 1** seasoned with or containing spice. **2** highly flavoured; pungent. **3** *Inf.* suggestive of scandal or sensation.
▸**'spicily** *adv* ▸**'spiciness** *n*

spider ('spaɪdə) *n* **1** any of various predatory silk-producing arachnids, having four pairs of legs and a rounded unsegmented body. **2** any of various similar or related arachnids. **3** any implement or tool having the shape of a spider. **4** any part of a machine having a number of radiating spokes, tines, or arms. **5** Also called: **octopus.** *Brit.* a cluster of elastic straps fastened at a central point and used to hold a load on a car rack, motorcycle, etc. **6** *Snooker, etc.* a rest having long legs, used to raise the cue above the level of the height of the ball. [OE *spīthra*]
▸**'spidery** *adj*

spider crab *n* any of various crabs having a small triangular body and very long legs.

spiderman ('spaɪdəˌmæn) *n, pl* **spidermen.** *Inf., chiefly Brit.* a person who erects the steel structure of a building.

spider mite *n* any of various plant-feeding mites, esp. the **red spider mite,** which is a serious orchard pest.

spider monkey *n* **1** any of several arboreal New World monkeys of Central and South America, having very long legs, a long prehensile tail, and a small head. **2 woolly spider monkey.** a rare related monkey of SE Brazil.

spider plant *n* a house plant having long narrow leaves with a light central stripe.

spiderwort ('spaɪdəˌwɜːt) *n* **1** any of various American plants having blue, purplish, or pink flowers and widely grown as house plants. See also **tradescantia. 2** any of various similar or related plants.

spiel ❶ (ʃpiːl) *n* **1** glib plausible talk, associated esp. with salesmen. ◆ *vb* **2** (*intr*) to deliver a prepared spiel. **3** (*tr;* usually foll. by *off*) to recite (a prepared oration). [C19: from G *Spiel* play]
▸**'spieler** *n*

spier ('spaɪə) *n Arch.* a person who spies or scouts.

THESAURUS

spew *vb* **1** = **vomit**, barf (*US sl.*), belch forth, chuck (up) (*sl., chiefly US*), chunder (*sl., chiefly Austral.*), disgorge, do a technicolour yawn (*sl.*), puke (*sl.*), regurgitate, spit out, throw up (*inf.*), toss one's cookies (*US sl.*)

sphere *n* **2** = **ball**, circle, globe, globule, orb **6** = **field**, capacity, compass, department, domain, employment, function, patch, province, range, realm, scope, territory, turf (*US sl.*), walk of life **7** = **rank**, station, stratum

spherical *adj* **1** = **round**, globe-shaped, globular, orbicular, rotund

spice *n* **1** = **seasoning**, relish, savour **2** = **excitement**, colour, gusto, kick (*inf.*), pep, piquancy, tang, zest, zing (*inf.*), zip (*inf.*)

spick-and-span *adj* **1** = **neat**, clean, fresh as paint, immaculate, impeccable, in apple-pie order (*inf.*), shipshape, spotless, spruce, tidy, trim

spicy *adj* **2** = **hot**, aromatic, flavoursome, piquant, pungent, savoury, seasoned, tangy **3** *Informal* = **scandalous**, broad, hot (*inf.*), improper, indecorous, indelicate, off-colour, racy, ribald, risqué, sensational, suggestive, titillating, unseemly

spiel *n* **1** = **patter**, harangue, pitch, recital, sales patter, sales talk, speech

spiffing ('spɪfɪŋ) *adj Brit. sl., old-fashioned.* excellent; splendid. [C19: prob. from dialect *spiff* spruce, smart]

spiffy ('spɪfɪ) *adj* **spiffier, spiffiest.** *US & Canad. sl.* smart; stylish. [C19: from dialect *spiff* smartly dressed]
▸**'spiffily** *adv*

spigot ('spɪgət) *n* **1** a stopper for the vent hole of a cask. **2** a tap, usually of wood, fitted to a cask. **3** a US name for **tap**[2] (sense 1). **4** a short projection on one component designed to fit into a hole on another, esp. the male part of a joint between two pipes. [C14: prob. from OProvençal *espiga* a head of grain, from L *spīca* a point]

spike[1] ⓣ (spaɪk) *n* **1** a sharp point. **2** any sharp-pointed object, esp. one made of metal. **3** a long metal nail. **4** (*pl*) shoes with metal projections on the sole and heel for greater traction, as used by athletes. **5** *Brit. sl.* another word for **dosshouse.** ◆ *vb* **spikes, spiking, spiked.** (*tr*) **6** to secure or supply with or as with spikes. **7** to render ineffective or block the intentions of; thwart. **8** to impale on a spike. **9** to add alcohol to (a drink). **10** *Volleyball.* to hit (a ball) sharply downwards with an overarm motion from the front of one's own court into the opposing court. **11** (formerly) to render (a cannon) ineffective by blocking its vent with a spike. **12 spike (someone's) guns.** to thwart (someone's) purpose. [C13 *spyk*]
▸**'spiky** *adj*

spike[2] (spaɪk) *n Bot.* **1** an inflorescence consisting of a raceme of sessile flowers. **2** an ear of wheat, etc. [C14: from L *spīca* ear of corn]

spikelet ('spaɪklɪt) *n Bot.* a small spike, esp. the inflorescence of most grasses and sedges.

spikenard ('spaɪknɑːd, 'spaɪkəˌnɑːd) *n* **1** an aromatic Indian plant, having rose-purple flowers. **2** an aromatic ointment obtained from this plant. **3** any of various similar or related plants. **4** a North American plant having small green flowers and an aromatic root. ◆ Also called (for senses 1, 2): **nard.** [C14: from Med. L *spīca nardī;* see SPIKE[2], NARD]

spile (spaɪl) *n* **1** a heavy timber stake or pile. **2** *US.* a spout for tapping sap from the sugar maple tree. **3** a plug or spigot. ◆ *vb* **spiles, spiling, spiled.** (*tr*) **4** to provide or support with a spile. **5** *US.* to tap (a tree) with a spile. [C16: prob. from MDu. *spile* peg]

spill[1] ⓣ (spɪl) *vb* **spills, spilling; spilt** *or* **spilled.** (*mainly tr*) **1** (when *intr*, usually foll. by *from, out of,* etc.) to fall or cause to fall from or as from a container, esp. unintentionally. **2** to disgorge (contents, occupants, etc.) or (of contents, occupants, etc.) to be disgorged. **3** to shed (blood). **4** Also: **spill the beans.** *Inf.* to divulge something confidential. **5** *Naut.* to let (wind) escape from a sail or (of the wind) to escape from a sail. ◆ *n* **6** *Inf.* a fall or tumble. **7** short for **spillway. 8** a spilling of liquid, etc., or the amount spilt. **9** *Austral.* the declaring of several political jobs vacant when one higher up becomes so. [OE *spillan* to destroy]
▸**'spillage** *n* ▸**'spiller** *n*

spill[2] (spɪl) *n* a splinter of wood or strip of twisted paper with which pipes, fires, etc., are lit. [C13: of Gmc origin]

spillikin, spilikin ('spɪlɪkɪn), *or* **spellican** ('spelɪkən) *n* a thin strip of wood, cardboard, or plastic, esp. one used in spillikins.

spillikins ('spɪlɪkɪnz) *n* (*functioning as sing*) *Brit.* a game in which players try to pick each spillikin from a heap without moving any of the others. Also called: **jackstraws.**

spill over *vb* **1** (*intr, adv*) to overflow or be forced out of an area, container, etc. ◆ *n* **spillover.** *Chiefly US & Canad.* **2** the act of spilling over. **3** the excess part of something.

spillway ('spɪlˌweɪ) *n* a channel that carries away surplus water, as from a dam.

spilt (spɪlt) *vb* a past tense and past participle of **spill**[1].

spin ⓣ (spɪn) *vb* **spins, spinning, spun. 1** to rotate or cause to rotate rapidly, as on an axis. **2a** to draw out and twist (natural fibres, as of silk or cotton) into a long continuous thread. **2b** to make such a thread or filament from (synthetic resins, etc.), usually by forcing through a nozzle. **3** (of spiders, silkworms, etc.) to form (webs, cocoons, etc.) from a silky fibre exuded from the body. **4** (*tr*) to shape (metal) into a rounded form on a lathe. **5** (*tr*) *Inf.* to tell (a tale, story, etc.) by drawing it out at great length (esp. in **spin a yarn**). **6** to bowl, pitch, hit, or kick (a ball) so that it rotates in the air and changes direction or speed on bouncing, or (of a ball) to be projected in this way. **7** (*intr*) (of wheels) to revolve rapidly without causing propulsion. **8** to cause (an aircraft) to dive in a spiral descent or (of an aircraft) to dive in a spiral descent. **9** (*intr;* foll. by *along*) to drive or travel swiftly. **10** (*tr*) Also: **spin-dry.** to rotate (clothes) in a washing machine in order to extract surplus water. **11** (*intr*) to reel or grow dizzy, as from turning around: *my head is spinning.* **12** (*intr*) to fish by drawing a revolving lure through the water. **13** (*intr*) *Inf.* to present news or information in a way that creates a favourable impression. ◆ *n* **14** a swift rotating motion; instance of spinning. **15** *Physics.* **15a** the intrinsic angular momentum of an elementary particle or atomic nucleus. **15b** a quantum number determining values of this angular momentum. **16** a condition of loss of control of an aircraft or an intentional flight manoeuvre in which the aircraft performs a continuous spiral descent. **17** a spinning motion imparted to a ball, etc. **18** *Inf.* a short or fast drive, ride, etc., esp. in a car, for pleasure. **19 flat spin.** *Inf., chiefly Brit.* a state of agitation or confusion. **20** *Austral. & NZ inf.* a period of a specified kind of fortune: *a bad spin.* **21** *Inf.* the practice of presenting news or information in a way that creates a favourable impression. ◆ See also **spin out.** [OE *spinnan*]

spina bifida ('spaɪnə 'bɪfɪdə) *n* a congenital condition in which the meninges of the spinal cord protrude through a gap in the backbone, sometimes causing enlargement of the skull and paralysis. [NL; see SPINE, BIFID]

spinach ('spɪnɪdʒ, -ɪtʃ) *n* **1** an annual plant cultivated for its dark green edible leaves. **2** the leaves, eaten as a vegetable. [C16: from OF *espinache,* from OSp., from Ar. *isfānākh,* from Persian]

spinal ('spaɪnᵊl) *adj* **1** of or relating to the spine or the spinal cord. ◆ *n* **2** short for **spinal anaesthesia.**
▸**'spinally** *adv*

spinal anaesthesia *n* **1** anaesthesia of the lower half of the body produced by injecting an anaesthetic beneath the arachnoid membrane. Cf. **epidural** (sense 2). **2** loss of sensation in part of the body as the result of injury of the spinal cord.

spinal canal *n* the passage through the spinal column that contains the spinal cord.

spinal column *n* a series of contiguous or interconnecting bony or cartilaginous segments that surround and protect the spinal cord. Also called: **spine, vertebral column.** Nontechnical name: **backbone.**

spinal cord *n* the thick cord of nerve tissue within the spinal canal, which together with the brain forms the central nervous system.

spin bowler *n* another name for **spinner** (sense 2b).

spindle ('spɪndᵊl) *n* **1** a rod or stick that has a notch in the top, used to draw out natural fibres for spinning into thread, and a long narrow body around which the thread is wound when spun. **2** one of the thin rods or pins bearing bobbins upon which spun thread is wound in a spinning machine. **3** any of various parts in the form of a rod, esp. a rotating rod that acts as an axle, etc. **4** a piece of wood that has been turned, such as a table leg. **5** a small square metal shaft that passes through the lock of a door and to which the door knobs or handles are fixed. **6** *Biol.* a spindle-shaped structure formed in a cell during mitosis or meiosis which draws the duplicated chromosomes apart during cell division. **7** a device consisting of a sharp upright spike on a pedestal on which bills, order forms, etc., are impaled. ◆ *vb* **spindles, spindling, spindled. 8** (*tr*) to form into a spindle or equip with spindles. **9** (*intr*) *Rare.* (of a plant, stem, shoot, etc.) to grow rapidly and become elongated and thin. [OE *spinel*]

spindlelegs ('spɪndᵊlˌlegz) *or* **spindleshanks** *n* **1** (*functioning as pl*) long thin legs. **2** (*functioning as sing*) a person who has such legs.

spindle tree *n* any of various shrubs or trees of Europe and W Asia, typically having red fruits and yielding a hard wood formerly used in making spindles.

spindly ⓣ ('spɪndlɪ) *adj* **spindlier, spindliest.** tall, slender, and frail; attenuated.

spin doctor *n Inf.* a person who provides a favourable slant to an item of news, potentially unpopular policy, etc., esp. on behalf of a political personality or party. [C20: from the spin given to a ball in various sports to make it go in the desired direction]

spindrift ('spɪnˌdrɪft) *n* spray blown up from the sea. Also: **spoondrift.** [C16: Scot. var. of *spoondrift,* from *spoon* to scud + DRIFT]

spin-dry *vb* **spin-dries, spin-drying, spin-dried.** (*tr*) to extract water from (wet washing) by spinning in a washing machine or spin-dryer.

spin-dryer *n* a device that extracts water from clothes, etc., by spinning them in a perforated drum.

spine ⓣ (spaɪn) *n* **1** the spinal column. **2** the sharply pointed tip or outgrowth of a leaf, stem, etc. **3** *Zool.* a hard pointed process or structure, such as the quill of a porcupine. **4** the back of a book, record sleeve, etc. **5** a ridge, esp. of a hill. **6** strength of endurance, will, etc. **7** anything resembling the spinal column in function or importance; main support or feature. [C14: from OF *espine* spine, from L *spīna* thorn, backbone]
▸**spined** *adj*

spine-chiller ⓣ *n* a book, film, etc., that arouses terror.
▸**'spine-ˌchilling** *adj*

spinel (spɪ'nel) *n* any of a group of hard glassy minerals of variable colour consisting of oxides of aluminium, magnesium, iron, zinc, or manganese: used as gemstones. [C16: from F *spinelle,* from It. *spinella,* dim. of *spina* a thorn, from L; so called from the shape of the crystals]

THESAURUS

spike[1] *n* **1, 2** = **point**, barb, prong, spine ◆ *vb* **8** = **impale**, spear, spit, stick

spill[1] *vb* **1, 2** = **pour**, discharge, disgorge, overflow, scatter, shed, slop over, spill *or* run over, teem, throw off, upset **4 spill the beans** *Informal* = **betray a secret**, blab, blow the gaff (*Brit. sl.*), give the game away, grass (*Brit. sl.*), inform, let the cat out of the bag, shop (*sl., chiefly Brit.*), sing (*sl., chiefly US*), spill one's guts (*sl.*), split (*sl.*), squeal (*sl.*), talk out of turn, tattle, tell all ◆ *n* **6** *Informal* = **fall**, accident, cropper (*inf.*), tumble

spin *vb* **1** = **revolve**, birl (*Scot.*), gyrate, pirouette, reel, rotate, turn, twirl, twist, wheel, whirl **5** *As in* **spin a yarn** = **tell**, concoct, develop, invent, narrate, recount, relate, unfold **11** = **reel**, be giddy, be in a whirl, grow dizzy, swim, whirl ◆ *n* **14** = **revolution**, gyration, roll, twist, whirl **18** *Informal* = **drive**, hurl (*Scot.*), joy ride (*inf.*), ride, turn, whirl **19 flat spin** *Informal* = **panic**, agitation, commotion, flap (*inf.*), state (*inf.*), tizwoz (*inf.*), tizzy (*inf.*)

spindly *adj* = **lanky**, attenuated, gangling, gangly, leggy, spidery, spindle-shanked, twiggy

spine *n* **1** = **backbone**, spinal column, vertebrae, vertebral column **3** = **barb**, needle, quill, rachis, ray, spike, spur

spine-chilling *adj* = **frightening**, bloodcurdling, eerie, hair-raising, horrifying, scary (*inf.*), spooky (*inf.*), terrifying

spineless ⓣ ('spaɪnlɪs) *adj* **1** lacking a backbone. **2** having no spiny processes: *spineless stems*. **3** lacking character, resolution, or courage.
▸**'spinelessly** *adv* ▸**'spinelessness** *n*

spinet (spɪ'nɛt, 'spɪnɪt) *n* a small type of harpsichord having one manual. [C17: from It. *spinetta*, ? from Giovanni *Spinetti*, 16th-cent. It. maker of musical instruments & its supposed inventor]

spinifex ('spɪnɪˌfɛks) *n* **1** any of various Australian grasses having pointed leaves and spiny seed heads. **2** Also called: **porcupine grass.** *Austral.* any of various coarse spiny-leaved inland grasses. [C19: from NL, from L *spīna* a thorn + *-fex* maker, from *facere* to make]

spinnaker ('spɪnəkə; *Naut.* 'spæŋkə) *n* a large light triangular racing sail set from the foremast of a yacht. [C19: prob. from SPIN + (MO)NIKER, but traditionally from *Sphinx*, the yacht that first adopted this type of sail]

spinner ('spɪnə) *n* **1** a person or thing that spins. **2** *Cricket.* **2a** a ball that is bowled with a spinning motion. **2b** a bowler who specializes in bowling such balls. **3** a streamlined fairing that fits over the hub of an aircraft propeller. **4** a fishing lure with a fin or wing that revolves.

spinneret ('spɪnəˌrɛt) *n* **1** any of several organs in spiders and certain insects through which silk threads are exuded. **2** a finely perforated dispenser through which a liquid is extruded in the production of synthetic fibres.

spinney ('spɪnɪ) *n Chiefly Brit.* a small wood or copse. [C16: from OF *espinei*, from *espine* thorn, from L *spīna*]

spinning ('spɪnɪŋ) *n* **1** the act or process of spinning. **2** the act or technique of casting and drawing a revolving lure through the water so as to imitate a live fish, etc.

spinning jenny *n* an early type of spinning frame with several spindles, invented in 1764.

spinning wheel *n* a wheel-like machine for spinning at home, having one hand- or foot-operated spindle.

spin-off *n* **1** any product or development derived incidentally from the application of existing knowledge or enterprise. **2** a book, film, or television series derived from a similar successful book, film, or television series.

spinose ('spaɪnəʊs, spaɪ'nəʊs) *adj* (esp. of plants) bearing many spines. [C17: from L *spīnōsus* prickly, from *spīna* a thorn]

spin out ⓣ *vb (tr, adv)* **1** to extend or protract (a story, etc.) by including superfluous detail. **2** to spend or pass (time). **3** to contrive to cause (money, etc.) to last as long as possible.

spinster ('spɪnstə) *n* **1** an unmarried woman. **2** a woman regarded as being beyond the age of marriage. **3** (formerly) a woman who spins thread for her living. [C14 (in the sense: a person, esp. a woman, whose occupation is spinning; C17: a woman still unmarried): from SPIN + -STER]
▸**'spinsterˌhood** *n* ▸**'spinsterish** *adj*

spiny ('spaɪnɪ) *adj* **spinier, spiniest. 1** (of animals) having or covered with quills or spines. **2** (of plants) covered with spines; thorny. **3** troublesome; puzzling.
▸**'spininess** *n*

spiny anteater *n* another name for **echidna.**

spiny-finned *adj* (of certain fishes) having fins that are supported by stiff bony spines.

spiny lobster *n* any of various large edible marine decapod crustaceans having a very tough spiny carapace. Also called: **rock lobster, crawfish, langouste.**

spiracle ('spaɪərək$^{\partial}$l, 'spaɪrə-) *n* **1** any of several paired apertures in the cuticle of an insect, by which air enters and leaves the trachea. **2** a small paired rudimentary gill slit in skates, rays, and related fishes. **3** any similar respiratory aperture, such as the blowhole in whales. [C14 (orig.: breath): from L *spīrāculum* vent, from *spīrāre* to breathe]
▸**spiracular** (spɪ'rækjʊlə) *adj* ▸**spi'raculate** *adj*

spiraea *or esp. US* **spirea** (spaɪ'rɪə) *n* any of various rosaceous plants having sprays of small white or pink flowers. See also **meadowsweet** (sense 2). [C17: via L from Gk *speiraia*, from *speira* SPIRE[2]]

spiral ⓣ ('spaɪərəl) *n* **1** *Geom.* one of several plane curves formed by a point winding about a fixed point at an ever-increasing distance from it. **2** a curve that lies on a cylinder or cone, at a constant angle to the line segments making up the surface; helix. **3** something that pursues a winding, usually upward, course or that displays a twisting form or shape. **4** a flight manoeuvre in which an aircraft descends describing a helix of comparatively large radius with the angle of attack within the normal flight range. **5** *Econ.* a continuous upward or downward movement in economic activity or prices, caused by interaction between prices, wages, demand, and production. ◆ *adj* **6** having the shape of a spiral. ◆ *vb* **spirals, spiralling, spiralled** *or US* **spirals, spiraling, spiraled. 7** to assume or cause to assume a spiral course or shape. **8** *(intr)* to increase or decrease with steady acceleration: *prices continue to spiral.* [C16: via F from Med. L *spīrālis*, from L *spīra* a coil; see SPIRE[2]]
▸**'spirally** *adv*

spiral galaxy *n* a galaxy consisting of an ellipsoidal nucleus of old stars from opposite sides of which arms, containing younger stars, spiral outwards around the nucleus.

spirant ('spaɪrənt) *adj* **1** *Phonetics.* another word for **fricative.** ◆ *n* **2** a fricative consonant. [C19: from L *spīrāns* breathing, from *spīrāre* to breathe]

spire[1] ('spaɪə) *n* **1** Also called: **steeple.** a tall structure that tapers upwards to a point, esp. one on a tower or roof or one that forms the upper part of a steeple. **2** a slender tapering shoot or stem, such as a blade of grass. **3** the apical part of any tapering formation; summit. ◆ *vb* **spires, spiring, spired. 4** *(intr)* to assume the shape of a spire; point up. **5** *(tr)* to furnish with a spire or spires. [OE *spīr* blade]
▸**'spiry** *adj*

spire[2] ('spaɪə) *n* **1** any of the coils or turns in a spiral structure. **2** the apical part of a spiral shell. [C16: from L *spīra* a coil, from Gk *speira*]

spirillum (spaɪ'rɪləm) *n, pl* **spirilla** (-lə). **1** any bacterium having a curved or spirally twisted rodlike body. **2** any bacterium of the genus *Spirillum*, such as *S. minus*, which causes ratbite fever. [C19: from NL, lit.: a little coil, from *spīra* a coil]

spirit[1] ⓣ ('spɪrɪt) *n* **1** the force or principle of life that animates the body of living things. **2** temperament or disposition: *truculent in spirit.* **3** liveliness; mettle: *they set to it with spirit.* **4** the fundamental, emotional, and activating principle of a person; will: *the experience broke his spirit.* **5** a sense of loyalty or dedication: *team spirit.* **6** the prevailing element; feeling: *a spirit of joy pervaded the atmosphere.* **7** state of mind or mood; attitude: *he did it in the wrong spirit.* **8** *(pl)* an emotional state, esp. with regard to exaltation or dejection: *in high spirits.* **9** a person characterized by some activity, quality, or disposition: *a leading spirit of the movement.* **10** the deeper more significant meaning as opposed to a pedantic interpretation: *the spirit of the law.* **11** a person's intangible being as contrasted with his physical presence: *I shall be with you in spirit.* **12a** an incorporeal being, esp. the soul of a dead person. **12b** *(as modifier): spirit world.* ◆ *vb (tr)* **13** (usually foll. by *away* or *off*) to carry off mysteriously or secretly. **14** (often foll. by *up*) to impart animation or determination to. [C13: from OF *esperit*, from L *spīritus* breath, spirit]
▸**'spiritless** *adj*

spirit[2] ⓣ ('spɪrɪt) *n* **1** *(often pl)* any distilled alcoholic liquor, such as whisky or gin. **2** *Chem.* **2a** an aqueous solution of ethanol, esp. one obtained by distillation. **2b** the active principle or essence of a substance, extracted as a liquid, esp. by distillation. **3** *Pharmacol.* a solution of a volatile substance, esp. a volatile oil, in alcohol. **4** *Alchemy.* any of the four substances sulphur, mercury, sal ammoniac, or arsenic. [C14: special use of SPIRIT[1], name applied to alchemical substances (as in sense 4), hence extended to distilled liquids]

Spirit ('spɪrɪt) *n* **the. a** another name for the **Holy Spirit. b** God, esp. when regarded as transcending material limitations.

spirited ⓣ ('spɪrɪtɪd) *adj* **1** displaying animation, vigour, or liveliness. **2** *(in combination)* characterized by mood, temper, or disposition as specified: *high-spirited; public-spirited.*
▸**'spiritedly** *adv* ▸**'spiritedness** *n*

spirit gum *n* a glue made from gum dissolved in ether used to affix a false beard, etc.

spiritism ('spɪrɪˌtɪzəm) *n* a less common word for **spiritualism.**
▸**'spiritist** *n* ▸**ˌspirit'istic** *adj*

spirit lamp *n* a lamp that burns methylated or other spirits instead of oil.

spirit level *n* a device for setting horizontal surfaces, consisting of a block of material in which a sealed tube partially filled with liquid is set so that the air bubble rests between two marks on the tube when the block is horizontal.

spiritous ('spɪrɪtəs) *adj* a variant of **spirituous.**

THESAURUS

spineless *adj* **3** = **weak**, boneless, cowardly, faint-hearted, feeble, gutless (*inf.*), inadequate, ineffective, irresolute, lily-livered, pathetic, soft, spiritless, squeamish, submissive, vacillating, weak-kneed (*inf.*), weak-willed, without a will of one's own, yellow (*inf.*)
Antonyms *adj* bold, brave, courageous, gritty, strong, strong-willed

spin out *vb* **1** = **prolong**, amplify, delay, drag out, draw out, extend, lengthen, pad out, prolongate, protract

spiral *n* **3** = **coil**, corkscrew, curlicue, gyre (*literary*), helix, screw, volute, whorl ◆ *adj* **6** = **coiled**, circular, cochlear, cochleate (*Biology*), corkscrew, helical, scrolled, voluted, whorled, winding

spirit[1] *n* **1** = **life force**, air, breath, life, psyche, soul, vital spark **2** = **temperament**, attitude, character, complexion, disposition, essence, humour, outlook, quality, temper **3** = **liveliness**, animation, ardour, brio, earnestness, energy, enterprise, enthusiasm, fire, force, life, mettle, resolution, sparkle, vigour, warmth, zest **4** = **will**, motivation, resolution, resolve, willpower **5** = **courage**, backbone, dauntlessness, gameness, grit, guts (*inf.*), spunk (*inf.*), stoutheartedness **6** = **feeling**, atmosphere, gist, humour, tenor, tone **8** *plural* = **mood**, feelings, frame of mind, humour, morale **10** = **intention**, essence, intent, meaning, purport, purpose, sense, substance **12** = **ghost**, apparition, eidolon, phantom, shade (*literary*), shadow, spectre, spook (*inf.*), sprite, vision ◆ *vb* **13** *with* **away** *or* **off** = **remove**, abduct, abstract, carry, convey, make away with, purloin, seize, snaffle (*Brit. inf.*), steal, whisk

spirit[2] *n, often plural* = **alcohol**, firewater, liquor, strong liquor, the hard stuff (*inf.*)

spirited *adj* **1** = **lively**, active, animated, ardent, bold, courageous, energetic, feisty (*inf., chiefly US & Canad.*), game, have-a-go (*inf.*), high-spirited, mettlesome, plucky, sparkling, sprightly, spunky (*inf.*), vigorous, vivacious
Antonyms *adj* apathetic, bland, calm, dispirited, dull, feeble, half-hearted, lacklustre, lifeless, low-key, spiritless, timid, token, unenthusiastic, weary

spiritless *adj* **3, 5** = **lifeless**, apathetic, dejected, depressed, despondent, dispirited, droopy, dull, lacklustre, languid, listless, low (*inf.*), melancholic, melancholy, mopy, torpid, unenthusiastic, unmoved

spirits of ammonia *n* (*functioning as sing or pl*) another name for **sal volatile.**

spirits of hartshorn *n* (*functioning as sing or pl*) a solution of ammonia gas in water. See **ammonium hydroxide.** Also called: **aqueous ammonia.**

spirits of salt *n* (*functioning as sing or pl*) a solution of hydrochloric acid in water.

spiritual Ⓣ (ˈspɪrɪtjʊəl) *adj* **1** relating to the spirit or soul and not to physical nature or matter; intangible. **2** of or relating to sacred things, the Church, religion, etc. **3** standing in a relationship based on communication between souls or minds: *a spiritual father.* **4** having a mind or emotions of a high and delicately refined quality. ◆ *n* **5** Also called: **Negro spiritual.** a type of religious song originating among Black slaves in the American South. **6** (*often pl*) the sphere of religious, spiritual, or ecclesiastical matters, or such matters in themselves.
▸ˌ**spirituˈality** *n* ▸ˈ**spiritually** *adv*

spiritualism (ˈspɪrɪtjʊəˌlɪzəm) *n* **1** the belief that the disembodied spirits of the dead, surviving in another world, can communicate with the living in this world, esp. through mediums. **2** the doctrines and practices associated with this belief. **3** *Philosophy.* the belief that because reality is to some extent immaterial it is therefore spiritual. **4** any doctrine that prefers the spiritual to the material.
▸ˈ**spiritualist** *n*

spiritualize *or* **spiritualise** (ˈspɪrɪtjʊəˌlaɪz) *vb* **spiritualizes, spiritualizing, spiritualized** *or* **spiritualises, spiritualising, spiritualised.** (*tr*) to make spiritual or infuse with spiritual content.
▸ˌ**spiritualiˈzation** *or* ˌ**spiritualiˈsation** *n* ▸ˈ**spiritualˌizer** *or* ˈ**spiritualˌiser** *n*

spirituel (ˌspɪrɪtjʊˈɛl) *adj* having a refined and lively mind or wit. Also (fem): **spirituelle.** [C17: from F]

spirituous (ˈspɪrɪtjʊəs) *adj* **1** characterized by or containing alcohol. **2** (of a drink) being a spirit.
▸**spirituosity** (ˌspɪrɪtjʊˈɒsɪtɪ) *or* ˈ**spirituousness** *n*

spirochaete *or US* **spirochete** (ˈspaɪrəʊˌkiːt) *n* any of a group of spirally coiled rodlike bacteria that includes the causative agent of syphilis. [C19: from NL, from *spiro-*, from L *spira*, from Gk *speira* a coil + *chaeta*, from Gk *khaitē* long hair]

spirograph (ˈspaɪrəˌgrɑːf) *n Med.* an instrument for recording the movements of breathing. [C20: NL, from *spiro-*, from L *spīrāre* to breathe + -GRAPH]
▸ˌ**spiroˈgraphic** *adj*

spirogyra (ˌspaɪrəˈdʒaɪrə) *n* any of various green freshwater multicellular algae containing spirally coiled chloroplasts. [C20: from NL, from *spiro-*, from L *spīra*, from Gk *speira* a coil + Gk *guros* a circle]

spirt (spɜːt) *n* a variant spelling of **spurt.**

spiry (ˈspaɪərɪ) *adj Poetic.* of spiral form; helical.

spit[1] Ⓣ (spɪt) *vb* **spits, spitting, spat** *or* **spit. 1** (*intr*) to expel saliva from the mouth; expectorate. **2** (*intr*) *Inf.* to show disdain or hatred by spitting. **3** (of a fire, hot fat, etc.) to eject (sparks, etc.) violently and with an explosive sound. **4** (*intr*) to rain very lightly. **5** (*tr; often foll. by out*) to eject or discharge (something) from the mouth: *he spat the food out.* **6** (*tr; often foll. by out*) to utter (short sharp words or syllables), esp. in a violent manner. **7 spit it out!** *Brit. inf.* a command given to someone that he should speak forthwith. ◆ *n* **8** another name for **spittle. 9** a light or brief fall of rain, snow, etc. **10** the act or an instance of spitting. **11** *Inf., chiefly Brit.* another word for **spitting image.** [OE *spittan*]
▸ˈ**spitter** *n*

spit[2] (spɪt) *n* **1** a pointed rod on which meat is skewered and roasted before or over an open fire. **2** Also called: **rotisserie, rotating spit.** a similar device fitted onto a cooker. **3** an elongated often hooked strip of sand or shingle projecting from a shore. ◆ *vb* **spits, spitting, spitted. 4** (*tr*) to impale on or transfix with or as if with a spit. [OE *spitu*]

spit and polish *n Inf.* punctilious attention to neatness, discipline, etc., esp. in the armed forces.

spite Ⓣ (spaɪt) *n* **1** maliciousness; venomous ill will. **2** an instance of such malice; grudge. **3 in spite of.** (*prep*) in defiance of; regardless of; notwithstanding. ◆ *vb* **spites, spiting, spited.** (*tr*) **4** to annoy in order to vent spite. [C13: var. of DESPITE]
▸ˈ**spiteful** *adj*

spitfire (ˈspɪtˌfaɪə) *n* a person given to outbursts of spiteful temper, esp. a woman or girl.

spitting image Ⓣ *n Inf.* a person who bears a strong physical resemblance to another. Also called: **spit, spit and image.** [C19: modification of *spit and image*, from SPIT[1] (as in *the very spit of* the exact likeness of)]

spitting snake *n* another name for the **rinkhals.**

spittle (ˈspɪtᵊl) *n* **1** the fluid secreted in the mouth; saliva. **2** Also called: **cuckoo spit, frog spit.** the frothy substance secreted on plants by the larvae of certain froghoppers. [OE *spǣtl* saliva]

spittoon (spɪˈtuːn) *n* a receptacle for spittle, usually in a public place.

spitz (spɪts) *n* any of various breeds of dog characterized by a stocky build, a pointed muzzle, erect ears, and a tightly-curled tail. [C19: from G *Spitz*, from *spitz* pointed]

spiv (spɪv) *n Brit. sl.* a person who makes a living by underhand dealings or swindling; black marketeer. [C20: back formation from dialect *spiving* smart]
▸ˈ**spivvy** *adj*

splake (spleɪk) *n* a type of hybrid trout bred by Canadian zoologists. [from *sp(eckled)* + *lake (trout)*]

splanchnic (ˈsplæŋknɪk) *adj* of or relating to the viscera: *a splanchnic nerve.* [C17: from NL *splanchnicus*, from Gk, from *splankhna* the entrails]

splash Ⓣ (splæʃ) *vb* **1** to scatter (liquid) about in blobs; spatter. **2** to descend or cause to descend upon in scattered blobs: *he splashed his jacket; rain splashed against the window.* **3** to make (one's way) by or as if by splashing: *he splashed through the puddle.* **4** (*tr*) to print (a story or photograph) prominently in a newspaper. ◆ *n* **5** an instance or sound of splashing. **6** an amount splashed. **7** a mark or patch created by or as if by splashing. **8** *Inf.* an extravagant display, usually for effect (esp. in **make a splash**). **9** a small amount of soda water, etc., added to an alcoholic drink. [C18: alteration of PLASH]
▸ˈ**splashy** *adj*

splashdown (ˈsplæʃˌdaʊn) *n* **1** the controlled landing of a spacecraft on water at the end of a space flight. **2** the time scheduled for this event. ◆ *vb* **splash down. 3** (*intr, adv*) (of a spacecraft) to make a splashdown.

splat[1] (splæt) *n* a wet slapping sound. [C19: imit.]

splat[2] (splæt) *n* a wide flat piece of wood, esp. one that is the upright central part of a chair back. [C19: ? rel. to OE *splātan* to split]

splatter (ˈsplætə) *vb* **1** to splash with small blobs. ◆ *n* **2** a splash of liquid, mud, etc.

splatter movie *n Sl.* a film in which the main feature is the graphic and gory murder of numerous victims.

splay (spleɪ) *adj* **1** spread out; broad and flat. **2** turned outwards in an awkward manner. ◆ *vb* **3** to spread out; turn out or expand. ◆ *n* **4** a surface of a wall that forms an oblique angle to the main flat surfaces, esp. at a doorway or window opening. [C14: short for DISPLAY]

splayfoot (ˈspleɪˌfʊt) *n, pl* **splayfeet.** *Pathol.* another word for **flatfoot.**
▸ˈ**splayˌfooted** *adj*

spleen Ⓣ (spliːn) *n* **1** a spongy highly vascular organ situated near the stomach in man. It forms lymphocytes, produces antibodies, and filters bacteria and foreign particles from the blood. **2** the corresponding organ in other animals. **3** spitefulness or ill humour: *to vent one's spleen.* **4** *Arch.* the organ in the human body considered to be the seat of the emotions. **5** *Arch.* another word for **melancholy.** [C13: from OF *esplen*, from L *splēn*, from Gk]
▸ˈ**spleenish** *or* ˈ**spleeny** *adj*

spleenwort (ˈspliːnˌwɜːt) *n* any of various ferns that often grow on walls.

splendent (ˈsplendənt) *adj Arch.* **1** shining brightly; lustrous: *a splendent sun.* **2** famous; illustrious. [C15: from L *splendēns* brilliant, from *splendēre* to shine]

splendid Ⓣ (ˈsplɛndɪd) *adj* **1** brilliant or fine, esp. in appearance. **2**

THESAURUS

spiritual *adj* **1 = nonmaterial**, ethereal, ghostly, immaterial, incorporeal **2 = sacred**, devotional, divine, holy, religious **4 = otherworldly**, pure
Antonyms *adj* ≠ **nonmaterial:** concrete, corporeal, material, nonspiritual, palpable, physical, substantial, tangible

spit[1] *vb* **1, 3, 5 = eject**, discharge, expectorate, hiss, spew, splutter, sputter, throw out ◆ *n* **8 = saliva**, dribble, drool, slaver, spittle, sputum

spite *n* **1 = malice**, animosity, bitchiness (*sl.*), gall, grudge, hate, hatred, ill will, malevolence, malignity, pique, rancour, spitefulness, spleen, venom **3 in spite of = despite**, (even) though, in defiance of, notwithstanding, regardless of ◆ *vb* **4 = annoy**, discomfit, gall, harm, hurt, injure, needle (*inf.*), nettle, offend, pique, provoke, put out, put (someone's) nose out of joint (*inf.*), vex
Antonyms *n* ≠ **malice:** benevolence, big-heartedness, charity, compassion, generosity of spirit, goodwill, kindliness, kindness, love, warm-heartedness ◆ *vb* ≠ **annoy:** aid, benefit, encourage, go along with, help, please, serve, support

spiteful *adj* **1 = malicious**, barbed, bitchy (*inf.*), catty (*inf.*), cruel, ill-disposed, ill-natured, malevolent, malignant, nasty, rancorous, shrewish, snide, splenetic, venomous, vindictive

spitting image *n* **= double**, clone, (dead) ringer (*sl.*), likeness, living image, lookalike, picture, replica, spit (*inf., chiefly Brit.*), spit and image (*inf.*)

splash *vb* **1 = scatter**, bespatter, shower, slop, slosh (*inf.*), spatter, splodge, spray, spread, sprinkle, squirt, strew, wet **2 = dash**, batter, break, buffet, plash, plop, smack, strike, surge, wash **3 = wade**, bathe, dabble, paddle, plunge, wallow **4 = publicize**, blazon, broadcast, flaunt, headline, plaster, tout, trumpet ◆ *n* **6, 7 = dash**, burst, patch, spattering, splodge, touch **8** *Informal* **= display**, effect, impact, sensation, splurge, stir **8 make a splash** *Informal* **= cause a stir**, be ostentatious, cut a dash, go overboard (*inf.*), go to town, splurge

spleen *n* **3 = spite**, acrimony, anger, animosity, animus, bad temper, bile, bitterness, gall, hatred, hostility, ill humour, ill will, malevolence, malice, malignity, peevishness, pique, rancour, resentment, spitefulness, venom, vindictiveness, wrath

splendid *adj* **2 = magnificent**, costly, dazzling, gorgeous, grand, imposing, impressive, lavish, luxurious, ornate, resplendent, rich, splendiferous (*facetious*), sumptuous, superb **3 = glorious**, admirable, brilliant, exceptional, grand, heroic, illustrious, magnificent, outstanding, rare, remarkable, renowned, sterling, sublime, superb, supreme **4 = radiant**, beaming, bright, brilliant, glittering, glowing, lustrous, refulgent **5 = excellent**, awesome (*sl.*), bodacious (*sl., chiefly US*), boffo (*sl.*), brill, chillin' (*US sl.*), cracking (*Brit. inf.*), crucial (*sl.*), def (*sl.*), fantastic (*inf.*), fine, first-class, glorious, great (*inf.*), marvellous, mean (*sl.*), mega (*sl.*), sovereign, topping (*Brit. sl.*), wonderful
Antonyms *adj* ≠ **magnificent:** beggarly, drab, dull, low, mean, plain, poor, poverty-stricken, sordid, squalid ≠ **glorious:** ignoble, ignominious ≠ **radiant:** tarnished ≠ **excellent:** depressing, disgusting, lacklustre, mediocre, miserable, no great shakes

characterized by magnificence. **3** glorious or illustrious: *a splendid reputation.* **4** brightly gleaming; radiant: *splendid colours.* **5** very good or satisfactory: *a splendid time.* [C17: from L *splendidus,* from *splendēre* to shine]
▸'**splendidly** *adv* ▸'**splendidness** *n*

splendiferous (splɛn'dɪfərəs) *adj Facetious.* grand; splendid: *a really splendiferous meal.* [C15: from Med. L *splendiferus,* from L *splendor* radiance + *ferre* to bring]

splendour ❶ *or US* **splendor** ('splɛndə) *n* **1** the state or quality of being splendid. **2 sun in splendour.** *Heraldry.* a representation of the sun with rays and a human face.

splenetic ❶ (splɪ'nɛtɪk) *adj* **1** of or relating to the spleen. **2** spiteful or irritable; peevish. ◆ *n* **3** a spiteful or irritable person.
▸**sple'netically** *adv*

splenic ('splɛnɪk, 'spliː-) *adj* **1** of, relating to, or in the spleen. **2** having a disease or disorder of the spleen.

splenius ('spliːnɪəs) *n, pl* **splenii** (-nɪ,aɪ). either of two muscles at the back of the neck that rotate, flex, and extend the head and neck. [C18: via NL from Gk *splēnion* a plaster]
▸'**splenial** *adj*

splenomegaly (,spliːnəʊ'mɛgəlɪ) *n* abnormal enlargement of the spleen. [C20: NL, from Gk *splēn* spleen + *megal-,* stem of *megas* big]

splice ❶ (splaɪs) *vb* **splices, splicing, spliced.** (*tr*) **1** to join (two ropes) by intertwining the strands. **2** to join up the trimmed ends of (two pieces of wire, film, etc.) with solder or an adhesive material. **3** to join (timbers) by overlapping and binding or bolting the ends together. **4** (*passive*) *Inf.* to enter into marriage: *the couple got spliced.* **5 splice the mainbrace.** *Naut. hist.* to issue and partake of an extra allocation of alcoholic spirits. ◆ *n* **6** a join made by splicing. **7** the place where such a join occurs. **8** the wedge-shaped end of a cricket-bat handle that fits into the blade. [C16: prob. from MDu. *splissen*]
▸'**splicer** *n*

spline (splaɪn) *n* **1** any one of a series of narrow keys formed longitudinally around a shaft that fit into corresponding grooves in a mating part: used to prevent movement between two parts, esp. in transmitting torque. **2** a long narrow strip of wood, metal, etc.; slat. **3** a thin narrow strip made of wood, metal, or plastic fitted into a groove in the edge of a board, tile, etc., to connect it to another. ◆ *vb* **splines, splining, splined. 4** (*tr*) to provide (a shaft, part, etc.) with splines. [C18: East Anglian dialect; ? rel. to OE *splin* spindle]

splint (splɪnt) *n* **1** a rigid support for restricting movement of an injured part, esp. a broken bone. **2** a thin sliver of wood, esp. one used to light cigars, a fire, etc. **3** a thin strip of wood woven with others to form a chair seat, basket, etc. **4** *Vet. science.* a bony enlargement of the cannon bone of a horse. ◆ *vb* **5** to apply a splint to (a broken arm, etc.). [C13: from MLow G *splinte*]

splinter ❶ ('splɪntə) *n* **1** a small thin sharp piece of wood, glass, etc., broken off from a whole. **2** a metal fragment from a shell, bomb, etc., thrown out during an explosion. ◆ *vb* **3** to reduce or be reduced to sharp fragments. **4** to break or be broken off in small sharp fragments. [C14: from MDu. *splinter;* see SPLINT]
▸'**splintery** *adj*

splinter group *n* a number of members of an organization, political party, etc., who split from the main body and form an independent association of their own.

split ❶ (splɪt) *vb* **splits, splitting, split. 1** to break or cause to break, esp. forcibly, by cleaving into separate pieces, often into two roughly equal pieces. **2** to separate or be separated from a whole: *he split a piece of wood from the block.* **3** to separate or be separated into factions, usually through discord. **4** (often foll. by *up*) to separate or cause to separate through a disagreement. **5** (when *tr,* often foll. by *up*) to divide or be divided among two or more persons: *split up the pie among us.* **6** *Sl.* to depart; leave: *let's split.* **7** (*tr*) to separate (something) into its components by interposing something else: *to split a word with hyphens.* **8** (*intr;* usually foll. by *on*) *Sl.* to betray; inform: *he split on me to the cops.* **9** (*tr*) *US politics.* to mark (a ballot, etc.) so as to vote for the candidates of more than one party: *he split the ticket.* **10 split one's sides.** to laugh very heartily. ◆ *n* **11** the act or process of splitting. **12** a gap or rift caused or a piece removed by the process of splitting. **13** a breach or schism in a group or the faction resulting from such a breach. **14** a dessert of sliced fruit and ice cream, covered with whipped cream, nuts, etc.: *banana split.* **15** See **Devonshire split. 16** *Tenpin bowling.* a formation of the pins after the first bowl in which there is a large gap between two pins or groups of pins. **17** *Inf.* an arrangement or process of dividing up loot or money. ◆ *adj* **18** having been split; divided: *split logs.* **19** having a split or splits: *hair with split ends.* ◆ See also **splits, split up.** [C16: from MDu. *splitten* to cleave]
▸'**splitter** *n*

split infinitive *n* (in English grammar) an infinitive used with another word between *to* and the verb itself, as in *to really finish it.*

> **USAGE NOTE** The traditional rule against placing an adverb between *to* and its verb is gradually disappearing. Although it is true that a split infinitive may result in a clumsy sentence (*he decided to firmly and definitively deal with the problem*), this is not enough to justify the absolute condemnation that this practice has attracted. Indeed, very often the most natural position of the adverb is between *to* and the verb (*he decided to really try next time*) and to change it would result in an artificial and awkward construction (*he decided really to try next time*). The current view is therefore that the split infinitive is not a grammatical error. Nevertheless, many writers prefer to avoid splitting infinitives in formal written English, since readers with a more traditional point of view are likely to interpret this type of construction as incorrect.

split-level *adj* (of a house, room, etc.) having the floor level of one part about half a storey above the floor level of an adjoining part.

split pea *n* a pea dried and split and used in soups, pease pudding, or as a vegetable.

split personality *n* **1** the tendency to change rapidly in mood or temperament. **2** a nontechnical term for **multiple personality.**

split pin *n* a metal pin made by bending double a wire, often of hemispherical section, so that it can be passed through a hole in a nut, shaft, etc., to secure another part by bending back the ends of the wire.

split ring *n* a steel ring having two helical turns, often used as a key ring.

splits (splɪts) *n* (*functioning as sing*) (in gymnastics, etc.) the act of sinking to the floor to achieve a sitting position in which both legs are straight, pointing in opposite directions, and at right angles to the body.

split-screen technique *n* a cinematic device by which two or more complete images are projected simultaneously onto separate parts of the screen. Also called: **split screen.**

split second *n* **1** an extremely small period of time; instant. ◆ *adj* **split-second.** (*prenominal*) **2** made or arrived at in an extremely short time: *a split-second decision.* **3** depending upon minute precision: *split-second timing.*

split shift *n* a work period divided into two parts that are separated by an interval longer than a normal rest period.

splitting ('splɪtɪŋ) *adj* **1** (of a headache) intolerably painful; acute. **2** (of the head) assailed by an overpowering unbearable pain.

split up ❶ *vb* (*adv*) **1** (*tr*) to separate out into parts; divide. **2** (*intr*) to become parted through disagreement: *they split up after years of marriage.* **3** to break down or be capable of being broken down into constituent parts. ◆ *n* **split-up. 4** the act or an instance of separating.

splodge (splɒdʒ) *n* **1** a large irregular spot or blot. ◆ *vb* **splodges, splodging, splodged. 2** (*tr*) to mark (something) with such a blot or blots. [C19: alteration of earlier SPLOTCH]
▸'**splodgy** *adj*

splotch (splɒtʃ) *n, vb* the usual US word for **splodge.** [C17: ? a blend of SPOT + BLOTCH]
▸'**splotchy** *adj*

splurge (splɜːdʒ) *n* **1** an ostentatious display, esp. of wealth. **2** a bout of unrestrained extravagance. ◆ *vb* **splurges, splurging, splurged. 3** (often foll. by *out*) to spend (money) extravagantly. [C19: from ?]

splutter ('splʌtə) *vb* **1** to spit out (saliva, food particles, etc.) from the mouth in an explosive manner, as through choking or laughing. **2** to utter (words) with spitting sounds, as through rage or choking. **3** to eject or be ejected in an explosive manner: *sparks spluttered from the fire.* **4** (*tr*) to bespatter (a person) with tiny particles explosively ejected. ◆ *n* **5** the process or noise of spluttering. **6** spluttering incoherent speech. **7** anything ejected through spluttering. [C17: var. of SPUTTER, infl. by SPLASH]
▸'**splutterer** *n*

THESAURUS

(*inf.*), ordinary, pathetic, poor, rotten, run-of-the-mill, tawdry, undistinguished, unexceptional

splendour *n* **2** = **magnificence**, ceremony, display, éclat, gorgeousness, grandeur, majesty, pomp, resplendence, richness, show, solemnity, spectacle, stateliness, sumptuousness
Antonyms *n* ≠ **magnificence:** lacklustreness, meanness, ordinariness, plainness, poverty, simplicity, squalor, tawdriness

splenetic *adj* **2** *Literary* = **irritable**, acid, bad-tempered, bitchy (*inf.*), choleric, churlish, crabbed, crabby, cross, envenomed, fretful, irascible, morose, peevish, petulant, rancorous, ratty (*Brit. & NZ inf.*), sour, spiteful, sullen, testy, tetchy, touchy

splice *vb* **1-3** = **join**, braid, entwine, graft, interlace, intertwine, intertwist, interweave, knit, marry, mesh, plait, unite, wed, yoke

splinter *n* **1, 2** = **sliver**, chip, flake, fragment, needle, paring, shaving ◆ *vb* **3, 4** = **shatter**, break into fragments, disintegrate, fracture, shiver, split

split *vb* **1** = **break**, break up, burst, come apart, come undone, crack, gape, give way, open, rend, rip, slash, slit, snap, splinter **3** = **separate**, bifurcate, branch, cleave, disband, disunite, diverge, fork, go separate ways, part, pull apart **5** = **share out**, allocate, allot, apportion, carve up, distribute, divide, divvy up (*inf.*), dole out, halve, parcel out, partition, slice up **8** *foll. by* **on** *Slang* = **betray**, give away, grass (*Brit. sl.*), inform on, peach (*sl.*), shop (*sl., chiefly Brit.*), sing (*sl., chiefly US*), spill one's guts (*sl.*), squeal (*sl.*) ◆ *n* **11** = **division**, breach, break, break-up, difference, discord, disruption, dissension, disunion, divergence, estrangement, partition, rift, rupture, schism **12** = **crack**, breach, damage, division, fissure, gap, rent, rip, separation, slash, slit, tear ◆ *adj* **18, 19** = **divided**, ambivalent, bisected, broken, cleft, cracked, dual, fractured, ruptured, twofold

split up *vb* **1, 2** = **separate**, break up, disband, divorce, go separate ways, part, part company

spode (spəʊd) *n* (*sometimes cap.*) china or porcelain manufactured by Josiah Spode (1754–1827), English potter, or his company.

spoil Ⓣ (spɔɪl) *vb* **spoils, spoiling, spoilt** *or* **spoiled. 1** (*tr*) to cause damage to (something), in regard to its value, beauty, usefulness, etc. **2** (*tr*) to weaken the character of (a child) by complying unrestrainedly with its desires. **3** (*intr*) (of perishable substances) to become unfit for consumption or use. **4** (*intr*) *Sport.* to disrupt the play or style of an opponent, as to prevent him from settling into a rhythm. **5** *Arch.* to strip (a person or place) of (property) by force. **6 be spoiling for.** to have an aggressive desire for (a fight, etc.). ◆ *n* **7** waste material thrown up by an excavation. **8** any treasure accumulated by a person. **9** *Obs.* the act of plundering. ◆ See also **spoils.** [C13: from OF *espoillier*, from L *spoliāre* to strip, from *spolium* booty]

spoilage (ˈspɔɪlɪdʒ) *n* **1** the act or an instance of spoiling or the state or condition of being spoilt. **2** an amount of material that has been wasted by being spoilt: *considerable spoilage.*

spoiler (ˈspɔɪlə) *n* **1** a plunderer or robber. **2** a person or thing that causes spoilage or corruption. **3** a device fitted to an aircraft wing to increase drag and reduce lift. **4** a similar device fitted to a car. **5** *Sport.* a competitor who adopts spoiling tactics. **6** a magazine, newspaper, etc., produced specifically to coincide with the production of a rival magazine, newspaper, etc., in order to divert public interest and reduce its sales.

spoils Ⓣ (spɔɪlz) *pl n* **1** (*sometimes sing*) valuables seized by violence, esp. in war. **2** *Chiefly US.* the rewards and benefits of public office regarded as plunder for the winning party or candidate. See also **spoils system.**

spoilsport Ⓣ (ˈspɔɪlˌspɔːt) *n Inf.* a person who spoils the pleasure of other people.

spoils system *n Chiefly US.* the practice of filling appointive public offices with friends and supporters of the ruling political party.

spoilt (spɔɪlt) *vb* a past tense and past participle of **spoil.**

spoke[1] (spəʊk) *vb* **1** the past tense of **speak. 2** *Arch. or dialect.* a past participle of **speak.**

spoke[2] (spəʊk) *n* **1** a radial member of a wheel, joining the hub to the rim. **2** a radial projection from the rim of a wheel, as in a ship's wheel. **3** a rung of a ladder. **4 put a spoke in someone's wheel.** *Brit.* to thwart someone's plans. ◆ *vb* **spokes, spoking, spoked. 5** (*tr*) to equip with or as if with spokes. [OE *spaca*]

spoken Ⓣ (ˈspəʊkən) *vb* **1** the past participle of **speak.** ◆ *adj* **2** uttered in speech. **3** (*in combination*) having speech as specified: *soft-spoken.* **4 spoken for.** engaged or reserved.

spokeshave (ˈspəʊkˌʃeɪv) *n* a small plane with two handles, one on each side of its blade, used for shaping or smoothing cylindrical wooden surfaces, such as spokes.

spokesman (ˈspəʊksmən), **spokesperson** Ⓣ (ˈspəʊksˌpɜːsᵊn), *or* **spokeswoman** (ˈspəʊksˌwʊmən) *n, pl* **spokesmen, spokespersons** *or* **spokespeople,** *or* **spokeswomen.** a person authorized to speak on behalf of another person or group.

spoliation (ˌspəʊlɪˈeɪʃən) *n* **1** the act or an instance of despoiling or plundering. **2** the authorized plundering of neutral vessels on the seas by a belligerent state in time of war. **3** *Law.* the material alteration of a document so as to render it invalid. **4** *English ecclesiastical law.* the taking of the fruits of a benefice by a person not entitled to them. [C14: from L *spoliātiō*, from *spoliāre* to SPOIL]
▸**spoliatory** (ˈspəʊlɪətərɪ, -trɪ) *adj*

spondee (ˈspɒndiː) *n Prosody.* a metrical foot consisting of two long syllables (ˉˉ). [C14: from OF *spondée*, from L *spondēus*, from Gk, from *spondē* ritual libation; from use of spondee in the music for such ceremonies]
▸**spondaic** (spɒnˈdeɪɪk) *adj*

spondylitis (ˌspɒndɪˈlaɪtɪs) *n* inflammation of the vertebrae. [C19: from NL, from Gk *spondulos* vertebra; see -ITIS]

sponge Ⓣ (spʌndʒ) *n* **1** any of various multicellular typically marine animals, usually occurring in complex sessile colonies, in which the porous body is supported by a fibrous, calcareous, or siliceous skeletal framework. **2** a piece of the light porous highly absorbent elastic skeleton of certain sponges, used in bathing, cleaning, etc. **3** any of a number of light porous elastic materials resembling a sponge. **4** another word for **sponger** (sense 1). **5** *Inf.* a person who indulges in heavy drinking. **6** leavened dough, esp. before kneading. **7** See **sponge cake. 8** Also called: **sponge pudding.** *Brit.* a light steamed or baked spongy pudding. **9** porous metal capable of absorbing large quantities of gas: *platinum sponge.* **10** a rub with a sponge. **11 throw in the sponge** (*or* **towel**). See **throw in** (sense 3). ◆ *vb* **sponges, sponging, sponged. 12** (*tr;* often foll. by *off* or *down*) to clean (something) by wiping or rubbing with a damp or wet sponge. **13** (*tr;* usually foll. by *off, away, out,* etc.) to remove (marks, etc.) by rubbing with a damp or wet sponge or cloth. **14** (when *tr,* often foll. by *up*) to absorb (liquids, esp. when spilt) in the manner of a sponge. **15** (*intr*) to go collecting sponges. **16** (foll. by *off*) to get (something) from someone by presuming on his generosity: *to sponge a meal off someone.* **17** (foll. by *off* or *on*) to obtain one's subsistence, etc., unjustifiably (from): *he sponges off his friends.* [OE, from L *spongia*, from Gk]
▸ˈ**spongy** *adj*

sponge bag *n* a small waterproof bag made of plastic, etc., that holds toilet articles, used esp. when travelling.

sponge bath *n* a washing of the body with a wet sponge or cloth, without immersion in water.

sponge cake *n* a light porous cake, made of eggs, sugar, flour, and flavourings, without any fat.

sponger Ⓣ (ˈspʌndʒə) *n* **1** *Inf.* a person who lives off other people by continually taking advantage of their generosity; parasite or scrounger. **2** a person or ship employed in collecting sponges.

spongiform (ˈspʌndʒɪˌfɔːm) *adj* **1** resembling a sponge in appearance, esp. in having many holes. **2** denoting diseases characterized by this appearance of affected tissues.

sponsion (ˈspɒnʃən) *n* **1** the act or process of becoming surety; sponsorship. **2** (*often pl*) *International law.* an unauthorized agreement made by a public officer, requiring ratification by his government. **3** any act or promise, esp. one made on behalf of someone else. [C17: from L *sponsiō*, from *spondēre* to pledge]

sponson (ˈspɒnsən) *n* **1** *Naval.* an outboard support for a gun, etc. **2** a structural projection from the side of a paddle steamer for supporting a paddle wheel. **3** a float or flotation chamber along the gunwale of a boat or ship. **4** a structural unit attached to a helicopter fuselage by struts, housing the landing gear and flotation bags. [C19: ?from EXPANSION]

sponsor Ⓣ (ˈspɒnsə) *n* **1** a person or group that promotes either another person or group in an activity or the activity itself, either for profit or for charity. **2** *Chiefly US & Canad.* a person or business firm that pays the costs of a radio or television programme in return for advertising time. **3** a legislator who presents and supports a bill, motion, etc. **4** Also called: **godparent. 4a** an authorized witness who makes the required promises on behalf of a person to be baptized and thereafter assumes responsibility for his Christian upbringing. **4b** a person who presents a candidate for confirmation. ◆ *vb* **5** (*tr*) to act as a sponsor for. [C17: from L, from *spondēre* to promise solemnly]
▸**sponsorial** (spɒnˈsɔːrɪəl) *adj* ▸ˈ**sponsor,ship** *n*

sponsored (ˈspɒnsəd) *adj* denoting an activity organized to raise money for a charity in which sponsors agree to donate money on completion of the activity by participants.

spontaneity (ˌspɒntəˈniːɪtɪ, -ˈneɪ-) *n, pl* **spontaneities. 1** the state or quality of being spontaneous. **2** (*often pl*) the exhibiting of spontaneous actions, impulses, or behaviour.

spontaneous Ⓣ (spɒnˈteɪnɪəs) *adj* **1** occurring, produced, or performed through natural processes without external influence. **2** arising from an unforced personal impulse; voluntary; unpremeditated. **3** (of plants) growing naturally; indigenous. [C17: from LL *spontāneus*, from L *sponte* voluntarily]
▸**sponˈtaneously** *adv* ▸**sponˈtaneousness** *n*

spontaneous combustion *n* the ignition of a substance or body as a result of internal oxidation processes, without the application of an external source of heat.

spontaneous generation *n* another name for **abiogenesis.**

spoof Ⓣ (spuːf) *Inf.* ◆ *n* **1** a mildly satirical mockery or parody; lampoon. **2** a good-humoured deception or trick. ◆ *vb* **3** to indulge in a spoof of (a person or thing). [C19: coined by A. Roberts (1852–1933), E comedian]
▸ˈ**spoofer** *n*

THESAURUS

spoil *vb* **1 = ruin,** blemish, blow (*sl.*), damage, debase, deface, destroy, disfigure, harm, impair, injure, mar, mess up, put a damper on, scar, total (*sl.*), trash (*sl.*), undo, upset, wreck **2 = overindulge,** baby, cocker (*rare*), coddle, cosset, indulge, kill with kindness, mollycoddle, pamper, spoon-feed **3 = go bad,** addle, become tainted, curdle, decay, decompose, go off (*Brit. inf.*), mildew, putrefy, rot, turn **6 be spoiling for = be eager for,** be bent upon, be desirous of, be enthusiastic about, be keen to, be looking for, be out to get (*inf.*), be raring to
Antonyms *vb* ≠ **ruin:** augment, conserve, enhance, improve, keep, preserve, save ≠ **overindulge:** be strict with, deprive, ignore, pay no attention to, treat harshly

spoils *pl n* **1 = booty,** boodle (*sl., chiefly US*), gain, loot, pickings, pillage, plunder, prey, prizes, rapine, swag (*sl.*)

spoilsport *n Informal* **= killjoy,** damper, dog in the manger, misery (*Brit. inf.*), party-pooper (*US sl.*), wet blanket (*inf.*)

spoken *adj* **2 = said,** by word of mouth, expressed, oral, phonetic, put into words, told, unwritten, uttered, verbal, viva voce, voiced

spokesperson *n* **= speaker,** mouthpiece, official, spin doctor (*inf.*), spokesman *or* spokeswoman, voice

sponger *n* **1** *Informal* **= scrounger** (*inf.*), bloodsucker (*inf.*), cadge, cadger, freeloader (*sl.*), hanger-on, leech, parasite

spongy *adj* **2, 3 = porous,** absorbent, cushioned, cushiony, elastic, light, springy

sponsor *n* **1, 3, 4a = backer,** angel (*inf.*), godparent, guarantor, patron, promoter ◆ *vb* **5 = back,** finance, fund, guarantee, lend one's name to, patronize, promote, put up the money for, subsidize

spontaneous *adj* **2 = unplanned,** extempore, free, impromptu, impulsive, instinctive, natural, unbidden, uncompelled, unconstrained, unforced, unpremeditated, unprompted, voluntary, willing
Antonyms *adj* arranged, calculated, contrived, deliberate, forced, mannered, orchestrated, planned, prearranged, premeditated, preplanned, stage-managed, studied

spontaneously *adv* **2 = of one's own accord,** extempore, freely, impromptu, impulsively, instinctively, in the heat of the moment, off one's own bat, off the cuff (*inf.*), on impulse, quite unprompted, voluntarily

spoof *n Informal* **1 = parody,** burlesque, caricature, lampoon, mockery, satire, send-up (*Brit. inf.*), take-off (*inf.*), travesty **2 = trick,** bluff, canard, deception, game, hoax, joke, leg-pull (*Brit. inf.*), prank

spook Ⓣ (spu:k) *Inf.* ◆ *n* **1** a ghost. **2** *US & Canad.* a spy. **3** a strange or frightening person. ◆ *vb* (*tr*) *US & Canad.* **4** to frighten: *to spook horses; to spook a person.* **5** (of a ghost) to haunt. [C19: Du. *spook,* from MLow G *spōk* ghost]
▸**'spooky** *adj*

spool (spu:l) *n* **1** a device around which magnetic tape, film, cotton, etc., can be wound, with plates at top and bottom to prevent it from slipping off. **2** anything round which other materials, esp. thread, are wound. ◆ *vb* **3** (sometimes foll. by *up*) to wind or be wound onto a spool. [C14: of Gmc origin]

spoon (spu:n) *n* **1** a utensil having a shallow concave part, usually elliptical in shape, attached to a handle, used in eating or serving food, stirring, etc. **2** Also called: **spoonbait.** an angling lure consisting of a bright piece of metal which swivels on a trace to which are attached a hook or hooks. **3** *Golf.* a former name for a No. 3 wood. **4 be born with a silver spoon in one's mouth.** to inherit wealth or social standing. **5** *Rowing.* a type of oar blade that is curved at the edges and tip. ◆ *vb* **6** (*tr*) to scoop up or transfer (food, liquid, etc.) from one container to another with or as if with a spoon. **7** (*intr*) *Old-fashioned sl.* to kiss and cuddle. **8** *Sport.* to hit (a ball) with a weak lifting motion, as in golf, cricket, etc. [OE *spōn* splinter]

spoonbill ('spu:n,bɪl) *n* any of several wading birds of warm regions, having a long horizontally flattened bill.

spoondrift ('spu:n,drɪft) *n* a less common spelling of **spindrift.**

spoonerism ('spu:nə,rɪzəm) *n* the transposition of the initial consonants or consonant clusters of a pair of words, often resulting in an amusing ambiguity, such as *hush my brat* for *brush my hat.* [C20: after W. A. *Spooner* (1844–1930), E clergyman renowned for this]

spoon-feed Ⓣ *vb* **spoon-feeds, spoon-feeding, spoon-fed.** (*tr*) **1** to feed with a spoon. **2** to overindulge or spoil. **3** to provide (a person) with ready-made opinions, judgments, etc.

spoonful ('spu:n,fʊl) *n, pl* **spoonfuls. 1** the amount that a spoon is able to hold. **2** a small quantity.

spoony *or* **spooney** ('spu:nɪ) *Inf., old-fashioned.* ◆ *adj* **spoonier, spooniest. 1** foolishly or stupidly amorous. ◆ *n, pl* **spoonies. 2** a fool or silly person, esp. one in love.

spoor (spʊə, spɔ:) *n* **1** the trail of an animal or person, esp. as discernible to the eye. ◆ *vb* **2** to track (an animal) by following its trail. [C19: from Afrik., from MDu. *spor;* rel. to OE *spor* track]

sporadic Ⓣ (spə'rædɪk) *adj* **1** occurring at irregular points in time; intermittent: *sporadic firing.* **2** scattered; isolated: *a sporadic disease.* [C17: from Med. L *sporadicus,* from Gk, from *sporas* scattered]
▸**spo'radically** *adv*

sporangium (spə'rændʒɪəm) *n, pl* **sporangia** (-dʒɪə). any organ, esp. in fungi, in which asexual spores are produced. [C19: from NL, from SPORO- + Gk *angeion* receptacle]
▸**spo'rangial** *adj*

spore (spɔ:) *n* **1** a reproductive body, produced by bacteria, fungi, some protozoans and many plants, that develops into a new individual. A **sexual spore** is formed after the fusion of gametes and an **asexual spore** is the result of asexual reproduction. **2** a germ cell, seed, dormant bacterium, or similar body. ◆ *vb* **spores, sporing, spored. 3** (*intr*) to produce, carry, or release spores. [C19: from NL *spora,* from Gk: a sowing; rel. to Gk *speirein* to sow]

spore case *n* the nontechnical name for **sporangium.**

sporo- *or before a vowel* **spor-** *combining form.* spore: *sporophyte.* [from NL *spora*]

sporogenesis (,spɔ:rəʊ'dʒenɪsɪs, ,spɒ-) *n* the process of spore formation in plants and animals.
▸**sporogenous** (spɔ:'rɒdʒɪnəs, spɒ-) *adj*

sporogonium (,spɔ:rəʊ'gəʊnɪəm, ,spɒ-) *n, pl* **sporogonia** (-nɪə). a structure in mosses and liverworts consisting of a spore-bearing capsule on a short stalk that arises from the parent plant.

sporophyll *or* **sporophyl** ('spɔ:rəʊfɪl, 'spɒ-) *n* a leaf in mosses, ferns, and related plants that bears the sporangia.

sporophyte ('spɔ:rəʊ,faɪt, 'spɒ-) *n* the diploid form of plants that have alternation of generations. It produces asexual spores.
▸**sporophytic** (,spɔ:rə'fɪtɪk, ,spɒ-) *adj*

-sporous *adj combining form.* (in botany) having a specified type or number of spores.

sporozoan (,spɔ:rə'zəʊən, ,spɒ-) *n* **1** any parasitic protozoan of a phylum that includes the malaria parasite. ◆ *adj* **2** of or relating to the sporozoans.

sporran ('spɒrən) *n* a large pouch, usually of fur, worn hanging from a belt in front of the kilt in Scottish Highland dress. [C19: from Scot. Gaelic *sporan* purse]

sport Ⓣ (spɔ:t) *n* **1** an individual or group activity pursued for exercise or pleasure, often taking a competitive form. **2** such activities considered collectively. **3** any pastime indulged in for pleasure. **4** the pleasure derived from a pastime, esp. hunting, shooting, or fishing. **5** playful or good-humoured joking: *to say a thing in sport.* **6** derisive mockery or the object of such mockery: *to make sport of someone.* **7** someone or something that is controlled by external influences: *the sport of fate.* **8** *Inf.* (sometimes qualified by *good, bad,* etc.) a person who reacts cheerfully in the face of adversity, esp. a good loser. **9** *Inf.* a person noted for being scrupulously fair and abiding by the rules of a game. **10** *Inf.* a person who leads a merry existence, esp. a gambler: *he's a bit of a sport.* **11** *Austral. & NZ inf.* a form of address used esp. between males. **12** *Biol.* **12a** an animal or plant that differs conspicuously from other organisms of the same species, usually because of a mutation. **12b** an anomalous characteristic of such an organism. ◆ *vb* **13** (*tr*) *Inf.* to wear or display in an ostentatious or proud manner: *she was sporting a new hat.* **14** (*intr*) to skip about or frolic happily. **15** to amuse (oneself), esp. in outdoor physical recreation. **16** (*intr;* often foll. by *with*) *Arch.* to make fun (of). **17** (*intr*) *Biol.* to produce or undergo a mutation. ◆ See also **sports.** [C15 *sporten,* var. of *disporten* to DISPORT]
▸**'sporter** *n* ▸**'sportful** *adj* ▸**'sportfully** *adv* ▸**'sportfulness** *n*

sporting Ⓣ ('spɔ:tɪŋ) *adj* **1** (*prenominal*) of, relating to, or used or engaged in a sport or sports. **2** relating or conforming to sportsmanship; fair. **3** of or relating to gambling. **4** willing to take a risk.
▸**'sportingly** *adv*

sportive Ⓣ ('spɔ:tɪv) *adj* **1** playful or joyous. **2** done in jest rather than seriously.
▸**'sportively** *adv* ▸**'sportiveness** *n*

sports (spɔ:ts) *n* **1** (*modifier*) relating to, concerned with, or used in sports: *sports equipment.* **2** Also called: **sports day.** *Brit.* a meeting held at a school or college for competitions in various athletic events.

sports car *n* a production car designed for speed and manoeuvrability, having a low body and usually seating only two persons.

sportscast ('spɔ:ts,kɑ:st) *n US.* a broadcast consisting of sports news.
▸**'sports,caster** *n*

sports jacket *n* a man's informal jacket, made esp. of tweed. Also called (US, Austral., and NZ): **sports coat.**

sportsman ('spɔ:tsmən) *n, pl* **sportsmen. 1** a man who takes part in sports, esp. of the outdoor type. **2** a person who exhibits fairness, generosity, observance of the rules, and good humour when losing.
▸**'sportsman-,like** *or* **'sportsmanly** *adj* ▸**'sportsman,ship** *n*

sports medicine *n* the branch of medicine concerned with injuries sustained through sport.

sportswear ('spɔ:ts,wɛə) *n* clothes worn for sport or outdoor leisure wear.

sportswoman ('spɔ:ts,wʊmən) *n, pl* **sportswomen.** a woman who takes part in sports, esp. of the outdoor type.

sporty Ⓣ ('spɔ:tɪ) *adj* **sportier, sportiest. 1** (of a person) fond of sport or outdoor activities. **2** (of clothes) having the appearance of sportswear. **3** (of a car) having the performance or appearance of a sports car.
▸**'sportily** *adv* ▸**'sportiness** *n*

sporule ('spɒru:l) *n* a very small spore. [C19: from NL *sporula*]

spot Ⓣ (spɒt) *n* **1** a small mark on a surface, such as a circular patch or stain, differing in colour or texture from its surroundings. **2** a location: *this is the exact spot.* **3** a blemish of the skin, esp. a pimple or one occurring through some disease. **4** a blemish on the character of a person; moral flaw. **5** *Inf.* a place of entertainment: *a night spot.* **6** *Inf., chiefly Brit.* a small quantity or amount: *a spot of lunch.* **7** *Inf.* an awkward situation: *that puts me in a spot.* **8** a short period between regular television or radio programmes that is used for advertising. **9** a position or length of time in a show assigned to a specific performer. **10** short for **spotlight. 11** (in billiards) **11a** Also called: **spot ball.** the white ball that is distinguished from the plain by a mark or spot. **11b** the player using this ball. **12** *Billiards, snooker, etc.* one of the marked places where the ball is placed. **13** (*modifier*) **13a** denoting or relating to goods, currencies, or securities available for immediate delivery and payment: *spot goods.* See also **spot price. 13b** involving immediate cash payment: *spot sales.* **14 change one's spots.** (*used mainly in negative constructions*) to reform one's character. **15 high spot.** an outstanding

THESAURUS

spooky *adj* **1** = **eerie**, chilling, creepy (*inf.*), frightening, ghostly, mysterious, scary (*inf.*), spine-chilling, supernatural, uncanny, unearthly, weird

spoon-feed *vb* **2** = **mollycoddle**, baby, cosset, featherbed, overindulge, overprotect, spoil, wrap up in cotton wool (*inf.*)

sporadic *adj* **1, 2** = **intermittent**, infrequent, irregular, isolated, occasional, on and off, random, scattered, spasmodic
Antonyms *adj* consistent, frequent, recurrent, regular, set, steady, systematic

sport *n* **1-3** = **game**, amusement, diversion, entertainment, exercise, pastime, physical activity, play, recreation **5** = **fun**, badinage, banter, frolic, jest, joking, josh (*sl., chiefly US & Canad.*), kidding (*inf.*), merriment, mirth, raillery, ridicule, teasing **6** = **mockery**, derision **6** = **butt**, buffoon, fair game, laughing stock, plaything ◆ *vb* **13** *Informal* = **wear**, display, exhibit, show off **14** = **frolic**, caper, disport, gambol, play, romp **16 sport with** *Archaic* = **make fun of**, amuse oneself with, dally with, flirt with, fool around with, play with, take advantage of, toy with, treat lightly *or* cavalierly, trifle with

sporting *adj* **2** = **fair**, game (*inf.*), gentlemanly, sportsmanlike
Antonyms *adj* unfair, unsporting, unsportsmanlike

sportive *adj* **1, 2** = **playful**, coltish, frisky, frolicsome, full of beans (*inf.*), full of fun, gamesome, gay, joyous, kittenish, lively, merry, prankish, rollicking, skittish, sprightly

sporty *adj* **1** = **athletic**, energetic, hearty, outdoor

spot *n* **1** = **mark**, blemish, blot, blotch, daub, discoloration, flaw, scar, smudge, speck, speckle, stain, taint **2** = **place**, locality, location, point, position, scene, site, situation **3** = **pimple**, plook (*Scot.*), pustule, zit (*sl.*) **6** *Informal, chiefly Brit.* = **bit**, little, morsel, splash **7** *Informal* = **predicament**, difficulty, hot water (*inf.*), mess, plight, quandary, tight spot, trouble ◆ *vb* **20** = **see**, behold (*arch. or literary*), catch sight of, descry, detect, discern, espy, identify, make out, observe, pick out, recognize, sight

event: *the high spot of the holiday.* **16 knock spots off.** to outstrip or outdo with ease. **17 on the spot. 17a** immediately. **17b** at the place in question. **17c** in the best position to deal with a situation. **17d** in an awkward predicament. **17e** (*as modifier*): *our on-the-spot reporter.* **18 tight spot.** a serious, difficult, or dangerous situation. **19 weak spot. 19a** some aspect of a character or situation that is susceptible to criticism. **19b** a flaw in a person's knowledge. ◆ *vb* **spots, spotting, spotted. 20** (*tr*) to observe or perceive suddenly; discern. **21** to put stains or spots upon (something). **22** (*intr*) (of some fabrics) to be susceptible to spotting by or as if by water: *silk spots easily.* **23** *Billiards.* to place (a ball) on one of the spots. **24** to look out for and note (trains, talent, etc.). **25** (*intr*) to rain slightly; spit. [C12 (in the sense: moral blemish): from G]
▸ **'spotless** *adj* ▸ **'spotlessly** *adv* ▸ **'spotlessness** *n*

spot check *n* **1** a quick random examination. **2** a check made without prior warning. ◆ *vb* **spot-check. 3** (*tr*) to perform a spot check on.

spot height *n* a mark on a map indicating the height of a hill, mountain, etc.

spotlight Ⓣ ('spɒt,laɪt) *n* **1** a powerful light focused so as to illuminate a small area. **2 the.** the focus of attention. ◆ *vb* **spotlights, spotlighting, spotlit** *or* **spotlighted.** (*tr*) **3** to direct a spotlight on. **4** to focus attention on.

spot-on Ⓣ *adj Brit. inf.* absolutely correct; very accurate.

spot price *n* the price of goods, currencies, or securities that are offered for immediate delivery and payment.

spotted Ⓣ ('spɒtɪd) *adj* **1** characterized by spots or marks, esp. in having a pattern of spots. **2** stained or blemished; soiled or bespattered.

spotted dick *or* **dog** *n Brit.* a steamed or boiled suet pudding containing dried fruit and shaped into a roll.

spotted fever *n* any of various severe febrile diseases characterized by small irregular spots on the skin.

spotted gum *n* **1** an Australian eucalyptus tree. **2** the wood of this tree, used for shipbuilding, sleepers, etc.

spotter ('spɒtə) *n* **1a** a person or thing that watches or observes. **1b** (*as modifier*): *a spotter plane.* **2** a person who makes a hobby of watching for and noting numbers or types of trains, buses, etc.: *a train spotter.* **3** *Mil.* a person who advises adjustment of fire on a target by observations. **4** a person, esp. one engaged in civil defence, who watches for enemy aircraft.

spottie ('spɒtɪ) *n NZ.* a young deer of up to three months of age.

spotty Ⓣ ('spɒtɪ) *adj* **spottier, spottiest. 1** abounding in or characterized by spots or marks, esp. on the skin. **2** not consistent or uniform; irregular or uneven.
▸ **'spottily** *adv* ▸ **'spottiness** *n*

spot-weld *vb* **1** (*tr*) to join (two pieces of metal) by small circular welds by means of heat, usually electrically generated, and pressure. ◆ *n* **2** a weld so formed.
▸ **'spot-,welder** *n*

spousal ('spaʊzᵊl) *n* **1** (*often pl*) **1a** the marriage ceremony. **1b** a wedding. ◆ *adj* **2** of or relating to marriage.
▸ **'spousally** *adv*

spouse Ⓣ *n* (spaʊs, spaʊz). **1** a person's partner in marriage. Related adj: **spousal.** ◆ *vb* (spaʊz, spaʊs), **spouses, spousing, spoused. 2** (*tr*) *Obs.* to marry. [C12: from OF *spus* (masc), *spuse* (fem), from L *sponsus, sponsa* betrothed man or woman, from *spondēre* to promise solemnly]

spout Ⓣ (spaʊt) *vb* **1** to discharge (a liquid) in a continuous jet or in spurts, esp. through a narrow gap or under pressure, or (of a liquid) to gush thus. **2** (of a whale, etc.) to discharge air through the blowhole in a spray at the surface of the water. **3** *Inf.* to utter (a stream of words) on a subject. ◆ *n* **4** a tube, pipe, chute, etc., allowing the passage or pouring of liquids, grain, etc. **5** a continuous stream or jet of liquid. **6** short for **waterspout. 7 up the spout.** *Sl.* **7a** ruined or lost: *any hope of rescue is right up the spout.* **7b** pregnant. [C14: ?from MDu. *spouten*, from ON *spyta* to spit]
▸ **'spouter** *n*

spouting ('spaʊtɪŋ) *n NZ.* **a** a rainwater downpipe on the exterior of a building. **b** such pipes collectively.

SPQR *abbrev. for* Senatus Populusque Romanus. [L: the Senate and People of Rome]

sprag (spræg) *n* **1** a chock or steel bar used to prevent a vehicle from running backwards on an incline. **2** a support or post used in mining. [C19: from ?]

sprain (spreɪn) *vb* **1** (*tr*) to injure (a joint) by a sudden twisting or wrenching of its ligaments. ◆ *n* **2** the injury, characterized by swelling and temporary disability. [C17: from ?]

sprang (spræŋ) *vb* a past tense of **spring.**

sprat (spræt) *n* **1** Also called: **brisling.** a small marine food fish of the herring family. **2** any of various small or young herrings. [C16: var. of OE *sprott*]

sprawl Ⓣ (sprɔːl) *vb* **1** (*intr*) to sit or lie in an ungainly manner with one's limbs spread out. **2** to fall down or knock down with the limbs spread out in an ungainly way. **3** to spread out or cause to spread out in a straggling fashion: *his handwriting sprawled all over the paper.* ◆ *n* **4** the act or an instance of sprawling. **5** a sprawling posture or arrangement of items. **6a** the urban area formed by the expansion of a town or city into surrounding countryside: *the urban sprawl.* **6b** the process by which this has happened. [OE *spreawlian*]
▸ **'sprawling** *or* **'sprawly** *adj*

spray[1] Ⓣ (spreɪ) *n* **1** fine particles of a liquid. **2a** a liquid, such as perfume, paint, etc., designed to be discharged from an aerosol or atomizer: *hair spray.* **2b** the aerosol or atomizer itself. **3** a quantity of small objects flying through the air: *a spray of bullets.* ◆ *vb* **4** to scatter (liquid) in the form of fine particles. **5** to discharge (a liquid) from an aerosol or atomizer. **6** (*tr*) to treat or bombard with a spray: *to spray the lawn.* [C17: from MDu. *spraien*]
▸ **'sprayer** *n*

spray[2] Ⓣ (spreɪ) *n* **1** a single slender shoot, twig, or branch that bears buds, leaves, flowers, or berries. **2** an ornament or floral design like this. [C13: of Gmc origin]

spray gun *n* a device that sprays a fluid in a finely divided form by atomizing it in an air jet.

spread Ⓣ (spred) *vb* **spreads, spreading, spread. 1** to extend or unfold or be extended or unfolded to the fullest width: *she spread the map.* **2** to extend or cause to extend over a larger expanse: *the milk spread all over the floor; the political unrest spread over several years.* **3** to apply or be applied in a coating: *butter does not spread very well when cold.* **4** to distribute or be distributed over an area or region. **5** to display or be displayed in its fullest extent: *the landscape spread before us.* **6** (*tr*) to prepare (a table) for a meal. **7** (*tr*) to lay out (a meal) on a table. **8** to send or be sent out in all directions; disseminate or be disseminated: *someone was spreading rumours; the disease spread quickly.* **9** (of rails, wires, etc.) to force or be forced apart. **10** to increase the breadth of (a part), esp. to flatten the head of a rivet by pressing, hammering, or forging. **11** (*tr*) *Agriculture.* **11a** to lay out (hay) in a relatively thin layer to dry. **11b** to scatter (seed, manure, etc.) over an area. **12** (*tr; often foll. by around*) *Inf.* to make (oneself) agreeable to a large number of people. ◆ *n* **13** the act or process of spreading; diffusion, dispersion, expansion, etc. **14** *Inf.* the wingspan of an aircraft. **15** an extent of space or time; stretch: *a spread of 50 years.* **16** *Inf., chiefly US & Canad.* a ranch or large tract of land. **17** the limit of something fully extended: *the spread of a bird's wings.* **18** a covering for a table or bed. **19** *Inf.* a large meal or feast, esp. when it is laid out on a table. **20** a food which can be spread on bread, etc.: *salmon spread.* **21** two facing pages in a book or other publication. **22** a widening of the hips and waist: *middle-age spread.* ◆ *adj* **23** extended or stretched out, esp. to the fullest extent. [OE *sprǣdan*]
▸ **'spreadable** *adj* ▸ **'spreader** *n*

spread betting *n* a form of gambling in which stakes are placed not on the results of contests but on the number of points scored, etc. Winnings and losses are calculated according to the accuracy or inaccuracy of the prediction.

spread eagle *n* **1** the representation of an eagle with outstretched wings, used as an emblem of the US. **2** an acrobatic skating figure.

spread-eagle *adj also* **spread-eagled. 1** lying or standing with arms and legs outstretched. ◆ *vb* **spread-eagles, spread-eagling, spread-eagled. 2** to assume or cause to assume the shape of a spread eagle. **3** (*intr*) *Skating.* to execute a spread eagle.

spreadsheet ('spred,ʃiːt) *n* a computer program that allows easy entry

THESAURUS

spotless *adj* **1** = **clean**, faultless, flawless, gleaming, immaculate, impeccable, pure, shining, snowy, unblemished, unstained, unsullied, untarnished, virgin, virginal, white **4** = **blameless**, above reproach, chaste, innocent, irreproachable, squeaky-clean, unimpeachable
Antonyms *adj* ≠ **clean:** besmirched, bespattered, blemished, defiled, dirty, filthy, flawed, impure, messy, soiled, spotted, stained, sullied, tainted, tarnished, unchaste ≠ **blameless:** notorious, reprehensible

spotlight *n* **2** = **attention**, fame, interest, limelight, notoriety, public attention, public eye ◆ *vb* **4** = **highlight**, accentuate, draw attention to, feature, focus attention on, give prominence to, illuminate, point up, throw into relief

spot-on *adj Informal* = **accurate**, correct, exact, hitting the nail on the head (*inf.*), on the bull's-eye (*inf.*), on the money (*US*), precise, punctual (to the minute), right, unerring

spotted *adj* **1** = **speckled**, dappled, dotted, flecked, mottled, pied, polka-dot, specked

spotty *adj* **1** = **pimply**, blotchy, pimpled, plooky-faced (*Scot.*), poor-complexioned **2** = **inconsistent**, erratic, fluctuating, irregular, patchy, sporadic, uneven

spouse *n* **1** = **partner**, better half (*humorous*), companion, consort, helpmate, her indoors (*Brit. sl.*), husband *or* wife, mate, significant other (*US inf.*)

spout *vb* **1** = **stream**, discharge, emit, erupt, gush, jet, shoot, spray, spurt, squirt, surge **3** *Informal* = **hold forth**, declaim, expatiate, go on (*inf.*), orate, pontificate, rabbit (on) (*Brit. inf.*), ramble (on), rant, speechify, spiel (*inf.*), talk

sprawl *vb* **1** = **loll**, flop, lounge, slouch, slump **3** = **spread**, ramble, straggle, trail

spray[1] *n* **1** = **droplets**, drizzle, fine mist, moisture, spindrift, spoondrift **2b** = **aerosol**, atomizer, sprinkler ◆ *vb* **4** = **scatter**, atomize, diffuse, shower, sprinkle

spray[2] *n* = **sprig**, bough, branch, corsage, floral arrangement, shoot

spread *vb* **1** = **open (out)**, be displayed, bloat, broaden, dilate, expand, extend, fan out, sprawl, stretch, swell, unfold, unfurl, unroll, widen **6, 7** = **lay out**, arrange, array, cover, furnish, prepare, set **8** = **circulate**, advertise, blazon, broadcast, bruit, cast, cover, diffuse, disseminate, distribute, make known, make public, proclaim, promulgate, propagate, publicize, publish, radiate, scatter, shed, strew, transmit ◆ *n* **13** = **increase**, advance, advancement, development, diffusion, dispersal, dissemination, escalation, expansion, proliferation, spreading, suffusion, transmission **15** = **extent**, compass, period, reach, span, stretch, sweep, term **19** *Informal* = **feast**, array, banquet, blowout (*sl.*), repast and manipulation of figures, equations, and text: used esp. for financial planning.

sprechgesang (*German* 'ʃprɛçgəzaŋ) *n Music.* a type of vocalization between singing and recitation. [C20: from G *Sprechgesang*, lit.: speak-ing-song]

spree ❶ (spriː) *n* **1** a session of considerable overindulgence, esp. in drinking, squandering money, etc. **2** a romp. [C19: ? changed from Scot. *spreath* plundered cattle, ult. from L *praeda* booty]

sprig (sprɪg) *n* **1** a shoot, twig, or sprout of a tree, shrub, etc.; spray. **2** an ornamental device resembling a spray of leaves or flowers. **3** Also called: **dowel pin.** a small wire nail without a head. **4** *Inf., rare.* a youth. **5** *Inf., rare.* a person considered as the descendant of an established family, social class, etc. **6** *NZ.* another word for **stud**[1] (sense 5). ◆ *vb* **sprigs, sprigging, sprigged.** (*tr*) **7** to fasten or secure with sprigs. **8** to ornament (fabric, etc.) with a design of sprigs. [C15: prob. of Gmc origin]
▸**'sprigger** *n* ▸**'spriggy** *adj*

sprightly ❶ ('spraɪtlɪ) *adj* **sprightlier, sprightliest. 1** full of vitality; lively and active. ◆ *adv* **2** *Obs.* in an active or lively manner. [C16: from *spright*, var. of SPRITE + -LY[1]]
▸**'sprightliness** *n*

spring ❶ (sprɪŋ) *vb* **springs, springing, sprang** *or* **sprung; sprung. 1** to move or cause to move suddenly upwards or forwards in a single motion. **2** to release or be released from a forced position by elastic force: *the bolt sprang back.* **3** (*tr*) to leap or jump over. **4** (*intr*) to come or arise suddenly. **5** (*intr*) (of a part of a mechanism, etc.) to jump out of place. **6** to make (wood, etc.) warped or split or (of wood, etc.) to become warped or split. **7** to happen or cause to happen unexpectedly: *to spring a surprise.* **8** (*intr;* usually foll. by *from*) to originate; be descended: *the idea sprang from a chance meeting; he sprang from peasant stock.* **9** (*intr;* often foll. by *up*) to come into being or appear suddenly: *factories springing up.* **10** (*tr*) (of a gundog) to rouse (game) from cover. **11** (*intr*) (of game or quarry) to start or rise suddenly from cover. **12** to explode (a mine) or (of a mine) to explode. **13** (*tr*) to provide with a spring or springs. **14** (*tr*) *Inf.* to arrange the escape of (someone) from prison. **15** (*intr*) *Arch. or poetic.* (of daylight or dawn) to begin to appear. ◆ *n* **16** the act or an instance of springing. **17** a leap, jump, or bound. **18a** the quality of resilience; elasticity. **18b** (*as modifier*): *spring steel.* **19** the act or an instance of moving rapidly back from a position of tension. **20a** a natural outflow of ground water, as forming the source of a stream. **20b** (*as modifier*): *spring water.* **21a** a device, such as a coil or strip of steel, that stores potential energy when it is compressed, stretched, or bent and releases it when the restraining force is removed. **21b** (*as modifier*): *a spring mattress.* **22** a structural defect such as a warp or bend. **23a** (*sometimes cap.*) the season of the year between winter and summer, astronomically from the March equinox to the June solstice in the N hemisphere and from the September equinox to the December solstice in the S hemisphere. **23b** (*as modifier*): *spring showers.* Related adj: **vernal. 24** the earliest or freshest time of something. **25** a source or origin. **26** Also called: **spring line.** *Naut.* a mooring line, usually one of a pair that cross amidships. [OE *springan*]
▸**'springless** *adj* ▸**'spring,like** *adj*

spring balance *or esp. US* **spring scale** *n* a device in which an object to be weighed is attached to the end of a helical spring, the extension of which indicates the weight of the object on a calibrated scale.

springboard ('sprɪŋ,bɔːd) *n* **1** a flexible board, usually projecting low over the water, used for diving. **2** a similar board used for gaining height or momentum in gymnastics. **3** *Austral. & NZ.* a board inserted into the trunk of a tree at some height above the ground on which a lumberjack stands to chop down the tree. **4** anything that serves as a point of departure or initiation.

springbok ('sprɪŋ,bʌk) *n, pl* **springbok** *or* **springboks.** an antelope of semidesert regions of southern Africa, which moves in leaps. [C18: from Afrik., from Du. *springen* to spring + *bok* goat]

Springbok ('sprɪŋ,bʌk, -,bɒk) *n* a person who has represented South Africa in a national sports team.

spring chicken *n* **1** *Chiefly US.* a young chicken, tender for cooking, esp. one from two to ten months old. **2 he** *or* **she is no spring chicken.** *Inf.* he or she is no longer young.

spring-clean *vb* **1** to clean (a house) thoroughly: traditionally at the end of winter. ◆ *n* **2** an instance of this.
▸**,spring-'cleaning** *n*

springe (sprɪndʒ) *n* **1** a snare set to catch small wild animals or birds and consisting of a loop attached to a bent twig or branch under tension. ◆ *vb* **springes, springeing, springed. 2** (*tr*) to catch (animals or birds) with this. [C13: rel. to OE *springan* to spring]

springer ('sprɪŋə) *n* **1** a person or thing that springs. **2** short for **springer spaniel. 3** *Archit.* **3a** the first and lowest stone of an arch. **3b** the impost of an arch.

springer spaniel *n* either of two breeds of spaniel with a slightly domed head and ears of medium length.

springhaas ('sprɪŋ,hɑːs) *n, pl* **springhaas** *or* **springhase** (-,hɑːzə). a small S and E African nocturnal kangaroo-like rodent. [from Afrik.: spring hare]

springing ('sprɪŋɪŋ) *n Archit.* the level where an arch or vault rises from a support.

spring lock *n* a type of lock having a spring-loaded bolt, a key being required only to unlock it.

spring onion *n* an immature form of the onion, widely cultivated for its tiny bulb and long green leaves which are eaten in salads, etc. Also called: **scallion.**

spring roll *n* a Chinese dish consisting of a savoury mixture rolled up in a thin pancake and fried.

springtail ('sprɪŋ,teɪl) *n* any of various primitive wingless insects having a forked springing organ.

spring tide *n* **1** either of the two tides that occur at or just after new moon and full moon: the greatest rise and fall in tidal level. Cf. **neap tide. 2** any great rush or flood.

springtime ('sprɪŋ,taɪm) *n* **1** Also called: **springtide.** the season of spring. **2** the earliest, usually the most attractive, period of the existence of something.

springy ❶ ('sprɪŋɪ) *adj* **springier, springiest. 1** possessing or characterized by resilience or bounce. **2** (of a place) having many springs of water.
▸**'springily** *adv* ▸**'springiness** *n*

sprinkle ❶ ('sprɪŋkəl) *vb* **sprinkles, sprinkling, sprinkled. 1** to scatter (liquid, powder, etc.) in tiny particles or droplets over (something). **2** (*tr*) to distribute over (something): *the field was sprinkled with flowers.* **3** (*intr*) to drizzle slightly. ◆ *n* **4** the act or an instance of sprinkling or a quantity that is sprinkled. **5** a slight drizzle. [C14: prob. from MDu. *sprenkelen*]
▸**'sprinkler** *n*

sprinkler system *n* a fire-extinguishing system that releases water from overhead nozzles opened automatically by a temperature rise.

sprinkling ❶ ('sprɪŋklɪŋ) *n* a small quantity or amount: *a sprinkling of common sense.*

sprint ❶ (sprɪnt) *n* **1** *Athletics.* a short race run at top speed. **2** a fast finishing speed at the end of a longer race, as in running or cycling, etc. **3** any quick run. ◆ *vb* **4** (*intr*) to go at top speed, as in running, cycling, etc. [C16: of Scand. origin]
▸**'sprinter** *n*

sprit (sprɪt) *n Naut.* a light spar pivoted at the mast and crossing a fore-and-aft quadrilateral sail diagonally to the peak. [OE *spreot*]

sprite ❶ (spraɪt) *n* **1** (in folklore) a nimble elflike creature, esp. one associated with water. **2** a small dainty person. [C13: from OF *esprit*, from L *spīritus* SPIRIT[1]]

spritsail ('sprɪt,seɪl; *Naut.* 'sprɪtsəl) *n Naut.* a sail mounted on a sprit or bowsprit.

spritzer ('sprɪtsə) *n* a drink, usually white wine, with soda water added. [from G *spritzen* to splash]

sprocket ('sprɒkɪt) *n* **1** Also called: **sprocket wheel.** a relatively thin wheel having teeth projecting radially from the rim, esp. one that drives or is driven by a chain. **2** an individual tooth on such a wheel. **3** a cylindrical wheel with teeth on one or both rims for pulling film through a camera or projector. [C16: from ?]

sprout ❶ (spraʊt) *vb* **1** (of a plant, seed, etc.) to produce (new leaves, shoots, etc.). **2** (*intr;* often foll. by *up*) to begin to grow or develop. ◆ *n* **3** a new shoot or bud. **4** something that grows like a sprout. **5** See **Brussels sprout.** [OE *sprūtan*]

spruce[1] (spruːs) *n* **1** any coniferous tree of a N temperate genus, cultivated for timber and for ornament. They grow in a pyramidal shape and have needle-like leaves and light-coloured wood. See also **Norway spruce. 2** the wood of any of these trees. [C17: short for *Spruce fir*, from C14 *Spruce* Prussia, changed from *Pruce*, via OF from L *Prussia*]

spruce[2] ❶ (spruːs) *adj* neat, smart, and trim. [C16: ?from *Spruce leather*, a fashionable leather imported from Prussia; see SPRUCE[1]]
▸**'sprucely** *adv* ▸**'spruceness** *n*

THESAURUS

Antonyms *vb* ≠ **circulate:** contain, control, curb, hold back, hold in, repress, restrain, stifle

spree *n* **1** = **binge** (*inf.*), bacchanalia, beano (*Brit. sl.*), bender (*inf.*), carousal, carouse, debauch, fling, jag (*sl.*), junketing, orgy, revel, splurge

sprightly *adj* **1** = **lively**, active, agile, airy, alert, animated, blithe, bright-eyed and bushy-tailed, brisk, cheerful, energetic, frolicsome, gay, jaunty, joyous, nimble, perky, playful, spirited, sportive, spry, vivacious
Antonyms *adj* dull, inactive, lethargic, sedentary, sluggish, torpid, unenergetic

spring *vb* **1-3** = **jump**, bounce, bound, hop, leap, rebound, recoil, vault **8** *usually with* **from** = **originate**, arise, be derived, be descended, come, derive, descend, emanate, emerge, grow, issue, proceed, start, stem **9** *often with* **up** = **appear**, burgeon, come into existence *or* being, develop, mushroom, shoot up ◆ *n* **16, 17** = **jump**, bound, buck, hop, leap, saltation, vault **18a** = **elasticity**, bounce, bounciness, buoyancy, flexibility, give (*inf.*), recoil, resilience, springiness ◆ *modifier* **23b** = **vernal**, springlike ◆ *n* **25** = **source**, beginning, cause, fount, fountainhead, origin, root, well, wellspring

springy *adj* **1** = **elastic**, bouncy, buoyant, flexible, resilient, rubbery, spongy

sprinkle *vb* **1** = **scatter**, dredge, dust, pepper, powder, shower, spray, strew

sprinkling *n* = **scattering**, admixture, dash, dusting, few, handful, scatter, smattering, sprinkle

sprint *vb* **4** = **race**, barrel (along) (*inf., chiefly US & Canad.*), dart, dash, go at top speed, go like a bomb (*Brit. & NZ inf.*), hare (*Brit. inf.*), hotfoot, put on a burst of speed, scamper, shoot, tear, whizz (*inf.*)

sprite *n* **1** = **spirit**, apparition, brownie, dryad, elf, fairy, goblin, imp, leprechaun, naiad, nymph, Oceanid (*Greek myth*), peri, pixie, sylph

sprout *vb* **1, 2** = **grow**, bud, develop, germinate, push, shoot, spring, vegetate

spruce[2] *adj* = **smart**, as if one had just stepped out of a bandbox, dainty, dapper, elegant, natty (*inf.*), neat, soigné *or* soignée, trig (*arch. or dialect*), trim, well-groomed, well turned out

spruce beer *n* an alcoholic drink made of fermented molasses flavoured with spruce twigs and cones.

spruce up ❶ *vb* **spruces, sprucing, spruced.** (*adv*) to make (oneself, a person, or thing) smart and neat.

sprue[1] (spru:) *n* **1** a vertical channel in a mould through which plastic or molten metal is introduced or out of which it flows when the mould is filled. **2** plastic or metal that solidifies in a sprue. [C19: from ?]

sprue[2] (spru:) *n* a chronic disease, esp. of tropical climates, characterized by diarrhoea and emaciation. [C19: from Du. *spruw*]

spruik ('spru:ɪk) *vb* (*intr*) *Austral. sl.* to describe or hold forth like a salesman; spiel or advertise loudly. [C20: from ?]
▸ **'spruiker** *n*

spruit (spreɪt) *n S. African.* a small tributary stream or watercourse. [Afrik. *sprint* offshoot, tributary]

sprung (sprʌŋ) *vb* a past tense and past participle of **spring.**

sprung rhythm *n Prosody.* a type of poetic rhythm characterized by metrical feet of irregular composition, each having one strongly stressed syllable, often the first, and an indefinite number of unstressed syllables.

spry ❶ (spraɪ) *adj* **spryer, spryest** *or* **sprier, spriest.** active and brisk; nimble. [C18: ? of Scand. origin]
▸ **'spryly** *adv* ▸ **'spryness** *n*

spud (spʌd) *n* **1** an informal word for **potato. 2** a narrow-bladed spade for cutting roots, digging up weeds, etc. ◆ *vb* **spuds, spudding, spudded. 3** (*tr*) to eradicate (weeds) with a spud. **4** (*intr*) to drill the first foot of an oil well. [C15 *spudde* short knife, from ?; applied later to a digging tool, & hence to a potato]

spue (spju:) *vb* **spues, spuing, spued.** an archaic spelling of **spew.**
▸ **'spuer** *n*

spume (spju:m) *n* **1** foam or surf, esp. on the sea; froth. ◆ *vb* **spumes, spuming, spumed. 2** (*intr*) to foam or froth. [C14: from OF *espume*, from L *spūma*]
▸ **'spumous** *or* **'spumy** *adj*

spun (spʌn) *vb* **1** the past tense and past participle of **spin.** ◆ *adj* **2** formed or manufactured by spinning: *spun gold; spun glass.*

spunk ❶ (spʌŋk) *n* **1** *Inf.* courage or spirit. **2** *Brit. taboo sl.* semen. **3** touchwood or tinder. [C16 (in the sense: a spark): from Scot. Gaelic *spong* tinder, sponge, from L *spongia* sponge]
▸ **'spunky** *adj* ▸ **'spunkily** *adv*

spun silk *n* shiny yarn or fabric made from silk waste.

spur ❶ (spɜ:) *n* **1** a pointed device or sharp spiked wheel fixed to the heel of a rider's boot to enable him to urge his horse on. **2** anything serving to urge or encourage. **3** a sharp horny projection from the leg in male birds, such as the domestic cock. **4** a pointed process in any of various animals. **5** a tubular extension at the base of the corolla in flowers such as larkspur. **6** a short or stunted branch of a tree. **7** a ridge projecting laterally from a mountain or mountain range. **8** another name for **groyne. 9** Also called: **spur track.** a railway branch line or siding. **10** a short side road leading off a main road. **11** a sharp cutting instrument attached to the leg of a gamecock. **12 on the spur of the moment.** on impulse. **13 win one's spurs. 13a** to prove one's ability; gain distinction. **13b** *History.* to earn knighthood. ◆ *vb* **spurs, spurring, spurred. 14** (*tr*) to goad or urge with or as if with spurs. **15** (*intr*) to go or ride quickly; press on. **16** (*tr*) to provide with a spur or spurs. [OE *spura*]

spurge (spɜ:dʒ) *n* any of various plants that have milky sap and small flowers typically surrounded by conspicuous bracts. [C14: from OF *espurge*, from *espurgier* to purge, from L *expurgāre* to cleanse]

spur gear *or* **wheel** *n* a gear having involuted teeth either straight or helically cut on a cylindrical surface.

spurious ❶ ('spjʊərɪəs) *adj* **1** not genuine or real. **2** (of a plant part or organ) resembling another part in appearance only; false: *a spurious fruit.* **3** *Rare.* illegitimate. [C17: from L *spurius* of illegitimate birth]
▸ **'spuriously** *adv* ▸ **'spuriousness** *n*

spurn ❶ (spɜ:n) *vb* **1** to reject (a person or thing) with contempt. **2** (when *intr*, often foll. by *against*) *Arch.* to kick (at). ◆ *n* **3** an instance of spurning. **4** *Arch.* a kick or thrust. [OE *spurnan*]
▸ **'spurner** *n*

spurt ❶ *or* **spirt** (spɜ:t) *vb* **1** to gush or cause to gush forth in a sudden stream or jet. **2** (*intr*) to make a sudden effort. ◆ *n* **3** a sudden stream or jet. **4** a short burst of activity, speed, or energy. [C16: ? rel. to MHG *sprützen* to squirt]

Sputnik ('spʊtnɪk, 'spʌt-) *n* any of a series of Soviet artificial satellites, **Sputnik 1** (launched in 1957) being the first man-made satellite to orbit the earth. [C20: from Russian, lit.: fellow traveller, from *s*- with + *put* path + *-nik*, suffix indicating agent]

sputter ('spʌtə) *vb* **1** another word for **splutter** (senses 1–3). **2** *Physics.* **2a** to undergo or cause to undergo a process in which atoms of a solid are removed from its surface by the impact of high-energy ions. **2b** to coat (a metal) onto (a solid surface) by this process. ◆ *n* **3** the process or noise of sputtering. **4** incoherent stammering speech. **5** something ejected while sputtering. [C16: from Du. *sputteren*, imit.]
▸ **'sputterer** *n*

sputum ('spju:təm) *n, pl* **sputa** (-tə). saliva ejected from the mouth, esp. mixed with mucus. [C17: from L: spittle, from *spuere* to spit out]

spy ❶ (spaɪ) *n, pl* **spies. 1** a person employed by a state or institution to obtain secret information from rival countries, organizations, companies, etc. **2** a person who keeps secret watch on others. **3** *Obs.* a close view. ◆ *vb* **spies, spying, spied. 4** (*intr*; usually foll. by *on*) to keep a secret or furtive watch (on). **5** (*intr*) to engage in espionage. **6** (*tr*) to catch sight of; descry. [C13 *spien*, from OF *espier*, of Gmc origin]

spyglass ('spaɪ,glɑ:s) *n* a small telescope.

spy out *vb* (*tr, adv*) **1** to discover by careful observation. **2** to make a close scrutiny of.

sq. *abbrev. for:* **1** sequence. **2** square. **3** (*pl* **sqq.**) the following one. [from L *sequens*]

Sq. *abbrev. for:* **1** Squadron. **2** Square.

SQL *abbrev. for* structured query language: a computer programming language used for database management.

squab (skwɒb) *n, pl* **squabs** *or* **squab. 1** a young unfledged bird, esp. a pigeon. **2** a short fat person. **3a** a well-stuffed bolster or cushion. **3b** a sofa. ◆ *adj* **4** (of birds) unfledged. **5** short and fat. [C17: prob. of Gmc origin]
▸ **'squabby** *adj*

squabble ❶ ('skwɒbᵊl) *vb* **squabbles, squabbling, squabbled. 1** (*intr*) to quarrel over a small matter. ◆ *n* **2** a petty quarrel. [C17: prob. of Scand. origin]
▸ **'squabbler** *n*

squad ❶ (skwɒd) *n* **1** the smallest military formation, typically a dozen soldiers, esp. a drill formation. **2** any small group of people engaged in a common pursuit. **3** *Sport.* a number of players from which a team is to be selected. [C17: from OF *esquade*, from OSp. *escuadra*, from *escuadrar* to SQUARE, from the square formations used]

squaddie *or* **squaddy** ('skwɒdɪ) *n, pl* **squaddies.** *Brit. sl.* a private soldier. [C20: from SQUAD]

squadron ('skwɒdrən) *n* **1** a subdivision of a naval fleet detached for a particular task. **2** a cavalry unit comprising two or more troops. **3** the basic tactical and administrative air force unit comprising two or more flights. [C16: from It. *squadrone* soldiers drawn up in square formation, from *squadro* square]

squadron leader *n* an officer holding commissioned rank, between flight lieutenant and wing commander in the air forces of Britain and certain other countries.

squalene ('skweɪ,li:n) *n Biochemistry.* a terpene first found in the liver of sharks but also present in the livers of most higher animals. [C20: from NL *squalus*, genus name of the shark]

squalid ❶ ('skwɒlɪd) *adj* **1** dirty and repulsive, esp. as a result of neglect or poverty. **2** sordid. [C16: from L *squālidus*, from *squālēre* to be stiff with dirt]
▸ **squa'lidity** *or* **'squalidness** *n* ▸ **'squalidly** *adv*

squall[1] ❶ (skwɔ:l) *n* **1** a sudden strong wind or brief turbulent storm. **2**

THESAURUS

Antonyms *adj* bedraggled, disarrayed, dishevelled, frowsy, messy, rumpled, uncombed, unkempt, untidy

spruce up *vb* = **smarten up**, groom, have a wash and brush-up (*Brit.*), tidy, titivate

spry *adj* = **active**, agile, alert, brisk, nimble, nippy (*Brit. inf.*), quick, ready, sprightly, supple
Antonyms *adj* awkward, decrepit, doddering, inactive, lethargic, slow, sluggish, stiff

spunk *n* **1** *Old-fashioned, informal* = **courage**, backbone, balls (*taboo sl.*), ballsiness (*taboo sl.*), bottle (*Brit. sl.*), gameness, grit, gumption (*inf.*), guts (*inf.*), mettle, nerve, pluck, resolution, spirit, toughness

spur *n* **1** = **goad**, prick, rowel **2** = **stimulus**, impetus, impulse, incentive, incitement, inducement, kick up the backside (*inf.*), motive **12 on the spur of the moment** = **on impulse**, impetuously, impromptu, impulsively, on the spot, unpremeditatedly, unthinkingly, without planning, without thinking ◆ *vb* **14** = **incite**, animate, drive, goad, impel, press, prick, prod, prompt, put a bomb under (*inf.*), stimulate, urge

spurious *adj* **1** = **false**, artificial, bogus, contrived, counterfeit, deceitful, ersatz, fake, feigned, forged, imitation, mock, phoney *or* phony (*inf.*), pretended, pseudo (*inf.*), sham, simulated, specious, unauthentic
Antonyms *adj* authentic, bona fide, genuine, honest, kosher (*inf.*), legitimate, real, sound, unfeigned, valid

spurn *vb* **1** = **reject**, cold-shoulder, contemn, despise, disdain, disregard, kick in the teeth (*sl.*), put down, rebuff, repulse, scorn, slight, snub, turn one's nose up at (*inf.*)
Antonyms *vb* embrace, grasp, seize, take up, welcome

spurt *vb* **1** = **gush**, burst, erupt, jet, shoot, spew, squirt, surge ◆ *n* **4** = **burst**, access, fit, rush, spate, surge

spy *n* **1** = **undercover agent**, double agent, fifth columnist, foreign agent, mole, nark (*Brit., Austral., & NZ sl.*), secret agent, secret service agent ◆ *vb* **4** *usually with* **on** = **watch**, follow, keep under surveillance, keep watch on, shadow, tail (*inf.*), trail **6** = **catch sight of**, behold (*arch. or literary*), descry, espy, glimpse, notice, observe, set eyes on, spot

spying *n* **5** = **espionage**, secret service

squabble *vb* **1** = **quarrel**, argue, bicker, brawl, clash, dispute, fall out (*inf.*), fight, fight like cat and dog, go at it hammer and tongs, have words, row, scrap (*inf.*), spar, wrangle ◆ *n* **2** = **quarrel**, argument, barney (*inf.*), difference of opinion, disagreement, dispute, fight, row, scrap (*inf.*), set-to (*inf.*), spat, tiff

squad *n* **1-3** = **team**, band, company, crew, force, gang, group, troop

squalid *adj* **1, 2** = **dirty**, broken-down, decayed, disgusting, fetid, filthy, foul, low, nasty, poverty-stricken, repulsive, run-down, seedy, sleazy, slovenly, slummy, sordid, unclean, yucky *or* yukky (*sl.*)
Antonyms *adj* attractive, clean, hygienic, in good condition, pleasant, salubrious, spick-and-span, spotless, tidy, well-kempt, well looked-after

any sudden commotion. ◆ *vb* **3** (*intr*) to blow in a squall. [C18: ? a special use of SQUALL[2]]
►'**squally** *adj*

squall[2] (skwɔːl) *vb* **1** (*intr*) to cry noisily; yell. ◆ *n* **2** a shrill or noisy yell or howl. [C17: prob. of Scand. origin]
►'**squaller** *n*

squalor ❶ ('skwɒlə) *n* the condition or quality of being squalid; disgusting filth. [C17: from L]

squama ('skweɪmə) *n, pl* **squamae** (-miː). *Biol.* a scale or scalelike structure. [C18: from L]
►**squamate** ('skweɪmeɪt) *adj* ►**squa'mation** *n* ►'**squamose** *or* '**squamous** *adj*

squander ❶ ('skwɒndə) *vb* (*tr*) to spend wastefully or extravagantly; dissipate. [C16: from ?]
►'**squanderer** *n*

square ❶ (skweə) *n* **1** a plane geometric figure having four equal sides and four right angles. **2** any object, part, or arrangement having this or a similar shape. **3** an open area in a town, sometimes including the surrounding buildings, which may form a square. **4** *Maths.* the product of two equal factors; the second power: *9 is the square of 3, written* 3^2. **5** an instrument having two strips of wood, metal, etc., set in the shape of a T or L, used for constructing or testing right angles. **6** *Cricket.* the closely-cut area in the middle of a ground on which wickets are prepared. **7** *Inf.* a person who is old-fashioned in views, customs, appearance, etc. **8** *Obs.* a standard, pattern, or rule. **9 back to square one.** indicating a return to the starting point because of failure, lack of progress, etc. **10 on the square. 10a** at right angles. **10b** *Inf.* honestly and openly. **11 out of square. 11a** not at right angles or not having a right angle. **11b** not in order or agreement. ◆ *adj* **12** being a square in shape or section. **13** having or forming one or more right angles or being at right angles to something. **14a** (*prenominal*) denoting a measure of area of any shape: *a circle of four square feet.* **14b** (*immediately postpositive*) denoting a square having a specified length on each side: *a board four feet square.* **15** fair and honest (esp. in **a square deal**). **16** straight, even, or level: *a square surface.* **17** *Cricket.* at right angles to the wicket: *square leg.* **18** *Soccer, hockey, etc.* in a straight line across the pitch: *a square pass.* **19** *Naut.* (of the sails of a square-rigged ship) set at right angles to the keel. **20** *Inf.* old-fashioned. **21** stocky or sturdy: *square shoulders.* **22** (*postpositive*) having no remaining debts or accounts to be settled. **23** (*prenominal*) unequivocal or straightforward: *a square contradiction.* **24** (*postpositive*) neat and tidy. **25** *Maths.* (of a matrix) having the same number of rows and columns. **26 all square.** on equal terms; even in score. **27 square peg (in a round hole).** *Inf.* a person or thing that is a misfit. ◆ *vb* **squares, squaring, squared.** (*mainly tr*) **28** to make into a square or similar shape. **29** *Maths.* to raise (a number or quantity) to the second power. **30** to test or adjust for deviation with respect to a right angle, plane surface, etc. **31** (sometimes foll. by *off*) to divide into squares. **32** to position so as to be rectangular, straight, or level: *to square the shoulders.* **33** (sometimes foll. by *up*) to settle (debts, accounts, etc.). **34** to level (the score) in a game, etc. **35** (*also intr; often foll. by with*) to agree or cause to agree: *your ideas don't square with mine.* **36** to arrange (something) or come to an arrangement with (someone) as by bribery. **37 square the circle.** to attempt the impossible (in reference to the insoluble problem of constructing a square having exactly the same area as a given circle). ◆ *adv* **38** in order to be square. **39** at right angles. **40** *Soccer, hockey, etc.* in a straight line across the pitch: *to pass the ball square.* **41** *Inf.* squarely. ◆ See also **square away, square off, square up.** [C13: from OF *esquare,* from Vulgar L *exquadra* (unattested), from L *quadrāre* to make square]
►'**squareness** *n* ►'**squarer** *n*

square away *vb* (*adv*) **1** to set the sails of (a square-rigged ship) at right angles to the keel. **2** (*tr*) *US & Canad.* to make neat and tidy.

square-bashing *n Brit. mil. sl.* drill on a barracks square.

square bracket *n* **1** either of a pair of characters [ ], used to enclose a section of writing or printing to separate it from the main text. **2** Also called: **bracket.** either of these characters used as a sign of aggregation in mathematical or logical expressions.

square dance *n* **1** any of various formation dances in which the couples form squares. ◆ *vb* **square-dance, square-dances, square-dancing, square-danced. 2** (*intr*) to perform such a dance.
►'**square-ˌdancer** *n*

square knot *n* another name for **reef knot.**

square leg *n Cricket.* **1** a fielding position on the on side approximately at right angles to the batsman. **2** a person who fields in this position.

squarely ('skwɛəlɪ) *adv* **1** in a direct way; straight: *he hit me squarely on the nose.* **2** in an honest, frank, and just manner. **3** at right angles.

square meal *n* a substantial meal consisting of enough to satisfy.

square measure *n* a unit or system of units for measuring areas.

square number *n* an integer, such as 1, 4, 9, or 16, that is the square of an integer.

square off *vb* (*intr, adv*) to assume a posture of offence or defence, as in boxing.

square of opposition *n Logic.* the diagrammatic representation of the relationships between the four types of proposition found in the syllogism.

square-rigged *adj Naut.* rigged with square sails. See **square sail.**

square root *n* a number or quantity that when multiplied by itself gives a given number or quantity: *the square roots of 4 are 2 and −2.*

square sail *n Naut.* a rectangular or square sail set on a horizontal yard rigged more or less at right angles to the keel.

square shooter *n Inf., chiefly US.* an honest or frank person.
►**square shooting** *adj*

square up *vb* (*adv*) **1** to pay or settle (bills, debts, etc.). **2** *Inf.* to arrange or be arranged satisfactorily. **3** (*intr; foll. by to*) to prepare to be confronted (with), esp. courageously. **4** (*tr; foll. by to*) to adopt a position of readiness to fight (an opponent). **5** *Scot.* to tidy up.

squarrose ('skwærəʊz, 'skwɒ-) *adj* **1** *Biol.* having a rough surface, caused by projecting hairs, scales, etc. **2** *Bot.* having or relating to overlapping parts that are pointed or recurved. [C18: from L *squarrōsus* scabby]

squash[1] ❶ (skwɒʃ) *vb* **1** to press or squeeze or be pressed or squeezed in or down so as to crush, distort, or pulp. **2** (*tr*) to suppress or overcome. **3** (*tr*) to humiliate or crush (a person), esp. with a disconcerting retort. **4** (*intr*) to make a sucking, splashing, or squelching sound. **5** (often foll. by *in* or *into*) to enter or insert in a confined space. ◆ *n* **6** *Brit.* a still drink made from fruit juice or fruit syrup diluted with water. **7** a crush, esp. of people in a confined space. **8** something squashed. **9** the act or sound of squashing or the state of being squashed. **10** Also called: **squash rackets.** a game for two or four players played in an enclosed court with a small rubber ball and light long-handled rackets. **11** Also called: **squash tennis.** a similar game played with larger rackets and a larger pneumatic ball. [C16: from OF *esquasser,* from Vulgar L *exquassāre* (unattested), from L EX-[1] + *quassāre* to shatter]
►'**squasher** *n*

squash[2] (skwɒʃ) *n, pl* **squashes** *or* **squash.** *US & Canad.* **1** any of various marrow-like plants, the fruits of which have a hard rind surrounding edible flesh. **2** the fruit, eaten as a vegetable. [C17: of Amerind origin, from *askutasquash,* lit.: green vegetable eaten green]

squashy ❶ ('skwɒʃɪ) *adj* **squashier, squashiest. 1** easily squashed; pulpy: *a squashy peach.* **2** soft and wet; marshy: *squashy ground.*
►'**squashily** *adv* ►'**squashiness** *n*

squat (skwɒt) *vb* **squats, squatting, squatted.** (*intr*) **1** to rest in a crouching position with the knees bent and the weight on the feet. **2** to crouch down, esp. in order to hide. **3** *Law.* to occupy land or property to which the occupant has no legal title. ◆ *adj* **4** Also: **squatty.** short and broad. ◆ *n* **5** a squatting position. **6** a house occupied by squatters. [C13: from OF *esquater,* from *es-* EX-[1] + *catir* to press together, from Vulgar L *coactīre* (unattested), from L *cōgere* to compress]
►'**squatly** *adv* ►'**squatness** *n*

squatter ('skwɒtə) *n* **1** a person who occupies property or land to which he has no legal title. **2** (in Australia) **2a** a grazier with extensive holdings. **2b** *History.* a person occupying land as tenant of the Crown. **3** (in New Zealand) a 19th-century settler who took up large acreage on a crown lease.

squat thrust *n* an exercise in which the hands are kept on the floor with the arms held straight while the legs are straightened out behind and quickly drawn in towards the body again.

squattocracy (skwɒ'tɒkrəsɪ) *n Austral.* squatters collectively, regarded as rich and influential. See **squatter** (sense 2a). [C19: from SQUATTER + -CRACY]

squaw (skwɔː) *n* **1** *Offens.* a North American Indian woman. **2** *Sl., usually facetious.* a woman or wife. [C17: of Amerind origin]

squawk ❶ (skwɔːk) *n* **1** a loud raucous cry; screech. **2** *Inf.* a loud complaint. ◆ *vb* **3** to utter (with) a squawk. **4** (*intr*) *Inf.* to complain loudly. [C19: imit.]
►'**squawker** *n*

squaw man *n Derog.* a White man married to a North American Indian woman.

THESAURUS

squally[1] *adj* = **stormy,** blustery, gusty, inclement, rough, tempestuous, turbulent, wild, windy

squalor *n* = **filth,** decay, foulness, meanness, sleaziness, slumminess, squalidness, wretchedness
Antonyms *n* beauty, cleanliness, fine condition, luxury, neatness, order, pleasantness, splendour

squander *vb* = **waste,** be prodigal with, blow, consume, dissipate, expend, fritter away, frivol away, lavish, misspend, misuse, run through, scatter, spend, spend like water, throw away
Antonyms *vb* be frugal, be thrifty, economize, keep, put aside for a rainy day, save, store

square *n* **7** *Informal* = **(old) fogey,** antediluvian, back number (*inf.*), conservative, die-hard, dinosaur, fuddy-duddy (*inf.*), old buffer (*Brit. inf.*), stick-in-the-mud (*inf.*), traditionalist ◆ *adj* **15** = **honest,** above board, decent, equitable, ethical, fair, fair and square, genuine, just, kosher (*inf.*), on the level (*inf.*), on the up and up, straight, straightforward, upfront (*inf.*), upright **20** *Informal* = **old-fashioned,** behind the times, bourgeois, conservative, conventional, dated, out of date, out of the ark (*inf.*), Pooterish, straight (*sl.*), strait-laced, stuffy ◆ *vb* **32** = **even up,** accommodate, adapt, adjust, align, level, regulate, suit, tailor, true (up) **33** *sometimes with* **up** = **pay off,** balance, clear (up), discharge, liquidate, make even, quit, satisfy, settle **35** *often with* **with** = **agree,** accord, conform, correspond, fit, harmonize, match, reconcile, tally **36** *Slang* = **bribe,** buy off, corrupt, fix (*inf.*), rig, suborn
Antonyms *adj* ≠ **old-fashioned:** fashionable, in vogue, modern, modish, stylish, trendy (*Brit. inf.*), voguish

squash[1] *vb* **1** = **crush,** compress, distort, flatten, mash, pound, press, pulp, smash, stamp on, trample down **3** = **suppress,** annihilate, crush, humiliate, put down (*sl.*), put (someone) in his (*or* her) place, quash, quell, silence, sit on (*inf.*)

squashy *adj* **1, 2** = **soft,** mushy, pappy, pulpy, spongy, yielding

squawk *vb* **3** = **cry,** cackle, crow, hoot, screech, yelp **4** *Informal* = **complain,** kick up a fuss (*inf.*), protest, raise Cain (*sl.*), squeal (*inf., chiefly Brit.*)

squeak ❶ (skwiːk) *n* **1** a short shrill cry or high-pitched sound. **2** *Inf.* an escape (esp. in **narrow squeak, near squeak**). **3** *Inf.* (*usually used with a negative*) a word; a slight sound. ◆ *vb* **4** to make or cause to make a squeak. **5** (*intr;* usually foll. by *through* or *by*) to pass with only a narrow margin: *to squeak through an examination.* **6** (*intr*) *Inf.* to confess information about oneself or another. **7** (*tr*) to utter with a squeak. [C17: prob. of Scand. origin]
▸**'squeaky** *adj* ▸**'squeakily** *adv* ▸**'squeakiness** *n*

squeaky-clean *adj* **1** (of hair) washed so clean that wet strands squeak when rubbed. **2** completely clean. **3** *Inf., derog.* (of a person) cultivating a virtuous and wholesome image.

squeal ❶ (skwiːl) *n* **1** a high shrill yelp, as of pain. **2** a screaming sound. ◆ *vb* **3** to utter (with) a squeal. **4** (*intr*) *Sl.* to confess information about another. **5** (*intr*) *Inf., chiefly Brit.* to complain loudly. [C13 *squelen,* imit.]
▸**'squealer** *n*

squeamish ❶ ('skwiːmɪʃ) *adj* **1** easily sickened or nauseated. **2** easily shocked; prudish. **3** easily frightened: *squeamish about spiders.* [C15: from Anglo-F *escoymous,* from ?]
▸**'squeamishly** *adv* ▸**'squeamishness** *n*

squeegee ('skwiːdʒiː) *n* **1** an implement with a rubber blade used for wiping away surplus water from a surface, such as a windowpane. **2** any of various similar devices used in photography for pressing water out of wet prints or negatives or for squeezing prints onto a glazing surface. ◆ *vb* **squeegees, squeegeeing, squeegeed. 3** to remove (liquid) from (something) by use of a squeegee. [C19: prob. imit., infl. by SQUEEZE]

squeeze ❶ (skwiːz) *vb* **squeezes, squeezing, squeezed.** (*mainly tr*) **1** to grip or press firmly, esp. so as to crush or distort. **2** to crush or press (something) so as to extract (a liquid): *to squeeze juice from an orange; to squeeze an orange.* **3** to apply gentle pressure to, as in affection or reassurance: *he squeezed her hand.* **4** to push or force in a confined space: *to squeeze six lettuces into one box; to squeeze through a crowd.* **5** to hug closely. **6** to oppress with exacting demands, such as excessive taxes. **7** to exert pressure on (someone) in order to extort (something): *to squeeze money out of a victim by blackmail.* **8** *Bridge, whist.* to lead a card that forces (opponents) to discard potentially winning cards. ◆ *n* **9** the act or an instance of squeezing or of being squeezed. **10** a hug or handclasp. **11** a crush of people in a confined space. **12** *Chiefly Brit.* a condition of restricted credit imposed by a government to counteract price inflation. **13** an amount extracted by squeezing: *a squeeze of lemon juice.* **14** *Inf.* pressure brought to bear in order to extort something (esp. in **put the squeeze on**). **15** *Commerce.* any action taken by a trader or traders on a market that forces buyers to make purchases and prices to rise. **16** Also called: **squeeze play.** *Bridge, whist.* a manoeuvre that forces opponents to discard potentially winning cards. [C16: from ME *queysen* to press, from OE *cwȳsan*]
▸**'squeezable** *adj* ▸**'squeezer** *n*

squelch (skwɛltʃ) *vb* **1** (*intr*) to walk laboriously through soft wet material or with wet shoes, making a sucking noise. **2** (*intr*) to make such a noise. **3** (*tr*) to crush completely; squash. **4** (*tr*) *Inf.* to silence, as by a crushing retort. ◆ *n* **5** a squelching sound. **6** something that has been squelched. **7** *Inf.* a crushing remark. [C17: imit.]
▸**'squelcher** *n* ▸**'squelchy** *adj*

squib (skwɪb) *n* **1** a firework that burns with a hissing noise and culminates in a small explosion. **2** a short witty attack; lampoon. **3 damp squib.** something intended but failing to impress. ◆ *vb* **squibs, squibbing, squibbed. 4** (*intr*) to sound, move, or explode like a squib. **5** (*intr*) to let off or shoot a squib. **6** to write a squib against (someone). [C16: prob. imit. of a light explosion]

squid (skwɪd) *n, pl* **squid** *or* **squids.** any of various ten-limbed pelagic cephalopod molluscs of most seas, having a torpedo-shaped body ranging from about 10 centimetres to 16.5 metres long. See also **cuttlefish.** [C17: from ?]

squiffy ('skwɪfɪ) *adj* **squiffier, squiffiest.** *Brit. inf.* slightly drunk. [C19: from ?]

squiggle ('skwɪgᵊl) *n* **1** a mark or movement in the form of a wavy line; curlicue. **2** an illegible scrawl. ◆ *vb* **squiggles, squiggling, squiggled. 3** (*intr*) to wriggle. **4** (*intr*) to form or draw squiggles. **5** (*tr*) to make into squiggles. [C19: ? a blend of SQUIRM + WIGGLE]
▸**'squiggler** *n* ▸**'squiggly** *adj*

squilgee ('skwɪldʒiː) *n* a variant spelling of **squeegee.** [C19: ?from SQUEEGEE, infl. by SQUELCH]

squill (skwɪl) *n* **1** Also called: **sea squill.** a Mediterranean plant of the lily family. **2** any of various related Old World plants. **3** Also called: **scilla.** the bulb of the sea squill, which is sliced, dried, and used medicinally, as an expectorant. [C14: from L *squilla* sea onion, from Gk *skilla,* from ?]

squinch (skwɪntʃ) *n* a small arch, corbelling, etc., across an internal corner of a tower, used to support a spire, etc. Also called: **squinch arch.** [C15: from obs. *scunch,* from ME *sconcheon,* from OF *escoinson,* from *es-* EX-[1] + *coin* corner]

squint ❶ (skwɪnt) *vb* **1** (*usually intr*) to cross or partly close (the eyes). **2** (*intr*) to have a squint. **3** (*intr*) to look or glance sideways or askance. ◆ *n* **4** the nontechnical name for **strabismus. 5** the act or an instance of squinting; glimpse. **6** a narrow oblique opening in a wall or pillar of a church to permit a view of the main altar from a side aisle or transept. **7** *Inf.* a quick look; glance. ◆ *adj* **8** having a squint. **9** *Inf.* askew; crooked. [C14: short for ASQUINT]
▸**'squinter** *n* ▸**'squinty** *adj*

squire ❶ ('skwaɪə) *n* **1** a country gentleman in England, esp. the main landowner in a rural community. **2** *Feudal history.* a young man of noble birth, who attended upon a knight. **3** *Rare.* a man who courts or escorts a woman. **4** *Inf., chiefly Brit.* a term of address used by one man to another. ◆ *vb* **squires, squiring, squired. 5** (*tr*) (of a man) to escort (a woman). [C13: from OF *esquier;* see ESQUIRE]

squirearchy *or* **squirarchy** ('skwaɪəˌrɑːkɪ) *n, pl* **squirearchies** *or* **squirarchies. 1** government by squires. **2** squires collectively, esp. as a political or social force.
▸**squire'archal, squir'archal** *or* **squire'archical, squir'archical** *adj*

squireen (skwaɪ'riːn) *or* **squireling** ('skwaɪəlɪŋ) *n Rare.* a petty squire. [C19: from SQUIRE + *-een,* Anglo-Irish dim. suffix]

squirm ❶ (skwɜːm) *vb* (*intr*) **1** to move with a wriggling motion; writhe. **2** to feel deep mental discomfort, guilt, embarrassment, etc. ◆ *n* **3** a squirming movement. [C17: imit. (? infl. by WORM)]
▸**'squirmer** *n* ▸**'squirmy** *adj*

squirrel ('skwɪrəl) *n, pl* **squirrels** *or* **squirrel. 1** any of various arboreal rodents having a bushy tail and feeding on nuts, seeds, etc. **2** any of various related rodents, such as a ground squirrel or a marmot. **3** the fur of such an animal. **4** *Inf.* a person who hoards things. ◆ *vb* **squirrels, squirrelling, squirrelled** *or US* **squirrels, squirreling, squirreled. 5** (*tr ;* usually foll. by *away*) *Inf.* to store for future use; hoard. [C14: from OF *esquireul,* from LL *sciūrus,* from Gk *skiouros,* from *skia* shadow + *oura* tail]

squirrel cage *n* **1** a cage consisting of a cylindrical framework that is made to rotate by a small animal running inside the framework. **2** a repetitive purposeless task, way of life, etc. **3** Also called: **squirrel-cage motor.** *Electrical engineering.* the rotor of an induction motor with a cylindrical winding having copper bars around the periphery parallel to the axis.

squirt (skwɜːt) *vb* **1** to force (a liquid) or (of a liquid) to be forced out of a narrow opening. **2** (*tr*) to cover or spatter with liquid so ejected. ◆ *n* **3** a jet or amount of liquid so ejected. **4** the act or an instance of squirting. **5** an instrument used for squirting. **6** *Inf.* **6a** a person regarded as insignificant or contemptible. **6b** a short person. [C15: imit.]
▸**'squirter** *n*

squirting cucumber *n* a hairy plant of the Mediterranean region, having a fruit that discharges seeds explosively when ripe.

squish (skwɪʃ) *vb* **1** (*tr*) to crush, esp. so as to make a soft splashing noise. **2** (*intr*) (of mud, etc.) to make a splashing noise. ◆ *n* **3** a soft squashing sound. [C17: imit.]
▸**'squishy** *adj*

squit (skwɪt) *n Brit. sl.* **1** an insignificant person. **2** nonsense. [C19: var. of SQUIRT]

squiz (skwɪz) *n, pl* **squizzes.** *Austral. & NZ sl.* a look or glance, esp. an inquisitive one. [C20: ? blend of SQUINT + QUIZ]

sr *Maths. abbrev. for* steradian.

Sr *abbrev. for:* **1** (after a name) senior. **2** Señor. **3** Sir. **4** Sister (religious). **5** *the chemical symbol for* strontium.

Sra *abbrev. for* Señora.

SRC (in Britain) *abbrev. for* Science Research Council.

Sri Lankan (srɪ'læŋkən) *adj* **1** of Sri Lanka, a republic in S Asia, or its inhabitants. ◆ *n* **2** an inhabitant of Sri Lanka.

SRN (formerly, in Britain) *abbrev. for* State Registered Nurse.

SRO *abbrev. for:* **1** standing room only. **2** (in Britain) Statutory Rules and Orders. **3** self-regulatory organization.

Srta *abbrev. for* Señorita.

SS *abbrev. for:* **1** Saints. **2** a paramilitary organization within the Nazi party that provided Hitler's bodyguard, security forces, concentration-camp guards, etc. [G *Schutzstaffel* protection squad] **3** steamship.

THESAURUS

squeak *vb* **4** = **peep**, pipe, shrill, squeal, whine, yelp

squeal *n, vb* **3** = **scream**, screech, shriek, wail, yell, yelp, yowl **4** *Slang* = **inform on**, betray, blab, blow the gaff (*Brit. sl.*), grass (*Brit. sl.*), peach (*sl.*), rat on (*inf.*), sell (someone) down the river (*inf.*), shop (*sl., chiefly Brit.*), sing (*sl., chiefly US*), snitch (*sl.*), spill one's guts (*sl.*), spill the beans (*inf.*), tell all **5** *Informal, chiefly Brit.* = **complain**, kick up a fuss (*inf.*), moan, protest, squawk (*inf.*)

squeamish *adj* **1** = **queasy**, nauseous, qualmish, queer, sick, sickish **2** = **fastidious**, delicate, finicky, nice (*rare*), particular, prissy (*inf.*), prudish, punctilious, scrupulous, strait-laced
Antonyms *adj* ≠ **queasy:** strong-stomached ≠ **fastidious:** bold, brassy, brazen, coarse, earthy, immodest, indifferent, tough, wanton

squeeze *vb* **1** = **press**, clutch, compress, crush, grip, nip, pinch, squash, wring **4** = **cram**, crowd, force, jam, jostle, pack, press, ram, stuff, thrust, wedge **5** = **hug**, clasp, cuddle, embrace, enfold, hold tight **7** = **extort**, bleed (*inf.*), bring pressure to bear on, lean on (*inf.*), milk, oppress, pressurize, put the screws on (*inf.*), put the squeeze on (*inf.*), wrest ◆ *n* **10** = **hug**, clasp, embrace, handclasp, hold **11** = **crush**, congestion, crowd, jam, press, squash

squint *adj* **9** *Informal* = **crooked**, askew, aslant, awry, cockeyed, oblique, off-centre, skew-whiff (*inf.*)
Antonyms *adj* aligned, even, horizontal, in line, level, perpendicular, plum, square, straight, true, vertical

squire *vb* **5** *Old-fashioned* = **escort**, accompany, attend, companion

squirm *vb* **1** = **wriggle**, fidget, flounder, shift, twist, wiggle, writhe

SSE *symbol for* south-southeast.
ssp. (*pl* **sspp.**) *Biol. abbrev. for* subspecies.
SSR (formerly) *abbrev. for* Soviet Socialist Republic.
SSRC (formerly in Britain) *abbrev. for* Social Science Research Council.
SST *abbrev. for* supersonic transport.
SSW *symbol for* south-southwest.
St *abbrev. for:* **1** Saint (all entries that are usually preceded by *St* are in this dictionary listed alphabetically under **Saint**). **2** statute. **3** Strait. **4** Street.
st. *abbrev. for:* **1** stanza. **2** statute. **3** stone. **4** *Cricket.* stumped by.
s.t. *abbrev. for* short ton.
-st *suffix.* a variant of **-est**[2].
Sta (in the names of places or churches) *abbrev. for* Saint (female). [It. *Santa*]
stab ➊ (stæb) *vb* **stabs, stabbing, stabbed. 1** (*tr*) to pierce or injure with a sharp pointed instrument. **2** (*tr*) (of a sharp pointed instrument) to pierce or wound. **3** (when *intr*, often foll. by *at*) to make a thrust (at); jab. **4** (*tr*) to inflict with a sharp pain. **5 stab in the back. 5a** (*vb*) to damage the reputation of (a person, esp. a friend) in a surreptitious way. **5b** (*n*) a treacherous action or remark that causes the downfall of or injury to a person. ◆ *n* **6** the act or an instance of stabbing. **7** an injury or rift made by stabbing. **8** a sudden sensation, esp. an unpleasant one: *a stab of pity.* **9** *Inf.* an attempt (esp. in **make a stab at**). [C14: from *stabbe* stab wound]
▸**'stabber** *n*
Stabat Mater ('sta:bæt 'ma:tə) *n* **1** *RC Church.* a Latin hymn commemorating the sorrows of the Virgin Mary at the crucifixion. **2** a musical setting of this hymn. [from opening words, lit.: the mother was standing]
stabile ('steɪbaɪl) *n* **1** *Arts.* a stationary abstract construction, usually of wire, metal, wood, etc. ◆ *adj* **2** fixed; stable. **3** resistant to chemical change. [C18: from L *stabilis*]
stability ➊ (stə'bɪlɪtɪ) *n, pl* **stabilities. 1** the quality of being stable. **2** the ability of an aircraft to resume its original flight path after inadvertent displacement.
stabilize *or* **stabilise** ('steɪbɪˌlaɪz) *vb* **stabilizes, stabilizing, stabilized** *or* **stabilises, stabilising, stabilised. 1** to make or become stable or more stable. **2** to keep or be kept stable. **3** (*tr*) to put or keep (an aircraft, vessel, etc.) in equilibrium by one or more special devices or (of an aircraft, etc.) to become stable.
▸**ˌstabili'zation** *or* **ˌstabili'sation** *n*
stabilizer *or* **stabiliser** ('steɪbɪˌlaɪzə) *n* **1** any device for stabilizing an aircraft. **2** a substance added to something to maintain it in a stable or unchanging state, such as an additive that preserves the texture of food. **3** *Naut.* **3a** a system of pairs of fins projecting from the hull of a ship and controllable to counteract roll. **3b** See **gyrostabilizer. 4** either of a pair of small wheels fitted to the back wheel of a bicycle to help a beginner to maintain balance. **5** *Econ.* a measure, such as progressive taxation, interest-rate control, or unemployment benefit, used to restrict swings in prices, employment, production, etc., in a free economy. **6** a person or thing that stabilizes.
stable[1] ('steɪb^{ə}l) *n* **1** a building, usually consisting of stalls, for the lodging of horses or other livestock. **2** the animals lodged in such a building, collectively. **3a** the racehorses belonging to a particular establishment or owner. **3b** the establishment itself. **3c** (*as modifier*): *stable companion.* **4** *Inf.* a source of training, such as a school, theatre, etc.: *the two athletes were out of the same stable.* **5** a number of people considered as a source of a particular talent: *a stable of writers.* **6** (*modifier*) of, relating to, or suitable for a stable: *stable door.* ◆ *vb* **stables, stabling, stabled. 7** to put, keep, or be kept in a stable. [C13: from OF *estable* cowshed, from L *stabulum* shed, from *stāre* to stand]
stable[2] ➊ ('steɪb^{ə}l) *adj* **1** steady in position or balance; firm. **2** lasting: *a stable relationship.* **3** steadfast or firm of purpose. **4** (of an elementary particle, etc.) not undergoing decay; not radioactive. **5** (of a chemical compound) not readily partaking in a chemical change. [C13: from OF *estable*, from L *stabilis* steady, from *stāre* to stand]
▸**'stableness** *n* ▸**'stably** *adv*
stableboy ('steɪb^{ə}lˌbɔɪ), **stablegirl** ('steɪb^{ə}lˌgɜl), *or* **stableman** ('steɪb^{ə}lˌmæn, -mən) *n, pl* **stableboys, stablegirls,** *or* **stablemen.** a boy, girl, or man who works in a stable.
stable door *n* a door with an upper and lower leaf that may be opened separately. US and Canad. equivalent: **Dutch door.**
Stableford ('steɪb^{ə}lfəd) *n Golf.* **a** a scoring system in which points are awarded according to the number of strokes taken at each hole, whereby a hole completed in one stroke over par counts as one point, a hole completed in level par counts as two points, etc. **b** (*as modifier*): *a Stableford competition.* ◆ Cf. **match play, stroke play.** [C20: after its inventor Dr Frank *Stableford* (1870–1959), E amateur golfer]
stable lad *n* a person who looks after the horses in a racing stable.
stabling ('steɪblɪŋ) *n* stable buildings or accommodation.
stablish ('stæblɪʃ) *vb* an archaic variant of **establish.**
staccato (stə'ka:təʊ) *adj* **1** *Music.* (of notes) short, clipped, and separate. **2** characterized by short abrupt sounds, as in speech: *a staccato command.* ◆ *adv* **3** (esp. used as a musical direction) in a staccato manner. [C18: from It., from *staccare* to detach, shortened from *distaccare*]
stachys ('stækɪs) *n* any plant of the herbaceous genus *Stachys.* See also **woundwort.** [C16: from L, from Gk: ear of corn]
stack ➊ (stæk) *n* **1** an ordered pile or heap. **2** a large orderly pile of hay, straw, etc., for storage in the open air. **3** (*often pl*) compactly spaced bookshelves, used to house collections of books in an area usually prohibited to library users. **4** a number of aircraft circling an airport at different altitudes, awaiting their signal to land. **5** a large amount. **6** *Mil.* a pile of rifles or muskets in the shape of a cone. **7** *Brit.* a measure of coal or wood equal to 108 cubic feet. **8** See **chimney stack, smokestack. 9** a vertical pipe, such as the funnel of a ship or the soil pipe attached to the side of a building. **10** a high column of rock, esp. one isolated from the mainland by the erosive action of the sea. **11** an area in a computer memory for temporary storage. ◆ *vb* (*tr*) **12** to place in a stack; pile. **13** to load or fill up with piles of something: *to stack a lorry with bricks.* **14** to control a number of aircraft waiting to land at an airport so that each flies at a different altitude. **15 stack the cards.** to prearrange the order of a pack of cards secretly so as to cheat. [C13: from ON *stakkr* haystack, of Gmc origin]
▸**'stackable** *adj* ▸**'stacker** *n*
stacked (stækt) *adj Sl.* a variant of **well-stacked.**
stadholder *or* **stadtholder** ('stædˌhəʊldə) *n* **1** the chief magistrate of the former Dutch republic or any of its provinces (from about 1580 to 1802). **2** a viceroy or governor of a province. [C16: from Du. *stad houder*, from *stad* city + *houder* holder]
stadia[1] ('steɪdɪə) *n* **1** measurement of distance using a telescopic surveying instrument and a graduated staff calibrated to correspond with the distance from the observer. **2** the two parallel cross hairs or **stadia hairs** in the eyepiece of the instrument used. **3** the staff used. [C19: prob. from STADIA[2]]
stadia[2] ('steɪdɪə) *n* a plural of **stadium.**
stadium ('steɪdɪəm) *n, pl* **stadiums** *or* **stadia. 1** a sports arena with tiered seats for spectators. **2** (in ancient Greece) a course for races, usually located between two hills providing slopes for tiers of seats. **3** an ancient Greek measure of length equivalent to about 607 feet or 184 metres. [C16: via L from Gk *stadion*, changed from *spadion* racecourse, from *spān* to pull; infl. by Gk *stadios* steady]
staff[1] ➊ (sta:f) *n, pl* **staffs** *for senses 1–4;* **staffs** *or* **staves** *for senses 5–9.* **1** a group of people employed by a company, individual, etc., for executive, clerical, sales work, etc. **2** (*modifier*) attached to or provided for the staff of an establishment: *a staff doctor.* **3** the body of teachers or lecturers of an educational institution. **4** *Mil.* the officers appointed to assist a commander, service, or central headquarters organization. **5** a stick with some special use, such as a walking stick or an emblem of authority. **6** something that sustains or supports: *bread is the staff of life.* **7** a pole on which a flag is hung. **8** *Chiefly Brit.* a graduated rod used in surveying, esp. for sighting to with a levelling instrument. **9** Also called: **stave.** *Music.* **9a** the system of horizontal lines grouped into sets of five (four in plainsong) upon which music is written. The spaces between them are employed in conjunction with a clef in order to give a graphic indication of pitch. **9b** any set of five lines in this system together with its clef: *the treble staff.* ◆ *vb* **10** (*tr*) to provide with a staff. [OE *stæf*]
staff[2] (sta:f) *n US.* a mixture of plaster and hair used to cover the external surface of temporary structures and for decoration. [C19: from ?]
staff corporal *n* a noncommissioned rank in the British Army above that of staff sergeant and below that of warrant officer.
staff nurse *n* a qualified nurse ranking immediately below a sister.
staff officer *n* a commissioned officer serving on the staff of a commander, service, or central headquarters.
Staffordshire bull terrier ('stæfədˌʃɪə, -ʃə) *n* a breed of smooth-coated terrier with a stocky frame and generally a pied or brindled coat.
Staffs. (stæfs) *abbrev. for* Staffordshire.
staff sergeant *n Mil.* **1** *Brit.* a noncommissioned officer holding a rank between sergeant and warrant officer and employed on administrative duties. **2** *US.* a noncommissioned officer who ranks: **2a** (in the Army) above sergeant and below sergeant first class. **2b** (in the Air

THESAURUS

stab *vb* **1, 2 = pierce,** bayonet, cut, gore, impale, injure, jab, knife, puncture, run through, spear, spill blood, stick, thrust, transfix, wound **5a stab in the back = betray,** break faith with, deceive, do the dirty on (*Brit. sl.*), double-cross (*inf.*), give the Judas kiss to, inform on, let down, play false, sell, sell out (*inf.*), slander ◆ *n* **7 = wound,** gash, incision, jab, puncture, rent, thrust **8 = twinge,** ache, pang, prick **9** *Informal* **= attempt,** crack (*inf.*), endeavour, essay (*inf.*), go, shot (*inf.*), try

stability *n* **1 = firmness,** constancy, durability, permanence, solidity, soundness, steadfastness, steadiness, strength
Antonyms *n* changeableness, fickleness, fragility, frailty, inconstancy, instability, unpredictability, unreliability, unsteadiness

stable[2] *adj* **1 = firm,** abiding, constant, deep-rooted, durable, enduring, established, fast, fixed, immovable, immutable, invariable, lasting, permanent, secure, sound, strong, sturdy, unalterable, unchangeable, unwavering, well-founded **3 = steady,** reliable, staunch, steadfast, sure
Antonyms *adj* ≠ **firm:** changeable, erratic, inconstant, insecure, irresolute, mercurial, mutable, shaky, shifting, temperamental, uncertain, unpredictable, unreliable, unstable, variable, volatile, wavering ≠ **steady:** unsteady, unsure

stack *n* **1, 2 = pile,** clamp (*Brit. agriculture*), cock, heap, hoard, load, mass, mound, mountain, rick ◆ *vb* **12, 13 = pile,** accumulate, amass, assemble, bank up, heap up, load, stockpile

staff[1] *n* **1 = workers,** employees, lecturers, officers, organization, personnel, teachers, team, workforce **5 = stick,** cane, crook, pole, prop, rod, sceptre, stave, wand

Force) above airman first class and below technical sergeant. **2c** (in the Marine Corps) above sergeant and below gunnery sergeant.

stag (stæg) *n* **1** the adult male of a deer. **2** a man unaccompanied by a woman at a social gathering. **3** *Stock Exchange, Brit.* a speculator who applies for shares in a new issue in anticipation of a rise in its price and thus a quick profit on resale. **4** (*modifier*) (of a social gathering) attended by men only. ◆ *adv* **5** without a female escort. ◆ *vb* **stags, stagging, stagged.** (*tr*) **6** *Stock Exchange.* to apply for (shares in a new issue) with the intention of selling them for a quick profit when trading commences. [OE *stagga* (unattested); rel. to ON *steggr* male bird]

stag beetle *n* any of various beetles, the males of which have large branched mandibles.

stage ❶ (steɪdʒ) *n* **1** a distinct step or period of development, growth, or progress. **2** a raised area or platform. **3** the platform in a theatre where actors perform. **4 the.** the theatre as a profession. **5** any scene regarded as a setting for an event or action. **6** a portion of a journey or a stopping place after such a portion. **7** short for **stagecoach. 8** *Brit.* a division of a bus route for which there is a fixed fare. **9** one of the separate propulsion units of a rocket that can be jettisoned when it has burnt out. **10** a small stratigraphical unit; a subdivision of a rock series or system. **11** the platform on a microscope on which the specimen is mounted for examination. **12** *Electronics.* a part of a complex circuit, esp. a transistor with the associated elements required to amplify a signal in an amplifier. **13 by** *or* **in easy stages.** not hurriedly: *he learned French by easy stages.* ◆ *vb* **stages, staging, staged.** (*tr*) **14** to perform (a play), esp. on a stage: *to stage "Hamlet"*. **15** to set the action of (a play) in a particular time or place. **16** to plan, organize, and carry out (an event). [C13: from OF *estage* position, from Vulgar L *staticum* (unattested), from L *stāre* to stand]

stagecoach ('steɪdʒˌkəʊtʃ) *n* a large four-wheeled horse-drawn vehicle formerly used to carry passengers, mail, etc., on a regular route.

stagecraft ('steɪdʒˌkrɑːft) *n* skill in or the art of writing or staging plays.

stage direction *n* an instruction to an actor or director, written into the script of a play.

stage door *n* a door at a theatre leading backstage.

stage fright *n* nervousness or panic that may beset a person about to appear in front of an audience.

stagehand ('steɪdʒˌhænd) *n* a person who sets the stage, moves props, etc., in a theatrical production.

stage left *n* the part of the stage to the left of a performer facing the audience.

stage-manage *vb* **stage-manages, stage-managing, stage-managed. 1** to work as stage manager (for a play, etc.). **2** (*tr*) to arrange, present, or supervise from behind the scenes.

stage manager *n* a person who supervises the stage arrangements of a theatrical production.

stager ('steɪdʒə) *n* **1** a person of experience; veteran (esp. in **old stager**). **2** an archaic word for **actor.**

stage right *n* the part of the stage to the right of a performer facing the audience.

stage-struck *adj* infatuated with the glamour of theatrical life, esp. with the desire to act.

stage whisper *n* **1** a loud whisper from one actor to another onstage intended to be heard by the audience. **2** any loud whisper that is intended to be overheard.

stagflation (stæg'fleɪʃən) *n* a situation in which inflation is combined with stagnant or falling output and employment. [C20: blend of *stagnation* + *inflation*]

stagger ❶ ('stægə) *vb* **1** (*usually intr*) to walk or cause to walk unsteadily as if about to fall. **2** (*tr*) to astound or overwhelm, as with shock: *I am staggered by his ruthlessness.* **3** (*tr*) to place or arrange in alternating or overlapping positions or time periods to prevent confusion or congestion: *a staggered junction; to stagger holidays.* **4** (*intr*) to falter or hesitate: *his courage staggered in the face of the battle.* ◆ *n* **5** the act or an instance of staggering. [C13: from dialect *stacker,* from ON *staka* to push]

▸**'staggerer** *n* ▸**'staggering** *adj* ▸**'staggeringly** *adv*

staggered directorships *pl n Business.* a defence against unwelcome takeover bids in which a company resolves that its directors should serve staggered terms of office and that no director can be removed from office without just cause, thus preventing a bidder from controlling the board for some years.

staggers ('stægəz) *n* (*functioning as sing or pl*) **1** a form of vertigo associated with decompression sickness. **2** Also called: **blind staggers.** a disease of horses and some other domestic animals characterized by a swaying unsteady gait, caused by infection or lesions of the central nervous system.

staging ('steɪdʒɪŋ) *n* any temporary structure used in the process of building, esp. the horizontal platforms supported by scaffolding.

staging area *n* a checkpoint or regrouping area for military formations in transit.

staging post *n* a place where a journey is usually broken, esp. a stopover on a flight.

stagnant ❶ ('stægnənt) *adj* **1** (of water, etc.) standing still; without flow or current. **2** brackish and foul from standing still. **3** stale, sluggish, or dull from inaction. **4** not growing or developing; static. [C17: from L *stagnāns,* from *stagnāre* to be stagnant, from *stagnum* a pool]

▸**'stagnancy** *n*

stagnate ❶ (stæg'neɪt) *vb* **stagnates, stagnating, stagnated.** (*intr*) to be or become stagnant.

▸**stag'nation** *n*

stag night *or* **party** *n* a party for men only, esp. one held for a man just before he is married.

stagy *or US* **stagey** ('steɪdʒɪ) *adj* **stagier, stagiest.** excessively theatrical or dramatic.

▸**'stagily** *adv* ▸**'staginess** *n*

staid ❶ (steɪd) *adj* of a settled, sedate, and steady character. [C16: obs. p.p. of STAY[1]]

▸**'staidly** *adv* ▸**'staidness** *n*

stain ❶ (steɪn) *vb* (*mainly tr*) **1** to mark or discolour with patches of something that dirties. **2** to dye with a penetrating dyestuff or pigment. **3** to bring disgrace or shame on: *to stain one's honour.* **4** to colour (specimens) for microscopic study by treatment with a dye or similar reagent. **5** (*intr*) to produce indelible marks or discoloration: *does ink stain?* ◆ *n* **6** a spot, mark, or discoloration. **7** a moral taint; blemish or slur. **8** a dye or similar reagent, used to colour specimens for microscopic study. **9** a solution or liquid used to penetrate the surface of a material, esp. wood, and impart a rich colour without covering up the surface or grain. **10** any dye used to colour textiles and hides. [C14 *steynen* (vb), shortened from *disteynen* to remove colour from, from OF *desteindre* to discolour, ult. from L *tingere* to tinge]

▸**'stainable** *adj* ▸**ˌstaina'bility** *n* ▸**'stainer** *n*

stained glass *n* **a** glass that has been coloured, as by fusing with a film of metallic oxide or burning pigment into the surface. **b** (*as modifier*): *a stained-glass window.*

stainless ('steɪnlɪs) *adj* **1** resistant to discoloration, esp. that resulting from corrosion; rust-resistant: *stainless steel.* **2** having no blemish: *stainless reputation.*

▸**'stainlessly** *adv*

stainless steel *n* **a** a type of steel resistant to corrosion as a result of the presence of large amounts of chromium. **b** (*as modifier*): *stainless-steel cutlery.*

stair (stɛə) *n* **1** one of a flight of stairs. **2** a series of steps: *a narrow stair.* ◆ See also **stairs.** [OE *stæger*]

staircase ('stɛəˌkeɪs) *n* a flight of stairs, its supporting framework, and, usually, a handrail or banisters.

stairs (stɛəz) *pl n* **1** a flight of steps leading from one storey or level to another, esp. indoors. **2 below stairs.** *Brit.* in the servants' quarters.

stairway ('stɛəˌweɪ) *n* a means of access consisting of stairs; staircase or flight of steps.

stairwell ('stɛəˌwel) *n* a vertical shaft or opening that contains a staircase.

stake[1] ❶ (steɪk) *n* **1** a stick or metal bar driven into the ground as a marker, part of a fence, support for a plant, etc. **2** one of a number of vertical posts that fit into sockets around a flat truck or railway wagon to hold the load in place. **3** a method or the practice of executing a person by binding him to a stake in the centre of a pile of wood that is then set on fire. **4 pull up stakes.** to leave one's home or resting place and move on. ◆ *vb* **stakes, staking, staked.** (*tr*) **5** to tie, fasten, or tether with or to a stake. **6** (often foll. by *out* or *off*) to fence or surround with stakes. **7** (often foll. by *out*) to lay (a claim) to land, rights, etc. **8** to support with a stake. [OE *staca* pin]

stake[2] ❶ (steɪk) *n* **1** the money or valuables that a player must hazard in order to buy into a gambling game or make a bet. **2** an interest, often financial, held in something: *a stake in the company's future.* **3** (*often pl*) the money that a player has available for gambling. **4** (*often pl*) a prize in a race, etc., esp. one made up of contributions from con-

THESAURUS

stage *n* **1** = **step**, division, juncture, lap, leg, length, level, period, phase, point ◆ *vb* **14** = **present**, do, give, perform, play, produce, put on **16** = **organize**, arrange, engineer, lay on, mount, orchestrate

stagger *vb* **1** = **totter**, falter, lurch, reel, sway, teeter, waver, wobble **2** = **astound**, amaze, astonish, bowl over (*inf.*), confound, dumbfound, flabbergast, give (someone) a shock, nonplus, overwhelm, shake, shock, strike (someone) dumb, stun, stupefy, surprise, take (someone) aback, take (someone's) breath away, throw off balance **3** = **alternate**, overlap, step, zigzag

stagnant *adj* **1, 2** = **stale**, brackish, motionless, quiet, sluggish, standing, still

Antonyms *adj* clear, flowing, fresh, moving, pure, running, unpolluted

stagnate *vb* = **vegetate**, decay, decline, deteriorate, fester, go to seed, idle, languish, lie fallow, rot, rust, stand still

staid *adj* = **sedate**, calm, composed, decorous, demure, grave, quiet, self-restrained, serious, set in one's ways, sober, solemn, steady

Antonyms *adj* adventurous, capricious, demonstrative, exuberant, flighty, giddy, indecorous, lively, rowdy, sportive, wild

stain *vb* **1** = **mark**, blemish, blot, dirty, discolour, smirch, soil, spot, tarnish, tinge **2** = **dye**, colour, tint **3** = **disgrace**, besmirch, blacken, contaminate, corrupt, defile, deprave, drag through the mud, sully, taint ◆ *n* **6** = **mark**, blemish, blot, discoloration, smirch, spot **7** = **stigma**, blemish, blot on the escutcheon, disgrace, dishonour, infamy, reproach, shame, slur **9, 10** = **dye**, colour, tint

stake[1] *n* **1** = **pole**, pale, paling, palisade, picket, post, spike, stave, stick ◆ *vb* **7** *often with* **out** = **lay claim to**, define, delimit, demarcate, mark out, outline, reserve **8** = **support**, brace, prop, secure, tether, tie up

stake[2] *n* **1** = **bet**, ante, chance, hazard, peril, pledge, risk, venture, wager **2** = **interest**, claim, concern, investment, involvement, share ◆ *vb* **9** = **bet**, chance, gamble, hazard, imperil, jeopardize, pledge, put on, risk, venture, wager testants or owners. **5** (*pl*) a horse race in which all owners of competing horses contribute to the prize. **6** *US & Canad. inf.* short for **grubstake. 7 at stake.** at risk: *lives are at stake.* **8 raise the stakes. 8a** to increase the amount of money or valuables hazarded in a gambling game. **8b** to increase the costs, risks, or considerations involved in taking an action or reaching a conclusion. ◆ *vb* **stakes, staking, staked.** (*tr*) **9** to hazard (money, etc.) on a result. **10** to invest in or support with money, etc.: *to stake a business.* [C16: from ?]

stakeholder ('steɪkˌhəʊldə) *n* **1** a person or group owning a significant percentage of a company's shares. **2** a person or group not owning shares in an enterprise but affected by or having an interest in its operations, such as the employees, customers, local community, etc. ◆ *adj* **3** of or relating to policies intended to allow people to participate in and benefit from decisions made by enterprises in which they have a stake: *a stakeholder economy.*

stakeout ('steɪkaʊt) *Chiefly US & Canad. sl.* ◆ *n* **1** a police surveillance. **2** an area or house kept under such surveillance. ◆ *vb* **stake out. 3** (*tr, adv*) to keep under surveillance.

Stakhanovism (stæ'kænəˌvɪzəm) *n* (in the former Soviet Union) a system designed to raise production by offering incentives to efficient workers. [C20: after A. G. *Stakhanov* (1906–77), Soviet miner, the worker first awarded benefits under the system in 1935]
▸**Sta'khanovˌite** *n, adj*

stalactite ('stæləkˌtaɪt) *n* a cylindrical mass of calcium carbonate hanging from the roof of a limestone cave: formed by precipitation from continually dripping water. Cf. **stalagmite.** [C17: from NL *stalactites,* from Gk *stalaktos* dripping, from *stalassein* to drip]
▸**stalactiform** (stə'læktɪˌfɔːm) *adj* ▸**stalactitic** (ˌstælək'tɪtɪk) *or* ˌ**stalac'titical** *adj*

stalag ('stælæg) *n* a German prisoner-of-war camp in World War II, esp. for men from the ranks. [short for *Stammlager* base camp]

stalagmite ('stæləgˌmaɪt) *n* a cylindrical mass of calcium carbonate projecting upwards from the floor of a limestone cave: formed by precipitation from continually dripping water. Cf. **stalactite.** [C17: from NL *stalagmites,* from Gk *stalagmos* dripping; rel. to Gk *stalassein* to drip]
▸**stalagmitic** (ˌstæləg'mɪtɪk) *or* ˌ**stalag'mitical** *adj*

stale[1] ❶ (steɪl) *adj* **1** (esp. of food) hard, musty, or dry from being kept too long. **2** (of beer, etc.) flat and tasteless from being kept open too long. **3** (of air) stagnant; foul. **4** uninteresting from overuse: *stale clichés.* **5** no longer new: *stale news.* **6** lacking in energy or ideas through overwork or lack of variety. **7** *Banking.* (of a cheque) not negotiable by a bank as a result of not having been presented within six months of being written. **8** *Law.* (of a claim, etc.) having lost its effectiveness or force, as by failure to act or by the lapse of time. ◆ *vb* **stales, staling, staled. 9** to make or become stale. [C13 (orig. applied to liquor in the sense: well matured): prob. from OF *estale* (unattested) motionless, of Frankish origin]
▸**'staleness** *n*

stale[2] (steɪl) *vb* **stales, staling, staled. 1** (*intr*) (of livestock) to urinate. ◆ *n* **2** the urine of horses or cattle. [C15: ?from OF *estaler* to stand in one position]

stale bull *n Business.* a dealer or speculator who holds unsold commodities after a rise in market prices but who cannot trade because there are no buyers at the new levels and because his financial commitments prevent him from making further purchases.

stalemate ❶ ('steɪlˌmeɪt) *n* **1** a chess position in which any of a player's possible moves would place his king in check: in this position the game ends in a draw. **2** a situation in which two opposing forces find that further action is impossible or futile; deadlock. ◆ *vb* **stalemates, stalemating, stalemated. 3** (*tr*) to subject to a stalemate. [C18: from obs. *stale,* from OF *estal* STALL[1] + (CHECK)MATE]

Stalinism ('stɑːlɪˌnɪzəm) *n* the theory and form of government associated with Joseph Stalin (1879–1953), general secretary of the Communist Party of the Soviet Union 1922–53: a variant of Marxism-Leninism characterized by totalitarianism, rigid bureaucracy, and loyalty to the state.

stalk[1] (stɔːk) *n* **1** the main stem of a herbaceous plant. **2** any of various subsidiary plant stems, such as a leafstalk or flower stalk. **3** a slender supporting structure in animals such as crinoids and barnacles. **4** any long slender supporting shaft or column. [C14: prob. dim. from OE *stalu* upright piece of wood]
▸**stalked** *adj* ▸**'stalkˌlike** *adj*

stalk[2] ❶ (stɔːk) *vb* **1** to follow or approach (game, prey, etc.) stealthily and quietly. **2** to pursue persistently and, sometimes, attack (a person with whom one is obsessed, often a celebrity). **3** to spread over (a place) in a menacing or grim manner: *fever stalked the camp.* **4** (*intr*) to walk in a haughty, stiff, or threatening way. **5** to search (a piece of land) for prey. ◆ *n* **6** the act of stalking. **7** a stiff or threatening stride. [OE *bestealcian* to walk stealthily]
▸**'stalker** *n*

stalk-and-slash movie *n* another name for **slasher movie.**

stalking-horse *n* **1** a horse or an imitation one used by a hunter to hide behind while stalking. **2** something serving as a means of concealing plans; pretext. **3** a candidate put forward to divide the opposition or mask the candidacy of another person for whom the stalking-horse would then withdraw.

stalky ('stɔːkɪ) *adj* **stalkier, stalkiest. 1** like a stalk; slender and tall. **2** having or abounding in stalks.
▸**'stalkily** *adv* ▸**'stalkiness** *n*

stall[1] (stɔːl) *n* **1a** a compartment in a stable or shed for a single animal. **1b** another name for **stable**[1] (sense 1). **2** a small often temporary stand or booth for the sale of goods. **3** (in a church) **3a** one of a row of seats usually divided by armrests or a small screen, for the choir or clergy. **3b** a pen. **4** an instance of an engine stalling. **5** a condition of an aircraft in flight in which a reduction in speed or an increase in the aircraft's angle of attack causes a sudden loss of lift resulting in a downward plunge. **6** any small room or compartment. **7** *Brit.* **7a** a seat in a theatre or cinema, usually fixed to the floor. **7b** (*pl*) the area of seats on the ground floor of a theatre or cinema nearest to the stage or screen. **8** a tubelike covering for a finger. **9** (*pl*) short for **starting stalls.** ◆ *vb* **10** to cause (a motor vehicle or its engine) to stop, usually by incorrect use of the clutch or incorrect adjustment of the fuel mixture, or (of an engine or motor vehicle) to stop, usually for these reasons. **11** to cause (an aircraft) to go into a stall or (of an aircraft) to go into a stall. **12** to stick or cause to stick fast, as in mud or snow. **13** (*tr*) to confine (an animal) in a stall. [OE *steall* a place for standing]

stall[2] ❶ (stɔːl) *vb* **1** to employ delaying tactics towards (someone); be evasive. ◆ *n* **2** an evasive move; pretext. [C16: from Anglo-F *estale* bird used as a decoy, infl. by STALL[1]]

stall-feed *vb* **stall-feeds, stall-feeding, stall-fed.** (*tr*) to keep and feed (an animal) in a stall, esp. as an intensive method of fattening it for slaughter.

stallholder ('stɔːlˌhəʊldə) *n* a person who sells goods at a market stall.

stallion ('stæljən) *n* an uncastrated male horse, esp. one used for breeding. [C14 *staloun,* from OF *estalon,* of Gmc origin]

stalwart ❶ ('stɔːlwət) *adj* **1** strong and sturdy; robust. **2** solid, dependable, and courageous. **3** resolute and firm. ◆ *n* **4** a stalwart person, esp. a supporter. [OE *stælwirthe* serviceable, from *stǣl,* from *stathol* support + *wierthe* WORTH]
▸**'stalwartly** *adv* ▸**'stalwartness** *n*

stamen ('steɪmɛn) *n, pl* **stamens** *or* **stamina.** the male reproductive organ of a flower, consisting of a stalk (filament) bearing an anther in which pollen is produced. [C17: from L: the warp in an upright loom, from *stāre* to stand]
▸**staminiferous** (ˌstæmɪ'nɪfərəs) *adj*

stamina[1] ❶ ('stæmɪnə) *n* enduring energy, strength, and resilience. [C19: identical with STAMINA[2], from L *stāmen* thread, hence the threads of life spun out by the Fates, hence energy, etc.]

stamina[2] ('stæmɪnə) *n* a plural of **stamen.**

staminate ('stæmɪnɪt, -ˌneɪt) *adj* (of plants) having stamens, esp. having stamens but no carpels; male.

stammer ❶ ('stæmə) *vb* **1** to speak or say (something) in a hesitant way, esp. as a result of a speech disorder or through fear, stress, etc. ◆ *n* **2** a speech disorder characterized by involuntary repetitions and hesitations. [OE *stamerian*]
▸**'stammerer** *n* ▸**'stammering** *n, adj*

stamp ❶ (stæmp) *vb* **1** (when *intr,* often foll. by *on*) to bring (the foot) down heavily (on the ground, etc.). **2** (*intr*) to walk with heavy or noisy footsteps. **3** (*intr;* foll. by *on*) to repress or extinguish: *he stamped on criticism.* **4** (*tr*) to impress or mark (a device or sign) on (something). **5** to mark (something) with an official seal or device: *to stamp a passport.* **6** (*tr*) to fix or impress permanently: *the date was stamped on her memory.* **7** (*tr*) to affix a postage stamp to. **8** (*tr*) to distinguish or reveal: *that behaviour stamps him as a cheat.* **9** to pound or crush (ores, etc.). ◆ *n* **10** the act or an instance of stamping. **11a** See **postage stamp. 11b** a mark applied to postage stamps for cancellation. **12** a similar piece of gummed paper used for commercial or trading purposes. **13** a block, die, etc., used for imprinting a design or device. **14** a design, device, or mark that has been stamped. **15** a characteristic feature or trait; hallmark: *the stamp of authenticity.* **16** a piece of gummed paper or other mark applied to official documents to indicate payment, validity,

THESAURUS

stale[1] *adj* **1-3 = old,** decayed, dry, fetid, flat, fusty, hard, insipid, musty, sour, stagnant, tasteless **4 = unoriginal,** antiquated, banal, cliché-ridden, common, commonplace, drab, effete, flat, hackneyed, insipid, old hat, overused, platitudinous, repetitious, stereotyped, threadbare, trite, worn-out
Antonyms *adj* ≠ **old:** crisp, fresh ≠ **unoriginal:** different, imaginative, innovative, lively, new, novel, original, refreshing

stalemate *n* **2 = deadlock,** draw, impasse, standstill, tie

stalk[2] *vb* **1 = pursue,** creep up on, follow, haunt, hunt, shadow, tail (*inf.*), track **4 = strut,** flounce, march, pace, stride

stall[2] *vb* **1 = play for time,** beat about the bush (*inf.*), hedge, stonewall, temporize

stalwart *adj* **1 = strong,** athletic, beefy (*inf.*), brawny, hefty (*inf.*), husky (*inf.*), lusty, manly, muscular, robust, rugged, sinewy, stout, strapping, sturdy, vigorous **2, 3 = loyal,** courageous, daring, dependable, firm, indomitable, intrepid, redoubtable, reliable, resolute, staunch, valiant
Antonyms *adj* ≠ **strong:** feeble, frail, infirm, namby-pamby, puny, shilpit (*Scot.*), sickly, weak ≠ **courageous:** faint-hearted, timid

stamina[1] *n* = **staying power,** endurance, energy, force, grit, indefatigability, lustiness, power, power of endurance, resilience, resistance, strength, tenacity, vigour

stammer *vb* **1 = stutter,** falter, hem and haw, hesitate, pause, splutter, stumble

stamp *vb* **1 = trample,** beat, crush **4 = imprint,** engrave, fix, impress, inscribe, mark, mould, print **8 = identify,** betray, brand, categorize, exhibit, label, mark, pronounce, reveal, show to be, typecast ◆ *n* **13 = imprint,** brand, cast, earmark, hallmark, mark, mould, signature **18 = type,** breed, cast, character, cut, description, fashion, form, kind, sort

ownership, etc. **17** *Brit. inf.* a national insurance contribution, formerly recorded by means of a stamp on an official card. **18** type or class: *men of his stamp.* **19** an instrument or machine for crushing or pounding ores, etc., or the pestle in such a device. ◆ See also **stamp out.** [OE *stampe*]
▸ **'stamper** *n*

stamp duty *or* **tax** *n* a tax on legal documents, publications, etc., the payment of which is certified by the attaching or impressing of official stamps.

stampede Ⓣ (stæm'piːd) *n* **1** an impulsive headlong rush of startled cattle or horses. **2** headlong rush of a crowd. **3** any sudden large-scale action, such as a rush of people to support a candidate. **4** *W US & Canad.* a rodeo event featuring fairground and social elements. ◆ *vb* **stampedes, stampeding, stampeded. 5** to run away or cause to run away in a stampede. [C19: from American Sp. *estampida,* from Sp.: a din, from *estampar* to stamp, of Gmc origin]
▸ **stam'peder** *n*

stamping ground *n* a habitual or favourite meeting or gathering place.

stamp mill *n* a machine for crushing ore.

stamp out Ⓣ *vb (tr, adv)* **1** to put out or extinguish by stamping: *to stamp out a fire.* **2** to suppress by force: *to stamp out a rebellion.*

stance Ⓣ (stæns, stɑːns) *n* **1** the manner and position in which a person or animal stands. **2** *Sport.* the posture assumed when about to play the ball, as in golf, cricket, etc. **3** emotional or intellectual attitude: *a leftist stance.* **4** *Chiefly Scot.* a place where a vehicle waits: *taxi stance.* [C16: via F from It. *stanza* place for standing, from L *stāns,* from *stāre* to stand]

stanch Ⓣ (stɑːntʃ) *vb* a variant of **staunch**[2].

stanchion ('stɑːnʃən) *n* **1** any vertical pole, beam, rod, etc., used as a support. ◆ *vb* **2** *(tr)* to provide or support with a stanchion or stanchions. [C15: from OF *estanchon,* from *estance,* from Vulgar L *stantia* (unattested) a standing, from L *stāre* to stand]

stand Ⓣ (stænd) *vb* **stands, standing, stood.** *(mainly intr)* **1** *(also tr)* to be or cause to be in an erect or upright position. **2** to rise to, assume, or maintain an upright position. **3** *(copula)* to have a specified height when standing: *to stand six feet tall.* **4** to be situated or located: *the house stands in the square.* **5** to be in a specified state or condition: *to stand in awe of someone.* **6** to adopt or remain in a resolute position or attitude. **7** *(may take an infinitive)* to be in a specified position: *I stand to lose money in this venture.* **8** to remain in force or continue in effect: *my orders stand.* **9** to come to a stop or halt, esp. temporarily. **10** (of water, etc.) to collect and remain without flowing. **11** (often foll. by *at*) (of a score, account, etc.) to indicate the specified position: *the score stands at 20 to 1.* **12** *(also tr;* when *intr,* foll. by *for)* to tolerate or bear: *I won't stand for your nonsense; I can't stand spiders.* **13** *(tr)* to resist; survive: *to stand the test of time.* **14** *(tr)* to submit to: *to stand trial.* **15** (often foll. by *for) Chiefly Brit.* to be or become a candidate: *stand for Parliament.* **16** to navigate in a specified direction: *we were standing for Madeira.* **17** (of a gun dog) to point at game. **18** to halt, esp. to give action, repel attack, or disrupt an enemy advance when retreating. **19** *(tr) Inf.* to bear the cost of; pay for: *to stand someone a drink.* **20 stand a chance.** to have a hope or likelihood of winning, succeeding, etc. **21 stand fast.** to maintain one's position firmly. **22 stand one's ground.** to maintain a stance or position in the face of opposition. **23 stand still. 23a** to remain motionless. **23b** (foll. by *for) US.* to tolerate: *I won't stand still for your threats.* **24 stand to (someone).** *Irish inf.* to be useful to (someone): *your knowledge of English will stand to you.* ◆ *n* **25** the act or an instance of standing. **26** an opinion, esp. a resolutely held one: *he took a stand on capital punishment.* **27** a halt or standstill. **28** a place where a person or thing stands. **29** *Austral. & NZ.* **29a** a position on the floor of a shearing shed allocated to one shearer. **29b** the shearer's equipment. **30** a structure on which people can sit or stand. **31** a frame or rack on which such articles as coats and hats may be hung. **32** a small table or piece of furniture where articles may be placed or stored: *a music stand.* **33** a supporting framework, esp. for a tool or instrument. **34** a stall, booth, or counter from which goods may be sold. **35** a halt to give action, etc., esp. during a retreat and having some duration or success. **36** *Cricket.* an extended period at the wicket by two batsmen. **37** a growth of plants in a particular area, esp. trees in a forest or a crop in a field. **38** a stop made by a touring theatrical company, pop group, etc., to give a performance (esp. in **one-night stand**). **39** (of a gun dog) the act of pointing at game. ◆ See also **stand by, stand down,** etc. [OE *standan*]
▸ **'stander** *n*

standard Ⓣ ('stændəd) *n* **1** an accepted or approved example of something against which others are judged or measured. **2** *(often pl)* a principle of propriety, honesty, and integrity. **3** a level of excellence or quality. **4** any distinctive flag or device, etc., as of a nation, sovereign, or special cause, etc., or the colours of a cavalry regiment. **5** a flag or emblem formerly used to show the central or rallying point of an army in battle. **6** the commodity or commodities in which is stated the value of a basic monetary unit: *the gold standard; the silver standard.* **7** an authorized model of a unit of measure or weight. **8** a unit of board measure equal to 1980 board feet. **9** (in coinage) the prescribed proportion by weight of precious metal and base metal that each coin must contain. **10** an upright pole or beam, esp. one used as a support. **11a** a piece of furniture consisting of an upright pole or beam on a base or support. **11b** *(as modifier): a standard lamp.* **12a** a plant, esp. a fruit tree, that is trained so that it has an upright stem free of branches. **12b** *(as modifier): a standard cherry.* **13** a song or piece of music that has remained popular for many years. **14** a form or grade in an elementary school. ◆ *adj* **15** of the usual, regularized, medium, or accepted kind: *a standard size.* **16** of recognized authority, competence, or excellence: *the standard work on Greece.* **17** denoting or characterized by idiom, vocabulary, etc., that is regarded as correct and acceptable by educated native speakers. **18** *Brit.* (formerly) (of eggs) of a size that is smaller than *large* and larger than *medium.* [C12: from OF *estandart* gathering place, flag to mark such a place, prob. of Gmc origin]

standard assessment tasks *pl n Brit. education.* the formal name for assessment tests. Acronym: **SATs.**

standard-bearer *n* **1** a man who carries a standard. **2** a leader of a cause or party.

standard cell *n* a voltaic cell producing a constant and accurately known electromotive force that can be used to calibrate voltage-measuring instruments.

standard cost *n* the predetermined budgeted cost of a manufacturing process against which actual costs are compared.

standard deviation *n Statistics.* a measure of dispersion obtained by extracting the square root of the mean of the squared deviations of the observed values from their mean in a frequency distribution.

standard error of the mean *n Statistics.* the standard deviation of the distribution of means of samples chosen from a larger population; equal to the standard deviation of the whole population divided by the square root of the sample size.

standard function *n Computing.* a subprogram provided by a translator that carries out a task, for example the computation of a mathematical function, such as sine, square root, etc.

standard gauge *n* **1** a railway track with a distance of 4 ft. 8½ in. (1.435 m) between the lines; used on most railways. ◆ *adj* **standard-gauge** *or* **standard-gauged. 2** of, relating to, or denoting a railway with a standard gauge.

Standard Grade *n* (in Scotland) an examination designed to test skills and the application of knowledge, which is replaced O grade.

standardize Ⓣ *or* **standardise** ('stændəˌdaɪz) *vb* **standardizes, standardizing, standardized** *or* **standardises, standardising, standardised. 1** to make or become standard. **2** *(tr)* to test by or compare with a standard.
▸ **ˌstandardi'zation** *or* **ˌstandardi'sation** *n* ▸ **'standardˌizer** *or* **'standardˌiser** *n*

standard model *n Physics.* a theory of fundamental interactions in which the electromagnetic, weak, and strong interactions are described in terms of the exchange of virtual particles.

standard of living *n* a level of subsistence or material welfare of a community, class, or person.

standard time *n* the official local time of a region or country determined by the distance from Greenwich of a line of longitude passing through the area.

stand by Ⓣ *vb (intr)* **1** *(adv)* to be available and ready to act if needed. **2** *(adv)* to be present as an onlooker or without taking any action: *he stood by at the accident.* **3** *(prep)* to be faithful to: *to stand by one's principles.* ◆ *n* **stand-by. 4a** a person or thing that is ready for use or can be relied on in an emergency. **4b** *(as modifier): stand-by provisions.* **5 on stand-by.** in a state of readiness for action or use. ◆ *adj* **stand-by. 6** not booked in advance but awaiting or subject to availability: *a stand-by ticket.*

stand down *vb (adv)* **1** *(intr)* to resign or withdraw, esp. in favour of an-

THESAURUS

stampede *n* **1, 2 = rush,** charge, flight, rout, scattering

stamp out *vb* **1, 2 = eliminate,** crush, destroy, eradicate, extinguish, extirpate, put down, put out, quell, quench, scotch, suppress

stance *n* **1 = posture,** bearing, carriage, deportment **3 = attitude,** position, stand, standpoint, viewpoint

stanch *see* **staunch**[2]

stand *vb* **1, 2 = be upright,** be erect, be vertical, rise **8 = exist,** be in force, belong, be situated *or* located, be valid, continue, halt, hold, obtain, pause, prevail, remain, rest, stay, stop **12 = tolerate,** abide, allow, bear, brook, cope with, countenance, endure, experience, hack *(sl.),* handle, put up with *(inf.),* stomach, submit to, suffer, support, sustain, take, thole *(dialect),* undergo, wear *(Brit. sl.),* weather, withstand ◆ *n* **26 = position,** attitude, determination, firm stand, opinion, stance, standpoint **27 = stop,** halt, rest, standstill, stay, stopover **30 = grandstand 31 = support,** base, bracket, dais, frame, place, platform, rack, rank, stage, staging, stance *(chiefly Scot.),* tripod, trivet **32 = stall,** booth, table

standard *n* **1 = criterion,** average, benchmark, example, guide, guideline, model, norm, par, pattern, sample, touchstone, yardstick **2** *often plural* **= principles,** canon, code of honour, ethics, ideals, moral principles, morals, rule **3 = level,** gauge, grade, measure **5 = flag,** banner, colours, ensign, pennant, pennon, streamer ◆ *adj* **15 = usual,** average, basic, customary, normal, orthodox, popular, prevailing, regular, set, staple, stock, typical **16 = accepted,** approved, authoritative, classic, definitive, established, official, recognized
Antonyms *adj* ≠ **usual:** abnormal, atypical, exceptional, extraordinary, irregular, singular, strange, uncommon, unusual ≠ **accepted:** unauthorised, unconventional, unofficial

standardize *vb* **1 = bring into line,** assimilate, institutionalize, mass-produce, regiment, stereotype

stand by *vb* **1 = be prepared,** wait, wait in the wings **3 = support,** back, befriend, be loyal to, champion, defend, stick up for *(inf.),* take (someone's) part, uphold other. **2** (*intr*) to leave the witness box in a court of law after giving evidence. **3** *Chiefly Brit.* to go or be taken off duty.

stand for ⊕ *vb* (*intr, prep*) **1** to represent or mean. **2** *Chiefly Brit.* to be or become a candidate for. **3** to support or recommend. **4** *Inf.* to tolerate or bear: *he won't stand for it.*

stand in ⊕ *vb* **1** (*intr, adv;* usually foll. by *for*) to act as a substitute. **2** **stand (someone) in good stead.** to be of benefit or advantage to (someone). ◆ *n* **stand-in. 3a** a person or thing that serves as a substitute. **3b** (*as modifier*): *a stand-in teacher.* **4** a person who substitutes for an actor during intervals of waiting or in dangerous stunts.

standing ⊕ ('stændɪŋ) *n* **1** social or financial position, status, or reputation: *a man of some standing.* **2** length of existence, experience, etc. **3** (*modifier*) used to stand in or on: *standing room.* ◆ *adj* **4** *Athletics.* **4a** (of the start of a race) begun from a standing position. **4b** (of a jump, leap, etc.) performed from a stationary position without a run-up. **5** (*prenominal*) permanent, fixed, or lasting. **6** (*prenominal*) still or stagnant: *a standing pond.* **7** *Printing.* (of type) set and stored for future use.

standing army *n* a permanent army of paid soldiers maintained by a nation.

standing order *n* **1** Also called: **banker's order.** an instruction to a bank by a depositor to pay a stated sum at regular intervals. Cf. **direct debit. 2** a rule or order governing the procedure, conduct, etc., of an organization. **3** *Mil.* one of a number of orders which have long-term validity.

standing rigging *n* the stays, shrouds, and other more or less fixed, though adjustable, ropes that support the masts of a sailing vessel.

standing wave *n Physics.* a wave that has unchanging amplitude at each point along its axis. Also called: **stationary wave.**

standoff ('stænd,ɒf) *n* **1** *US & Canad.* the act or an instance of standing off or apart. **2** a deadlock or stalemate. **3** *Rugby.* short for **stand-off half.** ◆ *vb* **stand off.** (*adv*) **4** (*intr*) to navigate a vessel so as to avoid the shore, an obstruction, etc. **5** (*tr*) to keep or cause to keep at a distance. **6** (*intr*) to reach a deadlock or stalemate. **7** (*tr*) to dismiss (workers), esp. temporarily.

stand-off half *n Rugby.* **1** a player who acts as a link between his scrum half and three-quarter backs. **2** this position. ◆ Also called: **fly half.**

standoffish ⊕ (,stænd'ɒfɪʃ) *adj* reserved, haughty, or aloof.
▶,**stand'offishness** *n*

stand on *vb* (*intr*) **1** (*adv*) to continue to navigate a vessel on the same heading. **2** (*prep*) to insist on: *to stand on ceremony.*

stand out ⊕ *vb* (*intr, adv*) **1** to be distinctive or conspicuous. **2** to refuse to agree or comply: *they stood out for a better price.* **3** to protrude or project. **4** to navigate a vessel away from a port, harbour, etc. ◆ *n* **standout. 5** *Inf.* **5a** a person or thing that is distinctive or outstanding. **5b** (*as modifier*): *the standout track from the album.*

stand over *vb* (*tr, prep*) **1** to supervise closely. **2** *Austral. & NZ inf.* to threaten or intimidate.

standover man ('stænd,əʊvə) *n Austral.* a person who extorts money by intimidation.

standpipe ('stænd,paɪp) *n* **1** a vertical pipe, open at the upper end, attached to a pipeline or tank serving to limit the pressure head to that of the height of the pipe. **2** a temporary freshwater outlet installed in a street when household water supplies are cut off.

standpoint ⊕ ('stænd,pɔɪnt) *n* a physical or mental position from which things are viewed.

standstill ('stænd,stɪl) *n* a complete cessation of movement; halt: *come to a standstill.*

stand to *vb* **1** (*adv*) *Mil.* to assume positions or cause to assume positions to resist a possible attack. **2** **stand to reason.** to conform with the dictates of reason: *it stands to reason.*

stand up ⊕ *vb* (*adv*) **1** (*intr*) to rise to the feet. **2** (*intr*) to resist or withstand wear, criticism, etc. **3** (*tr*) *Inf.* to fail to keep an appointment with, esp. intentionally. **4** **stand up for.** to support, side with, or defend. **5** **stand up to. 5a** to confront or resist courageously. **5b** to withstand or endure (wear, criticism, etc.). ◆ *adj* **stand-up.** (*prenominal*) **6** having or being in an erect position: *a stand-up collar.* **7** done, taken, etc., while standing: *a stand-up meal.* **8** (of comedy or a comedian) performed or performing solo. ◆ *n* **stand-up. 9** a stand-up comedian. **10** stand-up comedy.

Stanford-Binet test (-bɪ'neɪ) *n Psychol.* a revision, esp. for US use, of the Binet-Simon scale designed to measure mental ability by comparing the performance of an individual with the average performance for his age group. See also **Binet-Simon scale, intelligence test.** [C20: after *Stanford University,* California, & Alfred *Binet* (1857–1911), F psychologist]

stanhope ('stænəp) *n* a light one-seater carriage with two or four wheels. [C18: after Fitzroy *Stanhope* (1787–1864), E clergyman for whom it was first built]

stank (stæŋk) *vb* a past tense of **stink.**

Stanley knife *n Trademark.* a type of knife used for carpet fitting, etc., consisting of a thick hollow metal handle with a short, very sharp, replaceable blade inserted in one end. [C19: after F. T. *Stanley,* US businessman and founder of the Stanley Rule and Level Company]

stann- *combining form.* denoting tin: *stannite.* [from LL *stannum* tin]

Stannaries ('stænərɪz) *n* (*sometimes functioning as sing*) **the.** a former tin-mining district of Devon and Cornwall, under the jurisdiction of special courts.

stannary ('stænərɪ) *n, pl* **stannaries.** a place or region where tin is mined or worked. [C15: from Med. L *stannāria,* from LL *stannum* tin]

stannic ('stænɪk) *adj* of or containing tin, esp. in the tetravalent state; designating a tin(IV) compound. [C18: from LL *stannum* tin]

stannite ('stænaɪt) *n* a grey metallic mineral that consists of a sulphide of tin, copper, and iron and is a source of tin. Formula: Cu_2FeSnS_4. [C19: from LL *stannum* tin + -ITE[1]]

stannous ('stænəs) *adj* of or containing tin, esp. in the divalent state; designating a tin(II) compound.

stanza ('stænzə) *n* **1** *Prosody.* a fixed number of verse lines arranged in a definite metrical pattern, forming a unit of a poem. **2** *US & Austral.* a half or a quarter in a football match. [C16: from It.: halting place, from Vulgar L *stantia* (unattested) station, from L *stāre* to stand]
▶**'stanzaed** *adj* ▶**stanzaic** (stæn'zeɪɪk) *adj*

stapelia (stə'piːlɪə) *n* any of various fleshy cactus-like leafless African plants having large fetid flowers. [C18: from NL, after J. B. van *Stapel* (died 1636), Du. botanist]

stapes ('steɪpiːz) *n, pl* **stapes** *or* **stapedes** (stæ'piːdiːz). the stirrup-shaped bone that is the innermost of three small bones in the middle ear of mammals. Nontechnical name: **stirrup bone.** Cf. **incus, malleus.** [C17: via NL from Med. L, ? var. of *stapeda* stirrup, infl. by L *stāre* to stand + *pēs* a foot]

staphylo- *combining form.* **1** uvula: *staphyloplasty.* **2** resembling a bunch of grapes: *staphylococcus.* [from Gk *staphulē* bunch of grapes, uvula]

staphylococcus (,stæfɪləʊ'kɒkəs) *n, pl* **staphylococci** (-'kɒkaɪ; *US* -'kɒksaɪ). any spherical Gram-positive bacterium of the genus *Staphylococcus,* typically occurring in clusters and causing boils, infection in wounds, and septicaemia. Often shortened to **staph.**
▶,**staphylo'coccal** *adj*

staphyloplasty ('stæfɪləʊ,plæstɪ) *n* plastic surgery or surgical repair involving the soft palate or the uvula.
▶,**staphylo'plastic** *adj*

staple[1] ('steɪpᵊl) *n* **1** a short length of thin wire bent into a square U-shape, used to fasten papers, cloth, etc. **2** a short length of stiff wire formed into a U-shape with pointed ends, used for holding a hasp to a post, securing electric cables, etc. ◆ *vb* **staples, stapling, stapled. 3** (*tr*) to secure (papers, wire, etc.) with staples. [OE *stapol* prop, of Gmc origin]
▶**'stapler** *n*

staple[2] ⊕ ('steɪpᵊl) *adj* **1** of prime importance; principal: *staple foods.* **2** (of a commodity) forming a predominant element in the product, consumption, or trade of a nation, region, etc. ◆ *n* **3** a staple commodity. **4** a main constituent; integral part. **5** *Chiefly US & Canad.* a principal raw material produced or grown in a region. **6** the fibre of wool, cotton, etc., graded as to length and degree of fineness. ◆ *vb* **staples, stapling, stapled. 7** (*tr*) to arrange or sort (wool, cotton, etc.) according to length and fineness. [C15: from MDu. *stapel* warehouse]

staple gun *n* a mechanism that fixes staples to a surface.

star ⊕ (stɑː) *n* **1** any of a vast number of celestial objects visible in the clear night sky as points of light. **2a** a hot gaseous mass, such as the sun, that radiates energy, esp. as light and infrared radiation, and in some cases as ultraviolet, radio waves, and X-rays. **2b** (*as modifier*): *a star catalogue.* Related adjs.: **astral, sidereal, stellar. 3** *Astrol.* **3a** a celestial body, esp. a planet, supposed to influence events, personalities, etc. **3b** (*pl*) another name for **horoscope** (sense 1). **4** an emblem shaped like a conventionalized star, often used as a symbol of rank, an award, etc. **5** a small white blaze on the forehead of an animal, esp. a horse. **6a** a distinguished or glamorous celebrity, often from the entertainment world. **6b** (*as modifier*): *star quality.* **7** another word for **asterisk. 8** **see stars.** to see or seem to see bright moving pinpoints of light, as from a blow on the head, increased blood pressure, etc. ◆ *vb* **stars, starring, starred. 9** (*tr*) to mark or decorate with a star or stars. **10** to feature or be

THESAURUS

stand for *vb* **1** = **represent**, betoken, denote, exemplify, indicate, mean, signify, symbolize **4** *Informal* = **tolerate**, bear, brook, endure, lie down under (*inf.*), put up with, suffer, wear (*Brit. inf.*)

stand in *vb* **1** *usually with* **for** = **be a substitute for**, cover for, deputize for, do duty for, hold the fort for, replace, represent, take the place of, understudy ◆ *n* **stand-in 3a** = **substitute**, deputy, locum, replacement, reserve, stopgap, surrogate, understudy

standing *n* **1** = **status**, condition, credit, eminence, estimation, footing, position, rank, reputation, repute, station **2** = **duration**, continuance, existence, experience ◆ *adj* **5** = **permanent**, fixed, lasting, perpetual, regular, repeated

standoffish *adj* = **reserved**, aloof, cold, distant, haughty, remote, unapproachable, unsociable
Antonyms *adj* affable, approachable, congenial, cordial, friendly, open, sociable, warm

stand out *vb* **1** = **be conspicuous**, attract attention, be distinct, be highlighted, be obvious, be prominent, be striking, be thrown into relief, bulk large, catch the eye, leap to the eye, project, stare one in the face (*inf.*), stick out a mile (*inf.*), stick out like a sore thumb (*inf.*)

standpoint *n* = **point of view**, angle, position, post, stance, station, vantage point, viewpoint

stand up for *vb* **4** = **support**, champion, come to the defence of, defend, side with, stick up for (*inf.*), uphold

stand up to *vb* **5a** = **resist**, brave, confront, defy, oppose, tackle **5b** = **withstand**, endure

staple[2] *adj* **1** = **principal**, basic, chief, essential, fundamental, key, main, predominant, primary

star *n* **1** = **heavenly body 6a** = **celebrity**, big name, celeb (*inf.*), draw, idol, lead, leading man or lady, luminary, main attraction, megastar (*inf.*), name ◆ *adj* **6b** = **leading**, brilliant, celebrated, illustrious, major, paramount, principal, prominent, talented, well-known

featured as a star: *"Greed" starred Erich von Stroheim; Olivier starred in "Hamlet".* [OE *steorra*]
▸ **'starless** *adj* ▸ **'star,like** *adj*

starboard ('stɑːbəd, -ˌbɔːd) *n* **1** the right side of an aeroplane or vessel when facing the nose or bow. Cf. **port**² (sense 1). ◆ *adj* **2** relating to or on the starboard. ◆ *vb* **3** to turn or be turned towards the starboard. [OE *stēorbord*, lit.: steering side, from *stēor* steering paddle + *bord* side; from the fact that boats were formerly steered by a paddle held over the right-hand side]

starburst ('stɑːˌbɜːst) *n* **1** a pattern of rays or lines radiating from a light source. **2** *Photog.* a lens attachment which produces a starburst effect.

starch (stɑːtʃ) *n* **1** a polysaccharide composed of glucose units that occurs widely in plant tissues in the form of storage granules. **2** a starch obtained from potatoes and some grain: it is fine white powder that, in solution with water, is used to stiffen fabric. **3** any food containing a large amount of starch, such as rice and potatoes. **4** stiff or pompous formality. ◆ *vb* **5** (*tr*) to stiffen with or soak in starch. [OE *stercan* (unattested except by the p.p. *sterced*) to stiffen]
▸ **'starcher** *n*

Star Chamber *n* **1** *English history.* the Privy Council sitting as a court of equity; abolished 1641. **2** (*sometimes not caps.*) any arbitrary tribunal dispensing summary justice. **3** (*sometimes not caps.*) (in Britain, in a Conservative government) a group of senior ministers who make the final decision on the public spending of each government department.

starch-reduced *adj* (of food, esp. bread) having the starch content reduced, as in proprietary slimming products.

starchy ❶ ('stɑːtʃɪ) *adj* **starchier, starchiest. 1** of or containing starch. **2** extremely formal, stiff, or conventional: *a starchy manner.* **3** stiffened with starch.
▸ **'starchily** *adv* ▸ **'starchiness** *n*

star connection *n* a connection used in a polyphase electrical device or system of devices in which the windings each have one end connected to a common junction, the **star point**, and the other end to a separate terminal.

star-crossed *adj* dogged by ill luck; destined to misfortune.

stardom ('stɑːdəm) *n* **1** the fame and prestige of being a star in films, sport, etc. **2** the world of celebrities.

stardust ('stɑːˌdʌst) *n* **1** a large number of distant stars appearing to the observer as a cloud of dust. **2** a dreamy romantic or sentimental quality or feeling.

stare ❶ (steə) *vb* **stares, staring, stared. 1** (*intr*) (often foll. by *at*) to look or gaze fixedly, often with hostility or rudeness. **2** (*intr*) to stand out as obvious; glare. **3 stare one in the face.** to be glaringly obvious or imminent. ◆ *n* **4** the act or an instance of staring. [OE *starian*]
▸ **'starer** *n*

starfish ('stɑːˌfɪʃ) *n, pl* **starfish** *or* **starfishes.** any of various echinoderms, typically having a flattened body covered with a flexible test and five arms radiating from a central disc.

star fruit *n* another name for **carambola.**

stargaze ('stɑːˌgeɪz) *vb* **stargazes, stargazing, stargazed.** (*intr*) **1** to observe the stars. **2** to daydream.
▸ **'star,gazer** *n* ▸ **'star,gazing** *n, adj*

stark ❶ (stɑːk) *adj* **1** (*usually prenominal*) devoid of any elaboration; blunt: *the stark facts.* **2** grim; desolate: *a stark landscape.* **3** (*usually prenominal*) utter; absolute: *stark folly.* **4** *Arch.* severe; violent. **5** *Arch. or poetic.* rigid, as in death (esp. in **stiff and stark, stark dead**). **6** short for **stark-naked.** ◆ *adv* **7** completely: *stark mad.* **8** *Rare.* starkly. [OE *stearc* stiff]
▸ **'starkly** *adv* ▸ **'starkness** *n*

stark-naked ❶ *adj* completely naked. Informal word (*postpositive*): **starkers.** [C13 *stert naket*, lit.: tail naked; *stert*, from OE *steort* tail]

starlet ('stɑːlɪt) *n* **1** a young actress who is projected as a potential star. **2** a small star.

starlight ('stɑːˌlaɪt) *n* **1** the light emanating from the stars. ◆ *adj also* **starlighted. 2** of or like starlight. **3** Also: **starlit** ('stɑːˌlɪt). illuminated by starlight.

starling ('stɑːlɪŋ) *n* any gregarious passerine songbird of an Old World family, esp. the **common starling,** which has a blackish iridescent plumage and a short tail. [OE *stærlinc*, from *stær* starling + *-line* -LING¹]

star-of-Bethlehem *n* **1** Also: **starflower.** a Eurasian liliaceous plant having narrow leaves and starlike white flowers. **2** any of several similar and related plants.

Star of David *n* an emblem symbolizing Judaism and consisting of a six-pointed star formed by superimposing one inverted equilateral triangle upon another of equal size.

starry ('stɑːrɪ) *adj* **starrier, starriest. 1** filled, covered with, or illuminated by stars. **2** of, like, or relating to a star or stars.
▸ **'starriness** *n*

starry-eyed *adj* given to naive wishes, judgments, etc.; full of unsophisticated optimism.

Stars and Stripes *n* (*functioning as sing*) **the.** the national flag of the United States of America, consisting of 50 white stars representing the present states on a blue field and seven red and six white horizontal stripes representing the original states. Also called: the **Star-Spangled Banner.**

star sapphire *n* a sapphire showing a starlike figure in reflected light because of its crystalline structure.

star sign *n* another name for **sign of the zodiac.**

Star-Spangled Banner *n* **the. 1** the national anthem of the United States of America. **2** another term for the **Stars and Stripes.**

star stream *n* one of two main streams of stars that, because of the rotation of the Milky Way, appear to move in opposite directions.

star-studded *adj* featuring a large proportion of well-known performers: *a star-studded cast.*

start ❶ (stɑːt) *vb* **1** to begin or cause to begin (something or to do something); come or cause to come into being, operation, etc.: *he started a quarrel; they started to work.* **2** (when *intr*, sometimes foll. by *on*) to make or cause to make a beginning of (a process, series of actions, etc.): *they started on the project.* **3** (sometimes foll. by *up*) to set or be set in motion: *he started up the machine.* **4** (*intr*) to make a sudden involuntary movement, as from fright; jump. **5** (*intr;* sometimes foll. by *up, away,* etc.) to spring or jump suddenly from a position or place. **6** to establish or be established; set up: *to start a business.* **7** (*tr*) to support (someone) in the first part of a venture, career, etc. **8** to work or cause to work loose. **9** to enter or be entered in a race. **10** (*intr*) to flow violently from a source: *wine started from a hole in the cask.* **11** (*tr*) to rouse (game) from a hiding place, lair, etc. **12** (*intr*) (esp. of eyes) to bulge; pop. **13** (*intr*) *Brit. inf.* to commence quarrelling or causing a disturbance. **14 to start with.** in the first place. ◆ *n* **15** the beginning or first part of a journey, series of actions or operations, etc. **16** the place or time of starting, as of a race or performance. **17** a signal to proceed, as in a race. **18** a lead or advantage, either in time or distance, in a competitive activity: *he had an hour's start on me.* **19** a slight involuntary movement, as through fright, surprise, etc.: *she gave a start as I entered.* **20** an opportunity to enter a career, undertake a project, etc. **21** *Inf.* a surprising incident. **22 for a start.** in the first place. ◆ See also **start in, start off,** etc. [OE *styrtan*]

starter ('stɑːtə) *n* **1** Also called: **self-starter.** a device for starting an internal-combustion engine, usually consisting of a powerful electric motor that engages with the flywheel. **2** a person who supervises and signals the start of a race. **3** a competitor who starts in a race or contest. **4** *Inf., chiefly Austral.* an acceptable or practicable proposition, plan, idea, etc. **5** *Chiefly Brit.* the first course of a meal. **6** (*modifier*) designed to be used by a novice: *a starter kit.* **7 for starters.** *Sl.* in the first place. **8 under starter's orders. 8a** (of horses in a race) awaiting the start signal. **8b** (of a person) eager or ready to begin.

starter home *n* a compact flat or house marketed by price and size specifications to suit the requirements of first-time home buyers.

start in *vb* (*adv*) to undertake (something or doing something); commence or begin.

starting block *n* one of a pair of adjustable devices with pads or blocks against which a sprinter braces his feet in crouch starts.

starting gate *n* **1** a movable barrier so placed on the starting line of a racecourse that the raising of it releases all the contestants simultaneously. **2** the US name for **starting stalls.**

starting grid *n Motor racing.* a marked section of the track at the start where the cars line up according to their times in practice, the fastest occupying the front position.

starting price *n* (esp. in horse racing) the latest odds offered by bookmakers at the start of a race.

starting stalls *pl n Brit.* a line of stalls in which horses are enclosed at

THESAURUS

starchy *adj* **2** = **formal**, ceremonious, conventional, precise, prim, punctilious, stiff, stuffy

stare *vb* **1** = **gaze**, eyeball (*sl.*), gape, gawk, gawp (*Brit. sl.*), goggle, look, ogle, rubberneck (*sl.*), watch

stark *adj* **1** = **absolute**, arrant, bald, bare, blunt, consummate, downright, entire, flagrant, out-and-out, palpable, patent, pure, sheer, simple, unalloyed, unmitigated, utter **2** = **harsh**, austere, bare, barren, bleak, cold, depressing, desolate, dreary, forsaken, godforsaken, grim, hard, plain, severe, solitary, unadorned ◆ *adv* **7** = **absolutely**, altogether, clean, completely, entirely, quite, utterly, wholly

stark-naked *adj* = **undressed**, buck naked, in a state of nature, in one's birthday suit (*inf.*), in the altogether (*inf.*), in the bare scud (*sl.*), in the buff (*inf.*), in the raw (*inf.*), naked, naked as the day one was born (*inf.*), nude, stark, starkers (*inf.*), stripped, unclad, without a stitch on (*inf.*)

start *vb* **1** = **begin**, appear, arise, come into being, come into existence, commence, first see the light of day, get under way, go ahead, issue, originate **2** = **set about**, embark upon, make a beginning, put one's hand to the plough, take the first step, take the plunge (*inf.*) **3** = **set in motion**, activate, engender, enter upon, get going, get (something) off the ground, get *or* set *or* start the ball rolling, initiate, instigate, kick off (*inf.*), kick-start, open, originate, trigger, turn on **4** = **jump**, blench, flinch, jerk, recoil, shy, twitch **6** = **establish**, begin, create, father, found, inaugurate, initiate, institute, introduce, launch, lay the foundations of, pioneer, set up ◆ *n* **15** = **beginning**, birth, commencement, dawn, first step(s), foundation, inauguration, inception, initiation, kickoff (*inf.*), onset, opening, opening move, outset **18** = **advantage**, edge, head start, lead **19** = **jump**, convulsion, jar, spasm, twitch **20** = **opportunity**, backing, break (*inf.*), chance, helping hand, introduction, opening, sponsorship

Antonyms *vb* ≠ **begin, set about, set in motion:** abandon, bring to an end, call it a day (*inf.*), cease, conclude, delay, desist, end, finish, give up, put aside, put off, quit, stop, switch off, terminate, turn off, wind up ◆ *n* ≠ **beginning:** cessation, conclusion, denouement, end, finale, finish, outcome, result, stop, termination, turning off, wind-up the start of a race and from which they are released by the simultaneous springing open of retaining barriers at the front of each stall.

startle ➊ (ˈstɑːtᵊl) *vb* **startles, startling, startled.** to be or cause to be surprised or frightened, esp. so as to start involuntarily. [OE *steartlian* to stumble]
▸ˈ**startler** *n* ▸ˈ**startling** *adj*

start off *vb* (*adv*) **1** (*intr*) to set out on a journey. **2** to be or make the first step in (an activity); initiate: *he started the show off with a lively song.* **3** (*tr*) to cause (a person) to act or do something, such as to laugh, to tell stories, etc.

start on *vb* (*intr, prep*) *Brit. inf.* to pick a quarrel with; upbraid.

start out *vb* (*intr, adv*) **1** to set out on a journey. **2** to take the first steps, as in life, one's career, etc.: *he started out as a salesman.* **3** to take the first actions in an activity in a particular way or with a specified aim: *they started out wanting a house, but eventually bought a flat.*

start up *vb* (*adv*) **1** to come or cause to come into being for the first time; originate. **2** (*intr*) to spring or jump suddenly. **3** to set in or go into motion, activity, etc.: *he started up the engine.* ◆ *adj* **start-up. 4** of or relating to input, usually financial, made to establish a new project or business: *a start-up mortgage.*

starve ➊ (stɑːv) *vb* **starves, starving, starved. 1** to die or cause to die from lack of food. **2** to deprive (a person or animal) or (of a person, etc.) to be deprived of food. **3** (*intr*) *Inf.* to be very hungry. **4** (foll. by *of* or *for*) to deprive or be deprived (of something), esp. so as to cause suffering or malfunctioning: *the engine was starved of fuel.* **5** (*tr;* foll. by *into*) to bring (to) a specified condition by starving: *to starve someone into submission.* **6** *Arch. or dialect.* to be or cause to be extremely cold. [OE *steorfan* to die]
▸**star**ˈ**vation** *n*

starveling (ˈstɑːvlɪŋ) *Arch.* ◆ *n* **1a** a starving or poorly fed person, animal, etc. **1b** (*as modifier*): *a starveling child.* ◆ *adj* **2** insufficient; meagre; scant.

Star Wars *n* (*functioning as sing*) (in the US) a proposed system of artificial satellites armed with lasers to destroy enemy missiles in space. [C20: popularly named after the science-fiction film *Star Wars* (1977)]

starwort (ˈstɑːˌwɜːt) *n* **1** any of several plants with star-shaped flowers, esp. the stitchwort. **2** any of several aquatic plants having a star-shaped rosette of floating leaves.

stash ➊ (stæʃ) *vb* **1** (*tr;* often foll. by *away*) *Inf.* to put or store (money, valuables, etc.) in a secret place, as for safekeeping. ◆ *n* **2** *Inf., chiefly US & Canad.* a secret store or the place where this is hidden. **3** *Sl.* drugs kept for personal consumption. [C20: from ?]

stasis (ˈsteɪsɪs) *n* **1** *Pathol.* a stagnation in the normal flow of bodily fluids, such as the blood or urine. **2** a state or condition in which there is no action or progress. [C18: via NL from Gk: a standing, from *histanai* to cause to stand]

-stat *n combining form.* indicating a device that causes something to remain stationary or constant: *thermostat.* [from Gk *-statēs,* from *histanai* to cause to stand]

state ➊ (steɪt) *n* **1** the condition of a person, thing, etc., with regard to main attributes. **2** the structure or form of something: *a solid state.* **3** any mode of existence. **4** position in life or society; estate. **5** ceremonious style, as befitting wealth or dignity: *to live in state.* **6** a sovereign political power or community. **7** the territory occupied by such a community. **8** the sphere of power in such a community: *affairs of state.* **9** (*often cap.*) one of a number of areas or communities having their own governments and forming a federation under a sovereign government, as in the US. **10** (*often cap.*) the body politic of a particular sovereign power, esp. as contrasted with a rival authority such as the Church. **11** *Obs.* a class or order; estate. **12** *Inf.* a nervous, upset, or excited condition (esp. in **in a state**). **13 lie in state.** (of a body) to be placed on public view before burial. **14 state of affairs.** a situation; circumstances or condition. ◆ *modifier.* **15** controlled or financed by a state: *state university.* **16** of, relating to, or concerning the State: *State trial.* **17** involving ceremony or concerned with a ceremonious occasion: *state visit.* ◆ *vb* **states, stating, stated.** (*tr; may take a clause as object*) **18** to articulate in words; utter. **19** to declare formally or publicly. [C13: from OF *estat,* from L *status* a standing, from *stāre* to stand]
▸ˈ**statable** *or* ˈ**stateable** *adj* ▸ˈ**statehood** *n*

state bank *n* (in the US) a commercial bank incorporated under a State charter and not required to be a member of the Federal Reserve System.

statecraft (ˈsteɪtˌkrɑːft) *n* the art of conducting public affairs; statesmanship.

state duma *n* another name for **duma** (sense 3).

state house *n NZ.* a house built by the government and rented to a **state tenant.** Brit. equivalent: **council house.**

Statehouse (ˈsteɪtˌhaʊs) *n* (in the US) the building which houses a state legislature.

stateless (ˈsteɪtlɪs) *adj* **1** without nationality: *stateless persons.* **2** without a state or states.
▸ˈ**statelessness** *n*

stately ➊ (ˈsteɪtlɪ) *adj* **statelier, stateliest. 1** characterized by a graceful, dignified, and imposing appearance or manner. ◆ *adv* **2** in a stately manner.
▸ˈ**stateliness** *n*

stately home *n Brit.* a large mansion, esp. one open to the public.

statement ➊ (ˈsteɪtmənt) *n* **1** the act of stating. **2** something that is stated, esp. a formal prepared announcement or reply. **3** *Law.* a declaration of matters of fact. **4** an account containing a summary of bills or invoices and displaying the total amount due. **5** an account prepared by a bank for a client, usually at regular intervals, to show all credits and debits and the balance at the end of the period. **6** a computer instruction written in a source language, such as FORTRAN, which is converted into one or more machine-code instructions by a compiler. **7** *Logic.* the content of a sentence that affirms or denies something and may be true or false. **8** *Brit. education.* a legally binding account of the provisions that will be made to meet the needs of a pupil with special educational needs.

statement of attainment *n Brit. education.* a programme of specific objectives that pupils should achieve within their own levels of attainment in a particular subject.

statement of claim *n Law.* (in England) the first pleading made by the plaintiff in a High Court action.

state of the art ➊ *n* **1** the level of knowledge and development achieved in a technique, science, etc., esp. at present. ◆ *adj* **state-of-the-art.** (*prenominal*) **2** the most recent and therefore considered the best; up-to-the-minute: *a state-of-the-art amplifier.*

State Registered Nurse *n* (formerly, in Britain) a nurse who had extensive training and was qualified to perform all nursing services. See **Registered General Nurse.**

stateroom (ˈsteɪtˌruːm, -ˌrʊm) *n* **1** a private cabin or room on a ship, train, etc. **2** *Chiefly Brit.* a large room in a palace or other building for use on state occasions.

States (steɪts) *n* (*functioning as sing or pl*) **the.** an informal name for the United States of America.

state school *n* any school maintained by the state, in which education is free.

stateside (ˈsteɪtˌsaɪd) *adj, adv* (*sometimes cap.*) *US.* of, in, to, or towards the US.

statesman (ˈsteɪtsmən) *n, pl* **statesmen. 1** a political leader whose wisdom, integrity, etc., win great respect. **2** a person active and influential in the formulation of high government policy.
▸ˈ**statesman-**ˌ**like** *or* ˈ**statesmanly** *adj* ▸ˈ**statesmanship** *n* ▸ˈ**states-**ˌ**woman** *fem n*

state socialism *n* a variant of socialism in which the power of the state is employed for the purpose of creating an egalitarian society by means of public control of major industries, banks, etc.
▸**state socialist** *n*

state trooper *n US.* a state policeman.

static ➊ (ˈstætɪk) *adj also* **statical. 1** not active or moving; stationary. **2** (of a weight, force, or pressure) acting but causing no movement. **3** of or concerned with forces that do not produce movement. **4** relating to or causing stationary electric charges; electrostatic. **5** of or relating to interference in the reception of radio or television transmissions. **6** of or concerned with statics. **7** *Computing.* (of a memory) not needing its contents refreshed periodically. ◆ *n* **8** random hissing or crackling or a speckled picture caused by interference in the reception of radio or television transmissions. **9** electric sparks or crackling produced by friction. [C16: from NL *staticus,* from Gk *statikos* causing to stand, from *histanai* to stand]
▸ˈ**statically** *adv*

statice (ˈstætɪsɪ) *n* another name for **sea lavender.**

THESAURUS

startle *vb* = **surprise**, agitate, alarm, amaze, astonish, astound, frighten, give (someone) a turn (*inf.*), make (someone) jump, scare, shock, take (someone) aback

startling *adj* = **surprising**, alarming, astonishing, astounding, extraordinary, jaw-dropping, shocking, staggering, sudden, unexpected, unforeseen

starving *adj* **3** = **hungry**, esurient, faint from lack of food, famished, hungering, ravenous, ready to eat a horse (*inf.*), sharp-set, starved

stash *vb* **1** *Informal* = **store**, cache, hide, hoard, lay up, put aside for a rainy day, salt away, save up, secrete, stockpile, stow

state *n* **1** = **condition**, case, category, circumstances, equation, mode, pass, plight, position, predicament, shape, situation, state of affairs **5** = **ceremony**, dignity, display, glory, grandeur, majesty, pomp, splendour, style **6, 7** = **country**, body politic, commonwealth, federation, government, kingdom, land, nation, republic, territory **12 in a state** *Informal* = **distressed**, agitated, all steamed up (*sl.*), anxious, disturbed, flustered, het up, panic-stricken, ruffled, upset, uptight (*inf.*) ◆ *vb* **18, 19** = **express**, affirm, articulate, assert, asseverate, aver, declare, enumerate, explain, expound, present, propound, put, report, say, specify, utter, voice

stately *adj* **1** = **grand**, august, ceremonious, deliberate, dignified, elegant, imperial, imposing, impressive, lofty, majestic, measured, noble, pompous, regal, royal, solemn
Antonyms *adj* common, humble, lowly, modest, simple, undignified, undistinguished, unimpressive

statement *n* **2** = **account**, announcement, communication, communiqué, declaration, explanation, proclamation, recital, relation, report, testimony, utterance

state-of-the-art *adj* **2** = **latest**, newest, up-to-date, up-to-the-minute
Antonyms *adj* obsolescent, obsolete, old-fashioned, outdated, outmoded, out of date, out of the ark (*inf.*)

static *adj* **1** = **stationary**, changeless, constant, fixed, immobile, inert, motionless, stagnant, still, stock-still, unmoving, unvarying
Antonyms *adj* active, dynamic, kinetic, lively, mobile, moving, travelling, varied

static electricity *n* electricity that is not dynamic or flowing as a current.

statics ('stætɪks) *n* (*functioning as sing*) the branch of mechanics concerned with the forces that produce a state of equilibrium in a system.

station ➊ ('steɪʃən) *n* **1** the place or position at which a thing or person stands. **2a** a place along a route or line at which a bus, train, etc., stops for fuel or to pick up or let off passengers or goods, esp. one with ancillary buildings and services. **2b** (*as modifier*): *a station buffet.* **3a** the headquarters or local offices of an organization such as the police or fire services. **3b** (*as modifier*): *a station sergeant.* See **police station, fire station.** **4** a building, depot, etc., with special equipment for some particular purpose: *power station; petrol station.* **5** *Mil.* a place of duty: *an action station.* **6** *Navy.* **6a** a location to which a ship or fleet is assigned for duty. **6b** an assigned location for a member of a ship's crew. **7** a television or radio channel. **8** a position or standing, as in a particular society or organization. **9** the type of one's occupation; calling. **10** (in British India) a place where the British district officials or garrison officers resided. **11** *Biol.* the habitat occupied by a particular animal or plant. **12** *Austral. & NZ.* a large sheep or cattle farm. **13** (*sometimes cap.*) *RC Church.* **13a** one of the stations of the Cross. **13b** any of the churches (**station churches**) in Rome used as points of assembly for religious processions and ceremonies on particular days (**station days**). ◆ *vb* **14** (*tr*) to place in or assign to a station. [C14: via OF from L *statiō* a standing still, from *stāre* to stand]

stationary ➊ ('steɪʃənərɪ) *adj* **1** not moving; standing still. **2** not able to be moved. **3** showing no change: *the doctors said his condition was stationary.* **4** tending to remain in one place. [C15: from L *statiōnārius,* from *statiō* STATION]

> **USAGE NOTE** Avoid confusion with **stationery.**

stationary orbit *n Astronautics.* a synchronous orbit lying in or approximately in the plane of the equator.

stationary wave *n* another name for **standing wave.**

stationer ('steɪʃənə) *n* a person who sells stationery or a shop where stationery is sold. [C14: from Med. L *stationarius* a person having a regular station, hence a shopkeeper (esp. a bookseller) as distinguished from an itinerant tradesman; see STATION]

stationery ('steɪʃənərɪ) *n* any writing materials, such as paper, envelopes, pens, ink, rulers, etc.

> **USAGE NOTE** Avoid confusion with **stationary.**

station house *n Chiefly US.* a house that is situated by or serves as a station, esp. as a police or fire station.

stationmaster ('steɪʃən,mɑːstə) *n* the senior official in charge of a railway station.

Stations of the Cross *pl n RC Church.* **1** a series of 14 crosses, often accompanied by 14 pictures or carvings, arranged around the walls of a church, to commemorate 14 stages in Christ's journey to Calvary. **2** a devotion of 14 prayers relating to each of these stages.

station wagon *n* another name (less common in Britain) for **estate car.**

statism ('steɪtɪzəm) *n* the theory or practice of concentrating economic and political power in the state.
▸ **'statist** *n*

statistic (stə'tɪstɪk) *n* a datum capable of exact numerical representation, such as the correlation coefficient of two series or the standard deviation of a sample.
▸ **sta'tistical** *adj* ▸ **sta'tistically** *adv* ▸ **statistician** (,stætɪ'stɪʃən) *n*

statistical mechanics *n* (*functioning as sing*) the study of the properties of physical systems as predicted by the statistical behaviour of their constituent particles.

statistics (stə'tɪstɪks) *n* **1** (*functioning as sing*) a science concerned with the collection, classification, and interpretation of quantitative data and with the application of probability theory to the analysis and estimation of population parameters. **2** the quantitative data themselves. [C18 (orig. "science dealing with facts of a state"): via G *Statistik,* from NL *statisticus* concerning state affairs, from L *status* STATE]

stator ('steɪtə) *n* the stationary part of a rotary machine or device, esp. of a motor or generator. [C20: from L: one who stands (by), from *stāre* to stand]

statoscope ('stætə,skəʊp) *n* a very sensitive form of aneroid barometer used to detect and measure small variations in atmospheric pressure, such as one used in an aircraft to indicate small changes in altitude.

statuary ('stætjʊərɪ) *n* **1** statues collectively. **2** the art of making statues. ◆ *adj* **3** of or for statues. [C16: from L *statuārius*]

statue ('stætjuː) *n* a wooden, stone, metal, plaster, or other sculpture of a human or animal figure, usually life-size or larger. [C14: via OF from L *statua,* from *statuere* to set up; cf. STATUTE]

statuesque ➊ (,stætjʊ'ɛsk) *adj* like a statue, esp. in possessing great formal beauty or dignity.
▸ **,statu'esquely** *adv* ▸ **,statu'esqueness** *n*

statuette (,stætjʊ'ɛt) *n* a small statue.

stature ➊ ('stætʃə) *n* **1** height, esp. of a person or animal when standing. **2** the degree of development of a person: *the stature of a champion.* **3** intellectual or moral greatness: *a man of stature.* [C13: via OF from L *statūra,* from *stāre* to stand]

status ➊ ('steɪtəs) *n, pl* **statuses. 1** a social or professional position, condition, or standing. **2** the relative position or standing of a person or thing. **3** a high position or standing: *he has acquired a new status in that job.* **4** the legal standing or condition of a person. **5** a state of affairs. [C17: from L: posture, from *stāre* to stand]

status quo (kwəʊ) *n* (usually preceded by *the*) the existing state of affairs. [lit.: the state in which]

status symbol *n* a possession which is regarded as proof of the owner's social position, wealth, prestige, etc.

statute ➊ ('stætjuːt) *n* **1a** an enactment of a legislative body expressed in a formal document. **1b** this document. **2** a permanent rule made by a body or institution. [C13: from OF *estatut,* from LL *statūtum,* from L *statuere* to set up, decree, ult. from *stāre* to stand]

statute book *n Chiefly Brit.* a register of enactments passed by the legislative body of a state: *not on the statute book.*

statute law *n* **1** a law enacted by a legislative body. **2** a particular example of this. ◆ Cf. **common law, equity.**

statute mile *n* a legal or formal name for **mile** (sense 1).

statute of limitations *n* a legislative enactment prescribing the period of time within which proceedings must be instituted to enforce a right or bring an action at law.

statutory ('stætjʊtərɪ, -trɪ) *adj* **1** of, relating to, or having the nature of a statute. **2** prescribed or authorized by statute. **3** (of an offence) **3a** recognized by statute. **3b** subject to a punishment or penalty prescribed by statute.
▸ **'statutorily** *adv*

statutory order *n* a statute that applies further legislation to an existing act.

staunch[1] ➊ (stɔːntʃ) *adj* **1** loyal, firm, and dependable: *a staunch supporter.* **2** solid or substantial in construction. **3** *Rare.* (of a ship, etc.) watertight; seaworthy. [C15 (orig.: watertight): from OF *estanche,* from *estanchier* to STANCH]
▸ **'staunchly** *adv* ▸ **'staunchness** *n*

staunch[2] ➊ (stɔːntʃ) *or* **stanch** (stɑːntʃ) *vb* **1** to stem the flow of (a liquid, esp. blood) or (of a liquid) to stop flowing. **2** to prevent the flow of a liquid, esp. blood, from (a hole, wound, etc.). [C14: from OF *estanchier,* from Vulgar L *stanticāre* (unattested) to cause to stand, from L *stāre* to halt]
▸ **'staunchable** *or* **'stanchable** *adj* ▸ **'stauncher** *or* **'stancher** *n*

stave (steɪv) *n* **1** any one of a number of long strips of wood joined together to form a barrel, bucket, boat hull, etc. **2** any of various bars, slats, or rods, usually of wood, such as a rung of a ladder. **3** any stick, staff, etc. **4** a stanza or verse of a poem. **5** *Music.* **5a** *Brit.* an individual group of five lines and four spaces used in staff notation. **5b** another word for **staff**[1] (sense 9). ◆ *vb* **staves, staving, staved** *or* **stove. 6** (often foll. by *in*) to break or crush (the staves of a boat, barrel, etc.) or (of the staves of a boat) to be broken or crushed. **7** (*tr;* usually foll. by *in*) to burst or force (a hole in something). **8** (*tr*) to provide (a ladder, chair, etc.) with staves. [C14: back formation from *staves,* pl. of STAFF[1]]

stave off ➊ *vb* (*tr, adv*) to avert or hold off, esp. temporarily: *to stave off hunger.*

staves (steɪvz) *n* a plural of **staff**[1] or **stave.**

stavesacre ('steɪvz,eɪkə) *n* **1** a Eurasian ranunculaceous plant having poisonous seeds. **2** the seeds, which have strong emetic and cathartic properties. [C14 *staphisagre,* from L *staphis agria,* from Gk, from *staphis* raisin + *agria* wild]

stay[1] ➊ (steɪ) *vb* **1** (*intr*) to continue or remain in a certain place, position, etc.: *to stay outside.* **2** (*copula*) to continue to be; remain: *to stay awake.* **3** (*intr;* often foll. by *at*) to reside temporarily: *to stay at a hotel.* **4** (*tr*) to remain for a specified period: *to stay the weekend.* **5** (*intr*) *Scot. & S.*

THESAURUS

station *n* **1** = **place**, location, position, post, seat, situation **3a** = **headquarters**, base, depot **8** = **position**, grade, post, rank, situation, sphere, standing, status **9** = **occupation**, appointment, business, calling, employment ◆ *vb* **14** = **assign**, establish, fix, garrison, install, locate, post, set

stationary *adj* **1** = **motionless**, at a standstill, fixed, inert, moored, parked, standing, static, stock-still, unmoving
Antonyms *adj* changeable, changing, inconstant, mobile, moving, shifting, travelling, unstable, variable, varying, volatile

statuesque *adj* = **well-proportioned**, dignified, imposing, Junoesque, majestic, regal, stately

stature *n* **1-3** = **importance**, consequence, eminence, high station, prestige, prominence, rank, size, standing

status *n* **1-3** = **position**, condition, consequence, degree, distinction, eminence, grade, prestige, rank, standing

statute *n* **1** = **law**, act, decree, edict, enactment, ordinance, regulation, rule

staunch[1] *adj* **1** = **loyal**, constant, dependable, faithful, firm, immovable, reliable, resolute, sound, stalwart, steadfast, stout, strong, sure, tried and true, true, true-blue, trustworthy, trusty

staunch[2] *vb* **1, 2** = **stop**, arrest, check, dam, halt, plug, stay, stem

stave off *vb* = **hold off**, avert, evade, fend off, foil, keep at arm's length, keep at bay, parry, ward off

stay[1] *vb* **1** = **remain**, abide, bide, continue, delay, establish oneself, halt, hang around (*inf.*), hang in the air, hover, linger, loiter, pause, put down roots, reside, settle, stand, stay put, stop, tarry, wait **3** *often with* **at** = **lodge**, be accommodated at, put up at, sojourn, visit **8** = **delay**, arrest, check, curb, detain, hinder,

African. to reside permanently or habitually; live. **6** *Arch.* to stop or cause to stop. **7** (*intr*) to wait, pause, or tarry. **8** (*tr*) to delay or hinder. **9** (*tr*) **9a** to discontinue or suspend (a judicial proceeding). **9b** to hold in abeyance or restrain from enforcing (an order, decree, etc.). **10** to endure (something testing or difficult, such as a race): *stay the course.* **11** (*tr*) to hold back or restrain: *to stay one's anger.* **12** (*tr*) to satisfy or appease (an appetite, etc.) temporarily. ◆ *n* **13** the act of staying or sojourning in a place or the period during which one stays. **14** the act of stopping or restraining or state of being stopped, etc. **15** the suspension of a judicial proceeding, etc.: *stay of execution.* [C15 *staien*, from Anglo-F *estaier* to stay, from OF *ester* to stay, from L *stāre* to stand]
▸**'stayer** *n*

stay[2] ➊ (steɪ) *n* **1** anything that supports or steadies, such as a prop or buttress. **2** a thin strip of metal, plastic, bone, etc., used to stiffen corsets, etc. See also **stays** (sense 1). ◆ *vb* (*tr*) *Arch.* **3** (often foll. by *up*) to prop or hold. **4** (often foll. by *up*) to comfort or sustain. **5** (foll. by *on* or *upon*) to cause to rely or depend. [C16: from OF *estaye*, of Gmc origin]

stay[3] (steɪ) *n* a rope, cable, or chain, usually one of a set, used for bracing uprights, such as masts, funnels, flagpoles, chimneys, etc.; guy. ◆ See also **stays** (senses 2, 3). [OE *stæg*]

stay-at-home *adj* **1** (of a person) enjoying a quiet, settled, and unadventurous use of leisure. ◆ *n* **2** a stay-at-home person.

staying power ➊ *n* endurance; stamina.

stays (steɪz) *pl n* **1** old-fashioned corsets with bones in them. **2** a position of a sailing vessel relative to the wind so that the sails are luffing or aback. **3 miss** *or* **refuse stays.** (of a sailing vessel) to fail to come about.

staysail ('steɪ,seɪl; *Naut.* 'steɪsᵊl) *n* an auxiliary sail, often triangular, set on a stay.

STD *abbrev. for:* **1** Doctor of Sacred Theology. **2** sexually transmitted disease. **3** subscriber trunk dialling.

STD code *n Brit.* a code of four or more digits, other than those comprising a subscriber's local telephone number, that determines the routing of a call. [C20: *s*(*ubscriber*) *t*(*runk*) *d*(*ialling*)]

Ste *abbrev. for* Saint (female). [F *Sainte*]

stead (stɛd) *n* **1** (preceded by *in*) *Rare.* the place, function, or position that should be taken by another: *to come in someone's stead.* **2 stand (someone) in good stead.** to be useful or of good service to (someone). ◆ *vb* **3** (*tr*) *Arch.* to help or benefit. [OE *stede*]

steadfast ➊ *or* **stedfast** ('stɛdfəst, -,fɑːst) *adj* **1** (esp. of a person's gaze) fixed in intensity or direction; steady. **2** unwavering or determined in purpose, loyalty, etc.: *steadfast resolve.*
▸**'steadfastly** *or* **'stedfastly** *adv* ▸**'steadfastness** *or* **'stedfastness** *n*

steading ('stɛdɪŋ) *n* another name for **farmstead.**

steady ➊ ('stɛdɪ) *adj* **steadier, steadiest. 1** not able to be moved or disturbed easily; stable. **2** free from fluctuation. **3** not easily excited; imperturbable. **4** staid; sober. **5** regular; habitual: *a steady drinker.* **6** continuous: *a steady flow.* **7** *Naut.* (of a vessel) keeping upright, as in heavy seas. ◆ *vb* **steadies, steadying, steadied. 8** to make or become steady. ◆ *adv* **9** in a steady manner. **10 go steady.** *Inf.* to date one person regularly. ◆ *n, pl* **steadies. 11** *Inf.* one's regular boyfriend or girlfriend. ◆ *interj* **12** *Naut.* an order to the helmsman to stay on a steady course. **13** a warning to keep calm, be careful, etc. **14** *Brit.* a command to get set to start, as in a race: *ready, steady, go!* [C16: from STEAD + -Y[1]]
▸**'steadily** *adv* ▸**'steadiness** *n* ▸**'steadying** *adj*

steady state *n Physics.* the condition of a system when some or all of the quantities describing it are independent of time but not necessarily in thermodynamic or chemical equilibrium.

steady-state theory *n* a theory postulating that the universe exists throughout time in a steady state such that the average density of matter does not vary with distance or time. Matter is continuously created in the space left by the receding stars and galaxies of the expanding universe. Cf. **big-bang theory.**

steak (steɪk) *n* **1** See **beefsteak. 2** any of various cuts of beef, for braising, stewing, etc. **3** a thick slice of pork, veal, cod, salmon, etc. **4** minced meat prepared in the same way as steak: *hamburger steak.* [C15: from ON *steik* roast]

steakhouse ('steɪk,haʊs) *n* a restaurant that has steaks as its speciality.

steak tartare (tɑː'tɑː) *or* **tartar** *n* raw minced steak, mixed with onion, seasonings, and raw egg. Also called: **tartare steak, tartar steak.**

steal ➊ (stiːl) *vb* **steals, stealing, stole, stolen. 1** to take (something) from someone, etc., without permission or unlawfully, esp. in a secret manner. **2** (*tr*) to obtain surreptitiously. **3** (*tr*) to appropriate (ideas, etc.) without acknowledgment, as in plagiarism. **4** to move or convey stealthily: *they stole along the corridor.* **5** (*intr*) to pass unnoticed: *the hours stole by.* **6** (*tr*) to win or gain by strategy or luck, as in various sports: *to steal a few yards.* ◆ *n Inf.* **7** the act of stealing. **8** something stolen or acquired easily or at little cost. [OE *stelan*]
▸**'stealer** *n*

stealth ➊ (stɛlθ) *n* **1** the act or characteristic of moving with extreme care and quietness, esp. so as to avoid detection. **2** cunning or underhand procedure or dealing. [C13 *stelthe*; see STEAL, -TH[1]]
▸**'stealthy** *adj*

Stealth (stɛlθ) *n* (*modifier*) *Inf.* denoting or referring to technology that aims to reduce the radar, thermal, and acoustic recognizability of aircraft and missiles.

Stealth bomber *or* **plane** *n* a type of US military aircraft using advanced technology to render it virtually undetectable to sight, radar, or infrared sensors. Also called: **B-2.**

steam (stiːm) *n* **1** the gas or vapour into which water is changed when boiled. **2** the mist formed when such gas or vapour condenses in the atmosphere. **3** any vaporous exhalation. **4** *Inf.* power, energy, or speed. **5 get up steam. 5a** (of a ship, etc.) to work up a sufficient head of steam in a boiler to drive an engine. **5b** *Inf.* to go quickly. **6 let off steam.** *Inf.* to release pent-up energy, feelings, etc. **7 under one's own steam.** without the assistance of others. **8** (*modifier*) driven, operated, heated, powered, etc., by steam: *a steam radiator.* **9** (*modifier*) treated by steam: *steam-ironed.* **10** (*modifier*) *Humorous.* old-fashioned; outmoded: *steam radio.* ◆ *vb* **11** to emit or be emitted as steam. **12** (*intr*) to generate steam, as a boiler, etc. **13** (*intr*) to move or travel by steam power, as a ship, etc. **14** (*intr*) *Inf.* to proceed quickly and sometimes forcefully. **15** to cook or be cooked in steam. **16** (*tr*) to treat with steam or apply steam to, as in cleaning, pressing clothes, etc. ◆ See also **steam up.** [OE]

steam bath *n* **1** a room or enclosure that can be filled with steam in which people bathe to induce sweating and refresh or cleanse themselves. **2** an act of taking such a bath.

steamboat ('stiːm,bəʊt) *n* a boat powered by a steam engine.

steam boiler *n* a vessel in which water is boiled to generate steam.

steam engine *n* an engine that uses steam to produce mechanical work, esp. one in which steam from a boiler is expanded in a cylinder to drive a reciprocating piston.

steamer ('stiːmə) *n* **1** a boat or ship driven by steam engines. **2** a vessel used to cook food by steam. **3** *Austral. sl.* a rough clash between sports teams.

steaming ('stiːmɪŋ) *adj* **1** very hot. **2** *Inf.* angry. **3** *Sl.* drunk. ◆ *n* **4** *Inf.* robbery, esp. of passengers in a railway carriage or bus, by a large gang of armed youths.

steam iron *n* an electric iron that emits steam from channels in the iron face to facilitate pressing and ironing, the steam being produced from water contained within the iron.

steam jacket *n Engineering.* a jacket containing steam that surrounds and heats a cylinder.

steam organ *n* a type of organ powered by steam, once common at fairgrounds, played either by a keyboard or by a moving punched card. US name: **calliope.**

steam point *n* the temperature at which the maximum vapour pressure of water is equal to one atmosphere (1.01325×10^5 N/m^2). It has the value of 100° on the Celsius scale.

steam reforming *n Chem.* a process in which methane from natural gas is heated, with steam, usually with a catalyst, to produce a mixture of carbon monoxide and hydrogen used in organic synthesis and as a fuel.

steamroller ('stiːm,rəʊlə) *n* **1a** a steam-powered vehicle with heavy rollers used for compressing road surfaces during road-making. **1b** another word for **roadroller. 2a** an overpowering force or person that

THESAURUS

hold, impede, obstruct, prevent **9 = suspend**, adjourn, defer, discontinue, hold in abeyance, hold over, prorogue, put off ◆ *n* **13 = visit**, holiday, sojourn, stop, stopover **14 = postponement**, deferment, delay, halt, pause, remission, reprieve, stopping, suspension
Antonyms *vb* ≠ **remain:** abandon, depart, exit, go, leave, move on, pack one's bags (*inf.*), pass through, quit, withdraw

stay[2] *n* **1 = support**, brace, buttress, prop, reinforcement, shoring, stanchion

staying power *n* **= endurance**, stamina, strength, toughness

steadfast *adj* **1, 2 = firm**, constant, dedicated, dependable, established, faithful, fast, fixed, immovable, intent, loyal, persevering, reliable, resolute, single-minded, stable, stalwart, staunch, steady, unfaltering, unflinching, unswerving, unwavering
Antonyms *adj* capricious, faint-hearted, faltering, fickle, flagging, half-hearted, inconstant, irresolute, uncommitted, undependable, unreliable, unstable, vacillating, wavering

steady *adj* **1 = firm**, fixed, immovable, on an even keel, safe, secure, stable, substantial, unchangeable, uniform **4 = dependable**, balanced, calm, equable, having both feet on the ground, imperturbable, level-headed, reliable, sedate, sensible, serene, serious-minded, settled, sober, staid, staunch, steadfast **6 = continuous**, ceaseless, confirmed, consistent, constant, even, habitual, incessant, nonstop, persistent, regular, rhythmic, unbroken, unfaltering, unfluctuating, uninterrupted, unremitting, unvarying, unwavering ◆ *vb* **8 = stabilize**, balance, brace, secure, support
Antonyms *adj* ≠ **firm:** insecure, unsettled, unstable, unsteady ≠ **continuous:** changeable, faltering, fluctuating, inconsistent, infrequent, intermittent, irregular, occasional, sporadic ≠ **dependable:** careless, fickle, half-hearted, in two minds, uncommitted, unconscientious, undependable, unpredictable, unreliable, vacillating, wavering ◆ *vb* ≠ **stabilize:** agitate, shake, tilt, upset

steal *vb* **1-3 = take**, appropriate, be light-fingered, blag (*sl.*), cabbage (*Brit. sl.*), embezzle, filch, half-inch (*old-fashioned sl.*), heist (*US sl.*), lift (*inf.*), misappropriate, nick (*sl., chiefly Brit.*), peculate, pilfer, pinch (*inf.*), pirate, plagiarize, poach, prig (*Brit. sl.*), purloin, shoplift, snitch (*sl.*), swipe (*sl.*), thieve, walk *or* make off with **4 = sneak**, creep, flit, insinuate oneself, slink, slip, tiptoe

stealing *n* **1-3 = theft**, embezzlement, larceny, misappropriation, pilferage, pilfering, plagiarism, robbery, shoplifting, thievery, thieving

stealth *n* **1, 2 = secrecy**, furtiveness, slyness, sneakiness, stealthiness, surreptitiousness, unobtrusiveness

stealthy *adj* **1, 2 = secret**, clandestine, covert, furtive, secretive, skulking, sly, sneaking, sneaky, surreptitious, underhand overcomes all opposition. **2b** (*as modifier*): *steamroller tactics.* ◆ *vb* **3** (*tr*) to crush (opposition, etc.) by overpowering force.

steamship ('stiːmˌʃɪp) *n* a ship powered by one or more steam engines.

steam shovel *n* a steam-driven mechanical excavator.

steam turbine *n* a turbine driven by steam.

steam up *vb* (*adv*) **1** to cover (windows, etc.) or (of windows, etc.) to become covered with a film of condensed steam. **2** (*tr; usually passive*) *Sl.* to excite or make angry: *he's all steamed up about the delay.*

steamy ❶ ('stiːmɪ) *adj* **steamier, steamiest. 1** of, resembling, full of, or covered with steam. **2** *Inf.* lustful or erotic: *steamy nightlife.*
▸ **'steaminess** *n*

steapsin (stɪ'æpsɪn) *n Biochem.* a pancreatic lipase. [C19: from Gk *stear* fat + PEPSIN]

stearic (stɪ'ærɪk) *adj* **1** of or relating to suet or fat. **2** of, consisting of, containing, or derived from stearic acid.

stearic acid *n* a colourless odourless insoluble waxy carboxylic acid used for making candles and suppositories. Formula: $CH_3(CH_2)_{16}COOH$. Systematic name: **octadecanoic acid.**

stearin *or* **stearine** ('stɪərɪn) *n* **1** Also called: **tristearin.** a colourless crystalline ester of glycerol and stearic acid, present in fats and used in soap and candles. **2** another name for **stearic acid. 3** fat in its solid form. [C19: from F *stéarine,* from Gk *stear* fat + -IN]

steatite ('stɪəˌtaɪt) *n* another name for **soapstone.** [C18: from L *steatītes,* from Gk *stear* fat + -ITE[1]]
▸ **steatitic** (ˌstɪə'tɪtɪk) *adj*

steato- *combining form.* denoting fat. [from Gk *stear, steat-* fat, tallow]

steatolysis (ˌstɪə'tɒlɪsɪs) *n Physiol.* **1** the digestive process whereby fats are emulsified and then hydrolysed to fatty acids and glycerine. **2** the breaking down of fat.

steatopygia (ˌstɪətəʊ'pɪdʒɪə, -'paɪ-) *or* **steatopyga** (ˌstɪətəʊ'paɪgə) *n* excessive fatness of the buttocks. [C19: from NL, from STEATO- + Gk *pugē* the buttocks]
▸ **ˌsteato'pygic** *or* **steatopygous** (ˌstɪə'tɒpɪgəs) *adj*

stedfast ('stɛdfəst, -ˌfɑːst) *adj* a less common spelling of **steadfast.**

steed (stiːd) *n Arch. or literary.* a horse, esp. one that is spirited or swift. [OE *stēda* stallion]

steel ❶ (stiːl) *n* **1a** any of various alloys based on iron containing carbon and often small quantities of other elements such as sulphur, manganese, chromium, and nickel. Steels exhibit a variety of properties, such as strength, malleability, etc., depending on their composition and the way they have been treated. **1b** (*as modifier*): *steel girders.* See also **stainless steel. 2** something that is made of steel. **3** a steel stiffener in a corset, etc. **4** a ridged steel rod used for sharpening knives. **5** the quality of hardness, esp. with regard to a person's character or attitudes. **6** *Canad.* a railway track or line. **7 cold steel.** bladed weapons. ◆ *vb* (*tr*) **8** to fit, plate, edge, or point with steel. **9** to make hard and unfeeling: *he steeled his heart against her sorrow; he steeled himself for the blow.* [OE *stēli*]
▸ **'steely** *adj* ▸ **'steeliness** *n*

steel band *n Music.* a type of band, popular in the Caribbean Islands, consisting mainly of percussion instruments made from oil drums, hammered or embossed to obtain different notes.

steel blue *n* **a** a dark bluish-grey colour. **b** (*as adj*): *steel-blue eyes.*

steel engraving *n* **a** a method or art of engraving (letters, etc.) on a steel plate. **b** a print made from such a plate.

steel grey *n* **a** a dark grey colour, usually slightly purple. **b** (*as adj*): *a steel-grey suit.*

steelhead ('stiːlˌhɛd) *n, pl* **steelheads** *or* **steelhead.** a silvery North Pacific variety of the rainbow trout.

steel wool *n* a tangled or woven mass of fine steel fibres, used for cleaning or polishing.

steelworks ('stiːlˌwɜːks) *n* (*functioning as sing or pl*) a plant in which steel is made from iron ore and rolled or forged into bars, sheets, etc.
▸ **'steelˌworker** *n*

steelyard ('stiːlˌjɑːd) *n* a portable balance consisting of a pivoted bar with two unequal arms. The load is suspended from the shorter one and the bar is returned to the horizontal by sliding a weight along the longer, graduated arm.

steenbok ('stiːnˌbɒk) *n, pl* **steenboks** *or* **steenbok.** a small antelope of central and southern Africa, having a reddish-brown coat and straight horns. [C18: from Afrik., from Du. *steen* stone + *bok* BUCK[1]]

steep[1] ❶ (stiːp) *adj* **1a** having or being a slope or gradient approaching the perpendicular. **1b** (*as n*): *the steep.* **2** *Inf.* (of a fee, price, demand, etc.) unduly high; unreasonable (esp. in **that's a bit steep**). **3** *Inf.* excessively demanding or ambitious: *a steep task.* **4** *Brit. inf.* (of a statement) extreme or far-fetched. [OE *steap*]
▸ **'steeply** *adv* ▸ **'steepness** *n*

steep[2] ❶ (stiːp) *vb* **1** to soak or be soaked in a liquid in order to soften, cleanse, extract an element, etc. **2** (*tr; usually passive*) to saturate; imbue: *steeped in ideology.* ◆ *n* **3** an instance or the process of steeping or the condition of being steeped. **4** a liquid or solution used for the purpose of steeping something. [OE *stēpan*]
▸ **'steeper** *n*

steepen ('stiːpᵊn) *vb* to become or cause to become steep or steeper.

steeple ('stiːpᵊl) *n* **1** a tall ornamental tower that forms the superstructure of a church, temple, etc. **2** such a tower with the spire above it. **3** any spire or pointed structure. [OE *stēpel*]
▸ **'steepled** *adj*

steeplechase ('stiːpᵊlˌtʃeɪs) *n* **1** a horse race over a course equipped with obstacles to be jumped. **2** a track race in which the runners have to leap hurdles, a water jump, etc. **3** *Arch.* **3a** a horse race across a stretch of open countryside including obstacles to be jumped. **3b** a rare word for **point-to-point.** ◆ *vb* **steeplechases, steeplechasing, steeplechased. 4** (*intr*) to take part in a steeplechase.
▸ **'steepleˌchaser** *n* ▸ **'steepleˌchasing** *n*

steeplejack ('stiːpᵊlˌdʒæk) *n* a person trained and skilled in the construction and repair of steeples, chimneys, etc.

steer[1] ❶ (stɪə) *vb* **1** to direct the course of (a vehicle or vessel) with a steering wheel, rudder, etc. **2** (*tr*) to guide with tuition: *his teachers steered him through his exams.* **3** (*tr*) to direct the movements or course of (a person, conversation, etc.). **4** to pursue (a specified course). **5** (*intr*) (of a vessel, vehicle, etc.) to admit of being guided in a specified fashion: *this boat does not steer properly.* **6 steer clear of.** to keep away from; shun. ◆ *n* **7** *Chiefly US.* guidance; information (esp. in **a bum steer**). [OE *stieran*]
▸ **'steerable** *adj* ▸ **'steerer** *n*

steer[2] (stɪə) *n* a castrated male ox or bull; bullock. [OE *stēor*]

steerage ('stɪərɪdʒ) *n* **1** the cheapest accommodation on a passenger ship, originally the compartments containing steering apparatus. **2** an instance or the practice of steering and its effect on a vessel or vehicle.

steerageway ('stɪərɪdʒˌweɪ) *n Naut.* enough forward movement to allow a vessel to be steered.

steering committee *n* a committee set up to prepare and arrange topics to be discussed, the order of business, etc., for a legislative assembly or other body.

steering wheel *n* a wheel turned by the driver of a motor vehicle, ship, etc., when he wishes to change direction.

steersman ❶ ('stɪəzmən) *n, pl* **steersmen.** the helmsman of a vessel.

stegosaur ('stɛgəˌsɔː) *or* **stegosaurus** (ˌstɛgə'sɔːrəs) *n* any of various quadrupedal herbivorous dinosaurs of Jurassic and early Cretaceous times, having an armour of bony plates. [C19: from Gk *stegos* roof + -SAUR]

stein (staɪn) *n* an earthenware beer mug, esp. of a German design. [from G *Stein,* lit.: stone]

steinbok ('staɪnˌbɒk) *n, pl* **steinboks** *or* **steinbok.** a variant of **steenbok.**

stele ('stiːlɪ, stiːl) *n, pl* **stelae** ('stiːliː) *or* **steles. 1** an upright stone slab or column decorated with figures or inscriptions, common in prehistoric times. **2** a prepared vertical surface that has a commemorative inscription or design, esp. one on the face of a building. **3** the conducting tissue of the stems and roots of plants, which is in the form of a cylinder. ◆ Also called (for senses 1, 2): **stela.** [C19: from Gk *stēlē*]
▸ **'stelar** *adj*

stellar ('stɛlə) *adj* **1** of, relating to, or resembling a star or stars. **2** of or relating to star entertainers. **3** *Inf.* outstanding or immense: *companies are registering stellar profits.* [C17: from LL *stellāris,* from L *stella* star]

stellar evolution *n Astron.* the sequence of changes that occurs in a star as it ages.

stellate ('stɛlɪt, -eɪt) *or* **stellated** *adj* resembling a star in shape; radiating from the centre: *a stellate arrangement of petals.* [C16: from L *stellātus* starry, from *stellāre* to stud with stars, from *stella* a star]
▸ **'stellately** *adv*

stellular ('stɛljʊlə) *adj* **1** displaying or abounding in small stars: *a stellular pattern.* **2** resembling a little star or little stars. [C18: from LL *stellula,* dim. of L *stella* star]
▸ **'stellularly** *adv*

stem[1] ❶ (stɛm) *n* **1** the main axis of a plant, which bears the leaves, axillary buds, and flowers and contains a hollow cylinder of vascular tissue. **2** any similar subsidiary structure in such plants that bears a flower, fruit, or leaf. **3** a corresponding structure in algae and fungi. **4** any long slender part, such as the hollow part of a tobacco pipe between the bit and the bowl. **5** the main line of descent or branch of a family. **6** any shank or cylindrical pin or rod, such as the pin that carries the winding knob on a watch. **7** *Linguistics.* the form of a word that remains after removal of all inflectional affixes. **8** the main, usually vertical, stroke of a letter or of a musical note such as a minim. **9a**

THESAURUS

steamy *adj* **2** *Informal* = **erotic,** carnal, hot (*sl.*), lascivious, lewd, lubricious (*formal or literary*), lustful, prurient, raunchy (*sl.*), sensual, sexy (*inf.*), titillating

steel oneself *vb* **9** = **brace oneself,** fortify oneself, grit one's teeth, harden oneself, make up one's mind

steep[1] *adj* **1a** = **sheer,** abrupt, headlong, precipitous **2** *Informal* = **high,** excessive, exorbitant, extortionate, extreme, overpriced, stiff, uncalled-for, unreasonable

Antonyms *adj* ≠ **sheer:** easy, gentle, gradual, moderate, slight ≠ **high:** fair, moderate, reasonable

steep[2] *vb* **1** = **soak,** damp, drench, imbrue (*rare*), immerse, macerate, marinate (*Cookery*), moisten, souse, submerge **2** = **saturate,** fill, imbue, infuse, permeate, pervade, suffuse

steer[1] *vb* **1** = **drive,** control, direct, guide, handle, pilot **2, 3** = **direct,** administer, be in the driver's seat, conduct, control, govern **6 steer clear of** = **avoid,** body-swerve (*Scot.*), circumvent, eschew, evade, give a wide berth to, sheer off, shun

steersman *n* = **pilot,** cox, coxswain, helmsman

stem[1] *n* **1-3** = **stalk,** axis, branch, peduncle, shoot, stock, trunk ◆ *vb* **10 stem from** = **originate from,** arise from, be bred by, be brought about by, be caused by, be generated by, derive from, develop from, emanate from, flow from, issue forth from

the main upright timber or structure at the bow of a vessel. **9b** the very forward end of a vessel (esp. in **from stem to stern**). ◆ *vb* **stems, stemming, stemmed. 10** (*intr;* usually foll. by *from*) to be derived; originate. **11** (*tr*) to make headway against (a tide, wind, etc.). **12** (*tr*) to remove or disengage the stem or stems from. [OE *stemn*]
▸**'stem,like** *adj*

stem² ❶ (stɛm) *vb* **stems, stemming, stemmed. 1** (*tr*) to restrain or stop (the flow of something) by or as if by damming up. **2** (*tr*) to pack tightly or stop up. **3** *Skiing.* to manoeuvre (a ski or skis), as in performing a stem. ◆ *n* **4** *Skiing.* a technique in which the heel of one ski or both skis is forced outwards from the direction of movement in order to slow down or turn. [C15 *stemmen,* from ON *stemma*]

stem cell *n Histology.* an undifferentiated cell that gives rise to specialized cells, such as blood cells.

stem ginger *n* choice pieces of the underground stem of the ginger plant which are crystallized or preserved in syrup and eaten as a sweetmeat.

stemma ('stɛmə) *n* a family tree; pedigree. [C19: via L from Gk *stema* garland, wreath, from *stephein* to crown, wreathe]

stemmed (stɛmd) *adj* **1a** having a stem. **1b** (*in combination*): *a long-stemmed glass.* **2** having had the stem or stems removed.

stem turn *n Skiing.* a turn in which the heel of one ski is stemmed and the other ski is brought parallel. Also called: **stem.**

stench ❶ (stɛntʃ) *n* a strong and extremely offensive odour; stink. [OE *stenc*]

stencil ('stɛnsᵊl) *n* **1** a device for applying a design, characters, etc., to a surface, consisting of a thin sheet of plastic, metal, etc., in which the design or characters have been cut so that ink or paint can be applied through the incisions onto the surface. **2** a design or characters produced in this way. ◆ *vb* **stencils, stencilling, stencilled** *or US* **stencils, stenciling, stenciled.** (*tr*) **3** to mark (a surface) with a stencil. **4** to produce (characters or a design) with a stencil. [C14 *stanselen* to decorate with bright colours, from OF *estenceler,* from *estencele* a spark, from L *scintilla*]

Sten gun (stɛn) *n* a light 9mm sub-machine-gun formerly used in the British Army. [C20: from *S* & *T* (initials of Shepherd & Turpin, the inventors) + *-en,* as in BREN GUN]

steno- *or before a vowel* **sten-** *combining form.* indicating narrowness or contraction: *stenography; stenosis.* [from Gk *stenos* narrow]

stenograph ('stɛnə,grɑːf) *n* **1** any of various keyboard machines for writing in shorthand. **2** any character used in shorthand. ◆ *vb* **3** (*tr*) to record (minutes, letters, etc.) in shorthand.

stenographer (stə'nɒgrəfə) *n* the US & Canad. name for **shorthand typist.**

stenography (stə'nɒgrəfɪ) *n* **1** the act or process of writing in shorthand by hand or machine. **2** matter written in shorthand.
▸**stenographic** (,stɛnə'græfɪk) *adj*

stenosis (stɪ'nəʊsɪs) *n, pl* **stenoses** (-siːz). *Pathol.* an abnormal narrowing of a bodily canal or passage. [C19: via NL from Gk *stenōsis,* ult. from *stenos* narrow]
▸**stenotic** (stɪ'nɒtɪk) *adj*

Stenotype ('stɛnə,taɪp) *n* **1** *Trademark.* a machine with a keyboard for recording speeches, etc., in a phonetic shorthand. **2** any machine resembling this. **3** the phonetic symbol typed in one stroke of such a machine.

stenotypy ('stɛnə,taɪpɪ) *n* a form of shorthand in which alphabetic combinations are used to represent groups of sounds or short common words.
▸**'steno,typist** *n*

Stentor ('stɛntɔː) *n* **1** *Greek myth.* a Greek herald with a powerful voice who died after he lost a shouting contest with Hermes, herald of the gods. **2** (*not cap.*) any person with an unusually loud voice.

stentorian (stɛn'tɔːrɪən) *adj* (of the voice, etc.) uncommonly loud: *stentorian tones.* [C17: after STENTOR]

step ❶ (stɛp) *n* **1** the act of raising the foot and setting it down again in coordination with the transference of the weight of the body. **2** the distance or space covered by such a motion. **3** the sound made by such a movement. **4** the impression made by such movement of the foot; footprint. **5** the manner of walking or moving the feet; gait: *a proud step.* **6** a sequence of foot movements that make up a particular dance or part of a dance: *the steps of the waltz.* **7** any of several paces or rhythmic movements in marching, dancing, etc.: *the goose step.* **8** (*pl*) a course followed by a person in walking or as walking: *they followed in their leader's steps.* **9** one of a sequence of separate consecutive stages in the progression towards some goal. **10** a rank or grade in a series or scale. **11** an object or device that offers support for the foot when ascending or descending. **12** (*pl*) a flight of stairs, esp. out of doors. **13** (*pl*) another name for **stepladder. 14** a very short easily walked distance: *it is only a step.* **15** *Music.* a melodic interval of a second. **16** an offset or change in the level of a surface similar to the step of a stair. **17** a strong block or frame bolted onto the keel of a vessel and fitted to receive the base of a mast. **18** a ledge cut in mining or quarrying excavations. **19 break step.** to cease to march in step. **20 in step. 20a** marching, dancing, etc., in conformity with a specified pace or moving in unison with others. **20b** *Inf.* in agreement or harmony. **21 keep step.** to remain walking, marching, dancing, etc., in unison or in a specified rhythm. **22 out of step. 22a** not moving in conformity with a specified pace or in accordance with others. **22b** *Inf.* not in agreement; out of harmony. **23 step by step.** with care and deliberation; gradually. **24 take steps.** to undertake measures (to do something). **25 watch one's step. 25a** *Inf.* to conduct oneself with caution and good behaviour. **25b** to walk or move carefully. ◆ *vb* **steps, stepping, stepped. 26** (*intr*) to move by raising the foot and then setting it down in a different position, transferring the weight of the body to this foot and repeating the process with the other foot. **27** (*intr;* often foll. by *in, out,* etc.) to move or go on foot, esp. for a short distance: *step this way.* **28** (*intr*) *Inf., chiefly US.* to move, often in an attractive graceful manner, as in dancing: *he can really step around.* **29** (*intr;* usually foll. by *on* or *upon*) to place or press the foot; tread: *to step on the accelerator.* **30** (*intr;* usually foll. by *into*) to enter (into a situation) apparently with ease: *she stepped into a life of luxury.* **31** (*tr*) to walk or take (a number of paces, etc.): *to step ten paces.* **32** (*tr*) to perform the steps of: *they step the tango well.* **33** (*tr*) to set or place (the foot). **34** (*tr;* usually foll. by *off* or *out*) to measure (some distance of ground) by stepping. **35** (*tr*) to arrange in or supply with a series of steps so as to avoid coincidence or symmetry. **36** (*tr*) to raise (a mast) and fit it into its step. ◆ See also **step down, step in,** etc. [OE *stepe, stæpe*]
▸**'step,like** *adj*

Step (stɛp) *n* **a** a set of aerobic exercises designed to improve the cardiovascular system, which consists of stepping on and off a special box of adjustable height. **b** (*as modifer*): *Step aerobics.*

step- *combining form.* indicating relationship through the previous marriage of a spouse or parent: *stepson; stepfather.* [OE *stēop-*]

stepbrother ('stɛp,brʌðə) *n* a son of one's stepmother or stepfather by a union with someone other than one's father or mother.

stepchild ('stɛp,tʃaɪld) *n, pl* **stepchildren.** a stepson or stepdaughter.

stepdaughter ('stɛp,dɔːtə) *n* a daughter of one's husband or wife by a former union.

step down ❶ *vb* (*adv*) **1** (*tr*) to reduce gradually. **2** (*intr*) *Inf.* to resign or abdicate (from a position). **3** (*intr*) *Inf.* to assume an inferior or less senior position. ◆ *adj* **step-down.** (*prenominal*) **4** (of a transformer) reducing a high voltage to a lower voltage. Cf. **step-up** (sense 3). ◆ *n* **step-down. 5** *Inf.* a decrease in quantity or size.

stepfather ('stɛp,fɑːðə) *n* a man who has married one's mother after the death or divorce of one's father.

stephanotis (,stɛfə'nəʊtɪs) *n* any of various climbing shrubs of Madagascar and Malaya, cultivated for their fragrant white waxy flowers. [C19: via NL from Gk: fit for a crown, from *stephanos* a crown]

step in ❶ *vb* **1** (*intr, adv*) *Inf.* to intervene or involve oneself. ◆ *adj* **step-in. 2** (*prenominal*) (of garments, etc.) put on by being stepped into; without fastenings. **3** (of a ski binding) engaging automatically when the boot is positioned on the ski. ◆ *n* **step-in. 4** (*often pl*) a step-in garment, esp. underwear.

stepladder ('stɛp,lædə) *n* a folding portable ladder that is made of broad flat steps fixed to a supporting frame hinged at the top to another supporting frame.

stepmother ('stɛp,mʌðə) *n* a woman who has married one's father after the death or divorce of one's mother.

step on *vb* (*intr, prep*) **1** to place or press the foot on. **2** *Inf.* to behave harshly or contemptuously towards. **3 step on it.** *Inf.* to go more quickly; hurry up.

step out *vb* (*intr, adv*) **1** to go outside or leave a room, etc., esp. briefly. **2** to begin to walk more quickly and take longer strides. **3** *US & Canad. inf.* to withdraw from involvement.

step-parent ('stɛp,pɛərənt) *n* a stepfather or stepmother.
▸**'step-,parenting** *n*

steppe (stɛp) *n* (*often pl*) an extensive grassy plain usually without trees. [C17: from ORussian *step* lowland]

stepper ('stɛpə) *n* a person who or animal that steps, esp. a horse or a dancer.

stepping stone *n* **1** one of a series of stones acting as footrests for crossing streams, marshes, etc. **2** a circumstance that assists progress towards some goal.

stepsister ('stɛp,sɪstə) *n* a daughter of one's stepmother or stepfather by a union with someone other than one's father or mother.

stepson ('stɛp,sʌn) *n* a son of one's husband or wife by a former union.

THESAURUS

stem² *vb* **1** = **stop,** bring to a standstill, check, contain, curb, dam, hold back, oppose, resist, restrain, stanch, staunch, stay (*arch.*), withstand

stench *n* = **stink,** foul smell, malodour, mephitis, niff (*Brit. sl.*), noisomeness, pong (*Brit. inf.*), reek, whiff (*Brit. sl.*)

step *n* **1** = **footstep,** footfall, footprint, impression, pace, print, stride, trace, track **5** = **gait,** walk **9** = **stage,** advance, advancement, move, phase, point, process, progression **10** = **degree,** level, rank, remove **11** = **stair,** doorstep, round, rung, tread **20 in step** *Informal* = **in agreement,** coinciding, conforming, in conformity, in harmony, in line, in unison **22 out of step** *Informal* = **in disagreement,** erratic, incongruous, out of harmony, out of line, out of phase, pulling different ways **24 take steps** = **take action,** act, intervene, move in, prepare, take measures, take the initiative **25 watch one's step** *Informal* = **be careful,** be canny, be cautious, be discreet, be on one's guard, have one's wits about one, look out, mind how one goes, mind one's p's and q's, take care, take heed, tread carefully ◆ *vb* **26** = **walk,** move, pace, tread

step down *vb* **2** *Informal* = **resign,** abdicate, bow out, give up, hand over, leave, pull out, quit, retire

step in *vb* **1** *Informal* = **intervene,** become involved, chip in (*inf.*), intercede, take action, take a hand

step up ⓘ *vb (adv) Inf.* **1** (*tr*) to increase or raise by stages; accelerate. **2** (*intr*) to make progress or effect an advancement; be promoted. ◆ *adj* **step-up.** (*prenominal*) **3** (of a transformer) increasing a low voltage to a higher voltage. Cf. **step-down** (sense 4). ◆ *n* **step-up. 4** *Inf.* an increment in quantity, size, etc.

-ster *suffix forming nouns.* **1** indicating a person who is engaged in a certain activity: *prankster; songster.* **2** indicating a person associated with or being something specified: *mobster; youngster.* [OE *-estre*]

steradian (stəˈreɪdɪən) *n* an SI unit of solid angle; the angle that, having its vertex in the centre of a sphere, cuts off an area of the surface of the sphere equal to the square of the length of the radius. Symbol: sr [C19: from STEREO- + RADIAN]

stercoraceous (ˌstɜːkəˈreɪʃəs) *adj* of, relating to, or consisting of dung or excrement. [C18: from L *stercus* dung + -ACEOUS]

stere (stɪə) *n* a unit used to measure volumes of stacked timber equal to one cubic metre (35.315 cubic feet). [C18: from F *stère,* from Gk *stereos* solid]

stereo (ˈsterɪəʊ, ˈstɪər-) *adj* **1** short for **stereophonic** or **stereoscopic.** ◆ *n, pl* **stereos. 2** stereophonic sound: *to broadcast in stereo.* **3** a stereophonic record player, tape recorder, etc. **4** *Photog.* **4a** stereoscopic photography. **4b** a stereoscopic photograph. **5** *Printing.* short for **stereotype.** [C20: shortened form]

stereo- *or sometimes before a vowel* **stere-** *combining form.* indicating three-dimensional quality or solidity: *stereoscope.* [from Gk *stereos* solid]

stereochemistry (ˌsterɪəʊˈkemɪstrɪ, ˌstɪər-) *n* the study of the spatial arrangement of atoms in molecules and its effect on chemical properties.

stereograph (ˈsterɪəˌgrɑːf, ˈstɪər-) *n* two almost identical pictures, or one special picture, that when viewed through special glasses or a stereoscope form a single three-dimensional image. Also called: **stereogram.**

stereoisomer (ˌsterɪəʊˈaɪsəmə, ˌstɪər-) *n Chem.* an isomer that exhibits stereoisomerism.

stereoisomerism (ˌsterɪəʊaɪˈsɒməˌrɪzəm, ˌstɪər-) *n Chem.* isomerism caused by differences in the spatial arrangement of atoms in molecules.

stereophonic (ˌsterɪəˈfɒnɪk, ˌstɪər-) *adj* (of a system for recording, reproducing, or broadcasting sound) using two or more separate microphones to feed two or more loudspeakers through separate channels in order to give a spatial effect to the sound. Often shortened to **stereo.**
▸ˌ**stereoˈphonically** *adv* ▸**stereophony** (ˌsterɪˈɒfənɪ, ˌstɪər-) *n*

stereoscope (ˈsterɪəˌskəʊp, ˈstɪər-) *n* an optical instrument for viewing two-dimensional pictures, giving an illusion of depth and relief. It has a binocular eyepiece through which two slightly different pictures of an object are viewed, one with each eye.
▸**stereoscopic** (ˌsterɪəˈskɒpɪk, ˌstɪər-) *adj*

stereoscopy (ˌsterɪˈɒskəpɪ, ˌstɪər-) *n* **1** the viewing or appearance of objects in or as if in three dimensions. **2** the study and use of the stereoscope.
▸ˌ**stereˈoscopist** *n*

stereospecific (ˌsterɪəʊspɪˈsɪfɪk, ˌstɪər-) *adj Chem.* relating to or having fixed position in space, as in the spatial arrangements of atoms in certain polymers.

stereotype ⓘ (ˈsterɪəˌtaɪp, ˈstɪər-) *n* **1a** a method of producing cast-metal printing plates from a mould made from a forme of type. **1b** the plate so made. **2** another word for **stereotypy. 3** an idea, convention, etc., that has grown stale through fixed usage. **4** a standardized image or conception of a type of person, etc. ◆ *vb* **stereotypes, stereotyping, stereotyped.** (*tr*) **5a** to make a stereotype of. **5b** to print from a stereotype. **6** to impart a fixed usage or convention to.
▸ˈ**stereoˌtyper** *or* ˈ**stereoˌtypist** *n*

stereotyped ⓘ (ˈsterɪəˌtaɪpt, ˈstɪər-) *adj* **1** lacking originality or individuality; conventional; trite. **2** reproduced from or on a stereotype printing plate.

stereotypy (ˈsterɪəˌtaɪpɪ, ˈstɪər-) *n* **1** the act or process of making stereotype printing plates. **2** a tendency to think or act in rigid, repetitive, and often meaningless patterns.

stereovision (ˈsterɪəʊˌvɪʒən, ˈstɪər-) *n* the perception or exhibition of three-dimensional objects in three dimensions.

steric (ˈsterɪk, ˈstɪər-) *or* **sterical** *adj Chem.* of or caused by the spatial arrangement of atoms in a molecule. [C19: from STEREO- + -IC]

sterile ⓘ (ˈsteraɪl) *adj* **1** unable to produce offspring; permanently infertile. **2** free from living, esp. pathogenic, microorganisms. **3** (of plants or their parts) not producing or bearing seeds, fruit, spores, stamens, or pistils. **4** lacking inspiration or vitality; fruitless. [C16: from L *sterilis*]
▸ˈ**sterilely** *adv* ▸**sterility** (steˈrɪlɪtɪ) *n*

sterilize ⓘ *or* **sterilise** (ˈsterɪˌlaɪz) *vb* **sterilizes, sterilizing, sterilized** *or* **sterilises, sterilising, sterilised.** (*tr*) to render sterile; make infertile or barren.
▸ˌ**steriliˈzation** *or* ˌ**steriliˈsation** *n* ▸ˈ**steriˌlizer** *or* ˈ**steriˌliser** *n*

sterling ⓘ (ˈstɜːlɪŋ) *n* **1a** British money: *pound sterling.* **1b** (*as modifier*): *sterling reserves.* **2** the official standard of purity of British coins. **3a** short for **sterling silver. 3b** (*as modifier*): *a sterling bracelet.* **4** an article or articles manufactured from sterling silver. ◆ *adj* **5** (*prenominal*) genuine and reliable: first-class: *sterling quality.* [C13: prob. from OE *steorra* star + -LING[1]; referring to a small star on early Norman pennies]

sterling area *n* a group of countries that use sterling as a medium of international payments. Also called: **scheduled territories.**

sterling silver *n* **1** an alloy containing not less than 92.5 per cent of silver. **2** sterling-silver articles collectively.

stern[1] ⓘ (stɜːn) *adj* **1** showing uncompromising or inflexible resolve; firm or authoritarian. **2** lacking leniency or clemency. **3** relentless; unyielding: *the stern demands of parenthood.* **4** having an austere or forbidding appearance or nature. [OE *styrne*]
▸ˈ**sternly** *adv* ▸ˈ**sternness** *n*

stern[2] (stɜːn) *n* **1** the rear or after part of a vessel, opposite the bow or stem. **2** the rear part of any object. ◆ *adj* **3** relating to or located at the stern. [C13: from ON *stjórn* steering]

sternforemost (ˈstɜːnˈfɔːməʊst) *adv Naut.* backwards.

sternmost (ˈstɜːnˌməʊst) *adj Naut.* **1** farthest to the stern; aftmost. **2** nearest the stern.

sternpost (ˈstɜːnˌpəʊst) *n Naut.* the main upright timber or structure at the stern of a vessel.

stern sheets *pl n Naut.* the part of an open boat near the stern.

sternum (ˈstɜːnəm) *n, pl* **sterna** (-nə) *or* **sternums. 1** (in man) a long flat vertical bone in front of the thorax, to which are attached the collarbone and the first seven pairs of ribs. Nontechnical name: **breastbone. 2** the corresponding part in many other vertebrates. [C17: via NL from Gk *sternon* breastbone]
▸ˈ**sternal** *adj*

sternutation (ˌstɜːnjuˈteɪʃən) *n* a sneeze or the act of sneezing. [C16: from LL *sternūtāre* to sneeze, from *sternuere* to sputter (of a light)]

sternutator (ˈstɜːnjuˌteɪtə) *n* a substance that causes sneezing, coughing, and tears; used in chemical warfare.
▸**sternutatory** (stɜːˈnjuːtətərɪ, -trɪ) *adj, n*

sternwards (ˈstɜːnwədz) *or* **sternward** *adv Naut.* towards the stern; astern.

sternway (ˈstɜːnˌweɪ) *n Naut.* movement of a vessel sternforemost.

stern-wheeler *n* a vessel, esp. a river boat, propelled by a large paddle wheel at the stern.

steroid (ˈstɪərɔɪd, ˈster-) *n Biochem.* any of a large group of organic compounds containing a characteristic chemical ring system, including sterols, bile acids, many hormones, and the D vitamins. [C20: from STEROL + -OID]
▸**steˈroidal** *adj*

sterol (ˈsterɒl) *n Biochem.* any of a group of natural steroid alcohols, such as cholesterol and ergosterol, that are waxy insoluble substances. [C20: shortened from CHOLESTEROL, ERGOSTEROL, etc.]

stertorous (ˈstɜːtərəs) *adj* **1** marked by heavy snoring. **2** breathing in this way. [C19: from L *stertere* to snore]
▸ˈ**stertorously** *adv* ▸ˈ**stertorousness** *n*

stet (stet) *n* **1** a word or mark indicating that certain deleted typeset or written matter is to be retained. ◆ *vb* **stets, stetting, stetted. 2** (*tr*) to mark (matter) thus. [L, lit.: let it stand]

stethoscope (ˈsteθəˌskəʊp) *n Med.* an instrument for listening to the sounds made within the body, typically consisting of a hollow disc that transmits the sound through hollow tubes to earpieces. [C19: from F, from Gk *stēthos* breast + -SCOPE]
▸**stethoscopic** (ˌsteθəˈskɒpɪk) *adj* ▸**stethoscopy** (steˈθɒskəpɪ) *n*

Stetson (ˈstetsᵊn) *n Trademark.* a type of felt hat with a broad brim and high crown, worn mainly by cowboys. [C20: after John *Stetson* (1830–1906), US hat-maker]

stevedore (ˈstiːvɪˌdɔː) *n* **1** a person employed to load or unload ships. ◆ *vb* **stevedores, stevedoring, stevedored. 2** to load or unload (a ship, ship's cargo, etc.). [C18: from Sp. *estibador* a packer, from *estibar* to load (a ship), from L *stīpāre* to pack full]

stew[1] ⓘ (stjuː) *n* **1a** a dish of meat, fish, or other food, cooked by stewing. **1b** (*as modifier*): *stew pot.* **2** *Inf.* a difficult or worrying situation or a troubled state (esp. in **in a stew**). **3** a heterogeneous mixture: *a stew of*

THESAURUS

step up *vb* **1** *Informal* = **increase**, accelerate, augment, boost, escalate, intensify, raise, speed up, up

stereotype *n* **3** = **formula**, mould, pattern, received idea ◆ *vb* **6** = **categorize**, conventionalize, dub, ghettoize, pigeonhole, standardize, take to be, typecast

stereotyped *adj* **1** = **unoriginal**, banal, cliché-ridden, conventional, corny (*sl.*), hackneyed, mass-produced, overused, platitudinous, played out, stale, standard, standardized, stock, threadbare, tired, trite

sterile *adj* **1** = **barren**, abortive, bare, dry, empty, fruitless, infecund, unfruitful, unproductive, unprofitable, unprolific **2** = **germ-free**, antiseptic, aseptic, disinfected, sterilized
Antonyms *adj* ≠ **barren**: fecund, fertile, fruitful, productive, prolific ≠ **germ-free**: contaminated, dirty, germ-ridden, infected, insanitary, unhygienic, unsterile

sterilize *vb* = **disinfect**, autoclave, fumigate, purify

sterling *adj* **5** = **excellent**, authentic, fine, first-class, genuine, pure, real, sound, standard, substantial, superlative, true

stern[1] *adj* **1-3** = **strict**, austere, authoritarian, cruel, drastic, grim, hard, harsh, inflexible, relentless, rigid, rigorous, unrelenting, unsparing, unyielding **4** = **severe**, flinty, forbidding, frowning, serious, steely
Antonyms *adj* ≠ **strict**: compassionate, flexible, gentle, kind, lenient, liberal, permissive, soft, sympathetic, tolerant ≠ **severe**: amused, approachable, friendly, warm

stew[1] *n* **1b** = **hash**, goulash, olio, olla, olla podrida, potpourri, ragout **2 in a stew** *Informal* = **troubled**, anxious, concerned, fretting, in a lather (*inf.*), in a panic, worrying **3** = **mixture**, blend, hash, hodgepodge (*US & Canad.*), hotchpotch, medley, miscellany, mix, olio, olla, potpourri people of every race. **4** (*usually pl*) *Arch.* a brothel. ◆ *vb* **5** to cook or cause to cook by long slow simmering. **6** (*intr*) *Inf.* to be troubled or agitated. **7** (*intr*) *Inf.* to be oppressed with heat or crowding. **8** to cause (tea) to become bitter or (of tea) to become bitter through infusing for too long. **9 stew in one's own juice.** to suffer unaided the consequences of one's actions. [C14 *stuen* to take a very hot bath, from OF *estuver*, from Vulgar L *extūfāre* (unattested), from EX-[1] + (unattested) *tūfus* vapour, from Gk *tuphos*]

stew[2] (stju:) *n Brit.* **1** a fishpond or fishtank. **2** an artificial oyster bed. [C14: from OF *estui*, from *estoier* to confine, ult. from L *studium* STUDY]

steward (stjuəd) *n* **1** a person who administers the property, house, finances, etc., of another. **2** a person who manages the eating arrangements, staff, or service at a club, hotel, etc. **3** a waiter on a ship or aircraft. **4** a mess attendant in a naval mess. **5** a person who helps to supervise some event or proceedings in an official capacity. **6** short for **shop steward.** ◆ *vb* **7** to act or serve as a steward (of something). [OE *stigweard*, from *stig* hall + *weard* WARD]
▸**'stewardship** *n*

stewardess ('stjuədɪs, ˌstjuə'dɛs) *n* a woman steward on an aircraft or ship.

stewed (stju:d) *adj* **1** (of meat, fish, etc.) cooked by stewing. **2** *Brit.* (of tea) bitter through having been left to infuse for too long. **3** a slang word for **drunk** (sense 1).

stg *abbrev. for* sterling.

sthenic ('sθɛnɪk) *adj* abounding in energy or bodily strength; active or strong. [C18: from NL *sthenicus*, from Gk *sthenos* force, on the model of *asthenic*]

stibine ('stɪbaɪn) *n* **1** a colourless poisonous gas with an offensive odour: made by the action of hydrochloric acid on an alloy of antimony and zinc. **2** any one of a class of stibine derivatives in which one or more hydrogen atoms have been replaced by organic groups. [C19: from L *stibium* antimony + -INE[2]]

stibnite ('stɪbnaɪt) *n* a soft greyish mineral consisting of antimony sulphide in crystalline form: the chief ore of antimony. [C19: from obs. *stibine* stibnite + -ITE[1]]

-stichous *adj combining form.* having a certain number of rows. [from LL *-stichus*, from Gk *-stikhos*, from *stikhos* row]

stick[1] ➊ (stɪk) *n* **1** a small thin branch of a tree. **2a** any long thin piece of wood. **2b** such a piece of wood having a characteristic shape for a special purpose: *a walking stick; a hockey stick.* **2c** a baton, wand, staff, or rod. **3** an object or piece shaped like a stick: *a stick of celery.* **4** In full: **control stick.** the lever by which a pilot controls the movements of an aircraft. **5** *Inf.* the lever used to change gear in a motor vehicle. **6** *Naut.* a mast or yard. **7a** a group of bombs arranged to fall at intervals across a target. **7b** a number of paratroops jumping in sequence. **8** *Sl.* **8a** verbal abuse, criticism: *I got some stick for that blunder.* **8b** physical power, force (esp. in **give it some stick**). **9** (*usually pl*) a piece of furniture: *these few sticks are all I have.* **10** (*pl*) *Inf.* a rural area considered remote or backward (esp. in **in the sticks**). **11** (*pl*) *Hockey.* a declaration made by the umpire if a player's stick is above the shoulders. **12** (*pl*) goalposts. **13** *Inf.* a dull boring person. **14** (usually preceded by *old*) *Inf.* a familiar name for a person: *not a bad old stick.* **15** punishment; beating. **16 in a cleft stick.** in a difficult position. **17 wrong end of the stick.** a complete misunderstanding of a situation, explanation, etc. ◆ *vb* **sticks, sticking, sticked. 18** to support (a plant) with sticks; stake. [OE *sticca*]

stick[2] ➊ (stɪk) *vb* **sticks, sticking, stuck. 1** (*tr*) to pierce or stab with or as if with something pointed. **2** to thrust or push (a sharp or pointed object) or (of a sharp or pointed object) to be pushed into or through another object. **3** (*tr*) to fasten in position by pushing or forcing a point into something: *to stick a peg in a hole.* **4** (*tr*) to fasten in position by or as if by pins, nails, etc.: *to stick a picture on the wall.* **5** (*tr*) to transfix or impale on a pointed object. **6** (*tr*) to cover with objects piercing or set in the surface. **7** (when *intr*, foll. by *out, up, through*, etc.) to put forward or be put forward; protrude or cause to protrude: *to stick one's head out.* **8** (*tr*) *Inf.* to place or put in a specified position: *stick your coat on this chair.* **9** to fasten or be fastened by or as if by an adhesive substance: *stick the pages together; they won't stick.* **10** (*tr*) *Inf.* to cause to become sticky. **11** (when *tr*, *usually passive*) to come or cause to come to a standstill: *stuck in a traffic jam; the wheels stuck.* **12** (*intr*) to remain for a long time: *the memory sticks in my mind.* **13** (*tr*) *Sl., chiefly Brit.* to tolerate; abide: *I can't stick that man.* **14** (*intr*) to be reluctant. **15** (*tr; usually passive*) *Inf.* to cause to be at a loss; baffle or puzzle: *I was totally stuck for an answer.* **16** (*tr*) *Sl.* to force or impose something unpleasant on: *they stuck me with the bill.* **17** (*tr*) to kill by piercing or stabbing. **18 stick to the ribs.** *Inf.* (of food) to be hearty and satisfying. ◆ *n* **19** the state or condition of adhering. **20** *Inf.* a substance causing adhesion. **21** *Obs.* something that causes delay or stoppage. ◆ See also **stick around, stick by,** etc. [OE *stician*]

stick around *or* **about** *vb* (*intr, adv*) *Inf.* to remain in a place, esp. awaiting something.

stick by *vb* (*intr, prep*) to remain faithful to; adhere to.

sticker ('stɪkə) *n* **1** an adhesive label, poster, or paper. **2** a person or thing that sticks. **3** a persevering or industrious person. **4** something prickly, such as a thorn, that clings to one's clothing, etc. **5** *Inf.* something that perplexes. **6** *Inf.* a knife used for stabbing or piercing.

stickhandle ('stɪkˌhænd[ə]l) *vb* **stickhandles, stickhandling, stickhandled.** *Ice hockey.* to manoeuvre (the puck) deftly.

sticking plaster *n* a thin cloth with an adhesive substance on one side, used for covering slight or superficial wounds.

stick insect *n* any of various mostly tropical insects that have an elongated cylindrical body and long legs and resemble twigs.

stick-in-the-mud ➊ *n Inf.* a conservative person who lacks initiative or imagination.

stickle ('stɪk[ə]l) *vb* **stickles, stickling, stickled.** (*intr*) **1** to dispute stubbornly, esp. about minor points. **2** to refuse to agree or concur, esp. by making petty stipulations. [C16 *stightle* (in the sense: to arbitrate): frequentative of OE *stihtan* to arrange]

stickleback ('stɪk[ə]lˌbæk) *n* any of various small fishes that have a series of spines along the back and occur in cold and temperate northern regions. [C15: from OE *stickel* prick, sting + BACK]

stickler ➊ ('stɪklə) *n* **1** (usually foll. by *for*) a person who makes insistent demands: *a stickler for accuracy.* **2** a problem or puzzle.

stick out ➊ *vb* (*adv*) **1** to project or cause to project. **2** (*tr*) *Inf.* to endure (something disagreeable) (esp. in **stick it out**). **3 stick out a mile** *or* **like a sore thumb.** *Inf.* to be extremely obvious. **4 stick out for.** to insist on (a demand), refusing to yield until it is met.

stick shift *n US & Canad.* **1a** a manually operated transmission system in a motor vehicle. **1b** a motor vehicle having manual transmission. **2** a gear lever.

stick to ➊ *vb* (*prep, mainly intr*) **1** (*also tr*) to adhere or cause to adhere to. **2** to continue constantly at. **3** to remain faithful to. **4** not to move or digress from: *the speaker stuck closely to his subject.* **5 stick to someone's fingers.** *Inf.* to be stolen by someone.

stick-up ➊ *n* **1** *Sl., chiefly US.* a robbery at gunpoint; hold-up. ◆ *vb* **stick up.** (*adv*) **2** (*tr*) *Sl., chiefly US.* to rob, esp. at gunpoint. **3** (*intr;* foll. by *for*) *Inf.* to support or defend: *stick up for oneself.*

sticky ➊ ('stɪkɪ) *adj* **stickier, stickiest. 1** covered or daubed with an adhesive or viscous substance: *sticky fingers.* **2** having the property of sticking to a surface. **3** (of weather or atmosphere) warm and humid; muggy. **4** *Inf.* difficult, awkward, or painful: *a sticky business.* ◆ *vb* **stickies, stickying, stickied. 5** (*tr*) *Inf.* to make sticky.
▸**'stickily** *adv* ▸**'stickiness** *n*

stickybeak ('stɪkɪˌbi:k) *Austral. & NZ inf.* ◆ *n* **1** an inquisitive person. ◆ *vb* **2** (*intr*) to pry.

sticky end *n Inf.* an unpleasant finish or death (esp. in **come to** *or* **meet a sticky end**).

sticky wicket *n* **1** a cricket pitch that is rapidly being dried by the sun after rain and is particularly conducive to spin. **2** *Inf.* a difficult or awkward situation.

stiff ➊ (stɪf) *adj* **1** not easily bent; rigid; inflexible. **2** not working or moving easily or smoothly: *a stiff handle.* **3** difficult to accept in its severity or harshness: *a stiff punishment.* **4** moving with pain or difficulty; not supple: *a stiff neck.* **5** difficult; arduous: *a stiff climb.* **6** unrelaxed or awkward; formal. **7** firmer than liquid in consistency; thick or viscous. **8** powerful; strong: *a stiff breeze; a stiff drink.* **9** exces-

THESAURUS

stick[1] *n* **1-3** = **cane**, baton, birch, crook, pole, rod, sceptre, staff, stake, switch, twig, wand **8a** *Slang* = **abuse**, blame, criticism, flak (*inf.*), hostility, punishment **13** *Informal* = **(old) fogey**, dinosaur, fuddy-duddy (*inf.*), pain (*inf.*), prig, stick-in-the-mud (*inf.*)

stick[2] *vb* **1** = **poke**, dig, gore, insert, jab, penetrate, pierce, pin, prod, puncture, spear, stab, thrust, transfix **7** *with* **out, up, through** *etc.* = **protrude**, bulge, extend, jut, obtrude, poke, project, show **8** *Informal* = **put**, deposit, drop, fix, install, lay, place, plant, plonk, position, set, store, stuff **9** = **fasten**, adhere, affix, attach, bind, bond, cement, cleave, cling, fix, fuse, glue, hold, hold on, join, paste, weld **11** = **catch**, be bogged down, become immobilized, be embedded, clog, come to a standstill, jam, lodge, snag, stop **12** = **stay**, linger, persist, remain **13** *Slang* = **tolerate**, abide, bear up under, endure, get on with, hack (*sl.*), stand, stomach, take

stick-in-the-mud *n Informal* = **(old) fogey**, Colonel Blimp, conservative, die-hard, dinosaur, fuddy-duddy (*inf.*), reactionary, sobersides, stick (*inf.*)

stickler *n* **1** = **fanatic**, fusspot (*Brit. inf.*), hard taskmaster, maniac (*inf.*), martinet, nut (*sl.*), pedant, perfectionist, purist

stick out *vb* **2** *Informal* = **endure**, bear, grin and bear it (*inf.*), last out, put up with (*inf.*), see through, soldier on, take it (*inf.*), weather

stick to *vb* **1-4** = **remain faithful**, adhere to, cleave to, continue in, honour, keep, persevere in, remain loyal, remain true, stick at

stick up for *vb* **3** *Informal* = **defend**, champion, stand up for, support, take the part *or* side of, uphold

sticky *adj* **1** = **tacky**, adhesive, claggy, clinging, gluey, glutinous, gooey (*inf.*), gummy, syrupy, tenacious, viscid, viscous **3** = **humid**, clammy, close, muggy, oppressive, sultry, sweltering **4** *Informal* = **difficult**, awkward, delicate, discomforting, embarrassing, hairy (*sl.*), nasty, painful, thorny, tricky, unpleasant

stiff *adj* **1** = **inflexible**, brittle, firm, hard, hardened, inelastic, rigid, solid, solidified, taut, tense, tight, unbending, unyielding **3** = **severe**, austere, cruel, drastic, extreme, great, hard, harsh, heavy, inexorable, oppressive, pitiless, rigorous, sharp, strict, stringent **4** = **unsupple**, arthritic, creaky (*inf.*), rheumaticky **5** = **difficult**, arduous, exacting, fatiguing, formidable, hard, laborious, tough, trying, uphill **6** = **unrelaxed**, artificial, austere, ceremonious, chilly, cold, constrained, forced, formal, laboured, mannered, pompous, priggish, prim, punctilious, standoffish, starchy (*inf.*), stilted, uneasy, unnatural, wooden **8** = **powerful**, brisk, fresh, strong, vigorous **10** = **awkward**, clumsy, crude, graceless, inelegant, jerky (*inf.*), ungainly, ungraceful

Antonyms *adj* ≠ **inflexible:** bendable, ductile, elastic, flexible, pliable, pliant, yielding ≠ **unsupple:** flexible, limber, lissom(e), lithe, supple ≠ **unrelaxed:** casual, easy, informal, laid-back, natural, relaxed, spontaneous, unceremonious, unofficial

sively high: *a stiff price.* **10** lacking grace or attractiveness. **11** stubborn or stubbornly maintained: *a stiff fight.* **12** *Obs.* tightly stretched; taut. **13** *Sl.* intoxicated. **14 stiff with.** *Inf.* amply provided with. ◆ *n* **15** *Sl.* a corpse. **16** *Sl.* anything thought to be a loser or a failure; flop. ◆ *adv* **17** completely or utterly: *bored stiff; frozen stiff.* ◆ *vb* **18** (*intr*) *Sl.* to fail: *the film stiffed.* **19** (*tr*) *Sl., chiefly US.* to cheat or swindle. [OE *stīf*]
▸ **'stiffish** *adj* ▸ **'stiffly** *adv* ▸ **'stiffness** *n*

stiffen Ⓣ ('stɪfᵊn) *vb* **1** to make or become stiff or stiffer. **2** (*intr*) to become suddenly tense or unyielding.
▸ **'stiffener** *n*

stiff-necked Ⓣ *adj* haughtily stubborn or obstinate.

stifle Ⓣ ('staɪfᵊl) *vb* **stifles, stifling, stifled. 1** (*tr*) to smother or suppress: *stifle a cough.* **2** to feel or cause to feel discomfort and difficulty in breathing. **3** to prevent or be prevented from breathing so as to cause death. **4** (*tr*) to crush or stamp out. [C14: var. of *stuflen,* prob. from OF *estouffer* to smother]

stigma Ⓣ ('stɪgmə) *n, pl* **stigmas** *or* **stigmata** ('stɪgmətə, stɪg'mɑːtə). **1** a distinguishing mark of social disgrace: *the stigma of having been in prison.* **2** a small scar or mark such as a birthmark. **3** *Pathol.* any mark on the skin, such as one characteristic of a specific disease. **4** *Bot.* the terminal part of the ovary, at the end of the style, where deposited pollen enters the gynoecium. **5** *Zool.* **5a** a pigmented eyespot in some invertebrates. **5b** the spiracle of an insect. **6** *Arch.* a mark branded on the skin. **7** (*pl*) *Christianity.* marks resembling the wounds of the crucified Christ, believed to appear on the bodies of certain individuals. [C16: via L from Gk: brand, from *stizein* to tattoo]

stigmatic (stɪg'mætɪk) *adj* **1** relating to or having a stigma or stigmata. **2** another word for **anastigmatic.** ◆ *n also* **stigmatist** ('stɪgmətɪst). **3** *Chiefly RC Church.* a person marked with the stigmata.

stigmatism ('stɪgmə,tɪzəm) *n* **1** *Physics.* the state or condition of being anastigmatic. **2** *Pathol.* the condition resulting from or characterized by stigmata.

stigmatize Ⓣ *or* **stigmatise** ('stɪgmə,taɪz) *vb* **stigmatizes, stigmatizing, stigmatized** *or* **stigmatises, stigmatising, stigmatised.** (*tr*) **1** to mark out or describe (as something bad). **2** to mark with a stigma or stigmata.
▸ **,stigmati'zation** *or* **,stigmati'sation** *n* ▸ **'stigma,tizer** *or* **'stigma,tiser** *n*

stilbene ('stɪlbiːn) *n* a colourless or slightly yellow crystalline unsaturated hydrocarbon used in the manufacture of dyes. [C19: from Gk *stilbos* glittering + -ENE]

stilboestrol *or US* **stilbestrol** (stɪl'biːstrəl) *n* a synthetic hormone having derivatives with oestrogenic properties. Also called: **diethylstilboestrol.** [C20: from STILBENE + OESTRUS + -OL[1]]

stile[1] (staɪl) *n* **1** a set of steps or rungs in a wall or fence to allow people, but not animals, to pass over. **2** short for **turnstile.** [OE *stigel*]

stile[2] (staɪl) *n* a vertical framing member in a door, window frame, etc. [C17: prob. from Du. *stijl* pillar, ult. from L *stilus* writing instrument]

stiletto (stɪ'lɛtəʊ) *n, pl* **stilettos. 1** a small dagger with a slender tapered blade. **2** a sharply pointed tool used to make holes in leather, cloth, etc. **3** Also called: **spike heel, stiletto heel.** a very high heel on a woman's shoe, tapering to a very narrow tip. ◆ *vb* **stilettoes, stilettoeing, stilettoed. 4** (*tr*) to stab with a stiletto. [C17: from It., from *stilo* a dagger, from L *stilus* a stake, pen]

still[1] Ⓣ (stɪl) *adj* **1** (*usually predicative*) motionless; stationary. **2** undisturbed or tranquil; silent and calm. **3** not sparkling or effervescent. **4** gentle or quiet; subdued. **5** *Obs.* (of a child) dead at birth. ◆ *adv* **6** continuing now or in the future as in the past: *do you still love me?* **7** up to this or that time; yet: *I still don't know your name.* **8** (often used with a comparative) even or yet: *still more insults.* **9** quietly or without movement: *sit still.* **10** *Poetic & dialect.* always. ◆ *n* **11** *Poetic.* silence or tranquillity: *the still of the night.* **12a** a still photograph, esp. of a scene from a film. **12b** (*as modifier*): *a still camera.* ◆ *vb* **13** to make or become still, quiet, or calm. **14** (*tr*) to allay or relieve: *her fears were stilled.* ◆ *sentence connector.* **15** even then; nevertheless: *the child has some new toys and still cries.* [OE *stille*]
▸ **'stillness** *n*

still[2] (stɪl) *n* an apparatus for carrying out distillation, used esp. in the manufacture of spirits. [C16: from OF *stiller* to drip, from L *stillāre,* from *stilla* a drip]

stillage ('stɪlɪdʒ) *n* **1** a frame or stand for keeping things off the ground, such as casks in a brewery. **2** a container in which goods, machinery, etc., are transported. [C16: prob. from Du. *stillagie* frame, scaffold, from *stellen* to stand; see -AGE]

stillborn ('stɪl,bɔːn) *adj* **1** (of a fetus) dead at birth. **2** (of an idea, plan, etc.) fruitless; abortive; unsuccessful.
▸ **'still,birth** *n*

still life *n, pl* **still lifes. 1a** a painting or drawing of inanimate objects, such as fruit, flowers, etc. **1b** (*as modifier*): *a still-life painting.* **2** the genre of such paintings.

still room *n Brit.* **1** a room in which distilling is carried out. **2** a pantry or storeroom, as in a large house.

Stillson wrench ('stɪlsᵊn) *n Trademark.* a large wrench having adjustable jaws that tighten as the pressure on the handle is increased.

stilly *adv* ('stɪllɪ). **1** *Arch. or literary.* quietly or calmly. ◆ *adj* ('stɪlɪ). **2** *Poetic.* still, quiet, or calm.

stilt (stɪlt) *n* **1** either of a pair of two long poles with footrests on which a person stands and walks, as used by circus clowns. **2** a long post or column that is used with others to support a building above ground level. **3** any of several shore birds similar to the avocets but having a straight bill. ◆ *vb* **4** (*tr*) to raise or place on or as if on stilts. [C14 (in the sense: crutch, handle of a plough): rel. to Low G *stilte* pole]

stilted Ⓣ ('stɪltɪd) *adj* **1** (of speech, writing, etc.) formal, pompous, or bombastic. **2** not flowing continuously or naturally: *stilted conversation.* **3** *Archit.* (of an arch) having vertical piers between the impost and the springing.
▸ **'stiltedly** *adv* ▸ **'stiltedness** *n*

Stilton ('stɪltən) *n Trademark.* either of two rich cheeses, blue-veined (**blue Stilton**) or white (**white Stilton**), both very strong in flavour. [C18: named after *Stilton,* Cambridgeshire, where it was orig. sold]

stimulant Ⓣ ('stɪmjʊlənt) *n* **1** a drug or similar substance that increases physiological activity, esp. of a particular organ. **2** any stimulating agent or thing. ◆ *adj* **3** stimulating. [C18: from L *stimulāns* goading, from *stimulāre* to urge on]

stimulate Ⓣ ('stɪmjʊ,leɪt) *vb* **stimulates, stimulating, stimulated. 1** (*tr*) to arouse or quicken the activity or senses of. **2** (*tr*) *Physiol.* to excite (a nerve, organ, etc.) with a stimulus. **3** (*intr*) to act as a stimulant or stimulus. [C16: from L *stimulāre*]
▸ **'stimu,lating** *adj* ▸ **,stimu'lation** *n* ▸ **'stimulative** *adj, n* ▸ **'stimu,lator** *n*

stimulus Ⓣ ('stɪmjʊləs) *n, pl* **stimuli** (-,laɪ, -,liː). **1** something that stimulates or acts as an incentive. **2** any drug, agent, electrical impulse, or other factor able to cause a response in an organism. [C17: from L: a cattle goad]

sting Ⓣ (stɪŋ) *vb* **stings, stinging, stung. 1** (of certain animals and plants) to inflict a wound on (an organism) by the injection of poison. **2** to feel or cause to feel a sharp mental or physical pain. **3** (*tr*) to goad or incite (esp. in **sting into action**). **4** (*tr*) *Inf.* to cheat, esp. by overcharging. ◆ *n* **5** a skin wound caused by the poison injected by certain insects or plants. **6** pain caused by or as if by the sting of a plant or animal. **7** a mental pain or pang: *a sting of conscience.* **8** a sharp pointed organ, such as the ovipositor of a wasp, by which poison can be injected. **9** the ability to sting: *a sharp sting in his criticism.* **10** something as painful or swift of action as a sting: *the sting of death.* **11** a sharp stimulus or incitement. **12** *Sl.* a swindle or fraud. **13** *Sl.* a police trap, esp. one whereby a person is enticed into committing a crime for which he is then arrested. [OE *stingan*]
▸ **'stinger** *n* ▸ **'stinging** *adj*

stinging nettle *n* See **nettle** (sense 1).

stingray ('stɪŋ,reɪ) *n* any of various rays having a whiplike tail bearing a serrated venomous spine capable of inflicting painful weals.

stingy[1] Ⓣ ('stɪndʒɪ) *adj* **stingier, stingiest. 1** unwilling to spend or give. **2** insufficient or scanty. [C17 (? in the sense: ill-tempered): ?from *stinge,* dialect var. of STING]
▸ **'stingily** *adv* ▸ **'stinginess** *n*

THESAURUS

stiffen *vb* **1 = brace**, reinforce, starch, tauten, tense **2 = set**, coagulate, congeal, crystallize, harden, jell, solidify, thicken

stiff-necked *adj* **= stubborn**, boneheaded (*sl.*), contumacious, haughty, obstinate, opinionated, uncompromising, unreceptive

stifle *vb* **1 = suppress**, check, choke back, cover up, curb, extinguish, gag, hush, muffle, prevent, repress, restrain, silence, smother, stop **3 = suffocate**, asphyxiate, choke, smother, strangle

stigma *n* **1 = disgrace**, blot, brand, dishonour, imputation, mark, reproach, shame, slur, smirch, spot, stain

stigmatize *vb* **1 = brand**, cast a slur upon, defame, denounce, discredit, label, mark, pillory

still[1] *adj* **1 = motionless**, at rest, calm, inert, lifeless, pacific, peaceful, placid, restful, serene, smooth, stationary, tranquil, undisturbed, unruffled, unstirring **2 = silent**, hushed, noiseless, quiet, stilly (*poetic*) ◆ *n* **11** *Poetic* **= stillness**, hush, peace, quiet, silence, tranquillity ◆ *vb* **12 = quieten**, allay, alleviate, appease, calm, hush, lull, pacify, quiet, settle, silence, smooth, smooth over, soothe, subdue, tranquillize ◆ *sentence connector* **15 = however**, but, for all that, nevertheless, notwithstanding, yet
Antonyms *adj* ≠ **motionless:** active, agitated, astir, bustling, busy, humming, lively, moving, restless, turbulent ≠ **silent:** noisy ◆ *n* ≠ **stillness:** bustle, clamour, hubbub, noise, uproar ◆ *vb* ≠ **quieten:** aggravate, agitate, exacerbate, increase, inflame, rouse, stir up

stilted *adj* **1, 2 = stiff**, artificial, arty-farty (*inf.*), bombastic, constrained, forced, fustian, grandiloquent, high-flown, high-sounding, inflated, laboured, pedantic, pompous, pretentious, unnatural, wooden
Antonyms *adj* flowing, fluid, free, natural, spontaneous, unaffected, unpretentious

stimulant *n* **1 = pick-me-up** (*inf.*), analeptic, bracer (*inf.*), energizer, excitant, pep pill (*inf.*), restorative, reviver, tonic, upper (*sl.*)
Antonyms *n* depressant, downer (*sl.*), sedative, tranquilliser

stimulate *vb* **1, 3 = encourage**, animate, arouse, fan, fire, foment, gee up, goad, impel, incite, inflame, inspire, instigate, prod, prompt, provoke, quicken, rouse, spur, turn on (*sl.*), urge, whet

stimulating *adj* **1, 3 = exciting**, exhilarating, galvanic, inspiring, intriguing, provocative, provoking, rousing, stirring, thought-provoking
Antonyms *adj* as dry as dust, boring, dull, mind-numbing, unexciting, unimaginative, uninspiring, uninteresting, unstimulating

stimulus *n* **1 = incentive**, clarion call, encouragement, fillip, geeing-up, goad, impetus, incitement, inducement, provocation, shot in the arm (*inf.*), spur

sting *vb* **1 = hurt**, burn, pain, smart, tingle, wound **2 = anger**, gall, incense, inflame, infuriate, nettle, pique, provoke, rile **4** *Informal* **= cheat**, defraud, do (*sl.*), fleece, overcharge, rip off (*sl.*), skin (*sl.*), stiff (*sl.*), swindle, take for a ride (*inf.*)

stingy[1] *adj* **1 = mean**, avaricious, cheeseparing, close-fisted, covetous, illiberal, mingy (*Brit.*

stingy[2] ('stɪŋɪ) *adj* **stingier, stingiest.** *Inf.* stinging or capable of stinging.

stink ⓣ (stɪŋk) *n* **1** a strong foul smell; stench. **2** *Sl.* a great deal of trouble (esp. in **make** *or* **raise a stink**). **3 like stink.** intensely; furiously. ◆ *vb* **stinks, stinking, stank** *or* **stunk; stunk.** (*mainly intr*) **4** to emit a foul smell. **5** *Sl.* to be thoroughly bad or abhorrent: *this town stinks.* **6** *Inf.* to have a very bad reputation: *his name stinks.* **7** to be of poor quality. **8** (foll. by *of* or *with*) *Sl.* to have or appear to have an excessive amount (of money). **9** (*tr;* usually foll. by *up*) *Inf.* to cause to stink. ◆ See also **stink out.** [OE *stincan*]
▸ **'stinky** *adj*

stink bomb *n* a small glass globe used by practical jokers: it releases a liquid with an offensive smell when broken.

stinker ⓣ ('stɪŋkə) *n* **1** a person or thing that stinks. **2** *Sl.* a difficult or very unpleasant person or thing. **3** *Sl.* something of very poor quality. **4** *Inf.* any of several fulmars or related birds that feed on carrion.

stinkhorn ('stɪŋk,hɔːn) *n* any of various fungi having an unpleasant odour.

stinking ⓣ ('stɪŋkɪŋ) *adj* **1** having a foul smell. **2** *Inf.* unpleasant or disgusting. **3** (*postpositive*) *Sl.* very drunk. **4 cry stinking fish.** to decry something, esp. one's own products. ◆ *adv* **5** *Inf.* (intensifier, expressing contempt): *stinking rich.*
▸ **'stinkingly** *adv* ▸ **'stinkingness** *n*

stinko ('stɪŋkəʊ) *adj* (*postpositive*) *Sl.* drunk.

stink out *vb* (*tr, adv*) **1** to drive out or away by a foul smell. **2** *Brit.* to cause to stink: *the smell of orange peel stinks out the room.*

stinkweed ('stɪŋk,wiːd) *n* **1** Also called: **wall mustard.** a cruciferous plant, naturalized in Britain and S and central Europe, having pale yellow flowers and a disagreeable smell when bruised. **2** any of various other ill-smelling plants.

stinkwood ('stɪŋk,wʊd) *n* **1** any of various trees having offensive-smelling wood, esp. a southern African lauraceous tree yielding a hard wood used for furniture. **2** the heavy durable wood of any of these trees.

stint[1] ⓣ (stɪnt) *vb* **1** to be frugal or miserly towards (someone) with (something). **2** *Arch.* to stop or check (something). ◆ *n* **3** an allotted or fixed amount of work. **4** a limitation or check. [OE *styntan* to blunt]
▸ **'stinter** *n*

stint[2] (stɪnt) *n* any of various small sandpipers of a chiefly northern genus. [OE]

stipe (staɪp) *n* **1** a stalk in plants that bears reproductive structures, esp. the stalk bearing the cap of a mushroom. **2** the stalk that bears the leaflets of a fern or the thallus of a seaweed. **3** *Zool.* any stalklike part; stipes. [C18: via F from L *stīpes* tree trunk]

stipel ('staɪpᵊl) *n* a small paired leaflike structure at the base of certain leaflets; secondary stipule. [C19: via NL from L *stipula,* dim. of *stīpes* a log]
▸ **stipellate** (staɪ'pelɪt, -eɪt) *adj*

stipend ('staɪpend) *n* a fixed or regular amount of money paid as a salary or allowance, as to a clergyman. [C15: from OF *stipende,* from L *stīpendium* tax, from *stips* a contribution + *pendere* to pay out]

stipendiary (staɪ'pendɪərɪ) *adj* **1** receiving or working for regular pay: *a stipendiary magistrate.* **2** paid for by a stipend. ◆ *n, pl* **stipendiaries. 3** a person who receives regular payment. [C16: from L *stīpendiārius* concerning tribute, from *stīpendium* STIPEND]

stipes ('staɪpiːz) *n, pl* **stipites** ('stɪpɪ,tiːz). *Zool.* **1** the second maxillary segment in insects and crustaceans. **2** the eyestalk of a crab or similar crustacean. **3** any similar stemlike structure. [C18: from L; see STIPE]
▸ **stipiform** ('staɪpɪ,fɔːm) *or* **stipitiform** ('stɪpɪtɪ,fɔːm) *adj*

stipple ('stɪpᵊl) *vb* **stipples, stippling, stippled.** (*tr*) **1** to draw, engrave, or paint using dots or flecks. **2** to apply paint, powder, etc., to (something) with many light dabs. ◆ *n also* **stippling. 3** the technique of stippling or a picture produced by or using stippling. [C18: from Du. *stippelen,* from *stippen* to prick, from *stip* point]
▸ **'stippler** *n*

stipulate ⓣ ('stɪpjʊ,leɪt) *vb* **stipulates, stipulating, stipulated. 1** (*tr; may take a clause as object*) to specify, often as a condition of an agreement. **2** (*intr;* foll. by *for*) to insist (on) as a term of an agreement. **3** (*tr; may take a clause as object*) to guarantee or promise. [C17: from L *stipulārī,* prob. from OL *stipulus* firm]
▸ **,stipu'lation** *n* ▸ **'stipu,lator** *n*

stipule ('stɪpjuːl) *n* a small paired usually leaflike outgrowth occurring at the base of a leaf or its stalk. [C18: from L; see STIPE]
▸ **stipular** ('stɪpjʊlə) *adj*

stir[1] ⓣ (stɜː) *vb* **stirs, stirring, stirred. 1** to move an implement such as a spoon around in (a liquid) so as to mix up the constituents. **2** to change or cause to change position; disturb or be disturbed. **3** (*intr;* often foll. by *from*) to venture or depart (from one's usual or preferred place). **4** (*intr*) to be active after a rest; be up and about. **5** (*tr*) to excite or stimulate, esp. emotionally. **6** to move (oneself) briskly or vigorously; exert (oneself). **7** (*tr*) to rouse or awaken: *to stir someone from sleep; to stir memories.* **8** (when *tr,* foll. by *up*) to cause or incite others to cause (trouble, arguments, etc.). **9 stir one's stumps.** to move or become active. ◆ *n* **10** the act or an instance of stirring or the state of being stirred. **11** a strong reaction, esp. of excitement: *his publication caused a stir.* **12** a slight movement. **13** *NZ inf.* a noisy party. ◆ See also **stir up.** [OE *styrian*]

stir[2] (stɜː) *n* **1** a slang word for **prison:** *in stir.* **2 stir-crazy.** *Sl., chiefly US & Canad.* mentally disturbed as a result of being in prison. [C19: from ?]

stir-fry *vb* **stir-fries, stir-frying, stir-fried. 1** to cook (chopped meat, vegetables, etc.) rapidly by stirring them in a wok or frying pan over a high heat. ◆ *n, pl* **stir-fries. 2** a dish cooked in this way.

stirk (stɜːk) *n* **1** a heifer of 6 to 12 months old. **2** a yearling heifer or bullock. [OE *stierc*]

stirps (stɜːps) *n, pl* **stirpes** ('stɜːpiːz). **1** *Genealogy.* a line of descendants from an ancestor. **2** *Bot.* a race or variety. [C17: from L: root, family origin]

stirrer ('stɜːrə) *n* **1** a person or thing that stirs. **2** *Inf.* a person who deliberately causes trouble. **3** *Austral. & NZ inf.* a political activist or agitator.

stirring ⓣ ('stɜːrɪŋ) *adj* **1** exciting the emotions; stimulating. **2** active, lively, or busy.
▸ **'stirringly** *adv*

stirrup ('stɪrəp) *n* **1** Also called: **stirrup iron.** either of two metal loops on a riding saddle, with a flat footpiece through which a rider puts his foot for support. They are attached to the saddle by **stirrup leathers. 2** a U-shaped support or clamp. **3** *Naut.* one of a set of ropes fastened to a yard at one end and having a thimble at the other through which a footrope is reeved for support. [OE *stigrāp,* from *stīg* step + *rāp* rope]

stirrup cup *n* a cup containing an alcoholic drink offered to a horseman ready to ride away.

stirrup pump *n* a hand-operated pump, the base of the cylinder of which is placed in a bucket of water: used in fighting fires.

stir up *vb* (*tr, adv*) to set in motion; instigate: *he stirred up trouble.*

stitch (stɪtʃ) *n* **1** a link made by drawing a thread through material by means of a needle. **2** a loop of yarn formed around an implement used in knitting, crocheting, etc. **3** a particular method of stitching or shape of stitch. **4** a sharp spasmodic pain in the side resulting from running or exercising. **5** (*usually used with a negative*) *Inf.* the least fragment of clothing: *he wasn't wearing a stitch.* **6** *Agriculture.* the ridge between two furrows. **7 drop a stitch.** to allow a loop of wool to fall off a knitting needle accidentally while knitting. **8 in stitches.** *Inf.* laughing uncontrollably. ◆ *vb* **9** (*tr*) to sew, fasten, etc., with stitches. **10** (*intr*) to be engaged in sewing. **11** (*tr*) to bind together (the leaves of a book, pamphlet, etc.) with wire staples or thread. ◆ *n, vb* **12** an informal word for **suture** (senses 1b, 5). [OE *stice* sting]
▸ **'stitcher** *n*

stitch up *vb* (*tr, adv*) **1** to join or mend by means of stitches or sutures. **2** *Sl.* **2a** to incriminate (someone) on a false charge by manufacturing evidence. **2b** to betray, cheat, or defraud. **3** *Sl.* to prearrange (some-

THESAURUS

inf.), miserly, near, niggardly, parsimonious, penny-pinching (*inf.*), penurious, scrimping, tight-arse (*taboo sl.*), tight-arsed (*taboo sl.*), tight as a duck's arse (*taboo sl.*), tight-ass (*US taboo sl.*), tight-assed (*US taboo sl.*), tightfisted, ungenerous **2** = **insufficient**, inadequate, meagre, measly (*inf.*), on the small side, pathetic, scant, scanty, skimpy, small

stink *n* **1** = **stench**, fetor, foulness, foul smell, malodour, noisomeness, pong (*Brit. inf.*) **2** *Slang As in* **make, create** *or* **kick up a stink** = **fuss**, brouhaha, commotion, deal of trouble (*inf.*), disturbance, hubbub, row, rumpus, scandal, stir, to-do, uproar, upset ◆ *vb* **4** = **reek**, offend the nostrils, pong (*Brit. inf.*), stink to high heaven (*inf.*), whiff (*Brit. sl.*) **5** *Slang* = **be bad**, be abhorrent, be detestable, be held in disrepute, be no good, be offensive, be rotten, have a bad name

stinker *n Slang* **2** = **scoundrel**, bounder (*old-fashioned Brit. sl.*), cad (*Brit. inf.*), cur, dastard (*arch.*), heel, nasty piece of work (*inf.*), rotter (*sl., chiefly Brit.*), scab, sod (*sl.*), swine **2** = **problem**, affliction, beast, difficulty, fine how-do-you-do (*inf.*), horror, impediment, plight, poser, predicament, shocker

stinking *adj* **1** = **foul-smelling**, fetid, ill-smelling, malodorous, mephitic, niffy (*Brit. sl.*), noisome, olid, pongy (*Brit. inf.*), reeking, smelly, whiffy (*Brit. sl.*) **2** *Informal* = **rotten**, contemptible, disgusting, low, low-down (*inf.*), mean, shitty (*taboo sl.*), unpleasant, vile, wretched

stint[1] *vb* **1** = **be mean**, be frugal, begrudge, be mingy (*Brit. inf.*), be parsimonious, be sparing, economize, hold back, save, scrimp, skimp on, spoil the ship for a ha'porth of tar, withhold ◆ *n* **3** = **share**, assignment, bit, period, quota, shift, spell, stretch, term, time, tour, turn

stipulate *vb* **1** = **specify**, agree, contract, covenant, engage, guarantee, insist upon, lay down, lay down *or* impose conditions, make a point of, pledge, postulate, promise, require, settle

stipulation *n* **1** = **condition**, agreement, clause, contract, engagement, precondition, prerequisite, provision, proviso, qualification, requirement, restriction, rider, settlement, *sine qua non*, specification, term

stir[1] *vb* **1** = **mix**, agitate, beat, disturb, flutter, move, quiver, rustle, shake, tremble **4** = **get moving**, bestir oneself, be up and about (*inf.*), budge, exert oneself, get a move on (*inf.*), hasten, look lively (*inf.*), make an effort, mill about, move, shake a leg (*inf.*) **5** = **stimulate**, affect, animate, arouse, awaken, electrify, excite, fire, incite, inflame, inspire, instigate, kindle, move, prod, prompt, provoke, quicken, raise, rouse, spur, thrill, touch, urge ◆ *n* **11** = **commotion**, activity, ado, agitation, bustle, disorder, disturbance, excitement, ferment, flurry, fuss, movement, to-do, tumult, uproar
Antonyms *vb* ≠ **stimulate**: check, curb, dampen, inhibit, restrain, stifle, suppress, throw cold water on (*inf.*)

stirring *adj* **1** = **exciting**, animating, dramatic, emotive, exhilarating, heady, impassioned, inspiring, intoxicating, lively, moving, rousing, spirited, stimulating, thrilling thing) in a clandestine manner. ♦ *n* **stitch-up. 4** *Sl.* a matter that has been prearranged clandestinely.

stitchwort ('stɪtʃ,wɜːt) *n* any of several low-growing N temperate herbaceous plants having small white star-shaped flowers.

stiver ('staɪvə) *n* **1** a former Dutch coin worth one twentieth of a guilder. **2** a small amount, esp. of money. [C16: from Du. *stuiver*]

stoa ('stəʊə) *n, pl* **stoae** ('stəʊiː) *or* **stoas.** a covered walk that has a colonnade on one or both sides, esp. as in ancient Greece. [C17: from Gk]

stoat (stəʊt) *n* a small Eurasian mammal, closely related to the weasels, having a brown coat and a black-tipped tail: in the northern parts of its range it has a white winter coat and is then known as an ermine. [C15: from ?]

stochastic (stɒ'kæstɪk) *adj* **1** *Statistics.* **1a** (of a random variable) having a probability distribution, usually with finite variance. **1b** (of a process) involving a random variable the successive values of which are not independent. **1c** (of a matrix) square with non-negative elements that add to unity in each row. **2** *Rare.* involving conjecture. [C17: from Gk *stokhastikos* capable of guessing, from *stokhazesthai* to aim at, conjecture, from *stokhos* a target]

stock ⓣ (stɒk) *n* **1a** (*sometimes pl*) the total goods or raw material kept on the premises of a shop or business. **1b** (*as modifier*): *a stock book.* **2** a supply of something stored for future use. **3** *Finance.* **3a** the capital raised by a company through the issue and subscription of shares entitling their holders to dividends, partial ownership, and usually voting rights. **3b** the proportion of such capital held by an individual shareholder. **3c** the shares of a specified company or industry. **4** standing or status. **5a** farm animals, such as cattle and sheep, bred and kept for their meat, skins, etc. **5b** (*as modifier*): *stock farming.* **6** the trunk or main stem of a tree or other plant. **7** *Horticulture.* **7a** a rooted plant into which a scion is inserted during grafting. **7b** a plant or stem from which cuttings are taken. **8** the original type from which a particular race, family, group, etc., is derived. **9** a race, breed, or variety of animals or plants. **10** (*often pl*) a small pen in which a single animal can be confined. **11** a line of descent. **12** any of the major subdivisions of the human species; race or ethnic group. **13** the part of a rifle, etc., into which the barrel is set: held by the firer against the shoulder. **14** the handle of something, such as a whip or fishing rod. **15** the main body of a tool, such as the block of a plane. **16** short for **diestock, gunstock,** or **rolling stock. 17** (formerly) the part of a plough to which the irons and handles were attached. **18** the main upright part of a supporting structure. **19** a liquid or broth in which meat, fish, bones, or vegetables have been simmered for a long time. **20** film material before exposure and processing. **21** Also called: **gillyflower.** any of several cruciferous plants such as **evening** or **night-scented stock**, of the Mediterranean region: cultivated for their brightly coloured flowers. **22 Virginian stock.** a similar and related North American plant. **23** a long usually white neckcloth wrapped around the neck, worn in the 18th century and as part of modern riding dress. **24a** the repertoire of plays available to a repertory company. **24b** (*as modifier*): *a stock play.* **25** a log or block of wood. **26** See **laughing stock. 27 in stock. 27a** stored on the premises or available for sale or use. **27b** supplied with goods of a specified kind. **28 out of stock. 28a** not immediately available for sale or use. **28b** not having goods of a specified kind immediately available. **29 take stock. 29a** to make an inventory. **29b** to make a general appraisal, esp. of prospects, resources, etc. **30 take stock in.** to attach importance to. ♦ *adj* **31** staple; standard: *stock sizes in clothes.* **32** (*prenominal*) being a cliché; hackneyed: *a stock phrase.* ♦ *vb* **33** (*tr*) to keep (goods) for sale. **34** (*intr; usually foll. by up or up on*) to obtain a store of (something) for future use or sale: *to stock up on beer.* **35** (*tr*) to supply with live animals, fish, etc.: *to stock a farm.* **36** (*intr*) (of a plant) to put forth new shoots. **37** (*tr*) *Obs.* to punish by putting in the stocks. ♦ See also **stocks.** [OE *stocc* trunk (of a tree), stem, stick (the various senses developed from these meanings, as trunk of a tree, hence line of descent; structures made of timber; a store of timber or other goods for future use, hence an aggregate of goods, animals, etc.)]
▸'**stocker** *n*

stockade (stɒ'keɪd) *n* **1** an enclosure or barrier of stakes and timbers. ♦ *vb* **stockades, stockading, stockaded. 2** (*tr*) to surround with a stockade. [C17: from Sp. *estacada*, from *estaca* a stake, of Gmc origin]

stockbreeder ('stɒk,briːdə) *n* a person who breeds or rears livestock as an occupation.
▸'**stock,breeding** *n*

stockbroker ('stɒk,brəʊkə) *n* a person who buys and sells securities on a commission basis for customers.
▸'**stock,brokerage** *or* '**stock,broking** *n*

stockbroker belt *n Brit. inf.* the area outside a city, esp. London, in which rich commuters live.

stock car *n* **1** a car, usually a production saloon, strengthened and modified for a form of racing in which the cars often collide. **2** *US & Canad.* a railway wagon for carrying livestock.

stock dove *n* a European dove, smaller than the wood pigeon and having a grey plumage.

stock exchange *n* **1a** a highly organized market facilitating the purchase and sale of securities and operated by professional stockbrokers and market makers according to fixed rules. **1b** a place where securities are regularly traded. **1c** (*as modifier*): *a stock-exchange operator; stock-exchange prices.* **2** the prices or trading activity of a stock exchange: *the stock exchange fell heavily today.* ♦ Also called: **stock market.**

stockfish ('stɒk,fɪʃ) *n, pl* **stockfish** *or* **stockfishes.** fish cured by splitting and drying in the air.

stockholder ('stɒk,həʊldə) *n* **1** an owner of corporate capital stock. **2** *Austral.* a person who keeps livestock.
▸'**stock,holding** *n*

stockhorse ('stɒk,hɔːs) *n Austral.* a stockman's horse.

stockinet (,stɒkɪ'nɛt) *n* a machine-knitted elastic fabric used, esp. formerly, for stockings, underwear, etc. [C19: ?from earlier *stocking-net*]

stocking ('stɒkɪŋ) *n* **1** one of a pair of close-fitting garments made of knitted yarn to cover the foot and part or all of the leg. **2** something resembling this in position, function, etc. **3 in (one's) stocking** *or* **stockinged feet.** wearing stockings or socks but no shoes. [C16: from dialect *stock* stocking + -ING[1]]
▸'**stockinged** *adj*

stocking cap *n* a conical knitted cap, often with a tassel.

stocking filler *n Brit.* a present of a size suitable for inclusion in a Christmas stocking.

stock in trade *n* **1** goods in stock necessary for carrying on a business. **2** anything constantly used by someone as a part of his profession, occupation, or trade: *friendliness is the salesman's stock in trade.*

stockist ('stɒkɪst) *n Commerce, Brit.* a dealer who undertakes to maintain stocks of a specified product at or above a certain minimum in return for favourable buying terms granted by the manufacturer of the product.

stockjobber ('stɒk,dʒɒbə) *n* **1** *Brit.* (formerly) a wholesale dealer on a stock exchange who sold securities to brokers without transacting directly with the public. See **market maker. 2** *US, disparaging.* a stockbroker, esp. one dealing in worthless securities.
▸'**stock,jobbery** *or* '**stock,jobbing** *n*

stockman ('stɒkmən, -,mæn) *n, pl* **stockmen. 1a** a man engaged in the rearing or care of farm livestock, esp. cattle. **1b** an owner of cattle or other livestock. **2** *US & Canad.* a man employed in a warehouse or stockroom.

stock market *n* another name for **stock exchange.**

stockpile ('stɒk,paɪl) *vb* **stockpiles, stockpiling, stockpiled. 1** to acquire and store a large quantity of (something). ♦ *n* **2** a large store or supply accumulated for future use.
▸'**stock,piler** *n*

stockpot ('stɒk,pɒt) *n Chiefly Brit.* a pot in which stock for soup, etc., is made or kept.

stockroom ('stɒk,ruːm, -,rʊm) *n* a room in which a stock of goods is kept, as in a shop or factory.

stock route *n Austral. & NZ.* a route designated for droving sheep or cattle.

stocks (stɒks) *pl n* **1** *History.* an instrument of punishment consisting of a heavy wooden frame with holes in which the feet, hands, or head of an offender were locked. **2** a frame used to support a boat while under construction. **3** *Naut.* a vertical post or shaft at the forward edge of a rudder, extended upwards for attachment to the steering controls. **4 on the stocks.** in preparation or under construction.

stock-still *adv* absolutely still; motionless.

stocktaking ('stɒk,teɪkɪŋ) *n* **1** the examination, counting, and valuing of goods on hand in a shop or business. **2** a reassessment of one's current situation, progress, prospects, etc.

stock watering *n Business.* the creation of more new shares in a company than is justified by its assets.

stock whip *n* a whip with a long lash and a short handle, used to herd cattle, etc.

stocky ⓣ ('stɒkɪ) *adj* **stockier, stockiest.** (usually of a person) thickset; sturdy.
▸'**stockily** *adv* ▸'**stockiness** *n*

stockyard ('stɒk,jɑːd) *n* a large yard with pens or covered buildings where farm animals are assembled, sold, etc.

stodge (stɒdʒ) *Inf.* ♦ *n* **1** heavy filling starchy food. **2** a dull person or subject. ♦ *vb* **stodges, stodging, stodged. 3** to stuff (oneself or another) with food. [C17: ? blend of STUFF + *podge*, from *podgy* fat]

stodgy ⓣ ('stɒdʒɪ) *adj* **stodgier, stodgiest. 1** (of food) heavy or uninteresting. **2** excessively formal and conventional. [C19: from STODGE]
▸'**stodgily** *adv* ▸'**stodginess** *n*

THESAURUS

stock *n* **1** = **goods**, array, assortment, cache, choice, commodities, inventory, merchandise, range, selection, variety, wares **2** = **supply**, fund, hoard, reserve, reservoir, stockpile, store **3a** = **property**, assets, capital, funds, investment **5a** = **livestock**, beasts, cattle, domestic animals **11** = **lineage**, ancestry, background, breed, descent, extraction, family, forebears, house, line, line of descent, parentage, pedigree, race, strain, type, variety **29b take stock** = **review the situation**, appraise, estimate, see how the land lies, size up (*inf.*), weigh up ♦ *adj* **31** = **standard**, basic, commonplace, conventional, customary, formal, ordinary, regular, routine, run-of-the-mill, set, staple, traditional, usual **32** = **hackneyed**, banal, overused, stereotyped, trite, worn-out ♦ *vb* **33** = **sell**, deal in, handle, keep, supply, trade in **34** *foll. by* **up, up on** = **store (up)**, accumulate, amass, buy up, gather, hoard, lay in, put away, replenish, save, supply **35** = **provide with**, equip, fill, fit out, furnish, kit out, provision, supply

stocky *adj* = **thickset**, chunky, dumpy, mesomorphic, solid, stubby, stumpy, sturdy

stodgy *adj* **1** = **heavy**, filling, leaden, starchy, substantial **2** = **dull**, boring, dull as ditchwater, formal, fuddy-duddy (*inf.*), heavy going, ho-hum, laboured, staid, stuffy, tedious, tiresome, turgid, unexciting, unimaginative, uninspired
Antonyms *adj* ≠ **heavy**: appetizing, fluffy, insub-

stoep (stu:p) *n S. African.* a veranda. [from Afrik., from Du.]
stoic ('stəʊɪk) *n* **1** a person who maintains stoical qualities. ◆ *adj* **2** a variant of **stoical.**
Stoic ('stəʊɪk) *n* **1** a member of the ancient Greek school of philosophy founded by Zeno of Citium (?336–?264 B.C.), holding that virtue and happiness can be attained only by submission to destiny and the natural law. ◆ *adj* **2** of or relating to the doctrines of the Stoics. [C16: via L from Gk *stōikos,* from *stoa,* the porch in Athens where Zeno taught]
stoical ⓣ ('stəʊɪkᵊl) *adj* characterized by impassivity or resignation.
▸**'stoically** *adv*
stoichiometry *or* **stoicheiometry** (ˌstɔɪkɪ'ɒmɪtrɪ) *n* the branch of chemistry concerned with the proportions in which elements are combined in compounds and the quantitative relationships between reactants and products in chemical reactions. [C19: from Gk *stoikheion* element + -METRY]
▸**ˌstoichio'metric** *or* **ˌstoicheio'metric** *adj*
stoicism ⓣ ('stəʊɪˌsɪzəm) *n* **1** indifference to pleasure and pain. **2** (*cap.*) the philosophy of the Stoics.
stoke (stəʊk) *vb* **stokes, stoking, stoked. 1** to feed, stir, and tend (a fire, furnace, etc.). **2** (*tr*) to tend the furnace of; act as a stoker for. [C17: back formation from STOKER]
stokehold ('stəʊkˌhəʊld) *n Naut.* **1** a coal bunker for a ship's furnace. **2** the hold for a ship's boilers; fire room.
stokehole ('stəʊkˌhəʊl) *n* **1** another word for **stokehold. 2** a hole in a furnace through which it is stoked.
stoker ('stəʊkə) *n* a person employed to tend a furnace, as on a steamship. [C17: from Du., from *stoken* to stoke]
stoke up *vb* (*adv*) **1** to feed and tend (a fire, etc.) with fuel. **2** (*intr*) to fill oneself with food.
STOL (stɒl) *n* **1** a system in which an aircraft can take off and land in a short distance. **2** an aircraft using this system. Cf. **VTOL** [C20: *s(hort) t(ake)o(ff and) l(anding)*]
stole[1] (stəʊl) *vb* the past tense of **steal.**
stole[2] (stəʊl) *n* **1** a long scarf or shawl, worn by women. **2** a long narrow scarf worn by various officiating clergymen. [OE *stole,* from L *stola,* from Gk *stolē* clothing]
stolen ⓣ ('stəʊlən) *vb* the past participle of **steal.**
stolid ⓣ ('stɒlɪd) *adj* showing little or no emotion or interest. [C17: from L *stolidus* dull]
▸**stolidity** (stɒ'lɪdɪtɪ) *or* **'stolidness** *n* ▸**'stolidly** *adv*
stolon ('stəʊlən) *n* **1** another name for **runner** (sense 9). **2** a branching structure in lower animals, esp. the anchoring rootlike part of colonial organisms. [C17: from L *stolō* shoot]
▸**stoloniferous** (ˌstəʊlə'nɪfərəs) *adj*
stoma ('stəʊmə) *n, pl* **stomata. 1** *Bot.* an epidermal pore in plant leaves, that controls the passage of gases into and out of a plant. **2** *Zool., anat.* a mouth or mouthlike part. **3** *Surgery.* an artificial opening made in a tubular organ, esp. the colon or ileum. See **colostomy, ileostomy.** [C17: via NL from Gk: mouth]
stomach ⓣ ('stʌmək) *n* **1** (in vertebrates) the enlarged muscular saclike part of the alimentary canal in which food is stored until it has been partially digested. Related adj: **gastric. 2** the corresponding organ in invertebrates. **3** the abdominal region. **4** desire, appetite, or inclination: *I have no stomach for arguments.* ◆ *vb* (*tr; used mainly in negative constructions*) **5** to tolerate; bear: *I can't stomach his bragging.* **6** to eat or digest: *he cannot stomach oysters.* [C14: from OF *stomaque,* from L *stomachus,* from Gk *stomakhos,* from *stoma* mouth]
stomachache ('stʌməkˌeɪk) *n* pain in the stomach, as from acute indigestion. Also called: **stomach upset, upset stomach.**
stomacher ('stʌməkə) *n* a decorative V-shaped panel of stiff material worn over the chest and stomach by men and women in the 16th century, later only by women.
stomachic (stə'mækɪk) *adj also* **stomachical. 1** stimulating gastric activity. **2** of or relating to the stomach. ◆ *n* **3** a stomachic medicine.
stomach pump *n Med.* a suction device for removing stomach contents by a tube inserted through the mouth.
stomata ('stəʊmətə, 'stɒm-, stəʊ'mɑ:tə) *n* the plural of **stoma.**
stomatitis (ˌstəʊmə'taɪtɪs, ˌstɒm-) *n* inflammation of the mouth.
▸**stomatitic** (ˌstəʊmə'tɪtɪk, ˌstɒm-) *adj*
stomato- *or before a vowel* **stomat-** *combining form.* indicating the mouth or a mouthlike part: *stomatology.* [from Gk *stoma, stomat-*]
stomatology (ˌstəʊmə'tɒlədʒɪ) *n* the branch of medicine concerned with the mouth.
▸**stomatological** (ˌstəʊmətə'lɒdʒɪkᵊl) *adj*
-stome *n combining form.* indicating a mouth or opening resembling a mouth: *peristome.* [from Gk *stoma* mouth, & *stomion* little mouth]
-stomous *adj combining form.* having a specified type of mouth.
stomp (stɒmp) *vb* **1** (*intr*) to tread or stamp heavily. ◆ *n* **2** a rhythmic stamping jazz dance. [var. of STAMP]
▸**'stomper** *n*
-stomy *n combining form.* indicating a surgical operation performed to make an artificial opening into or for a specified part: *cytostomy.* [from Gk *-stomia,* from *stoma* mouth]
stone (stəʊn) *n* **1** the hard compact nonmetallic material of which rocks are made. **2** a small lump of rock; pebble. **3** short for **gemstone. 4a** a piece of rock designed or shaped for some particular purpose. **4b** (*in combination*): *gravestone; millstone.* **5a** something that resembles a stone. **5b** (*in combination*): *hailstone.* **6** the woody central part of such fruits as the peach and plum, that contains the seed; endocarp. **7** any similar hard part of a fruit, such as the stony seed of a date. **8** (*pl* **stone**) *Brit.* a unit of weight, used esp. to express human body weight, equal to 14 pounds or 6.350 kilograms. **9** Also called: **granite.** the rounded heavy mass of granite or iron used in the game of curling. **10** *Pathol.* a nontechnical name for **calculus. 11** *Printing.* a table with a very flat iron or stone surface upon which pages are composed. **12** (*modifier*) relating to or made of stone: *a stone house.* **13** (*modifier*) made of stoneware: *a stone jar.* **14 cast a stone (at).** cast aspersions (upon). **15 heart of stone.** an obdurate or unemotional nature. **16 leave no stone unturned.** to do everything possible to achieve an end. ◆ *vb* **stones, stoning, stoned.** (*tr*) **17** to throw stones at, esp. to kill. **18** to remove the stones from. **19** to furnish or provide with stones. [OE *stān*]
▸**'stoner** *n*
stone- *prefix* very, completely: *stone-blind, stone-cold.* [from STONE in sense of "like a stone"]
Stone Age *n* **1** a period in human culture identified by the use of stone implements. ◆ *modifier.* **Stone-Age. 2** (*sometimes not caps.*) of or relating to this period.
stone-blind *adj* completely blind. Cf. **sand-blind.**
stonechat ('stəʊnˌtʃæt) *n* an Old World songbird having a black plumage with a reddish-brown breast. [C18: from its cry, which sounds like clattering pebbles]
stone-cold *adj* **1** completely cold. **2 stone-cold sober.** completely sober.
stonecrop ('stəʊnˌkrɒp) *n* any of various N temperate plants having fleshy leaves and typically red, yellow, or white flowers.
stone curlew *n* any of several brownish shore birds having a large head and eyes. Also called: **thick-knee.**
stonecutter ('stəʊnˌkʌtə) *n* **1** a person who is skilled in cutting and carving stone. **2** a machine used to dress stone.
▸**'stoneˌcutting** *n*
stoned (stəʊnd) *adj Sl.* under the influence of drugs or alcohol.
stone-deaf *adj* completely deaf.
stonefish ('stəʊnˌfɪʃ) *n, pl* **stonefish** *or* **stonefishes.** a venomous tropical marine fish that resembles a piece of rock on the seabed.
stonefly ('stəʊnˌflaɪ) *n, pl* **stoneflies.** any of various insects, in which the larvae are aquatic, living beneath stones.
stone fruit *n* the nontechnical name for **drupe.**
stonemason ('stəʊnˌmeɪsᵊn) *n* a person who is skilled in preparing stone for building.
▸**'stoneˌmasonry** *n*
stone pine *n* a pine tree with a short bole and radiating branches forming an umbrella shape.
stone's throw *n* a short distance.
stonewall (ˌstəʊn'wɔ:l) *vb* **1** (*intr*) *Cricket.* (of a batsman) to play defensively. **2** to obstruct (an investigation, etc.), esp. by giving uncommunicative answers to questioning. **3** to obstruct or hinder (parliamentary business).
▸**ˌstone'waller** *n*
stoneware ('stəʊnˌwɛə) *n* **1** a hard opaque pottery, fired at a very high temperature. ◆ *adj* **2** made of stoneware.
stonewashed ('stəʊnˌwɒʃt) *adj* (of clothes or fabric) given a worn faded look by being subjected to the abrasive action of many small pieces of pumice.
stonework ('stəʊnˌwɜ:k) *n* **1** any structure or part of a building made of stone. **2** the process of dressing or setting stones.
▸**'stoneˌworker** *n*
stonkered ('stɒŋkəd) *adj Sl.* completely exhausted or beaten. [C20: from *stonker* to beat, from ?]
stony ⓣ *or* **stoney** ('stəʊnɪ) *adj* **stonier, stoniest. 1** of or resembling stone. **2** abounding in stone or stones. **3** unfeeling or obdurate. **4** short for **stony-broke.**
▸**'stonily** *adv* ▸**'stoniness** *n*
stony-broke *adj Brit. sl.* completely without money; penniless.
stony-hearted *adj* unfeeling; hardhearted.
▸**ˌstony-'heartedness** *n*
stood (stʊd) *vb* the past tense and past participle of **stand.**

THESAURUS

stantial, light ≠ **dull:** animated, exciting, fashionable, fresh, interesting, light, lively, readable, stimulating, trendy (*Brit. inf.*), up-to-date
stoical *adj* **2** = **resigned**, calm, cool, dispassionate, impassive, imperturbable, indifferent, long-suffering, philosophic, phlegmatic, stoic, stolid
stoicism *n* **1** = **resignation**, acceptance, calmness, dispassion, fatalism, forbearance, fortitude, impassivity, imperturbability, indifference, long-suffering, patience, stolidity
stolen *adj* = **hot** (*sl.*), bent (*sl.*), hooky (*sl.*)
stolid *adj* = **apathetic**, bovine, doltish, dozy (*Brit. inf.*), dull, heavy, lumpish, obtuse, slow, stupid, unemotional, wooden
Antonyms *adj* acute, animated, bright, emotional, energetic, excitable, intelligent, interested, lively, passionate, sharp, smart
stomach *n* **1** = **belly**, abdomen, breadbasket (*sl.*), gut (*inf.*), inside(s) (*inf.*), paunch, pot, potbelly, spare tyre (*inf.*), tummy (*inf.*) **4** = **inclination**, appetite, desire, mind, relish, taste ◆ *vb* **5** = **bear**, abide, endure, hack (*sl.*), put up with (*inf.*), reconcile *or* resign oneself to, submit to, suffer, swallow, take, tolerate
stony *adj* **3** = **cold**, adamant, blank, callous, chilly, expressionless, frigid, hard, harsh, heartless, hostile, icy, indifferent, inexorable, merciless, obdurate, pitiless, unfeeling, unforgiving, unresponsive

stooge ❶ (stu:dʒ) *n* **1** an actor who feeds lines to a comedian or acts as his butt. **2** *Sl.* someone who is taken advantage of by another. ◆ *vb* **stooges, stooging, stooged. 3** (*intr*) *Sl.* to act as a stooge. [C20: from ?]

stook (stu:k) *n* **1** a number of sheaves set upright in a field to dry with their heads together. ◆ *vb* **2** (*tr*) to set up (sheaves) in stooks. [C15: var. of *stouk*, of Gmc origin]
▸**ˈstooker** *n*

stool (stu:l) *n* **1** a backless seat or footrest consisting of a small flat piece of wood, etc., resting on three or four legs, a pedestal, etc. **2** a rootstock or base of a plant from which shoots, etc., are produced. **3** a cluster of shoots growing from such a base. **4** *Chiefly US.* a decoy used in hunting. **5** waste matter evacuated from the bowels. **6** a lavatory seat. **7** (in W Africa, esp. Ghana) a chief's throne. **8 fall between two stools. 8a** to fail through vacillation between two alternatives. **8b** to be in an unsatisfactory situation through not belonging to either of two categories or groups. ◆ *vb* (*intr*) **9** (of a plant) to send up shoots from the base of the stem, rootstock, etc. **10** to lure wildfowl with a decoy. [OE *stōl*]

stool ball *n* a game resembling cricket, still played by girls and women in Sussex, England.

stool pigeon *n* **1** an informer for the police. **2** *Sl.* a person acting as a decoy. [C19: from use of pigeon fixed to a stool as a decoy]

stoop[1] ❶ (stu:p) *vb* (*mainly intr*) **1** (*also tr*) to bend (the body) forward and downward. **2** to carry oneself with head and shoulders habitually bent forward. **3** (often foll. by *to*) to abase or degrade oneself. **4** (often foll. by *to*) to condescend; deign. **5** (of a bird of prey) to swoop down. ◆ *n* **6** the act, position, or characteristic of stooping. **7** a lowering from a position of dignity or superiority. **8** a downward swoop, esp. of a bird of prey. [OE *stūpan*]
▸**ˈstooping** *adj*

stoop[2] (stu:p) *n US.* an open porch or small platform with steps leading up to it at the entrance to a building. [C18: from Du. *stoep*, of Gmc origin]

stop ❶ (stɒp) *vb* **stops, stopping, stopped. 1** to cease from doing or being (something); discontinue. **2** to cause (something moving) to halt or (of something moving) to come to a halt. **3** (*tr*) to prevent the continuance or completion of. **4** (*tr;* often foll. by *from*) to prevent or restrain: *to stop George from fighting.* **5** (*tr*) to keep back: *to stop supplies.* **6** (*tr*) to intercept or hinder in transit: *to stop a letter.* **7** (*tr;* often foll. by *up*) to block or plug, esp. so as to close: *to stop up a pipe.* **8** (*tr;* often foll. by *up*) to fill a hole or opening in: *to stop up a wall.* **9** (*tr*) to staunch or stem: *to stop a wound.* **10** (*tr*) to instruct a bank not to honour (a cheque). **11** (*tr*) to deduct (money) from pay. **12** (*tr*) *Brit.* to provide with punctuation. **13** (*tr*) *Boxing.* to beat (an opponent) by a knockout. **14** (*tr*) *Inf.* to receive (a blow, hit, etc.). **15** (*intr*) to stay or rest: *we stopped at the Robinsons'.* **16** (*tr*) *Rare.* to defeat, beat, or kill. **17** (*tr*) *Music.* **17a** to alter the vibrating length of (a string on a violin, guitar, etc.) by pressing down on it at some point with the finger. **17b** to alter the vibrating length of an air column in a wind instrument by closing (a finger hole, etc.). **17c** to produce (a note) in this manner. **18** *Bridge.* to have a protecting card or winner in (a suit in which one's opponents are strong). **19 stop at nothing.** to be prepared to do anything; be unscrupulous or ruthless. ◆ *n* **20** an arrest of movement or progress. **21** the act of stopping or the state of being stopped. **22** a place where something halts or pauses: *a bus stop.* **23** a stay in or as if in the course of a journey. **24** the act or an instance of blocking or obstructing. **25** a plug or stopper. **26** a block, screw, etc., that prevents, limits, or terminates the motion of a mechanism or moving part. **27** *Brit.* a punctuation mark, esp. a full stop. **28** *Music.* **28a** the act of stopping the string, finger hole, etc., of an instrument. **28b** a set of organ pipes or harpsichord strings that may be allowed to sound as a group by muffling or silencing all other such sets. **28c** a knob, lever, or handle on an organ, etc., that is operated to allow sets of pipes to sound. **28d** an analogous device on a harpsichord or other instrument with variable registers, such as an electronic instrument. **29 pull out all the stops. 29a** to play at full volume. **29b** to spare no effort. **30** Also called: **stop consonant.** *Phonetics.* any of a class of consonants articulated by first making a complete closure at some point of the vocal tract and then releasing it abruptly with audible plosion. **31** Also called: **f-stop.** *Photog.* **31a** a setting of the aperture of a camera lens, calibrated to the corresponding f-number. **31b** another name for **diaphragm** (sense 4). **32** Also called: **stopper.** *Bridge.* a protecting card or winner in a suit in which one's opponents are strong. ◆ See also **stop off, stop out, stopover.** [C14: from OE *stoppian* (unattested), as in *forstoppian* to plug the ear, ult. from LL *stuppāre* to stop with tow, from L *stuppa* tow, from Gk *stuppē*]
▸**ˈstoppable** *adj*

stopbank (ˈstɒpbæŋk) *n NZ.* an embankment to prevent flooding.

stop bath *n* a weakly acidic solution used to stop the action of a developer on a film, plate, or paper before the material is immersed in fixer.

stopcock (ˈstɒpˌkɒk) *n* a valve used to control or stop the flow of a fluid in a pipe.

stope (stəup) *n* **1** a steplike excavation made in a mine to extract ore. ◆ *vb* **stopes, stoping, stoped. 2** to mine (ore, etc.) in stopes. [C18: prob. from Low G *stope*]

stopgap ❶ (ˈstɒpˌgæp) *n* **a** a temporary substitute. **b** (*as modifier*): *a stopgap programme.*

stop-go *adj Brit.* (of economic policy) characterized by deliberate alternate expansion and contraction of aggregate demand in an effort to curb inflation and eliminate balance-of-payments deficits, and yet maintain full employment.

stoplight (ˈstɒpˌlaɪt) *n* **1** a red light on a traffic signal indicating that vehicles or pedestrians coming towards it should stop. **2** another word for **brake light.**

stop-loss *adj Business.* of or relating to an order to a broker in a commodity or security market to close an open position at a specified price in order to limit any loss.

stop off *vb also* **stop in,** (esp. US) **stop by. 1** (*intr, adv;* often foll. by *at*) to halt and call somewhere, as on a visit or errand, esp. en route to another place. ◆ *n* **stopoff. 2a** a break in a journey. **2b** (*as modifier*): *stopoff point.*

stop out *vb* (*adv*) **1** (*tr*) to cover (part of the area) of a piece of cloth, printing plate, etc., to prevent it from being dyed, etched, etc. **2** (*intr*) to remain out of a house, esp. overnight.

stopover (ˈstɒpˌəuvə) *n* **1** a stopping place on a journey. ◆ *vb* **stop over. 2** (*intr, adv*) to make a stopover.

stoppage ❶ (ˈstɒpɪdʒ) *n* **1** the act of stopping or the state of being stopped. **2** something that stops or blocks. **3** a deduction of money, as from pay. **4** an organized cessation of work, as during a strike.

stoppage time *n Soccer, rugby, etc.* another name for **injury time.**

stopped (stɒpt) *adj* (of a pipe, esp. an organ pipe) closed at one end and thus sounding an octave lower than an open pipe of the same length.

stopper (ˈstɒpə) *n* **1** Also called: **stopple.** a plug or bung for closing a bottle, pipe, duct, etc. **2** a person or thing that stops or puts an end to something. **3** *Bridge.* another name for **stop** (sense 32). ◆ *vb* **4** (*tr*) Also: **stopple.** to close or fit with a stopper.

stopping (ˈstɒpɪŋ) *n* **1** *Brit. inf.* a dental filling. ◆ *adj* **2** *Chiefly Brit.* making many stops in a journey: *a stopping train.*

stop press *n Brit.* **1** news items inserted into a newspaper after the printing has been started. **2** the space regularly left blank for this.

stopwatch (ˈstɒpˌwɒtʃ) *n* a type of watch used for timing sporting events, etc., accurately, having a device for stopping the hands instantly.

storage (ˈstɔ:rɪdʒ) *n* **1** the act of storing or the state of being stored. **2** space or an area reserved for storing. **3** a charge made for storing. **4** *Computing.* **4a** the act or process of storing information in a computer memory or on a disk, etc. **4b** (*as modifier*): *storage capacity.*

storage battery *n* another name (esp. US) for **accumulator** (sense 1).

storage capacity *n* the maximum number of bits, bytes, words, etc., that can be held in a memory system such as that of a computer or of the brain.

storage device *n* a piece of computer equipment, such as a magnetic tape, disk, drum, etc., in or on which information can be stored.

storage heater *n* an electric device capable of accumulating and radiating heat generated by off-peak electricity.

storax (ˈstɔ:ræks) *n* **1** any of numerous trees or shrubs of tropical and subtropical regions, having drooping showy white flowers. **2** a vanilla-scented solid resin obtained from one of these trees, formerly used as incense and in perfumery and medicine. **3** a liquid aromatic balsam obtained from liquidambar trees and used in perfumery and medicine. [C14: via LL from Gk *sturax*]

store ❶ (stɔ:) *vb* **stores, storing, stored. 1** (*tr*) to keep, set aside, or accumulate for future use. **2** (*tr*) to place in a warehouse, depository, etc., for safekeeping. **3** (*tr*) to supply, provide, or stock. **4** (*intr*) to be put into

THESAURUS

stooge *n* **1, 2** = **pawn**, butt, dupe, fall guy (*inf.*), foil, henchman, lackey, patsy (*sl., chiefly US & Canad.*), puppet

stoop[1] *vb* **1** = **bend**, be bowed *or* round-shouldered, bow, crouch, descend, duck, hunch, incline, kneel, lean, squat **3, 4** *foll. by* **to** = **lower oneself by**, condescend to, deign to, demean oneself by, descend to, resort to, sink to ◆ *n* **6** = **slouch**, bad posture, droop, round-shoulderedness, sag, slump

stop *vb* **1** = **halt**, axe (*inf.*), belay (*Nautical*), be over, break off, bring *or* come to a halt *or* standstill, call it a day (*inf.*), cease, come to an end, conclude, cut out (*inf.*), cut short, desist, discontinue, draw up, end, finish, leave off, pack in (*Brit. inf.*), pause, peter out, pull up, put an end to, quit, refrain, run down, run its course, shut down, stall, terminate **3** = **prevent**, arrest, bar, break, check, close, forestall, frustrate, hinder, hold back, impede, intercept, interrupt, nip (something) in the bud, rein in, repress, restrain, silence, suspend **7** = **plug**, block, bung, obstruct, seal, staunch, stem **15** = **stay**, break one's journey, lodge, put up, rest, sojourn, tarry ◆ *n* **20** = **block**, bar, break, check, control, hindrance, impediment, plug, stoppage **21** = **end**, cessation, conclusion, discontinuation, finish, halt, standstill **22** = **station**, depot, destination, halt, stage, termination, terminus **23** = **stay**, break, rest, sojourn, stopover, visit
Antonyms *vb* ≠ **halt**: advance, begin, commence, continue, get going, get under way, give the go ahead, go, institute, keep going, keep on, kick off (*inf.*), proceed, set in motion, set off, start ≠ **prevent**: assist, boost, encourage, expedite, facilitate, further, gee up, hasten, promote, push ◆ *n* ≠ **end**: beginning, commencement, kick-off (*inf.*), start ≠ **block**: boost, encouragement, geeing-up, incitement

stopgap *n* **a** = **makeshift**, improvisation, resort, shift, substitute, temporary expedient ◆ *modifier* **b** = **makeshift**, emergency, impromptu, improvised, provisional, rough-and-ready, temporary

stoppage *n* **1** = **stopping**, abeyance, arrest, close, closure, cutoff, deduction, discontinuance, halt, hindrance, lay-off, shutdown, standstill **2** = **blockage**, check, curtailment, interruption, obstruction, occlusion, stopping up

store *vb* **1** = **put by**, accumulate, deposit, garner, hoard, husband, keep, keep in reserve, lay by *or*

storage. **5** *Computing.* to enter or retain (information) in a storage device. ◆ *n* **6a** an establishment for the retail sale of goods and services. **6b** (*in combination*): *storefront.* **7** a large supply or stock kept for future use. **8** short for **department store. 9a** a storage place such as a warehouse or depository. **9b** (*in combination*): *storeman.* **10** the state of being stored (esp. in **in store**). **11** a large amount or quantity. **12** *Computers, chiefly Brit.* another name for **memory** (sense 7). **13 in store.** forthcoming or imminent. **14 lay, put,** *or* **set store by.** to value or reckon as important. ◆ *adj* **15** (of cattle, sheep, etc.) bought lean to be fattened up for market. ◆ See also **stores.** [C13: from OF *estor,* from *estorer* to restore, from L *instaurāre* to refresh]
▸ **'storable** *adj*

store card *n* another name for **charge card.**

storehouse ('stɔːˌhaʊs) *n* a place where things are stored.

storekeeper ('stɔːˌkiːpə) *n* a manager, owner, or keeper of a store.
▸ **'storeˌkeeping** *n*

store of value *n Econ.* the function of money that enables goods and services to be paid for a considerable time after they have been acquired.

storeroom ('stɔːˌruːm, -ˌrʊm) *n* **1** a room in which things are stored. **2** room for storing.

stores (stɔːz) *pl n* supply or stock of something, esp. essentials, for a specific purpose.

storey *or esp. US* **story** ('stɔːrɪ) *n, pl* **storeys** *or* **stories. 1** a floor or level of a building. **2** a set of rooms on one level. [C14: from Anglo-L *historia,* picture, from L: narrative, prob. from the pictures on medieval windows]

storeyed *or US* **storied** ('stɔːrɪd) *adj* **a** having a storey or storeys. **b** (*in combination*): *a two-storeyed house.*

storied ('stɔːrɪd) *adj* **1** recorded in history or in a story. **2** decorated with narrative scenes.

stork (stɔːk) *n* any of a family of large wading birds, chiefly of warm regions of the Old World, having very long legs and a long stout pointed bill, and typically having a white-and-black plumage. [OE *storc*]

storksbill ('stɔːksˌbɪl) *n* a plant related to the geranium, having pink or reddish-purple flowers and fruits with a beaklike process.

storm 🅣 (stɔːm) *n* **1a** a violent weather condition of strong winds, rain, hail, thunder, lightning, blowing sand, snow, etc. **1b** (*as modifier*): *storm cloud.* **1c** (*in combination*): *stormproof.* **2** *Meteorol.* a wind of force 10 on the Beaufort scale, reaching speeds of 55 to 63 mph. **3** a strong or violent reaction: *a storm of protest.* **4** a direct assault on a stronghold. **5** a heavy discharge or rain, as of bullets or missiles. **6** short for **storm window. 7 storm in a teacup.** *Brit.* a violent fuss or disturbance over a trivial matter. **8 take by storm. 8a** to capture or overrun by a violent assault. **8b** to overwhelm and enthral. ◆ *vb* **9** to attack or capture (something) suddenly and violently. **10** (*intr*) to be vociferously angry. **11** (*intr*) to move or rush violently or angrily. **12** (*intr; with it as subject*) to rain, hail, or snow hard and be very windy, often with thunder and lightning. [OE]

stormbound ('stɔːmˌbaʊnd) *adj* detained or harassed by storms.

storm centre *n* **1** the centre of a cyclonic storm, etc., where pressure is lowest. **2** the centre of any disturbance or trouble.

storm cloud *n* **1** a heavy dark cloud presaging rain or a storm. **2** a herald of disturbance, anger, etc.: *the storm clouds of war.*

storm-cock *n* another name for **mistle thrush.**

storm cone *n Brit.* a canvas cone hoisted as a warning of high winds.

storm door *n* an additional door outside an ordinary door, providing extra insulation against wind, cold, rain, etc.

storming ('stɔːmɪŋ) *adj Inf.* characterized by or displaying dynamism, speed, and energy: *a storming performance.*

storm lantern *n* another name for **hurricane lamp.**

storm trooper *n* **1** a member of the Nazi SA. **2** a member of a force of shock troops.

storm window *n* **1** an additional window fitted outside an ordinary window to provide insulation against wind, cold, rain, etc. **2** a type of dormer window.

stormy 🅣 ('stɔːmɪ) *adj* **stormier, stormiest. 1** characterized by storms. **2** involving or characterized by violent disturbance or emotional outburst.
▸ **'stormily** *adv* ▸ **'storminess** *n*

stormy petrel *n* **1** Also called: **storm petrel.** any of various small petrels typically having dark plumage and paler underparts. **2** a person who brings or portends trouble.

Storting *or* **Storthing** ('stɔːtɪŋ) *n* the parliament of Norway. [C19: Norwegian, from *stor* great + *thing* assembly]

story[1] 🅣 ('stɔːrɪ) *n, pl* **stories. 1** a narration of a chain of events told or written in prose or verse. **2** Also called: **short story.** a piece of fiction, briefer and usually less detailed than a novel. **3** Also called: **story line.** the plot of a book, film, etc. **4** an event that could be the subject of a narrative. **5** a report or statement on a matter or event. **6** the event or material for such a report. **7** *Inf.* a lie, fib, or untruth. **8 cut** (*or* **make**) **a long story short.** to leave out details in a narration. **9 the same old story.** *Inf.* the familiar or regular course of events. **10 the story goes.** it is commonly said or believed. ◆ *vb* **stories, storying, storied.** (*tr*) **11** to decorate (a pot, wall, etc.) with scenes from history or legends. [C13: from Anglo-F *estorie,* from L *historia;* see HISTORY]

story[2] ('stɔːrɪ) *n, pl* **stories.** another spelling (esp. US) of **storey.**

storyboard ('stɔːrɪˌbɔːd) *n* (in films, television, etc.) a series of sketches or photographs showing the sequence of shots or images planned for a film.

storybook ('stɔːrɪˌbʊk) *n* **1** a book containing stories, esp. for children. ◆ *adj* **2** unreal or fantastic: *a storybook world.*

storyteller 🅣 ('stɔːrɪˌtelə) *n* **1** a person who tells stories. **2** *Inf.* a liar.
▸ **'storyˌtelling** *n*

Stoss (*German* ʃtoːs) *n* **Viet** (faɪət). ?1445–1533, German Gothic sculptor and woodcarver. His masterpiece is the high altar in the Church of St Mary, Cracow (1477–89).

stoup *or* **stoop** (stuːp) *n* **1** a small basin for holy water. **2** *Dialect.* a bucket or cup. [C14 (in the sense: bucket): from ON]

stoush (staʊʃ) *Austral. & NZ sl.* ◆ *vb* **1** (*tr*) to hit or punch. ◆ *n* **2** fighting, violence, or a fight. [C19: from ?]

stout 🅣 (staʊt) *adj* **1** solidly built or corpulent. **2** (*prenominal*) resolute or valiant: *stout fellow.* **3** strong, substantial, and robust. **4 a stout heart.** courage; resolution. ◆ *n* **5** strong porter highly flavoured with malt. [C14: from OF *estout* bold, of Gmc origin]
▸ **'stoutly** *adv* ▸ **'stoutness** *n*

stouthearted 🅣 (ˌstaʊt'hɑːtɪd) *adj* valiant; brave.
▸ **ˌstout'heartedly** *adv* ▸ **ˌstout'heartedness** *n*

stove[1] (stəʊv) *n* **1** another word for **cooker** (sense 1). **2** any heating apparatus, such as a kiln. [OE *stofa* bathroom]

stove[2] (stəʊv) *vb* a past tense and past participle of **stave.**

stove enamel *n* a type of enamel made heatproof by treatment in a stove.

stovepipe ('stəʊvˌpaɪp) *n* **1** a pipe that serves as a flue to a stove. **2** Also called: **stovepipe hat.** a man's tall silk hat.

stow 🅣 (stəʊ) *vb* (*tr*) **1** (often foll. by *away*) to pack or store. **2** to fill by packing. **3** *Naut.* to pack or put away (cargo, sails, etc.). **4** to have enough room for. **5** (*usually imperative*) *Brit. sl.* to cease from: *stow your noise!* [OE *stōwian* to keep, from *stōw* a place]

Stow (stəʊ) *n* **John.** 1525–1605, English antiquary, noted for his *Survey of London and Westminster* (1598; 1603).

stowage ('stəʊɪdʒ) *n* **1** space, room, or a charge for stowing goods. **2** the act or an instance of stowing or the state of being stowed. **3** something that is stowed.

stowaway ('stəʊəˌweɪ) *n* **1** a person who hides aboard a vehicle, ship, or aircraft in order to gain free passage. ◆ *vb* **stow away. 2** (*intr, adv*) to travel in such a way.

STP *abbrev. for:* **1** Professor of Sacred Theology. [from L: *Sanctae Theologiae Professor*] **2** *Trademark.* scientifically treated petroleum: an oil substitute promising renewed power for an internal-combustion engine. **3** standard temperature and pressure. ◆ *n* **4** a synthetic hallucinogenic drug related to mescaline. [from humorous reference to the extra power resulting from scientifically treated petroleum]

THESAURUS

in, lock away, put aside, put aside for a rainy day, put in storage, reserve, salt away, save, stash (*inf.*), stock, stockpile ◆ *n* **6a** = **shop**, chain store, department store, emporium, hypermarket, market, mart, outlet, supermarket **7** = **supply**, abundance, accumulation, cache, fund, hoard, lot, mine, plenty, plethora, provision, quantity, reserve, reservoir, stock, stockpile, wealth **9a** = **repository**, depository, depot, storehouse, storeroom, warehouse **14 lay store by** = **value**, appreciate, esteem, hold in high regard, prize, think highly of

storm *n* **1a** = **tempest**, blast, blizzard, cyclone, gale, gust, hurricane, squall, tornado, whirlwind **3** = **outburst**, agitation, anger, clamour, commotion, disturbance, furore, hubbub, outbreak, outcry, passion, roar, row, rumpus, stir, strife, tumult, turmoil, violence **4** = **attack**, assault, blitz, blitzkrieg, offensive, onset, onslaught, rush ◆ *vb* **9** = **attack**, assail, assault, beset, charge, rush, take by storm **10** = **rage**, bluster, complain, fly off the handle, fume, go ballistic (*sl., chiefly US*), rant, rave, scold, thunder, wig out (*sl.*) **11** = **rush**, flounce, fly, stalk, stamp, stomp (*inf.*)

stormy *adj* **1** = **wild**, blustering, blustery, dirty, foul, gusty, inclement, raging, rough, squally, tempestuous, turbulent, windy

story[1] *n* **1** = **tale**, account, anecdote, chronicle, fictional account, history, legend, narration, narrative, novel, recital, record, relation, romance, urban legend, urban myth, version, yarn **5** = **report**, article, feature, news, news item, scoop **7** *Informal* = **lie**, falsehood, fib, fiction, pork pie (*Brit. sl.*), porky (*Brit. sl.*), untruth, white lie

storyteller *n* **1** = **raconteur**, anecdotist, author, bard, chronicler, fabulist, narrator, novelist, romancer, spinner of yarns

stout *adj* **1** = **fat**, big, bulky, burly, corpulent, fleshy, heavy, obese, on the large *or* heavy side, overweight, plump, portly, rotund, substantial, tubby **2** = **brave**, bold, courageous, dauntless, doughty, fearless, gallant, indomitable, intrepid, lion-hearted, manly, plucky, resolute, valiant, valorous **3** = **strong**, able-bodied, athletic, beefy (*inf.*), brawny, hardy, hulking, husky (*inf.*), lusty, muscular, robust, stalwart, strapping, sturdy, substantial, thickset, tough, vigorous

Antonyms *adj* ≠ **fat**: insubstantial, lanky, lean, skin-and-bones (*inf.*), skinny, slender, slight, slim ≠ **strong**: feeble, flimsy, frail, insubstantial, puny ≠ **brave**: cowardly, faint-hearted, fearful, irresolute, shrinking, soft, spineless, timid, weak

stouthearted *adj Old-fashioned* = **brave**, ballsy (*taboo sl.*), bold, courageous, dauntless, doughty, fearless, great-hearted, gutsy (*sl.*), heroic, indomitable, intrepid, lion-hearted, plucky, spirited, stalwart, valiant, valorous

stow *vb* **1, 2** = **pack**, bundle, cram, deposit, jam, load, put away, secrete, stash (*inf.*), store, stuff, tuck

strabismus (strəˈbɪzməs) *n* abnormal alignment of one or both eyes, characterized by a turning inwards or outwards from the nose: caused by paralysis of an eye muscle, etc. Also called: **squint.** [C17: via NL from Gk *strabismos*, from *strabizein* to squint, from *strabos* cross-eyed] ▸**straˈbismal, straˈbismic,** *or* **straˈbismical** *adj*

straddle (ˈstrædᵊl) *vb* **straddles, straddling, straddled. 1** *(tr)* to have one leg, part, or support on each side of. **2** *(tr) US & Canad. inf.* to be in favour of both sides of (something). **3** *(intr)* to stand, walk, or sit with the legs apart. **4** *(tr)* to spread (the legs) apart. **5** *Gunnery.* to fire a number of shots slightly beyond and slightly short of (a target) to determine the correct range. **6** *(intr)* (in poker, of the second player after the dealer) to double the ante before looking at one's cards. ◆ *n* **7** the act or position of straddling. **8** a noncommittal attitude or stand. **9** *Business.* a contract or option permitting its purchaser either to sell or buy securities or commodities within a specified period of time at specified prices. **10** *Athletics.* a high-jumping technique in which the body is parallel with the bar and the legs straddle it at the highest point of the jump. **11** (in poker) the stake put up after the ante in poker by the second player after the dealer. [C16: from obs. *strad-* (OE *strode*), past stem of STRIDE] ▸**ˈstraddler** *n*

Stradivarius (ˌstrædɪˈvɛərɪəs) *n* any of a number of violins manufactured in Italy by Antonio Stradivari (?1644–1737) or his family. Often shortened to (informal): **Strad.**

strafe (streɪf, strɑːf) *vb* **strafes, strafing, strafed.** *(tr)* **1** to machine-gun (troops, etc.) from the air. **2** *Sl.* to punish harshly. ◆ *n* **3** an act or instance of strafing. [C20: from G *strafen* to punish] ▸**ˈstrafer** *n*

straggle ❶ (ˈstrægᵊl) *vb* **straggles, straggling, straggled.** *(intr)* **1** to go, come, or spread in a rambling or irregular way. **2** to linger behind or wander from a main line or part. [C14: from ?] ▸**ˈstraggler** *n* ▸**ˈstraggly** *adj*

straight ❶ (streɪt) *adj* **1** not curved or crooked; continuing in the same direction without deviating. **2** straightforward, outright, or candid: *a straight rejection.* **3** even, level, or upright. **4** in keeping with the facts; accurate. **5** honest, respectable, or reliable. **6** accurate or logical: *straight reasoning.* **7** continuous; uninterrupted. **8** (esp. of an alcoholic drink) undiluted; neat. **9** not crisp, kinked, or curly: *straight hair.* **10** correctly arranged; orderly. **11** (of a play, acting style, etc.) straightforward or serious. **12** *Boxing.* (of a blow) delivered with an unbent arm: *a straight left.* **13** (of the cylinders of an internal-combustion engine) in line, rather than in a V-formation or in some other arrangement: *a straight eight.* **14** a slang word for **heterosexual. 15** *Inf.* no longer owing or being owed something: *if you buy the next round we'll be straight.* **16** *Sl.* conventional in views, customs, appearance, etc. **17** *Sl.* not using narcotics. ◆ *adv* **18** in a straight line or direct course. **19** immediately; at once: *he came straight back.* **20** in an even, level, or upright position. **21** without cheating, lying, or unreliability: *tell it to me straight.* **22** continuously; uninterruptedly. **23** (often foll. by *out*) frankly; candidly: *he told me straight out.* **24 go straight.** *Inf.* to reform after having been dishonest or a criminal. ◆ *n* **25** the state of being straight. **26** a straight line, form, part, or position. **27** *Brit.* a straight part of a racetrack. **28** *Poker.* **28a** five cards that are in sequence irrespective of suit. **28b** a hand containing such a sequence. **28c** *(as modifier): a straight flush.* **29** *Sl.* a conventional person. **30** a slang word for a **heterosexual. 31** *Sl.* a cigarette containing only tobacco, without marijuana, etc. [C14: from p.p. of OE *streccan* to stretch] ▸**ˈstraightly** *adv* ▸**ˈstraightness** *n*

straight and narrow *n Inf.* the proper, honest, and moral path of behaviour.

straight angle *n* an angle of 180°.

straightaway ❶ *adv* (ˌstreɪtəˈweɪ). *also* **straight away. 1** at once. ◆ *n* (ˈstreɪtəˌweɪ). **2** the US word for **straight** (sense 27).

straight chair *n* a straight-backed side chair.

straightedge (ˈstreɪtˌɛdʒ) *n* a stiff strip of wood or metal with one edge straight, used for ruling and testing straight lines.

straighten ❶ (ˈstreɪtᵊn) *vb* (sometimes foll. by *up* or *out*) **1** to make or become straight. **2** *(tr)* to make neat or tidy. ▸**ˈstraightener** *n*

straighten out ❶ *vb (adv)* **1** to make or become less complicated or confused. **2** *US & Canad.* to reform or become reformed.

straight face *n* a serious facial expression, esp. one that conceals the impulse to laugh. ▸**ˈstraight-ˈfaced** *adj*

straight fight *n* a contest between two candidates only.

straight flush *n* (in poker) five consecutive cards of the same suit.

straightforward ❶ (ˌstreɪtˈfɔːwəd) *adj* **1** (of a person) honest, frank, or simple. **2** *Chiefly Brit.* (of a task, etc.) simple; easy. ◆ *adv, adj* **3** in a straight course. ▸**ˌstraightˈforwardly** *adv* ▸**ˌstraightˈforwardness** *n*

straightjacket (ˈstreɪtˌdʒækɪt) *n* a less common spelling of **straitjacket.**

straight-laced *adj* a variant spelling of **strait-laced.**

straight man *n* a subsidiary actor who acts as stooge to a comedian.

straight-out *adj US inf.* **1** complete; thoroughgoing. **2** frank or honest.

straight razor *n* another name for **cut-throat** (sense 2).

straightway (ˈstreɪtˌweɪ) *adv Arch.* at once.

strain[1] ❶ (streɪn) *vb* **1** to draw or be drawn taut; stretch tight. **2** to exert, tax, or use (resources) to the utmost extent. **3** to injure or damage or be injured or damaged by overexertion: *he strained himself.* **4** to deform or be deformed as a result of a stress. **5** *(intr)* to make intense or violent efforts; strive. **6** to subject or be subjected to mental tension or stress. **7** to pour or pass (a substance) or (of a substance) to be poured or passed through a sieve, filter, or strainer. **8** *(tr)* to draw off or remove (one part of a substance or mixture from another) by or as if by filtering. **9** *(tr)* to clasp tightly; hug. **10** *(intr;* foll. by *at)* to push, pull, or work with violent exertion (upon). ◆ *n* **11** the act or an instance of straining. **12** the damage resulting from excessive exertion. **13** an intense physical or mental effort. **14** *(often pl) Music.* a theme, melody, or tune. **15** a great demand on the emotions, resources, etc. **16** a way of speaking; tone of voice: *don't go on in that strain.* **17** tension or tiredness resulting from overwork, worry, etc.; stress. **18** *Physics.* the change in dimension of a body under load expressed as the ratio of the total deflection or change in dimension to the original unloaded dimension. [C13: from OF *estreindre* to press together, from L *stringere* to bind tightly]

strain[2] ❶ (streɪn) *n* **1** the main body of descendants from one ancestor. **2** a group of organisms within a species or variety, distinguished by one or more minor characteristics. **3** a variety of bacterium or fungus, esp. one used for a culture. **4** a streak; trace. **5** *Arch.* a kind, type, or sort. [OE *strēon*]

strained ❶ (streɪnd) *adj* **1** (of an action, expression, etc.) not natural or spontaneous. **2** (of an atmosphere, relationship, etc.) not relaxed; tense.

strainer (ˈstreɪnə) *n* **1** a sieve used for straining sauces, vegetables, tea, etc. **2** a gauze or simple filter used to strain liquids.

THESAURUS

straggle *vb* **1** = **spread**, drift, lag, loiter, ramble, range, roam, rove, stray, string out, trail, wander

straggly *adj* **1** = **spread out**, aimless, disorganized, drifting, irregular, loose, rambling, random, spreading, straggling, straying, untidy

straight *adj* **1** = **direct**, near, short, undeviating, unswerving **2** = **frank**, blunt, bold, candid, downright, forthright, honest, outright, plain, point-blank, straightforward, unqualified, upfront (*inf.*) **3** = **level**, aligned, even, horizontal, in line, perpendicular, plumb, right, smooth, square, true, upright, vertical **4** = **accurate**, authentic, fair, honest, reliable, trustworthy **5** = **honest**, above board, decent, equitable, fair, fair and square, honourable, just, law-abiding, reliable, respectable, trustworthy, upright **7** = **successive**, consecutive, continuous, nonstop, running, solid, sustained, through, uninterrupted, unrelieved **8** = **undiluted**, neat, pure, unadulterated, unmixed **10** = **orderly**, arranged, in order, neat, organized, put to rights, shipshape, sorted out, tidy **16** *Slang* = **conventional**, bourgeois, conservative, orthodox, Pooterish, square (*inf.*), traditional ◆ *adv* **18** = **directly**, as the crow flies, at once, immediately, instantly **23** = **frankly**, candidly, honestly, in plain English, point-blank, pulling no punches (*inf.*), with no holds barred
Antonyms *adj* ≠ **direct:** circuitous, indirect, roundabout, winding, zigzag ≠ **level:** askew, bent, crooked, curved, skewwhiff (*Brit. inf.*), twisted, uneven ≠ **frank:** ambiguous, cryptic, equivocal, evasive, indirect, vague ≠ **successive:** broken, discontinuous, interrupted, non-consecutive ≠ **orderly:** confused, disorderly, disorganized, in disarray, messy, untidy ≠ **honest:** bent (*sl.*), crooked (*inf.*), dishonest, dishonourable, shady (*inf.*), unlawful ≠ **conventional:** cool, fashionable, trendy (*Brit. inf.*), voguish

straight away *adv* **1** = **immediately**, at once, directly, instantly, now, on the spot, right away, straightway (*arch.*), there and then, this minute, without any delay, without more ado

straighten *vb* **2** = **neaten**, arrange, order, put in order, set *or* put to rights, smarten up, spruce up, tidy (up)

straighten out *vb* **1** = **make clear**, clear up, correct, disentangle, put right, rectify, regularize, resolve, settle, sort out, unsnarl, work out

straightforward *adj* **1** = **honest**, above board, candid, direct, forthright, genuine, guileless, open, sincere, truthful, upfront (*inf.*) **2** *Chiefly Brit.* = **simple**, clear-cut, easy, easy-peasy (*sl.*), elementary, routine, uncomplicated, undemanding
Antonyms *adj* ≠ **honest:** devious, disingenuous, roundabout, shady, sharp, unscrupulous ≠ **simple:** complex, complicated, confused, convoluted, unclear

strain[1] *vb* **1** = **stretch**, distend, draw tight, extend, tauten, tighten **2** = **strive**, bend over backwards (*inf.*), break one's back *or* neck (*inf.*), bust a gut (*inf.*), do one's damnedest (*inf.*), endeavour, give it one's all (*inf.*), give it one's best shot (*inf.*), go all out for (*inf.*), go for broke (*sl.*), go for it (*inf.*), knock oneself out (*inf.*), labour, make an all-out effort (*inf.*), rupture oneself (*inf.*), struggle **3** = **overexert**, drive, exert, fatigue, injure, overtax, overwork, pull, push to the limit, sprain, tax, tear, test, tire, twist, weaken, wrench **7** = **sieve**, filter, percolate, purify, riddle, screen, seep, separate, sift ◆ *n* **12** = **injury**, pull, sprain, tautness, tension, tensity (*rare*), wrench **13** = **exertion**, effort, force, struggle **14** *often plural* = **tune**, air, lay, measure (*poetic*), melody, song, theme **15** = **stress**, anxiety, burden, pressure, tension
Antonyms *n* ≠ **stress, exertion:** ease, effortlessness, lack of tension, relaxation ◆ *vb* ≠ **strive, overexert:** idle, loose, pamper, relax, rest, slacken, take it easy, yield

strain[2] *n* **1** = **breed**, ancestry, blood, descent, extraction, family, lineage, pedigree, race, stock **4** = **trace**, streak, suggestion, suspicion, tendency, trait

strained *adj* **1** = **forced**, artificial, false, laboured, put on, unnatural **2** = **tense**, awkward, constrained, difficult, embarrassed, self-conscious, stiff, uncomfortable, uneasy, unrelaxed
Antonyms *adj* ≠ **forced:** natural ≠ **tense:** comfortable, relaxed

strait 🅣 (streɪt) *n* **1** (*often pl*) a narrow channel of the sea linking two larger areas of sea. **2** (*often pl*) a position of acute difficulty (often in **in dire** *or* **desperate straits**). **3** *Arch.* a narrow place or passage. ◆ *adj* **4** *Arch.* (of spaces, etc.) affording little room. [C13: from OF *estreit* narrow, from L *strictus* constricted, from *stringere* to bind tightly]
▸**'straitly** *adv* ▸**'straitness** *n*

straiten ('streɪtᵊn) *vb* **1** (*tr; usually passive*) to embarrass or distress, esp. financially. **2** (*tr*) to limit, confine, or restrict. **3** *Arch.* to make or become narrow.

straitjacket ('streɪtˌdʒækɪt) *n* **1** Also: **straightjacket.** a jacket made of strong canvas material with long sleeves for binding the arms of violent prisoners or mental patients. **2** a restriction or limitation. ◆ *vb* **3** (*tr*) to confine in or as if in a straitjacket.

strait-laced 🅣 *or* **straight-laced** *adj* prudish or puritanical.

strake (streɪk) *n* **1a** a curved metal plate forming part of the metal rim on a wooden wheel. **1b** any metal plate let into a rubber tyre. **2** Also called: **streak.** *Naut.* one of a continuous range of planks or plates forming the side of a vessel. [C14: rel. to OE *streccan* to stretch]

stramonium (strə'məʊnɪəm) *n* **1** a preparation of the dried leaves and flowers of the thorn apple, containing hyoscyamine and used as a drug to treat nervous disorders. **2** another name for **thorn apple** (sense 1). [C17: from NL, from ?]

strand[1] 🅣 (strænd) *vb* **1** to leave or drive (ships, fish, etc.) aground or ashore or (of ships, etc.) to be left or driven ashore. **2** (*tr; usually passive*) to leave helpless, as without transport, money, etc. ◆ *n* **3** *Chiefly poetic.* a shore or beach. [OE]

strand[2] 🅣 (strænd) *n* **1** a set of or one of the individual fibres or threads of string, wire, etc., that form a rope, cable, etc. **2** a single length of string, hair, wool, wire, etc. **3** a string of pearls or beads. **4** a constituent element of something. ◆ *vb* **5** (*tr*) to form (a rope, cable, etc.) by winding strands together. [C15: from ?]

strange 🅣 (streɪndʒ) *adj* **1** odd, unusual, or extraordinary; peculiar. **2** not known, seen, or experienced before; unfamiliar. **3** not easily explained. **4** (usually foll. by *to*) inexperienced (in) or unaccustomed (to): *strange to a task.* **5** not of one's own kind, locality, etc.; alien; foreign. **6** shy; distant; reserved. **7 strange to say.** it is unusual or surprising (that). **8** *Physics.* **8a** denoting a particular flavour of quark. **8b** denoting or relating to a hypothetical form of matter composed of such quarks: *strange matter; a strange star.* ◆ *adv* **9** *Not standard.* in a strange manner. [C13: from OF *estrange*, from L *extrāneus* foreign; see EXTRANEOUS]
▸**'strangely** *adv*

strangeness ('streɪndʒnɪs) *n* **1** the state or quality of being strange. **2** *Physics.* a property of certain elementary particles characterized by a quantum number (**strangeness number**) conserved in strong but not in weak interactions.

stranger 🅣 ('streɪndʒə) *n* **1** any person whom one does not know. **2** a person who is new to a particular locality, from another region, town, etc. **3** a guest or visitor. **4** (foll. by *to*) a person who is unfamiliar (with) or new (to) something: *he is no stranger to computing.*

strangle 🅣 ('stræŋgᵊl) *vb* **strangles, strangling, strangled.** (*tr*) **1** to kill by compressing the windpipe; throttle. **2** to prevent or inhibit the growth or development of: *to strangle originality.* **3** to suppress (an utterance) by or as if by swallowing suddenly: *to strangle a cry.* ◆ See also **strangles.** [C13: via OF, ult. from Gk *strangalē* a halter]
▸**'strangler** *n*

stranglehold ('stræŋgᵊlˌhəʊld) *n* **1** a wrestling hold in which a wrestler's arms are pressed against his opponent's windpipe. **2** complete power or control over a person or situation.

strangles ('stræŋgᵊlz) *n* (*functioning as sing*) an acute infectious bacterial disease of horses, characterized by inflammation of the respiratory tract. Also called: **equine distemper.**

strangulate ('stræŋgjʊˌleɪt) *vb* **strangulates, strangulating, strangulated.** (*tr*) **1** to constrict (a hollow organ, vessel, etc.) so as to stop the flow of air, blood, etc., through it. **2** another word for **strangle.**
▸**ˌstrangu'lation** *n*

strangury ('stræŋgjʊrɪ) *n* *Pathol.* painful excretion of urine, drop by drop. [C14: from L *strangūria*, from Gk, from *stranx* a drop squeezed out + *ouron* urine]

strap 🅣 (stræp) *n* **1** a long strip of leather or similar material, for binding trunks, baggage, etc. **2** a strip of leather or similar material used for carrying, lifting, or holding. **3** a loop of leather, rubber, etc., suspended from the roof in a bus or train for standing passengers to hold on to. **4** a razor strop. **5** short for **shoulder strap. 6** *Business.* a triple option on a security or commodity consisting of one put option and two call options at the same price and for the same period. Cf. **strip**[2] (sense 4). **7** *Irish, derog. sl.* a shameless or promiscuous woman. **8 the strap.** a beating with a strap as a punishment. ◆ *vb* **straps, strapping, strapped.** (*tr*) **9** to tie or bind with a strap. **10** to beat with a strap. **11** to sharpen with a strap or strop. [C16: var. of STROP]

straphanger ('stræpˌhæŋə) *n* *Inf.* a passenger in a bus, train, etc., who has to travel standing, esp. holding on to a strap.
▸**'strapˌhanging** *n*

strapping 🅣 ('stræpɪŋ) *adj* (*prenominal*) tall and sturdy. [C17: from STRAP (in the arch. sense: to work vigorously)]

strapwork ('stræpˌwɜːk) *n* *Archit.* decorative work resembling interlacing straps.

strata ('strɑːtə) *n* a plural of **stratum.**

> **USAGE NOTE** *Strata* is sometimes wrongly used as a singular noun: *this stratum* (not *strata*) *of society is often disregarded.*

stratagem 🅣 ('strætɪdʒəm) *n* a plan or trick, esp. to deceive an enemy. [C15: ult. from Gk *stratēgos* a general, from *stratos* an army + *agein* to lead]

strategic 🅣 (strə'tiːdʒɪk) *or* **strategical** *adj* **1** of or characteristic of strategy. **2** important to strategy. **3** (of weapons, esp. missiles) directed against an enemy's homeland rather than used on a battlefield. Cf. **tactical.**
▸**stra'tegically** *adv*

strategics (strə'tiːdʒɪks) *n* (*functioning as sing*) strategy, esp. in a military sense.

strategist ('strætɪdʒɪst) *n* a specialist or expert in strategy.

strategy 🅣 ('strætɪdʒɪ) *n, pl* **strategies. 1** the art or science of the planning and conduct of a war. **2** a particular long-term plan for success, esp. in politics, business, etc. **3** a plan or stratagem. [C17: from F *stratégie*, from Gk *stratēgia* function of a general; see STRATAGEM]

strath (stræθ) *n* *Scot.* a flat river valley. [C16: from Scot. & Irish Gaelic *srath*]

strathspey (stræθ'speɪ) *n* **1** a Scottish dance with gliding steps, slower than a reel. **2** a piece of music composed for or in the rhythm of this dance. [after *Strathspey*, valley of the river Spey]

strati- *combining form.* indicating stratum or strata: *stratigraphy.*

straticulate (strə'tɪkjʊlɪt, -ˌleɪt) *adj* (of a rock formation) composed of very thin even strata. [C19: from NL *strāticulum* (unattested), dim. of L *strātum* something strewn; see STRATUS]
▸**straˌticu'lation** *n*

stratify ('strætɪˌfaɪ) *vb* **stratifies, stratifying, stratified. 1** to form or be formed in layers or strata. **2** *Sociol.* to divide (a society) into status groups or (of a society) to develop such groups. [C17: from F *stratifier*, from NL *stratificāre*, from L STRATUM]
▸**ˌstratifi'cation** *n* ▸**'stratiˌfied** *adj*

stratigraphy (strə'tɪgrəfɪ) *n* **1** the study of the composition, relative positions, etc., of rock strata in order to determine their geological history. **2** *Archaeol.* a vertical section through the earth showing the relative positions of the human artefacts and therefore the chronology of successive levels of occupation.
▸**stratigraphic** (ˌstrætɪ'græfɪk) *or* **ˌstrati'graphical** *adj*

stratocumulus (ˌstrætəʊ'kjuːmjʊləs) *n, pl* **stratocumuli** (-ˌlaɪ). *Meteorol.* a uniform stretch of cloud containing dark grey globular masses.

stratopause ('strætəˌpɔːz) *n* *Meteorol.* the transitional zone of maximum temperature between the stratosphere and the mesosphere.

stratosphere ('strætəˌsfɪə) *n* the atmospheric layer lying between the troposphere and the mesosphere, in which temperature generally increases with height.
▸**stratospheric** (ˌstrætə'sferɪk) *or* **ˌstrato'spherical** *adj*

stratum 🅣 ('strɑːtəm) *n, pl* **strata** *or* **stratums. 1** (*usually pl*) any of the dis-

THESAURUS

strait *n* **1** *often plural* = **channel**, narrows, sound **2** *often plural* = **difficulty**, crisis, dilemma, distress, embarrassment, emergency, extremity, hardship, hole (*sl.*), mess, panic stations (*inf.*), pass, perplexity, plight, predicament, pretty *or* fine kettle of fish (*inf.*)

strait-laced *adj* = **puritanical**, moralistic, narrow, narrow-minded, niminy-piminy, of the old school, old-maidish (*inf.*), overscrupulous, prim, proper, prudish, strict, Victorian
Antonyms *adj* broad-minded, earthy, immoral, loose, relaxed, uninhibited, unreserved

strand[2] *n* **1, 2** = **filament**, fibre, length, lock, rope, string, thread, tress, twist, wisp

stranded *adj* **1** = **beached**, aground, ashore, cast away, grounded, marooned, shipwrecked **2** = **helpless**, abandoned, high and dry, homeless, left in the lurch, penniless

strange *adj* **1** = **odd**, abnormal, astonishing, bizarre, curious, curiouser and curiouser, eccentric, exceptional, extraordinary, fantastic, funny, irregular, left-field (*inf.*), marvellous, mystifying, oddball (*inf.*), off-the-wall (*sl.*), out-of-the-way, outré, peculiar, perplexing, queer, rare, remarkable, rum (*Brit. sl.*), singular, unaccountable, uncanny, uncommon, unheard-of, weird, wonderful **2** = **unfamiliar**, alien, exotic, foreign, new, novel, outside one's experience, remote, unexplored, unknown, untried **4 strange to** = **unaccustomed to**, a stranger to, ignorant of, inexperienced in, new to, unpractised in, unseasoned in, unused to, unversed in
Antonyms *adj* ≠ **odd:** accustomed, bog-standard (*Brit. & Irish sl.*), common, commonplace, conventional, familiar, habitual, ordinary, regular, routine, run-of-the-mill, standard, typical, unexceptional, usual, well-known ≠ **unfamiliar:** accustomed, familiar, habitual

stranger *n* **1-3** = **newcomer**, alien, foreigner, guest, incomer, new arrival, outlander, unknown, visitor

strangle *vb* **1** = **throttle**, asphyxiate, choke, garrotte, smother, strangulate, suffocate **3** = **suppress**, gag, inhibit, repress, stifle

strap *n* **1** = **belt**, leash, thong, tie ◆ *vb* **2** = **fasten**, bind, buckle, lash, secure, tie, truss **10** = **beat**, belt (*inf.*), flog, lash, scourge, whip

strapping *adj* = **well-built**, beefy, big, brawny, burly, hefty (*inf.*), hulking, husky (*inf.*), powerful, robust, stalwart, sturdy, well set-up

stratagem *n* = **trick**, artifice, device, dodge, feint, intrigue, manoeuvre, plan, plot, ploy, ruse, scheme, subterfuge, wile

strategic *adj* **1** = **tactical**, calculated, deliberate, diplomatic, planned, politic **2** = **crucial**, cardinal, critical, decisive, important, key, vital

strategy *n* **2, 3** = **plan**, approach, grand design, manoeuvring, planning, policy, procedure, programme, scheme

stratum *n* **1, 3, 4** = **layer**, bed, level, lode, seam, stratification, table, tier, vein **5** = **class**, bracket, caste, category, estate, grade, group, level, rank, station

tinct layers into which sedimentary rocks are divided. **2** *Biol.* a single layer of tissue or cells. **3** a layer of any material, esp. one of several parallel layers. **4** a layer of ocean or atmosphere either naturally or arbitrarily demarcated. **5** a level of a social hierarchy. [C16: via NL from L: something strewn, from *sternere* to scatter]
▸'**stratal** *adj*

stratus ('streɪtəs) *n, pl* **strati** (-taɪ). a grey layer cloud. [C19: via NL from L: strewn, from *sternere* to extend]

straw (strɔː) *n* **1a** stalks of threshed grain, esp. of wheat, rye, oats, or barley, used in plaiting hats, baskets, etc., or as fodder. **1b** (*as modifier*): *a straw hat.* **2** a single dry or ripened stalk, esp. of a grass. **3** a long thin hollow paper or plastic tube, used for sucking up liquids into the mouth. **4** (*usually used with a negative*) anything of little value or importance: *I wouldn't give a straw for our chances.* **5** a measure or remedy that one turns to in desperation (esp. in **clutch** *or* **grasp at a straw** *or* **straws**). **6a** a pale yellow colour. **6b** (*as adj*): *straw hair.* **7 draw the short straw.** to be the person to whom an unpleasant task falls. **8 straw in the wind.** a hint or indication. **9 the last straw.** a small incident, setback, etc., that coming after others proves insufferable. [OE *streaw*]
▸'**strawy** *adj*

strawberry ('strɔːbərɪ, -brɪ) *n, pl* **strawberries. 1** any of various low-growing rosaceous plants which have red edible fruits and spread by runners. **2a** the fruit of any of these plants, consisting of a sweet fleshy receptacle bearing small seedlike parts (the true fruits). **2b** (*as modifier*): *strawberry ice cream.* **3a** a purplish-red colour. **3b** (*as adj*): *strawberry shoes.* [OE *streawberige;* ?from the strawlike appearance of the runners]

strawberry blonde *adj* **1** (of hair) reddish blonde. ◆ *n* **2** a woman with such hair.

strawberry mark *n* a soft vascular red birthmark. Also called: **strawberry.**

strawberry tomato *n* **1** a tropical annual plant having bell-shaped whitish-yellow flowers and small edible round yellow berries. **2** the fruit of this plant, eaten fresh or made into preserves or pickles. ◆ Also called: **Cape gooseberry.**

strawberry tree *n* a S European evergreen tree having white or pink flowers and red strawberry-like berries. See also **arbutus.**

strawboard ('strɔːˌbɔːd) *n* a board made of compressed straw and adhesive.

strawflower ('strɔːˌflauə) *n* an Australian plant in which the coloured bracts retain their colour when the plant is dried. See also **immortelle.**

straw man *n Chiefly US.* **1** a figure of a man made from straw. **2** a person of little substance. **3** a person used as a cover for some dubious plan or enterprise.

straw poll *or esp. US, Canad., & NZ.* **vote** *n* an unofficial poll or vote taken to determine the opinion of a group or the public on some issue.

strawweight ('strɔːˌweɪt) *n* **a** a professional boxer weighing not more than 47.6 kg (105 pounds). **b** (*as modifier*): *the strawweight title.* ◆ Also called: **mini-flyweight.**

stray ❶ (streɪ) *vb* (*intr*) **1** to wander away, as from the correct path or from a given area. **2** to wander haphazardly. **3** to digress from the point, lose concentration, etc. **4** to deviate from certain moral standards. ◆ *n* **5a** a domestic animal, fowl, etc., that has wandered away from its place of keeping and is lost. **5b** (*as modifier*): *stray dogs.* **6** a lost or homeless person, esp. a child: *waifs and strays.* **7** an occurrence, specimen, etc., that is out of place or outside the usual pattern. ◆ *adj* **8** scattered, random, or haphazard. [C14: from OF *estraier,* from Vulgar L *estragāre* (unattested), from L *extrā-* outside + *vagāri* to roam]
▸'**strayer** *n*

strays (streɪz) *pl n* **1** Also called: **stray capacitance.** *Electronics.* undesired capacitance in equipment. **2** another word for **static** (sense 8).

streak ❶ (striːk) *n* **1** a long thin mark, stripe, or trace of some contrasting colour. **2** (of lightning) a sudden flash. **3** an element or trace, as of some quality or characteristic. **4** a strip, vein, or layer. **5** a short stretch or run, esp. of good or bad luck. **6** *Inf.* an act or the practice of running naked through a public place. ◆ *vb* **7** (*tr*) to mark or daub with a streak or streaks. **8** (*intr*) to form streaks or become streaked. **9** (*intr*) to move rapidly in a straight line. **10** (*intr*) *Inf.* to run naked through a public place in order to shock or amuse. [OE *strica*]
▸**streaked** *adj* ▸'**streaker** *n* ▸'**streak,like** *adj*

streaky ('striːkɪ) *adj* **streakier, streakiest. 1** marked with streaks. **2** occurring in streaks. **3** (of bacon) having alternate layers of meat and fat. **4** of varying or uneven quality.
▸'**streakiness** *n*

stream ❶ (striːm) *n* **1** a small river; brook. **2** any steady flow of water or other fluid. **3** something that resembles a stream in moving continuously in a line or particular direction. **4** a rapid or unbroken flow of speech, etc.: *a stream of abuse.* **5** *Brit., Austral., & NZ.* any of several parallel classes of schoolchildren, or divisions of children within a class, grouped together because of similar ability. **6 go** (*or* **drift**) **with the stream.** to conform to the accepted standards. **7 on** (*or* **off**) **stream.** (of an industrial plant, manufacturing process, etc.) in (*or* not in) operation or production. ◆ *vb* **8** to emit or be emitted in a continuous flow: *his nose streamed blood.* **9** (*intr*) to move in unbroken succession, as a crowd of people, vehicles, etc. **10** (*intr*) to float freely or with a waving motion: *bunting streamed in the wind.* **11** (*tr*) to unfurl (a flag, etc.). **12** *Brit. education.* to group or divide (children) in streams. [OE]
▸'**streamlet** *n*

streamer ❶ ('striːmə) *n* **1** a long narrow flag or part of a flag. **2** a long narrow coiled ribbon of coloured paper that becomes unrolled when tossed. **3** a stream of light, esp. one appearing in some forms of the aurora. **4** *Journalism.* a large heavy headline printed across the width of a page. **5** *Computing.* another word for **tape streamer.**

streamline ('striːmˌlaɪn) *n* **1** a contour on a body that offers the minimum resistance to a gas or liquid flowing around it. ◆ *vb* **streamlines, streamlining, streamlined. 2** (*tr*) to make streamlined.

streamlined ❶ ('striːmˌlaɪnd) *adj* **1** offering or designed to offer the minimum resistance to the flow of a gas or liquid. **2** made more efficient, esp. by simplifying.

stream of consciousness *n* **1** *Psychol.* the continuous flow of ideas, thoughts, and feelings forming the content of an individual's consciousness. **2** a literary technique that reveals the flow of thoughts and feelings of characters through long passages of soliloquy.

streamy ('striːmɪ) *adj* **streamier, streamiest.** *Chiefly poetic.* **1** (of an area, land, etc.) having many streams. **2** flowing or streaming.

street ❶ (striːt) *n* **1a** a public road that is usually lined with buildings, esp. in a town: *Oxford Street.* **1b** (*as modifier*): *a street directory.* **2** the buildings lining a street. **3** the part of the road between the pavements, used by vehicles. **4** the people living, working, etc., in a particular street. **5** (*modifier*) of or relating to the urban counterculture. **6 on the streets. 6a** earning a living as a prostitute. **6b** homeless. **7** (**right**) **up one's street.** *Inf.* (just) what one knows or likes best. **8 streets ahead of.** *Inf.* superior to, more advanced than, etc. **9 streets apart.** *Inf.* markedly different. [OE *strǣt,* from L *via strāta* paved way (*strāta,* from *strātus,* p.p. of *sternere* to stretch out)]

street Arab *n Literary & old-fashioned.* a homeless child, esp. one who survives by begging and stealing; urchin.

streetcar ('striːtˌkɑː) *n* the usual US and Canad. name for **tram** (sense 1).

street credibility *n* a command of the style, knowledge, etc., associated with urban counter-culture. Often shortened to **street cred.**
▸ˌ**street-'credible** *adj*

street cry *n* (*often pl*) the cry of a street hawker.

street furniture *n* pieces of equipment, such as street lights and pillar boxes, placed in the street for the benefit of the public.

street value *n* the monetary worth of a commodity, usually an illicit one, considered as the price it would fetch when sold to the ultimate user.

streetwalker ('striːtˌwɔːkə) *n* a prostitute who solicits on the streets.
▸'**street,walking** *n, adj*

streetwise ('striːtˌwaɪz) *adj* adept at surviving in an urban, poor, and often criminal environment.

strelitzia (strɛ'lɪtsɪə) *n* any of various southern African perennial herbaceous plants, cultivated for their showy flowers: includes the bird-of-paradise flower. [C18: after Charlotte of Mecklenburg-*Strelitz* (1744–1818), queen of Great Britain & Ireland]

strength ❶ (strɛŋθ) *n* **1** the state or quality of being physically or mentally strong. **2** the ability to withstand or exert great force, stress, or pressure. **3** something regarded as beneficial or a source of power: *their chief strength is technology.* **4** potency, as of a drink, drug, etc. **5** power to convince; cogency: *the strength of an argument.* **6** degree of intensity or concentration of colour, light, sound, flavour, etc. **7** the full or part of the full complement as specified: *at full strength; below strength.* **8 from strength to strength.** with ever-increasing success. **9 in strength.** in large numbers. **10 on the strength of.** on the basis of or relying

THESAURUS

stray *vb* **1 = wander,** be abandoned *or* lost, drift, err, go astray, lose one's way, meander, range, roam, rove, straggle **2 = digress,** deviate, diverge, get off the point, get sidetracked, go off at a tangent, ramble ◆ *modifier* **5b = lost,** abandoned, homeless, roaming, vagrant ◆ *adj* **8 = random,** accidental, chance, erratic, freak, odd, scattered

streak *n* **1 = band,** layer, line, slash, smear, strip, stripe, stroke, vein **3 = trace,** dash, element, strain, touch, vein ◆ *vb* **7 = band,** daub, fleck, slash, smear, striate, stripe **9 = speed,** barrel (along), burn rubber (*inf.*), dart, flash, fly, hurtle, move like greased lightning (*inf.*), sprint, sweep, tear, whistle, whizz (*inf.*), zoom

stream *n* **1 = river,** bayou, beck, brook, burn (*Scot.*), creek (*US*), freshet, rill, rivulet, tributary, undertow **2 = flow,** course, current, drift, outpouring, run, rush, surge, tide, tideway, torrent ◆ *vb* **9 = flow,** cascade, course, emit, flood, glide, gush, issue, pour, run, shed, spill, spout

streamer *n* **1 = banner,** colours, ensign, flag, gonfalon, pennant, pennon, ribbon, standard

streamlined *adj* **2 = efficient,** modernized, organized, rationalized, sleek, slick, smooth, smooth-running, time-saving, well-run

street *n* **1 = road,** avenue, boulevard, lane, roadway, row, terrace, thoroughfare **7 (right) up one's street** *Informal* **= to one's liking,** acceptable, compatible, congenial, familiar, one's cup of tea (*inf.*), pleasing, suitable, to one's taste

strength *n* **1 = might,** backbone, brawn, brawniness, courage, firmness, fortitude, health, lustiness, muscle, robustness, sinew, stamina, stoutness, sturdiness, toughness, wellness **3 = strong point,** advantage, anchor, asset, mainstay, security, succour, tower of strength **5 = power,** cogency, concentration, effectiveness, efficacy, energy, force, intensity, potency, resolution, spirit, vehemence, vigour, virtue (*arch.*)

Antonyms *n* ≠ **might:** debility, feebleness, frailty, infirmity, powerlessness, weakness ≠ **strong point:** Achilles heel, chink in one's armour, defect, failing, flaw, shortcoming, weakness ≠ **power:** feebleness, impotence, powerlessness, weakness upon. **11 the strength of.** *Austral. & NZ inf.* the essential facts about. [OE *strengthu*]

strengthen ● ('streŋθən) *vb* to make or become stronger.
▸**'strengthener** *n*

strenuous ● ('strɛnjʊəs) *adj* **1** requiring or involving the use of great energy or effort. **2** characterized by great activity, effort, or endeavour. [C16: from L *strēnuus* brisk]
▸**'strenuously** *adv* ▸**'strenuousness** *n*

strep (strɛp) *n Inf.* short for **streptococcus.**

strepitoso (ˌstrɛpɪ'təʊsəʊ) *adv Music.* boisterously. [It.]

strepto- *combining form.* **1** indicating a shape resembling a twisted chain: *streptococcus.* **2** indicating streptococcus. [from Gk *streptos* twisted, from *strephein* to twist]

streptocarpus (ˌstrɛptəʊ'kɑːpəs) *n* any of various mostly African plants having spirally-twisted capsules. [C19: from NL, from Gk *streptos* twisted + *karpos* fruit]

streptococcus (ˌstrɛptəʊ'kɒkəs) *n, pl* **streptococci** (-'kɒkaɪ; *US* -'kɒksaɪ). any spherical bacterium of the genus *Streptococcus,* typically occurring in chains and including many pathogenic species. Often shortened to **strep.**
▸**streptococcal** (ˌstrɛptəʊ'kɒkᵊl) *or* **streptococcic** (ˌstrɛptəʊ'kɒksɪk) *adj*

streptomycin (ˌstrɛptəʊ'maɪsɪn) *n* an antibiotic obtained from the bacterium *Streptomyces griseus:* used in the treatment of tuberculosis and other bacterial infections.

streptothricin (ˌstrɛptəʊ'θraɪsɪn) *n* an antibiotic produced by the bacterium *Streptomyces lavendulae.*

stress ● (strɛs) *n* **1** special emphasis or significance. **2** mental, emotional, or physical strain or tension. **3** emphasis placed upon a syllable by pronouncing it more loudly than those that surround it. **4** such emphasis as part of a rhythm in music or poetry. **5** a syllable so emphasized. **6** *Physics.* **6a** force or a system of forces producing deformation or strain. **6b** the force acting per unit area. ◆ *vb (tr)* **7** to give emphasis or prominence to. **8** to pronounce (a word or syllable) more loudly than those that surround it. **9** to subject to stress. [C14 *stresse,* shortened from DISTRESS]
▸**'stressful** *adj*

-stress *suffix forming nouns.* indicating a woman who performs or is engaged in a certain activity: *songstress; seamstress.* [from -ST(E)R + -ESS]

stretch ● (strɛtʃ) *vb* **1** to draw out or extend or be drawn out or extended in length, area, etc. **2** to extend or be extended to an undue degree, esp. so as to distort or lengthen permanently. **3** to extend (the limbs, body, etc.). **4** *(tr)* to reach or suspend (a rope, etc.) from one place to another. **5** *(tr)* to draw tight; tighten. **6** (often foll. by *out, forward,* etc.) to reach or hold (out); extend. **7** *(intr;* usually foll. by *over)* to extend in time: *the course stretched over three months.* **8** *(intr;* foll. by *for, over,* etc.) (of a region, etc.) to extend in length or area. **9** *(intr)* (esp. of a garment) to be capable of expanding, as to a larger size: *socks that will stretch.* **10** *(tr)* to put a great strain upon or extend to the limit. **11** to injure (a muscle, tendon, etc.) by means of a strain or sprain. **12** *(tr;* often foll. by *out)* to make do with (limited resources): *to stretch one's budget.* **13** *(tr) Inf.* to expand or elaborate (a story, etc.) beyond what is credible or acceptable. **14** *(tr; often passive)* to extend, as to the limit of one's abilities or talents. **15** *Arch. or sl.* to hang or be hanged by the neck. **16 stretch a point. 16a** to make a concession or exception not usually made. **16b** to exaggerate. ◆ *n* **17** the act of stretching or state of being stretched. **18** a large or continuous expanse or distance: *a stretch of water.* **19** extent in time, length, area, etc. **20a** capacity for being stretched, as in some garments. **20b** *(as modifier): stretch pants.* **21** the section or sections of a racecourse that are straight, esp. the final section leading to the finishing line. **22** *Sl.* a term of imprisonment. **23 at a stretch.** *Chiefly Brit.* **23a** with some difficulty; by making a special effort. **23b** if really necessary or in extreme circumstances. **23c** at one time: *he sometimes read for hours at a stretch.* [OE *streccan*]
▸**'stretchable** *adj* ▸ˌ**stretcha'bility** *n*

stretcher ('strɛtʃə) *n* **1** a device for transporting the ill, wounded, or dead, consisting of a frame covered by canvas or other material. **2** a strengthening often decorative member joining the legs of a chair, table, etc. **3** the wooden frame on which canvas is stretched and fixed for oil painting. **4** a tie beam or brace used in a structural framework. **5** a brick or stone laid horizontally with its length parallel to the length of a wall. **6** *Rowing.* a fixed board across a boat on which an oarsman braces his feet. **7** *Austral. & NZ.* a camp bed. ◆ *vb (tr)* **8** to transport (a sick or injured person) on a stretcher.

stretcher-bearer *n* a person who helps to carry a stretcher, esp. in wartime.

stretch limo *n Inf.* a limousine that has been lengthened to provide extra seating accommodation and more legroom. In full: **stretch limousine.**

stretchmarks ('strɛtʃˌmɑːks) *pl n* marks that remain visible on the abdomen after its distension in pregnancy.

stretchy ('strɛtʃɪ) *adj* **stretchier, stretchiest.** characterized by elasticity.
▸**'stretchiness** *n*

stretto ('strɛtəʊ) *n, pl* **strettos** *or* **stretti** (-tiː). **1** (in a fugue) the close overlapping of two parts or voices, the second one entering before the first has completed its statement. **2** Also called: **stretta.** a concluding passage, played at a faster speed than earlier material. [C17: from It., from L *strictus* tightly bound; see STRICT]

strew ● (struː) *vb* **strews, strewing, strewed; strewn** *or* **strewed.** to spread or scatter or be spread or scattered, as over a surface or area. [OE *streowian*]
▸**'strewer** *n*

strewth (struːθ) *interj* an expression of surprise or dismay. [C19: alteration of *God's truth*]

stria ('straɪə) *n, pl* **striae** ('straɪiː). *(often pl)* **1** Also called: **striation.** *Geol.* any of the parallel scratches or grooves on the surface of a rock over which a glacier has flowed or on the surface of a crystal. **2** *Biol., anat.* a narrow band of colour or a ridge, groove, or similar linear mark. **3** *Archit.* a narrow channel, such as a flute on the shaft of a column. [C16: from L: a groove]

striate *adj* ('straɪɪt), *also* **striated. 1** marked with striae; striped. ◆ *vb* ('straɪeɪt), **striates, striating, striated. 2** *(tr)* to mark with striae. [C17: from L *striāre* to make grooves]

striation (straɪ'eɪʃən) *n* **1** an arrangement or pattern of striae. **2** the condition of being striate. **3** another word for **stria** (sense 1).

stricken ● ('strɪkən) *adj* **1** laid low, as by disease or sickness. **2** deeply affected, as by grief, love, etc. **3** *Arch.* wounded or injured. **4 stricken in years.** made feeble by age. [C14: p.p. of STRIKE]
▸**'strickenly** *adv*

strict ● (strɪkt) *adj* **1** adhering closely to specified rules, ordinances, etc. **2** complied with or enforced stringently; rigorous: *a strict code of conduct.* **3** severely correct in attention to conduct or morality: *a strict teacher.* **4** (of a punishment, etc.) harsh; severe. **5** *(prenominal)* complete; absolute: *strict secrecy.* [C16: from L *strictus,* from *stringere* to draw tight]
▸**'strictly** *adv* ▸**'strictness** *n*

strict implication *n Logic.* a form of implication in which the proposition "if A then B" is true only when B is deducible from A.

stricture ● ('strɪktʃə) *n* **1** a severe criticism; censure. **2** *Pathol.* an abnormal constriction of a tubular organ or part. [C14: from L *strictūra* contraction; see STRICT]
▸**'strictured** *adj*

stride (straɪd) *n* **1** a long step or pace. **2** the space measured by such a step. **3** a striding gait. **4** an act of forward movement by an animal. **5** progress or development (esp. in **make rapid strides**). **6** a regular pace or rate of progress: *to get into one's stride; to be put off one's stride.* **7** Also: **stride piano.** *Jazz.* a piano style characterized by single bass notes on the first and third beats and chords on the second and fourth. **8** *(pl) Inf., chiefly Austral. & NZ.* men's trousers. **9 take (something) in one's stride.** to do (something) without difficulty or effort. ◆ *vb* **strides, striding, strode, stridden** ('strɪdᵊn). **10** *(intr)* to walk with long regular or measured paces, as in haste, etc. **11** *(tr)* to cover or traverse by striding: *he strode thirty miles.* **12** (often foll. by *over, across,* etc.) to cross (over a space, obstacle, etc.) with a stride. **13** *Arch. or poetic.* to straddle or bestride. [OE *strīdan*]
▸**'strider** *n*

strident ● ('straɪdᵊnt) *adj* **1** (of a shout, voice, etc.) loud or harsh. **2** urgent, clamorous, or vociferous: *strident demands.* [C17: from L *strīdēns,* from *strīdēre* to make a grating sound]
▸**'stridence** *or* **'stridency** *n* ▸**'stridently** *adv*

stridor ('straɪdɔː) *n* **1** *Pathol.* a high-pitched whistling sound made dur-

THESAURUS

strengthen *vb* = **fortify**, animate, brace up, consolidate, encourage, gee up, give new energy to, harden, hearten, invigorate, nerve, nourish, rejuvenate, restore, stiffen, toughen
Antonyms *vb* crush, debilitate, destroy, dilute, enervate, render impotent, sap, subvert, undermine, weaken

strenuous *adj* **1** = **demanding**, arduous, exhausting, hard, Herculean, laborious, taxing, toilsome, tough, tough going, unrelaxing, uphill **2** = **tireless**, active, bold, determined, eager, earnest, energetic, persistent, resolute, spirited, strong, vigorous, zealous
Antonyms *adj* ≠ **demanding:** easy, effortless, relaxing, undemanding, untaxing ≠ **tireless:** relaxed, unenergetic

stress *n* **1** = **emphasis**, force, importance, significance, urgency, weight **2** = **strain**, anxiety, burden, hassle (*inf.*), nervous tension, oppression, pressure, tension, trauma, worry **3-5** = **accent**, accentuation, beat, emphasis, ictus ◆ *vb* **7** = **emphasize**, accentuate, belabour, dwell on, harp on, lay emphasis upon, point up, repeat, rub in, underline, underscore

stressful *adj* **2** = **worrying**, agitating, anxious, tense, traumatic

stretch *vb* **1** = **extend**, cover, put forth, reach, spread, unfold, unroll **2** = **pull**, distend, draw out, elongate, expand, inflate, lengthen, pull out of shape, rack, strain, swell, tighten ◆ *n* **18** = **expanse**, area, distance, extent, spread, sweep, tract **19** = **period**, bit, run, space, spell, stint, term, time

strew *vb* = **scatter**, bestrew, disperse, litter, spread, sprinkle, toss

stricken *adj* **1** = **affected**, afflicted, hit, injured, laid low, smitten, struck, struck down

strict *adj* **1** = **exact**, accurate, close, faithful, meticulous, particular, precise, religious, scrupulous, true **3, 4** = **severe**, austere, authoritarian, firm, harsh, no-nonsense, rigid, rigorous, stern, stringent **5** = **absolute**, complete, perfect, total, utter
Antonyms *adj* ≠ **severe:** easy-going, easy-oasy (*sl.*), flexible, laid-back (*inf.*), lax, mild, moderate, soft, tolerant

stricture *n* **1** *Formal* = **criticism**, animadversion, bad press, blame, censure, flak (*inf.*), rebuke, stick (*sl.*)

strident *adj* **1** = **harsh**, clamorous, clashing, discordant, grating, jangling, jarring, rasping, raucous, screeching, shrill, stridulant, stridulous, unmusical ing respiration, caused by obstruction of the air passages. **2** *Chiefly literary.* a harsh or shrill sound. [C17: from L; see STRIDENT]

stridulate ('strɪdjʊ,leɪt) *vb* **stridulates, stridulating, stridulated.** (*intr*) (of insects such as the cricket) to produce sounds by rubbing one part of the body against another. [C19: back formation from *stridulation,* from L *strīdulus* creaking, from *strīdēre* to make a harsh noise] ▸**,stridu'lation** *n* ▸**'stridu,lator** *n*

stridulous ('strɪdjʊləs) *or* **stridulant** *adj* **1** making a harsh, shrill, or grating noise. **2** *Pathol.* of, relating to, or characterized by stridor. ▸**'stridulousness** *or* **'stridulance** *n*

strife ➊ (straɪf) *n* **1** angry or violent struggle; conflict. **2** rivalry or contention, esp. of a bitter kind. **3** *Austral. & NZ inf.* trouble or discord of any kind. **4** *Arch.* striving. [C13: from OF *estrif,* prob. from *estriver* to STRIVE]

strigil ('strɪdʒɪl) *n* a curved blade used by the ancient Romans and Greeks to scrape the body after bathing. [C16: from L *strigilis,* from *stringere* to graze]

strigose ('straɪgəʊs) *adj* **1** *Bot.* bearing stiff hairs or bristles. **2** *Zool.* marked with fine closely set grooves or ridges. [C18: via NL *strigōsus,* from *striga* a bristle, from L: grain cut down]

strike ➊ (straɪk) *vb* **strikes, striking, struck. 1** to deliver (a blow or stroke) to (a person). **2** to come or cause to come into sudden or violent contact (with). **3** (*tr*) to make an attack on. **4** to produce (fire, sparks, etc.) or (of fire, sparks, etc.) to be produced by ignition. **5** to cause (a match) to light by friction or (of a match) to be lighted. **6** to press (the key of a piano, organ, etc.) or to sound (a specific note) in this or a similar way. **7** to indicate (a specific time) by the sound of a hammer striking a bell or by any other percussive sound. **8** (of a venomous snake) to cause injury by biting. **9** (*tr*) to affect or cause to affect deeply, suddenly, or radically: *her appearance struck him as strange.* **10** (*past participle* **struck** *or* **stricken**) (*tr; passive;* usually foll. by *with*) to render incapable or nearly so: *stricken with grief.* **11** (*tr*) to enter the mind of: *it struck me that he had become very quiet.* **12** (*past participle* **struck** *or* **stricken**) to render: *struck dumb.* **13** (*tr*) to be perceived by; catch: *the glint of metal struck his eye.* **14** to arrive at or come upon (something), esp. suddenly or unexpectedly: *to strike the path for home; to strike upon a solution.* **15** (*intr;* sometimes foll. by *out*) to set (out) or proceed, esp. upon a new course: *to strike out for the coast.* **16** (*tr; usually passive*) to afflict with a disease, esp. unexpectedly: *he was struck with polio.* **17** (*tr*) to discover or come upon a source of (ore, petroleum, etc.). **18** (*tr*) (of a plant) to produce or send down (a root or roots). **19** (*tr*) to take apart or pack up; break (esp. in **strike camp**). **20** (*tr*) to take down or dismantle (a stage set, etc.). **21** (*tr*) *Naut.* **21a** to lower or remove (a specified piece of gear). **21b** to haul down or dip (a flag, sail, etc.) in salute or in surrender. **22** to attack (an objective). **23** to impale the hook in the mouth of (a fish) by suddenly tightening or jerking the line after the bait has been taken. **24** (*tr*) to form or impress (a coin, metal, etc.) by or as if by stamping. **25** to level (a surface) by use of a flat board. **26** (*tr*) to assume or take up (an attitude, posture, etc.). **27** (*intr*) (of workers in a factory, etc.) to cease work collectively as a protest against working conditions, low pay, etc. **28** (*tr*) to reach by agreement: *to strike a bargain.* **29** (*tr*) to form (a jury, esp. a special jury) by cancelling certain names among those nominated for jury service until only the requisite number remains. **30 strike home. 30a** to deliver an effective blow. **30b** to achieve the intended effect. **31 strike it rich.** *Inf.* **31a** to discover an extensive deposit of a mineral, petroleum, etc. **31b** to have an unexpected financial success. ◆ *n* **32** an act or instance of striking. **33** a cessation of work, as a protest against working conditions or low pay: *on strike.* **34** a military attack, esp. an air attack on a surface target: *air strike.* **35** *Baseball.* a pitched ball judged good but missed or not swung at, three of which cause a batter to be out. **36** Also called: **ten-strike.** *Tenpin bowling.* **36a** the act or an instance of knocking down all the pins with the first bowl of a single frame. **36b** the score thus made. **37** a sound made by striking. **38** the mechanism that makes a clock strike. **39** the discovery of a source of ore, petroleum, etc. **40** the horizontal direction of a fault, rock stratum, etc. **41** *Angling.* the act or an instance of striking. **42** *Inf.* an unexpected or complete success, esp. one that brings financial gain. **43 take strike.** *Cricket.* (of a batsman) to prepare to play a ball delivered by the bowler. ◆ See also **strike down, strike off,** etc. [OE *strīcan*]

strikebound ('straɪk,baʊnd) *adj* (of a factory, etc.) closed or made inoperative by a strike.

strikebreaker ('straɪk,breɪkə) *n* a person who tries to make a strike ineffectual by working or by taking the place of those on strike. ▸**'strike,breaking** *n, adj*

strike down ➊ *vb* (*tr, adv*) to cause to die, esp. suddenly: *he was struck down in his prime.*

strike off *vb* (*tr*) **1** to remove or erase from (a list, record, etc.) by or as if by a stroke of the pen. **2** (*adv*) to cut off or separate by or as if by a blow: *she was struck off from the inheritance.*

strike out ➊ *vb* (*adv*) **1** (*tr*) to remove or erase. **2** (*intr*) to start out or begin: *to strike out on one's own.* **3** *Baseball.* to put out or be put out on strikes. **4** (*intr*) *US inf.* to fail utterly.

strike pay *n* money paid to strikers from the funds of a trade union.

striker ('straɪkə) *n* **1** a person who is on strike. **2** the hammer in a timepiece that rings a bell or alarm. **3** any part in a mechanical device that strikes something, such as the firing pin of a gun. **4** *Soccer, inf.* an attacking player, esp. one who generally positions himself near his opponent's goal in the hope of scoring. **5** *Cricket.* the batsman who is about to play a ball.

strike up *vb* (*adv*) **1** (of a band, orchestra, etc.) to begin to play or sing. **2** (*tr*) to bring about; cause to begin: *to strike up a friendship.*

striking ➊ ('straɪkɪŋ) *adj* **1** attracting attention; fine; impressive: *a striking beauty.* **2** conspicuous; noticeable: *a striking difference.* ▸**'strikingly** *adv* ▸**'strikingness** *n*

striking circle *n Hockey.* the semicircular area in front of each goal, which an attacking player must have entered before scoring a goal.

Strimmer ('strɪmə) *n Trademark.* an electrical tool for trimming the edges of lawns.

Strine (straɪn) *n* a humorous transliteration of Australian pronunciation, as in *Gloria Soame* for *glorious home.* [C20: a jocular rendering of the Australian pronunciation of *Australian*]

string ➊ (strɪŋ) *n* **1** a thin length of cord, twine, fibre, or similar material used for tying, hanging, binding, etc. **2** a group of objects threaded on a single strand: *a string of beads.* **3** a series or succession of things, events, etc.: *a string of oaths.* **4** a number, chain, or group of similar things, animals, etc., owned by or associated with one person or body: *a string of girlfriends.* **5** a tough fibre or cord in a plant. **6** *Music.* a tightly stretched wire, cord, etc., found on stringed instruments, such as the violin, guitar, and piano. **7** short for **bowstring. 8** *Archit.* short for **string course** or **stringer** (sense 1). **9** (*pl; usually preceded by the*) **9a** violins, violas, cellos, and double basses collectively. **9b** the section of a symphony orchestra constituted by such instruments. **10** a group of characters that can be treated as a unit by a computer program. **11** *Physics.* a one-dimensional entity postulated to be a fundamental component of matter in some theories of particle physics. See also **cosmic string. 12** (*pl*) complications or conditions (esp. in **no strings attached**). **13** (*modifier*) composed of stringlike strands woven in a large mesh: *a string bag; a string vest.* **14 first** (**second,** etc.) **string.** a person or thing regarded as a primary (secondary, etc.) source of strength. **15 keep on a string.** to have control or a hold over (a person), esp. emotionally. **16 pull strings.** *Inf.* to exert power or influence, esp. secretly or unofficially. **17 pull the strings.** to have real or ultimate control of something. ◆ *vb* **strings, stringing, strung. 18** (*tr*) to provide with a string or strings. **19** (*tr*) to suspend or stretch from one point to another. **20** (*tr*) to thread on a string. **21** (*tr*) to form or extend in a line or series. **22** (foll. by *out*) to space or spread out at intervals. **23** (*tr; usually foll. by up*) *Inf.* to kill (a person) by hanging. **24** (*tr*) to remove the stringy parts from (vegetables, esp. beans). **25** (*intr*) (esp. of viscous liquids) to become stringy or ropey. **26** (*tr; often foll. by up*) to cause to be tense or nervous. [OE *streng*] ▸**'string,like** *adj*

string along ➊ *vb* (*adv*) *Inf.* **1** (*intr; often foll. by with*) to agree or appear to be in agreement (with). **2** (*intr; often foll. by with*) to accompany. **3** to deceive or hoax, esp. in order to gain time.

stringboard ('strɪŋ,bɔːd) *n* a skirting that covers the ends of the steps in a staircase. Also called: **stringer.**

string course *n Archit.* an ornamental projecting band or continuous moulding along a wall. Also called: **cordon.**

stringed (strɪŋd) *adj* (of musical instruments) having or provided with strings.

stringendo (strɪn'dʒendəʊ) *adj, adv Music.* to be performed with increasing speed. [It., from *stringere* to compress, from L: to draw tight]

THESAURUS

Antonyms *adj* dulcet, gentle, harmonious, mellifluous, mellow, quiet, soft, soothing, sweet

strife *n* **1, 2 = conflict**, animosity, battle, bickering, clash, clashes, combat, contention, contest, controversy, discord, dissension, friction, quarrel, rivalry, row, squabbling, struggle, warfare, wrangling

strike *vb* **1 = hit**, bang, beat, box, buffet, chastise, chin (*sl.*), clobber (*sl.*), clout (*inf.*), clump (*sl.*), cuff, deck (*sl.*), hammer, knock, lambast(e), lay a finger on (*inf.*), lay one on (*sl.*), pound, punch, punish, slap, smack, smite, sock (*sl.*), swipe, thump, wallop (*inf.*) **2 = collide with**, be in collision with, bump into, clash, come into contact with, dash, hit, knock into, run into, smash into, touch **9 = affect**, hit, make an impact on, reach, register (*inf.*) **11 = occur to**, come to, come to the mind of, dawn on *or* upon, hit, register (*inf.*), seem **14** *sometimes with* **upon = discover**, arrive at, come upon *or* across, encounter, find, happen *or* chance upon, hit upon, light upon, reach, stumble upon *or* across, turn up, uncover, unearth **22 = attack**, affect, assail, assault, deal a blow to, devastate, fall upon, hit, invade, set upon, smite **27 = walk out**, down tools, mutiny, revolt

strike down *vb* **= kill**, afflict, bring low, deal a deathblow to, destroy, ruin, slay, smite

strike out *vb* **1 = score out**, cancel, cross out, delete, efface, erase, excise, expunge, remove **2 = begin**, get under way, set out, start out

striking *adj* **1, 2 = impressive**, astonishing, conspicuous, dazzling, dramatic, drop-dead (*sl.*), extraordinary, forcible, jaw-dropping, memorable, noticeable, out of the ordinary, outstanding, stunning (*inf.*), wonderful

Antonyms *adj* average, dull, indifferent, undistinguished, unexceptional, unextraordinary, unimpressive, uninteresting, vanilla (*inf.*)

string *n* **1 = cord**, fibre, twine **3 = series**, chain, file, line, procession, queue, row, sequence, strand, succession **12** *plural* **= conditions**, catches (*inf.*), complications, obligations, prerequisites, provisos, qualifications, requirements, riders, stipulations ◆ *vb* **19 = hang**, festoon, link, loop, sling, stretch, suspend, thread **22 = spread out**, disperse, extend, fan out, lengthen, protract, space out, straggle

string along *vb* **2** *often with* **with = accompany**, go along with **3 = deceive**, bluff, dupe, fool, hoax, kid (*inf.*), play fast and loose with (someone) (*inf.*), play (someone) false, put one

stringent ➊ (ˈstrɪndʒənt) *adj* **1** requiring strict attention to rules, procedure, detail, etc. **2** *Finance.* characterized by or causing a shortage of credit, loan capital, etc. [C17: from L *stringere* to bind]
▸ˈ**stringency** *n* ▸ˈ**stringently** *adv*

stringer (ˈstrɪŋə) *n* **1** *Archit.* **1a** a long horizontal beam that is used for structural purposes. **1b** another name for **stringboard. 2** *Naut.* a longitudinal structural brace for strengthening the hull of a vessel. **3** a journalist retained by a newspaper or news service on a part-time basis to cover a particular town or area.

stringhalt (ˈstrɪŋˌhɔːlt) *n Vet. science.* a sudden spasmodic lifting of the hind leg of a horse. Also called: **springhalt.** [C16: prob. STRING + HALT[2]]

stringpiece (ˈstrɪŋˌpiːs) *n* a long horizontal timber beam used to strengthen or support a framework.

string quartet *n Music.* **1** an instrumental ensemble consisting of two violins, one viola, and one cello. **2** a piece of music for such a group.

string tie *n* a very narrow tie.

stringy ➊ (ˈstrɪŋɪ) *adj* **stringier, stringiest. 1** made of strings or resembling strings. **2** (of meat, etc.) fibrous. **3** (of a person's build) wiry; sinewy. **4** (of liquids) forming in strings.
▸ˈ**stringily** *adv* ▸ˈ**stringiness** *n*

stringy-bark *n Austral.* any of several eucalyptus trees having fibrous bark.

strip[1] ➊ (strɪp) *vb* **strips, stripping, stripped. 1** to take or pull (the covering, clothes, etc.) off (oneself, another person, or thing). **2** (*intr*) **2a** to remove all one's clothes. **2b** to perform a striptease. **3** (*tr*) to denude or empty completely. **4** (*tr*) to deprive: *he was stripped of his pride.* **5** (*tr*) to rob or plunder. **6** (*tr*) to remove (paint, etc.) from (a surface, furniture, etc.): *stripped pine.* **7** (*tr*) to pull out the old coat of hair from (dogs of certain long- and wire-haired breeds). **8a** to remove the leaves from the stalks of (tobacco, etc.). **8b** to separate the leaves from the stems of (tobacco, etc.). **9** (*tr*) *Agriculture.* to draw the last milk from (a cow). **10** to dismantle (an engine, mechanism, etc.). **11** to tear off or break (the thread) from (a screw, bolt, etc.) or (the teeth) from (a gear). **12** (often foll. by *down*) to remove the accessories from (a motor vehicle): *his car was stripped down.* ◆ *n* **13** the act or an instance of undressing or of performing a striptease. [OE *bestriepan* to plunder]

strip[2] ➊ (strɪp) *n* **1** a relatively long, flat, narrow piece of something. **2** short for **airstrip. 3** the clothes worn by the members of a team, esp. a football team. **4** *Business.* a triple option on a security or commodity consisting of one call option and two put options at the same price and for the same period. Cf. **strap** (sense 6). **5 tear (someone) off a strip.** *Inf.* to rebuke (someone) angrily. ◆ *vb* **strips, stripping, stripped. 6** to cut or divide into strips. [C15: from MDu. *strīpe* STRIPE[1]]

strip cartoon *n* a sequence of drawings in a newspaper, magazine, etc., relating a humorous story or an adventure. Also called: **comic strip.**

strip club *n* a small club in which striptease performances take place.

stripe[1] (straɪp) *n* **1** a relatively long band of colour or texture that differs from the surrounding material or background. **2** a fabric having such bands. **3** a strip, band, or chevron worn on a uniform, etc., esp. to indicate rank. **4** *Chiefly US & Canad.* kind; type: *a man of a certain stripe.* ◆ *vb* **stripes, striping, striped. 5** (*tr*) to mark with stripes. [C17: prob. from MDu. *strīpe*]
▸**striped** *adj*

stripe[2] (straɪp) *n* a stroke from a whip, rod, cane, etc. [C15: ?from MLow G *strippe*]

striped muscle *n* a type of contractile tissue that is marked by transverse striations. Also called: **striated muscle.**

strip lighting *n* electric lighting by means of long glass tubes that are fluorescent lamps or that contain long filaments.

stripling ➊ (ˈstrɪplɪŋ) *n* a lad. [C13: from STRIP[2] + -LING[1]]

strip mining *n* another term (esp. US) for **opencast mining.**

stripper (ˈstrɪpə) *n* **1** a striptease artiste. **2** a person or thing that strips. **3** a device or substance for removing paint, varnish, etc.

strip-search *vb* **1** (*tr*) (of police, customs officials, etc.) to strip (a prisoner or suspect) naked to search him or her for contraband, narcotics, etc. ◆ *n* **2** a search that involves stripping a person naked.
▸ˈ**strip-**ˌ**searching** *n*

striptease (ˈstrɪpˌtiːz) *n* **a** a form of erotic entertainment in which a person gradually undresses to music. **b** (*as modifier*): *a striptease club.*
▸ˈ**strip**ˌ**teaser** *n*

stripy *or* **stripey** (ˈstraɪpɪ) *adj* **stripier, stripiest.** marked by or with stripes; striped.

strive ➊ (straɪv) *vb* **strives, striving, strove, striven** (ˈstrɪvᵊn). **1** (*may take a clause as object or an infinitive*) to make a great and tenacious effort. **2** (*intr*) to fight; contend. [C13: from OF *estriver,* of Gmc origin]
▸ˈ**striver** *n*

strobe (strəʊb) *n* short for **strobe lighting** or **stroboscope.**

strobe lighting *n* **1** a high-intensity flashing beam of light produced by rapid electrical discharges in a tube or by a perforated disc rotating in front of an intense light source. **2** the use of or the apparatus for producing such light. Sometimes shortened to **strobe.**

strobilus (ˈstrəʊbɪləs) *or* **strobile** (ˈstrəʊbaɪl) *n, pl* **strobiluses, strobili** (-bɪlaɪ), *or* **strobiles.** *Bot.* the technical name for **cone** (sense 3). [C18: via LL from Gk *strobilos* a fir cone]

stroboscope (ˈstrəʊbəˌskəʊp) *n* **1** an instrument producing an intense flashing light, the frequency of which can be synchronized with some multiple of the frequency of rotation, vibration, or operation of an object, etc., making it appear stationary. Sometimes shortened to **strobe. 2** a similar device synchronized with the shutter of a camera so that a series of still photographs can be taken of a moving object. [C19: from *strobo-,* from Gk *strobos* a whirling + -SCOPE]
▸**stroboscopic** (ˌstrəʊbəˈskɒpɪk) *or* ˌ**strobo**ˈ**scopical** *adj* ▸ˌ**strobo**ˈ**scopically** *adv*

strode (strəʊd) *vb* the past tense of **stride.**

stroganoff (ˈstrɒgəˌnɒf) *n* a dish of sliced beef cooked with onions and mushrooms, served in a sour-cream sauce. Also called: **beef stroganoff.** [C19: after Count *Stroganoff,* 19th-century Russian diplomat]

stroke ➊ (strəʊk) *n* **1** the act or an instance of striking; a blow, knock, or hit. **2** a sudden action, movement, or occurrence: *a stroke of luck.* **3** a brilliant or inspired act or feat: *a stroke of genius.* **4** *Pathol.* apoplexy; rupture of a blood vessel in the brain resulting in loss of consciousness, often followed by paralysis, or embolism or thrombosis affecting a cerebral vessel. **5a** the striking of a clock. **5b** the hour registered by this: *on the stroke of three.* **6** a mark made by a writing implement. **7** another name for **solidus** (sense 1), used esp. when dictating or reading aloud. **8** a light touch or caress, as with the fingers. **9** a pulsation, esp. of the heart. **10** a single complete movement or one of a series of complete movements. **11** *Sport.* the act or manner of striking the ball with a club, bat, etc. **12** any one of the repeated movements used by a swimmer. **13** a manner of swimming, esp. one of several named styles such as the crawl. **14a** any one of a series of linear movements of a reciprocating part, such as a piston. **14b** the distance travelled by such a part from one end of its movement to the other. **15** a single pull on an oar or oars in rowing. **16** manner or style of rowing. **17** the oarsman who sits nearest the stern of a shell, facing the cox, and sets the rate of rowing. **18 a stroke (of work).** (*usually used with a negative*) a small amount of work. **19 at a stroke.** with one action. **20 off one's stroke.** performing or working less well than usual. **21 on the stroke.** punctually. ◆ *vb* **strokes, stroking, stroked. 22** (*tr*) to touch, brush, etc. lightly or gently. **23** (*tr*) to mark a line or a stroke on or through. **24** to act as the stroke of (a racing shell). **25** (*tr*) *Sport.* to strike (a ball) with a smooth swinging blow. [OE *strācian*]

stroke play *n Golf.* **a** scoring by counting the strokes taken. **b** (*as modifier*): *a strokeplay tournament.* ◆ Also called: **medal play.** Cf. **match play, Stableford.**

stroll ➊ (strəʊl) *vb* **1** to walk about in a leisurely manner. **2** (*intr*) to wander about. ◆ *n* **3** a leisurely walk. [C17: prob. from dialect G *strollen,* from ?]

stroller (ˈstrəʊlə) *n* the usual US, Canad., and Austral. word for **pushchair.**

stroma (ˈstrəʊmə) *n, pl* **stromata** (-mətə). *Biol.* **1** the dense colourless framework of a chloroplast and certain cells. **2** the fibrous connective tissue forming the matrix of the mammalian ovary and testis. **3** a dense mass of hyphae that is produced by certain fungi and gives rise to spore-producing bodies. [C19: via NL from LL: a mattress, from Gk]
▸**stromatic** (strəʊˈmætɪk) *or* ˈ**stromatous** *adj*

Strombolian (strɒmˈbəʊlɪən) *adj* relating to or denoting a type of volcanic eruption characterized by repeated small explosions caused by gas escaping through lava. [from *Stromboli,* island with a famous active volcano, off the N coast of Sicily]

strong ➊ (strɒŋ) *adj* **stronger** (ˈstrɒŋgə), **strongest** (ˈstrɒŋgɪst). **1** involving or possessing strength. **2** solid or robust; not easily broken or injured. **3** resolute or morally firm. **4** intense in quality; not faint or feeble: *a strong voice; a strong smell.* **5** easily defensible; incontestable or formidable. **6** concentrated; not weak or diluted. **7a** (*postpositive*) containing or having a specified number: *a navy 40 000 strong.* **7b** (*in combination*): *a 40 000-strong navy.* **8** having an unpleasantly powerful taste or smell. **9**

THESAURUS

over on (someone) (*inf.*), take (someone) for a ride (*inf.*)

stringent *adj* **1** = **strict,** binding, demanding, exacting, inflexible, rigid, rigorous, severe, tight, tough
Antonyms *adj* equivocal, flexible, inconclusive, lax, loose, relaxed, slack, unrigorous, vague

stringy *adj* = **fibrous,** chewy, gristly, sinewy, tough, wiry

strip[1] *vb* **1, 2a** = **undress,** disrobe, unclothe, uncover **3, 4, 5** = **plunder,** bare, denude, deprive, despoil, dismantle, divest, empty, gut, lay bare, loot, peel, pillage, ransack, rob, sack, skin, spoil

strip[2] *n* **1** = **piece,** band, belt, bit, fillet, ribbon, shred, slip, swathe, tongue

stripling *n* = **boy,** adolescent, fledgling, hobbledehoy (*arch.*), lad, shaver (*inf.*), young fellow, youngster, youth

strive *vb* **1, 2** = **try,** attempt, bend over backwards, bust a gut (*inf.*), compete, contend, do all one can, do one's best, do one's damnedest (*inf.*), do one's utmost, endeavour, exert oneself, fight, give it one's all (*inf.*), give it one's best shot (*inf.*), go all out (*inf.*), go for broke (*sl.*), go for it (*inf.*), jump through hoops (*inf.*), knock oneself out (*inf.*), labour, make an all-out effort (*inf.*), make every effort, strain, struggle, toil, try hard

stroke *n* **1** = **blow,** hit, knock, pat, rap, swipe, thump **3** = **feat,** accomplishment, achievement, flourish, move, movement **4** = **apoplexy,** attack, collapse, fit, seizure, shock ◆ *vb* **8** = **caress,** fondle, pat, pet, rub

stroll *vb* **1, 2** = **walk,** amble, make one's way, mooch (*sl.*), mosey (*inf.*), promenade, ramble, saunter, stooge (*sl.*), stretch one's legs, take a turn, toddle, wander ◆ *n* **3** = **walk,** airing, breath of air, constitutional, excursion, promenade, ramble, turn

strong *adj* **1** = **powerful,** athletic, beefy (*inf.*),

having an extreme or drastic effect: *strong discipline*. **10** emphatic or immoderate: *strong language*. **11** convincing, effective, or cogent. **12** (of a colour) having a high degree of saturation or purity; produced by a concentrated quantity of colouring agent. **13** *Grammar*. **13a** of or denoting a class of verbs, in certain languages including the Germanic languages, whose conjugation shows vowel gradation, as *sing, sang, sung*. **13b** belonging to any part-of-speech class, in various languages, whose inflections follow the less regular of two possible patterns. Cf. **weak** (sense 10). **14** (of a wind, current, etc.) moving fast. **15** (of a syllable) accented or stressed. **16** (of an industry, etc.) firm in price or characterized by firm or increasing prices. **17** (of certain acids and bases) producing high concentrations of hydrogen or hydroxide ions in aqueous solution. **18 have a strong stomach.** not to be prone to nausea. ◆ *adv* **19** *Inf.* in a strong way; effectively: *going strong*. **20 come on strong.** to make a forceful or exaggerated impression. [OE *strang*]
▸ **'strongly** *adv* ▸ **'strongness** *n*

strong-arm ⓣ *Inf.* ◆ *n* **1** (*modifier*) of or involving physical force or violence: *strong-arm tactics*. ◆ *vb* **2** (*tr*) to show violence towards.

strongbox ('strɒŋˌbɒks) *n* a box or safe in which valuables are locked for safety.

strong breeze *n Meteorol.* a wind of force 6 on the Beaufort scale, reaching speeds of 25 to 31 mph.

strong drink *n* alcoholic drink.

strong-eye dog *n NZ.* See **eye dog.**

strong gale *n Meteorol.* a wind of force 9 on the Beaufort scale, reaching speeds of 47 to 54 mph.

stronghold ⓣ ('strɒŋˌhəʊld) *n* **1** a defensible place; fortress. **2** a major centre or area of predominance.

strong interaction *or* **force** *n Physics.* an interaction between elementary particles responsible for the forces between nucleons in the nucleus. Also called: **strong nuclear interaction** *or* **force.** See **interaction** (sense 2). Cf. **weak interaction.**

strong-minded ⓣ *adj* having strength of mind; firm, resolute, and determined.
▸ **ˌstrong-'mindedly** *adv* ▸ **ˌstrong-'mindedness** *n*

strong point ⓣ *n* something at which one excels; forte.

strongroom ('strɒŋˌruːm, -ˌrʊm) *n* a specially designed room in which valuables are locked for safety.

strong-willed *adj* having strength of will.

strontium ('strɒntɪəm) *n* a soft silvery-white element of the alkaline earth group of metals. The radioisotope **strontium-90,** with a half-life of 28.1 years, is used in nuclear power sources and is a hazardous nuclear fallout product. Symbol: Sr; atomic no.: 38; atomic wt.: 87.62. [C19: from NL, after *Strontian*, in the Highlands of Scotland, where discovered]

strontium unit *n* a unit expressing the concentration of strontium-90 in an organic medium, such as soil, bone, etc., relative to the concentration of calcium in the medium.

strop (strɒp) *n* **1** a leather strap or an abrasive strip for sharpening razors. **2** a rope or metal band around a block or deadeye for support. ◆ *vb* **strops, stropping, stropped. 3** (*tr*) to sharpen (a razor, etc.) on a strop. [C14 (in nautical use: a strip of rope): via MLow G or MDu. *strop*, ult. from L *stroppus*, from Gk *strophos* cord]

strophanthin (strəʊ'fænθɪn) *n* a toxic glycoside or mixture of glycosides obtained from the ripe seeds of certain species of strophanthus. [C19: NL, from STROPHANTH(US) + -IN]

strophanthus (strəʊ'fænθəs) *n* **1** any of various small trees or shrubs of tropical Africa and Asia, having strap-shaped twisted petals. **2** the seeds of any of these plants. [C19: NL, from Gk *strophos* twisted cord + *anthos* flower]

strophe ('strəʊfɪ) *n Prosody.* (in ancient Greek drama) **a** the first of two movements made by a chorus during the performance of a choral ode. **b** the first part of a choral ode sung during this movement. ◆ See **antistrophe, epode.** [C17: from Gk: a verse, lit.: a turning, from *strephein* to twist]
▸ **strophic** ('strɒfɪk, 'strəʊ-) *adj*

stroppy ⓣ ('strɒpɪ) *adj* **stroppier, stroppiest.** *Brit. inf.* angry or awkward. [C20: changed & shortened from OBSTREPEROUS]
▸ **'stroppily** *adv* ▸ **'stroppiness** *n*

strove (strəʊv) *vb* the past tense of **strive.**

strow (strəʊ) *vb* **strows, strowing, strowed; strown** *or* **strowed.** an archaic variant of **strew.**

struck (strʌk) *vb* **1** the past tense and past participle of **strike.** ◆ *adj* **2** *Chiefly US & Canad.* (of an industry, factory, etc.) shut down or otherwise affected by a labour strike.

structural ('strʌktʃərəl) *adj* **1** of, relating to, or having structure or a structure. **2** of, relating to, or forming part of the structure of a building. **3** of or relating to the structure of the earth's crust. **4** of or relating to the structure of organisms. **5** *Chem.* of or involving the arrangement of atoms in molecules.
▸ **'structurally** *adv*

structural formula *n* a chemical formula showing the composition and structure of a molecule.

structuralism ('strʌktʃərəˌlɪzəm) *n* **1** an approach to social sciences and to literature in terms of oppositions, contrasts, and hierarchical structures, esp. as they might reflect universal mental characteristics or organizing principles. **2** an approach to linguistics that analyses and describes the structure of language, as distinguished from its comparative and historical aspects.
▸ **'structuralist** *n, adj*

structural linguistics *n* (*functioning as sing*) a descriptive approach to an analysis of language on the basis of its structure as reflected by irreducible units of phonological, morphological, and semantic features.

structural unemployment *n Econ.* unemployment resulting from changes in the structure of an industry as a result of changes in either technology or taste.

structure ⓣ ('strʌktʃə) *n* **1** a complex construction or entity. **2** the arrangement and interrelationship of parts in a construction. **3** the manner of construction or organization. **4** *Chem.* the arrangement of atoms in a molecule of a chemical compound. **5** *Geol.* the way in which a mineral, rock, etc., is made up of its component parts. ◆ *vb* **structures, structuring, structured.** (*tr*) **6** to impart a structure to. [C15: from L *structūra*, from *struere* to build]

structured interview *n Marketing.* an interview in which the respondent answers only "yes", "no", or "don't know".

strudel ('struːdəl) *n* a thin sheet of filled dough rolled up and baked: *apple strudel*. [G, from MHG *strodel* whirlpool, from the way the pastry is rolled]

struggle ⓣ ('strʌgᵊl) *vb* **struggles, struggling, struggled.** (*intr*) **1** (usually foll. by *for* or *against; may take an infinitive*) to exert strength, energy, and force; work or strive. **2** to move about strenuously so as to escape from something confining. **3** to contend, battle, or fight. **4** to go or progress with difficulty. ◆ *n* **5** a laboured or strenuous exertion or effort. **6** a fight or battle. **7** the act of struggling. [C14: from ?]
▸ **'struggling** *adj*

strum (strʌm) *vb* **strums, strumming, strummed. 1** to sound (the strings of a guitar, etc.) with a downward or upward sweep of the thumb or of a plectrum. **2** to play (chords, a tune, etc.) in this way. [C18: prob. imit.]
▸ **'strummer** *n*

struma ('struːmə) *n, pl* **strumae** (-miː). **1** an abnormal enlargement of the thyroid gland; goitre. **2** *Bot.* a swelling, esp. at the base of a moss capsule. **3** another word for **scrofula.** [C16: from L: scrofulous tumour, from *struere* to heap up]
▸ **strumous** ('struːməs) *or* **strumose** ('struːməʊs) *adj*

strumpet ('strʌmpɪt) *n Arch.* a prostitute or promiscuous woman. [C14: from ?]

strung (strʌŋ) *vb* **1** a past tense and past participle of **string.** ◆ *adj* **2a** (of a piano, etc.) provided with strings. **2b** (*in combination*): *gut-strung*. **3 highly strung.** very nervous or volatile in character.

THESAURUS

brawny, burly, capable, fighting fit, fit, fit as a fiddle, hale, hardy, healthy, Herculean, lusty, muscular, robust, sinewy, sound, stalwart, stout, strapping, sturdy, tough, virile **2** = **durable**, hard-wearing, heavy-duty, on a firm foundation, reinforced, sturdy, substantial, well-armed, well-built, well-protected **3** = **self-confident**, aggressive, brave, courageous, determined, feisty (*inf., chiefly US & Canad.*), firm in spirit, forceful, hard as nails, hard-nosed (*inf.*), high-powered, plucky, resilient, resolute, resourceful, self-assertive, steadfast, stout-hearted, tenacious, tough, unyielding **4** = **distinct**, clear, marked, overpowering, unmistakable **6, 8** = **pungent**, biting, concentrated, heady, highly-flavoured, highly-seasoned, hot, intoxicating, piquant, powerful, pure, sharp, spicy, undiluted **9** = **extreme**, Draconian, drastic, forceful, severe **11** = **persuasive**, clear, clear-cut, cogent, compelling, convincing, effective, formidable, great, overpowering, potent, redoubtable, sound, telling, trenchant, urgent, weighty, well-established, well-founded **12** = **bright**, bold, brilliant, dazzling, glaring, loud, stark

Antonyms *adj* ≠ **powerful:** delicate, feeble, frail, ineffectual, namby-pamby, puny, weak ≠ **self-confident:** characterless, faint-hearted, lacking drive, spineless, timid, unassertive, uncommitted, unimpassioned ≠ **distinct:** delicate, faint, slight ≠ **pungent:** bland, mild, tasteless, vapid, weak ≠ **bright:** dull, insipid, pale, pastel, washed-out

strong-arm *adj* **1** *Informal* = **bullying**, aggressive, coercive, forceful, high-pressure, terror, terrorizing, threatening, thuggish, violent

stronghold *n* **1** = **fortress**, bastion, bulwark, castle, citadel, fastness, fort, keep, refuge

strong-minded *adj* = **determined**, firm, independent, iron-willed, resolute, strong-willed, unbending, uncompromising

strong point *n* = **forte**, advantage, asset, long suit (*inf.*), métier, speciality, strength, strong suit

stroppy *adj Brit. informal* = **awkward**, bloody-minded (*Brit. inf.*), cantankerous, destructive, difficult, litigious, obstreperous, perverse, quarrelsome, uncooperative, unhelpful

structure *n* **1** = **building**, construction, edifice, erection, pile **2** = **arrangement**, configuration, conformation, construction, design, fabric, form, formation, interrelation of parts, make, make-up, organization ◆ *vb* **6** = **arrange**, assemble, build up, design, organize, put together, shape

struggle *vb* **1** = **strive**, bend over backwards, break one's neck (*inf.*), bust a gut (*inf.*), do one's damnedest (*inf.*), exert oneself, give it one's all (*inf.*), give it one's best shot (*inf.*), go all out (*inf.*), go for broke (*sl.*), go for it (*inf.*), knock oneself out (*inf.*), labour, make an all-out effort (*inf.*), make every effort, rupture oneself (*inf.*), strain, toil, work, work like a Trojan **3** = **fight**, battle, compete, contend, grapple, lock horns, scuffle, wrestle ◆ *n* **5** = **effort**, exertion, grind (*inf.*), labour, long haul, pains, scramble, toil, work **6** = **fight**, battle, brush, clash, combat, conflict, contest, encounter, hostilities, skirmish, strife, tussle

strung up Ⓣ *adj (postpositive) Inf.* tense or nervous.

strut Ⓣ (strʌt) *vb* **struts, strutting, strutted. 1** *(intr)* to walk in a pompous manner; swagger. **2** *(tr)* to support or provide with struts. ◆ *n* **3** a structural member, esp. as part of a framework. **4** an affected, proud, or stiff walk. [C14 *strouten* (in the sense: swell, stand out; C16: to walk stiffly), from OE *strūtian* to stand stiffly]
▸**ˈstrutter** *n* ▸**ˈstrutting** *adj* ▸**ˈstruttingly** *adv*

struthious (ˈstruːθɪəs) *adj* **1** (of birds) related to or resembling the ostrich. **2** of, relating to, or designating all flightless birds. [C18: from LL *strūthiō*, from Gk *strouthiōn*, from *strouthos* ostrich]

strychnine (ˈstrɪkniːn) *n* a white crystalline very poisonous alkaloid, obtained from the plant nux vomica: formerly used in small quantities as a stimulant. [C19: via F from NL *Strychnos*, from Gk *strukhnos* nightshade]

Stuart (ˈstjuət) *adj* of or relating to the royal house that ruled Scotland from 1371 to 1714 and England from 1603 to 1714.

stub Ⓣ (stʌb) *n* **1** a short piece remaining after something has been cut, removed, etc.: *a cigar stub*. **2** the residual piece or section of a receipt, ticket, cheque, etc. **3** the usual US and Canad. word for **counterfoil. 4** any short projection or blunted end. **5** the stump of a tree or plant. ◆ *vb* **stubs, stubbing, stubbed.** *(tr)* **6** to strike (one's toe, foot, etc.) painfully against a hard surface. **7** (usually foll. by *out*) to put (out a cigarette or cigar) by pressing the end against a surface. **8** to clear (land) of stubs. **9** to dig up (the roots) of (a tree or bush). [OE *stubb*]

stub axle *n* a short axle that carries one of the front steered wheels of a motor vehicle.

stubble (ˈstʌbᵊl) *n* **1a** the stubs of stalks left in a field where a crop has been harvested. **1b** *(as modifier)*: *a stubble field*. **2** any bristly growth. [C13: from OF *estuble*, from L *stupula*, var. of *stipula* stalk]
▸**ˈstubbled** *or* **ˈstubbly** *adj*

stubble-jumper *n Canad. sl.* a prairie grain farmer.

stubborn Ⓣ (ˈstʌbᵊn) *adj* **1** refusing to comply, agree, or give in. **2** difficult to handle, treat, or overcome. **3** persistent and dogged. [C14 *stoborne*, from ?]
▸**ˈstubbornly** *adv* ▸**ˈstubbornness** *n*

stubby Ⓣ (ˈstʌbɪ) *adj* **stubbier, stubbiest. 1** short and broad; stumpy or thickset. **2** bristling and stiff. ◆ *n* **3** *Austral. sl.* Also: **stubbie.** a small bottle of beer.
▸**ˈstubbily** *adv* ▸**ˈstubbiness** *n*

stucco (ˈstʌkəu) *n, pl* **stuccoes** *or* **stuccos. 1** a weather-resistant mixture of dehydrated lime, powdered marble, and glue, used in decorative mouldings on buildings. **2** any of various types of cement or plaster used for coating outside walls. **3** Also called: **stuccowork.** decorative work moulded in stucco. ◆ *vb* **stuccoes** *or* **stuccos, stuccoing, stuccoed. 4** *(tr)* to apply stucco to. [C16: from It., of Gmc origin]

stuck Ⓣ (stʌk) *vb* **1** the past tense and past participle of **stick**[2]. ◆ *adj* **2** *Inf.* baffled or nonplussed. **3** (foll. by *on*) *Sl.* keen (on) or infatuated (with). **4 get stuck in** *or* **into.** *Inf.* **4a** to perform (a task) with determination. **4b** to attack (a person).

stuck-up Ⓣ *adj Inf.* conceited, arrogant, or snobbish.
▸**ˈstuck-ˈupness** *n*

stud[1] Ⓣ (stʌd) *n* **1** a large-headed nail or other projection protruding from a surface, usually as decoration. **2** a type of fastener consisting of two discs at either end of a short shank, used to fasten shirtfronts, collars, etc. **3** a vertical member used with others to construct the framework of a wall. **4** the crossbar in the centre of a link of a heavy chain. **5** one of a number of rounded projections on the sole of a boot or shoe to give better grip, as on a football boot. ◆ *vb* **studs, studding, studded.** *(tr)* **6** to provide, ornament, or make with studs. **7** to dot or cover (with): *the park was studded with daisies*. **8** to provide or support (a wall, partition, etc.) with studs. [OE *studu*]

stud[2] (stʌd) *n* **1** a group of pedigree animals, esp. horses, kept for breeding purposes. **2** any male animal kept principally for breeding purposes, esp. a stallion. **3** a farm or stable where a stud is kept. **4** the state or condition of being kept for breeding purposes: *at stud; put to stud*. **5** *(modifier)* of or relating to such animals or the place where they are kept: *a stud farm; a stud horse*. **6** *Sl.* a virile or sexually active man. **7** short for **stud poker.** [OE *stōd*]

studbook (ˈstʌd,buk) *n* a written record of the pedigree of a purebred stock, esp. of racehorses.

studding (ˈstʌdɪŋ) *n* **1** studs collectively, esp. as used to form a wall or partition. **2** material used to form or serve as studs.

studdingsail (ˈstʌdɪŋ,seɪl; *Naut.* ˈstʌnsᵊl) *n Naut.* a light auxiliary sail set outboard on spars on either side of a square sail. Also called: **stunsail, stuns'l.** [C16: *studding*, ?from MLow G, MDu. *stōtinge*, from *stōten* to thrust]

student Ⓣ (ˈstjuːdᵊnt) *n* **1a** a person following a course of study, as in a school, college, university, etc. **1b** *(as modifier)*: *student teacher*. **2** a person who makes a thorough study of a subject. [C15: from L *studēns* diligent, from *studēre* to be zealous]

Student's t *n* a statistic often used to test the hypothesis that a random sample of normally distributed observations has a given mean. [after *Student*, pen name of W. S. Gosset (1876–1937), Brit. mathematician]

studhorse (ˈstʌd,hɔːs) *n* another word for **stallion.**

studied Ⓣ (ˈstʌdɪd) *adj* carefully practised, designed, or premeditated: *a studied reply*.
▸**ˈstudiedly** *adv* ▸**ˈstudiedness** *n*

studio Ⓣ (ˈstjuːdɪəu) *n, pl* **studios. 1** a room in which an artist, photographer, or musician works. **2** a room used to record television or radio programmes, make films, etc. **3** *(pl)* the premises of a radio, television, or film company. [C19: from It., lit.: study, from L *studium* diligence]

studio couch *n* an upholstered couch, usually backless, convertible into a double bed.

studio flat *n* a flat with one main room.

studious Ⓣ (ˈstjuːdɪəs) *adj* **1** given to study. **2** of a serious, thoughtful, and hard-working character. **3** showing deliberation, care, or precision. [C14: from L *studiōsus* devoted to, from *studium* assiduity]
▸**ˈstudiously** *adv* ▸**ˈstudiousness** *n*

stud poker *n* a variety of poker in which the first card is dealt face down before each player and the next four are dealt face up (**five-card stud**) or in which the first two cards and the last card are dealt face down and the intervening four cards are dealt face up (**seven-card stud**).

study Ⓣ (ˈstʌdɪ) *vb* **studies, studying, studied. 1** to apply the mind to the learning or understanding of (a subject), esp. by reading. **2** *(tr)* to investigate or examine, as by observation, research, etc. **3** *(tr)* to look at minutely; scrutinize. **4** *(tr)* to give much careful or critical thought to. **5** to take a course in (a subject), as at a college. **6** *(tr)* to try to memorize: *to study a part for a play*. **7** *(intr)* to meditate or contemplate; reflect. ◆ *n, pl* **studies. 8a** the act or process of studying. **8b** *(as modifier)*: *study group*. **9** a room used for studying, reading, writing, etc. **10** *(often pl)* work relating to a particular discipline: *environmental studies*. **11** an investigation and analysis of a subject, institution etc. **12** a product of studying, such as a written paper or book. **13** a drawing, sculpture, etc., executed for practice or in preparation for another work. **14** a musical composition intended to develop one aspect of performing technique. **15** *Inf.* **in a brown study.** in a reverie or daydream. [C13: from OF *estudie*, from L *studium* zeal, from *studēre* to be diligent]

stuff Ⓣ (stʌf) *vb (mainly tr)* **1** to pack or fill completely; cram. **2** *(intr)* to eat large quantities. **3** to force, shove, or squeeze: *to stuff money into a pocket*. **4** to fill (food such as poultry or tomatoes) with a stuffing. **5** to fill (an animal's skin) with material so as to restore the shape of the live animal. **6** *Taboo sl.* to have sexual intercourse with (a woman). **7** *US & Canad.* to fill (a ballot box) with fraudulent votes. **8** *Sl.* to ruin, frustrate, or defeat. ◆ *n* **9** the raw material or fabric of something. **10**

THESAURUS

strung up *adj Informal* = **tense**, a bundle of nerves *(inf.)*, edgy, jittery *(inf.)*, keyed up, nervous, on edge, on tenterhooks, twitchy *(inf.)*, under a strain, uptight *(inf.)*, wired *(sl.)*

strut *vb* **1** = **swagger**, parade, peacock, prance, stalk

stub *n* **1** = **butt**, dog-end *(inf.)*, end, fag end *(inf.)*, remnant, stump, tail, tail end **2** = **counterfoil**

stubborn *adj* **1, 3** = **obstinate**, bull-headed, contumacious, cross-grained, dogged, dour, fixed, headstrong, inflexible, intractable, mulish, obdurate, opinionated, persistent, pig-headed, recalcitrant, refractory, self-willed, stiff-necked, tenacious, unbending, unmanageable, unshakable, unyielding, wilful
Antonyms *adj* biddable, compliant, docile, flexible, half-hearted, irresolute, malleable, manageable, pliable, pliant, tractable, vacillating, wavering, yielding

stubby *adj* **1** = **stocky**, chunky, dumpy, fubsy *(arch. or dialect)*, short, squat, stumpy, thickset

stuck *adj* **1** = **fastened**, cemented, fast, firm, fixed, glued, joined **2** *Informal* = **baffled**, at a loss, at a standstill, at one's wits' end, beaten, bereft of ideas, nonplussed, stumped, up against a brick wall *(inf.)* **3** *Slang foll. by* **on** = **infatuated with**, crazy about, for, *or* over *(inf.)*, enthusiastic about, hung up on, keen on, mad about, obsessed with, wild about *(inf.)* **4 get stuck in** *Informal* = **set about**, get down to, make a start on, tackle, take the bit between one's teeth

stuck-up *adj Informal* = **snobbish**, arrogant, bigheaded *(inf.)*, conceited, condescending, haughty, high and mighty *(inf.)*, hoity-toity *(inf.)*, patronizing, proud, snooty *(inf.)*, swollen-headed, toffee-nosed *(sl., chiefly Brit.)*, uppish *(Brit. inf.)*, uppity *(inf.)*

stud[1] *vb* **6, 7** = **ornament**, bejewel, bespangle, dot, fleck, spangle, speckle, spot, sprinkle

student *n* **1a, 2** = **learner**, apprentice, disciple, observer, pupil, scholar, trainee, undergraduate

studied *adj* = **planned**, calculated, conscious, deliberate, intentional, premeditated, purposeful, well-considered, wilful
Antonyms *adj* impulsive, natural, spontaneous, spur-of-the-moment, unplanned, unpremeditated

studio *n* **1** = **workshop**, atelier

studious *adj* **1, 2** = **scholarly**, academic, assiduous, bookish, diligent, eager, earnest, hard-working, intellectual, meditative, reflective, sedulous, serious, thoughtful **3** = **careful**, attentive, deliberate, precise
Antonyms *adj* ≠ **scholarly:** frivolous, idle, lazy, loafing, unacademic, unintellectual, unscholarly ≠ **careful:** careless, inattentive, indifferent, negligent

study *vb* **1** = **learn**, bone up on *(inf.)*, burn the midnight oil, cram *(inf.)*, hammer away at, lucubrate *(rare)*, mug up *(Brit. sl.)*, read up, swot (up) *(Brit. inf.)* **2** = **contemplate**, apply oneself (to), cogitate, con *(arch.)*, consider, examine, go into, meditate, ponder, pore over, read **3** = **examine**, analyse, deliberate, investigate, look into, peruse, research, scrutinize, survey, work over ◆ *n* **8a** = **learning**, academic work, application, book work, cramming *(inf.)*, lessons, reading, research, school work, swotting *(Brit. inf.)*, thought **11** = **examination**, analysis, attention, cogitation, consideration, contemplation, inquiry, inspection, investigation, perusal, review, scrutiny, survey

stuff *vb* **1** = **cram**, compress, crowd, fill, force, jam, load, pack, pad, push, ram, shove, squeeze, stow, wedge **2** = **gorge**, gobble, gor-

woollen cloth or fabric. **11** any general or unspecified substance or accumulation of objects. **12** stupid or worthless actions, speech, etc. **13** subject matter, skill, etc.: *he knows his stuff.* **14** a slang word for **money.** **15** *Sl.* a drug, esp. cannabis. **16** *Inf.* **do one's stuff.** to do what is expected of one. **17 that's the stuff.** that is what is needed. **18** *Brit. sl.* a girl or woman considered sexually (esp. in **bit of stuff**). [C14: from OF *estoffe,* from *estoffer* to furnish, of Gmc origin]
▸'**stuffer** *n*

stuffed (stʌft) *adj* **1** filled with something, esp. (of poultry and other food) filled with stuffing. **2** (foll. by *up*) having the nasal passages blocked with mucus. **3 get stuffed!** *Brit. taboo sl.* an exclamation of contemptuous anger or annoyance against another person.

stuffed shirt *n Inf.* a pompous person.

stuff gown *n Brit.* a woollen gown worn by a barrister who has not taken silk.

stuffing ➊ ('stʌfɪŋ) *n* **1** the material with which something is stuffed. **2** a mixture of ingredients with which poultry, meat, etc., is stuffed before cooking. **3 knock the stuffing out of (someone).** to defeat (someone) utterly.

stuffing box *n* a small chamber in which packing is compressed around a reciprocating or rotating rod or shaft to form a seal.

stuffy ➊ ('stʌfɪ) *adj* **stuffier, stuffiest. 1** lacking fresh air. **2** excessively dull, staid, or conventional. **3** (of the nasal passages) blocked with mucus.
▸'**stuffily** *adv* ▸'**stuffiness** *n*

stultify ('stʌltɪˌfaɪ) *vb* **stultifies, stultifying, stultified.** (*tr*) **1** to make useless, futile, or ineffectual, esp. by routine. **2** to cause to appear absurd or inconsistent. [C18: from L *stultus* stupid + *facere* to make]
▸ˌ**stultifi'cation** *n* ▸'**stultiˌfier** *n*

stum (stʌm) (in wine-making) ◆ *n* **1** a less common word for **must**[2]. **2** partly fermented wine added to fermented wine as a preservative. ◆ *vb* **stums, stumming, stummed. 3** to preserve (wine) by adding stum. [C17: from Du. *stom* dumb]

stumble ➊ ('stʌmbᵊl) *vb* **stumbles, stumbling, stumbled.** (*intr*) **1** to trip or fall while walking or running. **2** to walk in an awkward, unsteady, or unsure way. **3** to make mistakes or hesitate in speech or actions. **4** (foll. by *across* or *upon*) to come (across) by accident. ◆ *n* **5** a false step, trip, or blunder. **6** the act of stumbling. [C14: rel. to Norwegian *stumla,* Danish dialect *stumle*]
▸'**stumbler** *n* ▸'**stumbling** *adj* ▸'**stumblingly** *adv*

stumbling block ➊ *n* any impediment or obstacle.

stumer ('stju:mə) *n* **1** *Sl.* a forgery or cheat. **2** *Irish dialect.* a poor bargain. **3** *Scot.* a stupid person. **4 come a stumer.** *Austral. sl.* to crash financially. [from ?]

stump ➊ (stʌmp) *n* **1** the base of a tree trunk left standing after the tree has been felled or has fallen. **2** the part of something, such as a tooth, limb, or blade, that remains after a larger part has been removed. **3** (*often pl*) *Inf., facetious.* a leg (esp. in **stir one's stumps**). **4** *Cricket.* any of three upright wooden sticks that, with two bails laid across them, form a wicket (the **stumps**). **5** Also called: **tortillon.** a short sharply-pointed stick of cork or rolled paper or leather, used in drawing and shading. **6** a heavy tread or the sound of heavy footsteps. **7** a platform used by an orator when addressing a meeting. ◆ *vb* **8** (*tr*) to stop, confuse, or puzzle. **9** (*intr*) to plod or trudge heavily. **10** (*tr*) *Cricket.* to dismiss (a batsman) by breaking his wicket with the ball or with the ball in the hand while he is out of his crease. **11** *Chiefly US & Canad.* to campaign or canvass (an area), esp. by political speech- making. [C14: from MLow G *stump*]
▸'**stumper** *n*

stump up ➊ *vb* (*adv*) *Brit. inf.* to give (the money required).

stumpy ➊ ('stʌmpɪ) *adj* **stumpier, stumpiest. 1** short and thickset like a stump; stubby. **2** full of stumps.
▸'**stumpiness** *n*

stun ➊ (stʌn) *vb* **stuns, stunning, stunned.** (*tr*) **1** to render unconscious, as by a heavy blow or fall. **2** to shock or overwhelm. **3** to surprise or astound. ◆ *n* **4** the state or effect of being stunned. [C13 *stunen,* from OF *estoner* to daze, ult. from L EX-[1] + *tonāre* to thunder]

stung ➊ (stʌŋ) *vb* the past tense and past participle of **sting.**

stunk (stʌŋk) *vb* a past tense and past participle of **stink.**

stunner ➊ ('stʌnə) *n Inf.* a person or thing of great beauty, quality, size, etc.

stunning ➊ ('stʌnɪŋ) *adj Inf.* very attractive, impressive, astonishing, etc.
▸'**stunningly** *adv*

stunsail *or* **stuns'l** ('stʌnsᵊl) *n* another word for **studdingsail.**

stunt[1] ➊ (stʌnt) *vb* **1** (*tr*) to prevent or impede (the growth or development) of (a plant, animal, etc.). ◆ *n* **2** the act or an instance of stunting. **3** a person, animal, or plant that has been stunted. [C17 (as vb: to check the growth of): ?from C15 *stont* of short duration, from OE *stunt* foolish; sense prob. infl. by ON *stuttr* dwarfed]
▸'**stunted** *adj* ▸'**stuntedness** *n*

stunt[2] ➊ (stʌnt) *n* **1** a feat of daring or skill. **2a** an acrobatic or dangerous piece of action in a film, etc. **2b** (*as modifier*): *a stunt man.* **3** anything spectacular or unusual done for attention. ◆ *vb* **4** (*intr*) to perform a stunt or stunts. [C19: US student slang, from ?]

stupa ('stu:pə) *n* a domed edifice housing Buddhist or Jain relics. [C19: from Sansk.: dome]

stupe (stju:p) *n Med.* a hot damp cloth, usually sprinkled with an irritant, applied to the body to relieve pain by counterirritation. [C14: from L *stuppa* flax, from Gk *stuppē*]

stupefacient (ˌstju:pɪ'feɪʃɪənt) *n* **1** a drug that causes stupor. ◆ *adj* **2** of, relating to, or designating this type of drug. [C17: from L *stupefaciēns,* from *stupēre* to be stunned + *facere* to make]

stupefaction ➊ (ˌstju:pɪ'fækʃən) *n* **1** astonishment. **2** the act of stupefying or the state of being stupefied.

stupefy ➊ ('stju:pɪˌfaɪ) *vb* **stupefies, stupefying, stupefied.** (*tr*) **1** to render insensitive or lethargic. **2** to confuse or astound. [C16: from OF *stupefier,* from L *stupefacere;* see STUPEFACIENT]
▸'**stupeˌfying** *adj*

stupendous ➊ (stju:'pendəs) *adj* astounding, wonderful, huge, etc. [C17: from L *stupēre* to be amazed]
▸**stu'pendously** *adv* ▸**stu'pendousness** *n*

stupid ➊ ('stju:pɪd) *adj* **1** lacking in common sense, perception, or intelligence. **2** (*usually postpositive*) dazed or stupefied: *stupid from lack of sleep.* **3** slow-witted. **4** trivial, silly, or frivolous. ◆ *n* **5** *Inf.* a stupid person. [C16: from F *stupide,* from L *stupidus* silly, from *stupēre* to be amazed]
▸**stu'pidity** *or* '**stupidness** *n*

THESAURUS

mandize, guzzle, make a pig of oneself (*inf.*), overindulge, pig out (*sl.*), sate, satiate ◆ *n* **9** = **substance,** essence, matter, pith, quintessence, staple **10** = **material,** cloth, fabric, raw material, textile **11** = **things,** belongings, bits and pieces, clobber, effects, equipment, gear, goods and chattels, impedimenta, junk, kit, luggage, materials, objects, paraphernalia, possessions, tackle, trappings **12** = **nonsense,** balderdash, baloney (*inf.*), bosh (*inf.*), bunk (*inf.*), bunkum, claptrap (*inf.*), foolishness, humbug, poppycock (*inf.*), rot, rubbish, stuff and nonsense, tommyrot, trash, tripe (*inf.*), twaddle, verbiage

stuffing *n* **1** = **filling,** kapok, packing, quilting, wadding **2** = **forcemeat,** farce, farcemeat

stuffy *adj* **1** = **airless,** close, fetid, frowsty, fuggy, heavy, muggy, oppressive, stale, stifling, suffocating, sultry, unventilated **2** *Informal* = **staid,** as dry as dust, conventional, deadly, dreary, dull, fusty, humourless, musty, niminy-piminy, old-fashioned, old-fogeyish, pompous, priggish, prim, prim and proper, stilted, stodgy, strait-laced, uninteresting
Antonyms *adj* ≠ **airless:** airy, breezy, cool, draughty, fresh, gusty, pleasant, well-ventilated

stumble *vb* **1** = **trip,** blunder about, come a cropper (*inf.*), fall, falter, flounder, lose one's balance, lurch, reel, slip, stagger **3** = **falter,** fluff (*inf.*), hesitate, stammer, stutter **4** *with* **across, on** *or* **upon** = **discover,** blunder upon, chance upon, come across, encounter, find, happen upon, light upon, run across, turn up

stumbling block *n* = **obstacle,** bar, barrier, difficulty, hazard, hindrance, hurdle, impediment, obstruction, snag

stump *vb* **8** = **baffle,** bewilder, bring (someone) up short, confound, confuse, dumbfound, flummox, foil, mystify, nonplus, outwit, perplex, puzzle, snooker, stop, stymie **9** = **stamp,** clomp, clump, lumber, plod, stomp (*inf.*), trudge

stumped *adj* = **baffled,** at a loss, at one's wits' end, at sea, brought to a standstill, floored (*inf.*), flummoxed, in despair, nonplussed, perplexed, stymied, uncertain which way to turn

stump up *vb Brit. informal* = **pay,** chip in (*inf.*), come across with (*inf.*), contribute, cough up (*inf.*), donate, fork out (*sl.*), hand over, shell out (*inf.*)

stumpy *adj* **1** = **stocky,** chunky, dumpy, fubsy (*arch. or dialect*), heavy, short, squat, stubby, thick, thickset

stun *vb* **1** = **knock out,** daze **2, 3** = **overcome,** amaze, astonish, astound, bewilder, confound, confuse, dumbfound, flabbergast (*inf.*), hit (someone) like a ton of bricks (*inf.*), knock (someone) for six (*inf.*), overpower, shock, stagger, strike (someone) dumb, stupefy, take (someone's) breath away

stung *adj* = **goaded,** angered, exasperated, hurt, incensed, nettled, piqued, resentful, roused, wounded

stunner *n Informal* = **beauty,** charmer, dazzler, dish (*inf.*), dolly (*sl.*), eyeful (*inf.*), glamour puss, good-looker, heart-throb, honey (*inf.*), humdinger (*sl.*), knockout (*inf.*), looker (*inf., chiefly US*), lovely (*sl.*), peach (*inf.*), sensation, smasher (*inf.*), wow (*sl., chiefly US*)

stunning *adj Informal* = **wonderful,** beautiful, brilliant, dazzling, devastating (*inf.*), dramatic, drop-dead (*sl.*), gorgeous, great (*inf.*), heavenly, impressive, jaw-dropping, lovely, marvellous, out of this world (*inf.*), ravishing, remarkable, sensational (*inf.*), smashing (*inf.*), spectacular, striking
Antonyms *adj* average, dreadful, horrible, mediocre, no great shakes (*inf.*), ordinary, plain, poor, rotten, run-of-the-mill, ugly, unattractive, unimpressive, uninspiring, unremarkable

stunt[2] *n* **1** = **feat,** act, deed, exploit, feature, gest (*arch.*), *tour de force,* trick

stunted *adj* **1** = **undersized,** diminutive, dwarfed, dwarfish, little, small, tiny

stupefaction *n* **1** = **astonishment,** amazement, awe, wonder, wonderment

stupefy *vb* **1, 2** = **astound,** amaze, bewilder, confound, daze, dumbfound, knock senseless, numb, shock, stagger, stun

stupendous *adj* = **wonderful,** amazing, astounding, breathtaking, brilliant, colossal, enormous, fabulous (*inf.*), fantastic (*inf.*), gigantic, jaw-dropping, marvellous, mega (*sl.*), mind-blowing (*inf.*), mind-boggling (*inf.*), out of this world (*inf.*), overwhelming, phenomenal, prodigious, sensational (*inf.*), staggering, stunning (*inf.*), superb, surpassing belief, surprising, tremendous (*inf.*), vast, wondrous (*arch. or literary*)
Antonyms *adj* ≠ **wonderful:** average, mediocre, modest, no great shakes (*inf.*), ordinary, petty, unexciting, unimpressive, unremarkable, unsurprising ≠ **huge:** diminutive, puny, tiny

stupid *adj* **1, 3** = **unintelligent,** Boeotian, braindead (*inf.*), brainless, crass, cretinous, dead from the neck up, deficient, dense, dim, dolt-

stupor ➊ ('stjuːpə) *n* **1** a state of unconsciousness. **2** mental dullness; torpor. [C17: from L, from *stupēre* to be aghast]
▸**'stuporous** *adj*

sturdy ➊ ('stɜːdɪ) *adj* **sturdier, sturdiest. 1** healthy, strong, and vigorous. **2** strongly built; stalwart. [C13 (in the sense: rash, harsh): from OF *estordi* dazed, from *estordir* to stun]
▸**'sturdily** *adv* ▸**'sturdiness** *n*

sturgeon ('stɜːdʒən) *n* any of various primitive bony fishes of temperate waters of the N hemisphere, having an elongated snout and rows of spines along the body. [C13: from OF *estourgeon*, of Gmc origin]

Sturt's desert pea (stɜːts) *n* another name for **desert pea.**

stutter ➊ ('stʌtə) *vb* **1** to speak (a word, phrase, etc.) with recurring repetition of consonants, esp. initial ones. **2** to make (an abrupt sound) repeatedly: *the gun stuttered.* ◆ *n* **3** the act or habit of stuttering. **4** a stuttering sound. [C16]
▸**'stutterer** *n* ▸**'stuttering** *n, adj* ▸**'stutteringly** *adv*

sty (staɪ) *n, pl* **sties. 1** a pen in which pigs are housed. **2** any filthy or corrupt place. ◆ *vb* **sties, stying, stied. 3** to enclose or be enclosed in a sty. [OE *stig*]

stye *or* **sty** (staɪ) *n, pl* **styes** *or* **sties.** inflammation of a sebaceous gland of the eyelid. [C15 *styanye* (mistaken as *sty on eye*), from OE *stīgend* rising, hence swelling, + *ye* eye]

Stygian ('stɪdʒɪən) *adj* **1** of or relating to the Styx, a river in Hades. **2** *Chiefly literary.* dark, gloomy, or hellish. [C16: from L *Stygius*, from Gk *Stugios*, from *Stux* Styx]

style ➊ (staɪl) *n* **1** a form of appearance, design, or production; type or make. **2** the way in which something is done: *good style.* **3** the manner in which something is expressed or performed, considered as separate from its intrinsic content, meaning, etc. **4** a distinctive, formal, or characteristic manner of expression in words, music, painting, etc. **5** elegance or refinement of manners, dress, etc. **6** prevailing fashion in dress, looks, etc. **7** a fashionable or ostentatious mode of existence: *to live in style.* **8** the particular mode of orthography, punctuation, design, etc., followed in a book, journal, etc., or in a printing or publishing house. **9** *Chiefly Brit.* the distinguishing title or form of address of a person or firm. **10** *Bot.* the long slender extension of the ovary, bearing the stigma. **11** a method of expressing or calculating dates. See **Old Style, New Style. 12** another word for **stylus** (sense 1). **13** the arm of a sundial. ◆ *vb* **styles, styling, styled.** (*mainly tr*) **14** to design, shape, or tailor: *to style hair.* **15** to adapt or make suitable for. **16** to make consistent or correct according to a printing or publishing style. **17** to name or call; designate: *to style a man a fool.* [C13: from L *stylus, stilus* writing implement, hence characteristics of the writing, style]
▸**'stylar** *adj* ▸**'styler** *n*

stylebook ('staɪl,bʊk) *n* a book containing rules and examples of punctuation, typography, etc., for the use of writers, editors, and printers.

stylet ('staɪlɪt) *n Surgery.* **1** a wire for insertion into a catheter, etc., to maintain its rigidity during passage. **2** a slender probe. [C17: from F *stilet*, from OIt. STILETTO; infl. by L *stylus* style]

styling mousse *n* a light foamy substance applied to the hair before styling in order to retain the style.

stylish ➊ ('staɪlɪʃ) *adj* having style; smart; fashionable.
▸**'stylishly** *adv* ▸**'stylishness** *n*

stylist ('staɪlɪst) *n* **1** a person who performs, writes, or acts with attention to style. **2** a designer of clothes, décor, etc. **3** a hairdresser who styles hair.

stylistic (staɪ'lɪstɪk) *adj* of or relating to style, esp. artistic or literary style.
▸**sty'listically** *adv*

stylite ('staɪlaɪt) *n Christianity.* one of a class of recluses who in ancient times lived on the top of high pillars. [C17: from LGk *stulitēs*, from Gk *stulos* a pillar]
▸**stylitic** (staɪ'lɪtɪk) *adj*

stylize *or* **stylise** ('staɪlaɪz) *vb* **stylizes, stylizing, stylized** *or* **stylises, stylising, stylised.** (*tr*) to give a conventional or established stylistic form to.
▸,**styli'zation** *or* ,**styli'sation** *n*

stylo- *or before a vowel* **styl-** *combining form.* **1** (in biology) a style. **2** indicating a column or point: *stylobate; stylograph.* [from Gk *stulos* column]

stylobate ('staɪlə,beɪt) *n* a continuous horizontal course of masonry that supports a colonnade. [C17: from L *stylobatēs*, from Gk *stulos* pillar + *-batēs*, from *bainein* to walk]

stylograph ('staɪlə,grɑːf) *n* a fountain pen having a fine hollow tube as the writing point instead of a nib. [C19: from STYL(US) + -GRAPH]

styloid ('staɪlɔɪd) *adj* **1** resembling a stylus. **2** *Anat.* of or relating to a projecting process of the temporal bone. [C18: from NL *styloides*, from Gk *stuloeidēs* like a stylus; infl. by Gk *stulos* pillar]

stylops ('staɪlɒps) *n, pl* **stylopes** (-lə,piːz). any of various insects living as a parasite in other insects, esp. bees and wasps. [C19: NL, from Gk, from *stulos* a pillar + *ōps* an eye, from the fact that the male has stalked eyes]

stylus ('staɪləs) *n, pl* **styli** (-laɪ) *or* **styluses. 1** Also called: **style.** a pointed instrument for engraving, drawing, or writing. **2** a tool used in ancient times for writing on wax tablets, which was pointed at one end and blunt at the other for erasing. **3** Also called: **needle.** a device attached to the cartridge in the pick-up arm of a record player that rests in the groove in the record, transmitting the vibrations to the sensing device in the cartridge. [C18: from L, var. of *stilus* writing implement]

stymie ➊ *or* **stymy** ('staɪmɪ) *vb* **stymies, stymieing** *or* **stymying, stymied.** (*tr; often passive*) **1** to hinder or thwart. **2** *Golf.* (formerly) to impede with a stymie. ◆ *n, pl* **stymies. 3** *Golf.* (formerly) a situation in which an opponent's ball is blocking the line between the hole and the ball about to be played. **4** a situation of obstruction. [C19: from ?]

styptic ('stɪptɪk) *adj* **1** contracting the blood vessels or tissues. ◆ *n* **2** a styptic drug. [C14: via LL, from Gk *stuptikos* capable of contracting, from *stuphein* to contract]

styrene ('staɪriːn) *n* a colourless oily volatile flammable liquid made from ethylene and benzene. It readily polymerizes and is used in making synthetic plastics and rubbers. Formula: $C_6H_5CH{:}CH_2$. Systematic name: **phenylethene.** [C20: from Gk *sturax* tree of the genus *Styrax* + -ENE]

suable ('sjuːəbᵊl) *adj* liable to be sued in a court.
▸,**sua'bility** *n*

suasion ('sweɪʒən) *n* a rare word for **persuasion.** [C14: from L *suāsiō*, from *suādēre* to PERSUADE]
▸**'suasive** *adj*

suave ➊ (swɑːv) *adj* (esp. of a man) displaying smoothness and sophistication in manner; urbane. [C16: from L *suāvis* sweet]
▸**'suavely** *adv* ▸**suavity** ('swɑːvɪtɪ) *or* **'suaveness** *n*

sub (sʌb) *n* **1** short for several words beginning with *sub-*, such as **subeditor, submarine, subordinate, subscription,** and **substitute. 2** *Brit. inf.* an advance payment of wages or salary. Formal term: **subsistence allowance.** ◆ *vb* **subs, subbing, subbed. 3** (*intr*) to serve or act as a substitute. **4** *Brit. inf.* to grant or receive (an advance payment of wages or salary). **5** (*tr*) *Inf.* short for **subedit.**

sub. *abbrev. for:* **1** subeditor. **2** *Music.* subito. **3** subscription. **4** substitute.

sub- *prefix* **1** situated under or beneath: *subterranean.* **2** secondary in rank; subordinate: *subeditor.* **3** falling short of; less than or imperfectly: *subarctic; subhuman.* **4** forming a subdivision or subordinate part: *subcommittee.* **5** (in chemistry) **5a** indicating that a compound contains a relatively small proportion of a specified element: *suboxide.* **5b** indicating that a salt is basic salt: *subacetate.* [from L *sub*]

subacid (sʌb'æsɪd) *adj* (esp. of some fruits) moderately acid or sour.
▸**subacidity** (,sʌbə'sɪdɪtɪ) *or* **sub'acidness** *n*

subadar *or* **subahdar** ('suːbə,dɑː) *n* (formerly) the chief native officer

THESAURUS

ish, dopey (*inf.*), dozy (*Brit. inf.*), dull, dumb (*inf.*), dumb-ass (*sl.*), gullible, half-witted, moronic, naive, obtuse, simple, simple-minded, slow, slow on the uptake (*inf.*), slow-witted, sluggish, stolid, thick, thick as mince (*Scot. inf.*), thickheaded, witless, woodenheaded (*inf.*) **2** = **dazed**, groggy, in a daze, insensate, punch-drunk, semiconscious, senseless, stunned, stupefied **4** = **silly**, asinine, crackbrained, crackpot (*inf.*), daft (*inf.*), foolish, futile, half-baked (*inf.*), idiotic, ill-advised, imbecilic, inane, irresponsible, laughable, ludicrous, meaningless, mindless, nonsensical, pointless, puerile, rash, senseless, short-sighted, trivial, unintelligent, unthinking
Antonyms *adj* ≠ **unintelligent:** astute, brainy, bright, brilliant, clear-headed, clever, intelligent, lucid, on the ball (*inf.*), quick, quick on the uptake, quick-witted, sensible, sharp, shrewd, smart, wise ≠ **silly:** astute, prudent, realistic, reasonable, sensible, shrewd, thoughtful, well-thought-out, wise

stupidity *n* **1** = **lack of intelligence**, asininity, brainlessness, denseness, dimness, dopiness (*sl.*), doziness (*Brit. inf.*), dullness, dumbness (*inf.*), feeble-mindedness, imbecility, lack of brain, naivety, obtuseness, simplicity, slowness, thickheadedness, thickness **4** = **silliness**, absurdity, fatuity, fatuousness, folly, foolhardiness, foolishness, futility, idiocy, impracticality, inanity, irresponsibility, ludicrousness, lunacy, madness, pointlessness, puerility, rashness, senselessness

stupor *n* **1, 2** = **daze**, coma, inertia, insensibility, lethargy, numbness, stupefaction, torpor, trance, unconsciousness

sturdy *adj* **1** = **robust**, athletic, brawny, firm, hardy, hearty, lusty, muscular, powerful, stalwart, staunch, thickset, vigorous **2** = **substantial**, built to last, durable, secure, solid, well-built, well-made
Antonyms *adj* ≠ **robust:** feeble, infirm, puny, skinny, weak, weakly ≠ **substantial:** flimsy, frail, rickety, unsubstantial

stutter *vb* **1** = **stammer**, falter, hesitate, speak haltingly, splutter, stumble

style *n* **1** = **design**, appearance, category, characteristic, cut, form, genre, kind, manner, pattern, sort, spirit, strain, tenor, tone, type, variety **2, 3** = **manner**, approach, custom, method, mode, technique, way **4** = **mode of expression**, diction, expression, phraseology, phrasing, treatment, turn of phrase, vein, wording **5** = **elegance**, *bon ton*, chic, cosmopolitanism, dash, dressiness (*inf.*), élan, fashionableness, flair, grace, panache, polish, refinement, savoir-faire, smartness, sophistication, stylishness, taste, urbanity **6** = **fashion**, mode, rage, trend, vogue **7** = **luxury**, affluence, comfort, ease, elegance, gracious living, grandeur ◆ *vb* **14** = **design**, adapt, arrange, cut, dress, fashion, shape, tailor **17** = **call**, address, christen, denominate, designate, dub, entitle, label, name, term

stylish *adj* = **smart**, à la mode, chic, classy (*sl.*), dapper, dressy (*inf.*), fashionable, in fashion, in vogue, modish, natty (*inf.*), polished, snappy, snazzy (*inf.*), trendy (*Brit. inf.*), urbane, voguish, well turned-out
Antonyms *adj* badly-tailored, naff (*Brit. sl.*), old-fashioned, outmoded, out-of-date, passé, scruffy, shabby, slovenly, tacky, tawdry, unfashionable, unstylish, untrendy (*Brit. inf.*)

stymie *vb* **1** = **frustrate**, balk, confound, defeat, flummox, foil, hinder, mystify, nonplus, puzzle, snooker, spike (someone's) guns, stump, throw a spanner in the works (*Brit. inf.*), thwart

suave *adj* = **smooth**, affable, agreeable, bland, charming, civilized, cool, courteous, debonair, diplomatic, gracious, obliging, pleasing, polite, of a company of Indian soldiers in the British service. [C17: via Urdu from Persian, from *sūba* province + *-dār* holding]

subalpine (sʌbˈælpaɪn) *adj* **1** situated in or relating to the regions at the foot of mountains. **2** (of plants) growing below the tree line in mountainous regions.

subaltern (ˈsʌbᵊltən) *n* **1** a commissioned officer below the rank of captain in certain armies, esp. the British. ◆ *adj* **2** of inferior position or rank. **3** *Logic.* (of a proposition) particular, esp. in relation to a universal of the same quality. [C16: from LL *subalternus,* from L SUB- + *alternus* alternate, from *alter* the other]

subalternation (ˌsʌbɔːltəˈneɪʃən) *n Logic.* the relation between a universal and a particular proposition of the same quality where the universal proposition implies the particular proposition.

subantarctic (ˌsʌbæntˈɑːktɪk) *adj* of or relating to latitudes immediately north of the Antarctic Circle.

subaqua (ˌsʌbˈækwə) *adj* of or relating to underwater sport: *subaqua swimming.*

subaqueous (sʌbˈeɪkwɪəs, -ˈækwɪ-) *adj* occurring, formed, or used under water.

subarctic (sʌbˈɑːktɪk) *adj* of or relating to latitudes immediately south of the Arctic Circle.

subatomic (ˌsʌbəˈtɒmɪk) *adj* **1** of, relating to, or being a particle making up an atom or a process occurring within atoms. **2** having dimensions smaller than atomic dimensions.

subbasement (ˈsʌbˌbeɪsmənt) *n* a storey of a building beneath the main basement.

subclass (ˈsʌbˌklɑːs) *n* **1** a principal subdivision of a class. **2** *Biol.* a taxonomic group that is a subdivision of a class. **3** *Maths.* another name for **subset.**

subclavian (sʌbˈkleɪvɪən) *adj Anat.* (of an artery, vein, etc.) below the clavicle. [C17: from NL *subclāvius,* from L SUB- + *clavis* key]

subclinical (sʌbˈklɪnɪkᵊl) *adj Med.* of or relating to the stage in the course of a disease before the symptoms are first noted.
▸**subˈclinically** *adv*

subconscious (sʌbˈkɒnʃəs) *adj* **1** acting or existing without one's awareness. ◆ *n* **2** *Psychol.* that part of the mind on the fringe of consciousness which contains material it is possible to become aware of by redirecting attention.
▸**subˈconsciously** *adv* ▸**subˈconsciousness** *n*

subcontinent (sʌbˈkɒntɪnənt) *n* a large land mass that is a distinct part of a continent, such as India is of Asia.
▸**subcontinental** (ˌsʌbkɒntɪˈnentᵊl) *adj*

subcontract *n* (sʌbˈkɒntrækt). **1** a subordinate contract under which the supply of materials, labour, etc., is let out to someone other than a party to the main contract. ◆ *vb* (ˌsʌbkənˈtrækt). **2** (*intr; often foll. by for*) to enter into or make a subcontract. **3** (*tr*) to let out (work) on a subcontract.
▸ˌ**subconˈtractor** *n*

subcontrary (sʌbˈkɒntrərɪ) *Logic.* ◆ *adj* **1** (of a pair of propositions) related such that they cannot both be false at once, although they may be true together. ◆ *n, pl* **subcontraries. 2** a statement which cannot be false when a given statement is false.

subcritical (sʌbˈkrɪtɪkᵊl) *adj Physics.* (of a nuclear reaction, power station, etc.) having or involving a chain reaction that is not self- sustaining; not yet critical.

subculture (ˈsʌbˌkʌltʃə) *n* a subdivision of a national culture or an enclave within it with a distinct integrated network of behaviour, beliefs, and attitudes.
▸**subˈcultural** *adj*

subcutaneous (ˌsʌbkjuːˈteɪnɪəs) *adj Med.* situated, used, or introduced beneath the skin.
▸ˌ**subcuˈtaneously** *adv*

subdeacon (ˌsʌbˈdiːkən) *n Chiefly RC Church.* **1** a cleric who assists at High Mass. **2** (formerly) a person ordained to the lowest of the major orders.
▸**subdeaconate** (sʌbˈdiːkənɪt) *n*

subdivide (ˌsʌbdɪˈvaɪd, ˈsʌbdɪˌvaɪd) *vb* **subdivides, subdividing, subdivided.** to divide (something) resulting from an earlier division.
▸ˈ**subdiˌvision** *n*

subdominant (sʌbˈdɒmɪnənt) *Music.* ◆ *n* **1** the fourth degree of a major or minor scale. **2** a key or chord based on this. ◆ *adj* **3** of or relating to the subdominant.

subdue (səbˈdjuː) *vb* **subdues, subduing, subdued.** (*tr*) **1** to establish ascendancy over by force. **2** to overcome and bring under control, as by intimidation or persuasion. **3** to hold in check or repress (feelings, etc.). **4** to render less intense or less conspicuous. [C14 *sobdue,* from OF *soduire* to mislead, from L *subdūcere* to remove; infl. by L *subdere* to subject]
▸**subˈduable** *adj* ▸**subˈdual** *n*

subdued (səbˈdjuːd) *adj* **1** cowed, passive, or shy. **2** gentle or quiet: *a subdued whisper.* **3** (of colours, lighting, etc.) not harsh or bright.

subdural (sʌbˈdjʊərəl) *adj Anat.* between the dura mater and the arachnoid: *subdural haematoma.*

subedit (sʌbˈedɪt) *vb* **subedits, subediting, subedited.** to edit and correct (written or printed material).

subeditor (sʌbˈedɪtə) *n* a person who checks and edits copy, esp. on a newspaper.

subequatorial (sʌbˌekwəˈtɔːrɪəl) *adj* in or characteristic of regions immediately north or south of equatorial regions.

suberose (ˈsjuːbəˌrəʊs), **subereous** (sjuːˈberɪəs), *or* **suberic** (sjuːˈberɪk) *adj Bot.* relating to, resembling, or consisting of cork; corky. [C19: from L *sūber* cork + -OSE[1]]

subfamily (ˈsʌbˌfæmɪlɪ) *n, pl* **subfamilies. 1** *Biol.* a taxonomic group that is a subdivision of a family. **2** a subdivision of a family of languages.

subfusc (ˈsʌbfʌsk) *adj* **1** devoid of brightness or appeal; drab, dull, or dark. ◆ *n* **2** (at Oxford University) formal academic dress. [C18: from L *subfuscus* dusky, from *fuscus* dark]

subgenus (ˈsʌbˌdʒiːnəs, -ˌdʒen-) *n, pl* **subgenera** (-ˈdʒenərə) *or* **subgenuses.** *Biol.* a subdivision of a genus that is of higher rank than a species.
▸**subgeneric** (ˌsʌbdʒəˈnerɪk) *adj*

subheading (ˈsʌbˌhedɪŋ) *or* **subhead** *n* **1** the heading or title of a subdivision or subsection of a printed work. **2** a division subordinate to a main heading or title.

subhuman (sʌbˈhjuːmən) *adj* **1** of or designating animals below man (*Homo sapiens*) in evolutionary development. **2** less than human.

subindex (sʌbˈɪndeks) *n, pl* **subindices** (-dɪˌsiːz) *or* **subindexes.** another word for **subscript** (sense 2).

subitize *or* **subitise** (ˈsʌbɪˌtaɪz) *vb* **subitizes, subitizing, subitized** *or* **subitises, subitising, subitised.** *Psychol.* to perceive the number of (a group of items) at a glance and without counting: *the maximum number of items that can be subitized is about five.* [C20: from L *subitus* sudden + -IZE]

subito (ˈsuːbɪˌtəʊ) *adv Music.* suddenly; immediately. [C18: via It. from L: suddenly, from *subitus* sudden, from *subīre* to approach]

subj. *abbrev. for:* **1** subject. **2** subjective(ly). **3** subjunctive.

subjacent (sʌbˈdʒeɪsᵊnt) *adj* **1** forming a foundation; underlying. **2** lower than. [C16: from L *subjacēre* to lie close, be under]
▸**subˈjacency** *n* ▸**subˈjacently** *adv*

subject *n* (ˈsʌbdʒɪkt). **1** the predominant theme or topic, as of a book, discussion, etc. **2** any branch of learning considered as a course of study. **3** *Grammar, logic.* a word, phrase, etc., about which something is predicated or stated in a sentence; for example, *the cat* in the sentence *The cat catches mice.* **4** a person or thing that undergoes experiment, treatment, etc. **5** a person under the rule of a monarch, government, etc. **6** an object, figure, scene, etc., as portrayed by an artist or photographer. **7** *Philosophy.* **7a** that which thinks or feels as opposed to the object of thinking and feeling; the self or the mind. **7b** a substance as opposed to its attributes. **8** Also called: **theme.** *Music.* the principal motif of a fugue, the basis from which the musical material is derived in a sonata-form movement, or the recurrent figure in a rondo. **9** *Logic.* the term of a proposition about which something is asserted. **10** an originating motive. **11 change the subject.** to select a new topic of conversation. ◆ *adj* (ˈsʌbdʒɪkt). (*usually postpositive;* foll. by *to*) **12** being under the power or sovereignty of a ruler, government, etc.: *subject peoples.* **13** showing a tendency (towards): *a child subject to indiscipline.* **14** exposed or vulnerable: *subject to ribaldry.* **15** conditional upon: *the results are subject to correction.* ◆ *adv* (ˈsʌbdʒɪkt). **16 subject to.** (*prep*) under the condition that: *we accept, subject to her agreement.* ◆ *vb* (səbˈdʒekt). (*tr*) **17** (foll. by *to*) to cause to undergo: *they subjected him to torture.* **18** (*often passive;* foll. by *to*) to expose or render vulnerable or liable (to some experience): *he was subjected to great danger.* **19** (foll. by *to*) to bring under the control or authority (of): *to subject a soldier to discipline.* **20** *Rare.* to present for consideration; submit. [C14: from L *subjectus* brought under, from *subicere* to place under, from SUB- + *jacere* to throw]
▸**subˈjectable** *adj* ▸**subˈjection** *n*

subjective (səbˈdʒektɪv) *adj* **1** of, proceeding from, or relating to the

THESAURUS

smooth-tongued, sophisticated, svelte, urbane, worldly

subconscious *adj* **1 = hidden,** inner, innermost, intuitive, latent, repressed, subliminal, suppressed
Antonyms *adj* aware, conscious, knowing, sensible, sentient

subdue *vb* **1, 2 = overcome,** beat down, break, conquer, control, crush, defeat, discipline, gain ascendancy over, get the better of, get the upper hand over, get under control, humble, master, overpower, overrun, put down, quell, tame, trample, triumph over, vanquish **3, 4 = moderate,** check, control, mellow, quieten down, repress, soften, suppress, tone down
Antonyms *vb* **≠ moderate:** agitate, arouse, awaken, incite, provoke, stir up, waken, whip up

subdued *adj* **1 = quiet,** chastened, crestfallen, dejected, downcast, down in the mouth, grave, out of spirits, repentant, repressed, restrained, sad, sadder and wiser, serious, sobered, solemn **3 = soft,** dim, hushed, low-key, muted, quiet, shaded, sober, subtle, toned down, unobtrusive
Antonyms *adj* **≠ quiet:** cheerful, enthusiastic, full of beans (*inf.*), happy, lively, vivacious **≠ soft:** bright, loud, strident

subject *n* **1 = topic,** affair, business, field of inquiry *or* reference, issue, matter, object, point, question, subject matter, substance, theme **4 = participant,** case, client, guinea pig (*inf.*), patient, victim **5 = citizen,** dependant, liegeman, national, subordinate, vassal ◆ *adj* **12 = subordinate,** captive, dependent, enslaved, inferior, obedient, satellite, subjugated, submissive, subservient **13 = liable to,** disposed to, prone to **14 = vulnerable,** exposed, in danger, open, susceptible **16 subject to = conditional on,** contingent on, dependent on ◆ *vb* **17, 18 = put through,** expose, lay open, make liable, submit, treat

subjective *adj* **2 = personal,** biased, emotional, idiosyncratic, instinctive, intuitive, nonobjective, prejudiced
Antonyms *adj* concrete, detached, disinterested,

mind of the thinking subject and not the nature of the object being considered. **2** of, relating to, or emanating from a person's emotions, prejudices, etc. **3** relating to the inherent nature of a person or thing; essential. **4** existing only as perceived and not as a thing in itself. **5** *Med.* (of a symptom, condition, etc.) experienced only by the patient and incapable of being recognized or studied by anyone else. **6** *Grammar.* denoting a case of nouns and pronouns, esp. in languages having only two cases, that identifies the subject of a finite verb and (in formal use in English) is selected for predicate complements, as in *It is I.* ◆ *n* **7** *Grammar.* **7a** the subjective case. **7b** a subjective word or speech element. Cf. **objective.**
▸**sub'jectively** *adv* ▸**,subjec'tivity** *or* **sub'jectiveness** *n*

subjectivism (səb'dʒɛktɪ,vɪzəm) *n Philosophy.* the doctrine that there are no absolute moral values but that these are variable in the same way that taste is.
▸**sub'jectivist** *n*

subjoin (sʌb'dʒɔɪn) *vb* (*tr*) to add or attach at the end of something spoken, written, etc. [C16: from F *subjoindre*, from L *subjungere* to add to, from *sub-* in addition + *jungere* to join]
▸**sub'joinder** *n*

sub judice ('dʒuːdɪsɪ) *adj* (*usually postpositive*) before a court of law or a judge; under judicial consideration. [L]

subjugate ⓣ ('sʌbdʒʊ,geɪt) *vb* **subjugates, subjugating, subjugated.** (*tr*) **1** to bring into subjection. **2** to make subservient or submissive. [C15: from LL *subjugāre* to subdue, from L SUB- + *jugum* yoke]
▸**'subjugable** *adj* ▸**,subju'gation** *n* ▸**'subju,gator** *n*

subjunctive (səb'dʒʌŋktɪv) *Grammar.* ◆ *adj* **1** denoting a mood of verbs used when the content of the clause is being doubted, supposed, feared true, etc., rather than being asserted. In the following sentence, *were* is in the subjunctive: *I'd think seriously about it if I were you.* Cf. **indicative.** ◆ *n* **2a** the subjunctive mood. **2b** a verb in this mood. [C16: via LL *subjunctīvus*, from L *subjungere* to SUBJOIN]
▸**sub'junctively** *adv*

sublease *n* ('sʌb,liːs). **1** a lease of property made by a lessee or tenant of that property. ◆ *vb* (sʌb'liːs), **subleases, subleasing, subleased. 2** to grant a sublease of (property); sublet. **3** (*tr*) to obtain or hold by sublease.
▸**sublessee** (,sʌblɛ'siː) *n* ▸**sublessor** (,sʌblɛ'sɔː) *n*

sublet (sʌb'lɛt) *vb* **sublets, subletting, sublet. 1** to grant a sublease of (property). **2** to let out (work, etc.) under a subcontract.

sublieutenant (,sʌblə'tɛnənt) *n* the most junior commissioned officer in the Royal Navy and certain other navies.
▸**,sublieu'tenancy** *n*

sublimate ⓣ ('sʌblɪ,meɪt) *vb* **sublimates, sublimating, sublimated. 1** *Psychol.* to direct the energy of (a primitive impulse) into activities that are socially more acceptable. **2** (*tr*) to make purer; refine. ◆ *n* **3** *Chem.* the material obtained when a substance is sublimed. [C16: from L *sublīmāre* to elevate, from *sublīmis* lofty; see SUBLIME]
▸**,subli'mation** *n*

sublime ⓣ (sə'blaɪm) *adj* **1** of high moral, intellectual, or spiritual value; noble; exalted. **2** inspiring deep veneration or awe. **3** unparalleled; supreme. **4** *Poetic.* of proud bearing or aspect. **5** *Arch.* raised up. ◆ *n* **the sublime. 6** something that is sublime. **7** the ultimate degree or perfect example: *the sublime of folly.* ◆ *vb* **sublimes, subliming, sublimed. 8** (*tr*) to make higher or purer. **9** to change or cause to change directly from a solid to a vapour or gas without first melting. **10** to undergo or cause to undergo this process followed by a reverse change directly from a vapour to a solid: *to sublime iodine onto glass.* [C14: from L *sublīmis* lofty, ?from *sub-* up to + *līmen* lintel]
▸**sub'limely** *adv* ▸**sublimity** (sə'blɪmɪtɪ) *n*

subliminal ⓣ (sʌb'lɪmɪnᵊl) *adj* **1** resulting from processes of which the individual is not aware. **2** (of stimuli) less than the minimum intensity or duration required to elicit a response. [C19: from L *sub-* below + *līmen* threshold]
▸**sub'liminally** *adv*

subliminal advertising *n* advertising on film or television that employs subliminal images to influence the viewer unconsciously.

sublingual (sʌb'lɪŋgwəl) *adj Anat.* situated beneath the tongue.

sublunary (sʌb'luːnərɪ) *adj* **1** between the moon and the earth. **2** of or relating to the earth. [C16: via LL, from L SUB- + *lūna* moon]

sub-machine-gun *n* a portable automatic or semiautomatic light gun with a short barrel, designed to be fired from the hip or shoulder.

submarginal (sʌb'mɑːdʒɪnᵊl) *adj* **1** below the minimum requirements. **2** (of land) infertile and unprofitable.
▸**sub'marginally** *adv*

submarine ('sʌbmə,riːn, ,sʌbmə'riːn) *n* **1** a vessel, esp. a warship, capable of operating below the surface of the sea. **2** (*modifier*) **2a** of or relating to a submarine: *a submarine captain.* **2b** below the surface of the sea: *a submarine cable.*
▸**submariner** (sʌb'mærɪnə) *n*

submaxillary gland (,sʌbmæk'sɪlərɪ) *n* (in mammals) either of a pair of salivary glands situated on each side behind the lower jaw.

submediant (sʌb'miːdɪənt) *Music.* ◆ *n* **1** the sixth degree of a major or minor scale. **2** a key or chord based on this. ◆ *adj* **3** of or relating to the submediant.

submerge ⓣ (səb'mɜːdʒ) *or* **submerse** (səb'mɜːs) *vb* **submerges, submerging, submerged** *or* **submerses, submersing, submersed. 1** to plunge, sink, or dive or cause to plunge, sink, or dive below the surface of water, etc. **2** (*tr*) to cover with water or other liquid. **3** (*tr*) to hide; suppress. **4** (*tr*) to overwhelm, as with work, etc. [C17: from L *submergere*]
▸**sub'mergence** *or* **sub'mersion** *n*

submersible (səb'mɜːsɪbᵊl) *or* **submergible** (səb'mɜːdʒɪbᵊl) *adj* **1** able to be submerged. **2** capable of operating under water, etc. ◆ *n* **3** a vessel designed to operate under water for short periods. **4** a submarine designed and equipped to carry out work below the level that divers can work.
▸**sub,mersi'bility** *or* **sub,mergi'bility** *n*

subminiature (sʌb'mɪnɪətʃə) *adj* smaller than miniature.

subminiature camera *n* a pocket-sized camera, usually using 16 millimetre film.

submission ⓣ (səb'mɪʃən) *n* **1** an act or instance of submitting. **2** something submitted; a proposal, etc. **3** the quality or condition of being submissive. **4** the act of referring a document, etc., for the consideration of someone else.

submissive ⓣ (səb'mɪsɪv) *adj* of, tending towards, or indicating submission, humility, or servility.
▸**sub'missively** *adv* ▸**sub'missiveness** *n*

submit ⓣ (səb'mɪt) *vb* **submits, submitting, submitted. 1** (often foll. by *to*) to yield (oneself), as to the will of another person, a superior force, etc. **2** (foll. by *to*) to subject or be voluntarily subjected (to analysis, treatment, etc.). **3** (*tr; often foll. by to*) to refer (something to someone) for judgment or consideration. **4** (*tr; may take a clause as object*) to state, contend, or propose deferentially. **5** (*intr;* often foll. by *to*) to defer or accede (to the decision, etc., of another). [C14: from L *submittere* to place under]
▸**sub'mittable** *or* **sub'missible** *adj* ▸**sub'mittal** *n* ▸**sub'mitter** *n*

submultiple (sʌb'mʌltɪpᵊl) *n* **1** a number that can be divided into another number an integral number of times without a remainder: *three is a submultiple of nine.* ◆ *adj* **2** being a submultiple of a quantity or number.

subnormal ⓣ (sʌb'nɔːməl) *adj* **1** less than the normal. **2** having a low intelligence. ◆ *n* **3** a subnormal person.
▸**subnormality** (,sʌbnɔː'mælɪtɪ) *n*

subnuclear (sʌb'njuːklɪə) *adj* in or smaller than the nucleus of an atom.

suborbital (sʌb'ɔːbɪtᵊl) *adj* **1** (of a rocket, missile, etc.) having a flight path that is less than an orbit of the earth or other celestial body. **2** *Anat.* situated beneath the orbit of the eye.

suborder ('sʌb,ɔːdə) *n Biol.* a subdivision of an order.
▸**sub'ordinal** *adj*

subordinate ⓣ *adj* (sə'bɔːdɪnɪt). **1** of lesser order or importance. **2** under the authority or control of another: *a subordinate functionary.* ◆ *n* (sə'bɔːdɪnɪt). **3** a person or thing that is subordinate. ◆ *vb* (sə'bɔːdɪ,neɪt), **subordinates, subordinating, subordinated.** (*tr;* usually foll. by *to*) **4** to put in a lower rank or position (than). **5** to make subservient: *to subordinate mind to heart.* [C15: from Med. L *subordināre*, from L SUB- + *ordō* rank]
▸**sub'ordinately** *adv* ▸**sub,ordi'nation** *n* ▸**sub'ordinative** *adj*

THESAURUS

dispassionate, impartial, impersonal, objective, open-minded, unbiased

subjugate *vb* **1, 2 = conquer**, bring (someone) to his knees, bring to heel, bring under the yoke, crush, defeat, enslave, hold sway over, lick (*inf.*), master, overcome, overpower, overthrow, put down, quell, reduce, rule over, subdue, suppress, tame, vanquish

sublimate *vb* **1 = channel**, divert, redirect, transfer, turn

sublime *adj* **1 = noble**, elevated, eminent, exalted, glorious, grand, great, high, imposing, lofty, magnificent, majestic, transcendent
Antonyms *adj* bad, commonplace, lowly, mundane, ordinary, poor, ridiculous, worldly

subliminal *adj* **1 = subconscious**, unconscious

submerge *vb* **1, 2 = immerse**, deluge, dip, drown, duck, dunk, engulf, flood, inundate, overflow, overwhelm, plunge, sink, swamp

submission *n* **1 = surrender**, acquiescence, assent, capitulation, cave-in (*inf.*), giving in, yielding **2 = proposal**, argument, contention **3 = meekness**, compliance, deference, docility, obedience, passivity, resignation, submissiveness, tractability, unassertiveness **4 = presentation**, entry, handing in, submitting, tendering

submissive *adj* **= meek**, abject, accommodating, acquiescent, amenable, biddable, bootlicking (*inf.*), compliant, deferential, docile, dutiful, humble, ingratiating, lowly, malleable, obedient, obeisant, obsequious, passive, patient, pliant, resigned, subdued, tractable, uncomplaining, unresisting, yielding
Antonyms *adj* awkward, difficult, disobedient, headstrong, intractable, obstinate, stubborn, uncooperative, unyielding

submit *vb* **1 = surrender**, accede, acquiesce, agree, bend, bow, capitulate, cave in (*inf.*), comply, defer, endure, give in, hoist the white flag, knuckle under, lay down arms, put up with, resign oneself, stoop, succumb, throw in the sponge, toe the line, tolerate, yield **3 = present**, commit, hand in, proffer, put forward, refer, table, tender **4 = suggest**, advance, argue, assert, claim, contend, move, propose, propound, put, state, volunteer

subnormal *adj* **2 = retarded**, cretinous, E.S.N., feeble-minded, imbecilic, mentally defective, moronic, simple, slow

subordinate *adj* **1 = lesser**, dependent, inferior, junior, lower, minor, secondary, subject, subservient **2 = auxiliary**, ancillary, subsidiary, supplementary ◆ *n* **3 = inferior**, aide, assistant, attendant, dependant, junior, second, subaltern, underling
Antonyms *adj* ≠ **lesser**: central, essential, greater, higher, key, main, necessary, predominant, senior, superior, vital ◆ *n* ≠ **inferior**: boss (*inf.*), captain, chief, commander, head, leader, master, principal, senior, superior

subordinate clause *n Grammar.* a clause with an adjectival, adverbial, or nominal function, rather than one that functions as a separate sentence in its own right.

subordinating conjunction *n* a conjunction that introduces subordinate clauses, such as *if, because, although,* and *until.*

suborn (sə'bɔːn) *vb* (*tr*) **1** to bribe, incite, or instigate (a person) to commit a wrongful act. **2** *Law.* to induce (a witness) to commit perjury. [C16: from L *subornāre,* from *sub-* secretly + *ornāre* to furnish] ▸**subornation** (ˌsʌbɔː'neɪʃən) *n* ▸**subornative** (sʌ'bɔːnətɪv) *adj* ▸**sub'orner** *n*

suboxide (sʌb'ɒksaɪd) *n* an oxide of an element containing less oxygen than the common oxide formed by the element: *carbon suboxide,* C_2O_3.

subplot ('sʌbˌplɒt) *n* a subordinate or auxiliary plot in a novel, play, film, etc.

subpoena (səb'piːnə) *n* **1** a writ issued by a court of justice requiring a person to appear before the court at a specified time. ◆ *vb* **subpoenas, subpoenaing, subpoenaed. 2** (*tr*) to serve with a subpoena. [C15: from L: under penalty]

subrogate ('sʌbrəˌgeɪt) *vb* **subrogates, subrogating, subrogated.** (*tr*) *Law.* to put (one person or thing) in the place of another in respect of a right or claim. [C16: from L *subrogāre,* from *sub-* in place of + *rogāre* to ask] ▸ˌ**subro'gation** *n*

sub rosa ('rəʊzə) *adv* in secret. [L, lit.: under the rose; from use of the rose in ancient times as a token of secrecy]

subroutine ('sʌbruːˌtiːn) *n* a section of a computer program that is stored only once but can be used at several different points in the program. Also called: **procedure.**

sub-Saharan *adj* in, of, or relating to Africa south of the Sahara desert.

subscribe ➊ (səb'skraɪb) *vb* **subscribes, subscribing, subscribed. 1** (usually foll. by *to*) to pay or promise to pay (money) as a contribution (to a fund, for a magazine, etc.), esp. at regular intervals. **2** to sign (one's name, etc.) at the end of a document. **3** (*intr;* foll. by *to*) to give support or approval: *to subscribe to the theory of reincarnation.* [C15: from L *subscrībere* to write underneath] ▸**sub'scriber** *n*

subscriber trunk dialling *n Brit.* a service by which telephone subscribers can obtain trunk calls by dialling direct without the aid of an operator. Abbrev.: **STD.**

subscript ('sʌbskrɪpt) *Printing.* ◆ *adj* **1** (of a character) written or printed below the base line. Cf. **superscript.** ◆ *n* **2** Also called: **subindex.** a subscript character.

subscription ➊ (səb'skrɪpʃən) *n* **1** a payment or promise of payment for consecutive issues of a magazine, newspaper, book, etc., over a specified period of time. **2a** the advance purchase of tickets for a series of concerts, etc. **2b** (*as modifier*): *a subscription concert.* **3** money paid or promised, as to a charity, or the fund raised in this way. **4** an offer to buy shares or bonds issued by a company. **5** the act of signing one's name to a document, etc. **6** a signature or other appendage attached to the bottom of a document, etc. **7** agreement or acceptance expressed by or as if by signing one's name. **8** a signed document, statement, etc. **9** *Chiefly Brit.* the membership dues or fees paid to a society or club. **10** an advance order for a new product. **11a** the sale of books, etc., prior to publishing. **11b** (*as modifier*): *a subscription edition.* ▸**sub'scriptive** *adj* ▸**sub'scriptively** *adv*

subsequence ('sʌbsɪkwəns) *n* **1** the fact or state of being subsequent. **2** a subsequent incident or occurrence.

subsequent ➊ ('sʌbsɪkwənt) *adj* occurring after; succeeding. [C15: from L *subsequēns* following on, from *subsequī,* from *sub-* near + *sequī* to follow] ▸**'subsequently** *adv* ▸**'subsequentness** *n*

subserve (səb'sɜːv) *vb* **subserves, subserving, subserved.** (*tr*) to be helpful or useful to. [C17: from L *subservīre* to be subject to, from SUB- + *servīre* to serve]

subservient ➊ (səb'sɜːvɪənt) *adj* **1** obsequious. **2** serving as a means to an end. **3** a less common word for **subordinate** (sense 2). [C17: from L *subserviēns* complying with, from *subservīre* to SUBSERVE] ▸**sub'serviently** *adv* ▸**sub'servience** *or* **sub'serviency** *n*

subset ('sʌbˌset) *n* a mathematical set contained within a larger set.

subshrub ('sʌbˌʃrʌb) *n* a small bushy plant that is woody except for the tips of the branches.

subside ➊ (səb'saɪd) *vb* **subsides, subsiding, subsided.** (*intr*) **1** to become less loud, excited, violent, etc.; abate. **2** to sink or fall to a lower level. **3** (of the surface of the earth, etc.) to cave in; collapse. **4** (of sediment, etc.) to sink or descend to the bottom; settle. [C17: from L *subsīdere* to settle down] ▸**sub'sider** *n*

subsidence ➊ (səb'saɪdᵊns, 'sʌbsɪdᵊns) *n* **1** the act or process of subsiding or the condition of having subsided. **2** *Geol.* the gradual sinking of landforms to a lower level.

subsidiarity (səbˌsɪdɪ'ærɪtɪ) *n* the principle of devolving political decisions to the lowest practical level.

subsidiary ➊ (səb'sɪdɪərɪ) *adj* **1** serving to aid or supplement; auxiliary. **2** of lesser importance; subordinate. ◆ *n, pl* **subsidiaries. 3** a subsidiary person or thing. **4** Also called: **subsidiary company.** a company with at least half of its capital stock owned by another company. [C16: from L *subsidiārius* supporting, from *subsidium* SUBSIDY] ▸**sub'sidiarily** *adv* ▸**sub'sidiariness** *n*

subsidize ➊ *or* **subsidise** ('sʌbsɪˌdaɪz) *vb* **subsidizes, subsidizing, subsidized** *or* **subsidises, subsidising, subsidised.** (*tr*) **1** to aid or support with a subsidy. **2** to obtain the aid of by means of a subsidy. ▸ˌ**subsidi'zation** *or* ˌ**subsidi'sation** *n* ▸**'subsiˌdizer** *or* **'subsiˌdiser** *n*

subsidy ➊ ('sʌbsɪdɪ) *n, pl* **subsidies. 1** a financial aid supplied by a government, as to industry, for public welfare, the balance of payments, etc. **2** *English history.* a financial grant made originally for special purposes by Parliament to the Crown. **3** any monetary aid, grant, or contribution. [C14: from Anglo-Norman *subsidie,* from L *subsidium* assistance, from *subsidēre* to remain, from *sub-* down + *sedēre* to sit]

subsist ➊ (səb'sɪst) *vb* (*mainly intr*) **1** (often foll. by *on*) to be sustained; manage to live: *to subsist on milk.* **2** to continue in existence. **3** (foll. by *in*) to lie or reside by virtue (of); consist. **4** (*tr*) *Obs.* to provide with support. [C16: from L *subsistere* to stand firm] ▸**sub'sistent** *adj*

subsistence ➊ (səb'sɪstəns) *n* **1** the means by which one maintains life. **2** the act or condition of subsisting.

subsistence farming *n* a type of farming in which most of the produce (**subsistence crop**) is consumed by the farmer and his family.

subsistence level *n* a standard of living barely adequate to support life.

subsistence wage *n* the lowest wage upon which a worker and his family can survive.

subsoil ('sʌbˌsɔɪl) *n* **1** Also called: **undersoil.** the layer of soil beneath the surface soil and overlying the bedrock. ◆ *vb* **2** (*tr*) to plough (land) to a depth so as to break up the subsoil.

subsonic (sʌb'sɒnɪk) *adj* being, having, or travelling at a velocity below that of sound.

subspecies ('sʌbˌspiːʃiːz) *n, pl* **subspecies.** *Biol.* a subdivision of a species: usually occurs because of isolation within a species.

substance ➊ ('sʌbstəns) *n* **1** the tangible basic matter of which a thing consists. **2** a specific type of matter, esp. a homogeneous material with definite or fairly definite chemical composition. **3** the essence, meaning, etc., of a discourse, thought, or written article. **4** solid or meaningful quality: *an education of substance.* **5** material density or body: *free space has no substance.* **6** material possessions or wealth: *a man of substance.* **7** *Philosophy.* the supposed immaterial substratum of anything that can receive modifications and in which attributes and accidents inhere. **8 in substance.** with regard to the salient points. [C13: via OF from L *substantia,* from *substāre,* from SUB- + *stāre* to stand]

substandard ➊ (sʌb'stændəd) *adj* **1** below an established or required standard. **2** another word for **nonstandard.**

substantial ➊ (səb'stænʃəl) *adj* **1** of a considerable size or value: *sub-*

THESAURUS

subordination *n* **4, 5** = **inferiority**, inferior or secondary status, servitude, subjection

subscribe *vb* **1** = **contribute**, chip in, donate, give, offer, pledge, promise **3** = **support**, acquiesce, advocate, agree, consent, countenance, endorse

subscription *n* **1** *Chiefly Brit.* = **membership fee**, annual payment, dues **3** = **contribution**, donation, gift, offering

subsequent *adj* = **following**, after, consequent, consequential, ensuing, later, succeeding, successive
Antonyms *adj* antecedent, earlier, erstwhile, former, one-time, past, preceding, previous, prior

subsequently *adv* = **later**, afterwards, at a later date, consequently, in the aftermath (of), in the end

subservient *adj* **1** = **servile**, abject, bootlicking (*inf.*), deferential, inferior, obsequious, slavish, subject, submissive, sycophantic, truckling **2** = **subordinate**, accessory, ancillary, auxiliary, conducive, subsidiary
Antonyms *adj* ≠ **servile:** bolshie, bossy, disobedient, domineering, overbearing, overriding, rebellious, superior, wilful

subside *vb* **1** = **decrease**, abate, de-escalate, diminish, dwindle, ease, ebb, lessen, let up, level off, melt away, moderate, peter out, quieten, recede, slacken, wane **2** = **drop**, decline, descend, ebb, fall **3, 4** = **collapse**, cave in, drop, lower, settle, sink
Antonyms *vb* ≠ **decrease, drop:** escalate, grow, heighten, increase, inflate, intensify, mount, rise, soar, swell, tumefy, wax

subsidence *n* **1** = **decrease**, abatement, de-escalation, diminution, easing off, lessening, slackening **1** = **drop**, decline, descent, ebb **2** = **sinking**, collapse, settlement, settling

subsidiary *adj* **1, 2** = **lesser**, aiding, ancillary, assistant, auxiliary, contributory, cooperative, helpful, minor, secondary, subordinate, subservient, supplemental, supplementary, useful
Antonyms *adj* central, chief, head, key, leading, main, major, primary, principal, vital

subsidize *vb* **1** = **fund**, finance, promote, put up the money for, sponsor, support, underwrite

subsidy *n* **3** = **aid**, allowance, assistance, contribution, financial aid, grant, help, stipend, subvention, support

subsist *vb* **1, 2** = **stay alive**, be, continue, eke out an existence, endure, exist, keep going, keep one's head above water, last, live, make ends meet, remain, survive, sustain oneself

subsistence *n* **1** = **food**, aliment, provision, rations, sustenance, victuals **2** = **living**, existence, keep, livelihood, maintenance, support, survival, upkeep

substance *n* **1** = **material**, body, element, fabric, stuff, texture **3** = **meaning**, burden, essence, gist, gravamen, import, main point, matter, pith, significance, subject, sum and substance, theme **5** = **reality**, actuality, concreteness, entity, force **6** = **wealth**, affluence, assets, estate, means, property, resources

substandard *adj* **1** = **inferior**, damaged, imperfect, inadequate, second-rate, shoddy, unacceptable

substantial *adj* **1** = **big**, ample, considerable, generous, goodly, important, large, significant,

stantial funds. **2** worthwhile; important; telling: *a substantial reform.* **3** having wealth or importance: *a substantial member of the community.* **4** (of food or a meal) sufficient and nourishing. **5** solid or strong: *a substantial door.* **6** real; actual; true: *substantial evidence.* **7** of or relating to the basic or fundamental substance or aspects of a thing. ◆ *n* **8** (*often pl*) *Rare.* an essential or important element.
▸**substantiality** (səbˌstænʃɪ'ælɪtɪ) *or* **sub'stantialness** *n* ▸**sub'stantially** *adv*

substantialism (səb'stænʃəˌlɪzəm) *n Philosophy.* the doctrine that a substantial reality underlies phenomena.
▸**sub'stantialist** *n*

substantiate ➊ (səb'stænʃɪˌeɪt) *vb* **substantiates, substantiating, substantiated.** (*tr*) **1** to establish as valid or genuine. **2** to give form or real existence to. [C17: from NL *substantiāre*, from L *substantia* SUBSTANCE]
▸**subˌstanti'ation** *n*

substantive ('sʌbstəntɪv) *n* **1** *Grammar.* a noun or pronoun used in place of a noun. ◆ *adj* **2** of, relating to, containing, or being the essential element of a thing. **3** having independent function, resources, or existence. **4** of substantial quantity. **5** solid in foundation or basis. **6** *Grammar.* denoting, relating to, or standing in place of a noun. **7** (səb'stæntɪv). (of a dye or colour) staining the material directly without use of a mordant. [C15: from LL *substantīvus*, from L *substāre* to stand beneath]
▸**substantival** (ˌsʌbstən'taɪvᵊl) *adj* ▸ˌ**substan'tivally** *adv* ▸'**substantively** *adv*

substantive rank *n* a permanent rank in the armed services.

substation ('sʌbˌsteɪʃən) *n* **1** a subsidiary station. **2** an installation at which electrical energy is received from one or more power stations for conversion from alternating to direct current, stepping down the voltage, or switching before distribution by a low-tension network.

substituent (sʌb'stɪtjuənt) *n* **1** *Chem.* an atom or group that replaces another atom or group in a molecule or can be regarded as replacing an atom in a parent compound. ◆ *adj* **2** substituted or substitutable. [C19: from L *substituere* to SUBSTITUTE]

substitute ➊ ('sʌbstɪˌtjuːt) *vb* **substitutes, substituting, substituted. 1** (often foll. by *for*) to serve or cause to serve in place of another person or thing. **2** *Chem.* to replace (an atom or group in a molecule) with (another atom or group). ◆ *n* **3a** a person or thing that serves in place of another, such as a player in a game who takes the place of an injured colleague. **3b** (*as modifier*): *a substitute goalkeeper.* [C16: from L *substituere*, from *sub-* in place of + *statuere* to set up]
▸ˌ**substi'tutable** *adj* ▸'**substiˌtutive** *adj*

> **USAGE NOTE** *Substitute* is sometimes wrongly used where *replace* is meant: *he replaced* (not *substituted*) *the worn tyre with a new one.*

substitution ➊ (ˌsʌbstɪ'tjuːʃən) *n* **1** the act of substituting or state of being substituted. **2** something or someone substituted.

substrate ('sʌbstreɪt) *n* **1** *Biochem.* the substance upon which an enzyme acts. **2** another word for **substratum.**

substratum (sʌb'strɑːtəm, -'streɪ-) *n, pl* **substrata** (-'strɑːtə, -'streɪtə). **1** any layer or stratum lying underneath another. **2** a basis or foundation; groundwork. [C17: from NL, from L *substrātus* strewn beneath, from *substernere* to spread under]
▸**sub'strative** *or* **sub'stratal** *adj*

substructure ('sʌbˌstrʌktʃə) *n* **1** a structure, pattern, etc., that forms the basis of anything. **2** a structure forming a foundation or framework for a building or other construction.
▸**sub'structural** *adj*

subsume (səb'sjuːm) *vb* **subsumes, subsuming, subsumed.** (*tr*) **1** to incorporate (an idea, case, etc.) under a comprehensive or inclusive classification. **2** to consider (an instance of something) as part of a general rule. [C16: from NL *subsumere*, from L SUB- + *sumere* to take]
▸**sub'sumable** *adj* ▸**subsumption** (səb'sʌmpʃən) *n*

subtemperate (sʌb'tempərɪt) *adj* of or relating to the colder temperate regions.

subtenant (sʌb'tenənt) *n* a person who rents or leases property from a tenant.
▸**sub'tenancy** *n*

subtend (səb'tend) *vb* (*tr*) **1** *Geom.* to be opposite to and delimit (an angle or side). **2** (of a bract, stem, etc.) to have (a bud or similar part) growing in its axil. [C16: from L *subtendere* to extend beneath]

subterfuge ➊ ('sʌbtəˌfjuːdʒ) *n* a stratagem employed to conceal something, evade an argument, etc. [C16: from LL *subterfugium*, from L *subterfugere* to escape by stealth, from *subter* secretly + *fugere* to flee]

subterminal (sʌb'tɜːmɪnᵊl) *adj* almost at an end.

subterranean (ˌsʌbtə'reɪnɪən) *adj* **1** Also: **subterraneous, subterrestrial.** situated, living, or operating below the surface of the earth. **2** existing or operating in concealment. [C17: from L *subterrāneus*, from SUB- + *terra* earth]
▸ˌ**subter'raneanly** *or* ˌ**subter'raneously** *adv*

subtext ('sʌbˌtekst) *n* **1** an underlying theme in a piece of writing. **2** a message which is not stated directly but can be inferred.

subtile ('sʌtᵊl) *adj* a rare spelling of **subtle.**
▸'**subtilely** *adv* ▸**subtility** (sʌb'tɪlɪtɪ) *or* '**subtileness** *n* ▸'**subtilty** *n*

subtilize *or* **subtilise** ('sʌtɪˌlaɪz) *vb* **subtilizes, subtilizing, subtilized** *or* **subtilises, subtilising, subtilised. 1** (*tr*) to bring to a purer state; refine. **2** to debate subtly. **3** (*tr*) to make (the mind, etc.) keener.
▸ˌ**subtili'zation** *or* ˌ**subtili'sation** *n*

subtitle ('sʌbˌtaɪtᵊl) *n* **1** an additional subordinate title given to a literary or other work. **2** (*often pl*) **2a** text superimposed on a film or television broadcast, either a translation of foreign dialogue or as an aid for the hard of hearing. **2b** Also called: **caption.** explanatory text on a silent film. ◆ *vb* **subtitles, subtitling, subtitled. 3** (*tr; usually passive*) to provide a subtitle for.

subtle ➊ ('sʌtᵊl) *adj* **1** not immediately obvious or comprehensible. **2** difficult to detect or analyse, often through being delicate or highly refined: *a subtle scent.* **3** showing or making or capable of showing or making fine distinctions of meaning. **4** marked by or requiring mental acuteness or ingenuity; discriminating. **5** delicate or faint: *a subtle shade.* **6** cunning or wily: *a subtle rogue.* **7** operating or executed in secret: *a subtle intrigue.* [C14: from OF *soutil*, from L *subtīlis* finely woven]
▸'**subtleness** *n* ▸'**subtly** *adv*

subtlety ➊ ('sʌtᵊltɪ) *n, pl* **subtleties. 1** the state or quality of being subtle; delicacy. **2** a fine distinction. **3** something subtle.

subtonic (sʌb'tɒnɪk) *n Music.* the seventh degree of a major or minor scale.

subtotal (sʌb'təutᵊl, 'sʌbˌtəutᵊl) *n* **1** the total made up by a column of figures, etc., forming part of the total made up by a larger column. ◆ *vb* **subtotals, subtotalling, subtotalled** *or US* **subtotals, subtotaling, subtotaled. 2** to work out a subtotal for (a column, etc.).

subtract ➊ (səb'trækt) *vb* **1** to calculate the difference between (two numbers or quantities) by subtraction. **2** to remove (a part of a thing, quantity, etc.) from the whole. [C16: from L *subtractus* withdrawn, from *subtrahere* to draw away from beneath]
▸**sub'tracter** *n* ▸**sub'tractive** *adj*

subtraction (səb'trækʃən) *n* **1** the act or process of subtracting. **2** a mathematical operation in which the difference between two numbers or quantities is calculated.

subtrahend ('sʌbtrəˌhend) *n* the number to be subtracted from another number (the **minuend**). [C17: from L *subtrahendus*, from *subtrahere* to SUBTRACT]

subtropics (sʌb'trɒpɪks) *pl n* the region lying between the tropics and temperate lands.
▸**sub'tropical** *adj*

subulate ('suːbjəlɪt, -ˌleɪt) *adj* (esp. of plant parts) tapering to a point; awl-shaped. [C18: from NL *subulatus* like an awl, from L *sūbula* awl]

suburb ➊ ('sʌbɜːb) *n* a residential district situated on the outskirts of a city or town. [C14: from L *suburbium*, from *sub-* close to + *urbs* a city]

suburban (sə'bɜːbᵊn) *adj* **1** of, in, or inhabiting a suburb or the suburbs. **2** characteristic of a suburb or the suburbs. **3** *Mildly derog.* narrow or unadventurous in outlook.
▸**su'burbanˌite** *n* ▸**su'burbanˌize** *or* **su'burbanˌise** *vb* (*tr*)

THESAURUS

sizable *or* sizeable, tidy (*inf.*), worthwhile **5** = **solid**, bulky, durable, firm, hefty, massive, sound, stout, strong, sturdy, well-built **6** *Formal* = **real**, actual, existent, material, positive, true, valid, weighty
Antonyms *adj* ≠ **big:** inadequate, inconsiderable, insignificant, insubstantial, meagre, niggardly, pathetic, poor, skimpy, small ≠ **solid:** feeble, frail, infirm, insubstantial, jerry-built, light-weight, rickety, weak ≠ **real:** fictitious, imaginary, imagined, insubstantial, nonexistent, unreal

substantially *adv* **7** = **essentially**, in essence, in essentials, in substance, in the main, largely, materially, to a large extent

substantiate *vb* **1** = **support**, affirm, attest to, authenticate, bear out, confirm, corroborate, establish, prove, validate, verify
Antonyms *vb* confute, contradict, controvert, disprove, expose, invalidate, make a nonsense of, negate, prove false, rebut, refute

substitute *vb* **1** *often foll. by* **for** = **stand in for**, act for, be in place of, cover for, deputize for, double for, fill in for, hold the fort for, relieve, take over from ◆ *n* **3a** = **replacement**, agent, depute (*Scot.*), deputy, equivalent, expedient, locum, locum tenens, makeshift, proxy, relief, representative, reserve, stand-by, stopgap, sub, supply, surrogate, temp (*inf.*), temporary ◆ *modifier* **3b** = **replacement**, acting, additional, alternative, fall-back, proxy, reserve, second, surrogate, temporary

substitution *n* **1, 2** = **replacement**, change, exchange, interchange, swap, switch

subterfuge *n* = **trick**, artifice, deception, deviousness, dodge, duplicity, evasion, excuse, machination, manoeuvre, ploy, pretence, pretext, quibble, ruse, shift, stall, stratagem

subtle *adj* **1, 2** = **faint**, delicate, implied, indirect, insinuated, slight, understated **3, 4** = **sophisticated**, delicate, discriminating, nice, refined **6** = **crafty**, artful, astute, cunning, designing, devious, ingenious, intriguing, keen, Machiavellian, scheming, shrewd, sly, wily
Antonyms *adj* ≠ **faint:** overwhelming, strong ≠ **crafty:** artless, blunt, direct, downright, guileless, obvious, simple, straightforward ≠ **sophisticated:** crass, heavy-handed, lacking finesse, tactless, unsophisticated, unsubtle

subtlety *n* **1** = **discrimination**, delicacy, discernment, finesse, refinement, sophistication **1** = **cunning**, acumen, acuteness, artfulness, astuteness, cleverness, craftiness, deviousness, guile, ingenuity, sagacity, skill, slyness, wiliness **2** = **fine point**, intricacy, nicety

subtract *vb* **2** = **take away**, deduct, detract, diminish, remove, take from, take off, withdraw
Antonyms *vb* add, add to, append, increase by, supplement

suburb *n* = **residential area**, dormitory area (*Brit.*), environs, faubourgs, neighbourhood, outskirts, precincts, purlieus, suburbia

suburbia (sə'bɜːbɪə) *n* **1** suburbs or the people living in them considered as an identifiable community or class in society. **2** the life, customs, etc., of suburbanites.

subvention (səb'venʃən) *n* **1** a grant, aid, or subsidy, as from a government. **2** *Sport.* a fee paid indirectly to a supposedly amateur athlete for appearing at a meeting. [C15: from LL *subventiō* assistance, from L *subvenīre,* from *sub-* under + *venīre* to come]

subversion (səb'vɜːʃən) *n* **1** the act or an instance of subverting a legally constituted government, institution, etc. **2** the state of being subverted; destruction or ruin. [C14: from LL *subversiō* destruction, from L *subvertere* to overturn]

subversive ❶ (səb'vɜːsɪv) *adj* **1** liable to subvert or overthrow a government, legally constituted institution, etc. ◆ *n* **2** a person engaged in subversive activities, etc.
▸**sub'versively** *adv* ▸**sub'versiveness** *n*

subvert ❶ (səb'vɜːt) *vb* (*tr*) **1** to bring about the complete downfall or ruin of (something existing by a system of law, etc.). **2** to undermine the moral principles of (a person, etc.). [C14: from L *subvertere* to overturn]
▸**sub'verter** *n*

subway ('sʌbˌweɪ) *n* **1** *Brit.* an underground tunnel enabling pedestrians to cross a road, railway, etc. **2** an underground tunnel for traffic, power supplies, etc. **3** an underground railway.

succedaneum (ˌsʌksɪ'deɪnɪəm) *n, pl* **succedanea** (-nɪə). something that is used as a substitute, esp. any medical drug or agent that may be taken or prescribed in place of another. [C17: from L *succēdāneus* following after; see SUCCEED]
▸ˌ**succe'daneous** *adj*

succeed ❶ (sək'siːd) *vb* **1** (*intr*) to accomplish an aim, esp. in the manner desired. **2** (*intr*) to happen in the manner desired: *the plan succeeded.* **3** (*intr*) to acquit oneself satisfactorily or do well, as in a specified field. **4** (when *intr,* often foll. by *to*) to come next in order (after someone or something). **5** (when *intr,* often foll. by *to*) to take over an office, post, etc. (from a person). **6** (*intr;* usually foll. by *to*) to come into possession (of property, etc.); inherit. **7** (*intr*) to have a result according to a specified manner: *the plan succeeded badly.* [C15: from L *succēdere* to follow after]
▸**suc'ceeder** *n* ▸**suc'ceedingly** *adv*

success ❶ (sək'ses) *n* **1** the favourable outcome of something attempted. **2** the attainment of wealth, fame, etc. **3** an action, performance, etc., that is characterized by success. **4** a person or thing that is successful. [C16: from L *successus* an outcome; see SUCCEED]

successful ❶ (sək'sesfʊl) *adj* **1** having succeeded in one's endeavours. **2** marked by a favourable outcome. **3** having obtained fame, wealth, etc.
▸**suc'cessfully** *adv* ▸**suc'cessfulness** *n*

succession ❶ (sək'seʃən) *n* **1** the act or an instance of one person or thing following another. **2** a number of people or things following one another in order. **3** the act, process, or right by which one person succeeds to the office, etc., of another. **4** the order that determines how one person or thing follows another. **5** a line of descent to a title, etc. **6 in succession.** in a manner such that one thing is followed uninterruptedly by another. [C14: from L *successio;* see SUCCEED]
▸**suc'cessional** *adj*

successive ❶ (sək'sesɪv) *adj* **1** following another without interruption. **2** of or involving succession: *a successive process.*
▸**suc'cessively** *adv* ▸**suc'cessiveness** *n*

successor (sək'sesə) *n* a person or thing that follows, esp. a person who succeeds another.

succinct ❶ (sək'sɪŋkt) *adj* marked by brevity and clarity; concise. [C15: from L *succinctus* girt about, from *succingere* to gird from below]
▸**suc'cinctly** *adv* ▸**suc'cinctness** *n*

succinic acid (sʌk'sɪnɪk) *n* a colourless odourless water-soluble acid found in plant and animal tissues, deriving from amber. Formula: $HOOC(CH_2)_2COOH$. Systematic name: **butanedioic acid.** [C19: from L *succinum* amber]

succotash ('sʌkəˌtæʃ) *n US & Canad.* a mixture of cooked sweet corn kernels and lima beans, served as a vegetable. [C18: of Amerind origin, from *msiquatash,* lit.: broken pieces]

succour ❶ *or US* **succor** ('sʌkə) *n* **1** help or assistance, esp. in time of difficulty. **2** a person or thing that provides help. ◆ *vb* **3** (*tr*) to give aid to. [C13: from OF *sucurir,* from L *succurrere* to hurry to help]

succubus ('sʌkjʊbəs) *n, pl* **succubi** (-ˌbaɪ). **1** Also called: **succuba.** a female demon fabled to have sexual intercourse with sleeping men. Cf. **incubus. 2** any evil demon. [C16: from Med. L, from LL *succuba* harlot, from L *succubāre* to lie beneath]

succulent ❶ ('sʌkjʊlənt) *adj* **1** juicy. **2** (of plants) having thick fleshy leaves or stems. ◆ *n* **3** a plant that can exist in arid conditions by using water stored in its fleshy tissues. [C17: from L *succulentus,* from *sūcus* juice]
▸**'succulence** *or* **'succulency** *n* ▸**'succulently** *adv*

succumb ❶ (sə'kʌm) *vb* (*intr;* often foll. by *to*) **1** to give way to the force (of) or desire (for). **2** to be fatally overwhelmed (by disease, etc.); die (of). [C15: from L *succumbere* to be overcome, from SUB- + *-cumbere,* from *cubāre* to lie down]

succursal (sʌ'kɜːsᵊl) *adj* **1** (esp. of a religious establishment) subsidiary. ◆ *n* **2** a subsidiary establishment. [C19: from F, from Med. L *succursus,* from L *succurrere* to SUCCOUR]

such (sʌtʃ) (often foll. by a corresponding subordinate clause introduced by *that* or *as*) ◆ *determiner* **1a** of the sort specified or understood: *such books.* **1b** (*as pronoun*): *such is life; robbers, rapists, and such.* **2** so great; so much: *such a help.* **3 as such. 3a** in the capacity previously specified or understood: *a judge as such hasn't so much power.* **3b** in itself or themselves: *intelligence as such can't guarantee success.* **4 such and such.** specific, but not known or named: *at such and such a time.* **5 such as. 5a** for example: *animals, such as tigers.* **5b** of a similar kind as; like: *people such as your friend.* **5c** of the (usually small) amount, etc.: *the food, such as there was, was excellent.* **6 such that.** so that: used to express purpose or result: *power such that it was effortless.* ◆ *adv* **7** (intensifier): *such a nice person.* [OE *swilc*]

suchlike ('sʌtʃˌlaɪk) *adj* **1** (*prenominal*) of such a kind; similar: *John, Ken, and other suchlike idiots.* ◆ *n* **2** such or similar persons or things: *hyenas, jackals, and suchlike.*

suck (sʌk) *vb* **1** to draw (a liquid or other substance) into the mouth by creating a partial vacuum in the mouth. **2** to draw in (fluid, etc.) by or as if by a similar action: *plants suck moisture from the soil.* **3** to drink milk from (a mother's breast); suckle. **4** (*tr*) to extract fluid content from (a solid food): *to suck a lemon.* **5** (*tr*) to take into the mouth and moisten, dissolve, or roll around with the tongue: *to suck one's thumb.* **6** (*tr;* often foll. by *down, in,* etc.) to draw by using irresistible force. **7** (*intr*) (of a pump) to draw in air because of a low supply level or leaking valves, etc. **8** (*tr*) to assimilate or acquire (knowledge, comfort, etc.). **9** (*intr*) *Sl.* to be contemptible or disgusting. ◆ *n* **10** the act or an instance of sucking. **11** something that is sucked, esp. milk from the mother's breast. **12 give suck to.** to give (a baby or young animal) milk from the breast or udder. **13** an attracting or sucking force. **14** a sound caused by sucking. ◆ See also **suck in, sucks, suck up to.** [OE *sūcan*]

sucker ❶ ('sʌkə) *n* **1** a person or thing that sucks. **2** *Sl.* a person who is

THESAURUS

subversive *adj* **1** = **seditious**, destructive, incendiary, inflammatory, insurrectionary, overthrowing, perversive, riotous, treasonous, underground, undermining ◆ *n* **2** = **dissident**, deviationist, fifth columnist, insurrectionary, quisling, saboteur, seditionary, seditionist, terrorist, traitor

subvert *vb* **1** = **overturn**, demolish, destroy, invalidate, raze, ruin, sabotage, undermine, upset, wreck **2** = **corrupt**, confound, contaminate, debase, demoralize, deprave, pervert, poison, vitiate

succeed *vb* **1-3** = **make it** (*inf.*), arrive (*inf.*), be successful, bring home the bacon (*inf.*), carry all before one, come off (*inf.*), crack it (*inf.*), cut it (*inf.*), do all right for oneself (*inf.*), do the trick (*inf.*), do well, flourish, gain one's end, get to the top, go down a bomb (*inf., chiefly Brit.*), go like a bomb (*Brit. & NZ inf.*), hit the jackpot (*inf.*), make good, make one's mark (*inf.*), make the grade (*inf.*), prosper, thrive, triumph, turn out well, work **4** = **follow**, be subsequent, come next, ensue, result, supervene **6** = **take over**, accede, assume the office of, come into, come into possession of, enter upon, fill (someone's) boots, inherit, replace, step into (someone's) boots
Antonyms *vb* ≠ **make it:** be unsuccessful, collapse, come a cropper (*inf.*), fail, fall by the wayside, fall flat, fall short, flop (*inf.*), go belly up (*inf.*), go by the board, not make the grade, not manage ≠ **follow:** be a precursor of, come before, go ahead of, go before, pave the way, precede

success *n* **1, 2** = **favourable outcome**, ascendancy, eminence, fame, fortune, happiness, luck, prosperity, triumph **4** = **hit** (*inf.*), best seller, big name, celebrity, market leader, megastar (*inf.*), sensation, smash (*inf.*), smash hit (*inf.*), somebody, star, V.I.P., winner, wow (*sl.*)
Antonyms *n* ≠ **favourable outcome:** collapse, disaster, downfall, failure, misfortune ≠ **hit:** dead duck (*sl.*), fiasco, flop (*inf.*), loser, nobody, no-hoper, washout

successful *adj* **2** = **thriving**, acknowledged, best-selling, booming, efficacious, favourable, flourishing, fortunate, fruitful, going places, home and dry (*Brit. inf.*), lucky, lucrative, moneymaking, on a roll, out in front (*inf.*), paying, profitable, rewarding, top, unbeaten, victorious **3** = **prosperous**, at the top of the tree, wealthy
Antonyms *adj* ≠ **thriving:** defeated, failed, ineffective, losing, luckless, uneconomic, unprofitable, unsuccessful, useless

successfully *adv* **2** = **well**, famously (*inf.*), favourably, in triumph, swimmingly, victoriously, with flying colours

succession *n* **2** = **series**, chain, continuation, course, cycle, flow, order, procession, progression, run, sequence, train **3** = **taking over**, accession, assumption, elevation, entering upon, inheritance **5** = **lineage**, descendants, descent, line, race **6 in succession** = **one after the other**, consecutively, one behind the other, on the trot (*inf.*), running, successively

successive *adj* **1** = **consecutive**, following, in a row, in succession, sequent, succeeding

succinct *adj* = **brief**, compact, compendious, concise, condensed, gnomic, in a few well-chosen words, laconic, pithy, summary, terse, to the point
Antonyms *adj* circuitous, circumlocutory, diffuse, discursive, long-winded, prolix, rambling, verbose, wordy

succour *n* **1** = **help**, aid, assistance, comfort, relief, support ◆ *vb* **3** = **help**, aid, assist, befriend, comfort, encourage, foster, give aid and encouragement to, minister to, nurse, relieve, render assistance to, support

succulent *adj* **1** = **juicy**, luscious, lush, mellow, moist, mouthwatering, rich

succumb *vb* **1** = **surrender**, capitulate, cave in (*inf.*), give in, give way, go under, knuckle under, submit, yield **2** = **die**, fall, fall victim to
Antonyms *vb* ≠ **surrender:** beat, conquer, get the better of, master, overcome, rise above, surmount, triumph over

sucker *n* **2** *Slang* = **fool**, butt, cat's paw, dupe, easy game *or* mark (*inf.*), mug (*Brit. sl.*), nerd *or* easily deceived or swindled. **3** *Sl.* a person who cannot resist the attractions of a particular type of person or thing: *he's a sucker for blondes.* **4** a young animal that is not yet weaned. **5** *Zool.* an organ specialized for sucking or adhering. **6** a cup-shaped device, generally made of rubber, that may be attached to articles allowing them to adhere to a surface by suction. **7** *Bot.* **7a** a strong shoot that arises in a mature plant from a root, rhizome, or the base of the main stem. **7b** a short branch of a parasitic plant that absorbs nutrients from the host. **8** a pipe or tube through which a fluid is drawn by suction. **9** any of various small mainly North American cyprinoid fishes having a large sucking mouth. **10** any of certain fishes that have sucking discs, esp. the sea snail. **11** a piston in a suction pump or the valve in such a piston. ♦ *vb* **12** (*tr*) to strip the suckers from (a plant). **13** (*intr*) (of a plant) to produce suckers.

suck in *vb* (*adv*) **1** (*tr*) to attract by using an inexorable force, inducement, etc. **2** to draw in (one's breath) sharply.

suckle (ˈsʌkᵊl) *vb* **suckles, suckling, suckled. 1** to give (a baby or young animal) milk from the breast or (of a baby, etc.) to suck milk from the breast. **2** (*tr*) to bring up; nurture. [C15: prob. back formation from SUCKLING]
▸ **ˈsuckler** *n*

suckling (ˈsʌklɪŋ) *n* **1** an infant or young animal that is still taking milk from the mother. **2** a very young child. [C15: see SUCK, -LING[1]]

sucks (sʌks) *interj Sl.* **1** an expression of disappointment. **2** an exclamation of defiance or derision (esp. in **yah boo sucks to you**).

suck up to 🅣 *vb* (*intr, adv + prep*) *Inf.* to flatter for one's own profit; toady.

sucrase (ˈsjuːkreɪz) *n* another name for **invertase.** [C19: from F *sucre* sugar + -ASE]

sucre (*Spanish* ˈsukre) *n* the standard monetary unit of Ecuador. [C19: after Antonio José de *Sucre* (1795–1830), S American liberator]

sucrose (ˈsjuːkrəʊz, -krəʊs) *n* the technical name for **sugar** (sense 1). [C19: F *sucre* sugar + -OSE[2]]

suction (ˈsʌkʃən) *n* **1** the act or process of sucking. **2** the force produced by a pressure difference, as the force holding a sucker onto a surface. **3** the act or process of producing such a force. [C17: from LL *suctiō* a sucking, from L *sūgere* to suck]
▸ **ˈsuctional** *adj*

suction pump *n* a pump for raising water or a similar fluid by suction. It usually consists of a cylinder containing a piston fitted with a flap valve.

suctorial (sʌkˈtɔːrɪəl) *adj* **1** specialized for sucking or adhering. **2** relating to or possessing suckers or suction. [C19: from NL *suctōrius,* from L *sūgere* to suck]

Sudanese (ˌsuːdᵊˈniːz) *adj* **1** of or relating to the Sudan, in NE Africa. ♦ *n* **2** a native or inhabitant of the Sudan.

sudarium (sjuˈdɛərɪəm) *n, pl* **sudaria** (-ˈdɛərɪə). another word for **sudatorium.** [C17: from L, from *sūdāre* to sweat]

sudatorium (ˌsjuːdəˈtɔːrɪəm) *or* **sudatory** *n, pl* **sudatoria** (-ˈtɔːrɪə) *or* **sudatories.** a room, esp. in a Roman bathhouse, where sweating is induced by heat. [C18: from L, from *sūdāre* to sweat]

sudatory (ˈsjuːdətərɪ, -trɪ) *adj* **1** relating to or producing sweating. ♦ *n, pl* **sudatories. 2** a sudatory agent. **3** another word for **sudatorium.**

sudd (sʌd) *n* floating masses of reeds and weeds that occur on the White Nile and obstruct navigation. [C19: from Ar., lit.: obstruction]

sudden 🅣 (ˈsʌdᵊn) *adj* **1** occurring or performed quickly and without warning. **2** marked by haste; abrupt. **3** *Rare.* rash; precipitate. ♦ *n* **4** *Arch.* an abrupt occurrence (in **on a sudden**). **5 all of a sudden.** without warning; unexpectedly. [C13: via F from LL *subitāneus,* from L *subitus* unexpected, from *subīre* to happen unexpectedly, from *sub-* secretly + *īre* to go]
▸ **ˈsuddenly** *adv* ▸ **ˈsuddenness** *n*

sudden death *n* **1** (in sports, etc.) an extra game or contest to decide the winner of a tied competition. **2** an unexpected or quick death.

sudden infant death syndrome *n* a technical name for **cot death.** Abbrev.: **SIDS.**

sudor (ˈsjuːdɔː) *n* a technical name for **sweat.** [L]
▸ **sudoral** (ˈsjuːdərəl) *adj*

sudoriferous (ˌsjuːdəˈrɪfərəs) *adj* producing or conveying sweat. Also: **ˌsudoˈriparous.** [C16: via NL from SUDOR + L *ferre* to bear]
▸ **ˌsudorˈiferousness** *n*

sudorific (ˌsjuːdəˈrɪfɪk) *adj* **1** producing or causing sweating. ♦ *n* **2** a sudorific agent. [C17: from NL *sūdōrificus,* from SUDOR + L *facere* to make]

suds (sʌdz) *pl n* **1** the bubbles on the surface of water in which soap, detergents, etc., have been dissolved; lather. **2** soapy water. [C16: prob. from MDu. *sudse* marsh]
▸ **ˈsudsy** *adj*

sue 🅣 (sjuː, suː) *vb* **sues, suing, sued. 1** to institute legal proceedings (against). **2** to make suppliant requests of (someone for something). [C13: from OF *sivre,* from L *sequī* to follow]
▸ **ˈsuer** *n*

suede (sweɪd) *n* **a** a leather with a fine velvet-like nap on the flesh side, produced by abrasive action. **b** (*as modifier*): *a suede coat.* [C19: from F *gants de Suède,* lit.: gloves from Sweden]

suet (ˈsuːɪt, ˈsjuːɪt) *n* a hard waxy fat around the kidneys and loins in sheep, cattle, etc., used in cooking and making tallow. [C14: from OF *seu,* from L *sēbum*]
▸ **ˈsuety** *adj*

suet pudding *n Brit.* any of a variety of puddings made with suet and steamed or boiled.

suffer 🅣 (ˈsʌfə) *vb* **1** to undergo or be subjected to (pain, punishment, etc.). **2** (*tr*) to undergo or experience (anything): *to suffer a change of management.* **3** (*intr*) to be set at a disadvantage: *this author suffers in translation.* **4** (*tr*) *Arch.* to tolerate; permit (someone to do something): *suffer the little children to come unto me.* **5 suffer from. 5a** to be ill with, esp. recurrently. **5b** to be given to: *he suffers from a tendency to exaggerate.* [C13: from OF *soffrir,* from L *sufferre,* from SUB- + *ferre* to bear]
▸ **ˈsufferer** *n* ▸ **ˈsuffering** *n*

sufferable (ˈsʌfərəbᵊl, ˈsʌfrə-) *adj* able to be tolerated or suffered; endurable.

sufferance (ˈsʌfərəns, ˈsʌfrəns) *n* **1** tolerance arising from failure to prohibit; tacit permission. **2** capacity to endure pain, injury, etc. **3** the state or condition of suffering. **4 on sufferance.** tolerated with reluctance. [C13: via OF from LL *sufferentia* endurance, from L *sufferre* to SUFFER]

suffice 🅣 (səˈfaɪs) *vb* **suffices, sufficing, sufficed. 1** to be adequate or satisfactory for (something). **2 suffice it to say that.** (*takes a clause as object*) let us say no more than that; I shall just say that. [C14: from OF *suffire,* from L *sufficere* from *sub-* below + *facere* to make]

sufficiency (səˈfɪʃənsɪ) *n, pl* **sufficiencies. 1** the quality or condition of being sufficient. **2** an adequate amount. **3** *Arch.* efficiency.

sufficient 🅣 (səˈfɪʃənt) *adj* **1** enough to meet a need or purpose; adequate. **2** *Logic.* (of a condition) assuring the truth of a statement; requiring but not necessarily caused by some other state of affairs. Cf. **necessary** (sense 3b). **3** *Arch.* competent; capable. ♦ *n* **4** a sufficient quantity. [C14: from L *sufficiens* supplying the needs of, from *sufficere* to SUFFICE]
▸ **sufˈficiently** *adv*

suffix *n* (ˈsʌfɪks). **1** *Grammar.* an affix that follows the stem to which it is attached, as for example *-s* and *-ness* in *dogs* and *softness.* Cf. **prefix** (sense 1). **2** anything added at the end of something else. ♦ *vb* (ˈsʌfɪks, səˈfɪks). **3** (*tr*) *Grammar.* to add (a morpheme) as a suffix to a word. [C18: from NL *suffixum,* from L *suffixus* fastened below, from *suffigere* to fasten below]

suffocate 🅣 (ˈsʌfəˌkeɪt) *vb* **suffocates, suffocating, suffocated. 1** to kill or be killed by the deprivation of oxygen, as by obstruction of the air passage. **2** to block the air passages or have the air passages blocked. **3** to feel or cause to feel discomfort from heat and lack of air. [C16: from L *suffōcāre,* from SUB- + *faucēs* throat]
▸ **ˈsuffoˌcating** *adj* ▸ **ˌsuffoˈcation** *n*

Suffolk punch (ˈsʌfək) *n* a breed of draught horse with a chestnut coat and short legs.

suffragan (ˈsʌfrəgən) *adj* **1a** (of any bishop of a diocese) subordinate to and assisting his superior archbishop or metropolitan. **1b** (of any assistant bishop) assisting the bishop of his diocese but having no ordinary jurisdiction in that diocese. ♦ *n* **2** a suffragan bishop. [C14: from Med. L *suffrāgāneus,* from *suffrāgium* assistance, from L: suffrage]
▸ **ˈsuffraganship** *n*

suffrage (ˈsʌfrɪdʒ) *n* **1** the right to vote, esp. in public elections; franchise. **2** the exercise of such a right; casting a vote. **3** a short intercessory prayer. [C14: from L *suffrāgium*]

suffragette (ˌsʌfrəˈdʒɛt) *n* a female advocate of the extension of the franchise to women, esp. a militant one, as in Britain at the beginning of the 20th century. [C20: from SUFFRAG(E) + -ETTE]

THESAURUS

nurd (*sl.*), pushover (*sl.*), sap (*sl.*), sitting duck (*inf.*), sitting target, victim

suck up to *vb Informal* = **ingratiate oneself with**, brown-nose (*taboo sl.*), butter up, curry favour with, dance attendance on, fawn on, flatter, get on the right side of, keep in with (*inf.*), kiss (someone's) ass (*US & Canad. taboo sl.*), lick (someone's) boots, pander to, play up to (*inf.*), toady, truckle, worm oneself into (someone's) favour

sudden *adj* **1, 2** = **quick**, abrupt, hasty, hurried, impulsive, rapid, rash, swift, unexpected, unforeseen, unusual
Antonyms *adj* anticipated, deliberate, expected, foreseen, gentle, gradual, slow, unhasty

suddenly *adv* **1, 2** = **abruptly**, all at once, all of a sudden, on the spur of the moment, out of the blue (*inf.*), unexpectedly, without warning

sue *vb* **1** *Law* = **take (someone) to court**, bring an action against (someone), charge, have the law on (someone) (*inf.*), indict, institute legal proceedings against (someone), prefer charges against (someone), prosecute, summon **2** = **appeal for**, beg, beseech, entreat, petition, plead, solicit, supplicate

suffer *vb* **1** = **be affected**, ache, agonize, be in pain, be racked, feel wretched, go through a lot (*inf.*), go through the mill (*inf.*), grieve, have a bad time, hurt **2** = **undergo**, bear, endure, experience, feel, go through, sustain **3** = **be shown to disadvantage**, appear in a poor light, be handicapped **4** *Archaic* = **tolerate**, allow, let, permit, put up with (*inf.*), support

suffering *n* **1** = **pain**, affliction, agony, anguish, discomfort, distress, hardship, martyrdom, misery, ordeal, torment, torture

suffice *vb* **1** = **be enough**, answer, be adequate, be sufficient, content, do, fill the bill (*inf.*), meet requirements, satisfy, serve

sufficient *adj* **1** = **adequate**, competent, enough, enow (*arch.*), satisfactory
Antonyms *adj* deficient, inadequate, insufficient, meagre, not enough, poor, scant, short, sparse

suffocate *vb* **1, 2** = **choke**, asphyxiate, smother, stifle, strangle

suffragist ('sʌfrədʒɪst) *n* an advocate of the extension of the franchise, esp. to women.
▸**'suffragism** *n*

suffruticose (sə'fruːtɪˌkəʊz) *adj* (of a plant) having a permanent woody base and herbaceous branches. [C18: from NL *suffruticōsus,* from L SUB- + *frutex* shrub]

suffuse ❶ (sə'fjuːz) *vb* **suffuses, suffusing, suffused.** (*tr; usually passive*) to spread or flood through or over (something). [C16: from L *suffūsus* overspread with, from *suffundere,* from SUB- + *fundere* to pour]
▸**suffusion** (sə'fjuːʒən) *n* ▸**suf'fusive** *adj*

Sufi ('suːfɪ) *n, pl* **Sufis.** an adherent of any of various Muslim mystical orders or teachings, which emphasize the direct personal experience of God. [C17: from Ar. *sūfīy,* lit.: (man) of wool; prob. from the ascetic's woollen garments]
▸**'Sufic** *adj* ▸**'Sufism** *n*

sugar ('ʃʊgə) *n* **1** Also called: **sucrose, saccharose.** a white crystalline sweet carbohydrate, a disaccharide, found in many plants: used esp. as a sweetening agent in food and drinks. Related adj: **saccharine. 2** any of a class of simple water-soluble carbohydrates, such as sucrose, lactose, and fructose. **3** *Inf., chiefly US & Canad.* a term of affection, esp. for one's sweetheart. ◆ *vb* **4** (*tr*) to add sugar to; make sweet. **5** (*tr*) to cover or sprinkle with sugar. **6** (*intr*) to produce sugar. **7 sugar the pill** *or* **medicine.** to make something unpleasant more agreeable by adding something pleasant. [C13 *suker,* from OF *çucre,* from Med. L *zuccārum,* ult. from Sansk. *śarkarā*]
▸**'sugared** *adj*

sugar beet *n* a variety of beet cultivated for its white roots from which sugar is obtained.

sugar candy *n* **1** Also called: **rock candy.** large crystals of sugar formed by suspending strings in a strong sugar solution that hardens on the strings, used chiefly for sweetening coffee. **2** *Chiefly US.* confectionery; sweets.

sugar cane *n* a coarse perennial grass of Old World tropical regions, having tall stout canes that yield sugar: cultivated chiefly in the Caribbean and the southern US.

sugar-coat *vb* (*tr*) **1** to coat or cover with sugar. **2** to cause to appear more attractive.

sugar diabetes *n* an informal name for **diabetes mellitus** (see **diabetes**).

sugar glider *n* a common Australian phalanger that glides from tree to tree feeding on insects and nectar.

sugaring off *n Canad.* the boiling down of maple sap to produce sugar, traditionally a social event in early spring.

sugar loaf *n* **1** a large conical mass of hard refined sugar. **2** something resembling this.

sugar maple *n* a North American maple tree, grown as a source of sugar, which is extracted from the sap, and for its hard wood.

sugar of lead (lɛd) *n* another name for **lead acetate.**

sugarplum ('ʃʊgəˌplʌm) *n* a crystallized plum.

sugary ('ʃʊgərɪ) *adj* **1** of, like, or containing sugar. **2** excessively sweet. **3** deceptively pleasant; insincere.
▸**'sugariness** *n*

suggest ❶ (sə'dʒɛst) *vb* (*tr; may take a clause as object*) **1** to put forward (a plan, idea, etc.) for consideration: *I suggest Smith for the post; a plan suggested itself.* **2** to evoke (a person, thing, etc.) in the mind by the association of ideas: *that painting suggests home to me.* **3** to give an indirect or vague hint of: *his face always suggests his peace of mind.* [C16: from L *suggerere* to bring up]
▸**sug'gester** *n*

suggestible ❶ (sə'dʒɛstɪb^{ə}l) *adj* **1** easily influenced by ideas provided by other persons. **2** characteristic of something that can be suggested.
▸**sugˌgesti'bility** *n*

suggestion ❶ (sə'dʒɛstʃən) *n* **1** something that is suggested. **2** a hint or indication: *a suggestion of the odour of violets.* **3** *Psychol.* the process whereby the mere presentation of an idea to a receptive individual leads to the acceptance of that idea. See also **autosuggestion.**

suggestive ❶ (sə'dʒɛstɪv) *adj* **1** (*postpositive; foll. by of*) conveying a hint (of something). **2** tending to suggest something improper or indecent.
▸**sug'gestively** *adv* ▸**sug'gestiveness** *n*

suicidal (ˌsuːɪ'saɪd^{ə}l, ˌsjuː-) *adj* **1** involving, indicating, or tending towards suicide. **2** liable to result in suicide: *a suicidal attempt.* **3** liable to destroy one's own interests or prospects; dangerously rash.
▸**ˌsui'cidally** *adv*

suicide ('suːɪˌsaɪd, 'sjuː-) *n* **1** the act or an instance of killing oneself intentionally. **2** the self-inflicted ruin of one's own prospects or interests: *a merger would be financial suicide.* **3** a person who kills himself intentionally. **4** (*modifier*) reckless; extremely dangerous: *a suicide mission.* **5** (*modifier*) (of an action) undertaken or (of a person) undertaking an action in the knowledge that it will result in the death of the person performing it in order that maximum damage may be inflicted: *suicide bomber.* [C17: from NL *suīcīdium,* from L *suī* of oneself + *-cīdium,* from *caedere* to kill]

sui generis (ˌsuːaɪ 'dʒɛnərɪs) *adj* unique. [L, lit.: of its own kind]

suint ('suːɪnt, swɪnt) *n* a water-soluble substance found in the fleece of sheep, formed from dried perspiration. [C18: from F *suer* to sweat, from L *sūdāre*]

suit ❶ (suːt, sjuːt) *n* **1** any set of clothes of the same or similar material designed to be worn together, now usually (for men) a jacket with matching trousers or (for women) a jacket with matching or contrasting skirt or trousers. **2** (*in combination*) any outfit worn for a specific purpose: *a spacesuit.* **3** any set of items, such as parts of personal armour. **4** any of the four sets of 13 cards in a pack of playing cards, being spades, hearts, diamonds, and clubs. **5** a civil proceeding; lawsuit. **6** the act or process of suing in a court of law. **7** a petition or appeal made to a person of superior rank or status or the act of making such a petition. **8** a man's courting of a woman. **9** *Sl.* an executive, manager, or bureaucrat, esp. one considered faceless or dull. **10 follow suit. 10a** to play a card of the same suit as the card played immediately before it. **10b** to act in the same way as someone else. **11 strong** *or* **strongest suit.** something that one excels in. ◆ *vb* **12** to make or be fit or appropriate for: *that dress suits your figure.* **13** to meet the requirements or standards (of). **14** to be agreeable or acceptable to (someone). **15 suit oneself.** to pursue one's own intentions without reference to others. [C13: from OF *sieute* set of things, from *sivre* to follow]

suitable ❶ ('suːtəb^{ə}l, 'sjuːt-) *adj* appropriate; proper; fit.
▸**ˌsuita'bility** *or* **'suitableness** *n* ▸**'suitably** *adv*

suitcase ('suːtˌkeɪs, 'sjuːt-) *n* a portable rectangular travelling case for clothing, etc.

suite ❶ (swiːt) *n* **1** a series of items intended to be used together; set. **2** a set of connected rooms in a hotel. **3** a matching set of furniture, esp. of two armchairs and a settee. **4** a number of attendants or followers. **5** *Music.* **5a** an instrumental composition consisting of several movements in the same key based on or derived from dance rhythms, esp. in the baroque period. **5b** an instrumental composition in several movements less closely connected than a sonata. [C17: from F, from OF *sieute;* see SUIT]

suiting ('suːtɪŋ, 'sjuːt-) *n* a fabric used for suits.

suitor ❶ ('suːtə, 'sjuːt-) *n* **1** a man who courts a woman; wooer. **2** *Law.* a person who brings a suit in a court of law; plaintiff. [C13: from Anglo-Norman *suter,* from L *secūtor* follower, from *sequī* to follow]

sukiyaki (ˌsuːkɪ'jɑːkɪ) *n* a Japanese dish consisting of very thinly sliced beef or other meat, vegetables, and seasonings cooked together quickly, usually at the table. [from Japanese]

Sukkoth *or* **Succoth** ('sʊkəʊt, -kəʊθ; *Hebrew* suː'kɔt) *n* an eight-day Jewish harvest festival beginning on Tishri 15, which commemorates the period when the Israelites lived in the wilderness. Also called: **Feast of Tabernacles.** [from Heb., lit.: tabernacles]

sulcate ('sʌlkeɪt) *adj Biol.* marked with longitudinal parallel grooves. [C18: via L *sulcātus* from *sulcāre* to plough, from *sulcus* a furrow]

sulcus ('sʌlkəs) *n, pl* **sulci** (-saɪ). **1** a linear groove, furrow, or slight depression. **2** any of the narrow grooves on the surface of the brain that mark the cerebral convolutions. [C17: from L]

sulf- *combining form.* a US variant of **sulph-.**

sulfur ('sʌlfə) *n* the US spelling of **sulphur.**

sulk ❶ (sʌlk) *vb* **1** (*intr*) to be silent and resentful because of a wrong done to one; brood sullenly: *the child sulked after being slapped.* ◆ *n* **2** (*often pl*) a state or mood of feeling resentful or sullen: *he's in a sulk; he's got the sulks.* **3** Also: **sulker.** a person who sulks. [C18: ? back formation from SULKY[1]]

sulky[1] ❶ ('sʌlkɪ) *adj* **sulkier, sulkiest. 1** sullen, withdrawn, or moody,

THESAURUS

suffuse *vb* = **spread through** *or* **over**, bathe, cover, flood, imbue, infuse, mantle, overspread, permeate, pervade, steep, transfuse

suggest *vb* **1** = **recommend**, advise, advocate, move, offer a suggestion, prescribe, propose, put forward **2** = **bring to mind**, connote, evoke, put one in mind of **3** = **hint**, imply, indicate, insinuate, intimate, lead one to believe

suggestible *adj* **1** = **impressionable**, accessible, amenable, influencable, malleable, open, open-minded, persuadable, pervious, pliant, receptive, susceptible, tractable
Antonyms *adj* firm, headstrong, impervious, obdurate, single-minded, unwavering

suggestion *n* **1** = **recommendation**, motion, plan, proposal, proposition **2** = **hint**, breath, indication, insinuation, intimation, suspicion, trace, whisper

suggestive *adj* **1** *foll. by* **of** = **evocative of**, expressing, indicative of, redolent of, reminiscent of **2** = **smutty**, bawdy, blue, immodest, improper, indecent, indelicate, off colour, provocative, prurient, racy, ribald, risqué, rude, spicy (*inf.*), titillating, unseemly

suit *n* **1** = **outfit**, clothing, costume, dress, ensemble, habit **5** = **lawsuit**, action, case, cause, industrial tribunal, proceeding, prosecution, trial **7** = **appeal**, addresses, entreaty, invocation, petition, prayer, request **8** = **courtship**, attentions **10b follow suit** = **copy**, accord with, emulate, run with the herd, take one's cue from ◆ *vb* **12** = **befit**, agree, agree with, become, be seemly, conform to, correspond, go with, harmonize, match, tally **12** = **fit**, accommodate, adapt, adjust, customize, fashion, modify, proportion, tailor **14** = **be acceptable to**, answer, do, gratify, please, satisfy

suitability *n* = **appropriateness**, aptness, fitness, opportuneness, rightness, timeliness

suitable *adj* = **appropriate**, acceptable, applicable, apposite, apt, becoming, befitting, convenient, cut out for, due, fit, fitting, in character, in keeping, opportune, pertinent, proper, relevant, right, satisfactory, seemly, suited
Antonyms *adj* discordant, inapposite, inappropriate, incorrect, inopportune, jarring, out of character, out of keeping, unbecoming, unfitting, unseemly, unsuitable, unsuited

suite *n* **1** = **set**, collection, series **2** = **rooms**, apartment **3** = **furniture** **4** = **attendants**, entourage, escort, followers, retainers, retinue, train

suitor *n* **1** *Old-fashioned* = **admirer**, beau, follower (*obs.*), swain (*arch.*), wooer, young man

sulk *vb* **1** = **be sullen**, be in a huff, be put out, brood, have the hump (*Brit. inf.*), pout

sulky[1] *adj* **1** = **huffy**, aloof, churlish, cross, dis-

through or as if through resentment. **2** dull or dismal: *sulky weather.* [C18: ?from obs. *sulke* sluggish]
▸**'sulkily** *adv* ▸**'sulkiness** *n*

sulky[2] ('sʌlkɪ) *n, pl* **sulkies.** a light two-wheeled vehicle for one person, usually drawn by one horse. [C18: from SULKY[1]]

sullage ('sʌlɪdʒ) *n* **1** filth or waste, esp. sewage. **2** sediment deposited by running water. [C16: ?from F *souiller* to sully]

sullen ● ('sʌlən) *adj* **1** unwilling to talk or be sociable; sulky; morose. **2** sombre; gloomy: *a sullen day.* ◆ *n* **3** *(pl) Arch.* a sullen mood. [C16: ?from Anglo-F *solain* (unattested), ult. rel. to L *sōlus* alone]
▸**'sullenly** *adv* ▸**'sullenness** *n*

sully ● ('sʌlɪ) *vb* **sullies, sullying, sullied.** *(tr)* to stain or tarnish (a reputation, etc.) or (of a reputation) to become stained or tarnished. [C16: prob. from F *souiller* to soil]

sulph- *or US* **sulf-** *combining form.* containing sulphur: *sulphate.*

sulpha *or US* **sulfa drug** ('sʌlfə) *n* any of a group of sulphonamides that inhibit the activity of bacteria and are used to treat bacterial infections.

sulphadiazine *or US* **sulfadiazine** (ˌsʌlfə'daɪəˌziːn) *n* an important sulpha drug used chiefly in combination with an antibiotic. [from SULPH- + DIAZ(O) + -INE[2]]

sulphanilamide *or US* **sulfanilamide** (ˌsʌlfə'nɪləˌmaɪd) *n* a white crystalline compound formerly used in the treatment of bacterial infections. [from SULPH- + ANIL(INE) + AMIDE]

sulphate *or US* **sulfate** ('sʌlfeɪt) *n* **1** any salt or ester of sulphuric acid. ◆ *vb* **sulphates, sulphating, sulphated** *or US* **sulfates, sulfating, sulfated. 2** *(tr)* to treat with a sulphate or convert into a sulphate. **3** to undergo or cause to undergo the formation of a layer of lead sulphate on the plates of an accumulator. [C18: from NL *sulfātum*]
▸**sul'phation** *or US* **sul'fation** *n*

sulphide *or US* **sulfide** ('sʌlfaɪd) *n* a compound of sulphur with a more electropositive element.

sulphite *or US* **sulfite** ('sʌlfaɪt) *n* any salt or ester of sulphurous acid.
▸**sulphitic** *or US* **sulfitic** (sʌl'fɪtɪk) *adj*

sulphonamide *or US* **sulfonamide** (sʌl'fɒnəˌmaɪd) *n* any of a class of organic compounds that are amides of sulphonic acids containing the group $-SO_2NH_2$ or a group derived from this. An important class of sulphonamides are the sulpha drugs.

sulphone *or US* **sulfone** ('sʌlfəʊn) *n* any of a class of organic compounds containing the divalent group SO_2 linked to two other organic groups.

sulphonic *or US* **sulfonic acid** (sʌl'fɒnɪk) *n* any of a large group of strong organic acids that contain the group $-SO_2OH$ and are used in the manufacture of dyes and drugs.

sulphonmethane *or US* **sulfonmethane** (ˌsʌlfɒn'miːθeɪn) *n* a colourless crystalline compound used medicinally as a hypnotic. Formula: $C_7H_{16}O_4S_2$.

sulphur *or US* **sulfur** ('sʌlfə) *n* **a** an allotropic nonmetallic element, occurring free in volcanic regions and in combined state in gypsum, pyrite, and galena. It is used in the production of sulphuric acid, in the vulcanization of rubber, and in fungicides. Symbol: S; atomic no.: 16; atomic wt.: 32.066. **b** *(as modifier)*: *sulphur springs.* [C14 *soufre*, from OF, from L *sulfur*]
▸**sulphuric** *or US* **sulfuric** (sʌl'fjʊərɪk) *adj*

sulphurate *or US* **sulfurate** ('sʌlfjʊˌreɪt) *vb* **sulphurates, sulphurating, sulphurated.** *(tr)* to combine or treat with sulphur or a sulphur compound.
▸**ˌsulphu'ration** *or US* **ˌsulfu'ration** *n*

sulphur-bottom *n* another name for **blue whale.**

sulphur dioxide *n* a colourless soluble pungent gas. It is both an oxidizing and a reducing agent and is used in the manufacture of sulphuric acid, the preservation of foodstuffs (**E 220**), bleaching, and disinfecting. Formula: SO_2. Systematic name: **sulphur(IV) oxide.**

sulphureous *or US* **sulfureous** (sʌl'fjʊərɪəs) *adj* **1** another word for **sulphurous** (sense 1). **2** of the yellow colour of sulphur.

sulphuretted *or US* **sulfureted hydrogen** ('sʌlfjʊˌrɛtɪd) *n* another name for **hydrogen sulphide.**

sulphuric acid *n* a colourless dense oily corrosive liquid used in accumulators and in the manufacture of fertilizers, dyes, and explosives. Formula: H_2SO_4. Systematic name: **tetraoxosulphuric(VI) acid.**

sulphurize, sulphurise, *or US* **sulfurize** ('sʌlfjʊˌraɪz) *vb* **sulphurizes, sulphurizing, sulphurized, sulphurises, sulphurising, sulphurised** *or US* **sulfurizes, sulfurizing, sulfurized.** *(tr)* to combine or treat with sulphur or a sulphur compound.
▸**ˌsulphuri'zation, ˌsulphuri'sation,** *or US* **ˌsulfuri'zation** *n*

sulphurous *or US* **sulfurous** ('sʌlfərəs) *adj* **1** Also: **sulphureous.** of, relating to, or resembling sulphur: *a sulphurous colour.* **2** (sʌl'fjʊərəs). of or containing sulphur with an oxidation state of 4: *sulphurous acid.* **3** of or relating to hellfire. **4** hot-tempered.
▸**'sulphurously** *or US* **'sulfurously** *adv* ▸**'sulphurousness** *or US* **'sulfurousness** *n*

sulphurous acid *n* an unstable acid produced when sulphur dioxide dissolves in water: used as a preservative for food and a bleaching agent. Formula: H_2SO_3. Systematic name: **sulphuric(IV) acid.**

sulphur trioxide *n* a colourless reactive fuming solid that forms sulphuric acid with water. Formula: SO_3. Systematic name: **sulphur(VI) oxide.**

sultan ('sʌltən) *n* **1** the sovereign of a Muslim country, esp. of the former Ottoman Empire. **2** a small domestic fowl with a white crest and heavily feathered legs and feet: originated in Turkey. [C16: from Med. L *sultānus*, from Ar. *sultān* rule, from Aramaic *salita* to rule]

sultana (sʌl'tɑːnə) *n* **1a** the dried fruit of a small white seedless grape, originally produced in SW Asia; seedless raisin. **1b** the grape itself. **2** Also called: **sultaness.** a wife, concubine, or female relative of a sultan. **3** a mistress; concubine. [C16: from It., fem of *sultano* SULTAN]

sultanate ('sʌltəˌneɪt) *n* **1** the territory or a country ruled by a sultan. **2** the office, rank, or jurisdiction of a sultan.

sultry ● ('sʌltrɪ) *adj* **sultrier, sultriest. 1** (of weather or climate) oppressively hot and humid. **2** characterized by or emitting oppressive heat. **3** displaying or suggesting passion; sensual: *sultry eyes.* [C16: from obs. *sulter* to swelter + -Y[1]]
▸**'sultrily** *adv* ▸**'sultriness** *n*

sum ● (sʌm) *n* **1** the result of the addition of numbers, quantities, objects, etc. **2** one or more columns or rows of numbers to be added, subtracted, multiplied, or divided. **3** *Maths.* the limit of the first *n* terms of a converging infinite series as *n* tends to infinity. **4** a quantity, esp. of money: *he borrows enormous sums.* **5** the essence or gist of a matter (esp. in **in sum, in sum and substance**). **6** a less common word for **summary. 7** *(modifier)* complete or final (esp. in **sum total**). ◆ *vb* **sums, summing, summed. 8** (often foll. by *up*) to add or form a total of (something). **9** *(tr)* to calculate the sum of (the terms in a sequence). ◆ See also **sum up.** [C13 *summe*, from OF, from L *summa* the top, sum, from *summus* highest, from *super* above]

sumach *or US* **sumac** ('suːmæk, 'ʃuː-) *n* **1** any of various temperate or subtropical shrubs or small trees, having compound leaves and red hairy fruits. See also **poison sumach. 2** a preparation of powdered leaves of certain species of sumach, used in dyeing and tanning. **3** the wood of any of these plants. [C14: via OF from Ar. *summāq*]

Sumerian (suː'mɪərɪən, -'mɛər-) *n* **1** a member of a people who established a civilization in Sumer, in W Asia, during the 4th millennium B.C. **2** the extinct language of this people. ◆ *adj* **3** of or relating to ancient Sumer, its inhabitants, or their language or civilization.

summa cum laude ('sʊmɑː kʊm 'laʊdeɪ) *adv, adj Chiefly US.* with the utmost praise: the highest designation for achievement in examinations. In Britain it is sometimes used to designate a first-class honours degree. [from L]

summarize ● *or* **summarise** ('sʌməˌraɪz) *vb* **summarizes, summarizing, summarized** *or* **summarises, summarising, summarised.** *(tr)* to make or be a summary of; express concisely.
▸**ˌsummari'zation** *or* **ˌsummari'sation** *n* ▸**'summaˌrizer, 'summaˌriser,** *or* **'summarist** *n*

summary ● ('sʌmərɪ) *n, pl* **summaries. 1** a brief account giving the main points of something. ◆ *adj (usually prenominal).* **2** performed arbitrarily and quickly, without formality: *a summary execution.* **3** (of legal proceedings) short and free from the complexities and delays of a full trial. **4 summary jurisdiction.** the right a court has to adjudicate immediately upon some matter. **5** giving the gist or essence. [C15: from L *summārium*, from *summa* SUM]
▸**'summarily** *adv* ▸**'summariness** *n*

summary offence *n* an offence that is triable in a magistrates' court.

summation (sʌ'meɪʃən) *n* **1** the act or process of determining a sum; addition. **2** the result of such an act or process. **3** a summary. **4** *US law.* the concluding statements made by opposing counsel in a case before a court. [C18: from Med. L *summātiō*, from *summāre* to total, from L *summa* SUM]
▸**sum'mational** *adj* ▸**'summative** *adj*

summative assessment *n Brit. education.* general assessment of a pupil's achievements over a range of subjects by means of a combined appraisal of formative assessments.

summer ('sʌmə) *n* **1** *(sometimes cap.)* **1a** the warmest season of the year, between spring and autumn, astronomically from the June solstice to

THESAURUS

gruntled, ill-humoured, in the sulks, moody, morose, perverse, petulant, put out, querulous, resentful, sullen, vexed

sullen *adj* **1 = morose,** brooding, cheerless, cross, dismal, dour, gloomy, glowering, moody, obstinate, out of humour, perverse, silent, sour, stubborn, sulky, surly, unsociable **2 = dull,** gloomy, heavy, sombre
Antonyms *adj* ≠ **morose:** amiable, bright, cheerful, cheery, chirpy *(inf.)*, genial, good-humoured, good-natured, pleasant, sociable, sunny, warm, warm-hearted

sullenness *n* **1 = moroseness,** glumness, ill humour, moodiness, sourness, sulkiness, sulks

sully *vb* **= dishonour,** besmirch, disgrace, ruin, smirch, tarnish

sultry *adj* **1 = humid,** close, hot, muggy, oppressive, sticky, stifling, stuffy, sweltering **3 = seductive,** amorous, come-hither *(inf.)*, erotic, passionate, provocative, sensual, sexy *(inf.)*, voluptuous
Antonyms *adj* ≠ **humid:** cool, fresh, invigorating, refreshing

sum *n* **1 = total,** aggregate, amount, entirety, quantity, reckoning, score, sum total, tally, totality, whole

summarily *adv* **2 = immediately,** arbitrarily, at short notice, expeditiously, forthwith, on the spot, peremptorily, promptly, speedily, swiftly, without delay, without wasting words

summarize *vb* **= sum up,** abridge, condense, encapsulate, epitomize, give a rundown of, give the main points of, outline, précis, put in a nutshell, recap, recapitulate, review

summary *n* **1 = synopsis,** abridgment, abstract, compendium, digest, epitome, essence, extract, outline, précis, recapitulation, résumé, review, rundown, summing-up ◆ *adj* **2 = hasty,** arbitrary, cursory, perfunctory **5 = succinct,** brief, compact, compendious, concise, condensed, laconic, pithy

the September equinox in the N hemisphere and at the opposite time of year in the S hemisphere. **1b** (*as modifier*): *summer flowers.* Related adj: **aestival. 2** the period of hot weather associated with the summer. **3** a time of blossoming, greatest happiness, etc. **4** *Chiefly poetic.* a year represented by this season: *a child of nine summers.* ◆ *vb* **5** (*intr*) to spend the summer (at a place). **6** (*tr*) to keep or feed (farm animals) during the summer: *they summered their cattle on the mountain slopes.* [OE *sumor*]
▸ **'summerly** *adj* ▸ **'summery** *adj*

summerhouse ('sʌmə,haʊs) *n* a small building in a garden or park, used for shade or recreation in the summer.

summer pudding *n Brit.* a pudding made by filling a bread-lined basin with a purée of fruit.

summersault ('sʌmə,sɔːlt) *n, vb* a variant spelling of **somersault.**

summer school *n* a school, academic course, etc., held during the summer.

summer solstice *n* **1** the time at which the sun is at its northernmost point in the sky (southernmost point in the S hemisphere). It occurs about June 21 (December 22 in the S hemisphere). **2** *Astron.* the point on the celestial sphere, opposite the **winter solstice,** at which the ecliptic is furthest north from the celestial equator.

summertime ('sʌmə,taɪm) *n* the period or season of summer.

summer time *n Brit.* any daylight-saving time, esp. British Summer Time.

summerweight ('sʌmə,weɪt) *adj* (of clothes) suitable in weight for wear in the summer.

summing-up *n* **1** a review or summary of the main points of an argument, speech, etc. **2** concluding statements made by a judge to the jury before they retire to consider their verdict.

summit ➊ ('sʌmɪt) *n* **1** the highest point or part, esp. of a mountain; top. **2** the highest possible degree or state; peak or climax: *the summit of ambition.* **3** the highest level, importance, or rank: *a meeting at the summit.* **4a** a meeting of chiefs of governments or other high officials. **4b** (*as modifier*): *a summit conference.* [C15: from OF *somet,* dim. of *som,* from L *summum;* see SUM]

summon ➊ ('sʌmən) *vb* (*tr*) **1** to order to come; send for, esp. to attend court, by issuing a summons. **2** to order or instruct (to do something) or call (to something): *the bell summoned them to their work.* **3** to call upon to meet or convene. **4** (often foll. by *up*) to muster or gather (one's strength, courage, etc.). **5** *Arch.* to call upon to surrender. [C13: from L *summonēre* to give a discreet reminder, from *monēre* to advise]

summons ('sʌmənz) *n, pl* **summonses. 1** a call, signal, or order to do something, esp. to attend at a specified place or time. **2a** an official order requiring a person to attend court, either to answer a charge or to give evidence. **2b** the writ making such an order. **3** a call or command given to the members of an assembly to convene a meeting. ◆ *vb* **4** to take out a summons against (a person). [C13: from OF *somonse,* from *somondre* to SUMMON]

summum bonum *Latin.* ('sʊmʊm 'bɒnʊm) *n* the principle of goodness in which all moral values are included or from which they are derived; highest or supreme good.

sumo ('suːməʊ) *n* the national style of wrestling of Japan, in which two contestants of great height and weight attempt to force each other to touch the ground with any part of the body except the soles of the feet or to step out of the ring. [from Japanese *sumō*]

sump (sʌmp) *n* **1** a receptacle, as in the crankcase of an internal-combustion engine, into which liquids, esp. lubricants, can drain to form a reservoir. **2** another name for **cesspool** (sense 1). **3** *Mining.* a depression at the bottom of a shaft where water collects. [C17: from MDu. *somp* marsh]

sumpter ('sʌmptə) *n Arch.* a packhorse, mule, or other beast of burden. [C14: from OF *sometier* driver of a baggage horse, from Vulgar L *sagmatārius* (unattested), from LL *sagma* packsaddle]

sumptuary ('sʌmptjʊərɪ) *adj* relating to or controlling expenditure or extravagance. [C17: from L *sumptuārius* concerning expense, from *sumptus* expense, from *sūmere* to spend]

sumptuous ➊ ('sʌmptjʊəs) *adj* **1** expensive or extravagant: *sumptuous costumes.* **2** magnificent; splendid: *a sumptuous scene.* [C16: from OF *somptueux,* from L *sumptuōsus* costly, from *sumptus;* see SUMPTUARY]
▸ **'sumptuously** *adv* ▸ **'sumptuousness** *n*

sum up ➊ *vb* (*adv*) **1** to summarize (the main points of an argument, etc.). **2** (*tr*) to form a quick opinion of: *I summed him up in five minutes.*

sun ➊ (sʌn) *n* **1** the star that is the source of heat and light for the planets in the solar system. Related adj: **solar. 2** any star around which a planetary system revolves. **3** the sun as it appears at a particular time or place: *the winter sun.* **4** the radiant energy, esp. heat and light, received from the sun; sunshine. **5** a person or thing considered as a source of radiant warmth, glory, etc. **6** a pictorial representation of the sun, often depicted with a human face. **7** *Poetic.* a year or a day. **8** *Poetic.* a climate. **9** *Arch.* sunrise or sunset (esp. in **from sun to sun**). **10 catch the sun.** to become slightly sunburnt. **11 place in the sun.** a prominent or favourable position. **12 take** *or* **shoot the sun.** *Naut.* to measure the altitude of the sun in order to determine latitude. **13 touch of the sun.** slight sunstroke. **14 under** *or* **beneath the sun.** on earth; at all: *nobody under the sun eats more than you.* ◆ *vb* **suns, sunning, sunned. 15** to expose (oneself) to the sunshine. **16** (*tr*) to expose to the sunshine in order to warm, etc. [OE *sunne*]

Sun. *abbrev. for* Sunday.

sunbaked ('sʌn,beɪkt) *adj* **1** (esp. of roads, etc.) dried or cracked by the sun's heat. **2** baked hard by the heat of the sun: *sunbaked bricks.*

sun bath *n* the exposure of the body to the rays of the sun or a sun lamp, esp. in order to get a suntan.

sunbathe ('sʌn,beɪð) *vb* **sunbathes, sunbathing, sunbathed.** (*intr*) to bask in the sunshine, esp. in order to get a suntan.
▸ **'sun,bather** *n*

sunbeam ('sʌn,biːm) *n* a beam, ray, or stream of sunlight.
▸ **'sun,beamed** *or* **'sun,beamy** *adj*

sunbird ('sʌn,bɜːd) *n* any of various small songbirds of tropical regions of the Old World, esp. Africa, having a long slender curved bill and a bright plumage in the males.

sunbonnet ('sʌn,bɒnɪt) *n* a hat that shades the face and neck from the sun, esp. one of cotton with a projecting brim, now worn esp. by babies.

sunburn ➊ ('sʌn,bɜːn) *n* **1** inflammation of the skin caused by overexposure to the sun. **2** another word for **suntan.**
▸ **'sun,burnt** *or* **'sun,burned** *adj*

sunburst ('sʌn,bɜːst) *n* **1** a burst of sunshine, as through a break in the clouds. **2** a pattern or design resembling that of the sun. **3** a jewelled brooch with this pattern.

sun-cured *adj* cured or preserved by exposure to the sun.

sundae ('sʌndɪ, -deɪ) *n* ice cream topped with a sweet sauce, nuts, whipped cream, etc. [C20: from ?]

Sunday ('sʌndɪ) *n* the first day of the week and the Christian day of worship. [OE *sunnandæg,* translation of L *diēs sōlis* day of the sun, translation of Gk *hēmera hēliou*]

Sunday best *n* one's best clothes, esp. regarded as those most suitable for churchgoing.

Sunday school *n* **1a** a school for the religious instruction of children on Sundays, usually held in a church hall. **1b** (*as modifier*): *a Sunday-school outing.* **2** the members of such a school.

sunder ('sʌndə) *Arch. or literary.* ◆ *vb* **1** to break or cause to break apart or in pieces. ◆ *n* **2 in sunder.** into pieces; apart. [OE *sundrian*]

sundew ('sʌn,djuː) *n* any of several bog plants having leaves covered with sticky hairs that trap and digest insects. [C16: translation of L *ros solis*]

sundial ('sʌn,daɪəl) *n* a device indicating the time during the hours of sunlight by means of a stationary arm (the **gnomon**) that casts a shadow onto a plate or surface marked in hours.

sun disc *n* a disc symbolizing the sun, esp. one flanked by two serpents and the extended wings of a vulture: a religious figure in ancient Egypt.

sundog ('sʌn,dɒg) *n* another word for **parhelion.**

sundown ('sʌn,daʊn) *n* another name for **sunset.**

sundowner ('sʌn,daʊnə) *n* **1** *Austral. sl.* a tramp, esp. one who seeks food and lodging at sundown when it is too late to work. **2** *Inf., chiefly Brit.* an alcoholic drink taken at sunset.

sundress ('sʌn,dres) *n* a dress for hot weather that exposes the shoulders, arms, and back.

sun-dried *adj* dried or preserved by exposure to the sun.

sundry ➊ ('sʌndrɪ) *determiner* **1** several or various; miscellaneous. ◆ *pron* **2 all and sundry.** everybody, individually and collectively. ◆ *n, pl* **sundries. 3** (*pl*) miscellaneous unspecified items. **4** the Austral. term for **extra** (sense 6). [OE *syndrig* separate]

sunfast ('sʌn,fɑːst) *adj Chiefly US & Canad.* not fading in sunlight.

sunfish ('sʌn,fɪʃ) *n, pl* **sunfish** *or* **sunfishes. 1** any of various large fishes of temperate and tropical seas, esp. one which has a large rounded compressed body, long pointed dorsal and anal fins, and a fringelike tail fin. **2** any of various small predatory North American freshwater percoid fishes, typically having a compressed brightly coloured body.

sunflower ('sʌn,flaʊə) *n* **1** any of several American plants having very tall thick stems, large flower heads with yellow rays, and seeds used as food, esp. for poultry. See also **Jerusalem artichoke. 2 sunflower seed oil.** the oil extracted from sunflower seeds, used as a salad oil, in margarine, etc.

THESAURUS

summit *n* **2** = **peak,** acme, apex, crest, crown, crowning point, culmination, head, height, pinnacle, top, zenith
Antonyms *n* base, bottom, depths, foot, lowest point, nadir

summon *vb* **3** = **send for,** arouse, assemble, bid, call, call together, cite, convene, convoke, invite, rally, rouse **4** *often with* **up** = **gather,** call into action, draw on, invoke, mobilize, muster

sumptuous *adj* **1, 2** = **luxurious,** costly, dear, de luxe, expensive, extravagant, gorgeous, grand, lavish, magnificent, opulent, palatial, plush (*inf.*), posh (*inf., chiefly Brit.*), rich, ritzy (*sl.*), splendid, splendiferous (*facetious*), superb
Antonyms *adj* austere, basic, cheap, frugal, inexpensive, meagre, mean, miserly, plain, shabby, wretched

sum up *vb* **1** = **summarize,** close, conclude, put in a nutshell, recapitulate, review **2** = **form an opinion of,** estimate, get the measure of, size up (*inf.*)

sun *n* **1** = **Sol** (*Roman myth*), daystar (*poetic*), eye of heaven, Helios (*Greek myth*), Phoebus (*Greek myth*), Phoebus Apollo (*Greek myth*) ◆ *vb* **15 sun oneself** = **sunbathe,** bake, bask, tan

sunburnt *adj* **1** = **tanned,** bronzed, brown, brown as a berry, burnt, burnt to a crisp, like a lobster, peeling, red, ruddy, scarlet

sundry *determiner* **1** = **various,** assorted, different, divers (*arch.*), miscellaneous, several, some, varied

sung (sʌŋ) *vb* **1** the past participle of **sing.** ◆ *adj* **2** produced by singing: *a sung syllable.*

USAGE NOTE See at **ring**[2].

sunglass ('sʌn,glɑːs) *n* another name for **burning glass.**
sunglasses ('sʌn,glɑːsɪz) *pl n* glasses with darkened or polarizing lenses that protect the eyes from the sun's glare.
sun-god *n* **1** the sun considered as a personal deity. **2** a deity associated with the sun or controlling its movements.
sunk ❶ (sʌŋk) *vb* **1** a past participle of **sink.** ◆ *adj* **2** *Inf.* with all hopes dashed; ruined.
sunken ❶ ('sʌŋkən) *vb* **1** a past participle of **sink.** ◆ *adj* **2** unhealthily hollow: *sunken cheeks.* **3** situated at a lower level than the surrounding or usual one: *a sunken bath.* **4** situated under water; submerged. **5** depressed; low: *sunken spirits.*
sunk fence *n* another name for **ha-ha**[2].
sun lamp *n* **1** a lamp that generates ultraviolet rays, used for obtaining an artificial suntan, for muscular therapy, etc. **2** a lamp used in film studios, etc., to give an intense beam of light by means of parabolic mirrors.
sunless ❶ ('sʌnlɪs) *adj* **1** without sun or sunshine. **2** gloomy; depressing.
▸**'sunlessly** *adv*
sunlight ('sʌnlaɪt) *n* **1** the light emanating from the sun. **2** an area or the time characterized by sunshine.
▸**'sunlit** *adj*
sun lounge *or US* **sun parlor** *n* a room with large windows positioned to receive as much sunlight as possible.
Sunna ('sʌnə) *n* the body of traditional Islamic law accepted by most orthodox Muslims as based on the words and acts of Mohammed. [C18: from Ar. *sunnah* rule]
Sunni ('sʌnɪ) *n* **1** one of the two main branches of orthodox Islam (the other being the Shiah), consisting of those who acknowledge the authority of the Sunna. **2** (*pl* **Sunni**) a less common word for **Sunnite.**
Sunnite ('sʌnaɪt) *n* an adherent of the Sunni.
sunny ❶ ('sʌnɪ) *adj* **sunnier, sunniest. 1** full of or exposed to sunlight. **2** radiating good humour. **3** of or resembling the sun.
▸**'sunnily** *adv* ▸**'sunniness** *n*
sunrise ❶ ('sʌn,raɪz) *n* **1** the daily appearance of the sun above the horizon. **2** the atmospheric phenomena accompanying this appearance. **3** Also called (esp. US): **sunup.** the time at which the sun rises at a particular locality.
sunrise industry *n* any of the high-technology industries, such as electronics, that hold promise of future development.
sunroof ('sʌn,ruːf) *or* **sunshine roof** *n* a panel, often translucent, that may be opened in the roof of a car.
sunset ❶ ('sʌn,set) *n* **1** the daily disappearance of the sun below the horizon. **2** the atmospheric phenomena accompanying this disappearance. **3** Also called: **sundown.** the time at which the sun sets at a particular locality. **4** the final stage or closing period, as of a person's life.
sunshade ('sʌn,ʃeɪd) *n* a device, esp. a parasol or awning, serving to shade from the sun.
sunshine ('sʌn,ʃaɪn) *n* **1** the light received directly from the sun. **2** the warmth from the sun. **3** a sunny area. **4** a light-hearted or ironic term of address.
▸**'sun,shiny** *adj*
sun sign *n* another name for **sign of the zodiac.**
sunspot ('sʌn,spɒt) *n* **1** any of the dark cool patches that appear on the surface of the sun and last about a week. **2** *Inf.* a sunny holiday resort. **3** *Austral.* a small cancerous spot produced by overexposure to the sun.
sunstroke ('sʌn,strəʊk) *n* heatstroke caused by prolonged exposure to intensely hot sunlight.
sunsuit ('sʌn,suːt, -,sjuːt) *n* a child's outfit consisting of a brief top and shorts or skirt.
suntan ('sʌn,tæn) *n* **a** a brownish colouring of the skin caused by the formation of the pigment melanin within the skin on exposure to the ultraviolet rays of the sun or a sun lamp. Often shortened to **tan. b** (*as modifier*): *suntan oil.*
▸**'sun,tanned** *adj*
suntrap ('sʌn,træp) *n* a very sunny sheltered place.
sunward ('sʌnwəd) *adj* **1** directed or moving towards the sun. ◆ *adv* **2** Also: **sunwards.** towards the sun.
sup[1] (sʌp) *vb* **sups, supping, supped.** (*intr*) *Arch.* to have supper. [C13: from OF *soper*]
sup[2] (sʌp) *vb* **sups, supping, supped. 1** to partake of (liquid) by swallowing a little at a time. **2** *Scot. & N English dialect.* to drink. ◆ *n* **3** a sip. [OE *sūpan*]
sup. *abbrev. for:* **1** above. [from L *supra*] **2** superior. **3** *Grammar.* superlative. **4** supplement. **5** supplementary. **6** supply.
super ❶ (suːpə) *adj* **1** *Inf.* outstanding; exceptional. ◆ *n* **2** petrol with a high octane rating. **3** *Inf.* a supervisor. **4** *Austral. & NZ inf.* superannuation benefits. **5** *Austral & NZ inf.* superphosphate. ◆ *interj* **6** *Brit. inf.* an enthusiastic expression of approval. [from L: above]
super. *abbrev. for:* **1** superfine. **2** superior.
super- *prefix* **1** placed above or over: *superscript.* **2** surpassing others; outstanding: *superstar.* **3** of greater size, extent, quality, etc.: *supermarket.* **4** beyond a standard or norm: *supersonic.* **5** indicating that a chemical compound contains a specified element in a higher proportion than usual: *superphosphate.* [from L *super* above]
superable ('suːpərəbᵊl) *adj* able to be surmounted or overcome. [C17: from L *superābilis*, from *superāre* to overcome]
▸**,supera'bility** *or* **'superableness** *n* ▸**'superably** *adv*
superannuate (,suːpər'ænjʊ,eɪt) *vb* **superannuates, superannuating, superannuated.** (*tr*) **1** to pension off. **2** to discard as obsolete or old-fashioned.
superannuated ❶ (,suːpər'ænjʊ,eɪtɪd) *adj* **1** discharged, esp. with a pension, owing to age or illness. **2** too old to serve usefully. **3** obsolete. [C17: from Med. L *superannātus* aged more than one year, from L SUPER- + *annus* a year]
superannuation (,suːpər,ænjʊ'eɪʃən) *n* **1a** the amount deducted regularly from employees' incomes in a contributory pension scheme. **1b** the pension finally paid. **2** the act or process of superannuating or the condition of being superannuated.
superb ❶ (sʊ'pɜːb, sjʊ-) *adj* **1** surpassingly good; excellent. **2** majestic or imposing. **3** magnificently rich; luxurious. [C16: from OF *superbe*, from L *superbus* distinguished, from *super* above]
▸**su'perbly** *adv* ▸**su'perbness** *n*
Super Bowl *n American football.* the championship game held annually between the best team of the American Football Conference and that of the National Football Conference.
supercalender (,suːpə'kæləndə) *n* **1** a calender that gives a high gloss to paper. ◆ *vb* **2** (*tr*) to finish (paper) in this way.
▸**,super'calendered** *adj*
supercargo (,suːpə'kɑːgəʊ) *n, pl* **supercargoes.** an officer on a merchant ship who supervises commercial matters and is in charge of the cargo. [C17: changed from Sp. *sobrecargo*, from *sobre* over + *cargo* CARGO]
supercharge ('suːpə,tʃɑːdʒ) *vb* **supercharges, supercharging, supercharged.** (*tr*) **1** to increase the intake pressure of (an internal-combustion engine) with a supercharger; boost. **2** to charge (the atmosphere, a remark, etc.) with an excess amount of (tension, emotion, etc.). **3** to apply pressure to (a fluid); pressurize.
supercharger ('suːpə,tʃɑːdʒə) *n* a device that increases the mass of air drawn into an internal-combustion engine by raising the intake pressure. Also called: **blower, booster.**
superciliary (,suːpə'sɪlɪərɪ) *adj* over the eyebrow or a corresponding region in lower animals. [C18: from NL *superciliaris*, from L, from SUPER- + *cilium* eyelid]
supercilious ❶ (,suːpə'sɪlɪəs) *adj* displaying arrogant pride, scorn, or indifference. [C16: from L, from *supercilium* eyebrow]
▸**,super'ciliously** *adv* ▸**,super'ciliousness** *n*
superclass ('suːpə,klɑːs) *n* a taxonomic group that is a subdivision of a subphylum.
supercolumnar (,suːpəkə'lʌmnə) *adj Archit.* **1** having one colonnade above another. **2** placed above a colonnade or a column.
▸**,supercol,umni'ation** *n*
superconductivity (,suːpə,kɒndʌk'tɪvɪtɪ) *n Physics.* the property of

THESAURUS

sunk *adj* **2** = **ruined**, all washed up (*inf.*), done for (*inf.*), finished, lost, on the rocks, up the creek without a paddle (*inf.*)
sunken *adj* **2** = **hollow**, concave, drawn, haggard, hollowed **3** = **lower**, at a lower level, below ground, buried, depressed, immersed, recessed, submerged
sunless *adj* **1** = **cloudy**, dark, gloomy, grey, hazy, overcast **2** = **depressing**, bleak, cheerless, gloomy, sombre
sunny *adj* **1** = **bright**, brilliant, clear, fine, luminous, radiant, summery, sunlit, sunshiny, unclouded, without a cloud in the sky **2** = **cheerful**, beaming, blithe, buoyant, cheery, chirpy (*inf.*), genial, happy, joyful, light- hearted, optimistic, pleasant, smiling
Antonyms *adj* ≠ **bright:** cloudy, depressing, dreary, dreich (*Scot.*), dull, gloomy, murky, overcast, rainy, shaded, shadowy, sunless, wet, wintry ≠ **cheerful:** doleful, down in the dumps (*inf.*), gloomy, miserable, morbid, unsmiling
sunrise *n* **1** = **dawn**, aurora (*poetic*), break of day, cockcrow, daybreak, daylight, dayspring (*poetic*), sunup
sunset *n* **1** = **nightfall**, close of (the) day, dusk, eventide, gloaming (*Scot. or poetic*), sundown
super *adj* **1** *Informal* = **excellent**, awesome (*sl.*), brill (*inf.*), cracking (*Brit. inf.*), glorious, incomparable, magnificent, marvellous, matchless, mega (*sl.*), out of this world (*inf.*), outstanding, peerless, sensational (*inf.*), smashing (*inf.*), sovereign, superb, terrific (*inf.*), top-notch (*inf.*), wonderful
superannuated *adj* **1** = **retired**, discharged, pensioned off, put out to grass (*inf.*) **2, 3** = **obsolete**, aged, antiquated, decrepit, old, past it (*inf.*), senile, unfit
superb *adj* **1** = **splendid**, awesome (*sl.*), brill (*inf.*), choice, divine, excellent, exquisite, fine, first-rate, gorgeous, marvellous, mega (*sl.*), of the first water, superior, superlative, topping (*Brit. sl.*), unrivalled, world-class
Antonyms *adj* abysmal, awful, bad, disappointing, dreadful, inferior, mediocre, no great shakes (*inf.*), pathetic, poor quality, run-of-the-mill, terrible, third-rate, uninspired, woeful
supercilious *adj* = **scornful**, arrogant, condescending, contemptuous, disdainful, haughty, high and mighty (*inf.*), hoity-toity (*inf.*), imperious, insolent, lofty, lordly, overbearing, patronizing, proud, snooty (*inf.*), stuck-up (*inf.*), toffee-nosed (*sl., chiefly Brit.*), uppish (*Brit. inf.*), vainglorious
Antonyms *adj* deferential, generous, humble, meek, modest, obsequious, self-effacing, submissive, unassuming, unpretentious, warm-hearted

certain substances that have no electrical resistance. In metals it occurs at very low temperatures; higher-temperature superconductivity occurs in some ceramic materials.
▸**superconduction** (ˌsuːpəkənˈdʌkʃən) *n* ▸**ˌsuperconˈductive** *or* **ˌsuperconˈducting** *adj* ▸**ˌsuperconˈductor** *n*

supercontinent (ˈsuːpəˌkɒntɪnənt) *n* a great landmass thought to have existed in the geological past and to have split into smaller landmasses, which drifted and formed the present continents.

supercool (ˌsuːpəˈkuːl) *vb Chem.* to cool or be cooled without freezing or crystallization to a temperature below that at which freezing or crystallization should occur.

supercritical (ˌsuːpəˈkrɪtɪkᵊl) *adj* **1** *Physics.* (of a fluid) brought to a temperature and pressure higher than its critical temperature and pressure, so that its physical and chemical properties change. **2** *Nuclear physics.* of or containing more than the critical mass.

superdense theory (ˌsuːpəˈdɛns) *n Astron.* another name for the **big-bang theory.**

super-duper (ˈsuːpəˈduːpə) *adj Inf.* extremely pleasing, impressive, etc.: often used as an exclamation.

superego (ˌsuːpərˈiːgəʊ, -ˈɛgəʊ) *n, pl* **superegos.** *Psychoanal.* that part of the unconscious mind that acts as a conscience for the ego.

superelevation (ˌsuːpərˌɛlɪˈveɪʃən) *n* **1** another name for **bank**[2] (sense 8). **2** the difference between the heights of the sides of a road or railway track on a bend.

supereminent (ˌsuːpərˈɛmɪnənt) *adj* of distinction, dignity, or rank superior to that of others; pre-eminent.
▸**ˌsuperˈeminence** *n* ▸**ˌsuperˈeminently** *adv*

supererogation (ˌsuːpərˌɛrəˈgeɪʃən) *n* **1** the performance of work in excess of that required or expected. **2** *RC Church.* supererogatory prayers, devotions, etc.

supererogatory (ˌsuːpərɛˈrɒgətərɪ, -trɪ) *adj* **1** performed to an extent exceeding that required or expected. **2** exceeding what is needed; superfluous. **3** *RC Church.* of or relating to prayers, good works, etc., performed over and above those prescribed as obligatory. [C16: from Med. L *superērogātōrius,* from L *superērogāre* to spend over and above]

superfamily (ˈsuːpəˌfæmɪlɪ) *n, pl* **superfamilies. 1** *Biol.* a subdivision of a suborder. **2** any analogous group, such as a group of related languages.

superfecundation (ˌsuːpəˌfiːkənˈdeɪʃən) *n Physiol.* the fertilization of two or more ova, produced during the same menstrual cycle, by sperm ejaculated during two or more acts of sexual intercourse.

superfetation (ˌsuːpəfiːˈteɪʃən) *n Physiol.* the presence in the uterus of two fetuses developing from ova fertilized at different times. [C17 *superfetate,* from L *superfētāre* to fertilize when already pregnant, from *fētus* offspring]

superficial ➊ (ˌsuːpəˈfɪʃəl) *adj* **1** of, near, or forming the surface: *superficial bruising.* **2** displaying a lack of thoroughness or care: *a superficial inspection.* **3** only outwardly apparent rather than genuine or actual: *the similarity was merely superficial.* **4** of little substance or significance: *superficial differences.* **5** lacking profundity: *the film's plot was quite superficial.* **6** (of measurements) involving only the surface area. [C14: from LL *superficiālis* of the surface, from L SUPERFICIES]
▸**superficiality** (ˌsuːpəˌfɪʃɪˈælɪtɪ) *n* ▸**ˌsuperˈficially** *adv*

superficies (ˌsuːpəˈfɪʃiːz) *n, pl* **superficies. 1** a surface or outer face. **2** the outward form of a thing. [C16: from L: upper side]

superfine (ˌsuːpəˈfaɪn) *adj* **1** of exceptional fineness or quality. **2** excessively refined.
▸**ˌsuperˈfineness** *n*

superfix (ˈsuːpəˌfɪks) *n Linguistics.* a type of feature distinguishing the meaning or grammatical function of one word or phrase from that of another, as stress does for example between the noun *conduct* and the verb *conduct.*

superfluid (ˌsuːpəˈfluːɪd) *n* **1** *Physics.* a fluid in a state characterized by a very low viscosity, high thermal conductivity, high capillarity, etc. The only known example is that of liquid helium at temperatures close to absolute zero. ◆ *adj* **2** being or relating to a superfluid.
▸**ˌsuperfluˈidity** *n*

superfluity ➊ (ˌsuːpəˈfluːɪtɪ) *n* **1** the condition of being superfluous. **2** a quantity or thing that is in excess of what is needed. **3** a thing that is not needed. [C14: from OF *superfluité,* via LL from L *superfluus* SUPERFLUOUS]

superfluous ➊ (suːˈpɜːfluəs) *adj* **1** exceeding what is sufficient or required. **2** not necessary or relevant; uncalled for. [C15: from L *superfluus* overflowing, from *fluere* to flow]
▸**suˈperfluously** *adv* ▸**suˈperfluousness** *n*

Super-G *n Skiing.* a type of slalom in which the course is shorter than in a standard slalom and the obstacles are farther apart than in a giant slalom. [C20: from SUPER- + G(IANT)]

supergiant (ˈsuːpəˌdʒaɪənt) *n* any of a class of extremely bright stars which have expanded to a large diameter and are eventually likely to explode as supernovas.

superglue (ˈsuːpəˌgluː) *n* any of various adhesives that quickly make an exceptionally strong bond.

supergrass (ˈsuːpəˌgrɑːs) *n* an informer whose information implicates a large number of people.

supergravity (ˌsuːpəˈgrævɪtɪ) *n Physics.* any of various theories in which supersymmetry is applied to the theory of gravitation.

superheat (ˌsuːpəˈhiːt) *vb* (*tr*) **1** to heat (a vapour, esp. steam) to a temperature above its saturation point for a given pressure. **2** to heat (a liquid) to a temperature above its boiling point without boiling occurring. **3** to heat excessively; overheat.
▸**ˌsuperˈheater** *n*

superheavy (ˌsuːpəˈhɛvɪ) *adj Physics.* denoting or relating to elements of high atomic number (above 109) postulated to exist with special stability as a consequence of the shell model of the nucleus.

superheterodyne receiver (ˌsuːpəˈhɛtərəˌdaɪn) *n* a radio receiver that combines two radio-frequency signals by heterodyne action, to produce a signal above the audible frequency limit. Sometimes shortened to **superhet.** [C20: from SUPER(SONIC) + HETERODYNE]

superhigh frequency (ˈsuːpəˌhaɪ) *n* a radio-frequency band or radio frequency lying between 30 000 and 3000 megahertz.

superhuman ➊ (ˌsuːpəˈhjuːmən) *adj* **1** having powers above and beyond those of mankind. **2** exceeding normal human ability or experience.
▸**ˌsuperˈhumanly** *adv*

superimpose (ˌsuːpərɪmˈpəʊz) *vb* **superimposes, superimposing, superimposed.** (*tr*) **1** to set or place on or over something else. **2** (usually foll. by *on* or *upon*) to add (to).
▸**ˌsuperˌimpoˈsition** *n*

superinduce (ˌsuːpərɪnˈdjuːs) *vb* **superinduces, superinducing, superinduced.** (*tr*) to introduce as an additional feature, factor, etc.
▸**superinduction** (ˌsuːpərɪnˈdʌkʃən) *n*

superintend ➊ (ˌsuːpərɪnˈtɛnd) *vb* to undertake the direction or supervision (of); manage. [C17: from Church L *superintendere,* from L SUPER- + *intendere* to give attention to]
▸**ˌsuperinˈtendence** *n*

superintendent ➊ (ˌsuːpərɪnˈtɛndənt) *n* **1** a person who directs and manages an organization, office, etc. **2** (in Britain) a senior police officer higher in rank than an inspector but lower than a chief superintendent. **3** (in the US) the head of a police department. **4** *Chiefly US & Canad.* a caretaker, esp. of a block of apartments. ◆ *adj* **5** of or relating to supervision; superintending. [C16: from Church L *superintendens* overseeing]
▸**ˌsuperinˈtendency** *n*

superior ➊ (suːˈpɪərɪə) *adj* **1** greater in quality, quantity, etc. **2** of high or extraordinary worth, merit, etc. **3** higher in rank or status. **4** displaying a conscious sense of being above or better than others; supercilious. **5** (*often postpositive;* foll. by *to*) not susceptible (to) or influenced (by). **6** placed higher up; further from the base. **7** *Astron.* (of a planet) having an orbit further from the sun than the orbit of the earth. **8** (of a plant ovary) situated above the calyx and other floral parts. **9** *Printing.* (of a character) written or printed above the line; superscript. ◆ *n* **10** a person or thing of greater rank or quality. **11** *Printing.* a character set in a superior position. **12** (*often cap.*) the head of a community in a religious order. [C14: from L, from *superus* placed above, from *super* above]
▸**suˈperioress** *fem n* ▸**superiority** (suːˌpɪərɪˈɒrɪtɪ) *n*

> **USAGE NOTE** *Superior* should not be used with *than: he is a better* (not *a superior*) *poet than his brother; his poetry is superior to* (not *superior than*) *his brother's.*

THESAURUS

superficial *adj* **1** = **surface,** cosmetic, exterior, external, on the surface, peripheral, skin-deep, slight **2** = **hasty,** casual, cursory, desultory, facile, hurried, inattentive, nodding, passing, perfunctory, sketchy, slapdash **3** = **outward,** apparent, evident, ostensible, seeming **5** = **shallow,** empty, empty-headed, frivolous, lightweight, silly, trivial
Antonyms ≠ **surface:** deep, profound *adj* ≠ **hasty:** complete, comprehensive, detailed, exhaustive, in depth, major, penetrating, probing, substantial, thorough ≠ **shallow:** earnest, serious

superficiality *n* **4, 5** = **shallowness,** emptiness, lack of depth, lack of substance, triviality

superficially *adv* **3** = **at first glance,** apparently, at face value, externally, on the surface, ostensibly, to the casual eye

superfluity *n* **1** = **excess,** exuberance, glut, plethora, redundancy, superabundance, surfeit, surplus

superfluous *adj* **1** = **excess,** excessive, extra, in excess, left over, needless, on one's hands, pleonastic (*Rhetoric*), redundant, remaining, residuary, spare, superabundant, supererogatory, supernumerary, surplus, surplus to requirements, uncalled-for, unnecessary, unneeded, unrequired
Antonyms *adj* called for, essential, imperative, indispensable, necessary, needed, requisite, vital, wanted

superhuman *adj* **1** = **heroic,** herculean, phenomenal, prodigious, stupendous, valiant **2** = **supernatural,** divine, paranormal, preternatural

superintend *vb* = **supervise,** administer, control, direct, handle, inspect, look after, manage, overlook, oversee, run

superintendence *n* = **supervision,** care, charge, control, direction, government, guidance, inspection, management, surveillance

superintendent *n* **1** = **supervisor,** administrator, chief, conductor, controller, director, governor, inspector, manager, overseer

superior *adj* **1** = **better,** grander, greater, higher, more advanced, more expert, more extensive, more skilful, paramount, predominant, preferred, prevailing, surpassing, unrivalled **2** = **first-class,** a cut above, admirable, choice, de luxe, distinguished, excellent, exceptional, exclusive, fine, first-rate, good, good quality, high calibre, high-class, of the first order, running rings around (*inf.*), streets ahead (*inf.*), world-class **4** = **supercilious,** airy, condescending, disdainful, haughty, lofty, lordly, on one's high horse (*inf.*), patronizing, pretentious, snobbish,

superior court *n* **1** (in England) a higher court not subject to control by any other court except by way of appeal. See also **Supreme Court of Judicature. 2** (in several states of the US) a court of general jurisdiction ranking above the inferior courts and below courts of last resort.

superiority complex *n Inf.* an inflated estimate of one's own merit, usually manifested in arrogance.

superior planet *n* any of the six planets (Mars, Jupiter, Saturn, Uranus, Neptune, and Pluto) whose orbit lies outside that of the earth.

superl. *abbrev. for* superlative.

superlative Ⓣ (suːˈpɜːlətɪv) *adj* **1** of outstanding quality, degree, etc.; supreme. **2** *Grammar.* denoting the form of an adjective or adverb that expresses the highest or a very high degree of quality. In English this is usually marked by the suffix *-est* or the word *most,* as in *loudest* or *most loudly.* **3** (of language or style) excessive; exaggerated. ◆ *n* **4** a thing that excels all others or is of the highest quality. **5** *Grammar.* the superlative form of an adjective or adverb. **6** the highest degree; peak. [C14: from OF *superlatif,* via LL from L *superlātus* extravagant, from *superferre* to carry beyond]
▸**suˈperlatively** *adv* ▸**suˈperlativeness** *n*

superlunar (ˌsuːpəˈluːnə) *adj* beyond the moon; celestial.
▸**ˌsuperˈlunary** *adj*

superman (ˈsuːpəˌmæn) *n, pl* **supermen. 1** (in the philosophy of Nietzsche) an ideal man who would rise above good and evil and who represents the goal of human evolution. **2** any man of apparently superhuman powers.

supermarket (ˈsuːpəˌmɑːkɪt) *n* a large self-service store selling food and household supplies.

supermembrane (ˌsuːpəˈmɛmbreɪn) *n Physics.* a type of membrane postulated in certain theories of elementary particles that involve supersymmetry.

supermundane (ˌsuːpəˈmʌndeɪn) *adj* elevated above earthly things.

supernal (suːˈpɜːnᵊl, sjuː-) *adj Literary.* **1** divine; celestial. **2** of, from above, or from the sky. [C15: from Med. L *supernālis,* from L *supernus* that is on high, from *super* above]
▸**suˈpernally** *adv*

supernatant (ˌsuːpəˈneɪtᵊnt) *adj* **1** floating on the surface or over something. **2** *Chem.* (of a liquid) lying above a sediment or precipitate. [C17: from L *supernatāre* to float, from SUPER- + *natāre* to swim]
▸**ˌsupernaˈtation** *n*

supernatural Ⓣ (ˌsuːpəˈnætʃərəl) *adj* **1** of or relating to things that cannot be explained according to natural laws. **2** of or caused as if by a god; miraculous. **3** of or involving occult beings. **4** exceeding the ordinary; abnormal. ◆ *n* **5 the supernatural.** supernatural forces, occurrences, and beings collectively.
▸**ˌsuperˈnaturally** *adv* ▸**ˌsuperˈnaturalness** *n*

supernaturalism (ˌsuːpəˈnætʃərəlɪzəm) *n* **1** the quality or condition of being supernatural. **2** belief in supernatural forces or agencies as producing effects in this world.
▸**ˌsuperˈnaturalist** *n, adj* ▸**ˌsuperˌnaturalˈistic** *adj*

supernormal (ˌsuːpəˈnɔːməl) *adj* greatly exceeding the normal.
▸**supernormality** (ˌsuːpənɔːˈmælɪtɪ) *n* ▸**ˌsuperˈnormally** *adv*

supernova (ˌsuːpəˈnəʊvə) *n, pl* **supernovae** (-viː) *or* **supernovas.** a star that explodes owing to instabilities following the exhaustion of its nuclear fuel, becoming for a few days up to one hundred million times brighter than the sun. Cf. **nova.**

supernumerary Ⓣ (ˌsuːpəˈnjuːmərərɪ) *adj* **1** exceeding a regular or proper number; extra. **2** functioning as a substitute or assistant with regard to a regular body or staff. ◆ *n, pl* **supernumeraries. 3** a person or thing that exceeds the required or regular number. **4** a substitute or assistant. **5** an actor who has no lines, esp. a nonprofessional one. [C17: from LL *supernumerārius,* from L SUPER- + *numerus* number]

superorder (ˈsuːpərˌɔːdə) *n Biol.* a subdivision of a subclass.

superordinate (ˌsuːpərˈɔːdɪnɪt) *adj* **1** of higher status or condition. ◆ *n* **2** a person or thing that is superordinate. **3** a word the meaning of which includes the meaning of another word or words: *"red" is the superordinate of "scarlet" and "crimson".*

superphosphate (ˌsuːpəˈfɒsfeɪt) *n* **1** a mixture of the diacid calcium salt of orthophosphoric acid with calcium sulphate and small quantities of other phosphates: used as a fertilizer. **2** a salt of phosphoric acid formed by incompletely replacing its acidic hydrogen atoms.

superpose (ˌsuːpəˈpəʊz) *vb* **superposes, superposing, superposed.** (*tr*) *Geom.* to transpose (the coordinates of one geometric figure) to coincide with those of another. [C19: from F *superposer,* from L *superpōnere,* from *pōnere* to place]

superposition (ˌsuːpəpəˈzɪʃən) *n* **1** the act of superposing or state of being superposed. **2** *Geol.* the principle that in any sequence of sedimentary rocks that has not been disturbed the lowest strata are the oldest.

superpower (ˈsuːpəˌpaʊə) *n* **1** an extremely powerful state, such as the US. **2** extremely high power, esp. electrical or mechanical.
▸**ˈsuperˌpowered** *adj*

supersaturated (ˌsuːpəˈsætʃəˌreɪtɪd) *adj* **1** (of a solution) containing more solute than a saturated solution. **2** (of a vapour) containing more material than a saturated vapour.
▸**ˌsuperˌsatuˈration** *n*

superscribe (ˌsuːpəˈskraɪb) *vb* **superscribes, superscribing, superscribed.** (*tr*) to write (an inscription, name, etc.) above, on top of, or outside. [C16: from L *superscrībere,* from *scrībere* to write]
▸**superscription** (ˌsuːpəˈskrɪpʃən) *n*

superscript (ˈsuːpəˌskrɪpt) *Printing.* ◆ *adj* **1** (of a character) written or printed above the line; superior. Cf. **subscript.** ◆ *n* **2** a superscript or superior character. [C16: from L *superscriptus*]

supersede Ⓣ (ˌsuːpəˈsiːd) *vb* **supersedes, superseding, superseded.** (*tr*) **1** to take the place of (something old-fashioned or less appropriate); supplant. **2** to replace in function, office, etc.; succeed. **3** to discard or set aside or cause to be set aside as obsolete or inferior. [C15: via OF from L *supersedēre* to sit above]
▸**ˌsuperˈsedence** *n* ▸**supersedure** (ˌsuːpəˈsiːdʒə) *n* ▸**supersession** (ˌsuːpəˈsɛʃən) *n*

supersex (ˈsuːpəˌsɛks) *n Genetics.* a sterile organism in which the ratio between the sex chromosomes is disturbed.

supersonic (ˌsuːpəˈsɒnɪk) *adj* being, having, or capable of a velocity in excess of the velocity of sound.
▸**ˌsuperˈsonically** *adv*

supersonics (ˌsuːpəˈsɒnɪks) *n* (*functioning as sing*) **1** the study of supersonic motion. **2** a less common name for **ultrasonics.**

superstar (ˈsuːpəˌstɑː) *n* an extremely popular film star, pop star, etc.
▸**ˈsuperˌstardom** *n*

superstition (ˌsuːpəˈstɪʃən) *n* **1** irrational belief usually founded on ignorance or fear and characterized by obsessive reverence for omens, charms, etc. **2** a notion, act, or ritual that derives from such belief. **3** any irrational belief, esp. with regard to the unknown. [C15: from L *superstitiō,* from *superstāre* to stand still by something (as in amazement)]

superstitious (ˌsuːpəˈstɪʃəs) *adj* **1** disposed to believe in superstition. **2** of or relating to superstition.
▸**ˌsuperˈstitiously** *adv* ▸**ˌsuperˈstitiousness** *n*

superstore (ˈsuːpəˌstɔː) *n* a large supermarket.

superstratum (ˌsuːpəˈstrɑːtəm, -ˈstreɪ-) *n, pl* **superstrata** (-tə) *or* **superstratums.** *Geol.* a layer or stratum overlying another layer or similar structure.

superstring (ˈsuːpəˌstrɪŋ) *n Physics.* a type of string postulated in certain theories of elementary particles that involve supersymmetry.

superstructure (ˈsuːpəˌstrʌktʃə) *n* **1** the part of a building above its foundation. **2** any structure or concept erected on something else. **3** *Naut.* any structure above the main deck of a ship with sides flush with the sides of the hull. **4** the part of a bridge supported by the piers and abutments.
▸**ˈsuperˌstructural** *adj*

supersymmetry (ˌsuːpəˈsɪmɪtrɪ) *n Physics.* a symmetry of elementary particles having a higher order than that in the standard model, postulated to encompass the behaviour of both bosons and fermions.

supertanker (ˈsuːpəˌtæŋkə) *n* a large fast tanker of more than 275 000 tons capacity.

supertax (ˈsuːpəˌtæks) *n* a tax levied in addition to the basic tax, esp. on incomes above a certain level.

supertonic (ˌsuːpəˈtɒnɪk) *n Music.* **1** the second degree of a major or minor scale. **2** a key or chord based on this.

supervene (ˌsuːpəˈviːn) *vb* **supervenes, supervening, supervened.** (*intr*) **1** to follow closely; ensue. **2** to occur as an unexpected or extraneous development. [C17: from L *supervenīre* to come upon]
▸**ˌsuperˈvenience** *or* **supervention** (ˌsuːpəˈvɛnʃən) *n* ▸**ˌsuperˈvenient** *adj*

supervise Ⓣ (ˈsuːpəˌvaɪz) *vb* **supervises, supervising, supervised.** (*tr*) **1** to direct or oversee the performance or operation of. **2** to watch over so as to maintain order, etc. [C16: from Med. L *supervidēre,* from L SUPER- + *vidēre* to see]
▸**supervision** (ˌsuːpəˈvɪʒən) *n*

supervisor Ⓣ (ˈsuːpəˌvaɪzə) *n* **1** a person who manages or supervises. **2**

THESAURUS

stuck-up (*inf.*) ◆ *n* **10** = **boss** (*inf.*), chief, director, manager, principal, senior, supervisor
Antonyms *adj* ≠ **better:** inferior, less, lesser, lower, not as good, poorer, worse ≠ **first-class:** average, inferior, mediocre, no great shakes (*inf.*), ordinary, second-class, second-rate, substandard, unremarkable ◆ *n* ≠ **boss:** assistant, cohort (*chiefly US*), dogsbody, inferior, junior, lackey, minion, subordinate, underling

superiority *n* **1** = **supremacy,** advantage, ascendancy, excellence, lead, predominance, pre-eminence, preponderance, prevalence

superlative *adj* **1** = **supreme,** consummate, crack (*sl.*), excellent, greatest, highest, magnificent, matchless, of the first water, of the highest order, outstanding, peerless, stellar (*inf.*), surpassing, transcendent, unparalleled, unrivalled, unsurpassed
Antonyms *adj* abysmal, appalling, average, dreadful, easily outclassed, inferior, ordinary, poor, rotten, run-of-the-mill, undistinguished, unexceptional, uninspired, unspectacular

supernatural *adj* **1-4** = **paranormal,** abnormal, dark, ghostly, hidden, miraculous, mysterious, mystic, occult, phantom, preternatural, psychic, spectral, uncanny, unearthly, unnatural

supernumerary *adj* **1** = **extra,** excess, excessive, in excess, odd, redundant, spare, superfluous, surplus, unrequired

supersede *vb* **1, 2** = **replace,** displace, fill *or* step into (someone's) boots, oust, remove, supplant, take over, take the place of, usurp **3** = **set aside,** annul, overrule

supervise *vb* **1, 2** = **oversee,** administer, be on duty at, be responsible for, conduct, control, direct, handle, have *or* be in charge of, inspect, keep an eye on, look after, manage, preside over, run, superintend

supervision *n* **1, 2** = **superintendence,** administration, auspices, care, charge, control, direction, guidance, instruction, management, oversight, stewardship, surveillance

supervisor *n* **1, 2** = **boss** (*inf.*), administrator, chief, foreman, gaffer (*inf., chiefly Brit.*), inspec-

a foreman or forewoman. 3 (in some British universities) a tutor supervising the work, esp. research work, of a student. 4 (in some US schools) an administrator running a department of teachers.
▸'**super,visorship** *n* ▸'**super,visory** *adj*

supinate ('suːpɪ,neɪt, 'sjuː-) *vb* **supinates, supinating, supinated.** to turn (the hand and forearm) so that the palm faces up or forwards. [C19: from L *supīnāre* to lay on the back, from *supīnus* supine]
▸**,supi'nation** *n*

supine ❶ *adj* (suː'paɪn, sjuː-; 'suːpaɪn, 'sjuː-). **1** lying or resting on the back with the face, palm, etc., upwards. **2** displaying no interest or animation; lethargic. ◆ *n* ('suːpaɪn, 'sjuː-). **3** *Grammar.* a noun form derived from a verb in Latin, often used to express purpose with verbs of motion. [C15: from L *supīnus* rel. to *sub* under, up; (in grammatical sense) from L *verbum supīnum* supine word (from ?)]
▸**su'pinely** *adv* ▸**su'pineness** *n*

supp. *or* **suppl.** *abbrev. for* supplement(ary).

supper ('sʌpə) *n* **1** an evening meal, esp. a light one. **2** an evening social event featuring a supper. **3 sing for one's supper.** to obtain something by performing a service. [C13: from OF *soper*]
▸'**supperless** *adj*

supplant ❶ (sə'plɑːnt) *vb* (*tr*) to take the place of, often by trickery or force. [C13: via OF from L *supplantāre* to trip up, from *sub-* from below + *planta* sole of the foot]
▸**sup'planter** *n*

supple ❶ ('sʌpᵊl) *adj* **1** bending easily without damage. **2** capable of or showing easy or graceful movement; lithe. **3** mentally flexible; responding readily. **4** disposed to agree, sometimes to the point of servility. ◆ *vb* **supples, suppling, suppled. 5** *Rare.* to make or become supple. [C13: from OF *souple,* from L *supplex* bowed]
▸'**suppleness** *n*

supplejack ('sʌpᵊl,dʒæk) *n* **1** a North American twining woody vine that has greenish-white flowers and purple fruits. **2** a bush plant of New Zealand having tough climbing vines. **3** a tropical American woody vine having strong supple wood. **4** any of various other vines with strong supple stems. **5** *US.* a walking stick made from the wood of the tropical supplejack.

supplement ❶ *n* ('sʌplɪmənt). **1** an addition designed to complete, make up for a deficiency, etc. **2** a section appended to a publication to supply further information, correct errors, etc. **3** a magazine or section inserted into a newspaper or periodical, such as one issued every week. **4** *Geom.* **4a** either of a pair of angles whose sum is 180°. **4b** an arc of a circle that when added to another arc forms a semicircle. ◆ *vb* ('sʌplɪ,mɛnt). **5** (*tr*) to provide a supplement to, esp. in order to remedy a deficiency. [C14: from L *supplēmentum,* from *supplēre* to SUPPLY]
▸**,supplemen'tation** *n*

supplementary ❶ (,sʌplɪ'mɛntərɪ) *adj* **1** Also (*less commonly*): **supplemental** (,sʌplə'mɛntᵊl). forming or acting as a supplement. ◆ *n, pl* **supplementaries. 2** a person or thing that is a supplement.
▸**,supple'mentarily** *or* (*less commonly*) **,supple'mentally** *adv*

supplementary angle *n* either of two angles whose sum is 180°. Cf. **complementary angle.**

suppliant ('sʌplɪənt) *adj* **1** expressing entreaty or supplication. ◆ *n, adj* **2** another word for **supplicant.** [C15: from F *supplier* to beseech, from L *supplicāre* to kneel in entreaty]
▸'**suppliantly** *adv*

supplicant ❶ ('sʌplɪkənt) *or* **suppliant** *n* **1** a person who supplicates. ◆ *adj* **2** entreating humbly; supplicating. [C16: from L *supplicāns* beseeching]

supplicate ❶ ('sʌplɪ,keɪt) *vb* **supplicates, supplicating, supplicated. 1** to make a humble request to (someone); plead. **2** (*tr*) to ask for or seek humbly. [C15: from L *supplicāre* to beg on one's knees]
▸**,suppli'cation** *n* ▸'**suppli,catory** *adj*

supply[1] ❶ (sə'plaɪ) *vb* **supplies, supplying, supplied. 1** (*tr;* often foll. by *with*) to furnish with something required. **2** (*tr;* often foll. by *to* or *for*) to make available or provide (something desired or lacking): *to supply books to the library.* **3** (*tr*) to provide for adequately; satisfy: *who will supply their needs?* **4** to serve as a substitute, usually temporary, in (another's position, etc.): *there are no clergymen to supply the pulpit.* **5** (*tr*) *Brit.* to fill (a vacancy, position, etc.). ◆ *n, pl* **supplies. 6a** the act of providing or something provided. **6b** (*as modifier*): *a supply dump.* **7** (*often pl*) an amount available for use; stock. **8** (*pl*) food, equipment, etc., needed for a campaign or trip. **9** *Econ.* **9a** willingness and ability to offer goods and services for sale. **9b** the amount of a commodity that producers are willing and able to offer for sale at a specified price. Cf. **demand** (sense 9). **10** *Mil.* **10a** the management and disposal of food and equipment. **10b** (*as modifier*): *supply routes.* **11** (*often pl*) a grant of money voted by a legislature for government expenses. **12** (in Parliament and similar legislatures) the money voted annually for the expenses of the civil service and armed forces. **13a** a person who acts as a temporary substitute. **13b** (*as modifier*): *a supply vicar.* **14** a source of electricity, gas, etc. [C14: from OF *souppleier,* from L *supplēre* to complete, from *sub-* up + *plēre* to fill]
▸**sup'pliable** *adj* ▸**sup'plier** *n*

supply[2] ('sʌplɪ) *or* **supplely** ('sʌpᵊlɪ) *adv* in a supple manner.

supply-side economics (sə'plaɪ-) *n* (*functioning as sing*) a school of economic thought that emphasizes the importance to a strong economy of policies that remove impediments to supply.

support ❶ (sə'pɔːt) *vb* (*tr*) **1** to carry the weight of. **2** to bear (pressure, weight, etc.). **3** to provide the necessities of life for (a family, person, etc.). **4** to tend to establish (a theory, statement, etc.) by providing new facts. **5** to speak in favour of (a motion). **6** to give aid or courage to. **7** to give approval to (a cause, principle, etc.); subscribe to. **8** to endure with forbearance: *I will no longer support bad behaviour.* **9** to give strength to; maintain: *to support a business.* **10** (in a concert) to perform earlier than (the main attraction). **11** *Films, theatre.* **11a** to play a subordinate role to. **11b** to accompany (the feature) in a film programme. **12** to act or perform (a role or character). ◆ *n* **13** the act of supporting or the condition of being supported. **14** a thing that bears the weight or part of the weight of a construction. **15** a person who or thing that furnishes aid. **16** the means of maintenance of a family, person, etc. **17** a band or entertainer not topping the bill. **18** (often preceded by *the*) an actor or group of actors playing subordinate roles. **19** *Med.* an appliance worn to ease the strain on an injured bodily structure or part. **20** Also: **athletic support.** a more formal term for **jockstrap.** [C14: from OF *supporter,* from L *supportāre* to bring, from *sub-* up + *portāre* to carry]
▸**sup'portable** *adj* ▸**sup'portive** *adj*

supporter ❶ (sə'pɔːtə) *n* **1** a person who or thing that acts as a support. **2** a person who backs a sports team, politician, etc. **3** a garment or device worn to ease the strain on or restrict the movement of a bodily structure or part. **4** *Heraldry.* a figure or beast in a coat of arms depicted as holding up the shield.

supporting (sə'pɔːtɪŋ) *adj* **1** (of a role) being a fairly important but not leading part. **2** (of an actor or actress) playing a supporting role.

suppose ❶ (sə'pəʊz) *vb* **supposes, supposing, supposed.** (*tr; may take a clause as object*) **1** to presume (something) to be true without certain knowledge: *I suppose he meant to kill her.* **2** to consider as a possible sug-

THESAURUS

tor, manager, overseer, steward, superintendent

supervisory *adj* **1** = **managerial**, administrative, executive, overseeing, superintendent

supine *adj* **1** = **flat on one's back**, flat, horizontal, recumbent **2** = **lethargic**, apathetic, careless, heedless, idle, incurious, indifferent, indolent, inert, languid, lazy, listless, lymphatic, negligent, passive, slothful, sluggish, spineless, spiritless, torpid, uninterested
Antonyms *adj* ≠ **flat on one's back:** lying on one's face, prone, prostrate

supplant *vb* = **replace**, displace, oust, overthrow, remove, supersede, take over, take the place of, undermine, unseat

supple *adj* **1** = **pliant**, bending, elastic, plastic, pliable **2** = **flexible**, limber, lissom(e), lithe, loose-limbed
Antonyms ≠ **pliant:** firm, inflexible, rigid, stiff, taut, unbending, unyielding *adj* ≠ **flexible:** awkward, creaky (*inf.*), graceless, inflexible, stiff, unsupple

supplement *n* **1** = **addition**, added feature, addendum, add-on, appendix, codicil, complement, extra, insert, postscript, pull-out, sequel ◆ *vb* **5** = **add**, augment, complement, extend, fill out, reinforce, supply, top up

supplementary *adj* **1** = **additional**, accompanying, add-on, ancillary, auxiliary, complementary, extra, secondary, supplemental

supplicant *n* **1** = **petitioner**, applicant, suitor, suppliant ◆ *adj* **2** = **imploring**, begging, beseeching, craving, entreating, importunate, on bended knee

supplication *n* **1** = **plea**, appeal, entreaty, invocation, petition, pleading, prayer, request, solicitation, suit

supply[1] *vb* **1-3** = **provide**, afford, cater to *or* for, come up with, contribute, endow, equip, fill, furnish, give, grant, minister, outfit, produce, purvey, replenish, satisfy, stock, store, victual, yield ◆ *n* **7** = **store**, cache, fund, hoard, quantity, reserve, reservoir, source, stock, stockpile **8** *plural* = **provisions**, equipment, food, foodstuff, items, materials, necessities, provender, rations, stores

support *vb* **1, 2** = **bear**, bolster, brace, buttress, carry, hold, hold up, prop, reinforce, shore up, sustain, underpin, uphold **3** = **provide for**, cherish, finance, foster, fund, keep, look after, maintain, nourish, subsidize, sustain, take care of, underwrite **4** = **bear out**, attest to, authenticate, confirm, corroborate, document, endorse, lend credence to, substantiate, verify **5-7** = **help**, advocate, aid, assist, back, be a source of strength to, boost (someone's) morale, buoy up, champion, defend, encourage, espouse, forward, go along with, hold (someone's) hand, promote, second, side with, stand behind, stand up for, stick up for (*inf.*), strengthen, succour, take (someone's) part, take up the cudgels for, uphold **8** = **tolerate**, bear, brook, countenance, endure, put up with (*inf.*), stand (for), stomach, submit, suffer, thole (*dialect*), undergo ◆ *n* **13** = **help**, aid, approval, assistance, backing, blessing, championship, comfort, encouragement, espousal, friendship, furtherance, loyalty, moral support, patronage, promotion, protection, relief, succour, sustenance **14** = **prop**, abutment, back, brace, foundation, lining, pillar, post, shore, stanchion, stay, stiffener, underpinning **15** = **supporter**, backbone, backer, comforter, mainstay, prop, second, stay, tower of strength **16** = **upkeep**, keep, livelihood, maintenance, subsistence, sustenance
Antonyms *vb* ≠ **provide for:** live off, sponge off ≠ **bear out:** challenge, contradict, deny, refute ≠ **help:** go against, hinder, hold out against, oppose, reject, stab in the back, turn one's back on, undermine, walk away from ◆ *n* ≠ **help:** burden, denial, encumbrance, hindrance, impediment, opposition, refutation, rejection, undermining ≠ **supporter:** antagonist

supporter *n* **2** = **follower**, adherent, advocate, ally, apologist, champion, co-worker, defender, fan, friend, helper, henchman, patron, protagonist, sponsor, upholder, well-wisher
Antonyms *n* adversary, antagonist, challenger, competitor, foe, opponent, rival

supportive *adj* **6** = **helpful**, caring, encouraging, reassuring, sympathetic, understanding

suppose *vb* **1** = **presume**, assume, calculate (*US dialect*), conjecture, dare say, expect, guess

gestion for the sake of discussion, etc.: *suppose that he wins.* **3** (of theories, etc.) to imply the inference or assumption (of): *your policy supposes full employment.* [C14: from OF *supposer,* from Med. L *suppōnere,* from L: to substitute, from SUB- + *pōnere* to put]
▸**sup'posable** *adj* ▸**sup'poser** *n*

supposed ❶ (sə'pəʊzd, -'pəʊzɪd) *adj* **1** (*prenominal*) presumed to be true without certain knowledge. **2** (*prenominal*) believed to be true on slight grounds; highly doubtful. **3** (sə'pəʊzd). (*postpositive;* foll. by *to*) expected or obliged (to): *I'm supposed to be there.* **4** (sə'pəʊzd). (*postpositive; used in negative;* foll. by *to*) expected or obliged not (to): *you're not supposed to walk on the grass.*
▸**supposedly** (sə'pəʊzɪdlɪ) *adv*

supposition ❶ (ˌsʌpə'zɪʃən) *n* **1** the act of supposing. **2** a fact, theory, etc., that is supposed.
▸ˌ**suppo'sitional** *adj* ▸ˌ**suppo'sitionally** *adv*

suppositious (ˌsʌpə'zɪʃəs) *adj* deduced from supposition; hypothetical.
▸ˌ**suppo'sitiously** *adv* ▸ˌ**suppo'sitiousness** *n*

supposititious (səˌpɒzɪ'tɪʃəs) *adj* substituted with intent to mislead or deceive.
▸**supˌposi'titiously** *adv* ▸**supˌposi'titiousness** *n*

suppositive (sə'pɒzɪtɪv) *adj* **1** of, involving, or arising out of supposition. **2** *Grammar.* denoting a conjunction introducing a clause expressing a supposition, as for example *if, supposing,* or *provided that.* ◆ *n* **3** *Grammar.* a suppositive conjunction.
▸**sup'positively** *adv*

suppository (sə'pɒzɪtərɪ, -trɪ) *n, pl* **suppositories.** *Med.* a solid medication for insertion into the vagina, rectum, or urethra, where it melts and releases the active substance. [C14: from Med. L *suppositōrium,* from L *suppositus* placed beneath]

suppress ❶ (sə'prɛs) *vb* (*tr*) **1** to put an end to; prohibit. **2** to hold in check; restrain: *I was obliged to suppress a smile.* **3** to withhold from circulation or publication: *to suppress seditious pamphlets.* **4** to stop the activities of; crush: *to suppress a rebellion.* **5** *Electronics.* **5a** to reduce or eliminate (unwanted oscillations) in a circuit. **5b** to eliminate (a particular frequency or frequencies) in a signal. **6** *Psychiatry.* to resist consciously (an idea or a desire entering one's mind). [C14: from L *suppressus* held down, from *supprimere* to restrain, from *sub-* down + *premere* to press]
▸**sup'pressible** *adj* ▸**sup'pressive** *adj* ▸**sup'presser** *n*

suppressant (sə'prɛsənt) *adj* **1** tending to suppress or restrain an action or condition. ◆ *n* **2** a suppressant drug or agent: *a cough suppressant.*

suppression ❶ (sə'prɛʃən) *n* **1** the act or process of suppressing or the condition of being suppressed. **2** *Psychiatry.* the conscious avoidance of unpleasant thoughts.

suppressor (sə'prɛsə) *n* **1** a person or thing that suppresses. **2** a device fitted to an electrical appliance to suppress unwanted electrical interference to audiovisual signals.

suppurate ❶ ('sʌpjʊˌreɪt) *vb* **suppurates, suppurating, suppurated.** (*intr*) *Pathol.* (of a wound, sore, etc.) to discharge pus; fester. [C16: from L *suppūrāre,* from SUB- + *pūs* pus]
▸ˌ**suppu'ration** *n* ▸**'suppurative** *adj*

supra- *prefix* over, above, beyond, or greater than: *supranational.* [from L *suprā* above]

supraliminal (ˌsuːprə'lɪmɪnᵊl, ˌsjuː-) *adj* of or relating to any stimulus that is above the threshold of sensory awareness.
▸ˌ**supra'liminally** *adv*

supramolecular (ˌsuːprəmə'lɛkjʊlə, ˌsjuː-) *adj* **1** more complex than a molecule. **2** consisting of more than one molecule.

supranational (ˌsuːprə'næʃnᵊl, ˌsjuː-) *adj* beyond the authority or jurisdiction of one national government: *the supranational institutions of the EU.*
▸ˌ**supra'nationalism** *n*

supraorbital (ˌsuːprə'ɔːbɪtᵊl, ˌsjuː-) *adj Anat.* situated above the orbit.

suprarenal (ˌsuːprə'riːnᵊl, ˌsjuː-) *adj Anat.* situated above a kidney.

suprarenal gland *n* another name for **adrenal gland.**

supremacist (sʊ'prɛməsɪst, sjʊ-) *n* **1** a person who promotes or advocates the supremacy of any particular group. ◆ *adj* **2** characterized by belief in the supremacy of any particular group.
▸**su'prematism** *n*

supremacy ❶ (sʊ'prɛməsɪ, sjʊ-) *n* **1** supreme power; authority. **2** the quality or condition of being supreme.

supreme ❶ (sʊ'priːm, sjʊ-) *adj* **1** of highest status or power. **2** (*usually prenominal*) of highest quality, importance, etc. **3** greatest in degree; extreme: *supreme folly.* **4** (*prenominal*) final or last, ultimate: *the supreme judgment.* [C16: from L *suprēmus* highest, from *superus* that is above, from *super* above]
▸**su'premely** *adv*

Supreme Being *n* God.

Supreme Court *n* (in the US) **1** the highest Federal court. **2** (in many states) the highest state court.

Supreme Court of Judicature *n* (in England) a court formed in 1873 by the amalgamation of several superior courts into two divisions, the High Court of Justice and the Court of Appeal.

supreme sacrifice *n* **the.** the sacrifice of one's life.

Supreme Soviet *n* (in the former Soviet Union) **1** the bicameral legislature, comprising the **Soviet of the Union** and the **Soviet of the Nationalities. 2** a similar legislature in each former Soviet republic.

supremo ❶ (sʊ'priːməʊ, sjʊ-) *n, pl* **supremos.** *Brit. inf.* a person in overall authority. [C20: from SUPREME]

Supt *or* **supt** *abbrev. for* superintendent.

sur-[1] *prefix* over; above; beyond: *surcharge; surrealism.* Cf. **super-.** [from OF, from L SUPER-]

sur-[2] *prefix* a variant of **sub-** before *r: surrogate.*

sura ('sʊərə) *n* any of the 114 chapters of the Koran. [C17: from Ar. *sūrah* section]

surah ('sʊərə) *n* a twill-weave fabric of silk or rayon. [C19: from F pronunciation of *Surat,* a port in W India where orig. made]

sural ('sjʊərəl) *adj Anat.* of or relating to the calf of the leg. [C17: via NL from L *sūra* calf]

surbase ('sɜːˌbeɪs) *n* the uppermost part, such as a moulding, of a pedestal, base, or skirting.

surcease (sɜː'siːs) *Arch.* ◆ *n* **1** cessation or intermission. ◆ *vb* **surceases, surceasing, surceased. 2** to desist from (some action). **3** to cease or cause to cease. [C16: from earlier *sursesen,* from OF *surseoir,* from L *supersedēre* to sit above]

surcharge *n* ('sɜːˌtʃɑːdʒ). **1** a charge in addition to the usual payment, tax, etc. **2** an excessive sum charged, esp. when unlawful. **3** an extra and usually excessive burden or supply. **4** an overprint that alters the face value of a postage stamp. ◆ *vb* (sɜː'tʃɑːdʒ, 'sɜːˌtʃɑːdʒ), **surcharges, surcharging, surcharged.** (*tr*) **5** to charge an additional sum, tax, etc. **6** to overcharge (a person) for something. **7** to put an extra physical burden upon; overload. **8** to fill to excess; overwhelm. **9** *Law.* to insert credits that have been omitted in (an account). **10** to overprint a surcharge on (a stamp).

surcingle ('sɜːˌsɪŋgᵊl) *n* a girth for a horse which goes around the body, used esp. with a racing saddle. [C14: from OF *surcengle,* from *sur-* over + *cengle* a belt, from L *cingulum*]

surcoat ('sɜːˌkəʊt) *n* **1** a tunic, often embroidered with heraldic arms, worn by a knight over his armour during the Middle Ages. **2** (formerly) an outer coat or other garment.

surculose ('sɜːkjʊˌləʊs) *adj* (of a plant) bearing suckers. [C19: from L *surculōsus* woody, from *surculus* twig, from *sūrus* a branch]

surd (sɜːd) *n* **1** *Maths.* a number containing an irrational root, such as $2\sqrt{3}$; irrational number. **2** *Phonetics.* a voiceless consonant, such as (t). ◆ *adj* **3** of or relating to a surd. [C16: from L *surdus* muffled]

sure ❶ (ʃʊə, ʃɔː) *adj* **1** (sometimes foll. by *of*) free from hesitancy or uncertainty (with regard to a belief, conviction, etc.): *we are sure of the accuracy of the data; I am sure that he is lying.* **2** (foll. by *of*) having no

THESAURUS

(*inf., chiefly US & Canad.*), imagine, infer, judge, opine, presuppose, surmise, take as read, take for granted, think **2 = imagine,** believe, conceive, conclude, conjecture, consider, fancy, hypothesize, postulate, pretend

supposed *adj* **1 = presumed,** accepted, alleged, assumed, hypothetical, presupposed, professed, putative, reputed, rumoured **3** *usually with* **to = meant,** expected, obliged, required

supposedly *adv* **1 = presumably,** allegedly, at a guess, avowedly, by all accounts, hypothetically, ostensibly, professedly, purportedly, theoretically
Antonyms *adv* absolutely, actually, certainly, in actuality, in fact, really, surely, truly, undoubtedly, without a doubt

supposition *n* **1 = guess,** conjecture, doubt, guesswork, hypothesis, idea, notion, postulate, presumption, speculation, surmise, theory

suppress *vb* **2 = restrain,** conceal, contain, cover up, curb, hold in *or* back, hold in check, keep secret, muffle, muzzle, repress, silence, smother, stifle, sweep under the carpet (*inf.*), withhold **4 = stop,** beat down, check, clamp down on, conquer, crack down on, crush, drive underground, extinguish, overpower, overthrow, put an end to, quash, quell, quench, snuff out, stamp out, subdue, trample on
Antonyms *vb* encourage, foster, further, gee up, incite, inflame, promote, rouse, spread, stimulate, stir up, whip up

suppression *n* **1 = elimination,** check, clampdown, crackdown, crushing, dissolution, extinction, prohibition, quashing, termination **2 = inhibition,** smothering

suppurate *vb Pathology* **= discharge,** fester, gather, maturate, ooze, weep

supremacy *n* **2 = domination,** absolute rule, ascendancy, dominance, dominion, lordship, mastery, paramountcy, predominance, pre-eminence, primacy, sovereignty, supreme power, sway

supreme *adj* **1-4 = highest,** cardinal, chief, crowning, culminating, extreme, final, first, foremost, greatest, head, incomparable, leading, matchless, mother of all (*inf.*), paramount, peerless, predominant, pre-eminent, prevailing, prime, principal, sovereign, superlative, surpassing, top, ultimate, unsurpassed, utmost
Antonyms *adj* least, least successful, lowest, most inferior, most minor, most subordinate, most trivial, poorest, worst

supremo *n Brit. informal* **= head,** boss (*inf.*), commander, director, governor, leader, master, principal, ruler

sure *adj* **1 = certain,** assured, clear, confident, convinced, decided, definite, free from doubt, persuaded, positive, satisfied **3-6 = reliable,** accurate, dependable, effective, foolproof, honest, indisputable, infallible, never-failing, precise, sure-fire (*inf.*), tried and true, trustworthy, trusty, undeniable, undoubted, unerring, unfailing, unmistakable, well-proven **8 = inevitable,** assured, bound, guaranteed, ineluctable, inescapable, in the bag (*sl.*), irrevocable **10 = secure,** fast, firm, fixed, safe, solid, stable, staunch, steady
Antonyms *adj* ≠ **certain:** distrustful, doubtful, dubious, sceptical, unassured, uncertain, unconvinced, uneasy, unsure ≠ **reliable:** dodgy (*Brit., Austral., & NZ inf.*), dubious, fallible, iffy (*inf.*), un-

doubt, as of the occurrence of a future state or event: *sure of success.* **3** always effective; unfailing: *a sure remedy.* **4** reliable in indication or accuracy: *a sure criterion.* **5** (of persons) worthy of trust or confidence: *a sure friend.* **6** not open to doubt: *sure proof.* **7** admitting of no vacillation or doubt: *he is sure in his beliefs.* **8** bound to be or occur; inevitable: *victory is sure.* **9** (*postpositive*) bound inevitably (to be or do something); certain: *she is sure to be there.* **10** physically secure or dependable: *a sure footing.* **11 be sure.** (*usually imperative or dependent imperative; takes a clause as object or an infinitive,* sometimes with *to* replaced by *and*) to be careful or certain: *be sure and shut the door; be sure to shut the door.* **12 for sure.** without a doubt; surely. **13 make sure. 13a** (*takes a clause as object*) to make certain; ensure. **13b** (foll. by *of*) to establish or confirm power or possession (over). **14 sure enough.** *Inf.* as might have been confidently expected; definitely: often used as a sentence substitute. **15 to be sure. 15a** without doubt; certainly. **15b** it has to be acknowledged; admittedly. ◆ *adv* **16** (*sentence modifier*) *US & Canad. inf.* without question; certainly. ◆ *sentence substitute.* **17** *US & Canad. inf.* willingly; yes. [C14: from OF *seur,* from L *sēcūrus* SECURE]
►**'sureness** *n*

sure-fire *adj* (*usually prenominal*) *Inf.* certain to succeed or meet expectations; assured.

sure-footed *adj* **1** unlikely to fall, slip, or stumble. **2** not likely to err or fall.
►**,sure-'footedly** *adv* ►**,sure-'footedness** *n*

surely ➊ ('ʃʊəlɪ, 'ʃɔː-) *adv* **1** without doubt; assuredly. **2** without fail; inexorably (esp. in **slowly but surely**). **3** (*sentence modifier*) am I not right in thinking that?; I am sure that: *surely you don't mean it?* **4** *Rare.* in a sure manner. **5** *Arch.* safely; securely. ◆ *sentence substitute.* **6** *Chiefly US & Canad.* willingly; yes.

sure thing *Inf.* ◆ *sentence substitute.* **1** *Chiefly US.* used to express enthusiastic assent. ◆ *n* **2** something guaranteed to be successful.

surety ➊ ('ʃʊətɪ, 'ʃʊərɪtɪ) *n, pl* **sureties. 1** a person who assumes legal responsibility for another's debt or obligation and himself becomes liable if the other defaults. **2** security given against loss or damage or as a guarantee that an obligation will be met. **3** *Obs.* the quality or condition of being sure. **4 stand surety.** to act as a surety. [C14: from OF *seurte,* from L *sēcūritās* security]
►**'suretyship** *n*

surf (sɜːf) *n* **1** waves breaking on the shore or on a reef. **2** foam caused by the breaking of waves. ◆ *vb* (*intr*) **3** to take part in surfing. **4** to move rapidly and easily through a particular medium: *surfing the Internet.* **5** *Inf.* to be carried on top of something: *that guy's surfing the audience.* [C17: prob. var. of SOUGH]

surface ➊ ('sɜːfɪs) *n* **1a** the exterior face of an object or one such face. **1b** (*as modifier*): *surface gloss.* **2** the area or size of such a face. **3** material resembling such a face, with length and width but without depth. **4a** the superficial appearance as opposed to the real nature. **4b** (*as modifier*): *a surface resemblance.* **5** *Geom.* **5a** the complete boundary of a solid figure. **5b** a continuous two-dimensional configuration. **6a** the uppermost level of the land or sea. **6b** (*as modifier*): *surface transportation.* **7 come to the surface.** to emerge; become apparent. **8 on the surface.** to all appearances. ◆ *vb* **surfaces, surfacing, surfaced. 9** to rise or cause to rise to or as if to the surface (of water, etc.). **10** (*tr*) to treat the surface of, as by polishing, smoothing, etc. **11** (*tr*) to furnish with a surface. **12** (*intr*) to become apparent; emerge. **13** (*intr*) *Inf.* **13a** to wake up. **13b** to get up. [C17: from F, from *sur* on + *face* FACE]
►**'surfacer** *n*

surface-active *adj* (of a substance, esp. a detergent) capable of lowering the surface tension of a liquid. See also **surfactant.**

surface mail *n* mail transported by land or sea. Cf. **airmail.**

surface structure *n Generative grammar.* a representation of a string of words or morphemes as they occur in a sentence, together with labels and brackets that represent syntactic structure. Cf. **deep structure.**

surface tension *n* **1** a property of liquids caused by intermolecular forces near the surface leading to the apparent presence of a surface film and to capillarity, etc. **2** a measure of this.

surface-to-air *adj* of or relating to a missile launched from the surface of the earth against airborne targets.

surfactant (sɜː'fæktənt) *n* **1** Also called: **surface-active agent.** a substance, such as a detergent, that can reduce the surface tension of a liquid and thus allow it to foam or penetrate solids; a wetting agent. ◆ *adj* **2** having the properties of a surfactant. [C20: *surf(ace)-act(ive) a(ge)nt*]

surfboard ('sɜːf,bɔːd) *n* a long narrow board used in surfing.

surfboat ('sɜːf,bəʊt) *n* a boat with a high bow and stern and flotation chambers, equipped for use in rough surf.

surfcasting ('sɜːf,kɑːstɪŋ) *n* fishing from the shore by casting into the surf.
►**'surf,caster** *n*

surfeit ➊ ('sɜːfɪt) *n* **1** (usually foll. by *of*) an excessive amount. **2** overindulgence, esp. in eating or drinking. **3** disgust, nausea, etc., caused by such overindulgence. ◆ *vb* **4** (*tr*) to supply or feed excessively; satiate. **5** (*intr*) *Arch.* to eat, drink, or be supplied to excess. [C13: from F *sourfait,* from *sourfaire* to overdo, from SUR-[1] + *faire,* from L *facere* to do]

surfie ('sɜːfɪ) *n Austral. & NZ sl.* a young person whose main interest in life is surfing.

surfing ('sɜːfɪŋ) *n* the sport of riding towards shore on the crest of a wave by standing or lying on a surfboard.
►**'surfer** *or* **'surf,rider** *n*

surf mat *n Austral. inf.* a small inflatable rubber mattress used to ride on waves.

surg. *abbrev. for:* **1** surgeon. **2** surgery. **3** surgical.

surge ➊ (sɜːdʒ) *n* **1** a strong rush or sweep; sudden increase: *a surge of anger.* **2** the rolling swell of the sea. **3** a heavy rolling motion or sound: *the surge of the trumpets.* **4** an undulating rolling surface, as of hills. **5** a billowing cloud or volume. **6** *Naut.* a temporary release or slackening of a rope or cable. **7** a large momentary increase in the voltage or current in an electric circuit. **8** an instability or unevenness in the power output of an engine. ◆ *vb* **surges, surging, surged. 9** (*intr*) (of waves, the sea, etc.) to rise or roll with a heavy swelling motion. **10** (*intr*) to move like a heavy sea. **11** *Naut.* to slacken or temporarily release (a rope or cable) from a capstan or (of a rope, etc.) to be slackened or released and slip back. **12** (*intr*) (of an electric current or voltage) to undergo a large momentary increase. **13** (*tr*) *Rare.* to cause to move in or as if in a wave or waves. [C15: from L *surgere* to rise, from *sub-* up + *regere* to lead]
►**'surger** *n*

surgeon ('sɜːdʒən) *n* **1** a medical practitioner who specializes in surgery. **2** a medical officer in the Royal Navy. [C14: from Anglo-Norman *surgien,* from OF *cirurgien;* see SURGERY]

surgeonfish ('sɜːdʒən,fɪʃ) *n, pl* **surgeonfish** *or* **surgeonfishes.** any of various tropical marine spiny-finned fishes, having a compressed brightly coloured body with knifelike spines at the base of the tail.

surgeon general *n, pl* **surgeons general. 1** (esp. in the British and US armies and navies) the senior officer of the medical service. **2** the head of the US public health service.

surgery ('sɜːdʒərɪ) *n, pl* **surgeries. 1** the branch of medicine concerned with manual or operative procedures, esp. incision into the body. **2** the performance of such procedures by a surgeon. **3** *Brit.* a place where, or time when, a doctor, dentist, etc., can be consulted. **4** *Brit.* an occasion when an MP, lawyer, etc., is available for consultation. **5** *US & Canad.* an operating theatre. [C14: via OF from L *chirurgia,* from Gk *kheirurgia,* from *kheir* hand + *ergon* work]

surgical ('sɜːdʒɪkᵊl) *adj* of, relating to, involving, or used in surgery.
►**'surgically** *adv*

surgical boot *n* a specially designed boot or shoe that compensates for deformities of the foot or leg.

surgical spirit *n* methylated spirit used medically for sterilizing.

suricate ('sjʊərɪ,keɪt) *n* another name for **slender-tailed meerkat** (see **meerkat**). [C18: from F *surikate,* prob. from a native South African word]

surly ➊ ('sɜːlɪ) *adj* **surlier, surliest. 1** sullenly ill-tempered or rude. **2** (of an animal) ill-tempered or refractory. [C16: from obs. *sirly* haughty]
►**'surlily** *adv* ►**'surliness** *n*

surmise ➊ *vb* (sɜː'maɪz), **surmises, surmising, surmised. 1** (when *tr, may take a clause as object*) to infer (something) from incomplete or uncertain evidence. ◆ *n* (sɜː'maɪz, 'sɜːmaɪz). **2** an idea inferred from inconclusive evidence. [C15: from OF, from *surmettre* to accuse, from L *supermittere* to throw over]
►**surmisedly** (sɜː'maɪzɪdlɪ) *adv*

surmount ➊ (sɜː'maʊnt) *vb* (*tr*) **1** to prevail over; overcome. **2** to ascend and cross to the opposite side of. **3** to lie on top of or rise above. **4** to put something on top of or above. [C14: from OF *surmonter,* from SUR-[1] + *monter* to mount]
►**sur'mountable** *adj*

surname ('sɜː,neɪm) *n* **1** Also called: **last name, second name.** a family name as opposed to a first or Christian name. **2** (formerly) a descrip-

THESAURUS

dependable, unreliable, untrustworthy, vague ≠ **inevitable:** touch-and-go, unsure ≠ **secure:** insecure

surely *adv* **1, 2 = undoubtedly,** assuredly, beyond the shadow of a doubt, certainly, come what may, definitely, doubtlessly, for certain, indubitably, inevitably, inexorably, unquestionably, without doubt, without fail

surety *n* **1 = guarantor,** bondsman, hostage, mortgagor, sponsor **2 = security,** bail, bond, deposit, guarantee, indemnity, insurance, pledge, safety, warranty

surface *n* **1a = outside,** covering, exterior, façade, face, facet, plane, side, skin, superficies (*rare*), top, veneer ◆ *modifier* **4b = outward,** apparent, exterior, external, superficial ◆ *n* **8 on the surface = at first glance,** apparently, ostensibly, outwardly, seemingly, superficially, to all appearances, to the casual eye ◆ *vb* **12 = appear,** arise, come to light, come up, crop up (*inf.*), emerge, materialize, transpire

surfeit *n* **1, 2 = excess,** glut, overindulgence, plethora, satiety, superabundance, superfluity ◆ *vb* **4 = glut,** cram, fill, gorge, overfeed, overfill, satiate, stuff
Antonyms *n* ≠ **excess:** dearth, deficiency, insufficiency, lack, scarcity, shortage, shortness, want

surge *n* **1 = rush,** flood, flow, gush, outpouring, uprush, upsurge **2 = wave,** billow, breaker, efflux, roller, swell ◆ *vb* **9 = rush,** gush, rise, swell, tower, well forth **10 = roll,** billow, eddy, heave, swirl, undulate

surly *adj* **1 = ill-tempered,** bearish, brusque, churlish, crabbed, cross, crusty, curmudgeonly, grouchy (*inf.*), gruff, morose, perverse, shrewish, sulky, sullen, testy, uncivil, ungracious
Antonyms *adj* agreeable, cheerful, cheery, genial, good-natured, happy, pleasant, sunny

surmise *vb* **1 = guess,** come to the conclusion, conclude, conjecture, consider, deduce, fancy, hazard a guess, imagine, infer, opine, presume, speculate, suppose, suspect ◆ *n* **2 = guess,** assumption, conclusion, conjecture, deduction, hypothesis, idea, inference, notion, possibility, presumption, speculation, supposition, suspicion, thought

surmount *vb* **1 = overcome,** conquer, exceed,

tive epithet attached to a person's name to denote a personal characteristic, profession, etc.; nickname. ◆ *vb* **surnames, surnaming, surnamed.** **3** (*tr*) to furnish with or call by a surname.
▸**'sur,namer** *n*

surpass Ⓣ (sɜː'pɑːs) *vb* (*tr*) **1** to be greater than in degree, extent, etc. **2** to be superior to in achievement or excellence. **3** to overstep the limit or range of: *the theory surpasses my comprehension.* [C16: from F *surpasser,* from SUR-[1] + *passer* to PASS]
▸**sur'passable** *adj*

surpassing Ⓣ (sɜː'pɑːsɪŋ) *adj* **1** exceptional; extraordinary. ◆ *adv* **2** *Obs. or poetic.* (intensifier): *surpassing fair.*
▸**sur'passingly** *adv*

surplice ('sɜːplɪs) *n* a loose wide-sleeved liturgical vestment of linen, reaching to the knees, worn over the cassock by clergymen, choristers, and acolytes. [C13: from OF *sourpelis,* from Med. L *superpellīcium,* from SUPER- + *pellīcium* coat made of skins, from L *pellis* a skin]

surplus Ⓣ ('sɜːpləs) *n, pl* **surpluses. 1** a quantity or amount in excess of what is required. **2** *Accounting.* **2a** an excess of total assets over total liabilities. **2b** an excess of actual net assets over the nominal value of capital stock. **2c** an excess of revenues over expenditures. **3** *Econ.* **3a** an excess of government revenues over expenditures. **3b** an excess of receipts over payments on the balance of payments. ◆ *adj* **4** being in excess; extra. [C14: from OF, from Med. L *superplūs,* from L SUPER- + *plūs* more]

surprise Ⓣ (sə'praɪz) *vb* **surprises, surprising, surprised.** (*tr*) **1** to cause to feel amazement or wonder. **2** to encounter or discover unexpectedly or suddenly. **3** to capture or assault suddenly and without warning. **4** to present with something unexpected, such as a gift. **5** (foll. by *into*) to provoke (someone) to unintended action by a trick, etc. **6** (often foll. by *from*) to elicit by unexpected behaviour or by a trick: *to surprise information from a prisoner.* ◆ *n* **7** the act or an instance of surprising; the act of taking unawares. **8** a sudden or unexpected event, gift, etc. **9** the feeling or condition of being surprised; astonishment. **10** (*modifier*) causing, characterized by, or relying upon surprise: *a surprise move.* **11 take by surprise. 11a** to come upon suddenly and without warning. **11b** to capture unexpectedly or catch unprepared. **11c** to astonish; amaze. [C15: from OF, from *surprendre* to overtake, from SUR-[1] + L *prehendere* to grasp]
▸**sur'prisal** *n* ▸**sur'prised** *adj* ▸**surprisedly** (sə'praɪzɪdlɪ) *adv*

surprising Ⓣ (sə'praɪzɪŋ) *adj* causing surprise; unexpected or amazing.
▸**sur'prisingly** *adv*

surra ('sʊərə) *n* a tropical febrile disease of cattle, horses, camels, and dogs. [from Marathi, a language of India]

surrealism (sə'rɪə,lɪzəm) *n* (*sometimes cap.*) a movement in art and literature in the 1920s, which developed esp. from Dada, characterized by the evocative juxtaposition of incongruous images in order to include unconscious and dream elements. [C20: from F *surréalisme,* from SUR-[1] + *réalisme* realism]
▸**sur'real** *adj* ▸**sur'realist** *n, adj* ▸**sur,real'istic** *adj*

surrebutter (,sɜːrɪ'bʌtə) *n Law.* (in pleading) the plaintiff's reply to the defendant's rebutter.
▸**,surre'buttal** *n*

surrejoinder (,sɜːrɪ'dʒɔɪndə) *n Law.* (in pleading) the plaintiff's reply to the defendant's rejoinder.

surrender Ⓣ (sə'rɛndə) *vb* **1** (*tr*) to relinquish to another under duress or on demand: *to surrender a city.* **2** (*tr*) to relinquish or forego (an office, position, etc.), esp. as a voluntary concession to another: *he surrendered his place to a lady.* **3** to give (oneself) up physically, as to an enemy. **4** to allow (oneself) to yield, as to a temptation, influence, etc. **5** (*tr*) to give up (hope, etc.). **6** (*tr*) *Law.* to give up or restore (an estate), esp. to give up a lease before expiration of the term. **7 surrender to bail.** to present oneself at court at the appointed time after having been on bail. ◆ *n* **8** the act or instance of surrendering. **9** *Insurance.* the voluntary discontinuation of a life policy by its holder in return for a consideration (the **surrender value**). **10** *Law.* **10a** the yielding up or restoring of an estate, esp. the giving up of a lease before its term has expired. **10b** the giving up to the appropriate authority of a fugitive from justice. **10c** the act of surrendering or being surrendered to bail. **10d** the deed by which a legal surrender is effected. [C15: from OF *surrendre* to yield]

surreptitious Ⓣ (,sʌrəp'tɪʃəs) *adj* **1** done, acquired, etc., in secret or by improper means. **2** operating by stealth. [C15: from L *surreptīcius* furtive, from *surripere* to steal, from *sub-* secretly + *rapere* to snatch]
▸**,surrep'titiously** *adv* ▸**,surrep'titiousness** *n*

surrey ('sʌrɪ) *n* a light four-wheeled horse-drawn carriage having two or four seats. [C19: from *Surrey cart,* after *Surrey* where orig. made]

surrogate Ⓣ *n* ('sʌrəgɪt). **1** a person or thing acting as a substitute. **2** *Chiefly Brit.* a deputy, such as a clergyman appointed to deputize for a bishop in granting marriage licences. **3** (in some US states) a judge with jurisdiction over the probate of wills, etc. **4** (*modifier*) of, relating to, or acting as a surrogate: *a surrogate pleasure.* ◆ *vb* ('sʌrə,geɪt), **surrogates, surrogating, surrogated.** (*tr*) **5** to put in another's position as a deputy, substitute, etc. [C17: from L *surrogāre* to substitute]
▸**'surrogateship** *n* ▸**,surro'gation** *n*

surrogate motherhood *or* **surrogacy** ('sʌrəgəsɪ) *n* the role of a woman who bears a child on behalf of a childless couple, either by artificial insemination or implantation of an embryo.
▸**surrogate mother** *n*

surround Ⓣ (sə'raʊnd) *vb* (*tr*) **1** to encircle or enclose or cause to be encircled or enclosed. **2** to deploy forces on all sides of (a place or military formation), so preventing access or retreat. **3** to exist around: *the people who surround her.* ◆ *n* **4** *Chiefly Brit.* a border, esp. the area of uncovered floor between the walls of a room and the carpet or around an opening or panel. **5** *Chiefly US.* **5a** a method of capturing wild beasts by encircling the area in which they are believed to be. **5b** the area so encircled. [C15 *surrounden* to overflow, from OF *suronder,* from LL, from L SUPER- + *undāre* to abound, from *unda* a wave]
▸**sur'rounding** *adj*

surroundings Ⓣ (sə'raʊndɪŋz) *pl n* the conditions, scenery, etc., around a person, place, or thing; environment.

sursum corda ('sɜːsəm 'kɔːdə) *n* **1** *RC Church.* a Latin versicle meaning *Lift up your hearts,* said by the priest at Mass. **2** a cry of exhortation, hope, etc.

surtax ('sɜː,tæks) *n* **1** a tax, usually highly progressive, levied on the amount by which a person's income exceeds a specific level. **2** an additional tax on something that has already been taxed. ◆ *vb* **3** (*tr*) to assess for liability to surtax; charge with an extra tax.

surtitles ('sɜː,taɪtᵊlz) *pl n* brief translations of the text of an opera or play that is being sung or spoken in a foreign language, projected above the stage.

surtout ('sɜːtuː) *n* a man's overcoat resembling a frock coat, popular in the late 19th century. [C17: from F, from *sur* over + *tout* all]

surveillance Ⓣ (sɜː'veɪləns) *n* close observation or supervision over a person, group, etc., esp. one in custody or under suspicion. [C19: from F, from *surveiller* to watch over, from SUR-[1] + *veiller* to keep watch (from L *vigilāre;* see VIGIL)]
▸**sur'veillant** *adj, n*

survey Ⓣ *vb* (sɜː'veɪ, 'sɜːveɪ). **1** (*tr*) to view or consider in a comprehensive or general way. **2** (*tr*) to examine carefully, in order to or as if to appraise condition and value. **3** to plot a detailed map of (an area of land) by measuring or calculating distances and height. **4** *Brit.* to inspect a building to determine its condition and value. **5** to examine a vessel thoroughly in order to determine its seaworthiness. **6** (*tr*) to run a statistical survey on (incomes, opinions, etc.). ◆ *n* ('sɜːveɪ). **7** a comprehensive or general view. **8** a critical, detailed, and formal inspec-

THESAURUS

master, overpower, pass, prevail over, surpass, triumph over, vanquish

surpass *vb* **2** = **outdo**, beat, best, cap (*inf.*), eclipse, exceed, excel, go one better than (*inf.*), outshine, outstrip, override, overshadow, put in the shade, top, tower above, transcend

surpassing *adj* **1** = **supreme**, exceptional, extraordinary, incomparable, matchless, outstanding, phenomenal, rare, stellar (*inf.*), transcendent, unrivalled

surplus *n* **1** = **excess**, balance, remainder, residue, superabundance, superfluity, surfeit ◆ *adj* **4** = **extra**, excess, in excess, left over, odd, remaining, spare, superfluous, unused
Antonyms *n* ≠ **excess:** dearth, deficiency, deficit, insufficiency, lack, paucity, shortage, shortfall ◆ *adj* ≠ **extra:** deficient, falling short, inadequate, insufficient, lacking, limited, scant, scanty, scarce

surprise *vb* **1** = **amaze**, astonish, astound, bewilder, bowl over (*inf.*), confuse, disconcert, flabbergast (*inf.*), leave open-mouthed, nonplus, stagger, stun, take aback, take (someone's) breath away **2** = **catch unawares** *or* **off-guard**, burst in on, catch in the act *or* red-handed, catch napping, catch on the hop (*inf.*), come down on like a bolt from the blue, discover, spring upon, startle ◆ *n* **8** = **shock**, bolt from the blue, bombshell, eye-opener (*inf.*), jolt, revelation, start (*inf.*), turn-up for the books (*inf.*) **9** = **amazement**, astonishment, bewilderment, incredulity, stupefaction, wonder

surprised *adj* **1** = **amazed**, astonished, at a loss, disconcerted, incredulous, nonplussed, open-mouthed, speechless, startled, taken aback, thunderstruck, unable to believe one's eyes **2** = **taken by surprise**, caught on the hop, caught on the wrong foot (*inf.*)

surprising *adj* = **amazing**, astonishing, astounding, bewildering, extraordinary, incredible, jaw-dropping, marvellous, remarkable, staggering, startling, unexpected, unlooked-for, unusual, wonderful

surrender *vb* **1** = **give up**, abandon, cede, concede, deliver up, forego, part with, relinquish, renounce, resign, waive, yield **3** = **give in**, capitulate, cave in (*inf.*), give oneself up, give way, lay down arms, quit, show the white flag, submit, succumb, throw in the towel, yield ◆ *n* **8** = **submission**, capitulation, cave-in (*inf.*), relinquishment, renunciation, resignation, yielding
Antonyms *vb* ≠ **give in:** defy, fight (on), make a stand against, oppose, resist, stand up to, withstand

surreptitious *adj* **1, 2** = **secret**, clandestine, covert, fraudulent, furtive, sly, sneaking, stealthy, unauthorized, underhand, veiled
Antonyms *adj* blatant, conspicuous, frank, honest, manifest, obvious, open, overt, unconcealed, undisguised

surrogate *n* **1, 2** = **substitute**, deputy, proxy, representative, stand-in

surround *vb* **1** = **enclose**, close in on, encircle, encompass, envelop, environ, enwreath, fence in, girdle, hem in, ring **2** *Military* = **besiege**, beset, invest (*rare*), lay siege to

surrounding *adj* **3** = **nearby**, neighbouring

surroundings *pl n* = **environment**, background, environs, location, milieu, neighbourhood, setting

surveillance *n* = **observation**, care, control, direction, inspection, scrutiny, superintendence, supervision, vigilance, watch

survey *vb* **1** = **look over**, contemplate, examine, eyeball (*sl.*), eye up, inspect, observe, recce (*sl.*), reconnoitre, scan, scrutinize, supervise, view **2** = **estimate**, appraise, assess, eye up, measure, plan, plot, prospect, size up, take stock of, triangulate ◆ *n* **8** = **examination**, inspection, once-over (*inf.*), overview, perusal, scrutiny tion. **9** *Brit.* an inspection of a building to determine its condition and value. **10** a report incorporating the results of such an inspection. **11a** a body of surveyors. **11b** an area surveyed. [C15: from F *surveoir,* from SUR-[1] + *veoir* to see, from L *vidēre*]

surveying (sɜːˈveɪɪŋ) *n* **1** the study or practice of making surveys of land. **2** the setting out on the ground of the positions of proposed construction or engineering works.

surveyor (sɜːˈveɪə) *n* **1** a person whose occupation is to survey land or buildings. See also **quantity surveyor. 2** *Chiefly Brit.* a person concerned with the official inspection of something for purposes of measurement and valuation. **3** a person who carries out surveys, esp. of ships (**marine surveyor**) to determine seaworthiness, etc. **4** a customs official. **5** *Arch.* a supervisor.
▸**surˈveyorship** *n*

surveyor's measure *n* the system of measurement based on the **surveyor's chain** (66 feet) as a unit.

survival (səˈvaɪvᵊl) *n* **1** a person or thing that survives, such as a custom. **2a** the act or fact of surviving or condition of having survived. **2b** (*as modifier*): *survival kit.*

survival bag *n* a large plastic bag carried by climbers for use in an emergency as protection against exposure.

survivalist (səˈvaɪvəlɪst) *n Chiefly US.* **a** a person who believes in ensuring his personal survival of a catastrophic event by arming himself and often by living in the wild. **b** (*as modifier*): *survivalist weapons.*
▸**surˈvivalˌism** *n*

survival of the fittest *n* a popular term for **natural selection.**

survive ➊ (səˈvaɪv) *vb* **survives, surviving, survived. 1** (*tr*) to live after the death of (another). **2** to continue in existence or use after (a passage of time, adversity, etc.). **3** *Inf.* to endure (something): *I don't know how I survive such an awful job.* [C15: from OF *sourvivre,* from L *supervīvere,* from SUPER- + *vīvere* to live]
▸**surˈvivor** *n*

sus (sʌs) *Brit. sl.* ◆ *n* **1** short for **suspicion,** with reference to former police powers (**sus laws**) of detaining for questioning, searching, etc., any person suspected of criminal intent: *he was picked up on sus.* ◆ *vb* **susses, sussing, sussed. 2** a variant spelling of **suss** (sense 2).

susceptance (səˈsɛptəns) *n Physics.* the imaginary component of the admittance. [C19: from *suscept(ibility)* + -ANCE]

susceptibility ➊ (səˌsɛptəˈbɪlɪtɪ) *n, pl* **susceptibilities. 1** the quality or condition of being susceptible. **2** the ability or tendency to be impressed by emotional feelings. **3** (*pl*) emotional sensibilities; feelings. **4** *Physics.* **4a** Also called: **electric susceptibility.** (of a dielectric) the amount by which the relative permittivity differs from unity. **4b** Also called: **magnetic susceptibility.** (of a magnetic medium) the amount by which the relative permeability differs from unity.

susceptible ➊ (səˈsɛptəbᵊl) *adj* **1** (*postpositive;* foll. by *of* or *to*) yielding readily (to); capable (of): *hypotheses susceptible of refutation; susceptible to control.* **2** (*postpositive;* foll. by *to*) liable to be afflicted (by): *susceptible to colds.* **3** easily impressed emotionally. [C17: from LL *susceptibilis,* from L *suscipere* to take up]
▸**susˈceptibly** *adv*

sushi (ˈsuːʃɪ) *n* a Japanese dish consisting of small cakes of cold rice with a topping, esp. of raw fish. [Japanese]

suslik (ˈsʌslɪk) *or* **souslik** *n* a central Eurasian ground squirrel having large eyes and small ears. [from Russian]

suspect ➊ *vb* (səˈspɛkt). **1** (*tr*) to believe guilty of a specified offence without proof. **2** (*tr*) to think false, questionable, etc.: *she suspected his sincerity.* **3** (*tr; may take a clause as object*) to surmise to be the case; think probable: *to suspect fraud.* **4** (*intr*) to have suspicion. ◆ *n* (ˈsʌspɛkt). **5** a person under suspicion. ◆ *adj* (ˈsʌspɛkt). **6** causing or open to suspicion. [C14: from L *suspicere* to mistrust, from SUB- + *specere* to look]

suspend ➊ (səˈspɛnd) *vb* **1** (*tr*) to hang from above. **2** (*tr; passive*) to cause to remain floating or hanging: *a cloud of smoke was suspended over the town.* **3** (*tr*) to render inoperative or cause to cease, esp. temporarily. **4** (*tr*) to hold in abeyance; postpone action on. **5** (*tr*) to debar temporarily from privilege, office, etc., as a punishment. **6** (*tr*) *Chem.* to cause (particles) to be held in suspension in a fluid. **7** (*tr*) *Music.* to continue (a note) until the next chord is sounded, with which it usually forms a dissonance. See **suspension** (sense 11). **8** (*intr*) to cease payment, as from incapacity to meet financial obligations. [C13: from L *suspendere* from SUB- + *pendere* to hang]
▸**susˈpendible** *or* **susˈpensible** *adj* ▸**susˌpendiˈbility** *n*

suspended animation *n* a temporary cessation of the vital functions, as by freezing an organism.

suspended sentence *n* a sentence of imprisonment that is not served by an offender unless he commits a further offence during its currency.

suspender (səˈspɛndə) *n* **1** (*often pl*) *Brit.* **1a** an elastic strap attached to a belt or corset having a fastener at the end, for holding up women's stockings. **1b** a similar fastener attached to a garter worn by men in order to support socks. **2** (*pl*) the US and Canad. name for **braces. 3** a person or thing that suspends, such as one of the vertical cables in a suspension bridge.

suspender belt *n* a belt with suspenders hanging from it to hold up women's stockings.

suspense ➊ (səˈspɛns) *n* **1** the condition of being insecure or uncertain. **2** mental uncertainty; anxiety: *their father's illness kept them in a state of suspense.* **3** excitement felt at the approach of the climax: *a play of terrifying suspense.* **4** the condition of being suspended. [C15: from Med. L *suspensum* delay, from L *suspendere* to hang up]
▸**susˈpenseful** *adj*

suspense account *n Book-keeping.* an account in which entries are made until determination of their proper disposition.

suspension ➊ (səˈspɛnʃən) *n* **1** an interruption or temporary revocation: *the suspension of a law.* **2** a temporary debarment, as from position, privilege, etc. **3** a deferment, esp. of a decision, judgment, etc. **4** *Law.* a postponement of execution of a sentence or the deferring of a judgment, etc. **5** cessation of payment of business debts, esp. as a result of insolvency. **6** the act of suspending or the state of being suspended. **7** a system of springs, shock absorbers, etc., that supports the body of a wheeled or tracked vehicle and insulates it from shocks transmitted by the wheels. **8** a device or structure, usually a wire or spring, that serves to suspend or support something, such as the pendulum of a clock. **9** *Chem.* a dispersion of fine solid or liquid particles in a fluid, the particles being supported by buoyancy. See also **colloid. 10** the process by which eroded particles of rock are transported in a river. **11** *Music.* one or more notes of a chord that are prolonged until a subsequent chord is sounded, usually to form a dissonance.

suspension bridge *n* a bridge suspended from cables or chains that hang between two towers and are anchored at both ends.

suspensive (səˈspɛnsɪv) *adj* **1** having the power of deferment; effecting suspension. **2** causing, characterized by, or relating to suspense.
▸**susˈpensively** *adv* ▸**susˈpensiveness** *n*

suspensory (səˈspɛnsərɪ) *n, pl* **suspensories. 1** Also called: **suspensor.** *Anat.* a ligament or muscle that holds a structure or part in position. **2** *Med.* a bandage, sling, etc., for supporting a dependent part. ◆ *adj* **3** suspending or supporting. **4** *Anat.* (of a ligament or muscle) supporting or holding a structure or part in position.

suspicion ➊ (səˈspɪʃən) *n* **1** the act or an instance of suspecting; belief without sure proof, esp. that something is wrong. **2** the feeling of mistrust of a person who suspects. **3** the state of being suspected: *to be shielded from suspicion.* **4** a slight trace. **5 above suspicion.** in such a position that no guilt may be thought or implied, esp. through having an unblemished reputation. **6 on suspicion.** as a suspect. **7 under suspicion.** regarded with distrust. [C14: from OF *sospeçon,* from L *suspīciō* distrust, from *suspicere;* see SUSPECT]
▸**susˈpicional** *adj*

suspicious ➊ (səˈspɪʃəs) *adj* **1** exciting or liable to excite suspicion;

THESAURUS

survive *vb* **1-3** = **remain alive,** be extant, endure, exist, fight for one's life, hold out, keep body and soul together (*inf.*), keep one's head above water, last, live, live on, outlast, outlive, pull through, subsist

susceptibility *n* **1, 2** = **vulnerability,** liability, predisposition, proneness, propensity, responsiveness, sensitivity, suggestibility, weakness

susceptible *adj* **1, 2** *usually with* **to** = **liable,** disposed, given, inclined, open, predisposed, prone, subject, vulnerable **3** = **impressionable,** alive to, easily moved, receptive, responsive, sensitive, suggestible, tender
Antonyms *adj* ≠ **liable:** immune, insusceptible, invulnerable, resistant, unaffected by ≠ **impressionable:** insensitive, unaffected by, unmoved by, unresponsive

suspect *vb* **2** = **distrust,** doubt, harbour suspicions about, have one's doubts about, mistrust, smell a rat (*inf.*) **3** = **believe,** conclude, conjecture, consider, fancy, feel, guess, have a sneaking suspicion, hazard a guess, speculate, suppose, surmise, think probable ◆ *adj* **6** = **dubious,** dodgy, doubtful, fishy (*inf.*), iffy (*inf.*), open to suspicion, questionable
Antonyms ≠ **distrust:** have faith in, think innocent, trust *vb* ≠ **believe:** accept, be certain, be confident of, believe, buy (*sl.*), know, swallow (*inf.*) ◆ *adj* ≠ **dubious:** above suspicion, innocent, reliable, straightforward, trustworthy, trusty

suspend *vb* **1** = **hang,** append, attach, dangle, swing **3-5** = **postpone,** adjourn, arrest, cease, cut short, debar, defer, delay, discontinue, hold off, interrupt, lay aside, pigeonhole, put in cold storage, put off, shelve, stay, withhold
Antonyms *vb* ≠ **postpone:** carry on, continue, re-establish, reinstate, restore, resume, return

suspense *n* **1, 2** = **uncertainty,** anticipation, anxiety, apprehension, doubt, expectancy, expectation, indecision, insecurity, irresolution, tension, wavering

suspenseful *adj* **3** = **thrilling,** cliffhanging, exciting, gripping, hair-raising, spine-chilling

suspension *n* **1-3** = **postponement,** abeyance, adjournment, break, breaking off, deferment, delay, disbarment, discontinuation, interruption, moratorium, remission, respite, stay

suspicion *n* **1** = **idea,** conjecture, guess, gut feeling (*inf.*), hunch, impression, notion, supposition, surmise **2** = **distrust,** bad vibes (*sl.*), chariness, doubt, dubiety, funny feeling (*inf.*), jealousy, lack of confidence, misgiving, mistrust, qualm, scepticism, wariness **4** = **trace,** glimmer, hint, shade, shadow, *soupçon,* strain, streak, suggestion, tinge, touch **5 above suspicion** = **blameless,** above reproach, honourable, like Caesar's wife, pure, sinless, unimpeachable, virtuous

suspicious *adj* **1** = **suspect,** dodgy (*Brit., Austral., & NZ inf.*), doubtful, dubious, fishy (*inf.*), funny, irregular, of doubtful honesty, open to doubt *or* misconstruction, queer, questionable, shady (*inf.*) **2** = **distrustful,** apprehensive, doubtful, jealous, leery (*sl.*), mistrustful, sceptical, suspecting, unbelieving, wary
Antonyms *adj* ≠ **suspect:** above board, beyond suspicion, not open to question, open, straight, straightforward, unquestionable, upright ≠ **dis-**

questionable. **2** disposed to suspect something wrong. **3** indicative or expressive of suspicion.
▸**sus'piciously** *adv* ▸**sus'piciousness** *n*

suss ❶ (sʌs) *Sl.* ◆ *vb* (*tr*) **1** (often foll. by *out*) to attempt to work out (a situation, person's character, etc.), esp. using one's intuition. **2** Also: **sus.** to become aware of; suspect (esp. in **suss it**). ◆ *n* **3** sharpness of mind; social astuteness. [C20: shortened from SUSPECT]

sustain ❶ (sə'steɪn) *vb* (*tr*) **1** to hold up under; withstand: *to sustain great provocation.* **2** to undergo (an injury, loss, etc.); suffer: *to sustain a broken arm.* **3** to maintain or prolong: *to sustain a discussion.* **4** to support physically from below. **5** to provide for or give support to, esp. by supplying necessities: *to sustain one's family.* **6** to keep up the vitality or courage of. **7** to uphold or affirm the justice or validity of: *to sustain a decision.* **8** to establish the truth of; confirm. ◆ *n* **9** *Music.* the prolongation of a note, by playing technique or electronics. [C13: via OF from L *sustinēre* to hold up]
▸**sus'tained** *adj* ▸**sustainedly** (sə'steɪnɪdlɪ) *adv* ▸**sus'tainer** *n* ▸**sus'taining** *adj* ▸**sus'tainment** *n*

sustainable (sə'steɪnəbᵊl) *adj* **1** capable of being sustained. **2** (of economic development, energy sources, etc.) capable of being maintained at a steady level without exhausting natural resources or causing severe ecological damage: *sustainable development.*

sustaining pedal *n Music.* a foot-operated lever on a piano that keeps the dampers raised from the strings when keys are released, allowing them to continue to vibrate.

sustenance ❶ ('sʌstənəns) *n* **1** means of sustaining health or life; nourishment. **2** means of maintenance; livelihood. **3** Also: **sustention** (sə'stɛnʃən). the act or process of sustaining or the quality of being sustained. [C13: from OF *sostenance*, from *sustenir* to SUSTAIN]

sustentation (ˌsʌstɛn'teɪʃən) *n* a less common word for **sustenance.** [C14: from L *sustentātio*, from *sustentāre*, frequentative of *sustinēre* to SUSTAIN]

susurrate ('sjuːsəˌreɪt) *vb* **susurrates, susurrating, susurrated.** (*intr*) *Literary.* to make a soft rustling sound; whisper; murmur. [C17: from L *susurrāre* to whisper]
▸ˌ**susur'ration** *or* **susurrus** (sjuː'sʌrəs) *n*

sutler ('sʌtlə) *n* (formerly) a merchant who accompanied an army in order to sell provisions to the soldiers. [C16: from obs. Du. *soeteler*, ult. from MHG *sudelen* to do dirty work]

sutra ('suːtrə) *n* **1** *Hinduism.* Sanskrit sayings or collections of sayings on Vedic doctrine dating from about 200 A.D. onwards. **2** (*modifier*) *Hinduism.* **2a** of or relating to the last of the Vedic literary periods, from about 500 to 100 B.C.: *the sutra period.* **2b** of or relating to the sutras or compilations of sutras of about 200 A.D. onwards. **3** *Buddhism.* collections of dialogues and discourses of classic Mahayana Buddhism dating from the 2nd to the 6th century A.D. [C19: from Sansk.: list of rules]

suttee (sʌ'tiː, 'sʌtiː) *n* **1** the former Hindu custom whereby a widow burnt herself to death on her husband's funeral pyre. **2** a widow performing this. [C18: from Sansk. *satī* virtuous woman, from *sat* good]
▸**sut'teeism** *n*

suture ('suːtʃə) *n* **1** *Surgery.* **1a** catgut, silk thread, or wire used to stitch together two bodily surfaces. **1b** the surgical seam formed after stitching. **2** *Anat.* a type of immovable joint, esp. between the bones of the skull (**cranial suture**). **3** a seam or joining, as in sewing. **4** *Zool.* a line of junction in a mollusc shell. ◆ *vb* **sutures, suturing, sutured. 5** (*tr*) *Surgery.* to join (the edges of a wound, etc.) by means of sutures. [C16: from L *sūtūra*, from *suere* to sew]
▸**'sutural** *adj*

suzerain ('suːzəˌreɪn) *n* **1a** a state or sovereign exercising some degree of dominion over a dependent state, usually controlling its foreign affairs. **1b** (*as modifier*): *a suzerain power.* **2a** a feudal overlord. **2b** (*as modifier*): *suzerain lord.* [C19: from F, from *sus* above (from L *sursum* turned upwards) + *-erain*, as in *souverain* sovereign]

suzerainty ('suːzərəntɪ) *n, pl* **suzerainties. 1** the position, power, or dignity of a suzerain. **2** the relationship between suzerain and subject.

sv *abbrev. for:* **1** sailing vessel. **2** side valve. **3** sub verbo *or* voce. [L: under the word *or* voice]

svelte ❶ (svɛlt, sfɛlt) *adj* attractively or gracefully slim; slender. [C19: from F, from It. *svelto*, from *svellere* to pull out, from L *ēvellere*]

Svengali (svɛn'gɑːlɪ) *n* a person who controls another's mind, usually with sinister intentions. [after a character in George Du Maurier's novel *Trilby* (1894)]

SW 1 *symbol for* southwest(ern). **2** *abbrev. for* short wave.

Sw. *abbrev. for:* **1** Sweden. **2** Swedish.

swab (swɒb) *n* **1** *Med.* **1a** a small piece of cotton, gauze, etc., for use in applying medication, cleansing a wound, or obtaining a specimen of a secretion, etc. **1b** the specimen so obtained. **2** a mop for cleaning floors, decks, etc. **3** a brush used to clean a firearm's bore. **4** *Sl.* an uncouth or worthless fellow. ◆ *vb* **swabs, swabbing, swabbed. 5** (*tr*) to clean or medicate with or as if with a swab. **6** (*tr;* foll. by *up*) to take up with a swab. [C16: prob. from MDu. *swabbe* mop]
▸**'swabber** *n*

swaddle ('swɒdᵊl) *vb* **swaddles, swaddling, swaddled.** (*tr*) **1** to wind a bandage round. **2** to wrap (a baby) in swaddling clothes. **3** to restrain as if by wrapping with bandages; smother. ◆ *n* **4** *Chiefly US.* swaddling clothes. [C15: from OE *swæthel* swaddling clothes]

swaddling clothes *pl n* **1** long strips of linen or other cloth formerly wrapped round a newly born baby. **2** restrictions or supervision imposed on the immature.

swaddy *or* **swaddie** ('swɒdɪ) *n Brit. sl., old-fashioned.* a soldier. [C19: from E dialect *swad* country bumpkin, soldier]

swag (swæg) *n* **1** *Sl.* property obtained by theft or other illicit means. **2** *Sl.* goods; valuables. **3** an ornamental festoon of fruit, flowers, or drapery or a representation of this. **4** a swaying movement; lurch. **5** *Austral. & NZ inf.* a swagman's pack containing personal belongings, etc. **6 swags of.** *Austral. & NZ inf.* lots of. ◆ *vb* **swags, swagging, swagged. 7** *Chiefly Brit.* to lurch or sag or cause to lurch or sag. **8** (*tr*) to adorn or arrange with swags. [C17: ? of Scand. origin]

swage (sweɪdʒ) *n* **1** a shaped tool or die used in forming cold metal by hammering, pressing, etc. ◆ *vb* **swages, swaging, swaged. 2** (*tr*) to form (metal) with a swage. [C19: from F *souage*, from ?]
▸**'swager** *n*

swage block *n* an iron block with holes, grooves, etc., to assist in the cold-working of metal.

swagger ❶ ('swægə) *vb* **1** (*intr*) to walk or behave in an arrogant manner. **2** (*intr;* often foll. by *about*) to brag loudly. ◆ *n* **3** an arrogant gait or manner. ◆ *adj* **4** *Brit. inf., rare.* elegantly fashionable. [C16: prob. from SWAG]
▸**'swaggerer** *n* ▸**'swaggering** *adj* ▸**'swaggeringly** *adv*

swagger stick *or esp. Brit.* **swagger cane** *n* a short cane or stick carried on occasion mainly by army officers.

swaggie ('swægɪ) *n Austral. sl.* short for **swagman.**

swagman ('swægˌmæn, -mən) *n, pl* **swagmen.** *Austral. & NZ inf.* a tramp or vagrant worker who carries his possessions on his back. Also called: **swaggie.**

Swahili (swɑː'hiːlɪ) *n* **1** a language of E Africa that is an official language of Kenya and Tanzania and is widely used as a lingua franca throughout E and central Africa. Also called: **Kiswahili. 2** (*pl* **Swahilis** *or* **Swahili**) a member of a people speaking this language, living chiefly in Zanzibar. Also called: **Mswahili** (*pl* **Waswahili**). ◆ *adj* **3** of or relating to the Swahilis or their language. [C19: from Ar. *sawāhil* coasts]
▸**Swa'hilian** *adj*

swain (sweɪn) *n Arch. or poetic.* **1** a male lover or admirer. **2** a country youth. [OE *swān* swineherd]

swallow[1] ❶ ('swɒləʊ) *vb* (*mainly tr*) **1** to pass (food, drink, etc.) through the mouth to the stomach by means of the muscular action of the oesophagus. **2** (often foll. by *up*) to engulf or destroy as if by ingestion. **3** *Inf.* to believe gullibly: *he will never swallow such an excuse.* **4** to refrain from uttering or manifesting: *to swallow one's disappointment.* **5** to endure without retaliation. **6** to enunciate (words, etc.) indistinctly; mutter. **7** (often foll. by *down*) to eat or drink reluctantly. **8** (*intr*) to perform or simulate the act of swallowing, as in gulping. ◆ *n* **9** the act of swallowing. **10** the amount swallowed at any single time; mouthful. **11** *Rare.* another word for **throat** or **gullet.** [OE *swelgan*]
▸**'swallowable** *adj* ▸**'swallower** *n*

swallow[2] ('swɒləʊ) *n* any of various passerine songbirds having long pointed wings, a forked tail, short legs, and a rapid flight. [OE *swealwe*]

swallow dive *n* a type of dive in which the diver arches back while in the air, keeping his legs straight and together and his arms outstretched, finally entering the water headfirst. US and Canad. equivalent: **swan dive.**

swallow hole *n Chiefly Brit.* another word for **sinkhole** (sense 1).

swallowtail ('swɒləʊˌteɪl) *n* **1** any of various butterflies of Europe, having a tail-like extension of each hind wing. **2** the forked tail of a swallow or similar bird. **3** short for **swallow-tailed coat.**
▸**'swallow-ˌtailed** *adj*

swallow-tailed coat *n* another name for **tail coat.**

THESAURUS

trustful: believing, credulous, gullible, trustful, trusting, unsuspecting, unsuspicious

suss *vb* **1** *often foll. by* **out** *Brit. & NZ slang* = **work out**, calculate, clear up, figure out, find out, puzzle out, resolve, solve

sustain *vb* **1, 2** = **suffer**, bear, bear up under, endure, experience, feel, undergo, withstand **3** = **maintain**, continue, keep alive, keep going, keep up, prolong, protract **4** = **support**, bear, carry, keep from falling, keep up, uphold **5** = **keep alive**, aid, assist, comfort, foster, help, nourish, nurture, provide for, relieve **7, 8** = **uphold**, approve, confirm, endorse, ratify, validate, verify

sustained *adj* **3** = **continuous**, constant, nonstop, perpetual, prolonged, steady, unremitting
Antonyms *adj* broken, discontinuous, intermittent, irregular, periodic, spasmodic, sporadic

sustenance *n* **1** = **nourishment**, aliment, comestibles, daily bread, eatables, edibles, food, provender, provisions, rations, refection, refreshments, victuals **2** = **livelihood**, maintenance, subsistence, support

svelte *adj* = **slender**, graceful, lissom(e), lithe, slinky, sylphlike, willowy

swagger *vb* **1, 2** = **show off** (*inf.*), bluster, boast, brag, bully, gasconade (*rare*), hector, hot-dog (*chiefly US*), parade, prance, strut, swank (*inf.*) ◆ *n* **3** = **ostentation**, arrogance, bluster, braggadocio, display, gasconade (*rare*), pomposity, show, showing off (*inf.*), swank (*inf.*), swashbuckling

swallow[1] *vb* **1** = **gulp**, absorb, consume, devour, down (*inf.*), drink, eat, ingest, swig (*inf.*), swill, wash down **2** *often foll. by* **up** = **absorb**, assimilate, consume, engulf, envelop, overrun, overwhelm, use up **3** *Informal* = **believe**, accept, buy (*sl.*), fall for, take (something) as gospel **4** = **hold in**, choke back, repress

swam (swæm) *vb* the past tense of **swim**.
swami ('swɑːmɪ) *n, pl* **swamies** *or* **swamis**. (in India) a title of respect for a Hindu saint or religious teacher. [C18: from Hindi *svāmī*, from Sansk. *svāmin* master, from *sva* one's own]
swamp ❶ (swɒmp) *n* **1** permanently waterlogged ground that is usually overgrown and sometimes partly forested. Cf. **marsh**. ◆ *vb* **2** to drench or submerge or be drenched or submerged. **3** *Naut.* to cause (a boat) to sink or fill with water or (of a boat) to sink or fill with water. **4** to overburden or overwhelm or be overburdened or overwhelmed, as by excess work or great numbers. **5** (*tr*) to render helpless. [C17: prob. from MDu. *somp*]
▸ **'swampy** *adj*
swamp boat *n* a shallow-draught boat powered by an aeroplane engine mounted on a raised structure for use in swamps. Also called: **airboat**.
swamp cypress *n* a North American deciduous coniferous tree that grows in swamps. Also called: **bald cypress**.
swamp fever *n* **1** Also called: **equine infectious anaemia**. a viral disease of horses. **2** *US.* another name for **malaria**.
swampland ('swɒmpˌlænd) *n* a permanently waterlogged area; marshland.
swan (swɒn) *n* **1** any of various large aquatic birds having a long neck and usually a white plumage. **2** *Rare, literary.* **2a** a poet. **2b** (*cap. when part of a title or epithet*): *the Swan of Avon* (Shakespeare). ◆ *vb* **swans, swanning, swanned. 3** (*intr;* usually foll. by *around* or *about*) *Inf.* to wander idly. [OE]
▸ **'swanˌlike** *adj*
swan dive *n* the US and Canad. name for **swallow dive**.
swank ❶ (swæŋk) *Inf.* ◆ *vb* **1** (*intr*) to show off or swagger. ◆ *n* **2** Also called: **swankpot**. *Brit.* a swaggering or conceited person. **3** *Chiefly US.* showy elegance or style. **4** swagger; ostentation. ◆ *adj* **5** another word (esp. US) for **swanky**. [C19: ?from MHG *swanken* to sway]
swanky ❶ ('swæŋkɪ) *adj* **swankier, swankiest**. *Inf.* **1** expensive and showy; stylish: *a swanky hotel.* **2** boastful or conceited.
▸ **'swankily** *adv* ▸ **'swankiness** *n*
swan neck *n* a tube, rail, etc., curved like a swan's neck.
swannery ('swɒnərɪ) *n, pl* **swanneries**. a place where swans are kept and bred.
swan's-down *n* **1** the fine soft down feathers of a swan, used to trim powder puffs, clothes, etc. **2** a thick soft fabric of wool with silk, cotton, or rayon, used for infants' clothing, etc. **3** a cotton fabric with a heavy nap.
swan song *n* **1** the last act, publication, etc., of a person before retirement or death. **2** the song that a dying swan is said to sing.
swan-upping *n Brit.* **1** the practice or action of marking nicks in swans' beaks as a sign of ownership. **2** the annual swan-upping of royal cygnets on the River Thames.
swap ❶ *or* **swop** (swɒp) *vb* **swaps, swapping, swapped** *or* **swops, swopping, swopped. 1** to trade or exchange (something or someone) for another. ◆ *n* **2** an exchange. **3** something that is exchanged. **4** *Finance.* Also called: **swap option, swaption**. a contract in which the parties to it exchange liabilities on outstanding debts, often exchanging fixed-interest-rate for floating-rate debts (**debt swap**), either as a means of debt management or in trading (**swap trading**). [C14 (in the sense: to shake hands on a bargain, strike): prob. imit.]
▸ **'swapper** *or* **'swopper** *n*
SWAPO *or* **Swapo** ('swɑːpəʊ) *n acronym for* South-West Africa People's Organization.
swaption ('swɒpʃən) *n* another name for **swap** (sense 4).
swaraj (swə'rɑːdʒ) *n* (in British India) self-government; independence. [C20: from Sansk. *svarāj*, from *sva* self + *rājya* rule]
▸ **swa'rajism** *n* ▸ **swa'rajist** *n, adj*
sward (swɔːd) *n* **1** turf or grass or a stretch of turf or grass. ◆ *vb* **2** to cover or become covered with grass. [OE *sweard* skin]
swarf (swɔːf, swɑːf) *n* material removed by cutting or grinding tools in the machining of metals, stone, etc. [C16: of Scand. origin]
swarm[1] ❶ (swɔːm) *n* **1** a group of bees, led by a queen, that has left the parent hive to start a new colony. **2** a large mass of small animals, esp. insects. **3** a throng or mass, esp. when moving or in turmoil. ◆ *vb* **4** (*intr*) (of small animals, esp. bees) to move in or form a swarm. **5** (*intr*) to congregate, move about or proceed in large numbers. **6** (when *intr*, often foll. by *with*) to overrun or be overrun (with): *swarming with rats.* **7** (*tr*) to cause to swarm. [OE *swearm*]
swarm[2] (swɔːm) *vb* (when *intr*, usually foll. by *up*) to climb (a ladder, etc.) by gripping with the hands and feet: *the boys swarmed up the rigging.* [C16: from ?]
swart (swɔːt) *or* **swarth** (swɔːθ) *adj Arch. or dialect.* swarthy. [OE *sweart*]
swarthy ❶ ('swɔːðɪ) *adj* **swarthier, swarthiest**. dark-hued or dark-complexioned. [C16: from obs. *swarty*]
▸ **'swarthily** *adv* ▸ **'swarthiness** *n*
swash (swɒʃ) *vb* **1** (*intr*) (esp. of water or things in water) to wash or move with noisy splashing. **2** (*tr*) to dash (a liquid, esp. water) against or upon. **3** (*intr*) *Arch.* to swagger. ◆ *n* **4** Also called: **send**. the dashing movement or sound of water, as of waves on a beach. **5** Also called: **swash channel**. a channel of moving water cutting through or running behind a sandbank. **6** *Arch.* swagger or bluster. [C16: prob. imit.]
swashbuckler ❶ ('swɒʃˌbʌklə) *n* **1** a swaggering or flamboyant adventurer. **2** a film, book, play, etc., depicting excitement and adventure, esp. in a historical setting. [C16: from SWASH (in archaic sense: to make the noise of a sword striking a shield) + BUCKLER]
▸ **'swashˌbuckling** *adj*
swash letter *n Printing.* a decorative letter, esp. an ornamental italic capital. [C17: from *aswash* aslant]
swastika ❶ ('swɒstɪkə) *n* **1** a primitive religious symbol or ornament in the shape of a Greek cross, usually having the ends of the arms bent at right angles. **2** this symbol with clockwise arms, the emblem of Nazi Germany. [C19: from Sansk. *svastika*, from *svasti* prosperity; from belief that it brings good luck]
swat (swɒt) *vb* **swats, swatting, swatted**. (*tr*) **1** to strike or hit sharply: *to swat a fly.* ◆ *n* **2** a sharp or violent blow. ◆ Also: **swot**. [C17: N English dialect & US var. of SQUAT]
▸ **'swatter** *n*
swatch (swɒtʃ) *n* **1** a sample of cloth or other material. **2** a number of such samples, usually fastened together in book form. [C16: Scot. & N English, from ?]
swath (swɔːθ) *or* **swathe** (sweɪð) *n, pl* **swaths** (swɔːðz) *or* **swathes**. **1** the width of one sweep of a scythe or of the blade of a mowing machine. **2** the strip cut by these in one course. **3** the quantity of cut grass, hay, etc., left in one such course. **4** a long narrow strip or belt. [OE *swæth*]
swathe ❶ (sweɪð) *vb* **swathes, swathing, swathed**. (*tr*) **1** to bandage (a wound, limb, etc.), esp. completely. **2** to wrap a band, garment, etc., around, esp. so as to cover completely; swaddle. **3** to envelop. ◆ *n* **4** a bandage or wrapping. **5** a variant spelling of **swath**. [OE *swathian*]
sway ❶ (sweɪ) *vb* **1** (*usually intr*) to swing or cause to swing to and fro: *the door swayed in the wind.* **2** (*usually intr*) to lean or incline or cause to lean or incline to one side or in different directions in turn. **3** (*usually intr*) to vacillate or cause to vacillate between two or more opinions. **4** to be influenced or swerve or influence or cause to swerve to or from a purpose or opinion. **5** *Arch. or poetic.* to rule or wield power (over). ◆ *n* **6** control; power. **7** a swinging or leaning movement. **8** *Arch.* dominion; governing authority. **9 hold sway**. to be master; reign. [C16: prob. from ON *sveigja* to bend]
sway-back *n* an abnormal sagging or concavity of the spine in horses. ▸ **'sway-ˌbacked** *adj*
swear ❶ (swɛə) *vb* **swears, swearing, swore, sworn**. **1** to declare or affirm (a statement) as true, esp. by invoking a deity, etc., as witness. **2** (foll. by *by*) **2a** to invoke (a deity, etc.) by name as a witness or guarantee to an oath. **2b** to trust implicitly; have complete confidence (in). **3** (*intr;* often foll. by *at*) to curse, blaspheme, or use swearwords. **4** (when *tr*, *may take a clause as object or an infinitive*) to promise solemnly on oath; vow. **5** (*tr*) to assert or affirm with great emphasis or earnestness. **6**

THESAURUS

swamp *n* **1** = **bog**, everglade(s) (*US*), fen, marsh, mire, morass, moss (*Scot. & N English dialect*), quagmire, slough ◆ *vb* **3** *Nautical* = **flood**, capsize, drench, engulf, inundate, overwhelm, sink, submerge, swallow up, upset, wash over, waterlog **4** = **overwhelm**, beset, besiege, deluge, engulf, flood, inundate, overload, snow under, submerge
swampy *adj* **1** = **boggy**, fenny, marish (*obs.*), marshy, miry, quaggy, waterlogged, wet
swank *Informal* ◆ *vb* **1** = **show off** (*inf.*), give oneself airs, hot-dog (*chiefly US*), posture, put on side (*Brit. sl.*), swagger ◆ *n* **2** = **show-off** (*inf.*), attitudinizer, braggadocio, hot dog (*chiefly US*), poser, poseur, swankpot (*inf.*), swashbuckler **4** = **boastfulness**, display, ostentation, show, swagger, vainglory
swanky *adj* **1** *Informal* = **ostentatious**, de luxe, exclusive, expensive, fancy, fashionable, flash, flashy, glamorous, glitzy (*sl.*), gorgeous, grand, lavish, luxurious, plush (*inf.*), posh (*inf., chiefly Brit.*), rich, ritzy (*sl.*), showy, smart, stylish, sumptuous, swish (*inf., chiefly Brit.*)
Antonyms *adj* discreet, humble, inconspicuous, low-key, low-profile, modest, subdued, unassuming, unostentatious, unpretentious
swap *vb* **1** = **exchange**, bandy, barter, interchange, switch, trade, traffic
swarm[1] *n* **3** = **multitude**, army, bevy, concourse, crowd, drove, flock, herd, horde, host, mass, myriad, shoal, throng ◆ *vb* **5** = **crowd**, congregate, flock, mass, stream, throng **6** = **teem**, abound, be alive, be infested, be overrun, bristle, crawl
swarthy *adj* = **dark-skinned**, black, brown, dark, dark-complexioned, dusky, swart (*arch.*), tawny
swashbuckling *adj* **1** = **dashing**, bold, daredevil, flamboyant, gallant, mettlesome, roisterous, spirited, swaggering
swastika *n* **1** = **crooked cross**, fylfot
swathe *vb* **1-3** = **wrap**, bandage, bind, bundle up, cloak, drape, envelop, enwrap, fold, furl, lap, muffle up, sheathe, shroud, swaddle
sway *vb* **1** = **bend**, fluctuate, incline, lean, lurch, oscillate, rock, roll, swing, wave **4** = **influence**, affect, control, direct, dominate, govern, guide, induce, persuade, prevail on, win over ◆ *n* **6** = **power**, ascendency, authority, clout (*inf.*), command, control, dominion, government, influence, jurisdiction, predominance, rule, sovereignty **9 hold sway** = **prevail**, predominate, reign, rule, run
swear *vb* **2b** *with* **by** = **trust**, depend on, have confidence in, rely on **3** = **curse**, be foul-mouthed, blaspheme, cuss (*inf.*), imprecate, take the Lord's name in vain, turn the air blue (*inf.*), utter profanities **4** = **vow**, attest, avow, depose, give one's word, pledge oneself, promise, state under oath, take an oath, testify, warrant **5** = **declare**, affirm, assert, asseverate, swear blind

(*intr*) to give evidence or make any statement or solemn declaration on oath. **7** to take an oath in order to add force or solemnity to (a statement or declaration). ◆ *n* **8** a period of swearing. [OE *swerian*]
▸ **'swearer** *n*

swear in *vb* (*tr, adv*) to administer an oath to (a person) on his assuming office, entering the witness box to give evidence, etc.

swear off *vb* (*intr, prep*) to promise to abstain from something: *to swear off drink.*

swearword ❶ ('swɛə,wɜːd) *n* a socially taboo word of a profane, obscene, or insulting character.

sweat ❶ (swɛt) *n* **1** the secretion from the sweat glands, esp. when profuse and visible, as during strenuous activity, from excessive heat, etc.; perspiration. **2** the act or process of secreting this fluid. **3** the act of inducing the exudation of moisture. **4** drops of moisture given forth or gathered on the surface of something. **5** *Inf.* a state or condition of worry or eagerness (esp. in **in a sweat**). **6** *Sl.* drudgery or hard labour: *mowing lawns is a real sweat!* **7** *Sl., chiefly Brit.* a soldier, esp. one who is old and experienced. **8 no sweat!** *Sl.* an expression conveying consent or assurance. ◆ *vb* **sweats, sweating, sweat** *or* **sweated. 9** to secrete (sweat) through the pores of the skin, esp. profusely; perspire. **10** (*tr*) to make wet or stain with perspiration. **11** to give forth or cause to give forth (moisture) in droplets: *the maple sweats sap.* **12** (*intr*) to collect and condense moisture on an outer surface: *a glass of beer sweating.* **13** (*intr*) (of a liquid) to pass through a porous surface in droplets. **14** (of tobacco leaves, hay, etc.) to exude moisture and, sometimes, begin to ferment or to cause (tobacco leaves, etc.) to exude moisture. **15** (*tr*) to heat (food, esp. vegetables) slowly in butter in a tightly closed saucepan. **16** (*tr*) to join (pieces of metal) by pressing together and heating. **17** (*tr*) to heat (solder) until it melts. **18** (*tr*) to heat (partially fused metal) to extract an easily fusible constituent. **19** *Inf.* to suffer anxiety, impatience, or distress. **20** *Inf.* to overwork or be overworked. **21** (*tr*) *Inf.* to employ at very low wages and under bad conditions. **22** (*tr*) *Inf.* to extort, esp. by torture: *to sweat information out of a captive.* **23** (*intr*) *Inf.* to suffer punishment: *you'll sweat for this!* **24 sweat blood.** *Inf.* **24a** to work very hard. **24b** to be filled with anxiety or impatience. ◆ See also **sweat off, sweat out, sweats.** [OE *swætan* to sweat, from *swāt* sweat]

sweatband ('swɛt,bænd) *n* **1** a band of material set in a hat or cap to protect it from sweat. **2** a piece of cloth tied around the forehead to keep sweat out of the eyes or around the wrist to keep the hands dry, as in sports.

sweated ('swɛtɪd) *adj* **1** made by exploited labour: *sweated goods.* **2** (of workers, etc.) forced to work in poor conditions for low pay.

sweater ('swɛtə) *n* **1** a garment made of knitted or crocheted material covering the upper part of the body, esp. a heavy one worn for warmth. **2** a person or thing that sweats. **3** an employer who overworks and underpays his employees.

sweat gland *n* any of the coiled tubular subcutaneous glands that secrete sweat.

sweating sickness *n* an acute infectious febrile disease that was widespread in Europe during the late 15th century, characterized by profuse sweating.

sweat off *or* **away** *vb* (*tr, adv*) *Inf.* to get rid of (weight) by strenuous exercise or sweating.

sweat out ❶ *vb* (*tr, adv*) **1** to cure or lessen the effects of (a cold, respiratory infection, etc.) by sweating. **2** *Inf.* to endure (hardships) for a time (often in **sweat it out**). **3 sweat one's guts out.** *Inf.* to work extremely hard.

sweats (swɛts) *pl n* sweatshirts and sweat-suit trousers: *jeans and sweats.*

sweatshirt ('swɛt,ʃɜːt) *n* a long-sleeved knitted cotton sweater worn by athletes, etc.

sweatshop ('swɛt,ʃɒp) *n* a workshop where employees work long hours under bad conditions for low wages.

sweat suit *n* a suit worn by athletes for training comprising knitted cotton trousers and a light cotton sweater.

sweaty ❶ ('swɛtɪ) *adj* **sweatier, sweatiest. 1** covered with perspiration; sweating. **2** smelling of or like sweat. **3** causing sweat.
▸ **'sweatily** *adv* ▸ **'sweatiness** *n*

swede (swiːd) *n* **1** a Eurasian plant cultivated for its bulbous edible root, which is used as a vegetable and as cattle fodder. **2** the root of this plant. ◆ Also called: **Swedish turnip.** [C19: so called after being introduced into Scotland from Sweden in the 18th century]

Swede (swiːd) *n* a native, citizen, or inhabitant of Sweden, a kingdom in NW Europe.

Swedish ('swiːdɪʃ) *adj* **1** of, relating to, or characteristic of Sweden, its people, or their language. ◆ *n* **2** the official language of Sweden.

sweep ❶ (swiːp) *vb* **sweeps, sweeping, swept. 1** to clean or clear (a space, chimney, etc.) with a brush, broom, etc. **2** (often foll. by *up*) to remove or collect (dirt, rubbish, etc.) with a brush, broom, etc. **3** to move in a smooth or continuous manner, esp. quickly or forcibly: *cars swept along the road.* **4** to move in a proud or dignified fashion: *she swept past.* **5** to spread or pass rapidly across, through, or along (a region, area, etc.): *the news swept through the town.* **6** (*tr*) to direct (the gaze, line of fire, etc.) over; survey. **7** (*tr;* foll. by *away* or *off*) to overwhelm emotionally: *she was swept away by his charm.* **8** to brush or lightly touch (a surface, etc.): *the dress swept along the ground.* **9** (*tr;* often foll. by *away*) to convey, clear, or abolish, esp. with strong or continuous movements: *the sea swept the sandcastle away; secondary modern schools were swept away.* **10** (*intr*) to extend gracefully or majestically, esp. in a wide circle: *the plains sweep down to the sea.* **11** to search (a body of water) for mines, etc., by dragging. **12** (*tr*) to win overwhelmingly, esp. in an election: *Labour swept the country.* **13** (*tr*) to propel (a boat) with sweeps. **14 sweep the board. 14a** (in gambling) to win all the cards or money. **14b** to win every event or prize in a contest. **15 sweep (something) under the carpet.** to conceal (something, esp. a problem) in the hope that it will be overlooked by others. ◆ *n* **16** the act or an instance of sweeping; removal by or as if by a brush or broom. **17** a swift or steady movement, esp. in an arc. **18** the distance, arc, etc., through which something, such as a pendulum, moves. **19** a wide expanse or scope: *the sweep of the plains.* **20** any curving line or contour. **21** short for **sweepstake. 22a** a long oar used on an open boat. **22b** *Austral.* a person steering a surf boat with such an oar at the stern. **23** any of the sails of a windmill. **24** *Electronics.* a steady horizontal or circular movement of an electron beam across or around the fluorescent screen of a cathode-ray tube. **25** a curving driveway. **26** *Chiefly Brit.* See **chimney sweep. 27** another name for **swipe** (sense 6). **28 clean sweep. 28a** an overwhelming victory or success. **28b** a complete change; purge: *to make a clean sweep.* [C13 *swepen*]
▸ **'sweepy** *adj*

sweeper ('swiːpə) *n* **1** a person employed to sweep, such as a roadsweeper. **2** any device for sweeping: *a carpet sweeper.* **3** *Inf., soccer.* a player who supports the main defenders, as by intercepting loose balls, etc.

sweep hand *n Horology.* a long hand that registers seconds or fractions of seconds on the perimeter of the dial.

sweeping ❶ ('swiːpɪŋ) *adj* **1** comprehensive and wide-ranging: *sweeping reforms.* **2** indiscriminate or without reservations: *sweeping statements.* **3** decisive or overwhelming: *a sweeping victory.* **4** taking in a wide area: *a sweeping glance.* **5** driving steadily onwards, esp. over a large area: *a sweeping attack.*
▸ **'sweepingly** *adv* ▸ **'sweepingness** *n*

sweep-saw *n* a saw with a thin blade that can be used for cutting curved shapes.

sweepstake ('swiːp,steɪk) *or esp. US* **sweepstakes** *n* **1a** a lottery in which the stakes of the participants constitute the prize. **1b** the prize itself. **2** any event involving such a lottery, esp. a horse race. ◆ Often shortened to **sweep.** [C15: orig. referring to someone who *sweeps* or takes all the stakes in a game]

sweet ❶ (swiːt) *adj* **1** having or denoting a pleasant taste like that of sugar. **2** agreeable to the senses or the mind: *sweet music.* **3** having pleasant manners; gentle: *a sweet child.* **4** (of wine, etc.) having a relatively high sugar content; not dry. **5** (of foods) not decaying or rancid: *sweet milk.* **6** not salty: *sweet water.* **7** free from unpleasant odours: *sweet air.* **8** containing no corrosive substances: *sweet soil.* **9** (of petrol) containing no sulphur compounds. **10** sentimental or unrealistic. **11** *Jazz.* performed with a regular beat, with the emphasis on clearly outlined melody and little improvisation. **12** *Arch.* respected; dear (used in polite forms of address): *sweet sir.* **13** smooth and precise; perfectly executed: *a sweet shot.* **14 at one's own sweet will.** as it suits oneself alone. **15 keep (someone) sweet.** to ingratiate oneself in order to ensure cooperation. **16 sweet on.** fond of or infatuated with. ◆ *adv* **17** *Inf.* in a sweet manner. ◆ *n* **18** a sweet taste or smell; sweetness in general. **19** (*often pl*) *Brit.* any of numerous kinds of confectionery consisting

THESAURUS

swearword *n* = **oath**, curse, cuss (*inf.*), expletive, four-letter word, obscenity, profanity

sweat *n* **1** = **perspiration**, diaphoresis (*Medical*), exudation, sudor (*Medical*) **5** *Informal* = **worry**, agitation, anxiety, distress, flap, panic, strain **6** *Slang* = **labour**, backbreaking task, chore, drudgery, effort, toil ◆ *vb* **9** = **perspire**, break out in a sweat, exude moisture, glow **19** *Informal* = **worry**, agonize, be on pins and needles (*inf.*), be on tenterhooks, chafe, fret, lose sleep over, suffer, torture oneself

sweat out *vb* **2** *Informal, as in* **sweat it out** = **endure**, see (something) through, stay the course, stick it out (*inf.*)

sweaty *adj* **1** = **perspiring**, bathed *or* drenched *or* soaked in perspiration, clammy, glowing, sticky, sweating

sweep *vb* **1, 2** = **clear**, brush, clean, remove **3, 4** = **sail**, flounce, fly, glide, hurtle, pass, scud, skim, tear, zoom ◆ *n* **17** = **arc**, bend, curve, gesture, move, movement, stroke, swing **18, 19** = **extent**, compass, range, scope, span, stretch, vista **21** = **lottery**, draw, raffle, sweepstake

sweeping *adj* **1** = **wide-ranging**, all-embracing, all-inclusive, broad, comprehensive, extensive, global, overarching, radical, thoroughgoing, wide **2** = **indiscriminate**, across-the-board, blanket, exaggerated, overdrawn, overstated, unqualified, wholesale
Antonyms *adj* ≠ **wide-ranging:** constrained, limited, minor, modest, narrow, restricted, token, unimportant

sweet *adj* **1** = **sugary**, cloying, honeyed, luscious, melting, saccharine, sweetened, syrupy, toothsome, treacly **2** = **delightful**, appealing, attractive, beautiful, cute, engaging, fair, likable *or* likeable, lovable, taking, winning, winsome **2** = **melodious**, dulcet, euphonic, euphonious, harmonious, mellow, musical, silver-toned, silvery, soft, sweet-sounding, tuneful **3** = **charming**, affectionate, agreeable, amiable, gentle, kind, sweet-tempered, tender, unselfish **7** = **fragrant**, aromatic, balmy, clean, fresh, new, perfumed, pure, redolent, sweet-smelling, wholesome **12** = **beloved**, cherished, darling, dear, dearest, pet, precious, treasured **16 sweet on** = **in love with**, enamoured of, fond of, gone on (*sl.*), head over heels in love with, infatuated with, keen on, obsessed *or* bewitched by, taken wholly or partly of sugar, esp. of sugar boiled and crystallized (**boiled sweets**). **20** *Brit.* any sweet dish served as a dessert. **21** dear; sweetheart (used as a form of address). **22** anything that is sweet. **23** (*often pl*) a pleasurable experience, state, etc.: *the sweets of success.* [OE *swēte*] ▸**'sweetish** *adj* ▸**'sweetly** *adv* ▸**'sweetness** *n*

sweet alyssum *n* a Mediterranean plant having clusters of small fragrant white or violet flowers. See also **alyssum.**

sweet-and-sour *adj* (of food) cooked in a sauce made from sugar and vinegar and other ingredients.

sweet bay *n* a small tree of SE North America, belonging to the magnolia family and having large fragrant white flowers. Sometimes shortened to **bay.**

sweetbread ('swi:tˌbrɛd) *n* the pancreas or the thymus gland of an animal, used for food. [C16: SWEET + BREAD, ? from OE *brǣd* meat]

sweetbrier ('swi:tˌbraɪə) *n* a Eurasian rose having a tall bristly stem, fragrant leaves, and single pink flowers. Also called: **eglantine.**

sweet cherry *n* either of two types of cherry tree that are cultivated for their edible sweet fruit.

sweet chestnut *n* See **chestnut** (sense 1).

sweet cicely ('sɪsəlɪ) *n* **1** Also called: **myrrh.** an aromatic European plant, having compound leaves and clusters of small white flowers. **2** the leaves, formerly used in cookery for their flavour of aniseed. **3** any of various related plants of Asia and America, having aromatic roots.

sweet corn *n* **1** a variety of maize whose kernels are rich in sugar and eaten as a vegetable when young. **2** the unripe ears of maize, esp. the sweet kernels removed from the cob, cooked as a vegetable.

sweeten ● ('swi:tᵊn) *vb* (*mainly tr*) **1** (*also intr*) to make or become sweet or sweeter. **2** to mollify or soften (a person). **3** to make more agreeable. **4** (*also intr*) *Chem.* to free or be freed from unpleasant odours, acidic or corrosive substances, or the like.

sweetener ('swi:tᵊnə) *n* **1** a sweetening agent, esp. one that does not contain sugar. **2** *Inf.* a bribe. **3** *Inf.* a financial inducement.

sweetening ('swi:tᵊnɪŋ) *n* something that sweetens.

sweet flag *n* an aroid marsh plant, having swordlike leaves, small greenish flowers, and aromatic roots. Also called: **calamus.**

sweet gale *n* a shrub of northern swamp regions, having yellow catkin-like flowers and aromatic leaves. Also called: **bog myrtle.** Often shortened to **gale.**

sweet gum *n* **1** a North American liquidambar tree, having prickly spherical fruit clusters and fragrant sap: the wood (called **satin walnut**) is used to make furniture. **2** the sap of this tree. ◆ Also called: **red gum.**

sweetheart ● ('swi:tˌhɑ:t) *n* **1** a person loved by another. **2** *Inf.* a lovable, generous, or obliging person. **3** a term of endearment.

sweetheart agreement *n Austral. inf.* an industrial agreement on pay and conditions concluded without resort to arbitration.

sweetie ('swi:tɪ) *n Inf.* **1** sweetheart; darling: used as a term of endearment. **2** *Brit.* another word for **sweet** (sense 19). **3** *Chiefly Brit.* an endearing person. **4** a large seedless variety of grapefruit that has a green-to-yellow rind and juicy sweet pulp.

sweeting ('swi:tɪŋ) *n* **1** a variety of sweet apple. **2** an archaic word for **sweetheart.**

sweet marjoram *n* another name for **marjoram** (sense 1).

sweetmeat ('swi:tˌmi:t) *n* a sweetened delicacy, such as a preserve, sweet, or, formerly, a cake or pastry.

sweet pea *n* a climbing plant of S Europe, widely cultivated for its butterfly-shaped fragrant flowers of delicate pastel colours.

sweet pepper *n* **1** a pepper plant with large bell-shaped fruits that are eaten unripe (**green pepper**) or ripe (**red pepper**). **2** the fruit of this plant.

sweet potato *n* **1** a twining plant of tropical America, cultivated in the tropics for its edible fleshy yellow root. **2** the root of this plant.

sweet shop *n Chiefly Brit.* a shop solely or largely selling sweets, esp. boiled sweets.

sweetsop ('swi:tˌsɒp) *n* **1** a small West Indian tree, having yellowish-green fruit. **2** the fruit, which has a sweet edible pulp. ◆ Also called: **custard apple.**

sweet spot *n Sport.* the centre area of a racket, golf club, etc., from which the cleanest shots are made.

sweet-talk ● *Inf.* ◆ *vb* **1** to coax, flatter, or cajole (someone). ◆ *n* **sweet talk. 2** cajolery; coaxing.

sweet tooth *n* a strong liking for sweet foods.

sweetveld ('swi:tˌfelt) *n* (in South Africa) a type of grazing characterized by high-quality grass. [pron. from Afrik. *soetveld*]

sweet william ('wɪljəm) *n* a widely cultivated Eurasian plant with flat clusters of white, pink, red, or purple flowers.

swell ● (swɛl) *vb* **swells, swelling, swelled; swollen** *or* **swelled. 1** to grow or cause to grow in size, esp. as a result of internal pressure. **2** to expand or cause to expand at a particular point or above the surrounding level; protrude. **3** to grow or cause to grow in size, amount, intensity, or degree: *the party is swelling with new recruits.* **4** to puff or be puffed up with pride or another emotion. **5** (*intr*) (of seas or lakes) to rise in waves. **6** (*intr*) to well up or overflow. **7** (*tr*) to make (a musical phrase) increase gradually in volume and then diminish. ◆ *n* **8a** the undulating movement of the surface of the open sea. **8b** a succession of waves or a single large wave. **9** a swelling or being swollen; expansion. **10** an increase in quantity or degree; inflation. **11** a bulge; protuberance. **12** a gentle hill. **13** *Inf.* a person very fashionably dressed. **14** *Inf.* a man of high social or political standing. **15** *Music.* a crescendo followed by an immediate diminuendo. **16** Also called: **swell organ.** *Music.* **16a** a set of pipes on an organ housed in a box (**swell box**) fitted with a shutter operated by a pedal, which can be opened or closed to control the volume. **16b** the manual on an organ controlling this. ◆ *adj* **17** *Inf.* stylish or grand. **18** *Sl.* excellent; first-class. [OE *swellan*]

swelled head *or* **swollen head** *Inf.* ◆ *n* **1** an inflated view of one's own worth, often caused by sudden success. ◆ *adj* **swelled-headed, swell-headed,** *or* **swollen-headed. 2** conceited.

swelling ● ('swɛlɪŋ) *n* **1** the act of expansion or inflation. **2** the state of being or becoming swollen. **3** a swollen or inflated part or area. **4** an abnormal enlargement of a bodily structure or part, esp. as the result of injury. ◆ Related adj: **tumescent.**

swelter ('swɛltə) *vb* **1** (*intr*) to suffer under oppressive heat, esp. to perspire and feel faint. **2** (*tr*) *Rare.* to cause to suffer under oppressive heat. ◆ *n* **3** a sweltering condition (esp. in **in a swelter**). **4** oppressive humid heat. [C15 *swelten*, from OE *sweltan* to die]

sweltering ● ('swɛltərɪŋ) *adj* oppressively hot and humid: *a sweltering day.*
▸**'swelteringly** *adv*

swept (swɛpt) *vb* the past tense and past participle of **sweep.**

sweptback ('swɛptˌbæk) *adj* (of an aircraft wing) inclined backwards towards the rear of the fuselage.

sweptwing ('swɛptˌwɪŋ) *adj* (of an aircraft, etc.) having wings swept (usually) backwards.

swerve ● (swɜ:v) *vb* **swerves, swerving, swerved. 1** to turn or cause to turn aside, usually sharply or suddenly, from a course. ◆ *n* **2** the act, instance, or degree of swerving. [OE *sweorfan* to scour]
▸**'swervable** *adj* ▸**'swerver** *n* ▸**'swerving** *adj*

SWG *abbrev. for* Standard Wire Gauge; a notation for the diameters of metal rods or thickness of metal sheet ranging from 16 mm to 0.02 mm or from 0.5 inch to 0.001 inch.

swift ● (swɪft) *adj* **1** moving or able to move quickly; fast. **2** occurring or performed quickly or suddenly; instant. **3** (*postpositive;* foll. by *to*) prompt to act or respond: *swift to take revenge.* ◆ *adv* **4a** swiftly or quickly. **4b** (*in combination*): *swift-moving.* ◆ *n* **5** any of various insectivorous birds of the Old World. They have long narrow wings and spend most of the time on the wing. **6** any of certain North American

THESAURUS

with, wild *or* mad about (*inf.*) ◆ *n* **19** *usually plural* = **confectionery**, bonbon, candy (*US*), sweetie, sweetmeats **20** *Brit.* = **dessert**, afters (*Brit. inf.*), pudding, sweet course
Antonyms *adj* ≠ **sugary:** acerbic, acetic, acid, bitter, savoury, sharp, sour, tart, vinegary ≠ **delightful:** hated, loathsome, nasty, objectionable, obnoxious, unappealing, unattractive, unlovable, unpleasant, unwanted ≠ **melodious:** cacophonous, discordant, grating, harsh, shrill, strident, unharmonious, unmusical, unpleasant ≠ **charming:** bad-tempered, disagreeable, grouchy (*inf.*), grumpy, ill-tempered, nasty, obnoxious ≠ **fragrant:** fetid, foul, noisome, rank, stinking

sweeten *vb* **1** = **sugar**, honey, sugar-coat **2, 3** = **mollify**, alleviate, appease, pacify, soften up, soothe, sugar the pill

sweetheart *n* **1** = **love**, admirer, beau, beloved, boyfriend *or* girlfriend, darling, dear, flame (*inf.*), follower (*obs.*), inamorata *or* inamorato, leman (*arch.*), lover, steady (*inf.*), suitor, swain (*arch.*), sweetie (*inf.*), truelove, valentine

sweet-talk *vb* **1** *Informal* = **flatter**, beguile, blandish, cajole, chat up, coax, dupe, entice, inveigle, manoeuvre, mislead, palaver, persuade, seduce, soft-soap (*inf.*), tempt, wheedle

swell *vb* **1** = **expand**, balloon, become bloated *or* distended, become larger, be inflated, belly, billow, bloat, bulge, dilate, distend, enlarge, extend, fatten, grow, increase, protrude, puff up, rise, round out, tumefy, well up **3** = **increase**, add to, aggravate, augment, enhance, heighten, intensify, mount, surge ◆ *n* **8** = **wave**, billow, rise, surge, undulation **13, 14** *Old-fashioned, informal* = **dandy**, beau, blade (*arch.*), cockscomb (*inf.*), fashion plate, fop, nob (*sl.*), toff (*Brit. sl.*) ◆ *adj* **18** *Slang* = **grand**, de luxe, exclusive, fashionable, plush *or* plushy (*inf.*), posh (*inf., chiefly Brit.*), ritzy (*sl.*), smart, stylish
Antonyms *vb* ≠ **expand:** become smaller, contract, deflate, shrink ≠ **increase:** decrease, diminish, ebb, fall, go down, lessen, reduce, wane ◆ *adj* ≠ **grand:** common, grotty (*sl.*), ordinary, plebeian, poor, run down, seedy, shabby, sordid, tatty, unimpressive, vulgar

swelling *n* **4** = **enlargement**, blister, bruise, bulge, bump, dilation, distension, inflammation, lump, protuberance, puffiness, tumescence

sweltering *adj* = **hot**, airless, baking, boiling, burning, humid, oppressive, roasting, scorching, steaming, stifling, sultry, torrid

swerve *vb* **1** = **veer**, bend, deflect, depart from, deviate, diverge, incline, sheer off, shift, skew, stray, swing, turn, turn aside, wander, wind

swift *adj* **1-3** = **quick**, abrupt, expeditious, express, fast, fleet, fleet-footed, flying, hurried, nimble, nippy (*Brit. inf.*), prompt, quickie (*inf.*), rapid, ready, short, short-lived, spanking, speedy, sudden, winged
Antonyms *adj* lead-footed, lingering, plodding, ponderous, slow, sluggish, tardy, tortoise-like, unhurried

swiftly *adv* **1** = **quickly**, apace, as fast as one's legs can carry one, (at) full tilt, double-quick, fast, hell for leather, hotfoot, hurriedly, in less than no time, like greased lightning (*inf.*), like lightning, like the clappers, nippily (*Brit. inf.*), posthaste, promptly, pronto (*inf.*), rapidly, speedily, without losing time

swiftness *n* **1** = **speed**, alacrity, celerity,

lizards of the iguana family that can run very rapidly. **7** the main cylinder in a carding machine. **8** an expanding circular frame used to hold skeins of silk, wool, etc. [OE, from *swīfan* to turn]
▸**'swiftly** *adv* ▸**'swiftness** *n*

swiftlet ('swɪftlɪt) *n* any of various small swifts of an Asian genus that often live in caves and use echolocation.

swig (swɪg) *Inf.* ◆ *n* **1** a large swallow or deep drink, esp. from a bottle. ◆ *vb* **swigs, swigging, swigged. 2** to drink (some liquid) deeply, esp. from a bottle. [C16: from ?]
▸**'swigger** *n*

swill ❶ (swɪl) *vb* **1** to drink large quantities of (liquid, esp. alcoholic drink); guzzle. **2** (*tr*; often foll. by *out*) *Chiefly Brit.* to drench or rinse in large amounts of water. **3** (*tr*) to feed swill to (pigs, etc.). ◆ *n* **4** wet feed, esp. for pigs, consisting of kitchen waste, skimmed milk, etc. **5** refuse, esp. from a kitchen. **6** a deep drink, esp. beer. **7** any liquid mess. **8** the act of swilling. [OE *swilian* to wash out]
▸**'swiller** *n*

swim (swɪm) *vb* **swims, swimming, swam, swum. 1** (*intr*) to move along in water by means of movements of the body, esp. the arms and legs, or (in the case of fish) tail and fins. **2** (*tr*) to cover (a distance or stretch of water) in this way. **3** (*tr*) to compete in (a race) in this way. **4** (*intr*) to be supported by and on a liquid; float. **5** (*tr*) to use (a particular stroke) in swimming. **6** (*intr*) to move smoothly, usually through air or over a surface. **7** (*intr*) to reel or seem to reel: *my head swam; the room swam around me.* **8** (*intr*; often foll. by *in* or *with*) to be covered or flooded with water or other liquid. **9** (*intr*; often foll. by *in*) to be liberally supplied (with): *he's swimming in money.* **10** (*tr*) to cause to float or swim. **11 swim with** (*or* **against**) **the stream** *or* **tide.** to conform to (or resist) prevailing opinion. ◆ *n* **12** the act, an instance, or period of swimming. **13** any graceful gliding motion. **14** a condition of dizziness; swoon. **15** a pool in a river good for fishing. **16 in the swim.** *Inf.* fashionable or active in social or political activities. [OE *swimman*]
▸**'swimmable** *adj* ▸**'swimmer** *n* ▸**'swimming** *n, adj*

swim bladder *n Ichthyol.* another name for **air bladder** (sense 1).

swimmeret ('swɪmə,rɛt) *n* any of the small paired appendages on the abdomen of crustaceans, used chiefly in locomotion.

swimming bath *n* (*often pl*) an indoor swimming pool.

swimming costume *or* **bathing costume** *n Chiefly Brit.* any garment worn for swimming or sunbathing, such as a woman's one-piece garment covering most of the torso but not the limbs.

swimmingly ❶ ('swɪmɪŋlɪ) *adv* successfully, effortlessly, or well (esp. in **go swimmingly**).

swimming pool *n* an artificial pool for swimming.

swimsuit ('swɪm,suːt, -,sjuːt) *n* a woman's one-piece swimming garment that leaves the arms and legs bare.

swindle ❶ ('swɪndᵊl) *vb* **swindles, swindling, swindled. 1** to cheat (someone) of money, etc.; defraud. **2** (*tr*) to obtain (money, etc.) by fraud. ◆ *n* **3** a fraudulent scheme or transaction. [C18: back formation from G *Schwindler*, from *schwindeln*, from OHG *swintilōn*, from *swintan* to disappear]
▸**'swindler** *n*

swindle sheet *n* a slang term for **expense account.**

swine (swaɪn) *n* **1** (*pl* **swine** *or* **swines**). a coarse or contemptible person. **2** (*pl* **swine**). another name for a **pig.** [OE *swīn*]
▸**'swinish** *adj* ▸**'swinishly** *adv* ▸**'swinishness** *n*

swine fever *n* an infectious viral disease of pigs, characterized by fever and diarrhoea.

swineherd ('swaɪn,hɜːd) *n Arch.* a person who looks after pigs.

swing ❶ (swɪŋ) *vb* **swings, swinging, swung. 1** to move or cause to move rhythmically to and fro, as a free-hanging object; sway. **2** (*intr*) to move, walk, etc., with a relaxed and swaying motion. **3** to pivot or cause to pivot, as on a hinge. **4** to move or cause to move in a curve: *the car swung around the bend.* **5** to move or cause to move by suspending or being suspended. **6** to hang or be hung so as to be able to turn freely. **7** (*intr*) *Sl.* to be hanged: *he'll swing for it.* **8** to alter or cause to alter habits, a course, etc. **9** (*tr*) *Inf.* to influence or manipulate successfully: *I hope he can swing the deal.* **10** (*tr*; foll. by *up*) to raise or hoist, esp. in a sweeping motion. **11** (*intr*; often foll. by *at*) to hit out or strike (at), esp. with a sweeping motion. **12** (*tr*) to wave (a weapon, etc.) in a sweeping motion; flourish. **13** to arrange or play (music) with the rhythmically flexible and compulsive quality associated with jazz. **14** (*intr*) (of popular music, esp. jazz, or of the musicians who play it) to have this quality. **15** *Sl.* to be lively and modern. **16** (*intr*) *Cricket.* to bowl (a ball) with swing or (of a ball) to move with a swing. **17 swing the lead.** *Inf.* to malinger or make up excuses. ◆ *n* **18** the act or manner of swinging or the distance covered while swinging: *a wide swing.* **19** a sweeping stroke or blow. **20** *Boxing.* a wide punch from the side similar to but longer than a hook. **21** *Cricket.* the lateral movement of a bowled ball through the air. **22** any free-swaying motion. **23** any curving movement; sweep. **24** something that swings or is swung, esp. a suspended seat on which a person may swing back and forth. **25** a kind of popular dance music influenced by jazz, usually played by big bands and originating in the 1930s. **26** *Prosody.* a steady distinct rhythm or cadence in prose or verse. **27** *Inf.* the normal round or pace: *the swing of things.* **28a** a fluctuation, as in some business activity, voting pattern, etc. **28b** (*modifier*) able to bring about a swing in a voting pattern. **29** *Canad.* (in the North) a train of freight sleighs or canoes. **30** *Chiefly US.* a circular tour. **31 go with a swing.** to go well; be successful. **32 in full swing.** at the height of activity. **33 swings and roundabouts.** equal advantages and disadvantages. [OE *swingan*]

swingboat ('swɪŋ,bəʊt) *n* a piece of fairground equipment consisting of a boat-shaped carriage for swinging in.

swing bridge *n* a low bridge that can be rotated about a vertical axis to permit the passage of ships, etc.

swinge (swɪndʒ) *vb* **swinges, swingeing** *or* **swinging, swinged.** (*tr*) *Arch.* to beat, flog, or punish. [OE *swengan*]

swingeing ❶ ('swɪndʒɪŋ) *adj Chiefly Brit.* punishing; severe.

swinger ('swɪŋə) *n Sl.* **1** a person regarded as being modern and lively. **2** a person who swaps sexual partners in a group, esp. habitually.
▸**'swinging** *adj* ▸**'swingingly** *adv*

swingle ('swɪŋgᵊl) *n* **1** a flat-bladed wooden instrument used for beating and scraping flax or hemp to remove coarse matter from it. ◆ *vb* **swingles, swingling, swingled. 2** (*tr*) to use a swingle on. [OE *swingel* stroke]

swingletree ('swɪŋgᵊl,triː) *n* a crossbar in a horse's harness to which the ends of the traces are attached. Also called: **whippletree.**

swing shift *n US & Canad. inf.* the usual US and Canad. term for **back shift.**

swing-wing *adj* **1** of or relating to a variable-geometry aircraft. ◆ *n* **2a** such an aircraft. **2b** either of the two wings of such an aircraft.

swipe ❶ (swaɪp) *vb* **swipes, swiping, swiped. 1** (when *intr*, usually foll. by *at*) *Inf.* to hit hard with a sweeping blow. **2** (*tr*) *Sl.* to steal. **3** (*tr*) to pass a machine-readable card, such as a credit card, debit card, etc., through a machine that electronically interprets the information encoded on it, usu. in a magnetic strip. ◆ *n* **4** *Inf.* a hard blow. **5** an unexpected criticism of someone or something while discussing another subject. **6** Also called: **sweep.** a type of lever for raising and lowering a weight, such as a bucket in a well. [C19: ? rel. to SWEEP]

swirl ❶ (swɜːl) *vb* **1** to turn or cause to turn in a twisting spinning fashion. **2** (*intr*) to be dizzy; swim: *my head was swirling.* ◆ *n* **3** a whirling or spinning motion, esp. in water. **4** a whorl; curl. **5** the act of swirling or stirring. **6** dizzy confusion or disorder. [C15: prob. from Du. *zwirrelen*]
▸**'swirling** *adj* ▸**'swirly** *adj*

swish ❶ (swɪʃ) *vb* **1** to move with or make or cause to move with or make a whistling or hissing sound. **2** (*intr*) (esp. of fabrics) to rustle. **3** (*tr*) *Sl., now rare.* to whip; flog. **4** (*tr*; foll. by *off*) to cut with a swishing blow. ◆ *n* **5** a hissing or rustling sound or movement. **6** a rod for flogging or a blow from this. ◆ *adj* **7** *Inf., chiefly Brit.* fashionable; smart. [C18: imit.]
▸**'swishy** *adj*

Swiss (swɪs) *adj* **1** of, relating to, or characteristic of Switzerland, a republic in W central Europe, its inhabitants, or their dialects of German, French, and Italian. ◆ *n, pl* **Swiss. 2** a native, inhabitant, or citizen of Switzerland.

Swiss chard *n* another name for **chard.**

Swiss cheese plant *n* See **monstera.**

THESAURUS

dispatch, expedition, fleetness, promptness, quickness, rapidity, speediness, velocity

swill *vb* **1** = **drink**, bend the elbow (*inf.*), bevvy (*dialect*), consume, drain, gulp, guzzle, imbibe, pour down one's gullet, quaff, swallow, swig (*inf.*), toss off **2** *Chiefly Brit. often with* **out** = **rinse**, drench, flush, sluice, wash down, wash out ◆ *n* **4** = **waste**, hogwash, mash, mush, pigswill, scourings, slops

swimmingly *adv* = **successfully**, as planned, cosily, effortlessly, like a dream, like clockwork, smoothly, very well, with no trouble, without a hitch

swindle *vb* **1** = **cheat**, bamboozle (*inf.*), bilk (of), con, cozen, deceive, defraud, diddle (*inf.*), do (*sl.*), dupe, fleece, overcharge, pull a fast one (on someone) (*inf.*), put one over on (someone) (*inf.*), rip (someone) off (*sl.*), rook (*sl.*), skin (*sl.*), stiff (*sl.*), sting (*inf.*), take (someone) for a ride (*inf.*), take to the cleaners (*inf.*), trick ◆ *n* **3** = **fraud**, con trick (*inf.*), deceit, deception, double-dealing, fiddle (*Brit. inf.*), imposition, knavery, racket, rip-off (*sl.*), roguery, scam (*sl.*), sharp practice, sting (*inf.*), swizz (*Brit. inf.*), swizzle (*Brit. inf.*), trickery

swindler *n* **1** = **cheat**, charlatan, chiseller (*inf.*), confidence trickster, con man (*inf.*), fraud, fraudster, hustler (*US inf.*), impostor, knave (*arch.*), mountebank, rascal, rogue, rook (*sl.*), shark, sharper, trickster

swing *vb* **1** = **sway**, fluctuate, oscillate, rock, vary, veer, vibrate, wave **3, 4** *usually with* **round** = **turn**, curve, pivot, rotate, swivel, turn on one's heel, wheel **5, 6** = **hang**, be pendent, be suspended, dangle, move back and forth, suspend ◆ *n* **18** = **swaying**, fluctuation, oscillation, stroke, sway, vibration **32 in full swing** = **at its height**, animated, lively, on the go (*inf.*), under way

swingeing *adj Chiefly Brit.* = **severe**, daunting, Draconian, drastic, excessive, exorbitant, harsh, heavy, huge, oppressive, punishing, stringent

swipe *vb* **1** *Informal* = **hit**, chin (*sl.*), clip (*inf.*), deck (*sl.*), fetch (someone) a blow, lash out at, lay one on (*sl.*), slap, slosh (*Brit. sl.*), sock (*sl.*), strike, wallop (*inf.*) **2** *Slang* = **steal**, appropriate, cabbage (*Brit. sl.*), filch, lift (*inf.*), make off with, nick, pilfer, pinch (*inf.*), purloin, snaffle (*Brit. inf.*) ◆ *n* **4** = **blow**, clip (*inf.*), clout (*inf.*), clump (*sl.*), cuff, slap, smack, thump, wallop (*inf.*)

swirl *vb* **1** = **whirl**, agitate, boil, churn, eddy, spin, surge, twirl, twist

swish *adj* **7** *Informal, chiefly Brit.* = **smart**, de luxe, elegant, exclusive, fashionable, grand, plush *or* plushy (*inf.*), posh (*inf., chiefly Brit.*), ritzy (*sl.*), sumptuous, swell (*inf.*)

swiss roll *n* a sponge cake spread with jam, cream, or some other filling, and rolled up.

switch ❶ (swɪtʃ) *n* **1** a mechanical, electrical, or electronic device for opening or closing a circuit or for diverting a current from one part of a circuit to another. **2** a swift and usually sudden shift or change. **3** an exchange or swap. **4** a flexible rod or twig, used esp. for punishment. **5** the sharp movement or blow of such an instrument. **6** a tress of false hair used to give added length or bulk to a woman's own hair-style. **7** the tassel-like tip of the tail of cattle and certain other animals. **8** any of various card games in which the suit is changed during play. **9** *US & Canad.* a railway siding. **10** *US & Canad.* a railway point. **11** *Austral. inf.* short for **switchboard** (sense 1). ◆ *vb* **12** to shift, change, turn aside, or change the direction of (something). **13** to exchange (places); replace (something by something else). **14** *Chiefly US & Canad.* to transfer (rolling stock) from one railway track to another. **15** (*tr*) to cause (an electric current) to start or stop flowing or to change its path by operating a switch. **16** (*tr*) to lash or whip with or as if with a switch. ◆ See also **switch off, switch on.** [C16: ?from MDu. *swijch* twig]
▸**'switcher** *n*

switchback ('swɪtʃ,bæk) *n* **1** a mountain road, railway, or track which rises and falls sharply many times or a sharp rise and fall on such a road, railway, or track. **2** another word (esp. Brit.) for **big dipper.**

switchblade *or* **switchblade knife** ('swɪtʃ,bleɪd) *n* another name (esp. US and Canad.) for **flick knife.**

switchboard ('swɪtʃ,bɔːd) *n* **1** an installation in a telephone exchange, office, etc., at which the interconnection of telephone lines is manually controlled. **2** an assembly of switchgear for the control of power supplies in an installation or building.

switchgear ('swɪtʃ,gɪə) *n Electrical engineering.* any of several devices used for opening and closing electric circuits, esp. those that pass high currents.

switchman ('swɪtʃmən) *n, pl* **switchmen.** the US and Canad. name for **pointsman.**

switch off *vb* (*adv*) **1** to cause (a device) to stop operating as by moving a switch, knob, etc. **2** *Inf.* to cease to interest or be interested; make or become bored, alienated, etc.

switch on *vb* (*adv*) **1** to cause (a device) to operate as by moving a switch, knob, or lever. **2** (*tr*) *Inf.* to produce (charm, tears, etc.) suddenly or automatically. **3** (*tr*) *Inf.* (now dated) to make up-to-date, esp. in outlook, dress, etc.

swither ('swɪðə) *Scot.* ◆ *vb* (*intr*) **1** to hesitate; vacillate; be perplexed. ◆ *n* **2** hesitation; perplexity; agitation. [C16: from ?]

Switzer ('swɪtsə) *n* a less common word for **Swiss.** [C16: from MHG, from *Swīz* Switzerland]

swivel ❶ ('swɪvᵊl) *n* **1** a coupling device which allows an attached object to turn freely. **2** such a device made of two parts which turn independently, such as a compound link of a chain. **3a** a pivot on which is mounted a gun that may be swung horizontally from side to side. **3b** Also called: **swivel gun.** the gun itself. ◆ *vb* **swivels, swivelling, swivelled** *or US* **swivels, swiveling, swiveled.** **4** to turn or swing on or as if on a pivot. **5** (*tr*) to provide with, secure by, or support with a swivel. [C14: from OE *swīfan* to turn]

swivel chair *n* a chair, the seat of which is joined to the legs by a swivel and which thus may be spun round.

swivel pin *n* another name for **kingpin** (sense 2).

swiz *or* **swizz** (swɪz) *n Brit. inf.* a swindle or disappointment; swizzle.

swizzle ('swɪzᵊl) *n* **1** an alcoholic drink containing gin or rum. **2** *Brit. inf.* a swiz. ◆ *vb* **swizzles, swizzling, swizzled.** **3** (*tr*) to stir a swizzle stick in (a drink). **4** *Brit. inf.* to swindle; cheat. [C19: from ?]

swizzle stick *n* a small rod used to agitate an effervescent drink to facilitate the escape of carbon dioxide.

swob (swɒb) *n, vb* **swobs, swobbing, swobbed.** a less common word for **swab.**

swollen ❶ ('swəʊlən) *vb* **1** a past participle of **swell.** ◆ *adj* **2** tumid or enlarged as by swelling. **3** turgid or bombastic.
▸**'swollenness** *n*

swoon (swuːn) *vb* (*intr*) **1** a literary word for **faint. 2** to become ecstatic. ◆ *n* **3** an instance of fainting. ◆ Also (archaic or dialect): **swound** (swaʊnd). [OE *geswōgen* insensible, p.p. of *swōgan* (unattested except in compounds) suffocate]
▸**'swooning** *adj*

swoop ❶ (swuːp) *vb* **1** (*intr;* usually foll. by *down, on,* or *upon*) to sweep or pounce suddenly. **2** (*tr;* often foll. by *up, away,* or *off*) to seize or scoop suddenly. ◆ *n* **3** the act of swooping. **4** a swift descent. [OE *swāpan* to sweep]

swoosh (swʊʃ) *vb* **1** to make or cause to make a rustling or swirling sound, esp. when moving or pouring out. ◆ *n* **2** a swirling or rustling sound or movement. [C20: imit.]

swop (swɒp) *vb* **swops, swopping, swopped,** *n* a variant spelling of **swap.**

sword ❶ (sɔːd) *n* **1** a thrusting, striking, or cutting weapon with a long blade having one or two cutting edges, a hilt, and usually a crosspiece or guard. **2** such a weapon worn on ceremonial occasions as a symbol of authority. **3** something resembling a sword, such as the snout of a swordfish. **4 the sword. 4a** violence or power, esp. military power. **4b** death; destruction: *to put to the sword.* [OE *sweord*]

swordbearer ('sɔːd,beərə) *n* an official who carries a ceremonial sword.

sword dance *n* a dance in which the performers dance nimbly over swords on the ground or brandish them in the air.
▸**sword dancer** *n* ▸**sword dancing** *n*

swordfish ('sɔːd,fɪʃ) *n, pl* **swordfish** *or* **swordfishes.** a large fish with a very long upper jaw: valued as a food and game fish.

sword grass *n* any of various grasses and other plants having sword-shaped sharp leaves.

sword knot *n* a loop on the hilt of a sword by which it was attached to the wrist, now purely decorative.

sword lily *n* another name for **gladiolus.**

Sword of Damocles ('dæmə,kliːz) *n* a closely impending disaster. [after a sycophant forced by Dionysius, tyrant of ancient Syracuse, to sit under a sword suspended by a hair]

swordplay ('sɔːd,pleɪ) *n* **1** the action or art of fighting with a sword. **2** verbal sparring.

swordsman ('sɔːdzmən) *n, pl* **swordsmen.** one who uses or is skilled in the use of a sword.
▸**'swordsmanship** *n*

swordstick ('sɔːd,stɪk) *n* a hollow walking stick containing a short sword or dagger.

swordtail ('sɔːd,teɪl) *n* any of several small freshwater fishes of Central America having a long swordlike tail.

swore (swɔː) *vb* the past tense of **swear.**

sworn (swɔːn) *vb* **1** the past participle of **swear.** ◆ *adj* **2** bound, pledged, or made inveterate, by or as if by an oath: *a sworn statement; he was sworn to God.*

swot[1] ❶ (swɒt) *Brit. inf.* ◆ *vb* **swots, swotting, swotted. 1** (often foll. by *up*) to study (a subject) intensively, as for an examination; cram. ◆ *n* **2** Also called: **swotter.** a person who works or studies hard. **3** hard work or grind. ◆ Also: **swat.** [C19: var. of SWEAT (n)]

swot[2] (swɒt) *vb* **swots, swotting, swotted,** *n* a variant of **swat.**

SWOT (swɒt) *n acronym for* strengths, weaknesses, opportunities, and threats: an analysis of a product made before it is marketed.

swounds *or* **'swounds** (zwaʊndz, zaʊndz) *interj Arch.* less common spellings of **zounds.**

swum (swʌm) *vb* the past participle of **swim.**

swung (swʌŋ) *vb* the past tense and past participle of **swing.**

swy (swaɪ) *n Austral.* another name for **two-up.** [C20: from G *zwei* two]

sybarite ❶ ('sɪbə,raɪt) *n* **1** (*sometimes cap.*) a devotee of luxury and the sensual vices. ◆ *adj* **2** luxurious; sensuous. [C16: from L *Sybarīta,* from Gk *Subaritēs* inhabitant of *Sybaris,* Gk colony in S Italy, famed for its luxury]
▸**sybaritic** (,sɪbə'rɪtɪk) *adj* ▸**,syba'ritically** *adv* ▸**'sybaritism** *n*

sycamore ('sɪkə,mɔː) *n* **1** a Eurasian maple tree, naturalized in Britain and North America, having five-lobed leaves and two-winged fruits. **2** *US & Canad.* an American plane tree. See **plane tree. 3** a tree of N Africa and W Asia, having an edible figlike fruit. [C14: from OF *sicamor,* from L *sȳcomorus,* from Gk, from *sukon* fig + *moron* mulberry]

syconium (saɪ'kəʊnɪəm) *n, pl* **syconia** (-nɪə). *Bot.* the fleshy fruit of the fig, consisting of an enlarged receptacle. [C19: from NL, from Gk *sukon* fig]

sycophant ❶ ('sɪkəfənt) *n* a person who uses flattery to win favour from individuals wielding influence; toady. [C16: from L *sȳcophanta,* from Gk *sukophantēs,* lit.: person showing a fig, apparently referring to the fig sign used in accusation, from *sukon* fig + *phainein* to show; sense prob. developed from "accuser" to "informer, flatterer"]
▸**'sycophancy** *n* ▸**sycophantic** (,sɪkə'fæntɪk) *adj* ▸**,syco'phantically** *adv*

THESAURUS

switch *n* **2** = **change,** about-turn, alteration, change of direction, reversal, shift **3** = **exchange,** substitution, swap ◆ *vb* **12** = **change,** change course, deflect, deviate, divert, shift, turn aside **13** = **exchange,** interchange, rearrange, replace by, substitute, swap, trade

swivel *vb* **4** = **turn,** pirouette, pivot, revolve, rotate, spin, swing round

swollen *adj* **2** = **enlarged,** bloated, distended, dropsical, edematous, inflamed, oedematous, puffed up, puffy, tumescent, tumid

swoop *vb* **1** = **pounce,** descend, dive, rush, stoop, sweep ◆ *n* **3, 4** = **pounce,** descent, drop, lunge, plunge, rush, stoop, sweep

sword *n* **1** = **blade,** brand (*arch.*), trusty steel **4 the sword: a** = **military power,** aggression, arms, war **b** = **death,** butchery, massacre, murder, slaying, violence

swot[1] *vb* **1** *Informal* = **study,** apply oneself to, bone up on (*inf.*), burn the midnight oil, cram (*inf.*), get up (*inf.*), lucubrate (*rare*), mug up (*Brit. sl.*), pore over, revise, toil over, work

sybarite *n* **1** = **hedonist,** epicure, epicurean, playboy, sensualist, voluptuary

sybaritic *adj* **1** = **pleasure-loving,** bacchanalian, epicurean, hedonistic, Lucullan, luxurious, luxury-loving, self-indulgent, sensual, voluptuous

sycophancy *n* = **obsequiousness,** adulation, bootlicking (*inf.*), cringing, fawning, flattery, grovelling, kowtowing, servility, slavishness, toadyism, truckling

sycophant *n* = **crawler,** apple polisher (*US sl.*), ass-kisser (*US & Canad. taboo sl.*), bootlicker (*inf.*), brown-noser (*taboo sl.*), cringer, fawner, flatterer, hanger-on, lickspittle, parasite, slave, sponger, toadeater (*rare*), toady, truckler, yes man

sycophantic *adj* = **obsequious,** all over (some-one) (*inf.*), arse-licking (*taboo sl.*), bootlicking (*inf.*), crawling, cringing, fawning, flattering, grovelling, ingratiating, parasitical,

sycosis (saɪˈkəʊsɪs) *n* chronic inflammation of the hair follicles, esp. those of the beard. [C16: via NL from Gk *sukōsis,* from *sukon* fig]

Sydenham's chorea (ˈsɪdᵊnəmz) *n* a form of chorea affecting children, often associated with rheumatic fever. Nontechnical name: **Saint Vitus's dance.** [after T. *Sydenham* (1624–89), E physician]

syenite (ˈsaɪəˌnaɪt) *n* a light-coloured coarse-grained igneous rock consisting of feldspars with hornblende. [C18: from F, from L *syēnītēs lapis* stone from *Syene* (Aswan), Egypt, where orig. quarried]
▸**syenitic** (ˌsaɪəˈnɪtɪk) *adj*

syllabary (ˈsɪləbərɪ) *n, pl* **syllabaries. 1** a table or list of syllables. **2** a set of symbols used in certain writing systems, such as one used for Japanese, in which each symbol represents a spoken syllable. [C16: from NL *syllabārium,* from L *syllaba* SYLLABLE]

syllabi (ˈsɪləˌbaɪ) *n* a plural of **syllabus.**

syllabic (sɪˈlæbɪk) *adj* **1** of or relating to syllables or the division of a word into syllables. **2** denoting a kind of verse line based on a specific number of syllables rather than being regulated by stresses or quantities. **3** (of a consonant) constituting a syllable. ◆ *n* **4** a syllabic consonant.
▸**sylˈlabically** *adv*

syllabify (sɪˈlæbɪˌfaɪ) *or* **syllabicate** *vb* **syllabifies, syllabifying, syllabified** *or* **syllabicates, syllabicating, syllabicated.** (*tr*) to divide (a word) into its constituent syllables.
▸**sylˌlabifiˈcation** *or* **sylˌlabiˈcation** *n*

syllable (ˈsɪləbᵊl) *n* **1** a combination or set of one or more units of sound in a language that must consist of a sonorous element (a sonant or vowel) and may or may not contain less sonorous elements (consonants or semivowels) flanking it: for example "paper" has two syllables. **2** (in the writing systems of certain languages, esp. ancient ones) a symbol or set of symbols standing for a syllable. **3** the least mention: *don't breathe a syllable of it.* **4 in words of one syllable.** simply; bluntly. ◆ *vb* **syllables, syllabling, syllabled. 5** to pronounce syllables of (a text); articulate. **6** (*tr*) to write down in syllables. [C14: via OF from L *syllaba,* from Gk *sullabē,* from *sullambanein* to collect together]

syllabub *or* **sillabub** (ˈsɪləˌbʌb) *n* **1** a spiced drink made of milk with rum, port, brandy, or wine, often hot. **2** *Brit.* a cold dessert made from milk or cream beaten with sugar, wine, and lemon juice. [C16: from ?]

syllabus ⓘ (ˈsɪləbəs) *n, pl* **syllabuses** *or* **syllabi** (-ˌbaɪ). **1** an outline of a course of studies, text, etc. **2** *Brit., Austral., & NZ.* **2a** the subjects studied for a particular course. **2b** a list of these subjects. [C17: from LL, erroneously from L *sittybus* parchment strip giving title and author, from Gk *sittuba*]

syllepsis (sɪˈlɛpsɪs) *n, pl* **syllepses** (-siːz). **1** (in grammar or rhetoric) the use of a single sentence construction in which a verb, adjective, etc., is made to cover two syntactical functions, as *have* in *she and they have promised to come.* **2** another word for **zeugma.** [C16: from LL, from Gk *sullēpsis,* from *sul-* SYN- + *lēpsis,* from *lambanein* to take]
▸**sylˈleptic** *adj* ▸**sylˈleptically** *adv*

syllogism (ˈsɪləˌdʒɪzəm) *n* **1** a deductive inference consisting of two premises and a conclusion, all of which are categorical propositions. The subject of the conclusion is the **minor term** and its predicate the **major term;** the **middle term** occurs in both premises but not the conclusion. There are 256 such arguments but only 24 are valid. *Some men are mortal; some men are angelic; so some mortals are angelic* is invalid, while *some temples are in ruins; all ruins are fascinating; so some temples are fascinating* is valid. Here *fascinating, in ruins,* and *temples* are respectively major, middle, and minor terms. **2** a piece of deductive reasoning from the general to the particular. [C14: via L from Gk *sullogismos,* from *sullogizesthai* to reckon together, from *logos* a discourse]
▸**ˌsylloˈgistic** *adj* ▸**ˈsylloˌgize** *or* **ˈsylloˌgise** *vb*

sylph ⓘ (sɪlf) *n* **1** a slender graceful girl or young woman. **2** any of a class of imaginary beings assumed to inhabit the air. [C17: from NL *sylphus,* prob. coined from L *silva* wood + Gk *numphē* nymph]
▸**ˈsylphˌlike** *adj*

sylva *or* **silva** (ˈsɪlvə) *n, pl* **sylvas** *or* **sylvae** (-viː). the trees growing in a particular region. [C17: from L *silva* a wood]

sylvan *or* **silvan** (ˈsɪlvən) *Chiefly poetic.* ◆ *adj* **1** of or consisting of woods or forests. **2** in woods or forests. **3** idyllically rural or rustic. ◆ *n* **4** an inhabitant of the woods, esp. a spirit. [C16: from L *silvānus,* from *silva* forest]

sylvanite (ˈsɪlvəˌnaɪt) *n* a silver-white mineral consisting of a compound of tellurium with gold and silver in the form of elongated crystals. [C18: from (*Tran*)*sylvan*(*ia*), Romania, + -ITE[1], with reference to the region where first found]

sylviculture (ˈsɪlvɪˌkʌltʃə) *n* a variant spelling of **silviculture.**

sym- *prefix* a variant of **syn-** before *b, p,* and *m.*

symbiont (ˈsɪmbɪˌɒnt) *n* an organism living in a state of symbiosis. [C19: from Gk *sumbioun* to live together, from *bioun* to live]
▸**ˌsymbiˈontic** *adj* ▸**ˌsymbiˈontically** *adv*

symbiosis (ˌsɪmbɪˈəʊsɪs) *n* **1** a close association of two interdependent animal or plant species. **2** a similar relationship between persons or groups. [C19: via NL from Gk: a living together]
▸**ˌsymbiˈotic** *adj*

symbol ⓘ (ˈsɪmbᵊl) *n* **1** something that represents or stands for something else, usually by convention or association, esp. a material object used to represent something abstract. **2** an object, person, etc., used in a literary work, film, etc., to stand for or suggest something else with which it is associated. **3** a letter, figure, or sign used in mathematics, music, etc., to represent a quantity, phenomenon, operation, function, etc. ◆ *vb* **symbols, symbolling, symbolled** *or US* **symbols, symboling, symboled. 4** (*tr*) another word for **symbolize.** [C15: from Church L *symbolum,* from Gk *sumbolon* sign, from *sumballein* to throw together, from SYN- + *ballein* to throw]

symbolic ⓘ (sɪmˈbɒlɪk) *or* **symbolical** *adj* **1** of or relating to a symbol or symbols. **2** serving as a symbol. **3** characterized by the use of symbols or symbolism.
▸**symˈbolically** *adv*

symbolic logic *n* another name for **formal logic.**

symbolism (ˈsɪmbəˌlɪzəm) *n* **1** the representation of something in symbolic form or the attribution of symbolic character to something. **2** a system of symbols or symbolic representation. **3** a symbolic significance or quality. **4** (*often cap.*) a late 19th-century movement in art that sought to express mystical or abstract ideas through the symbolic use of images.

symbolist (ˈsɪmbəlɪst) *n* **1** a person who uses or can interpret symbols, esp. as a means to revealing aspects of truth and reality. **2** an artist or writer who practises symbolism in his work. **3** (*usually cap.*) a writer associated with the symbolist movement. **4** (*often cap.*) an artist associated with the symbolist movement. ◆ *adj* **5** of, relating to, or characterizing symbolism or symbolists.
▸**ˌsymbolˈistic** *adj* ▸**ˌsymbolˈistically** *adv*

symbolist movement *n* (*usually cap.*) a movement beginning in French and Belgian poetry towards the end of the 19th century with Mallarmé, Valéry, Verlaine, Rimbaud, and others, and seeking to express states of mind rather than objective reality by the power of words and images to suggest as well as denote.

symbolize ⓘ *or* **symbolise** (ˈsɪmbəˌlaɪz) *vb* **symbolizes, symbolizing, symolized** *or* **symbolises, symbolising, symbolised. 1** (*tr*) to serve as or be a symbol of. **2** (*tr;* usually foll. by *by*) to represent by a symbol or symbols. **3** (*intr*) to use symbols. **4** (*tr*) to treat or regard as symbolic.
▸**ˌsymboliˈzation** *or* **ˌsymboliˈsation** *n*

symbol retailer *n* any member of a voluntary group of independent retailers, often using a common name or symbol, formed to obtain better prices from wholesalers or manufacturers in competition with supermarket chains. Also called: **voluntary retailer.**

symmetrical ⓘ (sɪˈmɛtrɪkᵊl) *adj* possessing or displaying symmetry.

symmetry ⓘ (ˈsɪmɪtrɪ) *n, pl* **symmetries. 1** similarity, correspondence, or balance among systems or parts of a system. **2** *Maths.* an exact correspondence in position or form about a given point, line, or plane. **3** beauty or harmony of form based on a proportionate arrangement of parts. [C16: from L *symmetria,* from Gk *summetria* proportion, from SYN- + *metron* measure]

sympathectomy (ˌsɪmpəˈθɛktəmɪ) *n, pl* **sympathectomies.** the surgical excision or chemical destruction (**chemical sympathectomy**) of one or more parts of the sympathetic nervous system. [C20: from SYMPATHETIC + -ECTOMY]

sympathetic ⓘ (ˌsɪmpəˈθɛtɪk) *adj* **1** characterized by, feeling, or showing sympathy; understanding. **2** in accord with the subject's personality or mood; congenial: *a sympathetic atmosphere.* **3** (when *postpositive,* often foll. by *to* or *towards*) showing agreement (with) or favour (towards). **4** *Anat., physiol.* of or relating to the division of the autonomic nervous system that acts in opposition to the parasympathetic system accelerating the heartbeat, dilating the bronchi, inhib-

THESAURUS

servile, slavish, slimy, smarmy (*Brit. inf.*), time-serving, toadying, unctuous

syllabus *n* 1 = **course of study**, curriculum

sylphlike *adj* 1 = **slender**, graceful, lithe, svelte, willowy

symbol *n* 1-3 = **sign**, badge, emblem, figure, glyph, image, logo, mark, representation, token, type

symbolic *adj* 2, 3 = **representative**, allegorical, emblematic, figurative, significant, token, typical

symbolize *vb* 1 = **represent**, betoken, body forth, connote, denote, exemplify, mean, personify, signify, stand for, typify

symmetrical *adj* = **balanced**, in proportion, proportional, regular, well-proportioned
Antonyms *adj* asymmetrical, disorderly, irregular, lopsided, unbalanced, unequal, unsymmetrical

symmetry *n* 1 = **balance**, agreement, correspondence, evenness, form, harmony, order, proportion, regularity

sympathetic *adj* 1 = **caring**, affectionate, commiserating, compassionate, concerned, condoling, feeling, interested, kind, kindly, pitying, responsive, supportive, tender, understanding, warm, warm-hearted 2 = **like-minded**, agreeable, appreciative, companionable, compatible, congenial, friendly, responsive, well-intentioned 3 *often foll. by* **to** = **favourably disposed towards**, agreeable with, approving of, encouraging, friendly to, in sympathy with, pro, well-disposed towards
Antonyms *adj* ≠ **caring**: apathetic, callous, cold, cold-hearted, disinterested, indifferent, inhumane, insensitive, steely, uncaring, uncompassionate, unfeeling, uninterested, unmoved, unsympathetic ≠ **like-minded**: uncongenial, unresponsive

sympathetically *adv* 1 = **feelingly**, appreciatively, kindly, perceptively, responsively, sensitively, understandingly, warm-heartedly, warmly, with compassion, with feeling, with interest

iting the smooth muscles of the digestive tract, etc. Cf. **parasympathetic.** 5 relating to vibrations occurring as a result of similar vibrations in a neighbouring body: *sympathetic strings on a sitar.*
▸ **ˌsympaˈthetically** *adv*

sympathetic magic *n* a type of magic in which it is sought to produce a large-scale effect, often at a distance, by performing some small-scale ceremony resembling it, such as the pouring of water on an altar to induce rainfall.

sympathize ❶ *or* **sympathise** (ˈsɪmpəˌθaɪz) *vb* **sympathizes, sympathizing, sympathized** *or* **sympathises, sympathising, sympathised.** (*intr;* often foll. by *with*) **1** to feel or express compassion or sympathy (for); commiserate: *he sympathized with my troubles.* **2** to share or understand the sentiments or ideas (of); be in sympathy (with).
▸ **ˈsympaˌthizer** *or* **ˈsympaˌthiser** *n*

sympatholytic (ˌsɪmpəθəʊˈlɪtɪk) *Med.* ◆ *adj* **1a** inhibiting or antagonistic to nerve impulses of the sympathetic nervous system. **1b** of or relating to such inhibition. ◆ *n* **2** a sympatholytic drug. Cf. **sympathomimetic.** [C20: from SYMPATH(ETIC) + -LYTIC]

sympathomimetic (ˌsɪmpəθəʊmɪˈmetɪk) *Med.* ◆ *adj* **1** causing a physiological effect similar to that produced by stimulation of the sympathetic nervous system. ◆ *n* **2** a sympathomimetic drug. Cf. **sympatholytic.** [C20: from SYMPATH(ETIC) + MIMETIC]

sympathy ❶ (ˈsɪmpəθɪ) *n, pl* **sympathies. 1** the sharing of another's emotions, esp. of sorrow or anguish; compassion. **2** affinity or harmony, usually of feelings or interests, between persons or things: *to be in sympathy with someone.* **3** mutual affection or understanding arising from such a relationship. **4** the condition of a physical system or body when its behaviour is similar or corresponds to that of a different system that influences it, such as the vibration of sympathetic strings. **5** (*sometimes pl*) a feeling of loyalty, support, or accord, as for an idea, cause, etc. **6** *Physiol.* the relationship between two organs or parts whereby a change in one affects the other. [C16: from L *sympathīa,* from Gk, from *sumpathēs,* from SYN- + *pathos* suffering]

sympathy strike *n* a strike organized in support of another strike or cause. Also called: **sympathetic strike.**

symphonic poem *n Music.* an extended orchestral composition, originated by Liszt (1811–86), Hungarian composer, based on nonmusical material, such as a work of literature or folk tale. Also called: **tone poem.**

symphony (ˈsɪmfənɪ) *n, pl* **symphonies. 1** an extended large-scale orchestral composition, usually with several movements, at least one of which is in sonata form. **2** a piece of instrumental music in up to three very short movements, used as an overture to or interlude in a baroque opera. **3** any purely orchestral movement in a vocal work, such as a cantata or oratorio. **4** short for **symphony orchestra. 5** anything distinguished by a harmonious composition: *the picture was a symphony of green.* **6** *Arch.* harmony in general; concord. [C13: from OF *symphonie,* from L *symphōnia* concord, from Gk, from SYN- + *phōnē* sound]
▸ **symphonic** (sɪmˈfɒnɪk) *adj* ▸ **symˈphonically** *adv*

symphony orchestra *n Music.* an orchestra capable of performing symphonies, esp. a large orchestra comprising strings, brass, woodwind, harp and percussion.

symphysis (ˈsɪmfɪsɪs) *n, pl* **symphyses** (-ˌsiːz). **1** *Anat., bot.* a growing together of parts or structures, such as two bony surfaces joined by an intermediate layer of fibrous cartilage. **2** a line marking this growing together. **3** *Pathol.* an abnormal adhesion of two or more parts or structures. [C16: via NL from Gk *sumphusis,* from *sumphuein,* from SYN- + *phuein* to grow]
▸ **symphysial** *or* **symphyseal** (sɪmˈfɪzɪəl) *adj*

sympodium (sɪmˈpəʊdɪəm) *n, pl* **sympodia** (-dɪə). the main axis of growth in the grapevine and similar plants: a number of lateral branches that arise from just behind the apex of the main stem, which ceases to grow. [C19: from NL, from SYN- + Gk *podion* a little foot]
▸ **symˈpodial** *adj* ▸ **symˈpodially** *adv*

symposium (sɪmˈpəʊzɪəm) *n, pl* **symposiums** *or* **symposia** (-zɪə). **1** a conference or meeting for the discussion of some subject, esp. an academic topic or social problem. **2** a collection of scholarly contributions on a given subject. **3** (in classical Greece) a drinking party with intellectual conversation, music, etc. [C16: via L from Gk *sumposion,* from *sumpinein* to drink together]

symptom ❶ (ˈsɪmptəm) *n* **1** *Med.* any sensation or change in bodily function experienced by a patient that is associated with a particular disease. **2** any phenomenon or circumstance accompanying something and regarded as evidence of its existence; indication. [C16: from LL *symptōma,* from Gk *sumptōma* chance, from *sumpiptein* to occur, from SYN- + *piptein* to fall]

symptomatic ❶ (ˌsɪmptəˈmætɪk) *adj* **1** (often foll. by *of*) being a symptom; indicative: *symptomatic of insanity.* **2** of, relating to, or according to symptoms: *a symptomatic analysis.*
▸ **ˌsymptoˈmatically** *adv*

symptomatology (ˌsɪmptəməˈtɒlədʒɪ) *n* the branch of medicine concerned with the study and classification of the symptoms of disease.

syn. *abbrev. for* synonym(ous).

syn- *prefix* **1** with or together: *synecology.* **2** fusion: *syngamy.* [from Gk *sun* together]

synaeresis (sɪˈnɪərɪsɪs) *n* a variant spelling of **syneresis.**

synaesthesia *or US* **synesthesia** (ˌsɪniːsˈθiːzɪə) *n* **1** *Physiol.* a sensation experienced in a part of the body other than the part stimulated. **2** *Psychol.* the subjective sensation of a sense other than the one being stimulated. [C19: from NL, from SYN- + *-esthesia,* from Gk *aisthēsis* sensation]
▸ **synaesthetic** *or US* **synesthetic** (ˌsɪniːsˈθetɪk) *adj*

synagogue (ˈsɪnəˌgɒg) *n* **1a** a building for Jewish religious services and religious instruction. **1b** (*as modifier*): *synagogue services.* **2** a congregation of Jews who assemble for worship or religious study. **3** the religion of Judaism as organized in such congregations. [C12: from OF, from LL *synagōga,* from Gk *sunagōgē* a gathering, from *sunagein* to bring together]
▸ **synagogical** (ˌsɪnəˈgɒdʒɪkᵊl) *or* **synagogal** (ˈsɪnəˌgɒgᵊl) *adj*

synapse (ˈsaɪnæps) *n* the point at which a nerve impulse is relayed from the terminal portion of an axon to the dendrites of an adjacent neuron.

synapsis (sɪˈnæpsɪs) *n, pl* **synapses** (-siːz). **1** *Cytology.* the association in pairs of homologous chromosomes at the start of meiosis. **2** another word for **synapse.** [C19: from NL, from Gk *sunapsis* junction, from *sunaptein* to join together]
▸ **synaptic** (sɪˈnæptɪk) *adj* ▸ **synˈaptically** *adv*

synarthrosis (ˌsɪnɑːˈθrəʊsɪs) *n, pl* **synarthroses** (-siːz). *Anat.* any of various joints which lack a synovial cavity and are virtually immovable; a fixed joint. [C16: via NL from Gk *sunarthrōsis,* from *sunarthrousthai* to be connected by joints, from *sun-* SYN- + *arthron* a joint]
▸ **ˌsynarˈthrodial** *adj*

sync *or* **synch** (sɪŋk) *Films, television, computing.* ◆ *vb* **1** an informal word for **synchronize.** ◆ *n* **2** an informal word for **synchronization** (esp. in **in** *or* **out of sync**).

syncarp (ˈsɪnkɑːp) *n Bot.* a fleshy multiple fruit, formed from two or more carpels of one flower or the aggregated fruits of several flowers. [C19: from NL *syncarpium,* from SYN- + Gk *karpos* fruit]

syncarpous (sɪnˈkɑːpəs) *adj* **1** (of the ovaries of certain flowering plants) consisting of united carpels. **2** of or relating to a syncarp.

synchro (ˈsɪŋkrəʊ) *n, pl* **synchros. 1** Also called: **selsyn.** any of a number of electrical devices in which the angular position of a rotating part is transformed into a voltage, or vice versa. **2** short for **synchronized swimming.**

synchro- *combining form.* indicating synchronization: *synchromesh.*

synchrocyclotron (ˌsɪŋkrəʊˈsaɪkləˌtrɒn) *n* a cyclotron in which the frequency of the electric field is modulated to allow for relativistic effects at high velocities and thus produce higher energies.

synchromesh (ˈsɪŋkrəʊˌmeʃ) *adj* **1** (of a gearbox, etc.) having a system of clutches that synchronizes the speeds of the driving and driven members before engagement to avoid shock in gear changing and to reduce noise and wear. ◆ *n* **2** a gear system having these features. [C20: shortened from *synchronized mesh*]

synchronic (sɪnˈkrɒnɪk) *adj* **1** concerned with the events or phenomena at a particular period without considering historical antecedents: *synchronic linguistics.* Cf. **diachronic. 2** synchronous.
▸ **synˈchronically** *adv* ▸ **synchronicity** (ˌsɪnkrəˈnɪsɪtɪ) *n*

synchronicity (ˌsɪŋkrəˈnɪsɪtɪ) *n* an apparently meaningful coincidence in time of two or more similar or identical events that are causally unrelated. [C20: coined by Carl *Jung* (1875–1961), Swiss psychologist, from SYNCHRONIC + -ITY]

synchronism (ˈsɪŋkrəˌnɪzəm) *n* **1** the quality or condition of being synchronous. **2** a chronological list of historical persons and events, arranged to show parallel or synchronous occurrence. **3** the representation in a work of art of one or more incidents that occurred at separate times. [C16: from Gk *sunkhronismos*]
▸ **ˌsynchroˈnistic** *or* **ˌsynchroˈnistical** *adj* ▸ **ˌsynchroˈnistically** *adv*

synchronize *or* **synchronise** (ˈsɪŋkrəˌnaɪz) *vb* **synchronizes, synchronizing, synchronized** *or* **synchronises, synchronising, synchronised. 1** (when *intr,* usually foll. by *with*) to occur or recur or cause to occur or recur at the same time or in unison. **2** to indicate or cause to indicate the same time: *synchronize your watches.* **3** (*tr*) *Films.* to establish (the picture and soundtrack records) in their correct relative position. **4** (*tr*) to designate (events) as simultaneous.
▸ **ˌsynchroniˈzation** *or* **ˌsynchroniˈsation** *n* ▸ **ˈsynchroˌnizer** *or* **ˈsynchroˌniser** *n*

THESAURUS

sympathize *vb* **1** = **feel for,** bleed for, commiserate, condole, empathize, feel one's heart go out to, grieve with, have compassion, offer consolation, pity, share another's sorrow **2** = **agree,** be in accord, be in sympathy, go along with, identify with, side with, understand
Antonyms *vb* ≠ **feel for:** disdain, disregard, have no feelings for, mock, scorn ≠ **agree:** disagree, fail to understand, misunderstand, oppose, reject

sympathizer *n* **2** = **supporter,** fellow traveller, partisan, protagonist, well-wisher

sympathy *n* **1** = **compassion,** commiseration, condolence(s), empathy, pity, tenderness, thoughtfulness, understanding **2** = **affinity,** agreement, congeniality, correspondence, fellow feeling, harmony, rapport, union, warmth
Antonyms *n* ≠ **compassion:** callousness, coldness, disdain, hard-heartedness, indifference, insensitivity, lack of feeling *or* understanding *or* sympathy, pitilessness, scorn ≠ **affinity:** antagonism, disapproval, hostility, opposition, resistance, unfriendliness

synchronized swimming *n* a sport in which swimmers move in patterns in time to music. Sometimes shortened to **synchro** *or* **synchro swimming.**

synchronous ('sɪŋkrənəs) *adj* **1** occurring at the same time. **2** *Physics.* (of periodic phenomena, such as voltages) having the same frequency and phase. **3** occurring or recurring exactly together and at the same rate. [C17: from LL *synchronus,* from Gk *sunkhronos,* from SYN- + *khronos* time]
▸**'synchronously** *adv* ▸**'synchronousness** *n*

synchronous machine *n* an electrical machine whose rotating speed is proportional to the frequency of the alternating-current supply and independent of the load.

synchronous motor *n* an alternating-current motor that runs at a speed that is equal to or is a multiple of the frequency of the supply.

synchrony ('sɪŋkrənɪ) *n* the state of being synchronous; simultaneity.

synchrotron ('sɪŋkrəˌtrɒn) *n* a particle accelerator having an electric field of fixed frequency and a changing magnetic field. [C20: from SYNCHRO- + (ELEC)TRON]

syncline ('sɪŋklaɪn) *n* a downward fold of stratified rock in which the strata slope towards a vertical axis. [C19: from SYN- + Gk *klīnein* to lean]
▸**syn'clinal** *adj*

Syncom ('sɪnˌkɒm) *n* a communications satellite in stationary orbit. [C20: from *syn(chronous) com(munication)*]

syncopate ('sɪŋkəˌpeɪt) *vb* **syncopates, syncopating, syncopated.** (*tr*) **1** *Music.* to modify or treat (a beat, rhythm, note, etc.) by syncopation. **2** to shorten (a word) by omitting sounds or letters from the middle. [C17: from Med. L *syncopāre* to omit a letter or syllable, from LL *syncopa* SYNCOPE]
▸**'syncoˌpator** *n*

syncopation (ˌsɪŋkə'peɪʃən) *n* **1** *Music.* **1a** the displacement of the usual rhythmic accent away from a strong beat onto a weak beat. **1b** a note, beat, rhythm, etc., produced by syncopation. **2** another word for **syncope** (sense 2).

syncope ('sɪŋkəpɪ) *n* **1** a technical word for a **faint. 2** the omission of sounds or letters from the middle of a word. [C16: from LL *syncopa,* from Gk *sunkopē* a cutting off, from SYN- + *koptein* to cut]
▸**syncopic** (sɪŋ'kɒpɪk) *or* **'syncopal** *adj*

syncretism ('sɪŋkrɪˌtɪzəm) *n* **1** the tendency to syncretize. **2** the historical tendency of languages to reduce their use of inflection, as in the development of Old English into Modern English. [C17: from NL *syncrētismus,* from Gk *sunkrētismos* alliance of Cretans, from *sunkrētizein* to join forces (in the manner of the Cretan towns), from SYN- + *Krēs* a Cretan]
▸**syncretic** (sɪŋ'kretɪk) *or* ˌ**syncre'tistic** *adj* ▸**'syncretist** *n*

syncretize *or* **syncretise** ('sɪŋkrɪˌtaɪz) *vb* **syncretizes, syncretizing, syncretized** *or* **syncretises, syncretising, syncretised.** to attempt to combine the characteristic teachings, beliefs, or practices of (differing systems of religion or philosophy).
▸ˌ**syncreti'zation** *or* ˌ**syncreti'sation** *n*

syndactyl (sɪn'dæktɪl) *adj* **1** (of certain animals) having two or more digits growing fused together. ◆ *n* **2** an animal with this arrangement of digits.
▸**syn'dactylism** *n*

syndesmosis (ˌsɪndes'məʊsɪs) *n, pl* **syndesmoses** (-siːz). *Anat.* a type of joint in which the articulating bones are held together by a ligament of connective tissue. [C18: NL, from Gk *sundein* to bind together]
▸**syndesmotic** (ˌsɪndes'mɒtɪk) *adj*

syndetic (sɪn'detɪk) *adj* denoting a grammatical construction in which two clauses are connected by a conjunction. [C17: from Gk *sundetikos,* from *sundetos* bound together]
▸**syndesis** (sɪn'diːsɪs) *n* ▸**syn'detically** *adv*

syndic ('sɪndɪk) *n* **1** *Brit.* a business agent of some universities or other bodies. **2** (in several countries) a government administrator or magistrate with varying powers. [C17: via OF from LL *syndicus,* from Gk *sundikos* defendant's advocate, from SYN- + *dikē* justice]
▸**'syndical** *adj*

syndicalism ('sɪndɪkəˌlɪzəm) *n* **1** a revolutionary movement and theory advocating seizure of the means of production and distribution by syndicates of workers, esp. by a general strike. **2** an economic system resulting from such action.
▸**'syndical** *adj* ▸**'syndicalist** *adj, n* ▸ˌ**syndical'istic** *adj*

syndicate *n* ('sɪndɪkɪt). **1** an association of business enterprises or individuals organized to undertake a joint project. **2** a news agency that sells articles, photographs, etc., to a number of newspapers for simultaneous publication. **3** any association formed to carry out an enterprise of common interest to its members. **4** a board of syndics or the office of syndic. ◆ *vb* ('sɪndɪˌkeɪt) **syndicates, syndicating, syndicated. 5** (*tr*) to sell (articles, photographs, etc.) to several newspapers for simultaneous publication. **6** (*tr*) *US.* to sell (a programme or programmes) to several local commercial stations. **7** to form a syndicate of (people). [C17: from OF *syndicat* office of a SYNDIC]
▸ˌ**syndi'cation** *n*

syndicated research *n Marketing.* a large-scale marketing research project undertaken without being commissioned and subsequently offered to interested parties.

syndrome ('sɪndrəʊm) *n* **1** *Med.* any combination of signs and symptoms that are indicative of a particular disease or disorder. **2** a symptom, characteristic, or set of symptoms or characteristics indicating the existence of a condition, problem, etc. [C16: via NL from Gk *sundromē,* lit.: a running together, from SYN- + *dramein* to run]
▸**syndromic** (sɪn'drɒmɪk) *adj*

syne *or* **syn** (saɪn) *adv, prep, conj* a Scottish word for **since.** [C14: prob. rel. to OE *sīth* since]

synecdoche (sɪn'ekdəkɪ) *n* a figure of speech in which a part is substituted for a whole or a whole for a part, as in *50 head of cattle* for *50 cows,* or *the army* for *a soldier.* [C14: via L from Gk *sunekdokhē,* from SYN- + *ekdokhē* interpretation, from *dekhesthai* to accept]
▸**synecdochic** (ˌsɪnek'dɒkɪk) *or* ˌ**synec'dochical** *adj*

synecious (sɪ'niːʃəs) *adj* a variant spelling of **synoecious.**

synecology (ˌsɪnɪ'kɒlədʒɪ) *n* the ecological study of communities of plants and animals.
▸**synecologic** (sɪnˌekə'lɒdʒɪk) *or* **synˌeco'logical** *adj* ▸**synˌeco'logically** *adv*

syneresis *or* **synaeresis** (sɪ'nɪərɪsɪs) *n* **1** *Chem.* the process in which a gel contracts on standing and exudes liquid, as in the separation of whey in cheese-making. **2** the contraction of two vowels into a diphthong. [C16: via LL from Gk *sunairesis* a shortening, from *sunairein* to draw together, from SYN- + *hairein* to take]

synergism ('sɪnəˌdʒɪzəm, sɪ'nɜː-) *n* **1** Also called: **synergy.** the working together of two or more drugs, muscles, etc., to produce an effect greater than the sum of their individual effects. **2** another name for **synergy** (sense 1). [C18: from NL *synergismus,* from Gk *sunergos,* from SYN- + *ergon* work]
▸ˌ**syner'getic** *adj* ▸**'synergist** *n, adj*

synergy ('sɪnədʒɪ) *n, pl* **synergies. 1** Also called: **synergism.** the potential ability of individual organizations or groups to be more successful or productive as a result of a merger. **2** another name for **synergism** (sense 1). [C19: from NL *synergia,* from Gk *sunergos;* see SYNERGISM]
▸**sy'nergic** *adj*

synesis ('sɪnɪsɪs) *n* a grammatical construction in which the inflection or form of a word is conditioned by the meaning rather than the syntax, as for example the plural form *have* with the singular noun *group* in the sentence *the group have already assembled.* [via NL from Gk *sunesis* union, from *sunienai* to bring together, from SYN- + *hienai* to send]

synesthesia (ˌsɪniːs'θiːzɪə) *n* the usual US spelling of **synaesthesia.**

syngamy ('sɪŋgəmɪ) *or* **syngenesis** (sɪn'dʒenɪsɪs) *n* reproduction involving the fusion of a male and female haploid gamete. Also called: **sexual reproduction.**
▸**syngamic** (sɪŋ'gæmɪk) *or* **syngamous** ('sɪŋgəməs) *adj*

synod ('sɪnəd, 'sɪnɒd) *n* **1** a special ecclesiastical council, esp. of a diocese, formally convened to discuss ecclesiastical affairs. **2** *Rare.* any council, esp. for discussion. [C14: from LL *synodus,* from Gk SYN- + *hodos* a way]
▸**'synodal** *adj*

synodic (sɪ'nɒdɪk) *adj* relating to or involving a conjunction or two successive conjunctions of the same star, planet, or satellite.

synodic month *n* See **month** (sense 6).

synoecious *or* **synecious** (sɪ'niːʃəs) *adj* (of plants) having male and female organs on the same flower or structure. [C19: SYN- + *-oecious,* from Gk *oikion* dim. of *oikos* house]

synonym ('sɪnənɪm) *n* **1** a word that means the same or nearly the same as another word, such as *bucket* and *pail.* **2** a word or phrase used as another name for something, such as *Hellene* for a *Greek.*
▸ˌ**syno'nymic** *or* ˌ**syno'nymical** *adj* ▸ˌ**syno'nymity** *n*

synonymous ❶ (sɪ'nɒnɪməs) *adj* **1** (often foll. by *with*) being a synonym (of). **2** (*postpositive;* foll. by *with*) closely associated (with) or suggestive (of): *his name was synonymous with greed.*
▸**syn'onymously** *adv* ▸**syn'onymousness** *n*

synonymy (sɪ'nɒnɪmɪ) *n, pl* **synonymies. 1** the study of synonyms. **2** the character of being synonymous; equivalence. **3** a list or collection of synonyms, esp. one in which their meanings are discriminated.

synopsis ❶ (sɪ'nɒpsɪs) *n, pl* **synopses** (-siːz). a brief review of a subject; summary. [C17: via LL from Gk *sunopsis,* from SYN- + *opsis* view]

synopsize *or* **synopsise** (sɪ'nɒpsaɪz) *vb* **synopsizes, synopsizing, synopsized** *or* **synopsises, synopsising, synopsised.** (*tr*) **1** *US.* variants of **epitomize. 2** *US & Canad.* to make a synopsis of.

synoptic (sɪ'nɒptɪk) *adj* **1** of or relating to a synopsis. **2** (*often cap.*) *Bible.* **2a** (of the Gospels of Matthew, Mark, and Luke) presenting the narrative of Christ's life, ministry, etc., from a point of view held in common by all three, and with close similarities in content, order, etc. **2b**

THESAURUS

symptom *n* **2** = **sign**, expression, indication, mark, note, syndrome, token, warning

symptomatic *adj* **1** = **indicative**, characteristic, suggestive

synonymous *adj* **1** = **equivalent**, equal, identical, identified, interchangeable, one and the same, similar, tantamount, the same

synopsis *n* = **summary**, abridgment, abstract, *aperçu*, compendium, condensation, conspectus, digest, epitome, outline, outline sketch, précis, résumé, review, rundown

of or relating to these three Gospels. **3** *Meteorol.* concerned with the distribution of meteorological conditions over a wide area at a given time: *a synoptic chart.* ◆ *n* **4** (*often cap.*) *Bible.* **4a** any of the three synoptic Gospels. **4b** any of the authors of these. [C18: from Gk *sunoptikos*]
▸**syn'optically** *adv* ▸**syn'optist** *n*

synovia (saɪ'nəʊvɪə, sɪ-) *n* a transparent viscid lubricating fluid, secreted by the membrane lining joints, tendon sheaths, etc. [C17: from NL, prob. from SYN- + L *ōvum* egg]
▸**syn'ovial** *adj*

synovitis (ˌsaɪnəʊ'vaɪtɪs, ˌsɪn-) *n* inflammation of the membrane surrounding a joint.
▸**synovitic** (ˌsaɪnəʊ'vɪtɪk, ˌsɪn-) *adj*

synroc ('sɪnˌrɒk) *n* a titanium-ceramic substance that can incorporate nuclear waste in its crystals. [from *syn(thetic)* + *roc(k)*]

syntactics (sɪn'tæktɪks) *n* (*functioning as sing*) the branch of semiotics that deals with the formal properties of symbol systems; proof theory.

syntagma (sɪn'tægmə) *or* **syntagm** ('sɪnˌtæm) *n, pl* **syntagmata** (-'tægmətə) *or* **syntagms. 1** a word or phrase forming a syntactic unit. **2** a systematic collection of statements or propositions. [C17: from LL, from Gk, from *suntassein* to put in order; see SYNTAX]
▸ˌ**syntag'matic** *adj*

syntax ('sɪntæks) *n* **1** the branch of linguistics that deals with the grammatical arrangement of words and morphemes in sentences. **2** the totality of facts about the grammatical arrangement of words in a language. **3** a systematic statement of the rules governing the grammatical arrangement of words and morphemes in a language. **4** a systematic statement of the rules governing the properly formed formulas of a logical system. [C17: from LL *syntaxis*, from Gk *suntaxis*, from *suntassein* to put in order, from SYN- + *tassein* to arrange]
▸**syn'tactic** *or* **syn'tactical** *adj* ▸**syn'tactically** *adv*

synth (sɪnθ) *n* short for **synthesizer.**

synthesis ❶ ('sɪnθɪsɪs) *n, pl* **syntheses** (-ˌsiːz). **1** the process of combining objects or ideas into a complex whole. **2** the combination or whole produced by such a process. **3** the process of producing a compound by a chemical reaction or series of reactions, usually from simpler starting materials. **4** *Linguistics.* the use of inflections rather than word order and function words to express the syntactic relations in a language. [C17: via L from Gk *sunthesis*, from *suntithenai* to put together, from SYN- + *tithenai* to place]
▸'**synthesist** *n*

synthesis gas *n Chem.* **1** a mixture of carbon dioxide, carbon monoxide, and hydrogen formerly made by reacting water gas with steam to enrich the proportion of hydrogen in the synthesis of ammonia. **2** a similar mixture of gases made by steam reforming natural gas, used for synthesizing organic chemicals and as a fuel.

synthesize ('sɪnθɪˌsaɪz), **synthetize,** *or* **synthesise, synthetise** *vb* **synthesizes, synthesizing, synthesized; synthetizes, synthetizing, synthetized** *or* **synthesises, synthesising, synthesised; synthetises, synthetising, synthetised. 1** to combine or cause to combine into a whole. **2** (*tr*) to produce by synthesis.
▸ˌ**synthesi'zation,** ˌ**syntheti'zation** *or* ˌ**synthesi'sation,** ˌ**syntheti'sation** *n*

synthesizer ('sɪnθɪˌsaɪzə) *n* **1** an electronic musical instrument, usually operated by means of a keyboard, in which sounds are produced by oscillators, filters, and amplifiers. **2** a person or thing that synthesizes.

synthetic ❶ (sɪn'θetɪk) *adj also* **synthetical. 1** (of a substance or material) made artificially by chemical reaction. **2** not genuine; insincere: *synthetic compassion.* **3** denoting languages, such as Latin, whose morphology is characterized by synthesis. **4** *Philosophy.* **4a** (of a proposition) having a truth-value that is not determined solely by virtue of the meanings of the words, as in *all men are arrogant.* **4b** contingent. ◆ *n* **5** a synthetic substance or material. [C17: from NL *syntheticus*, from Gk *sunthetikos* expert in putting together, from *suntithenai* to put together; see SYNTHESIS]
▸**syn'thetically** *adv*

syphilis ('sɪfɪlɪs) *n* a sexually transmitted disease caused by infection with the microorganism *Treponema pallidum:* characterized by an ulcerating chancre, usually on the genitals and progressing through the lymphatic system to nearly all tissues of the body, producing serious clinical manifestations. [C18: from NL *Syphilis* (*sive Morbus Gallicus*) "Syphilis (or the French disease)", title of a poem (1530) by G. Fracastoro, It. physician and poet, in which a shepherd *Syphilus* is portrayed as the first victim of the disease]
▸**syphilitic** (ˌsɪfɪ'lɪtɪk) *adj* ▸'**syphiˌloid** *adj*

syphon ('saɪfᵊn) *n, vb* a variant spelling of **siphon.**

Syriac ('sɪrɪˌæk) *n* a dialect of Aramaic spoken in Syria until about the 13th century A.D.

Syrian ('sɪrɪən) *adj* **1** of or relating to Syria, a republic in W Asia, its people, or their dialect of Arabic. ◆ *n* **2** a native or inhabitant of Syria.

syringa (sɪ'rɪŋgə) *n* another name for **mock orange** (sense 1) or **lilac** (sense 1). [C17: from NL, from Gk *surinx* tube, from use of its hollow stems for pipes]

syringe ('sɪrɪndʒ, sɪ'rɪndʒ) *n* **1** *Med.* a hypodermic syringe or a rubber ball with a slender nozzle, for use in withdrawing or injecting fluids, cleaning wounds, etc. **2** any similar device for injecting, spraying, or extracting liquids by means of pressure or suction. ◆ *vb* **syringes, syringing, syringed. 3** (*tr*) to cleanse, inject, or spray with a syringe. [C15: from LL, from L: SYRINX]

syringomyelia (səˌrɪŋgəʊmaɪ'iːlɪə) *n* a chronic progressive disease of the spinal cord in which cavities form in the grey matter: characterized by loss of the sense of pain and temperature. [C19: *syringo-*, from Gk: SYRINX + *-myelia* from Gk *muelos* marrow]
▸**syringomyelic** (səˌrɪŋgəʊmaɪ'elɪk) *adj*

syrinx ('sɪrɪŋks) *n, pl* **syringes** (sɪ'rɪndʒiːz) *or* **syrinxes. 1** the vocal organ of a bird, situated in the lower part of the trachea. **2** (in classical Greek music) a panpipe or set of panpipes. [C17: via L from Gk *surinx* pipe]
▸**syringeal** (sɪ'rɪndʒɪəl) *adj*

syrup ('sɪrəp) *n* **1** a solution of sugar dissolved in water and often flavoured with fruit juice: used for sweetening fruit, etc. **2** any of various thick sweet liquids prepared for cooking or table use from molasses, sugars, etc. **3** *Inf.* cloying sentimentality. **4** a liquid medicine containing a sugar solution for flavouring or preservation. ◆ Also: **sirup.** [C15: from Med. L *syrupus*, from Ar. *sharāb* a drink, from *shariba* to drink]
▸'**syrupy** *adj*

syssarcosis (ˌsɪsɑː'kəʊsɪs) *n, pl* **syssarcoses** (-siːz). *Anat.* the union or articulation of bones by muscle. [C17: from NL, from Gk *sussarkōsis*, from *sus-* SYN- + *sarkoun* to become fleshy, from *sarx* flesh]
▸**syssarcotic** (ˌsɪsɑː'kɒtɪk) *adj*

systaltic (sɪ'stæltɪk) *adj* (esp. of the action of the heart) of, relating to, or characterized by alternate contractions and dilations; pulsating. [C17: from LL *systalticus*, from Gk, from *sustellein* to contract, from SYN- + *stellein* to place]

system ❶ ('sɪstəm) *n* **1** a group or combination of interrelated, interdependent, or interacting elements forming a collective entity; a methodical or coordinated assemblage of parts, facts, etc. **2** any scheme of classification or arrangement. **3** a network of communications, transportation, or distribution. **4** a method or complex of methods: *he has a perfect system at roulette.* **5** orderliness; an ordered manner. **6 the system.** (*often cap.*) society seen as an environment exploiting, restricting, and repressing individuals. **7** an organism considered as a functioning entity. **8** any of various bodily parts or structures that are anatomically or physiologically related: *the digestive system.* **9** one's physiological or psychological constitution: *get it out of your system.* **10** any assembly of electronic, mechanical, etc., components with interdependent functions, usually forming a self-contained unit: *a brake system.* **11** a group of celestial bodies that are associated as a result of natural laws, esp. gravitational attraction: *the solar system.* **12** a point of view or doctrine used to interpret a branch of knowledge. **13** *Mineralogy.* one of a group of divisions into which crystals may be placed on the basis of the lengths and inclinations of their axes. **14** *Geol.* a stratigraphical unit for the rock strata formed during a period of geological time. [C17: from F, from LL *systēma*, from Gk *sustēma*, from SYN- + *histanai* to cause to stand]

systematic ❶ (ˌsɪstɪ'mætɪk) *adj* **1** characterized by the use of order and planning; methodical: *a systematic administrator.* **2** comprising or resembling a system: *systematic theology.* **3** Also: **systematical.** *Biol.* of or relating to taxonomic classification.
▸ˌ**system'atically** *adv* ▸'**systemaˌtism** *n* ▸'**systematist** *n*

systematics (ˌsɪstɪ'mætɪks) *n* (*functioning as sing*) the study of systems and the principles of classification and nomenclature.

systematize ❶ ('sɪstɪməˌtaɪz), **systemize** *or* **systematise, system-**

THESAURUS

synthesis *n* **1 = combining,** amalgamation, coalescence, integration, unification, welding **2 = combination,** amalgam, blend, composite, compound, fusion, meld, union

synthetic *adj* **1 = artificial,** ersatz, fake, man-made, manufactured, mock, pseudo (*inf.*), sham, simulated
Antonyms *adj* authentic, genuine, kosher (*inf.*), natural, pure, real

system *n* **1 = method,** fixed order, frame of reference, methodology, modus operandi, practice, procedure, routine, technique, theory, usage **2 = arrangement,** classification, combination, coordination, organization, scheme, set-up (*inf.*), structure **5 = orderliness,** definite plan, logical process, method, methodicalness, regularity, systematization

systematic *adj* **1 = methodical,** businesslike, efficient, orderly, organized, precise, standardized, systematized, well-ordered
Antonyms *adj* arbitrary, cursory, disorderly, disorganized, haphazard, indiscriminate, random, slapdash, unbusinesslike, unmethodical, unpremeditated, unsystematic

systematize *vb* **= arrange,** classify, dispose, make uniform, methodize, organize, put in order, rationalize, regulate, schematize, sequence, standardize, tabulate

ise *vb* **systematizes, systematizing, systematized; systemizes, systemizing, systemized** *or* **systematises, systematising, systematised; systemises, systemising, systemised.** (*tr*) to arrange in a system.
▸**ˌsystematiˈzation, ˌsystematiˈsation** *or* **ˌsystemiˈzation, ˌsystemiˈsation** *n* ▸**ˈsystemaˌtizer, ˈsystemaˌtiser** *or* **ˈsysteˌmizer, ˈsysteˌmiser** *n*

system building *n* a method of building in which prefabricated components are used to speed the construction of buildings.
▸**ˌsystem ˈbuilt** *adj*

Système International d'Unités (*French* sistɛm ɛ̃tɛrnasjɔnal dynite) *n* the International System of units. See **SI unit.**

systemic (sɪˈstɛmɪk, -ˈstiː-) *adj* **1** another word for **systematic** (senses 1, 2). **2** *Physiol.* (of a poison, disease, etc.) affecting the entire body. **3** (of an insecticide, fungicide, etc.) designed to be absorbed by a plant into its tissues. ◆ *n* **4** a systemic insecticide, fungicide, etc.
▸**sysˈtemically** *adv*

systems analysis *n* the analysis of the requirements of a task and the expression of these in a form that permits the assembly of computer hardware and software to perform the task.
▸**systems analyst** *n*

systems engineering *n* the branch of engineering, based on systems analysis and information theory, concerned with the design of integrated systems.

systole (ˈsɪstəlɪ) *n* contraction of the heart, during which blood is pumped into the aorta and the arteries. Cf. **diastole.** [C16: via LL from Gk *sustolē*, from *sustellein* to contract; see SYSTALTIC]
▸**systolic** (sɪˈstɒlɪk) *adj*

syzygy (ˈsɪzɪdʒɪ) *n, pl* **syzygies. 1** either of the two positions (conjunction or opposition) of a celestial body when sun, earth, and the body lie in a straight line: *the moon is at syzygy when full.* **2** *Rare.* any pair, usually of opposites. [C17: from LL, from Gk *suzugia*, from *suzugos* yoked together, from SYN- + *zugon* a yoke]
▸**syzygial** (sɪˈzɪdʒɪəl), **syzygetic** (ˌsɪzɪˈdʒɛtɪk), *or* **syzygal** (ˈsɪzɪgᵊl) *adj*
▸**ˌsyzyˈgetically** *adv*

Tt

t *or* **T** (tiː) *n, pl* **t's, T's,** *or* **Ts. 1** the 20th letter of the English alphabet. **2** a speech sound represented by this letter. **3** something shaped like a T. **4 to a T.** in every detail; perfectly.
t *symbol for:* **1** *Statistics.* distribution. **2** tonne(s). **3** troy (weight).
T *symbol for:* **1** absolute temperature. **2** surface tension. **3** tera-. **4** tesla. **5** *Chem.* tritium. **6** *Biochem.* thymine.
t. *abbrev. for:* **1** *Commerce.* tare. **2** teaspoon(ful). **3** temperature. **4** *Music.* tempo. **5** *Music.* Also: **T.** tenor. **6** *Grammar.* tense. **7** ton(s). **8** transitive.
't *contraction of* it.
ta (tɑː) *interj Brit. inf.* thank you. [C18: imit. of baby talk]
Ta *the chemical symbol for* tantalum.
TA (in Britain) *abbrev. for* Territorial Army (now superseded by **TAVR**).
taal (tɑːl) *n S. African* language: usually, by implication, Afrikaans. [Afrik. from Du.]
tab[1] Ⓣ (tæb) *n* **1** a small flap of material, esp. one on a garment for decoration or for fastening to a button. **2** any similar flap, such as a piece of paper attached to a file for identification. **3** *Brit. mil.* the insignia on the collar of a staff officer. **4** *Chiefly US & Canad.* a bill, esp. for a meal or drinks. **5 keep tabs on.** *Inf.* to keep a watchful eye on. ◆ *vb* **tabs, tabbing, tabbed. 6** *(tr)* to supply with a tab or tabs. [C17: from ?]
tab[2] (tæb) *n* short for **tabulator** or **tablet.**
TAB *abbrev. for:* **1** *Austral. & NZ.* Totalizator Agency Board. **2** typhoid-paratyphoid A and B (vaccine).
tabard ('tæbəd) *n* a sleeveless or short-sleeved jacket, esp. one worn by a herald, bearing a coat of arms, or by a knight over his armour. [C13: from OF *tabart,* from ?]
tabaret ('tæbərɪt) *n* a hard-wearing fabric of silk or similar cloth with stripes of satin or moire, used esp. for upholstery. [C19: ? from TABBY[1]]
Tabasco (tə'bæskəʊ) *n Trademark.* a very hot red sauce made from matured capsicums.
tabby[1] ('tæbɪ) *n* a fabric with a watered pattern, esp. silk or taffeta. [C17: from OF *tabis* silk cloth, from Ar. *al-'attabiya,* lit.: the quarter of (Prince) 'Attab, the part of Baghdad where the fabric was first made]
tabby[2] Ⓣ ('tæbɪ) *adj* **1** (esp. of cats) brindled with dark stripes or wavy markings on a lighter background. **2** having a wavy or striped pattern, particularly in colours of grey and brown. ◆ *n, pl* **tabbies. 3** a tabby cat. **4** any female domestic cat. [C17: from *Tabby,* pet form of the girl's name *Tabitha,* prob. infl. by TABBY[1]]
tabernacle ('tæbəˌnækᵊl) *n* **1** *(often cap.) Old Testament.* **1a** the portable sanctuary in which the ancient Israelites carried the Ark of the Covenant. **1b** the Jewish Temple. **2** any place of worship that is not called a church. **3** *RC Church.* a receptacle in which the Blessed Sacrament is kept. **4** *Chiefly RC Church.* a canopied niche. **5** *Naut.* a strong framework for holding the foot of a mast, allowing it to be swung down to pass under low bridges, etc. [C13: from L *tabernāculum* a tent, from *taberna* a hut]
▸ˌ**taber'nacular** *adj*
tabes ('teɪbiːz) *n, pl* **tabes. 1** a wasting of a bodily organ or part. **2** short for **tabes dorsalis.** [C17: from L: a wasting away]
▸**tabetic** (tə'bɛtɪk) *adj*
tabescent (tə'bɛsᵊnt) *adj* **1** progressively emaciating; wasting away. **2** of, relating to, or having tabes. [C19: from L *tābēscere,* from TABES]
▸**ta'bescence** *n*
tabes dorsalis (dɔː'sɑːlɪs) *n* a form of late syphilis that attacks the spinal cord causing degeneration of the nerve fibres, paralysis of the leg muscles, acute abdominal pain, etc. [NL, lit.: tabes of the back]
tabla ('tʌblə, 'tɑːblɑː) *n* a musical instrument of India consisting of a pair of drums whose pitches can be varied. [Hindu, from Ar. *tabla* drum]
tablature ('tæblətʃə) *n Music.* any of a number of forms of musical notation, esp. for playing the lute, consisting of letters and signs indicating rhythm and fingering. [C16: from F, ult. from L *tabulātum* wooden floor, from *tabula* a plank]
table Ⓣ ('teɪbᵊl) *n* **1** a flat horizontal slab or board, usually supported by one or more legs. **2a** such a slab or board on which food is served. **2b** *(as modifier): table linen.* **3** food as served in a particular household, etc.: *a good table.* **4** such a piece of furniture specially designed for any of various purposes: *a bird table.* **5a** a company of persons assembled for a meal, game, etc. **5b** *(as modifier): table talk.* **6** any flat or level area, such as a plateau. **7** a rectangular panel set below or above the face of a wall. **8** *Archit.* another name for **string course. 9** any of various flat surfaces, as an upper horizontal facet of a cut gem. **10** *Music.* the sounding board of a violin, guitar, etc. **11a** an arrangement of words, numbers, or signs, usually in parallel columns. **11b** See **multiplication table. 12** a tablet on which laws were inscribed by the ancient Romans, the Hebrews, etc. **13 turn the tables.** to cause a complete reversal of circumstances. **14 under the table. 14a (under-the-table** *when prenominal)* done illicitly and secretly. **14b** *Sl.* drunk. ◆ *vb* **tables, tabling, tabled.** *(tr)* **15** to place on a table. **16** *Brit.* to submit (a bill, etc.) for consideration by a legislative body. **17** *US.* to suspend discussion of (a bill, etc.) indefinitely. **18** to enter in or form into a list. [C12: via OF from L *tabula* a writing tablet]
tableau Ⓣ ('tæbləʊ) *n, pl* **tableaux** (-ləʊ, -ləʊz) *or* **tableaus. 1** See ***tableau vivant.*** **2** a pause on stage when all the performers briefly freeze in position. **3** any dramatic group or scene. [C17: from F, from OF *tablel* a picture, dim. of TABLE]
tableau vivant *French.* (tablo vivɑ̃) *n, pl* ***tableaux vivants*** (tablo vivɑ̃). a representation of a scene by a person or group posed silent and motionless. [C19, lit.: living picture]
tablecloth ('teɪbᵊlˌklɒθ) *n* a cloth for covering the top of a table, esp. during meals.
table d'hôte ('tɑːbᵊl 'dəʊt) *adj* **1** (of a meal) consisting of a set number of courses with limited choice of dishes offered at a fixed price. Cf. **à la carte.** ◆ *n, pl* **tables d'hôte** ('tɑːbᵊlz 'dəʊt). **2** a table d'hôte meal or menu. [C17: from F, lit.: the host's table]
tableland Ⓣ ('teɪbᵊlˌlænd) *n* flat elevated land.
table licence *n* a licence authorizing the sale of alcoholic drinks with meals only.
tablespoon ('teɪbᵊlˌspuːn) *n* **1** a spoon, larger than a dessertspoon, used for serving food, etc. **2** Also called: **tablespoonful.** the amount contained in such a spoon. **3** a unit of capacity used in cooking, etc., equal to half a fluid ounce.
tablet ('tæblɪt) *n* **1** a pill made of a compressed medicinal substance. **2** a flattish cake of some substance, such as soap. **3** a slab of stone, wood, etc., esp. one used for inscriptions. **4a** a rigid sheet, as of bark, etc., used for similar purposes. **4b** *(often pl)* a set of these fastened together. **5** a pad of writing paper. **6** *Scot.* a sweet made from butter, sugar, and condensed milk, usually shaped into flat oblong cakes. [C14: from OF *tablete* a little table, from L *tabula* a board]
table tennis *n* a miniature form of tennis played on a table with bats and a hollow ball.
table-turning *n* the movement of a table attributed by spiritualists to the power of spirits.
tableware ('teɪbᵊlˌwɛə) *n* articles such as dishes, plates, knives, forks, etc., used at meals.
tabloid ('tæblɔɪd) *n* **1** a newspaper with pages about 30 cm (12 inches) by 40 cm (16 inches), usually with many photographs and a concise and often sensational style. **2** *(modifier)* designed to appeal to a mass audience or readership; sensationalist: *the tabloid press; tabloid television.* [C20: from earlier *Tabloid,* a trademark for a medicine in tablet form]
taboo Ⓣ *or* **tabu** (tə'buː) *adj* **1** forbidden or disapproved of: *taboo words.* **2** (in Polynesia) marked off as sacred and forbidden. ◆ *n, pl* **taboos** *or* **tabus. 3** any prohibition resulting from social or other conventions. **4** ritual restriction or prohibition, esp. of something that is considered holy or unclean. ◆ *vb* **5** *(tr)* to place under a taboo. [C18: from Tongan *tapu*]
tabor *or* **tabour** ('teɪbə) *n* a small drum used esp. in the Middle Ages, struck with one hand while the other held a pipe. [C13: from OF *tabour,* ?from Persian *tabīr*]
taboret *or* **tabouret** ('tæbərɪt) *n* **1** a low stool. **2** a frame for stretching out cloth while it is being embroidered. **3** a small tabor. [C17: from F *tabouret,* dim. of TABOR]
tabular ('tæbjʊlə) *adj* **1** arranged in systematic or table form. **2** calculated from or by means of a table. **3** like a table in form; flat. [C17: from L *tabulāris* concerning boards, from *tabula* a board]
▸**'tabularly** *adv*
tabula rasa ('tæbjʊlə 'rɑːsə) *n, pl* **tabulae rasae** ('tæbjʊliː 'rɑːsiː). **1** the mind in its uninformed original state. **2** an opportunity for a fresh start; clean slate. [L: a scraped tablet]
tabulate Ⓣ *vb* ('tæbjʊˌleɪt), **tabulates, tabulating, tabulated.** *(tr)* **1** to set out, arrange, or write in tabular form. **2** to form or cut with a flat surface.

THESAURUS

tab[1] *n* **1, 2** = **flap,** flag, label, marker, sticker, tag, ticket
tabby[2] *adj* **2** = **striped,** banded, brindled, streaked, stripy, wavy
table *n* **1** = **counter,** bench, board, slab, stand **3** *Formal* = **food,** board, diet, fare, spread *(inf.),* victuals **6** = **plateau,** flat, flatland, mesa, plain, tableland **11a** = **list,** agenda, catalogue, chart, diagram, digest, graph, index, inventory, plan, record, register, roll, schedule, synopsis, tabulation ◆ *vb* **16** *Brit.* = **submit,** enter, move, propose, put forward, suggest
tableau *n* **3** = **picture,** representation, scene, spectacle
tableland *n* = **plateau,** flat, flatland, mesa, plain, table
taboo *adj* **1** = **forbidden,** anathema, banned, beyond the pale, disapproved of, frowned on, not allowed, not permitted, off limits, outlawed, prohibited, proscribed, ruled out, unacceptable, unmentionable, unthinkable ◆ *n* **3** = **prohibition,** anathema, ban, disapproval, interdict, proscription, restriction
Antonyms *adj* ≠ **forbidden:** acceptable, allowed, permitted, sanctioned
tabulate *vb* **1** = **arrange,** catalogue, categorize, chart, classify, codify, index, list, order, range, systematize, tabularize

◆ *adj* ('tæbjʊlɪt, -ˌleɪt). **3** having a flat surface. [C18: from L *tabula* a board]
▸ **'tabulable** *adj* ▸ **ˌtabu'lation** *n*

tabulator ('tæbjʊˌleɪtə) *n* **1** a device for setting the stops that locate the column margins on a typewriter. **2** *Computing.* a machine that reads data from one medium, such as punched cards, producing lists, tabulations, or totals.

tacamahac ('tækəməˌhæk) *or* **tacmahack** *n* **1** any of several strong-smelling resinous gums used in ointments, incense, etc. **2** any tree yielding this resin. [C16: from Sp. *tacamahaca,* from Nahuatl *tecomahca* aromatic resin]

tacet ('teɪsɛt, 'tæs-) *vb* (*intr*) (on a musical score) a direction indicating that a particular instrument or singer does not take part. [C18: from L: it is silent, from *tacēre* to be quiet]

tacheometer (ˌtækɪ'ɒmɪtə) *or* **tachymeter** *n Surveying.* a type of theodolite designed for the rapid measurement of distances, elevations, and directions.
▸ **ˌtache'ometry** *n*

tachisme ('tɑːʃɪzəm) *n* a type of action painting in which haphazard dabs and blots of colour are treated as a means of unconscious expression. [C20: F, from *tache* stain]

tachistoscope (tæ'kɪstəˌskəʊp) *n* an instrument for displaying visual images for very brief intervals, usually a fraction of a second. [C20: from Gk *takhistos* swiftest + -SCOPE]
▸ **tachistoscopic** (tæˌkɪstə'skɒpɪk) *adj*

tacho- *combining form.* speed: *tachograph; tachometer.* [from Gk *takhos*]

tachograph ('tækəˌgrɑːf) *n* a tachometer that produces a record (**tachogram**) of its readings, esp. a device for recording the speed of and distance covered by a vehicle. Often shortened to **tacho.**

tachometer (tæ'kɒmɪtə) *n* any device for measuring speed, esp. the rate of revolution of a shaft. Tachometers are often fitted to cars to indicate the number of revolutions per minute of the engine.
▸ **ta'chometry** *n*

tachy- *or* **tacheo-** *combining form.* swift or accelerated: *tachyon.* [from Gk *takhus* swift]

tachycardia (ˌtækɪ'kɑːdɪə) *n* abnormally rapid beating of the heart.

tachygraphy (tæ'kɪgrəfɪ) *n* shorthand, esp. as used in ancient Rome or Greece.

tachymeter (tæ'kɪmɪtə) *n* another name for **tacheometer.**

tachyon ('tækɪˌɒn) *n Physics.* a hypothetical elementary particle capable of travelling faster than the velocity of light. [C20: from TACHY- + -ON]

tachyphylaxis (ˌtækɪfɪ'læksɪs) *n* very rapid development of tolerance or immunity to the effects of a drug. [NL, from TACHY- + *phylaxis* on the model of *prophylaxis;* see PROPHYLACTIC]

tacit ⓣ ('tæsɪt) *adj* implied or inferred without direct expression; understood: *a tacit agreement.* [C17: from L *tacitus,* p.p. of *tacēre* to be silent]
▸ **'tacitly** *adv*

taciturn ⓣ ('tæsɪˌtɜːn) *adj* habitually silent, reserved, or uncommunicative. [C18: from L *taciturnus,* from *tacēre* to be silent]
▸ **ˌtaci'turnity** *n* ▸ **'taciˌturnly** *adv*

tack[1] ⓣ (tæk) *n* **1** a short sharp-pointed nail, with a large flat head. **2** *Brit.* a long loose temporary stitch used in dressmaking, etc. **3** See **tailor's-tack. 4** a temporary fastening. **5** stickiness. **6** *Naut.* the heading of a vessel sailing to windward, stated in terms of the side of the sail against which the wind is pressing. **7** *Naut.* **7a** a course sailed with the wind blowing from forward of the beam. **7b** one such course or a zigzag pattern of such courses. **8** *Naut.* **8a** a sheet for controlling the weather clew of a course. **8b** the weather clew itself. **9** *Naut.* the forward lower clew of a fore-and-aft sail. **10** a course of action or policy. **11 on the wrong tack.** under a false impression. ◆ *vb* **12** (*tr*) to secure by a tack or tacks. **13** *Brit.* to sew (something) with long loose temporary stitches. **14** (*tr*) to attach or append. **15** *Naut.* to change the heading of (a sailing vessel) to the opposite tack. **16** *Naut.* to steer (a sailing vessel) on alternate tacks. **17** (*intr*) *Naut.* (of a sailing vessel) to proceed on a different tack or to alternate tacks. **18** (*intr*) to follow a zigzag route; keep changing one's course of action. [C14 *tak* fastening, nail]
▸ **'tacker** *n*

tack[2] (tæk) *n* riding harness for horses, such as saddles, bridles, etc. [C20: shortened from TACKLE]

tack hammer *n* a light hammer for driving tacks.

tackies *or* **takkies** ('tækɪz) *pl n, sing* **tacky.** *S. African inf.* tennis shoes or plimsolls. [C20: prob. from TACKY[1], from their nonslip rubber soles]

tackle ⓣ ('tæk^{ə}l) *n* **1** an arrangement of ropes and pulleys designed to lift heavy weights. **2** the equipment required for a particular occupation, etc. **3** *Naut.* the halyards and other running rigging aboard a vessel. **4** *Sport.* a physical challenge to an opponent, as to prevent his progress with the ball. **5** *American football.* a defensive lineman. ◆ *vb* **tackles, tackling, tackled. 6** (*tr*) to undertake (a task, etc.). **7** (*tr*) to confront (esp. an opponent) with a difficult proposition. **8** *Sport.* to challenge (an opponent) with a tackle. [C13: rel. to MLow G *takel* ship's rigging]
▸ **'tackler** *n*

tack rag *n Building trades.* a cotton cloth impregnated with an oil, used to remove dust from a surface prior to painting.

tacky[1] ⓣ ('tækɪ) *adj* **tackier, tackiest.** slightly sticky or adhesive. [C18: from TACK[1] (in the sense: stickiness)]
▸ **'tackily** *adv* ▸ **'tackiness** *n*

tacky[2] ⓣ ('tækɪ) *adj* **tackier, tackiest.** *Inf.* **1** shabby or shoddy. **2** ostentatious and vulgar. **3** *US.* (of a person) dowdy; seedy. [C19: from dialect *tacky* an inferior horse, from ?]
▸ **'tackiness** *n*

tacnode ('tækˌnəʊd) *n* another name for **osculation** (sense 1). [C19: from L *tactus* touch (from *tangere* to touch) + NODE]

tact ⓣ (tækt) *n* **1** a sense of what is fitting and considerate in dealing with others, so as to avoid giving offence. **2** skill in handling difficult situations; diplomacy. [C17: from L *tactus* a touching, from *tangere* to touch]
▸ **'tactful** *adj* ▸ **'tactfulness** *n* ▸ **'tactless** *adj* ▸ **'tactlessness** *n*

tactic ⓣ ('tæktɪk) *n* a piece of tactics; tactical move. See also **tactics.**

-tactic *adj combining form.* having a specified kind of pattern or arrangement or having an orientation determined by a specified force: *syndiotactic; phototactic.* [from Gk *taktikos* relating to order; see TACTICS]

tactical ⓣ ('tæktɪk^{ə}l) *adj* **1** of, relating to, or employing tactics: *a tactical error.* **2** (of missiles, bombing, etc.) for use in or supporting limited military operations; short-range. **3** skilful, adroit, or diplomatic.
▸ **'tactically** *adv*

tactical voting *n* (in an election) the practice of casting one's vote not for the party of one's choice but for the second strongest contender in a constituency in order to defeat the likeliest winner.

tactics ⓣ ('tæktɪks) *pl n* **1** (*functioning as sing*) *Mil.* the art and science of the detailed direction and control of movement of forces in battle to achieve an aim or task. **2** the manoeuvres used to achieve an aim or task. **3** plans followed to achieve a particular short-term aim. [C17: from NL *tactica,* from Gk, from *taktikos* concerning arrangement, from *taktos* arranged (for battle), from *tassein* to arrange]
▸ **tac'tician** *n*

tactile ('tæktaɪl) *adj* **1** of, relating to, affecting, or having a sense of touch. **2** *Now rare.* tangible. [C17: from L *tactilis, from tangere* to touch]
▸ **tactility** (tæk'tɪlɪtɪ) *n*

tadpole ('tædˌpəʊl) *n* the aquatic larva of frogs, toads, etc., which develops from a limbless tailed form with external gills into a form with internal gills, limbs, and a reduced tail. [C15 *taddepol,* from *tadde* toad + *pol* head]

taedium vitae ('tiːdɪəm 'viːtaɪ, 'vaɪtiː) *n* the feeling that life is boring and dull. [L, lit.: weariness of life]

tae kwon do ('taɪ 'kwɒn 'dəʊ, 'teɪ) *n* a Korean martial art that resembles karate. [C20: Korean *tae* kick + *kwon* fist + *do* way, method]

tael (teɪl) *n* **1** a unit of weight, used in the Far East. **2** (formerly) a Chi-

THESAURUS

tacit *adj* = **implied**, implicit, inferred, silent, taken for granted, undeclared, understood, unexpressed, unspoken, unstated, wordless
Antonyms *adj* explicit, express, spelled-out, spoken, stated

taciturn *adj* = **uncommunicative**, aloof, antisocial, close-lipped, cold, distant, dumb, mute, quiet, reserved, reticent, silent, tight-lipped, unforthcoming, withdrawn
Antonyms *adj* blethering, chatty, communicative, forthcoming, garrulous, loquacious, open, outgoing, prattling, sociable, talkative, unreserved, verbose, voluble, wordy

tack[1] *n* **1** = **nail**, drawing pin, pin, staple, thumbtack (*US*), tintack ◆ *vb* **12** = **fasten**, affix, attach, fix, nail, pin, staple **13** *Brit.* = **stitch**, baste, sew **14 tack on** = **append**, add, annex, attach, tag

tackle *n* **2** = **equipment**, accoutrements, apparatus, gear, implements, outfit, paraphernalia, rig, rigging, tools, trappings **4** = **challenge**, block, stop ◆ *vb* **6** = **deal with**, apply oneself to, attempt, begin, come *or* get to grips with, embark upon, engage in, essay, get stuck into (*inf.*), have a go *or* stab at (*inf.*), set about, sink one's teeth into, take on, take the bit between one's teeth, try, turn one's hand to, undertake, wade into **7** = **confront**, block, bring down, challenge, clutch, grab, grasp, halt, intercept, seize, stop, take hold of, throw

tacky[1] *adj* = **sticky**, adhesive, gluey, gummy, wet

tacky[2] *adj* **1** = **shabby**, seedy, shoddy, tatty **2** = **vulgar**, naff (*Brit. sl.*), nasty, sleazy, tasteless

tact *n* **1, 2** = **diplomacy**, address, adroitness, consideration, delicacy, discretion, finesse, judgment, perception, savoir-faire, sensitivity, skill, thoughtfulness, understanding
Antonyms *n* awkwardness, clumsiness, gaucherie, heavy-handedness, indiscretion, insensitivity, lack of consideration, lack of discretion, tactlessness

tactful *adj* **1, 2** = **diplomatic**, careful, considerate, delicate, discreet, judicious, perceptive, polished, polite, politic, prudent, sensitive, subtle, thoughtful, treating with kid gloves, understanding
Antonyms *adj* awkward, clumsy, gauche, inconsiderate, indiscreet, insensitive, tactless, tasteless, thoughtless, undiplomatic, unsubtle, untoward

tactic *n* = **policy**, approach, course, device, line, manoeuvre, means, method, move, ploy, scheme, stratagem, tack, trick, way

tactical *adj* **3** = **strategic**, adroit, artful, clever, cunning, diplomatic, foxy, politic, shrewd, skilful, smart
Antonyms *adj* blundering, clumsy, gauche, impolitic, inept

tactics *n* **1-3** = **strategy**, campaigning, generalship, manoeuvres, plans

tactless *adj* **1, 2** = **insensitive**, blundering, boorish, careless, clumsy, discourteous, gauche, harsh, impolite, impolitic, imprudent, inconsiderate, indelicate, indiscreet, inept, injudicious, maladroit, rough, rude, sharp, thoughtless, uncivil, undiplomatic, unfeeling, unkind, unsubtle nese monetary unit. [C16: from Port., from Malay *tahil* weight, ?from Sansk.]

ta'en (teɪn) *vb* a Scot. or poetic contraction of **taken.**

taenia *or US* **tenia** ('tiːnɪə) *n, pl* **taeniae** *or US* **teniae** (-nɪˌiː). **1** (in ancient Greece) a headband. **2** *Archit.* the fillet between the architrave and frieze of a Doric entablature. **3** *Anat.* any bandlike structure or part. **4** any of a genus of tapeworms. [C16: via L from Gk *tainia* narrow strip]

taeniasis *or US* **teniasis** (tiːˈnaɪəsɪs) *n Pathol.* infestation with tapeworms of the genus *Taenia.*

taffeta ('tæfɪtə) *n* a thin crisp lustrous plain-weave fabric of silk, etc., used esp. for women's clothes. [C14: from Med. L *taffata,* from Persian *tāftah* spun, from *tāftan* to spin]

taffrail ('tæfˌreɪl) *n Naut.* a rail at the stern of a vessel. [C19: changed from earlier *tafferel,* from Du. *taffereel* panel (hence applied to the part of a vessel decorated with carved panels), from *tafel* table]

Taffy ('tæfɪ) *n, pl* **Taffies.** a slang word or nickname for a **Welshman.** [C17: from the supposed Welsh pronunciation of *Davy* (from *David,* Welsh *Dafydd*), a common Welsh Christian name]

tafia *or* **taffia** ('tæfɪə) *n* a type of rum, esp. from Guyana or the Caribbean. [C18: from F, from West Indian Creole, prob. from RATAFIA]

tag[1] ❶ (tæg) *n* **1** a piece of paper, leather, etc., for attaching to something as a mark or label: *a price tag.* **2** Also called: **electronic tag.** an electronic device worn by an offender serving a noncustodial sentence, which monitors the offender's whereabouts by means of a link to a central computer through the telephone system. **3** a small piece of material hanging from a part or piece. **4** a point of metal, etc., at the end of a cord or lace. **5** an epithet or verbal appendage, the refrain of a song, the moral of a fable, etc. **6** a brief quotation. **7** an ornamental flourish. **8** the tip of an animal's tail. **9** a matted lock of wool or hair. **10** *Sl.* a graffito consisting of a nickname or personal symbol. ◆ *vb* **tags, tagging, tagged.** (*mainly tr*) **11** to mark with a tag. **12** to monitor the whereabouts of (an offender) by means of an electronic tag. **13** to add or append as a tag. **14** to supply (prose or blank verse) with rhymes. **15** (*intr; usually foll. by on or along*) to trail (behind). **16** to name or call (someone something). **17** to cut the tags of wool or hair from (an animal). [C15: from ?]

tag[2] (tæg) *n* **1** Also called: **tig.** a children's game in which one player chases the others in an attempt to catch one of them who will then become the chaser. **2** the act of tagging one's partner in tag wrestling. **3** (*modifier*) denoting a wrestling contest between two teams of two wrestlers, in which only one from each team may be in the ring at one time. The contestant outside the ring may change places with his team-mate inside the ring after touching his hand. ◆ *vb* **tags, tagging, tagged.** (*tr*) **4** to catch (another child) in the game of tag. **5** (in tag wrestling) to touch the hand of (one's partner). [C18: ?from TAG[1]]

Tagalog (təˈgɑːlɒg) *n* **1** (*pl* **Tagalogs** *or* **Tagalog**) a member of a people of the Philippines. **2** the language of this people. ◆ *adj* **3** of or relating to this people or their language.

tag end *n* **1** the last part of something. **2** a loose end of cloth, thread, etc.

tagetes (tæˈdʒiːtiːz) *n, pl* **tagetes.** any of a genus of plants with yellow or orange flowers, including the French and African marigolds. [from NL, from *Tages,* an Etruscan god]

tagliatelle (ˌtæljəˈtelɪ) *n* a form of pasta made in narrow strips. [It., from *tagliare* to cut]

tag line *n* **1** an amusing or memorable phrase designed to catch attention in an advert. **2** another name for **punch line.**

tahr *or* **thar** (tɑː) *n* any of several goatlike mammals of S and SW Asia, having a shaggy coat and curved horns. [from Nepali *thār*]

tahsil (təˈsiːl) *n* an administrative division in certain states in India. [Urdu, from Ar.: collection]

Tai (taɪ) *adj, n* a variant spelling of **Thai.**

taiaha ('taɪəˌhɑː) *n NZ.* a carved weapon in the form of a staff, now used in Maori ceremonial oratory. [from Maori]

t'ai chi ch'uan ('taɪ dʒiː 'tʃwɑːn) *n* a Chinese system of callisthenics characterized by coordinated and rhythmic movements. Often shortened to **t'ai chi** ('taɪ 'dʒiː). [Chinese, lit.: great art of boxing]

taiga ('taɪgɑː) *n* the coniferous forests extending across much of subarctic North America and Eurasia. [from Russian, of Turkic origin]

taihoa ('taɪhəʊə) *sentence substitute. NZ.* hold on! no hurry! [Maori]

tail[1] ❶ (teɪl) *n* **1** the rear part of the vertebrate body that contains an elongation of the vertebral column, esp. forming a flexible appendage. **2** anything resembling such an appendage; the bottom, lowest, or rear part. **3** the last part or parts: *the tail of the storm.* **4** the rear part of an aircraft including the fin, tailplane, and control surfaces. **5** *Astron.* the luminous stream of gas and dust particles driven from the head of a comet when close to the sun. **6** the rear portion of a bomb, rocket, missile, etc., usually fitted with guiding or stabilizing vanes. **7** a line of people or things. **8** a long braid or tress of hair: *a pigtail.* **9** a final short line in a stanza. **10** *Inf.* a person employed to follow and spy upon another. **11** an informal word for **buttocks. 12** *Taboo sl.* **12a** the female genitals. **12b** a woman considered sexually (esp. in **piece of tail, bit of tail**). **13** the foot of a page. **14** the lower end of a pool or part of a stream. **15** *Inf.* the course or track of a fleeing person or animal. **16** (*modifier*) coming from or situated in the rear: *a tail wind.* **17 turn tail.** to run away; escape. **18 with one's tail between one's legs.** in a state of utter defeat or confusion. ◆ *vb* **19** to form or cause to form the tail. **20** to remove the tail of (an animal). **21** (*tr*) to remove the stalk of. **22** (*tr*) to connect (objects, ideas, etc.) together by or as if by the tail. **23** (*tr*) *Inf.* to follow stealthily. **24** (*intr*) (of a vessel) to assume a specified position, as when at a mooring. **25** to build the end of (a brick, joist, etc.) into a wall or (of a brick, etc.) to have one end built into a wall. ◆ See also **tail off, tail out, tails.** [OE *tægel*]

▸ **'tailless** *adj*

tail[2] (teɪl) *Law.* ◆ *n* **1** the limitation of an estate or interest to a person and the heirs of his body. ◆ *adj* **2** (*immediately postpositive*) limited in this way. [C15: from OF *taille* a division; see TAILOR]

▸ **'tailless** *adj*

tailback ('teɪlˌbæk) *n* a queue of traffic stretching back from an obstruction.

tailboard ('teɪlˌbɔːd) *n* a board at the rear of a lorry, etc., that can be removed or let down.

tail coat *n* **1** a man's black coat having a horizontal cut over the hips and a tapering tail with a vertical slit up to the waist. **2** a cutaway frock coat, part of morning dress.

tail covert *n* any of the covert feathers of a bird covering the bases of the tail feathers.

tail end *n* the last, endmost, or final part.

tailgate ('teɪlˌgeɪt) *n* **1** another name for **tailboard. 2** a door at the rear of a hatchback vehicle. ◆ *vb* **tailgates, tailgating, tailgated. 3** to drive very close behind (a vehicle).

▸ **'tailˌgater** *n*

tail gate *n* a gate that is used to control the flow of water at the lower end of a lock.

tailing ('teɪlɪŋ) *n* the part of a beam, rafter, projecting brick, etc., embedded in a wall.

tailings ('teɪlɪŋz) *pl n* waste left over after certain processes, such as from an ore-crushing plant or in milling grain.

tail-light ('teɪlˌlaɪt) *or* **tail lamp** *n* other names for **rear light.**

tail off ❶ *or* **away** *vb* (*adv; usually intr*) to decrease or cause to decrease in quantity, degree, etc., esp. gradually.

tailor ❶ ('teɪlə) *n* **1** a person who makes, repairs, or alters outer garments, esp. menswear. Related adj: **sartorial. 2** a voracious and active marine food fish of Australia. ◆ *vb* **3** to cut or style (material, etc.) to satisfy certain requirements. **4** (*tr*) to adapt so as to make suitable. **5** (*intr*) to work as a tailor. [C13: from Anglo-Norman *taillour,* from OF *taillier* to cut, from L *tālea* a cutting]

▸ **'tailored** *adj*

tailorbird ('teɪləˌbɜːd) *n* any of several tropical Asian warblers that build nests by sewing together large leaves using plant fibres.

tailor-made ❶ *adj* **1** made by a tailor to fit exactly. **2** perfectly meeting a particular purpose. ◆ *n* **3** a tailor-made garment. **4** *Inf.* a factory-made cigarette.

tailor's chalk *n* pipeclay used by tailors and dressmakers to mark seams, darts, etc., on material.

tailor's-tack *n* one of a series of loose looped stitches used to transfer markings for seams, darts, etc., from a paper pattern to material.

tail out *vb* (*tr, adv*) *NZ.* to guide (timber) as it emerges from a circular saw.

tailpiece ('teɪlˌpiːs) *n* **1** an extension or appendage that lengthens or completes something. **2** a decorative design at the foot of a page or end of a chapter. **3** *Music.* a piece of wood to which the strings of a violin, etc., are attached at their lower end. **4** a short beam or rafter that has one end embedded in a wall.

tailpipe ('teɪlˌpaɪp) *n* a pipe from which exhaust gases are discharged, esp. the terminal pipe of the exhaust system of a motor vehicle.

tailplane ('teɪlˌpleɪn) *n* a small horizontal wing at the tail of an aircraft to provide longitudinal stability. Also called (esp. US): **horizontal stabilizer.**

tailrace ('teɪlˌreɪs) *n* a channel that carries water away from a water wheel, turbine, etc.

tail rotor *n* a small propeller fitted to the rear of a helicopter to coun-

THESAURUS

Antonyms *adj* considerate, diplomatic, discreet, polite, subtle, tactful

tag[1] *n* **1** = **label,** docket, flag, flap, identification, mark, marker, note, slip, sticker, tab, ticket ◆ *vb* **11** = **label,** earmark, flag, identify, mark, ticket **13** *with* **on** = **add,** adjoin, affix, annex, append, fasten, tack **15** *with* **along** *or* **on** = **accompany,** attend, dog, follow, shadow, tail (*inf.*), trail **16** = **name,** call, christen, dub, label, nickname, style, term

tail[1] *n* **2** = **extremity,** appendage, conclusion, empennage, end, rear end, tailpiece, train **7** = **line,** file, queue, tailback, train **8** = **braid,** pigtail, plait, ponytail, tress **11** *Informal* = **buttocks,** arse, ass (*US & Canad. taboo sl.*), backside (*inf.*), behind (*inf.*), bottom, bum (*Brit. sl.*), buns (*US sl.*), butt (*US & Canad. inf.*), croup, derrière (*euphemistic*), jacksy (*Brit. sl.*), posterior, rear (*inf.*), rear end, rump **17 turn tail** = **run away,** cut and run, escape, flee, hook it (*sl.*), make off, retreat, run for it (*inf.*), run off, scarper (*Brit. sl.*), show a clean pair of heels, skedaddle (*inf.*), take off (*inf.*), take to one's heels ◆ *vb* **23** *Informal* = **follow,** dog the footsteps of, keep an eye on, shadow, stalk, track, trail

tail off *vb* = **decrease,** die out, drop, dwindle, fade, fall away, peter out, wane

Antonyms *vb* grow, increase, intensify, wax

tailor *n* **1** = **outfitter,** clothier, costumier, couturier, dressmaker, garment maker, seamstress ◆ *vb* **4** = **adapt,** accommodate, adjust, alter, convert, customize, cut, fashion, fit, modify, mould, shape, style, suit

tailor-made *adj* **1** = **made-to-measure,** cut to fit, fitted, made to order **2** = **perfect,** custom-made, ideal, just right, right, right up one's street (*inf.*), suitable, up one's alley teract the torque reaction of the main rotor and thus prevent the body of the helicopter from rotating in an opposite direction.

tails (teɪlz) *pl n* **1** an informal name for **tail coat.** ◆ *interj, adv* **2** with the reverse side of a coin uppermost.

tailskid ('teɪl,skɪd) *n* **1** a runner under the tail of an aircraft. **2** a rear-wheel skid of a motor vehicle.

tailspin ('teɪl,spɪn) *n* **1** *Aeronautics.* another name for **spin** (sense 16). **2** *Inf.* a state of confusion or panic.

tailstock ('teɪl,stɒk) *n* a casting that slides on the bed of a lathe and is locked in position to support the free end of a workpiece.

tailwind ('teɪl,wɪnd) *n* a wind blowing in the same direction as the course of an aircraft or ship.

Taino ('taɪnəʊ) *n* **1** (*pl* **Tainos** *or* **Taino**) a member of an extinct American Indian people of the West Indies. **2** the language of this people.

taint Ⓣ (teɪnt) *vb* **1** to affect or be affected by pollution or contamination. **2** to tarnish (someone's reputation, etc.). ◆ *n* **3** a defect or flaw. **4** a trace of contamination or infection. [C14: (infl. by *attaint* infected, from ATTAIN) from OF *teindre* to dye, from L *tingere*]

▸ **'taintless** *adj*

taipan ('taɪ,pæn) *n* a large highly venomous Australian snake. [C20: from Abor.]

Taisho (taɪ'ʃəʊ) *n* **1** the period of Japanese history and artistic style associated with the reign of Emperor Yoshihito (1912–26). **2** the throne name of Yoshihito (1879–1926), emperor of Japan (1912–26).

taj (tɑːdʒ) *n* a tall conical cap worn as a mark of distinction by Muslims. [via Ar. from Persian: crown]

takahe ('tɑːkə,hiː) *n* a rare flightless New Zealand rail. Also called: **notornis.** [from Maori]

take Ⓣ (teɪk) *vb* **takes, taking, took, taken.** (*mainly tr*) **1** (*also intr*) to gain possession of (something) by force or effort. **2** to appropriate or steal. **3** to receive or accept into a relationship with oneself: *to take a wife.* **4** to pay for or buy. **5** to rent or lease. **6** to obtain by regular payment. **7** to win. **8** to obtain or derive from a source. **9** to assume the obligations of: *to take office.* **10** to endure, esp. with fortitude: *to take punishment.* **11** to adopt as a symbol of duty, etc.: *to take the veil.* **12** to receive in a specified way: *she took the news very well.* **13** to adopt as one's own: *to take someone's part in a quarrel.* **14** to receive and make use of: *to take advice.* **15** to receive into the body, as by eating, inhaling, etc. **16** to eat, drink, etc., esp. habitually. **17** to have or be engaged in for one's benefit or use: *to take a rest.* **18** to work at or study: *to take economics at college.* **19** to make, do, or perform (an action). **20** to make use of: *to take an opportunity.* **21** to put into effect: *to take measures.* **22** (*also intr*) to make a photograph of or admit of being photographed. **23** to act or perform. **24** to write down or copy: *to take notes.* **25** to experience or feel: *to take offence.* **26** to consider or regard: *I take him to be honest.* **27** to accept as valid: *I take your point.* **28** to hold or maintain in the mind: *his father took a dim view of his career.* **29** to deal or contend with. **30** to use as a particular case: *take hotels for example.* **31** (*intr;* often foll. by *from*) to diminish or detract: *the actor's bad performance took from the effect of the play.* **32** to confront successfully: *the horse took the jump at the third attempt.* **33** (*intr*) to have or produce the intended effect: *her vaccination took.* **34** (*intr*) (of plants, etc.) to start growing successfully. **35** to aim or direct: *he took a swipe at his opponent.* **36** to deal a blow to in a specified place. **37** *Arch.* to have sexual intercourse with (a woman). **38** to remove from a place. **39** to carry along or have in one's possession. **40** to convey or transport. **41** to use as a means of transport: *I shall take the bus.* **42** to conduct or lead. **43** to escort or accompany. **44** to bring or deliver to a state, position, etc.: *his ability took him to the forefront.* **45** to seek: *to take cover.* **46** to ascertain by measuring, etc.: *to take a pulse.* **47** (*intr*) (of a mechanism) to catch or engage (a part). **48** to put an end to: *she took her own life.* **49** to come upon unexpectedly. **50** to contract: *he took a chill.* **51** to affect or attack: *the fever took him one night.* **52** (*copula*) to become suddenly or be rendered (ill): *he was taken sick.* **53** (*also intr*) to absorb or become absorbed by something: *to take a polish.* **54** (*usually passive*) to charm: *she was very taken with the puppy.* **55** (*intr*) to be or become popular; win favour. **56** to require: *that task will take all your time.* **57** to subtract or deduct. **58** to hold: *the suitcase won't take all your clothes.* **59** to quote or copy. **60** to proceed to occupy: *to take a seat.* **61** (often foll. by *to*) to use or employ: *to take steps to ascertain the answer.* **62** to win or capture (a trick, piece, etc.). **63** *Sl.* to cheat, deceive, or victimize. **64 take five** (*or* **ten**). *Inf., chiefly US & Canad.* to take a break of five (or ten) minutes. **65 take it. 65a** to assume; believe. **65b** *Inf.* to stand up to or endure criticism, harsh treatment, etc. **66 take one's time.** to use as much time as is needed. **67 take (someone's) name in vain. 67a** to use a name, esp. of God, disrespectfully or irreverently. **67b** *Jocular.* to say (someone's) name. **68 take upon oneself.** to assume the right to do or responsibility for something. ◆ *n* **69** the act of taking. **70** the number of quarry killed or captured. **71** *Inf., chiefly US.* the amount of anything taken, esp. money. **72** *Films, music.* **72a** one of a series of recordings from which the best will be selected. **72b** the process of taking one such recording. **72c** a scene photographed without interruption. **73** *Inf., chiefly US.* a version or interpretation: *Cronenberg's harsh take on the sci-fi story.* ◆ See also **take after, take against,** etc. [OE *tacan*]

▸ **'takable** *or* **'takeable** *adj* ▸ **'taker** *n*

take after *vb* (*intr, prep*) to resemble in appearance, character, behaviour, etc.

take against *vb* (*intr, prep*) to start to dislike, esp. without good reason.

take apart *vb* (*tr, adv*) **1** to separate (something) into component parts. **2** to criticize severely.

take away *vb* (*tr, adv*) **1** to subtract: *take away four from nine to leave five.* ◆ *prep* **2** minus: *nine take away four is five.* ◆ *adj* **takeaway.** *Brit., Austral., & NZ.* **3** sold for consumption away from the premises: *a takeaway meal.* **4** selling food for consumption away from the premises: *a takeaway Indian restaurant.* ◆ *n* **takeaway.** *Brit., Austral., & NZ.* **5** a shop or restaurant that sells such food. **6** a meal bought at such a shop or restaurant: *we'll have a Chinese takeaway tonight.* ◆ Scot. word (for senses 3–6): **carry out.** US and Canad. word (for senses 3–6): **takeout.**

take back Ⓣ *vb* (*adv, mainly tr*) **1** to retract or withdraw (something said, promised, etc.). **2** to regain possession of. **3** to return for exchange. **4** to accept (someone) back (into one's home, affections, etc.). **5** to remind one of the past: *that tune really takes me back.* **6** (*also intr*) *Printing.* to move (copy) to the previous line.

take down Ⓣ *vb* (*tr, adv*) **1** to record in writing. **2** to dismantle or tear down. **3** to lower or reduce in power, arrogance, etc. (esp. in **take down a peg**). ◆ *adj* **take-down. 4** made or intended to be disassembled.

take for *vb* (*tr, prep*) *Inf.* to consider or suppose to be, esp. mistakenly: *the fake coins were taken for genuine; who do you take me for?*

take-home pay *n* the remainder of one's pay after all income tax and other compulsory deductions have been made.

take in Ⓣ *vb* (*tr, adv*) **1** to understand. **2** to include. **3** to receive into one's house in exchange for payment: *to take in lodgers.* **4** to make (clothing, etc.) smaller by altering seams. **5** *Inf.* to cheat or deceive. **6** *US.* to go to: *let's take in a movie tonight.*

taken ('teɪkən) *vb* **1** the past participle of **take.** ◆ *adj* **2** (*postpositive;* foll. by *with*) enthusiastically impressed (by); infatuated (with).

take off Ⓣ *vb* (*adv*) **1** (*tr*) to remove (a garment). **2** (*intr*) (of an aircraft) to become airborne. **3** *Inf.* to set out or cause to set out on a journey: *they took off for Spain.* **4** (*tr*) (of a disease) to kill. **5** (*tr*) *Inf.* to mimic. **6** (*intr*) *Inf.* to become successful or popular. ◆ *n* **takeoff. 7** the act or process of making an aircraft airborne. **8** the stage of a country's eco-

THESAURUS

taint *vb* **1** = **spoil**, adulterate, besmirch, blemish, blight, blot, contaminate, corrupt, damage, defile, dirty, foul, infect, muddy, poison, pollute, ruin, smear, smirch, soil, stain, sully, tarnish, vitiate **2** = **disgrace**, blacken, brand, dishonour, ruin, shame, stigmatize ◆ *n* **3** = **stain**, black mark, blemish, blot, defect, demerit, fault, flaw, smear, smirch, spot **4** = **contamination**, contagion, infection, pollution

Antonyms *vb* ≠ **spoil:** clean, cleanse, decontaminate, disinfect, purify

take *vb* **1** = **obtain**, acquire, capture, carry off, cart off (*sl.*), catch, clutch, gain possession of, get, get hold of, grasp, grip, have, help oneself to, lay hold of, receive, secure, seize, win **2** = **steal**, abstract, appropriate, blag (*sl.*), cabbage (*Brit. sl.*), carry off, filch, misappropriate, nick (*sl., chiefly Brit.*), pinch (*inf.*), pocket, purloin, run off with, swipe (*sl.*), walk off with **4, 5** = **choose**, book, buy, engage, hire, lease, pay for, pick, purchase, rent, reserve, select **9** = **accept**, adopt, assume, enter upon, undertake **10** = **tolerate**, abide, bear, brave, brook, endure, go through, hack (*sl.*), pocket, put up with (*inf.*), stand, stomach, submit to, suffer, swallow, thole (*Scot.*), undergo, weather, withstand **15, 16** = **consume**, drink, eat, imbibe, ingest, inhale, swallow **17, 21** = **perform**, do, effect, execute, have, make **26** = **assume**, believe, consider, deem, hold, interpret as, perceive, presume, receive, regard, see as, think of as, understand **33** = **work**, be efficacious, do the trick (*inf.*), have effect, operate, succeed **40** = **carry**, bear, bring, cart, convey, ferry, fetch, haul, tote (*inf.*), transport **42, 43** = **accompany**, bring, conduct, convoy, escort, guide, hold (someone's) hand, lead, usher **54, 55** = **charm**, attract, become popular, captivate, delight, enchant, fascinate, please, win favour **56** = **require**, call for, demand, necessitate, need **57** = **subtract**, deduct, eliminate, remove **58** = **have room for**, accept, accommodate, contain, hold **63** *Slang* = **cheat**, bilk, con (*inf.*), deceive, defraud, do (*sl.*), dupe, fiddle (*inf.*), gull (*arch.*), pull a fast one on (*inf.*), stiff (*sl.*), swindle ◆ *n* **71** = **takings**, gate, haul, proceeds, profits, receipts, return, revenue, yield

Antonyms *vb* ≠ **capture:** free, let go, release ≠ **steal:** give, give back, hand over, restore, return, surrender, yield ≠ **accept:** decline, dismiss, eschew, ignore, refuse, reject, scorn, spurn ≠ **tolerate:** avoid, dodge, give in, give way ≠ **work:** fail, flop (*inf.*) ≠ **carry:** send ≠ **subtract:** add, put

take back *vb* **1** = **retract**, disavow, disclaim, recant, renege, renounce, unsay, withdraw **2** = **regain**, get back, recapture, reclaim, reconquer, repossess, retake **3** = **give one a refund for**, accept back, exchange

take down *vb* **1** = **make a note of**, minute, note, put on record, record, set down, transcribe, write down **2** = **dismantle**, demolish, disassemble, level, raze, take apart, take to pieces, tear down **3** = **humble**, deflate, humiliate, mortify, put down (*sl.*)

take in *vb* **1** = **understand**, absorb, assimilate, comprehend, digest, get the hang of (*inf.*), grasp **2** = **include**, comprise, contain, cover, embrace, encompass **3** = **let in**, accommodate, admit, receive **5** = **deceive**, bilk, cheat, con, cozen, do (*sl.*), dupe, fool, gull (*arch.*), hoodwink, mislead, pull the wool over (someone's) eyes (*inf.*), stiff (*sl.*), swindle, trick

take off *vb* **1** = **remove**, discard, divest oneself of, doff, drop, peel off, strip off **2** = **lift off**, become airborne, leave the ground, take to the air **3** *Informal* = **depart**, abscond, beat it (*sl.*), decamp, disappear, go, hit the road (*sl.*), hook it (*sl.*), leave, pack one's bags (*inf.*), set out, slope off, split (*sl.*), strike out **5** *Informal* = **parody**, caricature, hit off, imitate, lampoon, mimic, mock, satirize, send up (*Brit. inf.*), spoof (*inf.*), take the piss (out of) (*taboo sl.*), travesty ◆ *n* **takeoff 7** = **departure**, launch, liftoff **9** *Informal* = **parody**, caricature, imitation, lampoon, mocking, satire, send-up (*Brit. inf.*), spoof (*inf.*), travesty nomic development when rapid and sustained economic growth is first achieved. **9** *Inf.* an act of mimicry.

take on ➊ *vb* (*adv, mainly tr*) **1** to employ or hire. **2** to assume or acquire: *his voice took on a plaintive note.* **3** to agree to do; undertake. **4** to compete against; fight. **5** (*intr*) *Inf.* to exhibit great emotion, esp. grief.

take out *vb* (*tr, adv*) **1** to extract or remove. **2** to obtain or secure (a licence, patent, etc.). **3** to go out with; escort. **4** *Bridge.* to bid a different suit from (one's partner) in order to rescue him from a difficult contract. **5** *Sl.* to kill or destroy. **6** *Austral. inf.* to win, esp. in sport. **7 take it** *or* **a lot out of.** *Inf.* to sap the energy or vitality of. **8 take out on.** *Inf.* to vent (anger, etc.) on. **9 take someone out of himself.** *Inf.* to make someone forget his anxieties, problems, etc. ◆ *adj* **takeout. 10** *Bridge.* of or designating a conventional informatory bid, asking one's partner to bid another suit. ◆ *adj, n* **takeout. 11** the US and Canad. word for **takeaway** (senses 3–6).

take over ➊ *vb* (*adv*) **1** to assume the control or management of. **2** *Printing.* to move (copy) to the next line. ◆ *n* **takeover. 3** the act of seizing or assuming power, control, etc.

take to ➊ *vb* (*intr, prep*) **1** to make for; flee to: *to take to the hills.* **2** to form a liking for. **3** to have recourse to: *to take to the bottle.*

take up ➊ *vb* (*adv, mainly tr*) **1** to adopt the study, practice, or activity of: *to take up gardening.* **2** to shorten (a garment). **3** to pay off (a note, mortgage, etc.). **4** to agree to or accept (an invitation, etc.). **5** to pursue further or resume (something): *he took up French where he left off.* **6** to absorb (a liquid). **7** to act as a patron to. **8** to occupy or fill (space or time). **9** to interrupt, esp. in order to contradict or criticize. **10** *Austral. & NZ.* to occupy and break in (uncultivated land): *he took up some hundreds of acres in the back country.* **11 take up on. 11a** to argue with (someone): *can I take you up on two points in your talk?* **11b** to accept what is offered by (someone): *let me take you up on your invitation.* **12 take up with. 12a** to discuss with (someone); refer to. **12b** (*intr*) to begin to keep company or associate with. ◆ *n* **take-up. 13a** the claiming of something, esp. a state benefit. **13b** (*as modifier*): *take-up rate.*

takin ('tɑːkiːn) *n* a massive bovid mammal of S Asia, having a shaggy coat, short legs, and horns. [C19: from Tibetan native name]

taking ➊ ('teɪkɪŋ) *adj* **1** charming, fascinating, or intriguing. **2** *Inf.* infectious; catching. ◆ *n* **3** something taken. **4** (*pl*) receipts; earnings.
▸ **'takingly** *adv* ▸ **'takingness** *n*

talapoin ('tæləˌpɔɪn) *n* **1** a small W African monkey. **2** (in Myanmar and Thailand) a Buddhist monk. [C16: from F, lit.: Buddhist monk, from Port. *talapão;* orig. jocular, from the appearance of the monkey]

talaria (tə'lɛərɪə) *pl n Greek myth.* winged sandals. [C16: from L, from *tālāris* belonging to the ankle, from *tālus* ankle]

talc (tælk) *n also* **talcum. 1** See **talcum powder. 2** a soft mineral, consisting of magnesium silicate, used in the manufacture of ceramics and paints and as a filler in talcum powder, etc. ◆ *vb* **talcs, talcking, talcked** *or* **talcs, talcing, talced. 3** (*tr*) to apply talc to. [C16: from Med. L *talcum,* from Ar. *talq* mica, from Persian *talk*]
▸ **'talcose** *or* **'talcous** *adj*

talcum powder ('tælkəm) *n* a powder made of purified talc, usually scented, used for perfuming the body and for absorbing excess moisture. Often shortened to **talcum** or **talc.**

tale ➊ (teɪl) *n* **1** a report, narrative, or story. **2** one of a group of short stories. **3a** a malicious or meddlesome rumour or piece of gossip. **3b** (*in combination*): *talebearer; taleteller.* **4** a fictitious or false statement. **5 tell tales. 5a** to tell fanciful lies. **5b** to report malicious stories, trivial complaints, etc., esp. to someone in authority. **6 tell a tale.** to reveal something important. **7 tell its own tale.** to be self-evident. **8** *Arch.* a number; amount. [OE *talu* list]

talent ➊ ('tælənt) *n* **1** innate ability, aptitude, or faculty; above average ability: *a talent for cooking; a child with talent.* **2** a person or persons possessing such ability. **3** any of various ancient units of weight and money. **4** *Inf.* members of the opposite sex collectively: *the local talent.* [OE *talente,* from L *talenta,* pl. of *talentum* sum of money, from Gk *talanton* unit of money; in Med. L the sense was extended to ability through the infl. of the parable of the talents (Matthew 25:14–30)]
▸ **'talented** *adj*

talent scout *n* a person whose occupation is the search for talented sportsmen, performers, etc., for engagements as professionals.

tales ('teɪliːz) *n Law.* **1** (*functioning as pl*) a group of persons summoned to fill vacancies on a jury panel. **2** (*functioning as sing*) the writ summoning such jurors. [C15: from Med. L *tālēs dē circumstantibus* such men from among the bystanders, from L *tālis* such]
▸ **'talesman** *n*

Taliban *or* **Taleban** ('tælɪˌbæn) *n* a militant Islamic organization in Afghanistan. [C20: from Ar. *tāliban* seekers]

taligrade ('tælɪˌgreɪd) *adj* (of mammals) walking on the outer side of the foot. [C20: from NL, from L *tālus* ankle, heel + -GRADE]

talion ('tælɪən) *n* the system or legal principle of making the punishment correspond to the crime; retaliation. [C15: via OF from L *tāliō,* from *tālis* such]

talipes ('tælɪˌpiːz) *n* **1** a congenital deformity of the foot by which it is twisted in any of various positions. **2** a technical name for **club foot.** [C19: NL, from L *tālus* ankle + *pēs* foot]

talipot *or* **talipot palm** ('tælɪˌpɒt) *n* a palm tree of the East Indies, having large leaves that are used for fans, thatching houses, etc. [C17: from Bengali: palm leaf, from Sansk. *tālī* fan palm + *pattra* leaf]

talisman ➊ ('tælɪzmən) *n, pl* **talismans. 1** a stone or other small object, usually inscribed or carved, believed to protect the wearer from evil influences. **2** anything thought to have magical or protective powers. [C17: via F or Sp. from Ar. *tilsam,* from Med. Gk *telesma* ritual, from Gk: consecration, from *telein* to perform a rite, complete]
▸ **talismanic** (ˌtælɪz'mænɪk) *adj*

talk ➊ (tɔːk) *vb* **1** (*intr;* often foll. by *to* or *with*) to express one's thoughts, feelings, or desires by means of words (to). **2** (*intr*) to communicate by other means: *lovers talk with their eyes.* **3** (*intr;* usually foll. by *about*) to exchange ideas or opinions (about). **4** (*intr*) to articulate words. **5** (*tr*) to give voice to; utter: *to talk rubbish.* **6** (*tr*) to discuss: *to talk business.* **7** (*intr*) to reveal information. **8** (*tr*) to know how to communicate in (a language or idiom): *he talks English.* **9** (*intr*) to spread rumours or gossip. **10** (*intr*) to make sounds suggestive of talking. **11** (*intr*) to be effective or persuasive: *money talks.* **12 now you're talking.** *Inf.* at last you're saying something agreeable. **13 talk big.** to boast. **14 you can talk.** *Inf.* **14a** you don't have to worry about doing a particular thing yourself. **14b** Also: **you can't talk.** you yourself are guilty of offending in the very matter you are upholding or decrying. ◆ *n* **15** a speech or lecture. **16** an exchange of ideas or thoughts. **17** idle chatter, gossip, or rumour. **18** a subject of conversation; theme. **19** (*often pl*) a conference, discussion, or negotiation. **20** a specific manner of speaking: *children's talk.* ◆ See also **talk about, talk back,** etc. [C13 *talkien*]
▸ **'talker** *n*

talk about *vb* (*intr, prep*) **1** to discuss. **2** used informally and often ironically to add emphasis to a statement: *all his plays have such ridiculous plots – talk about good drama!*

talkative ➊ ('tɔːkətɪv) *adj* given to talking a great deal.
▸ **'talkatively** *adv* ▸ **'talkativeness** *n*

talk back *vb* (*intr, adv*) **1** to answer boldly or impudently. **2** *NZ.* to conduct a telephone dialogue for immediate transmission over the air. ◆ *n* **talkback. 3** *Television, radio.* a system of telephone links enabling spoken directions to be given during the production of a programme. **4** *NZ.* a broadcast telephone dialogue.

talk down *vb* (*adv*) **1** (*intr;* often foll. by *to*) to behave (towards) in a superior manner. **2** (*tr*) to override (a person) by continuous or loud

THESAURUS

take on *vb* **1 = engage,** employ, enlist, enrol, hire, retain **2 = acquire,** assume, come to have **3 = accept,** address oneself to, agree to do, have a go at (*inf.*), tackle, undertake **4 = compete against,** contend with, enter the lists against, face, fight, match oneself against, oppose, pit oneself against, vie with **5** *Informal* **= get upset,** break down, get excited, give way, make a fuss

take over *vb* **1 = gain control of,** assume control of, become leader of, come to power, take command of ◆ *n* **takeover 3 = merger,** change of leadership, coup, incorporation

take to *vb* **1 = head for,** flee to, make for, run for **2 = like,** become friendly with, be pleased by, be taken with, conceive an affection for, get on with, warm to **3 = start,** have recourse to, make a habit of, resort to

take up *vb* **1 = start,** adopt, assume, become involved in, engage in **5 = resume,** begin again, carry on, continue, follow on, go on, pick up, proceed, recommence, restart **8 = occupy,** absorb, consume, cover, extend over, fill, use up

taking *adj* **1 = charming,** attractive, beguiling, captivating, compelling, cute, delightful, enchanting, engaging, fascinating, fetching (*inf.*), intriguing, likable *or* likeable, pleasing, prepossessing, winning **2** *Informal* **= infectious,** catching, contagious ◆ *n* **4** *plural* **= revenue,** earnings, gain, gate, income, pickings, proceeds, profits, receipts, returns, take, yield
Antonyms *adj* ≠ **charming:** abhorrent, loathsome, offensive, repulsive, unattractive, unpleasant

tale *n* **1 = story,** account, anecdote, *conte,* fable, fiction, legend, narration, narrative, novel, relation, report, romance, saga, short story, spiel (*inf.*), urban legend, urban myth, yarn (*inf.*) **3a = lie,** cock-and-bull story (*inf.*), fabrication, falsehood, fib, gossip, rigmarole, rumour, spiel (*inf.*), tall story (*inf.*), untruth

talent *n* **1 = ability,** aptitude, bent, capacity, endowment, faculty, flair, forte, genius, gift, knack, parts, power

talented *adj* **1 = gifted,** able, artistic, brilliant, well-endowed

talisman *n* **1, 2 = charm,** amulet, fetish, juju, lucky charm, mascot, periapt (*rare*)

talk *vb* **1, 4 = speak,** articulate, chat, chatter, communicate, converse, crack (*Scot. & Irish*), express oneself, gab (*inf.*), give voice to, gossip, natter, prate, prattle, rap (*sl.*), run off at the mouth (*sl.*), say, shoot the breeze (*US sl.*), spout, utter, verbalize, witter (*inf.*) **3 = discuss,** chew the rag *or* fat (*sl.*), confabulate, confer, have a confab (*inf.*), hold discussions, negotiate, palaver, parley **7 = inform,** blab, crack, give the game away, grass (*Brit. sl.*), let the cat out of the bag, reveal information, shop (*sl., chiefly Brit.*), sing (*sl., chiefly US*), spill one's guts (*sl.*), spill the beans (*inf.*), squeak (*inf.*), squeal (*sl.*), tell all **13 talk big = boast,** blow one's own trumpet, bluster, brag, crow, exaggerate, vaunt ◆ *n* **15 = speech,** address, discourse, disquisition, dissertation, harangue, lecture, oration, sermon **16 = discussion,** confab (*inf.*), confabulation, conference, consultation, dialogue **17 = conversation,** blather, blether, chat, chatter, chitchat, crack (*Scot. & Irish*), gossip, hearsay, rumour, tittle-tattle **19 = meeting,** colloquy, conclave, conference, congress, negotiation, palaver, parley, seminar, symposium **20 = language,** argot, dialect, jargon, lingo (*inf.*), patois, slang, speech, words

talkative *adj* **= loquacious,** big-mouthed (*sl.*), chatty, effusive, gabby (*inf.*), garrulous, gossipy, long-winded, mouthy, prolix, verbose, voluble, wordy
Antonyms *adj* quiet, reserved, reticent, silent, taciturn, tight-lipped, uncommunicative, un- forthcoming

talker *n* **15, 17 = speaker,** chatterbox, conversationalist, lecturer, orator, speechmaker talking. **3** (*tr*) to give instructions to (an aircraft) by radio to enable it to land.

talkie ('tɔ:kɪ) *n Inf.* an early film with a soundtrack. Full name: **talking picture.**

Talking Book *n Trademark.* a recording of a book, designed to be used by blind people.

talking head *n* (on television) a person, shown only from the shoulders up, who speaks without illustrative material.

talking-to Ⓣ *n Inf.* a session of criticism, as of a subordinate by a person in authority.

talk into Ⓣ *vb* (*tr, prep*) to persuade to by talking: *I talked him into buying the house.*

talk out *vb* (*tr, adv*) **1** to resolve or eliminate by talking. **2** *Brit.* to block (a bill, etc.) in a legislative body by lengthy discussion. **3 talk out of.** to dissuade from by talking.

talk round *vb* **1** (*tr, adv*) Also: **talk over.** to persuade to one's opinion. **2** (*intr, prep*) to discuss (a subject), esp. without coming to a conclusion.

talk shop *vb* to talk about one's profession, esp. at a social occasion.

talk show *n* another name for **chat show.**

tall Ⓣ (tɔ:l) *adj* **1** of more than average height. **2** (*postpositive*) having a specified height: *five feet tall.* [C14 (in the sense: big, comely, valiant)]
▸**'tallness** *n*

tallage ('tælɪdʒ) *n English history.* **a** a tax levied by kings on Crown lands and royal towns. **b** a toll levied by a lord upon his tenants or by a feudal lord upon his vassals. [C13: from OF *taillage,* from *taillier* to cut; see TAILOR]

tallboy ('tɔ:l,bɔɪ) *n* **1** a high chest of drawers made in two sections placed one on top of the other. **2** a fitting on the top of a chimney to prevent downdraughts.

tallith ('tælɪθ) *n* a shawl with fringed corners worn by Jewish males, esp. during religious services. [C17: from Heb. *tallīt*]

tall order *n Inf.* a difficult or unreasonable request.

tallow ('tæləʊ) *n* **1** a fatty substance extracted chiefly from the suet of sheep and cattle: used for making soap, candles, food, etc. ◆ *vb* **2** (*tr*) to cover or smear with tallow. [OE *tælg,* a dye]
▸**'tallowy** *adj*

tallowwood ('tæləʊ,wʊd) *n Austral.* a tall eucalyptus tree having soft fibrous bark and a greasy timber.

tall poppy *n Austral. inf.* a prominent or highly paid person.

tall poppy syndrome *n Austral. inf.* a tendency to disparage any person who has achieved great prominence or wealth.

tall ship *n* any square-rigged sailing ship.

tall story *n Inf.* an exaggerated or incredible account.

tally Ⓣ ('tælɪ) *vb* **tallies, tallying, tallied. 1** (*intr*) to correspond one with the other: *the two stories don't tally.* **2** (*tr*) to supply with an identifying tag. **3** (*intr*) to keep score. **4** (*tr*) *Obs.* to record or mark. ◆ *n, pl* **tallies. 5** any record of debit, credit, the score in a game, etc. **6** *Austral. & NZ.* the number of sheep shorn in a specified period. **7** an identifying label or mark. **8** a counterpart or duplicate of something. **9** a stick used (esp. formerly) as a record of the amount of a debt according to the notches cut in it. **10** a notch or mark made on such a stick. **11** a mark used to represent a certain number in counting. [C15: from Med. L *tālea,* from L: cutting]

tally clerk *n Austral. & NZ.* a person, esp. on a wharf or in an airport, who checks the count of goods being loaded or unloaded.

tally-ho (,tælɪ'həʊ) *interj* **1** the cry of a participant at a hunt when the quarry is sighted. ◆ *n, pl* **tally-hos. 2** an instance of crying tally-ho. **3** another name for a **four-in-hand** (sense 1). ◆ *vb* **tally-hos, tally-hoing, tally-hoed** *or* **tally-ho'd. 4** (*intr*) to make the cry of tally-ho. [C18: ?from F *taïaut* cry used in hunting]

tallyman ('tælɪmən) *n, pl* **tallymen. 1** a scorekeeper or recorder. **2** *Dialect.* a travelling salesman for a firm specializing in hire-purchase.
▸**'tally,woman** *fem n*

Talmud ('tælmʊd) *n Judaism.* the primary source of Jewish religious law, consisting of the Mishnah and the Gemara. [C16: from Heb. *talmūdh,* lit.: instruction, from *lāmadh* to learn]
▸**Tal'mudic** *or* **Tal'mudical** *adj* ▸**'Talmudism** *n* ▸**'Talmudist** *n*

talon ('tælən) *n* **1** a sharply hooked claw, esp. of a bird of prey. **2** anything resembling this. **3** the part of a lock that the key presses on when it is turned. **4** *Piquet, etc.* the pile of cards left after the deal. **5** *Archit.* another name for **ogee. 6** *Stock Exchange.* a printed slip attached to some bearer bonds to enable the holder to apply for a new sheet of coupons. [C14: from OF: heel, from L *tālus*]
▸**'taloned** *adj*

talus[1] ('teɪləs) *n, pl* **tali** (-laɪ). the bone of the ankle that articulates with the leg bones to form the ankle joint; anklebone. [C18: from L: ankle]

talus[2] ('teɪləs) *n, pl* **taluses. 1** *Geol.* another name for **scree. 2** *Fortifications.* the sloping side of a wall. [C17: from F, from L *talūtium* slope, ? of Iberian origin]

tam (tæm) *n* short for **tam-o'-shanter.**

tamale (tə'mɑ:lɪ) *n* a Mexican dish made of minced meat mixed with crushed maize and seasonings, wrapped in maize husks and steamed. [C19: erroneously for *tamal,* from Mexican Sp., from Nahuatl *tamalli*]

tamandua (,tæmən'duə) *n* a small arboreal mammal of Central and South America, having a tubular mouth specialized for feeding on termites. Also called: **lesser anteater.** [C17: via Port. from Tupi: ant trapper, from *taixi* ant + *mondê* to catch]

tamarack ('tæmə,ræk) *n* **1** any of several North American larches. **2** the wood of any of these trees. [C19: of Amerind origin]

tamari (tə'mɑ:rɪ) *n* a Japanese variety of soy sauce. [Japanese]

tamarillo (,tæmə'rɪləʊ) *n, pl* **tamarillos.** another name for **tree tomato.**

tamarin ('tæmərɪn) *n* any of numerous small monkeys of South and Central American forests; similar to the marmosets. [C18: via F, of Amerind origin]

tamarind ('tæmərɪnd) *n* **1** a tropical evergreen tree having yellow flowers and brown pods. **2** the fruit of this tree, used as a food and to make beverages and medicines. **3** the wood of this tree. [C16: from Med. L *tamarindus,* ult. from Ar. *tamr hindī* Indian date]

tamarisk ('tæmərɪsk) *n* any of a genus of trees and shrubs of the Mediterranean region and S and SE Asia, having scalelike leaves, slender branches, and feathery flower clusters. [C15: from LL *tamariscus,* from L *tamarix*]

tambour ('tæmbʊə) *n* **1** *Real Tennis.* the sloping buttress on one side of the receiver's end of the court. **2** a small embroidery frame, consisting of two hoops over which the fabric is stretched while being worked. **3** embroidered work done on such a frame. **4** a sliding door on desks, cabinets, etc., made of thin strips of wood glued onto a canvas backing. **5** *Archit.* a wall that is circular in plan, esp. one that supports a dome or one that is surrounded by a colonnade. **6** a drum. ◆ *vb* **7** to embroider on a tambour. [C15: from F, from *tabour* TABOR]

tamboura (tæm'bʊərə) *n* a stringed instrument with a long neck used in Indian music to provide a drone. [from Persian *tanbūr,* from Ar. *tunbūr*]

tambourin ('tæmbʊrɪn) *n* **1** an 18th-century Provençal folk dance. **2** a piece of music composed for or in the rhythm of this dance. **3** a small drum. [C18: from F: a little drum]

tambourine (,tæmbə'ri:n) *n Music.* a percussion instrument consisting of a single drumhead of skin stretched over a circular wooden frame hung with pairs of metal discs that jingle when it is struck or shaken. [C16: from MFlemish *tamborijn* a little drum, from OF: TAMBOURIN]
▸**,tambou'rinist** *n*

tame Ⓣ (teɪm) *adj* **1** changed by man from a wild state into a domesticated or cultivated condition. **2** (of animals) not fearful of human contact. **3** meek or submissive. **4** flat, insipid, or uninspiring. ◆ *vb* **tames, taming, tamed.** (*tr*) **5** to make tame; domesticate. **6** to break the spirit of, subdue, or curb. **7** to tone down, soften, or mitigate. [OE *tam*]
▸**'tamable** *or* **'tameable** *adj* ▸**'tamely** *adv* ▸**'tameness** *n* ▸**'tamer** *n*

Tamil ('tæmɪl) *n* **1** (*pl* **Tamils** *or* **Tamil**) a member of a mixed Dravidian and Caucasoid people of S India and Sri Lanka. **2** the language of this people. ◆ *adj* **3** of or relating to this people or their language.

tammy[1] ('tæmɪ) *n, pl* **tammies.** another word for **tam-o'-shanter.**

tammy[2] ('tæmɪ) *n, pl* **tammies.** (esp. formerly) a woollen cloth used for straining sauces, soups, etc. [C18: changed from F *tamis,* ? of Celtic origin]

tam-o'-shanter (,tæmə'ʃæntə) *n* a Scottish brimless wool or cloth cap with a bobble in the centre. [C19: after the hero of Burns's poem *Tam o' Shanter* (1790)]

tamoxifen (tə'mɒksɪ,fen) *n* a drug that antagonizes the action of oestrogen and is used to treat breast cancer and some types of infertility in women. [C20: from T(RANS-) + AM(INE) + OXY-[2] + PHEN(OL)]

tamp (tæmp) *vb* (*tr*) **1** to force or pack down firmly by repeated blows. **2** to pack sand, earth, etc., into (a drill hole) over an explosive. [C17: prob. back formation from *tampin* (obs. var. of TAMPION), taken as a present participle *tamping*]

THESAURUS

talking-to *n Informal* = **reprimand**, criticism, dressing-down (*inf.*), lecture, rap on the knuckles, rebuke, reproach, reproof, row, scolding, telling-off (*inf.*), ticking-off (*inf.*), wigging (*Brit. sl.*)
Antonyms *n* acclaim, approbation, commendation, encouragement, praise

talk into *vb* = **persuade**, bring round (*inf.*), convince, prevail on *or* upon, sway, win over

tall *adj* **1** = **high**, big, elevated, giant, lanky, lofty, soaring, towering
Antonyms *adj* ≠ **high:** fubsy (*arch. or dialect*), short, small, squat, stumpy, tiny, wee ≠ **implausible:** accurate, believable, plausible, realistic, reasonable, true, unexaggerated

tally *vb* **1** = **agree**, accord, coincide, concur, conform, correspond, fit, harmonize, jibe (*inf.*), match, parallel, square, suit **3** = **keep score**, compute, count up, total **4** = **record**, mark, reckon, register ◆ *n* **5** = **record**, count, mark, reckoning, running total, score, total **8** = **counterpart**, counterfoil, duplicate, match, mate, stub
Antonyms *vb* ≠ **agree:** clash, conflict, contradict, differ, disagree

tame *adj* **1** = **domesticated**, amenable, broken, cultivated, disciplined, docile, gentle, obedient, tractable **2** = **unafraid**, fearless, used to human contact **3** = **submissive**, compliant, docile, manageable, meek, obedient, spiritless, subdued, unresisting **4** = **unexciting**, bland, boring, dull, flat, humdrum, insipid, lifeless, prosaic, tedious, tiresome, uninspiring, uninteresting, vapid, wearisome ◆ *vb* **5** = **domesticate**, break in, gentle, house-train, make tame, pacify, train **6** = **subdue**, break the spirit of, bridle, bring to heel, conquer, curb, discipline, enslave, humble, master, repress, subjugate, suppress
Antonyms *adj* ≠ **domesticated:** aggressive, feral, ferocious, savage, undomesticated, untamed, wild ≠ **submissive:** aggressive, argumentative, obdurate, strong-willed, stubborn, unmanageable ≠ **unexciting:** exciting, frenzied, hot, interesting, lively, stimulating ◆ *vb* ≠ **domesticate:** make fiercer ≠ **subdue:** arouse, incite, intensify

tamper[1] ● ('tæmpə) *vb* (*intr*) **1** (usually foll. by *with*) to interfere or meddle. **2** to use bribery or blackmail. **3** (usually foll. by *with*) to attempt to influence, esp. by bribery. [C16: alteration of TEMPER (vb)]
▸ **'tamperer** *n*

tamper[2] ('tæmpə) *n* **1** a person or thing that tamps, esp. an instrument for packing down tobacco in a pipe. **2** a casing around the core of a nuclear weapon to increase its efficiency by reflecting neutrons and delaying the expansion.

tampion ('tæmpɪən) *or* **tompion** *n* a plug placed in a gun's muzzle when the gun is not in use. [C15: from F: TAMPON]

tampon ('tæmpɒn) *n* **1** a plug of lint, cotton wool, etc., inserted into a wound or body cavity to stop the flow of blood, absorb secretions, etc. ◆ *vb* **2** (*tr*) to plug (a wound, etc.) with a tampon. [C19: via F from OF *tapon* a little plug, of Gmc origin]
▸ **tamponage** ('tæmpənɪdʒ) *n*

tam-tam *n* another name for **gong** (sense 1). [from Hindi; see TOM-TOM]

tan[1] (tæn) *n* **1** the brown colour produced by the skin after exposure to ultraviolet rays, esp. those of the sun. **2** a yellowish-brown colour. **3** short for **tanbark**. ◆ *vb* **tans, tanning, tanned. 4** to go brown or cause to go brown after exposure to ultraviolet rays. **5** to convert (a skin or hide) into leather by treating it with a tanning agent. **6** (*tr*) *Sl.* to beat or flog. ◆ *adj* **tanner, tannest. 7** of the colour tan. [OE *tannian* (unattested as infinitive, attested as *getanned*, p.p.), from Med. L *tannāre*, from *tannum* tanbark, ? of Celtic origin]
▸ **'tannable** *adj* ▸ **'tannish** *adj*

tan[2] (tæn) *abbrev. for* tangent (sense 2).

tanager ('tænədʒə) *n* any of a family of American songbirds having a short thick bill and, in the male, a brilliantly coloured plumage. [C19: from NL *tanagra*, based on Amerind *tangara*]

tanbark ('tænˌbɑːk) *n* the bark of certain trees, esp. the oak, used as a source of tannin.

tandem ('tændəm) *n* **1** a bicycle with two sets of pedals and two saddles, arranged one behind the other for two riders. **2** a two-wheeled carriage drawn by two horses harnessed one behind the other. **3** a team of two horses so harnessed. **4** any arrangement of two things in which one is placed behind the other. **5 in tandem.** together or in conjunction. ◆ *adj* **6** *Brit.* used as, used in, or routed through an intermediate automatic telephone exchange. ◆ *adv* **7** one behind the other. [C18: whimsical use of L *tandem* at length, to indicate a long vehicle]

tandoori (tæn'dʊərɪ) *n* an Indian method of cooking meat or vegetables on a spit in a clay oven. [from Urdu, from *tandoor* an oven]

tang ● (tæŋ) *n* **1** a strong taste or flavour. **2** a pungent or characteristic smell. **3** a trace, touch, or hint of something. **4** the pointed end of a tool, such as a chisel, file, knife, etc., which is fitted into a handle, shaft, or stock. [C14: from ON *tangi* point]

tangent ('tændʒənt) *n* **1** a geometric line, curve, plane, or curved surface that touches another curve or surface at one point but does not intersect it. **2** (of an angle) a trigonometric function that in a right-angled triangle is the ratio of the length of the opposite side to that of the adjacent side; the ratio of sine to cosine. Abbrev.: **tan. 3** *Music.* a small piece of metal that strikes the string of a clavichord. **4 on** *or* **at a tangent.** on a completely different or divergent course, esp. of thought. ◆ *adj* **5a** of or involving a tangent. **5b** touching at a single point. **6** touching. [C16: from L *līnea tangēns* the touching line, from *tangere* to touch]
▸ **'tangency** *n*

tangent galvanometer *n* a galvanometer having a vertical coil of wire with a horizontal magnetic needle at its centre. The current to be measured is passed through the coil and produces a proportional magnetic field which deflects the needle.

tangential (tæn'dʒɛnʃəl) *adj* **1** of, being, or in the direction of a tangent. **2** *Astron.* (of velocity) in a direction perpendicular to the line of sight of a celestial object. **3** of superficial relevance only; digressive.
▸ **tanˌgenti'ality** *n* ▸ **tan'gentially** *adv*

tangerine (ˌtændʒə'riːn) *n* **1** an Asian citrus tree cultivated for its small orange-like fruits. **2** the fruit of this tree, having sweet spicy flesh. **3a** a reddish-orange colour. **3b** (*as adj*): *a tangerine door.* [C19: from *Tangier*, a port in N Morocco]

tangi ('tæŋiː) *n NZ.* **1** a Maori funeral ceremony. **2** *Inf.* a lamentation.

tangible ● ('tændʒɪbᵊl) *adj* **1** capable of being touched or felt. **2** capable of being clearly grasped by the mind. **3** having a physical existence: *tangible assets.* [C16: from LL *tangibilis*, from L *tangere* to touch]
▸ **ˌtangi'bility** *or* **'tangibleness** *n* ▸ **'tangibly** *adv*

tangle ● ('tæŋgᵊl) *n* **1** a confused or complicated mass of hairs, lines, fibres, etc., knotted or coiled together. **2** a complicated problem, condition, or situation. ◆ *vb* **tangles, tangling, tangled. 3** to become or cause to become twisted together in a confused mass. **4** (*intr*; often foll. by *with*) to come into conflict; contend. **5** (*tr*) to involve in matters which hinder or confuse. **6** (*tr*) to ensnare or trap, as in a net. [C14 *tangilen*, var. of *tagilen*, prob. from ON]
▸ **'tangled** *or* **'tangly** *adj*

tango ('tæŋgəʊ) *n, pl* **tangos. 1** a Latin-American dance characterized by long gliding steps and sudden pauses. **2** a piece of music composed for or in the rhythm of this dance. ◆ *vb* **tangoes, tangoing, tangoed. 3** (*intr*) to perform this dance. [C20: from American Sp., prob. of Niger-Congo origin]

tangram ('tæŋgræm) *n* a Chinese puzzle in which a square, cut into a parallelogram, a square, and five triangles, is formed into figures. [C19: ?from Chinese *t'ang* Chinese + -GRAM]

tangy ● ('tæŋɪ) *adj* **tangier, tangiest.** having a pungent, fresh, or briny flavour or aroma.

tanh (θæn, tænʃ) *n* hyperbolic tangent; a hyperbolic function that is the ratio of sinh to cosh. [C20: from TAN(GENT) + H(YPERBOLIC)]

tank (tæŋk) *n* **1** a large container or reservoir for liquids or gases. **2** an armoured combat vehicle moving on tracks and armed with guns, etc. **3** *Brit. or US dialect.* a reservoir, lake, or pond. **4** *Sl., chiefly US.* a jail. **5** Also called: **tankful.** the quantity contained in a tank. **6** *Austral.* a reservoir formed by excavation and damming. ◆ *vb* **7** (*tr*) to put or keep in a tank. **8** *Sl.* to defeat heavily. ◆ See also **tank up.** [C17: from Gujarati (a language of W India) *tānkh* artificial lake, but infl. also by Port. *tanque*, from *estanque* pond, ult. from Vulgar L *stanticāre* (unattested) to block]

tanka ('tɑːŋkə) *n, pl* **tankas** *or* **tanka.** a Japanese verse form consisting of five lines, the first and third having five syllables, the others seven. [C19: from Japanese, from *tan* short + *ka* verse]

tankage ('tæŋkɪdʒ) *n* **1** the capacity or contents of a tank or tanks. **2** the act of storing in a tank or tanks, or a fee charged for this. **3** *Agriculture.* **3a** fertilizer consisting of the dried and ground residues of animal carcasses. **3b** a protein supplement feed for livestock.

tankard ('tæŋkəd) *n* a large one-handled drinking vessel sometimes fitted with a hinged lid. [C14]

tank engine *or* **locomotive** *n* a steam locomotive that carries its water supply in tanks mounted around its boiler.

tanker ('tæŋkə) *n* a ship, lorry, or aeroplane designed to carry liquid in bulk, such as oil.

tank farming *n* another name for **hydroponics.**
▸ **tank farmer** *n*

tank top *n* a sleeveless upper garment with wide shoulder straps and a low neck. [C20: after *tank suits*, one-piece bathing costumes of the 1920s worn in tanks or swimming pools]

tank up *vb* (*adv*) *Chiefly Brit.* **1** to fill the tank of (a vehicle) with petrol. **2** *Sl.* to imbibe or cause to imbibe a large quantity of alcoholic drink.

tank wagon *or esp. US & Canad.* **tank car** *n* a form of railway wagon carrying a tank for the transport of liquids.

tanner[1] ('tænə) *n* a person who tans skins and hides.

tanner[2] ('tænə) *n Brit.* an informal word for **sixpence.** [C19: from ?]

tannery ('tænərɪ) *n, pl* **tanneries.** a place or building where skins and hides are tanned.

tannic ('tænɪk) *adj* of, relating to, containing, or produced from tan, tannin, or tannic acid.

tannin ('tænɪn) *n* any of a class of yellowish compounds found in many plants and used as tanning agents, mordants, medical astringents, etc. Also called: **tannic acid.** [C19: from F *tanin*, from TAN[1]]

Tannoy ('tænɔɪ) *n Trademark.* a type of public-address system.

Tans (tænz) *pl n* **the.** *Irish inf.* short for the **Black and Tans.**

tansy ('tænzɪ) *n, pl* **tansies.** any of numerous plants having yellow flowers in flat-topped clusters and formerly used in medicine and for seasoning. [C15: from OF *tanesie*, from Med. L *athanasia* (from its alleged power to prolong life) from Gk: immortality]

tantalite ('tæntəˌlaɪt) *n* a heavy brownish mineral: it occurs in coarse granite and is an ore of tantalum. [C19: from TANTALUM + -ITE[1]]

tantalize ● *or* **tantalise** ('tæntəˌlaɪz) *vb* **tantalizes, tantalizing, tantalized** *or* **tantalises, tantalising, tantalised.** (*tr*) to tease or make frustrated, as by tormenting with the sight of something desired but inaccessible. [C16: from *Tantalus*, a king in Gk mythology condemned to stand in water that receded when he tried to drink it and under fruit that moved away when he tried to reach for it]

THESAURUS

tamper[1] *vb* **1 = interfere**, alter, damage, fiddle (*inf.*), fool about (*inf.*), intrude, meddle, mess about, monkey around, muck about (*Brit. sl.*), poke one's nose into (*inf.*), tinker **2, 3 = influence**, bribe, corrupt, fix (*inf.*), get at, manipulate, rig

tang *n* **1, 2 = taste**, aroma, bite, flavour, odour, piquancy, reek, savour, scent, smack, smell **3 = trace**, hint, suggestion, tinge, touch, whiff

tangible *adj* **1-3 = definite**, actual, concrete, corporeal, discernible, evident, manifest, material, objective, palpable, perceptible, physical, positive, real, solid, substantial, tactile, touchable
Antonyms *adj* abstract, disembodied, ethereal, immaterial, impalpable, imperceptible, indiscernible, insubstantial, intangible, theoretical, unreal

tangle *n* **1 = knot**, coil, entanglement, jungle, mass, mat, mesh, ravel, snarl, twist, web **2 = confusion**, complication, entanglement, fix (*inf.*), imbroglio, jam, labyrinth, maze, mess, mix-up ◆ *vb* **3 = twist**, coil, confuse, entangle, interlace, interlock, intertwist, interweave, jam, kink, knot, mat, mesh, ravel, snarl **4** *often with* **with = come into conflict**, come up against, contend, contest, cross swords, dispute, lock horns **5 = involve**, drag into, embroil, implicate **6 = catch**, enmesh, ensnare, entangle, entrap
Antonyms *vb* ≠ **twist:** disentangle, extricate, free, straighten out, unravel, untangle

tangled *adj* **1 = twisted**, entangled, jumbled, knotted, knotty, matted, messy, scrambled, snarled, tousled **2 = complicated**, complex, confused, convoluted, involved, knotty, messy, mixed-up

tangy *adj* **= sharp**, biting, briny, fresh, piquant, pungent, spicy, tart

tantalize *vb* **= torment**, baffle, balk, disappoint, entice, frustrate, keep (someone) hanging on, lead on, make (someone's) mouth water, provoke, taunt, tease, thwart, titillate, torture

▸ˌ**tantaliˈzation** *or* ˌ**tantaliˈsation** *n* ▸ˈ**tantaˌlizing** *or* ˈ**tantaˌlising** *adj* ▸ˈ**tantaˌlizingly** *or* ˈ**tantaˌlisingly** *adv*

tantalum (ˈtæntələm) *n* a hard greyish-white metallic element: used in electrolytic rectifiers and in alloys to increase hardness and chemical resistance, esp. in surgical instruments. Symbol: Ta; atomic no.: 73; atomic wt.: 180.95. [C19: after *Tantalus* (see TANTALIZE), from the metal's incapacity to absorb acids]

tantalus (ˈtæntələs) *n Brit.* a case in which bottles may be locked with their contents tantalizingly visible.

tantamount ⓣ (ˈtæntəˌmaʊnt) *adj* (*postpositive; foll. by to*) as good (as); equivalent in effect (to). [C17: from Anglo-F *tant amunter* to amount to as much]

tantara (ˈtæntərə, tænˈtɑːrə) *n* a fanfare or blast, as on a trumpet or horn. [C16: from L *taratantara*, imit. of the sound of the tuba]

tantivy (tænˈtɪvɪ) *adv* **1** at full speed; rapidly. ◆ *n, pl* **tantivies**, *sentence substitute.* **2** a hunting cry, esp. at full gallop. [C17: ? imit. of galloping hooves]

tant mieux *French.* (tɑ̃ mjø) so much the better.

tanto (ˈtæntəʊ) *adv Music.* too much; excessively. [It.]

tant pis *French.* (tɑ̃ pi) so much the worse.

Tantrism (ˈtæntrɪzəm) *n* **1** a movement within Hinduism combining magical and mystical elements and with sacred writings of its own (**the Tantra**). **2** a similar movement within Buddhism. [C18: from Sansk. *tantra*, lit.: warp, hence doctrine]
▸ˈ**Tantric** *adj* ▸ˈ**Tantrist** *n*

tantrum ⓣ (ˈtæntrəm) *n* (*often pl*) a childish fit of rage; outburst of bad temper. [C18: from ?]

Tao (taʊ) *n* (in the philosophy of Taoism) **1** that in virtue of which all things happen or exist. **2** the rational basis of human conduct. **3** the course of life and its relation to eternal truth. [Chinese, lit.: path, way]

Taoiseach (ˈtiːʃæx) *n* the prime mininster of the Irish Republic. [from Irish, lit.: leader]

Taoism (ˈtaʊɪzəm) *n* a system of religion and philosophy based on the teachings of Lao Zi, 6th-century B.C. Chinese philosopher, and advocating a simple honest life and noninterference with the course of natural events.
▸ˈ**Taoist** *n, adj* ▸ˌ**Taoˈistic** *adj*

taonga (tɑˈɔŋgə) *n NZ.* anything highly prized. [Maori]

tap[1] ⓣ (tæp) *vb* **taps, tapping, tapped. 1** to strike (something) lightly and usually repeatedly. **2** (*tr*) to produce by striking in this way: *to tap a rhythm.* **3** (*tr*) to strike lightly with (something): *to tap one's finger on the desk.* **4** (*intr*) to walk with a tapping sound. **5** (*tr*) to attach reinforcing pieces to (the toe or heel of a shoe). ◆ *n* **6** a light blow or knock, or the sound made by it. **7** the metal piece attached to the toe or heel of a shoe used for tap-dancing. **8** short for **tap-dancing.** ◆ See also **taps.** [C13 *tappen*, prob. from OF *taper*, of Gmc origin]

tap[2] ⓣ (tæp) *n* **1** a valve by which a fluid flow from a pipe can be controlled. US names: **faucet, spigot. 2** a stopper to plug a cask or barrel. **3** a particular quality of alcoholic drink, esp. when contained in casks: *an excellent tap.* **4** *Brit.* short for **taproom. 5** the withdrawal of fluid from a bodily cavity. **6** a tool for cutting female screw threads. **7** *Electronics, chiefly US & Canad.* a connection made at some point between the end terminals of an inductor, resistor, etc. Usual Brit. name: **tapping. 8** *Stock Exchange.* **8a** an issue of a government security released slowly onto the market when its market price reaches a predetermined level. **8b** (*as modifier*): *tap stock; tap issue.* **9** a concealed listening or recording device connected to a telephone or telegraph wire. **10 on tap. 10a** *Inf.* ready for use. **10b** (of drinks) on draught. ◆ *vb* **taps, tapping, tapped.** (*tr*) **11** to furnish with a tap. **12** to draw off with or as if with a tap. **13** to cut into (a tree) and draw off sap from it. **14** *Brit. inf.* **14a** to ask (someone) for money: *he tapped me for a fiver.* **14b** to obtain (money) from someone. **15** to connect a tap to (a telephone or telegraph wire). **16** to make a connection to (a pipe, drain, etc.). **17** to cut a female screw thread in (an object or material) by use of a tap. **18** *Inf.* (of a sports team or an employer) to make an illicit attempt to recruit (a player or employee bound by an existing contract). [OE *tæppa*]
▸ˈ**tapper** *n*

tapa (ˈtɑːpə) *n* **1** the inner bark of the paper mulberry. **2** a cloth made from this in the Pacific islands. [C19: from native Polynesian name]

tapas (ˈtæpəs) *pl n* **a** light snacks or appetizers, usually eaten with drinks. **b** (*as modifier*): *a tapas bar.* [from Sp. *tapa* cover, lid]

tap dance *n* **1** a step dance in which the performer wears shoes equipped with taps that make a rhythmic sound on the stage as he dances. ◆ *vb* **tap-dance, tap-dances, tap-dancing, tap-danced.** (*intr*) **2** to perform a tap dance.
▸ˈ**tap-ˌdancer** *n* ▸ˈ**tap-ˌdancing** *n*

tape ⓣ (teɪp) *n* **1** a long thin strip of cotton, linen, etc., used for binding, fastening, etc. **2** a long narrow strip of paper, metal, etc. **3** a string stretched across the track at the end of a race course. **4** See **magnetic tape, ticker tape, paper tape, tape recording.** ◆ *vb* **tapes, taping, taped.** (*mainly tr*) **5** (*also intr*) Also: **tape record.** to record (speech, music, etc.). **6** to furnish with tapes. **7** to bind, measure, secure, or wrap with tape. **8** (*usually passive*) *Brit. inf.* to take stock of (a person or situation). [OE *tæppe*]
▸ˈ**tapeˌlike** *adj* ▸ˈ**taper** *n*

tape deck *n* **1** a tape recording unit in a hi-fi system. **2** the platform supporting the spools, cassettes, or cartridges of a tape recorder, incorporating the motor and the playback, recording, and erasing heads.

tape machine *n* **1** another word for **tape recorder. 2** a telegraphic device that records current stock quotations electronically or on ticker tape. US equivalent: **ticker.**

tape measure *n* a tape or length of metal marked off in inches, centimetres, etc., used for measuring. Also called (esp. US): **tapeline.**

tapenade (ˈtæpənɑːd) *n* a savoury paste made from capers, olives, and anchovies, with olive oil and lemon juice. [C20: F, from Provençal *tapéo* capers]

taper ⓣ (ˈteɪpə) *vb* **1** to become or cause to become narrower towards one end. **2** (*often foll. by off*) to become or cause to become smaller or less significant. ◆ *n* **3** a thin candle. **4** a thin wooden or waxed strip for transferring a flame; spill. **5** a narrowing. **6** any feeble light. [OE *tapor*, prob. from L *papȳrus* papyrus (from its use as a wick)]
▸ˈ**taperer** *n* ▸ˈ**tapering** *adj*

tape recorder *n* an electrical device used for recording sounds on magnetic tape and usually also for reproducing them.

tape recording *n* **1** the act of recording on magnetic tape. **2** the magnetized tape used for this. **3** the speech, music, etc., so recorded.

tape streamer *n Computing.* an electromechanical device that enables data to be copied byte by byte from a hard disk onto magnetic tape for security or storage.

tapestry (ˈtæpɪstrɪ) *n, pl* **tapestries. 1** a heavy woven fabric, often in the form of a picture, used for wall hangings, furnishings, etc. **2** another word for **needlepoint** (sense 1). **3** a colourful and complicated situation: *the rich tapestry of life.* [C15: from OF *tapisserie* carpeting, from OF *tapiz*; see TAPIS]
▸ˈ**tapestried** *adj*

tapeworm (ˈteɪpˌwɜːm) *n* any of a class of parasitic ribbon-like flatworms. The adults inhabit the intestines of vertebrates.

taphole (ˈtæpˌhəʊl) *n* a hole in a furnace for running off molten metal or slag.

taphouse (ˈtæpˌhaʊs) *n Now rare.* an inn.

tapioca (ˌtæpɪˈəʊkə) *n* a beadlike starch obtained from cassava root, used in cooking as a thickening agent, esp. in puddings. [C18: via Port. from Tupi *tipioca* pressed-out juice, from *tipi* residue + *ok* to squeeze out]

tapir (ˈteɪpə) *n, pl* **tapirs** *or* **tapir.** any of various mammals of South and Central America and SE Asia, having an elongated snout, three-toed hind legs, and four-toed forelegs. [C18: from Tupi *tapiira*]

tapis (ˈtæpiː) *n, pl* **tapis. 1** tapestry or carpeting, esp. as formerly used to cover a table. **2 on the tapis.** currently under consideration. [C17: from F, from OF *tapiz*, from Gk *tapētion* rug, from *tapēs* carpet]

tappet (ˈtæpɪt) *n* a mechanical part that reciprocates to receive or transmit intermittent motion. [C18: from TAP[1] + -ET]

taproom (ˈtæpˌruːm, -ˌrʊm) *n* a bar, as in a hotel or pub.

taproot (ˈtæpˌruːt) *n* the main root of plants such as the dandelion, which grows vertically downwards and bears smaller lateral roots.

taps (tæps) *n* (*functioning as sing*) **1** *Chiefly US.* **1a** (in army camps, etc.) a signal given on a bugle, drum, etc., indicating that lights are to be put out. **1b** any similar signal, as at a military funeral. **2** (in the Guide movement) a closing song sung at an evening camp fire or at the end of a meeting.

tapster (ˈtæpstə) *n* **1** *Rare.* a barman. **2** (in W Africa) a man who taps palm trees. [OE *tæppestre*, fem. of *tæppere*, from *tappian* to TAP[2]]

tap water *n* water drawn off through taps from pipes in a house, as distinguished from distilled water, mineral water, etc.

tar[1] (tɑː) *n* **1** any of various dark viscid substances obtained by the destructive distillation of organic matter such as coal, wood, or peat. **2** another name for **coal tar.** ◆ *vb* **tars, tarring, tarred.** (*tr*) **3** to coat with tar. **4 tar and feather.** to punish by smearing tar and feathers over (someone). **5 tarred with the same brush.** regarded as having the same faults. [OE *teoru*]
▸ˈ**tarry** *adj* ▸ˈ**tarriness** *n*

tar[2] (tɑː) *n* an informal word for **seaman.** [C17: short for TARPAULIN]

taradiddle (ˈtærəˌdɪdᵊl) *n* a variant spelling of **tarradiddle.**

tarakihi *or* **terakihi** (ˈtærəˌkiːhiː) *n, pl* **tarakihis.** a common edible sea fish of New Zealand waters. [from Maori]

taramasalata (ˌtærəməsəˈlɑːtə) *n* a creamy pale pink paté, made from

THESAURUS

tantamount *adj, foll. by* **to** = **equivalent to,** as good as, commensurate with, equal to, synonymous with, the same as

tantrum *n* = **outburst,** bate (*Brit. sl.*), fit, flare-up, hysterics, ill humour, paddy (*Brit. inf.*), paroxysm, storm, temper, wax (*inf., chiefly Brit.*)

tap[1] *vb* **1** = **knock,** beat, drum, pat, rap, strike, touch ◆ *n* **6** = **knock,** beat, light blow, pat, rap, touch

tap[2] *n* **1** = **valve,** faucet (*US*), spigot, spout, stopcock **2** = **stopper,** bung, plug, spile **9** = **bug** (*inf.*), listening device **10 on tap: a** *Informal* = **ready,** at hand, in reserve, on hand **b** = **on draught** ◆ *vb* **12** = **draw off,** bleed, broach, drain, open, pierce, siphon off

tape *n* **1, 2** = **strip,** band, ribbon ◆ *vb* **5** = **record,** tape-record, video **7** = **bind,** seal, secure, stick, wrap

taper *vb* **1** = **narrow,** come to a point, thin **2** *often foll. by* **off** = **decrease,** die away, die out, dwindle, fade, lessen, reduce, subside, thin out, wane, weaken, wind down
Antonyms *vb* ≠ **decrease:** grow, increase, intensify, step up, strengthen, swell, widen

the roe of grey mullet or smoked cod and served as an hors d'oeuvre. [C20: from Mod. Gk, from *tarama* cod's roe]

tarantass (ˌtɑːrən'tæs) *n* a four-wheeled Russian carriage without springs. [C19: from Russian *tarantas*]

tarantella (ˌtærən'tɛlə) *n* **1** a peasant dance from S Italy. **2** a piece of music composed for or in the rhythm of this dance. [C18: from It., from *Taranto,* port in SE Italy]

tarantism ('tærənˌtɪzəm) *n* a nervous disorder marked by uncontrollable bodily movement, widespread in S Italy during the 15th to 17th centuries: popularly thought to be caused by the bite of a tarantula. [C17: from NL *tarantismus,* from *Taranto;* see TARANTULA, TARANTELLA]

tarantula (tə'ræntjulə) *n, pl* **tarantulas** *or* **tarantulae** (-ˌliː). **1** any of various large hairy spiders of tropical America. **2** a large hairy spider of S Europe. [C16: from Med. L, from OIt. *tarantola,* from *Taranto;* see TARANTELLA]

taraxacum (tə'ræksəkəm) *n* **1** any of a genus of perennial plants of the composite family, such as the dandelion. **2** the dried root of the dandelion, used as a laxative, diuretic, and tonic. [C18: from Med. L, from Ar. *tarakhshaqūn* wild chicory, ? of Persian origin]

tarboosh (tɑː'buːʃ) *n* a felt or cloth brimless cap, usually red and often with a silk tassel, worn by Muslim men. [C18: from Ar. *tarbūsh*]

tarboy ('tɑːˌbɔɪ) *n Austral. & NZ inf.* a boy who applies tar to the skin of sheep cut during shearing.

Tardenoisian (ˌtɑːdə'nɔɪzɪən) *adj* of or referring to a Mesolithic culture characterized by small flint instruments. [C20: after *Tardenois,* France, where implements were found]

tardigrade ('tɑːdɪˌgreɪd) *n* any of various minute aquatic segmented eight-legged invertebrates occurring in soil, ditches, etc. Popular name: **water bear.** [C17: via L *tardigradus,* from *tardus* sluggish + *gradī* to walk]

tardy Ⓣ ('tɑːdɪ) *adj* **tardier, tardiest. 1** occurring later than expected. **2** slow in progress, growth, etc. [C15: from OF *tardif,* from L *tardus* slow]
▸ **'tardily** *adv* ▸ **'tardiness** *n*

tare[1] (tɛə) *n* **1** any of various vetch plants of Eurasia and N Africa. **2** the seed of any of these plants. **3** *Bible.* a weed, thought to be the darnel. [C14: from ?]

tare[2] (tɛə) *n* **1** the weight of the wrapping or container in which goods are packed. **2** a deduction from gross weight to compensate for this. **3** the weight of an unladen vehicle. ◆ *vb* **tares, taring, tared. 4** *(tr)* to weigh (a package, etc.) in order to calculate the amount of tare. [C15: from OF: waste, from Med. L *tara,* from Ar. *tarhah* something discarded, from *taraha* to reject]

targe (tɑːdʒ) *n* an archaic word for **shield.** [C13: from OF, of Gmc origin]

target Ⓣ ('tɑːgɪt) *n* **1a** an object or area at which an archer or marksman aims, usually a round flat surface marked with concentric rings. **1b** *(as modifier): target practice.* **2a** any point or area aimed at. **2b** *(as modifier): target area; target company.* **3** a fixed goal or objective. **4** a person or thing at which an action or remark is directed or the object of a person's feelings. **5** a joint of lamb consisting of the breast and neck. **6** (formerly) a small round shield. **7** *Physics, electronics.* **7a** a substance subjected to bombardment by electrons or other particles, or to irradiation. **7b** an electrode in a television camera tube whose surface is scanned by the electron beam. **8** *Electronics.* an object detected by the reflection of a radar or sonar signal, etc. ◆ *vb* **targets, targeting, targeted.** *(tr)* **9** to make a target of. **10** to direct or aim: *to target benefits at those most in need.* [C14: from OF *targette* a little shield, from OF TARGE]

tariff Ⓣ ('tærɪf) *n* **1a** a tax levied by a government on imports or occasionally exports. **1b** a system or list of such taxes. **2** any schedule of prices, fees, fares, etc. **3** *Chiefly Brit.* **3a** a method of charging for the supply of services such as gas and electricity. **3b** a schedule of such charges. **4** *Chiefly Brit.* a bill of fare with prices listed; menu. ◆ *vb (tr)* **5** to set a tariff on. **6** to price according to a schedule of tariffs. [C16: from It. *tariffa,* from Ar. *ta'rīfa* to inform]

tariff office *n Insurance.* a company whose premiums are based on a tariff agreed with other insurance companies.

tarlatan ('tɑːlətən) *n* an open-weave cotton fabric, used for stiffening garments. [C18: from F *tarlatane,* var. of *tarnatane* type of muslin, ? of Indian origin]

Tarmac ('tɑːmæk) *n* **1** *Trademark.* *(often not cap.)* a paving material that consists of crushed stone rolled and bound with a mixture of tar and bitumen, esp. as used for a road, airport runway, etc. Full name: **Tarmacadam** (ˌtɑːmə'kædəm). See also **macadam.** ◆ *vb* **Tarmacs, Tarmacking, Tarmacked.** *(tr)* **2** *(usually not cap.)* to apply Tarmac to.

tarn (tɑːn) *n* a small mountain lake or pool. [C14: from ON]

tarnation (tɑː'neɪʃən) *n* a euphemism for **damnation.**

tarnish Ⓣ ('tɑːnɪʃ) *vb* **1** to lose or cause to lose the shine, esp. by exposure to air or moisture resulting in surface oxidation; discolour. **2** to stain or become stained; taint. ◆ *n* **3** a tarnished condition, surface, or film. [C16: from OF *ternir* to make dull, from *terne* lustreless of Gmc origin]
▸ **'tarnishable** *adj*

taro ('tɑːrəʊ) *n, pl* **taros. 1** a plant cultivated in the tropics for its large edible rootstock. **2** the rootstock of this plant. ◆ Also called: **eddo.** [C18: from Tahitian & Maori]

tarot ('tærəʊ) *n* **1** one of a special pack of cards, now used mainly for fortune-telling. **2** a card in a tarot pack with distinctive symbolic design. ◆ *adj* **3** relating to tarot cards. [C16: from F, from OIt. *tarocco,* from ?]

tarpan ('tɑːpæn) *n* a European wild horse, now extinct. [from Tatar]

tarpaulin (tɑː'pɔːlɪn) *n* **1** a heavy waterproof fabric made of canvas or similar material coated with tar, wax, or paint. **2** a sheet of this fabric. **3** a hat made of or covered with this fabric, esp. a sailor's hat. **4** a rare word for **seaman.** [C17: prob. from TAR[1] + PALL[1] + -ING[1]]

tarpon ('tɑːpən) *n, pl* **tarpons** *or* **tarpon.** a large silvery game fish of warm oceans. [C17: ?from Du. *tarpoen,* from ?]

tarradiddle ('tærəˌdɪdᵊl) *n* **1** a trifling lie. **2** nonsense; twaddle. [C18: from ?]

tarragon ('tærəgən) *n* **1** an aromatic plant of the Old World, having leaves which are used as seasoning. **2** the leaves of this plant. [C16: from OF *targon,* from Med. L *tarcon,* ? ult. from Gk *drakontion* adderwort]

tarry Ⓣ ('tærɪ) *vb* **tarries, tarrying, tarried. 1** *(intr)* to delay; linger. **2** *(intr)* to remain temporarily or briefly. **3** *(intr)* to wait or stay. **4** *(tr) Arch. or poetic.* to await. [C14 *tarien,* from ?]
▸ **'tarrier** *n*

tarsal ('tɑːsᵊl) *adj* **1** of the tarsus or tarsi. ◆ *n* **2** a tarsal bone.

tarseal ('tɑːˌsiːl) *n NZ.* **1** the bitumen surface of a road. **2 the tarseal.** the main highway.

tarsia ('tɑːsɪə) *n* another term for **intarsia.** [C17: from It., from Ar. *tarsī'*]

tarsier ('tɑːsɪə) *n* any of several nocturnal arboreal primates of Indonesia and the Philippines, having huge eyes, long hind legs, and digits ending in pads to facilitate climbing. [C18: from F, from *tarse* the flat of the foot; see TARSUS]

tarsus ('tɑːsəs) *n, pl* **tarsi** (-saɪ). **1** the bones of the ankle and heel, collectively. **2** the corresponding part in other mammals and in amphibians and reptiles. **3** the connective tissue supporting the free edge of each eyelid. **4** the part of an insect's leg that lies distal to the tibia. [C17: from NL, from Gk *tarsos* flat surface, instep]

tart[1] Ⓣ (tɑːt) *n* a pastry case often having no top crust, with a filling of fruit, custard, etc. [C14: from OF *tarte,* from ?]

tart[2] Ⓣ (tɑːt) *adj* **1** (of a flavour, etc.) sour; acid. **2** cutting; sharp: *a tart remark.* [OE *teart* rough]
▸ **'tartly** *adv* ▸ **'tartness** *n*

tart[3] Ⓣ (tɑːt) *n Inf.* a promiscuous woman, esp. a prostitute. See also **tart up.** [C19: shortened from SWEETHEART]
▸ **'tarty** *adj*

tartan ('tɑːtᵊn) *n* **1a** a design of straight lines, crossing at right angles to give a chequered appearance, esp. the distinctive design or designs associated with each Scottish clan. **1b** *(as modifier): a tartan kilt.* **2** a fabric or garment with this design. [C16: ?from OF *tertaine* linsey-woolsey, from OSp. *tiritaña* a fine silk fabric, from *tiritar* to rustle]
▸ **'tartaned** *adj*

tartar[1] ('tɑːtə) *n* **1** a hard deposit on the teeth, consisting of food, cellular debris, and mineral salts. **2** a brownish-red substance consisting mainly of potassium hydrogen tartrate, deposited during the fermentation of wine. [C14: from Med. L *tartarum,* from Med. Gk *tartaron*]

tartar[2] ('tɑːtə) *n (sometimes cap.)* a fearsome or formidable person. [C16: special use of TARTAR]

Tartar ('tɑːtə) *n, adj* a variant spelling of **Tatar.**

Tartarean (tɑː'tɛərɪən) *adj Literary.* of or relating to Tartarus, in Greek mythology an abyss below Hades; infernal.

tartar emetic *n* antimony potassium tartrate, a poisonous, crystalline salt used as a mordant and in medicine.

tartaric (tɑː'tærɪk) *adj* of, containing, or derived from tartar or tartaric acid.

THESAURUS

tardiness *n* **1, 2** = **lateness**, belatedness, delay, dilatoriness, procrastination, slowness, unpunctuality

tardy *adj* **1** = **late**, behindhand, belated, overdue **2** = **slow**, backward, dawdling, dilatory, loitering, procrastinating, retarded, slack, sluggish, unpunctual

target *n* **1a, 2a, 3** = **goal**, aim, ambition, bull's-eye, end, Holy Grail *(inf.)*, intention, mark, object, objective **4** = **victim**, butt, quarry, scapegoat

tariff *n* **1** = **tax**, assessment, duty, excise, impost, levy, rate, toll **2** = **price list**, bill of fare, charges, menu, schedule

tarnish *vb* **1** = **stain**, befoul, blemish, blot, darken, dim, discolour, dull, lose lustre *or* shine, rust, soil, spot **2** = **damage**, blacken, drag through the mud, smirch, sully, taint ◆ *n* **3** = **stain**, blemish, blot, discoloration, rust, spot, taint
Antonyms *vb* ≠ **stain:** brighten, enhance, polish up, shine ≠ **damage:** enhance

tarry *vb Old-fashioned* **1, 3** = **linger**, bide, dally, dawdle, delay, drag one's feet *or* heels, hang around, loiter, lose time, pause, remain, take one's time, wait **2** = **stay**, abide, dwell, lodge, rest, sojourn
Antonyms *vb* ≠ **linger:** hasten, hurry, move on, rush, scoot, step on it *(inf.)*

tart[1] *n* = **pie**, pastry, tartlet

tart[2] *adj* **1** = **sharp**, acid, acidulous, astringent, bitter, piquant, pungent, sour, tangy, vinegary **2** = **cutting**, acrimonious, astringent, barbed, biting, caustic, crusty, harsh, hurtful, mordacious, mordant, nasty, scathing, sharp, short, snappish, testy, trenchant, vitriolic, wounding
Antonyms *adj* ≠ **sharp:** honeyed, sugary, sweet, syrupy, toothsome ≠ **cutting:** agreeable, delightful, gentle, kind, pleasant

tart[3] *n* = **slut**, call girl, fallen woman, *fille de joie,* floozy *(sl.)*, harlot, hooker, loose woman, prostitute, scrubber *(Brit. & Austral. sl.)*, slag *(Brit. sl.)*, streetwalker, strumpet, trollop, whore, woman of easy virtue, working girl *(facetious sl.)*

tartaric acid *n* a colourless crystalline acid which is found in many fruits: used as a food additive (**E334**) in soft drinks, confectionery, and baking powders, and in tanning and photography. Formula: $(CHOH)_2(COOH)_2$. Systematic name: **2,3-dihydroxybutanedioic acid.**

tartar sauce *n* a mayonnaise sauce mixed with hard-boiled egg yolks, chopped herbs, capers, etc. [from F *sauce tartare,* from TARTAR]

tartlet ('tɑ:tlɪt) *n Brit.* an individual pastry case with a sweet or savoury filling.

tartrate ('tɑ:treɪt) *n* any salt or ester of tartaric acid.

tartrated ('tɑ:treɪtɪd) *adj* being in the form of a tartrate.

tartrazine ('tɑ:trəˌzi:n, -zɪn) *n* an azo dye that produces a yellow colour: used as a food additive (**E102**), in drugs, and to dye textiles.

tart up *vb* (*tr; adv*) *Brit. inf.* **1** to dress and make (oneself) up in a provocative or promiscuous way. **2** to decorate or improve the appearance of: *to tart up a bar.*

tarwhine ('tɑ:ˌwaɪn) *n* any of various Australian marine food fishes, esp. the sea bream. [?from Abor.]

Tarzan ('tɑ:zən) *n* (*sometimes not cap.*) *Inf., often ironical.* a man with great physical strength, agility, and virility. [C20: after the hero of a series of stories by E. R. *Burroughs* 1875–1950]

Tas. *abbrev. for* Tasmania.

tasimeter (tə'sɪmɪtə) *n* a device for measuring small temperature changes. It depends on the changes of pressure resulting from expanding or contracting solids. [C19 *tasi-,* from Gk *tasis* tension + -METER]
▸**tasimetric** (ˌtæsɪ'metrɪk) *adj* ▸**ta'simetry** *n*

task Ⓣ (tɑ:sk) *n* **1** a specific piece of work required to be done. **2** an unpleasant or difficult job or duty. **3** any piece of work. **4 take to task.** to criticize or reprove. ◆ *vb* (*tr*) **5** to assign a task to. **6** to subject to severe strain; tax. [C13: from OF *tasche,* from Med. L *tasca,* from *taxa* tax, from L *taxāre* to TAX]

task force *n* **1** a temporary grouping of military units formed to undertake a specific mission. **2** any organization set up to carry out a continuing task.

taskmaster ('tɑ:skˌmɑ:stə) *n* a person, discipline, etc., that enforces work, esp. hard or continuous work.
▸**'taskˌmistress** *fem n*

taskwork ('tɑ:skˌwɜ:k) *n* **1** hard or unpleasant work. **2** a rare word for **piecework.**

Tasmanian devil (tæz'meɪnɪən) *n* a small ferocious carnivorous marsupial of Tasmania.

Tasmanian wolf *or* **tiger** *n* other names for **thylacine.**

tass (tæs) *or* **tassie** ('tæsɪ) *n Scot. & N English dialect.* **1** a cup or glass. **2** its contents. [C15: from OF *tasse* cup, from Ar. *tassah* basin, from Persian *tast*]

Tass (tæs) *n* (formerly) the principal news agency of the Soviet Union: replaced in 1992 by Itar Tass. [*T(elegrafnoye) a(gentstvo) S(ovetskogo) S(oyuza)* Telegraphic Agency of the Soviet Union]

tassel ('tæs^{ə}l) *n* **1** a tuft of loose threads secured by a knot or knob, used to decorate soft furnishings, clothes, etc. **2** anything resembling this, esp. the tuft of stamens at the tip of a maize inflorescence. ◆ *vb* **tassels, tasselling, tasselled** *or US* **tassels, tasseling, tasseled. 3** (*tr*) to adorn with tassels. **4** (*intr*) (of maize) to produce stamens in a tuft. [C13: from OF, from Vulgar L *tassellus* (unattested), changed from L *taxillus* a small die]

Tassie *or* **Tassy** ('tæzɪ) *n, Austral. inf.* **1** Tasmania. **2** (*pl* **Tassies**) a native or inhabitant of Tasmania.

taste Ⓣ (teɪst) *n* **1** the sense by which the qualities and flavour of a substance are distinguished by the taste buds. **2** the sensation experienced by means of the taste buds. **3** the act of tasting. **4** a small amount eaten, drunk, or tried on the tongue. **5** a brief experience of something: *a taste of the whip.* **6** a preference or liking for something. **7** the ability to make discerning judgments about aesthetic, artistic, and intellectual matters. **8** judgment of aesthetic or social matters according to a generally accepted standard: *bad taste.* **9** discretion; delicacy: *that remark lacks taste.* ◆ *vb* **tastes, tasting, tasted. 10** to distinguish the taste of (a substance) by means of the taste buds. **11** (*usually tr*) to take a small amount of (a food, liquid, etc.) into the mouth, esp. in order to test the quality. **12** (often foll. by *of*) to have a specific flavour or taste. **13** (when *intr,* usually foll. by *of*) to have an experience of (something): *to taste success.* **14** (*tr*) an archaic word for **enjoy.** [C13: from OF *taster,* ult. from L *taxāre* to appraise]
▸**'tastable** *adj*

taste bud *n* any of the elevated sensory organs on the surface of the tongue, by means of which the sensation of taste is experienced.

tasteful Ⓣ ('teɪstfʊl) *adj* indicating good taste: *a tasteful design.*
▸**'tastefully** *adv* ▸**'tastefulness** *n*

tasteless Ⓣ ('teɪstlɪs) *adj* **1** lacking in flavour; insipid. **2** lacking social or aesthetic taste.
▸**'tastelessly** *adv* ▸**'tastelessness** *n*

taster ('teɪstə) *n* **1** a person who samples food or drink for quality. **2** any device used in tasting or sampling. **3** a person employed, esp. formerly, to taste food and drink prepared for a king, etc., to test for poison. **4** a sample or preview of a product, experience, etc., intended to stimulate interest in the product, experience, etc., itself: *the single serves as a taster for the band's new album.*

tasty Ⓣ ('teɪstɪ) *adj* **tastier, tastiest.** having a pleasant flavour.
▸**'tastily** *adv* ▸**'tastiness** *n*

tat[1] (tæt) *vb* **tats, tatting, tatted.** to make (something) by tatting. [C19: from ?]

tat[2] (tæt) *n* **1** tatty articles or a tatty condition. **2** tasteless articles. **3** a tangled mass. [C20: back formation from TATTY]

tat[3] (tæt) *n* See **tit for tat.**

ta-ta (tæ'tɑ:) *sentence substitute. Brit. inf.* goodbye; farewell. [C19: from ?]

Tatar *or* **Tartar** ('tɑ:tə) *n* **1a** a member of a Mongoloid people who established a powerful state in central Asia in the 13th century. **1b** a descendant of this people, now scattered throughout Russia and N central Asia. **2** any of the Turkic languages spoken by the present-day Tatars. ◆ *adj* **3** of or relating to the Tatars. [C14: from OF *Tartare,* from Med. L *Tartarus* (associated with L *Tartarus* the underworld), from Persian *Tātār*]
▸**Tatarian** (tɑ:'teərɪən), **Tar'tarian** *or* **Tataric** (tɑ:'tærɪk), **Tar'taric** *adj*

tater ('teɪtə) *n* a dialect word for **potato.**

tatouay ('tætʊˌeɪ) *n* a large armadillo of South America. [C16: from Sp. *tatuay,* from Guarani, from *tatu* armadillo + *ai* worthless (because inedible)]

tatter Ⓣ ('tætə) *vb* **1** to make or become ragged or worn to shreds. ◆ *n* **2** a torn or ragged piece, esp. of material. [C14: from ON]

tatterdemalion (ˌtætədɪ'meɪljən) *n Rare.* a person dressed in ragged clothes. [C17: from TATTER + *-demalion,* from ?]

tattersall ('tætəˌsɔ:l) *n* a fabric having stripes or bars in a checked or squared pattern. [C19: after *Tattersall's,* a horse market in London founded by Richard *Tattersall* (died 1795), Brit. horseman; the horse blankets at the market orig. had this pattern]

Tattersall's ('tætəˌsɔ:lz) *n Austral.* **1** Also called (inf.): **Tatt's.** a lottery now based in Melbourne. **2** a name used for sportsmen's clubs. [after *Tattersall's* horse market; see TATTERSALL]

tatting ('tætɪŋ) *n* **1** an intricate type of lace made by looping a thread of cotton or linen by means of a hand shuttle. **2** the act or work of producing this. [C19: from ?]

tattle Ⓣ ('tæt^{ə}l) *vb* **tattles, tattling, tattled. 1** (*intr*) to gossip about another's personal matters. **2** (*tr*) to reveal by gossiping. **3** (*intr*) to talk idly; chat. ◆ *n* **4** the act or an instance of tattling. **5** a scandalmonger; gossip. [C15 (in the sense: to stammer, hesitate): from MDu. *tatelen* to prate, imit.]
▸**'tattler** *n*

THESAURUS

task *n* **1-3** = **job**, assignment, business, charge, chore, duty, employment, enterprise, exercise, labour, mission, occupation, toil, undertaking, work **4 take to task** = **criticize**, bawl out (*inf.*), blame, blast, carpet (*inf.*), censure, lambast(e), lecture, read the riot act, rebuke, reprimand, reproach, reprove, scold, tear into (*inf.*), tear (someone) off a strip (*Brit. inf.*), tell off (*inf.*), upbraid ◆ *vb* **5** = **assign to**, charge, entrust **6** = **strain**, burden, exhaust, load, lumber (*Brit. inf.*), oppress, overload, push, saddle, tax, test, weary

taste *n* **2** = **flavour**, relish, savour, smack, tang **4** = **bit**, bite, dash, drop, morsel, mouthful, nip, sample, sip, *soupçon*, spoonful, swallow, titbit, touch **6** = **liking**, appetite, bent, desire, fancy, fondness, inclination, leaning, palate, partiality, penchant, predilection, preference, relish **7** = **refinement**, appreciation, cultivation, culture, discernment, discrimination, elegance, grace, judgment, perception, polish, sophistication, style **8, 9** = **propriety**, correctness, decorum, delicacy, discretion, nicety, politeness, restraint, tact, tactfulness ◆ *vb* **10** = **distinguish**, differentiate, discern, perceive **11** = **sample**, assay, nibble, relish, savour, sip, test, try **12** = **have a flavour of**, savour of, smack of **13** = **experience**, come up against, encounter, feel, have knowledge of, know, meet with, partake of, undergo
Antonyms *n* ≠ **flavour:** blandness, insipidity, tastelessness ≠ **liking:** disinclination, dislike, distaste, hatred, loathing ≠ **refinement:** lack of discernment, lack of judgment, mawkishness, tackiness, tastelessness ≠ **propriety:** bawdiness, blueness, coarseness, crudeness, impropriety, indelicacy, obscenity (*inf.*), tactlessness, unsubtlety ◆ *vb* ≠ **distinguish:** fail to discern ≠ **experience:** fail to achieve, miss, remain ignorant of

tasteful *adj* = **refined**, aesthetically pleasing, artistic, beautiful, charming, cultivated, cultured, delicate, discriminating, elegant, exquisite, fastidious, graceful, handsome, harmonious, in good taste, polished, restrained, smart, stylish, urbane
Antonyms *adj* brash, flashy, garish, gaudy, inelegant, loud, objectionable, offensive, showy, sick, tacky (*inf.*), tasteless, tawdry, twee, uncultured, unrefined, vulgar

tasteless *adj* **1** = **insipid**, bland, boring, dull, flat, flavourless, mild, stale, tame, thin, uninspired, uninteresting, vapid, watered-down, weak **2** = **vulgar**, cheap, coarse, crass, crude, flashy, garish, gaudy, graceless, gross, impolite, improper, indecorous, indelicate, indiscreet, inelegant, low, naff (*Brit. sl.*), rude, tacky (*inf.*), tactless, tawdry, uncouth, unseemly
Antonyms *adj* ≠ **insipid:** appetizing, delectable, delicious, flavoursome, savoury, scrumptious (*inf.*), tasty ≠ **vulgar:** elegant, graceful, refined, tasteful

tasty *adj* = **delicious**, appetizing, delectable, flavourful, flavoursome, full-flavoured, good-tasting, luscious, palatable, sapid, savoury, scrumptious (*inf.*), toothsome, yummy (*sl.*)
Antonyms *adj* bland, flavourless, insipid, tasteless, unappetizing, unsavoury

tatter *n* **2** = **rag**, bit, piece, scrap, shred

tattle *vb* **1, 3** = **gossip**, babble, blab, blather, blether, chat, chatter, jabber, natter, prate, prattle, run off at the mouth (*sl.*), spread rumours, talk idly, tell tales, tittle-tattle, yak (*sl.*) ◆ *n* **4** = **gossip**, babble, blather, blether, chat, chatter, chitchat, hearsay, idle talk, jabber, prattle, small talk, tittle-tattle, yak (*sl.*), yap (*sl.*)

tattler *n* **1** = **gossip**, bigmouth (*sl.*), quidnunc,

tattletale ('tæt°l,teɪl) *Chiefly US & Canad. n* **1** a scandalmonger or gossip. **2** another word for **telltale** (sense 1).

tattoo[1] (tæ'tu:) *n, pl* **tattoos. 1** (formerly) a signal by drum or bugle ordering the military to return to their quarters. **2** a military display or pageant. **3** any similar beating on a drum, etc. [C17: from Du. *taptoe,* from *tap toe!* turn off the taps! from *tap* tap of a barrel + *toe* to shut]

tattoo[2] (tæ'tu:) *vb* **tattoos, tattooing, tattooed. 1** to make (pictures or designs) on (the skin) by pricking and staining with indelible colours. ◆ *n, pl* **tattoos. 2** a design made by this process. **3** the practice of tattooing. [C18: from Tahitian *tatau*]
▸**tat'tooer** *or* **tat'tooist** *n*

tatty ⓣ ('tætɪ) *adj* **tattier, tattiest.** *Chiefly Brit.* worn out, shabby, or unkempt. [C16: of Scot. origin]
▸**'tattily** *adv* ▸**'tattiness** *n*

tau (tɔ:, taʊ) *n* the 19th letter in the Greek alphabet (Τ or τ). [C13: from Gk]

tau cross *n* a cross shaped like the Greek letter tau. Also called: **Saint Anthony's cross.**

taught (tɔ:t) *vb* the past tense and past participle of **teach.**

taunt ⓣ (tɔ:nt) *vb* (*tr*) **1** to provoke or deride with mockery, contempt, or criticism. **2** to tease; tantalize. ◆ *n* **3** a jeering remark. [C16: from F *tant pour tant* like for like]
▸**'taunting** *adj*

tau particle *n Physics.* a type of elementary particle classified as a lepton.

taupe (təʊp) *n* **a** a brownish-grey colour. **b** (*as adj*): *a taupe coat.* [C20: from F, lit.: mole, from L *talpa*]

taurine ('tɔ:raɪn) *adj* of or resembling a bull. [C17: from L *taurīnus,* from *taurus* a bull]

tauromachy (tɔ:'rɒməkɪ) *n* the art or act of bullfighting. [C19: Gk *tauromakhia,* from *tauros* bull + *makhē* fight]

Taurus ('tɔ:rəs) *n* **1** *Astron.* a constellation in the N hemisphere. **2** *Astrol.* Also called: the **Bull.** the second sign of the zodiac. The sun is in this sign between about April 20 and May 20. [C14: from L: bull]

taut ⓣ (tɔ:t) *adj* **1** tightly stretched; tense. **2** showing nervous strain; stressed. **3** *Chiefly naut.* in good order; neat. [C14 *toght*]
▸**'tautly** *adv* ▸**'tautness** *n*

tauten ('tɔ:t°n) *vb* to make or become taut.

tauto- *or before a vowel* **taut-** *combining form.* identical or same: *tautology.* [from Gk *tauto,* from *to auto*]

tautog (tɔ:'tɒg) *n* a large dark-coloured food fish of the North American coast of the Atlantic Ocean. [C17: from Narraganset *tautauog,* pl. of *tautau* sheepshead]

tautology ⓣ (tɔ:'tɒlədʒɪ) *n, pl* **tautologies. 1** the use of words that merely repeat elements of the meaning already conveyed, as in *Will these supplies be adequate enough?* in place of *Will these supplies be adequate?* **2** *Logic.* a statement that is always true, as in *either the sun is out or the sun is not out.* [C16: from LL *tautologia,* from Gk, from *tautologos*]
▸**tautological** (,tɔ:t°'lɒdʒɪk°l) *or* **tau'tologous** *adj*

tautomerism (tɔ:'tɒmə,rɪzəm) *n* the ability of certain chemical compounds to exist as a mixture of two interconvertible isomers in equilibrium. [C19: from TAUTO- + ISOMERISM]
▸**tautomer** ('tɔ:təmə) *n* ▸**tautomeric** (,tɔ:tə'merɪk) *adj*

tautonym ('tɔ:tənɪm) *n Biol.* a taxonomic name in which the generic and specific components are the same, as in *Rattus rattus* (black rat).
▸**,tauto'nymic** *or* **tautonymous** (tɔ:'tɒnɪməs) *adj* ▸**tau'tonymy** *n*

tavern ⓣ ('tævən) *n* **1** a less common word for **pub. 2** *US, E Canad., & NZ.* a place licensed for the sale and consumption of alcoholic drink. [C13: from OF *taverne,* from L *taberna* hut]

taverna (tə'vɜ:nə) *n* **1** (in Greece) a guesthouse that has its own bar. **2** a Greek restaurant. [C20: Mod. Gk, from L *taberna*]

TAVR *abbrev. for* Territorial and Army Volunteer Reserve.

taw[1] (tɔ:) *n* **1** a large marble used for shooting. **2** a game of marbles. **3** the line from which the players shoot in marbles. **4 back to taws.** *Austral. inf.* back to the beginning. [C18: from ?]

taw[2] (tɔ:) *vb* (*tr*) to convert (skins) into leather by treatment with alum and salt rather than by normal tanning processes. [OE *tawian*]
▸**'tawer** *n*

tawa ('tɑ:wə) *n* a New Zealand timber tree with edible berries. [from Maori]

tawdry ⓣ ('tɔ:drɪ) *adj* **tawdrier, tawdriest.** cheap, showy, and of poor quality: *tawdry jewellery.* [C16 *tawdry lace,* shortened & altered from *Seynt Audries lace,* finery sold at the fair of St Audrey (Etheldrida), 7th-century queen of Northumbria]
▸**'tawdrily** *adv* ▸**'tawdriness** *n*

tawny ('tɔ:nɪ) *n* **a** a light brown to brownish-orange colour. **b** (*as adj*): *tawny port.* [C14: from OF *tané,* from *taner* to tan]
▸**'tawniness** *n*

tawny owl *n* a European owl having a reddish-brown plumage and a round head.

tawse *or* **taws** (tɔ:z) *n Chiefly Scot.* a leather strap having one end cut into thongs, formerly used as an instrument of punishment by a schoolteacher. [C16: prob. pl of obs. *taw* strip of leather; see TAW[2]]

tax ⓣ (tæks) *n* **1** a compulsory financial contribution imposed by a government to raise revenue, levied on income or property, on the prices of goods and services, etc. **2** a heavy demand on something; strain. ◆ *vb* (*tr*) **3** to levy a tax on (persons, companies, etc.). **4** to make heavy demands on; strain. **5** to accuse or blame. **6** *Law.* to determine (the amount legally chargeable or allowable to a party to a legal action): *to tax costs.* **7** *Sl.* to demand money or goods from (someone) with menaces. [C13: from OF *taxer,* from L *taxāre* to appraise, from *tangere* to touch]
▸**'taxable** *adj* ▸**'taxer** *n*

taxation (tæk'seɪʃən) *n* **1** the act or principle of levying taxes or the condition of being taxed. **2a** an amount assessed as tax. **2b** a tax rate. **3** revenue from taxes.
▸**tax'ational** *adj*

tax avoidance *n* reduction or minimization of tax liability by lawful methods.

tax-deductible *adj* legally deductible from income or wealth before tax assessment.

tax disc *n* a paper disc displayed on the windscreen of a motor vehicle showing that the tax due on it has been paid.

taxeme ('tæksi:m) *n Linguistics.* any element of speech that may differentiate one utterance from another with a different meaning, such as the occurrence of a particular phoneme, the presence of a certain intonation, or a distinctive word order. [C20: from Gk *taxis* order, arrangement + -EME]
▸**tax'emic** *adj*

tax evasion *n* reduction or minimization of tax liability by illegal methods.

tax exile *n* a person having a high income who chooses to live abroad so as to avoid paying high taxes.

tax haven *n* a country or state having a lower rate of taxation than elsewhere.

tax holiday *n* a period during which tax concessions are made for some reason; examples include an export incentive or an incentive to start a new business given by some governments, in which a company is excused all or part of its tax liability.

taxi ('tæksɪ) *n, pl* **taxis** *or* **taxies. 1** Also called: **cab, taxicab.** a car, usually fitted with a taximeter, that may be hired, along with its driver, to carry passengers to any specified destination. ◆ *vb* **taxis** *or* **taxies, taxiing** *or* **taxying, taxied. 2** to cause (an aircraft) to move along the ground, esp. before takeoff and after landing, or (of an aircraft) to move along the ground in this way. **3** (*intr*) to travel in a taxi. [C20: shortened from *taximeter cab*]

taxidermy ('tæksɪ,dɜ:mɪ) *n* the art or process of preparing, stuffing, and mounting animal skins so that they have a lifelike appearance. [C19: from Gk *taxis* arrangement + *-dermy,* from Gk *derma* skin]
▸**,taxi'dermal** *or* **,taxi'dermic** *adj* ▸**'taxi,dermist** *n*

taximeter ('tæksɪ,mi:tə) *n* a meter fitted to a taxi to register the fare, based on the length of the journey. [C19: from F *taximètre;* see TAX, -METER]

taxing ⓣ ('tæksɪŋ) *adj* demanding, onerous, and wearing.
▸**'taxingly** *adv*

taxi rank *n* a place where taxis wait to be hired.

taxis ('tæksɪs) *n* **1** the movement of an organism in response to an ex-

THESAURUS

rumourmonger, scandalmonger, talebearer, taleteller, telltale

tatty *adj Chiefly Brit.* = **shabby,** bedraggled, dilapidated, down at heel, frayed, having seen better days, neglected, poor, ragged, rumpled, run-down, scruffy, seedy, tattered, tawdry, the worse for wear, threadbare, unkempt, worn, worn out
Antonyms *adj* good, new, smart, well-preserved

taunt *vb* **1** = **jeer,** deride, flout, gibe, guy (*inf.*), insult, mock, provoke, revile, ridicule, sneer, take the piss (out of) (*taboo sl.*), tease, torment, twit ◆ *n* **3** = **jeer,** barb, cut, derision, dig, gibe, insult, provocation, ridicule, sarcasm, teasing

taut *adj* **1** = **tight,** flexed, rigid, strained, stressed, stretched, tense **3** *Nautical* = **neat,** in good order, orderly, shipshape, spruce, tidy, tight, trim, well-ordered, well-regulated
Antonyms *adj* ≠ **tight:** loose, relaxed, slack

tautological *adj* **1** = **repetitive,** iterative, pleonastic, prolix, redundant, repetitious, verbose

tautology *n* **1** = **repetition,** iteration, pleonasm, prolixity, redundancy, repetitiousness, repetitiveness, verbiage, verbosity

tavern *n* **1, 2** = **inn,** alehouse (*arch.*), bar, boozer (*Brit., Austral., & NZ inf.*), hostelry, pub (*inf., chiefly Brit.*), public house, taproom, watering hole (*facetious sl.*)

tawdry *adj* = **vulgar,** brummagem, cheap, cheap-jack (*inf.*), flashy, gaudy, gimcrack, glittering, meretricious, naff (*Brit. sl.*), plastic (*sl.*), raffish, showy, tacky (*inf.*), tasteless, tatty, tinsel, tinselly
Antonyms *adj* elegant, graceful, plain, refined, simple, stylish, tasteful, unflashy, unostentatious, well-tailored

tax *n* **1** = **charge,** assessment, contribution, customs, duty, excise, imposition, impost, levy, rate, tariff, tithe, toll, tribute **2** = **strain,** burden, demand, drain, load, pressure, weight ◆ *vb* **3** = **charge,** assess, demand, exact, extract, impose, levy a tax on, rate, tithe **4** = **strain,** burden, drain, enervate, exhaust, load, make heavy demands on, overburden, push, put pressure on, sap, stretch, task, test, try, weaken, wear out, weary, weigh heavily on **5** = **accuse,** arraign, blame, charge, impeach, impugn, incriminate, lay at one's door
Antonyms *vb* ≠ **accuse:** acquit, clear, exculpate, exonerate, vindicate

taxing *adj* = **demanding,** burdensome, enervating, exacting, heavy, onerous, punishing, sapping, stressful, tiring, tough, trying, wearing, wearisome
Antonyms *adj* easy, easy-peasy (*sl.*), effortless, light, unburdensome, undemanding

ternal stimulus. **2** *Surgery.* the repositioning of a displaced part by manual manipulation only. [C18: via NL from Gk: arrangement, from *tassein* to place in order]

-taxis *or* **-taxy** *n combining form.* **1** indicating movement towards or away from a specified stimulus: *thermotaxis.* **2** order or arrangement: *phyllotaxis.* [from NL, from Gk *taxis* order]
▸**-tactic** *or* **-taxic** *adj combining form.*

taxiway ('tæksɪˌweɪ) *n* a marked path along which aircraft taxi to or from a runway, parking area, etc.

tax loss *n* a loss sustained by a company that can be set against future profits for tax purposes.

taxman ('tæksˌmæn) *n, pl* **-men. 1** a collector of taxes. **2** *Inf.* a tax-collecting body personified: *he was convicted of conspiring to cheat the taxman of five million pounds.*

taxon ('tæksɒn) *n, pl* **taxa** ('tæksə). *Biol.* any taxonomic group or rank. [C20: back formation from TAXONOMY]

taxonomy (tæk'sɒnəmɪ) *n* **1** the branch of biology concerned with the classification of organisms into groups based on similarities of structure, origin, etc. **2** the science or practice of classification. [C19: from F *taxonomie,* from Gk *taxis* order + -NOMY]
▸**taxonomic** (ˌtæksə'nɒmɪk) *or* ˌ**taxo'nomical** *adj* ▸ˌ**taxo'nomically** *adv* ▸**tax'onomist** *n*

taxpayer ('tæksˌpeɪə) *n* a person or organization that pays taxes.

tax relief *n* remission of income tax due on a proportion of income earned.

tax return *n* a declaration of personal income used as a basis for assessing an individual's liability for taxation.

tax shelter *n* a form into which business activities may be organized to minimize taxation.

-taxy *n combining form.* a variant of **-taxis.**

Tay-Sachs disease (ˌteɪ'sæks) *n* an inherited disorder, caused by a faulty recessive gene, in which lipids accumulate in the brain, leading to mental retardation and blindness. [C20: after W. *Tay* (1843–1927), Brit. physician, and B. *Sachs* (1858–1944), US neurologist]

tazza ('tætsə) *n* a wine cup with a shallow bowl and a circular foot. [C19: from It., prob. from Ar. *tassah* bowl]

Tb *the chemical symbol for* terbium.

TB *abbrev. for:* **1** torpedo boat. **2** Also: **tb.** tuberculosis.

T-bar *n* **1** a T-shaped wrench for use with a socket. **2** a T-shaped bar on a ski tow which skiers hold on to while being pulled up slopes.

T-bone steak *n* a large choice steak cut from the sirloin of beef, containing a T-shaped bone.

tbs. *or* **tbsp.** *abbrev. for* tablespoon(ful).

TBT *abbrev. for* tri-*n*-butyl tin: a biocide used in marine paints to prevent fouling.

Tc *the chemical symbol for* technetium.

T-cell *n* a type of lymphocyte that matures in the thymus gland and is responsible for killing cells infected by a virus. Also called: **T-lymphocyte.**

t.d.c. *abbrev. for* top dead-centre.

t distribution *n* See **Student's t.**

te *or* **ti** (tiː) *n Music.* (in tonic sol-fa) the syllable used for the seventh note or subtonic of any scale. [later variant of *si;* see GAMUT]

Te *the chemical symbol for* tellurium.

tea (tiː) *n* **1** an evergreen shrub of tropical and subtropical Asia, having white fragrant flowers: family *Theaceae.* **2a** the dried leaves of this shrub, used to make a beverage by infusion in boiling water. **2b** such a beverage, served hot or iced. **3a** any of various similar plants or any plants that are used to make a tealike beverage. **3b** any such beverage. **4** *Chiefly Brit.* **4a** Also called: **afternoon tea.** a light meal eaten in mid-afternoon, usually consisting of tea and cakes, etc. **4b** Also called: **high tea.** afternoon tea that also includes a light cooked dish. **5** *Brit., Austral., & NZ.* the main evening meal. **6** *US & Canad. dated sl.* marijuana. **7 tea and sympathy.** *Inf.* a caring attitude, esp. to someone in trouble. [C17: from Chinese (Amoy) *t'e,* from Ancient Chinese *d'a*]

tea bag *n* a small bag containing tea leaves, infused in boiling water to make tea.

tea ball *n Chiefly US.* a perforated metal ball filled with tea leaves and used to make tea.

tea break *n* a short rest period during working hours during which tea, coffee, etc., is drunk.

teacake ('tiːˌkeɪk) *n Brit.* a flat bun, usually eaten toasted and buttered.

teach 🅣 (tiːtʃ) *vb* **teaches, teaching, taught. 1** (*tr; may take a clause as object or an infinitive;* often foll. by *how*) to help to learn; tell or show (how). **2** to give instruction or lessons in (a subject) to (a person or animal). **3** (*tr; may take a clause as object or an infinitive*) to cause to learn or understand: *experience taught him that he could not be a journalist.* [OE *tǣcan*]
▸'**teachable** *adj*

teacher 🅣 ('tiːtʃə) *n* a person whose occupation is teaching others, esp. children.

teach-in *n* an informal conference, esp. on a topical subject, usually held at a university or college and involving a panel of visiting speakers, lecturers, students, etc.

teaching ('tiːtʃɪŋ) *n* **1** the art or profession of a teacher. **2** (*sometimes pl*) something taught; precept. **3** (*modifier*) denoting a person or institution that teaches: *a teaching hospital.* **4** (*modifier*) used in teaching: *teaching aids.*

teaching machine *n* a machine that presents information and questions to the user, registers the answers, and indicates whether these are correct or acceptable.

tea cloth *n* another name for **tea towel.**

tea cosy *n* a covering for a teapot to keep the contents hot.

teacup ('tiːˌkʌp) *n* **1** a cup out of which tea may be drunk. **2** Also called: **teacupful.** the amount a teacup will hold, about four fluid ounces.

tea dance *n* a dance held in the afternoon at which tea is served.

teahouse ('tiːˌhaʊs) *n* a restaurant, esp. in Japan or China, where tea and light refreshments are served.

teak (tiːk) *n* **1** a large tree of the East Indies. **2** the hard resinous yellowish-brown wood of this tree, used for furniture making, etc. [C17: from Port. *teca,* from Malayalam *tēkka*]

teakettle ('tiːˌketᵊl) *n* a kettle for boiling water to make tea.

teal (tiːl) *n, pl* **teals** *or* **teal. 1** any of various small freshwater ducks that are related to the mallard. **2** a greenish-blue colour. [C14]

tea lady *n* a woman employed in a factory, office, etc., to make tea during a tea break.

tea leaf *n* **1** the dried leaf of the tea shrub, used to make tea. **2** (*usually pl*) shredded parts of these leaves, esp. after infusion.

team 🅣 (tiːm) *n* (*sometimes functioning as pl*) **1** a group of people organized to work together. **2** a group of players forming one of the sides in a sporting contest. **3** two or more animals working together, as to pull a vehicle. **4** such animals and the vehicle. ◆ *vb* **5** (when *intr,* often foll. by *up*) to make or cause to make a team. **6** (*tr*) *US & Canad.* to drag or transport in or by a team. **7** (*intr*) *US & Canad.* to drive a team. [OE *team* offspring]

tea-maker *n* a spoon with a perforated cover used to infuse tea in a cup of boiling water.

team-mate *n* a fellow member of a team.

team spirit *n* willingness to cooperate as part of a team.

teamster ('tiːmstə) *n* **1** a driver of a team of horses. **2** *US & Canad.* the driver of a lorry.

team teaching *n* a system whereby two or more teachers pool their skills, knowledge, etc., to teach combined classes.

teamwork 🅣 ('tiːmˌwɜːk) *n* **1** the cooperative work done by a team. **2** the ability to work efficiently as a team.

teapot ('tiːˌpɒt) *n* a container with a lid, spout, and handle, in which tea is made and from which it is served.

teapoy ('tiːpɔɪ) *n* a small table with a tripod base. [C19: from Hindi *tipāī,* from Sansk. *tri* three + *pāda* foot]

tear[1] (tɪə) *n* **1** a drop of the secretion of the lacrimal glands. See **tears. 2** something shaped like a hanging drop: *a tear of amber.* ◆ Also called: **teardrop.** [OE *tēar*]
▸'**tearless** *adj*

tear[2] 🅣 (tɛə) *vb* **tears, tearing, tore, torn. 1** to cause to come apart or to come apart; rip. **2** (*tr*) to make (a hole or split) in (something). **3** (*intr;* often foll. by *along*) to hurry or rush. **4** (*tr;* usually foll. by *away* or *from*) to remove or take by force. **5** (when *intr,* often foll. by *at*) to cause pain, distress, or anguish (to). **6 tear one's hair.** *Inf.* to be angry, frustrated, very worried, etc. ◆ *n* **7** a hole, cut, or split. **8** the act of tearing. ◆ See also **tear away, tear down,** etc. [OE *teran*]
▸'**tearable** *adj* ▸'**tearer** *n*

tear away 🅣 (tɛə) *vb* **1** (*tr, adv*) to persuade (oneself or someone else) to leave. ◆ *n* **tearaway. 2** *Brit.* a reckless impetuous unruly person.

tear down (tɛə) *vb* (*tr, adv*) to destroy or demolish: *to tear down an argument.*

tear duct (tɪə) *n* a short tube in the inner corner of the eyelid through which tears drain into the nose. Technical name: **lacrimal duct.**

tearful 🅣 ('tɪəfʊl) *adj* **1** crying or about to cry. **2** tending to produce tears; sad.
▸'**tearfully** *adv* ▸'**tearfulness** *n*

tear gas (tɪə) *n* a gas that makes the eyes smart and water, causing temporary blindness; used in warfare and to control riots.

THESAURUS

teach *vb* **1-3** = **instruct,** advise, coach, demonstrate, direct, discipline, drill, edify, educate, enlighten, give lessons in, guide, impart, implant, inculcate, inform, instil, school, show, train, tutor

teacher *n* = **instructor,** coach, dominie (*Scot.*), don, educator, guide, guru, handler, lecturer, master *or* mistress, mentor, pedagogue, professor, schoolmaster *or* schoolmistress, schoolteacher, trainer, tutor

team *n* **1** = **group,** band, body, bunch, company, crew, gang, line-up, posse (*inf.*), set, side, squad, troupe **3** = **pair,** span, yoke ◆ *vb* **5** *often with* **up** = **join,** band together, cooperate, couple, get together, link, unite, work together, yoke

teamwork *n* **1** = **cooperation,** collaboration, concert, coordination, esprit de corps, fellowship, harmony, joint action, unity

tear[2] *vb* **1** = **rip,** divide, rend, rive, run, rupture, scratch, shred, split, sunder **3** = **rush,** barrel (along) (*inf., chiefly US & Canad.*), belt, bolt, burn rubber (*inf.*), career, charge, dart, dash, fly, gallop, hurry, race, run, shoot, speed, sprint, zoom **4** = **seize,** grab, pluck, pull, rip, snatch, wrench, wrest, yank ◆ *n* **7** = **hole,** laceration, rent, rip, run, rupture, scratch, split

tear away *n* **tearaway 2** *Brit.* = **hooligan,** daredevil, delinquent, good-for-nothing, madcap, rough (*inf.*), roughneck (*sl.*), rowdy, ruffian, tough

tearful *adj* **1** = **weeping,** blubbering, crying, in tears, lachrymose, sobbing, weepy (*inf.*), whimpering **2** = **sad,** distressing, dolorous, harrowing, lamentable, mournful, pathetic, pitiable, pitiful, poignant, sorrowful, upsetting, woeful

tearing ('tɛərɪŋ) *adj* violent or furious (esp. in **tearing hurry** *or* **rush**).
tear into (tɛə) *vb (intr, prep) Inf.* to attack vigorously and damagingly.
tear-jerker ('tɪəˌdʒɜːkə) *n Inf.* an excessively sentimental film, play, book, etc.
tearoom ('tiːˌruːm, -ˌrʊm) *n Brit.* a restaurant where tea and light refreshments are served. Also called: **teashop.**
tea rose *n* any of several varieties of hybrid rose that have pink or yellow flowers with a scent resembling that of tea.
tears 🅣 (tɪəz) *pl n* **1** the clear salty solution secreted by the lacrimal glands that lubricates and cleanses the surface of the eyeball. **2** a state of intense frustration (esp. in **bored to tears**). **3 in tears.** weeping.
tear sheet (tɛə) *n* a page in a newspaper or periodical that is cut or perforated so that it can be easily torn out.
tease 🅣 (tiːz) *vb* **teases, teasing, teased. 1** to annoy (someone) by deliberately offering something with the intention of delaying or withdrawing the offer. **2** to vex (someone) maliciously or playfully. **3** *(tr)* to separate the fibres of; comb; card. **4** *(tr)* to raise the nap of (a fabric) with a teasel. **5** another word (esp. US and Canad.) for **backcomb. 6** *(tr)* to loosen or pull apart (biological tissues, etc.). ◆ *n* **7** a person or thing that teases. **8** the act of teasing. ◆ See also **tease out.** [OE *tǣsan*]
▸**'teasing** *adj* ▸**'teasingly** *adv*
teasel, teazel, *or* **teazle** ('tiːzᵊl) *n* **1** any of various plants (esp. the **fuller's teasel**) of Eurasia and N Africa, having prickly leaves and prickly heads of yellow or purple flowers. **2a** the dried flower head of the fuller's teasel, used for teasing. **2b** any implement used for the same purpose. ◆ *vb* **teasels, teaselling, teaselled** *or US* **teasels, teaseling, teaseled. 3** *(tr)* to tease (a fabric). [OE *tǣsel*]
▸**'teaseller** *n*
tease out *vb (tr, adv)* to extract (information) with difficulty.
teaser ('tiːzə) *n* **1** a person who teases. **2** a difficult question. **3** a preliminary advertisement in a campaign that attracts attention by making people curious to know what product is being advertised.
tea service *or* **set** *n* the china or pottery articles used in serving tea, including a teapot, cups, saucers, etc.
teashop ('tiːˌʃɒp) *n Brit.* another name for **tearoom.**
teaspoon ('tiːˌspuːn) *n* **1** a small spoon used for stirring tea, etc. **2** Also called: **teaspoonful** the amount contained in such a spoon. **3** a unit of capacity used in cooking, medicine, etc., equal to about 5 ml.
teat (tiːt) *n* **1a** the nipple of a mammary gland. **1b** (in cows, etc.) any of the projections from the udder. **2** something resembling a teat such as the rubber mouthpiece of a feeding bottle. [C13: from OF *tete,* of Gmc origin]
tea towel *or* **cloth** *n* a towel for drying dishes, etc. US name: **dishtowel.**
tea tree *n* any of various trees of Australia and New Zealand that yield an oil used as an antiseptic.
tea trolley *n Brit.* a trolley from which tea is served.
TEC (tɛk) *n acronym for* Training and Enterprise Council. See **Training Agency.**
tech (tɛk) *n Inf.* a technical college.
tech. *abbrev. for:* **1** technical. **2** technology.
technetium (tɛk'niːʃɪəm) *n* a silvery-grey metallic element, artificially produced by bombardment of molybdenum by deuterons. The radioisotope **technetium-99m** is used in radiotherapy. Symbol: Tc; atomic no.: 43; half-life of most stable isotope, ^{97}Tc: 2.6×10^6 years. [C20: NL, from Gk *tekhnētos* manmade, from *tekhnasthai* to devise artificially, from *tekhnē* skill]
technic *n* **1** (tɛk'niːk). another word for **technique. 2** ('tɛknɪk). another word for **technics.** [C17: from L *technicus,* from Gk *tekhnikos,* from *tekhnē* skill]
technical 🅣 ('tɛknɪkᵊl) *adj* **1** of or specializing in industrial, practical, or mechanical arts and applied sciences. **2** skilled in practical arts rather than abstract thinking. **3** relating to a particular field of activity: *the technical jargon of linguistics.* **4** existing by virtue of a strict application of the rules or a strict interpretation of the wording: *a technical loophole in the law.* **5** of or showing technique: *technical brilliance.*
▸**'technically** *adv* ▸**'technicalness** *n*
technical college *n Brit.* an institution for further education that provides courses in technology, art, secretarial skills, agriculture, etc.
technical drawing *n* the study and practice of the basic techniques of draughtsmanship, as employed in mechanical drawing, architecture, etc.
technicality (ˌtɛknɪ'kælɪtɪ) *n, pl* **technicalities. 1** a petty formal point arising from a strict interpretation of rules, etc. **2** the state or quality of being technical. **3** technical methods and vocabulary.
technical knockout *n Boxing.* a judgment of a knockout given when a boxer is in the referee's opinion too badly beaten to continue without risk of serious injury.
technician (tɛk'nɪʃən) *n* **1** a person skilled in mechanical or industrial techniques or in a particular technical field. **2** a person employed in a laboratory, etc., to do mechanical and practical work. **3** a person having specific artistic or mechanical skill, esp. if lacking flair.
Technicolor ('tɛknɪˌkʌlə) *n Trademark.* the process of producing colour film by means of superimposing synchronized films of the same scene, each of which has a different colour filter.
technics ('tɛknɪks) *n (functioning as sing)* the study or theory of industry and industrial arts; technology.
technique 🅣 (tɛk'niːk) *n* **1** a practical method, skill, or art applied to a particular task. **2** proficiency in a practical or mechanical skill. **3** special facility; knack. [C19: from F, from *technique* (adj): see TECHNIC]
techno ('tɛknəʊ) *n* a type of fast disco music, using electronic sounds and having a strong technological influence.
techno- *combining form.* **1** craft or art: *technology; technography.* **2** technological or technical: *technocracy.* [from Gk *tekhnē* skill]
technocracy (tɛk'nɒkrəsɪ) *n, pl* **technocracies.** government by scientists, engineers, and other such experts.
▸**technocrat** ('tɛknəˌkræt) *n* ▸**ˌtechno'cratic** *adj*
technology (tɛk'nɒlədʒɪ) *n, pl* **technologies. 1** the application of practical or mechanical sciences to industry or commerce. **2** the methods, theory, and practices governing such application. **3** the total knowledge and skills available to any human society. [C17: from Gk *tekhnologia* systematic treatment, from *tekhnē* skill]
▸**technological** (ˌtɛknə'lɒdʒɪkᵊl) *adj* ▸**tech'nologist** *n*
technophile ('tɛknəʊˌfaɪl) *n* **1** a person who is enthusiastic about technology. ◆ *adj* **2** enthusiastic about technology.
technophobe (ˌtɛknəʊ'fəʊb) *n* **1** someone who fears the effects of technological development on society or the environment. **2** someone who is afraid of using technological devices, such as computing.
techy ('tɛtʃɪ) *adj* **techier, techiest.** a variant spelling of **tetchy.**
▸**'techily** *adv* ▸**'techiness** *n*
tectonic (tɛk'tɒnɪk) *adj* **1** denoting or relating to building. **2** *Geol.* **2a** (of landforms, etc.) resulting from distortion of the earth's crust due to forces within it. **2b** (of processes, movements, etc.) occurring within the earth's crust and causing structural deformation. [C17: from LL *tectonicus,* from Gk *tektonikos* belonging to carpentry, from *tektōn* a builder]
tectonics (tɛk'tɒnɪks) *n (functioning as sing)* **1** the art and science of construction or building. **2** the study of the processes by which the earth's surface has attained its present structure.
tectrix ('tɛktrɪks) *n, pl* **tectrices** ('tɛktrɪˌsiːz). *(usually pl) Ornithol.* another name for **covert** (sense 5). [C19: NL, from L *tector* plasterer, from *tegere* to cover]
▸**tectricial** (tɛk'trɪʃəl) *adj*
ted[1] (tɛd) *vb* **teds, tedding, tedded.** to shake out (hay), so as to dry it. [C15: from ON *tethja*]
ted[2] (tɛd) *n Inf.* short for **teddy boy.**
tedder ('tɛdə) *n* **1** a machine equipped with a series of small rotating forks for tedding hay. **2** a person who teds.
teddy ('tɛdɪ) *n, pl* **teddies.** a woman's one-piece undergarment, incorporating a chemise top and panties.
teddy bear *n* a stuffed toy bear. Often shortened to **teddy.** [C20: from *Teddy,* from *Theodore,* after Theodore Roosevelt (1858–1919), US president, well known as a hunter of bears]
teddy boy *n* **1** (in Britain, esp. in the mid-1950s) one of a cult of youths who wore mock Edwardian fashions. **2** any tough or delinquent youth. [C20: from *Teddy,* from *Edward,* referring to the Edwardian dress]
Te Deum (ˌtiː 'diːəm) *n* **1** an ancient Latin hymn in rhythmic prose. **2** a musical setting of this hymn. **3** a service of thanksgiving in which the recital of this hymn forms a central part. [from the L canticle beginning *Tē Deum laudāmus,* lit.: Thee, God, we praise]
tedious 🅣 ('tiːdɪəs) *adj* causing fatigue or tedium; monotonous.
▸**'tediousness** *n*
tedium 🅣 ('tiːdɪəm) *n* the state of being bored or the quality of being boring; monotony. [C17: from L *taedium,* from *taedēre* to weary]
tee[1] (tiː) *n* **1** a pipe fitting in the form of a letter T, used to join three pipes. **2** a metal section with a cross section in the form of a letter T.
tee[2] (tiː) *Golf.* ◆ *n* **1** an area from which the first stroke of a hole is made. **2** a support for a golf ball, usually a small wooden or plastic peg, used when teeing off or in long grass, etc. ◆ *vb* **tees, teeing, teed. 3** (when *intr,* often foll. by *up*) to position (the ball) ready for striking, on or as if on a tee. ◆ See also **tee off.** [C17 *teaz,* from ?]

THESAURUS

tears *pl n* **3 in tears = weeping,** blubbering, crying, distressed, sobbing, visibly moved, whimpering
tease *vb* **1 = tantalize,** lead on **2 = mock,** aggravate (*inf.*), annoy, badger, bait, bedevil, bother, chaff, gibe, goad, guy (*inf.*), needle (*inf.*), pester, plague (*inf.*), provoke, pull someone's leg (*inf.*), rag, rib (*inf.*), ridicule, take the mickey (*inf.*), take the piss (out of) (*taboo sl.*), taunt, torment, twit, vex, wind up (*Brit. sl.*), worry
technical *adj* **1 = scientific,** hi-tech *or* high-tech, skilled, specialist, specialized, technological
technique *n* **1 = method,** approach, course, fashion, manner, means, mode, modus operandi, procedure, style, system, way **2, 3 = skill,** address, adroitness, art, artistry, craft, craftsmanship, delivery, execution, facility, knack, know-how (*inf.*), performance, proficiency, touch
tedious *adj* **= boring,** annoying, banal, deadly dull, drab, dreary, dreich (*Scot.*), dull, fatiguing, ho-hum (*inf.*), humdrum, irksome, laborious, lifeless, long-drawn-out, mind-numbing, monotonous, prosaic, prosy, soporific, tiresome, tiring, unexciting, uninteresting, vapid, wearisome
Antonyms *adj* enjoyable, enthralling, exciting, exhilarating, imaginative, inspiring, interesting, quickly finished, short, stimulating
tedium *n* **= boredom,** banality, deadness, drabness, dreariness, dullness, ennui, lifelessness, monotony, routine, sameness, tediousness, the doldrums
Antonyms *n* challenge, excitement, exhilaration, fascination, interest, liveliness, stimulation

tee[3] (tiː) *n* a mark used as a target in certain games such as curling and quoits. [C18: ?from T-shaped marks, which may have orig. been used in curling]

tee-hee *or* **te-hee** (ˈtiːˈhiː) *interj* **1** an exclamation of laughter, esp. when mocking. ◆ *n* **2** a chuckle. ◆ *vb* **tee-hees, tee-heeing, tee-heed** *or* **te-hees, te-heeing, te-heed. 3** (*intr*) to snigger or laugh, esp. derisively. [C14: imit.]

teem[1] (tiːm) *vb* (*intr; usually foll. by with*) to be prolific or abundant (in). [OE *tēman* to produce offspring; rel. to West Saxon *tīeman;* see TEAM]

teem[2] (tiːm) *vb* **1** (*intr; often foll. by down* or *with rain*) to pour in torrents. **2** (*tr*) to pour or empty out. [C15 *temen* to empty, from ON *tœma*]

teen (tiːn) *adj Inf.* another word for **teenage.**

teenage (ˈtiːnˌeɪdʒ) *adj* (*prenominal*) of or relating to the time in a person's life between the ages of 13 and 19. Also: **teenaged.**

teenager (ˈtiːnˌeɪdʒə) *n* a person between the ages of 13 and 19 inclusive.

teens (tiːnz) *pl n* **1** the years of a person's life between the ages of 13 and 19 inclusive. **2** all the numbers that end in *-teen.*

teeny (ˈtiːnɪ) *adj* **teenier, teeniest.** *Inf.* extremely small; tiny. Also: **teeny-weeny** (ˈtiːnɪˈwiːnɪ) *or* **teensy-weensy** (ˈtiːnzɪˈwiːnzɪ). [C19: var. of TINY]

teenybopper (ˈtiːnɪˌbɒpə) *n Sl.* a young teenager, usually a girl, who avidly follows fashions in clothes and pop music. [C20: *teeny,* from teenage + *-bopper;* see BOP]

tee off *vb* (*adv*) **1** *Golf.* to strike (the ball) from a tee. **2** *Inf.* to begin; start.

teepee (ˈtiːpiː) *n* a variant spelling of **tepee.**

tee shirt *n* a variant of **T-shirt.**

teeter (ˈtiːtə) *vb* **1** to move or cause to move unsteadily; wobble. ◆ *n, vb* **2** another word for **seesaw.** [C19: from ME *titeren*]

teeth (tiːθ) *n* **1** the plural of **tooth. 2** the most violent part: *the teeth of the gale.* **3** the power to produce a desired effect: *that law has no teeth.* **4 get one's teeth into.** to become engrossed in. **5 in the teeth of.** in direct opposition to; against. **6 to the teeth.** to the greatest possible degree: *armed to the teeth.* **7 show one's teeth.** to threaten.

teethe (tiːð) *vb* **teethes, teething, teethed.** (*intr*) to cut one's baby (deciduous) teeth.

teething ring *n* a hard ring on which babies may bite while teething.

teething troubles *pl n* the problems that arise during the initial stages of a project, etc.

teetotal (tiːˈtəʊtᵊl) *adj* **1** of or practising abstinence from alcoholic drink. **2** *Dialect.* complete. [C19: allegedly coined in 1833 by Richard Turner, E advocate of total abstinence from alcohol; prob. from TOTAL, with emphatic reduplication]
▸**teeˈtotaller** *n* ▸**teeˈtotalism** *n*

teetotum (tiːˈtəʊtəm) *n Arch.* a spinning top bearing letters of the alphabet on its four sides. [C18: from *T totum,* from *T* initial on one of the faces + *totum* the name of the toy, from L *tōtum* the whole]

teff (tɛf) *n* an annual grass of NE Africa, grown for its grain. [C18: from Amharic *tēf*]

TEFL (ˈtɛfᵊl) *acronym for* Teaching (of) English as a Foreign Language.

Teflon (ˈtɛflɒn) *n* a trademark for **polytetrafluoroethylene.**

teg (tɛg) *n* **1** a two-year-old sheep. **2** the fleece of a two-year-old sheep. [C16: from ?]

tegmen (ˈtɛgmən) *n, pl* **tegmina** (-mənə). **1** either of the leathery forewings of the cockroach and related insects. **2** the delicate inner covering of a seed. **3** any similar covering or layer. [C19: from L: a cover, from *tegere* to cover]
▸**ˈtegminal** *adj*

tegument (ˈtɛgjʊmənt) *n* a less common word for **integument.** [C15: from L *tegumentum* a covering, from *tegere* to cover]

te-hee (tiːˈhiː) *interj, n, vb* a variant of **tee-hee.**

te igitur *Latin.* (teɪ ˈɪgɪˌtʊə; *English* tiː ˈɪdʒɪtʊə) *n RC Church.* the first prayer of the canon of the Mass, which begins *Te igitur clementissime Pater* (Thee, therefore, most merciful Father).

tektite (ˈtɛktaɪt) *n* a small dark glassy object found in several areas around the world, thought to be a product of meteorite impact. [C20: from Gk *tēktos* molten]

tel. *abbrev. for:* **1** telegram. **2** telegraph(ic). **3** telephone.

tel- *combining form.* a variant of **tele-** and **telo-** before a vowel.

telaesthesia *or US* **telesthesia** (ˌtɛlɪsˈθiːzɪə) *n* the alleged perception of events that are beyond the normal range of perceptual processes.
▸**telaesthetic** *or US* **telesthetic** (ˌtɛlɪsˈθɛtɪk) *adj*

telamon (ˈtɛləmən) *n, pl* **telamones** (ˌtɛləˈməʊniːz) *or* **telamons.** a column in the form of a male figure, used to support an entablature. [C18: via L from Gk, from *tlēnai* to bear]

telangiectasis (tɪˌlændʒɪˈɛktəsɪs) *or* **telangiectasia** (tɪˌlændʒɪɛkˈteɪzɪə) *n, pl* **telangiectases** (-ˌsiːz). *Pathol.* an abnormal dilation of the capillaries or terminal arteries producing blotched red spots, esp. on the face or thighs. [C19: NL, from Gk *telos* end + *angeion* vessel + *ektasis* dilation]
▸**telangiectatic** (tɪˌlændʒɪɛkˈtætɪk) *adj*

tele- *combining form.* **1** at or over a distance; distant: *telescope; telekinesis.* **2** television: *telecast.* **3** by means of or via telephone or television: *telesales.* [from Gk *tele* far]

telecast (ˈtɛləˌkɑːst) *vb* **telecasts, telecasting, telecast** *or* **telecasted. 1** to broadcast by television. ◆ *n* **2** a television broadcast.
▸**ˈteleˌcaster** *n*

telecom (ˈtɛlɪˌkɒm) *or* **telecoms** (ˈtɛlɪˌkɒmz) *n* (*functioning as sing*) short for **telecommunications.**

telecommunications (ˌtɛlɪkəˌmjuːnɪˈkeɪʃənz) *n* (*functioning as sing*) the science and technology of communications by telephony, radio, television, etc.

telecommuting (ˌtɛlɪkəˈmjuːtɪŋ) *n* another name for **teleworking.**
▸**ˌtelecomˈmuter** *n*

teledu (ˈtɛlɪˌduː) *n* a badger of SE Asia and Indonesia, having dark brown hair with a white stripe along the back and producing a fetid secretion when attacked. [C19: from Malay]

telegenic (ˌtɛlɪˈdʒɛnɪk) *adj* having or showing a pleasant television image. [C20: from TELE(VISION) + (PHOTO)GENIC]
▸**ˌteleˈgenically** *adv*

telegnosis (ˌtɛləˈnəʊsɪs, ˌtɛləg-) *n* knowledge about distant events alleged to have been obtained without the use of any normal sensory mechanism. [C20: from TELE- + *-gnosis,* from Gk *gnōsis* knowledge]

telegony (tɪˈlɛgənɪ) *n Genetics.* the supposed influence of a previous sire on offspring borne by a female to other sires.
▸**telegonic** (ˌtɛlɪˈgɒnɪk) *or* **teˈlegonous** *adj*

telegram (ˈtɛlɪˌgræm) *n* a communication transmitted by telegraph.

telegraph (ˈtɛlɪˌgrɑːf) *n* **1a** a device, system, or process by which information can be transmitted over a distance, esp. using radio signals or coded electrical signals sent along a transmission line. **1b** (*as modifier*): *telegraph pole.* ◆ *vb* **2** to send a telegram to (a person or place); wire. **3** (*tr*) to transmit or send by telegraph. **4** (*tr*) to give advance notice of (anything), esp. unintentionally. **5** (*tr*) *Canad. inf.* to cast (votes) illegally by impersonating registered voters.
▸**telegraphist** (tɪˈlɛgrəˌfɪst) *or* **telegrapher** (tɪˈlɛgrəfə) *n* ▸**ˌteleˈgraphic** *adj*

telegraph plant *n* a small tropical Asian shrub having small leaflets that turn in various directions during the day and droop at night.

telegraphy (tɪˈlɛgrəfɪ) *n* **1** a system of telecommunications involving any process providing reproduction at a distance of written, printed, or pictorial matter. **2** the skill or process of operating a telegraph.

Telegu (ˈtɛləˌguː) *n, adj* a variant spelling of **Telugu.**

telekinesis (ˌtɛlɪkaɪˈniːsɪs) *n* **1** the movement of a body caused by thought or willpower without the application of a physical force. **2** the ability to cause such movement.
▸**telekinetic** (ˌtɛlɪkɪˈnɛtɪk) *adj*

telemark (ˈtɛlɪˌmɑːk) *n Skiing.* a turn in which one ski is placed far forward of the other and turned gradually inwards. [C20: after *Telemark,* county in Norway]

telemarketing (ˈtɛlɪˌmɑːkɪtɪŋ) *n* another name for **telesales.**
▸**ˈteleˌmarketer** *n*

telemedicine (ˈtɛlɪˌmɛdɪsɪn, -ˌmɛdsɪn) *n* the treatment of disease or injury by consultation with a specialist in a distant place, esp. by means of a computer or satellite link.

Telemessage (ˈtɛlɪˌmɛsɪdʒ) *n Trademark.* a message sent by telephone or telex and delivered in printed form.

telemeter (tɪˈlɛmɪtə) *n* **1** any device for recording or measuring a distant event and transmitting the data to a receiver. **2** any device used to measure a distance without directly comparing it with a measuring rod, etc. ◆ *vb* **3** (*tr*) to obtain and transmit (data) from a distant source.
▸**telemetric** (ˌtɛlɪˈmɛtrɪk) *adj*

telemetry (tɪˈlɛmɪtrɪ) *n* **1** the use of radio waves, telephone lines, etc., to transmit the readings of measuring instruments to a device on which the readings can be indicated or recorded. **2** the measurement of linear distance using a tellurometer.

telencephalon (ˌtɛlɛnˈsɛfəˌlɒn) *n* the cerebrum together with related parts of the hypothalamus and the third ventricle.
▸**telencephalic** (ˈtɛlɛnsɪˈfælɪk) *adj*

teleology (ˌtɛlɪˈɒlədʒɪ, ˌtiːlɪ-) *n* **1** *Philosophy.* **1a** the doctrine that there is evidence of purpose or design in the universe, and esp. that this provides proof of the existence of a Designer. **1b** the belief that certain phenomena are best explained in terms of purpose rather than cause. **2** *Biol.* the belief that natural phenomena have a predetermined purpose and are not determined by mechanical laws. [C18: from NL *teleologia,* from Gk *telos* end + -LOGY]
▸**teleological** (ˌtɛlɪəˈlɒdʒɪkᵊl, ˌtiːlɪ-) *adj* ▸**ˌteleˈologist** *n*

teleost (ˈtɛlɪˌɒst, ˈtiːlɪ-) *n* any of a subclass of bony fishes having rayed fins and a swim bladder, as herrings, carps, eels, cod, perches, etc.

THESAURUS

teem[1] *vb* = **be full of,** abound, be abundant, bear, be crawling with, be prolific, brim, bristle, burst at the seams, overflow, produce, pullulate, swarm

teem[2] *vb* **1** = **pour,** belt (*sl.*), bucket down (*inf.*), lash, pelt (down), rain cats and dogs (*inf.*), stream

teenage *adj* = **youthful,** adolescent, immature, juvenile

teenager *n* = **youth,** adolescent, boy, girl, juvenile, minor

teeny *adj Informal* = **tiny,** diminutive, microscopic, miniature, minuscule, minute, teensy-weensy, teeny-weeny, wee

teeter *vb* **1, 2** = **wobble,** balance, pivot, rock, seesaw, stagger, sway, totter, tremble, waver

teetotaller *n* **1** = **abstainer,** nondrinker, Rechabite

telegram *n* = **cable,** radiogram, telegraph, telex, wire (*inf.*)

telegraph *n* **1** = **cable,** radiogram, telegram,

[C19: from NL *teleosteī* (pl) creatures having complete skeletons, from Gk *teleos* complete + *osteon* bone]

telepathy ❶ (tɪˈlɛpəθɪ) *n* the communication between people of thoughts, feelings, etc., involving mechanisms that cannot be understood in terms of known scientific laws.
▸**telepathic** (ˌtɛlɪˈpæθɪk) *adj* ▸**teˈlepathist** *n* ▸**teˈlepaˌthize** *or* ▸**teˈlepaˌthise** *vb (intr)*

telephone ❶ (ˈtɛlɪˌfəʊn) *n* **1** an electrical device for transmitting speech, consisting of a microphone and receiver mounted on a handset. **2a** a worldwide system of communications using telephones. The microphone in one telephone converts sound waves into electrical signals that are transmitted along a telephone wire or by radio to one or more distant sets. **2b** (*as modifier*): *a telephone exchange.* ◆ *vb* **3** to call or talk to (a person) by telephone. **4** to transmit (a message, etc.) by telephone.
▸ˈ**teleˌphoner** *n* ▸**telephonic** (ˌtɛlɪˈfɒnɪk) *adj*

telephone banking *n* a facility enabling customers to make use of banking services, such as oral payment instructions, account movements, raising loans, etc., over the telephone rather than by personal visit.

telephone box *n* an enclosure from which a paid telephone call can be made. Also called: **telephone kiosk, telephone booth.**

telephone directory *n* a book listing the names, addresses, and telephone numbers of subscribers in a particular area.

telephone number *n* **1** a set of figures identifying the telephone of a particular subscriber, and used in making connections to that telephone. **2** (*pl*) extremely large numbers, esp. in reference to salaries or prices.

telephone selling *n* another name for **telesales.**

telephonist (tɪˈlɛfənɪst) *n Brit.* a person who operates a telephone switchboard. Also called (esp. US): **telephone operator.**

telephony (tɪˈlɛfənɪ) *n* a system of telecommunications for the transmission of speech or other sounds.

telephotography (ˌtɛlɪfəˈtɒgrəfɪ) *n* the process or technique of photographing distant objects using a telephoto lens.

telephoto lens (ˈtɛlɪˌfəʊtəʊ) *n* a compound camera lens in which the focal length is greater than that of a simple lens and thus produces a magnified image of a distant object.

teleprinter (ˈtɛlɪˌprɪntə) *n* **1** a telegraph apparatus consisting of a keyboard transmitter, which converts a typed message into coded pulses for transmission along a wire or cable, and a printing receiver, which converts incoming signals and prints out the message. US name: **teletypewriter. 2** a network of such devices: no longer widely used. **3** a similar device used for direct input/output of data into a computer at a distant location.

Teleprompter (ˈtɛlɪˌprɒmptə) *n Trademark.* a device for displaying a television script so that the speaker can read it while appearing to look at the camera.

Teleran (ˈtɛləˌræn) *n Trademark.* an electronic navigational aid in which the image of a ground-based radar system is televised to aircraft. [C20: from *Tele(vision) R(adar) A(ir) N(avigation)*]

telesales (ˈtɛlɪˌseɪlz) *n (functioning as sing)* the selling or attempted selling of a particular commodity or service by a salesman who makes his initial approach by telephone. Also called: **telemarketing, telephone selling.**

telescope ❶ (ˈtɛlɪˌskəʊp) *n* **1** an optical instrument for making distant objects appear closer by use of a combination of lenses (**refracting telescope**) or lenses and curved mirrors (**reflecting telescope**). **2** any instrument, such as a radio telescope, for collecting, focusing, and detecting electromagnetic radiation from space. ◆ *vb* **telescopes, telescoping, telescoped. 3** to crush together or be crushed together, as in a collision. **4** to fit together like a set of cylinders that slide into one another, thus allowing extension and shortening. **5** to make or become smaller or shorter. [C17: from It. *telescopio* or NL *telescopium*, lit.: far-seeing instrument]

telescopic (ˌtɛlɪˈskɒpɪk) *adj* **1** of or relating to a telescope. **2** seen through or obtained by means of a telescope. **3** visible only with a telescope. **4** able to see far. **5** having parts that telescope.
▸ˌ**teleˈscopically** *adv*

telescopic sight *n* a telescope mounted on a rifle, etc., used for sighting.

telescopy (tɪˈlɛskəpɪ) *n* the branch of astronomy concerned with the use and design of telescopes.

telespectroscope (ˌtɛlɪˈspɛktrəˌskəʊp) *n* a combination of a telescope and a spectroscope, used for spectroscopic analysis of radiation from stars and other celestial bodies.

telestereoscope (ˌtɛlɪˈstɪərɪəˌskəʊp, -ˈstɛrɪə-) *n* an optical instrument for obtaining stereoscopic images of distant objects.

telestich (tɪˈlɛstɪk, ˈtɛlɪˌstɪk) *n* a short poem in which the last letters of each successive line form a word. [C17: from Gk *telos* end + *stikhos* row]

Teletext (ˈtɛlɪˌtɛkst) *n Trademark.* a form of Videotex in which information is broadcast by a television station and received on an adapted television set. **Ceefax** is provided by the BBC and **Oracle** by ITV.

telethon (ˈtɛlɪˌθɒn) *n* a lengthy television programme to raise charity funds, etc. [C20: from TELE- + MARATHON]

Teletype (ˈtɛlɪˌtaɪp) *n* **1** *Trademark.* a type of teleprinter. **2** (*sometimes not cap.*) a network of such devices. ◆ *vb* **Teletypes, Teletyping, Teletyped. 3** (*sometimes not cap.*) to transmit (a message) by Teletype.

teletypewriter (ˌtɛlɪˈtaɪpˌraɪtə, ˈtɛlɪˌtaɪp-) *n* a US name for **teleprinter.**

televangelist (ˌtɛlɪˈvændʒəlɪst) *n US.* an evangelical preacher who appears regularly on television, preaching the gospel and appealing for donations from viewers. [C20: from TELE(VISION + E)VANGELIST]

televise (ˈtɛlɪˌvaɪz) *vb* **televises, televising, televised. 1** to put on television. **2** (*tr*) to transmit by television.

television ❶ (ˈtɛlɪˌvɪʒən) *n* **1** the system or process of producing on a distant screen a series of transient visible images, usually with an accompanying sound signal. Electrical signals, converted from optical images by a camera tube, are transmitted by radio waves or by cable and reconverted into optical images by means of a television tube inside a television set. **2** Also called: **television set.** a device designed to receive and convert incoming electrical signals into a series of visible images on a screen together with accompanying sound. **3** the content, etc., of television programmes. **4** the occupation or profession concerned with any aspect of the broadcasting of television programmes. **5** (*modifier*) of, relating to, or used in the transmission or reception of video and audio UHF or VHF radio signals: *a television transmitter.* ◆ Abbrev.: **TV.**

television tube *n* a cathode-ray tube designed for the reproduction of television pictures. Sometimes shortened to **tube.**

televisual (ˌtɛlɪˈvɪʒʊəl, -zjʊ-) *adj* relating to or suitable for production on television.
▸ˌ**teleˈvisually** *adv*

teleworking (ˈtɛlɪˌwɜːkɪŋ) *n* the use of home computers, telephones, etc., to enable a person to work from home while maintaining contact with colleagues, customers, or a central office. Also called: **telecommuting.**
▸ˈ**teleˌworker** *n*

telex (ˈtɛlɛks) *n* **1** an international telegraph service in which teleprinters are rented out to subscribers. **2** a teleprinter used in such a service. **3** a message transmitted or received by telex. ◆ *vb* **4** to transmit (a message) to (a person, etc.) by telex. [C20: from *tel(eprinter) ex(change)*]

Telidon (ˈtɛlɪˌdɒn) *n Trademark.* a Canadian interactive viewdata service.

tell[1] ❶ (tɛl) *vb* **tells, telling, told. 1** (when *tr, may take a clause as object*) to let know or notify. **2** (*tr*) to order or instruct. **3** (when *intr*, usually foll. by *of*) to give an account or narration (of). **4** (*tr*) to communicate by words: *tell lies.* **5** (*tr*) to make known: *to tell fortunes.* **6** (*intr;* often foll. by *of*) to serve as an indication: *her blush told of her embarrassment.* **7** (*tr;* used with *can*, etc.; *may take a clause as object*) to discover or discern: *I can tell what is wrong.* **8** (*tr;* used with *can*, etc.) to distinguish or discriminate: *he couldn't tell chalk from cheese.* **9** (*intr*) to have or produce an impact, effect, or strain: *every step told on his bruised feet.* **10** (*intr;* sometimes foll. by *on*) *Inf.* to reveal secrets or gossip (about). **11** (*tr*) to assure: *I tell you, I've had enough!* **12** (*tr*) to count (votes). **13 tell the time.** to read the time from a clock. **14 you're telling me.** *Sl.* I know that very well. ◆ See also **tell apart, tell off.** [OE *tellan*]
▸ˈ**tellable** *adj*

tell[2] (tɛl) *n* a large mound resulting from the accumulation of rubbish on a long-settled site, esp. in the Middle East. [C19: from Ar. *tall*]

tell apart *vb (tr, adv)* to distinguish between.

teller (ˈtɛlə) *n* **1** a bank cashier. **2** a person appointed to count votes. **3** a person who tells; narrator.

telling ❶ (ˈtɛlɪŋ) *adj* **1** having a marked effect or impact. **2** revealing.
▸ˈ**tellingly** *adv*

THESAURUS

telex, wire (*inf.*) ◆ *vb* **2** = **cable**, send, telex, transmit, wire (*inf.*)

telepathy *n* = **mind-reading**, sixth sense, thought transference

telephone *n* **1** = **phone**, blower, dog and bone (*sl.*), handset, line, mobile (phone) ◆ *vb* **3** = **call**, buzz (*inf.*), call up, dial, get on the blower (*inf.*), give (someone) a bell (*Brit. sl.*), give (someone) a buzz (*inf.*), give (someone) a call, give (someone) a ring (*inf., chiefly Brit.*), give someone a tinkle (*Brit. inf.*), phone, ring (*chiefly Brit.*)

telescope *n* **1** = **glass**, spyglass ◆ *vb* **3** = **crush**, concertina, squash **5** = **shorten**, abbreviate, abridge, capsulize, compress, condense, consolidate, contract, curtail, cut, shrink, tighten, trim, truncate
Antonyms *vb* ≠ **shorten:** amplify, draw out, elongate, extend, flesh out, lengthen, protract, spread out

television *n* **2** = **TV**, gogglebox (*Brit. sl.*), idiot box (*sl.*), receiver, small screen (*inf.*), telly (*Brit. inf.*), the box, the tube (*sl.*), TV set

tell[1] *vb* **1** = **inform**, acquaint, announce, apprise, communicate, confess, disclose, divulge, express, get off one's chest (*inf.*), impart, let know, make known, mention, notify, proclaim, reveal, say, speak, state, utter **2** = **instruct**, authorize, bid, call upon, command, direct, enjoin, order, require, summon **3** = **describe**, chronicle, depict, give an account of, narrate, portray, recount, rehearse, relate, report **7** = **see**, comprehend, discern, discover, make out, understand **8** = **distinguish**, differentiate, discern, discriminate, identify **9** = **have** *or* **take effect**, carry weight, count, have force, make its presence felt, register, take its toll, weigh **12** = **count**, calculate, compute, enumerate, number, reckon, tally

telling *adj* **1** = **effective**, considerable, decisive, effectual, forceful, forcible, impressive, influential, marked, potent, powerful, significant, solid, striking, trenchant, weighty
Antonyms *adj* easily ignored, inconsequential, indecisive, ineffectual, insignificant, lightweight, minor, negligible, slight, trivial, unimportant

tell off Ⓣ *vb* (*tr, adv*) **1** *Inf.* to reprimand; scold. **2** to count and select for duty.

telltale ('tɛl,teɪl) *n* **1** a person who tells tales about others. **2a** an outward indication of something concealed. **2b** (*as modifier*): *a telltale paw mark.* **3** a device used to monitor a process, machine, etc.

tellurian (tɛ'lʊərɪən) *adj* **1** of the earth. ◆ *n* **2** (esp. in science fiction) an inhabitant of the earth. [C19: from L *tellūs* the earth]

telluric[1] (tɛ'lʊərɪk) *adj* of or originating on or in the earth or soil; terrestrial. [C19: from L *tellūs* the earth]

telluric[2] (tɛ'lʊərɪk) *adj* of or containing tellurium, esp. in a high valence state. [C20: from TELLUR(IUM) + -IC]

tellurion *or* **tellurian** (tɛ'lʊərɪən) *n* an instrument that shows how day and night, etc., result from the earth's rotation on its axis, etc. [C19: from L *tellūs* the earth]

tellurium (tɛ'lʊərɪəm) *n* a brittle silvery-white nonmetallic element. Symbol: Te; atomic no.: 52; atomic wt.: 127.60. [C19: NL, from L *tellūs* the earth, by analogy with URANIUM]

tellurometer (,tɛljʊ'rɒmɪtə) *n Surveying.* an electronic instrument for measuring distances by the transmission of radio waves. [C20: from L *tellūs* the earth + -METER]

telly ('tɛlɪ) *n, pl* **tellies.** *Inf., chiefly Brit.* short for **television.**

telo- *or before a vowel* **tel-** *combining form.* **1** complete; final; perfect. **2** end; at the end. [from Gk *telos* end]

telpherage ('tɛlfərɪdʒ) *n* an overhead transport system in which an electrically driven truck runs along a rail or cable, the load being suspended in a car beneath. Also called: **telpher.** [C19: changed from *telephore,* from TELE- + -PHORE + -AGE]

telson ('tɛlsən) *n* the last segment or an appendage on the last segment of the body of crustaceans and arachnids. [C19: from Gk: a boundary]

Telugu *or* **Telegu** ('tɛlə,guː) *n* **1** a language of SE India, belonging to the Dravidian family of languages. **2** (*pl* **Telugus** *or* **Telugu**) a member of the people who speak this language. ◆ *adj* **3** of or relating to this people or their language.

temazepam (tə'mæzə,pæm) *n* a sedative in the form of a gel-like capsule, which is taken orally or melted and injected by drug users.

temblor ('tɛmblə, -blɔː) *n, pl* **temblors** *or* **temblores** (tɛm'blɔːreɪz). *Chiefly US.* an earthquake or earth tremor. [C19: American Sp., from Sp. *temblar* to shake, tremble]

temerity Ⓣ (tɪ'mɛrɪtɪ) *n* rashness or boldness. [C15: from L *temeritās* accident, from *temere* at random]
▸**temerarious** (,tɛmə'rɛərɪəs) *adj*

temp (tɛmp) *Inf.* ◆ *n* **1** a person, esp. a typist or other office worker, employed on a temporary basis. ◆ *vb* (*intr*) **2** to work as a temp.

temp. *abbrev. for:* **1** temperature. **2** temporary. **3** tempore. [L: in the time of]

temper Ⓣ ('tɛmpə) *n* **1** a frame of mind; mood or humour. **2** a sudden outburst of anger. **3** a tendency to exhibit anger; irritability. **4** a mental condition of moderation and calm (esp. in **keep one's temper** *or* **lose one's temper**). **5** the degree of hardness, elasticity, etc., of a metal. ◆ *vb* (*tr*) **6** to make more acceptable or suitable by adding something else; moderate: *he tempered his criticism with sympathy.* **7** to reduce the brittleness of (a hardened metal) by reheating it and allowing it to cool. **8** *Music.* **8a** to adjust the frequency differences between the notes of a scale on (a keyboard instrument). **8b** to make such an adjustment to the pitches of notes in (a scale). [OE *temprian* to mingle, from L *temperāre* to mix, prob. from *tempus* time]
▸'**temperable** *adj* ▸'**temperer** *n*

tempera ('tɛmpərə) *n* **1** a painting medium for powdered pigments, consisting usually of egg yolk and water. **2a** any emulsion used as a painting medium, with casein, glue, wax, etc., as a base. **2b** the paint made from this. **3** the technique of painting with tempera. [C19: from It. *pingere a tempera* painting in tempera, from *temperare* to mingle; see TEMPER]

temperament Ⓣ ('tɛmpərəmənt) *n* **1** a person's character, disposition, and tendencies. **2** excitability, moodiness, or anger. **3** the characteristic way an individual behaves, esp. towards other people. **4a** an adjustment made to the frequency differences between notes on a keyboard instrument to allow modulation to other keys. **4b** any of several systems of such adjustment, esp. **equal temperament,** a system giving a scale based on an octave divided into twelve exactly equal semitones. **5** *Obs.* the characteristic way an individual behaves, viewed as the result of the influence of the four humours. [C15: from L *temperāmentum* a mixing in proportion, from *temperāre* to TEMPER]

temperamental Ⓣ (,tɛmpərə'mɛnt°l) *adj* **1** easily upset or irritated; excitable. **2** of or caused by temperament. **3** *Inf.* working erratically and inconsistently; unreliable.
▸,**tempera'mentally** *adv*

temperance Ⓣ ('tɛmpərəns) *n* **1** restraint or moderation, esp. in yielding to one's appetites or desires. **2** abstinence from alcoholic drink. [C14: from L *temperantia,* from *temperāre* to regulate]

temperate Ⓣ ('tɛmpərɪt) *adj* **1** having a climate intermediate between tropical and polar; moderate or mild in temperature. **2** mild in quality or character; exhibiting temperance. [C14: from L *temperātus*]
▸'**temperately** *adv* ▸'**temperateness** *n*

Temperate Zone *n* those parts of the earth's surface lying between the Arctic Circle and the tropic of Cancer and between the Antarctic Circle and the tropic of Capricorn.

temperature ('tɛmprɪtʃə) *n* **1** the degree of hotness of a body, substance, or medium, esp. as measured on a scale that has one or more fixed reference points. **2** *Inf.* a body temperature in excess of the normal. [C16 (orig.: a mingling): from L *temperātūra* proportion, from *temperāre* to TEMPER]

temperature gradient *n* the rate of change in temperature in a given direction.

temperature-humidity index *n* an index of the effect on human comfort of temperature and humidity levels, 65 being the highest comfortable level.

tempered ('tɛmpəd) *adj* **1** *Music.* adjusted in accordance with a system of temperament. **2** (*in combination*) having a temper or temperament as specified: *ill-tempered.*

tempest Ⓣ ('tɛmpɪst) *n* **1** *Chiefly literary.* a violent wind or storm. **2** a violent commotion, uproar, or disturbance. [C13: from OF *tempeste,* from L *tempestās* storm, from *tempus* time]

tempestuous Ⓣ (tɛm'pɛstjʊəs) *adj* **1** of or relating to a tempest. **2** violent or stormy.
▸**tem'pestuously** *adv* ▸**tem'pestuousness** *n*

tempi ('tɛmpiː) *n* (in musical senses) the plural of **tempo.**

Templar ('tɛmplə) *n* **1** a member of a military order (**Knights of the Temple of Solomon**) founded by Crusaders in Jerusalem around 1118; suppressed in 1312. **2** (*sometimes not cap.*) *Brit.* a lawyer who has chambers in the Temple in London. [C13: from Med. L *templārius* of the TEMPLE; applied to the order because their house adjoined the site of the Temple of Solomon]

template *or* **templet** ('tɛmplɪt) *n* **1** a gauge or pattern, cut out in wood or metal, used in woodwork, etc., to help shape something accurately. **2** a pattern cut out in card or plastic, used to reproduce shapes. **3** a short beam that is used to spread a load, as over a doorway. **4** *Biochem.* the molecular structure of a compound that serves as a pattern for the production of another compound. [C17 *templet* (later spelling infl. by PLATE), prob. from F, dim. of TEMPLE[3]]

temple[1] Ⓣ ('tɛmp°l) *n* **1** a building or place dedicated to the worship of

THESAURUS

tell off *vb* **1** = **reprimand,** berate, carpet (*inf.*), censure, chide, give (someone) a piece of one's mind, haul over the coals (*inf.*), lecture, read the riot act, rebuke, reproach, reprove, scold, take to task, tear (someone) off a strip (*Brit. inf.*), tick off (*inf.*), upbraid

temerity *n* = **audacity,** assurance, boldness, brass neck (*Brit. inf.*), cheek, chutzpah (*US & Canad. inf.*), effrontery, foolhardiness, forwardness, front, gall (*inf.*), heedlessness, impudence, impulsiveness, intrepidity, nerve (*inf.*), pluck, rashness, recklessness, sassiness (*US inf.*)

temper *n* **1** = **frame of mind,** attitude, character, constitution, disposition, humour, mind, mood, nature, temperament, tenor, vein **2** = **rage,** bate (*Brit. sl.*), fit of pique, fury, gall, paddy (*Brit. inf.*), passion, tantrum, wax (*inf., chiefly Brit.*) **3** = **irritability,** anger, annoyance, heat, hot-headedness, ill humour, irascibility, irritation, passion, peevishness, petulance, resentment, surliness **4** = **self-control,** calm, calmness, composure, cool (*sl.*), coolness, equanimity, good humour, moderation, tranquillity ◆ *vb* **6** = **moderate,** abate, admix, allay, assuage, calm, lessen, mitigate, mollify, palliate, restrain, soften, soft-pedal (*inf.*), soothe, tone down **7** = **strengthen,** anneal, harden, toughen
Antonyms *n* ≠ **irritability:** contentment, goodwill ≠ **self-control:** agitation, anger, bad mood, excitability, foul humour, fury, grumpiness, indignation, irascibility, irritation, pique, vexation, wrath ◆ *vb* ≠ **moderate:** aggravate, arouse, excite, heighten, intensify, provoke, stir ≠ **strengthen:** soften

temperament *n* **1** = **nature,** bent, cast of mind, character, complexion, constitution, disposition, frame of mind, humour, make-up, mettle, outlook, personality, quality, soul, spirit, stamp, temper, tendencies, tendency **2** = **excitability,** anger, explosiveness, hot-headedness, impatience, mercurialness, moodiness, moods, petulance, volatility

temperamental *adj* **1** = **moody,** capricious, easily upset, emotional, erratic, excitable, explosive, fiery, highly strung, hot-headed, hypersensitive, impatient, irritable, mercurial, neurotic, passionate, petulant, sensitive, touchy, volatile **2** = **natural,** congenital, constitutional, inborn, ingrained, inherent, innate **3** *Informal* = **unreliable,** erratic, inconsistent, inconstant, undependable, unpredictable
Antonyms *adj* ≠ **moody:** calm, cool-headed, easy-going, even-tempered, level-headed, phlegmatic, unexcitable, unflappable, unperturbable ≠ **unreliable:** constant, dependable, reliable, stable, steady

temperance *n* **1** = **moderation,** continence, discretion, forbearance, restraint, self-control, self-discipline, self-restraint **2** = **teetotalism,** abstemiousness, abstinence, prohibition, sobriety
Antonyms *n* ≠ **moderation:** excess, immoderation, intemperance, overindulgence, prodigality

temperate *adj* **1** = **mild,** agreeable, balmy, calm, clement, cool, fair, gentle, moderate, pleasant, soft **2** = **moderate,** calm, composed, dispassionate, equable, even-tempered, mild, reasonable, self-controlled, self-restrained, sensible, stable
Antonyms *adj* ≠ **mild:** extreme, harsh, inclement, intemperate, severe, torrid ≠ **moderate:** intemperate, uncontrolled, undisciplined, unreasonable, unrestrained, wild

tempest *n* **1** *Literary* = **storm,** cyclone, gale, hurricane, squall, tornado, typhoon **2** = **uproar,** commotion, disturbance, ferment, furore, storm, tumult, upheaval
Antonyms *n* ≠ **uproar:** calm, peace, quiet, serenity, stillness, tranquillity

tempestuous *adj* **2** = **stormy,** agitated, blustery, boisterous, breezy, furious, gusty, inclement, intense, raging, squally, turbulent, uncontrolled, violent, wild, windy
Antonyms *adj* ≠ **passionate:** calm, peaceful, quiet, serene, still, tranquil, undisturbed, unruffled

temple[1] *n* **1** = **shrine,** church, holy place, place of worship, sanctuary a deity or deities. **2** a Mormon church. **3** *US.* another name for a **synagogue.** **4** a Christian church. **5** any place or object regarded as a shrine where God makes himself present. **6** a building regarded as the focus of an activity, interest, or practice: *a temple of the arts.* [OE *tempel,* from L *templum*]

temple[2] ('temp°l) *n* the region on each side of the head in front of the ear and above the cheek bone. [C14: from OF *temple,* from L *tempora* the temples, from *tempus* temple of the head]

temple[3] ('temp°l) *n* the part of a loom that keeps the cloth being woven stretched to the correct width. [C15: from F, from L *templum* a small timber]

Temple ('tɛmpəl) *n* **1** a building in London that belonged to the Templars: it now houses two law societies. **2** any of three buildings erected by the Jews in ancient Jerusalem for the worship of Jehovah.

tempo ➊ ('tɛmpəu) *n, pl* **tempos** *or* **tempi** (-piː). **1** the speed at which a piece of music is meant to be played. **2** rate or pace. [C18: from It., from L *tempus* time]

temporal[1] ➊ ('tɛmpərəl) *adj* **1** of or relating to time. **2** of secular as opposed to spiritual or religious affairs. **3** lasting for a relatively short time. **4** *Grammar.* of or relating to tense or the linguistic expression of time. [C14: from L *temporālis,* from *tempus* time]
▸ **'temporally** *adv*

temporal[2] ('tɛmpərəl) *adj Anat.* of or near the temple or temples. [C16: from LL *temporālis* belonging to the temples; see TEMPLE[2]]

temporal bone *n* either of two compound bones forming the sides of the skull.

temporality (ˌtɛmpə'rælɪtɪ) *n, pl* **temporalities. 1** the state or quality of being temporal. **2** something temporal. **3** (*often pl*) a secular possession or revenue belonging to a Church.

temporal lobe *n* the laterally protruding portion of each cerebral hemisphere, situated below the parietal lobe and associated with sound perception and interpretation.

temporary ➊ ('tɛmpərərɪ) *adj* **1** not permanent; provisional. **2** lasting only a short time. ◆ *n, pl* **temporaries. 3** a person employed on a temporary basis. [C16: from L *temporārius,* from *tempus* time]
▸ **'temporarily** *adv* ▸ **'temporariness** *n*

temporize ➊ *or* **temporise** ('tɛmpəˌraɪz) *vb* **temporizes, temporizing, temporized** *or* **temporises, temporising, temporised.** (*intr*) **1** to delay, act evasively, or protract a negotiation, etc., esp. in order to gain time or effect a compromise. **2** to adapt oneself to the circumstances, as by temporary or apparent agreement. [C16: from F *temporiser,* from Med. L *temporizāre,* from L *tempus* time]
▸ **ˌtempori'zation** *or* **ˌtempori'sation** *n* ▸ **'tempoˌrizer** *or* **'tempoˌriser** *n*

tempt ➊ (tɛmpt) *vb* (*tr*) **1** to entice to do something, esp. something morally wrong or unwise. **2** to allure or attract. **3** to give rise to a desire in (someone) to do something; dispose. **4** to risk provoking (esp. in **tempt fate**). [C13: from OF *tempter,* from L *temptāre* to test]
▸ **'temptable** *adj* ▸ **'tempter** *n* ▸ **'temptress** *fem n*

temptation ➊ (tɛmp'teɪʃən) *n* **1** the act of tempting or the state of being tempted. **2** a person or thing that tempts.

tempting ➊ ('tɛmptɪŋ) *adj* attractive or inviting: *a tempting meal.*
▸ **'temptingly** *adv*

tempus fugit *Latin.* ('tɛmpəs 'fjuːdʒɪt) time flies.

ten (tɛn) *n* **1** the cardinal number that is the sum of nine and one. It is the base of the decimal number system and the base of the common logarithm. **2** a numeral, 10, X, etc., representing this number. **3** something representing or consisting of ten units. **4** Also called: **ten o'clock.** ten hours after noon or midnight. ◆ *determiner* **5** amounting to ten. ◆ Related adj: **decimal.** [OE *tēn*]

ten. *Music. abbrev. for:* **1** tenor. **2** tenuto.

tenable ➊ ('tɛnəb°l) *adj* able to be upheld, believed, maintained, or defended. [C16: from OF, from *tenir* to hold, from L *tenēre*]
▸ **ˌtena'bility** *or* **'tenableness** *n* ▸ **'tenably** *adv*

tenace ('tɛneɪs) *n Bridge, whist.* a holding of two nonconsecutive high cards of a suit, such as the ace and queen. [C17: from F, from Sp. *tenaza* forceps, ult. from L *tenāx* holding fast, from *tenēre* to hold]

tenacious ➊ (tɪ'neɪʃəs) *adj* **1** holding firmly: *a tenacious grip.* **2** retentive: *a tenacious memory.* **3** stubborn or persistent. **4** holding together firmly; cohesive. **5** tending to stick or adhere. [C16: from L *tenāx,* from *tenēre* to hold]
▸ **te'naciously** *adv* ▸ **te'naciousness** *or* **tenacity** (tɪ'næsɪtɪ) *n*

tenaculum (tɪ'nækjuləm) *n, pl* **tenacula** (-lə). a hooked surgical instrument for grasping and holding parts. [C17: from LL, from L *tenēre* to hold]

tenancy ➊ ('tɛnənsɪ) *n, pl* **tenancies. 1** the temporary possession or holding by a tenant of lands or property owned by another. **2** the period of holding or occupying such property. **3** the period of holding office, a position, etc.

tenant ➊ ('tɛnənt) *n* **1** a person who holds, occupies, or possesses land or property, esp. from a landlord. **2** a person who has the use of a house, etc., subject to the payment of rent. **3** any holder or occupant. ◆ *vb* **4** (*tr*) to hold as a tenant. [C14: from OF, lit.: (one who is) holding, from *tenir* to hold, from L *tenēre*]
▸ **'tenantable** *adj* ▸ **'tenantless** *adj*

tenant farmer *n* a person who farms land rented from another, the rent usually taking the form of crops or livestock.

tenantry ('tɛnəntrɪ) *n* **1** tenants collectively. **2** the status or condition of being a tenant.

tench (tɛntʃ) *n* a European freshwater game fish of the carp family. [C14: from OF *tenche,* from LL *tinca*]

Ten Commandments *pl n* **the.** *Old Testament.* the commandments summarizing the basic obligations of man towards God and his fellow men, delivered to Moses on Mount Sinai engraved on two tables of stone (Exodus 20:1–17).

tend[1] ➊ (tɛnd) *vb* (when *intr,* usually foll. by *to* or *towards*) **1** (when *tr, takes an infinitive*) to have a general disposition (to do something); be inclined: *children tend to prefer sweets to meat.* **2** (*intr*) to have or be an influence (towards a specific result). **3** (*intr*) to go or move (in a particular direction): *to tend to the south.* [C14: from OF *tendre,* from L *tendere* to stretch]

tend[2] ➊ (tɛnd) *vb* **1** (*tr*) to care for. **2** (when *intr,* often foll. by *on* or *to*) to attend (to). **3** (*tr*) to handle or control. **4** (*intr;* often foll. by *to*) *Inf., chiefly US & Canad.* to pay attention. [C14: var. of ATTEND]

tendency ➊ ('tɛndənsɪ) *n, pl* **tendencies. 1** (often foll. by *to*) an inclination, predisposition, propensity, or leaning. **2** the general course, purport, or drift of something, esp. a written work. [C17: from Med. L *tendentia,* from L *tendere* to TEND[1]]

tendentious *or* **tendencious** (tɛn'dɛnʃəs) *adj* having or showing an intentional tendency or bias, esp. a controversial one. [C20: from TENDENCY]
▸ **ten'dentiously** *or* **ten'denciously** *adv* ▸ **ten'dentiousness** *or* **ten'denciousness** *n*

THESAURUS

tempo *n* **1, 2** = **pace**, beat, cadence, measure (*Prosody*), metre, pulse, rate, rhythm, speed, time

temporal[1] *adj* **2** = **secular**, carnal, civil, earthly, fleshly, lay, material, mortal, mundane, profane, sublunary, terrestrial, worldly **3** = **temporary**, evanescent, fleeting, fugacious, fugitive, impermanent, momentary, passing, short-lived, transient, transitory

temporarily *adv* **2** = **briefly**, fleetingly, for a little while, for a moment, for a short time, for a short while, for the moment, for the nonce, for the time being, momentarily, pro tem

temporary *adj* **1, 2** = **impermanent**, brief, ephemeral, evanescent, fleeting, fugacious, fugitive, here today and gone tomorrow, interim, momentary, passing, pro tem, *pro tempore*, provisional, short-lived, transient, transitory
Antonyms *adj* durable, enduring, eternal, everlasting, long-lasting, long-term, permanent

temporize *vb* **1** = **play for time**, beat about the bush, be evasive, delay, equivocate, gain time, hum and haw, play a waiting game, procrastinate, stall, tergiversate

tempt *vb* **1** = **entice**, coax, decoy, inveigle, invite, lead on, lure, seduce, tantalize, woo **2** = **attract**, allure, appeal to, draw, make one's mouth water, whet the appetite of **4** = **provoke**, bait, dare, fly in the face of, risk, test, try
Antonyms *vb* ≠ **entice:** deter, discourage, dissuade, hinder, inhibit, put off

temptation *n* **1, 2** = **enticement**, allurement, appeal, attraction, attractiveness, bait, coaxing, come-on (*inf.*), decoy, draw, inducement, invitation, lure, pull, seduction, snare, tantalization

tempting *adj* = **inviting**, alluring, appetizing, attractive, enticing, mouthwatering, seductive, tantalizing
Antonyms *adj* off-putting (*Brit. inf.*), unappetizing, unattractive, undesirable, uninviting, untempting

tenable *adj* = **sound**, arguable, believable, defendable, defensible, justifiable, maintainable, plausible, rational, reasonable, viable
Antonyms *adj* indefensible, insupportable, unjustifiable, untenable

tenacious *adj* **1** = **firm**, clinging, fast, forceful, immovable, iron, strong, tight, unshakable **2** = **retentive**, unforgetful **3** = **stubborn**, adamant, determined, dogged, firm, immovable, inflexible, intransigent, obdurate, obstinate, persistent, pertinacious, resolute, staunch, steadfast, stiff-necked, strong-willed, sure, unswerving, unyielding **4** = **cohesive**, coherent, solid, strong, tough **5** = **adhesive**, clinging, gluey, glutinous, mucilaginous, sticky
Antonyms *adj* ≠ **stubborn:** changeable, flexible, irresolute, vacillating, wavering, yielding

tenacity *n* **1** = **firmness**, fastness, force, forcefulness, power, strength **2** = **retentiveness**, firm grasp, retention **3** = **perseverance**, application, determination, diligence, doggedness, firmness, inflexibility, intransigence, obduracy, obstinacy, persistence, pertinacity, resoluteness, resolution, resolve, staunchness, steadfastness, strength of purpose, strength of will, stubbornness **4** = **cohesiveness**, coherence, solidity, solidness, strength, toughness **5** = **adhesiveness**, clingingness, stickiness
Antonyms *n* ≠ **firmness:** looseness, powerlessness, slackness, weakness

tenancy *n* **1** = **lease**, holding, occupancy, occupation, possession, renting, residence **3** = **period of office**, incumbency, tenure, time in office

tenant *n* **1-3** = **leaseholder**, holder, inhabitant, lessee, occupant, occupier, renter, resident

tend[1] *vb* **1** = **be inclined**, be apt, be biased, be disposed, be liable, be likely, gravitate, have a leaning, have an inclination, have a tendency, incline, lean, trend **2** = **influence**, be conducive, conduce, contribute **3** = **go**, aim, bear, head, lead, make for, move, point

tend[2] *vb* **1-3** = **take care of**, attend, care for, cater for, control, cultivate, feed, guard, handle, keep, keep an eye on, look after, maintain, manage, minister to, nurse, nurture, protect, see to, serve, wait on, watch, watch over
Antonyms *vb* disregard, ignore, neglect, overlook, shirk

tendency *n* **1** = **inclination**, bent, disposition, leaning, liability, partiality, penchant, predilection, predisposition, proclivity, proneness, propensity, readiness, susceptibility **2** = **course**, bearing, bias, direction, drift, drive, heading, movement, purport, tenor, trend, turning

tender[1] ❶ ('tɛndə) *adj* **1** easily broken, cut, or crushed; soft. **2** easily damaged; vulnerable or sensitive: *at a tender age.* **3** having or expressing warm feelings. **4** kind or sympathetic: *a tender heart.* **5** arousing warm feelings; touching. **6** gentle and delicate: *a tender breeze.* **7** requiring care in handling: *a tender question.* **8** painful or sore. **9** sensitive to moral or spiritual feelings. **10** (*postpositive;* foll. by *of*) protective: *tender of one's emotions.* [C13: from OF *tendre,* from L *tener* delicate]
▸ **'tenderly** *adv* ▸ **'tenderness** *n*

tender[2] ❶ ('tɛndə) *vb* **1** (*tr*) to give, present, or offer: *to tender a bid.* **2** (*intr;* foll. by *for*) to make a formal offer or estimate (for a job or contract). **3** (*tr*) *Law.* to offer (money or goods) in settlement of a debt or claim. ◆ *n* **4** the act or an instance of tendering; offer. **5** a formal offer to supply specified goods or services at a stated cost or rate. **6** something, esp. money, used as an official medium of payment: *legal tender.* [C16: from Anglo-F *tendre,* from L *tendere* to extend]
▸ **'tenderer** *n*

tender[3] ('tɛndə) *n* **1** a small boat towed or carried by a ship. **2** a vehicle drawn behind a steam locomotive to carry the fuel and water. **3** a person who tends. [C15: var. of *attender*]

tenderfoot ('tɛndə,fʊt) *n, pl* **tenderfoots** *or* **tenderfeet.** **1** a newcomer, esp. to the mines or ranches of the southwestern US. **2** (formerly) a beginner in the Scouts or Guides.

tenderhearted ❶ (,tɛndə'hɑːtɪd) *adj* having a compassionate, kindly, or sensitive disposition.

tenderize *or* **tenderise** ('tɛndə,raɪz) *vb* **tenderizes, tenderizing, tenderized** *or* **tenderises, tenderising, tenderised.** (*tr*) to make (meat) tender, as by pounding it or adding a substance to break down the fibres.
▸ **,tenderi'zation** *or* **,tenderi'sation** *n* ▸ **'tender,izer** *or* **'tender,iser** *n*

tenderloin ('tɛndə,lɔɪn) *n* a tender cut of pork or other meat from between the sirloin and ribs.

tendon ('tɛndən) *n* a cord or band of tough tissue that attaches a muscle to a bone or some other part; sinew. [C16: from Med. L *tendō,* from L *tendere* to stretch]

tendril ('tɛndrɪl) *n* a threadlike leaf or stem that attaches climbing plants to a support by twining or adhering. [C16: ?from OF *tendron* tendril (confused with OF *tendron* bud), from Med. L *tendō* TENDON]

tenebrism ('tɛnə,brɪzəm) *n* (*sometimes cap.*) a school, style, or method of painting, adopted chiefly by 17th-century Spanish and Neapolitan painters, characterized by large areas of dark colours, usually relieved with a shaft of light.
▸ **'tenebrist** *n, adj*

tenebrous ('tɛnəbrəs) *or* **tenebrious** (tə'nebrɪəs) *adj* gloomy, shadowy, or dark. [C15: from L *tenebrōsus* from *tenebrae* darkness]

tenement ('tɛnəmənt) *n* **1** Also called: **tenement building.** a large building divided into rooms or flats. **2** a dwelling place or residence. **3** *Chiefly Brit.* a room or flat for rent. **4** *Property law.* any form of permanent property, such as land, dwellings, offices, etc. [C14: from Med. L *tenementum,* from L *tenēre* to hold]
▸ **tenemental** (,tɛnə'mɛntᵊl) *adj*

tenesmus (tɪ'nɛzməs) *n* an ineffective painful straining to empty the bowels or bladder. [C16: from Med. L, from L *tēnesmos,* from Gk, from *teinein* to strain]
▸ **te'nesmic** *adj*

tenet ❶ ('tɛnɪt, 'tiːnɪt) *n* a belief, opinion, or dogma. [C17: from L, lit.: he (it) holds, from *tenēre* to hold]

tenfold ('tɛn,fəʊld) *adj* **1** equal to or having 10 times as many or as much. **2** composed of 10 parts. ◆ *adv* **3** by or up to 10 times as many or as much.

ten-gallon hat *n* (in the US) a cowboy's broad-brimmed felt hat with a very high crown.

Ten Gurus *pl n* the ten leaders of the Sikh religion, from its founder Guru Nanak (1469–1539) to Guru Govind Singh (1666–1708).

tenner ('tɛnə) *n Inf.* **1** *Brit.* **1a** a ten-pound note. **1b** the sum of ten pounds. **2** *US.* a ten-dollar bill.

tennis ('tɛnɪs) *n* **a** a racket game played between two players or pairs of players who hit a ball to and fro over a net on a rectangular court of grass, asphalt, clay, etc. See also **lawn tennis, real tennis, table tennis.** **b** (*as modifier*): *tennis court; tennis racket.* [C14: prob. from Anglo-F *tenetz* hold (imperative), from OF *tenir* to hold, from L *tenēre*]

tennis elbow *n* inflammation of the elbow caused by exertion in playing tennis, etc.

tennis shoe *n* a rubber-soled canvas shoe tied with laces.

Tennysonian (,tɛnɪ'səʊnɪən) *adj* of or in the style of Alfred, Lord Tennyson (1809–92), British poet.

teno- *or before a vowel* **ten-** *combining form.* tendon: *tenosynovitis.* [from Gk *tenōn*]

tenon ('tɛnən) *n* **1** the projecting end of a piece of wood formed to fit into a corresponding mortise in another piece. ◆ *vb* (*tr*) **2** to form a tenon on (a piece of wood). **3** to join with a tenon and mortise. [C15: from OF, from *tenir* to hold, from L *tenēre*]
▸ **'tenoner** *n*

tenon saw *n* a small fine-toothed saw with a strong back, used esp. for cutting tenons.

tenor ❶ ('tɛnə) *n* **1** *Music.* **1a** the male voice intermediate between alto and baritone. **1b** a singer with such a voice. **1c** a saxophone, horn, etc., intermediate between the alto and baritone or bass. **2** general drift of thought; purpose. **3** a settled course of progress. **4** *Arch.* general tendency. **5** *Finance.* the time required for a bill of exchange or promissory note to become due for payment. **6** *Law.* **6a** the exact words of a deed, etc. **6b** an exact copy. [C13 (orig.: general sense): from OF *tenour,* from L *tenor* a holding to a course, from *tenēre* to hold; musical sense via It. *tenore,* referring to the voice part that was continuous, that is, to which the melody was assigned]

tenor clef *n* the clef that establishes middle C as being on the fourth line of the staff.

tenorrhaphy (tɪ'nɒrəfɪ) *n, pl* **tenorrhaphies.** *Surgery.* the union of torn or divided tendons by means of sutures. [C19: from TENO- + Gk *raphē* a sewing]

tenosynovitis ('tɛnəʊ,saɪnəʊ'vaɪtɪs) *n* painful swelling and inflammation of tendons, usually of the wrist, often the result of repetitive movements such as typing.

tenotomy (tə'nɒtəmɪ) *n, pl* **tenotomies.** surgical division of a tendon.
▸ **te'notomist** *n*

tenpin bowling ('tɛn,pɪn) *n* a bowling game in which bowls are rolled down a lane to knock over the ten target pins. Also called (esp. US and Canad.): **tenpins.**

tenrec ('tɛnrɛk) *n* any of a family of small mammals of Madagascar resembling hedgehogs or shrews. [C18: via F from Malagasy *tràndraka*]

tense[1] ❶ (tɛns) *adj* **1** stretched or stressed tightly; taut or rigid. **2** under mental or emotional strain. **3** producing mental or emotional strain: *a tense day.* **4** *Phonetics.* Also: **narrow.** pronounced with considerable muscular effort, as the vowel (iː) in "beam". ◆ *vb* **tenses, tensing, tensed.** (often foll. by *up*) **5** to make or become tense. [C17: from L *tensus* taut, from *tendere* to stretch]
▸ **'tensely** *adv* ▸ **'tenseness** *n*

tense[2] (tɛns) *n Grammar.* a category of the verb or verbal inflections, such as present, past, and future, that expresses the temporal relations between what is reported in a sentence and the time of its utterance. [C14: from OF *tens* time, from L *tempus*]
▸ **'tenseless** *adj*

tense logic *n Logic.* the study of temporal relations between propositions, usually pursued by considering the logical properties of symbols representing the tenses of natural languages.

tensile ('tɛnsaɪl) *adj* **1** of or relating to tension. **2** sufficiently ductile to be stretched or drawn out. [C17: from NL *tensilis,* from L *tendere* to stretch]
▸ **tensility** (tɛn'sɪlɪtɪ) *or* **'tensileness** *n*

tensile strength *n* a measure of the ability of a material to withstand a longitudinal stress, expressed as the greatest stress that the material can stand without breaking.

tensimeter (tɛn'sɪmɪtə) *n* a device that measures differences in vapour pressures. [C20: from TENSI(ON) + -METER]

THESAURUS

tender[1] *adj* **1** = **fragile**, breakable, delicate, feeble, frail, soft, weak **2** = **vulnerable**, impressionable, raw, sensitive **3, 4** = **gentle**, affectionate, amorous, benevolent, caring, compassionate, considerate, fond, humane, kind, loving, merciful, pitiful, sentimental, softhearted, sympathetic, tenderhearted, touchy-feely (*inf.*), warm, warm-hearted **5** = **touching**, emotional, evocative, moving, poignant, romantic **7** = **difficult**, complicated, dangerous, risky, sensitive, ticklish, touchy, tricky **8** = **sensitive**, aching, acute, bruised, inflamed, irritated, painful, raw, smarting, sore
Antonyms *adj* ≠ **fragile:** hard, leathery, strong, tough ≠ **vulnerable:** sophisticated, worldly, worldly-wise ≠ **gentle:** brutal, cold-hearted, cruel, hard, hard-hearted, inhuman, insensitive, pitiless, tough, uncaring, unkind, unsympathetic

tender[2] *vb* **1** = **offer**, extend, give, hand in, present, proffer, propose, put forward, submit, suggest, volunteer ◆ *n* **4** = **offer**, bid, estimate, proffer, proposal, submission, suggestion

tenderhearted *adj* = **kind**, affectionate, benevolent, benign, caring, compassionate, considerate, fond, gentle, humane, kind-hearted, kindly, loving, merciful, mild, responsive, sensitive, sentimental, softhearted, sympathetic, touchy-feely (*inf.*), warm, warm-hearted

tenderness *n* **1** = **fragility**, delicateness, feebleness, frailness, sensitiveness, sensitivity, softness, vulnerability, weakness **2** = **vulnerability**, impressionableness, rawness, sensitivity **3, 4** = **gentleness**, affection, amorousness, attachment, benevolence, care, compassion, consideration, devotion, fondness, humaneness, humanity, kindness, liking, love, mercy, pity, sentimentality, softheartedness, sympathy, tender-heartedness, warm-heartedness, warmth **8** = **soreness**, ache, aching, bruising, inflammation, irritation, pain, painfulness, rawness, sensitiveness, sensitivity, smart
Antonyms *n* ≠ **gentleness:** cruelty, hardness, harshness, indifference, insensitivity, unkindness

tenet *n* = **principle**, article of faith, belief, canon, conviction, creed, doctrine, dogma, maxim, opinion, precept, rule, teaching, thesis, view

tenor *n* **2, 3** = **direction**, aim, burden, course, drift, evolution, intent, meaning, path, purport, purpose, sense, substance, tendency, theme, trend, way

tense[1] *adj* **1** = **tight**, rigid, strained, stretched, taut **2** = **nervous**, anxious, apprehensive, edgy, fidgety, jittery, jumpy, keyed up, on edge, on tenterhooks, overwrought, restless, strained, strung up (*inf.*), twitchy (*inf.*), under pressure, uptight (*inf.*), wired (*sl.*), wound up (*inf.*), wrought up **3** = **exciting**, moving, nerve-racking, stressful, worrying ◆ *vb* **5** = **tighten**, brace, flex, strain, stretch, tauten
Antonyms *adj* ≠ **tight:** flaccid, flexible, limp, loose, pliant, relaxed ≠ **nervous:** calm, collected, cool-headed, easy-going, self-possessed, serene, unconcerned, unruffled, unworried ≠ **exciting:** boring, dull, uninteresting ◆ *vb* ≠ **tighten:** loosen, relax, slacken

tensiometer (ˌtɛnsɪˈɒmɪtə) *n* **1** an instrument for measuring the tensile strength of a wire, beam, etc. **2** an instrument used to compare the vapour pressures of two liquids. **3** an instrument for measuring the surface tension of a liquid. **4** an instrument for measuring the moisture content of soil.

tension ➊ (ˈtɛnʃən) *n* **1** the act of stretching or the state or degree of being stretched. **2** mental or emotional strain; stress. **3** a situation or condition of hostility, suspense, or uneasiness. **4** *Physics.* a force that tends to produce an elongation of a body or structure. **5** *Physics.* voltage, electromotive force, or potential difference. **6** a device for regulating the tension in a part, string, thread, etc., as in a sewing machine. **7** the degree of tightness or looseness with which a person knits. [C16: from L *tensiō*, from *tendere* to strain]
▸ˈ**tensional** *adj* ▸ˈ**tensionless** *adj*

tensor (ˈtɛnsə, -sɔː) *n* **1** *Anat.* any muscle that can cause a part to become firm or tense. **2** *Maths.* a set of components, functions of the coordinates of any point in space, that transform linearly between coordinate systems. [C18: from NL, lit.: a stretcher]
▸**tensorial** (tɛnˈsɔːrɪəl) *adj*

tent (tɛnt) *n* **1** a portable shelter of canvas, plastic, etc., supported on poles and fastened to the ground by pegs and ropes. **2** something resembling this in function or shape. ◆ *vb* **3** (*intr*) to camp in a tent. **4** (*tr*) to cover with or as if with a tent or tents. **5** (*tr*) to provide with a tent as shelter. [C13: from OF *tente*, from L *tentōrium* something stretched out, from *tendere* to stretch]
▸ˈ**tentage** *n* ▸ˈ**tented** *adj*

tentacle (ˈtɛntəkᵊl) *n* **1** any of various elongated flexible organs that occur near the mouth in many invertebrates and are used for feeding, grasping, etc. **2** any of the hairs on the leaf of an insectivorous plant that are used to capture prey. **3** something resembling a tentacle, esp. in its ability to reach out or grasp. [C18: from NL *tentāculum*, from L *tentāre*, var. of *temptāre* to feel]
▸ˈ**tentacled** *adj* ▸**tentacular** (tɛnˈtækjʊlə) *adj*

tentation (tɛnˈteɪʃən) *n* a method of achieving the correct adjustment of a mechanical device by a series of trials. [C14: from L *tentātiō*, variant of *temptātiō* TEMPTATION]

tentative ➊ (ˈtɛntətɪv) *adj* **1** provisional or experimental. **2** hesitant, uncertain, or cautious. [C16: from Med. L *tentātīvus*, from L *tentāre* to test]
▸ˈ**tentatively** *adv* ▸ˈ**tentativeness** *n*

tenter (ˈtɛntə) *n* **1** a frame on which cloth is stretched in order that it may retain its shape while drying. **2** a person who stretches cloth on a tenter. ◆ *vb* **3** (*tr*) to stretch (cloth) on a tenter. [C14: from Med. L *tentōrium*, from L *tentus* stretched, from *tendere* to stretch]

tenterhook (ˈtɛntəˌhʊk) *n* **1** one of a series of hooks used to hold cloth on a tenter. **2** **on tenterhooks.** in a state of tension or suspense.

tenth (tɛnθ) *adj* **1** (*usually prenominal*) **1a** coming after the ninth in numbering, position, etc.; being the ordinal number of *ten*: often written 10th. **1b** (*as n*): *see you on the tenth.* ◆ *n* **2a** one of 10 equal parts of something. **2b** (*as modifier*): *a tenth part.* **3** the fraction equal to one divided by ten (1/10). ◆ *adv* **4** Also: **tenthly.** after the ninth person, position, event, etc. [C12 *tenthe*, from OE *tēotha*]

tent stitch *n* another term for **petit point.** [C17: from ?]

tenuis (ˈtɛnjʊɪs) *n, pl* **tenues** (ˈtɛnjʊˌiːz). (in classical Greek) a voiceless stop (k, p, t). [C17: from L: thin]

tenuous ➊ (ˈtɛnjʊəs) *adj* **1** insignificant or flimsy: *a tenuous argument.* **2** slim, fine, or delicate: *a tenuous thread.* **3** diluted or rarefied in consistency or density: *a tenuous fluid.* [C16: from L *tenuis*]
▸**tenuity** (tɛˈnjuːɪtɪ) *or* ˈ**tenuousness** *n* ▸ˈ**tenuously** *adv*

tenure ➊ (ˈtɛnjʊə, ˈtɛnjə) *n* **1** the possession or holding of an office or position. **2** the length of time an office, position, etc., lasts. **3** *Chiefly US & Canad.* the improved security status of a person after having been in the employ of the same company or institution for a specified period. **4** the right to permanent employment until retirement, esp. for teachers, etc. **5a** the holding of property, esp. realty, in return for services rendered, etc. **5b** the duration of such holding. [C15: from OF, from Med. L *tenitūra*, ult. from L *tenēre* to hold]
▸**tenˈurial** *adj*

tenuto (tɪˈnjuːtəʊ) *adj, adv Music.* (of a note) to be held for or beyond its full time value. [from It., lit.: held, from *tenere* to hold, from L *tenēre*]

teocalli (ˌtiːəʊˈkælɪ) *n, pl* **teocallis.** any of various truncated pyramids built by the Aztecs as bases for their temples. [C17: from Nahuatl, from *teotl* god + *calli* house]

tepee *or* **teepee** (ˈtiːpiː) *n* a cone-shaped tent of animal skins used by American Indians. [C19: from Siouan *tīpī*, from *ti* to dwell + *pi* used for]

tephra (ˈtɛfrə) *n Chiefly US.* solid matter ejected during a volcanic eruption. [C20: Gk, lit.: ashes]

tepid ➊ (ˈtɛpɪd) *adj* **1** slightly warm; lukewarm. **2** relatively unenthusiastic or apathetic. [C14: from L *tepidus*, from *tepēre* to be lukewarm]
▸**tepidity** (tɛˈpɪdɪtɪ) *or* ˈ**tepidness** *n* ▸ˈ**tepidly** *adv*

tequila (tɪˈkiːlə) *n* **1** a spirit that is distilled in Mexico from an agave plant and forms the basis of many mixed drinks. **2** the plant from which this drink is made. [C19: from Mexican Sp., from *Tequila*, region of Mexico]

ter. *abbrev. for:* **1** terrace. **2** territory.

ter- *combining form.* three, third, or three times. [from L *ter* thrice]

tera- *prefix* denoting 10^{12}: *terameter.* Symbol: T [from Gk *teras* monster]

terat- *or* **terato-** *combining form.* indicating a monster or something abnormal: *teratism.* [from Gk *terat-*, *teras* monster, prodigy]

teratism (ˈtɛrəˌtɪzəm) *n* a malformed animal or human, esp. in the fetal stage; monster.

teratogen (ˈtɛrətədʒən, tɪˈrætə-) *n* any substance, organism, or process that causes malformations in a fetus. Teratogens include certain drugs (such as thalidomide), infections (such as German measles), and ionizing radiation.
▸ˌ**teratoˈgenic** *adj*

teratoid (ˈtɛrəˌtɔɪd) *adj Biol.* resembling a monster.

teratology (ˌtɛrəˈtɒlədʒɪ) *n* **1** the branch of medical science concerned with the development of physical abnormalities during the fetal or early embryonic stage. **2** the branch of biology concerned with the structure, development, etc., of monsters. **3** a collection of tales about mythical or fantastic creatures, monsters, etc.
▸ˌ**teraˈtologist** *n*

teratoma (ˌtɛrəˈtəʊmə) *n, pl* **teratomata** (-mətə) *or* **teratomas.** a tumour composed of tissue foreign to the site of growth.

terbium (ˈtɜːbɪəm) *n* a soft malleable silvery-grey element of the lanthanide series of metals. Symbol: Tb; atomic no.: 65; atomic wt.: 158.925. [C19: from NL, after *Ytterby*, Sweden, village where discovered]
▸ˈ**terbic** *adj*

terbium metal *n Chem.* any of a group of related lanthanides, including terbium, europium, and gadolinium.

terce (tɜːs) *or* **tierce** *n Chiefly RC Church.* the third of the seven canonical hours, originally fixed at the third hour of the day, about 9 a.m. [C14: var. of TIERCE]

tercel (ˈtɜːsᵊl) *or* **tiercel** *n* a male falcon or hawk, esp. as used in falconry. [C14: from OF, from Vulgar L *tertiolus* (unattested), from L *tertius* third, from the tradition that only one egg in three hatched a male chick]

tercentenary (ˌtɜːsɛnˈtiːnərɪ) *or* **tercentennial** *adj* **1** of a period of 300 years. **2** of a 300th anniversary. ◆ *n, pl* **tercentenaries** *or* **tercentennials. 3** an anniversary of 300 years.

tercet (ˈtɜːsɪt, tɜːˈsɛt) *n* a group of three lines of verse that rhyme together or are connected by rhyme with adjacent groups of three lines. [C16: from F, from It. *terzetto*, dim. of *terzo* third, from L *tertius*]

terebene (ˈtɛrəˌbiːn) *n* a mixture of hydrocarbons prepared from oil of turpentine and sulphuric acid, used to make paints and varnishes and medicinally as an expectorant and antiseptic. [C19: from TEREB(INTH) + -ENE]

terebinth (ˈtɛrɪbɪnθ) *n* a small Mediterranean tree that yields a turpentine. [C14: from L *terebinthus*, from Gk *terebinthos* turpentine tree]

terebinthine (ˌtɛrɪˈbɪnθaɪn) *adj* **1** of or relating to terebinth or related plants. **2** of, consisting of, or resembling turpentine.

teredo (tɛˈriːdəʊ) *n, pl* **teredos** *or* **teredines** (-dɪˌniːz). any of a genus of marine bivalve molluscs. See **shipworm.** [C17: via L from Gk *terēdōn* wood-boring worm]

terete (ˈtɛriːt) *adj* (esp. of plant parts) cylindrical and tapering. [C17: from L *teres* smooth, from *terere* to rub]

tergiversate (ˈtɜːdʒɪvəˌseɪt) *vb* **tergiversates, tergiversating, tergiversated.** (*intr*) **1** to change sides or loyalties. **2** to be evasive or ambiguous. [C17: from L *tergiversārī* to turn one's back, from *tergum* back + *vertere* to turn]
▸ˌ**tergiverˈsation** *n* ▸ˈ**tergiverˌsator** *n*

tergum (ˈtɜːgəm) *n, pl* **terga** (-gə). a cuticular plate covering the dorsal surface of a body segment of an arthropod. [C19: from L: the back]
▸ˈ**tergal** *adj*

term ➊ (tɜːm) *n* **1** a name, expression, or word used for some particular thing, esp. in a specialized field of knowledge: *a medical term.* **2** any

THESAURUS

tension *n* **1** = **tightness**, pressure, rigidity, stiffness, straining, stress, stretching, tautness **2, 3** = **strain**, anxiety, apprehension, edginess, hostility, ill feeling, nervousness, pressure, restlessness, stress, suspense, the jitters (*inf.*), unease
Antonyms *n* ≠ **strain:** calmness, peacefulness, relaxation, restfulness, serenity, tranquillity

tentative *adj* **1** = **unconfirmed**, conjectural, experimental, indefinite, provisional, speculative, unsettled **2** = **hesitant**, backward, cautious, diffident, doubtful, faltering, timid, uncertain, undecided, unsure
Antonyms *adj* ≠ **unconfirmed:** conclusive, confirmed, decisive, definite, final, fixed, resolved, settled ≠ **hesitant:** assured, bold, certain, confident, unhesitating

tenuous *adj* **1** = **slight**, doubtful, dubious, flimsy, insignificant, insubstantial, nebulous, questionable, shaky, sketchy, weak **2** = **fine**, attenuated, delicate, gossamer, slim
Antonyms *adj* ≠ **slight:** significant, solid, sound, strong, substantial

tenure *n* **1, 2** = **holding**, incumbency, occupancy, occupation, possession, proprietorship, residence, tenancy, term, time

tepid *adj* **1** = **lukewarm**, slightly warm, warmish **2** = **half-hearted**, apathetic, cool, half-arsed (*Brit. sl.*), half-assed (*US & Canad. sl.*), indifferent, lukewarm, unenthusiastic
Antonyms *adj* ≠ **half-hearted:** animated, eager, enthusiastic, excited, keen, passionate, vibrant, zealous

term *n* **1, 2** = **word**, appellation, denomination, designation, expression, locution, name, phrase, title **3** = **period**, duration, interval, season, space, span, spell, time, while **4** = **session**, course **5** = **end**, bound, boundary, close, conclusion, confine, culmination, finish, fruition, limit, terminus ◆ *vb* **11** = **call**, denominate, designate, dub, entitle, label, name, style

word or expression. **3** a limited period of time: *a prison term.* **4** any of the divisions of the academic year during which a school, college, etc., is in session. **5** a point in time determined for an event or for the end of a period. **6** the period at which childbirth is imminent. **7** *Law.* **7a** an estate or interest in land limited to run for a specified period. **7b** the duration of an estate, etc. **7c** (formerly) a period of time during which sessions of courts of law are held. **7d** time allowed to a debtor to settle. **8** *Maths.* any distinct quantity making up a fraction or proportion, or contained in a polynominal, sequence, series, etc. **9** *Logic.* **9a** the word or phrase that forms either the subject or predicate of a proposition. **9b** a name or variable, as opposed to a predicate. **9c** any of the three subjects or predicates occurring in a syllogism. **10** *Archit.* a sculptured post, esp. one in the form of an armless bust or an animal on the top of a square pillar. ◆ *vb* **11** (*tr*) to designate; call: *he was termed a thief.* ◆ See also **terms.** [C13: from OF *terme,* from L *terminus* end]
▸**'termly** *adj, adv*

termagant ('tɜːməgənt) *n* a shrewish woman; scold. [C13: from earlier *Tervagaunt,* from OF *Tervagan,* from It. *Trivigante;* after an arrogant character in medieval mystery plays who was supposed to be a Muslim deity]

-termer *n* (*in combination*) a person serving a specified length of time in prison: *a short-termer.*

terminable ('tɜːmɪnəbᵊl) *adj* **1** able to be terminated. **2** terminating after a specific period or event.
▸**,termina'bility** *or* **'terminableness** *n* ▸**'terminably** *adv*

terminal ❶ ('tɜːmɪnᵊl) *adj* **1** of, being, or situated at an end, terminus, or boundary. **2** of or occurring after or in a term: *terminal examinations.* **3** (of a disease) terminating in death. **4** *Inf.* extreme: *terminal boredom.* **5** of or relating to the storage or delivery of freight at a warehouse. ◆ *n* **6** a terminating point, part, or place. **7a** a point at which current enters or leaves an electrical device, such as a battery or a circuit. **7b** a conductor by which current enters or leaves at such a point. **8** *Computing.* a device having input/output links with a computer. **9** *Archit.* **9a** an ornamental carving at the end of a structure. **9b** another name for **term** (sense 10). **10a** a point or station at the end of the line of a railway or at an airport, serving as an important access point for passengers or freight. **10b** a less common name for **terminus** (sense 2). **11** a reception and departure building at the terminus of a bus, sea, or air transport route. **12** a site where raw material is unloaded and processed, esp. an onshore installation designed to receive offshore oil or gas. [C15: from L *terminālis,* from *terminus* end]
▸**'terminally** *adv*

terminal market *n* a commodity market in a trading centre rather than at a producing centre.

terminal velocity *n* **1** the constant maximum velocity reached by a body falling under gravity through a fluid, esp. the atmosphere. **2** the velocity of a missile or projectile when it reaches its target. **3** the maximum velocity attained by a rocket, missile, or shell flying in a parabolic flight path. **4** the maximum velocity that an aircraft can attain.

terminate ❶ ('tɜːmɪ,neɪt) *vb* **terminates, terminating, terminated.** (when *intr,* often foll. by *in* or *with*) to form, be, or put an end (to); conclude. [C16: from L *terminātus* limited, from *termināre* to set boundaries, from *terminus* end]
▸**'terminative** *adj* ▸**'termi,nator** *n*

termination ❶ (,tɜːmɪ'neɪʃən) *n* **1** the act of terminating or the state of being terminated. **2** something that terminates. **3** a final result.

terminology ❶ (,tɜːmɪ'nɒlədʒɪ) *n, pl* **terminologies. 1** the body of specialized words relating to a particular subject. **2** the study of terms. [C19: from Med. L *terminus* term from L: end]
▸**terminological** (,tɜːmɪnə'lɒdʒɪkᵊl) *adj* ▸**,termi'nologist** *n*

term insurance *n* life assurance, usually low in cost and offering no cash value, that provides for the payment of a specified sum of money only if the insured dies within a stipulated time.

terminus ❶ ('tɜːmɪnəs) *n, pl* **termini** (-naɪ) *or* **terminuses. 1** the last or final part or point. **2** either end of a railway, bus route, etc., or a station or town at such a point. **3** a goal aimed for. **4** a boundary or boundary marker. **5** *Archit.* another name for **term** (sense 10). [C16: from L: end]

terminus ad quem *Latin.* ('tɜːmɪ,nʊs æd 'kwem) *n* the aim or terminal point. [lit.: the end to which]

terminus a quo *Latin.* ('tɜːmɪ,nʊs ɑː 'kwəʊ) *n* the starting point; beginning. [lit.: the end from which]

termitarium (,tɜːmɪ'teərɪəm) *n, pl* **termitaria** (-ɪə). the nest of a termite colony. [C20: from TERMITE + -ARIUM]

termite ('tɜːmaɪt) *n* any of an order of whitish antlike social insects of warm and tropical regions. Some species feed on wood, causing damage to buildings, trees, etc. [C18: from NL *termitēs* white ants, pl of *termes,* from L: a woodworm]
▸**termitic** (tɜː'mɪtɪk) *adj*

termless ('tɜːmlɪs) *adj* **1** without limit or boundary. **2** unconditional. **3** an archaic word for **indescribable.**

termor *or* **termer** ('tɜːmə) *n Property law.* a person who holds an estate for a term of years or until he dies.

terms ❶ (tɜːmz) *pl n* **1** (usually specified prenominally) the actual language or mode of presentation used: *he described the project in loose terms.* **2** conditions of an agreement. **3** a sum of money paid for a service. **4** (usually preceded by *on*) mutual relationship or standing: *they are on affectionate terms.* **5 bring to terms.** to cause to agree or submit. **6 come to terms.** to reach acceptance or agreement. **7 in terms of.** as expressed by; regarding: *in terms of money he was no better off.*

terms of trade *pl n Economics, Brit.* the ratio of export prices to import prices.

tern (tɜːn) *n* any of several aquatic birds related to the gulls, having a forked tail, long narrow wings, and a typically black-and-white plumage. [C18: from ON *therna*]

ternary ('tɜːnərɪ) *adj* **1** consisting of three or groups of three. **2** *Maths.* (of a number system) to the base three. [C14: from L *ternārius,* from *ternī* three each]

ternary form *n* a musical structure consisting of two contrasting sections followed by a repetition of the first; the form *aba.*

ternate ('tɜːnɪt, -neɪt) *adj* **1** (esp. of a leaf) consisting of three leaflets or other parts. **2** (esp. of plants) having groups of three members. [C18: from NL *ternātus,* from Med. L *ternāre* to increase threefold]
▸**'ternately** *adv*

terne (tɜːn) *n* **1** an alloy of lead containing tin and antimony. **2** Also called: **terne plate.** steel plate coated with this alloy. [C16: ?from F *terne* dull, from OF *ternir* to TARNISH]

terotechnology (,tɪərəʊtɛk'nɒlədʒɪ, tɛr-) *n* a branch of technology that utilizes management, financial, and engineering expertise in the installation, efficient operation, and maintenance of equipment and machinery. [C20: from Gk *tērein* to care for + TECHNOLOGY]

terpene ('tɜːpiːn) *n* any one of a class of unsaturated hydrocarbons, such as pinene and the carotenes, that are found in the essential oils of many plants, esp. conifers. [C19: *terp-* from obs. *terpentine* turpentine + -ENE]

terpineol (tɜː'pɪnɪ,ɒl) *n* a terpene alcohol with an odour of lilac, existing in three isomeric forms that occur in several essential oils. [C20: from TERPENE + -INE² + -OL¹]

Terpsichore (tɜːp'sɪkərɪ) *n* the Muse of the dance and of choral song. [C18: via L from Gk, from *terpsikhoros* delighting in the dance, from *terpein* to delight + *khoros* dance]

Terpsichorean (,tɜːpsɪkə'rɪən, -'kɔːrɪən) *Often used facetiously.* ◆ *adj also* **Terpsichoreal. 1** of or relating to dancing. ◆ *n* **2** a dancer.

terra ('tɛrə) *n* (in legal contexts) earth or land. [from L]

terra alba ('ælbə) *n* **1** a white finely powdered form of gypsum, used to make paints, paper, etc. **2** any of various other white earthy substances, such as kaolin, pipeclay, and magnesia. [from L, lit.: white earth]

terrace ('tɛrəs) *n* **1** a horizontal flat area of ground, often one of a series in a slope. **2a** a row of houses, usually identical and having common dividing walls, or the street onto which they face. **2b** (*cap. when part of a street name*): *Grosvenor Terrace.* **3** a paved area alongside a building, serving partly as a garden. **4** a balcony or patio. **5** the flat roof of a house built in a Spanish or Oriental style. **6** a flat area bounded by a short steep slope formed by the down-cutting of a river or by erosion. **7** (*usually pl*) unroofed tiers around a football pitch on which the spectators stand. ◆ *vb* **terraces, terracing, terraced. 8** (*tr*) to make into or provide with a terrace or terraces. [C16: from OF *terrasse,* from OProvençal *terrassa* pile of earth, from *terra* earth, from L]

terraced house *n Brit.* a house that is part of a terrace. US and Canad. name: **row house.**

terracing ('tɛrəsɪŋ) *n* **1** a series of terraces, esp. one dividing a slope into a steplike system of flat narrow fields. **2** the act of making a terrace or terraces. **3** another name for **terrace** (sense 7).

terra cotta ('kɒtə) *n* **1** a hard unglazed brownish-red earthenware, or the clay from which it is made. **2** something made of terra cotta, such as a sculpture. **3** a strong reddish-brown to brownish-orange colour. [C18: from It., lit.: baked earth]
▸**'terra-'cotta** *adj*

terra firma ('fɜːmə) *n* the solid earth; firm ground. [C17: from L]

THESAURUS

terminal *adj* **1** = **final**, bounding, concluding, extreme, last, limiting, ultimate, utmost **3** = **fatal**, deadly, incurable, killing, lethal, mortal ◆ *n* **6** = **end**, boundary, extremity, limit, termination, terminus **10** = **terminus**, depot, end of the line, station
Antonyms *adj* ≠ **final:** beginning, commencing, first, initial, introductory, opening

terminate *vb* = **end**, abort, axe (*inf.*), belay, bring *or* come to an end, cease, close, complete, conclude, cut off, discontinue, expire, finish, issue, lapse, pull the plug on (*inf.*), put an end to, result, run out, stop, wind up
Antonyms *vb* begin, commence, inaugurate, initiate, instigate, introduce, open, start

termination *n* **1-3** = **ending**, abortion, cessation, close, completion, conclusion, consequence, cut-off point, discontinuation, effect, end, expiry, finale, finis, finish, issue, result, wind-up
Antonyms *n* beginning, commencement, inauguration, initiation, opening, start

terminology *n* **1** = **language**, argot, cant, jargon, lingo (*inf.*), nomenclature, patois, phraseology, terms, vocabulary

terminus *n* **1, 3, 4** = **end**, boundary, close, extremity, final point, goal, limit, target, termination **2** = **end of the line**, depot, garage, last stop, station

terms *pl n* **1** = **language**, manner of speaking, phraseology, terminology **2** = **conditions**, particulars, premises (*Law*), provisions, provisos, qualifications, specifications, stipulations **3** = **price**, charges, fee, payment, rates **4** = **relationship**, footing, position, relations, standing, status **6 come to terms** = **learn to live with**, be reconciled, come to accept, come to an understanding, conclude agreement, reach acceptance, reach agreement

terrain Ⓣ (tə'reɪn) *n* a piece of ground, esp. with reference to its physical character or military potential: *a rocky terrain.* [C18: from F, ult. from L *terrēnum* ground, from *terra* earth]

terra incognita *Latin.* ('tɛrə ɪn'kɒgnɪtə) *n* an unexplored or unknown land, region, or area.

Terramycin (ˌtɛrə'maɪsɪn) *n Trademark.* a broad-spectrum antibiotic used in treating various infections.

terrapin ('tɛrəpɪn) *n* any of various web-footed reptiles that live on land and in fresh water and feed on small aquatic animals. Also called: **water tortoise.** [C17: of Amerind origin]

terrarium (tɛ'rɛərɪəm) *n, pl* **terrariums** *or* **terraria** (-'rɛərɪə). **1** an enclosure for small land animals. **2** a glass container, often a globe, in which plants are grown. [C19: NL, from L *terra* earth]

terra sigillata (ˌsɪdʒɪ'lɑːtə) *n* **1** a reddish-brown clayey earth found on the Aegean island of Lemnos: formerly used as an astringent and in the making of earthenware pottery. **2** any similar earth resembling this. **3** earthenware pottery made from this or a similar earth, esp. Samian ware. [from L: sealed earth]

terrazzo (tɛ'rætsəʊ) *n, pl* **terrazzos.** a floor made by setting marble chips into a layer of mortar and polishing the surface. [C20: from It.: TERRACE]

terrene (tɛ'riːn) *adj* **1** of the earth; worldly; mundane. **2** *Rare.* of earth; earthy. ◆ *n* **3** a land. **4** a rare word for **earth.** [C14: from Anglo-Norman, from L *terrēnus,* from *terra* earth]

terreplein ('tɛəˌpleɪn) *n* the top of a rampart where guns are placed behind the parapet. [C16: from F, from Med. L *terrā plēnus* filled with earth]

terrestrial Ⓣ (tə'rɛstrɪəl) *adj* **1** of the earth. **2** of the land as opposed to the sea or air. **3** (of animals and plants) living or growing on the land. **4** earthly, worldly, or mundane. **5** *Television.* denoting or using signals sent over the earth's surface from a transmitter on land, rather than by satellite. ◆ *n* **6** an inhabitant of the earth. [C15: from L *terrestris,* from *terra* earth]
▸**ter'restrially** *adv* ▸**ter'restrialness** *n*

terrestrial telescope *n* a telescope for use on earth rather than for making astronomical observations. Such telescopes contain an additional lens or prism system to produce an erect image.

terret ('tɛrɪt) *n* **1** either of the two rings on a harness through which the reins are passed. **2** the ring on a dog's collar for attaching the lead. [C15: var. of *toret,* from OF, dim. of *tor* loop]

terre-verte ('tɛəˌvɜːt) *n* **1** a greyish-green pigment used in paints. It is made from a mineral found in greensand and similar rocks. ◆ *adj* **2** of a greyish-green colour. [C17: from F, lit.: green earth]

terrible Ⓣ ('tɛrəbᵊl) *adj* **1** very serious or extreme. **2** *Inf.* of poor quality; unpleasant or bad. **3** causing terror. **4** causing awe. [C15: from L *terribilis,* from *terrēre* to terrify]
▸**'terribleness** *n* ▸**'terribly** *adv*

terricolous (tɛ'rɪkələs) *adj* living on or in the soil. [C19: from L *terricola,* from *terra* earth + *colere* to inhabit]

terrier[1] ('tɛrɪə) *n* any of several usually small, active, and short-bodied breeds of dog, originally trained to hunt animals living underground. [C15: from OF *chien terrier* earth dog, from Med. L *terrārius* belonging to the earth, from L *terra* earth]

terrier[2] ('tɛrɪə) *n English legal history.* a register or survey of land. [C15: from OF, from Med. L *terrārius* of the land, from L *terra* land]

terrific Ⓣ (tə'rɪfɪk) *adj* **1** very great or intense. **2** *Inf.* very good; excellent. **3** very frightening. [C17: from L *terrificus,* from *terrēre* to frighten]
▸**ter'rifically** *adv*

terrify Ⓣ ('tɛrɪˌfaɪ) *vb* **terrifies, terrifying, terrified.** (*tr*) to inspire fear or dread in; frighten greatly. [C16: from L *terrificāre,* from *terrēre* to alarm + *facere* to cause]
▸**'terriˌfying** *adj* ▸**'terriˌfyingly** *adv*

terrigenous (tɛ'rɪdʒɪnəs) *adj* **1** of or produced by the earth. **2** (of geological deposits) formed in the sea from material derived from the land by erosion. [C17: from L *terrigenus,* from *terra* earth + *gignere* to beget]

terrine (tɛ'riːn) *n* **1** an oval earthenware cooking dish with a tightly fitting lid used for pâtés, etc. **2** the food cooked or served in such a dish, esp. pâté. [C18: earlier form of TUREEN]

territorial (ˌtɛrɪ'tɔːrɪəl) *adj* **1** of or relating to a territory or territories. **2** restricted to or owned by a particular territory. **3** local or regional. **4** *Zool.* establishing and defending a territory. **5** pertaining to a territorial army, providing a reserve of trained men for use in emergency.
▸ˌ**terriˌtori'ality** *n* ▸ˌ**terri'torially** *adv*

Territorial (ˌtɛrɪ'tɔːrɪəl) *n* a member of a Territorial Army.

Territorial Army *n* (in Britain) a standing reserve army originally organized between 1907 and 1908. Full name: **Territorial and Volunteer Reserve.**

Territorial Council *n* (in Canada) an elected body responsible for local government in the Northwest Territories or the Yukon.

territorial waters *pl n* the waters over which a nation exercises jurisdiction and control.

territory Ⓣ ('tɛrɪtərɪ) *n, pl* **territories.** **1** any tract of land; district. **2** the geographical domain under the jurisdiction of a political unit, esp. of a sovereign state. **3** the district for which an agent, etc., is responsible. **4** an area inhabited and defended by an animal or a pair of animals. **5** an area of knowledge. **6** (in football, hockey, etc.) the area defended by a team. **7** (*often cap.*) a region of a country, esp. of a federal state, that enjoys less autonomy and a lower status than most constituent parts of the state. **8** (*often cap.*) a protectorate or other dependency of a country. [C15: from L *territōrium* land surrounding a town, from *terra* land]

terror Ⓣ ('tɛrə) *n* **1** great fear, panic, or dread. **2** a person or thing that inspires great dread. **3** *Inf.* a troublesome person or thing, esp. a child. **4** terrorism. [C14: from OF *terreur,* from L *terror,* from *terrēre* to frighten]
▸**'terrorful** *adj* ▸**'terrorless** *adj*

terrorism ('tɛrəˌrɪzəm) *n* **1** the systematic use of violence and intimidation to achieve some goal. **2** the act of terrorizing. **3** the state of being terrorized.
▸**'terrorist** *n, adj*

terrorize Ⓣ *or* **terrorise** ('tɛrəˌraɪz) *vb* **terrorizes, terrorizing, terrorized** *or* **terrorises, terrorising, terrorised.** (*tr*) **1** to coerce or control by violence, fear, threats, etc. **2** to inspire with dread; terrify.
▸ˌ**terrori'zation** *or* ˌ**terrori'sation** *n* ▸**'terrorˌizer** *or* **'terrorˌiser** *n*

terror-stricken *or* **terror-struck** *adj* in a state of terror.

terry ('tɛrɪ) *n, pl* **terries.** **1** an uncut loop in the pile of towelling or a similar fabric. **2** a fabric with such a pile. [C18: ? var. of TERRET]

terse Ⓣ (tɜːs) *adj* **1** neatly brief and concise. **2** curt; abrupt. [C17: from L *tersus* precise, from *tergēre* to polish]
▸**'tersely** *adv* ▸**'terseness** *n*

tertial ('tɜːʃəl) *adj, n* another word for **tertiary** (senses 5, 6). [C19: from L *tertius* third, from *ter* thrice, from *trēs* three]

tertian ('tɜːʃən) *adj* **1** (of a fever) occurring every other day. ◆ *n* **2** a tertian fever. [C14: from L *febris tertiāna* fever occurring every third day, from *tertius* third]

tertiary ('tɜːʃərɪ) *adj* **1** third in degree, order, etc. **2** (of an industry) involving services as opposed to extraction or manufacture, such as transport, finance, etc. **3** *RC Church.* of or relating to a Third Order. **4** *Chem.* **4a** (of an organic compound) having a functional group attached to a carbon atom that is attached to three other groups. **4b** (of an amine) having three organic groups attached to a nitrogen atom. **4c** (of a salt) derived from a tribasic acid by replacement of all its acidic hydrogen atoms with metal atoms or electropositive groups. **5** *Ornithol., rare.* of or designating any of the small flight feathers at-

THESAURUS

terrain *n* = **ground,** country, going, land, landscape, topography

terrestrial *adj* **1, 4** = **earthly,** global, mundane, sublunary, tellurian, terrene, worldly ◆ *n* **6** = **earthling,** earthman, earthwoman, human

terrible *adj* **1** = **serious,** bad, dangerous, desperate, extreme, severe **2** *Informal* = **bad,** abhorrent, abysmal, awful, beastly (*inf.*), dire, dreadful, duff (*Brit. inf.*), foul, frightful, from hell (*inf.*), hateful, hideous, loathsome, obnoxious, obscene, odious, offensive, poor, repulsive, revolting, rotten (*inf.*), shitty (*taboo sl.*), unpleasant, vile **3** = **fearful,** appalling, awful, dread, dreaded, dreadful, frightful, gruesome, harrowing, hellacious (*US sl.*), horrendous, horrible, horrid, horrifying, monstrous, shocking, terrifying, unspeakable
Antonyms *adj* ≠ **serious:** harmless, insignificant, mild, moderate, paltry, small ≠ **bad:** admirable, brilliant, delightful, excellent, fine, great, magic, noteworthy, pleasant, remarkable, super, superb, terrific, very good, wonderful ≠ **fearful:** calming, comforting, encouraging, reassuring, settling, soothing

terribly *adv* **1** = **extremely,** awfully (*inf.*), decidedly, desperately, exceedingly, gravely, greatly, much, seriously, thoroughly, very

terrific *adj* **1** = **great,** awesome, awful, dreadful, enormous, excessive, extreme, fearful, fierce, gigantic, harsh, horrific, huge, intense, monstrous, severe, terrible, tremendous **2** *Informal* = **excellent,** ace (*inf.*), amazing, awesome (*sl.*), breathtaking, brill (*inf.*), brilliant, cracking, fabulous (*inf.*), fantastic (*inf.*), fine, great (*inf.*), jim-dandy (*sl.*), magnificent, marvellous, outstanding, sensational (*inf.*), smashing (*inf.*), stupendous, super (*inf.*), superb, very good, wonderful
Antonyms *adj* ≠ **great:** insignificant, mild, moderate, paltry ≠ **excellent:** appalling, awful, bad, dreadful, terrible

terrified *adj* = **frightened,** alarmed, appalled, awed, dismayed, frightened out of one's wits, horrified, horror-struck, intimidated, panic-stricken, petrified, scared, scared shitless (*taboo sl.*), scared stiff, scared to death, shit-scared (*taboo sl.*), shocked, terror-stricken

terrify *vb* = **frighten,** alarm, appal, awe, dismay, fill with terror, frighten out of one's wits, horrify, intimidate, make one's blood run cold, make one's flesh creep, make one's hair stand on end, petrify, put the fear of God into, scare, scare to death, shock, terrorize

territory *n* **1-3** = **district,** area, bailiwick, country, domain, land, patch, province, region, sector, state, terrain, tract, turf (*US sl.*), zone

terror *n* **1** = **fear,** alarm, anxiety, awe, consternation, dismay, dread, fear and trembling, fright, horror, intimidation, panic, shock **2** = **scourge,** bogeyman, bugbear, devil, fiend, monster

terrorize *vb* **1** = **oppress,** browbeat, bully, coerce, intimidate, menace, strong-arm (*inf.*), threaten **2** = **terrify,** alarm, appal, awe, dismay, fill with terror, frighten, frighten out of one's wits, horrify, inspire panic in, intimidate, make one's blood run cold, make one's flesh creep, make one's hair stand on end, petrify, put the fear of God into, scare, scare to death, shock, strike terror into

terse *adj* **1** = **concise,** aphoristic, brief, clipped, compact, condensed, crisp, elliptical, epigrammatic, gnomic, incisive, laconic, monosyllabic, neat, pithy, sententious, short, succinct, summary, to the point **2** = **curt,** abrupt, brusque, short, snappy
Antonyms *adj* ≠ **concise:** circumlocutory, confused, discursive, lengthy, long-winded, rambling, roundabout, vague, verbose, wordy ≠ **curt:** chatty, polite

tached to the part of the humerus nearest to the body. ◆ *n, pl* **tertiaries. 6** *Ornithol., rare.* any of the tertiary feathers. **7** *RC Church.* a member of a Third Order. [C16: from L *tertiārius* containing one third, from *tertius* third]

Tertiary ('tɜːʃərɪ) *adj* **1** of, denoting, or formed in the first period of the Cenozoic era. ◆ *n* **2 the.** the Tertiary period or rock system.

tertiary college *n Brit.* a college system incorporating the secondary school sixth form and vocational courses.

tertiary colour *n* a colour formed by mixing two secondary colours.

tertium quid ('tɜːtɪəm) *n* an unknown or indefinite thing related in some way to two known or definite things, but distinct from both. [C18: from LL, rendering Gk *triton ti* some third thing]

tervalent (tɜː'veɪlənt) *adj Chem.* another word for **trivalent.**
▸**ter'valency** *n*

Terylene ('terɪˌliːn) *n Trademark.* a synthetic polyester fibre or fabric. US name (trademark): **Dacron.**

terza rima ('teətsə 'riːmə) *n, pl* **terze rime** ('teətseɪ 'riːmeɪ). a verse form consisting of a series of tercets in which the middle line of one tercet rhymes with the first and third lines of the next. [C19: from It., lit.: third rhyme]

TESL ('tesᵊl) *acronym for* Teaching (of) English as a Second Language.

tesla ('teslə) *n* the derived SI unit of magnetic flux density equal to a flux of 1 weber in an area of 1 square metre. Symbol: T [C20: after Nikola *Tesla* (1857–1943), US electrical engineer & inventor]

tesla coil *n* a step-up transformer with an air core, used for producing high voltages at high frequencies.

Tessa ('tesə) *n* (in Britain) *acronym for* Tax Exempt Special Savings Account; a savings scheme introduced in 1991 enabling interest on up to £1800 p.a. to be paid tax free if the capital remains intact for five years.

tessellate ('tesɪˌleɪt) *vb* **tessellates, tessellating, tessellated. 1** *(tr)* to construct, pave, or inlay with a mosaic of small tiles. **2** *(intr)* (of identical shapes) to fit together exactly. [C18: from L *tessellātus* checked, from *tessella* small stone cube, from TESSERA]

tessera ('tesərə) *n, pl* **tesserae** (-səˌriː). **1** a small square tile of stone, glass, etc., used in mosaics. **2** a die, tally, etc., used in classical times, made of bone or wood. [C17: from L, from Ionic Gk *tesseres* four]
▸**'tesseral** *adj*

tessitura (ˌtesɪ'tʊərə) *n Music.* the general pitch level of a piece of vocal music. [It.: texture, from L *textura;* see TEXTURE]

test[1] ● (test) *vb* **1** to ascertain (the worth, capability, or endurance) of (a person or thing) by subjection to certain examinations, etc.; try. **2** (often foll. by *for*) to carry out an examination on (a substance, material, or system) to indicate the presence of a substance or the possession of a property: *to test food for arsenic.* **3** *(tr)* to put under severe strain: *the long delay tested my patience.* **4** *(intr)* to achieve a specified result in a test: *he tested positive for the AIDS virus.* ◆ *n* **5** a method, practice, or examination designed to test a person or thing. **6** a series of questions or problems designed to test a specific skill or knowledge. **7** a standard of judgment; criterion. **8a** a chemical reaction or physical procedure for testing a substance, material, etc. **8b** a chemical reagent used in such a procedure. **8c** the result of the procedure or the evidence gained from it. **9** *Sport.* See **test match. 10** *Arch.* a declaration of truth, loyalty, etc. **11** *(modifier)* performed as a test: *test drive.* [C14 (in the sense: vessel used in treating metals): from L *testum* earthen vessel]
▸**'testable** *adj* ▸**'testing** *adj*

test[2] (test) *n* the hard outer covering of certain invertebrates and tunicates. [C19: from L *testa* shell]

testa ('testə) *n, pl* **testae** (-tiː). the hard outer layer of a seed. [C18: from L: shell]

testaceous (te'steɪʃəs) *adj Biol.* **1** of or possessing a test or testa. **2** of the reddish-brown colour of terra cotta. [C17: from L *testācens,* from TESTA]

testament ● ('testəmənt) *n* **1** *Law.* a will (esp. in **last will and testament**). **2** a proof, attestation, or tribute. **3a** a covenant instituted between God and man. **3b** a copy of either the Old or the New Testament, or of the complete Bible. [C14: from L *testamentum* a will, from *testārī* to bear witness, from *testis* a witness]
▸ˌ**testa'mental** *adj* ▸ˌ**testa'mentary** *adj*

Testament ('testəmənt) *n* **1** either of the two main parts of the Bible; the Old Testament or the New Testament. **2** the New Testament as distinct from the Old.

testate ('testeɪt, 'testɪt) *adj* **1** having left a legally valid will at death. ◆ *n* **2** a person who dies testate. [C15: from L *testārī* to make a will; see TESTAMENT]
▸**testacy** ('testəsɪ) *n*

testator (te'steɪtə) *or (fem)* **testatrix** (te'steɪtrɪks) *n* a person who makes a will, esp. one who dies testate. [C15: from Anglo-F *testatour,* from LL *testātor,* from L *testārī* to make a will]

test ban *n* an agreement among nations to forgo tests of nuclear weapons.

test-bed *n Engineering.* an area used for testing machinery, etc., under working conditions.

test card *or* **pattern** *n* a complex pattern used to test the characteristics of a television transmission system.

test case *n* a legal action that serves as a precedent in deciding similar succeeding cases.

test-drive *vb* **test-drives, test-driving, test-drove, test-driven.** *(tr)* to drive (a car or other motor vehicle) for a limited period in order to assess it.

tester[1] ('testə) *n* a person or thing that tests.

tester[2] ('testə) *n* a canopy over a bed. [C14: from Med. L *testerium,* from LL *testa* a skull, from L: shell]

testes ('testiːz) *n* the plural of **testis.**

testicle ('testɪkᵊl) *n* either of the two male reproductive glands, in most mammals enclosed within the scrotum, that produce spermatozoa. [C15: from L *testiculus,* dim. of *testis*]
▸**testicular** (te'stɪkjʊlə) *adj*

testiculate (te'stɪkjʊlɪt) *adj Bot.* having an oval shape: *the testiculate tubers of certain orchids.* [C18: from LL *testiculātus;* see TESTICLE]

testify ● ('testɪˌfaɪ) *vb* **testifies, testifying, testified. 1** (when *tr, may take a clause as object*) to state (something) formally as a declaration of fact. **2** *Law.* to declare or give (evidence) under oath, esp. in court. **3** (when *intr,* often foll. by *to*) to be evidence (of); serve as witness (to). **4** *(tr)* to declare or acknowledge openly. [C14: from L *testificārī,* from *testis* witness]
▸ˌ**testifi'cation** *n* ▸**'testiˌfier** *n*

testimonial ● (ˌtestɪ'məʊnɪəl) *n* **1a** a recommendation of the character, ability, etc., of a person or of the quality of a product or service. **1b** *(as modifier)*: *testimonial advertising.* **2** a formal statement of truth or fact. **3** a tribute given for services or achievements. **4** a sports match to raise money for a particular player. ◆ *adj* **5** of or relating to a testimony or testimonial.

> **USAGE NOTE** *Testimonial* is sometimes wrongly used where *testimony* is meant: *his re-election is a testimony* (not *a testimonial*) *to his popularity with his constituents.*

testimony ● ('testɪmənɪ) *n, pl* **testimonies. 1** a declaration of truth or fact. **2** *Law.* evidence given by a witness, esp. in court under oath. **3** evidence testifying to something: *her success was a testimony to her good luck.* **4** *Old Testament.* the Ten Commandments. [C15: from L *testimōnium,* from *testis* witness]

testis ('testɪs) *n, pl* **testes.** another word for **testicle.** [C17: from L, lit.: witness (to masculinity)]

test match *n* (in various sports, esp. cricket) an international match, esp. one of a series.

testosterone (te'stostəˌrəʊn) *n* a potent steroid hormone secreted mainly by the testes. [C20: from TESTIS + STEROL + -ONE]

test paper *n* **1** *Chem.* paper impregnated with an indicator for use in chemical tests. **2a** the question sheet of a test. **2b** the paper completed by a test candidate.

test pilot *n* a pilot who flies aircraft of new design to test their performance in the air.

test tube *n* **1** a cylindrical round-bottomed glass tube open at one end: used in scientific experiments. **2** *(modifier)* made synthetically in, or as if in, a test tube: *a test-tube product.*

test-tube baby *n* **1** a fetus that has developed from an ovum fertilized in an artificial womb. **2** a baby conceived by artificial insemination.

testudinal (te'stjuːdɪnᵊl) *adj* of or resembling a tortoise. [C19: from L TESTUDO]

testudo (te'stjuːdəʊ) *n, pl* **testudines** (-dɪˌniːz). a form of shelter used by the ancient Roman Army as protection against attack from above, consisting of a mobile arched structure or of overlapping shields held by the soldiers over their heads. [C17: from L: a tortoise, from *testa* a shell]

testy ('testɪ) *adj* **testier, testiest.** irritable or touchy. [C14: from Anglo-Norman *testif* headstrong, from OF *teste* head, from LL *testa* skull, from L: shell]
▸**'testily** *adv* ▸**'testiness** *n*

tetanus ('tetənəs) *n* **1** Also called: **lockjaw.** an acute infectious disease in which sustained muscular spasm, contraction, and convulsion are caused by the release of toxins from a bacterium. **2** *Physiol.* any tense contraction of a muscle. [C16: via L from Gk *tetanos,* ult. from *teinein* to stretch]
▸**'tetanal** *adj* ▸**'tetaˌnoid** *adj*

THESAURUS

test *vb* **1 = check,** analyse, assay, assess, examine, experiment, investigate, prove, put through their paces, put to the proof, put to the test, research, try, try out, verify, work over ◆ *n* **5 = examination,** acid test, analysis, assessment, attempt, catechism, check, evaluation, investigation, ordeal, probation, proof, research, trial

testament *n* **1 = will,** last wishes **2 = proof,** attestation, demonstration, earnest, evidence, exemplification, testimony, tribute, witness

testify *vb* **1 = bear witness,** affirm, assert, asseverate, attest, certify, corroborate, declare, depone (*Scots Law*), depose (*Law*), evince, give testimony, show, state, swear, vouch, witness
Antonyms *vb* belie, contradict, controvert, disprove, dispute, gainsay (*arch. or literary*), oppose

testimonial *n* **1a, 3 = tribute,** certificate, character, commendation, credential, endorsement, recommendation, reference

testimony *n* **2 = evidence,** affidavit, affirmation, attestation, avowal, confirmation, corroboration, declaration, deposition, information, profession, statement, submission, witness **3 = proof,** corroboration, demonstration, evidence, indication, manifestation, support, verification

testing *adj* **3 = difficult,** arduous, challenging, demanding, exacting, formidable, rigorous, searching, strenuous, taxing, tough, trying
Antonyms *adj* easy, friendly, gentle, mild, simple, straightforward, undemanding

tetany ('tɛtənɪ) *n* an abnormal increase in the excitability of nerves and muscles caused by a deficiency of parathyroid secretion. [C19: from F; see TETANUS]

tetchy ('tɛtʃɪ) *adj* **tetchier, tetchiest.** being or inclined to be cross, irritable, or touchy. [C16: prob. from obs. *tetch* defect, from OF *tache* spot, of Gmc origin]
▸ **'tetchily** *adv* ▸ **'tetchiness** *n*

tête-à-tête (,teɪtə'teɪt) *n, pl* **tête-à-têtes** *or* **tête-à-tête. 1a** a private conversation between two people. **1b** *(as modifier): a tête-à-tête conversation.* **2** a small sofa for two people, esp. one that is S-shaped in plan so that the sitters are almost face to face. ◆ *adv* **3** intimately; in private. [C17: from F, lit.: head to head]

tête-bêche (tɛt'bɛʃ) *adj Philately.* (of an unseparated pair of stamps) printed so that one is inverted in relation to the other. [C19: from F, from *tête* head + *bêche*, from obs. *béchevet* double-headed (orig. of a bed)]

tether ('tɛðə) *n* **1** a rope, chain, etc., by which an animal is tied to a particular spot. **2** the range of one's endurance, etc. **3 at the end of one's tether.** distressed or exasperated to the limit of one's endurance. ◆ *vb* **4** *(tr)* to tie with or as if with a tether. [C14: from ON *tjothr*]

Tethys ('ti:θɪs, 'tɛθ-) *n* the sea that lay between the two ancient supercontinents, Laurasia and Gondwanaland, and which can be regarded as the predecessor of today's smaller Mediterranean.

tetra- *or before a vowel* **tetr-** *combining form.* four: *tetrameter.* [from Gk]

tetrabasic (,tɛtrə'beɪsɪk) *adj* (of an acid) containing four replaceable hydrogen atoms.
▸ **tetrabasicity** (,tɛtrəbeɪ'sɪsɪtɪ) *n*

tetrachloromethane ('tɛtrəklɔ:rəʊ,mi:θeɪn) *n* the systematic name for **carbon tetrachloride.**

tetrachord ('tɛtrə,kɔ:d) *n Music.* any of several groups of four notes in descending order, in which the first and last notes form a perfect fourth. [C17: from Gk *tetrakhordos* four-stringed]
▸ **,tetra'chordal** *adj*

tetracyclic (,tɛtrə'saɪklɪk) *adj Chem.* containing four rings in its molecular structure.

tetracycline (,tɛtrə'saɪklaɪn, -klɪn) *n* an antibiotic synthesized from chlortetracycline or derived from a bacterium. [C20: from TETRA- + CYCL(IC) + -INE[2]]

tetrad ('tɛtræd) *n* a group or series of four. [C17: from Gk *tetras*, from *tettares* four]

tetraethyl lead (,tɛtrə'i:θaɪl lɛd) *n* a colourless oily insoluble liquid used in petrol to prevent knocking. Systematic name: **lead tetraethyl.**

tetrafluoroethene ('tɛtrə,flʊərəʊ'ɛθi:n) *n Chem.* a dense colourless gas that is polymerized to make polytetrafluorethene (PTFE). Formula: $F_2C{:}CF_2$. Also called: **tetrafluoroethylene.** [C20: from TETRA- + FLUORO- + ETHENE]

tetragon ('tɛtrə,gɒn) *n* a less common name for **quadrilateral** (sense 2). [C17: from Gk *tetragōnon*]

tetragonal (tɛ'trægən[ə]l) *adj* **1** *Crystallog.* relating or belonging to the crystal system characterized by three mutually perpendicular axes of which only two are equal. **2** of or shaped like a quadrilateral.
▸ **te'tragonally** *adv*

Tetragrammaton (,tɛtrə'græmət[ə]n) *n Bible.* the Hebrew name for God consisting of the four consonants Y H V H (or Y H W H). It is usually transliterated as *Jehovah* or *Yahweh*. Sometimes shortened to **Tetragram.** [C14: from Gk, from *tetragrammatos* having four letters]

tetrahedron (,tɛtrə'hi:drən) *n, pl* **tetrahedrons** *or* **tetrahedra** (-drə). a solid figure having four triangular plane faces. A **regular tetrahedron** has faces that are equilateral triangles. [C16: from NL, from LGk *tetraedron*]
▸ **,tetra'hedral** *adj*

tetralogy (tɛ'trælədʒɪ) *n, pl* **tetralogies.** a series of four related works, as in drama or opera. [C17: from Gk *tetralogia*]

tetramerous (tɛ'træmərəs) *adj Biol.* having or consisting of four parts. [C19: from NL *tetramerus*, from Gk *tetramerēs*]

tetrameter (tɛ'træmɪtə) *n Prosody.* **1** a line of verse consisting of four metrical feet. **2** a verse composed of such lines.

tetraplegia (,tɛtrə'pli:dʒɪə) *n* another name for **quadriplegia.**
▸ **,tetra'plegic** *adj*

tetraploid ('tɛtrə,plɔɪd) *Genetics.* ◆ *adj* **1** having four times the haploid number of chromosomes in the nucleus. ◆ *n* **2** a tetraploid organism, nucleus, or cell.

tetrapod ('tɛtrə,pɒd) *n* **1** any vertebrate that has four limbs. **2** a device consisting of four arms radiating from a central point: three arms form a supporting tripod and the fourth is vertical.

tetrapterous (tɛ'træptərəs) *adj* having four wings. [C19: from NL *tetrapterus*, from Gk *tetrapteros*, from TETRA- + *pteron* wing]

tetrarch ('tɛtrɑ:k) *n* **1** the ruler of one fourth of a country. **2** a subordinate ruler. **3** any of four joint rulers. [C14: from Gk *tetrarkhēs*; see TETRA-, -ARCH]
▸ **tetrarchate** (tɛ'trɑ:,keɪt, -kɪt) *n* ▸ **te'trarchic** *adj* ▸ **'tetrarchy** *n*

tetrastich ('tɛtrə,stɪk) *n* a poem, stanza, or strophe that consists of four lines. [C16: via L from Gk *tetrastikhon*, from TETRA- + *stikhos* row]
▸ **tetrastichic** (,tɛtrə'stɪkɪk) *or* **tetrastichal** (tɛ'træstɪk[ə]l) *adj*

tetravalent (,tɛtrə'veɪlənt) *adj Chem.* **1** having a valency of four. **2** Also: **quadrivalent.** having four valencies.
▸ **,tetra'valency** *n*

tetrode ('tɛtrəʊd) *n* an electronic valve having four electrodes.

tetroxide (tɛ'trɒksaɪd) *n* any oxide that contains four oxygen atoms per molecule.

tetryl ('tɛtrɪl) *n* a yellow crystalline explosive solid, trinitrophenylmethylnitramine, used in detonators.

Teucrian ('tju:krɪən) *n, adj* another word for **Trojan.**

Teut. *abbrev. for* Teuton(ic).

Teuton ('tju:tən) *n* **1** a member of an ancient Germanic people from Jutland who migrated to S Gaul in the 2nd century B.C. **2** a member of any people speaking a Germanic language, esp. a German. ◆ *adj* **3** Teutonic. [C18: from L *Teutonī* the Teutons, of Gmc origin]

Teutonic (tju:'tɒnɪk) *adj* **1** characteristic of or relating to the German people. **2** of the ancient Teutons. **3** (not used in linguistics) of or relating to the Germanic languages.

Tex-Mex ('tɛks,mɛks) *adj* of, relating to, or denoting the Texan version of something Mexican, such as music, food, or language.

text (tɛkst) *n* **1** the main body of a printed or written work as distinct from commentary, notes, illustrations, etc. **2** the words of something printed, written, or displayed on a visual display unit. **3** the original exact wording of a work as distinct from a revision or translation. **4** a short passage of the Bible used as a starting point for a sermon. **5** the topic or subject of a discussion or work. **6** short for **textbook. 7** any novel, play, etc., prescribed as part of a course of study. [C14: from Med. L *textus* version, from L *textus* texture, from *texere* to compose]

textbook ('tɛkst,bʊk) *n* a book used as a standard source of information on a particular subject.
▸ **'text,bookish** *adj*

textile ('tɛkstaɪl) *n* **1** any fabric or cloth, esp. woven. **2** raw material suitable to be made into cloth. ◆ *adj* **3** of or relating to fabrics. [C17: from L *textilis* woven, from *texere* to weave]

textual ('tɛkstjʊəl) *adj* **1** of or relating to a text or texts. **2** based on a text.
▸ **'textually** *adv*

textual criticism *n* **1** the scholarly study of manuscripts, esp. of the Bible, in an effort to establish the original text. **2** literary criticism emphasizing a close analysis of the text.

textualism ('tɛkstjʊə,lɪzəm) *n* **1** doctrinaire adherence to a text, esp. of the Bible. **2** textual criticism, esp. of the Bible.
▸ **'textualist** *n, adj*

texture ('tɛkstʃə) *n* **1** the surface of a material, esp. as perceived by the sense of touch. **2** the structure, appearance, and feel of a woven fabric. **3** the general structure and disposition of the constituent parts of something: *the texture of a cake.* **4** the distinctive character or quality of something: *the texture of life in America.* ◆ *vb* **textures, texturing, textured. 5** *(tr)* to give a distinctive texture to. [C15: from L *textūra* web, from *texere* to weave]
▸ **'textural** *adj* ▸ **'texturally** *adv*

TGAT ('ti:gæt) *n* (in Britain) *acronym for* Task Group on Assessment and Testing: a group that advises on assessment and testing within the National Curriculum.

TGV (,ti:dʒi:'vi:, *French* teʒeve) (in France) *abbrev. for* train à grande vitesse: a high-speed passenger train.

TGWU (in Britain) *abbrev. for* Transport and General Workers' Union.

Th *the chemical symbol for* thorium.

Th. *abbrev. for* Thursday.

-th[1] *suffix forming nouns.* **1** *(from verbs)* indicating an action or its consequence: *growth.* **2** *(from adjectives)* indicating a quality: *width.* [from OE *-thu, -tho*]

-th[2] *or* **-eth** *suffix.* forming ordinal numbers: *fourth; thousandth.* [from OE *-(o)tha, -(o)the*]

Thai (taɪ) *adj* **1** of Thailand, its people, or their language. ◆ *n* **2** *(pl* **Thais** *or* **Thai)** a native or inhabitant of Thailand. **3** the language of Thailand, sometimes classified as belonging to the Sino-Tibetan family.

thalamus ('θæləməs) *n, pl* **thalami** (-,maɪ). **1** either of the two contiguous egg-shaped masses of grey matter at the base of the brain. **2** both of these masses considered as a functional unit. **3** the receptacle or torus of a flower. [C18: from L, from Gk *thalamos* inner room]
▸ **thalamic** (θə'læmɪk) *adj*

thalassaemia *or US* **thalassemia** (,θælə'si:mɪə) *n* a hereditary disease resulting from defects in the synthesis of the red blood pigment haemoglobin. [NL, from Gk *thalassa* sea + -AEMIA, it being esp. prevalent round the eastern Mediterranean]

thalassic (θə'læsɪk) *adj* of or relating to the sea, esp. to small or inland seas. [C19: from F *thalassique*, from Gk *thalassa* sea]

THESAURUS

tetchy *adj* = **irritable**, bad-tempered, cantankerous, captious, crabbed, cross, fretful, grumpy, impatient, irascible, liverish, peevish, peppery, petulant, quarrelsome, quick-tempered, ratty (*Brit. & NZ inf.*), short-tempered, snappish, snappy, splenetic, sullen, testy, touchy, waspish

tête-à-tête *n* **1a** = **private conversation**, chat, confab (*inf.*), cosy chat, parley, private word, talk ◆ *adv* **3** = **in private**, intimately, privately

tether *n* **1** = **rope**, bond, chain, fastening, fetter, halter, lead, leash, restraint, shackle **3 at the end of one's tether** = **exasperated**, at one's wits' end, at the limit of one's endurance, exhausted, finished, out of patience ◆ *vb* **4** = **tie**, bind, chain, fasten, fetter, leash, manacle, picket, restrain, rope, secure, shackle

text *n* **1** = **contents**, body, main body, matter **2** = **words**, wording **4** = **passage**, paragraph, sentence, verse **5** = **subject**, argument, matter, motif, theme, topic **6** = **reference book**, reader, source, textbook

texture *n* **1-4** = **feel**, character, composition, consistency, constitution, fabric, grain, make, quality, structure, surface, tissue, weave

thaler ('tɑːlə) *n, pl* **thaler** *or* **thalers.** a former German, Austrian, or Swiss silver coin. [from G; see DOLLAR]

Thalia (θə'laɪə) *n Greek myth.* **1** the Muse of comedy and pastoral poetry. **2** one of the three Graces, the others are Aglaia and Euphrosyne. [C17: via L from Gk, from *thaleia* blooming]

thalidomide (θə'lɪdəˌmaɪd) *n* **a** a drug formerly used as a sedative and hypnotic but withdrawn from use when found to cause abnormalities in developing fetuses. **b** (*as modifier*): *a thalidomide baby.* [C20: from *thali(mi)do(glutari)mide*]

thallium ('θælɪəm) *n* a soft malleable highly toxic white metallic element. Symbol: Tl; atomic no.: 81; atomic wt.: 204.37. [C19: from NL, from Gk *thallos* a green shoot; from the green line in its spectrum]

thallus ('θæləs) *n, pl* **thalli** ('θælaɪ) *or* **thalluses.** the undifferentiated vegetative body of algae, fungi, and lichens. [C19: from L, from Gk *thallos* green shoot, from *thallein* to bloom]
▸ **'thalloid** *adj*

thalweg *or* **talweg** ('tɑːlveg) *n Geog., rare.* **1** the longitudinal outline of a riverbed from source to mouth. **2** the line of steepest descent from any point on the land surface. [C19: from G *Thal* or *Tal* valley + *Weg* way]

than (ðæn; *unstressed* ðən) *conj* (*coordinating*), *prep* **1** used to introduce the second element of a comparison, the first element of which expresses difference: *shorter than you.* **2** used after adverbs such as *rather* or *sooner* to introduce a rejected alternative in an expression of preference: *rather than be imprisoned, I shall die.* [OE *thanne*]

> **USAGE NOTE** In formal English, *than* is usually regarded as a conjunction governing an unexpressed verb: *he does it far better than I (do).* The case of any pronoun therefore depends on whether it is the subject or object of the unexpressed verb: *she likes him more than I (like him); she likes him more than (she likes) me.* However in ordinary speech and writing *than* is usually treated as a preposition and is followed by the object form of a pronoun: *my brother is younger than me.*

thanatology (ˌθænə'tɒlədʒɪ) *n* the scientific study of death and its related phenomena. [C19: from Gk *thanatos* death + -LOGY]

thanatopsis (ˌθænə'tɒpsɪs) *n* a meditation on death, as in a poem. [C19: from Gk *thanatos* death + *opsis* a view]

thane *or* (*less commonly*) **thegn** (θeɪn) *n* **1** (in Anglo-Saxon England) a member of an aristocratic class who held land from the king or from another nobleman in return for certain services. **2** (in medieval Scotland) a person of rank holding land from the king. [OE *thegn*]
▸ **thanage** ('θeɪnɪdʒ) *n*

thank ❶ (θæŋk) *vb* (*tr*) **1** to convey feelings of gratitude to. **2** to hold responsible: *he has his creditors to thank for his bankruptcy.* [OE *thancian*]

thankful ❶ ('θæŋkful) *adj* grateful and appreciative.
▸ **'thankfully** *adv* ▸ **'thankfulness** *n*

> **USAGE NOTE** The use of *thankfully* to mean *fortunately* was formerly considered incorrect by many people, but has now become acceptable in informal contexts.

thankless ❶ ('θæŋklɪs) *adj* **1** receiving no thanks or appreciation. **2** ungrateful.
▸ **'thanklessly** *adv* ▸ **'thanklessness** *n*

thanks ❶ (θæŋks) *pl n* **1** an expression of appreciation or gratitude. **2** **thanks to.** because of: *thanks to him we lost the match.* ◆ *interj* **3** *Inf.* an exclamation expressing gratitude.

thanksgiving ('θæŋksˌgɪvɪŋ; *US* θæŋks'gɪv-) *n* **1** the act of giving thanks. **2** a formal public expression of thanks to God.

Thanksgiving Day *n* an annual day of holiday celebrated in thanksgiving to God on the fourth Thursday of November in the United States, and on the second Monday of October in Canada. Often shortened to **Thanksgiving.**

thar (tɑː) *n* a variant spelling of **tahr.**

that (ðæt; *unstressed* ðət) *determiner* (*used before a sing n*) **1a** used preceding a noun that has been mentioned or is understood: *that idea of yours.* **1b** (*as pronoun*): *don't eat that.* **2a** used preceding a noun that denotes something more remote or removed: *that building over there is for sale.* **2b** (*as pronoun*): *that is John and this is his wife.* **3** used to refer to something that is familiar: *that old chap from across the street.* **4 and (all) that.** *Inf.* everything connected with the subject mentioned: *he knows a lot about building and that.* **5 at that.** (*completive-intensive*) additionally, all things considered, or nevertheless: *I might decide to go at that.* **6 like that. 6a** effortlessly: *he gave me the answer just like that.* **6b** of such a nature, character, etc.: *he paid for all our tickets — he's like that.* **7 that is. 7a** to be precise. **7b** in other words. **7c** for example. **8 that's that.** there is no more to be done, discussed, etc. ◆ *conj* (*subordinating*) **9** used to introduce a noun clause: *I believe that you'll come.* **10** used to introduce: **10a** a clause of purpose: *they fought that others might have peace.* **10b** a clause of result: *he laughed so hard that he cried.* **10c** a clause after an understood sentence expressing desire, indignation, or amazement: *oh, that I had never lived!* ◆ *adv* **11** used to reinforce the specification of a precise degree already mentioned: *go just that fast and you should be safe.* **12** Also: **all that.** (*usually used with a negative*) *Inf.* (intensifier): *he wasn't that upset at the news.* **13** *Dialect.* (intensifier): *the cat was that weak after the fight.* ◆ *pron* **14** used to introduce a restrictive relative clause: *the book that we want.* **15** used to introduce a clause with the verb *to be* to emphasize the extent to which the preceding noun is applicable: *genius that she is, she outwitted the computer.* [OE *thæt*]

> **USAGE NOTE** Precise stylists maintain a distinction between *that* and *which*: *that* is used as a relative pronoun in restrictive clauses and *which* in nonrestrictive clauses. In *the book that is on the table is mine,* the clause *that is on the table* is used to distinguish one particular book (the one on the table) from another or others (which may be anywhere, but not on the table). In *the book, which is on the table, is mine,* the *which* clause is merely descriptive or incidental. The more formal the level of language, the more important it is to preserve the distinction between the two relative pronouns; but in informal or colloquial usage, the words are often used interchangeably.

thatch (θætʃ) *n* **1a** Also called: **thatching.** a roofing material that consists of straw, reed, etc. **1b** a roof made of such a material. **2** anything resembling this, such as the hair of the head. **3** Also called: **thatch palm.** any of various palms with leaves suitable for thatching. ◆ *vb* **4** to cover with thatch. [OE *theccan* to cover]
▸ **'thatcher** *n*

Thatcherism ('θætʃəˌrɪzəm) *n* the policies of monetarism, privatization, and self-help promoted by Margaret Thatcher, British prime minister (1979–90).
▸ **'Thatcherˌite** *n, adj*

thaumatology (ˌθɔːmə'tɒlədʒɪ) *n* the study of or a treatise on miracles. [C19: from Gk *thaumato-* combining form of *thauma* a wonder, marvel + -LOGY]

thaumatrope ('θɔːməˌtrəʊp) *n* a toy in which partial pictures on the two sides of a card appear to merge when the card is twirled rapidly. [C19: from Gk *thaumato-* (see THAUMATOLOGY) + -TROPE]
▸ **thaumatropical** (ˌθɔːmə'trɒpɪkᵊl) *adj*

thaumaturge ('θɔːməˌtɜːdʒ) *n Rare.* a performer of miracles; magician. [C18: from Med. L *thaumaturgus,* from Gk *thaumatourgos* miracle-working]
▸ **ˌthauma'turgic** *adj* ▸ **'thaumaˌturgy** *n*

thaw ❶ (θɔː) *vb* **1** to melt or cause to melt: *the snow thawed.* **2** to become or cause to become unfrozen; defrost. **3** (*intr*) to be the case that the ice or snow is melting: *it's thawing fast.* **4** (*intr*) to become more relaxed or friendly. ◆ *n* **5** the act or process of thawing. **6** a spell of relatively warm weather, causing snow or ice to melt. **7** an increase in relaxation or friendliness. [OE *thawian*]

ThD *abbrev. for* Doctor of Theology.

the[1] (*stressed or emphatic* ðiː; *unstressed before a consonant* ðə; *unstressed before a vowel* ðɪ) *determiner* (*article*) **1** used preceding a noun that has been previously specified: *the pain should disappear soon.* Cf. **a**[1]. **2** used to indicate a particular person, object, etc.: *ask the man standing outside.* Cf. **a**[1]. **3** used preceding certain nouns associated with one's culture, society, or community: *to go to the doctor; to listen to the news.* **4** used preceding present participles and adjectives when they function as nouns: *the singing is awful.* **5** used preceding titles and certain uniquely specific or proper nouns: *the United States; the Chairman.* **6** used preceding a qualifying adjective or noun in certain names or titles: *Edward the First.* **7** used preceding a noun to make it refer to its class generically: *the white seal is hunted for its fur.* **8** used instead of *my, your, her,* etc., with parts of the body: *take me by the hand.* **9** (usually stressed) the best, only, or most remarkable: *Harry's is the club in this town.* **10** used with proper nouns when qualified: *written by the young Hardy.* **11** another word for **per:** *fifty pence the pound.* **12** *Often facetious or derog.* my; our: *the wife goes out on Thursdays.* **13** used preceding a unit of time in phrases or titles indicating an outstanding person, event, etc.: *housewife of the year.* [ME, from OE *thē,* a demonstrative adjective that later superseded *sē* (masculine singular) and *sēo, sio* (feminine singular)]

the[2] (ðə, ðɪ) *adv* **1** (often foll. by *for*) used before comparative adjectives or adverbs for emphasis: *she looks the happier for her trip.* **2** used correlatively before each of two comparative adjectives or adverbs to indicate equality: *the sooner you come, the better; the more I see you, the more I love you.* [OE *thī, thȳ*]

theanthropism (θiː'ænθrəˌpɪzəm) *n* **1** the ascription of human traits or characteristics to a god or gods. **2** *Christian theol.* the doctrine of the union of the divine and human natures in the single person of Christ. [C19: from Ecclesiastical Gk *theanthrōpos* (from *theos* god + *anthrōpos* man) + -ISM]
▸ **theanthropic** (ˌθiːæn'θrɒpɪk) *adj*

THESAURUS

thank *vb* **1** = **say thank you,** express gratitude, show gratitude, show one's appreciation

thankful *adj* = **grateful,** appreciative, beholden, indebted, in (someone's) debt, obliged, pleased, relieved
Antonyms *adj* thankless, unappreciative, ungrateful

thankless *adj* **1** = **unrewarding,** fruitless, unappreciated, unprofitable, unrequited, useless
Antonyms *adj* fruitful, productive, profitable, rewarding, useful, worthwhile

thanks *pl n* **1** = **gratitude,** acknowledgment, appreciation, Brownie points, credit, gratefulness, recognition, thanksgiving **2 thanks to** = **because of,** as a result of, by reason of, due to, owing to, through

thaw *vb* **1, 2** = **melt,** defrost, dissolve, liquefy, soften, unfreeze, warm
Antonyms *vb* chill, congeal, freeze, harden, solidify, stiffen

thearchy ('θiːɑːkɪ) *n, pl* **thearchies.** rule or government by God or gods; theocracy. [C17: from Church Gk *thearkhia;* see THEO-, -ARCHY]

theatre *or US* **theater** ('θɪətə) *n* **1** a building designed for the performance of plays, operas, etc. **2** a large room or hall, usually with a raised platform and tiered seats for an audience. **3** a room in a hospital equipped for surgical operations. **4** plays regarded collectively as a form of art. **5 the theatre.** the world of actors, theatrical companies, etc. **6** a setting for dramatic or important events. **7** writing that is suitable for dramatic presentation: *a good piece of theatre.* **8** *US, Austral., & NZ.* the usual word for **cinema** (sense 1). **9** a major area of military activity. **10** a circular or semicircular open-air building with tiers of seats. [C14: from L *theātrum,* from Gk *theatron* place for viewing, from *theasthai* to look at]

theatre-in-the-round *n, pl* **theatres-in-the-round.** a theatre with seats arranged around a central acting area.

theatre of cruelty *n* a type of theatre that seeks to communicate a sense of pain, suffering, and evil, using gesture, movement, sound, and symbolism rather than language.

theatre of the absurd *n* drama in which normal conventions and dramatic structure are modified in order to present life as irrational.

theatrical ❶ (θɪ'ætrɪkᵊl) *adj* **1** of or relating to the theatre or dramatic performances. **2** exaggerated and affected in manner or behaviour; histrionic.
▸**the,atri'cality** *or* **the'atricalness** *n* ▸**the'atrically** *adv*

theatricals (θɪ'ætrɪkᵊlz) *pl n* dramatic performances, esp. as given by amateurs.

theatrics (θɪ'ætrɪks) *n* (*functioning as sing*) **1** the art of staging plays. **2** exaggerated mannerisms or displays of emotions.

thebaine ('θiːbə,iːn) *n* a poisonous white crystalline alkaloid, extracted from opium. [C19: from NL *thebaia* opium of Thebes (with reference to Egypt as a chief source of opium) + -INE[2]]

Theban ('θiːbən) *adj* **1** of or relating to Thebes, (in ancient Greece) the chief city of Boeotia, or (in ancient Egypt) a city on the Nile, at various times the capital. ◆ *n* **2** a native or inhabitant of either of these cities.

theca ('θiːkə) *n, pl* **thecae** (-siː). **1** *Bot.* an enclosing organ, cell, or spore case. **2** *Zool.* a hard outer covering, such as the container of a coral polyp. [C17: from L *thēca,* from Gk *thēkē* case]
▸**'thecate** *adj*

thecodont ('θiːkə,dɒnt) *adj* **1** (of mammals and certain reptiles) having teeth that grow in sockets. **2** of or relating to teeth of this type. ◆ *n* **3** any of various extinct reptiles of Triassic times, having teeth set in sockets: they gave rise to the dinosaurs, crocodiles, pterodactyls, and birds. [C20: NL *Thecodontia,* from Gk *thēkē* case + -ODONT]

thé dansant *French.* (te dɑ̃sɑ̃) *n, pl* **thés dansant** (te dɑ̃sɑ̃). a dance held while afternoon tea is served, popular in the 1920s and 1930s. [lit.: dancing tea]

thee (ðiː) *pron* **1** the objective form of **thou**[1]. **2** (*subjective*) *Rare.* refers to the person addressed: used mainly by members of the Society of Friends. [OE *thē*]

theft ❶ (θɛft) *n* **1** the dishonest taking of property belonging to another person with the intention of depriving the owner permanently of its possession. **2** *Rare.* something stolen. [OE *thēofth*]

thegn (θeɪn) *n* a less common variant of **thane.**

theine ('θiːiːn, -ɪn) *n* caffeine, esp. when present in tea. [C19: from NL *thea* tea + -INE[2]]

their (ðɛə) *determiner* **1** of or associated in some way with them: *their own clothes; she tried to combat their mocking her.* **2** belonging to or associated with people in general: *in many countries they wash their clothes in the river.* **3** belonging to or associated with an indefinite antecedent such as *one, whoever,* or *anybody: everyone should bring their own lunch.* [C12: from ON *theira*]

> **USAGE NOTE** See at **they.**

theirs (ðɛəz) *pron* **1** something or someone belonging to or associated with them: *theirs is difficult.* **2** something or someone belonging to or associated with an indefinite antecedent such as *one, whoever,* or *anybody: everyone thinks theirs is best.* **3 of theirs.** belonging to or associated with them.

theism ('θiːɪzəm) *n* **1** the belief in one God as the creator and ruler of the universe. **2** the belief in the existence of a God or gods. [C17: from Gk *theos* god + -ISM]
▸**'theist** *n, adj* ▸**the'istic** *or* **the'istical** *adj*

them (ðɛm; *unstressed* ðəm) *pron* **1** (*objective*) refers to things or people other than the speaker or people addressed: *I'll kill them; what happened to them?* ◆ *determiner* **2** a nonstandard word for **those:** *three of them oranges.* [OE *thǣm,* infl. by ON *theim*]

> **USAGE NOTE** See at **me**[1], **they.**

thematic apperception test *n Psychol.* a projective test in which drawings of interacting people are shown and the person being tested is asked to make up a story about them.

theme ❶ (θiːm) *n* **1** an idea or topic expanded in a discourse, discussion, etc. **2** (in literature, music, art, etc.) a unifying idea, image, or motif, repeated or developed throughout a work. **3** *Music.* a group of notes forming a recognizable melodic unit, often used as the basis of the musical material in a composition. **4** a short essay, esp. one set as an exercise for a student. **5** *Grammar.* another word for **root**[1] (sense 8) or **stem**[1] (sense 7). **6** (*modifier*) planned or designed round one unifying subject, image, etc.: *a theme holiday.* ◆ *vb* **themes, theming, themed.** (*tr*) **7** to design, decorate, etc., in accordance with a theme. [C13: from L *thema,* from Gk: deposit, from *tithenai* to lay down]
▸**thematic** (θɪ'mætɪk) *adj*

theme park *n* an area planned as a leisure attraction, in which all the displays, buildings, activities, etc., are based on one subject.

theme song *n* **1** a melody used, esp. in a film score, to set a mood, introduce a character, etc. **2** another term for **signature tune.**

themselves (ðəm'sɛlvz) *pron* **1a** the reflexive form of *they* or *them.* **1b** (intensifier): *the team themselves voted on it.* **2** (*preceded by a copula*) their normal or usual selves: *they don't seem themselves any more.* **3** Also: **themself.** *Not standard.* a reflexive form of an indefinite antecedent such as *one, whoever,* or *anybody: everyone has to look after themselves.*

then (ðɛn) *adv* **1** at that time; over that period of time. **2** (*sentence modifier*) in that case; that being so: *then why don't you ask her? go on then, take it.* ◆ *sentence connector.* **3** after that; with that: *then John left the room.* ◆ *n* **4** that time: *from then on.* ◆ *adj* **5** (*prenominal*) existing, functioning, etc., at that time: *the then prime minister.* [OE *thenne*]

thenar ('θiːnɑː) *n* **1** the palm of the hand. **2** the fleshy area of the palm at the base of the thumb. [C17: via NL from Gk]

thence (ðɛns) *adv* **1** from that place. **2** Also: **thenceforth** ('ðɛns'fɔːθ). from that time or event; thereafter. **3** therefore. [C13 *thannes,* from *thanne,* from OE *thanon*]

thenceforward ('ðɛns'fɔːwəd) *or* **thenceforwards** *adv* from that time or place on.

theo- *or before a vowel* **the-** *combining form.* indicating God or gods: *theology.* [from Gk *theos* god]

theobromine (,θiːəʊ'brəʊmiːn, -mɪn) *n* a white crystalline alkaloid that occurs in tea and cacao: used to treat coronary heart disease and headaches. [C18: from NL *theobroma* genus of trees, lit.: food of the gods]

theocentric (,θɪə'sɛntrɪk) *adj Theol.* having God as the focal point of attention.

theocracy (θɪ'ɒkrəsɪ) *n, pl* **theocracies. 1** government by a deity or by a priesthood. **2** a community under such government.
▸**'theo,crat** *n* ▸**,theo'cratic** *adj*

theocrasy (θɪ'ɒkrəsɪ) *n* **1** a mingling into one of deities or divine attributes previously regarded as distinct. **2** the union of the soul with God in mysticism. [C19: from Gk *theokrasia,* from THEO- + *-krasia* from *krasis* a blending]

theodicy (θɪ'ɒdɪsɪ) *n, pl* **theodicies.** the branch of theology concerned with defending the attributes of God against objections resulting from the existence of physical and moral evil. [C18: coined by Leibnitz in F as *théodicée,* from THEO- + Gk *dikē* justice]
▸**the,odi'cean** *adj*

theodolite (θɪ'ɒdə,laɪt) *n* a surveying instrument for measuring horizontal and vertical angles, consisting of a small tripod-mounted telescope. Also called (in the US and Canada): **transit.** [C16: from NL *theodolitus,* from ?]
▸**theodolitic** (θɪ,ɒdə'lɪtɪk) *adj*

theogony (θɪ'ɒgənɪ) *n, pl* **theogonies. 1** the origin and descent of the gods. **2** an account of this. [C17: from Gk *theogonia*]
▸**theogonic** (,θɪə'gɒnɪk) *adj* ▸**the'ogonist** *n*

theol. *abbrev. for:* **1** theologian. **2** theological. **3** theology.

theologian (,θɪə'ləʊdʒɪən) *n* a person versed in or engaged in the study of theology.

theological ❶ (,θɪə'lɒdʒɪkᵊl) *adj* of, relating to, or based on theology.
▸**,theo'logically** *adv*

theological virtues *pl n* those virtues that are infused into man by a special grace of God, specifically faith, hope, and charity.

theologize *or* **theologise** (θɪ'ɒlə,dʒaɪz) *vb* **theologizes, theologizing, theologized** *or* **theologises, theologising, theologised. 1** (*intr*) to speculate upon theological subjects or engage in theological study or discussion. **2** (*tr*) to render theological or treat from a theological point of view.
▸**the,ologi'zation** *or* **the,ologi'sation** *n* ▸**the'olo,gizer** *or* **the'olo,giser** *n*

theology (θɪ'ɒlədʒɪ) *n, pl* **theologies. 1** the systematic study of the existence and nature of the divine and its relationship to other beings. **2** the systematic study of Christian revelation concerning God's nature and purpose. **3** a specific system, form, or branch of this study. [C14: from LL *theologia,* from L]
▸**the'ologist** *n*

THESAURUS

theatrical *adj* **1** = **dramatic,** dramaturgic, scenic, Thespian **2** = **exaggerated,** actorly *or* actressy, affected, artificial, camp (*inf.*), ceremonious, dramatic, hammy (*inf.*), histrionic, mannered, melodramatic, ostentatious, overdone, pompous, showy, stagy, stilted, unreal

Antonyms *adj* ≠ **exaggerated:** natural, plain, simple, straightforward, unaffected, unassuming, unexaggerated, unpretentious, unsophisticated

theft *n* **1** = **stealing,** embezzlement, fraud, larceny, pilfering, purloining, rip-off (*sl.*), robbery, swindling, thievery, thieving

theme *n* **1** = **subject,** argument, burden, idea, keynote, matter, subject matter, text, thesis, topic **2** = **motif,** leitmotif, recurrent image, unifying idea **4** = **essay,** composition, dissertation, exercise, paper

theological *adj* = **religious,** divine, doctrinal, ecclesiastical

theomachy (θɪˈɒməkɪ) *n, pl* **theomachies.** a battle among the gods or against them. [C16: from Gk *theomakhia,* from THEO- + *makhē* battle]

theomancy (ˈθiːəʊˌmænsɪ) *n* divination or prophecy by an oracle or by people directly inspired by a god.

theomania (ˌθɪəˈmeɪnɪə) *n* religious madness, esp. when it takes the form of believing oneself to be a god.
▸ **ˌtheoˈmaniˌac** *n*

theophany (θɪˈɒfənɪ) *n, pl* **theophanies.** a visible manifestation of a deity to man. [C17: from LL *theophania,* from LGk, from THEO- + *phainein* to show]
▸ **theophanic** (ˌθɪəˈfænɪk) *adj*

theophylline (ˌθɪəˈfɪliːn, -ɪn) *n* a white crystalline alkaloid that is an isomer of theobromine: it occurs in plants such as tea. [C19: from THEO(BROMINE) + PHYLLO- + -INE[2]]

theorem Ⓣ (ˈθɪərəm) *n* a statement or formula that can be deduced from the axioms of a formal system by means of its rules of inference. [C16: from LL *theōrēma,* from Gk: something to be viewed, from *theōrein* to view]
▸ **theorematic** (ˌθɪərəˈmætɪk) *or* **theoremic** (ˌθɪəˈrɛmɪk) *adj*

theoretical Ⓣ (ˌθɪəˈrɛtɪkᵊl) *or* **theoretic** *adj* **1** of or based on theory. **2** lacking practical application or actual existence; hypothetical. **3** using or dealing in theory; impractical.
▸ **ˌtheoˈretically** *adv*

theoretician (ˌθɪərɪˈtɪʃən) *n* a student or user of the theory rather than the practical aspects of a subject.

theoretics (ˌθɪəˈrɛtɪks) *n (functioning as sing or pl)* the theory of a particular subject.

theorize Ⓣ *or* **theorise** (ˈθɪəˌraɪz) *vb* **theorizes, theorizing, theorized** *or* **theorises, theorising, theorised.** *(intr)* to produce or use theories; speculate.
▸ **ˈtheorist** *n* ▸ **ˌtheoriˈzation** *or* **ˌtheoriˈsation** *n* ▸ **ˈtheoˌrizer** *or* **ˈtheoˌriser** *n*

theory Ⓣ (ˈθɪərɪ) *n, pl* **theories. 1** a system of rules, procedures, and assumptions used to produce a result. **2** abstract knowledge or reasoning. **3** a conjectural view or idea: *I have a theory about that.* **4** an ideal or hypothetical situation (esp. in **in theory**). **5** a set of hypotheses related by logical or mathematical arguments to explain a wide variety of connected phenomena in general terms: *the theory of relativity.* **6** a nontechnical name for **hypothesis.** [C16: from LL *theōria,* from Gk: a sight, from *theōrein* to gaze upon]

theory of games *n* a mathematical theory concerned with the optimum choice of strategy in situations involving a conflict of interest. Also called: **game theory.**

theosophy (θɪˈɒsəfɪ) *n* **1** any of various religious or philosophical systems claiming to be based on or to express an intuitive insight into the divine nature. **2** the system of beliefs of the Theosophical Society founded in 1875, claiming to be derived from the sacred writings of Brahmanism and Buddhism. [C17: from Med. L *theosophia,* from LGk; see THEO-, -SOPHY]
▸ **theosophical** (ˌθɪəˈsɒfɪkᵊl) *or* **ˌtheoˈsophic** *adj* ▸ **theˈosophist** *n*

therapeutic Ⓣ (ˌθɛrəˈpjuːtɪk) *adj* **1** of or relating to the treatment of disease; curative. **2** serving or performed to maintain health: *therapeutic abortion.* [C17: from NL *therapeuticus,* from Gk, from *therapeuein* to minister to, from *theraps* an attendant]
▸ **ˌtheraˈpeutically** *adv*

therapeutics (ˌθɛrəˈpjuːtɪks) *n (functioning as sing)* the branch of medicine concerned with the treatment of disease.

therapy Ⓣ (ˈθɛrəpɪ) *n, pl* **therapies. a** the treatment of physical, mental, or social disorders or disease. **b** *(in combination): physiotherapy.* [C19: from NL *therapia,* from Gk *therapeia* attendance; see THERAPEUTIC]
▸ **ˈtherapist** *n*

Theravada (ˌθɛrəˈvɑːdə) *n* the southern school of Buddhism, the name preferred by Hinayana Buddhists. [from Pali: doctrine of the elders]

there (ðɛə) *adv* **1** in, at, or to that place, point, case, or respect: *we never go there; I agree with you there.* ◆ *pron* **2** used as a grammatical subject with some verbs, esp. *be,* when the true subject follows the verb: *there is a girl in that office.* ◆ *adj* **3** *(postpositive)* who or which is in that place or position: *that boy there did it.* **4 all there.** *(predicative)* of normal intelligence. **5 so there.** an exclamation that usually follows a declaration of refusal or defiance. **6 there you are. 6a** an expression used when handing a person something requested or desired. **6b** an exclamation of triumph. ◆ *n* **7** that place: *near there.* ◆ *interj* **8** an expression of sympathy, as in consoling a child: *there, there, dear.* [OE *thǣr*]

> **USAGE NOTE** In correct usage, the verb should agree with the number of the subject in such constructions as *there is a man waiting* and *there are several people waiting.* However, where the subject is compound, it is common in speech to use the singular as in *there's a police car and an ambulance outside.*

thereabouts (ˈðɛərəˌbaʊts) *or US* **thereabout** *adv* near that place, time, amount, etc.

thereafter (ˌðɛərˈɑːftə) *adv* from that time on or after that time.

thereat (ˌðɛərˈæt) *adv Rare.* **1** at that point or time. **2** for that reason.

thereby (ˌðɛəˈbaɪ, ˈðɛəˌbaɪ) *adv* **1** by that means; because of that. **2** *Arch.* thereabouts.

therefor (ˌðɛəˈfɔː) *adv Arch.* for this, that, or it.

therefore Ⓣ (ˈðɛəˌfɔː) *sentence connector.* **1** thus; hence: *those people have their umbrellas up; therefore, it must be raining.* **2** consequently; as a result.

therefrom (ˌðɛəˈfrɒm) *adv Arch.* from that or there: *the roads that lead therefrom.*

therein (ˌðɛərˈɪn) *adv Formal or law.* in or into that place, thing, etc.

thereinto (ˌðɛərˈɪntuː) *adv Formal or law.* into that place, circumstance, etc.

thereof (ˌðɛərˈɒv) *adv Formal or law.* **1** of or concerning that or it. **2** from or because of that.

thereon (ˌðɛərˈɒn) *adv Arch.* thereupon.

thereto (ˌðɛəˈtuː) *adv* **1** *Formal or law.* to that or it. **2** *Obs.* in addition to that.

theretofore (ˌðɛətʊˈfɔː) *adv Formal or law.* before that time; previous to that.

thereunder (ˌðɛərˈʌndə) *adv Formal or law.* **1** (in documents, etc.) below that or it; subsequently in that; thereafter. **2** under the terms or authority of that.

thereupon (ˌðɛərəˈpɒn) *adv* **1** immediately after that; at that point. **2** *Formal or law.* upon that thing, point, subject, etc.

therewith (ˌðɛəˈwɪθ, -ˈwɪð) *or* **therewithal** *adv* **1** *Formal or law.* with or in addition to that. **2** a less common word for **thereupon** (sense 1). **3** *Arch.* by means of or on account of that.

therianthropic (ˌθɪərɪənˈθrɒpɪk) *adj* **1** (of certain mythical creatures or deities) having a partly animal, partly human form. **2** of or relating to such creatures or deities. [C19: from Gk *thērion* wild animal + *anthrōpos* man]
▸ **therianthropism** (ˌθɪərɪˈænθrəˌpɪzəm) *n*

theriomorphic (ˌθɪərɪəʊˈmɔːfɪk) *adj* (esp. of a deity) possessing or depicted in the form of a beast. [C19: from Gk *thēriomorphos,* from *thērion* wild animal + *morphē* shape]

therm (θɜːm) *n Brit.* a unit of heat equal to 100 000 British thermal units. One therm is equal to 1.055 056 × 10^8 joules. [C19: from Gk *thermē* heat]

thermae (ˈθɜːmiː) *pl n* public baths or hot springs, esp. in ancient Greece or Rome. [C17: from L, from Gk *thermai,* pl. of *thermē* heat]

thermal (ˈθɜːməl) *adj* **1** Also: **thermic.** of, caused by, or generating heat. **2** hot or warm: *thermal baths.* **3** (of garments) specially made so as to have exceptional heat-retaining qualities: *thermal underwear.* ◆ *n* **4** a column of rising air caused by local unequal heating of the land surface, and used by gliders and birds to gain height. **5** *(pl)* thermal garments, esp. underclothes.
▸ **ˈthermally** *adv*

thermal barrier *n* an obstacle to flight at very high speeds as a result of the heating effect of air friction. Also called: **heat barrier.**

thermal conductivity *n* a measure of the ability of a substance to conduct heat.

thermal efficiency *n* the ratio of the work done by a heat engine to the energy supplied to it.

thermal equator *n* an imaginary line round the earth running through the point on each meridian with the highest average temperature.

thermal imaging *n* the use of heat-sensitive equipment to detect or provide images of people or things.

thermalize *or* **thermalise** (ˈθɜːməˌlaɪz) *vb* **thermalizes, thermalizing, thermalized** *or* **thermalises, thermalising, thermalised.** *Physics.* to undergo or cause to undergo a process in which neutrons lose energy in a moderator and become thermal neutrons.
▸ **ˌthermaliˈzation** *or* **ˌthermaliˈsation** *n*

thermal neutrons *pl n* slow neutrons that are approximately in thermal equilibrium with a moderator.

thermal reactor *n* a nuclear reactor in which most of the fission is caused by thermal neutrons.

thermal shock *n* a fluctuation in temperature causing stress in a material. It often results in fracture, esp. in brittle materials such as ceramics.

thermion (ˈθɜːmɪən) *n Physics.* an electron or ion emitted by a body at high temperature.

thermionic (ˌθɜːmɪˈɒnɪk) *adj* of, relating to, or operated by electrons emitted from materials at high temperatures: *a thermionic valve.*

THESAURUS

theorem *n* = **proposition**, deduction, dictum, formula, hypothesis, principle, rule, statement

theoretical *adj* **1-3** = **abstract**, academic, conjectural, hypothetical, ideal, impractical, notional, pure, speculative
Antonyms *adj* applied, experiential, factual, practical, realistic

theorize *vb* = **speculate**, conjecture, formulate, guess, hypothesize, project, propound, suppose

theory *n* **1** = **system**, philosophy, plan, proposal, scheme **2** = **hypothesis**, assumption, conjecture, guess, presumption, speculation, supposition, surmise, thesis
Antonyms *n* ≠ **hypothesis:** certainty, experience, fact, practice, reality

therapeutic *adj* **1-2** = **beneficial**, ameliorative, analeptic, corrective, curative, good, healing, remedial, restorative, salubrious, salutary, sanative
Antonyms *adj* adverse, damaging, destructive, detrimental, harmful

therapist *n* = **healer**, physician

therapy *n* = **remedy**, cure, healing, remedial treatment, treatment

therefore *sentence connector* **1, 2** = **consequently**, accordingly, as a result, ergo, for that reason, hence, so, then, thence, thus, whence

thermionic current *n* an electric current produced between two electrodes as a result of electrons emitted by thermionic emission.
thermionic emission *n* the emission of electrons from very hot solids or liquids.
thermionics (ˌθɜːmɪˈɒnɪks) *n* (*functioning as sing*) the branch of electronics concerned with the emission of electrons by hot bodies and with devices based on this effect.
thermionic valve *or esp. US & Canad.* **tube** *n* an electronic valve in which electrons are emitted from a heated rather than a cold cathode.
thermistor (θɜːˈmɪstə) *n* a semiconductor device having a resistance that decreases rapidly with an increase in temperature. It is used for temperature measurement and control. [C20: from THERMO- + (RES)ISTOR]
Thermit (ˈθɜːmɪt) *or* **Thermite** (ˈθɜːmaɪt) *n Trademark.* a mixture of aluminium powder and a metal oxide, which when ignited produces great heat: used for welding and in incendiary bombs.
thermo- *or before a vowel* **therm-** *combining form.* related to, caused by, or measuring heat: *thermodynamics; thermophile.* [from Gk *thermos* hot, *thermē* heat]
thermobarograph (ˌθɜːməʊˈbærəˌgrɑːf) *n* a device that simultaneously records the temperature and pressure of the atmosphere.
thermobarometer (ˌθɜːməʊbəˈrɒmɪtə) *n* an apparatus that provides an accurate measurement of pressure by observation of the change in the boiling point of a fluid.
thermochemistry (ˌθɜːməʊˈkɛmɪstrɪ) *n* the branch of chemistry concerned with the study and measurement of the heat evolved or absorbed during chemical reactions.
▸ **ˌthermoˈchemical** *adj* ▸ **ˌthermoˈchemist** *n*
thermocline (ˈθɜːməʊˌklaɪn) *n* a temperature gradient in a thermally stratified body of water, such as a lake.
thermocouple (ˈθɜːməʊˌkʌpᵊl) *n* **1** a device for measuring temperature consisting of a pair of wires of different metals or semiconductors joined at both ends. One junction is at the temperature to be measured, the second at a fixed temperature. The electromotive force generated depends upon the temperature difference. **2** a similar device with only one junction between two dissimilar metals or semiconductors.
thermodynamic (ˌθɜːməʊdaɪˈnæmɪk) *or* **thermodynamical** *adj* **1** of or concerned with thermodynamics. **2** determined by or obeying the laws of thermodynamics.
thermodynamic equilibrium *n* the condition of a system in which the quantities that specify its properties, such as pressure, temperature, etc., all remain unchanged.
thermodynamics (ˌθɜːməʊdaɪˈnæmɪks) *n* (*functioning as sing*) the branch of physical science concerned with the interrelationship and interconversion of different forms of energy.
thermodynamic temperature *n* temperature defined in terms of the laws of thermodynamics rather than of the properties of a real material: expressed in kelvins.
thermoelectric (ˌθɜːməʊɪˈlɛktrɪk) *or* **thermoelectrical** *adj* **1** of, relating to, used in, or operated by the conversion of heat energy to electrical energy. **2** of, relating to, used in, or operated by the conversion of electrical energy.
thermoelectric effect *n* another name for the **Seebeck effect**.
thermoelectricity (ˌθɜːməʊɪlɛkˈtrɪsɪtɪ) *n* **1** electricity generated by a thermocouple. **2** the study of the relationship between heat and electrical energy.
thermoelectron (ˌθɜːməʊɪˈlɛktrɒn) *n* an electron emitted at high temperature, as in a thermionic valve.
thermogenesis (ˌθɜːməʊˈdʒɛnɪsɪs) *n* the production of heat by metabolic processes.
thermogram (ˈθɜːməʊˌgræm) *n* **1** *Med.* a picture produced by thermography, using film sensitive to infrared radiation. **2** the record produced by a thermograph.
thermograph (ˈθɜːməʊˌgrɑːf, -ˌgræf) *n* a type of thermometer that produces a continuous record of a fluctuating temperature.
thermography (θɜːˈmɒgrəfɪ) *n* **1** any writing, printing, or recording process involving the use of heat. **2** *Med.* the measurement and recording of heat produced by a part of the body: used in the diagnosis of tumours, esp. of the breast (**mammothermography**), which have increased blood supply and therefore generate more heat than normal tissue. See also **thermogram**.
▸ **therˈmographer** *n* ▸ **thermographic** (ˌθɜːməʊˈgræfɪk) *adj*
thermojunction (ˌθɜːməʊˈdʒʌŋkʃən) *n* a point of electrical contact between two dissimilar metals across which a voltage appears, the magnitude of which depends on the temperature of the contact and the nature of the metals.
thermolabile (ˌθɜːməʊˈleɪbɪl) *adj* easily decomposed or subject to a loss of characteristic properties by the action of heat.
thermoluminescence (ˌθɜːməʊˌluːmɪˈnɛsəns) *n* phosphorescence of certain materials or objects as a result of heating.
thermolysis (θɜːˈmɒlɪsɪs) *n* **1** *Physiol.* loss of heat from the body. **2** the dissociation of a substance as a result of heating.
▸ **thermolytic** (ˌθɜːməʊˈlɪtɪk) *adj*
thermomagnetic (ˌθɜːməʊmægˈnɛtɪk) *adj* of or concerned with the relationship between heat and magnetism, esp. the change in temperature of a body when it is magnetized or demagnetized.
thermometer (θəˈmɒmɪtə) *n* an instrument used to measure temperature, esp. one in which a thin column of liquid, such as mercury, expands and contracts within a graduated sealed tube.
▸ **therˈmometry** *n*
thermonuclear (ˌθɜːməʊˈnjuːklɪə) *adj* **1** involving nuclear fusion. **2** involving thermonuclear weapons.
thermonuclear reaction *n* a nuclear fusion reaction occurring at a very high temperature: responsible for the energy produced in the sun, nuclear weapons, and fusion reactors.
thermophile (ˈθɜːməʊˌfaɪl) *or* **thermophil** (ˈθɜːməʊˌfɪl) *n* **1** an organism, esp. a bacterium or plant, that thrives under warm conditions. ◆ *adj* **2** thriving under warm conditions.
▸ **ˌthermoˈphilic** *adj*
thermopile (ˈθɜːməʊˌpaɪl) *n* an instrument for detecting and measuring heat radiation or for generating a thermoelectric current. It consists of a number of thermocouple junctions.
thermoplastic (ˌθɜːməʊˈplæstɪk) *adj* **1** (of a material, esp. a synthetic plastic) becoming soft when heated and rehardening on cooling without appreciable change of properties. ◆ *n* **2** a synthetic plastic or resin, such as polystyrene, with these properties.
Thermos *or* **Thermos flask** (ˈθɜːməs) *n Trademark.* a type of stoppered vacuum flask used to preserve the temperature of its contents.
thermosetting (ˌθɜːməʊˈsɛtɪŋ) *adj* (of a material, esp. a synthetic plastic) hardening permanently after one application of heat and pressure.
thermosiphon (ˌθɜːməʊˈsaɪfən) *n* a system in which a coolant is circulated by convection caused by a difference in density between the hot and cold portions of the liquid.
thermosphere (ˈθɜːməˌsfɪə) *n* an atmospheric layer lying between the mesosphere and the exosphere.
thermostable (ˌθɜːməʊˈsteɪbᵊl) *adj* capable of withstanding moderate heat without loss of characteristic properties.
thermostat (ˈθɜːməˌstæt) *n* **1** a device that maintains a system at a constant temperature. **2** a device that sets off a sprinkler, etc., at a certain temperature.
▸ **ˌthermoˈstatic** *adj* ▸ **ˌthermoˈstatically** *adv*
thermostatics (ˌθɜːməˈstætɪks) *n* (*functioning as sing*) the branch of science concerned with thermal equilibrium.
thermotaxis (ˌθɜːməʊˈtæksɪs) *n* the directional movement of an organism in response to the stimulus of heat.
▸ **ˌthermoˈtaxic** *adj*
thermotropism (ˌθɜːməʊˈtrəʊpɪzəm) *n* the directional growth of a plant in response to the stimulus of heat.
▸ **ˌthermoˈtropic** *adj*
-thermy *n combining form.* indicating heat: *diathermy.* [from NL *-thermia,* from Gk *thermē*]
▸ **-thermic** *or* **-thermal** *adj combining form.*
theroid (ˈθɪərɔɪd) *adj* of, relating to, or resembling a beast. [C19: from Gk *thēroeidēs,* from *thēr* wild animal; see -OID]
thesaurus ❶ (θɪˈsɔːrəs) *n, pl* **thesauruses** *or* **thesauri** (-raɪ). **1** a book containing systematized lists of synonyms and related words. **2** a dictionary of selected words or topics. **3** *Rare.* a treasury. [C18: from L, Gk: TREASURE]
these (ðiːz) *determiner* **a** the form of **this** used before a plural noun: *these men.* **b** (*as pronoun*): *I don't much care for these.*
thesis ❶ (ˈθiːsɪs) *n, pl* **theses** (-siːz). **1** a dissertation resulting from original research, esp. when submitted for a degree or diploma. **2** a doctrine maintained in argument. **3** a subject for a discussion or essay. **4** an unproved statement put forward as a premise in an argument. [C16: via LL from Gk: a placing, from *tithenai* to place]
Thespian (ˈθɛspɪən) *adj* **1** of or relating to Thespis, 6th-century B.C. Greek poet. **2** (*usually not cap.*) of or relating to drama and the theatre; dramatic. ◆ *n* (*usually not cap.*) **3** *Often facetious.* an actor or actress.
Thess. *Bible. abbrev. for* Thessalonians.
theta (ˈθiːtə) *n* the eighth letter of the Greek alphabet (Θ, θ). [C17: from Gk]
theurgy (ˈθiːˌɜːdʒɪ) *n, pl* **theurgies**. **1** the intervention of a divine or supernatural agency in the affairs of man. **2** beneficent magic as taught by Egyptian Neoplatonists. [C16: from LL *theūrgia,* from LGk *theourgia* the practice of magic, from *theo-* THEO- + *-urgia,* from *ergon* work]
▸ **theˈurgic** *or* **theˈurgical** *adj* ▸ **ˈtheurgist** *n*
thew (θjuː) *n* **1** muscle, esp. if strong or well-developed. **2** (*pl*) muscular strength. [OE *thēaw*]
▸ **ˈthewless** *adj* ▸ **ˈthewy** *adj*
they (ðeɪ) *pron* (*subjective*) **1** refers to people or things other than the speaker or people addressed: *they fight among themselves.* **2** refers to people in general: *in Australia they have Christmas in the summer.* **3** refers to an indefinite antecedent such as *one, whoever,* or *anybody: if anyone objects, they can go.* [C12 *thei* from ON *their,* masc. nominative pl, equivalent to OE *thā*]

THESAURUS

thesaurus *n* **1-3** = **wordbook**, dictionary, encyclopedia, repository, storehouse, treasury, wordfinder
thesis *n* **1** = **dissertation**, composition, disquisition, essay, monograph, paper, treatise **2** = **proposition**, contention, hypothesis, idea, line of argument, opinion, proposal, theory, view **3** = **subject**, area, theme, topic **4** *Logic* = **premise**, assumption, postulate, proposition, statement, supposition, surmise

> **USAGE NOTE** It was formerly considered correct to use *he, him,* or *his* after pronouns such as *everyone, no-one, anyone,* or *someone* as in *everyone did his best,* but it is now more common to use *they, them,* or *their,* and this use has become acceptable in all but the most formal contexts: *everyone did their best.*

they'd (ðeɪd) *contraction of* they would *or* they had.
they'll (ðeɪl) *contraction of* they will *or* they shall.
they're (ðeə, 'ðeɪə) *contraction of* they are.
they've (ðeɪv) *contraction of* they have.
thi- *combining form.* a variant of **thio-**.
thiamine ('θaɪə,mi:n, -mɪn) *or* **thiamin** ('θaɪəmɪn) *n* a white crystalline vitamin that occurs in the outer coat of rice and other grains. It forms part of the vitamin B complex: deficiency leads to nervous disorders and to the disease beriberi. Also called: **vitamin B_1, aneurin.** [C20: THIO- + (VIT)AMIN]
thiazine ('θaɪə,zi:n, -,zaɪn) *n* any of a group of organic compounds containing a ring system composed of four carbon atoms, a sulphur atom, and a nitrogen atom.
thiazole ('θaɪə,zəʊl) *n* **1** a colourless liquid that contains a ring system composed of three carbon atoms, a sulphur atom, and a nitrogen atom. **2** any of a group of compounds derived from this substance that are used in dyes.
thick ❶ (θɪk) *adj* **1** of relatively great extent from one surface to the other: *a thick slice of bread.* **2a** (*postpositive*) of specific fatness: *ten centimetres thick.* **2b** (*in combination*): *a six-inch-thick wall.* **3** having a dense consistency: *thick soup.* **4** abundantly covered or filled: *a piano thick with dust.* **5** impenetrable; dense: *a thick fog.* **6** stupid, slow, or insensitive. **7** throaty or badly articulated: *a voice thick with emotion.* **8** (of accents, etc.) pronounced. **9** *Inf.* very friendly (esp. in **thick as thieves**). **10 a bit thick.** *Brit.* unfair or excessive. ◆ *adv* **11** in order to produce something thick: *to slice bread thick.* **12** profusely; in quick succession (esp. in **thick and fast**). **13 lay it on thick.** *Inf.* **13a** to exaggerate a story, etc. **13b** to flatter excessively. ◆ *n* **14** a thick piece or part. **15 the thick.** the busiest or most intense part. **16 through thick and thin.** in good times and bad. [OE *thicce*]
▸ **'thickish** *adj* ▸ **'thickly** *adv*
thicken ❶ ('θɪkən) *vb* **1** to make or become thick or thicker. **2** (*intr*) to become more involved: *the plot thickened.*
▸ **'thickener** *n*
thickening ('θɪkənɪŋ) *n* **1** something added to a liquid to thicken it. **2** a thickened part or piece.
thicket ❶ ('θɪkɪt) *n* a dense growth of small trees, shrubs, and similar plants. [OE *thiccet*]
thickhead ❶ ('θɪk,hɛd) *n* **1** a stupid or ignorant person; fool. **2** any of a family of Australian and SE Asian songbirds.
▸ **,thick'headed** *adj*
thickie *or* **thicky** ('θɪkɪ) *n, pl* **thickies.** *Brit. sl.* a variant of **thicko.**
thick-knee *n* another name for **stone curlew.**
thickness ('θɪknɪs) *n* **1** the state or quality of being thick. **2** the dimension through an object, as opposed to length or width. **3** a layer.
thicko ('θɪkəʊ) *n, pl* **thickos** *or* **thickoes.** *Brit. sl.* a slow-witted unintelligent person. Also: **thickie, thicky.**
thickset ❶ (,θɪk'sɛt) *adj* **1** stocky in build; sturdy. **2** densely planted or placed. ◆ *n* **3** a rare word for **thicket.**
thick-skinned ❶ *adj* insensitive to criticism or hints; not easily upset or affected.
thick-witted *or* **thick-skulled** *adj* stupid, dull, or slow to learn.
▸ **,thick-'wittedly** *adv* ▸ **,thick-'wittedness** *n*
thief ❶ (θi:f) *n, pl* **thieves** (θi:vz). a person who steals something from another. [OE *thēof*]
▸ **'thievish** *adj*
thieve ❶ (θi:v) *vb* **thieves, thieving, thieved.** to steal (someone's possessions). [OE *thēofian,* from *thēof* thief]
▸ **'thievery** *n* ▸ **'thieving** *adj*
thigh (θaɪ) *n* **1** the part of the leg between the hip and the knee in man. **2** the corresponding part in other vertebrates and insects. ◆ Related adj: **femoral.** [OE *thēh*]
thighbone ('θaɪ,bəʊn) *n* a nontechnical name for the **femur.**
thimble ('θɪmb^{ə}l) *n* **1** a cap of metal, plastic, etc., used to protect the end of the finger when sewing. **2** any small metal cap resembling this. **3** *Naut.* a loop of metal having a groove at its outer edge for a rope or cable. [OE *thȳmel* thumbstall, from *thūma* thumb]
thimbleful ❶ ('θɪmb^{ə}l,fʊl) *n* a very small amount, esp. of a liquid.
thimblerig ('θɪmb^{ə}l,rɪg) *n* a game in which the operator rapidly moves about three inverted thimbles, often with sleight of hand, one of which conceals a token, the other player betting on which thimble the token is under. [C19: from THIMBLE + RIG (in obs. sense meaning a trick, scheme)]
▸ **'thimble,rigger** *n*
thin ❶ (θɪn) *adj* **thinner, thinnest. 1** of relatively small extent from one side or surface to the other. **2** slim or lean. **3** sparsely placed; meagre: *thin hair.* **4** of low density: *a thin liquid.* **5** weak; poor: *a thin disguise.* **6 thin on the ground.** few in number; scarce. ◆ *adv* **7** in order to produce something thin: *to cut bread thin.* ◆ *vb* **thins, thinning, thinned. 8** to make or become thin or sparse. [OE *thynne*]
▸ **'thinly** *adv* ▸ **'thinness** *n*
thine (ðaɪn) *determiner Arch.* **a** (*preceding a vowel*) of or associated with you (thou): *thine eyes.* **b** (*as pronoun*): *thine is the greatest burden.* [OE *thīn*]
thin-film *adj* (of an electronic component, etc.) composed of one or more extremely thin layers of metal, semiconductor, etc.
thing ❶ (θɪŋ) *n* **1** an object, fact, affair, circumstance, or concept considered as being a separate entity. **2** any inanimate object. **3** an object or entity that cannot or need not be precisely named. **4** *Inf.* a person or animal: *you poor thing.* **5** an event or act. **6** a thought or statement. **7** *Law.* property. **8** a device, means, or instrument. **9** (*often pl*) a posses-

THESAURUS

thick *adj* **1** = **wide**, broad, bulky, deep, fat, solid, substantial **3, 5** = **dense**, close, clotted, coagulated, compact, concentrated, condensed, crowded, deep, heavy, impenetrable, opaque **4** = **full**, abundant, brimming, bristling, bursting, chock-a-block, chock-full, covered, crawling, frequent, numerous, packed, replete, swarming, teeming **6** *Informal* = **stupid**, blockheaded, braindead (*inf.*), brainless, dense, dim-witted (*inf.*), dopey (*inf.*), dozy, dull, insensitive, moronic, obtuse, slow, slow-witted, thickheaded **7** = **hoarse**, distorted, guttural, husky, inarticulate, indistinct, throaty **8** = **strong**, broad, decided, distinct, marked, pronounced, rich **9** *As in* **thick as thieves** *Informal* = **friendly**, buddy-buddy (*sl., chiefly US & Canad.*), chummy (*inf.*), close, confidential, devoted, familiar, hand in glove, inseparable, intimate, matey *or* maty (*Brit. inf.*), on good terms, pally (*inf.*), palsy-walsy (*inf.*), well in (*inf.*) **10 a bit thick** *Brit. informal* = **unreasonable**, excessive, over the score (*inf.*), too much, unfair, unjust
Antonyms *adj* ≠ **wide:** narrow, slight, slim, thin ≠ **dense:** clear, diluted, runny, thin, watery, weak ≠ **full:** bare, clear, devoid of, empty, free from, sparse, thin ≠ **stupid:** articulate, brainy, bright, clever, intellectual, intelligent, quick-witted, sharp, smart ≠ **hoarse:** articulate, clear, distinct, sharp, shrill, thin ≠ **strong:** faint, slight, vague, weak ≠ **friendly:** antagonistic, distant, hostile, unfriendly

thicken *vb* **1** = **set**, cake, clot, coagulate, condense, congeal, deepen, gel, inspissate (*arch.*), jell
Antonyms *vb* dilute, thin, water down, weaken

thicket *n* = **wood**, brake, clump, coppice, copse, covert, grove, hurst (*arch.*), spinney (*Brit.*), woodland

thickhead *n* **1** *Slang* = **idiot**, berk (*Brit. sl.*), blockhead, bonehead (*sl.*), chump, clot (*Brit. inf.*), dimwit (*inf.*), dipstick, divvy (*Brit. sl.*), dolt, dope (*inf.*), dummy (*sl.*), dunce, dunderhead, fathead (*inf.*), fool, imbecile, lamebrain (*inf.*), moron, numbskull *or* numskull, pillock (*Brit. sl.*), pinhead (*sl.*), plank (*Brit. sl.*)

thickheaded *adj* **1** = **idiotic**, blockheaded, braindead (*inf.*), brainless, dense, dim-witted (*inf.*), doltish, dopey (*inf.*), dozy (*Brit. inf.*), moronic, obtuse, slow, slow-witted, stupid, thick

thickset *adj* **1** = **stocky**, beefy (*inf.*), brawny, bulky, burly, heavy, muscular, powerfully built, strong, stubby, sturdy, well-built **2** = **dense**, closely packed, densely planted, solid, thick
Antonyms *adj* ≠ **stocky:** angular, bony, gangling, gaunt, lanky, rawboned, scraggy, scrawny, weedy (*inf.*)

thick-skinned *adj* = **insensitive**, callous, case-hardened, hard-boiled (*inf.*), hardened, impervious, stolid, tough, unfeeling, unsusceptible
Antonyms *adj* concerned, feeling, sensitive, tender, thin-skinned, touchy

thief *n* = **robber**, bandit, burglar, cheat, cracksman (*sl.*), crook (*inf.*), embezzler, footpad (*arch.*), housebreaker, larcenist, mugger (*inf.*), pickpocket, pilferer, plunderer, purloiner, shoplifter, stealer, swindler

thieve *vb* = **steal**, blag (*sl.*), filch, knock off (*sl.*), lift (*inf.*), misappropriate, nick (*sl., chiefly Brit.*), peculate, pilfer, pinch (*inf.*), plunder, poach, purloin, rob, run off with, snitch (*sl.*), swipe (*sl.*)

thievery *n* = **stealing**, banditry, burglary (*inf.*), larceny, pilfering, plundering, robbery, shoplifting, theft, thieving

thieving *adj* = **thievish**, larcenous, light-fingered, predatory, rapacious, sticky-fingered (*inf.*)

thimbleful *n* = **drop**, capful, dab, dash, dram, jot, modicum, nip, pinch, sip, *soupçon,* spoonful, spot, taste, toothful

thin *adj* **1** = **narrow**, attenuate, attenuated, fine, threadlike **2** = **slim**, bony, emaciated, lank, lanky, lean, light, meagre, scraggy, scrawny, skeletal, skin and bone, skinny, slender, slight, spare, spindly, thin as a rake, undernourished, underweight **3** = **meagre**, deficient, scanty, scarce, scattered, skimpy, sparse, wispy **4** = **fine**, delicate, diaphanous, filmy, flimsy, gossamer, see-through, sheer, translucent, transparent, unsubstantial **4** = **watery**, dilute, diluted, rarefied, runny, weak, wishy-washy (*inf.*) **5** = **unconvincing**, feeble, flimsy, inadequate, insufficient, lame, poor, scant, scanty, shallow, slight, superficial, unsubstantial, weak ◆ *vb* **8** = **reduce**, attenuate, cut back, dilute, diminish, emaciate, prune, rarefy, refine, trim, water down, weaken, weed out
Antonyms *adj* ≠ **narrow:** heavy, thick ≠ **slim:** bulky, corpulent, fat, heavy, obese, stout ≠ **meagre:** abundant, adequate, plentiful, profuse ≠ **fine:** bulky, dense, heavy, strong, substantial, thick ≠ **watery:** concentrated, dense, strong, thick, viscous ≠ **unconvincing:** adequate, convincing, strong, substantial

thing *n* **1** = **object**, affair, article, being, body, circumstance, concept, entity, fact, matter, part, portion, something, substance **5** = **happening**, act, deed, event, eventuality, feat, incident, occurrence, phenomenon, proceeding **8** = **device**, apparatus, contrivance, gadget, implement, instrument, machine, means, mechanism, tool **9** *often plural* = **possessions**, baggage, belongings, bits and pieces, clobber (*Brit. sl.*), clothes, effects, equipment, gear, goods, impedimenta, luggage, odds and ends, paraphernalia, stuff **10** *Informal* = **obsession**, attitude, bee in one's bonnet, fetish, fixation, hang-up (*inf.*), *idée fixe,* mania, phobia, preoccupation, quirk sion, article of clothing, etc. **10** *Inf.* a preoccupation or obsession (esp. in **have a thing about**). **11** an activity or mode of behaviour satisfying to one's personality (esp. in **do one's (own) thing**). **12 make a thing of.** exaggerate the importance of. **13 the thing.** the latest fashion. [OE *thing* assembly]

thing-in-itself *n* (in the philosophy of Immanuel Kant (1724–1804), German idealist philosopher) reality regarded apart from human knowledge and perception.

thingumabob *or* **thingamabob** ('θɪŋəmə,bɒb) *n Inf.* a person or thing the name of which is unknown, temporarily forgotten, or deliberately overlooked. Also: **thingumajig, thingamajig,** *or* **thingummy.** [C18: from THING, with humorous suffix]

think ❶ (θɪŋk) *vb* **thinks, thinking, thought. 1** (*tr; may take a clause as object*) to consider, judge, or believe: *he thinks my ideas impractical.* **2** (*intr;* often foll. by *about*) to exercise the mind as in order to make a decision; ponder. **3** (*intr*) to be capable of conscious thought: *man is the only animal that thinks.* **4** to remember; recollect. **5** (*intr;* foll. by *of*) to make the mental choice (of): *think of a number.* **6** (*may take a clause as object or an infinitive*) **6a** to expect; suppose. **6b** to be considerate enough (to do something): *he did not think to thank them.* **7** (*intr*) to focus the attention on being: *think big.* **8 think twice.** to consider carefully before deciding. ◆ *n* **9** *Inf.* a careful, open-minded assessment. **10** (*modifier*) *Inf.* characterized by or involving thinkers, thinking, or thought. ◆ See also **think over, think up.** [OE *thencan*]
▸ **'thinkable** *adj* ▸ **'thinker** *n*

thinking ❶ ('θɪŋkɪŋ) *n* **1** opinion or judgment. **2** the process of thought. ◆ *adj* **3** (*prenominal*) using or capable of using intelligent thought: *thinking people.* **4 put on one's thinking cap.** to ponder a matter or problem.

think over ❶ *vb* (*tr, adv*) to ponder or consider.

think-tank *n Inf.* a group of specialists commissioned to undertake intensive study and research into specified problems.

think up ❶ *vb* (*tr, adv*) to invent or devise.

thinner ('θɪnə) *n* (*often pl, functioning as sing*) a solvent, such as turpentine, added to paint or varnish to dilute it, reduce its opacity or viscosity, or increase its penetration.

thin-skinned ❶ *adj* sensitive to criticism or hints; easily upset or affected.

thio- *or before a vowel* **thi-** *combining form.* sulphur, esp. denoting the replacement of an oxygen atom with a sulphur atom: *thiol; thiosulphate.* [from Gk *theion* sulphur]

thiol ('θaɪɒl) *n* any of a class of sulphur-containing organic compounds with the formula RSH, where R is an organic group.

thionine ('θaɪəʊ,ni:n, -,naɪn) *or* **thionin** ('θaɪənɪn) *n* **1** a crystalline derivative of thiazine used as a violet dye to stain microscope specimens. **2** any of a class of related dyes. [C19: by shortening, from *ergothioneine*]

thiopentone sodium (,θaɪəʊ'pɛntəʊn) *or* **thiopental sodium** (,θaɪəʊ'pɛntæl) *n* a barbiturate drug used as an intravenous general anaesthetic. Also called: **Sodium Pentothal.**

thiophen ('θaɪəʊ,fɛn) *or* **thiophene** ('θaɪəʊ,fi:n) *n* a colourless liquid heterocyclic compound found in the benzene fraction of coal tar and manufactured from butane and sulphur.

thiosulphate (,θaɪəʊ'sʌlfeɪt) *n* any salt of thiosulphuric acid.

thiosulphuric acid (,θaɪəʊsʌl'fjʊərɪk) *n* an unstable acid known only in solutions and in the form of its salts. Formula: $H_2S_2O_3$.

thiouracil (,θaɪəʊ'jʊərəsɪl) *n* a white crystalline water-insoluble substance with an intensely bitter taste, used in medicine to treat hyperthyroidism. [from THIO- + *uracil* (URO- + AC(ETIC) + -IL(E))]

thiourea (,θaɪəʊ'jʊərɪə) *n* a white crystalline substance used in photographic fixing, rubber vulcanization, and the manufacture of synthetic resins.

third (θɜ:d) *adj* (*usually prenominal*) **1a** coming after the second in numbering, position, etc.; being the ordinal number of *three:* often written 3rd. **1b** (*as n*): *the third got a prize.* **2** rated, graded, or ranked below the second level. **3** denoting the third from lowest forward ratio of a gearbox in a motor vehicle. ◆ *n* **4a** one of three equal parts of an object, quantity, etc. **4b** (*as modifier*): *a third part.* **5** the fraction equal to one divided by three (1/3). **6** the forward ratio above second of a gearbox in a motor vehicle. **7a** the interval between one note and another three notes away from it counting inclusively along the diatonic scale. **7b** one of two notes constituting such an interval in relation to the other. **8** *Brit.* an honours degree of the third and usually the lowest class. Full term: **third class honours degree.** ◆ *adv* **9** Also: **thirdly.** in the third place. [OE *thirda,* var. of *thridda;* rel. to OFrisian *thredda,* OSaxon *thriddio*]
▸ **'thirdly** *adv*

Third Age *n* **the.** old age, esp. when viewed as a period of opportunity for learning something new or for other new developments: *University of the Third Age.*

third class *n* **1** the class or grade next in value, quality, etc., to the second. ◆ *adj* (**third-class** *when prenominal*). **2** of the class or grade next in value, quality, etc., to the second. ◆ *adv* **3** by third-class transport, etc.

third degree *n Inf.* torture or bullying, esp. used to extort confessions or information.

third-degree burn *n Pathol.* the most severe type of burn, involving the destruction of both epidermis and dermis.

third dimension *n* the dimension of depth by which a solid object may be distinguished from a two-dimensional drawing or picture of it.

third eyelid *n* another name for **nictitating membrane.**

Third International *n* another name for **Comintern.**

third-line forcing *n* the deprecated practice of forcing a buyer to purchase a supply of a product that he does not want as a condition of supplying him with the product he does want.

third man *n Cricket.* **a** a fielding position on the off side near the boundary behind the batsman's wicket. **b** a fielder in this position.

Third Market *n Stock Exchange.* a new small market designed to meet the needs of young growing British companies for raising capital.

Third Order *n RC Church.* a religious society of laymen affiliated to one of the religious orders and following a mitigated form of religious rule.

third party *n* **1** a person who is involved by chance or only incidentally in a legal proceeding, agreement, or other transaction. ◆ *adj* **2** *Insurance.* providing protection against liability caused by accidental injury or death of other persons.

third person *n* a grammatical category of pronouns and verbs used when referring to objects or individuals other than the speaker or his addressee or addressees.

third-rate ❶ *adj* mediocre or inferior.

third reading *n* (in a legislative assembly) **1** *Brit.* the process of discussing the committee's report on a bill. **2** *US.* the final consideration of a bill.

Third World *n* the less economically and industrially advanced countries of Africa, Asia, and Latin America collectively. Also called: **developing world.**

thirst ❶ (θɜ:st) *n* **1** a craving to drink, accompanied by a feeling of dryness in the mouth and throat. **2** an eager longing, craving, or yearning. ◆ *vb* (*intr*) **3** to feel a thirst. [OE *thyrstan,* from *thurst*]

thirsty ❶ ('θɜ:stɪ) *adj* **thirstier, thirstiest. 1** feeling a desire to drink. **2** dry; arid. **3** (foll. by *for*) feeling an eager desire. **4** causing thirst.
▸ **'thirstily** *adv* ▸ **'thirstiness** *n*

thirteen ('θɜ:'ti:n) *n* **1** the cardinal number that is the sum of ten and three and is a prime number. **2** a numeral, 13, XIII, etc., representing this number. **3** something representing or consisting of 13 units. ◆ *determiner* **4a** amounting to thirteen. **4b** (*as pronoun*): *thirteen of them fell.* [OE *threotēne*]
▸ **'thir'teenth** *adj, n*

thirteenth chord *n* a chord much used in jazz and pop, consisting of a major or minor triad upon which are superimposed the seventh, ninth, eleventh, and thirteenth above the root. Often shortened to **thirteenth.**

thirty ('θɜ:tɪ) *n, pl* **thirties. 1** the cardinal number that is the product of ten and three. **2** a numeral, 30, XXX, etc., representing this number. **3** (*pl*) the numbers 30-39, esp. the 30th to the 39th year of a person's life or of a century. **4** the amount or quantity that is three times as big as ten. **5** something representing or consisting of 30 units. ◆ *determiner* **6a** amounting to thirty. **6b** (*as pronoun*): *thirty are broken.* [OE *thrītig*]
▸ **'thirtieth** *adj, n*

Thirty-nine Articles *pl n* a set of formulas defining the doctrinal position of the Church of England, drawn up in the 16th century.

THESAURUS

think *vb* **1** = **believe**, conceive, conclude, consider, deem, determine, esteem, estimate, guess (*inf., chiefly US & Canad.*), hold, imagine, judge, reckon, regard, suppose, surmise **2** = **ponder**, brood, cerebrate, chew over (*inf.*), cogitate, consider, contemplate, deliberate, have in mind, meditate, mull over, muse, obsess, rack one's brains, reason, reflect, revolve, ruminate, turn over in one's mind, weigh up **4** = **remember**, call to mind, recall, recollect **6a** = **anticipate**, envisage, expect, foresee, imagine, plan for, presume, suppose ◆ *n* **9** *Informal* = **consideration**, assessment, contemplation, deliberation, look, reflection

thinkable *adj* **2** = **possible**, conceivable, feasible, imaginable, likely, reasonable, within the bounds of possibility
Antonyms *adj* absurd, impossible, inconceivable, not on (*inf.*), out of the question, unlikely, unreasonable, unthinkable

thinking *n* **1** = **reasoning**, assessment, conclusions, conjecture, idea, judgment, opinion, outlook, philosophy, position, theory, thoughts, view ◆ *adj* **3** = **thoughtful**, contemplative, cultured, intelligent, meditative, philosophical, ratiocinative, rational, reasoning, reflective, sophisticated

think over *vb* = **consider**, chew over (*inf.*), consider the pros and cons of, contemplate, give thought to, mull over, ponder, rack one's brains, reflect upon, turn over in one's mind, weigh up

think up *vb* = **devise**, come up with, concoct, contrive, create, dream up, imagine, improvise, invent, manufacture, trump up, visualize

thin-skinned *adj* = **easily hurt**, hypersensitive, quick to take offence, sensitive, soft, susceptible, tender, touchy, vulnerable
Antonyms *adj* callous, hard, heartless, insensitive, obdurate, stolid, thick-skinned, tough, unfeeling

third-rate *adj* = **mediocre**, bad, cheap-jack, duff (*Brit. inf.*), indifferent, inferior, low-grade, no great shakes (*inf.*), not much cop (*inf.*), poor, poor-quality, ropey *or* ropy (*Brit. inf.*), shoddy

thirst *n* **1** = **thirstiness**, craving to drink, drought, dryness **2** = **craving**, ache, appetite, desire, eagerness, hankering, hunger, keenness, longing, lust, passion, yearning, yen (*inf.*)
Antonyms *n* ≠ **craving**: apathy, aversion, disinclination, dislike, distaste, loathing, revulsion

thirsty *adj* **2** = **parched**, arid, dehydrated, dry **3** *with* **for** = **eager**, athirst, avid, burning, craving, desirous, dying, greedy, hankering, hungry, itching, longing, lusting, thirsting, yearning

thirty-second note *n* the usual US and Canad. name for **demisemiquaver.**

thirty-twomo (ˌθɜːtɪˈtuːməʊ) *n, pl* **thirty-twomos.** a book size resulting from folding a sheet of paper into 32 leaves or 64 pages.

this (ðɪs) *determiner (used before a sing n)* **1a** used preceding a noun referring to something or someone that is closer: *look at this picture.* **1b** *(as pronoun): take this.* **2a** used preceding a noun that has just been mentioned or is understood: *this plan of yours won't work.* **2b** *(as pronoun): I first saw this on Sunday.* **3a** used to refer to something about to be said, read, etc.: *consider this argument.* **3b** *(as pronoun): listen to this.* **4a** the present or immediate: *this time you'll know better.* **4b** *(as pronoun): before this, I was mistaken.* **5** *Inf.* an emphatic form of **a** or **the**[1]: *I saw this big brown bear.* **6 this and that.** various unspecified and trivial actions, matters, objects, etc. **7 with** *(or* **at***)* **this.** after this. ◆ *adv* **8** used with adjectives and adverbs to specify a precise degree that is about to be mentioned: *go just this fast and you'll be safe.* [OE *thēs, thēos, this* (masc, fem, neuter sing)]

thistle (ˈθɪsᵊl) *n* **1** any of a genus of plants of the composite family, having prickly-edged leaves, dense flower heads, and feathery hairs on the seeds: the national emblem of Scotland. **2** any of various similar or related plants. [OE *thīstel*]
▸ **ˈthistly** *adj*

thistledown (ˈθɪsᵊlˌdaʊn) *n* the mass of feathery plumed seeds produced by a thistle.

thither (ˈðɪðə) *or* **thitherward** *adv Obs. or formal.* to or towards that place; in that direction. [OE *thider*, var. of *thæder*, infl. by *hider* hither]

thitherto (ˌðɪðəˈtuː, ˈðɪðəˌtuː) *adv Obs. or formal.* until that time.

thixotropic (ˌθɪksəˈtrɒpɪk) *adj* (of fluids and gels) having a reduced viscosity when stress is applied, as when stirred: *thixotropic paints.* [C20: from Gk *thixis* the act of touching + -TROPIC]
▸ **thixotropy** (θɪkˈsɒtrəpɪ) *n* ▸ **thixotrope** (ˈθɪksəˌtrəʊp) *n*

tho' *or* **tho** (ðəʊ) *conj, adv US or poetic.* a variant spelling of **though.**

thole[1] (θəʊl) *or* **tholepin** (ˈθəʊlˌpɪn) *n* a wooden pin or one of a pair, set upright in the gunwales of a rowing boat to serve as a fulcrum in rowing. [OE *tholl*]

thole[2] (θəʊl) *vb* **tholes, tholing, tholed. 1** *(tr) Scot. & N English dialect.* to put up with; bear. **2** an archaic word for **suffer.** [OE *tholian*]

tholos (ˈθəʊlɒs) *n, pl* **tholoi** (-lɔɪ). a dry-stone beehive-shaped tomb associated with the Mycenaean culture of Greece from the 16th to the 12th centuries B.C. [C17: from Gk]

Thomism (ˈtəʊmɪzəm) *n* the system of philosophy and theology developed by Saint Thomas Aquinas in the 13th century.

Thompson sub-machine-gun (ˈtɒmsən) *n Trademark.* a .45 calibre sub-machine-gun. [C20: after John T. *Thompson* (1860–1940), US Army officer, its co-inventor]

-thon *suffix forming nouns.* indicating a large-scale event or operation of a specified kind: *telethon.* [C20: on the pattern of MARATHON]

thong (θɒŋ) *n* **1** a thin strip of leather or other material. **2** a whip or whiplash, esp. one made of leather. **3** *US, Canad., Austral., & NZ.* the usual name for **flip-flop** (sense 5). [OE *thwang*]

thoracic (θɔːˈræsɪk) *adj* of, near, or relating to the thorax.

thoracic duct *n* the major duct of the lymphatic system, beginning below the diaphragm and ascending in front of the spinal column to the base of the neck.

thoraco- *or before a vowel* **thorac-** *combining form.* thorax: *thoracotomy.*

thoracoplasty (ˈθɔːrəkəʊˌplæstɪ) *n, pl* **thoracoplasties. 1** plastic surgery of the thorax. **2** surgical removal of several ribs or a part of them to permit the collapse of a diseased lung.

thorax (ˈθɔːræks) *n, pl* **thoraxes** *or* **thoraces** (ˈθɔːrəˌsiːz, θɔːˈreɪsiːz). **1** the part of the human body enclosed by the ribs. **2** the corresponding part in other vertebrates. **3** the part of an insect's body between the head and abdomen. [C16: via L from Gk *thōrax* breastplate, chest]

thorium (ˈθɔːrɪəm) *n* a silvery-white radioactive metallic element. It is used in electronic equipment and as a nuclear power source. Symbol: Th; atomic no.: 90; atomic wt.: 232.04. [C19: NL, *Thor* Norse god of thunder + -IUM]
▸ **ˈthoric** *adj*

thorium dioxide *n* a white powder used in incandescent mantles. Also called: **thoria.**

thorium series *n* a radioactive series that starts with thorium–232 and ends with lead–208.

thorn ➊ (θɔːn) *n* **1** a sharp pointed woody extension of a stem or leaf. Cf. **prickle** (sense 1). **2** any of various trees or shrubs having thorns, esp. the hawthorn. **3** a Germanic character of runic originus (þ) used in Icelandic to represent the sound of *th*, as in *thin, bath.* **4** this same character as used in Old and Middle English to represent this sound. **5** a source of irritation (esp. in **a thorn in one's side** *or* **flesh**). [OE]
▸ **ˈthornless** *adj*

thorn apple *n* **1** a poisonous plant of the N hemisphere, having white funnel-shaped flowers and spiny fruits. US name: **jimson weed. 2** the fruit of certain types of hawthorn.

thornbill (ˈθɔːnˌbɪl) *n* **1** any of various South American hummingbirds having a thornlike bill. **2** Also called: **thornbill warbler.** any of various Australasian wrens. **3** any of various other birds with thornlike bills.

thorny ➊ (ˈθɔːnɪ) *adj* **thornier, thorniest. 1** bearing or covered with thorns. **2** difficult or unpleasant. **3** sharp.
▸ **ˈthornily** *adv* ▸ **ˈthorniness** *n*

thoron (ˈθɔːrɒn) *n* a radioisotope of radon that is a decay product of thorium. Symbol: Tn or ^{220}Rn; atomic no.: 86; half-life: 54.5s. [C20: from THORIUM + -ON]

thorough ➊ (ˈθʌrə) *adj* **1** carried out completely and carefully. **2** *(prenominal)* utter: *a thorough bore.* **3** painstakingly careful. [OE *thurh*]
▸ **ˈthoroughly** *adv* ▸ **ˈthoroughness** *n*

thorough bass (beɪs) *n* a bass part underlying a piece of concerted music. Also called: **basso continuo, continuo.** See also **figured bass.**

thoroughbred ➊ (ˈθʌrəˌbrɛd) *adj* **1** purebred. ◆ *n* **2** a pedigree animal; purebred. **3** a person regarded as being of good breeding.

Thoroughbred (ˈθʌrəˌbrɛd) *n* a British breed of horse the ancestry of which can be traced to English mares and Arab sires.

thoroughfare ➊ (ˈθʌrəˌfɛə) *n* **1** a road from one place to another, esp. a main road. **2** way through, access, or passage: *no thoroughfare.*

thoroughgoing (ˈθʌrəˌgəʊɪŋ) *adj* **1** extremely thorough. **2** *(usually prenominal)* absolute; complete: *thoroughgoing incompetence.*

thoroughpaced (ˈθʌrəˌpeɪst) *adj* **1** (of a horse) showing performing ability in all paces. **2** thoroughgoing.

thorp *or* **thorpe** (θɔːp) *n Obs. except in place names.* a small village. [OE]

those (ðəʊz) *determiner* the form of **that** used before a plural noun. [OE *thās*, pl. of THIS]

thou[1] (ðaʊ) *pron (subjective)* **1** *Arch. or dialect.* refers to the person addressed: used mainly in familiar address. **2** *(usually cap.)* refers to God when addressed in prayer, etc. [OE *thū*]

thou[2] (θaʊ) *n, pl* **thous** *or* **thou. 1** one thousandth of an inch. **2** *Inf.* short for **thousand.**

though ➊ (ðəʊ) *conj (subordinating)* **1** (sometimes preceded by *even*) despite the fact that: *though he tries hard, he always fails.* ◆ *adv* **2** nevertheless; however: *he can't dance; he sings well, though.* [OE *theah*]

thought ➊ (θɔːt) *vb* **1** the past tense and past participle of **think.** ◆ *n* **2** the act or process of thinking. **3** a concept, opinion, or idea. **4** ideas typical of a particular time or place: *German thought in the 19th century.* **5** application of mental attention; consideration. **6** purpose or intention: *I have no thought of giving up.* **7** expectation: *no thought of reward.* **8** a small amount; trifle: *you could be a thought more enthusiastic.* **9** kindness or regard. [OE *thōht*]

thoughtful ➊ (ˈθɔːtfʊl) *adj* **1** considerate in the treatment of other people. **2** showing careful thought. **3** pensive; reflective.
▸ **ˈthoughtfully** *adv* ▸ **ˈthoughtfulness** *n*

THESAURUS

thorn *n* **1** = **prickle**, barb, spike, spine **5** *As in* **thorn in one's side** *or* **flesh** = **irritation**, affliction, annoyance, bane, bother, curse, hassle *(inf.)*, irritant, nuisance, pest, plague, scourge, torment, torture, trouble

thorny *adj* **1** = **prickly**, barbed, bristling with thorns, bristly, pointed, sharp, spiky, spinous, spiny **2** = **troublesome**, awkward, difficult, harassing, hard, irksome, problematic(al), sticky *(inf.)*, ticklish, tough, trying, unpleasant, upsetting, vexatious, worrying

thorough *adj* **1** = **careful**, all-embracing, all-inclusive, assiduous, complete, comprehensive, conscientious, efficient, exhaustive, full, in-depth, intensive, leaving no stone unturned, meticulous, painstaking, scrupulous, sweeping **2** = **complete**, absolute, arrant, deep-dyed *(usually derogatory)*, downright, entire, out-and-out, outright, perfect, pure, sheer, total, unmitigated, unqualified, utter
Antonyms *adj* ≠ **careful:** careless, cursory, half-hearted, haphazard, lackadaisical, sloppy ≠ **complete:** imperfect, incomplete, partial, superficial

thoroughbred *adj* **1** = **purebred**, blood, full-blooded, of unmixed stock, pedigree, pure-blooded
Antonyms *adj* crossbred, crossed, half-breed, hybrid, mongrel, of mixed breed

thoroughfare *n* **1.** **2** = **road**, access, avenue, highway, passage, passageway, roadway, street, way

thoroughly *adv* **1** = **carefully**, assiduously, completely, comprehensively, conscientiously, efficiently, exhaustively, from top to bottom, fully, inside out, intensively, leaving no stone unturned, meticulously, painstakingly, scrupulously, sweepingly, through and through, throughout **2** = **completely**, absolutely, downright, entirely, perfectly, quite, totally, to the full, to the hilt, utterly, without reservation
Antonyms *adv* ≠ **carefully:** carelessly, cursorily, half-heartedly, haphazardly, lackadaisically, sloppily ≠ **completely:** imperfectly, incompletely, in part, partly, somewhat, superficially

though *conj* **1** = **although**, albeit, allowing, despite the fact that, even if, even supposing, even though, granted, notwithstanding, tho' *(US or poetic)*, while ◆ *adv* **2** = **nevertheless**, all the same, for all that, however, nonetheless, notwithstanding, still, yet

thought *n* **2** = **thinking**, brainwork, cerebration, cogitation, consideration, contemplation, deliberation, introspection, meditation, musing, navel-gazing *(sl.)*, reflection, regard, rumination **3** = **idea**, assessment, belief, concept, conception, conclusion, conjecture, conviction, estimation, judgment, notion, opinion, thinking, view **5** = **consideration**, attention, heed, regard, scrutiny, study **6** = **intention**, aim, design, idea, notion, object, plan, purpose **7** = **expectation**, anticipation, aspiration, dream, hope, prospect **8** = **little**, dash, jot, small amount, *soupçon*, touch, trifle, whisker *(inf.)* **9** = **kindness**, anxiety, attentiveness, care, compassion, concern, regard, solicitude, sympathy, thoughtfulness

thoughtful *adj* **1** = **considerate**, attentive, caring, helpful, kind, kindly, solicitous, unselfish **2** = **well-thought-out**, astute, canny, careful, cautious, circumspect, deliberate, discreet, heedful, mindful, prudent, wary **3** = **reflective**, contemplative, deliberative, in a brown study, introspective, lost in thought, meditative, musing, pensive, rapt, ruminative, serious, studious, thinking, wistful
Antonyms *adj* ≠ **considerate:** cold-hearted, impolite, inconsiderate, insensitive, neglectful, selfish, uncaring ≠ **well-thought-out:** flippant, heedless,

DICTIONARY

thoughtless 🅣 ('θɔːtlɪs) *adj* **1** inconsiderate. **2** having or showing lack of thought.
▸'**thoughtlessly** *adv* ▸'**thoughtlessness** *n*

thought-out *adj* conceived and developed by careful thought: *a well thought-out scheme.*

thought transference *n Psychol.* another name for **telepathy.**

thousand ('θaʊzənd) *n* **1** the cardinal number that is the product of 10 and 100. **2** a numeral, 1000, 10^3, M, etc., representing this number. **3** (*often pl*) a very large but unspecified number, amount, or quantity. **4** something representing or consisting of 1000 units. ◆ *determiner* **5a** amounting to a thousand. **5b** (*as pronoun*): *a thousand is hardly enough.* ◆ Related adj: **millenary.** [OE *thūsend*]
▸'**thousandth** *adj, n*

Thousand Guineas *n* (*functioning as sing*), usually written **1,000 Guineas.** an annual horse race, restricted to fillies, run at Newmarket in England since 1814.

Thousand Island dressing *n* a salad dressing made from mayonnaise with ketchup, chopped gherkins, etc.

Thracian ('θreɪʃɪən) *n* **1** a member of an ancient Indo-European people who lived in Thrace, an ancient country in the SE corner of the Balkan Peninsula. **2** the ancient language spoken by this people. ◆ *adj* **3** of or relating to Thrace, its inhabitants, or the extinct Thracian language.

thrall 🅣 (θrɔːl) *n* **1** Also: **thraldom** *or US* **thralldom** ('θrɔːldəm). the state or condition of being in the power of another person. **2** a person who is in such a state. **3** a person totally subject to some need, desire, appetite, etc. ◆ *vb* **4** (*tr*) to enslave or dominate. [OE *thrǣl* slave]

thrash 🅣 (θræʃ) *vb* **1** (*tr*) to beat soundly, as with a whip or stick. **2** (*tr*) to defeat totally; overwhelm. **3** (*intr*) to beat or plunge about in a wild manner. **4** to sail (a boat) against the wind or tide or (of a boat) to sail in this way. **5** another word for **thresh.** ◆ *n* **6** the act of thrashing; beating. **7** *Inf.* a party. ◆ See also **thrash out.** [OE *threscan*]

thrasher[1] ('θræʃə) *n* another name for **thresher** (the shark).

thrasher[2] ('θræʃə) *n* any of various brown thrushlike American songbirds.

thrashing 🅣 ('θræʃɪŋ) *n* a physical assault; flogging.

thrash metal *n* a type of very fast very loud rock music that combines elements of heavy metal and punk rock. Often shortened to **thrash.**

thrash out 🅣 *vb* (*tr, adv*) to discuss fully or vehemently, esp. in order to come to an agreement.

thrasonical (θrəˈsɒnɪkəl) *adj Rare.* bragging; boastful. [C16: from L *Thrasō* name of boastful soldier in *Eunuchus,* a play by Terence, from Gk *Thrasōn,* from *thrasus* forceful]
▸**thra'sonically** *adv*

thrawn (θrɔːn) *adj Scot. & N English dialect.* **1** crooked or twisted. **2** stubborn; perverse. [N English dialect, var. of *thrown,* from OE *thrāwan* to twist about, throw]

thread 🅣 (θrɛd) *n* **1** a fine strand, filament, or fibre of some material. **2** a fine cord of twisted filaments, esp. of cotton, used in sewing, etc. **3** any of the filaments of which a spider's web is made. **4** any fine line, stream, mark, or piece. **5** the helical ridge on a screw, bolt, nut, etc. **6** a very thin seam of coal or vein of ore. **7** something acting as the continuous link or theme of a whole: *the thread of the story.* **8** the course of an individual's life believed in Greek mythology to be spun, measured, and cut by the Fates. ◆ *vb* **9** (*tr*) to pass (thread, film, tape, etc.) through (something). **10** (*tr*) to string on a thread: *she threaded the beads.* **11** to make (one's way) through or over (something). **12** (*tr*) to produce a screw thread. **13** (*tr*) to pervade: *hysteria threaded his account.* **14** (*intr*) (of boiling syrup) to form a fine thread when poured from a spoon. ◆ See also **threads.** [OE *thrǣd*]
▸'**threader** *n* ▸'**thread,like** *adj*

threadbare 🅣 ('θrɛd,bɛə) *adj* **1** (of cloth, clothing, etc.) having the nap worn off so that the threads are exposed; worn out. **2** meagre or poor. **3** hackneyed: *a threadbare argument.* **4** wearing threadbare clothes; shabby.

thread mark *n* a mark put into paper money to prevent counterfeiting, consisting of a pattern of silk fibres.

threads (θrɛdz) *pl n Sl.* clothes.

threadworm ('θrɛd,wɜːm) *n* any of various nematodes, esp. the pinworm.

thready ('θrɛdɪ) *adj* **threadier, threadiest. 1** of or resembling a thread. **2** (of the pulse) barely perceptible; weak. **3** sounding thin, weak, or reedy.
▸'**threadiness** *n*

threat 🅣 (θrɛt) *n* **1** a declaration of the intention to inflict harm, pain, or misery. **2** an indication of imminent harm, danger, or pain. **3** a person or thing that is regarded as dangerous or likely to inflict pain or misery. [OE]

threaten 🅣 ('θrɛtən) *vb* **1** (*tr*) to be a threat to. **2** to be a menacing indication of (something); portend. **3** (when *tr, may take a clause as object*) to express a threat to (a person or people).
▸'**threatening** *adj* ▸'**threateningly** *adv*

three (θriː) *n* **1** the cardinal number that is the sum of two and one and is a prime number. **2** a numeral, 3, III, (iii), representing this number. **3** something representing or consisting of three units. **4** Also called: **three o'clock.** three hours after noon or midnight. ◆ *determiner* **5a** amounting to three. **5b** (*as pronoun*): *three were killed.* ◆ Related adjs.: **ternary, tertiary, treble, triple.** [OE *thrēo*]

three-card trick *n* a game in which players bet on which of three playing cards is the queen.

three-colour *adj* of or comprising a colour print or a photomechanical process in which a picture is reproduced by superimposing three prints from half-tone plates in inks corresponding to the three primary colours.

three-D *or* **3-D** *n* a three-dimensional effect.

three-decker *n* **1a** anything having three levels or layers. **1b** (*as modifier*): *a three-decker sandwich.* **2** a warship with guns on three decks.

three-dimensional *adj* **1** of, having, or relating to three dimensions. **2** simulating the effect of depth. **3** having volume. **4** lifelike.

threefold ('θriː,fəʊld) *adj* **1** equal to or having three times as many or as much; triple. **2** composed of three parts. ◆ *adv* **3** by or up to three times as many or as much.

three-legged race *n* a race in which pairs of competitors run with their adjacent legs tied together.

threepenny bit *or* **thrupenny bit** ('θrʌpnɪ, -ənɪ, 'θrɛp-) *n* a twelve-sided British coin valued at three old pence, obsolete since 1971.

three-phase *adj* (of an electrical circuit, etc.) having or using three alternating voltages of the same frequency, displaced in phase by 120°.

three-ply *adj* **1** having three layers or thicknesses. **2** (of wool, etc.) three-stranded.

three-point landing *n* an aircraft landing in which the main wheels and the nose or tail wheel touch the ground simultaneously.

three-point turn *n* a complete turn of a motor vehicle using forward and reverse gears alternately, and completed after only three movements.

three-quarter *adj* **1** being three quarters of something. **2** being of three quarters the normal length. ◆ *n* **3** *Rugby.* any of the four players between the fullback and the halfbacks.

three-ring circus *n US.* **1** a circus with three rings for simultaneous performances. **2** a situation of confusion, characterized by a bewildering variety of events or activities.

three Rs *pl n* **the.** the three skills regarded as the fundamentals of education; reading, writing, and arithmetic. [from the humorous spelling *reading, 'riting,* and *'rithmetic*]

threescore ('θriːˈskɔː) *determiner* an archaic word for **sixty.**

threesome 🅣 ('θriːsəm) *n* **1** a group of three. **2** *Golf.* a match in which a

THESAURUS

irresponsible, rash, thoughtless, unthinking ≠ **reflective:** extrovert, shallow, superficial

thoughtless *adj* **1** = **inconsiderate**, impolite, indiscreet, insensitive, rude, selfish, tactless, uncaring, undiplomatic, unkind **2** = **unthinking**, absent-minded, careless, ditsy *or* ditzy (*sl.*), foolish, heedless, ill-considered, imprudent, inadvertent, inattentive, injudicious, mindless, neglectful, negligent, rash, reckless, regardless, remiss, silly, slapdash, slipshod, stupid, unmindful, unobservant
Antonyms *adj* ≠ **inconsiderate:** attentive, considerate, diplomatic, tactful, thoughtful, unselfish ≠ **unthinking:** considered, intelligent, prudent, smart, well-advised, well-thought-out, wise

thrall *n* **1** = **slavery**, bondage, enslavement, serfdom, servitude, subjection, subjugation, thraldom, vassalage **2** = **slave**, bondservant, bondsman, serf, subject, varlet (*arch.*), vassal

thrash *vb* **1** = **beat**, belt (*inf.*), birch, cane, chastise, clobber (*sl.*), drub, flagellate, flog, give (someone) a (good) hiding (*inf.*), hide (*inf.*), horsewhip, lambast(e), leather, lick (*inf.*), paste (*sl.*), punish, scourge, spank, take a stick to, tan (*sl.*), whip **2** = **defeat**, beat, beat (someone) hollow (*Brit. inf.*), blow out of the water (*sl.*), clobber (*sl.*), crush, drub, hammer (*inf.*), lick (*inf.*), make mincemeat of (*inf.*), maul, overwhelm, paste (*sl.*), rout, run rings around (*inf.*), slaughter (*inf.*), stuff (*sl.*), tank (*sl.*), trounce, wipe the floor with (*inf.*) **3** = **thresh**, flail, heave, jerk, plunge, squirm, toss, toss and turn, writhe

thrashing *n* = **beating**, belting (*inf.*), caning, chastisement, drubbing, flogging, hiding (*inf.*), lashing, pasting (*sl.*), punishment, tanning (*sl.*), whipping

thrash out *vb* = **settle**, argue out, debate, discuss, have out, resolve, solve, talk over

thread *n* **1, 2** = **strand**, cotton, fibre, filament, line, string, yarn **7** = **theme**, course, direction, drift, motif, plot, story line, strain, tenor, train of thought ◆ *vb* **10** = **string 11** = **pass**, ease, inch, loop, meander, pick (one's way), squeeze through

threadbare *adj* **1** = **shabby**, down at heel, frayed, old, ragged, scruffy, tattered, tatty, used, worn, worn-out **3** = **hackneyed**, clichéd, cliché-ridden, common, commonplace, conventional, corny, familiar, overused, stale, stereotyped, stock, tired, trite, well-worn
Antonyms *adj* ≠ **shabby:** brand-new, good, new, smart, unused, well-preserved ≠ **hackneyed:** different, fresh, new, novel, original, unconventional, unfamiliar, unusual

threat *n* **1** = **menace**, commination, intimidatory remark, threatening remark **2** = **warning**, foreboding, foreshadowing, omen, portent, presage, writing on the wall **3** = **danger**, hazard, menace, peril, risk

threaten *vb* **1** = **endanger**, imperil, jeopardize, put at risk, put in jeopardy, put on the line **2** = **foreshadow**, be imminent, be in the air, be in the offing, forebode, hang over, hang over (someone's) head, impend, loom over, portend, presage, warn **3** = **intimidate**, browbeat, bully, cow, lean on (*sl.*), make threats to, menace, pressurize, terrorize, warn
Antonyms *vb* ≠ **intimidate, endanger:** defend, guard, protect, safeguard, shelter, shield

threatening *adj* **2** = **ominous**, baleful, forbidding, grim, inauspicious, sinister **3** = **menacing**, bullying, comminatory, intimidatory, minatory, terrorizing
Antonyms *adj* ≠ **ominous:** auspicious, bright, comforting, encouraging, favourable, promising, propitious, reassuring

threesome *n* **1** = **trio**, triad, trilogy, trine, trinity, triple, triplet, triplex, triptych, triumvirate, triune, troika single player playing his own ball competes against two others playing on the same ball. **3** any game, etc., for three people. **4** (*modifier*) performed by three.

thremmatology (ˌθrɛməˈtɒlədʒɪ) *n* the science of breeding domesticated animals and plants. [C19: from Gk *thremma* nursling + -LOGY]

threnody (ˈθrɛnədɪ, ˈθriː-) *or* **threnode** (ˈθriːnəʊd, ˈθrɛn-) *n, pl* **threnodies** *or* **threnodes.** an ode, song, or speech of lamentation, esp. for the dead. [C17: from Gk *thrēnōidia*, from *thrēnos* dirge + *ōidē* song]
▸**threnodic** (θrɪˈnɒdɪk) *adj* ▸**threnodist** (ˈθrɛnədɪst, ˈθriː-) *n*

thresh (θrɛʃ) *vb* **1** to beat stalks of ripe corn, etc., either with a hand implement or a machine to separate the grain from the husks and straw. **2** (*tr*) to beat or strike. **3** (*intr; often foll. by about*) to toss and turn; thrash. [OE *threscan*]

thresher (ˈθrɛʃə) *n* **1** a person who threshes. **2** short for **threshing machine. 3** any of a genus of large sharks occurring in tropical and temperate seas. They have a very long whiplike tail.

threshing machine *n* a machine for threshing crops.

threshold ❶ (ˈθrɛʃəʊld, ˈθrɛʃˌhəʊld) *n* **1** a sill, esp. one made of stone or hardwood, placed at a doorway. **2** any doorway or entrance. **3** the starting point of an experience, event, or venture. **4** *Psychol.* the strength at which a stimulus is just perceived: *the threshold of consciousness.* **5a** a point at which something would stop, take effect, etc. **5b** (*as modifier*): *threshold price; threshold effect.* **6** the minimum intensity or value of a signal, etc., that will produce a response or specified effect. **7** (*modifier*) of a pay agreement, clause, etc., that raises wages to compensate for increases in the cost of living. ◆ Related adj: **liminal.** [OE *therscold*]

threshold agreement *n* an agreement between an employer and employees or their union to increase wages by a specified sum if inflation exceeds a specified level in a specified time.

threw (θruː) *vb* the past tense of **throw.**

thrice (θraɪs) *adv* **1** three times. **2** threefold. **3** *Arch.* greatly. [OE *thrīwa, thrīga*]

thrift ❶ (θrɪft) *n* **1** wisdom and caution in the management of money. **2** Also called: **sea pink.** any of a genus of perennial low-growing plants of Europe, W Asia, and North America, having narrow leaves and round heads of pink or white flowers. [C13: from ON: success; see THRIVE]
▸ˈ**thriftless** *adj* ▸ˈ**thriftlessly** *adv*

thrifty ❶ (ˈθrɪftɪ) *adj* **thriftier, thriftiest. 1** showing thrift; economical or frugal. **2** *Rare.* thriving or prospering.
▸ˈ**thriftily** *adv* ▸ˈ**thriftiness** *n*

thrill ❶ (θrɪl) *n* **1** a sudden sensation of excitement and pleasure. **2** a situation producing such a sensation. **3** a trembling sensation caused by fear or emotional shock. **4** *Pathol.* an abnormal slight tremor. ◆ *vb* **5** to feel or cause to feel a thrill. **6** to tremble or cause to tremble; vibrate or quiver. [OE *thyrlian* to pierce, from *thyrel* hole]
▸ˈ**thrilling** *adj*

thriller (ˈθrɪlə) *n* a book, film, play, etc., depicting crime, mystery, or espionage in an atmosphere of excitement and suspense.

thrips (θrɪps) *n, pl* **thrips.** any of various small slender-bodied insects typically having piercing mouthparts and feeding on plant sap. [C18: via NL from Gk: woodworm]

thrive ❶ (θraɪv) *vb* **thrives, thriving; thrived** *or* **throve; thrived** *or* **thriven** (ˈθrɪvᵊn). (*intr*) **1** to grow strongly and vigorously. **2** to do well; prosper. [C13: from ON *thrīfask* to grasp for oneself, from ?]

thro' *or* **thro** (θruː) *prep, adv Inf. or poetic.* variant spellings of **through.**

throat (θrəʊt) *n* **1a** that part of the alimentary and respiratory tracts extending from the back of the mouth to just below the larynx. **1b** the front part of the neck. **2** something resembling a throat, esp. in shape or function: *the throat of a chimney.* **3 cut one's (own) throat.** to bring about one's own ruin. **4 ram** *or* **force (something) down someone's throat.** to insist that someone listen to or accept (something). ◆ Related adjs.: **guttural, laryngeal.** [OE *throtu*]

throaty ❶ (ˈθrəʊtɪ) *adj* **throatier, throatiest. 1** indicating a sore throat; hoarse: *a throaty cough.* **2** of or produced in the throat. **3** deep, husky, or guttural.
▸ˈ**throatily** *adv*

throb ❶ (θrɒb) *vb* **throbs, throbbing, throbbed.** (*intr*) **1** to pulsate or beat repeatedly, esp. with increased force. **2** (of engines, drums, etc.) to have a strong rhythmic vibration or beat. ◆ *n* **3** a throbbing, esp. a rapid pulsation as of the heart: *a throb of pleasure.* [C14: ? imit.]

throes ❶ (θrəʊz) *pl n* **1** a condition of violent pangs, pain, or convulsions: *death throes.* **2 in the throes of.** struggling with great effort with. [OE *thrāwu* threat]

thrombin (ˈθrɒmbɪn) *n Biochem.* an enzyme that acts on fibrinogen in blood causing it to clot. [C19: from THROMB(US) + -IN]

thrombocyte (ˈθrɒmbəˌsaɪt) *n* another name for **platelet.**
▸**thrombocytic** (ˌθrɒmbəˈsɪtɪk) *adj*

thromboembolism (ˌθrɒmbəʊˈɛmbəˌlɪzəm) *n* the obstruction of a blood vessel by a thrombus that has become detached from its original site.

thrombose (ˈθrɒmbəʊz) *vb* **thromboses, thrombosing, thrombosed.** to become or affect with a thrombus. [C19: back formation from THROMBOSIS]

thrombosis (θrɒmˈbəʊsɪs) *n, pl* **thromboses** (-siːz). **1** the formation or presence of a thrombus. **2** *Inf.* short for **coronary thrombosis.** [C18: from NL, from Gk: curdling, from *thrombousthai* to clot, from *thrombos* THROMBUS]
▸**thrombotic** (θrɒmˈbɒtɪk) *adj*

thrombus (ˈθrɒmbəs) *n, pl* **thrombi** (-baɪ). a clot of coagulated blood that forms within a blood vessel or inside the heart, often impeding the flow of blood. [C17: from NL, from Gk *thrombos* lump, from ?]

throne (θrəʊn) *n* **1** the ceremonial seat occupied by a monarch, bishop, etc., on occasions of state. **2** the power or rank ascribed to a royal person. **3** a person holding royal rank. **4** (*pl; often cap.*) the third of the nine orders into which the angels are divided in medieval angelology. ◆ *vb* **thrones, throning, throned. 5** to place or be placed on a throne. [C13: from OF *trone*, from L *thronus*, from Gk *thronos*]

throng ❶ (θrɒŋ) *n* **1** a great number of people or things crowded together. ◆ *vb* **2** to gather in or fill (a place) in large numbers; crowd. **3** (*tr*) to hem in (a person); jostle. [OE *gethrang*]

throstle (ˈθrɒsᵊl) *n* **1** a poetic name for the **song thrush. 2** a spinning machine for wool or cotton in which the fibres are twisted and wound continuously. [OE]

throttle ❶ (ˈθrɒtᵊl) *n* **1** Also called: **throttle valve.** any device that controls the quantity of fuel or fuel and air mixture entering an engine. **2** an informal or dialect word for **throat.** ◆ *vb* **throttles, throttling, throttled.** (*tr*) **3** to kill or injure by squeezing the throat. **4** to suppress. **5** to control or restrict (a flow of fluid) by means of a throttle valve. [C14: *throtelen*, from *throte* THROAT]
▸ˈ**throttler** *n*

through ❶ (θruː) *prep* **1** going in at one side and coming out at the other side of: *a path through the wood.* **2** occupying or visiting several points scattered around in (an area). **3** as a result of; by means of. **4** *Chiefly US.* up to and including: *Monday through Friday.* **5** during: *through the night.* **6** at the end of; having completed. **7 through with.** having finished with (esp. when dissatisfied with). ◆ *adj* **8** (*postpositive*) having successfully completed some specified activity. **9** (on a telephone line) connected. **10** (*postpositive*) no longer able to function successfully in some specified capacity: *as a journalist, you're through.* **11** (*prenominal*) (of a route, journey, etc.) continuous or unbroken: *a through train.* ◆ *adv* **12** through some specified thing, place, or period of time. **13 through and through.** thoroughly; completely. [OE *thurh*]

through bridge *n Civil engineering.* a bridge in which the track is carried by the lower horizontal members.

throughout ❶ (θruːˈaʊt) *prep* **1** right through; through the whole of (a

THESAURUS

threshold *n* **1, 2** = **entrance**, door, doorsill, doorstep, doorway, sill **3** = **start**, beginning, brink, dawn, inception, opening, outset, starting point, verge **5a** = **minimum**, lower limit
Antonyms *n* ≠ **start:** close, decline, end, finish, twilight

thrift *n* **1** = **economy**, carefulness, frugality, good husbandry, parsimony, prudence, saving, thriftiness
Antonyms *n* carelessness, extravagance, prodigality, profligacy, recklessness, squandering, waste

thriftless *adj* **1** = **spendthrift**, extravagant, improvident, imprudent, lavish, prodigal, profligate, unthrifty, wasteful
Antonyms *adj* careful, economical, frugal, provident, prudent, sparing, thrifty

thrifty *adj* **1** = **economical**, careful, frugal, parsimonious, provident, prudent, saving, sparing
Antonyms *adj* extravagant, free-spending, generous, improvident, prodigal, spendthrift, wasteful

thrill *n* **1** = **pleasure**, buzz (*sl.*), charge (*sl.*), flush of excitement, glow, kick (*inf.*), sensation, stimulation, tingle, titillation **3** = **trembling**, flutter, fluttering, quiver, shudder, throb, tremor, vibration ◆ *vb* **5** = **excite**, arouse, electrify, flush, get a charge (*sl.*), get a kick (*inf.*), move, send (*sl.*), stimulate, stir, tingle, titillate **6** = **tremble**, flutter, quake, quiver, shake, shudder, throb, vibrate
Antonyms *n* ≠ **pleasure:** boredom, dreariness, dullness, ennui, monotony, tedium

thrilling *adj* **1** = **exciting**, electrifying, gripping, hair-raising, rip-roaring (*inf.*), riveting, rousing, sensational, sexy (*inf.*), stimulating, stirring
Antonyms *adj* ≠ **exciting:** boring, dreary, dull, monotonous, quiet, staid, tedious, tiresome, uninteresting, unmoving

thrive *vb* **1, 2** = **prosper**, advance, bloom, boom, burgeon, develop, do well, flourish, get on, grow, grow rich, increase, succeed, wax
Antonyms *vb* decline, droop, fail, languish, perish, shrivel, stagnate, wane, wilt, wither

throaty *adj* **3** = **hoarse**, deep, gruff, guttural, husky, low, thick

throb *vb* **1** = **pulsate**, beat, palpitate, pound, pulse, thump, vibrate ◆ *n* **3** = **pulse**, beat, palpitation, pounding, pulsating, thump, thumping, vibration

throes *pl n* **1** = **pains**, convulsions, fit, pangs, paroxysm, spasms, stabs **2 in the throes of** = **struggling with**, agonized by, anguished by, in the midst of, in the pangs of, in the process of, suffering from, toiling with, wrestling with

throng *n* **1** = **crowd**, assemblage, concourse, congregation, crush, horde, host, jam, mass, mob, multitude, pack, press, swarm ◆ *vb* **2** = **crowd**, bunch, congregate, converge, cram, fill, flock, hem in, herd, jam, mill around, pack, press, swarm around, troop
Antonyms *vb* ≠ **crowd:** break up, disband, dispel, disperse, scatter, separate, spread out

throttle *vb* **3** = **strangle**, choke, garrotte, strangulate **4** = **suppress**, control, gag, inhibit, silence, stifle

through *prep* **1** = **from one side to the other of**, between, by, from end to end of, in and out of, past **3** = **because of**, as a consequence or result of, by means of, by virtue of, by way of, using, via, with the help of **5** = **during**, in, in the middle of, throughout ◆ *adj* **7 through with** = **finished**, done, having had enough of **8** = **completed**, done, ended, finished, terminated ◆ *adv* **13 through and through** = **completely**, altogether, entirely, fully, thoroughly, totally, to the core, unreservedly, utterly, wholly

throughout *prep* **1** = **through the whole of**, all over, all through, during the whole of, everyplace or a period of time): *throughout the day.* ◆ *adv* **2** through the whole of some specified period or area.

throughput ('θruːˌpʊt) *n* the quantity of raw material or information processed or communicated in a given period, esp. by a computer.

throughway ('θruːˌweɪ) *n US.* a thoroughfare, esp. a motorway.

throve (θrəʊv) *vb* a past tense of **thrive.**

throw ❶ (θrəʊ) *vb* **throws, throwing, threw, thrown.** (*mainly tr*) **1** (*also intr*) to project (something) through the air, esp. with a rapid motion of the arm. **2** (foll. by *in, on, onto,* etc.) to put or move suddenly, carelessly, or violently. **3** to bring to or cause to be in a specified state or condition, esp. suddenly: *the news threw them into a panic.* **4** to direct or cast (a shadow, light, etc.). **5** to project (the voice) so as to make it appear to come from other than its source. **6** to give or hold (a party). **7** to cause to fall or be upset: *the horse threw his rider.* **8a** to tip (dice) out onto a flat surface. **8b** to obtain (a specified number) in this way. **9** to shape (clay) on a potter's wheel. **10** to move (a switch or lever) to engage or disengage a mechanism. **11** to be subjected to (a fit). **12** to turn (wood, etc.) on a lathe. **13** *Inf.* to baffle or astonish; confuse: *the question threw me.* **14** *Boxing.* to deliver (a punch). **15** *Wrestling.* to hurl (an opponent) to the ground. **16** *Inf.* to lose (a contest, etc.) deliberately. **17a** to play (a card). **17b** to discard (a card). **18** (of an animal) to give birth to (young). **19** to twist or spin (filaments) into thread. **20** *Austral. inf.* (often foll. by *at*) to mock or poke fun. **21 throw oneself at.** to strive actively to attract the attention or affection of. **22 throw oneself into.** to involve oneself enthusiastically in. **23 throw oneself on.** to rely entirely upon. ◆ *n* **24** the act or an instance of throwing. **25** the distance over which anything may be thrown: *a stone's throw.* **26** *Inf.* a chance or try. **27** an act or result of throwing dice. **28a** the eccentricity of a cam. **28b** the radial distance between the central axis of a crankshaft and the axis of a crankpin forming part of the shaft. **29** a decorative blanket or cover. **30** *Geol.* the vertical displacement of rock strata at a fault. **31** *Physics.* the deflection of a measuring instrument as a result of a fluctuation. ◆ See also **throwaway, throwback, throw in,** etc. [OE *thrāwan* to turn, torment]
▸ **'thrower** *n*

throwaway ❶ ('θrəʊəˌweɪ) *adj* (*prenominal*) **1** said or done incidentally, esp. for rhetorical effect; casual: *a throwaway remark.* **2** designed to be discarded after use rather than reused, refilled, etc.: *a throwaway carton.* ◆ *n* **3** *Chiefly US & Canad.* a handbill. ◆ *vb* **throw away.** (*tr, adv*) **4** to get rid of; discard. **5** to fail to make good use of; waste.

throwback ('θrəʊˌbæk) *n* **1a** a person, animal, or plant that has the characteristics of an earlier or more primitive type. **1b** a reversion to such an organism. ◆ *vb* **throw back.** (*adv*) **2** (*intr*) to revert to an earlier or more primitive type. **3** (*tr;* foll. by *on*) to force to depend (on): *the crisis threw her back on her faith in God.*

throw in *vb* (*tr, adv*) **1** to add at no additional cost. **2** to contribute or interpose (a remark, argument, etc.). **3 throw in the sponge** (*or* **towel**). to give in; accept defeat. ◆ *n* **throw-in. 4** *Soccer, etc.* the method of putting the ball into play after it has gone into touch by throwing it to a team-mate.

thrown (θrəʊn) *vb* the past participle of **throw.**

throw off ❶ *vb* (*mainly tr, adv*) **1** to free oneself of; discard. **2** to produce or utter in a casual manner. **3** to escape from or elude. **4** to confuse or disconcert. **5** (*intr;* often foll. by **at**) *Austral. & NZ inf.* to deride or ridicule.

throw out ❶ *vb* (*tr, adv*) **1** to discard or reject. **2** to expel or dismiss, esp. forcibly. **3** to construct (something projecting or prominent). **4** to put forward or offer. **5** to utter in a casual or indirect manner. **6** to confuse or disconcert. **7** to give off or emit. **8** *Cricket.* (of a fielder) to put (the batsman) out by throwing the ball to hit the wicket. **9** *Baseball.* to make a throw to a team-mate who in turn puts out (a base runner).

throw over ❶ *vb* (*tr, adv*) to forsake or abandon; jilt.

throw together *vb* (*tr, adv*) **1** to assemble hurriedly. **2** to cause to become casually acquainted.

throw up ❶ *vb* (*adv, mainly tr*) **1** to give up; abandon. **2** to construct hastily. **3** to reveal; produce. **4** (*also intr*) *Inf.* to vomit.

thru (θruː) *prep, adv, adj Chiefly US.* a variant spelling of **through.**

thrum[1] (θrʌm) *vb* **thrums, thrumming, thrummed. 1** to strum rhythmically but without expression on (a musical instrument). **2** (*intr*) to drum incessantly: *rain thrummed on the roof.* ◆ *n* **3** a repetitive strumming. [C16: imit.]

thrum[2] (θrʌm) *n* **1a** any of the unwoven ends of warp thread remaining on the loom when the web has been removed. **1b** such ends of thread collectively. **2** a fringe or tassel of short unwoven threads. ◆ *vb* **thrums, thrumming, thrummed. 3** (*tr*) to trim with thrums. [C14: from OE]

thrush[1] (θrʌʃ) *n* any of a subfamily of songbirds, esp. those having a brown plumage with a spotted breast, such as the mistle thrush and song thrush. [OE *thrȳsce*]

thrush[2] (θrʌʃ) *n* **1** a fungal disease, esp. of infants, characterized by the formation of whitish spots. **2** a genital infection caused by the same fungus. **3** a softening of the frog of a horse's hoof characterized by inflammation and a thick foul discharge. [C17: from ?]

thrust ❶ (θrʌst) *vb* **thrusts, thrusting, thrust. 1** (*tr*) to push (someone or something) with force. **2** (*tr*) to force upon (someone) or into (some condition or situation): *they thrust responsibilities upon her.* **3** (*tr;* foll. by *through*) to pierce; stab. **4** (*intr;* usually foll. by *through* or *into*) to force a passage. **5** to make a stab or lunge at. ◆ *n* **6** a forceful drive, push, stab, or lunge. **7** a force, esp. one that produces motion. **8a** a propulsive force produced by the fluid pressure or the change of momentum of the fluid in a jet engine, rocket engine, etc. **8b** a similar force produced by a propeller. **9** a continuous pressure exerted by one part of an object, structure, etc., against another. **10** force, impetus, or drive. **11** the essential or most forceful part: *the thrust of the argument.* [C12: from ON *thrysta*]

thruster ('θrʌstə) *n* **1** a person or thing that thrusts. **2** a small rocket engine, esp. one used to correct the altitude or course of a spacecraft.

thrust fault *n* a fault in which the rocks on the lower side of an inclined fault plane have been displaced downwards; a reverse fault.

thud ❶ (θʌd) *n* **1** a dull heavy sound. **2** a blow or fall that causes such a sound. ◆ *vb* **thuds, thudding, thudded. 3** to make or cause to make such a sound. [OE *thyddan* to strike]

thug ❶ (θʌg) *n* **1** a tough and violent man, esp. a criminal. **2** (*sometimes cap.*) (formerly) a member of an organization of robbers and assassins in India. [C19: from Hindi *thag* thief, from Sansk. *sthaga* scoundrel, from *sthagati* to conceal]
▸ **'thuggery** *n* ▸ **'thuggish** *adj*

thuja *or* **thuya** ('θuːjə) *n* any of a genus of coniferous trees of North America and East Asia, having scalelike leaves, small cones, and an aromatic wood. [C18: from NL, from Med. L *thuia,* ult. from Gk *thua* an African tree]

thulium ('θjuːlɪəm) *n* a malleable ductile silvery-grey element. The radioisotope **thulium-170** is used as an electron source in portable X-ray units. Symbol: Tm; atomic no.: 69; atomic wt.: 168.93. [C19: NL, from *Thule* a region thought, by ancient geographers, to be northernmost in the world + -IUM]

thumb ❶ (θʌm) *n* **1** the first and usually shortest and thickest of the digits of the hand. **2** the corresponding digit in other vertebrates. **3** the part of a glove shaped to fit the thumb. **4 all thumbs.** clumsy. **5 thumbs down.** an indication of refusal or disapproval. **6 thumbs up.** an indication of encouragement or approval. **7 under someone's thumb.** at

THESAURUS

where in, for the duration of, from end to end of, over the length and breadth of, right through ◆ *adv* **2** = **from start to finish,** all the time, all through, from beginning to end, from the start, in every nook and cranny, right through, the whole time

throw *vb* **1** = **hurl,** cast, chuck (*inf.*), fling, heave, launch, lob (*inf.*), pitch, project, propel, put, send, shy, sling, toss **7** = **bring down,** dislodge, fell, floor, hurl to the ground, overturn, unseat, upset **13** *Informal* = **confuse,** astonish, baffle, confound, disconcert, dumbfound, faze, put one off one's stroke, throw off, throw one off one's stride, throw out ◆ *n* **24** = **toss,** cast, fling, heave, lob, pitch, projection, put, shy, sling **26** *Informal* = **try,** attempt, chance, essay, gamble, hazard, venture, wager

throwaway *adj* **1** = **casual,** careless, offhand, passing, understated ◆ *vb* **throw away 4** = **discard,** axe (*inf.*), bin (*inf.*), cast off, chuck (*inf.*), dispense with, dispose of, ditch (*sl.*), dump (*inf.*), get rid of, jettison, junk (*inf.*), reject, scrap, throw out **5** = **waste,** blow (*sl.*), fail to make use of, fritter away, lose, make poor use of, squander
Antonyms *vb* ≠ **discard:** conserve, keep, preserve, rescue, retain, retrieve, salvage, save

throw off *vb* **1** *Literary* = **free oneself of,** abandon, cast off, discard, drop, rid oneself of, shake off **3** = **escape from,** elude, evade, get away from, give (someone) the slip, leave behind, lose, outdistance, outrun, shake off, show a clean pair of heels to **4** = **disconcert,** confuse, disturb, faze, put one off one's stroke, throw (*inf.*), throw one off one's stride, unsettle, upset

throw out *vb* **1** = **discard,** bin (*inf.*), cast off, chuck (*inf.*), dispense with, ditch (*sl.*), dump (*inf.*), jettison, junk (*inf.*), reject, relegate, scrap, throw away, turn down **2** = **expel,** dismiss, eject, evict, get rid of, give the bum's rush (*sl.*), kick out (*inf.*), oust, show one the door, turf out (*Brit. inf.*) **6** = **disconcert,** confuse, disturb, put one off one's stroke, throw (*inf.*), throw one off one's stride, unsettle, upset **7** = **emit,** diffuse, disseminate, give off, put forth, radiate

throw over *vb Old-fashioned* = **abandon,** break with, chuck (*inf.*), desert, discard, drop (*inf.*), finish with, forsake, jilt, leave, quit, split up with, walk out on (*inf.*)

throw up *vb* **1** = **give up,** abandon, chuck (*inf.*), jack in, leave, quit, relinquish, renounce, resign from, step down from (*inf.*) **2** = **throw together,** jerry-build, run up, slap together **3** = **produce,** bring forward, bring to light, bring to notice, bring to the surface, reveal **4** *Informal* = **vomit,** barf (*US sl.*), be sick, bring up, chuck (up), chunder (*sl., chiefly Austral.*), disgorge, heave, puke (*sl.*), regurgitate, retch, spew

thrust *vb* **1** = **push,** butt, drive, force, impel, jam, plunge, poke, press, prod, propel, ram, shove, urge **3** = **stab,** jab, lunge, pierce, stick **4** = **shove,** elbow *or* shoulder one's way, push ◆ *n* **6** = **push,** drive, lunge, poke, prod, shove, stab **7** = **momentum,** impetus, motive force, motive power, propulsive force

thud *n, vb* **1-3** = **thump,** clonk, clump, clunk, crash, knock, smack, wallop (*inf.*)

thug *n* **1** = **ruffian,** assassin, bandit, bruiser (*inf.*), bully boy, cut-throat, gangster, heavy (*sl.*), hooligan, killer, mugger (*inf.*), murderer, robber, tough, tsotsi (*S. Afr.*)

thumb *n* **1** = **pollex 4 all thumbs** = **clumsy,** butterfingered, cack-handed (*inf.*), ham-fisted (*inf.*), inept, maladroit **5 thumbs down** = **disapproval,** negation, no, rebuff, refusal, rejection **6 thumbs up** = **approval,** acceptance, affirmation, encouragement, go-ahead (*inf.*), green light, O.K. *or* okay (*inf.*), yes ◆ *vb* **8** = **handle,** dog-ear, finger, mark **9** = **hitch** (*inf.*), hitchhike **10** *often foll. by* **through** = **flick through,** browse through, flip through, glance at, leaf through, riffle through, run one's eye over, scan the pages of, skim through, turn over **11 thumb one's nose at** = **show contempt for,** be contemptuous of, cock a snook at, deride, flout, jeer at, laugh at, laugh in the face of, mock, ridicule, show disrespect to someone's mercy or command. ◆ *vb* **8** (*tr*) to touch, mark, or move with the thumb. **9** to attempt to obtain (a lift or ride) by signalling with the thumb. **10** (when *intr*, often foll. by *through*) to flip the pages of (a book, etc.) in order to glance at the contents. **11 thumb one's nose at.** to deride or mock, esp. by placing the thumb on the nose with fingers extended. [OE *thūma*]

thumb index *n* **1** a series of indentations cut into the fore-edge of a book to facilitate quick reference. ◆ *vb* **thumb-index. 2** (*tr*) to furnish with a thumb index.

thumbnail Ⓣ (ˈθʌm,neɪl) *n* **1** the nail of the thumb. **2** (*modifier*) concise and brief: *a thumbnail sketch.*

thumbnut (ˈθʌm,nʌt) *n* a wing nut.

thumb piano *n* another name for **mbira.**

thumbscrew (ˈθʌm,skruː) *n* **1** an instrument of torture that pinches or crushes the thumbs. **2** a screw with projections on its head enabling it to be turned by the thumb and forefinger.

thumbtack (ˈθʌm,tæk) *n* the US and Canad. name for **drawing pin.**

thump Ⓣ (θʌmp) *n* **1** the sound of a heavy solid body hitting a comparatively soft surface. **2** a heavy blow with the hand. ◆ *vb* **3** (*tr*) to strike or beat heavily; pound. **4** (*intr*) to throb, beat, or pound violently. [C16]
▸ **ˈthumper** *n*

thumping Ⓣ (ˈθʌmpɪŋ) *adj* (*prenominal*) *Sl.* huge or excessive: *a thumping loss.*

thunbergia (θʌnˈbɜːdʒɪə) *n* any of various climbing or dwarf plants of tropical and subtropical Africa and Asia. [C19: after K. P. *Thunberg* (1743-1822), Swedish botanist]

thunder Ⓣ (ˈθʌndə) *n* **1** a loud cracking or deep rumbling noise caused by the rapid expansion of atmospheric gases which are suddenly heated by lightning. **2** any loud booming sound. **3** *Rare.* a violent threat or denunciation. **4 steal someone's thunder.** to lessen the effect of someone's idea or action by anticipating it. ◆ *vb* **5** to make (a loud sound) or utter (words) in a manner suggesting thunder. **6** (*intr; with it as subject*) to be the case that thunder is being heard. **7** (*intr*) to move fast and heavily: *the bus thundered downhill.* **8** (*intr*) to utter vehement threats or denunciation; rail. [OE *thunor*]
▸ **ˈthundery** *adj* ▸ **ˈthunderer** *n*

thunderbolt (ˈθʌndə,bəʊlt) *n* **1** a flash of lightning accompanying thunder. **2** the imagined agency of destruction produced by a flash of lightning. **3** (in mythology) the destructive weapon wielded by several gods, esp. the Greek god Zeus. **4** something very startling.

thunderclap (ˈθʌndə,klæp) *n* **1** a loud outburst of thunder. **2** something as violent or unexpected as a clap of thunder.

thundercloud (ˈθʌndə,klaʊd) *n* a towering electrically charged cumulonimbus cloud associated with thunderstorms.

thunderhead (ˈθʌndə,hɛd) *n Chiefly US.* the anvil-shaped top of a cumulonimbus cloud.

thundering Ⓣ (ˈθʌndərɪŋ) *adj* (*prenominal*) *Sl.* very great or excessive: *a thundering idiot.*

thunderous Ⓣ (ˈθʌndərəs) *adj* **1** threatening; angry. **2** resembling thunder, esp. in loudness.

thunderstorm (ˈθʌndə,stɔːm) *n* a storm with thunder and lightning and usually heavy rain or hail.

thunderstruck Ⓣ (ˈθʌndə,strʌk) *or* **thunderstricken** (ˈθʌndə,strɪkən) *adj* **1** completely taken aback; amazed or shocked. **2** *Rare.* struck by lightning.

thurible (ˈθjʊərɪbᵊl) *n* another word for **censer.** [C15: from L *tūribulum* censer, from *tūs* incense]

Thurs. *abbrev. for* Thursday.

Thursday (ˈθɜːzdɪ) *n* the fifth day of the week; fourth day of the working week. [OE *Thursdæg*, lit.: Thor's day]

thus Ⓣ (ðʌs) *adv* **1** in this manner: *do it thus.* **2** to such a degree: *thus far and no further.* ◆ *sentence connector.* **3** therefore: *We have failed. Thus we have to take the consequences.* [OE]

thuya (ˈθuːjə) *n* a variant spelling of **thuja.**

thwack Ⓣ (θwæk) *vb* **1** to beat, esp. with something flat. ◆ *n* **2a** a blow with something flat. **2b** the sound made by it. [C16: imit.]

thwart Ⓣ (θwɔːt) *vb* **1** to oppose successfully or prevent; frustrate. **2** *Obs.* to be or move across. ◆ *n* **3** an oarsman's seat lying across a boat. ◆ *adj* **4** passing or being situated across. ◆ *prep, adv* **5** *Obs.* across. [C13: from ON *thvert*, from *thverr* transverse]

thy (ðaɪ) *determiner* (*usually preceding a consonant*) *Arch. or Brit. dialect.* belonging to or associated in some way with you (thou): *thy goodness.* [C12: var. of THINE]

thylacine (ˈθaɪlə,saɪn) *n* an extinct or rare doglike carnivorous marsupial of Tasmania. Also called: **Tasmanian wolf.** [C19: from NL *thȳlacīnus*, from Gk *thulakos* pouch]

thyme (taɪm) *n* any of various small shrubs having a strong odour, small leaves, and white, pink, or red flowers. [C14: from OF *thym*, from L *thymum*, from Gk, from *thuein* to make a burnt offering]
▸ **ˈthymy** *adj*

-thymia *n combining form.* indicating a certain emotional condition, mood, or state of mind: *cyclothymia.* [NL, from Gk *thumos* temper]

thymine (ˈθaɪmiːn) *n* a white crystalline base found in DNA. [C19: from THYMIC (see THYMUS) + -INE^{2}]

thymol (ˈθaɪmɒl) *n* a white crystalline substance obtained from thyme and used as a fungicide, antiseptic, etc. [C19: from THYME + -OL^{2}]

thymus (ˈθaɪməs) *n, pl* **thymuses** *or* **thymi** (-maɪ). a glandular organ of vertebrates, consisting in man of two lobes situated below the thyroid. It atrophies with age and is almost nonexistent in the adult. [C17: from NL, from Gk *thumos* sweetbread]
▸ **ˈthymic** *adj*

thyratron (ˈθaɪrə,trɒn) *n Electronics.* a gas-filled tube that has three electrodes and can be switched between an 'off' state and an 'on' state. It has been superseded by the thyristor. [C20: orig. a trademark, from Gk *thura* door, valve + -TRON]

thyristor (θaɪˈrɪstə) *n* any of a group of semiconductor devices, such as the silicon-controlled rectifier, that can be switched between two states. [C20: from THYR(ATRON) + (TRANS)ISTOR]

thyroid (ˈθaɪrɔɪd) *adj* **1** of or relating to the thyroid gland. **2** of or relating to the largest cartilage of the larynx. ◆ *n* **3** See **thyroid gland. 4** a preparation of the thyroid gland of certain animals, used to treat hypothyroidism. [C18: from NL *thyroidēs*, from Gk *thureoeidēs*, from *thureos* oblong (lit.: door-shaped), from *thura* door]

thyroid gland *n* an endocrine gland of vertebrates, consisting in man of two lobes near the base of the neck. It secretes hormones that control metabolism and growth.

thyrotropin (,θaɪrəʊˈtrəʊpɪn) *or* **thyrotrophin** *n* a hormone secreted by the pituitary gland: it stimulates the activity of the thyroid gland. [C20: from *thyro-* thyroid + -TROPE + -IN]

thyroxine (θaɪˈrɒksiːn, -sɪn) *or* **thyroxin** (θaɪˈrɒksɪn) *n* the principal hormone produced by the thyroid gland. [C19: from *thyro-* thyroid + OXY-^{2} + -INE^{2}]

thyrse (θɜːs) *or* **thyrsus** (ˈθɜːsəs) *n, pl* **thyrses** *or* **thyrsi** (ˈθɜːsaɪ). *Bot.* a type of inflorescence, occurring in the lilac and grape, in which the main branch is racemose and the lateral branches cymose. [C17: from F: THYRSUS]

thyrsus (ˈθɜːsəs) *n, pl* **thyrsi** (-saɪ). **1** *Greek myth.* a staff, usually one tipped with a pine cone, borne by Dionysus (Bacchus) and his followers. **2** a variant spelling of **thyrse.** [C18: from L, from Gk *thursos* stalk]

thyself (ðaɪˈsɛlf) *pron Arch.* **a** the reflexive form of *thou* or *thee.* **b** (intensifier): *thou, thyself, wouldst know.*

ti (tiː) *n Music.* a variant spelling of **te.**

Ti *the chemical symbol for* titanium.

tiara (tɪˈɑːrə) *n* **1** a woman's semicircular jewelled headdress for formal occasions. **2** a high headdress worn by Persian kings in ancient times. **3** a headdress worn by the pope, consisting of a beehive-shaped diadem surrounded by three coronets. [C16: via L from Gk, of Oriental origin]
▸ **tiˈaraed** *adj*

Tibetan (tɪˈbɛtᵊn) *adj* **1** of or characteristic of Tibet, its people, or their language. ◆ *n* **2** a native or inhabitant of Tibet. **3** the language of Tibet.

tibia (ˈtɪbɪə) *n, pl* **tibiae** (ˈtɪbɪ,iː) *or* **tibias. 1** the inner and thicker of the two bones of the human leg below the knee; shinbone. **2** the corresponding bone in other vertebrates. **3** the fourth segment of an insect's leg. [C16: from L: leg, pipe]
▸ **ˈtibial** *adj*

THESAURUS

thumbnail *modifier* **2** = **brief**, compact, concise, pithy, quick, short, succinct

thump *n* **1** = **thud**, bang, clunk, crash, thwack **2** = **blow**, clout (*inf.*), knock, punch, rap, smack, swipe, wallop (*inf.*), whack ◆ *vb* **3** = **strike**, batter, beat, belabour, chin (*sl.*), clobber (*sl.*), clout (*inf.*), deck (*sl.*), hit, knock, lambast(e), lay one on (*sl.*), pound, punch, rap, smack, swipe, thrash, wallop (*inf.*), whack **4** = **throb**, beat

thumping *adj Slang* = **huge**, colossal, elephantine, enormous, excessive, exorbitant, gargantuan, gigantic, great, humongous *or* humungous (*US sl.*), impressive, mammoth, massive, monumental, stellar (*inf.*), terrific, thundering (*sl.*), titanic, tremendous, whopping (*inf.*)
Antonyms *adj* inconsequential, insignificant, meagre, measly (*inf.*), negligible, paltry, petty, piddling (*inf.*), trifling, trivial

thunder *n* **1, 2** = **rumble**, boom, booming, cracking, crash, crashing, detonation, explosion, pealing, rumbling ◆ *vb* **5** = **rumble**, bark, bellow, blast, boom, clap, crack, crash, detonate, explode, peal, resound, reverberate, roar, shout, yell **8** = **rail**, curse, denounce, fulminate, threaten, utter threats

thundering *adj Old-fashioned slang* = **great**, decided, enormous, excessive, monumental, remarkable, unmitigated, utter

thunderous *adj* **2** = **loud**, booming, deafening, ear-splitting, noisy, resounding, roaring, tumultuous

thunderstruck *adj* **1** = **amazed**, aghast, astonished, astounded, bowled over (*inf.*), dazed, dumbfounded, flabbergasted (*inf.*), floored (*inf.*), flummoxed, gobsmacked (*Brit. sl.*), knocked for six (*inf.*), left speechless, nonplussed, open-mouthed, paralysed, petrified, rooted to the spot, shocked, staggered, struck dumb, stunned, taken aback

thus *adv* **1, 2** = **in this way**, as follows, in this fashion, in this manner, like so, like this, so, to such a degree ◆ *sentence connector* **3** = **therefore**, accordingly, consequently, ergo, for this reason, hence, on that account, so, then

thwack *vb* **1** = **smack**, bash (*inf.*), beat, chin (*sl.*), clout (*inf.*), deck (*sl.*), flog, hit, lambast(e), lay one on (*sl.*), swipe, thump, wallop (*inf.*), whack ◆ *n* **2** = **smack**, bash (*inf.*), blow, clout (*inf.*), swipe, thump, wallop (*inf.*), whack

thwart *vb* **1** = **frustrate**, baffle, balk, check, cook (someone's) goose (*inf.*), defeat, foil, hinder, impede, obstruct, oppose, outwit, prevent, put a spoke in someone's wheel (*inf.*), snooker, stop, stymie
Antonyms *vb* aggravate, aid, assist, encourage, exacerbate, facilitate, hasten, help, intensify, support

tic ● (tɪk) *n* spasmodic twitching of a particular group of muscles. [C19: from F, from ?]
tic douloureux (ˈtɪk ˌduːləˈruː) *n* a condition of momentary stabbing pain along the trigeminal nerve. [C19: from F, lit.: painful tic]
tick[1] ● (tɪk) *n* **1** a recurrent metallic tapping or clicking sound, such as that made by a clock. **2** *Brit. inf.* a moment or instant. **3** a mark (✓) used to check off or indicate the correctness of something. **4** *Commerce.* the smallest increment by which a price can fluctuate in a commodity or financial futures market. ◆ *vb* **5** to produce a recurrent tapping sound or indicate by such a sound: *the clock ticked the minutes away.* **6** (when *tr*, often foll. by *off*) to mark or check with a tick. **7 what makes someone tick.** *Inf.* the basic drive or motivation of a person. ◆ See also **tick off, tick over.** [C13: from Low G *tikk* touch]
tick[2] (tɪk) *n* any of a large group of small parasitic arachnids typically living on the skin of warm-blooded animals and feeding on the blood, etc., of their hosts. [OE *ticca*]
tick[3] (tɪk) *n* **1** the strong covering of a pillow, mattress, etc. **2** *Inf.* short for **ticking.** [C15: prob. from MDu. *tīke*]
tick[4] ● (tɪk) *n Brit. inf.* account or credit (esp. in **on tick**). [C17: shortened from TICKET]
tick bird *n* another name for **oxpecker.**
ticker (ˈtɪkə) *n* **1** *Sl.* **1a** the heart. **1b** a watch. **2** a person or thing that ticks. **3** the US word for **tape machine.**
ticker tape *n* a continuous paper ribbon on which a tape machine prints current stock quotations.
ticket ● (ˈtɪkɪt) *n* **1a** a piece of paper, cardboard, etc., showing that the holder is entitled to certain rights, such as travel on a train or bus, entry to a place of public entertainment, etc. **1b** (*modifier*) concerned with the issue, sale, or checking of tickets: *a ticket collector.* **2** a piece of card, cloth, etc., attached to an article showing information such as its price, size, etc. **3** a summons served for a parking or traffic offence. **4** *Inf.* the certificate of competence issued to a ship's captain or an aircraft pilot. **5** *Chiefly US & NZ.* the group of candidates nominated by one party in an election; slate. **6** *Chiefly US.* the declared policy of a political party at an election. **7** *Brit. inf.* a certificate of discharge from the armed forces. **8** *Inf.* the right or appropriate thing: *that's the ticket.* **9 have (got) tickets on oneself.** *Austral. inf.* to be conceited. ◆ *vb* **tickets, ticketing, ticketed.** (*tr*) **10** to issue or attach a ticket or tickets to. [C17: from OF *etiquet,* from *estiquier* to stick on, from MDu. *steken* to stick]
ticket day *n Stock Exchange.* the day before settling day, when the stockbrokers are given the names of the purchasers.
ticket of leave *n* (formerly, in Britain) a permit allowing a convict (**ticket-of-leave man**) to leave prison, after serving only part of his sentence, with certain restrictions placed on him.
tick fever *n* any acute infectious febrile disease caused by the bite of an infected tick.
ticking (ˈtɪkɪŋ) *n* a strong cotton fabric, often striped, used esp. for mattress and pillow covers. [C17: from TICK[3]]
tickle ● (ˈtɪkᵊl) *vb* **tickles, tickling, tickled. 1** to touch or stroke, so as to produce pleasure, laughter, or a twitching sensation. **2** (*tr*) to excite pleasurably; gratify. **3** (*tr*) to delight or entertain (often in **tickle one's fancy**). **4** (*intr*) to itch or tingle. **5** (*tr*) to catch (a fish, esp. a trout) with the hands. **6 tickle pink** *or* **to death.** *Inf.* to please greatly. ◆ *n* **7** a sensation of light stroking or itching. **8** the act of tickling. **9** *Canad.* (in the Atlantic Provinces) a narrow strait. [C14]
tickler (ˈtɪklə) *n* **1** *Inf., chiefly Brit.* a difficult problem. **2** Also called: **tickler file.** *US.* a memorandum book. **3** a person or thing that tickles.
ticklish ● (ˈtɪklɪʃ) *adj* **1** sensitive to being tickled. **2** delicate or difficult. **3** easily upset or offended.
▸ **ˈticklishly** *adv* ▸ **ˈticklishness** *n*
tick off ● *vb* (*tr, adv*) **1** to mark with a tick. **2** *Inf., chiefly Brit.* to scold; reprimand.
tick over *vb* (*intr, adv*) **1** Also: **idle.** *Brit.* (of an engine) to run at low speed with the throttle control closed and the transmission disengaged. **2** to run smoothly without any major changes.
ticktack (ˈtɪkˌtæk) *n* **1** *Brit.* a system of sign language, mainly using the hands, by which bookmakers transmit their odds to each other at race courses. **2** *US.* a ticking sound. [from TICK[1]]
ticktock (ˈtɪkˌtɒk) *n* **1** a ticking sound as made by a clock. ◆ *vb* **2** (*intr*) to make a ticking sound.
tidal (ˈtaɪdᵊl) *adj* **1** relating to, characterized by, or affected by tides. **2** dependent on the tide: *a tidal ferry.*
▸ **ˈtidally** *adv*
tidal energy *n* energy obtained by harnessing tidal power.
tidal volume *n* **1** the volume of water associated with a rising tide. **2** *Physiol.* the amount of air passing into and out of the lungs during normal breathing.
tidal wave *n* **1** a name (not in technical usage) for **tsunami. 2** an unusually large incoming wave, often caused by high winds and spring tides. **3** a forceful and widespread movement in public opinion, action, etc.
tidbit (ˈtɪdˌbɪt) *n* the usual US spelling of **titbit.**
tiddler (ˈtɪdlə) *n Brit. inf.* **1** a very small fish, esp. a stickleback. **2** a small child. [C19: from *tittlebat,* childish var. of STICKLEBACK, infl. by TIDDLY[1]]
tiddly[1] (ˈtɪdlɪ) *adj* **tiddlier, tiddliest.** *Brit.* small; tiny. [C19: childish var. of LITTLE]
tiddly[2] (ˈtɪdlɪ) *adj Sl., chiefly Brit.* slightly drunk. [C19 (meaning: a drink): from ?]
tiddlywinks (ˈtɪdlɪˌwɪŋks) *n* (*functioning as sing*) a game in which players try to flick discs of plastic into a cup by pressing them with other larger discs. [C19: prob. from TIDDLY[1] + dialect *wink,* var. of WINCH[1]]
tide ● (taɪd) *n* **1** the cyclic rise and fall of sea level caused by the gravitational pull of the sun and moon. There are usually two high tides and two low tides in each lunar day. **2** the current, ebb, or flow of water at a specified place resulting from these changes in level. **3** See **ebb** (sense 3) and **flood** (sense 3). **4** a widespread tendency or movement. **5** a critical point in time; turning point. **6** *Arch. except in combination.* a season or time: *Christmastide.* **7** *Arch.* a favourable opportunity. **8 the tide is in** (*or* **out**). the sea has reached its highest (*or* lowest) level. ◆ *vb* **tides, tiding, tided. 9** to carry or be carried with or as if with the tide. **10** (*intr*) to ebb and flow like the tide. [OE *tīd* time]
▸ **ˈtideless** *adj*
tideland (ˈtaɪdˌlænd) *n US.* land between high-water and low-water marks.
tideline (ˈtaɪdˌlaɪn) *n* the mark or line left by the tide when it retreats from its highest point.
tidemark (ˈtaɪdˌmɑːk) *n* **1** a mark left by the highest or lowest point of a tide. **2** *Chiefly Brit.* a mark showing a level reached by a liquid: *a tidemark on the bath.* **3** *Inf., chiefly Brit.* a dirty mark on the skin, indicating the extent to which someone has washed.
tide over ● *vb* (*tr, adv*) to help to get through (a period of difficulty, distress, etc.).
tide-rip *n* another word for **riptide** (sense 1).
tidewaiter (ˈtaɪdˌweɪtə) *n* (formerly) a customs officer who boarded and inspected incoming ships.
tidewater (ˈtaɪdˌwɔːtə) *n* **1** water that advances and recedes with the tide. **2** *US.* coastal land drained by tidal streams.
tideway (ˈtaɪdˌweɪ) *n* a strong tidal current or its channel, esp. the tidal part of a river.
tidings ● (ˈtaɪdɪŋz) *pl n* information or news. [OE *tīdung*]
tidy ● (ˈtaɪdɪ) *adj* **tidier, tidiest. 1** characterized by or indicating neatness and order. **2** *Inf.* considerable: *a tidy sum of money.* ◆ *vb* **tidies, tidying, tidied. 3** (when *intr,* usually foll. by *up*) to put (things) in order; neaten. ◆ *n, pl* **tidies. 4a** a small container for odds and ends. **4b sink tidy.** a container to retain rubbish that might clog the plughole. **5** *Chiefly US & Canad.* an ornamental protective covering for the back or arms of a chair. [C13 (in the sense: timely, excellent): from TIDE + -Y[1]]
▸ **ˈtidily** *adv* ▸ **ˈtidiness** *n*
tie ● (taɪ) *vb* **ties, tying, tied. 1** (when *tr*, often foll. by *up*) to fasten or be fastened with string, thread, etc. **2** to make (a knot or bow) in (something). **3** (*tr*) to restrict or secure. **4** to equal (the score) of a competitor, etc. **5** (*tr*) *Inf.* to unite in marriage. **6** *Music.* **6a** to execute (two

THESAURUS

tic *n* = **twitch**, jerk, spasm
tick[1] *n* **1** = **tapping**, clack, click, clicking, tap, ticktock **2** *Brit. informal* = **moment**, flash, half a mo (*Brit. inf.*), instant, jiffy, minute, sec (*inf.*), second, shake (*inf.*), split second, trice, twinkling, two shakes of a lamb's tail (*inf.*) **3** = **mark**, dash, stroke ◆ *vb* **5** = **tap**, clack, click, ticktock **6** = **mark**, check off, choose, indicate, mark off, select **7 what makes someone tick** *Informal* = **motivation**, drive, motive, *raison d'être*
tick[4] *n Brit. informal* = **credit**, account, deferred payment, the slate (*Brit. inf.*)
ticket *n* **1a** = **voucher**, card, certificate, coupon, pass, slip, token **2** = **label**, card, docket, marker, slip, sticker, tab, tag
tickle *vb* **2** = **amuse**, delight, divert, entertain, excite, gratify, please, thrill, titillate
Antonyms *vb* annoy, bore, bother, irritate, pester, trouble, vex, weary
ticklish *adj* **2** = **difficult**, awkward, critical, delicate, nice, risky, sensitive, thorny, touchy, tricky, uncertain, unstable, unsteady
tick off *vb* **1** = **mark off**, check off, put a tick at **2** *Informal* = **scold**, carpet (*inf.*), censure, chide, lecture, read the riot act, rebuke, reprimand, reproach, reprove, take to task, tell off (*inf.*), upbraid
tide *n* **2** = **current**, course, ebb, flow, stream, tideway, undertow **4** = **tendency**, course, current, direction, drift, movement, trend
tide over *vb* = **keep one going**, aid, assist, bridge the gap, help, keep one's head above water, keep the wolf from the door, see one through
tidings *pl n* = **news**, advice, bulletin, communication, gen (*Brit. inf.*), information, intelligence, latest (*inf.*), message, report, word
tidy *adj* **1** = **neat**, businesslike, clean, cleanly, in apple-pie order (*inf.*), methodical, ordered, orderly, shipshape, spick-and-span, spruce, systematic, trig (*arch. or dialect*), trim, well-groomed, well-kept, well-ordered **2** *Informal* = **considerable**, ample, fair, generous, good, goodly, handsome, healthy, large, largish, respectable, sizable *or* sizeable, substantial ◆ *vb* **3** = **neaten**, clean, groom, order, put in order, put in trim, put to rights, spruce up, straighten
Antonyms *adj* ≠ **neat:** careless, dirty, dishevelled, disordered, disorderly, filthy, in disarray, messy, scruffy, sloppy, slovenly, unbusinesslike, unkempt, unmethodical, unsystematic, untidy ≠ **considerable:** inconsiderable, insignificant, little, small, tiny ◆ *vb* ≠ **neaten:** dirty, dishevel, disorder, mess, mess up
tie *vb* **1** = **fasten**, attach, bind, connect, interlace, join, knot, lash, link, make fast, moor, rope, secure, tether, truss, unite **3** = **restrict**, bind, confine, hamper, hinder, hold, limit, restrain **4** = **draw**, be even, be neck and neck, equal, match ◆ *n* **7, 9** = **fastening**, band, bond, connection, cord, fetter, joint, knot, ligature, link, rope, string **8** = **encumbrance**, hindrance, limitation, restraint, restriction **11** = **draw**, dead heat, deadlock, stalemate **13** *Brit.* = **match**, contest, fixture, game
Antonyms *vb* ≠ **fasten:** free, loose, release, separate, undo, unfasten, unhitch, unknot, untie ≠ **restrict:** free, release

successive notes) as though they formed one note. **6b** to connect (two printed notes) with a tie. ◆ *n* **7** a bond, link, or fastening. **8** a restriction or restraint. **9** a string, wire, etc., with which something is tied. **10** a long narrow piece of material worn, esp. by men, under the collar of a shirt, tied in a knot close to the throat with the ends hanging down the front. US name: **necktie. 11a** an equality in score, attainment, etc., in a contest. **11b** the match or competition in which such a result is attained. **12** a structural member such as a tie beam or tie rod. **13** *Sport, Brit.* a match or game in an eliminating competition: *a cup tie.* **14** (*usually pl*) a shoe fastened by means of laces. **15** the US and Canad. name for **sleeper** (on a railway track). **16** *Music.* a slur connecting two notes of the same pitch indicating that the sound is to be prolonged for their joint time value. ◆ See also **tie in, tie up.** [OE *tigan* to tie]

tie beam *n* a horizontal beam that serves to prevent two other structural members from separating, esp. one that connects two corresponding rafters in a roof or roof truss.

tie-break *or* **tie-breaker** *n* **1** *Tennis.* an extra game played to decide the result of a set when the score is 6–6. **2** any method of deciding quickly the result of a drawn contest, esp. an extra game, question, etc.

tie clasp *n* a clip which holds a tie in place against a shirt. Also called: **tie clip.**

tied (taɪd) *adj Brit.* **1** (of a public house, retail shop, etc.) obliged to sell only the beer, products, etc. of a particular producer: *a tied house; tied outlet.* **2** (of a house) rented out to the tenant for as long as he is employed by the owner. **3** (of a loan) made by one nation to another on condition that the money is spent on goods or services provided by the lending nation.

tie-dyeing, tie-dye *or* **tie and dye** *n* a method of dyeing textiles to produce patterns by tying sections of the cloth together so that they will not absorb the dye.
▸ **'tie-ˌdyed** *adj*

tie in ➊ *vb* (*adv*) **1** to come or bring into a certain relationship; coordinate. ◆ *n* **tie-in. 2** a link, relationship, or coordination. **3** publicity material, a book, etc., linked to a film, etc. **4** *US.* **4a** a sale or advertisement offering products of which a purchaser must buy one or more in addition to his purchase. **4b** an item sold or advertised in this way. **4c** (*as modifier*): *a tie-in sale.*

tie line *n* a telephone line between two private branch exchanges or private exchanges that may or may not pass through a main exchange.

tiepin ('taɪˌpɪn) *n* an ornamental pin of various shapes used to pin the two ends of a tie to a shirt.

tier[1] ➊ (tɪə) *n* **1** one of a set of rows placed one above and behind the other, such as theatre seats. **2a** a layer or level. **2b** (*in combination*): *a three-tier cake.* ◆ *vb* **3** to be or arrange in tiers. [C16: from OF *tire* rank, of Gmc origin]

tier[2] ('taɪə) *n* a person or thing that ties.

tierce (tɪəs) *n* **1** a variant of **terce. 2** the third of eight positions from which a parry or attack can be made in fencing. **3** (tɜːs). a sequence of three cards. **4** an obsolete measure of capacity equal to 42 wine gallons. [C15: from OF, fem of *tiers* third, from L *tertius*]

tiercel ('tɪəsᵊl) *n* a variant of **tercel.**

tie up ➊ *vb* (*adv*) **1** (*tr*) to bind securely with or as if with string, rope, etc. **2** to moor (a vessel). **3** (*tr; often passive*) to engage the attentions of. **4** (*tr; often passive*) to conclude (the organization of something). **5** to come or bring to a complete standstill. **6** (*tr*) to commit (funds, etc.) and so make unavailable for other uses. **7** (*tr*) to subject (property) to conditions that prevent sale, alienation, etc. ◆ *n* **tie-up. 8** a link or connection. **9** *Chiefly US & Canad.* a standstill. **10** *Chiefly US & Canad.* an informal term for **traffic jam.**

tiff ➊ (tɪf) *n* **1** a petty quarrel. **2** a fit of ill humour. ◆ *vb* **3** (*intr*) to have or be in a tiff. [C18: from ?]

tiffany ('tɪfənɪ) *n, pl* **tiffanies.** a sheer fine gauzy fabric. [C17 (in the sense: a fine dress worn on Twelfth Night): from OF *tifanie,* from ecclesiastical L *theophania* Epiphany]

tiffin ('tɪfɪn) *n* (in India) a light meal, esp. at midday. [C18: prob. from obs. *tiffing,* from *tiff* to sip]

tig (tɪg) *n, vb* **tigs, tigging, tigged.** another word for **tag**[2] (senses 1, 4).

tiger ('taɪgə) *n* **1** a large feline mammal of forests in most of Asia, having a tawny yellow coat with black stripes. **2** a dynamic, forceful, or cruel person. **3a** a country, esp. in E Asia, that is achieving rapid economic growth. **3b** (*as modifier*): *a tiger economy.* [C13: from OF *tigre,* from L *tigris,* from Gk, of Iranian origin]
▸ **'tigerish** *or* **'tigrish** *adj*

Tiger ('taɪgə) *n* a variant of **TIGR.**

tiger beetle *n* any of a family of active predatory beetles, chiefly of warm dry regions, having powerful mandibles and long legs.

tiger cat *n* a medium-sized feline mammal of Central and South America, having a dark-striped coat.

tiger lily *n* a lily plant of China and Japan cultivated for its flowers, which have black-spotted orange petals.

tiger moth *n* any of various moths having wings that are conspicuously marked with stripes and spots.

tiger's-eye *or* **tigereye** ('taɪgərˌaɪ) *n* a semiprecious golden-brown stone.

tiger shark *n* a voracious omnivorous requiem shark of tropical waters, having a striped or spotted body.

tiger snake *n* a highly venomous and aggressive Australian snake, usually with dark bands on the back.

tight ➊ (taɪt) *adj* **1** stretched or drawn so as not to be loose; taut. **2** fitting in a close manner. **3** held, made, fixed, or closed firmly and securely: *a tight knot.* **4a** of close and compact construction or organization, esp. so as to be impervious to water, air, etc. **4b** (*in combination*): *airtight.* **5** unyielding or stringent. **6** cramped or constricted: *a tight fit.* **7** mean or miserly. **8** difficult and problematic: *a tight situation.* **9** hardly profitable: *a tight bargain.* **10** *Econ.* **10a** (of a commodity) difficult to obtain. **10b** (of funds, money, etc.) difficult and expensive to borrow. **10c** (of markets) characterized by excess demand or scarcity. **11** (of a match or game) very close or even. **12** (of a team or group, esp. of a pop group) playing well together, in a disciplined coordinated way. **13** *Inf.* drunk. **14** *Inf.* (of a person) showing tension. ◆ *adv* **15** in a close, firm, or secure way. [C14: prob. var. of *thight,* from ON *thēttr* close]
▸ **'tightly** *adv* ▸ **'tightness** *n*

tightass ('taɪtˌæs) *n Sl., chiefly US.* an inhibited or excessively self-controlled person.
▸ **'tightˌassed** *adj*

tighten ➊ ('taɪtᵊn) *vb* to make or become tight or tighter.

tightfisted ➊ (ˌtaɪt'fɪstɪd) *adj* mean; miserly.

tight head *n Rugby.* the prop on the hooker's right in the front row of a scrum. Cf. **loose head.**

tightknit (ˌtaɪt'nɪt) *adj* **1** closely integrated: *a tightknit community.* **2** organized carefully.

tight-lipped ➊ *adj* **1** secretive or taciturn. **2** with the lips pressed tightly together, as through anger.

tightrope ('taɪtˌrəʊp) *n* a rope stretched taut on which acrobats walk or perform balancing feats.
▸ **tightrope walker** *n*

tights (taɪts) *pl n* **1a** Also called: (US) **panty hose,** (Canad. and NZ) **pantyhose,** (Austral. and NZ) **pantihose.** a one-piece clinging garment covering the body from the waist to the feet, worn by women and also by acrobats, dancers, etc. **1b** *US & Canad.* Also called: **leotards.** a similar, tight-fitting garment worn instead of trousers by either sex. **2** a similar garment formerly worn by men, as in the 16th century with a doublet.

tiglic acid ('tɪglɪk) *n* a syrupy liquid or crystalline unsaturated carboxylic acid, found in croton oil and used in perfumery. [C19 *tiglic,* from NL *Croton tiglium* (the croton plant), from ?]

tigon ('taɪgən) *or* **tiglon** ('tɪglɒn) *n* the hybrid offspring of a male tiger and a female lion.

TIGR *abbrev. for* Treasury Investment Growth Receipts: a bond denominated in dollars and linked to US treasury bonds, the yield on which is taxed in the UK as income when it is cashed or redeemed. Also called: **Tiger.**

THESAURUS

tie in *vb* **1** = **link,** be relevant, come in, connect, coordinate, fit in, have bearing, relate ◆ *n* **tie-in 2** = **link,** association, connection, coordination, hook-up, liaison, relation, relationship, tie-up

tier[1] *n* **1, 2a** = **row,** bank, echelon, file, layer, level, line, order, rank, series, storey, stratum

tie up *vb* **1** = **bind,** attach, pinion, restrain, tether, truss **2** = **moor,** lash, make fast, rope, secure **3** = **occupy,** engage, engross, keep busy **4** = **conclude,** bring to a close, end, finish off, settle, terminate, wind up, wrap up (*inf.*) ◆ *n* **tie-up 8** = **link,** association, connection, coordination, hook-up, liaison, linkup, relation, relationship, tie-in

tiff *n* **1** = **quarrel,** difference, disagreement, dispute, falling-out (*inf.*), petty quarrel, row, scrap (*inf.*), squabble, words **2** = **temper,** bad mood, fit of ill humour, fit of pique, huff, ill humour, pet, sulk, tantrum, wax (*inf., chiefly Brit.*)

tight *adj* **1** = **taut,** rigid, stiff, stretched, tense **2** = **close-fitting,** close, compact, constricted, cramped, narrow, snug **3** = **secure,** fast, firm, fixed **4a** = **sealed,** hermetic, impervious, proof, sound, watertight **5** = **strict,** harsh, inflexible, rigid, rigorous, severe, stern, stringent, tough, uncompromising, unyielding **7** *Informal* = **miserly,** close, grasping, mean, niggardly, parsimonious, penurious, sparing, stingy, tight-arsed (*taboo sl.*), tightfisted **8** = **difficult,** dangerous, hazardous, perilous, precarious, problematic, sticky (*inf.*), ticklish, tough, tricky, troublesome, worrisome **11** = **close,** even, evenly-balanced, near, well-matched **13** *Informal* = **drunk,** blotto, Brahms and Liszt (*sl.*), half cut (*Brit. sl.*), inebriated, in one's cups, intoxicated, legless (*inf.*), out of it (*sl.*), out to it (*Austral. & NZ sl.*), pickled (*inf.*), pie-eyed (*sl.*), pissed (*taboo sl.*), plastered (*sl.*), rat-arsed (*taboo sl.*), smashed (*sl.*), sozzled (*inf.*), three sheets in the wind (*sl.*), tiddly (*sl., chiefly Brit.*), tipsy, under the influence (*inf.*)
Antonyms *adj* ≠ **taut:** relaxed, slack ≠ **close-fitting:** loose, spacious ≠ **sealed:** loose, open, porous ≠ **strict:** easy, easy-going, generous, lax, lenient, liberal, relaxed, soft, undemanding ≠ **miserly:** abundant, extravagant, generous, lavish, munificent, open, prodigal, profuse, spendthrift ≠ **difficult:** easy ≠ **close:** easy, landslide, overwhelming, runaway, uneven ≠ **drunk:** sober

tighten *vb* = **stretch,** rigidify, stiffen, tauten, tense = **squeeze,** close, constrict, cramp, narrow = **fasten,** fix, screw, secure
Antonyms *vb* ≠ **stretch:** loosen, relax, slacken, weaken ≠ **squeeze:** ease off, let out, slacken ≠ **fasten:** unbind, unfasten, unscrew

tightfisted *adj* = **miserly,** close, close-fisted, grasping, mean, mingy (*Brit. inf.*), niggardly, parsimonious, penurious, sparing, stingy, tight, tight-arsed (*taboo sl.*)

tight-lipped *adj* **1** = **secretive,** close-lipped, close-mouthed, mum, mute, quiet, reserved, reticent, silent, taciturn, uncommunicative, unforthcoming

tigress ('taɪgrɪs) *n* **1** a female tiger. **2** a fierce, cruel, or wildly passionate woman.

tigridia (taɪ'grɪdɪə) *n* any of various bulbous plants of Mexico, Central America, and tropical S America. [C19: from Mod. L, from Gk *tigris* tiger (alluding to the spotted flowers of these plants)]

tike (taɪk) *n* a variant spelling of **tyke.**

tiki ('tiːkiː) *n* a Maori greenstone neck ornament in the form of a fetus. Also called: **heitiki.** [from Maori *heitiki* figure worn round neck]

tikka ('tiːkə) *adj* (*immediately postpositive*) *Indian cookery*. (of meat, esp. chicken or lamb) marinated in spices and then dry-roasted, usually in a clay oven.

tilak ('tɪlək) *n, pl* **tilak** *or* **tilaks.** a coloured spot or mark worn by Hindus, esp. on the forehead, often indicating membership of a religious sect, caste, etc., or (in the case of a woman) marital status. [from Sansk. *tilaka*]

tilbury ('tɪlbərɪ, -brɪ) *n, pl* **tilburies.** a light two-wheeled horse-drawn open carriage, seating two people. [C19: prob. after the inventor]

tilde ('tɪldə) *n* the diacritical mark (~) placed over a letter to indicate a nasal sound, as in Spanish *señor.* [C19: from Sp., from L *titulus* title]

tile (taɪl) *n* **1** a thin slab of fired clay, rubber, linoleum, etc., used with others to cover a roof, floor, wall, etc. **2** a short pipe made of earthenware, plastic, etc., used with others to form a drain. **3** tiles collectively. **4** a rectangular block used as a playing piece in mah jong and other games. **5 on the tiles.** *Inf.* on a spree, esp. of drinking or debauchery. ◆ *vb* **tiles, tiling, tiled. 6** (*tr*) to cover with tiles. [OE *tīgele*, from L *tēgula*]

▸ **'tiler** *n*

tiling ('taɪlɪŋ) *n* **1** tiles collectively. **2** something made of or surfaced with tiles.

till[1] (tɪl) *conj, prep* short for **until.** Also (not standard): **'til.** [OE *til*]

> **USAGE NOTE** *Till* is a variant of *until* that is acceptable at all levels of language. *Until* is, however, often preferred at the beginning of a sentence in formal writing: *until his behaviour improves, he cannot become a member.*

till[2] ⓣ (tɪl) *vb* (*tr*) **1** to cultivate and work (land) for the raising of crops. **2** to plough. [OE *tilian* to try, obtain]

▸ **'tillable** *adj* ▸ **'tiller** *n*

till[3] ⓣ (tɪl) *n* a box, case, or drawer into which money taken from customers is put, now usually part of a cash register. [C15 *tylle*, from ?]

till[4] (tɪl) *n* a glacial deposit consisting of rock fragments of various sizes. The most common is boulder clay. [C17: from ?]

tillage ('tɪlɪdʒ) *n* **1** the act, process, or art of tilling. **2** tilled land.

tiller[1] ('tɪlə) *n Naut.* a handle fixed to the top of a rudderpost to serve as a lever in steering it. [C14: from Anglo-F *teiler* beam of a loom, from Med. L *tēlārium*, from L *tēla* web]

▸ **'tillerless** *adj*

tiller[2] ('tɪlə) *n* **1** a shoot that arises from the base of the stem in grasses. **2** a less common name for **sapling.** ◆ *vb* **3** (*intr*) (of a plant) to produce tillers. [OE *telgor* twig]

tilt ⓣ (tɪlt) *vb* **1** to incline or cause to incline at an angle. **2** (*usually intr*) to attack or overthrow (a person) in a tilt or joust. **3** (when *intr*, often foll. by *at*) to aim or thrust: *to tilt a lance.* **4** (*tr*) to forge with a tilt hammer. ◆ *n* **5** a slope or angle: *at a tilt.* **6** the act of tilting. **7** (esp. in medieval Europe) **7a** a jousting contest. **7b** a thrust with a lance or pole delivered during a tournament. **8** an attempt to win a contest. **9** See **tilt hammer. 10 (at) full tilt.** at full speed or force. [OE *tealtian*]

▸ **'tilter** *n*

tilth (tɪlθ) *n* **1** the act or process of tilling land. **2** the condition of soil or land that has been tilled. [OE *tilthe*]

tilt hammer *n* a drop hammer with a heavy head; used in forging.

tiltyard ('tɪltˌjɑːd) *n* (formerly) an enclosed area for tilting.

Tim. *Bible. abbrev. for* Timothy.

timbal *or* **tymbal** ('tɪmbᵊl) *n Music.* a type of kettledrum. [C17: from F *timbale*, from OF *tamballe*, (associated also with *cymbale* cymbal), from OSp. *atabal*, from Ar. *at-tabl* the drum]

timbale (tæm'bɑːl) *n* **1** a mixture of meat, fish, etc., cooked in a mould lined with potato or pastry. **2** a straight-sided mould in which such a dish is prepared. [C19: from F: kettledrum]

timber ⓣ ('tɪmbə) *n* **1a** wood, esp. when regarded as a construction material. Usual US and Canad. word: **lumber. 1b** (*as modifier*): *a timber cottage.* **2a** trees collectively. **2b** *Chiefly US.* woodland. **3** a piece of wood used in a structure. **4** *Naut.* a frame in a wooden vessel. ◆ *vb* **5** (*tr*) to provide with timbers. ◆ *sentence substitute.* **6** a lumberjack's shouted warning when a tree is about to fall. [OE]

▸ **'timbered** *adj* ▸ **'timbering** *n*

timber hitch *n* a knot used for tying a rope round a spar, log, etc., for haulage.

timber limit *n Canad.* **1** the area to which rights of cutting timber, granted by a government licence, are limited. **2** another term for **timber line.**

timber line *n* the altitudinal or latitudinal limit of normal tree growth. See also **tree line.**

timber wolf *n* a wolf with a grey brindled coat found in forested northern regions, esp. of North America.

timberyard ('tɪmbəˌjɑːd) *n Brit., Austral., & NZ.* an establishment where timber, etc., is stored or sold. US and Canad. word: **lumberyard.**

timbre ⓣ ('tɪmbə, 'tæmbə) *n* **1** *Phonetics.* the distinctive tone quality differentiating one vowel or sonant from another. **2** *Music.* tone colour or quality of sound. [C19: from F: note of a bell, from OF: drum, from Med. Gk *timbanon*, from Gk *tumpanon*]

timbrel ('tɪmbrəl) *n Chiefly biblical.* a tambourine. [C16: from OF; see TIMBRE]

Timbuktu (ˌtɪmbʌk'tuː) *n* any distant or outlandish place: *from here to Timbuktu.* [from *Timbuktu*, town in Africa: terminus of a trans-Saharan caravan route]

time ⓣ (taɪm) *n* **1** the continuous passage of existence in which events pass from a state of potentiality in the future, through the present, to a state of finality in the past. Related adj: **temporal. 2** *Physics.* a quantity measuring duration, usually with reference to a periodic process such as the rotation of the earth or the vibration of electromagnetic radiation emitted from certain atoms. Time is considered as a fourth coordinate required to specify an event. See **space-time continuum. 3** a specific point on this continuum expressed in hours and minutes: *the time is four o'clock.* **4** a system of reckoning for expressing time: *Greenwich Mean Time.* **5a** a definite and measurable portion of this continuum. **5b** (*as modifier*): *time limit.* **6a** an accepted period such as a day, season, etc. **6b** (*in combination*): *springtime.* **7** an unspecified interval; a while. **8** (*often pl*) a period or point marked by specific attributes or events: *the Victorian times.* **9** a sufficient interval or period: *have you got time to help me?* **10** an instance or occasion: *I called you three times.* **11** an occasion or period of specified quality: *have a good time.* **12** the duration of human existence. **13** the heyday of human life: *in her time she was a great star.* **14** a suitable moment: *it's time I told you.* **15** the expected interval in which something is done. **16** a particularly important moment, esp. childbirth or death: *her time had come.* **17** (*pl*) indicating a degree or amount calculated by multiplication with the number specified: *ten times three is thirty.* **18** (*often pl*) the fashions, thought, etc., of the present age (esp. in **ahead of one's time, behind the times**). **19** *Brit.* Also: **closing time.** the time at which bars, pubs, etc., are legally obliged to stop selling alcoholic drinks. **20** *Inf.* a term in jail (esp. in **do time**). **21a** a customary or full period of work. **21b** the rate of pay for this period. **22** Also (esp. US): **metre. 22a** the system of combining beats or pulses in music into successive groupings by which the rhythm of the music is established. **22b** a specific system having a specific number of beats in each grouping or bar: *duple time.* **23** *Music.* short for **time value. 24 against time.** in an effort to complete something in a limited period. **25 ahead of time.** before the deadline. **26 at one time. 26a** once; formerly. **26b** simultaneously. **27 at the same time. 27a** simultaneously. **27b** nevertheless; however. **28 at times.** sometimes. **29 beat time.** to indicate the tempo of a piece of music by waving a baton, hand, etc. **30 for the time being.** for the moment; temporarily. **31 from time to time.** at intervals; occasionally. **32 have no time for.** to have no patience with; not tolerate. **33 in good time. 33a** early. **33b** quickly. **34 in no time.** very quickly. **35 in one's own time. 35a** outside paid working hours. **35b** at one's own rate. **36 in time. 36a** early or at the appointed time. **36b** eventually. **36c** *Music.* at a correct metrical or rhythmic pulse. **37 keep time.** to observe correctly the accent or rhythmic pulse of a piece of music in relation to tempo. **38 make time. 38a** to find an opportunity. **38b** (often foll. by *with*) *US inf.* to succeed in seducing. **39 on time.**

THESAURUS

till[2] *vb* **1, 2** = **cultivate**, dig, plough, turn over, work

till[3] *n* = **cash register**, cash box, cash drawer

tilt *vb* **1** = **slant**, cant, heel, incline, lean, list, slope, tip **2** = **joust**, attack, break a lance, clash, contend, cross swords, duel, encounter, fight, lock horns, spar ◆ *n* **5** = **slope**, angle, cant, inclination, incline, list, pitch, slant **7a** *Medieval history* = **joust**, clash, combat, duel, encounter, fight, lists, set-to (*inf.*), tournament, tourney **10 (at) full tilt** = **full speed**, for dear life, full force, headlong, like a bat out of hell (*sl.*), like the clappers (*Brit. inf.*)

timber *n* **1a** = **wood**, beams, boards, logs, planks **2a** = **trees**, forest

timbre *n* **2** = **tone**, colour, quality of sound, resonance, ring, tonality, tone colour

time *n* **5a, 7** = **period**, age, chronology, date, duration, epoch, era, generation, hour, interval, season, space, span, spell, stretch, term, while **10** = **occasion**, instance, juncture, point, stage **12** = **lifetime**, allotted span, day, duration, life, life span, season **13** = **heyday**, hour, peak **22** = **tempo**, beat, measure, metre, rhythm **26 at one time: a** = **once**, for a while, formerly, hitherto, once upon a time, previously **b** = **simultaneously**, all at once, at the same time, together **28 at times** = **sometimes**, every now and then, every so often, from time to time, now and then, occasionally, once in a while, on occasion **30 for the time being** = **for now**, for the moment, for the nonce, for the present, in the meantime, meantime, meanwhile, pro tem, temporarily **31 from time to time** = **occasionally**, at times, every now and then, every so often, now and then, once in a while, on occasion, sometimes **33 in good time: a** = **on time**, early, with time to spare **b** = **quickly**, rapidly, speedily, swiftly, with dispatch **34 in no time** = **quickly**, apace, before one knows it, before you can say Jack Robinson, in a flash, in a jiffy (*inf.*), in a moment, in an instant, in a trice, in two shakes of a lamb's tail (*inf.*), rapidly, speedily, swiftly **36 in time: a** = **on time**, at the appointed time, early, in good time, on schedule, with time to spare **b** = **eventually**, by and by, in the fullness of time, one day, someday, sooner or later, ultimately **39a on time** = **punctually**, in good time, on the dot **41 time and again** = **frequently**, many times, often, on many occasions, over and over again, repeatedly, time after time ◆ *vb* **46** = **measure**, clock, count, judge **47** = **schedule**, set **48** = **regulate**, control

39a at the expected or scheduled time. **39b** *US.* payable in instalments. **40 pass the time of day.** to exchange casual greetings (with an acquaintance). **41 time and again.** frequently. **42 time off.** a period when one is absent from work for a holiday, through sickness, etc. **43 time of one's life.** a memorably enjoyable time. **44 time out of mind.** from time immemorial. **45** (*modifier*) operating automatically at or for a set time: *time lock; time switch.* ◆ *vb* **times, timing, timed.** (*tr*) **46** to ascertain the duration or speed of. **47** to set a time for. **48** to adjust to keep accurate time. **49** to pick a suitable time for. **50** *Sport.* to control the execution or speed of (an action). ◆ *sentence substitute.* **51** the word called out by a publican signalling that it is closing time. [OE *tīma*]

time and a half *n* the rate of pay equalling one and a half times the normal rate, often offered for overtime work.

time and motion study *n* the analysis of industrial or work procedures to determine the most efficient methods of operation. Also: **time and motion, time study, motion study.**

time bomb *n* a bomb containing a timing mechanism that determines the time at which it will detonate.

time capsule *n* a container holding articles, documents, etc., representative of the current age, buried for discovery in the future.

time charter *n* the hire of a ship or aircraft for a specified period. Cf. **voyage charter.**

time clock *n* a clock which records, by punching or stamping **timecards** inserted into it, the time of arrival or departure of people, such as employees in a factory.

time-consuming *adj* taking up or involving a great deal of time.

time exposure *n* **1** an exposure of a photographic film for a relatively long period, usually a few seconds. **2** a photograph produced by such an exposure.

time-honoured ❶ *adj* having been observed for a long time and sanctioned by custom.

time immemorial *n* the distant past beyond memory or record.

timekeeper ('taɪm,kiːpə) *n* **1** a person or thing that keeps or records time. **2** an employee who maintains a record of the hours worked by the other employees. **3** an employee whose record of punctuality is of a specified nature: *a bad timekeeper.*
▸**'time,keeping** *n*

time-lag *n* an interval between two connected events.

time-lapse photography *n* the technique of recording a very slow process on film by exposing single frames at regular intervals. The film is then projected at normal speed.

timeless ❶ ('taɪmlɪs) *adj* **1** unaffected or unchanged by time; ageless. **2** eternal.
▸**'timelessly** *adv* ▸**'timelessness** *n*

timely ❶ ('taɪmlɪ) *adj* **timelier, timeliest,** *adv* at the right or an opportune or appropriate time.

time machine *n* (in science fiction) a machine in which people or objects can be transported into the past or the future.

time-out *n Chiefly US & Canad.* **1** *Sport.* an interruption in play during which players rest, discuss tactics, etc. **2** a period of rest; break. **3** *Computing.* a condition that occurs when the amount of time a computer has been instructed to wait for another device to perform a task has expired, usually indicated by an error message. ◆ *vb* **time out. 4** (of a computer) to stop operating because of a time-out.

timepiece ('taɪm,piːs) *n* any of various devices, such as a clock, watch, or chronometer, which measure and indicate time.

timer ('taɪmə) *n* **1** a device for measuring, recording, or indicating time. **2** a switch or regulator that causes a mechanism to operate at a specific time. **3** a person or thing that times.

time-saving *adj* shortening the length of time required for an operation, activity, etc.
▸**time-saver** *n*

timescale ('taɪm,skeɪl) *n* the span of time within which certain events occur or are scheduled in relation to any broader period of time.

time-served *adj* (of a craftsman or tradesman) having completed an apprenticeship; fully trained and competent.

timeserver ❶ ('taɪm,sɜːvə) *n* a person who compromises and changes his opinions, way of life, etc., to suit the current fashions.

time sharing *n* **1** a system of part ownership of a property for use as a holiday home whereby each participant owns the property for a particular period every year. **2** a system by which users at different terminals of a computer can, because of its high speed, apparently communicate with it at the same time.

time signal *n* an announcement of the correct time, esp. on radio or television.

time signature *n Music.* a sign usually consisting of two figures, one above the other, the upper figure representing the number of beats per bar and the lower one the time value of each beat: it is placed after the key signature.

timetable ❶ ('taɪm,teɪbᵊl) *n* **1** a list or table of events arranged according to the time when they take place; schedule. ◆ *vb* **timetables, timetabling, timetabled.** (*tr*) **2** to include in or arrange according to a timetable.

time value *n Music.* the duration of a note relative to other notes in a composition and considered in relation to the basic tempo.

time warp *n* an imagined distortion of the progress of time so that, for instance, events from the past may appear to be happening in the present.

timeworn ❶ ('taɪm,wɔːn) *adj* **1** showing the adverse effects of overlong use or of old age. **2** hackneyed; trite.

time zone *n* a region throughout which the same standard time is used. There are 24 time zones in the world, demarcated approximately by meridians at 15° intervals, an hour apart.

timid ❶ ('tɪmɪd) *adj* **1** easily frightened or upset, esp. by human contact; shy. **2** indicating shyness or fear. [C16: from L *timidus,* from *timēre* to fear]
▸**ti'midity** *or* **'timidness** *n* ▸**'timidly** *adv*

timing ('taɪmɪŋ) *n* the regulation of actions or remarks in relation to others to produce the best effect, as in music, the theatre, etc.

timocracy (taɪ'mɒkrəsɪ) *n, pl* **timocracies. 1** a political system in which possession of property is a requirement for participation in government. **2** a political system in which love of honour is deemed the guiding principle of government. [C16: from OF *tymocracie,* ult. from Gk *timokratia,* from *timē* worth, honour, + -CRACY]

timorous ❶ ('tɪmərəs) *adj* **1** fearful or timid. **2** indicating fear or timidity. [C15: from OF *temoros,* from Med. L, from L *timor* fear, from *timēre* to be afraid]
▸**'timorously** *adv* ▸**'timorousness** *n*

timothy grass *or* **timothy** ('tɪməθɪ) *n* a perennial grass of temperate regions having erect stiff stems: grown for hay and pasture. [C18: apparently after a *Timothy Hanson,* who brought it to colonial Carolina]

timpani *or* **tympani** ('tɪmpənɪ) *pl n* (*sometimes functioning as sing*) a set of kettledrums. [from It., pl of *timpano* kettledrum, from L: TYMPANUM]
▸**'timpanist** *or* **'tympanist** *n*

tin (tɪn) *n* **1** a malleable silvery-white metallic element. It is used extensively in alloys, esp. bronze and pewter, and as a noncorroding coating for steel. Symbol: Sn; atomic no.: 50; atomic wt.: 118.69. Related adjs.: **stannic, stannous. 2** Also called (esp. US and Canad.): **can.** an airtight sealed container of thin sheet metal coated with tin, used for preserving and storing food or drink. **3** any container made of metallic tin. **4** Also called: **tinful.** the contents of a tin. **5** *Brit., Austral., & NZ.* galvanized iron: *a tin roof.* **6** any metal regarded as cheap or flimsy. **7** *Brit.* a loaf of bread with a rectangular shape. **8** *NZ.* a receptacle for home-baked biscuits, etc. (esp. in **fill her tins** to bake a supply of biscuits, etc.). ◆ *vb* **tins, tinning, tinned.** (*tr*) **9** to put (food, etc.) into a tin or tins; preserve in a tin. **10** to plate or coat with tin. **11** to prepare (a metal) for soldering or brazing by applying a thin layer of solder to the surface. [OE]

tinamou ('tɪnə,muː) *n* any of various birds of Central and South America, having small wings and a heavy body. [C18: via F from Carib *tinamu*]

tin can *n* a metal food container, esp. when empty.

tinctorial (tɪŋk'tɔːrɪəl) *adj* of or relating to colouring, staining, or dyeing. [C17: from L *tinctōrius,* from *tingere* to tinge]

tincture ❶ ('tɪŋktʃə) *n* **1** a medicinal extract in a solution of alcohol. **2** a tint, colour, or tinge. **3** a slight flavour, aroma, or trace. **4** a colour or metal used on heraldic arms. **5** *Obs.* a dye. ◆ *vb* **tinctures, tincturing, tinctured. 6** (*tr*) to give a tint or colour to. [C14: from L *tinctūra* a dyeing, from *tingere* to dye]

tinder ('tɪndə) *n* **1** dry wood or other easily combustible material used for lighting a fire. **2** anything inflammatory or dangerous. [OE *tynder*]
▸**'tindery** *adj*

THESAURUS

time-honoured *adj* = **long-established**, age-old, ancient, conventional, customary, established, fixed, old, traditional, usual, venerable

timeless *adj* **1, 2** = **eternal**, abiding, ageless, ceaseless, changeless, deathless, endless, enduring, everlasting, immortal, immutable, imperishable, indestructible, lasting, permanent, persistent, undying
Antonyms *adj* ephemeral, evanescent, momentary, mortal, passing, temporal, temporary, transitory

timely *adj* = **opportune**, appropriate, at the right time, convenient, judicious, prompt, propitious, punctual, seasonable, suitable, well-timed
Antonyms *adj* ill-timed, inconvenient, inopportune, late, tardy, unseasonable, untimely

timeserver *n* = **opportunist**, hypocrite, self-seeker, trimmer, Vicar of Bray, weathercock

timetable *n* **1** = **schedule**, agenda, calendar, curriculum, diary, list, order of the day, programme

timeworn *adj* **1** = **decrepit**, aged, ancient, broken-down, dog-eared, lined, ragged, run-down, shabby, the worse for wear, weathered, worn, wrinkled **2** = **hackneyed**, ancient, clichéd, dated, hoary, old hat, out of date, outworn, passé, stale, stock, threadbare, tired, trite, well-worn

timid *adj* **1** = **fearful**, afraid, apprehensive, bashful, cowardly, coy, diffident, faint-hearted, irresolute, modest, mousy, nervous, pusillanimous, retiring, shrinking, shy, timorous
Antonyms *adj* aggressive, arrogant, ballsy (*taboo sl.*), bold, brave, confident, daring, fearless, fierce, forceful, forward, presumptuous, self-assured, self-confident, shameless, unabashed

timorous *adj* **1** *Literary* = **timid**, afraid, apprehensive, bashful, cowardly, coy, diffident, faint-hearted, fearful, frightened, irresolute, mousy, nervous, pusillanimous, retiring, shrinking, shy, trembling
Antonyms *adj* assertive, assured, audacious, bold, confident, courageous, daring, fearless

tincture *n* **2, 3** = **tinge**, aroma, colour, dash, flavour, hint, hue, seasoning, shade, smack, *soupçon,* stain, suggestion, tint, touch, trace ◆ *vb* **6** = **tinge**, colour, dye, flavour, scent, season, stain, tint

tinderbox ('tɪndəˌbɒks) *n* **1** a box used formerly for holding tinder, esp. one fitted with a flint and steel. **2** a person or thing that is particularly touchy or explosive.

tine (taɪn) *n* **1** a slender prong, esp. of a fork. **2** any of the sharp terminal branches of a deer's antler. [OE *tind*]
▸**tined** *adj*

tinea ('tɪnɪə) *n* any fungal skin disease, esp. ringworm. [C17: from L: worm]
▸'**tineal** *adj*

tinfoil ('tɪnˌfɔɪl) *n* **1** thin foil made of tin or an alloy of tin and lead. **2** thin foil made of aluminium; used for wrapping foodstuffs.

ting (tɪŋ) *n* **1** a high metallic sound such as that made by a small bell. ◆ *vb* **2** to make or cause to make such a sound. [C15: imit.]

ting-a-ling ('tɪŋəˈlɪŋ) *n* the sound of a small bell.

tinge 🅣 (tɪndʒ) *n* **1** a slight tint or colouring. **2** any slight addition. ◆ *vb* **tinges, tingeing** *or* **tinging, tinged.** (*tr*) **3** to colour or tint faintly. **4** to impart a slight trace to: *her thoughts were tinged with nostalgia.* [C15: from L *tingere* to colour]

tingle 🅣 ('tɪŋgᵊl) *vb* **tingles, tingling, tingled. 1** (*usually intr*) to feel or cause to feel a prickling, itching, or stinging sensation of the flesh, as from a cold plunge. ◆ *n* **2** a sensation of tingling. [C14: ? a var. of TINKLE]
▸'**tingler** *n* ▸'**tingling** *adj* ▸'**tingly** *adj*

tin god *n* **1** a self-important person. **2** a person erroneously regarded as holy or venerable.

tin hat *n Inf.* a steel helmet worn by military personnel.

tinker 🅣 ('tɪŋkə) *n* **1** (esp. formerly) a travelling mender of pots and pans. **2** a clumsy worker. **3** the act of tinkering. **4** *Scot. & Irish.* a Gypsy. ◆ *vb* **5** (*intr;* foll. by *with*) to play, fiddle, or meddle (with machinery, etc.), esp. while undertaking repairs. **6** to mend (pots and pans) as a tinker. [C13 *tinkere*, ?from *tink* tinkle, imit.]
▸'**tinkerer** *n*

tinker's damn *or* **cuss** *n Sl.* the slightest heed (esp. in **not give a tinker's damn** *or* **cuss**).

tinkle ('tɪŋkᵊl) *vb* **tinkles, tinkling, tinkled. 1** to ring with a high tinny sound like a small bell. **2** (*tr*) to announce or summon by such a ringing. **3** (*intr*) *Brit. inf.* to urinate. ◆ *n* **4** a high clear ringing sound. **5** the act of tinkling. **6** *Brit. inf.* a telephone call. [C14: imit.]
▸'**tinkly** *adj*

tin lizzie ('lɪzɪ) *n Inf.* an old or decrepit car.

tinned (tɪnd) *adj* **1** plated, coated, or treated with tin. **2** *Chiefly Brit.* preserved or stored in airtight tins. **3** coated with a layer of solder.

tinnitus (tɪˈnaɪtəs) *n Pathol.* a ringing, hissing, or booming sensation in one or both ears, caused by infection of the ear, a side effect of certain drugs, etc. [C19: from L, from *tinnīre* to ring]

tinny ('tɪnɪ) *adj* **tinnier, tinniest. 1** of or resembling tin. **2** cheap or shoddy. **3** (of a sound) high, thin, and metallic. **4** (of food or drink) flavoured with metal, as from a container. **5** *Austral. & NZ sl.* lucky. ◆ *n, pl* **tinnies. 6** *Austral. sl.* a can of beer.
▸'**tinnily** *adv* ▸'**tinniness** *n*

tin-opener *n* a small tool for opening tins.

Tin Pan Alley *n* **1** originally, a district in New York concerned with the production of popular music. **2** the commercial side of show business and pop music.

tin plate *n* **1** thin steel sheet coated with a layer of tin that protects the steel from corrosion. ◆ *vb* **tin-plate, tin-plates, tin-plating, tin-plated. 2** (*tr*) to coat with a layer of tin.

tinpot 🅣 ('tɪnˌpɒt) *adj* (*prenominal*) *Brit. inf.* **1** inferior, cheap, or worthless. **2** petty; unimportant.

tinsel 🅣 ('tɪnsəl) *n* **1** a decoration consisting of a piece of string with thin strips of metal foil attached along its length. **2** a yarn or fabric interwoven with strands of glittering thread. **3** anything cheap, showy, and gaudy. ◆ *vb* **tinsels, tinselling, tinselled** *or US* **tinsels, tinseling, tinseled.** (*tr*) **4** to decorate with or as if with tinsel: *snow tinsels the trees.* **5** to give a gaudy appearance to. ◆ *adj* **6** made of or decorated with tinsel. **7** showily but cheaply attractive; gaudy. [C16: from OF *estincele* a spark, from L *scintilla*]
▸'**tinselly** *adj*

Tinseltown ('tɪnsəlˌtaʊn) *n* an informal name for **Hollywood**, esp. as the home of the film industry. [C20: from the insubstantial glitter of the film world]

tinsmith ('tɪnˌsmɪθ) *n* a person who works with tin or tin plate.

tin soldier *n* a miniature toy soldier, usually made of lead.

tinstone ('tɪnˌstəʊn) *n* another name for **cassiterite.**

tint 🅣 (tɪnt) *n* **1** a shade of a colour, esp. a pale one. **2** a colour that is softened by the addition of white. **3** a tinge. **4** a dye for the hair. **5** a trace or hint. **6** *Engraving.* uniform shading, produced esp. by hatching. ◆ *vb* **7** (*tr*) to colour or tinge. **8** (*intr*) to acquire a tint. [C18: from earlier *tinct*, from L *tingere* to colour]
▸'**tinter** *n*

tintinnabulation (ˌtɪntɪˌnæbjʊˈleɪʃən) *n* the act or an instance of the ringing or pealing of bells. [from L, from *tintinnāre* to tinkle, from *tinnīre* to ring]

tinware ('tɪnˌwɛə) *n* objects made of tin plate.

tin whistle *n* another name for **penny whistle.**

tinworks ('tɪnˌwɜːks) *n* (*functioning as sing or pl*) a place where tin is mined, smelted, or rolled.

tiny 🅣 ('taɪnɪ) *adj* **tinier, tiniest.** very small. [C16 *tine*, from ?]
▸'**tinily** *adv* ▸'**tininess** *n*

-tion *suffix forming nouns.* indicating state, condition, action, process, or result: *election; prohibition.* [from OF, from L *-tiō, -tiōn-*]

tip[1] 🅣 (tɪp) *n* **1** a narrow or pointed end of something. **2** the top or summit. **3** a small piece forming an end: *a metal tip on a cane.* ◆ *vb* **tips, tipping, tipped.** (*tr*) **4** to adorn or mark the tip of. **5** to cause to form a tip. [C15: from ON *typpa*]
▸'**tipless** *adj*

tip[2] 🅣 (tɪp) *vb* **tips, tipping, tipped. 1** to tilt or cause to tilt. **2** (usually foll. by *over* or *up*) to tilt or cause to tilt, so as to overturn or fall. **3** *Brit.* to dump (rubbish, etc.). **4 tip one's hat.** to raise one's hat in salutation. ◆ *n* **5** a tipping or being tipped. **6** *Brit.* a dump for refuse, etc. [C14: from ?]
▸'**tipper** *n*

tip[3] 🅣 (tɪp) *n* **1** a payment given for services in excess of the standard charge; gratuity. **2** a helpful hint or warning. **3** a piece of inside information, esp. in betting or investing. ◆ *vb* **tips, tipping, tipped. 4** to give a tip to. [C18: ?from TIP[4]]
▸'**tipper** *n*

tip[4] (tɪp) *vb* **tips, tipping, tipped.** (*tr*) **1** to hit or strike lightly. ◆ *n* **2** a light blow. [C13: ?from Low G *tippen*]

tip-off 🅣 *n* **1** a warning or hint, esp. given confidentially and based on inside information. **2** *Basketball.* the act or an instance of putting the ball in play by the referee throwing it high between two opposing players. ◆ *vb* **tip off. 3** (*tr, adv*) to give a hint or warning to.

tipper truck *or* **lorry** *n* a truck or lorry the rear platform of which can be raised at the front end to enable the load to be discharged.

tippet ('tɪpɪt) *n* **1** a woman's fur cape for the shoulders. **2** the long stole of Anglican clergy worn during a service. **3** a long streamer-like part to a sleeve, hood, etc., esp. in the 16th century. [C14: ?from TIP[1]]

tipple 🅣 ('tɪpᵊl) *vb* **tipples, tippling, tippled. 1** to make a habit of taking (alcoholic drink), esp. in small quantities. ◆ *n* **2** alcoholic drink. [C15: back formation from obs. *tippler* tapster, from ?]
▸'**tippler** *n*

tipstaff ('tɪpˌstɑːf) *n* **1** a court official. **2** a metal-tipped staff formerly used as a symbol of office. [C16 *tipped staff*]

tipster ('tɪpstə) *n* a person who sells tips on horse racing, the stock market, etc.

tipsy 🅣 ('tɪpsɪ) *adj* **tipsier, tipsiest. 1** slightly drunk. **2** slightly tilted or tipped; askew. [C16: from TIP[2]]
▸'**tipsily** *adv* ▸'**tipsiness** *n*

tipsy cake *n Brit.* a kind of trifle made from a sponge cake soaked with wine or sherry and decorated with almonds and crystallized fruit.

tiptoe ('tɪpˌtəʊ) *vb* **tiptoes, tiptoeing, tiptoed.** (*intr*) **1** to walk with the heels off the ground. **2** to walk silently or stealthily. ◆ *n* **3 on tiptoe. 3a** on the tips of the toes or on the ball of the foot and the toes. **3b** eagerly

THESAURUS

tinge *n* **1** = **tint**, cast, colour, dye, shade, stain, tincture, wash **2** = **bit**, dash, drop, pinch, smack, smattering, *soupçon*, sprinkling, suggestion, touch, trace ◆ *vb* **3** = **tint**, colour, dye, imbue, shade, stain, suffuse

tingle *vb* **1** = **prickle**, have goose pimples, itch, sting, tickle ◆ *n* **2** = **quiver**, goose pimples, itch, itching, pins and needles (*inf.*), prickling, shiver, stinging, thrill, tickle, tickling

tinker *vb* **5** = **meddle**, dabble, fiddle (*inf.*), mess about, monkey, muck about (*Brit. sl.*), play, potter, toy

tinpot *adj* **1** *Brit. informal* = **worthless**, inferior, Mickey Mouse (*sl.*), miserable, paltry, pathetic, poxy (*sl.*), second-class, second-rate, two-bit (*US & Canad. sl.*), twopenny-halfpenny, unimportant, wretched

tinsel *adj* **7** = **showy**, brummagem, cheap, flashy, gaudy, gimcrack, meretricious, ostentatious, pinchbeck, plastic (*sl.*), sham, specious, superficial, tawdry, trashy

tint *n* **1** = **shade**, cast, colour, hue, tone **3, 5** = hint, shade, suggestion, tinge, touch, trace **4** = **dye**, rinse, stain, tincture, tinge, wash ◆ *vb* **7** = **dye**, colour, rinse, stain, tincture, tinge

tiny *adj* = **small**, diminutive, dwarfish, infinitesimal, insignificant, Lilliputian, little, microscopic, mini, miniature, minute, negligible, petite, pint-sized (*inf.*), puny, pygmy *or* pigmy, slight, teensy-weensy, teeny-weeny, trifling, wee

Antonyms *adj* colossal, enormous, extra-large, gargantuan, giant, gigantic, great, huge, immense, mammoth, massive, monstrous, titanic, vast

tip[1] *n* **2** = **end**, apex, cap, crown, extremity, head, peak, pinnacle, point, summit, top ◆ *vb* **4** = **cap**, crown, finish, surmount, top

tip[2] *vb* **1** = **tilt**, cant, capsize, incline, lean, list, overturn, slant, spill, topple over, upend, upset **3** *Brit.* = **dump**, ditch (*sl.*), empty, pour out, unload ◆ *n* **6** *Brit.* = **dump**, midden (*dialect*), refuse heap, rubbish heap

tip[3] *n* **1** = **gratuity**, baksheesh, gift, perquisite, *pourboire* **2** = **hint**, gen (*Brit. inf.*), information, inside information, pointer, suggestion ◆ *vb* **4** = **reward**, remunerate **4** = **advise**, give a clue, give a hint, suggest, tip (someone) the wink (*Brit. inf.*)

tip-off *n* **1** = **hint**, clue, forecast, gen (*Brit. inf.*), information, inside information, pointer, suggestion, warning, word, word of advice ◆ *vb* **tip off 3** = **advise**, caution, forewarn, give a clue, give a hint, suggest, tip (someone) the wink (*Brit. inf.*), warn

tipple *vb* **1** = **drink**, bend the elbow, bevvy (*dialect*), imbibe, indulge (*inf.*), quaff, swig, take a drink, tope ◆ *n* **2** = **alcohol**, booze (*inf.*), drink, John Barleycorn, liquor, poison (*inf.*)

tippler *n* **1** = **drinker**, bibber, boozer (*inf.*), drunk, drunkard, inebriate, soak (*sl.*), sot, sponge (*inf.*), toper

tipsy *adj* **1** = **tiddly** (*sl., chiefly Brit.*), babalas (*S. Afr.*), elevated (*inf.*), fuddled, happy (*inf.*), mellow, merry (*Brit. inf.*), slightly drunk, woozy (*inf.*)

anticipating something. **3c** stealthily or silently. ◆ *adv* **4** on tiptoe. ◆ *adj* **5** walking or standing on tiptoe.

tiptop (ˌtɪp'tɒp) *adj, adv* **1** at the highest point of health, excellence, etc. **2** at the topmost point. ◆ *n* **3** the best in quality. **4** the topmost point.

tip-up *adj* (*prenominal*) able to be turned upwards around a hinge or pivot: *a tip-up seat.*

TIR *abbrev. for* Transports Internationaux Routiers. [F: International Road Transport]

tirade ⓘ (taɪ'reɪd) *n* a long angry speech or denunciation. [C19: from F, lit.: a pulling, from It. *tirata*, from *tirare* to pull, from ?]

tire[1] ⓘ ('taɪə) *vb* **tires, tiring, tired. 1** (*tr*) to reduce the energy of, esp. by exertion; weary. **2** (*tr; often passive*) to reduce the tolerance of; bore or irritate: *I'm tired of the children's chatter.* **3** (*intr*) to become wearied or bored; flag. [OE *tēorian*, from ?]
▸ **'tiring** *adj*

tire[2] ('taɪə) *n, vb* the US spelling of **tyre**.

tired ⓘ ('taɪəd) *adj* **1** weary; fatigued. **2** no longer fresh; hackneyed. **3 tired and emotional.** *Euphemistic.* drunk.
▸ **'tiredness** *n*

tireless ⓘ ('taɪəlɪs) *adj* unable to be tired.
▸ **'tirelessly** *adv* ▸ **'tirelessness** *n*

tiresome ⓘ ('taɪəsəm) *adj* boring and irritating.
▸ **'tiresomely** *adv* ▸ **'tiresomeness** *n*

tirewoman ('taɪəˌwʊmən) *n, pl* **tirewomen.** an obsolete term for a lady's maid. [C17: from *tire* (obs.) to ATTIRE]

tiring room ('taɪərɪŋ) *n Arch.* a dressing room.

tiro ('taɪrəʊ) *n, pl* **tiros.** a variant spelling of **tyro.**

'tis (tɪz) *Poetic or dialect. contraction of* it is.

tisane (tɪ'zæn) *n* an infusion of leaves or flowers. [C19: from F, from L *ptisana* barley water]

Tishri *Hebrew.* (tɪʃ'riː) *n* (in the Jewish calendar) the seventh month of the year according to biblical reckoning and the first month of the civil year, falling in September and October. [C19: from Heb.]

tissue ⓘ ('tɪsjuː, 'tɪʃuː) *n* **1** a part of an organism consisting of a large number of cells having a similar structure and function: nerve tissue. **2** a thin piece of soft absorbent paper used as a disposable handkerchief, towel, etc. **3** See **tissue paper. 4** an interwoven series: *a tissue of lies.* **5** a woven cloth, esp. of a light gauzy nature. ◆ *vb* **tissues, tissuing, tissued.** (*tr*) **6** to decorate or clothe with tissue or tissue paper. [C14: from OF *tissu* woven cloth, from *tistre* to weave, from L *texere*]

tissue culture *n* **1** the growth of small pieces of animal or plant tissue in a sterile controlled medium. **2** the tissue produced.

tissue paper *n* very thin soft delicate paper used to wrap breakable goods, as decoration, etc.

tit[1] (tɪt) *n* any of numerous small active Old World songbirds, esp. the bluetit, great tit, etc. They have a short bill and feed on insects and seeds. [C16: ? imit., applied to small animate or inanimate objects]

tit[2] (tɪt) *n* **1** *Sl.* a female breast. **2** a teat or nipple. **3** *Derog.* a young woman. **4** *Taboo sl.* a despicable or unpleasant person. [OE *titt*]

Tit. *Bible. abbrev. for* Titus.

titan ⓘ ('taɪtᵊn) *n* a person of great strength or size. [after *Titans*, a family of gods in Gk myth]

titanic ⓘ (taɪ'tænɪk) *adj* possessing or requiring colossal strength: *a titanic battle.*

titanium (taɪ'teɪnɪəm) *n* a strong malleable white metallic element, which is very corrosion-resistant. It is used in the manufacture of strong lightweight alloys, esp. aircraft parts. Symbol: Ti; atomic no.: 22; atomic wt.: 47.88. [C18: NL; see TITAN, -IUM]

titanium dioxide *n* a white powder used chiefly as a pigment. Formula: TiO_2. Also called: **titanium oxide, titanic oxide, titania.**

titbit ⓘ ('tɪtˌbɪt) *or esp. US* **tidbit** *n* **1** a tasty small piece of food; dainty. **2** a pleasing scrap of anything, such as scandal. [C17: ?from dialect *tid* tender, from ?]

titchy *or* **tichy** ('tɪtʃɪ) *adj* **titchier, titchiest** *or* **tichier, tichiest.** *Brit. sl.* very small; tiny. [C20: from *tich* or *titch* a small person, from *Little Tich*, stage name of Harry Relph (1867–1928), E actor noted for his small stature]

titfer ('tɪtfə) *n Brit. sl.* a hat. [from rhyming slang *tit for tat*]

tit for tat ⓘ *n* an equivalent given in return or retaliation; blow for blow. [C16: from earlier *tip for tap*]

tithe ⓘ (taɪð) *n* **1** (*often pl*) a tenth part of produce, income, or profits, contributed for the support of the church or clergy. **2** any levy, esp. of one tenth. **3** a tenth or a very small part of anything. ◆ *vb* **tithes, tithing, tithed. 4** (*tr*) **4a** to exact or demand a tithe from. **4b** to levy a tithe upon. **5** (*intr*) to pay a tithe or tithes. [OE *teogoth*]
▸ **'tithable** *adj*

tithe barn *n* a large barn where, formerly, the agricultural tithe of a parish was stored.

titi ('tiːtiː) *n, pl* **titis.** any of a genus of small New World monkeys of South America, having beautifully coloured fur and a long nonprehensile tail. [via Sp. from Aymara, lit.: little cat]

Titian red ('tɪʃən) *n* a reddish-yellow colour, as in the hair colour in many of the works of Titian (?1490–1576), Italian painter.

titillate ⓘ ('tɪtɪˌleɪt) *vb* **titillates, titillating, titillated.** (*tr*) **1** to arouse or excite pleasurably. **2** to cause a tickling or tingling sensation in, esp. by touching. [C17: from L *tītillāre*]
▸ **'titilˌlating** *adj* ▸ **ˌtitil'lation** *n*

titivate ⓘ *or* **tittivate** ('tɪtɪˌveɪt) *vb* **titivates, titivating, titivated** *or* **tittivates, tittivating, tittivated.** to smarten up; spruce up. [C19: earlier *tidivate*, ? based on TIDY & CULTIVATE]
▸ **ˌtiti'vation** *or* **ˌtitti'vation** *n*

titlark ('tɪtˌlɑːk) *n* another name for **pipit**, esp. the meadow pipit. [C17: from TIT[1] + LARK[1]]

title ⓘ ('taɪtᵊl) *n* **1** the distinctive name of a work of art, musical or literary composition, etc. **2** a descriptive name or heading of a section of a book, speech, etc. **3** See **title page. 4** a name or epithet signifying rank, office, or function. **5** a formal designation, such as *Mr.* **6** an appellation designating nobility. **7** *Films.* **7a** short for **subtitle. 7b** written material giving credits in a film or television programme. **8** *Sport.* a championship. **9** *Law.* **9a** the legal right to possession of property, esp. real property. **9b** the basis of such right. **9c** the documentary evidence of such right: *title deeds.* **10a** any customary or established right. **10b** a claim based on such a right. **11** a definite spiritual charge or office in the church as a prerequisite for ordination. **12** *RC Church.* a titular church. ◆ *vb* **titles, titling, titled. 13** (*tr*) to give a title to. [C13: from OF, from L *titulus*]

title deed *n* a document evidencing a person's legal right or title to property, esp. real property.

titleholder ('taɪtᵊlˌhəʊldə) *n* a person who holds a title, esp. a sporting championship.

title page *n* the page in a book that gives the title, author, publisher, etc.

title role *n* the role of the character after whom a play, etc., is named.

titmouse ('tɪtˌmaʊs) *n, pl* **titmice.** another name for **tit**[1]. [C14 *titemous*, from *tite* (see TIT[1]) + MOUSE]

titrate ('taɪtreɪt) *vb* **titrates, titrating, titrated.** (*tr*) to measure the volume or

THESAURUS

tirade *n* = **outburst**, abuse, denunciation, diatribe, fulmination, harangue, invective, lecture, philippic

tire[1] *vb* **1** = **exhaust**, drain, enervate, fag (*inf.*), fatigue, knacker (*sl.*), take it out of (*inf.*), wear down, wear out, weary, whack (*Brit. inf.*) **2** *usually passive* = **bore**, aggravate (*inf.*), annoy, exasperate, get on one's nerves (*inf.*), harass, hassle (*inf.*), irk, irritate, piss one off (*taboo sl.*), weary **3** = **flag**, droop, fail
Antonyms *vb* ≠ **exhaust:** energize, enliven, exhilarate, invigorate, liven up, pep up, refresh, restore, revive

tired *adj* **1** = **exhausted**, all in (*sl.*), asleep *or* dead on one's feet, clapped out (*Austral. & NZ inf.*), dead beat (*inf.*), dog-tired (*inf.*), done in (*inf.*), drained, drooping, drowsy, enervated, fagged (*inf.*), fatigued, flagging, knackered (*sl.*), ready to drop, sleepy, spent, weary, whacked (*Brit. inf.*), worn out, zonked (*sl.*) **2** = **hackneyed**, clichéd, conventional, corny (*sl.*), familiar, old, outworn, stale, stock, threadbare, trite, well-worn
Antonyms *adj* ≠ **exhausted:** alive and kicking, energetic, fresh, full of beans (*inf.*), lively, refreshed, rested, wide-awake ≠ **hackneyed:** innovative, original

tireless *adj* = **energetic**, determined, indefatigable, industrious, resolute, unflagging, untiring, unwearied, vigorous
Antonyms *adj* drained, exhausted, fatigued, flagging, tired, weak, weary, worn out

tiresome *adj* = **boring**, annoying, dull, exasperating, flat, irksome, irritating, laborious, monotonous, tedious, trying, uninteresting, vexatious, wearing, wearisome
Antonyms *adj* exhilarating, inspiring, interesting, refreshing, rousing, stimulating

tiring *adj* **1** = **exhausting**, arduous, demanding, enervative, exacting, fatiguing, laborious, strenuous, tough, wearing, wearying

tissue *n* **2** = **paper**, paper handkerchief, wrapping paper **4** = **series**, accumulation, chain, collection, combination, concatenation, conglomeration, fabrication, mass, network, pack, web **5** = **fabric**, gauze, mesh, structure, stuff, texture, web

titan *n* = **giant**, colossus, leviathan, ogre, superman

titanic *adj* = **gigantic**, Brobdingnagian, colossal, elephantine, enormous, giant, herculean, huge, humongous *or* humungous (*US sl.*), immense, jumbo (*inf.*), mammoth, massive, mighty, monstrous, mountainous, prodigious, stellar (*inf.*), stupendous, towering, vast

titbit *n* **1** = **delicacy**, *bonne bouche*, choice item, dainty, goody, juicy bit, morsel, scrap, snack, treat

tit for tat *n* = **retaliation**, an eye for an eye, as good as one gets, a tooth for a tooth, blow for blow, like for like, measure for measure

tithe *n* **2** = **tax**, assessment, duty, impost, levy, tariff, tenth, toll, tribute ◆ *vb* **4b** = **tax**, assess, charge, levy, rate **5** = **pay a tithe on**, give up, pay, render, surrender, turn over

titillate *vb* **1** = **excite**, arouse, interest, provoke, stimulate, tantalize, tease, thrill, tickle, turn on (*sl.*)

titillating *adj* **1** = **exciting**, arousing, interesting, lewd, lurid, provocative, sensational, stimulating, suggestive, teasing, thrilling

titivate *vb* = **smarten up**, doll up (*sl.*), do up (*inf.*), make up, prank, preen, primp, prink, refurbish, tart up (*Brit. sl.*), touch up

title *n* **1** = **name**, appellation, denomination, designation, epithet, handle (*sl.*), moniker *or* monicker (*sl.*), nickname, nom de plume, pseudonym, sobriquet, term **2** = **heading**, caption, inscription, label, legend, name, style **8** *Sport* = **championship**, crown, laurels **9a** *Law* = **ownership**, claim, entitlement, prerogative, privilege, right ◆ *vb* **13** = **name**, call, designate, label, style, term

the concentration of (a solution) by titration. [C19: from F *titrer;* see TITRE]
▸**ti'tratable** *adj*

titration (taɪ'treɪʃən) *n* an operation in which a measured amount of one solution is added to a known quantity of another solution until the reaction between the two is complete. If the concentration of one solution is known, that of the other can be calculated.

titre *or US* **titer** ('taɪtə) *n* the concentration of a solution as determined by titration. [C19: from F *titre* proportion of gold or silver in an alloy, from OF *title* TITLE]

titter ❶ ('tɪtə) *vb* (*intr*) **1** to snigger, esp. derisively or in a suppressed way. ◆ *n* **2** a suppressed laugh, chuckle, or snigger. [C17: imit.]
▸**'titterer** *n* ▸**'tittering** *adj*

tittle ❶ ('tɪtᵊl) *n* **1** a small mark in printing or writing, esp. a diacritic. **2** a jot; particle. [C14: from Med. L *titulus* label, from L: title]

tittle-tattle ❶ *n* **1** idle chat or gossip. ◆ *vb* **tittle-tattles, tittle-tattling, tittle-tattled. 2** (*intr*) to chatter or gossip.
▸**'tittle-,tattler** *n*

tittup ('tɪtəp) *vb* **tittups, tittupping, tittupped** *or US* **tittups, tittuping, tittuped. 1** (*intr*) to prance or frolic. ◆ *n* **2** a caper. [C18 (in the sense: a horse's gallop): prob. imit.]

titubation (,tɪtjʊ'beɪʃən) *n Pathol.* a disordered gait characterized by stumbling or staggering, often caused by a lesion of the cerebellum. [C17: from L *titubātiō,* from *titubāre* to reel]

titular ❶ ('tɪtjʊlə) *adj* **1** of, relating to, or of the nature of a title. **2** in name only. **3** bearing a title. **4** *RC Church.* designating any of certain churches in Rome to whom cardinals or bishops are attached as their nominal incumbents. ◆ *n* **5** the bearer of a title. **6** the bearer of a nominal office. [C18: from F *titulaire,* from L *titulus* title]

tizzy ('tɪzɪ) *n, pl* **tizzies.** *Inf.* a state of confusion or excitement. Also called: **tizz, tiz-woz.** [C19: from ?]

T-junction *n* a road junction in which one road joins another at right angles but does not cross it.

TKO *Boxing. abbrev. for* technical knockout.

Tl *the chemical symbol for* thallium.

Tm *the chemical symbol for* thulium.

TM *abbrev. for* transcendental meditation.

tmesis (tə'miːsɪs) *n* interpolation of a word or words between the parts of a compound word, as in *every-blooming-where.* [C16: via L from Gk, lit.: a cutting, from *temnein* to cut]

TNT *n* 2,4,6-trinitrotoluene; a yellow solid: used chiefly as a high explosive.

T-number *or* **T number** *n Photog.* a function of the f-number of a lens that takes into account the light transmitted by the lens. [from *T(otal Light Transmission) Number*]

to (tuː; *unstressed* tʊ, tə) *prep* **1** used to indicate the destination of the subject or object of an action: *he climbed to the top.* **2** used to mark the indirect object of a verb: *telling stories to children.* **3** used to mark the infinitive of a verb: *he wanted to go.* **4** as far as; until: *working from Monday to Friday.* **5** used to indicate equality: *16 ounces to the pound.* **6** against; upon; onto: *put your ear to the wall.* **7** before the hour of: *five minutes to four.* **8** accompanied by: *dancing to loud music.* **9** as compared with, as against: *the score was eight to three.* **10** used to indicate a resulting condition: *they starved to death.* ◆ *adv* **11** towards a fixed position, esp. (of a door) closed. [OE *tō*]

toad (təʊd) *n* **1** any of a group of amphibians similar to frogs but more terrestrial, having a drier warty skin. **2** a loathsome person. [OE *tādige,* from ?]
▸**'toadish** *adj*

toadfish ('təʊd,fɪʃ) *n, pl* **toadfish** *or* **toadfishes.** any of various spiny-finned marine fishes of tropical and temperate seas.

toadflax ('təʊd,flæks) *n* a perennial plant having narrow leaves and spurred two-lipped yellow-orange flowers. Also called: **butter-and-eggs.**

toad-in-the-hole *n Brit. & Austral.* a dish made of sausages baked in a batter.

toadstone ('təʊd,stəʊn) *n* an intrusive volcanic rock occurring in limestone. [C18: ?from a supposed resemblance to a toad's spotted skin]

toadstool ('təʊd,stuːl) *n* (*not in technical use*) any basidiomycetous fungus with a capped spore-producing body that is poisonous. Cf. **mushroom.**

toady ❶ ('təʊdɪ) *n, pl* **toadies. 1** Also: **toadeater.** a person who flatters and ingratiates himself in a servile way; sycophant. ◆ *vb* **toadies, toadying, toadied. 2** to fawn on and flatter (someone). [C19: shortened from *toadeater,* orig. a quack's assistant who pretended to eat toads, hence a flatterer]
▸**'toadyish** *adj* ▸**'toadyism** *n*

to and fro *adv,* **to-and-fro** *adj* **1** back and forth. **2** here and there.
▸**'toing and 'froing** *n*

toast[1] ❶ (təʊst) *n* **1a** sliced bread browned by exposure to heat. **1b** (*as modifier*): *a toast rack.* ◆ *vb* **2** (*tr*) to brown under a grill or over a fire: *to toast cheese.* **3** to warm or be warmed: *to toast one's hands by the fire.* [C14: from OF *toster,* from L *tōstus* parched, from *torrēre* to dry with heat]

toast[2] ❶ (təʊst) *n* **1** a tribute or proposal of health, success, etc., given to a person or thing and marked by people raising glasses and drinking together. **2** a person or thing honoured by such a tribute or proposal. **3** (esp. formerly) an attractive woman to whom such tributes are frequently made. ◆ *vb* **4** to propose or drink a toast to (a person or thing). **5** (*intr*) to add vocal effects to a prerecorded track: a disc-jockey technique. [C17 (in the sense: a lady to whom the company is asked to drink): from TOAST[1], from the idea that the name of the lady would flavour the drink like a piece of spiced toast]
▸**'toaster** *n*

toaster ('təʊstə) *n* a device, esp. an electrical device, for toasting bread.

toastmaster ('təʊst,mɑːstə) *n* a person who introduces speakers, proposes toasts, etc., at public dinners.
▸**'toast,mistress** *fem n*

toasty *or* **toastie** ('təʊstɪ) *n, pl* **toasties.** a toasted sandwich.

Tob. *abbrev. for* Tobit.

tobacco (tə'bækəʊ) *n, pl* **tobaccos** *or* **tobaccoes. 1** any of a genus of plants having mildly narcotic properties, one species of which is cultivated as the chief source of commercial tobacco. **2** the leaves of certain of these plants dried and prepared for snuff, chewing, or smoking. [C16: from Sp. *tabaco,* ?from Taino: leaves rolled for smoking, assumed by the Spaniards to be the name of the plant]

tobacco mosaic virus *n* the virus that causes mosaic disease in tobacco and related plants: its discovery provided the first evidence of the existence of viruses. Abbrev.: **TMV.**

tobacconist (tə'bækənɪst) *n Chiefly Brit.* a person or shop that sells tobacco, cigarettes, pipes, etc.

-to-be *adj* (*in combination*) about to be; future: *a mother-to-be; the bride-to-be.*

toboggan (tə'bɒgən) *n* **1** a light wooden frame on runners used for sliding over snow and ice. **2** a long narrow sledge made of a thin board curved upwards at the front. ◆ *vb* **toboggans, tobogganing, tobogganed.** (*intr*) **3** to ride on a toboggan. [C19: from Canad. F, of Amerind origin]
▸**to'bogganer** *or* **to'bogganist** *n*

toby ('təʊbɪ) *n, pl* **tobies.** *NZ.* a water stopcock at the boundary of a street and house section.

toby jug ('təʊbɪ) *n* a beer mug or jug in the form of a stout seated man wearing a three-cornered hat and smoking a pipe. Also called: **toby.** [C19: from the familiar form of the name *Tobias*]

toccata (tə'kɑːtə) *n* a rapid keyboard composition for organ, harpsichord, etc., usually in a rhythmically free style. [C18: from It., lit.: touched, from *toccare* to play (an instrument)]

Toc H ('tɒk 'eɪtʃ) *n* a society formed after World War I to encourage Christian comradeship. [C20: from the obs. telegraphic code for *T.H.,* initials of *Talbot House,* Poperinge, Belgium, the original headquarters of the society]

Tocharian *or* **Tokharian** (tɒ'kɑːrɪən) *n* **1** a member of an Asian people who lived in the Tarim Basin until around 800 A.D. **2** the language of this people, known from records in a N Indian script of the 7th and 8th centuries A.D. [C20: ult. from Gk *Tokharoi,* from ?]

tocopherol (tɒ'kɒfə,rɒl) *n* any of a group of fat-soluble alcohols that occur in wheat-germ oil, lettuce, egg yolk, etc. Also called: **vitamin E.** [C20: from *toco-,* from Gk *tokos* offspring + *-pher-,* from *pherein* to bear + -OL[1]]

tocsin ('tɒksɪn) *n* **1** an alarm or warning signal, esp. one sounded on a bell. **2** an alarm bell. [C16: from F, from OF *toquassen,* from OProvençal, from *tocar* to touch + *senh* bell, from L *signum*]

tod (tɒd) *n* **on one's tod.** *Brit. sl.* on one's own. [C19: rhyming sl. *Tod Sloan/alone,* after *Tod* Sloan, a jockey]

today (tə'deɪ) *n* **1** this day, as distinct from yesterday or tomorrow. **2** the present age. ◆ *adv* **3** during or on this day. **4** nowadays. [OE *tō dæge,* lit.: on this day]

toddle ('tɒdᵊl) *vb* **toddles, toddling, toddled.** (*intr*) **1** to walk with short unsteady steps, as a child. **2** (foll. by *off*) *Jocular.* to depart. **3** (foll. by *round, over,* etc.) *Jocular.* to stroll. ◆ *n* **4** the act or an instance of toddling. [C16 (Scot. & N English): from ?]

toddler ('tɒdlə) *n* a young child, usually between the ages of one and two and a half.

toddy ('tɒdɪ) *n, pl* **toddies. 1** a drink made from spirits, esp. whisky, hot

THESAURUS

titter *vb* **1 = snigger,** chortle (*inf.*), chuckle, giggle, laugh, tee-hee, te-hee

tittle *n* **2 = bit,** atom, dash, drop, grain, iota, jot, mite, particle, scrap, shred, speck, whit

tittle-tattle *n* **1 = gossip,** babble, blather, blether, cackle, chatter, chitchat, clishmaclaver (*Scot.*), dirt (*US sl.*), hearsay, idle chat, jaw (*sl.*), natter, prattle, rumour, twaddle, yackety-yak (*sl.*), yatter (*inf.*) ◆ *vb* **2 = gossip,** babble, blather, blether, cackle, chat, chatter, chitchat, jaw (*sl.*), natter, prattle, run off at the mouth (*sl.*), witter (*inf.*), yak (*sl.*), yatter (*inf.*)

titular *adj* **2 = in name only,** honorary, nominal, puppet, putative, so-called, theoretical, token
Antonyms *adj* actual, effective, functioning, real, true

toady *n* **1 = sycophant,** apple polisher (*US sl.*), ass-kisser (*US & Canad. taboo sl.*), bootlicker (*inf.*), brown-noser (*taboo sl.*), crawler (*sl.*), creep (*sl.*), fawner, flatterer, flunkey, groveller, hanger-on, jackal, lackey, lickspittle, minion, parasite, spaniel, truckler, yes man ◆ *vb* **2 = fawn on,** be obsequious to, bow and scrape, brown-nose (*taboo sl.*), butter up, crawl, creep, cringe, curry favour with, flatter, grovel, kiss the feet of, kowtow to, lick (someone's) boots, pander to, suck up to (*inf.*)
Antonyms *vb* ≠ **fawn on:** confront, defy, oppose, rebel, resist, stand against, withstand

toast[1] *vb* **2 = brown,** grill, roast **3 = warm,** heat

toast[2] *n* **1 = tribute,** compliment, drink, health, pledge, salutation, salute **2, 3 = favourite,** darling, hero *or* heroine ◆ *vb* **4 = drink to,** drink (to) the health of, pledge, salute water, sugar, and usually lemon juice. **2** the sap of various palm trees used as a beverage. [C17: from Hindi *tārī* juice of the palmyra palm, from *tār* palmyra palm, from Sansk. *tāra*]

to-do ➊ (tə'du:) *n, pl* **to-dos.** a commotion, fuss, or quarrel.

toe ➊ (təʊ) *n* **1** any one of the digits of the foot. **2** the corresponding part in other vertebrates. **3** the part of a shoe, etc., covering the toes. **4** anything resembling a toe in shape or position. **5 on one's toes.** alert. **6 tread on someone's toes.** to offend a person, esp. by trespassing on his field of responsibility. ◆ *vb* **toes, toeing, toed. 7** (*tr*) to touch, kick, or mark with the toe. **8** (*tr*) to drive (a nail, etc.) obliquely. **9** (*intr*) to walk with the toes pointing in a specified direction: *to toe inwards.* **10 toe the line** *or* **mark.** to conform to expected attitudes, standards, etc. [OE *tā*]

toe and heel *n* a technique used by racing drivers on sharp bends, in which the brake and accelerator are operated simultaneously by the toe and heel of the right foot.

toecap ('təʊˌkæp) *n* a reinforced covering for the toe of a boot or shoe.

toed (təʊd) *adj* **1** having a part resembling a toe. **2** fixed by nails driven in at the foot. **3** (*in combination*) having a toe or toes as specified: *five-toed; thick-toed.*

toehold ('təʊˌhəʊld) *n* **1** a small foothold to facilitate climbing. **2** any means of gaining access, support, etc. **3** a wrestling hold in which the opponent's toe is held and his leg twisted.

toe-in *n* a slight forward convergence given to the wheels of motor vehicles to improve steering.

toenail ('təʊˌneɪl) *n* **1** a thin horny translucent plate covering part of the surface of the end joint of each toe. **2** *Carpentry.* a nail driven obliquely. ◆ *vb* **3** (*tr*) *Carpentry.* to join (beams) by driving nails obliquely.

toerag ('təʊˌræg) *n Brit. sl.* a contemptible or despicable person. [C20: orig., a beggar, tramp: from the rags wrapped round their feet]

toey ('təʊɪ) *adj Austral. sl.* nervous and restless; anxious.

toff (tɒf) *n Brit. sl.* a well-dressed or upper-class person, esp. a man. [C19: ? var. of TUFT, nickname for a titled student at Oxford University, wearing a cap with a gold tassel]

toffee *or* **toffy** ('tɒfɪ) *n, pl* **toffees** *or* **toffies. 1** a sweet made from sugar or treacle boiled with butter, nuts, etc. **2 for toffee.** (preceded by *can't*) *Inf.* to be incompetent at: *he can't sing for toffee.* [C19: var. of earlier *taffy*]

toffee-apple *n* an apple fixed on a stick and coated with a thin layer of toffee.

toffee-nosed *adj Sl., chiefly Brit.* pretentious or supercilious; used esp. of snobbish people.

toft (tɒft) *n Brit. history.* **1** a homestead. **2** a homestead and its arable land. [OE]

tofu ('təʊˌfu:) *n* unfermented soya-bean curd, a food with a soft cheese-like consistency. [from Japanese]

tog[1] (tɒg) *Inf.* ◆ *vb* **togs, togging, togged. 1** (often foll. by *up* or *out*) to dress oneself, esp. in smart clothes. ◆ *n* **2** See **togs.** [C18: ?from obs. cant *togemans* coat, from L *toga* TOGA + *-mans,* from ?]

tog[2] (tɒg) *n* **a** a unit of thermal resistance used to measure the power of insulation of a fabric, garment, quilt, etc. **b** (*as modifier*): *tog-rating.* [C20: arbitrary coinage from TOG[1] (n)]

toga ('təʊgə) *n* **1** a garment worn by citizens of ancient Rome, consisting of a piece of cloth draped around the body. **2** a robe of office. [C16: from L]
▸**togaed** ('təʊgəd) *adj*

together ➊ (tə'geðə) *adv* **1** with cooperation and interchange between constituent elements, members, etc.: *we worked together.* **2** in or into contact with each other: *to stick papers together.* **3** in or into one place; with each other: *the people are gathered together.* **4** at the same time. **5** considered collectively: *all our wages put together couldn't buy that car.* **6** continuously: *working for eight hours together.* **7** closely or compactly united or held: *water will hold the dough together.* **8** mutually or reciprocally: *to multiply seven and eight together.* **9** *Inf.* organized: *to get things together.* ◆ *adj* **10** *Sl.* self-possessed, competent, and well-organized. **11 together with.** (*prep*) in addition to. [OE *tōgædre*]

USAGE NOTE See at **plus.**

togetherness (tə'geðənɪs) *n* a feeling of closeness or affection from being united with other people.

toggery ('tɒgərɪ) *n Inf.* clothes; togs.

toggle ('tɒg[ə]l) *n* **1** a peg or rod at the end of a rope, chain, or cable, for fastening by insertion through an eye in another rope, chain, etc. **2** a bar-shaped button inserted through a loop for fastening. **3** a toggle joint or a device having such a joint. ◆ *vb* **toggles, toggling, toggled. 4** (*tr*) to supply or fasten with a toggle. [C18: from ?]

toggle joint *n* a device consisting of two arms pivoted at a common joint and at their outer ends and used to apply pressure by straightening the angle between the two arms.

toggle switch *n* **1** an electric switch having a projecting lever that is manipulated in a particular way to open or close a circuit. **2** a computer device used to turn a feature on or off.

togs (tɒgz) *pl n Inf.* **1** clothes. **2** *Austral., NZ, & Irish.* a swimming costume. [from TOG[1]]

toheroa (ˌtəʊə'rəʊə) *n* a large edible bivalve mollusc of New Zealand with a distinctive flavour. [from Maori]

tohunga ('tɒhʊŋə) *n NZ.* a Maori priest, the repository of traditional lore.

toil[1] ➊ (tɔɪl) *n* **1** hard or exhausting work. ◆ *vb* (*intr*) **2** to labour. **3** to progress with slow painful movements. [C13: from Anglo-F *toiler* to struggle, from OF *toeillier* to confuse, from L *tudiculāre* to stir, ult. from *tundere* to beat]
▸**'toiler** *n*

toil[2] (tɔɪl) *n* **1** (*often pl*) a net or snare. **2** *Arch.* a trap for wild beasts. [C16: from OF *toile,* from L *tēla* loom]

toile (twɑ:l) *n* **1** a transparent linen or cotton fabric. **2** a garment of exclusive design made up in cheap cloth so that alterations can be made. [C19: from F, from L *tēla* a loom]

toilet ➊ ('tɔɪlɪt) *n* **1** another word for **lavatory. 2** *Old-fashioned.* the act of dressing and preparing oneself. **3** *Old-fashioned.* a dressing table. **4** *Rare.* costume. **5** the cleansing of a wound, etc., after an operation or childbirth. [C16: from F *toilette* dress, from TOILE]

toilet paper *or* **tissue** *n* thin absorbent paper, often wound in a roll round a cardboard cylinder (**toilet roll**), used for cleaning oneself after defecation or urination.

toiletry ('tɔɪlɪtrɪ) *n, pl* **toiletries.** an object or cosmetic used in making up, dressing, etc.

toilet set *n* a matching set consisting of a hairbrush, comb, mirror, and clothes brush.

toilette (twɑ:'let) *n* another word for **toilet** (sense 2). [C16: from F; see TOILET]

toilet water *n* a form of liquid perfume lighter than cologne.

toilsome ➊ ('tɔɪlsəm) *or* **toilful** *adj* laborious.
▸**'toilsomely** *adv* ▸**'toilsomeness** *n*

toitoi ('tɔɪtɔɪ) *n* a tall New Zealand grass with feathery seed-heads. [from Maori]

tokamak ('təʊkəˌmæk) *n Physics.* a toroidal reactor used in thermonuclear experiments, in which strong axial magnetic fields keep the plasma from contacting the external walls. [C20: from Russian acronym, from *to(roidál'naya) kám(era s) ak(siál'nym magnitnym pólem),* toroidal chamber with magnetic field]

Tokay (təʊ'keɪ) *n* **1** a sweet wine made near Tokaj, Hungary. **2** a variety of grape used to make this. **3** a similar wine made elsewhere.

token ➊ ('təʊkən) *n* **1** an indication, warning, or sign of something. **2** a symbol or visible representation of something. **3** something that indicates authority, proof, etc. **4** a metal or plastic disc, such as a substitute for currency for use in slot machines. **5** a memento. **6** a gift voucher that can be used as payment for goods of a specified value. **7** (*modifier*) as a matter of form only; nominal: *a token increase in salary.* ◆ *vb* **8** (*tr*) to act or serve as a warning or symbol of; betoken. [OE *tācen*]

tokenism ('təʊkəˌnɪzəm) *n* the practice of making only a token effort or doing no more than the minimum, esp. in order to comply with a law.
▸**'tokeˌnist** *adj*

token money *n* coins having greater face value than the value of their metal content.

token strike *n* a brief strike intended to convey strength of feeling on a disputed issue.

token vote *n* a Parliamentary vote of money in which the amount quoted is not binding.

THESAURUS

to-do *n* = **fuss**, agitation, bother, brouhaha, bustle, commotion, disturbance, excitement, flap (*inf.*), furore, hoo-ha, hue and cry, performance (*inf.*), quarrel, ruction (*inf.*), rumpus, stir, tumult, turmoil, unrest, upheaval, uproar

toe *n* **6 tread on someone's toes** = **offend**, affront, annoy, bruise, disgruntle, get someone's back up, hurt, hurt someone's feelings, infringe, injure, irk, vex

together *adv* **1** = **collectively**, as a group, as one, cheek by jowl, closely, hand in glove, hand in hand, in a body, in concert, in cooperation, in unison, jointly, mutually, shoulder to shoulder, side by side **4** = **at the same time**, all at once, as one, at one fell swoop, concurrently, contemporaneously, en masse, in unison, simultaneously, with one accord **6** *Old-fashioned* = **in succession**, consecutively, continuously, in a row, one after the other, on end, successively, without a break, without interruption **9** *Informal* = **organized**, arranged, fixed, ordered, settled, sorted out, straight, to rights ◆ *adj* **10** *Slang* = **self-possessed**, calm, composed, cool, stable, well-adjusted, well-balanced, well-organized
Antonyms *adv* ≠ **collectively:** alone, apart, independently, individually, one at a time, one by one, separately, singly

toil[1] *n* **1** = **hard work**, application, blood, sweat, and tears (*inf.*), donkey-work, drudgery, effort, elbow grease (*inf.*), exertion, graft (*inf.*), industry, labour, pains, slog, sweat, travail ◆ *vb* **2** = **labour**, bust a gut (*inf.*), graft (*inf.*), grind (*inf.*), grub, knock oneself out (*inf.*), make an all-out effort (*inf.*), push oneself, slave, slog, strive, struggle, sweat (*inf.*), work, work like a dog, work like a Trojan, work one's fingers to the bone
Antonyms *n* ≠ **hard work:** idleness, inactivity, indolence, inertia, laziness, sloth, torpor

toilet *n* **1** = **lavatory**, ablutions (*Military inf.*), bathroom, bog (*sl.*), can (*US & Canad. sl.*), closet, convenience, gents *or* ladies, john (*sl., chiefly US & Canad.*), ladies' room, latrine, little boy's *or* little girl's room (*inf.*), loo (*Brit. inf.*), outhouse, powder room, privy, throne (*inf.*), urinal, washroom, water closet, W.C. **2** *Old-fashioned* = **dressing**, ablutions, bathing, grooming, toilette

toilsome *adj Literary* = **laborious**, arduous, backbreaking, difficult, fatiguing, hard, herculean, painful, severe, strenuous, taxing, tedious, tiresome, tough, wearisome

token *n* **1-3** = **symbol**, badge, clue, demonstra-

tokoloshe (ˌtɒkɒˈlɒʃ, -ˈlɒʃɪ) *n* (in Bantu folklore) a malevolent mythical manlike animal. Also called: **tikoloshe.** [from Xhosa *uthikoloshe*]
toktokkie (ˈtɒkˌtɒkɪ) *n* a large S. African beetle. [from Afrik., from Du. *tokken* to tap]
tolbooth (ˈtəʊlˌbuːθ, -ˌbuːð, ˈtɒl-) *n* **1** *Chiefly Scot.* a town hall. **2** a variant spelling of **tollbooth.**
tolbutamide (tɒlˈbjuːtəˌmaɪd) *n* a synthetic crystalline compound used in the treatment of diabetes to lower blood glucose levels. [C20: from TOL(UENE) + BUT(YRIC ACID) + AMIDE]
told (təʊld) *vb* **1** the past tense and past participle of **tell**[1]. ◆ *adj* **2** See **all told.**
tole (təʊl) *n* enamelled or lacquered metal ware, popular in the 18th century. [from F *tôle* sheet metal, from F (dialect): table, from L *tabula* table]
Toledo (tɒˈleɪdəʊ) *n* a fine-tapered sword or sword blade. [C16: from *Toledo*, city in Spain]
tolerable ➊ (ˈtɒlərəbᵊl) *adj* **1** able to be tolerated; endurable. **2** permissible. **3** *Inf.* fairly good.
▸ˌ**toleraˈbility** *n* ▸ˈ**tolerably** *adv*
tolerance ➊ (ˈtɒlərəns) *n* **1** the state or quality of being tolerant. **2** capacity to endure something, esp. pain or hardship. **3** the permitted variation in some characteristic of an object or workpiece. **4** the capacity to endure the effects of a poison or other substance, esp. after it has been taken over a prolonged period.
tolerant ➊ (ˈtɒlərənt) *adj* **1** able to tolerate the beliefs, actions, etc., of others. **2** permissive. **3** able to withstand extremes. **4** exhibiting tolerance to a drug.
▸ˈ**tolerantly** *adv*
tolerate ➊ (ˈtɒləˌreɪt) *vb* **tolerates, tolerating, tolerated.** (*tr*) **1** to treat with indulgence or forbearance. **2** to permit. **3** to be able to bear; put up with. **4** to have tolerance for (a drug, etc.). [C16: from L *tolerāre* to sustain]
toleration ➊ (ˌtɒləˈreɪʃən) *n* **1** the act or practice of tolerating. **2** freedom to hold religious opinions that differ from the established religion of a country.
▸ˌ**tolerˈationist** *n*
toll[1] ➊ (təʊl) *vb* **1** to ring slowly and recurrently. **2** (*tr*) to summon or announce by tolling. **3** *US & Canad.* to decoy (game, esp. ducks). ◆ *n* **4** the act or sound of tolling. [C15: ? rel. to OE *-tyllan*, as in *fortyllan* to attract]
toll[2] ➊ (təʊl, tɒl) *n* **1a** an amount of money levied, esp. for the use of certain roads, bridges, etc. **1b** (*as modifier*): *toll road; toll bridge.* **2** loss or damage incurred through a disaster, etc.: *the war took its toll of the inhabitants.* **3** (formerly) the right to levy a toll. [OE *toln*]
tollbooth *or* **tolbooth** (ˈtəʊlˌbuːθ, -ˌbuːð, ˈtɒl-) *n* a booth or kiosk at which a toll is collected.
tollgate (ˈtəʊlˌgeɪt, ˈtɒl-) *n* a gate across a toll road or bridge at which travellers must pay.
tollhouse (ˈtəʊlˌhaʊs, ˈtɒl-) *n* a small house at a tollgate occupied by a toll collector.
tollie (ˈtɒlɪ) *n, pl* **tollies.** *S. African.* a castrated calf. [C19: from Xhosa *ithole* calf on which the horns have begun to appear]
Toltec (ˈtɒltɛk) *n, pl* **Toltecs** *or* **Toltec. 1** a member of a Central American Indian people who dominated the valley of Mexico until they were overrun by the Aztecs. ◆ *adj also* **Toltecan. 2** of or relating to this people.
tolu (tɒˈluː) *n* an aromatic balsam obtained from a South American tree. [C17: after *Santiago de Tolu*, Colombia, from which it was exported]
toluene (ˈtɒljʊˌiːn) *n* a colourless volatile flammable liquid obtained from petroleum and coal tar and used as a solvent and in the manufacture of many organic chemicals. [C19: from TOLU + -ENE, since it was previously obtained from tolu]
toluic acid (tɒˈluːɪk) *n* a white crystalline derivative of toluene used in synthetic resins and as an insect repellent. [C19: from TOLU(ENE) + -IC]
toluidine (tɒˈljuːɪˌdiːn) *n* an amine derived from toluene, used in making dyes. [C19: from TOLU(ENE) + -IDE + -INE[2]]
tom (tɒm) *n* **a** the male of various animals, esp. the cat. **b** (*as modifier*): *a tom turkey.* **c** (*in combination*): *a tomcat.* [C16: special use of the short form of *Thomas*, applied to any male, often implying a common or ordinary type of person, etc.]
tomahawk (ˈtɒməˌhɔːk) *n* a fighting axe with a stone or iron head, used by the North American Indians. [C17: from Algonquian *tamahaac*]
tomato (təˈmɑːtəʊ) *n, pl* **tomatoes. 1** a South American plant widely cultivated for its red fleshy many-seeded fruits. **2** the fruit of this plant, eaten in salads, as a vegetable, etc. [C17 *tomate*, from Sp., from Nahuatl *tomatl*]
tomb ➊ (tuːm) *n* **1** a place, esp. a vault beneath the ground, for the burial of a corpse. **2** a monument to the dead. **3 the tomb.** a poetic term for death. [C13: from OF *tombe*, from LL *tumba* burial mound, from Gk *tumbos*]
tombac (ˈtɒmbæk) *n* any of various alloys containing copper and zinc: used for making cheap jewellery, etc. [C17: from F, from Du. *tombak*, from Malay *tambâga* copper, apparently from Sansk. *tāmraka*, from *tāmra* dark coppery red]
tombola (tɒmˈbəʊlə) *n Brit.* a type of lottery, esp. at a fête, in which tickets are drawn from a revolving drum. [C19: from It., from *tombolare* to somersault]
tomboy (ˈtɒmˌbɔɪ) *n* a girl who acts or dresses in a boyish way, liking rough outdoor activities.
▸ˈ**tomˌboyish** *adj* ▸ˈ**tomˌboyishly** *adv*
tombstone ➊ (ˈtuːmˌstəʊn) *n* another word for **gravestone.**
Tom Collins *n* a long drink consisting of gin, lime or lemon juice, sugar, and soda water.
Tom, Dick, and (or) Harry *n* an ordinary, undistinguished, or common person (esp. in **every Tom, Dick, and Harry; any Tom, Dick, or Harry).**
tome ➊ (təʊm) *n* **1** a large weighty book. **2** one of the several volumes of a work. [C16: from F, from L *tomus* section of larger work, from Gk *tomos* a slice, from *temnein* to cut]
-tome *n combining form.* indicating an instrument for cutting: *osteotome.* [from Gk *tomē* a cutting, *tomos* a slice, from *temnein* to cut]
tomentum (təˈmɛntəm) *n, pl* **tomenta** (-tə). **1** a covering of downy hairs on leaves and other plant parts. **2** a network of minute blood vessels occurring in the human brain. [C17: NL, from L: stuffing for cushions]
▸**toˈmentose** *adj*
tomfool ➊ (ˌtɒmˈfuːl) *n* **a** a fool. **b** (*as modifier*): *tomfool ideas.*
▸ˌ**tomˈfoolishness** *n*
tomfoolery ➊ (ˌtɒmˈfuːlərɪ) *n, pl* **tomfooleries. 1** foolish behaviour. **2** utter nonsense; rubbish.
tommy (ˈtɒmɪ) *n, pl* **tommies.** (*often cap.*) *Brit. inf.* a private in the British Army. [C19: orig. *Thomas Atkins*, name representing typical private in specimen forms]
Tommy gun *n* an informal name for **Thompson sub-machine-gun.**
tommyrot (ˈtɒmɪˌrɒt) *n* utter nonsense.
tomography (təˈmɒgrəfɪ) *n* a technique used to obtain an X-ray pho-

THESAURUS

tion, earnest, evidence, expression, index, indication, manifestation, mark, note, proof, representation, sign, warning **5** = **memento**, keepsake, memorial, remembrance, reminder, souvenir ◆ *modifier* **7** = **nominal**, hollow, minimal, perfunctory, superficial, symbolic
tolerable *adj* **1** = **bearable**, acceptable, allowable, endurable, sufferable, supportable **3** *Informal* = **fair**, acceptable, adequate, all right, average, fairly good, fair to middling, good enough, indifferent, middling, not bad (*inf.*), O.K. *or* okay (*inf.*), ordinary, passable, run-of-the-mill, so-so (*inf.*), unexceptional
Antonyms *adj* ≠ **bearable:** insufferable, intolerable, unacceptable, unbearable, unendurable ≠ **fair:** awful, bad, dreadful, rotten
tolerance *n* **1** = **broad-mindedness**, charity, forbearance, indulgence, lenity, magnanimity, open-mindedness, patience, permissiveness, sufferance, sympathy **2** = **endurance**, fortitude, hardiness, hardness, resilience, resistance, stamina, staying power, toughness **3** = **variation**, fluctuation, play, swing
Antonyms *n* ≠ **broad-mindedness:** bigotry, discrimination, intolerance, narrow-mindedness, prejudice, sectarianism
tolerant *adj* **1** = **broad-minded**, catholic, charitable, fair, forbearing, latitudinarian, liberal, long-suffering, magnanimous, open-minded, patient, sympathetic, unbigoted, understanding, unprejudiced **2** = **permissive**, complaisant, easy-going, easy-oasy (*sl.*), free and easy, indulgent, kind-hearted, lax, lenient, soft
Antonyms *adj* ≠ **broad-minded:** biased, bigoted, dogmatic, illiberal, intolerant, narrow-minded, prejudiced, sectarian, uncharitable ≠ **permissive:** authoritarian, despotic, dictatorial, intolerant, repressive, rigid, stern, strict, tyrannical
tolerate *vb* **1, 2** = **allow**, accept, admit, brook, condone, countenance, indulge, permit, pocket, put up with (*inf.*), receive, sanction, take, turn a blind eye to, wink at **3** = **endure**, abide, bear, hack (*sl.*), put up with (*inf.*), stand, stomach, submit to, suffer, swallow, take, thole (*Scot.*), undergo
Antonyms *vb* ≠ **allow:** ban, disallow, disapprove, forbid, outlaw, preclude, prohibit, veto
toleration *n* **1** = **acceptance**, allowance, condonation, endurance, indulgence, permissiveness, sanction, sufferance **2** = **religious freedom**, freedom of conscience, freedom of worship
toll[1] *vb* **1** = **ring**, chime, clang, knell, peal, sound, strike **2** = **announce**, call, signal, summon, warn ◆ *n* **4** = **ringing**, chime, clang, knell, peal, ring, tolling
toll[2] *n* **1a** = **charge**, assessment, customs, demand, duty, fee, impost, levy, payment, rate, tariff, tax, tribute **2** = **damage**, cost, inroad, loss, penalty
tomb *n* **1** = **grave**, burial chamber, catacomb, crypt, mausoleum, sarcophagus, sepulchre, vault
tombstone *n* = **gravestone**, headstone, marker, memorial, monument
tome *n* **1, 2** = **book**, title, volume, work
tomfool *n* **a** = **fool**, ass, berk (*Brit. sl.*), blockhead, chump (*inf.*), clown, dipstick (*Brit. sl.*), divvy (*Brit. sl.*), dolt, dork (*sl.*), idiot, nincompoop, ninny, nitwit (*inf.*), numbskull *or* numskull, pillock (*Brit. sl.*), plank (*Brit. sl.*), plonker (*sl.*), simpleton, twit (*inf., chiefly Brit.*), wally (*sl.*) ◆ *modifier* **b** = **idiotic**, asinine, crackbrained, crazy, daft (*inf.*), dumb-ass (*sl.*), foolish, half-witted, harebrained, inane, rash, senseless, silly, stupid
tomfoolery *n* **1** = **foolishness**, buffoonery, childishness, clowning, fooling around (*inf.*), horseplay, idiocy, larks (*inf.*), messing around (*inf.*), shenanigans (*inf.*), silliness, skylarking (*inf.*), stupidity **2** = **nonsense**, balderdash, baloney (*inf.*), bilge (*inf.*), bosh, bunk (*inf.*), bunkum *or* buncombe (*chiefly US*), claptrap (*inf.*), hogwash, hooey (*sl.*), inanity, poppycock (*inf.*), rot, rubbish, stuff and nonsense, tommyrot, tosh (*sl., chiefly Brit.*), trash, twaddle
Antonyms *n* ≠ **foolishness:** demureness, gravity, heaviness, reserve, sedateness, seriousness, sobriety, solemnity, sternness

tograph of a plane section of the human body or some other object. [C20: from Gk *tomē* a cutting + -GRAPHY]

tomorrow (tə'mɒrəʊ) *n* **1** the day after today. **2** the future. ◆ *adv* **3** on the day after today. **4** at some time in the future. [OE *tō morgenne,* from *tō* on + *morgenne,* dative of *morgen* morning]

Tom Thumb *n* a dwarf; midget. [after *Tom Thumb,* the tiny hero of several E folk tales]

tomtit ('tɒm,tɪt) *n Brit.* any of various tits, esp. the bluetit.

tom-tom *n* a drum usually beaten with the hands as a signalling instrument. [C17: from Hindi *tamtam,* imit.]

-tomy *n combining form.* indicating a surgical cutting of a specified part or tissue: *lobotomy.* [from Gk *-tomia*]

ton[1] (tʌn) *n* **1** Also called: **long ton.** *Brit.* a unit of weight equal to 2240 pounds or 1016.046 909 kilograms. **2** Also called: **short ton, net ton.** *US & Canad.* a unit of weight equal to 2000 pounds or 907.184 kilograms. **3** See **metric ton, tonne.** a unit of weight equal to 1000 kilograms. **4** Also called: **freight ton, measurement ton.** a unit of volume or weight used for charging or measuring freight in shipping. It is usually equal to 40 cubic feet, 1 cubic metre, or 1000 kilograms. **5** Also called: **displacement ton.** a unit used for measuring the displacement of a ship, equal to 35 cubic feet of sea water or 2240 pounds. **6** Also called: **register ton.** a unit of internal capacity of ships equal to 100 cubic feet. ◆ *adv* **7** **tons.** (intensifier): *the new flat is tons better than the old one.* [C14: var. of TUN]

ton[2] (tʌn) *n Sl., chiefly Brit.* a score or achievement of a hundred, esp. a hundred miles per hour, as on a motorcycle. [C20: special use of TON[1] applied to quantities of one hundred]

tonal ('təʊnᵊl) *adj* **1** of or relating to tone. **2** of or utilizing the diatonic system; having an established key. **3** (of an answer in a fugue) not having the same melodic intervals as the subject, so as to remain in the original key.
▸**'tonally** *adv*

tonality (təʊ'nælɪtɪ) *n, pl* **tonalities. 1** *Music.* **1a** the presence of a musical key in a composition. **1b** the system of major and minor keys prevalent in Western music. **2** the overall scheme of colours and tones in a painting.

tondo ('tɒndəʊ) *n, pl* **tondi** (-diː). a circular easel painting or relief carving. [C19: from It.: a circle, shortened from *rotondo* round]

tone ❶ (təʊn) *n* **1** sound with reference to quality, pitch, or volume. **2** short for **tone colour. 3** *US & Canad.* another word for **note** (sense 10). **4** an interval of a major second; whole tone. **5** Also called: **Gregorian tone.** any of several plainsong melodies or other chants used in the singing of psalms. **6** *Linguistics.* any of the pitch levels or pitch contours at which a syllable may be pronounced, such as high tone, falling tone, etc. **7** the quality or character of a sound: *a nervous tone of voice.* **8** general aspect, quality, or style. **9** high quality or style: *to lower the tone of a place.* **10** the quality of a given colour, as modified by mixture with white or black; shade; tint. **11** *Physiol.* **11a** the normal tension of a muscle at rest. **11b** the natural firmness of the tissues and normal functioning of bodily organs in health. **12** the overall effect of the colour values and gradations of light and dark in a picture. **13** *Photog.* a colour of a particular area on a negative or positive that can be distinguished from surrounding areas. ◆ *vb* **tones, toning, toned. 14** (*intr;* often foll. by *with*) to be of a matching or similar tone (to). **15** (*tr*) to give a tone to or correct the tone of. **16** (*tr*) *Photog.* to soften or change the colour of the tones of (a photographic image). ◆ See also **tone down, tone up.** [C14: from L *tonus,* from Gk *tonos* tension, tone, from *teinein* to stretch]
▸**'toneless** *adj* ▸**'tonelessly** *adv*

tone arm *n* another name for **pick-up.**

tone colour *n* the quality of a musical sound that is conditioned or distinguished by the upper partials or overtones present in it.

tone-deaf *adj* unable to distinguish subtle differences in musical pitch.
▸**tone deafness** *n*

tone down ❶ *vb* (*adv*) to moderate or become moderated in tone: *to tone down an argument.*

tone language *n* a language, such as Chinese, in which differences in tone may make differences in meaning.

toneme ('təʊniːm) *n Linguistics.* a phoneme that is distinguished from another phoneme only by its tone. [C20]
▸**to'nemic** *adj*

tone poem *n* another term for **symphonic poem.**

toner ('təʊnə) *n* **1** a person or thing that tones. **2** a cosmetic preparation that is applied to produce a desired effect, such as to reduce the oiliness of the skin. **3** *Photog.* a chemical solution that softens or alters the tones of a photographic image. **4** a powdered chemical used in photocopying machines, which adheres to electrostatically charged areas of a plate or roller and is then transferred onto the paper to form the copy.

tone row *or* **series** *n Music.* a group of notes having a characteristic pattern that forms the basis of the musical material in a serial composition, esp. one consisting of the twelve notes of the chromatic scale.

tone up ❶ *vb* (*adv*) to make or become more vigorous, healthy, etc.

tong (tɒŋ) *n* (formerly) a secret society of Chinese Americans. [C20: from Chinese (Cantonese) *t'ong* meeting place]

tonga ('tɒŋgə) *n* a light two-wheeled vehicle used in rural areas of India. [C19: from Hindi *tāngā*]

Tongan ('tɒŋən) *adj* **1** of or relating to Tonga, a kingdom occupying an archipelago in the SW Pacific. ◆ *n* **2** a native or inhabitant of Tonga. **3** the Polynesian language of the Tongans.

Tongchak (,tɒŋ'tʃæk) *n* the former name for **Chondokyo.**

tongs (tɒŋz) *pl n* a tool for grasping or lifting, consisting of a hinged, sprung, or pivoted pair of arms or levers, joined at one end. Also called: **pair of tongs.** [pl. of OE *tange*]

tongue ❶ (tʌŋ) *n* **1** a movable mass of muscular tissue attached to the floor of the mouth in most vertebrates. It is used in tasting, eating, and (in man) speaking. Related adj: **lingual. 2** an analogous organ in invertebrates. **3** the tongue of certain animals used as food. **4** a language, dialect, or idiom: *the English tongue.* **5** the ability to speak: *to lose one's tongue.* **6** a manner of speaking: *a glib tongue.* **7** utterance or voice (esp. in **give tongue**). **8** anything which resembles a tongue in shape or function. **9** a promontory or spit of land. **10** a flap of leather on a shoe. **11** *Music.* the reed of an oboe or similar instrument. **12** the clapper of a bell. **13** the harnessing pole of a horse-drawn vehicle. **14** a projection on a machine part that serves as a guide for assembly, etc. **15** a projecting strip along an edge of a board that is made to fit a groove in another board. **16 hold one's tongue.** to keep quiet. **17 on the tip of one's tongue.** about to come to mind. **18 with (one's) tongue in (one's) cheek.** Also: **tongue in cheek.** with insincere or ironical intent. ◆ *vb* **tongues, tonguing, tongued. 19** to articulate (notes on a wind instrument) by tonguing. **20** (*tr*) to lick, feel, or touch with the tongue. **21** (*tr*) to provide (a board) with a tongue. **22** (*intr*) (of a piece of land) to project into a body of water. [OE *tunge*]
▸**'tongueless** *adj* ▸**'tongue,like** *adj*

tongue-and-groove joint *n* a joint made between two boards by means of a tongue along the edge of one board that fits into a groove along the edge of the other board.

tongued (tʌŋd) *adj* **1** having a tongue or tongues. **2** (*in combination*) having a manner of speech as specified: *sharp-tongued.*

tongue-lash ❶ *vb* (*tr*) to reprimand severely; scold.
▸**'tongue-,lashing** *n, adj*

tongue-tie *n* a congenital condition in which the tongue has restricted mobility as the result of an abnormally short fraenum.

tongue-tied ❶ *adj* **1** speechless, esp. with embarrassment or shyness. **2** having a condition of tongue-tie.

tongue twister *n* a sentence or phrase that is difficult to articulate clearly and quickly, such as *Peter Piper picked a peck of pickled pepper.*

tonguing ('tʌŋɪŋ) *n* a technique of playing (any nonlegato passage) on a wind instrument by obstructing and uncovering the air passage through the lips with the tongue.

tonic ❶ ('tɒnɪk) *n* **1** a medicinal preparation that improves the functioning of the body or increases the feeling of wellbeing. **2** anything that enlivens or strengthens. **3** Also called: **tonic water.** a mineral water, usually carbonated and containing quinine and often mixed with gin or other alcoholic drinks. **4** *Music.* **4a** the first degree of a major or minor scale and the tonal centre of a piece composed in a particular key. **4b** a key or chord based on this. ◆ *adj* **5** serving to enliven and invigorate: *a tonic wine.* **6** of or relating to a tone or tones. **7** *Music.* of the first degree of a major or minor scale. **8** of or denoting the general effect of colour and light and shade in a picture. **9** *Physiol.* of or affecting normal muscular or bodily tone: *a tonic spasm.* [C17: from NL *tonicus,* from Gk *tonikos* concerning tone, from *tonos* TONE]
▸**'tonically** *adv*

tonic accent *n* **1** emphasis imparted to a note by virtue of its having a higher pitch. **2** (in some languages) an accent in which emphatic syllables are pronounced on a higher musical pitch.

tonicity (təʊ'nɪsɪtɪ) *n* **1** the condition or quality of being tonic. **2** another name for **tonus.**

tonic sol-fa *n* a method of teaching music, by which syllables are used as names for the notes of the major scale in any key.

tonight (tə'naɪt) *n* **1** the night or evening of this present day. ◆ *adv* **2** in or during the night or evening of this day. **3** *Obs.* last night. [OE *tōniht*]

toning table *n* an exercise table, parts of which move mechanically

THESAURUS

tone *n* **1** = **pitch**, accent, emphasis, force, inflection, intonation, modulation, strength, stress, timbre, tonality, volume **8** = **character**, air, approach, aspect, attitude, drift, effect, feel, frame, grain, manner, mood, note, quality, spirit, style, temper, tenor, vein **10** = **colour**, cast, hue, shade, tinge, tint ◆ *vb* **14** = **harmonize**, blend, go well with, match, suit

tone down *vb* = **moderate**, dampen, dim, mitigate, modulate, play down, reduce, restrain, soften, soft-pedal (*inf.*), subdue, temper

tone up *vb* = **get into condition**, freshen, get in shape, invigorate, limber up, shape up, sharpen up, trim, tune up

tongue *n* **4** = **language**, argot, dialect, idiom, lingo (*inf.*), parlance, patois, speech, talk, vernacular **7** *As in* **give tongue** = **utterance**, articulation, speech, verbal expression, voice

tongue-lashing *n* = **scolding**, dressing-down (*inf.*), lecture, rebuke, reprimand, reproach, reproof, slating (*inf.*), talking-to (*inf.*), telling-off (*inf.*), ticking-off (*inf.*), wigging (*Brit. sl.*)

tongue-tied *adj* **1** = **speechless**, at a loss for words, dumb, dumbstruck, inarticulate, mute, struck dumb
Antonyms *adj* articulate, chatty, effusive, garrulous, loquacious, talkative, verbose, voluble, wordy

tonic *n* **2** = **stimulant**, analeptic, boost, bracer (*inf.*), cordial, fillip, livener, pick-me-up (*inf.*), refresher, restorative, roborant, shot in the arm (*inf.*)

for a set time in order to exercise specific parts of the body of the person lying on it.

tonka bean ('tɒŋkə) *n* **1** a tall tree of tropical America. **2** the seeds of this tree, used in the manufacture of perfumes, snuff, etc. [C18: prob. from Tupi *tonka*]

tonnage *or* **tunnage** ('tʌnɪdʒ) *n* **1** the capacity of a merchant ship expressed in tons. **2** the weight of the cargo of a merchant ship. **3** the total amount of shipping of a port or nation. **4** a duty on ships based either on their capacity or their register tonnage. [C15: from OF, from *tonne* barrel]

tonne (tʌn) *n* a unit of mass equal to 1000 kg or 2204.6 pounds. Also called (not in technical use): **metric ton.** [from F]

tonneau ('tɒnəʊ) *n, pl* **tonneaus** *or* **tonneaux** (-nəʊ, -nəʊz). **1** a detachable cover to protect empty passenger seats in an open vehicle. **2** *Rare.* the part of an open car in which the rear passengers sit. [C20: from F: special type of vehicle body, from OF *tonnel* cask, from *tonne* tun]

tonometer (təʊ'nɒmɪtə) *n* **1** an instrument for measuring the pitch of a sound, esp. one consisting of a set of tuning forks. **2** any of various types of instrument for measuring pressure or tension, such as the blood pressure, vapour pressure, etc. [C18: from Gk *tonos* TONE + -METER]

▸**tonometric** (ˌtɒnə'mɛtrɪk, ˌtəʊ-) *adj*

tonsil ('tɒnsəl) *n* either of two small masses of lymphatic tissue situated one on each side of the back of the mouth. [C17: from L *tōnsillae* (pl) tonsils, from ?]

▸**'tonsillar** *adj*

tonsillectomy (ˌtɒnsɪ'lɛktəmɪ) *n, pl* **tonsillectomies.** surgical removal of the tonsils.

tonsillitis (ˌtɒnsɪ'laɪtɪs) *n* inflammation of the tonsils.

▸**tonsillitic** (ˌtɒnsɪ'lɪtɪk) *adj*

tonsorial (tɒn'sɔːrɪəl) *adj Often facetious.* of barbering or hairdressing. [C19: from L *tōnsōrius* concerning shaving, from *tondēre* to shave]

tonsure ('tɒnʃə) *n* **1** (in certain religions and monastic orders) **1a** the shaving of the head or the crown of the head only. **1b** the part of the head left bare by shaving. ◆ *vb* **tonsures, tonsuring, tonsured. 2** (*tr*) to shave the head of. [C14: from L *tōnsūra* a clipping, from *tondēre* to shave]

▸**'tonsured** *adj*

tontine ('tɒntiːn, tɒn'tiːn) *n* an annuity scheme by which several subscribers accumulate and invest a common fund out of which they receive an annuity that increases as subscribers die until the last survivor takes the whole. [C18: from F, after Lorenzo *Tonti*, Neapolitan banker who devised the scheme]

ton-up *Brit. inf.* ◆ *adj* (*prenominal*) **1** (esp. of a motorcycle) capable of speeds of a hundred miles per hour or more. **2** liking to travel at such speeds: *a ton-up boy.* ◆ *n* **3** a person who habitually rides at such speeds.

tonus ('təʊnəs) *n* the normal tension of a muscle at rest; tone. [C19: from L, from Gk *tonos* TONE]

too ❶ (tuː) *adv* **1** as well; in addition; also: *can I come too?* **2** in or to an excessive degree: *I have too many things to do.* **3** extremely: *you're too kind.* **4** *US & Canad. inf.* indeed: used to reinforce a command: *you will too do it!* [OE *tō*]

> **USAGE NOTE** See at **very.**

took (tʊk) *vb* the past tense of **take.**

tool ❶ (tuːl) *n* **1a** an implement, such as a hammer, saw, or spade, that is used by hand. **1b** a power-driven instrument; machine tool. **1c** (*in combination*): *a toolkit.* **2** the cutting part of such an instrument. **3** any of the instruments used by a bookbinder to impress a design on a book cover. **4** anything used as a means of achieving an end. **5** a person used to perform dishonourable or unpleasant tasks for another. **6** a necessary medium for or adjunct to one's profession: *numbers are the tools of the mathematician's trade.* ◆ *vb* **7** to work, cut, or form (something) with a tool. **8** (*tr*) to decorate (a book cover) with a bookbinder's tool. **9** (*tr; often foll. by up*) to furnish with tools. [OE *tōl*]

▸**'tooler** *n*

tooling ('tuːlɪŋ) *n* **1** any decorative work done with a tool, esp. a design stamped onto a book cover, etc. **2** the selection, provision, and setting up of tools for a machining operation.

tool-maker *n* a person who specializes in the production or reconditioning of precision tools, cutters, etc.

▸**'tool-ˌmaking** *n*

tool pusher *n* a foreman who supervises drilling operations on an oil rig.

toolroom ('tuːlruːm, -rʊm) *n* a room, such as in a machine shop, where tools are made, stored, etc.

toot (tuːt) *vb* **1** to give or cause to give (a short blast, hoot, or whistle). ◆ *n* **2** the sound made by or as if by a horn, whistle, etc. **3** *Sl.* any drug for snorting, esp. cocaine. **4** *US & Canad. sl.* a drinking spree. **5** *Austral. sl.* a lavatory. [C16: from MLow G *tuten*, imit.]

▸**'tooter** *n*

tooth (tuːθ) *n, pl* **teeth** (tiːθ). **1** any of various bonelike structures set in the jaws of most vertebrates and used for biting, tearing, or chewing. Related adj: **dental. 2** any of various similar structures in invertebrates. **3** anything resembling a tooth in shape, prominence, or function: *the tooth of a comb.* **4** any of the indentations on the margin of a leaf, petal, etc. **5** any of the projections on a gear, sprocket, rack, etc. **6** taste or appetite (esp. in **sweet tooth**). **7 long in the tooth.** old or ageing. **8 tooth and nail.** with ferocity and force. ◆ *vb* (tuːð, tuːθ). **9** (*tr*) to provide with a tooth or teeth. **10** (*intr*) (of two gearwheels) to engage. [OE *tōth*]

▸**'toothless** *adj* ▸**'tooth,like** *adj*

toothache ('tuːθˌeɪk) *n* a pain in or about a tooth. Technical name: **odontalgia.**

toothbrush ('tuːθˌbrʌʃ) *n* a small brush, usually with a long handle, for cleaning the teeth.

toothed (tuːθt) *adj* **a** having a tooth or teeth. **b** (*in combination*): *sabre-toothed; six-toothed.*

toothed whale *n* any of a suborder of whales having simple teeth and feeding on fish, smaller mammals, etc.: includes dolphins and porpoises.

toothpaste ('tuːθˌpeɪst) *n* a paste used for cleaning the teeth, applied with a toothbrush.

toothpick ('tuːθˌpɪk) *n* a small sharp sliver of wood, plastic, etc., used for extracting pieces of food from between the teeth.

tooth powder *n* a powder used for cleaning the teeth, applied with a toothbrush.

tooth shell *n* another name for the **tusk shell.**

toothsome ❶ ('tuːθsəm) *adj* of delicious or appetizing appearance, flavour, or smell.

toothwort ('tuːθˌwɜːt) *n* **1** a European plant having scaly stems and pinkish flowers and a rhizome covered with toothlike scales. **2** any of a genus of North American or Eurasian plants having rhizomes covered with toothlike projections.

toothy ('tuːθɪ) *adj* **toothier, toothiest.** having or showing numerous, large, or projecting teeth: *a toothy grin.*

▸**'toothily** *adv* ▸**'toothiness** *n*

tootle ('tuːtᵊl) *vb* **tootles, tootling, tootled. 1** to toot or hoot softly or repeatedly. ◆ *n* **2** a soft hoot or series of hoots. [C19: from TOOT]

▸**'tootler** *n*

top[1] ❶ (tɒp) *n* **1** the highest or uppermost part of anything: *the top of a hill.* **2** the most important or successful position: *the top of the class.* **3** the part of a plant that is above ground: *carrot tops.* **4** a thing that forms or covers the uppermost part of anything, esp. a lid or cap. **5** the highest degree or point: *at the top of his career.* **6** the most important person. **7** the best part of anything. **8** the loudest or highest pitch (esp. in **top of one's voice**). **9** another name for **top gear** (sense 1). **10** *Cards.* the highest card of a suit in a player's hand. **11** *Sport.* **11a** a stroke that hits the ball above its centre. **11b** short for **topspin. 12** a platform around the head of a lower mast of a sailing vessel. **13** a garment, esp. for a woman, that extends from the shoulders to the waist or hips. **14 off the top of one's head.** with no previous preparation; extempore. **15 on top of. 15a** in addition to. **15b** *Inf.* in complete control of (a difficult situation, etc.). **16 over the top. 16a** over the parapet or leading edge of a trench. **16b** over the limit; lacking restraint or a sense of proportion. **17 the top of the morning.** a morning greeting regarded as characteristic of Irishmen. ◆ *adj* **18** of, relating to, serving as, or situated on the top. ◆ *vb* **tops, topping, topped.** (*mainly tr*) **19** to form a top on (something): *to top a cake with cream.* **20** to remove the top of or from. **21** to reach or pass the top of. **22** to be at the top of: *he tops the team.* **23** to exceed or surpass. **24** *Sl.* to kill, esp. by hanging. **25** (*also intr*) *Sport.* **25a** to hit (a ball) above the centre. **25b** to make (a stroke) by hitting the ball in this way. **26 top and tail. 26a** to trim off the ends of (fruit or vegetables) before cooking them. **26b** to wash a baby's face and bottom without immersion in a bath. ◆ See also **top off, top out, tops, top up.** [OE *topp*]

top[2] (tɒp) *n* **1** a toy that is spun on its pointed base. **2 sleep like a top.** to sleep very soundly. [OE, from ?]

THESAURUS

too *adv* **1** = **also**, as well, besides, further, in addition, into the bargain, likewise, moreover, to boot **2, 3** = **excessively**, exorbitantly, extremely, immoderately, inordinately, over-, overly, unduly, unreasonably, very

tool *n* **1a** = **implement**, apparatus, appliance, contraption, contrivance, device, gadget, instrument, machine, utensil **4** = **means**, agency, agent, intermediary, medium, vehicle, wherewithal **5** = **puppet**, cat's-paw, creature, dupe, flunkey, hireling, jackal, lackey, minion, pawn, stooge (*sl.*) ◆ *vb* **7** = **make**, chase, cut, decorate, ornament, shape, work

toothsome *adj* = **appetizing**, agreeable, dainty, delectable, delicious, luscious, mouthwatering, nice, palatable, savoury, scrumptious (*inf.*), sweet, tasty, tempting, yummy (*sl.*)

top[1] *n* **1** = **peak**, acme, apex, apogee, crest, crown, culmination, head, height, high point, meridian, pinnacle, summit, vertex, zenith **2** = **first place**, head, highest rank, lead **4** = **lid**, cap, cork, cover, stopper **16b over the top** = **excessive**, a bit much (*inf.*), going too far, immoderate, inordinate, over the limit, too much, uncalled-for ◆ *adj* **18** = **leading**, best, chief, crack, crowning, culminating, dominant, elite, finest, first, foremost, greatest, head, highest, lead, pre-eminent, prime, principal, ruling, sovereign, superior, topmost, upper, uppermost ◆ *vb* **19** = **cover**, cap, crown, finish, garnish, roof, tip **21** = **reach the top of**, ascend, climb, crest, scale, surmount **22** = **lead**, be first, be in charge of, command, head, rule **23** = **surpass**, beat, best, better, eclipse, exceed, excel, go beyond, outdo, outshine, outstrip, transcend

Antonyms *n* ≠ **peak:** base, bottom, foot, nadir, underneath, underside ◆ *adj* ≠ **leading:** amateurish, bottom, incompetent, inept, inferior, least, lower, lowest, second-rate, unknown, unranked, worst ◆ *vb* ≠ **surpass:** fail to equal, fall short of, not be as good as

topaz ('təʊpæz) *n* **1** a hard glassy mineral consisting of a silicate of aluminium and fluorine in crystalline form. It is yellow, pink, or colourless, and is a valuable gemstone. **2 oriental topaz.** a yellowish-brown variety of sapphire. **3 false topaz.** another name for **citrine. 4a** a yellowish-brown colour, as in some varieties of topaz. **4b** (*as adj*): *topaz eyes.* **5** either of two South American hummingbirds. [C13: from OF *topaze,* from L *topazus,* from Gk *topazos*]

top boot *n* a high boot, often with a decorative or contrasting upper section.

top brass *n* (*functioning as pl*) *Inf.* the most important or high-ranking officials or leaders.

topcoat ('tɒpˌkəʊt) *n* an outdoor coat worn over a suit, etc.

top dog *n Inf.* the leader or chief of a group.

top dollar *n Inf.* the highest level of payment.

top drawer *n* people of the highest standing, esp. socially (esp. in **out of the top drawer**).

top dressing *n* a surface application of some material, such as fertilizer.
▸ **'top-ˌdress** *vb* (*tr*)

tope[1] (təʊp) *vb* **topes, toping, toped.** to consume (alcoholic drink) as a regular habit, usually in large quantities. [C17: from F *toper* to keep an agreement, from Sp. *topar* to take a bet; prob. because a wager was generally followed by a drink]
▸ **'toper** *n*

tope[2] (təʊp) *n* a small grey shark of European coastal waters. [C17: from ?]

topee *or* **topi** ('təʊpiː, -pɪ) *n, pl* **topees** *or* **topis.** another name for **pith helmet.** [C19: from Hindi *topī* hat]

top-flight *adj* of superior or excellent quality.

topgallant (ˌtɒp'gælənt; *Naut.* tə'gælənt) *n* **1** a mast on a square-rigger above a topmast or an extension of a topmast. **2** a sail set on a yard of a topgallant mast. **3** (*modifier*) of or relating to a topgallant.

top gear *n* **1** Also called: **top.** the highest forward ratio of a gearbox in a motor vehicle. **2** the highest speed, greatest energy, etc.

top hat *n* a man's hat with a tall cylindrical crown and narrow brim, often made of silk, now worn for some formal occasions.

top-hat scheme *n Inf.* a pension scheme for the senior executives of an organization.

top-heavy *adj* **1** unstable through being overloaded at the top. **2** *Finance.* characterized by too much debt capital in relation to revenue or profit; overcapitalized.

tophus ('təʊfəs) *n, pl* **tophi** (-faɪ). a deposit of sodium urate in the ear or surrounding a joint: a diagnostic of gout. [C16: from L, var. of *tōfus* TUFA, TUFF]

topi[1] ('təʊpiː, -pɪ) *n, pl* **topis.** another name for **pith helmet.** [C19: from Hindi: hat]

topi[2] ('təʊpɪ) *n, pl* **topi** *or* **topis.** a glossy brown African antelope. [C19: from Swahili]

topiary ('təʊpɪərɪ) *adj* **1** of, relating to, or characterized by the trimming or training of trees or bushes into artificial decorative shapes. ◆ *n, pl* **topiaries. 2a** topiary work. **2b** a topiary garden. **3** the art of topiary. [C16: from F *topiaire,* from L *topia* decorative garden work, from Gk *topion* little place, from *topos* place]
▸ **'topiarist** *n*

topic **T** ('tɒpɪk) *n* **1** a subject or theme of a speech, book, etc. **2** a subject of conversation. [C16: from L *topica* translating Gk *ta topika,* lit.: matters relating to commonplaces, title of a treatise by Aristotle, from *topoi,* pl. of *topos* place]

topical **T** ('tɒpɪkᵊl) *adj* **1** of, relating to, or constituting current affairs. **2** relating to a particular place; local. **3** of or relating to a topic or topics. **4** (of a drug, ointment, etc.) for application to the body surface; local.
▸ **topicality** (ˌtɒpɪ'kælɪtɪ) *n* ▸ **'topically** *adv*

topknot ('tɒpˌnɒt) *n* **1** a crest, tuft, chignon, etc., on top of the head. **2** any of several European flatfishes.

topless ('tɒplɪs) *adj* **1** having no top. **2a** denoting a costume which has no covering for the breasts. **2b** wearing such a costume.

top-level *n* (*modifier*) of, involving, or by those on the highest level of influence or authority: *top-level talks.*

toplofty ('tɒpˌlɒftɪ) *adj Inf.* haughty or pretentious.
▸ **'topˌloftiness** *n*

topmast ('tɒpˌmɑːst; *Naut.* 'tɒpməst) *n* the mast next above a lower mast on a sailing vessel.

topmost **T** ('tɒpˌməʊst) *adj* at or nearest the top.

top-notch ('tɒp'nɒtʃ) *adj Inf.* excellent; superb.
▸ **'top-'notcher** *n*

topo- *or before a vowel* **top-** *combining form.* indicating place or region: *topography.* [from Gk *topos* a place]

top off *vb* (*tr, adv*) to finish or complete, esp. with some decisive action.

topography (tə'pɒgrəfɪ) *n, pl* **topographies. 1** the study or detailed description of the surface features of a region. **2** the detailed mapping of the configuration of a region. **3** the land forms or surface configuration of a region. **4** the surveying of a region's surface features. **5** the study or description of the configuration of any object.
▸ **to'pographer** *n* ▸ **topographic** (ˌtɒpə'græfɪk) *or* ˌ**topo'graphical** *adj*

topological group *n Maths.* a group, such as the set of all real numbers, that constitutes a topological space and in which multiplication and inversion are continuous.

topological space *n Maths.* a set *S* with an associated family of subsets τ that is closed under set union and finite intersection.

topology (tə'pɒlədʒɪ) *n* **1** the branch of mathematics concerned with generalization of the concepts of continuity, limit, etc. **2** a branch of geometry describing the properties of a figure that are unaffected by continuous distortion. **3** *Maths.* a family of subsets of a given set *S,* such that *S* is a topological space. **4** the study of the topography of a given place. **5** the anatomy of any specific bodily area, structure, or part.
▸ **topologic** (ˌtɒpə'lɒdʒɪk) *or* ˌ**topo'logical** *adj* ▸ ˌ**topo'logically** *adv* ▸ **to'pologist** *n*

top out *vb* (*adv*) to place the highest part of a building in position.

topper ('tɒpə) *n* **1** an informal name for **top hat. 2** a person or thing that tops or excels.

topping ('tɒpɪŋ) *n* **1** something that tops something else, esp. a sauce or garnish for food. ◆ *adj* **2** high or superior in rank, degree, etc. **3** *Brit. sl.* excellent; splendid.

topple **T** ('tɒpᵊl) *vb* **topples, toppling, toppled. 1** to tip over or cause to tip over, esp. from a height. **2** (*intr*) to lean precariously or totter. [C16: frequentative of TOP[1] (vb)]

tops (tɒps) *Sl.* ◆ *n* **1 the tops.** a person or thing of top quality. ◆ *adj* **2** (*postpositive*) excellent.

topsail ('tɒpˌseɪl; *Naut.* 'tɒpsəl) *n* a square sail carried on a yard set on a topmast.

top-secret *adj* classified as needing the highest level of secrecy and security.

topside ('tɒpˌsaɪd) *n* **1** the uppermost side of anything. **2** *Brit. & NZ.* a lean cut of beef from the thigh containing no bone. **3** (*often pl*) **3a** the part of a ship's sides above the water line. **3b** the parts of a ship above decks.

topsoil ('tɒpˌsɔɪl) *n* the surface layer of soil.

topspin ('tɒpˌspɪn) *n Tennis, etc.* a spin imparted to make a ball bounce or travel exceptionally far, high, or quickly.

topsy-turvy **T** ('tɒpsɪ'tɜːvɪ) *adj* **1** upside down. **2** in a state of confusion. ◆ *adv* **3** in a topsy-turvy manner. ◆ *n* **4** a topsy-turvy state. [C16: prob. from *tops,* pl. of TOP[1] + obs. *tervy* to turn upside down]

top up **T** *vb* (*tr, adv*) *Brit.* **1** to raise the level of (a liquid, powder, etc.) in (a container), usually bringing it to the brim of the container. **2a** to increase the benefits from (an insurance scheme), esp. to increase a pension when a salary rise enables higher premiums to be paid. **2b** to add money to (a loan, bank account, etc.) in order to keep it at a constant or acceptable level. ◆ *n* **top-up. 3a** an amount added to something in order to raise it to or maintain it at a desired level. **3b** (*as modifier*): *a top-up loan; a top-up policy.*

toque (təʊk) *n* **1** a woman's small round brimless hat. **2** a chef's tall white hat. **3** *Canad.* a variant spelling of **tuque** (sense 2). **4** a small plumed hat popular in the 16th century. [C16: from F, from OSp. *toca* headdress, prob. from Basque *tauka* hat]

tor (tɔː) *n* a high hill, esp. a bare rocky one. [OE *torr*]

Torah ('tɔːrə) *n* **1a** the Pentateuch. **1b** the scroll on which this is written. **2** the whole body of traditional Jewish teaching, including the Oral Law. [C16: from Heb.: precept, from *yārāh* to instruct]

torc (tɔːk) *n* a variant of **torque** (sense 1).

torch (tɔːtʃ) *n* **1** a small portable electric lamp powered by batteries. US and Canad. word: **flashlight. 2** a wooden or tow shaft dipped in wax or tallow and set alight. **3** anything regarded as a source of enlightenment, guidance, etc. **4** any apparatus with a hot flame for welding, brazing, etc. **5 carry a torch for.** to be in love with, esp. unrequitedly. ◆ *vb* **6** (*tr*) to set fire to, esp. deliberately as an act of arson. [C13: from OF *torche* handful of twisted straw, from Vulgar L *torca* (unattested), from L *torquēre* to twist]

torchbearer ('tɔːtʃˌbeərə) *n* **1** a person or thing that carries a torch. **2** a person who leads or inspires.

torchère (tɔː'ʃeə) *n* a tall stand for holding a candelabrum. [C20: from F, from *torche* TORCH]

torchier *or* **torchiere** ('tɔːtʃɪə) *n* a standing lamp with a bowl for casting light upwards. [C20: from TORCHÈRE]

torch song *n* a sentimental song, usually sung by a woman. [C20: from *to carry a torch for* (*someone*)]
▸ **torch singer** *n*

tore (tɔː) *vb* the past tense of **tear**[2].

toreador ('tɒrɪəˌdɔː) *n* a bullfighter. [C17: from Sp., from *torear* to take part in bullfighting, from *toro* a bull, from L *taurus*]

torero (tɒ'reərəʊ) *n, pl* **toreros.** a bullfighter, esp. one who fights on foot. [C18: from Sp., from LL *taurārius,* from L *taurus* a bull]

toric lens ('tɒrɪk) *n* a lens used to correct astigmatism, having one of its

THESAURUS

topic *n* **1** = **subject**, issue, matter, point, question, subject matter, text, theme, thesis

topical *adj* **1** = **current**, contemporary, newsworthy, popular, up-to-date, up-to-the-minute

topmost *adj* = **highest**, dominant, foremost, leading, loftiest, paramount, principal, supreme, top, upper, uppermost

Antonyms *adj* base, basic, bottom, bottommost, last, lowest, undermost

topple *vb* **1** = **fall over**, capsize, collapse, fall, fall headlong, keel over, knock down, knock over, overbalance, overturn, tip over, totter, tumble, upset

topsy-turvy *adj* **2** = **confused**, chaotic, disarranged, disorderly, disorganized, inside-out, jumbled, messy, mixed-up, untidy, upside-down

Antonyms *adj* neat, ordered, orderly, organized, shipshape, systematic, tidy

top up *vb* **2** = **supplement**, add to, augment, boost, enhance, fill out *or* up surfaces shaped like part of a torus so that its focal lengths are different in different meridians.

torii ('tɔːrɪˌiː) *n, pl* **torii.** a gateway at the entrance to a Shinto temple. [C19: from Japanese, lit.: a perch for birds]

torment 🅣 *vb* (tɔː'mɛnt). (*tr*) **1** to afflict with great pain, suffering, or anguish; torture. **2** to tease or pester in an annoying way. ◆ *n* ('tɔːmɛnt). **3** physical or mental pain. **4** a source of pain, worry, annoyance, etc. [C13: from OF, from L *tormentum*, from *torquēre*]
▸**tor'mented** *adj* ▸**tor'menting** *adj, n* ▸**tor'mentor** *n*

tormentil ('tɔːməntɪl) *n* a perennial plant of Europe and W Asia, having yellow flowers, and an astringent root used in medicine, tanning, and dyeing. [C15: from OF *tormentille*, from Med. L *tormentilla*, from L *tormentum* agony; from its use in relieving pain]

torn 🅣 (tɔːn) *vb* **1** the past participle of **tear**[2]. **2 that's torn it.** *Brit. sl.* an unexpected event or circumstance has upset one's plans. ◆ *adj* **3** split or cut. **4** divided or undecided, as in preference: *torn between staying and leaving*.

tornado 🅣 (tɔː'neɪdəʊ) *n, pl* **tornadoes** *or* **tornados. 1** a violent storm with winds whirling around a small area of extremely low pressure, usually characterized by a dark funnel-shaped cloud causing damage along its path. **2** a small but violent squall or whirlwind. **3** any violently active or destructive person or thing. [C16: prob. alteration of Sp. *tronada* thunderstorm (from *tronar* to thunder, from L *tonāre*) through infl. of *tornar* to turn, from L *tornāre* to turn in a lathe]
▸**tornadic** (tɔː'nædɪk) *adj*

toroid ('tɔːrɔɪd) *n* **1** *Geom.* a surface generated by rotating a closed plane curve about a coplanar line that does not intersect the curve. **2** the solid enclosed by such a surface. See also **torus.**
▸**to'roidal** *adj*

torpedo (tɔː'piːdəʊ) *n, pl* **torpedoes. 1** a cylindrical self-propelled weapon carrying explosives that is launched from aircraft, ships, or submarines and follows an underwater path to hit its target. **2** *Obs.* a submarine mine. **3** *US & Canad.* a firework with a percussion cap. **4** an electric ray. ◆ *vb* **torpedoes, torpedoing, torpedoed.** (*tr*) **5** to attack or hit (a ship, etc.) with one or a number of torpedoes. **6** to destroy or wreck: *to torpedo the administration's plan.* [C16: from L: crampfish (whose electric discharges can cause numbness), from *torpēre* to be inactive]
▸**tor'pedo-ˌlike** *adj*

torpedo boat *n* (formerly) a small high-speed warship designed to carry out torpedo attacks.

torpedo tube *n* the tube from which a torpedo is discharged from submarines or ships.

torpid 🅣 ('tɔːpɪd) *adj* **1** apathetic; sluggish. **2** (of a hibernating animal) dormant. **3** unable to move or feel. [C17: from L *torpidus*, from *torpēre* to be numb]
▸**tor'pidity** *n* ▸**'torpidly** *adv*

torpor 🅣 ('tɔːpə) *n* a state of torpidity. [C17: from L: inactivity, from *torpēre* to be motionless]

torque (tɔːk) *n* **1** a necklace or armband made of twisted metal. **2** any force that causes rotation. [C19: from L *torquēs* necklace & *torquēre* to twist]

torque converter *n* a device for the transmission of power in which an engine-driven impeller transmits its momentum to a fluid held in a sealed container, which in turn drives a rotor. Also called: **hydraulic coupling.**

torques ('tɔːkwiːz) *n* a distinctive band of hair, feathers, skin, or colour around the neck of an animal; a collar. [C17: from L: necklace, from *torquēre* to twist]
▸**torquate** ('tɔːkwɪt, -kweɪt) *adj*

torque wrench *n* a type of wrench with a gauge attached to indicate the torque applied.

torr (tɔː) *n, pl* **torr.** a unit of pressure equal to one millimetre of mercury (133.322 newtons per square metre). [C20: after E. *Torricelli* (1608–47), It. physicist]

torrefy ('tɒrɪˌfaɪ) *vb* **torrefies, torrefying, torrefied.** (*tr*) to dry (drugs, ores, etc.) by heat. [C17: from F *torréfier*, from L *torrefacere*, from *torrēre* to parch + *facere* to make]
▸**torrefaction** (ˌtɒrɪ'fækʃən) *n*

Torrens title ('tɒrənz) *n Austral.* legal title to land based on record of registration rather than on title deeds. [from Sir Robert Richard *Torrens* (1814–84), who introduced the system as premier of South Australia in 1857]

torrent 🅣 ('tɒrənt) *n* **1** a fast or violent stream, esp. of water. **2** an overwhelming flow of thoughts, words, sound, etc. [C17: from F, from L *torrēns* (n), from *torrēns* (adj) burning, from *torrēre* to burn]
▸**torrential** (tɒ'rɛnʃəl) *adj*

Torricellian tube (ˌtɒrɪ'sɛlɪən) *n* a vertical glass tube partly evacuated and partly filled with mercury, used to measure atmospheric pressure. [C17: after E. *Torricelli*; see TORR]

torrid 🅣 ('tɒrɪd) *adj* **1** so hot and dry as to parch or scorch. **2** arid or parched. **3** highly charged emotionally: *a torrid love scene.* [C16: from L *torridus*, from *torrēre* to scorch]
▸**tor'ridity** *or* **'torridness** *n* ▸**'torridly** *adv*

Torrid Zone *n Rare.* that part of the earth's surface lying between the tropics of Cancer and Capricorn.

torsion ('tɔːʃən) *n* **1a** the twisting of a part by application of equal and opposite torques. **1b** the condition of twist and shear stress produced by a torque on a part or component. **2** a twisting or being twisted. [C15: from OF, from Medical L *torsiō* griping pains, from L *torquēre* to twist, torture]
▸**'torsional** *adj* ▸**'torsionally** *adv*

torsion balance *n* an instrument used to measure small forces, esp. electric or magnetic forces, by the torsion they produce in a thin wire.

torsion bar *n* a metal bar acting as a torsional spring.

torsk (tɔːsk) *n, pl* **torsks** *or* **torsk.** a food fish of northern coastal waters. Usual US name: **cusk.** [C17: of Scand. origin]

torso ('tɔːsəʊ) *n, pl* **torsos** *or* **torsi** (-sɪ). **1** the trunk of the human body. **2** a statue of a nude human trunk, esp. without the head or limbs. [C18: from It.: stalk, stump, from L: THYRSUS]

tort (tɔːt) *n Law.* a civil wrong or injury arising out of an act or failure to act, independently of any contract, for which an action for damages may be brought. [C14: from OF, from Med. L *tortum*, lit.: something twisted, from L *torquēre* to twist]

torte (tɔːt) *n* a rich cake usually decorated or filled with cream, fruit, etc. [C16: ult. ?from LL *tōrta* a round loaf, from ?]

torticollis (ˌtɔːtɪ'kɒlɪs) *n Pathol.* an abnormal position of the head, usually with the neck bent to one side. [C19: NL, from L *tortus* twisted (from *torquēre* to twist) + *collum* neck]

tortilla (tɔː'tiːə) *n Mexican cookery.* a kind of thin pancake made from corn meal. [C17: from Sp.: a little cake, from *torta* a round cake, from LL]

tortoise ('tɔːtəs) *n* **1** any of a family of herbivorous reptiles having a heavy dome-shaped shell and clawed limbs. **2** a slow-moving person. **3** another word for **testudo.** [C15: prob. from OF *tortue* (infl. by L *tortus* twisted), from Med. L *tortūca*, from LL *tartarūcha* coming from Tartarus (in the underworld), from Gk *tartaroukhos;* from belief that the tortoise originated in the underworld]

tortoiseshell ('tɔːtəsˌʃɛl) *n* **1** the horny yellow-and-brown mottled shell of the hawksbill turtle: used for making ornaments, jewellery, etc. **2** a similar synthetic substance. **3** a breed of domestic cat having black, cream, and brownish markings. **4** any of several butterflies having orange-brown wings with black markings. **5a** a yellowish-brown mottled colour. **5b** (*as adj*): *a tortoiseshell décor.* **6** (*modifier*) made of tortoiseshell.

tortricid ('tɔːtrɪsɪd) *n* any of a family of moths, the larvae of which live in leaves, which they roll or tie together. [C19: from NL *Tortrīcidae*, from *tortrix*, fem. of *tortor*, lit.: twister, from the leaf-rolling of the larvae, from *torquēre* to twist]

tortuous 🅣 ('tɔːtjʊəs) *adj* **1** twisted or winding. **2** devious or cunning. **3** intricate.
▸**tortuosity** (ˌtɔːtjʊ'ɒsɪtɪ) *n* ▸**'tortuously** *adv* ▸**'tortuousness** *n*

torture 🅣 ('tɔːtʃə) *vb* **tortures, torturing, tortured.** (*tr*) **1** to cause extreme physical pain to, esp. to extract information, etc.: *to torture prisoners.* **2** to give mental anguish to. **3** to twist into a grotesque form. ◆ *n* **4** physical or mental anguish. **5** the practice of torturing a person. **6** a

THESAURUS

torment *vb* **1** = **torture**, afflict, agonize, crucify, distress, excruciate, harrow, pain, rack **2** = **tease**, aggravate (*inf.*), annoy, bedevil, bother, chivvy, devil (*inf.*), harass, harry, hassle (*inf.*), hound, irritate, lead (someone) a merry dance (*Brit. inf.*), nag, persecute, pester, plague, provoke, trouble, vex, worry ◆ *n* **3** = **suffering**, agony, anguish, distress, hell, misery, pain, torture **4** = **trouble**, affliction, annoyance, bane, bother, harassment, hassle (*inf.*), irritation, nag, nagging, nuisance, pain in the neck (*inf.*), persecution, pest, plague, provocation, scourge, thorn in one's flesh *or* side, vexation, worry
Antonyms *vb* ≠ **torture:** comfort, delight, ease, encourage, make happy, put at ease, reassure, soothe ◆ *n* ≠ **suffering:** bliss, comfort, ease, ecstasy, encouragement, happiness, joy, reassurance, rest

torn *adj* **3** = **cut**, lacerated, ragged, rent, ripped, slit, split **4** = **undecided**, divided, in two minds (*inf.*), irresolute, split, uncertain, unsure, vacillating, wavering

tornado *n* **1, 2** = **whirlwind**, cyclone, gale, hurricane, squall, storm, tempest, twister, typhoon, windstorm

torpid *adj* **1** = **inactive**, apathetic, benumbed, drowsy, dull, indolent, inert, lackadaisical, languid, languorous, lazy, lethargic, listless, lymphatic, motionless, numb, passive, slothful, slow, slow-moving, sluggish, somnolent, stagnant

torpor *n* = **inactivity**, accidie, acedia, apathy, drowsiness, dullness, inanition, indolence, inertia, inertness, languor, laziness, lethargy, listlessness, numbness, passivity, sloth, sluggishness, somnolence, stagnancy, stupor, torpidity
Antonyms *n* animation, energy, get-up-and-go (*inf.*), go, liveliness, pep, vigour

torrent *n* **1** = **stream**, cascade, deluge, downpour, effusion, flood, flow, gush, outburst, rush, spate, tide

torrid *adj* **1** = **hot**, blistering, boiling, broiling, burning, dry, fiery, flaming, parching, scorching, sizzling, stifling, sultry, sweltering, tropical **2** = **arid**, dried, parched, scorched **3** = **passionate**, ardent, erotic, fervent, flaming, hot, intense, sexy (*inf.*), steamy (*inf.*)

tortuous *adj* **1** = **winding**, bent, circuitous, convoluted, crooked, curved, indirect, mazy, meandering, serpentine, sinuous, twisted, twisting, twisty, zigzag **2** = **complicated**, ambiguous, convoluted, cunning, deceptive, devious, indirect, involved, mazy, misleading, roundabout, tricky
Antonyms *adj* ≠ **complicated:** candid, direct, honest, ingenuous, open, reliable, straightforward, upright

torture *vb* **1, 2** = **torment**, afflict, agonize, crucify, distress, excruciate, harrow, lacerate, martyr, pain, persecute, put on the rack, rack ◆ *n* **4, 5** = **agony**, affliction, anguish, distress, hell, laceration, martyrdom, misery, pain, pang(s), persecution, rack, suffering, torment
Antonyms *vb* ≠ **torment:** alleviate, comfort, con-

cause of mental agony. [C16: from LL *tortūra* a twisting, from *torquēre* to twist]
▸**'torturer** *n* ▸**'torturous** *adj* ▸**'torturously** *adv*

> **USAGE NOTE** The adjective *torturous* is sometimes confused with *tortuous*. One speaks of a *torturous* experience, i.e. one that involves pain or suffering, but of a *tortuous* road, i.e. one that winds or twists.

torus ('tɔːrəs) *n, pl* **tori** (-raɪ). **1** a large convex moulding semicircular in cross section, esp. one used on the base of a column. **2** *Geom.* a ring-shaped surface generated by rotating a circle about a coplanar line that does not intersect the circle. **3** *Bot.* another name for **receptacle** (sense 2). [C16: from L: a swelling, from ?]
▸**toric** ('tɒrɪk) *adj*

Tory ('tɔːrɪ) *n, pl* **Tories. 1** a member or supporter of the Conservative Party in Great Britain or Canada. **2** a member of the English political party that opposed the exclusion of James, Duke of York from the royal succession (1679–80). Tory remained the label for conservative interests until they gave birth to the Conservative Party in the 1830s. **3** an American supporter of the British cause; loyalist. Cf. **Whig. 4** (*sometimes not cap.*) an ultraconservative or reactionary. ◆ *adj* **5** of, characteristic of, or relating to Tories. **6** (*sometimes not cap.*) ultraconservative or reactionary. [C17: from Irish *tōraidhe* outlaw, from MIrish *tōir* pursuit]
▸**'Toryish** *adj* ▸**'Toryism** *n*

tosa ('təʊsə) *n* a large dog, usually red in colour, that is a cross between a mastiff and a Great Dane: originally developed for dog-fighting; it is not recognized as a breed by kennel clubs outside Japan. [C20: from the name of a province of Japan]

tosh (tɒʃ) *n Sl., chiefly Brit.* nonsense; rubbish. [C19: from ?]

toss ❶ (tɒs) *vb* **1** (*tr*) to throw lightly, esp. with the palm of the hand upwards. **2** to fling or be flung about, esp. in an agitated or violent way: *a ship tosses in a storm.* **3** to discuss or put forward for discussion in an informal way. **4** (*tr*) (of a horse, etc.) to throw (its rider). **5** (*tr*) (of an animal) to butt with the head or the horns and throw into the air. **6** (*tr*) to shake or disturb. **7** to toss up a coin with (someone) in order to decide something. **8** (*intr*) to move away angrily or impatiently. ◆ *n* **9** an abrupt movement. **10** a rolling or pitching motion. **11** the act or an instance of tossing. **12** the act of tossing up a coin. See **toss up. 13** a fall from a horse. [C16: of Scand. origin]

tosser ('tɒsə) *n Brit. sl.* a stupid or despicable person. [C20: probably from TOSS OFF (to masturbate)]

toss off *vb* (*adv*) **1** (*tr*) to perform, write, etc., quickly and easily. **2** (*tr*) to drink at one draught. **3** (*intr*) *Brit. taboo.* to masturbate.

toss up *vb* (*adv*) **1** to spin (a coin) in the air in order to decide between alternatives by guessing which side will fall uppermost. ◆ *n* **toss-up. 2** an instance of tossing up a coin. **3** *Inf.* an even chance or risk.

tot[1] ❶ (tɒt) *n* **1** a young child; toddler. **2** *Chiefly Brit.* a small amount of anything. **3** a small measure of spirits. [C18: ? short for *totterer;* see TOTTER]

tot[2] ❶ (tɒt) *vb* **tots, totting, totted.** (usually foll. by *up*) *Chiefly Brit.* to total; add. [C17: shortened from TOTAL or from L *totum* all]

total ❶ ('təʊtᵊl) *n* **1** the whole, esp. regarded as the complete sum of a number of parts. ◆ *adj* **2** complete; absolute. **3** (*prenominal*) being or related to a total. ◆ *vb* **totals, totalling, totalled** *or US* **totals, totaling, totaled. 4** (when *intr,* sometimes foll. by *to*) to amount: *to total six pounds.* **5** (*tr*) to add up. **6** (*tr*) *Sl.* to kill or destroy. [C14: from OF, from Med. L *tōtālis,* from L *tōtus* all]
▸**'totally** *adv*

total football *n* an attacking style of play, popularized by the Dutch national team of the 1970s, in which there are no fixed positions and every outfield player can join in the attack.

total internal reflection *n Physics.* the complete reflection of a light ray at the boundary of two media, when the ray is in the medium with greater refractive index.

totalitarian ❶ (təʊˌtælɪ'tɛərɪən) *adj* **1** of, denoting, relating to, or characteristic of a dictatorial one-party state that regulates every realm of life. ◆ *n* **2** a person who advocates or practises totalitarian policies.
▸**toˌtali'tarianism** *n*

totality ❶ (təʊ'tælɪtɪ) *n, pl* **totalities. 1** the whole amount. **2** the state of being total.

totalizator ('təʊtᵊlaɪˌzeɪtə), **totalizer** *or* **totalisator, totaliser** *n* **1** a system of betting on horse races in which the aggregate stake, less tax, etc., is paid out to winners in proportion to their stake. **2** the machine that records bets in this system and works out odds, pays out winnings, etc. ◆ US and Canad. term: **pari-mutuel.**

total quality management *n* an approach to the management of an organization that integrates the needs of customers with a deep understanding of the technical details, costs, and human-resource relationships of the organization. Abbrev.: **TQM.**

totaquine ('təʊtəˌkwiːn, -kwɪn) *n* a mixture of quinine and other alkaloids derived from cinchona bark, used as a substitute for quinine in treating malaria. [C20: from NL *tōtaquīna,* from TOTA(L) + Sp. *quina* cinchona bark; see QUININE]

totara ('təʊtərə) *n* a tall coniferous forest tree of New Zealand with durable wood.

tote[1] (təʊt) *Inf.* ◆ *vb* **totes, toting, toted. 1** (*tr*) to carry, convey, or drag. ◆ *n* **2** the act of or an instance of toting. **3** something toted. [C17: from ?]
▸**'toter** *n*

tote[2] (təʊt) *n* (usually preceded by *the*) *Inf.* short for **totalizator.**

tote bag *n* a large handbag or shopping bag.

totem ('təʊtəm) *n* **1** (in some societies, esp. among North American Indians) an object, animal, plant, etc., symbolizing a clan, family, etc., often having ritual associations. **2** a representation of such an object. [C18: from Ojibwa *nintōtēm* mark of my family]
▸**totemic** (təʊ'temɪk) *adj* ▸**'totemˌism** *n*

totem pole *n* a pole carved or painted with totemic figures set up by certain North American Indians as a tribal symbol, etc.

tother *or* **t'other** ('tʌðə) *adj, n Arch. or dialect.* the other. [C13 *the tother,* by mistaken division from *thet other* (*thet,* from OE *thæt,* neuter of THE[1])]

totipalmate (ˌtəʊtɪ'pælmɪt, -ˌmeɪt) *adj* (of certain birds) having all four toes webbed. [C19: from L *tōtus* entire + *palmate,* from *palmātus* shaped like a hand, from *palma* PALM[1]]

totter ❶ ('tɒtə) *vb* (*intr*) **1** to move in an unsteady manner. **2** to sway or shake as if about to fall. **3** to be failing, unstable, or precarious. ◆ *n* **4** the act or an instance of tottering. [C12: ?from OE *tealtrian* to waver, & MDu. *touteren* to stagger]
▸**'totterer** *n* ▸**'tottery** *adj*

totting ('tɒtɪŋ) *n Brit.* the practice of searching through rubbish for usable or saleable items. [C19: from ?]

toucan ('tuːkən) *n* any of a family of tropical American fruit-eating birds having a large brightly coloured bill and a bright plumage. [C16: from F, from Port. *tucano,* from Tupi *tucana,* prob. imit. of its cry]

touch ❶ (tʌtʃ) *n* **1** the sense by which the texture and other qualities of objects can be experienced when they come in contact with a part of the body surface, esp. the tips of the fingers. Related adj: **tactile. 2** the quality of an object as perceived by this sense; feel; feeling. **3** the act or an instance of something coming into contact with the body. **4** a gentle push, tap, or caress. **5** a small amount; hint: *a touch of sarcasm.* **6** a noticeable effect; influence: *the house needed a woman's touch.* **7** any slight stroke or mark. **8** characteristic manner or style. **9** a detail of some work: *she added a few finishing touches to the book.* **10** a slight attack, as of a disease. **11** a specific ability or facility. **12** the state of being aware of a situation or in contact with someone. **13** the state of being in physical contact. **14** a trial or test (esp. in **put to the touch**). **15** *Rugby, soccer, etc.* the area outside the touchlines, beyond which the ball is out of play (esp. in **in touch**). **16** a scoring hit in fencing. **17** an estimate of the amount of gold in an alloy as obtained by use of a touchstone. **18** the technique of fingering a keyboard instrument. **19** the quality of the

THESAURUS

sole, ease, mollify, relieve, salve, solace, soothe ◆ *n* ≠ **agony:** amusement, bliss, delight, enjoyment, happiness, joy, pleasure, well-being

toss *vb* **1** = **throw**, cast, chuck, fling, flip, hurl, launch, lob (*inf.*), pitch, project, propel, shy, sling **2** = **heave**, labour, lurch, pitch, roll, wallow **6** = **thrash**, agitate, disturb, jiggle, joggle, jolt, rock, roll, shake, tumble, wriggle, writhe ◆ *n* **11** = **throw**, cast, fling, lob (*inf.*), pitch, shy

tot[1] *n* **1** = **infant**, ankle-biter (*Austral. sl.*), baby, child, little one, mite, rug rat (*sl.*), sprog (*sl.*), toddler, wean (*Scot.*) **3** = **measure**, dram, finger, nip, shot (*inf.*), slug, snifter (*inf.*), toothful

tot[2] *vb, usually foll. by* **up** = **add up**, calculate, count up, reckon, sum (up), tally, total

total *n* **1** = **whole**, aggregate, all, amount, entirety, full amount, mass, sum, totality ◆ *adj* **2** = **complete**, absolute, all-out, arrant, comprehensive, consummate, deep-dyed (*usually derogatory*), downright, entire, full, gross, integral, out-and-out, outright, overarching, perfect, sheer, sweeping, thorough, thoroughgoing, unconditional, undisputed, undivided, unmitigated, unqualified, utter, whole ◆ *vb* **4** = **amount to**, come to, mount up to, reach **5** = **add up**, reckon, sum up, tot up
Antonyms *n* ≠ **whole:** individual amount, part, subtotal ◆ *adj* ≠ **complete:** conditional, fragmentary, incomplete, limited, mixed, part, partial, qualified, restricted, uncombined ◆ *vb* ≠ **add up:** deduct, subtract

totalitarian *adj* **1** = **dictatorial**, authoritarian, despotic, monolithic, one-party, oppressive, tyrannous, undemocratic
Antonyms *adj* autonomous, democratic, egalitarian, popular, self-governing

totality *n* **1** = **whole**, aggregate, all, entirety, everything, sum, total **2** = **completeness**, entireness, fullness, wholeness

totally *adv* **2** = **completely**, absolutely, comprehensively, consummately, entirely, fully, one hundred per cent, perfectly, quite, thoroughly, to the hilt, unconditionally, unmitigatedly, utterly, wholeheartedly, wholly
Antonyms *adv* incompletely, in part, partially, partly, somewhat, to a certain extent

totter *vb* **1, 2** = **stagger**, falter, lurch, quiver, reel, rock, shake, stumble, sway, teeter, tremble, walk unsteadily, waver, wobble

touch *n* **2** = **feeling**, feel, handling, palpation, physical contact, tactility **4** = **tap**, brush, caress, fondling, pat, stroke **5** = **bit**, dash, detail, drop, hint, intimation, jot, pinch, smack, small amount, smattering, *soupçon,* speck, spot, suggestion, suspicion, taste, tincture, tinge, trace, whiff **6** = **influence**, direction, effect, hand **8** = **style**, approach, characteristic, handiwork, manner, method, technique, trademark, way **11** = **skill**, ability, adroitness, art, artistry, command, craft, deftness, facility, flair, knack, mastery, virtuosity **12** = **communication**, acquaintance, awareness, contact, correspondence, familiarity, understanding ◆ *vb* **21** = **handle**, brush, caress, contact, feel, finger, fondle, graze, lay a finger on, palpate, stroke **22** = **tap**, hit, pat, push, strike **23, 24** = **come into con-**

action of a keyboard instrument with regard to the ease with which the keys may be depressed. **20** *Sl.* **20a** the act of asking for money, often by devious means. **20b** the money received. **20c** a person asked for money in this way. ◆ *vb* **21** (*tr*) to cause or permit a part of the body to come into contact with. **22** (*tr*) to tap, feel, or strike. **23** to come or cause to come into contact with. **24** (*intr*) to be in contact. **25** (*tr; usually used with a negative*) to take hold of (a person or thing), esp. in violence. **26** to be adjacent to (each other). **27** (*tr*) to move or disturb by handling. **28** (*tr*) to have an effect on. **29** (*tr*) to produce an emotional response in. **30** (*tr*) to affect; concern. **31** (*tr; usually used with a negative*) to partake of, eat, or drink. **32** (*tr; usually used with a negative*) to handle or deal with: *I wouldn't touch that business.* **33** (when *intr*, often foll. by *on*) to allude (to) briefly or in passing. **34** (*tr*) to tinge or tint slightly: *brown hair touched with gold.* **35** (*tr*) to spoil slightly: *blackfly touched the flowers.* **36** (*tr*) to mark, as with a brush or pen. **37** (*tr*) to compare to in quality or attainment. **38** (*tr*) to reach or attain: *he touched the high point in his career.* **39** (*intr*) to dock or stop briefly: *the ship touches at Tenerife.* **40** (*tr*) *Sl.* to ask for a loan or gift of money from. ◆ See also **touchdown, touch off, touch up.** [C13: from OF *tochier*, from Vulgar L *toccāre* (unattested) to strike, prob. imit. of a tapping sound]
▸'**touchable** *adj* ▸'**toucher** *n*

touch and go Ⓣ *adj* (**touch-and-go** *when prenominal*) risky or critical.

touchdown ('tʌtʃˌdaʊn) *n* **1** the moment at which a landing aircraft or spacecraft comes into contact with the landing surface. **2** *Rugby.* the act of placing or touching the ball on the ground behind the goal line, as in scoring a try. **3** *American football.* a scoring play worth six points, achieved by being in possession of the ball in the opposing team's end zone. Abbrev.: **TD.** ◆ *vb* **touch down.** (*intr, adv*) **4** (of an aircraft, etc.) to land. **5** *Rugby.* to place the ball behind the goal line, as when scoring a try.

touché (tuː'ʃeɪ) *interj* **1** an acknowledgment of a scoring hit in fencing. **2** an acknowledgment of the striking home of a remark, witty reply, etc. [from F, lit.: touched]

touched Ⓣ (tʌtʃt) *adj* (*postpositive*) **1** moved to sympathy or emotion. **2** showing slight insanity.

touchhole ('tʌtʃˌhəʊl) *n* a hole in the breech of early cannon and firearms through which the charge was ignited.

touching Ⓣ ('tʌtʃɪŋ) *adj* **1** evoking or eliciting tender feelings. ◆ *prep* **2** on the subject of; relating to.
▸'**touchingly** *adv*

touch judge *n* one of the two linesmen in rugby.

touchline ('tʌtʃˌlaɪn) *n* either of the lines marking the side of the playing area in certain games, such as rugby.

touchmark ('tʌtʃˌmɑːk) *n* a maker's mark stamped on pewter objects.

touch-me-not *n* an impatiens with yellow spurred flowers and seed pods that burst open at a touch when ripe. Also called: **noli-me-tangere.**

touch off Ⓣ *vb* (*tr, adv*) **1** to cause to explode, as by touching with a match. **2** to cause (a disturbance, violence, etc.) to begin.

touchpaper ('tʌtʃˌpeɪpə) *n* paper soaked in saltpetre for lighting fireworks or firing gunpowder.

touchstone Ⓣ ('tʌtʃˌstəʊn) *n* **1** a criterion or standard. **2** a hard dark stone that is used to test gold and silver from the streak they produce on it.

touch-tone *adj* of or relating to a telephone dialling system in which each dialling button pressed generates a different pitch, which is transmitted to the exchange.

touch-type *vb* **touch-types, touch-typing, touch-typed.** (*intr*) to type without looking at the keyboard.
▸'**touch-ˌtypist** *n*

touch up Ⓣ *vb* (*tr, adv*) **1** to put extra or finishing touches to. **2** to enhance, renovate, or falsify by putting extra touches to. **3** *Brit. sl.* to touch or caress (someone).

touchwood ('tʌtʃˌwʊd) *n* something, esp. dry wood or fungus material, used as tinder. [C16: TOUCH (in the sense: to kindle) + WOOD]

touchy Ⓣ ('tʌtʃɪ) *adj* **touchier, touchiest. 1** easily upset or irritated. **2** extremely risky. **3** easily ignited.
▸'**touchily** *adv* ▸'**touchiness** *n*

touchy-feely ('tʌtʃɪˌfiːlɪ) *adj Inf., sometimes derog.* sensitive and caring.

tough Ⓣ (tʌf) *adj* **1** strong or resilient; durable. **2** not tender. **3** hardy and fit. **4** rough or pugnacious. **5** resolute or intractable. **6** difficult or troublesome to do or deal with: *a tough problem.* **7** *Inf.* unfortunate or unlucky: *it's tough on him.* ◆ *n* **8** a rough, vicious, or pugnacious person. ◆ *adv* **9** *Inf.* violently, aggressively, or intractably: *to treat someone tough.* ◆ *vb* (*tr*) **10** *Sl.* to stand firm, hold out against (a difficulty or difficult situation) (esp. in **tough it out**). [OE *tōh*]
▸'**toughly** *adv* ▸'**toughness** *n*

toughen ('tʌfən) *vb* to make or become tough or tougher.
▸'**toughener** *n*

tough love *n* the practice of taking a stern attitude towards a relative or friend suffering from an addiction, etc., to help the addict overcome the problem.

tough-minded *adj* practical, unsentimental, or intractable.
▸ˌ**tough-'mindedness** *n*

toupee ('tuːpeɪ) *n* a hairpiece worn by men to cover a bald place. [C18: apparently from F *toupet* forelock, from OF *toup* top, of Gmc origin]

tour Ⓣ (tʊə) *n* **1** an extended journey visiting places of interest along the route. **2** *Mil.* a period of service, esp. in one place. **3** a short trip, as for inspection. **4** a trip made by a theatre company, orchestra, etc., to perform in several places. **5** an overseas trip made by a cricket or rugby team, etc., to play in several places. ◆ *vb* **6** to make a tour of (a place). [C14: from OF: a turn, from L *tornus* a lathe, from Gk *tornos*]

touraco *or* **turaco** ('tʊərəˌkəʊ) *n, pl* **touracos** *or* **turacos.** any of a family of brightly coloured crested African birds. [C18: of West African origin]

tour de force *French.* (tur də fɔrs) *n, pl* ***tours de force*** (tur). a masterly or brilliant stroke, creation, effect, or accomplishment. [lit.: feat of skill or strength]

tourer ('tʊərə) *n* a large open car with a folding top, usually seating a driver and four passengers. Also called (esp. US): **touring car.**

tourism ('tʊərɪzəm) *n* tourist travel, esp. when regarded as an industry.

tourist Ⓣ ('tʊərɪst) *n* **1a** a person who travels for pleasure, usually sightseeing and staying in hotels. **1b** (*as modifier*): *tourist attractions.* **2** a person on an excursion or sightseeing tour. **3** a member of a touring team. **4** Also called: **tourist class.** the lowest class of accommodation on a passenger ship or aircraft. ◆ *adj* **5** of or relating to tourist accommodation.
▸**tour'istic** *adj*

touristy ('tʊərɪstɪ) *adj Inf., often derog.* abounding in or designed for tourists.

tourmaline ('tʊəməˌliːn) *n* any of a group of hard glassy minerals of variable colour consisting of a complex silicate of boron and aluminium in crystalline form: used in jewellery and optical and electrical equipment. [C18: from G *Turmalin*, from Sinhalese *toramalli* carnelian]

tournament Ⓣ ('tʊənəmənt) *n* **1** a sporting competition in which contestants play a series of games to determine an overall winner. **2** a meeting for athletic or other sporting contestants: *an archery tournament.* **3** *Medieval history.* a martial sport or contest in which mounted combatants fought for a prize. [C13: from OF *torneiement*, from

THESAURUS

tact, abut, adjoin, be in contact, border, brush, come together, contact, converge, graze, impinge upon, meet **28** = **affect**, get through to, get to (*inf.*), have an effect on, impress, influence, inspire, make an impression on, mark, strike **29** = **move**, disturb, melt, soften, stir, tug at (someone's) heartstrings (*often facetious*), upset **30** = **concern**, bear upon, have to do with, interest, pertain to, regard **31** = **consume**, drink, eat, partake of **32** = **get involved in**, be a party to, concern oneself with, deal with, handle, have to do with, use, utilize **33** *often foll. by* **on** = **refer to**, allude to, bring in, cover, deal with, mention, speak of **37** = **match**, be a match for, be in the same league as, be on a par with, come near, come up to, compare with, equal, hold a candle to (*inf.*), parallel, rival **38** = **reach**, arrive at, attain, come to

touch and go *adj* = **risky**, close, critical, dangerous, hairy, hazardous, near, nerve-racking, parlous, perilous, precarious, sticky (*inf.*), tricky

touched *adj* **1** = **moved**, affected, disturbed, impressed, melted, softened, stirred, swayed, upset **2** = **moved**, daft (*inf.*), loopy (*inf.*), not all there, not right in the head, out to lunch (*inf.*), soft in the head (*inf.*)

touchiness *n* **1** = **irritability**, bad temper, crabbedness, fretfulness, grouchiness (*inf.*), irascibility, peevishness, pettishness, petulance, surliness, testiness, tetchiness, ticklishness

touching *adj* **1** = **moving**, affecting, emotive, heartbreaking, melting, pathetic, piteous, pitiable, pitiful, poignant, sad, stirring, tender

touch off *vb* **1** = **ignite**, fire, light, put a match to, set off **2** = **trigger (off)**, arouse, begin, cause, foment, give rise to, initiate, provoke, set in motion, spark off

touchstone *n* **1** = **standard**, criterion, gauge, measure, norm, par, yardstick

touch up *vb* **1** = **finish off**, perfect, put the finishing touches to, round off **2** = **enhance**, brush up, fake (up), falsify, give a face-lift to, gloss over, improve, patch up, polish up, renovate, retouch, revamp, titivate, whitewash (*inf.*)

touchy *adj* **1** = **oversensitive**, bad-tempered, captious, crabbed, cross, easily offended, grouchy (*inf.*), grumpy, irascible, irritable, peevish, pettish, petulant, querulous, quick-tempered, ratty (*Brit. & NZ inf.*), splenetic, surly, testy, tetchy, thin-skinned, ticklish
Antonyms *adj* affable, cheerful, easy-going, genial, good-humoured, imperious, indifferent, insensitive, light-hearted, pleasant, sunny, sweet, thick-skinned, unconcerned

tough *adj* **1** = **resilient**, cohesive, durable, firm, hard, inflexible, leathery, resistant, rigid, rugged, solid, stiff, strong, sturdy, tenacious **3** = **strong**, brawny, fit, hard as nails, hardened, hardy, resilient, seasoned, stalwart, stout, strapping, sturdy, vigorous **4** = **rough**, hard-bitten, pugnacious, ruffianly, ruthless, vicious, violent **5** = **strict**, adamant, exacting, firm, hard, inflexible, intractable, merciless, resolute, severe, stern, unbending, unforgiving, unyielding **6** = **difficult**, arduous, baffling, exacting, exhausting, hard, irksome, knotty, laborious, perplexing, puzzling, strenuous, thorny, troublesome, uphill **7** *Informal* = **unlucky**, bad, lamentable, regrettable, too bad (*inf.*), unfortunate ◆ *n* **8** = **ruffian**, bravo, bruiser (*inf.*), brute, bully, bully boy, heavy, hooligan, rough (*inf.*), roughneck (*sl.*), rowdy, thug, tsotsi (*S. Afr.*)
Antonyms *adj* ≠ **resilient:** delicate, flexible, flimsy, fragile, soft, tender, weak ≠ **strong:** delicate, soft, weak ≠ **rough:** civilized, gentle, humane, soft, tender ≠ **strict:** accommodating, benign, compassionate, considerate, easy, flexible, gentle, humane, indulgent, kind, lenient, merciful, mild, soft, sympathetic, tender, unexacting ≠ **difficult:** easy, easy-peasy (*sl.*), unexacting

tour *n* **1** = **journey**, excursion, expedition, jaunt, outing, peregrination, progress, trip ◆ *vb* **6** = **visit**, explore, go on the road, go round, holiday in, journey, sightsee, travel round, travel through

tourist *n* **1a, 2** = **traveller**, excursionist, globetrotter, holiday-maker, journeyer, sightseer, tripper, voyager

tournament *n* **1, 2** = **competition**, contest, event, match, meeting, series **3** *Medieval* = **joust**, the lists, tourney *torneier* to fight on horseback, lit.: to turn, from the constant wheeling round of the combatants; see TOURNEY]

tournedos ('tʊənəˌdəʊ) *n, pl* **tournedos** (-ˌdəʊz). a thick round steak of beef. [from F, from *tourner* to TURN + *dos* back]

tourney ('tʊənɪ, 'tɔː-) *Medieval history.* ◆ *n* **1** a knightly tournament. ◆ *vb* **2** (*intr*) to engage in a tourney. [C13: from OF *torneier*, from Vulgar L *tornidiāre* (unattested) to turn constantly, from L *tornāre* to TURN (in a lathe); see TOURNAMENT].

tourniquet ('tʊənɪˌkeɪ) *n Med.* any device for constricting an artery of the arm or leg to control bleeding. [C17: from F: device that operates by turning, from *tourner* to TURN]

tour operator *n* a person or company that specializes in providing package holidays.

tousle ⓣ ('taʊzᵊl) *vb* **tousles, tousling, tousled.** (*tr*) **1** to tangle, ruffle, or disarrange. **2** to treat roughly. ◆ *n* **3** a disorderly, tangled, or rumpled state. **4** a dishevelled or disordered mass, esp. of hair. [C15: from Low G *tūsen* to shake]

tout ⓣ (taʊt) *vb* **1** to solicit (business, customers, etc.) or hawk (merchandise), esp. in a brazen way. **2** (*intr*) **2a** to spy on racehorses being trained in order to obtain information for betting purposes. **2b** to sell such information or to take bets, esp. in public places. ◆ *n* **3** a person who touts. **4** Also: **ticket tout.** a person who sells tickets for a heavily booked event at inflated prices. [C14 (in the sense: to peer, look out): rel. to OE *tȳtan* to peep out]
▸ **'touter** *n*

tout à fait *French.* (tut a fɛ) *adv* completely.

tout de suite *French.* (tud sɥit) *adv* at once.

tout le monde *French.* (tu lə mɔ̃d) *n* all the world; everyone.

tovarisch, tovarich, *or* **tovarish** (təˈvɑːrɪʃ) *n* comrade: a term of address. [from Russian]

tow¹ ⓣ (təʊ) *vb* **1** (*tr*) to pull or drag (a vehicle, boat, etc.), esp. by means of a rope or cable. ◆ *n* **2** the act or an instance of towing. **3** the state of being towed (esp. in **in tow, on tow**). **4** something towed. **5** something used for towing. **6 in tow.** in one's charge or under one's influence. **7** short for **ski tow.** [OE *togian*]
▸ **'towable** *adj* ▸ **'towage** *n*

tow² (təʊ) *n* the coarse and broken fibres of hemp, flax, jute, etc., prepared for spinning. [OE *tōw*]
▸ **'towy** *adj*

toward *adj* ('təʊəd). **1** *Now rare.* in progress; afoot. **2** *Obs.* about to happen; imminent. **3** *Obs.* promising or favourable. ◆ *prep* (təˈwɔːd, tɔːd). **4** a variant of **towards.** [OE *tōweard*]

towards ⓣ (təˈwɔːdz, tɔːdz) *prep* **1** in the direction or vicinity of: *towards London.* **2** with regard to: *her feelings towards me.* **3** as a contribution or help to: *money towards a new car.* **4** just before: *towards noon.* ◆ Also: **toward.**

towbar ('təʊˌbɑː) *n* a rigid metal bar or frame used for towing vehicles.

towboat ('təʊˌbəʊt) *n* another word for **tug** (sense 4).

tow-coloured *adj* pale yellow; flaxen.

towel ('taʊəl) *n* **1** a piece of absorbent cloth or paper used for drying things. **2 throw in the towel.** See **throw in** (sense 3). ◆ *vb* **towels, towelling, towelled** *or US* **towels, toweling, toweled. 3** (*tr*) to dry or wipe with a towel. **4** (*tr*; often foll. by *up*) *Austral. sl.* to assault or beat (a person). [C13: from OF *toaille*, of Gmc origin]

towelling ('taʊəlɪŋ) *n* an absorbent fabric used for making towels, bathrobes, etc.

tower ⓣ ('taʊə) *n* **1** a tall, usually square or circular structure, sometimes part of a larger building and usually built for a specific purpose. **2** a place of defence or retreat. **3 tower of strength.** a person who gives support, comfort, etc. ◆ *vb* **4** (*intr*) to be or rise like a tower; loom. [C12: from OF *tur*, from L *turris*, from Gk]

towering ⓣ ('taʊərɪŋ) *adj* **1** very tall; lofty. **2** outstanding, as in importance or stature. **3** (*prenominal*) very intense: *a towering rage.*

towhead ('təʊˌhɛd) *n* **1** a person with blond or yellowish hair. **2** a head of such hair. [from TOW² (flax)]
▸ ˌ**tow'headed** *adj*

towhee ('taʊˌhiː, 'təʊ-) *n* any of various North American brownish-coloured sparrows. [C18: imit.]

towline ('təʊˌlaɪn) *n* another name for **towrope.**

town (taʊn) *n* **1** a densely populated urban area, typically smaller than a city and larger than a village. **2** a city, borough, or other urban area. **3** (in the US) a territorial unit of local government that is smaller than a county; township. **4** the nearest town or commercial district. **5** London or the chief city of an area. **6** the inhabitants of a town. **7 go to town. 7a** to make a supreme or unrestricted effort. **7b** *Austral. & NZ inf.* to lose one's temper. **8 on the town.** seeking out entertainments and amusements. [OE *tūn* village]
▸ **'townish** *adj*

town clerk *n* **1** (in Britain until 1974) the secretary and chief administrative officer of a town or city. **2** (in the US) the official who keeps the records of a town.

town crier *n* (formerly) a person employed to make public announcements in the streets.

town gas *n* coal gas manufactured for domestic and industrial use.

town hall *n* the chief building in which municipal business is transacted, often with a hall for public meetings.

town house *n* **1** a terraced house in an urban area, esp. a fashionable one. **2** a person's town residence as distinct from his country residence.

townie ('taʊnɪ) *or* **townee** (taʊˈniː) *n Inf., often disparaging.* a permanent resident in a town, esp. as distinct from country dwellers or students.

townland ('taʊnlænd) *n Irish.* a division of land of various sizes.

town planning *n* the comprehensive planning of the physical and social development of a town. US term: **city planning.**

townscape ('taʊnskeɪp) *n* **1** a view of an urban scene. **2** an extensive area of urban development.

township ('taʊnʃɪp) *n* **1** a small town. **2** (in the Scottish Highlands) a small crofting community. **3** (in the US and Canada) a territorial area, esp. a subdivision of a county: often organized as a unit of local government. **4** (in Canada) a land-survey area, usually 36 square miles (93 square kilometres). **5** (formerly, in South Africa) a planned urban settlement of Black Africans or Coloured people. **6** *English history.* **6a** any of the local districts of a large parish. **6b** the parish itself.

townsman ('taʊnzmən) *n, pl* **townsmen. 1** an inhabitant of a town. **2** a person from the same town as oneself.
▸ **'towns,woman** *fem n*

townspeople ('taʊnzˌpiːpᵊl) *or* **townsfolk** ('taʊnzˌfəʊk) *pl n* the inhabitants of a town; citizens.

towpath ('təʊˌpɑːθ) *n* a path beside a canal or river, used by people or animals towing boats. Also called: **towing path.**

towrope ('təʊˌrəʊp) *n* a rope or cable used for towing a vehicle or vessel. Also called: **towline.**

tox-, toxic- *or before a consonant* **toxo-, toxico-** *combining form.* indicating poison: *toxaemia.* [from L *toxicum*]

toxaemia *or US* **toxemia** (tɒkˈsiːmɪə) *n* **1** a condition characterized by the presence of bacterial toxins in the blood. **2** the condition in pregnancy of pre-eclampsia or eclampsia.
▸ **tox'aemic** *or US* **tox'emic** *adj*

toxic ⓣ ('tɒksɪk) *adj* **1** of or caused by a toxin or poison. **2** harmful or deadly. [C17: from Medical L *toxicus*, from L *toxicum* poison, from Gk *toxikon (pharmakon)* (poison) used on arrows, from *toxon* arrow]
▸ **'toxically** *adv* ▸ **toxicity** (tɒkˈsɪsɪtɪ) *n*

toxicant ('tɒksɪkənt) *n* **1** a toxic substance; poison. ◆ *adj* **2** poisonous; toxic. [C19: from Med. L *toxicāre* to poison]

toxicology (ˌtɒksɪˈkɒlədʒɪ) *n* the branch of science concerned with poisons, their effects, antidotes, etc.
▸ **toxicological** (ˌtɒksɪkəˈlɒdʒɪkᵊl) *or* ˌ**toxico'logic** *adj* ▸ ˌ**toxi'cologist** *n*

toxic shock syndrome *n* a potentially fatal condition in women, characterized by fever, stomachache, a painful rash, and a drop in blood pressure, that is caused by staphylococcal blood poisoning, commonly from a retained tampon.

toxin ('tɒksɪn) *n* **1** any of various poisonous substances produced by microorganisms that stimulate the production of neutralizing substances (antitoxins) in the body. **2** any other poisonous substance of plant or animal origin.

toxin-antitoxin *n* a mixture of a toxin and antitoxin. The diphtheria toxin-antitoxin was formerly used for immunization.

toxocariasis (ˌtɒksəkəˈraɪəsɪs) *n* the infection of humans with the larvae of a genus of roundworms, *Toxocara*, of dogs and cats.

toxoid ('tɒksɔɪd) *n* a toxin that has been treated to reduce its toxicity and is used in immunization to stimulate production of antitoxins.

toxophilite (tɒkˈsɒfɪˌlaɪt) *Formal.* ◆ *n* **1** an archer. ◆ *adj* **2** of archery. [C18: from *Toxophilus*, the title of a book (1545) by Ascham, designed to mean: a lover of the bow, from Gk *toxon* bow + *philos* loving]
▸ **tox'ophily** *n*

toxoplasmosis (ˌtɒksəʊplæzˈməʊsɪs) *n* a protozoal disease characterized by jaundice and convulsions.
▸ ˌ**toxo'plasmic** *adj*

toy ⓣ (tɔɪ) *n* **1** an object designed to be played with. **2a** something that is a nonfunctioning replica of something else, esp. a miniature one.

THESAURUS

tousle *vb* **1 = dishevel**, disarrange, disarray, disorder, mess up, ruffle, rumple, tangle

tout *vb* **1 = solicit**, bark (*US inf.*), canvass, drum up, spiel ◆ *n* **3 = seller**, barker, canvasser, solicitor

tow¹ *vb* **1 = drag**, draw, hale, haul, lug, pull, trail, trawl, tug, yank

towards *prep* **1 = in the direction of**, en route for, for, in the vicinity of, on the road to, on the way to, to **2 = regarding**, about, concerning, for, with regard to, with respect to **4 = just before**, almost, close to, coming up to, getting on for, nearing, nearly, not quite, shortly before

tower *n* **1 = column**, belfry, obelisk, pillar, skyscraper, steeple, turret **2 = stronghold**, castle, citadel, fort, fortification, fortress, keep, refuge ◆ *vb* **4 = rise**, ascend, dominate, loom, mount, overlook, overtop, rear, soar, surpass, top, transcend

towering *adj* **1 = tall**, colossal, elevated, gigantic, great, high, lofty, soaring **2 = impressive**, extraordinary, imposing, magnificent, outstanding, paramount, prodigious, stellar (*inf.*), striking, sublime, superior, supreme, surpassing, transcendent **3 = intense**, burning, excessive, extreme, fiery, immoderate, inordinate, intemperate, mighty, passionate, vehement, violent

toxic *adj* **2 = poisonous**, baneful (*arch.*), deadly, harmful, lethal, noxious, pernicious, pestilential, septic
Antonyms *adj* harmless, invigorating, nonpoisonous, nontoxic, safe, salubrious

toy *n* **1 = plaything**, doll, game **3 = trinket**, bauble, gewgaw, knick-knack, trifle ◆ *vb* **5** *usually foll. by* **with = play**, amuse oneself with, dally with, fiddle (*inf.*), flirt with, fool (about *or* around) with, play fast and loose (*inf.*), sport, trifle, wanton

2b (*as modifier*): *a toy guitar.* **3** any small thing of little value; trifle. **4a** something small or miniature, esp. a miniature variety of a breed of dog. **4b** (*as modifier*): *a toy poodle.* ◆ *vb* **5** (*intr; usually foll. by with*) to play, fiddle, or flirt. [C16 (in the sense: amorous dalliance): from ?]

toy boy *n* the much younger male lover of an older woman.

TPI *abbrev. for* tax and price index: a measure of the increase in taxable income needed to compensate for an increase in retail prices.

TQM *abbrev. for* total quality management.

tr *abbrev. for* treasurer.

tr. *abbrev. for:* **1** transitive. **2** translated. **3** translator. **4** *Music.* trill. **5** trustee.

trabeated ('treɪbɪˌeɪtɪd) *or* **trabeate** ('treɪbɪɪt, -ˌeɪt) *adj Archit.* constructed with horizontal beams as opposed to arches. [C19: back formation from *trabeation*, from L *trabs* a beam]

trabecula (trə'bɛkjʊlə) *n, pl* **trabeculae** (-ˌliː). *Anat., bot.* any of various rod-shaped structures that support other organs. [C19: via NL from L: a little beam, from *trabs* a beam]
▸**tra'becular** *or* **tra'beculate** *adj*

trace[1] ❶ (treɪs) *n* **1** a mark or other sign that something has been in a place. **2** a scarcely detectable amount or characteristic. **3** a footprint or other indication of the passage of an animal or person. **4** any line drawn by a recording instrument or a record consisting of a number of such lines. **5** something drawn, such as a tracing. **6** *Chiefly US.* a beaten track or path. ◆ *vb* **traces, tracing, traced. 7** (*tr*) to follow, discover, or ascertain the course or development of (something). **8** (*tr*) to track down and find, as by following a trail. **9** to copy (a design, map, etc.) by drawing over the lines visible through a superimposed sheet of transparent paper. **10** (*tr; often foll. by out*) **10a** to draw or delineate a plan or diagram of. **10b** to outline or sketch (an idea, etc.). **11** (*tr*) to decorate with tracery. **12** (usually foll. by *back*) to follow or be followed to source; date back: *his ancestors trace back to the 16th century.* [C13: from F *tracier*, from Vulgar L *tractiāre* (unattested) to drag, from L *tractus*, from *trahere*]
▸**'traceable** *adj* ▸**ˌtracea'bility** *or* **'traceableness** *n* ▸**'traceably** *adv*

trace[2] (treɪs) *n* **1** either of the two side straps that connect a horse's harness to the swingletree. **2** *Angling.* a length of nylon or, formerly, gut attaching a hook or fly to a line. **3 kick over the traces.** to escape or defy control. [C14 *trais*, from OF *trait*, ult. from L *trahere* to drag]

trace element *n* any of various chemical elements, such as iron, manganese, zinc, copper, and iodine, that occur in very small amounts in organisms and are essential for many physiological and biochemical processes.

trace fossil *n* the fossilized remains of a track, trail, footprint, burrow, etc., of an organism.

tracer ('treɪsə) *n* **1** a person or thing that traces. **2** a projectile that can be observed when in flight by the burning of chemical substances in its base. **3** *Med.* any radioactive isotope introduced into the body to study metabolic processes, etc., by following its progress with a gamma counter or other detector. **4** an investigation to trace missing cargo, mail, etc.

tracer bullet *n* a round of small arms ammunition containing a tracer.

tracery ('treɪsərɪ) *n, pl* **traceries. 1** a pattern of interlacing ribs, esp. as used in the upper part of a Gothic window, etc. **2** any fine pattern resembling this.
▸**'traceried** *adj*

trachea (trə'kiːə) *n, pl* **tracheae** (-'kiːiː). **1** *Anat., zool.* the tube that conveys inhaled air from the larynx to the bronchi. **2** any of the tubes in insects and related animals that convey air from the spiracles to the tissues. [C16: from Med. L, from Gk *trakheia*, shortened from (*artēria*) *trakheia* rough (artery), from *trakhus* rough]
▸**tra'cheal** *or* **tra'cheate** *adj*

tracheitis (ˌtreɪkɪ'aɪtɪs) *n* inflammation of the trachea.

tracheo- *or before a vowel* **trache-** *combining form.* denoting the trachea.

tracheotomy (ˌtrækɪ'ɒtəmɪ) *n, pl* **tracheotomies.** surgical incision into the trachea, as performed when the air passage has been blocked.

trachoma (trə'kəʊmə) *n* a chronic contagious disease of the eye caused by a species of chlamydia: a severe form of conjunctivitis that can result in scarring and blindness. [C17: from NL, from Gk *trakhōma* roughness, from *trakhus* rough]
▸**trachomatous** (trə'kɒmətəs) *adj*

trachyte ('treɪkaɪt, 'træ-) *n* a light-coloured fine-grained volcanic rock. [C19: from F, from Gk *trakhutēs*, from *trakhus* rough]

tracing ('treɪsɪŋ) *n* **1** a copy made by tracing. **2** the act of making a trace. **3** a record made by an instrument.

track ❶ (træk) *n* **1** the mark or trail left by something that has passed by. **2** any road or path, esp. a rough one. **3** a rail or pair of parallel rails on which a vehicle, such as a locomotive, runs. **4** a course of action, thought, etc.: *don't start on that track again!* **5** a line of motion or travel, such as flight. **6** an endless band on the wheels of a tank, tractor, etc., to enable it to move across rough ground. **7a** a course for running or racing. **7b** (*as modifier*): *track events.* **8** *US & Canad.* **8a** sports performed on a track. **8b** track and field events as a whole. **9** a path on a magnetic recording medium, esp. magnetic tape, on which music or speech is recorded. **10** any of a number of separate sections in the recording on a record, CD, or cassette. **11** the distance between the points of contact with the ground of a pair of wheels, as of a motor vehicle. **12 keep** (*or* **lose**) **track of.** to follow (or fail to follow) the passage, course, or progress of. **13 off the track.** away from what is correct or true. **14 on the track of.** on the scent or trail of; pursuing. ◆ *vb* **15** to follow the trail of (a person, animal, etc.). **16** to follow the flight path of (a satellite, etc.) by picking up signals transmitted or reflected by it. **17** *US railways.* **17a** to provide with a track. **17b** to run on a track of (a certain width). **18** (of a camera or camera-operator) to follow (a moving object) while operating. **19** to follow a track through (a place): *to track the jungles.* **20** (*intr*) (of the pick-up, stylus, etc., of a record player) to follow the groove of a record. ◆ See also **tracks.** [C15: from OF *trac*, prob. of Gmc origin]
▸**'tracker** *n*

track down ❶ *vb* (*tr, adv*) to find by tracking or pursuing.

tracker dog *n* a dog specially trained to search for missing people.

track event *n* a competition in athletics, such as relay running or sprinting, that takes place on a running track.

tracking ('trækɪŋ) *n* **1** the act or process of following something or someone. **2** *Electrical engineering.* a leakage of electric current between two insulated points caused by dirt, carbon particles, moisture, etc.

tracking shot *n* a camera shot in which the cameraman follows a specific person or event in the action.

tracking station *n* a station that can use a radio or radar beam to follow the path of an object in space or in the atmosphere.

tracklaying ('trækˌleɪɪŋ) *adj also* **tracked.** (of a vehicle) having an endless jointed metal band around the wheels.

track record *n Inf.* the past record of the accomplishments and failures of a person, business, etc.

track rod *n* the rod connecting the two front wheels of a motor vehicle.

tracks ❶ (træks) *pl n* **1** (*sometimes sing*) marks, such as footprints, etc., left by someone or something that has passed. **2 in one's tracks.** on the very spot where one is standing. **3 make tracks.** to leave or depart. **4 make tracks for.** to go or head towards.

track shoe *n* either of a pair of light running shoes fitted with steel spikes for better grip.

tracksuit ('trækˌsuːt) *n* a warm suit worn by athletes, etc., esp. during training.

tract[1] ❶ (trækt) *n* **1** an extended area, as of land. **2** *Anat.* a system of organs, glands, etc., that has a particular function: *the digestive tract.* **3** *Arch.* an extended period of time. [C15: from L *tractus* a stretching out, from *trahere* to drag]

tract[2] ❶ (trækt) *n* a treatise or pamphlet, esp. a religious or moralistic one. [C15: from L *tractātus* TRACTATE]

tractable ❶ ('træktəbᵊl) *adj* **1** easily controlled or persuaded. **2** readily worked; malleable. [C16: from L *tractābilis*, from *tractāre* to manage, from *trahere* to draw]
▸**ˌtracta'bility** *or* **'tractableness** *n* ▸**'tractably** *adv*

Tractarianism (træk'tɛərɪəˌnɪzəm) *n* another name for the **Oxford Movement.** [after the series of tracts, *Tracts for the Times* published between 1833 and 1841, in which the principles of the movement were presented]
▸**Trac'tarian** *n, adj*

tractate ('trækteɪt) *n* a treatise. [C15: from L *tractātus*, from *tractāre* to handle; see TRACTABLE]

traction ❶ ('trækʃən) *n* **1** the act of drawing or pulling, esp. by motive power. **2** the state of being drawn or pulled. **3** *Med.* the application of a steady pull on a limb, etc., using a system of weights and pulleys or splints. **4** adhesive friction, as between a wheel of a motor vehicle and

THESAURUS

trace[1] *n* **1** = **remnant**, evidence, indication, mark, record, relic, remains, sign, survival, token, vestige **2** = **bit**, dash, drop, hint, iota, jot, shadow, *soupçon*, suggestion, suspicion, tincture, tinge, touch, trifle, whiff **3** = **track**, footmark, footprint, footstep, path, slot, spoor, trail ◆ *vb* **7** = **find**, ascertain, detect, determine, discover, ferret out, follow, hunt down, pursue, search for, seek, shadow, stalk, track, trail, unearth **9** = **copy 10** *often foll. by* **out** = **outline**, chart, delineate, depict, draw, map, mark out, show, sketch

track *n* **1** = **trail**, footmark, footprint, footstep, mark, path, scent, slipstream, slot, spoor, trace, wake **3** = **line**, permanent way, rail, rails **5** = **path**, course, flight path, line, orbit, pathway, road, trajectory, way **12 keep track of** = **keep up with**, follow, keep an eye on, keep in sight, keep in touch with, keep up to date with, monitor, oversee, watch **12 lose track of** = **lose**, lose sight of, misplace ◆ *vb* **15** = **follow**, chase, dog, follow the trail of, hunt down, pursue, shadow, stalk, tail (*inf.*), trace, trail

track down *vb* = **find**, apprehend, bring to light, capture, catch, dig up, discover, expose, ferret out, hunt down, run to earth *or* ground, sniff out, trace, unearth

tracks *pl n* **1** = **trail**, footprints, impressions, imprints, tyre marks, tyre prints, wheel marks **4 make tracks** = **leave**, beat it (*sl.*), depart, disappear, get going, get moving, go, head off, hit the road (*sl.*), pack one's bags (*inf.*), set out, split (*sl.*), take off (*inf.*)

tract[1] *n* **1** = **area**, district, estate, expanse, extent, lot, plot, quarter, region, stretch, territory, zone

tract[2] *n* = **treatise**, booklet, brochure, disquisition, dissertation, essay, homily, leaflet, monograph, pamphlet, tractate

tractable *adj Formal* **1** = **manageable**, amenable, biddable, compliant, controllable, docile, governable, obedient, persuadable, submissive, tame, willing, yielding **2** = **malleable**, ductile, fictile, plastic, pliable, pliant, tensile, tractile, workable
Antonyms *adj* ≠ **manageable:** defiant, headstrong, obstinate, refractory, stiff-necked, stubborn, unruly, wilful

traction *n* **1** = **pulling**, drag, draught, drawing, haulage, pull **4** = **grip**, adhesion, friction, purchase, resistance

the road. [C17: from Med. L *tractiō*, from L *tractus* dragged, from *trahere* to drag]
▸ **'tractional** *adj* ▸**tractive** ('træktɪv) *adj*

traction engine *n* a steam-powered locomotive used, esp. formerly, for drawing heavy loads along roads or over rough ground.

traction load *n Geol.* the solid material that is carried along the bed of a river.

tractor ('træktə) *n* **1** a motor vehicle with large rear wheels or endless belt treads, used to pull heavy loads, esp. farm machinery. **2** a short vehicle with a driver's cab, used to pull a trailer, as in an articulated lorry. [C18: from LL: one who pulls, from *trahere* to drag]

trad (træd) *n* **1** *Chiefly Brit.* traditional jazz. ◆ *adj* **2** short for **traditional.**

trade ❶ (treɪd) *n* **1** the act or an instance of buying and selling goods and services. **2** a personal occupation, esp. a craft requiring skill. **3** the people and practices of an industry, craft, or business. **4** exchange of one thing for something else. **5** the regular clientele of a firm or industry. **6** amount of custom or commercial dealings; business. **7** a specified market or business: *the tailoring trade.* **8** an occupation in commerce, as opposed to a profession. ◆ *vb* **trades, trading, traded. 9** (*tr*) to buy and sell (merchandise). **10** to exchange (one thing) for another. **11** (*intr*) to engage in trade. **12** (*intr*) to deal or do business (with). ◆ See also **trade-in, trade on.** [C14 (in the sense: track, hence, a regular business)]
▸ **'tradable** *or* **'tradeable** *adj*

trade agreement *n* a commercial treaty between two or more nations.

trade association *n* an association of organizations in the same trade formed to further their collective interests, esp. in negotiating with governments, trade unions, etc.

trade cycle *n* the recurrent fluctuation between boom and depression in the economic activity of a capitalist country.

trade discount *n* a sum or percentage deducted from the list price of a commodity allowed to a retailer or by one enterprise to another in the same trade.

traded option *n Stock Exchange.* an option that can itself be bought and sold on a stock exchange. Cf. **traditional option.**

trade down *vb* (*intr, adv*) to sell a large or relatively expensive house, car, etc., and replace it with a smaller or less expensive one.

trade gap *n* the amount by which the value of a country's visible imports exceeds that of visible exports; an unfavourable balance of trade.

trade-in *n* **1a** a used article given in part payment for the purchase of a new article. **1b** a transaction involving such part payment. **1c** the valuation put on the article traded in. ◆ *vb* **trade in. 2** (*tr, adv*) to give (a used article) as part payment for a new article.

trademark ('treɪd,mɑːk) *n* **1a** the name or other symbol used by a manufacturer or dealer to distinguish his products from those of competitors. **1b Registered Trademark.** one that is officially registered and legally protected. **2** any distinctive sign or mark of the presence of a person or animal. ◆ *vb* (*tr*) **3** to label with a trademark. **4** to register as a trademark.

trade name *n* **1** the name used by a trade to refer to a commodity, service, etc. **2** the name under which a commercial enterprise operates in business.

trade-off *n* an exchange, esp. as a compromise.

trade on *vb* (*intr, prep*) to exploit or take advantage of: *he traded on her endless patience.*

trade plate *n* a numberplate attached temporarily to a vehicle by a dealer, etc., before the vehicle has been registered.

trader ❶ ('treɪdə) *n* **1** a person who engages in trade. **2** a vessel regularly employed in trade. **3** *Stock Exchange, US.* a member who operates mainly on his own account.

trade reference *n* a reference in which one trader gives his opinion as to the credit worthiness of another trader in the same trade, esp. to a supplier.

tradescantia (,trædes'kænʃɪə) *n* any of a genus of plants widely cultivated for their striped variegated leaves. [C18: NL, after John *Tradescant* (1608–62), E botanist]

Trades Council *n* (in Britain) an association of the different trade unions in one town or area.

trade secret *n* a secret formula, technique, process, etc., known and used to advantage by only one manufacturer.

tradesman ❶ ('treɪdzmən) *n, pl* **tradesmen. 1** a man engaged in trade, esp. a retail dealer. **2** a skilled worker.
▸ **'trades,woman** *fem n*

tradespeople ('treɪdz,piːpᵊl) *or* **tradesfolk** ('treɪdz,fəʊk) *pl n Chiefly Brit.* people engaged in trade, esp. shopkeepers.

Trades Union Congress *n* the major association of British trade unions, which includes all the larger unions. Abbrev.: **TUC**

trade union *or* **trades union** *n* an association of employees formed to improve their incomes and working conditions by collective bargaining.
▸**trade unionism** *or* **trades unionism** *n* ▸**trade unionist** *or* **trades unionist** *n*

trade up *vb* (*intr, adv*) to sell a small or relatively inexpensive house, car, etc., and replace it with a larger or more expensive one.

trade wind (wɪnd) *n* a wind blowing obliquely towards the equator either from the northeast in the N hemisphere or the southeast in the S hemisphere, between latitudes 30° N and S. [C17: from *to blow trade* to blow steadily in one direction, from *trade* in the obs. sense: a track]

trading estate *n Chiefly Brit.* a large area in which a number of commercial or industrial firms are situated. Also called: **industrial estate.**

trading post *n* a general store in an unsettled or thinly populated region.

tradition ❶ (trə'dɪʃən) *n* **1** the handing down from generation to generation of customs, beliefs, etc. **2** the body of customs, thought, etc., belonging to a particular country, people, family, or institution over a long period. **3** a specific custom or practice of long standing. **4** *Christianity.* a doctrine regarded as having been established by Christ or the apostles though not contained in Scripture. **5** (*often cap.*) *Judaism.* a body of laws regarded as having been handed down from Moses orally. **6** the beliefs and customs of Islam supplementing the Koran. **7** *Law, chiefly Roman & Scots.* the act of formally transferring ownership of movable property. [C14: from L *trāditiō* a handing down, surrender, from *trādere* to give up, transmit, from TRANS- + *dāre* to give]
▸**tra'ditionless** *adj*

traditional ❶ (trə'dɪʃənᵊl) *adj* **1** of, relating to, or being a tradition. **2** of the style of jazz originating in New Orleans, characterized by collective improvisation by a front line of trumpet, trombone, and clarinet.
▸**tra'ditionally** *adv*

traditionalism (trə'dɪʃənᵊ,lɪzəm) *n* **1** the doctrine that all knowledge originates in divine revelation and is perpetuated by tradition. **2** adherence to tradition, esp. in religion.
▸**tra'ditionalist** *n, adj* ▸**tra,ditional'istic** *adj*

traditional logic *n* the logic of the late Middle Ages, derived from Aristotelian logic, and concerned esp. with the study of the syllogism.

traditional option *n Stock Exchange.* an option that once purchased cannot be resold. Cf. **traded option.**

traduce ❶ (trə'djuːs) *vb* **traduces, traducing, traduced.** (*tr*) to speak badly or maliciously of. [C16: from L *trādūcere* to lead over, disgrace]
▸**tra'ducement** *n* ▸**tra'ducer** *n*

traffic ❶ ('træfɪk) *n* **1a** the vehicles coming and going in a street, town, etc. **1b** (*as modifier*): *traffic lights.* **2** the movement of vehicles, people, etc., in a particular place or for a particular purpose: *sea traffic.* **3** (usually foll. by *with*) dealings or business. **4** trade, esp. of an illicit kind: *drug traffic.* **5** the aggregate volume of messages transmitted through a communications system in a given period. **6** *Chiefly US.* the number of customers patronizing a commercial establishment in a given time period. ◆ *vb* **traffics, trafficking, trafficked.** (*intr*) **7** (often foll. by *in*) to carry on trade or business, esp. of an illicit kind. **8** (usually foll. by *with*) to have dealings. [C16: from OF *trafique,* from OIt. *traffico,* from *trafficare* to engage in trade]
▸ **'trafficker** *n*

trafficator ('træfɪ,keɪtə) *n* (formerly) an illuminated arm on a motor vehicle raised to indicate a left or right turn.

traffic calming *n* the use of a series of devices, such as bends and humps in the road, to slow down traffic, esp. in residential areas.

traffic island *n* a raised area in the middle of a road designed as a guide for traffic flow and to provide a stopping place for pedestrians crossing.

traffic jam *n* a number of vehicles so obstructed that they can scarcely move.

traffic light *or* **signal** *n* one of a set of coloured lights at crossroads or junctions, to control the flow of traffic.

traffic pattern *n* a pattern of permitted lanes in the air around an airport to which an aircraft is restricted.

traffic warden *n Brit.* a person who is appointed to supervise road traffic and report traffic offences.

tragacanth ('trægə,kænθ) *n* **1** any of various spiny plants that yield a

THESAURUS

trade *n* **1** = **commerce,** barter, business, buying and selling, dealing, exchange, traffic, transactions, truck **2** = **job,** avocation, business, calling, craft, employment, line, line of work, métier, occupation, profession, pursuit, skill **4** = **exchange,** deal, interchange, swap **5** = **customers,** clientele, custom, market, patrons, public ◆ *vb* **9, 12** = **deal,** bargain, barter, buy and sell, cut a deal, do business, exchange, have dealings, peddle, traffic, transact, truck **10** = **exchange,** barter, swap, switch

trader *n* **1** = **dealer,** broker, buyer, marketer, merchandiser, merchant, purveyor, seller, supplier

tradesman *n* **1** = **shopkeeper,** dealer, merchant, purveyor, retailer, seller, supplier, vendor **2** = **craftsman,** artisan, journeyman, skilled worker, workman

tradition *n* **1, 2** = **custom,** convention, customs, established practice, folklore, habit, institution, lore, praxis, ritual, unwritten law, usage

traditional *adj* **1** = **customary,** accustomed, ancestral, conventional, established, fixed, folk, historic, long-established, old, oral, time-honoured, transmitted, unwritten, usual
Antonyms *adj* avant-garde, contemporary, ground-breaking, innovative, modern, new, novel, off-the-wall (*sl.*), original, revolutionary, unconventional, unusual

traduce *vb Formal* = **malign,** abuse, asperse, bad-mouth (*sl., chiefly US & Canad.*), blacken, calumniate, decry, defame, denigrate, deprecate, depreciate, detract, disparage, drag through the mud, knock (*inf.*), misrepresent, revile, rubbish (*inf.*), run down, slag (off) (*sl.*), slander, smear, speak ill of, vilify

traffic *n* **2** = **transport,** coming and going, freight, movement, passengers, transportation, vehicles **3, 4** = **trade,** barter, business, buying and selling, commerce, communication, dealing, dealings, doings, exchange, intercourse, peddling, relations, truck ◆ *vb* **7, 8** = **trade,** bargain, barter, buy and sell, cut a deal, deal, do business, exchange, have dealings, have transactions, market, peddle, truck substance that is made into a gum. **2** the gum obtained from these plants, used in the manufacture of pills and lozenges and in calico printing. [C16: from F *tragacante*, from L *tragacantha* goat's thorn, from Gk, from *tragos* goat + *akantha* thorn]

tragedian (trəˈdʒiːdɪən) *or (fem)* **tragedienne** (trəˌdʒiːdɪˈɛn) *n* **1** an actor who specializes in tragic roles. **2** a writer of tragedy.

tragedy Ⓣ (ˈtrædʒɪdɪ) *n, pl* **tragedies. 1** a play in which the protagonist falls to disaster through the combination of a personal failing and circumstances with which he cannot deal. **2** any dramatic or literary composition dealing with serious or sombre themes and ending with disaster. **3** the branch of drama dealing with such themes. **4** the unfortunate aspect of something. **5** a shocking or sad event; disaster. [C14: from OF *tragédie*, from L *tragoedia*, from Gk, from *tragos* goat + *ōidē* song; ?from the goat-satyrs of Peloponnesian plays]

tragic Ⓣ (ˈtrædʒɪk) *or (less commonly)* **tragical** *adj* **1** of, relating to, or characteristic of tragedy. **2** mournful or pitiable.
▸**ˈtragically** *adv*

tragic flaw *n* the failing of character in a tragic hero.

tragic irony *n* the use of dramatic irony in a tragedy so that the audience is aware that a character's words or actions will bring about a tragic or fatal result, while the character himself is not.

tragicomedy (ˌtrædʒɪˈkɒmɪdɪ) *n, pl* **tragicomedies. 1** a drama in which aspects of both tragedy and comedy are found. **2** an event or incident having both comic and tragic aspects. [C16: from F, ult. from LL *tragicōmoedia*]
▸**ˌtragiˈcomic** *or* **ˌtragiˈcomical** *adj*

tragopan (ˈtræɡəˌpæn) *n* any of a genus of pheasants of S and SE Asia, having brightly coloured fleshy processes on the head. [C19: via L from Gk, from *tragos* goat + *Pan*, ancient Gk god, represented as a man with goat's legs, horns, and ears]

tragus (ˈtreɪɡəs) *n, pl* **tragi** (-dʒaɪ). the fleshy projection that partially covers the entrance to the external ear. [C17: from LL, from Gk *tragos* hairy projection of the ear, lit.: goat]

trail Ⓣ (treɪl) *vb* **1** to drag, stream, or permit to drag or stream along a surface, esp. the ground. **2** to make (a track) through (a place). **3** to follow or hunt (an animal or person) by following marks or tracks. **4** (when *intr*, often foll. by *behind*) to lag or linger behind (a person or thing). **5** (*intr*) (esp. of plants) to extend or droop over or along a surface. **6** (*intr*) to be falling behind in a race: *the favourite is trailing at the last fence.* **7** (*tr*) to tow (a caravan, etc.) behind a motor vehicle. **8** (*tr*) to carry (a rifle) at the full length of the right arm in a horizontal position, with the muzzle to the fore. **9** (*intr*) to move wearily or slowly. **10** (*tr*) (on television or radio) to advertise (a future programme) with short extracts. ◆ *n* **11** a print, mark, or scent made by a person, animal, or object. **12** the act or an instance of trailing. **13** a path, track, or road, esp. one roughly blazed. **14** something that trails behind or trails in loops or strands. **15** the part of a towed gun carriage and limber that connects the two when in movement and rests on the ground as a partial support when unlimbered. [C14: from OF *trailler* to tow, from Vulgar L *tragulāre* (unattested), from L *trāgula* dragnet, from *trahere* to drag]

trail away Ⓣ *or* **off** *vb (intr, adv)* to make or become fainter, quieter, or weaker.

trailblazer (ˈtreɪlˌbleɪzə) *n* **1** a leader or pioneer in a particular field. **2** a person who blazes a trail.
▸**ˈtrailˌblazing** *adj, n*

trailer (ˈtreɪlə) *n* **1** a road vehicle, usually two-wheeled, towed by a motor vehicle: used for transporting boats, etc. **2** the rear section of an articulated lorry. **3** a series of short extracts from a film, used to advertise it in a cinema or on television. **4** a person or thing that trails. **5** the US and Canad. name for **caravan** (sense 1).

trailing edge *n* the rear edge of a propeller blade or aerofoil. Cf. **leading edge.**

train Ⓣ (treɪn) *vb* **1** (*tr*) to guide or teach (to do something), as by subjecting to various exercises or experiences. **2** (*tr*) to control or guide towards a specific goal: *to train a plant up a wall.* **3** (*intr*) to do exercises and prepare for a specific purpose. **4** (*tr*) to improve or curb by subjecting to discipline: *to train the mind.* **5** (*tr*) to focus or bring to bear (on something): *to train a telescope on the moon.* ◆ *n* **6** a line of coaches or wagons coupled together and drawn by a railway locomotive. **7** a sequence or series: *a train of disasters.* **8** a procession of people, vehicles, etc., travelling together, such as one carrying equipment in support of a military operation. **9** a series of interacting parts through which motion is transmitted: *a train of gears.* **10** a fuse or line of gunpowder to an explosive charge, etc. **11** something drawn along, such as the long back section of a dress that trails along the floor. **12** a retinue or suite. [C14: from OF *trahiner*, from Vulgar L *tragīnāre* (unattested) to draw]
▸**ˈtrainable** *adj*

trainband (ˈtreɪnˌbænd) *n* a company of English militia from the 16th to the 18th century. [C17: altered from *trained band*]

trainbearer (ˈtreɪnˌbɛərə) *n* an attendant who holds up the train of a dignitary's robe or bride's gown.

trainee (treɪˈniː) *n* **a** a person undergoing training. **b** (*as modifier*): *a trainee journalist.*

trainer Ⓣ (ˈtreɪnə) *n* **1** a person who trains athletes. **2** a piece of equipment employed in training, such as a simulated aircraft cockpit. **3** a person who schools racehorses. **4** (*pl*) another name for **training shoes.**

training Ⓣ (ˈtreɪnɪŋ) *n* **1a** the process of bringing a person, etc., to an agreed standard of proficiency, etc., by practice and instruction. **1b** (*as modifier*): *training college.* **2 in training. 2a** undergoing physical training. **2b** physically fit. **3 out of training.** physically unfit.

Training Agency *n* (in Britain) an organization established in 1989 to replace the **Training Commission**; it provides training and retraining for adult workers and operates the Youth Training Scheme, in England and Wales working through the local **Training and Enterprise Councils** (TECs) and in Scotland through the **Local Enterprise Companies** (LECs) set up in 1990.

training shoes *pl n* **1** running shoes for sports training, esp. in contrast to studded or spiked shoes worn for the sport itself. **2** shoes in the style of those used for sports training. ◆ Also called: **trainers.**

train oil *n* whale oil obtained from blubber. [C16: from earlier *train* or *trane*, from MLow G *trān*, or MDu. *traen* tear, drop]

train spotter *n* **1** a person who collects the numbers of railway locomotives. **2** *Inf.* a person who is obsessed with trivial details, esp. of a subject generally considered uninteresting.

traipse Ⓣ *or* **trapes** (treɪps) *Inf.* ◆ *vb* **traipses, traipsing, traipsed** *or* **trapeses, trapesing, trapesed. 1** (*intr*) to walk heavily or tiredly. ◆ *n* **2** a long or tiring walk; trudge. [C16: from ?]

trait Ⓣ (treɪt, treɪ) *n* **1** a characteristic feature or quality distinguishing a particular person or thing. **2** *Rare.* a touch or stroke. [C16: from F, from OF: a pulling, from L *tractus*, from *trahere* to drag]

traitor Ⓣ (ˈtreɪtə) *n* a person who is guilty of treason or treachery, in betraying friends, country, a cause, etc. [C13: from OF *traitour*, from L *trāditor*, from *trādere* to hand over]
▸**ˈtraitorous** *adj* ▸**ˈtraitress** *fem n*

trajectory Ⓣ (trəˈdʒɛktərɪ) *n, pl* **trajectories. 1** the path described by an object moving in air or space, esp. the curved path of a projectile. **2** *Geom.* a curve that cuts a family of curves or surfaces at a constant angle. [C17: from L *trājectus* cast over, from *trāicere* to throw across]

tram (træm) *n* **1** Also called: **tramcar.** an electrically driven public transport vehicle that runs on rails let into the surface of the road. US and Canad. names: **streetcar, trolley car. 2** a small vehicle on rails for carrying loads in a mine; tub. [C16 (in the sense: shaft of a cart): prob. from Low G *traam* beam]
▸**ˈtramless** *adj*

tramline (ˈtræmˌlaɪn) *n* **1** (*often pl*) Also called: **tramway.** the tracks on which a tram runs. **2** the route taken by a tram. **3** (*often pl*) the outer markings along the sides of a tennis or badminton court.

trammel Ⓣ (ˈtræməl) *n* **1** (*often pl*) a hindrance to free action or move-

THESAURUS

tragedy *n* **5** = **disaster**, adversity, affliction, calamity, catastrophe, grievous blow, misfortune, whammy (*inf., chiefly US*)
Antonyms *n* fortune, happiness, joy, prosperity, success

tragic *adj* **1** = **distressing**, appalling, awful, calamitous, catastrophic, deadly, dire, disastrous, dreadful, fatal, grievous, ill-fated, ill-starred, lamentable, ruinous, sad, shocking, unfortunate, woeful, wretched **2** = **sad**, anguished, dismal, doleful, heartbreaking, heart-rending, miserable, mournful, pathetic, pitiable, sorrowful
Antonyms *adj* ≠ **distressing:** beneficial, fortunate, lucky, satisfying, worthwhile ≠ **sad:** cheerful, comic, happy, joyful

trail *vb* **1** = **drag**, dangle, draw, hang down, haul, pull, stream, tow **3** = **follow**, chase, hunt, pursue, shadow, stalk, tail (*inf.*), trace, track **4** = **lag**, bring up the rear, dawdle, drag oneself, fall behind, follow, hang back, linger, loiter, straggle, traipse (*inf.*) ◆ *n* **11** = **tracks**, footprints, footsteps, mark, marks, path, scent, slipstream, spoor, trace, wake **13** = **path**, beaten track, footpath, road, route, track, way **14** = **stream**, appendage, tail, train

trail away *vb* = **fade away** *or* **out**, decrease, die away, diminish, dwindle, fall away, grow faint, grow weak, lessen, peter out, shrink, sink, subside, tail off, taper off, weaken

train *vb* **1** = **instruct**, coach, discipline, drill, educate, guide, improve, prepare, rear, rehearse, school, teach, tutor **3** = **exercise**, prepare, work out **5** = **aim**, bring to bear, direct, focus, level, line up, point ◆ *n* **6** = **convoy**, caravan, column, file, procession **7** = **sequence**, chain, concatenation, course, order, progression, series, set, string, succession **11** = **tail**, appendage, trail **12** = **retinue**, attendants, cortege, court, entourage, followers, following, household, staff, suite

trainer *n* **1, 3** = **coach**, handler

training *n* **1a** = **instruction**, coaching, discipline, education, grounding, guidance, schooling, teaching, tuition, tutelage, upbringing

traipse *vb Informal* **1** = **trudge**, drag oneself, footslog, slouch, trail, tramp ◆ *n Informal* **2** = **trudge**, long walk, slog, tramp, trek

trait *n* **1** = **characteristic**, attribute, feature, idiosyncrasy, lineament, mannerism, peculiarity, quality, quirk

traitor *n* = **betrayer**, apostate, back-stabber, deceiver, defector, deserter, double-crosser (*inf.*), fifth columnist, informer, Judas, miscreant, quisling, rebel, renegade, snake in the grass (*inf.*), turncoat
Antonyms *n* defender, loyalist, patriot, supporter

traitorous *adj* = **treacherous**, apostate, disloyal, double-crossing, double-dealing, faithless, false, perfidious, renegade, seditious, treasonable, unfaithful, untrue
Antonyms *adj* constant, faithful, loyal, patriotic, staunch, steadfast, true, trusty

trajectory *n* **1** = **path**, course, flight, flight path, line, route, track

trammel *n* **1** *often pl* = **restrictions**, bars, blocks, bonds, chains, checks, curbs, fetters, handicaps, hazards, hindrances, impediments, obstacles, reins, shackles, stumbling blocks ◆ *vb* **8, 9** = **hinder**, bar, block, capture, catch, check, clog, curb, enmesh, ensnare, entrap, fetter, ment. 2 Also called: **trammel net.** a fishing net in three sections, the two outer nets having a large mesh and the middle one a fine mesh. 3 *Rare.* a fowling net. 4 *US.* a shackle for a horse. 5 a device for drawing ellipses consisting of a flat sheet having a cruciform slot in which run two pegs attached to a beam. 6 (*sometimes pl*) a beam compass. 7 a device set in a fireplace to support cooking pots. ◆ *vb* **trammels, trammelling, trammelled** *or US* **trammels, trammeling, trammeled.** (*tr*) 8 to hinder or restrain. 9 to catch or ensnare. [C14: from OF *tramail* three-mesh net, from LL *trēmaculum,* from L *trēs* three + *macula* mesh in a net]

tramontane (trəˈmɒnteɪn) *adj* 1 being or coming from the far side of the mountains, esp. from the other side of the Alps as seen from Italy. ◆ *n* 2 an inhabitant of a tramontane country. 3 Also called: **tramontana.** a cold dry wind blowing south or southwest from the mountains in Italy and the W Mediterranean. [C16: from It. *tramontano,* from L *trānsmontānus,* from TRANS- + *montānus,* from *mōns* mountain]

tramp ❶ (træmp) *vb* 1 (*intr*) to walk long and far; hike. 2 to walk heavily or firmly across or through (a place). 3 (*intr*) to wander about as a vagabond or tramp. 4 (*tr*) to traverse on foot, esp. laboriously or wearily. 5 (*intr*) to tread or trample. ◆ *n* 6 a person who travels about on foot, living by begging or doing casual work. 7 a long hard walk; hike. 8 a heavy or rhythmic tread. 9 the sound of heavy treading. 10 a merchant ship that does not run on a regular schedule but carries cargo wherever the shippers desire. 11 *Sl., chiefly US & Canad.* a prostitute or promiscuous girl or woman. [C14: prob. from MLow G *trampen*]
▸ **ˈtrampish** *adj*

tramper (ˈtræmpə) *n NZ.* a person who tramps, or walks long distances, in the bush.

tramping (ˈtræmpɪŋ) *n NZ.* 1 the leisure activity of walking in the bush. 2 (*as modifier*): *tramping boots.*

trample ❶ (ˈtræmpᵊl) *vb* **tramples, trampling, trampled.** (when *intr,* usually foll. by *on, upon,* or *over*) 1 to stamp or walk roughly (on). 2 to encroach (upon) so as to violate or hurt. ◆ *n* 3 the action or sound of trampling. [C14: frequentative of TRAMP]
▸ **ˈtrampler** *n*

trampoline (ˈtræmpəlɪn, -ˌliːn) *n* 1 a tough canvas sheet suspended by springs or cords from a frame, used by acrobats, gymnasts, etc. ◆ *vb* **trampolines, trampolining, trampolined.** 2 (*intr*) to exercise on a trampoline. [C18: via Sp. from It. *trampolino,* from *trampoli* stilts, of Gmc origin]
▸ **ˈtrampoliner** *or* **ˈtrampolinist** *n*

trance ❶ (trɑːns) *n* 1 a hypnotic state resembling sleep. 2 any mental state in which a person is unaware of the environment, characterized by loss of voluntary movement, rigidity, and lack of sensitivity to external stimuli. 3 a dazed or stunned state. 4 a state of ecstasy or mystic absorption so intense as to cause a temporary loss of consciousness at the earthly level. 5 *Spiritualism.* a state in which a medium can supposedly be controlled by an intelligence from without as a means of communication with the dead. ◆ *vb* **trances, trancing, tranced.** 6 (*tr*) to put into or as into a trance. [C14: from OF *transe,* from *transir* to faint, from L *trānsīre* to go over]
▸ **ˈtranceˌlike** *adj*

tranche (trɑːnʃ) *n* an instalment or portion, esp. of a loan or share issue. [F, lit.: slice]

trannie *or* **tranny** (ˈtrænɪ) *n, pl* **trannies.** *Inf., chiefly Brit.* a transistor radio.

tranquil ❶ (ˈtræŋkwɪl) *adj* calm, peaceful, or quiet. [C17: from L *tranquillus*]
▸ **ˈtranquilly** *adv*

tranquillity ❶ *or US* (*sometimes*) **tranquility** (træŋˈkwɪlɪtɪ) *n* a state of calm or quietude.

tranquillize ❶**, tranquillise,** *or US* **tranquilize** (ˈtræŋkwɪˌlaɪz) *vb* **tranquillizes, tranquillizing; tranquillized, tranquillises, tranquillising, tranquillised,** *or US* **tranquilizes, tranquilizing, tranquilized.** to make or become calm or calmer.
▸ **ˌtranquilliˈzation, ˌtranquilliˈsation,** *or US* **ˌtranquiliˈzation** *n*

tranquillizer ❶**, tranquilliser,** *or US* **tranquilizer** (ˈtræŋkwɪˌlaɪzə) *n* 1 a drug that calms a person. 2 anything that tranquillizes.

tranquillo (ˌtræŋˈkwiːləʊ) *adj Music.* calm; tranquil. [It.]

trans. *abbrev. for:* 1 transaction. 2 transferred. 3 transitive. 4 translated. 5 translator. 6 transport(ation). 7 transverse.

trans- *prefix* 1 across, beyond, crossing, on the other side: *transatlantic.* 2 changing thoroughly: *transliterate.* 3 transcending: *transubstantiation.* 4 transversely: *transect.* 5 (*often in italics*) indicating that a chemical compound has a molecular structure in which two identical groups or atoms are on opposite sides of a double bond: *trans-butadiene.* [from L *trāns* across, through, beyond]

transact ❶ (trænˈzækt) *vb* to do, conduct, or negotiate (business, a deal, etc.). [C16: from L *trānsactus,* from *trānsigere,* lit.: to drive through]
▸ **transˈactor** *n*

transactinide (trænsˈæktɪˌnaɪd) *n* any artificially produced element with an atomic number greater than 103. [C20]

transaction ❶ (trænˈzækʃən) *n* 1 something that is transacted, esp. a business deal. 2 a transacting or being transacted. 3 (*pl*) the records of the proceedings of a society, etc.
▸ **transˈactional** *adj*

transalpine (trænzˈælpaɪn) *adj* (*prenominal*) 1 situated in or relating to places beyond the Alps, esp. from Italy. 2 passing over the Alps.

transaminase (trænzˈæmɪˌneɪz, -ˌneɪs) *n Biochem.* an enzyme that catalyses the transfer of an amino group from one molecule, esp. an amino acid, to another, esp. a keto acid, in the process of **transamination.**

transatlantic (ˌtrænzətˈlæntɪk) *adj* 1 on or from the other side of the Atlantic. 2 crossing the Atlantic.

transceiver (trænˈsiːvə) *n* a device which transmits and receives radio or electronic signals. [C20: from TRANS(MITTER) + (RE)CEIVER]

transcend ❶ (trænˈsɛnd) *vb* 1 to go above or beyond (a limit, expectation, etc.), as in degree or excellence. 2 (*tr*) to be superior to. [C14: from L *trānscendere* to climb over]

transcendent ❶ (trænˈsɛndənt) *adj* 1 exceeding or surpassing in degree or excellence. 2 (in the philosophy of Kant) beyond or before experience. 3 *Theol.* (of God) having existence outside the created world. 4 free from the limitations inherent in matter. ◆ *n* 5 *Philosophy.* a transcendent thing.
▸ **tranˈscendence** *or* **tranˈscendency** *n* ▸ **tranˈscendently** *adv*

transcendental (ˌtrænsɛnˈdɛntᵊl) *adj* 1 transcendent, superior, or surpassing. 2 (in the philosophy of Kant) 2a (of a judgment or logical deduction) being both synthetic and a priori. 2b of or relating to knowledge of the presuppositions of thought. 3 *Philosophy.* beyond our experience of phenomena, although not beyond potential knowledge. 4 *Theol.* supernatural or mystical. 5 *Maths.* 5a (of a number or quantity) not being a root of any polynomial with rational coefficients. 5b (of a function) not capable of expression in terms of a finite number of arithmetical operations.
▸ **ˌtranscenˈdentally** *adv*

transcendentalism (ˌtrænsɛnˈdɛntəˌlɪzəm) *n* 1a any system of philosophy, esp. that of Kant, holding that the key to knowledge of the nature of reality lies in the critical examination of the processes of reason on which depends the nature of experience. 1b any system of philosophy, esp. that of Emerson, that emphasizes intuition as a means to knowledge or the importance of the search for the divine. 2 vague philosophical speculation. 3 the state of being transcendental. 4 something, such as thought or language, that is transcendental.
▸ **ˌtranscenˈdentalist** *n, adj*

transcendental meditation *n* a technique, based on Hindu traditions, for relaxing and refreshing the mind and body through the silent repetition of a mantra.

transcontinental (ˌtrænzkɒntɪˈnɛntᵊl) *adj* 1 crossing a continent. 2 on or from the far side of a continent.
▸ **ˌtranscontiˈnentally** *adv*

transcribe ❶ (trænˈskraɪb) *vb* **transcribes, transcribing, transcribed.** (*tr*) 1 to write, type, or print out fully from speech, notes, etc. 2 to transliterate or translate. 3 to make an electrical recording of (a programme or speech) for a later broadcast. 4 *Music.* to rewrite (a piece of music)

THESAURUS

hamper, handicap, impede, net, restrain, restrict, snag, tie
Antonyms *vb* ≠ **hinder:** advance, assist, expedite, facilitate, foster, further, promote, support

tramp *vb* 1 = **hike,** footslog, march, ramble, range, roam, rove, slog, trek, walk, yomp 2 = **trudge,** march, plod, stamp, stump, toil, traipse (*inf.*), walk heavily 5 = **trample,** crush, stamp, stomp (*inf.*), tread, walk over ◆ *n* 6 = **vagrant,** bag lady (*chiefly US*), bum (*inf.*), derelict, dosser (*Brit. sl.*), down-and-out, drifter, hobo (*chiefly US*), vagabond 7 = **hike,** march, ramble, slog, trek 8 = **tread,** footfall, footstep, stamp

trample *vb* 1 *often with* **on** = **crush,** flatten, run over, squash, stamp, tread, walk over 2 *usually with* **on** = **show no consideration for,** hurt, ride roughshod over

trance *n* 1-4 = **daze,** abstraction, dream, ecstasy, hypnotic state, muse, rapture, reverie, spell, stupor, unconsciousness

tranquil *adj* = **calm,** at peace, composed, cool, pacific, peaceful, placid, quiet, restful, sedate, serene, still, undisturbed, unexcited, unperturbed, unruffled, untroubled
Antonyms *adj* agitated, busy, confused, disturbed, excited, hectic, restless, troubled

tranquillity *n* = **calm,** ataraxia, calmness, composure, coolness, equanimity, hush, imperturbability, peace, peacefulness, placidity, quiet, quietness, quietude, repose, rest, restfulness, sedateness, serenity, stillness
Antonyms *n* agitation, commotion, confusion, disturbance, excitement, noise, restlessness, turmoil, upset

tranquillize *vb* = **calm,** compose, lull, pacify, quell, quiet, relax, sedate, settle one's nerves, soothe
Antonyms *vb* agitate, confuse, distress, disturb, harass, perturb, ruffle, trouble, upset

tranquillizer *n* 1 = **sedative,** barbiturate, bromide, downer (*sl.*), opiate, red (*sl.*)

transact *vb* = **carry out,** accomplish, carry on, conclude, conduct, discharge, do, enact, execute, handle, manage, negotiate, perform, prosecute, see to, settle, take care of

transaction *n* 1 = **deal,** action, affair, bargain, business, coup, deed, enterprise, event, matter, negotiation, occurrence, proceeding, undertaking 3 *plural* = **records,** affairs, annals, doings, goings-on (*inf.*), minutes, proceedings

transcend *vb* 1 = **surpass,** eclipse, exceed, excel, go above, go beyond, leave behind, leave in the shade (*inf.*), outdo, outrival, outshine, outstrip, overstep, rise above

transcendence *n* 1 = **greatness,** ascendancy, excellence, incomparability, matchlessness, paramountcy, pre-eminence, sublimity, superiority, supremacy

transcendent *adj* 1 = **unparalleled,** consummate, exceeding, extraordinary, incomparable, matchless, peerless, pre-eminent, second to none, sublime, superior, transcendental, unequalled, unique, unrivalled

transcribe *vb* 1 = **write out,** copy out, engross, note, reproduce, rewrite, set out, take down,

for an instrument or medium other than that originally intended; arrange. **5** *Computing.* **5a** to transfer (information) from one storage device to another. **5b** to transfer (information) from a computer to an external storage device. [C16: from L *trānscrībere*]
▸**tran'scribable** *adj* ▸**tran'scriber** *n*

transcript ➊ ('trænskrɪpt) *n* **1** a written, typed, or printed copy or manuscript made by transcribing. **2** *Chiefly US & Canad.* an official record of a student's school progress. **3** any reproduction or copy. [C13: from L *trānscrīptum,* from *trānscrībere* to transcribe]

transcriptase (træn'skrɪpteɪz) *n* See **reverse transcriptase.**

transcription (træn'skrɪpʃən) *n* **1** the act or an instance of transcribing or the state of being transcribed. **2** something transcribed. **3** a representation in writing of the actual pronunciation of a speech sound, word, etc., using phonetic symbols.
▸**tran'scriptional** *or* **tran'scriptive** *adj*

transducer (trænz'dju:sə) *n* any device, such as a microphone or electric motor, that converts one form of energy into another. [C20: from L *trānsducere* to lead across]

transect *vb* (træn'sɛkt). *(tr)* **1** to cut or divide crossways. ◆ *n* ('trænsɛkt). **2** a sample strip of land used to monitor plant distribution, animal populations, or some other feature, within a given area. [C17: from L TRANS- + *secāre* to cut]
▸**tran'section** *n*

transept ('trænsɛpt) *n* either of the two wings of a cruciform church at right angles to the nave. [C16: from Anglo-L *trānseptum,* from L TRANS- + *saeptum* enclosure]
▸**tran'septal** *adj*

trans-fatty acid *n* a polyunsaturated fatty acid that has been converted from the cis-form by hydrogenation: used in the manufacture of margarine.

transfer ➊ *vb* (træns'fɜ:), **transfers, transferring, transferred. 1** to change or go or cause to change or go from one thing, person, or point to another. **2** to change (buses, trains, etc.). **3** *Law.* to make over (property, etc.) to another; convey. **4** to displace (a drawing, design, etc.) from one surface to another. **5** (of a football player) to change clubs or (of a club, manager, etc.) to sell or release (a player) to another club. **6** to leave one school, college, etc., and enrol at another. **7** to change (the meaning of a word, etc.), esp. by metaphorical extension. ◆ *n* ('trænsfɜ:). **8** the act, process, or system of transferring, or the state of being transferred. **9** a person or thing that transfers or is transferred. **10** a design or drawing that is transferred from one surface to another. **11** *Law.* the passing of title to property or other right from one person to another; conveyance. **12** any document or form effecting or regulating a transfer. **13** *Chiefly US & Canad.* a ticket that allows a passenger to change routes. [C14: from L *trānsferre,* from TRANS- + *ferre* to carry]
▸**trans'ferable** *or* **trans'ferrable** *adj* ▸**transference** ('trænsfərəns) *n*

transferable vote *n* a vote that is transferred to a second candidate indicated by the voter if the first is eliminated from the ballot.

transferee (,trænsfə'ri:) *n* **1** *Property law.* a person to whom property is transferred. **2** a person who is transferred.

transfer fee *n* a sum of money paid by one football club to another for a transferred player.

transferrin (træns'fɜ:rɪn) *n Biochem.* any of a group of blood proteins that transport iron. [C20: from TRANS- + FERRO- + -IN]

transfer RNA *n Biochem.* any of several soluble forms of RNA of low molecular weight, each of which transports a specific amino acid to a ribosome during protein synthesis.

transfiguration (,trænsfɪgju'reɪʃən) *n* a transfiguring or being transfigured.

Transfiguration (,trænsfɪgju'reɪʃən) *n* **1** *New Testament.* the change in the appearance of Christ that took place before three disciples (Matthew 17:1–9). **2** the Church festival held in commemoration of this on Aug. 6.

transfigure ➊ (træns'fɪgə) *vb* **transfigures, transfiguring, transfigured.** *(usually tr)* **1** to change or cause to change in appearance. **2** to become or cause to become more exalted. [C13: from L *trānsfigūrāre,* from TRANS- + *figūra* appearance]
▸**trans'figurement** *n*

transfinite number (træns'faɪnaɪt) *n* a cardinal or ordinal number used in the comparison of infinite sets for which several types of infinity can be classified.

transfix ➊ (træns'fɪks) *vb* **transfixes, transfixing, transfixed** *or* **transfixt.** *(tr)* **1** to render motionless, esp. with horror or shock. **2** to impale or fix with a sharp weapon or other device. [C16: from L *trānsfīgere* to pierce through]
▸**transfixion** (træns'fɪkʃən) *n*

transform ➊ *vb* (træns'fɔ:m). **1** to alter or be altered in form, function, etc. **2** *(tr)* to convert (one form of energy) to another form. **3** *(tr) Maths.* to change the form of (an equation, etc.) by a mathematical transformation. **4** *(tr)* to change (an alternating current or voltage) using a transformer. ◆ *n* ('træns,fɔ:m). **5** *Maths.* the result of a mathematical transformation. [C14: from L *trānsformāre*]
▸**trans'formable** *adj* ▸**trans'formative** *adj*

transformation ➊ (,trænsfə'meɪʃən) *n* **1** a change or alteration, esp. a radical one. **2** a transforming or being transformed. **3** *Maths.* **3a** a change in position or direction of the reference axes in a coordinate system without an alteration in their relative angle. **3b** an equivalent change in an expression or equation resulting from the substitution of one set of variables by another. **4** *Physics.* a change in an atomic nucleus to a different nuclide as the result of the emission of either an alpha-particle or a beta-particle. **5** *Linguistics.* another word for **transformational rule. 6** an apparently miraculous change in the appearance of a stage set.
▸**,transfor'mational** *adj*

transformational grammar *n* a grammatical description of a language making essential use of transformational rules.

transformational rule *n Generative grammar.* a rule that converts one phrase marker into another. Taken together, these rules convert the deep structures of sentences into their surface structures.

transformer (træns'fɔ:mə) *n* **1** a device that transfers an alternating current from one circuit to one or more other circuits, usually with a change of voltage. **2** a person or thing that transforms.

transfuse ➊ (træns'fju:z) *vb* **transfuses, transfusing, transfused.** *(tr)* **1** to permeate or infuse. **2a** to inject (blood, etc.) into a blood vessel. **2b** to give a transfusion to (a patient). [C15: from L *trānsfundere* to pour out]
▸**trans'fuser** *n* ▸**trans'fusible** *or* **trans'fusable** *adj* ▸**trans'fusive** *adj*

transfusion (træns'fju:ʒən) *n* **1** a transfusing. **2** the injection of blood, blood plasma, etc., into the blood vessels of a patient.

transgenic (trænz'dʒɛnɪk) *adj* (of an animal or plant) containing genetic material artificially transferred from another species.

transgress ➊ (trænz'grɛs) *vb* **1** to break (a law, etc.). **2** to go beyond or overstep (a limit). [C16: from L *trānsgredī,* from TRANS- + *gradī* to step]
▸**trans'gressive** *adj* ▸**trans'gressor** *n*

transgression ➊ (trænz'grɛʃən) *n* **1** a breach of a law, etc.; sin or crime. **2** a transgressing.

tranship (træn'ʃɪp) *vb* **tranships, transhipping, transhipped.** a variant spelling of **transship.**

transhumance (træns'hju:məns) *n* the seasonal migration of livestock to suitable grazing grounds. [C20: from F, from *transhumer* to change one's pastures, from Sp. *trashumar,* from L TRANS- + *humus* ground]
▸**trans'humant** *adj*

transient ➊ ('trænzɪənt) *adj* **1** for a short time only; temporary or transitory. ◆ *n* **2** a transient person or thing. [C17: from L *trānsiēns* going over, from *trānsīre* to pass over]
▸**'transiently** *adv* ▸**'transience** *or* **'transiency** *n*

transistor (træn'zɪstə) *n* **1** a semiconductor device, having three or more terminals attached to electrode regions, in which current flowing between two electrodes is controlled by a voltage or current applied to one or more specified electrodes. The device has replaced the valve in most circuits since it is much smaller and works at a much lower voltage. **2** *Inf.* a transistor radio. [C20: orig. a trademark, from TRANSFER + RESISTOR, from the transfer of electric signals across a resistor]

transistorize *or* **transistorise** (træn'zɪstə,raɪz) *vb* **transistorizes, transistorizing, transistorized** *or* **transistorises, transistorising, transistorised. 1** to

THESAURUS

transfer **2** = **translate**, interpret, render, transliterate **3** = **record**, tape, tape-record

transcript *n* **1** = **copy**, carbon, carbon copy, duplicate, manuscript, note, notes, record, reproduction, transcription, translation, transliteration, version

transfer *vb* **1** = **move**, carry, change, consign, convey, displace, hand over, make over, pass on, relocate, remove, shift, translate, transmit, transplant, transport, transpose, turn over ◆ *n* **8** = **move**, change, displacement, handover, relocation, removal, shift, transference, translation, transmission, transposition

transfigure *vb* **1** = **change**, alter, convert, metamorphose, transform, transmute **2** = **exalt**, apotheosize, glorify, idealize

transfix *vb* **1** = **stun**, engross, fascinate, halt *or* stop in one's tracks, hold, hypnotize, mesmerize, paralyse, petrify, rivet the attention of, root to the spot, spellbind, stop dead **2** = **pierce**, fix, impale, puncture, run through, skewer, spear, spit, transpierce
Antonyms *vb* ≠ **stun:** bore, fatigue, tire, weary

transform *vb* **1** = **change**, alter, convert, make over, metamorphose, reconstruct, remodel, renew, revolutionize, transfigure, translate, transmogrify (*jocular*), transmute

transformation *n* **1** = **change**, alteration, conversion, metamorphosis, radical change, renewal, revolution, revolutionary change, sea change, transfiguration, transmogrification (*jocular*), transmutation

transfuse *vb* **1** = **permeate**, instil, pervade, spread over, suffuse

transgress *vb Formal* **1** = **break**, be out of order, break the law, contravene, defy, disobey, do *or* go wrong, err, fall from grace, go astray, infringe, lapse, misbehave, offend, sin, trespass, violate **2** = **go beyond**, encroach, exceed, overstep

transgression *n* **1** = **crime**, breach, contravention, encroachment, error, fault, infraction, infringement, iniquity, lapse, misbehaviour, misdeed, misdemeanour, offence, peccadillo, sin, trespass, violation, wrong, wrongdoing

transgressor *n* **1** = **criminal**, culprit, delinquent, evildoer, felon, lawbreaker, malefactor, miscreant, offender, sinner, trespasser, villain, wrongdoer

transience *n* **1** = **briefness**, brevity, ephemerality, evanescence, fleetingness, fugacity, fugitiveness, impermanence, momentariness, shortness, transitoriness

transient *adj* **1** = **brief**, ephemeral, evanescent, fleeting, flying, fugacious, fugitive, here today and gone tomorrow, impermanent, momentary, passing, short, short-lived, short-term, temporary, transitory
Antonyms *adj* abiding, constant, durable, enduring, eternal, imperishable, long-lasting, long-term, permanent, perpetual, persistent, undying

convert to the use or manufacture of transistors and other solid-state components. **2** (*tr*) to equip with transistors and other solid-state components.

transit ❶ ('trænsɪt, 'trænz-) *n* **1a** the passage or conveyance of goods or people. **1b** (*as modifier*): *a transit visa.* **2** a change or transition. **3** a route. **4** *Astron.* **4a** the passage of a celestial body or satellite across the face of a larger body as seen from the earth. **4b** the apparent passage of a celestial body across the meridian. **5 in transit.** while being conveyed; during passage. ◆ *vb* **6** to make a transit through or over (something). [C15: from L *trānsitus* a going over, from *trānsīre* to pass over]

transit camp *n* a camp in which refugees, soldiers, etc., live temporarily.

transit instrument *n* an astronomical instrument used to time the transit of a star, etc., across the meridian.

transition ❶ (træn'zɪʃən) *n* **1** change or passage from one state or stage to another. **2** the period of time during which something changes. **3** *Music.* **3a** a movement from one key to another; modulation. **3b** a linking passage between two divisions in a composition; bridge. **4** a style of architecture in the late 11th and early 12th centuries, characterized by late Romanesque forms combined with early Gothic details. **5** *Physics.* a change in the configuration of an atomic nucleus, involving either a change in energy level or a transformation to another element or isotope. **6** a sentence, passage, etc., that links sections of a written work. [C16: from L *transitio*; see TRANSIENT]
▸**tran'sitional** *adj* ▸**tran'sitionally** *adv*

transition element *or* **metal** *n Chem.* any element belonging to one of three series of elements with atomic numbers between 21 and 30, 39 and 48, and 57 and 80. They have an incomplete penultimate electron shell and tend to form complexes.

transition temperature *n* the temperature at which a sudden change of physical properties occurs.

transitive ('trænsɪtɪv) *adj* **1** *Grammar.* **1a** denoting an occurrence of a verb when it requires a direct object or denoting a verb that customarily requires a direct object: *"to find" is a transitive verb.* **1b** (*as n*): *these verbs are transitives.* **2** *Logic, maths.* having the property that if one object bears a relationship to a second object that also bears the same relationship to a third object, then the first object bears this relationship to the third object: *if x = y and y = z then x = z.* ◆ Cf. **intransitive.** [C16: from LL *trānsitīvus*, from L *trānsitus* a going over; see TRANSIENT]
▸**'transitively** *adv* ▸**,transi'tivity** *or* **'transitiveness** *n*

transitory ❶ ('trænsɪtərɪ, -trɪ) *adj* of short duration; transient or ephemeral. [C14: from Church L *trānsitōrius* passing, from L *trānsitus* a crossing over]
▸**'transitoriness** *n*

transit theodolite *n* a theodolite the telescope of which can be rotated completely about its horizontal axis.

transl. *abbrev. for:* **1** translated. **2** translator.

translate ❶ (træns'leɪt, trænz-) *vb* **translates, translating, translated. 1** to express or be capable of being expressed in another language. **2** (*intr*) to act as translator. **3** (*tr*) to express or explain in simple or less technical language. **4** (*tr*) to interpret or infer the significance of (gestures, symbols, etc.). **5** (*tr*) to transform or convert: *to translate hope into reality.* **6** to transfer from one place or position to another. **7** (*tr*) *Theol.* to transfer (a person) from one place or plane of existence to another, as from earth to heaven. **8** (*tr*) *Maths, physics.* to move (a figure or body) laterally, without rotation, dilation, or angular displacement. [C13: from L *trānslātus* carried over, from *trānsferre* to TRANSFER]
▸**trans'latable** *adj* ▸**trans'lator** *n*

translation (træns'leɪʃən, trænz-) *n* **1** something that is or has been translated. **2** a translating or being translated. **3** *Maths.* a transformation in which the origin of a coordinate system is moved to another position so that each axis retains the same direction.
▸**trans'lational** *adj*

transliterate (trænz'lɪtə,reɪt) *vb* **transliterates, transliterating, transliterated.** (*tr*) to transcribe (a word, etc.) into corresponding letters of another alphabet. [C19: TRANS- + *-literate*, from L *līttera* letter]
▸**,translitera'ation** *n* ▸**trans'liter,ator** *n*

translocation (,trænzləʊ'keɪʃən) *n* **1** *Genetics.* the transfer of one part of a chromosome to another part of the same or a different chromosome. **2** *Bot.* the transport of minerals, sugars, etc., in solution within a plant. **3** a movement from one position or place to another.

translucent ❶ (trænz'luːsᵊnt) *adj* allowing light to pass through partially or diffusely; semitransparent. [C16: from L *trānslūcēre* to shine through]
▸**trans'lucence** *or* **trans'lucency** *n* ▸**trans'lucently** *adv*

translunar (trænz'luːnə) *or* **translunary** (trænz'luːnərɪ) *adj* **1** lying beyond the moon. **2** unworldly or ethereal.

transmigrate ❶ (,trænzmaɪ'greɪt) *vb* **transmigrates, transmigrating, transmigrated.** (*intr*) **1** to move from one place, state, or stage to another. **2** (of souls) to pass from one body into another at death.
▸**,transmi'gration** *n* ▸**trans'migratory** *adj*

transmission ❶ (trænz'mɪʃən) *n* **1** the act or process of transmitting. **2** something that is transmitted. **3** the extent to which a body or medium transmits light, sound, etc. **4** the transference of motive force or power. **5** a system of shafts, gears, etc., that transmits power, esp. the arrangement of such parts that transmits the power of the engine to the driving wheels of a motor vehicle. **6** the act or process of sending a message, picture, or other information by means of radio waves, electrical signals, light signals, etc. **7** a radio or television broadcast. [C17: from L *trānsmissiō* a sending across]
▸**trans'missible** *adj* ▸**trans'missive** *adj*

transmission density *n Physics.* a measure of the extent to which a substance transmits light or other electromagnetic radiation.

transmission line *n* a coaxial cable, waveguide, etc., that transfers electrical signals from one location to another.

transmissivity (,trænzmɪ'sɪvɪtɪ) *n Physics.* a measure of the ability of a material to transmit radiation.

transmit ❶ (trænz'mɪt) *vb* **transmits, transmitting, transmitted. 1** (*tr*) to pass or cause to go from one place or person to another; transfer. **2** (*tr*) to pass on or impart (a disease, etc.). **3** (*tr*) to hand down to posterity. **4** (*tr; usually passive*) to pass (an inheritable characteristic) from parent to offspring. **5** to allow the passage of (particles, energy, etc.): *radio waves are transmitted through the atmosphere.* **6a** to send out (signals) by means of radio waves or along a transmission line. **6b** to broadcast (a radio or television programme). **7** (*tr*) to transfer (a force, motion, etc.) from one part of a mechanical system to another. [C14: from L *trānsmittere* to send across]
▸**trans'mittable** *adj* ▸**trans'mittal** *n*

transmittance (trænz'mɪtᵊns) *n* **1** the act of transmitting. **2** Also called: **transmission factor.** *Physics.* a measure of the ability of anything to transmit radiation, equal to the ratio of the transmitted flux to the incident flux.

transmitter (trænz'mɪtə) *n* **1** a person or thing that transmits. **2** the equipment used for generating and amplifying a radio-frequency carrier, modulating the carrier with information, and feeding it to an aerial for transmission. **3** the microphone in a telephone that converts sound waves into audio-frequency electrical signals. **4** a device that converts mechanical movements into coded electrical signals transmitted along a telegraph circuit. **5** a substance released by nerve endings that transmits impulses across synapses.

transmogrify (trænz'mɒgrɪ,faɪ) *vb* **transmogrifies, transmogrifying, transmogrified.** (*tr*) *Jocular.* to change or transform into a different shape, esp. a grotesque or bizarre one. [C17: from ?]
▸**trans,mogrifi'cation** *n*

transmontane (,trænzmɒn'teɪn) *adj, n* another word for **tramontane.**

transmutation (,trænzmjuː'teɪʃən) *n* **1** the act or an instance of transmuting. **2** the change of one chemical element into another by a nuclear reaction. **3** the attempted conversion, by alchemists, of base metals into gold or silver.
▸**,transmu'tational** *or* **trans'mutative** *adj*

transmute ❶ (trænz'mjuːt) *vb* **transmutes, transmuting, transmuted.** (*tr*) **1** to change the form, character, or substance of. **2** to alter (an element, metal, etc.) by alchemy. [C15: via OF from L *trānsmūtāre* to shift, from TRANS- + *mūtāre* to change]
▸**trans,muta'bility** *n* ▸**trans'mutable** *adj*

transnational (trænz'næʃənəl) *adj* extending beyond the boundaries, etc., of a single nation.

transoceanic (trænz,əʊʃɪ'ænɪk) *adj* **1** on or from the other side of an ocean. **2** crossing an ocean.

transom ('trænsəm) *n* **1** a horizontal member across a window. **2** a hori-

THESAURUS

transit *n* **1a** = **movement**, carriage, conveyance, crossing, motion, passage, portage, shipment, transfer, transport, transportation, travel, traverse **2** = **change**, alteration, changeover, conversion, shift, transition **5 in transit** = **en route**, during passage, on the journey, on the move, on the road, on the way, while travelling ◆ *vb* **6** = **move**, cross, journey, pass, travel, traverse

transition *n* **1** = **change**, alteration, changeover, conversion, development, evolution, flux, metamorphosis, metastasis, passage, passing, progression, shift, transit, transmutation, upheaval

transitional *adj* **1** = **changing**, developmental, fluid, intermediate, passing, provisional, temporary, transitionary, unsettled

transitory *adj* = **short-lived**, brief, ephemeral, evanescent, fleeting, flying, fugacious, here today and gone tomorrow, impermanent, momentary, passing, short, short-term, temporary, transient
Antonyms *adj* abiding, enduring, eternal, everlasting, lasting, long-lived, long-term, permanent, perpetual, persistent, undying

translate *vb* **1** = **interpret**, construe, convert, decipher, decode, paraphrase, render, transcribe, transliterate **3** = **put in plain English**, elucidate, explain, make clear, paraphrase, simplify, spell out, state in layman's language **5** = **convert**, alter, change, metamorphose, transfigure, transform, transmute, turn **6** = **transfer**, carry, convey, move, remove, send, transplant, transport, transpose

translator *n* **1** = **interpreter**, linguist

translucent *adj* = **semitransparent**, clear, diaphanous, limpid, lucent, pellucid

transmigration *n* **1, 2** = **reincarnation**, journey, metempsychosis, migration, movement, passage, rebirth, travel

transmission *n* **1** = **transfer**, carriage, communication, conveyance, diffusion, dispatch, dissemination, remission, sending, shipment, spread, transference, transport **6** = **broadcasting**, dissemination, putting out, relaying, sending, showing **7** = **programme**, broadcast, show

transmit *vb* **1-5** = **pass on**, bear, carry, communicate, convey, diffuse, dispatch, disseminate, forward, hand down, hand on, impart, remit, send, spread, take, transfer, transport **6b** = **broadcast**, disseminate, put on the air, radio, relay, send, send out

transmute *vb* **1, 2** = **transform**, alchemize, alter, change, convert, metamorphose, remake, transfigure

zontal member that separates a door from a window over it. **3** the usual US name for **fanlight**. **4** *Naut.* **4a** a surface forming the stern of a vessel. **4b** any of several transverse beams used for strengthening the stern of a vessel. [C14: earlier *traversayn*, from OF *traversin*, from TRAVERSE]
▸ **'transomed** *adj*

transonic (træn'sɒnɪk) *adj* of or relating to conditions when travelling at or near the speed of sound.

transparency ❶ (træns'pærənsɪ) *n, pl* **transparencies. 1** Also called: **transparence**. the state of being transparent. **2** Also called: **slide**. a positive photograph on a transparent base, usually mounted in a frame or between glass plates. It can be viewed by means of a slide projector.

transparent ❶ (træns'pærənt) *adj* **1** permitting the uninterrupted passage of light; clear. **2** easy to see through, understand, or recognize; obvious. **3** permitting the free passage of electromagnetic radiation. **4** candid, open, or frank. [C15: from Med. L *trānspārēre* to show through, from L TRANS- + *pārēre* to appear]
▸ **trans'parently** *adv* ▸ **trans'parentness** *n*

transpire ❶ (træn'spaɪə) *vb* **transpires, transpiring, transpired. 1** (*intr*) to come to light; be known. **2** (*intr*) *Inf.* to happen or occur. **3** *Physiol.* to give off or exhale (water or vapour) through the skin, a mucous membrane, etc. **4** (of plants) to lose (water), esp. through the stomata of the leaves. [C16: from Med. L *trānspīrāre*, from L TRANS- + *spīrāre* to breathe]
▸ **transpiration** (ˌtrænspə'reɪʃən) *n* ▸ **tran'spiratory** *adj*

USAGE NOTE It is often maintained that *transpire* should not be used to mean happen or occur, as in *the event transpired late in the evening*, and that the word is properly used to mean become known, as in *it transpired later that the thief had been caught*. The word is, however, widely used in the former sense, esp. in spoken English.

transplant ❶ *vb* (træns'plɑːnt). **1** (*tr*) to remove or transfer (esp. a plant) from one place to another. **2** (*intr*) to be capable of being transplanted. **3** *Surgery*. to transfer (an organ or tissue) from one part of the body or from one person to another. ◆ *n* ('træns,plɑːnt). **4** *Surgery*. **4a** the procedure involved in such a transfer. **4b** the organ or tissue transplanted.
▸ **trans'plantable** *adj* ▸ ˌ**transplan'tation** *n*

transponder (træn'spɒndə) *n* **1** a type of radio or radar transmitter-receiver that transmits signals automatically when it receives predetermined signals. **2** the receiver and transmitter in a communications satellite, relaying signals back to earth. [C20: from TRANSMITTER + RESPONDER]

transport ❶ *vb* (træns'pɔːt). (*tr*) **1** to carry or cause to go from one place to another, esp. over some distance. **2** to deport or exile to a penal colony. **3** (*usually passive*) to have a strong emotional effect on. ◆ *n* ('træns,pɔːt). **4a** the business or system of transporting goods or people. **4b** (*as modifier*): *a modernized transport system*. **5** *Brit.* freight vehicles generally. **6a** a vehicle used to transport goods or people, esp. troops. **6b** (*as modifier*): *a transport plane*. **7** a transporting or being transported. **8** ecstasy, rapture, or any powerful emotion. **9** a convict sentenced to be transported. [C14: from L *trānsportāre*, from TRANS- + *portāre* to carry]
▸ **trans'portable** *adj* ▸ **trans'porter** *n*

transportation (ˌtrænspɔː'teɪʃən) *n* **1** a means or system of transporting. **2** the act of transporting or the state of being transported. **3** (esp. formerly) deportation to a penal colony.

transport café ('træns,pɔːt) *n Brit.* an inexpensive eating place on a main route, used mainly by long-distance lorry drivers.

transpose ❶ (træns'pəʊz) *vb* **transposes, transposing, transposed. 1** (*tr*) to alter the positions of; interchange, as words in a sentence. **2** *Music*. to play (notes, music, etc.) in a different key from that originally intended. **3** (*tr*) *Maths.* to move (a term) from one side of an equation to the other with a corresponding reversal in sign. [C14: from OF *transposer*, from L *trānspōnere* to remove]
▸ **trans'posable** *adj* ▸ **trans'posal** *n* ▸ **trans'poser** *n* ▸ **transposition** (ˌtrænspə'zɪʃən) *n*

transposing instrument *n* a musical instrument, esp. a horn or clarinet, pitched in a key other than C major, but whose music is written down as if its basic scale were C major.

transposon (træns'pəuzɒn) *n Genetics*. a fragment of bacterial nucleic acid that can move from one site in a chromosome to another site in the same or a different chromosome and thus alter the genetic constitution of the bacterium. [C20: TRANSPOS(E) + -ON]

transputer (trænz'pjuːtə) *n Computing*. a type of fast powerful microchip that is the equivalent of a 32-bit microprocessor with its own RAM facility. [C20: from TRANS(ISTOR) + (COM)PUTER]

transsexual *or* **transexual** (trænz'sɛksjuəl) *n* **1** a person who completely identifies with the opposite sex. **2** a person who has undergone medical procedures to alter sexual characteristics to those of the opposite sex.

transship (træns'ʃɪp) *or* **tranship** *vb* **transships, transshipping, transshipped** *or* **tranships, transhipping, transhipped.** to transfer or be transferred from one vessel or vehicle to another.
▸ **trans'shipment** *or* **tran'shipment** *n*

transubstantiation (ˌtrænsəbˌstænʃɪ'eɪʃən) *n* **1** (esp. in Roman Catholic theology) **1a** the doctrine that the whole substance of the bread and wine changes into the substance of the body and blood of Christ when consecrated in the Eucharist. **1b** the mystical process by which this is believed to take place during consecration. Cf. **consubstantiation**. **2** a substantial change; transmutation.
▸ ˌ**transubˌstanti'ationalist** *n*

transude (træn'sjuːd) *vb* **transudes, transuding, transuded.** (of a fluid) to ooze or pass through interstices, pores, or small holes. [C17: from NL *trānsūdāre*, from L TRANS- + *sūdāre* to sweat]
▸ **transudation** (ˌtrænsjʊ'deɪʃən) *n*

transuranic (ˌtrænzjʊ'rænɪk), **transuranian** (ˌtrænzjʊ'reɪnɪən), *or* **transuranium** *adj* **1** (of an element) having an atomic number greater than that of uranium. **2** of or having the behaviour of transuranic elements. [C20]

transversal (trænz'vɜːsᵊl) *n* **1** *Geom.* a line intersecting two or more other lines. ◆ *adj* **2** a less common word for **transverse**.
▸ **trans'versally** *adv*

transverse ❶ (trænz'vɜːs) *adj* **1** crossing from side to side; athwart; crossways. ◆ *n* **2** a transverse piece or object. [C16: from L *trānsversus*, from *trānsvertere* to turn across]
▸ **trans'versely** *adv*

transverse colon *n Anat.* the part of the large intestine passing transversely in front of the liver and stomach.

transverse wave *n* a wave, such as an electromagnetic wave, that is propagated in a direction perpendicular to the displacement of the transmitting field or medium.

transvestite (trænz'vɛstaɪt) *n* a person who seeks sexual pleasure from wearing clothes of the opposite sex. [C19: from G *Transvestit*, from TRANS- + L *vestītus* clothed, from *vestīre* to clothe]
▸ **trans'vestism** *or* **trans'vestitism** *n*

trap[1] ❶ (træp) *n* **1** a mechanical device or enclosed place or pit in which something, esp. an animal, is caught or penned. **2** any device or plan for tricking a person or thing into being caught unawares. **3** anything resembling a trap or prison. **4** a fitting for a pipe in the form of a U-shaped or S-shaped bend that contains standing water to prevent the passage of gases. **5** any similar device. **6** a device that hurls clay pigeons into the air to be fired at by trapshooters. **7** *Greyhound racing*. any one of a line of boxlike stalls in which greyhounds are enclosed before the start of a race. **8** See **trap door**. **9** a light two-wheeled carriage. **10** a slang word for **mouth**. **11** *Golf*. an obstacle or hazard, esp. a bunker. **12** (*pl*) *Jazz sl.* percussion instruments. **13** (*usually pl*) *Austral. sl.* a policeman. ◆ *vb* **traps, trapping, trapped. 14** to catch, take, or pen in or as if in a trap. **15** (*tr*) to ensnare by trickery; trick. **16** (*tr*) to provide (a pipe) with a trap. **17** to set traps in (a place), esp. for animals. [OE *træppe*]
▸ **'trapˌlike** *adj*

trap[2] (træp) *vb* **traps, trapping, trapped.** (*tr*; often foll. by *out*) to dress or adorn. ◆ See also **traps**. [C11: prob. from OF *drap* cloth]

trap[3] (træp) *or* **traprock** ('træp,rɒk) *n* **1** any fine-grained often columnar dark igneous rock, esp. basalt. **2** any rock in which oil or gas has

THESAURUS

transparency *n* **1** = **clarity**, clearness, diaphaneity, diaphanousness, filminess, gauziness, limpidity, limpidness, pellucidity, pellucidness, sheerness, translucence, translucency, transparence **1** = **obviousness**, apparentness, distinctness, explicitness, patentness, perspicuousness, plainness, unambiguousness **1** = **frankness**, candour, directness, forthrightness, openness, straightforwardness **2** = **photograph**, slide
Antonyms *n* ≠ **clarity**: cloudiness, murkiness, opacity, unclearness ≠ **obviousness**: obscurity, unclearness, vagueness ≠ **frankness**: ambiguity, vagueness

transparent *adj* **1** = **clear**, crystal clear, crystalline, diaphanous, filmy, gauzy, limpid, lucent, lucid, pellucid, see-through, sheer, translucent, transpicuous **2** = **obvious**, apparent, as plain as the nose on one's face (*inf.*), bold, distinct, easy, evident, explicit, manifest, patent, perspicuous, plain, recognizable, unambiguous, understandable, undisguised, visible **4** = **frank**, candid, direct, forthright, open, plain-spoken, straight, straightforward, unambiguous, unequivocal
Antonyms *adj* ≠ **clear**: cloudy, muddy, opaque, thick, turbid, unclear ≠ **obvious**: hidden, mysterious, opaque, uncertain, unclear, vague ≠ **frank**: ambiguous, deceptive, disingenuous, mysterious, unclear, vague

transpire *vb* **1** = **become known**, be disclosed, be discovered, be made public, come out, come to light, emerge **2** = **happen**, arise, befall, chance, come about, come to pass (*arch.*), occur, take place, turn up

transplant *vb* **1** = **transfer**, displace, relocate, remove, resettle, shift, uproot

transport *vb* **1** = **convey**, bear, bring, carry, fetch, haul, move, remove, run, ship, take, transfer **2** *History* = **exile**, banish, deport, sentence to transportation **3** = **enrapture**, captivate, carry away, delight, electrify, enchant, entrance, move, ravish, spellbind ◆ *n* **4a** = **transference**, carriage, conveyance, removal, shipment, shipping, transportation **6a** = **vehicle**, conveyance, transportation, wheels (*inf.*) **8** = **ecstasy**, bliss, cloud nine (*inf.*), delight, enchantment, euphoria, happiness, heaven, rapture, ravishment, seventh heaven
Antonyms *n* ≠ **ecstasy**: blues (*inf.*), depression, despondency, doldrums, dumps (*inf.*), melancholy

transpose *vb* **1** = **interchange**, alter, change, exchange, move, rearrange, relocate, reorder, shift, substitute, swap, switch, transfer

transverse *adj* **1** = **crossways**, athwart, crosswise, diagonal, oblique

trap[1] *n* **1** = **snare**, ambush, gin, net, noose, pitfall, springe, toils **2** = **trick**, ambush, artifice, deception, device, ruse, stratagem, subterfuge, wile ◆ *vb* **14** = **catch**, corner, enmesh, ensnare, entrap, snare, take **15** = **trick**, ambush, beguile, deceive, dupe, ensnare, inveigle accumulated. [C18: from Swedish *trappa* stair (from its steplike formation)]

trap door *n* a door or flap flush with and covering an opening, esp. in a ceiling.

trap-door spider *n* any of various spiders that construct a silk-lined hole in the ground closed by a hinged door of earth and silk.

trapes (treɪps) *vb, n* a less common spelling of **traipse**.

trapeze (trəˈpiːz) *n* a free-swinging bar attached to two ropes, used by circus acrobats, etc. [C19: from F *trapèze,* from NL; see TRAPEZIUM]

trapezium (trəˈpiːzɪəm) *n, pl* **trapeziums** *or* **trapezia** (-zɪə). **1** *Chiefly Brit.* a quadrilateral having two parallel sides of unequal length. Usual US and Canad. name: **trapezoid. 2** *Chiefly US & Canad.* a quadrilateral having neither pair of sides parallel. [C16: via LL from Gk *trapezion,* from *trapeza* table]
▸**traˈpezial** *adj*

trapezius (trəˈpiːzɪəs) *n, pl* **trapeziuses.** either of two flat triangular muscles that rotate the shoulder blades. [C18: from NL *trapezius (musculus)* trapezium-shaped (muscle)]

trapezoid (ˈtræpɪˌzɔɪd) *n* **1** a quadrilateral having neither pair of sides parallel. **2** the usual US and Canad. name for **trapezium.** [C18: from NL *trapezoidēs,* from LGk *trapezoeidēs* trapezium-shaped, from *trapeza* table]

trapper (ˈtræpə) *n* a person who traps animals, esp. for their furs or skins.

trappings ❶ (ˈtræpɪŋz) *pl n* **1** the accessories and adornments that symbolize a condition, office, etc.: *the trappings of success.* **2** ceremonial harness for a horse or other animal. [C16: from TRAP[2]]

Trappist (ˈtræpɪst) *n* **a** a member of a branch of the Cistercian order of Christian monks, which originated at La Trappe in France in 1664. They are noted for their rule of silence. **b** *(as modifier): a Trappist monk.*

traps (træps) *pl n* belongings; luggage. [C19: prob. shortened from TRAPPINGS]

trapshooting (ˈtræpˌʃuːtɪŋ) *n* the sport of shooting at clay pigeons thrown up by a trap.
▸ˈ**trapˌshooter** *n*

trash ❶ (træʃ) *n* **1** foolish ideas or talk; nonsense. **2** *Chiefly US & Canad.* useless or unwanted matter or objects; rubbish. **3** a literary or artistic production of poor quality. **4** *Chiefly US & Canad.* a poor or worthless person or a group of such people. **5** bits that are broken or lopped off, esp. the trimmings from trees or plants. **6** the dry remains of sugar cane after the juice has been extracted. ◆ *vb* **7** to remove the outer leaves and branches from (growing plants, esp. sugar cane). **8** *Sl.* to attack or destroy (someone or something) wilfully or maliciously. [C16: from ?]

trashy ❶ (ˈtræʃɪ) *adj* **trashier, trashiest.** cheap, worthless, or badly made.
▸ˈ**trashily** *adv* ▸ˈ**trashiness** *n*

trass (træs) *n* a volcanic rock used to make a hydraulic cement. [C18: from Du. *tras, tarasse,* from It. *terrazza* worthless earth; see TERRACE]

trattoria (ˌtrætəˈrɪə) *n* an Italian restaurant. [C19: from It., from *trattore* innkeeper, from F *traiteur,* from OF *tretier* to TREAT]

trauma ❶ (ˈtrɔːmə) *n, pl* **traumata** (-mətə) *or* **traumas. 1** *Psychol.* a powerful shock that may have long-lasting effects. **2** *Pathol.* any bodily injury or wound. [C18: from Gk: a wound]
▸**traumatic** (trɔːˈmætɪk) *adj* ▸**trauˈmatically** *adv*

traumatize *or* **traumatise** (ˈtrɔːməˌtaɪz) *vb* **traumatizes, traumatizing, traumatized** *or* **traumatises, traumatising, traumatised. 1** *(tr)* to wound or injure (the body). **2** to subject or be subjected to mental trauma.
▸ˌ**traumatiˈzation** *or* ˌ**traumatiˈsation** *n*

travail ❶ (ˈtræveɪl) *Literary.* ◆ *n* **1** painful or excessive labour or exertion. **2** the pangs of childbirth; labour. ◆ *vb* **3** *(intr)* to suffer or labour painfully, esp. in childbirth. [C13: from OF *travaillier,* from Vulgar L *tripaliāre* (unattested) to torture, from LL *trepālium* instrument of torture, from L *tripālis* having three stakes]

travel ❶ (ˈtræv[ə]l) *vb* **travels, travelling, travelled** *or US* **travels, traveling, traveled.** *(mainly intr)* **1** to go, move, or journey from one place to another. **2** *(tr)* to go, move, or journey through or across (an area, region, etc.). **3** to go, move, or cover a distance. **4** to go from place to place as a salesman. **5** (esp. of perishable goods) to withstand a journey. **6** (of light, sound, etc.) to be transmitted or move. **7** to progress or advance. **8** *Basketball.* to take an excessive number of steps while holding the ball. **9** (of part of a mechanism) to move in a fixed path. **10** *Inf.* to move rapidly. ◆ *n* **11a** the act of travelling. **11b** *(as modifier): a travel brochure.* Related adj: **itinerant. 12** *(usually pl)* a tour or journey. **13** the distance moved by a mechanical part, such as the stroke of a piston. **14** movement or passage. [C14 *travaillen* to make a journey, from OF *travaillier* to TRAVAIL]

travel agency *or* **bureau** *n* an agency that arranges and negotiates flights, holidays, etc., for travellers.
▸**travel agent** *n*

travelled *or US* **traveled** (ˈtr[æ]vəld) *adj* having experienced or undergone much travelling.

traveller ❶ (ˈtrævələ, ˈtrævlə) *n* **1** a person who travels, esp. habitually. **2** See **travelling salesman. 3** a part of a mechanism that moves in a fixed course. **4** *Austral.* a swagman.

traveller's cheque *n* a cheque sold by a bank, etc., to the bearer, who signs it on purchase and can cash it abroad by signing it again.

traveller's joy *n* a ranunculaceous Old World climbing plant having white flowers and heads of feathery plumed fruits; wild clematis.

travelling people *or* **folk** *pl n (sometimes caps.) Brit.* Gypsies or other itinerant people: a term used esp. by such people of themselves.

travelling salesman *n* a salesman who travels within an assigned territory in order to sell merchandise or to solicit orders for the commercial enterprise he represents by direct personal contact with customers.

travelling wave *n* **a** a wave carrying energy away from its source. **b** *(as modifier): a travelling-wave aerial.*

travelogue *or US (sometimes)* **travelog** (ˈtræv[ə]lɒg) *n* a film, lecture, or brochure on travels and travelling.

traverse ❶ (ˈtrævɜːs, trəˈvɜːs) *vb* **traverses, traversing, traversed. 1** to pass or go over or back and forth over (something); cross. **2** *(tr)* to go against; oppose. **3** to move sideways or crosswise. **4** *(tr)* to extend or reach across. **5** to turn (an artillery gun) laterally or (of an artillery gun) to turn laterally. **6** *(tr)* to examine carefully. **7** *(tr) Law.* to deny (an allegation). **8** *Mountaineering.* to move across (a face) horizontally. ◆ *n* **9** something being or lying across, such as a transom. **10** a gallery or loft inside a building that crosses it. **11** an obstruction. **12** a protective bank or other barrier across a trench or rampart. **13** a railing, screen, or curtain. **14** the act or an instance of traversing or crossing. **15** *Mountaineering.* the act or an instance of moving horizontally across a face. **16** a path or road across. **17** *Naut.* the zigzag course of a vessel tacking frequently. **18** *Law.* the formal denial of a fact alleged in the opposite party's pleading. **19** *Surveying.* a survey consisting of a series of straight lines, the length of each and the angle between them being measured. ◆ *adj* **20** being or lying across; transverse. [C14: from OF *traverser,* from LL *trānsversāre,* from L *trānsversus* TRANSVERSE]
▸**traˈversal** *n* ▸ˈ**traverser** *n*

travertine (ˈtrævətɪn) *n* a porous rock consisting of calcium carbonate, used for building. [C18: from It. *travertino* (infl. by *tra-* TRANS-), from L *lapis Tīburtīnus* Tiburtine stone, from *Tībur*s the district around Tibur (now Tivoli)]

travesty ❶ (ˈtrævɪstɪ) *n, pl* **travesties. 1** a farcical or grotesque imitation; mockery. ◆ *vb* **travesties, travestying, travestied.** *(tr)* **2** to make or be a travesty of. [C17: from F *travesti* disguised, from *travestir* to disguise, from It. *travestire,* from *tra-* TRANS- + *vestire* to clothe]

travois (trəˈvɔɪ) *n, pl* **travois** (-ˈvɔɪz). **1** *History.* a sled formerly used by the Plains Indians of North America, consisting of two poles joined by a frame and pulled by an animal. **2** *Canad.* a similar sled used for dragging logs. [from Canad. F, from F *travail* beam, from L *trabs*]

THESAURUS

trappings *pl n* **1** = **accessories**, accoutrements, adornments, bells and whistles, decorations, dress, equipment, finery, fittings, fixtures, fripperies, furnishings, gear, livery, ornaments, panoply, paraphernalia, raiment (*arch. or poetic*), things, trimmings

trash *n* **1** = **nonsense**, balderdash, balls (*taboo sl.*), bilge (*inf.*), bosh (*inf.*), bull (*sl.*), bullshit (*taboo sl.*), bunkum *or* buncombe (*chiefly US*), cobblers (*Brit. taboo sl.*), crap (*sl.*), drivel, eyewash (*inf.*), foolish talk, garbage (*inf.*), guff (*sl.*), hogwash, hokum (*sl., chiefly US & Canad.*), hot air (*inf.*), moonshine, pap, piffle (*inf.*), poppycock (*inf.*), rot, rubbish, tommyrot, tosh (*sl., chiefly Brit.*), tripe (*inf.*), trumpery, twaddle **2** *Chiefly U.S. & Canad.* = **litter**, dreck (*sl., chiefly US*), dregs, dross, garbage, junk (*inf.*), offscourings, refuse, rubbish, sweepings, waste
Antonyms *n* ≠ **nonsense:** logic, reason, sense, significance

trashy *adj* = **worthless**, brummagem, catchpenny, cheap, cheap-jack (*inf.*), crappy (*sl.*), flimsy, inferior, meretricious, of a sort *or* of sorts, poxy (*sl.*), rubbishy, shabby, shoddy, tawdry, thrown together, tinsel
Antonyms *adj* A1 *or* A-one (*inf.*), excellent, exceptional, first-class, first-rate, outstanding, superlative

trauma *n* **1** = **shock**, anguish, disturbance, jolt, ordeal, pain, strain, suffering, torture, upheaval, upset **2** = **injury**, agony, damage, hurt, wound

traumatic *adj* **1** = **shocking**, disturbing, painful, scarring, upsetting **2** = **wounding**, agonizing, damaging, hurtful, injurious
Antonyms *adj* ≠ **shocking:** calming, relaxing, therapeutic ≠ **wounding:** healing, helpful, therapeutic, wholesome

travail *n Literary* **1** = **toil**, distress, drudgery, effort, exertion, grind, hardship, hard work, labour, pain, slavery, slog, strain, stress, suffering, sweat, tears **2** = **labour pains**, birth pangs, childbirth, labour ◆ *vb* **3** = **toil**, drudge, grind (*inf.*), labour, slave, slog, suffer, sweat

travel *vb* **1, 2** = **go**, cross, journey, make a journey, make one's way, move, proceed, progress, ramble, roam, rove, take a trip, tour, traverse, trek, voyage, walk, wander, wend **6** = **be transmitted**, carry, get through, move ◆ *n* **12** *usually plural* = **journey**, excursion, expedition, globetrotting, movement, passage, peregrination, ramble, tour, touring, trip, voyage, walk, wandering

traveller *n* **1** = **voyager**, excursionist, explorer, globetrotter, gypsy, hiker, holiday-maker, journeyer, migrant, nomad, passenger, tourist, tripper, wanderer, wayfarer **2** = **travelling salesman**, agent, commercial traveller, rep, representative, salesman, sales rep

traverse *vb* **1** = **cross**, bridge, cover, cut across, go across, go over, make one's way across, negotiate, pass over, ply, range, roam, span, travel over, wander **2** = **oppose**, balk, contravene, counter, counteract, deny, frustrate, go against, hinder, impede, obstruct, thwart **6** = **examine**, check, consider, eye, inspect, investigate, look into, look over, pore over, range over, review, scan, scrutinize, study

travesty *n* **1** = **mockery**, burlesque, caricature, distortion, lampoon, parody, perversion, send-up (*Brit. inf.*), sham, spoof (*inf.*), takeoff (*inf.*) ◆ *vb* **2** = **mock**, burlesque, caricature, deride, distort, lampoon, make a mockery of, make fun of, parody, pervert, ridicule, send up (*Brit. inf.*), sham, spoof (*inf.*), take off (*inf.*)

trawl (trɔːl) *n* **1** Also called: **trawl net.** a large net, usually in the shape of a sock or bag, drawn at deep levels behind special boats (trawlers). **2** Also called: **trawl line.** a long line to which numerous shorter hooked lines are attached, suspended between buoys. **3** the act of trawling. ◆ *vb* **4** to catch (fish) with a trawl net or trawl line. **5** (*intr*; foll. by *for*) to seek or gather (information, etc.) from a wide variety of sources. [C17: from MDu. *traghelen* to drag, from L *trāgula* dragnet; see TRAIL]

trawler ('trɔːlə) *n* **1** a vessel used for trawling. **2** a person who trawls.

tray (treɪ) *n* **1** a thin flat board or plate of metal, plastic, etc., usually with a raised edge, on which things can be carried. **2** a shallow receptacle for papers, etc., sometimes forming a drawer in a cabinet or box. [OE *trieg*]

treacherous ❶ ('tretʃərəs) *adj* **1** betraying or likely to betray faith or confidence. **2** unstable, unreliable, or dangerous.
▸ **'treacherously** *adv* ▸ **'treacherousness** *n*

treachery ❶ ('tretʃərɪ) *n, pl* **treacheries. 1** the act or an instance of wilful betrayal. **2** the disposition to betray. [C13: from OF *trecherie*, from *trechier* to cheat]

treacle ('triːkᵊl) *n* **1** Also called: **black treacle,** (US and Canad.) **molasses.** *Brit.* a dark viscous syrup obtained during the refining of sugar. **2** *Brit.* another name for **golden syrup. 3** anything sweet and cloying. [C14: from OF *triacle*, from L *thēriaca* antidote to poison]
▸ **'treacly** *adj*

tread ❶ (tred) *vb* **treads, treading, trod; trodden** *or* **trod. 1** to walk or trample in, on, over, or across (something). **2** (when *intr*, foll. by *on*) to crush or squash by or as if by treading. **3** (*intr*; sometimes foll. by *on*) to subdue or repress. **4** (*tr*) to do by walking or dancing: *to tread a measure.* **5** (*tr*) (of a male bird) to copulate with (a female bird). **6 tread lightly.** to proceed with delicacy or tact. **7 tread water.** to stay afloat in an upright position by moving the legs in a walking motion. ◆ *n* **8** a manner or style of walking, dancing, etc.: *a light tread.* **9** the act of treading. **10** the top surface of a step in a staircase. **11** the outer part of a tyre or wheel that makes contact with the road, esp. the grooved surface of a pneumatic tyre. **12** the part of a rail that wheels touch. **13** the part of a shoe that is generally in contact with the ground. [OE *tredan*]
▸ **'treader** *n*

treadle ('tredᵊl) *n* **1** a lever operated by the foot to drive a machine. ◆ *vb* **treadles, treadling, treadled. 2** to work (a machine) with a treadle. [OE *tredel*, from *trǣde* something firm, from *tredan* to tread]

treadmill ('tred,mɪl) *n* **1** Also called: **treadwheel.** (formerly) an apparatus turned by the weight of men or animals climbing steps on the periphery of a cylinder or wheel. **2** a dreary round or routine. **3** an exercise machine that consists of a continuous moving belt on which to walk or jog.

treas. *abbrev. for:* **1** treasurer. **2** treasury.

treason ❶ ('triːzᵊn) *n* **1** betrayal of one's sovereign or country, esp. by attempting to overthrow the government. **2** any treachery or betrayal. [C13: from OF *traïson*, from L *trāditiō* a handing over; see TRADITION]
▸ **'treasonable** *or* **'treasonous** *adj* ▸ **'treasonably** *adv*

treasure ❶ ('treʒə) *n* **1** wealth and riches, usually hoarded, esp. in the form of money, precious metals, or gems. **2** a thing or person that is highly prized or valued. ◆ *vb* **treasures, treasuring, treasured.** (*tr*) **3** to prize highly as valuable, rare, or costly. **4** to store up and save; hoard. [C12: from OF *tresor*, from L *thēsaurus* anything hoarded, from Gk *thēsauros*]

treasure hunt *n* a game in which players act upon successive clues to find a hidden prize.

treasurer ('treʒərə) *n* a person appointed to look after the funds of a society, company, city, or other governing body.
▸ **'treasurership** *n*

Treasurer ('treʒərə) *n* (in Australia) the minister of finance.

treasure-trove *n* **1** *Brit. Law.* valuable articles, such as coins, etc., found hidden and of unknown ownership. **2** any valuable discovery. [C16: from Anglo-F *tresor trové* treasure found, from OF *tresor* TREASURE + *trover* to find]

treasury ❶ ('treʒərɪ) *n, pl* **treasuries. 1** a storage place for treasure. **2** the revenues or funds of a government, private organization, or individual. **3** a place where funds are kept and disbursed. **4** a person or thing regarded as a valuable source of information. **5** a collection of highly valued poems, etc.; anthology. **6** Also: **treasure house.** a source of valuable items: *a treasury of information.* [C13: from OF *tresorie*, from *tresor* TREASURE]

Treasury ('treʒərɪ) *n* (in various countries) the government department in charge of finance.

Treasury Bench *n* (in Britain) the front bench to the right of the Speaker in the House of Commons, traditionally reserved for members of the Government.

treasury note *n* a note issued by a government treasury and generally receivable as legal tender for any debt.

treat ❶ (triːt) *n* **1** a celebration, entertainment, gift, or feast given for or to someone and paid for by another. **2** any delightful surprise or specially pleasant occasion. **3** the act of treating. ◆ *vb* **4** (*tr*) to deal with or regard in a certain manner: *she treats school as a joke.* **5** (*tr*) to apply treatment to. **6** (*tr*) to subject to a process or to the application of a substance. **7** (often foll. by *to*) to provide (someone) (with) as a treat. **8** (*intr*; usually foll. by *of*) to deal (with), as in writing or speaking. **9** (*intr*) to discuss settlement; negotiate. [C13: from OF *tretier*, from L *tractāre* to manage, from *trahere* to drag]
▸ **'treatable** *adj* ▸ **'treater** *n*

treatise ❶ ('triːtɪz) *n* a formal work on a subject, esp. one that deals systematically with its principles and conclusions. [C14: from Anglo-F *tretiz*, from OF *tretier* to TREAT]

treatment ❶ ('triːtmənt) *n* **1** the application of medicines, surgery, etc., to a patient. **2** the manner of handling a person or thing, as in a literary or artistic work. **3** the act, practice, or manner of treating. **4 the treatment.** *Sl.* the usual manner of dealing with a particular type of person (esp. in **give someone the (full) treatment**).

treaty ❶ ('triːtɪ) *n, pl* **treaties. 1a** a formal agreement between two or more states, such as an alliance or trade arrangement. **1b** the document in which such a contract is written. **2** any pact or agreement. **3** an agreement between two parties concerning the purchase of property at a price privately agreed between them. [C14: from OF *traité*, from Med. L *tractātus*, from L: discussion, from *tractāre* to manage; see TREAT]

treaty port *n History.* (in China, Japan, and Korea) a city, esp. a port, in which foreigners, esp. Westerners, were allowed by treaty to conduct trade.

treble ('trebᵊl) *adj* **1** threefold; triple. **2** of or denoting a soprano voice or part or a high-pitched instrument. ◆ *n* **3** treble the amount, size, etc. **4** a soprano voice or part or a high-pitched instrument. **5** the highest register of a musical instrument. **6** the high-frequency response of an audio amplifier, esp. in a record player or tape recorder. **7a** the narrow inner ring on a dartboard. **7b** a hit on this ring. ◆ *vb* **trebles, trebling, trebled. 8** to make or become three times as much. [C14: from OF, from L *triplus* threefold]
▸ **'trebly** *adv, adj*

treble chance *n* a method of betting in football pools in which the chances of winning are related to the number of draws and the number of home and away wins forecast by the competitor.

treble clef *n Music.* the clef that establishes G a fifth above middle C as being on the second line of the staff. Symbol: 𝄞

trebuchet ('trebjʊ,ʃet) *or* **trebucket** ('triː,bʌkɪt) *n* a large medieval siege engine consisting of a sling on a pivoted wooden arm set in motion by the fall of a weight. [C13: from OF, from *trebuchier* to stumble, from *tre-* TRANS- + *-buchier*, from *buc* trunk of the body, of Gmc origin]

trecento (treɪ'tʃentəʊ) *n* the 14th century, esp. with reference to Italian art and literature. [C19: shortened from It. *mille trecento* one thousand three hundred]
▸ **tre'centist** *n*

tree (triː) *n* **1** any large woody perennial plant with a distinct trunk giv-

THESAURUS

treacherous *adj* **1** = **disloyal**, deceitful, double-crossing (*inf.*), double-dealing, duplicitous, faithless, false, perfidious, recreant (*arch.*), traitorous, treasonable, unfaithful, unreliable, untrue, untrustworthy **2** = **dangerous**, deceptive, hazardous, icy, perilous, precarious, risky, slippery, slippy (*inf. or dialect*), tricky, unreliable, unsafe, unstable
Antonyms *adj* ≠ **disloyal**: dependable, faithful, loyal, reliable, true, trustworthy ≠ **dangerous**: reliable, safe

treachery *n* **1, 2** = **betrayal**, disloyalty, double-cross (*inf.*), double-dealing, duplicity, faithlessness, infidelity, perfidiousness, perfidy, stab in the back, treason
Antonyms *n* allegiance, dependability, faithfulness, fealty, fidelity, loyalty, reliability

tread *vb* **1** = **step**, hike, march, pace, plod, stamp, stride, tramp, trudge, walk **2** = **crush underfoot**, squash, trample **3** = **repress**, bear down, crush, oppress, quell, ride roughshod over, subdue, subjugate, suppress ◆ *n* **8** = **step**, footfall, footstep, gait, pace, stride, walk

treason *n* **1, 2** = **disloyalty**, disaffection, duplicity, lese-majesty, mutiny, perfidy, sedition, subversion, traitorousness, treachery
Antonyms *n* allegiance, faithfulness, fealty, fidelity, loyalty, patriotism

treasonable *adj* **1, 2** = **disloyal**, false, mutinous, perfidious, seditious, subversive, traitorous, treacherous, treasonous
Antonyms *adj* dependable, faithful, loyal, patriotic, reliable, trustworthy

treasure *n* **1** = **riches**, cash, fortune, funds, gold, jewels, money, valuables, wealth **2** *Informal* = **darling**, apple of one's eye, gem, jewel, nonpareil, paragon, pearl, precious, pride and joy, prize ◆ *vb* **3** = **prize**, adore, cherish, dote upon, esteem, hold dear, idolize, love, revere, value, venerate, worship **4** = **hoard**, accumulate, cache, collect, garner, husband, lay up, salt away, save, stash (away) (*inf.*), store up

treasury *n* **1** = **storehouse**, bank, cache, hoard, repository, store, vault **2** = **funds**, assets, capital, coffers, exchequer, finances, money, resources, revenues

treat *n* **1** = **entertainment**, banquet, celebration, feast, gift, party, refreshment **2** = **pleasure**, delight, enjoyment, fun, gratification, joy, satisfaction, surprise, thrill ◆ *vb* **4** = **behave towards**, act towards, consider, deal with, handle, look upon, manage, regard, use **5** = **take care of**, apply treatment to, attend to, care for, doctor, medicate, nurse **7** = **provide**, buy for, entertain, feast, foot *or* pay the bill, give, lay on, pay for, regale, stand (*inf.*), take out, wine and dine **8** *usually foll. by* **of** = **deal with**, be concerned with, contain, discourse upon, discuss, go into, touch upon **9** = **negotiate**, bargain, come to terms, confer, have talks, make terms, parley

treatise *n* = **paper**, disquisition, dissertation, essay, exposition, monograph, pamphlet, study, thesis, tract, work, writing

treatment *n* **1** = **care**, cure, healing, medication, medicine, remedy, surgery, therapy **2** = **handling**, action, behaviour, conduct, dealing, management, manipulation, reception, usage

treaty *n* **1a, 2** = **agreement**, alliance, bargain, bond, compact, concordat, contract, convention, covenant, entente, pact

ing rise to branches. Related adj: **arboreal.** **2** any plant that resembles this. **3** a wooden post, bar, etc. **4** See **family tree, shoetree, saddletree.** **5** *Chem.* a treelike crystal growth. **6** a branching diagrammatic representation of something. **7 at the top of the tree.** in the highest position of a profession, etc. **8 up a tree.** *US & Canad. inf.* in a difficult situation; trapped or stumped. ◆ *vb* **trees, treeing, treed.** (*tr*) **9** to drive or force up a tree. **10** to stretch on a shoetree. [OE *treo*]
▸ **'treeless** *adj* ▸ **'treelessness** *n* ▸ **'tree,like** *adj*

tree creeper *n* any of a family of small songbirds of the N hemisphere, having a slender downward-curving bill. They creep up trees to feed on insects.

tree diagram *n* a diagram in which relationships are represented by lines and nodes having other lines branching off from them.

tree fern *n* any of numerous large tropical ferns having a trunklike stem.

tree frog *n* any of various arboreal frogs of SE Asia, Australia, and America.

treehopper ('tri:ˌhɒpə) *n* any of a family of insects which live among trees and have a large hoodlike thoracic process curving backwards over the body.

tree kangaroo *n* any of several arboreal kangaroos of New Guinea and N Australia, having hind legs and forelegs of a similar length.

tree line *n* the zone, at high altitudes or high latitudes, beyond which no trees grow. Trees growing between the timber line and the tree line are typically stunted.

treen ('tri:ən) *adj* **1** made of wood; wooden. ◆ *n* **2** dishes and other utensils made of wood. [OE *trēowen*, from *trēow* tree]
▸ **'treen,ware** *n*

treenail *or* **trenail** ('tri:neɪl, 'trenᵊl) *n* a dowel used for pinning planks or timbers together.

tree of heaven *n* another name for **ailanthus.**

tree shrew *n* any of a family of small arboreal mammals of SE Asia having large eyes and resembling squirrels.

tree sparrow *n* **1** a small European weaverbird similar to the house sparrow but having a brown head. **2** a small North American finch.

tree surgery *n* the treatment of damaged trees by filling cavities, applying braces, etc.
▸ **tree surgeon** *n*

tree toad *n* a less common name for **tree frog.**

tree tomato *n* **1** an arborescent shrub of South America bearing red egg-shaped edible fruit. **2** the fruit of this plant. ◆ Also called: **tamarillo.**

tref (treɪf) *adj Judaism.* ritually unfit to be eaten. [Yiddish, from Heb. *terēphāh*, lit.: torn (i.e., animal meat torn by beasts), from *tāraf* to tear]

trefoil ('trefɔɪl) *n* **1** any of a genus of leguminous plants having leaves divided into three leaflets. **2** any of various related plants having similar leaves. **3** a flower or leaf having three lobes. **4** *Archit.* an ornament in the form of three arcs arranged in a circle. [C14: from Anglo-F *trifoil*, from L *trifolium* three-leaved herb]
▸ **'trefoiled** *adj*

trek ❶ (trek) *n* **1** a long and often difficult journey. **2** *S. African.* a journey or stage of a journey, esp. a migration by ox wagon. ◆ *vb* **treks, trekking, trekked.** **3** (*intr*) to make a trek. [C19: from Afrik., from MDu. *trekken* to travel]

trellis ('trelɪs) *n* **1** a structure of latticework, esp. one used to support climbing plants. ◆ *vb* (*tr*) **2** to interweave (strips of wood, etc.) to make a trellis. **3** to provide or support with a trellis. [C14: from OF *treliz* fabric of open texture, from LL *trilīcius* woven with three threads, from L TRI- + *līcium* thread]
▸ **'trellis,work** *n*

trematode ('tremәˌtәud, 'tri:-) *n* any of a class of parasitic flatworms, which includes the flukes. [C19: from NL *Trematoda*, from Gk *trēmatōdēs* full of holes, from *trēma* hole]

tremble ❶ ('trembᵊl) *vb* **trembles, trembling, trembled.** (*intr*) **1** to vibrate with short slight movements; quiver. **2** to shake involuntarily, as with cold or fear; shiver. **3** to experience fear or anxiety. ◆ *n* **4** the act or an instance of trembling. [C14: from OF *trembler*, from Med. L *tremulāre*, from L *tremulus* quivering, from *tremere* to quake]
▸ **'trembling** *adj* ▸ **'trembly** *adj*

trembler ('tremblə) *n* a device that vibrates to make or break an electrical circuit.

trembles ('trembᵊlz) *n* (*functioning as sing*) a disease of cattle and sheep characterized by trembling.

trembling poplar *n* another name for **aspen.**

tremendous ❶ (trɪ'mendəs) *adj* **1** vast; huge. **2** *Inf.* very exciting or unusual. **3** *Inf.* (intensifier): *a tremendous help.* **4** *Arch.* terrible or dreadful. [C17: from L *tremendus* terrible, lit.: that is to be trembled at, from *tremere* to quake]
▸ **tre'mendously** *adv* ▸ **tre'mendousness** *n*

tremolo ('treməˌləʊ) *n, pl* **tremolos.** *Music.* **1** (in playing the violin, cello, etc.) the rapid reiteration of a note or notes to produce a trembling effect. **2** (in singing) a fluctuation in pitch. **3** a device, as on an organ, that produces a tremolo effect. [C19: from It.: quavering, from Med. L *tremulāre* to TREMBLE]

tremor ❶ ('tremə) *n* **1** an involuntary shudder or vibration. **2** any trembling movement. **3** a vibrating or trembling effect, as of sound or light. **4** a minor earthquake. ◆ *vb* **5** (*intr*) to tremble. [C14: from L: a shaking, from *tremere* to tremble]
▸ **'tremorous** *adj*

tremulous ❶ ('tremjʊləs) *adj* **1** vibrating slightly; quavering; trembling. **2** showing or characterized by fear, anxiety, excitement, etc. [C17: from L *tremulus*, from *tremere* to shake]
▸ **'tremulously** *adv* ▸ **'tremulousness** *n*

trenail ('tri:neɪl, 'trenᵊl) *n* a variant spelling of **treenail.**

trench ❶ (trentʃ) *n* **1** a deep ditch. **2** a ditch dug as a fortification, having a parapet of earth. ◆ *vb* **3** to make a trench in (a place). **4** (*tr*) to fortify with a trench. **5** to slash or be slashed. **6** (*intr*; foll. by *on* or *upon*) to encroach or verge. [C14: from OF *trenche* something cut, from *trenchier* to cut, from L *truncāre* to cut off]

trenchant ❶ ('trentʃənt) *adj* **1** keen or incisive: *trenchant criticism.* **2** vigorous and effective: *a trenchant foreign policy.* **3** distinctly defined. **4** *Arch. or poetic.* sharp. [C14: from OF *trenchant* cutting, from *trenchier* to cut; see TRENCH]
▸ **'trenchancy** *n* ▸ **'trenchantly** *adv*

trench coat *n* a belted waterproof coat resembling a military officer's coat.

trencher ('trentʃə) *n* **1** (esp. formerly) a wooden board on which food was served or cut. **2** Also called: **trencher cap.** a mortarboard. [C14 *trenchour* knife, plate for carving on, from OF *trencheoir*, from *trenchier* to cut; see TRENCH]

trencherman ('trentʃəmən) *n, pl* **trenchermen.** a person who enjoys food; hearty eater.

trench fever *n* an acute infectious disease characterized by fever and muscular aches and pains and transmitted by lice.

trench foot *n* a form of frostbite affecting persons standing for long periods in cold water.

trench mortar *or* **gun** *n* a portable mortar used in trench warfare to shoot projectiles at a high trajectory over a short range.

trench warfare *n* a type of warfare in which opposing armies face each other in entrenched positions.

trend ❶ (trend) *n* **1** general tendency or direction. **2** fashion; mode. ◆ *vb* **3** (*intr*) to take a certain trend. [OE *trendan* to turn]

trendsetter ❶ ('trendˌsetə) *n* a person or thing that creates, or may create, a new fashion.
▸ **'trend,setting** *adj*

trendy ❶ ('trendɪ) *Brit. inf.* ◆ *adj* **trendier, trendiest.** **1** consciously fashionable. ◆ *n, pl* **trendies.** **2** a trendy person.
▸ **'trendily** *adv* ▸ **'trendiness** *n*

trente et quarante (*French* trɑ̃t e karɑ̃t) *n Cards.* another name for **rouge et noir.** [C17: F, lit.: thirty and forty; from the rule that forty is the maximum number that may be dealt and the winning colour is the one closest to thirty-one]

trepan (trɪ'pæn) *n* **1** *Surgery.* an instrument resembling a carpenter's

THESAURUS

trek *n* **1 = journey**, expedition, footslog, hike, long haul, march, odyssey, safari, slog, tramp ◆ *vb* **3 = journey**, footslog, hike, march, plod, range, roam, rove, slog, traipse (*inf.*), tramp, trudge, yomp

tremble *vb* **1, 2 = shake**, oscillate, quake, quake in one's boots, quiver, rock, shake in one's boots *or* shoes, shiver, shudder, teeter, totter, vibrate, wobble ◆ *n* **4 = shake**, oscillation, quake, quiver, shiver, shudder, tremor, vibration, wobble

tremendous *adj* **1 = huge**, awesome, colossal, enormous, formidable, gargantuan, gigantic, great, immense, mammoth, monstrous, prodigious, stellar (*inf.*), stupendous, terrific, titanic, towering, vast, whopping (*inf.*) **2 = excellent**, amazing, awesome (*sl.*), exceptional, extraordinary, fabulous (*inf.*), fantastic (*inf.*), great, incredible, marvellous, sensational (*inf.*), terrific (*inf.*), wonderful **4** *Archaic* **= dreadful**, appalling, awful, fearful, frightful, terrible
Antonyms *adj* ≠ **huge**: diminutive, little, minuscule, minute, small, tiny ≠ **excellent**: abysmal, appalling, average, awful, dreadful, mediocre, no great shakes (*inf.*), ordinary, rotten, run-of-the-mill, so-so, terrible

tremor *n* **1, 2 = shake**, agitation, quaking, quaver, quiver, quivering, shaking, shiver, tremble, trembling, vibration, wobble **4 = earthquake**, quake (*inf.*), shock

tremulous *adj* **1, 2 = trembling**, aflutter, afraid, agitated, agog, anxious, aquiver, excited, fearful, frightened, jittery (*inf.*), jumpy, nervous, quavering, quivering, quivery, scared, shaking, shivering, timid, vibrating, wavering

trench *n* **1 = ditch**, channel, cut, drain, earthwork, entrenchment, excavation, fosse, furrow, gutter, pit, trough, waterway

trenchant *adj* **1 = scathing**, acerbic, acid, acidulous, acute, astringent, biting, caustic, cutting, hurtful, incisive, keen, mordacious, mordant, penetrating, piquant, pointed, pungent, sarcastic, severe, sharp, tart, vitriolic **2 = effective**, driving, effectual, emphatic, energetic, forceful, potent, powerful, strong, vigorous **3 = clear**, clear-cut, crisp, distinct, distinctly defined, explicit, salient, unequivocal, well-defined
Antonyms *adj* ≠ **scathing**: appeasing, kind, mollifying, soothing ≠ **clear**: ill-defined, indistinct, nebulous, obscure, unclear, vague, woolly

trend *n* **1 = tendency**, bias, course, current, direction, drift, flow, inclination, leaning **2 = fashion**, craze, fad (*inf.*), look, mode, rage, style, thing, vogue ◆ *vb* **3 = tend**, bend, flow, head, incline, lean, run, stretch, swing, turn, veer

trendsetter *n* **= leader of fashion**, arbiter of taste, avant-gardist, pacemaker, pacesetter

trendy *adj Brit. informal* **1 = fashionable**, flash (*inf.*), in (*sl.*), in fashion, in vogue, latest, modish, now (*inf.*), stylish, up to the minute, voguish, with it (*inf.*) ◆ *n Brit. informal* **2 = poser** (*inf.*), pseud (*inf.*)

brace and bit formerly used to remove circular sections of bone from the skull. **2** a tool for cutting out circular blanks or for making grooves around a fixed centre. ◆ *vb* **trepans, trepanning, trepanned.** *(tr)* **3** to cut (a hole or groove) with a trepan. **4** *Surgery.* another word for **trephine.** [C14: from Med. L *trepanum* rotary saw, from Gk *trupanon* auger, from *trupan* to bore, from *trupa* a hole]
▸**trepanation** (ˌtrɛpəˈneɪʃən) *n*

trepang (trɪˈpæŋ) *n* any of various large sea cucumbers of tropical Oriental seas, the body walls of which are used as food by the Japanese and Chinese. [C18: from Malay *těripang*]

trephine (trɪˈfiːn) *n* **1** a surgical sawlike instrument for removing circular sections of bone esp. from the skull. ◆ *vb* **trephines, trephining, trephined. 2** *(tr)* to remove a circular section of bone from (esp. the skull). [C17: from F *tréphine,* from obs. E *trefine* TREPAN, allegedly from L *trēs fīnēs,* lit.: three ends]
▸**trephination** (ˌtrɛfɪˈneɪʃən) *n*

trepidation Ⓣ (ˌtrɛpɪˈdeɪʃən) *n* **1** a state of fear or anxiety. **2** a condition of quaking or palpitation, esp. one caused by anxiety. [C17: from L *trepidātiō,* from *trepidāre* to be in a state of alarm]

trespass Ⓣ (ˈtrɛspəs) *vb (intr)* **1** (often foll. by *on* or *upon*) to go or intrude (on the property, privacy, or preserves of another) with no right or permission. **2** *Law.* to commit trespass. **3** *Arch.* (often foll. by *against*) to sin or transgress. ◆ *n* **4** *Law.* **4a** any unlawful act committed with force, which causes injury to another person, his property or his rights. **4b** a wrongful entry upon another's land. **5** an intrusion on another's privacy or preserves. **6** a sin or offence. [C13: from OF *trespas* a passage, from *trespasser* to pass through, ult. from L *passus* PACE[1]]
▸ˈ**trespasser** *n*

tress Ⓣ (trɛs) *n* **1** *(often pl)* a lock of hair, esp. a long lock of woman's hair. **2** a plait or braid of hair. ◆ *vb (tr)* **3** to arrange in tresses. [C13: from OF *trece,* from ?]
▸ˈ**tressy** *adj*

trestle (ˈtrɛsᵊl) *n* **1** a framework in the form of a horizontal member supported at each end by a pair of splayed legs, used to carry scaffold boards, a table top, etc. **2a** a framework of timber, metal, or reinforced concrete that is used to support a bridge or ropeway. **2b** a bridge constructed of such frameworks. [C14: from OF *trestel,* ult. from L *trānstrum* transom]

trestlework (ˈtrɛsᵊlˌwɜːk) *n* an arrangement of trestles, esp. one that supports a bridge.

trevally (trɪˈvælɪ) *n, pl* **trevallies.** *Austral. & NZ.* any of various food and game fishes of the genus *Caranx.* [C19: prob. alteration of *cavally,* from *cavalla* species of tropical fish, from Sp. *caballa* horse]

trews (truːz) *pl n Chiefly Brit.* close-fitting trousers of tartan cloth. [C16: from Scot. Gaelic *triubhas,* from OF *trebus*]

trey (treɪ) *n* any card or dice throw with three spots. [C14: from OF *treis* three, from L *trēs*]

tri- *prefix* **1** three or thrice: *triaxial; trigon; trisect.* **2** occurring every three: *trimonthly.* [from L *trēs,* Gk *treis*]

triable (ˈtraɪəbᵊl) *adj* **1** subject to trial in a court of law. **2** *Rare.* able to be tested.

triacid (traɪˈæsɪd) *adj* capable of reacting with three molecules of a monobasic acid.

triad Ⓣ (ˈtraɪæd) *n* **1** a group of three; trio. **2** *Chem.* an atom, element, group, or ion that has a valency of three. **3** *Music.* a three-note chord consisting of a note and the third and fifth above it. **4** an aphoristic literary form used in medieval Welsh and Irish literature. [C16: from LL *trias,* from Gk]
▸**triˈadic** *adj* ▸ˈ**triadism** *n*

Triad (ˈtraɪæd) *n* any of several Chinese secret societies, esp. one involved in criminal activities, such as drug trafficking.

triage (ˈtraɪɪdʒ) *n* **1** the action of sorting casualties, patients, etc. according to priority. **2** the allocating of limited resources on a basis of expediency rather than moral principles. [C18: from F; see TRY, -AGE]

trial Ⓣ (ˈtraɪəl, traɪl) *n* **1a** the act or an instance of trying or proving; test or experiment. **1b** *(as modifier): a trial run.* **2** *Law.* **2a** the judicial examination and determination of the issues in a civil or criminal cause by a competent tribunal. **2b** the determination of an accused person's guilt or innocence after hearing evidence and the judicial examination of the issues involved. **2c** *(as modifier): trial proceedings.* **3** an effort or attempt to do something. **4** trouble or grief. **5** an annoying or frustrating person or thing. **6** *(often pl)* a competition for individuals: *sheepdog trials.* **7** a motorcycling competition in which the skills of the riders are tested over rough ground. **8 on trial. 8a** undergoing trial, esp. before a court of law. **8b** being tested, as before a commitment to purchase. ◆ *vb* **trials, trialling, trialled. 9** to test or make experimental use of (something): *the idea has been trialled in several schools.* [C16: from Anglo-F, from *trier* to TRY]
▸ˈ**trialling** *n*

trial and error *n* a method of discovery, solving problems, etc., based on practical experiment and experience rather than on theory: *he learned to cook by trial and error.*

trial balance *n Book-keeping.* a statement of all the debit and credit balances in the ledger of a double-entry system, drawn up to test their equality.

triallist *or* **trialist** (ˈtraɪəlɪst, ˈtraɪlɪst) *n* **1** a person who takes part in a competition, esp. a motorcycle trial. **2** *Sport.* a person who takes part in a preliminary match or heat held to determine selection for an event, a team, etc.

triangle (ˈtraɪˌæŋgᵊl) *n* **1** *Geom.* a three-sided polygon that can be classified by angle, as in an acute triangle, or by side, as in an equilateral triangle. **2** any object shaped like a triangle. **3** any situation involving three parties or points of view. **4** *Music.* a percussion instrument consisting of a sonorous metal bar bent into a triangular shape, beaten with a metal stick. **5** a group of three. [C14: from L *triangulum* (n), from *triangulus* (adj), from TRI- + *angulus* corner]
▸**triangular** (traɪˈæŋgjʊlə) *adj*

triangle of forces *n Physics.* a triangle whose sides represent the magnitudes and directions of three forces in equilibrium.

triangulate *vb* (traɪˈæŋgjʊˌleɪt), **triangulates, triangulating, triangulated.** *(tr)* **1a** to survey by the method of triangulation. **1b** to calculate trigonometrically. **2** to divide into triangles. **3** to make triangular. ◆ *adj* (traɪˈæŋgjʊlɪt, -ˌleɪt). **4** marked with or composed of triangles.
▸**triˈangulately** *adv*

triangulation (traɪˌæŋgjʊˈleɪʃən) *n* a method of surveying in which an area is divided into triangles, one side (the base line) and all angles of which are measured and the lengths of the other lines calculated trigonometrically.

triangulation station *n* a point on a hilltop, etc., used for triangulation by a surveyor.

Triassic (traɪˈæsɪk) *adj* **1** of or formed in the first period of the Mesozoic era. ◆ *n* **2 the.** Also called: **Trias.** the Triassic period or rock system. [C19: from L *trias* triad, from the three subdivisions]

triathlon (traɪˈæθlɒn) *n* an athletic contest in which each athlete competes in three different events, swimming, cycling, and running. [C20: from TRI- + Gk *athlon* contest]
▸ˌ**triˈathlete** *n*

triatomic (ˌtraɪəˈtɒmɪk) *adj Chem.* having three atoms in the molecule.

tribade (ˈtrɪbɑːd) *n* a lesbian who practises tribadism. [C17: from L *tribas,* from Gk *tribein* to rub]

tribadism (ˈtrɪbədɪzəm) *n* a lesbian practice in which one partner lies on top of the other and simulates the male role in heterosexual intercourse.

tribalism (ˈtraɪbəˌlɪzəm) *n* **1** the state of existing as a tribe. **2** the customs and beliefs of a tribal society. **3** loyalty to a tribe.
▸ˈ**tribalist** *n, adj* ▸ˌ**tribalˈistic** *adj*

tribasic (traɪˈbeɪsɪk) *adj* **1** (of an acid) containing three replaceable hydrogen atoms in the molecule. **2** (of a molecule) containing three monovalent basic atoms or groups.

tribe Ⓣ (traɪb) *n* **1** a social division of a people, esp. of a preliterate people, defined in terms of common descent, territory, culture, etc. **2** an ethnic or ancestral division of ancient cultures, esp.: **2a** one of the political divisions of the Roman people. **2b** any of the 12 divisions of ancient Israel, each of which was believed to be descended from one of the 12 patriarchs. **3** *Inf.* **3a** a large number of persons, animals, etc. **3b** a specific class or group of persons. **3c** a family, esp. a large one. **4** *Biol.* a taxonomic group that is a subdivision of a subfamily. [C13: from L *tribus*]
▸ˈ**tribal** *adj*

tribesman (ˈtraɪbzmən) *n, pl* **tribesmen.** a member of a tribe.

tribo- *combining form.* indicating friction: *triboelectricity.* [from Gk *tribein* to rub]

triboelectricity (ˌtraɪbəʊɪlɛkˈtrɪsɪtɪ, -ˌiːlɛk-) *n* electricity generated by friction.

THESAURUS

trepidation *n* **1, 2** *Formal* = **anxiety**, agitation, alarm, apprehension, blue funk *(inf.)*, butterflies *(inf.)*, cold feet *(inf.)*, cold sweat *(inf.)*, consternation, dismay, disquiet, disturbance, dread, emotion, excitement, fear, fright, jitters *(inf.)*, nervousness, palpitation, perturbation, quivering, shaking, the heebie-jeebies *(sl.)*, trembling, tremor, uneasiness, worry
Antonyms *n* aplomb, calm, composure, confidence, coolness, equanimity, self-assurance

trespass *vb* **1** = **intrude**, encroach, infringe, invade, obtrude, poach **3** *Archaic* = **sin**, offend, transgress, violate, wrong ◆ *n* **5** = **intrusion**, encroachment, infringement, invasion, poaching, unlawful entry, wrongful entry **6** *Old-fashioned* = **sin**, breach, crime, delinquency, error, evil-doing, fault, infraction, iniquity, injury, misbehaviour, misconduct, misdeed, misdemeanour, offence, transgression, wrongdoing

trespasser *n* **5** = **intruder**, infringer, interloper, invader, poacher, unwelcome visitor **6** *Archaic* = **sinner**, criminal, delinquent, evildoer, malefactor, offender, transgressor, wrongdoer

tress *n* **1, 2** = **hair**, braid, curl, lock, pigtail, plait, ringlet

triad *n* **1** = **threesome**, trilogy, trine, trinity, trio, triple, triplet, triptych, triumvirate, triune

trial *n* **1a** = **test**, assay, audition, check, dry run *(inf.)*, examination, experience, experiment, probation, proof, testing, test-run ◆ *modifier* **1b** = **experimental**, exploratory, pilot, probationary, provisional, testing ◆ *n* **2a** *Law* = **hearing**, contest, industrial tribunal, judicial examination, litigation, tribunal **3** = **attempt**, crack *(inf.)*, effort, endeavour, go *(inf.)*, shot *(inf.)*, stab *(inf.)*, try, venture, whack *(inf.)* **4** = **hardship**, adversity, affliction, burden, cross to bear, distress, grief, hard times, load, misery, ordeal, pain, suffering, tribulation, trouble, unhappiness, vexation, woe, wretchedness **5** = **nuisance**, bane, bother, drag *(inf.)*, hassle *(inf.)*, irritation, pain in the arse *(taboo sl.)*, pain in the neck *(inf.)*, pest, plague *(inf.)*, thorn in one's flesh *or* side, vexation

tribe *n* **1** = **race**, blood, caste, clan, class, division, dynasty, ethnic group, family, gens, house, people, seed *(chiefly Biblical)*, sept, stock

tribology (traɪˈbɒlədʒɪ) *n* the study of friction, lubrication, and wear between moving surfaces.

triboluminescence (ˌtraɪbəʊˌluːmɪˈnesəns) *n* luminescence produced by friction, such as the emission of light when certain crystals are crushed.
▸ **ˌtriboˌlumiˈnescent** *adj*

tribrach (ˈtraɪbræk, ˈtrɪb-) *n* a metrical foot of three short syllables. [C16: from L *tribrachys,* from Gk, from TRI- + *brakhus* short]

tribromoethanol (traɪˌbrəʊməʊˈɛθəˌnɒl) *n* a soluble white crystalline compound with a slight aromatic odour, used as a general anaesthetic.

tribulation ❶ (ˌtrɪbjʊˈleɪʃən) *n* **1** a cause of distress. **2** a state of suffering or distress. [C13: from OF, from Church L *trībulātiō,* from L *trībulāre* to afflict, from *trībulum* a threshing board, from *terere* to rub]

tribunal ❶ (traɪˈbjuːnᵊl, trɪ-) *n* **1** a court of justice. **2** (in England) a special court, convened by the government to inquire into a specific matter. **3** a raised platform containing the seat of a judge. [C16: from L *tribūnus* TRIBUNE[1]]

tribune[1] (ˈtrɪbjuːn) *n* **1** (in ancient Rome) **1a** an officer elected by the plebs to protect their interests. **1b** a senior military officer. **2** a person who upholds public rights. [C14: from L *tribunus,* prob. from *tribus* tribe]
▸ **tribunate** (ˈtrɪbjunɪt) *or* **ˈtribuneship** *n*

tribune[2] (ˈtrɪbjuːn) *n* **1a** the apse of a Christian basilica that contains the bishop's throne. **1b** the throne itself. **2** a gallery or raised area in a church. **3** *Rare.* a raised platform; dais. [C17: via F from It. *tribuna,* from Med. L *tribūna,* var. of L *tribūnal* TRIBUNAL]

tributary (ˈtrɪbjutərɪ) *n, pl* **tributaries. 1** a stream, river, or glacier that feeds another larger one. **2** a person, nation, or people that pays tribute. ◆ *adj* **3** (of a stream, etc.) feeding a larger stream. **4** given or owed as a tribute. **5** paying tribute.
▸ **ˈtributarily** *adv*

tribute ❶ (ˈtrɪbjuːt) *n* **1** a gift or statement made in acknowledgment, gratitude, or admiration. **2** a payment by one ruler or state to another, usually as an acknowledgment of submission. **3** the obligation to pay tribute. [C14: from L *tribūtum,* from *tribuere* to grant (orig.: to distribute among the tribes), from *tribus* tribe]

trice ❶ (traɪs) *n* a moment; instant (esp. in **in a trice**). [C15 (in *at* or *in a trice,* in the sense: at one tug): apparent substantive use of *trice* to haul up, from MDu. *trīse* pulley]

tricentenary (ˌtraɪsɛnˈtiːnərɪ) *or* **tricentennial** (ˌtraɪsɛnˈtɛnɪəl) *adj* **1** of a period of 300 years. **2** of a 300th anniversary. ◆ *n, pl* **tricentenaries** *or* **tricentennials. 3** an anniversary of 300 years.

triceps (ˈtraɪsɛps) *n, pl* **tricepses** (-sɛpsɪz) *or* **triceps.** any muscle having three heads, esp. the one that extends the forearm. [C16: from L, from TRI- + *caput* head]

trichiasis (trɪˈkaɪəsɪs) *n Pathol.* an abnormal position of the eyelashes that causes irritation when they rub against the eyeball. [C17: via LL from Gk *trikhiasis,* from *thrix* a hair]

trichina (trɪˈkaɪnə) *n, pl* **trichinae** (-niː). a parasitic nematode worm occurring in the intestines of pigs, rats, and man and producing larvae that form cysts in skeletal muscle. [C19: from NL, from Gk *trikhinos* relating to hair, from *thrix* a hair]
▸ **trichinous** (ˈtrɪkɪnəs) *adj*

trichinosis (ˌtrɪkɪˈnəʊsɪs) *n* a disease characterized by nausea, fever, diarrhoea, and swelling of the muscles, caused by ingestion of pork infected with trichina larvae. [C19: from NL TRICHINA]

trichloride (traɪˈklɔːraɪd) *n* any compound that contains three chlorine atoms per molecule.

tricho- *or before a vowel* **trich-** *combining form.* indicating hair or a part resembling hair: *trichocyst.* [from Gk *thrix* (genitive *trikhos*) hair]

trichology (trɪˈkɒlədʒɪ) *n* the branch of medicine concerned with the hair and its diseases.
▸ **triˈchologist** *n*

trichomoniasis (ˌtrɪkəʊməˈnaɪəsɪs) *n* inflammation of the vagina caused by infection with parasitic protozoa. [C19: NL]

trichopteran (traɪˈkɒptərən) *n* **1** any insect of the order *Trichoptera,* which comprises the caddis flies. ◆ *adj* **2** Also: **trichopterous** (trɪˈkɒptərəs). of or belonging to the order *Trichoptera.* [C19: from NL *Trichoptera,* lit.: having hairy wings, from Gk *thrix* a hair + *pteron* wing]

trichosis (trɪˈkəʊsɪs) *n* any abnormal condition or disease of the hair. [C19: via NL from Gk *trikhōsis* growth of hair]

trichotomy (traɪˈkɒtəmɪ) *n, pl* **trichotomies. 1** division into three categories. **2** *Theol.* the division of man into body, spirit, and soul. [C17: prob. from NL *trichotomia,* from Gk *trikhotomein* to divide into three]
▸ **trichotomic** (ˌtrɪkəˈtɒmɪk) *or* **triˈchotomous** *adj*

trichroism (ˈtraɪkrəʊˌɪzəm) *n* a property of biaxial crystals as a result of which they show a difference in colour when viewed along three different axes. [C19: from Gk *trikhroos* three-coloured, from TRI- + *khrōma* colour]

trichromatic (ˌtraɪkrəʊˈmætɪk) *or* **trichromic** (traɪˈkrəʊmɪk) *adj* **1** involving the combination of three primary colours. **2** of or having normal colour vision. **3** having or involving three colours.
▸ **triˈchromaˌtism** *n*

trick ❶ (trɪk) *n* **1** a deceitful or cunning action or plan. **2a** a mischievous, malicious, or humorous action or plan; joke. **2b** (*as modifier*): *a trick spider.* **3** an illusory or magical feat. **4** a simple feat learned by an animal or person. **5** an adroit or ingenious device; knack: *a trick of the trade.* **6** a habit or mannerism. **7** a turn of duty. **8** *Cards.* a batch of cards containing one from each player, usually played in turn and won by the player or side that plays the card with the highest value. **9 can't take a trick.** *Austral. sl.* to be consistently unsuccessful or unlucky. **10 do the trick.** *Inf.* to produce the desired result. **11 how's tricks?** *Sl.* how are you? **12 turn a trick.** *Sl.* (of a prostitute) to gain a customer. ◆ *vb* **13** (*tr*) to defraud, deceive, or cheat (someone). ◆ See also **trick out.** [C15: from OF *trique,* from *trikier* to deceive, ult. from L *trīcārī* to play tricks]

trick cyclist *n* **1** a cyclist who performs tricks, such as in a circus. **2** a slang term for **psychiatrist.**

trickery ❶ (ˈtrɪkərɪ) *n, pl* **trickeries.** the practice or an instance of using tricks.

trickle ❶ (ˈtrɪkᵊl) *vb* **trickles, trickling, trickled. 1** to run or cause to run in thin or slow streams. **2** (*intr*) to move gradually: *the crowd trickled away.* ◆ *n* **3** a thin, irregular, or slow flow of something. **4** the act of trickling. [C14: ? imit.]
▸ **ˈtrickling** *adj*

trickle charger *n* a small mains-operated battery charger, esp. one used by car owners.

trickle-down *adj* of or concerning the theory that granting concessions such as tax cuts to the rich will benefit all levels of society by stimulating the economy.

trick or treat *sentence substitute. Chiefly US & Canad.* a customary cry used by children at Halloween when they call at houses in disguise, indicating that they want a present of sweets, apples, or money and, if refused, will play a trick on the householder.

trick out ❶ *or* **up** *vb* (*tr, adv*) to dress up; deck out: *tricked out in frilly dresses.*

trickster ❶ (ˈtrɪkstə) *n* a person who deceives or plays tricks.

tricksy (ˈtrɪksɪ) *adj* **tricksier, tricksiest. 1** playing tricks habitually; mischievous. **2** crafty or difficult to deal with.
▸ **ˈtricksiness** *n*

tricky ❶ (ˈtrɪkɪ) *adj* **trickier, trickiest. 1** involving snags or difficulties. **2** needing careful handling. **3** sly; wily: *a tricky dealer.*
▸ **ˈtrickily** *adv* ▸ **ˈtrickiness** *n*

THESAURUS

tribulation *n* **1, 2 = trouble,** adversity, affliction, bad luck, blow, bummer (*sl.*), burden, care, cross to bear, curse, distress, grief, hardship, hassle (*inf.*), heartache, ill fortune, misery, misfortune, ordeal, pain, reverse, sorrow, suffering, trial, unhappiness, vexation, woe, worry, wretchedness
Antonyms *n* blessing, bliss, ease, good fortune, happiness, joy, pleasure, rest

tribunal *n* **1 = hearing,** bar, bench, court, industrial tribunal, judgment seat, judicial examination, trial

tribute *n* **1 = accolade,** acknowledgment, applause, commendation, compliment, encomium, esteem, eulogy, gift, gratitude, honour, laudation, panegyric, praise, recognition, respect, testimonial **2 = tax,** charge, contribution, customs, duty, excise, homage, impost, offering, payment, ransom, subsidy, toll
Antonyms *n* ≠ **accolade:** blame, complaint, condemnation, criticism, disapproval, reproach, reproof

trice *n As in* **in a trice = moment,** bat of an eye (*inf.*), flash, instant, jiffy (*inf.*), minute, second, shake (*inf.*), split second, tick (*Brit. inf.*), twinkling, twinkling of an eye, two shakes of a lamb's tail (*inf.*)

trick *n* **1 = deception,** artifice, canard, con (*sl.*), deceit, device, dodge, feint, fraud, gimmick, hoax, imposition, imposture, manoeuvre, ploy, ruse, scam (*sl.*), sting (*inf.*), stratagem, subterfuge, swindle, trap, wile **2a = joke,** antic, cantrip (*Scot.*), caper, frolic, gag, gambol, jape, leg-pull (*Brit. inf.*), practical joke, prank, put-on (*sl.*), stunt **3 = sleight of hand,** device, feat, juggle, legerdemain **5 = secret,** art, command, craft, device, expertise, gift, hang (*inf.*), knack, know-how (*inf.*), skill, technique **6 = mannerism,** characteristic, crotchet, foible, habit, idiosyncrasy, peculiarity, practice, quirk, trait **10 do the trick** *Informal* **= work,** be effective *or* effectual, have effect, produce the desired result ◆ *vb* **13 = deceive,** bamboozle (*inf.*), cheat, con, defraud, delude, dupe, fool, gull (*arch.*), have (someone) on, hoax, hoodwink, impose upon, kid (*inf.*), mislead, pull a fast one on (*inf.*), pull the wool over (someone's) eyes, put one over on (someone) (*inf.*), stiff (*sl.*), sting (*inf.*), swindle, take in (*inf.*), trap

trickery *n* **= deception,** cheating, chicanery, con (*inf.*), deceit, dishonesty, double-dealing, fraud, funny business, guile, hanky-panky (*inf.*), hoax, hokum (*sl., chiefly US & Canad.*), imposture, jiggery-pokery (*inf., chiefly Brit.*), monkey business (*inf.*), pretence, skulduggery (*inf.*), swindling
Antonyms *n* artlessness, candour, directness, frankness, honesty, openness, straightforwardness, uprightness

trickle *vb* **1 = dribble,** crawl, creep, drip, drop, exude, ooze, percolate, run, seep, stream ◆ *n* **3 = dribble,** drip, seepage

trick out *vb* **= dress up,** adorn, array, attire, bedeck, deck out, doll up (*sl.*), do up (*inf.*), get up (*inf.*), ornament, prank, prink

trickster *n* **= deceiver,** cheat, chiseller (*inf.*), con man (*inf.*), fraud, fraudster, hoaxer, hustler (*US inf.*), impostor, joker, practical joker, pretender, swindler

tricky *adj* **1, 2 = difficult,** complicated, delicate, knotty, problematic, risky, sticky (*inf.*), thorny, ticklish, touch-and-go **3 = crafty,** artful, cunning, deceitful, deceptive, devious, foxy, scheming, slippery, sly, subtle, wily
Antonyms *adj* ≠ **difficult:** clear, easy, obvious, simple, straightforward, uncomplicated ≠ **crafty:** above board, artless, direct, genuine, honest, ingenuous, open, sincere, truthful

triclinic (traɪˈklɪnɪk) *adj* of the crystal system characterized by three unequal axes, no pair of which are perpendicular.
triclinium (traɪˈklɪnɪəm) *n, pl* **triclinia** (-ɪə). (in ancient Rome) **1** an arrangement of three couches around a table for reclining upon while dining. **2** a dining room. [C17: from L, from Gk *triklinion,* from TRI- + *klinē* a couch]
tricolour *or US* **tricolor** (ˈtrɪkələ, ˈtraɪˌkʌlə) *adj also* **tricoloured** *or US* **tricolored** (ˈtraɪˌkʌləd). **1** having or involving three colours. ◆ *n* **2** (*often cap.*) the French flag, having three stripes in blue, white, and red. **3** any flag, badge, etc., with three colours.
tricorn (ˈtraɪˌkɔːn) *n also* **tricorne. 1** a cocked hat with the brim turned up on three sides. ◆ *adj also* **tricornered. 2** having three horns or corners. [C18: from L *tricornis,* from TRI- + *cornu* horn]
tricot (ˈtrɪkəʊ, ˈtriː-) *n* **1** a thin rayon or nylon fabric knitted or resembling knitting, used for dresses, etc. **2** a type of ribbed dress fabric. [C19: from F, from *tricoter* to knit, from ?]
tricuspid (traɪˈkʌspɪd) *Anat.* ◆ *adj also* **tricuspidal. 1** having three points, cusps, or segments: *a tricuspid tooth; a tricuspid valve.* ◆ *n* **2** a tooth having three cusps.
tricycle (ˈtraɪsɪkᵊl) *n* a three-wheeled cycle, esp. one driven by pedals.
▸ **ˈtricyclist** *n*
trident (ˈtraɪdᵊnt) *n* a three-pronged spear. [C16: from L *tridēns* three-pronged, from TRI- + *dēns* tooth]
Trident (ˈtraɪdᵊnt) *n* a type of US submarine-launched ballistic missile with independently targetable warheads.
tridentate (traɪˈdenteɪt) *or* **tridental** *adj* having three prongs, teeth, or points.
Tridentine (traɪˈdentaɪn) *adj* **1a** *History.* of the Council of Trent in the 16th century. **1b** in accord with Tridentine doctrine: *Tridentine mass.* ◆ *n* **2** an orthodox Roman Catholic. [C16: from Med. L *Tridentīnus,* from *Tridentum* Trent]
tried (traɪd) *vb* the past tense and past participle of **try**.
triella (traɪˈɛlə) *n* a cumulative bet on horses in three specified races.
triennial (traɪˈɛnɪəl) *adj* **1** relating to, lasting for, or occurring every three years. ◆ *n* **2** a third anniversary. **3** a triennial period, thing, or occurrence. [C17: from L TRIENNIUM]
▸ **triˈennially** *adv*
triennium (traɪˈɛnɪəm) *n, pl* **trienniums** *or* **triennia** (-nɪə). a period or cycle of three years. [C19: from L, from TRI- + *annus* a year]
trier (ˈtraɪə) *n* a person or thing that tries.
trifacial (traɪˈfeɪʃəl) *adj* another word for **trigeminal.**
trifecta (traɪˈfɛktə) *n Austral.* a form of betting in which punters select first-, second-, and third-place winners in the correct order.
trifid (ˈtraɪfɪd) *adj* divided or split into three parts or lobes. [C18: from L *trifidus,* from TRI- + *findere* to split]
trifle ❶ (ˈtraɪfᵊl) *n* **1** a thing of little or no value or significance. **2** a small amount; bit: *a trifle more enthusiasm.* **3** *Brit.* a cold dessert made with sponge cake spread with jam or fruit, soaked in sherry, covered with custard and cream. ◆ *vb* **trifles, trifling, trifled. 4** (*intr;* usually foll. by *with*) to deal (with) as if worthless; dally: *to trifle with a person's affections.* **5** to waste (time) frivolously. [C13: from OF *trufle* mockery, from *trufler* to cheat]
▸ **ˈtrifler** *n*
trifling ❶ (ˈtraɪflɪŋ) *adj* **1** insignificant or petty. **2** frivolous or idle.
▸ **ˈtriflingly** *adv*
trifocal *adj* (traɪˈfəʊkᵊl). **1** having three focuses. **2** having three focal lengths. ◆ *n* (traɪˈfəʊkᵊl, ˈtraɪˌfəʊkᵊl). **3** (*pl*) glasses that have trifocal lenses.
triforium (traɪˈfɔːrɪəm) *n, pl* **triforia** (-rɪə). an arcade above the arches of the nave, choir, or transept of a church. [C18: from Anglo-L, apparently from L TRI- + *foris* a doorway; from the fact that each bay had three openings]
trifurcate (ˈtraɪfɜːkɪt, -ˌkeɪt) *or* **trifurcated** *adj* having three branches or forks. [C19: from L *trifurcus,* from TRI- + *furca* a fork]
trig (trɪg) *Arch. or dialect.* ◆ *adj* **1** neat or spruce. ◆ *vb* **trigs, trigging, trigged. 2** to make or become trim or spruce. [C12 (orig.: trusty): from ON]
▸ **ˈtrigly** *adv* ▸ **ˈtrigness** *n*
trig. *abbrev. for:* **1** trigonometrical. **2** trigonometry.
trigeminal (traɪˈdʒɛmɪnᵊl) *adj Anat.* of or relating to the trigeminal nerve. [C19: from L *trigeminus* triplet, from TRI- + *geminus* twin]
trigeminal nerve *n* either one of the fifth pair of cranial nerves, which supply the muscles of the mandible and maxilla. Their ophthalmic branches supply the area around the orbit of the eye, the nasal cavity, and the forehead.
trigeminal neuralgia *n Pathol.* another name for **tic douloureux.**
trigger ❶ (ˈtrɪgə) *n* **1** a small lever that activates the firing mechanism of a firearm. **2** a device that releases a spring-loaded mechanism. **3** any event that sets a course of action in motion. ◆ *vb* (*tr*) **4** (usually foll. by *off*) to give rise (to); set off. **5** to fire or set in motion by or as by pulling a trigger. [C17 *tricker,* from Du. *trekker,* from *trekken* to pull]
triggerfish (ˈtrɪgəˌfɪʃ) *n, pl* **triggerfish** *or* **triggerfishes.** any of a family of fishes of tropical and temperate seas. They have erectile spines in the first dorsal fin.
trigger-happy *adj Inf.* **1** tending to resort to the use of firearms or violence irresponsibly. **2** tending to act rashly.
triglyceride (traɪˈglɪsəˌraɪd) *n* any ester of glycerol and one or more carboxylic acids, in which each glycerol molecule has combined with three carboxylic acid molecules.
triglyph (ˈtraɪˌglɪf) *n Archit.* a stone block in a Doric frieze, having three vertical channels. [C16: via L from Gk *trigluphos,* from TRI- + *gluphē* carving]
trigonal (ˈtrɪgənᵊl) *adj* **1** triangular. **2** of the crystal system characterized by three equal axes that are equally inclined and not perpendicular to each other. [C16: via L from Gk *trigōnon* triangle]
trigonometric function *n* any of a group of functions of an angle expressed as a ratio of two of the sides of a right-angled triangle containing the angle. The group includes sine, cosine, tangent, etc.
trigonometry (ˌtrɪgəˈnɒmɪtrɪ) *n* the branch of mathematics concerned with the properties of trigonometric functions and their application to the determination of the angles and sides of triangles: used in surveying, navigation, etc. [C17: from NL *trigōnometria,* from Gk *trigōnon* triangle]
▸ **trigonometric** (ˌtrɪgənəˈmetrɪk) *or* **ˌtrigonoˈmetrical** *adj*
trig point *n* an informal name for **triangulation station.** [from *trigonometric*]
trigraph (ˈtraɪˌgrɑːf) *n* a combination of three letters used to represent a single speech sound or phoneme, such as *eau* in French *beau.*
trihedral (traɪˈhiːdrəl) *adj* **1** having three plane faces. ◆ *n* **2** a figure formed by the intersection of three lines in different planes.
trihedron (traɪˈhiːdrən) *n, pl* **trihedrons** *or* **trihedra** (-drə). a figure determined by the intersection of three planes.
trike (traɪk) *n* short for **tricycle.**
trilateral (traɪˈlætərəl) *adj* having three sides.
trilby (ˈtrɪlbɪ) *n, pl* **trilbies.** a man's soft felt hat with an indented crown. [C19: after *Trilby,* the heroine of a dramatized novel (1893) of that title by George Du Maurier]
trilingual (traɪˈlɪŋgwəl) *adj* **1** able to speak three languages fluently. **2** expressed or written in three languages.
▸ **triˈlingualism** *n*
trilithon (traɪˈlɪθɒn) *or* **trilith** (ˈtraɪlɪθ) *n* a structure consisting of two upright stones with a third placed across the top, as at Stonehenge. [C18: from Gk]
▸ **trilithic** (traɪˈlɪθɪk) *adj*
trill (trɪl) *n* **1** *Music.* a rapid alternation between a principal note and the note above it. **2** a shrill warbling sound, esp. as made by some birds. **3** the articulation of an (r) sound produced by the rapid vibration of the tongue or the uvula. ◆ *vb* **4** to sound, sing, or play (a trill or with a trill). **5** (*tr*) to pronounce (an (r) sound) by the production of a trill. [C17: from It. *trillo,* from *trillare,* apparently from MDu. *trillen* to vibrate]
trillion (ˈtrɪljən) *n* **1** the number represented as one followed by twelve zeros (10^{12}); a million million. **2** (formerly, in Britain) the number represented as one followed by eighteen zeros (10^{18}); a million million million. ◆ *determiner* **3** (preceded by *a* or a numeral) amounting to a trillion. [C17: from F, on the model of *million*]
▸ **ˈtrillionth** *n, adj*
trillium (ˈtrɪljəm) *n* any of a genus of herbaceous plants of Asia and North America, having a whorl of three leaves at the top of the stem with a single white, pink, or purple three-petalled flower. [C18: from NL, modification by Linnaeus of Swedish *trilling* triplet]
trilobate (traɪˈləʊbeɪt, ˈtraɪləˌbeɪt) *adj* (esp. of a leaf) consisting of or having three lobes or parts.
trilobite (ˈtraɪləˌbaɪt) *n* any of various extinct marine arthropods abundant in Palaeozoic times, having a segmented exoskeleton divided into three parts. [C19: from NL *Trilobītēs,* from Gk *trilobos* having three lobes]
▸ **trilobitic** (ˌtraɪləˈbɪtɪk) *adj*
trilogy (ˈtrɪlədʒɪ) *n, pl* **trilogies. 1** a series of three related works, esp. in literature, etc. **2** (in ancient Greece) a series of three tragedies performed together. [C19: from Gk *trilogia*]
trim ❶ (trɪm) *adj* **trimmer, trimmest. 1** neat and spruce in appearance. **2** slim; slender. **3** in good condition. ◆ *vb* **trims, trimming, trimmed.** (*mainly tr*) **4** to put in good order, esp. by cutting or pruning. **5** to shape and finish (timber). **6** to adorn or decorate. **7** (sometimes foll. by *off* or *away*) to cut so as to remove: *to trim off a branch.* **8** to cut down to the desired size or shape. **9** *Naut.* **9a** (*also intr*) to adjust the balance of (a vessel) or (of a vessel) to maintain an even balance, by distribu-

THESAURUS

trifle *n* **1 = knick-knack,** bagatelle, bauble, child's play (*inf.*), gewgaw, nothing, plaything, toy, triviality **2 = little,** bit, dash, drop, jot, pinch, spot, touch, trace ◆ *vb* **4** *usually foll. by* **with = toy,** amuse oneself, coquet, dally, flirt, mess about, palter, play, play fast and loose (*inf.*), wanton **5 = waste time,** dawdle, fritter, idle, waste
trifler *n* **5 = idler,** dilettante, good-for-nothing, layabout, loafer, ne'er-do-well, skiver (*Brit. sl.*), waster
trifling *adj* **1, 2 = insignificant,** empty, footling (*inf.*), frivolous, idle, inconsiderable, measly, minuscule, negligible, nickel-and-dime (*US sl.*), paltry, petty, piddling (*inf.*), puny, shallow, silly, slight, small, tiny, trivial, unimportant, valueless, worthless
Antonyms *adj* considerable, crucial, important, large, major, serious, significant, vital, weighty
trigger *vb* **4 = set off,** activate, bring about, cause, elicit, generate, give rise to, produce, prompt, provoke, set in motion, spark off, start
Antonyms *vb* bar, block, hinder, impede, inhibit, obstruct, prevent, repress, stop
trim *adj* **1 = neat,** compact, dapper, natty (*inf.*), nice, orderly, shipshape, smart, soigné *or* soignée, spick-and-span, spruce, tidy, trig (*arch. or dialect*), well-groomed, well-ordered, well turned-out **2 = slender,** fit, shapely, sleek,

tion of ballast, cargo, etc. **9b** (*also intr*) to adjust (a vessel's sails) to take advantage of the wind. **10** to balance (an aircraft) before flight by adjusting the position of the load or in flight by the use of trim tabs, fuel transfer, etc. **11** (*also intr*) to modify (one's opinions, etc.) for expediency. **12** *Inf.* to thrash or beat. **13** *Inf.* to rebuke. ◆ *n* **14** a decoration or adornment. **15** the upholstery and decorative facings of a car's interior. **16** proper order or fitness; good shape. **17** a haircut that neatens but does not alter the existing hairstyle. **18** *Naut.* **18a** the general set and appearance of a vessel. **18b** the difference between the draught of a vessel at the bow and at the stern. **18c** the fitness of a vessel. **18d** the position of a vessel's sails relative to the wind. **19** dress or equipment. **20** *US.* window-dressing. **21** the attitude of an aircraft in flight when the pilot allows the main control surfaces to take up their own positions. **22** material that is trimmed off. **23** decorative mouldings, such as architraves, picture rails, etc. [OE *trymman* to strengthen]
▸ **'trimly** *adv* ▸ **'trimness** *n*

trimaran ('traɪmə,ræn) *n* a vessel, usually of shallow draught, with two hulls flanking the main hull. [C20: from TRI- + (CATA)MARAN]

trimer ('traɪmə) *n* a polymer or a molecule of a polymer consisting of three identical monomers.

trimerous ('trɪmərəs) *adj* **1** having parts in groups of three. **2** having three parts.

trimester (traɪ'mɛstə) *n* **1** a period of three months. **2** (in some US and Canad. universities or schools) any of the three academic sessions. [C19: from F *trimestre*, from L *trimēstris* of three months]
▸**tri'mestral** *or* **tri'mestrial** *adj*

trimeter ('trɪmɪtə) *Prosody.* ◆ *n* **1** a verse line consisting of three metrical feet. ◆ *adj* **2** designating such a line.

trimethadione (,traɪmeθə'daɪəʊn) *n* a crystalline compound with a camphor-like odour, used in the treatment of epilepsy.

trimetric projection (traɪ'mɛtrɪk) *n* a geometric projection, used in mechanical drawing, in which the three axes are at arbitrary angles, often using different linear scales.

trimmer ('trɪmə) *n* **1** a beam attached to truncated joists in order to leave an opening for a staircase, chimney, etc. **2** a machine for trimming timber. **3** a variable capacitor of small capacitance used for making fine adjustments, etc. **4** a person who alters his opinions on the grounds of expediency. **5** a person who fits out motor vehicles.

trimming **T** ('trɪmɪŋ) *n* **1** an extra piece used to decorate or complete. **2** (*pl*) usual or traditional accompaniments: *roast turkey with all the trimmings.* **3** (*pl*) parts that are cut off.

trimolecular (,traɪmə'lɛkjʊlə) *adj Chem.* of, formed from, or involving three molecules.

trimonthly (traɪ'mʌnθlɪ) *adj, adv* every three months.

trimorphism (traɪ'mɔ:fɪzəm) *n* **1** *Biol.* the property exhibited by certain species of having or occurring in three different forms. **2** the property of certain minerals of existing in three crystalline forms.

trinary ('traɪnərɪ) *adj* **1** made up of three parts; ternary. **2** going in threes. [C15: from LL *trīnārius* of three sorts, from L *trīnī* three each, from *trēs* three]

trine (traɪn) *n* **1** *Astrol.* an aspect of 120° between two planets. **2** anything comprising three parts. ◆ *adj* **3** of or relating to a trine. **4** threefold; triple. [C14: from OF *trin*, from L *trīnus* triple, from *trēs* three]
▸ **'trinal** *adj*

Trinitarian (,trɪnɪ'tɛərɪən) *n* **1** a person who believes in the doctrine of the Trinity. ◆ *adj* **2** of or relating to the doctrine of the Trinity or those who uphold it.
▸ **,Trini'tarian,ism** *n*

trinitroglycerine (traɪ,naɪtrəʊ'glɪsərɪn) *n* the full name for **nitroglycerine**.

trinitrotoluene (traɪ,naɪtrəʊ'tɒljʊ,i:n) *or* **trinitrotoluol** (traɪ,naɪtrəʊ'tɒljʊ,ɒl) *n* the full name for **TNT**.

trinity **T** ('trɪnɪtɪ) *n, pl* **trinities. 1** a group of three. **2** the state of being threefold. [C13: from OF *trinite*, from LL *trīnitās*, from L *trīnus* triple]

Trinity ('trɪnɪtɪ) *n Christian theol.* the union of three persons, the Father, Son, and Holy Spirit, in one Godhead.

Trinity Brethren *pl n* the members of Trinity House.

Trinity House *n* an association that provides lighthouses, buoys, etc., around the British coast.

Trinity Sunday *n* the Sunday after Whit Sunday.

Trinity term *n* the summer term at the Inns of Court and certain universities.

trinket **T** ('trɪŋkɪt) *n* **1** a small or worthless ornament or piece of jewellery. **2** a trivial object; trifle. [C16: ? from earlier *trenket* little knife, via OF, from L *truncāre* to lop]

trinomial (traɪ'nəʊmɪəl) *adj* **1** consisting of three terms. ◆ *n* **2** *Maths.* a polynomial consisting of three terms, such as $ax^2 + bx + c$. **3** *Biol.* the three-part name of an organism that incorporates its genus, species, and subspecies. [C18: TRI- + *-nomial* on the model of *binomial*]

trio **T** ('tri:əʊ) *n, pl* **trios. 1** a group of three. **2** *Music.* **2a** a group of three singers or instrumentalists or a piece of music composed for such a group. **2b** a subordinate section in a scherzo, minuet, etc. [C18: from It., ult. from L *trēs* three]

triode ('traɪəʊd) *n* **1** an electronic valve having three electrodes, a cathode, an anode, and a grid. **2** any electronic device having three electrodes. [C20: TRI- + ELECTRODE]

trioecious *or* **triecious** (traɪ'i:ʃəs) *adj* (of a plant species) having male, female, and hermaphrodite flowers in three different plants. [C18: from NL *trioecia*, from Gk TRI- + *oikos* house]

triolein (traɪ'əʊlɪɪn) *n* a naturally occurring glyceride of oleic acid, found in fats and oils.

triolet ('tri:əʊ,lɛt) *n* a verse form of eight lines, having the first line repeated as the fourth and seventh and the second line as the eighth, rhyming a b a a a b a b. [C17: from F: a little TRIO]

trioxide (traɪ'ɒksaɪd) *n* any oxide that contains three oxygen atoms per molecule.

trip **T** (trɪp) *n* **1** an outward and return journey, often for a specific purpose. **2** any journey. **3** a false step; stumble. **4** any slip or blunder. **5** a light step or tread. **6** a manoeuvre or device to cause someone to trip. **7** Also called: **tripper.** any catch on a mechanism that acts as a switch. **8** *Inf.* a hallucinogenic drug experience. **9** *Inf.* any stimulating, profound, etc., experience. ◆ *vb* **trips, tripping, tripped. 10** (often foll. by *up*, or when *intr*, by *on* or *over*) to stumble or cause to stumble. **11** to make or cause to make a mistake. **12** (*tr*; often foll. by *up*) to trap or catch in a mistake. **13** (*intr*) to go on a short journey. **14** (*intr*) to move or tread lightly. **15** (*intr*) *Inf.* to experience the effects of a hallucinogenic drug. **16** (*tr*) to activate a mechanical trip. [C14: from OF *triper* to tread, of Gmc origin]

tripartite (traɪ'pɑ:taɪt) *adj* **1** divided into or composed of three parts. **2** involving three participants. **3** (esp. of leaves) consisting of three parts formed by divisions extending almost to the base.
▸**tri'partitely** *adv*

tripe **T** (traɪp) *n* **1** the stomach lining of an ox, cow, etc., prepared for cooking. **2** *Inf.* something silly; rubbish. [C13: from OF, from ?]

triphammer ('trɪp,hæmə) *n* a power hammer that is raised or tilted by a cam and allowed to fall under gravity.

triphibious (traɪ'fɪbɪəs) *adj* (esp. of military operations) occurring on land, at sea, and in the air. [C20: from TRI- + (AM)PHIBIOUS]

triphthong ('trɪfθɒŋ, 'trɪp-) *n* **1** a composite vowel sound during the articulation of which the vocal organs move from one position through a second, ending in a third, as in *fire.* **2** a trigraph representing such a composite vowel sound. [C16: via NL from Med. Gk *triphthongos*, from TRI- + *phthongos* sound]
▸**triph'thongal** *adj*

tripinnate (traɪ'pɪnɪt, -eɪt) *adj* (of a leaf) having pinnate leaflets that are bipinnately arranged.

triplane ('traɪ,pleɪn) *n* an aeroplane having three wings arranged one above the other.

triple **T** ('trɪpᵊl) *adj* **1** consisting of three parts; threefold. **2** (of musical time or rhythm) having three beats in each bar. **3** three times as great or as much. ◆ *n* **4** a threefold amount. **5** a group of three. ◆ *vb* **triples, tripling, tripled. 6** to increase threefold; treble. [C16: from L *triplus*]
▸ **'triply** *adv*

triple A *n Mil.* anti-aircraft artillery. [referring to the abbrev. AAA]

triple jump *n* an athletic event in which the competitor has to per-

THESAURUS

slim, streamlined, svelte, willowy ◆ *vb* **4** = **cut**, barber, clip, crop, curtail, cut back, dock, even up, lop, pare, prune, shave, shear, tidy **6** = **decorate**, adorn, array, beautify, bedeck, deck out, dress, embellish, embroider, garnish, ornament, trick out **9** = **adjust**, arrange, balance, distribute, order, prepare, settle ◆ *n* **14** = **decoration**, adornment, border, edging, embellishment, frill, fringe, garnish, ornamentation, piping, trimming **16** = **condition**, fettle, fitness, form, health, order, repair, shape (*inf.*), situation, state, wellness **17** = **cut**, clipping, crop, pruning, shave, shearing, tidying up, trimming
Antonyms *adj* ≠ **neat**: disarrayed, disorderly, messy, scruffy, shabby, sloppy, ungroomed, unkempt, untidy

trimming *n* **1** = **decoration**, adornment, border, braid, edging, embellishment, festoon, frill, fringe, garnish, ornamentation, piping **2** *pl* = **extras**, accessories, accompaniments, appurtenances, frills, garnish, ornaments, paraphernalia, trappings **3** *pl* = **clippings**, brash, cuttings, ends, parings, shavings

trinity *n* **1** = **threesome**, triad, trilogy, trine, trio, triple, triplet, triptych, triumvirate, triune

trinket *n* **1, 2** = **ornament**, bagatelle, bauble, bibelot, gewgaw, gimcrack, kickshaw, knick-knack, nothing, piece of bric-a-brac, toy, trifle

trio *n* **1** = **threesome**, triad, trilogy, trine, trinity, triple, triplet, triptych, triumvirate, triune

trip *n* **1, 2** = **journey**, errand, excursion, expedition, foray, jaunt, outing, ramble, run, tour, travel, voyage **3** = **stumble**, blunder, fall, false move, false step, misstep, slip **4** = **blunder**, bloomer (*Brit. inf.*), boob (*Brit. sl.*), error, faux pas, indiscretion, lapse, slip ◆ *vb* **10** = **stumble**, fall, lose one's balance, lose one's footing, make a false move, misstep, slip, tumble **11** = **blunder**, boob (*Brit. sl.*), err, go wrong, lapse, make a faux pas, miscalculate, slip up (*inf.*) **12** = **catch out**, confuse, disconcert, put off one's stride, throw off, trap, unsettle **13** = **journey**, go, ramble, tour, travel, voyage **14** = **skip**, caper, dance, flit, frisk, gambol, hop, spring, tread lightly **15** *Informal* = **take drugs**, get high (*inf.*), get stoned (*sl.*), turn on (*sl.*) **16** = **activate**, engage, flip, pull, release, set off, switch on, throw, turn on

tripe 2 *n Informal* = **nonsense**, balderdash, bollocks (*Brit. taboo sl.*), bull (*sl.*), bullshit (*taboo sl.*), bunkum *or* buncombe (*chiefly US*), claptrap (*inf.*), cobblers (*Brit. taboo sl.*), crap (*sl.*), drivel, eyewash (*inf.*), garbage (*inf.*), guff (*sl.*), hogwash, hokum (*sl., chiefly US & Canad.*), inanity, moonshine, pap, piffle (*inf.*), poppycock (*inf.*), rot, rubbish, tommyrot, tosh (*sl., chiefly Brit.*), trash, trumpery, twaddle

triple *adj* **1** = **threefold**, three times as much, three-way, tripartite ◆ *n* **5** = **threesome**, triad, trilogy, trine, trinity, trio, triplet, triumvirate, triune ◆ *vb* **6** = **treble**, increase threefold, triplicate form successively a hop, a step, and a jump in continuous movement.

triple point *n Chem.* the temperature and pressure at which the three phases of a substance are in equilibrium.

triplet Ⓣ ('trɪplɪt) *n* **1** a group or set of three similar things. **2** one of three offspring born at one birth. **3** *Music.* a group of three notes played in a time value of two, four, etc. **4** *Chem.* a state of a molecule or free radical in which there are two unpaired electrons. [C17: from TRIPLE, on the model of *doublet*]

Triplex ('trɪplɛks) *n Brit. trademark.* a laminated safety glass, as used in car windows.

triplicate *adj* ('trɪplɪkɪt). **1** triple. ◆ *vb* ('trɪplɪˌkeɪt), **triplicates, triplicating, triplicated. 2** to multiply or be multiplied by three. ◆ *n* ('trɪplɪkɪt). **3a** a group of three things. **3b** one of such a group. **4 in triplicate.** written out three times. [C15: from L *triplicāre* to triple]
▸ˌ**tripli'cation** *n*

triploid ('trɪplɔɪd) *adj* **1** having or relating to three times the haploid number of chromosomes: *a triploid organism.* ◆ *n* **2** a triploid organism. [C19: from Gk *tripl(oos)* triple + (HAPL)OID]

tripod ('traɪpɒd) *n* **1** a three-legged stand to which a camera, etc., can be attached to hold it steady. **2** a stand or table having three legs.
▸**tripodal** ('trɪpədᵊl) *adj*

tripoli ('trɪpəlɪ) *n* a lightweight porous siliceous rock used in a powdered form as a polish. [C17: after *Tripoli*, in Libya or in Lebanon]

tripos ('traɪpɒs) *n Brit.* the final honours degree examinations at Cambridge University. [C16: from L *tripūs*, infl. by Gk noun ending *-os*]

tripper Ⓣ ('trɪpə) *n* **1** *Chiefly Brit.* a tourist. **2** another word for **trip** (sense 7). **3** any device that causes a trip to operate.

trippy ('trɪpɪ) *adj* **trippier, trippiest.** *Inf.* suggestive of or resembling the effect produced by a hallucinogenic drug.

triptane ('trɪpteɪn) *n* a liquid hydrocarbon used in aviation fuel. [C20: shortened & altered from *trimethylbutane*]

triptych ('trɪptɪk) *n* **1** a set of three pictures or panels, usually hinged so that the two wing panels fold over the larger central one: often used as an altarpiece. **2** a set of three hinged writing tablets. [C18: from Gk *triptukhos*, from TRI- + *ptux* plate]

triptyque (trɪp'tiːk) *n* a customs permit for the temporary importation of a motor vehicle. [C20: from F: TRIPTYCH (from its three sections)]

tripwire ('trɪpˌwaɪə) *n* a wire that activates a trap, mine, etc., when tripped over.

trireme ('traɪriːm) *n* an ancient Greek galley with three banks of oars on each side. [C17: from L *trirēmis*, from TRI- + *rēmus* oar]

trisect (traɪ'sɛkt) *vb* (*tr*) to divide into three parts, esp. three equal parts. [C17: TRI- + *-sect* from L *secāre* to cut]
▸**trisection** (traɪ'sɛkʃən) *n*

trishaw ('traɪˌʃɔː) *n* another name for **rickshaw** (sense 2). [C20: from TRI- + RICKSHAW]

triskelion (trɪ'skɛlɪˌɒn) *n, pl* **triskelia** (trɪ'skɛlɪə). a symbol consisting of three bent limbs or lines radiating from a centre. [C19: from Gk *triskelēs* three-legged]

trismus ('trɪzməs) *n Pathol.* the state of being unable to open the mouth because of sustained contractions of the jaw muscles, caused by tetanus. Nontechnical name: **lockjaw.** [C17: from NL, from Gk *trismos* a grinding]

triste (triːst) *adj* an archaic word for **sad.** [from F]

trisyllable (traɪ'sɪləbᵊl) *n* a word of three syllables.
▸**trisyllabic** (ˌtraɪsɪ'læbɪk) *adj*

trite Ⓣ (traɪt) *adj* hackneyed; dull: *a trite comment.* [C16: from L *trītus* worn down, from *terere* to rub]
▸'**tritely** *adv* ▸'**triteness** *n*

tritheism ('traɪθɪˌɪzəm) *n Theol.* belief in three gods, esp. in the Trinity as consisting of three distinct gods.
▸'**tritheist** *n, adj*

triticum ('trɪtɪkəm) *n* any of a genus of cereal grasses which includes the wheats. [C19: L, lit.: wheat, prob. from *tritum*, supine of *terere* to grind]

tritium ('trɪtɪəm) *n* a radioactive isotope of hydrogen. Symbol: T or ^{3}H; half-life: 12.5 years. [C20: NL, from Gk *tritos* third]

triton[1] ('traɪtᵊn) *n* any of various chiefly tropical marine gastropod molluscs having large spiral shells. [C16: via L from Gk *tritōn*]

triton[2] ('traɪtɒn) *n Physics.* a nucleus of an atom of tritium, containing two neutrons and one proton. [C20: from TRIT(IUM) + -ON]

Triton ('traɪtᵊn) *n Greek myth.* a sea god depicted as having the upper parts of a man with a fish's tail.

tritone ('traɪˌtəʊn) *n* a musical interval consisting of three whole tones.

triturate ('trɪtjʊˌreɪt) *vb* **triturates, triturating, triturated. 1** (*tr*) to grind or rub into a fine powder or pulp. ◆ *n* **2** the powder or pulp resulting from this. [C17: from LL *trītūrāre* to thresh, from L *trītūra* a threshing, from *terere* to grind]
▸ˌ**tritu'ration** *n*

triumph Ⓣ ('traɪəmf) *n* **1** the feeling of exultation and happiness derived from a victory or major achievement. **2** the act or condition of being victorious; victory. **3** (in ancient Rome) a procession held in honour of a victorious general. ◆ *vb* (*intr*) **4** (often foll. by *over*) to win a victory or control: *to triumph over one's weaknesses.* **5** to rejoice over a victory. **6** to celebrate a Roman triumph. [C14: from OF *triumphe*, from L *triumphus*, from OL *triumpus*]
▸**triumphal** (traɪ'ʌmfəl) *adj*

triumphant Ⓣ (traɪ'ʌmfənt) *adj* **1** experiencing or displaying triumph. **2** exultant through triumph.
▸**tri'umphantly** *adv*

triumvir (traɪ'ʌmvə) *n, pl* **triumvirs** *or* **triumviri** (-vɪˌriː). (esp. in ancient Rome) a member of a triumvirate. [C16: from L: one of three administrators, from *trium virōrum* of three men, from *trēs* three + *vir* man]
▸**tri'umviral** *adj*

triumvirate (traɪ'ʌmvɪrɪt) *n* **1** (in ancient Rome) a board of three officials jointly responsible for some task. **2** joint rule by three men. **3** any group of three men associated in some way. **4** the office of a triumvir.

triune ('traɪjuːn) *adj* constituting three in one, esp. the three persons in one God of the Trinity. [C17: TRI- + *-une*, from L *ūnus* one]
▸**tri'unity** *n*

trivalent (traɪ'veɪlənt, 'trɪvələnt) *adj Chem.* **1** having a valency of three. **2** having three valencies. ◆ Also: **tervalent.**
▸**tri'valency** *n*

trivet ('trɪvɪt) *n* **1** a stand, usually three-legged and metal, on which cooking vessels are placed over a fire. **2** a short metal stand on which hot dishes are placed on a table. **3 as right as a trivet.** in perfect health. [OE *trefet* (infl. by OE *thrifēte* having three feet), from L *tripēs* having three feet]

trivia Ⓣ ('trɪvɪə) *n* (*functioning as sing or pl*) petty details or considerations; trifles; trivialities. [from NL, pl of L *trivium* junction of three roads]

trivial Ⓣ ('trɪvɪəl) *adj* **1** of little importance; petty or frivolous: *trivial complaints.* **2** ordinary or commonplace; trite: *trivial conversation.* **3** *Biol., chem.* denoting the common name of an organism or substance. **4** *Biol.* denoting the specific name of an organism in binomial nomenclature. [C15: from L *triviālis* belonging to the public streets, common, from *trivium* junction of three roads]
▸'**trivially** *adv* ▸'**trivialness** *n*

triviality Ⓣ (ˌtrɪvɪ'ælɪtɪ) *n, pl* **trivialities. 1** the state or quality of being trivial. **2** something, such as a remark, that is trivial.

trivialize Ⓣ *or* **trivialise** ('trɪvɪəˌlaɪz) *vb* **trivializes, trivializing, trivialized** *or* **trivialises, trivialising, trivialised.** (*tr*) to cause to seem trivial or more trivial; minimize.
▸ˌ**triviali'zation** *or* ˌ**triviali'sation** *n*

trivium ('trɪvɪəm) *n, pl* **trivia** (-ɪə). (in medieval learning) the arts of grammar, rhetoric, and logic. Cf. **quadrivium.** [C19: from Med. L, from L: crossroads]

-trix *suffix forming nouns.* indicating a feminine agent, corresponding to nouns ending in *-tor: executrix.* [from L]

t-RNA *abbrev. for* transfer RNA.

trocar ('trəʊkɑː) *n* a surgical instrument for removing fluid from bodily cavities. [C18: from F *trocart*, lit.: with three sides, from *trois* three + *carre* side]

trochal ('trəʊkᵊl) *adj Zool.* shaped like a wheel. [C19: from Gk *trokhos* wheel]

THESAURUS

triplet *n* **1 = threesome**, triad, trilogy, trine, trinity, trio, triple, triumvirate, triune

tripper *n* **1** *Chiefly Brit.* **= tourist**, excursionist, holiday-maker, journeyer, sightseer, voyager

trite *adj* **= unoriginal**, banal, bromidic, clichéd, common, commonplace, corny (*sl.*), dull, hack, hackneyed, ordinary, pedestrian, routine, run-of-the-mill, stale, stereotyped, stock, threadbare, tired, uninspired, worn
Antonyms *adj* exciting, fresh, interesting, new, novel, original, out-of-the-ordinary, uncommon, unexpected, unfamiliar

triumph *n* **1 = joy**, elation, exultation, happiness, jubilation, pride, rejoicing **2 = success**, accomplishment, achievement, attainment, conquest, coup, feat, feather in one's cap, hit (*inf.*), mastery, sensation, smash (*inf.*), smash hit (*inf.*), *tour de force*, victory, walkover (*inf.*) ◆ *vb* **4** *often with* **over = succeed**, best, carry the day, come out on top (*inf.*), dominate, flourish, get the better of, overcome, overwhelm, prevail, prosper, subdue, take the honours, thrive, vanquish, win **5 = rejoice**, celebrate, crow, drool, exult, gloat, glory, jubilate, revel, swagger
Antonyms *n* ≠ **success:** catastrophe, defeat, disaster, failure, fiasco, flop (*inf.*), washout (*inf.*) ◆ *vb* ≠ **succeed:** come a cropper (*inf.*), fail, fall, flop (*inf.*), lose

triumphant *adj* **1 = victorious**, boastful, cock-a-hoop, conquering, dominant, elated, exultant, glorious, proud, successful, swaggering, undefeated, winning **2 = celebratory**, jubilant, rejoicing, triumphal
Antonyms *adj* ≠ **victorious:** beaten, defeated, embarrassed, humbled, humiliated, shamed, unsuccessful

trivia *n* **= minutiae**, details, petty details, trifles, trivialities
Antonyms *n* basics, brass tacks (*inf.*), core, essentials, fundamentals, nitty-gritty (*inf.*), rudiments

trivial *adj* **1, 2 = unimportant**, commonplace, everyday, frivolous, incidental, inconsequential, inconsiderable, insignificant, little, meaningless, minor, negligible, nickel-and-dime (*US sl.*), paltry, petty, puny, slight, small, trifling, trite, valueless, worthless
Antonyms *adj* considerable, crucial, essential, important, profound, serious, significant, uncommon, unusual, vital, weighty, worthwhile

triviality *n* **1 = insignificance**, frivolity, inconsequentiality, littleness, meaninglessness, much ado about nothing, negligibility, paltriness, pettiness, slightness, smallness, triteness, unimportance, valuelessness, worthlessness **2 = trifle**, detail, no big thing, no great matter, nothing, petty detail, technicality
Antonyms *n* ≠ **insignificance:** consequence, importance, significance, value, worth ≠ **trifle:** essential, rudiment

trivialize *vb* **= undervalue**, belittle, laugh off, make light of, minimize, play down, scoff at, underestimate, underplay

trochanter (trəʊ'kæntə) *n* **1** any of several processes on the upper part of the vertebrate femur, to which muscles are attached. **2** the third segment of an insect's leg. [C17: via F from Gk *trokhantēr*, from *trekhein* to run]

troche (trəʊʃ) *n Med.* another name for **lozenge** (sense 1). [C16: from F *trochisque*, from LL *trochiscus*, from Gk *trokhiskos* little wheel, from *trokhos* wheel]

trochee ('trəʊkiː) *n* a metrical foot of two syllables, the first long and the second short. [C16: via L from Gk *trokhaios pous*, lit.: a running foot, from *trekhein* to run]
▸**trochaic** (trəʊ'keɪɪk) *adj*

trochlea ('trɒklɪə) *n, pl* **trochleae** (-lɪ,iː). any bony or cartilaginous part with a grooved surface over which a bone, etc., may slide or articulate. [C17: from L, from Gk *trokhileia* a sheaf of pulleys]

trochlear nerve ('trɒklɪə) *n* either one of the fourth pair of cranial nerves, which supply the superior oblique muscle of the eye.

trochoid ('trəʊkɔɪd) *n* **1** the curve described by a fixed point on the radius of a circle as the circle rolls along a straight line. ◆ *adj also* **trochoidal. 2** rotating about a central axis. **3** *Anat.* (of a structure or part) resembling or functioning as a pivot or pulley. [C18: from Gk *trokhoeidēs* circular, from *trokhos* wheel]

trod (trɒd) *vb* the past tense and a past participle of **tread.**

trodden ('trɒdən) *vb* a past participle of **tread.**

trode (trəʊd) *vb Arch.* a past tense of **tread.**

troglodyte ('trɒglə,daɪt) *n* **1** a cave dweller, esp. of prehistoric times. **2** *Inf.* a person who lives alone and appears eccentric. [C16: via L from Gk *trōglodutēs* one who enters caves, from *trōglē* hole + *duein* to enter]
▸**troglodytic** (,trɒglə'dɪtɪk) *adj*

trogon ('trəʊgɒn) *n* any of an order of birds of tropical regions of America, Africa, and Asia, having a brilliant plumage and long tail. See also **quetzal** (sense 1). [C18: from NL, from Gk *trōgōn*, from *trōgein* to gnaw]

troika ('trɔɪkə) *n* **1** a Russian vehicle drawn by three horses abreast. **2** three horses harnessed abreast. **3** a triumvirate. [C19: from Russian, from *troe* three]

Trojan ('trəʊdʒən) *n* **1** a native or inhabitant of ancient Troy. **2** a person who is hard-working and determined. ◆ *adj* **3** of or relating to ancient Troy or its inhabitants.

Trojan Horse *n* **1** *Greek myth.* the huge wooden hollow figure of a horse left outside Troy by the Greeks and dragged inside by the Trojans. The men concealed inside it opened the city to the final Greek assault. **2** a trap intended to undermine an enemy. **3** *Computing.* a bug inserted into a program or system designed to be activated after a certain time or a certain number of operations.

troll[1] (trəʊl) *vb* **1** *Angling.* **1a** to draw (a baited line, etc.) through the water. **1b** to fish (a stretch of water) by trolling. **1c** to fish (for) by trolling. **2** to roll or cause to roll. **3** *Arch.* to sing (a refrain, chorus, etc.) in a loud hearty voice. **4** (*intr*) *Brit. inf.* to walk or stroll. ◆ *n* **5** a trolling. **6** *Angling.* a bait or lure used in trolling. [C14: from OF *troller* to run about]
▸**'troller** *n*

troll[2] (trəʊl) *n* (in Scandinavian folklore) one of a class of supernatural creatures that dwell in caves or mountains and are depicted either as dwarfs or as giants. [C19: from ON: demon]

trolley ('trɒlɪ) *n* **1** a small table on casters used for conveying food, etc. **2** *Chiefly Brit.* a wheeled cart or stand used for moving heavy items, such as shopping in a supermarket or luggage at a railway station. **3** *Brit.* (in a hospital) a bed mounted on casters and used for moving patients who are unconscious, etc. **4** *Brit.* See **trolleybus. 5** *US & Canad.* See **trolley car. 6** a device that collects the current from an overhead wire, third rail, etc., to drive the motor of an electric vehicle. **7** a pulley or truck that travels along an overhead wire in order to support a suspended load. **8** *Chiefly Brit.* a low truck running on rails, used in factories, mines, etc. **9** a truck, cage, or basket suspended from an overhead track or cable for carrying loads in a mine, etc. [C19: prob. from TROLL[1]]

trolleybus ('trɒlɪ,bʌs) *n* an electrically driven public-transport vehicle that does not run on rails but takes its power from two overhead wires.

trolley car *n* a US and Canad. name for **tram** (sense 1).

trollius ('trəʊlɪəs) *n* another name for **globeflower.** [from G *Trollblume* globeflower]

trollop Ⓣ ('trɒləp) *n* **1** a promiscuous woman, esp. a prostitute. **2** an untidy woman; slattern. [C17: ?from G dialect *Trolle* prostitute]
▸**'trollopy** *adj*

trombone (trɒm'bəʊn) *n* a brass instrument, a low-pitched counterpart of the trumpet, consisting of a tube the effective length of which is varied by means of a U-shaped slide. [C18: from It., from *tromba* a trumpet, from OHG *trumba*]
▸**trom'bonist** *n*

trommel ('trɒməl) *n* a revolving cylindrical sieve used to screen crushed ore. [C19: from G: a drum]

trompe (trɒmp) *n* an apparatus for supplying the blast of air in a forge, consisting of a thin column down which water falls, drawing in air through side openings. [C19: from F, lit.: trumpet]

trompe l'oeil (*French* trɔ̃p lœj) *n, pl* **trompe l'oeils** (trɔ̃p lœj). **1** a painting, etc., giving a convincing illusion of reality. **2** an effect of this kind. [from F, lit.: deception of the eye]

-tron *suffix forming nouns.* **1** indicating a vacuum tube. **2** indicating an instrument for accelerating atomic particles. [from Gk, suffix indicating instrument]

tronc (trɒŋk) *n* a pool into which waiters, etc., pay their tips for later distribution to staff by a **tronc master**, according to agreed percentages. [C20: from F: collecting box]

tronk (trɒŋk) *n S. African inf.* a prison. [Afrik.]

troop Ⓣ (truːp) *n* **1** a large group or assembly. **2** a subdivision of a cavalry squadron or artillery battery of about platoon size. **3** (*pl*) armed forces; soldiers. **4** a large group of Scouts comprising several patrols. ◆ *vb* **5** (*intr*) to gather, move, or march in or as if in a crowd. **6** (*tr*) *Mil., chiefly Brit.* to parade (the colour or flag) ceremonially. [C16: from F *troupe*, from *troupeau* flock, of Gmc origin]

trooper ('truːpə) *n* **1** a soldier in a cavalry regiment. **2** *US & Austral.* a mounted policeman. **3** *US.* a state policeman. **4** a cavalry horse. **5** *Inf., chiefly Brit.* a troopship.

troopship ('truːp,ʃɪp) *n* a ship used to transport military personnel.

tropaeolum (trəʊ'piːələm) *n, pl* **tropaeolums** *or* **tropaeola** (-lə). any of a genus of garden plants, esp. the nasturtium. [C18: from NL, from L *tropaeum* TROPHY; from the shield-shaped leaves and helmet-shaped flowers]

trope (trəʊp) *n* a word or expression used in a figurative sense. [C16: from L *tropus* figurative use of a word, from Gk *tropos* style, turn]

-trope *n combining form.* indicating a turning towards, development in the direction of, or affinity to: *heliotrope.* [from Gk *tropos* a turn]

trophic ('trɒfɪk) *adj* of nutrition. [C19: from Gk *trophikos*, from *trophē* food, from *trephein* to feed]

tropho- *or before a vowel* **troph-** *combining form.* indicating nourishment or nutrition: *trophozoite.* [from Gk *trophē* food, from *trephein* to feed]

trophoblast ('trɒfə,blæst) *n* a membrane that encloses the embryo of mammals and absorbs nourishment from the uterine fluids.

trophozoite (,trɒfə'zəʊaɪt) *n* the form of a sporozoan protozoan, esp. of certain parasites, in the feeding stage.

trophy Ⓣ ('trəʊfɪ) *n, pl* **trophies. 1** an object such as a silver cup that is symbolic of victory in a contest, esp. a sporting contest; prize. **2** a memento of success, esp. one taken in war or hunting. **3** (in ancient Greece and Rome) a memorial to a victory, usually consisting of captured arms raised on the battlefield or in a public place. **4** an ornamental carving that represents a group of weapons, etc. [C16: from F *trophée*, from L *tropaeum*, from Gk *tropaion*, from *tropē* a turning, defeat of the enemy]

-trophy *n combining form.* indicating a certain type of nourishment or growth: *dystrophy.* [from Gk *-trophia*, from *trophē* nourishment]
▸**-trophic** *adj combining form.*

tropic ('trɒpɪk) *n* **1** (*sometimes cap.*) either of the parallel lines of latitude at about 23½°N (**tropic of Cancer**) and 23½°S (**tropic of Capricorn**) of the equator. **2 the tropics.** (*often cap.*) that part of the earth's surface between the tropics of Cancer and Capricorn. **3** *Astron.* either of the two parallel circles on the celestial sphere having the same latitudes and names as the lines on the earth. ◆ *adj* **4** tropical. [C14: from LL *tropicus* belonging to a turn, from Gk *tropikos*, from *tropos* a turn; from the belief that the sun turned back at the solstices]

-tropic *adj combining form.* turning or developing in response to a certain stimulus: *heliotropic.* [from Gk *tropos* a turn]

tropical Ⓣ ('trɒpɪkəl) *adj* **1** situated in, used in, characteristic of, or relating to the tropics. **2** (of weather) very hot, esp. when humid. **3** of a trope.
▸,**tropi'cality** *n* ▸**'tropically** *adv*

tropicbird ('trɒpɪk,bɜːd) *n* any of various tropical aquatic birds having long tail feathers and a white plumage with black markings.

tropism ('trəʊpɪzəm) *n* the response of an organism, esp. a plant, to an external stimulus by growth in a direction determined by the stimulus. [from Gk *tropos* a turn]
▸,**tropis'matic** *adj*

-tropism *or* **-tropy** *n combining form.* indicating a tendency to turn or develop in response to a stimulus: *phototropism.* [from Gk *tropos* a turn]

tropo- *combining form.* indicating change or a turning: *tropophyte.* [from Gk *tropos* a turn]

tropopause ('trɒpə,pɔːz) *n Meteorol.* the plane of discontinuity between the troposphere and the stratosphere, characterized by a sharp change in the lapse rate.

troposphere ('trɒpə,sfɪə) *n* the lowest atmospheric layer, about 18 kilometres (11 miles) thick at the equator to about 6 km (4 miles) at the Poles, in which air temperature decreases normally with height at about 6.5°C per km.
▸**tropospheric** (,trɒpə'sferɪk) *adj*

THESAURUS

trollop *n* **1** *Derogatory* = **slut**, fallen woman, floozy (*sl.*), harlot, hussy, loose woman, prostitute, scrubber (*Brit. & Austral. sl.*), slag (*Brit. sl.*), streetwalker, strumpet, tart (*inf.*), wanton, whore, working girl (*facetious sl.*)

troop *n* **1** = **group**, assemblage, band, bevy, body, bunch (*inf.*), company, contingent, crew (*inf.*), crowd, drove, flock, gang, gathering, herd, horde, multitude, pack, posse (*inf.*), squad, swarm, team, throng, unit **3** *pl* = **soldiers**, armed forces, army, fighting men, men, military, servicemen, soldiery ◆ *vb* **5** = **flock**, crowd, march, parade, stream, swarm, throng, traipse (*inf.*)

trophy *n* **1, 2** = **prize**, award, bays, booty, cup, laurels, memento, souvenir, spoils

tropical *adj* **2** = **hot**, humid, lush, steamy, stifling, sultry, sweltering, torrid
Antonyms *adj* arctic, chilly, cold, cool, freezing, frosty, frozen, parky (*Brit. inf.*)

-tropous *adj combining form.* indicating a turning away: *anatropous.* [from Gk *-tropos* concerning a turn]
troppo[1] ('trɒpəʊ) *adv Music.* too much; excessively. See **non troppo.** [It.]
troppo[2] ('trɒpəʊ) *adj Austral. sl.* mentally affected by a tropical climate.
trot ➊ (trɒt) *vb* **trots, trotting, trotted. 1** to move or cause to move at a trot. ◆ *n* **2** a gait of a horse in which diagonally opposite legs come down together. **3** a steady brisk pace. **4** (in harness racing) a race for horses that have been trained to trot fast. **5** *Chiefly Brit.* a small child. **6** *US sl.* a student's crib. **7 on the trot.** *Inf.* **7a** one after the other: *to read two books on the trot.* **7b** busy, esp. on one's feet. **8 the trots.** *Inf.* **8a** diarrhoea. **8b** *NZ.* trotting races. ◆ See also **trot out.** [C13: from OF *trot,* from *troter* to trot, of Gmc origin]
Trot (trɒt) *n Inf.* a follower of Trotsky; Trotskyist.
troth (trəʊθ) *n Arch.* **1** a pledge of fidelity, esp. a betrothal. **2** truth (esp. in **in troth**). **3** loyalty; fidelity. [OE *trēowth*]
trotline ('trɒt,laɪn) *n Angling.* a long line suspended across a stream, river, etc., to which shorter hooked and baited lines are attached.
trot out ➊ *vb (tr, adv) Inf.* to bring forward, as for approbation or admiration, esp. repeatedly.
Trotskyism ('trɒtskɪ,ɪzəm) *n* the theory of communism of Leon Trotsky (1879–1940), Russian revolutionary and writer, in which he called for immediate worldwide revolution by the proletariat.
▸ **'Trotsky,ite** *or* **'Trotskyist** *n, adj*
trotter ('trɒtə) *n* **1** a horse that is specially trained to trot fast. **2** (*usually pl*) the foot of certain animals, esp. of pigs.
troubadour ➊ ('tru:bə,dʊə) *n* any of a class of lyric poets who flourished principally in Provence and N Italy from the 11th to the 13th century, writing chiefly on courtly love. [C18: from F, from OProvençal *trobador,* from *trobar* to write verses, ? ult. from L *tropus* TROPE]
trouble ➊ ('trʌbᵊl) *n* **1** a state of mental distress or anxiety. **2** a state of disorder or unrest: *industrial trouble.* **3** a condition of disease, pain, or malfunctioning: *liver trouble.* **4** a cause of distress, disturbance, or pain. **5** effort or exertion taken to do something. **6** liability to suffer punishment or misfortune (esp. in **be in trouble**): *he's in trouble with the police.* **7** a personal weakness or cause of annoyance: *his trouble is he's too soft.* **8** political unrest. **9** the condition of an unmarried girl who becomes pregnant (esp. in **in trouble**). ◆ *vb* **troubles, troubling, troubled. 10** (*tr*) to cause trouble to. **11** (*intr;* usually with a negative and foll. by *about*) to put oneself to inconvenience; be concerned: *don't trouble about me.* **12** (*intr;* usually with a negative) to take pains; exert oneself. **13** (*tr*) to cause inconvenience or discomfort to. **14** (*tr; usually passive*) to agitate or make rough: *the seas were troubled.* **15** (*tr*) *Caribbean.* to interfere with. [C13: from OF *troubler,* from Vulgar L *turbulāre* (unattested), from LL *turbidāre,* ult. from *turba* commotion]
▸ **'troubler** *n*
troublemaker ➊ ('trʌbᵊl,meɪkə) *n* a person who makes trouble, esp. between people.
▸ **'trouble,making** *adj, n*
troubleshooter ('trʌbᵊl,ʃu:tə) *n* a person who locates the cause of trouble and removes or treats it.
▸ **'trouble,shooting** *n, adj*
troublesome ➊ ('trʌbᵊlsəm) *adj* **1** causing trouble. **2** characterized by violence; turbulent.
▸ **'troublesomeness** *n*
troublous ('trʌbləs) *adj Arch. or literary.* unsettled; agitated.
▸ **'troublously** *adv*
trough ➊ (trɒf) *n* **1** a narrow open container, esp. one in which food or water for animals is put. **2** a narrow channel, gutter, or gulley. **3** a narrow depression, as between two waves. **4** *Meteorol.* an elongated area of low pressure. **5** a single or temporary low point; depression. **6** *Physics.* the portion of a wave in which the amplitude lies below its average value. **7** *Econ.* the lowest point of the trade cycle. [OE *trōh*]
trounce ➊ (traʊns) *vb* **trounces, trouncing, trounced.** (*tr*) to beat or defeat utterly; thrash. [C16: from ?]
troupe ➊ (tru:p) *n* **1** a company of actors or other performers, esp. one that travels. ◆ *vb* **troupes, trouping, trouped. 2** (*intr*) (esp. of actors) to move or travel in a group. [C19: from F; see TROOP]
trouper ➊ ('tru:pə) *n* **1** a member of a troupe. **2** a dependable worker or associate.
trouser ('traʊzə) *n* (*modifier*) of or relating to trousers: *trouser buttons.*
trousers ('traʊzəz) *pl n* a garment shaped to cover the body from the waist to the ankles or knees with separate tube-shaped sections for both legs. [C17: from earlier *trouse,* var. of TREWS, infl. by DRAWERS]
trousseau ('tru:səʊ) *n, pl* **trousseaux** *or* **trousseaus** (-səʊz). the clothes, linen, etc., collected by a bride for her marriage. [C19: from OF, lit.: a little bundle; see TRUSS]
trout (traʊt) *n, pl* **trout** *or* **trouts.** any of various game fishes, mostly of fresh water in northern regions. They are related to the salmon but are smaller and spotted. [OE *trūht,* from LL *tructa,* from Gk *troktēs* sharp-toothed fish]
trouvère (tru:'vɛə) *n* any of a group of poets of N France during the 12th and 13th centuries who composed chiefly narrative works. [C19: from F, from OF *troveor,* from *trover* to compose]
trove (trəʊv) *n* See **treasure-trove.**
trow (trəʊ) *vb Arch.* to think, believe, or trust. [OE *treow*]
trowel ('traʊəl) *n* **1** any of various small hand tools having a flat metal blade attached to a handle, used for scooping or spreading plaster or similar materials. **2** a similar tool with a curved blade used by gardeners for lifting plants, etc. ◆ *vb* **trowels, trowelling, trowelled** *or US* **trowels, troweling, troweled. 3** (*tr*) to use a trowel on. [C14: from OF *truele,* from L *trulla* a scoop, from *trua* a stirring spoon]
troy weight *or* **troy** (trɔɪ) *n* a system of weights used for precious metals and gemstones, based on the grain. 24 grains = 1 pennyweight; 20 pennyweights = 1 (troy) ounce; 12 ounces = 1 (troy) pound. [C14: after the city of *Troyes,* France, where first used]
trs *Printing. abbrev. for* transpose.
truant ➊ ('tru:ənt) *n* **1** a person who is absent without leave, esp. from school. ◆ *adj* **2** being or relating to a truant. ◆ *vb* **3** (*intr*) to play truant. [C13: from OF: vagabond, prob. of Celtic origin]
▸ **'truancy** *n*
truce ➊ (tru:s) *n* **1** an agreement to stop fighting, esp. temporarily. **2** temporary cessation of something unpleasant. [C13: from pl of OE *treow* trow]
truck[1] (trʌk) *n* **1** *Brit.* a vehicle for carrying freight on a railway; wagon. **2** another name (esp. US, Canad., Austral., and NZ) for **lorry. 3** Also called: **truckload.** the amount carried by a truck. **4** a frame carrying two or more pairs of wheels attached under an end of a railway coach, etc. **5** *Naut.* a disc-shaped block fixed to the head of a mast having holes for receiving halyards. **6** any wheeled vehicle used to move goods. ◆ *vb* **7** to convey (goods) in a truck. **8** (*intr*) *Chiefly US & Canad.* to drive a truck. [C17: ? shortened from *truckle* a small wheel]
truck[2] ➊ (trʌk) *n* **1** commercial goods. **2** dealings (esp. in **have no truck with**). **3** commercial exchange. **4** *Arch.* payment of wages in kind. **5**

THESAURUS

trot *vb* **1 = run,** canter, go briskly, jog, lope, scamper ◆ *n* **3 = run,** brisk pace, canter, jog, lope **7a on the trot** *Informal* **= one after the other,** consecutively, in a row, in succession, without break, without interruption
trot out *vb Informal* **= repeat,** bring forward, bring up, come out with, drag up, exhibit, recite, rehearse, reiterate, relate
troubadour *n* **= minstrel,** balladeer, jongleur, lyric poet, poet, singer
trouble *n* **1 = distress,** agitation, annoyance, anxiety, bummer, disquiet, grief, hardship, hassle (*inf.*), heartache, irritation, misfortune, pain, sorrow, suffering, torment, tribulation, vexation, woe, worry **2 = disorder,** agitation, bother (*inf.*), commotion, discontent, discord, dissatisfaction, disturbance, hassle (*inf.*), Pandora's box, row, strife, tumult, unrest **3 = ailment,** complaint, defect, disability, disease, disorder, failure, illness, malfunction, upset **5 = effort,** attention, bother, care, exertion, inconvenience, labour, pains, struggle, thought, work **6 = difficulty,** bother, concern, danger, deep water, dilemma, dire straits, hassle (*inf.*), hot water (*inf.*), mess, nuisance, pest, pickle (*inf.*), predicament, problem, scrape (*inf.*), spot (*inf.*), tight spot ◆ *vb* **10 = bother,** afflict, agitate, annoy, discompose, disconcert, disquiet, distress, disturb, faze, fret, grieve, harass, hassle (*inf.*), pain, perplex, perturb, pester, plague, put *or* get someone's back up, sadden, torment, upset, vex, worry **12 = take pains,** exert oneself, go to the effort of, make an effort, take the time **13 = inconvenience,** bother, burden, cause discomfort, discommode, disturb, impose upon, incommode, put out
Antonyms *n* ≠ **distress:** comfort, contentment, good fortune, happiness, pleasure, tranquillity ≠ **disorder:** agreement, contentment, harmony, peace, tranquillity, unity ≠ **effort:** convenience, ease, facility ◆ *vb* ≠ **bother:** appease, calm, mollify, please, relieve, soothe ≠ **take pains:** avoid, dodge ≠ **inconvenience:** relieve
troublemaker *n* **= mischief-maker,** *agent provocateur,* agitator, bad apple (*US inf.*), firebrand, incendiary, instigator, meddler, rabble-rouser, rotten apple (*Brit. inf.*), stirrer (*inf.*), stormy petrel
Antonyms *n* appeaser, arbitrator, conciliator, pacifier, peace-maker
troublesome *adj* **1 = bothersome,** annoying, arduous, burdensome, demanding, difficult, harassing, hard, importunate, inconvenient, irksome, irritating, laborious, oppressive, pestilential, plaguy (*inf.*), taxing, tiresome, tricky, trying, upsetting, vexatious, wearisome, worrisome, worrying **2 = disorderly,** insubordinate, rebellious, recalcitrant, refractory, rowdy, turbulent, uncooperative, undisciplined, unruly, violent
Antonyms *adj* ≠ **bothersome:** agreeable, calming, congenial, easy, pleasant, simple, soothing, undemanding ≠ **disorderly:** disciplined, eager-to-please, obedient, well-behaved
trough *n* **1 = manger,** crib, water trough **2 = channel,** canal, depression, ditch, duct, flume, furrow, gully, gutter, trench, watercourse
trounce *vb* **= defeat heavily** *or* **utterly,** beat, blow out of the water, clobber (*sl.*), crush, drub, give a hiding (*inf.*), hammer (*inf.*), lick (*inf.*), make mincemeat of, overwhelm, paste (*sl.*), rout, slaughter (*inf.*), stuff (*sl.*), tank (*sl.*), thrash, walk over (*inf.*), wipe the floor with (*inf.*)
troupe *n* **1 = company,** band, cast
trouper *n* **1 = performer,** actor, artiste, entertainer, player, theatrical, thespian
truancy *n* **2 = absence,** absence without leave, malingering, shirking, skiving (*Brit. sl.*)
truant *n* **1 = absentee,** delinquent, deserter, dodger, malingerer, runaway, shirker, skiver (*Brit. sl.*), straggler ◆ *adj* **2 = absent,** absent without leave, A.W.O.L., missing, skiving (*Brit. sl.*) ◆ *vb* **3 = absent oneself,** bob off (*Brit. sl.*), bunk off (*sl.*), desert, dodge, go missing, malinger, play truant, run away, shirk, skive (*Brit. sl.*), wag (*dialect*)
truce *n* **1, 2 = ceasefire,** armistice, break, cessation, cessation of hostilities, intermission, interval, let-up (*inf.*), lull, moratorium, peace, respite, rest, stay, treaty
truck[2] *n* **1 = commercial goods,** commodities, goods, merchandise, stock, stuff, wares **2, 3 = dealings,** barter, business, buying and selling, commerce, communication, connection, contact, exchange, relations, trade, traffic ◆ *vb* **8, 9 = buy and sell,** bargain, barter, cut a deal, deal,

miscellaneous articles. **6** *Inf.* rubbish. **7** *US & Canad.* vegetables grown for market. ◆ *vb* **8** *Arch.* to exchange (goods); barter. **9** (*intr*) to traffic or negotiate. [C13: from OF *troquer* (unattested) to barter, equivalent to Med. L *trocare*, from ?]

trucker ('trʌkə) *n Chiefly US & Canad.* **1** a lorry driver. **2** a person who arranges for the transport of goods by lorry.

truck farm *n US & Canad.* a market garden.
▸**truck farmer** *n* ▸**truck farming** *n*

truckie ('trʌkɪ) *n Austral. & NZ inf.* a truck driver.

trucking ('trʌkɪŋ) *n Chiefly US & Canad.* the transportation of goods by lorry.

truckle ⓣ ('trʌkᵊl) *vb* **truckles, truckling, truckled.** (*intr;* usually foll. by *to*) to yield weakly; give in. [C17: from obs. *truckle* to sleep in a truckle bed]
▸**'truckler** *n*

truckle bed *n* a low bed on wheels, stored under a larger bed. [C17: from *truckle* small wheel, ult. from L *trochlea* sheaf of a pulley]

truck system *n* a system during the early years of the Industrial Revolution of forcing workers to accept payment of wages in kind.

truculent ⓣ ('trʌkjulənt) *adj* **1** defiantly aggressive, sullen, or obstreperous. **2** *Arch.* savage, fierce, or harsh. [C16: from L *truculentus*, from *trux* fierce]
▸**'truculence** *or* **'truculency** *n* ▸**'truculently** *adv*

trudge ⓣ (trʌdʒ) *vb* **trudges, trudging, trudged. 1** (*intr*) to walk or plod heavily or wearily. **2** (*tr*) to pass through or over by trudging. ◆ *n* **3** a long tiring walk. [C16: from ?]
▸**'trudger** *n*

trudgen ('trʌdʒən) *n* a type of swimming stroke that uses overarm action, as in the crawl, and a scissors kick. [C19: after John *Trudgen*, E swimmer, who introduced it]

true ⓣ (truː) *adj* **truer, truest. 1** not false, fictional, or illusory; factual; conforming with reality. **2** (*prenominal*) real; not synthetic. **3** faithful and loyal. **4** conforming to a required standard, law, or pattern: *a true aim.* **5** exactly in tune. **6** (of a compass bearing) according to the earth's geographical rather than magnetic poles: *true north.* **7** *Biol.* conforming to the typical structure of a designated type. **8** *Physics.* not apparent or relative. ◆ *n* **9** correct alignment (esp. in **in true, out of true**). ◆ *adv* **10** truthfully; rightly. **11** precisely or unswervingly. ◆ *vb* **trues, truing, trued. 12** (*tr*) to adjust so as to make true. [OE *triewe*]
▸**'trueness** *n*

true bill *n* (formerly in Britain; now US) the endorsement made on a bill of indictment by a grand jury certifying it to be supported by sufficient evidence to warrant a trial.

true-blue ⓣ *adj* **1** unwaveringly or staunchly loyal. ◆ *n* **true blue. 2** *Chiefly Brit.* a staunch royalist or Conservative.

true-life *adj* directly comparable to reality: *a true-life story.*

truelove ('truː,lʌv) *n* **1** someone truly loved; sweetheart. **2** another name for **herb Paris.**

truelove knot *or* **true-lovers' knot** *n* a complicated bowknot that is hard to untie, symbolizing ties of love.

true north *n* the direction from any point along a meridian towards the North Pole. Also called: **geographic north.** Cf. **magnetic north.**

true rib *n* any of the upper seven pairs of ribs in man.

true time *n* the time shown by a sundial.

truffle ('trʌfᵊl) *n* **1** any of various edible subterranean European fungi. They have a tuberous appearance and are regarded as a delicacy. **2** Also called: **rum truffle.** *Chiefly Brit.* a sweet resembling this fungus in shape, flavoured with chocolate or rum. [C16: from F *truffe*, from OProvençal *trufa*, ult. from L *tūber*]

trug (trʌg) *n* a long shallow basket for carrying flowers, fruit, etc. [C16: ? var. of TROUGH]

trugo ('truːgəʊ) *n Austral.* a game similar to croquet, originally improvised in Victoria from the rubber discs used as buffers on railway carriages. [from *true go*, when the wheel is hit between the goalposts]

truism ⓣ ('truːɪzəm) *n* an obvious truth; platitude.
▸**tru'istic** *adj*

trull (trʌl) *n Arch.* a prostitute; harlot. [C16: from G *Trulle*]

truly ⓣ ('truːlɪ) *adv* **1** in a true, just, or faithful manner. **2** (intensifier): *a truly great man.* **3** indeed; really.

trumeau (truˈməʊ) *n, pl* **trumeaux** (-məʊz). *Archit.* a section of a wall or pillar between two openings. [from F]

trump[1] ⓣ (trʌmp) *n* **1** Also called: **trump card. 1a** any card from the suit chosen as trumps. **1b** this suit itself; trumps. **2** a decisive or advantageous move, resource, action, etc. **3** *Inf.* a fine or reliable person. ◆ *vb* **4** to play a trump card on (a suit, or a particular card of a suit, that is not trumps). **5** (*tr*) to outdo or surpass. ◆ See also **trumps, trump up.** [C16: var. of TRIUMPH]

trump[2] (trʌmp) *n Arch. or literary.* **1** a trumpet or the sound produced by one. **2 the last trump.** the final trumpet call on the Day of Judgment. [C13: from OF *trompe*, from OHG *trumpa* trumpet]

trumpery ⓣ ('trʌmpərɪ) *n, pl* **trumperies. 1** foolish talk or actions. **2** a useless or worthless article; trinket. ◆ *adj* **3** useless or worthless. [C15: from OF *tromperie* deceit, from *tromper* to cheat]

trumpet ⓣ ('trʌmpɪt) *n* **1** a valved brass instrument of brilliant tone consisting of a narrow tube ending in a flared bell. **2** any similar instrument, esp. a straight instrument used for fanfares, signals, etc. **3** a loud sound such as that of a trumpet, esp. when made by an animal. **4** an eight-foot reed stop on an organ. **5** something resembling a trumpet in shape. **6** short for **ear trumpet. 7 blow one's own trumpet.** to boast about one's own skills or good qualities. ◆ *vb* **trumpets, trumpeting, trumpeted. 8** to proclaim or sound loudly. [C13: from OF *trompette* a little TRUMP[2]]

trumpeter ('trʌmpɪtə) *n* **1** a person who plays the trumpet, esp. one whose duty it is to play fanfares, signals, etc. **2** any of three birds of South America, having a rounded body, long legs, and a glossy blackish plumage. **3** (*sometimes cap.*) a breed of domestic fancy pigeon with a long ruff. **4** a large silvery-grey Australian marine food and game fish that grunts when taken from the water.

trumpeter swan *n* a large swan of W North America, having a white plumage and black bill.

trumps (trʌmps) *pl n* **1** (*sometimes sing*) *Cards.* any one of the four suits that outranks all the other suits for the duration of a deal or game. **2 turn up trumps.** (of a person) to bring about a happy or successful conclusion, esp. unexpectedly.

trump up ⓣ *vb* (*tr, adv*) to invent (a charge, accusation, etc.) so as to deceive.

truncate ⓣ *vb* (trʌŋˈkeɪt, 'trʌŋkeɪt), **truncates, truncating, truncated. 1** (*tr*) to shorten by cutting. ◆ *adj* ('trʌŋkeɪt). **2** cut short; truncated. **3** *Biol.* having a blunt end. [C15: from L *truncāre* to lop]
▸**trun'cation** *n*

truncated (trʌŋˈkeɪtɪd) *adj* **1** (of a cone, prism, etc.) having an apex or end removed by a plane intersection. **2** shortened by or as if by cutting off; truncate.

THESAURUS

do business, exchange, have dealings, negotiate, swap, trade, traffic, transact business

truckle *vb* = **give in**, bend the knee, bow and scrape, concede, cringe, crouch, defer, fawn, give way, knuckle under, kowtow, lick (someone's) boots, pander to, stoop, submit, toady, yield

truculent *adj* **1** = **hostile**, aggressive, antagonistic, bad-tempered, bellicose, belligerent, combative, contentious, cross, defiant, ill-tempered, itching *or* spoiling for a fight (*inf.*), obstreperous, pugnacious, scrappy (*inf.*), sullen
Antonyms *adj* agreeable, amiable, civil, co-operative, gentle, good-natured, peaceable, placid

trudge *vb* **1** = **plod**, clump, drag oneself, footslog, hike, lumber, march, slog, stump, traipse (*inf.*), tramp, trek, walk heavily, yomp ◆ *n* **3** = **tramp**, footslog, haul, hike, march, slog, traipse (*inf.*), trek, yomp

true *adj* **1, 2** = **correct**, accurate, actual, authentic, bona fide, exact, factual, genuine, legitimate, natural, precise, pure, real, right, truthful, valid, veracious, veritable **3** = **faithful**, confirmed, constant, dedicated, devoted, dutiful, fast, firm, honest, honourable, loyal, pure, reliable, sincere, staunch, steady, true-blue, trustworthy, trusty, unswerving, upright **4** = **exact**, accurate, correct, on target, perfect, precise, proper, spot-on (*Brit. inf.*), unerring ◆ *adv* **10** = **truthfully**, honestly, rightly, veraciously, veritably **11** = **precisely**, accurately, correctly, on target, perfectly, properly, unerringly
Antonyms *adj* ≠ **correct:** abnormal, artificial, atypical, bogus, counterfeit, erroneous, fake, false, fictional, fictitious, illegitimate, imaginary, inaccurate, incorrect, made-up, make-believe, phoney *or* phony (*inf.*), pretended, self-styled, spurious, unofficial, untrue, untruthful ≠ **faithful:** deceitful, disloyal, faithless, false, treacherous, unreliable, untrue, untrustworthy ≠ **exact:** askew, awry, inaccurate, incorrect

true-blue *adj* **1** = **staunch**, confirmed, constant, dedicated, devoted, dyed-in-the-wool, faithful, loyal, orthodox, trusty, uncompromising, unwavering

truism *n* = **cliché**, axiom, bromide, commonplace, platitude, stock phrase, trite saying

truly *adv* **1** = **correctly**, accurately, authentically, beyond doubt, beyond question, confirmedly, exactly, factually, firmly, genuinely, honestly, in actuality, in fact, in reality, in truth, legitimately, precisely, really, rightly, sincerely, truthfully, veraciously, veritably, without a doubt **3** = **really**, exceptionally, extremely, greatly, indeed, of course, seriously (*inf.*), to be sure, verily, very
Antonyms *adv* ≠ **correctly:** doubtfully, falsely, fraudulently, inaccurately, incorrectly, mistakenly

trump[1] *vb* **5** = **outdo**, cap, excel, score points off, surpass, top

trumpery *n* **1** = **nonsense**, balderdash, bilge (*inf.*), bosh (*inf.*), bullshit (*taboo sl.*), bunkum *or* buncombe (*chiefly US*), claptrap (*inf.*), cobblers (*Brit. taboo sl.*), drivel, eyewash (*inf.*), foolishness, foolish talk, garbage (*inf.*), guff (*sl.*), hogwash, hokum (*sl., chiefly US & Canad.*), hot air (*inf.*), idiocy, inanity, moonshine, pap, piffle (*inf.*), poppycock (*inf.*), stuff, tommyrot, tosh (*sl., chiefly Brit.*), tripe (*inf.*), twaddle **2** = **trifle**, bagatelle, bauble, gewgaw, kickshaw, knick-knack, toy, trinket ◆ *adj* **3** = **trifle**, brummagem, cheap, flashy, meretricious, nasty, rubbishy, shabby, shoddy, tawdry, trashy, trifling, useless, valueless, worthless

trumpet *n* **2** = **horn**, bugle, clarion **3** = **roar**, bay, bellow, call, cry **7 blow one's own trumpet** = **boast**, brag, crow, sing one's own praises, vaunt ◆ *vb* **8** = **proclaim**, advertise, announce, broadcast, crack up (*inf.*), extol, noise abroad, publish, shout from the rooftops, sound loudly, tout (*inf.*)
Antonyms *vb* ≠ **proclaim:** conceal, hide, hush up, keep secret, make light of, play down, soft pedal (*inf.*)

trump up *vb* = **invent**, concoct, contrive, cook up (*inf.*), create, fabricate, fake, make up, manufacture

truncate *vb* **1** = **shorten**, abbreviate, clip, crop, curtail, cut, cut short, dock, lop, pare, prune, trim
Antonyms *vb* drag out, draw out, extend, lengthen, prolong, protract, spin out, stretch

truncheon ◐ ('trʌntʃən) *n* **1** *Chiefly Brit.* a club or cudgel carried by a policeman. **2** a baton of office. [C16: from OF *tronchon* stump, from L *truncus* trunk; see TRUNCATE]

trundle ('trʌndᵊl) *vb* **trundles, trundling, trundled. 1** to move heavily on or as if on wheels: *the bus trundled by.* ◆ *n* **2** a trundling. **3** a small wheel or roller. [OE *tryndel*]

trundle bed *n* a less common word for **truckle bed.**

trundler ('trʌndlə) *n NZ.* **1** a trolley for shopping or one for golf clubs. **2** a child's pushchair.

trunk ◐ (trʌŋk) *n* **1** the main stem of a tree. **2** a large strong case or box used to contain clothes, etc., when travelling and for storage. **3** the body excluding the head, neck, and limbs; torso. **4** the elongated nasal part of an elephant. **5** the US and Canad. name for **boot**[1] (sense 2). **6** the main stem of a nerve, blood vessel, etc. **7** *Naut.* a watertight boxlike cover within a vessel, such as one used to enclose a centreboard. **8** an enclosed duct or passageway for ventilation, etc. **9** (*modifier*) of a main road, railway, etc., in a network: *a trunk line.* ◆ See also **trunks.** [C15: from OF *tronc,* from L *truncus,* from *truncus* (adj) lopped]

trunk call *n Chiefly Brit.* a long-distance telephone call.

trunk curl *n* another name for **sit-up.**

trunkfish ('trʌŋk,fɪʃ) *n, pl* **trunkfish** *or* **trunkfishes.** any of a family of fishes having the body encased in bony plates.

trunk hose *n* a man's puffed-out breeches reaching to the thighs and worn with tights in the 16th century.

trunking ('trʌŋkɪŋ) *n* **1** *Telecomm.* the cables that take a common route through a telephone exchange building. **2** plastic housing used to conceal wires, etc.; casing. **3** the delivery of goods over long distances, esp. by road vehicles to local distribution centres.

trunk line *n* **1** a direct link between two telephone exchanges or switchboards that are a considerable distance apart. **2** the main route or routes on a railway.

trunk road *n Brit.* a main road, esp. one that is suitable for heavy vehicles.

trunks (trʌŋks) *pl n* **1** a man's garment worn for swimming, extending from the waist to the thigh. **2** shorts worn for some sports. **3** *Chiefly Brit.* men's underpants with legs that reach midthigh.

trunnion ('trʌnjən) *n* one of a pair of coaxial projections attached to opposite sides of a container, cannon, etc., to provide a support about which it can turn. [C17: from OF *trognon* trunk]

truss ◐ (trʌs) *vb* (*tr*) **1** (sometimes foll. by *up*) to tie, bind, or bundle. **2** to bind the wings and legs of (a fowl) before cooking. **3** to support or stiffen (a roof, bridge, etc.) with structural members. **4** *Med.* to supply or support with a truss. ◆ *n* **5** a structural framework of wood or metal used to support a roof, bridge, etc. **6** *Med.* a device for holding a hernia in place, typically consisting of a pad held in position by a belt. **7** a cluster of flowers or fruit growing at the end of a single stalk. **8** *Naut.* a metal fitting fixed to a yard at its centre for holding it to a mast. **9** another name for **corbel. 10** a bundle or pack. **11** *Chiefly Brit.* a bundle of hay or straw, esp. one having a fixed weight of 36, 56, or 60 pounds. [C13: from OF *trousse,* from *trousser,* apparently from Vulgar L *torciāre* (unattested), from *torca* (unattested) a bundle]

trust ◐ (trʌst) *n* **1** reliance on and confidence in the truth, worth, reliability, etc., of a person or thing; faith. Related adj: **fiducial. 2** a group of commercial enterprises combined to control the market for any commodity. **3** the obligation of someone in a responsible position. **4** custody, charge, or care. **5** a person or thing in which confidence or faith is placed. **6** commercial credit. **7a** an arrangement whereby a person to whom the legal title to property is conveyed (the trustee) holds such property for the benefit of those entitled to the beneficial interest. **7b** property that is the subject of such an arrangement. Related adj: **fiduciary. 8** (in the British National Health Service) a self-governing hospital, group of hospitals, or other body providing health-care services, which operates as an independent commercial unit within the NHS. **9** (*modifier*) of or relating to a trust or trusts. ◆ *vb* **10** (*tr; may take a clause as object*) to expect, hope, or suppose. **11** (when *tr, may take an infinitive;* when *intr,* often foll. by *in* or *to*) to place confidence in (someone to do something); rely (upon). **12** (*tr*) to consign for care. **13** (*tr*) to allow (someone to do something) with confidence in his or her good sense or honesty. **14** (*tr*) to extend business credit to. [C13: from ON *traust*]
▸ **'trustable** *adj* ▸ **'truster** *n*

trust account *n* **1** Also called: **trustee account.** a savings account deposited in the name of a trustee who controls it during his lifetime, after which the balance is payable to a prenominated beneficiary. **2** property under the control of a trustee or trustees.

trustee (trʌ'stiː) *n* **1** a person to whom the legal title to property is entrusted. **2** a member of a board that manages the affairs of an institution or organization.

trustee in bankruptcy *n* a person entrusted with the administration of a bankrupt's affairs and with realizing his assets for the benefit of the creditors.

trustee investment *n Stock Exchange.* an investment in which trustees are authorized to invest money belonging to a trust fund.

trusteeship (trʌ'stiːʃɪp) *n* **1** the office or function of a trustee. **2a** the administration or government of a territory by a foreign country under the supervision of the **Trusteeship Council** of the United Nations. **2b** (*often cap.*) any such dependent territory; trust territory.

trustful ◐ ('trʌstfʊl) *or* **trusting** *adj* characterized by a tendency or readiness to trust others.
▸ **'trustfully** *or* **'trustingly** *adv*

trust fund *n* money, securities, etc., held in trust.

trust territory *n* (*sometimes cap.*) another name for a **trusteeship** (sense 2b).

trustworthy ◐ ('trʌst,wɜːðɪ) *adj* worthy of being trusted; honest, reliable, or dependable.
▸ **'trust,worthily** *adv* ▸ **'trust,worthiness** *n*

trusty ◐ ('trʌstɪ) *adj* **trustier, trustiest. 1** faithful or reliable. ◆ *n, pl* **trusties. 2** a trustworthy convict given special privileges.
▸ **'trustily** *adv* ▸ **'trustiness** *n*

truth ◐ (truːθ) *n* **1** the quality of being true, genuine, actual, or factual. **2** something that is true as opposed to false. **3** a proven or verified fact, principle, etc.: *the truths of astronomy.* **4** (*usually pl*) a system of concepts purporting to represent some aspect of the world: *the truths of religion.* **5** fidelity to a standard or law. **6** faithful reproduction or portrayal. **7** honesty. **8** accuracy, as in the setting of a mechanical instrument. **9** loyalty. ◆ Related adjs.: **veritable, veracious.** [OE *triewth*]
▸ **'truthless** *adj*

truth drug *or* **serum** *n Inf.* any of various drugs supposed to have the property of making people tell the truth, as by relaxing them.

truthful ◐ ('truːθfʊl) *adj* **1** telling the truth; honest. **2** realistic: *a truthful portrayal of the king.*
▸ **'truthfully** *adv* ▸ **'truthfulness** *n*

truth-function *n Logic.* a function that determines the truth-value of a complex sentence solely in terms of the truth-values of the component sentences without reference to their meaning.

truth set *n Logic, maths.* the set of values that satisfy an open sentence, equation, inequality, etc., having no unique solution. Also called: **solution set.**

truth table *n* **1** a table, used in logic, indicating the truth-value of a compound statement for every truth-value of its component propositions. **2** a similar table, used in transistor technology, to indicate the value of the output signal of a logic circuit for every value of input signal.

truth-value *n Logic.* either of the values, true or false, that may be taken by a statement.

THESAURUS

truncheon *n* **1** *Chiefly Brit.* = **club**, baton, cudgel, staff

trunk *n* **1** = **stem**, bole, stalk, stock **2** = **chest**, bin, box, case, casket, coffer, crate, kist (*Scot. & N English dialect*), locker, portmanteau **3** = **body**, torso **4** = **snout**, proboscis

truss *vb* **1** = **tie**, bind, bundle, fasten, make fast, pack, pinion, secure, strap, tether **4** *Medical* = **support**, bandage ◆ *n* **5** = **joist**, beam, brace, buttress, prop, shore, stanchion, stay, strut, support

trust *n* **1** = **confidence**, assurance, belief, certainty, certitude, conviction, credence, credit, expectation, faith, hope, reliance **3** = **responsibility**, duty, obligation **4** = **custody**, care, charge, guard, guardianship, protection, safekeeping, trusteeship ◆ *vb* **10** = **expect**, assume, believe, hope, presume, suppose, surmise, think likely **11** = **believe in**, bank on, count on, depend on, have faith in, lean on, pin one's faith on, place confidence in, place one's trust in, place reliance on, rely upon, swear by, take as gospel, take at face value **12** = **entrust**, assign, command, commit, confide, consign, delegate, give, put into the hands of, sign over, turn over
Antonyms *n* ≠ **confidence:** distrust, doubt, fear, incredulity, lack of faith, mistrust, scepticism, suspicion, uncertainty, wariness ◆ *vb* ≠ **believe in:** be sceptical of, beware, disbelieve, discredit, distrust, doubt, lack confidence in, lack faith in, mistrust, suspect

trustful *adj* = **unsuspecting**, confiding, credulous, gullible, innocent, naive, optimistic, simple, unguarded, unsuspicious, unwary
Antonyms *adj* cagey (*inf.*), cautious, chary, distrustful, guarded, on one's guard, suspicious, wary

trustworthy *adj* = **dependable**, ethical, honest, honourable, level-headed, mature, principled, reliable, reputable, responsible, righteous, sensible, staunch, steadfast, to be trusted, true, trusty, truthful, upright
Antonyms *adj* deceitful, dishonest, disloyal, irresponsible, treacherous, undependable, unethical, unprincipled, unreliable, untrustworthy

trusty *adj* **1** = **reliable**, dependable, faithful, firm, honest, responsible, solid, staunch, steady, straightforward, strong, true, trustworthy, upright
Antonyms *adj* dishonest, irresolute, irresponsible, undependable, unfaithful, unreliable

truth *n* **1** = **truthfulness**, accuracy, actuality, exactness, fact, factuality, factualness, genuineness, legitimacy, naturalism, precision, reality, validity, veracity, verity **3** = **fact**, axiom, certainty, law, maxim, proven principle, reality, truism, verity **7** = **honesty**, candour, frankness, integrity, realism, uprightness **9** = **loyalty**, constancy, dedication, devotion, dutifulness, faith, faithfulness, fidelity
Antonyms *n* ≠ **truthfulness:** error, falsity, inaccuracy ≠ **fact:** delusion, fabrication, falsehood, fiction, invention, legend, lie, make-believe, myth, old wives' tale, untruth ≠ **honesty:** deceit, deception, dishonesty

truthful *adj* **1** = **honest**, candid, faithful, forthright, frank, plain-spoken, reliable, sincere, straight, straightforward, true, trustworthy, upfront (*inf.*), veracious **2** = **true**, accurate, correct, exact, literal, naturalistic, precise, realistic, veritable
Antonyms *adj* ≠ **honest:** deceptive, dishonest, false, insincere, lying, untruthful ≠ **true:** fabricated, false, fictional, fictitious, inaccurate, incorrect, made-up, untrue, untruthful

truthless *adj* **1** = **untrue**, deceitful, deceptive, dishonest, faithless, false, fraudulent, insincere, lying, mendacious, perjured, treacherous, untrustworthy

try ❶ (traɪ) *vb* **tries, trying, tried. 1** (when *tr, may take an infinitive,* sometimes with *to* replaced by *and*) to make an effort or attempt. **2** (*tr; often foll. by out*) to sample, test, or give experimental use to (something). **3** (*tr*) to put strain or stress on: *he tries my patience.* **4** (*tr; often passive*) to give pain, affliction, or vexation to. **5a** to examine and determine the issues involved in (a cause) in a court of law. **5b** to hear evidence in order to determine the guilt or innocence of (an accused). **6** (*tr*) to melt (fat, lard, etc.) in order to separate out impurities. ◆ *n, pl* **tries. 7** an experiment or trial. **8** an attempt or effort. **9** *Rugby.* the act of an attacking player touching the ball down behind the opposing team's goal line. **10** *American football.* an attempt made after a touchdown to score an extra point, as by kicking a goal. ◆ See also **try on, try out.** [C13: from OF *trier* to sort, from ?]

USAGE NOTE The use of *and* instead of *to* after *try* is very common, but should be avoided in formal writing: *we must try to prevent* (not *try and prevent*) *this happening.*

trying ❶ ('traɪɪŋ) *adj* upsetting, difficult, or annoying.
▸**'tryingly** *adv*

trying plane *n* a plane with a long body for planing the edges of long boards. Also called: **try plane.**

try on *vb* (*tr, adv*) **1** to put on (a garment) to find out whether it fits, etc. **2 try it on.** *Inf.* to attempt to deceive or fool someone. ◆ *n* **try-on. 3** *Brit. inf.* something done to test out a person's tolerance, etc.

try out ❶ *vb* (*adv*) **1** (*tr*) to test or put to experimental use. **2** (when *intr,* usually foll. by *for*) *US & Canad.* (of an athlete, actor, etc.) to undergo a test or to submit (an athlete, actor, etc.) to a test in order to determine suitability for a place in a team, an acting role, etc. ◆ *n* **tryout. 3** *Chiefly US & Canad.* a trial or test, as of an athlete or actor.

trypanosome ('trɪpənəˌsəʊm) *n* any parasitic flagellate protozoan that lives in the blood of vertebrates and causes sleeping sickness and certain other diseases. [C19: from NL *Trypanosoma,* from Gk *trupanon* borer + *sōma* body]

trypanosomiasis (ˌtrɪpənəsə'maɪəsɪs) *n* any infection of an animal or human with a trypanosome.

trypsin ('trɪpsɪn) *n* a digestive enzyme in the pancreatic juice: it catalyses the hydrolysis of proteins to peptides. [C19 *tryp-,* from Gk *tripsis* a rubbing, from *tribein* to rub + -IN; from the fact that it was orig. produced by rubbing the pancreas with glycerine]
▸**tryptic** ('trɪptɪk) *adj*

tryptophan ('trɪptəˌfæn) *n* an essential amino acid; a component of proteins necessary for growth. [C20: from *trypt(ic),* from TRYPSIN + *-o-* + *-phan,* var. of -PHANE]

trysail ('traɪˌseɪl; *Naut.* 'traɪsᵊl) *n* a small fore-and-aft sail set on a sailing vessel in foul weather to help keep her head to the wind.

try square *n* a device for testing or laying out right angles, usually consisting of a metal blade fixed at right angles to a wooden handle.

tryst (trɪst, traɪst) *n Arch. or literary.* **1** an appointment to meet, esp. secretly. **2** the place of such a meeting or the meeting itself. [C14: from OF *triste* lookout post, apparently from ON]

tsar ❶ *or* **czar** (zɑː) *n* **1** (until 1917) the emperor of Russia. **2** a tyrant; autocrat. **3** *Inf.* a person in authority. [C17: from Russian *tsar,* via Gothic *kaisar* from L: CAESAR]
▸**'tsardom** *or* **'czardom** *n*

tsarevitch *or* **czarevitch** ('zɑːrəvɪtʃ) *n* a son of a Russian tsar, esp. the eldest son. [from Russian *tsarevich,* from TSAR + *-evich,* masc. patronymic suffix]

tsarevna *or* **czarevna** (zɑː'revnə) *n* **1** a daughter of a Russian tsar. **2** the wife of a Russian tsarevitch. [from Russian, from TSAR + *-evna,* fem. patronymic suffix]

tsarina, czarina (zɑː'riːnə) *or* **tsaritsa, czaritza** (zɑː'rɪtsə) *n* the wife of a Russian tsar; Russian empress. [from It., Sp. *czarina,* from G *Czarin*]

tsarism *or* **czarism** ('zɑːrɪzəm) *n* a system of government by a tsar.
▸**'tsarist** *or* **'czarist** *n, adj*

TSE (in Canada) *abbrev. for* Toronto Stock Exchange.

tsetse fly *or* **tzetze fly** ('tsetsɪ) *n* any of various bloodsucking African dipterous flies which transmit various diseases, esp. sleeping sickness. [C19: via Afrik. from Tswana]

T-shirt *or* **tee-shirt** *n* a lightweight simple garment for the upper body, usually short-sleeved. [from T-shape formed when laid out flat]

tsotsi ('tsɒtsɪ) *n, pl* **tsotsis.** *S. African inf.* a Black street thug or gang member; wide boy. [C20: ?from Nguni *tsotsa* to dress flashily]

tsp. *abbrev. for* teaspoon.

T-square *n* a T-shaped ruler used for drawing horizontal lines and to support set squares when drawing vertical and inclined lines.

T-stop *n* a setting of the lens aperture on a camera calibrated photometrically and assigned a T-number.

tsunami (tsʊ'nɑːmɪ) *n, pl* **tsunamis** *or* **tsunami.** a large, often destructive sea wave produced by a submarine earthquake, subsidence, or volcanic eruption. [from Japanese, from *tsu* port + *nami* wave]

tsutsugamushi disease (ˌtsutsugə'muʃɪ) *n* one of the five major groups of acute infectious rickettsial diseases affecting man, common in Asia. It is transmitted by the bite of mites. [from Japanese, from *tsutsuga* disease + *mushi* insect]

Tswana ('tswɑːnə) *n* **1** (*pl* **Tswana** *or* **Tswanas**) a member of a mixed Negroid and Bushman people of southern Africa, living chiefly in Botswana. **2** the language of this people.

TT *abbrev. for:* **1** teetotal. **2** teetotaller. **3** telegraphic transfer: a method of sending money abroad by cabled transfer between banks. **4** Tourist Trophy (annual motorcycle races held in the Isle of Man). **5** tuberculin-tested.

TTL *abbrev. for:* **1** transistor transistor logic: a method of constructing electronic logic circuits. **2** through-the-lens: denoting a system of light metering in cameras.

TU *abbrev. for* trade union.

Tu. *abbrev. for* Tuesday.

tuatara (ˌtuːə'tɑːrə) *n* a lizard-like reptile occurring on certain islands near New Zealand. [C19: from Maori, from *tua* back + *tara* spine]

tub (tʌb) *n* **1** a low wide open container, typically round: used in a variety of domestic and industrial situations. **2** a small plastic or cardboard container of similar shape for ice cream, margarine, etc. **3** another word (esp. US) for **bath** (sense 1). **4** Also called: **tubful.** the amount a tub will hold. **5** a clumsy slow boat or ship. **6a** a small vehicle on rails for carrying loads in a mine. **6b** a container for lifting coal or ore up a mine shaft. ◆ *vb* **tubs, tubbing, tubbed. 7** *Brit. inf.* to wash (oneself) in a tub. **8** (*tr*) to keep or put in a tub. [C14: from MDu. *tubbe*]
▸**'tubbable** *adj* ▸**'tubber** *n*

tuba ('tjuːbə) *n, pl* **tubas** *or* **tubae** (-biː). **1** a valved brass instrument of bass pitch, in which the bell points upwards and the mouthpiece projects at right angles. **2** a powerful reed stop on an organ. [L]

tubal ('tjuːbᵊl) *adj* **1** of or relating to a tube. **2** of, relating to, or developing in a Fallopian tube.

tubby ❶ ('tʌbɪ) *adj* **tubbier, tubbiest. 1** plump. **2** shaped like a tub.
▸**'tubbiness** *n*

tube (tjuːb) *n* **1** a long hollow cylindrical object, used for the passage of fluids or as a container. **2** a collapsible cylindrical container of soft metal or plastic closed with a cap, used to hold viscous liquids or pastes. **3** *Anat.* **3a** short for **Eustachian tube** or **Fallopian tube. 3b** any hollow cylindrical structure. **4** (*sometimes cap.*) *Brit.* **4a the tube.** an underground railway system, esp. that in London. US and Canad. equivalent: **subway. 4b** the tunnels through which the railway runs. **5** *Electronics.* **5a** another name for **valve** (sense 3). **5b** See **electron tube, cathode-ray tube, television tube. 6** *Sl., chiefly US.* a television set. **7** *Austral. sl.* a bottle or can of beer. **8** *Surfing.* the cylindrical passage formed when a wave breaks and the crest tips forward. ◆ *vb* **tubes, tubing, tubed.** (*tr*) **9** to supply with a tube. **10** to convey in a tube. **11** to shape like a tube. [C17: from L *tubus*]
▸**'tubeless** *adj*

tube foot *n* any of numerous tubular outgrowths of most echinoderms that are used for locomotion, to aid ingestion of food, etc.

tubeless tyre *n* a pneumatic tyre in which the outer casing makes an airtight seal with the rim of the wheel so that an inner tube is unnecessary.

tuber ('tjuːbə) *n* **1** a fleshy underground stem or root. **2** *Anat.* a raised area; swelling. [C17: from L *tūber* hump]

tubercle ('tjuːbəkᵊl) *n* **1** any small rounded nodule or elevation, esp. on the skin, on a bone, or on a plant. **2** any small rounded pathological lesion, esp. one characteristic of tuberculosis. [C16: from L *tūberculum* a little swelling]

tubercle bacillus *n* a rodlike bacterium that causes tuberculosis.

tubercular (tjʊ'bɜːkjʊlə) *adj also* **tuberculous. 1** of or symptomatic of tuberculosis. **2** of or relating to a tubercle. **3** characterized by the presence of tubercles. ◆ *n* **4** a person with tuberculosis.

tuberculate (tjʊ'bɜːkjʊlɪt) *adj* covered with tubercles.
▸**tuˌbercu'lation** *n*

tuberculin (tjʊ'bɜːkjʊlɪn) *n* a sterile liquid prepared from cultures of attenuated tubercle bacillus and used in the diagnosis of tuberculosis.

tuberculin-tested *adj* (of milk) produced by cows that have been certified as free of tuberculosis.

tuberculosis (tjʊˌbɜːkjʊ'ləʊsɪs) *n* a communicable disease caused by infection with the tubercle bacillus, most frequently affecting the lungs. [C19: from NL]

THESAURUS

try *vb* **1 = attempt,** aim, do one's best, do one's damnedest (*inf.*), endeavour, essay, exert oneself, give it one's best shot (*inf.*), have a crack (*inf.*), have a go, have a shot (*inf.*), have a stab (*inf.*), make an all-out effort (*inf.*), make an attempt, make an effort, move heaven and earth, seek, strive, struggle, undertake **2 = test,** appraise, check out, evaluate, examine, experiment, inspect, investigate, prove, put to the test, sample, taste **3, 4 = strain,** afflict, annoy, inconvenience, irk, irritate, pain, plague, stress, tax, tire, trouble, upset, vex, weary **5a = judge,** adjudge, adjudicate, examine, hear ◆ *n* **7 = test,** appraisal, evaluation, experiment, inspection, sample, taste, trial **8 = attempt,** crack (*inf.*), effort, endeavour, essay, go (*inf.*), shot (*inf.*), stab (*inf.*)

trying *adj* **= annoying,** aggravating, arduous, bothersome, difficult, exasperating, fatiguing, hard, irksome, irritating, stressful, taxing, tiresome, tough, troublesome, upsetting, vexing, wearisome

Antonyms *adj* calming, easy, no bother, no trouble, painless, simple, straightforward, undemanding

try out *vb* **1 = test,** appraise, check out, evaluate, experiment with, inspect, put into practice, put to the test, sample, taste

tsar *n* **2, 3** *Informal* **= head,** autocrat, despot, emperor, leader, overlord, ruler, sovereign, tyrant

tubby *adj* **1 = fat,** chubby, corpulent, obese, overweight, paunchy, plump, podgy, portly, roly-poly, stout

tuberose ('tju:bə,rəuz) *n* a perennial Mexican agave plant having a tuberous root and fragrant white flowers. [C17: from L *tūberōsus* full of lumps; from its root]

tuberous ('tju:bərəs) *or* **tuberose** ('tju:bə,rəus) *adj* **1** (of plants) forming, bearing, or resembling a tuber or tubers. **2** *Anat.* of or having warty protuberances or tubers. [C17: from L *tūberōsus* full of knobs]

tube worm *n* any of various worms that construct and live in a tube of sand, lime, etc.

tubifex ('tju:bɪ,fɛks) *n, pl* **tubifex** *or* **tubifexes.** any of a genus of small reddish freshwater worms. [C19: from NL, from L *tubus* tube + *facere* to make]

tubing ('tju:bɪŋ) *n* **1** tubes collectively. **2** a length of tube. **3** a system of tubes. **4** fabric in the form of a tube.

tub-thumper *n* a noisy, violent, or ranting public speaker.
▸**'tub-,thumping** *adj, n*

tubular ('tju:bjʊlə) *adj* **1** Also: **tubiform** ('tju:bɪ,fɔ:m). having the form of a tube or tubes. **2** of or relating to a tube or tubing.

tubular bells *pl n* a set of long tubes of brass tuned for use in an orchestra and struck with a mallet to simulate the sound of bells.

tubule ('tju:bju:l) *n* any small tubular structure, esp. in an animal body. [C17: from L *tubulus* a little TUBE]

TUC (in Britain) *abbrev. for* Trades Union Congress.

tuck ❶ (tʌk) *vb* **1** (*tr*) to push or fold into a small confined space or concealed place or between two surfaces. **2** (*tr*) to thrust the loose ends or sides of (something) into a confining space, so as to make neat and secure. **3** to make a tuck or tucks in (a garment). **4** (*usually tr*) to draw together, contract, or pucker. ◆ *n* **5** a tucked object or part. **6** a pleat or fold in a part of a garment, usually stitched down. **7** the part of a vessel where the planks meet at the sternpost. **8** *Brit. inf.* **8a** food, esp. cakes and sweets. **8b** (*as modifier*): *a tuck box.* **9** a position of the body, as in certain dives, in which the legs are bent with the knees drawn up against the chest and tightly clasped. ◆ See also **tuck away, tuck in.** [C14: from OE *tūcian* to torment]

tuck away *vb* (*tr, adv*) *Inf.* **1** to eat (a large amount of food). **2** to store, esp. in a place difficult to find.

tucker[1] ('tʌkə) *n* **1** a person or thing that tucks. **2** a detachable yoke of lace, linen, etc., often white, worn over the breast, as of a low-cut dress. **3** *Austral. & NZ. old-fashioned* an informal word for **food.**

tucker[2] ('tʌkə) *vb* (*tr; often passive;* usually foll. by *out*) *Inf., chiefly US & Canad.* to weary or tire.

tucker-bag *or* **tuckerbox** ('tʌkə,bɒks) *n Austral. old-fashioned sl.* a bag or box in which food is carried or stored.

tucket ('tʌkɪt) *n Arch.* a flourish on a trumpet. [C16: from OF *toquer* to sound (on a drum)]

tuck in ❶ *vb* (*adv*) **1** (*tr*) Also: **tuck into.** to put to bed and make snug. **2** (*tr*) to thrust the loose ends or sides of (something) into a confining space: *tuck the blankets in.* **3** (*intr*) Also: **tuck into.** *Inf.* to eat, esp. heartily. ◆ *n* **tuck-in. 4** *Brit. inf.* a meal, esp. a large one.

tuck shop *n Chiefly Brit.* a shop, esp. one near a school, where cakes and sweets are sold.

-tude *suffix forming nouns.* indicating state or condition: *plenitude.* [from L *-tūdō*]

Tudor ('tju:də) *adj* **1** of or relating to the English royal house ruling from 1485 to 1603. **2** characteristic of or happening in this period. **3** denoting a style of architecture characterized by half-timbered houses.

Tues. *abbrev. for* Tuesday.

Tuesday ('tju:zdɪ) *n* the third day of the week; second day of the working week. [OE *tīwesdæg*]

tufa ('tju:fə) *n* a porous rock formed of calcium carbonate deposited from springs. [C18: from It. *tufo,* from LL *tōfus*]
▸**tufaceous** (tju:'feɪʃəs) *adj*

tuff (tʌf) *n* a hard volcanic rock consisting of consolidated fragments of lava. [C16: from OF *tuf,* from It. *tufo;* see TUFA]
▸**tuffaceous** (tʌ'feɪʃəs) *adj*

tuffet ('tʌfɪt) *n* a small mound or low seat. [C16: alteration of TUFT]

tuft ❶ (tʌft) *n* **1** a bunch of feathers, grass, hair, etc., held together at the base. **2** a cluster of threads drawn tightly through upholstery, a quilt, etc., to secure the padding. **3** a small clump of trees or bushes. **4** (formerly) a gold tassel on the cap worn by titled undergraduates at English universities. ◆ *vb* **5** (*tr*) to provide or decorate with a tuft or tufts. **6** to form or be formed into tufts. **7** to secure with tufts. [C14: ?from OF *tufe,* of Gmc origin]
▸**'tufted** *adj* ▸**'tufty** *adj*

tufted duck *n* a European lake-dwelling duck, the male of which has a black plumage with white underparts and a long black drooping crest.

tug ❶ (tʌg) *vb* **tugs, tugging, tugged. 1** (when *intr,* sometimes foll. by *at*) to pull or drag with sharp or powerful movements. **2** (*tr*) to tow (a vessel) by means of a tug. ◆ *n* **3** a strong pull or jerk. **4** Also called: **tugboat.** a boat with a powerful engine, used for towing barges, ships, etc. **5** a hard struggle or fight. [C13: rel. to OE *tēon* to TOW[1]]
▸**'tugger** *n*

tug-of-love *n* a conflict over custody of a child between divorced parents or between natural parents and foster or adoptive parents.

tug-of-war *n* **1** a contest in which two people or teams pull opposite ends of a rope in an attempt to drag the opposition over a central line. **2** any hard struggle between two factions.

tui ('tu:i:) *n, pl* **tuis.** a New Zealand songbird with white feathers at the throat. Also called: **parson bird.** [from Maori]

tuition ❶ (tju:'ɪʃən) *n* **1** instruction, esp. that received individually or in a small group. **2** the payment for instruction, esp. in colleges or universities. [C15: from OF *tuicion,* from L *tuitiō* a guarding, from *tuērī* to watch over]
▸**tu'itional** *adj*

tularaemia *or US* **tularemia** (,tu:lə'ri:mɪə) *n* an infectious disease of rodents, transmitted to man by infected ticks or flies or by handling contaminated flesh. [C19/20: from NL, from *Tulare,* county in California where first observed]
▸**,tula'raemic** *or US* **,tula'remic** *adj*

tulip ('tju:lɪp) *n* **1** any of various spring-blooming bulb plants having long broad pointed leaves and single showy bell-shaped flowers. **2** the flower or bulb. [C17: from NL *tulipa,* from Turkish *tülbend* turban, which the opened bloom was thought to resemble]

tulip tree *n* **1** Also called: **tulip poplar.** a North American tree having tulip-shaped greenish-yellow flowers and long conelike fruits. **2** any of various other trees with tulip-shaped flowers, such as the magnolia.

tulipwood ('tju:lɪp,wʊd) *n* **1** the light soft wood of the tulip tree, used in making furniture and veneer. **2** any of several woods having streaks of colour.

tulle (tju:l) *n* a fine net fabric of silk, rayon, etc. [C19: from F, from *Tulle,* city in S central France, where first manufactured]

tumble ❶ ('tʌmb[ə]l) *vb* **tumbles, tumbling, tumbled. 1** to fall or cause to fall, esp. awkwardly, precipitately, or violently. **2** (*intr;* usually foll. by *about*) to roll or twist, esp. in playing. **3** (*intr*) to perform leaps, somersaults, etc. **4** to move in a heedless or hasty way. **5** (*tr*) to polish (gemstones) in a tumbler. **6** (*tr*) to disturb, rumple, or toss around. ◆ *n* **7** a tumbling. **8** a fall or toss. **9** an acrobatic feat, esp. a somersault. **10** a state of confusion. **11** a confused heap or pile. ◆ See also **tumble to.** [OE *tumbian*]

tumbledown ❶ ('tʌmb[ə]l,daʊn) *adj* falling to pieces; dilapidated; crumbling.

tumble dryer *or* **tumble drier** *n* a machine that dries wet laundry by rotating it in warmed air inside a metal drum. Also called: **tumbler dryer, tumbler.**

tumbler ('tʌmblə) *n* **1a** a flat-bottomed drinking glass with no handle or stem. **1b** Also called: **tumblerful.** its contents. **2** a person who performs somersaults and other acrobatic feats. **3** another name for **tumble dryer. 4** a box or drum rotated so that the contents (usually gemstones) become smooth and polished. **5** the part of a lock that retains or releases the bolt and is moved by the action of a key. **6** a lever in a gunlock that receives the action of the mainspring when the trigger is pressed and thus forces the hammer forwards. **7** a part that moves a gear in a train of gears into and out of engagement.

tumbler switch *n* a small electrical switch incorporating a spring, widely used in lighting.

tumble to *vb* (*intr, prep*) *Inf.* to understand; become aware of: *she tumbled to his plan quickly.*

tumbleweed ('tʌmb[ə]l,wi:d) *n* any of various densely branched American and Australian plants that break off near the ground on withering and are rolled about by the wind.

tumbrel *or* **tumbril** ('tʌmbrəl) *n* **1** a farm cart, esp. one that tilts backwards to deposit its load. A cart of this type was used to take condemned prisoners to the guillotine during the French Revolution. **2** (formerly) a covered cart used to carry ammunition, tools, etc. [C14 *tumberell* ducking stool, from Med. L *tumbrellum,* from OF *tumberel* dump cart, ult. of Gmc origin]

tumefacient (,tju:mɪ'feɪʃənt) *adj* producing or capable of producing swelling: *a tumefacient drug.* [C16: from L *tumefacere* to cause to swell]

tumefy ('tju:mɪ,faɪ) *vb* **tumefies, tumefying, tumefied.** to make or become tumid; swell or puff up. [C16: from F *tuméfier,* from L *tumefacere*]
▸**,tume'faction** *n*

tumescent (tju:'mɛsənt) *adj* swollen or becoming swollen. [C19: from L *tumescere* to begin to swell, from *tumēre*]
▸**tu'mescence** *n*

tumid ❶ ('tju:mɪd) *adj* **1** enlarged or swollen. **2** bulging. **3** pompous or fulsome in style. [C16: from L *tumidus,* from *tumēre* to swell]
▸**tu'midity** *or* **'tumidness** *n* ▸**'tumidly** *adv*

THESAURUS

tuck *vb* **1 = push**, fold, gather, insert ◆ *n* **6 = fold**, gather, pinch, pleat **8a** *Brit. informal* **= food**, comestibles, eats (*sl.*), grub (*sl.*), nosebag (*sl.*), nosh (*sl.*), scoff (*sl.*), tack (*inf.*), victuals, vittles (*obs. or dialect*)

tuck in *vb* **1 = make snug**, bed down, enfold, fold under, put to bed, swaddle, wrap up **3** *Informal* **= eat up**, chow down (*sl.*), eat heartily, fall to, get stuck in (*inf.*)

tuft *n* **1-3 = clump**, bunch, cluster, collection, knot, shock, topknot, tussock

tug *vb* **1 = pull**, drag, draw, haul, heave, jerk, lug, tow, wrench, yank ◆ *n* **3 = pull**, drag, haul, heave, jerk, tow, traction, wrench, yank

tuition *n* **1 = training**, education, instruction, lessons, schooling, teaching, tutelage, tutoring

tumble *vb* **1 = fall**, drop, fall end over end, fall headlong, fall head over heels, flop, lose one's footing, pitch, plummet, roll, stumble, topple, toss, trip up ◆ *n* **8 = fall**, collapse, drop, flop, headlong fall, plunge, roll, spill, stumble, toss, trip

tumbledown *adj* **= dilapidated**, crumbling, decrepit, disintegrating, falling to pieces, ramshackle, rickety, ruined, shaky, tottering
Antonyms *adj* durable, firm, solid, sound, stable, sturdy, substantial, well-kept

tumid *adj* **1, 2 = swollen**, bloated, bulging, distended, enlarged, inflated, protuberant, puffed

tummy ⓣ ('tʌmɪ) *n, pl* **tummies.** an informal or childish word for **stomach.** Also called: **tum.**

tummy tuck *n Inf.* the surgical removal of abdominal fat and skin for cosmetic purposes.

tumour ⓣ *or US* **tumor** ('tjuːmə) *n Pathol.* **a** any abnormal swelling. **b** a mass of tissue formed by a new growth of cells. [C16: from L, from *tumēre* to swell]
▸ **'tumorous** *adj*

tumult ⓣ ('tjuːmʌlt) *n* **1** a loud confused noise, as of a crowd; commotion. **2** violent agitation or disturbance. **3** great emotional agitation. [C15: from L *tumultus,* from *tumēre* to swell up]

tumultuous ⓣ (tjuː'mʌltjʊəs) *adj* **1** uproarious, riotous, or turbulent. **2** greatly agitated, confused, or disturbed. **3** making a loud or unruly disturbance.
▸ **tu'multuously** *adv* ▸ **tu'multuousness** *n*

tumulus ('tjuːmjʊləs) *n, pl* **tumuli** (-liː). *Archaeol. (no longer in technical usage)* another word for **barrow**[2]. [C17: from L: a hillock, from *tumēre* to swell up]

tun (tʌn) *n* **1** a large beer cask. **2** a measure of capacity, usually equal to 252 wine gallons. ◆ *vb* **tuns, tunning, tunned. 3** *(tr)* to put into or keep in tuns. [OE *tunne*]

tuna[1] ('tjuːnə) *n, pl* **tuna** *or* **tunas.** another name for **tunny** (sense 1). [C20: from American Sp., from Sp. *atún,* from Ar. *tūn,* from L *thunnus* tunny, from Gk]

tuna[2] ('tjuːnə) *n* any of various tropical American prickly pear cacti. [C16: via Sp. from Taino]

tunable *or* **tuneable** ('tjuːnəbᵊl) *adj* able to be tuned.

tundra ('tʌndrə) *n* a vast treeless zone lying between the ice cap and the timber line of North America and Eurasia and having a permanently frozen subsoil. [C19: from Russian, from Lapp *tundar* hill]

tune ⓣ (tjuːn) *n* **1** a melody, esp. one for which harmony is not essential. **2** the condition of producing accurately pitched notes, intervals, etc. (esp. in **in tune, out of tune**). **3** accurate correspondence of pitch and intonation between instruments (esp. in **in tune, out of tune**). **4** the correct adjustment of a radio, television, etc., with respect to the required frequency. **5** a frame of mind; mood. **6 call the tune.** to be in control of the proceedings. **7 change one's tune.** to alter one's attitude or tone of speech. **8 to the tune of.** *Inf.* to the amount or extent of. ◆ *vb* **tunes, tuning, tuned. 9** to adjust (a musical instrument) to a certain pitch. **10** to adjust (a note, etc.) so as to bring it into harmony or concord. **11** *(tr)* to adapt or adjust (oneself); attune. **12** *(tr;* often foll. by *up)* to make fine adjustments to (an engine, machine, etc.) to obtain optimum performance. **13** *Electronics.* to adjust (one or more circuits) for resonance at a desired frequency. ◆ See also **tune in, tune up.** [C14: var. of TONE]
▸ **'tuner** *n*

tuneful ⓣ ('tjuːnfʊl) *adj* **1** having a pleasant tune; melodious. **2** producing a melody or music.
▸ **'tunefully** *adv* ▸ **'tunefulness** *n*

tune in *vb (adv;* often foll. by *to)* **1** to adjust (a radio or television) to receive (a station or programme). **2** *Sl.* to make or become more aware, knowledgeable, etc. (about).

tuneless ⓣ ('tjuːnlɪs) *adj* having no melody or tune.
▸ **'tunelessly** *adv* ▸ **'tunelessness** *n*

tune up *vb (adv)* **1** to adjust (a musical instrument) to a particular pitch. **2** to tune (instruments) to a common pitch. **3** *(tr)* to adjust (an engine) in (a car, etc.) to improve performance. ◆ *n* **tune-up. 4** adjustments made to an engine to improve its performance.

tung oil (tʌŋ) *n* a fast-drying oil obtained from the seeds of an Asian tree, used in paints, varnishes, etc. [partial translation of Chinese *yu t'ung* tung tree oil, from *yu* oil + *t'ung* tung tree]

tungsten ('tʌŋstən) *n* a hard malleable ductile greyish-white element. It is used in lamp filaments, electrical contact points, X-ray targets, and, alloyed with steel, in high-speed cutting tools. Symbol: W; atomic no.: 74; atomic wt.: 183.85. Also called: **wolfram.** [C18: from Swedish *tung* heavy + *sten* stone]

tungsten lamp *n* a lamp in which light is produced by a tungsten filament heated to incandescence by an electric current. Sometimes small amounts of a halogen, such as iodine, are added to improve the intensity (**tungsten-halogen lamp**).

tungsten steel *n* any of various hard steels containing tungsten and traces of carbon.

Tungusic (tʊŋ'gʊsɪk) *n* a branch or subfamily of the Altaic family of languages, some of which are spoken in NE Asia.

tunic ('tjuːnɪk) *n* **1** any of various hip-length or knee-length garments, such as the loose sleeveless garb worn in ancient Greece or Rome, the jacket of some soldiers, or a woman's hip-length garment, worn with a skirt or trousers. **2** a covering, lining, or enveloping membrane of an organ or part. **3** Also called: **tunicle.** a short vestment worn by a bishop or subdeacon. [OE *tunice* (unattested except in the accusative case), from L *tunica*]

tunicate ('tjuːnɪkɪt, -ˌkeɪt) *n* **1** any of various minute primitive marine animals having a saclike unsegmented body enclosed in a cellulose-like outer covering. ◆ *adj also* **tunicated. 2** (esp. of a bulb) having concentric layers of tissue. [C18: from L *tunicātus* clad in a TUNIC]

tuning ('tjuːnɪŋ) *n Music.* **1** a set of pitches to which the open strings of a guitar, violin, etc., are tuned. **2** the accurate pitching of notes and intervals by a choir, orchestra, etc.; intonation.

tuning fork *n* a two-pronged metal fork that when struck produces a pure note of constant specified pitch. It is used to tune musical instruments and in acoustics.

tunnage ('tʌnɪdʒ) *n* a variant spelling of **tonnage.**

tunnel ⓣ ('tʌnᵊl) *n* **1** an underground passageway, esp. one for trains or cars. **2** any passage or channel through or under something. ◆ *vb* **tunnels, tunnelling, tunnelled** *or US* **tunnels, tunneling, tunneled. 3** *(tr)* to make or force (a way) through or under (something). **4** *(intr;* foll. by *through, under,* etc.) to make or force a way (through or under something). [C15: from OF *tonel* cask, from *tonne* tun, from Med. L *tonna* barrel, of Celtic origin]
▸ **'tunneller** *or US* **'tunneler** *n*

tunnel diode *n* an extremely stable semiconductor diode, having a very narrow highly doped p-n junction, in which electrons travel across the junction by means of the tunnel effect. Also called: **Esaki diode.**

tunnel effect *n Physics.* the phenomenon in which an object, usually an elementary particle, tunnels through a potential barrier even though it does not have sufficient energy to surmount it.

tunnel vision *n* **1** a condition in which peripheral vision is greatly restricted. **2** narrowness of viewpoint resulting from concentration on a single idea, opinion, etc.

tunny ('tʌnɪ) *n, pl* **tunnies** *or* **tunny. 1** Also called: **tuna.** any of a genus of large marine spiny-finned fishes, chiefly of warm waters. They are important food fishes. **2** any of various similar and related fishes. [C16: from OF *thon,* from OProvençal *ton,* from L *thunnus,* from Gk]

tup (tʌp) *n* **1** *Chiefly Brit.* a male sheep; ram. **2** the head of a pile-driver or steam hammer. ◆ *vb* **tups, tupping, tupped. 3** *(tr)* (of a ram) to mate with (a ewe). [C14: from ?]

Tupamaro (ˌtuːpə'mɑːrəʊ) *n, pl* **Tupamaros.** any of a group of Marxist urban guerrillas in Uruguay. [C20: after *Tupac Amaru,* 18th-century Peruvian Indian who led a rebellion against the Spaniards]

tupelo ('tjuːpɪˌləʊ) *n, pl* **tupelos. 1** any of several gum trees of the southern US. **2** the light strong wood of any of these trees. [C18: from Creek *ito opilwa,* from *ito* tree + *opilwa* swamp]

Tupi (tuː'piː) *n* **1** *(pl* **Tupis** *or* **Tupi)** a member of a South American Indian people of Brazil and Paraguay. **2** their language.
▸ **Tu'pian** *adj*

tupik ('tuːpək) *n Canad.* a tent of seal or caribou skin used for shelter by the Inuit in summer. [from Eskimo]

tuppence ('tʌpəns) *n Brit.* a variant spelling of **twopence.**
▸ **'tuppenny** *adj*

Tupperware ('tʌpəweə) *n Trademark.* a range of plastic containers used for storing food. [C20: *Tupper,* US manufacturing company + WARE[1]]

tuque (tuːk) *n Canad.* **1** a knitted cap with a long tapering end. **2** Also called: **toque.** a close-fitting knitted hat often with a tassel or pompom. [C19: from Canad. F, from F: TOQUE]

turaco ('tʊərəˌkəʊ) *n, pl* **turacos.** a variant spelling of **touraco.**

THESAURUS

up, puffy, tumescent **3** = **pompous,** arty-farty (*inf.*), bombastic, flowery, fulsome, fustian, grandiloquent, grandiose, high-flown, inflated, magniloquent, orotund, overblown, pretentious, sesquipedalian, stilted, turgid

tummy *n Informal* = **stomach,** abdomen, belly, breadbasket (*sl.*), corporation (*inf.*), gut (*inf.*), inside(s) (*inf.*), paunch, pot, potbelly, spare tyre, tum (*inf.*)

tumour *n* **a** = **growth,** cancer, carcinoma (*Pathology*), lump, neoplasm (*Medical*), sarcoma (*Medical*), swelling

tumult *n* **1-3** = **commotion,** ado, affray (*Law*), agitation, altercation, bedlam, brawl, brouhaha, clamour, din, disorder, disturbance, excitement, fracas, hubbub, hullabaloo, outbreak, pandemonium, quarrel, racket, riot, row, ruction (*inf.*), stir, stramash (*Scot.*), strife, turmoil, unrest, upheaval, uproar
Antonyms *n* calm, hush, peace, quiet, repose, serenity, silence, stillness

tumultuous *adj* **1-3** = **turbulent,** agitated, boisterous, clamorous, confused, disorderly, disturbed, excited, fierce, full-on (*inf.*), hectic, irregular, lawless, noisy, obstreperous, passionate, raging, restless, riotous, rowdy, rumbustious, stormy, unrestrained, unruly, uproarious, violent, vociferous, wild
Antonyms *adj* calm, hushed, peaceful, quiet, restful, serene, still, tranquil

tune *n* **1** = **melody,** air, melody line, motif, song, strain, theme **3** = **concord,** agreement, concert, consonance, euphony, harmony, pitch, sympathy, unison **5** = **frame of mind,** attitude, demeanour, disposition, mood **6 call the tune** = **be in control,** be in charge, be in command, call the shots (*sl.*), command, dictate, govern, lead, rule, rule the roost **7 change one's tune** = **change one's attitude,** change one's mind, do an about-face, have a change of heart, reconsider, take a different tack, think again ◆ *vb* **9-11** = **adjust,** adapt, attune, bring into harmony, harmonize, pitch, regulate
Antonyms *n* ≠ **concord:** clashing, conflict, contention, disagreement, discord, discordance, disharmony, disunity, friction

tuneful *adj* **1** = **melodious,** catchy, consonant, easy on the ear (*inf.*), euphonic, euphonious, harmonious, mellifluous, melodic, musical, pleasant, symphonic
Antonyms *adj* cacophonous, clashing, discordant, dissonant, harsh, jangly, tuneless, unmelodious

tuneless *adj* = **discordant,** atonal, cacophonous, clashing, dissonant, harsh, unmelodic, unmelodious, unmusical
Antonyms *adj* harmonious, melodious, musical, pleasing, sonorous, symphonic, tuneful

tunnel *n* **1** = **passage,** burrow, channel, hole, passageway, shaft, subway, underpass ◆ *vb* **3, 4** = **dig,** burrow, dig one's way, excavate, mine, penetrate, scoop out, undermine

Turanian (tjʊ'reɪnɪən) *n, adj* another name for **Ural-Altaic.**
turban ('tɜːbᵊn) *n* **1** a man's headdress, worn esp. by Muslims, Hindus, and Sikhs, made by swathing a length of linen, silk, etc., around the head or around a caplike base. **2** a woman's brimless hat resembling this. **3** any headdress resembling this. [C16: from Turkish *tülbend,* from Persian *dulband*]
▸**'turbaned** *adj*
turbary ('tɜːbərɪ) *n, pl* **turbaries. 1** land where peat or turf is cut. **2** the legal right to cut peat for fuel on a common. [C14: from OF *turbarie,* from Med. L *turbāria,* from *turba* peat]
turbellarian (ˌtɜːbɪ'leərɪən) *n* **1** any of a class of flatworms having a ciliated epidermis and a simple life cycle. ◆ *adj* **2** of or belonging to this class of flatworms. [C19: from NL *Turbellāria,* from L *turbellae* (pl) bustle, from *turba* brawl, referring to the swirling motion created in the water]
turbid ('tɜːbɪd) *adj* **1** muddy or opaque, as a liquid clouded with a suspension of particles. **2** dense, thick, or cloudy: *turbid fog.* **3** in turmoil or confusion. [C17: from L *turbidus,* from *turbāre* to agitate, from *turba* crowd]
▸**tur'bidity** *or* **'turbidness** *n* ▸**'turbidly** *adv*
turbinate ('tɜːbɪnɪt, -ˌneɪt) *or* **turbinal** ('tɜːbɪnᵊl) *adj also* **turbinated. 1** *Anat.* of any of the scroll-shaped bones on the walls of the nasal passages. **2** shaped like a spiral or scroll. **3** shaped like an inverted cone. ◆ *n* **4** a turbinate bone. **5** a turbinate shell. [C17: from L *turbō* spinning top]
▸**ˌturbi'nation** *n*
turbine ('tɜːbɪn, -baɪn) *n* any of various types of machine in which the kinetic energy of a moving fluid, as water, steam, air, etc., is converted into mechanical energy by causing a bladed rotor to rotate. [C19: from F, from L *turbō* whirlwind, from *turbāre* to throw into confusion]
turbine blade *n* any of a number of bladelike vanes assembled around the periphery of a turbine rotor to guide the steam or gas flow.
turbit ('tɜːbɪt) *n* a crested breed of domestic pigeon. [C17: from L *turbō* spinning top, from the bird's shape]
turbo- *combining form.* of, relating to, or driven by a turbine: *turbofan.*
turbocharger ('tɜːbəʊˌtʃɑːdʒə) *n* a centrifugal compressor which boosts the intake pressure of an internal-combustion engine, driven by an exhaust-gas turbine fitted to the engine's exhaust manifold.
turbofan (ˌtɜːbəʊ'fæn) *n* **1** a type of bypass engine in which a large fan driven by a turbine forces air rearwards around the exhaust gases in order to increase the propulsive thrust. **2** an aircraft driven by turbofans. **3** the fan in such an engine.
turbogenerator (ˌtɜːbəʊ'dʒenəˌreɪtə) *n* an electrical generator driven by a steam turbine.
turbojet (ˌtɜːbəʊ'dʒet) *n* **1** a turbojet engine. **2** an aircraft powered by turbojet engines.
turbojet engine *n* a gas turbine in which the exhaust gases provide the propulsive thrust to drive an aircraft.
turboprop (ˌtɜːbəʊ'prɒp) *n* **1** an aircraft propulsion unit where a propeller is driven by a gas turbine. **2** an aircraft powered by turboprops.
turbosupercharger (ˌtɜːbəʊ'suːpəˌtʃɑːdʒə) *n Obs.* a supercharging device for an internal-combustion engine, consisting of a turbine driven by the exhaust gases.
turbot ('tɜːbət) *n, pl* **turbot** *or* **turbots. 1** a European flatfish having a speckled scaleless body covered with tubercles. It is highly valued as a food fish. **2** any of various similar or related fishes. [C13: from OF *tourbot,* from Med. L *turbō,* from L: spinning top, from a fancied similarity in shape]
turbulence ❶ ('tɜːbjʊləns) *n* **1** a state or condition of confusion, movement, or agitation. **2** *Meteorol.* instability in the atmosphere causing gusty air currents and cumulonimbus clouds.
turbulent ❶ ('tɜːbjʊlənt) *adj* **1** being in a state of turbulence. **2** wild or insubordinate; unruly. [C16: from L *turbulentus,* from *turba* confusion]
▸**'turbulently** *adv*
turd (tɜːd) *n Taboo.* **1** a piece of excrement. **2** *Sl.* a contemptible person or thing. [OE *tord*]
tureen (tə'riːn) *n* a large deep usually rounded dish with a cover, used for serving soups, stews, etc. [C18: from F *terrine* earthenware vessel, from *terrin* made of earthenware, from Vulgar L *terrīnus* (unattested), from L *terra* earth]
turf ❶ (tɜːf) *n, pl* **turfs** *or* **turves. 1** the surface layer of fields and pastures, consisting of earth containing a dense growth of grasses with their roots; sod. **2** a piece cut from this layer. **3 the turf. 3a** a track where horse races are run. **3b** horse racing as a sport or industry. **4** an area of knowledge or influence: *he's on home turf when it comes to music.* **5** another word for **peat.** ◆ *vb* **6** (*tr*) to cover with pieces of turf. ◆ See also **turf out.** [OE]
turf accountant *n Brit.* a formal name for a **bookmaker.**
turfman ('tɜːfmən) *n, pl* **turfmen.** *Chiefly US.* a person devoted to horse racing.
turf out ❶ *vb* (*tr, adv*) *Brit. inf.* to throw out or dismiss; eject.
turgescent (tɜː'dʒesᵊnt) *adj* becoming or being swollen; inflated; tumid.
▸**tur'gescence** *n*
turgid ❶ ('tɜːdʒɪd) *adj* **1** swollen and distended. **2** (of language) pompous; bombastic. [C17: from L *turgidus,* from *turgēre* to swell]
▸**tur'gidity** *or* **'turgidness** *n* ▸**'turgidly** *adv*
turgor ('tɜːgə) *n* the normal rigid state of a cell, caused by pressure of the cell contents against the cell wall or membrane. [C19: from LL: a swelling, from L *turgēre* to swell]
Turing machine ('tjʊərɪŋ) *n* a hypothetical universal computing machine able to modify its original instructions by reading, erasing, or writing a new symbol on a moving tape that acts as its program. [C20: after Alan Mathison *Turing* (1912–54), Brit. mathematician]
turion ('tʊərɪən) *n* a scaly shoot produced by many aquatic plants: it detaches from the parent plant and remains dormant until the following spring. [C17: from F *turion,* from L *turio* shoot]
Turk (tɜːk) *n* **1** a native, inhabitant, or citizen of Turkey. **2** a native speaker of any Turkic language. **3** *Obs., derog.* a brutal or domineering person. See also **Young Turk.**
Turk. *abbrev. for:* **1** Turkey. **2** Turkish.
turkey ('tɜːkɪ) *n, pl* **turkeys** *or* **turkey. 1** a large bird of North America, having a bare wattled head and neck and a brownish plumage. The male has a fan-shaped tail. A domesticated variety is bred for its flesh. **2** *Inf.* something, esp. a film or theatrical production, that fails. **3** See **cold turkey. 4 talk turkey.** *Sl., chiefly US & Canad.* to discuss frankly and practically. [C16: shortened from *Turkey cock* (*hen*), used at first to designate the African guinea fowl (apparently because the bird was brought through Turkish territory), later applied by mistake to the American bird]
turkey buzzard *or* **vulture** *n* a New World vulture having a naked red head.
turkey cock *n* **1** a male turkey. **2** an arrogant person.
turkey nest *n Austral.* a small earth dam adjacent to, and higher than, a larger earth dam, to feed water by gravity to a cattle trough, etc.
Turkey red *n* **1a** a moderate or bright red colour. **1b** (*as adj*): *a Turkey-red fabric.* **2** a cotton fabric of a bright red colour.
Turki ('tɜːkɪ) *adj* **1** of or relating to the Turkic languages. **2** of or relating to speakers of these languages. ◆ *n* **3** these languages collectively.
Turkic ('tɜːkɪk) *n* a branch of the Altaic family of languages, including Turkish, Tatar, etc., members of which are found from Turkey to NE China, esp. in Soviet central Asia.
Turkish ('tɜːkɪʃ) *adj* **1** of Turkey, its people, or their language. ◆ *n* **2** the official language of Turkey, belonging to the Turkic branch of the Altaic family.
Turkish bath *n* **1** a type of bath in which the bather sweats freely in hot dry air, is then washed, often massaged, and has a cold plunge or shower. **2** (*sometimes pl*) an establishment where such a bath is obtainable.
Turkish coffee *n* very strong black coffee.
Turkish delight *n* a jelly-like sweet flavoured with flower essences, usually cut into cubes and covered in icing sugar.
Turkish towel *n* a rough loose-piled towel.
Turk's-cap lily *n* any of several cultivated lilies that have brightly coloured flowers with reflexed petals.
Turk's-head *n* an ornamental turban-like knot.
turmeric ('tɜːmərɪk) *n* **1** a tropical Asian plant, *Curcuma longa,* having yellow flowers and an aromatic underground stem. **2** the powdered stem of this plant, used as a condiment and as a yellow dye. [C16: from OF *terre merite,* from Med. L *terra merita,* lit.: meritorious earth, name applied for obscure reasons to curcuma]
turmeric paper *n Chem.* paper impregnated with turmeric used as a test for alkalis and for boric acid.
turmoil ❶ ('tɜːmɔɪl) *n* violent or confused movement; agitation; tumult. [C16: ?from TURN + MOIL]
turn ❶ (tɜːn) *vb* **1** to move around an axis: *to turn a knob.* **2** (sometimes

THESAURUS

turbulence *n* **1 = confusion,** agitation, boiling, commotion, disorder, instability, pandemonium, roughness, storm, tumult, turmoil, unrest, upheaval
Antonyms *n* calm, peace, quiet, repose, rest, stillness
turbulent *adj* **1 = agitated,** blustery, boiling, choppy, confused, disordered, foaming, furious, raging, rough, tempestuous, tumultuous, unsettled, unstable **2 = wild,** agitated, anarchic, boisterous, disorderly, insubordinate, lawless, mutinous, obstreperous, rebellious, refractory, riotous, rowdy, seditious, tumultuous, unbridled, undisciplined, ungovernable, unruly, uproarious, violent
Antonyms *adj* ≠ **agitated:** calm, glassy, peaceful, quiet, smooth, still, unruffled
turf *n* **1 = grass,** clod, divot, green, sod, sward **3 the turf = horse-racing,** racecourse, racetrack, racing, the flat
turf out *vb Brit. informal* **= throw out,** banish, bounce (*sl.*), cast out, chuck out (*inf.*), discharge, dismiss, dispossess, eject, evict, expel, fire (*inf.*), fling out, give one the bum's rush (*sl.*), give one the sack (*inf.*), kick out (*inf.*), kiss off (*sl., chiefly US & Canad.*), oust, relegate, sack (*inf.*), show one the door
turgid *adj* **1 = swollen,** bloated, bulging, congested, distended, inflated, protuberant, puffed up, puffy, tumescent, tumid **2 = pompous,** arty-farty (*inf.*), bombastic, flowery, fulsome, fustian, grandiloquent, grandiose, high-flown, inflated, magniloquent, orotund, ostentatious, overblown, pretentious, sesquipedalian, stilted, tumid, windy
turmoil *n* **= confusion,** agitation, bedlam, brouhaha, bustle, chaos, commotion, disarray, disorder, disturbance, ferment, flurry, hubbub, noise, pandemonium, row, stir, strife, trouble, tumult, turbulence, upheaval, uproar, violence
Antonyms *n* calm, peace, quiet, repose, rest, serenity, stillness, tranquillity
turn *vb* **2 = rotate,** circle, go round, gyrate, move in a circle, pivot, revolve, roll, spin, swivel, twirl, twist, wheel, whirl **3 = change**

foll. by *round*) to change or cause to change positions by moving through an arc of a circle: *he turned the chair to face the light.* **3** to change or cause to change in course, direction, etc. **4** to go or pass to the other side of (a corner, etc.). **5** to assume or cause to assume a rounded, curved, or folded form: *the road turns here.* **6** to reverse or cause to reverse position. **7** (*tr*) to perform or do by a rotating movement: *to turn a somersault.* **8** (*tr*) to shape or cut a thread in (a workpiece) by rotating it on a lathe against a cutting tool. **9** (when *intr*, foll. by *into* or *to*) to change or convert or be changed or converted. **10** (foll. by *into*) to change or cause to change in nature, character, etc.: *the frog turned into a prince.* **11** (*copula*) to change so as to become: *he turned nasty.* **12** to cause (foliage, etc.) to change colour or (of foliage, etc.) to change colour. **13** to cause (milk, etc.) to become rancid or sour or (of milk, etc.) to become rancid or sour. **14** to change or cause to change in subject, trend, etc.: *the conversation turned to fishing.* **15** to direct or apply or be directed or applied: *he turned his attention to the problem.* **16** (*intr*; usually foll. by *to*) to appeal or apply (to) for help, advice, etc. **17** to reach, pass, or progress beyond in age, time, etc.: *she has just turned twenty.* **18** (*tr*) to cause or allow to go: *to turn an animal loose.* **19** to affect or be affected with nausea. **20** to affect or be affected with giddiness: *my head is turning.* **21** (*tr*) to affect the mental or emotional stability of (esp. in **turn (someone's) head**). **22** (*tr*) to release from a container. **23** (*tr*) to render into another language. **24** (usually foll. by *against* or *from*) to transfer or reverse (one's loyalties, affections, etc.). **25** (*tr*) to cause (an enemy agent) to become a double agent working for one's own side. **26** (*tr*) to bring (soil) from lower layers to the surface. **27** to blunt (an edge) or (of an edge) to become blunted. **28** (*tr*) to give a graceful form to: *to turn a compliment.* **29** (*tr*) to reverse (a cuff, collar, etc.). **30** (*intr*) *US.* to be merchandised as specified: *shirts are turning well this week.* **31** *Cricket.* to spin (the ball) or (of the ball) to spin. **32 turn a trick.** *Sl.* (of a prostitute) to gain a customer. **33 turn one's hand to.** to undertake (something practical). ◆ *n* **34** a turning or being turned. **35** a movement of complete or partial rotation. **36** a change of direction or position. **37** direction or drift: *his thoughts took a new turn.* **38** a deviation from a course or tendency. **39** the place, point, or time at which a deviation or change occurs. **40** another word for **turning** (sense 1). **41** the right or opportunity to do something in an agreed order or succession: *now it's George's turn.* **42** a change in nature, condition, etc.: *his illness took a turn for the worse.* **43** a period of action, work, etc. **44** a short walk, ride, or excursion. **45** natural inclination: *a speculative turn of mind.* **46** distinctive form or style: *a neat turn of phrase.* **47** requirement, need, or advantage: *to serve someone's turn.* **48** a deed that helps or hinders someone. **49** a twist, bend, or distortion in shape. **50** *Music.* a melodic ornament that makes a turn around a note, beginning with the note above, in a variety of sequences. **51** a short theatrical act. **52** *Stock Exchange, Brit.* the difference between a market maker's bid and offer prices, representing the market maker's profit. **53** *Inf.* a shock or surprise. **54 by turns.** one after another; alternately. **55 turn and turn about.** one after another; alternately. **56 to a turn.** to the proper amount; perfectly. ◆ See also **turn down, turn in,** etc. [OE *tyrnian,* from OF *torner,* from L *tornāre* to turn in a lathe, from *tornus* lathe, from Gk *tornos* dividers]
▸ **'turner** *n*

turnabout ('tɜːnəˌbaut) *n* **1** the act of turning so as to face a different direction. **2** a change or reversal of opinion, attitude, etc.

turnaround ('tɜːnəˌraund) *n* **1a** the act or process in which a ship, aircraft, etc., unloads at the end of a trip and reloads for the next trip. **1b** the time taken for this. **2** the total time taken by a vehicle in a round trip. **3** a complete reversal of a situation.

turnbuckle ('tɜːnˌbʌkᵊl) *n* an open mechanical sleeve usually having a swivel at one end and a thread at the other to enable a threaded wire or rope to be tightened.

turncoat 🅣 ('tɜːnˌkəut) *n* a person who deserts one cause or party for the opposite faction.

turncock ('tɜːnˌkɒk) *n* (formerly) an official employed to turn on the water for the mains supply.

turn down 🅣 *vb* (*tr, adv*) **1** to reduce (the volume or brightness) of (something). **2** to reject or refuse. **3** to fold down (a collar, sheets, etc.). ◆ *adj* **turndown. 4** (*prenominal*) designed to be folded down.

turn in 🅣 *vb* (*adv*) *Inf.* **1** (*intr*) to go to bed for the night. **2** (*tr*) to hand in; deliver. **3** (*tr*) to give up or conclude (something). **4** (*tr*) to record (a score, etc.). **5 turn in on oneself.** to become preoccupied with one's own problems.

turning 🅣 ('tɜːnɪŋ) *n* **1** a road, river, or path that turns off the main way. **2** the point where such a way turns off. **3** a bend in a straight course. **4** an object made on a lathe. **5** the process or skill of turning objects on a lathe. **6** (*pl*) the waste produced in turning on a lathe.

turning circle *n* the smallest circle in which a vehicle can turn.

turning point 🅣 *n* **1** a moment when the course of events is changed. **2** a point at which there is a change in direction or motion.

turnip ('tɜːnɪp) *n* **1** a widely cultivated plant of the cabbage family with a large yellow or white edible root. **2** the root of this plant, which is eaten as a vegetable. [C16: from earlier *turnepe,* ?from TURN (indicating its rounded shape) + *nepe,* from L *nāpus* turnip]

turnkey ('tɜːnˌkiː) *n* **1** *Arch.* a keeper of the keys, esp. in a prison; warder or jailer. ◆ *adj* **2** denoting a project, as in civil engineering, in which a single contractor has responsibility for the complete job from the start to the time of installation or occupancy.

turn off 🅣 *vb* **1** (*intr*) to leave (a road, etc.). **2** (*intr*) (of a road, etc.) to deviate from (another road, etc.). **3** (*tr, adv*) to cause (something) to cease operating by turning a knob, pushing a button, etc. **4** (*tr*) *Inf.* to cause (a person, etc.) to feel dislike or distaste for (something): *this music turns me off.* **5** (*tr, adv*) *Brit. inf.* to dismiss from employment. ◆ *n* **turn-off. 6** a road or other way branching off from the main thoroughfare. **7** *Inf.* a person or thing that elicits dislike or distaste.

turn on 🅣 *vb* **1** (*tr, adv*) to cause (something) to operate by turning a knob, etc. **2** (*intr, prep*) to depend or hinge on: *the success of the party turns on you.* **3** (*prep*) to become hostile or to retaliate: *the dog turned on the children.* **4** (*tr, adv*) *Inf.* to produce (charm, tears, etc.) suddenly or automatically. **5** (*tr, adv*) *Sl.* to arouse emotionally or sexually. **6** (*intr, adv*) *Sl.* to take or become intoxicated by drugs. **7** (*tr, adv*) *Sl.* to introduce (someone) to drugs. ◆ *n* **turn-on. 8** *Sl.* a person or thing that causes emotional or sexual arousal.

turn out 🅣 *vb* (*adv*) **1** (*tr*) to cause (something, esp. a light) to cease operating by or as if by turning a knob, etc. **2** (*tr*) to produce by an effort or process. **3** (*tr*) to dismiss, discharge, or expel. **4** (*tr*) to empty the contents of, esp. in order to clean, tidy, or rearrange. **5** (*copula*) to prove to be as specified. **6** to end up; result: *it all turned out well.* **7** (*tr*) to fit as with clothes: *that woman turns her children out well.* **8** (*intr*) to assemble or gather. **9** (of a soldier) to parade or to call (a soldier) to pa-

THESAURUS

course, change position, go back, move, return, reverse, shift, swerve, switch, veer, wheel **4** = **go round**, arc, come round, corner, negotiate, pass, pass around, take a bend **7, 8** = **shape**, construct, execute, fashion, frame, make, mould, perform **9, 10** = **change**, adapt, alter, become, convert, divert, fashion, fit, form, metamorphose, mould, mutate, remodel, shape, transfigure, transform, transmute **13** = **go bad**, become rancid, curdle, go off (*Brit. inf.*), go sour, make rancid, sour, spoil, taint **16** *usually foll. by* **to** = **appeal**, apply, approach, go, have recourse, look, resort **19** = **sicken**, nauseate, upset **24** = **change sides**, apostatize, change one's mind, defect, desert, go over, renege, retract ◆ *n* **35** = **rotation**, bend, change, circle, curve, cycle, gyration, pivot, reversal, revolution, spin, swing, turning, twist, whirl **36** = **change of direction**, bend, change of course, curve, departure, deviation, shift **37** = **direction**, bias, drift, heading, tendency, trend **41** = **opportunity**, chance, crack, fling, go, period, round, shift, shot (*inf.*), spell, stint, succession, time, try, whack (*inf.*) **44** = **excursion**, airing, circuit, constitutional, drive, jaunt, outing, promenade, ride, saunter, spin (*inf.*), stroll, walk **45** = **inclination**, affinity, aptitude, bent, bias, flair, gift, knack, leaning, propensity, talent **46** = **style**, cast, fashion, form, format, guise, make-up, manner, mode, mould, shape, way **48** = **act**, action, deed, favour, gesture, service **49** = **twist**, bend, distortion, warp **53** *Informal* = **shock**, fright, scare, start, surprise **54 by turns** = **alternately**, in succession, one after another, reciprocally, turn and turn about **56 to a turn** *Informal* = **perfectly**, correctly, exactly, just right, precisely

turncoat *n* = **traitor**, apostate, backslider, defector, deserter, rat (*inf.*), recreant (*arch.*), renegade, seceder, tergiversator

turn down *vb* **1** = **lower**, diminish, lessen, muffle, mute, quieten, reduce the volume of, soften **2** = **refuse**, abstain from, decline, rebuff, reject, repudiate, say no to, spurn, throw out
Antonyms *vb* ≠ **lower**: amplify, augment, boost, increase, raise, strengthen, swell, turn up ≠ **refuse**: accede, accept, acquiesce, agree, receive, take

turn in *vb Informal* **1** = **go to bed**, go to sleep, hit the hay (*sl.*), hit the sack (*sl.*), retire for the night **2** = **hand in**, deliver, give back, give up, hand over, return, submit, surrender, tender

turning *n* **1, 2** = **turn-off**, bend, crossroads, curve, junction, side road, turn

turning point *n* **1** = **crossroads**, change, climacteric, crisis, critical moment, crux, decisive moment, moment of decision, moment of truth, point of no return

turn off *vb* **1** = **branch off**, change direction, depart from, deviate, leave, quit, take another road, take a side road **3** = **stop**, cut out, kill, put out, shut down, switch off, turn out, unplug **4** *Informal* = **put off**, alienate, bore, disenchant, disgust, displease, gross out (*US sl.*), irritate, lose one's interest, nauseate, offend, repel, sicken ◆ *n* **turn-off 6** = **turning**, branch, exit, side road, turn

turn on *vb* **1** = **start**, activate, energize, ignite, kick-start, put on, set in motion, start up, switch on **2** = **depend on**, balance on, be contingent on, be decided by, hang on, hinge on, pivot on, rest on **3** = **attack**, assail, assault, fall on, lose one's temper with, round on **5** *Informal* = **arouse**, arouse one's desire, attract, excite, please, press one's buttons (*sl.*), ring (someone's) bell (*US sl.*), stimulate, thrill, titillate, work up **7** *Slang* = **introduce**, expose, get one started with, inform, initiate, show
Antonyms *vb* ≠ **start**: cut out, put out, shut off, stop, switch off, turn off

turn out *vb* **1** = **turn off**, put out, switch off, unplug **2** = **produce**, bring out, fabricate, finish, make, manufacture, process, put out **3** = **expel**, banish, cashier, cast out, deport, discharge, dismiss, dispossess, drive out, drum out, evict, kick out (*inf.*), kiss off (*sl., chiefly US & Canad.*), oust, put out, show one the door, throw out, turf out (*Brit. inf.*), unseat **4** = **empty**, clean out, clear, discharge, take out the contents of **5** = **prove to be**, come to light, crop up (*inf.*), develop, emerge, happen **6** = **end up**, become, come about, come to be, eventuate, evolve, result, transpire (*inf.*), work out **7** = **dress**, accoutre, apparel (*arch.*), attire, clothe, fit, outfit, rig out **8** = **come**, appear, assemble, attend, be present, gather, go, put in an appearance, show up (*inf.*), turn up ◆ *n* **turn-out 12** = **attendance**, assemblage, assembly, audience, congregation, crowd, gate, number, throng **13** = **output**, amount produced, outturn (*rare*), production, production quota, productivity, turnover, volume, yield **14** = **outfit**, array, attire, costume, dress, equipage, equipment, gear (*inf.*), get-up (*inf.*), rigout (*inf.*)

rade. **10** (*intr*) *Inf.* to get out of bed. **11** (*intr*; foll. by *for*) *Inf.* to make an appearance, esp. in a sporting competition: *he was asked to turn out for Liverpool.* ◆ *n* **turnout. 12** the body of people appearing together at a gathering. **13** the quantity or amount produced. **14** an array of clothing or equipment.

turn over ⓣ *vb* (*adv*) **1** to change or cause to change position, esp. so as to reverse top and bottom. **2** to start (an engine), esp. with a starting handle, or (of an engine) to start or function correctly. **3** to shift or cause to shift position, as by rolling from side to side. **4** (*tr*) to deliver; transfer. **5** (*tr*) to consider carefully. **6** (*tr*) **6a** to sell and replenish (stock in trade). **6b** to transact business and so generate gross revenue of (a specified sum). **7** (*tr*) to invest and recover (capital). **8** (*tr*) *Sl.* to rob. ◆ *n* **turnover. 9a** the amount of business transacted during a specified period. **9b** (*as modifier*): *a turnover tax.* **10** the rate at which stock in trade is sold and replenished. **11** a change or reversal of position. **12** a small pastry case filled with fruit, jam, etc. **13a** the number of workers employed by a firm in a given period to replace those who have left. **13b** the ratio between this number and the average number of employees during the same period. **14** *Banking.* the amount of capital funds loaned on call during a specified period. ◆ *adj* **turnover. 15** (*prenominal*) designed to be turned over.

turnpike ('tɜːnˌpaɪk) *n* **1** *History.* **1a** a barrier set across a road to prevent passage until a toll had been paid. **1b** a road on which a turnpike was operated. **2** an obsolete word for **turnstile. 3** *US.* a motorway for use of which a toll is charged. [C15: from TURN + PIKE[2]]

turnround ('tɜːnˌraʊnd) *n* another word for **turnaround.**

turnspit ('tɜːnˌspɪt) *n* **1** (formerly) a servant or small dog whose job was to turn a spit. **2** a spit that can be so turned.

turnstile ('tɜːnˌstaɪl) *n* a mechanical barrier with arms that are turned to admit one person at a time.

turnstone ('tɜːnˌstəʊn) *n* a shore bird, related to the plovers and sandpipers, that lifts up stones in search of food.

turntable ('tɜːnˌteɪbᵊl) *n* **1** the circular platform that rotates a gramophone record while it is being played. **2** a circular platform used for turning locomotives and cars. **3** the revolvable platform on a microscope on which specimens are examined.

turntable ladder *n Brit.* a power-operated extending ladder mounted on a fire engine. US and Canad. name: **aerial ladder.**

turn to *vb* (*intr, adv*) to set about a task.

turn up ⓣ *vb* (*adv*) **1** (*intr*) to arrive or appear. **2** to find or be found, esp. by accident. **3** (*tr*) to increase the flow, volume, etc., of. ◆ *n* **turn-up. 4** (*often pl*) *Brit.* the turned-up fold at the bottom of some trouser legs. US, Canad. and Austral. name: **cuff. 5** *Inf.* an unexpected or chance occurrence.

turpentine ('tɜːpᵊnˌtaɪn) *n* **1** Also called: **gum turpentine.** any of various oleoresins obtained from various coniferous trees and used as the main source of commercial turpentine. **2** a sticky oleoresin that exudes from the terebinth tree. **3** Also called: **oil of turpentine, spirits of turpentine.** a colourless volatile oil distilled from turpentine oleoresin. It is used as a solvent for paints and in medicine. **4** Also called: **turpentine substitute, white spirit.** (*not in technical usage*) any one of a number of thinners for paints and varnishes, consisting of fractions of petroleum. Related adj: **terebinthine.** ◆ *vb* **turpentines, turpentining, turpentined.** (*tr*) **5** to treat or saturate with turpentine. [C14 *terebentyne*, from Med. L, from L *terebinthīna* turpentine, from *terebinthus* the turpentine tree]

turpentine tree *n* **1** a tropical African tree yielding a hard dark wood and a useful resin. **2** either of two Australian evergreen trees that yield resin.

turpeth ('tɜːpɪθ) *n* **1** an East Indian plant having roots with purgative properties. **2** the root of this plant or the drug obtained from it. [C14: from Med. L *turbithum*, ult. from Ar. *turbid*]

turpitude ⓣ ('tɜːpɪˌtjuːd) *n* base character or action; depravity. [C15: from L *turpitūdō* ugliness, from *turpis* base]

turps (tɜːps) *n* (*functioning as sing*) *Brit.* short for **turpentine** (sense 3).

turquoise ('tɜːkwɔɪz, -kwɑːz) *n* **1** a greenish-blue fine-grained mineral consisting of hydrated copper aluminium phosphate. It is used as a gemstone. **2a** the colour of turquoise. **2b** (*as adj*): *a turquoise dress.* [C14: from OF *turqueise* Turkish (stone)]

turret ('tʌrɪt) *n* **1** a small tower that projects from the wall of a building, esp. a castle. **2a** a self-contained structure, capable of rotation, in which weapons are mounted, esp. in tanks and warships. **2b** a similar structure on an aircraft. **3** (on a machine tool) a turret-like steel structure with tools projecting radially that can be indexed round to bring each tool to bear on the work. [C14: from OF *torete*, from *tor* tower, from L *turris*]
▸**'turreted** *adj*

turret lathe *n* another name for **capstan lathe.**

turtle[1] ('tɜːtᵊl) *n* **1** any of various aquatic reptiles, esp. those having a flattened shell enclosing the body and flipper-like limbs adapted for swimming. **2 turn turtle.** to capsize. [C17: from F *tortue* TORTOISE (infl. by TURTLE[2])]

turtle[2] ('tɜːtᵊl) *n* an archaic name for **turtledove.** [OE *turtla*, from L *turtur*, imit.]

turtleback ('tɜːtᵊlˌbæk) *n* an arched projection over the upper deck of a ship for protection in heavy seas.

turtledove ('tɜːtᵊlˌdʌv) *n* **1** any of several Old World doves having a brown plumage with speckled wings and a long dark tail. **2** a gentle or loving person. [see TURTLE[2]]

turtleneck ('tɜːtᵊlˌnɛk) *n* a round high close-fitting neck on a sweater or the sweater itself.

turves (tɜːvz) *n* a plural of **turf.**

Tuscan ('tʌskən) *adj* **1** of or relating to Tuscany, a region of central Italy, its inhabitants, or their dialect of Italian. **2** of or denoting one of the five classical orders of architecture: characterized by a column with an unfluted shaft and a capital and base with mouldings but no decoration. ◆ *n* **3** a native or inhabitant of Tuscany. **4** any of the dialects of Italian spoken in Tuscany.

tusche (tʊʃ) *n* a substance used in lithography for drawing the design and as a resist in silk-screen printing and lithography. [from G, from *tuschen* to touch up with colour, from F *toucher* to touch]

tush (tʌʃ) *interj Arch.* an exclamation of disapproval or contempt. [C15: imit.]

tusk (tʌsk) *n* **1** a pointed elongated usually paired tooth in the elephant, walrus, and certain other mammals. **2** a tusklike tooth or part. **3** a sharp pointed projection. ◆ *vb* **4** to stab, tear, or gore with the tusks. [OE *tūsc*]
▸**tusked** *adj*

tusker ('tʌskə) *n* any animal with long tusks.

tusk shell *n* any of various burrowing seashore molluscs that have a long narrow tubular shell open at both ends.

tussis ('tʌsɪs) *n* the technical name for a **cough.** See **pertussis.** [L: cough]
▸**'tussive** *adj*

tussle ⓣ ('tʌsᵊl) *vb* **tussles, tussling, tussled. 1** (*intr*) to fight or wrestle in a vigorous way. ◆ *n* **2** a vigorous fight; scuffle; struggle. [C15]

tussock ('tʌsək) *n* **1** a dense tuft of vegetation, esp. of grass. **2** *Austral. & NZ.* **2a** short for **tussock grass. 2b the.** country where tussock grass grows. [C16: from ?]
▸**'tussocky** *adj*

tussock grass *n* any of several pasture grasses.

tussore (tu'sɔː, 'tʌsə), **tusser** ('tʌsə), *or* (*Chiefly US*) **tussah** ('tʌsə) *n* **1** Also called: **wild silk.** a coarse silk obtained from an oriental silkworm. **2** the silkworm producing this. [C17: from Hindi *tasar* shuttle, from Sansk. *tasara* a wild silkworm]

tut (tʌt) *interj, n, vb* **tuts, tutting, tutted.** short for **tut-tut.**

tutelage ⓣ ('tjuːtɪlɪdʒ) *n* **1** the act or office of a guardian or tutor. **2** instruction or guidance, esp. by a tutor. **3** the condition of being under the supervision of a guardian or tutor. [C17: from L *tūtēla* a caring for, from *tuērī* to watch over]

tutelary ('tjuːtɪlərɪ) *or* **tutelar** ('tjuːtɪlə) *adj* **1** invested with the role of guardian or protector. **2** of or relating to a guardian. ◆ *n, pl* **tutelaries** *or* **tutelars. 3** a tutelary person, deity, etc.

tutor ⓣ ('tjuːtə) *n* **1** a teacher, usually instructing individual pupils. **2** (at universities, colleges, etc.) a member of staff responsible for the teaching and supervision of a certain number of students. ◆ *vb* **3** to act as a tutor to (someone). **4** (*tr*) to act as guardian to. [C14: from L: a watcher, from *tuērī* to watch over]
▸**'tutorage** *or* **'tutorship** *n*

tutorial ⓣ (tjuː'tɔːrɪəl) *n* **1** a period of intensive tuition given by a tutor to an individual student or to a small group of students. ◆ *adj* **2** of or relating to a tutor.

tutsan ('tʌtsən) *n* a woodland shrub of Europe and W Asia, having yel-

THESAURUS

turn over *vb* **1** = **overturn**, capsize, flip over, keel over, reverse, tip over, upend, upset **2** = **start up**, activate, crank, press the starter button, set going, set in motion, switch on, switch on the ignition, warm up **4** = **hand over**, assign, commend, commit, deliver, give over, give up, pass on, render, surrender, transfer, yield **5** = **consider**, contemplate, deliberate, give thought to, mull over, ponder, reflect on, revolve, ruminate about, think about, think over, wonder about ◆ *n* **turnover 9a** = **output**, business, flow, outturn (*rare*), production, productivity, volume, yield **13a** = **movement**, change, coming and going, replacement

turn up *vb* **1** = **arrive**, appear, attend, come, put in an appearance, show (*inf.*), show one's face, show up (*inf.*) **2** = **find**, bring to light, come up with, dig up, disclose, discover, expose, reveal, unearth **2** = **come to light**, appear, become known, be found, come to pass, crop up (*inf.*), pop up, transpire **3** = **increase**, amplify, boost, enhance, increase the volume of, intensify, make louder, raise
Antonyms *vb* ≠ **find**: hide ≠ **come to light**: disappear, evaporate, fade, vanish ≠ **increase**: diminish, lessen, lower, reduce, soften, turn down

turpitude *n Formal* = **wickedness**, badness, baseness, corruption, criminality, degeneracy, depravity, evil, foulness, immorality, iniquity, nefariousness, sinfulness, viciousness, vileness, villainy

tussle *vb* **1** = **fight**, battle, brawl, contend, grapple, scrap (*inf.*), scuffle, struggle, vie, wrestle ◆ *n* **2** = **fight**, battle, bout, brawl, competition, conflict, contention, contest, fracas, fray, punch-up (*Brit. inf.*), scrap (*inf.*), scrimmage, scuffle, set-to (*inf.*), shindig (*inf.*), shindy (*inf.*), struggle

tutelage *n Formal* **1, 2** = **guidance**, care, charge, custody, dependence, education, guardianship, instruction, patronage, preparation, protection, schooling, teaching, tuition, wardship

tutor *n* **1, 2** = **teacher**, coach, educator, governor, guardian, guide, guru, instructor, lecturer, master *or* mistress, mentor, preceptor, schoolmaster *or* schoolmistress ◆ *vb* **3** = **teach**, coach, direct, discipline, drill, edify, educate, guide, instruct, lecture, school, train

tutorial *n* **1** = **seminar**, individual instruction, lesson ◆ *adj* **2** = **teaching**, coaching, guiding, instructional low flowers and reddish-purple fruits. [C15: from OF *toute-saine* (unattested), lit.: all healthy]

tutti ('tʊtɪ) *adj, adv Music.* to be performed by the whole orchestra, choir, etc. [C18: from It., pl of *tutto* all, from L *tōtus*]

tutti-frutti ('tu:tɪ'fru:tɪ) *n* **1** (*pl* **tutti-fruttis**) an ice cream or a confection containing small pieces of candied or fresh fruits. **2** a preserve of chopped mixed fruits. **3** a flavour like that of many fruits combined. [from It., lit.: all the fruits]

tut-tut ('tʌt'tʌt) *interj* **1** an exclamation of mild reprimand, disapproval, or surprise. ◆ *vb* **tut-tuts, tut-tutting, tut-tutted. 2** (*intr*) to express disapproval by the exclamation of "tut-tut". ◆ *n* **3** the act of tut-tutting.

tutty ('tʌtɪ) *n* impure zinc oxide used as a polishing powder. [C14: from OF *tutie,* from Ar. *tūtiyā*, prob. from Persian, from Sansk. *tuttha*]

tutu ('tu:tu:) *n* a very short skirt worn by ballerinas, made of projecting layers of stiffened material. [from F, changed from the nursery word *cucu* backside, from L *cūlus* the buttocks]

tu-whit tu-whoo (tə'wɪt tə'wu:) *interj* an imitation of the sound made by an owl.

tuxedo (tʌk'si:dəʊ) *n, pl* **tuxedos.** the usual US and Canad. name for **dinner jacket.** [C19: after a country club in *Tuxedo Park*, New York]

tuyère ('twi:ɛə, 'twaɪə) *or* **twyer** ('twaɪə) *n* a water-cooled nozzle through which air is blown into a cupola, blast furnace, or forge. [C18: from F, from *tuyau* pipe, from OF *tuel,* prob. of Gmc origin]

TV Ⓣ *abbrev. for* television.

TVEI (in Britain) *abbrev. for* technical and vocational educational initiative: a national educational scheme in which pupils gain practical experience in technology and industry often through work placement.

TVP *abbrev. for* textured vegetable protein: protein from soya beans or other vegetables spun into fibres and flavoured: used esp. as a substitute for meat.

TVR *abbrev. for* television rating: a measurement of the popularity of a TV programme based on a survey.

TVRO *abbrev. for* television receive only: an antenna and associated apparatus for reception from a broadcasting satellite.

twaddle Ⓣ ('twɒdᵊl) *n* **1** silly, trivial, or pretentious talk or writing. ◆ *vb* **twaddles, twaddling, twaddled. 2** (*intr*) to talk or write in a silly or pretentious way. [C16 *twattle*, var. of *twittle* or *tittle*]
▸**'twaddler** *n*

twain (tweɪn) *determiner, n* an archaic word for **two.** [OE *twēgen*]

twang (twæŋ) *n* **1** a sharp ringing sound produced by or as if by the plucking of a taut string. **2** the act of plucking a string to produce such a sound. **3** a strongly nasal quality in a person's speech. ◆ *vb* **4** to make or cause to make a twang. **5** to strum (music, a tune, etc.). **6** to speak with a nasal voice. **7** (*intr*) to be released or move with a twang: *the arrow twanged away.* [C16: imit.]
▸**'twangy** *adj*

'twas (twɒz; *unstressed* twəz) *Poetic or dialect. contraction of* it was.

twat (twæt, twɒt) *n Taboo sl.* **1** the female genitals. **2** a foolish person. [from ?]

twayblade ('tweɪˌbleɪd) *n* any of various orchids having a basal pair of unstalked leaves arranged opposite each other. [C16: translation of Med. L *bifolium* having two leaves, from obs. *tway* two + BLADE]

tweak Ⓣ (twi:k) *vb* (*tr*) **1** to twist or pinch with a sharp or sudden movement. **2** *Inf.* to make a minor alteration. ◆ *n* **3** a tweaking. **4** *Inf.* a minor alteration. [OE *twiccian*]

twee Ⓣ (twi:) *adj Brit. inf.* excessively sentimental, sweet, or pretty. [C19: from *tweet*, mincing or affected pronunciation of *sweet*]
▸**'tweely** *adv*

tweed (twi:d) *n* **1** a thick woollen cloth produced originally in Scotland. **2** (*pl*) clothes made of this. **3** (*pl*) *Austral. inf.* trousers. [C19: prob. from *tweel*, Scot. var. of TWILL, infl. by *Tweed*, a Scot. river]

Tweedledum and Tweedledee (ˌtwi:dᵊl'dʌm; ˌtwi:dᵊl'di:) *n* any two persons or things that differ only slightly from each other; two of a kind. [C19: from the proverbial names of Handel and the rival musician Buononcini. The names were popularized by Lewis Carroll's use of them in *Through the Looking Glass* (1872)]

tweedy ('twi:dɪ) *adj* **tweedier, tweediest. 1** of, made of, or resembling tweed. **2** showing a fondness for a hearty outdoor life, usually associated with wearers of tweeds.

'tween (twi:n) *Poetic or dialect. contraction of* between.

'tween deck *or* **decks** *n Naut.* a space between two continuous decks of a vessel.

tweet (twi:t) *interj* **1** an imitation of the thin chirping sound made by small birds. ◆ *vb* **2** (*intr*) to make this sound. [C19: imit.]

tweeter ('twi:tə) *n* a loudspeaker used in high-fidelity systems for the reproduction of high audio frequencies. It is usually employed in conjunction with a woofer. [C20: from TWEET]

tweezers ('twi:zəz) *pl n* a small pincer-like instrument for handling small objects, plucking out hairs, etc. Also called: **pair of tweezers, tweezer** (esp. US). [C17: pl of *tweezer* (on the model of *scissors*, etc.), from *tweeze* case of instruments, from F *étuis*, from OF *estuier* to preserve, ult. from L *studēre* to care about]

Twelfth Day *n* Jan. 6, the twelfth day after Christmas and the feast of the Epiphany.

twelfth man *n* a reserve player in a cricket team.

Twelfth Night *n* **a** the evening of Jan. 5, the eve of Twelfth Day. **b** the evening of Twelfth Day itself.

twelve (twɛlv) *n* **1** the cardinal number that is the sum of ten and two. **2** a numeral, 12, XII, etc., representing this number. **3** something representing or consisting of 12 units. **4** Also called: **twelve o'clock.** noon or midnight. ◆ *determiner* **5a** amounting to twelve. **5b** (*as pronoun*): *twelve have arrived.* ◆ Related adj: **duodecimal.** [OE *twelf*]
▸**twelfth** *adj, n*

twelve-inch *n* a gramophone record 12 inches in diameter and played at 45 revolutions per minute, usually containing an extended remix of a single.

twelvemo ('twɛlvməʊ) *n, pl* **twelvemos.** *Bookbinding.* another word for **duodecimo.**

twelvemonth ('twɛlvˌmʌnθ) *n Chiefly Brit.* an archaic or dialect word for a **year.**

twelve-tone *adj* of or denoting the type of serial music which uses as musical material a tone row formed by the 12 semitones of the chromatic scale. See **serialism.**

twenty ('twɛntɪ) *n, pl* **twenties. 1** the cardinal number that is the product of ten and two. **2** a numeral, 20, XX, etc., representing this number. **3** something representing or consisting of 20 units. ◆ *determiner* **4a** amounting to twenty: *twenty questions.* **4b** (*as pronoun*): *to order twenty.*
▸**'twentieth** *adj, n* [OE *twēntig*]

twenty-six counties *pl n* the counties of the Republic of Ireland.

twenty-twenty *adj Med.* (of vision) being of normal acuity: usually written 20/20.

'twere (twɜ:; *unstressed* twə) *Poetic or dialect. contraction of* it were.

twerp *or* **twirp** (twɜ:p) *n Inf.* a silly, weak-minded, or contemptible person. [C20: from ?]

twibill *or* **twibil** ('twaɪˌbɪl) *n* **1** a mattock with a blade shaped like an adze at one end and like an axe at the other. **2** *Arch.* a double-bladed battle-axe. [OE, from *twi-* double + *bill* sword]

twice (twaɪs) *adv* **1** two times; on two occasions or in two cases. **2** double in degree or quantity: *twice as long.* [OE *twiwa*]

twiddle Ⓣ ('twɪdᵊl) *vb* **twiddles, twiddling, twiddled. 1** (when *intr*, often foll. by *with*) to twirl or fiddle (with), often in an idle way. **2 twiddle one's thumbs.** to do nothing; be unoccupied. **3** (*intr*) to turn, twirl, or rotate. **4** (*intr*) *Rare.* to be occupied with trifles. ◆ *n* **5** an act or instance of twiddling. [C16: prob. a blend of TWIRL + FIDDLE]
▸**'twiddler** *n*

twig¹ Ⓣ (twɪg) *n* **1** any small branch or shoot of a tree. **2** something resembling this, esp. a minute branch of a blood vessel. [OE *twigge*]
▸**'twiggy** *adj*

twig² Ⓣ (twɪg) *vb* **twigs, twigging, twigged.** *Brit. inf.* **1** to understand (something). **2** to find out or suddenly comprehend (something): *he hasn't twigged yet.* [C18: ?from Scot. Gaelic *tuig* I understand]

twilight Ⓣ ('twaɪˌlaɪt) *n* **1** the soft diffused light occurring when the sun is just below the horizon, esp. following sunset. **2** the period in which this light occurs. **3** any faint light. **4** a period in which strength, importance, etc., are waning. **5** (*modifier*) **5a** of or relating to the period towards the end of the day: *the twilight shift.* **5b** of or relating to the final phase of a particular era: *the twilight days of the Bush presidency.* **5c** denoting irregularity and obscurity: *a twilight existence.* [C15: lit.: half light (between day and night), from OE *twi-* half + LIGHT¹]
▸**twilit** ('twaɪˌlɪt) *adj*

Twilight of the Gods *n* another term for **Götterdämmerung.**

twilight sleep *n Med.* a state of partial anaesthesia in which the patient retains a slight degree of consciousness.

twilight zone *n* **1** any indefinite or transitional condition or area. **2** an inner-city area where houses have become dilapidated.

THESAURUS

TV *n* = **television**, gogglebox (*Brit. sl.*), idiot box (*sl.*), receiver, small screen (*inf.*), television set, telly (*Brit. inf.*), the box (*Brit. inf.*), the tube (*sl.*), TV set

twaddle *n* **1** = **nonsense**, balderdash, blather, bull (*sl.*), bullshit (*taboo sl.*), bunkum *or* buncombe (*chiefly US*), chatter, claptrap (*inf.*), cobblers (*Brit. taboo sl.*), crap (*sl.*), drivel, eyewash (*inf.*), foolish talk, gabble, garbage (*inf.*), gossip, guff (*sl.*), hogwash, hokum (*sl., chiefly US & Canad.*), hot air (*inf.*), inanity, moonshine, pap, piffle (*inf.*), poppycock (*inf.*), rigmarole, rot, rubbish, tattle, tommyrot, tosh (*sl., chiefly Brit.*), trash, tripe (*inf.*), trumpery, verbiage, waffle (*inf., chiefly Brit.*) ◆ *vb* **2** = **talk nonsense**, blather, chatter, gabble, gossip, prattle, rattle on, talk through one's hat, tattle, waffle (*inf., chiefly Brit.*)

tweak *vb, n* **1, 3** = **twist**, jerk, nip, pinch, pull, squeeze, twitch

twee *adj Informal* = **sweet**, bijou, cute, dainty, precious, pretty, quaint, sentimental

twiddle *vb* **1** = **fiddle** (*inf.*), adjust, finger, jiggle, juggle, monkey with (*inf.*), play with, twirl, wiggle **2 twiddle one's thumbs** = **be idle**, be unoccupied, do nothing, have nothing to do, malinger, mark time, sit around

twig¹ *n* = **branch**, offshoot, shoot, spray, sprig, stick, withe

twig² *vb* **1, 2** *Brit. informal* = **understand**, catch on, comprehend, fathom, find out, get, grasp, make out, rumble (*Brit. inf.*), see, tumble to (*inf.*)

twilight *n* **1** = **dusk**, dimness, evening, gloaming (*Scot. or poetic*), gloom, half-light, sundown, sunset **4** = **decline**, ebb, last phase ◆ *modifier* **5a** = **evening**, crepuscular, darkening, dim ◆ *adj* **5b** = **declining**, dying, ebbing, final, last

Antonyms *n* ≠ **dusk**: dawn, daybreak, morning,

twill (twɪl) *adj* **1** (in textiles) of a weave in which the yarns are worked to produce an effect of parallel diagonal lines or ribs. ◆ *n* **2** any fabric so woven. ◆ *vb* **3** (*tr*) to weave in this fashion. [OE *twilic* having a double thread]

'twill (twɪl) *Poetic or dialect. contraction of* it will.

twin Ⓣ (twɪn) *n* **1a** either of two persons or animals conceived at the same time. **1b** (*as modifier*): *a twin brother.* See also **identical** (sense 3), **fraternal** (sense 3). **2a** either of two persons or things that are identical or very similar. **2b** (*as modifier*): *twin carburettors.* **3** Also called: **macle.** a crystal consisting of two parts each of which has a definite orientation to the other. ◆ *vb* **twins, twinning, twinned. 4** to pair or be paired together; couple. **5** (*intr*) to bear twins. **6** (*intr*) (of a crystal) to form into a twin. **7a** (*tr*) to create a reciprocal relation between (two towns in different countries); pair (a town) with another in a different country. **7b** (*intr*) (of a town) to be paired in a town in a different country. [OE *twinn*]
▸**'twinning** *n*

twin bed *n* one of a pair of matching single beds.

twine Ⓣ (twaɪn) *n* **1** string made by twisting together fibres of hemp, cotton, etc. **2** a twining. **3** something produced or characterized by twining. **4** a twist, coil, or convolution. **5** a knot or tangle. ◆ *vb* **twines, twining, twined. 6** (*tr*) to twist together; interweave. **7** (*tr*) to form by or as if by twining. **8** (when *intr*, often foll. by *around*) to wind or cause to wind, esp. in spirals. [OE *twīn*]
▸**'twiner** *n*

twin-engined *adj* (of an aeroplane) having two engines.

twinge Ⓣ (twɪndʒ) *n* **1** a sudden brief darting or stabbing pain. **2** a sharp emotional pang. ◆ *vb* **twinges, twinging, twinged. 3** to have or cause to have a twinge. [OE *twengan* to pinch]

twinkle Ⓣ ('twɪŋkəl) *vb* **twinkles, twinkling, twinkled.** (*mainly intr*) **1** to emit or reflect light in a flickering manner; shine brightly and intermittently; sparkle. **2** (of the eyes) to sparkle, esp. with amusement or delight. **3** *Rare.* to move about quickly. ◆ *n* **4** a flickering brightness; sparkle. **5** an instant. [OE *twinclian*]
▸**'twinkler** *n*

twinkling Ⓣ ('twɪŋklɪŋ) *or* **twink** (twɪŋk) *n* a very short time; instant; moment. Also called: **twinkling of an eye.**

Twins (twɪnz) *pl n* **the.** the constellation Gemini, the third sign of the zodiac.

twin-screw *adj* (of a vessel) having two propellers.

twinset ('twɪn,sɛt) *n Brit.* a matching jumper and cardigan.

twin town *n* a town that has civic associations, such as reciprocal visits and cultural exchanges, with a foreign town.

twin-tub *n* a type of washing machine that has two revolving drums, one for washing and the other for spin-drying.

twirl Ⓣ (twɜːl) *vb* **1** to move around rapidly and repeatedly in a circle. **2** (*tr*) to twist, wind, or twiddle, often idly: *she twirled her hair around her finger.* **3** (*intr;* often foll. by *around* or *about*) to turn suddenly to face another way. ◆ *n* **4** a rotating or being rotated; whirl or twist. **5** something wound around or twirled; coil. **6** a written flourish. [C16: ? a blend of TWIST + WHIRL]
▸**'twirler** *n*

twirp (twɜːp) *n* a variant spelling of **twerp.**

twist Ⓣ (twɪst) *vb* **1** to cause (one end or part) to turn or (of one end or part) to turn in the opposite direction from another; coil or spin. **2** to distort or be distorted. **3** to wind or twine. **4** to force or be forced out of the natural form or position. **5** to change for the worse in character, meaning, etc.; pervert: *she twisted the statement.* **6** to revolve; rotate. **7** (*tr*) to wrench with a turning action. **8** (*intr*) to follow a winding course. **9** (*intr*) to squirm, as with pain. **10** (*intr*) to dance the twist. **11** (*tr*) *Brit. inf.* to cheat; swindle. **12 twist someone's arm.** to persuade or coerce someone. ◆ *n* **13** a twisting. **14** something formed by or as if by twisting. **15** a decisive change of direction, aim, meaning, or character. **16** (in a novel, play, etc.) an unexpected event, revelation, etc. **17** a bend: *a twist in the road.* **18** a distortion of the original shape or form. **19** a jerky pull, wrench, or turn. **20** a strange personal characteristic, esp. a bad one. **21** a confused tangle made by twisting. **22** a twisted thread used in sewing where extra strength is needed. **23 the twist.** a dance popular in the 1960s, in which dancers vigorously twist the hips. **24** a loaf or roll made of pieces of twisted dough. **25** a thin sliver of peel from a lemon, lime, etc., twisted and added to a drink. **26a** a cigar made by twisting three cigars around one another. **26b** chewing tobacco made in the form of a roll by twisting the leaves together. **27** *Physics.* torsional deformation or shear stress or strain. **28** *Sport, chiefly US & Canad.* spin given to a ball in various games. **29 round the twist.** *Brit. sl.* mad; eccentric. [OE]
▸**'twisty** *adj*

twist drill *n* a drill bit having two helical grooves running from the point along the shank to clear swarf and cuttings.

twister Ⓣ ('twɪstə) *n* **1** *Brit.* a swindling or dishonest person. **2** a person or thing that twists. **3** *US & Canad.* an informal name for **tornado. 4** a ball moving with a twisting motion.

twist grip *n* a handlebar control in the form of a ratchet-controlled rotating grip.

twit[1] Ⓣ (twɪt) *vb* **twits, twitting, twitted. 1** (*tr*) to tease, taunt, or reproach, often in jest. ◆ *n* **2** *US & Canad. inf.* a nervous or excitable state. **3** *Rare.* a reproach; taunt. [OE *ætwītan,* from *æt* against + *wītan* to accuse]

twit[2] Ⓣ (twɪt) *n Inf., chiefly Brit.* a foolish or stupid person; idiot. [C19: from TWIT[1] (orig. in the sense: a person given to twitting)]

twitch Ⓣ (twɪtʃ) *vb* **1** to move in a jerky spasmodic way. **2** (*tr*) to pull (something) with a quick jerky movement. **3** (*intr*) to hurt with a sharp spasmodic pain. ◆ *n* **4** a sharp jerking movement. **5** a mental or physical twinge. **6** a sudden muscular spasm, esp. one caused by a nervous condition. **7** a loop of cord used to control a horse by drawing it tight about its upper lip. [OE *twiccian* to pluck]

twitcher ('twɪtʃə) *n* **1** a person or thing that twitches. **2** *Inf.* a bird-watcher who tries to spot as many rare varieties as possible.

twitch grass *n* another name for **couch grass.** Sometimes shortened to **twitch.** [C16: var. of QUITCH GRASS]

twite (twaɪt) *n* a N European finch with a brown streaked plumage. [C16: imit. of its cry]

twitter Ⓣ ('twɪtə) *vb* **1** (*intr*) (esp. of a bird) to utter a succession of chirping sounds. **2** (*intr*) to talk or move rapidly and tremulously. **3** (*intr*) to giggle. **4** (*tr*) to utter in a chirping way. ◆ *n* **5** a twittering sound. **6** the act of twittering. **7** a state of nervous excitement (esp. in **in a twitter**). [C14: imit.]
▸**'twitterer** *n* ▸**'twittery** *adj*

'twixt *or* **twixt** (twɪkst) *Poetic or dialect. contraction of* betwixt.

two (tuː) *n* **1** the cardinal number that is the sum of one and one. **2** a numeral, 2, II, (ii), etc., representing this number. **3** something representing or consisting of two units. **4** Also called: **two o'clock.** two hours after noon or midnight. **5 in two.** in or into two parts. **6 put two and two together.** to make an inference from available evidence, esp. an obvious inference. **7 that makes two of us.** the same applies to me. ◆ *determiner* **8a** amounting to two: *two nails.* **8b** (*as pronoun*): *he bought two.* ◆ Related adjs.: **binary, double, dual.** [OE *twā* (fem)]

THESAURUS

sunrise, sunup ≠ **decline:** climax, crowning moment, height, peak

twin *n* **2a** = **double,** clone, corollary, counterpart, duplicate, fellow, likeness, lookalike, match, mate, ringer (*sl.*) ◆ *modifier* **2b** = **identical,** corresponding, double, dual, duplicate, geminate, matched, matching, paired, parallel, twofold ◆ *vb* **4** = **pair,** couple, join, link, match, yoke

twine *n* **1** = **string,** cord, yarn **4** = **coil,** convolution, interlacing, twist, whorl **5** = **tangle,** knot, snarl ◆ *vb* **6** = **twist together,** braid, entwine, interlace, interweave, knit, plait, splice, twist, weave **8** = **coil,** bend, curl, encircle, loop, meander, spiral, surround, twist, wind, wrap, wreathe

twinge *n* **1** = **pain,** bite, gripe, pang, pinch, prick, sharp pain, spasm, stab, stitch, throb, throe (*rare*), tic, tweak, twist, twitch

twinkle *vb* **1** = **sparkle,** blink, coruscate, flash, flicker, gleam, glint, glisten, glitter, scintillate, shimmer, shine, wink ◆ *n* **4** = **sparkle,** blink, coruscation, flash, flicker, gleam, glimmer, glistening, glittering, light, scintillation, shimmer, shine, spark, wink **5** = **moment,** flash, instant, jiffy (*inf.*), second, shake (*inf.*), split second, tick (*Brit. inf.*), trice, twinkling, two shakes of a lamb's tail (*inf.*)

twinkling *n* = **moment,** bat of an eye (*inf.*), flash, instant, jiffy, second, shake (*inf.*), split second, tick (*Brit. inf.*), trice, twinkle, two shakes of a lamb's tail (*inf.*)

twirl *vb* **1** = **turn,** gyrate, pirouette, pivot, revolve, rotate, spin, turn on one's heel, twiddle, twist, wheel, whirl, wind ◆ *n* **4** = **turn,** gyration, pirouette, revolution, rotation, spin, twist, wheel, whirl **5** = **coil,** spiral, twist

twist *vb* **1, 3** = **wind,** coil, corkscrew, curl, encircle, entwine, intertwine, screw, spin, swivel, twine, weave, wrap, wreathe, wring **2** = **distort,** contort, screw up **5** = **misrepresent,** alter, change, distort, falsify, garble, misquote, pervert, warp **7** = **sprain,** rick, turn, wrench **9** = **squirm,** wriggle, writhe **12 twist someone's arm** = **force,** bully, coerce, persuade, pressurize, talk into ◆ *n* **13** = **wind,** coil, curl, spin, swivel, twine **14** = **coil,** braid, curl, hank, plug, quid, roll **16** = **development,** change, revelation, slant, surprise, turn, variation **17** = **curve,** arc, bend, convolution, meander, turn, undulation, zigzag **18** = **distortion,** defect, deformation, flaw, imperfection, kink, warp **19** = **jerk,** pull, sprain, turn, wrench **20** = **trait,** aberration, bent, characteristic, crotchet, eccentricity, fault, foible, idiosyncrasy, oddity, peculiarity, proclivity, quirk **21** = **tangle,** confusion, entanglement, kink, knot, mess, mix-up, ravel, snarl **29 round the twist** *Brit. slang* = **mad,** barmy (*sl.*), batty (*sl.*), bonkers (*sl., chiefly Brit.*), crazy, cuckoo (*inf.*), daft (*inf.*), insane, loopy (*inf.*), not all there, not right in the head, nuts (*sl.*), nutty (*sl.*), off one's rocker (*sl.*), off one's trolley (*sl.*), out to lunch (*inf.*)
Antonyms *vb* ≠ **distort:** straighten, untwist ≠ **wind:** straighten, uncoil, unravel, unroll, untwist, unwind

twister *n* **1** *Brit.* = **swindler,** cheat, chiseller (*inf.*), con man (*inf.*), crook (*inf.*), deceiver, fraud, fraudster, hustler (*US inf.*), rogue, trickster

twit[1] *vb* **1** = **make fun of,** banter, deride, jeer, poke fun at, scorn, taunt, tease **1** = **reproach,** berate, blame, censure, upbraid

twit[2] *n Informal, chiefly Brit.* = **fool,** airhead (*sl.*), ass, berk, blockhead, charlie (*Brit. inf.*), chump (*inf.*), clown, divvy (*Brit. sl.*), dope (*inf.*), dork (*sl.*), dumb-ass (*sl.*), geek (*sl.*), halfwit, idiot, nincompoop, ninny, nitwit (*inf.*), numbskull *or* numskull, pillock (*Brit. sl.*), plank (*Brit. sl.*), plonker (*sl.*), schmuck (*US sl.*), silly-billy (*inf.*), simpleton, wally (*sl.*)

twitch *vb* **1** = **jerk,** blink, flutter, jump, squirm **2** = **pull,** pluck, snatch, tug, yank ◆ *n* **4, 5** = **jerk,** blink, flutter, jump, spasm, tic, tremor, twinge

twitter *vb* **1** = **chirrup,** chatter, cheep, chirp, trill, tweet, warble, whistle **2** = **chatter,** prattle **3** = **giggle,** simper, snigger, titter ◆ *n* **5** = **chirrup,** call, chatter, cheep, chirp, cry, song, trill, tweet, warble, whistle **7** *As in* **in a twitter** = **nervousness,** agitation, anxiety, bustle, dither (*chiefly Brit.*), excitement, flurry, fluster, flutter, tizzy (*inf.*), whirl

two-by-four *n* **1** a length of untrimmed timber with a cross section that measures 2 inches by 4 inches. **2** a trimmed timber joist with a cross section that measures 1½ inches by 3½ inches.
twoccing *or* **twocking** ('twɒkɪŋ) *n Brit. sl.* the act of breaking into a motor vehicle and driving it away. [C20: from *T(aking) W(ithout) O(wner's) C(onsent),* the legal offence with which car thieves may be charged]
▸ **'twoccer** *or* **'twocker** *n*
two-dimensional *adj* **1** of or having two dimensions. **2** having an area but not enclosing any volume. **3** lacking in depth.
two-edged ❶ *adj* **1** having two cutting edges. **2** (esp. of a remark) having two interpretations, such as *she looks nice when she smiles.*
two-faced ❶ *adj* deceitful; hypocritical.
twofold ('tuːˌfəʊld) *adj* **1** equal to twice as many or twice as much. **2** composed of two parts. ◆ *adv* **3** doubly.
two-handed *adj* **1** requiring the use of both hands. **2** ambidextrous. **3** requiring the participation or cooperation of two people.
two-pack *adj* (of a paint, filler, etc.) supplied as two separate components, for example a base and a catalyst, that are mixed together immediately before use.
twopence *or* **tuppence** ('tʌpəns) *n Brit.* **1** the sum of two pennies. **2** (*used with a negative*) something of little value (in **not care** *or* **give twopence**). **3** a former British silver coin.
twopenny *or* **tuppenny** ('tʌpənɪ) *adj Chiefly Brit.* **1** Also: **twopenny-halfpenny.** cheap or tawdry. **2** (intensifier): *a twopenny damn.* **3** worth two pence.
two-phase *adj* (of an electrical circuit, device, etc.) generating or using two alternating voltages of the same frequency, displaced in phase by 90°.
two-piece *adj* **1** consisting of two separate parts, usually matching, as of a garment. ◆ *n* **2** such an outfit.
two-ply *adj* **1** made of two thicknesses, layers, or strands. ◆ *n, pl* **two-plies. 2** a two-ply wood, knitting yarn, etc.
two-sided *adj* **1** having two sides or aspects. **2** controversial; debatable.
twosome ('tuːsəm) *n* **1** two together, esp. two people. **2** a match between two people.
two-step *n* **1** an old-time dance in duple time. **2** a piece of music composed for or in the rhythm of this dance.
two-stroke *adj* of an internal-combustion engine whose piston makes two strokes for every explosion. US and Canad. word: **two-cycle.**
Two Thousand Guineas *n* (*functioning as sing*), *usually written* **2000 Guineas. the.** an annual horse race run at Newmarket since 1809.
two-time *vb* **two-times, two-timing, two-timed.** *Inf.* to deceive (someone, esp. a lover) by carrying on a relationship with another.
▸ **ˌtwo-'timer** *n*
two-tone *adj* **1** of two colours or two shades of the same colour. **2** (esp. of sirens, car horns, etc.) producing or consisting of two notes.
'twould (twʊd) *Poetic or dialect. contraction of* it would.
two-up *n Chiefly Austral.* a illegal gambling game in which two coins are tossed or spun.
two-way *adj* **1** moving, permitting movement, or operating in either of two opposite directions. **2** involving two participants. **3** involving reciprocal obligation or mutual action. **4** (of a radio, telephone, etc.) allowing communications in two directions using both transmitting and receiving equipment.
two-way mirror *n* a half-silvered sheet of glass that functions as a mirror when viewed from one side but is translucent from the other.
-ty[1] *suffix of numerals.* denoting a multiple of ten: *sixty; seventy.* [from OE *-tig*]
-ty[2] *suffix forming nouns.* indicating state, condition, or quality: *cruelty.* [from OF *-te, -tet,* from L *-tās, -tāt-*]
Tyburn ('taɪbɜːn) *n* (formerly) a place of execution in London, on the River Tyburn.
tychism ('taɪkɪzəm) *n Philosophy.* the theory that chance is an objective reality at work in the universe. [from Gk *tukhē* chance]
tycoon ❶ (taɪ'kuːn) *n* **1** a businessman of great wealth and power. **2** an archaic name for a **shogun.** [C19: from Japanese *taikun,* from Chinese *ta* great + *chün* ruler]
tyke *or* **tike** (taɪk) *n* **1** a dog, esp. a mongrel. **2** *Inf.* a small or cheeky child. **3** *Brit. dialect.* a rough ill-mannered person. **4** *Brit. sl. often offens.* a person from Yorkshire. **5** *Austral. sl., offens.* a Roman Catholic. [C14: from ON *tīk* bitch]
tylopod ('taɪləʊˌpɒd) *n* a mammal having padded, rather than hoofed, digits, such as camels and llamas. [C19: from NL, from Gk *tulos* knob or *tulē* cushion + -POD]
tympan ('tɪmpən) *n* **1** a membrane stretched over a frame or cylinder. **2** *Printing.* packing interposed between the platen and the paper to be printed in order to provide an even impression. **3** *Archit.* another name for **tympanum.** [OE *timpana,* from L; see TYMPANUM]
tympani ('tɪmpənɪ) *pl n* a variant spelling of **timpani.**
tympanic bone (tɪm'pænɪk) *n* the part of the temporal bone that surrounds the auditory canal.
tympanic membrane *n* the thin membrane separating the external ear from the middle ear. It transmits vibrations, produced by sound waves, to the cochlea. Nontechnical name: **eardrum.**
tympanites (ˌtɪmpə'naɪtiːz) *n* distension of the abdomen caused by an accumulation of gas in the intestinal or peritoneal cavity. Also called: **meteorism, tympany.** [C14: from LL, from Gk *tumpanitēs* concerning a drum, from *tumpanon* drum]
▸ **tympanitic** (ˌtɪmpə'nɪtɪk) *adj*
tympanitis (ˌtɪmpə'naɪtɪs) *n* inflammation of the eardrum.
tympanum ('tɪmpənəm) *n, pl* **tympanums** *or* **tympana** (-nə). **1a** the cavity of the middle ear. **1b** another name for **tympanic membrane. 2** any diaphragm resembling that in the middle ear in function. **3** *Archit.* **3a** the recessed space bounded by the cornices of a pediment, esp. one that is triangular in shape. **3b** the recessed space bounded by an arch and the lintel of a doorway or window below it. **4** *Music.* a tympan or drum. **5** a scoop wheel for raising water. [C17: from L, from Gk *tumpanon* drum]
▸ **tympanic** (tɪm'pænɪk) *adj*
Tyndall effect *n* the phenomenon in which light is scattered by particles of matter in its path. [C19: after John *Tyndall* (1820–93), Irish physicist]
Tynwald ('tɪnwəld, 'taɪn-) *n* **the.** the Parliament of the Isle of Man. [C15: from ON *thingvollr,* from *thing* assembly + *vollr* field]
typ., typo., *or* **typog.** *abbrev. for:* **1** typographer. **2** typographic(al). **3** typography.
typal ('taɪpᵊl) *adj* a rare word for **typical.**
type ❶ (taɪp) *n* **1** a kind, class, or category, the constituents of which share similar characteristics. **2** a subdivision of a particular class; sort: *what type of shampoo do you use?* **3** the general form, plan, or design distinguishing a particular group. **4** *Inf.* a person who typifies a particular quality: *he's the administrative type.* **5** *Inf.* a person, esp. of a specified kind: *he's a strange type.* **6a** a small block of metal or more rarely wood bearing a letter or character in relief for use in printing. **6b** such pieces collectively. **7** characters printed from type; print. **8** *Biol.* **8a** the taxonomic group the characteristics of which are used for defining the next highest group. **8b** (*as modifier*): *a type genus.* **9** See **type specimen. 10** the characteristic device on a coin. **11** *Chiefly Christian theol.* a figure, episode, or symbolic factor resembling some future reality in such a way as to foreshadow or prefigure it. ◆ *vb* **types, typing, typed. 12** to write (copy) on a typewriter. **13** (*tr*) to be a symbol of; typify. **14** (*tr*) to decide the type of. **15** (*tr*) *Med.* to determine the blood group of (a blood sample). **16** (*tr*) *Chiefly Christian theol.* to foreshadow or serve as a symbol of (some future reality). [C15: from L *typus* figure, from Gk *tupos* image, from *tuptein* to strike]
-type *n combining form.* **1** type or form: *archetype.* **2** printing type or photographic process: *collotype.* [from L *-typus,* from Gk *-typos,* from *tupos* TYPE]
typecast ('taɪpˌkɑːst) *vb* **typecasts, typecasting, typecast.** (*tr*) to cast (an actor) in the same kind of role continually, esp. because of his physical appearance or previous success in such roles.
typeface ('taɪpˌfeɪs) *n* another name for **face** (sense 14).
type founder *n* a person who casts metallic printer's type.
▸ **type foundry** *n*
type metal *n Printing.* an alloy of tin, lead, and antimony, from which type is cast.
typescript ('taɪpˌskrɪpt) *n* **1** a typed copy of a document, etc. **2** any typewritten material.
typeset ('taɪpˌsɛt) *vb* **typesets, typesetting, typeset.** (*tr*) *Printing.* to set (textual matter) in type.
typesetter ('taɪpˌsɛtə) *n* **1** a person who sets type; compositor. **2** a typesetting machine.
type specimen *n Biol.* the original specimen from which a description of a new species is made.
typewrite ('taɪpˌraɪt) *vb* **typewrites, typewriting, typewrote, typewritten.** to write by means of a typewriter; type.
▸ **'typeˌwriting** *n*
typewriter ('taɪpˌraɪtə) *n* a keyboard machine for writing mechanically in characters resembling print.
typhlitis (tɪf'laɪtɪs) *n* inflammation of the caecum. [C19: from NL, from Gk *tuphlon* the caecum, from *tuphlos* blind]
▸ **typhlitic** (tɪf'lɪtɪk) *adj*
typhoid ('taɪfɔɪd) *Pathol.* ◆ *adj also* **typhoidal. 1** resembling typhus. ◆ *n* **2** short for **typhoid fever.** [C19: from TYPHUS + -OID]
typhoid fever *n* an acute infectious disease characterized by high fever, spots, abdominal pain, etc. It is caused by a bacillus ingested with food or water.
typhoon ❶ (taɪ'fuːn) *n* a violent tropical storm or cyclone, esp. in the China Seas and W Pacific. [C16: from Chinese *tai fung* great wind; infl. by Gk *tuphōn* whirlwind]
▸ **typhonic** (taɪ'fɒnɪk) *adj*

THESAURUS

two-edged *adj* **2** = **ambiguous,** ambivalent, backhanded, double-edged, equivocal
two-faced *adj* = **hypocritical,** deceitful, deceiving, dissembling, double-dealing, duplicitous, false, insincere, Janus-faced, perfidious, treacherous, untrustworthy
Antonyms *adj* artless, candid, frank, genuine, honest, ingenuous, sincere, trustworthy
tycoon *n* **1** = **magnate,** baron, big cheese (*sl., old-fashioned*), big noise (*inf.*), capitalist, captain of industry, fat cat (*sl., chiefly US*), financier, industrialist, merchant prince, mogul, plutocrat, potentate, wealthy businessman
type *n* **1, 2** = **kind,** breed, category, class, classification, form, genre, group, ilk, kidney, order, sort, species, stamp, strain, style, subdivision, variety **4** = **epitome,** archetype, essence, example, exemplar, model, norm, original, paradigm, pattern, personification, prototype, quintessence, specimen, standard **7** = **print,** case, characters, face, font, fount, printing
typhoon *n* = **storm,** cyclone, squall, tempest, tornado, tropical storm

typhus ('taɪfəs) *n* any one of a group of acute infectious rickettsial diseases characterized by high fever, skin rash, and severe headache. Also called: **typhus fever.** [C18: from NL *týphus,* from Gk *tuphos* fever]
▸**'typhous** *adj*

typical ❶ ('tɪpɪkᵊl) *adj* **1** being or serving as a representative example of a particular type; characteristic. **2** considered to be an example of some undesirable trait: *that is typical of you!* **3** of or relating to a representative specimen or type. **4** conforming to a type. **5** *Biol.* having most of the characteristics of a particular taxonomic group. [C17: from Med. L *typicālis,* from LL *typicus* figurative, from Gk *tupikos,* from *tupos* TYPE]
▸**'typically** *adv* ▸**'typicalness** *or* **,typi'cality** *n*

typify ❶ ('tɪpɪ,faɪ) *vb* **typifies, typifying, typified.** (*tr*) **1** to be typical of; characterize. **2** to symbolize or represent completely, by or as if by a type. [C17: from L *typus* TYPE]
▸**,typifi'cation** *n*

typist ('taɪpɪst) *n* a person who types, esp. for a living.

typo ('taɪpəʊ) *n, pl* **typos.** *Inf.* a typographical error. Also called (Brit.): **literal.**

typographer (taɪ'pɒgrəfə) *n* **1** a person skilled in typography. **2** a compositor.

typography (taɪ'pɒgrəfɪ) *n* **1** the art, craft, or process of composing type and printing from it. **2** the planning, selection, and setting of type for a printed work.
▸**typographical** (,taɪpə'græfɪkᵊl) *or* **,typo'graphic** *adj* ▸**,typo'graphically** *adv*

typology (taɪ'pɒlədʒɪ) *n* **1** the study of types in archaeology, biology, etc. **2** *Christian theol.* the doctrine that symbols for events, figures, etc., in the New Testament can be found in the Old Testament.
▸**typological** (,taɪpə'lɒdʒɪkᵊl) *adj* ▸**ty'pologist** *n*

tyrannical ❶ (tɪ'rænɪkᵊl) *or* **tyrannic** *adj* characteristic of or relating to a tyrant or to tyranny; oppressive.
▸**ty'rannically** *adv*

tyrannicide (tɪ'rænɪ,saɪd) *n* **1** the killing of a tyrant. **2** a person who kills a tyrant.

tyrannize ❶ *or* **tyrannise** ('tɪrə,naɪz) *vb* **tyrannizes, tyrannizing, tyrannized** or **tyrannises, tyrannising, tyrannised.** (when *intr,* often foll. by *over*) to rule or exercise power (over) in a cruel or oppressive manner.
▸**'tyran,nizer** *or* **'tyran,niser** *n*

tyrannosaurus (tɪ,rænə'sɔːrəs) *or* **tyrannosaur** (tɪ'rænə,sɔː) *n* any of various large carnivorous two-footed dinosaurs common in North America in Upper Jurassic and Cretaceous times. [C19: from NL, from Gk *turannos* tyrant + -SAUR]

tyranny ❶ ('tɪrənɪ) *n, pl* **tyrannies. 1a** government by a tyrant; despotism. **1b** oppressive and unjust government by more than one person. **2** arbitrary, unreasonable, or despotic behaviour or use of authority. **3** a tyrannical act. [C14: from OF *tyrannie,* from Med. L *tyrannia,* from L *tyrannus* TYRANT]
▸**'tyrannous** *adj*

tyrant ❶ ('taɪrənt) *n* **1** a person who governs oppressively, unjustly, and arbitrarily; despot. **2** any person who exercises authority in a tyrannical manner. [C13: from OF *tyrant,* from L *tyrannus,* from Gk *turannos*]

tyre *or US* **tire** ('taɪə) *n* **1** a rubber ring placed over the rim of a wheel of a road vehicle to provide traction and reduce road shocks, esp. a hollow inflated ring (**pneumatic tyre**) consisting of a reinforced outer casing enclosing an inner tube. **2** a metal band or hoop attached to the rim of a wooden cartwheel. [C18: var. of C15 *tire,* prob. from archaic var. of ATTIRE]

Tyrian ('tɪrɪən) *n* **1** a native or inhabitant of ancient Tyre, a port in S Lebanon and centre of ancient Phoenician culture. ◆ *adj* **2** of or relating to ancient Tyre.

Tyrian purple *n* **1** a deep purple dye obtained from certain molluscs and highly prized in antiquity. **2a** a vivid purplish-red colour. **2b** (*as adj*): *a Tyrian-purple robe.*

tyro ❶ *or* **tiro** ('taɪrəʊ) *n, pl* **tyros** *or* **tiros.** a novice or beginner. [C17: from L *tīrō* recruit]

tyrosinase (,taɪrəʊsɪ'neɪz) *n* an enzyme that is a catalyst in the conversion of tyrosine to the pigment melanin.

tyrosine ('taɪrə,siːn, -sɪn, 'tɪrə-) *n* an amino acid that is a precursor of the hormones adrenaline and thyroxine and of the pigment melanin. [C19: from Gk *turos* cheese + -INE²]

tyrothricin (,taɪrəʊ'θraɪsɪn) *n* an antibiotic, obtained from a soil bacterium: applied locally for the treatment of ulcers and abscesses. [C20: from NL *Tyrothrix* (genus name), from Gk *turos* cheese + *thrix* hair]

tzar (zɑː) *n* a less common spelling of **tsar.**

tzatziki (tsæt'sɪkɪ) *n* a Greek dip made from yogurt, chopped cucumber, and mint. [C20: from Mod. Gk]

tzetze fly ('tsetsɪ) *n* a variant spelling of **tsetse fly.**

Tzigane (tsɪ'gɑːn, sɪ-) *n* **a** a Gypsy, esp. a Hungarian one. **b** (*as modifier*): *Tzigane music.* [C19: via F from Hungarian *czigány* Gypsy, from ?]

THESAURUS

typical *adj* **1 = characteristic,** archetypal, average, bog-standard, classic, conventional, essential, illustrative, in character, indicative, in keeping, model, normal, orthodox, representative, standard, stock, true to type, usual
Antonyms *adj* atypical, exceptional, out of keeping, out of the ordinary, singular, uncharacteristic, unconventional, unexpected, unique, unrepresentative, unusual

typify *vb* **1, 2 = represent,** characterize, embody, epitomize, exemplify, illustrate, incarnate, personify, sum up, symbolize

tyrannical *adj* **= oppressive,** absolute, arbitrary, authoritarian, autocratic, coercive, cruel, despotic, dictatorial, domineering, high-handed, imperious, inhuman, magisterial, overbearing, overweening, peremptory, severe, tyrannous, unjust, unreasonable
Antonyms *adj* democratic, easy-going, lax, lenient, liberal, reasonable, tolerant, understanding

tyrannize *vb* **= oppress,** browbeat, bully, coerce, dictate, domineer, enslave, have (someone) under one's thumb, intimidate, ride roughshod over, rule with an iron hand, subjugate, terrorize

tyranny *n* **1, 2 = oppression,** absolutism, authoritarianism, autocracy, coercion, cruelty, despotism, dictatorship, harsh discipline, high-handedness, imperiousness, peremptoriness, reign of terror, unreasonableness
Antonyms *n* democracy, ease, laxity, leniency, liberality, mercy, relaxation, tolerance, understanding

tyrant *n* **1, 2 = dictator,** absolutist, authoritarian, autocrat, bully, despot, Hitler, martinet, oppressor, slave-driver

tyro *n* **= beginner,** apprentice, catechumen, greenhorn (*inf.*), initiate, learner, neophyte, novice, novitiate, pupil, student, trainee

Uu

u *or* **U** (ju:) *n, pl* **u's, U's,** *or* **Us. 1** the 21st letter and fifth vowel of the English alphabet. **2** any of several speech sounds represented by this letter, as in *mute, cut,* or *minus.* **3a** something shaped like a U. **3b** (*in combination*): *a U-bolt.*

U *symbol for:* **1** united. **2** unionist. **3** university. **4** (in Britain) **4a** universal (used to describe a category of film certified as suitable for viewing by anyone). **4b** (*as modifier*): *a U certificate film.* **5** *Chem.* uranium. **6** *Biochem.* uracil. ◆ *adj* **7** *Brit. inf.* (esp. of language habits) characteristic of or appropriate to the upper class.

U. *abbrev. for:* **1** *Maths.* union. **2** unit. **3** united. **4** university. **5** upper.

UAE *abbrev. for* United Arab Emirates.

UB40 *n* (in Britain) **1** a registration card issued by the Department of Employment to a person registering as unemployed. **2** *Inf.* a person registered as unemployed.

U-bend *n* a U-shaped bend in a pipe that traps water in the lower part of the U and prevents the escape of noxious fumes; trap.

uberrima fides (ju'bɛrɪmə 'faɪdi:z) *n* another name for **utmost good faith.** [L: utmost good faith]

ubiety (ju:'baɪɪtɪ) *n* the condition of being in a particular place. [C17: from L *ubī* where + *-ety,* on the model of *society*]

ubiquitarian (ju:ˌbɪkwɪ'tɛərɪən) *n* **1** a member of the Lutheran church who holds that Christ is no more present in the elements of the Eucharist than elsewhere, as he is present in all places at all times. ◆ *adj* **2** denoting or holding this belief. [C17: from L *ubīque* everywhere]

▸**uˌbiqui'tarianˌism** *n*

ubiquitous ❶ (ju:'bɪkwɪtəs) *adj* having or seeming to have the ability to be everywhere at once. [C14: from L *ubīque* everywhere, from *ubī* where]

▸**u'biquitously** *adv* ▸**u'biquity** *n*

U-boat *n* a German submarine, esp. in World Wars I and II. [from G *U-Boot,* short for *Unterseeboot,* lit.: undersea boat]

UBR *abbrev. for* uniform business rate.

u.c. *Printing. abbrev. for* upper case.

UCATT (in Britain) *abbrev. for* Union of Construction, Allied Trades and Technicians.

UCCA ('ʌkə) *n* (formerly, in Britain) *acronym for* Universities Central Council on Admissions.

UDA *abbrev. for* Ulster Defence Association.

udal ('ju:dᵊl) *n Law.* a form of freehold possession of land existing in northern Europe before the introduction of the feudal system and still used in Orkney and Shetland. [C16: Orkney & Shetland dialect, from ON *othal*]

UDC (in Britain) *abbrev. for* Urban District Council.

udder ('ʌdə) *n* the large baglike mammary gland of cows, sheep, etc., having two or more teats. [OE *ūder*]

UDI *abbrev. for* Unilateral Declaration of Independence.

UDM (in Britain) *abbrev. for* Union of Democratic Mineworkers.

udometer (ju:'dɒmɪtə) *n* another term for **rain gauge.** [C19: from F, from L *ūdus* damp]

UDR *abbrev. for* Ulster Defence Regiment.

UEFA (ju:'eɪfə, 'ju:fə) *n acronym for* Union of European Football Associations.

uey ('ju:ɪ) *n, pl* **ueys.** *Austral. sl.* a U-turn.

UFO (*sometimes* 'ju:fəʊ) *abbrev. for* unidentified flying object.

ufology (ˌju:'fɒlədʒɪ) *n* the study of UFOs.

▸**u'fologist** *n*

Ugaritic (ˌu:gə'rɪtɪk) *n* **1** an extinct Semitic language of N Syria. ◆ *adj* **2** of or relating to this language. [C19: after *Ugarit* (modern name: Ras Shamra), an ancient Syrian city-state]

UGC (in Britain) *abbrev. for* University Grants Committee.

ugh (ʊx, ʊh, ʌx) *interj* an exclamation of disgust, annoyance, or dislike.

UGLI ('ʌglɪ) *n, pl* **UGLIS** *or* **UGLIES.** *Trademark.* a large juicy yellow-skinned citrus fruit of the Caribbean: a cross between a tangerine, grapefruit, and orange. Also called: **UGLI fruit.** [C20: prob. an alteration of UGLY, from its wrinkled skin]

uglify ('ʌglɪˌfaɪ) *vb* **uglifies, uglifying, uglified.** to make or become ugly or more ugly.

▸**ˌuglifi'cation** *n*

ugly ❶ ('ʌglɪ) *adj* **uglier, ugliest. 1** of unpleasant or unsightly appearance. **2** repulsive or displeasing: *war is ugly.* **3** ominous or menacing: *an ugly situation.* **4** bad-tempered or sullen: *an ugly mood.* [C13: from ON *uggligr* dreadful, from *ugga* fear]

▸**'uglily** *adv* ▸**'ugliness** *n*

ugly duckling *n* a person or thing, initially ugly or unpromising, that changes into something beautiful or admirable. [from *The Ugly Duckling* by Hans Christian Andersen]

Ugrian ('u:grɪən, 'ju:-) *adj* **1** of or relating to a subdivision of the Turanian people, who include the Samoyeds and Magyars. ◆ *n* **2** a member of this group. **3** another word for **Ugric.** [C19: from ORussian *Ugre* Hungarians]

Ugric ('u:grɪk, 'ju:-) *n* **1** one of the two branches of the Finno-Ugric family of languages, including Hungarian and some languages of NW Siberia. ◆ *adj* **2** of or relating to this group of languages or their speakers.

UHF *Radio. abbrev. for* ultrahigh frequency.

uh-huh ('ʌhʌ) *sentence substitute. Inf.* a less emphatic variant of **yes.**

uhlan ('u:lɑ:n) *n History.* a member of a body of lancers first employed in the Polish army and later in W European armies. [C18: via G from Polish *ulan,* from Turkish *ōlan* young man]

UHT *abbrev. for* ultra-heat-treated (milk or cream).

uhuru (u:'hu:ru:) *n* (esp. in E Africa) **1** national independence. **2** freedom. [C20: from Swahili]

uillean pipes ('u:lɪən) *pl n* bagpipes developed in Ireland and operated by squeezing bellows under the arm. Also called: **Irish pipes, union pipes.** [C19: Irish *píob uilleann,* from *píob* pipe + *uilleann* genitive sing of *uille* elbow]

uitlander ('eɪtˌlandə, -ˌlæn-) *n* (*sometimes cap.*) *S. African.* a foreigner. [C19: Afrik.: outlander]

UK *abbrev. for* United Kingdom.

ukase (ju:'keɪz) *n* **1** (in imperial Russia) an edict of the tsar. **2** a rare word for **edict.** [C18: from Russian *ukaz,* from *ukazat* to command]

UKCC *abbrev. for* United Kingdom Central Council for Nursing, Midwifery, and Health Visiting.

Ukrainian (ju:'kreɪnɪən) *adj* **1** of or relating to the Ukraine, its people, or their language. ◆ *n* **2** the official language of the Ukraine: an East Slavonic language closely related to Russian. **3** a native or inhabitant of the Ukraine.

ukulele *or* **ukelele** (ˌju:kə'leɪlɪ) *n* a small four-stringed guitar, esp. of Hawaii. [C19: from Hawaiian, lit.: jumping flea]

ulcer ❶ ('ʌlsə) *n* **1** a disintegration of the surface of the skin or a mucous membrane resulting in an open sore that heals very slowly. **2** a source or element of corruption or evil. [C14: from L *ulcus*]

ulcerate ('ʌlsəˌreɪt) *vb* **ulcerates, ulcerating, ulcerated.** to make or become ulcerous.

▸**ˌulce'ration** *n* ▸**'ulcerative** *adj*

ulcerous ❶ ('ʌlsərəs) *adj* **1** relating to or characterized by ulcers. **2** being or having a corrupting influence.

▸**'ulcerously** *adv*

-ule *suffix forming nouns.* indicating smallness: *globule.* [from L *-ulus,* dim. suffix]

ulema ('u:lɪmə) *n* **1** a body of Muslim scholars or religious leaders. **2** a member of this body. [C17: from Ar. *'ulamā* scholars, from *'alama* to know]

-ulent *suffix forming adjectives.* abundant or full of: *fraudulent.* [from L *-ulentus*]

ullage ('ʌlɪdʒ) *n* **1** the volume by which a liquid container falls short of being full. **2a** the quantity of liquid lost from a container due to leakage or evaporation. **2b** (in customs terminology) the amount of liquid remaining in a container after such loss. [C15: from OF *ouillage* filling of a cask, from *ouil* eye, from L *oculus* eye]

ulna ('ʌlnə) *n, pl* **ulnae** (-ni:) *or* **ulnas. 1** the inner and longer of the two bones of the human forearm. **2** the corresponding bone in other vertebrates. [C16: from L: elbow]

▸**'ulnar** *adj*

ulnar nerve *n* a nerve situated along the inner side of the arm and passing close to the surface of the skin near the elbow.

ulotrichous (ju:'lɒtrɪkəs) *adj* having woolly or curly hair. [C19: from NL *Ulotrichī* (classification applied to humans having this type of hair), from Gk *oulothrix,* from *oulos* curly + *thrix* hair]

ulster ('ʌlstə) *n* a man's heavy double-breasted overcoat with a belt or half-belt. [C19: from *Ulster,* the northernmost province of Ireland]

Ulster Defence Association *n* (in Northern Ireland) a Loyalist paramilitary organization. Abbrev.: **UDA.**

Ulster Democratic Unionist Party *n* a Northern Irish political party advocating the maintenance of the Union with Great Britain.

Ulsterman ('ʌlstəmən) *n, pl* **Ulstermen.** a native or inhabitant of Ulster.

▸**'Ulsterˌwoman** *fem n*

THESAURUS

ubiquitous *adj* = **everywhere,** all-over, ever-present, omnipresent, pervasive, universal

ugly *adj* **1** = **unattractive,** hard-favoured, hard-featured, homely, ill-favoured, misshapen, no oil painting (*inf.*), not much to look at, plain, unlovely, unprepossessing, unsightly **2** = **unpleasant,** disagreeable, disgusting, distasteful, frightful, hideous, horrid, monstrous, objectionable, obscene, offensive, repugnant, repulsive, revolting, shocking, terrible, vile **3** = **ominous,** baleful, dangerous, forbidding, menacing, sinister, threatening **4** = **bad-tempered,** angry, dark, evil, malevolent, nasty, spiteful, sullen, surly

Antonyms *adj* ≠ **unattractive:** attractive, beautiful, cute, good-looking, gorgeous, handsome, lovely, pretty ≠ **unpleasant:** agreeable, pleasant ≠ **ominous:** auspicious, promising ≠ **bad-tempered:** friendly, good-humoured, good-natured, peaceful

ulcer *n* **1** = **sore,** abscess, boil, fester, gathering, gumboil, peptic ulcer, pustule

ulcerous *adj* **1** = **festering,** cankered, cankerous, suppurative, ulcerative

Ulster Unionist Council *n* a Northern Irish political party advocating the maintenance of the Union with Great Britain.

ult. *abbrev. for:* **1** ultimate(ly). **2** ultimo.

ulterior 🅣 (ʌl'tɪərɪə) *adj* **1** lying beneath or beyond what is revealed or supposed: *ulterior motives.* **2** succeeding, subsequent, or later. **3** lying beyond a certain line or point. [C17: from L: further, from *ulter* beyond]
▸**ul'teriorly** *adv*

ultima ('ʌltɪmə) *n* the final syllable of a word. [from L: the last]

ultimate 🅣 ('ʌltɪmɪt) *adj* **1** conclusive in a series or process; final: *an ultimate question.* **2** the highest or most significant: *the ultimate goal.* **3** elemental, fundamental, or essential. **4** most extreme: *the ultimate abuse of human rights.* **5** final or total: *the ultimate cost.* ◆ *n* **6** the most significant, highest, or greatest thing. [C17: from LL *ultimāre* to come to an end, from L *ultimus* last, from *ulter* distant]
▸**'ultimately** *adv* ▸**'ultimateness** *n*

ultima Thule ('θju:lɪ) *n* **1** a region believed by ancient geographers to be the northernmost land. **2** any distant or unknown region. **3** a remote goal or aim. [L: the most distant Thule]

ultimatum (ˌʌltɪ'meɪtəm) *n, pl* **ultimatums** *or* **ultimata** (-tə). **1** a final communication by a party setting forth conditions on which it insists, as during negotiations on some topic. **2** any final or peremptory demand or proposal. [C18: from NL, neuter of *ultimatus* ULTIMATE]

ultimo ('ʌltɪˌməʊ) *adv Now rare except when abbreviated in formal correspondence.* in or during the previous month: *a letter of the 7th ultimo.* Abbrev.: **ult.** [C16: from L *ultimō* on the last]

ultimogeniture (ˌʌltɪməʊ'dʒenɪtʃə) *n Law.* a principle of inheritance whereby the youngest son succeeds to the estate of his ancestor. [C19: *ultimo-* from L *ultimus* last + LL *genitūra* a birth]

ultra ('ʌltrə) *adj* **1** extreme or immoderate, esp. in beliefs or opinions. ◆ *n* **2** an extremist. [C19: from L: beyond, from *ulter* distant]

ultra- 🅣 *prefix* **1** beyond or surpassing a specified extent, range, or limit: *ultramicroscopic.* **2** extreme or extremely: *ultramodern.* [from L *ultrā* beyond]

ultracentrifuge (ˌʌltrə'sentrɪˌfju:dʒ) *n Chem.* a high-speed centrifuge used to separate colloidal solutions.

ultraconservative (ˌʌltrəkən'sɜ:vətɪv) *adj* **1** highly reactionary. ◆ *n* **2** a reactionary person.

ultra-distance *n (modifier) Athletics.* covering a distance in excess of 30 miles, often as part of a longer race or competition: *an ultra-distance runner.*

ultrafiche ('ʌltrəˌfi:ʃ) *n* a sheet of film, usually the size of a filing card, that is similar to a microfiche but has a much larger number of microcopies. [C20: from ULTRA- + F *fiche* small card]

ultrahigh frequency ('ʌltrəˌhaɪ) *n* a radio-frequency band or radio frequency lying between 3000 and 300 megahertz. Abbrev.: **UHF.**

ultraism ('ʌltrəˌɪzəm) *n* extreme philosophy, belief, or action.
▸**'ultraist** *n, adj*

ultramarine (ˌʌltrəmə'ri:n) *n* **1** a blue pigment obtained by powdering natural lapis lazuli or made synthetically: used in paints, printing ink, plastics, etc. **2** a vivid blue colour. ◆ *adj* **3** of the colour ultramarine. **4** from across the seas. [C17: from Med. L *ultramarinus,* from *ultrā* beyond + *mare* sea; so called because the lapis lazuli from which the pigment was made was imported from Asia]

ultramicroscope (ˌʌltrə'maɪkrəˌskəʊp) *n* a microscope used for studying colloids, in which the sample is illuminated from the side and colloidal particles are seen as bright points on a dark background.

ultramicroscopic (ˌʌltrəˌmaɪkrə'skɒpɪk) *adj* **1** too small to be seen with an optical microscope. **2** of or relating to an ultramicroscope.

ultramodern 🅣 (ˌʌltrə'mɒdən) *adj* extremely modern.
▸**ˌultra'modernism** *n* ▸**ˌultra'modernist** *n* ▸**ˌultraˌmodern'istic** *adj*

ultramontane (ˌʌltrəmɒn'teɪn) *adj* **1** on the other side of the mountains, esp. the Alps, from the speaker or writer. **2** of or relating to a movement in the Roman Catholic Church which favours the centralized authority and influence of the pope as opposed to local independence. ◆ *n* **3** a person from beyond the mountains, esp. the Alps. **4** a member of the ultramontane party of the Roman Catholic Church.

ultramundane (ˌʌltrə'mʌndeɪn) *adj* extending beyond the world, this life, or the universe.

ultranationalism (ˌʌltrə'næʃnəˌlɪzəm) *n* extreme devotion to one's own nation.
▸**ˌultra'national** *adj* ▸**ˌultra'nationalist** *adj, n*

ultrashort (ˌʌltrə'ʃɔ:t) *adj* (of a radio wave) having a wavelength shorter than 10 metres.

ultrasonic (ˌʌltrə'sɒnɪk) *adj* of, concerned with, or producing waves with the same nature as sound waves but frequencies above audio frequencies.
▸**ˌultra'sonically** *adv*

ultrasonics (ˌʌltrə'sɒnɪks) *n (functioning as sing)* the branch of physics concerned with ultrasonic waves. Also called: **supersonics.**

ultrasound ('ʌltrəˌsaʊnd) *n* ultrasonic waves at frequencies above the audible range (above about 20 kHz), used in cleaning metallic parts, echo sounding, medical diagnosis and therapy, etc.

ultrasound scanner *n* a device used to examine an internal bodily structure by the use of ultrasonic waves, esp. for the diagnosis of abnormality in a fetus.

ultrastructure ('ʌltrəˌstrʌktʃə) *n* the minute structure of an organ, tissue, or cell, as revealed by microscopy.

ultraviolet (ˌʌltrə'vaɪəlɪt) *n* **1** the part of the electromagnetic spectrum with wavelengths shorter than light but longer than X-rays; in the range 0.4×10^{-6} and 1×10^{-8} metres. ◆ *adj* **2** of, relating to, or consisting of radiation lying in the ultraviolet: *ultraviolet radiation; ultraviolet spectroscopy.* Abbrev.: **UV.**

ultraviolet astronomy *n* the study of radiation from celestial sources in the wavelength range 91.2 to 320 nanometres.

ultra vires ('vaɪri:z) *adv, adj (predicative) Law.* beyond the legal power of a person, corporation, agent, etc. [L, lit.: beyond strength]

ultravirus (ˌʌltrə'vaɪrəs) *n* a virus small enough to pass through the finest filter.

ululate ('ju:ljʊˌleɪt) *vb* **ululates, ululating, ululated.** *(intr)* to howl or wail, as with grief. [C17: from L *ululāre* to howl, from *ulula* screech owl]
▸**'ululant** *adj* ▸**ˌulu'lation** *n*

Uluru (ˌu:lə'ru:) *n* the world's largest monolith, in the Northern Territory of Australia. Height: 330 m (1100 ft). Base circumference: 9 km (5.6 miles). Former name: **Ayers Rock.**

umbel ('ʌmbᵊl) *n* a racemose inflorescence, characteristic of umbelliferous plants, in which the flowers arise from the same point in the main stem and have stalks of the same length, to give a cluster with the youngest flowers at the centre. [C16: from L *umbella* a sunshade, from *umbra* shade]
▸**umbellate** ('ʌmbɪlɪt, -ˌleɪt) *or* **umbellar** (ʌm'belə) *adj* ▸**umbellule** (ʌm'belju:l) *n*

umbelliferous (ˌʌmbɪ'lɪfərəs) *adj* of or belonging to a family of herbaceous plants and shrubs, typically having hollow stems, divided or compound leaves, and flowers in umbels: includes fennel, parsley, carrot, and parsnip. [C17: from NL, from L *umbella* sunshade + *ferre* to bear]
▸**um'bellifer** *n*

umber ('ʌmbə) *n* **1** any of various natural brown earths containing ferric oxide together with lime and oxides of aluminium, manganese, and silicon. **2** any of the dark brown to greenish-brown colours produced by this pigment. **3** *Obs.* shade. ◆ *adj* **4** of, relating to, or stained with umber. [C16: from F *(terre d')ombre* or It. *(terra di) ombra* shadow (earth), from L *umbra* shade]

umbilical (ʌm'bɪlɪkᵊl, ˌʌmbɪ'laɪkᵊl) *adj* **1** of, relating to, or resembling the umbilicus or the umbilical cord. **2** in the region of the umbilicus: *an umbilical hernia.*

umbilical cord *n* **1** the long flexible tubelike structure connecting a fetus with the placenta. **2** any flexible cord, tube, or cable, as between an astronaut walking in space and his spacecraft.

umbilicate (ʌm'bɪlɪkɪt, -ˌkeɪt) *adj* **1** having an umbilicus. **2** having a central depression: *an umbilicate leaf.* **3** shaped like a navel, as some bacterial colonies.
▸**umˌbili'cation** *n*

umbilicus (ʌm'bɪlɪkəs, ˌʌmbɪ'laɪkəs) *n, pl* **umbilici** (-'bɪlɪˌsaɪ, -bɪ'laɪsaɪ). **1** *Biol.* a hollow or navel-like structure, such as the cavity at the base of a gastropod shell. **2** *Anat.* a technical name for the **navel.** [C18: from L: navel, centre]

umble pie ('ʌmbᵊl) *n* See **humble pie** (sense 1).

umbles ('ʌmbᵊlz) *pl n* See **numbles.**

umbo ('ʌmbəʊ) *n, pl* **umbones** (ʌm'bəʊni:z) *or* **umbos. 1** *Bot., anat.* a small hump, prominence, or convex area, as in certain mushrooms, bivalve molluscs, and the outer surface of the eardrum. **2** a large projecting central boss on a shield, esp. on a Saxon shield. [C18: from L: projecting piece]
▸**umbonate** ('ʌmbənɪt, -ˌneɪt), **umbonal** ('ʌmbənᵊl), *or* **umbonic** (ʌm'bɒnɪk) *adj*

umbra ('ʌmbrə) *n, pl* **umbrae** (-bri:) *or* **umbras. 1** a region of complete shadow resulting from the obstruction of light by an opaque object, esp. the shadow cast by the moon onto the earth during a solar eclipse. **2** the darker inner region of a sunspot. [C16: from L: shade]
▸**'umbral** *adj*

umbrage 🅣 ('ʌmbrɪdʒ) *n* **1** displeasure or resentment; offence (in **give** *or* **take umbrage**). **2** the foliage of trees, considered as providing shade. **3** *Rare.* shadow or shade. [C15: from OF, from L *umbrāticus* relating to shade, from *umbra* shade]

THESAURUS

ulterior *adj* **1 = hidden,** concealed, covert, personal, secondary, secret, selfish, undisclosed, unexpressed
Antonyms *adj* apparent, declared, manifest, obvious, overt, plain

ultimate *adj* **1 = final,** conclusive, decisive, end, eventual, extreme, furthest, last, terminal **2 = supreme,** extreme, greatest, highest, maximum, most significant, paramount, superlative, topmost, utmost **3 = fundamental,** basic, elemental, primary, radical ◆ *n* **6 = epitome,** culmination, extreme, greatest, height, mother of all (*inf.*), peak, perfection, summit, the last word

ultimately *adv* **1 = finally,** after all, at last, at the end of the day, eventually, in due time, in the end, in the fullness of time, sooner or later **3 = fundamentally,** basically

ultra- *prefix* **2 = extremely,** excessively, fanatically, immoderately, rabidly, radically

ultramodern *adj* **= advanced,** ahead of its time, avant-garde, futuristic, modernistic, neoteric (*rare*), progressive, way-out (*inf.*)

umbrage *n* **1** *As in* **take umbrage = offence,** anger, chagrin, displeasure, grudge, high dudgeon, huff, indignation, pique, resentment, sense of injury
Antonyms *n* amity, cordiality, goodwill, harmony, pleasure, understanding

DICTIONARY

umbrageous (ʌm'breɪdʒəs) *adj* **1** shady or shading. **2** *Rare.* easily offended.

umbrella Ⓣ (ʌm'brɛlə) *n* **1** a portable device used for protection against rain, snow, etc., and consisting of a light canopy supported on a collapsible metal frame mounted on a central rod. **2** the flattened cone-shaped body of a jellyfish. **3** a protective shield or screen, esp. of aircraft or gunfire. **4** anything that has the effect of a protective screen, general cover, or organizing agency. [C17: from It. *ombrella*, dim. of *ombra* shade; see UMBRA]
▸**um'brella-,like** *adj*

umbrella pine *n* another name for **stone pine.**

umbrella stand *n* an upright rack or stand for umbrellas.

umbrella tree *n* **1** a North American magnolia having long leaves clustered into an umbrella formation at the ends of the branches and having unpleasant-smelling white flowers. **2** Also called: **umbrella bush.** any of various trees or shrubs having umbrella-shaped leaves or growing in an umbrella-like cluster.

Umbrian ('ʌmbrɪən) *adj* **1** of or relating to Umbria, in Italy, its inhabitants, or the ancient language once spoken there. **2** of or relating to a Renaissance school of painting that included Raphael. ◆ *n* **3** a native or inhabitant of Umbria. **4** an extinct language of ancient S Italy.

umfazi (,ʊm'fɑːzɪ) *n S. African.* a Black married woman. [from Bantu]

umiak *or* **oomiak** ('uːmɪ,æk) *n* a large open boat made of stretched skins, used by Eskimos. [C18: from Eskimo: boat for the use of women]

umlaut ('ʊmlaʊt) *n* **1** the mark (¨) placed over a vowel in some languages, such as German, indicating modification in the quality of the vowel. **2** (esp. in Germanic languages) the change of a vowel within a word brought about by the assimilating influence of a vowel or semivowel in a preceding or following syllable. [C19: G, from *um* around (in the sense of changing places) + *Laut* sound]

umlungu (,ʊm'lʊŋgʊ) *n S. African.* a White man: used esp. as a term of address. [from Bantu]

umpire Ⓣ ('ʌmpaɪə) *n* **1** an official who rules on the playing of a game, as in cricket. **2** a person who rules on or judges disputes between contesting parties. ◆ *vb* **umpires, umpiring, umpired. 3** to act as umpire in (a game, dispute, or controversy). [C15: by mistaken division from *a noumpere*, from OF *nomper* not one of a pair, from *nom-, non-* not + *per* equal]

umpteen Ⓣ (,ʌmp'tiːn) *determiner Inf.* **a** very many: *umpteen things to do.* **b** (*as pronoun*): *umpteen of them came.* [C20: from *umpty* a great deal (?from *-enty* as in *twenty*) + *-teen* ten]
▸**,ump'teenth** *n, adj*

UN *abbrev. for* United Nations.

un-[1] *prefix* (*freely used with adjectives, participles, and their derivative adverbs and nouns: less frequently used with certain other nouns*) not; contrary to; opposite of: *uncertain; untidiness; unbelief; untruth.* [from OE *on-, un-*]

un-[2] *prefix forming verbs.* **1** denoting reversal of an action or state: *uncover; untangle.* **2** denoting removal from, release, or deprivation: *unharness; unthrone.* **3** (intensifier): *unloose.* [from OE *un-, on-*]

'un *or* **un** (ən) *pron* a spelling of **one** intended to reflect a dialectal or informal pronunciation: *that's a big 'un.*

unable Ⓣ (ʌn'eɪbᵊl) *adj* (*postpositive;* foll. by *to*) lacking the necessary power, ability, or authority (to do something); not able.

unaccented (,ʌnæk'sɛntɪd) *adj* not stressed or emphasized in pronunciation.

unaccountable Ⓣ (,ʌnə'kaʊntəbᵊl) *adj* **1** allowing of no explanation; inexplicable. **2** extraordinary: *an unaccountable fear of heights.* **3** not accountable or answerable to.
▸**,unac,counta'bility** *n* ▸**,unac'countably** *adv*

unaccustomed Ⓣ (,ʌnə'kʌstəmd) *adj* **1** (foll. by *to*) not used (to): *unaccustomed to pain.* **2** not familiar.
▸**,unac'customedness** *n*

una corda ('uːnə 'kɔːdə) *adj, adv Music.* (of the piano) to be played with the soft pedal depressed. [It., lit.: one string; the pedal moves the mechanism so that only one string of the three tuned to each note is struck by the hammer]

unadopted (,ʌnə'dɒptɪd) *adj* **1** (of a child) not adopted. **2** *Brit.* (of a road, etc.) not maintained by a local authority.

unadvised Ⓣ (,ʌnəd'vaɪzd) *adj* **1** rash or unwise. **2** not having received advice.
▸**unadvisedly** (,ʌnəd'vaɪzɪdlɪ) *adv* ▸**,unad'visedness** *n*

unaffected[1] Ⓣ (,ʌnə'fɛktɪd) *adj* unpretentious, natural, or sincere.
▸**,unaf'fectedly** *adv* ▸**,unaf'fectedness** *n*

unaffected[2] Ⓣ (,ʌnə'fɛktɪd) *adj* not affected.

unalienable (ʌn'eɪljənəbᵊl) *adj Law.* a variant of **inalienable.**

un-American *adj* **1** not in accordance with the aims, ideals, customs, etc., of the US. **2** against the interests of the US.
▸**,un-A'mericanism** *n*

unanimous Ⓣ (juː'nænɪməs) *adj* **1** in complete agreement. **2** characterized by complete agreement: *a unanimous decision.* [C17: from L, from *ūnus* one + *animus* mind]
▸**u'nanimously** *adv* ▸**unanimity** (,juːnə'nɪmɪtɪ) *n*

unapproachable Ⓣ (,ʌnə'prəʊtʃəbᵊl) *adj* **1** discouraging intimacy, friendliness, etc.; aloof. **2** inaccessible. **3** not to be rivalled.
▸**,unap'proachableness** *n* ▸**,unap'proachably** *adv*

unappropriated (,ʌnə'prəʊprɪ,eɪtɪd) *adj* **1** not set aside for specific use. **2** *Accounting.* designating that portion of the profits of a business enterprise that is retained in the business and not withdrawn by the proprietor. **3** (of property) not having been taken into any person's possession or control.

unapt (ʌn'æpt) *adj* **1** (*usually postpositive;* often foll. by *for*) not suitable or qualified; unfitted. **2** mentally slow. **3** (*postpositive; may take an infinitive*) not disposed or likely (to).
▸**un'aptly** *adv* ▸**un'aptness** *n*

unarm (ʌn'ɑːm) *vb* a less common word for **disarm.**

unarmed Ⓣ (ʌn'ɑːmd) *adj* **1** without weapons. **2** (of animals and plants) having no claws, prickles, spines, thorns, or similar structures.

unassailable Ⓣ (,ʌnə'seɪləbᵊl) *adj* **1** not able to be attacked. **2** undeniable or irrefutable.
▸**,unas'sailableness** *n* ▸**,unas'sailably** *adv*

unassuming Ⓣ (,ʌnə'sjuːmɪŋ) *adj* modest or unpretentious.
▸**,unas'sumingly** *adv* ▸**,unas'sumingness** *n*

unattached Ⓣ (,ʌnə'tætʃt) *adj* **1** not connected with any specific thing, body, group, etc. **2** not engaged or married. **3** (of property) not seized or held as security.

THESAURUS

umbrella *n* **1 = brolly** (*Brit. inf.*), gamp (*Brit. inf.*) **4 = cover**, aegis, agency, patronage, protection

umpire *n* **1, 2 = referee**, adjudicator, arbiter, arbitrator, judge, moderator, ref (*inf.*) ◆ *vb* **3 = referee**, adjudicate, arbitrate, call (*Sport*), judge, mediate, moderate

umpteen *determiner* **a** *Informal* **= very many**, a good many, a thousand and one, considerable, countless, ever so many, millions, n, numerous

unable *adj* **= incapable**, impotent, inadequate, ineffectual, no good, not able, not equal to, not up to, powerless, unfit, unfitted, unqualified
Antonyms *adj* able, adept, adequate, capable, competent, effective, potent, powerful

unaccountable *adj* **1 = inexplicable**, baffling, incomprehensible, inscrutable, mysterious, odd, peculiar, puzzling, strange, unexplainable, unfathomable, unintelligible **3 = not answerable**, clear, exempt, free, not responsible, unliable
Antonyms *adj* ≠ **inexplicable:** accountable, comprehensible, explicable, intelligible, understandable

unaccustomed *adj* **1 unaccustomed to = not used to**, a newcomer to, a novice at, green, inexperienced at, not given to, unfamiliar with, unpractised in, unused to, unversed in **2 = unfamiliar**, new, out of the ordinary, remarkable, special, strange, surprising, uncommon, unexpected, unprecedented, unusual, unwonted
Antonyms *adj* ≠ **unfamiliar:** accustomed, familiar, ordinary, regular, usual ≠ **not used to:** experienced at, given to, practised in, used to, well-versed in

unadvised *adj* **1 = rash**, careless, hasty, heedless, ill-advised, imprudent, inadvisable, indiscreet, injudicious, reckless, unwary, unwise **2 = uninformed**, ignorant, in the dark, not in the loop (*inf.*), unaware, unknowing, unsuspecting, unwarned

unaffected[1] *adj* **= natural**, artless, genuine, honest, ingenuous, naive, plain, simple, sincere, straightforward, unassuming, unpretentious, unsophisticated, unspoilt, unstudied, without airs
Antonyms *adj* affected, assumed, designing, devious, insincere, mannered, pretentious, put-on, snobbish, sophisticated

unaffected[2] *adj* **= impervious**, aloof, not influenced, proof, unaltered, unchanged, unimpressed, unmoved, unresponsive, unstirred, untouched
Antonyms *adj* affected, changed, concerned, disrupted, hard-hit, influenced, interested, responsive, sympathetic, touched

unanimity *n* **1, 2 = agreement**, accord, assent, chorus, concert, concord, concurrence, consensus, harmony, like-mindedness, one mind, unison, unity
Antonyms *n* difference, disagreement, discord, disunity, division, variance

unanimous *adj* **1 = agreed**, agreeing, at one, common, concerted, concordant, harmonious, in agreement, in complete accord, like-minded, of one mind, united
Antonyms *adj* differing, discordant, dissident, disunited, divided, schismatic, split

unanimously *adv* **2 = without exception**, by common consent, nem. con., unitedly, unopposed, with one accord, without opposition

unapproachable *adj* **1 = unfriendly**, aloof, chilly, cool, distant, frigid, offish, remote, reserved, standoffish, unsociable, withdrawn **2 = inaccessible**, out of reach, out-of-the-way, remote, un-get-at-able (*inf.*), unreachable
Antonyms *adj* ≠ **unfriendly:** affable, approachable, congenial, cordial, friendly, sociable

unarmed *adj* **1, 2 = defenceless**, assailable, exposed, helpless, open, open to attack, unarmoured, unprotected, weak, weaponless, without arms
Antonyms *adj* armed, equipped, fortified, protected, ready, strengthened

unassailable *adj* **1 = impregnable**, invincible, invulnerable, secure, well-defended **2 = undeniable**, absolute, conclusive, incontestable, incontrovertible, indisputable, irrefutable, positive, proven, sound
Antonyms *adj* ≠ **undeniable:** debatable, doubtful, dubious, inconclusive, uncertain, unfounded, unproven, unsound

unassuming *adj* **= modest**, diffident, humble, meek, quiet, reserved, retiring, self-effacing, simple, unassertive, unobtrusive, unostentatious, unpretentious
Antonyms *adj* assuming, audacious, conceited, ostentatious, overconfident, presumptuous, pretentious

unattached *adj* **1 = free**, autonomous, independent, nonaligned, unaffiliated, uncommitted **2 = single**, a free agent, available, by oneself, footloose and fancy-free, left on the shelf, not spoken for, on one's own, unengaged, unmarried
Antonyms *adj* ≠ **free:** affiliated, aligned, attached, committed, dependent, implicated, involved

unavailing ➊ (ˌʌnəˈveɪlɪŋ) *adj* useless or futile.
▸ˌ**unaˈvailingly** *adv*
unavoidable ➊ (ˌʌnəˈvɔɪdəbᵊl) *adj* **1** unable to be avoided. **2** *Law.* not capable of being declared null and void.
▸ˌ**unaˌvoidaˈbility** *or* ˌ**unaˈvoidableness** *n* ▸ˌ**unaˈvoidably** *adv*
unaware ➊ (ˌʌnəˈwɛə) *adj* **1** (*postpositive*) not aware or conscious (of): *unaware of the danger he ran across the road.* ◆ *adv* **2** a variant of **unawares.**
▸ˌ**unaˈwareness** *n*
unawares ➊ (ˌʌnəˈwɛəz) *adv* **1** without prior warning or plan: *she caught him unawares.* **2** without knowing: *he lost it unawares.*
unbacked (ʌnˈbækt) *adj* **1** (of a book, chair, etc.) not having a back. **2** bereft of support, esp. on a financial basis. **3** not supported by bets.
unbalance (ʌnˈbæləns) *vb* **unbalances, unbalancing, unbalanced.** (*tr*) **1** to upset the equilibrium or balance of. **2** to disturb the mental stability of (a person or his mind). ◆ *n* **3** imbalance or instability.
unbalanced ➊ (ʌnˈbælənst) *adj* **1** lacking balance. **2** irrational or unsound; erratic. **3** mentally disordered or deranged. **4** biased; one-sided: *unbalanced reporting.* **5** (in double-entry book-keeping) not having total debit balances equal to total credit balances.
unbar (ʌnˈbɑː) *vb* **unbars, unbarring, unbarred.** (*tr*) **1** to take away a bar or bars from. **2** to unfasten bars, locks, etc., from (a door); open.
unbearable ➊ (ʌnˈbɛərəbᵊl) *adj* not able to be borne or endured.
▸**unˈbearably** *adv*
unbeatable ➊ (ʌnˈbiːtəbᵊl) *adj* unable to be defeated or outclassed; surpassingly excellent.
unbeaten ➊ (ʌnˈbiːtᵊn) *adj* **1** having suffered no defeat. **2** not worn down; untrodden. **3** not mixed or stirred by beating: *unbeaten eggs.*
unbecoming ➊ (ˌʌnbɪˈkʌmɪŋ) *adj* **1** unsuitable or inappropriate, esp. through being unattractive: *an unbecoming hat.* **2** (when *postpositive,* usually foll. by *of* or an object) not proper or seemly (for): *manners unbecoming a lady.*
▸ˌ**unbeˈcomingly** *adv* ▸ˌ**unbeˈcomingness** *n*
unbeknown (ˌʌnbɪˈnəʊn) *adv* (*sentence modifier;* foll. by *to*) without the knowledge (of a person): *unbeknown to him she had left the country.* Also (esp. Brit.): **unbeknownst.** [C17: from arch. *beknown* known]
unbelief ➊ (ˌʌnbɪˈliːf) *n* disbelief or rejection of belief.
unbelievable ➊ (ˌʌnbɪˈliːvəbᵊl) *adj* unable to be believed; incredible.
▸ˌ**unbeˌlievaˈbility** *n* ▸ˌ**unbeˈlievably** *adv*
unbeliever ➊ (ˌʌnbɪˈliːvə) *n* a person who does not believe, esp. in religious matters.
unbelieving ➊ (ˌʌnbɪˈliːvɪŋ) *adj* **1** not believing; sceptical. **2** proceeding from or characterized by scepticism.
▸ˌ**unbeˈlievingly** *adv*
unbend ➊ (ʌnˈbɛnd) *vb* **unbends, unbending, unbent. 1** to release or be released from the restraints of formality and ceremony. **2** *Inf.* to relax (the mind) or (of the mind) to become relaxed. **3** to straighten out from an originally bent shape. **4** (*tr*) *Naut.* **4a** to remove (a sail) from a stay, mast, etc. **4b** to untie (a rope, etc.) or cast (a cable) loose.
unbending ➊ (ʌnˈbɛndɪŋ) *adj* **1** rigid or inflexible. **2** characterized by sternness or severity: *an unbending rule.*
▸**unˈbendingly** *adv* ▸**unˈbendingness** *n*
unbent (ʌnˈbɛnt) *vb* **1** the past tense and past participle of **unbend.** ◆ *adj* **2** not bent or bowed. **3** not compelled to give way by force.
unbidden ➊ (ʌnˈbɪdᵊn) *adj* **1** not ordered or commanded; voluntary or spontaneous. **2** not invited or asked.
unbind ➊ (ʌnˈbaɪnd) *vb* **unbinds, unbinding, unbound.** (*tr*) **1** to set free from restraining bonds or chains. **2** to unfasten or make loose (a bond, etc.).
unblessed (ʌnˈblɛst) *adj* **1** deprived of blessing. **2** cursed or evil. **3** unhappy or wretched.
▸**unblessedness** (ʌnˈblɛsɪdnɪs) *n*
unblushing ➊ (ʌnˈblʌʃɪŋ) *adj* immodest or shameless.
▸**unˈblushingly** *adv*
unbolt (ʌnˈbəʊlt) *vb* (*tr*) **1** to unfasten a bolt of (a door). **2** to undo (the nut) on a bolt.
unbolted (ʌnˈbəʊltɪd) *adj* (of grain, meal, or flour) not sifted.
unborn ➊ (ʌnˈbɔːn) *adj* **1** not yet born or brought to birth. **2** still to come in the future: *the unborn world.*
unbosom ➊ (ʌnˈbʊzəm) *vb* (*tr*) to relieve (oneself) of (secrets, etc.) by telling someone. [C16: from UN-² + BOSOM (in the sense: seat of the emotions)]
unbounded ➊ (ʌnˈbaʊndɪd) *adj* having no boundaries or limits.
▸**unˈboundedly** *adv* ▸**unˈboundedness** *n*
unbowed (ʌnˈbaʊd) *adj* **1** not bowed or bent. **2** free or unconquered.
unbridled ➊ (ʌnˈbraɪdᵊld) *adj* **1** with all restraints removed. **2** (of a horse) wearing no bridle.
▸**unˈbridledly** *adv* ▸**unˈbridledness** *n*
unbroken ➊ (ʌnˈbrəʊkən) *adj* **1** complete or whole. **2** continuous or incessant. **3** undaunted in spirit. **4** (of animals, esp. horses) not tamed; wild. **5** not disturbed or upset: *the unbroken quiet of the afternoon.* **6** (of a record, esp. at sport) not improved upon.
▸**unˈbrokenly** *adv* ▸**unˈbrokenness** *n*
unbundling (ʌnˈbʌndlɪŋ) *n Commerce.* the takeover of a large conglomerate with a view to retaining the core business and selling off some of the subsidiaries to help finance the takeover.
unburden ➊ (ʌnˈbɜːdᵊn) *vb* (*tr*) **1** to remove a load or burden from. **2** to

THESAURUS

unavailing *adj* = **useless**, abortive, bootless, fruitless, futile, idle, ineffective, ineffectual, of no avail, pointless, to no purpose, unproductive, unsuccessful, vain
Antonyms *adj* effective, fruitful, productive, rewarding, successful, useful, worthwhile
unavoidable *adj* **1** = **inevitable**, bound to happen, certain, compulsory, fated, ineluctable, inescapable, inexorable, necessary, obligatory, sure
unaware *adj* **1** = **ignorant**, heedless, incognizant, not in the loop (*inf.*), oblivious, unconscious, unenlightened, uninformed, unknowing, unmindful, unsuspecting
Antonyms *adj* attentive, aware, conscious, informed, in the loop (*inf.*), knowing, mindful
unawares *adv* **1** = **by surprise**, aback, abruptly, caught napping, off guard, on the hop (*Brit. inf.*), suddenly, unexpectedly, unprepared, without warning **2** = **unknowingly**, accidentally, by accident, by mistake, inadvertently, mistakenly, unconsciously, unintentionally, unwittingly
Antonyms *adv* ≠ **by surprise:** forewarned, on the lookout, prepared ≠ **unknowingly:** deliberately, knowingly, on purpose, wittingly
unbalanced *adj* **1** = **shaky**, asymmetrical, irregular, lopsided, not balanced, unequal, uneven, unstable, unsymmetrical, wobbly **3** = **deranged**, barking (*sl.*), barking mad (*sl.*), crazy, demented, disturbed, doolally (*sl.*), eccentric, erratic, insane, irrational, loopy (*inf.*), lunatic, mad, *non compos mentis,* not all there, not the full shilling (*inf.*), off one's trolley (*sl.*), out to lunch (*inf.*), touched, unhinged, unsound, unstable, up the pole (*inf.*) **4** = **biased**, inequitable, one-sided, partial, partisan, prejudiced, unfair, unjust
Antonyms *adj* ≠ **shaky:** balanced, equal, even, stable, symmetrical
unbearable *adj* = **intolerable**, insufferable, insupportable, oppressive, too much (*inf.*), unacceptable, unendurable
Antonyms *adj* acceptable, bearable, endurable, supportable, tolerable
unbeatable *adj* = **invincible**, indomitable, more than a match for, unconquerable, unstoppable, unsurpassable
unbeaten *adj* **1** = **undefeated**, triumphant, unbowed, unsubdued, unsurpassed, unvanquished, victorious, winning
unbecoming *adj* **1** = **unattractive**, ill-suited, inappropriate, incongruous, unbefitting, unfit, unflattering, unsightly, unsuitable, unsuited **2** = **unseemly**, discreditable, improper, indecorous, indelicate, offensive, tasteless
Antonyms *adj* ≠ **unseemly:** becoming, decent, decorous, delicate, proper, seemly
unbelief *n* = **scepticism**, atheism, disbelief, distrust, doubt, incredulity
Antonyms *n* belief, credence, credulity, faith, trust
unbelievable *adj* = **incredible**, astonishing, beyond belief, cock-and-bull (*inf.*), far-fetched, implausible, impossible, improbable, inconceivable, jaw-dropping, outlandish, preposterous, questionable, staggering, unconvincing, unimaginable, unthinkable
Antonyms *adj* ≠ **incredible:** authentic, believable, credible, likely, plausible, possible, probable, trustworthy
unbeliever *n* = **atheist**, agnostic, disbeliever, doubting Thomas, infidel, sceptic
unbelieving *adj* **1** = **sceptical**, disbelieving, distrustful, doubtful, doubting, dubious, incredulous, suspicious, unconvinced
Antonyms *adj* believing, convinced, credulous, trustful, undoubting, unsuspicious
unbend *vb* **1** = **relax**, be informal, calm down, chill out (*sl., chiefly US*), cool it (*sl.*), ease up, let it all hang out (*sl.*), let oneself go, let up, lighten up (*sl.*), loosen up, slacken, slow down, take it easy, unbutton (*inf.*), unwind **3** = **straighten**, put straight, uncoil, uncurl
unbending *adj* **1, 2** = **inflexible**, firm, hardline, intractable, resolute, rigid, severe, strict, stubborn, tough, uncompromising, unyielding
unbidden *adj* **1** = **voluntary**, free, spontaneous, unforced, unprompted, willing **2** = **uninvited**, unasked, unwanted, unwelcome
unbind *vb* **1, 2** = **free**, loosen, release, set free, unbridle, unchain, unclasp, undo, unfasten, unfetter, unloose, unshackle, unstrap, untie, unyoke
Antonyms *vb* bind, chain, fasten, fetter, restrain, shackle, tie, yoke
unblushing *adj* = **shameless**, amoral, bold, brazen, forward, immodest, unabashed, unashamed, unembarrassed
unborn *adj* **1, 2** = **expected**, awaited, embryonic, *in utero*
unbosom *vb* = **confide**, admit, confess, disburden, disclose, divulge, get (something) off one's chest (*inf.*), get (something) out of one's system, lay bare, let out, reveal, spill one's guts about (*sl.*), tell, unburden
Antonyms *vb* conceal, cover up, guard, hold back, suppress, withhold
unbounded *adj* = **unlimited**, absolute, boundless, endless, immeasurable, infinite, lavish, limitless, unbridled, unchecked, unconstrained, uncontrolled, unrestrained, vast
Antonyms *adj* bounded, confined, constrained, curbed, limited, restricted
unbridled *adj* **1** = **unrestrained**, excessive, full-on (*inf.*), intemperate, licentious, rampant, riotous, unchecked, unconstrained, uncontrolled, uncurbed, ungovernable, ungoverned, unruly, violent, wanton
unbroken *adj* **1** = **intact**, complete, entire, solid, total, unimpaired, whole **2** = **continuous**, ceaseless, constant, endless, incessant, progressive, serried, successive, uninterrupted, unremitting **5** = **undisturbed**, deep, fast, profound, sound, unruffled, untroubled **4** = **untamed**, unbowed, unsubdued
Antonyms *adj* ≠ **intact:** broken, cracked, damaged, fragmented, in pieces, shattered ≠ **continuous:** erratic, fitful, intermittent, interrupted, irregular, occasional, off-and-on, uneven
unburden *vb* **1** = **unload**, disburden, discharge, disencumber, ease the load, empty, lighten, relieve **2** = **confess**, come clean (*inf.*), confide, disclose, get (something) off one's chest (*inf.*), lay bare, make a clean breast of, re-

relieve or make free (one's mind, oneself, etc.) of a worry, trouble, etc., by revelation or confession.

unbutton (ʌn'bʌt(ə)n) *vb* to undo by unfastening (the buttons) of (a garment).

unbuttoned (ʌn'bʌt(ə)nd) *adj* **1** with buttons not fastened. **2** *Inf.* uninhibited; unrestrained: *hours of unbuttoned self-revelation.*

uncalled-for Ⓣ (ˌʌn'kɔːldfɔː) *adj* unnecessary or unwarranted.

uncanny Ⓣ (ʌn'kænɪ) *adj* **1** characterized by apparently supernatural wonder, horror, etc. **2** beyond what is normal: *uncanny accuracy.*
▸**un'cannily** *adv* ▸**un'canniness** *n*

uncap (ʌn'kæp) *vb* **uncaps, uncapping, uncapped. 1** (*tr*) to remove a cap or top from (a container): *to uncap a bottle.* **2** to remove a cap from (the head).

uncared-for (ˌʌn'kɛədfɔː) *adj* not cared for; neglected.

unceremonious (ˌʌnserɪ'məʊnɪəs) *adj* without ceremony; informal, abrupt, rude, or undignified.
▸ˌ**uncere'moniously** *adv* ▸ˌ**uncere'moniousness** *n*

uncertain Ⓣ (ʌn'sɜːt(ə)n) *adj* **1** not able to be accurately known or predicted: *the issue is uncertain.* **2** (when *postpositive,* often foll. by *of*) not sure or confident (about): *he was uncertain of the date.* **3** not precisely determined or decided: *uncertain plans.* **4** not to be depended upon: *an uncertain vote.* **5** liable to variation; changeable: *the weather is uncertain.* **6 in no uncertain terms. 6a** unambiguously. **6b** forcefully.
▸**un'certainly** *adv*

uncertainty Ⓣ (ʌn'sɜːt(ə)ntɪ) *n, pl* **uncertainties. 1** Also: **uncertainness.** the state or condition of being uncertain. **2** an uncertain matter, contingency, etc.

uncertainty principle *n* **the.** the principle that energy and time or position and momentum, cannot both be accurately measured simultaneously. Also called: **Heisenberg uncertainty principle, indeterminacy principle.**

uncharted Ⓣ (ʌn'tʃɑːtɪd) *adj* (of a physical or nonphysical region or area) not yet mapped, surveyed, or investigated: *uncharted waters; the uncharted depths of the mind.*

unchartered (ʌn'tʃɑːtəd) *adj* **1** not authorized by charter; unregulated. **2** unauthorized, lawless, or irregular.

> **USAGE NOTE** Care should be taken not to use *unchartered* where *uncharted* is meant: *uncharted* (not *unchartered*) *territory.*

unchristian (ʌn'krɪstjən) *adj* **1** not in accordance with the principles or ethics of Christianity. **2** non-Christian or pagan.
▸**un'christianly** *adv*

unchurch (ʌn'tʃɜːtʃ) *vb* (*tr*) **1** to excommunicate. **2** to remove church status from (a building).

uncial ('ʌnsɪəl) *adj* **1** of, relating to, or written in majuscule letters, as used in Greek and Latin manuscripts of the third to ninth centuries, that resemble modern capitals, but are characterized by much greater curvature. ◆ *n* **2** an uncial letter or manuscript. [C17: from LL *unciāles litterae* letters an inch long, from L *unciālis,* from *uncia* one twelfth, inch]
▸'**uncially** *adv*

uncinate ('ʌnsɪnɪt, -ˌneɪt) *adj Biol.* shaped like a hook: *the uncinate process of the ribs of certain vertebrates.* [C18: from L *uncīnātus,* from *uncīnus* a hook, from *uncus*]

uncircumcised (ʌn'sɜːkəmˌsaɪzd) *adj* **1** not circumcised. **2** not Jewish; gentile. **3** spiritually unpurified.
▸ˌ**uncircum'cision** *n*

uncivil Ⓣ (ʌn'sɪvəl) *adj* **1** lacking civility or good manners. **2** an obsolete word for **uncivilized.**
▸**uncivility** (ˌʌnsɪ'vɪlɪtɪ) *n* ▸**un'civilly** *adv*

uncivilized Ⓣ *or* **uncivilised** (ʌn'sɪvɪˌlaɪzd) *adj* **1** (of a tribe or people) not yet civilized, esp. not having developed a written language. **2** lacking culture or sophistication.
▸**un'civilˌizedness** *or* **un'civilˌisedness** *n*

unclad Ⓣ (ʌn'klæd) *adj* having no clothes on; naked.

unclasp (ʌn'klɑːsp) *vb* **1** (*tr*) to unfasten the clasp of (something). **2** to release one's grip (upon an object).

uncle ('ʌŋk(ə)l) *n* **1** a brother of one's father or mother. **2** the husband of one's aunt. **3** a term of address sometimes used by children for a male friend of their parents. **4** *Sl.* a pawnbroker. ◆ Related adj: **avuncular.** [C13: from OF *oncle,* from L *avunculus*]

unclean Ⓣ (ʌn'kliːn) *adj* lacking moral, spiritual, or physical cleanliness.
▸**un'cleanness** *n*

uncleanly[1] (ʌn'kliːnlɪ) *adv* in an unclean manner.

uncleanly[2] (ʌn'klenlɪ) *adj* characterized by an absence of cleanliness.
▸**un'cleanliness** *n*

Uncle Sam (sæm) *n* a personification of the government of the United States. [C19: apparently a humorous interpretation of the letters stamped on army supply boxes during the War of 1812: *US*]

Uncle Tom (tɒm) *n Inf., derog.* a Black person whose behaviour towards White people is regarded as servile. [C20: after the main character of H. B. Stowe's novel *Uncle Tom's Cabin* (1852)]
▸'**Uncle 'Tomˌism** *n*

unclose (ʌn'kləʊz) *vb* **uncloses, unclosing, unclosed. 1** to open or cause to open. **2** to come or bring to light.

unclothe (ʌn'kləʊð) *vb* **unclothes, unclothing, unclothed** *or* **unclad.** (*tr*) **1** to take off garments from; strip. **2** to uncover or lay bare.

uncoil (ʌn'kɔɪl) *vb* to unwind or become unwound; untwist.

uncomfortable Ⓣ (ʌn'kʌmftəb(ə)l) *adj* **1** not comfortable. **2** feeling or causing discomfort or unease; disquieting.
▸**un'comfortableness** *n* ▸**un'comfortably** *adv*

uncommitted Ⓣ (ˌʌnkə'mɪtɪd) *adj* not bound or pledged to a specific opinion, course of action, or cause.

uncommon Ⓣ (ʌn'kɒmən) *adj* **1** outside or beyond normal experience, etc. **2** in excess of what is normal: *an uncommon liking for honey.* ◆ *adv* **3** an archaic word for **uncommonly** (sense 2).
▸**un'commonness** *n*

uncommonly Ⓣ (ʌn'kɒmənlɪ) *adv* **1** in an uncommon or unusual manner or degree; rarely. **2** (intensifier): *you're uncommonly friendly.*

uncommunicative Ⓣ (ˌʌnkə'mjuːnɪkətɪv) *adj* disinclined to talk or give information or opinions.
▸ˌ**uncom'municatively** *adv* ▸ˌ**uncom'municativeness** *n*

THESAURUS

veal, spill one's guts about (*sl.*), tell all, unbosom

uncalled-for *adj* = **unnecessary,** gratuitous, inappropriate, needless, undeserved, unjust, unjustified, unprovoked, unwarranted, unwelcome
Antonyms *adj* appropriate, deserved, just, justified, necessary, needed, provoked, warranted

uncanny *adj* **1** = **weird,** creepy (*inf.*), eerie, eldritch (*poetic*), mysterious, preternatural, queer, spooky (*inf.*), strange, supernatural, unearthly, unnatural **2** = **extraordinary,** astonishing, astounding, exceptional, fantastic, incredible, inspired, miraculous, prodigious, remarkable, singular, unheard-of, unusual

uncertain *adj* **1** = **unpredictable,** ambiguous, chancy, conjectural, doubtful, iffy (*inf.*), incalculable, indefinite, indeterminate, indistinct, questionable, risky, speculative, undetermined, unforeseeable **2** = **unsure,** ambivalent, at a loss, doubtful, dubious, hazy, in the balance, in two minds, irresolute, unclear, unconfirmed, undecided, undetermined, unfixed, unresolved, unsettled, up in the air, vacillating, vague **5** = **changeable,** erratic, fitful, hesitant, iffy (*inf.*), inconstant, insecure, irregular, precarious, unpredictable, unreliable, vacillating, variable, wavering
Antonyms *adj* ≠ **unpredictable:** certain, clear, clear-cut, decided, definite, firm, fixed, known, predictable, unambiguous ≠ **unsure:** certain, positive, resolute, settled, sure, unhesitating ≠ **changeable:** certain, reliable, unvarying, unwavering

uncertainty *n* = **doubt,** bewilderment, confusion, dilemma, dubiety, hesitancy, hesitation, indecision, irresolution, lack of confidence, misgiving, mystification, perplexity, puzzlement, qualm, quandary, scepticism, vagueness
Antonyms ≠ **doubt:** assurance, certainty, confidence, decision, resolution, sureness, trust

uncharted *adj* = **unexplored,** not mapped, strange, undiscovered, unfamiliar, unknown, unplumbed, virgin

uncivil *adj* **1** = **impolite,** bad-mannered, bearish, boorish, brusque, churlish, discourteous, disrespectful, gruff, ill-bred, ill-mannered, rude, surly, uncouth, unmannerly
Antonyms *adj* civil, courteous, mannerly, polished, polite, refined, respectful, well-bred, well-mannered

uncivilized *adj* **1** = **primitive,** barbarian, barbaric, barbarous, illiterate, savage, wild **2** = **uncouth,** beyond the pale, boorish, brutish, churlish, coarse, gross, philistine, uncultivated, uncultured, uneducated, unmannered, unpolished, unsophisticated, vulgar

unclad *adj* = **naked,** bare, buck naked (*sl.*), in one's birthday suit (*inf.*), in the altogether (*inf.*), in the bare scud, in the buff (*inf.*), in the raw (*inf.*), naked as the day one was born (*inf.*), nude, starkers (*inf.*), stripped, unclothed, undressed, with nothing on, without a stitch on (*inf.*)

unclean *adj* = **dirty,** contaminated, corrupt, defiled, evil, filthy, foul, impure, nasty, polluted, scuzzy (*sl., chiefly US*), soiled, spotted, stained, sullied, tainted
Antonyms *adj* clean, faultless, flawless, pure, spotless, unblemished, unstained, unsullied

uncomfortable *adj* **1** = **painful,** awkward, causing discomfort, cramped, disagreeable, hard, ill-fitting, incommodious, irritating, rough, troublesome **2** = **uneasy,** awkward, confused, discomfited, disquieted, distressed, disturbed, embarrassed, ill at ease, like a fish out of water, out of place, self-conscious, troubled
Antonyms *adj* ≠ **uneasy:** at ease, at home, comfortable, easy, relaxed, serene, untroubled

uncommitted *adj* = **uninvolved,** floating, free, free-floating, neutral, nonaligned, nonpartisan, not involved, (sitting) on the fence, unattached

uncommon *adj* **1** = **rare,** bizarre, curious, few and far between, infrequent, novel, odd, out of the ordinary, peculiar, queer, scarce, singular, strange, thin on the ground, unfamiliar, unusual **2** = **extraordinary,** distinctive, exceptional, incomparable, inimitable, notable, noteworthy, outstanding, rare, remarkable, singular, special, superior, unparalleled, unprecedented
Antonyms *adj* ≠ **rare:** common, familiar, frequent, regular, routine, usual ≠ **extraordinary:** average, banal, commonplace, everyday, humdrum, mundane, ordinary, run-of-the-mill

uncommonly *adv* **1** = **rarely,** hardly ever, infrequently, not often, occasionally, only now and then, scarcely ever, seldom **2** = **exceptionally,** extremely, particularly, peculiarly, remarkably, seriously (*inf.*), strangely, to the nth degree, unusually, very

uncommunicative *adj* = **reticent,** close, curt, guarded, reserved, retiring, secretive, short, shy, silent, taciturn, tight-lipped, unforthcoming, unresponsive, unsociable, withdrawn
Antonyms *adj* chatty, communicative, forthcom-

uncompromising ⓣ (ʌnˈkɒmprəˌmaɪzɪŋ) *adj* not prepared to give ground or to compromise.
▸**unˈcompro͵misingly** *adv*
unconcern ⓣ (ˌʌnkənˈsɜːn) *n* apathy or indifference.
unconcerned ⓣ (ˌʌnkənˈsɜːnd) *adj* **1** lacking in concern or involvement. **2** untroubled.
▸**unconcernedly** (ˌʌnkənˈsɜːnɪdlɪ) *adv*
unconditional ⓣ (ˌʌnkənˈdɪʃənᵊl) *adj* without conditions or limitations; total: *unconditional surrender.*
▸**͵unconˈditionally** *adv*
unconditioned (ˌʌnkənˈdɪʃənd) *adj* **1** *Psychol.* characterizing an innate reflex and the stimulus and response that form parts of it. **2** *Metaphysics.* unrestricted by conditions; absolute. **3** without limitations.
▸**͵unconˈditionedness** *n*
unconformable (ˌʌnkənˈfɔːməbᵊl) *adj* **1** not conformable or conforming. **2** (of rock strata) consisting of a series of recent strata resting on different, much older rocks.
▸**͵uncon͵formaˈbility** *or* **͵unconˈformableness** *n* ▸**͵unconˈformably** *adv* ▸**͵unconˈformity** *n*
unconscionable ⓣ (ʌnˈkɒnʃənəbᵊl) *adj* **1** unscrupulous or unprincipled: *an unconscionable liar.* **2** immoderate or excessive: *unconscionable demands.*
▸**unˈconscionably** *adv*
unconscious ⓣ (ʌnˈkɒnʃəs) *adj* **1** lacking normal sensory awareness of the environment; insensible. **2** not aware of one's actions, behaviour, etc.: *unconscious of his bad manners.* **3** characterized by lack of awareness or intention: *an unconscious blunder.* **4** coming from or produced by the unconscious: *unconscious resentment.* ◆ *n* **5** *Psychoanal.* the part of the mind containing instincts, impulses, images, and ideas that are not available for direct examination.
▸**unˈconsciously** *adv*
unconstitutional (ˌʌnkɒnstɪˈtjuːʃənᵊl) *adj* at variance with or not permitted by a constitution.
▸**͵unconsti͵tutionˈality** *n*
unconventional ⓣ (ˌʌnkənˈvenʃənᵊl) *adj* not conforming to accepted rules or standards.
▸**͵uncon͵ventionˈality** *n* ▸**͵unconˈventionally** *adv*
uncool (ʌnˈkuːl) *adj Sl.* **1** unsophisticated; unfashionable. **2** excitable; tense; not cool.
uncork (ʌnˈkɔːk) *vb* (*tr*) **1** to draw the cork from (a bottle, etc.). **2** to release or unleash (emotions, etc.).
uncountable (ʌnˈkaʊntəbᵊl) *adj* **1** too many to be counted; innumerable. **2** *Linguistics.* denoting a noun that does not refer to an isolable object. See **mass noun**.
uncounted ⓣ (ʌnˈkaʊntɪd) *adj* **1** unable to be counted; innumerable. **2** not counted.
uncouple (ʌnˈkʌpᵊl) *vb* **uncouples, uncoupling, uncoupled. 1** to disconnect or unfasten or become disconnected or unfastened. **2** (*tr*) to set loose; release.
uncouth ⓣ (ʌnˈkuːθ) *adj* lacking in good manners, refinement, or grace. [OE *uncūth*, from UN-[1] + *cūth* familiar]
▸**unˈcouthly** *adv* ▸**unˈcouthness** *n*
uncover ⓣ (ʌnˈkʌvə) *vb* **1** (*tr*) to remove the cover, cap, top, etc., from. **2** (*tr*) to reveal or disclose: *to uncover a plot.* **3** to take off (one's head covering), esp. as a mark of respect.
uncovered (ʌnˈkʌvəd) *adj* **1** not covered; revealed or bare. **2** not protected by insurance, security, etc. **3** with hat off, as a mark of respect.
UNCTAD *abbrev. for* United Nations Conference on Trade and Development.
unction (ˈʌŋkʃən) *n* **1** *Chiefly RC & Eastern Churches.* the act of anointing with oil in sacramental ceremonies, in the conferring of holy orders. **2** excessive suavity or affected charm. **3** an ointment or unguent. **4** anything soothing. [C14: from L *unctiō* an anointing, from *ungere* to anoint]
▸**ˈunctionless** *adj*
unctuous ⓣ (ˈʌŋktjʊəs) *adj* **1** slippery or greasy. **2** affecting an oily charm. [C14: from Med. L *unctuōsus*, from L *unctum* ointment, from *ungere* to anoint]
▸**unctuosity** (ˌʌŋktjʊˈɒsɪtɪ) *or* **ˈunctuousness** *n* ▸**ˈunctuously** *adv*
uncut (ʌnˈkʌt) *adj* **1** (of a book) not having the edges of its pages trimmed or slit. **2** (of a gemstone) not cut and faceted. **3** not abridged.
undamped (ʌnˈdæmpt) *adj* **1** (of an oscillating system) having unrestricted motion; not damped. **2** not repressed, discouraged, or subdued.
undaunted ⓣ (ʌnˈdɔːntɪd) *adj* not put off, discouraged, or beaten.
▸**unˈdauntedly** *adv* ▸**unˈdauntedness** *n*
undecagon (ʌnˈdekəˌgɒn) *n* a polygon having eleven sides. [C18: from L *undecim* eleven + -GON]
undeceive ⓣ (ˌʌndɪˈsiːv) *vb* **undeceives, undeceiving, undeceived.** (*tr*) to reveal the truth to (someone previously misled or deceived).
▸**͵undeˈceivable** *adj* ▸**͵undeˈceiver** *n*
undecidability (ˌʌndɪˌsaɪdəˈbɪlɪtɪ) *n, pl* **undecidabilities.** *Maths, logic.* the condition of not being open to formal proof or disproof by logical deduction from the axioms of a system.
undecided ⓣ (ˌʌndɪˈsaɪdɪd) *adj* **1** not having made up one's mind. **2** (of an issue, problem, etc.) not agreed or decided upon.
▸**͵undeˈcidedly** *adv* ▸**͵undeˈcidedness** *n*
undeniable(ˌʌndɪˈnaɪəbᵊl) *adj* **1** unquestionably or obviously true. **2** of unquestionable excellence: *a man of undeniable character.* **3** unable to be resisted or denied.
▸**͵undeˈniableness** *n* ▸**͵undeˈniably** *adv*
under ⓣ (ˈʌndə) *prep* **1** directly below; on, to, or beneath the underside or base of: *under one's feet.* **2** less than: *under forty years.* **3** lower in rank than: *under a corporal.* **4** subject to the supervision, jurisdiction, control, or influence of. **5** subject to (conditions); in (certain circumstances). **6** within a classification of: *a book under theology.* **7** known by: *under an assumed name.* **8** planted with: *a field under corn.* **9** powered by: *under sail.* **10** *Astrol.* during the period that the sun is in (a sign of the zodiac): *born under Aries.* ◆ *adv* **11** below; to a position underneath something. [OE]
under- *prefix* **1** below or beneath: *underarm; underground.* **2** of lesser importance or lower rank: *undersecretary.* **3** insufficient or insufficiently: *underemployed.* **4** indicating secrecy or deception: *underhand.*
underachieve (ˌʌndərəˈtʃiːv) *vb* **underachieves, underachieving, under-**

THESAURUS

ing, garrulous, loquacious, responsive, talkative, voluble
uncompromising *adj* = **inflexible**, decided, die-hard, firm, hardline, inexorable, intransigent, obdurate, obstinate, rigid, steadfast, stiff-necked, strict, stubborn, tough, unbending, unyielding
unconcern *n* = **indifference**, aloofness, apathy, detachment, insouciance, lack of interest, nonchalance, remoteness, uninterestedness
unconcerned *adj* **1** = **indifferent**, aloof, apathetic, cool, detached, dispassionate, distant, incurious, oblivious, uninterested, uninvolved, unmoved, unsympathetic **2** = **untroubled**, blithe, callous, carefree, careless, easy, insouciant, nonchalant, not bothered, not giving a toss (*inf.*), relaxed, serene, unperturbed, unruffled, unworried
Antonyms *adj* ≠ **indifferent:** avid, curious, eager, interested, involved ≠ **untroubled:** agitated, anxious, concerned, distressed, perturbed, uneasy, worried
unconditional *adj* = **absolute**, arrant, categorical, complete, downright, entire, explicit, full, out-and-out, outright, plenary, positive, thoroughgoing, total, unlimited, unqualified, unreserved, unrestricted, utter
Antonyms *adj* conditional, limited, partial, qualified, reserved, restricted
unconscionable *adj* **1** = **unscrupulous**, amoral, criminal, unethical, unfair, unjust, unprincipled **2** = **excessive**, exorbitant, extravagant, extreme, immoderate, inordinate, outrageous, preposterous, unreasonable
unconscious *adj* **1** = **senseless**, blacked out, comatose, dead to the world (*inf.*), insensible, knocked out, numb, out, out cold, out for the count (*Boxing*), stunned **2** = **unaware**, blind to, deaf to, heedless, ignorant, in ignorance, lost to, oblivious, unknowing, unmindful, unsuspecting **3** = **unintentional**, accidental, inadvertent, unintended, unpremeditated, unwitting **4** = **subconscious**, automatic, gut (*inf.*), inherent, innate, instinctive, involuntary, latent, reflex, repressed, subliminal, suppressed, unrealized
Antonyms *adj* ≠ **senseless:** awake, conscious, sensible ≠ **unaware:** alert, aware, conscious, sensible ≠ **unintentional:** calculated, conscious, deliberate, intentional, planned, studied, wilful
unconventional *adj* = **unusual**, atypical, bizarre, bohemian, different, eccentric, far-out (*sl.*), freakish, idiosyncratic, individual, individualistic, informal, irregular, left-field (*inf.*), nonconformist, odd, oddball (*inf.*), offbeat, off-the-wall (*sl.*), original, out of the ordinary, outré, uncustomary, unorthodox, way-out (*inf.*)
Antonyms *adj* conventional, normal, ordinary, orthodox, proper, regular, typical, usual
uncounted *adj* = **innumerable**, countless, infinite, legion, multitudinous, myriad, numberless, unnumbered, untold
uncouth *adj* = **coarse**, awkward, barbaric, boorish, clownish, clumsy, crude, gawky, graceless, gross, ill-mannered, loutish, lubberly, oafish, rough, rude, rustic, uncivilized, uncultivated, ungainly, unrefined, unseemly, vulgar
Antonyms *adj* civilized, courteous, cultivated, elegant, graceful, refined, seemly, well-mannered
uncover *vb* **1** = **open**, bare, lay open, lift the lid, show, strip, unwrap **2** = **reveal**, blow wide open (*sl.*), bring to light, disclose, discover, divulge, expose, lay bare, make known, take the wraps off, unearth, unmask
Antonyms *vb* ≠ **reveal:** conceal, cover, cover up, hide, keep under wraps, suppress
unctuous *adj* **1** = **greasy**, oily, oleaginous, slippery, slithery **2** = **obsequious**, fawning, glib, gushing, ingratiating, insincere, oily, plausible, slick, smarmy (*Brit. inf.*), smooth, suave, sycophantic
undaunted *adj* = **undeterred**, bold, brave, courageous, dauntless, fearless, gallant, gritty, indomitable, intrepid, not discouraged, nothing daunted, not put off, resolute, steadfast, undiscouraged, undismayed, unfaltering, unflinching, unshrinking
undeceive *vb* = **enlighten**, be honest with, correct, disabuse, disillusion, open (someone's) eyes (to), put (someone) right, set (someone) straight, shatter (someone's) illusions
undecided *adj* **1** = **unsure**, ambivalent, dithering (*chiefly Brit.*), doubtful, dubious, hesitant, in two minds, irresolute, swithering (*Scot.*), torn, uncertain, uncommitted, wavering **2** = **unsettled**, debatable, iffy (*inf.*), indefinite, in the balance, moot, open, pending, tentative, unconcluded, undetermined, up in the air, vague
Antonyms *adj* ≠ **unsure:** certain, committed, decided, resolute, sure ≠ **unsettled:** decided, definite, determined, resolved, settled
undeniable *adj* **1** = **certain**, beyond (a) doubt, beyond question, clear, evident, incontestable, incontrovertible, indisputable, indubitable, irrefutable, manifest, obvious, patent, proven, sound, sure, unassailable, undoubted, unquestionable
Antonyms *adj* debatable, deniable, doubtful, dubious, questionable, uncertain, unproven
under *prep* **1** = **below**, beneath, on the bottom

achieved. (*intr*) to fail to achieve a performance appropriate to one's age or talents.
▸ ˌunderaˈchievement *n* ▸ ˌunderaˈchiever *n*

underact (ˌʌndərˈækt) *vb Theatre.* to play (a role) without adequate emphasis.

underage (ˌʌndərˈeɪdʒ) *adj* below the required or standard age, esp. below the legal age for voting or drinking.

underarm (ˈʌndərˌɑːm) *adj* **1** (of a measurement) extending along the arm from wrist to armpit. **2** *Cricket, tennis, etc.* denoting a style of throwing, bowling, or serving in which the hand is swung below shoulder level. **3** below the arm. ◆ *adv* **4** in an underarm style.

underbelly (ˈʌndəˌbelɪ) *n, pl* **underbellies. 1** the part of an animal's belly nearest to the ground. **2** a vulnerable or unprotected part, aspect, or region.

underbid (ˌʌndəˈbɪd) *vb* **underbids, underbidding, underbid. 1** (*tr*) to submit a bid lower than that of (others). **2** (*tr*) to submit an excessively low bid for. **3** *Bridge.* to bid (one's hand) at a lower level than the strength of the hand warrants: *he underbid his hand.*

underbidder (ˈʌndəˌbɪdə) *n* **1** the person who makes the highest bid below the top bidder, esp. in an auction. **2** a person who underbids.

underbody (ˈʌndəˌbɒdɪ) *n, pl* **underbodies.** the underpart of a body, as of an animal or motor vehicle.

underbred (ˌʌndəˈbrɛd) *adj* of impure stock; not thoroughbred.
▸ ˌunderˈbreeding *n*

underbuy (ˌʌndəˈbaɪ) *vb* **underbuys, underbuying, underbought. 1** to buy (stock in trade) in amounts lower than required. **2** (*tr*) to buy at a price below that paid by (others). **3** (*tr*) to pay a price less than the true value for.

undercapitalize *or* **undercapitalise** (ˌʌndəˈkæpɪtəˌlaɪz) *vb* **undercapitalizes, undercapitalizing, undercapitalized** *or* **undercapitalises, undercapitalising, undercapitalised.** to provide or issue capital for (a commercial enterprise) in an amount insufficient for efficient operation.

undercarriage (ˈʌndəˌkærɪdʒ) *n* **1** Also called: **landing gear.** the assembly of wheels, shock absorbers, struts, etc., that supports an aircraft on the ground and enables it to take off and land. **2** the framework that supports the body of a vehicle, carriage, etc.

undercharge (ˌʌndəˈtʃɑːdʒ) *vb* **undercharges, undercharging, undercharged. 1** to charge too little for something. **2** (*tr*) to load (a gun, cannon, etc.) with an inadequate charge.

underclass (ˈʌndəˌklɑːs) *n* a class beneath the usual social scale consisting of the most disadvantaged people, such as the long-term unemployed.

underclothes ❶ (ˈʌndəˌkləʊðz) *pl n* a variant of **underwear.** Also called: **underclothing.**

undercoat (ˈʌndəˌkəʊt) *n* **1** a coat of paint or other substance applied before the top coat. **2** a coat worn under an overcoat. **3** *Zool.* another name for **underfur.** ◆ *vb* **4** (*tr*) to apply an undercoat to (a surface).

undercover ❶ (ˌʌndəˈkʌvə) *adj* done or acting in secret: *undercover operations.*

undercroft (ˈʌndəˌkrɒft) *n* an underground chamber, such as a church crypt, often with a vaulted ceiling. [C14: from *croft* a vault, cavern, ult. from L *crypta* CRYPT]

undercurrent ❶ (ˈʌndəˌkʌrənt) *n* **1** a current that is not apparent at the surface or lies beneath another current. **2** an opinion, emotion, etc., lying beneath apparent feeling or meaning. ◆ Also called: **underflow.**

undercut ❶ *vb* (ˌʌndəˈkʌt), **undercuts, undercutting, undercut. 1** to charge less than (a competitor) in order to obtain trade. **2** to cut away the under part of (something). **3** *Golf, tennis, etc.* to hit (a ball) in such a way as to impart backspin. ◆ *n* (ˈʌndəˌkʌt). **4** the act of cutting underneath. **5** a part that is cut away underneath. **6** a tenderloin of beef. **7** *Forestry, chiefly US & Canad.* a notch cut in a tree trunk, to ensure a clean break in felling. **8** *Tennis, golf, etc.* a stroke that imparts backspin to the ball.

underdevelop (ˌʌndədɪˈvɛləp) *vb* (*tr*) *Photog.* to process (a film, plate, or paper) in developer for less than the required time, or at too low a temperature, or in an exhausted solution.

underdeveloped (ˌʌndədɪˈvɛləpt) *adj* **1** immature or undersized. **2** relating to societies in which both the surplus capital and the social organization necessary to advance are lacking. **3** *Photog.* (of a film, etc.) processed in developer for less than the required time.

underdog ❶ (ˈʌndəˌdɒg) *n* **1** the losing competitor in a fight or contest. **2** a person in adversity or a position of inferiority.

underdone (ˌʌndəˈdʌn) *adj* insufficiently or lightly cooked.

underdressed (ˌʌndəˈdrɛst) *adj* wearing clothes that are not elaborate or formal enough for a particular occasion.

underemployed (ˌʌndərɪmˈplɔɪd) *adj* not fully or adequately employed.

underestimate ❶ *vb* (ˌʌndərˈɛstɪˌmeɪt), **underestimates, underestimating, underestimated.** (*tr*) **1** to make too low an estimate of: *he underestimated the cost.* **2** to think insufficiently highly of: *to underestimate a person.* ◆ *n* (ˌʌndərˈɛstɪmɪt). **3** too low an estimate.
▸ ˌunderˌestiˈmation *n*

> **USAGE NOTE** *Underestimate* is sometimes wrongly used where *overestimate* is meant: *the importance of his work cannot be overestimated* (not *cannot be underestimated*).

underexpose (ˌʌndərɪkˈspəʊz) *vb* **underexposes, underexposing, underexposed.** (*tr*) **1** *Photog.* to expose (a film, plate, or paper) for too short a period or with insufficient light so as not to produce the required effect. **2** (*often passive*) to fail to subject to appropriate or expected publicity.
▸ ˌunderexˈposure *n*

underfeed (ˌʌndəˈfiːd) *vb* **underfeeds, underfeeding, underfed.** (*tr*) **1** to give too little food to. **2** to supply (a furnace, engine, etc.) with fuel from beneath.

underfelt (ˈʌndəˌfɛlt) *n* thick felt laid between floorboards and carpet to increase insulation.

underfloor (ˈʌndəˌflɔː) *adj* situated beneath the floor: *underfloor heating.*

underfoot (ˌʌndəˈfʊt) *adv* **1** underneath the feet; on the ground. **2** in a position of subjugation. **3** in the way.

underfur (ˈʌndəˌfɜː) *n* the layer of dense soft fur occurring beneath the outer coarser fur in certain mammals, such as the otter and seal. Also called: **undercoat.**

undergarment (ˈʌndəˌgɑːmənt) *n* any garment worn under the visible outer clothes, usually next to the skin.

undergird (ˌʌndəˈgɜːd) *vb* **undergirds, undergirding, undergirded** *or* **undergirt.** (*tr*) to strengthen or reinforce by passing a rope, cable, or chain around the underside of (an object, load, etc.). [C16: from UNDER- + GIRD[1]]

underglaze (ˈʌndəˌgleɪz) *adj* **1** *Ceramics.* applied to pottery or porcelain before the application of glaze. ◆ *n* **2** a pigment, etc., applied in this way.

undergo ❶ (ˌʌndəˈgəʊ) *vb* **undergoes, undergoing, underwent, undergone.** (*tr*) to experience, endure, or sustain: *to undergo a change of feelings.* [OE]
▸ ˈunderˌgoer *n*

undergraduate (ˌʌndəˈgrædjʊɪt) *n* a person studying in a university for a first degree. Sometimes shortened to **undergrad.**

underground ❶ *adj* (ˈʌndəˌgraʊnd), *adv* (ˌʌndəˈgraʊnd). **1** occurring, situated, used, or going below ground level: *an underground explosion.* **2** secret; hidden: *underground activities.* ◆ *n* (ˈʌndəˌgraʊnd). **3** a space or region below ground level. **4a** a movement dedicated to overthrowing a government or occupation forces, as in the European countries occupied by the German army in World War II. **4b** (*as modifier*): *an underground group.* **5** (often preceded by *the*) an electric passenger railway operated in underground tunnels. US and Canad. equivalent: **subway. 6** (usually preceded by *the*) **6a** any avant-garde, experimental, or subversive movement in popular art, films, music, etc. **6b** (*as modifier*): *the underground press.*

underground railroad *n* (*often cap.*) (in the pre-Civil War US) the system established by abolitionists to aid escaping slaves.

undergrowth ❶ (ˈʌndəˌgrəʊθ) *n* small trees, bushes, ferns, etc., growing beneath taller trees in a wood or forest.

underhand ❶ (ˈʌndəˌhænd) *adj also* **underhanded. 1** clandestine, deceptive, or secretive. **2** *Sport.* another word for **underarm.** ◆ *adv* **3** in an underhand manner or style.

THESAURUS

of, underneath **3, 4 = subject to,** directed by, governed by, inferior to, junior to, reporting to, secondary to, subordinate to, subservient to **6 = included in,** belonging to, comprised in, subsumed under ◆ *adv* **11 = below,** beneath, down, downward, lower, to the bottom
Antonyms *prep* ≠ **below:** above, over, up, upper, upward ◆ *adv* ≠ **below:** above, over, up, upward

underclothes *pl n* **= underwear,** lingerie, smalls (*inf.*), underclothing, undergarments, underlinen, underthings, undies (*inf.*), unmentionables (*humorous*)

undercover *adj* **= secret,** clandestine, concealed, confidential, covert, hidden, hush-hush (*inf.*), intelligence, private, spy, surreptitious, underground
Antonyms *adj* manifest, open, overt, plain, unconcealed, visible

undercurrent *n* **1 = undertow,** crosscurrent, rip, rip current, riptide, tideway, underflow **2 = undertone,** atmosphere, aura, drift, feeling, flavour, hidden feeling, hint, murmur, overtone, sense, suggestion, tendency, tenor, tinge, trend, vibes (*sl.*), vibrations

undercut *vb* **1 = underprice,** sacrifice, sell at a loss, sell cheaply, undercharge, undersell **2 = cut away,** cut out, excavate, gouge out, hollow out, mine, undermine

underdog *n* **1, 2 = weaker party,** fall guy, little fellow (*inf.*), loser, outsider, victim

underestimate *vb* **2 = underrate,** belittle, hold cheap, minimize, miscalculate, misprize, not do justice to, rate too low, sell short, set no store by, think too little of, undervalue
Antonyms *vb* exaggerate, inflate, overdo, overestimate, overrate, overstate

undergo *vb* **= experience,** bear, be subjected to, endure, go through, stand, submit to, suffer, sustain, weather, withstand

underground *adj* **1 = subterranean,** below ground, below the surface, buried, covered **2 = secret,** clandestine, concealed, covert, hidden, surreptitious, undercover ◆ *n* **4a = the Resistance,** partisans, the Maquis **5 the underground = the tube** (*Brit.*), the metro, the subway ◆ *modifier* **6b = avant-garde,** alternative, experimental, radical, revolutionary, subversive

undergrowth *n* **= scrub,** bracken, brambles, briars, brush, brushwood, underbrush, underbush, underwood

underhand *adj* **1 = sly,** below the belt (*inf.*), clandestine, crafty, crooked (*inf.*), deceitful, deceptive, devious, dishonest, dishonourable, fraudulent, furtive, secret, secretive, sneaky, stealthy, surreptitious, treacherous, underhanded, unethical, unscrupulous

underhanded (ˌʌndəˈhændɪd) *adj* another word for **underhand** or **short-handed.**

underhung (ˌʌndəˈhʌŋ) *adj* **1** (of the lower jaw) projecting beyond the upper jaw; undershot. **2** (of a sliding door, etc.) supported at its lower edge by a track or rail.

underlay *vb* (ˌʌndəˈleɪ), **underlays, underlaying, underlaid.** (*tr*) **1** to place (something) under or beneath. **2** to support by something laid beneath. **3** to achieve the correct printing pressure all over (a forme block) or to bring (a block) up to type height by adding material, such as paper, beneath it. ◆ *n* (ˈʌndəˌleɪ). **4** a lining, support, etc., laid underneath something else. **5** *Printing.* material, such as paper, used to underlay a forme or block. **6** felt, rubber, etc., laid beneath a carpet to increase insulation and resilience.

underlie (ˌʌndəˈlaɪ) *vb* **underlies, underlying, underlay, underlain.** (*tr*) **1** to lie or be placed under or beneath. **2** to be the foundation, cause, or basis of: *careful planning underlies all our decisions.* **3** to be the root or stem from which (a word) is derived: *"happy" underlies "happiest".*
▸ **ˈunderˌlier** *n*

underline ❶ (ˌʌndəˈlaɪn) *vb* **underlines, underlining, underlined.** (*tr*) **1** to put a line under. **2** to state forcibly; emphasize.

underlinen (ˈʌndəˌlɪnən) *n* underclothes, esp. when made of linen.

underling ❶ (ˈʌndəlɪŋ) *n* a subordinate or lackey.

underlying ❶ (ˌʌndəˈlaɪɪŋ) *adj* **1** concealed but detectable: *underlying guilt.* **2** fundamental; basic. **3** lying under. **4** *Finance.* (of a claim, liability, etc.) taking precedence; prior.

undermentioned (ˈʌndəˌmɛnʃənd) *adj* mentioned below or subsequently.

undermine ❶ (ˌʌndəˈmaɪn) *vb* **undermines, undermining, undermined.** (*tr*) **1** (of the sea, wind, etc.) to wear away the bottom or base of (land, cliffs, etc.). **2** to weaken gradually or insidiously: *insults undermined her confidence.* **3** to tunnel or dig beneath.
▸ **ˌunderˈminer** *n*

undermost (ˈʌndəˌməʊst) *adj* **1** being the furthest under; lowest. ◆ *adv* **2** in the lowest place.

underneath (ˌʌndəˈniːθ) *prep, adv* **1** under; beneath. ◆ *adj* **2** lower. ◆ *n* **3** a lower part, surface, etc. [OE *underneothan*, from UNDER + *neothan* below]

undernourish (ˌʌndəˈnʌrɪʃ) *vb* (*tr*) to deprive of or fail to provide with nutrients essential for health and growth.
▸ **ˌunderˈnourishment** *n*

underpants (ˈʌndəˌpænts) *pl n* a man's undergarment covering the body from the waist or hips to the thighs or ankles. Often shortened to **pants.**

underpass (ˈʌndəˌpɑːs) *n* **1** a section of a road that passes under another road, railway line, etc. **2** another word for **subway** (sense 1).

underpay (ˌʌndəˈpeɪ) *vb* **underpays, underpaying, underpaid.** to pay (someone) insufficiently.
▸ **ˌunderˈpayment** *n*

underpin (ˌʌndəˈpɪn) *vb* **underpins, underpinning, underpinned.** (*tr*) **1** to support from beneath, esp. by a prop, while avoiding damaging or weakening the superstructure: *to underpin a wall.* **2** to give corroboration, strength, or support to.

underpinning ❶ (ˈʌndəˌpɪnɪŋ) *n* a structure of masonry, concrete, etc., placed beneath a wall to provide support.

underplay (ˌʌndəˈpleɪ) *vb* **1** to play (a role) with restraint or subtlety. **2** to achieve (an effect) by deliberate lack of emphasis. **3** (*intr*) *Cards.* to lead or follow suit with a lower card when holding a higher one.

underprivileged ❶ (ˌʌndəˈprɪvɪlɪdʒd) *adj* lacking the rights and advantages of other members of society; deprived.

underproduction (ˌʌndəprəˈdʌkʃən) *n Commerce.* production below full capacity or below demand.

underproof (ˌʌndəˈpruːf) *adj* (of a spirit) containing less than 57.1 per cent alcohol by volume.

underquote (ˌʌndəˈkwəʊt) *vb* **underquotes, underquoting, underquoted. 1** to offer for sale (securities, goods, or services) at a price lower than the market price. **2** (*tr*) to quote a price lower than that quoted by (another).

underrate ❶ (ˌʌndəˈreɪt) *vb* **underrates, underrating, underrated.** (*tr*) to underestimate.

underscore (ˌʌndəˈskɔː) *vb* **underscores, underscoring, underscored.** (*tr*) **1** to draw or score a line or mark under. **2** to stress or reinforce.

undersea (ˈʌndəˌsiː) *adj, adv also* **underseas** (ˌʌndəˈsiːz). below the surface of the sea.

underseal (ˈʌndəˌsiːl) *Brit.* ◆ *n* **1** a coating of a tar, etc., applied to the underside of a motor vehicle to retard corrosion. ◆ *vb* **2** (*tr*) to apply a coating of underseal to (a vehicle).

undersecretary (ˌʌndəˈsɛkrətrɪ) *n, pl* **undersecretaries. 1** (in Britain) **1a** any of various senior civil servants in certain government departments. **1b** short for **undersecretary of state:** any of various high officials subordinate only to the minister in charge of a department. **2** (in the US) a high government official subordinate only to the secretary in charge of a department.

undersell ❶ (ˌʌndəˈsɛl) *vb* **undersells, underselling, undersold. 1** to sell for less than the usual price. **2** (*tr*) to sell at a price lower than that of (another seller). **3** (*tr*) to advertise (merchandise) with moderation or restraint.
▸ **ˌunderˈseller** *n*

undersexed (ˌʌndəˈsɛkst) *adj* having weaker sex urges or responses than is considered normal.

undershirt (ˈʌndəˌʃɜːt) *n* the US and Canad. name for **vest** (sense 1).

undershoot (ˌʌndəˈʃuːt) *vb* **undershoots, undershooting, undershot. 1** (of a pilot) to cause (an aircraft) to land short of (a runway) or (of an aircraft) to land in this way. **2** to shoot a projectile so that it falls short of (a target).

undershorts (ˈʌndəˌʃɔːts) *pl n* another word for **shorts** (sense 2).

undershot (ˈʌndəˌʃɒt) *adj* **1** (of the lower jaw) projecting beyond the upper jaw; underhung. **2** (of a water wheel) driven by a flow of water that passes under the wheel rather than over it.

underside (ˈʌndəˌsaɪd) *n* the bottom or lower surface.

undersigned (ˈʌndəˌsaɪnd) *n* **1 the.** the person or persons who have signed at the foot of a document, statement, etc. ◆ *adj* **2** having signed one's name at the foot of a document, statement, etc.

undersized ❶ (ˌʌndəˈsaɪzd) *adj* of less than usual size.

underskirt (ˈʌndəˌskɜːt) *n* any skirtlike garment worn under a skirt or dress; petticoat.

underslung (ˌʌndəˈslʌŋ) *adj* suspended below a supporting member, esp. (of a motor vehicle chassis) suspended below the axles.

understand ❶ (ˌʌndəˈstænd) *vb* **understands, understanding, understood. 1** (*may take a clause as object*) to know and comprehend the nature or meaning of: *I understand you.* **2** (*may take a clause as object*) to realize or grasp (something): *he understands your position.* **3** (*tr; may take a clause as object*) to assume, infer, or believe: *I understand you are thinking of marrying.* **4** (*tr*) to know how to translate or read: *can you understand Spanish?* **5** (*tr; may take a clause as object; often passive*) to accept as a condition or proviso: *it is understood that children must be kept quiet.* **6** (*tr*) to be sympathetic to or compatible with: *we understand each other.* [OE *understandan*]
▸ **ˌunderˈstandable** *adj* ▸ **ˌunderˈstandably** *adv*

understanding ❶ (ˌʌndəˈstændɪŋ) *n* **1** the ability to learn, judge, make decisions, etc. **2** personal opinion or interpretation of a subject: *my understanding of your predicament.* **3** a mutual agreement or compact, esp. an informal or private one. **4** *Chiefly Brit.* an unofficial engagement to be married. **5 on the understanding that.** providing. ◆ *adj* **6** sym-

THESAURUS

Antonyms *adj* above board, frank, honest, honourable, legal, open, outright, principled, scrupulous

underline *vb* **1 = underscore**, italicize, mark, rule a line under **2 = emphasize**, accentuate, bring home, call *or* draw attention to, give emphasis to, highlight, point up, stress
Antonyms *vb* ≠ **emphasize:** gloss over, make light of, minimize, play down, soft-pedal (*inf.*)

underling *n Derogatory* = **subordinate**, cohort (*chiefly US*), flunky, hireling, inferior, lackey, menial, minion, nonentity, retainer, servant, slave, understrapper

underlying *adj* **1 = hidden**, concealed, latent, lurking, veiled **2 = fundamental**, basal, basic, elementary, essential, intrinsic, primary, prime, radical, root

undermine *vb* **1 = wear away**, dig out, eat away at, erode, excavate, mine, tunnel, undercut **2 = weaken**, debilitate, disable, impair, sabotage, sap, subvert, threaten
Antonyms *vb* ≠ **weaken:** fortify, promote, reinforce, strengthen, sustain ≠ **wear away:** buttress, fortify, reinforce, strengthen, sustain

underpinning *n* = **support**, base, footing, foundation, groundwork, substructure

underprivileged *adj* = **disadvantaged**, badly off, deprived, destitute, impoverished, in need, in want, needy, on the breadline, poor

underrate *vb* = **underestimate**, belittle, discount, disparage, fail to appreciate, misprize, not do justice to, set (too) little store by, undervalue
Antonyms *vb* exaggerate, overestimate, overprize, overrate, overvalue

undersell *vb* **1, 2 = undercut**, cut, mark down, reduce, slash, undercharge **3 = understate**, play down

undersized *adj* = **stunted**, atrophied, dwarfish, miniature, pygmy *or* pigmy, runtish, runty, small, squat, teensy-weensy, teeny-weeny, tiny, underdeveloped, underweight
Antonyms *adj* big, colossal, giant, huge, massive, oversized, overweight

understand *vb* **1 = comprehend**, appreciate, apprehend, be aware, catch on (*inf.*), conceive, cotton on (*inf.*), discern, fathom, follow, get, get one's head round, get the hang of (*inf.*), get to the bottom of, grasp, know, make head or tail of (*inf.*), make out, penetrate, perceive, realize, recognize, savvy (*sl.*), see, see the light, take in, tumble to (*inf.*), twig (*Brit. inf.*) **3 = believe**, assume, be informed, conclude, gather, hear, learn, presume, suppose, take it, think **6 = sympathize with**, accept, appreciate, be able to see, commiserate, empathize with, show compassion for, tolerate

understandable *adj* **2 = reasonable**, justifiable, legitimate, logical, natural, normal, to be expected

understanding *n* **1 = perception**, appreciation, awareness, comprehension, discernment, grasp, insight, intelligence, judgment, knowledge, penetration, sense **2 = interpretation**, belief, conclusion, estimation, idea, judgment, notion, opinion, perception, view, viewpoint **3 = agreement**, accord, common view, gentlemen's agreement, pact ◆ *adj* **6 = sympathetic**, accepting, compassionate, considerate, discerning, forbearing, forgiving, kind, kindly, patient, perceptive, responsive, sensitive, tolerant
Antonyms *n* ≠ **perception:** ignorance, incomprehension, insensitivity, misapprehension, misunderstanding, obtuseness ≠ **agreement:** disagreement, dispute ◆ *adj* ≠ **sympathetic:** inconsiderate, insensitive, intolerant, strict, unfeeling, unsympathetic

DICTIONARY

pathetic, tolerant, or wise towards people. **7** possessing judgment and intelligence.
▸ˌ**under'standingly** *adv*

understate (ˌʌndəˈsteɪt) *vb* **understates, understating, understated. 1** to state (something) in restrained terms, often to obtain an ironic effect. **2** to state that (something, such as a number) is less than it is.
▸ˌ**under'statement** *n*

understeer (ˌʌndəˈstɪə) *vb* (*intr*) (of a vehicle) to turn less sharply, for a particular movement of the steering wheel, than anticipated.

understood ❶ (ˌʌndəˈstʊd) *vb* **1** the past tense and past participle of **understand.** ◆ *adj* **2** implied or inferred. **3** taken for granted.

understudy ❶ (ˈʌndəˌstʌdɪ) *vb* **understudies, understudying, understudied. 1** (*tr*) to study (a role or part) so as to be able to replace the usual actor or actress if necessary. **2** to act as understudy to (an actor or actress). ◆ *n, pl* **understudies. 3** an actor or actress who studies a part so as to be able to replace the usual actor or actress if necessary. **4** anyone who is trained to take the place of another in case of need.

undertake ❶ (ˌʌndəˈteɪk) *vb* **undertakes, undertaking, undertook, undertaken.** (*tr*) **1** to contract to or commit oneself to (something) or (to do something): *to undertake a job.* **2** to attempt to; agree to start. **3** to take (someone) in charge. **4** to promise.

undertaker ❶ (ˈʌndəˌteɪkə) *n* a person whose profession is the preparation of the dead for burial or cremation and the management of funerals; funeral director.

undertaking ❶ (ˈʌndəˌteɪkɪŋ) *n* **1** a task, venture, or enterprise. **2** an agreement to do something. **3** the business of an undertaker.

underthings (ˈʌndəˌθɪŋz) *pl n* girls' or women's underwear.

underthrust (ˈʌndəˌθrʌst) *n Geol.* a reverse fault in which the rocks on the lower surface of a fault plane have moved under the relatively static rocks on the upper surface.

undertone ❶ (ˈʌndəˌtəʊn) *n* **1** a quiet or hushed tone of voice. **2** an underlying suggestion in words or actions: *his offer has undertones of dishonesty.*

undertow (ˈʌndəˌtəʊ) *n* **1** the seaward undercurrent following the breaking of a wave on the beach. **2** any strong undercurrent flowing in a different direction from the surface current.

undertrick (ˈʌndəˌtrɪk) *n Bridge.* a trick by which a declarer falls short of making his or her contract.

undervalue ❶ (ˌʌndəˈvæljuː) *vb* **undervalues, undervaluing, undervalued.** (*tr*) to value at too low a level or price.
▸ˌ**underˌvalu'ation** *n* ▸ˌ**under'valuer** *n*

undervest (ˈʌndəˌvest) *n Brit.* another name for **vest** (sense 1).

underwater ❶ (ˈʌndəˈwɔːtə) *adj* **1** being, occurring, or going under the surface of the water, esp. the sea: *underwater exploration.* **2** *Naut.* below the water line of a vessel. ◆ *adv* **3** beneath the surface of the water.

under way ❶ *adj* (*postpositive*) **1** in progress; in operation: *the show was under way.* **2** *Naut.* in motion.

underwear ❶ (ˈʌndəˌwɛə) *n* clothing worn under the outer garments, usually next to the skin.

underweight ❶ (ˌʌndəˈweɪt) *adj* weighing less than is average, expected, or healthy.

underwent (ˌʌndəˈwent) *vb* the past tense of **undergo.**

underwhelm (ˌʌndəˈwelm) *vb* (*tr*) to make no positive impact on; disappoint. [C20: orig. a humorous coinage based on *overwhelm*]
▸ˌ**under'whelming** *adj*

underwing (ˈʌndəˌwɪŋ) *n* **1** the hind wing of an insect. **2** See **red underwing, yellow underwing.**

underwood (ˈʌndəˌwʊd) *n* a less common word for **undergrowth.**

underworld ❶ (ˈʌndəˌwɜːld) *n* **1a** criminals and their associates. **1b** (*as modifier*): *underworld connections.* **2** *Greek & Roman myth.* the regions below the earth's surface regarded as the abode of the dead. **3** the antipodes.

underwrite ❶ (ˈʌndəˌraɪt, ˌʌndəˈraɪt) *vb* **underwrites, underwriting, underwrote, underwritten.** (*tr*) **1** *Finance.* to undertake to purchase at an agreed price any unsold portion of (a public issue of shares, etc.). **2** to accept financial responsibility for (a commercial project or enterprise). **3** *Insurance.* **3a** to sign and issue (an insurance policy) thus accepting liability. **3b** to insure (a property or risk). **3c** to accept liability up to (a specified amount) in an insurance policy. **4** to write (words, a signature, etc.) beneath (other written matter). **5** to support.

underwriter (ˈʌndəˌraɪtə) *n* **1** a person or enterprise that underwrites public issues of shares, bonds, etc. **2a** a person or enterprise that underwrites insurance policies. **2b** an employee or agent of an insurance company who determines the premiums payable.

undesirable ❶ (ˌʌndɪˈzaɪərəbᵊl) *adj* **1** not desirable or pleasant; objectionable. ◆ *n* **2** a person or thing considered undesirable.
▸ˌ**undeˌsira'bility** *or* ˌ**unde'sirableness** *n* ▸ˌ**unde'sirably** *adv*

undetermined (ˌʌndɪˈtɜːmɪnd) *adj* **1** not yet resolved; undecided. **2** not known or discovered.

undies (ˈʌndɪz) *pl n Inf.* women's underwear.

undine (ˈʌndiːn) *n* any of various female water spirits. [C17: from NL *undina,* from L *unda* a wave]

undisputed world champion *n Boxing.* a boxer who holds the World Boxing Association and the World Boxing Council world championship titles simultaneously.

undistributed (ˌʌndɪˈstrɪbjʊtɪd) *adj* **1** *Logic.* (of a term) referring only to some members of the class designated by the term, as *doctors* in *some doctors are overworked.* **2** *Business.* (of a profit) not paid in dividends to the shareholders of a company but retained to help finance its trading.

undo ❶ (ʌnˈduː) *vb* **undoes, undoing, undid, undone.** (*mainly tr*) **1** (*also intr*) to untie, unwrap, or open or become untied, unwrapped, etc. **2** to reverse the effects of. **3** to cause the downfall of.

undoing ❶ (ʌnˈduːɪŋ) *n* **1** ruin; downfall. **2** the cause of downfall: *drink was his undoing.*

undone[1] ❶ (ʌnˈdʌn) *adj* not done or completed; unfinished.

undone[2] ❶ (ʌnˈdʌn) *adj* **1** ruined; destroyed. **2** unfastened; untied.

undoubted ❶ (ʌnˈdaʊtɪd) *adj* beyond doubt; certain or indisputable.
▸**un'doubtedly** *adv*

undreamed (ʌnˈdriːmd) *or* **undreamt** (ʌnˈdremt) *adj* (often foll. by *of*) not thought of, conceived, or imagined.

undress ❶ (ʌnˈdres) *vb* **1** to take off clothes from (oneself or another). **2** (*tr*) to strip of ornamentation. **3** (*tr*) to remove the dressing from (a wound). ◆ *n* **4** partial or complete nakedness. **5** informal or normal working clothes or uniform.

undressed (ʌnˈdrest) *adj* **1** partially or completely naked. **2** (of an animal hide) not fully processed. **3** (of food, esp. salad) not prepared with sauce or dressing.

undue ❶ (ʌnˈdjuː) *adj* **1** excessive or unwarranted. **2** unjust, improper, or illegal. **3** (of a debt, bond, etc.) not yet payable.

> **USAGE NOTE** The use of *undue* in sentences such as *there is no cause for undue alarm* is redundant and should be avoided.

THESAURUS

understood *adj* **2** = **implied**, implicit, inferred, tacit, unspoken, unstated **3** = **assumed**, accepted, axiomatic, presumed, taken for granted

understudy *n* **3, 4** = **stand-in**, double, fill-in, replacement, reserve, sub, substitute

undertake *vb* **1** = **agree**, bargain, commit oneself, contract, covenant, engage, guarantee, pledge, promise, stipulate, take upon oneself **2** = **take on**, attempt, begin, commence, embark on, endeavour, enter upon, set about, tackle, try

undertaker *n* = **funeral director**, mortician (*US*)

undertaking *n* **1** = **task**, affair, attempt, business, effort, endeavour, enterprise, game, operation, project, venture **2** = **promise**, assurance, commitment, pledge, solemn word, vow, word, word of honour

undertone *n* **1** = **murmur**, low tone, subdued voice, whisper **2** = **undercurrent**, atmosphere, feeling, flavour, hint, suggestion, tinge, touch, trace, vibes (*sl.*)

undervalue *vb* = **underrate**, depreciate, hold cheap, look down on, make light of, minimize, misjudge, misprize, set no store by, underestimate
Antonyms *vb* exaggerate, overestimate, overrate, overvalue

underwater *adj* **1** = **submerged**, submarine, sunken, undersea

under way *adj* **1** = **in progress**, afoot, begun, going on, in business, in motion, in operation, started

underwear *n* = **underclothes**, lingerie, smalls (*inf.*), underclothing, undergarments, underlinen, underthings, undies (*inf.*), unmentionables (*humorous*)

underweight *adj* = **skinny**, emaciated, half-starved, puny, skin and bone, undernourished, undersized

underworld *n* **1a** = **criminals**, criminal element, gangland (*inf.*), gangsters, organized crime **2** = **nether world**, abode of the dead, Hades, hell, infernal region, nether regions, the inferno

underwrite *vb* **1** = **finance**, back, fund, guarantee, insure, provide security, sponsor, subsidize **3a** = **sign**, countersign, endorse, initial, subscribe **5** = **support**, agree to, approve, consent, O.K. *or* okay, sanction

undesirable *adj* **1** = **objectionable**, disagreeable, disliked, distasteful, dreaded, for the birds (*inf.*), obnoxious, offensive, out of place, repugnant, strictly for the birds (*inf.*), (to be) avoided, unacceptable, unattractive, unpleasing, unpopular, unsavoury, unsuitable, unwanted, unwelcome, unwished-for
Antonyms *adj* acceptable, agreeable, appealing, attractive, desirable, inviting, pleasing, popular, welcome

undo *vb* **1** = **open**, disengage, disentangle, loose, loosen, unbutton, unclasp, unfasten, unlock, unstrap, untie, unwrap **2** = **reverse**, annul, cancel, invalidate, neutralize, nullify, offset, wipe out **3** = **ruin**, bring to naught, defeat, destroy, impoverish, mar, overturn, quash, shatter, subvert, undermine, upset, wreck

undoing *n* **1** = **ruin**, collapse, defeat, destruction, disgrace, downfall, humiliation, overthrow, overturn, reversal, ruination, shame **2** = **downfall**, affliction, blight, curse, fatal flaw, misfortune, the last straw, trial, trouble, weakness

undone[1] *adj* = **unfinished**, incomplete, left, neglected, not completed, not done, omitted, outstanding, passed over, unattended to, unfulfilled, unperformed
Antonyms *adj* accomplished, attended to, complete, done, finished, fulfilled, performed

undone[2] *adj* = **ruined**, betrayed, destroyed, forlorn, hapless, overcome, prostrate, wretched

undoubted *adj* = **certain**, acknowledged, definite, evident, incontrovertible, indisputable, indubitable, obvious, sure, undisputed, unquestionable, unquestioned

undoubtedly *adv* = **certainly**, assuredly, beyond a shadow of (a) doubt, beyond question, come hell or high water (*inf.*), definitely, doubtless, of course, surely, undeniably, unmistakably, unquestionably, without doubt

undress *vb* **1** = **strip**, disrobe, divest oneself of, peel off (*sl.*), shed, take off one's clothes ◆ *n* **4** = **nakedness**, deshabille, disarray, nudity

undue *adj* **1** = **excessive**, disproportionate, extravagant, extreme, immoderate, improper, in-

undulant ('ʌndjulənt) *adj Rare.* resembling waves; undulating.
▸**'undulance** *n*

undulant fever *n* another name for **brucellosis.** [C19: so called because the fever symptoms are intermittent]

undulate ❶ *vb* ('ʌndjuˌleɪt), **undulates, undulating, undulated. 1** to move or cause to move in waves or as if in waves. **2** to have or provide with a wavy form or appearance. ◆ *adj* ('ʌndjulɪt, -ˌleɪt). **3** having a wavy or rippled appearance, margin, or form: *an undulate leaf.* [C17: from L from *unda* a wave]
▸**'unduˌlator** *n* ▸**'undulatory** *adj*

undulation (ˌʌndju'leɪʃən) *n* **1** the act or an instance of undulating. **2** any wave or wavelike form, line, etc.

unduly ❶ (ʌn'djuːlɪ) *adv* excessively.

undying ❶ (ʌn'daɪɪŋ) *adj* unending; eternal.
▸**un'dyingly** *adv*

unearned (ʌn'ɜːnd) *adj* **1** not deserved. **2** not yet earned.

unearned income *n* income from property, investment, etc., comprising rent, interest, and dividends.

unearth ❶ (ʌn'ɜːθ) *vb* (*tr*) **1** to dig up out of the earth. **2** to reveal or discover, esp. by exhaustive searching.

unearthly ❶ (ʌn'ɜːθlɪ) *adj* **1** ghostly; eerie: *unearthly screams.* **2** heavenly; sublime: *unearthly music.* **3** ridiculous or unreasonable (esp. in **unearthly hour**).
▸**un'earthliness** *n*

uneasy ❶ (ʌn'iːzɪ) *adj* **1** (of a person) anxious; apprehensive. **2** (of a condition) precarious: *an uneasy truce.* **3** (of a thought, etc.) disquieting.
▸**un'ease** *n* ▸**un'easily** *adv* ▸**un'easiness** *n*

uneatable (ʌn'iːtəbᵊl) *adj* (of food) not fit or suitable for eating, esp. because it is rotten or unattractive.

uneconomic ❶ (ˌʌniːkə'nɒmɪk, ˌʌnɛkə-) *adj* not economic; not profitable.

uneconomical (ˌʌniːkə'nɒmɪkᵊl, -ɛkə-) *adj* not economical; wasteful.

unemployable (ˌʌnɪm'plɔɪəbᵊl) *adj* unable or unfit to keep a job.
▸**ˌunemˌployaˈbility** *n*

unemployed ❶ (ˌʌnɪm'plɔɪd) *adj* **1a** without remunerative employment; out of work. **1b** (*as collective n; preceded by the*): *the unemployed.* **2** not being used; idle.

unemployment (ˌʌnɪm'plɔɪmənt) *n* **1** the condition of being unemployed. **2** the number of unemployed workers, often as a percentage of the total labour force.

unemployment benefit *n* (in Britain, formerly) a regular payment to a person who is out of work: replaced by jobseeker's allowance in 1996. Informal term: **dole.**

unequal ❶ (ʌn'iːkwəl) *adj* **1** not equal in quantity, size, rank, value, etc. **2** (foll. by *to*) inadequate; insufficient. **3** not evenly balanced. **4** (of character, quality, etc.) irregular; inconsistent. **5** (of a contest, etc.) having competitors of different ability.

unequalled ❶ *or US* **unequaled** (ʌn'iːkwəld) *adj* not equalled; unrivalled; supreme.

unequivocal ❶ (ˌʌnɪ'kwɪvəkᵊl) *adj* not ambiguous; plain.
▸**ˌune'quivocally** *adv* ▸**ˌune'quivocalness** *n*

unerring ❶ (ʌn'ɜːrɪŋ) *adj* **1** not missing the mark or target. **2** consistently accurate; certain.
▸**un'erringly** *adv* ▸**un'erringness** *n*

UNESCO (juː'nɛskəʊ) *n acronym for* United Nations Educational, Scientific, and Cultural Organization.

uneven ❶ (ʌn'iːvən) *adj* **1** (of a surface, etc.) not level or flat. **2** spasmodic or variable. **3** not parallel, straight, or horizontal. **4** not fairly matched: *an uneven race.* **5** *Arch.* not equal.
▸**un'evenly** *adv* ▸**un'evenness** *n*

uneventful ❶ (ˌʌnɪ'vɛntfʊl) *adj* ordinary, routine, or quiet.
▸**ˌune'ventfully** *adv* ▸**ˌune'ventfulness** *n*

unexampled ❶ (ˌʌnɪg'zɑːmpᵊld) *adj* without precedent or parallel.

unexceptionable (ˌʌnɪk'sɛpʃənəbᵊl) *adj* beyond criticism or objection.
▸**ˌunex'ceptionably** *adv*

unexceptional ❶ (ˌʌnɪk'sɛpʃənᵊl) *adj* **1** usual, ordinary, or normal. **2** subject to or allowing no exceptions.
▸**ˌunex'ceptionally** *adv*

unexcited (ˌʌnɪk'saɪtɪd) *adj* **1** not aroused to pleasure, interest, agitation, etc. **2** (of an atom, molecule, etc.) remaining in its ground state.

unexpected ❶ (ˌʌnɪk'spɛktɪd) *adj* surprising or unforeseen.
▸**ˌunex'pectedly** *adv* ▸**ˌunex'pectedness** *n*

unfailing ❶ (ʌn'feɪlɪŋ) *adj* **1** not failing; unflagging. **2** continuous. **3** sure; certain.
▸**un'failingly** *adv* ▸**un'failingness** *n*

unfair ❶ (ʌn'fɛə) *adj* **1** characterized by inequality or injustice. **2** dishonest or unethical.
▸**un'fairly** *adv* ▸**un'fairness** *n*

unfaithful ❶ (ʌn'feɪθfʊl) *adj* **1** not true to a promise, vow, etc. **2** not true to a wife, husband, lover, etc., esp. in having sexual intercourse

THESAURUS

appropriate, inordinate, intemperate, needless, overmuch, too great, too much, uncalled-for, undeserved, unjustified, unnecessary, unseemly, unsuitable, unwarranted
Antonyms *adj* appropriate, due, fitting, justified, necessary, proper, suitable, well-considered

undulate *vb* **1** = **wave**, billow, heave, ripple, rise and fall, roll, surge, swell

unduly *adv* = **excessively**, disproportionately, extravagantly, immoderately, improperly, inordinately, out of all proportion, overly, overmuch, unjustifiably, unnecessarily, unreasonably
Antonyms *adv* duly, justifiably, moderately, ordinately, properly, proportionately, reasonably

undying *adj* = **eternal**, constant, continuing, deathless, everlasting, imperishable, indestructible, inextinguishable, infinite, perennial, permanent, perpetual, sempiternal (*literary*), undiminished, unending, unfading
Antonyms *adj* ephemeral, finite, fleeting, impermanent, inconstant, momentary, mortal, perishable, short-lived

unearth *vb* **1** = **dig up**, disinter, dredge up, excavate, exhume **2** = **discover**, bring to light, expose, ferret out, find, reveal, root up, turn up, uncover

unearthly *adj* **1** = **eerie**, eldritch (*poetic*), ghostly, haunted, nightmarish, phantom, preternatural, spectral, spooky (*inf.*), strange, supernatural, uncanny, weird **3** = **unreasonable**, abnormal, absurd, extraordinary, ridiculous, strange, ungodly (*inf.*), unholy (*inf.*)

uneasiness *n* **1-3** = **anxiety**, agitation, alarm, apprehension, apprehensiveness, disquiet, doubt, dubiety, misgiving, nervousness, perturbation, qualms, suspicion, trepidation, worry
Antonyms *n* calm, composure, cool, ease, peace, quiet, serenity

uneasy *adj* **1** = **anxious**, agitated, apprehensive, discomposed, disturbed, edgy, ill at ease, impatient, jittery (*inf.*), like a fish out of water, nervous, on edge, perturbed, restive, restless, troubled, twitchy (*inf.*), uncomfortable, unsettled, upset, wired (*sl.*), worried **2** = **precarious**, awkward, constrained, insecure, shaky, strained, tense, uncomfortable, unstable **3** = **disturbing**, bothering, dismaying, disquieting, troubling, upsetting, worrying
Antonyms *adj* ≠ **anxious**: at ease, calm, comfortable, relaxed, tranquil, unfazed (*inf.*), unflustered, unperturbed, unruffled

uneconomic *adj* = **unprofitable**, loss-making, nonpaying, non-profit-making, nonviable
Antonyms *adj* economic, money-making, productive, profitable, remunerative, viable

unemployed *adj* **1a** = **out of work**, idle, jobless, laid off, on the dole (*Brit. inf.*), out of a job, redundant, resting (*of an actor*), workless

unequal *adj* **1** = **different**, differing, disparate, dissimilar, not uniform, unlike, unmatched, variable, varying **2** *with* **to** = **inadequate for**, found wanting, insufficient for, not up to **3** = **disproportionate**, asymmetrical, ill-matched, irregular, unbalanced, uneven
Antonyms *adj* ≠ **different**: equal, equivalent, identical, like, matched, similar, uniform

unequalled *adj* = **incomparable**, beyond compare, inimitable, matchless, nonpareil, paramount, peerless, pre-eminent, second to none, supreme, transcendent, unmatched, unparalleled, unrivalled, unsurpassed, without equal

unequivocal *adj* = **clear**, absolute, black-and-white, certain, clear-cut, cut-and-dried (*inf.*), decisive, definite, direct, evident, explicit, incontrovertible, indubitable, manifest, plain, positive, straight, unambiguous, uncontestable, unmistakable
Antonyms *adj* ambiguous, doubtful, equivocal, evasive, indecisive, noncommittal, vague

unerring *adj* = **accurate**, certain, exact, faultless, impeccable, infallible, perfect, sure, unfailing

uneven *adj* **1** = **rough**, bumpy, not flat, not level, not smooth **2** = **variable**, broken, changeable, fitful, fluctuating, intermittent, irregular, jerky, patchy, spasmodic, unsteady **3** = **unbalanced**, asymmetrical, lopsided, not parallel, odd, out of true **4** = **unequal**, disparate, ill-matched, one-sided, unfair
Antonyms *adj* ≠ **rough**: even, flat, level, plane, smooth

uneventful *adj* = **humdrum**, boring, commonplace, dull, ho-hum, monotonous, ordinary, quiet, routine, tedious, unexceptional, unexciting, uninteresting, unmemorable, unremarkable, unvaried
Antonyms *adj* eventful, exceptional, exciting, interesting, memorable, momentous, remarkable

unexampled *adj* = **unprecedented**, unequalled, unheard-of, unique, unmatched, unparalleled

unexceptional *adj* **1** = **ordinary**, bog-standard (*Brit. & Irish sl.*), common or garden (*inf.*), commonplace, conventional, insignificant, mediocre, no great shakes (*inf.*), normal, nothing to write home about (*inf.*), pedestrian, run-of-the-mill, undistinguished, unimpressive, unremarkable, usual
Antonyms *adj* distinguished, exceptional, impressive, notable, noteworthy, outstanding, remarkable, significant, unusual

unexpected *adj* = **unforeseen**, abrupt, accidental, astonishing, chance, fortuitous, not bargained for, out of the blue, startling, sudden, surprising, unanticipated, unlooked-for, unpredictable
Antonyms *adj* anticipated, awaited, expected, foreseen, normal, planned, predictable

unfailing *adj* **1, 2** = **continuous**, bottomless, boundless, ceaseless, continual, endless, inexhaustible, never-failing, persistent, unflagging, unlimited **3** = **reliable**, certain, constant, dependable, faithful, infallible, loyal, staunch, steadfast, sure, tried and true, true
Antonyms *adj* ≠ **reliable**: disloyal, fallible, inconstant, uncertain, unfaithful, unreliable, unsure, untrustworthy

unfair *adj* **1** = **biased**, arbitrary, bigoted, discriminatory, inequitable, one-sided, partial, partisan, prejudiced, unjust **2** = **unscrupulous**, crooked (*inf.*), dishonest, dishonourable, uncalled-for, unethical, unprincipled, unsporting, unwarranted, wrongful
Antonyms *adj* ≠ **unscrupulous**: ethical, fair, honest, just, principled, scrupulous

unfaithful *adj* **1** = **disloyal**, deceitful, faithless, false, false-hearted, perfidious, recreant (*arch.*), traitorous, treacherous, treasonable, unreliable, untrustworthy **2** = **faithless**, adulterous, fickle, inconstant, two-timing (*inf.*), unchaste, untrue

DICTIONARY

with someone else. **3** inaccurate; untrustworthy: *unfaithful copy.* **4** *Obs.* not having religious faith.
▸**un'faithfully** *adv* ▸**un'faithfulness** *n*

unfamiliar Ⓣ (ˌʌnfəˈmɪljə) *adj* **1** not known or experienced; strange. **2** (*postpositive;* foll. by *with*) not familiar.
▸**unfamiliarity** (ˌʌnfəˌmɪlɪˈærɪtɪ) *n* ▸**un,fa'miliarly** *adv*

unfasten Ⓣ (ʌnˈfɑːsᵊn) *vb* to undo, untie, or open or become undone, untied, or opened.

unfathered (ʌnˈfɑːðəd) *adj* **1** having no known father. **2** of unknown or uncertain origin.

unfathomable Ⓣ (ʌnˈfæðəməbᵊl) *adj* **1** incapable of being fathomed; immeasurable. **2** incomprehensible.
▸**un'fathomableness** *n* ▸**un'fathomably** *adv*

unfavourable Ⓣ *or US* **unfavorable** (ʌnˈfeɪvərəbᵊl) *adj* not favourable; adverse or inauspicious.
▸**un'favourably** *or US* **un'favorably** *adv*

unfazed (ʌnˈfeɪzd) *adj Inf.* not disconcerted; unperturbed.

unfeeling Ⓣ (ʌnˈfiːlɪŋ) *adj* **1** without sympathy; callous. **2** without physical feeling or sensation.
▸**un'feelingly** *adv* ▸**un'feelingness** *n*

unfinished Ⓣ (ʌnˈfɪnɪʃt) *adj* **1** incomplete or imperfect. **2** (of paint, polish, varnish, etc.) without an applied finish; rough. **3** (of fabric) unbleached or not processed.

unfit Ⓣ (ʌnˈfɪt) *adj* **1** (*postpositive;* often foll. by *for*) unqualified, incapable, or incompetent: *unfit for military service.* **2** (*postpositive;* often foll. by *for*) unsuitable or inappropriate: *the ground was unfit for football.* **3** in poor physical condition. ◆ *vb* **unfits, unfitting, unfitted. 4** (*tr*) *Rare.* to render unfit.
▸**un'fitly** *adv* ▸**un'fitness** *n*

unfix (ʌnˈfɪks) *vb* (*tr*) **1** to unfasten, detach, or loosen. **2** to unsettle or disturb.

unflappable Ⓣ (ʌnˈflæpəbᵊl) *adj Inf.* hard to upset; calm; composed.
▸**un,flappa'bility** *n* ▸**un'flappably** *adv*

unfledged Ⓣ (ʌnˈflɛdʒd) *adj* **1** (of a young bird) not having developed adult feathers. **2** immature and undeveloped.

unflinching Ⓣ (ʌnˈflɪntʃɪŋ) *adj* not shrinking from danger, difficulty, etc.
▸**un'flinchingly** *adv*

unfold Ⓣ (ʌnˈfəʊld) *vb* **1** to open or spread out or be opened or spread out from a folded state. **2** to reveal or be revealed: *the truth unfolds.* **3** to develop or expand or be developed or expanded.
▸**un'folder** *n*

unfortunate Ⓣ (ʌnˈfɔːtʃənɪt) *adj* **1** causing or attended by misfortune. **2** unlucky or unhappy: *an unfortunate character.* **3** regrettable or unsuitable: *an unfortunate speech.* ◆ *n* **4** an unlucky person.
▸**un'fortunately** *adv*

unfounded Ⓣ (ʌnˈfaʊndɪd) *adj* **1** (of ideas, allegations, etc.) baseless; groundless. **2** not yet founded or established.
▸**un'foundedly** *adv* ▸**un'foundedness** *n*

unfranked income (ʌnˈfræŋkt) *n* any income from an investment that does not qualify as franked investment income.

unfreeze (ʌnˈfriːz) *vb* **unfreezes, unfreezing, unfroze, unfrozen. 1** to thaw or cause to thaw. **2** (*tr*) to relax governmental restrictions on (wages, prices, credit, etc.) or on the manufacture or sale of (goods, etc.).

unfriended (ʌnˈfrɛndɪd) *adj Now rare.* without a friend or friends; friendless.

unfriendly Ⓣ (ʌnˈfrɛndlɪ) *adj* **unfriendlier, unfriendliest. 1** not friendly; hostile. **2** unfavourable or disagreeable. ◆ *adv* **3** *Rare.* in an unfriendly manner.
▸**un'friendliness** *n*

unfrock (ʌnˈfrɒk) *vb* (*tr*) to deprive (a person in holy orders) of ecclesiastical status.

unfunded debt (ʌnˈfʌndɪd) *n* a short-term floating debt not represented by bonds.

unfurl (ʌnˈfɜːl) *vb* to unroll, unfold, or spread out or be unrolled, unfolded, or spread out from a furled state.

ungainly Ⓣ (ʌnˈgeɪnlɪ) *adj* **ungainlier, ungainliest. 1** lacking grace when moving. **2** difficult to move or use; unwieldy. [C17: from UN-[1] + obs. or dialect *gainly* graceful]
▸**un'gainliness** *n*

ungodly Ⓣ (ʌnˈgɒdlɪ) *adj* **ungodlier, ungodliest. 1a** wicked, sinful. **1b** (*as collective n;* preceded by *the*): *the ungodly.* **2** *Inf.* unseemly; outrageous (esp. in **an ungodly hour**).
▸**un'godliness** *n*

ungovernable Ⓣ (ʌnˈgʌvənəbᵊl) *adj* not able to be disciplined, restrained, etc.: *an ungovernable temper.*
▸**un'governableness** *n* ▸**un'governably** *adv*

ungual (ˈʌŋgwəl) *adj* **1** of, relating to, or affecting the fingernails or toenails. **2** of or relating to an unguis. [C19: from L *unguis* nail]

unguarded Ⓣ (ʌnˈgɑːdɪd) *adj* **1** unprotected; vulnerable. **2** open; frank. **3** incautious.
▸**un'guardedly** *adv* ▸**un'guardedness** *n*

unguent (ˈʌŋgwənt) *n* a less common name for an **ointment.** [C15: from L, from *unguere* to anoint]

unguiculate (ʌŋˈgwɪkjʊlɪt, -ˌleɪt) *adj* **1** (of mammals) having claws or

THESAURUS

3 = **inaccurate,** distorted, erroneous, imperfect, imprecise, inexact, unreliable, untrustworthy
Antonyms *adj* ≠ **faithless:** constant, faithful ≠ **disloyal:** faithful, loyal, steadfast, true, trustworthy ≠ **inaccurate:** accurate, exact, perfect, precise, reliable

unfamiliar *adj* **1** = **strange,** alien, beyond one's ken, curious, different, little known, new, novel, out-of-the-way, unaccustomed, uncommon, unknown, unusual **2 unfamiliar with** = **unacquainted with,** a stranger to, inexperienced in, unaccustomed to, unconversant with, uninformed about, uninitiated in, unpractised in, unskilled at, unversed in
Antonyms *adj* ≠ **strange:** accustomed, average, common, commonplace, everyday, familiar, normal, unexceptional, usual, well-known ≠ **unacquainted with:** accustomed to, acquainted with, conversant with, experienced in, familiar with, knowledgeable about, well-versed in

unfasten *vb* = **undo,** detach, disconnect, let go, loosen, open, separate, unclasp, uncouple, unlace, unlock, unstrap, untie

unfathomable *adj* **1** = **immeasurable,** bottomless, unmeasured, unplumbed, unsounded **2** = **baffling,** abstruse, deep, esoteric, impenetrable, incomprehensible, indecipherable, inexplicable, profound, unknowable

unfavourable *adj* = **adverse,** bad, contrary, disadvantageous, ill-suited, inauspicious, infelicitous, inopportune, ominous, threatening, unfortunate, unlucky, unpromising, unpropitious, unseasonable, unsuited, untimely, untoward

unfeeling *adj* **1** = **callous,** apathetic, cold, cruel, hardened, hardhearted, heartless, inhuman, insensitive, pitiless, stony, uncaring, unsympathetic **2** = **numb,** insensate, insensible, sensationless
Antonyms *adj* ≠ **callous:** benevolent, caring, concerned, feeling, gentle, humane, kind, sensitive, sympathetic

unfinished *adj* **1** = **incomplete,** deficient, half-done, imperfect, in the making, lacking, unaccomplished, uncompleted, undone, unfulfilled, wanting **2** = **rough,** bare, crude, natural, raw, sketchy, unpolished, unrefined, unvarnished
Antonyms *adj* ≠ **rough:** finished, flawless, perfected, polished, refined, smooth, varnished

unfit *adj* **1** = **incapable,** ill-equipped, inadequate, incompetent, ineligible, no good, not cut out for, not equal to, not up to, unprepared, unqualified, untrained, useless **2** = **unsuitable,** ill-adapted, inadequate, inappropriate, ineffective, not designed, not fit, unsuited, useless **3** = **out of shape,** debilitated, decrepit, feeble, flabby, in poor condition, out of kelter, out of trim, unhealthy
Antonyms *adj* ≠ **incapable:** able, capable, competent, equipped, qualified, ready ≠ **unsuitable:** acceptable, adequate, appropriate, suitable ≠ **out of shape:** fit, healthy, in good condition, strong, sturdy, well

unflappable *adj Informal* = **imperturbable,** calm, collected, composed, cool, impassive, level-headed, not given to worry, self-possessed, unfazed (*inf.*), unruffled
Antonyms *adj* excitable, flappable, hot-headed, nervous, temperamental, twitchy (*inf.*), volatile

unfledged *adj* **2** = **inexperienced,** callow, green, immature, raw, undeveloped, untried, young

unflinching *adj* = **determined,** bold, constant, firm, immovable, resolute, stalwart, staunch, steadfast, steady, unfaltering, unshaken, unshrinking, unswerving, unwavering
Antonyms *adj* cowed, faltering, scared, shaken, shrinking, wavering

unfold *vb* **1** = **open,** disentangle, expand, flatten, spread out, straighten, stretch out, undo, unfurl, unravel, unroll, unwrap **2** = **reveal,** clarify, describe, disclose, divulge, explain, illustrate, make known, present, show, uncover **3** = **develop,** bear fruit, blossom, evolve, expand, grow, mature

unfortunate *adj* **1** = **disastrous,** adverse, calamitous, ill-fated, ill-starred, infelicitous, inopportune, ruinous, unfavourable, untimely, untoward **2** = **unlucky,** cursed, doomed, hapless, hopeless, luckless, out of luck, poor, star-crossed, unhappy, unprosperous, unsuccessful, wretched **3** = **regrettable,** deplorable, ill-advised, inappropriate, lamentable, unbecoming, unsuitable
Antonyms *adj* ≠ **disastrous:** auspicious, felicitous, fortuitous, fortunate, opportune, timely ≠ **unlucky:** fortunate, happy, lucky, successful ≠ **regrettable:** appropriate, becoming, unsuitable

unfounded *adj* **1** = **groundless,** baseless, fabricated, false, idle, spurious, trumped up, unjustified, unproven, unsubstantiated, vain, without basis, without foundation
Antonyms *adj* attested, confirmed, factual, justified, proven, substantiated, verified

unfriendly *adj* **1** = **hostile,** aloof, antagonistic, chilly, cold, disagreeable, distant, ill-disposed, inhospitable, not on speaking terms, quarrelsome, sour, surly, uncongenial, unneighbourly, unsociable **2** = **unfavourable,** alien, hostile, inauspicious, inhospitable, inimical, unpropitious
Antonyms *adj* ≠ **hostile:** affable, amiable, convivial, friendly, hospitable, sociable, warm ≠ **unfavourable:** auspicious, congenial, hospitable, propitious

ungainly *adj* **1** = **awkward,** clumsy, gangling, gawky, inelegant, loutish, lubberly, lumbering, slouching, uncoordinated, uncouth, ungraceful
Antonyms *adj* attractive, comely, elegant, graceful, pleasing

ungodly *adj* **1a** = **wicked,** blasphemous, corrupt, depraved, godless, immoral, impious, irreligious, profane, sinful, vile **2** *Informal* = **unreasonable,** dreadful, horrendous, intolerable, outrageous, unearthly, unholy (*inf.*), unseemly

ungovernable *adj* = **uncontrollable,** unmanageable, unruly, wild

unguarded *adj* **1** = **unprotected,** defenceless, open to attack, undefended, unpatrolled, vulnerable **2** = **frank,** artless, candid, direct, guileless, open, straightforward **3** = **careless,** foolhardy, heedless, ill-considered, impolitic, imprudent, incautious, indiscreet, rash, thoughtless, uncircumspect, undiplomatic, unthinking, unwary
Antonyms *adj* ≠ **careless:** cagey (*inf.*), careful, cautious, diplomatic, discreet, guarded, prudent, wary

nails. **2** (of petals) having a clawlike base. ◆ *n* **3** an unguiculate mammal. [C19: from NL *unguiculātus,* from L *unguiculus,* dim. of *unguis* nail]

unguis ('ʌŋgwɪs) *n, pl* **ungues** (-gwiːz). **1** a nail, claw, or hoof, or the part of the digit giving rise to it. **2** the clawlike base of a petal. [C18: from L]

ungulate ('ʌŋgjʊlɪt, -ˌleɪt) *n* any of a large group of mammals all of which have hooves: divided into odd-toed ungulates (see **perissodactyl**) and even-toed ungulates (see **artiodactyl**). [C19: from LL *ungulātus* having hooves, from *ungula* hoof]

unhallowed ❶ (ʌn'hæləʊd) *adj* **1** not consecrated or holy: *unhallowed ground.* **2** sinful.

unhand (ʌn'hænd) *vb* (*tr*) *Arch. or literary.* to release from the grasp.

unhappy ❶ (ʌn'hæpɪ) *adj* **unhappier, unhappiest. 1** not joyful; sad or depressed. **2** unfortunate or wretched: *an unhappy fellow.* **3** tactless or inappropriate: *an unhappy remark.*
▸**un'happily** *adv* ▸**un'happiness** *n*

UNHCR *abbrev. for* United Nations High Commissioner for Refugees.

unhealthy ❶ (ʌn'hɛlθɪ) *adj* **unhealthier, unhealthiest. 1** characterized by ill health; sick. **2** characteristic of, conducive to, or resulting from ill health: *an unhealthy complexion.* **3** morbid or unwholesome. **4** *Inf.* dangerous; risky.
▸**un'healthily** *adv* ▸**un'healthiness** *n*

unheard (ʌn'hɜːd) *adj* **1** not heard; not perceived by the ear. **2** not listened to: *his warning went unheard.* **3** *Arch.* unheard-of.

unheard-of ❶ *adj* **1** previously unknown: *an unheard-of actress.* **2** without precedent: *an unheard-of treatment.* **3** highly offensive: *unheard-of behaviour.*

unhinge ❶ (ʌn'hɪndʒ) *vb* **unhinges, unhinging, unhinged.** (*tr*) **1** to remove (a door, etc.) from its hinges. **2** to derange or unbalance (a person, his mind, etc.). **3** to disrupt or unsettle (a process or state of affairs).

unholy ❶ (ʌn'həʊlɪ) *adj* **unholier, unholiest. 1** not holy or sacred. **2** immoral or depraved. **3** *Inf.* outrageous or unnatural: *an unholy alliance.*
▸**un'holiness** *n*

unhook (ʌn'hʊk) *vb* **1** (*tr*) to remove (something) from a hook. **2** (*tr*) to unfasten the hook of (a dress, etc.). **3** (*intr*) to become unfastened or be capable of unfastening: *the dress wouldn't unhook.*

unhorse (ʌn'hɔːs) *vb* **unhorses, unhorsing, unhorsed.** (*tr*) **1** (*usually passive*) to knock or throw from a horse. **2** to overthrow or dislodge, as from a powerful position.

unhouseled (ʌn'haʊzəld) *adj Arch.* not having received the Eucharist. [C16: from *un-* + obs. *housel* to administer the sacrament, from OE *hūsl* (n), *hūslian* (vb), from ?]

uni ('juːnɪ) *n Inf.* short for **university.**

uni- *combining form.* consisting of, relating to, or having only one: *unilateral.* [from L *ūnus* one]

Uniat ('juːnɪˌæt) *or* **Uniate** ('juːnɪɪt, -ˌeɪt) *adj* **1** designating any of the Eastern Churches that retain their own liturgy but submit to papal authority. ◆ *n* **2** a member of one of these Churches. [C19: from Russian *uniyat,* from Polish *unja* union, from LL *ūniō;* see UNION]
▸**'Uniˌatism** *n*

uniaxial (ˌjuːnɪ'æksɪəl) *adj* **1** (esp. of plants) having an unbranched main axis. **2** (of a crystal) having only one direction along which double refraction of light does not occur.

unicameral (ˌjuːnɪ'kæmərəl) *adj* of or characterized by a single legislative chamber.
▸ˌ**uni'cameralism** *n* ▸ˌ**uni'cameralist** *n* ▸ˌ**uni'camerally** *adv*

UNICEF ('juːnɪˌsɛf) *n acronym for* United Nations Children's Fund (formerly, United Nations International Children's Emergency Fund).

unicellular (ˌjuːnɪ'sɛljʊlə) *adj* (of organisms, such as protozoans and certain algae) consisting of a single cell.
▸ˌ**uniˌcellu'larity** *n*

unicorn ('juːnɪˌkɔːn) *n* **1** an imaginary creature usually depicted as a white horse with one long spiralled horn growing from its forehead. **2** *Old Testament.* a two-horned animal: mistranslation in the Authorized Version of the original Hebrew. [C13: from OF, from L *ūnicornis* one-horned, from *ūnus* one + *cornu* a horn]

unicycle ('juːnɪˌsaɪkᵊl) *n* a one-wheeled vehicle driven by pedals, esp. one used in a circus, etc. Also called: **monocycle.** [from UNI- + CYCLE, on the model of TRICYCLE]
▸**'uniˌcyclist** *n*

unidirectional (ˌjuːnɪdɪ'rɛkʃənᵊl) *adj* having, moving in, or operating in only one direction.

UNIDO (juː'niːdəʊ) *n acronym for* United Nations Industrial Development Organization.

Unification Church *n* a religious sect founded in 1954 by Sun Myung Moon (born 1920), S Korean industrialist and religious leader.

unified field theory *n* any theory capable of describing in one set of equations the properties of gravitational fields, electromagnetic fields, and strong and weak nuclear interactions. No satisfactory theory has yet been found. See also **grand unified theory.**

uniform ❶ ('juːnɪˌfɔːm) *n* **1** a prescribed identifying set of clothes for the members of an organization, such as soldiers or schoolchildren. **2** a single set of such clothes. **3** a characteristic feature of some class or group. ◆ *adj* **4** unchanging in form, quality, etc.: *a uniform surface.* **5** alike or like: *a line of uniform toys.* ◆ *vb* (*tr*) **6** to fit out (a body of soldiers, etc.) with uniforms. **7** to make uniform. [C16: from L *ūniformis,* from *ūnus* one + *forma* shape]
▸**'uniˌformly** *adv* ▸**'uniˌformness** *n*

Uniform Business Rate *n* a local tax in the UK paid by businesses, based on a local valuation of their premises and a rate fixed by central government that applies throughout the country. Abbrev.: **UBR.**

uniformitarianism (ˌjuːnɪˌfɔːmɪ'tɛərɪəˌnɪzəm) *n* the concept that the earth's surface was shaped in the past by gradual processes, such as erosion, and by small sudden changes, such as earthquakes, rather than by sudden divine acts, such as Noah's flood.
▸ˌ**uniˌformi'tarian** *n, adj*

uniformity ❶ (ˌjuːnɪ'fɔːmɪtɪ) *n, pl* **uniformities. 1** a state or condition in which everything is regular, homogeneous, or unvarying. **2** lack of diversity or variation.

unify ❶ ('juːnɪˌfaɪ) *vb* **unifies, unifying, unified.** to make or become one; unite. [C16: from Med. L *ūnificāre,* from L *ūnus* one + *facere* to make]
▸**'uniˌfiable** *adj* ▸ˌ**unifi'cation** *n* ▸**'uniˌfier** *n*

unilateral (ˌjuːnɪ'lætərəl) *adj* **1** of, having, affecting, or occurring on only one side. **2** involving or performed by only one party of several: *unilateral disarmament.* **3** *Law.* (of contracts, obligations, etc.) made by, affecting, or binding one party only. **4** *Bot.* having or designating parts situated or turned to one side of an axis.
▸ˌ**uni'lateralism** *n* ▸ˌ**uni'laterally** *adv*

Unilateral Declaration of Independence *n* a declaration of independence made by a dependent state without the assent of the protecting state. Abbrev.: **UDI.**

unimpeachable ❶ (ˌʌnɪm'piːtʃəbᵊl) *adj* unquestionable as to honesty, truth, etc.
▸ˌ**unim'peachably** *adv*

unimproved (ˌʌnɪm'pruːvd) *adj* **1** not improved or made better. **2** (of land) not cleared, drained, cultivated, etc. **3** neglected; unused: *unimproved resources.*

THESAURUS

unhallowed *adj* **1** = **unconsecrated,** not sacred, unblessed, unholy, unsanctified **2** = **wicked,** damnable, evil, godless, irreverent, profane, sinful

unhappiness *n* **1, 2** = **sadness,** blues, dejection, depression, despondency, discontent, dissatisfaction, gloom, heartache, low spirits, melancholy, misery, sorrow, wretchedness

unhappy *adj* **1** = **sad,** blue, crestfallen, dejected, depressed, despondent, disconsolate, dispirited, down, downcast, down in the dumps (*inf.*), gloomy, long-faced, low, melancholy, miserable, mournful, sorrowful **2** = **unlucky,** cursed, hapless, ill-fated, ill-omened, luckless, unfortunate, wretched **3** = **inappropriate,** awkward, clumsy, gauche, ill-advised, ill-timed, inept, infelicitous, injudicious, malapropos, tactless, unsuitable, untactful
Antonyms *adj* ≠ **sad:** cheerful, chirpy (*inf.*), content, exuberant, genial, good-humoured, happy, joyful, light-hearted, overjoyed, over the moon (*inf.*), satisfied ≠ **unlucky:** fortunate, lucky ≠ **inappropriate:** apt, becoming, prudent, suitable, tactful

unhealthy *adj* **1** = **sick,** ailing, delicate, feeble, frail, infirm, in poor health, invalid, poorly (*inf.*), sickly, unsound, unwell, weak **2** = **harmful,** deleterious, detrimental, insalubrious, insanitary, noisome, noxious, unwholesome **3** = **unwholesome,** bad, baneful (*arch.*), corrupt, corrupting, degrading, demoralizing, morbid, negative, undesirable
Antonyms ≠ **sick:** fit, healthy, robust, well *adj* ≠ **unwholesome:** desirable, moral, positive ≠ **harmful:** beneficial, good, healthy, salubrious, salutary, wholesome

unheard-of *adj* **1** = **obscure,** little known, undiscovered, unfamiliar, unknown, unregarded, unremarked, unsung **2** = **unprecedented,** ground-breaking, inconceivable, never before encountered, new, novel, singular, unbelievable, undreamed of, unexampled, unique, unusual **3** = **shocking,** disgraceful, extreme, offensive, outlandish, outrageous, preposterous, unacceptable, unthinkable

unhinge *vb* **1** = **detach,** disconnect, disjoint, dislodge, remove **2** = **unbalance,** confound, confuse, craze, dement, derange, disorder, distemper (*arch.*), drive out of one's mind, madden, unsettle

unholy *adj* **2** = **evil,** base, corrupt, depraved, dishonest, heinous, immoral, iniquitous, irreligious, profane, sinful, ungodly, vile, wicked **3** *Informal* = **outrageous,** appalling, awful, dreadful, horrendous, shocking, unearthly, ungodly (*inf.*), unnatural, unreasonable
Antonyms *adj* ≠ **evil:** devout, faithful, godly, holy, pious, religious, saintly, virtuous

unification *n* = **union,** alliance, amalgamation, coalescence, coalition, combination, confederation, federation, fusion, merger, uniting

uniform *n* **1** = **outfit,** costume, dress, garb, habit, livery, regalia, regimentals, suit ◆ *adj* **4** = **unvarying,** consistent, constant, equable, even, regular, smooth, unbroken, unchanging, undeviating **5** = **alike,** equal, identical, like, same, selfsame, similar
Antonyms *adj* ≠ **unvarying:** changeable, changing, deviating, inconsistent, irregular, uneven, varying

uniformity *n* **1** = **regularity,** constancy, evenness, homogeneity, invariability, sameness, similarity **2** = **monotony,** drabness, dullness, flatness, lack of diversity, sameness, tedium

unify *vb* = **unite,** amalgamate, bind, bring together, combine, confederate, consolidate, federate, fuse, join, merge
Antonyms *vb* alienate, disconnect, disjoin, disunite, divide, separate, sever, split

unimpeachable *adj* = **beyond question,** above reproach, beyond criticism, blameless, faultless, impeccable, irreproachable, perfect, squeaky-clean, unassailable, unblemished, unchallengeable, unexceptionable, unquestionable
Antonyms *adj* blameworthy, faulty, imperfect, reprehensible, reproachable, shameful

unincorporated business (ˌʌnɪnˈkɔːpəreɪtɪd) *n* a privately owned business, often owned by one person who has unlimited liability as the business is not legally registered as a company.

uninterested ❶ (ʌnˈɪntrɪstɪd) *adj* indifferent.
▸**unˈinterestedly** *adv* ▸**unˈinterestedness** *n*

USAGE NOTE See at **disinterested.**

union ❶ (ˈjuːnjən) *n* **1** the condition of being united, the act of uniting, or a conjunction formed by such an act. **2** an association, alliance, or confederation of individuals or groups for a common purpose, esp. political. **3** agreement or harmony. **4** short for **trade union. 5** the act or state of marriage or sexual intercourse. **6** a device on a flag representing union, such as another flag depicted in the top left corner. **7** a device for coupling pipes. **8** (*often cap.*) **8a** an association of students at a university or college formed to look after the students' interests. **8b** the building or buildings housing the facilities of such an organization. **9** *Maths.* a set containing all members of two given sets. Symbol: ∪ **10** (in 19th-century England) a number of parishes united for the administration of poor relief. **11** *Textiles.* a piece of cloth or fabric consisting of two different kinds of yarn. **12** (*modifier*) of or related to a union, esp. a trade union. [C15: from Church L *ūniō* oneness, from L *ūnus* one]

Union (ˈjuːnjən) *n* **the. 1** *Brit.* **1a** the union of England and Wales from 1543. **1b** the union of the English and Scottish crowns (1603–1707). **1c** the union of England and Scotland from 1707. **1d** the political union of Great Britain and Ireland (1801–1920). **1e** the union of Great Britain and Northern Ireland from 1921. **2** *US.* **2a** the United States of America. **2b** the northern states of the US during the Civil War. **2c** (*as modifier*): *Union supporters.*

union catalogue *n* a catalogue listing every publication held at cooperating libraries.

Union flag *n* the national flag of the United Kingdom, being a composite design composed of Saint George's Cross (England), Saint Andrew's Cross (Scotland), and Saint Patrick's Cross (Ireland). Often called: **Union Jack.**

unionism (ˈjuːnjəˌnɪzəm) *n* **1** the principles of trade unions. **2** adherence to the principles of trade unions. **3** the principle or theory of any union.
▸**ˈunionist** *n, adj*

Unionist (ˈjuːnjənɪst) *n* **1** (*sometimes not cap.*) **1a** (before 1920) a supporter of the Union of all Ireland and Great Britain. **1b** (since 1920) a supporter of Union between Britain and Northern Ireland. **2** a supporter of the US federal Union, esp. during the Civil War. ◆ *adj* **3** of, resembling, or relating to Unionists.
▸**ˈUnionˌism** *n*

Unionist Party *n* (formerly, in Northern Ireland) the major Protestant political party, closely identified with the Union with Britain. See also **Ulster Democratic Unionist Party, Ulster Unionist Council.**

unionize *or* **unionise** (ˈjuːnjəˌnaɪz) *vb* **unionizes, unionizing, unionized** *or* **unionises, unionising, unionised. 1** to organize (workers) into a trade union. **2** to join or cause to join a trade union. **3** (*tr*) to subject to the rules or codes of a trade union.
▸ˌ**unioniˈzation** *or* ˌ**unioniˈsation** *n*

Union Jack *n* a common name for **Union flag.**

union pipes *pl n* another name for **uillean pipes.**

union shop *n* (formerly) an establishment whose employment policy is governed by a contract between employer and a trade union permitting the employment of nonunion labour only on the condition that such labour joins the union within a specified time period.

unipolar (ˌjuːnɪˈpəʊlə) *adj* **1** of, concerned with, or having a single magnetic or electric pole. **2** (of a nerve cell) having a single process. **3** (of a transistor) utilizing charge carriers of one polarity only, as in a field-effect transistor.
▸**unipolarity** (ˌjuːnɪpəʊˈlærɪtɪ) *n*

unique ❶ (juːˈniːk) *adj* **1** being the only one of a particular type. **2** without equal or like. **3** *Inf.* very remarkable. **4** *Maths.* **4a** leading to only one result: *the sum of two integers is unique.* **4b** having precisely one value: *the unique positive square root of 4 is 2.* [C17: via F from L *ūnicus* unparalleled, from *ūnus* one]
▸**uˈniquely** *adv* ▸**uˈniqueness** *n*

USAGE NOTE *Unique* is normally taken to describe an absolute state, i.e. one that cannot be qualified; thus something is either *unique* or *not unique*; it cannot be *rather unique* or *very unique.* However, *unique* is sometimes used informally to mean very remarkable or unusual and this makes it possible to use comparatives or intensifiers with it, although many people object to this use.

unisex (ˈjuːnɪˌsɛks) *adj* of or relating to clothing, a hairstyle, hairdressers, etc., that can be worn or used by either sex. [C20: from UNI- + SEX]

unisexual (ˌjuːnɪˈsɛksjʊəl) *adj* **1** of one sex only. **2** (of some organisms) having either male or female reproductive organs but not both.
▸ˌ**uniˌsexuˈality** *n* ▸ˌ**uniˈsexually** *adv*

unison ❶ (ˈjuːnɪsᵊn) *n* **1** *Music.* **1a** the interval between two sounds of identical pitch. **1b** (*modifier*) played or sung at the same pitch: *unison singing.* **2** complete agreement (esp. in **in unison**). [C16: from LL *ūnisonus,* from UNI- + *sonus* sound]
▸**uˈnisonous, uˈnisonal,** *or* **uˈnisonant** *adj*

unit ❶ (ˈjuːnɪt) *n* **1** a single undivided entity or whole. **2** any group or individual, esp. when regarded as a basic element of a larger whole. **3** a mechanical part or assembly of parts that performs a subsidiary function: *a filter unit.* **4** a complete system or establishment that performs a specific function: *a production unit.* **5** a subdivision of a larger military formation. **6** a standard amount of a physical quantity, such as length, mass, etc., multiples of which are used to express magnitudes of that physical quantity: *the second is a unit of time.* **7** the amount of a drug, vaccine, etc., needed to produce a particular effect. **8** a standard measure used in calculating alcohol intake and its effect. **9** the digit or position immediately to the left of the decimal point. **10** (*modifier*) having or relating to a value of one: *a unit vector.* **11** *NZ.* a self-propelled railcar. **12** *Austral. & NZ.* short for **home unit.** [C16: back formation from UNITY, ? on the model of *digit*]

unitarian (ˌjuːnɪˈtɛərɪən) *n* **1** a supporter of unity or centralization in politics. ◆ *adj* **2** of or relating to unity or centralization.

Unitarian (ˌjuːnɪˈtɛərɪən) *n* **1** a person who believes that God is one being and rejects the doctrine of the Trinity. **2** a member of the Church (**Unitarian Church**) that embodies this system of belief. ◆ *adj* **3** of or relating to Unitarians or Unitarianism.
▸ˌ**Uniˈtariaˌnism** *n*

unitary (ˈjuːnɪtərɪ, -trɪ) *adj* **1** of a unit or units. **2** based on or characterized by unity. **3** individual; whole.

unitary authority *n* (in Britain) a district administered by a single tier of local government.

unit character *n Genetics.* a character inherited as a single unit and dependent on a single gene.

unit cost *n* the actual cost of producing one article.

unite[1] ❶ (juːˈnaɪt) *vb* **unites, uniting, united. 1** to make or become an integrated whole or a unity. **2** to join, unify or be unified in purpose, action, beliefs, etc. **3** to enter or cause to enter into an association or alliance. **4** to adhere or cause to adhere; fuse. **5** (*tr*) to possess (qualities) in combination or at the same time: *he united charm with severity.* [C15: from LL *ūnīre,* from *ūnus* one]

unite[2] (ˈjuːnaɪt, juːˈnaɪt) *n* an English gold coin of the Stuart period, originally worth 20 shillings. [C17: from obs. *unite* joined, from the union of England & Scotland (1603)]

united ❶ (juːˈnaɪtɪd) *adj* **1** produced by two or more persons or things in combination or from their union or amalgamation: *a united effort.* **2** in agreement. **3** in association or alliance.
▸**uˈnitedly** *adv* ▸**uˈnitedness** *n*

United Empire Loyalist *n Canad. history.* an American colonist who settled in Canada during or after the War of American Independence because of loyalty to the British Crown.

United Kingdom overseas territory *n* any of the territories that are governed by the UK but lie outside the British Isles; many were formerly British **crown colonies:** includes Bermuda, Falkland Islands, Gibraltar, and Montserrat.

United Nations *n* (*functioning as sing or pl*) an international organization of independent states, with its headquarters in New York City, that was formed in 1945 to promote peace and international cooperation and security. Abbrev.: **UN.**

unitive (ˈjuːnɪtɪv) *adj* **1** tending to unite or capable of uniting. **2** characterized by unity.

unitize *or* **unitise** (ˈjuːnɪˌtaɪz) *vb* **unitizes, unitizing, unitized** *or* **unitises, uni-**

THESAURUS

uninterested *adj* = **indifferent,** apathetic, blasé, bored, distant, impassive, incurious, listless, unconcerned, uninvolved, unresponsive
Antonyms *adj* alert, concerned, curious, enthusiastic, interested, involved, keen, responsive

union *n* **1** = **joining,** amalgam, amalgamation, blend, combination, conjunction, fusion, mixture, synthesis, uniting **2** = **alliance,** association, Bund, coalition, confederacy, confederation, federation, league **3** = **agreement,** accord, concord, concurrence, harmony, unanimity, unison, unity **5** = **intercourse,** coition, coitus, copulation, coupling, marriage, matrimony, nookie (*sl.*), rumpy-pumpy (*sl.*), the other (*inf.*), wedlock

unique *adj* **1** = **single,** lone, one and only, only, solitary, sui generis **2** = **unparalleled,** incomparable, inimitable, matchless, nonpareil, peerless, unequalled, unexampled, unmatched, unrivalled, without equal

unison *n* **2** = **agreement,** accord, accordance, concert, concord, cooperation, harmony, unanimity, unity
Antonyms *n* disagreement, discord, disharmony, dissension, dissidence, dissonance

unit *n* **1** = **item,** entity, module, piece, portion, whole **2** = **part,** component, constituent, element, member, section, segment **4** = **system,** assembly **5** = **section,** detachment, group **6** = **measure,** measurement, quantity

unite[1] *vb* **1** = **join,** amalgamate, blend, coalesce, combine, consolidate, couple, fuse, incorporate, link, marry, meld, merge, unify, wed **2** = **cooperate,** ally, associate, band, close ranks, club together, collaborate, confederate, join forces, join together, league, pool, pull together
Antonyms *vb* ≠ **join:** break, detach, disunite, divide, part, separate, sever, split ≠ **cooperate:** break, divorce, part, separate, split

united *adj* **1** = **combined,** affiliated, allied, banded together, collective, concerted, in partnership, leagued, pooled, unified **2** = **in agreement,** agreed, in accord, like-minded, of like

tising, unitised. (*tr*) *Finance.* to convert (an investment trust) into a unit trust.
▸ **,uniti'zation** *or* **,uniti'sation** *n*
unit-linked policy *n* a life-assurance policy the benefits of which are directly in proportion to the number of units purchased on the policyholder's behalf.
unit of account *n* **1** *Econ.* the function of money that enables the user to keep accounts, value transactions, etc. **2** a monetary denomination used for accounting purposes, etc., but not necessarily corresponding to any real currency: *the ECU is the unit of account of the European Monetary Fund.* **3** the unit of currency of a country.
unit price *n* a price for foodstuffs, etc., stated or shown as the cost per unit, as per pound, per kilogram, per dozen, etc.
unit pricing *n* a system of pricing foodstuffs, etc., in which the cost of a single unit is shown to enable shoppers to see the advantage of buying multipacks.
unit trust *n Brit.* an investment trust that issues units for public sale, the holders of which are creditors and not shareholders with their interests represented by a trust company independent of the issuing agency. US and Canad. equivalent: **mutual fund.**
unity ❶ ('ju:nɪtɪ) *n, pl* **unities. 1** the state or quality of being one; oneness. **2** the act, state, or quality of forming a whole from separate parts. **3** something whole or complete that is composed of separate parts. **4** mutual agreement; harmony or concord: *the participants were no longer in unity.* **5** uniformity or constancy: *unity of purpose.* **6** *Maths.* **6a** the number or numeral one. **6b** a quantity assuming the value of one: *the area of the triangle was regarded as unity.* **6c** the element of a set producing no change in a number following multiplication. **7** any one of the three principles of dramatic structure by which the action of a play should be limited to a single plot (unity of action), a single location (unity of place), and a single day (unity of time). [C13: from OF *unité,* from L *ūnitās,* from *ūnus* one]
Univ. *abbrev. for* University.
univalent (,ju:nɪ'veɪlənt, ju:'nɪvələnt) *adj* **1** (of a chromosome during meiosis) not paired with its homologue. **2** *Chem.* another word for **monovalent.**
▸ **,uni'valency** *n*
univalve ('ju:nɪ,vælv) *Zool.* ◆ *adj* **1** relating to or possessing a mollusc shell that consists of a single piece (valve). ◆ *n* **2** a gastropod mollusc.
universal ❶ (,ju:nɪ'vɜ:s^{ə}l) *adj* **1** of or typical of the whole of mankind or of nature. **2** common to or proceeding from all in a particular group. **3** applicable to or affecting many individuals, conditions, or cases. **4** existing or prevailing everywhere. **5** applicable or occurring throughout or relating to the universe: *a universal constant.* **6** (esp. of a language) capable of being used and understood by all. **7** embracing or versed in many fields of knowledge, activity, interest, etc. **8** *Machinery.* designed or adapted for a range of sizes, fittings, or uses. **9** *Logic.* (of a statement or proposition) affirming or denying something about every member of a class, as in *all men are wicked.* Cf. **particular** (sense 6). **10** *Arch.* entire; whole. ◆ *n* **11** *Philosophy.* a general term or concept or the type such a term signifies. **12** *Logic.* a universal proposition, statement, or formula. **13** a characteristic common to every member of a particular culture or to every human being.

> **USAGE NOTE** The use of *more universal* as in *his writings have long been admired by fellow scientists, but his latest book should have more universal appeal* is acceptable in modern English usage.

universal class *or* **set** *n* (in Boolean algebra) the class containing all points and including all other classes.
universal gas constant *n* another name for **gas constant.**
universalism (,ju:nɪ'vɜ:sə,lɪzəm) *n* **1** a universal feature or characteristic. **2** another word for **universality.**
Universalism (,ju:nɪ'vɜ:sə,lɪzəm) *n* a system of religious beliefs maintaining that all men are predestined for salvation.
▸ **,Uni'versalist** *n, adj*
universality ❶ (,ju:nɪvɜ:'sælɪtɪ) *n* the state or quality of being universal.
universalize *or* **universalise** (,ju:nɪ'vɜ:sə,laɪz) *vb* **universalizes, universalizing, universalized** *or* **universalises, universalising, universalised.** (*tr*) to make universal.
▸ **,uni,versali'zation** *or* **,uni,versali'sation** *n*
universal joint *or* **coupling** *n* a form of coupling between two rotating shafts allowing freedom of movement in all directions.
universally ❶ (,ju:nɪ'vɜ:səlɪ) *adv* everywhere or in every case: *this principle applies universally.*
universal motor *n* an electric motor capable of working on either direct current or single-phase alternating current at approximately the same speed and output.
universal time *n* **1** (from 1928) name adopted internationally for Greenwich Mean Time (measured from Greenwich midnight), now split into several slightly different scales, one of which (UT1) is used by astronomers. Abbrev.: **UT. 2** Also called: **universal coordinated time.** an internationally agreed system for civil timekeeping introduced in 1960 and redefined in 1972 as an atomic timescale. Available from broadcast signals, it has a second equal to the International Atomic Time (TAI) second, the difference between UTC and TAI being an integral number of seconds with leap seconds inserted when necessary to keep it within 0.9 seconds of UT1. Abbrev.: **UTC.**
universe ❶ ('ju:nɪ,vɜ:s) *n* **1** *Astron.* the aggregate of all existing matter, energy, and space. **2** human beings collectively. **3** a province or sphere of thought or activity. [C16: from F, from L *ūniversum* the whole world, from *ūniversus* all together, from UNI- + *vertere* to turn]
universe of discourse *n Logic.* the complete range of objects, relations, ideas, etc., that are expressed or implied in a discussion.
university (,ju:nɪ'vɜ:sɪtɪ) *n, pl* **universities. 1** an institution of higher education having authority to award bachelors' and higher degrees, usually having research facilities. **2** the buildings, members, staff, or campus of a university. [C14: from OF, from Med. L *universitās* group of scholars, from LL: guild, body of men, from L: whole]
UNIX ('ju:nɪks) *n Trademark.* a multi-user operating system found on many types of computer.
unjust ❶ (ʌn'dʒʌst) *adj* not in accordance with accepted standards of fairness or justice; unfair.
▸ **un'justly** *adv* ▸ **un'justness** *n*
unkempt ❶ (ʌn'kɛmpt) *adj* **1** (of the hair) uncombed; dishevelled. **2** ungroomed; slovenly: *unkempt appearance.* [OE *uncembed;* from UN-[1] + *cembed,* p.p. of *cemban* to comb]
▸ **un'kemptly** *adv* ▸ **un'kemptness** *n*
unkind ❶ (ʌn'kaɪnd) *adj* lacking kindness; unsympathetic or cruel.
▸ **un'kindly** *adv* ▸ **un'kindness** *n*
unknowing (ʌn'nəʊɪŋ) *adj* **1** not knowing; ignorant. **2** (*postpositive;* often foll. by *of*) unaware (of).
▸ **un'knowingly** *adv*
unknown ❶ (ʌn'nəʊn) *adj* **1** not known, understood, or recognized. **2** not established, identified, or discovered: *an unknown island.* **3** not famous: *some unknown artist.* ◆ *n* **4** an unknown person, quantity, or thing. **5** *Maths.* a variable the value of which is to be discovered by solving an equation; a variable in a conditional equation.
▸ **un'knownness** *n*
Unknown Soldier *or* **Warrior** *n* (in various countries) an unidentified soldier who has died in battle and for whom a tomb is established as a memorial to the other unidentified dead of the nation's armed forces.
unlace (ʌn'leɪs) *vb* **unlaces, unlacing, unlaced.** (*tr*) **1** to loosen or undo the lacing of (shoes, etc.). **2** to unfasten or remove garments, etc., of (oneself or another) by or as if by undoing lacing.
unlawful assembly (ʌn'lɔ:fʊl) *n Law.* a meeting of three or more people with the intent of carrying out any unlawful purpose.
unlay (ʌn'leɪ) *vb* **unlays, unlaying, unlaid.** (*tr*) to untwist (a rope or cable) to separate its strands.
unleaded (ʌn'lɛdɪd) *adj* **1** (of petrol) containing a reduced amount of tetraethyl lead, in order to reduce environmental pollution. ◆ *n* **2** petrol containing a reduced amount of tetraethyl lead.
unlearn (ʌn'lɜ:n) *vb* **unlearns, unlearning, unlearnt** *or* **unlearned** (-'lɜ:nd). to try to forget (something learnt) or to discard (accumulated knowledge).

THESAURUS

mind, of one mind, of the same opinion, one, unanimous
unity *n* **1, 2** = **wholeness,** entity, integrity, oneness, singleness, undividedness, unification, union **4** = **agreement,** accord, assent, concord, concurrence, consensus, harmony, peace, solidarity, unanimity, unison
Antonyms *n* ≠ **wholeness:** disunity, division, heterogeneity, multiplicity, separation ≠ **agreement:** disagreement, discord, disunity, division, factionalism, ill will, independence, individuality, infighting, strife
universal *adj* **1-7** = **widespread,** all-embracing, catholic, common, ecumenical, entire, general, omnipresent, overarching, total, unlimited, whole, worldwide
universality *n* = **comprehensiveness,** all-inclusiveness, completeness, entirety, generality, generalization, totality, ubiquity
universally *adv* = **everywhere,** across the board, always, in all cases, in every instance, invariably, uniformly, without exception
universe *n* **1** = **cosmos,** creation, everything, macrocosm, nature, the natural world
unjust *adj* = **unfair,** biased, inequitable, one-sided, partial, partisan, prejudiced, undeserved, unjustified, unmerited, wrong, wrongful
Antonyms *adj* equitable, ethical, fair, impartial, just, justified, right, unbiased
unkempt *adj* **1** = **uncombed,** shaggy, tousled **2** = **untidy,** bedraggled, blowsy, disarranged, disarrayed, dishevelled, disordered, frowzy, messy, rumpled, scruffy, shabby, slatternly, sloppy (*inf.*), slovenly, sluttish, ungroomed
Antonyms *adj* ≠ **untidy:** neat, presentable, soigné *or* soignée, spruce, tidy, trim, well-groomed
unkind *adj* = **cruel,** hardhearted, harsh, inconsiderate, inhuman, insensitive, malicious, mean, nasty, spiteful, thoughtless, uncaring, uncharitable, unchristian, unfeeling, unfriendly, unsympathetic
Antonyms *adj* benevolent, caring, charitable, considerate, generous, kind, soft-hearted, sympathetic, thoughtful
unkindness *n* = **cruelty,** hardheartedness, harshness, ill will, inhumanity, insensitivity, malevolence, malice, maliciousness, meanness, spite, spitefulness, unfeeling
Antonyms *n* benevolence, charity, friendliness, generosity, goodwill, kindness, sympathy, thoughtfulness
unknown *adj* **1** = **hidden,** concealed, dark, mysterious, secret, unrecognized, unrevealed, untold **2** = **unidentified,** anonymous, beyond one's ken, nameless, uncharted, undiscovered, unexplored, unnamed **3** = **obscure,** humble, little known, undistinguished, unfamiliar, unheard-of, unrenowned, unsung
Antonyms *adj* ≠ **obscure:** celebrated, distin-

unlearned (ʌnˈlɜːnɪd) *adj* ignorant or untaught.
▸**unˈlearnedly** *adv*

unlearnt (ʌnˈlɜːnt) *or* **unlearned** (ʌnˈlɜːnd) *adj* **1** denoting knowledge or skills innately present and therefore not learnt. **2** not learnt or taken notice of: *unlearnt lessons.*

unleash ❶ (ʌnˈliːʃ) *vb* (*tr*) **1** to release from or as if from a leash. **2** to free from restraint.

unleavened (ʌnˈlɛvənd) *adj* (of bread, etc.) made from a dough containing no yeast or leavening.

unless (ʌnˈlɛs) *conj* (*subordinating*) except under the circumstances that; except on the condition that: *they'll sell it unless he hears otherwise.* [C14 *onlesse,* from *on* ON + *lesse* LESS]

unlettered (ʌnˈlɛtəd) *adj* uneducated; illiterate.

unlike ❶ (ʌnˈlaɪk) *adj* **1** not alike; dissimilar or unequal; different. ◆ *prep* **2** not like; not typical of: *unlike his father he lacks intelligence.*
▸**unˈlikeness** *n*

unlikely ❶ (ʌnˈlaɪklɪ) *adj* not likely; improbable.
▸**unˈlikeliness** *or* **unˈlikeliˌhood** *n*

unlimber (ʌnˈlɪmbə) *vb* **1** (*tr*) to disengage (a gun) from its limber. **2** to prepare (something) for use.

unlimited ❶ (ʌnˈlɪmɪtɪd) *adj* **1** without limits or bounds: *unlimited knowledge.* **2** not restricted, limited, or qualified: *unlimited power.*
▸**unˈlimitedly** *adv* ▸**unˈlimitedness** *n*

unlisted (ʌnˈlɪstɪd) *adj* **1** not entered on a list. **2** the US and Canad. word for **ex-directory.**

Unlisted Securities Market *n* a market on the London Stock Exchange for trading in shares of smaller companies, who do not wish to comply with the requirements for a full listing. Abbrev.: **USM.**

unload ❶ (ʌnˈləʊd) *vb* **1** to remove a load or cargo from (a ship, lorry, etc.). **2** to discharge (cargo, freight, etc.). **3** (*tr*) to relieve of a burden or troubles. **4** (*tr*) to give vent to (anxiety, troubles, etc.). **5** (*tr*) to get rid of or dispose of (esp. surplus goods). **6** (*tr*) to remove the charge of ammunition from (a firearm).
▸**unˈloader** *n*

unlock ❶ (ʌnˈlɒk) *vb* **1** (*tr*) to unfasten (a lock, door, etc.). **2** (*tr*) to release or let loose. **3** (*tr*) to provide the key to: *unlock a puzzle.* **4** (*intr*) to become unlocked.
▸**unˈlockable** *adj*

unlooked-for ❶ (ˌʌnˈlʊktfɔː) *adj* unexpected; unforeseen.

unloose (ʌnˈluːs) *or* **unloosen** *vb* **unlooses, unloosing, unloosed** *or* **unloosens, unloosening, unloosened.** (*tr*) **1** to set free; release. **2** to loosen or relax (a hold, grip, etc.). **3** to unfasten or untie.

unlovely (ʌnˈlʌvlɪ) *adj* unpleasant in appearance or character.
▸**unˈloveliness** *n*

unlucky ❶ (ʌnˈlʌkɪ) *adj* **1** characterized by misfortune or failure: *an unlucky chance.* **2** ill-omened; inauspicious: *an unlucky date.* **3** regrettable; disappointing.
▸**unˈluckily** *adv* ▸**unˈluckiness** *n*

unmake (ʌnˈmeɪk) *vb* **unmakes, unmaking, unmade.** (*tr*) **1** to undo or destroy. **2** to depose from office or authority. **3** to alter the nature of.

unman ❶ (ʌnˈmæn) *vb* **unmans, unmanning, unmanned.** (*tr*) **1** to cause to lose courage or nerve. **2** to make effeminate. **3** to remove the men from.

unmanly ❶ (ʌnˈmænlɪ) *adj* **1** not masculine or virile. **2** ignoble, cowardly, or dishonourable. ◆ *adv* **3** *Arch.* in an unmanly manner.
▸**unˈmanliness** *n*

unmanned (ʌnˈmænd) *adj* **1** lacking personnel or crew: *an unmanned ship.* **2** (of aircraft, spacecraft, etc.) operated by automatic or remote control. **3** uninhabited.

unmannered (ʌnˈmænəd) *adj* **1** without good manners; rude. **2** without mannerisms.

unmannerly ❶ (ʌnˈmænəlɪ) *adj* **1** lacking manners; discourteous. ◆ *adv* **2** *Arch.* rudely; discourteously.
▸**unˈmannerliness** *n*

unmask ❶ (ʌnˈmɑːsk) *vb* **1** to remove (the mask or disguise) from (someone or oneself). **2** to appear or cause to appear in true character.
▸**unˈmasker** *n*

unmeaning (ʌnˈmiːnɪŋ) *adj* **1** having no meaning. **2** showing no intelligence; vacant: *an unmeaning face.*
▸**unˈmeaningly** *adv* ▸**unˈmeaningness** *n*

unmeet (ʌnˈmiːt) *adj Literary or arch.* unsuitable.
▸**unˈmeetly** *adv* ▸**unˈmeetness** *n*

unmentionable ❶ (ʌnˈmɛnʃənəbᵊl) *adj* **a** unsuitable or forbidden as a topic of conversation. **b** (*as n*): *the unmentionable.*
▸**unˈmentionableness** *n* ▸**unˈmentionably** *adv*

unmentionables (ʌnˈmɛnʃənəbᵊlz) *pl n Chiefly humorous.* underwear.

unmerciful ❶ (ʌnˈmɜːsɪfʊl) *adj* **1** showing no mercy; relentless. **2** extreme or excessive.
▸**unˈmercifully** *adv* ▸**unˈmercifulness** *n*

unmindful ❶ (ʌnˈmaɪndfʊl) *adj* (*usually postpositive* and foll. by *of*) careless or forgetful.
▸**unˈmindfully** *adv* ▸**unˈmindfulness** *n*

unmissable (ʌnˈmɪsəbᵊl) *adj* (of a film, television programme, etc.) so good that it should not be missed.

unmistakable ❶ *or* **unmistakeable** (ˌʌnmɪsˈteɪkəbᵊl) *adj* not mistakable; clear or unambiguous.
▸**ˌunmisˈtakably** *or* **ˌunmisˈtakeably** *adv*

unmitigated ❶ (ʌnˈmɪtɪˌgeɪtɪd) *adj* **1** not diminished in intensity, severity, etc. **2** (*prenominal*) (intensifier): *an unmitigated disaster.*
▸**unˈmitiˌgatedly** *adv*

unmoral (ʌnˈmɒrəl) *adj* outside morality; amoral.
▸**unmorality** (ˌʌnməˈrælɪtɪ) *n* ▸**unˈmorally** *adv*

unmurmuring (ʌnˈmɜːmərɪŋ) *adj* not complaining.

unmuzzle (ʌnˈmʌzᵊl) *vb* **unmuzzles, unmuzzling, unmuzzled.** (*tr*) **1** to take the muzzle off (a dog, etc.). **2** to free from control or censorship.

unnatural ❶ (ʌnˈnætʃərəl) *adj* **1** contrary to nature; abnormal. **2** not in accordance with accepted standards of behaviour or right and wrong: *unnatural love.* **3** uncanny; supernatural: *unnatural phenomena.* **4** affected or forced: *an unnatural manner.* **5** inhuman or monstrous: *an unnatural crime.*
▸**unˈnaturally** *adv* ▸**unˈnaturalness** *n*

unnecessary ❶ (ʌnˈnɛsɪsərɪ) *adj* not necessary.
▸**unˈnecessarily** *adv* ▸**unˈnecessariness** *n*

THESAURUS

guished, familiar, known, recognized, renowned, well-known

unleash *vb* **1, 2 = release,** free, let go, let loose, unbridle, unloose, untie

unlike *adj* **= different,** as different as chalk and cheese (*inf.*), contrasted, dissimilar, distinct, divergent, diverse, ill-matched, incompatible, not alike, opposite, unequal, unrelated
Antonyms *adj* compatible, equal, like, matched, related, similar

unlikely *adj* **= improbable,** doubtful, faint, not likely, remote, slight, unimaginable

unlimited *adj* **1 = infinite,** boundless, countless, endless, extensive, great, illimitable, immeasurable, immense, incalculable, limitless, stellar (*inf.*), unbounded, vast **2 = total,** absolute, all-encompassing, complete, full, unconditional, unconstrained, unfettered, unqualified, unrestricted
Antonyms *adj* ≠ **infinite:** bounded, confined, finite, limited ≠ **total:** circumscribed, constrained, limited, restricted

unload *vb* **1, 2 = empty,** disburden, discharge, dump, lighten, off-load, relieve, unburden, unlade, unpack

unlock *vb* **1, 2 = open,** free, let loose, release, unbar, unbolt, undo, unfasten, unlatch

unlooked-for *adj* **= unexpected,** chance, fortuitous, out of the blue, surprise, surprising, unanticipated, undreamed of, unforeseen, unhoped-for, unpredicted, unthought-of

unlucky *adj* **1 = unfortunate,** cursed, disastrous, hapless, luckless, miserable, unhappy, unsuccessful, wretched **2 = ill-fated,** doomed, ill-omened, ill-starred, inauspicious, ominous, unfavourable, untimely
Antonyms *adj* ≠ **unfortunate:** blessed, favoured, fortunate, happy, lucky, prosperous

unman *vb* **1 = unnerve,** daunt, demoralize, discourage, dispirit, enervate, enfeeble, intimidate, psych out (*inf.*), weaken **2 = emasculate**

unmanly *adj* **1 = effeminate,** camp, feeble, sissy, soft (*inf.*), weak, womanish **2 = cowardly,** abject, chicken-hearted, craven, dishonourable, ignoble, weak-kneed (*inf.*), yellow (*inf.*)

unmannerly *adj* **1 = bad-mannered,** badly behaved, discourteous, disrespectful, ill-bred, ill-mannered, impolite, misbehaved, rude, uncivil, uncouth
Antonyms *adj* civil, courteous, mannerly, polite, respectful, well-behaved, well-bred, well-mannered

unmask *vb* **1, 2 = reveal,** bare, bring to light, disclose, discover, expose, lay bare, show up, uncloak, uncover, unveil

unmentionable *adj* **a = taboo,** disgraceful, disreputable, forbidden, frowned on, immodest, indecent, obscene, scandalous, shameful, shocking, unspeakable, unutterable, X-rated (*inf.*)

unmerciful *adj* **1 = merciless,** brutal, cruel, hard, heartless, implacable, inhumane, pitiless, relentless, remorseless, ruthless, uncaring, unfeeling, unsparing
Antonyms *adj* beneficent, caring, feeling, humane, merciful, pitying, sparing, tender-hearted

unmindful *adj* **= careless,** forgetful, heedless, inattentive, indifferent, lax, neglectful, negligent, oblivious, remiss, slack, unheeding
Antonyms *adj* alert, attentive, aware, careful, heedful, mindful, regardful, watchful

unmistakable *adj* **= clear,** blatant, certain, conspicuous, decided, distinct, evident, glaring, indisputable, manifest, obvious, palpable, patent, plain, positive, pronounced, sure, unambiguous, unequivocal
Antonyms *adj* ambiguous, dim, doubtful, equivocal, hidden, mistakable, obscure, uncertain, unclear, unsure

unmitigated *adj* **1 = unrelieved,** grim, harsh, intense, oppressive, persistent, relentless, unabated, unalleviated, unbroken, undiminished, unmodified, unqualified, unredeemed **2 = complete,** absolute, arrant, consummate, deep-dyed (*usually derogatory*), downright, out-and-out, outright, perfect, rank, sheer, thorough, thoroughgoing, utter

unnatural *adj* **1 = abnormal,** aberrant, anomalous, irregular, odd, perverse, perverted, unusual **3 = strange,** bizarre, extraordinary, freakish, outlandish, queer, supernatural, unaccountable, uncanny **4 = false,** affected, artificial, assumed, contrived, factitious, feigned, forced, insincere, laboured, mannered, phoney *or* phony (*inf.*), self-conscious, stagy, stiff, stilted, strained, studied, theatrical **5 = inhuman,** brutal, callous, cold-blooded, evil, fiendish, heartless, monstrous, ruthless, savage, unfeeling, wicked
Antonyms *adj* ≠ **strange, abnormal:** normal, ordinary, typical ≠ **false:** genuine, honest, natural, sincere, unaffected, unfeigned, unpretentious ≠ **inhuman:** caring, humane, loving, warm

unnecessary *adj* **= needless,** dispensable, expendable, inessential, nonessential, redundant, supererogatory, superfluous, surplus to requirements, uncalled-for, unneeded, unrequired, useless
Antonyms *adj* essential, indispensable, necessary, needed, required, vital

unnerve ⓘ (ʌnˈnɜːv) *vb* **unnerves, unnerving, unnerved.** (*tr*) to cause to lose courage, strength, confidence, self-control, etc.
unnumbered (ʌnˈnʌmbəd) *adj* **1** countless; innumerable. **2** not counted or assigned a number.
UNO *abbrev. for* United Nations Organization.
unoccupied ⓘ (ʌnˈɒkjʊˌpaɪd) *adj* **1** (of a building) without occupants. **2** unemployed or idle. **3** (of an area or country) not overrun by foreign troops.
unofficial ⓘ (ˌʌnəˈfɪʃəl) *adj* **1** not official or formal: *an unofficial engagement.* **2** not confirmed officially: *an unofficial report.* **3** (of a strike) not approved by the strikers' trade union.
▸**ˌunofˈficially** *adv*
unorganized *or* **unorganised** (ʌnˈɔːgəˌnaɪzd) *adj* **1** not arranged into an organized system, structure, or unity. **2** (of workers) not unionized. **3** nonliving; inorganic.
unowned (ʌnˈəʊnd) *adj* **1** unacknowledged. **2** without an owner.
unpack (ʌnˈpæk) *vb* **1** to remove the packed contents of (a case, trunk, etc.). **2** (*tr*) to take (something) out of a packed container. **3** (*tr*) to unload: *to unpack a mule.*
▸**unˈpacker** *n*
unpaged (ʌnˈpeɪdʒd) *adj* (of a book) having no page numbers.
unparalleled ⓘ (ʌnˈpærəˌlɛld) *adj* unmatched; unequalled.
unparliamentary (ˌʌnpɑːləˈmɛntərɪ) *adj* not consistent with parliamentary procedure or practice.
▸**ˌunparliaˈmentarily** *adv* ▸**ˌunparliaˈmentariness** *n*
unpeg (ʌnˈpɛg) *vb* **unpegs, unpegging, unpegged.** (*tr*) **1** to remove the peg from, esp. to unfasten. **2** to allow (prices, etc.) to rise and fall freely.
unpeople (ʌnˈpiːpᵊl) *vb* **unpeoples, unpeopling, unpeopled.** (*tr*) to empty of people.
unperson (ˈʌnpɜːsᵊn) *n* a person whose existence is officially denied or ignored.
unpick (ʌnˈpɪk) *vb* (*tr*) **1** to undo (the stitches) of (a piece of sewing). **2** to unravel or undo (a garment, etc.).
unpin (ʌnˈpɪn) *vb* **unpins, unpinning, unpinned.** (*tr*) **1** to remove a pin or pins from. **2** to unfasten by removing pins.
unpleasant ⓘ (ʌnˈplɛzᵊnt) *adj* not pleasant or agreeable.
▸**unˈpleasantly** *adv* ▸**unˈpleasantness** *n*
unplugged (ʌnˈplʌgd) *adj* (of a performer or performance of popular music) using acoustic rather than electric instruments: *Eric Clapton unplugged; an unplugged version of the song.*
unplumbed (ʌnˈplʌmd) *adj* **1** unfathomed; unsounded. **2** not understood in depth. **3** (of a building) having no plumbing.
unpolled (ʌnˈpəʊld) *adj* **1** not included in an opinion poll. **2** not having voted. **3** *Arch.* unshorn.
unpopular ⓘ (ʌnˈpɒpjʊlə) *adj* not popular with an individual or group of people.
▸**unpopularity** (ˌʌnpɒpjʊˈlærɪtɪ) *n* ▸**unˈpopularly** *adv*
unpractical (ʌnˈpræktɪkᵊl) *adj* another word for **impractical.**
▸**ˌunpractiˈcality** *n* ▸**unˈpractically** *adv*
unpractised *or US* **unpracticed** (ʌnˈpræktɪst) *adj* **1** without skill, training, or experience. **2** not used or done often or repeatedly. **3** not yet tested.
unprecedented ⓘ (ʌnˈprɛsɪˌdɛntɪd) *adj* having no precedent; unparalleled.
▸**unˈpreceˌdentedly** *adv*
unprejudiced ⓘ (ʌnˈprɛdʒʊdɪst) *adj* not prejudiced or biased; impartial.
▸**unˈprejudicedly** *adv*
unprincipled ⓘ (ʌnˈprɪnsɪpᵊld) *adj* lacking moral principles; unscrupulous.
▸**unˈprincipledness** *n*
unprintable (ʌnˈprɪntəbᵊl) *adj* unsuitable for printing for reasons of obscenity, libel, etc.
▸**unˈprintableness** *n* ▸**unˈprintably** *adv*
unprofessional ⓘ (ˌʌnprəˈfɛʃənᵊl) *adj* **1** contrary to the accepted code of conduct of a profession. **2** amateur. **3** not belonging to or having the required qualifications for a profession.
▸**ˌunproˈfessionally** *adv*
unprotected sex *n* an act of sexual intercourse or sodomy performed without the use of a condom thus involving the risk of sexually transmitted diseases.
unputdownable (ˌʌnpʊtˈdaʊnəbᵊl) *adj* (esp. of a novel) so gripping as to be read at one sitting.
unqualified ⓘ (ʌnˈkwɒlɪˌfaɪd) *adj* **1** lacking the necessary qualifications. **2** not restricted or modified: *an unqualified criticism.* **3** (*usually prenominal*) (intensifier): *an unqualified success.*
▸**unˈqualiˌfiable** *adj*
unquestionable ⓘ (ʌnˈkwɛstʃənəbᵊl) *adj* **1** indubitable or indisputable. **2** not admitting of exception: *an unquestionable ruling.*
▸**unˌquestionaˈbility** *n* ▸**unˈquestionably** *adv*
unquestioned (ʌnˈkwɛstʃənd) *adj* **1** accepted without question. **2** not admitting of doubt or question: *unquestioned power.* **3** not questioned or interrogated.
unquiet (ʌnˈkwaɪət) *Chiefly literary.* ◆ *adj* **1** characterized by disorder or tumult: *unquiet times.* **2** anxious; uneasy. ◆ *n* **3** a state of unrest.
▸**unˈquietly** *adv* ▸**unˈquietness** *n*
unquote (ʌnˈkwəʊt) *interj* **1** an expression used parenthetically to indicate that the preceding quotation is finished. ◆ *vb* **unquotes, unquoting, unquoted.** **2** to close (a quotation), esp. in printing.
unravel ⓘ (ʌnˈrævᵊl) *vb* **unravels, unravelling, unravelled** *or US* **unravels, unraveling, unraveled.** **1** (*tr*) to reduce (something knitted or woven) to separate strands. **2** (*tr*) to explain or solve: *the mystery was unravelled.* **3** (*intr*) to become unravelled.
unreactive (ˌʌnrɪˈæktɪv) *adj* (of a substance) not readily partaking in chemical reactions.
unread (ʌnˈrɛd) *adj* **1** (of a book, etc.) not yet read. **2** (of a person) having read little.
unreadable ⓘ (ʌnˈriːdəbᵊl) *adj* **1** illegible; undecipherable. **2** difficult or tedious to read.
▸**unˌreadaˈbility** *or* **unˈreadableness** *n*
unready (ʌnˈrɛdɪ) *adj* **1** not ready or prepared. **2** slow or hesitant to see or act.
▸**unˈreadily** *adv* ▸**unˈreadiness** *n*
unreal ⓘ (ʌnˈrɪəl) *adj* **1** imaginary or fanciful or seemingly so: *an unreal*

THESAURUS

unnerve *vb* = **intimidate**, confound, daunt, demoralize, disarm, disconcert, discourage, dishearten, dismay, dispirit, faze, fluster, frighten, psych out (*inf.*), rattle (*inf.*), shake, throw off balance, unhinge, unman, upset
Antonyms *vb* arm, brace, encourage, gee up, hearten, nerve, steel, strengthen, support
unoccupied *adj* **1** = **empty**, tenantless, uninhabited, untenanted, vacant **2** = **idle**, at a loose end, at leisure, disengaged, inactive, unemployed
unofficial *adj* = **unauthorized**, informal, off the record, personal, private, unconfirmed, wildcat
unparalleled *adj* = **unequalled**, beyond compare, consummate, exceptional, incomparable, matchless, peerless, rare, singular, superlative, unique, unmatched, unprecedented, unrivalled, unsurpassed, without equal
unpleasant *adj* = **nasty**, abhorrent, bad, disagreeable, displeasing, distasteful, horrid, ill-natured, irksome, objectionable, obnoxious, repulsive, troublesome, unattractive, unlikable *or* unlikeable, unlovely, unpalatable
Antonyms *adj* agreeable, congenial, delicious, good-natured, likable *or* likeable, lovely, nice, pleasant
unpleasantness *n* = **nastiness**, awfulness, disagreeableness, displeasure, dreadfulness, grimness, horridness, misery, trouble, ugliness, unacceptability, woe = **hostility**, abrasiveness, animosity, antagonism, argumentativeness, bad feeling, ill humour *or* will, malice, offensiveness, quarrelsomeness, rudeness, unfriendliness
Antonyms *n* ≠ **nastiness:** acceptability, agreeableness, amusement, congeniality, delectation, delight, enjoyment, pleasantness, pleasure ≠ **hostility:** friendliness, good humour *or* will, pleasantness
unpopular *adj* = **disliked**, avoided, detested, not sought out, out in the cold, out of favour, rejected, shunned, unattractive, undesirable, unloved, unwanted, unwelcome
Antonyms *adj* desirable, favoured, liked, loved, popular, wanted, welcome
unprecedented *adj* = **extraordinary**, abnormal, exceptional, freakish, ground-breaking, new, novel, original, remarkable, singular, unexampled, unheard-of, unparalleled, unrivalled, unusual
unprejudiced *adj* = **impartial**, balanced, even-handed, fair, fair-minded, just, nonpartisan, objective, open-minded, unbiased, uninfluenced
Antonyms *adj* biased, bigoted, influenced, narrow-minded, partial, prejudiced, unfair, unjust
unprincipled *adj* = **dishonest**, amoral, corrupt, crooked, deceitful, devious, dishonourable, immoral, sink, tricky, unconscionable, underhand, unethical, unprofessional, unscrupulous
Antonyms *adj* decent, ethical, honest, honourable, moral, righteous, scrupulous, upright, virtuous
unprofessional *adj* **1** = **unethical**, improper, lax, negligent, unfitting, unprincipled, unseemly, unworthy **3** = **amateurish**, amateur, cowboy (*inf.*), incompetent, inefficient, inexperienced, inexpert, slapdash, slipshod, untrained
Antonyms *adj* ≠ **amateurish:** adept, competent, efficient, experienced, expert, professional, skilful
unqualified *adj* **1** = **unfit**, ill-equipped, incapable, incompetent, ineligible, not equal to, not up to, unprepared **2** = **unconditional**, categorical, downright, outright, unmitigated, unreserved, unrestricted, without reservation **3** = **total**, absolute, arrant, complete, consummate, deep-dyed (*usually derogatory*), downright, out-and-out, outright, thorough, thoroughgoing, utter
unquestionable *adj* **1** = **certain**, absolute, beyond a shadow of doubt, clear, conclusive, definite, faultless, flawless, incontestable, incontrovertible, indisputable, indubitable, irrefutable, manifest, patent, perfect, self-evident, sure, undeniable, unequivocal, unmistakable
Antonyms *adj* ambiguous, doubtful, dubious, inconclusive, questionable, uncertain, unclear
unravel *vb* **1** = **undo**, disentangle, extricate, free, separate, straighten out, unknot, untangle, unwind **2** = **solve**, clear up, explain, figure out (*inf.*), get straight, get to the bottom of, interpret, make out, puzzle out, resolve, suss (out) (*sl.*), work out
unreadable *adj* **1** = **illegible**, crabbed, undecipherable **2** = **turgid**, badly written, dry as dust, heavy going
unreal *adj* **1** = **imaginary**, chimerical, dreamlike, fabulous, fanciful, fictitious, hypothetical, illusory, make-believe, mythical, phantasmagoric, storybook, visionary **2** = **insubstantial**, immaterial, impalpable, intangible, nebulous **3** = **fake**, artificial, false, insincere, mock, ostensible, pretended, seeming, sham
Antonyms *adj* ≠ **fake:** authentic, bona fide, genuine, real, realistic, sincere, true, veritable

situation. **2** having no actual existence or substance. **3** insincere or artificial.
▸**unreality** (ˌʌnrɪˈælɪtɪ) *n* ▸**un'really** *adv*

unreason (ʌnˈriːzᵊn) *n* **1** irrationality or madness. **2** something that lacks or is contrary to reason. **3** lack of order; chaos.

unreasonable ❶ (ʌnˈriːznəbᵊl) *adj* **1** immoderate: *unreasonable demands.* **2** refusing to listen to reason. **3** lacking judgment.
▸**un'reasonableness** *n* ▸**un'reasonably** *adv*

unreasoning (ʌnˈriːzənɪŋ) *adj* not controlled by reason; irrational.
▸**un'reasoningly** *adv*

unregenerate ❶ (ˌʌnrɪˈdʒɛnərɪt) *adj also* **unregenerated. 1** unrepentant; unreformed. **2** obstinately adhering to one's own views. ◆ *n* **3** an unregenerate person.
▸ˌ**unre'generacy** *n* ▸ˌ**unre'generately** *adv*

unrelenting ❶ (ˌʌnrɪˈlɛntɪŋ) *adj* **1** refusing to relent or take pity. **2** not diminishing in determination, speed, effort, force, etc.
▸ˌ**unre'lentingly** *adv* ▸ˌ**unre'lentingness** *n*

unreligious (ˌʌnrɪˈlɪdʒəs) *adj* **1** another word for **irreligious. 2** secular.
▸ˌ**unre'ligiously** *adv*

unremitting ❶ (ˌʌnrɪˈmɪtɪŋ) *adj* never slackening or stopping; unceasing; constant.
▸ˌ**unre'mittingly** *adv* ▸ˌ**unre'mittingness** *n*

unreserved ❶ (ˌʌnrɪˈzɜːvd) *adj* **1** without reserve; having an open manner. **2** without reservation. **3** not booked or bookable.
▸**unreservedly** (ˌʌnrɪˈzɜːvɪdlɪ) *adv* ▸ˌ**unre'servedness** *n*

unrest ❶ (ʌnˈrɛst) *n* **1** a troubled or rebellious state of discontent. **2** an uneasy or troubled state.

unriddle (ʌnˈrɪdᵊl) *vb* **unriddles, unriddling, unriddled.** (*tr*) to solve or puzzle out. [C16: from UN-[2] + RIDDLE[1]]
▸**un'riddler** *n*

unrig (ʌnˈrɪg) *vb* **unrigs, unrigging, unrigged. 1** (*tr*) to strip (a vessel) of standing and running rigging. **2** *Arch. or dialect.* to undress (someone or oneself).

unrighteous (ʌnˈraɪtʃəs) *adj* **1a** sinful; wicked. **1b** (*as collective n;* preceded by *the*): *the unrighteous.* **2** not fair or right; unjust.
▸**un'righteously** *adv* ▸**un'righteousness** *n*

unrip (ʌnˈrɪp) *vb* **unrips, unripping, unripped.** (*tr*) **1** to rip open. **2** *Obs.* to reveal; disclose.

unripe (ʌnˈraɪp) *or* **unripened** *adj* **1** not fully matured. **2** not fully prepared or developed; not ready.
▸**un'ripeness** *n*

unrivalled ❶ *or US* **unrivaled** (ʌnˈraɪvᵊld) *adj* having no equal; matchless.

unroll (ʌnˈrəʊl) *vb* **1** to open out or unwind (something rolled, folded, or coiled) or (of something rolled, etc.) to become opened out or unwound. **2** to make or become visible or apparent, esp. gradually; unfold.

unruffled ❶ (ʌnˈrʌfᵊld) *adj* **1** unmoved; calm. **2** still: *the unruffled seas.*
▸**un'ruffledness** *n*

unruly ❶ (ʌnˈruːlɪ) *adj* **unrulier, unruliest.** disposed to disobedience or indiscipline.
▸**un'ruliness** *n*

UNRWA (ˈʌnrə) *n acronym for* United Nations Relief and Works Agency.

unsaddle (ʌnˈsædᵊl) *vb* **unsaddles, unsaddling, unsaddled. 1** to remove the saddle from (a horse, mule, etc.). **2** (*tr*) to unhorse.

unsaddling enclosure *n* the area at a racecourse where horses are unsaddled after a race and often where awards are given to owners, trainers, and jockeys.

unsafe ❶ (ʌnˈseɪf) *adj* **1** not safe; perilous. **2** (of a criminal conviction) based on inadequate or false evidence.

unsaid ❶ (ʌnˈsɛd) *adj* not said or expressed; unspoken.

unsaturated (ʌnˈsætʃəˌreɪtɪd) *adj* **1** not saturated. **2** (of a chemical compound, esp. an organic compound) containing one or more double or triple bonds and thus capable of undergoing addition reactions. **3** (of a fat, esp. a vegetable fat) containing a high proportion of fatty acids having double bonds.
▸ˌ**unsatu'ration** *n*

unsavoury ❶ *or US* **unsavory** (ʌnˈseɪvərɪ) *adj* **1** objectionable or distasteful: *an unsavoury character.* **2** disagreeable in odour or taste.
▸**un'savourily** *or US* **un'savorily** *adv* ▸**un'savouriness** *or US* **un'savoriness** *n*

unsay (ʌnˈseɪ) *vb* **unsays, unsaying, unsaid.** (*tr*) to retract or withdraw (something said or written).

unscathed ❶ (ʌnˈskeɪðd) *adj* not harmed or injured.

unscramble (ʌnˈskræmbᵊl) *vb* **unscrambles, unscrambling, unscrambled.** (*tr*) **1** to resolve from confusion or disorderliness. **2** to restore (a scrambled message) to an intelligible form.
▸**un'scrambler** *n*

unscrew (ʌnˈskruː) *vb* **1** (*tr*) to remove a screw from (an object). **2** (*tr*) to loosen (a screw, lid, etc.) by rotating, usually in an anticlockwise direction. **3** (*intr*) (esp. of an engaged threaded part) to become loosened or separated.

unscripted (ʌnˈskrɪptɪd) *adj* (of a speech, play, etc.) not using or based on a script.

unscrupulous ❶ (ʌnˈskruːpjʊləs) *adj* without scruples; unprincipled.
▸**un'scrupulously** *adv* ▸**un'scrupulousness** *n*

unseal (ʌnˈsiːl) *vb* (*tr*) **1** to remove or break the seal of. **2** to free (something concealed or closed as if sealed): *to unseal one's lips.*

unsealed (ʌnˈsiːld) *adj Austral. & NZ.* (of a road) surfaced with road metal not bound by bitumen or other sealant.

unseam (ʌnˈsiːm) *vb* (*tr*) to open or undo the seam of.

unseasonable ❶ (ʌnˈsiːzənəbᵊl) *adj* **1** (esp. of the weather) inappropriate for the season. **2** untimely; inopportune.
▸**un'seasonableness** *n* ▸**un'seasonably** *adv*

unseat ❶ (ʌnˈsiːt) *vb* (*tr*) **1** to throw or displace from a seat, saddle, etc. **2** to depose from office or position.

unseeded (ʌnˈsiːdɪd) *adj* (of players in various sports) not assigned to a preferential position in the preliminary rounds of a tournament.

unseemly ❶ (ʌnˈsiːmlɪ) *adj* **1** not in good style or taste. **2** *Obs.* unattractive. ◆ *adv* **3** *Rare.* in an unseemly manner.
▸**un'seemliness** *n*

unseen ❶ (ʌnˈsiːn) *adj* **1** not observed or perceived; invisible. **2** (of passages of writing) not previously seen or prepared. ◆ *n* **3** *Chiefly Brit.* a

THESAURUS

unreasonable *adj* **1** = **excessive**, absurd, exorbitant, extortionate, extravagant, far-fetched, immoderate, irrational, preposterous, steep (*inf.*), too great, uncalled-for, undue, unfair, unjust, unwarranted **2** = **biased**, arbitrary, blinkered, capricious, erratic, headstrong, illogical, inconsistent, opinionated, quirky
Antonyms *adj* ≠ **excessive:** fair, just, justified, moderate, reasonable, temperate, warranted ≠ **biased:** fair-minded, flexible, open-minded

unregenerate *adj* **1, 2** = **unrepentant**, hardened, intractable, obdurate, obstinate, recalcitrant, refractory, self-willed, stubborn, unconverted, unreformed
Antonyms *adj* converted, reformed, regenerate, repentant

unrelenting *adj* **1** = **merciless**, cruel, implacable, inexorable, intransigent, pitiless, relentless, remorseless, ruthless, stern, tough, unsparing **2** = **steady**, ceaseless, constant, continual, continuous, endless, incessant, perpetual, unabated, unbroken, unremitting, unwavering

unremitting *adj* = **constant**, assiduous, continual, continuous, diligent, incessant, indefatigable, perpetual, relentless, remorseless, sedulous, unabated, unbroken, unceasing, unwavering, unwearied

unreserved *adj* **1** = **uninhibited**, demonstrative, extrovert, forthright, frank, free, open, open-hearted, outgoing, outspoken, unrestrained, unreticent **2** = **total**, absolute, complete, entire, full, unconditional, unlimited, unqualified, wholehearted, without reservation
Antonyms *adj* ≠ **uninhibited:** demure, inhibited, modest, reserved, restrained, reticent, shy, undemonstrative

unrest *n* **1** = **discontent**, agitation, disaffection, discord, dissatisfaction, dissension, protest, rebellion, sedition, strife, tumult, turmoil, upheaval **2** = **uneasiness**, agitation, anxiety, disquiet, distress, perturbation, restlessness, trepidation, worry
Antonyms *n* calm, contentment, peace, relaxation, rest, stillness, tranquillity

unrivalled *adj* = **unparalleled**, beyond compare, incomparable, matchless, nonpareil, peerless, supreme, unequalled, unexcelled, unmatched, unsurpassed, without equal

unruffled *adj* **1** = **calm**, collected, composed, cool, peaceful, placid, sedate, serene, tranquil, undisturbed, unfazed (*inf.*), unflustered, unmoved, unperturbed **2** = **smooth**, even, flat, level, unbroken

unruly *adj* = **uncontrollable**, disobedient, disorderly, fractious, headstrong, insubordinate, intractable, lawless, mutinous, obstreperous, rebellious, refractory, riotous, rowdy, turbulent, ungovernable, unmanageable, wayward, wild, wilful
Antonyms *adj* amenable, biddable, docile, governable, manageable, obedient, orderly, tractable

unsafe *adj* **1** = **dangerous**, hazardous, insecure, perilous, precarious, risky, threatening, treacherous, uncertain, unreliable, unsound, unstable
Antonyms *adj* certain, harmless, reliable, safe, secure, sound, stable, sure

unsaid *adj* = **unspoken**, left to the imagination, tacit, undeclared, unexpressed, unstated, unuttered, unvoiced

unsavoury *adj* **1** = **unpleasant**, distasteful, nasty, objectionable, obnoxious, offensive, repellent, repugnant, repulsive, revolting **2** = **unappetizing**, disagreeable, distasteful, nauseating, sickening, unpalatable
Antonyms *adj* ≠ **unappetizing:** agreeable, appetizing, palatable, pleasant, savoury, tasteful, tasty, toothsome

unscathed *adj* = **unharmed**, in one piece, safe, sound, unhurt, uninjured, unmarked, unscarred, unscratched, untouched, whole

unscrupulous *adj* = **unprincipled**, conscienceless, corrupt, crooked (*inf.*), dishonest, dishonourable, exploitative, immoral, improper, knavish, roguish, ruthless, sink, unconscientious, unconscionable, unethical
Antonyms *adj* ethical, honest, honourable, moral, principled, proper, scrupulous, upright

unseasonable *adj* **2** = **untimely**, ill-timed, inappropriate, inopportune, mistimed, out of keeping, unsuitable

unseat *vb* **1** = **throw**, unhorse, unsaddle **2** = **depose**, dethrone, discharge, dismiss, displace, oust, overthrow, remove

unseemly *adj* **1** = **improper**, discreditable, disreputable, inappropriate, indecorous, indelicate, in poor taste, out of keeping, out of place, unbecoming, unbefitting, undignified, unrefined, unsuitable
Antonyms *adj* acceptable, appropriate, becoming, decorous, fitting, proper, refined, seemly, suitable

unseen *adj* **1** = **hidden**, concealed, invisible, obscure, undetected, unnoticed, unobserved, unobtrusive, unperceived, veiled passage, not previously seen, that is presented to students for translation.

unselfish Ⓣ (ʌnˈsɛlfɪʃ) *adj* not selfish; generous.
▸**unˈselfishly** *adv* ▸**unˈselfishness** *n*

unsettle Ⓣ (ʌnˈsetᵊl) *vb* **unsettles, unsettling, unsettled. 1** (*usually tr*) to change or become changed from a fixed or settled condition. **2** (*tr*) to confuse or agitate (emotions, the mind, etc.).
▸**unˈsettlement** *n*

unsettled Ⓣ (ʌnˈsɛtᵊld) *adj* **1** lacking order or stability: *an unsettled era.* **2** unpredictable: *an unsettled climate.* **3** constantly changing or moving from place to place: *an unsettled life.* **4** (of controversy, etc.) not brought to an agreed conclusion. **5** (of debts, law cases, etc.) not disposed of.
▸**unˈsettledness** *n*

unsex (ʌnˈseks) *vb* (*tr*) *Chiefly literary.* to deprive (a person) of the attributes of his or her sex, esp. to make a woman more callous.

unshapen (ʌnˈʃeɪpᵊn) *adj* **1** having no definite shape; shapeless. **2** deformed; misshapen.

unsheathe (ʌnˈʃiːð) *vb* **unsheathes, unsheathing, unsheathed.** (*tr*) to draw or pull out (something, esp. a weapon) from a sheath.

unship (ʌnˈʃɪp) *vb* **unships, unshipping, unshipped. 1** to be or cause to be unloaded, discharged, or disembarked from a ship. **2** (*tr*) *Naut.* to remove from a regular place: *to unship oars.*

unsighted (ʌnˈsaɪtɪd) *adj* **1** not sighted. **2** not having a clear view. **3** (of a gun) not equipped with a sight.
▸**unˈsightedly** *adv*

unsightly Ⓣ (ʌnˈsaɪtlɪ) *adj* unpleasant or unattractive to look at; ugly.
▸**unˈsightliness** *n*

unskilful Ⓣ *or US* **unskillful** (ʌnˈskɪlfʊl) *adj* lacking dexterity or proficiency.
▸**unˈskilfully** *or US* **unˈskillfully** *adv* ▸**unˈskilfulness** *or US* **unˈskillfulness** *n*

unskilled Ⓣ (ʌnˈskɪld) *adj* **1** not having or requiring any special skill or training: *an unskilled job.* **2** having no skill; inexpert.

unsling (ʌnˈslɪŋ) *vb* **unslings, unslinging, unslung.** (*tr*) **1** to remove or release from a slung position. **2** to remove slings from.

unsnap (ʌnˈsnæp) *vb* **unsnaps, unsnapping, unsnapped.** (*tr*) to unfasten (the snap or catch) of (something).

unsnarl (ʌnˈsnɑːl) *vb* (*tr*) to free from a snarl or tangle.

unsociable Ⓣ (ʌnˈsəʊʃəbᵊl) *adj* **1** (of a person) disinclined to associate or fraternize with others. **2** unconducive to social intercourse: *an unsociable neighbourhood.*
▸**unˌsociaˈbility** *or* **unˈsociableness** *n*

unsocial (ʌnˈsəʊʃəl) *adj* **1** not social; antisocial. **2** (of the hours of work of certain jobs) falling outside the normal working day.

unsophisticated Ⓣ (ˌʌnsəˈfɪstɪˌkeɪtɪd) *adj* **1** lacking experience or worldly wisdom. **2** marked by a lack of refinement or complexity: *an unsophisticated machine.* **3** unadulterated or genuine.
▸**ˌunsoˈphistiˌcatedly** *adv* ▸**ˌunsoˈphistiˌcatedness** *or* **ˌunsoˌphistiˈcation** *n*

unsound Ⓣ (ʌnˈsaʊnd) *adj* **1** diseased or unstable: *of unsound mind.* **2** unreliable or fallacious: *unsound advice.* **3** lacking strength or firmness: *unsound foundations.* **4** of doubtful financial or commercial viability: *an unsound enterprise.*
▸**unˈsoundly** *adv* ▸**unˈsoundness** *n*

unsparing Ⓣ (ʌnˈspɛərɪŋ) *adj* **1** not sparing or frugal; lavish. **2** showing harshness or severity.
▸**unˈsparingly** *adv* ▸**unˈsparingness** *n*

unspeakable Ⓣ (ʌnˈspiːkəbᵊl) *adj* **1** incapable of expression in words: *unspeakable ecstasy.* **2** indescribably bad or evil. **3** not to be uttered: *unspeakable thoughts.*
▸**unˈspeakableness** *n* ▸**unˈspeakably** *adv*

unstable Ⓣ (ʌnˈsteɪbᵊl) *adj* **1** lacking stability, fixity, or firmness. **2** disposed to temperamental or psychological variability. **3** (of a chemical compound) readily decomposing. **4** *Physics.* **4a** (of an elementary particle) having a very short lifetime. **4b** spontaneously decomposing by nuclear decay: *an unstable nuclide.* **5** *Electronics.* (of an electrical circuit, etc.) having a tendency to self-oscillation.
▸**unˈstableness** *n* ▸**unˈstably** *adv*

unsteady Ⓣ (ʌnˈstɛdɪ) *adj* **1** not securely fixed: *an unsteady foothold.* **2** (of behaviour, etc.) erratic. **3** without regularity: *an unsteady rhythm.* **4** (of a manner of walking, etc.) precarious or staggering, as from intoxication.
▸**unˈsteadily** *adv* ▸**unˈsteadiness** *n*

unstep (ʌnˈstɛp) *vb* **unsteps, unstepping, unstepped.** (*tr*) *Naut.* to remove (a mast) from its step.

unstick (ʌnˈstɪk) *vb* **unsticks, unsticking, unstuck.** (*tr*) to free or loosen (something stuck).

unstop (ʌnˈstɒp) *vb* **unstops, unstopping, unstopped.** (*tr*) **1** to remove the stop or stopper from. **2** to free from any stoppage or obstruction. **3** to draw out the stops on (an organ).
▸**unˈstoppable** *adj* ▸**unˈstoppably** *adv*

unstopped (ʌnˈstɒpt) *adj* **1** not obstructed or stopped up. **2** *Phonetics.* denoting a speech sound for whose articulation the closure is not complete. **3** *Prosody.* (of verse) having the sense of the line carried over into the next. **4** (of an organ pipe or a string on a musical instrument) not stopped.

unstriated (ʌnˈstraɪˌeɪtɪd) *adj* (of muscle) composed of elongated cells that do not have striations; smooth.

unstring (ʌnˈstrɪŋ) *vb* **unstrings, unstringing, unstrung.** (*tr*) **1** to remove the strings of. **2** (of beads, etc.) to remove from a string. **3** to weaken emotionally (a person or his nerves).

unstriped (ʌnˈstraɪpt) *adj* (esp. of smooth muscle) not having stripes; unstriated.

unstructured (ʌnˈstrʌktʃəd) *adj* **1** without formal structure or systematic organization. **2** without a preformed shape; (esp. of clothes) loose; untailored.

unstrung (ʌnˈstrʌŋ) *adj* **1** emotionally distressed; unnerved. **2** (of a stringed instrument) with the strings detached.

unstuck (ʌnˈstʌk) *adj* **1** freed from being stuck, glued, fastened, etc. **2 come unstuck.** to suffer failure or disaster.

unstudied (ʌnˈstʌdɪd) *adj* **1** natural. **2** (foll. by *in*) without knowledge or training.

unsubstantial Ⓣ (ˌʌnsəbˈstænʃəl) *adj* **1** lacking weight or firmness. **2** (of an argument) of doubtful validity. **3** of no material existence.
▸**ˌunsubˌstantiˈality** *n* ▸**ˌunsubˈstantially** *adv*

unsung Ⓣ (ʌnˈsʌŋ) *adj* **1** not acclaimed or honoured: *unsung deeds.* **2** not yet sung.

THESAURUS

unselfish *adj* = **generous**, altruistic, charitable, devoted, disinterested, humanitarian, kind, liberal, magnanimous, noble, self-denying, selfless, self-sacrificing

unsettle *vb* **2** = **disturb**, agitate, bother, confuse, discompose, disconcert, disorder, faze, fluster, perturb, rattle (*inf.*), ruffle, throw (*inf.*), throw into confusion, throw into disorder, throw into uproar, throw off balance, trouble, unbalance, unnerve, upset

unsettled *adj* **1** = **unstable**, disorderly, insecure, shaky, unsteady **1** = **restless**, agitated, anxious, confused, disturbed, flustered, on edge, perturbed, restive, shaken, tense, troubled, uneasy, unnerved, wired (*sl.*) **2** = **inconstant**, changeable, changing, uncertain, unpredictable, variable **4** = **unresolved**, debatable, doubtful, moot, open, undecided, undetermined, up in the air **5** = **owing**, due, in arrears, outstanding, payable, pending

unsightly *adj* = **ugly**, disagreeable, hideous, horrid, repulsive, revolting (*inf.*), unattractive, unpleasant, unprepossessing
Antonyms *adj* agreeable, attractive, beautiful, comely, cute, handsome, pleasing, prepossessing, pretty

unskilful *adj* = **clumsy**, awkward, bungling, cowboy (*inf.*), fumbling, incompetent, inept, inexpert, maladroit, unhandy, unpractised, unworkmanlike

unskilled *adj* **2** = **unprofessional**, amateurish, cowboy (*inf.*), inexperienced, uneducated, unqualified, untalented, untrained
Antonyms *adj* adept, expert, masterly, professional, qualified, skilled, talented

unsociable *adj* **1** = **unfriendly**, chilly, cold, convivial, distant, hostile, inhospitable, introverted, reclusive, retiring, standoffish, uncongenial, unforthcoming, unneighbourly, unsocial, withdrawn
Antonyms *adj* congenial, convivial, friendly, gregarious, hospitable, neighbourly, outgoing, sociable

unsophisticated *adj* **1** = **natural**, artless, childlike, guileless, inexperienced, ingenuous, innocent, naive, unaffected, untutored, unworldly **2** = **simple**, plain, straightforward, uncomplex, uncomplicated, uninvolved, unrefined, unspecialized
Antonyms *adj* ≠ **simple:** advanced, complex, complicated, elegant, esoteric, intricate, sophisticated

unsound *adj* **1** = **unhealthy**, ailing, defective, delicate, deranged, diseased, frail, ill, in poor health, unbalanced, unhinged, unstable, unwell, weak **2** = **invalid**, defective, erroneous, fallacious, false, faulty, flawed, ill-founded, illogical, shaky, specious, unreliable, weak **3** = **unstable**, flimsy, insecure, not solid, rickety, shaky, tottering, unreliable, unsafe, unsteady, wobbly
Antonyms *adj* ≠ **unstable:** reliable, safe, solid, sound, stable, steady, strong, sturdy

unsparing *adj* **1** = **lavish**, abundant, bountiful, generous, liberal, munificent, open-handed, plenteous, prodigal, profuse, ungrudging, unstinting **2** = **severe**, cold-blooded, hard, harsh, implacable, inexorable, relentless, rigorous, ruthless, stern, stringent, uncompromising, unforgiving, unmerciful

unspeakable *adj* **1** = **indescribable**, beyond description, beyond words, inconceivable, ineffable, inexpressible, overwhelming, unbelievable, unimaginable, unutterable, wonderful **2** = **dreadful**, abominable, abysmal, appalling, awful, bad, evil, execrable, frightful, from hell (*inf.*), heinous, hellacious (*US sl.*), horrible, loathsome, monstrous, odious, repellent, shocking, too horrible for words

unstable *adj* **1** = **insecure**, not fixed, precarious, rickety, risky, shaky, tottering, unsettled, unsteady, wobbly **1** = **changeable**, fitful, fluctuating, inconstant, unpredictable, unsteady, variable, volatile **2** = **unpredictable**, capricious, changeable, erratic, inconsistent, irrational, temperamental, unreliable, untrustworthy, vacillating
Antonyms *adj* ≠ **changeable:** constant, predictable, stable, steady ≠ **unpredictable:** consistent, level-headed, rational, reliable, stable, trustworthy

unsteady *adj* **1** = **unstable**, infirm, insecure, precarious, reeling, rickety, shaky, tottering, treacherous, unsafe, wobbly **3** = **erratic**, changeable, flickering, flighty, fluctuating, inconstant, irregular, temperamental, unreliable, unsettled, vacillating, variable, volatile, wavering

unsubstantial *adj* **1** = **flimsy**, airy, fragile, frail, inadequate, light, slight, thin **2** = **unsound**, erroneous, full of holes, ill-founded, superficial, tenuous, unsupported, weak **3** = **immaterial**, dreamlike, fanciful, illusory, imaginary, impalpable, visionary

unsung *adj* **1** = **unacknowledged**, anonymous,

unsuspected (ˌʌnsəˈspɛktɪd) *adj* **1** not under suspicion. **2** not known to exist.
►**ˌunsusˈpectedly** *adv* ►**ˌunsusˈpectedness** *n*

unswerving Ⓣ (ʌnˈswɜːvɪŋ) *adj* not turning aside; constant.

untangle Ⓣ (ʌnˈtæŋgᵊl) *vb* **untangles, untangling, untangled.** (*tr*) **1** to free from a tangled condition. **2** to free from confusion.

untaught (ʌnˈtɔːt) *adj* **1** without training or education. **2** attained or achieved without instruction.

untenable Ⓣ (ʌnˈtɛnəbᵊl) *adj* **1** (of theories, etc.) incapable of being maintained or vindicated. **2** unable to be maintained against attack.
►**unˌtenaˈbility** *or* **unˈtenableness** *n* ►**unˈtenably** *adv*

unthinkable Ⓣ (ʌnˈθɪŋkəbᵊl) *adj* **1** not to be contemplated; out of the question. **2** unimaginable; inconceivable. **3** unreasonable; improbable.
►**unˈthinkably** *adv*

unthinking Ⓣ (ʌnˈθɪŋkɪŋ) *adj* **1** lacking thoughtfulness; inconsiderate. **2** heedless; inadvertent. **3** not thinking or able to think.
►**unˈthinkingly** *adv* ►**unˈthinkingness** *n*

unthread (ʌnˈθrɛd) *vb* (*tr*) **1** to draw out the thread or threads from (a needle, etc.). **2** to disentangle.

unthrone (ʌnˈθrəʊn) *vb* **unthrones, unthroning, unthroned.** (*tr*) a less common word for **dethrone.**

untidy Ⓣ (ʌnˈtaɪdɪ) *adj* **untidier, untidiest. 1** not neat; slovenly. ◆ *vb* **untidies, untidying, untidied. 2** (*tr*) to make untidy.
►**unˈtidily** *adv* ►**unˈtidiness** *n*

untie Ⓣ (ʌnˈtaɪ) *vb* **unties, untying, untied. 1** to unfasten or free (a knot or something that is tied) or (of a knot, etc.) to become unfastened. **2** (*tr*) to free from constraint or restriction.

until (ʌnˈtɪl) *conj* (*subordinating*) **1** up to (a time) that: *he laughed until he cried.* **2** (*used with a negative*) before (a time or event): *until you change, you can't go out.* ◆ *prep* **3** (often preceded by *up*) in or throughout the period before: *he waited until six.* **4** (*used with a negative*) earlier than; before: *he won't come until tomorrow.* [C13 *untill*; see TILL[1]]

> **USAGE NOTE** The use of *until such time as* (as in *industrial action will continue until such time as our demands are met*) is unnecessary and should be avoided: *industrial action will continue until our demands are met.* See also **till**[1].

untimely Ⓣ (ʌnˈtaɪmlɪ) *adj* **1** occurring before the expected, normal, or proper time: *an untimely death.* **2** inappropriate to the occasion, time, or season: *his joking at the funeral was most untimely.* ◆ *adv* **3** prematurely or inopportunely.
►**unˈtimeliness** *n*

unto (ˈʌntuː) *prep Arch.* to. [C13: from ON]

untogether (ˌʌntəˈgɛðə) *adj Sl.* incompetent or badly organized; mentally or emotionally unstable.

untold Ⓣ (ʌnˈtəʊld) *adj* **1** incapable of description: *untold suffering.* **2** incalculably great in number or quantity: *untold thousands.* **3** not told.

untouchable (ʌnˈtʌtʃəbᵊl) *adj* **1** lying beyond reach. **2** above reproach, suspicion, or impeachment. **3** unable to be touched. ◆ *n* **4** a member of the lowest class in India, whom those of the four main castes were formerly forbidden to touch.
►**unˌtouchaˈbility** *n*

untoward Ⓣ (ˌʌntəˈwɔːd) *adj* **1** characterized by misfortune or annoyance. **2** not auspicious; unfavourable. **3** unseemly. **4** out of the ordinary; out of the way. **5** *Arch.* perverse. **6** *Obs.* awkward.
►**ˌuntoˈwardly** *adv* ►**ˌuntoˈwardness** *n*

untrue Ⓣ (ʌnˈtruː) *adj* **1** incorrect or false. **2** disloyal. **3** diverging from a rule, standard, or measure; inaccurate.
►**unˈtruly** *adv*

untruss (ʌnˈtrʌs) *vb* **1** (*tr*) to release from or as if from a truss; unfasten. **2** *Obs.* to undress.

untruth Ⓣ (ʌnˈtruːθ) *n* **1** the state or quality of being untrue. **2** a statement, etc., that is not true.

untruthful Ⓣ (ʌnˈtruːθfʊl) *adj* **1** (of a person) given to lying. **2** diverging from the truth.
►**unˈtruthfully** *adv* ►**unˈtruthfulness** *n*

untuck (ʌnˈtʌk) *vb* to become or cause to become loose or not tucked in: *to untuck the blankets.*

untutored Ⓣ (ʌnˈtjuːtəd) *adj* **1** without formal education. **2** lacking sophistication or refinement.

unused Ⓣ *adj* **1** (ʌnˈjuːzd). not being or never having been made use of. **2** (ʌnˈjuːst). (*postpositive*; foll. by *to*) not accustomed or used (to something).

unusual Ⓣ (ʌnˈjuːʒʊəl) *adj* uncommon; extraordinary: *an unusual design.*
►**unˈusually** *adv*

unutterable Ⓣ (ʌnˈʌtərəbᵊl) *adj* incapable of being expressed in words.
►**unˈutterableness** *n* ►**unˈutterably** *adv*

unvarnished Ⓣ (ʌnˈvɑːnɪʃt) *adj* not elaborated upon or glossed; plain and direct: *the unvarnished truth.*

unveil Ⓣ (ʌnˈveɪl) *vb* **1** (*tr*) to remove the cover from, esp. in the ceremonial unveiling of a monument, etc. **2** to remove the veil from (one's own or another person's face). **3** (*tr*) to make (something concealed) known or public.

unveiling (ʌnˈveɪlɪŋ) *n* **1** a ceremony involving the removal of a veil covering a statue, etc., for the first time. **2** the presentation of something, esp. for the first time.

unvoice (ʌnˈvɔɪs) *vb* **unvoices, unvoicing, unvoiced.** (*tr*) *Phonetics.* **1** to pronounce without vibration of the vocal cords. **2** Also: **devoice.** to make (a voiced speech sound) voiceless.

unvoiced (ʌnˈvɔɪst) *adj* **1** not expressed or spoken. **2** articulated without vibration of the vocal cords; voiceless.

THESAURUS

disregarded, neglected, unacclaimed, unappreciated, uncelebrated, unhailed, unhonoured, unknown, unnamed, unrecognized

unswerving *adj* = **constant**, dedicated, devoted, direct, firm, resolute, single-minded, staunch, steadfast, steady, true, undeviating, unfaltering, unflagging, untiring, unwavering

untangle *vb* **1** = **disentangle**, extricate, unravel, unsnarl **2** = **solve**, clear up, explain, straighten out
Antonyms *vb* ≠ **disentangle:** enmesh, entangle, jumble, muddle, snarl, tangle ≠ **solve:** complicate, confuse, muddle, puzzle

untenable *adj* **1** = **unsustainable**, fallacious, flawed, groundless, illogical, indefensible, insupportable, shaky, unreasonable, unsound, weak
Antonyms *adj* defensible, justified, logical, rational, reasonable, sensible, sound, supportable, unarguable, uncontestable, valid, verifiable, well-grounded

unthinkable *adj* **1, 3** = **impossible**, absurd, illogical, improbable, not on (*inf.*), out of the question, preposterous, unlikely, unreasonable **2** = **inconceivable**, beyond belief, beyond the bounds of possibility, implausible, incredible, insupportable, unbelievable, unimaginable

unthinking *adj* **1** = **thoughtless**, blundering, inconsiderate, insensitive, rude, selfish, tactless, undiplomatic **2** = **unconscious**, careless, heedless, impulsive, inadvertent, instinctive, mechanical, negligent, oblivious, unmindful, unwitting
Antonyms *adj* ≠ **unconscious:** careful, conscious, deliberate, heedful, mindful, sensible, witting

untidy *adj* **1** = **messy**, bedraggled, chaotic, cluttered, disarrayed, disordered, higgledy-piggledy (*inf.*), jumbled, littered, muddled, muddly, mussy (*US inf.*), rumpled, shambolic, slatternly, slipshod, sloppy (*inf.*), slovenly, topsy-turvy, unkempt
Antonyms *adj* methodical, neat, orderly, presentable, ship-shape, spruce, systematic, tidy, well-kept

untie *vb* **1, 2** = **undo**, free, loosen, release, unbind, unbridle, unclasp, unfasten, unknot, unlace, unstrap

untimely *adj* **1** = **early**, premature, unseasonable **2** = **ill-timed**, awkward, badly timed, inappropriate, inauspicious, inconvenient, inopportune, mistimed, unfortunate, unsuitable
Antonyms *adj* ≠ **early:** seasonable, timely ≠ **ill-timed:** appropriate, auspicious, convenient, fortunate, opportune, suitable, welcome, well-timed

untold *adj* **1** = **indescribable**, inexpressible, undreamed of, unimaginable, unspeakable, unthinkable, unutterable **2** = **countless**, incalculable, innumerable, measureless, myriad, numberless, uncountable, uncounted, unnumbered **3** = **undisclosed**, hidden, private, secret, unknown, unpublished, unrecounted, unrelated, unrevealed

untoward *adj* **1** = **troublesome**, annoying, awkward, disastrous, ill-timed, inconvenient, inimical, irritating, unfortunate, vexatious **2** = **unfavourable**, adverse, contrary, inauspicious, inopportune, unlucky, untimely **3** = **unseemly**, improper, inappropriate, indecorous, out of place, unbecoming, unfitting, unsuitable

untrue *adj* **1** = **false**, deceptive, dishonest, erroneous, fallacious, inaccurate, incorrect, lying, misleading, mistaken, sham, spurious, untruthful, wrong **2** = **unfaithful**, deceitful, disloyal, faithless, false, forsworn, inconstant, perfidious, traitorous, treacherous, two-faced, untrustworthy
Antonyms *adj* ≠ **false:** accurate, correct, factual, right, true ≠ **unfaithful:** constant, dependable, faithful, honest, honourable, loyal

untruth *n* **1** = **untruthfulness**, deceitfulness, duplicity, falsity, inveracity (*rare*), lying, mendacity, perjury, truthlessness **2** = **lie**, deceit, fabrication, falsehood, falsification, fib, fiction, pork pie (*Brit. sl.*), porky (*Brit. sl.*), prevarication, story, tale, trick, whopper (*inf.*)

untruthful *adj* **1** = **dishonest**, crooked (*inf.*), deceitful, deceptive, dissembling, false, fibbing, hypocritical, lying, mendacious
Antonyms *adj* candid, honest, sincere, true, truthful, veracious

untutored *adj* **1** = **uneducated**, ignorant, illiterate, unlearned, unschooled, untrained, unversed **2** = **unsophisticated**, artless, inexperienced, simple, unpractised, unrefined

unused *adj* **1** = **unutilized**, available, extra, fresh, intact, left, leftover, new, pristine, remaining, unconsumed, unexhausted **2** *with* **to** = **unaccustomed to**, a stranger to, inexperienced in, new to, not ready for, not up to, unfamiliar with, unhabituated to

unusual *adj* = **extraordinary**, abnormal, atypical, bizarre, curious, different, exceptional, left-field (*inf.*), notable, odd, out of the ordinary, phenomenal, queer, rare, remarkable, singular, strange, surprising, uncommon, unconventional, unexpected, unfamiliar, unwonted
Antonyms *adj* average, banal, commonplace, conventional, everyday, familiar, normal, routine, traditional, typical, unremarkable, usual

unutterable *adj* = **indescribable**, beyond words, extreme, ineffable, overwhelming, unimaginable, unspeakable

unvarnished *adj* = **plain**, bare, candid, frank, honest, naked, pure, pure and simple, simple, sincere, stark, straightforward, unadorned, unembellished

unveil *vb* **3** = **reveal**, bare, bring to light, disclose, divulge, expose, lay bare, lay open, make known, make public, uncover
Antonyms *vb* cloak, conceal, cover, disguise, hide, mask, obscure, veil

unwaged (ʌn'weɪdʒd) *adj* of or denoting a person who is not receiving pay because of being unemployed or working in the home.
unwarrantable (ʌn'wɒrəntəbᵊl) *adj* incapable of vindication or justification.
▸**un'warrantableness** *n* ▸**un'warrantably** *adv*
unwarranted ❶ (ʌn'wɒrəntɪd) *adj* **1** lacking justification or authorization. **2** another word for **unwarrantable.**
unwary ❶ (ʌn'weərɪ) *adj* lacking caution or prudence.
▸**un'warily** *adv* ▸**un'wariness** *n*
unwearied (ʌn'wɪərɪd) *adj* **1** not abating or tiring. **2** not fatigued; fresh.
▸**un'weariedly** *adv* ▸**un'weariedness** *n*
unweighed (ʌn'weɪd) *adj* **1** (of quantities purchased, etc.) not measured for weight. **2** (of statements, etc.) not carefully considered.
unwell ❶ (ʌn'wel) *adj* (*postpositive*) not well; ill.
unwept (ʌn'wept) *adj* **1** not wept for or lamented. **2** *Rare.* (of tears) not shed.
unwholesome ❶ (ʌn'həʊlsəm) *adj* **1** detrimental to physical or mental health: *an unwholesome climate.* **2** morally harmful: *unwholesome practices.* **3** indicative of illness, esp. in appearance. **4** (esp. of food) of inferior quality.
▸**un'wholesomeness** *n*
unwieldy ❶ (ʌn'wi:ldɪ) *adj* **1** too heavy, large, or awkwardly shaped to be easily handled. **2** ungainly; clumsy.
▸**un'wieldily** *adv* ▸**un'wieldiness** *n*
unwilled (ʌn'wɪld) *adj* not intentional; involuntary.
unwilling ❶ (ʌn'wɪlɪŋ) *adj* **1** reluctant. **2** performed or said with reluctance.
▸**un'willingly** *adv* ▸**un'willingness** *n*
unwind ❶ (ʌn'waɪnd) *vb* **unwinds, unwinding, unwound. 1** to slacken, undo, or unravel or cause to slacken, undo, or unravel. **2** (*tr*) to disentangle. **3** to make or become relaxed: *he finds it hard to unwind.*
▸**un'windable** *adj*
unwise ❶ (ʌn'waɪz) *adj* lacking wisdom or prudence.
▸**un'wisely** *adv* ▸**un'wiseness** *n*
unwish (ʌn'wɪʃ) *vb* (*tr*) **1** to retract or revoke (a wish). **2** to desire (something) not to be or take place.
unwitting ❶ (ʌn'wɪtɪŋ) *adj* (*usually prenominal*) **1** not knowing or conscious. **2** not intentional; inadvertent. [OE *unwitende,* from UN-[1] + *witting,* present participle of *witan* to know]
▸**un'wittingly** *adv* ▸**un'wittingness** *n*
unwonted ❶ (ʌn'wəʊntɪd) *adj* **1** out of the ordinary; unusual. **2** (usually foll. by *to*) *Arch.* unaccustomed; unused.
▸**un'wontedly** *adv*
unworldly ❶ (ʌn'wɜ:ldlɪ) *adj* **1** not concerned with material values or pursuits. **2** lacking sophistication; naive. **3** not of this earth or world.
▸**un'worldliness** *n*
unworthy ❶ (ʌn'wɜ:ðɪ) *adj* **1** (often foll. by *of*) not deserving or worthy. **2** (often foll. by *of*) beneath the level considered befitting (to): *that remark is unworthy of you.* **3** lacking merit or value. **4** (of treatment) not warranted.
▸**un'worthily** *adv* ▸**un'worthiness** *n*
unwound (ʌn'waʊnd) *vb* the past tense and past participle of **unwind.**
unwrap (ʌn'ræp) *vb* **unwraps, unwrapping, unwrapped.** to remove the covering or wrapping from (something) or (of something wrapped) to have the covering come off.
unwritten ❶ (ʌn'rɪtᵊn) *adj* **1** not printed or in writing. **2** effective only through custom.
unwritten law *n* the law based upon custom, usage, and judicial decisions, as distinguished from the enactments of a legislature, orders or decrees in writing, etc.
unyoke (ʌn'jəʊk) *vb* **unyokes, unyoking, unyoked. 1** to release (an animal, etc.) from a yoke. **2** (*tr*) to set free; liberate. **3** (*tr*) to disconnect or separate.
unzip (ʌn'zɪp) *vb* **unzips, unzipping, unzipped.** to unfasten the zip of (a garment, etc.) or (of a zip or garment with a zip) to become unfastened: *her skirt unzipped as she sat down.*
up (ʌp) *prep* **1** indicating movement from a lower to a higher position: *climbing up a mountain.* **2** at a higher or further level or position in or on: *a shop up the road.* ◆ *adv* **3** (*often particle*) to an upward, higher, or erect position, esp. indicating readiness for an activity: *up and doing something.* **4** (*particle*) indicating intensity or completion of an action: *he tore up the cheque.* **5** to the place referred to or where the speaker is: *the man came up and asked the way.* **6a** to a more important place: *up to London.* **6b** to a more northerly place: *up to Scotland.* **6c** (of a member of some British universities) to or at university. **6d** in a particular part of the country: *up north.* **7** above the horizon: *the sun is up.* **8** appearing for trial: *up before the magistrate.* **9** having gained: *ten pounds up on the deal.* **10** higher in price: *coffee is up again.* **11** raised (for discussion, etc.): *the plan was up for consideration.* **12** taught: *well up in physics.* **13** (*functioning as imperative*) get, stand, etc., up: *up with you!* **14 all up with.** *Inf.* **14a** over; finished. **14b** doomed to die. **15 up with.** (*functioning as imperative*) wanting the beginning or continuation of: *up with the monarchy!* **16 something's up.** *Inf.* something strange is happening. **17 up against. 17a** touching. **17b** having to cope with: *look what we're up against now.* **18 up for.** as a candidate or applicant for: *he's up for re-election again.* **19 up to. 19a** devising or scheming: *she's up to no good.* **19b** dependent or incumbent upon: *the decision is up to you.* **19c** equal to (a challenge, etc.) or capable of (doing, etc.): *are you up to playing in the final?* **19d** as far as: *up to his waist in mud.* **19e** as many as: *up to two years' waiting time.* **f.** comparable with: *not up to your normal standard.* **20 up top.** *Inf.* in the head or mind. **21 up yours.** *Sl.* a vulgar expression of contempt or refusal. **22 what's up?** *Inf.* **22a** what is the matter? **22b** what is happening? ◆ *adj* **23** (*predicative*) of a high or higher position. **24** (*predicative*) out of bed: *the children aren't up yet.* **25** (*prenominal*) of or relating to a train or trains to a more important place or one regarded as higher: *the up platform.* **26** (*predicative*) over or completed: *their time was up.* **27** (*predicative*) beating one's opponent by a specified amount: *a goal up.* ◆ *vb* **ups, upping, upped. 28** (*tr*) to increase or raise. **29** (*intr;* foll. by *and* with a verb) *Inf.* to do (something) suddenly, etc.: *she upped and married someone else.* ◆ *n* **30** a high point (esp. in **ups and downs**). **31** *Sl.* another word (esp. US) for **upper** (sense 8). **32 on the up and up. 32a** trustworthy or honest. **32b** *Brit.* on the upward trend or movement: *our firm's on the up and up.* [OE *upp*]

> **USAGE NOTE** The use of *up* before *until* is redundant and should be avoided: *the talks will continue until* (not *up until*) *23rd March.*

up- *prefix* up, upper, or upwards: *uproot; upmost; upthrust; upgrade; uplift.*
up-anchor *vb* (*intr*) *Naut.* to weigh anchor.
up-and-coming ❶ *adj* promising continued or future success; enterprising.
up-and-down *adj* **1** moving or formed alternately upwards and downwards. ◆ *adv, prep* **up and down. 2** backwards and forwards (along).
up-and-over *adj* (of a door, etc.) opened by being lifted and moved into a horizontal position.

THESAURUS

unwarranted *adj* **1** = **unnecessary,** gratuitous, groundless, indefensible, inexcusable, uncalled-for, unjust, unjustified, unprovoked, unreasonable, wrong
unwary *adj* = **careless,** hasty, heedless, imprudent, incautious, indiscreet, rash, reckless, thoughtless, uncircumspect, unguarded, unwatchful
Antonyms *adj* cautious, chary, circumspect, discreet, guarded, prudent, wary, watchful
unwell *adj* = **ill,** ailing, at death's door, green about the gills, indisposed, in poor health, off colour, out of sorts, poorly (*inf.*), sick, sickly, under the weather (*inf.*), unhealthy
Antonyms *adj* fine, healthy, robust, sound, well
unwholesome *adj* **1** = **harmful,** deleterious, insalubrious, insanitary, junk (*inf.*), noxious, poisonous, tainted, unhealthy, unnourishing **2** = **wicked,** bad, corrupting, degrading, demoralizing, depraving, evil, immoral, maleficent, perverting **3** = **sickly,** anaemic, pale, pallid, pasty, wan
Antonyms *adj* ≠ **harmful:** beneficial, germ-free, healthy, hygienic, salubrious, sanitary, wholesome ≠ **wicked:** edifying, moral
unwieldy *adj* **1** = **awkward,** burdensome, cumbersome, inconvenient, unhandy, unmanageable **2** = **bulky,** clumsy, clunky (*inf.*), hefty, massive, ponderous, ungainly, weighty
unwilling *adj* **1** = **reluctant,** averse, demurring, disinclined, grudging, indisposed, laggard (*rare*), loath, not in the mood, opposed, resistant, unenthusiastic
Antonyms *adj* amenable, compliant, disposed, eager, enthusiastic, inclined, voluntary, willing
unwind *vb* **1, 2** = **unravel,** disentangle, slacken, uncoil, undo, unreel, unroll, untwine, untwist **3** = **relax,** calm down, let oneself go, loosen up, make oneself at home, mellow out, quieten down, sit back, slow down, take a break, take it easy, wind down
unwise *adj* = **foolish,** asinine, foolhardy, ill-advised, ill-considered, ill-judged, impolitic, improvident, imprudent, inadvisable, inane, indiscreet, injudicious, irresponsible, rash, reckless, senseless, short-sighted, silly, stupid
Antonyms *adj* discreet, judicious, politic, prudent, responsible, sensible, shrewd, wise
unwitting *adj* **1** = **unknowing,** ignorant, innocent, unaware, unconscious, unsuspecting **2** = **unintentional,** accidental, chance, inadvertent, involuntary, undesigned, unintended, unmeant, unplanned
Antonyms *adj* ≠ **unknowing:** conscious, deliberate, knowing, witting ≠ **unintentional:** deliberate, designed, intended, intentional, meant, planned
unwonted *adj* **1** = **unusual,** atypical, extraordinary, infrequent, out of the ordinary, peculiar, rare, seldom seen, singular, unaccustomed, uncommon, uncustomary, unexpected, unfamiliar, unheard-of
unworldly *adj* **1** = **spiritual,** abstract, celestial, metaphysical, nonmaterialistic, religious, transcendental **2** = **naive,** as green as grass, green, idealistic, inexperienced, innocent, raw, trusting, unsophisticated, wet behind the ears (*inf.*) **3** = **otherworldly,** ethereal, extraterrestrial, unearthly
unworthy *adj* **1** = **undeserving,** ineligible, not deserving of, not fit for, not good enough, not worth **2** *often foll. by* **of** = **unbefitting,** beneath, improper, inappropriate, out of character, out of place, unbecoming, unfitting, unseemly, unsuitable **3** = **dishonourable,** base, contemptible, degrading, discreditable, disgraceful, disreputable, ignoble, shameful
Antonyms *adj* ≠ **undeserving:** deserving, eligible, fit, meritorious, worthy ≠ **dishonourable:** commendable, creditable, honourable
unwritten *adj* **1** = **oral,** unrecorded, vocal, word-of-mouth **2** = **customary,** accepted, conventional, tacit, traditional, understood, unformulated
up-and-coming *adj* = **promising,** ambitious, eager, go-getting, on the make (*sl.*), pushing

up-and-under *n Rugby League.* a high kick forwards followed by a charge to the place where the ball lands.

Upanishad (uːˈpʌnɪʃəd) *n Hinduism.* any of a class of the Sanskrit sacred books probably composed between 400 and 200 B.C. and embodying the mystical and esoteric doctrines of ancient Hindu philosophy. [C19: from Sansk. *upanisad* a sitting down near something]

upas (ˈjuːpəs) *n* **1** a large tree of Java having whitish bark and poisonous milky sap. **2** the sap of this tree, used as an arrow poison. ◆ Also called: **antiar.** [C19: from Malay: poison]

upbeat (ˈʌpˌbiːt) *n* **1** *Music.* **1a** a usually unaccented beat, esp. the last in a bar. **1b** the upward gesture of a conductor's baton indicating this. ◆ *adj* **2** *Inf.* marked by cheerfulness or optimism.

upbraid (ʌpˈbreɪd) *vb (tr)* **1** to reprove or reproach angrily. **2** to find fault with. [OE *upbregdan*]
▸**upˈbraider** *n* ▸**upˈbraiding** *n*

upbringing (ˈʌpˌbrɪŋɪŋ) *n* the education of a person during his formative years.

upcast (ˈʌpˌkɑːst) *n* **1** material cast or thrown up. **2** a ventilation shaft through which air leaves a mine. **3** *Geol.* (in a fault) the section of strata that has been displaced upwards. ◆ *adj* **4** directed or thrown upwards. ◆ *vb* **upcasts, upcasting, upcast. 5** *(tr)* to throw or cast up.

upcountry (ʌpˈkʌntrɪ) *adj* **1** of or coming from the interior of a country or region. ◆ *n* **2** the interior part of a region or country. ◆ *adv* **3** towards, in, or into the interior part of a country or region.

update *vb* (ʌpˈdeɪt), **updates, updating, updated.** *(tr)* **1** to bring up to date. ◆ *n* (ˈʌpˌdeɪt). **2** the act of updating or something that is updated.
▸**upˈdateable** *adj* ▸**upˈdater** *n*

updraught *or US* **updraft** (ˈʌpˌdrɑːft) *n* an upward movement of air or other gas.

upend (ʌpˈɛnd) *vb* **1** to turn or set or become turned or set on end. **2** *(tr)* to affect or upset drastically.

upfront (ˈʌpˈfrʌnt) *adj* **1** open and frank. ◆ *adv, adj* **2** (of money) paid out at the beginning of a business arrangement.

upgrade *vb* (ʌpˈgreɪd), **upgrades, upgrading, upgraded.** *(tr)* **1** to assign or promote (a person or job) to a higher professional rank or position. **2** to raise in value, importance, esteem, etc. **3** to improve (a breed of livestock) by crossing with a better strain. ◆ *n* (ˈʌpˌgreɪd). **4** *US & Canad.* an upward slope. **5 on the upgrade.** improving or progressing, as in importance, status, health, etc.
▸**upˈgrader** *n*

upheaval (ʌpˈhiːvᵊl) *n* **1** a strong, sudden, or violent disturbance, as in politics. **2** *Geol.* another word for **uplift** (sense 7).

upheave (ʌpˈhiːv) *vb* **upheaves, upheaving, upheaved** *or* **uphove. 1** to heave or rise upwards. **2** *Geol.* to thrust (land) upwards or (of land) to be thrust upwards. **3** *(tr)* to throw into disorder.

upheld (ʌpˈhɛld) *vb* the past tense and past participle of **uphold.**

uphill (ˈʌpˈhɪl) *adj* **1** inclining, sloping, or leading upwards. **2** requiring protracted effort: *an uphill task.* ◆ *adv* **3** up an incline or slope. **4** against difficulties. ◆ *n* **5** a rising incline.

uphold (ʌpˈhəʊld) *vb* **upholds, upholding, upheld.** *(tr)* **1** to maintain or defend against opposition. **2** to give moral support to. **3** *Rare.* to support physically. **4** to lift up.
▸**upˈholder** *n*

upholster (ʌpˈhəʊlstə) *vb (tr)* to fit (chairs, sofas, etc.) with padding, springs, webbing, and covering.
▸**upˈholstery** *n*

upholsterer (ʌpˈhəʊlstərə) *n* a person who upholsters furniture as a profession. [C17: from *upholster* small furniture dealer]

upkeep (ˈʌpˌkiːp) *n* **1** the act or process of keeping something in good repair, esp. over a long period. **2** the cost of maintenance.

upland (ˈʌplənd) *n* **1** an area of high or relatively high ground. ◆ *adj* **2** relating to or situated in an upland.

uplift *vb* (ʌpˈlɪft). *(tr)* **1** to raise; lift up. **2** to raise morally, spiritually, etc. **3** *Scot. & NZ.* to collect; pick up (goods, documents, etc.). ◆ *n* (ˈʌpˌlɪft). **4** the act, process, or result of lifting up. **5** the act or process of bettering moral, social, or cultural conditions, etc. **6** *(modifier)* designating a brassiere for lifting and supporting the breasts: *an uplift bra.* **7** the process or result of land being raised to a higher level, as during a period of mountain building.
▸**upˈlifter** *n* ▸**upˈlifting** *adj*

uplighter (ˈʌpˌlaɪtə) *n* a lamp or wall light designed or positioned to cast its light upwards.

up-market *adj* relating to commercial products, services, etc., that are relatively expensive and of superior quality.

upmost (ˈʌpˌməʊst) *adj* another word for **uppermost.**

upon (əˈpɒn) *prep* **1** another word for **on. 2** indicating a position reached by going up: *climb upon my knee.* **3** imminent for: *the weekend was upon us again.* [C13: from UP + ON]

upper (ˈʌpə) *adj* **1** higher or highest in relation to physical position, wealth, rank, status, etc. **2** *(cap. when part of a name)* lying farther upstream, inland, or farther north: *the upper valley of the Loire.* **3** *(cap. when part of a name) Geol., archaeol.* denoting the late part or division of a period, system, etc.: *Upper Palaeolithic.* **4** *Maths.* (of a limit or bound) greater than or equal to one or more numbers or variables. ◆ *n* **5** the higher of two objects, people, etc. **6** the part of a shoe above the sole, covering the upper surface of the foot. **7 on one's uppers.** destitute. **8** *Sl.* any of various drugs having a stimulant effect.

upper atmosphere *n Meteorol.* that part of the atmosphere above the troposphere, esp. at heights that cannot be reached by balloon.

upper case *Printing.* ◆ *n* **1** the top half of a compositor's type case in which capital letters, reference marks, and accents are kept. ◆ *adj* **(upper-case** *when prenominal).* **2** of or relating to capital letters kept in this case and used in the setting or production of printed or typed matter.

upper chamber *n* another name for an **upper house.**

upper class *n* **1** the class occupying the highest position in the social hierarchy, esp. the aristocracy. ◆ *adj* **(upper-class** *when prenominal).* **2** of or relating to the upper class.

upper crust *n Inf.* the upper class.

uppercut (ˈʌpəˌkʌt) *n* **1** a short swinging upward blow with the fist delivered at an opponent's chin. ◆ *vb* **uppercuts, uppercutting, uppercut. 2** to hit (an opponent) with an uppercut.

upper hand *n* **the.** the position of control (esp. in **have** *or* **get the upper hand).**

upper house *n (often cap.)* one of the two houses of a bicameral legislature.

uppermost (ˈʌpəˌməʊst) *adj also* **upmost. 1** highest in position, power, importance, etc. ◆ *adv* **2** in or into the highest position, etc.

upper regions *pl n* **the.** *Chiefly literary.* the sky; heavens.

upper works *pl n Naut.* the parts of a vessel above the water line when fully laden.

uppish (ˈʌpɪʃ) *adj Brit. inf.* another word for **uppity** (sense 1). [C18: from UP + -ISH]
▸**ˈuppishly** *adv* ▸**ˈuppishness** *n*

uppity (ˈʌpɪtɪ) *adj Inf.* **1** snobbish, arrogant, or presumptuous. **2** offensively self-assertive. [from UP + fanciful ending, ? infl. by -ITY]

upraise (ʌpˈreɪz) *vb* **upraises, upraising, upraised.** *(tr) Chiefly literary.* to lift up; elevate.
▸**upˈraiser** *n*

uprear (ʌpˈrɪə) *vb (tr)* to lift up; raise.

upright (ˈʌpˌraɪt) *adj* **1** vertical or erect. **2** honest or just. ◆ *adv* **3** ver-

THESAURUS

upbeat *adj* **2** *Informal* = **cheerful**, buoyant, cheery, encouraging, favourable, forward-looking, heartening, hopeful, looking up, optimistic, positive, promising, rosy

upbraid *vb* **1** = **scold**, admonish, bawl out, berate, blame, carpet (*inf.*), castigate, censure, chew out (*US & Canad. inf.*), chide, condemn, dress down (*inf.*), excoriate, give (someone) a rocket (*Brit. & NZ inf.*), lecture, rap (someone) over the knuckles, read the riot act, rebuke, reprimand, reproach, reprove, slap on the wrist, take to task, tear into (*inf.*), tear (someone) off a strip (*Brit. inf.*), tell off (*inf.*), tick off (*inf.*)

upbringing *n* = **education**, breeding, bringing-up, care, cultivation, nurture, raising, rearing, tending, training

update *vb* **1** = **bring up to date**, amend, modernize, rebrand, renew, revise

upgrade *vb* **1, 2** = **promote**, advance, ameliorate, better, elevate, enhance, improve, raise
Antonyms *vb* degrade, demote, downgrade, lower

upheaval *n* **1** = **disturbance**, cataclysm, disorder, disruption, eruption, overthrow, revolution, turmoil, violent change

uphill *adj* **1** = **ascending**, climbing, mounting, rising **2** = **arduous**, difficult, exhausting, gruelling, hard, laborious, punishing, Sisyphean, strenuous, taxing, tough, wearisome
Antonyms *adj* ≠ **ascending:** descending, downhill, lowering

uphold *vb* **2** = **support**, advocate, aid, back, champion, defend, encourage, endorse, hold to, justify, maintain, promote, stand by, stick up for (*inf.*), sustain, vindicate

upkeep *n* **1** = **maintenance**, conservation, keep, preservation, repair, running, subsistence, support, sustenance **2** = **running costs**, expenditure, expenses, oncosts, operating costs, outlay, overheads

uplift *vb* **1** = **raise**, elevate, heave, hoist, lift up **2** = **improve**, advance, ameliorate, better, civilize, cultivate, edify, inspire, raise, refine, upgrade ◆ *n* **5** = **improvement**, advancement, betterment, cultivation, edification, enhancement, enlightenment, enrichment, refinement

upper *adj* **1** = **higher**, elevated, eminent, greater, high, important, loftier, superior, top, topmost
Antonyms *adj* ≠ **higher:** bottom, inferior, junior, low, lower

upper class *adj* **upper-class 2** = **aristocratic**, blue-blooded, highborn, high-class, noble, patrician, top-drawer, well-bred

upper hand *n* = **control**, advantage, ascendancy, dominion, edge, mastery, superiority, supremacy, sway, whip hand

uppermost *adj* **1** = **top**, chief, dominant, foremost, greatest, highest, leading, loftiest, main, most elevated, paramount, predominant, pre-eminent, primary, principal, supreme, topmost, upmost
Antonyms *adj* ≠ **top:** bottom, bottommost, humblest, least, lowermost, lowest, lowliest

uppish *adj Brit. informal* = **conceited**, affected, arrogant, cocky, high and mighty (*inf.*), hoity-toity (*inf.*), overweening, presumptuous, putting on airs, self-important, snobbish, stuck-up (*inf.*), supercilious, toffee-nosed (*sl., chiefly Brit.*), uppity (*inf.*)
Antonyms *adj* diffident, humble, lowly, meek, obsequious, servile, unaffected, unassertive

uppity *adj* **1, 2** *Informal* = **conceited**, bigheaded (*inf.*), bumptious, cocky, full of oneself, impertinent, on one's high horse (*inf.*), overweening, self-important, swanky (*inf.*), too big for one's boots *or* breeches (*inf.*), uppish (*Brit. inf.*)

upright *adj* **1** = **vertical**, erect, on end, per-

tically. ◆ *n* **4** a vertical support, such as a stake or post. **5** short for **upright piano.** **6** the state of being vertical.
▸ **'up,rightly** *adv* ▸ **'up,rightness** *n*

upright piano *n* a piano which has a rectangular vertical case.

uprise *vb* (ʌp'raɪz), **uprises, uprising, uprose, uprisen.** **1** (*tr*) to rise up. ◆ *n* ('ʌp,raɪz). **2** another word for **rise** (senses 23, 24).
▸ **up'riser** *n*

uprising ❶ ('ʌp,raɪzɪŋ, ʌp'raɪzɪŋ) *n* **1** a revolt or rebellion. **2** *Arch.* an ascent.

uproar ❶ ('ʌp,rɔː) *n* a commotion or disturbance characterized by loud noise and confusion.

uproarious ❶ (ʌp'rɔːrɪəs) *adj* **1** causing or characterized by an uproar. **2** extremely funny. **3** (of laughter, etc.) loud and boisterous.
▸ **up'roariously** *adv* ▸ **up'roariousness** *n*

uproot ❶ (ʌp'ruːt) *vb* (*tr*) **1** to pull up by or as if by the roots. **2** to displace (a person or persons) from native or habitual surroundings. **3** to remove or destroy utterly.
▸ **up'rooter** *n*

uprush ('ʌp,rʌʃ) *n* an upward rush, as of consciousness.

upsadaisy ('ʌpsə'deɪzɪ) *interj* a variant spelling of **upsy-daisy.**

ups and downs ❶ *pl n* alternating periods of good and bad fortune, high and low spirits, etc.

upscale ('ʌp'skeɪl) *adj Inf.* of or for the upper end of an economic or social scale; up-market.

upset ❶ *vb* (ʌp'sɛt), **upsets, upsetting, upset.** (*mainly tr*) **1** (*also intr*) to tip or be tipped over; overturn or spill. **2** to disturb the normal state or stability of: *to upset the balance of nature.* **3** to disturb mentally or emotionally. **4** to defeat or overthrow, usually unexpectedly. **5** to make physically ill: *seafood always upsets my stomach.* **6** to thicken or spread (the end of a bar, etc.) by hammering. ◆ *n* ('ʌp,sɛt). **7** an unexpected defeat or reversal, as in a contest or plans. **8** a disturbance or disorder of the emotions, body, etc. ◆ *adj* (ʌp'sɛt). **9** overturned or capsized. **10** emotionally or physically disturbed or distressed. **11** disordered; confused. **12** defeated or overthrown. [C14 (in the sense: to erect; C19 in the sense: to overthrow)]
▸ **up'setter** *n* ▸ **up'setting** *adj* ▸ **up'settingly** *adv*

upset price *n Chiefly Scot., US, & Canad.* the lowest price acceptable for something that is for sale, esp. a house. Cf. **reserve price.**

upshot ❶ ('ʌp,ʃɒt) *n* **1** the final result; conclusion; outcome. **2** *Archery.* the final shot in a match. [C16: from UP + SHOT[1]]

upside ('ʌp,saɪd) *n* the upper surface or part.

upside down ❶ *adj* **1** (*usually postpositive;* **upside-down** *when prenominal*) turned over completely; inverted. **2** (**upside-down** *when prenominal*) *Inf.* confused; topsy-turvy: *an upside-down world.* ◆ *adv* **3** in an inverted fashion. **4** in a chaotic manner. [C16: var., by folk etymology, of earlier *upsodown*]

upside-down cake *n* a sponge cake baked with fruit at the bottom, and inverted before serving.

upsides (,ʌp'saɪdz) *adv Inf., chiefly Brit.* (foll. by *with*) equal or level (with), as through revenge.

upsilon ('ʌpsɪ,lɒn) *n* **1** the 20th letter in the Greek alphabet (Υ or υ), a vowel transliterated as *y* or *u.* **2** a heavy short-lived subatomic particle produced by bombarding beryllium nuclei with high-energy protons. [C17: from Med. Gk *u psilon* simple *u,* name adopted for graphic *u* to avoid confusion with graphic *oi,* since pronunciation was the same for both in LGk]

upskill ('ʌp,skɪl) *vb* (*tr*) *NZ.* to improve a person's aptitude for work by additional training.

upstage ('ʌp'steɪdʒ) *adv* **1** on, at, or to the rear of the stage. ◆ *adj* **2** of or relating to the back half of the stage. **3** *Inf.* haughty. ◆ *vb* **upstages, upstaging, upstaged.** (*tr*) **4** to move upstage of (another actor), thus forcing him to turn away from the audience. **5** *Inf.* to draw attention to oneself from (someone else). **6** *Inf.* to treat haughtily.

upstairs ('ʌp'stɛəz) *adv* **1** up the stairs; to or on an upper floor. **2** *Inf.* to or into a higher rank or office. ◆ *n* (*functioning as sing or pl*) **3a** an upper floor. **3b** (*as modifier*): *an upstairs room.* **4** *Brit. inf., old-fashioned.* the masters and mistresses of a household collectively, esp. of a large house.

upstanding ❶ (ʌp'stændɪŋ) *adj* **1** of good character. **2** upright and vigorous in build. **3 be upstanding. 3a** (in a court of law) a direction to all persons present to rise to their feet before the judge enters or leaves the court. **3b** (at a formal dinner) a direction to all persons present to rise to their feet for a toast.

upstart ❶ ('ʌp,stɑːt) *n* **1a** a person, group, etc., that has risen suddenly to a position of power. **1b** (*as modifier*): *an upstart family.* **2a** an arrogant person. **2b** (*as modifier*): *his upstart ambition.*

upstate ('ʌp'steɪt) *US.* ◆ *adj, adv* **1** towards, in, or relating to the outlying or northern sections of a state. ◆ *n* **2** the outlying, esp. northern, sections of a state.
▸ **'up'stater** *n*

upstream ('ʌp'striːm) *adv, adj* **1** in or towards the higher part of a stream; against the current. Cf. **downstream. 2** (in the oil industry) of or for any of the stages prior to oil production, such as exploration or research.

upstretched (ʌp'strɛtʃt) *adj* (esp. of the arms) stretched or raised up.

upstroke ('ʌp,strəʊk) *n* **1a** an upward stroke or movement, as of a pen or brush. **1b** the mark produced by such a stroke. **2** the upward movement of a piston in a reciprocating engine.

upsurge *vb* (ʌp'sɜːdʒ), **upsurges, upsurging, upsurged.** **1** (*intr*) *Chiefly literary.* to surge up. ◆ *n* ('ʌp,sɜːdʒ). **2** a rapid rise or swell.

upsweep *n* ('ʌp,swiːp). **1** a curve or sweep upwards. ◆ *vb* (ʌp'swiːp), **upsweeps, upsweeping, upswept. 2** to sweep, curve, or brush or be swept, curved, or brushed upwards.

upswing ('ʌp,swɪŋ) *n* **1** *Econ.* a recovery period in the trade cycle. **2** an upward swing or movement or any increase or improvement.

upsy-daisy ('ʌpsɪ'deɪzɪ) *or* **upsadaisy** *interj* an expression, usually of reassurance, uttered as when someone, esp. a child, stumbles or is being lifted up. [C18 *up-a-daisy,* irregularly formed from UP (adv)]

uptake ('ʌp,teɪk) *n* **1** a pipe, shaft, etc., that is used to convey smoke or gases, esp. one that connects a furnace to a chimney. **2** lifting up. **3** the act of accepting something on offer. **4 quick** (*or* **slow**) **on the uptake.** *Inf.* quick (or slow) to understand or learn.

upthrow ('ʌp,θrəʊ) *n Geol.* the upward movement of rocks on one side of a fault plane relative to rocks on the other side.

upthrust ('ʌp,θrʌst) *n* **1** an upward push or thrust. **2** *Geol.* a violent upheaval of the earth's surface.

uptight ❶ (ʌp'taɪt) *adj Inf.* **1** displaying tense repressed nervousness, irritability, or anger. **2** unable to give expression to one's feelings.

uptime ('ʌp,taɪm) *n Commerce.* time during which a machine, such as a computer, actually operates.

up-to-date ❶ *adj* **a** modern or fashionable: *an up-to-date magazine.* **b** (*predicative*): *the magazine is up to date.*
▸ **'up-to-'dateness** *n*

THESAURUS

pendicular, straight **2** = **honest**, above board, conscientious, ethical, faithful, good, high-minded, honourable, incorruptible, just, principled, righteous, straightforward, true, trustworthy, unimpeachable, virtuous
Antonyms *adj* ≠ **vertical:** flat, horizontal, lying, prone, prostrate, supine ≠ **honest:** corrupt, devious, dishonest, dishonourable, unethical, unjust, untrustworthy, wicked

uprightness *n* **2** = **honesty**, fairness, faithfulness, goodness, high-mindedness, incorruptibility, integrity, justice, probity, rectitude, righteousness, straightforwardness, trustworthiness, virtue

uprising *n* **1** = **rebellion**, disturbance, insurgence, insurrection, mutiny, outbreak, putsch, revolt, revolution, rising, upheaval

uproar *n* = **commotion**, brawl, brouhaha, clamour, confusion, din, furore, hubbub, hullabaloo, hurly-burly, mayhem, noise, outcry, pandemonium, racket, riot, ruckus (*inf.*), ruction (*inf.*), rumpus, turbulence, turmoil

uproarious *adj* **1** = **riotous**, clamorous, confused, disorderly, loud, noisy, rowdy, tempestuous, tumultuous, turbulent, wild **2** = **hilarious**, convulsive (*inf.*), hysterical, killing (*inf.*), rib-tickling, rip-roaring (*inf.*), screamingly funny, side-splitting, very funny **3** = **boisterous**, gleeful, loud, rollicking, unrestrained
Antonyms ≠ **riotous:** inaudible, low-key, orderly, quiet, still *adj* ≠ **hilarious:** morose, mournful, sad, serious, sorrowful, tragic ≠ **boisterous:** peaceful, quiet

uproot *vb* **1** = **pull up**, deracinate, dig up, extirpate, grub up, pull out by the roots, rip up, root out, weed out **2** = **displace**, deracinate, disorient, exile **3** = **destroy**, do away with, eliminate, eradicate, extirpate, remove, wipe out

ups and downs *pl n* = **fluctuations**, changes, ebb and flow, moods, vicissitudes, wheel of fortune

upset *vb* **1** = **tip over**, capsize, knock over, overturn, spill, topple over **2** = **mess up**, change, disorder, disorganize, disturb, mix up, put out of order, spoil, turn topsy-turvy **3** = **distress**, agitate, bother, discompose, disconcert, dismay, disquiet, disturb, faze, fluster, grieve, hassle (*inf.*), perturb, ruffle, throw (someone) off balance, trouble, unnerve **4** = **defeat**, be victorious over, conquer, get the better of, overcome, overthrow, triumph over, win against the odds ◆ *n* **7** = **reversal**, defeat, shake-up (*inf.*), sudden change, surprise **8** = **distress**, agitation, bother, discomposure, disquiet, disturbance, hassle (*inf.*), shock, trouble, worry **8** = **illness**, bug (*inf.*), complaint, disorder, disturbance, indisposition, malady, queasiness, sickness ◆ *adj* **9** = **overturned**, capsized, spilled, tipped over, toppled, tumbled, upside down **10** = **distressed**, agitated, bothered, confused, disconcerted, dismayed, disquieted, disturbed, frantic, grieved, hassled (*inf.*), hurt, overwrought, put out, ruffled, troubled, worried **10** = **sick**, disordered, disturbed, gippy (*sl.*), ill, poorly (*inf.*), queasy **11** = **disordered**, at sixes and sevens, chaotic, confused, disarrayed, in disarray, in disorder, messed up, muddled, topsy-turvy **12** = **conquered**, beaten, defeated, overcome, overthrown, vanquished

upshot *n* **1** = **result**, conclusion, consequence, culmination, end, end result, event, finale, issue, outcome, payoff (*inf.*), sequel

upside down *adj* **1** = **inverted**, bottom up, on its head, overturned, upturned, wrong side up **2** *Informal* = **confused**, chaotic, disordered, higgledy-piggledy (*inf.*), in chaos, in confusion, in disarray, in disorder, jumbled, muddled, topsy-turvy

upstanding *adj* **1** = **honest**, ethical, good, honourable, incorruptible, moral, principled, true, trustworthy, upright **2** = **sturdy**, firm, hale and hearty, hardy, healthy, robust, stalwart, strong, upright, vigorous
Antonyms *adj* ≠ **honest:** bad, corrupt, dishonest, false, immoral, unethical, unprincipled, untrustworthy ≠ **sturdy:** delicate, feeble, frail, infirm, puny, unhealthy, weak

upstart *n* **1a** = **social climber**, arriviste, nobody, *nouveau riche,* parvenu, status seeker

uptight *adj* **1** *Informal* = **tense**, anxious, edgy, nervy (*Brit. inf.*), neurotic, on edge, on the defensive, prickly, uneasy, wired (*sl.*), withdrawn

up-to-date *adj* **a** = **modern**, à la mode, all the rage, contemporary, current, fashionable, happening (*inf.*), having one's finger on the pulse,

uptown ('ʌp'taʊn) *US & Canad.* ♦ *adj, adv* **1** towards, in, or relating to some part of a town that is away from the centre. ♦ *n* **2** such a part of a town, esp. a residential part.
▸**'up'towner** *n*

upturn ⓣ *vb* (ʌp'tɜːn). **1** to turn or cause to turn over or upside down. **2** (*tr*) to create disorder. **3** (*tr*) to direct upwards. ♦ *n* ('ʌpˌtɜːn). **4** an upward trend or improvement. **5** an upheaval.

UPVC *abbrev. for* unplasticized polyvinyl chloride. See also **PVC.**

upward ('ʌpwəd) *adj* **1** directed or moving towards a higher point or level. ♦ *adv* **2** a variant of **upwards.**
▸**'upwardly** *adv* ▸**'upwardness** *n*

upwardly mobile *adj* (of a person or social group) moving or aspiring to move to a higher social class or status.

upward mobility *n* movement from a lower to a higher economic and social status.

upwards ('ʌpwədz) *or* **upward** *adv* **1** from a lower to a higher place, level, condition, etc. **2** towards a higher level, standing, etc.

upwind ('ʌp'wɪnd) *adv* **1** into or against the wind. **2** towards or on the side where the wind is blowing; windward. ♦ *adj* **3** going against the wind: *the upwind leg of the course.* **4** on the windward side.

uracil ('jʊərəsɪl) *n Biochem.* a pyrimidine present in all living cells, usually in a combined form, as in RNA. [C20: from URO- + ACETIC + -ILE]

uraemia *or US* **uremia** (jʊ'riːmɪə) *n Pathol.* the accumulation of waste products, normally excreted in the urine, in the blood. [C19: from NL, from Gk *ouron* urine + *haima* blood]
▸**u'raemic** *or US* **u'remic** *adj*

uraeus (jʊ'riːəs) *n, pl* **uraeuses.** the sacred serpent represented on the headdresses of ancient Egyptian kings and gods. [C19: from NL, from Gk *ouraios,* from Egyptian *uro* asp]

Ural-Altaic ('jʊərəl-) *n* **1** a postulated group of related languages consisting of the Uralic and Altaic families of languages. ♦ *adj* **2** of or relating to this group of languages, characterized by agglutination and vowel harmony.

Uralic (jʊ'rælɪk) *or* **Uralian** (jʊ'reɪlɪən) *n* **1** a superfamily of languages consisting of the Finno-Ugric family together with Samoyed. See also **Ural-Altaic.** ♦ *adj* **2** of or relating to these languages.

uranalysis (ˌjʊərə'nælɪsɪs) *n, pl* **uranalyses** (-ˌsiːz). *Med.* a variant spelling of **urinalysis.**

uranide ('jʊərəˌnaɪd) *n* any element having an atomic number greater than that of protactinium.

uranism ('jʊərænɪzəm) *n Rare.* homosexuality (esp. male homosexuality). [C20: from G *Uranismus,* from Gk *ouranios* heavenly, i.e. spiritual]

uranium (jʊ'reɪnɪəm) *n* a radioactive silvery-white metallic element of the actinide series. It occurs in several minerals including pitchblende and is used chiefly as a source of nuclear energy by fission of the radioisotope **uranium-235.** Symbol: U; atomic no.: 92; atomic wt.: 238.03; half-life of most stable isotope, ^{238}U: 4.51×10^9 years. [C18: from NL, from URANUS²; from the fact that the element was discovered soon after the planet]

uranium series *n Physics.* a radioactive series that starts with uranium-238 and proceeds by radioactive decay to lead-206.

urano- *combining form.* denoting the heavens: *uranography.* [from Gk *ouranos*]

uranography (ˌjʊərə'nɒgrəfɪ) *n* the branch of astronomy concerned with the description and mapping of the stars, galaxies, etc.
▸ˌ**ura'nographer** *n* ▸**uranographic** (ˌjʊərənə'græfɪk) *adj*

Uranus¹ (jʊ'reɪnəs, 'jʊərənəs) *n Greek myth.* the personification of the sky, who, as a god, ruled the universe and fathered the Titans and Cyclopes; overthrown by his son Cronus.

Uranus² (jʊ'reɪnəs, 'jʊərənəs) *n* the seventh planet from the sun, sometimes visible to the naked eye. [C19: from L *Ūranus,* from Gk *Ouranos* heaven]

urate ('jʊəreɪt) *n* any salt or ester of uric acid.
▸**uratic** (jʊ'rætɪk) *adj*

urban ⓣ ('ɜːbᵊn) *adj* **1** of, relating to, or constituting a city or town. **2** living in a city or town. ♦ Cf. **rural.** [C17: from L *urbānus,* from *urbs* city]

urban area *n* (in population censuses) a city area considered as the inner city plus built-up environs, irrespective of local body administrative boundaries.

urban district *n* **1** (in England and Wales from 1888 to 1974 and Northern Ireland from 1898 to 1973) an urban division of an administrative county with an elected council in charge of housing and environmental services. **2** (in the Republic of Ireland) any of 49 medium-sized towns with their own elected councils.

urbane ⓣ (ɜː'beɪn) *adj* characterized by elegance or sophistication. [C16: from L *urbānus* of the town; see URBAN]
▸**ur'banely** *adv* ▸**ur'baneness** *n*

urban guerrilla *n* a guerrilla who operates in a town or city, engaging in terrorism, kidnapping, etc.

urbanism ('ɜːbəˌnɪzəm) *n Chiefly US.* **a** the character of city life. **b** the study of this.

urbanite ('ɜːbəˌnaɪt) *n* a resident of an urban community; city dweller.

urbanity ⓣ (ɜː'bænɪtɪ) *n, pl* **urbanities. 1** the quality of being urbane. **2** (*usually pl*) civilities or courtesies.

urbanize *or* **urbanise** ('ɜːbəˌnaɪz) *vb* **urbanizes, urbanizing, urbanized** *or* **urbanises, urbanising, urbanised.** (*tr*) (*usually passive*) **a** to make (esp. a predominantly rural area or country) more industrialized and urban. **b** to cause the migration of an increasing proportion of (rural dwellers) into cities.
▸ˌ**urbani'zation** *or* ˌ**urbani'sation** *n*

urban myth *or* **legend** *n* a story, esp. one with a shocking or amusing ending, related as having actually happened, usually to someone vaguely connected with the teller.

urban renewal *n* the process of redeveloping dilapidated or no longer functional urban areas.

urbi et orbi *Latin.* ('ɜːbɪ ɛt 'ɔːbɪ) *adv RC Church.* to the city and the world: a phrase qualifying the solemn papal blessing.

urceolate ('ɜːsɪəlɪt, -ˌleɪt) *adj Biol.* shaped like an urn or pitcher: *an urceolate corolla.* [C18: via NL from L *urceolus,* dim. of *urceus* a pitcher]

urchin ⓣ ('ɜːtʃɪn) *n* **1** a mischievous roguish child, esp. one who is young, small, or raggedly dressed. **2** See **sea urchin. 3** *Arch., dialect.* a hedgehog. **4** *Obs.* an elf or sprite. [C13 *urchon,* from OF *heriçon,* from L *ēricius* hedgehog]

Urdu ('ʊəduː, 'ɜː-) *n* an official language of Pakistan, also spoken in India. The script derives primarily from Persia. It belongs to the Indic branch of the Indo-European family of languages, being closely related to Hindi. [C18: from Hindustani (*zabāni*) *urdū* (language of the) camp, from Persian *urdū* camp, from Turkish *ordū*]

-ure *suffix forming nouns.* **1** indicating act, process, or result: *seizure.* **2** indicating function or office: *legislature; prefecture.* [from F, from L *-ūra*]

urea ('jʊərɪə) *n* a white water-soluble crystalline compound, produced by protein metabolism and excreted in urine. A synthetic form is used as a fertilizer and animal feed. Formula: $CO(NH_2)_2$. [C19: from NL, from F *urée,* from Gk *ouron* urine]
▸**u'real** *or* **u'reic** *adj*

urea-formaldehyde resin *n* any one of a class of rigid odourless synthetic materials that are made from urea and formaldehyde and are used in electrical fittings, adhesives, laminates, and finishes for textiles.

ureide ('jʊərɪˌaɪd) *n Chem.* **1** any of a class of organic compounds derived from urea by replacing one or more of its hydrogen atoms by organic groups. **2** any of a class of derivatives of urea and carboxylic acids, in which one or more of the hydrogen atoms have been replaced by acid radical groups.

-uret *suffix of nouns.* formerly used to form the names of binary chemical compounds. [from NL *-uretum*]

ureter (jʊ'riːtə) *n* the tube that conveys urine from the kidney to the urinary bladder or cloaca. [C16: via NL from Gk *ourētēr,* from *ourein* to urinate]
▸**u'reteral** *or* **ureteric** (ˌjʊərɪ'tɛrɪk) *adj*

urethane ('jʊərɪˌθeɪn) *or* **urethan** ('jʊərɪˌθæn) *n* short for **polyurethane.** [C19: from URO- + ETHYL + -ANE]

urethra (jʊ'riːθrə) *n, pl* **urethrae** (-θriː) *or* **urethras.** the canal that in most mammals conveys urine from the bladder out of the body. In human males it also conveys semen. [C17: via LL from Gk *ourēthra,* from *ourein* to urinate]
▸**u'rethral** *adj*

urethritis (ˌjʊərɪ'θraɪtɪs) *n* inflammation of the urethra. [C19: from NL, from LL URETHRA]
▸**urethritic** (ˌjʊərɪ'θrɪtɪk) *adj*

urethroscope (jʊ'riːθrəˌskəʊp) *n* a medical instrument for examining the urethra. [C20: see URETHRA, -SCOPE]
▸**urethroscopic** (jʊˌriːθrə'skɒpɪk) *adj* ▸**urethroscopy** (ˌjʊərɪ'θrɒskəpɪ) *n*

uretic (jʊ'rɛtɪk) *adj* of or relating to the urine. [C19: via LL from Gk *ourētikos,* from *ouron* urine]

urge ⓣ (ɜːdʒ) *vb* **urges, urging, urged.** (*tr*) **1** to plead, press, or move (someone to do something): *we urged him to surrender.* **2** (*may take a clause as object*) to advocate or recommend earnestly and persistently: *to urge the need for safety.* **3** to impel, drive, or hasten onwards: *he urged the horses on.* ♦ *n* **4** a strong impulse, inner drive, or yearning. [C16: from L *urgēre*]

THESAURUS

in, in vogue, newest, now (*inf.*), stylish, trendy (*Brit. inf.*), up-to-the-minute, with it (*inf.*)
Antonyms *adj* antiquated, dated, *démodé,* obsolete, old fashioned, outmoded, out of date, out of the ark (*inf.*), passé

upturn *n* **4** = **rise,** advancement, boost, improvement, increase, recovery, revival, upsurge, upswing

urban *adj* **1** = **civic,** city, inner-city, metropolitan, municipal, oppidan (*rare*), town

urbane *adj* = **sophisticated,** civil, civilized, cosmopolitan, courteous, cultivated, cultured, debonair, elegant, mannerly, polished, refined, smooth, suave, well-bred, well-mannered
Antonyms *adj* boorish, clownish, discourteous, gauche, impolite, rude, uncivilized, uncouth, uncultured

urbanity *n* **1** = **sophistication,** charm, civility, courtesy, culture, elegance, grace, mannerliness, polish, refinement, suavity, worldliness

urchin *n* **1** = **ragamuffin,** brat, gamin, guttersnipe, mudlark (*sl.*), street Arab (*offens.*), waif, young rogue

urge *vb* **1** = **beg,** appeal to, beseech, entreat, exhort, implore, plead, press, solicit **2** = **advocate,** advise, champion, counsel, insist on, push for, recommend, support **3** = **drive,** compel, constrain, egg on, encourage, force, gee up, goad, hasten, impel, incite, induce, instigate, press, prompt, propel, push, spur, stimulate ♦ *n* **4** = **impulse,** compulsion, desire, drive, fancy, itch, longing, thirst, wish, yearning, yen (*inf.*)
Antonyms *vb* ≠ **advocate, drive:** caution, deter, discourage, dissuade, warn ♦ *n* ≠ **impulse:** aversion, disinclination, distaste, indisposition, reluctance, repugnance

urgent ❶ ('ɜːdʒənt) *adj* **1** requiring or compelling speedy action or attention: *the matter is urgent.* **2** earnest and persistent. [C15: via F from L *urgent-, urgens,* present participle of *urgēre* to URGE]
▸**urgency** ('ɜːdʒənsɪ) *n* ▸'**urgently** *adv*

-urgy *n combining form.* indicating technology concerned with a specified material: *metallurgy.* [from Gk *-urgia,* from *ergon* work]

-uria *n combining form.* indicating a diseased or abnormal condition of the urine: *pyuria.* [from Gk *-ouria,* from *ouron* urine]
▸**-uric** *adj combining form.*

uric ('jʊərɪk) *adj* of, concerning, or derived from urine. [C18: from URO- + -IC]

uric acid *n* a white odourless tasteless crystalline product of protein metabolism, present in the blood and urine. Formula: $C_5H_4N_4O_3$.

uridine ('jʊərɪˌdiːn) *n Biochem.* a nucleoside present in all living cells in a combined form, esp. in RNA. [C20: from URO- + -IDE + -INE[2]]

urinal (jʊ'raɪnᵊl, 'jʊərɪ-) *n* **1** a sanitary fitting, esp. one fixed to a wall, used by men for urination. **2** a room containing urinals. **3** any vessel for holding urine prior to its disposal.

urinalysis (ˌjʊərɪ'nælɪsɪs) *n, pl* **urinalyses** (-ˌsiːz). *Med.* chemical analysis of the urine to test for the presence of disease.

urinary ('jʊərɪnərɪ) *adj* **1** *Anat.* of or relating to urine or to the organs and structures that secrete and pass urine. ◆ *n, pl* **urinaries. 2** a reservoir for urine.

urinary bladder *n* a distensible membranous sac in which the urine excreted from the kidneys is stored.

urinate ❶ ('jʊərɪˌneɪt) *vb* **urinates, urinating, urinated.** (*intr*) to excrete or void urine.
▸ˌ**uri'nation** *n* ▸'**urinative** *adj*

urine ('jʊərɪn) *n* the pale yellow slightly acid fluid excreted by the kidneys, containing waste products removed from the blood. It is stored in the urinary bladder and discharged through the urethra. [C14: via OF from L *ūrīna*]

urinogenital (ˌjʊərɪnəʊ'dʒenɪtᵊl) *adj* another word for **urogenital.**

URL *abbrev. for* uniform resource locator: a standardized address of a location on the Internet.

urn (ɜːn) *n* **1** a vaselike receptacle or vessel, esp. a large bulbous one with a foot. **2** a vase used as a receptacle for the ashes of the dead. **3** a large vessel, usually of metal, with a tap, used for making and holding tea, coffee, etc. [C14: from L *ūrna*]
▸'**urn**ˌ**like** *adj*

urnfield ('ɜːnˌfiːld) *n* **1** a cemetery full of individual cremation urns. ◆ *adj* **2** (of a number of Bronze Age cultures) characterized by cremation in urns, which began in E Europe about the second millennium B.C.

uro- *or before a vowel* **ur-** *combining form.* indicating urine or the urinary tract: *urogenital; urology.* [from Gk *ouron* urine]

urogenital (ˌjʊərəʊ'dʒenɪtᵊl) *or* **urinogenital** *adj* of or relating to the urinary and genital organs and their functions. Also: **genitourinary. urogenital system**

urogenital system *or* **tract** *n Anat.* the urinary tract and reproductive organs.

urolith ('jʊərəʊlɪθ) *n Pathol.* a calculus in the urinary tract.
▸ˌ**uro'lithic** *adj*

urology (jʊ'rɒlədʒɪ) *n* the branch of medicine concerned with the study and treatment of diseases of the urogenital tract.
▸**urologic** (ˌjʊərə'lɒdʒɪk) *adj* ▸**u'rologist** *n*

uropygial gland (ˌjʊərə'pɪdʒɪəl) *n* a gland, situated at the base of the tail in most birds, that secretes oil used in preening.

uropygium (ˌjʊərə'pɪdʒɪəm) *n* the hindmost part of a bird's body, from which the tail feathers grow. [C19: via NL from Gk *ouropugion,* from *oura* tail + *pugē* rump]
▸ˌ**uro'pygial** *adj*

uroscopy (jʊ'rɒskəpɪ) *n Med.* examination of the urine. See also **urinalysis.**
▸**uroscopic** (ˌjʊərə'skɒpɪk) *adj* ▸**u'roscopist** *n*

Ursa Major ('ɜːsə 'meɪdʒə) *n, Latin genitive* **Ursae Majoris** ('ɜːsiː mə'dʒɔːrɪs). an extensive conspicuous constellation in the N hemisphere. The seven brightest stars form the **Plough.** Also called: the **Great Bear,** the **Bear.** [L: greater bear]

Ursa Minor ('ɜːsə 'maɪnə) *n, Latin genitive* **Ursae Minoris** ('ɜːsiː mɪ'nɔːrɪs). a small faint constellation, the brightest star of which is the Pole Star. Also called: the **Little Bear,** the **Bear.** [L: lesser bear]

ursine ('ɜːsaɪn) *adj* of, relating to, or resembling a bear or bears. [C16: from L *ursus* a bear]

Ursprache *German.* ('uːrʃpraːxə) *n* any hypothetical extinct and unrecorded language reconstructed from groups of related recorded languages. For example, Indo-European is an Ursprache reconstructed by comparison of the Germanic group, Latin, Sanskrit, etc. [from *ur-* primeval + *Sprache* language]

Ursuline ('ɜːsjʊˌlaɪn) *n* **1** a member of an order of nuns devoted to teaching in the Roman Catholic Church: founded in 1537 at Brescia. ◆ *adj* **2** of or relating to this order. [C16: after St *Ursula,* patron saint of St Angela Merici, who founded the order]

Urtext *German.* ('uːrtekst) *n* **1** the earliest form of a text as established by linguistic scholars as a basis for variants in later texts still in existence. **2** an edition of a musical score showing the composer's intentions without later editorial interpolation. [from *ur-* original + TEXT]

urticaceous (ˌɜːtɪ'keɪʃəs) *adj* of or belonging to a family of plants having small flowers and, in many species, stinging hairs: includes the nettles and pellitory. [C18: via NL from L *urtīca* nettle, from *ūrere* to burn]

urticaria (ˌɜːtɪ'keərɪə) *n* a skin condition characterized by the formation of itchy red or whitish raised patches, usually caused by an allergy. Nontechnical names: **hives, nettle rash.** [C18: from NL, from L *urtīca* nettle]

urtication (ˌɜːtɪ'keɪʃən) *n* **1** a burning or itching sensation. **2** another name for **urticaria.**

urus ('jʊərəs) *n, pl* **uruses.** another name for the **aurochs.** [C17: from *ūrus,* of Gmc origin]

urushiol ('uːrʊʃɪˌɒl, uː'ruː-) *n* a poisonous pale yellow liquid occurring in poison ivy and the lacquer tree. [from Japanese *urushi* lacquer + -OL[2]]

us (ʌs) *pron* (*objective*) **1** refers to the speaker or writer and another person or other people: *don't hurt us.* **2** refers to all people or people in general: *this table shows us the tides.* **3** an informal word for **me:** *give us a kiss!* **4** a formal word for **me** used by editors, monarchs, etc. [OE *ūs*]

> **USAGE NOTE** See at **me**[1].

US *or* **U.S.** *abbrev. for* United States.

USA *abbrev. for:* **1.** Also: **U.S.A.** United States of America. **2** United States Army.

usable ❶ *or* **useable** ('juːzəbᵊl) *adj* able to be used.
▸ˌ**usa'bility** *or* ˌ**usea'bility** *n*

USAF *abbrev. for* United States Air Force.

usage ❶ ('juːsɪdʒ, -zɪdʒ) *n* **1** the act or a manner of using; use; employment. **2** constant use, custom, or habit. **3** something permitted or established by custom or practice. **4** what is actually said in a language, esp. as contrasted with what is prescribed. [C14: via OF from L *ūsus* USE (n)]

usance ('juːzəns) *n Commerce.* the period of time permitted by commercial usage for the redemption of foreign bills of exchange. [C14: from OF, from Med. L *ūsantia,* from *ūsāre* to USE]

USDAW ('ʌsdɔː) *n* (in Britain) *acronym for* Union of Shop, Distributive, and Allied Workers.

use ❶ *vb* (juːz), **uses, using, used.** (*tr*) **1** to put into service or action; employ for a given purpose: *to use a spoon to stir with.* **2** to make a practice or habit of employing; exercise: *he uses his brain.* **3** to behave towards in a particular way, esp. for one's own ends: *he uses people.* **4** to consume, expend, or exhaust: *the engine uses very little oil.* **5** to partake of (alcoholic drink, drugs, etc.) or smoke (tobacco, marijuana, etc.). ◆ *n* (juːs). **6** the act of using or the state of being used: *the carpet wore out through constant use.* **7** the ability or permission to use. **8** the occasion to use: *I have no use for this paper.* **9** an instance or manner of using. **10** usefulness; advantage: *it is of no use to complain.* **11** custom; habit: *long use has inured him to it.* **12** the purpose for which something is used; end. **13** *Christianity.* a distinctive form of liturgical or ritual observance, esp. one that is traditional. **14** the enjoyment of property, land, etc., by occupation or by deriving revenue from it. **15** *Law.* the beneficial enjoyment of property the legal title to which is held by another person as trustee. **16 have no use for. 16a** to have no need of. **16b** to have a contemptuous dislike for. **17 make use of. 17a** to employ; use. **17b** to exploit (a person). ◆ See also **use up.** [C13: from OF *user,* from L *ūsus* having used, from *ūtī* to use]

THESAURUS

urgency *n* **1** = **importance,** exigency, extremity, gravity, hurry, imperativeness, necessity, need, pressure, seriousness, stress

urgent *adj* **1** = **crucial,** compelling, critical, exigent, immediate, imperative, important, instant, not to be delayed, now or never, pressing, top-priority **2** = **insistent,** clamorous, earnest, importunate, intense, persistent, persuasive
Antonyms *adj* ≠ **crucial:** low-priority, minor, trivial, unimportant ≠ **insistent:** apathetic, casual, feeble, half-hearted, lackadaisical, perfunctory, weak

urinate *vb* = **pee** (*sl.*), leak (*sl.*), make water, micturate, pass water, piddle (*inf.*), piss (*taboo sl.*), spend a penny (*Brit. inf.*), tinkle (*Brit. inf.*), wee (*inf.*), wee-wee (*inf.*)

usable *adj* = **serviceable,** at one's disposal, available, current, fit for use, functional, in running order, practical, ready for use, utilizable, valid, working

usage *n* **1** = **use,** control, employment, handling, management, operation, regulation, running, treatment **2, 3** = **practice,** convention, custom, form, habit, matter of course, method, mode, procedure, regime, routine, rule, tradition, wont

use *vb* **1, 2** = **employ,** apply, avail oneself of, bring into play, exercise, exert, find a use for, make use of, operate, ply, practise, profit by, put to use, turn to account, utilize, wield, work **3** = **take advantage of,** act towards, behave towards, deal with, exploit, handle, manipulate, misuse, treat **4** = **consume,** exhaust, expend, run through, spend, waste ◆ *n* **6** = **usage,** application, employment, exercise, handling, operation, practice, service, treatment, wear and tear **10** = **good,** advantage, application, avail, benefit, help, mileage (*inf.*), point, profit, service, usefulness, utility, value, worth **11** = **custom,** habit, practice, usage, way, wont **12** = **purpose,** call, cause, end, necessity, need, object, occasion, point, reason

used ⓣ (juːzd) *adj* second-hand: *used cars.*
used to ⓣ (juːst) *adj* **1** accustomed to: *I am used to hitchhiking.* ◆ *vb (tr)* **2** (*takes an infinitive or implied infinitive*) used as an auxiliary to express habitual or accustomed actions, states, etc., taking place in the past but not continuing into the present: *I used to fish here every day.*

> **USAGE NOTE** The most common negative form of *used to* is *didn't used to* (or *didn't use to*), but in formal contexts *used not to* is preferred.

useful ⓣ (ˈjuːsfʊl) *adj* **1** able to be used advantageously, beneficially, or for several purposes. **2** *Inf.* commendable or capable: *a useful term's work.*
▸ **ˈusefully** *adv* ▸ **ˈusefulness** *n*
useless ⓣ (ˈjuːslɪs) *adj* **1** having no practical use or advantage. **2** *Inf.* ineffectual, weak, or stupid: *he's useless at history.*
▸ **ˈuselessly** *adv* ▸ **ˈuselessness** *n*
user (ˈjuːzə) *n* **1** *Law.* **1a** the continued exercise, use, or enjoyment of a right, esp. in property. **1b** a presumptive right based on long-continued use: *right of user.* **2** (*often in combination*) a person or thing that uses: *a road-user.* **3** *Inf.* a drug addict.
user-friendly *adj* (**user friendly** *when postpositive*) easy to familiarize oneself with, understand, or use.
use up ⓣ *vb (tr, adv)* **1** to finish (a supply); consume completely. **2** to exhaust; wear out.
usher ⓣ (ˈʌʃə) *n* **1** an official who shows people to their seats, as in a church or theatre. **2** a person who acts as doorkeeper, esp. in a court of law. **3** (in England) a minor official charged with maintaining order in a court of law. **4** an officer responsible for preceding persons of rank in a procession. **5** *Brit., obs.* a teacher. ◆ *vb (tr)* **6** to conduct or escort, esp. in a courteous or obsequious way. **7** (usually foll. by *in*) to be a precursor or herald (of). [C14: from OF *huissier* doorkeeper, from Vulgar L *ustiārius* (unattested), from L *ostium* door]
usherette (ˌʌʃəˈrɛt) *n* a woman assistant in a cinema, etc., who shows people to their seats.
USM *Stock Exchange. abbrev. for* unlisted securities market.
USN *abbrev. for* United States Navy.
USP *abbrev. for* unique selling proposition: a characteristic of a product that can be used in advertising to differentiate it from its competitors.
usquebaugh (ˈʌskwɪˌbɔː) *n* **1** *Irish.* the former name for **whiskey.** **2** *Scot.* the former name for **whisky.** [C16: from Irish Gaelic *uisce beathadh* or Scot. Gaelic *uisge beatha* water of life]
USS *abbrev. for:* **1** United States Senate. **2** United States Ship.
USSR *abbrev. for* (the former) Union of Soviet Socialist Republics.
usual ⓣ (ˈjuːʒʊəl) *adj* **1** of the most normal, frequent, or regular type: *that's the usual sort of application to send.* ◆ *n* **2** ordinary or commonplace events (esp. in **out of the usual**). **3 the usual.** *Inf.* the habitual or usual drink, etc. [C14: from LL *ūsuālis* ordinary, from L *ūsus* USE]
▸ **ˈusually** *adv* ▸ **ˈusualness** *n*
usufruct (ˈjuːsjʊˌfrʌkt) *n* the right to use and derive profit from a piece of property belonging to another, provided the property itself remains undiminished and uninjured in any way. [C17: from LL *ūsūfrūctus,* from L *ūsus* use + *frūctus* enjoyment]
▸ **ˌusuˈfructuary** *n, adj*
usurer (ˈjuːʒərə) *n* a person who lends funds at an exorbitant rate of interest.
usurp ⓣ (juːˈzɜːp) *vb* to seize or appropriate (land, a throne, etc.) without authority. [C14: from OF, from L *ūsūrpāre* to take into use, prob. from *ūsus* use + *rapere* to seize]
▸ **ˌusurˈpation** *n* ▸ **uˈsurper** *n*
usury (ˈjuːʒərɪ) *n, pl* **usuries. 1** the practice of loaning money at an exorbitant rate of interest. **2** an unlawfully high rate of interest. **3** *Obs.* moneylending. [C14: from Med. L, from L *ūsūra* usage, from *ūsus* USE]
▸ **usurious** (juːˈʒʊərɪəs) *adj*
USW *Radio. abbrev. for* ultrashort wave.
ut (ʌt, uːt) *n Music.* the syllable used in the fixed system of solmization for the note C. [C14: from L *ut;* see GAMUT]
UT *abbrev. for:* **1** universal time. **2** Utah.
UTC *abbrev. for* universal time coordinated. See **universal time.**
ute (juːt) *n Austral. & NZ inf.* short for **utility truck.**
utensil (juːˈtɛnsəl) *n* an implement, tool, or container for practical use: *writing utensils.* [C14 *utensele,* via OF from L *ūtēnsilia* necessaries, from *ūtēnsilis* available for use, from *ūtī* to use]
uterine (ˈjuːtəˌraɪn) *adj* **1** of, relating to, or affecting the uterus. **2** (of offspring) born of the same mother but not the same father.
uterus (ˈjuːtərəs) *n, pl* **uteri** (ˈjuːtəˌraɪ). **1** *Anat.* a hollow muscular organ lying within the pelvic cavity of female mammals. It houses the developing fetus. Nontechnical name: **womb. 2** the corresponding organ in other animals. [C17: from L]
utilidor (juːˈtɪlədə; *Canad.* -ˌdɒr) *n Canad.* above-ground insulated casing for pipes carrying water, etc., in permafrost regions.
utilitarian (juːˌtɪlɪˈtɛərɪən) *adj* **1** of or relating to utilitarianism. **2** designed for use rather than beauty. ◆ *n* **3** a person who believes in utilitarianism.
utilitarianism (juːˌtɪlɪˈtɛərɪəˌnɪzəm) *n Ethics.* **1** the doctrine that the morally correct course of action consists in the greatest good for the greatest number, that is, in maximizing the total benefit resulting, without regard to the distribution of benefits and burdens. **2** the theory that the criterion of virtue is utility.
utility ⓣ (juːˈtɪlɪtɪ) *n, pl* **utilities. 1a** the quality of practical use; usefulness. **1b** (*as modifier*): *a utility fabric.* **2** something useful. **3a** a public service, such as the bus system. **3b** (*as modifier*): *utility vehicle.* **4** *Econ.* the ability of a commodity to satisfy human wants. Cf. **disutility. 5** *Austral.* short for **utility truck. 6** *Computing.* a piece of software that performs a routine task. [C14: from OF *utelite,* from L *ūtilitās* usefulness, from *ūtī* to use]
utility function *n Econ.* a function relating specific goods and services in an economy to individual preferences.
utility player *n Sport.* a player who is capable of playing competently in any of several positions.
utility room *n* a room with equipment for domestic work like washing and ironing.
utility truck *n Austral. & NZ.* a small truck with an open body and low sides, often with a removable tarpaulin cover; pick-up truck.
utilize ⓣ *or* **utilise** (ˈjuːtɪˌlaɪz) *vb* **utilizes, utilizing, utilized** *or* **utilises, utilising, utilised.** (*tr*) to make practical or worthwhile use of.
▸ **ˈutiˌlizable** *or* **ˈutiˌlisable** *adj* ▸ **ˌutiliˈzation** *or* **ˌutiliˈsation** *n* ▸ **ˈutiˌlizer** *or* **ˈutiˌliser** *n*
utmost ⓣ (ˈʌtˌməʊst) *or* **uttermost** *adj* (*prenominal*) **1** of the greatest possible degree or amount: *the utmost degree.* **2** at the furthest limit: *the utmost town on the peninsula.* ◆ *n* **3** the greatest possible degree, extent, or amount: *he tried his utmost.* [OE *ūtemest,* from *ūte* out + *-mest* MOST]
utmost good faith *n* a principle used in insurance contracts, legally obliging all parties to reveal to the others any information that might influence the others' decision to enter into the contract. [from L *uberrima fides*]
Utopia ⓣ (juːˈtəʊpɪə) *n* (*sometimes not cap.*) any real or imaginary society, place, state, etc., considered to be perfect or ideal. [C16: from NL *Utopia* (coined by Sir Thomas More in 1516 as the title of his book that described an imaginary island representing the perfect society), lit.: no place, from Gk *ou* not + *topos* a place]
Utopian ⓣ (juːˈtəʊpɪən) (*sometimes not cap.*) ◆ *adj* **1** of or relating to a perfect or ideal existence. ◆ *n* **2** an idealistic social reformer.
▸ **Uˈtopianism** *n*

THESAURUS

used *adj* = **second-hand**, cast-off, hand-me-down (*inf.*), nearly new, not new, reach-me-down (*inf.*), shopsoiled, worn
Antonyms *adj* brand-new, fresh, intact, new, pristine, unused
used to *adj* **1** = **accustomed to,** at home in, attuned to, familiar with, given to, habituated to, hardened to, in the habit of, inured to, tolerant of, wont to
useful *adj* **1** = **helpful**, advantageous, all-purpose, beneficial, effective, fruitful, general-purpose, of help, of service, of use, practical, profitable, salutary, serviceable, valuable, worthwhile
Antonyms *adj* inadequate, ineffective, unbeneficial, unhelpful, unproductive, useless, vain, worthless
usefulness *n* **1** = **helpfulness**, benefit, convenience, effectiveness, efficacy, help, practicality, profit, service, use, utility, value, worth
useless *adj* **1** = **worthless**, bootless, disadvantageous, fruitless, futile, hopeless, idle, impractical, ineffective, ineffectual, of no use, pointless, profitless, unavailing, unproductive, unworkable, vain, valueless **2** *Informal* = **inept**, hopeless, incompetent, ineffectual, no good, stupid, weak
Antonyms *adj* ≠ **worthless:** advantageous, effective, fruitful, practical, productive, profitable, useful, valuable, workable, worthwhile
use up *vb* **1, 2** = **consume**, absorb, burn up, deplete, devour, drain, exhaust, finish, fritter away, run through, squander, swallow up, waste
usher *n* **1** = **attendant**, doorkeeper, doorman, escort, guide, usherette ◆ *vb* **6** = **escort**, conduct, direct, guide, lead, pilot, show in *or* out, steer **7** *usually with* **in** = **introduce**, bring in, herald, inaugurate, initiate, launch, open the door to, pave the way for, precede, ring in
usual *adj* **1** = **normal**, accustomed, bog-standard (*Brit. & Irish sl.*), common, constant, customary, everyday, expected, familiar, fixed, general, habitual, ordinary, regular, routine, standard, stock, typical, wonted
Antonyms *adj* exceptional, extraordinary, new, novel, off-beat, out of the ordinary, peculiar, rare, singular, strange, uncommon, unexpected, unhackneyed, unique, unorthodox, unusual
usually *adv* **1** = **normally**, as a rule, as is the custom, as is usual, by and large, commonly, for the most part, generally, habitually, in the main, mainly, mostly, most often, on the whole, ordinarily, regularly, routinely
usurp *vb* = **seize**, appropriate, arrogate, assume, commandeer, infringe upon, lay hold of, take, take over, wrest
utility *n* **1a** = **usefulness**, advantageousness, avail, benefit, convenience, efficacy, fitness, mileage, point, practicality, profit, service, serviceableness, use
utilize *vb* = **use**, appropriate, avail oneself of, employ, have recourse to, make the most of, make use of, profit by, put to use, resort to, take advantage of, turn to account
utmost *adj* **1** = **greatest**, chief, extreme, highest, maximum, paramount, pre-eminent, supreme **2** = **farthest**, extreme, final, last, most distant, outermost, remotest, uttermost ◆ *n* **3** = **greatest**, best, hardest, highest, most
Utopia *n* = **paradise**, bliss, Eden, Garden of Eden, Happy Valley, heaven, ideal life, perfect place, seventh heaven, Shangri-la
Utopian *adj* **1** = **perfect**, airy, chimerical, dream, fanciful, fantasy, ideal, idealistic, illusory, imaginary, impractical, romantic, visionary ◆ *n* **2** = **dreamer**, Don Quixote, idealist, romanticist, visionary

utricle ('ju:trɪkᵊl) *n* **1** *Anat.* the larger of the two parts of the membranous labyrinth of the internal ear. Cf. **saccule. 2** *Bot.* the bladder-like one-seeded indehiscent fruit of certain plants. [C18: from L *ūtriculus*, dim. of *ūter* bag]
▸**u'tricular** *adj*

utriculitis (ju:ˌtrɪkju'laɪtɪs) *n* inflammation of the inner ear.

utter[1] ⓣ ('ʌtə) *vb* **1** to give audible expression to (something): *to utter a growl.* **2** *Criminal law.* to put into circulation (counterfeit coin, forged banknotes, etc.). **3** (*tr*) to make publicly known; publish: *to utter slander.* [C14: prob. orig. a commercial term, from MDu. *ūteren* (modern Du. *uiteren*) to make known]
▸**'utterable** *adj* ▸**'utterableness** *n* ▸**'utterer** *n*

utter[2] ⓣ ('ʌtə) *adj* (*prenominal*) (intensifier): *an utter fool; the utter limit.* [C15: from OE *utera* outer, comp. of *ūte* out (adv)]
▸**'utterly** *adv*

utterance ⓣ ('ʌtərəns) *n* **1** something uttered, such as a statement. **2** the act or power of uttering or ability to utter.

utter barrister *n Law.* the full title of a barrister who is not a Queen's Counsel.

uttermost ⓣ ('ʌtəˌməust) *adj, n* a variant of **utmost**.

U-turn *n* **1** a turn made by a vehicle in the shape of a U, resulting in a reversal of direction. **2** a complete change in direction of political policy, etc.

UV *abbrev. for* ultraviolet.

UV-A *or* **UVA** *abbrev. for* ultraviolet radiation with a range of 320-380 nanometres.

uvarovite (u:'vɑ:rəˌvaɪt) *n* an emerald-green garnet found in chromium deposits. [C19: from G *Uvarovit*; after Count Sergei *Uvarov* (1785–1855), Russian author & statesman]

UV-B *or* **UVB** *abbrev. for* ultraviolet radiation with a range of 280-320 nanometres.

uvea ('ju:vɪə) *n* the part of the eyeball consisting of the iris, ciliary body, and choroid. [C16: from Med. L *ūvea*, from L *ūva* grape]
▸**'uveal** *adj*

UVF *abbrev. for* Ulster Volunteer Force.

uvula ('ju:vjʊlə) *n, pl* **uvulas** *or* **uvulae** (-ˌli:). a small fleshy flap of tissue that hangs in the back of the throat and is an extension of the soft palate. [C14: from Med. L, lit.: a little grape, from L *ūva* a grape]

uvular ('ju:vjʊlə) *adj* **1** of or relating to the uvula. **2** *Phonetics.* articulated with the uvula and the back of the tongue, such as the (r) sound of Parisian French. ◆ *n* **3** a uvular consonant.

uxorial (ʌk'sɔ:rɪəl) *adj* of or relating to a wife: *uxorial influence.* [C19: from L *uxor* wife]
▸**ux'orially** *adv*

uxoricide (ʌk'sɔ:rɪˌsaɪd) *n* **1** the act of killing one's wife. **2** a man who kills his wife. [C19: from L *uxor* wife + -CIDE]
▸**uxˌori'cidal** *adj*

uxorious (ʌk'sɔ:rɪəs) *adj* excessively attached to or dependent on one's wife. [C16: from L *uxōrius* concerning a wife, from *uxor* wife]
▸**ux'oriously** *adv* ▸**ux'oriousness** *n*

Uzbek ('uzbek, 'ʌz-) *n* **1** (*pl* **Uzbeks** *or* **Uzbek**) a member of a Mongoloid people of Uzbekistan in central Asia. **2** the language of this people.

THESAURUS

utter[1] *vb* **1** = **express**, articulate, enunciate, pronounce, put into words, say, speak, verbalize, vocalize, voice **3** = **publish**, declare, divulge, give expression to, make known, proclaim, promulgate, reveal, state

utter[2] *adj* = **absolute**, arrant, complete, consummate, deep-dyed (*usually derogatory*), downright, entire, out-and-out, outright, perfect, sheer, stark, thorough, thoroughgoing, total, unmitigated, unqualified

utterance *n* **1** = **speech**, announcement, declaration, expression, opinion, remark, statement, words **2** = **expression**, articulation, delivery, ejaculation, verbalization, vocalization, vociferation

utterly *adv* = **totally**, absolutely, completely, entirely, extremely, fully, one hundred per cent, perfectly, thoroughly, to the core, to the nth degree, wholly

uttermost *adj* = **farthest**, extreme, final, last, outermost, remotest, utmost

Vv

v *or* **V** (viː) *n, pl* **v's, V's,** *or* **Vs. 1** the 22nd letter of the English alphabet. **2** a speech sound represented by this letter, usually a voiced fricative, as in *vote*. **3a** something shaped like a V. **3b** (*in combination*): *a V neck.*

v *symbol. for:* **1** *Physics.* velocity. **2** specific volume (of a gas).

V *symbol for:* **1** *Chem.* vanadium. **2** (in transformational grammar) verb. **3** volume (capacity). **4** volt. **5** victory. **6** *the Roman numeral for* five.

v. *abbrev. for:* **1** ventral. **2** verb. **3** verse. **4** verso. **5** (*usually italic*) versus. **6** very. **7** vide [L: see]. **8** volume.

V. *abbrev. for:* **1** Venerable. **2** (in titles) Very. **3** (in titles) Vice. **4** Viscount.

V-1 *n* a robot bomb invented by the Germans in World War II: used esp. to bombard London. Also called: **doodlebug, buzz bomb, flying bomb.** [from G *Vergeltungswaffe* revenge weapon]

V-2 *n* a rocket-powered ballistic missile invented by the Germans in World War II: used esp. to bombard London. [see V-1]

V6 *n* a car or internal-combustion engine having six cylinders arranged in the form of a V.

V8 *n* a car or internal-combustion engine having eight cylinders arranged in the form of a V.

VA *abbrev. for:* **1** Vicar Apostolic. **2** (Order of) Victoria and Albert. **3** volt-ampere. **4** Virginia.

vac (væk) *n Brit. inf.* short for **vacation.**

vacancy ❶ (ˈveɪkənsɪ) *n, pl* **vacancies. 1** the state or condition of being vacant or unoccupied; emptiness. **2** an unoccupied post or office: *we have a vacancy in the accounts department.* **3** an unoccupied room in a hotel, etc.: *the manager put up the "No Vacancies" sign.* **4** lack of thought or intelligent awareness. **5** *Obs.* idleness or a period spent in idleness.

vacant ❶ (ˈveɪkənt) *adj* **1** without any contents; empty. **2** (*postpositive;* foll. by *of*) devoid (of something specified). **3** having no incumbent: *a vacant post.* **4** having no tenant or occupant: *a vacant house.* **5** characterized by or resulting from lack of thought or intelligent awareness. **6** (of time, etc.) not allocated to any activity: *it is pleasant to have a vacant hour in one's day.* **7** spent in idleness or inactivity: *a vacant life.* [C13: from L *vacāre* to be empty]
▸**ˈvacantly** *adv*

vacant possession *n* ownership of an unoccupied house or property, any previous owner or tenant having departed.

vacate ❶ (vəˈkeɪt) *vb* **vacates, vacating, vacated.** (*mainly tr*) **1** to cause (something) to be empty, esp. by departing from or abandoning it: *to vacate a room.* **2** (*also intr*) to give up the tenure, possession, or occupancy of (a place, post, etc.). **3** *Law.* **3a** to cancel. **3b** to annul.
▸**vaˈcatable** *adj*

vacation (vəˈkeɪʃən) *n* **1** *Chiefly Brit.* a period of the year when the law courts or universities are closed. **2** another word (esp. US. and Canad.) for **holiday** (sense 1). **3** the act of departing from or abandoning property, etc. ◆ *vb* **4** (*intr*) *US. & Canad.* to take a holiday. [C14: from L *vacātiō* freedom, from *vacāre* to be empty]
▸**vaˈcationer** *or* **vaˈcationist** *n*

vaccinate (ˈvæksɪˌneɪt) *vb* **vaccinates, vaccinating, vaccinated.** to inoculate (a person) with vaccine so as to produce immunity against a specific disease.
▸**ˈvacciˌnator** *n*

vaccination (ˌvæksɪˈneɪʃən) *n* **1** the act of vaccinating. **2** the scar left following inoculation with a vaccine.

vaccine (ˈvæksiːn) *n Med.* **1** a suspension of dead, attenuated, or otherwise modified microorganisms for inoculation to produce immunity to a disease by stimulating the production of antibodies. **2** a preparation of the virus of cowpox inoculated in humans to produce immunity to smallpox. **3** (*modifier*) of or relating to vaccination or vaccinia. **4** *Computing.* software designed to detect and remove computer viruses from a system. [C18: from NL *variolae vaccīnae* cowpox, title of medical treatise (1798) by Edward Jenner, from L *vacca* a cow]
▸**ˈvaccinal** *adj*

vaccinia (vækˈsɪnɪə) *n* a technical name for **cowpox.** [C19: NL, from L *vaccīnus* of cows]

vacherin *French.* (vaʃrɛ̃) *n* a dessert consisting of a meringue shell filled with whipped cream, ice cream, fruit, etc. [also in France a kind of cheese, from F *vache* cow, from L *vacca*]

vacillate ❶ (ˈvæsɪˌleɪt) *vb* **vacillates, vacillating, vacillated.** (*intr*) **1** to fluctuate in one's opinions. **2** to sway from side to side physically. [C16: from L *vacillāre* to sway, from ?]
▸**ˌvacilˈlation** *n* ▸**ˈvacilˌlator** *n*

vacua (ˈvækjʊə) *n* a plural of **vacuum.**

vacuity ❶ (væˈkjuːɪtɪ) *n, pl* **vacuities. 1** the state or quality of being vacuous. **2** an empty space or void. **3** a lack or absence of something specified: *a vacuity of wind.* **4** lack of normal intelligence or awareness. **5** a statement, saying, etc., that is inane or pointless. **6** (in customs terminology) the difference in volume between the actual contents of a container and its full capacity. [C16: from L *vacuitās* empty space, from *vacuus* empty]

vacuole (ˈvækjʊˌəʊl) *n Biol.* a fluid-filled cavity in a cell. [C19: from F, lit.: little vacuum, from L VACUUM]
▸**vacuolar** (ˌvækjʊˈəʊlə) *adj*

vacuous ❶ (ˈvækjʊəs) *adj* **1** empty. **2** bereft of ideas or intelligence. **3** characterized by or resulting from vacancy of mind: *a vacuous gaze.* **4** indulging in no useful mental or physical activity. [C17: from L *vacuus* empty]
▸**ˈvacuously** *adv*

vacuum ❶ (ˈvækjʊəm) *n, pl* **vacuums** *or* **vacua. 1** a region containing no free matter; in technical contexts now often called: **free space. 2** a region in which gas is present at a low pressure. **3** the degree of exhaustion of gas within an enclosed space: *a perfect vacuum.* **4** a feeling of emptiness: *his death left a vacuum in her life.* **5** short for **vacuum cleaner. 6** (*modifier*) of, containing, producing, or operated by a low gas pressure: *a vacuum brake.* ◆ *vb* **7** to clean (something) with a vacuum cleaner. [C16: from L: empty space, from *vacuus* empty]

vacuum cleaner *n* an electrical household appliance used for cleaning floors, carpets, etc., by suction.
▸**vacuum cleaning** *n*

vacuum distillation *n* distillation in which the liquid distilled is enclosed at a low pressure in order to reduce its boiling point.

vacuum flask *n* an insulating flask that has double walls, usually of silvered glass, with an evacuated space between them. It is used for maintaining substances at high or low temperatures. Also called: **Thermos.**

vacuum gauge *n* any of a number of instruments for measuring pressures below atmospheric pressure.

vacuum-packed *adj* packed in an airtight container or packet under low pressure in order to maintain freshness, prevent corrosion, etc.

vacuum pump *n* a pump for producing a low gas pressure.

vacuum tube *or* **valve** *n* the US. and Canad. name for **valve** (sense 3).

VAD *abbrev. for* **1** Voluntary Aid Detachment. ◆ *n* **2** a member of this organization.

vade mecum (ˈvɑːdɪ ˈmeɪkʊm) *n* a handbook or other aid carried on the person for immediate use when needed. [C17: from L, lit.: go with me]

vadose (ˈveɪdəʊs) *adj* of, designating, or derived from water occurring above the water table: *vadose deposits.* [C19: from L *vadōsus* full of shallows, from *vadum* a ford]

vagabond ❶ (ˈvægəˌbɒnd) *n* **1** a person with no fixed home. **2** an idle wandering beggar or thief. **3** (*modifier*) of or like a vagabond. [C15: from L *vagābundus* wandering, from *vagārī* to roam, from *vagus* VAGUE]
▸**ˈvagaˌbondage** *n*

vagal (ˈveɪgᵊl) *adj Anat.* of, relating to, or affecting the vagus nerve: *vagal inhibition.*

vagary ❶ (ˈveɪgərɪ, vəˈgeərɪ) *n, pl* **vagaries.** an erratic notion or action. [C16: prob. from L *vagārī* to roam; cf. L *vagus* VAGUE]

THESAURUS

vacancy *n* **1 = emptiness**, gap, space, vacuum, void **2 = job**, opening, opportunity, position, post, room, situation **4 = blankness**, absent-mindedness, abstraction, inanity, inattentiveness, incomprehension, incuriousness, lack of interest, vacuousness

vacant *adj* **1, 3, 4 = unoccupied**, available, disengaged, empty, free, idle, not in use, to let, unemployed, unengaged, unfilled, untenanted, void **5 = blank**, absent-minded, abstracted, ditzy *or* ditsy (*sl.*), dreaming, dreamy, expressionless, idle, inane, incurious, thoughtless, unthinking, vacuous, vague
Antonyms *adj* **≠ unoccupied:** busy, engaged, full, inhabited, in use, occupied, taken **≠ blank:** animated, engrossed, expressive, lively, reflective, thoughtful

vacate *vb* **1 = leave**, depart, evacuate, give up, go away, leave empty, move out of, quit, relinquish possession of, withdraw

vacillate *vb* **1, 2 = keep changing one's mind**, be irresolute *or* indecisive, blow hot and cold (*inf.*), chop and change, dither, fluctuate, haver, hesitate, oscillate, reel, rock, shillyshally (*inf.*), sway, swither (*Scot.*), waver

vacillating *adj* **1 = irresolute**, hesitant, in two minds (*inf.*), oscillating, shillyshallying (*inf.*), uncertain, unresolved, wavering

vacillation *n* **1 = indecisiveness**, dithering (*chiefly Brit.*), fluctuation, hesitation, inconstancy, irresoluteness, irresolution, shillyshallying (*inf.*), unsteadiness, wavering

vacuity *n* **1, 4 = unintelligence**, blankness, emptiness, inanity, incognizance, incomprehension, vacuousness **2 = emptiness**, nothingness, space, vacuum, void

vacuous *adj* **1 = emptiness**, empty, unfilled, vacant, void **2, 3 = unintelligent**, blank, inane, stupid, uncomprehending, vacant

vacuum *n* **1 = emptiness**, free space, gap, nothingness, space, vacuity, void

vagabond *n* **1 = vagrant**, bag lady, beggar, bum (*inf.*), down-and-out, hobo (*US*), itinerant, knight of the road, migrant, nomad, outcast, rascal, rover, tramp, wanderer, wayfarer ◆ *modifier* **3 = vagrant**, destitute, down and out, drifting, fly-by-night (*inf.*), footloose, homeless, idle, itinerant, journeying, nomadic, rootless, roving, shiftless, wandering

vagary *n* **= whim**, caprice, crotchet, fancy, humour, megrim (*arch.*), notion, whimsy

vagina ➊ (vəˈdʒaɪnə) *n, pl* **vaginas** *or* **vaginae** (-niː). **1** the canal in most female mammals that extends from the cervix of the uterus to an external opening between the labia minora. **2** *Anat., biol.* any sheath or sheathlike structure. [C17: from L: sheath]
▸**vagˈinal** *adj*

vaginate (ˈvædʒɪnɪt, -ˌneɪt) *adj* (esp. of plant parts) sheathed: *a vaginate leaf.*

vaginectomy (ˌvædʒɪˈnɛktəmɪ) *n, pl* **vaginectomies. 1** surgical removal of all or part of the vagina. **2** surgical removal of part of the serous sheath surrounding the testis and epididymis.

vaginismus (ˌvædʒɪˈnɪzməs) *n* painful spasm of the vagina. [C19: from NL, from VAGINA, + *-ismus;* see -ISM]

vaginitis (ˌvædʒɪˈnaɪtɪs) *n* inflammation of the vagina.

vagotomy (væˈgɒtəmɪ) *n, pl* **vagotomies.** surgical division of the vagus nerve, performed to limit gastric secretion in patients with severe peptic ulcers. [C19: from VAG(US) + -TOMY]

vagotonia (ˌveɪgəˈtəʊnɪə) *n* pathological overactivity of the vagus nerve, affecting various bodily functions controlled by this nerve. [C19: from VAG(US) + *-tonia,* from L *tonus* tension, TONE]

vagrancy (ˈveɪgrənsɪ) *n, pl* **vagrancies. 1** the state or condition of being a vagrant. **2** the conduct or mode of living of a vagrant.

vagrant ➊ (ˈveɪgrənt) *n* **1** a person of no settled abode, income, or job; tramp. ◆ *adj* **2** wandering about. **3** of or characteristic of a vagrant or vagabond. **4** moving in an erratic fashion; wayward. **5** (of plants) showing straggling growth. [C15: prob. from OF *waucrant* (from *wancrer* to roam, of Gmc origin), but also infl. by OF *vagant* vagabond, from L *vagārī* to wander]
▸**ˈvagrantly** *adv*

vague ➊ (veɪg) *adj* **1** (of statements, meaning, etc.) imprecise: *vague promises.* **2** not clearly perceptible or discernible: *a vague idea.* **3** not clearly established or known: *a vague rumour.* **4** (of a person or his expression) absent-minded. [C16: via F from L *vagus* wandering, from ?]
▸**ˈvaguely** *adv* ▸**ˈvagueness** *n*

vagus *or* **vagus nerve** (ˈveɪgəs) *n, pl* **vagi** (ˈveɪdʒaɪ) *or* **vagus nerves.** the tenth cranial nerve, which supplies the heart, lungs, and viscera. [C19: from L *vagus* wandering]
▸**ˈvagal** *adj*

vail (veɪl) *Obs.* ◆ *vb (tr)* **1** to lower (something, such as a weapon), esp. as a sign of deference. **2** to remove (the hat, etc.) as a mark of respect. ◆ *n* **3** a tip. [C14 *valen,* from obs. *avalen,* from OF *avaler* to let fall, from L *ad vallem,* lit.: to the valley, i.e., down]

vain ➊ (veɪn) *adj* **1** inordinately proud of one's appearance, possessions, or achievements. **2** given to ostentatious display. **3** worthless. **4** senseless or futile. ◆ *n* **5 in vain.** fruitlessly. [C13: via OF from L *vānus*]
▸**ˈvainly** *adv* ▸**ˈvainness** *n*

vainglory (ˌveɪnˈglɔːrɪ) *n* **1** boastfulness or vanity. **2** ostentation.
▸**ˌvainˈglorious** *adj*

vair (vɛə) *n* **1** a fur, probably Russian squirrel, used to trim robes in the Middle Ages. **2** a fur used on heraldic shields, conventionally represented by white and blue skins in alternate lines. [C13: from OF: of more than one colour, from L *varius* variegated]

Vaisya (ˈvaɪsjə, ˈvaɪʃjə) *n* the third of the four main Hindu castes, the traders. [C18: from Sansk., lit.: settler, from *viś* settlement]

valance (ˈvæləns) *n* a short piece of drapery hung along a shelf or bed to hide structural detail. [C15: ? after *Valence,* SE France, town noted for its textiles]
▸**ˈvalanced** *adj*

vale[1] (veɪl) *n* a literary word for **valley.** [C13: from OF *val,* from L *vallis* valley]

vale[2] *Latin.* (ˈvɑːleɪ) *sentence substitute.* farewell; goodbye.

valediction ➊ (ˌvælɪˈdɪkʃən) *n* **1** the act or an instance of saying goodbye. **2** any valedictory statement, etc. [C17: from L *valedīcere,* from *valē* farewell + *dīcere* to say]

valedictory ➊ (ˌvælɪˈdɪktərɪ) *adj* **1** saying goodbye. **2** of or relating to a farewell or an occasion of farewell. ◆ *n, pl* **valedictories. 3** a farewell address or speech.

valence (ˈveɪləns) *n Chem.* **1** another name (esp. US. and Canad.) for **valency. 2** the phenomenon of forming chemical bonds.

Valenciennes (ˌvælənsɪˈɛn) *n* a flat bobbin lace typically having scroll and floral designs and originally made of linen. [after *Valenciennes,* N France, where orig. made]

valency (ˈveɪlənsɪ) *or esp. US. & Canad.* **valence** *n, pl* **valencies** *or* **valences.** *Chem.* a property of atoms or groups equal to the number of atoms of hydrogen that the atom or group could combine with or displace in forming compounds. [C19: from L *valentia* strength, from *valēre* to be strong]

valency electron *n Chem.* an electron in the outer shell of an atom, responsible for forming chemical bonds.

valentine (ˈvælənˌtaɪn) *n* **1** a card or gift expressing love or affection, sent, often anonymously, on Saint Valentine's Day. **2** a sweetheart selected for such a greeting. [C15: after *St Valentine,* 3rd-century A.D. Christian martyr]

valerian (vəˈlɛərɪən) *n* **1** Also called: **allheal.** a Eurasian plant having small white or pinkish flowers and a medicinal root. **2** a sedative drug made from the dried roots of this plant. [C14: via OF from Med. L *valeriana (herba)* (herb) of *Valerius,* unexplained L personal name]

valeric (vəˈlɛrɪk, -ˈlɪərɪk) *adj* of, relating to, or derived from valerian.

valeric acid *n* another name for **pentanoic acid.**

valet (ˈvælɪt, ˈvæleɪ) *n* **1** a manservant who acts as personal attendant to his employer, looking after his clothing, serving his meals, etc. **2** a manservant who attends to the requirements of patrons in a hotel, etc.; steward. ◆ *vb* **valets, valeting, valeted. 3** to act as a valet for (a person). **4** *(tr)* to clean the bodywork and interior of (a car) as a professional service. [C16: from OF *vaslet* page, from Med. L *vassus* servant]

valeta *or* **veleta** (vəˈliːtə) *n* a ballroom dance in triple time. [from Sp.: weather vane]

valet de chambre *French.* (valɛ də ʃɑ̃brə) *n, pl* ***valets de chambre*** (valɛ də ʃɑ̃brə). the full French term for **valet** (sense 1).

valet parking *n* a system at hotels, airports, etc., in which patrons' cars are parked by a steward.

valetudinarian (ˌvælɪˌtjuːdɪˈnɛərɪən) *or* **valetudinary** (ˌvælɪˈtjuːdɪnərɪ) *n, pl* **valetudinarians** *or* **valetudinaries. 1** a person who is chronically sick. **2** a hypochondriac. ◆ *adj* **3** relating to or resulting from poor health. **4** being a valetudinarian. [C18: from L *valētūdō* state of health, from *valēre* to be well]
▸**ˌvaleˌtudiˈnarianism** *n*

valgus (ˈvælgəs) *adj Pathol.* twisted away from the midline of the body. [C19: from L: bow-legged]

Valhalla (vælˈhælə), **Walhalla, Valhall** (vælˈhæl, ˈvælhæl), *or* **Walhall** *n Norse myth.* the great hall of Odin where warriors who die as heroes in battle dwell eternally. [C18: from ON, from *valr* slain warriors + *höll* HALL]

valiant ➊ (ˈvæljənt) *adj* **1** courageous or intrepid. **2** marked by bravery or courage: *a valiant deed.* [C14: from OF, from *valoir* to be of value, from L *valēre* to be strong]
▸**ˈvaliantly** *adv*

valid ➊ (ˈvælɪd) *adj* **1** having some foundation; based on truth. **2** legally acceptable: *a valid licence.* **3a** having legal force. **3b** having legal authority. **4** having some force or cogency: *a valid point in a debate.* **5** *Logic.* (of an inference or argument) having premises and a conclusion so related that if the premises are true, the conclusion must be true. [C16: from L *validus* robust, from *valēre* to be strong]
▸**validity** (vəˈlɪdɪtɪ) *n* ▸**ˈvalidly** *adv*

THESAURUS

vagina *n* **1 = vulva,** beaver (*taboo sl.*), box (*taboo sl.*), crack (*taboo sl.*), cunt (*taboo*), fanny (*Brit. taboo sl.*), hole (*taboo sl.*), minge (*Brit. taboo*), muff (*taboo sl.*), pussy (*taboo sl.*), quim (*Brit. taboo*), snatch (*taboo sl.*), twat (*taboo sl.*), yoni

vagrant *n* **1 = tramp,** bag lady (*chiefly US*), beggar, bird of passage, bum (*inf.*), drifter, hobo (*US*), itinerant, person of no fixed address, rolling stone, wanderer ◆ *adj* **2 = itinerant,** nomadic, roaming, rootless, roving, unsettled, vagabond
Antonyms *adj* ≠ **itinerant:** established, fixed, purposeful, rooted, settled

vague *adj* **1 = unclear,** doubtful, generalized, hazy, imprecise, indefinite, loose, uncertain, unspecified, woolly **2 = indistinct,** amorphous, blurred, dim, fuzzy, hazy, ill-defined, indeterminate, nebulous, obscure, shadowy, unclear, unknown
Antonyms *adj* ≠ **unclear:** clear, clear-cut, definite, distinct, exact, explicit, precise, specific ≠ **indistinct:** clear, distinct, lucid, well-defined

vaguely *adv* **1 = imprecisely,** dimly, evasively, in a general way, obscurely, slightly **4 = absent-mindedly,** vacantly

vagueness *n* **1 = impreciseness,** ambiguity, inexactitude, lack of preciseness, looseness, obscurity, undecidedness, woolliness
Antonyms *n* clarity, clearness, definition, exactness, obviousness, preciseness, precision

vain *adj* **1, 2 = proud,** arrogant, bigheaded, cocky, conceited, egotistical, inflated, narcissistic, ostentatious, overweening, peacockish, pleased with oneself, self-important, stuck-up (*inf.*), swaggering, swanky (*inf.*), swollen-headed (*inf.*), vainglorious **3, 4 = futile,** abortive, empty, fruitless, hollow, idle, nugatory, pointless, senseless, time-wasting, trifling, trivial, unavailing, unimportant, unproductive, unprofitable, useless, worthless ◆ *n* **5 in vain = to no avail,** bootless(ly), fruitless(ly), ineffectual(ly), to no purpose, unsuccessful(ly), useless(ly), vain(ly), wasted, without success
Antonyms *adj* ≠ **proud:** bashful, humble, meek, modest, self-deprecating ≠ **futile:** fruitful, profitable, serious, successful, useful, valid, worthwhile, worthy

valediction *n* **1, 2 = farewell,** adieu, goodbye, leave-taking, sendoff (*inf.*), vale

valedictory *adj* **1 = farewell,** final, parting

valiant *adj* **1, 2 = brave,** bold, courageous, dauntless, doughty, fearless, gallant, heroic, indomitable, intrepid, lion-hearted, plucky, redoubtable, stouthearted, valorous, worthy
Antonyms *adj* cowardly, craven, fearful, shrinking, spineless, timid, weak

valid *adj* **1, 4 = sound,** acceptable, binding, cogent, conclusive, convincing, efficacious, efficient, good, just, logical, powerful, sensible, substantial, telling, weighty, well-founded, well-grounded **2, 3 = legal,** authentic, bona fide, genuine, in force, lawful, legally binding, legitimate, official, signed and sealed
Antonyms *adj* ≠ **sound:** baseless, bogus, fallacious, false, illogical, sham, spurious, unacceptable, unfounded, unrealistic, unrecognized, untrue, weak ≠ **legal:** illegal, inoperative, invalid, unlawful, unofficial

validate *vb* **1 = confirm,** certify, corroborate, prove, substantiate **2 = authorize,** authenticate, endorse, legalize, make legally binding, ratify, set one's seal on *or* to

validity *n* **3 = legality,** authority, lawfulness, legitimacy, right **4 = soundness,** cogency, force, foundation, grounds, point, power, strength, substance, weight

validate ❶ ('vælɪˌdeɪt) *vb* **validates, validating, validated.** (*tr*) **1** to confirm or corroborate. **2** to give legal force or official confirmation to.
▸ˌ**vali'dation** *n*

valine ('veɪliːn) *n* an essential amino acid: a component of proteins. [C19: from VAL(ERIC ACID) + -INE[2]]

valise (və'liːz) *n* a small overnight travelling case. [C17: via F from It. *valigia*, from ?]

Valium ('vælɪəm) *n Trademark.* a preparation of the drug diazepam used as a tranquillizer.

Valkyrie, Walkyrie (væl'kɪərɪ, 'vælkɪərɪ), *or* **Valkyr** ('vælkɪə) *n Norse myth.* any of the beautiful maidens who serve Odin and ride over battlefields to claim the dead heroes and take them to Valhalla. [C18: from ON *Valkyrja*, from *valr* slain warriors + *köri* to CHOOSE]
▸**Val'kyrian** *adj*

vallation (və'leɪʃən) *n* **1** the act or process of building fortifications. **2** a wall or rampart. [C17: from LL *vallātiō*, from L *vallum* rampart]

vallecula (və'lɛkjʊlə) *n, pl* **valleculae** (-ˌliː). **1** *Anat.* any of various natural depressions or crevices. **2** *Bot.* a groove or furrow. [C19: from LL: little valley, from L *vallis* valley]

valley ❶ ('vælɪ) *n* **1** a long depression in the land surface, usually containing a river, formed by erosion or by movements in the earth's crust. **2** the broad area drained by a single river system: *the Thames valley.* **3** any elongated depression resembling a valley. [C13: from OF *valee*, from L *vallis*]

vallum ('væləm) *n Archaeol.* a Roman rampart or earthwork.

valonia (və'ləʊnɪə) *n* the acorn cups and unripe acorns of the Eurasian oak, used in tanning, dyeing, and making ink. [C18: from It. *vallonia*, ult. from Gk *balanos* acorn]

valorize *or* **valorise** ('væləˌraɪz) *vb* **valorizes, valorizing, valorized** *or* **valorises, valorising, valorised.** (*tr*) to fix an artificial price for (a commodity) by governmental action. [C20: back formation from *valorization*; see VALOUR]
▸ˌ**valori'zation** *or* ˌ**valori'sation** *n*

valour ❶ *or US* **valor** ('vælə) *n* courage or bravery, esp. in battle. [C15: from LL *valor*, from *valēre* to be strong]
▸**'valorous** *adj*

valse *French.* (vals) *n* another word for **waltz.**

valuable ❶ ('væljʊəbᵊl) *adj* **1** having considerable monetary worth. **2** of considerable importance or quality: *valuable information.* **3** able to be valued. ◆ *n* **4** (*usually pl*) a valuable article of personal property, esp. jewellery.
▸**'valuably** *adv*

valuate ('væljʊˌeɪt) *vb* **valuates, valuating, valuated.** *US.* another word for **value** (senses 10, 12) or **evaluate.**
▸**'valuˌator** *n*

valuation (ˌvæljʊ'eɪʃən) *n* **1** the act of valuing, esp. a formal assessment of the worth of property, jewellery, etc. **2** the price arrived at by the process of valuing: *I set a high valuation on technical ability.*
▸ˌ**valu'ational** *adj*

value ❶ ('væljuː) *n* **1** the desirability of a thing, often in respect of some property such as usefulness or exchangeability. **2** an amount, esp. a material or monetary one, considered to be a fair exchange in return for a thing: *the value of the picture is £10 000.* **3** satisfaction: *value for money.* **4** precise meaning or significance. **5** (*pl*) the moral principles or accepted standards of a person or group. **6** *Maths.* a particular magnitude, number, or amount: *the value of the variable was 7.* **7** *Music.* short for **time value. 8** (in painting, drawing, etc.) **8a** a gradation of tone from light to dark. **8b** the relation of one of these elements to another or to the whole picture. **9** *Phonetics.* the quality of the speech sound associated with a written character representing it: *"g" has the value* (dʒ) *in English "gem".* ◆ *vb* **values, valuing, valued.** (*tr*) **10** to assess or estimate the worth, merit, or desirability of. **11** to have a high regard for, esp. in respect of worth, usefulness, merit, etc. **12** (foll. by *at*) to fix the financial or material worth of (a unit of currency, work of art, etc.). [C14: from OF, from *valoir*, from L *valēre* to be worth]
▸**'valued** *adj* ▸**'valueless** *adj* ▸**'valuer** *n*

value added *n* the difference between the total revenues of a firm, industry, etc., and its total purchases from other firms, industries, etc.

value-added tax *n* (in Britain) the full name for **VAT.**

valued policy *n* an insurance policy in which the amount payable in the event of a valid claim is agreed upon between the company and the policyholder when the policy is issued and is not related to the actual value of a loss.

value judgment *n* a subjective assessment based on one's own values or those of one's class.

Valuer General *n Austral.* a state official who values properties for rating purposes.

valuta (və'luːtə) *n Rare.* the value of one currency in terms of its exchange rate with another. [C20: from It., lit.: VALUE]

valvate ('vælveɪt) *adj* **1** furnished with a valve or valves. **2** *Bot.* **2a** taking place by means of valves: *valvate dehiscence.* **2b** (of petals) having the margins touching but not overlapping.

valve (vælv) *n* **1** any device that shuts off, starts, regulates, or controls the flow of a fluid. **2** *Anat.* a flaplike structure in a hollow organ, such as the heart, that controls the one-way passage of fluid through that organ. **3** Also called: **tube.** an evacuated electron tube containing a cathode, anode, and, usually, one or more additional control electrodes. When a positive potential is applied to the anode, it produces a one-way flow of current. **4** *Zool.* any of the separable pieces that make up the shell of a mollusc. **5** *Music.* a device on some brass instruments by which the effective length of the tube may be varied to enable a chromatic scale to be produced. **6** *Bot.* any of the several parts that make up a dry dehiscent fruit, esp. a capsule. [C14: from L *valva* a folding door]
▸**'valveless** *adj* ▸**'valveˌlike** *adj*

valve-in-head engine *n* the US name for **overhead-valve engine.**

valvular ('vælvjʊlə) *adj* **1** of, relating to, operated by, or having a valve or valves. **2** having the shape or function of a valve.

valvulitis (ˌvælvjʊ'laɪtɪs) *n* inflammation of a bodily valve, esp. a heart valve. [C19: from NL *valvula* dim. of VALVE + -ITIS]

vamoose ❶ (və'muːs) *vb* **vamooses, vamoosing, vamoosed.** (*intr*) *Sl., chiefly US.* to leave a place hurriedly; decamp. [C19: from Sp. *vamos* let us go, from L *vādere* to go, walk rapidly]

vamp[1] (væmp) *Inf.* ◆ *n* **1** a seductive woman who exploits men by use of her sexual charms. ◆ *vb* **2** to exploit (a man) in the fashion of a vamp. [C20: short for VAMPIRE]

vamp[2] (væmp) *n* **1** something patched up to make it look new. **2** the reworking of a story, etc. **3** an improvised accompaniment. **4** the front part of the upper of a shoe. ◆ *vb* **5** (*tr*; often foll. by *up*) to make a renovation of. **6** to improvise (an accompaniment) to (a tune). [C13: from OF *avantpié* the front part of a shoe (hence, something patched), from *avant-* fore- + *pié* foot, from L *pēs*]

vampire ('væmpaɪə) *n* **1** (in European folklore) a corpse that rises nightly from its grave to drink the blood of the living. **2** See **vampire bat. 3** a person who preys mercilessly upon others. [C18: from F, from G, from Magyar]
▸**vampiric** (væm'pɪrɪk) *adj* ▸**'vampirism** *n*

vampire bat *n* a bat of tropical regions of Central and South America, having sharp incisor and canine teeth and feeding on the blood of birds and mammals.

van[1] (væn) *n* **1** short for **caravan** (sense 1). **2** a motor vehicle for transporting goods, etc., by road. **3** *Brit.* a closed railway wagon in which the guard travels, for transporting goods, etc.

van[2] (væn) *n* short for **vanguard.**

van[3] (væn) *n Tennis, chiefly Brit.* short for **advantage** (sense 3).

van[4] (væn) *n* **1** any device for winnowing corn. **2** *Arch.* a wing. [C17: var. of FAN[1]]

vanadium (və'neɪdɪəm) *n* a toxic silvery-white metallic element used in steel alloys and as a catalyst. Symbol: V; atomic no.: 23; atomic wt.: 50.94. [C19: NL, from ON *Vanadis*, epithet of the goddess Freya + -IUM]

Van Allen belt *n* either of two regions of charged particles above the earth, the inner one extending from 2400 to 5600 kilometres above the earth and the outer one from 13 000 to 19 000 kilometres. [C20: after J. A. *Van Allen* (born 1914), US physicist]

V and A (in Britain) *abbrev. for* Victoria and Albert Museum.

vandal ❶ ('vændᵊl) *n* a person who deliberately causes damage to personal or public property. [C17: from VANDAL, from L *Vandallus*, of Gmc origin]

Vandal ('vændᵊl) *n* a member of a Germanic people that raided Roman provinces in the 3rd and 4th centuries A.D. before devastating Gaul, conquering Spain and N Africa, and sacking Rome.
▸**Vandalic** (væn'dælɪk) *adj*

THESAURUS

valley *n* **1** = **hollow**, coomb, cwm (*Welsh*), dale, dell, depression, dingle, glen, strath (*Scot.*), vale

valorous *adj* = **brave**, bold, courageous, dauntless, doughty, fearless, gallant, heroic, intrepid, lion-hearted, plucky, valiant

valour *n* = **bravery**, boldness, courage, derring-do (*arch.*), doughtiness, fearlessness, gallantry, heroism, intrepidity, lion-heartedness, spirit
Antonyms *n* cowardice, dread, fear, timidity, trepidation, weakness

valuable *adj* **1** = **precious**, costly, dear, expensive, high-priced **3** = **useful**, beneficial, cherished, esteemed, estimable, held dear, helpful, important, prized, profitable, serviceable, treasured, valued, worthwhile, worthy ◆ *n* **4** *usually plural* = **treasures**, heirlooms, jewellery
Antonyms *adj* ≠ **precious:** cheap, cheapo (*inf.*), inexpensive, worthless ≠ **useful:** insignificant, pointless, silly, trifling, trivial, unimportant, useless, worthless

value *n* **1** = **importance**, advantage, benefit, desirability, help, merit, mileage (*inf.*), profit, serviceableness, significance, use, usefulness, utility, worth **2** = **cost**, equivalent, market price, monetary worth, rate **5** *plural* = **principles**, code of behaviour, ethics, (moral) standards ◆ *vb* **10, 12** = **evaluate**, account, appraise, assess, compute, estimate, price, put a price on, rate, set at, survey **11** = **regard highly**, appreciate, cherish, esteem, hold dear, hold in high regard *or* esteem, prize, respect, set store by, treasure
Antonyms *n* ≠ **importance:** insignificance, unimportance, uselessness, worthlessness ◆ *vb* ≠ **regard highly:** disregard, have no time for, hold a low opinion of, underestimate, undervalue

valued *adj* **11** = **highly regarded**, cherished, dear, esteemed, loved, prized, treasured

valueless *adj* **1** = **worthless**, miserable, no good, of no earthly use, of no value, unsaleable, useless

vamoose *vb Slang, chiefly U.S.* = **go away**, clear off (*inf.*), decamp, do a bunk (*Brit. sl.*), hook it (*sl.*), make off, make oneself scarce (*inf.*), run away, scarper (*Brit. sl.*), scram (*inf.*), skedaddle (*inf.*), take flight, take oneself off

vandal *n* = **hooligan**, delinquent, graffiti artist, lager lout, rowdy, yob *or* yobbo (*Brit. sl.*)

vandalism (ˈvændəˌlɪzəm) *n* the deliberate destruction caused by a vandal or an instance of such destruction.
▸ˌvandalˈistic *adj*

vandalize *or* **vandalise** (ˈvændəˌlaɪz) *vb* **vandalizes, vandalizing, vandalized** *or* **vandalises, vandalising, vandalised.** (*tr*) to destroy or damage (something) by an act of vandalism.

Van de Graaff generator (ˈvæn də ˌɡrɑːf) *n* a device for producing high electrostatic potentials, consisting of a hollow metal sphere on which a charge is accumulated from a continuous moving belt of insulating material: used in particle accelerators. [C20: after R. J. *Van de Graaff* (1901–67), US physicist]

Vandyke beard (vænˈdaɪk) *n* a short pointed beard. Often shortened to **Vandyke.** [C18: after Sir Anthony *Van Dyck* (1599–1641), Flemish painter]

Vandyke collar *or* **cape** *n* a large white collar with several very deep points. Often shortened to **Vandyke.**

vane (veɪn) *n* **1** Also called: **weather vane.** a flat plate or blade of metal mounted on a vertical axis in an exposed position to indicate wind direction. **2** any one of the flat blades or sails forming part of the wheel of a windmill. **3** any flat or shaped plate used to direct fluid flow, esp. in a turbine, etc. **4** a fin or plate fitted to a projectile or missile to provide stabilization or guidance. **5** *Ornithol.* the flat part of a feather. **6** *Surveying.* **6a** a sight on a quadrant or compass. **6b** the movable marker on a levelling staff. [OE *fana*]
▸**vaned** *adj*

vanguard ❶ (ˈvænˌɡɑːd) *n* **1** the leading division or units of a military force. **2** the leading position in any movement or field, or the people who occupy such a position. [C15: from OF *avant-garde*, from *avant-* fore- + *garde* GUARD]

vanilla (vəˈnɪlə) *n* **1** any of a genus of tropical climbing orchids having spikes of large fragrant flowers and long fleshy pods containing the seeds (beans). **2** the pod or bean of certain of these plants, used to flavour food, etc. **3** a flavouring extract prepared from vanilla beans and used in cooking. ◆ *adj* **4** flavoured with or as with vanilla: *vanilla ice cream.* **5** *Sl.* ordinary or conventional: *a vanilla kind of guy.* [C17: from NL, from Sp. *vainilla* pod, from *vaina*, from L *vāgīna* sheath]
▸**vaˈnillic** *adj*

vanillin (ˈvænɪlɪn, vəˈnɪlɪn) *n* a white crystalline aldehyde found in vanilla and many natural balsams and resins. It is a by-product of paper manufacture and is used as a flavouring and in perfumes.

vanish ❶ (ˈvænɪʃ) *vb* (*intr*) **1** to disappear, esp. suddenly or mysteriously. **2** to cease to exist. **3** *Maths.* to become zero. [C14 *vanissen*, from OF *esvanir*, from L *ēvānēscere* to evaporate, from *ē-* EX-[1] + *vānēscere*, from *vānus* empty]
▸ˈ**vanisher** *n*

vanishing cream *n* a cosmetic cream that is colourless once applied, used as a foundation for powder or as a cleansing cream.

vanishing point *n* **1** the point to which parallel lines appear to converge in the rendering of perspective, usually on the horizon. **2** a point at which something disappears.

vanity ❶ (ˈvænɪtɪ) *n, pl* **vanities. 1** the state or quality of being vain. **2** ostentation occasioned by ambition or pride. **3** an instance of being vain or something about which one is vain. **4** the state or quality of being valueless or futile. [C13: from OF, from L *vānitās* emptiness, from *vānus* empty]

vanity bag, case, *or* **box** *n* a woman's small bag or hand case used to carry cosmetics, etc.

vanity unit *n* a hand basin built into a wooden Formica-covered or tiled top, usually with a built-in cupboard below it. Also called (trademark): **Vanitory unit.**

vanquish ❶ (ˈvæŋkwɪʃ) *vb* (*tr*) **1** to defeat or overcome in a battle, contest, etc. **2** to defeat in argument or debate. **3** to conquer (an emotion). [C14 *vanquisshen*, from OF *venquis*, from *veintre* to overcome, from L *vincere*]
▸ˈ**vanquishable** *adj* ▸ˈ**vanquisher** *n*

vantage (ˈvɑːntɪdʒ) *n* **1** a state, position, or opportunity affording superiority or advantage. **2** superiority or benefit accruing from such a position, etc. **3** *Tennis.* short for **advantage** (sense 3). [C13: from OF *avantage* ADVANTAGE]

vantage point *n* a position or place that allows one an overall view of a scene or situation.

vanward (ˈvænwəd) *adj, adv* in or towards the front.

vapid ❶ (ˈvæpɪd) *adj* **1** bereft of strength, sharpness, flavour, etc. **2** boring or dull. [C17: from L *vapidus*]
▸**vaˈpidity** *n* ▸ˈ**vapidly** *adv*

vapor (ˈveɪpə) *n* the US spelling of **vapour.**

vaporescence (ˌveɪpəˈrɛsəns) *n* the production or formation of vapour.
▸ˌ**vaporˈescent** *adj*

vaporetto (ˌveɪpəˈrɛtəʊ) *n, pl* **vaporetti** (-tɪ) *or* **vaporettos.** a steam-powered passenger boat, as used on the canals in Venice. [It., from *vapore* a steamboat]

vaporific (ˌveɪpəˈrɪfɪk) *adj* **1** producing, causing, or tending to produce vapour. **2** of, concerned with, or having the nature of vapour. **3** tending to become vapour; volatile. [C18: from NL *vaporificus*, from L *vapor* steam + *facere* to make]

vaporimeter (ˌveɪpəˈrɪmɪtə) *n* an instrument for measuring vapour pressure, used to determine the volatility of oils.

vaporize *or* **vaporise** (ˈveɪpəˌraɪz) *vb* **vaporizes, vaporizing, vaporized** *or* **vaporises, vaporising, vaporised. 1** to change or cause to change into vapour or into the gaseous state. **2** to evaporate or disappear or cause to evaporate or disappear, esp. suddenly. **3** to destroy or be destroyed by turning into a gas as a result of the extreme heat generated by a nuclear explosion.
▸ˌ**vaporiˈzation** *or* ˌ**vaporiˈsation** *n*

vaporizer *or* **vaporiser** (ˈveɪpəˌraɪzə) *n* **1** a substance that vaporizes or a device that causes vaporization. **2** *Med.* a device that produces steam or atomizes medication for inhalation.

vaporous (ˈveɪpərəs) *adj* **1** resembling or full of vapour. **2** lacking permanence or substance. **3** given to foolish imaginings.
▸**vaporosity** (ˌveɪpəˈrɒsɪtɪ) *n* ▸ˈ**vaporously** *adv*

vapour ❶ *or US* **vapor** (ˈveɪpə) *n* **1** particles of moisture or other substance suspended in air and visible as clouds, smoke, etc. **2** a gaseous substance at a temperature below its critical temperature. **3** a substance that is in a gaseous state at a temperature below its boiling point. **4 the vapours.** *Arch.* a depressed mental condition believed originally to be the result of vaporous exhalations from the stomach. ◆ *vb* **5** to evaporate or cause to evaporate. **6** (*intr*) to make vain empty boasts. [C14: from L *vapor*]
▸ˈ**vapourer** *or US* ˈ**vaporer** *n* ▸ˈ**vapourish** *or US* ˈ**vaporish** *adj* ▸ˈ**vapour-**ˌ**like** *or US* ˈ**vapor-**ˌ**like** *adj* ▸ˈ**vapoury** *or US* ˈ**vapory** *adj*

vapour density *n* the ratio of the density of a gas or vapour to that of hydrogen at the same temperature and pressure.

vapour lock *n* a stoppage in a pipe carrying a liquid caused by a bubble of gas, esp. in the pipe feeding the carburettor of an internal-combustion engine.

vapour pressure *n Physics.* the pressure exerted by a vapour in equilibrium with its solid or liquid phase at a particular temperature.

vapour trail *n* a visible trail left by an aircraft flying at high altitude or through supercold air caused by the deposition of water vapour in the engine exhaust as minute ice crystals.

var. *abbrev. for:* **1** variable. **2** variant. **3** variation. **4** variety. **5** various.

varactor (ˈveəˌræktə) *n* a semiconductor diode that acts as a voltage-dependent capacitor, being operated with a reverse bias. [C20: prob. a blend of *variable reactor*]

varec (ˈværɛk) *n* **1** another name for **kelp. 2** the ash obtained from kelp. [C17: from F, from ON *wrek* (unattested); see WRECK]

variable ❶ (ˈveərɪəbᵊl) *adj* **1** liable to or capable of change: *variable weather.* **2** (of behaviour, emotions, etc.) lacking constancy. **3** *Maths.* having a range of possible values. **4** (of a species, etc.) liable to deviate from the established type. **5** (of a wind) varying in direction and intensity. **6** (of an electrical component or device) designed so that a characteristic property, such as resistance, can be varied. ◆ *n* **7** something that is subject to variation. **8** *Maths.* **8a** an expression that can be assigned any of a set of values. **8b** a symbol, esp. *x, y,* or *z,* representing an unspecified member of a class of objects, numbers, etc. **9** *Logic.* a symbol, esp. *x, y,* or *z,* representing any member of a class of entities. **10** *Computing.* a named unit of storage that can be changed to any of a set of specified values during execution of a program. **11** *Astron.* See **variable star. 12** a variable wind. **13** (*pl*) a region where variable winds occur. [C14: from L *variābilis* changeable, from *variāre* to diversify]
▸ˌ**variaˈbility** *or* ˈ**variableness** *n* ▸ˈ**variably** *adv*

variable cost *n* a cost that varies directly with output.

variable-geometry *or* **variable-sweep** *adj* denoting an aircraft in which the wings are hinged to give the variable aspect ratio colloquially known as a **swing-wing.**

variable star *n* any star that varies considerably in brightness, either irregularly or in regular periods. **Intrinsic variables,** in which the variation is a result of internal changes, include novae and pulsating stars.

THESAURUS

vanguard *n* **1, 2 = forefront**, advance guard, cutting edge, forerunners, front, front line, front rank, leaders, spearhead, trailblazers, trendsetters, van
Antonyms *n* back, rear, rearguard, stern, tail, tail end

vanish *vb* **1, 2 = disappear**, become invisible, be lost to sight, die out, dissolve, evanesce, evaporate, exit, fade (away), melt (away), vanish off the face of the earth
Antonyms *vb* appear, arrive, become visible, come into view, materialize, pop up

vanity *n* **2, 3 = pride**, affected ways, airs, arrogance, bigheadedness, conceit, conceitedness, egotism, narcissism, ostentation, pretension, self-admiration, self-love, showing off (*inf.*), swollen-headedness (*inf.*), vainglory **4 = futility**, emptiness, frivolity, fruitlessness, hollowness, inanity, pointlessness, profitlessness, triviality, unproductiveness, unreality, unsubstantiality, uselessness, worthlessness
Antonyms *n* ≠ **pride:** humility, meekness, modesty, self-abasement, self-deprecation ≠ **futility:** importance, value, worth

vanquish *vb* **1, 2 = defeat**, beat, blow out of the water (*sl.*), clobber, conquer, crush, get the upper hand over, master, overcome, overpower, overwhelm, put down, put to flight, put to rout, quell, reduce, repress, rout, run rings around (*inf.*), stuff (*sl.*), subdue, subjugate, triumph over, undo

vapid *adj* **1, 2 = dull**, bland, boring, colourless, flat, insipid, limp, tame, uninspiring, uninteresting, weak, wishy-washy (*inf.*)

vapour *n* **1 = mist**, breath, dampness, exhalation, fog, fumes, haze, miasma, smoke, steam

variable *adj* **1, 2 = changeable**, capricious, chameleonic, fickle, fitful, flexible, fluctuating, inconstant, mercurial, mutable, protean, shifting, temperamental, uneven, unstable, unsteady, vacillating, wavering

variance Ⓣ ('vɛərɪəns) *n* **1** the act of varying or the quality, state, or degree of being divergent. **2** an instance of diverging; dissension. **3 at variance. 3a** (often foll. by *with*) (of facts, etc.) not in accord. **3b** (of persons) in a state of dissension. **4** *Statistics.* a measure of dispersion; the square of the standard deviations. **5** a difference or discrepancy between two steps in a legal proceeding, esp. between a statement and the evidence given to support it. **6** *Chem.* the number of degrees of freedom of a system, used in the phase rule.

variant Ⓣ ('vɛərɪənt) *adj* **1** liable to or displaying variation. **2** differing from a standard or type: *a variant spelling.* ◆ *n* **3** something that differs from a standard or type. **4** *Statistics.* another word for **variate.** [C14: via OF from L, from *variāre* to diversify, from *varius* VARIOUS]

variate ('vɛərɪɪt) *n Statistics.* a random variable or a numerical value taken by it. [C16: from L *variāre* to VARY]

variation Ⓣ (ˌvɛərɪ'eɪʃən) *n* **1** the act, process, condition, or result of changing or varying. **2** an instance of varying or the amount, rate, or degree of such change. **3** something that differs from a standard or convention. **4** *Music.* a repetition of a musical theme in which the rhythm, harmony, or melody is altered or embellished. **5** *Biol.* a marked deviation from the typical form or function. **6** *Astron.* any deviation from the mean motion or orbit of a planet, satellite, etc. **7** another word for **magnetic declination. 8** *Ballet.* a solo dance.
▸ **ˌvari'ational** *adj*

varicella (ˌværɪ'sɛlə) *n* the technical name for **chickenpox.** [C18: NL, irregular dim. of VARIOLA]
▸ **ˌvari'cellar** *adj*

varices ('værɪˌsiːz) *n* the plural of **varix.**

varico- *or before a vowel* **varic-** *combining form.* indicating a varix or varicose veins: *varicotomy.* [from L *varix, varic-* distended vein]

varicoloured *or US* **varicolored** ('vɛərɪˌkʌləd) *adj* having many colours.

varicose ('værɪˌkəʊs) *adj* of or resulting from varicose veins: *a varicose ulcer.* [C18: from L *varicōsus,* from VARIX]

varicose veins *pl n* a condition in which the superficial veins, esp. of the legs, become knotted and swollen.

varicosis (ˌværɪ'kəʊsɪs) *n Pathol.* any condition characterized by distension of the veins. [C18: from NL, from L: VARIX]

varicosity (ˌværɪ'kɒsɪtɪ) *n, pl* **varicosities.** *Pathol.* **1** the state, condition, or quality of being varicose. **2** an abnormally distended vein.

varicotomy (ˌværɪ'kɒtəmɪ) *n, pl* **varicotomies.** surgical excision of a varicose vein.

varied Ⓣ ('vɛərɪd) *adj* **1** displaying or characterized by variety; diverse. **2** modified or altered: *the amount may be varied.* **3** varicoloured; variegated.
▸ **'variedly** *adv*

variegate ('vɛərɪˌgeɪt) *vb* **variegates, variegating, variegated.** (*tr*) to alter the appearance of, esp. by adding different colours. [C17: from LL, from L *varius* diverse, VARIOUS + *agere* to make]
▸ **ˌvarie'gation** *n*

variegated Ⓣ ('vɛərɪˌgeɪtɪd) *adj* **1** displaying differently coloured spots., streaks, etc. **2** (of foliage) having pale patches.

varietal (və'raɪɪtᵊl) *adj* **1** of, characteristic of, designating, or forming a variety, esp. a biological variety. ◆ *n* **2** a wine labelled with the name of the grape from which it is pressed.
▸ **va'rietally** *adv*

variety Ⓣ (və'raɪɪtɪ) *n, pl* **varieties. 1** the quality or condition of being diversified or various. **2** a collection of unlike things, esp. of the same general group. **3** a different form or kind within a general category: *varieties of behaviour.* **4a** *Taxonomy.* a race whose distinct characters do not justify classification as a separate species. **4b** *Horticulture, stockbreeding.* a strain of animal or plant produced by artificial breeding. **5a** entertainment consisting of a series of short unrelated acts, such as comedy turns, songs, etc. **5b** (*as modifier*): *a variety show.* [C16: from L *varietās,* from VARIOUS]

variform ('vɛərɪˌfɔːm) *adj* varying in form or shape.
▸ **'variˌformly** *adv*

variola (və'raɪələ) *n* the technical name for **smallpox.** [C18: from Med. L: disease marked by little spots, from L *varius* spotted]
▸ **va'riolar** *adj*

variole ('vɛərɪˌəʊl) *n* any of the rounded masses that make up the rock variolite. [C19: from F, from Med. L; see VARIOLA]

variolite ('vɛərɪəˌlaɪt) *n* any basic igneous rock containing rounded bodies (varioles). [C18: from VARIOLA, referring to the pockmarked appearance of the rock]
▸ **variolitic** (ˌvɛərɪə'lɪtɪk) *adj*

variometer (ˌvɛərɪ'ɒmɪtə) *n* **1** an instrument for measuring variations in a magnetic field. **2** *Electronics.* a variable inductor consisting of a movable coil mounted inside and connected in series with a fixed coil.

variorum (ˌvɛərɪ'ɔːrəm) *adj* **1** containing notes by various scholars or various versions of the text. ◆ *n* **2** an edition or text of this kind. [C18: from L *ēditiō cum notīs variōrum* edition with the notes of various commentators]

various Ⓣ ('vɛərɪəs) *determiner* **1** several different: *he is an authority on various subjects.* ◆ *adj* **2** of different kinds, though often within the same general category: *his disguises are many and various.* **3** (*prenominal*) relating to a collection of separate persons or things: *the various members of the club.* **4** displaying variety; many-sided: *his various achievements.* [C16: from L *varius* changing]
▸ **'variously** *adv* ▸ **'variousness** *n*

> **USAGE NOTE** The use of *different* after *various* should be avoided: *the disease exists in various forms* (not *in various different forms*).

varistor (və'rɪstə) *n* a two-electrode semiconductor device having a voltage-dependent nonlinear resistance. [C20: a blend of *variable resistor*]

Varityper ('vɛərɪˌtaɪpə) *n Trademark.* a justifying typewriter used to produce copy in various type styles.

varix ('vɛərɪks) *n, pl* **varices.** *Pathol.* **a** a tortuous dilated vein. **b** a similar condition affecting an artery or lymphatic vessel. [C15: from L]

varlet ('vɑːlɪt) *n Arch.* **1** a menial servant. **2** a knight's page. **3** a rascal. [C15: from OF, var. of *vallet* VALET]
▸ **'varletry** *n*

varmint ('vɑːmɪnt) *n Inf.* an irritating or obnoxious person or animal. [C16: dialect var. of *varmin* VERMIN]

varna ('vɑːnə) *n* any of the four Hindu castes; Brahman, Kshatriya, Vaisya, or Sudra. [from Sansk.: class]

varnish Ⓣ ('vɑːnɪʃ) *n* **1** a preparation consisting of a solvent, a drying oil, and usually resin, rubber, etc., for application to a surface where it yields a hard glossy, usually transparent, coating. **2** a similar preparation consisting of a substance, such as shellac, dissolved in a volatile solvent, such as alcohol. It hardens to a film on evaporation of the solvent. **3** the sap of certain trees used to produce such a coating. **4** a smooth surface, coated with or as with varnish. **5** an artificial, superficial, or deceptively pleasing manner, covering, etc. **6** *Chiefly Brit.* another word for **nail polish.** ◆ *vb* (*tr*) **7** to cover with varnish. **8** to give a smooth surface to, as if by painting with varnish. **9** to impart a more attractive appearance to. [C14: from OF, from Med. L *veronix* sandarac, resin, from Med. Gk *berenikē,* ?from Gk *Berenikē,* city in Cyrenaica, Libya where varnishes were used]
▸ **'varnisher** *n*

varnish tree *n* any of various trees, such as the lacquer tree, yielding substances used to make varnish or lacquer.

varsity ('vɑːsɪtɪ) *n, pl* **varsities.** *Brit., S. African, & NZ inf.* short for **university.**

varus ('vɛərəs) *adj Pathol.* turned inwards towards the midline of the body. [C19: from L: crooked, bent]

varve (vɑːv) *n Geol.* a band of sediment deposited in glacial lakes, consisting of a light layer and a dark layer deposited at different seasons. [C20: from Swedish *varv* layer, from *varva,* from ON *hverfa* to turn]

vary Ⓣ ('vɛərɪ) *vb* **varies, varying, varied. 1** to undergo or cause to undergo change or modification in appearance, character, form, etc. **2** to be different or cause to be different; be subject to change. **3** (*tr*) to give variety to. **4** (*intr*; foll. by *from*) to differ, as from a convention, standard, etc. **5** (*intr*) to change in accordance with another variable: *her mood varies with the weather.* [C14: from L, from *varius* VARIOUS]
▸ **'varying** *adj*

THESAURUS

Antonyms *adj* constant, firm, fixed, settled, stable, steady, unalterable, unchanging

variance *n* **1, 2 = disagreement,** difference, difference of opinion, discord, discrepancy, dissension, dissent, divergence, inconsistency, lack of harmony, strife, variation **3 at variance = in disagreement,** at loggerheads, at odds, at sixes and sevens, conflicting, in opposition, out of harmony, out of line
Antonyms *n* ≠ **disagreement:** accord, agreement, congruity, correspondence, harmony, similarity, unison

variant *adj* **2 = different,** alternative, derived, divergent, exceptional, modified

variation *n* **1-3 = difference,** alteration, break in routine, change, departure, departure from the norm, deviation, discrepancy, diversification, diversity, innovation, modification, novelty, variety

Antonyms *n* dullness, monotony, sameness, tedium, uniformity

varied *adj* **1 = different,** assorted, diverse, heterogeneous, manifold, miscellaneous, mixed, motley, sundry, various
Antonyms *adj* homogeneous, repetitive, similar, standardized, uniform, unvarying

variegated *adj* **1 = mottled,** diversified, many-coloured, motley, parti-coloured, pied, streaked, varicoloured

variety *n* **1 = diversity,** change, difference, discrepancy, diversification, many-sidedness, multifariousness, variation **2 = range,** array, assortment, collection, cross section, intermixture, medley, miscellany, mixed bag (*inf.*), mixture, multiplicity **3 = type,** brand, breed, category, class, kind, make, order, sort, species, strain

Antonyms *n* ≠ **diversity:** homogeneity, invariability, monotony, similarity, similitude, uniformity

various *adj* **2-4 = different,** assorted, differing, disparate, distinct, divers (*arch.*), diverse, diversified, heterogeneous, manifold, many, many-sided, miscellaneous, several, sundry, varied, variegated
Antonyms *adj* alike, equivalent, matching, same, similar, uniform

varnish *n, vb* **1, 2, 7 = lacquer,** glaze, gloss, japan, polish, shellac ◆ *vb* **9 = adorn,** decorate, embellish, gild

vary *vb* **1 = change,** alter, fluctuate, transform **2 = differ,** be unlike, depart, disagree, diverge **3 = alternate,** diversify, intermix, permutate, reorder

varying *adj* **1 = changing,** fluctuating, inconsistent **2 = different,** distinct, distinguishable, diverse

vas (væs) *n, pl* **vasa** ('veɪsə). *Anat., zool.* a vessel or tube that carries a fluid. [C17: from L: vessel]

vascular ('væskjʊlə) *adj Biol., anat.* of, relating to, or having vessels that conduct and circulate liquids: *a vascular bundle.* [C17: from NL *vāsculāris,* from L *vāsculum,* dim. of *vās* vessel] ▸**vascularity** (ˌvæskjʊ'lærɪtɪ) *n* ▸**'vascularly** *adv*

vascular bundle *n* a longitudinal strand of vascular tissue in the stems and leaves of higher plants.

vascular tissue *n* tissue of plants occurring as a continuous system throughout the plant: it conducts water, mineral salts, and synthesized food, and provides mechanical support. Also called: **conducting tissue.**

vas deferens ('væs 'dɛfəˌrɛnz) *n, pl* **vasa deferentia** ('veɪsə ˌdɛfə'rɛnʃɪə). *Anat.* the duct that conveys spermatozoa from the epididymis to the urethra. [C16: from NL, from L *vās* vessel + *deferēns,* present participle of *deferre* to bear away]

vase (vɑːz) *n* a vessel used as an ornament or for holding cut flowers. [C17: via F from L *vās* vessel]

vasectomy (væ'sɛktəmɪ) *n, pl* **vasectomies.** surgical removal of all or part of the vas deferens, esp. as a method of contraception.

Vaseline ('væsɪˌliːn) *n* a trademark for **petrolatum.**

vaso- *or before a vowel* **vas-** *combining form.* **1** indicating a blood vessel: *vasodilator.* **2** indicating the vas deferens: *vasectomy.* [from L *vās* vessel]

vasoactive (ˌveɪzəʊ'æktɪv) *adj* affecting the diameter of blood vessels: *vasoactive peptides.*

vasoconstrictor (ˌveɪzəʊkən'strɪktə) *n* a drug, agent, or nerve that causes narrowing of the walls of blood vessels.

vasodilator (ˌveɪzəʊdaɪ'leɪtə) *n* a drug, agent, or nerve that can cause dilation of the walls of blood vessels.

vasoinhibitor (ˌveɪzəʊɪn'hɪbɪtə) *n* any of a group of drugs that reduce or inhibit the action of the vasomotor nerves.

vasomotor (ˌveɪzəʊ'məʊtə) *adj* (of a drug, nerve, etc.) relating to or affecting the diameter of blood vessels.

vasopressin (ˌveɪzəʊ'prɛsɪn) *n* a hormone secreted by the pituitary gland. It increases the reabsorption of water by the kidney tubules and increases blood pressure by constricting the arteries. Also called: **antidiuretic hormone.** [from *Vasopressin,* a trademark]

vasopressor ('veɪzəʊˌprɛsə) *Med.* ◆ *adj* **1** causing an increase in blood pressure by constricting the arteries. ◆ *n* **2** a substance that has such an effect.

vassal ❶ ('væsᵊl) *n* **1** (in feudal society) a man who entered into a relationship with a lord to whom he paid homage and fealty in return for protection and often a fief. **2a** a person, nation, etc., in a subordinate or dependent position relative to another. **2b** (*as modifier*): *vassal status.* ◆ *adj* **3** of or relating to a vassal. [C14: via OF from Med. L *vassallus,* from *vassus* servant, of Celtic origin] ▸**'vassalage** *n*

vast ❶ (vɑːst) *adj* **1** unusually large in size, degree, or number. **2** (*prenominal*) (intensifier): *in vast haste.* ◆ *n* **3 the vast.** *Chiefly poetic.* immense or boundless space. [C16: from L *vastus* deserted] ▸**'vastly** *adv* ▸**'vastness** *n*

vasty ('vɑːstɪ) *adj* **vastier, vastiest.** an archaic or poetic word for **vast.**

vat (væt) *n* **1** a large container for holding or storing liquids. **2** *Chem.* a preparation of reduced vat dye. ◆ *vb* **vats, vatting, vatted. 3** (*tr*) to place, store, or treat in a vat. [OE *fæt*]

VAT (*sometimes* væt) (in Britain) *abbrev. for* value-added tax: a tax levied on the difference between the cost of materials and the selling price of a commodity or service.

vat dye *n* a dye, such as indigo, that is applied by first reducing it to its base, which is soluble in alkali, and then regenerating the insoluble dye by oxidation in the fibres of the material. ▸**'vat-ˌdyed** *adj*

vatic ('vætɪk) *adj Rare.* of, relating to, or characteristic of a prophet; oracular. [C16: from L *vātēs* prophet]

Vatican ('vætɪkən) *n* **1a** the palace of the popes in Rome, which includes administrative offices and is attached to the basilica of St Peter's. **1b** (*as modifier*): *the Vatican Council.* **2a** the authority of the Pope and the papal curia. **2b** (*as modifier*): *a Vatican edict.* [C16: from L *Vāticānus mons* Vatican hill, on the western bank of the Tiber, of Etruscan origin]

vaudeville ('vəʊdəvɪl, 'vɔː-) *n* **1** *Chiefly US & Canad.* variety entertainment consisting of short acts such as acrobatic turns, song-and-dance routines, etc. Brit. name: **music hall. 2** a light or comic theatrical piece interspersed with songs and dances. [C18: from F, from *vaudevire* satirical folk song, shortened from *chanson du vau de Vire* song of the valley of Vire, a district in Normandy] ▸**ˌvaude'villian** *n, adj*

Vaudois ('vəʊdwɑː) *pl n, sing* **Vaudois. 1** another name for the **Waldenses. 2** the inhabitants of Vaud, in Switzerland.

vault[1] ❶ (vɔːlt) *n* **1** an arched structure that forms a roof or ceiling. **2** a room, esp. a cellar, having an arched roof down to floor level. **3** a burial chamber, esp. when underground. **4** a strongroom for the storage of valuables. **5** an underground room used for the storage of wine, food, etc. **6** *Anat.* any arched or domed bodily cavity or space: *the cranial vault.* **7** something suggestive of an arched structure, as the sky. ◆ *vb* **8** (*tr*) to furnish with or as if with an arched roof. **9** (*tr*) to construct in the shape of a vault. **10** (*intr*) to curve in the shape of a vault. [C14 *vaute,* from OF, from Vulgar L *volvita* (unattested) a turn, prob. from L *volvere* to roll]

vault[2] ❶ (vɔːlt) *vb* **1** to spring over (an object), esp. with the aid of a long pole or with the hands resting on the object. **2** (*intr*) to do, achieve, or attain something as if by a leap: *he vaulted to fame.* ◆ *n* **3** the act of vaulting. [C16: from OF *voulter* to turn from It. *voltare,* from Vulgar L *volvitāre* (unattested) to turn, leap; see VAULT[1]] ▸**'vaulter** *n*

vaulting[1] ('vɔːltɪŋ) *n* one or more vaults in a building or such structures considered collectively.

vaulting[2] ('vɔːltɪŋ) *adj* (*prenominal*) **1** excessively confident: *vaulting arrogance.* **2** used to vault: *a vaulting pole.*

vaunt ❶ (vɔːnt) *vb* **1** (*tr*) to describe, praise, or display (one's success, possessions, etc.) boastfully. **2** (*intr*) *Rare or literary.* to brag. ◆ *n* **3** a boast. [C14: from OF, from LL *vānitāre,* from L *vānus* VAIN] ▸**'vaunter** *n*

vavasor ('vævəˌsɔː) *or* **vavasour** ('vævəˌsʊə) *n* (in feudal society) the noble or knightly vassal of a baron or great lord who also has vassals himself. [C13: from OF *vavasour,* ?from Med. L *vassus vassōrum* vassal of vassals]

vb *abbrev. for* verb.

VC *abbrev. for:* **1** Vice-chairman. **2** Vice Chancellor. **3** Vice Consul. **4** Victoria Cross.

V-chip *n* a device within a television set that allows the set to be programmed not to receive transmissions that have been classified as containing sex, violence, or obscene language.

VCR *abbrev. for* video cassette recorder.

VD *abbrev. for* venereal disease.

V-Day *n* a day nominated to celebrate victory, as in V-E Day or V-J Day in World War II.

VDQS *abbrev. for* vins délimités de qualité supérieure: on a bottle of French wine, indicates that it contains high-quality wine from an approved regional vineyard: the second highest French wine classification. Cf. **AOC, vin de pays.**

VDU *Computing. abbrev. for* visual display unit.

've *contraction of* have: *I've; you've.*

veal (viːl) *n* the flesh of the calf used as food. [C14: from OF *veel,* from L *vitellus,* dim. of *vitulus* calf]

vealer ('viːlə) *n US, Canad., & Austral.* a calf bred for veal.

vector ('vɛktə) *n* **1** *Maths.* a variable quantity, such as force, that has magnitude and direction and can be resolved into components that are odd functions of the coordinates. **2** *Maths.* an element of a vector space. **3** Also called: **carrier.** *Pathol.* an organism, esp. an insect, that carries a disease-producing microorganism from one host to another. **4** Also called: **cloning vector.** *Genetics.* an agent, such as a bacteriophage or a plasmid, by means of which a fragment of foreign DNA is inserted into a host cell to produce a gene clone in genetic engineering. **5** the course or compass direction of an aircraft. ◆ *vb* (*tr*) **6** to direct or guide (a pilot, aircraft, etc.) by directions transmitted by radio. **7** to alter the direction of (the thrust of a jet engine) as a means of steering an aircraft. [C18: from L: carrier, from *vehere* to convey] ▸**vectorial** (vɛk'tɔːrɪəl) *adj*

vector field *n* a region of space under the influence of some vector quantity, such as magnetic field strength, in which each point can be described by a vector.

vector product *n* the product of two vectors that is a pseudovector, whose magnitude is the product of the magnitudes of the given vectors and the sine of the angle between them. Its axis is perpendicular to the plane of the given vectors.

vector sum *n* a vector whose length and direction are represented by the diagonal of a parallelogram whose sides represent the given vectors.

Veda ('veɪdə) *n* any or all of the most ancient sacred writings of Hinduism, esp. the Rig-Veda, Yajur-Veda, Sama-Veda, and Atharva-Veda. [C18: from Sansk.: knowledge]

vedalia (vɪ'deɪlɪə) *n* an Australian ladybird introduced elsewhere to control the scale insect, which is a pest of citrus fruits. [C20: from NL]

Vedanta (vɪ'dɑːntə) *n* one of the six main philosophical schools of

THESAURUS

Antonyms *adj* ≠ **changing:** consistent, fixed, monotonous, regular, settled, unchanging, unvarying

vassal *n* **1, 2** = **serf,** bondservant, bondsman, liegeman, retainer, slave, subject, thrall, varlet (*arch.*)

vassalage *n* **1, 2** = **serfdom,** bondage, dependence, servitude, slavery, subjection, thraldom

vast *adj* **1** = **huge,** astronomical, boundless, colossal, elephantine, enormous, extensive, gigantic, great, illimitable, immeasurable, immense, limitless, mammoth, massive, measureless, mega (*sl.*), monstrous, monumental, never-ending, prodigious, sweeping, tremendous, unbounded, unlimited, voluminous, wide

Antonyms *adj* bounded, limited, microscopic, narrow, negligible, paltry, puny, small, tiny, trifling

vault[1] *n* **1** = **arch,** ceiling, roof, span **3** = **crypt,** catacomb, cellar, charnel house, mausoleum, tomb, undercroft **4** = **strongroom,** depository, repository ◆ *vb* **10** = **arch,** bend, bow, curve, overarch, span

vault[2] *vb* **1** = **jump,** bound, clear, hurdle, leap, spring

vaunt *vb* **1** = **boast about,** brag about, crow about, exult in, flaunt, give oneself airs about, make a display of, make much of, parade, prate about, show off, talk big about (*inf.*)

Hinduism, expounding the monism regarded as implicit in the Veda in accordance with the doctrines of the Upanishads. [C19: from Sansk., from VEDA + ánta end]
▸**Ve'dantic** *adj* ▸**Ve'dantist** *n*

V-E Day *n* the day marking the Allied victory in Europe in World War II (May 8, 1945).

vedette (vɪ'dɛt) *n* **1** *Naval.* a small patrol vessel. **2** *Mil.* a mounted sentry posted forward of a formation's position. [C17: from F, from It. *vedetta* (infl. by *vedere* to see), from earlier *veletta,* ?from Sp., from L *vigilāre*]

Vedic ('veɪdɪk) *adj* **1** of or relating to the Vedas or the ancient form of Sanskrit in which they are written. ◆ *n* **2** the classical form of Sanskrit; the language of the Vedas.

veer ❶ (vɪə) *vb* **1** to alter direction (of). **2** (*intr*) to change from one position, opinion, etc., to another. **3** (*intr*) (of the wind) to change direction clockwise in the northern hemisphere and anticlockwise in the southern. ◆ *n* **4** a change of course or direction. [C16: from OF *virer,* prob. of Celtic origin]

veg (vɛdʒ) *n Inf.* a vegetable or vegetables.

Vega ('vi:gə) *n* the brightest star in the constellation Lyra and one of the most conspicuous in the N hemisphere. [C17: from Med. L, from Ar. *(al nasr) al wāqi,* lit.: the falling (vulture), i.e. the constellation Lyra]

vegan ('vi:gən) *n* a person who uses no animal products.

vegeburger *or* **veggieburger** ('vɛdʒɪ,bɜ:gə) *n* a flat cake of chopped seasoned vegetables and pulses that is grilled or fried and often served in a bread roll.

Vegemite ('vɛdʒɪ,maɪt) *n Austral. & NZ trademark.* a yeast extract used as a spread, flavouring for stews, etc.

vegetable ('vɛdʒtəbᵊl, 'vɛdʒətəbᵊl) *n* **1** any of various herbaceous plants having parts that are used as food, such as peas, potatoes, cauliflower, and onions. **2** *Inf.* a person who has lost control of his mental faculties, limbs, etc., as from an injury, mental disease, etc. **3** a dull inactive person. **4** (*modifier*) consisting of or made from edible vegetables: *a vegetable diet.* **5** (*modifier*) of, characteristic of, derived from, or consisting of plants or plant material: *the vegetable kingdom.* **6** *Rare.* any member of the plant kingdom. [C14 (adj): from LL *vegetābilis,* from *vegetāre* to enliven, from L *vegēre* to excite]

vegetable butter *n* any of a group of vegetable fats having the consistency of butter.

vegetable ivory *n* the hard whitish material obtained from the endosperm of the ivory nut: used to make buttons, ornaments, etc.

vegetable marrow *n* **1** a plant, probably native to America but widely cultivated for its oblong green striped fruit which is eaten as a vegetable. **2** the fruit of this plant. Often shortened to **marrow.**

vegetable oil *n* any of a group of oils that are obtained from plants.

vegetable oyster *n* another name for **salsify** (sense 1).

vegetable silk *n* any of various silky fibres obtained from the seed pods of certain plants.

vegetable wax *n* any of various waxes that occur on parts of certain plants, esp. the trunks of certain palms, and prevent loss of water.

vegetal ('vɛdʒɪtᵊl) *adj* **1** of or characteristic of vegetables or plant life. **2** vegetative. [C15: from LL *vegetāre* to quicken]

vegetarian (,vɛdʒɪ'tɛərɪən) *n* **1** a person who advocates or practises the exclusion of meat and fish, and sometimes eggs, milk, and cheese from the diet. ◆ *adj* **2** *Cookery.* strictly, consisting of vegetables and fruit only, but often including milk, cheese, eggs, etc.
▸,**vege'tarianism** *n*

vegetate ❶ ('vɛdʒɪ,teɪt) *vb* **vegetates, vegetating, vegetated.** (*intr*) **1** to grow like a plant. **2** to lead a life characterized by monotony, passivity, or mental inactivity. [C17: from LL *vegetāre* to invigorate]

vegetation (,vɛdʒɪ'teɪʃən) *n* **1** plant life as a whole, esp. the plant life of a particular region. **2** the process of vegetating.
▸,**vege'tational** *adj*

vegetative ('vɛdʒɪtətɪv) *adj* **1** of or concerned with plant life or plant growth. **2** (of reproduction) characterized by asexual processes. **3** of or relating to functions such as digestion and circulation rather than sexual reproduction. **4** (of a style of living, etc.) unthinking or passive.
▸'**vegetatively** *adv*

veggie ('vɛdʒɪ) *n, adj* an informal word for **vegetarian.**

veg out *vb* **vegges, vegging, vegged.** (*intr, adv*) *Sl., chiefly US.* to relax in an inert, passive way; vegetate: *vegging out in front of the television.*

vehement ❶ ('vi:ɪmənt) *adj* **1** marked by intensity of feeling or conviction. **2** (of actions, gestures, etc.) characterized by great energy, vigour, or force. [C15: from L *vehemēns* ardent]
▸'**vehemence** *n* ▸'**vehemently** *adv*

vehicle ❶ ('vi:ɪkᵊl) *n* **1** any conveyance in or by which people or objects are transported, esp. one fitted with wheels. **2** a medium for the expression or communication of ideas, power, etc. **3** *Pharmacol.* a therapeutically inactive substance mixed with the active ingredient to give bulk to a medicine. **4** Also called: **base.** a painting medium, such as oil, in which pigments are suspended. **5** (in the performing arts) a play, etc., that enables a particular performer to display his talents. [C17: from L *vehiculum,* from *vehere* to carry]
▸**vehicular** (vɪ'hɪkjʊlə) *adj*

veil ❶ (veɪl) *n* **1** a piece of more or less transparent material, usually attached to a hat or headdress, used to conceal or protect a woman's face and head. **2** part of a nun's headdress falling round the face onto the shoulders. **3** something that covers, conceals, or separates: *a veil of reticence.* **4 the veil.** the life of a nun in a religious order. **5 take the veil.** to become a nun. **6** Also called: **velum.** *Bot.* a membranous structure, esp. the thin layer of cells covering a young mushroom. ◆ *vb* **7** (*tr*) to cover, conceal, or separate with or as if with a veil. **8** (*intr*) to wear or put on a veil. [C13: from Norman F *veile,* from L *vēla,* pl of *vēlum* a covering]
▸'**veiler** *n* ▸'**veil-,like** *adj*

veiled ❶ (veɪld) *adj* **1** disguised: *a veiled insult.* **2** (of sound, tone, the voice, etc.) not distinct.
▸**veiledly** ('veɪlɪdlɪ) *adv*

veiling ('veɪlɪŋ) *n* a veil or the fabric used for veils.

vein ❶ (veɪn) *n* **1** any of the tubular vessels that convey oxygen-depleted blood to the heart. Cf. **pulmonary vein, artery** (sense 1). **2** any of the hollow branching tubes that form the supporting framework of an insect's wing. **3** any of the vascular bundles of a leaf. **4** a clearly defined mass of ore, mineral, etc. **5** an irregular streak of colour or alien substance in marble, wood, or other material. **6** a distinctive trait or quality in speech, writing, character, etc.: *a vein of humour.* **7** a temporary attitude or temper: *the debate entered a frivolous vein.* ◆ *vb* (*tr*) **8** to diffuse over or cause to diffuse over in streaked patterns. **9** to fill, furnish, or mark with or as if with veins. [C13: from OF, from L *vēna*]
▸'**veinless** *adj* ▸'**vein,like** *adj* ▸'**veiny** *adj*

veining ('veɪnɪŋ) *n* a pattern or network of veins or streaks.

veinlet ('veɪnlɪt) *n* any small vein or venule.

velamen (və'leɪmɛn) *n, pl* **velamina** (-'læmɪnə). **1** the thick layer of dead cells that covers the aerial roots of certain orchids. **2** *Anat.* another word for **velum.** [C19: from L: veil, from *vēlāre* to cover]

velar ('vi:lə) *adj* **1** of or attached to a velum: *velar tentacles.* **2** *Phonetics.* articulated with the soft palate and the back of the tongue, as in (k) or (ŋ). [C18: from L, from *vēlum* VEIL]

Velcro ('vɛlkrəʊ) *n Trademark.* a fastening consisting of two strips of nylon fabric, one having tiny hooked threads and the other a coarse surface, that form a strong bond when pressed together.

veld *or* **veldt** (fɛlt, vɛlt) *n* elevated open grassland in Southern Africa. See also **bushveld, highveld.** [C19: from Afrik., from earlier Du. *veldt* FIELD]

veldskoen ('fɛlt,skun, 'vɛlt-) *n* an ankle-length boot of soft but strong rawhide. [from Afrik., lit.: field shoe]

veleta (və'li:tə) *n* a variant spelling of **valeta.**

veliger ('vɛlɪdʒə) *n* the free-swimming larva of many molluscs, having a rudimentary shell and a ciliated velum used for feeding and locomotion. [C19: from NL, from VEL(UM) + -GER(OUS)]

vellum ('vɛləm) *n* **1** a fine parchment prepared from the skin of a calf, kid, or lamb. **2** a work printed or written on vellum. **3** a creamy coloured heavy paper resembling vellum. ◆ *adj* **4** made of or resembling vellum. [C15: from OF, from *velin* of a calf, from *veel* VEAL]

veloce (vɪ'ləʊtʃɪ) *adj, adv Music.* to be played rapidly. [from It., from L *vēlōx* quick]

velocipede (vɪ'lɒsɪ,pi:d) *n* an early form of bicycle, esp. one propelled by pushing along the ground with the feet. [C19: from F, from L *vēlōx* swift + *pēs* foot]
▸**ve'loci,pedist** *n*

velocity ❶ (vɪ'lɒsɪtɪ) *n, pl* **velocities. 1** speed of motion or operation; swiftness. **2** *Physics.* a measure of the rate of motion of a body expressed as the rate of change of its position in a particular direction with time. **3** *Physics.* (not in technical usage) another word for **speed** (sense 3). [C16: from L *vēlōcitās,* from *vēlōx* swift]

velocity of circulation *n Econ.* the average number of times a unit of

THESAURUS

veer *vb* **1-3 = change direction,** be deflected, change, change course, sheer, shift, swerve, tack, turn

vegetate *vb* **1 = grow,** burgeon, germinate, shoot, spring, sprout, swell **2 = stagnate,** be inert, deteriorate, exist, go to seed, idle, languish, loaf, moulder, veg out (*sl., chiefly US*)
Antonyms *vb* ≠ **stagnate:** accomplish, develop, grow, participate, perform, react, respond

vehemence *n* **1, 2 = forcefulness,** ardour, eagerness, earnestness, emphasis, energy, enthusiasm, fervency, fervour, fire, force, heat, intensity, keenness, passion, verve, vigour, violence, warmth, zeal
Antonyms *n* apathy, coolness, indifference, inertia, lethargy, listlessness, passivity, stoicism, torpor

vehement *adj* **1, 2 = strong,** ablaze, ardent, eager, earnest, emphatic, enthusiastic, fervent, fervid, fierce, flaming, forceful, forcible, impassioned, intense, passionate, powerful, violent, zealous
Antonyms *adj* apathetic, calm, cool, dispassionate, half-hearted, impassive, lukewarm, moderate

vehicle *n* **1 = transport,** conveyance, means of transport, transportation **2 = medium,** apparatus, channel, means, means of expression, mechanism, organ

veil *n* **1, 3 = cover,** blind, cloak, curtain, disguise, film, mask, screen, shade, shroud ◆ *vb* **7 = cover,** cloak, conceal, dim, disguise, hide, mantle, mask, obscure, screen, shield
Antonyms *vb* ≠ **cover:** disclose, display, divulge, expose, lay bare, reveal, uncover, unveil

veiled *adj* **1 = disguised,** concealed, covert, hinted at, implied, masked, suppressed

vein *n* **1 = blood vessel 4 = seam,** course, current, lode, stratum, streak, stripe **6 = trait,** dash, hint, strain, streak, thread **7 = mood,** attitude, bent, character, faculty, humour, mode, note, style, temper, tenor, tone, turn

velocity *n* **1 = speed,** celerity, fleetness, impetus, pace, quickness, rapidity, swiftness money is used in a given time, esp. calculated as the ratio of the total money spent in that time to the total amount of money in circulation.

velocity of light *n* a nontechnical name for **speed of light.**

velodrome ('vi:lə,drəʊm, 'vɛl-) *n* an arena with a banked track for cycle racing. [C20: from F *vélodrome,* from *vélo-* (from L *vēlōx* swift) + -DROME]

velour *or* **velours** (vəˈlʊə) *n* any of various fabrics with a velvet-like finish, used for upholstery, clothing, etc. [C18: from OF, from OProvençal *velos* velvet, from L, from *villus* shaggy hair]

velouté (vəˈlu:teɪ) *n* a rich white sauce or soup made from stock, egg yolks, and cream. [from F, lit.: velvety, from OF *velous;* see VELOUR]

velum ('vi:ləm) *n, pl* **vela** (-lə). **1** *Zool.* any of various membranous structures. **2** *Anat.* any of various veil-like bodily structures, esp. the soft palate. **3** *Bot.* another word for **veil** (sense 6). [C18: from L: veil]

velure (vəˈlʊə) *n* velvet or a similar fabric. [C16: from OF, from *velous;* see VELOUR]

velutinous (vəˈlu:tɪnəs) *adj* covered with short dense soft hairs. [C19: from NL *velūtīnus* like velvet]

velvet ❶ ('vɛlvɪt) *n* **1a** a fabric of silk, cotton, nylon, etc., with a thick close soft pile. **1b** (*as modifier*): *velvet curtains.* **2** anything with a smooth soft surface. **3a** smoothness. **3b** (*as modifier*): *a velvet night.* **4** the furry covering of the newly formed antlers of a deer. **5** *Sl., chiefly US.* **5a** gambling winnings. **5b** a gain. **6 on velvet.** *Sl.* in a condition of ease, advantage, or wealth. **7 velvet glove.** gentleness, often concealing strength or determination (esp. in **an iron hand in a velvet glove**). [C14 *veluet,* from OF, from *velu* hairy, from Vulgar L *villutus* (unattested), from L *villus* shaggy hair]
▸ **'velvet-,like** *adj* ▸ **'velvety** *adj*

velveteen (,vɛlvɪ'ti:n) *n* **1** a cotton fabric resembling velvet with a short thick pile, used for clothing, etc. **2** (*pl*) trousers made of velveteen.

Ven. *abbrev. for* Venerable.

vena ('vi:nə) *n, pl* **venae** (-ni:). *Anat.* a technical word for **vein.** [C15: from L *vēna* VEIN]

vena cava ('keɪvə) *n, pl* **venae cavae** ('keɪvi:). either one of two large veins that convey oxygen-depleted blood to the heart. [L: hollow vein]

venal ❶ ('vi:nᵊl) *adj* **1** easily bribed or corrupted: *a venal magistrate.* **2** characterized by corruption or bribery. [C17: from L *vēnālis,* from *vēnum* sale]
▸ **veˈnality** *n* ▸ **'venally** *adv*

venation (vi:'neɪʃən) *n* **1** the arrangement of the veins in a leaf or in the wing of an insect. **2** such veins collectively.
▸ **veˈnational** *adj*

vend (vɛnd) *vb* **1** to sell or be sold. **2** to sell (goods) for a living. [C17: from L *vendere,* from *vēnum dare* to offer for sale]

vendace ('vɛndeɪs) *n, pl* **vendaces** *or* **vendace.** either of two small whitefish occurring in lakes in Scotland and NW England. [C18: from NL *vandēsius,* from OF *vandoise,* prob. of Celtic origin]

vendee (vɛn'di:) *n Chiefly law.* a person to whom something, esp. real property, is sold.

vendetta ❶ (vɛn'dɛtə) *n* **1** a private feud, originally between Corsican or Sicilian families, in which the relatives of a murdered person seek vengeance by killing the murderer or some member of his family. **2** any prolonged feud. [C19: from It., from L *vindicta,* from *vindicāre* to avenge]
▸ **venˈdettist** *n*

vendible ('vɛndəbᵊl) *adj* **1** saleable or marketable. ◆ *n* **2** (*usually pl*) *Rare.* a saleable object.
▸ **,vendiˈbility** *n*

vending machine *n* a machine that automatically dispenses consumer goods such as cigarettes or food, when money is inserted.

vendor ('vɛndɔ:) *or* **vender** ('vɛndə) *n* **1** *Chiefly law.* a person who sells something, esp. real property. **2** another name for **vending machine.**

vendor placing *n Finance.* a method of financing the purchase of one company by another in which the purchasing company pays for the target company in its own shares, on condition that the vendor places these shares with investors for cash payment.

veneer ❶ (vɪ'nɪə) *n* **1** a thin layer of wood, plastic, etc., with a decorative or fine finish that is bonded to the surface of a less expensive material, usually wood. **2** a superficial appearance: *a veneer of gentility.* **3** any facing material that is applied to a different backing material. ◆ *vb* (*tr*) **4** to cover (a surface) with a veneer. **5** to conceal (something) under a superficially pleasant surface. [C17: from G *furnieren* to veneer, from OF *fournir* to FURNISH]
▸ **veˈneerer** *n*

veneering (vɪ'nɪərɪŋ) *n* material used as veneer or a veneered surface.

venepuncture ('vɛnɪ,pʌŋktʃə) *n* a variant spelling of **venipuncture.**

venerable ❶ ('vɛnərəbᵊl) *adj* **1** (esp. of a person) worthy of reverence on account of great age, religious associations, character, etc. **2** (of inanimate objects) hallowed on account of age or historical or religious association. **3** *RC Church.* a title bestowed on a deceased person when the first stage of his canonization has been accomplished. **4** *Church of England.* a title given to an archdeacon. [C15: from L *venerābilis,* from *venerārī* to venerate]
▸ **,veneraˈbility** *or* **'venerableness** *n* ▸ **'venerably** *adv*

venerate ❶ ('vɛnə,reɪt) *vb* **venerates, venerating, venerated.** (*tr*) **1** to hold in deep respect. **2** to honour in recognition of qualities of holiness, excellence, etc. [C17: from L *venerārī,* from *venus* love]
▸ **'vener,ator** *n*

veneration ❶ (,vɛnə'reɪʃən) *n* **1** a feeling or expression of awe or reverence. **2** the act of venerating or the state of being venerated.

venereal (vɪ'nɪərɪəl) *adj* **1** of or infected with venereal disease. **2** (of a disease) transmitted by sexual intercourse. **3** of or involving the genitals. **4** of or relating to sexual intercourse or erotic desire. [C15: from L *venereus,* from *venus* sexual love, from VENUS[1]]

venereal disease *n* another name for **sexually transmitted disease.** Abbrev.: **VD.**

venereology (vɪ,nɪərɪ'ɒlədʒɪ) *n* the branch of medicine concerned with the study and treatment of venereal disease.
▸ **ve,nereˈologist** *n*

venery[1] ('vɛnərɪ, 'vi:-) *n Arch.* the pursuit of sexual gratification. [C15: from Med. L *veneria,* from L *venus* love, VENUS[1]]

venery[2] ('vɛnərɪ, 'vi:-) *n* the art, sport, lore, or practice of hunting, esp. with hounds; the chase. [C14: from OF *venerie,* from *vener* to hunt, from L *vēnārī*]

venesection ('vɛnɪ,sɛkʃən) *n* surgical incision into a vein. [C17: from NL *vēnae sectiō;* see VEIN, SECTION]

Venetian (vɪ'ni:ʃən) *adj* **1** of, relating to, or characteristic of Venice, a port in NE Italy, or its inhabitants. ◆ *n* **2** a native or inhabitant of Venice. **3** See **Venetian blind.**

Venetian blind *n* a window blind consisting of a number of horizontal slats whose angle may be altered to let in more or less light.

Venetian red *n* **1** natural or synthetic ferric oxide used as a red pigment. **2a** a moderate to strong reddish-brown colour. **2b** (*as adj*): *a Venetian-red coat.*

vengeance ❶ ('vɛndʒəns) *n* **1** the act of or desire for taking revenge. **2 with a vengeance.** (intensifier): *he's a coward with a vengeance.* [C13: from OF, from *venger* to avenge, from L *vindicāre* to punish]

vengeful ❶ ('vɛndʒfʊl) *adj* **1** desiring revenge. **2** characterized by or indicating a desire for revenge. **3** inflicting or taking revenge: *with vengeful blows.*
▸ **'vengefully** *adv*

venial ❶ ('vi:nɪəl) *adj* easily excused or forgiven: *a venial error.* [C13: via OF from LL *veniālis,* from L *venia* forgiveness]
▸ **,veniˈality** *n* ▸ **'venially** *adv*

venial sin *n Christian theol.* a sin regarded as involving only a partial loss of grace.

venin ('vɛnɪn) *n* any of the poisonous constituents of animal venoms. [C20: from F *ven(in)* poison + -IN]

venipuncture *or* **venepuncture** ('vɛnɪ,pʌŋktʃə) *n Med.* the puncturing of a vein, esp. to take a sample of venous blood or inject a drug.

venison ('vɛnɪzᵊn, -sᵊn) *n* the flesh of a deer, used as food. [C13: from OF *venaison,* from L *vēnātiō* hunting, from *vēnārī* to hunt]

Venite (vɪ'naɪtɪ) *n* **1** the opening word of the 95th psalm, an invitatory prayer at matins. **2** a musical setting of this. [L: come ye]

Venn diagram (vɛn) *n Maths, logic.* a diagram in which mathematical sets or terms of a categorial statement are represented by overlapping circles within a boundary representing the universal set, so that all possible combinations of the relevant properties are represented by the various distinct areas in the diagram. [C19: after John *Venn* (1834–1923), Brit. logician]

venom ❶ ('vɛnəm) *n* **1** a poisonous fluid secreted by such animals as certain snakes and scorpions and usually transmitted by a bite or

THESAURUS

velvety *adj* **2** = **soft**, delicate, downy, mossy, smooth, velutinous, velvet-like

venal *adj* **1** = **corrupt**, bent (*sl.*), corruptible, crooked (*inf.*), dishonourable, grafting (*inf.*), mercenary, prostituted, purchasable, rapacious, simoniacal, sordid, unprincipled
Antonyms *adj* honest, honourable, incorruptible, law-abiding, principled, upright

vendetta *n* **1, 2** = **feud**, bad blood, blood feud, quarrel

veneer *n* **1** = **layer**, finish, gloss **2** = **mask**, appearance, façade, false front, front, guise, pretence, semblance, show

venerable *adj* **1** = **respected**, august, esteemed, grave, honoured, revered, reverenced, sage, sedate, wise, worshipped
Antonyms *adj* discredited, disdained, disgraced, dishonourable, disreputable, ignominious, inglorious, scorned

venerate *vb* **1, 2** = **respect**, adore, esteem, hold in awe, honour, look up to, revere, reverence, worship
Antonyms *vb* deride, dishonour, disregard, execrate, mock, scorn, spurn

veneration *n* **1, 2** = **respect**, adoration, awe, deference, esteem, reverence, worship

vengeance *n* **1** = **revenge**, an eye for an eye, avenging, lex talionis, reprisal, requital, retaliation, retribution, settling of scores **2 with a vengeance** = **to the utmost**, and no mistake, extremely, greatly, to the full, to the nth degree, with no holds barred
Antonyms *n* ≠ **revenge**: absolution, acquittal, exoneration, forbearance, forgiveness, mercy, pardon, remission

vengeful *adj* **1** = **unforgiving**, avenging, implacable, punitive, rancorous, relentless, retaliatory, revengeful, spiteful, thirsting for revenge, vindictive

venial *adj* = **forgivable**, allowable, excusable, insignificant, minor, pardonable, slight, trivial

venom *n* **1** = **poison**, bane, toxin **2** = **malice**, acidity, acrimony, bitterness, gall, grudge, hate, ill will, malevolence, maliciousness, masting. **2** malice; spite. [C13: from OF, from L *venēnum* poison, love potion]

▸**'venomous** *adj* ▸**'venomously** *adv* ▸**'venomousness** *n*

venose ('vi:nəus) *adj* **1** having veins; venous. **2** (of a plant) covered with veins or similar ridges. [C17: via L *venōsus,* from *vēna* a VEIN]

venosity (vɪ'nɒsɪtɪ) *n* **1** an excessive quantity of blood in the venous system or in an organ or part. **2** an unusually large number of blood vessels in an organ or part.

venous ('vi:nəs) *adj* **1** *Physiol.* of or relating to the blood circulating in the veins. **2** of or relating to the veins. [C17: see VENOSE]

vent[1] **T** (vɛnt) *n* **1** a small opening for the escape of fumes, liquids, etc. **2** the shaft of a volcano through which lava and gases erupt. **3** the external opening of the urinary or genital systems of lower vertebrates. **4** a small aperture at the breech of old guns through which the charge was ignited. **5 give vent to.** to release (an emotion, idea, etc.) in an outburst. ◆ *vb* (*mainly tr*) **6** to release or give expression or utterance to (an emotion, etc.): *he vents his anger on his wife.* **7** to provide a vent for or make vents in. **8** to let out (steam, etc.) through a vent. [C14: from OF *esventer* to blow out, from EX-[1] + *venter,* from Vulgar L *ventāre* (unattested), from L *ventus* wind]

vent[2] (vɛnt) *n* **1** a vertical slit at the back or both sides of a jacket. ◆ *vb* **2** (*tr*) to make a vent or vents in (a jacket). [C15: from OF *fente* slit, from *fendre* to split, from L *findere* to cleave]

venter ('vɛntə) *n* **1** *Anat., zool.* **1a** the belly or abdomen of vertebrates. **1b** a protuberant structure or part, such as the belly of a muscle. **2** *Bot.* the swollen basal region of an archegonium. **3** *Law.* the womb. [C16: from L]

ventilate T ('vɛntɪˌleɪt) *vb* **ventilates, ventilating, ventilated.** (*tr*) **1** to drive foul air out of (an enclosed area). **2** to provide with a means of airing. **3** to expose (a question, grievance, etc.) to public discussion. **4** *Physiol.* to oxygenate (the blood). [C15: from L *ventilāre* to fan, from *ventulus,* dim. of *ventus* wind]

▸**'ventilable** *adj* ▸**ˌventi'lation** *n*

ventilator ('vɛntɪˌleɪtə) *n* **1** an opening or device, such as a fan, used to ventilate a room, building, etc. **2** *Med.* a machine that maintains a flow of air into and out of the lungs of a patient unable to breathe normally.

ventral ('vɛntrəl) *adj* **1** relating to the front part of the body. **2** of or situated on the upper or inner side of a plant organ, esp. a leaf, that is facing the axis. [C18: from L *ventrālis,* from *venter* abdomen]

▸**'ventrally** *adv*

ventral fin *n* **1** another name for **pelvic fin. 2** any unpaired median fin situated on the undersurface of fishes.

ventricle ('vɛntrɪk^əl) *n Anat.* **1** a chamber of the heart that receives blood from the atrium and pumps it to the arteries. **2** any one of the four main cavities of the vertebrate brain. **3** any of various other small cavities in the body. [C14: from L *ventriculus,* dim. of *venter* belly]

▸**ven'tricular** *adj*

ventricose ('vɛntrɪˌkəus) *adj* **1** *Bot., zool., anat.* having a swelling on one side: *the ventricose corolla of many labiate plants.* **2** another word for **corpulent.** [C18: from NL, from L *venter* belly]

ventriculus (vɛn'trɪkjʊləs) *n, pl* **ventriculi** (-ˌlaɪ). **1** *Zool.* **1a** the midgut of an insect, where digestion takes place. **1b** the gizzard of a bird. **2** another word for **ventricle.** [C18: from L, dim. of *venter* belly]

ventriloquism (vɛn'trɪləˌkwɪzəm) *or* **ventriloquy** *n* the art of producing vocal sounds that appear to come from another source. [C18: from L *venter* belly + *loquī* to speak]

▸**ventriloquial** (ˌvɛntrɪ'ləukwɪəl) *adj* ▸**ˌventri'loquially** *adv* ▸**ven'triloquist** *n* ▸**ven'triloˌquize** *or* **ven'triloˌquise** *vb*

venture T ('vɛntʃə) *vb* **ventures, venturing, ventured. 1** (*tr*) to expose to danger: *he ventured his life.* **2** (*tr*) to brave the dangers of (something): *I'll venture the seas.* **3** (*tr*) to dare (to do something): *does he venture to object?* **4** (*tr; may take a clause as object*) to express in spite of possible criticism: *I venture that he is not that honest.* **5** (*intr;* often foll. by *out, forth,* etc.) to embark on a possibly hazardous journey, etc.: *to venture forth upon the high seas.* ◆ *n* **6** an undertaking that is risky or of uncertain outcome. **7** a commercial undertaking characterized by risk of loss as well as opportunity for profit. **8** something hazarded or risked in an adventure. **9 at a venture.** at random. [C15: var. of *aventure* ADVENTURE]

▸**'venturer** *n*

venture capital *n* another name for **risk capital.**

Venture Scout *or* **Venturer** *n Brit.* a person aged 16–20 who is a member of the senior branch of the Scouts.

venturesome T ('vɛntʃəsəm) *or* **venturous** ('vɛntʃərəs) *adj* **1** willing to take risks; daring. **2** hazardous.

Venturi tube (vɛn'tjuərɪ) *n Physics.* a device for measuring or controlling fluid flow, consisting of a tube so constricted that the pressure differential produced by fluid flowing through the constriction gives a measure of the rate of flow. [C19: after G. B. *Venturi* (1746–1822), It. physicist]

venue ('vɛnju:) *n* **1** *Law.* **1a** the place in which a cause of action arises. **1b** the place fixed for the trial of a cause. **1c** the locality from which the jurors must be summoned. **2** a meeting place. **3** any place where an organized gathering, such as a rock concert, is held. [C14: from OF, from *venir* to come, from L *venīre*]

venule ('vɛnju:l) *n* **1** *Anat.* any of the small branches of a vein that receives oxygen-depleted blood from the capillaries and returns it to the heart via the venous system. **2** any of the branches of a vein in an insect's wing. [C19: from L *vēnula,* dim. of *vēna* VEIN]

Venus[1] ('vi:nəs) *n* the Roman goddess of love. Greek counterpart: **Aphrodite.**

Venus[2] ('vi:nəs) *n* one of the inferior planets and the second nearest to the sun, visible as a bright morning or evening star.

▸**Venusian** (vɪ'nju:zɪən) *n, adj*

Venus's-flytrap *or* **Venus flytrap** *n* an insectivorous plant having hinged two-lobed leaves that snap closed when the sensitive hairs on the surface are touched.

Venus's looking glass *n* a purple-flowered plant of Europe, W Asia, and N Africa.

veracious T (vɛ'reɪʃəs) *adj* **1** habitually truthful or honest. **2** accurate. [C17: from L *vērax,* from *vērus* true]

▸**ve'raciously** *adv* ▸**ve'raciousness** *n*

veracity T (vɛ'ræsɪtɪ) *n, pl* **veracities. 1** truthfulness or honesty, esp. when consistent or habitual. **2** accuracy. **3** a truth. [C17: from Med. L *vērācitās,* from L *vērax;* see VERACIOUS]

veranda *or* **verandah** (və'rændə) *n* **1** a porch or portico, sometimes partly enclosed, along the outside of a building. **2** *NZ.* a continuous overhead canopy that gives shelter to pedestrians. [C18: from Port. *varanda* railing]

veratrine ('vɛrəˌtri:n) *or* **veratrin** ('vɛrətrɪn) *n* a white poisonous mixture obtained from sabadilla, consisting of various alkaloids: formerly used in medicine as a counterirritant. [C19: from L *vērātrum* hellebore + -INE[2]]

verb (vɜ:b) *n* **1** (in traditional grammar) any of a large class of words that serve to indicate the occurrence or performance of an action, the existence of a state, etc. Such words as *run, make, do,* etc., are verbs. **2** (in modern descriptive linguistic analysis) **2a** a word or group of words that functions as the predicate of a sentence or introduces the predicate. **2b** (*as modifier*): *a verb phrase.* ◆ Abbrev.: **vb, v.** [C14: from L *verbum* word]

verbal T ('vɜ:b^əl) *adj* **1** of, relating to, or using words: *merely verbal concessions.* **2** oral rather than written: *a verbal agreement.* **3** verbatim; literal: *an almost verbal copy.* **4** *Grammar.* of or relating to verbs or a verb. ◆ See also **verbals.**

▸**'verbally** *adv*

verbalism ('vɜ:bəˌlɪzəm) *n* **1** a verbal expression; phrase or word. **2** an exaggerated emphasis on the importance of words. **3** a statement lacking real content.

verbalist ('vɜ:bəlɪst) *n* **1** a person who deals with words alone, rather than facts, ideas, etc. **2** a person skilled in the use of words.

verbalize *or* **verbalise** ('vɜ:bəˌlaɪz) *vb* **verbalizes, verbalizing, verbalized** *or* **verbalises, verbalising, verbalised. 1** to express (an idea, etc.) in words. **2** to change (any word) into a verb or derive a verb from (any word). **3** (*intr*) to be verbose.

▸**ˌverbali'zation** *or* **ˌverbali'sation** *n*

verbal noun *n* a noun derived from a verb, such as *smoking* in the sentence *smoking is bad for you.*

verbals ('vɜ:b^əlz) *pl n Sl.* a criminal's admission of guilt on arrest.

verbascum (vɜ:'bæskəm) *n* any of a genus of hairy plants, mostly biennial, having spikes of yellow, purple, or red flowers. [L: mullein]

verbatim T (vɜ:'beɪtɪm) *adv, adj* using exactly the same words; word for word. [C15: from Med. L: word by word, from L *verbum* word]

verbena (vɜ:'bi:nə) *n* **1** any of a genus of plants of tropical and temperate America, having red, white, or purple fragrant flowers: much cultivated as garden plants. **2** any of various similar plants, esp. the lemon verbena. [C16: via Med. L, from L: sacred bough used by the priest in religious acts]

THESAURUS

lignity, pungency, rancour, spite, spitefulness, spleen, virulence

Antonyms *n* ≠ **malice:** benevolence, charity, compassion, favour, goodwill, kindness, love, mercy

venomous *adj* **1** = **poisonous,** baneful (*arch.*), envenomed, mephitic, noxious, poison, toxic, virulent **2** = **malicious,** baleful, hostile, malignant, rancorous, savage, spiteful, vicious, vindictive, virulent

Antonyms *adj* ≠ **poisonous:** harmless, nonpoisonous, nontoxic, nonvenomous ≠ **malicious:** affectionate, benevolent, compassionate, forgiving, harmless, loving, magnanimous

vent[1] *n* **1** = **outlet,** aperture, duct, hole, opening, orifice, split ◆ *vb* **6** = **express,** air, come out with, discharge, emit, empty, give expression to, give vent to, pour out, release, utter, voice

Antonyms *vb* ≠ **express:** bottle up, curb, hold back, inhibit, quash, quell, repress, stifle, subdue

ventilate *vb* **3** = **discuss,** air, bring out into the open, broadcast, debate, examine, make known, scrutinize, sift, talk about

venture *vb* **1** = **risk,** chance, endanger, hazard, imperil, jeopardize, put in jeopardy, speculate, stake, wager **4** = **dare,** advance, dare say, hazard, make bold, presume, stick one's neck out (*inf.*), take the liberty, volunteer **5** = **go,** embark on, plunge into, set out ◆ *n* **6** = **undertaking,** adventure, chance, endeavour, enterprise, fling, gamble, hazard, jeopardy, project, risk, speculation

venturesome *adj* **1** = **daring,** adventurous, bold, courageous, daredevil, doughty, enterprising, fearless, intrepid, plucky, spirited

veracious *adj* **1** = **truthful,** ethical, frank, high-principled, honest, trustworthy, veridical **2** = **accurate,** credible, dependable, factual, faithful, genuine, reliable, straightforward, true

veracity *n* **1** = **truthfulness,** candour, frankness, honesty, integrity, probity, rectitude, trustworthiness, uprightness **2** = **accuracy,** credibility, exactitude, precision, truth

verbal *adj* **2, 3** = **spoken,** literal, oral, unwritten, verbatim, word-of-mouth

verbally *adv* **2** = **orally,** by word of mouth

verbatim *adv* = **word for word,** exactly, precisely, to the letter

verbiage 🅣 ('vɜːbɪɪdʒ) *n* the excessive and often meaningless use of words. [C18: from F, from OF *verbier* to chatter, from *verbe* word, from L *verbum*]

verbose 🅣 (vɜː'bəʊs) *adj* using or containing an excess of words, so as to be pedantic or boring. [C17: from L, from *verbum* word]
▸**ver'bosely** *adv* ▸**verbosity** (vɜː'bɒsɪtɪ) *n*

verboten *German.* (fɛr'boːtən) *adj* forbidden.

verb phrase *n Grammar.* a constituent of a sentence that contains the verb and any direct and indirect objects but not the subject.

verdant 🅣 ('vɜːdᵊnt) *adj* **1** covered with green vegetation. **2** (of plants, etc.) green in colour. **3** unsophisticated; green. [C16: from OF, from *verdoyer* to become green, from OF *verd* green, from L *viridis*]
▸**'verdancy** *n* ▸**'verdantly** *adv*

verd antique (vɜːd) *n* **1** a dark green mottled impure variety of serpentine marble. **2** any of various similar marbles or stones. [C18: from F, from It. *verde antico* ancient green]

verdict 🅣 ('vɜːdɪkt) *n* **1** the findings of a jury on the issues of fact submitted to it for examination and trial. **2** any decision or conclusion. [C13: from Med. L *vērdictum*, from L *vērē dictum* truly spoken, from *vērus* true + *dīcere* to say]

verdigris ('vɜːdɪgrɪs) *n* **1** a green or bluish patina formed on copper, brass, or bronze. **2** a green or blue crystalline substance obtained by the action of acetic acid on copper and used as a fungicide and pigment. [C14: from OF *vert de Grice* green of Greece]

verdure ('vɜːdʒə) *n* **1** flourishing green vegetation or its colour. **2** a condition of freshness or healthy growth. [C14: from OF *verd* green, from L *viridis*]
▸**'verdured** *adj*

verge[1] 🅣 (vɜːdʒ) *n* **1** an edge or rim; margin. **2** a limit beyond which something occurs: *on the verge of ecstasy.* **3** *Brit.* a grass border along a road. **4** *Archit.* the edge of the roof tiles projecting over a gable. **5** *English legal history.* **5a** the area encompassing the royal court that is subject to the jurisdiction of the Lord High Steward. **5b** a rod or wand carried as a symbol of office or emblem of authority, as in the Church. ◆ *vb* **verges, verging, verged. 6** (*intr;* foll. by *on*) to be near (to): *to verge on chaos.* **7** (when *intr*, sometimes foll. by *on*) to serve as the edge of (something): *this narrow strip verges the road.* [C15: from OF, from L *virga* rod]

verge[2] (vɜːdʒ) *vb* **verges, verging, verged.** (*intr;* foll. by *to* or *towards*) to move or incline in a certain direction. [C17: from L *vergere*]

verger ('vɜːdʒə) *n Chiefly Church of England.* **1** a church official who acts as caretaker and attendant. **2** an official who carries the verge or rod of office before a bishop or dean in ceremonies and processions. [C15: from OF, from *verge*, from L *virga* rod, twig]

verglas ('vɛəglɑː) *n, pl* **verglases** (-glɑː, -glɑːz). a thin film of ice on rock. [from OF *verre-glaz*, from *verre* glass + *glaz* ice]

veridical (vɪ'rɪdɪkᵊl) *adj* **1** truthful. **2** *Psychol.* of revelations in dreams, etc., that appear to be confirmed by subsequent events. [C17: from L, from *vērus* true + *dīcere* to say]
▸**ve,ridi'cality** *n* ▸**ve'ridically** *adv*

veriest ('vɛrɪɪst) *adj Arch.* (intensifier): *the veriest coward.*

verification 🅣 (,vɛrɪfɪ'keɪʃən) *n* **1** establishment of the correctness of a theory, fact, etc. **2** evidence that provides proof of an assertion, theory, etc.
▸**'verifi,catory** *adj*

verify 🅣 ('vɛrɪ,faɪ) *vb* **verifies, verifying, verified.** (*tr*) **1** to prove to be true; confirm. **2** to check or determine the correctness or truth of by investigation, etc. **3** *Law.* to substantiate or confirm (an oath). [C14: from OF, from Med. L *vērificāre*, from L *vērus* true + *facere* to make]
▸**'veri,fiable** *adj* ▸**'veri,fiably** *adv* ▸**'veri,fier** *n*

verily ('vɛrɪlɪ) *adv* (*sentence modifier*) *Arch.* in truth; truly: *verily, thou art a man of God.* [C13: from VERY + -LY[2]]

verisimilar (,vɛrɪ'sɪmɪlə) *adj* probable; likely. [C17: from L, from *vērus* true + *similis* like]

verisimilitude 🅣 (,vɛrɪsɪ'mɪlɪ,tjuːd) *n* **1** the appearance or semblance of truth or reality. **2** something that merely seems to be true or real, such as a doubtful statement. [C17: from L, from *vērus* true + *similitūdō* SIMILITUDE]

verism ('vɪərɪzəm) *n* extreme naturalism in art or literature. [C19: from It. *verismo*, from *vero* true, from L *vērus*]
▸**'verist** *n, adj* ▸**ve'ristic** *adj*

verismo (vɛ'rɪzməʊ) *n Music.* a school of composition that originated in Italian opera towards the end of the 19th century, drawing its themes from real life. [C19: from It.; see VERISM]

veritable ('vɛrɪtəbᵊl) *adj* (*prenominal*) (intensifier; *usually qualifying a word used metaphorically*): *he's a veritable swine!* [C15: from OF, from *vérité* truth; see VERITY]
▸**'veritableness** *n* ▸**'veritably** *adv*

vérité ('vɛriː,teɪ; *French* verite) *adj* involving a high degree of realism or naturalism: *a vérité look at David Bowie.* See also **cinéma vérité.** [F, lit.: truth]

verity ('vɛrɪtɪ) *n, pl* **verities. 1** the quality or state of being true, real, or correct. **2** a true statement, idea, etc. [C14: from OF from L *vēritās*, from *vērus* true]

verjuice ('vɜː,dʒuːs) *n* **1** the acid juice of unripe grapes, apples, or crab apples, formerly much used in making sauces, etc. **2** *Rare.* sourness or sharpness of temper, looks, etc. [C14: from OF *vert jus* green (unripe) juice]

verkrampte (fə'kramtə) *n* (in South Africa during apartheid) **a** an Afrikaner Nationalist violently opposed to the end of apartheid and to liberalism in general. **b** (*as modifier*): *verkrampte politics.* [C20: from Afrik. (adj), lit.: restricted]

verligte (fə'ləxtə) *n* (in South Africa during apartheid) **a** a follower of any liberal White political party. **b** (*as modifier*): *verligte politics.* [C20: from Afrik. (adj), lit.: enlightened]

vermeil ('vɜːmeɪl) *n* **1** gilded silver, bronze, or other metal, used esp. in the 19th century. **2a** vermilion. **2b** (*as adj*): *vermeil shoes.* [C15: from OF, from LL *vermiculus* insect (of the genus *Kermes*) or the red dye prepared from it, from L: little worm]

vermi- *combining form.* worm: *vermicide; vermiform; vermifuge.* [from L *vermis* worm]

vermicelli (,vɜːmɪ'sɛlɪ, -'tʃɛlɪ) *n* **1** very fine strands of pasta, used in soups. **2** tiny chocolate strands used to coat cakes, etc. [C17: from It.: little worms, from *verme*, from L *vermis*]

vermicide ('vɜːmɪ,saɪd) *n* any substance used to kill worms.
▸**,vermi'cidal** *adj*

vermicular (vɜː'mɪkjʊlə) *adj* **1** resembling the form, motion, or tracks of worms. **2** of worms or wormlike animals. [C17: from Med. L, from L *vermiculus*, dim. of *vermis* worm]
▸**ver'miculate** *adj* ▸**ver,micu'lation** *n*

vermiculite (vɜː'mɪkjʊ,laɪt) *n* any of a group of micaceous minerals consisting mainly of hydrated silicate of magnesium, aluminium, and iron: on heating they expand and in this form are used in heat and sound insulation. [C19: from VERMICUL(AR) + -ITE[1]]

vermiform ('vɜːmɪ,fɔːm) *adj* resembling a worm.

vermiform appendix *n* a wormlike pouch extending from the lower end of the caecum in some mammals. Also called: **appendix.**

vermifuge ('vɜːmɪ,fjuːdʒ) *n* any drug or agent able to destroy or expel intestinal worms.
▸**vermifugal** (,vɜːmɪ'fjuːgᵊl) *adj*

vermilion (və'mɪljən) *n* **1a** a bright red to reddish-orange colour. **1b** (*as adj*): *a vermilion car.* **2** mercuric sulphide, esp. when used as a bright red pigment; cinnabar. [C13: from OF *vermeillon*, from *vermeil*, from L *vermiculus*, dim. of *vermis* worm]

vermin 🅣 ('vɜːmɪn) *n* **1** (*functioning as pl*) small animals collectively, esp. insects and rodents, that are troublesome to man, domestic animals, etc. **2** (*pl* **vermin**) an unpleasant person. [C13: from OF, from L *vermis* worm]
▸**'verminous** *adj*

vermis ('vɜːmɪs) *n, pl* **vermes** (-miːz). *Anat.* the middle lobe connecting the two halves of the cerebellum. [C19: via NL from L: worm]

vermouth ('vɜːməθ) *n* any of several wines containing aromatic herbs. [C19: from F, from G *Wermut* WORMWOOD (absinthe)]

vernacular 🅣 (və'nækjʊlə) *n* **1 the.** the commonly spoken language or dialect of a particular people or place. **2** a local style of architecture, in which ordinary houses are built: *a true English vernacular.* ◆ *adj* **3** relating to or in the vernacular. **4** designating or relating to the common name of an animal or plant. **5** built in the local style of ordinary houses. [C17: from L *vernāculus* belonging to a household slave, from *verna* household slave]
▸**ver'nacularly** *adv*

vernal ('vɜːnᵊl) *adj* **1** of or occurring in spring. **2** *Poetic.* of or characteristic of youth. [C16: from L, from *vēr* spring]
▸**'vernally** *adv*

vernal equinox *n* See at **equinox.**

vernal grass *n* any of a genus of Eurasian grasses, such as **sweet vernal grass**, having the fragrant scent of coumarin.

vernalize *or* **vernalise** ('vɜːnə,laɪz) *vb* **vernalizes, vernalizing, vernalized** *or* **vernalises, vernalising, vernalised.** to shorten the period between sowing

THESAURUS

verbiage *n* = **verbosity**, circumlocution, periphrasis, pleonasm, prolixity, redundancy, repetition, tautology

verbose *adj* = **long-winded**, circumlocutory, diffuse, garrulous, periphrastic, pleonastic, prolix, tautological, windy, wordy
Antonyms *adj* brief, brusque, concise, curt, quiet, reticent, short, succinct, terse, untalkative

verbosely *adv* = **at great length**, at undue length, long-windedly, wordily

verbosity *n* = **long-windedness**, garrulity, logorrhoea, loquaciousness, prolixity, rambling, verbiage, verboseness, windiness, wordiness

verdant *adj* **1** = **green**, flourishing, fresh, grassy, leafy, lush

verdict *n* **1, 2** = **decision**, adjudication, conclusion, finding, judgment, opinion, sentence

verge[1] *n* **1, 2** = **border**, boundary, brim, brink, edge, extreme, limit, lip, margin, roadside, threshold ◆ *vb* **6** *foll. by* **on** = **come near to**, approach, border

verification *n* **1** = **proof**, authentication, confirmation, corroboration, substantiation, validation

verify *vb* **1** = **prove**, attest, attest to, authenticate, bear out, confirm, corroborate, substantiate, support, validate **2** = **check**
Antonyms *vb* ≠ **prove:** deny, discount, discredit, dispute, invalidate, nullify, undermine, weaken

verisimilitude *n* **1** = **realism**, authenticity, colour, credibility, likeliness, likeness, plausibility, resemblance, semblance, show of

verminous *adj* **1** = **lousy**, alive, crawling, flea-ridden

vernacular *n* **1** = **dialect**, argot, cant, idiom, jargon, native language, parlance, patois, speech, vulgar tongue ◆ *adj* **3** = **colloquial**, common, indigenous, informal, local, mother, native, popular, vulgar

and flowering in (plants), esp. by subjection of the seeds to low temperatures before planting.
▸ **ˌvernaliˈzation** *or* **ˌvernaliˈsation** *n*

vernation (vɜːˈneɪʃən) *n* the way in which leaves are arranged in the bud. [C18: from NL, from L *vernāre* to be springlike, from *vēr* spring]

vernier (ˈvɜːnɪə) *n* **1** a small movable scale running parallel to the main graduated scale in certain measuring instruments, such as theodolites, used to obtain a fractional reading of one of the divisions on the main scale. **2** (*modifier*) relating to or fitted with a vernier: *a vernier scale.* [C18: after Paul *Vernier* (1580–1637), F mathematician, who described the scale]

vernissage (ˌvɜːnɪˈsɑːʒ) *n* a preview or the opening or the first day of an exhibition of paintings. [F, from *vernis* VARNISH]

Veronal (ˈverənˀl) *n* a trademark for **barbitone.**

veronica[1] (vəˈrɒnɪkə) *n* any plant of a genus, including the speedwells, of temperate and cold regions, having small blue, pink, or white flowers and flattened notched fruits. [C16: from Med. L, ?from the name *Veronica*]

veronica[2] (vəˈrɒnɪkə) *n Bullfighting.* a pass in which the matador slowly swings the cape away from the charging bull. [from Sp., from the name *Veronica*]

verruca (veˈruːkə) *n, pl* **verrucae** (-siː) *or* **verrucas. 1** *Pathol.* a wart, esp. one growing on the hand or foot. **2** *Biol.* a wartlike outgrowth. [C16: from L: wart]

verrucose (ˈverʊˌkəʊs) *or* **verrucous** (ˈverʊkəs, veˈruːkəs) *adj Bot.* covered with warty processes. [C17: from L *verrūcōsus* full of warts, from *verrūca* a wart]
▸ **verrucosity** (ˌveruˈkɒsɪtɪ) *n*

versant (ˈvɜːsˀnt) *n* **1** the side or slope of a mountain or mountain range. **2** the slope of a region. [C19: from F, from *verser* to turn, from L *versāre*]

versatile ❶ (ˈvɜːsəˌtaɪl) *adj* **1** capable of or adapted for many different uses, skills, etc. **2** variable. **3** *Bot.* (of an anther) attached to the filament by a small area so that it moves freely in the wind. **4** *Zool.* able to turn forwards and backwards. [C17: from L *versātilis* moving around, from *versāre* to turn]
▸ **ˈversaˌtilely** *adv* ▸ **versatility** (ˌvɜːsəˈtɪlɪtɪ) *n*

verse (vɜːs) *n* **1** (not in technical usage) a stanza of a poem. **2** poetry as distinct from prose. **3a** a series of metrical feet forming a rhythmic unit of one line. **3b** (*as modifier*): *verse line.* **4** a specified type of metre or metrical structure: *iambic verse.* **5** one of the series of short subsections into which most of the writings in the Bible are divided. **6** a poem. ◆ *vb* **verses, versing, versed. 7** a rare word for **versify.** [OE *vers,* from L *versus* furrow, lit.: a turning (of the plough), from *vertere* to turn]

versed ❶ (vɜːst) *adj* (*postpositive;* foll. by *in*) thoroughly knowledgeable (about), acquainted (with), or skilled (in).

versed sine *n* a trigonometric function equal to one minus the cosine of the specified angle. [C16: from NL, from SINE[1] + *versus,* from *vertere* to turn]

versicle (ˈvɜːsɪkˀl) *n* **1** a short verse. **2** a short sentence recited or sung by a minister and responded to by his congregation. [C14: from L *versiculus* a little line, from *versus* VERSE]

versicolour *or US* **versicolor** (ˈvɜːsɪˌkʌlə) *adj* of variable or various colours. [C18: from L *versicolor,* from *versāre* to turn + *color* COLOUR]

versification (ˌvɜːsɪfɪˈkeɪʃən) *n* **1** the technique or art of versifying. **2** the form or metrical composition of a poem. **3** a metrical version of a prose text.

versify (ˈvɜːsɪˌfaɪ) *vb* **versifies, versifying, versified. 1** (*tr*) to render (something) into verse. **2** (*intr*) to write in verse. [C14: from OF, from L, from *versus* VERSE + *facere* to make]
▸ **ˈversiˌfier** *n*

version ❶ (ˈvɜːʃən) *n* **1** an account of a matter from a certain point of view, as contrasted with others: *his version of the accident is different from the policeman's.* **2** a translation, esp. of the Bible, from one language into another. **3** a variant form of something. **4** an adaptation, as of a book or play into a film. **5** *Med.* manual turning of a fetus to correct an irregular position within the uterus. [C16: from Med. L *versiō* a turning, from L *vertere* to turn]
▸ **ˈversional** *adj*

vers libre *French.* (ver librə) *n* (in French poetry) another term for **free verse.**

verso (ˈvɜːsəʊ) *n, pl* **versos. 1a** the back of a sheet of printed paper. **1b** the left-hand pages of a book, bearing the even numbers. Cf. **recto** (sense 2). **2** the side of a coin opposite to the obverse. [C19: from NL *versō foliō* the leaf having been turned, from L *vertere* to turn + *folium* leaf]

verst (veəst, vɜːst) *n* a unit of length, used in Russia, equal to 1.067 kilometres (0.6629 miles). [C16: from F or G, from Russian *versta* line]

versus (ˈvɜːsəs) *prep* **1** (esp. in a competition or lawsuit) against. Abbrev.: **v.,** (esp. US) **vs. 2** in contrast with. [C15: from L: turned (in the direction of), opposite, from *vertere* to turn]

vertebra (ˈvɜːtɪbrə) *n, pl* **vertebrae** (-briː) *or* **vertebras.** one of the bony segments of the spinal column. [C17: from L: joint of the spine, from *vertere* to turn]
▸ **ˈvertebral** *adj* ▸ **ˈvertebrally** *adv*

vertebral column *n* another name for **spinal column.**

vertebrate (ˈvɜːtɪˌbreɪt, -brɪt) *n* **1** any animal of a subphylum characterized by a bony skeleton and a well-developed brain: the group contains fishes, amphibians, reptiles, birds, and mammals. ◆ *adj* **2** of or belonging to this subphylum.

vertebration (ˌvɜːtɪˈbreɪʃən) *n* the formation of vertebrae or segmentation resembling vertebrae.

vertex ❶ (ˈvɜːteks) *n, pl* **vertexes** *or* **vertices. 1** the highest point. **2** *Maths.* **2a** the point opposite the base of a figure. **2b** the point of intersection of two sides of a plane figure or angle. **2c** the point of intersection of a pencil of lines or three or more planes of a solid figure. **3** *Anat.* the crown of the head. [C16: from L: highest point, from *vertere* to turn]

vertical ❶ (ˈvɜːtɪkˀl) *adj* **1** at right angles to the horizon; upright: *a vertical wall.* **2** extending in a perpendicular direction. **3** directly overhead. **4** *Econ.* of or relating to associated or consecutive, though not identical, stages of industrial activity: *vertical integration.* **5** of or relating to the vertex. **6** *Anat.* of or situated at the top of the head (vertex). ◆ *n* **7** a vertical plane, position, or line. **8** a vertical post, pillar, etc. [C16: from LL *verticālis,* from L VERTEX]
▸ **ˌvertiˈcality** *n* ▸ **ˈvertically** *adv*

vertical angles *pl n Geom.* the pair of equal angles between a pair of intersecting lines.

vertical mobility *n Sociol.* the movement of individuals or groups to positions in society that involve a change in class, status, and power.

vertices (ˈvɜːtɪˌsiːz) *n* a plural of **vertex** (in technical and scientific senses only).

verticil (ˈvɜːtɪsɪl) *n Biol.* a circular arrangement of parts about an axis, esp. leaves around a stem. [C18: from L *verticillus* whorl (of a spindle), from VERTEX]
▸ **verˈticillate** *adj*

vertiginous (vɜːˈtɪdʒɪnəs) *adj* **1** of, relating to, or having vertigo. **2** producing dizziness. **3** whirling. **4** changeable; unstable. [C17: from L *vertīginōsus,* from VERTIGO]
▸ **verˈtiginously** *adv*

vertigo ❶ (ˈvɜːtɪgəʊ) *n, pl* **vertigoes** *or* **vertigines** (vɜːˈtɪdʒɪˌniːz). *Pathol.* a sensation of dizziness resulting from a disorder of the sense of balance. [C16: from L: a whirling round, from *vertere* to turn]

vertu (vɜːˈtuː) *n* a variant spelling of **virtu.**

vervain (ˈvɜːveɪn) *n* any of several plants of the genus *Verbena,* having square stems and long slender spikes of purple, blue, or white flowers. [C14: from OF *verveine,* from L *verbēna* sacred bough]

verve ❶ (vɜːv) *n* great vitality and liveliness. [C17: from OF: garrulity, from L *verba* words, chatter]

vervet (ˈvɜːvɪt) *n* a variety of a South African guenon monkey having dark hair on the hands and feet and a reddish patch beneath the tail. [C19: from F, from *vert* green]

very ❶ (ˈverɪ) *adv* **1** (intensifier) used to add emphasis to adjectives that are able to be graded: *very good; very tall.* ◆ *adj* (*prenominal*) **2** (intensifier) used with nouns preceded by a definite article or possessive determiner, in order to give emphasis to the significance or relevance of a noun in a particular context, or to give exaggerated intensity to certain nouns: *the very man I want to see; the very back of the room.* **3** (intensifier) used in metaphors to emphasize the applicability of the image to the situation described: *he was a very lion in the fight.* **4** *Arch.* genuine: *the very living God.* [C13: from OF *verai* true, from L *vērax,* from *vērus*]

USAGE NOTE In strict usage adverbs of degree such as *very, too, quite, really,* and *extremely* are used only to qualify adjectives: *he is very happy; she is too sad.* By this rule, these words should not be used to qualify past participles that follow the verb *to be,* since they would then be technically qualifying verbs. With the exception of certain participles, such as *tired* or *disappointed,* that have come to be regarded as adjectives, all other past participles are qualified by adverbs such as *much, greatly, seriously,* or *excessively: he has been much* (not *very*) *inconvenienced; she has been excessively* (not *too*) *criticized.*

THESAURUS

versatile *adj* **1, 2 = adaptable,** adjustable, all-purpose, all-round, all-singing, all-dancing, flexible, functional, handy, many-sided, multifaceted, protean, resourceful, variable
Antonyms *adj* fixed, inflexible, invariable, limited, one-sided, unadaptable

versed *adj* **= knowledgeable,** accomplished, acquainted, competent, conversant, experienced, familiar, practised, proficient, qualified, seasoned, skilled, well informed, well up in (*inf.*)
Antonyms *adj* callow, green, ignorant, inexperienced, new, raw, unacquainted, unfledged, unpractised, unschooled, unskilled, unversed

version *n* **1 = account,** interpretation, side, take (*inf., chiefly US*) **2, 4 = adaptation,** exercise, portrayal, reading, rendering, translation **3 = form,** design, kind, model, style, type, variant

vertex *n* **1 = top,** acme, apex, apogee, crest, crown, culmination, extremity, height, pinnacle, summit, zenith

vertical *adj* **1, 2 = upright,** erect, on end, perpendicular
Antonyms *adj* flat, horizontal, level, plane, prone

vertigo *n* **= dizziness,** giddiness, light-headedness, loss of equilibrium, swimming of the head

verve *n* **= enthusiasm,** animation, brio, dash, élan, energy, force, get-up-and-go (*inf.*), gusto, life, liveliness, pep, punch (*inf.*), sparkle, spirit, vigour, vim (*sl.*), vitality, vivacity, zeal, zip (*inf.*)
Antonyms *n* apathy, disdain, half-heartedness, indifference, inertia, lack of enthusiasm, languor, lethargy, lifelessness, reluctance, torpor

very *adv* **1 = extremely,** absolutely, acutely, awfully (*inf.*), decidedly, deeply, eminently,

very high frequency *n* a radio-frequency band or radio frequency lying between 30 and 300 megahertz. Abbrev.: **VHF.**

Very light ('vɛrɪ) *n* a coloured flare fired from a special pistol (**Very pistol**) for signalling at night, esp. at sea. [C19: after Edward W. *Very* (1852–1910), US naval ordnance officer]

very low frequency *n* a radio-frequency band or radio frequency lying between 3 and 30 kilohertz. Abbrev.: **VLF.**

vesica ('vɛsɪkə) *n, pl* **vesicae** (-,siː). *Anat.* a technical name for **bladder** (sense 1). [C17: from L: bladder, sac, blister]
▸ **'vesical** *adj* ▸ **vesiculate** (vɛ'sɪkju,leɪt, -lɪt) *vb, adj*

vesicant ('vɛsɪkənt) *or* **vesicatory** ('vɛsɪ,keɪtərɪ) *n, pl* **vesicants** *or* **vesicatories. 1** any substance that causes blisters. ◆ *adj* **2** acting as a vesicant. [C19: see VESICA]

vesicate ('vɛsɪ,keɪt) *vb* **vesicates, vesicating, vesicated.** to blister. [C17: from NL *vēsīcāre* to blister; see VESICA]
▸ **,vesi'cation** *n*

vesicle ('vɛsɪk°l) *n* **1** *Pathol.* **1a** any small sac or cavity, esp. one containing serous fluid. **1b** a blister. **2** *Geol.* a rounded cavity within a rock. **3** *Bot.* a small bladder-like cavity occurring in certain seaweeds. **4** any small cavity or cell. [C16: from L *vēsīcula*, dim. of VESICA]
▸ **vesicular** (vɛ'sɪkjulə) *adj*

vesper ('vɛspə) *n* **1** an evening prayer, service, or hymn. **2** *Arch.* evening. **3** (*modifier*) of or relating to vespers. ◆ See also **vespers.** [C14: from L: evening, the evening star]

vespers ('vɛspəz) *n* (*functioning as sing*) **1** *Chiefly RC Church.* the sixth of the seven canonical hours of the divine office. **2** another word for **evensong** (sense 1).

vespertine ('vɛspə,taɪn) *adj* **1** *Bot., zool.* appearing, opening, or active in the evening: *vespertine flowers.* **2** occurring in the evening or (esp. of stars) setting in the evening.

vespiary ('vɛspɪərɪ) *n, pl* **vespiaries.** a nest or colony of social wasps or hornets. [C19: from L *vespa* a wasp, on the model of *apiary*]

vespid ('vɛspɪd) *n* **1** any of a family of hymenopterous insects, including the common wasp. ◆ *adj* **2** of or belonging to this family. [C19: from NL, from L *vespa* a wasp]
▸ **'vespine** *adj*

vessel ❶ ('vɛs°l) *n* **1** any object used as a container, esp. for a liquid. **2** a passenger or freight-carrying ship, boat, etc. **3** *Anat.* a tubular structure that transports such body fluids as blood and lymph. **4** *Bot.* a tubular element of xylem tissue transporting water. **5** *Rare.* a person regarded as a vehicle for some purpose or quality. [C13: from OF, from LL *vascellum* urn, from L *vās* vessel]

vest ❶ (vɛst) *n* **1** an undergarment covering the body from the shoulders to the hips, made of cotton, nylon, etc. Austral. equivalent: **singlet.** US and Canad. equivalent: **undershirt. 2** *US, Canad., & Austral.* a waistcoat. **3** *Obs.* any form of dress. ◆ *vb* **4** (*tr;* foll. by *in*) to place or settle (power, rights, etc., in): *power was vested in the committee.* **5** (*tr;* foll. by *with*) to bestow or confer (on): *the company was vested with authority.* **6** (usually foll. by *in*) to confer (a right, title, etc., upon) or (of a right, title, etc.) to pass (to) or devolve (upon). **7** (*tr*) to clothe. **8** (*intr*) to put on clothes, ecclesiastical vestments, etc. [C15: from OF *vestir* to clothe, from L *vestīre*, from *vestis* clothing]

vesta ('vɛstə) *n* a short friction match, usually of wood. [C19: after *Vesta*, Roman goddess of the hearth]

vestal ('vɛst°l) *adj* **1** chaste or pure. **2** of or relating to the Roman goddess Vesta. ◆ *n* **3** a chaste woman, esp. a nun.

vestal virgin *n* (in ancient Rome) one of the virgin priestesses whose lives were dedicated to Vesta and to maintaining the sacred fire in her temple.

vested ('vɛstɪd) *adj Property law.* having a present right to the immediate or future possession and enjoyment of property.

vested interest *n* **1** *Property law.* an existing right to the immediate or future possession and enjoyment of property. **2** a strong personal concern in a state of affairs, etc. **3** a person or group that has such an interest.

vestiary ('vɛstɪərɪ) *n, pl* **vestiaries.** *Obs.* a room for storing clothes or dressing in, such as a vestry. [C17: from LL *vestiārius*, from *vestis* clothing]

vestibule ❶ ('vɛstɪ,bjuːl) *n* **1** a small entrance hall or anteroom. **2** any small bodily cavity at the entrance to a passage or canal. [C17: from L *vestibulum*]

vestige ❶ ('vɛstɪdʒ) *n* **1** a small trace; hint: *a vestige of truth.* **2** *Biol.* an organ or part of an organism that is a small nonfunctioning remnant of a functional organ in an ancestor. [C17: via F from L *vestīgium* track]
▸ **ves'tigial** *adj*

vestment ('vɛstmənt) *n* **1** a garment or robe, esp. one denoting office, authority, or rank. **2** any of various ceremonial garments worn by the clergy at religious services, etc. [C13: from OF *vestiment*, from L *vestīmentum*, from *vestīre* to clothe]
▸ **vestmental** (vɛst'mɛnt°l) *adj*

vest-pocket *n* (*modifier*) *Chiefly US.* small enough to fit into a waistcoat pocket.

vestry ('vɛstrɪ) *n, pl* **vestries. 1** a room in or attached to a church in which vestments, sacred vessels, etc., are kept. **2** a room in or attached to some churches, used for Sunday school, etc. **3a** *Church of England.* a meeting of all the members of a parish or their representatives, to transact the official and administrative business of the parish. **3b** the parish council. [C14: prob. from OF *vestiarie;* see VEST]
▸ **'vestral** *adj*

vestryman ('vɛstrɪmən) *n, pl* **vestrymen.** a member of a church vestry.

vesture ('vɛstʃə) *Arch.* ◆ *n* **1** a garment or something that seems like a garment: *a vesture of cloud.* ◆ *vb* **vestures, vesturing, vestured. 2** (*tr*) to clothe. [C14: from OF, from *vestir*, from L *vestīre*, from *vestis* clothing]
▸ **'vestural** *adj*

vet[1] ❶ (vɛt) *n* **1** short for **veterinary surgeon.** ◆ *vb* **vets, vetting, vetted. 2** (*tr*) *Chiefly Brit.* to make a prior examination and critical appraisal of (a person, document, etc.): *the candidates were well vetted.* **3** to examine or treat (an animal).

vet[2] (vɛt) *n US & Canad.* short for **veteran** (senses 2, 3).

vet. *abbrev. for:* **1** veteran. **2** veterinarian. **3** veterinary. ◆ Also (for senses 2, 3): **veter.**

vetch (vɛtʃ) *n* **1** any of various climbing plants having pinnate leaves, blue or purple flowers, and tendrils on the stems. **2** any of various similar and related plants, such as the kidney vetch. **3** the beanlike fruit of any of these plants. [C14 *fecche*, from OF *veche*, from L *vicia*]

vetchling ('vɛtʃlɪŋ) *n* any of various tendril-climbing plants, mainly of N temperate regions, having winged or angled stems and showy flowers. See also **sweet pea.**

veteran ❶ ('vɛtərən) *n* **1a** a person or thing that has given long service in some capacity. **1b** (*as modifier*): *veteran firemen.* **2** a soldier who has seen considerable active service. **3** *US & Canad.* a person who has served in the military forces. [C16: from L, from *vetus* old]

veteran car *n Brit.* a car constructed before 1919, esp. one constructed before 1905. Cf. **classic car, vintage car.**

veterinary ('vɛtərɪnərɪ) *adj* of or relating to veterinary medicine. [C18: from L *veterīnārius*, from *veterīnae* draught animals]

veterinary medicine *or* **science** *n* the branch of medicine concerned with the health of animals and the treatment of injuries or diseases that affect them.

veterinary surgeon *n Brit.* a person qualified to practise veterinary medicine. US and Canad. term: **veterinarian.**

veto ❶ ('viːtəu) *n, pl* **vetoes. 1** the power to prevent legislation or action proposed by others: *the presidential veto.* **2** the exercise of this power. ◆ *vb* **vetoes, vetoing, vetoed.** (*tr*) **3** to refuse consent to (a proposal, esp. a government bill). **4** to prohibit, ban, or forbid: *her parents vetoed her trip.* [C17: from L: I forbid, from *vetāre* to forbid]
▸ **'vetoer** *n*

vex ❶ (vɛks) *vb* (*tr*) **1** to anger or annoy. **2** to confuse; worry. **3** *Arch.* to agitate. [C15: from OF *vexer*, from L *vexāre* to jolt (in carrying), from *vehere* to convey]
▸ **'vexer** *n* ▸ **'vexing** *adj*

vexation ❶ (vɛk'seɪʃən) *n* **1** the act of vexing or the state of being vexed. **2** something that vexes.

vexatious ❶ (vɛk'seɪʃəs) *adj* **1** vexing or tending to vex. **2** vexed. **3** *Law.* (of a legal action or proceeding) instituted without sufficient grounds, esp. so as to cause annoyance to the defendant.
▸ **vex'atiously** *adv*

THESAURUS

exceedingly, excessively, greatly, highly, jolly (*Brit.*), noticeably, particularly, profoundly, really, remarkably, seriously (*inf.*), superlatively, surpassingly, terribly, truly, uncommonly, unusually, wonderfully ◆ *adj* **2 = exact**, actual, appropriate, express, identical, perfect, precise, real, same, selfsame, unqualified

vessel *n* **1 = container**, pot, receptacle, utensil **2 = ship**, barque, boat, craft

vest *vb* **4, 5** *with* **in** *or* **with = place**, authorize, be devolved upon, bestow, confer, consign, empower, endow, entrust, furnish, invest, lodge, put in the hands of, settle

vestibule *n* **1 = hall**, anteroom, entrance hall, foyer, lobby, porch, portico

vestige *n* **1 = trace**, evidence, glimmer, hint, indication, relic, remainder, remains, remnant, residue, scrap, sign, suspicion, token, track

vestigial *adj* **2 = rudimentary**, imperfect, incomplete, nonfunctional, surviving, undeveloped

Antonyms *adj* complete, developed, functional, perfect, practical, useful

vet[1] *vb* **2 = check**, appraise, check out, examine, investigate, look over, pass under review, review, scan, scrutinize, size up (*inf.*)

veteran *n* **1a, 2 = old hand**, master, old stager, old-timer, past master, pro (*inf.*), trouper, warhorse (*inf.*) ◆ *modifier* **1b = long-serving**, adept, battle-scarred, expert, old, proficient, seasoned

Antonyms *n* ≠ **old hand:** apprentice, beginner, freshman, initiate, neophyte, novice, recruit, tyro

veto *n* **2 = ban**, boycott, embargo, interdict, nonconsent, prohibition ◆ *vb* **3, 4 = ban**, boycott, disallow, forbid, give the thumbs down to, interdict, kill (*inf.*), negative, prohibit, put the kibosh on (*sl.*), refuse permission, reject, rule out, turn down

Antonyms *n* ≠ **ban:** approval, endorsement, go-ahead (*inf.*), ratification ◆ *vb* ≠ **ban:** approve, endorse, O.K. *or* okay (*inf.*), pass, ratify

vex *vb* **1, 2 = annoy**, afflict, aggravate (*inf.*), agitate, bother, bug (*inf.*), confuse, displease, distress, disturb, exasperate, fret, gall, grate on, harass, hassle (*inf.*), irritate, molest, needle (*inf.*), nettle, offend, peeve (*inf.*), perplex, pester, pique, plague, provoke, put out, rile, tease, torment, trouble, upset, worry

Antonyms *vb* allay, appease, comfort, console, gratify, hush, mollify, please, quiet, soothe

vexation *n* **1 = annoyance**, aggravation (*inf.*), chagrin, displeasure, dissatisfaction, exasperation, frustration, irritation, pique **2 = problem**, bother, difficulty, hassle, headache (*inf.*), irritant, misfortune, nuisance, thorn in one's flesh, trouble, upset, worry

vexatious *adj* **1 = annoying**, afflicting, aggravating (*inf.*), bothersome, burdensome,

vexed ⓘ (vɛkst) *adj* **1** annoyed, confused, or agitated. **2** much debated (esp. in **a vexed question**).
▸**vexedly** ('vɛksɪdlɪ) *adv*
vexillology (ˌvɛksɪ'lɒlədʒɪ) *n* the study and collection of information about flags. [C20: from L *vexillum* flag + -LOGY]
▸ˌ**vexil'lologist** *n*
vexillum (vɛk'sɪləm) *n, pl* **vexilla** (-lə). **1** *Ornithol.* the vane of a feather. **2** Also called: **standard.** *Bot.* the largest petal of a papilionaceous flower. [C18: from L: banner, ?from *vēlum* sail]
▸'**vexillate** *adj*
VF *abbrev. for* video frequency.
VFA (in Australia) *abbrev. for* Victorian Football Association.
vg *abbrev. for* very good.
VG *abbrev. for* Vicar General.
VGA *abbrev. for* video graphics array: a computing standard for spatial and colour resolution.
VHF *or* **vhf** *Radio. abbrev. for* very high frequency.
VHS *Trademark. abbrev. for* video home system: a video cassette recording system using ½″ magnetic tape.
VI *abbrev. for:* **1** Vancouver Island. **2** Virgin Islands.
v.i. *abbrev. for* vide infra (see **vide**).
via ('vaɪə) *prep* by way of; by means of; through: *to London via Paris.* [C18: from L *viā*, from *via* way]
viable ⓘ ('vaɪəbᵊl) *adj* **1** capable of becoming actual, etc.: *a viable proposition.* **2** (of seeds, eggs, etc.) capable of normal growth and development. **3** (of a fetus) having reached a stage of development at which further development can occur independently of the mother. [C19: from F, from *vie* life, from L *vīta*]
▸ˌ**via'bility** *n*
Via Dolorosa ('viːə ˌdɒlə'rəʊsə) *n* the route followed by Christ from the place of his condemnation to Calvary for his crucifixion. [L, lit.: sorrowful road]
viaduct ('vaɪəˌdʌkt) *n* a bridge, esp. for carrying a road or railway across a valley, etc. [C19: from L *via* way + *dūcere* to bring, on the model of *aqueduct*]
Viagra (vaɪ'ægrə, viː-) *n Trademark.* a drug that allows increased blood flow to the penis; used to treat impotence in men.
vial ('vaɪəl) *n* a less common variant of **phial.** [C14 *fiole*, from OF, ult. from Gk *phialē*; see PHIAL]
via media *Latin.* ('vaɪə 'miːdɪə) *n* a compromise between two extremes.
viand ('viːənd) *n* **1** a type of food, esp. a delicacy. **2** (*pl*) provisions. [C14: from OF, ult. from L *vīvenda* things to be lived on, from *vīvere* to live]
viatical (vaɪ'ætɪkᵊl) *adj* **1** of or denoting a road or a journey. **2** *Bot.* (of a plant) growing by the side of a road. [C19: from L *viāticus* belonging to a journey + -AL]
viatical settlement *n* the purchase by a charity of a life assurance policy owned by a person with only a short time to live, to enable that person to use the proceeds during his or her lifetime. See also **death futures.**
viaticum (vaɪ'ætɪkəm) *n, pl* **viatica** (-kə) *or* **viaticums. 1** *Christianity.* Holy Communion as administered to a person dying or in danger of death. **2** *Rare.* provisions or a travel allowance for a journey. [C16: from L, from *viāticus* belonging to a journey, from *via* way]
vibes ⓘ (vaɪbz) *pl n* **1** *Inf.* short for **vibraphone. 2** *Sl.* short for **vibrations.**
vibraculum (vaɪ'brækjʊləm) *n, pl* **vibracula** (-lə). *Zool.* any of the specialized bristle-like polyps in certain bryozoans, the actions of which prevent parasites from settling on the colony. [C19: from NL, from L *vibrāre* to brandish]
vibrant ⓘ ('vaɪbrənt) *adj* **1** characterized by or exhibiting vibration. **2** giving an impression of vigour and activity. **3** caused by vibration; resonant. [C16: from L *vibrāre* to agitate]
▸'**vibrancy** *n* ▸'**vibrantly** *adv*
vibraphone ('vaɪbrəˌfəʊn) *n* a percussion instrument consisting of a set of metal bars placed over tubular metal resonators, which are made to vibrate electronically.
▸'**vibraˌphonist** *n*
vibrate ⓘ (vaɪ'breɪt) *vb* **vibrates, vibrating, vibrated. 1** to move or cause to move back and forth rapidly. **2** (*intr*) to oscillate. **3** to resonate or cause to resonate. **4** (*intr*) to waver. **5** *Physics.* to undergo or cause to undergo an oscillatory process, as of an alternating current. **6** (*intr*) *Rare.* to respond emotionally; thrill. [C17: from L *vibrāre*]
▸**vibratile** ('vaɪbrəˌtaɪl) *adj* ▸**vi'brating** *adj* ▸**vibratory** ('vaɪbrətərɪ) *adj*
vibration ⓘ (vaɪ'breɪʃən) *n* **1** the act or an instance of vibrating. **2** *Physics.* **2a** a periodic motion about an equilibrium position, such as in the propagation of sound. **2b** a single cycle of such a motion. **3** the process or state of vibrating or being vibrated.
▸**vi'brational** *adj*
vibrations (vaɪ'breɪʃənz) *pl n Sl.* **1** instinctive feelings supposedly influencing human communication. **2** a characteristic atmosphere felt to be emanating from places or objects.
vibrato (vɪ'brɑːtəʊ) *n, pl* **vibratos.** *Music.* **1** a slight, rapid, and regular fluctuation in the pitch of a note produced on a stringed instrument by a shaking movement of the hand stopping the strings. **2** an oscillatory effect produced in singing by fluctuation in breath pressure or pitch. [C19: from It., from L *vibrāre* to VIBRATE]
vibrator (vaɪ'breɪtə) *n* **a** a device for producing a vibratory motion, such as one used in massage. **b** such a device with a vibrating part or tip, used as a dildo.
vibrissa (vaɪ'brɪsə) *n, pl* **vibrissae** (-siː). (*usually pl*) **1** any of the bristle-like sensitive hairs on the face of many mammals; a whisker. **2** any of the specialized bristle-like feathers around the beak in certain insectivorous birds. [C17: from L, prob. from *vibrāre* to shake]
▸**vi'brissal** *adj*
viburnum (vaɪ'bɜːnəm) *n* **1** any of various temperate and subtropical shrubs or trees having small white flowers and berry-like red or black fruits. **2** the dried bark of several species of this tree, sometimes used in medicine. [C18: from L: wayfaring tree]
Vic. *Austral. abbrev. for* Victoria (the state).
vicar ('vɪkə) *n* **1** *Church of England.* **1a** (in Britain) a clergyman appointed to act as priest of a parish from which, formerly, he did not receive tithes but a stipend. **1b** a clergyman who acts as assistant to or substitute for the rector of a parish at Communion. **2** *RC Church.* a bishop or priest representing the pope and exercising a limited jurisdiction. **3** Also called: **lay vicar, vicar choral.** *Church of England.* a member of a cathedral choir appointed to sing certain parts of the services. [C13: from OF, from L *vicārius* (n) a deputy, from *vicārius* (adj) VICARIOUS]
▸**vicarial** (vɪ'kɛərɪəl) *adj* ▸**vi'cariate** *n* ▸'**vicarly** *adj*
vicarage ('vɪkərɪdʒ) *n* the residence or benefice of a vicar.
vicar apostolic *n RC Church.* a titular bishop having jurisdiction in missionary countries.
vicar general *n, pl* **vicars general.** an official, usually a layman, appointed to assist the bishop of a diocese in discharging his administrative or judicial duties.
vicarious ⓘ (vɪ'kɛərɪəs, vaɪ-) *adj* **1** undergone at second hand through sympathetic participation in another's experiences. **2** undergone or done as the substitute for another: *vicarious punishment.* **3** delegated: *vicarious authority.* **4** taking the place of another. [C17: from L *vicārius* substituted, from *vicis* interchange]
▸**vi'cariously** *adv* ▸**vi'cariousness** *n*
Vicar of Christ *n RC Church.* the pope when regarded as Christ's earthly representative.
vice[1] ⓘ (vaɪs) *n* **1** an immoral, wicked, or evil habit, action, or trait. **2** frequent indulgence in immoral or degrading practices. **3** a specific form of pernicious conduct, esp. prostitution or sexual perversion. **4** an imperfection in character, conduct, etc.: *smoking is his only vice.* **5** a bad trick or disposition, as of horses, dogs, etc. [C13: via OF from L *vitium* a defect]
vice[2] *or US* (*often*) **vise** (vaɪs) *n* **1** an appliance for holding an object while work is done on it, usually having a pair of jaws. ◆ *vb* **2** (*tr*) to grip (something) with or as if with a vice. [C15: from OF *vis* a screw, from L *vītis* vine, plant with spiralling tendrils (hence the later meaning)]
vice[3] (vaɪs) *adj* **1a** (*prenominal*) serving in the place of. **1b** (*in combination*): *viceroy.* ◆ *n* **2** *Inf.* a person who serves as a deputy to another. [C18: from L, from *vicis* interchange]
vice[4] ('vaɪsɪ) *prep* instead of; as a substitute for. [C16: from L, ablative of *vicis* change]
vice admiral *n* a commissioned officer of flag rank in certain navies, junior to an admiral and senior to a rear admiral.
vice-chairman *n, pl* **vice-chairmen.** a person who deputizes for a chairman and serves in his place during his absence.
▸ˌ**vice-'chairmanship** *n*
vice chancellor *n* **1** the chief executive or administrator at some British universities. **2** (in the US) a judge in courts of equity subordinate to the chancellor. **3** (formerly in England) a senior judge of the court

THESAURUS

disagreeable, disappointing, distressing, exasperating, harassing, irksome, irritating, nagging, plaguy (*arch.*), provoking, teasing, tormenting, troublesome, trying, unpleasant, upsetting, worrisome, worrying
Antonyms *adj* agreeable, balmy, calming, comforting, pleasant, reassuring, relaxing, soothing

vexed *adj* **1** = **annoyed**, afflicted, aggravated (*inf.*), agitated, bothered, confused, displeased, distressed, disturbed, exasperated, fed up, harassed, irritated, miffed (*inf.*), nettled, out of countenance, peeved (*inf.*), perplexed, provoked, put out, riled, ruffled, tormented, troubled, upset, worried **2** = **controversial**, contested, disputed, moot, much debated

viable *adj* **1** = **workable**, applicable, feasible, operable, practicable, usable, within the bounds of possibility
Antonyms *adj* hopeless, impossible, impracticable, inconceivable, out of the question, unthinkable, unworkable

vibes *pl n Slang* **2** = **feelings**, emotions, reaction, response **2** = **atmosphere**, aura, emanation, vibrations

vibrant *adj* **2** = **energetic**, alive, animated, colourful, dynamic, electrifying, full of pep (*inf.*), responsive, sensitive, sparkling, spirited, storming, vigorous, vivacious, vivid

vibrate *vb* **1-3** = **shake**, fluctuate, judder (*inf.*), oscillate, pulsate, pulse, quiver, resonate, reverberate, shiver, sway, swing, throb, tremble, undulate

vibration *n* **1** = **shake**, judder (*inf.*), oscillation, pulsation, pulse, quiver, resonance, reverberation, throb, throbbing, trembling, tremor

vicarious *adj* **1** = **indirect**, at one remove, empathetic **2** = **substituted**, surrogate **3, 4** = **delegated**, acting, commissioned, deputed

vice[1] *n* **1** = **wickedness**, corruption, degeneracy, depravity, evil, evildoing, immorality, iniquity, profligacy, sin, turpitude, venality **4** = **fault**, blemish, defect, failing, imperfection, shortcoming, weakness
Antonyms *n* ≠ **wickedness:** honour, morality, virtue ≠ **fault:** gift, good point, strong point, talent

of chancery who acted as assistant to the Lord Chancellor. **4** a person serving as the deputy of a chancellor.
▸ˌ**vice-'chancellorship** *n*

vicegerent (ˌvaɪs'dʒɛrənt) *n* **1** a person appointed to exercise all or some of the authority of another. **2** *RC Church.* the pope or any other representative of God or Christ on earth, such as a bishop. ◆ *adj* **3** invested with or characterized by delegated authority. [C16: from NL, from VICE^{3} + L *gerere* to manage]
▸ˌ**vice'gerency** *n*

vicennial (vɪ'sɛnɪəl) *adj* **1** occurring every 20 years. **2** lasting for a period of 20 years. [C18: from LL *vīcennium* period of twenty years, from L *vīciēs* twenty times + *-ennium*, from *annus* year]

vice president *n* an officer ranking immediately below a president and serving as his deputy. A vice president takes the president's place during his absence or incapacity, after his death, and in certain other circumstances. Abbrev.: **VP.**
▸ˌ**vice-'presidency** *n*

viceregal (ˌvaɪs'riːgᵊl) *adj* **1** of or relating to a viceroy. **2** *Chiefly Austral. & NZ.* of or relating to a governor or governor general.
▸ˌ**vice'regally** *adv*

vicereine (ˌvaɪs'reɪn) *n* **1** the wife of a viceroy. **2** a female viceroy. [C19: from F, from VICE^{3} + *reine* queen, from L *rēgīna*]

viceroy ('vaɪsrɔɪ) *n* a governor of a colony, country, or province who acts for and rules in the name of his sovereign or government. Related adj: **viceregal.** [C16: from F, from VICE^{3} + *roy* king, from L *rex*]
▸**'viceroyship** *or* ˌ**vice'royalty** *n*

vice squad *n* a police division to which is assigned the enforcement of gaming and prostitution laws.

vice versa ❶ ('vaɪsɪ 'vɜːsə) *adv* the other way around. [C17: from L: relations being reversed, from *vicis* change + *vertere* to turn]

vichyssoise (*French* viʃiswaz) *n* a thick soup made from leeks, potatoes, chicken stock, and cream, usually served chilled. [F, from (*crème*) *vichyssoise* (*glacée*) (ice-cold cream) from Vichy]

vichy water ('viːʃiː) *n* **1** (*sometimes cap.*) a mineral water from springs at Vichy in France, reputed to be beneficial to health. **2** any sparkling mineral water resembling this.

vicinage ('vɪsnɪdʒ) *n Now rare.* **1** the residents of a particular neighbourhood. **2** a less common word for **vicinity.** [C14: from OF *vicenage*, from *vicin* neighbouring, from L *vīcīnus*]

vicinal ('vɪsɪnᵊl) *adj* **1** neighbouring. **2** (esp. of roads) of or relating to a locality. [C17: from L *vīcīnālis* nearby, from *vīcīnus*, from *vīcus* a neighbourhood]

vicinity ❶ (vɪ'sɪnɪtɪ) *n, pl* **vicinities. 1** a surrounding area; neighbourhood. **2** the fact or condition of being close in space or relationship. [C16: from L, from *vīcīnus* neighbouring, from *vīcus* village]

vicious ❶ ('vɪʃəs) *adj* **1** wicked or cruel: *a vicious thug.* **2** characterized by violence or ferocity: *a vicious blow.* **3** *Inf.* unpleasantly severe; harsh: *a vicious wind.* **4** characterized by malice: *vicious lies.* **5** (esp. of dogs, horses, etc.) ferocious. **6** characterized by or leading to vice. **7** invalidated by defects; unsound: *a vicious inference.* [C14: from OF, from L *vitiōsus* full of faults, from *vitium* defect]
▸**'viciously** *adv* ▸**'viciousness** *n*

vicious circle *n* **1** Also: **vicious cycle.** a situation in which an attempt to resolve one problem creates new problems that lead back to the original situation. **2** *Logic.* **2a** a form of reasoning in which a conclusion is inferred from premises the truth of which cannot be established independently of that conclusion. **2b** an explanation given in terms that cannot be understood independently of that which was to be explained.

vicissitude ❶ (vɪ'sɪsɪˌtjuːd) *n* **1** variation or mutability in nature or life, esp. successive alternation from one condition or thing to another. **2** a variation in circumstance, fortune, etc. [C16: from L *vicissitūdō*, from *vicis* change]
▸**viˌcissi'tudinous** *adj*

victim ❶ ('vɪktɪm) *n* **1** a person or thing that suffers harm, death, etc.: *victims of tyranny.* **2** a person who is tricked or swindled. **3** a living person or animal sacrificed in a religious rite. [C15: from L *victima*]

victimize ❶ *or* **victimise** ('vɪktɪˌmaɪz) *vb* **victimizes, victimizing, victimized** *or* **victimises, victimising, victimised.** (*tr*) **1** to punish or discriminate against unfairly. **2** to make a victim of.
▸ˌ**victimi'zation** *or* ˌ**victimi'sation** *n* ▸**'victimˌizer** *or* **'victimˌiser** *n*

victor ❶ ('vɪktə) *n* **1a** a person, nation, etc., that has defeated an adversary in war, etc. **1b** (*as modifier*): *the victor army.* **2** the winner of any contest, conflict, or struggle. [C14: from L, from *vincere* to conquer]

victoria (vɪk'tɔːrɪə) *n* **1** a light four-wheeled horse-drawn carriage with a folding hood, two passenger seats, and a seat in front for the driver. **2** Also called: **victoria plum.** *Brit.* a large sweet variety of plum, red and yellow in colour. [C19: both after Queen *Victoria*, (1819–1901), queen of the United Kingdom]

Victoria and Albert Museum *n* a museum of the fine and applied arts in London, originating from 1856 and given its present name and site in 1899. Abbrev.: **V and A.**

Victoria Cross *n* the highest decoration for gallantry in the face of the enemy awarded to the British and Commonwealth armed forces: instituted in 1856 by Queen Victoria.

Victoria Day *n* the Monday preceding May 24: observed in Canada as a national holiday in commemoration of the birthday of Queen Victoria.

Victorian (vɪk'tɔːrɪən) *adj* **1** of or characteristic of Victoria (1819–1901), queen of the United Kingdom, or the period of her reign. **2** exhibiting the characteristics popularly attributed to the Victorians, esp. prudery, bigotry, or hypocrisy. Cf. **Victorian values. 3** of or relating to Victoria (the state in Australia or any of the cities). ◆ *n* **4** a person who lived during the reign of Queen Victoria. **5** an inhabitant of Victoria (the state or any of the cities).
▸**Vic'torianˌism** *n*

Victoriana (vɪkˌtɔːrɪ'ɑːnə) *pl n* objects, ornaments, etc., of the Victorian period.

Victorian values *pl n* the qualities of enterprise and initiative, the importance of the family, and the development of charitable voluntary work considered to characterize the Victorian period. Cf. **Victorian** (sense 2).

victorious ❶ (vɪk'tɔːrɪəs) *adj* **1** having defeated an adversary: *the victorious nations.* **2** of, indicative of, or characterized by victory: *a victorious conclusion.*
▸**vic'toriously** *adv*

victory ❶ ('vɪktərɪ) *n, pl* **victories. 1** final and complete superiority in a war. **2** a successful military engagement. **3** a success attained in a contest or struggle or over an opponent, obstacle, or problem. **4** the act of triumphing or state of having triumphed. [C14: from OF *victorie*, from L *victōria*, from *vincere* to subdue]

victory roll *n* a rolling aircraft manoeuvre made by a pilot to announce or celebrate the shooting down of an enemy plane.

victual ('vɪtᵊl) *vb* **victuals, victualling, victualled** *or US* **victuals, victualing, victualed.** to supply with or obtain victuals. See also **victuals.** [C14: from OF *vitaille*, from LL *victuālia* provisions, from L *victus* sustenance, from *vīvere* to live]
▸**'victual-less** *adj*

victualler ('vɪtələ) *n* **1** a supplier of victuals, as to an army. **2** *Brit.* a licensed purveyor of spirits. **3** a supply ship, esp. one carrying foodstuffs.

victuals ❶ ('vɪtᵊlz) *pl n* (*sometimes sing*) food or provisions.

vicuña (vɪ'kuːnjə) *or* **vicuna** (vɪ'kjuːnə, -'kuːnjə) *n* **1** a tawny-coloured cud-chewing Andean mammal similar to the llama. **2** the fine light cloth made from the wool obtained from this animal. [C17: from Sp., from Quechuan *wikúña*]

vid (vɪd) *n Inf.* short for **video** (sense 4).

vide ('vaɪdɪ) (used to direct a reader to a specified place in a text, another book, etc.) refer to, see (often in **vide ante** (see before), **vide infra** (see below), **vide supra** (see above), etc.). Abbrev.: **v., vid.** [C16: from L]

videlicet (vɪ'diːlɪˌsɛt) *adv* namely: used to specify items, etc. Abbrev.: **viz.** [C15: from L]

video ('vɪdɪəʊ) *adj* **1** relating to or employed in the transmission or reception of a televised image. **2** of, concerned with, or operating at video frequencies. ◆ *n, pl* **videos. 3** the visual elements of a television broadcast. **4** a film recorded on a video cassette. **5** short for **video cassette, video cassette recorder. 6** *US.* an informal name for **television.** ◆ *vb*

THESAURUS

vice versa *adv* = **conversely**, contrariwise, in reverse, the other way round

vicinity *n* **1** = **neighbourhood**, area, district, environs, locality, neck of the woods (*inf.*), precincts, propinquity, proximity, purlieus

vicious *adj* **1, 2** = **savage**, abhorrent, atrocious, bad, barbarous, cruel, dangerous, diabolical, ferocious, fiendish, foul, heinous, monstrous, vile, violent **4** = **malicious**, backbiting, bitchy (*inf.*), cruel, defamatory, mean, rancorous, slanderous, spiteful, venomous, vindictive **6** = **depraved**, abandoned, corrupt, debased, degenerate, degraded, immoral, infamous, profligate, sinful, unprincipled, wicked, worthless, wrong
Antonyms *adj* ≠ **savage:** docile, friendly, gentle, good, honourable, kind, playful, tame, upright, virtuous ≠ **malicious:** appreciative, complimentary, congratulatory

viciousness *n* **1, 2** = **savagery**, cruelty, ferocity **4** = **malice**, bitchiness (*sl.*), rancour, spite, spitefulness, venom **6** = **depravity**, badness, corruption, immorality, profligacy, wickedness
Antonyms *n* ≠ **malice:** gentleness, goodness, goodwill, graciousness, kindness, mercy, virtue

vicissitude *n* **1** = **change of fortune**, alteration, life's ups and downs (*inf.*), shift **2** = **variation**, alternation, mutation

victim *n* **1** = **casualty**, fatality, injured party, martyr, sacrifice, scapegoat, sufferer **2** = **prey**, dupe, fall guy (*inf.*), gull (*arch.*), innocent, patsy (*sl., chiefly US & Canad.*), sitting duck (*inf.*), sitting target, sucker (*sl.*)
Antonyms *n* ≠ **casualty:** survivor ≠ **prey:** assailant, attacker, culprit, guilty party, offender

victimize *vb* **1** = **persecute**, demonize, discriminate against, have a down on (someone) (*inf.*), have it in for (someone) (*inf.*), have one's knife into (someone), pick on

victor *n* **1, 2** = **winner**, champ (*inf.*), champion, conquering hero, conqueror, first, prizewinner, top dog, vanquisher
Antonyms *n* also-ran, dud (*inf.*), failure, flop (*inf.*), loser, vanquished

victorious *adj* **1, 2** = **winning**, champion, conquering, first, prizewinning, successful, triumphant, vanquishing
Antonyms *adj* beaten, conquered, defeated, failed, losing, overcome, unsuccessful, vanquished

victory *n* **1, 3** = **win**, conquest, laurels, mastery, success, superiority, the palm, the prize, triumph
Antonyms *n* defeat, failure, loss

victuals *pl n* = **food**, bread, comestibles, eatables, eats (*sl.*), edibles, grub (*sl.*), meat, nosebag (*sl.*), nosh (*sl.*), provisions, rations, stores, supplies, tack (*inf.*), viands, vittles (*obs.*)

videos, videoing, videoed. **7** to record (a television programme, etc.) on a video cassette recorder. [C20: from L *vidēre* to see, on the model of AUDIO]

video cassette *n* a cassette containing video tape.

video cassette recorder *n* a tape recorder for vision and sound signals using magnetic tape in closed plastic cassettes: used for recording and playing back television programmes and films. Often shortened to **video** or **video recorder.**

videodisc (ˈvɪdɪəʊˌdɪsk) *n* another name for **optical disc.**

video frequency *n* the frequency of a signal conveying the image and synchronizing pulses in a television broadcasting system. It lies in the range from about 50 hertz to 8 megahertz.

video game *n* any of various games that can be played by using an electronic control to move graphical symbols on the screen of a visual display unit.

video jockey *n* a person who introduces and plays videos, esp. of pop songs, on a television programme.

video nasty *n, pl* **nasties.** a film, usually specially made for video, that is explicitly horrific and pornographic.

videophone (ˈvɪdɪəˌfəʊn) *n* a telephonic device through which there is both verbal and visual communication.

video recorder *n* short for **video cassette recorder.**

video tape *n* **1** magnetic tape used mainly for recording the sound and vision signals of a television programme or film for subsequent transmission. ◆ *vb* **video-tape, video-tapes, video-taping, video-taped.** **2** to record (a programme, etc.) on video tape.

video tape recorder *n* a tape recorder for visual signals and usually accompanying sound, using magnetic tape on open spools: used in television broadcasting.

Videotex (ˈvɪdɪəʊˌtɛks) *n Trademark.* an information system that displays information from a distant computer on a television screen. See also **Teletext, Viewdata.**

videotext (ˈvɪdɪəʊˌtɛkst) *n* a means of providing a written or graphical representation of computerized information on a television screen.

vidicon (ˈvɪdɪˌkɒn) *n* a small television camera tube, used in closed-circuit television and outside broadcasts, in which incident light forms an electric charge pattern on a photoconductive surface. [C20: from VID(EO) + ICON(OSCOPE)]

vie **T** (vaɪ) *vb* **vies, vying, vied.** (*intr;* foll. by *with* or *for*) to contend for superiority or victory (with) or strive in competition (for). [C15: prob. from OF *envier* to challenge, from L *invītāre* to INVITE]
▸ˈ**vier** *n* ▸ˈ**vying** *adj, n*

Viennese (ˌvɪəˈniːz) *adj* **1** of or relating to Vienna, capital of Austria. ◆ *n, pl* **Viennese.** **2** a native or inhabitant of Vienna.

vies (fɪs) *adj S. African sl.* angry, furious, or disgusted. [Afrik.]

Vietnamese (ˌvjetnəˈmiːz) *adj* **1** of or characteristic of Vietnam, in SE Asia, its people, or their language. ◆ *n* **2** (*pl* **Vietnamese**) a native or inhabitant of Vietnam. **3** the language of Vietnam.

vieux jeu *French.* (vjø ʒø) *adj* old-fashioned. [lit.: old game]

view **T** (vjuː) *n* **1** the act of seeing or observing. **2** vision or sight, esp. range of vision: *the church is out of view.* **3** a scene, esp. of a fine tract of countryside: *the view from the top was superb.* **4** a pictorial representation of a scene, such as a photograph. **5** (*sometimes pl*) opinion: *my own view on the matter differs from yours.* **6** (foll. by *to*) a desired end or intention: *he has a view to securing further qualifications.* **7** a general survey of a topic, subject, etc. **8** visual aspect or appearance: *they look the same in outward view.* **9** a sight of a hunted animal before or during the chase. **10 in view of.** taking into consideration. **11 on view.** exhibited to the public gaze. **12 take a dim** *or* **poor view of.** to regard (something) with disfavour. **13 with a view to. 13a** with the intention of. **13b** in anticipation or hope of. ◆ *vb* **14** (*tr*) to look at. **15** (*tr*) to consider in a specified manner: *they view Communism with horror.* **16** (*tr*) to examine or inspect carefully: *to view the accounts.* **17** (*tr*) to contemplate: *to view the difficulties.* **18** to watch (television). **19** (*tr*) to sight (a hunted animal) before or during the chase. [C15: from OF, from *veoir* to see, from L *vidēre*]
▸ˈ**viewable** *adj*

Viewdata (ˈvjuːˌdeɪtə) *n Trademark.* an interactive form of Videotext that sends information from a distant computer along telephone lines, enabling shopping, booking theatre and airline tickets, and banking transactions to be conducted from the home.

viewer **T** (ˈvjuːə) *n* **1** a person who views something, esp. television. **2** any optical device by means of which something is viewed, esp. one used for viewing photographic transparencies.

viewfinder (ˈvjuːˌfaɪndə) *n* a device on a camera, consisting of a lens system, enabling the user to see what will be included in his photograph.

view halloo *interj* a huntsman's cry uttered when the quarry is seen breaking cover or shortly afterwards.

viewing (ˈvjuːɪŋ) *n* **1** the act of watching television. **2** television programmes collectively: *late-night viewing.*

viewless (ˈvjuːlɪs) *adj* **1** (of windows, etc.) not affording a view. **2** having no opinions. **3** *Poetic.* invisible.

viewpoint **T** (ˈvjuːˌpɔɪnt) *n* **1** the mental attitude that determines a person's judgments. **2** a place from which something can be viewed.

vigesimal (vaɪˈdʒesɪməl) *adj* **1** relating to or based on the number 20. **2** taking place or proceeding in intervals of 20. **3** twentieth. [C17: from L *vīgēsimus,* var. (infl. by *vīgintī* twenty) of *vīcēsimus* twentieth]

vigia (ˈvɪdʒɪə) *n Naut.* a navigational hazard marked on a chart although its existence and nature has not been confirmed. [C19: from Sp. *vigía* reef, from L *vigilāre* to keep watch]

vigil (ˈvɪdʒɪl) *n* **1** a purposeful watch maintained, esp. at night, to guard, observe, pray, etc. **2** the period of such a watch. **3** *RC Church, Church of England.* the eve of certain major festivals, formerly observed as a night spent in prayer. [C13: from OF, from Med. L *vigilia* watch preceding a religious festival, from L, from *vigil* alert, from *vigēre* to be lively]

vigilance **T** (ˈvɪdʒɪləns) *n* **1** the fact, quality, or condition of being vigilant. **2** the abnormal state or condition of being unable to sleep.

vigilance committee *n* (in the US) a self-appointed body of citizens organized to maintain order, etc., where an efficient system of courts does not exist.

vigilant **T** (ˈvɪdʒɪlənt) *adj* keenly alert to or heedful of trouble or danger. [C15: from L *vigilāns,* from *vigilāre* to be watchful; see VIGIL]
▸ˈ**vigilantly** *adv*

vigilante (ˌvɪdʒɪˈlæntɪ) *n* **1** a self-appointed protector of public order. **2** *US.* a member of a vigilance committee. [C19: from Sp., from L *vigilāre* to keep watch]

vigilantism (ˌvɪdʒɪˈlæntɪzəm) *n US.* the methods, conduct, attitudes, etc., associated with vigilantes, esp. militancy or bigotry.

Vigil Mass *n RC Church.* a Mass held on Saturday evening, attendance at which fulfils one's obligation to attend Mass on Sunday.

vigneron (ˈviːnjərɒn; *French* viɲrɔ̃) *n* a person who grows grapes for winemaking. [F, from *vigne* vine]

vignette (vɪˈnjet) *n* **1** a small illustration placed at the beginning or end of a book or chapter. **2** a short graceful literary essay or sketch. **3** a photograph, drawing, etc., with edges that are shaded off. **4** any small endearing scene, view, etc. ◆ *vb* **vignettes, vignetting, vignetted.** (*tr*) **5** to finish (a photograph, etc.) with a fading border in the form of a vignette. **6** to portray in or as in a vignette. [C18: from F, lit.: little vine; with reference to the vine motif frequently used in embellishments to a text]
▸**viˈgnettist** *n*

vigoro (ˈvɪgəˌrəʊ) *n Austral.* a ball game combining elements of cricket and baseball. [C20: from VIGOUR]

vigorous **T** (ˈvɪgərəs) *adj* **1** endowed with bodily or mental strength or vitality. **2** displaying, characterized by, or performed with vigour: *vigorous growth.*
▸ˈ**vigorously** *adv*

vigour **T** *or US* **vigor** (ˈvɪgə) *n* **1** exuberant and resilient strength of body or mind. **2** substantial effective energy or force: *the vigour of the tempest.* **3** forcefulness: *I was surprised by the vigour of her complaints.* **4** the capacity for survival or strong healthy growth in a plant or animal. **5** the most active period or stage of life, manhood, etc. [C14: from OF, from L *vigor,* from *vigēre* to be lively]

THESAURUS

vie *vb* = **compete**, be rivals, contend, contest, match oneself against, strive, struggle

view *n* **1** = **look**, contemplation, display, examination, inspection, recce (*sl.*), scan, scrutiny, sight, survey, viewing **2** = **vision**, range *or* field of vision, sight **3** = **scene**, aspect, landscape, outlook, panorama, perspective, picture, prospect, spectacle, vista **5** *sometimes plural* = **opinion**, attitude, belief, conviction, feeling, impression, judgment, notion, point of view, sentiment, thought, way of thinking **13 with a view to** = **with the aim** *or* **intention of**, in order to, in the hope of, so as to ◆ *vb* **14, 16** = **look at**, behold, check, check out (*inf.*), clock (*Brit. sl.*), contemplate, examine, explore, eye, eyeball (*sl.*), gaze at, get a load of (*inf.*), inspect, observe, recce (*sl.*), regard, scan, spectate, stare at, survey, take a dekko at (*Brit. sl.*), watch, witness **15** = **regard**, consider, deem, judge, look on, think about

viewer *n* **1** = **watcher**, observer, one of an audience, onlooker, spectator, TV watcher

viewpoint *n* **1** = **attitude**, angle, frame of reference, perspective, point of view, position, slant, stance, standpoint, vantage point, way of thinking

vigilance *n* **1** = **watchfulness**, alertness, attentiveness, carefulness, caution, circumspection, observance

vigilant *adj* = **watchful**, alert, attentive, careful, cautious, circumspect, on one's guard, on one's toes, on the alert, on the lookout, sleepless, unsleeping, wakeful, wide awake
Antonyms *adj* careless, inattentive, lax, neglectful, negligent, remiss, slack

vigorous *adj* **1, 2** = **energetic**, active, alive and kicking, brisk, dynamic, effective, efficient, enterprising, fighting fit, fit as a fiddle (*inf.*), flourishing, forceful, forcible, full of beans (*inf.*), hale, hale and hearty, hardy, healthy, intense, lively, lusty, powerful, red-blooded, robust, sound, spanking, spirited, strenuous, strong, virile, vital, zippy (*inf.*)
Antonyms *adj* apathetic, effete, enervated, feeble, frail, inactive, indolent, lethargic, lifeless, spiritless, torpid, weak, weedy (*inf.*), wimpish *or* wimpy (*inf.*), wishy-washy

vigorously *adv* **1, 2** = **energetically**, all out, eagerly, forcefully, hammer and tongs, hard, like mad (*sl.*), lustily, strenuously, strongly, with a vengeance, with might and main

vigour *n* **1-3** = **energy**, activity, animation, brio, dash, dynamism, force, forcefulness, gusto, health, liveliness, might, oomph (*inf.*), pep, power, punch (*inf.*), robustness, snap (*inf.*), soundness, spirit, strength, verve, vim (*sl.*), virility, vitality, wellness, zip (*inf.*)
Antonyms *n* apathy, feebleness, fragility, frailty, impotence, inactivity, inertia, infirmity, lethargy, sluggishness, weakness

Viking ('vaɪkɪŋ) *n* (*sometimes not cap.*) **1** Also called: **Norseman, Northman.** any of the Danes, Norwegians, and Swedes who raided by sea most of N and W Europe from the 8th to the 11th centuries. **2** (*modifier*) of, relating to, or characteristic of a Viking or Vikings: *a Viking ship.* [C19: from ON *víkingr,* prob. from *vík* creek, sea inlet + *-ingr* (see -ING³)]

vile ❶ (vaɪl) *adj* **1** abominably wicked; shameful or evil. **2** morally despicable; ignoble: *vile accusations.* **3** disgusting to the senses or emotions; foul: *a vile smell.* **4** tending to humiliate or degrade: *only slaves would perform such vile tasks.* **5** unpleasant or bad: *vile weather.* [C13: from OF *vil,* from L *vīlis* cheap]
▸'**vilely** *adv* ▸'**vileness** *n*

vilify ❶ ('vɪlɪˌfaɪ) *vb* **vilifies, vilifying, vilified.** (*tr*) to revile with abusive language; malign. [C15: from LL, from L *vīlis* worthless + *facere* to make]
▸**vilification** (ˌvɪlɪfɪ'keɪʃən) *n* ▸'**viliˌfier** *n*

vilipend ('vɪlɪˌpɛnd) *vb* (*tr*) *Rare.* **1** to treat or regard with contempt. **2** to speak slanderously of. [C15: from LL, from L *vīlis* worthless + *pendere* to esteem]
▸'**viliˌpender** *n*

villa ('vɪlə) *n* **1** (in ancient Rome) a country house, usually consisting of farm buildings and residential quarters around a courtyard. **2** a large country residence. **3** *Brit.* a detached or semidetached suburban house. [C17: via It. from L]

village ('vɪlɪdʒ) *n* **1** a small group of houses in a country area, larger than a hamlet. **2** the inhabitants of such a community collectively. **3** an incorporated municipality smaller than a town in various parts of the US and Canada. **4** (*modifier*) of or characteristic of a village: *a village green.* [C15: from OF, from *ville* farm, from L: VILLA]
▸'**villager** *n*

villain ❶ ('vɪlən) *n* **1** a wicked or malevolent person. **2** (in a novel, play, etc.) the main evil character and antagonist to the hero. **3** *Often jocular.* a rogue. **4** *Obs.* an uncouth person; boor. [C14: from OF *vilein* serf, from LL *vīllānus* worker on a country estate, from L: VILLA]
▸'**villainess** *fem n*

villainous ❶ ('vɪlənəs) *adj* **1** of, like, or appropriate to a villain. **2** very bad or disagreeable: *a villainous climate.*
▸'**villainously** *adv* ▸'**villainousness** *n*

villainy ❶ ('vɪlənɪ) *n, pl* **villainies. 1** vicious behaviour or action. **2** an evil or criminal act or deed. **3** the fact or condition of being villainous.

villanelle (ˌvɪlə'nɛl) *n* a verse form of French origin consisting of 19 lines arranged in five tercets and a quatrain. [C16: from F, from It. *villanella,* from *villano* rustic]

-ville *n and adj combining form. Sl., chiefly US.* (denoting) a place, condition, or quality with a character as specified: *dragsville; squaresville.*

villein ('vɪlən) *n* (in medieval Europe) a peasant bound to his lord, to whom he paid dues and services in return for his land. [C14: from OF *vilein* serf; see VILLAIN]
▸'**villeinage** *n*

villiform ('vɪlɪˌfɔːm) *adj* having the form of a villus or a series of villi. [C19: from NL *villiformis,* from L *villus* shaggy hair + -FORM]

villus ('vɪləs) *n, pl* **villi** ('vɪlaɪ). (*usually pl*) **1** *Zool., anat.* any of the numerous finger-like projections of the mucous membrane lining the small intestine of many vertebrates. **2** any similar membranous process. **3** *Bot.* any of various hairlike outgrowths. [C18: from L: shaggy hair]
▸**villosity** (vɪ'lɒsɪtɪ) *n* ▸'**villous** *adj*

vim (vɪm) *n Sl.* exuberant vigour and energy. [C19: from L, from *vīs;* rel. to Gk *is* strength]

vimineous (vɪ'mɪnɪəs) *adj Bot.* having, producing, or resembling long flexible shoots. [C17: from L *vīmineus* made of osiers, from *vīmen* flexible shoot]

vina ('viːnə) *n* a stringed musical instrument, esp. of India, related to the sitar. [C18: from Hindi *bīnā,* from Sansk. *vīnā*]

vinaceous (vaɪ'neɪʃəs) *adj* **1** of, relating to, or containing wine. **2** having a colour suggestive of red wine. [C17: from LL *vīnāceus,* from L *vīnum* wine]

vinaigrette (ˌvɪneɪ'grɛt) *n* **1** Also called: **vinaigrette sauce.** a salad dressing made from oil and vinegar with seasonings; French dressing. **2** Also called: **vinegarette.** a small decorative bottle or box with a perforated top, used for holding smelling salts, etc. [C17: from F, from *vinaigre* VINEGAR]

Vincent's angina *or* **disease** ('vɪnsənts) *n* an ulcerative bacterial infection of the mouth, esp. involving the throat and tonsils. [C20: after J. H. *Vincent* (died 1950), F bacteriologist]

vincible ('vɪnsɪbᵊl) *adj Rare.* capable of being defeated. [C16: from L *vincibilis,* from *vincere* to conquer]
▸ˌ**vinci'bility** *n*

vincristine (vɪn'krɪstiːn) *n* an alkaloid used to treat leukaemia, derived from the tropical shrub Madagascar periwinkle. [C20: from NL *Vinca* genus name of the plant + L *crista* crest + -INE²]

vinculum ('vɪŋkjʊləm) *n, pl* **vincula** (-lə). **1** a horizontal line drawn above a group of mathematical terms, used as an alternative to parentheses in mathematical expressions, as in $x + \overline{y - z}$, which is equivalent to $x + (y - z)$. **2** *Anat.* any bandlike structure, esp. one uniting two or more parts. [C17: from L: bond, from *vincīre* to bind]

vindaloo (ˌvɪndə'luː) *n, pl* **vindaloos.** a type of very hot Indian curry. [C20: ? from Port. *vin d'alho* wine and garlic sauce]

vin de pays *French.* (vɛ̃ də pei) *n, pl* ***vins de pays*** (vɛ̃ də pei). the third highest French wine classification: indicates that the wine meets certain requirements concerning area of production, strength, etc. Also called: ***vin du pays.*** Abbrev.: **VDP.** Cf. **AOC, VDQS.** [lit.: local wine]

vindicable ('vɪndɪkəbᵊl) *adj* capable of being vindicated; justifiable.
▸ˌ**vindica'bility** *n*

vindicate ❶ ('vɪndɪˌkeɪt) *vb* **vindicates, vindicating, vindicated.** (*tr*) **1** to clear from guilt, blame, etc., as by evidence or argument. **2** to provide justification for: *his promotion vindicated his unconventional attitude.* **3** to uphold or defend (a cause, etc.): *to vindicate a claim.* [C17: from L *vindicāre,* from *vindex* claimant]
▸'**vindiˌcator** *n* ▸'**vindiˌcatory** *adj*

vindication ❶ (ˌvɪndɪ'keɪʃən) *n* **1** the act of vindicating or the condition of being vindicated. **2** a fact, evidence, etc., that serves to vindicate a claim.

vindictive ❶ (vɪn'dɪktɪv) *adj* **1** disposed to seek vengeance. **2** characterized by spite or rancour. **3** *English law.* (of damages) in excess of the compensation due to the plaintiff and imposed in punishment of the defendant. [C17: from L *vindicta* revenge, from *vindicāre* to VINDICATE]
▸**vin'dictively** *adv* ▸**vin'dictiveness** *n*

vin du pays *French.* (vɛ̃ du pei) *n, pl* ***vins du pays.*** a variant of ***vin de pays.***

vine (vaɪn) *n* **1** any of various plants, esp. the grapevine, having long flexible stems that creep along the ground or climb by clinging to a support by means of tendrils, leafstalks, etc. **2** the stem of such a plant. [C13: from OF, from L *vīnea* vineyard, from *vīnum* wine]
▸'**viny** *adj*

vinedresser ('vaɪnˌdrɛsə) *n* a person who prunes, tends, or cultivates grapevines.

vinegar ('vɪnɪgə) *n* **1** a sour-tasting liquid consisting of impure dilute acetic acid, made by fermentation of beer, wine, or cider. It is used as a condiment or preservative. **2** sourness or peevishness of temper, speech, etc. [C13: from OF, from *vin* WINE + *aigre* sour, from L *acer*]
▸'**vinegarish** *adj* ▸'**vinegary** *adj*

vinery ('vaɪnərɪ) *n, pl* **vineries. 1** a hothouse for growing grapes. **2** another name for a **vineyard. 3** vines collectively.

vineyard ('vɪnjəd) *n* a plantation of grapevines, esp. where wine grapes are produced. [OE *wīngeard;* see VINE, YARD²]

vingt-et-un *French.* (vɛ̃teœ̃) *n* another name for **pontoon**². [lit.: twenty-one]

vinho verde (ˌviːnjəʊ 'vɜːdɪ) *n* any of a variety of light sharp-tasting wines made from early-picked grapes of NW Portugal. [Port., lit.: green (or young) wine]

vini- *or before a vowel* **vin-** *combining form.* indicating wine: *viniculture.* [from L *vīnum*]

viniculture ('vɪnɪˌkʌltʃə) *n* the process or business of growing grapes and making wine.
▸ˌ**vini'cultural** *adj* ▸ˌ**vini'culturist** *n*

viniferous (vɪ'nɪfərəs) *adj* wine-producing.

THESAURUS

vile *adj* **1, 2, 4** = **wicked**, abandoned, abject, appalling, bad, base, coarse, contemptible, corrupt, debased, degenerate, degrading, depraved, despicable, disgraceful, evil, humiliating, ignoble, impure, loathsome, low, mean, miserable, nefarious, perverted, shocking, sinful, ugly, vicious, vulgar, worthless, wretched **3** = **disgusting**, foul, horrid, loathsome, nasty, nauseating, noxious, obscene, offensive, repellent, repugnant, repulsive, revolting, sickening, yucky *or* yukky (*sl.*)
Antonyms *adj* ≠ **wicked**: chaste, cultured, genteel, honourable, noble, polite, pure, refined, righteous, upright, worthy ≠ **disgusting**: agreeable, delicate, lovely, marvellous, pleasant, splendid, sublime

vileness *n* **1, 2** = **wickedness**, coarseness, corruption, degeneracy, depravity, dreadfulness, enormity, evil, heinousness, outrage, profanity, turpitude, ugliness **3** = **foulness**, noxiousness, offensiveness

vilification *n* = **denigration**, abuse, aspersion, calumniation, calumny, contumely, defamation, disparagement, invective, mudslinging, scurrility, vituperation

vilify *vb* = **malign**, abuse, asperse, berate, calumniate, debase, decry, defame, denigrate, disparage, knock (*inf.*), revile, rubbish (*inf.*), run down, slag (off) (*sl.*), slander, smear, speak ill of, traduce, vituperate
Antonyms *vb* adore, commend, esteem, exalt, glorify, honour, praise, revere, venerate

villain *n* **1** = **evildoer**, blackguard, caitiff (*arch.*), criminal, knave (*arch.*), libertine, malefactor, miscreant, profligate, rapscallion, reprobate, rogue, scoundrel, wretch **2** = **antihero**, baddy (*inf.*) **3** *Often jocular* = **scamp**, devil, monkey, rascal, rogue, scallywag (*inf.*)
Antonyms *n* ≠ **antihero**: goody, hero, heroine

villainous *adj* **1, 2** = **wicked**, atrocious, bad, base, blackguardly, criminal, cruel, debased, degenerate, depraved, detestable, diabolical, evil, fiendish, hateful, heinous, ignoble, infamous, inhuman, mean, nefarious, outrageous, ruffianly, scoundrelly, sinful, terrible, thievish, vicious, vile
Antonyms *adj* angelic, good, heroic, humane, moral, noble, righteous, saintly, virtuous

villainy *n* **1-3** = **wickedness**, atrocity, baseness, crime, criminality, delinquency, depravity, devilry, iniquity, knavery, rascality, sin, turpitude, vice

vindicate *vb* **1** = **clear**, absolve, acquit, exculpate, exonerate, free from blame, rehabilitate **2** = **justify**, defend, excuse **3** = **support**, advocate, assert, establish, maintain, uphold
Antonyms *vb* ≠ **clear**: accuse, blame, condemn, convict, incriminate, punish, reproach

vindication *n* **1** = **exoneration**, exculpating, exculpation **2** = **justification**, apology, defence, excuse

vindictive *adj* **1, 2** = **vengeful**, full of spleen, implacable, malicious, malignant, rancorous, relentless, resentful, revengeful, spiteful, unforgiving, unrelenting, venomous

vino ('vi:nəʊ) *n, pl* **vinos.** an informal word for **wine.** [jocular use of It. or Sp. *vino*]

vin ordinaire *French.* (vɛ̃n ɔrdinɛr) *n, pl* ***vins ordinaires*** (vɛ̃z ɔrdinɛr). cheap table wine, esp. French.

vinosity (vɪ'nɒsɪtɪ) *n* the distinctive and essential quality and flavour of wine. [C17: from LL *vīnōsitas,* from L *vīnōsus* VINOUS]

vinous ('vaɪnəs) *adj* **1** of or characteristic of wine. **2** indulging in or indicative of indulgence in wine. [C17: from L, from *vīnum* WINE]

vintage ❶ ('vɪntɪdʒ) *n* **1** the wine obtained from a harvest of grapes, esp. in an outstandingly good year. **2** the harvest from which such a wine is obtained. **3a** the harvesting of wine grapes. **3b** the season of harvesting these grapes or for making wine. **4** a time of origin: *a car of Edwardian vintage.* **5** *Inf.* a group of people or objects of the same period: *a fashion of last season's vintage.* ◆ *adj* **6** (of wine) of an outstandingly good year. **7** representative of the best and most typical: *vintage Shakespeare.* **8** of lasting interest and importance; classic: *vintage films.* **9** old-fashioned; dated. [C15: from OF *vendage* (infl. by *vintener* VINTNER), from L *vindēmia,* from *vīnum* WINE, grape + *dēmere* to take away]

vintage car *n Chiefly Brit.* an old car, esp. one constructed between 1919 and 1930. Cf. **classic car, veteran car.**

vintager ('vɪntɪdʒə) *n* a grape harvester.

vintner ('vɪntnə) *n* a wine merchant. [C15: from OF *vinetier,* from Med. L, from L *vīnētum* vineyard]

vinyl ('vaɪnɪl) *n* **1** (*modifier*) of or containing the monovalent group of atoms CH_2:CH–: *vinyl chloride.* **2** (*modifier*) of or made of a vinyl resin: *a vinyl raincoat.* **3** any vinyl resin or plastic, esp. PVC. **4** (collectively) conventional records made of vinyl as opposed to compact discs. [C19: from VINI- + -YL]

vinyl acetate *n* a colourless volatile liquid unsaturated ester that polymerizes readily in light and is used for making polyvinyl acetate.

vinyl chloride *n* a colourless flammable gaseous unsaturated compound made by the chlorination of ethylene and used as a refrigerant and in the manufacture of PVC.

vinyl resin *or* **polymer** *n* any one of a class of thermoplastic materials, esp. PVC and polyvinyl acetate, made by polymerizing vinyl compounds.

viol ('vaɪəl) *n* any of a family of stringed musical instruments that preceded the violin family, consisting of a fretted fingerboard, a body like that of a violin but having a flat back and six strings, played with a curved bow. [C15: from OF *viole,* from OProvençal *viola;* see VIOLA[1]]

viola[1] (vɪ'əʊlə) *n* **1** a bowed stringed instrument, the alto of the violin family; held beneath the chin when played. **2** any of various instruments of the viol family, such as the viola da gamba. [C18: from It., prob. from O Provençal]

viola[2] ('vaɪələ, vaɪ'əʊ-) *n* any of various temperate perennial herbaceous plants, the flowers of which have showy irregular petals, white, yellow, blue, or mauve in colour. [C15: from L: violet]

viola clef (vɪ'əʊlə) *n* another term for **alto clef.**

viola da gamba (vɪ'əʊlə də 'gæmbə) *n* the second largest and lowest member of the viol family. [C18: from It., lit.: viol for the leg]

viola d'amore (vɪ'əʊlə dæ'mɔːrɪ) *n* an instrument of the viol family having no frets, seven strings, and a set of sympathetic strings. [C18: from It., lit.: viol of love]

violate ❶ ('vaɪəˌleɪt) *vb* **violates, violating, violated.** (*tr*) **1** to break, disregard, or infringe (a law, agreement, etc.). **2** to rape or otherwise sexually assault. **3** to disturb rudely or improperly. **4** to treat irreverently or disrespectfully: *he violated a sanctuary.* [C15: from L *violāre* to do violence to, from *vīs* strength]
▸**'violable** *adj* ▸**ˌvio'lation** *n* ▸**'vioˌlator** *or* **'vioˌlater** *n*

violence ❶ ('vaɪələns) *n* **1** the exercise or an instance of physical force, usually effecting or intended to effect injuries, destruction, etc. **2** powerful, untamed, or devastating force: *the violence of the sea.* **3** great strength of feeling, as in language, etc. **4** an unjust, unwarranted, or unlawful display of force. **5 do violence to. 5a** to inflict harm upon: *they did violence to the prisoners.* **5b** to distort the sense or intention of: *the reporters did violence to my speech.* [C13: via OF from L *violentia* impetuosity, from *violentus* VIOLENT]

violent ❶ ('vaɪələnt) *adj* **1** marked or caused by great physical force or violence: *a violent stab.* **2** (of a person) tending to the use of violence, esp. in order to injure or intimidate others. **3** marked by intensity of any kind: *a violent clash of colours.* **4** characterized by an undue use of force. **5** caused by or displaying strong or undue mental or emotional force. [C14: from L *violentus,* prob. from *vīs* strength]
▸**'violently** *adv*

violent storm *n* a wind of force 11 on the Beaufort scale, reaching speeds of 64 to 72 mph.

violet ('vaɪəlɪt) *n* **1** any of various temperate perennial herbaceous plants of the genus *Viola,* such as the **sweet** (or **garden**) **violet,** having mauve or bluish flowers with irregular showy petals. **2** any other plant of the genus *Viola,* such as the wild pansy. **3** any of various similar but unrelated plants, such as the African violet. **4a** any of a group of colours that have a purplish-blue hue. They lie at one end of the visible spectrum. **4b** (*as adj*): *a violet dress.* **5** a dye or pigment of or producing these colours. **6** violet clothing: *dressed in violet.* [C14: from OF *violete* a little violet, from L *viola* violet]

violin (ˌvaɪə'lɪn) *n* a bowed stringed instrument, the highest member of the violin family, consisting of a fingerboard, a hollow wooden body with waisted sides, and a sounding board connected to the back by means of a soundpost that also supports the bridge. It has two f-shaped sound holes cut in the belly. [C16: from It. *violino* a little viola, from VIOLA[1]]

violinist (ˌvaɪə'lɪnɪst) *n* a person who plays the violin.

violist[1] (vɪ'əʊlɪst) *n* a person who plays the viola.

violist[2] ('vaɪəlɪst) *n* a person who plays the viol.

violoncello (ˌvaɪələn'tʃeləʊ) *n, pl* **violoncellos.** the full name for **cello.** [C18: from It., from *violone* large viol + *-cello,* dim. suffix]
▸**ˌviolon'cellist** *n*

VIP ❶ *abbrev. for* very important person.

viper ('vaɪpə) *n* **1** any of a family of venomous Old World snakes having hollow fangs in the upper jaw that are used to inject venom. **2** any of various other snakes, such as the horned viper. **3** a malicious or treacherous person. [C16: from L *vīpera,* ?from *vīvus* living + *parere* to bear, referring to a tradition that the viper was viviparous]

viperous ('vaɪpərəs) *or* **viperish** *adj* **1** Also: **viperine** ('vaɪpəˌraɪn). of or resembling a viper. **2** malicious.

viper's bugloss *n* **1** Also called (US): **blueweed.** a Eurasian weed, having blue flowers and pink buds. **2** a related plant that has purple flowers and is naturalized in Australia and New Zealand. Also called: (Austral.) **Paterson's curse, Salvation Jane.**

virago ❶ (vɪ'rɑːgəʊ) *n, pl* **viragoes** *or* **viragos.** **1** a loud, violent, and ill-tempered woman. **2** *Arch.* a strong or warlike woman. [OE, from L: a manlike maiden, from *vir* a man]
▸**vi'rago-ˌlike** *adj*

viral ('vaɪrəl) *adj* of or caused by a virus.

virelay ('vɪrɪˌleɪ) *n* an old French verse form, rarely used in English, having stanzas of short lines with two rhymes throughout and two opening lines recurring at intervals. [C14: from OF *virelai,* prob. from *vireli* (associated with *lai* LAY[4]), word used as a refrain]

vireo ('vɪrɪəʊ) *n, pl* **vireos.** any of a family of insectivorous American songbirds having an olive-grey back with pale underparts. [C19: from L: a bird, prob. a greenfinch; cf. *virēre* to be green]

vires ('vaɪriːz) *n* the plural of **vis.**

virescent (vɪ'resᵊnt) *adj* greenish or becoming green. [C19: from L *virescere,* from *virēre* to be green]
▸**vi'rescence** *n*

virgate[1] ('vɜːgɪt, -geɪt) *adj* long, straight, and thin; rod-shaped: *virgate stems.* [C19: from L *virgātus* made of twigs, from *virga* a rod]

virgate[2] ('vɜːgɪt, -geɪt) *n Brit.* an obsolete measure of land area, usually taken as 30 acres. [C17: from Med. L *virgāta* (*terrae*) a rod's measurement (of land), from L *virga* rod; translation of OE *gierd landes* a yard of land]

Virgilian *or* **Vergilian** (vɜː'dʒɪlɪən) *adj* of, relating to, or characteristic of Virgil (70–19 B.C.), Roman poet, or his style.

virgin ❶ ('vɜːdʒɪn) *n* **1** a person, esp. a woman, who has never had sexual intercourse. **2** an unmarried woman who has taken a religious vow of chastity. **3** any female animal that has never mated. **4** a female insect that produces offspring by parthenogenesis. ◆ *adj* (*usually prenominal*) **5** of, suitable for, or characteristic of a virgin or virgins. **6**

THESAURUS

Antonyms *adj* forgiving, generous, magnanimous, merciful, relenting, unvindictive

vintage *n* **2** = **harvest,** crop **4** = **era,** epoch, generation, time of origin, year ◆ *adj* **6-8** = **best,** choice, classic, mature, prime, rare, ripe, select, superior

violate *vb* **1** = **break,** contravene, disobey, disregard, encroach upon, infract, infringe, transgress **2** = **rape,** abuse, assault, debauch, ravish **4** = **desecrate,** abuse, befoul, defile, dishonour, invade, outrage, pollute, profane
Antonyms *vb* ≠ **break:** honour, obey, respect, uphold ≠ **desecrate:** defend, honour, protect, respect, revere, set on a pedestal

violation *n* **1** = **infringement,** abuse, breach, contravention, encroachment, infraction, transgression, trespass **4** = **desecration,** defilement, profanation, sacrilege, spoliation

violence *n* **1** = **force,** bestiality, bloodshed, bloodthirstiness, brutality, brute force, cruelty, destructiveness, ferocity, fierceness, fighting, frenzy, fury, murderousness, passion, rough handling, savagery, strong-arm tactics (*inf.*), terrorism, thuggery, vehemence, wildness **2** = **power,** boisterousness, raging, roughness, storminess, tumult, turbulence, wildness **3** = **intensity,** abandon, acuteness, fervour, force, harshness, severity, sharpness, vehemence

violent *adj* **1, 2** = **destructive,** berserk, bloodthirsty, brutal, cruel, fiery, flaming, forcible, furious, headstrong, homicidal, hot-headed, impetuous, intemperate, maddened, maniacal, murderous, passionate, powerful, raging, riotous, rough, savage, strong, tempestuous, uncontrollable, ungovernable, unrestrained, vehement, vicious, wild **3** = **intense,** acute, agonizing, biting, excruciating, extreme, harsh, inordinate, outrageous, painful, severe, sharp **4** = **powerful,** blustery, boisterous, devastating, full of force, gale force, raging, ruinous, storming, strong, tempestuous, tumultuous, turbulent, wild
Antonyms *adj* ≠ **destructive:** calm, composed, gentle, mild, peaceful, placid, quiet, rational, sane, serene, unruffled, well-behaved ≠ **powerful:** calm, gentle, mild, placid, serene

VIP *n* = **celebrity,** big hitter (*inf.*), big name, big noise (*inf.*), big shot, bigwig (*inf.*), heavy hitter (*inf.*), leading light (*inf.*), lion, luminary, notable, personage, public figure, somebody, star

virago *n* **1** = **harridan,** ballbreaker (*sl.*), battleaxe (*inf.*), fury, scold, shrew, termagant (*rare*), vixen, Xanthippe

virgin *n* **1, 2** = **maiden** (*arch.*), damsel (*arch.*), girl, maid (*arch.*), vestal, virgo intacta ◆ *adj* **6** = **pure,** chaste, immaculate, maidenly, modest, uncorrupted, undefiled, unsullied, vestal, virginal **7** = **fresh,** new, pristine, unsullied, untouched, unused
Antonyms *adj* ≠ **pure:** corrupted, defiled, impure ≠

pure and natural, uncorrupted or untouched: *virgin purity*. **7** not yet cultivated, explored, exploited, etc., by man: *virgin territories*. **8** being the first or happening for the first time. **9** (of a metal) made from an ore rather than from scrap. **10** occurring naturally in a pure and uncombined form: *virgin silver*. [C13: from OF *virgine*, from L *virgō* virgin]

Virgin[1] (ˈvɜːdʒɪn) *n* **1 the.** See **Virgin Mary. 2** a statue or other artistic representation of the Virgin Mary.

Virgin[2] (ˈvɜːdʒɪn) *n* **the.** the constellation Virgo, the sixth sign of the zodiac.

virginal[1] ❶ (ˈvɜːdʒɪnᵊl) *adj* **1** of, characterized by, or maintaining a state of virginity; chaste. **2** extremely pure or fresh. [C15: from L *virginālis* maidenly, from *virgō* virgin]
▸ **ˈvirginally** *adv*

virginal[2] (ˈvɜːdʒɪnᵊl) *n* (*often pl*) a smaller version of the harpsichord, but oblong in shape, having one manual and no pedals. [C16: prob. from L *virginālis* VIRGINAL[1], ? because it was played largely by young ladies]
▸ **ˈvirginalist** *n*

Virgin Birth *n* the doctrine that Jesus Christ was conceived by the intervention of the Holy Spirit so that Mary remained a virgin.

virgin forest *n* a forest in its natural state, before it has been explored or exploited by man.

Virginia creeper (vəˈdʒɪnɪə) *n* a woody vine of North America, having tendrils with adhesive tips, bluish-black berry-like fruits, and compound leaves that turn red in autumn: widely planted for ornament.

Virginia stock *n* a Mediterranean plant cultivated for its white and pink flowers.

virginity ❶ (vəˈdʒɪnɪtɪ) *n* **1** the condition or fact of being a virgin. **2** the condition of being untouched, unused, etc.

virginium (vəˈdʒɪnɪəm) *n Chem.* a former name for **francium.**

Virgin Mary *n* Mary, the mother of Christ. Also called: the **Virgin.**

virgin's-bower *n* any of several American varieties of clematis.

virgin soil *n* **1** soil that has not been cultivated before. **2** a person or thing that is as yet undeveloped.

virgin wool *n* wool that is being processed or woven for the first time.

Virgo (ˈvɜːgəʊ) *n, Latin genitive* **Virginis** (ˈvɜːdʒɪnɪs). **1** *Astron.* a large constellation on the celestial equator. **2** *Astrol.* Also called: **the Virgin.** the sixth sign of the zodiac. The sun is in this sign between about Aug. 23 and Sept. 22. [C14: from L]

virgo intacta (ˈvɜːgəʊ ɪnˈtæktə) *n* a girl or woman whose hymen is unbroken. [L, lit.: untouched virgin]

virgule (ˈvɜːgjuːl) *n Printing.* another name for **solidus.** [C19: from F: comma, from L *virgula* dim. of *virga* rod]

viridescent (ˌvɪrɪˈdesᵊnt) *adj* greenish or tending to become green. [C19: from LL *viridescere*, from L *viridis* green]
▸ **ˌviriˈdescence** *n*

viridian (vɪˈrɪdɪən) *n* a green pigment comprising a hydrated form of chromic oxide. [C19: from L *viridis* green]

viridity (vɪˈrɪdɪtɪ) *n* **1** the quality or state of being green. **2** innocence, youth, or freshness. [C15: from L *viriditās*, from *viridis* green]

virile ❶ (ˈvɪraɪl) *adj* **1** of or having the characteristics of an adult male. **2** (of a male) possessing high sexual drive and capacity for sexual intercourse. **3** of or capable of copulation or procreation. **4** strong, forceful, or vigorous. [C15: from L *virīlis* manly, from *vir* a man; rel. to OE *wer* man]
▸ **virility** (vɪˈrɪlɪtɪ) *n*

virilism (ˈvɪrɪˌlɪzəm) *n Med.* the abnormal development in a woman of male secondary sex characteristics.

virology (vaɪˈrɒlədʒɪ) *n* the branch of medicine concerned with the study of viruses.
▸ **virological** (ˌvaɪrəˈlɒdʒɪkᵊl) *adj*

virtu *or* **vertu** (vɜːˈtuː) *n* **1** a taste or love for curios or works of fine art. **2** such objects collectively. **3** the quality of being appealing to a connoisseur (esp. in **articles of virtu; objects of virtu**). [C18: from It. *virtù*; see VIRTUE]

virtual ❶ (ˈvɜːtʃʊəl) *adj* **1** having the essence or effect but not the appearance or form of: *a virtual revolution*. **2** *Physics.* being or involving a virtual image: *a virtual focus*. **3** *Computing.* of or relating to virtual storage: *virtual memory*. **4** of or relating to a computer technique by which a person, wearing a headset or mask, has the experience of being in an environment created by the computer, and of interacting with and causing changes within it. [C14: from Med. L *virtuālis* effective, from L *virtūs* VIRTUE]
▸ **ˌvirtuˈality** *n*

virtual image *n* an optical image formed by the apparent divergence of rays from a point, rather than their actual divergence from a point.

virtually ❶ (ˈvɜːtʃʊəlɪ) *adv* in effect though not in fact; practically; nearly.

virtual reality *n* a computer-generated environment that, to the person experiencing it, closely resembles reality. Abbrev.: **VR.** See also **virtual** (sense 4).

virtual storage *or* **memory** *n* a computer system in which the size of the memory is increased by transferring sections of a program from a large capacity backing store, such as a disk, into the smaller core memory as they are required.

virtue ❶ (ˈvɜːtjuː) *n* **1** the quality or practice of moral excellence or righteousness. **2** a particular moral excellence: *the virtue of tolerance*. **3** any of the cardinal virtues (prudence, justice, fortitude, and temperance) or theological virtues (faith, hope, and charity). **4** any admirable quality or trait. **5** chastity, esp. in women. **6** *Arch.* an effective, active, or inherent power. **7 by** *or* **in virtue of.** by reason of. **8 make a virtue of necessity.** to acquiesce in doing something unpleasant with a show of grace because one must do it in any case. [C13 *vertu*, from OF, from L *virtūs* manliness, courage]

virtuoso ❶ (ˌvɜːtjʊˈəʊzəʊ, -səʊ) *n, pl* **virtuosos** *or* **virtuosi** (-siː). **1** a consummate master of musical technique and artistry. **2** a person who has a masterly or dazzling skill or technique in any field of activity. **3** a connoisseur or collector of art objects. **4** (*modifier*) showing masterly skill or brilliance: *a virtuoso performance*. [C17: from It.: skilled, from LL *virtuōsus* good, virtuous]
▸ **virtuosic** (ˌvɜːtjʊˈɒsɪk) *adj* ▸ **ˌvirtuˈosity** *n*

virtuous ❶ (ˈvɜːtʃʊəs) *adj* **1** characterized by or possessing virtue or moral excellence. **2** (of women) chaste.
▸ **ˈvirtuously** *adv*

virulent ❶ (ˈvɪrʊlənt) *adj* **1a** (of a microorganism) extremely infective. **1b** (of a disease) having a violent effect. **2** extremely poisonous, injurious, etc. **3** extremely bitter, hostile, etc. [C14: from L *vīrulentus* full of poison, from *vīrus* poison]
▸ **ˈvirulence** *or* **ˈvirulency** *n* ▸ **ˈvirulently** *adv*

virus (ˈvaɪrəs) *n, pl* **viruses. 1** any of a group of submicroscopic entities consisting of a single nucleic acid surrounded by a protein coat and capable of replication only within the cells of animals and plants. **2** *Inf.* a disease caused by a virus. **3** any corrupting or infecting influence. **4** *Computing.* an unauthorized program that inserts itself into a computer system, and then propagates itself to other computers via networks or disks; when activated it interferes with the operation of the computer. [C16: from L: slime, poisonous liquid]

vis *Latin.* (vɪs) *n, pl* ***vires.*** power, force, or strength.

visa (ˈviːzə) *n, pl* **visas. 1** an endorsement in a passport or similar document, signifying that the document is in order and permitting its bearer to travel into or through the country of the government issuing it. ◆ *vb* **visas, visaing, visaed. 2** (*tr*) to enter a visa into (a passport). [C19: via F from L: things seen, from *vīsus*, p.p. of *vidēre* to see]

visage (ˈvɪzɪdʒ) *n Chiefly literary.* **1** face or countenance. **2** appearance. [C13: from OF: aspect, from *vis* face, from L *vīsus* appearance]

-visaged *adj* (*in combination*) having a visage as specified: *flat-visaged*.

vis-à-vis (ˌviːzɑːˈviː) *prep* **1** in relation to. **2** face to face with. ◆ *adv, adj* **3**

THESAURUS

fresh: contaminated, dirty, impure, polluted, spoiled, used

virginal[1] *adj* **1** = **pure,** celibate, chaste, immaculate, maidenly, uncorrupted, undefiled, virgin **2** = **fresh,** immaculate, pristine, pure, snowy, spotless, undisturbed, untouched, white

virginity *n* **1** = **chastity,** maidenhead, maidenhood

virile *adj* **1-4** = **manly,** forceful, lusty, macho, male, manlike, masculine, potent, red-blooded, robust, strong, vigorous
Antonyms *adj* camp (*inf.*), effeminate, emasculate, feminine, girlie, impotent, unmanly, weak, weedy (*inf.*), wimpish *or* wimpy (*inf.*)

virility *n* **1-4** = **masculinity,** machismo, manhood, potency, vigour
Antonyms *n* effeminacy, femininity, impotence, softness, unmanliness, weakness

virtual *adj* **1** = **practical,** essential, implicit, implied, in all but name, indirect, tacit, unacknowledged

virtually *adv* = **practically,** almost, as good as, effectually, for all practical purposes, in all but name, in effect, in essence, nearly, to all intents and purposes

virtue *n* **1** = **goodness,** ethicalness, excellence, high-mindedness, incorruptibility, integrity, justice, morality, probity, quality, rectitude, righteousness, uprightness, worth, worthiness **4** = **merit,** advantage, asset, attribute, credit, good point, good quality, plus (*inf.*), strength **5** = **chastity,** honour, innocence, purity, virginity **7 by virtue of** = **because of,** as a result of, by dint of, by reason of, in view of, on account of, owing to, thanks to
Antonyms *n* ≠ **goodness:** corruption, debauchery, depravity, dishonesty, dishonour, evil, immorality, sin, sinfulness, turpitude, vice ≠ **merit:** drawback, failing, frailty, shortcoming, weak point ≠ **chastity:** promiscuity, unchastity

virtuosity *n* **2** = **mastery,** brilliance, craft, éclat, expertise, finish, flair, panache, polish, skill

virtuoso *n* **1, 2** = **master,** artist, genius, grandmaster, maestro, magician, master hand, maven (*US*) ◆ *modifier* **4** = **masterly,** bravura (*Music*), brilliant, dazzling

virtuous *adj* **1** = **good,** blameless, ethical, excellent, exemplary, high-principled, honest, honourable, incorruptible, just, moral, praiseworthy, pure, righteous, squeaky-clean, upright, worthy **2** = **chaste,** celibate, clean-living, innocent, pure, spotless, virginal
Antonyms *adj* ≠ **good:** corrupt, debauched, depraved, dishonest, evil, immoral, sinful, unrighteous, vicious, wicked ≠ **chaste:** impure, loose, promiscuous, unchaste

virulence *n* **1, 2** = **deadliness,** harmfulness, hurtfulness, infectiousness, injuriousness, malignancy, noxiousness, poisonousness, toxicity, virulency **3** = **bitterness,** acrimony, antagonism, hatred, hostility, ill will, malevolence, malice, poison, pungency, rancour, resentment, spite, spleen, venom, viciousness, vindictiveness

virulent *adj* **1, 2** = **deadly,** baneful (*arch.*), infective, injurious, lethal, malignant, pernicious, poisonous, septic, toxic, venomous **3** = **bitter,** acrimonious, envenomed, hostile, malevolent, malicious, rancorous, resentful, spiteful, splenetic, venomous, vicious, vindictive
Antonyms *adj* ≠ **deadly:** harmless, innocuous, nonpoisonous, nontoxic ≠ **bitter:** amiable, benign, compassionate, kind, magnanimous, sympathetic, warm

face to face; opposite. ♦ *n, pl* **vis-à-vis. 4** a person or thing that is situated opposite to another. **5** a person who corresponds to another in office, capacity, etc. [C18: F, from *vis* face]

Visc. *abbrev. for* Viscount *or* Viscountess.

viscacha (vɪsˈkætʃə) *n* a gregarious burrowing rodent of southern South America, similar to but larger than the chinchillas. [C17: from Sp., from Quechuan *wiskácha*]

viscera (ˈvɪsərə) *pl n, sing* **viscus. 1** *Anat.* the large internal organs of the body collectively, esp. those in the abdominal cavity. **2** (less formally) the intestines; guts. [C17: from L: entrails, pl of *viscus* internal organ]

visceral (ˈvɪsərəl) *adj* **1** of or affecting the viscera. **2** characterized by instinct rather than intellect.
▸ **ˈviscerally** *adv*

viscid (ˈvɪsɪd) *adj* **1** cohesive and sticky. **2** (esp. of a leaf) covered with a sticky substance. [C17: from LL *viscidus* sticky, from L *viscum* mistletoe, birdlime]
▸ **visˈcidity** *n*

viscose (ˈvɪskəʊs) *n* **1a** a viscous orange-brown solution obtained by dissolving cellulose in sodium hydroxide and carbon disulphide. It can be converted back to cellulose by an acid, as in the manufacture of rayon and Cellophane. **1b** (*as modifier*): *viscose rayon.* **2** rayon made from this material. [C19: from LL *viscōsus* full of birdlime, sticky, from *viscum* birdlime]

viscosity (vɪsˈkɒsɪtɪ) *n, pl* **viscosities. 1** the state or property of being viscous. **2** *Physics.* **2a** the extent to which a fluid resists a tendency to flow. **2b** Also called: **absolute viscosity.** a measure of this resistance, measured in newton seconds per metre squared. Symbol: η

viscount (ˈvaɪkaʊnt) *n* **1** (in the British Isles) a nobleman ranking below an earl and above a baron. **2** (in various countries) a son or younger brother of a count. **3** (in medieval Europe) the deputy of a count. [C14: from OF, from Med. L, from LL *vice-* VICE[3] + *comes* COUNT[2]]
▸ **ˈviscountcy** *or* **ˈviscounty** *n*

viscountess (ˈvaɪkaʊntɪs) *n* **1** the wife or widow of a viscount. **2** a woman who holds the rank of viscount in her own right.

viscous ➊ (ˈvɪskəs) *adj* **1** (of liquids) thick and sticky. **2** having viscosity. [C14: from LL *viscōsus;* see VISCOSE]
▸ **ˈviscously** *adv*

viscus (ˈvɪskəs) *n* the singular of **viscera.**

vise (vaɪs) *n, vb* **vises, vising, vised.** *US.* a variant spelling of **vice**[2].

Vishnu (ˈvɪʃnuː) *n Hinduism.* the Pervader or Sustainer, originally a solar deity occupying a secondary place in the Hindu pantheon, later the saviour appearing in many incarnations. [C17: from Sansk. *Viṣṇu,* lit.: the one who works everywhere]
▸ **ˈVishnuism** *n*

visibility (ˌvɪzɪˈbɪlɪtɪ) *n* **1** the condition or fact of being visible. **2** clarity of vision or relative possibility of seeing. **3** the range of vision: *visibility is 500 yards.*

visible ➊ (ˈvɪzɪbᵊl) *adj* **1** capable of being perceived by the eye. **2** capable of being perceived by the mind: *no visible dangers.* **3** available: *the visible resources.* **4** of or relating to the balance of trade: *visible transactions.* [C14: from L *vīsibilis,* from *vidēre* to see]
▸ **ˈvisibly** *adv*

visible balance *n* another name for **balance of trade.**

visible radiation *n* electromagnetic radiation that causes the sensation of sight; light.

vision ➊ (ˈvɪʒən) *n* **1** the act, faculty, or manner of perceiving with the eye; sight. **2a** the image on a television screen. **2b** (*as modifier*): *vision control.* **3** the ability or an instance of great perception, esp. of future developments: *a man of vision.* **4** mystical or religious experience of seeing some supernatural event, person, etc.: *the vision of St John of the Cross.* **5** that which is seen, esp. in such a mystical experience. **6** (*sometimes pl*) a vivid mental image produced by the imagination: *he had visions of becoming famous.* **7** a person or thing of extraordinary beauty. [C13: from L *vīsiō* sight, from *vidēre* to see]

visionary ➊ (ˈvɪʒənərɪ) *adj* **1** marked by vision or foresight: *a visionary leader.* **2** incapable of being realized or effected. **3** (of people) characterized by idealistic or radical ideas, esp. impractical ones. **4** given to having visions. **5** of, of the nature of, or seen in visions. ♦ *n, pl* **visionaries. 6** a visionary person.

vision mixer *n Television.* **1** the person who selects and manipulates the television signals from cameras, film, etc., to make the composite programme. **2** the equipment used for vision mixing.

visit ➊ (ˈvɪzɪt) *vb* **visits, visiting, visited. 1** to go or come to see (a person, place, etc.). **2** to stay with (someone) as a guest. **3** to go or come to (an institution, place, etc.) for the purpose of inspecting or examining. **4** (*tr*) (of a disease, disaster, etc.) to afflict. **5** (*tr;* foll. by *upon* or *on*) to inflict (punishment, etc.). **6** (often foll. by *with*) *US & Canad. inf.* to chat (with someone). ♦ *n* **7** the act or an instance of visiting. **8** a stay as a guest. **9** a professional or official call. **10** a formal call for the purpose of inspection or examination. **11** *International law.* the right of an officer of a belligerent state to stop and search neutral ships in war to verify their nationality and ascertain whether they carry contraband. **12** *US & Canad. inf.* a chat. [C13: from L *vīsitāre* to go to see, from *vīsere* to examine, from *vidēre* to see]
▸ **ˈvisitable** *adj*

visitant (ˈvɪzɪtənt) *n* **1** a ghost; apparition. **2** a visitor or guest, usually from far away. **3** Also called: **visitor.** a migratory bird that is present in a particular region only at certain times: *a summer visitant.* [C16: from L *vīsitāns,* from *vīsitāre;* see VISIT]

visitation ➊ (ˌvɪzɪˈteɪʃən) *n* **1** an official call or visit for the purpose of inspecting or examining an institution. **2** a visiting of punishment or reward from heaven. **3** any disaster or catastrophe: *a visitation of the plague.* **4** an appearance or arrival of a supernatural being. **5** *Inf.* an unduly prolonged social call.

Visitation (ˌvɪzɪˈteɪʃən) *n* **1a** the visit made by the Virgin Mary to her cousin Elizabeth (Luke 1:39–56). **1b** the Church festival commemorating this, held on July 2. **2** a religious order of nuns, the **Order of the Visitation,** founded in 1610 and dedicated to contemplation.

visiting card *n Brit.* a small card bearing the name and usually the address of a person, esp. for giving to business or social acquaintances.

visiting fireman *n US inf.* a visitor whose presence is noticed because he is important, impressive, etc.

visitor ➊ (ˈvɪzɪtə) *n* **1** a person who pays a visit. **2** another name for **visitant** (sense 3).

visitor centre *n* another term for **interpretive centre.**

visitor's passport *n* (in Britain) a passport, valid for one year, that can be purchased from post offices. It grants entry to certain countries, usually for a restricted period of time. Also called: **British Visitor's Passport.**

visor *or* **vizor** (ˈvaɪzə) *n* **1** a transparent flap on a helmet that can be pulled down to protect the face. **2** a piece of armour fixed or hinged to the helmet to protect the face. **3** another name for **peak** (on a cap). **4** a small movable screen used as protection against glare from the sun, esp. one attached above the windscreen of a motor vehicle. **5** *Arch. or literary.* a mask or any other means of disguise. [C14: from Anglo-F *viser,* from OF *visiere,* from *vis* face; see VISAGE]
▸ **ˈvisored** *or* **ˈvizored** *adj*

vista ➊ (ˈvɪstə) *n* **1** a view, esp. through a long narrow avenue of trees, buildings, etc., or such a passage or avenue itself. **2** a comprehensive mental view of a distant time or a lengthy series of events. [C17: from It., from *vedere* to see, from L *vidēre*]
▸ **ˈvistaed** *adj*

visual ➊ (ˈvɪʒʊəl, -zjʊ-) *adj* **1** of, done by, or used in seeing: *visual powers.* **2** another word for **optical. 3** capable of being seen; visible. **4** of, occurring as, or induced by a mental image. ♦ *n* **5** a sketch to show the proposed layout of an advertisement, as in a newspaper. **6** (*often pl*) a photograph, film, or other display material. [C15: from LL *vīsuālis,* from L *vīsus* sight, from *vidēre* to see]
▸ **ˈvisually** *adv*

visual aids *pl n* devices, such as films, videos, slides, models, and blackboards, that display in visual form material to be understood or remembered.

visual display unit *n Computing.* a device that displays characters or graphics representing data in a computer memory. It usually has a keyboard for the input of information or inquiries. Abbrev.: **VDU.**

THESAURUS

viscous *adj* **1** = **thick,** adhesive, clammy, gelatinous, gluey, glutinous, gooey (*inf.*), gummy, mucilaginous, sticky, syrupy, tenacious, treacly, viscid

visible *adj* **1** = **apparent,** anywhere to be seen, bold, clear, conspicuous, detectable, discernible, discoverable, distinguishable, evident, in sight, in view, manifest, not hidden, noticeable, observable, obvious, palpable, patent, perceivable, perceptible, plain, salient, to be seen, unconcealed, unmistakable
Antonyms *adj* concealed, hidden, imperceptible, invisible, obscured, unnoticeable, unseen

vision *n* **1** = **sight,** eyes, eyesight, perception, seeing, view **3** = **foresight,** breadth of view, discernment, farsightedness, imagination, insight, intuition, penetration, prescience **4, 5** = **hallucination,** apparition, chimera, delusion, eidolon, ghost, illusion, mirage, phantasm, phantom, revelation, spectre, wraith **6** *sometimes plural* = **image,** castle in the air, concept, conception, daydream, dream, fantasy, idea, ideal, imago (*Psychoanalysis*), mental picture, pipe dream **7** = **picture,** dream, feast for the eyes, perfect picture, sight, sight for sore eyes, spectacle

visionary *adj* **3** = **idealistic,** dreaming, dreamy, impractical, quixotic, romantic, speculative, starry-eyed, unrealistic, unworkable, utopian, with one's head in the clouds **5** = **imaginary,** chimerical, delusory, fanciful, fantastic, ideal, idealized, illusory, imaginal (*Psychoanal.*), unreal **5** = **prophetic,** mystical ♦ *n* **6** = **idealist,** daydreamer, Don Quixote, dreamer, romantic, theorist, utopian, zealot **6** = **prophet,** mystic, seer
Antonyms *adj* ≠ **idealistic:** pragmatic, realistic ≠ **imaginary:** actual, mundane, real, unimaginary ♦ *n* ≠ **idealist:** cynic, pessimist, pragmatist, realist

visit *vb* **1, 2** = **call on,** be the guest of, call in, drop in on (*inf.*), go to see, inspect, look (someone) up, pay a call on, pop in (*inf.*), stay at, stay with, stop by, take in (*inf.*) **4** = **afflict,** assail, attack, befall, descend upon, haunt, smite, trouble **5** *foll. by* **on** *or* **upon** = **inflict,** bring down upon, execute, impose, wreak ♦ *n* **7, 8** = **call,** sojourn, stay, stop

visitation *n* **1** = **inspection,** examination, visit **2, 3** = **catastrophe,** bane, blight, calamity, cataclysm, disaster, infliction, ordeal, punishment, scourge, trial

visitor *n* **1** = **guest,** caller, company, visitant

vista *n* **1** = **view,** panorama, perspective, prospect

visual *adj* **1, 2** = **optical,** ocular, optic **3** = **observable,** discernible, perceptible, visible
Antonyms *adj* ≠ **observable:** imperceptible, indiscernible, invisible, out of sight, unnoticeable, unperceivable

visual field *n* the whole extent of the image falling on the retina when the eye is fixed on a given point.

visualize ❶ *or* **visualise** ('vɪʒʊəˌlaɪz) *vb* **visualizes, visualizing, visualized** *or* **visualises, visualising, visualised.** to form a mental image of (something incapable of being viewed or not at that moment visible).
▸ˌ**visualiˈzation** *or* ˌ**visualiˈsation** *n*

visual magnitude *n Astron.* the magnitude of a star as determined by visual observation.

visual purple *n* another name for **rhodopsin.**

visual violet *n* another name for **iodopsin.**

visual yellow *n* another name for **retinene.**

vital ❶ ('vaɪtᵊl) *adj* **1** essential to maintain life: *the lungs perform a vital function.* **2** forceful, energetic, or lively: *a vital person.* **3** of, having, or displaying life: *a vital organism.* **4** indispensable or essential: *books vital to this study.* **5** of great importance: *a vital game.* ◆ *n* **6** (*pl*) the bodily organs, such as the brain, liver, heart, lungs, etc., that are necessary to maintain life. **7** (*pl*) the essential elements of anything. [C14: via OF from L *vītālis*, from *vīta* life]
▸ˈ**vitally** *adv*

vital capacity *n Physiol.* the volume of air that can be exhaled from the lungs after the deepest possible breath has been taken.

vital force *n* (esp. in early biological theory) a hypothetical force, independent of physical and chemical forces, regarded as being the causative factor of the evolution of living organisms.

vitalism ('vaɪtəˌlɪzəm) *n* the philosophical doctrine that the phenomena of life cannot be explained in purely mechanical terms because there is something immaterial which distinguishes living from inanimate matter.
▸ˈ**vitalist** *n, adj* ▸ˌ**vitalˈistic** *adj*

vitality ❶ (vaɪˈtælɪtɪ) *n, pl* **vitalities. 1** physical or mental vigour, energy, etc. **2** the power or ability to continue in existence, live, or grow: *the vitality of a movement.*

vitalize *or* **vitalise** ('vaɪtəˌlaɪz) *vb* **vitalizes, vitalizing, vitalized** *or* **vitalises, vitalising, vitalised.** (*tr*) to make vital, living, or alive.
▸ˌ**vitaliˈzation** *or* ˌ**vitaliˈsation** *n*

vital staining *n* the technique of treating living cells and tissues with dyes that do not immediately kill them, facilitating observation under a microscope.

vital statistics *pl n* **1** quantitative data concerning human life or the conditions affecting it, such as the death rate. **2** *Inf.* the measurements of a woman's bust, waist, and hips.

vitamin ('vɪtəmɪn, 'vaɪ-) *n* any of a group of substances that are essential, in small quantities, for the normal functioning of metabolism in the body. They cannot usually be synthesized in the body but they occur naturally in certain foods. [C20: *vit-* from L *vīta* life + *-amin* from AMINE; so named by Casimir *Funk* (1884–1967), US biochemist, who believed the substances to be amines]
▸ˌ**vitaˈminic** *adj*

vitamin A *n* **1** Also called: **vitamin A$_1$, retinol.** a fat-soluble yellow unsaturated alcohol occurring in green and yellow vegetables, butter, egg yolk, and fish-liver oil. It is essential for the prevention of night blindness and the protection of epithelial tissue. **2** Also called: **vitamin A$_2$.** a vitamin that occurs in the tissues of freshwater fish and has a function similar to that of vitamin A$_1$.

vitamin B *n, pl* **B vitamins.** any of the vitamins in the vitamin B complex.

vitamin B complex *n* a large group of water-soluble vitamins occurring esp. in liver and yeast: includes thiamine (**vitamin B$_1$**), riboflavin (**vitamin B$_2$**), nicotinic acid, pyridoxine (**vitamin B$_6$**), pantothenic acid, biotin, choline, folic acid, and cyanocobalamin (**vitamin B$_{12}$**). Sometimes shortened to **B complex.**

vitamin C *n* another name for **ascorbic acid.**

vitamin D *n, pl* **D vitamins.** any of the fat-soluble vitamins, including calciferol (**vitamin D$_2$**) and cholecalciferol (**vitamin D$_3$**), occurring in fish-liver oils, milk, butter, and eggs: used in the treatment of rickets.

vitamin E *n* another name for **tocopherol.**

vitamin G *n* another name (esp. US and Canad.) for **riboflavin.**

vitamin H *n* another name (esp. US and Canad.) for **biotin.**

vitamin K *n, pl* **K vitamins.** any of the fat-soluble vitamins, including phylloquinone (**vitamin K$_1$**) and the menaquinones (**vitamin K$_2$**), which are essential for the normal clotting of blood.

vitamin P *n, pl* **P vitamins.** any of a group of water-soluble crystalline substances occurring mainly in citrus fruits, blackcurrants, and rosehips: they regulate the permeability of the blood capillaries.

vitellin (vɪˈtɛlɪn) *n Biochem.* a phosphoprotein that is the major protein in egg yolk. [C19: from VITELLUS + -IN]

vitelline membrane (vɪˈtɛlɪn) *n Zool.* a membrane that surrounds a fertilized ovum and prevents the entry of other spermatozoa.

vitellus (vɪˈtɛləs) *n, pl* **vitelluses** *or* **vitelli** (-laɪ). *Zool., rare.* the yolk of an egg. [C18: from L, lit.: little calf, later: yolk of an egg, from *vitulus* calf]

vitiate ('vɪʃɪˌeɪt) *vb* **vitiates, vitiating, vitiated.** (*tr*) **1** to make faulty or imperfect. **2** to debase or corrupt. **3** to destroy the force or legal effect of (a deed, etc.). [C16: from L *vitiāre* to injure, from *vitium* a fault]
▸ˌ**vitiˈation** *n* ▸ˈ**vitiˌator** *n*

viticulture ('vɪtɪˌkʌltʃə) *n* **1** the science, art, or process of cultivating grapevines. **2** the study of grapes and the growing of grapes. [C19: *viti-*, from L *vītis* vine]
▸ˌ**vitiˈculturist** *n*

vitreous ('vɪtrɪəs) *adj* **1** of or resembling glass. **2** made of or containing glass. **3** of or relating to the vitreous humour or vitreous body. [C17: from L *vitreus* made of glass, from *vitrum* glass]
▸ˈ**vitreously** *adv*

vitreous humour *or* **body** *n* a transparent gelatinous substance that fills the interior of the eyeball between the lens and the retina.

vitrescence (vɪˈtrɛsəns) *n* **1** the quality or condition of being or becoming vitreous. **2** the process of producing a glass or turning a crystalline material into glass.
▸**viˈtrescent** *adj*

vitrify ('vɪtrɪˌfaɪ) *vb* **vitrifies, vitrifying, vitrified.** to convert or be converted into glass or a glassy substance. [C16: from F, from L *vitrum* glass]
▸ˈ**vitriˌfiable** *adj* ▸**vitrification** (ˌvɪtrɪfɪˈkeɪʃən) *n*

vitrine ('vɪtriːn) *n* a glass display case or cabinet for works of art, curios, etc. [C19: from F, from *vitre* pane of glass, from L *vitrum* glass]

vitriol ('vɪtrɪˌɒl) *n* **1** another name for **sulphuric acid. 2** any one of a number of sulphate salts, such as ferrous sulphate (iron(II) sulphate; **green vitriol**), copper sulphate (**blue vitriol**), or zinc sulphate (**white vitriol**). **3** speech, writing, etc., displaying vituperation or bitterness. [C14: from Med. L *vitriolum*, from LL, from L *vitrum* glass, referring to the glossy appearance of the sulphates]

vitriolic ❶ (ˌvɪtrɪˈɒlɪk) *adj* **1** (of a strong acid) highly corrosive. **2** severely bitter or caustic.

vitriolize *or* **vitriolise** ('vɪtrɪəˌlaɪz) *vb* **vitriolizes, vitriolizing, vitriolized** *or* **vitriolises, vitriolising, vitriolised.** (*tr*) **1** to convert into or treat with vitriol. **2** to injure with vitriol.
▸ˌ**vitrioliˈzation** *or* ˌ**vitrioliˈsation** *n*

vittle ('vɪtᵊl) *n, vb* **vittles, vittling, vittled.** an obsolete or dialect spelling of **victual.**

vituperate (vɪˈtjuːpəˌreɪt) *vb* **vituperates, vituperating, vituperated.** to berate or rail (against) abusively; revile. [C16: from L *vituperāre* to blame, from *vitium* a defect + *parāre* to make]
▸**viˌtuperˈation** *n* ▸**viˈtuperˌator** *n*

viva[1] ('viːvə) *interj* long live; up with (a specified person or thing). [C17: from It., lit.: may (he) live! from *vivere* to live, from L *vīvere*]

viva[2] ('vaɪvə) *Brit.* ◆ *n* **1** an oral examination. ◆ *vb* **vivas, vivaing, vivaed.** (*tr*) **2** to examine orally. [shortened from VIVA VOCE]

vivace (vɪˈvɑːtʃɪ) *adj, adv Music.* to be performed in a brisk lively manner. [C17: from It., from L *vīvax* vigorous, from *vīvere* to live]

vivacious ❶ (vɪˈveɪʃəs) *adj* full of high spirits and animation. [C17: from L *vīvax* lively; see VIVACE]
▸**viˈvaciously** *adv* ▸**viˈvaciousness** *n*

vivacity ❶ (vɪˈvæsɪtɪ) *n, pl* **vivacities.** the quality or condition of being vivacious.

vivarium (vaɪˈvɛərɪəm) *n, pl* **vivariums** *or* **vivaria** (-ɪə). a place where live animals are kept under natural conditions for study, etc. [C16: from L: enclosure where live fish or game are kept, from *vīvus* alive]

viva voce ('vaɪvə 'vəʊtʃɪ) *adv, adj* **1** by word of mouth. ◆ *n, vb* **viva-voce, viva-voces, viva-voceing, viva-voced. 2** the full form of **viva**[2]. [C16: from Med. L, lit.: with living voice]

vive (viːv) *interj* long live; up with (a specified person or thing). [from F]

vivid ❶ ('vɪvɪd) *adj* **1** (of a colour) very bright; intense. **2** brilliantly coloured: *vivid plumage.* **3** conveying to the mind striking realism, freshness, or trueness to life: *a vivid account.* **4** (of a memory, etc.) remaining distinct in the mind. **5** (of the imagination, etc.) prolific in

THESAURUS

visualize *vb* = **picture**, conceive of, conjure up a mental picture of, envisage, imagine, see in the mind's eye

vital *adj* **1, 3** = **living**, alive, alive and kicking, animate, generative, invigorative, life-giving, live, quickening **2** = **lively**, animated, dynamic, energetic, forceful, full of beans (*inf.*), full of the joy of living, sparky, spirited, vibrant, vigorous, vivacious, zestful **4** = **essential**, basic, cardinal, fundamental, imperative, indispensable, necessary, radical, requisite **5** = **important**, critical, crucial, decisive, key, life-or-death, significant, urgent
Antonyms *adj* ≠ **living:** dead, dying, inanimate, moribund ≠ **lively:** apathetic, lethargic, listless, uninvolved ≠ **essential:** dispensable, inessential, nonessential, unnecessary ≠ **important:** minor, trivial, unimportant

vitality *n* **1** = **energy**, animation, brio, exuberance, go (*inf.*), life, liveliness, lustiness, pep, robustness, sparkle, stamina, strength, vigour, vim (*sl.*), vivaciousness, vivacity
Antonyms *n* apathy, inertia, lethargy, listlessness, sluggishness, weakness

vitriolic *adj* **2** = **bitter**, acerbic, acid, bitchy, caustic, destructive, dripping with malice, envenomed, sardonic, scathing, venomous, virulent, withering

vivacious *adj* = **lively**, animated, bubbling, cheerful, chirpy (*inf.*), ebullient, effervescent, frolicsome, full of beans (*inf.*), full of life, gay, high-spirited, jolly, light-hearted, merry, scintillating, sparkling, sparky, spirited, sportive, sprightly, upbeat (*inf.*), vital
Antonyms *adj* boring, dull, languid, lifeless, listless, melancholy, spiritless, unenthusiastic

vivacity *n* = **liveliness**, animation, brio, ebullience, effervescence, energy, gaiety, high spirits, life, pep, quickness, sparkle, spirit, sprightliness
Antonyms *n* apathy, ennui, fatigue, heaviness, inertia, languor, lethargy, listlessness, weariness

vivid *adj* **1** = **bright**, brilliant, clear, colourful, glowing, highly-coloured, intense, rich **3, 4** = **clear**, distinct, dramatic, graphic, lifelike, memorable, powerful, realistic, sharp, sharply-etched, stirring, strong, telling, true to life **6, 7** = **lively**, active, animated, dynamic, energetic,

the formation of lifelike images. **6** uttered, operating, or acting with vigour. **7** full of life or vitality: *a vivid personality*. [C17: from L *vīvidus* animated, from *vīvere* to live]
▸**'vividly** *adv* ▸**'vividness** *n*

vivify ('vɪvɪˌfaɪ) *vb* **vivifies, vivifying, vivified.** (*tr*) **1** to bring to life; animate. **2** to make more vivid or striking. [C16: from LL *vīvificāre*, from L *vīvus* alive + *facere* to make]
▸**ˌvivifi'cation** *n*

viviparous (vɪ'vɪpərəs) *adj* **1** (of most mammals) giving birth to living offspring that develop within the uterus of the mother. **2** (of seeds) germinating before separating from the parent plant. **3** (of plants) producing bulbils or young plants instead of flowers. [C17: from L, from *vīvus* alive + *parere* to bring forth]
▸**viviparity** (ˌvɪvɪ'pærɪtɪ) *or* **vi'viparousness** *n* ▸**vi'viparously** *adv*

vivisect ('vɪvɪˌsɛkt, ˌvɪvɪ'sɛkt) *vb* to subject (an animal) to vivisection. [C19: back formation from VIVISECTION]
▸**'viviˌsector** *n*

vivisection (ˌvɪvɪ'sɛkʃən) *n* the act or practice of performing experiments on living animals, involving cutting into or dissecting the body. [C18: from *vivi-*, from L *vīvus* living + SECTION, as in DISSECTION]
▸**ˌvivi'sectional** *adj*

vivisectionist (ˌvɪvɪ'sɛkʃənɪst) *n* a person who practises or advocates vivisection as being useful to science.

vivo ('viːvəʊ) *adj, adv Music.* (*in combination*) with life and vigour: *allegro vivo*. [It.: lively]

vixen ❶ ('vɪksən) *n* **1** a female fox. **2** a quarrelsome or spiteful woman. [C15 *fixen*; rel. to OE *fyxe*, fem. of FOX]
▸**'vixenish** *adj* ▸**'vixenly** *adv, adj*

Viyella (vaɪ'ɛlə) *n Trademark.* a soft fabric made of wool and cotton.

viz ❶ *abbrev. for* videlicet.

vizard ('vɪzəd) *n Arch. or literary.* a means of disguise. [C16: var. of VISOR]
▸**'vizarded** *adj*

vizier (vɪ'zɪə) *n* a high official in certain Muslim countries, esp. in the former Ottoman Empire. [C16: from Turkish *vezīr*, from Ar. *wazīr* porter, from *wazara* to bear a burden]
▸**vi'zierate** *n* ▸**vi'zierial** *adj* ▸**vi'ziership** *n*

vizor ('vaɪzə) *n* a variant spelling of **visor.**

vizsla ('vɪʒlə) *n* a breed of Hungarian hunting dog with a smooth rusty-gold coat. [C20: after *Vizsla*, town in Hungary]

VJ *abbrev. for* video jockey.

V-J Day *n* the day marking the Allied victory over Japan in World War II (Aug. 15, 1945).

VL *abbrev. for* Vulgar Latin.

vlei (fleɪ, vleɪ) *n S. African.* an area of low marshy ground, esp. one that feeds a stream. [C19: from Afrik.]

VLF *or* **vlf** *Radio. abbrev. for* very low frequency.

V neck *n* **a** a neck on a garment that comes down to a point, resembling the shape of the letter V. **b** a sweater with such a neck.
▸**'V-ˌneck** *or* **'V-ˌnecked** *adj*

voc. *or* **vocat.** *abbrev. for* vocative.

vocab ('vəʊkæb) *n* short for **vocabulary.**

vocable ('vəʊkəbᵊl) *n* any word, either written or spoken, regarded simply as a sequence of letters or spoken sounds. [C16: from L *vocābulum* a designation, from *vocāre* to call]
▸**'vocably** *adv*

vocabulary ❶ (və'kæbjʊlərɪ) *n, pl* **vocabularies. 1** a listing, either selective or exhaustive, containing the words and phrases of a language, with meanings or translations into another language. **2** the aggregate of words in the use or comprehension of a specified person, class, etc. **3** all the words contained in a language. **4** a range or system of symbols or techniques constituting a means of communication or expression, as any of the arts or crafts: *a wide vocabulary of textures and colours*. [C16: from Med. L *vocābulārium*, from L *vocābulum* VOCABLE]

vocal ❶ ('vəʊkᵊl) *adj* **1** of or designed for the voice: *vocal music*. **2** produced or delivered by the voice: *vocal noises*. **3** connected with the production of the voice: *vocal organs*. **4** frequently disposed to outspoken speech, criticism, etc.: *a vocal minority*. **5** full of sound or voices: *a vocal assembly*. **6** endowed with a voice. **7** *Phonetics*. **7a** of or relating to a speech sound. **7b** of or relating to a voiced speech sound, esp. a vowel. ◆ *n* **8** a piece of jazz or pop music that is sung. **9** a performance of such a piece of music. [C14: from L *vōcālis* possessed of a voice, from *vōx* voice]
▸**vocality** (vəʊ'kælɪtɪ) *n* ▸**'vocally** *adv*

vocal cords *pl n* either of two pairs of membranous folds in the larynx. The upper pair (**false vocal cords**) are not concerned with vocal production; the lower pair (**true vocal cords**) can be made to vibrate and produce sound when air from the lungs is forced over them.

vocalic (vəʊ'kælɪk) *adj Phonetics.* of, relating to, or containing a vowel or vowels.

vocalise (ˌvəʊkə'liːz) *n* a musical passage sung upon one vowel usually as an exercise to develop flexibility and control of pitch and tone.

vocalism ('vəʊkəˌlɪzəm) *n* **1** the exercise of the voice, as in singing or speaking. **2** *Phonetics*. **2a** a voiced speech sound, esp. a vowel. **2b** a system of vowels as used in a language.

vocalist ('vəʊkəlɪst) *n* a singer, esp. one who regularly appears with a jazz band or pop group.

vocalize *or* **vocalise** ('vəʊkəˌlaɪz) *vb* **vocalizes, vocalizing, vocalized** *or* **vocalises, vocalising, vocalised. 1** to express with or use the voice. **2** (*tr*) to make vocal or articulate. **3** (*tr*) *Phonetics.* to articulate (a speech sound) with voice. **4** another word for **vowelize. 5** (*intr*) to sing a melody on a vowel, etc.
▸**ˌvocali'zation** *or* **ˌvocali'sation** *n* ▸**'vocalˌizer** *or* **'vocalˌiser** *n*

vocal score *n* a musical score with voice parts in full and orchestral parts in the form of a piano transcription.

vocation ❶ (vəʊ'keɪʃən) *n* **1** a specified profession or trade. **2a** a special urge or predisposition to a particular calling or career, esp. a religious one. **2b** such a calling or career. [C15: from L *vocātiō*, from *vocāre* to call]

vocational (vəʊ'keɪʃənᵊl) *adj* **1** of or relating to a vocation or vocations. **2** of or relating to applied educational courses concerned with skills needed for an occupation, trade, or profession.

vocational guidance *n* a guidance service based on psychological tests and interviews to find out what career may best suit a person.

vocative ('vɒkətɪv) *Grammar.* ◆ *adj* **1** denoting a case of nouns, in some inflected languages, used when the referent of the noun is being addressed. ◆ *n* **2a** the vocative case. **2b** a vocative noun or speech element. [C15: from L *vocātīvus cāsus* the calling case, from *vocāre* to call]

voces ('vəʊsiːz) *n* the plural of **vox.**

vociferate (vəʊ'sɪfəˌreɪt) *vb* **vociferates, vociferating, vociferated.** to exclaim or cry out about (something) clamorously or insistently. [C17: from L *vōciferārī*, from *vōx* voice + *ferre* to bear]
▸**voˌcifer'ation** *n*

vociferous ❶ (vəʊ'sɪfərəs) *adj* **1** characterized by vehemence or noisiness: *vociferous protests*. **2** making an outcry: *a vociferous mob*.
▸**vo'ciferously** *adv* ▸**vo'ciferousness** *n*

vocoder ('vəʊˌkəʊdə) *n Music.* a type of synthesizer that uses the human voice as an oscillator.

vodka ('vɒdkə) *n* an alcoholic drink originating in Russia, made from grain, potatoes, etc., usually consisting only of rectified spirit and water. [C19: from Russian, dim. of *voda* water]

voe (vəʊ) *n* (in Orkney and Shetland) a small bay or narrow creek. [C17: from ON *vagr*]

voetsek ('futsɛk, 'vʊt-) *interj S. African sl.* an expression of dismissal or rejection. [C19: Afrik., from Du. *voort se ek* forward, I say, commonly applied to animals]

voetstoets *or* **voetstoots** ('futstʊts, 'vʊt-) *S. African.* ◆ *adj* **1** denoting a sale in which the vendor is freed from all responsibility for the condition of the goods being sold. ◆ *adv* **2** without responsibility for the condition of the goods sold. [from Afrik. *voetstoots* as it is]

vogue ❶ (vəʊg) *n* **1** the popular style at a specified time (esp. in **in vogue**). **2** a period of general or popular usage or favour: *the vogue for such dances is over*. ◆ *adj* **3** (*usually prenominal*) fashionable: *a vogue word*. [C16: from F: a rowing fashion, from OIt., from *vogare* to row, from ?]
▸**'voguish** *adj*

vogueing ('vəʊgɪŋ) *n* a dance style of the late 1980s, in which a fashion model's movements and postures are imitated in a highly stylized manner. [C20: from *Vogue* magazine]

voice ❶ (vɔɪs) *n* **1** the sound made by the vibration of the vocal cords, esp. when modified by the tongue and mouth. **2** the natural and distinctive tone of the speech sounds characteristic of a particular person. **3** the condition, quality, or tone of such sounds: *a hysterical voice*. **4** the musical sound of a singing voice, with respect to its quality or tone: *she has a lovely voice*. **5** the ability to speak, sing, etc.: *he has lost his voice*. **6** a sound resembling or suggestive of vocal utterance: *the*

THESAURUS

expressive, flamboyant, quick, spirited, storming, striking, strong, vigorous
Antonyms *adj* ≠ **bright:** colourless, cool, drab, dull, pale, pastel, sombre ≠ **clear:** unclear, unmemorable, vague ≠ **lively:** lifeless, nondescript, ordinary, quiet, routine, run-of-the-mill, unremarkable

vividness *n* **1** = **brightness**, brilliancy, glow, radiance, resplendence **3, 4** = **clarity**, distinctness, graphicness, immediacy, intensity, realism, sharpness, strength **6, 7** = **liveliness**

vixen *n* **2** = **shrew**, ballbreaker, fury, harpy, harridan, hellcat, scold, spitfire, termagant (*rare*), virago, Xanthippe

viz *adv* = **namely**, that is to say, to wit, videlicet

vocabulary *n* **1, 3** = **words**, dictionary, glossary, language, lexicon, wordbook, word hoard, word stock

vocal *adj* **2** = **spoken**, articulate, articulated, oral, put into words, said, uttered, voiced **4** = **outspoken**, articulate, blunt, clamorous, eloquent, expressive, forthright, frank, free-spoken, noisy, plain-spoken, strident, vociferous
Antonyms *adj* ≠ **outspoken:** inarticulate, quiet, reserved, reticent, retiring, shy, silent, uncommunicative

vocation *n* **1, 2** = **profession**, business, calling, career, employment, job, life's work, life work, métier, mission, office, post, pursuit, role, trade

vociferous *adj* **1, 2** = **noisy**, clamant, clamorous, loud, loudmouthed (*inf.*), obstreperous, outspoken, ranting, shouting, strident, uproarious, vehement, vocal
Antonyms *adj* hushed, muted, noiseless, quiet, silent, still

vogue *n* **1** = **fashion**, craze, custom, *dernier cri*, last word, mode, style, the latest, the rage, the thing (*inf.*), trend, way **2** = **popularity**, acceptance, currency, fashionableness, favour, prevalence, usage, use ◆ *adj* **3** = **fashionable**, in, modish, now (*inf.*), popular, prevalent, trendy (*Brit. inf.*), up-to-the-minute, voguish, with it (*inf.*)

voice *n* **1, 2, 5** = **sound**, articulation, language, power of speech, tone, utterance, words **7** = **say**, decision, expression, part, view, vote, will, wish **9** = **instrument**, agency, medium, mouth-

voice of hard experience. **7** written or spoken expression, as of feeling, opinion, etc. (esp. in **give voice to**). **8** a stated choice, wish, or opinion: *to give someone a voice in a decision.* **9** an agency through which is communicated another's purpose, etc.: *such groups are the voice of our enemies.* **10** *Music.* **10a** musical notes produced by vibrations of the vocal chords at various frequencies and in certain registers: *a tenor voice.* **10b** (in harmony) an independent melodic line or part: *a fugue in five voices.* **11** *Phonetics.* the sound characterizing the articulation of several speech sounds, including all vowels or sonants, that is produced when the vocal cords are set in vibration by the breath. **12** *Grammar.* a category of the verb that expresses whether the relation between the subject and the verb is that of agent and action, action and recipient, or some other relation. **13 in voice.** in a condition to sing or speak well. **14 with one voice.** unanimously. ◆ *vb* **voices, voicing, voiced.** (*tr*) **15** to give expression to: *to voice a complaint.* **16** to articulate (a speech sound) with voice. **17** *Music.* to adjust (a wind instrument or organ pipe) so that it conforms to the correct standards of tone colour, pitch, etc. [C13: from OF *voiz,* from L *vōx*]
▸ **'voicer** *n*

voice box *n* **1** another word for the **larynx. 2** Also called: **talkbox.** an electronic guitar attachment with a tube into the player's mouth to modulate the sound vocally.

voiced (vɔɪst) *adj* **1** declared or expressed by the voice. **2** (*in combination*) having a voice as specified: *loud-voiced.* **3** *Phonetics.* articulated with accompanying vibration of the vocal cords: *in English* (b) *is a voiced consonant.*

voice input *n* the control and operation of computer systems by spoken commands.

voiceless ('vɔɪslɪs) *adj* **1** without a voice. **2** not articulated: *voiceless misery.* **3** silent. **4** *Phonetics.* articulated without accompanying vibration of the vocal cords: *in English* (p) *is a voiceless consonant.*
▸ **'voicelessly** *adv*

voice mail *n* an electronic system for the transfer and storage of telephone messages, which can then be dealt with by the user at his or her convenience.

voice-over *n* the voice of an unseen commentator heard during a film, etc.

voiceprint ('vɔɪs,prɪnt) *n* a graphic representation of a person's voice recorded electronically, usually having time plotted along the horizontal axis and the frequency of the speech on the vertical axis.

void ❶ (vɔɪd) *adj* **1** without contents. **2** not legally binding: *null and void.* **3** (of an office, house, etc.) unoccupied. **4** (*postpositive; foll. by of*) destitute or devoid: *void of resources.* **5** useless: *all his efforts were rendered void.* **6** (of a card suit or player) having no cards in a particular suit: *his spades were void.* ◆ *n* **7** an empty space or area: *the huge desert voids of Asia.* **8** a feeling or condition of loneliness or deprivation. **9** a lack of any cards in one suit: *to have a void in spades.* ◆ *vb* (*mainly tr*) **10** to make ineffective or invalid. **11** to empty (contents, etc.) or make empty of contents. **12** (*also intr*) to discharge the contents of (the bowels or urinary bladder). [C13: from OF, from Vulgar L *vocītus* (untested), from L *vacuus,* from *vacāre* to be empty]
▸ **'voidable** *adj* ▸ **'voider** *n*

voidance ('vɔɪdᵊns) *n* **1** an annulment, as of a contract. **2** the condition of being vacant, as an office, benefice, etc. **3** the act of voiding or evacuating. [C14: var. of AVOIDANCE]

voile (vɔɪl) *n* a light semitransparent fabric of silk, rayon, cotton, etc., used for dresses, scarves, shirts, etc. [C19: from F: VEIL]

vol. *abbrev. for:* **1** volcano. **2** volume. **3** volunteer.

volant ('vəulənt) *adj* **1** (*usually postpositive*) *Heraldry.* in a flying position. **2** *Rare.* flying or capable of flight. [C16: from F, from *voler* to fly, from L *volāre*]

volar ('vəulə) *adj Anat.* of or relating to the palm of the hand or the sole of the foot. [C19: from L *vola* hollow of the hand, palm, sole of the foot]

volatile ❶ ('vɒlə,taɪl) *adj* **1** (of a substance) capable of readily changing from a solid or liquid form to a vapour. **2** (of persons) disposed to caprice or inconstancy. **3** (of circumstances) liable to sudden change. **4** lasting only a short time: *volatile business interests.* **5** *Computing.* (of a memory) not retaining stored information when the power supply is cut off. ◆ *n* **6** a volatile substance. [C17: from L *volātilis* flying, from *volāre* to fly]
▸ **'volatileness** *or* **volatility** (,vɒlə'tɪlɪtɪ) *n*

volatilize *or* **volatilise** (vɒ'lætɪ,laɪz) *vb* **volatilizes, volatilizing, volatilized** *or* **volatilises, volatilising, volatilised.** to change or cause to change from a solid or liquid to a vapour.
▸ **vo'lati,lizable** *or* **vo'lati,lisable** *adj* ▸ **vo,latiliz'ation** *or* **vo,latilis'ation** *n*

vol-au-vent (*French* vɔlovɑ̃) *n* a very light puff pastry case filled with a savoury mixture in a sauce. [C19: from F, lit.: flight in the wind]

volcanic (vɒl'kænɪk) *adj* **1** of, produced by, or characterized by the presence of volcanoes: *a volcanic region.* **2** suggestive of or resembling an erupting volcano: *a volcanic era.*
▸ **vol'canically** *adv* ▸ **volcanicity** (,vɒlkə'nɪsɪtɪ) *n*

volcanic glass *n* any of several glassy volcanic igneous rocks, such as obsidian.

volcanism ('vɒlkə,nɪzəm) *or* **vulcanism** *n* those processes collectively that result in the formation of volcanoes and their products.

volcano (vɒl'keɪnəu) *n, pl* **volcanoes** *or* **volcanos. 1** an opening in the earth's crust from which molten lava, rock fragments, ashes, dust, and gases are ejected from below the earth's surface. **2** a mountain formed from volcanic material ejected from a vent in a central crater. [C17: from It., from L *Volcānus* Vulcan, Roman god of fire and metal-working, whose forges were believed to be responsible for volcanic rumblings]

volcanology (,vɒlkə'nɒlədʒɪ) *or* **vulcanology** *n* the study of volcanoes and volcanic phenomena.
▸ **volcanological** (,vɒlkənə'lɒdʒɪkᵊl) *or* **,vulcano'logical** *adj*

vole (vəul) *n* any of various small rodents, mostly of Eurasia and North America, having a stocky body, short tail, and inconspicuous ears. [C19: short for *volemouse,* from ON *vollr* field + *mus* MOUSE]

volitant ('vɒlɪtənt) *adj* **1** flying or moving about rapidly. **2** capable of flying. [C19: from L *volitāre* to flit, from *volāre* to fly]

volition ❶ (və'lɪʃən) *n* **1** the act of exercising the will: *of one's own volition.* **2** the faculty of conscious choice, decision, and intention. **3** the resulting choice or resolution. [C17: from Med. L *volitiō,* from L *vol-* as in *volō* I will, present stem of *velle* to wish]
▸ **vo'litional** *adj*

volitive ('vɒlɪtɪv) *adj* of, relating to, or emanating from the will.

Volk (fɒlk) *n S. African.* the Afrikaner people. [from Afrik., from Du.]

Volksraad ('fɒlks,rɑːt) *n* (formerly, in South Africa) the Legislative Assemblies of the Transvaal and Orange Free State republics. [from Afrik., from Du. *volks* people's + *raad* council]

volley ❶ ('vɒlɪ) *n* **1** the simultaneous discharge of several weapons, esp. firearms. **2** the projectiles or missiles so discharged. **3** a burst of oaths, protests, etc., occurring simultaneously or in rapid succession. **4** *Sport.* a stroke, shot, or kick at a moving ball before it hits the ground. **5** *Cricket.* the flight of such a ball or the ball itself. ◆ *vb* **6** to discharge (weapons, etc.) in or as if in a volley or (of weapons, etc.) to be discharged. **7** (*tr*) to utter vehemently. **8** (*tr*) *Sport.* to strike or kick (a moving ball) before it hits the ground. [C16: from F *volée* a flight, from *voler* to fly, from L *volāre*]
▸ **'volleyer** *n*

volleyball ('vɒlɪ,bɔːl) *n* **1** a game in which two teams hit a large ball back and forth over a high net with their hands. **2** the ball used in this game.

volplane ('vɒl,pleɪn) *vb* **volplanes, volplaning, volplaned. 1** (*intr*) (of an aircraft) to glide without engine power. ◆ *n* **2** a glide by an aircraft. [C20: from F *vol plané* a gliding flight]

vols. *abbrev. for* volumes.

volt[1] (vəult) *n* the derived SI unit of electric potential; the potential difference between two points on a conductor carrying a current of 1 ampere, when the power dissipated between these points is 1 watt. Symbol: V [C19: after Count Alessandro *Volta* (1745–1827), It. physicist]

volt[2] *or* **volte** (vɒlt) *n* **1** a circle executed in dressage. **2** a leap made in fencing to avoid an opponent's thrust. [C17: from F, from It. *volta,* ult. from L *volvere* to turn]

volta ('vɒltə; *Italian* 'vɔlta) *n, pl* **volte** (*Italian* -te). **1** an Italian dance popular during the 16th and 17th centuries. **2** a piece of music for or in the rhythm of this dance. [C17: from It.: turn; see VOLT[2]]

voltage ('vəultɪdʒ) *n* an electromotive force or potential difference expressed in volts.

voltaic (vɒl'teɪɪk) *adj* another word for **galvanic** (sense 1).

voltaic cell *n* another name for **primary cell.**

voltaic couple *n Physics.* a pair of dissimilar metals in an electrolyte with a potential difference between the metals resulting from chemical action.

voltaic pile *n* an early form of battery consisting of a pile of paired plates of dissimilar metals, such as zinc and copper, each pair being separated from the next by a pad moistened with an electrolyte.

voltameter (vɒl'tæmɪtə) *n* a device for measuring electric charge.
▸ **voltametric** (,vɒltə'mɛtrɪk) *adj*

voltammeter (,vəult'æm,miːtə) *n* a dual-purpose instrument that can measure both potential difference and electric current, usually in volts and amperes respectively.

THESAURUS

piece, organ, spokesman, spokesperson, spokeswoman, vehicle ◆ *vb* **15, 16** = **express,** air, articulate, assert, come out with (*inf.*), declare, divulge, enunciate, give expression *or* utterance to, put into words, say, utter, ventilate

void *adj* **2, 5** = **invalid,** dead, ineffective, ineffectual, inoperative, nonviable, nugatory, null and void, unenforceable, useless, vain, worthless **3** = **empty,** bare, clear, drained, emptied, free, tenantless, unfilled, unoccupied, vacant **4** *foll. by* **of** = **devoid,** destitute, lacking, without ◆ *n* **7** = **emptiness,** blank, blankness, gap, lack, opening, space, vacuity, vacuum, want ◆ *vb* **10** = **invalidate,** abnegate, cancel, nullify, rescind **11, 12** = **empty,** discharge, drain, eject, eliminate (*Physiology*), emit, evacuate
Antonyms *adj* ≠ **empty:** abounding, complete, filled, full, occupied, replete, tenanted

volatile *adj* **1** = **changeable,** explosive, inconstant, unsettled, unstable, unsteady, variable **2** = **temperamental,** airy, erratic, fickle, flighty, gay, giddy, inconstant, lively, mercurial, sprightly, up and down (*inf.*), whimsical
Antonyms *adj* ≠ **changeable:** constant, inert, settled, stable, steady ≠ **temperamental:** calm, consistent, cool-headed, dependable, reliable, self-controlled, sober

volition *n* **1** = **free will,** choice, choosing, determination, discretion, election, option, preference, purpose, resolution, will

volley *n* **1, 3** = **barrage,** blast, bombardment, burst, cannonade, discharge, explosion, fusillade, hail, salvo, shower

volt-ampere ('vəʊlt'æmpeə) *n* the product of the potential in volts across an electrical circuit and the resultant current in amperes.

volte-face ('vɒlt'fɑːs) *n, pl* **volte-face. 1** a reversal, as in opinion. **2** a change of position so as to look, lie, etc., in the opposite direction. [C19: from F, from It., from *volta* turn + *faccia* face]

voltmeter ('vəʊlt,miːtə) *n* an instrument for measuring potential difference or electromotive force.

voluble ❶ ('vɒljubᵊl) *adj* **1** talking easily and at length. **2** *Arch.* easily turning or rotating. **3** *Rare.* (of a plant) twining or twisting. [C16: from L *volūbilis* turning readily, from *volvere* to turn]
▸,**volu'bility** *or* '**volubleness** *n* ▸'**volubly** *adv*

volume ❶ ('vɒljuːm) *n* **1** the magnitude of the three-dimensional space enclosed within or occupied by an object, geometric solid, etc. **2** a large mass or quantity: *the volume of protest.* **3** an amount or total: *the volume of exports.* **4** fullness of sound. **5** the control on a radio, etc., for adjusting the intensity of sound. **6** a bound collection of printed or written pages; book. **7** any of several books either bound in an identical format or part of a series. **8** the complete set of issues of a periodical over a specified period, esp. one year. **9** *History.* a roll of parchment, etc. **10 speak volumes.** to convey much significant information. [C14: from OF, from L *volūmen* a roll, from *volvere* to roll up]

volumetric (,vɒlju'mɛtrɪk) *adj* of, concerning, or using measurement by volume: *volumetric analysis.*
▸,**volu'metrically** *adv*

volumetric analysis *n Chem.* quantitative analysis of liquids or solutions by comparing the volumes that react with known volumes of standard reagents, usually by titration.

voluminous ❶ (və'luːmɪnəs) *adj* **1** of great size, quantity, or extent. **2** (of writing) consisting of or sufficient to fill volumes. [C17: from LL *volūminōsus* full of windings, from *volūmen* VOLUME]
▸**voluminosity** (və,luːmɪ'nɒsɪtɪ) *n* ▸**vo'luminously** *adv*

voluntarism ('vɒləntə,rɪzəm) *n* **1** *Philosophy.* the theory that the will rather than the intellect is the ultimate principle of reality. **2** a doctrine or system based on voluntary participation in a course of action. **3** another name for **voluntaryism.**
▸'**voluntarist** *n, adj*

voluntary ❶ ('vɒləntərɪ) *adj* **1** performed, undertaken, or brought about by free choice or willingly: *a voluntary donation.* **2** (of persons) serving or acting in a specified function without compulsion or promise of remuneration: *a voluntary social worker.* **3** done by, composed of, or functioning with the aid of volunteers: *a voluntary association.* **4** exercising or having the faculty of willing: *a voluntary agent.* **5** spontaneous: *voluntary laughter.* **6** *Law.* **6a** acting or done without legal obligation, compulsion, or persuasion. **6b** made without payment or recompense: *a voluntary conveyance.* **7** (of the muscles of the limbs, neck, etc.) having their action controlled by the will. **8** maintained by the voluntary actions or contributions of individuals and not by the state: *voluntary schools.* ◆ *n, pl* **voluntaries. 9** *Music.* a composition or improvisation, usually for organ, played at the beginning or end of a church service. [C14: from L *voluntārius,* from *voluntās* will, from *velle* to wish]
▸'**voluntarily** *adv*

voluntary arrangement *n Law.* a procedure enabling an insolvent company to come to an arrangement with its creditors and resolve its financial problems, often in compliance with a court order.

voluntaryism ('vɒləntərɪ,ɪzəm) *or* **voluntarism** *n* the principle of supporting churches, schools, and various other institutions by voluntary contributions rather than with state funds.
▸'**voluntaryist** *or* '**voluntarist** *n*

voluntary retailer *n* another name for **symbol retailer.**

volunteer ❶ (,vɒlən'tɪə) *n* **1a** a person who performs or offers to perform voluntary service. **1b** (*as modifier*): *a volunteer system.* **2** a person who freely undertakes military service. **3a** a plant that grows from seed that has not been deliberately sown. **3b** (*as modifier*): *a volunteer plant.* ◆ *vb* **4** to offer (oneself or one's services) for an undertaking by choice and without request or obligation. **5** (*tr*) to perform, give, or communicate voluntarily: *to volunteer help.* **6** (*intr*) to enlist voluntarily for military service. [C17: from F, from L *voluntārius;* see VOLUNTARY]

voluptuary ❶ (və'lʌptjʊərɪ) *n, pl* **voluptuaries. 1** a person devoted to luxury and sensual pleasures. ◆ *adj* **2** of or furthering sensual gratification or luxury. [C17: from LL *voluptuārius* delightful, from L *voluptās* pleasure]

voluptuous ❶ (və'lʌptjʊəs) *adj* **1** relating to, characterized by, or consisting of pleasures of the body or senses. **2** devoted or addicted to sensual indulgence or luxurious pleasures. **3** sexually alluring, esp. through shapeliness or fullness: *a voluptuous woman.* [C14: from L *voluptuōsus* full of gratification, from *voluptās* pleasure]
▸**vo'luptuously** *adv* ▸**vo'luptuousness** *n*

volute ('vɒljuːt, və'luːt) *n* **1** a spiral or twisting turn, form, or object. **2** Also called: **helix.** a carved ornament, esp. as used on an Ionic capital, that has the form of a spiral scroll. **3** any of the whorls of the spirally coiled shell of a snail or similar gastropod mollusc. **4** any of a family of tropical marine gastropod molluscs having a spiral shell with beautiful markings. ◆ *adj also* **voluted** (və'luːtɪd). **5** having the form of a volute; spiral. [C17: from L *volūta* spiral decoration, from *volūtus,* from *volvere* to roll up]
▸**vo'lution** *n*

vomer ('vəʊmə) *n* the thin flat bone forming part of the separation between the nasal passages in mammals. [C18: from L: ploughshare]

vomit ❶ ('vɒmɪt) *vb* **vomits, vomiting, vomited. 1** to eject (the contents of the stomach) through the mouth as the result of involuntary muscular spasms of the stomach and oesophagus. **2** to eject or be ejected forcefully. ◆ *n* **3** the matter ejected in vomiting. **4** the act of vomiting. **5** an emetic. [C14: from L *vomitāre* to vomit repeatedly, from *vomere* to vomit]
▸'**vomiter** *n*

vomitory ('vɒmɪtərɪ) *adj* **1** Also: **vomitive** ('vɒmɪtɪv). causing vomiting; emetic. ◆ *n, pl* **vomitories. 2** a vomitory agent. **3** Also called: **vomitorium** (,vɒmɪ'tɔːrɪəm). a passageway in an ancient Roman amphitheatre that connects an outside entrance to a tier of seats.

voodoo ('vuːduː) *n, pl* **voodoos. 1** Also called: **voodooism.** a religious cult involving witchcraft, common in Haiti and other Caribbean islands. **2** a person who practises voodoo. **3** a charm, spell, or fetish involved in voodoo worship. ◆ *adj* **4** relating to or associated with voodoo. ◆ *vb* **voodoos, voodooing, voodooed. 5** (*tr*) to affect by or as if by the power of voodoo. [C19: from Louisiana F *voudou,* ult. of West African origin]
▸'**voodooist** *n*

voorkamer ('fʊə,kɑːmə) *n S. African.* the front room of a house. [Afrik., from Du. *voor* fore + *kamer* chamber]

voorskot ('fʊə,skɒt) *n S. African.* advance payment made to a farmer for crops. Cf. **agterskot.** [C20: Afrik., from *voor* before + *skot* shot, payment]

Voortrekker ('fʊə,trɛkə) *n* (in South Africa) **1** one of the original Afrikaner settlers of the Transvaal and the Orange Free State who migrated from the Cape Colony in the 1830s. **2** a member of the Afrikaner youth movement founded in 1931. [C19: from Du., from *voor-* FORE- + *trekken* to TREK]

voracious ❶ (vɒ'reɪʃəs) *adj* **1** devouring or craving food in great quantities. **2** very eager or unremitting in some activity: *voracious reading.* [C17: from L *vorāx,* from *vorāre* to devour]
▸**voracity** (vɒ'ræsɪtɪ) *or* **vo'raciousness** *n*

-vorous *adj combining form.* feeding on or devouring: *carnivorous.* [from L *-vorus;* rel. to *vorāre* to swallow up]
▸ **-vore** *n combining form.*

vortex ❶ ('vɔːtɛks) *n, pl* **vortexes** *or* **vortices** (-tɪ,siːz). **1** a whirling mass or motion of liquid, gas, flame, etc., such as the spiralling movement of water around a whirlpool. **2** any activity or way of life regarded as irresistibly engulfing. [C17: from L: a whirlpool]
▸**vortical** ('vɔːtɪkᵊl) *adj*

vorticella (,vɔːtɪ'sɛlə) *n, pl* **vorticellae** (-liː). any of a genus of protozoans consisting of a goblet-shaped ciliated cell attached to the substratum

THESAURUS

volubility *n* **1** = **talkativeness**, fluency, garrulity, gift of the gab, glibness, loquaciousness, loquacity

voluble *adj* **1** = **talkative**, articulate, blessed with the gift of the gab, fluent, forthcoming, glib, loquacious
Antonyms *adj* hesitant, inarticulate, reticent, succinct, taciturn, terse, tongue-tied, unforthcoming

volume *n* **1** = **capacity**, compass, cubic content, dimensions **3** = **amount**, aggregate, body, bulk, mass, quantity, total **6** = **book**, publication, title, tome, treatise

voluminous *adj* **1** = **large**, ample, big, billowing, bulky, capacious, cavernous, full, massive, roomy, vast **2** = **copious**, prolific
Antonyms *adj* ≠ **large:** skimpy, slight, small, tiny ≠ **copious:** inadequate, insufficient, scanty

voluntarily *adv* **1** = **willingly**, by choice, freely, lief (*rare*), off one's own bat, of one's own accord, of one's own free will, on one's own initiative, without being asked, without prompting

voluntary *adj* **1, 2** = **unforced**, discretional, discretionary, free, gratuitous, honorary, intended, intentional, optional, spontaneous, uncompelled, unconstrained, unpaid, volunteer, willing
Antonyms *adj* automatic, conscripted, forced, instinctive, involuntary, obligatory, unintentional

volunteer *vb* **4** = **offer**, let oneself in for (*inf.*), need no invitation, offer one's services, present, proffer, propose, put oneself at (someone's) disposal, step forward **5** = **suggest**, advance, put forward, tender
Antonyms *vb* ≠ **offer:** begrudge, deny, keep, refuse, retain, withdraw, withhold

voluptuary *n* **1** = **sensualist**, *bon vivant*, epicurean, hedonist, luxury-lover, playboy, pleasure seeker, profligate, sybarite

voluptuous *adj* **1, 2** = **sensual**, bacchanalian, epicurean, hedonistic, licentious, luxurious, pleasure-loving, self-indulgent, sybaritic **3** = **buxom**, ample, curvaceous (*inf.*), enticing, erotic, full-bosomed, provocative, seductive, shapely
Antonyms *adj* ≠ **sensual:** abstemious, ascetic, celibate, rigorous, self-denying, Spartan

voluptuousness *n* **1, 2** = **sensuality**, carnality, licentiousness, opulence **3** = **curvaceousness** (*inf.*), seductiveness, shapeliness

vomit *vb* **1** = **be sick**, barf, belch forth, bring up, chuck (up) (*sl., chiefly US*), disgorge, eject, emit, heave, puke (*sl.*), regurgitate, retch, sick up (*inf.*), spew out *or* up, throw up (*inf.*)

voracious *adj* **1** = **gluttonous**, devouring, edacious, esurient, greedy, hungry, insatiable, omnivorous, ravening, ravenous **2** = **avid**, hungry, insatiable, prodigious, rapacious, uncontrolled, unquenchable
Antonyms *adj* ≠ **avid:** moderate, sated, satisfied, self-controlled, temperate

voracity *n* **1** = **greed**, edacity, hunger, ravenousness **2** = **avidity**, eagerness, hunger, rapacity

vortex *n* **1** = **whirlpool**, eddy, maelstrom

by a long contractile stalk. [C18: from NL, lit.: a little eddy, from VORTEX]

vorticism ('vɔːtɪˌsɪzəm) *n* an art movement in England combining the techniques of cubism with the concern for the problems of the machine age evinced in futurism. [C20: referring to the "vortices" of modern life on which the movement was based]
▸ **'vorticist** *n*

vostro account ('vɒstrəʊ) *n* a bank account held by a foreign bank with a British bank, usually in sterling. Cf. **nostro account.**

votary ❶ ('vəʊtərɪ) *n, pl* **votaries,** *also* **votarist. 1** *RC Church, Eastern Churches.* a person, such as a monk or nun, who has dedicated himself or herself to religion by taking vows. **2** a devoted adherent of a religion, cause, etc. ◆ *adj* **3** ardently devoted to the worship of God or a saint. [C16: from L *vōtum* a vow, from *vovēre* to vow]
▸ **'votaress** *fem n*

vote ❶ (vəʊt) *n* **1** an indication of choice, opinion, or will on a question, such as the choosing of a candidate: *10 votes for Jones.* **2** the opinion of a group of persons as determined by voting: *it was put to the vote.* **3** a body of votes or voters collectively: *the Jewish vote.* **4** the total number of votes cast. **5** the ticket, ballot, etc., by which a vote is expressed. **6a** the right to vote; franchise. **6b** a person regarded as the embodiment of this right. **7** a means of voting, such as a ballot. **8** *Chiefly Brit.* a grant or other proposition to be voted upon. ◆ *vb* **votes, voting, voted. 9** (when *tr, takes a clause as object or an infinitive*) to express or signify (one's preference or will) (for or against some question, etc.): *to vote by ballot.* **10** (*intr*) to declare oneself as being (something or in favour of something) by exercising one's vote: *to vote socialist.* **11** (*tr;* foll. by *into* or *out of,* etc.) to appoint or elect (a person to or from a particular post): *he was voted out of office.* **12** (*tr*) to determine the condition of in a specified way by voting: *the court voted itself out of existence.* **13** (*tr*) to authorize or allow by voting: *vote us a rise.* **14** (*tr*) *Inf.* to declare by common opinion: *the party was voted a failure.* [C15: from L *vōtum* a solemn promise, from *vovēre* to vow]
▸ **'votable** *or* **'voteable** *adj*

vote down *vb* (*tr, adv*) to decide against or defeat in a vote: *the bill was voted down.*

vote of no confidence *n Parliament.* a vote on a motion put by the Opposition censuring an aspect of the Government's policy; if the motion is carried the Government is obliged to resign. Also called: **vote of censure.**

voter ('vəʊtə) *n* a person who can or does vote.

voting machine *n* (esp. in the US) a machine at a polling station that voters operate to register their votes and that mechanically or electronically counts all votes cast.

votive ('vəʊtɪv) *adj* **1** given or dedicated in fulfilment of or in accordance with a vow. **2** *RC Church.* having the nature of a voluntary offering: *a votive Mass.* [C16: from L *vōtīvus* promised by a vow, from *vōtum* a vow]

vouch ❶ (vaʊtʃ) *vb* **1** (*intr;* usually foll. by *for*) to give personal assurance: *I'll vouch for his safety.* **2** (when *tr, usually takes a clause as object;* when *intr,* usually foll. by *for*) to furnish supporting evidence (for) or function as proof (of). **3** (*tr*) *Arch.* to cite (authors, principles, etc.) in support of something. [C14: from OF *vocher* to summon, ult. from L *vocāre* to call]

voucher ❶ ('vaʊtʃə) *n* **1** a document serving as evidence for some claimed transaction, as the receipt or expenditure of money. **2** *Brit.* a ticket or card serving as a substitute for cash: *a gift voucher.* **3** a person or thing that vouches for the truth of some statement, etc. [C16: from Anglo-F, noun use of OF *voucher* to summon; see VOUCH]

vouchsafe ❶ (ˌvaʊtʃ'seɪf) *vb* **vouchsafes, vouchsafing, vouchsafed.** (*tr*) **1** to give or grant or condescend to give or grant: *she vouchsafed no reply.* **2** (*may take a clause as object or an infinitive*) to agree, promise, or permit, often graciously or condescendingly: *he vouchsafed to come yesterday.* [C14 *vouchen sauf;* see VOUCH, SAFE]

voussoir (vuː'swɑː) *n* a wedge-shaped stone or brick that is used with others to construct an arch or vault. [C18: from F, from Vulgar L *volsōrium* (unattested), ult. from L *volvere* to turn, roll]

vow ❶ (vaʊ) *n* **1** a solemn or earnest pledge or promise binding the person making it to perform a specified act or behave in a certain way. **2** a solemn promise made to a deity or saint, by which the promiser pledges himself to some future act or way of life. **3 take vows.** to enter a religious order and commit oneself to its rule of life by the vows of poverty, chastity, and obedience. ◆ *vb* **4** (*tr; may take a clause as object or an infinitive*) to pledge, promise, or undertake solemnly: *he vowed to return.* **5** (*tr*) to dedicate or consecrate to God or a saint. **6** (*tr; usually takes a clause as object*) to assert or swear emphatically. **7** (*intr*) *Arch.* to declare solemnly. [C13: from OF *vou,* from L *vōtum;* see VOTE]
▸ **'vower** *n*

vowel ('vaʊəl) *n* **1** *Phonetics.* a voiced speech sound whose articulation is characterized by the absence of obstruction in the vocal tract, allowing the breath stream free passage. The timbre of a vowel is chiefly determined by the position of the tongue and the lips. **2** a letter or character representing a vowel. [C14: from OF, from L *vocālis littera* vowel, from *vocālis,* from *vox* voice]
▸ **'vowel-ˌlike** *adj*

vowel gradation *n* another name for **ablaut.** See **gradation** (sense 5).

vowelize *or* **vowelise** ('vaʊəˌlaɪz) *vb* **vowelizes, vowelizing, vowelized** *or* **vowelises, vowelising, vowelised.** (*tr*) to mark the vowel points in (a Hebrew word or text).
▸ **ˌvoweli'zation** *or* **ˌvoweli'sation** *n*

vowel mutation *n* another name for **umlaut.**

vowel point *n* any of several marks or points placed above or below consonants, esp. those evolved for Hebrew or Arabic, in order to indicate vowel sounds.

vox (vɒks) *n, pl* **voces.** a voice or sound. [L: voice]

vox pop *n* interviews with members of the public on a radio or television programme. [C20: shortened from VOX POPULI]

vox populi ('pɒpjʊˌlaɪ) *n* the voice of the people; popular or public opinion. [L]

voyage ❶ ('vɔɪɪdʒ) *n* **1** a journey, travel, or passage, esp. one to a distant land or by sea or air. ◆ *vb* **voyages, voyaging, voyaged. 2** to travel over or traverse (something): *we will voyage to Africa.* [C13: from OF *veiage,* from L *viāticum* provision for travelling, from *via* way]
▸ **'voyager** *n*

voyage charter *n* the hire of a ship or aircraft for a specific number of voyages. Cf. **time charter.**

voyageur (ˌvɔɪə'dʒɜː) *n* (in Canada) a woodsman, guide, trapper, boatman, or explorer, esp. in the North. [C19: F: traveller, from *voyager* to VOYAGE]

voyeur (vwaɪ'ɜː) *n* a person who obtains sexual pleasure from the observation of people undressing, having intercourse, etc. [C20: F, lit.: one who sees, from *voir* to see, from L *vidēre*]
▸ **vo'yeurism** *n* ▸ **ˌvoyeur'istic** *adj*

VP *abbrev. for:* **1** verb phrase. **2** Vice President.

VPL *Jocular abbrev. for* visible panty line.

VR *abbrev. for:* **1** variant reading. **2** Victoria Regina. [L: Queen Victoria] **3** virtual reality.

V. Rev. *abbrev. for* Very Reverend.

vrou (frəʊ) *n S. African.* an Afrikaner woman, esp. a married woman. [from Afrik., from Du.]

vrystater ('freɪˌstɑːtə) *n S. African.* a native inhabitant of the Free State, esp. one who is White. [from Afrik., from Du. *vrij* free + *staat* state]

vs *abbrev. for* versus.

VS *abbrev. for* Veterinary Surgeon.

v.s. *abbrev. for* vide supra (see **vide**).

V-sign *n* **1** (in Britain) an offensive gesture made by sticking up the index and middle fingers with the palm of the hand inwards. **2** a similar gesture with the palm outwards meaning victory or peace.

VSO *abbrev. for:* **1** very superior old: used to indicate that a brandy, port, etc., is between 12 and 17 years old. **2** (in Britain) Voluntary Service Overseas: an organization that sends young volunteers to use and teach their skills in developing countries.

VSOP *abbrev. for* very special (*or* superior) old pale: used to indicate that a brandy, port, etc., is between 20 and 25 years old.

VTOL ('viːtɒl) *n* vertical takeoff and landing; a system in which an aircraft can take off and land vertically. Cf. **STOL.**

VTR *abbrev. for* video tape recorder.

V-type engine *n* a type of internal-combustion engine having two cylinder blocks attached to a single crankcase, the angle between the two blocks forming a V.

vug (vʌg) *n Mining.* a small cavity in a rock or vein, usually lined with crystals. [C19: from Cornish *vooga* cave]
▸ **'vuggy** *adj*

vulcanian (vʌl'keɪnɪən) *adj Geol.* of or relating to a volcanic eruption characterized by the explosive discharge of gases, fine ash, and viscous lava that hardens in the crater. [C17: after *Vulcan,* Roman god of fire and metalworking]

vulcanism ('vʌlkəˌnɪzəm) *n* a variant spelling of **volcanism.**

vulcanite ('vʌlkəˌnaɪt) *n* a hard usually black rubber produced by vulcanizing natural rubber with sulphur. It is used for electrical insulators, etc. Also called: **ebonite.**

vulcanize *or* **vulcanise** ('vʌlkəˌnaɪz) *vb* **vulcanizes, vulcanizing, vulcanized** *or* **vulcanises, vulcanising, vulcanised.** (*tr*) **1** to treat (rubber) with sulphur under heat and pressure to improve elasticity and strength or to produce a hard substance such as vulcanite. **2** to treat (substances other than rubber) by a similar process in order to improve their properties.
▸ **ˌvulcani'zation** *or* **ˌvulcani'sation** *n*

vulcanology (ˌvʌlkə'nɒlədʒɪ) *n* a variant spelling of **volcanology.**

Vulg. *abbrev. for* Vulgate.

vulgar ❶ ('vʌlgə) *adj* **1** marked by lack of taste, culture, delicacy, man-

THESAURUS

votary *n* **2** = **devotee,** adherent, aficionado, believer, disciple, follower

vote *n* **1** = **poll,** ballot, franchise, plebiscite, referendum, show of hands **6a** = **right to vote,** suffrage ◆ *vb* **9** = **cast one's vote,** ballot, elect, go to the polls, opt, return **14** *Informal* = **declare,** judge, pronounce, propose, recommend, suggest

vouch *vb* **1** *usually foll. by* **for** = **guarantee,** answer for, asseverate, back, certify, give assurance of, go bail for, stand witness, swear to **2** *usually foll. by* **for** = **confirm,** affirm, assert, attest to, support, uphold

voucher *n* **2** = **ticket,** coupon, token

vouchsafe *vb* **1** = **grant,** accord, cede, condescend to give, confer, deign, favour (someone) with, yield

vow *n* **1** = **promise,** oath, pledge, troth (*arch.*) ◆ *vb* **4, 6** = **promise,** affirm, consecrate, dedicate, devote, pledge, swear, undertake solemnly

voyage *n* **1** = **journey,** crossing, cruise, passage, travels, trip

vulgar *adj* **1** = **crude,** blue, boorish, cheap and nasty, coarse, common, common as muck, dirty, flashy, gaudy, gross, ill-bred, impolite, improper, indecent, indecorous, indelicate, low, nasty, naughty, off colour, ribald, risqué,

ners, etc.: *vulgar language.* **2** (*often cap.; usually prenominal*) denoting a form of a language, esp. of Latin, current among common people, esp. at a period when the formal language is archaic. **3** *Arch.* of or current among the great mass of common people. [C14: from L *vulgāris*, from *vulgus* the common people]
▸ˈ**vulgarly** *adv*

vulgar fraction *n* another name for **simple fraction.**

vulgarian 🅣 (vʌlˈgɛərɪən) *n* a vulgar person, esp. one who is rich or has pretensions to good taste.

vulgarism (ˈvʌlgəˌrɪzəm) *n* **1** a coarse, crude, or obscene expression. **2** a word or phrase found only in the vulgar form of a language.

vulgarity 🅣 (vʌlˈgærɪtɪ) *n, pl* **vulgarities. 1** the condition of being vulgar; lack of good manners. **2** a vulgar action, phrase, etc.

vulgarize *or* **vulgarise** (ˈvʌlgəˌraɪz) *vb* **vulgarizes, vulgarizing, vulgarized** *or* **vulgarises, vulgarising, vulgarised.** (*tr*) **1** to make commonplace or vulgar. **2** to make (something little known or difficult to understand) widely known or popular among the public.
▸ˌ**vulgariˈzation** *or* ˌ**vulgariˈsation** *n*

Vulgar Latin *n* any of the dialects of Latin spoken in the Roman Empire other than classical Latin.

vulgate (ˈvʌlgeɪt, -gɪt) *n Rare.* **1** a commonly recognized text or version. **2** the vernacular.

Vulgate (ˈvʌlgeɪt, -gɪt) *n* **a** (from the 13th century onwards) the fourth-century Latin version of the Bible produced by Jerome. **b** (*as modifier*): *the Vulgate version.* [C17: from Med. L, from LL *vulgāta editiō* popular version (of the Bible), from L *vulgāre* to make common]

vulnerable 🅣 (ˈvʌlnərəbᵊl) *adj* **1** capable of being physically or emotionally wounded or hurt. **2** open to temptation, censure, etc. **3** *Mil.* exposed to attack. **4** *Bridge.* (of a side who have won one game towards rubber) subject to increased bonuses or penalties. [C17: from LL, from L *vulnerāre* to wound, from *vulnus* a wound]
▸ˌ**vulneraˈbility** *n* ▸ˈ**vulnerably** *adv*

vulnerary (ˈvʌlnərərɪ) *Med.* ◆ *adj* **1** of or used to heal a wound. ◆ *n, pl* **vulneraries. 2** a vulnerary drug or agent. [C16: from L *vulnerārius* from *vulnus* wound]

vulpine (ˈvʌlpaɪn) *adj* **1** of, relating to, or resembling a fox. **2** crafty, clever, etc. [C17: from L *vulpīnus* foxlike, from *vulpēs* fox]

vulture (ˈvʌltʃə) *n* **1** any of various very large diurnal birds of prey of Africa, Asia, and warm parts of Europe, typically having broad wings and soaring flight and feeding on carrion. **2** any similar bird of North, Central, and South America. **3** a person or thing that preys greedily and ruthlessly on others, esp. the helpless. [C14: from OF *voltour*, from L *vultur*]
▸**vulturine** (ˈvʌltʃəˌraɪn) *or* ˈ**vulturous** *adj*

vulva (ˈvʌlvə) *n, pl* **vulvae** (-viː) *or* **vulvas.** the external genitals of human females, including the labia, mons veneris, clitoris, and the vaginal orifice. [C16: from L: covering, womb, matrix]
▸ˈ**vulvar** *adj*

vulvitis (vʌlˈvaɪtɪs) *n* inflammation of the vulva.

vv *abbrev. for* vice versa.

vv. *abbrev. for:* **1** versus. **2** *Music.* volumes.

THESAURUS

rude, suggestive, tasteless, tawdry, uncouth, unmannerly, unrefined **2** = **vernacular**, general, native, ordinary, unrefined
Antonyms *adj* ≠ **crude:** aristocratic, classical, decorous, elegant, genteel, high-brow, polite, refined, sophisticated, tasteful, upper-class, urbane, well-mannered

vulgarian *n* = **upstart**, arriviste, boor, churl, *nouveau riche,* parvenu, philistine

vulgarity *n* **1** = **crudeness**, bad taste, coarseness, crudity, gaudiness, grossness, indecorum, indelicacy, lack of refinement, ribaldry, rudeness, suggestiveness, tastelessness, tawdriness
Antonyms *n* decorum, gentility, good breeding, good manners, good taste, refinement, sensitivity, sophistication, tastefulness

vulnerable *adj* **1** = **susceptible**, sensitive, tender, thin-skinned, weak **3** *Military* = **exposed**, accessible, assailable, defenceless, open to attack, unprotected, wide open
Antonyms *adj* ≠ **susceptible:** immune, impervious, insensitive, thick-skinned ≠ **exposed:** guarded, invulnerable, unassailable, well-protected

w *or* **W** ('dʌbᵊl,juː) *n, pl* **w's, W's,** *or* **Ws. 1** the 23rd letter of the English alphabet. **2** a speech sound represented by this letter, usually a bilabial semivowel, as in *web*.

W *symbol for:* **1** *Chem.* tungsten. [from NL *wolframium*, from G *Wolfram*] **2** watt. **3** West. **4** women's (size). **5** *Physics.* work.

w. *abbrev. for:* **1** week. **2** weight. **3** *Cricket.* **3a** wide. **3b** wicket. **4** width. **5** wife. **6** with.

W. *abbrev. for:* **1** Wales. **2** Welsh.

WA *abbrev. for:* **1** Washington (state). **2** Western Australia.

WAAAF (formerly) *abbrev. for* Women's Auxiliary Australian Air Force.

WAAC (wæk) *n* (formerly) **1** *acronym for* Women's Army Auxiliary Corps. **2** Also called: **Waac.** a member of this corps.

WAAF (wæf) *n* (formerly) **1** *acronym for* Women's Auxiliary Air Force. **2** Also called: **Waaf.** a member of this force.

wabble ('wɒbᵊl) *vb* **wabbles, wabbling, wabbled,** *n* a variant spelling of **wobble.**

wacke ('wækə) *n Obs.* any of various soft earthy rocks derived from basalt. [C18: from G: rock, gravel, basalt]

wacko ('wækəʊ) *Inf.* ◆ *adj* **1** mad or eccentric. ◆ *n, pl* **wackos. 2** a mad or eccentric person. [C20: back formation from WACKY]

wacky Ⓣ ('wækɪ) *adj* **wackier, wackiest.** *Sl.* eccentric or unpredictable. [C19 (in dialect sense: a fool): from WHACK (hence, a *whacky*, a person who behaves as if he had been whacked on the head)]
▸ **'wackily** *adv* ▸ **'wackiness** *n*

wad Ⓣ (wɒd) *n* **1** a small mass or ball of fibrous or soft material, such as cotton wool, used esp. for packing or stuffing. **2a** a plug of paper, cloth, leather, etc., pressed against a charge to hold it in place in a muzzle-loading cannon. **2b** a disc of paper, felt, etc., used to hold in place the powder and shot in a shotgun cartridge. **3** a roll or bundle of something, esp. of banknotes. ◆ *vb* **wads, wadding, wadded. 4** to form (something) into a wad. **5** (*tr*) to roll into a wad or bundle. **6** (*tr*) **6a** to hold (a charge) in place with a wad. **6b** to insert a wad into (a gun). **7** (*tr*) to pack or stuff with wadding. [C14: from LL *wadda*]

wadding Ⓣ ('wɒdɪŋ) *n* **1a** any fibrous or soft substance used as padding, stuffing, etc. **1b** a piece of this. **2** material for wads used in cartridges or guns.

waddle Ⓣ ('wɒdᵊl) *vb* **waddles, waddling, waddled.** (*intr*) **1** to walk with short steps, rocking slightly from side to side. ◆ *n* **2** a swaying gait or motion. [C16: prob. frequentative of WADE]
▸ **'waddler** *n* ▸ **'waddling** *adj*

waddy ('wɒdɪ) *n, pl* **waddies. 1** a heavy wooden club used as a weapon by native Australians. ◆ *vb* **waddies, waddying, waddied. 2** (*tr*) to hit with a waddy. [C19: from Abor., ? based on E WOOD]

wade Ⓣ (weɪd) *vb* **wades, wading, waded. 1** to walk with the feet immersed in (water, a stream, etc.). **2** (*intr;* often foll. by *through*) to proceed with difficulty: *to wade through a book.* **3** (*intr;* foll. by *in* or *into*) to attack energetically. ◆ *n* **4** the act or an instance of wading. [OE *wadan*]
▸ **'wadable** *or* **'wadeable** *adj*

wader ('weɪdə) *n* **1** a person or thing that wades. **2** Also called: **wading bird.** any of various long-legged birds, esp. herons, storks, etc., that live near water and feed on fish, etc. **3** a Brit. name for **shore bird.**

waders ('weɪdəz) *pl n* long waterproof boots, sometimes extending to the chest like trousers, worn by anglers.

wadi *or* **wady** ('wɒdɪ) *n, pl* **wadies.** a watercourse in N Africa and Arabia, dry except in the rainy season. [C19: from Ar.]

wafer ('weɪfə) *n* **1** a thin crisp sweetened biscuit, served with ice cream, etc. **2** *Christianity.* a thin disc of unleavened bread used in the Eucharist. **3** *Pharmacol.* an envelope of rice paper enclosing a medicament. **4** *Electronics.* a large single crystal of semiconductor material, such as silicon, on which numerous integrated circuits are manufactured and then separated. **5** a small thin disc of adhesive material used to seal letters, etc. ◆ *vb* **6** (*tr*) to seal or fasten with a wafer. [C14: from OF *waufre,* from MLow G *wāfel*]
▸ **'wafery** *adj*

waffle[1] ('wɒfᵊl) *n* **a** a crisp golden-brown pancake with deep indentations on both sides. **b** (*as modifier*): *waffle iron.* [C19: from Du. *wafel* (earlier *wæfel*), of Gmc origin]

waffle[2] Ⓣ ('wɒfᵊl) *Inf., chiefly Brit.* ◆ *vb* **waffles, waffling, waffled. 1** (*intr;* often foll. by *on*) to speak or write in a vague and wordy manner. ◆ *n* **2** vague and wordy speech or writing. [C19: from ?]
▸ **'waffling** *adj, n*

waft Ⓣ (wɑːft, wɒft) *vb* **1** to carry or be carried gently on or as if on the air or water. ◆ *n* **2** the act or an instance of wafting. **3** something, such as a scent, carried on the air. **4** *Naut.* (formerly) a signal flag hoisted furled to signify various messages depending on where it was flown. [C16 (in obs. sense: to convey by ship): back formation from C15 *wafter* a convoy vessel, from MDu. *wachter* guard]

wag[1] Ⓣ (wæg) *vb* **wags, wagging, wagged. 1** to move or cause to move rapidly and repeatedly from side to side or up and down. **2** to move (the tongue) or (of the tongue) to be moved rapidly in talking, esp. in gossip. **3** to move (the finger) or (of the finger) to be moved from side to side, in or as in admonition. **4** *Sl.* to play truant (esp. in **wag it**). ◆ *n* **5** the act or an instance of wagging. [C13: from OE *wagian* to shake]

wag[2] Ⓣ (wæg) *n* a humorous or jocular person; wit. [C16: from ?]
▸ **'waggish** *adj*

wage Ⓣ (weɪdʒ) *n* **1** (*often pl*) payment in return for work or services, esp. that made to workers on a daily, hourly, weekly, or piecework basis. Cf. **salary. 2** (*pl*) *Econ.* the portion of the national income accruing to labour as earned income, as contrasted with the unearned income accruing to capital in the form of rent, interest, and dividends. **3** (*often pl*) recompense, return, or yield. ◆ *vb* **wages, waging, waged.** (*tr*) **4** to engage in. [C14: from OF *wagier* to pledge, from *wage,* of Gmc origin]
▸ **'wageless** *adj*

wage differential *n* the difference in wages between workers with different skills in the same industry or between those with comparable skills in different industries or localities.

wage earner *n* **1** a person who works for wages. **2** the person who earns money to support a household by working.

wage freeze *n* a statutory restriction on wage increases.

wage indexation *n* a linking of wage rises to increases in the cost of living usually in order to maintain real wages during periods of high inflation.

wager Ⓣ ('weɪdʒə) *n* **1** an agreement to pay an amount of money as a result of the outcome of an unsettled matter. **2** an amount staked on the outcome of such an event. **3 wager of battle.** (in medieval Britain) a pledge to do battle to decide guilt or innocence by single combat. **4 wager of law.** *English legal history.* a form of trial in which the accused offered to make oath of his innocence, supported by the oaths of 11 of his neighbours declaring their belief in his statements. ◆ *vb* **5** (when *tr, may take a clause as object*) to risk or bet (something) on the outcome of an unsettled matter. [C14: from Anglo-F *wageure* a pledge, from OF *wagier* to pledge; see WAGE]
▸ **'wagerer** *n*

wages council *n* (formerly, in Britain) a statutory body empowered to fix minimum wages in an industry; abolished in 1994.

wage slave *n Ironical.* a person dependent on a wage or salary.

wagga ('wɒgə) *n Austral.* a blanket or bed covering of sacks stitched together. [C19: after *Wagga Wagga,* a city in SE Australia]

waggle Ⓣ ('wægᵊl) *vb* **waggles, waggling, waggled. 1** to move or cause to move with a rapid shaking or wobbling motion. ◆ *n* **2** a rapid shaking or wobbling motion. [C16: from WAG[1]]
▸ **'waggly** *adj*

waggon ('wægən) *n* a variant spelling (esp. Brit.) of **wagon.**

wag-n-bietjie ('vɑːxᵊn,bɪkɪ) *n S. African.* any of various thorn bushes or trees. [from Afrik. *wag* wait + *n* a + *bietjie* bit]

Wagnerian (vɑːg'nɪərɪən) *adj* **1** of or suggestive of the dramatic musical compositions of Richard Wagner (1813–83), German composer, their massive scale, dramatic and emotional intensity, etc. ◆ *n also* **Wagnerite** ('vɑːgnə,raɪt). **2** a follower or disciple of the music or theories of Richard Wagner.

THESAURUS

wacky *adj Slang* = **eccentric,** crazy, daft (*inf.*), erratic, irrational, loony (*sl.*), nutty (*sl.*), odd, oddball (*inf.*), off-the-wall (*sl.*), outré, screwy (*inf.*), silly, unpredictable, wild, zany

wad *n* **1-3** = **mass,** ball, block, bundle, chunk, hunk, lump, plug, roll

wadding *n* **1** = **padding,** filler, lining, packing, stuffing

waddle *vb* **1** = **shuffle,** rock, sway, toddle, totter, wobble

wade *vb* **1** = **walk through,** ford, paddle, splash **2** *often foll. by* **through** = **plough through,** drudge at, labour at, peg away at, toil at, work one's way through **3** *foll. by* **in** *or* **into** = **launch oneself at,** assail, attack, get stuck in (*inf.*), go for, light into (*inf.*), set about, tackle, tear into (*inf.*)

waffle[2] *vb* **1** = **prattle,** blather, jabber, prate, rabbit (on) (*Brit. inf.*), verbalize, witter on (*inf.*) ◆ *n* **2** = **verbosity,** blather, jabber, padding, prating, prattle, prolixity, verbiage, wordiness

waft *vb* **1** = **carry,** bear, be carried, convey, drift, float, ride, transmit, transport ◆ *n* **2** = **current,** breath, breeze, draught, puff, whiff

wag[1] *vb* **1** = **wave,** bob, flutter, nod, oscillate, quiver, rock, shake, stir, vibrate, waggle, wiggle ◆ *n* **5** = **wave,** bob, flutter, nod, oscillation, quiver, shake, toss, vibration, waggle, wiggle

wag[2] *n* = **joker,** card (*inf.*), clown, comedian, comic, humorist, jester, wit

wage *n* **1** = **payment,** allowance, compensation, earnings, emolument, fee, hire, pay, recompense, remuneration, reward, stipend ◆ *vb* **4** = **engage in,** carry on, conduct, practise, proceed with, prosecute, pursue, undertake

wager *n* **1, 2** = **bet,** flutter (*Brit. inf.*), gamble, pledge, punt (*chiefly Brit.*), stake, venture ◆ *vb* **5** = **bet,** chance, gamble, hazard, lay, pledge, punt (*chiefly Brit.*), put on, risk, speculate, stake, venture

waggish *adj* = **humorous,** amusing, comical, droll, facetious, funny, impish, jesting, jocose, jocular, merry, mischievous, playful, puckish, risible, sportive, witty

waggle *vb* **1** = **wag,** flutter, oscillate, shake, wave, wiggle, wobble

wagon *or* **waggon** ('wægən) *n* **1** any of various types of wheeled vehicles, ranging from carts to lorries, esp. a vehicle with four wheels drawn by a horse, tractor, etc., and used for carrying heavy loads. **2** *Brit.* a railway freight truck, esp. an open one. **3** an obsolete word for **chariot**. **4 on** (*or* **off**) **the wagon.** *Inf.* abstaining (*or* no longer abstaining) from alcohol. [C16: from Du. *wagen* WAIN]
►'**wagonless** *or* '**waggonless** *adj*

wagoner *or* **waggoner** ('wægənə) *n* a person who drives a wagon.

wagonette *or* **waggonette** (ˌwægə'nɛt) *n* a light four-wheeled horse-drawn vehicle with two lengthwise seats facing each other behind a crosswise driver's seat.

wagon-lit (*French* vagõli) *n, pl* **wagons-lits** (vagõli). **1** a sleeping car on a European railway. **2** a compartment on such a car. [C19: from F, from *wagon* railway coach + *lit* bed]

wagonload *or* **waggonload** ('wægənˌləʊd) *n* the load that is or can be carried by a wagon.

wagon train *n* a supply train of horses and wagons, esp. one going over rough terrain.

wagon vault *n* another name for **barrel vault**.

wagtail ('wægˌteɪl) *n* any of various passerine songbirds of Eurasia and Africa, having a very long tail that wags when the bird walks.

Wahhabi *or* **Wahabi** (wə'hɑːbɪ) *n, pl* **Wahhabis** *or* **Wahabis.** a member of a strictly conservative Muslim sect founded in the 18th century.
►**Wah'habism** *or* **Wa'habism** *n*

wahine (wɑː'hiːnɪ) *n* **1** *NZ.* a Maori woman. **2** a Polynesian woman. [from Maori & Hawaiian]

wahoo (wɑː'huː, 'wɑːhuː) *n, pl* **wahoos.** a large fast-moving food and game fish of tropical seas. [from ?]

wah-wah ('wɑːˌwɑː) *n* **1** the sound made by a trumpet, cornet, etc., when the bell is alternately covered and uncovered. **2** an electronic attachment for an electric guitar, etc., that simulates this effect. [C20: imit.]

waif ❶ (weɪf) *n* **1** a person, esp. a child, who is homeless, friendless, or neglected. **2** anything found and not claimed, the owner being unknown. [C14: from Anglo-Norman, var. of OF *gaif*, from ON]
►'**waifˌlike** *adj*

wail ❶ (weɪl) *vb* **1** (*intr*) to utter a prolonged high-pitched cry, as of grief or misery. **2** (*intr*) to make a sound resembling such a cry: *the wind wailed in the trees.* **3** (*tr*) to lament, esp. with mournful sounds. ◆ *n* **4** a prolonged high-pitched mournful cry or sound. [C14: from ON]
►'**wailer** *n*

wain (weɪn) *n Chiefly poetic.* a farm wagon or cart. [OE *wægn*]

wainscot ('weɪnskət) *n* **1** Also called: **wainscoting** *or* **wainscotting.** a lining applied to the walls of a room, esp. one of wood panelling. **2** the lower part of the walls of a room, esp. when finished in a material different from the upper part. **3** fine-quality oak used as wainscot. ◆ *vb* **4** (*tr*) to line (a wall of a room) with a wainscot. [C14: from MLow G *wagenschot*, ?from *wagen* WAGON + *schot* planking]

wainwright ('weɪnˌraɪt) *n* a person who makes wagons.

waist (weɪst) *n* **1** *Anat.* the constricted part of the trunk between the ribs and hips. **2** the part of a garment covering the waist. **3** the middle part of an object that resembles the waist in narrowness or position. **4** the middle part of a ship. **5** the middle section of an aircraft fuselage. **6** the constriction between the thorax and abdomen in wasps and similar insects. [C14: from ?]
►'**waistless** *adj*

waistband ('weɪstˌbænd) *n* an encircling band of material to finish and strengthen a skirt or trousers at the waist.

waistcoat ('weɪsˌkəʊt) *n* **1** a man's sleeveless waistlength garment worn under a suit jacket, usually buttoning up the front. **2** a similar garment worn by women. ◆ US and Canad. name: **vest.**
►'**waistˌcoated** *adj*

waistline ('weɪstˌlaɪn) *n* **1** a line around the body at the narrowest part of the waist. **2** the intersection of the bodice and the skirt of a dress, etc., or the level of this.

wait ❶ (weɪt) *vb* **1** (when *intr*, often foll. by *for, until,* or *to*) to stay in one place or remain inactive in expectation (of something). **2** to delay temporarily or be temporarily delayed: *that work can wait.* **3** (when *intr*, usually foll. by *for*) (of things) to be ready or at hand; be in store (for a person): *supper was waiting for them when they got home.* **4** (*intr*) to act as a waiter or waitress. ◆ *n* **5** the act or an instance of waiting. **6** a period of waiting. **7** (*pl*) *Rare.* a band of musicians who go around the streets, esp. at Christmas, singing and playing carols. **8 lie in wait.** to prepare an ambush (for someone). ◆ See also **wait on, wait up.** [C12: from OF *waitier*]

wait-a-bit *n* any of various mainly tropical plants having sharp hooked thorns.

Waitangi Day (waɪ'tʌŋiː) *n* the national day of New Zealand (Feb. 6), commemorating the signing of the **Treaty of Waitangi** (1840) by Maori chiefs and a representative of the British Government. The treaty provided the basis for the British annexation of New Zealand.

waiter ❶ ('weɪtə) *n* **1** a man whose occupation is to serve at table, as in a restaurant. **2** an attendant at the London stock exchange or Lloyd's who carries messages: the modern equivalent of waiters who performed these duties in the 17th-century London coffee houses in which these institutions originated. **3** a person who waits. **4** a tray or salver.

waiting game *n* the postponement of action or decision in order to gain the advantage.

waiting list *n* a list of people waiting to obtain some object, treatment, status, etc.

waiting room *n* a room in which people may wait, as at a railway station, doctor's or dentist's surgery, etc.

wait on ❶ *vb* (*intr, prep*) **1** to serve at the table of. **2** to act as an attendant to. ◆ *sentence substitute.* **3** *Austral. & NZ.* stop! hold on! ◆ Also (for senses 1, 2): **wait upon.**

waitress ('weɪtrɪs) *n* **1** a woman who serves at table, as in a restaurant. ◆ *vb* (*intr*) **2** to act as a waitress.

wait up *vb* (*intr, adv*) to delay going to bed in order to await some event.

waive ❶ (weɪv) *vb* **waives, waiving, waived.** (*tr*) **1** to set aside or relinquish: *to waive one's rights.* **2** to refrain from enforcing or applying (a law, penalty, etc.). **3** to defer. [C13: from OF *weyver*, from *waif* abandoned; see WAIF]

waiver ❶ ('weɪvə) *n* **1** the voluntary relinquishment, expressly or by implication, of some claim or right. **2** the act or an instance of relinquishing a claim or right. **3** a formal statement in writing of such relinquishment. [C17: from OF *weyver* to relinquish]

wake[1] ❶ (weɪk) *vb* **wakes, waking, woke, woken. 1** (often foll. by *up*) to rouse or become roused from sleep. **2** (often foll. by *up*) to rouse or become roused from inactivity. **3** (*intr;* often foll. by *to* or *up to*) to become conscious or aware: *at last he woke up to the situation.* **4** (*intr*) to be or remain awake. ◆ *n* **5** a watch or vigil held over the body of a dead person during the night before burial. **6** (in Ireland) festivities held after a funeral. **7** the patronal or dedication festival of English parish churches. **8** a solemn or ceremonial vigil. **9** (*usually pl*) an annual holiday in various towns in Northern England, when the local factories close. [OE *wacian*]
►'**waker** *n*

> **USAGE NOTE** Where there is an object and the sense is the literal one *wake* (*up*) and *waken* are the commonest forms: *I wakened him; I woke him* (*up*). Both verbs are also commonly used without an object: *I woke up. Awake* and *awaken* are preferred to other forms of *wake* where the sense is a figurative one: *he awoke to the danger.*

wake[2] ❶ (weɪk) *n* **1** the waves or track left by a vessel or other object moving through water. **2** the track or path left by anything that has passed: *wrecked houses in the wake of the hurricane.* [C16: of Scand. origin]

wakeful ❶ ('weɪkfʊl) *adj* **1** unable or unwilling to sleep. **2** sleepless. **3** alert.
►'**wakefully** *adv* ►'**wakefulness** *n*

wakeless ('weɪklɪs) *adj* (of sleep) unbroken.

waken ❶ ('weɪkən) *vb* to rouse or be roused from sleep or some other inactive state.

> **USAGE NOTE** See at **wake**[1].

THESAURUS

waif *n* **1** = **stray**, foundling, orphan

wail *vb* **1, 3** = **cry**, bawl, bemoan, bewail, deplore, grieve, howl, keen, lament, ululate, weep, yowl ◆ *n* **3** = **cry**, complaint, grief, howl, keen, lament, lamentation, moan, ululation, weeping, yowl

wait *vb* **1, 2** = **remain**, abide, bide one's time, cool one's heels, dally, delay, hang fire, hold back, hold on (*inf.*), kick one's heels, linger, mark time, pause, rest, stand by, stay, tarry ◆ *n* **5, 6** = **delay**, entr'acte, halt, hold-up, interval, pause, rest, stay
Antonyms *vb* ≠ **remain:** depart, go, go away, leave, move off, quit, set off, take off (*inf.*)

waiter *n* **1** = **attendant**, server, steward *or* stewardess

wait on *vb* **1, 2** = **serve**, attend, minister to, tend

waive *vb* **1, 2** = **set aside**, abandon, defer, dispense with, forgo, give up, postpone, put off, refrain from, relinquish, remit, renounce, resign, surrender
Antonyms *vb* claim, demand, insist, maintain, press, profess, pursue, uphold

waiver *n* **1** = **renunciation**, abandonment, abdication, disclaimer, giving up, relinquishment, remission, resignation, setting aside, surrender

wake[1] *vb* **1** = **awaken**, arise, awake, bestir, come to, get up, rouse, rouse from sleep, stir **2** = **activate**, animate, arouse, awaken, enliven, excite, fire, galvanize, kindle, provoke, quicken, rouse, stimulate, stir up ◆ *n* **5** = **vigil**, deathwatch, funeral, watch
Antonyms *vb* ≠ **awaken:** catnap, doze, drop off (*inf.*), hibernate, nod off (*inf.*), sleep, snooze (*inf.*), take a nap

wake[2] *n* **1, 2** = **slipstream**, aftermath, backwash, path, track, trail, train, wash, waves

wakeful *adj* **1, 2** = **sleepless**, insomniac, restless, unsleeping **3** = **watchful**, alert, alive, attentive, heedful, observant, on guard, on the alert, on the lookout, on the qui vive, unsleeping, vigilant, wary
Antonyms *adj* ≠ **sleepless:** asleep, dormant, dozing ≠ **watchful:** dreamy, drowsy, heedless, inattentive, off guard, sleepy

waken *vb* = **awaken**, activate, animate, arouse, awake, be roused, come awake, come to, enliven, fire, galvanize, get up, kindle, quicken, rouse, stimulate, stir
Antonyms *vb* be inactive, doze, lie dormant, nap, repose, sleep, slumber, snooze (*inf.*)

wake-robin *n* any of a genus of North American herbaceous plants having a whorl of three leaves and three-petalled solitary flowers.

wake-up *n* **a wake-up to.** *Austral. sl.* fully alert to (a person, thing, action, etc.).

Waldenses (wɒl'dɛnsiːz) *pl n* the members of a small sect founded as a reform movement within the Roman Catholic Church by Peter Waldo, a merchant of Lyons, in the late 12th century.
▸**Wal'densian** *n, adj*

waldo ('wɔːldəʊ) *n, pl* **waldos, waldoes.** a gadget for manipulating objects by remote control. [C20: after *Waldo* F. Jones, an inventor, in a science-fiction story by Robert Heinlein]

Waldorf salad ('wɔːldɔːf) *n* a salad of diced apples, celery, and walnuts mixed with mayonnaise.

waldsterben ('wɔːld,stɜːbən) *n Ecology.* the symptoms of tree decline in central Europe from the 1970s, considered to be caused by atmospheric pollution. [C20: from G *Wald* forest + *sterben* to die]

wale Ⓣ (weɪl) *n* **1** the raised mark left on the skin after the stroke of a rod or whip. **2** the weave or texture of a fabric, such as the ribs in corduroy. **3** *Naut.* a ridge of planking along the rail of a ship. ◆ *vb* **wales, waling, waled. 4** (*tr*) to raise a wale or wales on by striking. **5** to weave with a wale. [OE *walu* weal]

walk Ⓣ (wɔːk) *vb* **1** (*intr*) to move along or travel on foot at a moderate rate; advance in such a manner that at least one foot is always on the ground. **2** (*tr*) to pass through, on, or over on foot, esp. habitually. **3** (*tr*) to cause, assist, or force to move along at a moderate rate: *to walk a dog.* **4** (*tr*) to escort or conduct by walking: *to walk someone home.* **5** (*intr*) (of ghosts, spirits, etc.) to appear or move about in visible form. **6** (*intr*) to follow a certain course or way of life: *to walk in misery.* **7** (*tr*) to bring into a certain condition by walking: *I walked my shoes to shreds.* **8** to disappear or be stolen: *Where's my pencil? It seems to have walked.* **9 walk it.** to win easily. **10 walk on air.** to be delighted or exhilarated. **11 walk tall.** *Inf.* to have self-respect or pride. **12 walk the streets. 12a** to be a prostitute. **12b** to wander round a town, esp. when looking for work or when homeless. ◆ *n* **13** the act or an instance of walking. **14** the distance or extent walked. **15** a manner of walking; gait. **16** a place set aside for walking; promenade. **17** a chosen profession or sphere of activity (esp. in **walk of life**). **18a** an arrangement of trees or shrubs in widely separated rows. **18b** the space between such rows. **19** an enclosed ground for the exercise or feeding of domestic animals, esp. horses. **20** *Chiefly Brit.* the route covered in the course of work, as by a tradesman or postman. **21** a procession; march: *Orange walk.* **22** *Obs.* the section of a forest controlled by a keeper. ◆ See also **walk away, walk into,** etc. [OE *wealcan*]
▸**'walkable** *adj*

walkabout ('wɔːkə,baʊt) *n* **1** a periodic nomadic excursion into the Australian bush made by a native Australian. **2** an occasion when celebrities, royalty, etc., walk among and meet the public. **3 go walkabout.** *Austral.* **3a** to wander through the bush. **3b** *Inf.* to be lost or misplaced. **3c** *Inf.* to lose one's concentration.

walk away *vb* (*intr, adv*) **1** to leave, esp. disregarding someone else's distress. **2 walk away with.** to achieve or win easily.

walker Ⓣ ('wɔːkə) *n* **1** a person who walks. **2** Also called: **baby walker.** a tubular frame on wheels or casters to support a baby learning to walk. **3** a similar support for walking, often with rubber feet, for use by disabled or infirm people.

walkie-talkie *or* **walky-talky** (,wɔːkɪ'tɔːkɪ) *n, pl* **walkie-talkies.** a small combined radio transmitter and receiver that can be carried around by one person: widely used by the police, medical services, etc.

walk-in *adj* **1** (of a cupboard) large enough to allow a person to enter and move about in. **2** (of a flat or house) in a suitable condition for immediate occupation.

walking papers *pl n Sl., chiefly US & Canad.* notice of dismissal.

walking stick *n* **1** a stick or cane carried in the hand to assist walking. **2** the usual US name for **stick insect.**

walk into *vb* (*intr, prep*) to meet with unwittingly: *to walk into a trap.*

Walkman ('wɔːkmən) *n Trademark.* a small portable cassette player with headphones.

walk off *vb* **1** (*intr*) to depart suddenly. **2** (*tr, adv*) to get rid of by walking: *to walk off an attack of depression.* **3 walk (a person) off his** *or* **her feet.** to make (a person) walk so fast or far that he or she is exhausted. **4 walk off with. 4a** to steal. **4b** to win, esp. easily.

walk-on *n* **a** a small part in a play or theatrical entertainment, esp. one without any lines. **b** (*as modifier*): *a walk-on part.*

walk out Ⓣ *vb* (*intr, adv*) **1** to leave without explanation, esp. in anger. **2** to go on strike. **3 walk out on.** *Inf.* to abandon or desert. **4 walk out with.** *Brit., obs. or dialect.* to court or be courted by. ◆ *n* **walkout. 5** a strike by workers. **6** the act of leaving a meeting, conference, etc., as a protest.

walkover Ⓣ ('wɔːk,əʊvə) *n* **1** *Inf.* an easy or unopposed victory. **2** *Horse racing.* **2a** the running or walking over the course by the only contestant entered in a race at the time of starting. **2b** a race won in this way. ◆ *vb* **walk over.** (*intr, mainly prep*) **3** (*also adv*) to win a race by a walkover. **4** *Inf.* to beat (an opponent) conclusively or easily.

walk socks *pl n NZ.* knee-length, usually woollen, stockings.

walk through *Theatre.* ◆ *vb* **1** (*tr*) to act or recite (a part) in a perfunctory manner, as at a first rehearsal. ◆ *n* **walk-through. 2** a rehearsal of a part.

walkway ('wɔːk,weɪ) *n* **1** a path designed and sometimes landscaped for pedestrian use. **2** a passage or path, esp. one for walking over machinery, connecting buildings, etc.

wall Ⓣ (wɔːl) *n* **1a** a vertical construction made of stone, brick, wood, etc., with a length and height much greater than its thickness, used to enclose, divide, or support. **1b** (*as modifier*): *wall hangings.* Related adj: **mural. 2** (*often pl*) a structure or rampart built to protect and surround a position or place for defensive purposes. **3** *Anat.* any lining, membrane, or investing part that encloses or bounds a bodily cavity or structure: *abdominal wall.* Technical name: **paries.** Related adj: **parietal. 4** anything that suggests a wall in function or effect: *a wall of fire.* **5 drive** (*or* **push**) **to the wall.** to force into an awkward situation. **6 go to the wall.** *Inf.* to be ruined. **7 go** (*or* **drive**) **up the wall.** *Sl.* to become (*or* cause to become) crazy or furious. **8 have one's back to the wall.** to be in a difficult situation. ◆ *vb* (*tr*) **9** to protect, provide, or confine with or as if with a wall. **10** (often foll. by *up*) to block (an opening) with a wall. **11** (often foll. by *in* or *up*) to seal by or within a wall or walls. [OE *weall,* from L *vallum* palisade, from *vallus* stake]
▸**walled** *adj* ▸**'wall-less** *adj*

wallaby ('wɒləbɪ) *n, pl* **wallabies** *or* **wallaby.** any of various herbivorous marsupials of Australia and New Guinea, similar to but smaller than kangaroos. [C19: from Abor. *wolabā*]

Wallaby ('wɒləbɪ) *n, pl* **Wallabies.** a member of the international rugby union football team of Australia.

Wallace's line ('wɒlɪsɪz) *n* the hypothetical boundary between the Oriental and Australasian zoogeographical regions, which runs through Indonesia and SE of the Philippines. [C20: after A. R. *Wallace* (1823–1913), Brit. naturalist]

wallah *or* **walla** ('wɒlə) *n* (*usually in combination*) *Inf.* a person involved with or in charge of (a specified thing): *the book wallah.* [C18: from Hindi *-wālā* from Sansk. *pāla* protector]

wallaroo (,wɒlə'ruː) *n, pl* **wallaroos** *or* **wallaroo.** a large stocky Australian kangaroo of rocky or mountainous regions. [C19: from Abor. *wolarū*]

wall bars *pl n* a series of horizontal bars attached to a wall and used in gymnastics.

wallboard ('wɔːl,bɔːd) *n* a thin board made of materials, such as compressed wood fibres or gypsum plaster, between stiff paper, and used to cover walls, partitions, etc.

wall creeper *n* a pink-and-grey woodpecker-like songbird of Eurasian mountain regions.

walled plain *n* any of the largest of the lunar craters, having diameters between 50 and 300 kilometres.

wallet Ⓣ ('wɒlɪt) *n* **1** a small folding case, usually of leather, for holding paper money, documents, etc. **2** *Arch., chiefly Brit.* a rucksack or knapsack. [C14: of Gmc origin]

walleye ('wɔːl,aɪ) *n, pl* **walleyes** *or* **walleye. 1** a divergent squint. **2** opacity of the cornea. **3** an eye having a white or light-coloured iris. **4** Also called: **walleyed pike.** a North American pikeperch valued as a food and game fish. [back formation from earlier *walleyed,* from ON *vagleygr,* from *vage* ? a film over the eye + *-eygr* -eyed, from *auga* eye; infl. by WALL]
▸**'wall,eyed** *adj*

wallflower ('wɔːl,flaʊə) *n* **1** Also called: **gillyflower.** a cruciferous plant of S Europe, grown for its clusters of yellow, orange, brown, red, or purple fragrant flowers and naturalized on old walls, cliffs, etc. **2** *Inf.* a person who stays on the fringes of a dance or party on account of lacking a partner or being shy.

THESAURUS

wale *n* **1 = mark,** contusion, scar, streak, stripe, weal, welt, wheal

walk *vb* **1, 2 = go,** advance, amble, foot it, go by shanks's pony (*inf.*), go on foot, hike, hoof it (*sl.*), march, move, pace, perambulate, promenade, saunter, step, stride, stroll, traipse (*inf.*), tramp, travel on foot, tread, trek, trudge **4 = escort,** accompany, convoy, take ◆ *n* **13 = stroll,** constitutional, hike, march, perambulation, promenade, ramble, saunter, traipse (*inf.*), tramp, trek, trudge, turn **15 = gait,** carriage, manner of walking, pace, step, stride **16 = path,** aisle, alley, avenue, esplanade, footpath, lane, pathway, pavement, promenade, sidewalk, trail **17** *As in* **walk of life = profession,** area, arena, calling, career, course, field, line, métier, sphere, trade, vocation

walker *n* **1 = pedestrian,** footslogger, hiker, rambler, wayfarer

walk out *vb* **1 = leave suddenly,** flounce out, get up and go, storm out, take off (*inf.*), vote with one's feet **2 = go on strike,** down tools, stop work, strike, take industrial action, withdraw one's labour **3 walk out on** *Informal* **= abandon,** chuck (*inf.*), desert, forsake, jilt, leave, leave in the lurch, pack in (*inf.*), run away from, strand, throw over ◆ *n* **walkout 5 = strike,** industrial action, protest, stoppage
Antonyms *vb* ≠ **abandon:** be loyal to, defend, remain, stand by, stay, stick with, support, uphold

walkover *n* **1** *Informal* **= pushover** (*sl.*), breeze (*US & Canad. inf.*), cakewalk (*inf.*), child's play (*inf.*), cinch (*sl.*), doddle (*Brit. sl.*), easy victory, picnic (*inf.*), piece of cake (*inf.*), snap (*inf.*)
Antonyms *n* effort, grind (*inf.*), labour, ordeal, strain, struggle, trial

wall *n* **1 = partition,** divider, enclosure, panel, screen **2 = barricade,** breastwork, bulwark, embankment, fortification, palisade, parapet, rampart, stockade **6 go to the wall** *Informal* **= fail,** be ruined, collapse, fall, go bust (*inf.*), go under **7 drive up the wall** *Slang* **= infuriate,** aggravate (*inf.*), annoy, dement, derange, drive crazy (*inf.*), drive insane, exasperate, get on one's nerves (*inf.*), irritate, madden, send off one's head (*sl.*), try

wallet *n* **1 = holder,** case, notecase, pocketbook, pouch, purse

wall of death *n* (at a fairground) a giant cylinder round the inside vertical walls of which a motorcyclist rides.

Walloon (wɒˈluːn) *n* **1** a member of a French-speaking people living chiefly in S Belgium and adjacent parts of France. **2** the French dialect of Belgium. ◆ *adj* **3** of or characteristic of the Walloons or their dialect. [C16: from OF *Wallon*, from Med. L: foreigner, of Gmc origin]

wallop ❶ (ˈwɒləp) *vb* **wallops, walloping, walloped. 1** (*tr*) *Inf.* to beat soundly; strike hard. **2** (*tr*) *Inf.* to defeat utterly. **3** (*intr*) (of liquids) to boil violently. ◆ *n* **4** *Inf.* a hard blow. **5** *Inf.* the ability to hit powerfully, as of a boxer. **6** *Inf.* a forceful impression. **7** *Brit. sl.* beer. [C14: from OF *waloper* to gallop, from OF *galoper*, from ?]

walloper (ˈwɒləpə) *n* **1** a person or thing that wallops. **2** *Austral. sl.* a policeman.

walloping (ˈwɒləpɪŋ) *Inf.* ◆ *n* **1** a thrashing. ◆ *adj* **2** (intensifier): *a walloping drop in sales.*

wallow ❶ (ˈwɒləʊ) *vb* (*intr*) **1** (esp. of certain animals) to roll about in mud, water, etc., for pleasure. **2** to move about with difficulty. **3** to indulge oneself in possessions, emotion, etc.: *to wallow in self-pity.* ◆ *n* **4** the act or an instance of wallowing. **5** a muddy place where animals wallow. [OE *wealwian* to roll (in mud)]
▸ˈ**wallower** *n*

wallpaper (ˈwɔːlˌpeɪpə) *n* **1** paper usually printed or embossed with designs for pasting onto walls and ceilings. **2** *Computing.* a picture or pattern on a computer screen between and behind program icons and windows. ◆ *vb* **3** to cover (a surface) with wallpaper.

wall pepper *n* a small Eurasian plant having yellow flowers and acrid-tasting leaves.

wall plate *n* a horizontal timber member placed along the top of a wall to support the ends of joists, rafters, etc., and distribute the load.

wallposter (ˈwɔːlˌpəʊstə) *n* (in China) a bulletin or political message painted in large characters on a wall.

wall rocket *n* any of several yellow-flowered European cruciferous plants that grow on old walls and in waste places.

wall rue *n* a delicate fern that grows in rocky crevices and walls in North America and Eurasia.

Wall Street *n* a street in lower Manhattan, New York, where the Stock Exchange and major banks are situated, regarded as the embodiment of American finance.

wall-to-wall *adj* **1** (esp. of carpeting) completely covering a floor. **2** *Inf.* nonstop; widespread: *wall-to-wall sales.*

wally (ˈwɒlɪ) *n, pl* **wallies.** *Sl.* a stupid person. [C20: shortened from the name *Walter*]

walnut (ˈwɔːlˌnʌt) *n* **1** any of a genus of deciduous trees of America, SE Europe, and Asia. They have aromatic leaves and flowers in catkins and are grown for their edible nuts and for their wood. **2** the nut of any of these trees, having a wrinkled two-lobed seed and a hard wrinkled shell. **3** the wood of any of these trees, used in making furniture, etc. **4** a light yellowish-brown colour. ◆ *adj* **5** made from the wood of a walnut tree: *a walnut table.* **6** of the colour walnut. [OE *walh-hnutu*, lit.: foreign nut]

Walpurgis Night (vælˈpʊəgɪs) *n* the eve of May 1, believed in German folklore to be the night of a witches' sabbath on the Brocken, in the Harz Mountains. [C19: translation of G *Walpurgisnacht*, the eve of the feast day of St Walpurga, 8th-cent. abbess in Germany]

walrus (ˈwɔːlrəs, ˈwɒl-) *n, pl* **walruses** *or* **walrus.** a mammal of northern seas, having a tough thick skin, upper canine teeth enlarged as tusks, and coarse whiskers, and feeding mainly on shellfish. [C17: prob. from Du., of Scand. origin]

walrus moustache *n* a long thick moustache drooping at the ends.

waltz (wɔːls) *n* **1** a ballroom dance in triple time in which couples spin around as they progress round the room. **2** a piece of music composed for or in the rhythm of this dance. ◆ *vb* **3** to dance or lead (someone) in or as in a waltz. **4** (*intr*) to move in a sprightly and self-assured manner. **5** (*intr*) *Inf.* to succeed easily. **6 waltz Matilda** *Austral.* See **Matilda.** [C18: from G *Walzer*, from MHG *walzen* to roll]

waltzer (ˈwɔːlsə) *n* **1** a person who waltzes. **2** a fairground roundabout on which people are spun round and moved up and down as it revolves.

wampum (ˈwɒmpəm) *n* (formerly) money used by North American Indians, made of cylindrical shells strung or woven together. Also called: **peag, peage.** [C17: of Amerind origin, short for *wampumpeag*, from *wampompeag*, from *wampan* light + *api* string + *-ag* pl. suffix]

wan ❶ (wɒn) *adj* **wanner, wannest. 1** unnaturally pale, esp. from sickness, grief, etc. **2** suggestive of ill health, unhappiness, etc. **3** (of light, stars, etc.) faint or dim. [OE *wann* dark]
▸ˈ**wanly** *adv* ▸ˈ**wanness** *n*

wand ❶ (wɒnd) *n* **1** a slender supple stick or twig. **2** a thin rod carried as a symbol of authority. **3** a rod used by a magician, etc. **4** *Inf.* a conductor's baton. **5** *Archery.* a marker used to show the distance at which the archer stands from the target. [C12: from ON *vǫndr*]

wander ❶ (ˈwɒndə) *vb* (*mainly intr*) **1** (*also tr*) to move or travel about, in, or through (a place) without any definite purpose or destination. **2** to proceed in an irregular course. **3** to go astray, as from a path or course. **4** (of thoughts, etc.) to lose concentration. **5** to think or speak incoherently or illogically. ◆ *n* **6** the act or an instance of wandering. [OE *wandrian*]
▸ˈ**wanderer** *n* ▸ˈ**wandering** *adj, n*

wandering albatross *n* a large albatross having a very wide wingspan and a white plumage with black wings.

wandering Jew *n* any of several related creeping or trailing plants of tropical America, such as tradescantia.

Wandering Jew *n* (in medieval legend) a character condemned to roam the world eternally because he mocked Christ on the day of the Crucifixion.

wanderlust ❶ (ˈwɒndəˌlʌst) *n* a great desire to travel and rove about. [from G *Wanderlust*, lit.: wander desire]

wanderoo (ˌwɒndəˈruː) *n, pl* **wanderoos.** a macaque monkey of India and Sri Lanka, having black fur with a ruff of long greyish fur on each side of the face. [C17: from Sinhalese *vanduru* monkeys, lit.: forest-dwellers]

wandoo (wɒnˈduː) *n* a eucalyptus tree of W Australia, having white bark and durable wood. [from Abor.]

wane ❶ (weɪn) *vb* **wanes, waning, waned.** (*intr*) **1** (of the moon) to show a gradually decreasing portion of illuminated surface, between full moon and new moon. **2** to decrease gradually in size, strength, power, etc. **3** to draw to a close. ◆ *n* **4** a decrease, as in size, strength, power, etc. **5** the period during which the moon wanes. **6** a drawing to a close. **7** a rounded surface or defective edge of a plank, where the bark was. **8 on the wane.** in a state of decline. [OE *wanian* (vb)]
▸ˈ**waney** *or* ˈ**wany** *adj*

wangle ❶ (ˈwæŋgᵊl) *Inf.* ◆ *vb* **wangles, wangling, wangled. 1** (*tr*) to use devious methods to get or achieve (something) for (oneself or another): *he wangled himself a salary increase.* **2** to manipulate or falsify (a situation, etc.). ◆ *n* **3** the act or an instance of wangling. [C19: orig. printers' sl., ? a blend of WAGGLE & dialect *wankle* wavering, from OE *wancol*]
▸ˈ**wangler** *n*

wanigan *or* **wannigan** (ˈwɒnɪgən) *n Canad.* **1** a lumberjack's chest or box. **2** a cabin, caboose, or houseboat. [C19: from Algonquian]

wank (wæŋk) *Taboo sl.* ◆ *vb* **1** (*intr*) to masturbate. ◆ *n* **2** an instance of wanking. [from ?]

wankel engine (ˈwæŋkᵊl) *n* a type of rotary internal-combustion engine without reciprocating parts. It consists of a curved triangular-shaped piston rotating in an elliptical combustion chamber. [C20: after Felix *Wankel* (1902–88), G engineer who invented it]

wanker (ˈwæŋkə) *n Sl.* **1** *Taboo.* a person who wanks; masturbator. **2** *Derog.* a worthless fellow.

wannabe *or* **wannabee** (ˈwɒnəˌbiː) *n Inf.* **a** a person who desires to be, or be like, something or someone else. **b** (*as modifier*): *a wannabe film star.* [C20: phonetic shortening of *want to be*]

want ❶ (wɒnt) *vb* **1** (*tr*) to feel a need or longing for: *I want a new hat.* **2** (when *tr, may take a clause as object or an infinitive*) to wish, need, or de-

THESAURUS

wallop *Informal vb* **1** = **hit**, batter, beat, belt (*inf.*), buffet, chin (*sl.*), clobber (*sl.*), deck (*sl.*), lambast(e), lay one on (*sl.*), paste (*sl.*), pound, pummel, punch, slug, smack, strike, swipe, thrash, thump, whack **2** = **beat**, best, blow out of the water (*sl.*), clobber (*sl.*), crush, defeat, drub, hammer (*inf.*), lick (*inf.*), rout, run rings around (*inf.*), stuff (*sl.*), thrash, trounce, vanquish, wipe the floor with (*inf.*), worst ◆ *n* **4** = **blow**, bash, belt (*inf.*), haymaker (*sl.*), kick, punch, slug, smack, swipe, thump, thwack, whack

wallow *vb* **1** = **roll about**, lie, splash around, tumble, welter **3** = **revel**, bask, delight, glory, indulge oneself, luxuriate, relish, take pleasure
Antonyms *vb* ≠ **revel:** abstain, avoid, do without, eschew, forgo, give up, refrain

wan *adj* **1** = **pale**, anaemic, ashen, bloodless, cadaverous, colourless, discoloured, ghastly, like death warmed up (*inf.*), livid, pallid, pasty, sickly, washed out, waxen, wheyfaced, white **3** = **dim**, faint, feeble, pale, weak
Antonyms *adj* ≠ **pale:** blooming, bright, flourishing, glowing, healthy, roseate, rosy, rubicund, ruddy, vibrant

wand *n* **1-4** = **stick**, baton, rod, sprig, twig, withe, withy

wander *vb* **1, 2** = **roam**, cruise, drift, knock about *or* around, meander, mooch around (*sl.*), peregrinate, ramble, range, rove, straggle, stravaig (*Scot. & N English dialect*), stray, stroll, traipse (*inf.*) **3** = **deviate**, depart, digress, divagate (*rare*), diverge, err, get lost, go astray, go off at a tangent, go off course, lapse, lose concentration, lose one's train of thought, lose one's way, swerve, veer **5** = **rave**, babble, be delirious, be incoherent, ramble, speak incoherently, talk nonsense ◆ *n* **6** = **excursion**, cruise, meander, peregrination, ramble, traipse (*inf.*)
Antonyms *vb* ≠ **deviate:** comply, conform, fall in with, follow, run with the pack, toe the line

wanderer *n* **1** = **traveller**, bird of passage, drifter, gypsy, itinerant, nomad, rambler, ranger, rolling stone, rover, stroller, vagabond, vagrant, voyager

wandering *adj* **1** = **nomadic**, drifting, homeless, itinerant, migratory, peripatetic, rambling, rootless, roving, strolling, travelling, vagabond, vagrant, voyaging, wayfaring

wanderlust *n* = **restlessness**, itchy feet (*inf.*), urge to travel

wane *vb* **2, 3** = **decline**, abate, atrophy, decrease, die out, dim, diminish, draw to a close, drop, dwindle, ebb, fade, fade away, fail, lessen, sink, subside, taper off, weaken, wind down, wither ◆ *n* **8 on the wane** = **declining**, at its lowest ebb, dropping, dwindling, dying out, ebbing, fading, lessening, obsolescent, on its last legs, on the decline, on the way out, subsiding, tapering off, weakening, withering
Antonyms *vb* ≠ **decline:** blossom, brighten, develop, expand, grow, improve, increase, rise, strengthen, wax

wangle *vb* **1, 2** *Informal* = **contrive**, arrange, bring off, engineer, fiddle (*inf.*), finagle (*inf.*), fix (*inf.*), manipulate, manoeuvre, pull off, scheme, work (*inf.*)

want *vb* **1** = **desire**, covet, crave, eat one's heart out over, feel a need for, hanker after, have a

sire (something or to do something): *he wants to go home.* **3** (*intr;* usually used with a negative and often foll. by *for*) to be lacking or deficient (in something necessary or desirable): *the child wants for nothing.* **4** (*tr*) to feel the absence of: *lying on the ground makes me want my bed.* **5** (*tr*) to fall short by (a specified amount). **6** (*tr*) *Chiefly Brit.* to have need of or require (doing or being something): *your shoes want cleaning.* **7** (*intr*) to be destitute. **8** (*tr; often passive*) to seek or request the presence of: *you're wanted upstairs.* **9** (*tr; takes an infinitive*) *Inf.* should or ought (to do something): *you don't want to go out so late.* ◆ *n* **10** the act or an instance of wanting. **11** anything that is needed, desired, or lacked: *to supply someone's wants.* **12** a lack, shortage, or absence: *for want of common sense.* **13** the state of being in need: *the state should help those in want.* **14** a sense of lack; craving. [C12 (vb, in the sense: it is lacking), C13 (n): from ON *vanta* to be deficient]
▸ **'wanter** *n*

want ad *n Inf.* a classified advertisement in a newspaper, magazine, etc., for something wanted, such as property or employment.

wanting Ⓣ ('wɒntɪŋ) *adj* (*postpositive*) **1** lacking or absent. **2** not meeting requirements or expectations: *you have been found wanting.*

wanton Ⓣ ('wɒntən) *adj* **1** dissolute, licentious, or immoral. **2** without motive, provocation, or justification: *wanton destruction.* **3** maliciously and unnecessarily cruel. **4** unrestrained: *wanton spending.* **5** *Arch. or poetic.* playful or capricious. **6** *Arch.* (of vegetation, etc.) luxuriant. ◆ *n* **7** a licentious person, esp. a woman. ◆ *vb* **8** (*intr*) to behave in a wanton manner. [C13 *wantowen* (in the obs. sense: unruly): from *wan-* (prefix equivalent to UN-[1]) + *-towen*, from OE *togen* brought up, from *tēon* to bring up]
▸ **'wantonly** *adv* ▸ **'wantonness** *n*

wapentake ('wɒpən,teɪk, 'wæp-) *n English legal history.* a subdivision of certain shires or counties, esp. in the Midlands and North of England, corresponding to the hundred in other shires. [OE *wǣpen(ge)tæc*]

wapiti ('wɒpɪtɪ) *n, pl* **wapitis.** a large North American deer with large much-branched antlers, now also found in New Zealand. [C19: of Amerind origin, lit.: white deer, from *wap* (unattested) white; from the animal's white tail and rump]

war Ⓣ (wɔː) *n* **1** open armed conflict between two or more parties, nations, or states. Related adj: **belligerent** (see sense 2). **2** a particular armed conflict: *the 1973 war in the Middle East.* **3** the techniques of armed conflict as a study, science, or profession. **4** any conflict or contest: *the war against crime.* **5** (*modifier*) of, resulting from, or characteristic of war: *war damage; a war story.* **6 in the wars.** *Inf.* (esp. of a child) hurt or knocked about, esp. as a result of quarrelling and fighting. ◆ *vb* **wars, warring, warred. 7** (*intr*) to conduct a war. [C12: from ONorthern F *werre* (var. of OF *guerre*), of Gmc origin]

War. *abbrev. for* Warwickshire.

waratah ('wɒrətə) *n Austral.* a shrub having dark green leaves and clusters of crimson flowers. [from Abor.]

warble[1] Ⓣ ('wɔːbᵊl) *vb* **warbles, warbling, warbled. 1** to sing (words, songs, etc.) with trills, runs, and other embellishments. **2** (*tr*) to utter in a song. ◆ *n* **3** the act or an instance of warbling. [C14: via OF *werbler*, of Gmc origin]

warble[2] ('wɔːbᵊl) *n Vet. science.* **1** a small lumpy abscess under the skin of cattle caused by the larvae of the warble fly. **2** a hard lump of tissue on a horse's back, caused by prolonged friction of a saddle. [C16: from ?]

warble fly *n* any of a genus of hairy beelike dipterous flies, the larvae of which produce warbles in cattle.

warbler ('wɔːblə) *n* **1** a person or thing that warbles. **2** a small active passerine songbird of the Old World having a cryptic plumage and slender bill, that is an arboreal insectivore. **3** a small bird of an American family, similar to the Old World songbird but often brightly coloured.

war correspondent *n* a journalist who reports on a war from the scene of action.

war crime *n* a crime committed in wartime in violation of the accepted customs, such as ill-treatment of prisoners, etc.
▸ **war criminal** *n*

war cry Ⓣ *n* **1** a rallying cry used by combatants in battle. **2** a cry, slogan, etc., used to rally support for a cause.

ward Ⓣ (wɔːd) *n* **1** (in many countries) one of the districts into which a city, town, parish, or other area is divided for administration, election of representatives, etc. **2a** a room in a hospital, esp. one for patients requiring similar kinds of care: *a maternity ward.* **2b** (*as modifier*): *ward maid.* **3** one of the divisions of a prison. **4** an open space enclosed within the walls of a castle. **5** *Law.* Also called: **ward of court.** a person, esp. a minor or one legally incapable of managing his own affairs, placed under the control or protection of a guardian or of a court. **6** the state of being under guard or in custody. **7** a means of protection. **8a** an internal ridge or bar in a lock that prevents an incorrectly cut key from turning. **8b** a corresponding groove cut in a key. ◆ *vb* **9** (*tr*) *Arch.* to guard or protect. ◆ See also **ward off.** [OE *weard* protector]
▸ **'wardless** *adj*

-ward *suffix.* **1** (*forming adjectives*) indicating direction towards: *a backward step.* **2** (*forming adverbs*) a variant and the usual US and Canad. form of **-wards.** [OE *-weard* towards]

war dance *n* a ceremonial dance performed before going to battle or after victory, esp. by certain North American Indian peoples.

warden Ⓣ ('wɔːdᵊn) *n* **1** a person who has the charge or care of something, esp. a building, or someone. **2** a public official, esp. one responsible for the enforcement of certain regulations: *traffic warden.* **3** a person employed to patrol a national park or a safari park. **4** *Chiefly US & Canad.* the chief officer in charge of a prison. **5** *Brit.* the principal of any of various universities or colleges. **6** See **churchwarden** (sense 1). [C13: from OF *wardein*, from *warder* to guard, of Gmc origin]

warder Ⓣ ('wɔːdə) *or* (*fem*) **wardress** *n* **1** *Chiefly Brit.* an officer in charge of prisoners in a jail. **2** a person who guards or has charge of something. [C14: from Anglo-F *wardere*, from OF *warder* to guard, of Gmc origin]

ward heeler *n US politics, disparaging.* a party worker who canvasses votes and performs chores for a political boss. Also called: **heeler.**

ward off Ⓣ *vb* (*tr, adv*) to turn aside or repel.

wardrobe Ⓣ ('wɔːdrəʊb) *n* **1** a tall closet or cupboard, with a rail or hooks on which to hang clothes. **2** the total collection of articles of clothing belonging to one person. **3a** the collection of costumes belonging to a theatre or theatrical company. **3b** (*as modifier*): *wardrobe mistress.* [C14: from OF *warderobe*, from *warder* to guard + *robe* ROBE]

wardrobe trunk *n* a large upright rectangular travelling case, usually opening longitudinally, with one side having a hanging rail, the other having drawers or compartments.

wardroom ('wɔːd,ruːm, -,rʊm) *n* **1** the quarters assigned to the officers (except the captain) of a warship. **2** the officers of a warship collectively, excepting the captain.

-wards *or* **-ward** *suffix forming adverbs.* indicating direction towards: *a step backwards.* Cf. **-ward.** [OE *-weardes* towards]

wardship ('wɔːdʃɪp) *n* the state of being a ward.

ware[1] (wɛə) *n* (*often in combination*) **1** (*functioning as sing*) articles of the same kind or material: *silverware.* **2** porcelain or pottery of a specified type: *jasper ware.* ◆ See also **wares.** [OE *waru*]

ware[2] (wɛə) *vb Arch.* another word for **beware.** [OE *wær*. See AWARE, BEWARE]

THESAURUS

fancy for, have a yen for (*inf.*), hope for, hunger for, long for, pine for, set one's heart on, thirst for, wish, would give one's eyeteeth for, yearn for **2, 3 = need**, be able to do with, be deficient in, be short of, be without, call for, demand, fall short in, have need of, lack, miss, require, stand in need of ◆ *n* **10, 11, 14 = wish**, appetite, craving, demand, desire, fancy, hankering, hunger, longing, necessity, need, requirement, thirst, yearning, yen (*inf.*) **12 = lack**, absence, dearth, default, deficiency, famine, insufficiency, paucity, scantiness, scarcity, shortage **13 = poverty**, destitution, indigence, need, neediness, pauperism, penury, privation
Antonyms *vb* ≠ **desire:** detest, dislike, hate, loathe, reject, spurn ≠ **need:** be sated, have, own, possess ◆ *n* ≠ **lack:** abundance, adequacy, excess, plenty, sufficiency, surfeit, surplus ≠ **poverty:** comfort, ease, luxury, wealth

wanting *adj* **1 = lacking**, absent, incomplete, less, missing, short, shy **2 = inadequate**, defective, deficient, disappointing, faulty, imperfect, inferior, leaving much to be desired, not good enough, not up to expectations, not up to par, patchy, pathetic, poor, sketchy, substandard, unsound
Antonyms *adj* ≠ **lacking:** complete, full, replete, saturated ≠ **inadequate:** adequate, enough, satisfactory, sufficient

wanton *adj* **1 = promiscuous**, abandoned, dissipated, dissolute, fast, immoral, lecherous, lewd, libertine, libidinous, licentious, loose, lustful, of easy virtue, rakish, shameless, unchaste **2, 3 = unprovoked**, arbitrary, cruel, evil, gratuitous, groundless, malevolent, malicious, motiveless, needless, senseless, spiteful, uncalled-for, unjustifiable, unjustified, vicious, wicked, wilful **4 = reckless**, careless, devil-may-care, extravagant, heedless, immoderate, intemperate, lavish, outrageous, rash, unrestrained, wild ◆ *n* **7 = slut**, harlot, loose woman, prostitute, scrubber (*Brit. & Austral. sl.*), slag (*Brit. sl.*), strumpet, swinger (*inf.*), tart, trollop, whore, woman of easy virtue
Antonyms *adj* ≠ **promiscuous:** overmodest, priggish, prim, prudish, puritanical, rigid, strait-laced, stuffy, Victorian ≠ **unprovoked:** called-for, excusable, justified, legitimate, motivated, provoked, warranted ≠ **reckless:** cautious, circumspect, guarded, inhibited, moderate, prudent, reserved, restrained, temperate

war *n* **1, 2 = fighting**, armed conflict, battle, bloodshed, combat, conflict, contention, contest, enmity, hostilities, hostility, strife, struggle, warfare ◆ *vb* **7 = fight**, battle, campaign against, carry on hostilities, clash, combat, conduct a war, contend, contest, make war, strive, struggle, take up arms, wage war
Antonyms *n* ≠ **fighting:** accord, armistice, ceasefire, co-existence, compliance, co-operation, harmony, peace, peace-time, treaty, truce ◆ *vb* ≠ **fight:** call a ceasefire, co-exist, co-operate, make peace

warble[1] *vb* **1 = sing**, chirp, chirrup, quaver, trill, twitter ◆ *n* **3 = song**, call, chirp, chirrup, cry, quaver, trill, twitter

war cry *n* **1, 2 = battle cry**, rallying cry, slogan, war whoop

ward *n* **1 = district**, area, division, precinct, quarter, zone **2 = room**, apartment, cubicle **5 = dependant**, charge, minor, protégé, pupil

warden *n* **1 = keeper**, administrator, caretaker, curator, custodian, guardian, janitor, ranger, steward, superintendent, warder, watchman

warder *n* **1, 2 = jailer**, custodian, guard, keeper, prison officer, screw (*sl.*), turnkey (*arch.*)

ward off *vb* **= repel**, avert, avoid, beat off, block, deflect, fend off, forestall, keep at arm's length, keep at bay, parry, stave off, thwart, turn aside, turn away
Antonyms *vb* accept, admit, allow, embrace, permit, receive, take in, welcome

wardrobe *n* **1 = clothes cupboard**, closet, clothes-press **2 = clothes**, apparel, attire, collection of clothes, outfit

warehouse Ⓣ *n* ('wɛə,haus). **1** a place where goods are stored prior to their use, distribution, or sale. **2** See **bonded warehouse. 3** *Chiefly Brit.* a large commercial, esp. wholesale, establishment. ◆ *vb* ('wɛə,hauz, -,haus), **warehouses, warehousing, warehoused. 4** (*tr*) to store or place in a warehouse, esp. a bonded warehouse.
▸'**ware,houseman** *n*

warehousing ('wɛə,hauzɪŋ) *n Business.* an attempt to gain a significant stake in a company without revealing the identity of the purchaser by buying small quantities of shares in the name of nominees.

wares Ⓣ (wɛəz) *pl n* **1** articles of manufacture considered as being for sale. **2** any talent or asset regarded as a saleable commodity.

warfare Ⓣ ('wɔː,fɛə) *n* **1** the act, process, or an instance of waging war. **2** conflict or strife.

warfarin ('wɔːfərɪn) *n* a crystalline insoluble compound, used to kill rodents and, in the form of its sodium salt, as a medical anticoagulant. [C20: from the patent owners *W(isconsin) A(lumni) R(esearch) F(oundation)* + (COUM)ARIN]

war game *n* **1** a notional tactical exercise for training military commanders, in which no military units are actually deployed. **2** a game in which model soldiers are used to create battles, esp. past battles, in order to study tactics.

warhead ('wɔː,hɛd) *n* the part of the fore end of a missile or projectile that contains explosives.

warhorse ('wɔː,hɔːs) *n* **1** a horse used in battle. **2** *Inf.* a veteran soldier or politician.

warlike Ⓣ ('wɔː,laɪk) *adj* **1** of, relating to, or used in war. **2** hostile or belligerent. **3** fit or ready for war.

warlock Ⓣ ('wɔː,lɒk) *n* a man who practises black magic. [OE *wǣrloga* oath breaker, from *wǣr* oath + *-loga* liar, from *lēogan* to lie]

warlord ('wɔː,lɔːd) *n* a military leader of a nation or part of a nation: *the Chinese warlords.*

Warlpiri ('walpri) *n* an Aboriginal language of central Australia.

warm Ⓣ (wɔːm) *adj* **1** characterized by or having a moderate degree of heat. **2** maintaining or imparting heat: *a warm coat.* **3** having or showing ready affection, kindliness, etc.: *a warm personality.* **4** lively or passionate: *a warm debate.* **5** cordial or enthusiastic: *warm support.* **6** quickly or easily aroused: *a warm temper.* **7** (of colours) predominantly red or yellow in tone. **8** (of a scent, trail, etc.) recently made. **9** near to finding a hidden object or guessing facts, as in children's games. **10** *Inf.* uncomfortable or disagreeable, esp. because of the proximity of danger. ◆ *vb* **11** (sometimes foll. by *up*) to make or become warm or warmer. **12** (when *intr*, often foll. by *to*) to make or become excited, enthusiastic, etc. (about): *he warmed to the idea of buying a new car.* **13** (*intr*; often foll. by *to*) to feel affection, kindness, etc. (for someone): *I warmed to her mother from the start.* ◆ *n Inf.* **14** a warm place or area: *come into the warm.* **15** the act or an instance of warming or being warmed. ◆ See also **warm up.** [OE *wearm*]
▸'**warmer** *n* ▸'**warmish** *adj* ▸'**warmly** *adv* ▸'**warmness** *n*

warm-blooded Ⓣ *adj* **1** ardent, impetuous, or passionate. **2** (of birds and mammals) having a constant body temperature, usually higher than the temperature of the surroundings. Technical term: **homoiothermic.**
▸,**warm-'bloodedness** *n*

warm-down *n* light exercises performed to aid recovery from strenuous physical activity.

war memorial *n* a monument, usually an obelisk or cross, to those who die in a war, esp. those from a particular locality.

warm front *n Meteorol.* the boundary between a warm air mass and the cold air above which it is rising, at a less steep angle than at the cold front.

warm-hearted Ⓣ *adj* kindly, generous, or readily sympathetic.
▸,**warm-'heartedly** *adv* ▸,**warm-'heartedness** *n*

warming pan *n* a pan, often of copper and having a long handle, filled with hot coals and formerly drawn over the sheets to warm a bed.

warmonger Ⓣ ('wɔː,mʌŋgə) *n* a person who fosters warlike ideas or advocates war.
▸'**war,mongering** *n*

warmth Ⓣ (wɔːmθ) *n* **1** the state, quality, or sensation of being warm. **2** intensity of emotion: *he denied the accusation with some warmth.* **3** affection or cordiality.

warm up *vb* (*adv*) **1** to make or become warm or warmer. **2** (*intr*) to exercise immediately before a game, contest, or more vigorous exercise. **3** (*intr*) to get ready for something important; prepare. **4** to run (an engine, etc.) until the working temperature is attained, or (of an engine, etc.) to undergo this process. **5** to make or become more animated: *the party warmed up when Tom came.* **6** to reheat (already cooked food) or (of such food) to be reheated. ◆ *n* **warm-up. 7** the act or an instance of warming up. **8** a preparatory exercise routine.

warn Ⓣ (wɔːn) *vb* **1** to notify or make (someone) aware of danger, harm, etc. **2** (*tr; often takes a negative and an infinitive*) to advise or admonish (someone) as to action, conduct, etc.: *I warn you not to do that again.* **3** (*takes a clause as object or an infinitive*) to inform (someone) in advance: *he warned them that he would arrive late.* **4** (*tr*; usually foll. by *away, off*, etc.) to give notice to go away, be off, etc. [OE *wearnian*]
▸'**warner** *n*

warning Ⓣ ('wɔːnɪŋ) *n* **1** a hint, intimation, threat, etc., of harm or danger. **2** advice to beware or desist. **3** an archaic word for **notice** (sense 6). ◆ *adj* **4** (*prenominal*) intended or serving to warn: *a warning look.*
▸'**warningly** *adv*

War of American Independence *n* the conflict following the revolt of the North American colonies against British rule, particularly on the issue of taxation. Hostilities began in 1775 when British and American forces clashed at Lexington and Concord. Articles of Confederation agreed in the Continental Congress in 1777 provided for a confederacy to be known as the United States of America. The war was effectively ended with the surrender of the British at Yorktown in 1781 and peace was signed at Paris in Sept. 1783. Also called: **American Revolution** or **Revolutionary War.**

warp Ⓣ (wɔːp) *vb* **1** to twist or cause to twist out of shape, as from heat, damp, etc. **2** to turn or cause to turn from a true, correct, or proper course. **3** to pervert or be perverted. **4** *Naut.* to move (a vessel) by hauling on a rope fixed to a stationary object ashore or (of a vessel) to be moved thus. **5** (*tr*) to flood (land) with water from which alluvial matter is deposited. ◆ *n* **6** the state or condition of being twisted out of shape. **7** a twist, distortion, or bias. **8** a mental or moral deviation. **9** the yarns arranged lengthways on a loom, forming the threads through which the weft yarns are woven. **10** *Naut.* a rope used for warping a vessel. **11** alluvial sediment deposited by water. [OE *wearp* a throw]
▸'**warpage** *n* ▸**warped** *adj* ▸'**warper** *n*

war paint *n* **1** painted decoration of the face and body applied by certain North American Indians before battle. **2** *Inf.* finery or regalia. **3** *Inf.* cosmetics.

warpath ('wɔː,pɑːθ) *n* **1** the route taken by North American Indians on

THESAURUS

warehouse *n* **1** = **store**, depository, depot, stockroom, storehouse

wares *pl n* **1** = **goods**, commodities, lines, manufactures, merchandise, produce, products, stock, stuff

warfare *n* **1, 2** = **war**, armed conflict, armed struggle, arms, battle, blows, campaigning, clash of arms, combat, conflict, contest, discord, fighting, hostilities, passage of arms, strategy, strife, struggle
Antonyms *n* accord, amity, armistice, ceasefire, cessation of hostilities, conciliation, harmony, peace, treaty, truce

warily *adv* **1** = **cautiously**, cagily (*inf.*), carefully, charily, circumspectly, distrustfully, gingerly, guardedly, suspiciously, vigilantly, watchfully, with care
Antonyms *adv* carelessly, hastily, heedlessly, irresponsibly, rashly, recklessly, thoughtlessly, unwarily

wariness *n* **1** = **caution**, alertness, attention, caginess (*inf.*), care, carefulness, circumspection, discretion, distrust, foresight, heedfulness, mindfulness, prudence, suspicion, vigilance, watchfulness
Antonyms *n* carelessness, heedlessness, inattention, mindlessness, negligence, oblivion, recklessness, thoughtlessness

warlike *adj* **1, 2** = **belligerent**, aggressive, bellicose, bloodthirsty, combative, hawkish, hostile, inimical, jingoistic, martial, militaristic, military, pugnacious, sabre-rattling, unfriendly, warmongering
Antonyms *adj* amicable, conciliatory, friendly, nonbelligerent, pacific, peaceable, peaceful, placid, unwarlike

warlock *n* = **magician**, conjuror, enchanter, necromancer, sorcerer, witch, wizard

warm *adj* **1** = **heated**, balmy, lukewarm, moderately hot, pleasant, sunny, tepid, thermal **3** = **affectionate**, affable, amiable, amorous, cheerful, congenial, cordial, friendly, genial, happy, hearty, hospitable, kindly, likable *or* likeable, loving, pleasant, tender ◆ *vb* **11** = **heat**, heat up, melt, thaw, warm up **12** = **rouse**, animate, awaken, excite, get going, interest, make enthusiastic, put some life into, stimulate, stir, turn on (*sl.*)
Antonyms *adj* ≠ **heated:** chilly, cold, cool, freezing, icy ≠ **affectionate:** aloof, apathetic, cold, cool, distant, half-hearted, hostile, phlegmatic, remote, stand-offish, uncaring, unenthusiastic, unfriendly, unwelcoming ◆ *vb* ≠ **heat:** chill, cool, cool down, freeze ≠ **rouse:** alienate, depress, sadden

warm-blooded *adj* **1** = **passionate**, ardent, earnest, emotional, enthusiastic, excitable, fervent, impetuous, lively, rash, spirited, vivacious

warm-hearted *adj* = **kindly**, affectionate, compassionate, cordial, generous, kind-hearted, loving, sympathetic, tender, tender-hearted
Antonyms *adj* callous, cold, cold-hearted, hard, hard-hearted, harsh, heartless, insensitive, mean, merciless, unfeeling, unsympathetic

warmonger *n* = **hawk**, belligerent, jingo, militarist, sabre-rattler

warmth *n* **1** = **heat**, hotness, warmness **3** = **affection**, affability, amorousness, cheerfulness, cordiality, happiness, heartiness, hospitableness, kindliness, love, tenderness
Antonyms *n* ≠ **heat:** chill, chilliness, cold, coldness, coolness, iciness ≠ **affection:** aloofness, apathy, austerity, cold-heartedness, hard-heartedness, hostility, indifference, insincerity, lack of enthusiasm, remoteness, sternness

warn *vb* **1-3** = **notify**, admonish, advise, alert, apprise, caution, forewarn, give fair warning, give notice, inform, make (someone) aware, put one on one's guard, summon, tip off

warning *n* **1** = **caution**, admonition, advice, alarm, alert, augury, caveat, foretoken, hint, notice, notification, omen, premonition, presage, sign, signal, threat, tip, tip-off, token, word, word to the wise ◆ *adj* **4** = **cautionary**, admonitory, monitory, ominous, premonitory, threatening

warp *vb* **1** = **twist**, bend, contort, deform, deviate, distort, misshape, pervert, swerve, turn ◆ *n* **6-8** = **twist**, bend, bent, bias, contortion, deformation, deviation, distortion, kink, perversion, quirk, turn

a warlike expedition. **2 on the warpath. 2a** preparing to engage in battle. **2b** *Inf.* in a state of anger.
warplane ('wɔːˌpleɪn) *n* any aircraft designed for and used in warfare.
warrant ❶ ('wɒrənt) *n* **1** anything that gives authority for an action or decision; authorization. **2** a document that certifies or guarantees, such as a receipt for goods stored in a warehouse, a licence, or a commission. **3** *Law.* an authorization issued by a magistrate allowing a constable or other officer to search or seize property, arrest a person, or perform some other specified act. **4** (in certain armed services) the official authority for the appointment of warrant officers. **5** a security that functions as a stock option by giving the owner the right to buy ordinary shares in a company at a specified date, often at a specified price. ◆ *vb* (*tr*) **6** to guarantee the quality, condition, etc., of (something). **7** to give authority or power to. **8** to attest to the character, worthiness, etc., of. **9** to guarantee (a purchaser of merchandise) against loss of, damage to, or misrepresentation concerning the merchandise. **10** *Law.* to guarantee (the title to an estate or other property). **11** to declare confidently. [C13: from Anglo-F, var. of OF *guarant,* from *guarantir* to guarantee, of Gmc origin]
▸ **'warrantable** *adj* ▸ **ˌwarranta'bility** *n* ▸ **'warrantably** *adv* ▸ **'warranter** *n*
warrantee (ˌwɒrən'tiː) *n* a person to whom a warranty is given.
warrant officer *n* an officer in certain armed services who holds a rank between those of commissioned and noncommissioned officers. In the British army the rank has two classes: regimental sergeant major and company sergeant major.
Warrant of Fitness *n NZ.* a six-monthly certificate required for motor vehicles certifying mechanical soundness.
warrantor ('wɒrənˌtɔː) *n* an individual or company that provides a warranty.
warrant sale *n Scots Law.* a sale of someone's personal belongings or household effects that have been seized to meet unpaid debts.
warranty ❶ ('wɒrəntɪ) *n, pl* **warranties. 1** *Property law.* a covenant, express or implied, by which the vendor of real property vouches for the security of the title conveyed. **2** *Contract law.* an express or implied term in a contract collateral to the main purpose, such as an undertaking that goods contracted to be sold shall meet specified requirements as to quality, etc. **3** *Insurance law.* an undertaking by the party insured that the facts given regarding the risk are as stated. [C14: from Anglo-F *warantie,* from *warantir* to warrant, var. of OF *guarantir;* see WARRANT]
warren ('wɒrən) *n* **1** a series of interconnected underground tunnels in which rabbits live. **2** a colony of rabbits. **3** an overcrowded area or dwelling. **4** *Chiefly Brit.* an enclosed place where small game animals or birds are kept, esp. for breeding. [C14: from Anglo-F *warenne,* of Gmc origin]
warrigal ('wɒrɪgæl) *Austral.* ◆ *n* **1** a dingo. ◆ *adj* **2** untamed or wild. [C19: from Abor.]
warrior ❶ ('wɒrɪə) *n* **a** a person engaged in, experienced in, or devoted to war. **b** (*as modifier*): *a warrior nation.* [C13: from OF *werreieor,* from *werre* WAR]
Warsaw Pact ('wɔːsɔː) *n* a military treaty and association of E European countries (1955–91).
warship ('wɔːˌʃɪp) *n* a vessel armed, armoured, and otherwise equipped for naval warfare.
Wars of the Roses *pl n* the struggle for the throne in England (1455-85) between the House of York (symbolized by the white rose) and the House of Lancaster (symbolized by the red rose).
wart (wɔːt) *n* **1** *Pathol.* any firm abnormal elevation of the skin caused by a virus. **2** *Bot.* a small rounded outgrowth. **3 warts and all.** with all blemishes evident. [OE *weart(e)*]
▸ **'warty** *adj*
warthog ('wɔːthɒg) *n* a wild pig of S and E Africa, having heavy tusks, wartlike protuberances on the face, and a mane of coarse hair.
wartime ('wɔːˌtaɪm) *n* **a** a period or time of war. **b** (*as modifier*): *wartime conditions.*
war whoop *n* the yell or howl uttered, esp. by North American Indians, while making an attack.
wary ❶ ('wɛərɪ) *adj* **warier, wariest. 1** watchful, cautious, or alert. **2** characterized by caution or watchfulness. [C16: from WARE² + -Y¹]
▸ **'warily** *adv* ▸ **'wariness** *n*

was (wɒz; *unstressed* wəz) *vb* (used with *I, he, she, it,* and with singular nouns) **1** the past tense (indicative mood) of **be. 2** *Not standard.* a form of the subjunctive mood used in place of *were,* esp. in conditional sentences: *if the film was to be with you, would you be able to process it?* [OE *wæs,* from *wesan* to be]
wash ❶ (wɒʃ) *vb* **1** to apply water or other liquid, usually with soap, to (oneself, clothes, etc.) in order to cleanse. **2** (*tr;* often foll. by *away, from, off,* etc.) to remove by the application of water or other liquid and usually soap: *she washed the dirt from her clothes.* **3** (*intr*) to be capable of being washed without damage or loss of colour. **4** (of an animal such as a cat) to cleanse (itself or another animal) by licking. **5** (*tr*) to cleanse from pollution or defilement. **6** (*tr*) to make wet or moist. **7** (often foll. by *away,* etc.) to move or be moved by water: *the flood washed away the bridge.* **8** (esp. of waves) to flow or sweep against or over (a surface or object), often with a lapping sound. **9** to form by erosion or be eroded: *the stream washed a ravine in the hill.* **10** (*tr*) to apply a thin coating of paint, metal, etc., to. **11** (*tr*) to separate (ore, etc.) from (gravel, etc.) by immersion in water. **12** (*intr; usually used with a negative*) *Inf., chiefly Brit.* to admit of testing or proof: *your excuses won't wash.* ◆ *n* **13** the act or process of washing. **14** a quantity of articles washed together. **15** a preparation or thin liquid used as a coating or in washing: *a thin wash of paint.* **16** *Med.* **16a** any medicinal lotion for application to a part of the body. **16b** (*in combination*): *an eyewash.* **17a** the technique of making wash drawings. **17b** See **wash drawing. 18** the erosion of soil by the action of flowing water. **19** a mass of alluvial material transported and deposited by flowing water. **20** land that is habitually washed by tidal or river waters. **21** the disturbance in the air or water produced at the rear of an aircraft, boat, or other moving object. **22** gravel, earth, etc., from which valuable minerals may be washed. **23** waste liquid matter or liquid refuse, esp. as fed to pigs. **24** an alcoholic liquid resembling strong beer, resulting from the fermentation of wort in the production of whisky. **25 come out in the wash.** *Inf.* to become known or apparent in the course of time. ◆ See also **wash down, wash out, wash up.** [OE *wæscan, waxan*]
washable ('wɒʃəbᵊl) *adj* (esp. of fabrics or clothes) capable of being washed without deteriorating.
▸ **ˌwasha'bility** *n*
wash-and-wear *adj* (of fabrics, garments, etc.) requiring only light washing, short drying time, and little or no ironing.
washbasin ('wɒʃˌbeɪsᵊn) *n* **1** Also called: **washbowl.** a basin or bowl for washing the face and hands. **2** Also called: **wash-hand basin.** a bathroom fixture with taps, used for washing the face and hands.
washboard ('wɒʃˌbɔːd) *n* **1** a board having a surface, usually of corrugated metal, on which, esp. formerly, clothes were scrubbed. **2** such a board used as a rhythm instrument played with the fingers in skiffle, country-and-western music, etc. **3** *Naut.* a vertical planklike shield fastened to the gunwales of a boat to prevent water from splashing over the side.
washcloth ('wɒʃˌklɒθ) *n* **1** another term for **dishcloth. 2** the US and Canad. word for **face cloth.**
washday ('wɒʃˌdeɪ) *n* a day on which clothes and linen are washed.
wash down *vb* (*tr, adv*) **1** to wash completely, esp. from top to bottom. **2** to take drink with or after (food or another drink).
wash drawing *n* a pen-and-ink drawing that has been lightly brushed over with water to soften the lines.
washed out ❶ *adj* (**washed-out** *when prenominal*). **1** faded or colourless. **2** exhausted, esp. when being pale in appearance.
washed up *adj* (**washed-up** *when prenominal*). *Inf., chiefly US, Canad., & NZ.* no longer hopeful, etc.: *our hopes for the new deal are all washed up.*
washer ('wɒʃə) *n* **1** a person or thing that washes. **2** a flat ring or drilled disc of metal used under the head of a bolt or nut. **3** any flat ring of rubber, felt, metal, etc., used to provide a seal under a nut or in a tap or valve seat. **4** See **washing machine. 5** *Austral.* a face cloth; flannel.
washerwoman ('wɒʃəˌwʊmən) *or* (*masc*) **washerman** *n, pl* **washerwomen** *or* **washermen.** a person who washes clothes for a living.
washery ('wɒʃərɪ) *n, pl* **washeries.** a plant at a mine where water or other liquid is used to remove dirt from a mineral, esp. coal.
wash-hand basin *n* another name for **washbasin** (sense 2).
wash house *n* (formerly) an outbuilding in which clothes were washed.
washing ('wɒʃɪŋ) *n* **1** articles that have been or are to be washed to-

THESAURUS

warrant *n* **1** = **authorization**, assurance, authority, carte blanche, commission, guarantee, licence, permission, permit, pledge, sanction, security, warranty ◆ *vb* **6, 8** = **guarantee**, affirm, answer for, assure, attest, avouch, certify, declare, pledge, secure, stand behind, underwrite, uphold, vouch for **7** = **call for**, approve, authorize, commission, demand, deserve, empower, entail, entitle, excuse, give ground for, justify, license, necessitate, permit, require, sanction
warrantable *adj* **7** = **justifiable**, accountable, allowable, defensible, lawful, necessary, permissible, proper, reasonable, right
Antonyms *adj* indefensible, uncalled-for, undue, unjustifiable, unnecessary, unreasonable, unwarrantable, wrong
warranty *n* **1, 2** = **guarantee**, assurance, bond, certificate, contract, covenant, pledge
warring *adj* **7** = **fighting**, at daggers drawn, at war, belligerent, combatant, conflicting, contending, embattled, hostile, opposed
warrior *n* = **soldier**, champion, combatant, fighter, fighting man, gladiator, man-at-arms
wary *adj* **1** = **cautious**, alert, attentive, cagey (*inf.*), careful, chary, circumspect, distrustful, guarded, heedful, leery (*sl.*), on one's guard, on the lookout, on the qui vive, prudent, suspicious, vigilant, watchful, wide-awake
Antonyms *adj* careless, foolhardy, imprudent, negligent, rash, reckless, remiss, unguarded, unsuspecting, unwary
wash *vb* **1, 2, 5, 6** = **clean**, bath, bathe, cleanse, launder, moisten, rinse, scrub, shampoo, shower, wet **7** = **sweep away**, bear away, carry off, erode, move, wash off **12** *Informal, chiefly Brit.* = **be plausible**, bear scrutiny, be convincing, carry weight, hold up, hold water, stand up, stick ◆ *n* **13** = **cleaning**, ablution, bath, bathe, cleansing, laundering, rinse, scrub, shampoo, shower, washing **15** = **coat**, coating, film, layer, overlay, screen, stain, suffusion **21** = **swell**, ebb and flow, flow, roll, surge, sweep, wave
washed out *adj* **1** = **faded**, blanched, bleached, colourless, etiolated, flat, lacklustre, mat, pale **2** = **exhausted**, all in (*sl.*), dog-tired (*inf.*), done in, drained, drawn, fatigued, haggard, knackered (*sl.*), pale, spent, tired-out, wan, weary, wiped out (*inf.*), worn-out, zonked (*sl.*)
Antonyms *adj* ≠ **exhausted**: alert, chirpy, ener-

gether on a single occasion. **2** something, such as gold dust, that has been obtained by washing. **3** a thin coat of something applied in liquid form.

washing machine *n* a mechanical apparatus, usually powered by electricity, for washing clothing, linens, etc.

washing powder *n* powdered detergent for washing fabrics.

washing soda *n* crystalline sodium carbonate, esp. when used as a cleansing agent.

washing-up *n Brit.* **1** the washing of dishes, cutlery, etc., after a meal. **2** dishes and cutlery waiting to be washed up. **3** (*as modifier*): *a washing-up machine.*

wash out ⓣ *vb* (*adv*) **1** (*tr*) to wash (the inside of something) so as to remove (dirt). **2** Also: **wash off.** to remove or be removed by washing: *grass stains don't wash out easily.* ◆ *n* **washout. 3** *Geol.* **3a** erosion of the earth's surface by the action of running water. **3b** a narrow channel produced by this. **4** *Inf.* **4a** a total failure or disaster. **4b** an incompetent person.

washroom (ˈwɒʃˌruːm, -ˌrum) *n US & Canad.* a euphemism for **lavatory.**

washstand (ˈwɒʃˌstænd) *n* a piece of furniture designed to hold a basin, etc., for washing the face and hands.

washtub (ˈwɒʃˌtʌb) *n* a tub or large container used for washing anything, esp. clothes.

wash up *vb* (*adv*) **1** *Chiefly Brit.* to wash (dishes, cutlery, etc.) after a meal. **2** (*intr*) *US & Canad.* to wash one's face and hands. ◆ *n* **washup. 3** *Austral.* the end, outcome of a process: *in the washup, three were elected.*

washy ⓣ (ˈwɒʃɪ) *adj* **washier, washiest. 1** overdiluted, watery, or weak. **2** lacking intensity or strength.
▸ˈ**washiness** *n*

wasn't (ˈwɒzᵊnt) *contraction of* was not.

wasp (wɒsp) *n* **1** a social hymenopterous insect, such as the **common wasp,** having a black-and-yellow body and an ovipositor specialized for stinging. **2** any of various solitary hymenopterans, such as the digger wasp and gall wasp. [OE *wæsp*]
▸ˈ**waspˌlike** *adj* ▸ˈ**waspy** *adj* ▸ˈ**waspily** *adv* ▸ˈ**waspiness** *n*

Wasp *or* **WASP** (wɒsp) *n* (in the US) *acronym for* White Anglo-Saxon Protestant: a person descended from N European, usually Protestant stock, forming a group often considered the most dominant, privileged, and influential in American society.

waspish ⓣ (ˈwɒspɪʃ) *adj* **1** relating to or suggestive of a wasp. **2** easily annoyed or angered.
▸ˈ**waspishly** *adv*

wasp waist *n* a very slender waist, esp. one that is tightly corseted.
▸ˈ**wasp-ˌwaisted** *adj*

wassail (ˈwɒseɪl) *n* **1** (formerly) a toast or salutation made to a person at festivities. **2** a festivity when much drinking takes place. **3** alcoholic drink drunk at such a festivity, esp. spiced beer or mulled wine. ◆ *vb* **4** to drink the health of (a person) at a wassail. **5** (*intr*) to go from house to house singing carols at Christmas. [C13: from ON *ves heill* be in good health]
▸ˈ**wassailer** *n*

Wassermann test *or* **reaction** (ˈwæsəmən) *n Med.* a diagnostic test for syphilis. [C20: after August von *Wassermann* (1866–1925), G bacteriologist]

wast (wɒst; *unstressed* wəst) *vb Arch. or dialect.* (used with the pronoun *thou* or its relative equivalent) a singular form of the past tense (indicative mood) of **be.**

wastage (ˈweɪstɪdʒ) *n* **1** anything lost by wear or waste. **2** the process of wasting. **3** reduction in size of a workforce by retirement, etc. (esp. in **natural wastage**).

> **USAGE NOTE** *Waste* and *wastage* are to some extent interchangeable, but many people think that *wastage* should not be used to refer to loss resulting from human carelessness, inefficiency, etc.: *a waste* (not *a wastage*) *of time/money/effort*, etc.

waste ⓣ (weɪst) *vb* **wastes, wasting, wasted. 1** (*tr*) to use, consume, or expend thoughtlessly, carelessly, or to no avail. **2** (*tr*) to fail to take advantage of: *to waste an opportunity.* **3** (when *intr*, often foll. by *away*) to lose or cause to lose bodily strength, health, etc. **4** to exhaust or become exhausted. **5** (*tr*) to ravage. **6** (*tr*) *Sl.* to murder or kill. ◆ *n* **7** the act of wasting or state of being wasted. **8** a failure to take advantage of something. **9** anything unused or not used to full advantage. **10** anything or anyone rejected as useless, worthless, or in excess of what is required. **11** garbage, rubbish, or trash. **12** a land or region that is devastated or ruined. **13** a land or region that is wild or uncultivated. **14** *Physiol.* **14a** the useless products of metabolism. **14b** indigestible food residue. **15** *Law.* reduction in the value of an estate caused by act or neglect, esp. by a life tenant. ◆ *adj* **16** rejected as useless, unwanted, or worthless. **17** produced in excess of what is required. **18** not cultivated, inhabited, or productive: *waste land.* **19a** of or denoting the useless products of metabolism. **19b** of or denoting indigestible food residue. **20** destroyed, devastated, or ruined. **21 lay waste.** to devastate or destroy. [C13: from Anglo-F, from L *vastāre* to lay waste, from *vastus* empty]

wasted (ˈweɪstɪd) *adj* **1** not taken advantage of: *a wasted opportunity.* **2** unprofitable: *wasted effort.* **3** enfeebled and emaciated: *a thin wasted figure.* **4** *Sl.* showing signs of habitual drug abuse.

wasteful ⓣ (ˈweɪstful) *adj* **1** tending to waste or squander. **2** causing waste or devastation.
▸ˈ**wastefully** *adv* ▸ˈ**wastefulness** *n*

wasteland ⓣ (ˈweɪstˌlænd) *n* **1** a barren or desolate area of land. **2** a region, period in history, etc., that is considered spiritually, intellectually, or aesthetically barren or desolate.

wastepaper (ˈweɪstˌpeɪpə) *n* paper discarded after use.

wastepaper basket *or* **bin** *n* an open receptacle for paper and other dry litter. Usual US and Canad. word: **wastebasket.**

waste pipe *n* a pipe to take excess or used water away, as from a sink to a drain.

waster ⓣ (ˈweɪstə) *n* **1** a person or thing that wastes. **2** a ne'er-do-well; wastrel.

wasting (ˈweɪstɪŋ) *adj* (*prenominal*) reducing the vitality, strength, or robustness of the body: *a wasting disease.*
▸ˈ**wastingly** *adv*

wasting asset *n* an unreplaceable business asset of limited life, such as an oil well.

wastrel ⓣ (ˈweɪstrəl) *n* **1** a wasteful person; spendthrift; prodigal. **2** an idler or vagabond.

wat (wɑːt) *n* a Thai Buddhist monastery or temple. [Thai, from Sansk. *vāta* enclosure]

watap (wæˈtɑːp, wɑː-) *n* a stringy thread made by North American Indians from the roots of various conifers and used for weaving and sewing. [C18: from Canad. F, from Cree *watapiy*]

watch ⓣ (wɒtʃ) *vb* **1** to look at or observe closely or attentively. **2** (*intr*; foll. by *for*) to wait attentively. **3** to guard or tend (something) closely or carefully. **4** (*intr*) to keep vigil. **5** (*tr*) to maintain an interest in: *to watch the progress of a child at school.* **6 watch it!** be careful! ◆ *n* **7a** a small portable timepiece, usually worn strapped to the wrist (a **wristwatch**) or in a waistcoat pocket. **7b** (*as modifier*): *a watch spring.* **8** a watching. **9** a period of vigil, esp. during the night. **10** (formerly) one of a set of periods into which the night was divided. **11** *Naut.* **11a** any of the periods, usually of four hours, during which part of a ship's crew are on duty. **11b** those officers and crew on duty during a specified watch. **12** the period during which a guard is on duty. **13** (formerly) a watchman or band of watchmen. **14 on the watch.** on the lookout. ◆ See also **watch out.** [OE *wæccan* (vb), *wæcce* (n)]
▸ˈ**watcher** *n*

-watch *suffix of nouns.* indicating a regular television programme or newspaper feature on the topic specified: *Crimewatch.*

watchable (ˈwɒtʃəbᵊl) *adj* **1** capable of being watched. **2** interesting, enjoyable, or entertaining: *a watchable television documentary.*

watchcase (ˈwɒtʃˌkeɪs) *n* a protective case for a watch, generally of metal such as gold or silver.

watch chain *n* a chain used for fastening a pocket watch to the clothing. See also **fob**[1].

THESAURUS

getic, full of beans (*inf.*), full of pep (*inf.*), lively, perky, refreshed, sprightly, zippy (*inf.*)

washout *Informal n* **4a** = **failure**, disappointment, disaster, dud (*inf.*), fiasco, flop (*inf.*), mess **4b** = **loser**, failure, incompetent
Antonyms *n* ≠ **failure:** conquest, feat, success, triumph, victory, winner

washy *adj* **1, 2** = **watery**, attenuated, diluted, feeble, insipid, overdiluted, thin, watered-down, weak, wishy-washy (*inf.*)

waspish *adj* **2** = **bad-tempered**, cantankerous, captious, crabbed, crabby, cross, crotchety (*inf.*), fretful, grumpy, ill-tempered, irascible, irritable, liverish, peevish, peppery, pettish, petulant, snappish, splenetic, testy, tetchy, touchy
Antonyms *adj* affable, agreeable, cheerful, easy-going, genial, good-humoured, good-natured, jovial, pleasant

waste *vb* **1, 2** = **squander**, blow, dissipate, fritter away, frivol away (*inf.*), lavish, misuse, run through, throw away **3** *often foll. by* **away** = **decline**, atrophy, consume, corrode, crumble, debilitate, decay, deplete, disable, drain, dwindle, eat away, ebb, emaciate, enfeeble, exhaust, fade, gnaw, perish, sap the strength of, sink, undermine, wane, wear out, wither ◆ *n* **7, 8** = **squandering**, dissipation, expenditure, extravagance, frittering away, loss, lost opportunity, misapplication, misuse, prodigality, unthriftiness, wastefulness **12** = **rubbish**, debris, dregs, dross, garbage, leavings, leftovers, litter, offal, offscourings, refuse, scrap, sweepings, trash **13** = **desert**, solitude, void, wasteland, wild, wilderness ◆ *adj* **16** = **unwanted**, leftover, superfluous, supernumerary, unused, useless, worthless **18** = **uncultivated**, bare, barren, desolate, devastated, dismal, dreary, empty, uninhabited, unproductive, wild **21 lay waste** = **devastate**, depredate (*rare*), despoil, destroy, pillage, rape, ravage, raze, ruin, sack, spoil, total (*sl.*), trash (*sl.*), undo, wreak havoc upon
Antonyms *vb* ≠ **squander:** conserve, economize, husband, preserve, protect, save ≠ **decline:** build, develop, increase, rally, strengthen ◆ *n* ≠ **squandering:** economy, frugality, good housekeeping, saving, thrift ◆ *adj* ≠ **unwanted:** necessary, needed, utilized ≠ **uncultivated:** arable, developed, fruitful, habitable, in use, productive, verdant

wasteful *adj* **1** = **extravagant**, improvident, lavish, prodigal, profligate, ruinous, spendthrift, thriftless, uneconomical, unthrifty
Antonyms *adj* economical, frugal, money-saving, parsimonious, penny-wise, provident, sparing, thrifty

wasteland *n* **1** = **wilderness**, desert, void, waste, wild

waster *n* **2** = **layabout**, drone, good-for-nothing, idler, loafer, loser, malingerer, ne'er-do-well, shirker, skiver (*Brit. sl.*), wastrel

wastrel *n* **1** = **spendthrift**, prodigal, profligate, squanderer **2** = **layabout**, drone, good-for-nothing, idler, loafer, loser, malingerer, ne'er-do-well, shirker, skiver (*Brit. sl.*), waster

watch *vb* **1** = **look at**, check, check out (*inf.*), contemplate, eye, eyeball (*sl.*), feast one's eyes

Watch Committee *n Brit. history.* a local government committee responsible for the efficiency of the local police force.
watchdog ❶ ('wɒtʃ,dɒg) *n* **1** a dog kept to guard property. **2a** a person or group that acts as a protector against inefficiency, etc. **2b** (*as modifier*): *a watchdog committee.*
watch fire *n* a fire kept burning at night as a signal or for warmth and light by a person keeping watch.
watchful ❶ ('wɒtʃful) *adj* **1** vigilant or alert. **2** *Arch.* not sleeping.
▸'**watchfully** *adv* ▸'**watchfulness** *n*
watch-glass *n* **1** a curved glass disc that covers the dial of a watch. **2** a similarly shaped piece of glass used in laboratories for evaporating small samples of a solution, etc.
watchmaker ('wɒtʃ,meɪkə) *n* a person who makes or mends watches.
▸'**watch,making** *n*
watchman ❶ ('wɒtʃmən) *n, pl* **watchmen. 1** a person employed to guard buildings or property. **2** (formerly) a man employed to patrol or guard the streets at night.
watch night *n* (in Protestant churches) **1a** the night of December 24, during which a service is held to mark the arrival of Christmas Day. **1b** the night of December 31, during which a service is held to mark the passing of the old year. **2** the service held on either of these nights.
watch out ❶ *vb* (*intr, adv*) to be careful or on one's guard.
watchstrap ('wɒtʃ,stræp) *n* a strap of leather, cloth, etc., attached to a watch for fastening it around the wrist. Also called (US and Canad.): **watchband.**
watchtower ('wɒtʃ,tauə) *n* a tower on which a sentry keeps watch.
watchword ❶ ('wɒtʃ,wɜːd) *n* **1** another word for **password. 2** a rallying cry or slogan.
water ❶ ('wɔːtə) *n* **1** a clear colourless tasteless odourless liquid that is essential for plant and animal life and constitutes, in impure form, rain, oceans, rivers, lakes, etc. Formula: H_2O. Related adj: **aqueous. 2a** any body or area of this liquid, such as a sea, lake, river, etc. **2b** (*as modifier*): *water sports; a water plant.* Related adj: **aquatic. 3** the surface of such a body or area: *fish swam below the water.* **4** any form or variety of this liquid, such as rain. **5** See **high water, low water. 6** any of various solutions of chemical substances in water: *ammonia water.* **7** *Physiol.* **7a** any fluid secreted from the body, such as sweat, urine, or tears. **7b** (*usually pl*) the amniotic fluid surrounding a fetus in the womb. **8** a wavy lustrous finish on some fabrics, esp. silk. **9** *Arch.* the degree of brilliance in a diamond. **10** excellence, quality, or degree (in **of the first water**). **11** *Finance.* capital stock issued without a corresponding increase in paid-up capital. **12** (*modifier*) *Astrol.* of or relating to the three signs of the zodiac Cancer, Scorpio, and Pisces. **13 hold water.** to prove credible, logical, or consistent: *the alibi did not hold water.* **14 make water. 14a** to urinate. **14b** (of a boat, etc.) to let in water. **15 pass water.** to urinate. **16 water under the bridge.** events that are past and done with. ◆ *vb* **17** (*tr*) to sprinkle, moisten, or soak with water. **18** (*tr; often foll. by down*) to weaken by the addition of water. **19** (*intr*) (of the eyes) to fill with tears. **20** (*intr*) (of the mouth) to salivate, esp. in anticipation of food (esp. in **make one's mouth water**). **21** (*tr*) to irrigate or provide with water: *to water the land.* **22** (*intr*) to drink water. **23** (*intr*) (of a ship, etc.) to take in a supply of water. **24** (*tr*) *Finance.* to raise the par value of (issued capital stock) without a corresponding increase in the real value of assets. **25** (*tr*) to produce a wavy lustrous finish on (fabrics, esp. silk). ◆ See also **water down.** [OE *wæter*]
▸'**waterer** *n* ▸'**waterless** *adj*
water bag *n* a bag, sometimes made of skin, leather, etc., but in Australia usually canvas, for carrying water.
water bailiff *n* an official responsible for enforcing laws on shipping and fishing.
water bear *n* another name for a **tardigrade.**
water bed *n* a waterproof mattress filled with water.
water beetle *n* any of various beetles that live most of the time in freshwater ponds, rivers, etc.
water bird *n* any aquatic bird, including the wading and swimming birds.
water biscuit *n* a thin crisp plain biscuit, usually served with butter or cheese.
water blister *n* a blister containing watery or serous fluid, without any blood or pus.
water boatman *n* any of various aquatic bugs having a flattened body and oarlike hind legs, adapted for swimming.
waterborne ('wɔːtə,bɔːn) *adj* **1** floating or travelling on water. **2** (of a disease, etc.) transported or transmitted by water.
waterbuck ('wɔːtə,bʌk) *n* any of a genus of antelopes of swampy areas of Africa, having long curved ridged horns.
water buffalo *or* **ox** *n* a member of the cattle tribe of swampy regions of S Asia, having widely spreading back-curving horns. Domesticated forms are used as draught animals.
water bug *n* any of various heteropterous insects adapted to living in the water or on its surface, esp. any of the **giant water bugs** of North America, India, and southern Africa, which have flattened hairy legs.
water butt *n* a barrel for collecting rainwater, esp. from a drainpipe.
water cannon *n* an apparatus for pumping water through a nozzle at high pressure, used in quelling riots.
Water Carrier *or* **Bearer** *n* **the.** the constellation Aquarius, the 11th sign of the zodiac.
water chestnut *n* **1** a floating aquatic plant of Asia, having four-pronged edible nutlike fruits. **2 Chinese water chestnut.** a Chinese plant with an edible succulent corm. **3** the corm of the Chinese water chestnut, used in Oriental cookery.
water clock *or* **glass** *n* any of various devices for measuring time that use the escape of water as the motive force.
water closet *n* **1** a lavatory flushed by water. **2** a small room that has a lavatory. ◆ Usually abbreviated to **WC.**
watercolour *or US* **watercolor** ('wɔːtə,kʌlə) *n* **1** water-soluble pigment bound with gum arabic, applied in transparent washes and without the admixture of white pigment in the lighter tones. **2a** a painting done in watercolours. **2b** (*as modifier*): *a watercolour masterpiece.* **3** the art or technique of painting with such pigments.
▸'**water,colourist** *or US* '**water,colorist** *n*
water-cool *vb* (*tr*) to cool (an engine, etc.) by a flow of water circulating in an enclosed jacket.
▸'**water-,cooled** *adj*
water cooler *n* a device for cooling and dispensing drinking water.
watercourse ('wɔːtə,kɔːs) *n* **1** a stream, river, or canal. **2** the channel, bed, or route along which this flows.
watercraft ('wɔːtə,krɑːft) *n* **1** a boat or ship or such vessels collectively. **2** skill in handling boats or in water sports.
watercress ('wɔːtə,krɛs) *n* an Old World cruciferous plant of clear ponds and streams, having pungent leaves that are used in salads and as a garnish.
water cure *n Med.* a nontechnical name for **hydropathy** or **hydrotherapy.**
water cycle *n* the circulation of the earth's water, in which water evaporates from the sea into the atmosphere, where it condenses and falls as rain or snow, returning to the sea by rivers.
water diviner *n Brit.* a person able to locate the presence of water, esp. underground, with a divining rod.
water down ❶ *vb* (*tr, adv*) **1** to dilute or weaken with water. **2** to modify, esp. so as to omit anything unpleasant or offensive: *to water down the truth.*
▸,**watered-'down** *adj*
waterfall ❶ ('wɔːtə,fɔːl) *n* a cascade of falling water where there is a vertical or almost vertical step in a river.
water flea *n* any of numerous minute freshwater crustaceans which swim by means of hairy branched antennae. See also **daphnia.**
waterfowl ('wɔːtə,faul) *n* **1** any aquatic freshwater bird, esp. any species of the family Anatidae (ducks, geese, and swans). **2** such birds collectively.
waterfront ('wɔːtə,frʌnt) *n* the area of a town or city alongside a body of water, such as a harbour or dockyard.
water gap *n* a deep valley in a ridge, containing a stream.
water gas *n* a mixture of hydrogen and carbon monoxide produced by passing steam over hot carbon, used as a fuel and raw material.
water gate *n* **1** a gate in a canal, etc., that can be opened or closed to

THESAURUS

on, gaze at, get a load of (*inf.*), look, look on, mark, note, observe, pay attention, peer at, regard, see, stare at, view **3** = **guard**, keep, look after, mind, protect, superintend, take care of, tend **4** = **be vigilant**, attend, be on the alert, be on the lookout, be wary, be watchful, keep an eye open (*inf.*), look out, take heed, wait ◆ *n* **7** = **wristwatch**, chronometer, clock, pocket watch, timepiece **8, 9** = **lookout**, alertness, attention, eye, heed, inspection, notice, observation, supervision, surveillance, vigil, vigilance, watchfulness
watchdog *n* **1** = **guard dog 2** = **guardian**, custodian, inspector, monitor, protector, scrutineer
watcher *n* **1** = **viewer**, fly on the wall, looker-on, lookout, observer, onlooker, spectator, spy, witness
watchful *adj* **1** = **alert**, attentive, circumspect, guarded, heedful, observant, on one's guard, on one's toes, on the lookout, on the qui vive, on the watch, suspicious, vigilant, wary, wide awake
Antonyms *adj* careless, inattentive, reckless, thoughtless, unaware, unguarded, unmindful, unobservant, unwary
watchfulness *n* **1** = **vigilance**, alertness, attention, attentiveness, caution, cautiousness, circumspection, heedfulness, wariness
Antonyms *n* carelessness, heedlessness, inattention, indiscretion, irresponsibility, neglect, recklessness, thoughtlessness
watchman *n* **1** = **guard**, caretaker, custodian, security guard, security man
watch out *vb* = **be careful**, be alert, be on one's guard, be on the alert, be on (the) watch, be vigilant, be watchful, have a care, keep a sharp lookout, keep a weather eye open, keep one's eyes open, keep one's eyes peeled *or* skinned (*inf.*), look out, mind out, watch oneself
watchword *n* **1** = **password**, countersign, magic word, shibboleth **2** = **motto**, battle cry, byword, catch phrase, catchword, maxim, rallying cry, slogan, tag-line
water *n* **1** = **liquid**, Adam's ale *or* wine, aqua, H_2O **13 hold water** = **be sound**, bear examination *or* scrutiny, be credible, be logical, make sense, pass the test, ring true, work ◆ *vb* **17** = **moisten**, damp, dampen, douse, drench, flood, hose, irrigate, soak, souse, spray, sprinkle **18** = **dilute**, add water to, adulterate, put water in, thin, water down, weaken
water down *vb* **1** = **dilute**, add water to, adulterate, put water in, thin, water, weaken **2** = **weaken**, adulterate, mitigate, qualify, soften, tone down
Antonyms *vb* ≠ **dilute:** fortify, purify, strengthen, thicken
waterfall *n* = **cascade**, cataract, chute, fall, force (*N English dialect*), linn (*Scot.*)

control the flow of water. **2** a gate through which access may be gained to a body of water.

Watergate ('wɔːtəˌgeɪt) *n* **1** an incident during the 1972 US presidential campaign, when agents employed by the re-election organization of President Richard Nixon were caught breaking into the Democratic Party headquarters in the Watergate building, Washington, DC. The political scandal was exacerbated by attempts to conceal the fact that White House officials had approved the burglary, and eventually forced the resignation of President Nixon. **2** any similar public scandal, esp. involving politicians or a possible cover-up.

water gauge *n* an instrument that indicates the presence or the quantity of water in a tank, reservoir, or boiler feed. Also called: **water glass.**

water glass *n* **1** a viscous syrupy solution of sodium silicate in water: used as a protective coating for cement and a preservative, esp. for eggs. **2** another name for **water gauge.**

water gum *n* any of several Australian gum trees that grow in swampy ground and beside creeks and rivers.

water hammer *n* a sharp concussion produced when the flow of water in a pipe is suddenly blocked.

water hen *n* another name for **gallinule.**

water hole *n* **1** a depression, such as a pond or pool, containing water, esp. one used by animals as a drinking place. **2** a source of drinking water in a desert.

water hyacinth *n* a floating aquatic plant of tropical America, having showy bluish-purple flowers and swollen leafstalks. It forms dense masses in rivers, ponds, etc.

water ice *n* an ice cream made from a frozen sugar syrup flavoured with fruit juice or purée.

watering can *n* a container with a handle and a spout with a perforated nozzle used to sprinkle water over plants.

watering hole *n* **1** a pool where animals drink; water hole. **2** *Facetious sl.* a pub.

watering place *n* **1** a place where drinking water for people or animals may be obtained. **2** *Brit.* a spa. **3** *Brit.* a seaside resort.

water jacket *n* a water-filled envelope surrounding a machine or part for cooling purposes, esp. the casing around the cylinder block of a pump or internal-combustion engine.

water jump *n* a ditch or brook over which athletes or horses must jump in a steeplechase or similar contest.

water level *n* **1** the level reached by the surface of a body of water. **2** the water line of a boat or ship.

water lily *n* any of various aquatic plants of temperate and tropical regions, having large leaves and showy flowers that float on the surface of the water.

water line *n* **1** a line marked at the level around a vessel's hull to which the vessel will be immersed when afloat. **2** a line marking the level reached by a body of water.

waterlogged ❶ ('wɔːtəˌlɒgd) *adj* **1** saturated with water. **2** (of a vessel still afloat) having taken in so much water as to be unmanageable.

Waterloo (ˌwɔːtə'luː) *n* **1** a small town in Belgium south of Brussels: battle (1815) fought nearby in which British and Prussian forces under the Duke of Wellington and Blücher routed the French under Napoleon. **2** a total or crushing defeat (esp. in **meet one's Waterloo**).

water main *n* a principal supply pipe in an arrangement of pipes for distributing water.

waterman ('wɔːtəmən) *n, pl* **watermen.** a skilled boatman. ▸ **'waterman,ship** *n*

watermark ('wɔːtəˌmɑːk) *n* **1** a mark impressed on paper during manufacture, visible when the paper is held up to the light. **2** another word for **water line.** ◆ *vb (tr)* **3** to mark (paper) with a watermark.

water meadow *n* a meadow that remains fertile by being periodically flooded by a stream.

watermelon ('wɔːtəˌmelən) *n* **1** an African melon widely cultivated for its large edible fruit. **2** the fruit of this plant, which has a hard green rind and sweet watery reddish flesh.

water meter *n* a device for measuring the quantity or rate of water flowing through a pipe.

water milfoil *n* any of various pond plants having feathery underwater leaves and inconspicuous flowers.

water mill *n* a mill operated by a water wheel.

water moccasin *n* a large dark grey venomous snake of swamps in the southern US. Also called: **cottonmouth.**

water nymph *n* any fabled nymph of the water, such as the Naiad, Nereid, or Oceanid of Greek mythology.

water of crystallization *n* water present in the crystals of certain compounds. It is chemically combined in a specific amount but can often be easily expelled.

water ouzel *n* another name for **dipper** (the bird).

water paint *n* any water-based paint, such as an emulsion or an acrylic paint.

water pipe *n* **1** a pipe for water. **2** another name for **hookah.**

water pistol *n* a toy pistol that squirts a stream of water or other liquid.

water plantain *n* any of a genus of marsh plants of N temperate regions and Australia, having clusters of small white or pinkish flowers and broad pointed leaves.

water polo *n* a game played in water by two teams of seven swimmers in which each side tries to throw or propel an inflated ball into the opponents' goal.

water power *n* **1** the power latent in a dynamic or static head of water as used to drive machinery, esp. for generating electricity. **2** a source of such power, such as a drop in the level of a river, etc.

waterproof ('wɔːtəˌpruːf) *adj* **1** not penetrable by water. Cf. **water-repellent, water-resistant.** ◆ *n* **2** *Chiefly Brit.* a waterproof garment, esp. a raincoat. ◆ *vb (tr)* **3** to make (a fabric, etc.) waterproof.

water purslane *n* a marsh plant of temperate and warm regions, having reddish stems and small reddish flowers.

water rail *n* a large Eurasian rail of swamps, ponds, etc., having a long red bill.

water rat *n* **1** any of several small amphibious rodents, esp. the water vole or the muskrat. **2** any of various amphibious rats of New Guinea, the Philippines, and Australia.

water rate *n* a charge made for the public supply of water.

water-repellent *adj* (of fabrics, garments, etc.) having a finish that resists the absorption of water.

water-resistant *adj* (esp. of fabrics) designed to resist but not entirely prevent the penetration of water.

water scorpion *n* a long-legged aquatic insect that breathes by means of a long spinelike tube that projects from the rear of the body and penetrates the surface of the water.

watershed ('wɔːtəˌʃed) *n* **1** the dividing line between two adjacent river systems, such as a ridge. **2** an important period or factor that serves as a dividing line.

waterside ('wɔːtəˌsaɪd) *n* **a** the area of land beside a body of water. **b** *(as modifier): waterside houses.*

watersider ('wɔːtəˌsaɪdə) *n Austral. & NZ.* a dock labourer.

water-ski *n* **1** a type of ski used for planing or gliding over water. ◆ *vb* **water-skis, water-skiing, water-skied** *or* **water-ski'd. 2** *(intr)* to ride over water on water-skis while holding a rope towed by a speedboat. ▸ **'water-ˌskier** *n* ▸ **'water-ˌskiing** *n*

water snake *n* any of various snakes that live in or near water, esp. any of a genus of harmless North American snakes.

water softener *n* **1** any substance that lessens the hardness of water, usually by precipitating calcium and magnesium ions. **2** an apparatus that is used to remove chemicals that cause hardness.

water spaniel *n* either of two large curly-coated breeds of spaniel (the Irish and the American), which are used for hunting waterfowl.

water splash *n* a place where a stream runs over a road.

water sports *pl n* sports, such as swimming or windsurfing, that take place in or on water.

waterspout ('wɔːtəˌspaʊt) *n* **1** *Meteorol.* **1a** a tornado occurring over water that forms a column of water and mist. **1b** a sudden downpour of heavy rain. **2** a pipe or channel through which water is discharged.

water table *n* **1** the level below which the ground is saturated with water. **2** a string course that has a moulding designed to throw rainwater clear of the wall below.

water thrush *n* either of two North American warblers having brownish backs and striped underparts and occurring near water.

watertight ❶ ('wɔːtəˌtaɪt) *adj* **1** not permitting the passage of water either in or out: *a watertight boat.* **2** without loopholes: *a watertight argument.* **3** kept separate from other subjects or influences.

water tower ('taʊə) *n* a reservoir or storage tank mounted on a tower-like structure so that water can be distributed at a uniform pressure.

water vapour *n* water in the gaseous state, esp. when due to evaporation at a temperature below the boiling point.

water vole *n* a large amphibious vole of Eurasian river banks. Also called: **water rat.**

water wagtail *n* another name for **pied wagtail.**

waterway ('wɔːtəˌweɪ) *n* a river, canal, or other navigable channel used as a means of travel or transport.

waterweed ('wɔːtəˌwiːd) *n* any of various weedy aquatic plants.

water wheel *n* **1** a simple water-driven turbine consisting of a wheel having vanes set axially across its rim, used to drive machinery. **2** a wheel with buckets attached to its rim for raising water from a stream, pond, etc.

water wings *pl n* an inflatable rubber device shaped like a pair of wings, which is placed under the arms of a person learning to swim.

waterworks ('wɔːtəˌwɜːks) *n* **1** *(functioning as sing)* an establishment for storing, purifying, and distributing water for community supply. **2** *(functioning as pl)* a display of water in movement, as in fountains. **3** *(functioning as pl) Brit. inf., euphemistic.* the urinary system. **4** *(functioning as pl) Inf.* crying; tears.

waterworn ('wɔːtəˌwɔːn) *adj* worn smooth by the action or passage of water.

watery ❶ ('wɔːtərɪ) *adj* **1** relating to, containing, or resembling water. **2** discharging or secreting water or a water-like fluid. **3** tearful; weepy. **4** insipid, thin, or weak.

watt (wɒt) *n* the derived SI unit of power, equal to 1 joule per second;

THESAURUS

waterlogged *adj* **1** = **soaked**, drenched, dripping, droukit *or* drookit (*Scot.*), saturated, sodden, sopping, streaming, wet through, wringing wet

watertight *adj* **1** = **waterproof**, sound **2** = **foolproof**, airtight, firm, flawless, impregnable, incontrovertible, sound, unassailable
Antonyms *adj* ≠ **waterproof**: leaky ≠ **foolproof**: defective, flawed, questionable, shaky, tenuous, uncertain, unsound, weak

watery *adj* **1** = **wet**, aqueous, damp, fluid, humid, liquid, marshy, moist, soggy, squelchy the power dissipated by a current of 1 ampere flowing across a potential difference of 1 volt. Symbol: W [C19: after J. *Watt* (1736–1819), Scot. engineer & inventor]

wattage ('wɒtɪdʒ) *n* **1** power, esp. electric power, measured in watts. **2** the power rating, measured in watts, of an electrical appliance.

watt-hour *n* a unit of energy equal to a power of one watt operating for one hour.

wattle ('wɒtᵊl) *n* **1** a frame of rods or stakes interwoven with twigs, branches, etc., esp. when used to make fences. **2** the material used in such a construction. **3** a loose fold of skin, often brightly coloured, hanging from the neck or throat of certain birds, lizards, etc. **4** any of various chiefly Australian acacia trees having spikes of small brightly coloured flowers and flexible branches. ◆ *vb* **wattles, wattling, wattled.** (*tr*) **5** to construct from wattle. **6** to bind or frame with wattle. **7** to weave or twist (branches, twigs, etc.) into a frame. ◆ *adj* **8** made of, formed by, or covered with wattle. [OE *watol*]
▸'**wattled** *adj*

wattle and daub *n* a form of wall construction consisting of interwoven twigs plastered with a mixture of clay, water, and sometimes chopped straw.

wattmeter ('wɒt,miːtə) *n* a meter for measuring electric power in watts.

waul *or* **wawl** (wɔːl) *vb* (*intr*) to cry or wail plaintively like a cat. [C16: imit.]

wave **T** (weɪv) *vb* **waves, waving, waved. 1** to move or cause to move freely to and fro: *the banner waved in the wind.* **2** (*intr*) to move the hand to and fro as a greeting. **3** to signal or signify by or as if by waving something. **4** (*tr*) to direct to move by or as if by waving something: *he waved me on.* **5** to form or be formed into curves, undulations, etc. **6** (*tr*) to set waves in (the hair). ◆ *n* **7** one of a sequence of ridges or undulations that moves across the surface of a body of a liquid, esp. the sea. **8 the waves.** the sea. **9** any undulation on or at the edge of a surface reminiscent of a wave in the sea: *a wave across the field of corn.* **10** anything that suggests the movement of a wave, as by a sudden rise: *a crime wave.* **11** a widespread movement that advances in a body: *a wave of settlers.* **12** the act or an instance of waving. **13** *Physics.* an energy-carrying disturbance propagated through a medium or space by a progressive local displacement of the medium or a change in its physical properties, but without any overall movement of matter. **14** *Physics.* a graphical representation of a wave obtained by plotting the magnitude of the disturbance against time at a particular point in the medium or space. **15** a prolonged spell of some particular type of weather: *a heat wave.* **16** an undulating curve or series of curves or loose curls in the hair. **17 make waves.** to cause trouble; disturb the status quo. [OE *wafian* (vb); C16 (n) changed from earlier *wāwe*, prob. from OE *wǣg* motion]
▸'**waveless** *adj* ▸'**wave,like** *adj*

waveband ('weɪv,bænd) *n* a range of wavelengths or frequencies used for a particular type of radio transmission.

wave-cut platform *n* a flat surface at the base of a cliff formed by erosion by waves.

wave down *vb* (*tr, adv*) to signal with a wave to (a driver or vehicle) to stop.

wave energy *n* energy obtained by harnessing wave power.

wave equation *n Physics.* a partial differential equation describing wave motion.

waveform ('weɪv,fɔːm) *n Physics.* the shape of the graph of a wave or oscillation obtained by plotting the value of some changing quantity against time.

wavefront ('weɪv,frʌnt) *n Physics.* a surface associated with a propagating wave and passing through all points in the wave that have the same phase.

wave function *n Physics.* a mathematical function of position and sometimes time, used in wave mechanics to describe the state of a physical system. Symbol: ψ

waveguide ('weɪv,gaɪd) *n Electronics.* a solid rod of dielectric or a hollow metal tube, usually of rectangular cross section, used as a path to guide microwaves.

wavelength ('weɪv,leŋθ) *n* **1** the distance, measured in the direction of propagation, between two points of the same phase in consecutive cycles of a wave. Symbol: λ **2** the wavelength of the carrier wave used by a particular broadcasting station. **3 on someone's** (*or* **the same**) **wavelength.** *Inf.* having similar views, feelings, or thoughts (as someone else).

wavelet ('weɪvlɪt) *n* a small wave.

wave mechanics *n* (*functioning as sing*) *Physics.* the formulation of quantum mechanics in which the behaviour of systems, such as atoms, is described in terms of their wave functions.

wave number *n Physics.* the reciprocal of the wavelength of a wave.

waver **T** ('weɪvə) *vb* (*intr*) **1** to be irresolute; hesitate between two possibilities. **2** to become unsteady. **3** to fluctuate. **4** to move back and forth or one way and another. **5** (of light) to flicker or flash. ◆ *n* **6** the act or an instance of wavering. [C14: from ON *vafra* to flicker]
▸'**waverer** *n* ▸'**wavering** *adj* ▸'**waveringly** *adv*

wave theory *n* **1** the theory proposed by Huygens that light is transmitted by waves. **2** any theory that light or other radiation is transmitted as waves. ◆ Cf. **corpuscular theory.**

wavey ('weɪvɪ) *n Canad.* a snow goose or other wild goose. Also called: **wawa.** [via Canad. F from Algonquian (Cree *wehwew*)]

wavy ('weɪvɪ) *adj* **wavier, waviest. 1** abounding in or full of waves. **2** moving or proceeding in waves. **3** (of hair) set in or having waves.
▸'**wavily** *adv* ▸'**waviness** *n*

wax[1] (wæks) *n* **1** any of various viscous or solid materials of natural origin: characteristically lustrous, insoluble in water, and having a low softening temperature, they consist largely of esters of fatty acids. **2** any of various similar substances, such as paraffin wax, that have a mineral origin and consist largely of hydrocarbons. **3** short for **beeswax** or **sealing wax. 4** *Physiol.* another name for **cerumen. 5** a resinous preparation used by shoemakers to rub on thread. **6** any substance or object that is pliable or easily moulded: *he was wax in their hands.* **7** (*modifier*) made of or resembling wax: *a wax figure.* ◆ *vb* **8** (*tr*) to coat, polish, etc., with wax. [OE *weax*]
▸'**waxer** *n*

wax[2] **T** (wæks) *vb* (*intr*) **1** to become larger, more powerful, etc. **2** (of the moon) to show a gradually increasing portion of illuminated surface, between new moon and full moon. **3** to become: *to wax eloquent.* [OE *weaxan*]

wax[3] (wæks) *n Brit. inf., old-fashioned.* a fit of rage or temper: *he's in a wax today.* [from ?]

waxberry ('wæksbərɪ) *n, pl* **waxberries.** the waxy fruit of the wax myrtle or the snowberry.

waxbill ('wæks,bɪl) *n* any of various chiefly African finchlike weaverbirds having a brightly coloured bill and plumage.

wax cloth *n* **1** another name for **oilcloth. 2** (formerly) another name for **linoleum.**

waxen **T** ('wæksən) *adj* **1** made of, treated with, or covered with wax. **2** resembling wax in colour or texture.

waxeye ('wæks,aɪ) *n* a small New Zealand bird with a white circle around its eye. Also called: **silver-eye, blighty.**

wax flower *n Austral.* any of a genus of shrubs having waxy pink-white five-petalled flowers.

wax light *n* a candle or taper of wax.

wax myrtle *n* a shrub of SE North America, having evergreen leaves and a small berry-like fruit with a waxy coating. Also called: **bayberry, candleberry, waxberry.**

wax palm *n* **1** a tall Andean palm tree having pinnate leaves that yield a resinous wax used in making candles. **2** another name for **carnauba** (sense 1).

wax paper *n* paper treated or coated with wax or paraffin to make it waterproof.

waxplant ('wæks,plɑːnt) *n* a climbing shrub of E Asia and Australia, having fleshy leaves and clusters of small waxy white pink-centred flowers.

waxwing ('wæks,wɪŋ) *n* any of a genus of gregarious passerine songbirds having red waxy wing tips and crested heads.

waxwork ('wæks,wɜːk) *n* **1** an object reproduced in wax, esp. as an ornament. **2** a life-size lifelike figure, esp. of a famous person, reproduced in wax. **3** (*pl; functioning as sing or pl*) a museum or exhibition of wax figures.

waxy[1] ('wæksɪ) *adj* **waxier, waxiest. 1** resembling wax in colour, appearance, or texture. **2** made of, covered with, or abounding in wax.
▸'**waxily** *adv* ▸'**waxiness** *n*

waxy[2] ('wæksɪ) *adj* **waxier, waxiest.** *Brit. inf., old-fashioned.* bad-tempered or irritable; angry.

way **T** (weɪ) *n* **1** a manner, method, or means: *a way of life.* **2** a route or direction: *the way home.* **3a** a means or line of passage, such as a path or track. **3b** (*in combination*): *waterway.* **4** space or room for movement or activity (esp. in **make way, in the way, out of the way**). **5** distance, usu-

THESAURUS

2, 3 = tearful, rheumy, tear-filled, weepy **4 = diluted,** adulterated, dilute, flavourless, insipid, runny, tasteless, thin, washy, watered-down, waterish, weak, wishy-washy (*inf.*)
Antonyms *adj* ≠ **diluted:** concentrated, condensed, dense, fortified, solid, strong, thick

wave *vb* **1, 5 = brandish,** flap, flourish, flutter, move to and fro, oscillate, quiver, ripple, shake, stir, sway, swing, undulate, wag, waver, wield **2, 3 = signal,** beckon, direct, gesticulate, gesture, indicate, sign ◆ *n* **7 = ripple,** billow, breaker, comber, ridge, roller, sea surf, swell, undulation, unevenness **10, 11 = outbreak,** current, drift, flood, ground swell, movement, rash, rush, stream, surge, sweep, tendency, trend, upsurge

waver *vb* **1 = hesitate,** be indecisive, be irresolute, be unable to decide, be unable to make up one's mind, blow hot and cold (*inf.*), dither (*chiefly Brit.*), falter, fluctuate, hum and haw, seesaw, shillyshally (*inf.*), swither (*Scot.*), vacillate **2, 3, 5 = tremble,** flicker, fluctuate, quiver, reel, shake, sway, totter, undulate, vary, wave, weave, wobble
Antonyms *vb* ≠ **hesitate:** be decisive, be determined, be of fixed opinion, be resolute, determine, resolve, stand firm

wax[2] *vb* **1 = increase,** become fuller, become larger, develop, dilate, enlarge, expand, fill out, get bigger, grow, magnify, mount, rise, swell
Antonyms *vb* contract, decline, decrease, diminish, dwindle, fade, lessen, narrow, shrink, wane

waxen *adj* **2 = pale,** anaemic, ashen, bloodless, colourless, ghastly, pallid, wan, white, whitish

way *n* **1 = method,** approach, course of action, fashion, manner, means, mode, plan, practice, procedure, process, scheme, system, technique **2, 3, 10 = route,** access, avenue, channel, course, direction, highway, lane, path, pathway, road, street, thoroughfare, track, trail **4 = room,** elbowroom, opening, space **5 = distance,** journey, length, stretch, trail **6 = journey,** advance, approach, march, passage, progress **7, 8**

ally distance in general: *you've come a long way.* **6** a passage or journey: *on the way.* **7** characteristic style or manner: *I did it my way.* **8** (*often pl*) habit: *he has some offensive ways.* **9** an aspect of something; particular: *in many ways he was right.* **10a** a street in or leading out of a town. **10b** (*cap. when part of a street name*): *Icknield Way.* **11** something that one wants in a determined manner (esp. in **get** *or* **have one's (own) way**). **12** the experience or sphere in which one comes into contact with things (esp. in **come one's way**). **13** *Inf.* a state or condition, usually financial or concerning health (esp. in **in a good** (*or* **bad**) **way**). **14** *Inf.* the area or direction of one's home: *drop in if you're ever over my way.* **15** movement of a ship or other vessel. **16** a guide along which something can be moved, such as the surface of a lathe along which the tailstock slides. **17** (*pl*) the wooden or metal tracks down which a ship slides to be launched. **18** a course of life including experiences, conduct, etc.: *the way of sin.* **19 by the way.** incidentally. **20 by way of. 20a** via. **20b** serving as: *by way of introduction.* **20c** in the state or condition of: *by way of being an artist.* **21 each way.** (of a bet) laid on a horse, dog, etc., to win or gain a place. **22 give way. 22a** to collapse or break down. **22b** to yield. **23 give way to. 23a** to step aside for or stop for. **23b** to give full rein to (emotions, etc.). **24 go out of one's way.** to take considerable trouble or inconvenience oneself. **25 have a way with.** to have such a manner or skill as to handle successfully. **26 have it both ways.** to enjoy two things that would normally be mutually exclusive. **27 in a way.** in some respects. **28 in no way.** not at all. **29 lead the way. 29a** to go first. **29b** to set an example. **30 make one's way. 30a** to proceed or advance. **30b** to achieve success in life. **31 on the way out.** *Inf.* **31a** becoming unfashionable, etc. **31b** dying. **32 out of the way. 32a** removed or dealt with so as to be no longer a hindrance. **32b** remote. **32c** unusual and sometimes improper. **33 see one's way (clear).** to find it possible and be willing (to do something). **34 under way.** having started moving or making progress. ◆ *adv* **35** *Inf.* **35a** at a considerable distance or extent: *way over yonder.* **35b** very far: *they're way up the mountain.* **36** *Inf.* by far; considerably: *way better.* [OE *weg*]

waybill ('weɪˌbɪl) *n* a document attached to goods in transit specifying their nature, point of origin, and destination as well as the route to be taken and the rate to be charged.

wayfarer **T** ('weɪˌfɛərə) *n* a person who goes on a journey.
▸ **'wayˌfaring** *n, adj*

wayfaring tree *n* a shrub of Europe and W Asia, having white flowers and berries that turn from red to black.

waylay **T** (weɪ'leɪ) *vb* **waylays, waylaying, waylaid.** (*tr*) **1** to lie in wait for and attack. **2** to await and intercept unexpectedly.
▸ **way'layer** *n*

wayleave ('weɪˌliːv) *n* access to property granted by a landowner for payment, for example to allow a contractor access to a building site.

waymark ('weɪˌmɑːk) *n* a symbol or signpost marking the route of a footpath.
▸ **'wayˌmarked** *adj*

way-out **T** *adj Inf.* **1** extremely unconventional or experimental. **2** excellent or amazing.

-ways *suffix forming adverbs.* indicating direction or manner: *sideways.* [OE *weges,* lit.: of the way, from *weg* way]

ways and means **T** *pl n* **1** the revenues and methods of raising the revenues needed for the functioning of a state or other political unit. **2** the methods and resources for accomplishing some purpose.

wayside ('weɪˌsaɪd) *n* **1a** the side or edge of a road. **1b** (*modifier*) situated by the wayside: *a wayside inn.* **2 fall by the wayside.** to cease or fail to continue doing something: *of the nine starters, three fell by the wayside.*

wayward **T** ('weɪwəd) *adj* **1** wanting to have one's own way regardless of others. **2** capricious, erratic, or unpredictable. [C14: changed from *awayward* turned or turning away]
▸ **'waywardly** *adv* ▸ **'waywardness** *n*

wayworn ('weɪˌwɔːn) *adj Rare.* worn or tired by travel.

wb *abbrev. for:* **1** water ballast. **2** Also: **W/B, WB.** waybill. **3** westbound.

Wb *Physics. symbol for* weber.

WBA *abbrev. for* World Boxing Association.

WBC *abbrev. for* World Boxing Council.

WBU *abbrev. for* World Boxing Union.

WC *abbrev. for:* **1** Also: **wc.** water closet. **2** (in London postal code) West Central.

WD *abbrev. for:* **1** War Department. **2** Works Department.

we (wiː) *pron* (*subjective*) **1** refers to the speaker or writer and another person or other people: *we should go now.* **2** refers to all people or people in general: *the planet on which we live.* **3** a formal word for **I** used by editors or other writers, and formerly by monarchs. **4** *Inf.* used instead of *you* with a tone of condescension or sarcasm: *how are we today?* [OE *wē*]

WEA (in Britain) *abbrev. for* Workers' Educational Association.

weak **T** (wiːk) *adj* **1** lacking in physical or mental strength or force. **2** liable to yield, break, or give way: *a weak link in a chain.* **3** lacking in resolution or firmness of character. **4** lacking strength, power, or intensity: *a weak voice.* **5** lacking strength in a particular part: *a team weak in defence.* **6a** not functioning as well as is normal: *weak eyes.* **6b** easily upset: *a weak stomach.* **7** lacking in conviction, persuasiveness, etc.: *a weak argument.* **8** lacking in political or strategic strength: *a weak state.* **9** lacking the usual, full, or desirable strength of flavour: *weak tea.* **10** *Grammar.* **10a** denoting or belonging to a class of verbs, in Germanic languages, whose conjugation relies on inflectional endings rather than internal vowel gradation, as *look, looks, looking, looked.* **10b** belonging to any part-of-speech class, in any of various languages, whose inflections follow the more regular of two possible patterns. Cf. **strong** (sense 13). **11** (of a syllable) not accented or stressed. **12** (of an industry, market, securities, etc.) falling in price or characterized by falling prices. [OE *wāc* soft, miserable]
▸ **'weakish** *adj*

weaken **T** ('wiːkən) *vb* to become or cause to become weak or weaker.
▸ **'weakener** *n*

weak interaction *n Physics.* an interaction between elementary particles that is responsible for certain decay processes, operates at distances less than about 10^{-15} metres, and is 10^{12} times weaker than the strong interaction. Also called: **weak nuclear interaction** *or* **force.**

weak-kneed *adj Inf.* yielding readily to force, intimidation, etc.
▸ **ˌweak-'kneedly** *adv*

weakling **T** ('wiːklɪŋ) *n* a person or animal that is lacking in strength or weak in constitution or character.

weakly ('wiːklɪ) *adj* **weaklier, weakliest. 1** sickly; feeble. ◆ *adv* **2** in a weak or feeble manner.

weak-minded *adj* **1** lacking in stability of mind or character. **2** another word for **feeble-minded.**
▸ **ˌweak-'mindedly** *adv* ▸ **ˌweak-'mindedness** *n*

weakness **T** ('wiːknɪs) *n* **1** a being weak. **2** a failing, as in a person's character. **3** a self-indulgent liking: *a weakness for chocolates.*

THESAURUS

= **style**, characteristic, conduct, custom, habit, idiosyncrasy, manner, nature, personality, practice, trait, usage, wont **9** = **aspect**, detail, feature, particular, point, respect, sense **11** = **will**, aim, ambition, choice, demand, desire, goal, pleasure, wish **13** *Informal As in* **in a bad way** = **condition**, circumstance, fettle, shape (*inf.*), situation, state, status **19 by the way** = **incidentally**, by the bye, en passant, in parenthesis, in passing **22 give way: a** = **concede**, break down, cave in, crack, crumple, fall, fall to pieces, give, go to pieces, subside **b** accede, acknowledge defeat, acquiesce, back down, make concessions, withdraw, yield **34 under way** = **in progress**, afoot, begun, going, in motion, moving, on the go (*inf.*), on the move, started

wayfarer *n* = **traveller**, bird of passage, globetrotter, gypsy, itinerant, journeyer, nomad, rover, trekker, voyager, walker, wanderer

wayfaring *adj* = **roving**, drifting, itinerant, journeying, nomadic, peripatetic, rambling, travelling, voyaging, walking, wandering

waylay *vb* **1, 2** = **attack**, accost, ambush, catch, hold up, intercept, lie in wait for, pounce on, set upon, surprise, swoop down on

way-out *Informal adj* **1** = **outlandish**, advanced, avant-garde, bizarre, crazy, eccentric, experimental, far-out (*sl.*), freaky (*sl.*), oddball (*inf.*), offbeat, off-the-wall (*sl.*), outré, progressive, unconventional, unorthodox, weird, wild **2** = **wonderful**, amazing, awesome (*inf.*), brilliant, excellent, fantastic (*inf.*), great (*inf.*), marvellous, sensational (*inf.*), tremendous (*inf.*)

ways and means *pl n* **1, 2** = **capability**, ability, capacity, course, funds, methods, procedure, reserves, resources, tools, way, wherewithal

wayward *adj* **1, 2** = **erratic**, capricious, changeable, contrary, contumacious, cross-grained, disobedient, fickle, flighty, froward (*arch.*), headstrong, inconstant, incorrigible, insubordinate, intractable, mulish, obdurate, obstinate, perverse, rebellious, refractory, self-willed, stubborn, undependable, ungovernable, unmanageable, unpredictable, unruly, wilful
Antonyms *adj* complaisant, compliant, dependable, good-natured, malleable, manageable, obedient, obliging, predictable, reliable, submissive, tractable

weak *adj* **1** = **feeble**, anaemic, debilitated, decrepit, delicate, effete, enervated, exhausted, faint, fragile, frail, infirm, languid, puny, shaky, sickly, spent, tender, unsound, unsteady, wasted, weakly **2** = **deficient**, faulty, inadequate, lacking, pathetic, poor, substandard, under-strength, wanting **3** = **irresolute**, boneless, cowardly, impotent, indecisive, ineffectual, infirm, namby-pamby, pathetic, powerless, soft, spineless, timorous, weak-kneed (*inf.*) **4** = **faint**, distant, dull, imperceptible, low, muffled, poor, quiet, slight, small, soft **7** = **unconvincing**, feeble, flimsy, hollow, inconclusive, invalid, lame, pathetic, shallow, slight, unsatisfactory **9** = **tasteless**, diluted, insipid, milk-and-water, runny, thin, under-strength, waterish, watery, wishy-washy (*inf.*)
Antonyms *adj* ≠ **feeble:** energetic, hardy, healthy, hefty, mighty, strong, tough ≠ **deficient:** able, capable, effective ≠ **irresolute:** firm, resolute ≠ **unconvincing:** conclusive, convincing, forceful, incontrovertible, obvious, powerful, solid, trustworthy, valid ≠ **tasteless:** flavoursome, intoxicating, potent, tasty

weaken *vb* = **lessen**, abate, debilitate, depress, diminish, droop, dwindle, ease up, enervate, fade, fail, flag, give way, impair, invalidate, lower, mitigate, moderate, reduce, sap, sap the strength of, soften up, take the edge off, temper, tire, undermine, wane = **dilute**, adulterate, cut, debase, thin, thin out, water down
Antonyms *vb* ≠ **lessen:** boost, enhance, grow, improve, increase, invigorate, revitalize, strengthen

weakling *n* = **sissy**, coward, doormat (*sl.*), drip, jellyfish (*inf.*), milksop, mouse, wet (*Brit. inf.*), wimp (*inf.*)

weakness *n* **1** = **frailty**, debility, decrepitude, enervation, faintness, feebleness, fragility, impotence, infirmity, irresolution, powerlessness, vulnerability **2** = **failing**, Achilles heel, blemish, chink in one's armour, defect, deficiency, fault, flaw, imperfection, lack, shortcoming **3** = **liking**, fondness, inclination, partiality, passion, penchant, predilection, proclivity, proneness, soft spot
Antonyms *n* ≠ **frailty:** hardiness, health, impregnability, potency, power, stamina, sturdiness, valid-

weal[1] **T** (wiːl) *n* a raised mark on the skin produced by a blow. Also called: **welt.** [C19: var. of WALE, infl. in form by WHEAL]

weal[2] (wiːl) *n Arch.* prosperity or wellbeing (now esp. in **the public weal, the common weal**). [OE *wela*]

weald (wiːld) *n Brit. arch.* open or forested country. [OE]

Weald (wiːld) *n* **the.** a region of SE England, in Kent, Surrey, and Sussex between the North Downs and the South Downs: formerly forested.

wealth **T** (wɛlθ) *n* **1** a large amount of money and valuable material possessions. **2** the state of being rich. **3** a great profusion: *a wealth of gifts.* **4** *Econ.* all goods and services with monetary or productive value. [C13 *welthe,* from WEAL[2]]

wealth tax *n* a tax on personal property.

wealthy **T** (ˈwɛlθɪ) *adj* **wealthier, wealthiest. 1** possessing wealth; rich. **2** of or relating to wealth. **3** abounding: *wealthy in friends.*
▸ **ˈwealthily** *adv* ▸ **ˈwealthiness** *n*

wean[1] (wiːn) *vb (tr)* **1** to cause (a child or young mammal) to replace mother's milk by other nourishment. **2** (usually foll. by *from*) to cause to desert former habits, pursuits, etc. [OE *wenian* to accustom]

wean[2] (weɪn) *n Scot. & N English dialect.* a child. [? short form of WEANLING, or a contraction of *wee ane*]

weaner (ˈwiːnə) *n* **1** a person or thing that weans. **2** a pig that has just been weaned and weighs less than 40 kg. **3** *Austral. & NZ.* a lamb, pig, or calf in the year in which it is weaned.

weanling (ˈwiːnlɪŋ) *n* a child or young animal recently weaned. [C16: from WEAN[1] + -LING[1]]

weapon (ˈwɛpən) *n* **1** an object or instrument used in fighting. **2** anything that serves to get the better of an opponent: *his power of speech was his best weapon.* **3** any part of an animal that is used to defend itself, to attack prey, etc., such as claws or a sting. [OE *wǣpen*]
▸ **ˈweaponed** *adj* ▸ **ˈweaponless** *adj*

weaponry (ˈwɛpənrɪ) *n* weapons regarded collectively.

wear[1] **T** (wɛə) *vb* **wears, wearing, wore, worn. 1** *(tr)* to carry or have (a garment, etc.) on one's person as clothing, ornament, etc. **2** *(tr)* to carry or have on one's person habitually: *she wears a lot of red.* **3** *(tr)* to have in one's aspect: *to wear a smile.* **4** *(tr)* to display, show, or fly: *a ship wears its colours.* **5** to deteriorate or cause to deteriorate by constant use or action. **6** to produce or be produced by constant rubbing, scraping, etc.: *to wear a hole in one's trousers.* **7** to bring or be brought to a specified condition by constant use or action: *to wear a tyre to shreds.* **8** *(intr)* to submit to constant use or action in a specified way: *his suit wears well.* **9** *(tr)* to harass or weaken. **10** (when *intr,* often foll. by *on*) (of time) to pass or be passed slowly. **11** *(tr) Brit. inf.* to accept: *Larry won't wear that argument.* ◆ *n* **12** the act of wearing or state of being worn. **13a** anything designed to be worn: *leisure wear.* **13b** *(in combination): nightwear.* **14** deterioration from constant or normal use. **15** the quality of resisting the effects of constant use. ◆ See also **wear down, wear off, wear out.** [OE *werian*]
▸ **ˈwearer** *n*

wear[2] (wɛə) *vb* **wears, wearing, wore, worn.** *Naut.* to tack by gybing instead of by going through stays. [C17: from earlier *weare,* from ?]

wearable (ˈwɛərəbᵊl) *adj* suitable for wear or able to be worn.
▸ **ˌwearaˈbility** *n*

wear and tear *n* damage, depreciation, or loss resulting from ordinary use.

wear down **T** *vb (adv)* **1** to consume or be consumed by long or constant wearing, rubbing, etc. **2** to overcome or be overcome gradually by persistent effort.

wearing **T** (ˈwɛərɪŋ) *adj* causing fatigue or exhaustion; tiring.
▸ **ˈwearingly** *adv*

wearisome **T** (ˈwɪərɪsəm) *adj* causing fatigue or annoyance; tedious.
▸ **ˈwearisomely** *adv*

wear off **T** *vb (adv)* **1** *(intr)* to decrease in intensity gradually: *the pain will wear off in an hour.* **2** to disappear or cause to disappear gradually through exposure, use, etc.

wear out **T** *vb (adv)* **1** to make or become unfit or useless through wear. **2** *(tr)* to exhaust or tire.

weary **T** (ˈwɪərɪ) *adj* **wearier, weariest. 1** tired or exhausted. **2** causing fatigue or exhaustion. **3** caused by or suggestive of weariness: *a weary laugh.* **4** *(postpositive;* often foll. by *of* or *with)* discontented or bored. ◆ *vb* **wearies, wearying, wearied. 5** to make or become weary. **6** to make or become discontented or impatient. [OE *wērig*]
▸ **ˈweariless** *adj* ▸ **ˈwearily** *adv* ▸ **ˈweariness** *n* ▸ **ˈwearying** *adj*
▸ **ˈwearyingly** *adv*

weasand (ˈwiːzənd) *n* a former name for the **trachea.** [OE *wǣsend, wāsend*]

weasel (ˈwiːzᵊl) *n, pl* **weasels** *or* **weasel. 1** any of various small predatory mammals, such as the **European weasel,** having reddish-brown fur, an elongated body and neck, and short legs. **2** *Inf.* a sly or treacherous person. [OE *weosule, wesle*]
▸ **ˈweaselly** *adj*

weasel out *vb* **weasels, weaselling, weaselled** *or US* **weasels, weaseling, weaseled.** *(intr, adv) Inf., chiefly US & Canad.* **1** to go back on a commitment. **2** to evade a responsibility, esp. in a despicable manner.

weasel words *pl n Inf.* intentionally evasive or misleading speech; equivocation. [C20: from the weasel's supposed ability to suck an egg out of its shell without seeming to break the shell]

weather **T** (ˈwɛðə) *n* **1a** the day-to-day meteorological conditions, esp. temperature, cloudiness, and rainfall, affecting a specific place. **1b** *(modifier)* relating to the forecasting of weather: *a weather ship.* **2 make heavy weather. 2a** *Naut.* to roll and pitch in heavy seas. **2b** (foll. by *of*) *Inf.* to carry out with difficulty or unnecessarily great effort. **3 under the weather.** *Inf.* not in good health. ◆ *adj* **4** *(prenominal)* on or at the side or part towards the wind: *the weather anchor.* Cf. **lee** (sense 2). ◆ *vb* **5** to expose or be exposed to the action of the weather. **6** to undergo or cause to undergo changes, such as discoloration, due to the action of the weather. **7** *(intr)* to withstand the action of the weather. **8** (when *intr,* foll. by *through*) to endure (a crisis, danger, etc.). **9** *(tr)* to slope (a

THESAURUS

ity, vigour, virtue, vitality ≠ **failing:** advantage, forte, strength, strong point ≠ **liking:** aversion, dislike, hatred, loathing

weal[1] *n* = **mark,** contusion, ridge, scar, streak, stripe, wale, welt, wheal

wealth *n* **1, 2** = **riches,** affluence, assets, big money, capital, cash, estate, fortune, funds, goods, lucre, means, money, opulence, pelf, possessions, pretty penny (*inf.*), property, prosperity, resources, substance, tidy sum (*inf.*) **3** = **plenty,** abundance, bounty, copiousness, cornucopia, fullness, plenitude, profusion, richness, store
Antonyms *n* ≠ **riches:** deprivation, destitution, indigence, penury, poverty ≠ **plenty:** dearth, lack, need, paucity, poverty, scarcity, shortage, want

wealthy *adj* **1** = **rich,** affluent, comfortable, filthy rich, flush (*inf.*), in the money (*inf.*), loaded (*sl.*), made of money (*inf.*), moneyed, opulent, prosperous, quids in (*sl.*), rolling in it (*sl.*), stinking rich (*sl.*), well-heeled (*inf.*), well-off, well-to-do
Antonyms *adj* broke (*inf.*), deprived, destitute, dirt-poor (*inf.*), down and out, down at heel, flat broke (*inf.*), impoverished, indigent, needy, on the breadline, penniless, poor, poverty-stricken, short, skint (*Brit. sl.*)

wear[1] *vb* **1** = **be dressed in,** bear, be clothed in, carry, clothe oneself, don, dress in, have on, put on, sport (*inf.*) **4** = **show,** display, exhibit, fly **5** = **deteriorate,** abrade, consume, corrode, erode, fray, grind, impair, rub, use, wash away, waste **11** *Brit. informal* = **accept,** allow, brook, countenance, fall for, permit, put up with (*inf.*), stand for, stomach, swallow (*inf.*), take ◆ *n* **13** = **clothes,** apparel, attire, costume, dress, garb, garments, gear (*inf.*), habit, outfit, things, threads (*sl.*) **14** = **damage,** abrasion, attrition, corrosion, depreciation, deterioration, erosion, friction, use, wear and tear
Antonyms *n* ≠ **damage:** conservation, maintenance, preservation, repair, upkeep

wear down *vb* **1** = **erode,** abrade, be consumed, consume, corrode, grind down, rub away **2** = **undermine,** chip away at (*inf.*), fight a war of attrition against, overcome gradually, reduce

weariness *n* **1** = **tiredness,** drowsiness, enervation, exhaustion, fatigue, languor, lassitude, lethargy, listlessness, prostration
Antonyms *n* drive, energy, freshness, get-up-and-go (*inf.*), liveliness, stamina, vigour, vitality, zeal, zest

wearing *adj* = **tiresome,** exasperating, exhausting, fatiguing, irksome, oppressive, taxing, tiring, trying, wearisome
Antonyms *adj* easy, effortless, light, no bother, painless, refreshing, stimulating, undemanding

wearisome *adj* = **tedious,** annoying, boring, bothersome, burdensome, dull, exasperating, exhausting, fatiguing, humdrum, irksome, mind-numbing, monotonous, oppressive, pestilential, prosaic, tiresome, troublesome, trying, uninteresting, vexatious, wearing
Antonyms *adj* agreeable, delightful, enjoyable, exhilarating, interesting, invigorating, pleasurable, refreshing, stimulating

wear off *vb* **1** = **subside,** abate, decrease, diminish, disappear, dwindle, ebb, fade, lose effect, lose strength, peter out, wane, weaken **2** = **rub away,** abrade, disappear, efface, fade
Antonyms *vb* ≠ **subside:** grow, increase, intensify, magnify, persist, step up, strengthen, wax

wear out *vb* **1** = **deteriorate,** become useless, become worn, consume, erode, fray, impair, use up, wear through **2** = **exhaust,** enervate, fag out (*inf.*), fatigue, frazzle (*inf.*), knacker (*sl.*), prostrate, sap, tire, weary
Antonyms *vb* ≠ **exhaust:** buck up (*inf.*), energize, invigorate, pep up, perk up, refresh, revitalize, stimulate, strengthen

weary *adj* **1** = **tired,** all in (*sl.*), asleep *or* dead on one's feet (*inf.*), dead beat (*inf.*), dog-tired (*inf.*), done in (*inf.*), drained, drooping, drowsy, enervated, exhausted, fagged (*inf.*), fatigued, flagging, jaded, knackered (*sl.*), sleepy, spent, wearied, whacked (*Brit. inf.*), worn out **2** = **tiring,** arduous, enervative, irksome, laborious, taxing, tiresome, wearing, wearisome **4** = **fed up,** bored, browned-off (*inf.*), discontented, impatient, indifferent, jaded, sick (*inf.*), sick and tired (*inf.*) ◆ *vb* **5** = **tire,** burden, debilitate, drain, droop, enervate, fade, fag (*inf.*), fail, fatigue, grow tired, sap, take it out of (*inf.*), tax, tire out, wear out **6** = **bore,** annoy, become bored, exasperate, have had enough, irk, jade, make discontented, plague, sicken, try the patience of, vex
Antonyms *adj* ≠ **tired:** energetic, fresh, full of beans (*inf.*), full of get-up-and-go (*inf.*), invigorated, lively, refreshed, stimulated ≠ **tiring:** exciting, invigorating, original, refreshing ≠ **fed up:** amused, excited, forebearing, patient ◆ *vb* ≠ **tire:** enliven, invigorate, refresh, revive, stimulate ≠ **bore:** amuse, excite, interest

weather *n* **1** = **climate,** conditions **3** *Informal* **under the weather** = **ill,** ailing, below par, indisposed, nauseous, not well, off-colour, out of sorts, poorly (*inf.*), seedy (*inf.*), sick ◆ *vb* **5** = **toughen,** expose, harden, season **8** = **withstand,** bear up against, brave, come through, endure, get through, live through, make it (*inf.*), overcome, pull through, resist, ride out, rise above, stand, stick it out (*inf.*), suffer, surmount, survive
Antonyms *vb* ≠ **withstand:** cave in, collapse, fail, fall, give in, go under, succumb, surrender, yield

surface, such as a roof) so as to throw rainwater clear. **10** (*tr*) to sail to the windward of: *to weather a point.* [OE *weder*]
▸ **'weatherer** *n*

weather-beaten *adj* **1** showing signs of exposure to the weather. **2** tanned or hardened by exposure to the weather.

weatherboard ('wɛðə,bɔːd) *n* a timber board, with a groove (rabbet) along the front of its top edge and along the back of its lower edge, that is fixed horizontally with others to form an exterior covering on a wall or roof.
▸ **'weather,boarding** *n*

weather-bound *adj* (of a vessel, aircraft, etc.) delayed by bad weather.

weathercock ('wɛðə,kɒk) *n* **1** a weather vane in the form of a cock. **2** a person who is fickle or changeable.

weathered ('wɛðəd) *adj* **1** affected by exposure to the action of the weather. **2** (of rocks and rock formations) eroded, decomposed, or otherwise altered by the action of wind, frost, etc. **3** (of a sill, roof, etc.) having a sloped surface so as to allow rainwater to run off.

weather eye *n* **1** the vision of a person trained to observe changes in the weather. **2** *Inf.* an alert or observant gaze. **3 keep one's weather eye open.** to stay on the alert.

weatherglass ('wɛðə,glɑːs) *n* any of various instruments, esp. a barometer, that measure atmospheric conditions.

weather house *n* a model house, usually with two human figures, one that comes out to foretell bad weather and one that comes out to foretell good weather.

weathering ('wɛðərɪŋ) *n* the mechanical and chemical breakdown of rocks by the action of rain, snow, etc.

weatherly ('wɛðəlɪ) *adj* (of a sailing vessel) making very little leeway when close-hauled, even in a stiff breeze.
▸ **'weatherliness** *n*

weatherman ('wɛðə,mæn) *n, pl* **weathermen.** *Inf.* a person who forecasts the weather, esp. one who works in a meteorological office.

weather map *or* **chart** *n* a chart showing weather conditions, compiled from simultaneous observations taken at various weather stations.

weatherproof ('wɛðə,pruːf) *adj* **1** designed or able to withstand exposure to weather without deterioration. ◆ *vb* **2** (*tr*) to render (something) weatherproof.

weather station *n* one of a network of meteorological observation posts where weather data is recorded.

weather strip *n* a thin strip of compressible material, such as spring metal, felt, etc., that is fitted between the frame of a door or window and the opening part to exclude wind and rain. Also called: **weather-stripping.**

weather vane *n* a vane designed to indicate the direction in which the wind is blowing.

weather window *n* a limited interval when weather conditions can be expected to be suitable for a particular project.

weather-wise *adj* **1** skilful in predicting weather conditions. **2** skilful in predicting trends in opinion, reactions, etc.

weatherworn ('wɛðə,wɔːn) *adj* another word for **weather-beaten.**

weave ❶ (wiːv) *vb* **weaves, weaving, wove** *or* **weaved; woven** *or* **weaved. 1** to form (a fabric) by interlacing (yarn, etc.), esp. on a loom. **2** (*tr*) to make or construct by such a process: *to weave a shawl.* **3** to construct by interlacing (cane, twigs, etc.). **4** (of a spider) to make (a web). **5** (*tr*) to construct by combining separate elements into a whole. **6** (*tr; often foll. by in, into, through, etc.*) to introduce: *to weave factual details into a fiction.* **7** to create (a way, etc.) by moving from side to side: *to weave through a crowd.* **8 get weaving.** *Inf.* to hurry. ◆ *n* **9** the method or pattern of weaving or the structure of a woven fabric: *an open weave.* [OE *wefan*]

weaver ('wiːvə) *n* **1** a person who weaves, esp. as a means of livelihood. **2** short for **weaverbird.**

weaverbird ('wiːvə,bɜːd) *or* **weaver** *n* any of a family of small Old World passerine songbirds, having a short thick bill and a dull plumage and building covered nests: includes the house sparrow and whydahs.

web ❶ (wɛb) *n* **1** any structure, fabric, etc., formed by or as if by weaving or interweaving. **2** a mesh of fine tough threads built by a spider from a liquid secreted from its spinnerets and used to trap insects. **3** a similar network of threads spun by certain insect larvae, such as the silkworm. **4** a fabric, esp. one in the process of being woven. **5** a membrane connecting the toes of some aquatic birds or the digits of such aquatic mammals as the otter. **6** the vane of a bird's feather. **7** a thin piece of metal, esp. one connecting two thicker parts as in an H-beam or an I-beam. **8a** a continuous strip of paper as formed on a paper machine or fed from a reel into some printing presses. **8b** (*as modifier*): *web offset.* **9a** (*often cap.; preceded by the*) short for **World Wide Web. 9b** (*as modifier*): *web pages.* **10** any structure, construction, etc., that is intricately formed or complex: *a web of intrigue.* ◆ *vb* **webs, webbing, webbed. 11** (*tr*) to cover with or as if with a web. **12** (*tr*) to entangle or ensnare. **13** (*intr*) to construct a web. [OE *webb*]
▸ **'webless** *adj*

webbed (wɛbd) *adj* **1** (of the feet of certain animals) having the digits connected by a thin fold of skin. **2** having or resembling a web.

webbing ('wɛbɪŋ) *n* **1** a strong fabric of hemp, cotton, jute, etc., woven in strips and used under springs in upholstery or for straps, etc. **2** the skin that unites the digits of a webbed foot.

webby ('wɛbɪ) *adj* **webbier, webbiest.** of, relating to, resembling, or consisting of a web.

weber ('veɪbə) *n* the derived SI unit of magnetic flux; the flux that, when linking a circuit of one turn, produces in it an emf of 1 volt as it is reduced to zero at a uniform rate in one second. Symbol: Wb [C20: after W. E. *Weber* (1804–91), G physicist]

webfoot ('wɛb,fʊt) *n* **1** *Zool.* a foot having the toes connected by folds of skin. **2** *Anat.* a foot having an abnormal membrane connecting adjacent toes.

web-footed *or* **web-toed** *adj* (of certain animals) having webbed feet that facilitate swimming.

website ('wɛb,saɪt) *n* a group of connected pages on the World Wide Web containing information on a particular subject.

webwheel ('wɛb,wiːl) *n* **1** a wheel containing a plate or web instead of spokes. **2** a wheel of which the rim, spokes, and centre are in one piece.

wed ❶ (wɛd) *vb* **weds, wedding, wedded** *or* **wed. 1** to take (a person of the opposite sex) as a husband or wife; marry. **2** (*tr*) to join (two people) in matrimony. **3** (*tr*) to unite closely. [OE *weddian*]
▸ **'wedded** *adj*

we'd (wiːd; *unstressed* wɪd) *contraction of* we had *or* we would.

Wed. *abbrev. for* Wednesday.

wedding ❶ ('wɛdɪŋ) *n* **1a** the act of marrying or the celebration of a marriage. **1b** (*as modifier*): *wedding day.* **2** the anniversary of a marriage (in such combinations as **silver wedding** or **diamond wedding**).

wedding breakfast *n* the meal usually served after a wedding ceremony or just before the bride and bridegroom leave for their honeymoon.

wedding cake *n* a rich fruit cake, with one, two, or more tiers, covered with almond paste and decorated with royal icing, which is served at a wedding reception.

wedding ring *n* a band ring with parallel sides, typically of precious metal, worn to indicate married status.

wedge ❶ (wɛdʒ) *n* **1** a block of solid material, esp. wood or metal, that is shaped like a narrow V in cross section and can be pushed or driven between two objects or parts of an object in order to split or secure them. **2** any formation, structure, or substance in the shape of a wedge. **3** something such as an idea, action, etc., that tends to cause division. **4** a shoe with a wedge heel. **5** *Golf.* a club, a No. 10 iron with a face angle of more than 50°, used for bunker or pitch shots. **6** (formerly) a body of troops formed in a V-shape. **7 thin end of the wedge.** anything unimportant in itself that implies the start of something much larger. ◆ *vb* **wedges, wedging, wedged. 8** (*tr*) to secure with or as if with a wedge. **9** to squeeze or be squeezed like a wedge into a narrow space. **10** (*tr*) to force apart or divide with or as if with a wedge. [OE *wecg*]
▸ **'wedge,like** *adj* ▸ **'wedgy** *adj*

wedge heel *n* a raised shoe heel with the heel and sole forming a solid block.

wedge-tailed eagle *n* a large brown Australian eagle having a wedge-shaped tail. Also called: **eaglehawk,** (Inf.) **wedgie.**

Wedgwood ('wɛdʒwʊd) *Trademark.* ◆ *n* **1a** pottery produced at the Wedgwood factory, near Stoke-on-Trent. **1b** such pottery having applied decoration in white on a coloured ground. ◆ *adj* **2a** relating to pottery made at the Wedgwood factory. **2b** characteristic of such pottery: *Wedgwood blue.* [C18: after Josiah *Wedgwood* (1730–95), E potter]

wedlock ❶ ('wɛdlɒk) *n* **1** the state of being married. **2 born** *or* **conceived out of wedlock.** born or conceived when one's parents are not legally married. [OE *wedlāc*, from *wedd* pledge + *-lāc*, suffix denoting activity, ?from *lāc* game]

Wednesday ('wɛnzdɪ) *n* the fourth day of the week; third day of the working week. [OE *Wōdnes dæg* Woden's day, translation of L *mercurii dies* Mercury's day]

wee[1] ❶ (wiː) *adj* very small; tiny; minute. [C13: from OE *wǣg* weight]

wee[2] (wiː) *Inf., chiefly Brit.* ◆ *n* **1a** the act or an instance of urinating. **1b**

THESAURUS

weave *vb* **1, 3 = knit,** blend, braid, entwine, fuse, incorporate, interlace, intermingle, intertwine, introduce, mat, merge, plait, twist, unite **5 = create,** build, construct, contrive, fabricate, make, make up, put together, spin **7 = zigzag,** crisscross, move in and out, weave one's way, wind **8 get weaving** *Informal* **= start,** get a move on, get going, get one's finger out (*Brit. inf.*), get under way, hurry, make a start, shake a leg (*sl.*)

web *n* **1 = network,** interlacing, lattice, mesh, net, netting, screen, tangle, toils, weave, webbing **2 = spider's web,** cobweb **9 = World Wide Web,** information superhighway, Internet, net, WWW

wed *vb* **1 = marry,** become man and wife, be married to, espouse, get hitched, get married, join, make one, plight one's troth (*old-fashioned*), splice (*inf.*), take as one's husband, take as one's wife, take the plunge (*inf.*), take to wife, tie the knot (*inf.*), unite **3 = unite,** ally, blend, coalesce, combine, commingle, dedicate, fuse, interweave, join, link, marry, merge, unify, yoke

Antonyms *vb* ≠ **unite:** break up, disunite, divide, divorce, part, separate, sever, split

wedding *n* **1 = marriage,** espousals, marriage ceremony, nuptial rite, nuptials, wedlock

wedge *n* **1, 2 = block,** chock, chunk, lump, wodge (*Brit. inf.*) ◆ *vb* **8-10 = squeeze,** block, cram, crowd, force, jam, lodge, pack, ram, split, stuff, thrust

wedlock *n* **1 = marriage,** matrimony

wee[1] *adj* **= little,** diminutive, insignificant, itsy-bitsy (*inf.*), Lilliputian, microscopic, miniature, urine. ◆ *vb* **wees, weeing, weed. 2** (*intr*) to urinate. ◆ Also: **wee-wee.** [from ?]

weed (wi:d) *n* **1** any plant that grows wild and profusely, esp. one that grows among cultivated plants, depriving them of space, food, etc. **2** *Sl.* **2a the weed.** tobacco. **2b** marijuana. **3** *Inf.* a thin or unprepossessing person. **4** an inferior horse, esp. one showing signs of weakness. ◆ *vb* **5** to remove (useless or troublesome plants) from (a garden, etc.). [OE *weod*]
▸ **'weeder** *n* ▸ **'weedless** *adj*

weedkiller ('wi:d,kɪlə) *n* a substance, usually a chemical or hormone, used for killing weeds.

weed out ❶ *vb* (*tr, adv*) to separate out, remove, or eliminate (anything unwanted): *to weed out troublesome students.*

weeds (wi:dz) *pl n* a widow's black mourning clothes. Also called: **widow's weeds.** [C16: pl of *weed* (OE *wǣd, wēd*) a band worn in mourning]

weedy ❶ ('wi:dɪ) *adj* **weedier, weediest. 1** full of or containing weeds: *weedy land.* **2** (of a plant) resembling a weed in straggling growth. **3** *Inf.* thin or weakly in appearance.

week (wi:k) *n* **1** a period of seven consecutive days, esp. one beginning with Sunday. Related adj: **hebdomadal. 2** a period of seven consecutive days beginning from or including a specified day: *a week from Wednesday.* **3** the period of time within a week devoted to work. ◆ *adv* **4** *Chiefly Brit.* seven days before or after a specified day: *I'll visit you Wednesday week.* [OE *wice, wicu*]

weekday ('wi:k,deɪ) *n* any day of the week other than Sunday and, often, Saturday.

weekend *n* (,wi:k'ɛnd). **1a** the end of the week, esp. the period from Friday night until the end of Sunday. **1b** (*as modifier*): *a weekend party.* ◆ *vb* ('wi:k,ɛnd). **2** (*intr*) *Inf.* to spend or pass a weekend.

weekends (,wi:k'ɛndz) *adv Inf.* at the weekend, esp. regularly or during every weekend.

weekly ❶ ('wi:klɪ) *adj* **1** happening or taking place once a week or every week. **2** determined or calculated by the week. ◆ *adv* **3** once a week or every week. ◆ *n, pl* **weeklies. 4** a newspaper or magazine issued every week.

weeknight ('wi:k,naɪt) *n* the evening or night of a weekday.

ween (wi:n) *vb Arch.* to think or imagine (something). [OE *wēnan*]

weeny ('wi:nɪ) *adj* **weenier, weeniest.** *Inf.* very small; tiny. [C18: from WEE[1] with the ending *-ny* as in TINY]

weenybopper ('wi:nɪ,bɒpə) *n Inf.* a child of about 8 to 12 years who is a keen follower of pop music. [C20: formed on the model of TEENYBOPPER, from WEENY]

weep ❶ (wi:p) *vb* **weeps, weeping, wept. 1** to shed (tears). **2** (*tr;* foll. by *out*) to utter, shedding tears. **3** (when *intr*, foll. by *for*) to lament (for something). **4** to exude (drops of liquid). **5** (*intr*) (of a wound, etc.) to exude a watery fluid. ◆ *n* **6** a spell of weeping. [OE *wēpan*]

weeper ('wi:pə) *n* **1** a person who weeps, esp. a hired mourner. **2** something worn as a sign of mourning.

weeping ('wi:pɪŋ) *adj* (of plants) having slender hanging branches.
▸ **'weepingly** *adv*

weeping willow *n* a Chinese willow tree having long hanging branches.

weepy ❶ ('wi:pɪ) *Inf.* ◆ *adj* **weepier, weepiest. 1** liable or tending to weep. ◆ *n, pl* **weepies. 2** a sentimental film or book.
▸ **'weepily** *adv* ▸ **'weepiness** *n*

weever ('wi:və) *n* a small marine fish having venomous spines around the gills and the dorsal fin. [C17: from OF *wivre* viper, ult. from L *vīpera* VIPER]

weevil ('wi:vɪl) *n* any of numerous beetles, many having elongated snouts, that are pests, feeding on plants and plant products. [OE *wifel*]
▸ **'weevily** *adj*

wee-wee *n, vb* a variant of **wee**[2].

w.e.f. *abbrev. for* with effect from.

weft (wɛft) *n* the yarn woven across the width of the fabric through the lengthways warp yarn. Also called: **filling, woof.** [OE]

weigela (waɪ'gi:lə, -'dʒi:-) *n* a shrub of an Asian genus having clusters of showy bell-shaped flowers. [C19: from NL, after C. E. *Weigel* (1748–1831), G physician]

weigh[1] ❶ (weɪ) *vb* **1** (*tr*) to measure the weight of. **2** (*intr*) to have weight: *she weighs more than her sister.* **3** (*tr;* often foll. by *out*) to apportion according to weight. **4** (*tr*) to consider carefully: *to weigh the facts of a case.* **5** (*intr*) to be influential: *his words weighed little with the jury.* **6** (*intr;* often foll. by *on*) to be oppressive (to). **7 weigh anchor.** to raise a vessel's anchor or (of a vessel) to have its anchor raised preparatory to departure. ◆ See also **weigh down, weigh in,** etc. [OE *wegan*]
▸ **'weighable** *adj* ▸ **'weigher** *n*

weigh[2] (weɪ) *n* **under weigh.** a variant spelling of **under way.** [C18: var. due to the infl. of phrases such as *to weigh anchor*]

weighbridge ('weɪ,brɪdʒ) *n* a machine for weighing vehicles, etc., by means of a metal plate set into a road.

weigh down ❶ *vb* (*adv*) to press (a person, etc.) down by or as if by weight: *his troubles weighed him down.*

weigh in *vb* (*intr, adv*) **1a** (of a boxer or wrestler) to be weighed before a bout. **1b** (of a jockey) to be weighed after, or sometimes before, a race. **2** *Inf.* to contribute, as in a discussion, etc.: *he weighed in with a few sharp comments.* ◆ *n* **weigh-in. 3** the act of checking a competitor's weight, as in boxing, racing, etc.

weight ❶ (weɪt) *n* **1** a measure of the heaviness of an object; the amount anything weighs. **2** *Physics.* the vertical force experienced by a mass as a result of gravitation. **3** a system of units used to express weight: *troy weight.* **4** a unit used to measure weight: *the kilogram is the weight used in the metric system.* **5** any mass or heavy object used to exert pressure or weigh down. **6** an oppressive force: *the weight of cares.* **7** any heavy load: *the bag was such a weight.* **8** the main force; preponderance: *the weight of evidence.* **9** importance; influence: *his opinion carries weight.* **10** *Statistics.* one of a set of coefficients assigned to items of a frequency distribution that are analysed in order to represent the relative importance of the different items. **11** *Printing.* the apparent blackness of a printed typeface. **12 pull one's weight.** *Inf.* to do one's full or proper share of a task. **13 throw one's weight around.** *Inf.* to act in an overauthoritarian manner. ◆ *vb* (*tr*) **14** to add weight to. **15** to burden or oppress. **16** to add importance, value, etc., to (one side rather than another). **17** *Statistics.* to attach a weight or weights to. [OE *wiht*]
▸ **'weighter** *n*

weighted average *n Statistics.* a result produced by a technique designed to give recognition to the importance of certain factors when compiling the average of a group of values.

weighting ('weɪtɪŋ) *n* **1** a factor by which some quantity is multiplied in order to make it comparable with others. **2** an allowance paid to compensate for higher living costs: *a London weighting.*

weightlessness ('weɪtlɪsnɪs) *n* a state in which an object has no actual weight (because it is in space and unaffected by gravitational attraction) or no apparent weight (because the gravitational attraction equals the centripetal force and the object is in free fall).
▸ **'weightless** *adj*

weightlifting ('weɪt,lɪftɪŋ) *n* the sport of lifting barbells of specified weights in a prescribed manner.
▸ **'weight,lifter** *n*

weight training *n* physical exercise involving lifting weights, either heavy or light weights, as a way of improving muscle performance.

weight watcher *n* a person who tries to lose weight, esp. by dieting.

weighty ❶ ('weɪtɪ) *adj* **weightier, weightiest. 1** having great weight. **2** important. **3** causing worry.
▸ **'weightily** *adv* ▸ **'weightiness** *n*

weigh up *vb* (*tr, adv*) to make an assessment of (a person, situation, etc.); judge.

Weil's disease (vaɪlz) *n* another name for **leptospirosis.** [named after Adolf *Weil* (1848–1916), G physician]

Weimaraner ('vaɪmə,rɑ:nə, 'waɪmə,rɑ:-) *n* a breed of hunting dog, having a short grey coat and short tail. [C20: after *Weimar*, city in E central Germany, where the breed was developed]

weir (wɪə) *n* **1** a low dam that is built across a river to raise the water

THESAURUS

minuscule, minute, negligible, pygmy *or* pigmy, small, teensy-weensy, teeny, teeny-weeny, tiny

weed out *vb* = **eliminate**, dispense with, eradicate, extirpate, get rid of, remove, root out, separate out, shed, uproot

weedy *adj* **3** *Informal* = **weak**, feeble, frail, ineffectual, namby-pamby, nerdy *or* nurdy (*sl.*), puny, skinny, thin, undersized, weak-kneed (*inf.*)

weekly *adj* **1** = **once a week**, hebdomadal, hebdomadary ◆ *adv* **3** = **every week**, by the week, hebdomadally, once a week

weep *vb* **1-3** = **cry**, bemoan, bewail, blub (*sl.*), blubber, boohoo, complain, greet (*Scot. or arch.*), keen, lament, moan, mourn, shed tears, snivel, sob, ululate, whimper, whinge (*inf.*)
Antonyms *vb* be glad, celebrate, delight, exult, make merry, rejoice, revel, triumph

weepy *adj* **1** = **tearful**, blubbering, close to tears, crying, lachrymose, on the verge of tears, sobbing, weeping, whimpering ◆ *n* **2** = **tear-jerker** (*inf.*)

weigh[1] *vb* **1, 2** = **have a weight of**, measure the weight of, put on the scales, tip the scales at (*inf.*) **3** = **measure**, apportion, deal out, dole out **4** = **consider**, contemplate, deliberate upon, evaluate, examine, eye up, give thought to, meditate upon, mull over, ponder, reflect upon, study, think over **5** = **matter**, be influential, carry weight, count, cut any ice (*inf.*), have influence, impress, tell **6** *often foll. by* **on** = **oppress**, bear down, burden, prey

weigh down *vb* = **burden**, bear down, depress, get down, oppress, overburden, overload, press down, trouble, weigh upon, worry
Antonyms *vb* alleviate, ease, hearten, help, lift, lighten, refresh, relieve, unburden

weight *n* **1** = **heaviness**, avoirdupois, burden, gravity, heft (*inf.*), load, mass, poundage, pressure, tonnage **5** = **load**, ballast, heavy object, mass **6** = **burden**, albatross, load, millstone, oppression, pressure, strain **8** = **preponderance**, greatest force, main force, onus **9** = **importance**, authority, bottom, clout (*inf.*), consequence, consideration, efficacy, emphasis, impact, import, influence, moment, persuasiveness, power, significance, substance, value ◆ *vb* **14** = **load**, add weight to, ballast, charge, freight, increase the load on, increase the weight of, make heavier **15** = **burden**, encumber, handicap, impede, oppress, overburden, weigh down **16** = **bias**, load, slant, unbalance

weighty *adj* **1** = **heavy**, burdensome, cumbersome, dense, hefty (*inf.*), massive, ponderous **2** = **important**, consequential, considerable, critical, crucial, forcible, grave, momentous, portentous, serious, significant, solemn, substantial **3** = **onerous**, backbreaking, burdensome, crushing, demanding, difficult, exacting, oppressive, taxing, worrisome, worrying
Antonyms *adj* ≠ **important**: frivolous, immaterial, incidental, inconsequential, insignificant, minor, petty, trivial, unimportant

level, divert the water, or control its flow. **2** a series of traps or enclosures placed in a stream to catch fish. [OE *wer*]

weird Ⓣ (wɪəd) *adj* **1** suggestive of or relating to the supernatural; eerie. **2** strange or bizarre. **3** *Arch.* of or relating to fate or the Fates. ◆ *n* **4** *Arch., chiefly Scot.* **4a** fate or destiny. **4b** one of the Fates. [OE *(ge)wyrd* destiny]
▸ˈ**weirdly** *adv* ▸ˈ**weirdness** *n*

weirdo Ⓣ (ˈwɪədəʊ) *or* **weirdie** (ˈwɪədɪ) *n, pl* **weirdos** *or* **weirdies.** *Inf.* a person who behaves in a bizarre or eccentric manner.

Weismannism (ˈvaɪsmənˌɪzəm) *n* the theory that all inheritable characteristics are transmitted by the reproductive cells and that characteristics acquired during the lifetime of the organism are not inherited. [C19: after August *Weismann* (1834–1914), G biologist]

weka (ˈwɛkə) *n* a nocturnal flightless bird of New Zealand. Also called: **Maori hen, wood hen.** [from Maori]

welch (wɛlʃ) *vb* a variant spelling of **welsh.**

Welch (wɛlʃ) *adj, n* an archaic spelling of **Welsh.**

welcome Ⓣ (ˈwɛlkəm) *adj* **1** gladly and cordially received or admitted: *a welcome guest.* **2** bringing pleasure: *a welcome gift.* **3** freely permitted or invited: *you are welcome to call.* **4** under no obligation (only in such phrases as **you're welcome,** as conventional responses to thanks). ◆ *sentence substitute.* **5** an expression of cordial greeting. ◆ *n* **6** the act of greeting or receiving a person or thing; reception: *the new theory had a cool welcome.* **7 wear out** *or* **overstay one's welcome.** to come more often or stay longer than is pleasing. ◆ *vb* **welcomes, welcoming, welcomed.** (*tr*) **8** to greet the arrival of (guests, etc.) cordially. **9** to receive or accept, esp. gladly. [C12: changed (through infl. of WELL[1]) from OE *wilcuma* (agent n referring to a welcome guest), *wilcume* (a greeting of welcome), from *wil* WILL[2] + *cuman* to come]
▸ˈ**welcomely** *adv* ▸ˈ**welcomer** *n*

weld[1] Ⓣ (wɛld) *vb* **1** (*tr*) to unite (pieces of metal or plastic), as by softening with heat and hammering or by fusion. **2** to bring or admit of being brought into close union. ◆ *n* **3** a joint formed by welding. [C16: altered from obs. *well* to melt, weld]
▸ˈ**weldable** *adj* ▸ˌ**weldaˈbility** *n* ▸ˈ**welder** *or* ˈ**weldor** *n*

weld[2] (wɛld), **wold,** *or* **woald** (wəʊld) *n* a yellow dye obtained from the plant dyer's rocket. [C14: from Low G]

welfare Ⓣ (ˈwɛlˌfɛə) *n* **1** health, happiness, prosperity, and wellbeing in general. **2a** financial and other assistance given to people in need. **2b** (*as modifier*): *welfare services.* **3** Also called: **welfare work.** plans or work to better the social or economic conditions of various underprivileged groups. **4 on welfare.** *Chiefly US & Canad.* in receipt of financial aid from a government agency or other source. [C14: from *wel fare;* see WELL[1], FARE]

welfare economics *n* (*functioning as sing*) the aspects of economic theory concerned with the welfare of society and priorities to be observed in the allocation of resources.

welfare state *n* a system in which the government undertakes the chief responsibility for providing for the social and economic security of its population, usually through unemployment insurance, old age pensions, and other social-security measures.

welkin (ˈwɛlkɪn) *n Arch.* the sky, heavens, or upper air. [OE *wolcen, welcen*]

well[1] Ⓣ (wɛl) *adv* **better, best. 1** (*often used in combination*) in a satisfactory manner: *the party went very well.* **2** (*often used in combination*) in a skilful manner: *she plays the violin well; a well-chosen example.* **3** in a correct or careful manner: *listen well to my words.* **4** in a prosperous manner: *to live well.* **5** (*usually used with auxiliaries*) suitably; fittingly: *you can't very well say that.* **6** intimately: *I knew him well.* **7** in a kind or favourable manner: *she speaks well of you.* **8** fully: *to be well informed.* **9** by a considerable margin: *let me know well in advance.* **10** (preceded by *could, might,* or *may*) indeed: *you may well have to do it yourself.* **11** *Inf.* (intensifier): *well safe.* **12 all very well.** used ironically to express discontent, dissent, etc. **13 as well. 13a** in addition; too. **13b** (preceded by *may* or *might*) with equal effect: *you might as well come.* **14 as well as.** in addition to. **15** (**just**) **as well.** preferable or advisable: *it would be just as well if you paid me now.* **16 leave well** (**enough**) **alone.** to refrain from interfering with something that is satisfactory. **17 well and good.** used to indicate calm acceptance, as of a decision. **18 well up in.** well acquainted with (a particular subject); knowledgeable about. ◆ *adj* (*usually postpositive*) **19** (when *prenominal, usually used with a negative*) in good health: *I'm very well, thank you; he's not a well man.* **20** satisfactory or pleasing. **21** prudent; advisable: *it would be well to make no comment.* **22** prosperous or comfortable. **23** fortunate: *it is well that you agreed to go.* ◆ *interj* **24a** an expression of surprise, indignation, or reproof. **24b** an expression of anticipation in waiting for an answer or remark. ◆ *sentence connector.* **25** an expression used to preface a remark, gain time, etc.: *well, I don't think I will come.* [OE *wel*]

well[2] Ⓣ (wɛl) *n* **1** a hole or shaft bored into the earth to tap a supply of water, oil, gas, etc. **2** a natural pool where ground water comes to the surface. **3a** a cavity, space, or vessel used to contain a liquid. **3b** (*in combination*): *an inkwell.* **4** an open shaft through the floors of a building, such as one used for a staircase. **5** a deep enclosed space in a building or between buildings that is open to the sky. **6** a bulkheaded compartment built around a ship's pumps for protection and ease of access. **7** (in England) the open space in the centre of a law court. **8** an abundant source: *he is a well of knowledge.* ◆ *vb* **9** to flow or cause to flow upwards or outwards: *tears welled from her eyes.* [OE *wella*]

we'll (wiːl) *contraction of* we will *or* we shall.

well-advised *adj* (**well advised** *when postpositive*). **1** acting with deliberation or reason. **2** well thought out: *a well-advised plan.*

well-affected *adj* (**well affected** *when postpositive*). favourably disposed (towards); steadfast or loyal.

well-appointed *adj* (**well appointed** *when postpositive*). well equipped or furnished.

wellaway (ˈwɛləˈweɪ) *interj Arch.* woe! alas! [OE, from *wei lā wei,* var. of *wā lā wā,* lit.: woe! lo woe]

well-balanced Ⓣ *adj* (**well balanced** *when postpositive*). **1** having good balance or proportions. **2** sane or sensible.

wellbeing (ˈwɛlˈbiːɪŋ) *n* the condition of being contented, healthy, or successful; welfare.

well-bred Ⓣ *adj* (**well bred** *when postpositive*). **1** Also: **well-born.** of respected or noble lineage. **2** indicating good breeding: *well-bred manners.* **3** of good thoroughbred stock: *a well-bred spaniel.*

well-chosen *adj* (**well chosen** *when postpositive*). carefully selected to produce a desired effect; apt: *a few well-chosen words.*

well-connected *adj* (**well connected** *when postpositive*). having influential or important relatives or friends.

well-disposed *adj* (**well disposed** *when postpositive*). inclined to be sympathetic, kindly, or friendly.

well-done *adj* (**well done** *when postpositive*). **1** (of food, esp. meat) cooked thoroughly. **2** made or accomplished satisfactorily.

THESAURUS

weird *adj* **1, 2 = strange,** bizarre, creepy (*inf.*), eerie, eldritch (*poetic*), far-out, freakish, ghostly, grotesque, mysterious, odd, outlandish, queer, spooky (*inf.*), supernatural, uncanny, unearthly, unnatural
Antonyms *adj* common, mundane, natural, normal, ordinary, regular, typical, usual

weirdo *n Informal* **= eccentric,** crackpot (*inf.*), crank (*inf.*), freak (*inf.*), headbanger (*inf.*), headcase (*inf.*), loony (*sl.*), nut (*sl.*), nutcase (*sl.*), nutter (*Brit. sl.*), oddball (*inf.*), queer fish (*Brit. inf.*)

welcome *adj* **1, 2 = acceptable,** accepted, agreeable, appreciated, delightful, desirable, gladly received, gratifying, pleasant, pleasing, pleasurable, refreshing, wanted **3, 4 = free,** at home, invited, under no obligation ◆ *n* **6 = greeting,** acceptance, entertainment, hospitality, reception, salutation ◆ *vb* **8, 9 = greet,** accept gladly, bid welcome, embrace, hail, meet, offer hospitality to, receive, receive with open arms, roll out the red carpet for, usher in
Antonyms *adj* ≠ **acceptable:** disagreeable, excluded, rebuffed, rejected, unacceptable, undesirable, unpleasant, unwanted, unwelcome ◆ *n* ≠ **greeting:** cold shoulder, exclusion, ostracism, rebuff, rejection, slight, snub ◆ *vb* ≠ **greet:** exclude, rebuff, refuse, reject, slight, snub, spurn, turn away

weld[1] *vb* **1, 2 = join,** bind, bond, braze, cement, connect, fuse, link, solder, unite ◆ *n* **3 = joint,** bond, juncture, seam

welfare *n* **1 = wellbeing,** advantage, benefit, good, happiness, health, interest, profit, prosperity, success

well[1] *adv* **1 = satisfactorily,** agreeably, capitally, famously (*inf.*), happily, in a satisfactory manner, like nobody's business (*inf.*), nicely, pleasantly, smoothly, splendidly, successfully **2 = skilfully,** ably, adeptly, adequately, admirably, conscientiously, correctly, effectively, efficiently, expertly, proficiently, properly, with skill **3 = carefully,** accurately, attentively, closely **4 = prosperously,** comfortably, flourishingly **5 = suitably,** correctly, easily, fairly, fittingly, in all fairness, justly, properly, readily, rightly **6 = intimately,** closely, completely, deeply, fully, personally, profoundly, thoroughly **7 = favourably,** approvingly, glowingly, graciously, highly, kindly, warmly **8 = considerably,** abundantly, amply, completely, fully, greatly, heartily, highly, substantially, sufficiently, thoroughly, very much **13a as well = also,** besides, in addition, into the bargain, to boot, too **14 as well as = including,** along with, at the same time as, in addition to, over and above ◆ *adj* **19 = healthy,** able-bodied, alive and kicking, fighting fit (*inf.*), fit, fit as a fiddle, hale, hearty, in fine fettle, in good health, robust, sound, strong, up to par **20, 21 = satisfactory,** advisable, agreeable, bright, fine, fitting, flourishing, fortunate, good, happy, lucky, pleasing, profitable, proper, prudent, right, thriving, useful
Antonyms *adv* ≠ **satisfactorily:** badly, inadequately, poorly, wrongly ≠ **skilfully:** badly, ham-fistedly, incompetently, incorrectly, ineptly, inexpertly, sloppily, unskilfully ≠ **suitably:** unfairly, unjustly, unsuitably ≠ **intimately:** slightly, somewhat, vaguely ≠ **favourably:** coldly, disapprovingly, gracelessly, unkindly, unsympathetically ◆ *adj* ≠ **healthy:** ailing, at death's door, below par, feeble, frail, green about the gills, ill, infirm, poorly, run-down, sick, sickly, under-the-weather, unwell, weak ≠ **satisfactory:** going badly, improper, unfitting, unsatisfactory, unsuccessful, wrong

well[2] *n* **1 = hole,** bore, pit, shaft **2 = waterhole,** fount, fountain, pool, source, spring **8 = source,** fount, mine, repository, wellspring ◆ *vb* **9 = flow,** exude, gush, jet, ooze, pour, rise, run, seep, spout, spring, spurt, stream, surge, trickle

well-balanced *adj* **1 = well-proportioned,** graceful, harmonious, proportional, symmetrical **2 = sensible,** judicious, level-headed, rational, reasonable, sane, sober, sound, together (*sl.*), well-adjusted
Antonyms *adj* ≠ **sensible:** erratic, insane, irrational, neurotic, unbalanced, unreasonable, unsound, unstable, volatile

well-bred *adj* **1 = aristocratic,** blue-blooded, gentle, highborn, noble, patrician, well-born **2 = polite,** civil, courteous, courtly, cultivated, cultured, gallant, genteel, gentlemanly, ladylike, mannerly, polished, refined, sophisticated, urbane, well-brought-up, well-mannered
Antonyms *adj* ≠ **polite:** bad-mannered, base, coarse, discourteous, ill-bred, rude, uncivilized, uncouth, uncultured, vulgar

well dressing *n* the decoration of wells with flowers, etc.: a traditional annual ceremony of great antiquity in some parts of Britain, originally associated with the cult of water deities.
well-favoured ❶ *adj* (**well favoured** *when postpositive*). good-looking.
well-formed formula *n Logic.* a group of logical symbols that makes sense; a logical sentence.
well-found *adj* (**well found** *when postpositive*). furnished or supplied with all or most necessary things.
well-founded *adj* (**well founded** *when postpositive*). having good grounds: *well-founded rumours.*
well-groomed ❶ *adj* (**well groomed** *when postpositive*). having a tidy pleasing appearance.
well-grounded *adj* (**well grounded** *when postpositive*). **1** well instructed in the basic elements of a subject. **2** another term for **well-founded.**
wellhead ('wɛl,hɛd) *n* **1** the source of a well or stream. **2** a source, fountainhead, or origin.
well-heeled ❶ *adj* (**well heeled** *when postpositive*). *Inf.* rich; prosperous; wealthy.
wellies ('wɛlɪz) *pl n Brit. inf.* Wellington boots.
well-informed ❶ *adj* (**well informed** *when postpositive*). **1** having knowledge about a great variety of subjects: *he seems to be a well-informed person.* **2** possessing reliable information on a particular subject.
Wellington boots *pl n* **1** Also called: **gumboots.** *Brit.* knee-length or calf-length rubber boots, worn esp. in wet conditions. Often shortened to **wellingtons, wellies. 2** military leather boots covering the front of the knee but cut away at the back to allow easier bending of the knee. [C19: after the 1st Duke of *Wellington* (1769–1852), Brit. soldier & statesman]
wellingtonia (,wɛlɪŋ'təʊnɪə) *n* a giant Californian coniferous tree, often reaching 90 metres high. Also called: **big tree, sequoia.** [C19: after the 1st Duke of *Wellington*]
well-intentioned *adj* (**well intentioned** *when postpositive*). having benevolent intentions, usually with unfortunate results.
well-knit *adj* (**well knit** *when postpositive*). strong, firm, or sturdy.
well-known ❶ *adj* (**well known** *when postpositive*). **1** widely known; famous; celebrated. **2** known fully or clearly.
well-mannered ❶ *adj* (**well mannered** *when postpositive*). having good manners; polite.
well-meaning *adj* (**well meaning** *when postpositive*). having or indicating good intentions, usually with unfortunate results.
well-nigh ❶ *adv Arch. or poetic.* nearly; almost: *it's well-nigh three o'clock.*
well-off ❶ *adj* (**well off** *when postpositive*). **1** in a comfortable or favourable position or state. **2** financially well provided for; moderately rich.
well-oiled *adj* (**well oiled** *when postpositive*). *Inf.* drunk.
well-preserved *adj* (**well preserved** *when postpositive*). **1** kept in a good condition. **2** continuing to appear youthful: *she was a well-preserved old lady.*
well-read ('wɛl'rɛd) *adj* (**well read** *when postpositive*). having read widely and intelligently; erudite.
well-rounded *adj* (**well rounded** *when postpositive*). **1** rounded in shape or well developed: *a well-rounded figure.* **2** full, varied, and satisfying: *a well-rounded life.*
well-spoken *adj* (**well spoken** *when postpositive*). **1** having a clear, articulate, and socially acceptable accent and way of speaking. **2** spoken satisfactorily or pleasingly.
wellspring ❶ ('wɛl,sprɪŋ) *n* **1** the source of a spring or stream. **2** a source of abundant supply.
well-stacked *adj* (**well stacked** *when postpositive*). *Sl.* (of a woman) of voluptuous proportions.
well sweep *n* a device for raising buckets from and lowering them into a well, consisting of a long pivoted pole, the bucket being attached to one end by a long rope.
well-tempered *adj* (**well tempered** *when postpositive*). (of a musical scale or instrument) conforming to the system of equal temperament. See **temperament** (sense 4).
well-thought-of ❶ *adj* respected.
well-thumbed *adj* (**well thumbed** *when postpositive*). (of a book) having the pages marked from frequent turning.
well-to-do ❶ *adj* moderately wealthy.
well-turned *adj* (**well turned** *when postpositive*). **1** (of a phrase, etc.) apt and pleasing. **2** having a pleasing shape: *a well-turned leg.*
well-upholstered *adj* (**well upholstered** *when postpositive*). *Inf.* (of a person) fat.
well-wisher *n* a person who shows benevolence or sympathy towards a person, cause, etc.
▸ **'well-,wishing** *adj, n*
well-woman *n, pl* **well-women.** *Social welfare.* **a** a woman who attends a health-service clinic for preventive monitoring, health education, etc. **b** (*as modifier*): *well-woman clinic.*
well-worn ❶ *adj* (**well worn** *when postpositive*). **1** so much used as to be affected by wear: *a well-worn coat.* **2** hackneyed: *a well-worn phrase.*
welly ('wɛlɪ) *n* **1** (*pl* **wellies**) *Inf.* Also called: **welly boot.** a Wellington boot. **2** *Sl.* energy, concentration, or commitment (esp. in **give it some welly**).
welsh *or* **welch** (wɛlʃ) *vb* (*intr*; often foll. by *on*) **1** to fail to pay a gambling debt. **2** to fail to fulfil an obligation. [C19: from ?]
▸ **'welsher** *or* **'welcher** *n*
Welsh (wɛlʃ) *adj* **1** of, relating to, or characteristic of Wales, its people, their language, or their dialect of English. ◆ *n* **2** a language of Wales, belonging to the S Celtic branch of the Indo-European family. **3 the Welsh.** (*functioning as pl*) the natives or inhabitants of Wales. [OE *Wēlisc, Wǣlisc*]
Welsh corgi *n* another name for **corgi.**
Welsh dresser *n* a sideboard with drawers and cupboards below and open shelves above.
Welsh harp *n* a type of harp in which the strings are arranged in three rows.
Welshman ('wɛlʃmən) *or* (*fem*) **Welshwoman** *n, pl* **Welshmen** *or* **Welshwomen.** a native or inhabitant of Wales.
Welsh poppy *n* a perennial W European plant with large yellow flowers.
Welsh rabbit *n* a savoury dish consisting of melted cheese sometimes mixed with milk, seasonings, etc., on hot buttered toast. Also called: **Welsh rarebit, rarebit.** [C18: a fanciful coinage; *rarebit* is a later folk-etymological var.]
Welsh terrier *n* a wire-haired breed of terrier with a black-and-tan coat.
welt ❶ (wɛlt) *n* **1** a raised or strengthened seam in a garment. **2** another word for **weal**[1]. **3** (in shoemaking) a strip of leather, etc., put in between the outer sole and the inner sole and upper. ◆ *vb* (*tr*) **4** to put a welt in (a garment, etc.). **5** to beat soundly. [C15: from ?]
welter ❶ ('wɛltə) *vb* (*intr*) **1** to roll about, writhe, or wallow. **2** (esp. of the sea) to surge, heave, or toss. **3** to lie drenched in a liquid, esp. blood. ◆ *n* **4** a confused mass; jumble. [C13: from MLow G, MDu. *weltern*]
welterweight ('wɛltə,weɪt) *n* **1a** a professional boxer weighing 140–147 pounds (63.5–66.5 kg). **1b** an amateur boxer weighing 63.5–67 kg (140–148 pounds). **2a** a professional wrestler weighing 155–165 pounds (71–75 kg). **2b** an amateur wrestler weighing 69–74 kg (151–161 pounds).
wen[1] (wɛn) *n* **1** *Pathol.* a sebaceous cyst, esp. one occurring on the scalp. **2** a large overcrowded city (esp. London, **the great wen**). [OE *wenn*]
wen[2] (wɛn) *n* a rune having the sound of Modern English *w.* [OE *wen, wyn*]
wench (wɛntʃ) *n* **1** a girl or young woman: now used facetiously. **2** *Arch.* a female servant. **3** *Arch.* a prostitute. ◆ *vb* (*intr*) **4** *Arch.* to frequent the company of prostitutes. [OE *wencel* child, from *wancol* weak]
▸ **'wencher** *n*
wend ❶ (wɛnd) *vb* to direct (one's course or way); travel. [OE *wendan*]
Wend (wɛnd) *n* (esp. in medieval European history) a member of the Slavonic people who inhabited the area between the Rivers Saale and Oder, in central Europe, in the early Middle Ages. Also called: **Sorb.**
wendigo ('wɛndɪ,gəʊ) *n Canad.* **1** (*pl* **wendigos**) (among Algonquian In-

THESAURUS

well-favoured *adj* = **attractive**, beautiful, bonny, comely, fair, good-looking, handsome, lovely, nice-looking, pretty
well-groomed *adj* = **smart**, dapper, neat, soigné *or* soignée, spruce, tidy, trim, well-dressed, well turned out
well-heeled *adj Informal* = **prosperous**, affluent, comfortable, flush, in clover (*inf.*), in the money (*inf.*), loaded (*sl.*), moneyed, opulent, rich, wealthy, well-off, well-situated, well-to-do
well-informed *adj* **1, 2** = **educated**, acquainted, *au courant, au fait*, aware, clued-up (*inf.*), cognizant *or* cognisant, conversant, informed, in the know (*inf.*), in the loop (*inf.*), knowledgeable *or* knowledgable, understanding, well-educated, well-grounded, well-read, well-versed
well-known *adj* **1** = **famous**, celebrated, familiar, illustrious, notable, noted, on the map, popular, renowned, widely known
well-mannered *adj* = **polite**, civil, courteous, genteel, gentlemanly, gracious, ladylike, mannerly, respectful, well-bred
well-nigh *adv Archaic or poetic* = **almost**, all but, just about, more or less, nearly, next to, practically, virtually
well-off *adj* **1** = **fortunate**, comfortable, flourishing, lucky, successful, thriving **2** = **rich**, affluent, comfortable, flush, loaded (*sl.*), moneyed, prosperous, wealthy, well-heeled (*inf.*), well-to-do
Antonyms *adj* ≠ **rich:** badly off, broke (*inf.*), destitute, dirt-poor (*inf.*), down and out, down at heel, flat broke (*inf.*), hard up (*inf.*), impoverished, indigent, needy, on the breadline, on the rocks (*inf.*), penniless, poor, poverty-stricken, short, without two pennies to rub together (*inf.*)
wellspring *n* **1** = **fountainhead**, fount, origin, source, wellhead **2** = **supply**, fount, fund, mine, repository, reserve, reservoir, source, well
well-thought-of *adj* = **respected**, admired, esteemed, highly regarded, of good repute, reputable, revered, venerated
Antonyms *adj* abhorred, derided, despised, disdained, reviled, scorned, spurned
well-to-do *adj* = **prosperous**, affluent, comfortable, flush (*inf.*), moneyed, well-heeled (*inf.*), well-off
Antonyms *adj* bankrupt, broke (*inf.*), destitute, down at heel, hard up (*inf.*), indigent, insolvent, needy, on the breadline, poor, ruined
well-worn *adj* **2** = **stale**, banal, commonplace, hackneyed, overused, stereotyped, threadbare, timeworn, tired, trite
welt *n* **2** = **mark**, contusion, ridge, scar, streak, stripe, wale, weal, wheal
welter *vb* **1** = **roll**, flounder, lie, splash, tumble, wade, wallow, writhe **2** = **surge**, billow, heave, pitch, roll, swell, toss ◆ *n* **4** = **jumble**, confusion, hotchpotch, mess, muddle, tangle, web
wend *vb* = **go**, direct one's course, make for, move, proceed, progress, travel

dians) an evil spirit or cannibal. **2** (*pl* **wendigo** *or* **wendigos**) another name for **splake.** [from Algonquian: evil spirit or cannibal]

Wendy house ('wɛndɪ) *n* a small model house for children to play in. [C20: after the house built for *Wendy,* the girl in J. M. Barrie's play *Peter Pan* (1904)]

wensleydale ('wɛnzlɪˌdeɪl) *n* **1** a type of white cheese with a flaky texture. **2** a breed of sheep with long woolly fleece. [after *Wensleydale,* North Yorkshire]

went (wɛnt) *vb* the past tense of **go.** [C15: p.t. of WEND used as p.t. of *go*]

wentletrap ('wɛntᵊlˌtræp) *n* a marine gastropod mollusc having a long pointed pale-coloured longitudinally ridged shell. [C18: from Du. *winteltrap* spiral shell, from *wintel,* earlier *windel,* from *wenden* to wind + *trap* a step]

wept (wɛpt) *vb* the past tense and past participle of **weep.**

were (wɜː; *unstressed* wə) *vb* the plural form of the past tense (indicative mood) of **be** and the singular form used with *you.* It is also used as a subjunctive, esp. in conditional sentences. [OE *wērun, wǣron* p.t. pl of *wesan* to be]

> **USAGE NOTE** *Were,* as a remnant of the past subjunctive in English, is used in formal contexts in clauses expressing hypotheses (*if he were to die, she would inherit everything*), suppositions contrary to fact (*if I were you, I would be careful*), and desire (*I wish he were there now*). In informal speech, however, *was* is often used instead.

we're (wɪə) *contraction of* we are.

weren't (wɜːnt) *contraction of* were not.

werewolf ('wɪəˌwulf, 'wɛə-) *n, pl* **werewolves.** a person fabled in folklore and superstition to have been changed into a wolf by being bewitched or said to be able to assume wolf form at will. [OE *werewulf,* from *wer* man + *wulf* wolf]

wergild, weregild ('wɜːˌgɪld, 'wɛə-), *or* **wergeld** ('wɜːˌgeld, 'wɛə-) *n* the price set on a man's life in Anglo-Saxon and Germanic law, to be paid as compensation by his slayer. [OE *wergeld,* from *wer* man + *gield* tribute]

wert (wɜːt; *unstressed* wət) *vb Arch. or dialect.* (used with the pronoun *thou* or its relative equivalent) a singular form of the past tense (indicative mood) of **be.**

weskit ('wɛskɪt) *n* an informal name for **waistcoat.**

Wesleyan ('wɛzlɪən) *adj* **1** of or deriving from John Wesley (1703–91), British preacher who founded Methodism. **2** of or characterizing Methodism, esp. in its original form. ◆ *n* **3** a follower of John Wesley. **4** a member of the Methodist Church.
▸**'Wesleyanˌism** *n*

west (wɛst) *n* **1** the direction along a parallel towards the sunset, at 270° clockwise from north. **2 the west.** (*often cap.*) any area lying in or towards the west. Related adjs.: **Hesperian, Occidental. 3** (*usually cap.*) *Cards.* the player or position at the table corresponding to west on the compass. ◆ *adj* **4** situated in, moving towards, or facing the west. **5** (esp. of the wind) from the west. ◆ *adv* **6** in, to, or towards the west. **7 go west.** *Inf.* **7a** to be lost or destroyed. **7b** to die. [OE]

West (wɛst) *n* **the. 1** the western part of the world contrasted historically and culturally with the East or Orient. **2** the countries of western Europe and North America. **3** (in the US) that part of the US lying approximately to the west of the Mississippi. **4** (in the ancient and medieval world) the Western Roman Empire and, later, the Holy Roman Empire. ◆ *adj* **5** of or denoting the western part of a specified country, area, etc.

westbound ('wɛstˌbaʊnd) *adj* going or leading towards the west.

west by north *n* one point on the compass north of west.

west by south *n* one point on the compass south of west.

West Country *n* **the.** the southwest of England, esp. Cornwall, Devon, and Somerset.

West End *n* **the.** a part of W central London containing the main shopping and entertainment areas.

westering ('wɛstərɪŋ) *adj Poetic.* moving towards the west: *the westering star.*

Westerlies ('wɛstəlɪz) *pl n Meteorol.* the prevailing winds blowing from the west on the poleward sides of the horse latitudes, often bringing depressions and anticyclones.

westerly ('wɛstəlɪ) *adj* **1** of, relating to, or situated in the west. ◆ *adv, adj* **2** towards or in the direction of the west. **3** (esp. of the wind) from the west. ◆ *n, pl* **westerlies. 4** a wind blowing from the west.
▸**'westerliness** *n*

western ('wɛstən) *adj* **1** situated in or facing the west. **2** going or directed to or towards the west. **3** (of a wind, etc.) coming from the west. **4** native to the west. **5** *Music.* See **country and western.**
▸**'westernˌmost** *adj*

Western ('wɛstən) *adj* **1** of or characteristic of the West as opposed to the Orient. **2** of or characteristic of North America and western Europe. **3** of or characteristic of the western states of the US. ◆ *n* **4** (*often not cap.*) a film, book, etc., concerned with life in the western states of the US, esp. during the era of exploration.

Western Church *n* **1** the part of Christendom that derives its liturgy, discipline, and traditions principally from the patriarchate of Rome. **2** the Roman Catholic Church, sometimes together with the Anglican Communion of Churches.

westerner ('wɛstənə) *n* (*sometimes cap.*) a native or inhabitant of the west of any specific region.

western hemisphere *n* (*often caps.*) **1** that half of the globe containing the Americas, lying to the west of the Greenwich or another meridian. **2** the lands contained in this, esp. the Americas.

westernize *or* **westernise** ('wɛstəˌnaɪz) *vb* **westernizes, westernizing, westernized** *or* **westernises, westernising, westernised.** (*tr*) to influence or make familiar with the customs, practices, etc., of the West.
▸**ˌwesterniˈzation** *or* **ˌwesterniˈsation** *n*

Western Roman Empire *n* the westernmost of the two empires created by the division of the later Roman Empire, esp. after its final severance from the Eastern Roman Empire (395 A.D.). Also called: **Western Empire.**

westing ('wɛstɪŋ) *n Navigation.* movement, deviation, or distance covered in a westerly direction, esp. as expressed in the resulting difference in longitude.

Westminster ('wɛstˌmɪnstə) *n* **1** Also called: **City of Westminster.** a borough of Greater London, on the River Thames. **2** the Houses of Parliament at Westminster.

west-northwest *n* **1** the point on the compass or the direction midway between west and northwest, 292° 30′ clockwise from north. ◆ *adj, adv* **2** in, from, or towards this direction.

Weston standard cell ('wɛstən) *n* a primary cell used as a standard of emf: consists of a mercury anode and a cadmium amalgam cathode in an electrolyte of saturated cadmium sulphate. [C20: from a trademark]

west-southwest *n* **1** the point on the compass or the direction midway between southwest and west, 247° 30′ clockwise from north. ◆ *adj, adv* **2** in, from, or towards this direction.

westward ('wɛstwəd) *adj* **1** moving, facing, or situated in the west. ◆ *adv* **2** Also: **westwards.** towards the west. ◆ *n* **3** the westward part, direction, etc.
▸**'westwardly** *adj, adv*

wet ❶ (wɛt) *adj* **wetter, wettest. 1** moistened, covered, saturated, etc., with water or some other liquid. **2** not yet dry or solid: *wet varnish.* **3** rainy: *wet weather.* **4** employing a liquid, usually water: *a wet method of chemical analysis.* **5** *Chiefly US & Canad.* permitting the free sale of alcoholic beverages: *a wet state.* **6** *Brit. inf.* feeble or foolish. **7 wet behind the ears.** *Inf.* immature or inexperienced. ◆ *n* **8** wetness or moisture. **9** rainy weather. **10** *Brit. inf.* a feeble or foolish person. **11** (*often cap.*) *Brit. inf.* a Conservative politician who is not a hardliner. **12** *Chiefly US & Canad.* a person who advocates free sale of alcoholic beverages. **13 the wet.** *Austral.* (in northern and central Australia) the rainy season. ◆ *vb* **wets, wetting, wet** *or* **wetted. 14** to make or become wet. **15** to urinate on (something). **16** (*tr*) *Dialect.* to prepare (tea) by boiling or infusing. [OE *wǣt*]
▸**'wetly** *adv* ▸**'wetness** *n* ▸**'wettable** *adj* ▸**'wetter** *n* ▸**'wettish** *adj*

wet-and-dry-bulb thermometer *n* another name for **psychrometer.**

wet blanket *n Inf.* a person whose low spirits or lack of enthusiasm have a depressing effect on others.

wet cell *n* a primary cell in which the electrolyte is a liquid.

wet dream *n* an erotic dream accompanied by an emission of semen.

wet fly *n Angling.* an artificial fly designed to float or ride below the water surface.

wether ('wɛðə) *n* a male sheep, esp. a castrated one. [OE *hwæther*]

wetland ('wɛtlənd) *n* (*sometimes pl*) **a** an area of marshy land, esp. considered as part of an ecological system. **b** (*as modifier*): *wetland species.*

wet look *n* a shiny finish such as that given to certain clothing and footwear materials.

wet nurse *n* **1** a woman hired to suckle the child of another. ◆ *vb* **wet-nurse, wet-nurses, wet-nursing, wet-nursed.** (*tr*) **2** to act as a wet nurse to (a child). **3** *Inf.* to attend with great devotion.

wet pack *n Med.* a hot or cold damp sheet or blanket for wrapping around a patient.

wet rot *n* **1** a state of decay in timber caused by various fungi. The hyphal strands of the fungus are seldom visible, and affected timber turns dark brown. **2** any of the fungi causing this decay.

wet suit *n* a close-fitting rubber suit used by skin-divers, yachtsmen, etc., to retain body heat.

wetting agent *n Chem.* any substance added to a liquid to lower its

THESAURUS

wet *adj* **1** = **damp,** aqueous, dank, drenched, dripping, humid, moist, moistened, saturated, soaked, soaking, sodden, soggy, sopping, waterlogged, watery, wringing wet **3** = **rainy,** clammy, dank, drizzling, humid, misty, pouring, raining, showery, teeming **6** *Brit. informal* = **feeble,** boneless, effete, foolish, ineffectual, irresolute, namby-pamby, nerdy *or* nurdy (*sl.*), silly, soft, spineless, timorous, weak, weedy (*inf.*) **7 wet behind the ears** *Informal* = **naive,** as green as grass, born yesterday, callow, green, immature, inexperienced, innocent, new, raw ◆ *n* **8** = **moisture,** clamminess, condensation, damp, dampness, humidity, liquid, water, wetness **9** = **rain,** damp weather, drizzle, rains, rainy season, rainy weather **10** *Brit. informal* = **weakling,** drip (*inf.*), milksop, weed (*inf.*), wimp (*inf.*) ◆ *vb* **14** = **moisten,** damp, dampen, dip, douse, drench, humidify, irrigate, saturate, soak, splash, spray, sprinkle, steep, water

Antonyms *adj* ≠ **damp:** bone-dry, dried, dry, hardened, parched, set ≠ **rainy:** arid, dry, fine, sunny ◆ *n* ≠ **moisture:** dryness ≠ **rain:** dry weather, fine weather ◆ *vb* ≠ **moisten:** dehydrate, desiccate, dry, parch

wetness *n* **1** = **damp,** clamminess, condensation, dampness, humidity, liquid, moisture, sogginess, water, wet surface tension and thus increase its ability to spread across or penetrate a solid.

we've (wi:v) *contraction of* we have.

wf *Printing. abbrev. for* wrong fount.

WFF *Logic. abbrev. for* well-formed formula.

WFTU *abbrev. for* World Federation of Trade Unions.

W. Glam *abbrev. for* West Glamorgan.

whack Ⓣ (wæk) *vb (tr)* **1** to strike with a sharp resounding blow. **2** (*usually passive*) *Brit. inf.* to exhaust completely. ◆ *n* **3** a sharp resounding blow or the noise made by such a blow. **4** *Inf.* a share or portion. **5** *Inf.* a try or attempt (esp. in **have a whack at**). **6 out of whack.** *Inf.* out of order; unbalanced: *the whole system is out of whack.* [C18: ? var. of THWACK, ult. imit.]
▸'**whacker** *n*

whacking Ⓣ ('wækɪŋ) *Inf., chiefly Brit.* ◆ *adj* **1** enormous. ◆ *adv* **2** (intensifier): *a whacking big lie.*

whacky ('wækɪ) *adj* **whackier, whackiest.** *US sl.* a variant spelling of **wacky.**

whale[1] (weɪl) *n, pl* **whales** *or* **whale. 1** any of the larger cetacean mammals, excluding dolphins, porpoises, and narwhals. They have flippers, a streamlined body, and a horizontally flattened tail and breathe through a blowhole on the top of the head. **2 a whale of 2a** *Inf.* an exceptionally large, fine, etc., example of a (person or thing). [OE *hwæl*]

whale[2] (weɪl) *vb* **whales, whaling, whaled.** (*tr*) to beat or thrash soundly. [C18: var. of WALE]

whaleboat ('weɪl,bəʊt) *n* a narrow boat from 20 to 30 feet long having a sharp prow and stern, formerly used in whaling. Also called: **whaler.**

whalebone ('weɪl,bəʊn) *n* **1** Also called: **baleen.** a horny elastic material forming numerous thin plates that hang from the upper jaw in the toothless (whalebone) whales and strain plankton from water entering the mouth. **2** a strip of this substance, used in stiffening corsets, etc.

whalebone whale *n* any whale belonging to a cetacean suborder having a double blowhole and strips of whalebone between the jaws instead of teeth: includes the rorquals, right whales, and the blue whale.

whale oil *n* oil obtained either from the blubber of whales (train oil) or the head of the sperm whale (sperm oil).

whaler ('weɪlə) *n* **1** Also called (US): **whaleman.** a person employed in whaling. **2** a vessel engaged in whaling. **3** *Austral. obs. sl.* a tramp or sundowner. **4** an aggressive shark of Australian coastal waters.

whale shark *n* a large spotted whalelike shark of warm seas, that feeds on plankton and small animals.

whaling ('weɪlɪŋ) *n* the work or industry of hunting and processing whales for food, oil, etc.

wham Ⓣ (wæm) *n* **1** a forceful blow or impact or the sound produced by it. ◆ *vb* **whams, whamming, whammed. 2** to strike or cause to strike with great force. [C20: imit.]

whanau ('fɑ:naʊ) *n NZ.* a family, esp. an extended family. [Maori]

whang (wæŋ) *vb* **1** to strike or be struck so as to cause a resounding noise. ◆ *n* **2** the resounding noise produced by a heavy blow. **3** a heavy blow. [C19: imit.]

whangee (wæŋ'i:) *n* **1** a tall woody grass of an Asian genus, grown for its stems. **2** a cane or walking stick made from the stem of this plant. [C19: prob. from Chinese (Mandarin) *huangli,* from *huang* yellow + *li* bamboo cane]

whare ('wɔ:rɪ; *Maori* 'fɒrɛ) *n NZ.* **1** a Maori hut or dwelling place. **2** any simple dwelling place. [from Maori]

wharepuni ('fɒrɛ,puni) *n NZ.* in a Maori community, a lofty carved building that is used as a guesthouse. [from Maori WHARE + *puni* company]

wharf Ⓣ (wɔ:f) *n, pl* **wharves** (wɔ:vz) *or* **wharfs. 1** a platform built parallel to the waterfront at a harbour or navigable river for the docking, loading, and unloading of ships. ◆ *vb (tr)* **2** to moor or dock at a wharf. **3** to store or unload on a wharf. [OE *hwearf* heap]

wharfage ('wɔ:fɪdʒ) *n* **1** facilities for ships at wharves. **2** a charge for use of a wharf. **3** wharves collectively.

wharfie ('wɔ:fɪ) *n Austral. & NZ.* a wharf labourer; docker.

wharfinger ('wɔ:fɪndʒə) *n* an owner or manager of a wharf. [C16: prob. alteration of *wharfager*]

wharve (wɔ:v) *n* a wooden disc or wheel on a shaft serving as a flywheel or pulley. [OE *hweorfa,* from *hweorfan* to revolve]

what (wɒt; *unstressed* wət) *determiner* **1a** used with a noun in requesting further information about the identity or categorization of something: *what job does he do?* **1b** (*as pron*): *what is her address?* **1c** (*used in indirect questions*): *tell me what he said.* **2a** the (person, thing, persons, or things) that: *we photographed what animals we could see.* **2b** (*as pron*): *bring me what you've written.* **3** (intensifier; used in exclamations): *what a good book!* ◆ *adv* **4** in what respect? to what degree?: *what do you care?* **5 what about.** what do you think, know, etc., concerning? **6 what for. 6a** for what purpose? why? **6b** *Inf.* a punishment or reprimand (esp. in **give (a person) what for**). **7 what have you.** someone or something unknown or unspecified: *cars, motorcycles, or what have you.* **8 what if. 8a** what would happen if? **8b** what difference would it make if? **9 what matter.** what does it matter? **10 what's what.** *Inf.* the true state of affairs. [OE *hwæt*]

> **USAGE NOTE** The use of *are* in sentences such as *what we need are more doctors* is common, although many people think *is* should be used: *what we need is more doctors.*

whatever (wɒt'ɛvə, wət-) *pron* **1** everything or anything that: *do whatever he asks you to.* **2** no matter what: *whatever he does, he is forgiven.* **3** *Inf.* an unknown or unspecified thing or things: *take a hammer, chisel, or whatever.* **4** an intensive form of *what,* used in questions: *whatever can he have said to upset her so much?* ◆ *determiner* **5** an intensive form of *what: use whatever tools you can get hold of.* ◆ *adj* **6** (*postpositive*) absolutely; whatsoever: *I saw no point whatever in continuing.*

whatnot ('wɒt,nɒt) *n* **1** Also called: **what-d'you-call-it.** *Inf.* a person or thing the name of which is unknown or forgotten. **2** *Inf.* unspecified assorted material. **3** a portable stand with shelves for displaying ornaments, etc.

whatsit ('wɒtsɪt), **whatsitsname,** (*masc*) **whatshisname,** *or* (*fem*) **whatshername** *n Inf.* a person or thing the name of which is unknown or forgotten.

whatsoever (,wɒtsəʊ'ɛvə) *adj* **1** (*postpositive*) at all: used as an intensifier with indefinite pronouns and determiners such as *none, anybody,* etc. ◆ *pron* **2** an archaic word for **whatever.**

whaup (hwɔ:p) *n Chiefly Scot.* a popular name for the **curlew.** [C16: rel. to OE *huilpe,* ult. imit. of the bird's cry]

wheal (wi:l) *n* a variant spelling of **weal**[1].

wheat (wi:t) *n* **1** any of a genus of grasses, native to the Mediterranean region and W Asia but widely cultivated, having erect flower spikes and light brown grains. **2** the grain of any of these grasses, used in making flour, pasta, etc. ◆ See also **durum.** [OE *hwǣte*]

wheatbelt ('wi:t,bɛlt) *n* an area in which wheat is the chief agricultural product.

wheatear ('wi:t,ɪə) *n* a small northern songbird having a pale grey back, black wings and tail, white rump, and pale brown underparts. [C16: back formation from *wheatears* (wrongly taken as pl), prob. from WHITE + ARSE]

wheaten ('wi:tᵊn) *adj* **1** made of the grain or flour of wheat. **2** of a pale yellow colour.

wheat germ *n* the vitamin-rich embryo of the wheat kernel.

wheatmeal ('wi:t,mi:l) *n* **a** a brown flour intermediate between white flour and wholemeal flour. **b** (*as modifier*): *a wheatmeal loaf.*

Wheatstone bridge ('wi:tstən) *n* a device for determining the value of an unknown resistance by comparison with a known standard resistance. [C19: after Sir Charles *Wheatstone* (1802–75), Brit. physicist and inventor]

whee (wi:) *interj* an exclamation of joy, etc.

wheedle Ⓣ ('wi:dᵊl) *vb* **wheedles, wheedling, wheedled. 1** to persuade or try to persuade (someone) by coaxing words, flattery, etc. **2** (*tr*) to obtain thus: *she wheedled some money out of her father.* [C17: ?from G *wedeln* to wag one's tail, from OHG *wedil, wadil* tail]
▸'**wheedler** *n* ▸'**wheedling** *adj* ▸'**wheedlingly** *adv*

wheel Ⓣ (wi:l) *n* **1** a solid disc, or a circular rim joined to a hub by spokes, that is mounted on a shaft about which it can turn, as in vehicles. **2** anything like a wheel in shape or function. **3** a device consisting of or resembling a wheel: *a steering wheel; a water wheel.* **4** (usually preceded by *the*) a medieval torture in which the victim was tied to a wheel and then had his limbs struck and broken by an iron bar. **5** short for **wheel of fortune** or **potter's wheel. 6** the act of turning. **7** a pivoting movement of troops, ships, etc. **8** a type of firework coiled to make it rotate when let off. **9** a set of short rhyming lines forming the concluding part of a stanza. **10** *US & Canad.* an informal word for **bicycle. 11** *Inf., chiefly US & Canad.* a person of great influence (esp. in **big wheel**). **12 at the wheel. 12a** driving or steering a vehicle or vessel. **12b** in charge. ◆ *vb* **13** to turn or cause to turn on or as if on an axis. **14** (when *intr,* sometimes foll. by *about* or *around*) to move or cause to move on or as if on wheels; roll. **15** (*tr*) to perform with or in a circular movement. **16** (*tr*) to provide with a wheel or wheels. **17** (*intr;* often foll. by *about*) to change direction. **18 wheel and deal.** *Inf.* to operate free of restraint, esp. to advance one's own interests. ◆ See also **wheels.** [OE *hweol, hweowol*]

THESAURUS

whack *vb* **1** = **strike,** bang, bash (*inf.*), beat, belabour, belt (*inf.*), box, buffet, chin (*sl.*), clobber (*sl.*), clout (*inf.*), cuff, deck (*sl.*), hit, lambast(e), lay one on (*sl.*), rap, slap, slug, smack, sock (*sl.*), swipe, thrash, thump, thwack, wallop (*inf.*) ◆ *n* **3** = **blow,** bang, bash (*inf.*), belt (*inf.*), box, buffet, clout (*inf.*), cuff, hit, rap, slap, slug, smack, sock (*sl.*), stroke, swipe, thump, thwack, wallop (*inf.*), wham **4** *Informal* = **share,** allotment, bit, cut (*inf.*), part, portion, quota **5** *Informal As in* **have a whack** = **attempt,** bash (*inf.*), crack (*inf.*), go (*inf.*), shot (*inf.*), stab (*inf.*), try, turn

whacking *adj* **1** *Informal, chiefly Brit.* = **huge,** big, elephantine, enormous, extraordinary, giant, gigantic, great, humongous *or* humungous (*US sl.*), large, mammoth, monstrous, prodigious, tremendous, whopping (*inf.*)

wham *n* **1** = **blow,** bang, bash (*inf.*), concussion, impact, slam, smack, thump, thwack, wallop (*inf.*), whack, whang

wharf *n* **1** = **dock,** jetty, landing stage, pier, quay

wheedle *vb* **1, 2** = **coax,** butter up, cajole, charm, court, draw, entice, flatter, inveigle, persuade, talk into, worm

wheel *n* **2** = **circle,** gyration, pivot, revolution, roll, rotation, spin, turn, twirl, whirl **12 at the wheel** = **in control,** at the helm, driving, in charge, in command, in the driving seat, steering ◆ *vb* **13-15** = **turn,** circle, gyrate, orbit, pir-

wheel and axle *n* a simple machine for raising weights in which a rope unwinding from a wheel is wound onto a cylindrical drum or shaft coaxial with or joined to the wheel to provide mechanical advantage.

wheel animalcule *n* another name for **rotifer.**

wheelbarrow ('wiːlˌbærəʊ) *n* a simple vehicle for carrying small loads, typically being an open container supported by a wheel at the front and two legs behind.

wheelbase ('wiːlˌbeɪs) *n* the distance between the front and back axles of a motor vehicle.

wheelchair ('wiːlˌtʃɛə) *n* special chair on large wheels, for use by invalids or others for whom walking is impossible or inadvisable.

wheel clamp *n* a device fixed onto one wheel of an illegally parked car in order to immobilize it. The driver has to pay to have it removed.

wheeled (wiːld) *adj* **a** having a wheel or wheels. **b** (*in combination*): *four-wheeled.*

wheeler ('wiːlə) *n* **1** Also called: **wheel horse.** a horse or other draught animal nearest the wheel. **2** (*in combination*) something equipped with a specified sort or number of wheels: *a three-wheeler.* **3** a person or thing that wheels.

wheeler-dealer *n Inf.* a person who wheels and deals.

wheel horse *n* **1** another word for **wheeler** (sense 1). **2** *US & Canad.* a person who works steadily or hard.

wheelhouse ('wiːlˌhaʊs) *n* another term for **pilot house.**

wheelie ('wiːlɪ) *n* a manoeuvre on a bicycle or motorbike in which the front wheel is raised off the ground.

wheelie bin *or* **wheely bin** *n* a large container for rubbish, esp. one used by a household, mounted on wheels so that it can be moved more easily.

wheel lock *n* **1** a gunlock formerly in use in which the firing mechanism was activated by sparks produced by friction between a small steel wheel and a flint. **2** a gun having such a lock.

wheel of fortune *n* (in mythology and literature) a revolving device spun by a deity selecting random changes in the affairs of man.

wheels (wiːlz) *pl n* **1** the main directing force behind an organization, movement, etc.: *the wheels of government.* **2** an informal word for **car. 3 wheels within wheels.** a series of intricately connected events, plots, etc.

wheel window *n* another name for **rose window.**

wheel wobble *n* an oscillation of the front wheels of a vehicle caused by a defect in the steering gear, unbalanced wheels, etc.

wheelwright ('wiːlˌraɪt) *n* a person who makes or mends wheels as a trade.

wheeze Ⓣ (wiːz) *vb* **wheezes, wheezing, wheezed. 1** to breathe or utter (something) with a rasping or whistling sound. **2** (*intr*) to make or move with a noise suggestive of wheezy breathing. ◆ *n* **3** a husky, rasping, or whistling sound or breathing. **4** *Brit. sl.* a trick, idea, or plan. **5** *Inf.* a hackneyed joke or anecdote. [C15: prob. from ON *hvæsa* to hiss]
▸ **'wheezer** *n* ▸ **'wheezy** *adj* ▸ **'wheezily** *adv* ▸ **'wheeziness** *n*

whelk[1] (wɛlk) *n* a marine gastropod mollusc of coastal waters and intertidal regions, having a strong snail-like shell. [OE *weoloc*]

whelk[2] (wɛlk) *n* a raised lesion on the skin; wheal. [OE *hwylca,* from ?]
▸ **'whelky** *adj*

whelm (wɛlm) *vb* (*tr*) *Arch.* to engulf entirely; overwhelm. [C13 *whelmen* to turn over, from ?]

whelp (wɛlp) *n* **1** a young offspring of certain animals, esp. of a wolf or dog. **2** *Disparaging.* a youth. **3** *Jocular.* a young child. **4** *Naut.* any of the ridges, parallel to the axis, on the drum of a capstan to keep a rope, etc., from slipping. ◆ *vb* **5** (of an animal or, disparagingly, a woman) to give birth to (young). [OE *hwelp(a)*]

when (wɛn) *adv* **1a** at what time? over what period?: *when is he due?* **1b** (*used in indirect questions*): *ask him when he's due.* **2 say when.** to state when an action is to be stopped or begun, as when someone is pouring a drink. ◆ *conj* **3** (*subordinating*) at a time at which; just as; after: *I found it easy when I tried.* **4** although: *he drives when he might walk.* **5** considering the fact that: *how did you pass the exam when you hadn't worked for it?* ◆ *pron* **6** at which (time); over which (period): *an age when men were men.* ◆ *n* **7** a question as to the time of some occurrence. [OE *hwanne, hwænne*]

> **USAGE NOTE** *When* should not be used loosely as a substitute for *in which* after a noun which does not refer to a period of time: *paralysis is a condition in which* (not *when*) *parts of the body cannot be moved.*

whenas (wɛn'æz) *conj Arch.* **1a** when; whenever. **1b** inasmuch as; while. **2** although.

whence (wɛns) *Arch. or formal.* ◆ *adv* **1** from what place, cause, or origin? ◆ *pron* **2** (*subordinating*) from what place, cause, or origin. [C13 *whannes,* adv. genitive of OE *hwanon*]

> **USAGE NOTE** The expression *from whence* should be avoided, since *whence* already means from which place: *the tradition whence* (not *from whence*) *such ideas flowed.*

whencesoever (ˌwɛnssəʊ'ɛvə) *conj* (*subordinating*), *adv Arch.* from whatever place, cause, or origin.

whenever (wɛn'ɛvə) *conj* **1** (*subordinating*) at every or any time that; when: *I laugh whenever I see that.* ◆ *adv also* **when ever. 2** no matter when: *it'll be here, whenever you decide to come for it.* **3** *Inf.* at an unknown or unspecified time: *I'll take it if it comes today, tomorrow, or whenever.* **4** an intensive form of *when,* used in questions: *whenever did he escape?*

whensoever (ˌwɛnsəʊ'ɛvə) *conj, adv Rare.* an intensive form of **whenever.**

whenua (fɛn'ʊə) *n NZ.* land. [Maori]

where (wɛə) *adv* **1a** in, at, or to what place, point, or position?: *where are you going?* **1b** (*used in indirect questions*): *I don't know where they are.* ◆ *pron* **2** in, at, or to which (place): *the hotel where we spent our honeymoon.* ◆ *conj* **3** (*subordinating*) in the place at which: *where we live it's always raining.* ◆ *n* **4** a question as to the position, direction, or destination of something. [OE *hwǣr, hwār(a)*]

> **USAGE NOTE** It was formerly considered incorrect to use *where* as a substitute for *in which* after a noun which did not refer to a place or position, but this use has now become acceptable: *we have a situation where/in which no further action is needed.*

whereabouts Ⓣ ('wɛərəˌbaʊts) *adv* **1** at what approximate place; where: *whereabouts are you?* ◆ *n* **2** (*functioning as sing or pl*) the place, esp. the approximate place, where a person or thing is.

whereas (wɛər'æz) *conj* **1** (*coordinating*) but on the other hand: *I like to go swimming whereas Sheila likes to sail.* ◆ *sentence connector.* **2** (in formal documents) it being the case that; since.

whereat (wɛər'æt) *Arch.* ◆ *adv* **1** at or to which place. ◆ *sentence connector.* **2** upon which occasion.

whereby (wɛə'baɪ) *pron* by or because of which: *the means whereby he took his life.*

wherefore ('wɛəˌfɔː) *n* **1** (*usually pl*) an explanation or reason (esp. in **the whys and wherefores**). ◆ *adv* **2** *Arch.* why? ◆ *sentence connector.* **3** *Arch. or formal.* for which reason: used in legal preambles.

wherefrom (wɛə'frɒm) *Arch.* ◆ *adv* **1** from what or where? whence? ◆ *pron* **2** from which place; whence.

wherein (wɛər'ɪn) *Arch. or formal.* ◆ *adv* **1** in what place or respect? ◆ *pron* **2** in which place, thing, etc.

whereof (wɛər'ɒv) *Arch. or formal.* ◆ *adv* **1** of what or which person or thing? ◆ *pron* **2** of which (person or thing): *the man whereof I speak is no longer alive.*

whereon (wɛər'ɒn) *Arch.* ◆ *adv* **1** on what thing or place? ◆ *pron* **2** on which thing, place, etc.

wheresoever (ˌwɛəsəʊ'ɛvə) *conj* (*subordinating*), *adv, pron Rare.* an intensive form of **wherever.**

whereto (wɛə'tuː) *Arch. or formal.* ◆ *adv* **1** towards what (place, end, etc.)? ◆ *pron* **2** to which. ◆ Also (archaic): **whereunto.**

whereupon (ˌwɛərə'pɒn) *sentence connector.* at which; at which point; upon which.

wherever (wɛər'ɛvə) *pron* **1** at, in, or to every place or point which; where: *wherever she went, he would be there.* ◆ *conj* **2** (*subordinating*) in, to, or at whatever place: *wherever we go the weather is always bad.* ◆ *adv also* **where ever. 3** no matter where: *I'll find you, wherever you are.* **4** *Inf.* at, in, or to an unknown or unspecified place: *I'll go anywhere to escape: London, Paris, or wherever.* **5** an intensive form of *where,* used in questions: *wherever can they be?*

wherewith (wɛə'wɪθ, -'wɪð) *Arch. or formal.* ◆ *pron* **1** (*often foll. by an infinitive*) with or by which: *the pen wherewith I write.* **2** something with which: *I have not wherewith to buy my bread.* ◆ *adv* **3** with what? ◆ *sentence connector.* **4** with or after that; whereupon.

wherewithal Ⓣ *n* ('wɛəwɪðˌɔːl). **1 the wherewithal.** necessary funds, resources, or equipment: *these people lack the wherewithal for a decent existence.* ◆ *pron* (ˌwɛəwɪð'ɔːl). **2** a less common word for **wherewith.**

wherry ('wɛrɪ) *n, pl* **wherries. 1** any of certain kinds of half-decked commercial boats. **2** a light rowing boat. [C15: from ?]
▸ **'wherryman** *n*

whet Ⓣ (wɛt) *vb* **whets, whetting, whetted.** (*tr*) **1** to sharpen, as by grinding or friction. **2** to increase (the appetite, desire, etc.); stimulate. ◆ *n* **3** the act of whetting. **4** a person or thing that whets. [OE *hwettan*]
▸ **'whetter** *n*

whether ('wɛðə) *conj* **1** (*subordinating*) used to introduce an indirect question or a clause after a verb expressing or implying doubt or choice: *he doesn't know whether she's in Britain or whether she's gone to France.* **2** (*coordinating*) either: *any man, whether liberal or conservative,*

THESAURUS

ouette, revolve, roll, rotate, spin, swing, swivel, twirl, whirl

wheeze *vb* **1** = **gasp**, breathe roughly, catch one's breath, cough, hiss, rasp, whistle ◆ *n* **3** = **gasp**, cough, hiss, rasp, whistle **4** *Brit. slang* = **trick**, expedient, idea, plan, ploy, ruse, scheme, stunt, wrinkle (*inf.*) **5** *Informal* = **joke**, anecdote, chestnut (*inf.*), crack (*sl.*), gag (*inf.*), old joke, one-liner (*sl.*), story

whereabouts *n* **2** = **position**, location, site, situation

wherewithal *n* **1** = **resources**, capital, equipment, essentials, funds, means, money, ready (*inf.*), ready money, supplies

whet *vb* **1** = **sharpen**, edge, file, grind, hone, strop **2** = **stimulate**, animate, arouse, awaken, enhance, excite, incite, increase, kindle, pique, provoke, quicken, rouse, stir *would agree with me.* **3 whether or no.** in any case: *he will be here tomorrow, whether or no.* **4 whether...or (whether).** if on the one hand...or even if on the other hand: *you'll eat that, whether you like it or not.* [OE *hwæther, hwether*]

whetstone ('wɛtˌstəʊn) *n* **1** a stone used for sharpening edged tools, knives, etc. **2** something that sharpens.

whew (hwjuː) *interj* an exclamation or sharply exhaled breath expressing relief, delight, etc.

whey (weɪ) *n* the watery liquid that separates from the curd when milk is clotted, as in making cheese. [OE *hwǣg*]

wheyface ('weɪˌfeɪs) *n* **1** a pale bloodless face. **2** a person with such a face. ▸ **'wheyˌfaced** *adj*

which (wɪtʃ) *determiner* **1a** used with a noun in requesting that its referent be further specified, identified, or distinguished: *which house did you buy?* **1b** (*as pron*): *which did you find?* **1c** (*used in indirect questions*): *I wondered which apples were cheaper.* **2a** whatever of a class; whichever: *bring which car you want.* **2b** (*as pron*): *choose which of the cars suits you.* ◆ *pron* **3** used in relative clauses with inanimate antecedents: *the house, which is old, is in poor repair.* **4** as; and that: used in relative clauses with verb phrases or sentences as their antecedents: *he died of cancer, which is what I predicted.* **5 the which.** an archaic form of **which** often used as a sentence connector. [OE *hwelc, hwilc*]

> **USAGE NOTE** See at **that**.

whichever (wɪtʃ'ɛvə) *determiner* **1a** any (one, two, etc., out of several): *take whichever car you like.* **1b** (*as pron*): *choose whichever appeals to you.* **2a** no matter which (one or ones): *whichever card you pick you'll still be making a mistake.* **2b** (*as pron*): *it won't make any difference, whichever comes first.*

whichsoever (ˌwɪtʃsəʊ'ɛvə) *pron* an archaic or formal word for **whichever.**

whicker ('wɪkə) *vb* (*intr*) (of a horse) to whinny or neigh; nicker. [C17: imit.]

whidah ('wɪdə) *n* a variant spelling of **whydah.**

whiff ⓣ (wɪf) *n* **1** a passing odour. **2** a brief gentle gust of air. **3** a single inhalation or exhalation from the mouth or nose. ◆ *vb* **4** to puff or waft. **5** (*tr*) to sniff or smell. **6** (*intr*) *Brit. sl.* to stink. [C16: imit.]

whiffle ('wɪfᵊl) *vb* **whiffles, whiffling, whiffled. 1** (*intr*) to think or behave in an erratic or unpredictable way. **2** to blow or be blown fitfully or in gusts. **3** (*intr*) to whistle softly. [C16: frequentative of WHIFF]

whiffletree ('wɪfᵊlˌtriː) *n Chiefly US.* another word for **swingletree.** [C19: var. of WHIPPLETREE]

Whig (wɪg) *n* **1** a member of the English political party that opposed the succession to the throne of James, Duke of York (1679–80), on the grounds that he was a Catholic. Standing for a limited monarchy, the Whigs later represented the desires of industrialists and Dissenters for political and social reform, and provided the core of the Liberal Party. **2** (in the US) a supporter of the War of American Independence. Cf. **Tory. 3** a member of the American political party that opposed the Democrats from about 1834 to 1855 and represented propertied and professional interests. **4** *History.* a 17th-century Scottish Presbyterian, esp. one in rebellion against the Crown. ◆ *adj* **5** of, characteristic of, or relating to Whigs. [C17: prob. from *whiggamore*, one of a group of 17th-cent. Scottish rebels who joined in an attack on Edinburgh known as *the whiggamore raid;* prob. from Scot. *whig* to drive (from ?) + *more* horse] ▸ **'Whiggery** *or* **'Whiggism** *n* ▸ **'Whiggish** *adj*

while (waɪl) *conj also* **whilst. 1** (*subordinating*) at the same time that: *please light the fire while I'm cooking.* **2** (*subordinating*) all the time that: *I stay inside while it's raining.* **3** (*subordinating*) in spite of the fact that: *while I agree about his brilliance I still think he's rude.* **4** (*coordinating*) whereas; and in contrast: *houses are expensive, while flats are cheap.* ◆ *prep, conj* **5** *Scot. & N English dialect.* another word for **until:** *you'll have to wait while Monday.* ◆ *n* **6** (*usually used in adverbial phrases*) a period or interval of time: *once in a long while.* **7** trouble or time (esp. in **worth one's while**): *it's hardly worth your while to begin work today.* [OE *hwīl*]

> **USAGE NOTE** It was formerly considered incorrect to use *while* to mean *in spite of the fact that* or *whereas*, but these uses have become acceptable.

while away *vb* (*tr, adv*) to pass (time) idly and usually pleasantly.

whiles (waɪlz) *Arch. or dialect.* ◆ *adv* **1** at times; occasionally. ◆ *conj* **2** while; whilst.

whilom ('waɪləm) *Arch.* ◆ *adv* **1** formerly; once. ◆ *adj* **2** (*prenominal*) one-time; former. [OE *hwīlum*, dative pl of *hwīl* while]

whilst (waɪlst) *conj Chiefly Brit.* another word for **while** (senses 1–4). [C13: from WHILES + *-t* as in *amidst*]

whim ⓣ (wɪm) *n* **1** a sudden, passing, and often fanciful idea; impulsive or irrational thought. **2** a horse-drawn winch formerly used in mining to lift ore or water. [C17: from C16 *whim-wham*, from ?]

whimbrel ('wɪmbrəl) *n* a small European curlew with a striped head. [C16: from dialect *whimp* or from WHIMPER, from its cry]

whimper ⓣ ('wɪmpə) *vb* **1** (*intr*) to cry, sob, or whine softly or intermittently. **2** to complain or say (something) in a whining plaintive way. ◆ *n* **3** a soft plaintive whine. [C16: from dialect *whimp*, imit.] ▸ **'whimperer** *n* ▸ **'whimpering** *n, adj* ▸ **'whimperingly** *adv*

whimsical ⓣ ('wɪmzɪkᵊl) *adj* **1** spontaneously fanciful or playful. **2** given to whims; capricious. **3** quaint, unusual, or fantastic. ▸**whimsicality** (ˌwɪmzɪ'kælɪtɪ) *n* ▸ **'whimsically** *adv*

whimsy *or* **whimsey** ('wɪmzɪ) *n, pl* **whimsies** *or* **whimseys. 1** a capricious idea or notion. **2** light or fanciful humour. **3** something quaint or unusual. ◆ *adj* **whimsier, whimsiest. 4** quaint, comical, or unusual, often in a tasteless way. [C17: from WHIM]

whin[1] (wɪn) *n* another name for **gorse.** [C11: from ON]

whin[2] (wɪn) *n* short for **whinstone.** [C14 *quin*, from ?]

whinchat ('wɪnˌtʃæt) *n* an Old World songbird having a mottled brown-and-white plumage with pale cream underparts. [C17: from WHIN[1] + CHAT]

whine ⓣ (waɪn) *n* **1** a long high-pitched plaintive cry or moan. **2** a continuous high-pitched sound. **3** a peevish complaint, esp. one repeated. ◆ *vb* **whines, whining, whined. 4** to make a whine or utter in a whine. [OE *hwīnan*] ▸ **'whiner** *n* ▸ **'whining** *or* **'whiny** *adj* ▸ **'whiningly** *adv*

whinge ⓣ (wɪndʒ) *vb* **whinges, whingeing, whinged.** (*intr*) **1** to cry in a fretful way. **2** to complain. ◆ *n* **3** a complaint. [from Northern var. of OE *hwinsian* to whine] ▸ **'whingeing** *n, adj* ▸ **'whinger** *n*

whinny ('wɪnɪ) *vb* **whinnies, whinnying, whinnied.** (*intr*) **1** (of a horse) to neigh softly or gently. **2** to make a sound resembling a neigh, such as a laugh. ◆ *n, pl* **whinnies. 3** a gentle or low-pitched neigh. [C16: imit.]

whinstone ('wɪnˌstəʊn) *n* any dark hard fine-grained rock, such as basalt. [C16: from WHIN[2] + STONE]

whip ⓣ (wɪp) *vb* **whips, whipping, whipped. 1** to strike (a person or thing) with several strokes of a strap, rod, etc. **2** (*tr*) to punish by striking in this manner. **3** (*tr; foll. by out, away,* etc.) to pull, remove, etc., with sudden rapid motion: *to whip out a gun.* **4** (*intr; foll. by down, into, out of,* etc.) *Inf.* to come, go, etc., in a rapid sudden manner: *they whipped into the bar for a drink.* **5** to strike or be struck as if by whipping: *the tempest whipped the surface of the sea.* **6** (*tr*) to bring, train, etc., forcefully into a desired condition. **7** (*tr*) *Inf.* to overcome or outdo. **8** (*tr; often foll. by on, out,* or *off*) to drive, urge, compel, etc., by or as if by whipping. **9** (*tr*) to wrap or wind (a cord, thread, etc.) around (a rope, cable, etc.) to prevent chafing or fraying. **10** (*tr*) (in fly-fishing) to cast the fly repeatedly onto (the water) in a whipping motion. **11** (*tr*) (in sewing) to join, finish, or gather with whipstitch. **12** to beat (eggs, cream, etc.) with a whisk or similar utensil to incorporate air. **13** (*tr*) to spin (a top). **14** (*tr*) *Inf.* to steal: *he whipped her purse.* ◆ *n* **15** a device consisting of a lash or flexible rod attached at one end to a stiff handle and used for driving animals, inflicting corporal punishment, etc. **16** a whipping stroke or motion. **17** a person adept at handling a whip, as a coachman, etc. **18** (in a legislative body) **18a** a member of a party chosen to organize and discipline the members of his faction. **18b** a call issued to members of a party, insisting with varying degrees of urgency upon their presence or loyal voting behaviour. **18c** (in the Brit. Parliament) a schedule of business sent to members of a party each week. Each item on it is underlined to indicate its importance: three lines means that the item is very important and every member must attend and vote according to the party line. **19** an apparatus for hoisting, consisting of a rope, pulley, and snatch block. **20** any of a variety of desserts made from egg whites or cream beaten stiff. **21** See

THESAURUS

Antonyms *vb* ≠ **sharpen:** blunt, dull ≠ **stimulate:** blunt, dampen, deaden, depress, dull, numb, smother, stifle, subdue, suppress

whiff *n* **1-3** = **smell**, aroma, blast, breath, draught, gust, hint, niff (*Brit. sl.*), odour, puff, scent, sniff ◆ *vb* **6** *Brit. slang* = **stink**, hum (*sl.*), malodour, niff (*Brit. sl.*), pong (*Brit. inf.*), reek

whim *n* **1** = **impulse**, caprice, conceit, craze, crotchet, fad (*inf.*), fancy, freak, humour, notion, passing thought, quirk, sport, sudden notion, urge, vagary, whimsy

whimper *vb* **1, 2** = **cry**, blub (*sl.*), blubber, grizzle (*inf., chiefly Brit.*), mewl, moan, pule, snivel, sob, weep, whine, whinge (*inf.*) ◆ *n* **3** = **sob**, moan, snivel, whine

whimsical *adj* **1-3** = **fanciful**, capricious, chimerical, crotchety, curious, droll, eccentric, fantastic, fantastical, freakish, funny, mischievous, odd, peculiar, playful, quaint, queer, singular, unusual, waggish, weird

whine *n* **1** = **cry**, moan, plaintive cry, sob, wail, whimper **3** = **complaint**, beef, gripe (*inf.*), grouch (*inf.*), grouse, grumble, moan, whinge (*inf.*) ◆ *vb* **4** = **cry**, moan, sniffle, snivel, sob, wail, whimper

whinge *Informal vb* **2** = **complain**, beef, bellyache (*sl.*), bleat, carp, gripe (*inf.*), grizzle (*inf., chiefly Brit.*), grouch (*inf.*), grouse, grumble, kvetch (*US sl.*), moan ◆ *n* **3** = **complaint**, beef (*sl.*), gripe (*inf.*), grouch, grouse, grumble, moan, whine

whip *vb* **1, 2** = **lash**, beat, birch, cane, castigate, flagellate, flog, give a hiding (*inf.*), lambast(e), leather, lick (*inf.*), punish, scourge, spank, strap, switch, tan (*sl.*), thrash **3** *foll. by* **out, away** *etc.* = **pull out**, exhibit, flash, jerk, produce, remove, seize, show, snatch, whisk **4** *Informal* = **dash**, dart, dive, flit, flounce, fly, rush, shoot, tear, whisk **5** = **whisk**, beat **7** *Informal* = **beat**, best, clobber (*sl.*), conquer, defeat, drub, hammer (*inf.*), lick (*inf.*), outdo, overcome, overpower, overwhelm, rout, stuff (*sl.*), thrash, trounce, worst **8** = **incite**, agitate, compel, drive, foment, goad, hound, instigate, prick, prod, provoke, push, spur, stir, urge, work up ◆ *n* **15** = **lash**, birch, bullwhip, cane, cat-o'-nine-tails, crop, horsewhip, knout, rawhide, riding crop, scourge, switch, thong

whipper-in. 22 flexibility, as in the shaft of a golf club, etc. ◆ See also **whip-round, whip up, whips.** [C13: ?from MDu. *wippen* to swing]
▸ **'whip,like** *adj* ▸ **'whipper** *n*

whip bird *n Austral.* any of several birds having a whistle ending in a note sounding like the crack of a whip.

whipcord ('wɪpˌkɔːd) *n* **1** a strong worsted or cotton fabric with a diagonally ribbed surface. **2** a closely twisted hard cord used for the lashes of whips, etc.

whip graft *n Horticulture.* a graft made by inserting a tongue cut on the sloping base of the scion into a slit on the sloping top of the stock.

whip hand *n* (usually preceded by *the*) **1** (in driving horses) the hand holding the whip. **2** advantage or dominating position.

whiplash ('wɪpˌlæʃ) *n* a quick lash or stroke of a whip or like that of a whip.

whiplash injury *n Med. inf.* any injury to the neck resulting from a sudden thrusting forwards and snapping back of the unsupported head. Technical name: **hyperextension-hyperflexion injury.**

whipper-in *n, pl* **whippers-in.** a person employed to assist the huntsman managing the hounds.

whippersnapper ('wɪpəˌsnæpə) *n* an insignificant but pretentious or cheeky person, often a young one. Also called: **whipster.** [C17: prob. from *whipsnapper* a person who snaps whips, infl. by earlier *snippersnapper,* from ?]

whippet ('wɪpɪt) *n* a small slender breed of dog similar to a greyhound. [C16: from ?; ? based on *whip it!* move quickly!]

whipping 🅣 ('wɪpɪŋ) *n* **1** a thrashing or beating with a whip or similar implement. **2** cord or twine used for binding or lashing. **3** the binding formed by wrapping a rope, etc., with cord or twine.

whipping boy *n* a person of little importance who is blamed for the errors, incompetence, etc., of others, esp. his superiors; scapegoat. [C17: orig. referring to a boy who was educated with a prince and who received punishment for any faults committed by the prince]

whippletree ('wɪp^{ə}lˌtriː) *n* another name for **swingletree.** [C18: apparently from WHIP]

whippoorwill ('wɪpʊˌwɪl) *n* a nightjar of North and Central America, having a dark plumage with white patches on the tail. [C18: imit. of its cry]

whip-round *Inf., chiefly Brit.* ◆ *n* **1** an impromptu collection of money. ◆ *vb* **whip round. 2** (*intr, adv*) to make such a collection.

whips (wɪps) *pl n* (often foll. by *of*) *Austral. inf.* a large quantity: *I've got whips of cash at the moment.*

whipsaw ('wɪpˌsɔː) *n* **1** any saw with a flexible blade, such as a bandsaw. ◆ *vb* **whipsaws, whipsawing, whipsawed; whipsawed** *or* **whipsawn.** (*tr*) **2** to saw with a whipsaw. **3** *US.* to defeat in two ways at once.

whip scorpion *n* any of an order of nonvenomous arachnids, typically resembling a scorpion but lacking a sting.

whip snake *n* any of several long slender fast-moving nonvenomous snakes.

whipstitch ('wɪpˌstɪtʃ) *n* a sewing stitch passing over an edge.

whipstock ('wɪpˌstɒk) *n* a whip handle.

whip up 🅣 *vb* (*tr, adv*) **1** to excite; arouse: *to whip up a mob; to whip up discontent.* **2** *Inf.* to prepare quickly: *to whip up a meal.*

whir *or* **whirr** (wɜː) *n* **1** a prolonged soft swish or buzz, as of a motor working or wings flapping. **2** a bustle or rush. ◆ *vb* **whirs** *or* **whirrs, whirring, whirred. 3** to make or cause to make a whir. [C14: prob. from ON; see WHIRL]

whirl 🅣 (wɜːl) *vb* **1** to spin, turn, or revolve or cause to spin, turn, or revolve. **2** (*intr*) to turn around or away rapidly. **3** (*intr*) to have a spinning sensation, as from dizziness, etc. **4** to move or drive or be moved or driven at high speed. ◆ *n* **5** the act or an instance of whirling; swift rotation or a rapid whirling movement. **6** a condition of confusion or giddiness: *her accident left me in a whirl.* **7** a swift round, as of events, meetings, etc. **8** a tumult; stir. **9** *Inf.* a brief trip, dance, etc. **10 give (something) a whirl.** *Inf.* to attempt or give a trial to (something). [C13: from ON *hvirfla* to turn about]
▸ **'whirler** *n* ▸ **'whirling** *adj* ▸ **'whirlingly** *adv*

whirligig ('wɜːlɪˌɡɪɡ) *n* **1** any spinning toy, such as a top. **2** another name for **merry-go-round. 3** anything that whirls about, spins, or moves in a circular or giddy way: *the whirligig of social life.* [C15 *whirlegigge,* from WHIRL + GIG^{1}]

whirlpool ('wɜːlˌpuːl) *n* **1** a powerful circular current or vortex of water. **2** something resembling a whirlpool in motion or the power to attract into its vortex.

whirlwind 🅣 ('wɜːlˌwɪnd) *n* **1** a column of air whirling around and towards a more or less vertical axis of low pressure, which moves along the land or ocean surface. **2a** a motion or course resembling this, esp. in rapidity. **2b** (*as modifier*): *a whirlwind romance.* **3** an impetuously active person.

whirlybird ('wɜːlɪˌbɜːd) *n* an informal word for **helicopter.**

whish (wɪʃ) *n, vb* a less common word for **swish.**

whisht (hwɪʃt) *or* **whist** *Arch. or dialect, esp. Scot.* ◆ *interj* **1** hush! be quiet! ◆ *adj* **2** silent or still. [C14: cf. HIST]

whisk 🅣 (wɪsk) *vb* **1** (*tr;* often foll. by *away* or *off*) to brush, sweep, or wipe off lightly. **2** (*tr*) to move, carry, etc., with a light or rapid sweeping motion: *the taxi whisked us to the airport.* **3** (*intr*) to move, go, etc., quickly and nimbly: *to whisk downstairs for a drink.* **4** (*tr*) to whip (eggs, etc.) to a froth. ◆ *n* **5** the act of whisking. **6** a light rapid sweeping movement. **7** a utensil for whipping eggs, etc. **8** a small brush or broom. **9** a small bunch or bundle, as of grass, straw, etc. [C14: from ON *visk* wisp]

whisker ('wɪskə) *n* **1** any of the stiff sensory hairs growing on the face of a cat, rat, or other mammal. Technical name: **vibrissa. 2** any of the hairs growing on a man's face, esp. on the cheeks or chin. **3** (*pl*) a beard or that part of it growing on the sides of the face. **4** (*pl*) *Inf.* a moustache. **5** *Chem.* a very fine filamentary crystal having greater strength than the bulk material. **6** a person or thing that whisks. **7** a narrow margin or small distance: *he escaped death by a whisker.* [see WHISK]
▸ **'whiskered** *or* **'whiskery** *adj*

whiskey ('wɪskɪ) *n* the usual Irish and US spelling of **whisky.**

whiskey sour *n US.* a mixed drink of whisky and lime or lemon juice, sometimes sweetened.

whisky 🅣 ('wɪskɪ) *n, pl* **whiskies.** a spirit made by distilling fermented cereals, which is matured and often blended. [C18: shortened from *whiskybae,* from Scot. Gaelic *uisge beatha,* lit.: water of life; see USQUEBAUGH]

whisky-jack *n Canad.* another name for **Canada jay.**

whisky mac *n Brit.* a drink consisting of whisky and ginger wine.

whisper 🅣 ('wɪspə) *vb* **1** to speak or utter (something) in a soft hushed tone, esp. without vibration of the vocal cords. **2** (*intr*) to speak secretly or furtively, as in promoting intrigue, gossip, etc. **3** (*intr*) (of leaves, trees, etc.) to make a low soft rustling sound. **4** (*tr*) to utter or suggest secretly or privately: *to whisper treason.* ◆ *n* **5** a low soft voice: *to speak in a whisper.* **6** something uttered in such a voice. **7** a low soft rustling sound. **8** a trace or suspicion. **9** *Inf.* a rumour. [OE *hwisprian*]
▸ **'whisperer** *n*

whispering campaign *n* the organized diffusion of defamatory rumours to discredit a person, group, etc.

whispering gallery *n* a gallery or dome with acoustic characteristics such that a sound made at one point is audible at distant points.

whist^{1} (wɪst) *n* a card game for four in which the two sides try to win the balance of the 13 tricks: forerunner of bridge. [C17: ? changed from WHISK, referring to the sweeping up or whisking up of the tricks]

whist^{2} (hwɪst) *interj, adj* a variant of **whisht.**

whist drive *n* a social gathering where whist is played: the winners of each hand move to different tables to play the losers of the previous hand.

whistle ('wɪs^{ə}l) *vb* **whistles, whistling, whistled. 1** to produce (shrill or flutelike sounds), as by passing breath through a narrow constriction most easily formed by the pursed lips. **2** (*tr*) to signal or command by whistling or blowing a whistle: *the referee whistled the end of the game.* **3** (of a kettle, train, etc.) to produce (a shrill sound) caused by the emission of steam through a small aperture. **4** (*intr*) to move with a whistling sound caused by rapid passage through the air. **5** (of animals, esp. birds) to emit (a shrill sound) resembling human whistling. **6 whistle in the dark.** to try to keep up one's confidence in spite of fear. ◆ *n* **7** a device for making a shrill high-pitched sound by means of air or steam under pressure. **8** a shrill sound effected by whistling or blowing a whistle. **9** a whistling sound, as of a bird, bullet, the wind, etc. **10** a signal, etc., transmitted by or as if by a whistle. **11** the act of whistling. **12** an instrument, usually made of metal, that is blown down its end to produce a tune, signal, etc. **13 blow the whistle.** (usually foll. by *on*) *Inf.* **13a** to inform (on). **13b** to bring a stop (to). **14 clean as a**

THESAURUS

whipping *n* **1 = beating,** birching, caning, castigation, flagellation, flogging, hiding (*inf.*), lashing, leathering, punishment, spanking, tanning (*sl.*), the strap, thrashing

whip up *vb* **1 = arouse,** agitate, excite, foment, incite, inflame, instigate, kindle, provoke, rouse, stir up, work up

whirl *vb* **1 = spin,** circle, gyrate, pirouette, pivot, reel, revolve, roll, rotate, swirl, turn, twirl, twist, wheel **3 = feel dizzy,** reel, spin ◆ *n* **5 = revolution,** birl, circle, gyration, pirouette, reel, roll, rotation, spin, swirl, turn, twirl, twist, wheel **7 = bustle,** flurry, merry-go-round, round, series, succession **8 = confusion,** agitation, commotion, daze, dither (*chiefly Brit.*), giddiness, hurly-burly, spin, stir, tumult **10 give (something) a whirl** *Informal* **= attempt,** have a bash, have a crack (*inf.*), have a go (*inf.*), have a shot (*inf.*), have a stab (*inf.*), have a whack (*inf.*), try

whirlwind *n* **1 = tornado,** dust devil, waterspout ◆ *modifier* **2b = rapid,** hasty, headlong, impetuous, impulsive, lightning, quick, quickie (*inf.*), rash, short, speedy, swift
Antonyms *adj* ≠ **rapid:** calculated, cautious, considered, deliberate, measured, prudent, slow, unhurried

whisk *vb* **1 = flick,** brush, sweep, whip, wipe **3 = speed,** barrel (along) (*inf., chiefly US & Canad.*), burn rubber (*inf.*), dart, dash, fly, hasten, hurry, race, rush, shoot, sweep, tear **4 = beat,** fluff up, whip ◆ *n* **6 = flick,** brush, sweep, whip, wipe **7 = beater**

whisky *n* **= Scotch,** barley-bree, bourbon, firewater, John Barleycorn, malt, rye, usquebaugh (*Gaelic*)

whisper *vb* **1 = murmur,** breathe, say softly, speak in hushed tones, utter under the breath **2 = gossip,** hint, insinuate, intimate, murmur, spread rumours **3 = rustle,** hiss, murmur, sigh, sough, susurrate (*literary*), swish ◆ *n* **5 = murmur,** hushed tone, low voice, soft voice, undertone **7 = rustle,** hiss, murmur, sigh, sighing, soughing, susurration *or* susurrus (*literary*), swish **8 = hint,** breath, fraction, shadow, suggestion, suspicion, tinge, trace, whiff **9** *Informal* **= rumour,** buzz, dirt (*US sl.*), gossip, innuendo, insinuation, report, scuttlebutt (*US sl.*), word

whistle. perfectly clean or clear. **15 wet one's whistle.** *Inf.* to take an alcoholic drink. ◆ See also **whistle for, whistle up.** [OE *hwistlian*]
whistle-blower *n Inf.* a person who informs on someone or puts a stop to something.
whistle for *vb (intr, prep) Inf.* to seek or expect in vain.
whistler ('wɪslə) *n* **1** a person or thing that whistles. **2** *Radio.* an atmospheric disturbance picked up by radio receivers, caused by the electromagnetic radiation produced by lightning. **3** any of various birds having a whistling call, such as certain Australian flycatchers. **4** any of various North American marmots.
whistle stop *n* **1** *US & Canad.* **1a** a minor railway station where trains stop only on signal. **1b** a small town having such a station. **2a** a brief appearance in a town, esp. by a political candidate. **2b** *(as modifier): a whistle-stop tour.*
whistle up *vb (tr, adv)* to call or summon (a person or animal) by whistling.
whit ❶ (wɪt) *n (usually used with a negative)* the smallest particle; iota; jot: *he has changed not a whit.* [C15: prob. var. of WIGHT]
Whit (wɪt) *n* **1** See **Whitsuntide.** ◆ *adj* **2** of or relating to Whitsuntide.
white ❶ (waɪt) *adj* **1** having no hue, owing to the reflection of all or almost all incident light. **2** (of light, such as sunlight) consisting of all the colours of the spectrum or produced by certain mixtures of primary colours, as red, green, and blue. **3** comparatively white or whitish-grey or having parts of this colour: *white clover.* **4** (of an animal) having pale-coloured or white skin, fur, or feathers. **5** bloodless or pale, as from pain, emotion, etc. **6** (of hair, etc.) grey, usually from age. **7** benevolent or without malicious intent: *white magic.* **8** colourless or transparent: *white glass.* **9** capped with or accompanied by snow: *a white Christmas.* **10** blank, as an unprinted area of a page. **11** (of coffee or tea) with milk or cream. **12** (of wine) made from pale grapes or from black grapes separated from their skins. **13** denoting flour, or bread made from flour, that has had part of the grain removed. **14** *Physics.* having or characterized by a continuous distribution of energy, wavelength, or frequency: *white noise.* **15** *Inf.* honourable or generous. **16** *Poetic or arch.* having a fair complexion; blond. **17 bleed white.** to deprive slowly of resources. ◆ *n* **18** a white colour. **19** the condition of being white; whiteness. **20** the white or lightly coloured part of something. **21** (usually preceded by *the*) the viscous fluid that surrounds the yolk of a bird's egg, esp. a hen's egg; albumen. **22** *Anat.* the white part (sclera) of the eyeball. **23** any of various butterflies having white wings with scanty black markings. **24** *Chess, draughts.* **24a** a white or light-coloured piece or square. **24b** the player playing with such pieces. **25** anything that has or is characterized by a white colour, such as a white paint or white clothing. **26** *Inf.* white wine: *a bottle of white.* **27** *Archery.* the outer ring of the target, having the lowest score. ◆ *vb* **whites, whiting, whited.** **28** *Obs.* to make or become white. ◆ See also **white out, whites.** [OE *hwīt*]
▸'**whitely** *adv* ▸'**whiteness** *n* ▸'**whitish** *adj*
White (waɪt) *n* **1** a member of the Caucasoid race. **2** a person of European ancestry. ◆ *adj* **3** denoting or relating to a White or Whites.
white admiral *n* a butterfly of Eurasia having brown wings with white markings.
white ant *n* another name for **termite.**
whitebait ('waɪt,beɪt) *n* **1** the young of herrings, sprats, etc., cooked and eaten whole as a delicacy. **2** any of various small silvery fishes. [C18: from its formerly having been used as bait]
whitebeam ('waɪt,bi:m) *n* a N temperate tree having leaves that are densely hairy on the undersurface and hard timber.
white blood cell *n* a nontechnical name for **leucocyte.**
whitecap ('waɪt,kæp) *n* a wave with a white broken crest.
white cedar *n* either of two coniferous trees of North America, having scalelike leaves.
white clover *n* a Eurasian clover plant with rounded white flower heads: cultivated as a forage plant.
white coal *n* water, esp. when flowing and providing a potential source of usable power.
white-collar ❶ *adj* of or designating nonmanual and usually salaried workers employed in professional and clerical occupations.
white currant *n* a cultivated N temperate shrub having small rounded white edible berries.
whitedamp ('waɪt,dæmp) *n* a mixture of poisonous gases, mainly carbon monoxide, occurring in coal mines.
whited sepulchre *n* a hypocrite. [allusion to Matthew 23:27]
white dwarf *n* one of a large class of small faint stars of enormous density, thought to mark the final stage in the evolution of a sun-like star.
white elephant *n* **1** a rare albino variety of the Indian elephant, regarded as sacred in parts of S Asia. **2** a possession that is unwanted by its owner. **3** a rare or valuable possession the upkeep of which is very expensive.
White Ensign *n* the ensign of the Royal Navy and the Royal Yacht Squadron, having a red cross on a white background with the Union Jack at the upper corner of the vertical edge alongside the hoist.
white-eye *n* a songbird of Africa, Australia, New Zealand, and Asia, having a greenish plumage with a white ring around each eye.
white feather *n* **1** a symbol or mark of cowardice. **2 show the white feather.** to act in a cowardly manner. [from the belief that a white feather in a gamecock's tail was a sign of a poor fighter]
whitefish ('waɪt,fɪʃ) *n, pl* **whitefish** *or* **whitefishes.** a food fish typically of deep cold lakes of the N hemisphere, having large silvery scales and a small head.
white fish *n* (in the Brit. fishing industry) any edible marine fish or invertebrate excluding herrings but including trout, salmon, and all shellfish.
white flag *n* a white flag or a piece of white cloth hoisted to signify surrender or request a truce.
white flour *n* flour that consists substantially of the starchy endosperm of wheat, most of the bran and the germ having been removed by the milling process.
whitefly ('waɪt,flaɪ) *n, pl* **whiteflies.** any of a family of insects typically having a body covered with powdery wax. Many are pests of greenhouse crops.
white friar *n* a Carmelite friar, so called because of the white cloak that forms part of the habit of this order.
white gold *n* any of various white lustrous hard-wearing alloys containing gold together with platinum and palladium and sometimes smaller amounts of silver, nickel, or copper.
white goods *pl n* **1** household linen such as sheets, towels, tablecloths, etc. **2** large household appliances, such as refrigerators or cookers.
Whitehall (,waɪt'hɔ:l) *n* **1** a street in London stretching from Trafalgar Square to the Houses of Parliament: site of the main government offices. **2** the British Government.
white heat *n* **1** intense heat characterized by emission of white light. **2** *Inf.* a state of intense excitement or activity.
white hope *n Inf.* a person who is expected to bring honour or glory to his group, team, etc.
white horse *n* **1** the outline of a horse carved into the side of a chalk hill, usually dating to the Neolithic, Bronze, or Iron Ages. **2** *(usually pl)* a wave with a white broken crest.
white-hot *adj* **1** at such a high temperature that white light is emitted. **2** *Inf.* in a state of intense emotion.
White House *n* **the. 1** the official Washington residence of the president of the US. **2** the US presidency.
white knight *n* a champion or rescuer, esp. a person or organization that rescues a company from financial difficulties, an unwelcome takeover bid, etc.
white-knuckle *adj* causing or experiencing fear or anxiety: *a white-knuckle fairground ride.*
white lead (lɛd) *n* **1** a white solid usually regarded as a mixture of lead carbonate and lead hydroxide; basic lead carbonate: used in paint and in making putty and ointments for the treatment of burns. **2** either of two similar white pigments based on lead sulphate or lead silicate.
white leg *n* another name for **milk leg.**
white lie *n* a minor or unimportant lie, esp. one uttered in the interests of tact or politeness.
white light *n* light that contains all the wavelengths of visible light at approximately equal intensities, as in sunlight.
white-livered *adj* **1** lacking in spirit or courage. **2** pallid and unhealthy in appearance.
White man's burden *n* the supposed duty of the White race to bring education and Western culture to the non-White inhabitants of their colonies.
white matter *n* the whitish tissue of the brain and spinal cord, consisting mainly of nerve fibres covered with a protective white fatlike substance.
white meat *n* any meat that is light in colour, such as veal or the breast of turkey.
white metal *n* any of various alloys, such as Babbitt metal, used for bearings.
white meter *n Brit.* an electricity meter used to record the consumption of off-peak electricity.
whiten ❶ ('waɪtᵊn) *vb* to make or become white or whiter.
▸'**whitener** *n* ▸'**whitening** *n*
white noise *n* sound or electrical noise that has a relatively wide continuous range of frequencies of uniform intensity.
white oak *n* a large oak tree of E North America, having pale bark, leaves with rounded lobes, and heavy light-coloured wood.
white out *vb (adv)* **1** *(intr)* to lose or lack daylight visibility owing to snow or fog. **2** *(tr)* to create or leave white spaces in (printed or other matter). ◆ *n* **whiteout. 3** a polar atmospheric condition consisting of lack of visibility and sense of distance and direction due to a uniform whiteness of a heavy cloud cover and snow-covered ground, which reflects almost all the light it receives.
white paper *n (often caps.)* an official government report in any of a

THESAURUS

Antonyms *vb* ≠ **murmur:** bawl, bellow, clamour, roar, shout, thunder, yell
whit *n* = **bit,** atom, crumb, dash, drop, fragment, grain, iota, jot, least bit, little, mite, modicum, particle, piece, pinch, scrap, shred, speck, trace
white *adj* **5** = **pale,** ashen, bloodless, ghastly, grey, like death warmed up (*inf.*), pallid, pasty, wan, waxen, wheyfaced **6** = **silver,** grey, grizzled, hoary, snowy
Antonyms *adj* ≠ **pale:** black, dark
white-collar *adj* = **clerical,** executive, nonmanual, office, professional, salaried
whiten *vb* = **pale,** blanch, bleach, blench, etiolate, fade, go white, turn pale
Antonyms *vb* blacken, colour, darken

number of countries, which sets out the government's policy on a matter that is or will come before Parliament.

white pepper *n* a condiment, less pungent than black pepper, made from the husked dried beans of the pepper plant.

white pine *n* a North American coniferous tree having blue-green needle-like leaves, hanging brown cones, and rough bark.

white poplar *n* **1** Also called: **abele.** a Eurasian tree having leaves covered with dense silvery-white hairs. **2** another name for **tulipwood** (sense 1).

white rose *n English history.* an emblem of the House of York.

White Russian *adj, n* another term for **Belarussian.**

whites (waɪts) *pl n* **1** household linen or cotton goods, such as sheets. **2** white or off-white clothing, such as that worn for playing cricket.

white sale *n* a sale of household linens at reduced prices.

white sauce *n* a thick sauce made from flour, butter, seasonings, and milk or stock.

white settler *n* a well-off incomer to a district who takes advantage of what it has to offer without regard to the local inhabitants. **[**C20: from earlier colonial sense**]**

white slave *n* a girl or woman forced or sold into prostitution.
▸**white slavery** *n* ▸ˌ**white-ˈslaver** *n*

white spirit *n* a colourless liquid obtained from petroleum and used as a substitute for turpentine.

white spruce *n* a N North American spruce tree with grey bark.

white squall *n* a violent highly localized weather disturbance at sea, in which the surface of the water is whipped to a white spray by the winds.

whitethorn (ˈwaɪtˌθɔːn) *n* another name for **hawthorn.**

whitethroat (ˈwaɪtˌθrəʊt) *n* either of two Old World warblers having a greyish-brown plumage with a white throat and underparts.

white tie *n* **1** a white bow tie worn as part of a man's formal evening dress. **2a** formal evening dress for men. **2b** (*as modifier*): *a white-tie occasion.*

white trash *n Disparaging.* **a** poor White people living in the US, esp. the South. **b** (*as modifier*): *white-trash culture.*

whitewall (ˈwaɪtˌwɔːl) *n* a pneumatic tyre having white sidewalls.

whitewash Ⓣ (ˈwaɪtˌwɒʃ) *n* **1** a substance used for whitening walls and other surfaces, consisting of a suspension of lime or whiting in water. **2** *Inf.* deceptive or specious words or actions intended to conceal defects, gloss over failings, etc. **3** *Inf.* a defeat in a sporting contest in which the loser is beaten in every match, game, etc. in a series. ◆ *vb* (*tr*) **4** to cover with whitewash. **5** *Inf.* to conceal, gloss over, or suppress. **6** *Inf.* to defeat (an opponent or opposing team) by winning every match in a series.
▸ˈ**whiteˌwasher** *n*

white water *n* **1** a stretch of water with a broken foamy surface, as in rapids. **2** light-coloured sea water, esp. over shoals or shallows.

white whale *n* a small white toothed whale of northern waters. Also called: **beluga.**

whitewood (ˈwaɪtˌwʊd) *n* **1** any of various trees with light-coloured wood, such as the tulip tree, basswood, and cottonwood. **2** the wood of any of these trees.

whitey *or* **whity** (ˈwaɪtɪ) *n, pl* **whiteys** *or* **whities.** *Chiefly US.* (used contemptuously by Black people) a White man or White men collectively.

whither (ˈwɪðə) *Arch. or poetic.* ◆ *adv* **1** to what place? **2** to what end or purpose? ◆ *conj* **3** to whatever place, purpose, etc. **[**OE *hwider, hwæder;* Mod. E form infl. by HITHER**]**

whithersoever (ˌwɪðəsəʊˈɛvə) *adv, conj Arch. or poetic.* to whichever place.

whiting[1] (ˈwaɪtɪŋ) *n* **1** an important gadoid food fish of European seas, having a dark back with silvery sides and underparts. **2** any of various similar fishes. **[**C15: ?from OE *hwītling***]**

whiting[2] (ˈwaɪtɪŋ) *n* white chalk that has been ground and washed, used in making whitewash, metal polish, etc. Also called: **whitening.**

whitlow (ˈwɪtləʊ) *n* any pussy inflammation of the end of a finger or toe. **[**C14: changed from *whitflaw,* from WHITE + FLAW[1]**]**

Whitsun (ˈwɪtsᵊn) *n* **1** short for **Whitsuntide.** ◆ *adj* **2** of or relating to Whit Sunday or Whitsuntide.

Whitsunday (ˌhwɪtˈsʌndɪ, ˌwɪt-) *n* (in Scotland) May 15, one of the four quarter days.

Whit Sunday *n* the seventh Sunday after Easter, observed as a feast in commemoration of the descent of the Holy Spirit on the apostles. Also called: **Pentecost.** **[**OE *hwīta sunnandæg* white Sunday, prob. after the ancient custom of wearing white robes at or after baptism**]**

Whitsuntide (ˈwɪtsᵊnˌtaɪd) *n* the week that begins with Whit Sunday, esp. the first three days.

whittle Ⓣ (ˈwɪtᵊl) *vb* **whittles, whittling, whittled. 1** to cut or shave strips or pieces from (wood, a stick, etc.), esp. with a knife. **2** (*tr*) to make or shape by paring or shaving. **3** (*tr; often foll. by away, down, etc.*) to reduce, destroy, or wear away gradually. **[**C16: var. of C15 *thwittle* large knife, ult. from OE *thwītan* to cut**]**

whity (ˈwaɪtɪ) *n, pl* **whities. 1** *Inf.* a variant spelling of **whitey.** ◆ *adj* **2a** whitish in colour. **2b** (*in combination*): *whity-brown.*

whizz *or* **whiz** (wɪz) *vb* **whizzes, whizzing, whizzed. 1** to make or cause to make a loud humming or buzzing sound. **2** to move or cause to move with such a sound. **3** (*intr*) *Inf.* to move or go rapidly. ◆ *n, pl* **whizzes. 4** a loud humming or buzzing sound. **5** *Inf.* Also: **wizz.** a person who is extremely skilful at some activity. **6** a slang word for **amphetamine.** **[**C16: imit.**]**

whizz-bang *or* **whiz-bang** *n* **1** a World War I shell that travelled at such high velocity that the sound of its flight was heard only an instant before the sound of its explosion. **2** a type of firework that jumps around emitting a whizzing sound and occasional bangs.

whizz kid Ⓣ**, whiz kid,** *or* **wiz kid** *n Inf.* a person who is pushing, enthusiastic, and outstandingly successful for his or her age. **[**C20: from WHIZZ, ? infl. by WIZARD**]**

whizzy (ˈwɪzɪ) *adj* **whizzier, whizziest.** *Inf.* using sophisticated technology to produce vivid effects: *a whizzy new computer game.*

who (huː) *pron* **1** which person? what person? used in direct and indirect questions: *he can't remember who did it; who met you?* **2** used to introduce relative clauses with antecedents referring to human beings: *the people who lived here have left.* **3** the one or ones who; whoever: *bring who you want.* **[**OE *hwā***]**

> **USAGE NOTE** See at **whom.**

WHO *abbrev. for* World Health Organization.

whoa (wəʊ) *interj* a command used esp. to horses to stop or slow down. **[**C19: var. of HO**]**

who-does-what *adj* (of a dispute, strike, etc.) relating to the separation of kinds of work performed by different trade unions.

whodunnit *or* **whodunit** (huːˈdʌnɪt) *n Inf.* a novel, play, etc., concerned with a crime, usually murder.

whoever (huːˈɛvə) *pron* **1** any person who: *whoever wants it can have it.* **2** no matter who: *I'll come round tomorrow, whoever may be here.* **3** an intensive form of *who,* used in questions: *whoever could have thought that?* **4** *Inf.* an unspecified person: *give those to Cathy or whoever.*

whole Ⓣ (həʊl) *adj* **1** containing all the component parts necessary to form a total; complete: *a whole apple.* **2** constituting the full quantity, extent, etc. **3** uninjured or undamaged. **4** healthy. **5** having no fractional or decimal part; integral: *a whole number.* **6** designating a relationship by descent from the same parents; full: *whole brothers.* **7 out of whole cloth.** *US & Canad. inf.* entirely without a factual basis. ◆ *adv* **8** in an undivided or unbroken piece: *to swallow a plum whole.* ◆ *n* **9** all the parts, elements, etc., of a thing. **10** an assemblage of parts viewed together as a unit. **11** a thing complete in itself. **12 as a whole.** considered altogether; completely. **13 on the whole. 13a** taking all things into consideration. **13b** in general. **[**OE *hāl, hæl***]**
▸ˈ**wholeness** *n*

whole blood *n* blood for transfusion from which none of the elements has been removed.

wholefood (ˈhəʊlˌfuːd) *n* (*sometimes pl*) **a** food that has been refined or processed as little as possible and is eaten in its natural state, such as brown rice, wholemeal flour, etc. **b** (*as modifier*): *a wholefood restaurant.*

wholehearted Ⓣ (ˌhəʊlˈhɑːtɪd) *adj* done, acted, given, etc., with total sincerity, enthusiasm, or commitment.
▸ˌ**wholeˈheartedly** *adv*

whole hog *n Sl.* the whole or total extent (esp. in **go the whole hog**).

wholemeal (ˈhəʊlˌmiːl) *adj Brit.* (of flour, bread, etc.) made from the entire wheat kernel. Also called (esp. US and Canad.): **whole-wheat.**

whole milk *n* milk from which no constituent has been removed.

whole note *n* the usual US and Canad. name for **semibreve.**

whole number *n* **1** an integer. **2** a natural number.

wholesale Ⓣ (ˈhəʊlˌseɪl) *n* **1** the business of selling goods to retailers in larger quantities than they are sold to final consumers but in smaller

THESAURUS

whitewash *Informal n* **2** = **cover-up,** camouflage, concealment, deception, extenuation ◆ *vb* **5** = **cover up,** camouflage, conceal, extenuate, gloss over, make light of, suppress
Antonyms *vb* ≠ **cover up:** disclose, expose, lay bare, reveal, uncover, unmask, unveil

whittle *vb* **1, 2** = **carve,** cut, hew, pare, shape, shave, trim **3** *often foll. by* **away, down,** *etc.* = **reduce,** consume, destroy, eat away, erode, undermine, wear away

whizz kid *n Informal* = **prodigy,** child genius, genius, mastermind, talent, whizz (*inf.*), wonder kid, wunderkind

whole *adj* **1, 2** = **complete,** entire, full, in one piece, integral, total, unabridged, uncut, undivided **3** = **undamaged,** faultless, flawless, good, in one piece, intact, inviolate, mint, perfect, sound, unbroken, unharmed, unhurt, unimpaired, uninjured, unmutilated, unscathed, untouched **4** = **healthy,** able-bodied, better, cured, fit, hale, healed, in fine fettle, in good health, recovered, robust, sound, strong, well ◆ *adv* **8** = **in one piece,** in one ◆ *n* **9** = **total,** aggregate, all, everything, lot, sum total, the entire amount **10** = **totality,** ensemble, entirety, entity, fullness, piece, unit, unity **13 on the whole: a** = **generally,** all things considered, by and large, taking everything into consideration **b** = **as a rule,** for the most part, in general, in the main, mostly, predominantly
Antonyms *adj* ≠ **complete:** cut, divided, fragmented, incomplete, in pieces, partial ≠ **undamaged:** broken, damaged ≠ **healthy:** ailing, diseased, ill, sick, sickly, under-the-weather, unwell ◆ *n* ≠ **totality:** bit, component, constituent, division, element, fragment, part, piece, portion

wholehearted *adj* = **sincere,** committed, complete, dedicated, determined, devoted, earnest, emphatic, enthusiastic, genuine, heartfelt, hearty, real, true, unfeigned, unqualified, unreserved, unstinting, warm, zealous
Antonyms *adj* cool, grudging, half-hearted, insincere, qualified, reserved, unreal

wholesale *adj* **3** = **extensive,** all-inclusive, broad, comprehensive, far-reaching, indiscrim-

quantities than they are purchased from manufacturers. Cf. **retail** (sense 1). ◆ *adj* **2** of or engaged in such business. **3** made, done, etc., on a large scale or without discrimination. ◆ *adv* **4** on a large scale or without discrimination. ◆ *vb* **wholesales, wholesaling, wholesaled. 5** to sell (goods) at wholesale.
▸ **'whole,saler** *n*

wholesale price index *n* an indicator of price changes in the wholesale market.

wholesome ❶ ('həʊlsəm) *adj* **1** conducive to health or physical wellbeing. **2** conducive to moral wellbeing. **3** characteristic or suggestive of health or wellbeing, esp. in appearance. [C12: from WHOLE (healthy) + -SOME[1]]
▸ **'wholesomely** *adv* ▸ **'wholesomeness** *n*

whole tone *or US & Canad.* **whole step** *n* an interval of two semitones. Often shortened to **tone.**

whole-tone scale *n* either of two scales produced by commencing on one of any two notes a chromatic semitone apart and proceeding upwards or downwards in whole tones for an octave.

whole-wheat *adj* another term (esp. US and Canad.) for **wholemeal.**

who'll (hu:l) *contraction of* who will *or* who shall.

wholly ❶ ('həʊllɪ) *adv* **1** completely, totally, or entirely. **2** without exception; exclusively.

whom (hu:m) *pron* the objective form of *who,* used when *who* is not the subject of its own clause: *whom did you say you had seen? he can't remember whom he saw.* [OE *hwām,* dative of *hwā* who]

> **USAGE NOTE** It was formerly considered correct to use *whom* whenever the objective form of *who* was required. This is no longer thought to be necessary and the objective form *who* is now commonly used, even in formal writing: *there were several people there who he had met before. Who* cannot be used directly after a preposition – the preposition is usually displaced, as in *the man (who) he sold his car to.* In formal writing *whom* is preferred in sentences like these: *the man to whom he sold his car.* There are some types of sentence in which *who* cannot be used: *the refugees, many of whom were old and ill, were allowed across the border.*

whomever (hu:m'ɛvə) *pron* the objective form of *whoever: I'll hire whomever I can find.*

whoop ❶ (wu:p) *vb* **whoops, whooping, whooped. 1** to utter (speech) with loud cries, as of excitement. **2** (hu:p). *Med.* to cough convulsively with a crowing sound. **3** (of certain birds) to utter (a hooting cry). **4** (*tr*) to urge on or call with or as if with whoops. **5** (wʊp, wu:p). **whoop it up.** *Inf.* **5a** to indulge in a noisy celebration. **5b** *Chiefly US.* to arouse enthusiasm. ◆ *n* **6** a loud cry, esp. one expressing excitement. **7** (hu:p). *Med.* the convulsive crowing sound made during whooping cough. [C14: imit.]

whoopee *Inf.* ◆ *interj* (wʊ'pi:). **1** an exclamation of joy, excitement, etc. ◆ *n* ('wʊpi:). **2 make whoopee. 2a** to engage in noisy merrymaking. **2b** to make love.

whoopee cushion *n* a joke cushion that emits a sound like the breaking of wind when someone sits on it.

whooper *or* **whooper swan** ('wu:pə) *n* a large Old World swan having a black bill with a yellow base and a noisy whooping cry.

whooping cough ('hu:pɪŋ) *n* an acute infectious disease characterized by coughing spasms that end with a shrill crowing sound on inspiration. Technical name: **pertussis.**

whoops (wʊps) *interj* an exclamation of surprise or of apology.

whoosh *or* **woosh** (wʊʃ) *n* **1** a hissing or rushing sound. ◆ *vb* **2** (*intr*) to make or move with such a sound.

whop (wɒp) *Inf.* ◆ *vb* **whops, whopping, whopped. 1** (*tr*) to strike, beat, or thrash. **2** (*tr*) to defeat utterly. **3** (*intr*) to drop or fall. ◆ *n* **4** a heavy blow or the sound made by such a blow. [C14: var. of *wap,* ? imit.]

whopper ❶ ('wɒpə) *n Inf.* **1** anything uncommonly large of its kind. **2** a big lie. [C18: from WHOP]

whopping ❶ ('wɒpɪŋ) *adj Inf.* uncommonly large.

whore ❶ (hɔ:) *n* **1** a prostitute or promiscuous woman: often a term of abuse. ◆ *vb* **whores, whoring, whored.** (*intr*) **2** to be or act as a prostitute. **3** (of a man) to have promiscuous sexual relations, esp. with prostitutes. **4** (often foll. by *after*) to seek that which is immoral, idolatrous, etc. [OE *hōre*]
▸ **'whoredom** *n* ▸ **'whorish** *adj*

whorehouse ❶ ('hɔ:,haʊs) *n* another word for **brothel.**

whoremonger ('hɔ:,mʌŋgə) *n* a person who consorts with whores; lecher. Also called: **whoremaster.**
▸ **'whore,mongery** *n*

whoreson ('hɔ:sən) *Arch.* ◆ *n* **1** a bastard. **2** a scoundrel; wretch. ◆ *adj* **3** vile or hateful.

whorl ❶ (wɜ:l) *n* **1** *Bot.* a radial arrangement of petals, stamens, leaves, etc., around a stem. **2** *Zool.* a single turn in a spiral shell. **3** anything shaped like a coil. [C15: prob. var. of *wherville* whirl, infl. by Du. *worvel*]
▸ **whorled** *adj*

whortleberry ('wɜ:tᵊl,bɛrɪ) *n, pl* **whortleberries. 1** Also called: **bilberry, blaeberry, huckleberry.** a small Eurasian ericaceous shrub with greenish-pink flowers and edible sweet blackish berries. **2** the fruit of this shrub. **3 bog whortleberry.** a related plant of mountain regions, having pink flowers and black fruits. [C16: SW English dialect var. of *hurtleberry,* from ?]

who's (hu:z) *contraction of* who is *or* who has.

whose (hu:z) *determiner* **1a** of whom? belonging to whom? used in direct and indirect questions: *I told him whose fault it was; whose car is this?* **1b** (*as pron*): *whose is that?* **2** of whom; of which: used as a relative pronoun: *a house whose windows are broken; a man whose reputation has suffered.* [OE *hwæs,* genitive of *hwā* who & *hwæt* what]

whoso ('hu:səʊ) *pron* an archaic word for **whoever.**

whosoever (,hu:səʊ'ɛvə) *pron* an archaic or formal word for **whoever.**

who's who *n* a book or list containing the names and short biographies of famous people.

why (waɪ) *adv* **1a** for what reason?: *why are you here?* **1b** (*used in indirect questions*): *tell me why you're here.* ◆ *pron* **2** for or because of which: *there is no reason why he shouldn't come.* ◆ *n, pl* **whys. 3** (*usually pl*) the cause of something (esp. in **the whys and wherefores**). ◆ *interj* **4** an introductory expression of surprise, indignation, etc.: *why, don't be silly!* [OE *hwī*]

whydah *or* **whidah** ('wɪdə) *n* any of various predominantly black African weaverbirds, the males of which grow very long tail feathers in the breeding season. Also called: **whydah bird, whidah bird, widow bird.** [C18: after a town in Benin in W Africa]

WI *abbrev. for:* **1** West Indian. **2** West Indies. **3** Wisconsin. **4** (in Britain) Women's Institute.

Wicca ('wɪkə) *n* the cult or practice of witchcraft. [C20 revival of OE *wicca* witch]
▸ **'Wiccan** *n, adj*

wick[1] (wɪk) *n* **1** a cord or band of loosely twisted or woven fibres, as in a candle, that supplies fuel to a flame by capillary action. **2 get on (someone's) wick.** *Brit. sl.* to cause irritation to (someone). [OE *weoce*]

wick[2] (wɪk) *n Arch.* a village or hamlet. [OE *wīc;* rel. to *-wich* in place names]

wicked ❶ ('wɪkɪd) *adj* **1a** morally bad. **1b** (*as collective n;* preceded by *the*): *the wicked.* **2** mischievous or roguish in a playful way: *a wicked grin.* **3** causing injury or harm. **4** troublesome, unpleasant, or offensive. **5** *Sl.* very good. [C13: from dialect *wick,* from OE *wicca* sorcerer, *wicce* witch]
▸ **'wickedly** *adv* ▸ **'wickedness** *n*

THESAURUS

inate, mass, sweeping, wide-ranging ◆ *adv* **4** = **extensively,** all at once, comprehensively, indiscriminately, on a large scale, without exception
Antonyms *adj* ≠ **extensive:** confined, discriminate, limited, partial, restricted, selective

wholesome *adj* **1** = **healthy,** beneficial, good, healthful, health-giving, helpful, hygienic, invigorating, nourishing, nutritious, salubrious, salutary, sanitary, strengthening **2** = **moral,** apple-pie (*inf.*), clean, decent, edifying, ethical, exemplary, honourable, improving, innocent, nice, pure, respectable, righteous, squeaky-clean, uplifting, virtuous, worthy
Antonyms *adj* ≠ **healthy:** putrid, rotten, unhealthy, unhygienic, unwholesome ≠ **moral:** blue, corrupt, degrading, dirty, dishonest, evil, filthy, immoral, lewd, obscene, pernicious, pornographic, tasteless, trashy, unprincipled, unwholesome, X-rated (*inf.*)

wholly *adv* **1** = **completely,** all, altogether, comprehensively, entirely, fully, heart and soul, in every respect, one hundred per cent (*inf.*), perfectly, thoroughly, totally, utterly **2** = **solely,** exclusively, only, without exception
Antonyms *adv* ≠ **completely:** incompletely, in part, moderately, partially, partly, relatively, slightly, somewhat

whoop *n* **6** = **cry,** cheer, halloo, holler (*inf.*), hoot, hurrah, scream, shout, shriek, yell

whopper *Informal n* **1** = **giant,** colossus, crackerjack, jumbo (*inf.*), leviathan, mammoth, monster **2** = **big lie,** fable, fabrication, falsehood, tall story (*inf.*), untruth

whopping *adj Informal* = **gigantic,** big, elephantine, enormous, extraordinary, giant, great, huge, humongous *or* humungous (*US sl.*), large, mammoth, massive, monstrous, prodigious, tremendous, whacking (*inf.*)

whore *n* **1** = **prostitute,** call girl, cocotte, courtesan, demimondaine, demirep (*rare*), fallen woman, *fille de joie,* harlot, hooker (*US sl.*), hustler (*US & Canad. sl.*), lady of the night, loose woman, scrubber (*Brit. & Austral. sl.*), slag (*Brit. sl.*), streetwalker, strumpet, tart (*inf.*), trollop, woman of easy virtue, working girl (*facetious sl.*) ◆ *vb* **2** = **prostitute oneself,** be on the game (*sl.*), hustle (*US & Canad. sl.*), sell one's body, sell oneself, solicit, walk the streets **3** = **sleep around** (*inf.*), fornicate, lech *or* letch (*inf.*), wanton, wench (*arch.*), womanize

whorehouse *n* = **brothel,** bagnio, bordello, cathouse (*US sl.*), disorderly house, house of ill fame *or* repute, house of prostitution, knocking-shop (*Brit. sl.*)

whorl *n* **3** = **swirl,** coil, corkscrew, helix, spiral, twist, vortex

wicked *adj* **1** = **bad,** abandoned, abominable, amoral, atrocious, black-hearted, corrupt, debased, depraved, devilish, dissolute, egregious, evil, fiendish, flagitious, foul, guilty, heinous, immoral, impious, iniquitous, irreligious, maleficent, nefarious, scandalous, shameful, sinful, sink, unprincipled, unrighteous, vicious, vile, villainous, worthless **2** = **mischievous,** arch, impish, incorrigible, naughty, rascally, roguish **3** = **harmful,** acute, agonizing, awful, crashing, destructive, dreadful, fearful, fierce, gut-wrenching, injurious, intense, mighty, painful, severe, terrible **4** = **troublesome,** bothersome, difficult, distressing, galling, offensive, trying, unpleasant **5** *Slang* = **expert,** adept, adroit, deft, masterly, mighty, outstanding, powerful, skilful, strong
Antonyms *adj* ≠ **bad:** benevolent, ethical, good, honourable, moral, noble, principled, virtuous ≠ **mischievous:** good, mannerly, obedient, well-

wicker ('wɪkə) *n* **1** a slender flexible twig or shoot, esp. of willow. **2** short for **wickerwork.** ◆ *adj* **3** made of, consisting of, or constructed from wicker. [C14: from ON]

wickerwork ('wɪkə,wɜːk) *n* **a** a material consisting of woven wicker. **b** (*as modifier*): *a wickerwork chair.*

wicket ('wɪkɪt) *n* **1** a small door or gate, esp. one that is near to or part of a larger one. **2** *Chiefly US.* a small window or opening in a door, esp. one fitted with a grating or glass pane. **3** a small sluicegate. **4a** *Cricket.* either of two constructions, 22 yards apart, consisting of three stumps stuck in the ground with two wooden bails resting on top, at which the batsman stands. **4b** the strip of ground between these. **4c** a batsman's turn at batting or the period during which two batsmen bat. **4d** the act or instance of a batsman being got out: *the bowler took six wickets.* **5 keep wicket.** to act as a wicketkeeper. **6 on a good, sticky,** etc., **wicket.** *Inf.* in an advantageous, awkward, etc., situation. [C18: from OF *wiket*]

wicketkeeper ('wɪkɪt,kiːpə) *n Cricket.* the player on the fielding side positioned directly behind the wicket.

wickiup, wikiup, *or* **wickyup** ('wɪkɪ,ʌp) *n US & Canad.* a crude shelter made of brushwood or grass and having an oval frame, esp. of a kind used by nomadic Native Americans now in the Oklahoma area. [C19: of Amerind origin]

widdershins ('wɪdə,ʃɪnz) *adv Chiefly Scot.* a variant spelling of **withershins.**

wide ➊ (waɪd) *adj* **1** having a great extent from side to side. **2** spacious or extensive. **3a** (*postpositive*) having a specified extent, esp. from side to side: *two yards wide.* **3b** (*in combination*): extending throughout: *nationwide.* **4** remote from the desired point, mark, etc.: *your guess is wide of the mark.* **5** (of eyes) opened fully. **6** loose, full, or roomy: *wide trousers.* **7** exhibiting a considerable spread: *a wide variation.* **8** *Phonetics.* another word for **lax** (sense 4) or **open** (sense 32). ◆ *adv* **9** over an extensive area: *to travel far and wide.* **10** to the full extent: *he opened the door wide.* **11** far from the desired point, mark, etc. ◆ *n* **12** (in cricket) a bowled ball that is outside the batsman's reach and scores a run for the batting side. [OE *wīd*]
▸ **'widely** *adv* ▸ **'wideness** *n* ▸ **'widish** *adj*

wide-angle lens *n* a lens system on a camera that has a small focal length and therefore can cover an angle of view of 60° or more.

wide-awake ➊ *adj* (**wide awake** *when postpositive*). **1** fully awake. **2** keen, alert, or observant. ◆ *n* **3** Also called: **wide-awake hat.** a hat with a low crown and very wide brim.

wide-body *adj* (of an aircraft) having a wide fuselage, esp. wide enough to contain three rows of seats abreast.

wide boy *n Brit. sl.* a man who is prepared to use unscrupulous methods to progress or make money.

wide-eyed ➊ *adj* innocent or credulous.

widen ➊ ('waɪdᵊn) *vb* to make or become wide or wider.
▸ **'widener** *n*

wide-open ➊ *adj* (**wide open** *when postpositive*). **1** open to the full extent. **2** (*postpositive*) exposed to attack; vulnerable. **3** uncertain as to outcome. **4** *US inf.* (of a town or city) lax in the enforcement of certain laws, esp. those relating to the sale of alcohol, gambling, etc.

wide receiver *n American football.* a player whose function is to catch long passes from the quarterback.

widespread ➊ ('waɪd,sprɛd) *adj* **1** extending over a wide area. **2** accepted by or occurring among many people.

widgeon ('wɪdʒən) *n* a variant spelling of **wigeon.**

widget ('wɪdʒɪt) *n Inf.* any small mechanism or device, the name of which is unknown or temporarily forgotten. [C20: changed from GADGET]

widow ('wɪdəʊ) *n* **1** a woman whose husband has died, esp. one who has not remarried. **2** (*with a modifier*) *Inf.* a woman whose husband frequently leaves her alone while he indulges in a sport, etc.: *a golf widow.* **3** *Printing.* a short line at the end of a paragraph, esp. one that occurs as the top line of a page or column. **4** (in some card games) an additional hand or set of cards exposed on the table. ◆ *vb* (*tr; usually passive*) **5** to cause to become a widow. **6** to deprive of something valued. [OE *widuwe*]
▸ **'widowhood** *n*

widow bird *n* another name for **whydah.**

widower ('wɪdəʊə) *n* a man whose wife has died and who has not remarried.

widow's cruse *n* an endless or unfailing source of supply. [allusion to I Kings 17:16]

widow's mite *n* a small contribution by a person who has very little. [allusion to Mark 12:43]

widow's peak *n* a V-shaped point in the hairline in the middle of the forehead. [from the belief that it presaged early widowhood]

width ➊ (wɪdθ) *n* **1** the linear extent or measurement of something from side to side. **2** the state or fact of being wide. **3** a piece or section of something at its full extent from side to side: *a width of cloth.* **4** the distance across a rectangular swimming bath, as opposed to its length. [C17: from WIDE + -TH[1], analogous to BREADTH]

wield ➊ (wiːld) *vb* (*tr*) **1** to handle or use (a weapon, tool, etc.). **2** to exert or maintain (power or authority). [OE *wieldan, wealdan*]
▸ **'wieldable** *adj* ▸ **'wielder** *n*

wieldy ('wiːldɪ) *adj* **wieldier, wieldiest.** easily handled, used, or managed.

wiener ('wiːnə) *or* **wienerwurst** ('wiːnə,wɜːst) *n US & Canad.* a kind of smoked sausage, similar to a frankfurter. [C20: shortened from G *Wiener Wurst* Viennese sausage]

Wiener schnitzel ('viːnə 'ʃnɪtsəl) *n* a thin escalope of veal, fried in breadcrumbs. [G: Viennese cutlet]

wife ➊ (waɪf) *n, pl* **wives. 1** a man's partner in marriage; a married woman. Related adj: **uxorial. 2** an archaic or dialect word for **woman. 3 take to wife.** to marry (a woman). [OE *wīf*]
▸ **'wifehood** *n* ▸ **'wifely** *adj*

wig (wɪg) *n* **1** an artificial head of hair, either human or synthetic, worn to disguise baldness, as part of a theatrical or ceremonial dress, as a disguise, or for adornment. ◆ *vb* **wigs, wigging, wigged.** (*tr*) **2** *Brit. sl.* to berate severely. [C17: shortened from PERIWIG]
▸ **wigged** *adj* ▸ **'wigless** *adj*

wigeon *or* **widgeon** ('wɪdʒən) *n* **1** a Eurasian duck of marshes, swamps, etc., the male of which has a reddish-brown head and chest and grey-and-white back and wings. **2 American wigeon.** Also called: **baldpate.** a similar bird of North America, the male of which has a white crown. [C16: from ?]

wigging ('wɪgɪŋ) *n Brit. sl.* a reprimand.

wiggle ➊ ('wɪgᵊl) *vb* **wiggles, wiggling, wiggled. 1** to move or cause to move with jerky movements, esp. from side to side. ◆ *n* **2** the act of wiggling. [C13: from MLow G, MDu. *wiggelen*]
▸ **'wiggler** *n* ▸ **'wiggly** *adj*

wight (waɪt) *n Arch.* a human being. [OE *wiht*; rel. to OFrisian *āwet* something]

wigwag ('wɪg,wæg) *vb* **wigwags, wigwagging, wigwagged. 1** to move (something) back and forth. **2** to communicate with (someone) by means of a flag semaphore. ◆ *n* **3a** a system of communication by flag semaphore. **3b** the message signalled. [C16: from obs. *wig*, prob. short for WIGGLE + WAG[1]]
▸ **'wig,wagger** *n*

wigwam ('wɪg,wæm) *n* **1** any dwelling of the North American Indians, esp. one made of bark, rushes, or skins spread over a set of arched poles lashed together. **2** a similar structure for children. [from *wīkwām* (of Amerind origin), lit.: their abode]

wilco ('wɪlkəʊ) *interj* an expression in signalling, telecommunications, etc., indicating that a message just received will be complied with. [C20: abbrev. for *I will comply*]

wild ➊ (waɪld) *adj* **1** (of animals) living independently of man; not domesticated or tame. **2** (of plants) growing in a natural state; not cultivated. **3** uninhabited; desolate: *a wild stretch of land.* **4** living in a savage or uncivilized way: *wild tribes.* **5** lacking restraint or control: *wild merriment.* **6** of great violence: *a wild storm.* **7** disorderly or chaotic: *wild talk.* **8**

THESAURUS

behaved ≠ **harmful:** harmless, innocuous, mild, pleasant, wholesome

wide *adj* **1, 2** = **broad**, ample, catholic, comprehensive, distended, encyclopedic, expanded, expansive, extensive, far-reaching, general, immense, inclusive, large, overarching, sweeping, vast **4** = **distant**, away, off, off course, off target, remote **5** = **expanded**, dilated, distended, fully open, outspread, outstretched **6** = **spacious**, ample, baggy, capacious, commodious, full, loose, roomy ◆ *adv* **9, 10** = **fully**, as far as possible, completely, right out, to the furthest extent **11** = **off target**, astray, nowhere near, off course, off the mark, out
Antonyms *adj* ≠ **broad:** narrow, strict, tight ≠ **expanded:** closed, limited, restricted, shut ≠ **spacious:** confined, constricted, cramped, tight ◆ *adv* ≠ **fully:** narrowly, partially, partly

wide-awake *adj* **1** = **conscious**, fully awake, roused, wakened **2** = **alert**, aware, heedful, keen, observant, on one's toes, on the alert, on the ball (*inf.*), on the qui vive, vigilant, wary, watchful
Antonyms *adj* ≠ **alert:** distracted, dreamy, heedless, inattentive, negligent, oblivious, preoccupied, unaware, unobservant

wide-eyed *adj* = **naive**, as green as grass, credulous, green, impressionable, ingenuous, innocent, simple, trusting, unsophisticated, unsuspicious, wet behind the ears (*inf.*)

widen *vb* = **broaden**, dilate, enlarge, expand, extend, open out *or* up, open wide, spread, stretch
Antonyms *vb* compress, constrict, contract, cramp, diminish, narrow, reduce, shrink, tighten

wide-open *adj* **1** = **outspread**, fully extended, fully open, gaping, outstretched, splayed, spread **2** = **unprotected**, at risk, defenceless, exposed, in danger, in peril, open, susceptible, vulnerable **3** = **uncertain**, anybody's guess (*inf.*), indeterminate, unpredictable, unsettled, up for grabs (*inf.*)

widespread *adj* **1, 2** = **common**, broad, epidemic, extensive, far-flung, far-reaching, general, pervasive, popular, prevalent, rife, sweeping, universal, wholesale
Antonyms *adj* confined, exclusive, limited, local, narrow, rare, sporadic, uncommon

width *n* **1** = **breadth**, compass, diameter, extent, girth, measure, range, reach, scope, span, thickness, wideness

wield *vb* **1** = **brandish**, employ, flourish, handle, manage, manipulate, ply, swing, use **2** = **exert**, apply, be possessed of, command, control, exercise, have, have at one's disposal, hold, maintain, make use of, manage, possess, put to use, utilize

wife *n* **1** = **spouse**, better half (*humorous*), bride, helpmate, helpmeet, her indoors, little woman (*inf.*), mate, old lady (*inf.*), old woman (*inf.*), partner, significant other (*US inf.*), (the) missis *or* missus (*inf.*), woman (*inf.*)

wiggle *vb, n* **1, 2** = **jerk**, jiggle, shake, shimmy, squirm, twitch, wag, waggle, writhe

wild *adj* **1** = **untamed**, feral, ferocious, fierce, savage, unbroken, undomesticated **2** = **uncultivated**, free, indigenous, native, natural **3** = **desolate**, desert, deserted, empty, godforsaken, lonely, trackless, uncivilized, uncultivated, uninhabited, unpopulated, virgin **4** = **uncivilized**, barbaric, barbarous, brutish, ferocious, fierce, primitive, rude, savage **5** = **uncontrolled**, boister-

dishevelled; untidy: *wild hair*. **9** in a state of extreme emotional intensity: *wild with anger*. **10** reckless: *wild speculations*. **11** random: *a wild guess*. **12** (*postpositive*; foll. by *about*) *Inf.* intensely enthusiastic: *I'm wild about my new boyfriend*. **13** (of a card, such as a joker in some games) able to be given any value the holder pleases. **14 wild and woolly. 14a** rough; barbarous. **14b** (of theories, plans, etc.) not fully thought out. ◆ *adv* **15** in a wild manner. **16 run wild. 16a** to grow without cultivation or care: *the garden has run wild*. **16b** to behave without restraint: *he has let his children run wild*. ◆ *n* **17** (*often pl*) a desolate or uninhabited region. **18 the wild. 18a** a free natural state of living. **18b** the wilderness. [OE *wilde*] ▸ **'wildish** *adj* ▸ **'wildly** *adv* ▸ **'wildness** *n*

wild boar *n* a wild pig of parts of Europe and central Asia, having a pale grey to black coat and prominent tusks.

wild brier *n* another name for **wild rose**.

wild card *n* **1** See **wild** (sense 13). **2** *Sport.* a player or team that has not qualified for a competition but is allowed to take part, at the organizers' discretion, after all the regular places have been taken. **3** an unpredictable element in a situation. **4** *Computing.* a symbol that can represent any character or group of characters, as in a filename.

wild carrot *n* an umbelliferous plant of temperate regions, having clusters of white flowers and hooked fruits. Also called: **Queen Anne's lace**.

wildcat ('waɪldˌkæt) *n, pl* **wildcats** *or* **wildcat. 1** a wild European cat that resembles the domestic tabby but is larger and has a bushy tail. **2** any of various other felines, such as the lynx and the caracal. **3** *US & Canad.* another name for **bobcat**. **4** *Inf.* a savage or aggressive person. **5** an exploratory drilling for petroleum or natural gas. **6** (*modifier*) *Chiefly US.* involving risk, esp. financially or commercially unsound: *a wildcat project*. ◆ *vb* **wildcats, wildcatting, wildcatted. 7** (*intr*) to drill for petroleum or natural gas in an area having no known reserves. ▸ **'wildˌcatter** *n* ▸ **'wildˌcatting** *n, adj*

wildcat strike *n* a strike begun by workers spontaneously or without union approval.

wild cherry *n* another name for **gean**.

wild dog *n* another name for **dingo**.

wildebeest ('wɪldɪˌbiːst, 'vɪl-) *n, pl* **wildebeests** *or* **wildebeest.** another name for **gnu**. [C19: from Afrik., lit.: wild beast]

wilder ('wɪldə) *vb Arch.* **1** to lead or be led astray. **2** to bewilder or become bewildered. [C17: from ?]

wilderness ❶ ('wɪldənɪs) *n* **1** a wild uninhabited uncultivated region. **2** any desolate area. **3** a confused mass or collection. **4 a voice (crying) in the wilderness.** a person, group, etc., making a suggestion or plea that is ignored. [OE *wildēornes*, from *wildēor* wild beast + -NESS]

wild-eyed *adj* glaring in an angry, distracted, or wild manner.

wildfire ('waɪldˌfaɪə) *n* **1** a highly flammable material, such as Greek fire, formerly used in warfare. **2a** a raging and uncontrollable fire. **2b** anything that is disseminated quickly (esp. in **spread like wildfire**). **3** another name for **will-o'-the-wisp**.

wild flower *n* **1** any flowering plant that grows in an uncultivated state. **2** the flower of such a plant.

wildfowl ('waɪldˌfaʊl) *n* **1** any bird that is hunted by man, esp. any duck or similar aquatic bird. **2** such birds collectively. ▸ **'wildˌfowler** *n* ▸ **'wildˌfowling** *adj, n*

wild-goose chase *n* an absurd or hopeless pursuit, as of something unattainable.

wilding ('waɪldɪŋ) *n* **1** an uncultivated plant or a cultivated plant that has become wild. **2** a wild animal. ◆ Also called: **wildling**.

wildlife ❶ ('waɪldˌlaɪf) *n* wild animals and plants collectively: a term used esp. of fauna.

wild pansy *n* a Eurasian plant of the violet family having purple, yellow, and pale mauve spurred flowers. Also called: **heartsease, love-in-idleness**.

wild parsley *n* any of various uncultivated umbelliferous plants that resemble parsley.

wild rice *n* an aquatic North American grass with dark-coloured edible grain.

wild rose *n* any of numerous roses, such as the dogrose and sweetbrier, that grow wild and have flowers with only one whorl of petals.

wild rubber *n* rubber obtained from uncultivated rubber trees.

wild silk *n* **1** silk produced by wild silkworms. **2** a fabric made from this, or from short fibres of silk designed to imitate it.

wild type *n Biol.* the typical form of a species of organism resulting from breeding under natural conditions.

Wild West *n* the western US during its settlement, esp. with reference to its frontier lawlessness.

wildwood ('waɪldˌwʊd) *n Arch.* a wood or forest growing in a natural uncultivated state.

wile ❶ (waɪl) *n* **1** trickery, cunning, or craftiness. **2** (*usually pl*) an artful or seductive trick or ploy. ◆ *vb* **wiles, wiling, wiled. 3** (*tr*) to lure, beguile, or entice. [C12: from ON *vel* craft]

wilful ❶ *or US* **willful** ('wɪlfʊl) *adj* **1** intent on having one's own way; headstrong or obstinate. **2** intentional: *wilful murder*. ▸ **'wilfully** *or US* **'willfully** *adv* ▸ **'wilfulness** *or US* **'willfulness** *n*

will[1] (wɪl) *vb past* **would.** (takes an infinitive without *to* or an implied infinitive) used as an auxiliary. **1** (esp. with *you, he, she, it, they*, or a noun as subject) to make the future tense. Cf. **shall** (sense 1). **2** to express resolution on the part of the speaker: *I will buy that radio if it's the last thing I do*. **3** to indicate willingness or desire: *will you help me with this problem?* **4** to express commands: *you will report your findings to me tomorrow*. **5** to express ability: *this rope will support a load*. **6** to express probability or expectation: *that will be Jim telephoning*. **7** to express customary practice or inevitability: *boys will be boys*. **8** (*with the infinitive always implied*) to express desire: usually in polite requests: *stay if you will*. **9 what you will.** whatever you like. [OE *willan*]

> **USAGE NOTE** See at **shall**.

will[2] ❶ (wɪl) *n* **1** the faculty of conscious and deliberate choice of action. Related adj: **voluntary**. **2** the act or an instance of asserting a choice. **3a** the declaration of a person's wishes regarding the disposal of his property after his death. **3b** a document in which such wishes are expressed. **4** desire; wish. **5** determined intention: *where there's a will there's a way*. **6** disposition towards others: *he bears you no ill will*. **7 at will.** at one's own desire or choice. **8 with a will.** heartily; energetically. **9 with the best will in the world.** even with the best of intentions. ◆ *vb* (*mainly tr; often takes a clause as object or an infinitive*) **10** (*also intr*) to exercise the faculty of volition in an attempt to accomplish (something): *he willed his wife's recovery from her illness*. **11** to give (property) by will to a person, society, etc.: *he willed his art collection to the nation*. **12** (*also intr*) to order or decree: *the king wills that you shall die*. **13** to choose or prefer: *wander where you will*. [OE *willa*] ▸ **'willer** *n*

willed (wɪld) *adj* (*in combination*) having a will as specified: *weak-willed*.

willet ('wɪlɪt) *n* a large American shore bird having a grey plumage with black-and-white wings. [C19: imit. of its call]

willful ('wɪlfʊl) *adj* the US spelling of **wilful**.

willies ('wɪlɪz) *pl n* **the.** *Sl.* nervousness, jitters, or fright (esp. in **give** (*or* **get**) **the willies**). [C20: from ?]

willing ❶ ('wɪlɪŋ) *adj* **1** favourably disposed or inclined; ready. **2** cheerfully compliant. **3** done, given, accepted, etc., freely or voluntarily. ▸ **'willingly** *adv* ▸ **'willingness** *n*

THESAURUS

ous, chaotic, disorderly, impetuous, lawless, noisy, riotous, rough, rowdy, self-willed, turbulent, unbridled, undisciplined, unfettered, ungovernable, unmanageable, unrestrained, unruly, uproarious, violent, wayward **6** = **stormy**, blustery, choppy, furious, howling, intense, raging, rough, tempestuous, violent **8** = **dishevelled**, disordered, straggly, tousled, unkempt, untidy, windblown **9** = **excited**, agog, avid, crazy (*inf.*), daft (*inf.*), delirious, eager, enthusiastic, frantic, frenzied, hysterical, mad (*inf.*), nuts (*sl.*), potty (*Brit. inf.*), raving **10** = **outrageous**, extravagant, fantastic, flighty, foolhardy, foolish, giddy, ill-considered, impracticable, imprudent, madcap, preposterous, rash, reckless ◆ *adv* **16 run wild: a** = **go on the rampage**, ramble, spread, straggle **b** = **abandon all restraint**, cut loose, kick over the traces, rampage, run free, run riot, stray ◆ *n* **17** *often plural* = **wilderness**, back of beyond (*inf.*), desert, middle of nowhere (*inf.*), uninhabited area, wasteland
Antonyms *adj* ≠ **untamed:** broken, domesticated, tame ≠ **uncultivated:** cultivated, farmed, planted ≠ **desolate:** civilized, inhabited, populated, urban ≠ **uncivilized:** advanced, civilized ≠ **uncontrolled:** calm, careful, controlled, disciplined, domesticated, friendly, genteel, gentle, lawful, mild, ordered, orderly, peaceful, polite, quiet, restrained, self-controlled, thoughtful, well-behaved ≠ **excited:** unenthusiastic, uninterested ≠ **outrageous:** logical, practical, realistic, well-thought-out

wilderness *n* **1, 2** = **desert**, jungle, waste, wasteland, wilds **3** = **tangle**, clutter, confused mass, confusion, congeries, jumble, maze, muddle, welter

wildlife *n* = **flora and fauna**

wile *n* **1** = **trickery**, artfulness, artifice, cheating, chicanery, craft, craftiness, cunning, fraud, guile, slyness **2** *usually plural* = **ploys**, artifices, contrivances, devices, dodges, impositions, lures, manoeuvres, ruses, stratagems, subterfuges, tricks

wilful *adj* **1** = **obstinate**, adamant, bull-headed, determined, dogged, froward (*arch.*), headstrong, inflexible, intractable, intransigent, mulish, obdurate, persistent, perverse, pig-headed, refractory, self-willed, stiff-necked, stubborn, uncompromising, unyielding **2** = **intentional**, conscious, deliberate, intended, purposeful, volitional, voluntary, willed
Antonyms *adj* ≠ **obstinate:** biddable, complaisant, compromising, docile, flexible, good-natured, obedient, pliant, tractable, yielding ≠ **intentional:** accidental, involuntary, uncalculated, unconscious, unintentional, unplanned, unwitting

will[2] *n* **3** = **testament**, declaration, last wishes **4** = **wish**, choice, decision, decree, desire, fancy, inclination, mind, option, pleasure, preference, volition **5** = **determination**, aim, intention, purpose, resolution, resolve, willpower **7 at will** = **as one pleases**, as one thinks fit, as one wishes, at one's desire, at one's discretion, at one's inclination, at one's pleasure, at one's whim, at one's wish ◆ *vb* **10, 12** = **decree**, bid, bring about, cause, command, determine, direct, effect, ordain, order, resolve **11** = **bequeath**, confer, give, leave, pass on, transfer **13** = **wish**, choose, desire, elect, opt, prefer, see fit, want

willing *adj* **1, 2** = **ready**, agreeable, amenable, compliant, consenting, content, desirous, disposed, eager, enthusiastic, favourable, game (*inf.*), happy, inclined, in favour, in the mood, nothing loath, pleased, prepared, so-minded
Antonyms *adj* averse, disinclined, grudging, indisposed, loath, not keen, reluctant, unenthusiastic, unwilling

willingly *adv* **1-3** = **readily**, by choice, cheerfully, eagerly, freely, gladly, happily, lief (*rare*), of one's own accord, of one's own free will, voluntarily, with all one's heart, without hesitation, with pleasure
Antonyms *adv* grudgingly, hesitantly, involuntarily, reluctantly, unwillingly

willingness *n* **1, 2** = **inclination**, agreeableness, agreement, consent, desire, disposition,

williwaw ('wɪlɪ,wɔː) *n US & Canad.* **1** a sudden strong gust of cold wind blowing offshore from a mountainous coast, as in the Strait of Magellan. **2** a state of great turmoil. [C19: from ?]

will-o'-the-wisp (,wɪləðə'wɪsp) *n* **1** Also called: **friar's lantern, ignis fatuus, jack-o'-lantern.** a pale flame or phosphorescence sometimes seen over marshy ground at night. It is believed to be due to the spontaneous combustion of methane originating from decomposing organic matter. **2** a person or thing that is elusive or allures and misleads. [C17: from *Will*, short for *William* + *wisp*, in former sense of a twist of hay burning as a torch]

willow ('wɪləʊ) *n* **1** any of a large genus of trees and shrubs, such as the weeping willow and osiers of N temperate regions, which have graceful flexible branches and flowers in catkins. **2** the whitish wood of certain of these trees. **3** something made of willow wood, such as a cricket bat. [OE *welig*]

willowherb ('wɪləʊ,hɜːb) *n* **1** any of various temperate and arctic plants having narrow leaves and terminal clusters of pink, purplish, or white flowers. **2** short for **rosebay willowherb** (see **rosebay**).

willow pattern *n* **a** a pattern incorporating a willow tree, river, bridge, and figures, typically in blue on a white ground, used on porcelain, etc. **b** (*as modifier*): *a willow-pattern plate.*

willowy ➊ ('wɪləʊɪ) *adj* **1** slender and graceful. **2** flexible or pliant. **3** covered or shaded with willows.

willpower ➊ ('wɪl,paʊə) *n* **1** the ability to control oneself and determine one's actions. **2** firmness of will.

willy[1] ('wɪlɪ) *n, pl* **willies.** *Brit. inf.* a childish or jocular term for **penis.**

willy[2] ('wɪlɪ) *n Austral. sl.* a sudden loss of temper; fit: *to throw a willy.*

willy-nilly ➊ ('wɪlɪ'nɪlɪ) *adv* **1** whether desired or not. ◆ *adj* **2** occurring or taking place whether desired or not. [OE *wile hē, nyle hē*, lit.: will he or will he not]

willy wagtail *n* a black-and-white flycatcher found in Australasia and parts of Asia, having white feathers over the brows.

willy-willy ('wɪlɪ,wɪlɪ) *n, pl* **willy-willies.** *Austral.* a small sometimes violent upward-spiralling cyclone or dust storm. [from Abor.]

wilt[1] ➊ (wɪlt) *vb* **1** to become or cause to become limp or drooping: *insufficient water makes plants wilt.* **2** to lose or cause to lose courage, strength, etc. ◆ *n* **3** the act of wilting or state of becoming wilted. **4** any of various plant diseases characterized by permanent wilting. [C17: ? var. of *wilk* to wither, from MDu. *welken*]

wilt[2] (wɪlt) *vb Arch. or dialect.* (used with the pronoun *thou* or its relative equivalent) a singular form of the present tense (indicative mood) of **will**[1].

Wilton ('wɪltən) *n* a kind of carpet with a close velvet pile of cut loops. [after *Wilton*, town in Wiltshire, where first made]

Wilts (wɪlts) *abbrev. for* Wiltshire.

wily ➊ ('waɪlɪ) *adj* **wilier, wiliest.** sly or crafty.
▸'**wiliness** *n*

wimble ('wɪmbᵊl) *n* **1** any of a number of hand tools used for boring holes. ◆ *vb* **wimbles, wimbling, wimbled. 2** to bore (a hole) with a wimble. [C13: from MDu. *wimmel* auger]

wimp ➊ (wɪmp) *n Inf.* a feeble ineffective person. [C20: from ?]
▸'**wimpish** *or* '**wimpy** *adj*

WIMP (wɪmp) *n acronym for:* **1** windows, icons, menus (*or* mice), pointers: denoting a type of user-friendly screen display used on small computing. **2** *Physics.* weakly interacting massive particle.

wimple ('wɪmpᵊl) *n* **1** a piece of cloth draped around the head to frame the face, worn by women in the Middle Ages and still worn by some nuns. ◆ *vb* **wimples, wimpling, wimpled.** *Arch.* **2** (*tr*) to cover with or put a wimple on. **3** (esp. of a veil) to lie or cause to lie in folds or pleats. [OE *wimpel*]

wimp out *vb (intr, adv) Sl.* to fail to do or complete something through fear or lack of conviction.

win ➊ (wɪn) *vb* **wins, winning, won. 1** (*intr*) to achieve first place in a competition. **2** (*tr*) to gain (a prize, first place, etc.) in a competition. **3** (*tr*) to succeed in or gain (something) with an effort: *we won recognition.* **4** to gain victory or triumph in (a battle, argument, etc.). **5** (*tr*) to earn (a living, etc.) by work. **6** (*tr*) to capture: *the Germans never won Leningrad.* **7** (when *intr*, foll. by *out, through*, etc.) to reach with difficulty (a desired position) or become free, loose, etc., with effort: *the boat won the shore.* **8** (*tr*) to gain (the sympathy, loyalty, etc.) of someone. **9** (*tr*) to persuade (a woman, etc.) to marry one. **10** (*tr*) to extract (ore, coal, etc.) from a mine or (metal or other minerals) from ore. **11 you can't win.** *Inf.* an expression of resignation after an unsuccessful attempt to overcome difficulties. ◆ *n* **12** *Inf.* a success, victory, or triumph. **13** profit; winnings. ◆ See also **win over.** [OE *winnan*]
▸'**winnable** *adj*

wince[1] ➊ (wɪns) *vb* **winces, wincing, winced. 1** (*intr*) to start slightly, as with sudden pain; flinch. ◆ *n* **2** the act of wincing. [C18 (earlier (C13) meaning: to kick): via OF *wencier, guenchir* to avoid, of Gmc origin]
▸'**wincer** *n* ▸'**wincingly** *adv*

wince[2] (wɪns) *n* a roller for transferring pieces of cloth between dyeing vats. [C17: var. of WINCH[1]]

winceyette (,wɪnsɪ'ɛt) *n Brit.* a plain-weave cotton fabric with slightly raised two-sided nap. [from Scot. *wincey*, prob. altered from *woolsey* in *linsey-woolsey*, a fabric made of linen & wool]

winch[1] (wɪntʃ) *n* **1** a windlass driven by a hand- or power-operated crank. **2** a hand- or power-operated crank by which a machine is driven. ◆ *vb* **3** (*tr;* often foll. by *up* or *in*) to pull or lift using a winch. [OE *wince* pulley]

winch[2] (wɪntʃ) *vb (intr)* an obsolete word for **wince**[1].

Winchester rifle ('wɪntʃɪstə) *n Trademark.* a breech-loading lever-action repeating rifle. Often shortened to **Winchester.** [C19: after O. F. *Winchester* (1810–80), US manufacturer]

wind[1] ➊ (wɪnd) *n* **1** a current of air, sometimes of considerable force, moving generally horizontally from areas of high pressure to areas of low pressure. **2** *Chiefly poetic.* the direction from which a wind blows, usually a cardinal point of the compass. **3** air artificially moved, as by a fan, pump, etc. **4** a trend, tendency, or force: *the winds of revolution.* **5** *Inf.* a hint; suggestion: *we got wind that you were coming.* **6** something deemed insubstantial: *his talk was all wind.* **7** breath, as used in respiration or talk: *you're just wasting wind.* **8** (often used in sports) the power to breathe normally: *his wind is weak.* **9** *Music.* **9a** a wind instrument or wind instruments considered collectively. **9b** (*often pl*) the musicians who play wind instruments in an orchestra. **9c** (*modifier*) of or composed of wind instruments: *a wind ensemble.* **10** an informal name for **flatus. 11** the air on which the scent of an animal is carried to hounds or on which the scent of a hunter is carried to his quarry. **12 between wind and water. 12a** the part of a vessel's hull below the water line that is exposed by rolling or by wave action. **12b** any particularly susceptible point. **13 break wind.** to release intestinal gas through the anus. **14 get** *or* **have the wind up.** *Inf.* to become frightened. **15 how** *or* **which way the wind blows** *or* **lies.** what appears probable. **16 in the teeth** (*or* **eye**) **of the wind.** directly into the wind. **17 in the wind.** about to happen. **18 into the wind.** against the wind or upwind. **19 off the wind.** *Naut.* away from the direction from which the wind is blowing. **20 on the wind.** *Naut.* as near as possible to the direction from which the wind is blowing. **21 put the wind up.** *Inf.* to frighten or alarm. **22 raise the wind.** *Brit. inf.* to obtain the necessary funds. **23 sail close** *or* **near to the wind.** to come near the limits of danger or indecency. **24 take the wind out of someone's sails.** to disconcert or deflate someone. ◆ *vb* (*tr*) **25** to cause (someone) to be short of breath: *the blow winded him.* **26a** to detect the scent of. **26b** to pursue (quarry) by following its scent. **27** to cause (a baby) to bring up wind after feeding. **28** to expose to air, as in drying, etc. [OE]
▸'**windless** *adj*

wind[2] ➊ (waɪnd) *vb* **winds, winding, wound. 1** (often foll. by *around, about,* or *upon*) to turn or coil (string, cotton, etc.) around some object or point or (of string, etc.) to be turned, etc., around some object or point: *he wound a scarf around his head.* **2** (*tr*) to cover or wreathe by or as if by coiling, wrapping, etc.: *we wound the body in a shroud.* **3** (*tr;* often foll. by *up*) to tighten the spring of (a clockwork mechanism). **4** (*tr;* foll. by *off*) to remove by uncoiling or unwinding. **5** (*usually intr*) to move or cause to move in a sinuous, spiral, or circular course: *the river*

THESAURUS

enthusiasm, favour, goodwill, volition, will, wish
Antonyms *n* aversion, disagreement, disinclination, hesitation, loathing, reluctance, unwillingness

willowy *adj* **1, 2** = **slender,** graceful, limber, lissom(e), lithe, slim, supple, svelte, sylphlike

willpower *n* **1, 2** = **self-control,** determination, drive, firmness of purpose *or* will, fixity of purpose, force *or* strength of will, grit, resolution, resolve, self-discipline, single-mindedness
Antonyms *n* apathy, hesitancy, indecision, irresolution, languor, lethargy, shilly-shallying (*inf.*), torpor, uncertainty, weakness

willy-nilly *adv* **1** = **whether one likes it or not,** necessarily, *nolens volens,* of necessity, perforce, whether desired or not, whether or no

wilt[1] *vb* **1** = **droop,** become limp *or* flaccid, sag, shrivel, wither **2** = **weaken,** diminish, dwindle, ebb, fade, fail, flag, languish, lose courage, melt away, sag, sink, wane, wither

wily *adj* = **cunning,** arch, artful, astute, cagey (*inf.*), crafty, crooked, deceitful, deceptive, designing, fly (*sl.*), foxy, guileful, intriguing, scheming, sharp, shifty, shrewd, sly, tricky, underhand
Antonyms *adj* artless, candid, dull, guileless, honest, ingenuous, naive, simple, straightforward

wimp *n Informal* = **weakling,** coward, doormat (*sl.*), drip (*inf.*), milksop, mouse, sissy, softy *or* softie, wet (*Brit. sl.*)

win *vb* **1, 2, 4** = **triumph,** achieve first place, achieve mastery, be victorious, carry all before one, carry the day, come first, conquer, finish first, gain victory, overcome, prevail, succeed, sweep the board, take the prize **3** = **gain,** accomplish, achieve, acquire, attain, bag (*inf.*), catch, collect, come away with, earn, get, land, net, obtain, pick up, procure, receive, secure ◆ *n* **12** *Informal* = **victory,** conquest, success, triumph
Antonyms *vb* ≠ **triumph:** fail, fall, suffer defeat, suffer loss ≠ **gain:** forfeit, lose, miss ◆ *n* ≠ **victory:** beating, defeat, downfall, failure, loss, washout (*inf.*)

wince[1] *vb* **1** = **flinch,** blench, cower, cringe, draw back, quail, recoil, shrink, start ◆ *n* **2** = **flinch,** cringe, start

wind[1] *n* **1** = **air,** air-current, blast, breath, breeze, current of air, draught, gust, zephyr **5** *Informal* = **hint,** clue, inkling, intimation, notice, report, rumour, suggestion, tidings, warning, whisper **6** = **talk,** babble, blather, bluster, boasting, empty talk, gab (*inf.*), hot air, humbug, idle talk, verbalizing **7** = **breath,** puff, respiration **10** = **flatulence,** flatus, gas **14 get** *or* **have the wind up** *Informal* = **be afraid,** be alarmed, be frightened, be scared, fear, take fright **17 in the wind** = **imminent,** about to happen, approaching, close at hand, coming, impending, in the offing, near, on the cards (*inf.*), on the way **21 put the wind up** *Informal* = **scare,** alarm, discourage, frighten, frighten off, scare off

wind[2] *vb* **1, 2** = **coil,** curl, encircle, furl, loop, reel, roll, spiral, turn around, twine, twist, wreathe **5** = **meander,** bend, curve, deviate, ramble, snake, turn, twist, zigzag ◆ *n* **10** = **twist,** bend, curve, meander, turn, zigzag

winds through the hills. **6** (*tr*) to introduce indirectly or deviously: *he is winding his own opinions into the report.* **7** (*tr*) to cause to twist or revolve: *he wound the handle.* **8** (*tr*; usually foll. by *up* or *down*) to move by cranking: *please wind up the window.* ◆ *n* **9** the act of winding or state of being wound. **10** a single turn, bend, etc.: *a wind in the river.* ◆ See also **wind down, wind up.** [OE *windan*]
▸'**windable** *adj*

wind[3] (waınd) *vb* **winds, winding, winded** *or* **wound.** (*tr*) *Poetic.* to blow (a note or signal) on (a horn, bugle, etc.). [C16: special use of WIND[1]]

windage ('wındıdʒ) *n* **1a** a deflection of a projectile as a result of the effect of the wind. **1b** the degree of such deflection. **2** the difference between a firearm's bore and the diameter of its projectile. **3** *Naut.* the exposed part of the hull of a vessel responsible for wind resistance.

windbag ❶ ('wınd,bæg) *n* **1** *Sl.* a voluble person who has little of interest to communicate. **2** the bag in a set of bagpipes, which provides a continuous flow of air to the pipes.

windblown ('wınd,bləʊn) *adj* **1** blown by the wind. **2** (of trees, shrubs, etc.) growing in a shape determined by the prevailing winds.

wind-borne *adj* (esp. of plant seeds or pollen) transported by wind.

windbound ('wınd,baʊnd) *adj* (of a sailing vessel) prevented from sailing by an unfavourable wind.

windbreak ('wınd,breık) *n* a fence, line of trees, etc., serving as a protection from the wind by breaking its force.

windburn ('wınd,bɜːn) *n* irritation of the skin caused by prolonged exposure to winds of high velocity.

Windcheater ('wınd,tʃiːtə) *n Aust. trademark.* a warm jacket, usually with a close-fitting knitted neck, cuffs, and waistband.

wind chest (wınd) *n* a box in an organ in which air from the bellows is stored under pressure before being supplied to the pipes or reeds.

wind-chill ('wınd-) *n* **a** the serious chilling effect of wind and low temperature: measured on a scale that runs from hot to fatal to life. **b** (*as modifier*): *wind-chill factor.*

wind cone (wınd) *n* another name for **windsock.**

wind down ❶ (waınd) *vb* (*adv*) **1** (*tr*) to lower or move down by cranking. **2** (*intr*) (of a clock spring) to become slack. **3** (*intr*) to diminish gradually in power; relax.

winded ❶ ('wındıd) *adj* **1** out of breath, as from strenuous exercise. **2** (*in combination*) having breath or wind as specified: *broken-winded; short-winded.*

winder ('waındə) *n* **1** a person or device that winds. **2** an object, such as a bobbin, around which something is wound. **3** a knob or key used to wind up a clock, watch, or similar mechanism. **4** any plant that twists itself around a support. **5** a step of a spiral staircase. Cf. **flyer** (sense 4).

windfall ❶ ('wınd,fɔːl) *n* **1** a piece of unexpected good fortune, esp. financial gain. **2** something blown down by the wind, esp. a piece of fruit.

windfall tax *n* a tax levied on an organization considered to have made excessive profits, esp. a privatized utility company that has exploited a natural monopoly.

wind farm *n* a large group of wind-driven generators for electricity supply.

windflower ('wınd,flaʊə) *n* any of various anemone plants, such as the wood anemone.

wind gauge (wınd) *n* **1** another name for **anemometer. 2** a scale on a gun sight indicating the amount of deflection necessary to allow for windage. **3** *Music.* a device for measuring the wind pressure in the bellows of an organ.

wind harp (wınd) *n* a less common name for **aeolian harp.**

windhover ('wınd,hɒvə) *n Brit.* a dialect name for a **kestrel.**

winding ❶ ('waındıŋ) *n* **1** a curving or sinuous course or movement. **2** anything that has been wound or wrapped around something. **3** a particular manner or style in which something has been wound. **4** a curve, bend, or complete turn in wound material, a road, etc. **5** (*often pl*) devious thoughts or behaviour: *the tortuous windings of political argumentation.* **6** one or more turns of wire forming a continuous coil through which an electric current can pass, as used in transformers, generators, etc. ◆ *adj* **7** curving; sinuous: *a winding road.*
▸'**windingly** *adv*

winding sheet *n* a sheet in which a corpse is wrapped for burial; shroud.

winding-up *n* the process of finishing or closing something, esp. the process of closing down a business.

wind instrument (wınd) *n* any musical instrument sounded by the breath, such as the woodwinds and brass instruments of an orchestra.

windjammer ('wınd,dʒæmə) *n* a large merchant sailing ship.

windlass ('wındləs) *n* **1** a machine for raising weights by winding a rope or chain upon a barrel or drum driven by a crank, motor, etc. ◆ *vb* **2** (*tr*) to raise or haul (a weight, etc.) by means of a windlass. [C14: from ON *vindáss*, from *vinda* to WIND[2] + *ass* pole]

windlestraw ('wındᵊl,strɔː) *n Irish, Scot., & English dialect.* the dried stalk of any of various grasses. [OE *windelstrēaw*, from *windel* basket, from *windan* to wind + *strēaw* straw]

wind machine (wınd) *n* a machine used, esp. in the theatre, to produce a wind or the sound of wind.

windmill ('wınd,mıl, 'wın,mıl) *n* **1** a machine for grinding or pumping driven by a set of adjustable vanes or sails that are caused to turn by the force of the wind. **2** the set of vanes or sails that drives such a mill. **3** Also called: **whirligig.** *Brit.* a toy consisting of plastic or paper vanes attached to a stick in such a manner that they revolve like the sails of a windmill. **4** an imaginary opponent or evil (esp. in **tilt at** *or* **fight windmills**). ◆ *vb* **5** to move or cause to move like the arms of a windmill.

window ('wındəʊ) *n* **1** a light framework, made of timber, metal, or plastic, that contains glass or glazed opening frames and is placed in a wall or roof to let in light or air or to see through. Related adj: **fenestral. 2** an opening in the wall or roof of a building that is provided to let in light or air or to see through. **3** short for **windowpane. 4** the area behind a glass window in a shop used for display. **5** any opening or structure resembling a window in function or appearance, such as the transparent area of an envelope revealing an address within. **6** an opportunity to see or understand something usually unseen: *a window on the workings of Parliament.* **7** a period of unbooked time in a diary, schedule, etc. **8** short for **launch window** or **weather window. 9** *Physics.* a region of the spectrum in which a medium transmits electromagnetic radiation. **10** an area of a VDU display that can be manipulated separately from the rest of the display area. **11** (*modifier*) of or relating to a window or windows: *a window ledge.* ◆ *vb* **12** (*tr*) to furnish with or as if with windows. [C13: from ON *vindauga*, from *vindr* WIND[1] + *auga* eye]

window box *n* a long narrow box, placed on or outside a windowsill, in which plants are grown.

window-dresser *n* a person employed to design and build up a display in a shop window.

window-dressing *n* **1** the ornamentation of shop windows, designed to attract customers. **2** the pleasant aspect of an idea, etc., which is stressed to conceal the real nature.

windowpane ('wındəʊ,peın) *n* a sheet of glass in a window.

window sash *n* a glazed window frame, esp. one that opens.

window seat *n* **1** a seat below a window, esp. in a bay window. **2** a seat beside a window in a bus, train, etc.

window-shop *vb* **window-shops, window-shopping, window-shopped.** (*intr*) to look at goods in shop windows without intending to buy.
▸'**window-**,**shopper** *n* ▸'**window-**,**shopping** *n*

windowsill ('wındəʊ,sıl) *n* a sill below a window.

windpipe ('wınd,paıp) *n* a nontechnical name for **trachea** (sense 1).

wind rose (wınd) *n* a diagram with radiating lines showing the frequency and strength of winds from each direction affecting a specific place.

windrow ('wınd,rəʊ, 'wın,rəʊ) *n* **1** a long low ridge or line of hay or a similar crop, designed to achieve the best conditions for drying or curing. **2** a line of leaves, snow, dust, etc., swept together by the wind.

windscreen ('wınd,skriːn) *n Brit.* the sheet of flat or curved glass that forms a window of a motor vehicle, esp. the front window. US and Canad. name: **windshield.**

windscreen wiper *n Brit.* an electrically operated blade with a rubber edge that wipes a windscreen clear of rain, snow, etc. US and Canad. name: **windshield wiper.**

windshield ('wınd,ʃiːld) *n* the US and Canad. name for **windscreen.**

windsock ('wınd,sɒk) *n* a truncated cone of textile mounted on a mast so that it is free to rotate about a vertical axis: used, esp. at airports, to indicate the local wind direction. Also called: **air sock, drogue, wind sleeve, wind cone.**

Windsor ('wınzə) *adj* of or relating to the British royal family, whose official name this has been from 1917.

Windsor chair *n* a simple wooden chair, popular in England and America from the 18th century, usually having a shaped seat, splayed legs, and a back of many spindles.

Windsor knot *n* a wide triangular knot, produced by making extra turns in tying a tie.

windstorm ('wınd,stɔːm) *n* a storm consisting of violent winds.

wind-sucking *n* a harmful habit of horses in which the animal arches its neck and swallows a gulp of air.
▸'**wind**,**sucker** *n*

windsurfing ('wınd,sɜːfıŋ) *n* the sport of riding on water using a surfboard steered and propelled by an attached sail.

windswept ('wınd,swept) *adj* open to or swept by the wind.

wind tunnel (wınd) *n* a chamber for testing the aerodynamic properties of aircraft, aerofoils, etc., in which a current of air can be maintained at a constant velocity.

wind up ❶ (waınd) *vb* (*adv*) **1** to bring to or reach a conclusion: *he wound up the proceedings.* **2** (*tr*) to tighten the spring of (a clockwork

THESAURUS

windbag *n* **1** *Slang* = **bore**, bigmouth (*sl.*), blether (*Scot.*), blowhard, boaster, braggart, gasbag (*inf.*), gossip, loudmouth (*inf.*), prattler

wind down *vb* **3** = **subside**, cool off, decline, diminish, dwindle, lessen, reduce, relax, slacken, taper off, unwind
Antonyms *vb* accelerate, amplify, escalate, expand, heat up, increase, intensify, magnify, step up

winded *adj* **1** = **out of breath**, breathless, gasping for breath, out of puff, out of whack (*inf.*), panting, puffed, puffed out

windfall *n* **1** = **godsend**, bonanza, find, jackpot, manna from heaven, pot of gold at the end of the rainbow, stroke of luck
Antonyms *n* bad luck, disaster, infelicity, misadventure, mischance, misfortune, mishap

winding *n* **1, 4** = **twist**, bend, convolution, curve, meander, turn, undulation ◆ *adj* **7** = **twisting**, anfractuous, bending, circuitous, convoluted, crooked, curving, flexuous, indirect, meandering, roundabout, serpentine, sinuous, spiral, tortuous, turning, twisty
Antonyms *adj* ≠ **twisting**: direct, even, level, plumb, smooth, straight, undeviating, unswerving

wind up *vb* **1** = **end**, bring to a close, close,

mechanism). **3** (*tr; usually passive*) *Inf.* to make nervous, tense, etc.: *he was all wound up before the big fight.* **4** (*tr*) to roll (thread, etc.) into a ball. **5** an informal word for **liquidate** (sense 2). **6** (*intr*) *Inf.* to end up (in a specified state): *you'll wind up without any teeth.* **7** (*tr*) *Brit. sl.* to tease (someone). ◆ *n* **wind-up. 8** the act of concluding. **9** the end.

windward ('wɪndwəd) *Chiefly naut.* ◆ *adj* **1** of, in, or moving to the quarter from which the wind blows. ◆ *n* **2** the windward point. **3** the side towards the wind. ◆ *adv* **4** towards the wind. ◆ Cf. **leeward.**

windy ➊ ('wɪndɪ) *adj* **windier, windiest. 1** of, resembling, or relating to wind; stormy. **2** swept by or open to powerful winds. **3** marked by or given to prolonged and often boastful speech: *windy orations.* **4** void of substance. **5** an informal word for **flatulent. 6** *Sl.* frightened.
▸**'windily** *adv* ▸**'windiness** *n*

wine (waɪn) *n* **1a** an alcoholic drink produced by the fermenting of grapes with water and sugar. **1b** (*as modifier*): *the wine harvest.* **1c** an alcoholic drink produced in this way from other fruits, flowers, etc.: *elderberry wine.* **2a** a dark red colour, sometimes with a purplish tinge. **2b** (*as adj*): *wine-coloured.* **3** anything resembling wine in its intoxicating or invigorating effect. **4 new wine in old bottles.** something new added to or imposed upon an old or established order. ◆ *vb* **wines, wining, wined. 5** (*intr*) to drink wine. **6 wine and dine.** to entertain or be entertained with wine and fine food. [OE *wīn,* from L *vīnum*]
▸**'wineless** *adj*

wine bar *n* a bar in a restaurant, etc., or an establishment that specializes in serving wine and usually food.

winebibber ('waɪn,bɪbə) *n* a person who drinks a great deal of wine.
▸**'wine,bibbing** *n*

wine box *n* wine sold in a carton with a tap for pouring.

wine cellar *n* **1** a place, such as a dark cool cellar, where wine is stored. **2** the stock of wines stored there.

wine cooler *n* **1** a bucket-like vessel containing ice in which a bottle of wine is placed to be cooled. **2** the full name for **cooler** (sense 3).

wine gallon *n Brit.* a former unit of capacity equal to 231 cubic inches.

wineglass ('waɪn,glɑːs) *n* **1** a glass drinking vessel, typically having a small bowl on a stem, with a flared foot. **2** Also called: **wineglassful.** the amount that such a glass will hold.

wine grower *n* a person engaged in cultivating vines in order to make wine.
▸**wine growing** *n*

wine palm *n* any of various palm trees, the sap of which is used, esp. when fermented, as a drink. Also called: **toddy palm.**

winepress ('waɪn,prɛs) *n* any equipment used for squeezing the juice from grapes in order to make wine.

winery ('waɪnərɪ) *n, pl* **wineries.** *Chiefly US & Canad.* a place where wine is made.

wineskin ('waɪn,skɪn) *n* the skin of a sheep or goat sewn up and used as a holder for wine.

wing ➊ (wɪŋ) *n* **1** either of the modified forelimbs of a bird that are covered with large feathers and specialized for flight in most species. **2** one of the organs of flight of an insect, consisting of a membranous outgrowth from the thorax containing a network of veins. **3** either of the organs of flight in certain other animals, esp. the forelimb of a bat. **4a** a half of the main supporting surface on an aircraft, confined to one side of it. **4b** the full span of the main supporting surface on both sides of an aircraft. **5** an organ, structure, or apparatus resembling a wing. **6** anything suggesting a wing in form, function, or position, such as a sail of a windmill or a ship. **7** *Bot.* **7a** either of the lateral petals of a sweetpea or related flower. **7b** any of various outgrowths of a plant part, esp. the process on a wind-dispersed fruit or seed. **8** a means or cause of flight or rapid motion; flight: *fear gave wings to his feet.* **9** *Brit.* the part of a car body that surrounds the wheels. US and Canad. name: **fender. 10** *Soccer, hockey, etc.* **10a** either of the two sides of the pitch near the touchline. **10b** a player stationed in such a position; winger. **11** a faction or group within a political party or other organization. See also **left wing, right wing. 12** a part of a building that is subordinate to the main part. **13** (*pl*) the space offstage to the right or left of the acting area in a theatre. **14 in** *or* **on the wings.** ready to step in when needed. **15** either of the two pieces that project forwards from the sides of some chair backs. **16** (*pl*) an insignia in the form of stylized wings worn by a qualified aircraft pilot. **17** a tactical formation in some air forces, consisting of two or more squadrons. **18** any of various flattened organs or extensions in lower animals, esp. when used in locomotion. **19 clip (someone's) wings. 19a** to restrict (someone's) freedom. **19b** to thwart (someone's) ambitions. **20 on the wing. 20a** flying. **20b** travelling. **21 on wings.** flying or as if flying. **22 spread** *or* **stretch one's wings.** to make full use of one's abilities. **23 take wing. 23a** to lift off or fly away. **23b** to depart in haste. **23c** to become joyful. **24 under one's wing.** in one's care. ◆ *vb* (*mainly tr*) **25** (*also intr*) to make (one's way) swiftly on or as if on wings. **26** to shoot or wound (a bird, person, etc.) superficially, in the wing or arm, etc. **27** to cause to fly or move swiftly: *to wing an arrow.* **28** to provide with wings. [C12: from ON]
▸**winged** *adj* ▸**'wingless** *adj* ▸**'wing,like** *adj*

wing beat *or* **wing-beat** *n* a complete cycle of moving the wing by a bird when flying.

wing-case *n* the nontechnical name for **elytron.**

wing chair *n* an easy chair having wings on each side of the back.

wing collar *n* a stiff turned-up shirt collar worn with the points turned down over the tie.

wing commander *n* an officer holding commissioned rank in certain air forces, such as the Royal Air Force: junior to a group captain and senior to a squadron leader.

wing covert *n* any of the covert feathers of the wing of a bird, occurring in distinct rows.

wingding ('wɪŋ,dɪŋ) *n Sl., chiefly US & Canad.* **1** a noisy lively party or festivity. **2** a real or pretended fit or seizure. [C20: from ?]

winge (wɪndʒ) *vb, n Austral.* a variant spelling of **whinge.**

winger ('wɪŋə) *n Soccer, hockey, etc.* a player stationed on the wing.

wing loading *n* the total weight of an aircraft divided by its wing area.

wingman ('wɪŋmæn) *n pl* **wingmen.** a player in the wing position in Australian Rules.

wing nut *n* a threaded nut tightened by hand by means of two flat lugs or wings projecting from the central body. Also called: **butterfly nut.**

wingspan ('wɪŋ,spæn) *or* **wingspread** ('wɪŋ,sprɛd) *n* the distance between the wing tips of an aircraft, bird, etc.

wing tip *n* the outermost edge of a wing.

wink ➊ (wɪŋk) *vb* **1** (*intr*) to close and open one eye quickly, deliberately, or in an exaggerated fashion to convey friendliness, etc. **2** to close and open (an eye or the eyes) momentarily. **3** (*tr; foll. by away, back,* etc.) to force away (tears, etc.) by winking. **4** (*tr*) to signal with a wink. **5** (*intr*) (of a light) to gleam or flash intermittently. ◆ *n* **6** a winking movement, esp. one conveying a signal, etc., or such a signal. **7** an interrupted flashing of light. **8** a brief moment of time. **9** *Inf.* the smallest amount, esp. of sleep. **10 tip the wink.** *Brit. inf.* to give a hint. [OE *wincian*]

wink at ➊ *vb* (*intr, prep*) to connive at; disregard: *the authorities winked at corruption.*

winker ('wɪŋkə) *n* **1** a person or thing that winks. **2** *Dialect or US & Canad. sl.* an eye. **3** another name for **blinker**[1] (sense 1).

winkle ➊ ('wɪŋkᵊl) *n* **1** See **periwinkle**[1]. ◆ *vb* **winkles, winkling, winkled. 2** (*tr; usually foll. by out, out of,* etc.) *Inf., chiefly Brit.* to extract or prise out. [C16: shortened from PERIWINKLE[1]]

winkle-pickers *pl n* shoes or boots with very pointed narrow toes.

winner ➊ ('wɪnə) *n* **1** a person or thing that wins. **2** *Inf.* a person or thing that seems sure to win or succeed.

winning ➊ ('wɪnɪŋ) *adj* **1** (of a person, character, etc.) charming or attractive: *a winning smile.* **2** gaining victory: *the winning goal.* ◆ *n* **3** a shaft or seam of coal. **4** (*pl*) money, prizes, or valuables won, esp. in gambling.
▸**'winningly** *adv* ▸**'winningness** *n*

winning gallery *n Real Tennis.* the gallery farthest from the net on either side of the court, into which any shot played wins a point.

winning opening *n Real Tennis.* the grille or winning gallery, into which any shot played wins a point.

winning post *n* the post marking the finishing line on a racecourse.

Winnipeg couch ('wɪnɪ,pɛg) *n Canad.* a couch with no arms or back, opening out into a double bed. [after *Winnipeg,* city in S Canada]

winnow ➊ ('wɪnəʊ) *vb* **1** to separate (grain) from (chaff) by means of a

THESAURUS

close down, conclude, finalize, finish, liquidate, settle, terminate, tie up the loose ends (*inf.*), wrap up **3** *Informal* = **excite**, make nervous, make tense, put on edge, work up **6** *Informal* = **end up**, be left, end one's days, find oneself, finish up ◆ *n* **wind-up 9** = **end**, close, conclusion, culmination, denouement, finale, finish, termination

Antonyms *vb* ≠ **end**: begin, commence, embark on, initiate, instigate, institute, open, start

windy *adj* **1, 2** = **breezy**, blowy, blustering, blustery, boisterous, gusty, inclement, squally, stormy, tempestuous, wild, windswept **3** = **pompous**, boastful, bombastic, diffuse, empty, garrulous, long-winded, loquacious, meandering, prolix, rambling, turgid, verbose, wordy **6** *Slang* = **frightened**, afraid, chicken (*sl.*), cowardly, fearful, nervous, nervy (*inf.*), scared, timid

Antonyms *adj* ≠ **breezy**: becalmed, calm, motionless, smooth, still, windless ≠ **pompous**: modest, quiet, reserved, restrained, reticent, shy, taciturn, unforthcoming ≠ **frightened**: bold, brave, courageous, daring, fearless, gallant, unafraid, undaunted

wing *n* **1-3** = **organ of flight**, pennon (*poetic*), pinion (*poetic*) **11** = **faction**, arm, branch, cabal, circle, clique, coterie, group, grouping, schism, section, segment, set, side **12** = **annexe**, adjunct, ell, extension ◆ *vb* **25** = **fly**, glide, soar **26** = **wound**, clip, hit, nick **27** = **fly**, fleet, hasten, hurry, race, speed, zoom

wink *vb* **1, 2** = **blink**, bat, flutter, nictate, nictitate **5** = **twinkle**, flash, gleam, glimmer, sparkle ◆ *n* **6** = **blink**, flutter, nictation, nictitation **7** = **twinkle**, flash, gleam, glimmering, sparkle **8** = **moment**, instant, jiffy (*inf.*), second, split second, twinkling

wink at *vb* = **condone**, allow, blink at, connive at, disregard, ignore, overlook, pretend not to notice, put up with (*inf.*), shut one's eyes to, tolerate, turn a blind eye to

winkle *vb* **2** *Informal, chiefly Brit.* = **extract**, dig out, dislodge, draw out, extricate, force out, prise out, smoke out, worm out

winner *n* **1** = **victor**, champ (*inf.*), champion, conquering hero, conqueror, first, master, vanquisher

winning *adj* **1** = **charming**, alluring, amiable, attractive, bewitching, captivating, cute, delectable, delightful, disarming, enchanting, endearing, engaging, fascinating, fetching, likable *or* likeable, lovely, pleasing, prepossessing, sweet, taking, winsome **2** = **victorious**, conquering, successful, triumphant ◆ *n* **4** *plural* = **spoils**, booty, gains, prize, proceeds, profits, takings

Antonyms *adj* ≠ **charming**: disagreeable, irksome, offensive, repellent, tiresome, unappealing, unattractive, unpleasant

winnow *vb* **1** = **separate**, comb, cull, divide,

wind or current of air. **2** (*tr*) to examine in order to select the desirable elements. **3** (*tr*) *Rare.* to blow upon; fan. ◆ *n* **4a** a device for winnowing. **4b** the act or process of winnowing. [OE *windwian*]
▸'**winnower** *n*

wino ('waɪnəʊ) *n, pl* **winos.** *Inf.* a down-and-out who habitually drinks cheap wine.

win over ❶ *vb* (*tr, adv*) to gain the support or consent of (someone). Also: **win round.**

winsome ❶ ('wɪnsəm) *adj* charming; winning; engaging: *a winsome smile.* [OE *wynsum,* from *wynn* joy + *-sum* -SOME[1]]
▸'**winsomely** *adv*

winter ('wɪntə) *n* **1a** (*sometimes cap.*) the coldest season of the year, between autumn and spring, astronomically from the December solstice to the March equinox in the N hemisphere and at the opposite time of year in the S hemisphere. **1b** (*as modifier*): *winter pasture.* **2** the period of cold weather associated with the winter. **3** a time of decline, decay, etc. **4** *Chiefly poetic.* a year represented by this season: *a man of 72 winters.* ◆ Related adj: **hibernal.** ◆ *vb* **5** (*intr*) to spend the winter in a specified place. **6** to keep or feed (farm animals, etc.) during the winter or (of farm animals) to be kept or fed during the winter. [OE]
▸'**winterer** *n* ▸'**winterless** *adj*

winter aconite *n* a small Old World herbaceous plant cultivated for its yellow flowers, which appear early in spring.

winter cherry *n* **1** a Eurasian plant cultivated for its ornamental inflated papery orange-red calyx. **2** the calyx of this plant. ◆ See also **Chinese lantern.**

winter garden *n* **1** a garden of evergreen plants. **2** a conservatory in which flowers are grown in winter.

wintergreen ('wɪntəˌgriːn) *n* **1** any of a genus of evergreen ericaceous shrubs, esp. a subshrub of E North America, which has white bell-shaped flowers and edible red berries. **2 oil of wintergreen.** an aromatic compound, formerly made from this and various other plants but now synthesized: used medicinally and for flavouring. **3** any of a genus of plants, such as **common wintergreen,** of temperate and arctic regions, having rounded leaves and small pink globose flowers. **4 chickweed wintergreen.** a plant of N Europe and N Asia belonging to the primrose family, having white flowers and leaves arranged in a whorl. [C16: from Du. *wintergroen* or G *Wintergrün*]

winterize *or* **winterise** ('wɪntəˌraɪz) *vb* **winterizes, winterizing, winterized** *or* **winterises, winterising, winterised.** (*tr*) *US & Canad.* to prepare (a house, car, etc.) to withstand winter conditions.
▸ˌ**winteri'zation** *or* ˌ**winteri'sation** *n*

winter jasmine *n* a jasmine shrub widely cultivated for its winter-blooming yellow flowers.

winter solstice *n* the time at which the sun is at its southernmost point in the sky (northernmost point in the S hemisphere) appearing at noon at its lowest altitude above the horizon. It occurs about December 22 (June 21 in the S hemisphere).

winter sports *pl n* sports held in the open air on snow or ice, esp. skiing.

wintertime ('wɪntəˌtaɪm) *n* the winter season. Also (archaic): **wintertide.**

winterweight ('wɪntəˌweɪt) *adj* (of clothes) suitably heavy and warm for wear in the winter.

winter wheat *n* a type of wheat that is planted in the autumn and is harvested the following summer.

wintry ❶ ('wɪntrɪ) *or* **wintery** ('wɪntərɪ) *adj* **wintrier, wintriest. 1** (esp. of weather) of or characteristic of winter. **2** lacking cheer or warmth; bleak.
▸'**wintrily** *adv* ▸'**wintriness** *or* '**winteriness** *n*

winy ('waɪnɪ) *adj* **winier, winiest.** having the taste or qualities of wine; heady.

wipe ❶ (waɪp) *vb* **wipes, wiping, wiped.** (*tr*) **1** to rub (a surface or object) lightly, esp., with a cloth, hand, etc., as in removing dust, water, etc. **2** (usually foll. by *off, away, from, up,* etc.) to remove by or as if by rubbing lightly: *he wiped the dirt from his hands.* **3** to eradicate or cancel (a thought, memory, etc.). **4** to erase (a recording) from (a tape). **5** to apply (oil, etc.) by wiping. **6** *Austral. inf.* to abandon or reject (a person). **7 wipe the floor with (someone).** *Inf.* to defeat (someone) decisively. ◆ *n* **8** the act or an instance of wiping. **9** *Dialect.* a sweeping blow. [OE *wīpian*]

wipe out ❶ *vb* (*adv*) **1** (*tr*) to destroy completely. **2** (*tr*) *Inf.* to kill. **3** (*intr*) to fall off a surfboard. ◆ *n* **wipeout. 4** an act or instance of wiping out. **5** the interference of one radio signal by another so that reception is impossible.

wiper ('waɪpə) *n* **1** any piece of cloth, such as a handkerchief, etc., used for wiping. **2** a cam rotated to allow a part to fall under its own weight, as used in stamping machines, etc. **3** See **windscreen wiper. 4** *Electrical engineering.* a movable conducting arm that makes contact with a row or ring of contacts.

wire ('waɪə) *n* **1** a slender flexible strand or rod of metal. **2** a cable consisting of several metal strands twisted together. **3** a flexible metallic conductor, esp. one made of copper, usually insulated, and used to carry electric current in a circuit. **4** (*modifier*) of, relating to, or made of wire: *a wire fence.* **5** anything made of wire, such as wire netting. **6** a long continuous wire or cable connecting points in a telephone or telegraph system. **7** *Old-fashioned.* an informal name for **telegram** or **telegraph. 8** *US & Canad. horse racing.* the finishing line on a racecourse. **9** a snare made of wire for rabbits and similar animals. **10 get in under the wire.** *Inf., chiefly US & Canad.* to accomplish something with little time to spare. **11 get one's wires crossed.** *Inf.* to misunderstand. **12 pull wires.** *Chiefly US & Canad.* to exert influence behind the scenes; pull strings. ◆ *vb* **wires, wiring, wired.** (*mainly tr*) **13** (*also intr*) to send a telegram to (a person or place). **14** to send (news, a message, etc.) by telegraph. **15** to equip (an electrical system, circuit, or component) with wires. **16** to fasten or furnish with wire. **17** to snare with wire. **18 wire in.** *Inf.* to set about (something, esp. food) with enthusiasm. [OE *wīr*]
▸'**wireˌlike** *adj*

wire brush *n* a brush having wire bristles, used for cleaning metal, esp. for removing rust, or for brushing against cymbals.

wire cloth *n* a mesh or netting woven from fine wire, used in window screens, strainers, etc.

wiredraw ('waɪəˌdrɔː) *vb* **wiredraws, wiredrawing, wiredrew, wiredrawn.** to convert (metal) into wire by drawing through successively smaller dies.

wire-gauge *n* **1** a flat plate with slots in which standard wire sizes can be measured. **2** a standard system of sizes for measuring the diameters of wires.

wire gauze *n* a stiff meshed fabric woven of fine wires.

wire grass *n* any of various grasses that have tough wiry roots or rhizomes.

wire-guided *adj* (of a missile) able to be controlled in mid-flight by signals passed along a wire connecting the missile to the firer's control device.

wire-haired *adj* (of an animal) having a rough wiry coat.

wireless ('waɪəlɪs) *n, vb Chiefly Brit.* another word for **radio.**

wireless telegraphy *n* another name for **radiotelegraphy.**

wireless telephone *n* another name for **radiotelephone.**
▸**wireless telephony** *n*

wire netting *n* a net made of wire, often galvanized, that is used for fencing, etc.

wirepuller ('waɪəˌpʊlə) *n Chiefly US & Canad.* a person who uses private or secret influence for his own ends.
▸'**wireˌpulling** *n*

wire recorder *n* an early type of magnetic recorder in which sounds were recorded on a thin steel wire magnetized by an electromagnet.
▸**wire recording** *n*

wire service *n Chiefly US & Canad.* an agency supplying news, etc., to newspapers, radio, and television stations, etc.

wiretap ('waɪəˌtæp) *vb* **wiretaps, wiretapping, wiretapped. 1** (*intr*) to make a connection to a telegraph or telephone wire in order to obtain information secretly. **2** (*tr*) to tap (a telephone) or the telephone of (a person).
▸'**wireˌtapper** *n*

wire wheel *n* a wheel in which the rim is held to the hub by wire spokes, esp. one used on a sports car.

wire wool *n* a mass of fine wire used for cleaning and scouring.

wirework ('waɪəˌwɜːk) *n* **1** functional or decorative work made of wire. **2** objects made of wire, esp. netting.

wireworks ('waɪəˌwɜːks) *n* (*functioning as sing or pl*) a factory where wire or articles of wire are made.

wireworm ('waɪəˌwɜːm) *n* the wormlike larva of various beetles, which feeds on the roots of many plants and is a serious pest.

wiring ('waɪərɪŋ) *n* **1** the network of wires used in an electrical system, device, or circuit. ◆ *adj* **2** used in wiring.

wiry ❶ ('waɪərɪ) *adj* **wirier, wiriest. 1** (of people or animals) slender but strong in constitution. **2** made of or resembling wire, esp. in stiffness: *wiry hair.* **3** (of a sound) produced by or as if by a vibrating wire.
▸'**wirily** *adv* ▸'**wiriness** *n*

wis (wɪs) *vb Arch.* to know or suppose (something). [C17: a form derived from *iwis,* (from OE *gewiss* certain), mistakenly interpreted as *I wis* I know, as if from OE *witan* to know]

wisdom ❶ ('wɪzdəm) *n* **1** the ability or result of an ability to think and act utilizing knowledge, experience, understanding, common sense,

THESAURUS

fan, part, screen, select, separate the wheat from the chaff, sift, sort out

win over *vb* = **convince**, allure, attract, bring *or* talk round, charm, convert, disarm, influence, persuade, prevail upon, sway

winsome *adj* = **charming**, agreeable, alluring, amiable, attractive, bewitching, captivating, comely, cute, delectable, disarming, enchanting, endearing, engaging, fair, fascinating, fetching, likable *or* likeable, pleasant, pleasing, pretty, sweet, taking, winning

wintry *adj* **1** = **cold**, chilly, freezing, frosty, frozen, harsh, hibernal, hiemal, icy, snowy **2** = **bleak**, cheerless, cold, desolate, dismal

Antonyms *adj* balmy, bright, mild, pleasant, summery, sunny, warm

wipe *vb* **1** = **clean**, brush, dry, dust, mop, rub, sponge, swab **2** = **erase**, clean off, get rid of, remove, rub off, take away, take off ◆ *n* **8** = **rub**, brush, lick, swab

wipe out *vb* **1, 2** = **destroy**, annihilate, blot out, blow away, efface, eradicate, erase, expunge, exterminate, extirpate, kill to the last man, massacre, obliterate, take out (*sl.*), wipe from the face of the earth

wiry *adj* **1** = **lean**, sinewy, strong, tough **2** = **stiff**, bristly, kinky

Antonyms *adj* ≠ **lean:** fat, feeble, flabby, fleshy, frail, podgy, puny, spineless, weak

wisdom *n* **1, 2** = **understanding**, astuteness, circumspection, comprehension, discernment, enlightenment, erudition, foresight, insight, intelligence, judgment, judiciousness, knowledge, learning, penetration, prudence, reason, and insight. **2** accumulated knowledge or enlightenment. **3** *Arch.* a wise saying or wise sayings. ◆ Related adj: **sagacious.** [OE *wīsdōm*]

wisdom tooth *n* **1** any of the four molar teeth, one at the back of each side of the jaw, that are the last of the permanent teeth to erupt. Technical name: **third molar. 2 cut one's wisdom teeth.** to arrive at the age of discretion.

wise[1] ⓣ (waɪz) *adj* **1** possessing, showing, or prompted by wisdom or discernment. **2** prudent; sensible. **3** shrewd; crafty: *a wise plan.* **4** well-informed; erudite. **5** informed or knowing (esp. in **none the wiser**). **6** (*postpositive; often foll. by to*) *Sl.* in the know, esp. possessing inside information (about). **7** *Arch.* possessing powers of magic. **8 be** *or* **get wise.** (often foll. by *to*) *Inf.* to be or become aware or informed (of something). **9 put wise.** (often foll. by *to*) *Sl.* to inform or warn (of). ◆ *vb* **wises, wising, wised. 10** See **wise up.** [OE *wīs*]
▸ **'wisely** *adv* ▸ **'wiseness** *n*

wise[2] (waɪz) *n Arch.* way, manner, fashion, or respect (esp. in **any wise, in no wise**). [OE *wīse* manner]

-wise *adv combining form.* **1** indicating direction or manner: *clockwise; likewise.* **2** with reference to: *businesswise.* [OE *-wisan*; see WISE[2]]

wiseacre ('waɪzˌeɪkə) *n* **1** a person who wishes to seem wise. **2** a wise person: often used facetiously or contemptuously. [C16: from MDu. *wijsseggher* soothsayer. See WISE[1], SAY]

wisecrack ⓣ ('waɪzˌkræk) *Inf.* ◆ *n* **1** a flippant gibe or sardonic remark. ◆ *vb* (*intr*) **2** to make a wisecrack.
▸ **'wiseˌcracker** *n*

wise guy *n Inf.* a person who is given to making conceited, sardonic, or insolent comments.

wisent ('wiːzᵊnt) *n* another name for **European bison.** See **bison** (sense 2). [G, from OHG *wisunt* BISON]

wise up *vb* (*adv*) *Sl., chiefly US & Canad.* (often foll. by *to*) to become or cause to become aware or informed (of).

wish ⓣ (wɪʃ) *vb* **1** (when *tr, takes a clause as object or an infinitive;* when *intr,* often foll. by *for*) to want or desire (something, often that which cannot be or is not the case): *I wish I lived in Italy.* **2** (*tr*) to feel or express a desire or hope concerning the future or fortune of: *I wish you well.* **3** (*tr*) to desire or prefer to be as specified. **4** (*tr*) to greet as specified: *he wished us good afternoon.* ◆ *n* **5** the expression of some desire or mental inclination: *to make a wish.* **6** something desired or wished for: *he got his wish.* **7** (*usually pl*) expressed hopes or desire, esp. for someone's welfare, health, etc. **8** (*often pl*) *Formal.* a polite order or request. ◆ See also **wish on.** [OE *wȳscan*]
▸ **'wisher** *n*

wishbone ('wɪʃˌbəʊn) *n* the V-shaped bone above the breastbone in most birds consisting of the fused clavicles. [C17: from the custom of two people breaking apart the bone after eating: the person with the longer part makes a wish]

wishful ('wɪʃfʊl) *adj* having wishes or characterized by wishing.
▸ **'wishfully** *adv* ▸ **'wishfulness** *n*

wish fulfilment *n* (in Freudian psychology) any successful attempt to fulfil a wish stemming from the unconscious mind, whether in fact, in fantasy, or by disguised means.

wishful thinking *n* the erroneous belief that one's wishes are in accordance with reality.
▸ **wishful thinker** *n*

wish on *vb* (*tr, prep*) to hope that (someone or something) should be imposed (on someone); foist: *I wouldn't wish my cold on anyone.*

wishy-washy ⓣ ('wɪʃɪˌwɒʃɪ) *adj Inf.* **1** lacking in substance, force, colour, etc. **2** watery; thin.

wisp ⓣ (wɪsp) *n* **1** a thin, light, delicate, or fibrous piece or strand, such as a streak of smoke or a lock of hair. **2** a small bundle, as of hay or straw. **3** anything slender and delicate: *a wisp of a girl.* **4** a mere suggestion or hint. **5** a flock of birds, esp. snipe. [C14: var. of *wips,* from ?]
▸ **'wispˌlike** *adj* ▸ **'wispy** *adj*

wist (wɪst) *vb Arch.* the past tense and past participle of **wit**[2].

wisteria (wɪ'stɪərɪə) *n* any twining woody climbing plant of the genus *Wisteria,* of E Asia and North America, having blue, purple, or white flowers in large drooping clusters. [C19: from NL, after Caspar *Wistar* (1761–1818), US anatomist]

wistful ⓣ ('wɪstfʊl) *adj* sadly pensive, esp. about something yearned for.
▸ **'wistfully** *adv* ▸ **'wistfulness** *n*

wit[1] ⓣ (wɪt) *n* **1** the talent or quality of using unexpected associations between contrasting or disparate words or ideas to make a clever humorous effect. **2** speech or writing showing this quality. **3** a person possessing, showing, or noted for such an ability. **4** practical intelligence (esp. in **have the wit to**). **5** *Arch.* mental capacity or a person possessing it. ◆ See also **wits.** [OE *witt*]

wit[2] (wɪt) *vb* **wits, witting, wot, wist. 1** *Arch.* to be or become aware of (something). **2 to wit.** that is to say; namely (used to introduce statements, as in legal documents). [OE *witan*]

witan ('wɪtᵊn) *n* (in Anglo-Saxon England) **1** an assembly of higher ecclesiastics and important laymen that met to counsel the king on matters such as judicial problems. **2** the members of this assembly. ◆ Also called: **witenagemot.** [OE *witan,* pl. of *wita* wise man]

witblits ('vɪtˌblɪts) *n S. African.* alcoholic drink illegally distilled. [from Afrik. *wit* white + *blits* lightning]

witch[1] ⓣ (wɪtʃ) *n* **1** a person, usually female, who practises or professes to practise magic or sorcery, esp. black magic, or is believed to have dealings with the devil. **2** an ugly or wicked old woman. **3** a fascinating or enchanting woman. ◆ *vb* (*tr*) **4** a less common word for **bewitch.** [OE *wicca*]
▸ **'witchˌlike** *adj*

witch[2] (wɪtʃ) *n* a flatfish of N Atlantic coastal waters, having a narrow greyish-brown body marked with tiny black spots: related to the plaice, flounder, etc. [C19: ?from WITCH[1], from the appearance of the fish]

witchcraft ⓣ ('wɪtʃˌkrɑːft) *n* **1** the art or power of bringing magical or preternatural power to bear or the act or practice of attempting to do so. **2** the influence of magic or sorcery. **3** fascinating or bewitching influence or charm.

witch doctor *n* a man in certain societies, esp. preliterate ones, who appears to possess magical powers, used esp. to cure sickness but also to harm people. Also called: **shaman, medicine man.**

witch-elm *n* a variant spelling of **wych-elm.**

witchery ('wɪtʃərɪ) *n, pl* **witcheries. 1** the practice of witchcraft. **2** magical or bewitching influence or charm.

witches'-broom *n* a dense abnormal growth of shoots on a tree or other woody plant, usually caused by parasitic fungi.

witchetty grub ('wɪtʃɪtɪ) *n* the wood-boring edible caterpillar of an Australian moth. Also: **witchetty, witchety.** [C19 *witchetty,* from Abor.]

witch hazel *or* **wych-hazel** *n* **1** any of a genus of trees and shrubs of North America, having ornamental yellow flowers and medicinal properties. **2** an astringent medicinal solution containing an extract of the bark and leaves of one of these shrubs, applied to treat bruises, inflammation, etc.

witch-hunt *n* a rigorous campaign to expose dissenters on the pretext of safeguarding the public welfare.
▸ **'witch-ˌhunting** *n, adj*

witching ('wɪtʃɪŋ) *adj* **1** relating to or appropriate for witchcraft. **2** *Now rare.* bewitching.
▸ **'witchingly** *adv*

witching hour *n* **the.** the hour at which witches are supposed to appear, usually midnight.

witenagemot (ˌwɪtɪnəgɪ'məʊt) *n* another word for **witan.** [OE *witena,* genitive pl of *wita* councillor + *gemōt* meeting]

with ⓣ (wɪð, wɪθ) *prep* **1** using; by means of: *he killed her with an axe.* **2** accompanying; in the company of: *the lady you were with.* **3** possessing; having: *a man with a red moustache.* **4** concerning or regarding: *be patient with her.* **5** in spite of: *with all his talents, he was still humble.* **6** used to indicate a time or distance by which something is away from something else: *with three miles to go, he collapsed.* **7** in a manner char-

THESAURUS

sagacity, sapience, sense, smarts (*sl., chiefly US*), sound judgment
Antonyms *n* absurdity = **understanding,** daftness (*inf.*), folly, foolishness, idiocy, injudiciousness, nonsense, senselessness, silliness, stupidity

wise[1] *adj* **1-4** = **sensible,** aware, clever, clued-up (*inf.*), discerning, enlightened, erudite, informed, intelligent, in the loop (*inf.*), judicious, knowing, perceptive, politic, prudent, rational, reasonable, sagacious, sage, sapient, shrewd, sound, understanding, well-advised, well-informed **9 put wise** *Slang* = **inform,** alert, apprise, clue in *or* up (*inf.*), let (someone) into the secret, notify, tell, tip off, warn
Antonyms *adj* ≠ **sensible:** daft (*inf.*), foolish, injudicious, rash, silly, stupid, unintelligent, unwise

wisecrack *n* **1** = **joke,** barb, funny (*inf.*), gag (*inf.*), jest, jibe, pithy remark, quip, sally, sardonic remark, smart remark, witticism ◆ *vb* **2** = **joke,** be facetious, jest, jibe, quip, tell jokes

wish *vb* **1** = **want,** aspire, covet, crave, desiderate, desire, hanker, hope, hunger, long, need, set one's heart on, sigh for, thirst, yearn **3** = **require,** ask, bid, command, desire, direct, instruct, order **4** = **bid,** greet with ◆ *n* **5, 6** = **desire,** aspiration, hankering, hope, hunger, inclination, intention, liking, longing, thirst, urge, want, whim, will, yearning **8** *Formal* = **request,** bidding, command, desire, order, will
Antonyms *n* ≠ **desire:** aversion, disinclination, dislike, distaste, loathing, reluctance, repulsion, revulsion

wishy-washy *adj* **1, 2** *Informal* = **feeble,** bland, flat, ineffective, ineffectual, insipid, jejune, tasteless, thin, vapid, watered-down, watery, weak

wisp *n* **1** = **piece,** shred, snippet, strand, thread, twist

wispy *adj* **3** = **thin,** attenuate, attenuated, delicate, diaphanous, ethereal, faint, fine, flimsy, fragile, frail, gossamer, insubstantial, light, wisplike

wistful *adj* = **melancholy,** contemplative, disconsolate, dreaming, dreamy, forlorn, longing, meditative, mournful, musing, pensive, reflective, sad, thoughtful, yearning

wit[1] *n* **1, 2** = **humour,** badinage, banter, drollery, facetiousness, fun, jocularity, levity, pleasantry, raillery, repartee, wordplay **3** = **humorist,** card (*inf.*), comedian, epigrammatist, *farceur,* joker, punster, wag **4** = **cleverness,** acumen, brains, common sense, comprehension, discernment, ingenuity, insight, intellect, judgment, mind, nous (*Brit. sl.*), perception, practical intelligence, reason, sense, smarts (*sl., chiefly US*), understanding, wisdom
Antonyms *n* ≠ **humour:** dullness, gravity, humourlessness, seriousness, sobriety, solemnity ≠ **cleverness:** folly, foolishness, ignorance, lack of perception, obtuseness, silliness, stupidity

witch[1] *n* **1** = **enchantress,** crone, hag, magician, necromancer, occultist, sorceress

witchcraft *n* **1, 2** = **magic,** black magic, enchantment, incantation, necromancy, occultism, sorcery, sortilege, spell, the black art, the occult, voodoo, witchery, witching, wizardry

with *adj* **10 with it** *Informal* = **fashionable,** happening (*inf.*), in (*inf.*), latest (*inf.*), modern, modish, progressive, stylish, swinging (*sl.*), trendy (*Brit. inf.*), up-to-date, up-to-the-minute, vogue acterized by: *writing with abandon.* **8** caused or prompted by: *shaking with rage.* **9** often used with a verb indicating a reciprocal action or relation between the subject and the preposition's object: *agreeing with me.* **10 with it.** *Inf.* **10a** fashionable; in style. **10b** comprehending what is happening or being said. **11 with that.** after that. [OE]

withal (wɪ'ðɔːl) *adv* **1** *Literary.* as well. **2** *Arch.* therewith. ◆ *prep* **3** (*postpositive*) an archaic word for **with.** [C12: from WITH + ALL]

withdraw 🅣 (wɪð'drɔː) *vb* **withdraws, withdrawing, withdrew, withdrawn. 1** (*tr*) to take or draw back or away; remove. **2** (*tr*) to remove from deposit or investment in a bank, etc. **3** (*tr*) to retract or recall (a promise, etc.). **4** (*intr*) to retire or retreat: *the troops withdrew.* **5** (*intr;* often foll. by *from*) to depart (from): *he withdrew from public life.* **6** (*intr*) to detach oneself socially, emotionally, or mentally. [C13: from WITH (in the sense: away from) + DRAW]
▸**with'drawer** *n*

withdrawal 🅣 (wɪð'drɔːəl) *n* **1** an act or process of withdrawing. **2** the period a drug addict goes through following abrupt termination in the use of narcotics, usually characterized by physical and mental symptoms (**withdrawal symptoms**). **3** Also called: **withdrawal method, coitus interruptus.** the deliberate withdrawing of the penis from the vagina before ejaculation, as a method of contraception.

withdrawing room *n* an archaic term for **drawing room.**

withdrawn 🅣 (wɪð'drɔːn) *vb* **1** the past participle of **withdraw.** ◆ *adj* **2** unusually reserved or shy. **3** secluded or remote.

withe (wɪθ, wɪð, waɪð) *n* **1** a strong flexible twig, esp. of willow, suitable for binding things together; withy. **2** a band or rope of twisted twigs or stems. ◆ *vb* **withes, withing, withed. 3** (*tr*) to bind with withes. [OE *withthe*]

wither 🅣 ('wɪðə) *vb* **1** (*intr*) (esp. of a plant) to droop, wilt, or shrivel up. **2** (*intr;* often foll. by *away*) to fade or waste: *all hope withered away.* **3** (*intr*) to decay or disintegrate. **4** (*tr*) to cause to wilt or lose vitality. **5** (*tr*) to abash, esp. with a scornful look. [C14: ? var. of WEATHER (vb)]
▸**'witherer** *n* ▸**'withering** *adj* ▸**'witheringly** *adv*

withers ('wɪðəz) *pl n* the highest part of the back of a horse, behind the neck between the shoulders. [C16: short for *widersones,* from *wider* with + *-sones,* ? var. of SINEW]

withershins ('wɪðə,ʃɪnz) *or* **widdershins** *adv Chiefly Scot.* in the direction contrary to the apparent course of the sun; anticlockwise. [C16: from MLow G *weddersinnes,* from MHG, lit.: opposite course, from *wider* against + *sinnes,* genitive of *sin* course]

withhold 🅣 (wɪð'həʊld) *vb* **withholds, withholding, withheld. 1** (*tr*) to keep back: *he withheld his permission.* **2** (*tr*) to hold back; restrain. **3** (*intr;* usually foll. by *from*) to refrain or forbear.
▸**with'holder** *n*

within (wɪ'ðɪn) *prep* **1** in; inside; enclosed or encased by. **2** before (a period of time) has elapsed: *within a week.* **3** not differing by more than (a specified amount) from: *live within your means.* ◆ *adv* **4** *Formal.* inside; internally.

without (wɪ'ðaʊt) *prep* **1** not having: *a traveller without much money.* **2** not accompanied by: *he came without his wife.* **3** not making use of: *it is not easy to undo screws without a screwdriver.* **4** (*foll. by a verbal noun or noun phrase*) not, while not, or after not: *she can sing for two minutes without drawing breath.* **5** *Arch.* on the outside of: *without the city walls.* ◆ *adv* **6** *Formal.* outside.

withstand 🅣 (wɪð'stænd) *vb* **withstands, withstanding, withstood. 1** (*tr*) to resist. **2** (*intr*) to remain firm in endurance or opposition.
▸**with'stander** *n*

withy ('wɪðɪ) *n, pl* **withies.** a variant spelling of **withe** (senses 1, 2). [OE *wīdig(e)*]

witless 🅣 ('wɪtlɪs) *adj* lacking wit, intelligence, or sense.
▸**'witlessly** *adv* ▸**'witlessness** *n*

witling ('wɪtlɪŋ) *n Arch.* a person who thinks himself witty.

witness 🅣 ('wɪtnɪs) *n* **1** a person who has seen or can give first-hand evidence of some event. **2** a person or thing giving or serving as evidence. **3** a person who testifies, esp. in a court of law, to events or facts within his own knowledge. **4** a person who attests to the genuineness of a document, signature, etc., by adding his own signature. **5 bear witness to. 5a** to give written or oral testimony to. **5b** to be evidence or proof of. ◆ Related adj: **testimonial.** ◆ *vb* **6** (*tr*) to see, be present at, or know at first hand. **7** (*tr*) to give evidence of. **8** (*tr*) to be the scene or setting of: *this field has witnessed a battle.* **9** (*intr*) to testify, esp. in a court of law, to events within a person's own knowledge. **10** (*tr*) to attest to the genuineness of (a document, etc.) by adding one's own signature. [OE *witnes,* from *witan* to know + -NESS]
▸**'witnesser** *n*

witness box *or esp. US* **witness stand** *n* the place in a court of law in which witnesses stand to give evidence.

wits 🅣 (wɪts) *pl n* **1** (*sometimes sing*) the ability to reason and act, esp. quickly (esp. in **have one's wits about one**). **2** (*sometimes sing*) right mind, sanity (esp. in **out of one's wits**). **3 at one's wits' end.** at a loss to know how to proceed. **4 live by one's wits.** to gain a livelihood by craftiness rather than by hard work.

-witted *adj* (*in combination*) having wits or intelligence as specified: *slow-witted; dim-witted.*

witter 🅣 ('wɪtə) *vb* (*intr;* often foll. by *on*) *Inf.* to chatter or babble pointlessly or at unnecessary length. [C20: ?from obs. *whitter* to warble, twitter]

Wittgensteinian ('vɪtgən,ʃtaɪnɪən, -,staɪnɪən) *adj* (of a philosophical position or argument) derived from or related to the work of Wittgenstein (1889–1951), Brit. philosopher, and esp. the later work in which he attacks essentialism and stresses the open texture and variety of the use of ordinary language.

witticism 🅣 ('wɪtɪ,sɪzəm) *n* a clever or witty remark. [C17: from WITTY; coined by Dryden (1677) by analogy with *criticism*]

witting ('wɪtɪŋ) *adj Rare.* **1** deliberate; intentional. **2** aware.
▸**'wittingly** *adv*

witty 🅣 ('wɪtɪ) *adj* **wittier, wittiest. 1** characterized by clever humour or wit. **2** *Arch. or dialect.* intelligent.
▸**'wittily** *adv* ▸**'wittiness** *n*

wive (waɪv) *vb* **wives, wiving, wived.** *Arch.* **1** to marry (a woman). **2** (*tr*) to supply with a wife. [OE *gewīfian,* from *wīf* wife]

wivern ('waɪvən) *n* a less common spelling of **wyvern.**

wives (waɪvz) *n* **1** the plural of **wife. 2 old wives' tale.** a superstitious tradition, occasionally one that contains an element of truth.

wiz (wɪz) *n, pl* **wizzes.** *Inf.* a variant spelling of **whizz** (sense 5).

wizard 🅣 ('wɪzəd) *n* **1** a male witch or a man who practises or professes to practise magic or sorcery. **2** a person who is outstandingly clever in some specified field. **3** *Computing.* a program that guides a user through a complex task. ◆ *adj* **4** *Inf., chiefly Brit.* superb; outstanding. **5** of or relating to a wizard or wizardry. [C15: var. of *wissard,* from WISE[1] + -ARD]
▸**'wizardly** *adj*

THESAURUS

withdraw *vb* **1, 2 = remove,** draw back, draw out, extract, pull, pull out, take away, take off **3 = retract,** abjure, disavow, disclaim, recall, recant, rescind, revoke, take back, unsay **4, 5 = retreat,** absent oneself, back off, back out, cop out (*sl.*), depart, detach oneself, disengage, drop out, fall back, go, leave, make oneself scarce (*inf.*), pull back, pull out, retire, secede
Antonyms *vb* ≠ **retreat:** advance, forge ahead, go on, move forward, persist, press on, proceed, progress

withdrawal *n* **1 = removal,** extraction **1 = retraction,** abjuration, disavowal, disclaimer, recall, recantation, repudiation, rescission, revocation **1 = retreat,** departure, disengagement, exit, exodus, retirement, secession

withdrawn *adj* **2 = uncommunicative,** aloof, detached, distant, introverted, quiet, reserved, retiring, shrinking, shy, silent, taciturn, timorous, unforthcoming **3 = secluded,** hidden, isolated, out-of-the-way, private, remote, solitary
Antonyms *adj* ≠ **uncommunicative:** extrovert, forward, friendly, gregarious, open, outgoing, sociable ≠ **secluded:** easily accessible

wither *vb* **1-3 = wilt,** atrophy, blast, blight, decay, decline, desiccate, disintegrate, droop, dry, fade, languish, perish, shrink, shrivel, wane, waste **5 = humiliate,** abash, blast, mortify, put down, shame, snub
Antonyms *vb* ≠ **wilt:** bloom, blossom, develop, flourish, increase, prosper, succeed, thrive, wax

withhold *vb* **1, 2 = keep back,** check, conceal, deduct, hide, hold back, keep, keep secret, refuse, repress, reserve, resist, restrain, retain, sit on (*inf.*), suppress **3** *usually foll. by* **from = refrain,** forbear, keep oneself, stop oneself
Antonyms *vb* ≠ **keep back:** accord, expose, get off one's chest (*inf.*), give, grant, hand over, let go, release, relinquish, reveal

withstand *vb* **1, 2 = resist,** bear, brave, combat, confront, cope with, defy, endure, face, grapple with, hold off, hold out against, oppose, put up with (*inf.*), stand firm against, stand up to, suffer, take, take on, thwart, tolerate, weather
Antonyms *vb* capitulate, falter, give in, give way, relent, succumb, surrender, weaken, yield

witless *adj* **= foolish,** asinine, crackpot (*inf.*), crazy, daft (*inf.*), dull, empty-headed, goofy (*inf.*), halfwitted, idiotic, imbecilic, inane, loopy (*inf.*), moronic, obtuse, senseless, silly, stupid, unintelligent

witness *n* **1 = observer,** beholder, bystander, eyewitness, looker-on, onlooker, spectator, viewer, watcher **3 = testifier,** attestant, corroborator, deponent **5 bear witness: a = confirm,** depone, depose, give testimony, testify **b = be evidence of,** attest to, bear out, be proof of, betoken, constitute proof of, corroborate, demonstrate, evince, prove, show, testify to, vouch for ◆ *vb* **6 = see,** attend, behold (*arch. or literary*), be present at, look on, mark, note, notice, observe, perceive, view, watch **7, 9 = testify,** attest, authenticate, bear out, bear witness, confirm, corroborate, depone, depose, give evidence, give testimony **10 = sign,** countersign, endorse

wits *pl n* **1 = intelligence,** acumen, astuteness, brains, cleverness, comprehension, faculties, ingenuity, judgment, nous (*Brit. sl.*), reason, sense, smarts (*sl., chiefly US*), understanding **3 at one's wits' end = in despair,** at a loss, at the end of one's tether, baffled, bewildered, lost, stuck (*inf.*), stumped

witter *vb Informal* **= chatter,** babble, blab, blather, blether, burble, cackle, chat, clack, gab (*inf.*), gabble, jabber, prate, prattle, rabbit (on) (*Brit. inf.*), tattle, twaddle, waffle (*inf., chiefly Brit.*)

witticism *n* **= quip,** bon mot, clever remark, epigram, one-liner (*sl.*), play on words, pleasantry, pun, repartee, riposte, sally, witty remark

witty *adj* **1 = humorous,** amusing, brilliant, clever, droll, epigrammatic, facetious, fanciful, funny, gay, ingenious, jocular, lively, original, piquant, sparkling, waggish, whimsical
Antonyms *adj* boring, dull, humourless, stupid, tedious, tiresome, unamusing, uninteresting, witless

wizard *n* **1 = magician,** conjuror, enchanter, mage (*arch.*), magus, necromancer, occultist, shaman, sorcerer, thaumaturge (*rare*), warlock, witch **2 = virtuoso,** ace (*inf.*), adept, buff (*inf.*), expert, genius, guru, hotshot (*inf.*), maestro, master, maven (*US*), prodigy, star, whizz (*inf.*), whizz kid (*inf.*), wiz (*inf.*)

wizardry ➊ ('wɪzədrɪ) *n* the art, skills, and practices of a wizard, sorcerer, or magician.
wizen ('wɪzᵊn) *vb* **1** to make or become shrivelled. ◆ *adj* **2** a variant of **wizened.** [OE *wisnian*]
wizened ➊ ('wɪzᵊnd) *or* **wizen** *adj* shrivelled, wrinkled, or dried up, esp. with age.
wk *abbrev. for:* **1** (*pl* **wks**) week. **2** work.
wkly *abbrev. for* weekly.
w.l. *or* **WL** *abbrev. for* water line.
WMO *abbrev. for* World Meteorological Organization.
WNW *symbol for* west-northwest.
WO *abbrev. for:* **1** War Office. **2** Warrant Officer. **3** wireless operator.
woad (wəʊd) *n* **1** a European cruciferous plant, formerly cultivated for its leaves, which yield a blue dye. **2** the dye obtained from this plant, used esp. by the ancient Britons as a body dye. [OE *wād*]
wobbegong ('wɒbɪˌgɒŋ) *n* any of various sharks of Australian waters, having a richly patterned brown-and-white skin. [from Abor.]
wobble ➊ ('wɒbᵊl) *vb* **wobbles, wobbling, wobbled. 1** (*intr*) to move or sway unsteadily. **2** (*intr*) to shake: *her voice wobbled with emotion.* **3** (*intr*) to vacillate with indecision. **4** (*tr*) to cause to wobble. ◆ *n* **5** a wobbling movement or sound. [C17: var. of *wabble*, from Low G *wabbeln*]
▸'**wobbler** *n*
wobble board *n Austral.* a piece of fibreboard used as a rhythmic musical instrument, producing a characteristic sound when flexed.
wobbly ➊ ('wɒblɪ) *adj* **wobblier, wobbliest. 1** shaky, unstable, or unsteady. ◆ *n* **2 throw a wobbly.** *Sl.* to become suddenly very agitated or angry.
▸'**wobbliness** *n*
wodge (wɒdʒ) *n Brit. inf.* a thick lump or chunk cut or broken off something. [C20: alteration of WEDGE]
woe ➊ (wəʊ) *n* **1** *Literary.* intense grief. **2** (*often pl*) affliction or misfortune. **3 woe betide (someone).** misfortune will befall (someone): *woe betide you if you arrive late.* ◆ *interj* **4** Also: **woe is me.** *Arch.* an exclamation of sorrow or distress. [OE *wā, wǣ*]
woebegone ➊ ('wəʊbɪˌgɒn) *adj* sorrowful or sad in appearance. [C14: from a phrase such as *me is wo begon* woe has beset me]
woeful ➊ ('wəʊfᵊl) *adj* **1** expressing or characterized by sorrow. **2** bringing or causing woe. **3** pitiful; miserable: *a woeful standard of work.*
▸'**woefully** *adv* ▸'**woefulness** *n*
WOF (in New Zealand) *abbrev. for* Warrant of Fitness.
wog[1] (wɒg) *n Brit. sl., derog.* a person who is not White. [prob. from GOLLIWOG]
wog[2] (wɒg) *n Austral. sl.* any ailment or disease, such as influenza, a virus infection, etc. [C20: from ?]
woggle ('wɒgᵊl) *n* the ring of leather through which a Scout neckerchief is threaded. [C20: from ?]
wok (wɒk) *n* a large metal Chinese cooking pot having a curved base like a bowl: used esp. for stir-frying. [from Chinese (Cantonese)]
woke (wəʊk) *vb* the past tense of **wake**[1].
woken ('wəʊkən) *vb* the past participle of **wake**[1].
wokka board ('wɒkə) *n Austral.* another name for **wobble board.**
wold[1] (wəʊld) *n Chiefly literary.* a tract of open rolling country, esp. upland. [OE *weald* bush]
wold[2] (wəʊld) *n* a variant of **weld**[2].
Wolds (wəʊldz) *pl n* **the.** a range of chalk hills in NE England: consists of the **Yorkshire Wolds** to the north, separated from the **Lincolnshire Wolds** by the Humber estuary.
wolf ➊ (wʊlf) *n, pl* **wolves. 1** a predatory canine mammal which hunts in packs and was formerly widespread in North America and Eurasia but is now less common. Related adj: **lupine. 2** any of several similar and related canines, such as the red wolf and the coyote (**prairie wolf**). **3** the fur of any such animal. **4** a voracious or fiercely cruel person or thing. **5** *Inf.* a man who habitually tries to seduce women. **6** Also called: **wolf note.** *Music.* **6a** an unpleasant sound produced in some notes played on the violin, etc., owing to resonant vibrations of the belly. **6b** an out-of-tune effect produced on keyboard instruments accommodated esp. to the system of mean-tone temperament. **7 cry wolf.** to give a false alarm. **8 have** *or* **hold a wolf by the ears.** to be in a desperate situation. **9 keep the wolf from the door.** to ward off starvation or privation. **10 lone wolf.** a person or animal who prefers to be alone. **11 wolf in sheep's clothing.** a malicious person in a harmless or benevolent disguise. ◆ *vb* **12** (*tr;* often foll. by *down*) to gulp (down). **13** (*intr*) to hunt wolves. [OE *wulf*]
▸'**wolfish** *adj* ▸'**wolf,like** *adj*
Wolf Cub *n Brit.* the former name for **Cub Scout.**
wolffish ➊ ('wʊlfˌfɪʃ) *n, pl* **wolffish** *or* **wolffishes.** a large northern deep-sea fish. It has large sharp teeth and no pelvic fins and is used as a food fish. Also called: **catfish.**
wolfhound ('wʊlfˌhaʊnd) *n* the largest breed of dog, used formerly to hunt wolves.
wolfram ('wʊlfrəm) *n* another name for **tungsten.** [C18: from G, orig. ?from the proper name *Wolfram*, used pejoratively of tungsten because it was thought inferior to tin]
wolframite ('wʊlfrəˌmaɪt) *n* a black to reddish-brown mineral, a compound of tungsten, iron, and manganese: it is the chief ore of tungsten.
wolfsbane ('wʊlfsˌbeɪn) *or* **wolf's bane** *n* any of several poisonous N temperate plants of the ranunculaceous genus *Aconitum* having hoodlike flowers.
wolf spider *n* a spider which chases its prey to catch it. Also called: **hunting spider.**
wolf whistle *n* **1** a whistle made by a man to express admiration of a woman's appearance. ◆ *vb* **wolf-whistle, wolf-whistles, wolf-whistling, wolf-whistled. 2** (when *intr,* sometimes foll. by *at*) to make such a whistle (at someone).
Wolof ('wɒlɒf) *n* **1** (*pl* **Wolof** *or* **Wolofs**) a member of a Negroid people of W Africa living chiefly in Senegal. **2** the language of this people, belonging to the Niger-Congo family.
wolverine ('wʊlvəˌriːn) *n* a large musteline mammal of northern forests of Eurasia and North America having dark very thick water-resistant fur. Also called: **glutton.** [C16 *wolvering,* from WOLF + -ING[3] (later altered to *-ine*)]
wolves (wʊlvz) *n* the plural of **wolf.**
woman ➊ ('wʊmən) *n, pl* **women. 1** an adult female human being. **2** (*modifier*) female or feminine: *a woman politician.* **3** women collectively. **4** (usually preceded by *the*) feminine nature or feelings: *babies bring out the woman in him.* **5** a female servant or domestic help. **6** a man considered as having supposedly female characteristics, such as meekness. **7** *Inf.* a wife or girlfriend. **8 the little woman.** *Brit. inf., old-fashioned.* one's wife. **9 woman of the streets.** a prostitute. ◆ *vb* (*tr*) **10** *Obs.* to make effeminate. [OE *wīfmann, wimman*]
▸'**womanless** *adj* ▸'**woman-,like** *adj*
womanhood ('wʊmənˌhʊd) *n* **1** the state or quality of being a woman or being womanly. **2** women collectively.
womanish ('wʊmənɪʃ) *adj* **1** having qualities regarded as unsuitable to a man. **2** of or suitable for a woman.
▸'**womanishly** *adv* ▸'**womanishness** *n*
womanize ➊ *or* **womanise** ('wʊməˌnaɪz) *vb* **womanizes, womanizing, womanized** *or* **womanises, womanising, womanised. 1** (*intr*) (of a man) to indulge in casual affairs with women. **2** (*tr*) to make effeminate.
▸'**woman,izer** *or* '**woman,iser** *n*
womankind ('wʊmənˌkaɪnd) *n* the female members of the human race; women collectively.

THESAURUS

wizardry *n* = **magic**, conjuration, enchantment, necromancy, occultism, sorcery, sortilege, the black art, voodoo, witchcraft, witchery, witching

wizened *adj* = **wrinkled**, dried up, gnarled, lined, sere (*arch.*), shrivelled, shrunken, withered, worn
Antonyms *adj* bloated, plump, rounded, smooth, swollen, turgid

wobble *vb* **1, 2** = **shake**, quake, rock, seesaw, sway, teeter, totter, tremble, vibrate, waver **3** = **hesitate**, be unable to make up one's mind, be undecided, dither (*chiefly Brit.*), fluctuate, shilly-shally (*inf.*), swither (*Scot.*), vacillate, waver ◆ *n* **5** = **unsteadiness**, quaking, shake, tremble, tremor, vibration

wobbly *adj* **1** = **unsteady**, rickety, shaky, teetering, tottering, unbalanced, uneven, unsafe, unstable, wonky (*Brit. sl.*)

woe *n* **1, 2** = **grief**, adversity, affliction, agony, anguish, burden, curse, dejection, depression, disaster, distress, gloom, hardship, heartache, heartbreak, melancholy, misery, misfortune, pain, sadness, sorrow, suffering, trial, tribulation, trouble, unhappiness, wretchedness
Antonyms *n* bliss, elation, felicity, fortune, happiness, joy, jubilation, pleasure, prosperity, rapture

woebegone *adj* = **gloomy**, blue, chapfallen, cheerless, crestfallen, dejected, disconsolate, doleful, downcast, downhearted, forlorn, funereal, grief-stricken, hangdog, long-faced, low, lugubrious, miserable, mournful, sad, sorrowful, troubled, wretched

woeful *adj* **1** = **sad**, afflicted, agonized, anguished, calamitous, catastrophic, cruel, deplorable, disastrous, disconsolate, dismal, distressing, doleful, dreadful, gloomy, grieving, grievous, harrowing, heartbreaking, heart-rending, lamentable, miserable, mournful, pathetic, piteous, pitiable, pitiful, plaintive, sorrowful, tragic, unhappy, wretched **3** = **pitiful**, abysmal, appalling, awful, bad, deplorable, disappointing, disgraceful, dreadful, feeble, hopeless, inadequate, mean, miserable, paltry, pathetic, pitiable, poor, rotten (*inf.*), shocking, sorry, terrible, wretched
Antonyms *adj* ≠ **sad:** carefree, cheerful, chirpy (*inf.*), contented, delighted, glad, happy, jolly, joyful, jubilant, light-hearted ≠ **pitiful:** abundant, ample, bountiful, enviable, extensive, generous, lavish, luxurious, profuse, prosperous

wolf *n* **5** *Informal* = **womanizer**, Casanova, Don Juan, lady-killer, lech *or* letch (*inf.*), lecher, Lothario, philanderer, seducer ◆ *vb* **12** *often foll. by* **down** = **devour**, bolt, cram, eat like a horse, gobble, gollop, gorge, gulp, pack away (*inf.*), pig out (*sl.*), scoff (*sl.*), stuff
Antonyms *vb* ≠ **devour:** bite, nibble, nip, peck, pick at

wolfish *adj* **12** = **greedy**, avaricious, edacious, fierce, gluttonous, insatiable, predatory, rapacious, ravenous, savage, voracious

woman *n* **1** = **lady**, bird (*sl.*), chick (*sl.*), dame, female, gal (*sl.*), girl, lass, lassie (*inf.*), maid (*arch.*), maiden (*arch.*), miss, she, wench (*facetious*) **5** = **maid**, chambermaid, char (*inf.*), charwoman, domestic, female servant, handmaiden, housekeeper, lady-in-waiting, maidservant **7** *Informal* = **girlfriend**, bride, girl, ladylove, mate, mistress, old lady (*inf.*), partner, significant other (*US inf.*), spouse, sweetheart, wife
Antonyms *n* ≠ **lady:** bloke (*Brit. inf.*), boy, chap (*inf.*), gentleman, guy (*inf.*), lad, laddie, male, man

womanizer *n* **1** = **philanderer**, Casanova, Don Juan, lady-killer, lech *or* letch (*inf.*), lecher, Lothario, seducer, wolf (*inf.*)

womanly ➊ ('wʊmənlɪ) *adj* **1** possessing qualities, such as warmth, attractiveness, etc., generally regarded as typical of a woman. **2** of or belonging to a woman.

womb ➊ (wu:m) *n* **1** the nontechnical name for **uterus. 2** a hollow space enclosing something. **3** a place where something is conceived: *the Near East is the womb of western civilization.* **4** *Obs.* the belly. [OE *wamb*]
▸**wombed** *adj* ▸**'womb,like** *adj*

wombat ('wɒmbæt) *n* a burrowing herbivorous Australian marsupial having short limbs, a heavy body, and coarse dense fur. [C18: from Abor.]

women ('wɪmɪn) *n* the plural of **woman.**

womenfolk ('wɪmɪn,fəʊk) *pl n* **1** women collectively. **2** a group of women, esp. the female members of one's family.

Women's Institute *n* (in Britain and Commonwealth countries) a society for women interested in engaging in craft and cultural activities.

Women's Liberation *n* a movement directed towards the removal of attitudes and practices that preserve inequalities based upon the assumption that men are superior to women. Also called: **women's lib.**

Women's Movement *n* a grass-roots movement of women concerned with women's liberation. See **Women's Liberation.**

won (wʌn) *vb* the past tense and past participle of **win.**

wonder ➊ ('wʌndə) *n* **1** the feeling excited by something strange; a mixture of surprise, curiosity, and sometimes awe. **2** something that causes such a feeling, such as a miracle. **3** (*modifier*) exciting wonder by virtue of spectacular results achieved, feats performed, etc.: *a wonder drug.* **4 do** *or* **work wonders.** to achieve spectacularly fine results. **5 nine days' wonder.** a subject that arouses general surprise or public interest for a short time. **6 no wonder.** (*sentence connector*) (I am) not surprised at all (that): *no wonder he couldn't come.* **7 small wonder.** (*sentence connector*) (I am) hardly surprised (that): *small wonder he couldn't make it tonight.* ◆ *vb* (when *tr, may take a clause as object*) **8** (when *intr*, often foll. by *about*) to indulge in speculative inquiry: *I wondered about what she said.* **9** (when *intr*, often foll. by *at*) to be amazed (at something): *I wonder at your impudence.* [OE *wundor*]
▸**'wonderer** *n*

wonderful ➊ ('wʌndəful) *adj* **1** exciting a feeling of wonder. **2** extremely fine; excellent.
▸**'wonderfully** *adv*

wonderland ('wʌndə,lænd) *n* **1** an imaginary land of marvels or wonders. **2** an actual place or scene of great or strange beauty or wonder.

wonderment ('wʌndəmənt) *n* **1** rapt surprise; awe. **2** puzzled interest. **3** something that excites wonder.

wonderwork ('wʌndə,wɜ:k) *n* something done or made that excites wonder.
▸**'wonder-,worker** *n* ▸**'wonder-,working** *n, adj*

wondrous ('wʌndrəs) *Arch. or literary.* ◆ *adj* **1** exciting wonder; marvellous. ◆ *adv* **2** (intensifier): *wondrous cold.*
▸**'wondrously** *adv* ▸**'wondrousness** *n*

wonky ➊ ('wɒŋkɪ) *adj* **wonkier, wonkiest.** *Brit. sl.* **1** unsteady. **2** askew. **3** liable to break down. [C20: var. of dialect *wanky*, from OE *wancol*]

wont ➊ (wəʊnt) *adj* **1** (*postpositive*) accustomed (to doing something): *he was wont to come early.* ◆ *n* **2** a manner or action habitually employed by or associated with someone (often in **as is my wont, as is his wont,** etc.). ◆ *vb* **3** (when *tr, usually passive*) to become or cause to become accustomed. [OE *gewunod*, p.p. of *wunian* to be accustomed to]

won't (wəʊnt) *contraction of* will not.

wonted ➊ ('wəʊntɪd) *adj* **1** (*postpositive*) accustomed (to doing something). **2** (*prenominal*) usual: *she is in her wonted place.*

woo ➊ (wu:) *vb* **woos, wooing, wooed. 1** to seek the affection, favour, or love of (a woman) with a view to marriage. **2** (*tr*) to seek after zealously: *to woo fame.* **3** (*tr*) to beg or importune (someone). [OE *wōgian*, from ?]
▸**'wooer** *n* ▸**'wooing** *n*

wood ➊ (wʊd) *n* **1** the hard fibrous substance consisting of xylem tissue that occurs beneath the bark in trees, shrubs, and similar plants. **2** the trunks of trees that have been cut and prepared for use as a building material. **3** a collection of trees, shrubs, grasses, etc., usually dominated by one or a few species of tree: usually smaller than a forest: *an oak wood.* Related adj: **sylvan. 4** fuel; firewood. **5** *Golf.* **5a** a long-shafted club with a wooden head, used for driving. **5b** (*as modifier*): *a wood shot.* **6** *Tennis, etc.* the frame of a racket: *he hit a winning shot off the wood.* **7** one of the biased wooden bowls used in the game of bowls. **8** *Music.* short for **woodwind. 9 from the wood.** (of a beverage) from a wooden container rather than a metal or glass one. **10 out of the wood** *or* **woods.** clear of or safe from dangers or doubts: *we're not out of the wood yet.* **11 see the wood for the trees.** (*used with a negative*) to obtain a general view of a situation without allowing details to cloud one's analysis: *he can't see the wood for the trees.* **12** (*modifier*) made of, employing, or handling wood: *a wood fire.* **13** (*modifier*) dwelling in or situated in a wood: *a wood nymph.* ◆ *vb* **14** (*tr*) to plant a wood upon. **15** to supply or be supplied with firewood. ◆ See also **woods.** [OE *widu, wudu*]

wood alcohol *n* another name for **methanol.**

wood anemone *n* any of several woodland anemone plants having finely divided leaves and solitary white flowers. Also called: **windflower.**

wood avens *n* another name for **herb bennet.**

woodbine ('wu:d,baɪn) *n* **1** a honeysuckle of Europe, SW Asia, and N Africa, having fragrant yellow flowers. **2** *US.* another name for **Virginia creeper. 3** *Austral. sl.* an Englishman.

wood block *n* a small rectangular flat block of wood that is laid with others as a floor surface.

woodcarving ('wʊd,kɑ:vɪŋ) *n* **1** the act of carving wood. **2** a work of art produced by carving wood.
▸**'wood,carver** *n*

woodchuck ('wʊd,tʃʌk) *n* a North American marmot having coarse reddish-brown fur. Also called: **groundhog.** [C17: by folk etymology from Cree *otcheck* fisher]

woodcock ('wʊd,kɒk) *n* an Old World game bird resembling the snipe but larger and with shorter legs and neck.

woodcraft ('wʊd,krɑ:ft) *n Chiefly US & Canad.* **1** ability and experience in matters concerned with living in a forest. **2** ability or skill at woodwork, carving, etc.

woodcut ('wʊd,kʌt) *n* **1** a block of wood with a design, illustration, etc., from which prints are made. **2** a print from a woodcut.

woodcutter ('wʊd,kʌtə) *n* **1** a person who fells trees or chops wood. **2** a person who makes woodcuts.
▸**'wood,cutting** *n*

wooded ➊ ('wʊdɪd) *adj* **1** covered with or abounding in woods or trees. **2** (*in combination*) having wood of a specified character: *a soft-wooded tree.*

wooden ➊ ('wʊdᵊn) *adj* **1** made from or consisting of wood. **2** awkward or clumsy. **3** bereft of spirit or animation: *a wooden expression.* **4** obstinately unyielding: *a wooden attitude.* **5** mentally slow or dull. **6** not highly resonant: *a wooden thud.*
▸**'woodenly** *adv*

wood engraving *n* **1** the art of engraving pictures or designs on wood by incising them with a burin. **2** a block of wood so engraved or a print taken from it.
▸**wood engraver** *n*

woodenhead ('wʊdᵊn,hed) *n Inf.* a dull, foolish, or unintelligent person.
▸**,wooden'headed** *adj* ▸**,wooden'headedness** *n*

Wooden Horse *n* another name for the **Trojan Horse** (sense 1).

wooden spoon *n* a booby prize, esp. in sporting contests.

woodgrouse ('wʊd,graʊs) *n* another name for **capercaillie.**

woodland ('wʊdlənd) *n* **a** land that is mostly covered with woods or dense growths of trees and shrubs. **b** (*as modifier*): *woodland fauna.*
▸**'woodlander** *n*

woodlark ('wʊd,lɑ:k) *n* an Old World lark similar to but slightly smaller than the skylark.

woodlouse ('wʊd,laʊs) *n, pl* **woodlice** (-,laɪs). any of various small ter-

THESAURUS

womanly *adj* **1 = feminine,** female, ladylike, matronly, motherly, tender, warm

womb *n* **1 = uterus**

wonder *n* **1 = amazement,** admiration, astonishment, awe, bewilderment, curiosity, fascination, stupefaction, surprise, wonderment **2 = phenomenon,** curiosity, marvel, miracle, nonpareil, portent, prodigy, rarity, sight, spectacle, wonderment ◆ *vb* **8 = think,** ask oneself, be curious, be inquisitive, conjecture, cudgel one's brains, doubt, inquire, meditate, ponder, puzzle, query, question, speculate **9 = be amazed,** be astonished, be awed, be dumbstruck, be flabbergasted (*inf.*), boggle, gape, gawk, marvel, stand amazed, stare

wonderful *adj* **1 = remarkable,** amazing, astonishing, astounding, awe-inspiring, awesome, extraordinary, fantastic, incredible, jaw-dropping, marvellous, miraculous, odd, peculiar, phenomenal, staggering, startling, strange, surprising, unheard-of, wondrous (*arch. or literary*) **2 = excellent,** ace (*inf.*), admirable, brilliant, fabulous (*inf.*), fantastic (*inf.*), great (*inf.*), magnificent, marvellous, mean (*sl.*), out of this world (*inf.*), outstanding, sensational (*inf.*), smashing (*inf.*), sovereign, stupendous, super (*inf.*), superb, terrific, tremendous
Antonyms *adj* ≠ **remarkable:** common, commonplace, ordinary, run-of-the-mill, uninteresting, unremarkable, usual ≠ **excellent:** abominable, abysmal, appalling, average, awful, bad, depressing, dire, dreadful, frightful, grim, indifferent, mediocre, miserable, modest, rotten, terrible, unpleasant, vile

wonky *Brit. slang adj* **1 = shaky,** groggy (*inf.*), infirm, unsteady, weak, wobbly, woozy (*inf.*) **2 = askew,** awry, out of alignment, skewwhiff (*Brit. inf.*), squint (*inf.*)

wont *adj* **1 = accustomed,** given, in the habit of, used ◆ *n* **2 = habit,** custom, practice, rule, use, way

wonted *adj* **1 = in the habit of,** accustomed, given, habituated, used **2 = customary,** accustomed, common, conventional, familiar, frequent, habitual, normal, regular, usual

woo *vb* **1, 3 = court,** chase, cultivate, importune, pay court to, pay one's addresses to, pay suit to, press one's suit with, pursue, seek after, seek the hand of, seek to win, solicit the goodwill of, spark (*rare*)

wood *n* **2 = timber,** planks **3 = woodland,** coppice, copse, forest, grove, hurst (*arch.*), thicket, trees **10 out of the wood** *or* **woods = safe,** clear, home and dry (*Brit. sl.*), in the clear, out of danger, safe and sound, secure

wooded *adj* **1 = tree-covered,** forested, sylvan (*poetic*), timbered, tree-clad, woody

wooden *adj* **1 = woody,** ligneous, made of wood, of wood, timber **2 = awkward,** clumsy, gauche, gawky, graceless, inelegant, maladroit, rigid, stiff, ungainly **3 = expressionless,** blank, colourless, deadpan, dull, emotionless, empty, glassy, lifeless, spiritless, unemotional, unresponsive, vacant
Antonyms *adj* ≠ **awkward:** agile, comely, elegant, flexible, flowing, graceful, lissom(e), nimble, supple

restrial isopod crustaceans having a flattened segmented body and occurring in damp habitats.

woodman ('wʊdmən) *n, pl* **woodmen. 1** a person who looks after and fells trees used for timber. **2** another word for **woodsman.**

woodnote ('wʊd,nəʊt) *n* a natural musical note or song, like that of a wild bird.

wood nymph *n* one of a class of nymphs fabled to inhabit the woods, such as a dryad.

woodpecker ('wʊd,pɛkə) *n* a climbing bird, such as the **green woodpecker,** having a brightly coloured plumage and strong chisel-like bill with which it bores into trees for insects.

wood pigeon *n* a large Eurasian pigeon having white patches on the wings and neck. Also called: **ringdove, cushat.**

woodpile ('wʊd,paɪl) *n* a pile or heap of firewood.

wood preservative *n* a coating applied to timber as a protection against decay, insects, weather, etc.

wood pulp *n* **1** wood that has been ground to a fine pulp for use in making newsprint and other cheap forms of paper. **2** finely pulped wood that has been digested by a chemical, such as caustic soda: used in making paper.

woodruff ('wʊdrʌf) *n* any of several plants, esp. the sweet woodruff of Eurasia, which has small sweet-scented white flowers and whorls of narrow fragrant leaves used to flavour wine and liqueurs and in perfumery. [OE *wudurofe,* from WOOD + *rōfe*]

woods (wʊdz) *pl n* **1** closely packed trees forming a forest or wood, esp. a specific one. **2** another word for **backwoods** (sense 2). **3** the woodwind instruments in an orchestra.

woodscrew ('wʊd,skru:) *n* a metal screw that tapers to a point so that it can be driven into wood by a screwdriver.

woodshed ('wʊd,ʃɛd) *n* a small outbuilding where firewood, garden tools, etc., are stored.

woodsman ('wʊdzmən) *n, pl* **woodsmen.** a person who lives in a wood or who is skilled in woodcraft. Also called: **woodman.**

wood sorrel *n* a Eurasian plant having trifoliate leaves, an underground creeping stem, and white purple-veined flowers.

wood spirit *n Chem.* another name for **methanol.**

wood tar *n* any tar produced by the destructive distillation of wood.

wood warbler *n* **1** a European woodland warbler with a dull yellow plumage. **2** another name for the **American warbler.** See **warbler** (sense 3).

woodwind ('wʊd,wɪnd) *Music.* ◆ *adj* **1** of or denoting a type of wind instrument, formerly made of wood but now often made of metal, such as the flute. ◆ *n* **2** (*functioning as pl*) woodwind instruments collectively.

woodwork ('wʊd,wɜ:k) *n* **1** the art or craft of making things in wood. **2** components made of wood, such as doors, staircases, etc.

woodworking ('wʊd,wɜ:kɪŋ) *n* **1** the process of working wood. ◆ *adj* **2** of, relating to, or used in woodworking.
▸ **'wood,worker** *n*

woodworm ('wʊd,wɜ:m) *n* **1** any of various insect larvae that bore into wooden furniture, beams, etc., esp. the larvae of the furniture beetle and the deathwatch beetle. **2** the condition caused in wood by any of these larvae.

woody ('wʊdɪ) *adj* **woodier, woodiest. 1** abounding in or covered with forest or woods. **2** connected with, belonging to, or situated in a wood. **3** consisting of or containing wood or lignin: *woody tissue; woody stems.* **4** resembling wood in hardness or texture.
▸ **'woodiness** *n*

woodyard ('wʊd,jɑ:d) *n* a place where timber is cut and stored.

woody nightshade *n* a scrambling woody Eurasian plant, having purple flowers and producing poisonous red berry-like fruits. Also called: **bittersweet.**

woof[1] (wu:f) *n* **1** the crosswise yarns that fill the warp yarns in weaving; weft. **2** a woven fabric or its texture. [OE *ōwef,* from *ō-,* ?from ON, + *wef* web (see WEAVE); modern form infl. by WARP]

woof[2] (wʊf) *interj* **1** an imitation of the bark or growl of a dog. ◆ *vb* **2** (*intr*) (of dogs) to bark.

woofer ('wu:fə) *n* a loudspeaker used in high-fidelity systems for the reproduction of low audio frequencies.

woofter ('wʊftə, 'wu:f-) *n Derog. sl.* a male homosexual. [C20: altered from *poofter;* see POOF]

wool 🅣 (wʊl) *n* **1** the outer coat of sheep, yaks, etc., which consists of short curly hairs. **2** yarn spun from the coat of sheep, etc., used in weaving, knitting, etc. **3a** cloth or a garment made from this yarn. **3b** (*as modifier*): *a wool dress.* **4** any of certain fibrous materials: *glass wool; steel wool.* **5** *Inf.* short thick curly hair. **6** a tangled mass of soft fine hairs that occurs in certain plants. **7 keep one's wool on.** *Brit. inf.* to keep one's temper. **8 pull the wool over someone's eyes.** to deceive or delude someone. [OE *wull*]
▸ **'wool-,like** *adj*

wool clip *n Austral. & NZ.* the total amount of wool shorn from a particular flock in one year.

wool fat *or* **grease** *n* another name for **lanolin.**

woolfell ('wʊl,fɛl) *n Obs.* the skin of a sheep or similar animal with the fleece still attached.

woolgathering 🅣 ('wʊl,gæðərɪŋ) *n* idle or absent-minded daydreaming.

woolgrower ('wʊl,grəʊə) *n* a person who keeps sheep for their wool.
▸ **'wool,growing** *n*

woolled (wʊld) *adj* **1** (of animals) having wool. **2** (*in combination*) having wool as specified: *coarse-woolled.*

woollen *or US* **woolen** ('wʊlən) *adj* **1** relating to or consisting partly or wholly of wool. ◆ *n* **2** (*often pl*) a garment or piece of cloth made wholly or partly of wool, esp. a knitted one.

woolly 🅣 *or US* (*sometimes*) **wooly** ('wʊlɪ) *adj* **woollier, woolliest** *or US* (*sometimes*) **woolier, wooliest. 1** consisting of, resembling, or having the nature of wool. **2** covered or clothed in wool or something resembling it. **3** lacking clarity or substance: *woolly thinking.* **4** *Bot.* covered with long soft whitish hairs: *woolly stems.* ◆ *n, pl* **woollies** *or US* (*sometimes*) **woolies. 5** (*often pl*) a garment, such as a sweater, made of wool or something similar.
▸ **'woollily** *adv* ▸ **'woolliness** *n*

woolly bear *n* the caterpillar of any of various tiger moths, having a dense covering of soft hairs.

woolpack ('wʊl,pæk) *n* **1** the cloth wrapping used to pack a bale of wool. **2** a bale of wool.

woolsack ('wʊl,sæk) *n* **1** a sack containing or intended to contain wool. **2** (in Britain) the seat of the Lord Chancellor in the House of Lords, formerly made of a large square sack of wool.

woolshed ('wʊl,ʃɛd) *n Austral. & NZ.* a large building in which sheepshearing takes place.

wool stapler *n* a person who sorts wool into different grades or classifications.

woomera *or* **womera** ('wʊmərə) *n Austral.* a type of notched stick used by native Australians to increase leverage and propulsion in the throwing of a spear. [from Abor.]

Woop Woop ('wu:p ,wu:p) *n Austral. Sl.* a jocular name for any backward or remote town or district.

woozy 🅣 ('wu:zɪ) *adj* **woozier, wooziest.** *Inf.* **1** dazed or confused. **2** experiencing dizziness, nausea, etc. [C19: ? a blend of *woolly* + *muzzy* or *dizzy*]
▸ **'woozily** *adv* ▸ **'wooziness** *n*

wop (wɒp) *n Sl., derog.* a member of a Latin people, esp. an Italian. [C20: prob. from It. dialect *guappo* dandy, from Sp. *guapo*]

Worcester sauce *or* **Worcestershire sauce** *n* a commercially prepared piquant sauce, made from a basis of soy sauce, with vinegar, spices, etc.

Worcs *abbrev. for* Worcestershire.

word 🅣 (wɜ:d) *n* **1** one of the units of speech or writing that is the smallest isolable meaningful element of the language, although linguists would analyse these further into morphemes. **2** an instance of vocal intercourse; chat, talk, or discussion: *to have a word with someone.* **3** an utterance or expression, esp. a brief one: *a word of greeting.* **4** news or information: *he sent word that he would be late.* **5** a verbal signal for action; command: *when I give the word, fire!* **6** an undertaking or promise: *he kept his word.* **7** an autocratic decree; order: *his word must be obeyed.* **8** a watchword or slogan, as of a political party: *the word now is "freedom".* **9** *Computing.* a set of bits used to store, transmit, or operate upon an item of information in a computer. **10 as good as one's word.** doing what one has undertaken to do. **11 at a word.** at once. **12 by word of mouth.** orally rather than by written means. **13 in a word.** briefly or in short. **14 my word! 14a** an exclamation of surprise, annoyance, etc. **14b** *Austral.* an exclamation of agreement. **15 of one's word.** given to or noted for keeping one's promises: *I am a man of my word.* **16 put in a word** *or* **good word for.** to make favourable mention of (someone); recommend. **17 take someone at his** *or* **her word.** to assume that someone means, or will do, what he or she says: *when he told her to go, she took*

THESAURUS

wool *n* **1, 2** = **fleece,** hair, yarn **8 pull the wool over someone's eyes** = **deceive,** bamboozle, con (*sl.*), delude, dupe, fool, hoodwink, kid (*inf.*), lead (someone) up the garden path (*inf.*), pull a fast one (on someone) (*inf.*), put one over on (*sl.*), take in (*inf.*), trick

woolgathering *n* = **daydreaming,** absent-mindedness, abstraction, building castles in the air, dreaming, inattention, musing, preoccupation, reverie
Antonyms *n* alertness, attention, awareness, concentration, heed, observation, thoughtfulness, vigilance, watchfulness

woolly *adj* **1** = **fleecy,** flocculent, hairy, made of wool, shaggy, woollen **3** = **vague,** blurred, clouded, confused, foggy, fuzzy, hazy, ill-defined, indefinite, indistinct, muddled, nebulous, unclear
Antonyms *adj* ≠ **vague:** clear, clear-cut, definite, distinct, exact, obvious, precise, sharp, well-defined

woozy *adj* **1, 2** *Informal* = **dizzy,** befuddled, bemused, confused, dazed, nauseated, rocky (*inf.*), tipsy, unsteady, wobbly

word *n* **1** = **term,** expression, locution, name, vocable **2** = **chat,** brief conversation, chitchat, colloquy, confab (*inf.*), confabulation, consultation, discussion, talk, tête-à-tête **3** = **remark,** brief statement, comment, declaration, expression, utterance **4** = **message,** account, advice, bulletin, communication, communiqué, dispatch, gen (*Brit. inf.*), information, intelligence, intimation, latest (*inf.*), news, notice, report, tidings **6** = **promise,** affirmation, assertion, assurance, guarantee, oath, parole, pledge, solemn oath, solemn word, undertaking, vow, word of honour **7** = **command,** bidding, commandment, decree, edict, go-ahead (*inf.*), mandate, order, ukase (*rare*), will **13 in a word** = **briefly,** concisely, in a nutshell, in short, succinctly, to put it briefly, to sum up **19 last word: a** = **epitome,** finis, summation, ultimatum **b** = **latest,** *dernier cri,* fashion, newest, rage **c** = **best,** cream, *crème de la crème,* crown, mother of all (*inf.*), *ne plus ultra,* perfection, quintessence, ultimate ◆ *vb* **25** = **express,** couch, phrase, put, say, state, utter

him at his word and left. **18 take someone's word for it.** to accept or believe what someone says. **19 the last word. 19a** the closing remark of a conversation or argument, esp. a remark that supposedly settles an issue. **19b** the latest or most fashionable design, make, or model: *the last word in bikinis.* **19c** the finest example (of some quality, condition, etc.): *the last word in luxury.* **20 the word.** the proper or most fitting expression: *cold is not the word for it, it's freezing!* **21 upon my word! 21a** *Arch.* on my honour. **21b** an exclamation of surprise, annoyance, etc. **22 word for word.** (of a report, etc.) using exactly the same words as those employed in the situation being reported; verbatim. **23 word of honour.** a promise; oath. **24** (*modifier*) of, relating to, or consisting of words. ◆ *vb* **25** (*tr*) to state in words, usually specially selected ones; phrase. ◆ See also **words.** [OE]
▸ **'wordless** *adj* ▸ **'wordlessly** *adv*

Word (wɜːd) *n* **the. 1** *Christianity.* the 2nd person of the Trinity. **2** Scripture, the Bible, or the Gospels as embodying or representing divine revelation. Often called: **the Word of God.** [translation of Gk *logos*, as in John 1:1]

-word *n combining form.* (preceded by *the* and an initial letter) a euphemistic way of referring to a word by its first letter because it is considered unmentionable by the user: *the C-word* (meaning cancer).

wordage ('wɜːdɪdʒ) *n* words considered collectively, esp. a quantity of words.

word association *n* an early method of psychoanalysis in which the patient thinks of the first word that comes into consciousness on hearing a given word. In this way it was claimed that aspects of the unconscious could be revealed before defence mechanisms intervene.

word blindness *n* the nontechnical name for **alexia** and **dyslexia.**
▸ **'word-ˌblind** *adj*

wordbook ('wɜːdˌbʊk) *n* a book containing words, usually with their meanings.

word deafness *n* loss of ability to understand spoken words, esp. as the result of a cerebral lesion. Also called: **auditory aphasia.**

word game *n* any game involving the formation, discovery, or alteration of a word or words.

wording ❶ ('wɜːdɪŋ) *n* **1** the way in which words are used to express a statement, report, etc., esp. a written one. **2** the words themselves.

word order *n* the arrangement of words in a phrase, clause, or sentence.

word-perfect *or US* **letter-perfect** *adj* **1** correct in every detail. **2** (of a speaker, actor, etc.) knowing one's speech, role, etc., perfectly.

wordplay ❶ ('wɜːdˌpleɪ) *n* verbal wit based on the meanings of words; puns, repartee, etc.

word processing *n* the composition of documents using a computer system to input, edit, store, and print.

word processor *n* **a** a computer program that performs word processing. **b** a computer system designed for word processing.

words ❶ (wɜːdz) *pl n* **1** the text of a part of an actor, etc. **2** the text of a song, as opposed to the music. **3** angry speech (esp. in **have words with someone**). **4 eat** *or* **swallow one's words.** to retract a statement. **5 for words.** (preceded by *too* and an adj or adv) indescribably; extremely: *the play was too funny for words.* **6 have no words for.** to be incapable of describing. **7 in other words.** expressing the same idea but differently. **8 in so many words.** explicitly or precisely. **9 of many** (*or* **few**) **words.** (not) talkative. **10 put into words.** to express in speech or writing. **11 say a few words.** to give a brief speech. **12 take the words out of someone's mouth.** to say exactly what someone else was about to say. **13 words fail me.** I am too happy, sad, amazed, etc., to express my thoughts.

word square *n* a puzzle in which the player must fill a square grid with words that read the same across as down.

word wrapping *n Computing.* the automatic shifting of a word at the end of a line to a new line in order to keep within preset margins.

wordy ❶ ('wɜːdɪ) *adj* **wordier, wordiest.** using or containing an excess of words: *a wordy document.*
▸ **'wordily** *adv* ▸ **'wordiness** *n*

wore (wɔː) *vb* the past tense of **wear**[1] and **wear**[2].

work ❶ (wɜːk) *n* **1** physical or mental effort directed towards doing or making something. **2** paid employment at a job or a trade, occupation, or profession. **3** a duty, task, or undertaking. **4** something done, made, etc., as a result of effort or exertion: *a work of art.* **5** another word for **workmanship** (sense 3). **6** the place, office, etc., where a person is employed. **7a** decoration, esp. of a specified kind. **7b** (*in combination*): *wirework.* **8** an engineering structure such as a bridge, building, etc. **9** *Physics.* the transfer of energy expressed as the product of a force and the distance through which its point of application moves in the direction of the force. **10** a structure, wall, etc., built or used as part of a fortification system. **11 at work. 11a** at one's job or place of employment. **11b** in action; operating. **12 make short work of.** *Inf.* to dispose of very quickly. **13** (*modifier*) of, relating to, or used for work: *work clothes; a work permit; a work song.* ◆ *vb* **14** (*intr*) to exert effort in order to do, make, or perform something. **15** (*intr*) to be employed. **16** (*tr*) to carry on operations, activity, etc., in (a place or area): *that salesman works Yorkshire.* **17** (*tr*) to cause to labour or toil: *he works his men hard.* **18** to operate or cause to operate, esp. properly or effectively: *to work a lathe; that clock doesn't work.* **19** (*tr*) to till or cultivate (land). **20** to handle or manipulate or be handled or manipulated: *to work dough.* **21** to shape or process or be shaped or processed: *to work copper.* **22** to reach or cause to reach a specific condition, esp. gradually: *the rope worked loose.* **23** (*intr*) to move in agitation: *his face worked with anger.* **24** (*tr*; often foll. by *up*) to provoke or arouse: *to work someone into a frenzy.* **25** (*tr*) to effect or accomplish: *to work one's revenge.* **26** to make (one's way) with effort: *he worked his way through the crowd.* **27** (*tr*) to make or decorate by hand in embroidery, tapestry, etc.: *she was working a sampler.* **28** (*intr*) (of liquids) to ferment, as in brewing. **29** (*tr*) *Inf.* to manipulate or exploit to one's own advantage. ◆ See also **work in, work off,** etc., **works.** [OE *weorc* (n), *wircan, wyrcan* (vb)]
▸ **'workless** *adj*

workable ❶ ('wɜːkəbᵊl) *adj* **1** practicable or feasible. **2** able to be worked.
▸ **ˌworka'bility** *or* **'workableness** *n*

workaday ❶ ('wɜːkəˌdeɪ) *adj* (*usually prenominal*) **1** being a part of general human experience; ordinary. **2** suitable for working days; everyday or practical.

workaholic (ˌwɜːkə'hɒlɪk) *n* **a** a person obsessively addicted to work. **b** (*as modifier*): *workaholic behaviour.* [C20: from WORK + -HOLIC, coined in 1971 by US author Wayne Oates]

workbag ('wɜːkˌbæg) *n* a container for implements, tools, or materials, esp. sewing equipment. Also called: **work basket, workbox.**

workbench ('wɜːkˌbɛntʃ) *n* a heavy table at which work is done by a carpenter, mechanic, toolmaker, etc.

workbook ('wɜːkˌbʊk) *n* **1** an exercise book used for study, esp. with spaces for answers. **2** a book of instructions for some process. **3** a book in which is recorded all work done or planned.

work camp *n* a camp set up for young people who voluntarily do manual work on a worthwhile project.

workday ('wɜːkˌdeɪ) *n* **1** the usual US and Canad. term for **working day.** ◆ *adj* **2** another word for **workaday.**

worked (wɜːkt) *adj* made or decorated with evidence of workmanship; wrought, as with embroidery or tracery.

worked up *adj* excited or agitated.

worker ❶ ('wɜːkə) *n* **1** a person or thing that works, usually at a specific job: *a research worker.* **2** an employee, as opposed to an employer or manager. **3** a manual labourer working in a manufacturing industry. **4** any other member of the working class. **5** a sterile female member of a colony of bees, ants, or wasps that forages for food, cares for the larvae, etc.

worker director *n* (in certain British companies) an employee of a company chosen by his or her fellow workers to represent their interests on the board of directors. Also called: **employee director.**

worker-priest *n* a Roman Catholic priest who has employment in a secular job to be more in touch with the problems of the laity.

work ethic *n* a belief in the moral value of work.

workfare ('wɜːkˌfɛə) *n* a scheme under which the government of a country requires unemployed people to do community work or undergo job training in return for social-security payments. [C20: from WORK + (WEL)FARE]

THESAURUS

wording *n* **1, 2 = phraseology,** choice of words, language, mode of expression, phrasing, terminology, words

wordplay *n* **= puns,** punning, repartee, wit, witticisms

words *pl n* **1, 2 = text,** lyrics **3** *As in* **have words = argument,** altercation, angry exchange, angry speech, barney (*inf.*), bickering, disagreement, dispute, falling-out (*inf.*), quarrel, row, run-in (*inf.*), set-to (*inf.*), squabble

wordy *adj* **= long-winded,** diffuse, discursive, garrulous, loquacious, pleonastic, prolix, rambling, verbose, windy
Antonyms *adj* brief, concise, laconic, pithy, short, succinct, terse, to the point

work *n* **1 = effort,** drudgery, elbow grease (*facetious*), exertion, grind (*inf.*), industry, labour, slog, sweat, toil, travail (*literary*) **2 = employment,** bread and butter (*inf.*), business, calling, craft, duty, job, line, livelihood, métier, occupation, office, profession, pursuit, trade **3 = task,** assignment, chore, commission, duty, job, stint, undertaking **4 = creation,** achievement, composition, handiwork, *oeuvre*, opus, performance, piece, production ◆ *vb* **14 = labour,** break one's back, drudge, exert oneself, peg away, slave, slog (away), sweat, toil **15 = be employed,** be in work, do business, earn a living, have a job **18, 20 = operate,** act, control, direct, drive, handle, manage, manipulate, move, ply, use, wield **18 = function,** go, operate, perform, run **19 = cultivate,** dig, farm, till **21 = manipulate,** fashion, form, handle, knead, make, mould, process, shape **22 = progress,** force, make one's way, manoeuvre, move **23 = move,** be agitated, convulse, twitch, writhe **25 = accomplish,** achieve, bring about, carry out, cause, contrive, create, effect, encompass, execute, implement **29** *Informal* **= manipulate,** arrange, bring off, contrive, exploit, fiddle (*inf.*), fix (*inf.*), handle, pull off, swing (*inf.*)
Antonyms *n* **≠ effort:** ease, leisure, relaxation, rest **≠ employment:** entertainment, hobby, holiday, play, recreation, retirement, spare time, unemployment ◆ *vb* **≠ labour:** have fun, mark time, play, relax, skive (*Brit. sl.*), take it easy **≠ function:** be broken, be out of order

workable *adj* **1 = viable,** doable, feasible, possible, practicable, practical
Antonyms *adj* hopeless, impossible, impractical, inconceivable, unattainable, unthinkable, unworkable, useless

workaday *adj* **1, 2 = ordinary,** bog-standard (*Brit. & Irish sl.*), common, commonplace, everyday, familiar, humdrum, mundane, practical, prosaic, routine, run-of-the-mill
Antonyms *adj* atypical, different, exciting, extraordinary, rare, special, uncommon, unfamiliar, unusual

worker *n* **1-4 = employee,** artisan, craftsman, hand, labourer, proletarian, tradesman, wage earner, working man *or* working woman, workman

workforce ('wɜːk,fɔːs) *n* **1** the total number of workers employed by a company on a specific job, project, etc. **2** the total number of people who could be employed: *the country's workforce is growing.*

work function *n Physics.* the minimum energy required to transfer an electron from a point within a solid to a point just outside its surface. Symbol: ϕ or Φ

work-harden *vb (tr)* to increase the strength or hardness of (a metal) by a mechanical process, such as tension, compression, or torsion.

workhorse ('wɜːk,hɔːs) *n* **1** a horse used for nonrecreational activities. **2** *Inf.* a person who takes on the greatest amount of work in a project.

workhouse ('wɜːk,haʊs) *n* **1** (formerly in England) an institution maintained at public expense where able-bodied paupers did unpaid work in return for food and accommodation. **2** (in the US) a prison for petty offenders serving short sentences at manual labour.

work in *vb (adv)* **1** to insert or become inserted: *she worked the patch in carefully.* **2** *(tr)* to find space for: *I'll work this job in during the day.* ◆ *n* **work-in. 3** a form of industrial action in which a factory that is to be closed down is occupied and run by its workers.

working **T** ('wɜːkɪŋ) *n* **1** the operation or mode of operation of something. **2** the act or process of moulding something pliable. **3** a convulsive or jerking motion, as from excitement. **4** *(often pl)* a part of a mine or quarry that is being or has been worked. **5** a record of the steps by which the solution of a problem, calculation, etc., is obtained: *all working is to be submitted to the examiners.* ◆ *adj (prenominal)* **6** relating to or concerned with a person or thing that works: *a working man.* **7** concerned with, used in, or suitable for work: *working clothes.* **8** (of a meal or occasion) during which business discussions are carried on: *a working lunch.* **9** capable of being operated or used: *a working model; in working order.* **10** adequate for normal purposes: *a working majority; a working knowledge of German.* **11** (of a theory, etc.) providing a basis, usually a temporary one, on which operations or procedures may be carried out.

working bee *n NZ.* a voluntary group doing a job for charity.

working capital *n* **1** *Accounting.* current assets minus current liabilities. **2** current or liquid assets. **3** that part of the capital of a business enterprise available for operations.

working class *n* **1** Also called: **proletariat.** the social stratum, usually of low status, that consists of those who earn wages, esp. as manual workers. ◆ *adj* **working-class. 2** of, relating to, or characteristic of the working class.

working day *or esp. US & Canad.* **workday** *n* **1** a day on which work is done, esp. for an agreed or stipulated number of hours in return for a salary or wage. **2** the part of the day allocated to work. **3** *(often pl) Commerce.* any day of the week except Sunday, public holidays, and, in some cases, Saturday.

working drawing *n* a scale drawing of a part that provides a guide for manufacture.

working memory *n Psychol.* the current contents of consciousness.

working party *n* **1** a committee established to investigate a problem, question, etc. **2** a group of soldiers or prisoners assigned to perform a manual task or duty.

working week *or esp. US & Canad.* **workweek** *n* the number of hours or days in a week allocated to work.

work-in-progress *n Book-keeping.* the value of work begun but not completed, as shown in a profit-and-loss account.

workload ('wɜːk,ləʊd) *n* the amount of work to be done, esp. in a specified period.

workman **T** ('wɜːkmən) *n, pl* **workmen. 1** a man who is employed in manual labour or who works an industrial machine. **2** a craftsman of skill as specified: *a bad workman.*

workmanlike **T** ('wɜːkmən,laɪk) *or (less commonly)* **workmanly** *adj* appropriate to or befitting a good workman.

workmanship **T** ('wɜːkmənʃɪp) *n* **1** the art or skill of a workman. **2** the art or skill with which something is made or executed. **3** the degree of art or skill exhibited in the finished product. **4** the piece of work so produced.

workmate ('wɜːk,meɪt) *n* a person who works with another; fellow worker.

work of art *n* **1** a piece of fine art, such as a painting or sculpture. **2** something that may be likened to a piece of fine art, esp. in beauty, intricacy, etc.

work off *vb (tr, adv)* **1** to get rid of or dissipate, as by effort: *he worked off some of his energy by digging the garden.* **2** to discharge (a debt) by labour rather than payment.

work on *vb (intr, prep)* to persuade or influence or attempt to persuade or influence.

work out **T** *vb (adv)* **1** *(tr)* to achieve or accomplish by effort. **2** *(tr)* to solve or find out by reasoning or calculation: *to work out an answer; to work out a sum.* **3** *(tr)* to devise or formulate: *to work out a plan.* **4** *(intr)* to prove satisfactory: *did your plan work out?* **5** *(intr)* to happen as specified: *it all worked out well.* **6** *(intr)* to take part in physical exercise, as in training. **7** *(tr)* to remove all the mineral in (a mine, etc.) that can be profitably exploited. **8** *(intr;* often foll. by *to* or *at)* to reach a total: *your bill works out at a pound.* ◆ *n* **workout. 9** a session of physical exercise, esp. for training or to keep oneself fit.

work over *vb* **1** *(tr, adv)* to do again; repeat. **2** *(intr, prep)* to examine closely and thoroughly. **3** *(tr, adv) Sl.* to assault or thrash.

workpeople ('wɜːk,piːpᵊl) *pl n* the working members of a population.

workroom ('wɜːk,ruːm, -,rʊm) *n* **1** a room in which work, usually manual labour, is done. **2** a room in a house set aside for a hobby.

works **T** (wɜːks) *pl n* **1** *(often functioning as sing)* a place where a number of people are employed, such as a factory. **2** the sum total of a writer's or artist's achievements, esp. when considered together: *the works of Shakespeare.* **3** the deeds of a person, esp. virtuous or moral deeds: *works of charity.* **4** the interior parts of the mechanism of a machine, etc.: *the works of a clock.* **5 the works.** *Sl.* **5a** full or extreme treatment. **5b** a very violent physical beating: *to give someone the works.*

works council *n Chiefly Brit.* **1** a council composed of both employer and employees convened to discuss matters of common interest concerning a factory, plant, business policy, etc. **2** a body representing the workers of a plant, factory, etc., elected to negotiate with the management about working conditions, wages, etc. ◆ Also called: **works committee.**

worksheet ('wɜːk,ʃiːt) *n* **1** a sheet of paper used for the rough draft of a problem, design, etc. **2** a piece of paper recording work in progress.

workshop **T** ('wɜːk,ʃɒp) *n* **1** a room or building in which manufacturing or other forms of manual work are carried on. **2** a room in a private dwelling, school, etc., set aside for crafts. **3** a group of people engaged in study or work on a creative project or subject: *a music workshop.*

workshy ('wɜːk,ʃaɪ) *adj* not inclined to work.

work station *n* an area in an office where one person works.

work-study *n* an examination of ways of finding the most efficient method of doing a job.

worktable ('wɜːk,teɪbᵊl) *n* **a** any table at which writing, sewing, or other work may be done. **b** (in English cabinetwork) a small elegant table fitted with sewing accessories.

worktop ('wɜːk,tɒp) *n* a surface in a kitchen, often of heat-resistant plastic, used for food preparation.

work-to-rule *n* **1** a form of industrial action in which employees adhere strictly to all the working rules laid down by their employers, with the deliberate intention of reducing the rate of working. ◆ *vb* **work to rule. 2** *(intr)* to decrease the rate of working by this means.

work up **T** *vb* **1** *(tr, adv)* to arouse the feelings of; excite. **2** *(tr, adv)* to cause to grow or develop: *to work up a hunger.* **3** to move or cause to move gradually upwards. **4** *(tr, adv)* to manipulate or mix into a specified object or shape. **5** *(tr, adv)* to gain skill at (a subject). **6** *(adv)* (foll. by *to)* to develop gradually or progress (towards): *working up to a climax.*

world **T** (wɜːld) *n* **1** the earth as a planet, esp. including its inhabitants. **2** mankind; the human race. **3** people generally; the public: *in the eyes of the world.* **4** social or public life: *to go out into the world.* **5** the universe or cosmos; everything in existence. **6** a complex united whole re-

THESAURUS

working *n* **1 = operation**, action, functioning, manner, method, mode of operation, running **4** *often plural* **= mine**, digging, excavation, pit, quarry, shaft ◆ *adj* **6 = employed**, active, in a job, in work, labouring **9 = functioning**, going, operative, running **10 = effective**, practical, useful, viable

workman *n* **1, 2 = labourer**, artificer, artisan, craftsman, employee, hand, journeyman, mechanic, operative, tradesman, worker

workmanlike *adj* **= efficient**, adept, careful, expert, masterly, painstaking, professional, proficient, satisfactory, skilful, skilled, thorough
Antonyms *adj* amateurish, botchy, careless, clumsy, cowboy *(inf.)*, incompetent, slap-dash, slipshod, unprofessional, unskilful

workmanship *n* **1, 2 = skill**, art, artistry, craft, craftsmanship, execution, expertise, handicraft, handiwork, manufacture, technique, work

work out *vb* **2 = solve**, calculate, clear up, figure out, find out, puzzle out, resolve, suss (out) *(sl.)* **3 = plan**, arrange, construct, contrive, develop, devise, elaborate, evolve, form, formulate, put together **4 = succeed**, be effective, flourish, go as planned, go well, prosper, prove satisfactory **5 = happen**, come out, develop, evolve, go, pan out *(inf.)*, result, turn out **6 = exercise**, do exercises, drill, practise, train, warm up **8** *often foll. by* **to** *or* **at = amount to**, add up to, come to, reach, reach a total of ◆ *n* **workout 9 = exercise**, drill, exercise session, practice session, training, training session, warm-up

works *pl n* **1 = factory**, mill, plant, shop, workshop **2 = writings**, canon, *oeuvre*, output, productions **3 = deeds**, actions, acts, doings **4 = mechanism**, action, guts *(inf.)*, innards *(inf.)*, insides *(inf.)*, machinery, movement, moving parts, parts, workings

workshop *n* **1, 2 = studio**, atelier, factory, mill, plant, shop, workroom, works **3 = seminar**, class, discussion group, masterclass, study group

work up *vb* **1 = excite**, agitate, animate, arouse, enkindle, foment, generate, get (someone) all steamed up *(sl.)*, incite, inflame, instigate, move, rouse, spur, stir up, wind up *(inf.)*

world *n* **1 = earth**, earthly sphere, globe **2 = mankind**, everybody, everyone, humanity, humankind, human race, man, men, the public, the race of man **5 = universe**, cosmos, creation, existence, life, nature **7 = planet**, heavenly body, star **9 = sphere**, area, domain, environment, field, kingdom, province, realm, system **11 = period**, age, days, epoch, era, times **17 for all the world = exactly**, in every respect, in every way, just as if, just like, precisely, to all intents and purposes **22 on top of the world** *Informal* **= overjoyed**, beside oneself with joy, cock-a-hoop, ecstatic, elated, exultant, happy, in raptures, on cloud nine *(inf.)*, over the moon *(inf.)* **23 out of this world** *Informal* **= wonderful**, excellent, fabulous *(inf.)*, fantastic *(inf.)*, great *(inf.)*, incredible, indescribable, marvellous, superb, unbelievable garded as resembling the universe. **7** any star or planet, esp. one that might be inhabited. **8** (*often cap.*) a division or section of the earth, its history, or its inhabitants: *the Ancient World; the Third World.* **9** an area, sphere, or realm considered as a complete environment: *the animal world.* **10** any field of human activity or way of life or those involved in it: *the world of television.* **11** a period or state of existence: *the next world.* **12** the total circumstances and experience of an individual that make up his life: *you have shattered my world.* **13** a large amount, number, or distance: *worlds apart.* **14** worldly or secular life, ways, or people. **15 bring into the world. 15a** (of a midwife, doctor, etc.) to deliver (a baby). **15b** to give birth to. **16 come into the world.** to be born. **17 for all the world.** in every way; exactly. **18 for the world.** (*used with a negative*) for any inducement, however great. **19 in the world.** (intensifier; *usually used with a negative*): *no-one in the world can change things.* **20 man** (*or* **woman**) **of the world.** a man (or woman) experienced in social or public life. **21 not long for this world.** nearing death. **22 on top of the world.** *Inf.* elated or very happy. **23 out of this world.** *Inf.* wonderful; excellent. **24 set the world on fire.** to be exceptionally or sensationally successful. **25 the best of both worlds.** the benefits from two different ways of life, philosophies, etc. **26 think the world of.** to be extremely fond of or hold in very high esteem. **27 world of one's own.** a state of mental detachment from other people. **28 world without end.** forever. **29** (*modifier*) of or concerning most or all countries; worldwide: *world politics.* **30** (*in combination*) throughout the world: *world-famous.* [OE *w(e)orold,* from *wer* man + *ald* age, life]

World Bank *n* an international cooperative organization established in 1945 to assist economic development, esp. of backward nations, by the advance of loans guaranteed by member governments. Officially called: **International Bank for Reconstruction and Development.**

world-beater *n* a person or thing that surpasses all others in its category; champion.

world-class *adj* of or denoting someone with a skill or attribute that puts him or her in the highest class in the world: *a world-class swimmer.*

World Court *n* another name for **International Court of Justice.**

World Cup *n* an international competition held between national teams in various sports, most notably association football.

worldling ('wɜːldlɪŋ) *n* a person who is primarily concerned with worldly matters.

worldly ➊ ('wɜːldlɪ) *adj* **worldlier, worldliest. 1** not spiritual; mundane or temporal. **2** Also: **worldly-minded.** absorbed in material things. **3** Also: **worldly-wise.** versed in the ways of the world; sophisticated.
▸ **'worldliness** *n*

world music *n* popular music of various ethnic origins and styles.

world power *n* a state that possesses sufficient power to influence events throughout the world.

world-shaking *adj* of enormous significance.

World Trade Organization *n* an international body concerned with promoting and regulating trade between its member states; established in 1995 as a successor to GATT.

World War I *n* the war (1914–18), fought mainly in Europe and the Middle East, in which the Allies (principally France, Russia, Britain, Italy after 1915, and the US after 1917) defeated the Central Powers (principally Germany, Austria-Hungary, and Turkey). Also called: **First World War, Great War.**

World War II *n* the war (1939–45) in which the Allies (principally Britain, the Soviet Union, and the US) defeated the Axis powers (principally Germany, Italy, and Japan). Britain and France declared war on Germany (Sept. 3, 1939) as a result of the German invasion of Poland (Sept. 1, 1939). Italy entered the war on June 10, 1940 shortly before the collapse of France (armistice signed June 22, 1940). On June 22, 1941 Germany attacked the Soviet Union and on Dec. 7, 1941 the Japanese attacked the US at Pearl Harbor. On Sept. 8, 1943 Italy surrendered, the war in Europe ending on May 7, 1945 with the unconditional surrender of the Germans. The Japanese capitulated on Aug. 14, 1945. Also called: **Second World War.**

world-weary *adj* no longer finding pleasure in living.
▸ **'world-ˌweariness** *n*

worldwide ➊ ('wɜːld'waɪd) *adj* applying or extending throughout the world; universal.

World Wide Web *n Computing.* a vast network of linked hypertext files, stored on computers throughout the world, that can provide a computer user with information on a huge variety of subjects. Abbrev.: **WWW.**

worm (wɜːm) *n* **1** any of various invertebrates, esp. the annelids (earthworms, etc.), nematodes (roundworms), and flatworms, having a slender elongated body. **2** any of various insect larvae having an elongated body, such as the silkworm and wireworm. **3** any of various unrelated animals that resemble annelids, nematodes, etc., such as the glow-worm and shipworm. **4** a gnawing or insinuating force or agent that torments or slowly eats away. **5** a wretched or spineless person. **6** anything that resembles a worm in appearance or movement. **7** a shaft on which a helical groove has been cut, as in a gear arrangement in which such a shaft meshes with a toothed wheel. **8** a spiral pipe cooled by air or flowing water, used as a condenser in a still. **9** *Computing.* a program that duplicates itself many times in a network and prevents its destruction. It often carries a logic bomb or virus. ◆ *vb* **10** to move, act, or cause to move or act with the slow sinuous movement of a worm. **11** (foll. by *in, into, out of,* etc.) to make (one's way) slowly and stealthily; insinuate (oneself). **12** (*tr;* often foll. by *out of* or *from*) to extract (information, etc.) from by persistent questioning. **13** (*tr*) to free from worms. ◆ See also **worms.** [OE *wyrm*]
▸ **'wormer** *n* ▸ **'wormˌlike** *adj*

WORM (wɜːm) *n Computing. acronym for* write once read many times: an optical disk which enables users to store data but not change it.

wormcast ('wɜːmˌkɑːst) *n* a coil of earth or sand that has been excreted by a burrowing earthworm or lugworm.

worm-eaten *adj* **1** eaten into by worms: *a worm-eaten table.* **2** decayed; rotten. **3** old-fashioned; antiquated.

worm gear *n* **1** a device consisting of a threaded shaft (**worm**) that mates with a gear-wheel (**worm wheel**) so that rotary motion can be transferred between two shafts at right angles to each other. **2** Also called: **worm wheel.** a gear-wheel driven by a threaded shaft or worm.

wormhole ('wɜːmˌhəʊl) *n* a hole made by a worm in timber, plants, etc.
▸ **'wormˌholed** *adj*

worms (wɜːmz) *n* (*functioning as sing*) any disease or disorder, usually of the intestine, characterized by infestation with parasitic worms.

worm's eye view *n* a view seen from below or from a more lowly or humble point.

wormwood ('wɜːmˌwʊd) *n* **1** Also called: **absinthe.** any of various plants of a chiefly N temperate genus, esp. a European plant yielding a bitter extract used in making absinthe. **2** something that embitters, such as a painful experience. [C15: changed (through infl. of WORM & WOOD) from OE *wormōd, wermōd*]

wormy ('wɜːmɪ) *adj* **wormier, wormiest. 1** worm-infested or worm-eaten. **2** resembling a worm in appearance, ways, or condition. **3** (of wood) having irregular small tunnels bored into it and tracked over its surface, made by worms. **4** low or grovelling.
▸ **'worminess** *n*

worn ➊ (wɔːn) *vb* **1** the past participle of **wear**[1] and **wear**[2]. ◆ *adj* **2** affected, esp. adversely, by long use or action: *a worn suit.* **3** haggard; drawn. **4** exhausted; spent.
▸ **'wornness** *n*

worn-out ➊ *adj* (**worn out** *when postpositive*). **1** worn or used until threadbare, valueless, or useless. **2** exhausted; very weary.

worriment ('wʌrɪmənt) *n Inf., chiefly US.* anxiety or the trouble that causes it; worry.

worrisome ➊ ('wʌrɪsəm) *adj* **1** causing worry; vexing. **2** tending to worry.
▸ **'worrisomely** *adv*

worrit ('wʌrɪt) *vb* (*tr*) *Dialect.* to tease or worry. [prob. var. of WORRY]

worry ➊ ('wʌrɪ) *vb* **worries, worrying, worried. 1** to be or cause to be anxious or uneasy, esp. about something uncertain or potentially dangerous. **2** (*tr*) to disturb the peace of mind of; bother: *don't worry me with trivialities.* **3** (*intr;* often foll. by *along* or *through*) to proceed de-

THESAURUS

worldly *adj* **1 = earthly,** carnal, fleshly, lay, mundane, physical, profane, secular, sublunary, temporal, terrestrial **2 = materialistic,** avaricious, covetous, grasping, greedy, selfish, worldly-minded **3 = worldly-wise,** blasé, cosmopolitan, experienced, knowing, politic, sophisticated, urbane
Antonyms *adj* ≠ **earthly:** divine, ethereal, heavenly, immaterial, noncorporeal, spiritual, transcendental, unworldly ≠ **materialistic:** moral, nonmaterialistic, unworldly ≠ **worldly-wise:** ingenuous, innocent, naive, unsophisticated, unworldly

worldwide *adj* **= global,** general, international, omnipresent, pandemic, ubiquitous, universal
Antonyms *adj* confined, insular, limited, local, narrow, national, parochial, provincial, restricted

worn *adj* **2 = ragged,** frayed, shabby, shiny, tattered, tatty, the worse for wear, threadbare **3 = haggard,** careworn, drawn, lined, pinched, wizened **4 = exhausted,** fatigued, jaded, played-out (*inf.*), spent, tired, tired out, wearied, weary, worn-out

worn-out *adj* **1 = run-down,** broken-down, clapped out (*Brit., Austral., & NZ inf.*), decrepit, done, frayed, moth-eaten, on its last legs, ragged, shabby, tattered, tatty, threadbare, used, used-up, useless, worn **2 = exhausted,** all in (*sl.*), dead *or* out on one's feet (*inf.*), dog-tired (*inf.*), done in (*inf.*), fatigued, fit to drop, knackered (*sl.*), prostrate, spent, tired, tired out, weary, wiped out (*inf.*)
Antonyms *adj* ≠ **exhausted:** fresh, refreshed, relaxed, renewed, rested, restored, revived, strengthened

worried *adj* **1, 2 = anxious,** afraid, apprehensive, bothered, concerned, distracted, distraught, distressed, disturbed, fearful, fretful, frightened, hot and bothered, ill at ease, nervous, on edge, overwrought, perturbed, tense, tormented, troubled, uneasy, unquiet, upset, wired (*sl.*)
Antonyms *adj* calm, fearless, peaceful, quiet, tranquil, unafraid, unconcerned, unfazed (*inf.*), unworried

worrisome *adj* **1 = troublesome,** bothersome, disquieting, distressing, disturbing, irksome, perturbing, upsetting, vexing, worrying **2 = anxious,** apprehensive, fretful, insecure, jittery (*inf.*), nervous, neurotic, uneasy

worry *vb* **1 = be anxious,** agonize, brood, feel uneasy, fret, obsess **2 = trouble,** annoy, badger, bother, disquiet, distress, disturb, harass, harry, hassle (*inf.*), hector, importune, irritate, make anxious, perturb, pester, plague, tantalize, tease, torment, unsettle, upset, vex **5, 6 = attack,** bite, gnaw at, go for, harass, harry, kill, lacerate, savage, tear ◆ *n* **9 = anxiety,** annoyance, apprehension, care, concern, disturbance, fear, irritation, misery, misgiving, perplexity, torment, trepidation, trouble, un-

spite difficulties. **4** (*intr;* often foll. by *away*) to struggle or work: *to worry away at a problem.* **5** (*tr*) (of a dog, wolf, etc.) to lacerate or kill by biting, shaking, etc. **6** (when *intr,* foll. by *at*) to bite, tear, or gnaw (at) with the teeth: *a dog worrying a bone.* **7** (*tr*) to touch or poke repeatedly and idly. **8 not to worry.** *Inf.* you need not worry. ◆ *n, pl* **worries. 9** a state or feeling of anxiety. **10** a person or thing that causes anxiety. **11** an act of worrying. [OE *wyrgan*]
▸**'worried** *adj* ▸**'worriedly** *adv* ▸**'worrying** *adj* ▸**'worryingly** *adv*

worry beads *pl n* a string of beads that when fingered or played with supposedly relieves nervous tension.

worryguts ('wʌrɪˌgʌts) *n* (*functioning as sing*) *Inf.* a person who worries, esp. about insignificant matters.

worse (wɜːs) *adj* **1** the comparative of **bad**[1]. **2 none the worse for.** not harmed by (adverse events or circumstances). **3 the worse for wear. 3a** shabby or worn. **3b** a slang term for **drunk. 4 worse luck!** *Inf.* unhappily; unfortunately. **5 worse off.** (*postpositive*) in a worse, esp. a worse financial, condition. ◆ *n* **6** something that is worse. **7 for the worse.** into a less desirable or inferior state or condition: *a change for the worse.* ◆ *adv* **8** in a more severe or unpleasant manner. **9** in a less effective or successful manner. [OE *wiersa*]

worsen ❶ ('wɜːsᵊn) *vb* to grow or cause to grow worse.

worship ❶ ('wɜːʃɪp) *vb* **worships, worshipping, worshipped** *or US* **worships, worshiping, worshiped. 1** (*tr*) to show profound religious devotion and respect to; adore or venerate (God or any person or thing considered divine). **2** (*tr*) to be devoted to and full of admiration for. **3** (*intr*) to have or express feelings of profound adoration. **4** (*intr*) to attend services for worship. ◆ *n* **5** religious adoration or devotion. **6** the formal expression of religious adoration; rites, prayers, etc. **7** admiring love or devotion. [OE *weorthscipe*]
▸**'worshipper** *n*

Worship ('wɜːʃɪp) *n Chiefly Brit.* (preceded by *Your, His,* or *Her*) a title used to address or refer to a mayor, magistrate, etc.

worshipful ('wɜːʃɪpfʊl) *adj* **1** feeling or showing reverence or adoration. **2** (*often cap.*) *Chiefly Brit.* a title used to address or refer to various people or bodies of distinguished rank.
▸**'worshipfully** *adv* ▸**'worshipfulness** *n*

worst ❶ (wɜːst) *adj* **1** the superlative of **bad**[1]. ◆ *adv* **2** in the most extreme or bad manner or degree. **3** least well, suitably, or acceptably. **4** (*in combination*) in or to the smallest degree or extent; least: *worst-loved.* ◆ *n* **5 the worst.** the least good or most inferior person, thing, or part in a group, narrative, etc. **6** (often preceded by *at*) the most poor, unpleasant, or unskilled quality or condition: *television is at its worst these days.* **7** the greatest amount of damage or wickedness of which a person or group is capable: *the invaders came and did their worst.* **8** the weakest effort or poorest achievement that a person or group is capable of making: *the applicant did his worst at the test because he did not want the job.* **9 at worst. 9a** in the least favourable interpretation or view. **9b** under the least favourable conditions. **10 come off worst** *or* **get the worst of it.** to enjoy the least benefit from an issue or be defeated in it. **11 if the worst comes to the worst.** if all the more desirable alternatives become impossible or if the worst possible thing happens. ◆ *vb* **12** (*tr*) to get the advantage over; defeat or beat. [OE *wierrest*]

worsted ('wʊstɪd) *n* **1** a closely twisted yarn or thread made from combed long-staple wool. **2** a fabric made from this, with a hard smooth close-textured surface and no nap. **3** (*modifier*) made of this yarn or fabric: *a worsted suit.* [C13: after *Worstead,* a district in Norfolk]

wort (wɜːt) *n* **1** (*in combination*) any of various unrelated plants, esp. ones formerly used to cure diseases: *liverwort.* **2** the sweet liquid made from warm water and ground malt, used to make a malt liquor. [OE *wyrt* root]

worth ❶ (wɜːθ) *adj* (governing a noun with prepositional force) **1** worthy of; meriting or justifying: *it's not worth discussing.* **2** having a value of: *the book is worth £30.* **3 for all one is worth.** to the utmost. **4 worth one's weight in gold.** extremely helpful, kind, etc. ◆ *n* **5** high quality; excellence. **6** value; price. **7** the amount of something of a specified value: *five pounds' worth of petrol.* [OE *weorth*]

worthless ❶ ('wɜːθlɪs) *adj* **1** without value or usefulness. **2** without merit; good-for-nothing.
▸**'worthlessly** *adv* ▸**'worthlessness** *n*

worthwhile ❶ (ˌwɜːθ'waɪl) *adj* sufficiently important, rewarding, or valuable to justify time or effort spent.

worthy ❶ ('wɜːðɪ) *adj* **worthier, worthiest. 1** (*postpositive;* often foll. by *of* or an infinitive) having sufficient merit or value (for something or someone specified); deserving. **2** having worth, value, or merit. ◆ *n, pl* **worthies. 3** *Often facetious.* a person of merit or importance.
▸**'worthily** *adv* ▸**'worthiness** *n*

wot (wɒt) *vb Arch. or dialect.* (used with *I, she, he, it,* or a singular noun) a form of the present tense (indicative mood) of **wit**[2].

would (wʊd; *unstressed* wəd) *vb* (takes an infinitive without *to* or an implied infinitive) used as an auxiliary: **1** to form the past tense or subjunctive mood of **will**[1]. **2** (with *you, he, she, it, they,* or a noun as subject) to indicate willingness or desire in a polite manner: *would you help me, please?* **3** to describe a past action as being accustomed or habitual: *every day we would go for walks.* **4** I wish: *would that he were here.*

USAGE NOTE See at **should.**

would-be ❶ *adj* (*prenominal*) **1** *Usually derog.* wanting or professing to be: *a would-be politician.* **2** intended to be.

wouldn't ('wʊdᵊnt) *contraction of* would not.

wouldst (wʊdst) *vb Arch. or dialect.* (used with the pronoun *thou* or its relative equivalent) a singular form of the past tense of **will**[1].

Woulfe bottle (wʊlf) *n Chem.* a bottle with more than one neck, used for passing gases through liquids. [C18: after Peter *Woulfe* (?1727–1803), Brit. chemist]

wound[1] ❶ (wuːnd) *n* **1** any break in the skin or an organ or part as the result of violence or a surgical incision. **2** any injury or slight to the feelings or reputation. ◆ *vb* **3** to inflict a wound or wounds upon (someone or something). [OE *wund*]
▸**'wounding** *adj* ▸**'woundingly** *adv*

wound[2] (waʊnd) *vb* the past tense and past participle of **wind**[2] and **wind**[3].

wounded ('wuːndɪd) *adj* **1a** suffering from wounds; injured, esp. in a battle or fight. **1b** (*as collective n;* preceded by *the*): *the wounded.* **2** (of feelings) damaged or hurt.

woundwort ('wuːndˌwɜːt) *n* **1** any of various plants, such as field woundwort, having purple, scarlet, yellow, or white flowers and formerly used for dressing wounds. **2** any of various other plants used in this way.

wove (wəʊv) *vb* a past tense of **weave.**

woven ('wəʊvᵊn) *vb* a past participle of **weave.**

wove paper *n* paper with a very faint mesh impressed on it by the paper-making machine.

THESAURUS

ease, vexation, woe **10** = **problem**, annoyance, bother, care, hassle (*inf.*), irritation, pest, plague, torment, trial, trouble, vexation
Antonyms *vb* ≠ **be anxious**: be apathetic, be unconcerned, be unperturbed ≠ **trouble**: calm, comfort, console, solace, soothe ◆ *n* ≠ **anxiety**: calm, comfort, consolation, peace of mind, reassurance, serenity, solace, tranquillity

worsen *vb* = **aggravate**, damage, exacerbate = **deteriorate**, decay, decline, degenerate, get worse, go downhill (*inf.*), go from bad to worse, retrogress, sink, take a turn for the worse
Antonyms *vb* ≠ **aggravate**: ameliorate, enhance, improve, mend, rectify, upgrade ≠ **deteriorate**: be on the mend, improve, mend, recover

worship *vb* **1** = **praise**, adore, adulate, deify, exalt, glorify, honour, laud, pray to, respect, revere, reverence, venerate **2** = **love**, adore, idolize, put on a pedestal ◆ *n* **5** = **praise**, adoration, adulation, deification, devotion, exaltation, glorification, glory, homage, honour, laudation, love, prayer(s), regard, respect, reverence
Antonyms *vb* ≠ **praise**: blaspheme, deride, dishonour, flout, mock, revile, ridicule, scoff at ≠ **love**: despise, disdain, spurn

worst *vb* **12** = **beat**, best, blow out of the water (*sl.*), clobber (*sl.*), conquer, crush, defeat, gain the advantage over, get the better of, lick (*inf.*), master, overcome, overpower, overthrow, run rings around (*inf.*), subdue, subjugate, undo, vanquish

worth *n* **5** = **importance**, avail, benefit, credit, desert(s), estimation, excellence, goodness, help, merit, quality, usefulness, utility, value, virtue, worthiness **6** = **value**, cost, price, rate, valuation
Antonyms *n* ≠ **importance**: futility, insignificance, paltriness, triviality, unworthiness, uselessness, worthlessness, wretchedness

worthless *adj* **1** = **useless**, futile, ineffectual, insignificant, inutile, meaningless, measly, miserable, no use, nugatory, paltry, pointless, poor, poxy (*sl.*), rubbishy, trashy, trifling, trivial, two a penny (*inf.*), unavailing, unimportant, unusable, valueless, wretched **2** = **good-for-nothing**, abject, base, contemptible, depraved, despicable, ignoble, useless, vile
Antonyms *adj* ≠ **useless**: consequential, effective, fruitful, important, precious, productive, profitable, significant, useful, valuable, worthwhile ≠ **good-for-nothing**: decent, honourable, noble, upright, worthy

worthwhile *adj* = **useful**, beneficial, constructive, expedient, gainful, good, helpful, justifiable, productive, profitable, valuable, worthy
Antonyms *adj* inconsequential, pointless, trivial, unimportant, unworthy, useless, vain, valueless, wasteful, worthless

worthy *adj* **1, 2** = **praiseworthy**, admirable, commendable, creditable, decent, dependable, deserving, estimable, excellent, good, honest, honourable, laudable, meritorious, reliable, reputable, respectable, righteous, upright, valuable, virtuous, worthwhile ◆ *n* **3** *Often facetious* = **dignitary**, big hitter (*inf.*), big shot (*inf.*), bigwig (*inf.*), heavy hitter (*inf.*), luminary, notable, personage
Antonyms *adj* ≠ **praiseworthy**: demeaning, disreputable, dubious, ignoble, undeserving, unproductive, untrustworthy, unworthy, useless ◆ *n* ≠ **dignitary**: member of the rank and file, nobody, pleb, punter (*inf.*)

would-be *adj* **1** *Usually derogatory* = **budding**, dormant, latent, manqué, potential, professed, quasi-, self-appointed, self-styled, so-called, *soi-disant,* undeveloped, unfulfilled, unrealized, wannabe (*inf.*)

wound[1] *n* **1** = **injury**, cut, damage, gash, harm, hurt, laceration, lesion, slash, trauma (*Pathology*) **2** = **insult**, anguish, distress, grief, heartbreak, injury, offence, pain, pang, sense of loss, shock, slight, torment, torture, trauma ◆ *vb* **3** = **injure**, cut, damage, gash, harm, hit, hurt, irritate, lacerate, pierce, slash, wing **3** = **offend**, annoy, cut (someone) to the quick, distress, grieve, hurt, hurt the feelings of, mortify, pain, shock, sting, traumatize

wounding *adj* **3** = **hurtful**, acid, barbed, bitter, caustic, cruel, cutting, damaging, destructive, distressing, grievous, harmful, injurious, insulting, maleficent, malicious, mordacious, offensive, pernicious, pointed, savage, scathing, slighting, spiteful, stinging, trenchant, unkind, vitriolic

wow[1] (waʊ) *interj* **1** an exclamation of admiration, amazement, etc. ◆ *n* **2** *Sl.* a person or thing that is amazingly successful, attractive, etc. ◆ *vb* **3** (*tr*) *Sl.* to arouse great enthusiasm in. [C16: orig. Scot.]

wow[2] (waʊ, wəʊ) *n* a slow variation or distortion in pitch that occurs at very low audio frequencies in sound-reproducing systems. See also **flutter** (sense 12). [C20: imit.]

wowser (ˈwaʊzə) *n Austral. & NZ sl.* **1** a fanatically puritanical person. **2** a teetotaller. [C20: from E dialect *wow* to complain]

wp *abbrev. for* word processor.

wpb *abbrev. for* wastepaper basket.

WPC (in Britain) *abbrev. for* woman police constable.

wpm *abbrev. for* words per minute.

WRAAC *abbrev. for* Women's Royal Australian Army Corps.

WRAAF *abbrev. for* Women's Royal Australian Air Force.

WRAC (in Britain) *abbrev. for* Women's Royal Army Corps.

wrack[1] *or* **rack** (ræk) *n* **1** collapse or destruction (esp. in **wrack and ruin**). **2** something destroyed or a remnant of such. [OE *wræc* persecution, misery]

> **USAGE NOTE** The use of the spelling *wrack* rather than *rack* in sentences such as *she was wracked by grief* or *the country was wracked by civil war* is very common but is thought by many people to be incorrect.

wrack[2] (ræk) *n* **1** seaweed or other marine vegetation that is floating in the sea or has been cast ashore. **2** any of various seaweeds, such as serrated wrack. [C14 (in the sense: a wrecked ship, hence later applied to marine vegetation washed ashore): ?from MDu. *wrak* wreckage; the term corresponds to OE *wræc* WRACK[1]]

WRAF (in Britain) *abbrev. for* Women's Royal Air Force.

wraith 🅣 (reɪθ) *n* **1** the apparition of a person living or thought to be alive, supposed to appear around the time of his death. **2** any apparition. [C16: Scot., from ?]
▸**ˈwraith,like** *adj*

Wran (ræn) *n* a member of the Women's Royal Australian Naval Service.

wrangle 🅣 (ˈræŋgᵊl) *vb* **wrangles, wrangling, wrangled. 1** (*intr*) to argue, esp. noisily or angrily. **2** (*tr*) to encourage, persuade, or obtain by argument. **3** (*tr*) *Western US & Canad.* to herd (cattle or horses). ◆ *n* **4** a noisy or angry argument. [C14: from Low G *wrangeln*]

wrangler (ˈræŋglə) *n* **1** one who wrangles. **2** *Western US & Canad.* a herder; cowboy. **3** a person who handles or controls animals involved in the making of a film or television programme. **4** *Brit.* (at Cambridge University) a candidate who has obtained first-class honours in part II of the mathematics tripos. Formerly, the wrangler with the highest marks was called the **senior wrangler.**

WRANS *abbrev. for* Women's Royal Australian Naval Service. See also **Wran.**

wrap 🅣 (ræp) *vb* **wraps, wrapping, wrapped.** (*mainly tr*) **1** to fold or wind (paper, cloth, etc.) around (a person or thing) so as to cover. **2** (often foll. by *up*) to fold paper, etc., around to fasten securely. **3** to surround or conceal by surrounding. **4** to enclose, immerse, or absorb: *wrapped in joy.* **5** to fold, wind, or roll up. **6** to complete the filming of (a motion picture or television programme). **7** (*intr; often foll. by about, around,* etc.) to be or become wound or extended. **8** (often foll. by *up*) Also: **rap.** *Austral. inf.* to praise (someone). ◆ *n* **9** a garment worn wrapped around the body, esp. the shoulders, such as a shawl or cloak. **10a** the end of a working day during the filming of a motion picture or television programme. **10b** the completion of filming of a motion picture or television programme. **11** *Chiefly US.* wrapping or a wrapper. **12 keep under wraps.** to keep secret. **13 take the wraps off.** to reveal. **14** Also: **rap.** *Austral. inf.* a commendation. [C14: from ?]

wrapover (ˈræpˌəʊvə) *or* **wrapround** *adj* **1** (of a garment, esp. a skirt) not sewn up at one side, but worn wrapped round the body and fastened so that the open edges overlap. ◆ *n* **2** such a garment.

wrapped (ræpt) *vb* **1** the past tense and past participle of **wrap. 2 wrapped up in.** *Inf.* **2a** completely absorbed or engrossed in. **2b** implicated or involved in. ◆ *adj* **3** *Austral. inf.* a variant spelling of **rapt**[2].

wrapper 🅣 (ˈræpə) *n* **1** the cover, usually of paper or cellophane, in which something is wrapped. **2** a dust jacket of a book. **3** the firm tobacco leaf forming the outermost portion of a cigar. **4** a loose negligee or dressing gown.

wrapping (ˈræpɪŋ) *n* the material used to wrap something.

wrapround (ˈræpˌraʊnd) *or* **wraparound** *adj* **1** made so as to be wrapped round something: *a wrapround skirt.* **2** surrounding, curving round, or overlapping. **3** curving round in one continuous piece: *a wrapround windscreen.* ◆ *n* **4** *Printing.* a flexible plate of plastic, metal, or rubber that is made flat but used wrapped round the plate cylinder of a rotary press. **5** another name for **wrapover.**

wrap up 🅣 *vb* (*adv*) **1** (*tr*) to fold paper around. **2** to put warm clothes on. **3** (*intr; usually imperative*) *Sl.* to be silent. **4** (*tr*) *Inf.* **4a** to settle the final details of. **4b** to make a summary of.

wrasse (ræs) *n* a marine food fish of tropical and temperate seas, having thick lips, strong teeth, and usually a bright coloration. [C17: from Cornish *wrach*]

wrath 🅣 (rɒθ) *n* **1** angry, violent, or stern indignation. **2** divine vengeance or retribution. **3** *Arch.* a fit of anger or an act resulting from anger. [OE *wrǣththu*]

wrathful 🅣 (ˈrɒθfʊl) *adj* **1** full of wrath; raging or furious. **2** resulting from or expressing wrath.
▸**ˈwrathfully** *adv* ▸**ˈwrathfulness** *n*

wreak 🅣 (riːk) *vb* (*tr*) **1** to inflict (vengeance, etc.) or to cause (chaos, etc.): *to wreak havoc on the enemy.* **2** to express or gratify (anger, hatred, etc.). **3** *Arch.* to take vengeance for. [OE *wrecan*]
▸**ˈwreaker** *n*

> **USAGE NOTE** See at **wrought.**

wreath 🅣 (riːθ) *n, pl* **wreaths** (riːðz, riːθs). **1** a band of flowers or foliage intertwined into a ring, usually placed on a grave as a memorial or worn on the head as a garland or a mark of honour. **2** any circular or spiral band or formation. **3** (loosely) any floral design placed on a grave as a memorial. [OE *wrǣth, wrǣd*]
▸**ˈwreath,like** *adj*

wreathe 🅣 (riːð) *vb* **wreathes, wreathing, wreathed. 1** to form into or take the form of a wreath by intertwining or twisting together. **2** (*tr*) to decorate with wreaths. **3** to move or cause to move in a twisting way: *smoke wreathed up to the ceiling.* [C16: ? back formation from *wrēthen,* from OE *writhen,* p.p. of *wrīthan* to writhe]

wreck 🅣 (rɛk) *vb* **1** to involve in or suffer disaster or destruction. **2** (*tr*) to cause the wreck of (a ship). ◆ *n* **3a** the accidental destruction of a ship at sea. **3b** the ship so destroyed. **4** *Maritime law.* goods cast ashore from a wrecked vessel. **5** a person or thing that has suffered ruin or dilapidation. **6** Also called: **wreckage.** the remains of something that has been destroyed. **7** Also called: **wreckage.** the act of wrecking or the state of being wrecked. [C13: from ON]
▸**ˈwrecking** *n, adj*

wrecked (rɛkt) *adj Sl.* in a state of intoxication, stupor, or euphoria, induced by drugs or alcohol.

wrecker (ˈrɛkə) *n* **1** a person or thing that ruins or destroys. **2** *Chiefly US & Canad.* a person whose job is to demolish buildings or dismantle cars. **3** (formerly) a person who lures ships to destruction to plunder the wreckage. **4** a US and Canad. name for a breakdown van.

wrecking bar *n* a short crowbar, forked at one end and slightly angled at the other to make a fulcrum.

wren (rɛn) *n* **1** any small brown passerine songbird of a chiefly American family (in Britain **wren,** in the US and Canada **winter wren**). They have a slender bill and feed on insects. **2** any of various similar birds, such as the Australian warblers, New Zealand wrens, etc. [OE *wrenna, werna*]

Wren (rɛn) *n Inf.* (in Britain and certain other nations) a member of the Women's Royal Naval Service. [C20: from the abbrev. *WRNS*]

THESAURUS

wraith *n* **1** = **ghost,** apparition, eidolon, phantom, revenant, shade (*literary*), spectre, spirit, spook (*inf.*)

wrangle *vb* **1** = **argue,** altercate, bicker, brawl, contend, disagree, dispute, fall out (*inf.*), fight, have words, quarrel, row, scrap, spar, squabble ◆ *n* **4** = **argument,** altercation, angry exchange, argy-bargy (*Brit. inf.*), barney (*inf.*), bickering, brawl, clash, contest, controversy, dispute, falling-out (*inf.*), quarrel, row, set-to (*inf.*), slanging match (*Brit.*), squabble, tiff

wrap *vb* **1-5** = **cover,** absorb, bind, bundle up, cloak, encase, enclose, enfold, envelop, fold, immerse, muffle, pack, package, roll up, sheathe, shroud, surround, swathe, wind ◆ *n* **9** = **cloak,** cape, mantle, shawl, stole
Antonyms *vb* ≠ **cover:** disclose, open, strip, uncover, unfold, unpack, unwind, unwrap

wrapper *n* **1, 2** = **cover,** case, envelope, jacket, packaging, paper, sheath, sleeve, wrapping

wrap up *vb* **1** = **giftwrap,** bundle up, enclose, enwrap, pack, package **2** = **dress warmly,** muffle up, put warm clothes on, wear something warm **3** *Slang* = **be quiet,** be silent, button it (*sl.*), button one's lip (*sl.*), hold one's tongue, shut up **4a** *Informal* = **end,** bring to a close, conclude, finish off, polish off, round off, terminate, tidy up, wind up

wrath *n* **1** = **anger,** choler, displeasure, exasperation, fury, indignation, ire, irritation, passion, rage, resentment, temper
Antonyms *n* amusement, contentment, delight, enjoyment, gladness, gratification, happiness, joy, pleasure, satisfaction

wrathful *adj* **1** = **angry,** beside oneself with rage, choked, displeased, enraged, furious, incandescent, incensed, indignant, infuriated, irate, on the warpath (*inf.*), raging, wroth (*arch.*)
Antonyms *adj* amused, calm, contented, delighted, glad, gratified, happy, joyful, pleased, satisfied

wreak *vb* **1** = **create,** bring about, carry out, cause, effect, execute, exercise, inflict, visit, work **2** = **unleash,** express, give free rein to, give vent to, gratify, indulge, vent

wreath *n* **1** = **garland,** band, chaplet, coronet, crown, festoon, loop, ring

wreathe *vb* **1-3** = **surround,** adorn, coil, crown, encircle, enfold, engarland, entwine, envelop, enwrap, festoon, intertwine, interweave, twine, twist, wind, wrap, writhe

wreck *vb* **1** = **destroy,** blow (*sl.*), break, dash to pieces, demolish, devastate, mar, play havoc with, ravage, ruin, shatter, smash, spoil, total (*sl.*), trash (*sl.*), undo **2** = **go** *or* **run aground,** founder, run onto the rocks, shipwreck, strand ◆ *n* **3b** = **shipwreck,** derelict, hulk, sunken vessel **6** = **remains,** debris, fragments, hulk, pieces, rubble, ruin, wrack, wreckage **7** = **ruin,** desolation, destruction, devastation, disruption, mess, overthrow, undoing, wreckage
Antonyms *vb* ≠ **destroy:** build, conserve, create, fulfil, make possible, preserve, reconstruct, salvage, save ◆ *n* ≠ **ruin:** conservation, creation, formation, fulfilment, preservation, restoration, salvage, saving

wrench ❶ (rɛntʃ) *vb* **1** to give (something) a sudden or violent twist or pull, esp. so as to remove (something) from that to which it is attached: *to wrench a door off its hinges.* **2** (*tr*) to twist suddenly so as to sprain (a limb): *to wrench one's ankle.* **3** (*tr*) to give pain to. **4** (*tr*) to twist from the original meaning or purpose. **5** (*intr*) to make a sudden twisting motion. ◆ *n* **6** a forceful twist or pull. **7** an injury to a limb, caused by twisting. **8** sudden pain caused esp. by parting. **9** a parting that is difficult or painful to make. **10** a distorting of the original meaning or purpose. **11** a spanner, esp. one with adjustable jaws. See also **torque wrench.** [OE *wrencan*]

wrest ❶ (rɛst) *vb* (*tr*) **1** to take or force away by violent pulling or twisting. **2** to seize forcibly by violent or unlawful means. **3** to obtain by laborious effort. **4** to distort in meaning, purpose, etc. ◆ *n* **5** the act or an instance of wresting. **6** *Arch.* a small key used to tune a piano or harp. [OE *wræstan*]
▸ **'wrester** *n*

wrestle ❶ ('rɛsᵊl) *vb* **wrestles, wrestling, wrestled. 1** to fight (another person) by holding, throwing, etc., without punching with the closed fist. **2** (*intr*) to participate in wrestling. **3** (when *intr*, foll. by *with* or *against*) to fight with (a person, problem, or thing): *wrestle with one's conscience.* **4** (*tr*) to move laboriously, as with wrestling movements. ◆ *n* **5** the act of wrestling. **6** a struggle or tussle. [OE *wræstlian*]
▸ **'wrestler** *n*

wrestling ('rɛslɪŋ) *n* any of certain sports in which the contestants fight each other according to various rules governing holds and usually forbidding blows with the closed fist. The principal object is to overcome the opponent either by throwing or pinning him to the ground or by causing him to submit.

wrest pin *n* (on a piano, harp, etc.) a pin, embedded in the **wrest plank,** around which one end of a string is wound: it may be turned by means of a tuning key to alter the tension of the string.

wretch ❶ (rɛtʃ) *n* **1** a despicable person. **2** a person pitied for his misfortune. [OE *wrecca*]

wretched ❶ ('rɛtʃɪd) *adj* **1** in poor or pitiful circumstances. **2** characterized by or causing misery. **3** despicable; base. **4** poor, inferior, or paltry. **5** (*prenominal*) (intensifier qualifying something undesirable): *a wretched nuisance.*
▸ **'wretchedly** *adv* ▸ **'wretchedness** *n*

wrick (rɪk) *n* **1** a sprain or strain. ◆ *vb* **2** (*tr*) to sprain or strain.

wrier *or* **wryer** ('raɪə) *adj* the comparative of **wry.**

wriest *or* **wryest** ('raɪɪst) *adj* the superlative of **wry.**

wriggle ❶ ('rɪgᵊl) *vb* **wriggles, wriggling, wriggled. 1** to make or cause to make twisting movements. **2** (*intr*) to progress by twisting and turning. **3** (*intr;* foll. by *into* or *out of*) to manoeuvre oneself by clever or devious means: *wriggle out of an embarrassing situation.* ◆ *n* **4** a wriggling movement or action. **5** a sinuous marking or course. [C15: from MLow G]
▸ **'wriggler** *n* ▸ **'wriggly** *adj*

wright (raɪt) *n* (*now chiefly in combination*) a person who creates, builds, or repairs something specified: *a playwright; a shipwright.* [OE *wryhta, wyrhta*]

wring ❶ (rɪŋ) *vb* **wrings, wringing, wrung. 1** (often foll. by *out*) to twist and compress to squeeze (a liquid) from (cloth, etc.). **2** (*tr*) to twist forcibly: *wring its neck.* **3** (*tr*) to clasp and twist (one's hands), esp. in anguish. **4** (*tr*) to distress: *wring one's heart.* **5** (*tr*) to grip (someone's hand) vigorously in greeting. **6** (*tr*) to obtain as by forceful means: *wring information out of.* **7 wringing wet.** soaking; drenched. ◆ *n* **8** an act or the process of wringing. [OE *wringan*]

wringer ('rɪŋə) *n* another name for **mangle**[2] (sense 1).

wrinkle[1] ❶ ('rɪŋkᵊl) *n* **1** a slight ridge in the smoothness of a surface, such as a crease in the skin as a result of age. ◆ *vb* **wrinkles, wrinkling, wrinkled. 2** to make or become wrinkled, as by crumpling, creasing, or puckering. [C15: back formation from *wrinkled,* from OE *gewrinclod,* p.p. of *wrinclian* to wind around]
▸ **'wrinkly** *adj*

wrinkle[2] ❶ ('rɪŋkᵊl) *n Inf.* a clever or useful trick, hint, or dodge. [OE *wrenc* trick]

wrinklies ('rɪŋklɪz) *pl n Inf., derog.* old people.

wrist (rɪst) *n* **1** *Anat.* the joint between the forearm and the hand. Technical name: **carpus. 2** the part of a sleeve or glove that covers the wrist. **3** *Machinery.* **3a** See **wrist pin. 3b** a joint in which a wrist pin forms the pivot. [OE]

wristband ('rɪst,bænd) *n* **1** a band around the wrist, esp. one attached to a watch or forming part of a long sleeve. **2** a sweatband around the wrist.

wristlet ('rɪstlɪt) *n* a band or bracelet worn around the wrist.

wrist pin *n* **1** a cylindrical boss or pin attached to the side of a wheel parallel with the axis, esp. one forming a bearing for a crank. **2** the US and Canad. name for **gudgeon pin.**

wristwatch ('rɪst,wɒtʃ) *n* a watch worn strapped around the wrist.

wristy ('rɪstɪ) *adj* (of a player's style of hitting the ball in cricket, tennis, etc.) with much movement of the wrist.

writ ❶ (rɪt) *n* **1** a document under seal, issued in the name of the Crown or a court, commanding the person to whom it is addressed to do or refrain from doing some specified act. **2** *Arch.* a piece of writing: *Holy Writ.* [OE]

write ❶ (raɪt) *vb* **writes, writing, wrote, written. 1** to draw or mark (symbols, words, etc.) on a surface, usually paper, with a pen, pencil, or other instrument. **2** to describe or record (ideas, experiences, etc.) in writing. **3** to compose (a letter) to or correspond regularly with (a person, organization, etc.). **4** (*tr; may take a clause as object*) to say or communicate by letter: *he wrote that he was on his way.* **5** (*tr*) *Inf., chiefly US & Canad.* to send a letter to (a person, etc.). **6** to write (words) in cursive as opposed to printed style. **7** (*tr*) to be sufficiently familiar with (a specified style, language, etc.) to use it in writing. **8** to be the author or composer of (books, music, etc.). **9** (*tr*) to fill in the details for (a document, form, etc.). **10** (*tr*) to draw up or draft. **11** (*tr*) to produce by writing: *he wrote ten pages.* **12** (*tr*) to show clearly: *envy was written all over his face.* **13** (*tr*) to spell or inscribe. **14** (*tr*) to ordain or prophesy: *it is written.* **15** (*intr*) to produce writing as specified. **16** *Computing.* to record (data) in a location in a storage device. **17** (*tr*) See **underwrite** (sense 3a). ◆ See also **write down, write in,** etc. [OE *wrītan* (orig.: to scratch runes into bark)]
▸ **'writable** *adj*

write down *vb* (*adv*) **1** (*tr*) to set down in writing. **2** (*tr*) to harm or belittle by writing about (a person) in derogatory terms. **3** (*intr;* foll. by *to* or *for*) to write in a simplified way (to a supposedly less cultured readership). **4** (*tr*) *Accounting.* to decrease the book value of (an asset). ◆ *n* **write-down. 5** *Accounting.* a reduction made in the book value of an asset.

write in *vb* (*tr*) **1** to insert in (a document, form, etc.) in writing. **2** (*adv*) to write a letter to a company, institution, etc. **3** (*adv*) *US.* to vote for (a person not on a ballot) by inserting his name.

write off ❶ *vb* (*tr, adv*) **1** *Accounting.* **1a** to cancel (a bad debt or obsolete asset) from the accounts. **1b** to consider (a transaction, etc.) as a loss or set off (a loss) against revenues. **1c** to depreciate (an asset) by periodic charges. **1d** to charge (a specified amount) against gross profits as depreciation of an asset. **2** to cause or acknowledge the complete loss of. **3** to dismiss from consideration. **4** to send a written order (for something): *she wrote off for a brochure.* **5** *Inf.* to damage (something, esp. a car) beyond repair. ◆ *n* **write-off. 6** *Accounting.* **6a** the act of cancelling a bad debt or obsolete asset from the accounts. **6b** the bad debt or obsolete asset cancelled. **6c** the amount cancelled against gross profits, corresponding to the book value of the bad debt or obsolete asset. **7** *Inf.* something damaged beyond repair, esp. a car.

write out *vb* (*tr, adv*) **1** to put into writing or reproduce in full form in writing. **2** to exhaust (oneself or one's creativity) by excessive writing. **3** to remove (a character) from a television or radio series.

writer ❶ ('raɪtə) *n* **1** a person who writes books, articles, etc., esp. as an occupation. **2** the person who has written something specified. **3** a person who is able to write or write well. **4** a scribe or clerk. **5** a composer of music. **6 Writer to the Signet.** (in Scotland) a member of an ancient society of solicitors, now having the exclusive privilege of preparing crown writs.

THESAURUS

wrench *vb* **1** = **twist,** force, jerk, pull, rip, tear, tug, wrest, wring, yank **2** = **sprain,** distort, rick, strain ◆ *n* **6** = **twist,** jerk, pull, rip, tug, yank **7** = **sprain,** strain, twist **8** = **blow,** ache, pain, pang, shock, upheaval, uprooting **11** = **spanner,** adjustable spanner, shifting spanner

wrest *vb* **1-3** = **seize,** extract, force, pull, strain, take, twist, win, wrench, wring

wrestle *vb* **1-3** = **fight,** battle, combat, contend, grapple, scuffle, strive, struggle, tussle

wretch *n* **1** = **scoundrel,** bad egg (*old-fashioned inf.*), bastard (*offens.*), blackguard, cur, good-for-nothing, miscreant, outcast, profligate, rascal, rat (*inf.*), rogue, rotter (*sl., chiefly Brit.*), ruffian, swine, vagabond, villain, worm **2** = **poor thing,** poor soul, unfortunate

wretched *adj* **1** = **unhappy,** abject, broken-hearted, cheerless, comfortless, crestfallen, dejected, deplorable, depressed, disconsolate, dismal, distressed, doleful, downcast, forlorn, funereal, gloomy, hapless, hopeless, melancholy, miserable, pathetic, pitiable, pitiful, poor, sorry, unfortunate, woebegone, woeful, worthless **2, 4** = **worthless,** calamitous, deplorable, inferior, miserable, paltry, pathetic, poor, sorry **3** = **shameful,** base, contemptible, despicable, low, low-down (*inf.*), mean, paltry, poxy, scurvy, shabby, vile

Antonyms *adj* ≠ **unhappy:** carefree, cheerful, contented, happy, jovial, light-hearted, untroubled ≠ **worthless:** excellent, flourishing, great, splendid, successful, thriving ≠ **shameful:** admirable, decent, noble, worthy

wriggle *vb* **1** = **twist,** jerk, jiggle, squirm, turn, wag, waggle, wiggle, writhe **2** = **crawl,** slink, snake, twist and turn, worm, zigzag **3** = **manoeuvre,** crawl, dodge, extricate oneself, sneak, talk one's way out, worm ◆ *n* **4** = **twist,** jerk, jiggle, squirm, turn, wag, waggle, wiggle

wring *vb* **1, 6** = **twist,** coerce, extort, extract, force, screw, squeeze, wrench, wrest

wrinkle[1] *n* **1** = **crease,** corrugation, crinkle, crow's-foot, crumple, fold, furrow, gather, line, pucker, rumple ◆ *vb* **2** = **crease,** corrugate, crinkle, crumple, fold, furrow, gather, line, pucker, ruck, rumple

Antonyms *vb* ≠ **crease:** even out, flatten, iron, level, press, smooth, straighten, unfold

wrinkle[2] *n Informal* = **trick,** device, dodge, gimmick, idea, plan, ploy, ruse, scheme, stunt, tip, wheeze (*Brit. sl.*)

writ *n* **1** = **summons,** court order, decree, document

write *vb* **1, 8, 10** = **record,** author (*nonstandard*), commit to paper, compose, copy, correspond, create, draft, draw up, indite, inscribe, jot down, pen, put down in black and white, put in writing, scribble, set down, take down, tell, transcribe

write off *vb* **1, 2** = **cancel,** cross out, disregard, forget about, give up for lost, score out, shelve **5** *Informal* = **wreck,** crash, damage beyond repair, destroy, smash up, total (*sl.*), trash (*sl.*)

writer *n* **1** = **author,** columnist, essayist, hack, littérateur, man of letters, novelist, penman, penny-a-liner (*rare*), penpusher, scribbler, scribe, wordsmith

writer's cramp *n* a muscular spasm or temporary paralysis of the muscles of the thumb and first two fingers caused by prolonged writing.

write up *vb (tr, adv)* **1** to describe fully, complete, or bring up to date in writing: *write up a diary.* **2** to praise or bring to public notice in writing. **3** *Accounting.* **3a** to place an excessively high value on (an asset). **3b** to increase the book value of (an asset) in order to reflect more accurately its current worth in the market. ◆ *n* **write-up. 4** a published account of something, such as a review in a newspaper or magazine.

writhe ❶ (raɪð) *vb* **writhes, writhing, writhed. 1** to twist or squirm in or as if in pain. **2** *(intr)* to move with such motions. **3** *(intr)* to suffer acutely from embarrassment, revulsion, etc. ◆ *n* **4** the act of writhing. [OE *writhan*]
▸'**writher** *n*

writing ❶ ('raɪtɪŋ) *n* **1** a group of letters or symbols written or marked on a surface as a means of communicating. **2** short for **handwriting. 3** anything expressed in letters, esp. a literary composition. **4** the work of a writer. **5** literary style, art, or practice. **6** written form: *give it to me in writing.* **7** *(modifier)* related to or used in writing: *writing ink.* **8 writing on the wall.** a sign or signs of approaching disaster. [sense 8: allusion to Daniel 5:5]

writing desk *n* a piece of furniture with a writing surface and drawers and compartments for papers, etc.

writing paper *n* paper sized to take writing ink and used for letters and other manuscripts.

writ of execution *n Law.* a writ ordering that a judgment be enforced.

written ('rɪtᵊn) *vb* **1** the past participle of **write.** ◆ *adj* **2** taken down in writing; transcribed: *written evidence.*

WRNS *abbrev. for* Women's Royal Naval Service. See also **Wren.**

wrong ❶ (rɒŋ) *adj* **1** not correct or truthful: *the wrong answer.* **2** acting or judging in error: *you are wrong to think that.* **3** *(postpositive)* immoral; bad: *it is wrong to cheat.* **4** deviating from or unacceptable to correct or conventional laws, usage, etc. **5** not intended or wanted: *the wrong road.* **6** *(postpositive)* not working properly; amiss: *something is wrong with the engine.* **7** (of a side, esp. of a fabric) intended to face the inside so as not to be seen. **8 get on the wrong side of.** *Inf.* to come into disfavour with. **9 go down the wrong way.** (of food) to pass into the windpipe instead of the gullet. ◆ *adv* **10** in the wrong direction or manner. **11 get wrong. 11a** to fail to understand properly. **11b** to fail to provide the correct answer to. **12 go wrong. 12a** to turn out other than intended. **12b** to make a mistake. **12c** (of a machine, etc.) to cease to function properly. **12d** to go astray morally. ◆ *n* **13** a bad, immoral, or unjust thing or action. **14** *Law.* **14a** an infringement of another person's rights, rendering the offender liable to a civil action: *a private wrong.* **14b** a violation of public rights and duties, affecting the community as a whole and actionable at the instance of the Crown: *a public wrong.* **15 in the wrong.** mistaken or guilty. ◆ *vb (tr)* **16** to treat unjustly. **17** to malign or misrepresent. [OE *wrang* injustice]
▸'**wronger** *n* ▸'**wrongly** *adv* ▸'**wrongness** *n*

wrongdoer ❶ ('rɒŋˌduːə) *n* a person who acts immorally or illegally.
▸'**wrongˌdoing** *n*

wrong-foot *vb (tr)* **1** *Tennis, etc.* to play a shot in such a way as to cause (one's opponent) to be off balance. **2** to take by surprise so as to place in an embarrassing or disadvantageous situation.

wrongful ❶ ('rɒŋful) *adj* unjust or illegal.
▸'**wrongfully** *adv* ▸'**wrongfulness** *n*

wrong-headed ❶ *adj* **1** constantly wrong in judgment. **2** foolishly stubborn; obstinate.
▸ˌ**wrong-'headedly** *adv* ▸ˌ**wrong-'headedness** *n*

wrong number *n* a telephone number wrongly connected or dialled in error, or the person so contacted.

wrote (rəʊt) *vb* the past tense of **write.**

wroth (rəʊθ, rɒθ) *adj Arch. or literary.* angry; irate. [OE *wrāth*]

wrought (rɔːt) *vb* **1** *Arch.* a past tense and past participle of **work.** ◆ *adj* **2** *Metallurgy.* shaped by hammering or beating. **3** *(often in combination)* formed, fashioned, or worked as specified: *well-wrought.* **4** decorated or made with delicate care. [C16: var. of *worht,* from OE *geworht,* p.p. of *(ge)wyrcan* to work]

> **USAGE NOTE** *Wrought* is sometimes used as if it were the past tense and past participle of *wreak* as in *the hurricane wrought havoc in coastal areas.* Many people think this use is incorrect.

wrought iron *n* **a** a pure form of iron having a low carbon content: often used for decorative work. **b** *(as modifier): wrought-iron gates.*

wrought-up ❶ *adj* agitated or excited.

wrung (rʌŋ) *vb* the past tense and past participle of **wring.**

WRVS *abbrev. for* Women's Royal Voluntary Service.

wry ❶ (raɪ) *adj* **wrier, wriest** *or* **wryer, wryest. 1** twisted, contorted, or askew. **2** (of a facial expression) produced or characterized by contorting of the features. **3** drily humorous; sardonic. **4** warped, misdirected, or perverse. ◆ *vb* **wries, wrying, wried. 5** *(tr)* to twist or contort. [C16: from dialect *wry* to twist, from OE *wrīgian* to turn]
▸'**wryly** *adv* ▸'**wryness** *n*

wrybill ('raɪˌbɪl) *n* a New Zealand plover, having its bill deflected to one side enabling it to search for food beneath stones.

wryneck ('raɪˌnɛk) *n* **1** either of two cryptically coloured Old World woodpeckers, which do not drum on trees. **2** another name for **torticollis. 3** *Inf.* a person who has a twisted neck.

WSW *symbol for* west-southwest.

wt. *abbrev. for* weight.

WTO *abbrev. for* World Trade Organization.

wunderkind ('wʌndəˌkɪnd; *German* 'vʊndərˌkɪnt) *n, pl* **wunderkinds** *or* **wunderkinder** (*German* -ˌkɪndər) **1** a child prodigy. **2** a person who is extremely successful in his field while still young. [C20: from G *Wunderkind,* lit.: wonder child]

wurst (wɜːst, wʊəst, vʊəst) *n* a sausage, esp. of a type made in Germany, Austria, etc. [from G *Wurst,* lit.: something rolled]

wuthering ('wʌðərɪŋ) *adj N English dialect.* **1** (of a wind) blowing strongly with a roaring sound. **2** (of a place) characterized by such a sound. [var. of *whitherin,* from *whither* blow, from ON *hvithra*]

wuss (wʊs) *or* **wussy** ('wʊsɪ) *n, pl* **wusses** *or* **wussies.** *Sl., chiefly US.* a feeble or effeminate person. [C20: ?from PUSSY[1] (cat)]

WW1 *abbrev. for* World War One.

WW2 *abbrev. for* World War Two.

WWW *abbrev. for* World Wide Web.

wych-elm *or* **witch-elm** ('wɪtʃˌɛlm) *n* **1** a Eurasian elm tree, having a rounded shape, longish pointed leaves, clusters of small flowers, and winged fruits. **2** the wood of this tree. [C17: from OE *wice*]

wynd (waɪnd) *n Scot.* a narrow lane or alley. [C15: from the stem of WIND[2]]

WYSIWYG ('wɪzɪˌwɪg) *n, adj Computing. acronym for* what you see is what you get: referring to what is displayed on the screen being the same as what will be printed out.

wyvern *or* **wivern** ('waɪvən) *n* a heraldic beast having a serpent's tail and a dragon's head and a body with wings and two legs. [C17: var. of earlier *wyver,* from OF, from L *vīpera* VIPER]

THESAURUS

writhe *vb* **1 = squirm,** contort, convulse, distort, jerk, struggle, thrash, thresh, toss, twist, wiggle, wriggle

writing *n* **2 = script,** calligraphy, chirography, hand, handwriting, penmanship, print, scrawl, scribble **3 = document,** book, composition, letter, opus, publication, title, work **5 = literature,** belles-lettres, letters

wrong *adj* **1 = incorrect,** erroneous, fallacious, false, faulty, inaccurate, in error, mistaken, off base (*US & Canad. inf.*), off beam (*inf.*), off target, out, unsound, untrue, way off beam (*inf.*), wide of the mark **3 = bad,** blameworthy, criminal, crooked, dishonest, dishonourable, evil, felonious, illegal, illicit, immoral, iniquitous, not cricket (*inf.*), reprehensible, sinful, under-the-table, unethical, unfair, unjust, unlawful, wicked, wrongful **4 = inappropriate,** funny, improper, inapt, incongruous, incorrect, indecorous, infelicitous, malapropos, not done, unacceptable, unbecoming, unconventional, undesirable, unfitting, unhappy, unseemly, unsuitable **6 = defective,** amiss, askew, awry, faulty, not working, out of commission, out of order **7 = opposite,** inside, inverse, reverse ◆ *adv* **10 = incorrectly,** badly, erroneously, inaccurately, mistakenly, wrongly **10 = amiss,** askew, astray, awry **12 go wrong: a = lapse,** come to grief, come to nothing, fall through, flop (*inf.*), go pear-shaped (*inf.*), miscarry, misfire **b = err,** boob (*Brit. sl.*), go astray, slip up (*inf.*) **c = cease to function,** conk out (*inf.*), fail, go kaput (*inf.*), go on the blink (*sl.*), malfunction, misfire **d = go astray,** err, fall from grace, go off the straight and narrow (*inf.*), go to the bad, sin ◆ *n* **13 = offence,** abuse, bad *or* evil deed, crime, error, grievance, infraction, infringement, injury, injustice, misdeed, sin, transgression, trespass **15 in the wrong = guilty,** at fault, blameworthy, in error, mistaken, off beam (*inf.*), off course, off target, to be blamed ◆ *vb* **16, 17 = mistreat,** abuse, cheat, discredit, dishonour, harm, hurt, ill-treat, ill-use, impose upon, injure, malign, maltreat, misrepresent, oppress, take advantage of
Antonyms *adj* ≠ **incorrect:** accurate, correct, precise, right, true ≠ **bad:** ethical, fair, fitting, godly, honest, honourable, just, lawful, legal, moral, righteous, rightful, square, upright, virtuous ≠ **inappropriate:** appropriate, apt, becoming, commendable, correct, fitting, laudable, praiseworthy, proper, seemly, sensible, suitable ◆ *adv* ≠ **incorrectly:** accurately, correctly, exactly, precisely, properly, squarely, truly ◆ *n* ≠ **offence:** favour, good deed, good turn ◆ *vb* ≠ **mistreat:** aid, do a favour, help, support, treat well

wrongdoer *n* **= offender,** criminal, culprit, delinquent, evildoer, lawbreaker, malefactor, miscreant, sinner, transgressor, trespasser (*arch.*), villain

wrongful *adj* **= improper,** blameworthy, criminal, dishonest, dishonourable, evil, felonious, illegal, illegitimate, illicit, immoral, reprehensible, unethical, unfair, unjust, unlawful, wicked
Antonyms *adj* ethical, fair, honest, honourable, just, lawful, legal, legitimate, moral, proper, rightful

wrong-headed *adj* **1 = mistaken,** erroneous, fallacious, false, faulty, incorrect, in error, misguided, off target, unsound, wrong **2 = obstinate,** bull-headed, contrary, cross-grained, dogged, froward (*arch.*), inflexible, intransigent, mulish, obdurate, perverse, pig-headed, refractory, self-willed, stubborn, wilful

wrought-up *adj* **= worked-up,** agitated, animated, aroused, at fever pitch, beside oneself, excited, inflamed, keyed up, moved, overwrought, roused, stirred, strung up (*inf.*)

wry *adj* **1 = contorted,** askew, aslant, awry, crooked, deformed, distorted, off the level, skewwhiff (*Brit. inf.*), twisted, uneven, warped **3 = ironic,** droll, dry, mocking, mordacious, pawky (*Scot.*), sarcastic, sardonic
Antonyms *adj* ≠ **contorted:** aligned, even, level, smooth, straight, unbent

x *or* **X** (ɛks) *n, pl* **x's, X's,** *or* **Xs. 1** the 24th letter of the English alphabet. **2** a speech sound sequence represented by this letter, pronounced as *ks* or *gz* or, in initial position, *z*, as in *xylophone.*

x *symbol for:* **1** *Commerce, finance, etc.* ex. **2** *Maths.* the *x*-axis or a coordinate measured along the *x*-axis in a Cartesian coordinate system. **3** *Maths.* an algebraic variable. **4** multiplication.

X *symbol:* **1a** (in Britain, formerly) indicating a film that may not be publicly shown to anyone under 18. Since 1982 replaced by symbol 18. **1b** (*as modifier*): *an X film.* **2** denoting any unknown, unspecified, or variable factor, number, person, or thing. **3** (on letters, cards, etc.) denoting a kiss. **4** (on ballot papers, etc.) indicating choice. **5** (on examination papers, etc.) indicating error. **6** for Christ; Christian. [from the Gk letter khi (X), first letter of *Khristos* Christ] **7** *the Roman numeral for* ten. See **Roman numerals.**

xanthein ('zænθɪɪn) *n* the soluble part of the yellow pigment that is found in the cell sap of some flowers.

xanthene ('zænθiːn) *n* a yellowish crystalline compound used as a fungicide.

xanthic ('zænθɪk) *adj* **1** of, containing, or derived from xanthic acid. **2** *Bot., rare.* having a yellow colour.

xanthic acid *n* any of a class of sulphur-containing acids.

xanthine ('zænθiːn, -θaɪn) *n* **1** a crystalline compound found in urine, blood, certain plants, and certain animal tissues. Formula: $C_5H_4N_4O_2$. **2** any of three substituted derivatives of xanthine, which act as stimulants and diuretics.

Xanthippe (zæn'θɪpɪ) *or* **Xantippe** (zæn'tɪpɪ) *n* **1** the wife of Socrates (?470–399 BC) Greek philosopher, proverbial as scolding and quarrelsome. **2** any nagging, peevish, or irritable woman.

xantho- *or before a vowel* **xanth-** *combining form.* indicating yellow: *xanthophyll.* [from Gk *xanthos* yellow]

xanthochroism (zæn'θɒkrəʊˌɪzəm) *n* a condition in certain animals, esp. aquarium goldfish, in which all skin pigments other than yellow and orange disappear. [C19: from Gk *xanthokhro(os)* yellow-skinned + -ISM]

xanthoma (zæn'θəʊmə) *n Pathol.* the presence in the skin of fatty yellow or brownish plaques or nodules, esp. on the eyelids, caused by a disorder of lipid metabolism.

xanthophyll *or esp. US* **xanthophyl** ('zænθəʊfɪl) *n* any of a group of yellow carotenoid pigments occurring in plant and animal tissue.
▸ˌ**xantho'phyllous** *adj*

xanthous ('zænθəs) *adj* of, relating to, or designating races with yellowish hair and a light complexion.

***x*-axis** *n* a reference axis, usually horizontal, of a graph or two- or three-dimensional Cartesian coordinate system along which the *x*-coordinate is measured.

X-chromosome *n* the sex chromosome that occurs in pairs in the diploid cells of the females of many animals, including humans, and as one of a pair with the Y-chromosome in those of males. Cf. **Y-chromosome.**

Xe *the chemical symbol for* xenon.

xebec, zebec, *or* **zebeck** ('ziːbɛk) *n* a small three-masted Mediterranean vessel with both square and lateen sails, formerly used by Algerian pirates and later used for commerce. [C18: earlier *chebec* from F, ult. from Ar. *shabbāk;* present spelling infl. by Catalan *xabec,* Sp. *xabeque* (now *jabeque*)]

xeno- *or before a vowel* **xen-** *combining form.* indicating something strange, different, or foreign: *xenogamy.* [from Gk *xenos* strange]

xenogamy (zɛ'nɒgəmɪ) *n Bot.* another name for **cross-fertilization.**
▸**xe'nogamous** *adj*

xenogeneic (ˌzɛnəʊdʒɪ'neɪɪk) *adj Med.* derived from an individual of a different species: *a xenogeneic tissue graft.*

xenoglossia (ˌzɛnə'glɒsɪə) *n* an ability claimed by some mediums, clairvoyants, etc., to speak a language with which they are unfamiliar. [C20: from Gk, from XENO- + *glossa* language]

xenolith ('zɛnəlɪθ) *n* a fragment of rock differing in origin, composition, structure, etc., from the igneous rock enclosing it.
▸ˌ**xeno'lithic** *adj*

xenon ('zɛnɒn) *n* a colourless odourless gaseous element occurring in trace amounts in air; formerly considered inert, it is now known to form compounds and is used in radio valves, stroboscopic and bactericidal lamps, and bubble chambers. Symbol: Xe; atomic no.: 54; atomic wt.: 131.30. [C19: from Gk: something strange]

xenophile ('zɛnəˌfaɪl) *n* a person who likes foreigners or things foreign. [C19: from Gk, from XENO- + -PHILE]

xenophobia (ˌzɛnə'fəʊbɪə) *n* hatred or fear of foreigners or strangers or of their politics or culture. [C20: from Gk, from XENO- + -PHOBIA]
▸'**xenoˌphobe** *n* ▸ˌ**xeno'phobic** *adj*

xeric ('zɪərɪk) *adj Ecology.* of, relating to, or growing in dry conditions.
▸'**xerically** *adv*

xero- *or before a vowel* **xer-** *combining form.* indicating dryness: *xeroderma.* [from Gk *xēros* dry]

xeroderma (ˌzɪərəʊ'dɜːmə) *or* **xerodermia** (ˌzɪərəʊ'dɜːmɪə) *n Pathol.* **1** any abnormal dryness of the skin as the result of diminished secretions from the sweat or sebaceous glands. **2** another name for **ichthyosis.**
▸**xerodermatic** (ˌzɪərəʊdə'mætɪk) *or* ˌ**xero'dermatous** *adj*

xerography (zɪ'rɒgrəfɪ) *n* a photocopying process in which an electrostatic image is formed on a selenium plate or cylinder. The plate or cylinder is dusted with a resinous powder, which adheres to the charged regions, and the image is then transferred to a sheet of paper on which it is fixed by heating.
▸**xe'rographer** *n* ▸**xerographic** (ˌzɪərə'græfɪk) *adj* ▸ˌ**xero'graphically** *adv*

xerophilous (zɪ'rɒfɪləs) *adj* (of plants or animals) adapted for growing or living in dry surroundings.
▸**xerophile** ('zɪərəʊˌfaɪl) *n* ▸**xe'rophily** *n*

xerophthalmia (ˌzɪərɒf'θælmɪə) *n Pathol.* excessive dryness of the cornea and conjunctiva, caused by a deficiency of vitamin A. Also called: **xeroma** (zɪ'rəʊmə).
▸ˌ**xeroph'thalmic** *adj*

xerophyte ('zɪərəˌfaɪt) *n* a xerophilous plant, such as a cactus.
▸**xerophytic** (ˌzɪərə'fɪtɪk) *adj* ▸ˌ**xero'phytically** *adv* ▸'**xeroˌphytism** *n*

Xerox ('zɪərɒks) *n* **1** *Trademark.* **1a** a xerographic copying process. **1b** a machine employing this process. **1c** a copy produced by this process. ◆ *vb* **2** to produce a copy of (a document, illustration, etc.) by this process.

Xhosa ('kɔːsə) *n* **1** (*pl* **Xhosa** *or* **Xhosas**) a member of a cattle-rearing Negroid people of southern Africa, living chiefly in W South Africa. **2** the language of this people, belonging to the Bantu group and characterized by several clicks in its sound system.
▸'**Xhosan** *adj*

xi (zaɪ, saɪ, ksaɪ, ksiː) *n, pl* **xis.** the 14th letter in the Greek alphabet (Ξ, ξ).

xiphisternum (ˌzɪfɪ'stɜːnəm) *n, pl* **xiphisterna** (-nə). *Anat., zool.* the cartilaginous process forming the lowermost part of the breastbone (sternum). Also called: **xiphoid, xiphoid process.** [C19: from Gk *xiphos* sword + STERNUM]

xiphoid ('zɪfɔɪd) *adj* **1** *Biol.* shaped like a sword. **2** of or relating to the xiphisternum. ◆ *n* **3** Also called: **xiphoid process.** another name for **xiphisternum.** [C18: from NL, from Gk, from *xiphos* sword + *eidos* form]

Xmas ❶ ('ɛksməs, 'krɪsməs) *n Inf.* short for **Christmas.** [C18: from symbol X for Christ + -MAS]

X-ray ❶ *or* **x-ray** *n* **1a** electromagnetic radiation emitted when matter is bombarded with fast electrons. X-rays have wavelengths shorter than that of ultraviolet radiation, that is less than about 1×10^{-8} metres. Below about 1×10^{-11} metres they are often called gamma radiation or bremsstrahlung. **1b** (*as modifier*): *X-ray astronomy.* **2** a picture produced by exposing photographic film to X-rays: used in medicine as a diagnostic aid as parts of the body, such as bones, absorb X-rays and so appear as opaque areas on the picture. ◆ *vb* (*tr*) **3** to photograph (part of the body, etc.) using X-rays. **4** to treat or examine by means of X-rays. [C19: partial translation of G *X-Strahlen* (from *Strahl* ray), coined by W. K. Roentgen, G physicist who discovered it in 1895]

X-ray astronomy *n* the branch of astronomy concerned with the detection and measurement of X-rays emitted by certain celestial bodies, such as X-ray stars.

X-ray binary *n* a binary star that is an intense source of X-rays and is composed of a normal star in close orbit with a white dwarf, neutron star, or black hole.

X-ray crystallography *n* the study and practice of determining the structure of a crystal by passing a beam of X-rays through it and observing and analysing the diffraction pattern produced.

X-ray tube *n* an evacuated tube containing a metal target onto which is directed a beam of electrons at high energy for the generation of X-rays.

xylem ('zaɪləm, -lɛm) *n* a plant tissue that conducts water and mineral salts from the roots to all other parts, provides mechanical support, and forms the wood of trees and shrubs. [C19: from Gk *xulon* wood]

xylene ('zaɪliːn) *n* an aromatic hydrocarbon existing in three isomeric forms, all three being colourless flammable volatile liquids used as solvents and in the manufacture of synthetic resins, dyes, and insecticides. Formula: $(CH_3)_2C_6H_4$. Systematic name: **dimethyl benzene.**

THESAURUS

Xmas *n* = **Christmas,** Christmastide, festive season, Noel, Yule (*arch.*), Yuletide (*arch.*)

X-ray *n* = **Röntgen ray** (*old name*)

xylo- *or before a vowel* **xyl-** *combining form.* **1** indicating wood: *xylophone.* **2** indicating xylene: *xylidine.* [from Gk *xulon* wood]

xylocarp ('zaɪləˌkɑːp) *n Bot.* a fruit, such as a coconut, having a hard woody pericarp.
▸ˌ**xylo'carpous** *adj*

xylograph ('zaɪləˌgrɑːf) *n* **1** an engraving in wood. **2** a print taken from a wood block. ◆ *vb* **3** (*tr*) to print (a design, illustration, etc.) from a wood engraving.
▸**xylography** (zaɪ'lɒgrəfɪ) *n*

Xylonite ('zaɪlənaɪt) *n Trademark.* a thermoplastic of the cellulose nitrate type.

xylophagous (zaɪ'lɒfəgəs) *adj* (of certain insects, crustaceans, etc.) feeding on or living within wood.

xylophone ('zaɪləˌfəʊn) *n Music.* a percussion instrument consisting of a set of wooden bars of graduated length. It is played with hard-headed hammers.
▸**xylophonic** (ˌzaɪlə'fɒnɪk) *adj* ▸**xylophonist** (zaɪ'lɒfənɪst) *n*

xylose ('zaɪləuz, -ləus) *n* a white crystalline sugar found in wood and straw. It is extracted by hydrolysis with acids and used in dyeing, tanning, and in foods for diabetics.

xyster ('zɪstə) *n* a surgical instrument for scraping bone; surgical rasp or file. [C17: via NL from Gk: tool for scraping, from *xuein* to scrape]

y *or* **Y** (waɪ) *n, pl* **y's, Y's,** *or* **Ys. 1** the 25th letter of the English alphabet. **2** a speech sound represented by this letter, usually a semivowel, as in *yawn*, or a vowel, as in *symbol* or *shy*. **3** something shaped like a Y.

y *Maths. symbol for:* **1** the *y*-axis or a coordinate measured along the *y*-axis in a Cartesian coordinate system. **2** an algebraic variable.

Y *symbol for:* **1** any unknown or variable factor, number, or thing. **2** *Chem.* yttrium.

y. *abbrev. for* year.

-y[1] *or* **-ey** *suffix forming adjectives.* **1** (*from nouns*) characterized by; consisting of; filled with; resembling: *sunny; sandy; smoky; classy.* **2** (*from verbs*) tending to; acting or existing as specified: *leaky; shiny.* [from OE *-ig, -ǣg*]

-y[2], **-ie,** *or* **-ey** *suffix of nouns. Inf.* **1** denoting smallness and expressing affection and familiarity: *a doggy; Jamie.* **2** a person or thing concerned with or characterized by being: *a groupie; a goalie; a fatty.* [C14: from Scot. *-ie, -y*, familiar suffix orig. in names]

-y[3] *suffix forming nouns.* **1** (*from verbs*) indicating the act of doing what is indicated by the verbal element: *inquiry.* **2** (*esp. with combining forms of Greek, Latin, or French origin*) indicating state, condition, or quality: *geography; jealousy.* [from OF *-ie*, from L *-ia*]

Y2K *n Inf.* another name for the year 2000 A.D. (esp. referring to the millennium bug). [C20: Y(EAR) + 2 + K (in the sense: thousand)]

yabby *or* **yabbie** (ˈjæbɪ) *Austral.* ◆ *n, pl* **yabbies. 1** a small edible freshwater crayfish. **2** a saltwater prawn used as bait; nipper. ◆ *vb* **yabbies, yabbying, yabbied. 3** (*intr*) to fish for yabbies. [from Abor.]

yacht (jɒt) *n* **1** a vessel propelled by sail or power, used esp. for pleasure cruising, racing, etc. ◆ *vb* **2** (*intr*) to sail or cruise in a yacht. [C16: from obs. Du. *jaghte*, short for *jahtschip*, from *jagen* to chase + *schip* ship]

▸ˈ**yachting** *n, adj*

yachtie (ˈjɒtɪ) *n Austral. & NZ inf.* a yachtsman; sailing enthusiast.

yachtsman (ˈjɒtsmən) *or* (*fem*) **yachtswoman** *n, pl* **yachtsmen** *or* **yachtswomen.** a person who sails a yacht or yachts.

▸ˈ**yachtsmanship** *n*

yack (jæk) *n, vb* a variant spelling of **yak**[2].

yackety-yak (ˈjækɪtɪˈjæk) *n Sl.* noisy, continuous, and trivial talk or conversation. [imit.]

yaffle (ˈjæfᵊl) *n* another name for **green woodpecker** (see **woodpecker**). [C18: imit. of its cry]

Yagi aerial (ˈjɑːgɪ, ˈjægɪ) *n* a directional aerial, used esp. in television and radio astronomy, consisting of three or more elements lying parallel to each other, the principal direction of radiation being along the line of the centres. [C20: after Hidetsugu *Yagi* (1886–1976), Japanese engineer]

yah (jɑː, jeə) *sentence substitute.* **1** an informal word for **yes.** ◆ *interj* **2** an exclamation of derision or disgust.

yahoo 🅣 (jəˈhuː) *n, pl* **yahoos.** a crude, brutish, or obscenely coarse person. [C18: from a race of brutish creatures resembling men in Jonathan Swift's *Gulliver's Travels* (1726)]

▸**yaˈhoo,ism** *n*

Yahweh (ˈjɑːweɪ) *or* **Yahveh** (ˈjɑːveɪ) *n Old Testament.* a vocalization of the Tetragrammaton. [from Heb., from YHVH, with conjectural vowels; see also JEHOVAH]

Yahwism (ˈjɑːwɪzəm) *or* **Yahvism** (ˈjɑːvɪzəm) *n* the use of the name Yahweh, esp. in parts of the Old Testament, as the personal name of God.

Yahwist (ˈjɑːwɪst) *or* **Yahvist** (ˈjɑːvɪst) *n Bible.* **the.** the conjectured author or authors of the earliest sources of the Pentateuch in which God is called *Yahweh* throughout.

▸**Yahˈwistic** *or* **Yahˈvistic** *adj*

yak[1] (jæk) *n* an ox of Tibet having long shaggy hair. [C19: from Tibetan *gyag*]

yak[2] 🅣 (jæk) *Sl.* ◆ *n* **1** noisy, continuous, and trivial talk. ◆ *vb* **yaks, yakking, yakked. 2** (*intr*) to chatter or talk in this way. [C20: imit.]

yakka, yakker, *or* **yacker** (ˈjækə) *n Austral. & NZ inf.* work. [C19: from Abor.]

Yale lock (jeɪl) *n Trademark.* a type of cylinder lock using a flat serrated key. [C19: after L. *Yale* (1821–68), US inventor]

yam (jæm) *n* **1** any of various twining plants of tropical and subtropical regions, cultivated for their edible tubers. **2** the starchy tuber of any of these plants, eaten as a vegetable. **3** *Southern US.* the sweet potato. [C17: from Port. *inhame*, ult. of W African origin]

yammer (ˈjæmə) *Inf.* ◆ *vb* **1** to utter or whine in a complaining manner. **2** to make (a complaint) loudly or persistently. ◆ *n* **3** a yammering sound. **4** nonsense; jabber. [OE *geōmrian* to grumble]

▸ˈ**yammerer** *n*

Yang (jæŋ) *n* See **Yin and Yang.**

yank 🅣 (jæŋk) *vb* **1** to pull with a sharp movement; tug. ◆ *n* **2** a jerk. [C19: from ?]

Yank (jæŋk) *n* **1** a slang word for an **American. 2** *US inf.* short for **Yankee.**

Yankee (ˈjæŋkɪ) *or* (*inf.*) **Yank** *n* **1** *Often disparaging.* a native or inhabitant of the US; American. **2** a native or inhabitant of New England. **3** a native or inhabitant of the Northern US, esp. a Northern soldier in the Civil War. **4** *Finance.* a bond issued in the US by a foreign borrower. ◆ *adj* **5** of, relating to, or characteristic of Yankees. [C18: ?from Du. *Jan Kees* John Cheese, derisive nickname of Du. settlers for English colonists in Connecticut]

Yankee Doodle *n* **1** an American song, popularly regarded as a characteristically national melody. **2** another name for **Yankee.**

yap 🅣 (jæp) *vb* **yaps, yapping, yapped.** (*intr*) **1** (of a dog) to bark in quick sharp bursts; yelp. **2** *Inf.* to talk at length in an annoying or stupid way; jabber. ◆ *n* **3** a high-pitched or sharp bark; yelp. **4** *Sl.* annoying or stupid speech; jabber. **5** *Sl., chiefly US.* a derogatory word for **mouth.** [C17: imit.]

▸ˈ**yapper** *n* ▸ˈ**yappy** *adj*

yapok (jəˈpɒk) *n* an amphibious nocturnal opossum of Central and South America. Also called: **water opossum.** [C19: after *Oyapok*, a river flowing between French Guiana & Brazil]

yarborough (ˈjɑːbərə, -brə) *n Bridge, whist.* a hand of 13 cards in which no card is higher than nine. [C19: supposedly after the second Earl of *Yarborough* (d. 1897), said to have bet a thousand to one against its occurrence]

yard[1] (jɑːd) *n* **1** a unit of length equal to 3 feet and defined in 1963 as exactly 0.9144 metre. **2** a cylindrical wooden or hollow metal spar, slung from a mast of a vessel, and used for suspending a sail. [OE *gierd* rod, twig]

yard[2] (jɑːd) *n* **1** a piece of enclosed ground, often adjoining or surrounded by a building or buildings. **2a** an enclosed or open area used for some commercial activity, for storage, etc.: *a builder's yard.* **2b** (*in combination*): *a shipyard.* **3** a US and Canad. word for **garden** (sense 1). **4** an area having a network of railway tracks and sidings, used for storing rolling stock, making up trains, etc. **5** *US & Canad.* the winter pasture of deer, moose, and similar animals. **6** *NZ.* short for **stockyard.** [OE *geard*]

Yard (jɑːd) *n* **the.** *Brit. inf.* short for **Scotland Yard.**

yardage[1] (ˈjɑːdɪdʒ) *n* a length measured in yards.

yardage[2] (ˈjɑːdɪdʒ) *n* **1** the use of a railway yard for cattle. **2** the charge for this.

yardarm (ˈjɑːdˌɑːm) *n Naut.* the two tapering outer ends of a ship's yard.

yard grass *n* an Old World perennial grass with prostrate leaves, growing as a troublesome weed on open ground, yards, etc.

Yardie (ˈjɑːdɪ) *n* a member of a Black criminal syndicate originally based in Jamaica. [origin unknown]

yard of ale *n* **1** the beer or ale contained in a narrow horn-shaped drinking glass. **2** such a drinking glass itself.

yardstick 🅣 (ˈjɑːdˌstɪk) *n* **1** a measure or standard used for comparison. **2** a graduated stick, one yard long, used for measurement.

yarmulke (ˈjɑːməlkə) *n Judaism.* a skullcap worn by Orthodox male Jews at all times and by others during prayer. [from Yiddish, from Ukrainian & Polish *yarmulka* cap, prob. from Turkish *yağmurluk* raincoat, from *yağmur* rain]

yarn 🅣 (jɑːn) *n* **1** a continuous twisted strand of natural or synthetic fibres, used in weaving, knitting, etc. **2** *Inf.* a long and often involved story, usually of incredible or fantastic events. **3 spin a yarn.** *Inf.* **3a** to tell such a story. **3b** to make up a series of excuses. ◆ *vb* **4** (*intr*) to tell such a story or stories. [OE *gearn*]

yarn-dyed *adj* (of fabric) dyed while still in yarn form, before being woven.

yarran (ˈjærən) *n* a small hardy tree of inland Australia: useful as fodder and for firewood. [from Abor.]

yarrow (ˈjærəʊ) *n* any of several plants of the composite family of Eurasia, having finely dissected leaves and flat clusters of white flower heads. Also called: **milfoil.** [OE *gearwe*]

yashmak *or* **yashmac** (ˈjæʃmæk) *n* the face veil worn by Muslim women when in public. [C19: from Ar.]

THESAURUS

yahoo *n* = **philistine**, barbarian, beast, boor, brute, churl, lout, roughneck (*sl.*), rowdy, savage, yob *or* yobbo (*Brit. sl.*)

yak[2] *n* **1** = **gossip**, blather, chat, chinwag (*Brit. inf.*), confab (*inf.*), hot air (*inf.*), jaw (*sl.*), waffle (*inf., chiefly Brit.*), yackety-yak (*sl.*), yammer (*inf.*) ◆ *vb* **2** = **gossip**, blather, chatter, chew the fat *or* rag (*sl.*), gab (*inf.*), jabber, jaw (*sl.*), rabbit (on) (*Brit. inf.*), run off at the mouth (*sl.*), run on, spout, tattle, waffle (*inf., chiefly Brit.*), witter on (*inf.*), yap (*inf.*)

yank *vb* **1** = **pull**, hitch, jerk, snatch, tug, wrench ◆ *n* **2** = **pull**, hitch, jerk, snatch, tug, wrench

yap *vb* **1** = **yelp**, yammer (*inf.*) **2** *Informal* = **talk**, babble, blather, chatter, chew the fat *or* rag, go on, gossip, jabber, jaw (*sl.*), prattle, rabbit (on) (*Brit. inf.*), run off at the mouth (*sl.*), spout, tattle, waffle (*inf., chiefly Brit.*)

yardstick *n* **1** = **standard**, benchmark, criterion, gauge, measure, par, touchstone

yarn *n* **1** = **thread**, fibre **2** *Informal* = **story**, anecdote, cock-and-bull story, fable, tale, tall story, urban legend, urban myth

yataghan (ˈjætəgən) *n* a Turkish sword with a curved blade. [C19: from Turkish *yatağan*]

yaup (jɔːp) *vb, n* a variant spelling of **yawp**.
▸ˈ**yauper** *n*

yaw (jɔː) *vb* **1** (*intr*) (of an aircraft, etc.) to turn about its vertical axis. **2** (*intr*) (of a ship, etc.) to deviate temporarily from a straight course. **3** (*tr*) to cause (an aircraft, ship, etc.) to yaw. ◆ *n* **4** the movement of an aircraft, etc., about its vertical axis. **5** the deviation of a vessel from a straight course. [C16: from ?]

yawl (jɔːl) *n* **1** a two-masted sailing vessel with a small mizzenmast aft of the rudderpost. **2** a ship's small boat, usually rowed by four or six oars. [C17: from Du. *jol* or MLow G *jolle*, from ?]

yawn Ⓣ (jɔːn) *vb* **1** (*intr*) to open the mouth wide and take in air deeply, often as in involuntary reaction to sleepiness or boredom. **2** (*tr*) to express or utter while yawning. **3** (*intr*) to be open wide as if threatening to engulf (someone or something): *the mine shaft yawned below.* ◆ *n* **4** the act or an instance of yawning. [OE *gionian*]
▸ˈ**yawner** *n* ▸ˈ**yawning** *adj* ▸ˈ**yawningly** *adv*

yawp (jɔːp) *Dialect US & Canad. inf.* ◆ *vb* (*intr*) **1** to yawn, esp. audibly. **2** to shout, cry, or talk noisily. **3** to bark or yowl. ◆ *n* **4** a shout, bark, or cry. **5** a noisy, foolish, or raucous utterance. [C15 *yolpen*, prob. imit.]
▸ˈ**yawper** *n*

yaws (jɔːz) *n* (*usually functioning as sing*) an infectious disease of tropical climates characterized by red skin eruptions. [C17: of Carib origin]

***y*-axis** *n* a reference axis of a graph or two- or three-dimensional Cartesian coordinate system along which the *y*-coordinate is measured.

Yb *the chemical symbol for* ytterbium.

YC (in Britain) *abbrev. for* Young Conservative.

Y-chromosome *n* the sex chromosome that occurs as one of a pair with the X-chromosome in the diploid cells of the males of many animals, including humans. Cf. **X-chromosome**.

yclept (ɪˈklɛpt) *adj Obs.* having the name of; called. [OE *gecleopod*, p.p. of *cleopian* to call]

Y connection *n Electrical engineering.* a three-phase star connection.

yd *or* **yd.** *abbrev. for* yard (measure).

YDT (in Canada) *abbrev. for* Yukon Daylight Time.

ye[1] (jiː, *unstressed* jɪ) *pron* **1** *Arch. or dialect.* refers to more than one person including the person addressed. **2** Also: **ee** (iː). *Dialect.* refers to one person addressed: *I tell ye.* [OE *gē*]

ye[2] (ðiː, *spelling pron* jiː) *determiner* a form of **the**[1], used as a supposed archaism: *ye olde oake.* [from a misinterpretation of *the* as written in some ME texts. The runic letter thorn (þ, representing *th*) was incorrectly transcribed as *y* because of a resemblance in their shapes]

yea (jeɪ) *sentence substitute.* **1** a less common word for **aye** (yes). ◆ *adv* **2** (*sentence modifier*) *Arch. or literary.* indeed; truly: *yea, though they spurn me, I shall prevail.* [OE *gēa*]

yeah (jɛə) *sentence substitute.* an informal word for **yes**.

yean (jiːn) *vb* (of a sheep or goat) to give birth to (offspring). [OE *geēanian*]

yeanling (ˈjiːnlɪŋ) *n* the young of a goat or sheep.

year Ⓣ (jɪə) *n* **1** the period of time, the **calendar year**, containing 365 days or in a **leap year** 366 days. It is divided into 12 calendar months, and reckoned from January 1 to December 31. **2** a period of twelve months from any specified date. **3** a specific period of time, usually occupying a definite part or parts of a twelve-month period, used for some particular activity: *a school year.* **4** Also called: **astronomical year, tropical year.** the period of time, the **solar year**, during which the earth makes one revolution around the sun, measured between two successive vernal equinoxes: equal to 365.242 19 days. **5** the period of time, the **sidereal year**, during which the earth makes one revolution around the sun, measured between two successive conjunctions of a particular star: equal to 365.256 36 days. **6** the period of time, the **lunar year**, containing 12 lunar months and equal to 354.3671 days. **7** the period of time taken by a planet to complete one revolution around the sun. **8** (*pl*) age, esp. old age: *a man of his years should be more careful.* **9** (*pl*) time: *in years to come.* **10** a group of pupils or students, who are taught or study together. **11 the year dot.** *Inf.* as long ago as can be remembered. **12 year in, year out.** regularly or monotonously, over a long period. ◆ Related adj: **annual**. [OE *gear*]

> **USAGE NOTE** In writing spans of years, it is important to choose a style that avoids ambiguity. The practice adopted in this dictionary is, in four-figure dates, to specify the last two digits of the second date if it falls within the same century as the first: *1801–08; 1850–51; 1899–1901.* In writing three-figure B.C. dates, it is advisable to give both dates in full: *159–156* B.C., not *159–56* B.C. unless of course the span referred to consists of 103 years rather than three years. It is also advisable to specify B.C. or A.D. in years under 1000 unless the context makes this self-evident.

yearbook (ˈjɪəˌbʊk) *n* an almanac or other reference book published annually and containing details of events of the previous year.

yearling (ˈjɪəlɪŋ) *n* **1** the young of any of various animals, including the antelope and buffalo, between one and two years of age. **2** a thoroughbred racehorse counted as being one year old until the second January 1 following its birth. **3a** a bond intended to mature after one year. **3b** (*as modifier*): *yearling bonds.* ◆ *adj* **4** being a year old.

yearlong (ˈjɪəˈlɒŋ) *adj* throughout a whole year.

yearly Ⓣ (ˈjɪəlɪ) *adj* **1** occurring, done, appearing, etc., once a year or every year; annual. **2** lasting or valid for a year; annual: *a yearly fee.* ◆ *adv* **3** once a year; annually.

yearn Ⓣ (jɜːn) *vb* (*intr*) **1** (usually foll. by *for* or *after* or an infinitive) to have an intense desire or longing (for). **2** to feel tenderness or affection. [OE *giernan*]
▸ˈ**yearner** *n* ▸ˈ**yearning** *n, adj* ▸ˈ**yearningly** *adv*

year of grace *n* any year of the Christian era, as from the presumed date of Christ's birth.

year-round *adj* open, in use, operating, etc., throughout the year.

yeast (jiːst) *n* **1** any of various single-celled fungi which reproduce by budding and are able to ferment sugars: a rich source of vitamins of the B complex. **2** a commercial preparation containing yeast cells and inert material such as meal, used in raising dough for bread or for fermenting beer, whisky, etc. **3** a preparation containing yeast cells, used to treat diseases caused by vitamin B deficiency. **4** froth or foam, esp. on beer. ◆ *vb* **5** (*intr*) to froth or foam. [OE *giest*]
▸ˈ**yeastless** *adj* ▸ˈ**yeastˌlike** *adj*

yeasty (ˈjiːstɪ) *adj* **yeastier, yeastiest. 1** of, resembling, or containing yeast. **2** fermenting or causing fermentation. **3** tasting of or like yeast. **4** insubstantial or frivolous. **5** restless, agitated, or unsettled. **6** covered with or containing froth or foam.
▸ˈ**yeastily** *adv* ▸ˈ**yeastiness** *n*

yegg (jɛg) *n Sl., chiefly US.* a burglar or safe-breaker. [C20: ?from the surname of a burglar]

yell Ⓣ (jɛl) *vb* **1** to shout, scream, cheer, or utter in a loud or piercing way. ◆ *n* **2** a loud piercing inarticulate cry, as of pain, anger, or fear. **3** *US & Canad.* a rhythmic cry, used in cheering in unison. [OE *giellan*]
▸ˈ**yeller** *n*

yellow (ˈjɛləʊ) *n* **1** any of a group of colours such as that of a lemon or of gold, which vary in saturation but have the same hue. Yellow is the complementary colour of blue. Related adj: **xanthous**. **2** a pigment or dye of or producing these colours. **3** yellow cloth or clothing: *dressed in yellow.* **4** the yolk of an egg. **5** a yellow ball in snooker, etc. ◆ *adj* **6** of the colour yellow. **7** yellowish in colour or having parts or marks that are yellowish. **8** having a yellowish skin; Mongoloid. **9** *Inf.* cowardly or afraid. **10** offensively sensational, as a cheap newspaper (esp. in **yellow press**). ◆ *vb* **11** to make or become yellow. ◆ See also **yellows**. [OE *geolu*]
▸ˈ**yellowish** *adj* ▸ˈ**yellowly** *adv* ▸ˈ**yellowness** *n* ▸ˈ**yellowy** *adj*

yellow-belly *n, pl* **yellow-bellies.** a slang word for **coward**.
▸ˈ**yellow-ˌbellied** *adj*

yellow belly *n Austral.* any of several freshwater food fishes with yellow underparts.

yellow bile *n Arch.* one of the four bodily humours, choler.

yellow card *n Soccer.* a card of a yellow colour displayed by a referee to indicate that a player has been officially cautioned for some offence.

yellow fever *n* an acute infectious disease of tropical and subtropical climates, characterized by fever, haemorrhages, vomiting, and jaundice: caused by a virus transmitted by the bite of a certain mosquito. Also called: **yellow jack**.

yellowhammer (ˈjɛləʊˌhæmə) *n* a European bunting, having a yellowish head and body and brown-streaked wings and tail. [C16: from ?]

yellow jack *n* **1** *Pathol.* another name for **yellow fever**. **2** another name for **quarantine flag**. **3** any of certain large yellowish food fishes of warm and tropical Atlantic waters.

yellow jersey *n* (in the Tour de France) a yellow jersey awarded as a trophy to the cyclist with the fastest time in each stage of the race.

yellow journalism *n* the type of journalism that relies on sensationalism to attract readers. [C19: ? shortened from *Yellow Kid journalism*, referring to the *Yellow Kid*, a cartoon (1895) in the *New York World*, a newspaper having a reputation for sensationalism]

yellow line *n Brit.* a yellow line painted along the edge of a road indicating vehicle waiting restrictions.

yellow metal *n* **1** a type of brass having about 60 per cent copper and 40 per cent zinc. **2** another name for **gold**.

Yellow Pages *pl n Trademark.* a classified telephone directory or section of one, often on yellow paper, that lists subscribers by the business or service they provide.

yellow peril *n* the power or alleged power of Asiatic peoples, esp. the Chinese, to threaten or destroy White or Western civilization.

yellows (ˈjɛləʊz) *n* (*functioning as sing*) **1** any of various fungal or viral diseases of plants, characterized by yellowish discoloration and stunting. **2** *Vet. science.* another name for **jaundice**.

yellow spot *n Anat.* another name for **macula lutea**.

yellow streak *n Inf.* a cowardly or weak trait.

yellow underwing *n* any of several species of noctuid moths, the hind wings of which are yellow with a black bar.

yellowwood (ˈjɛləʊˌwʊd) *n* **1** any of several leguminous trees of the

THESAURUS

yawning *adj* **3** = **gaping**, cavernous, chasmal, vast, wide, wide-open

year *n* **8** *plural* = **old age**, age, dotage, eld, second childhood, senescence, senility **9** *plural* = **time**, days, generation(s), lifetime, span

yearly *adj* **1, 2** = **annual** ◆ *adv* **3** = **annually**, every year, once a year, per annum

yearn *vb* **1** = **long**, ache, covet, crave, desire, eat one's heart out over, hanker, have a yen for (*inf.*), hunger, itch, languish, lust, pant, pine, set one's heart upon, suspire (*arch. or poetic*), would give one's eyeteeth for

yell *vb* **1** = **scream**, bawl, holler (*inf.*), howl, screech, shout, shriek, squeal ◆ *n* **2** = **scream**, cry, howl, screech, shriek, whoop southeastern US, having clusters of white flowers and yellow wood yielding a yellow dye. **2** Also called: **West Indian satinwood.** a rutaceous tree of the West Indies, with smooth hard wood. **3** any of several other trees with yellow wood, esp. a conifer of southern Africa the wood of which is used for furniture and building. **4** the wood of any of these trees.

yelp ❶ (jɛlp) *vb* (*intr*) **1** (esp. of a dog) to utter a sharp or high-pitched cry or bark, often indicating pain. ◆ *n* **2** a sharp or high-pitched cry or bark. [OE *gielpan* to boast]
▸**'yelper** *n*

yen[1] (jɛn) *n, pl* **yen.** the standard monetary unit of Japan. [C19: from Japanese *en*, from Chinese *yüan* dollar]

yen[2] ❶ (jɛn) *Inf.* ◆ *n* **1** a longing or desire. ◆ *vb* **yens, yenning, yenned. 2** (*intr*) to yearn. [?from Chinese *yǎn* a craving]

yeoman ('jəʊmən) *n, pl* **yeomen. 1** *History.* **1a** a member of a class of small freeholders who cultivated their own land. **1b** an attendant or lesser official in a royal or noble household. **2** (in Britain) another name for **yeoman of the guard. 3** (*modifier*) characteristic of or relating to a yeoman. **4** a petty officer or noncommissioned officer in the Royal Navy or Marines in charge of signals. [C15: ?from *yongman* young man]

yeomanly ('jəʊmənlɪ) *adj* **1** of, relating to, or like a yeoman. **2** having the virtues attributed to yeomen, such as staunchness, loyalty, and courage. ◆ *adv* **3** in a yeomanly manner.

yeoman of the guard *n* a member of the ceremonial bodyguard (**Yeomen of the Guard**) of the British monarch.

yeomanry ('jəʊmənrɪ) *n* **1** yeomen collectively. **2** (in Britain) a volunteer cavalry force, organized in 1761 for home defence: merged into the Territorial Army in 1907.

yep (jɛp) *sentence substitute.* an informal word for **yes.**

yerba *or* **yerba maté** ('jɜːbə) *n* another name for **maté.** [from Sp. *yerba maté* herb maté]

yes (jɛs) *sentence substitute.* **1** used to express affirmation, consent, agreement, or approval or to answer when one is addressed. **2** used to signal someone to speak or keep speaking, enter a room, or do something. ◆ *n* **3** an answer or vote of *yes.* **4** (*often pl*) a person who votes in the affirmative. [OE *gēse*, from *iā sīe* may it be]

yeshiva (jə'ʃiːvə; *Hebrew* jə'ʃiːva) *n, pl* **yeshivahs** *or* **yeshivoth** (*Hebrew* -vɔt). **1** a traditional Jewish school devoted chiefly to the study of the Talmud. **2** a school run by Orthodox Jews for children of primary school age, providing both religious and secular instruction. [from Heb. *yĕshībhāh* a seat, hence, an academy]

yes man ❶ *n* a servile, submissive, or acquiescent subordinate, assistant, or associate.

yester ('jɛstə) *adj Arch.* of or relating to yesterday: *yester sun.* [OE *geostror*]

yester- *prefix* indicating a period of time before the present one: *yesteryear.* [OE *geostran*]

yesterday ('jɛstədɪ, -ˌdeɪ) *n* **1** the day immediately preceding today. **2** (*often pl*) the recent past. ◆ *adv* **3** on or during the day before today. **4** in the recent past.

yesteryear ('jɛstəˌjɪə) *Formal or literary.* ◆ *n* **1** last year or the past in general. ◆ *adv* **2** during last year or the past in general.

yestreen (jɛ'striːn) *adv Scot.* yesterday evening. [C14: from YEST(E)R- + E(V)EN[2]]

yet ❶ (jɛt) *sentence connector.* **1** nevertheless; still; in spite of that: *I want to and yet I haven't the courage.* ◆ *adv* **2** (*usually used with a negative or interrogative*) so far; up until then or now: *they're not home yet; is it teatime yet?* **3** (often preceded by *just; usually used with a negative*) now (as contrasted with later): *we can't stop yet.* **4** (*often used with a comparative*) even; still: *yet more old potatoes for sale.* **5** eventually in spite of everything: *we'll convince him yet.* **6 as yet.** so far; up until then or now. [OE *gēta*]

yeti ('jɛtɪ) *n* another term for **abominable snowman.** [C20: from Tibetan]

yew (juː) *n* **1** any coniferous tree of the Old World and North America having flattened needle-like leaves, fine-grained elastic wood, and cuplike red waxy cones resembling berries. **2** the wood of any of these trees, used to make bows for archery. **3** *Archery.* a bow made of yew. [OE *īw*]

Y-fronts *pl n Trademark.* boys' or men's underpants having a front opening within an inverted Y shape.

Yggdrasil *or* **Ygdrasil** ('ɪgdrəsɪl) *n Norse myth.* the ash tree that was thought to bind together earth, heaven, and hell with its roots and branches. [ON (prob. meaning: Uggr's horse), from *Uggr* a name of Odin, from *yggr, uggr* frightful + *drasill* horse, from ?]

YHA *abbrev. for* Youth Hostels Association.

YHVH *or* **YHWH** *Bible.* the letters of the **Tetragrammaton.**

yid (jɪd) *n Sl.* a derogatory word for a **Jew.** [C20: prob. from *Yiddish*, from MHG *Jude* JEW]

Yiddish ('jɪdɪʃ) *n* **1** a language spoken as a vernacular by Jews in Europe and elsewhere by Jewish emigrants, usually written in the Hebrew alphabet. It is a dialect of High German with an admixture of words of Hebrew, Romance, and Slavonic origin. ◆ *adj* **2** in or relating to this language. [C19: from G *jüdisch*, from *Jude* JEW]

Yiddisher ('jɪdɪʃə) *adj* **1** in or relating to Yiddish. **2** Jewish. ◆ *n* **3** a speaker of Yiddish; Jew.

yield ❶ (jiːld) *vb* **1** to give forth or supply (a product, result, etc.), esp. by cultivation, labour, etc.; produce or bear. **2** (*tr*) to furnish as a return: *the shares yielded three per cent.* **3** (*tr; often foll. by up*) to surrender or relinquish, esp. as a result of force, persuasion, etc. **4** (*intr; sometimes foll. by to*) to give way, submit, or surrender, as through force or persuasion: *she yielded to his superior knowledge.* **5** (*intr; often foll. by to*) to agree; comply; assent: *he eventually yielded to their request for money.* **6** (*tr*) to grant or allow; concede: *to yield right of way.* ◆ *n* **7** the result, product, or amount yielded. **8** the profit or return, as from an investment or tax. **9** the annual income provided by an investment. **10** the energy released by the explosion of a nuclear weapon expressed in terms of the amount of TNT necessary to produce the same energy. **11** *Chem.* the quantity of a specified product obtained in a reaction or series of reactions. [OE *gieldan*]
▸**'yieldable** *adj* ▸**'yielder** *n*

yielding ❶ ('jiːldɪŋ) *adj* **1** compliant, submissive, or flexible. **2** pliable or soft: *a yielding material.*

yield point *n* the stress at which an elastic material under increasing stress ceases to behave elastically; the elongation becomes greater than the increase in stress.

Yin and Yang (jɪn) *n* two complementary principles of Chinese philosophy: Yin is negative, dark, and feminine, Yang is positive, bright, and masculine. [from Chinese *yin* dark + *yang* bright]

yippee (jɪ'piː) *interj* an exclamation of joy, pleasure, anticipation, etc.

yips (jɪps) *pl n* **the.** *Inf.* (in sport) nervous twitching or tension that destroys concentration. [C20: from ?]

-yl *suffix forming nouns.* (in chemistry) indicating a group or radical: *methyl.* [from Gk *hulē* wood]

ylang-ylang ('iːlæŋ'iːlæŋ) *n* **1** an aromatic Asian tree with fragrant greenish-yellow flowers yielding a volatile oil. **2** the oil obtained from this tree, used in perfumery. [C19: from Tagalog *ilang-ilang*]

ylem ('aɪləm) *n* the original matter from which the basic elements are said to have been formed following the explosion postulated in the big-bang theory of cosmology. [ME, from OF *ilem*, from L *hȳlē* stuff, from Gk *hulē* wood]

YMCA *abbrev. for* Young Men's Christian Association.

-yne *suffix forming nouns.* denoting an organic chemical containing a triple bond: *alkyne.* [alteration of -INE[2]]

yo (jəʊ) *sentence substitute.* an expression used as a greeting, to attract someone's attention, etc. [C20: of unknown origin]

yob ❶ (jɒb) *or* **yobbo** ('jɒbəʊ) *n, pl* **yobs** *or* **yobbos.** *Brit. sl.* an aggressive and surly youth, esp. a teenager. [C19: ? back sl. for BOY]
▸**'yobbery** *n* ▸**'yobbish** *adj*

yodel ('jəʊdᵊl) *n* **1** an effect produced in singing by an abrupt change of register from the chest voice to falsetto, esp. in folk songs of the Swiss Alps. ◆ *vb* **yodels, yodelling, yodelled** *or US* **yodels, yodeling, yodeled. 2** to sing (a song) in which a yodel is used. [C19: from G *jodeln*, imit.]
▸**'yodeller** *n*

yoga ('jəʊgə) *n* (*often cap.*) **1** a Hindu system of philosophy aiming at the mystical union of the self with the Supreme Being in a state of complete awareness and tranquillity through certain physical and mental exercises. **2** any method by which such awareness and tranquillity are attained, esp. a course of related exercises and postures. [C19: from Sansk.: a yoking, from *yunakti* he yokes]
▸**yogic** ('jəʊgɪk) *adj*

yogh (jɒg) *n* **1** a character (ȝ) used in Old and Middle English to represent a palatal fricative very close to the semivowel sound of Modern English *y.* **2** this same character as used in Middle English for both the voiced and voiceless palatal fricatives; when final or in a closed syllable in medial position the sound approached that of German *ch* in *ich*, as in *knyȝt* (knight). [C14: ?from *yok* yoke, from the letter's shape]

THESAURUS

Antonyms *vb, n* ≠ **scream:** mumble, murmur, mutter, whisper

yelp *vb* **1** = **cry,** yammer (*inf.*), yap, yowl

yen[2] *n* **1** = **longing,** ache, craving, desire, hankering, hunger, itch, passion, thirst, yearning

yes man *n* = **sycophant,** ass-kisser (*US & Canad. taboo sl.*), bootlicker (*inf.*), bosses' lackey, company man, crawler, creature, minion, timeserver, toady

yet *sentence connector* **1** = **nevertheless,** however, notwithstanding, still ◆ *adv* **2** = **so far,** as yet, thus far, until now, up to now **3** = **now,** already, just now, right now, so soon **4** = **still,** additionally, as well, besides, further, in addition, into the bargain, moreover, over and above, to boot

yield *vb* **1, 2** = **produce,** afford, bear, bring forth, bring in, earn, furnish, generate, give, net, pay, provide, return, supply **3, 4** = **surrender,** abandon, abdicate, admit defeat, bow, capitulate, cave in (*inf.*), cede, cry quits, give in, give up the struggle, give way, knuckle under, lay down one's arms, lose, part with, raise the white flag, relinquish, resign, resign oneself, submit, succumb, throw in the towel **5, 6** = **comply,** accede, agree, allow, bow, concede, consent, go along with, grant, permit ◆ *n* **7** = **crop,** harvest, output, produce **8, 9** = **profit,** earnings, income, return, revenue, takings

Antonyms *vb* ≠ **produce:** consume, use, use up ≠ **surrender:** appropriate, commandeer, grab, hold on to, hold out, keep, maintain, reserve, retain, seize, struggle ≠ **comply:** combat, counterattack, defy, oppose, resist ◆ *n* ≠ **profit:** consumption, input, loss

yielding *adj* **1** = **submissive,** accommodating, acquiescent, biddable, compliant, docile, easy, flexible, obedient, pliant, tractable **2** = **soft,** elastic, pliable, quaggy, resilient, spongy, springy, supple, unresisting

Antonyms *adj* ≠ **submissive:** dogged, headstrong, mulish, obstinate, opinionated, perverse, stiff-necked, stubborn, tenacious, wilful

yob *n* = **thug,** heavy (*sl.*), hoodlum, hooligan,

yogi ('jəʊgɪ) *n, pl* **yogis** *or* **yogin** (-gɪn). a person who is a master of yoga.
yogurt *or* **yoghurt** ('jəʊgət, jɒg-) *n* a thick custard-like food prepared from milk curdled by bacteria, often sweetened and flavoured with fruit. [C19: from Turkish *yoğurt*]
yo-heave-ho (ˌjəʊhi:v'həʊ) *interj* a cry formerly used by sailors while pulling or lifting together in rhythm.
yohimbine (jəʊ'hɪmbi:n) *n* an alkaloid found in the bark of a West African tree and used in medicine. [C19: from Bantu *yohimbé* a tropical African tree + -INE[1]]
yo-ho-ho *interj* **1** an exclamation to call attention. **2** another word for **yo-heave-ho.**
yoicks (haɪk; *spelling pron* jɔɪks) *interj* a cry used by fox-hunters to urge on the hounds.
yoke ❶ (jəʊk) *n, pl* **yokes** *or* **yoke. 1** a wooden frame, usually consisting of a bar with an oxbow at either end, for attaching to the necks of a pair of draught animals, esp. oxen, so that they can be worked as a team. **2** something resembling a yoke in form or function, such as a frame fitting over a person's shoulders for carrying buckets. **3** a fitted part of a garment, esp. around the neck, shoulders, and chest or around the hips, to which a gathered, pleated, flared, or unfitted part is attached. **4** an oppressive force or burden: *under the yoke of a tyrant.* **5** a pair of oxen or other draught animals joined by a yoke. **6** a part that secures two or more components so that they move together. **7** (in the ancient world) a symbolic yoke, consisting of two upright spears with a third lashed across them, under which conquered enemies were compelled to march, esp. in Rome. **8** a mark, token, or symbol of slavery, subjection, or suffering. **9** *Now rare.* a link, tie, or bond: *the yoke of love.* ◆ *vb* **yokes, yoking, yoked. 10** (*tr*) to secure or harness (a draught animal) to (a plough, vehicle, etc.) by means of a yoke. **11** to join or be joined by means of a yoke; couple, unite, or link. [OE *geoc*]
yokel ❶ ('jəʊk[ə]l) *n Disparaging.* (used chiefly by townspeople) a person who lives in the country, esp. one who appears to be simple and old-fashioned. [C19: ?from dialect *yokel* green woodpecker]
yolk (jəʊk) *n* **1** the substance in an animal ovum that nourishes the developing embryo. **2** a greasy substance in the fleece of sheep. [OE *geoloca,* from *geolu* yellow]
▸'**yolky** *adj*
yolk sac *n Zool.* the membranous sac that is attached to the surface of the embryos of birds, reptiles, and some fishes, and contains yolk.
Yom Kippur (jɒm 'kɪpə; *Hebrew* jɔm ki'pur) *n* an annual Jewish day of fasting, on which prayers of penitence are recited in the synagogue. Also called: **Day of Atonement.** [from Heb., from *yōm* day + *kippūr* atonement]
yomp (jɒmp) *vb* (*intr*) to walk or trek laboriously, esp. over difficult terrain. [C20: mil. sl., from ?]
yon (jɒn) *determiner* **1** *Chiefly Scot. & N English.* **1a** an archaic or dialect word for **that:** *yon man.* **1b** (*as pronoun*): *yon's a fool.* **2** a variant of **yonder.** [OE *geon*]
yond (jɒnd) *Obs. or dialect.* ◆ *adj* **1** the farther, more distant. ◆ *determiner* **2** a variant of **yon.**
yonder ('jɒndə) *adv* **1** at, in, or to that relatively distant place; over there. ◆ *determiner* **2** being at a distance, either within view or as if within view: *yonder valleys.* [C13: from OE *geond* yond]
yoni ('jəʊnɪ) *n Hinduism.* **1** the female genitalia, regarded as a divine symbol of sexual pleasure and matrix of generation. **2** an image of these as an object of worship. [C18: from Sansk., lit.: vulva]
yonks (jɒŋks) *pl n Inf.* a very long time; ages: *I haven't seen him for yonks.* [C20: from ?]
yoo-hoo ('ju:ˌhu:) *interj* a call to attract a person's attention.
YOP (jɒp) *n* (formerly, in Britain) **a** *acronym for* Youth Opportunities Programme. **b** (*as modifier*): *a YOP scheme.*
yore (jɔ:) *n* **1** time long past (now only in **of yore**). ◆ *adv* **2** *Obs.* in the past; long ago. [OE *geāra,* genitive pl of *gēar* year]
york (jɔ:k) *vb* (*tr*) *Cricket.* to bowl (a batsman) by pitching the ball under or just beyond the bat. [C19: back formation from YORKER]
yorker ('jɔ:kə) *n Cricket.* a ball bowled so as to pitch just under or just beyond the bat. [C19: prob. after the *Yorkshire* County Cricket Club]
yorkie ('jɔ:kɪ) *n* short for **Yorkshire terrier.**
Yorkist ('jɔ:kɪst) *English history.* ◆ *n* **1** a member or adherent of the royal House of York, esp. during the Wars of the Roses. ◆ *adj* **2** of, belonging to, or relating to the supporters or members of the House of York.
Yorks (jɔ:ks) *abbrev. for* Yorkshire.
Yorkshire pudding ('jɔ:kʃɪə) *n Chiefly Brit.* a light puffy baked pudding made from a batter of flour, eggs, and milk, traditionally served with roast beef.
Yorkshire terrier *n* a very small breed of terrier with a long straight glossy coat of steel-blue and tan. Also called: **yorkie.**
Yoruba ('jɒrʊbə) *n* **1** (*pl* **Yorubas** *or* **Yoruba**) a member of a Negroid people of W Africa, living chiefly in the coastal regions of SW Nigeria. **2** the language of this people.
▸'**Yoruban** *adj*
you (ju:; *unstressed* jʊ) *pron* (*subjective or objective*) **1** refers to the person addressed or to more than one person including the person or persons addressed: *you know better; the culprit is among you.* **2** refers to an unspecified person or people in general: *you can't tell the boys from the girls.* ◆ *n* **3** *Inf.* the personality of the person being addressed: *that hat isn't really you.* **4 you know what** *or* **who.** a thing or person that the speaker does not want to specify. [OE *ēow,* dative & accusative of *gē* ye]

> **USAGE NOTE** See at **me**[1].

you'd (ju:d; *unstressed* jʊd) *contraction of* you had *or* you would.
you'll (ju:l; *unstressed* jʊl) *contraction of* you will *or* you shall.
young ❶ (jʌŋ) *adj* **younger** ('jʌŋgə), **youngest** ('jʌŋgɪst). **1a** having lived, existed, or been made or known for a relatively short time: *a young country.* **1b** (*as collective n;* preceded by *the*): *the young.* **2** youthful or having qualities associated with youth; vigorous or lively. **3** of or relating to youth: *in my young days.* **4** having been established or introduced for a relatively short time: *a young member.* **5** in an early stage of progress or development; not far advanced: *the day was young.* **6** (*often cap.*) of or relating to a rejuvenated group or movement or one claiming to represent the younger members of the population: *Young Socialists.* ◆ *n* **7** (*functioning as pl*) offspring, esp. young animals: *a rabbit with her young.* **8 with young.** (of animals) pregnant. [OE *geong*]
▸'**youngish** *adj*
young blood *n* young, fresh, or vigorous new people, ideas, attitudes, etc.
Young Fogey *n* a young person who adopts the conservative values of an older generation.
young lady *n* a girlfriend; sweetheart.
youngling ('jʌŋlɪŋ) *n Literary.* **a** a young person, animal, or plant. **b** (*as modifier*): *a youngling brood.* [OE *geongling*]
young man *n* a boyfriend; sweetheart.
young offender institution *n* (in Britain) a place where offenders aged 15 to 21 may be detained and given training, instruction, and work. Former names: **borstal, youth custody centre.**
Young Pretender *n* Charles Edward Stuart (1720–88), son of James Edward Stuart (see **Old Pretender**). He led the Jacobite Rebellion (1745–46) in an attempt to re-establish the Stuart succession to the British throne. Also known as **Bonnie Prince Charlie.**
Young's modulus (jʌŋz) *n* a modulus of elasticity, applicable to the stretching of a wire, etc., equal to the ratio of the applied load per unit area of cross section to the increase in length per unit length. [after Thomas *Young* (1773–1829), Brit. physicist]
youngster ❶ ('jʌŋstə) *n* **1** a young person; child or youth. **2** a young animal, esp. a horse.
Young Turk *n* **1** a progressive, revolutionary, or rebellious member of an organization, political party, etc. **2** a member of an abortive reform movement in the Ottoman Empire.
younker ('jʌŋkə) *n* **1** *Arch. or literary.* a young man; lad. **2** *Obs.* a young gentleman or knight. [C16: from Du. *jonker,* from MDu. *jonc* young]
your (jɔ:, jʊə; *unstressed* jə) *determiner* **1** of, belonging to, or associated with you: *your nose; your house.* **2** belonging to or associated with an unspecified person or people in general: *the path is on your left heading north.* **3** *Inf.* used to indicate all things or people of a certain type: *your part-time worker is a problem.* [OE *eower,* genitive of *gē* ye]
you're (jɔ:; *unstressed* jə) *contraction of* you are.
yours (jɔ:z, jʊəz) *pron* **1** something or someone belonging to or associated with you. **2** your family: *greetings to you and yours.* **3** used in conventional closing phrases at the end of a letter: *yours sincerely; yours faithfully.* **4 of yours.** belonging to or associated with you.
yourself (jɔ:'sɛlf, jʊə-) *pron, pl* **yourselves. 1a** the reflexive form of *you.* **1b** (intensifier): *you yourself control your fate.* **2** (*preceded by a copula*) your usual self: *you're not yourself.*
yours truly *pron* an informal term for *I* or *me.* [from the closing phrase of letters]
youth ❶ (ju:θ) *n, pl* **youths** (ju:ðz). **1** the quality or condition of being young, immature, or inexperienced: *his youth told against him in the contest.* **2** the period between childhood and maturity. **3** the freshness,

THESAURUS

lout, rough (*inf.*), roughneck (*sl.*), rowdy, ruffian, tough, tsotsi (*S. Afr.*), yahoo

yoke *n* **4** = **oppression,** bondage, burden, enslavement, helotry, serfdom, service, servility, servitude, slavery, thraldom, vassalage **6** = **bond,** chain, coupling, ligament, link, tie ◆ *vb* **11** = **link,** bracket, connect, couple, harness, hitch, join, tie, unite

yokel *n* = **peasant,** boor, bucolic, clodhopper (*inf.*), (country) bumpkin, country cousin, countryman, hayseed (*US & Canad. inf.*), hick (*inf., chiefly US & Canad.*), hillbilly, rustic

young *adj* **1** = **immature,** adolescent, callow, green, growing, infant, in the springtime of life, junior, juvenile, little, unfledged, youthful **5** = **new,** at an early stage, early, fledgling, newish, not far advanced, recent, undeveloped ◆ *n* **7** *functioning as plural* = **offspring,** babies, brood, family, issue, litter, little ones, progeny

Antonyms *adj* ≠ **immature:** adult, aged, elderly, full-grown, grown-up, mature, old, ripe, senior, venerable ≠ **new:** advanced, developed, old ◆ *n* ≠ **offspring:** adults, grown-ups, parents

youngster *n* **1** = **youth,** boy, cub, girl, juvenile, kid (*inf.*), lad, lass, pup (*inf., chiefly Brit.*), teenager, teenybopper (*sl.*), urchin, young person

youth *n* **2** = **immaturity,** adolescence, boyhood *or* girlhood, early life, girlhood, juvenescence, salad days, young days **5** = **boy,** adolescent, kid (*inf.*), lad, shaveling (*arch.*), stripling, teenager, young man, young shaver (*inf.*), youngster **6** = **young people,** teenagers, the rising generation, the young, the younger generation

Antonyms *n* ≠ **immaturity:** adulthood, age, later life, manhood *or* womanhood, maturity, old age ≠ **boy:** adult, grown-up, OAP, pensioner, senior citizen ≠ **young people:** the aged, the elderly, the old vigour, or vitality characteristic of young people. **4** any period of early development. **5** a young person, esp. a young man or boy. **6** young people collectively: *youth everywhere is rising in revolt.* [OE *geogoth*]

youth club *n* a centre providing leisure activities for young people.

youthful ⓣ ('ju:θfʊl) *adj* **1** of, relating to, possessing, or characteristic of youth. **2** fresh, vigorous, or active: *he's surprisingly youthful for his age.* **3** in an early stage of development: *a youthful culture.* **4** Also: **young.** (of a river, valley, or land surface) in the early stage of the cycle of erosion, characterized by steep slopes, lack of flood plains, and V-shaped valleys.
▸ **'youthfully** *adv* ▸ **'youthfulness** *n*

youth hostel *n* one of an organization of inexpensive lodging places for people travelling cheaply. Often shortened to **hostel.**

Youth Training Scheme *n* (formerly, in Britain) a scheme, run by the Training Agency, to provide vocational training for unemployed 16–17-year-olds. Abbrev.: **YTS.**

you've (ju:v; *unstressed* jʊv) *contraction of* you have.

yowl ⓣ (jaʊl) *vb* **1** to express with or produce a loud mournful wail or cry; howl. ◆ *n* **2** a wail or howl. [C13: from ON *gaula*]
▸ **'yowler** *n*

yo-yo ('jəʊjəʊ) *n, pl* **yo-yos. 1** a toy consisting of a spool attached to a string, the end of which is held while it is repeatedly spun out and reeled in. **2** *Sl., chiefly US.* a silly or insignificant person. ◆ *vb* **yo-yos, yo-yoing, yo-yoed.** (*intr*) **3** to change repeatedly from one position to another; fluctuate. [from Filipino *yo yo* come come, a weapon consisting of a spindle attached to a thong]

yr *abbrev. for:* **1** (*pl* **yrs**) year. **2** younger. **3** your.

yrs *abbrev. for:* **1** years. **2** yours.

YST (in Canada) *abbrev. for* Yukon Standard Time.

YT *abbrev. for* Yukon Territory.

YTS (in Britain) *abbrev. for* Youth Training Scheme.

ytterbia (ɪ'tɜ:bɪə) *n* another name for **ytterbium oxide.** [C19: NL; see YTTERBIUM]

ytterbium (ɪ'tɜ:bɪəm) *n* a soft malleable silvery element of the lanthanide series of metals that is used to improve the mechanical properties of steel. Symbol: Yb; atomic no.: 70; atomic wt.: 173.04. [C19: NL, after *Ytterby*, Swedish quarry where discovered]

ytterbium oxide *n* a weakly basic hygroscopic substance used in certain alloys and ceramics.

yttria ('ɪtrɪə) *n* another name for **yttrium oxide.** [C19: NL; see YTTERBIUM]

yttrium ('ɪtrɪəm) *n* a silvery metallic element used in various alloys, in lasers, and as a catalyst. Symbol: Y; atomic no.: 39; atomic wt.: 88.90. [C19: NL; see YTTERBIUM]

yttrium metal *n Chem.* any one of a group of elements including yttrium and the related lanthanides.

yttrium oxide *n* a colourless or white insoluble solid used in incandescent mantles.

yuan ('ju:'æn) *n, pl* **yuan.** the standard monetary unit of China. [from Chinese *yüan* round object; see YEN[1]]

Yuan Tan ('ju:'æn 'tæn) *n* an annual Chinese festival marking the Chinese New Year. It can last over three days and includes the exchange of gifts, firework displays, and dancing.

yucca ('jʌkə) *n* any of a genus of liliaceous plants of tropical and subtropical America, having stiff lancelike leaves and spikes of white flowers. [C16: from American Sp. *yuca*, ult. from Amerind]

yuck *or* **yuk** (jʌk) *interj Sl.* an exclamation indicating contempt, dislike, or disgust.

yucky ⓣ *or* **yukky** ('jʌkɪ) *adj* **yuckier, yuckiest** *or* **yukkier, yukkiest.** *Sl.* disgusting; nasty.

Yugoslav *or* **Jugoslav** ('ju:gəʊ,slɑ:v) *n* **1** a native or inhabitant of Yugoslavia. **2** (not in technical use) another name for **Serbo-Croat** (the language). ◆ *adj* **3** of, relating to, or characteristic of Yugoslavia or its people.

yulan ('ju:læn) *n* a Chinese magnolia that is often cultivated for its showy white flowers. [C19: from Chinese, from *yu* a gem + *lan* plant]

yule (ju:l) *n* (*sometimes cap.*) *Literary, arch., or dialect.* **a** Christmas or the Christmas season. **b** (*in combination*): *yuletide.* [OE *geōla*, orig. a pagan feast lasting 12 days]

yule log *n* a large log of wood traditionally used as the foundation of a fire at Christmas.

yummy ('jʌmɪ) *Sl.* ◆ *interj* **1** Also: **yum-yum.** an exclamation indicating pleasure or delight, as in anticipation of delicious food. ◆ *adj* **yummier, yummiest. 2** delicious, delightful, or attractive. [C20: from *yum-yum*, imit.]

yuppie *or* **yuppy** ('jʌpɪ) (*sometimes cap.*) ◆ *n* **1** an affluent young professional person. ◆ *adj* **2** typical of or reflecting the values characteristic of yuppies. [C20: from *y*(*oung*) *u*(*rban*) or *up*(*wardly mobile*) *p*(*rofessional*) + -IE]
▸ **'yuppiedom** *n*

yuppie disease *or* **flu** *n Inf., sometimes considered offens.* any of a number of debilitating long-lasting viral disorders associated with stress, such as chronic fatigue syndrome, whose symptoms include muscle weakness, chronic tiredness, and depression.

yuppify ('jʌpɪ,faɪ) *vb* **yuppifies, yuppifying, yuppified.** (*tr*) to make yuppie in nature.
▸ **,yuppifi'cation** *n*

yurt (jʊət) *n* a circular tent consisting of a framework of poles covered with felt or skins, used by Mongolian and Turkic nomads of E and central Asia. [from Russian *yurta*, of Turkic origin]

YWCA *abbrev. for* Young Women's Christian Association.

THESAURUS

youthful *adj* **1 = young**, boyish, childish, girlish, immature, inexperienced, juvenile, pubescent, puerile **2 = fresh**, active, spry, vigorous, young at heart, young looking
Antonyms *adj* ≠ **young:** adult, aged, ageing, elderly, grown-up, mature, old, senile ≠ **fresh:** aged, ancient, decaying, decrepit, hoary, over the hill, tired, waning, weary

yowl *vb* **1 = howl**, bawl, bay, caterwaul, cry, give tongue, screech, squall, ululate, wail, yell

yucky *adj* **= disgusting**, beastly, dirty, foul, grotty (*sl.*), horrible, messy, mucky, revolting (*inf.*), unpleasant

Zz

z *or* **Z** (zɛd; *US* zi:) *n, pl* **z's, Z's,** *or* **Zs. 1** the 26th and last letter of the English alphabet. **2** a speech sound represented by this letter. **3a** something shaped like a Z. **3b** *(in combination): a Z-bend in a road.*

z *Maths. symbol for:* **1** the *z*-axis or a coordinate measured along the *z*-axis in a Cartesian or cylindrical coordinate system. **2** an algebraic variable.

Z *symbol for:* **1** any unknown, variable, or unspecified factor, number, person, or thing. **2** *Chem.* atomic number. **3** *Physics.* impedance. **4** zone.

z. *abbrev. for:* **1** zero. **2** zone.

zabaglione (ˌzæbəˈljəʊnɪ) *n* a light foamy dessert made of egg yolks, sugar, and marsala, whipped together and served warm in a glass. [It.]

zaffer *or* **zaffre** (ˈzæfə) *n* impure cobalt oxide, used to impart a blue colour to enamels. [C17: from It. *zaffera*]

zaibatsu (ˈzaɪbætˈsu:) *n (functioning as sing or pl)* the group or combine comprising a few wealthy families that controls industry, business, and finance in Japan. [from Japanese, from *zai* wealth + *batsu* family, person of influence]

zakuski *or* **zakouski** (zæˈkuskɪ) *pl n, sing* **zakuska** *or* **zakouska** (-kə). *Russian cookery.* hors d'oeuvres, consisting of tiny open sandwiches spread with caviar, smoked sausage, etc., or a cold dish such as radishes in sour cream, all usually served with vodka. [Russian, from *zakusit'* to have a snack]

Zambian (ˈzæmbɪən) *adj* **1** of or relating to Zambia, a republic in central Africa. ◆ *n* **2** a native or inhabitant of Zambia.

zambuck *or* **zambuk** (ˈzæmbʌk) *n Austral. & NZ inf.* a first-aid attendant at a sports event. [from name of a proprietary ointment]

ZANU (ˈzɑ:nu:) *n acronym for* Zimbabwe African National Union.

zany ❶ (ˈzeɪnɪ) *adj* **zanier, zaniest. 1** comical in an endearing way; imaginatively funny or comical, esp. in behaviour. ◆ *n, pl* **zanies. 2** a clown or buffoon, esp. one in old comedies who imitated other performers with ludicrous effect. **3** a ludicrous or foolish person. [C16: from It. *zanni,* from dialect *Zanni,* nickname for *Giovanni* John; one of the traditional names for a clown]
▸ˈ**zanily** *adv* ▸ˈ**zaniness** *n*

zap (zæp) *Sl.* ◆ *vb* **zaps, zapping, zapped. 1** *(tr)* to attack, kill, or destroy, as with a sudden bombardment. **2** *(intr)* to move quickly. **3** *(tr) Computing.* **3a** to clear from the screen. **3b** to erase. **4** *(intr) Television.* to change channels rapidly by remote control. ◆ *n* **5** energy, vigour, or pep. ◆ *interj* **6** an exclamation used to express sudden or swift action. [C20: imit.]

zapateado *Spanish.* (ˌθapateˈaðo) *n, pl* **-dos** (-ðos). a Spanish dance with stamping and very fast footwork. [from *zapatear* to tap with the shoe, from *zapato* shoe]

zappy (ˈzæpɪ) *adj* **zappier, zappiest.** *Sl.* full of energy; zippy.

ZAPU (ˈzæpu:) *n acronym for* Zimbabwe African People's Union.

Zarathustrian (ˌzærəˈθu:strɪən) *adj, n* another name for **Zoroastrian.** [C19: from *Zarathustra* the Old Iranian form of Zoroaster]

zareba *or* **zareeba** (zəˈri:bə) *n* (in northern E Africa, esp. formerly) **1** a stockade or enclosure of thorn bushes around a village or camp site. **2** the area so protected or enclosed. [C19: from Ar. *zarībah* cattlepen, from *zarb* sheepfold]

zarf (zɑ:f) *n* (esp. in the Middle East) a holder, usually ornamental, for a hot coffee cup. [from Ar.: container]

zarzuela (zɑ:ˈzweɪlə) *n* **1** a type of Spanish vaudeville or operetta, usually satirical in nature. **2** a seafood stew. [from Sp., after *La Zarzuela,* the palace near Madrid where such vaudeville was first performed (1629)]

z-axis *n* a reference axis of a three-dimensional Cartesian coordinate system along which the *z*-coordinate is measured.

ZB station *n* (in New Zealand) a radio station of a commercial network.

Z chart *n Statistics.* a chart often used in industry and constructed by plotting on it three series: monthly, weekly, or daily data, the moving annual total, and the cumulative total dating from the beginning of the current year.

zeal ❶ (zi:l) *n* fervent or enthusiastic devotion, often extreme or fanatical in nature, as to a religious movement, political cause, ideal, or aspiration. [C14: from LL *zēlus,* from Gk *zēlos*]

zealot ❶ (ˈzɛlət) *n* an immoderate, fanatical, or extremely zealous adherent to a cause, esp. a religious one. [C16: from LL *zēlōtēs,* from Gk, from *zēloun* to be zealous, from *zēlos* zeal]
▸ˈ**zealotry** *n*

Zealot (ˈzɛlət) *n* any of the members of an extreme Jewish sect or political party that resisted all aspects of Roman rule in Palestine in the 1st century A.D.

zealous ❶ (ˈzɛləs) *adj* filled with or inspired by intense enthusiasm or zeal; ardent; fervent.
▸ˈ**zealously** *adv* ▸ˈ**zealousness** *n*

zebec *or* **zebeck** (ˈzi:bɛk) *n* variant spellings of **xebec.**

zebra (ˈzi:brə, ˈzɛbrə) *n, pl* **zebras** *or* **zebra.** any of several mammals of the horse family, such as the common zebra of southern and eastern Africa, having distinctive black-and-white striped hides. [C16: via It. from OSp.: wild ass, prob. from Vulgar L *eciferus* (unattested) wild horse, from L *equiferus,* from *equus* horse + *ferus* wild]
▸**zebrine** (ˈzi:braɪn, ˈzɛb-) *or* ˈ**zebroid** *adj*

Zebra (ˈzi:brə, ˈzɛbrə) *n Finance.* a noninterest-paying bond in which the accrued income is taxed annually rather than on redemption. Cf. **zero** (sense 10). [C20: from *zero-coupon bond*]

zebra crossing *n Brit.* a pedestrian crossing marked on a road by broad alternate black and white stripes. Once on the crossing the pedestrian has right of way.

zebra finch *n* any of various Australasian songbirds with zebra-like markings.

zebrawood (ˈzɛbrəˌwʊd, ˈzi:-) *n* **1** a tree of tropical America, Asia, and Africa, yielding striped hardwood used in cabinetwork. **2** any of various other trees or shrubs having striped wood. **3** the wood of any of these trees.

zebu (ˈzi:bu:) *n* a domesticated ox having a humped back, long horns, and a large dewlap: used in India and E Asia as a draught animal. [C18: from F *zébu,* ? of Tibetan origin]

Zech. *Bible. abbrev. for* Zechariah.

zed (zɛd) *n* the British spoken form of the letter *z.* [C15: from OF *zede,* via LL from Gk *zēta*]

zedoary (ˈzɛdəʊərɪ) *n* the dried rhizome of a tropical Asian plant, used as a stimulant and a condiment. [C15: from Med. L *zedoaria,* from Ar. *zadwār,* of Persian origin]

zee (zi:) *n* the US word for **zed** (letter *z*).

Zeeman effect (ˈzi:mən) *n* the splitting of a spectral line of a substance into several closely spaced lines when the substance is placed in a magnetic field. [C20: after Pieter *Zeeman* (1865–1943), Du. physicist]

zein (ˈzi:ɪn) *n* a protein occurring in maize and used in the manufacture of plastics, paper coatings, adhesives, etc. [C19: from NL *zēa* maize, from L: a kind of grain, from Gk *zeia* barley]

Zeitgeist *German.* (ˈtsaɪtˌgaɪst) *n* the spirit, attitude, or general outlook of a specific time or period, esp. as it is reflected in literature, philosophy, etc. [G, lit.: time spirit]

Zen (zɛn) *Buddhism. n* **1** a Japanese school, of 12th-century Chinese origin, teaching that contemplation of one's essential nature to the exclusion of all else is the only way of achieving pure enlightenment. **2** *(modifier)* of or relating to this school: *Zen Buddhism.* [from Japanese, from Chinese *ch'an* religious meditation, from Pali *jhāna,* from Sansk. *dhyāna*]
▸ˈ**Zenic** *adj* ▸ˈ**Zenist** *n*

zenana (zɛˈnɑ:nə) *n* (in the East, esp. in Muslim and Hindu homes) part of a house reserved for the women and girls of a household. [C18: from Hindi *zanāna,* from Persian, from *zan* woman]

Zend (zɛnd) *n* **1** a former name for **Avestan. 2** short for **Zend-Avesta. 3** an exposition of the Avesta in the Middle Persian language (Pahlavi). [C18: from Persian *zand* commentary, exposition; used specifically of the MPersian commentary on the Avesta, hence of the language of the Avesta itself]
▸ˈ**Zendic** *adj*

Zend-Avesta (ˌzɛndəˈvɛstə) *n* the Avesta together with the traditional interpretive commentary known as the Zend, esp. as preserved in the Avestan language among the Parsees. [from Avestan, representing *Avesta'-va-zend* Avesta with interpretation]

Zener diode (ˈzi:nə) *n* a semiconductor diode that exhibits a sharp increase in reverse current at a well-defined reverse voltage: used as a voltage regulator. [C20: after C. M. *Zener* (1905–93), US physicist]

zenith ❶ (ˈzɛnɪθ) *n* **1** *Astron.* the point on the celestial sphere vertically above an observer. **2** the highest point; peak; acme: *the zenith of some-*

THESAURUS

zany *adj* **1 = comical,** clownish, crazy, eccentric, funny, goofy (*inf.*), kooky (*US inf.*), loony (*sl.*), madcap, nutty (*sl.*), oddball (*inf.*), wacky (*sl.*) ◆ *n* **2 = clown,** buffoon, comedian, jester, joker, merry-andrew, nut (*sl.*), screwball (*sl., chiefly US & Canad.*), wag

zeal *n* **= enthusiasm,** ardour, devotion, eagerness, earnestness, fanaticism, fervency, fervour, fire, gusto, keenness, militancy, passion, spirit, verve, warmth, zest
Antonyms *n* apathy, coolness, indifference, passivity, stoicism, torpor, unresponsiveness

zealot *n* **= fanatic,** bigot, energumen, enthusiast, extremist, fiend (*inf.*), maniac, militant

zealous *adj* **= enthusiastic,** ablaze, afire, ardent, burning, devoted, eager, earnest, fanatical, fervent, fervid, impassioned, keen, militant, passionate, rabid, spirited
Antonyms *adj* apathetic, cold, cool, half-hearted, indifferent, lackadaisical, lacklustre, languorous, listless, low-key, sceptical, torpid, unenthusiastic, unimpassioned

zenith *n* **2 = height,** acme, apex, apogee, climax, crest, high noon, high point, meridian, peak, pinnacle, summit, top, vertex
Antonyms *n* base, bottom, depths, lowest point, nadir, rock bottom

one's achievements. [C17: from F *cenith,* from Med. L, from OSp. *zenit,* based on Ar. *samt,* as in *samt arrās* path over one's head]
▸**'zenithal** *adj*

zenithal projection *n* a type of map projection in which part of the earth's surface is projected onto a plane tangential to it, either at one of the poles (**polar zenithal**), at the equator (**equatorial zenithal**), or between (**oblique zenithal**).

zeolite ('ziːə,laɪt) *n* **1** any of a large group of glassy secondary minerals consisting of hydrated aluminium silicates of calcium, sodium, or potassium: formed in cavities in lava flows and plutonic rocks. **2** any of a class of similar synthetic materials used in ion exchange and as selective absorbents. [C18: *zeo-,* from Gk *zein* to boil + -LITE; from the swelling that occurs under the blowpipe]
▸**zeolitic** (,ziːə'lɪtɪk) *adj*

Zeph. *Bible. abbrev. for* Zephaniah.

zephyr ('zɛfə) *n* **1** a soft or gentle breeze. **2** any of several delicate soft yarns, fabrics, or garments, usually of wool. [C16: from L *zephyrus,* from Gk *zephuros* the west wind]

zeppelin ('zɛpəlɪn) *n* (*sometimes cap.*) a large cylindrical rigid airship built from 1900 to carry passengers and used in World War I for bombing and reconnaissance. [C20: after Count von *Zeppelin* (1838–1917), its G designer]

zero ● ('zɪərəʊ) *n, pl* **zeros** *or* **zeroes. 1** the symbol 0, indicating an absence of quantity or magnitude; nought. Former name: **cipher. 2** the integer denoted by the symbol 0; nought. **3** the cardinal number between +1 and –1. **4** nothing; nil. **5** a person or thing of no significance; nonentity. **6** the lowest point or degree: *his prospects were put at zero.* **7** the line or point on a scale of measurement from which the graduations commence. **8a** the temperature, pressure, etc., that registers a reading of zero on a scale. **8b** the value of a variable, such as temperature, obtained under specified conditions. **9** *Maths.* **9a** the cardinal number of a set with no members. **9b** the identity element of addition. **10** *Finance.* Also called: **zero-coupon bond.** a bond that pays no interest, the equivalent being paid in its redemption value. Cf. **Zebra.** ◆ *adj* **11** having no measurable quantity, magnitude, etc. **12** *Meteorol.* **12a** (of a cloud ceiling) limiting visibility to 15 metres (50 feet) or less. **12b** (of horizontal visibility) limited to 50 metres (165 feet) or less. ◆ *vb* **zeros** *or* **zeroes, zeroing, zeroed. 13** (*tr*) to adjust (an instrument, apparatus, etc.) so as to read zero or a position taken as zero. ◆ *determiner* **14** *Inf., chiefly US.* no (thing) at all: *this job has zero interest.* ◆ See also **zero in.** [C17: from It., from Med. L *zephirum,* from Ar. *sifr* empty]

zero gravity *n* the state or condition of weightlessness.

zero hour ● *n* **1** *Mil.* the time set for the start of an attack or the initial stage of an operation. **2** *Inf.* a critical time, esp. at the commencement of an action.

zero in ● *vb* (*adv*) **1** (often foll. by *on*) to bring (a weapon) to bear (on a target), as while firing repeatedly. **2** (*intr;* foll. by *on*) *Inf.* to bring one's attention to bear (on a problem, etc.). **3** (*intr;* foll. by *on*) *Inf.* to converge (upon): *the police zeroed in on the site of the crime.*

zero option *n* (in international nuclear arms negotiations) an offer to remove all shorter-range nuclear missiles or, in the case of the **zero-zero option** all intermediate-range nuclear missiles, if the other side will do the same.

zero-rated *adj* denoting goods on which the buyer pays no value-added tax although the seller can claim back any tax he has paid.

zero stage *n* a solid-propellant rocket attached to a liquid-propellant rocket to provide greater thrust at liftoff.

zeroth ('zɪərəʊθ) *adj* denoting a term in a series that precedes the term otherwise regarded as the first term. [C20: from ZERO + -TH[2]]

zero tolerance *n* the policy of applying laws or penalties to even minor infringements of a code in order to reinforce its overall importance.

zest ● (zɛst) *n* **1** invigorating or keen excitement or enjoyment: *a zest for living.* **2** added interest, flavour, or charm; piquancy: *her presence gave zest to the party.* **3** something added to give flavour or relish. **4** the peel or skin of an orange or lemon, used as flavouring in drinks, etc. ◆ *vb* **5** (*tr*) to give flavour, interest, or piquancy to. [C17: from F *zeste* peel of citrus fruits used as flavouring, from ?]
▸**'zestful** *adj* ▸**'zestfully** *adv* ▸**'zestfulness** *n* ▸**'zesty** *adj*

zeta ('ziːtə) *n* the sixth letter in the Greek alphabet (Z, ζ). [from Gk]

ZETA ('ziːtə) *n* a torus-shaped apparatus formerly used for research on controlled thermonuclear reactions. [C20: from *z(ero-)e(nergy) t(hermonuclear) a(pparatus)*]

zeugma ('zjuːgmə) *n* a figure of speech in which a word is used to modify or govern two or more words although appropriate to only one of them or making a different sense with each, as in *Mr Pickwick took his hat and his leave* (Charles Dickens). [C16: via L from Gk: a yoking, from *zeugnunai* to yoke]
▸**zeugmatic** (zjuːg'mætɪk) *adj*

zho (zəʊ) *n* a variant spelling of **zo.**

zibeline ('zɪbə,laɪn, -lɪn) *n* **1** a sable or the fur of this animal. **2** a thick cloth made of wool or other animal hair, having a long nap and a dull sheen. ◆ *adj* **3** of, relating to, or resembling a sable. [C16: from F, from OIt. *zibellino,* ult. of Slavonic origin]

zibet ('zɪbɪt) *n* a large civet of S and SE Asia, having tawny fur marked with black spots and stripes. [C16: from Med. L *zibethum,* from Ar. *zabād* civet]

zidovudine (zaɪ'dɒvjʊ,diːn) *n* a drug that prolongs life and alleviates symptoms among some AIDS sufferers. Also called: **AZT.**

ziff (zɪf) *n Austral. inf.* a beard. [C20: from ?]

ziggurat ('zɪgʊ,ræt) *n* a type of rectangular temple tower or tiered mound erected by the Sumerians, Akkadians, and Babylonians in Mesopotamia. [C19: from Assyrian *ziqqurati* summit]

zigzag ('zɪg,zæg) *n* **1** a line or course characterized by sharp turns in alternating directions. **2** one of the series of such turns. **3** something having the form of a zigzag. ◆ *adj* **4** (*usually prenominal*) formed in or proceeding in a zigzag. **5** (of a sewing machine) capable of producing stitches in a zigzag. ◆ *adv* **6** in a zigzag manner. ◆ *vb* **zigzags, zigzagging, zigzagged. 7** to proceed or cause to proceed in a zigzag. **8** (*tr*) to form into a zigzag. [C18: from F, from G *zickzack,* from *Zacke* point]

zigzagger ('zɪg,zægə) *n* **1** a person or thing that zigzags. **2** an attachment on a sewing machine for sewing zigzag stitches, as for joining two pieces of material.

zilch (zɪltʃ) *n Sl.* **1** nothing. **2** *US & Canad. sport.* nil. [C20: from ?]

zillion ('zɪljən) *Inf.* ◆ *n, pl* **zillions** *or* **zillion. 1** (*often pl*) an extremely large but unspecified number, quantity, or amount: *zillions of flies in this camp.* ◆ *determiner* **2** amounting to a zillion: *a zillion different problems.* [C20: coinage after MILLION]

Zimbabwean (zɪm'bɑːbwɪən) *adj* **1** of or relating to Zimbabwe, a republic in southern Africa. ◆ *n* **2** a native or inhabitant of Zimbabwe.

Zimmer ('zɪmə) *n Trademark.* Also: **Zimmer frame.** another name for **walker** (sense 3).

zinc (zɪŋk) *n* **1** a brittle bluish-white metallic element that is a constituent of several alloys, esp. brass and nickel-silver, and is used in die-casting, galvanizing metals, and in battery electrodes. Symbol: Zn; atomic no.: 30; atomic wt.: 65.37. **2** *Inf.* corrugated galvanized iron. [C17: from G *Zink,* ?from *Zinke* prong, from its jagged appearance in the furnace]
▸**'zincic, 'zincous,** *or* **'zincoid** *adj* ▸**'zincky, 'zincy,** *or* **'zinky** *adj*

zinc blende *n* another name for **sphalerite.**

zinc chloride *n* a white soluble poisonous granular solid used in manufacturing parchment paper and vulcanized fibre and in preserving wood. It is also a soldering flux, embalming agent, and medical astringent and antiseptic.

zincite ('zɪŋkaɪt) *n* a red or yellow mineral consisting of zinc oxide in hexagonal crystalline form. It occurs in metamorphosed limestone.

zincography (zɪŋ'kɒgrəfɪ) *n* the art or process of etching on zinc to form a printing plate.
▸**zincograph** ('zɪŋkə,grɑːf) *n* ▸**zin'cographer** *n*

zinc ointment *n* a medicinal ointment consisting of zinc oxide, petrolatum, and paraffin, used to treat certain skin diseases.

zinc oxide *n* a white insoluble powder used as a pigment in paints (**zinc white** or **Chinese white**), cosmetics, glass, and printing inks. It is an antiseptic and astringent and is used in making zinc ointment. Formula: ZnO. Also called: **flowers of zinc.**

zinc sulphate *n* a colourless soluble crystalline substance used as a mordant, in preserving wood and skins, and in the electrodeposition of zinc. Also called: **zinc vitriol.**

zine (ziːn) *n Inf.* a magazine or fanzine.

zing ● (zɪŋ) *n Inf.* **1** a short high-pitched buzzing sound, as of a bullet or vibrating string. **2** vitality; zest. ◆ *vb* **3** (*intr*) to make or move with or as if with a high-pitched buzzing sound. [C20: imit.]
▸**'zingy** *adj*

zinjanthropus (zɪn'dʒænθrəpəs) *n* a type of australopithecine, remains of which were discovered in the Olduvai Gorge in Tanzania in 1959. [C20: NL, from Ar. *Zinj* East Africa + Gk *anthrōpos* man]

zinnia ('zɪnɪə) *n* any of a genus of annual or perennial plants of the composite family, of tropical and subtropical America, having solitary heads of brightly coloured flowers. [C18: after J. G. *Zinn* (d. 1759), G botanist]

Zion ('zaɪən) *or* **Sion** *n* **1** the hill on which the city of Jerusalem stands. **2** *Judaism.* **2a** the ancient Israelites of the Bible. **2b** the modern Jewish nation. **2c** Israel as the national home of the Jewish people. **3** *Christianity.* heaven regarded as the city of God and the final abode of his elect.

Zionism ('zaɪə,nɪzəm) *n* **1** a political movement for the establishment and support of a national homeland for Jews in Palestine, now concerned chiefly with the development of the modern state of Israel. **2** a policy or movement for Jews to return to Palestine from the Diaspora.
▸**'Zionist** *n, adj* ▸**,Zion'istic** *adj*

zip ● (zɪp) *n* **1a** Also called: **zip fastener.** a fastening device operating by

THESAURUS

zero *n* **1-4** = **nothing,** cipher, naught, nil, nought **6** = **bottom,** lowest point *or* ebb, nadir, nothing, rock bottom

zero hour *n* **2** = **moment of truth,** appointed hour, crisis, moment of decision, turning point, vital moment

zero in *vb* **1, 2** = **home in,** aim, bring to bear, concentrate, converge, direct, focus, level, pinpoint, train

zest *n* **1** = **enjoyment,** appetite, delectation, gusto, keenness, relish, zeal, zing (*inf.*) **2** = **flavour,** charm, interest, kick (*inf.*), piquancy, pungency, relish, savour, smack, spice, tang, taste
Antonyms *n* ≠ **enjoyment:** abhorrence, apathy, aversion, disinclination, distaste, indifference, lack of enthusiasm, loathing, repugnance, weariness

zing *n* **2** *Informal* = **vitality,** animation, brio, dash, energy, go (*inf.*), life, liveliness, oomph (*inf.*), pep, pizzazz *or* pizazz (*inf.*), spirit, vigour, zest, zip (*inf.*)

zip *n* **3** *Informal* = **energy,** brio, drive, get-up-and-go (*inf.*), go (*inf.*), gusto, life, liveliness, oomph (*inf.*), pep, pizzazz *or* pizazz (*inf.*), punch (*inf.*), sparkle, spirit, verve, vigour, vim (*sl.*), vitality, zest, zing (*inf.*) ◆ *vb* **8** = **speed,** barrel (along) (*inf., chiefly US & Canad.*), burn rub-

means of two parallel rows of metal or plastic teeth on either side of a closure that are interlocked by a sliding tab. US and Canad. term: **zipper. 1b** (*modifier*) having such a device: *a zip bag.* **2** a short sharp whizzing sound, as of a passing bullet. **3** *Inf.* energy; vigour; vitality. **4** *US sl.* nothing. **5** *Sport, US & Canad. sl.* nil. ◆ *vb* **zips, zipping, zipped. 6** (*tr;* often foll. by *up*) to fasten (clothing, etc.) with a zip. **7** (*intr*) to move with a zip: *the bullet zipped past.* **8** (*intr;* often foll. by *along, through,* etc.) to hurry; rush. [C19: imit.]

zip code *n* the US equivalent of **postcode.** [C20: from *z(one) i(mprovement) p(lan)*]

zip gun *n US & Canad. sl.* a crude home-made pistol, esp. one powered by a spring or rubber band.

zipper ('zɪpə) *n* the US & Canad. word for **zip** (sense 1a).

zippy ('zɪpɪ) *adj* **zippier, zippiest.** *Inf.* full of energy; lively.

zircalloy (zɜːk'ælɔɪ) *n* an alloy of zirconium containing small amounts of tin, chromium, and nickel. It is used in pressurized-water reactors.

zircon ('zɜːkɒn) *n* a reddish-brown, grey, green, blue, or colourless hard mineral consisting of zirconium silicate: it is used as a gemstone and a refractory. [C18: from G *Zirkon,* from F *jargon,* via It. & Ar., from Persian *zargūn* golden]

zirconium (zɜː'kəʊnɪəm) *n* a greyish-white metallic element, occurring chiefly in zircon, that is exceptionally corrosion-resistant and has low neutron absorption. It is used as a coating in nuclear and chemical plants, as a deoxidizer in steel, and alloyed with niobium in superconductive magnets. Symbol: Zr; atomic no.: 40; atomic wt.: 91.22. [C19: from NL; see ZIRCON]
▸**zirconic** (zɜː'kɒnɪk) *adj*

zirconium oxide *n* a white amorphous powder that is insoluble in water and highly refractory, used as a pigment for paints, a catalyst, and an abrasive.

zit (zɪt) *n Sl.* a pimple. [from ?]

zither ('zɪðə) *n* a plucked musical instrument consisting of numerous strings stretched over a resonating box, a few of which may be stopped on a fretted fingerboard. [C19: from G, from L *cithara,* from Gk *kithara*]
▸**'zitherist** *n*

zloty ('zlɒtɪ) *n, pl* **zlotys** *or* **zloty.** the standard monetary unit of Poland. [from Polish: golden, from *złyoto* gold]

Zn *the chemical symbol for* zinc.

zo, zho, *or* **dzo** (zəʊ) *n, pl* **zos, zhos, dzos** *or* **zo, zho, dzo.** a Tibetan breed of cattle, developed by crossing the yak with common cattle. [C20: from Tibetan]

zo- *combining form.* a variant of **zoo-** before a vowel.

-zoa *suffix forming plural proper nouns.* indicating groups of animal organisms: *Metazoa.* [from NL, from Gk *zōia,* pl. of *zōion* animal]

zodiac ('zəʊdɪ,æk) *n* **1** an imaginary belt extending 8° either side of the ecliptic, which contains the 12 **zodiacal constellations** and within which the moon and planets appear to move. It is divided into 12 equal areas, called **signs of the zodiac,** each named after the constellation which once lay in it. **2** *Astrol.* a diagram, usually circular, representing this belt and showing the symbols, illustrations, etc., associated with each of the 12 signs of the zodiac, used to predict the future. [C14: from OF *zodiaque,* from L *zōdiacus,* from Gk *zōidiakos (kuklos)* (circle) of signs, from *zōidion* animal sign, from *zōion* animal]
▸**zodiacal** (zəʊ'daɪəkəl) *adj*

zodiacal constellation *n* any of the 12 constellations after which the signs of the zodiac are named: Aries, Taurus, Gemini, Cancer, Leo, Virgo, Libra, Scorpio, Sagittarius, Capricorn, Aquarius, or Pisces.

zodiacal light *n* a very faint cone of light in the sky, visible in the east just before sunrise and in the west just after sunset.

zoic ('zəʊɪk) *adj* **1** relating to or having animal life. **2** *Geol.* (of rocks, etc.) containing fossilized animals. [C19: from NL, from Gk *zōion* animal]

-zoic *adj and n combining form.* indicating a geological era: *Palaeozoic.* [from Gk *zōē* life + -IC]

Zollverein *German.* ('tsɔlfer,ain) *n* the customs union of German states organized in the early 1830s under Prussian auspices. [C19: from *Zoll* tax + *Verein* union]

zombie *or* **zombi** ('zɒmbɪ) *n, pl* **zombies** *or* **zombis. 1** a person who is or appears to be lifeless, apathetic, or totally lacking in independent judgment; automaton. **2** a supernatural spirit that reanimates a dead body. **3** a corpse brought to life in this manner. [from W African *zumbi* good-luck fetish]

zonation (zəʊ'neɪʃən) *n* arrangement in zones.

zone ❶ (zəʊn) *n* **1** a region, area, or section characterized by some distinctive feature or quality. **2** an area subject to a particular political, military, or government function, use, or jurisdiction: *a demilitarized zone.* **3** (*often cap.*) *Geog.* one of the divisions of the earth's surface, esp. divided into latitudinal belts according to temperature. See **Torrid Zone, Frigid Zone, Temperate Zone. 4** *Geol.* a distinctive layer or region of rock, characterized by particular fossils (**zone fossils**), etc. **5** *Ecology.* an area, esp. a belt of land, having a particular flora and fauna determined by the prevailing environmental conditions. **6** *Maths.* a portion of a sphere between two parallel planes intersecting the sphere. **7** *Sport.* **7a** a period during which a competitor is performing particularly well: *Hingis is in the zone at the moment.* **7b** (*modifier*) of or relating to competitive performance that depends on the mood or state of mind of the participant: *a zone player.* **8** *Arch. or literary.* a girdle or belt. **9** *NZ.* a section on a transport route; fare stage. **10** *NZ.* a catchment area for a specific school. ◆ *vb* **zones, zoning, zoned.** (*tr*) **11** to divide into zones, as for different use, jurisdiction, activities, etc. **12** to designate as a zone. **13** to mark with or divide into zones. [C15: from L *zōna* girdle, climatic zone, from Gk *zōnē*]
▸**'zonal** *adj* ▸**'zonated** *adj* ▸**'zoning** *n*

zone refining *n* a technique for producing solids of extreme purity, esp. for use in semiconductors. The material, in the form of a bar, is melted in one small region that is passed along the solid. Impurities concentrate in the melt and are moved to the end of the bar.

zonetime ('zəʊn,taɪm) *n* the standard time of the time zone in which a ship is located at sea, each zone extending 7½° to each side of a meridian.

zonked (zɒŋkt) *adj Sl.* **1** incapacitated by drugs or alcohol. **2** exhausted. [C20: imit.]

zonk out (zɒŋk) *vb* (*intr, adv*) *Sl.* to fall asleep, esp. from physical exhaustion or the effects of alcohol or drugs.

zoo (zuː) *n, pl* **zoos.** a place where live animals are kept, studied, bred, and exhibited to the public. Formal term: **zoological garden.** [C19: shortened from *zoological gardens* (orig. those in London)]

zoo- *or before a vowel* **zo-** *combining form.* indicating animals: *zooplankton.* [from Gk *zōion* animal]

zoogeography (,zəʊədʒɪ'ɒgrəfɪ) *n* the branch of zoology concerned with the geographical distribution of animals.
▸**,zooge'ographer** *n* ▸**zoogeographic** (,zəʊə,dʒɪə'græfɪk) *or* **,zoo,geo'graphical** *adj* ▸**,zoo,geo'graphically** *adv*

zoography (zəʊ'ɒgrəfɪ) *n* the branch of zoology concerned with the description of animals.
▸**zo'ographer** *n* ▸**zoographic** (,zəʊə'græfɪk) *or* **,zoo'graphical** *adj*

zooid ('zəʊɔɪd) *n* **1** any independent animal body, such as an individual of a coelenterate colony. **2** a motile cell or body, such as a gamete, produced by an organism.
▸**zo'oidal** *adj*

zool. *abbrev. for:* **1** zoological. **2** zoology.

zoolatry (zəʊ'ɒlətrɪ) *n* **1** (esp. in ancient or primitive religions) the worship of animals as the incarnations of certain deities, etc. **2** extreme or excessive devotion to animals, particularly domestic pets.
▸**zo'olatrous** *adj*

zoological garden *n* the formal term for **zoo.**

zoology (zəʊ'ɒlədʒɪ, zuː-) *n, pl* **zoologies. 1** the study of animals, including their classification, structure, physiology, and history. **2** the biological characteristics of a particular animal or animal group. **3** the fauna characteristic of a particular region.
▸**zoological** (,zəʊə'lɒdʒɪkᵊl, ,zuːə-) *adj* ▸**zo'ologist** *n*

zoom ❶ (zuːm) *vb* **1** to make or cause to make a continuous buzzing or humming sound. **2** to move or cause to move with such a sound. **3** (*intr*) to move very rapidly; rush: *we zoomed through town.* **4** to cause (an aircraft) to climb briefly at an unusually steep angle, or (of an aircraft) to climb in this way. **5** (*intr*) (of prices) to rise rapidly. ◆ *n* **6** the sound or act of zooming. **7** See **zoom lens.** [C19: imit.]

zoom in *or* **out** *vb* (*intr, adv*) *Photog., films, television.* to increase or decrease rapidly the magnification of the image of a distant object by means of a zoom lens.

zoom lens *n* a lens system that allows the focal length of a camera lens to be varied continuously without altering the sharpness of the image.

zoomorphism (,zəʊə'mɔːfɪzəm) *n* **1** the conception or representation of deities in the form of animals. **2** the use of animal forms or symbols in art, etc.
▸**,zoo'morphic** *adj*

-zoon *n combining form.* indicating an individual animal or an independently moving entity derived from an animal: *spermatozoon.* [from Gk *zōion* animal]

zoophilism (zəʊ'ɒfɪ,lɪzəm) *n* the tendency to be emotionally attached to animals.
▸**zoophile** ('zəʊə,faɪl) *n*

zoophobia (,zəʊə'fəʊbɪə) *n* an unusual or morbid dread of animals.
▸**zoophobous** (zəʊ'ɒfəbəs) *adj*

zoophyte ('zəʊə,faɪt) *n* any animal resembling a plant, such as a sea anemone.
▸**zoophytic** (,zəʊə'fɪtɪk) *or* **,zoo'phytical** *adj*

zooplankton (,zəʊə'plæŋktən) *n* the animal constituent of plankton, which consists mainly of small crustaceans and fish larvae.

zoospore ('zəʊə,spɔː) *n* an asexual spore of some algae and fungi that moves by means of flagella.
▸**,zoo'sporic** *or* **zoosporous** (zəʊ'ɒspərəs, ,zəʊə'spɔːrəs) *adj*

THESAURUS

ber, dash, flash, fly, hurry, rush, shoot, tear, whizz (*inf.*), zoom
Antonyms *n* ≠ **energy:** apathy, indifference, inertia, laziness, lethargy, listlessness, sloth, sluggishness

zone *n* **1, 2** = **area,** belt, district, region, section, sector, sphere

zoom *vb* **3** = **speed,** barrel (along), burn rubber (*inf.*), buzz, dash, dive, flash, fly, hare (*Brit. inf.*), hum (*sl.*), hurtle, pelt, rip (*inf.*), rush, shoot, streak, tear, whirl, whizz (*inf.*), zip (*inf.*)

zoosterol (zəʊ'ɒstəˌrɒl) *n* any of a group of animal sterols, such as cholesterol.

zootechnics (ˌzəʊə'tɛknɪks) *n* (*functioning as sing*) the science concerned with the domestication and breeding of animals.

zootomy (zəʊ'ɒtəmɪ) *n* the branch of zoology concerned with the dissection and anatomy of animals.
▸**zootomic** (ˌzəʊə'tɒmɪk) *or* ˌ**zoo'tomical** *adj* ▸ˌ**zoo'tomically** *adv* ▸**zo'otomist** *n*

zootoxin (ˌzəʊə'tɒksɪn) *n* a toxin, such as snake venom, that is produced by an animal.

zoot suit (zu:t) *n Sl.* a man's suit consisting of baggy tapered trousers and a long jacket with wide padded shoulders, popular esp. in the 1940s. [C20: from ?]

zoril *or* **zorille** (zə'rɪl) *n* a skunklike African mammal, having a long black-and-white coat. [C18: from F, from Sp. *zorrillo* a little fox, from *zorro* fox]

Zoroastrian (ˌzɒrəʊ'æstrɪən) *adj* **1** of or relating to Zoroastrianism. ◆ *n* **2** an adherent of Zoroastrianism.

Zoroastrianism (ˌzɒrəʊ'æstrɪənˌɪzəm) *or* **Zoroastrism** *n* the dualistic religion founded by the Persian prophet Zoroaster in the late 7th or early 6th century B.C. and set forth in the sacred writings of the Zend-Avesta. It is based on the concept of a continuous struggle between Ormazd (or Ahura Mazda), the god of creation, light, and goodness, and his archenemy, Ahriman, the spirit of evil and darkness.

zoster ('zɒstə) *n Pathol.* short for **herpes zoster.** [C18: from L: shingles, from Gk *zōster* girdle]

Zouave (zu:'ɑ:v, zwɑ:v) *n* **1** (formerly) a member of a body of French infantry composed of Algerian recruits noted for their dash, hardiness, and colourful uniforms. **2** a member of any body of soldiers wearing a similar uniform, esp. a volunteer in such a unit of the Union Army in the American Civil War. [C19: from F, from *Zwāwa,* tribal name in Algeria]

zouk (zu:k) *n* a style of dance music that combines African and Latin American rhythms and uses electronic instruments and modern studio technology. [C20: from West Indian Creole *zouk* to have a good time]

zounds (zaʊndz) *or* **swounds** (zwaʊndz, zaʊndz) *interj Arch.* a mild oath indicating surprise, indignation, etc. [C16: euphemistic shortening of *God's wounds*]

Zr *the chemical symbol for* zirconium.

zucchetto (tsu:'kɛtəʊ, su:-, zu:-) *n, pl* **zucchettos.** *RC Church.* a small round skullcap worn by certain ecclesiastics and varying in colour according to the rank of the wearer, the Pope wearing white, cardinals red, bishops violet, and others black. [C19: from It., from *zucca* a gourd, from LL *cucutia,* prob. from L *cucurbita*]

zucchini (tsu:'ki:nɪ, zu:-) *n, pl* **zucchini** *or* **zucchinis.** *Chiefly US, Canad., & Austral.* another name for **courgette.** [It., pl of *zucchino* a little gourd, from *zucca* gourd; see ZUCCHETTO]

zugzwang (*German* 'tsu:ktsvaŋ) *Chess.* ◆ *n* **1** a position in which one player can move only with loss or severe disadvantage. ◆ *vb* **2** (*tr*) to manoeuvre (one's opponent) into a zugzwang. [from G, from *Zug* a pull + *Zwang* force]

Zulu ('zu:lu, -lu:) *n* **1** (*pl* **Zulus** *or* **Zulu**) a member of a tall Negroid people of SE Africa, who became dominant during the 19th century due to a warrior-clan system organized by the powerful leader, Shaka. **2** the language of this people. [from Zulu *amaZulu* people of the sky]

Zuñi ('zu:nji:, 'su:-) *n* **1** (*pl* **Zuñis** *or* **Zuñi**) a member of a North American Indian people of W New Mexico. **2** the language of this people.
▸**'Zuñian** *adj, n*

zwieback ('zwi:ˌbæk; *German* 'tsvi:bak) *n* a small type of rusk, which has been baked first as a loaf, then sliced and toasted. [G: twice-baked]

Zwinglian ('zwɪŋglɪən, 'tsvɪŋ-) *n* **1** an upholder of the religious doctrines or movement of Zwingli (1484–1531), Swiss leader of the Reformation. ◆ *adj* **2** of or relating to Zwingli, his religious movement, or his doctrines.

zwitterion ('tsvɪtərˌaɪən) *n Chem.* an ion that carries both a positive and a negative charge. [C20: from G *Zwitter* bisexual + ION]

zygapophysis (ˌzɪgə'pɒfɪsɪs, ˌzaɪgə-) *n, pl* **zygapophyses** (-ˌsi:z). *Anat., zool.* one of several processes on a vertebra that articulates with the corresponding process on an adjacent vertebra. [from Gk ZYG- + *apophusis* a sideshoot]

zygo- *or before a vowel* **zyg-** *combining form.* indicating a pair or a union: *zygodactyl; zygospore.* [from Gk *zugon* yoke]

zygodactyl (ˌzaɪgəʊ'dæktɪl, ˌzɪgə-) *adj also* **zygodactylous. 1** (of the feet of certain birds) having the first and fourth toes directed backwards and the second and third forwards. ◆ *n* **2** a zygodactyl bird.

zygoma (zaɪ'gəʊmə, zɪ-) *n, pl* **zygomata** (-mətə). another name for **zygomatic arch.** [C17: via NL from Gk, from *zugon* yoke]
▸**zygomatic** (ˌzaɪgəʊ'mætɪk, ˌzɪg-) *adj*

zygomatic arch *n* the slender arch of bone that forms a bridge between the cheekbone and the temporal bone on each side of the skull of mammals. Also called: **zygoma.**

zygomatic bone *n* either of two bones, one on each side of the skull, that form part of the side wall of the eye socket and part of the zygomatic arch; cheekbone.

zygomorphic (ˌzaɪgəʊ'mɔ:fɪk, ˌzɪg-) *or* **zygomorphous** *adj* (of a flower) capable of being cut in only one plane so that the two halves are mirror images.

zygomycete (ˌzaɪgəʊ'maɪsi:t) *n* any of a phylum of fungi that reproduce sexually by means of zygospores. The group includes various moulds.
▸ˌ**zygomy'cetous** *adj*

zygophyte ('zaɪgəʊˌfaɪt, 'zɪg-) *n* a plant, such as an alga, that reproduces by means of zygospores.

zygospore ('zaɪgəʊˌspɔ:, 'zɪg-) *n* a thick-walled sexual spore formed from the zygote of some fungi and algae.
▸ˌ**zygo'sporic** *adj*

zygote ('zaɪgəʊt, 'zɪg-) *n* **1** the cell resulting from the union of an ovum and a spermatozoon. **2** the organism that develops from such a cell. [C19: from Gk *zugōtos* yoked, from *zugoun* to yoke]
▸**zygotic** (zaɪ'gɒtɪk, zɪ-) *adj* ▸**zy'gotically** *adv*

zymase ('zaɪmeɪs) *n* a mixture of enzymes that is obtained as an extract from yeast and ferments sugars.

zymo- *or before a vowel* **zym-** *combining form.* indicating fermentation: *zymology.* [from Gk *zumē* leaven]

zymogen ('zaɪməʊˌdʒɛn) *n Biochem.* any of a group of compounds that are inactive precursors of enzymes.

zymology (zaɪ'mɒlədʒɪ) *n* the chemistry of fermentation.
▸**zymologic** (ˌzaɪmə'lɒdʒɪk) *or* ˌ**zymo'logical** *adj* ▸**zy'mologist** *n*

zymolysis (zaɪ'mɒlɪsɪs) *n* the process of fermentation. Also called: **zymosis.**

zymosis (zaɪ'məʊsɪs) *n, pl* **zymoses** (-si:z). **1** *Med.* **1a** any infectious disease. **1b** the developmental process or spread of such a disease. **2** another name for **zymolysis.**

zymotic (zaɪ'mɒtɪk) *adj* **1** of, relating to, or causing fermentation. **2** relating to or caused by infection; denoting or relating to an infectious disease.
▸**zy'motically** *adv*

zymurgy ('zaɪmɜ:dʒɪ) *n* the branch of chemistry concerned with fermentation processes in brewing, etc.

W9-CHQ-671
WESTBOROUGH HIGH SCHOOL LIBRARY
WESTBOROUGH, MA 01581

Milenios de México

MILENIOS DE MÉXICO

HUMBERTO MUSACCHIO

RAYA
EN EL
AGUA

Milenios de México
Diccionario Enciclopédico de México

Dirección General: Consuelo Sáizar

Av. Cuauhtémoc 1430
Col. Santa Cruz Atoyac
03310 México, D.F.
5605-7600
5604-9553
mileniosdemexico@mail.internet.com.mx

Producción editorial: Diagrama Casa Editorial S.C.
Diseño: Adriana Díaz
Arte: Víctor Ornelas
Iconografía: Penélope Esparza y Soledad Ribó

Diseño de portada: Ana María Olabuenaga y José Brousset
Fotografía: Flavio Bizzarri
Printing and Binding by Sfera International S.r.l. - Milan Italy

ISBN Obra Completa: 968-6565-34-5
ISBN Tomo II: 968-6565-36-1

Impreso en Italia / *Printed in Italy*

ORMEÑO, WALTER ◆ n. en Perú (1928). Futbolista. Jugó como portero en varios equipos peruanos y alineó con la selección nacional de su país. En 1959 fue contratado por el club América del Distrito Federal. Después jugó para el Atlante y el Morelia. Ha sido director técnico de los equipos Atlante (1964-66), Universidad (1966-68), América (1968-69), Comunicaciones, de Guatemala (1970, 1972 y 1978), al que llevó al campeonato en tres ocasiones; Pachuca (1971), Tampico (1973), Guadalajara (1974), Veracruz (1976) y Atlético Español (1975 y 1980).

ORNELAS ◆ Cabecera del municipio michoacano de Marcos Castellanos (☛).

ORNELAS KUCHLE, OSCAR ◆ n. en Chihuahua, Chih. (1922). Licenciado en derecho por la UNAM (1944). Fundador, maestro y director de la Facultad de Derecho de la Universidad Autónoma de Chihuahua, de la que fue rector (1964-74). Ha sido secretario del Supremo Tribunal de Justicia de Chihuahua, secretario de asuntos educativos del Comité Directivo Estatal del PRI, presidente municipal de la capital del estado, secretario de Finanzas de la Confederación Nacional Campesina, senador de la República (1976-80), representante del Senado ante la Comisión Federal Electoral y gobernador de Chihuahua entre 1980 y 1985, año en que renunció.

ORO ◆ Río de Durango, también llamado Sestín. Nace en la sierra Madre Occidental, entre la sierra del Oso y la sierra de las Canoas, al sur de Hidalgo del Parral, Chihuahua, y al oeste-noroeste de Gómez Palacio. Corre hacia el sureste y desemboca en la presa Lázaro Cárdenas, al oeste de Gómez Palacio.

ORO ◆ Río de Guerrero. Nace en la sierra de la Cuchilla, corre por el noreste de esta formación hacia el oeste-suroeste hasta tributar en el río Balsas, en los límites con Michoacán.

ORO, EL ◆ Municipio de Durango situado al al noreste de Santiago Papasquiaro y al oeste de Gómez Palacio. Superficie: 3,458.8 km^2. Habitantes: 13,516, de los cuales 3,644 forman la población económicamente activa. Hablan tarahumara 23 personas mayores de cinco años. La cabecera municipal es Santa María del Oro.

ORO, EL ◆ Municipio del Estado de México situado en el noroccidente de la entidad, al oeste de Atlacomulco y en los límites con Michoacán. Superficie: 219.87 km^2. Habitantes: 29,466, de los cuales 5,786 forman la población económicamente activa. Hablan alguna lengua indígena 5,028 personas mayores de cinco años (mazahua 5,011). La cabecera municipal es El Oro de Hidalgo.

OROL, JUAN ◆ n. en España y m. en el DF (1897-1988). Se estableció en México hacia 1917. Fue policía del Servicio Secreto (1924-29), torero, actor, reportero, boxeador y director artístico de la radiodifusora del Partido Nacional Revolucionario. Tras un viaje a Hollywood fundó, en 1933, la compañía productora Aspa Films y produjo la película *Sagrario*, del cubano Ramón Peón, quien lo dirigió en esa cinta, y en *Mujeres sin alma* (1934). Dos años después, dice Emilio García Riera, "se convirtió en director de las películas por él producidas, que por largo tiempo serían vistas —con justicia— como grotescas y risibles, de tan mal hechas, y aun, en el futuro, con *snobismo*, como pruebas de un genio incomprendido." Es el realizador, y con frecuencia actor, de cintas como *Madre querida* (1935), *El calvario de una esposa* (1936), *Honrarás a tus padres* (1936), *El derecho y el deber* (1937), *Siboney* (1938), *Cruel destino* (1943), *Los misterios del hampa* (1944), *El amor de mi bohío* (1946), *El reino de los gángsters* (1947), *Gángsters contra charros* (1947), *El charro del arrabal* (1948), *Perdición de mujeres* (1950), *Sandra. La mujer de fuego* (1952), *El sindicato del crimen* (1953), *La mesera del café del puerto* (1954), *Zonga, el ángel diabólico* (1957), *Thaimí, la hija del pescador* (1958), *Bajo el manto de la noche* (1962), *El crimen de la hacienda* (1963), *La maldición de mi raza* (1964), *La virgen de la calle* (1965), *Organización criminal* (1968), *Historia de un gángster* (1968), *El fantástico mundo de los hippies* (1970) y *El tren de la Muerte* (1978), entre otras.

FOTO: JAVIER HINOJOSA

Juan Orol

ORONOZ, CARLOS ◆ n. y m. en Jalapa, Ver. (1820-1901). Combatió en las filas liberales durante las guerras de Reforma. General de brigada en 1858. Ese mismo año fue designado gobernador de Veracruz. Colaboró con los invasores franceses y el imperio de Maximiliano. A las órdenes de Leonardo Márquez combatió en Colima. En 1865 comandó la Tercera División Militar. Gobernador de Oaxaca en agosto de 1866. Dejó el cargo en octubre de ese año, cuando se rindió ante las fuerzas de Porfirio Díaz.

OROPEZA, AGUSTÍN ◆ n. Zacatlán de las Manzanas, Pue. y m. en el DF (1891-1991). Flautista. Comenzó sus estudios musicales de forma autodidacta a los ocho años de edad. Everardo Díaz le instruyó en solfeo. En 1902 se incorporó como flautista en la Orquesta de Manuel González Nieto. En 1908 ingresó al Conservatorio Nacional y se graduó en 1913. Miembro fundador de la Orquesta Beethoven, como flauta segunda. En 1914 partió a Mérida como flauta primera de la Orquesta de la Compañía de Ópera de Sigaldi. De 1924 a 1930 fue flauta primera de la Orquesta Sinfónica local de San Antonio. Realizó una gira por el país con la orquesta del Metropolitan Opera House de Nueva York. Fue segunda (1932-35) y primera (1935-48) flauta de la Orquesta Sinfónica de México. Perteneció a la Orquesta Sinfónica Nacional y fue maestro del Conservatorio Nacional. En Guadalajara dirigió la Escuela de Música de la Universidad y la Orquesta Sinfónica.

OROPEZA, RAFAEL ◆ n. en España y m. en el DF (?-1944). Desde su fundación, en 1936, dirigió la Banda Madrid, del Sindicato de Músicos de la capital española. A la caída de la República salió al exilio. Llegó a México a bordo del buque *Sinaia* en 1939. Grabó más de 100 discos de música española acompañado de su banda. Aquí compuso varios pasodobles, entre los que se cuentan *Mujer mexicana*, *Chiclanera* y *Morena*.

Oros Castillo, Gabriel ◆ n. en Tierra Nueva, SLP (1904). Durante 33 años (1936-1969) fue profesor en diversas poblaciones del país. Ha colaborado en *El Heraldo*, *El Sol de San Luis*, *Ferronales* y *Educación Interamericana*. Dirigió las revistas *La Voz de mi Escuela* y *Teatro Escolar*. Autor de poesía: *Preludios líricos* (1955), *Ritmos de ensueño* (1956), *Perfumes campestres* (1957), *Voces de la tarde* (1960) y *Sinfonías líricas* (1962). También ha escrito teatro y ensayo.

Orozco, Elena ◆ n. en Ciudad del Maíz, SLP (¿1906?). Hija de Wistano Luis Orozco. Colaboradora de las revistas *Plus Ultra*, de Tampico, y *Adelante*, de San Luis Potosí. Escribió *Wistano Luis Orozco, un precursor de la reforma agraria* (1968).

El Hombre, mural de José Clemente Orozco en el Hospicio Cabañas de Guadalajara, Jalisco

Foto: Carlos Hahn

Combate, óleo sobre tela de José Clemente Orozco

Orozco, Gabriel ◆ n. en Xalapa, Ver. (1962). Es egresado de la Escuela Nacional de Artes Plásticas de la UNAM, con estudios en el Círculo de Bellas Artes de Madrid y en Berlín. Reside en Nueva York, donde ha expuesto en el Museo de Arte Moderno y en otros recintos. También ha expuesto en el Museo de Arte Moderno de París y en el Museo de Arte Contemporáneo de Oaxaca. Ha llevado su obra a Madrid y Londres y ha sido uno de los pocos mexicanos, después de Rufino Tamayo, invitado al encuentro de arte alemán *Documenta*.

Orozco, Gladiola ◆ n. en León, Gto. (?). Estudió danza en la escuela de Martha Graham en Nueva York, EUA (1966). Trabajó en el Ballet Nacional de México. Fundó el Ballet Independiente de México que convirtió, en 1979, en el Ballet Teatro del Espacio. Ha sido maestra en la Escuela Nacional de Danza y consejera artística del Conjunto Nacional de Danza, ambos de Cuba. Una de sus coreografías es *Ícaro*.

Orozco, José Clemente ◆ n. en Zapotlán el Grande, actual Ciudad Guzman, Jal., y m. en el DF (1883-1949). A finales del siglo XIX se trasladó a la ciudad de México. Se tituló como perito agrícola en el Colegio de San Jacinto (1900). Pasó a la Escuela Nacional Preparatoria (1903). En los años noventa asistió como oyente a las clases nocturnas de la Escuela Nacional de Bellas Artes o Academia de San Carlos, donde luego hizo estudios formales. En 1904 tenía como maestros a Germán Gedovius y Leandro Izaguirre. En 1910 participó con algunos dibujos en la exposición organizada por la Sociedad de Alumnos, Pintores y Escultores de la misma Academia (1910) y al año siguiente intervino en la huelga de esa institución. En 1910 fue uno de los seis miembros del Centro Artístico que, dirigido por el *Dr. Atl*, trató sin éxito de conseguir muros públicos para pintar. Colaboró como caricaturista e ilustrador en *El Mundo Ilustrado* (1906), *Frivolidades* (1910), *Lo de Menos* (1910), *Testarudos* (1910-

Autorretrato de José Clemente Orozco

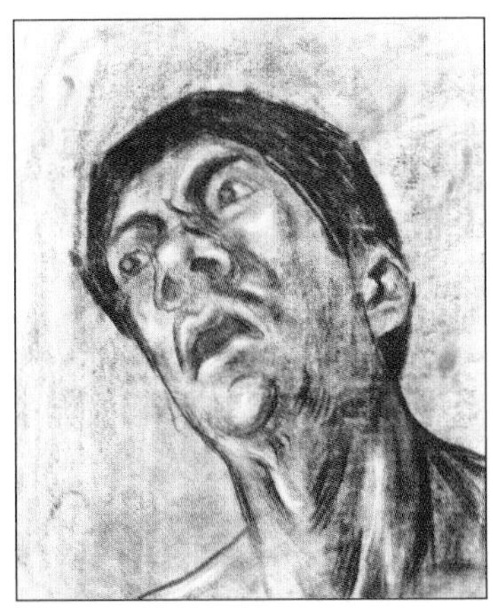

Cabeza de Fermín Chávez, dibujo al carbón de José Clemente Orozco

1912), *Panchito* (1911), *El Ahuizote* (1911), *El Hijo del Ahuizote* (1911-1912), *El Ojo Parado* (1912), *México* (1914), y *La Vanguardia*, periódico carrancista editado en Orizaba por el *Doctor Atl* (1915). En 1916 decoró el café de Los Monotes, propiedad de su hermano, y expuso individualmente, por primera vez, en la librería Biblos de la capital de la República. Al año siguiente viajó por Estados Unidos y se dedicó a hacer carteles de cine. En agosto de 1921, de nuevo establecido en la ciudad de México, fundó, con Lombardo Toledano, Diego Rivera y Jorge Juan Crespo de la Serna, entre otros, el Grupo Solidario del Movimiento Obrero. Ejecutó en 1922 sus primeros murales en la Escuela Nacional Preparatoria, los que borró años más tarde para realizar los murales definitivos. Hizo otro en la Casa de Los Azulejos (1925) y uno más en la Escuela Industrial de Orizaba (1926). Miembro fundador del Sindicato de Obreros Técnicos, Pintores y Escultores. Hizo caricaturas para el periódico sindical *El Machete*, que poco después se convirtió en órgano del Partido Comunista (1924-27). También fue cartonista de *El Heraldo de México* (1920) y la revista *L'ABC* (1925-26). Entre 1927 y 1934 vivió en Estados Unidos, donde presentó varias exposiciones de su obra y pintó murales en el Pomona College, en Clermont, California (1930), en la New School for Social Research, en Nueva York (1930), y en el Dartmouth College, en Hanover, New Hampshire (1932-34). En el mismo año de su retorno ejecutó un mural en el Palacio de Bellas Artes y luego se trasladó a Guadalajara, donde, entre 1936 y 1939, decoró la Universidad, el Palacio de Gobierno y el Hospicio Cabañas. Realizó, en 1940, un mural en la biblioteca Gabino Ortiz de Jiquilpan, Michoacán, y ese mismo año ejecutó otro, transportable, para el Museo de Arte Moderno de Nueva York. En 1941 terminó el de la Suprema Corte de Justicia de la Nación y, en 1944, el del ex templo del Hospital de Jesús. En 1943 figuró entre los miembros fundadores del Colegio Nacional y tres años más tarde recibió el Premio Nacional de Artes y Ciencias. En 1948 concluyó su trabajó en la Escuela Nacional de Maestros (tableros interiores y mural exterior), pintó un mural en el castillo de Chapultepec y al año siguiente inició uno en la bóveda de la Cámara de Diputados de Guadalajara y otro, el segundo exterior, en el multifamiliar Miguel Alemán del DF. Su *Autobiografía se publicó en 1954.*

OROZCO, JOSÉ MARÍA CAYETANO ◆ n. en Cocula, Jal., y m. en la ciudad de Mexico (?-1868). Realizó sus estudios en Guadalajara, en el Seminario Conciliar, hasta 1838. Después de ocuparse de algunos curatos, llegó a ser gobernador de la mitra de la capital jalisciense. Durante la guerra de Reforma, firmó un manifiesto contra las leyes promulgadas por Benito Juárez. En 1863 fue miembro de la Junta de Notables, creada al amparo del ejército francés de ocupación. Fue hecho prisionero al triunfo de la Republica. Escribió *Elementos de la física especial* (1844), *La religión del dinero* (1853) y *Contra las leyes de Reforma* (1859).

FOTO: FONDO EDITORIAL GRUPO AZABACHE

Murales de José Clemente Orozco en el Colegio de San Ildefonso, ciudad de México

FOTO: FONDO EDITORIAL GRUPO AZABACHE

Detalle del mural *Cortés y Malinche* de José Clemente Orozco en el Colegio de San Ildefonso de la ciudad de México

OROZCO, MARÍA ESTHER ◆ n. en San Isidro, Chihuahua (1945). Química bacterióloga parasitóloga graduada en la Universidad Autónoma de Chihuahua, maestra y doctora en ciencias y biología celular por el IPN. En el Cinvestav del IPN, trabaja desde 1981 en proyectos de biomedicina molecular de la multirresistencia a drogas de las cepas de amiba. Miembro del Sistema Nacional de Investigadores desde 1984. Ha publicado 95 artículos científicos y 12 capítulos en libros. Premio Nacional Miguel Otero 1985 de la SSA. Premio Dr. J. Rosenkranz 1991 de Syntex. Medalla Pasteur 1997 de la UNESCO y el Instituto Pasteur, Francia. Mujer Investigadora Internacional por el Instituto Howard Hughes de EUA (1991 y 1997).

Olga Orozco

Orozco, Olga ◆ n. y m. en Argentina (1920-1999). Poeta. Entre sus 12 libros de poesía se encuentran: *Desde lejos* (1946), *Las muertes* (1951), *Los juegos peligrosos* (1962), *Museo salvaje* (1974), *Veintinueve poemas* (1975) y *Obra poética* (1979). Recibió los premios nacionales de las Artes (1980), de Poesía (1988), el Gabriela Mistral (1995) y el de Literatura Latinoamericana y del Caribe Juan Rulfo (1998).

Pascual Orozco

Orozco, Pascual ◆ n. en la Hacienda de Santa Isabel, Chih., y m. en EUA (1882-1915). Hijo de Pascual Orozco Merino. Era simpatizante de los grupos magonistas y antirreelecionistas de Chihuahua. Se levantó en armas contra el gobierno de Porfirio Díaz el 19 de noviembre de 1910. En diciembre de ese año fue ascendido a coronel y se le nombró jefe de las fuerzas maderistas en Chihuahua. En mayo de 1911 tomó Ciudad Juárez, pese a las órdenes de Francisco I. Madero en sentido contrario, con lo que se aceleró la derrota del ejército federal. A la caída de la dictadura fue designado jefe de los Rurales de Chihuahua y más tarde de Sinaloa. En marzo de 1912, arguyendo el incumplimiento del Plan de San Luis, lanzó a su vez el Plan de la Empacadora y se levantó en armas contra el gobernador chihuahuense Abraham González y el presidente Madero. Derrotado por Victoriano Huerta, dispersó a sus tropas y viajó a Estados Unidos, donde permaneció, reclutando hombres y dinero, hasta la caída de Madero (febrero de 1913). Volvió a Mexico y se incorporó a las fuerzas huertistas. Encargado de defender Chihuahua, soportó el avance villista hasta enero de 1914, cuando se vió obligado a abandonar la capital del estado. Continuó peleando en Chihuahua, pero la renuncia de Huerta (en julio de 1914) lo obligó a exiliarse de nuevo en Estados Unidos. Se instaló en El Paso, Texas. Mientras organizaba, junto con Huerta, una incursión armada a México, fue detenido brevemente por la policía estadounidense. En agosto de 1915 fue ejecutado cuando intentaba robar unos caballos.

Orozco, Regina ◆ n. en el DF (1964). Realizó estudios en el Conservatorio Nacional, en la Escuela de Arte Teatral del INBA y en el Centro Universitario de Teatro de la UNAM. Hizo cursos de perfeccionamiento como cantante de ópera en la Julliard School de Nueva York, EUA. Participó como actriz en obras como *Doña Giovanni* y *Atracciones Fénix*, y en diversos cortometrajes de la realizadora Ximena Cuevas. Incursionó en el cine en la cinta *Sólo con tu pareja* (1990) y ha participado en *La vida conyugal* (1993), *Dama de noche* (1993), *De tripas corazón* (1994), *Mujeres insumisas* (1994), *Profundo carmesí* (1996) y *Santitos* (1999). También mantiene una carrera como cantante de ópera y en distintos espectáculos de cabaret.

Orozco, Wistano Luis ◆ n. en San Cristóbal de la Barranca y m. en Guadalajara, Jal. (1856-1927). Estudió en el Seminario Conciliar y en la Escuela de Derecho de Guadalajara. Se graduó en 1884. Por oponerse al gobernador porfirista, fue encarcelado. Se fugó y se estableció en el centro del país. Sus libros *Legislación y jurisprudencia sobre terrenos baldíos* (1895) y *La reforma agraria* (1911), contribuyeron al conocimiento de los problemas del campo. En 1914 fue nombrado secretario general de gobierno de Colima y, por ausencia del gobernador, se encargó del Poder Ejecutivo estatal entre el 7 de noviembre y el 1 de diciembre de ese año. Más tarde volvió a Guadalajara y se dedicó a la docencia.

Orozco Alfaro, José de Jesús ◆ n. en Colima (1956). Licenciado en Economía por la UNAM con posgrado en la Universidad de París. Pertenece al PRI, donde se ha desempeñado como director del CEPES, secretario de Planeación Política y secretario de Organización del CDE en Colima. Fue presidente municipal de Colima. Es senador de la República y miembro de la Gran Comisión (1994-2000).

Orozco y Berra, Fernando ◆ n. en San Felipe del Obraje, hoy del Progreso, Edo. Méx., y m. en la ciudad de México (1822-1851). Hermano de Manuel Orozco y Berra. Se graduó como médico en 1845, en Puebla. Editó un periódico teatral llamado *El Entreacto*. Posteriormente radicó en la ciudad de México, donde además de ejercer la medicina, colaboró en los periodicos *El Monitor Republicano*, *El Liceo Mexicano* y *El Siglo XIX*, entre otros. Escribió las siguientes obras de teatro: *Tres aspirantes* (1848), *Tres Patriotas* (1850), *La tienda de modas*, *Amistad* y *El novio y el alojado*. Es autor de la novela: *La guerra de treinta años* (1850).

Orozco y Berra, Manuel ◆ n. y m. en la ciudad de México (1816-1881). Ingeniero agrónomo por el Colegio de Minería de la ciudad de México (1830-34) y licenciado en derecho por el Seminario Palafoxiano de Puebla (1847). Fue secretario general de Gobierno del estado (1847-48), director del Archivo General de la Nación (1852-56), oficial mayor encargado de la Secretaría de Fomento durante el gobierno de Ignacio Comonfort (septiembre a octubre de 1857 y diciembre de 1857 a enero de 1858) y ministro de la Suprema Corte de Justicia de la Nación. Durante el imperio de Maximiliano, fue subsecretario de Fomento (1864-65), consejero de Estado (1865-66) y director del Museo Nacional (1866-67). Al triunfo de la República fue hecho prisionero, juzgado y condenado a cuatro años de prisión, pero debido a sus enfermedades se le liberó dos años más tarde. Autor de *Noticia histórica de la conjuración del Marqués del Valle* (1853), *Diccionario Universal de historia y Geografía* (10 t., entre 1853 y 1856), *Memoria para la carta hidrográfica del valle de México* (1864), *Geografía de las lenguas y carta etnográfica de México* (1864), *Memoria para el plano de la ciu-*

dad de México (1867), *Materiales para una cartografía mexicana* (1871), *Historia de la geografía en México* (1880), *Historia antigua y de la conquista de México* (4 t., 1881), *Apuntes para la historia de la geografía en México* (1881), e *Historia de la dominación española en México* (4 t., 1884).

OROZCO CAMACHO, MIGUEL ♦ n. en Zapopan, Jal., y m. en el DF (1887-1945). Durante la revolución formó parte del ejército del noroeste. Fue jefe de los departamentos de Infantería (1932-33) y de Ingenieros (1934-35); jefe del Estado Mayor del Ejército (1936-37), oficial mayor de la Secretaría de la Defensa Nacional (1937-41) y director del penal de las islas Marías.

OROZCO E., FERNANDO ♦ n. en Santo Tomás y m. en Chihuahua, Chih. (1886-1945). Dirigió el Partido Liberal Progresista Chihuahuense. En mayo de 1927 fue nombrado gobernador interino y más tarde provisional. Desempeñó el cargo hasta octubre de 1928.

OROZCO Y GÓMEZ, MANUEL ♦ n. y m. en Morelia, Mich. (1864-1889). Se graduó como abogado en 1887 en Morelia. Escribió el libro de poesía *Crepúsculo* y las obras de teatro *De abismo en abismo* y *Antonia*, entre otras.

OROZCO Y JIMÉNEZ, FRANCISCO ♦ n. en Zamora, Mich., y m. en Guadalajara, Jal. (1864-1936). Se ordenó sacerdote en Italia. Fue profesor del Colegio Josefino y del Seminario Conciliar de México, donde llegó a ser vicerrector. Fue también secretario de la Nueva Universidad Pontificia, obispo de Chiapas (1902-12) y arzobispo de Guadalajara (1912-36). Durante dos años (1914-16) vivió en Estados Unidos. En 1918, por oponerse a la Constitución, fue desterrado. Volvió al año siguiente y sostuvo duros enfrentamientos con el gobernador jalisciense José Guadalupe Zuno. Durante la guerra cristera se ocultó en las montañas y vivió entre grupos armados. Terminado el conflicto fue deportado a Estados Unidos (julio de 1929 a marzo de 1930), pues el gobierno temía la influencia de sus posiciones extremistas. En el exilio desaprobó el *modus vivendi* acordado entre el presidente Emilio Portes Gil y los dignatarios eclesiásticos Leopoldo Ruiz y Flores y Pascual Díaz. Reintegrado a su arquidiócesis, fue nuevamente expulsado del país. Radicó en Roma hasta que el presidente Lázaro Cárdenas permitió su retorno (1935).

OROZCO LOMELÍN, FRANCISCO ♦ n. en Lagos de Moreno, Jal., y m. en el DF (1917-1990). Se ordenó sacerdote en 1940. Desde 1952 fue obispo auxiliar de México, donde se encargaba de la vicaría episcopal de la VII zona pastoral y de la vicaría general de la arquidiócesis. El 3 de septiembre de 1968, como vocero oficial de la Mitra capitalina, negó que la Catedral hubiera sido profanada por los estudiantes, como decían algunos periódicos.

OROZCO LORETO, GUILLERMO ♦ n. en Guadalajara, Jal. (1954). Licenciado en economía por la Universidad de Guadalajara (1971-76). Priista desde 1980, ha sido subsecretario de Finanzas del CEN (1980) y secretario de Finanzas del Comité Distrital en el DF (1984-85). Subdirector general de Contraloría (1980) y subdirector de Contabilidad y Presupuesto (1980-81) de la Secretaría de la Reforma Agraria; director general de Evaluación y Control de la Secretaría del Trabajo (1981-82), secretario técnico de la Comisión Interna de Administración y Programación (1982-83) y gerente de Recursos Humanos (1983-84) de la Secretaría de Comunicaciones y Transportes; director general regional de la Zona Sur del DDF (1985-88) y delegado en Tlalpan (1988-90) y Cuauhtémoc (1990-92).

OROZCO MERINO, PASCUAL ♦ n. en el estado de Chihuahua y m. cerca de Cuautla, Mor. (1859-1913). Se dedicó al comercio hasta que se incorporó a la revolución, a las órdenes de su hijo Pascual Orozco, en cuyo ejército alcanzó el grado de coronel. Después del triunfo maderista fue diputado suplente en la legislatura del estado de Chihuahua. En 1912 desconoció al gobierno de Francisco I. Madero. Pasó a Estados Unidos, donde fue detenido algunos meses. Tras el asesinato del presidente, reconoció al gobierno de Victoriano Huerta y se incorporó a sus fuerzas. Al año siguiente fue enviado a Morelos para intentar una alianza con el Ejército Libertador del Sur. Fue fusilado por los zapatistas.

OROZCO MUÑOZ, FRANCISCO ♦ n. en San Francisco del Rincón, Gto., y m. en el DF (1884-1950). Estudió medicina en Bélgica. Durante la primera guerra mundial colaboró con la Cruz Roja. Fue diputado federal (1918-20), secretario de las representaciones mexicanas en Bélgica, España y Suiza; jefe del Departamento de Bibliotecas del Museo Nacional, director de la Escuela de Bibliotecarios y jefe del Departamento de Bibliotecas de la Secretaría de Educación Pública. Escribió *Invasión y conquista de la Bélgica mártir* (1915), *La Belgique Violée* (1917), *Bélgica en la paz* (1919), *¡Oh, tú, que comienzas a tener un pasado!* (1932) y *Renglones de Sevilla* (1947).

OROZCO PERALTA, JOSÉ ♦ n. en Veracruz, Ver. (1937). Estudió en la Escuela Naval Militar Antón Lizardo (1954-58) y en el Centro de Estudios Superiores Navales (1975-76). Obtuvo la maestría en guerra naval en el US Naval War College, EUA (1983-84). Fue profesor en la Academia Naval de Estados Unidos (1970-72) y en el Centro de Estudios Superiores Navales (1978-83). Ha sido agregado militar adjunto en la embajada mexicana en Washington (1970-72), jefe de ayudantes del secretario de Marina (1972-75), comandante del buque escuela M. Azueta (1977) y de la tercera flotilla (1977); director de Protección al Medio Ambiente Marino de la Armada de México (1982-83), jefe del Estado Mayor de la Quinta Zona Naval Militar (1984-85) y comandante del sector naval de Zihuatanejo (1985-86). En 1986 fue nombrado director de la Escuela Naval Militar Antón Lizardo.

OROZCO RIVERA, MARIO ♦ n. y m. en el DF (1930-1998). Estudió en la Escuela de Pintura y Escultura La Esmeralda. En 1953 expuso por

Mario Orozco Rivera

Fernando Orozco y Berra

Manuel Orozco y Berra

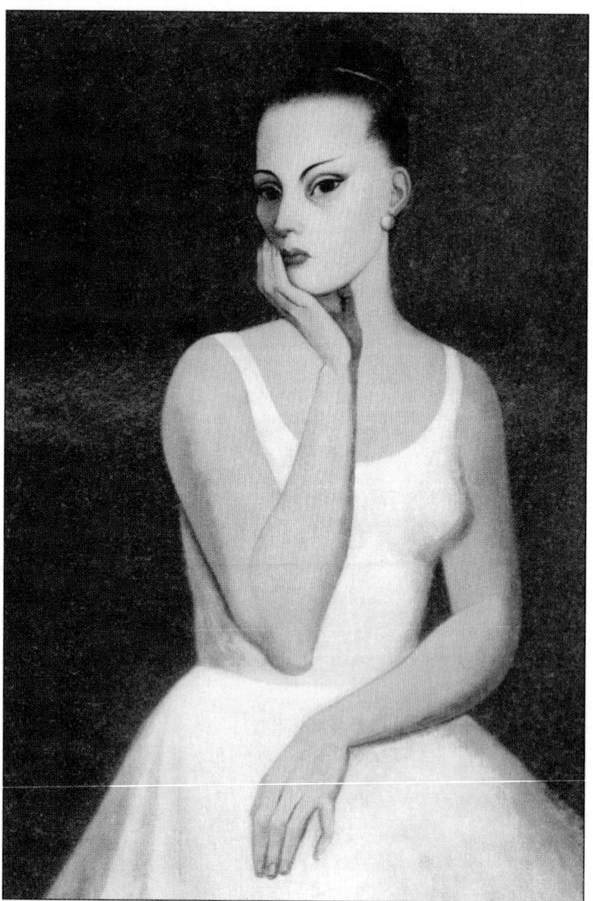

Retrato de María Marín, óleo sobre tela de Carlos Orozco Romero

primera vez, en el Círculo de Bellas Artes de México. Fue profesor de la UNAM, La Esmeralda y la Universidad Veracruzana. En esta fundó el Taller de Artes Plásticas (1963). Fue miembro del PCM (1947-81) y del PSUM (1981-87). Entre los murales que ejecutó se cuentan *Defensa, continuidad y destino de nuestra cultura*, en el Museo del Instituto de Antropología (1959), *Tríptico: lucha por la existencia y la creación en la naturaleza* en la Facultad de Veterinaria y Zootecnia (1960), *Veracruz revolucionario*, en la Biblioteca Central (1961), y *Microorganismos*, en la Facultad de Ciencias Químicas (1964), todos en la Universidad Veracruzana; *Lucha de clases*, en el edificio del Sindicato de Obreros Textiles, El Dique, en Jalapa, (1962); *Adolescencia*, en la Escuela Secundaria Antonio María Rivera (1963); *Carta abierta*, en el edificio del diario *El Mundo* de Córdoba (1963); *Cuauhnáhuac*, en el Hotel de México, en el Distrito Federal (1968); *De la agricultura a la industria*, en el Banco Agropecuario de Culiacán, Sinaloa (1969); otro en la embajada de Polonia en México y *La Universidad en la luchas del pueblo mexicano hacia su liberación*, en la Universidad Autónoma de Puebla (1979). Obtuvo el premio de Adquisición del Salón de la Plástica Mexicana, en 1955 y 1956. En 1957 recibió un premio en el Concurso Internacional de Pintura, en Moscú. También se dedicó a la composición de canciones políticas (1960-80).

Carlos Orozco Sosa

Orozco Romero, Alberto ◆ n. en Guadalajara, Jal. (1925). En 1950 se tituló como abogado en la Universidad de Guadalajara, donde ha sido profesor. Fue ministro de la Suprema Corte de Justicia de la Nación y presidente de la Cuarta Sala (1967-70). Gobernador constitucional de Jalisco (1971-77).

Orozco Romero, Carlos ◆ n. en Guadalajara, Jal., y m. en el DF (1898-1984). Fue miembro del llamado Centro Bohemio de Guadalajara, en el que participaban, hacia 1913, David Alfaro Siqueiros, Xavier Guerrero, Carlos Stahl y José Guadalupe Zuno. Al año siguiente se trasladó a la ciudad de México, donde colaboró como caricaturista en los periódicos *Excélsior*, *El Heraldo de México* y *El Universal Ilustrado*. Becado, hizo estudios en España y en Francia. En París, en 1922, expuso en el Salón de Otoño. En Guadalajara ejecutó tres murales: *Alfareros totonacas*, en el Museo Regional (1923), *Aplicación de las artes a la vida*, en la Biblioteca del Estado (1925), y *Hombre apisonando la tierra*, en la Dirección de Caminos (1926). Fundador, con Carlos Mérida, de la Galería del Palacio de Bellas Artes (1928-31) y de la Escuela de Danza del INBA (1932). A partir de 1934, con el mismo Mérida se dedicó al diseño gráfico, especialidad en la que trabajó en el Departamento Autónomo de Arte y Publicidad (1938). Fue miembro de la LEAR (1934-38). Cofundador de la Escuela de Pintura y Escultura La Esmeralda (1946), donde fue profesor 20 años. Director del Museo de Arte Moderno del DF (1946-61). Sus trabajos están publicados en *Los pequeños grabadores en madera* (1925) y *Tres aguafuertes en color con tres originales de Carlos Orozco Romero* (1938). Ingresó en la Academia de Artes en 1974. Fue becario de la Fundación Guggenheim (1940). En 1956 el Congreso de Jalisco le otorgó la insignia José Clemente Orozco y en 1980 recibió el Premio Nacional de Ciencias y Artes.

Orozco Sosa, Carlos ◆ n. en Morelia, Mich. (1930). Ingeniero petrolero por la UNAM (1952-56). Pertenece al PRI desde 1952. Trabajó en Pemex hasta llegar a subdirector técnico administrativo (1957-82). Ha sido subdirector administrativo de Aduanas de la Secretaría de Hacienda (1972-76), director general de Personal de la UNAM; asesor del director general y director de Puertos Industriales de Fondeport (1983-84). En Ferrocarriles Nacionales de México ha ocupado los cargos de subgerente de Administración (1986-87), subdirector general de Personal y Servicios Generales (1987-88) y director general (1988-92). Fue presidente del Colegio de Ingenieros Petroleros de México (1977-79).

Orquesta, La ◆ Periódico satírico publicado en la ciudad de México. El número inicial apareció el primero de marzo de 1861, con Carlos R. Casarín como redactor jefe, Constantino Escalante como caricaturista y Manuel C. de

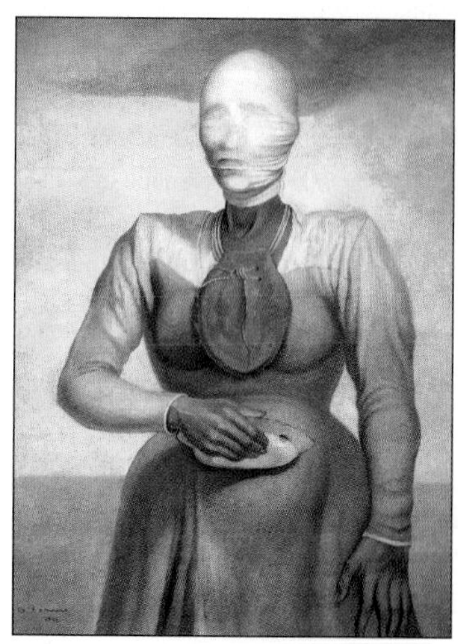

La manda, óleo sobre tela de Carlos Orozco Romero

Villegas, encargado de la edición y la administración. Los tres y el grabador Hesiquio Iriarte eran los propietarios. Esperamos, decían los editores, que el gobierno "oirá nuestras overturas (SIC) en pro de la protección al trabajo, a la industria; nuestros poutpurrís en cuanto a mejoras materiales y lo que cantemos en pro de lo que sea." La publicación, con cuatro páginas de texto y una caricatura en hoja aparte, salía puntualmente miércoles y sábados y fue tal su éxito que al año anunciaba que sólo en la capital circulaban 5,600 ejemplares y otros tantos en los estados. El blanco de sus críticas, en la primera etapa, fue el gobierno de Juárez. De la demolición de edificios eclesiásticos, realizada al amparo de las Leyes de Reforma, comentaban que "el romántico gobierno, para tener escena donde representar sus comedias, manda derribar los conventos para abrir nuevas calles y tener ruinas." En el primer año los editores debieron afrontar varias acusaciones de los que resultaron absueltos por los jurados populares que veían los llamados delitos de prensa. Al iniciarse la invasión francesa, Casarín se incorporó a las fuerzas de Ignacio Zaragoza hasta que, herido, volvió a la redacción. El mismo Casarín murió a principios de 1862, a consecuencia de un duelo a espada sostenido con un personaje conservador al que señaló como partidario de la intervención. En junio de 1864, al entrar los franceses en la capital del país, los editores de *La Orquesta* se ocultaron y Constantino Escalante logró huir a Pachuca, donde fue aprehendido y trasladado a la ciudad de México en una jaula, "encerrado como una fiera", según Hilarión Frías y Soto. De esta manera se vengaban los invasores del caricaturista, quien había dibujado a Saligny como borrachín, en un cartón que se reprodujo en Europa. En 1864 Escalante fue liberado y, al amparo de la Ley de Imprenta de 1855, entonces vigente, el periódico se volvió a publicar con Lorenzo Elízaga como redactor jefe, quien aclaró que la publicación "no ha variado ni variará nunca

La Orquesta

de casaca ni de tono." Elízaga fue sustituido por Juan A. Mateos, quien insertó un texto que despertó las iras del mariscal Bazaine, quien hizo detener a Villegas, el que acusó en el propio periódico a Mateos de denunciante, lo que sirvió para que éste se presentara a declarar su presunta culpa y pidiera la libertad de Villegas. El siguiente jefe de redacción, Luis Gonzaga Iza, fue en 1865 a la cárcel por defender las Leyes de Reforma y hacer una certera crítica de Félix Zuloaga. Iza tuvo el valor de enviar unos versos desde la prisión, a la que irónicamente llamó "Miramar", en referencia al castillo de Maximiliano en Trieste:

Desde este regio palacio
que me sirve ahora de asilo
y que el Sr. Juez Fernández
que es hombre caritativo
hace que me alquilen gratis
para bien de mi bolsillo.

En diciembre del mismo año, el entonces redactor jefe, Juan N. Berra, recibió siete puñaladas de unos desconocidos. En abril de 1866 los editores fueron obligados a insertar una primera advertencia "por haber violado los derechos sagrados del respeto (sic) del público". Una segunda advertencia, con suspensión por un mes, fue causada por una caricatura de los ministros de Maximiliano. La tercera, acompañada del cierre del periódico, fue por anunciar que el Emperador abdicaría en caso de no recibir un empréstito francés. A fines de junio de 1867, cinco días después de que las fuerzas republicanas habían recuperado la ciudad de México, se inició la tercera y última época del periódico, con el general Vicente Riva Palacio como redactor jefe, quien abogó por la amnistía general, "con señaladas excepciones que bien ha marcado la opinión pública", para los que habían colaborado con los invasores. En 1867 *La Orquesta* apoyó la candidatura de Porfirio Díaz a la Presidencia de la República. En 1869 murió Escalante y fue sustituido por Santiago Hernández, Jesús T. Alamilla y José María Villasana, con quienes el periódico se mantuvo dentro de una línea crítica hacia el gobierno de Juárez. Sin embargo, al morir el Benemérito, el periódico publicó: "Juárez ha muerto. Estas palabras deben de resonar en los oídos de todo el mundo, como el ruido que produce la caída de un gran monumento, de un coloso". Durante la presidencia de Lerdo de Tejada el periódico, abierto partidario de Díaz, continuó en el ejercicio de la crítica hacia el poder público hasta que por dificultades financieras cerró en 1874. Al triunfo de la asonada de Tuxtepec, se reinició la publicación con S. Mora como redactor en jefe y Villegas como editor. Pero se había iniciado el porfiriato y para el nuevo gobernante no era grata la crítica, ni siquiera la de sus antiguos simpatizantes. *La Orquesta*, desaparecida a fines de 1877, es, según Eduardo del Río *Rius*, "la gran revista de humor del siglo pasado. Es el gran ejemplo de prensa comprometida y de una calidad artística de primera clase."

ORQUESTA FILARMÓNICA DE QUERÉTARO ◆ Fundada en 1986, nació con el nombre de Filarmónica del Bajío, dentro del programa Nuevas Orquestas de la SEP, en colaboración con los estados de Querétaro, Guanajuato y Aguascalientes. Su proyecto era atender las necesidades musicales de esa región del país. Hasta 1994 había ofrecido 1,180 conciertos en 12 estados de la República y en Texas para 70,000 espectadores. Su director titular era Sergio Cárdenas.

Ofreció su primer concierto el 21 de agosto de 1986 en el Teatro Juárez de Guanajuato, que fue su sede. Por cinco años tuvo a su cargo la inauguración del Festival Internacional Cervantino. En 1991 el gobernador Carlos Medina Plascencia suspendió las subvenciones estatales a la orquesta, por lo que ésta se mudó a Querétaro y adoptó su actual nombre. El 10 de abril de 1992 ofreció su primer concierto en el Auditorio Josefa Ortiz de Domínguez, donde a partir de entonces estableció su sede. El 25 de mayo de 1992 se constituyó un patronato que apoya y sustenta las actividades de esta institución musical.

Aniceto Ortega

ORQUESTA SINFÓNICA DE XALAPA ◆ Fue fundada en 1929 por un grupo de profesores encabezados por el violinista Juan Lomán (☛). Durante la siguiente década tuvo serios problemas económicos. En 1944, el gobierno del estado de Veracruz encomendó a José Yves Limantour la reorganización del conjunto. Transformada, en poco tiempo se convirtió en una de las más importantes del país. Realizó giras por toda la República y presentó óperas, conciertos y otros géneros de grandes dimensiones. Por dificultades administrativas, cambió de sede en los años setenta, al norte del país, donde adoptó el nombre de Orquesta Sinfónica del Noroeste; de allí se trasladó a Guadalajara y, una vez resuelta la crisis, logró regresar a su sede original. Sus directores titulares (luego de Limantour) han sido Luis Ximénez Caballero, Francisco Savín, Luis Herrera de la Fuente, José Guadalupe Flores, Sergio Ortiz, Enrique Diemecke y nuevamente Francisco Savín.

Gregorio Ortega

ORQUESTA TÍPICA DE LA CIUDAD DE MÉXICO ◆ Se fundó en 1884 como la Orquesta Típica de Carlos Curi, quien adaptaba temas populares a la música de concierto e incorporaba instrumentos nacionales como la marimba, arpa, salterio y bandolón. Durante la administración de Porfirio Díaz fue bautizada como Orquesta Típica Mexicana y bajo la dirección de Miguel Lerdo de Tejada recibió su actual nombre. Por ella han pasado músicos como Pablo Mari, Ignacio Fernández Esperón *Tata Nacho*, Jesús Corona, Félix Santana, Jesús Galarza, Daniel Zaragoza, Mario Talavera y Alfonso Esparza Oteo y los cantantes Irma González, Cristina Ortega, Gilda Cruz Romo, Gil Mondragón, Tito Guízar, Pedro Vargas y José Mojica.

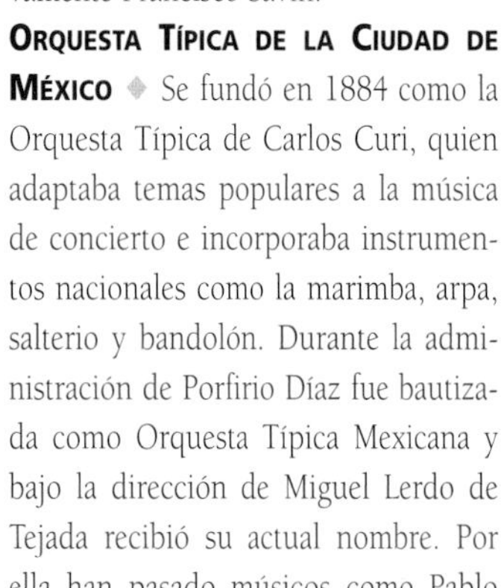

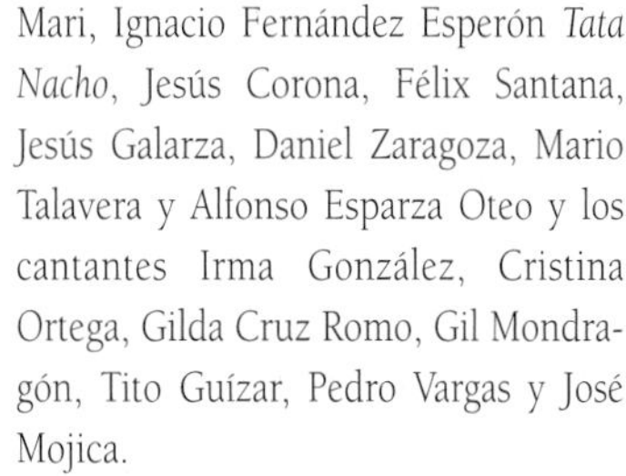

ORRANTIA, FRANCISCO ◆ n. y m. en Álamos, Son. (¿1770-1840?). Por ausencia de Francisco Iriarte, el Congreso local lo designó gobernador interino de Sonora en 1826.

ORRANTIA Y ANTELO, FRANCISCO ◆ n. y m. en Alamos, Son. (1803-¿1860?). Diputado local vocal de la junta departamental (1836-37) y gobernador interino de Sinaloa (junio de 1837 a enero de 1838). Más tarde fue elegido vicegobernador.

ORRICO DE LOS LLANOS, MIGUEL ◆ n. en San Juan Bautista, Tab. (1894-?). Se incorporó a la revolución constitucionalista en 1913. Después de la revolución continuó en el ejército, donde fue inspector de la Primera Zona Militar, jefe del Estado Mayor de las jefaturas de operaciones de Querétaro, Quintana Roo, Tlaxcala y Zacatecas, así como comandante de las zonas militares de Nuevo León y Sonora. General de división en 1952. Fue gobernador de Tabasco, en sustitución de Tomás Bartlett Bautista, de marzo de 1955 a diciembre de 1958, periodo en el que reanudó la celebración de la Exposición Regional, se puso en servicio el Museo de La Venta y Villahermosa quedó unida por carretera a Coatzacoalcos; reinstaló la biblioteca Martí, hizo construir el rastro municipal de Villahermosa y realizó otras obras de interés público en la capital tabasqueña.

ORRICO TOLEDO, RUBÉN DARÍO ◆ n. en el DF (1948). Licenciado en economía por la UNAM (1967-71), especializado en análisis económico y política financiera (1978) en el FMI. Pertenece al PRI desde 1968, donde ha sido secretario de afiliación juvenil (1969), miembro de la Comisión de Planeación del Programa de Gobierno (1981), asesor del director del IEPES (1982) y coordinador general de Presupuesto (1988). Se ha desempeñado como jefe del Departamento Técnico de Minería (1974), asesor del director de Estudios Económicos (1977) y subdirector de Evaluación Hacendaria (1978) de la Secretaría de Hacienda y Crédito Publico director de Presupuesto y Contabilidad de la SPP (1982) y director de Finanzas de la Presidencia de la República (1988-93).

ORTA, JORGE *CHAROLITO* ◆ n. en Mazatlán, Sin. (1950). Beisbolista. Jugó varias posiciones, especialmente la segunda base y los jardines. Desde 1972 jugó en equipos de las grandes ligas, como *Indios* de Cleveland y *Medias Blancas* de Chicago, entre otros, donde destacó como bateador.

ORTA MATA, MARÍA DE JESÚS ◆ n. en Cedral, SLP (1951). Profesora normalista por el Colegio Labastida (1976) y licenciada en administración pública por la Universidad Autónoma de Nuevo León (1983). De 1976 a 1982 fue maestra de primaria. Diputada federal del Partido Demócrata Mexicano (1982-85).

ORTEGA, ANICETO ◆ n. en Tulancingo, Hgo., y m. en la ciudad de México (1825-1875). Su segundo apellido era Del Villar. Primo de Francisco González Bocanegra. Se graduó como médico en 1845. Fue uno de los primeros obstetras mexicanos y, entre partos y consultas, escribía música, ámbito en el que también destacó. Su marcha *Zaragoza* (1863) era interpretada como himno nacional durante los gobiernos de Juárez, Lerdo de Tejada, el primer periodo de Porfirio Díaz y el de Manuel González. Entre sus obras más importantes están *Luna de miel*, *Invocación a Beethoven*, *Recuerdo de la amistad*, *Marcha Potosina*, *Marcha Republicana* y la ópera *Guatimotzín*, precursora del nacionalismo. Fue miembro del Consejo Superior de Salubridad de la ciudad de México y miembro fundador de la Sociedad Filarmónica de México (1866), que creó el Conservatorio Nacional de Música, del cual redactó su primer reglamento y fue profesor.

Ortega, Cristina ◆ n. en el DF (1940). Soprano. Estudió en el Conservatorio Nacional bajo la supervisión de Ángel R. Esquivel. Realizó su debut operístico en Monterrey (1963) con *Lucia di Lammermoor,* y un año después en el Palacio de Bellas Artes, con *La Traviata,* y actuó en el papel de Susana de *Las bodas de Fígaro.* Presentó la opereta *La viuda alegre* 138 veces en una sola temporada. Ha grabado numerosas canciones tradicionales de compositores mexicanos.

Ortega, Gregorio ◆ n. en el DF (1948). Estudió la licenciatura en letras francesas en la Universidad de París, Francia. Trabajó en la *Revista de América, El Nacional, Ovaciones, El Universal, Siempre!* y *unomásuno*, donde fue director del suplemento *Página Uno* (1993-98). Agregado cultural de la embajada en Suecia (1971-72), subdirector de Difusión (1972-73) y director de Administración del Programa Nacional de Mejoramiento Profesional del Magisterio (1976-77), gerente de difusión del Fonapas, (1978-79), asesor de difusión del Infonavit (1978-82), fundador y director de prensa de la Agencia Nacional para la Información de la Juventud (1979-80), coordinador de Difusión de la SPP (1980-81), secretario particular del subsecretario de Gobernación (1982-84), coordinador de investigadores para Asuntos Especiales de la Presidencia de la República (1984-88), secretario particular del director de la Comisión Nacional de los Libros de Texto Gratuitos (1984-92) y gerente de proyectos especiales de Taesa (1999-). Autor de ensayo: *El sindicalismo contemporáneo, ¿El fin de la Revolución Mexicana?, Casa Maya* y *Las muertas de Ciudad Juárez. El caso de Elizabeth Castro García y Abdel Latif Sharif* (1999); y novela: *Los círculos del poder, Estado de gracia, La maga* y *Crímenes de familia.* Coordinador de: *Fernando Gutiérrez Barrios. Diálogos con el hombre, el poder y la política, Salinas. La globalización del pánico* y *Cecilia Soto.* Premio de Periodismo José Pagés Llergo, en reportaje (1996).

Ortega, Héctor ◆ n. en el DF (1939). Actor y dramaturgo. Su nombre completo es Héctor Bernardo Ortega Gómez. Estudió teatro, danza y pantomima en el Teatro Estudio con Alejandro Jodorowsky, Carlos Ancira, Guillermo Arriaga y Juan José Arreola y formó parte de la primera compañía de mimos en México. En teatro, actuó en *La hermosa gente* (1957), *Fin de partida,* de Jodorowsky (premio Revelación Teatral de la Asociación de Críticos Teatrales, 1960), *¿Crimen, suicidio?* (1960), *El aguijón* (1960), *Las sillas,* de Ionesco (1960), *Penélope,* de Leonora Carrington; *La piel de nuestros dientes, Asesinato en la catedral, El alfarero y la apassionata, Hamlet, Romeo y Julieta, Escuela de bufones, El rey se muere, La muerte accidental de un anarquista* (premio al mejor actor de comedia, 1985), *El huevo de Colón* (1992) y *Molière,* de Sabina Berman (dir. Antonio Serrano, 1999). Autor de las obras: *Historia del oeste, Silencio hospital, hombres trabajando* (1966), *Cinco locos en uno* (1968), *¡Hay Cuauhtémoc, no te rajes!* (1985) y de la paráfrasis sobre la obra de T.S. Elliot *Muerte en la Catedral.* Ganó un Ariel para actor de cuadro por *Mariana, Mariana* (1987).

Ortega, Roberto Diego ◆ n. en el DF (1955). Escritor. Hijo de Vicente Ortega Colunga. Licenciado en periodismo por la UNAM. Formó parte del Taller de Poesía Sintética. Ha colaborado en los suplementos *La Cultura en México,* del semanario *Siempre!,* y *Sábado,* del diario *unomásuno*, así como en *Revista de la Universidad, As de Corazones, La Gaceta del FCE* y otras publicaciones. Fue jefe de redacción de *Nexos* y es director de *Su Otro Yo* y *Viva.* Autor del poemario *Línea del horizonte* (1979).

Ortega Arenas, Joaquín ◆ n. en el DF (1924). Sobrino bisnieto de León Guzmán. Licenciado en derecho por la UNAM. En 1944 se inició como litigante. En 1959 el Departamento Agrario reconoció a una empresa privada como propietaria de los terrenos en que se halla la ciudad de Tijuana, ante lo cual los habitantes recurrieron a su defensa. Ortega llevó a lo largo de una década el caso de los tijuanenses afectados y logró que la firma comercial aceptara una pequeña indemnización. Cuando se expropiaron terrenos comunales para el proyecto turístico de Bahías de Huatulco, se convirtió en abogado de los comuneros y logró que un juez diera entrada a la demanda de amparo contra el decreto presidencial expropiatorio; el juez fue trasladado a Cuernavaca, donde lo asesinaron, y perdió el asunto. En 1988 tramitó sin éxito 30,000 amparos contra la puesta en funciones de la planta nucleoeléctrica de Laguna Verde. Autor de la novela *Juan* (1990).

Ortega Arenas, Juan ◆ n. en Puebla, Pue. (1920). Estudió derecho, filosofía y economía en la UNAM, donde fue profesor hasta 1970. Es representante de organizaciones obreras desde 1935. Fue militante del Partido Comunista (1935-43). Expulsado del PCM junto a José Revueltas, Enrique Ramírez, Miguel Ángel Velasco, Ángel Olivo Solís y Genaro Carnero Checa, constituyó con ellos el Grupo Morelos. Creó el Partido de Liberación Nacional (1946-48) y fue cofundador del Partido Popular (1948), del que se separó para formar en 1949 el Frente Obrero, convertido en Frente Obrero Comunista de México en 1964, organismo que se extinguió hacia 1967. En 1951-52 participó en el Frente de Lucha por la Emancipación de la Clase Obrera. Con varios sindicatos a los que asesoraba, en 1972 constituyó Unidad Obrera Independiente, organización de la que es coordinador. Fundador del extinto Partido de Unidad Obrera Independiente, del que fue secretario general (1986-). Por motivos políticos ha estado en la cárcel en 1938, 1940, tres veces durante el sexenio de Manuel Ávila Camacho, en una ocasión en el periodo presidencial de Miguel Alemán (1946-47) y en otra con Gustavo Díaz Ordaz (1966-67). Es autor de numerosos folletos. Sus últimas publicaciones son *Instructivo obrero* (1984) y *Che marxista y la revolución proletaria* (1987).

Héctor Ortega

Joaquín Ortega Arenas

Ortega Bertrand, Tomás ◆ n. en el DF (1927). Almirante e ingeniero geógrafo por la Escuela Naval Militar Antón Lizardo de Veracruz (1945-50). Hizo cursos de posgrado en el Centro de Estudios Superiores Navales (1971-72). Ha sido profesor en la United States Naval Academy (1963-65), director de la Escuela de Grumetes (1968), profesor (1968-70) y director (1977-80) de la Escuela Naval Militar Antón Lizardo) director del Centro de Estudios Superiores Navales (1992-94); embajador en Noruega (1983-89) y agregado naval de la embajada en Inglaterra (1990-92). Autor de *Manual de entrenamiento para control de averías*, *Maniobra de buques* y *Estudio estratégico de la península de Yucatán*. En 1979 fue condecorado por el gobierno de España.

Ortega Camarena, Melchor ◆ n. en Comonfort, Gto., y m. en el estado de Guerrero (1896-1971). Se incorporó al constitucionalismo en 1914. Apoyó a Álvaro Obregón en la campaña presidencial en 1920. Combatió las rebeliones delahuertista (1923) y escobarista (1929). Asistió, como delegado de Guanajuato, a la fundación del Partido Nacional Revolucionario (1929), organismo que dirigió brevemente en 1933. Después de su retiro del ejército fue presidente municipal de Uruapan, Michoacán, diputado federal y gobernador de Guanajuato (1932-35). Acompañó al destierro a Plutarco Elías Calles. Volvió a México en 1940 y apoyó la candidatura de Juan Andrew Almazán. Fue presidente del Partido Democrático Revolucionario, cuyo candidato en las elecciones de 1945 fue Ezequiel Padilla. Seis años más tarde fundó el Sector Revolucionario Independiente, que se transformó en el Frente Cívico Mexicano de Afirmación Revolucionaria, de filiación anticomunista. Dirigió el Banco Nacional de Fomento Cooperativo. Murió en una emboscada entre Acapulco y Zihuatanejo.

Roberto Ortega Lomelín

Ortega Castillo, Romeo ◆ n. en Oaxaca, Oax. (1893-1958). Estudió derecho en la ciudad de México. Fue subsecretario de Gobernación, procurador general de la República, consejero de Plutarco Elías Calles y embajador en Cuba, Guatemala, Nicaragua y Suecia.

Ortega Castrejón, Félix ◆ n. en Tacámbaro, Mich., y m. en el estado de Morelos (1885-1915). Se trasladó a la ciudad de México hacia 1907 para estudiar ingeniería. Se graduó en 1911. Fundó la revista *Floreal* y dirigió *Prisma* y *Azul*. Incorporado al ejército constitucionalista, murió en combate contra las fuerzas de Emiliano Zapata.

Ortega Colunga, Vicente ◆ n. en Saltillo, Coah., y m. en el DF (1917-1985). Fue voceador en su infancia. Se inició en el periodismo como fotógrafo de *El Porvenir*, de Monterrey (1939). En 1941 pasó a la capital del país, donde fue reportero gráfico de la revista *Arena* y autor de la columna *Frente a mi cámara*, que se publicó en *Hoy*. Cofundador de los semanarios *Mañana*, *Impacto* y *Siempre!* Hacia 1956 hizo la fotonovela *La vida deslumbrante de María Félix* y al año siguiente *Vida y amores de Pedro Infante*, de la que llegó a editar 250,000 ejemplares cada semana. En 1958 fundó la Agencia Mexicana de Información. Dos años después inició la publicación del periódico *Pueblo*, en el que colaboraron Renato Leduc, José Alvarado, Víctor Rico Galán y José Natividad Rosales. Tambien editó las historietas *Islas Marías*, *Monstruos* y *Manicomio*, y las revistas *Latin Señoritas* y *Su otro yo*.

Ortega Cuevas, Joel ◆ n. en el DF (1961). Ingeniero electricista por el IPN. Ha sido profesor de la ESIME. Diputado federal (1985-88). Ha sido director de Concertación Política de la Dirección General de Gobierno, director de Proyectos de la Secretaría General Adjunta de Estudios y Proyectos Institucionales, director general regional Norte de la Secretaría General de Gobierno y la Dirección General de Autotransporte Urbano, en el DDF (1989-94). Director general del Servicio de Transportes Eléctricos de la ciudad de México (1997-99) y secretario de Transporte y Vialidad (1999-). Colaborador de *Excélsior* y de *Metro*.

Ortega Hernández, Gregorio ◆ n. en San Francisco Soyaniquilpan, Edo. de Méx., y m. en el DF (1888-1981). Periodista. Se inició en *El Universal Ilustrado*. En 1924 viajó a Europa y fue deportado de España por participar en manifestaciones antimonárquicas. En París vivió cuatro años dedicado al periodismo y logró un reconocimiento por su trabajo en el *Mercure de France*. A su regreso a México trabajó nuevamente en *El Universal*, colaboró en la revista *Hoy* y participó en la fundación de *Rotofoto*, con José Pagés Llergo, con quien hizo la revista *Cine*. Fue enviado por *El Universal* a cubrir las campañas presidenciales de Lázaro Cárdenas y Manuel Ávila Camacho. En 1942 fundó su primera publicación, la revista *Así*, y en 1944 la transformó en *Revista de América*, publicación que dirigió hasta su muerte. Mantuvo su colaboración en *El Universal* y *El Universal Gráfico*, donde publicaba la columna *Esa política*. Es autor del libro *Hombres, mujeres* (1924).

Ortega, J. Juan ◆ n. en Matehuala, SLP, y m. en el DF (1904-1996). Periodista y cineasta. Fue corresponsal, columnista y editorialista de varios periódicos. Colaboró en *Excélsior*. Fue uno de los promotores de la llamada Época de Oro del cine nacional. Entre las películas que produjo y dirigió están *Sendas del destino* (1939), *Flor de fango* (1941), *Lo que el hombre puede sufrir* (1942), *El abanico de Lady Windermere* (1944), *La casa de la zorra* (1945), *Lodo y armiño* (1959), *La mentira* (1959), *Piel canela* (1953). *Preciosa*, *frente al pecado* (1954), *Yo no creo en los hombres*, *Traición* y *La sombra del Tunco Maclovio*.

Ortega Lomelín, Roberto ◆ n. en Celaya, Gto. (1950). Licenciado en derecho por la UNAM (1969-73) y maestro en administración pública por la London School of Economics (1974-75). Es miembro del PRI desde 1971. Profesor de la UAM-A, de la UNAM y de la UAEM. Ha sido director general de Organización y Presupuesto (1977-82) y de Planeación de la Secretaría de Pesca (1982); subdirector de Programación y Presupuesto de la Subdirección General de Finanzas del ISSSTE (1983), director general de Planeación y Presupuesto de la SSA

(1983-85) y oficial mayor de la misma dependencia (1985-88), así como delegado del DDF en Benito Juárez (1989-94). Coautor de *Derecho federal mexicano* (1984), *La descentralización de los servicios de salud. El caso de México* (1986), *El refrendo y las relaciones entre el Congreso de la Unión y el Poder Ejecutivo* (1986) y de *75 años de constitucionalismo mexicano* (1988).

ORTEGA MARTÍNEZ, FRANCISCO ♦ n. y m. en la ciudad de México (1793-1849). Se recibió de abogado en el Seminario Palafoxiano de la ciudad de Puebla. Fue diputado al primer Congreso Nacional (1822) y se opuso a la coronación de Agustín de Iturbide; diputado por el Estado de México, senador (1837-41) y miembro de la Junta Nacional Legislativa de 1843. Colaboró en los periódicos capitalinos fundados por Quintana Roo *El Federalista* (1831) y *La Oposición* (1834), así como en *El Reformador*, de Toluca (1833). Es autor de *Poesías líricas* (1839), *Memoria sobre los medios de desterrar la embriaguez* (1847), *Disertación sobre los bienes eclesiásticos* y las obras de teatro *México libre* (1821), *Cacamatzin*, *Los misterios de la imprenta*, *La venida del Espíritu Santo* y *A los ojos de Delia*.

ORTEGA MARTÍNEZ, JESÚS ♦ n. en Aguascalientes, Ags. (1952). Es químico bacteriólogo por la Escuela Nacional de Ciencias Biológicas del IPN (1972-1978). Fue laboratorista químico de Ferronales (1974-76). Militó en el PST, de cuyo Comité Central fue secretario general (1987); en el PMS, en donde fue miembro del Comité Ejecutivo. Cofundador del PRD (1989), del que ha sido integrante del Consejo Nacional, secretario general del CEN (1996-99) y repersentante ante el IFE (1999-). Ha sido diputado federal LI Legislatura, 1979-82; LIV Legislatura (1988-91), LV1 Legislatura (1991-94) y secretario del Comité Directivo del DF.

ORTEGA MARTÍNEZ, LAURO ♦ n. en el DF y m. en Morelos (1910-1999). Médico cirujano por la UNAM (1935). Fundó en 1933 el Partido Estudiantil Cardenista. Fue secretario general de las Juventudes Socialistas Unificadas de México en los años treinta. Fue subsecretario de Ganadería de la Secretaría de Agricultura (1952-58), oficial mayor de la Secretaría de Salubridad y Asistencia (1938-40), secretario general de la Federación de Organizaciones Populares del Distrito Federal (1942-45), secretario general (1964-65) y presidente (1964-68) del Comité Ejecutivo Nacional del PRI; diputado federal (1946-49 y 1979-82) y gobernador constitucional del estado de Morelos (1982-88). Autor de unas *Memorias*.

ORTEGA Y MEDINA, JUAN ANTONIO ♦ n. en España y m. en el DF (1913-1992). Tras la derrota de la República Española se exilió en México (1940). En 1942 se naturalizó mexicano. Se especializó en historia en la Normal Superior y se doctoró en letras en la UNAM. Desde 1954 fue profesor e investigador de la misma universidad, donde en 1961 se convirtió en editor del *Anuario de Historia*, del Instituto de Investigaciones Históricas. Por encargo de la dirección de la Facultad de Filosofía y Letras, en 1966 redactó un nuevo plan de estudios para la carrera de historia. Entre 1969 y 1973 dirigió el Centro de Estudios Angloamericanos. Autor de *Ensayos, tareas y estudios históricos* (1962), *La evangelización puritana en Norteamérica* (1976) y *La idea colombina del descubrimiento desde México* (1987), entre otras obras. En 1951 ingresó en la Academia Mexicana de la Historia. Premio Nacional de Ciencias Sociales (1991).

Ensayo de Juan Antonio Ortega y Medina

ORTEGA MENDOZA, CEFERINO ♦ n. en Acamilpa y m. en Temimilcingo, Mor. (1890-1968). Se incorporó al Ejército Libertador del Sur en diciembre de 1911. En 1914 fue ascendido a general de brigada por su participación en la batalla de Cuernavaca. En 1920 se adhirió al Plan de Agua Prieta. Obtuvo su baja en 1925. Fue uno de los fundadores del Frente Zapatista, en el que fue presidente del comité estatal de Morelos y presidente del Comité Directivo Nacional (1966-68).

Jesús Ortega Martínez

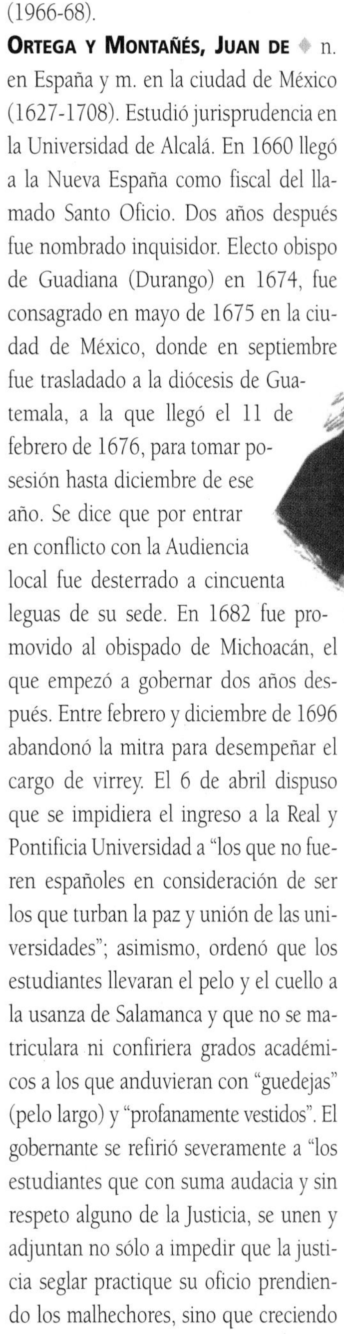

ORTEGA Y MONTAÑÉS, JUAN DE ♦ n. en España y m. en la ciudad de México (1627-1708). Estudió jurisprudencia en la Universidad de Alcalá. En 1660 llegó a la Nueva España como fiscal del llamado Santo Oficio. Dos años después fue nombrado inquisidor. Electo obispo de Guadiana (Durango) en 1674, fue consagrado en mayo de 1675 en la ciudad de México, donde en septiembre fue trasladado a la diócesis de Guatemala, a la que llegó el 11 de febrero de 1676, para tomar posesión hasta diciembre de ese año. Se dice que por entrar en conflicto con la Audiencia local fue desterrado a cincuenta leguas de su sede. En 1682 fue promovido al obispado de Michoacán, el que empezó a gobernar dos años después. Entre febrero y diciembre de 1696 abandonó la mitra para desempeñar el cargo de virrey. El 6 de abril dispuso que se impidiera el ingreso a la Real y Pontificia Universidad a "los que no fueren españoles en consideración de ser los que turban la paz y unión de las universidades"; asimismo, ordenó que los estudiantes llevaran el pelo y el cuello a la usanza de Salamanca y que no se matriculara ni confiriera grados académicos a los que anduvieran con "guedejas" (pelo largo) y "profanamente vestidos". El gobernante se refirió severamente a "los estudiantes que con suma audacia y sin respeto alguno de la Justicia, se unen y adjuntan no sólo a impedir que la justicia seglar practique su oficio prendiendo los malhechores, sino que creciendo sus atrevimientos han practicado quitar

Juan de Ortega y Montañés

los presos a los ministros, tan petulante y soberbiamente, que han pasado a perder el respeto a los Señores Alcaldes de esta Corte, como sucedió el día 27 de marzo, quitando un preso a los alguaciles, diciendo que era estudiante, procediendo a pegar fuego a la picota puesta para terror de los baratilleros". A la intromisión del virrey, el claustro universitario respondió que los hechos citados se habían producido "a ciencia y tolerancia de los señores virreyes y superiores" y que el caso competía al rector. Lo único que pudo hacer el gobernante fue suprimir el Baratillo, mercado popular de la Plaza Mayor donde presumiblemente se traficaba con objetos robados. En 1699 se le nombró arzobispo de México y tomó posesión el 24 de marzo de 1700. El 4 de noviembre de 1701 volvió a desempeñarse como virrey interino. Señalado como ostentoso por sus contemporáneos, en enero de 1701 ofreció un banquete en el que se sirvieron treinta platillos, "diez de pescado, diez de carne y diez de dulce", según algunos testigos, o cincuenta, de acuerdo con otros, todo acompañado por "diversos géneros de vinos y nevados". En esta gestión persiguió a los desempleados y llegó al extremo, el 2 de mayo de 1702, de hacer una visita sorpresiva a la Sala del Crimen, donde mandó cerrar las puertas y aprehender a los espectadores presentes por considerar que "no tenían ocupación". El 17 de noviembre de 1702 entregó el poder civil. Escribió *Regia y constituciones que por la autoridad apostólica deben observar las religiosas gerónymas del convento de San Lorenzo de la ciudad de México* y un *Informe del estado de la Nueva España* (1696).

Ortega Olaza, Fausto Manuel ♦ n. en Teziutlán y m. en Puebla, Pue. (1904-1971). Estudió en la Escuela Nacional de Agricultura. Fue delegado de la Secretaría de Comunicaciones en Puebla, tesorero general del estado, oficial mayor del gobierno de la entidad, presidente municipal de Teziutlán, diputado local (1939-42 y 1951-54), diputado federal (1947-50) y gobernador constitucional de Puebla (1957-63).

Ortega Orozco, Armando ♦ n. en el DF (1939). Estudió en la Escuela de Diseño y Artesanías (1958-60) y en la Academia de San Carlos. En 1961 ingresó al Taller de Gráfica Popular. En ese año realizó la escultura *Prometeo*, que se expuso en la Feria Mundial de Seattle, EUA, y que más tarde adquirió el Museo de Geografía y Estadística de Washington. Presentó su primera exposición individual en la Galería de Artes Plásticas de la ciudad de Oaxaca en 1964. Fundó el Taller Experimental de Escultura en Metal en la Escuela Nacional de Artes Plásticas (1965). Colaboró con David Alfaro Siqueiros en la realización del mural *La Marcha de la Humanidad*, del Polifórum Cultural Siqueiros. Es miembro fundador del grupo de escultores conocido como Tiempo IV. En 1974 realizó un monumento a Siqueiros que se encuentra en el Distrito Federal. Ha recibido el Premio Diego Rivera, el premio del Concurso de Escultura Mexicana Contemporánea (1960), el Premio Tolsá de la segunda Bienal de Escultura (1964) y el primer lugar en el concurso para la realización del monumento a Siqueiros (1974).

Ortega Ortega, Manuel Valerio ♦ n. en el DF (1930). Químico bacteriólogo parasitólogo por el Instituto Politécnico Nacional (1948-53) y doctor en bioquímica por el Massachusetts Institute of Technology, de Estados Unidos (1960). Fue profesor de la Escuela Nacional de Ciencias Biológicas (1960-62) y del CIEA del IPN (1961-83), así como de las facultades de Química (1975-77) y de Ciencias (1975-77) de la UNAM. Ha sido director de Apoyo al Sector Científico del Consejo Nacional de Ciencia y Tecnología (1975-77), director del Centro de Investigación y Estudios Avanzados del Instituto Politécnico Nacional (1978-82), subsecretario de Educación e Investigación Tecnológica de la Secretaría de Educación Pública (1982-88) y director general del Consejo Nacional de Ciencia y Tecnología (1988-). Pertenece a la Asociación Mexicana de Microbiología, a la Sociedad Mexicana de Bioquímica, de la que fue presidente (1980-82); a la American Chemical Society, The New York Academy of Sciences, a la American Association for the Advancement of Science, a la American Society of Microbiology, de Estados Unidos; y a la Sociedad Bioquímica de Gran Bretaña.

Ortega y Pérez Gallardo, Ricardo ♦ n. y m. en la ciudad de México (1863-1910). Se recibió de abogado en la Escuela Nacional de Jurisprudencia (1887). Después de ser juez durante cinco años (1890-95) se dedicó a la genealogía. Escribió *Estudios genealógicos* (1902) e *Historia y genealogía de las familias más antiguas de México* (3 t., 1908).

Ortega Ramírez, Toribio ♦ n. en Cuchillo Parado, municipio de Coyame, y m. en Chihuahua, Chih. (1870-1916). Era presidente del Club Antirreeleccionista de Cuchillo Parado cuando, el 14 de noviembre de 1910, se levantó en armas contra el gobierno de Porfirio Díaz. Combatió a las órdenes de Pascual Orozco y participó en la toma de Ciudad Juárez (mayo de 1911). En 1912 formó un grupo para comabtir la sublevación orozquista, que se convertiría, meses más tarde, en la brigada González Ortega de la División del Norte. Como general brigadier, participó en las tomas de Torreón y Zacatecas.

Ortega Velázquez, Sergio *Smaily* ♦ m. en el DF (1938-1986). Editor cinematográfico. Se inició profesionalmente en 1960. Trabajó en películas mexicanas y extranjeras. Colaboró con Alberto Mariscal en *Xoxontla* y *Blody Marlen* y con Sam Pekimpah en *Pat Garret y Billy the Kid* y *Tráiganme la cabeza de Alfredo García*. También intervino en el montaje de las cintas estadounidenses *Lets get Jarry* y *Rambo*.

Ortega Vila, Adriana ♦ n. en el DF (1954). Hija de Lauro Ortega Martínez. Licenciada en Historia por la UNAM (1974-78). Fue profesora del Instituto Matías Romero de Estudios Diplomáticos (1978-79). Ha sido investigadora de Asuntos Históricos de la Secretaría de Relaciones Exteriores (1978-79); jefa del Departamento de Procesamiento de Información (1980) y subdirectora de

Información de la SPP (1981); subsecretaria de Información y Propaganda del CEN del PRI (1981), partido al que pertenece desde 1972; secretaria de Documentación de la Confederación de Organizaciones Populares (1984), directora del Centro de Información y Documentación de la Secretaría de la Contraloría de la Federación (1983-85) y directora de Quejas de la Presidencia de la República (1985-88).

ORTEGA VILLA, MARGARITA ♦ n. en Mexicali, BC, y m. en el DF (1951-1996). Licenciada en sociología por la Universidad Autónoma de Baja California (1968-73), de la que fue profesora (1973-74 y 1978-80). Perteneció al PRI, en el que fue directora Femenil Estatal (1971-73), secretaria general de la Asociación Nacional Femenil Revolucionaria (1974-80), presidenta del Comité Municipal de Mexicali (1981-82), secretaria adjunta a la Presidencia (1983) y secretaria de Organización (1983-84) del Comité Directivo Estatal en Baja California. Fue diputada federal suplente (1973- 76 y 1982-85), diputada local (1974-77), coordinadora general de Catastro de la misma entidad (1983-85), directora del Programa Estatal de Fraccionamientos Populares BC (1984-85), diputada federal propietaria (1985-88) y senadora de la República (1988-89). Candidata del PRI a la gubernatura de Baja California (1989). Directora del Instituto Nacional del Consumidor (1989-92).

ORTEGA ZURITA, ANDRÉS ROBERTO ♦ n. en el DF (1957). Ingeniero electricista por la UNAM (1981). Miembro del PST y del PFCRN, en éste último fue secretario de Educación Ideológica (1988). Jefe de sección en la UNAM (1980-88), delegado sindical del STUNAM (1980- 87) y delegado del STUNAM al SUNTU (1987). Representante plurinominal a la primera Asamblea del Distrito Federal (1988-91).

ORTIGOSA Y DE LOS RÍOS, VICENTE ♦ n. en Tepic, Nay., y m. en Guadalajara, Jal. (1817-1877). Estudió en el Colegio Militar, en el Instituto Politécnico de París y en la Universidad de Leipzig, Alemania. Entre sus trabajos destacan los primeros experimentos con nicotina y cocaína y el proceso de envasamiento al alto vacío. Realizó investigaciones sobre el vuelo humano y fabricó ladrillos asfálticos. Fue miembro del Consejo de Estado de Maximiliano. Al triunfo de la República en 1867, tras un breve retiro, asesoró a los gobiernos de Benito Juárez y Sebastián Lerdo de Tejada en diversas obras de ingeniería. Presidió la Cámara de Comercio de Guadalajara (1874-77).

ORTIGOZA MENDOZA, GABRIELA ♦ n. en el DF (1962). Cursó la carrera de antropología social en la ENAH e hizo la maestría en comunicación social en la UNAM. Estudió con Gabriel García Márquez en la Escuela Internacional de Cuba. Ha impartido cursos en la UNAM, en el ITESM y en la Escuela de Escritores de la Sogem. En 1983 se inició como guionista y su primera telenovela se trasmitió en 1989 con la versión mexicana de *Simplemente María,* a la que siguieron *Alcanzar una Estrella, María José, Baila Conmigo, Agujetas de color de rosa, Sin ti, Camila* y *Por tu amor.* Ha escrito telenovelas para otros países como *Amor de papel* e *Isabela.* También ha incursionado en el cine con las películas *Tres son peor que una, Hay para todas, Pueblo viejo* y *la Segunda noche.*

ORTÍN, LEOPOLDO ♦ n. en Perú y m. en el DF (1893-1953). Vivió en México desde los ocho meses de edad. Participó en la revolución constitucionalista. Comenzó a hacer teatro al término de la lucha armada. Pasó al cine, en el que destacó como actor cómico. Trabajó en las películas *Chucho el Roto, Ora Ponciano* y *Los enredos de Papá*, entre otras.

ORTIZ, CARLOS RODRIGO ♦ n. en Álamos, Son., y m. en la ciudad de México (1851-1902). Se graduó como abogado en la ciudad de México, tras haber estudiado en Alemania. Diputado local en 1877 y federal en 1880, fue elegido gobernador de Sonora al año siguiente, para el periodo 1881-83, pero renunció en octubre de 1882 por sus diferencias con el jefe militar del estado. Durante su gestión impulsó la construcción de vías férreas y puso en servicio el Instituto Científico y Literario del estado (1882).

ORTIZ, EMILIO ♦ n. y m. en el DF (1936-1988). Expuso sus pinturas, por primera vez, en 1962. Más tarde estudió en la Escuela Slade, de Londres, y en el taller de Stanley Hitier, de París. Fue profesor visitante del Colegio de Arte y Diseño de Minneapolis, EUA (1970). Expuso en México, Estados Unidos, Francia, Gran Bretaña, Noruega y Argentina.

ORTIZ, ENCARNACIÓN ♦ n. en el rancho de La Pachona, Zac., y m. en la ciudad de México (?-1821). Acaudalado ranchero apodado *el Pachón*. En 1812 se incorporó a las fuerzas insurgentes. Combatió en San Luis Potosí, Zacatecas y Guanajuato, principalmente. En 1817 se unió a la fuerza expedicionaria de Francisco Javier Mina. Tras la captura y asesinato de éste, Ortiz reorganizó sus efectivos y continuó la lucha hasta fines de 1819. Fue indultado y se retiró a su rancho. En 1821 se volvió a levantar en armas, en apoyo del Plan de Iguala. Murió cerca de la ciudad de México, en uno de los últimos combates entre realistas e insurgentes.

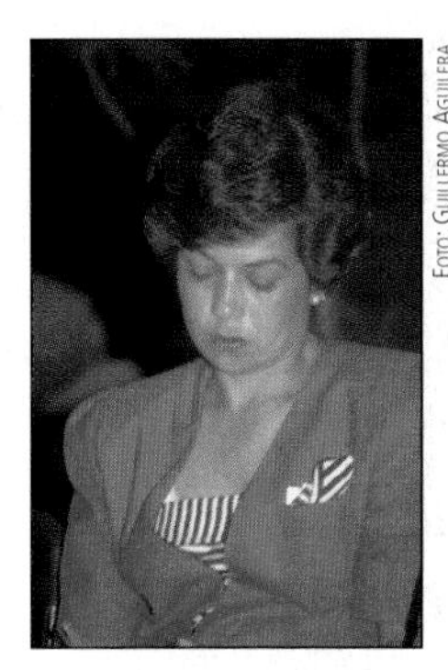

FOTO: GUILLERMO AGUILERA

Margarita Ortega Villa

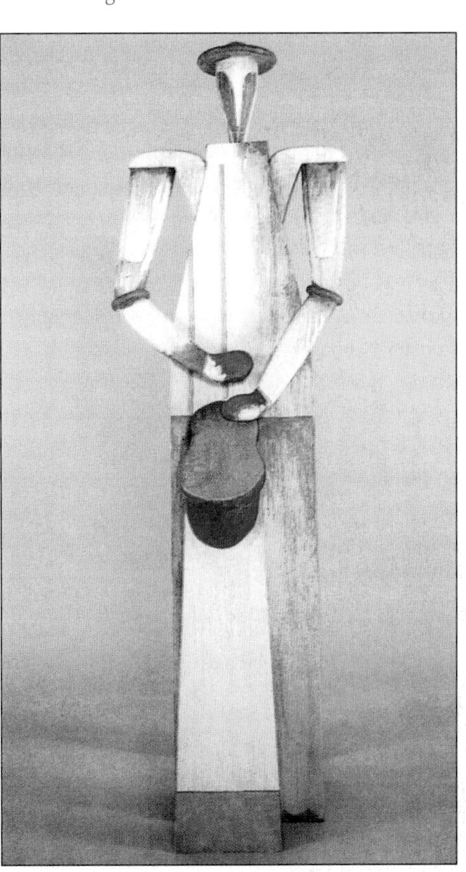

Personaje, obra de Emilio Ortiz

ORTIZ, GABINO ◆ n. en Jiquilpan y m. en Morelia, Mich. (1819-1885). Estudió jurisprudencia en el Seminario de Morelia. Se graduó en 1845. Acusado de editar el periódico *El Espectro*, fue desterrado por el gobierno de Antonio López de Santa Anna. Fue el primer juez del registro civil de Michoacán. Combatió contra la intervención francesa y al triunfo de la República combinó el periodismo con la docencia en el Colegió de San Nicolás en Morelia. Autor de *Perroblillos* (novela), *Por dinero baila el perro* (teatro) y *Un Chiarini* (zarzuela).

ORTIZ, GABRIELA ◆ n. en el DF (1964). Compositora. Realizó estudios musicales en el Conservatorio Nacional de Música del INBA con Mario Lavista y después en la Escuela Nacional de Música de la UNAM con Federico Ibarra. Posteriormente, cursó un posgrado en composición con Robert Saxton en la Guildhall Schooll of Music and Drama (Inglaterra). Se doctoró en electroacústica en The City University (Inglaterra). Además de su trabajo como compositora, ha sido maestra en residencia de los cursos Women in Music realizados en Spalding y Nueva Inglaterra, y asistente y maestra de composición en el área de música electroacústica en The City University. Obtuvo el primer lugar en el Concurso de Composición Alicia Urreta del INBA (1988) y la beca de Jóvenes Creadores del Fonca (1992). Perteneció al Sistema Nacional de Creadores del Fonca (1993-96). Ha escrito música para danza y cine.

ORTIZ, JOSÉ DEL CARMEN ◆ n. en el estado de Sonora y m. en EUA (?-1916). En 1911 se incorporó a la insurrección maderista. Formó parte de la escolta de Francisco Villa, conocida como Los Dorados. Murió durante la invasión a Columbus, Estados Unidos.

ORTIZ, JOSÉ DE JESÚS ◆ n. en Pátzcuaro, Mich., y m. en Guadalajara, Jal. (1849-1912). Estudió en el Colegio de San Nicolás de Hidalgo y fue profesor del Seminario Conciliar de Morelia. Se ordenó sacerdote en 1893. Fue obispo de Chihuahua (1893-01) y arzobispo de Guadalajara (1901-12).

ORTIZ, LUIS GONZAGA ◆ n. y m. en la ciudad de México (1825-1894). Poeta. Estudió en el Colegio de Minería y en el de San Juan de Letrán. Fue director del *Diario Oficial* y colaborador de los periódicos *El Renacimiento* y *El Nacional*. Autor de *Poesías* (1856), *Angélica: recuerdos de un viaje a Italia* (1871), *Ayes del alma* (1872), *Detrás de una nube un ángel* (1887) y *Algunas poesías líricas* (1895).

ORTIZ, MANUEL ◆ n. en Aguascalientes, Ags., y m. en EUA (1916-1970). Desde niño vivió en Estados Unidos, donde empezó a practicar el boxeo. En 1938 inició su carrera como boxeador profesional. Fue dos veces campeón mundial gallo: la primera de agosto de 1942 a enero de 1943 y la segunda de marzo de 1943 a mayo de 1950. Defendió el titulo en 22 ocasiones. Se retiró en 1955, tras una pelea en la Arena Coliseo de la ciudad de México. De las 122 peleas en que participó, en 92 obtuvo el triunfo (45 por nocaut y 47 por decisión), en 27 fue derrotado (una por nocaut y 26 por decisión) y empató en tres ocasiones.

ORTIZ, MARCIAL *EL RANCHERO* ◆ n. en Ahualulco de Mercado, Jal. (1910). Futbolista. Jugó en Guadalajara con los equipos Alianza y Atlas. De éste pasó en 1931 al Necaxa, del Distrito Federal, con el que integró el conjunto conocido como *los Once Hermanos*, en el cual se mantuvo hasta 1938. Fue seleccionado nacional en 1934-37, por lo que viajó a Roma en 1934, cuando en el encuentro para decidir la asistencia a la Copa del Mundo de ese año, el equipo mexicano fue eliminado por el de Estados Unidos. Asistió a los Juegos Centroamericanos de 1935 en El Salvador y de 1938 en Panamá. En 1942, cuando jugaba para el club León, dejó el futbol.

ORTIZ, MÁXIMO RAMÓN ◆ n. en Tehuantepec y m. en Santa María Jalapa del Marqués, Oax. (1816-1855). Estudió en el Instituto de Ciencias y Artes de Oaxaca, donde empezó a interesarse por la música y la política. Fue gobernador del territorio del Istmo de Tehuantepec durante el último periodo en el poder de Antonio López de Santa Anna (1853-55). Se opuso con las armas a la revolución de Ayutla y fue prontamente derrotado. Murió fusilado. Es el autor de *La Sandunga*.

ORTIZ, ORLANDO ◆ n. en Tampico, Tams. (1945). Estudió actuaría y letras hispánicas en la UNAM. Ha sido profesor, luchador y guionista de fotonovelas, radio y televisión. Fue miembro del Comité Central de los partidos Socialista Revolucionario (1977-80) y Socialista Unificado de México (1981-88). Coordina talleres literarios desde 1972. Ha colaborado en *Punto de Partida*, *Revista de la Universidad*, *El Cuento*, *Plural*, *Punto*, *El Sol de México*, *Así Es* y el suplemento *La Cultura en México*, en el que fue miembro del consejo de redacción (1987-88). Es autor de *En caso de duda* (1968), novela con la que ganó la beca Martín Luis Guzmán; los volúmenes de cuentos *Sin mirar a los lados* (1969), *Cuestión de calibres* (1982), *El desconocimiento de la necesidad* (1984) y *Secuelas* (1987); los ensayos *La violencia en México* (1971), *Jueves de Corpus* (1971) y *Genaro Vázquez* (1972); y los libros de historietas *Adiós mamá Carlota* (1981), *La decena trágica* (1982) y *Los dorados de Villa* (1982), *Recuento obligado* (antología personal, 1995) y *Entre el Pánuco y el Bravo* (antología de la literatura tamaulipeca, 1995).

ORTIZ, PASCUAL ◆ n. y m. en Morelia, Mich. (1833-1902). Estudió derecho en el Colegio de San Nicolás de Hidalgo. Fue secretario de Gobierno de Santos Degollado en Michoacán (1857). Participó en la guerra de los Tres Años y combatió la intervención francesa. Al triunfo de la República fue magistrado del Tribunal Superior de Justicia de Michoacán, diputado local, senador y rector del Colegio de San Nicolás de Hidalgo.

ORTIZ, VERÓNICA ◆ n. en el DF (1950). Su nombre completo es Verónica María Ortiz Lawrenz. En el Canal Once (1980-98) ha sido investigadora, guionista, conductora e investigadora en los programas sobre educación sexual: *La pareja humana*, *Hablemos de amor* y *Taller de* *sexualidad*, y de análisis político: *Reflexiones*. En Televisión Mexiquense de Toluca condujo el programa *Mujeres* (1989-91). Fundó y coordinó el Espacio del Lector de *El Financiero* (1990-98). En radio ha conducido y dirigido los programas *Palabras sin censura* y *Sexto sentido* en Grupo Radio Mil (1988-89), *Entre líneas* en Radio Centro (1990), *La hora de la verdad* en la XEX (con José Reveles, 1995-96), *De amores y desamores* en Radio UNAM (1988-95). Asesora en comunicación del Instituto Nacional Indigenista (1986-88). Fundadora y subdirectora de promoción de la revista *Este País* (1990-91). Directora de la Unidad de Información, Comunicación y Análisis de la Secretaría de Gobierno (1998-99) y asesora en comunicación de la jefa de gobierno (1999-) del DF. Colaboró en el Diccionario Inglés-Español-Chino del Instituto de Lenguas Extranjeras de China. Fue integrante de la Academia Mexicana de los Derechos Humanos (1989-90) y Servicio Desarrollo y Paz (1986-89). Ha ganado el Teponaxtli de Oro por *Reflexiones* y el Premio Nacional de Periodistas por *Taller de sexualidad* (1996).

Ortiz Arana, Fernando ◆ n. en Querétaro, Qro. (1944). Licenciado en derecho por la Universidad Autónoma de Querétaro, donde fue profesor y director de la biblioteca. Desde 1962 es miembro del PRI, en el que se ha desempeñado como coordinador juvenil (1962), secretario de Acción Electoral del Comité Ejecutivo Nacional (1987), presidente del Comité Directivo del Distrito Federal (1989-91) y del Comité Ejecutivo Nacional (1993-94). Ha sido juez municipal (1964), notario público (1968-73); oficial mayor (1973-76) y secretario de Gobierno de Querétaro (1976-79); director general de los fideicomisos federales de Tequesquitengo y Aguahedionda (1982), diputado federal en tres ocasiones (1979-82, 1985-88, 1991-94), director de Registro Patrimonial (1983-85), miembro de la Asamblea de Representantes del Distrito Federal, de la que fue líder de la mayoría (1988-91), senador de la República (1994-2000). En la LVI Legislatura fue presidente de la Gran Comisión y coordinador del grupo parlamentario del PRI. En 1997 fue candidato al gobierno del estado de Querétaro por el PRI.

Fernando Ortiz Arana

Ortiz Arana, José ◆ n. en Querétaro, Qro. (1943). Licenciado en derecho por la Universidad Autónoma de Querétaro (1962-66), de la que fue profesor (1967-73). Desde 1970 es miembro del PRI, en el que ha sido presidente del Comité Directivo Estatal de Querétaro (1973-80) y subsecretario general del Comité Ejecutivo Nacional (1979-80). Diputado federal (1973-76). En la Secretaría de Gobernación fue director general de Asuntos Jurídicos (1984) y director general de Asuntos Migratorios (1985-88). En 1997 renunció al PRI y fue candidato al gobierno del estado de Querétaro por el PT.

Ortiz Arreola, Andrés ◆ n. en Chihuahua, Chih., y m. en EUA (1890-1945). Ingeniero topógrafo e hidráulico (1913). Diputado federal (1917-18). Fue gobernador de Chihuahua entre noviembre de 1918 y febrero de 1920. Durante su gestión expidió un bando ofreciendo 50,000 pesos por la captura de Francisco Villa. Al triunfo de la rebelión de Agua Prieta tuvo que exiliarse en Estados Unidos. Volvió a México en 1930 y triunfó en las elecciones para la gubernatura, a la que renunció en noviembre de 1931. Más tarde fue director de Ferrocarriles Nacionales de México (de febrero de 1944 a enero de 1945).

Ortiz y Ayala, Simón Tadeo ◆ n. en Mascota, Jal., y m. en el golfo de México (¿1775?-1833). Al inicio de la guerra de independencia vivía en Europa y en 1814 fue recibido en Argentina como enviado especial de José María Morelos. Colaboró con el gobierno de Agustín de Iturbide. Murió en el barco que lo trasladaba de Veracruz a Nueva Orleans. Escribió un *Resumen de la estadística del Imperio Mexicano* (1822) y *México considerada como nación independiente y libre* (1832). En 1840 se editó un libro póstumo, llamado *Exposiciones dirigidas al supremo gobierno relativas a la seguridad de los límites de esta República*.

Ortiz Cedeño, Ignacio ◆ n. en la Piedad, Mich. (1934). Realizó sus primeros estudios en su tierra natal. Más tarde se trasladó a Monterrey. En 1952 ingresa por primera vez en la Escuela de Artes Plásticas de la UNL. Recibió una beca de la propia universidad para continuar sus estudios en la Escuela de Pintura y Escultura La Esmeralda en la ciudad de México, bajo la dirección de los maestros Carlos Orozco Romero, Ignacio Aguirre, Pablo O'Higgins, Guerrero Galván y Germán Cueto. En 1956 regresó a Monterrey para desempeñar el cargo de profesor en la Escuela de Artes Plásticas de la UNL. En 1958 recibió una beca del gobierno checoslovaco para hacer estudios de posgrado en la Escuela de Artes Industriales en Praga, Checoslovaquia. En 1961 regresó a Monterrey para desempeñar el cargo de profesor y director del Taller de Artes Plásticas de la UNL.

Ortiz de Castro, José Damián ◆ n. en Coatepec, Ver., y m. en la ciudad de México (1750-1793). Estudió arquitectura en la Academia de San Carlos de la ciudad de México. Construyó la fachada de la catedral de Tulancingo (1787) y en la ciudad de México dirigió el reempedrado de la Plaza Mayor (1790) y realizó una escultura que se encuentra en el atrio del templo de San Hipólito. A principios de la década de 1790 construyó las torres de la catedral metropolitana.

Ortiz de Domínguez, Josefa ◆ n. en Valladolid, hoy Morelia, Mich., y m. en la ciudad de México (1768-1829). Hasta 1791 permaneció al cuidado de las monjas del convento de Las Vizcaínas, en la ciudad de México. Dos años más tarde se casó con Miguel Domínguez, quien en 1803 fue nombrado corregidor de Querétaro. Participó en la conspiración encabezada por Miguel Hidalgo e Ignacio Allende. Al ser ésta descubierta, se lo comunicó a Hidalgo, con lo que se precipitó el inicio de la guerra de Independencia. Fue detenida y encarcelada en la capital del virreinato. En 1817 el virrey Apo-

Archivo General de la Nación
Josefa Ortiz de Domínguez

Foto: Carlos Hahn

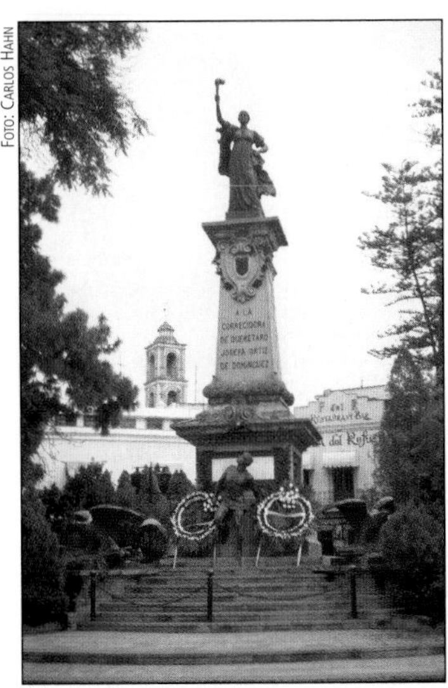

Estatua de Josefa Ortiz de Domínguez en el estado de Querétaro

daca la indultó, aunque le prohibió salir de la ciudad. Durante el imperio de Iturbide rehusó servir como dama de compañía de la emperatriz Ana Duarte. En los primeros años de la República mantuvo relaciones con los miembros del partido yorkino.

Ortiz Gallegos, Jorge Eugenio ◆ n. en Morelia, Mich. (1925). Licenciado en filosofía y letras por The Catholic University of America, de Washington, EUA. Hizo cursos de posgrado en administración y economía en el Instituto Tecnológico de Monterrey y en el Instituto Panamericano de Alta Dirección de Empresas. Ha sido profesor en diversas instituciones de enseñanza superior. Fue miembro del PAN de 1945 a 1992, partido en el que fue jefe de los grupos juveniles en Puebla (1946) y Nuevo León (1949), secretario del Comité Regional del partido en Puebla (1947), candidato a gobernador de Michoacán (1962), miembro del Consejo (1968) y del Comité Regional en Nuevo León (1972-92), miembro del Consejo Nacional (1974-92), jefe de la Comisión Política del Comité de Nuevo León (1978-92) y miembro del Comité Ejecutivo Nacional (1984-92). Diputado federal (1985-88). En 1992 renunció al PAN para integrarse al efímero Partido del Foro Doctrinario y Democrático (☛). Administra empresas de Monterrey y el Distrito Federal. Escribe desde 1945 para *La Nación*. Ha colaborado en *El Sol de Puebla* (1945-), *El Porvenir*, de Monterrey, *El Universal* y otras publicaciones. Fundó y dirigió las revistas *Rumbo* y *Reportajes*, ambas de Puebla (1949-50). Cofundador de *Fuensanta*. Autor de poesía: *Estación de amor* (1955), *Almena* (1959), *Noche de crucifixión* (1968), *Nueva York* (1976), *Del jengibre y de la rosa* (1977) y *Manifiesto al pueblo de Michoacán* (1984); novela: *Mono, perico y poblano* (1969); teatro: *Urías en Tlatelolco* (1978); ensayo: *Por la libertad y la justicia* (1979); y la semblanza *Carlos Septién García* (1957). Fue miembro de la Unión Social de Empresarios Mexicanos y es fundador de Causa Ciudadana.

Ortiz Garza, José Luis ◆ n. en Torreón, Coah. (1954). Licenciado en ciencias de la comunicación por el ITESM (1977). Desde 1977 vive en el DF y trabaja en el Instituto Panamericano de Alta Dirección de Empresa. Miembro del Consejo Directivo de Editora de Revistas y de la revista *Istmo* (1980-); miembro del Instituto de Estudios de Radio Fronteriza, con sede en Austin, Texas, y profesor en la Universidad Panamericana. Autor de *México en guerra. La historia secreta de los negocios entre empresarios mexicanos de la comunicación, los nazis y E.U.A.* (1989). *La guerra de las ondas* (1991) y *Una radio entre dos reinos* (1997).

Ortiz Garza, Nazario ◆ n. en Saltillo, Coah., y m. en el DF (1893-1991). Político y empresario. Se incorporó a las fuerzas del general Francisco Murguía en 1915 y dos años más tarde se convirtió en el proveedor de sus trenes militares. En 1918 instaló un negocio de intercambio cerealero en Torreón, de donde fue presidente municipal. Figuró entre los fundadores del Partido Nacional Revolucionario (1929) y fue gobernador constitucional de Coahuila (1929-33). Fundó la Compañía Vinícola de Saltillo (1933). Senador (1934-40), director de la Nacional Distribuidora y Reguladora (1943-46) y secretario de Agricultura y Ganadería en el gabinete del presidente Miguel Alemán (1946-52). En 1947 creó la Compañía Vinícola de Aguascalientes. Dirigió la Cámara Nacional de la Industria de la Transformación (1969-72) y desde 1971 hasta su muerte fue presidente vitalicio de la Asociación Nacional de Vitivinicultores. Obtuvo la Presea Saltillo en 1989. Aparecen sus memorias en el libro *Remembranzas, Visión de un luchador* (1992).

Ortiz González, Graciela ◆ n. en Chihuahua, Chih. (1954). Licenciada en Derecho, egresada de la Facultad de Derecho de la Universidad Autónoma de Chihuahua. Ha sido jefe de Comunicación Social del IMSS, diputada local a la LVII Legislatura y titular de la Secretaría de Desarrollo Social del Gobierno de Chihuahua.

Ortiz González, Horacio ◆ n. en el DF (1969). Estudió en la facultad de filosofía y letras. Asistente de investigaciones en la Fundación *Nexos* hasta 1992. Fue jefe del suplemento *Lectura* del periódico *El Nacional* y asesor editorial en la Secretaría de Desarrollo Social. Ha colaborado en *Casa del Tiempo*, *El Economista*, *Epitafios*, *Etcétera*, *Intermedios*, *La Jornada Semanal*, *El Nacional*, *Novedades*, *Sábado* y *Siempre!* Becario del Centro Mexicano de Escritores (1997-98).

Ortiz González, Patricio ◆ ☛ *Patricio.*

Ortiz Hernán, Gustavo ◆ n. en San Luis Potosí, SLP, y m. en el DF (1910-1978). Estudió en la Escuela Superior de Comercio y Administración de la ciudad de México, pero se dedicó al periodismo. Dirigió la *Gaceta Cultural de México* (1925), jefe de redacción de *El Nacional* (1929-35), jefe de prensa del Partido Nacional Revolucionario (1934-35), director de Talleres Gráficos de la Nación (1935-39), cónsul en Filadelfia (1939-45) y en San Antonio, Texas (1945-47); y director de los diarios capitalinos *Novedades* (1947) y *La Prensa* (1948), del que había sido cofundador (1927). Fue el primer embajador mexicano ante el gobierno de Israel (1956-58) y representó a México en Chile (1959-64). Subdirector de *El Nacional* (1969-71) y director de *El Universal Gráfico* y la *Revista Cultural de la Semana* de *El Universal* (1972-74). Es autor de la novela *Chimeneas* (1937).

Ortiz de Letona, Pascasio ◆ n. en Guatemala y m. en la ciudad de México (1775-1811). Se adhirió al movimiento independentista en noviembre de 1810, cuando el ejército de Miguel Hidalgo ocupó Guadalajara. En diciembre fue nombrado embajador de los insurgentes ante el gobierno de Estados Unidos. Cuando se dirigía a Veracruz para embarcarse, fue detenido en Molango, Hidalgo, y remitido a la ciudad de México. Se suicidó antes de llegar a la capital.

Ortiz y López, José Guadalupe ♦ n. en Momax, Zac., y m. en Guadalajara, Jal. (1867-1947). Estudió en los seminarios de Guadalajara, Monterrey y Zacatecas. Se ordenó sacerdote en 1891. Desempeñó diversos cargos en el arzobispado de Monterrey. Fue obispo de Tamaulipas (1919-23) y de Chilapa (1923-26) y arzobispo de Monterrey (1929-40).

Ortiz Macedo, Luis ♦ n. en el DF (1933). Se tituló como arquitecto en la UNAM (1960), donde obtuvo la maestría (1980) y ha sido profesor (1955-63 y 1977-) y secretario fundador del Seminario de Historia de la Arquitectura (1956-60). Ejerció la docencia en la Universidad Iberoamericana (1956-58). Hizo cursos de posgrado en Europa (1960-63). Fue director de la Escuela de Arquitectura de la Universidad de Guanajuato (1963-66) y, en el Instituto Nacional de Antropología Historia, jefe del Departamento de Monumentos Coloniales (1966-68), secretario general (1968-69) y director general (1971); subsecretario de Enseñanza Técnica y Superior (1969-70), director general del Instituto Nacional de Bellas Artes (1971-74), director de la Escuela de Arquitectura de la Universidad Anáhuac, director de Fomento Cultural Banamex (1982-84), vocal ejecutivo del Centro Histórico de la Ciudad de México (1984-88) y director del MAM (1989-). Colabora en *El Búho*, suplemento cultural del diario *Excélsior*. Coautor de *El mueble en México* (1985) y *Fachadas de México* (1989). Autor de *Cuarenta siglos de plástica mexicana* (1970), *El arte del México virreinal* (1971), *Los monumentos de México* (1984), *Nuestra pintura* (1985), *Nuestra pintura mexicana* (1986), *Ernesto Icaza, maestro del indigenismo mexicano* (1985). *Ernesto Icasza, el charro pintor* (1995). Ha presidido la sección mexicana del Consejo Internacional de Sitios y Monumentos (1977) y el Instituto Cultural Domecq. En 1985 ingresó en el Seminario de Cultura Mexicana. Miembro del SNI y honorario de la Sociedad Mexicana de Geografía y Estadística, que le otorgó la medalla Juárez en 1996.

Ortiz Martínez, Guillermo ♦ n. en el DF (1948). Licenciado en economía por la UNAM (1972), y maestro en economía (1977) y doctor en teoría monetaria, economía internacional y econometría (1977) por la Universidad de Stanford, de la que fue profesor (1975-76). Afiliado al PRI desde 1965. Ha sido asistente de investigación en la Secretaría de la Presidencia (1971-72), profesor en el ITAM (1977-83); economista (1977), subgerente (1980-82) y gerente (1982-84) de la Dirección de Investigación Económica del Banco de México; profesor en El Colegio de México (1983); director ejecutivo alterno (1984-86) y director ejecutivo (1986-88) del Fondo Monetario Internacional; subsecretario (1988-94) y secretario (1994-98) de Hacienda y Crédito Público; secretario de Comunicaciones y Transportes del primero al 28 de diciembre de 1994 y gobernador del Banco de México (1998-). Autor de *Acumulación de capital y crecimiento económico: una perspectiva financiera de México* (1977, tesis de doctorado). Premio Rodríguez Gómez de los Bancos Centrales de Latinoamérica-Cemla (1978).

Foto: Héctor Herrera

Guillermo Ortiz Martínez

Ortiz Mayagoitia, Guillermo Iberio ♦ n. en Misantla, Ver., (1941). Estudió licenciatura en derecho en la Universidad Veracruzana. Fue secretario de Acuerdos del Juzgado Primero de Primera Instancia en Poza Rica, Ver.; actuario y después secretario del Juzgado Tercero de Distrito, en Veracruz (actualmente quinto); secretario de Estudio y Cuenta de la Suprema Corte de Justicia de la Nación y juez de Distrito en el estado de Oaxaca y en el DF. Ocupó el cargo de magistrado de Circuito desde el 9 de marzo de 1981 hasta el 26 de enero de 1995. Con esta categoría estuvo adscrito en los Tribunales Colegiados de Villahermosa, Tab., de la ciudad y puerto de Veracruz, y al Segundo Tribunal Colegiado en Materia Administrativa en el DF. Es maestro del Instituto de Especialización Judicial de la H. Suprema Corte de Justicia de la Nación, donde imparte el curso de amparo en materia agraria. Fue designado magistrado de la Sala de Segunda Instancia del Tribunal Federal Electoral, por la Comisión Permanente del Congreso de la Unión, el 27 de octubre de 1993. Es ministro de la Suprema Corte de Justicia de la Nación desde 1995.

Ortiz Mena, Antonio ♦ n. en Hidalgo del Parral, Chih. (1907). Licenciado en derecho por la Escuela Nacional de Jurisprudencia (1930). También hizo estudios en la Facultad de Filosofía y Letras. Fue asesor del Departamento del Distrito Federal (1930-36). Colaboró con la dirección del Banco Nacional Hipotecario Urbano y de Obras Públicas (1936-45). Durante la segunda guerra mundial formó parte del Comité para la Defensa Política del Continente Americano. Fue director del Instituto Mexicano del Seguro Social en el sexenio de Adolfo Ruiz Cortines (1952-58). Ocupó la Secretaría de Hacienda y Crédito Público durante los periodos presidenciales de Adolfo López Mateos (1958-64) y Gustavo Díaz Ordaz (1964-70). En estos 12 años aplicó una política económica conocida como "desarrollo estabilizador". Presidió el Banco Interamericano de Desarrollo de 1971 a 1987, año en que renunció, pese a que había sido reelegido para continuar en el cargo hasta 1991. Durante su gestión,

Antonio Ortiz Mena

el número de países miembros pasó de 23 a 43 y el monto acumulado de los préstamos de 4,000 millones de dólares a 30,000 millones. En diciembre de 1988 fue designado director general de Banamex. *Doctor honoris causa* de la Universidad de las Américas. Es autor de *El desarrollo estabilizador* (1999).

Ortiz Mendoza, María de los Ángeles ◆ n. en el DF (1942). Cursó la licenciatura en Antropología Social, en la Escuela Nacional de Antropología e Historia (ENAH). Trabajó por varios años en admnistración pública teniendo a su cargo jefaturas y asesorías. En su actividad docente se desempeñó como investigadora de estudios agrarios del Centro de Estudios Políticos de la Facultad de Ciencias Políticas y Sociales de la UNAM. Colaboró como articulista en el periódico *unomásuno,* fundadora del colectivo de fotografía *Macro 78.* Fue subdirectora de la revista *México Agrario* (1971-82), y directora del mismo actualmente.

Ortiz Monasterio, Ángel ◆ n. y m. en la ciudad de México (1849-1922). Estudió en Cádiz, España, en la Escuela Naval de San Fernando y sirvió en la marina española hasta 1878, cuando ingresó a la Armada de México. Fue jefe del Departamento de Marina durante el porfiriato. Durante su gestión se crearon las escuelas navales de Mazatlán y Campeche. En 1885 dejó el cargo para convertirse en diputado. Fue después jefe del Estado Mayor Presidencial, cónsul en Belice y agregado naval en Estados Unidos. Entre 1896 y 1897 realizó un viaje alrededor del mundo al mando de la corbeta escuela *Zaragoza.*

Foto: Galería OMR

Fernando Ortiz Monasterio

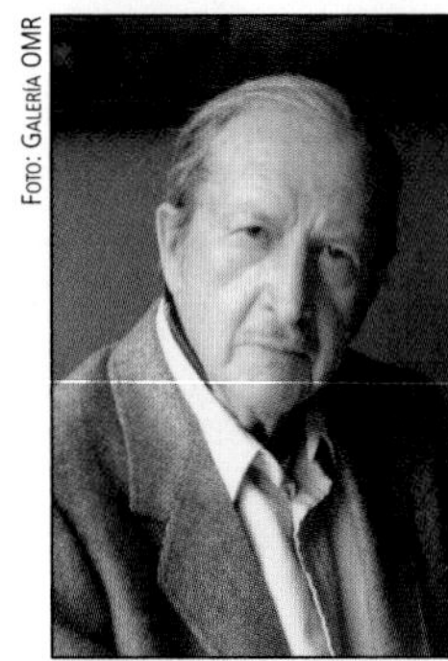

Foto: Galería OMR

José María Ortiz Monasterio

La nube, escultura en bronce de Luis Ortiz Monastério

Ortiz Monasterio, Fernando ◆ n. en el DF (1924). Médico cirujano por la UNAM (1946). Realizó estudios de posgrado en el Hospital General de México (1952) y su residencia, especializado en cirugía plástica y reconstructiva, en la Universidad de Texas (1954). Es profesor en la UNAM desde 1960. En el Hospital General de México ha sido médico adscrito (1950-52), jefe del servicio de cirugía plástica y reconstructiva (1960) y director general (1977). En 1959 fundó una clínica de cirugía craneofacial y otra para el estudio y tratamiento de pacientes con fisuras de labio y paladar. En 1988 trabajaba en el hospital Manuel Gea González, de la Secretaría de Salud.

Ortiz Monasterio, José María ◆ n. y m. en la ciudad de México (1807-1869). En la cartera de Relaciones Exteriores fue 16 veces oficial mayor encargado del despacho con los presidentes Bustamante (del 3 de junio al 29 de julio de 1831 y del 21 de mayo al 14 de agosto de 1832), Melchor Múzquiz (del 14 al 19 de agosto de 1832), Manuel Barragán (del 2 de junio al 8 de julio de 1835 y del 29 de octubre de 1835 al 27 de febrero de 1836), José Justo Corro (del 27 de febrero de 1836 al 18 de abril de 1837), de nuevo Bustamante (del 7 de noviembre de 1837 al 9 de enero de 1838 y del 6 de octubre de 1840 al 20 de mayo de 1841), Santa Anna (del 23 de julio al 5 de agosto de 1844), Paredes y Arrillaga (del 4 al 6 de enero de 1846), Nicolás Bravo (del 27 al 31 de julio de 1846), Mariano Salas (del 5 al 26 de agosto de 1846), Gómez Farías (del 22 de enero al 27 de febrero de 1847), Peña y Peña (del 16 al 26 de septiembre de 1847), José Joaquín Herrera (del 3 al 9 de mayo de 1848) y Mariano Arista (del 29 de abril al 9 de junio de 1851).

Ortiz Monasterio, Luis ◆ n. y m. en el DF (1906-1990). Escultor. Estudió en la Academia de San Carlos (1921-24). Fue profesor en la Escuela Nacional de Artes Plásticas de la UNAM (1939-62). Presentó su primera exposición en la Galería de Arte Mexicano (1935). Entre sus obras más conocidas están la fuente de entrada al teatro al aire libre del parque México (DF, 1929), *El Esclavo* de la colonia Michocán del DF (1936), los altorrelieves de la Escuela Nacional de Maestros (1948), el monumento a la Madre (en colaboración con el arquitecto José Villagrán, 1949), la fachada del Palacio Municipal de Jalapa, Veracruz (1954), la fuente de Nezahualcóyotl en Chapultepec (1956), diversas esculturas, fuentes y el pórtico de la Unidad Independencia (1962), la fuente de la Unidad de Congresos del Centro Médico Nacional (1963) y el altorrelieve del centro vacacional de Oaxtepec, Morelos (1964), todos del Seguro Social; y una escultura en bronce que se encuentra en el Centro Médico de Tlalnepantla. Participó en la transformación de la estructura del inconcluso palacio legislativo porfirista en monumento a la Revolución. Recibió el Premio de Escultura de la SEP (1946) y el Premio Nacional de Ciencias y Artes (1967). Autor del libro *Escultura* (1970). Pertenció al *Semanario de Cultura Mexicana*, del que fue director entre 1969 y 1971, y a la Academia de Artes de México, de la cual fue secretario en 1973.

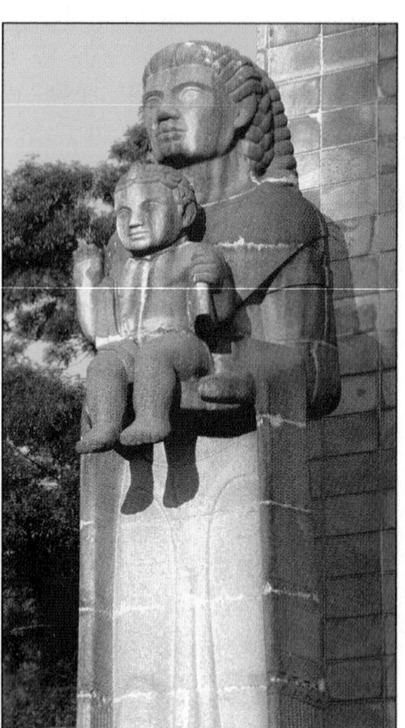

El monumento a la Madre, en el DF. obra de Luis Ortiz Monasterio y José Villagrán

Ortiz Monasterio, Luis ◆ n. en el DF (1942). Licenciado en relaciones internacionales por El Colegio de México (1960-63). Desde 1964 pertenece al PRI, en cuyo CEN se desempeñó como director de Documentación (1976-77) y subsecretario de Promoción y Gestoría (1987-88). Asesor del Congreso del Trabajo y de ASPA (1973-74). Ha sido profesor en el Icap, jefe del Departamento de Asuntos Norteamericanos de la SRE (1964-65), secretario de las embajadas de México en Cuba, Canadá, Costa Rica y la República Dominicana (1965-70), subdirector de Documentación e Informe Presidencial de la Secretaría de la Presidencia (1972-76), articulista en *Excélsior* (1973-76), director general de Programas Fronterizos de la SEP (1976-77), subdirector de Investigaciones Políticas y Sociales (1979-81) y coordinador general de la Comisión Mexicana para Ayuda a los Refugiados (1981-83), codirector fundador del periódico latinoamericano *Hora Cero* (1986), director general de Derechos Humanos de la Secretaría de Gobernación (1988-94), embajador en Jamaica (1994-96) y cónsul en Miami (1996-98) y Dallas (1998-). Miembro fundador del Centro Latinoamericano de Estudios Estratégicos (1982) y de la Academia Mexicana de Derechos Humanos (1985).

Ortiz Monasterio, Manuel ◆ n. en la ciudad de México (1893). Arquitecto. Se graduó en 1913. Fue profesor (1922-1924) y director (1929) de la Escuela Nacional de Arquitectura. Realizó, en Durango, el edificio de la estación ferroviaria (1918) y, en el Distrito Federal, el edificio de la compañía aseguradora La Nacional en el centro de la ciudad (1933-1940); los frontones y la alberca olímpica del Centro Deportivo Chapultepec (1941), el edificio de Nacional Finaciera (1942-45) y el edificio de la aseguradora La Comercial (1946-50). Colaboró en el diseño de la plaza de la Basílica de Guadalupe. Fue representante de la Liga de Propietarios (1939-40) y de la Confederación de Cámaras de Comercio en la Comisión de Planificación del Distrito Federal.

Ortiz Monasterio, Pablo ◆ n. en el DF (1952). Estudió economía en la UNAM (1974) y fotografía en el London College of Printing, Gran Bretaña (1976). Ha sido profesor de fotografía en la Universidad Autónoma Metropolitana. Fundador del Consejo Mexicano de Fotografía en 1977. Participó en la Sección

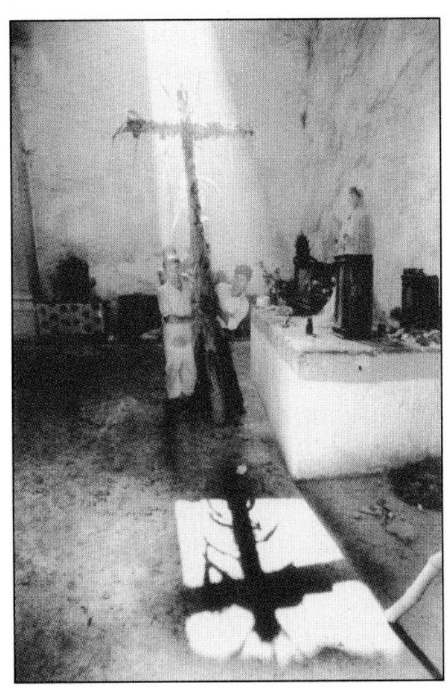

Viernes Santo, fotografía de Pablo Ortiz Monasterio

Bienal de Gráfica (1977 y 1979), en la primera Muestra Latinoamericana de Fotografía Contemporánea (1978), en la segunda Trienal de la Fotografía de Friburgo, Suiza (1978), en la exposición colectiva Hecho en Latinoamérica (Venecia, 1979), en la primera Bienal de Fotografía (1980) y en el segundo Coloquio Latinoamericano de la especialidad (1981). Ha expuesto en Estados Unidos, Gran Bretaña, Italia y Suiza. Es autor de los libros: *Los pueblos del viento* (1981), *Testigos y cómplices* (1982), *Tiempo acumulado. La ciudad de México en los 80* (1991), *Corazón de venado* (1992). Obtuvo el Premio Ojo de Oro en el Primer Festival de Fotografía de los Tres Continentes, en Nantes, Francia, por su libro *La última ciudad.*

Ortiz Monasterio Prieto, Fernando ◆ n. en el DF (1949). Ecologista. Ingeniero electromecánico por la Universidad Iberoamericana (1973) con estudios de posgrado en ingeniería ambiental en la Universidad de Londres (1975). Editor de las revistas *Posibilidades* (1971), *Medio Ambiente* (1973) y *Amnistía* (1977). Fue director de publicaciones de la Asociación Nacional de Energía Solar y responsable del grupo México-Medio Ambiente de la Comisión Latinoamericana de Ciencias Sociales. Director del Consejo de Salud y Emergencia Urbanas del Departamento del Distrito Federal (1988-1993). Es autor de *Introducción al estudio de la contaminación en la nave espacial Tierra* (1973) y coautor de *Tierra profanada. Historia ambiental de México* (1987).

Ortiz Monasterio Prieto, Leonor ◆ n. en el DF (1948). Licenciada en historia por la UNAM (1976). En Estados Unidos y en Francia ha hecho estudios sobre los archivos nacionales de esos países. Fue jefa de la Unidad de Archivos Incorporados (1977-78), jefa del Departamento de Investigación (1978-81) y directora del Archivo General de la Nación (1982-94). Entre 1975 y 1977 trabajó en el Archivo Histórico de la UNAM. Es miembro del Comité Mexicano de Ciencias Históricas y de la Sociedad Mexicana de Historia y Filosofía de la Medicina. En 1995, fue coodinadora de Atención Ciudadana de la Presidencia.

Ortiz de Montellano, Bernardo ◆ n. y m. en el DF (1899-1949). Estudió en la Escuela Nacional Preparatoria. Fue profesor de la Universidad Nacional. Fundador del Nuevo Ateneo de la Juventud (1918) y de la revista *Contemporáneos*, de la cual fue director (febrero de 1929 a diciembre de 1931). Colaboró en las revistas *El Hijo Pródigo* y *Letras de México*, la que dirigió en 1941. Escribió poesía: *Avidez* (1921), *El trompo de siete colores* (1925), *Red* (1928), *Primer sueño* (1931), *Sueños* (1933), *Muerte de cielo azul* (1937) y *Sueño y poesía* (1952); ensayo: *Esquema de la literatura mexicana moderna* (1931), *La poesía indígena de México* (1935), *Figura, amor y muerte de Amado Nervo* (1943) y *Literatura indígena y colonial mexicana* (1946); teatro: *Pantomima* (1930), *El sobrerón* (1931) y *La cabeza de Salomé* (1943); y cuento: *Cinco horas sin corazón* (1940), *El caso de mi amigo Alfazeta* (1946) y *Diario de mis sueños* (1952).

Ortiz Monteverde, Celedonio C. ◆ n. en Hermosillo, Son., y m. en la ciudad de México (1860-1919). Cuatro veces diputado local y oficial mayor (1895-97) y secretario (1897-99) del Gobierno de Sonora. Era vicegobernador cuando ocupó interinamente la gubernatura (1899). Dejó el cargo en

Foto: Rogelio Baeza

Luis Ortiz Monasterio, diplomático

Foto: Dante Bucio

Pablo Ortíz Monastério

Jorge Ortiz de Pinedo

Foto: La Jornada
José Agustín Ortiz Pinchetti

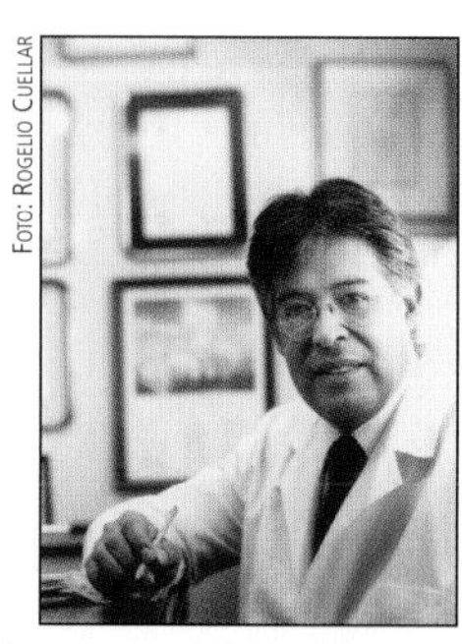
Foto: Rogelio Cuéllar
Federico Ortiz Quezada

1900. Fue oficial mayor del Congreso local hasta 1913.

Ortiz Partida, Víctor ◆ n. en Veracruz, Ver. (1970). Licenciado en letras por la Universidad de Guadalajara, donde ha sido auxiliar de investigaciones literarias. Ha colaborado en suplementos y revistas culturales como *Nostromo* y *Trashumancia*. Es autor de *Escrúpulo del minutero* (poesía 1994).

Ortiz Pérez, Tiburcio ◆ n. en Chinango, Oax. (1945). En la Academia de San Carlos tuvo como maestros a Elizabeth Cattlet, Fernando Castro Pacheco, Héctor Cruz y Adolfo Mexiac, entre otros. Fue profesor de los talleres de artes plásticas de la Universidad Obrera de México. Presentó su primera exposición individual en la galería de la Villa Olímpica en 1971. En 1967 ganó el primer premio en el concurso de escultura estudiantil.

Ortiz Pinchetti, Francisco ◆ n. en el DF (1944). Periodista egresado de la escuela Carlos Septién. Ha sido profesor en las universidades Autónoma Metropolitana (1984-87) e Iberoamericana (1985-). Cronista taurino de la segunda edición de *Ultimas Noticias* (1963-73) y de *El Día* (1968-72), colaborador de *Jueves de Excélsior* (1964-76), reportero de *Ultimas Noticias* y de *Excélsior* (1973-76), jefe de información de *Revista de Revistas* (1973-76), reportero fundador de *Proceso* (1976-). Coautor de *Petróleo y soberanía* (1979), *Los gobernadores* (1980), *El militarismo en América Latina* (1980), *Enriquecimiento inexplicable* (1981), *La Operación Cóndor* (1981) y *La sombra de Serrano* (1982). Autor de *Periodismo cultural* (1984). Miembro fundador de la Unión de Periodistas Democráticos, de cuya mesa directiva formó parte (1984-86). Medalla al mérito periodístico de la agrupación jalisciense Comunicación Cultural y Premio Nacional de Periodismo Rogelio Cantú, del periódico regiomontano *El Porvenir* (1986) y Premio Manuel Buendía (1990).

Ortiz Pinchetti, José Agustín ◆ n. en el DF (1937). Se tituló como abogado en la Escuela Libre de Derecho. Miembro del PRI, participó en el movimiento democratizador de Carlos Madrazo (1967-69). Ha sido profesor de la Universidad Iberoamericana (1961-) y asesor jurídico de las secretarías de Educación Pública, Agricultura y Ganadería, Hacienda y de Comercio y Fomento Industrial. Desde 1991 ha participado activamente en diversas organizaciones cívicas de lucha por la democracia, en las cuales ha realizado observaciones a más de 25 procesos electorales nacionales y extranjeros. Fue uno de los promotores de Los Veinte Compromisos por la Democracia, del plebiscito ciudadano del 21 de marzo de 1993 sobre la reforma política del DF y del seminario del Castillo de Chapultepec para discutir la agenda para la reforma electoral en 1995. Ha ocupado el cargo de consejero ciudadano del Consejo General del IFE (1994-1996). Fue integrante del grupo impulsor de la agrupación política "Causa Ciudadana", en donde partir del abril del 97 al enero del 98 fungió como coordinador general. En enero de 1998 fue nombrado secretario técnico de la Mesa de Participación Ciudadana en los trabajos de la reforma política para el Distrito Federal y, en marzo del mismo año, secretario técnico de la consulta ciudadana para la reforma integral del régimen jurídico del Gobierno de la ciudad de México. Colaborador de *Boletín Financiero*, *Novedades*, *unomásuno* y *Expansión*. Cofundador y colaborador del cotidiano *La Jornada*. Autor de *La democracia que viene* (1990) y de *Reflexiones privadas, testimonios públicos*. Secretario del Comité Directivo del Consejo Mexicano para la Democracia.

Ortiz de Pinedo, Jorge ◆ n. en el DF (1943). Actor. Estudió hasta el primer año de leyes en la Facultad de Derecho. Desde muy pequeño se vio envuelto en el medio artístico. Su primer participación en cine fue en la cinta *Dos angelitos negros*, en la que actuó al lado de su padre, don Óscar Ortiz de Pinedo, Pedro Vargas y Óscar Pulido, entre otros. En televisión participó por primera vez en la serie *Mamá*, al lado de María Douglas; posteriormente intervino en las telenovelas: *El medio pelo*, *Juventud divino tesoro*, *Gente sin historia*, *Una limosna de amor* y *La señora Robles y su hijo*, entre otras. Asimismo participó en los programas: *Hogar dulce hogar*, *Chespirito*, *La criada bien criada*, *Que lío con este trio*, *Dos mujeres en mi casa*, *Las suegras*, *Las aventuras de Chabelo*, *Los comediantes*, *El doctor Cándido Pérez*, *La Escuelita*, entre otros.

Ortiz de Pinedo, Óscar ◆ n. en Cuba y m. en el DF (1914-1978). Actor. Llegó a México con una compañía antillana y estableció su residencia en la capital del país. *El ciclón del Caribe* (1950) fue la primera película mexicana en que participó. Otras cintas en las que trabajó son *Arriba el telón*, *Apasionada*, *Escuela de vagabundos*, *La fuerza del deseo*, *Bodas de oro*, *El vividor*, *Te vi en TV*, *Mujer contra mujer*, *El medallón del crimen*, *El inocente* y otras que suman alrededor de 200. Se presentó también en teatro, cabaret y televisión. Autor de las comedias *Cleopatra era nerviosa* y *El pozo del amor*.

Ortiz Puga, José *Pepe* ◆ n. en Guadalajara, Jal., y m. en Atotonilco, Gto. (1902-1975). Se inició como novillero en 1922. Tres años después tomó la alternativa en la ciudad de México. Al año siguiente fue a España, donde permaneció hasta mediados de la década de 1930. Fue llamado *El Orfebre Tapatío*. Inventó varias suertes, entre otras *El quite de oro*, *La tapatía*, *La guadalupana* y *La orticina*. Se retiró del toreo en 1943 y trabajó en algunas películas como *El Tigre de Yautepec* (para la cual compuso la música), *Cielito Lindo*, *Oro, seda, sangre y sol*, *Al sonar el clarín*, *El bolero* y *La golondrina*, entre otras. Escribió el argumento de *Ora, Ponciano* y estableció su propia ganadería de reses bravas.

Ortiz Quesada, Federico ◆ n. en el DF (1935). Médico cirujano por la UNAM (1959). Hizo la residencia en la especialidad de urología en el Hospital General (1960-61) y en el New York Hospital-Cornell Medical Center (1962-63). Profesor de la UNAM, la Universidad Metropolitana y el Instituto Politécnico Nacional. En el Instituto Mexicano del Seguro Social ha sido coordinador del

Departamento de Servicios de Urología (1972) y coordinador del Sistema de Control y Evaluación Médica (1977-78); fue director del Banco de Riñones del DDF (1975), coordinador del Grupo de Nefrología y Urología del Cuadro Básico de Medicamentos (1976), director general de Medicina y Seguridad en el Trabajo de la Secretaría del Trabajo (1973-76), representante gubernamental ante diversas comisiones y asesor de varias dependencias del sector público. Presidió la Junta de Asistencia Humanitaria Pro Ayuda a Damnificados (1985). Colaborador de los diarios *unomásuno* (1980-83), *La Jornada* (1984) y *Excélsior* (1987-) y de las revistas *El Machete* (1980), *Punto* (1983-84) y *Mañana* (1986). Condujo el programa de televisión *Diagnóstico* (1983). Hasta septiembre de 1986 tenía más de 130 trabajos aparecidos en publicaciones especializadas. Director científico de la revista *Prescripción Médica* (1984-). Es profesor de la Facultad de Medicina y Filosofía y Letras de la UNAM, y desde enero de 1998 es profesor adjunto de la Universidad de George Washington, en Washington DC. Dirige la colección El Hombre y su Salud en Folios Ediciones. Es coautor de una veintena de libros, entre los que se cuenta el *Diccionario de terminología médica* (1971) y ha coordinado otros como *El hombre y su salud* (1982). Autor de los ensayos *Salud en la pobreza* (1985), *La enfermedad y el hombre* (1985), *Bacteriuria* (1985), *La medicina y el hombre* (1986), *Diagnóstico. La medicina y el hombre en el mundo moderno* (1988), *El trabajo del médico* (1997), y de las novelas *El adivinador de lo cierto* (1988), *La medicina está enferma* (1991), *Cartas a una Joven Doctora* (1998) y *Hospitales* (1998). Además dirigió el *Gallo Ilustrado* (1993). Miembro de la Sociedad Mexicana de Urología (1963-74), de la South Central Section of the American Urological Association (1964-), del Consejo Mexicano de Urología (1968-), de la Sociedad Mexicana de Nefrología (1969-), del American College of Surgeons (1969-), de las sociedades internacionales de Urología (1970-), Nefrología (1971-) y de Cirugía (1973-); miembro fundador y presidente de la Sociedad Médica del Hospital General del Centro Médico Nacional del IMSS (1972-73), del Colegio Mexicano de Urología (1972-) y de la Sociedad Médica del Hospital Humana del Pedregal (1985-86); miembro activo de la American Association of Clinical Urologists (1979-), miembro honorario de las sociedades Peruana (1968-) y Ecuatoriana (1976-) de Urología y de la Washington Urological Association, Inc. (1979-); miembro correspondiente de la Sociedad Colombiana de Urología y miembro numerario de la Sociedad Mexicana de Historia y Filosofía de la Medicina (1983-).

ORTIZ RAMOS, AGUSTÍN ◆ n. en Ahuehuetlán el Chico, Pue. (1890-?). Se incorporó a la revolución maderista en 1911, a las órdenes de Maurilio Mejía. Firmó el Plan de Ayala. Combatió en los estados de Puebla y Guerrero. Se retiró en 1920 con el grado de capitán primero y se dedicó a la agricultura.

ORTIZ RIVERA, ALICIA ◆ n. en el DF (1963). Hizo licenciatura y maestría en Sociología Política. Ha tomado cursos de especialización en Periodismo Económico y ha asistido a cursos y conferencias tanto políticos como económicos. Colaboradora en diversas revistas especializadas en información económica, política y temas de salud, especialmente en los periódicos *Reforma* y *El Universal*. Ha trabajado como reportera y editora de los periódicos *unomásuno*.(1983-89), *El Economista* (1989-92), *Reforma* (1993-96), Fue subdirectora de Información Económica y Financiera en Notimex (1992-93) y participó como entrevistadora en la investigación Identidad e Integración: América Latina a comienzos del siglo XXI, desarrollado por el Banco Interamericano de Desarrollo (BID), el INTAL y el Programa de las Naciones Unidas para el Desarrollo (PNUD). (1998-99). Ha publicado trabajos de investigación personal como *Los empresarios en la campaña presidencial de 1988* (1988), *La nueva pluralidad en el Senado* (1996) *Consejo Mexicano de Hombres de Negocios* (1998), *Alejandro Cervantes Delgado: Un guerrero sin violencia* (1999).

ORTIZ RODRÍGUEZ, JOSÉ ◆ n. en Taretán, Mich., y m. en el DF (1871-1962). Estudió derecho en el Seminario de Zamora y en el Colegio de San Nicolás, en Morelia. Fue secretario general de un grupo antirreeleccionista llamado Paz y Unión. Era diputado federal en 1913, cuando Victoriano Huerta disolvió las cámaras y lo hizo encarcelar con otros legisladores. En 1914 se incorporó a la División del Norte y fue subsecretario encargado del despacho de Relaciones en los gobiernos convencionistas de Eulalio Gutiérrez (31 de diciembre de 1914 al 16 de enero de 1915) y Roque González Garza (16 y 17 de enero de 1915). Entre 1920 y 1928 fue senador de la República y, de 1930 a 1952, juez del Tribunal Superior del Distrito y Territorios Federales.

ORTIZ RUBIO, PASCUAL ◆ n. en Morelia, Mich., y m. en el DF (1877-1963). Después de estudiar en el Colegio de San Nicolás, en Morelia, pasó a la Escuela Nacional de Ingenieros de la ciudad de México, donde se graduó como ingeniero topógrafo (1902). Volvió a Michoacán y se dedicó a su profesión hasta 1910, cuando se levantó en armas a las órdenes de Joaquín Mass. Diputado federal al triunfo de la insurrección maderista, fue encarcelado por Victoriano Huerta en 1913. En prisión

Pascual Ortiz Rubio

GABINETES DEL PRESIDENTE PASCUAL ORTIZ RUBIO
5 de febrero de 1930 al 3 de septiembre de 1932

GOBERNACIÓN	
EMILIO PORTES GIL	5 de febrero al 28 de abril de 1930
CARLOS RIVA PALACIO	29 de abril de 1930 al 10 de junio de 1931
OCTAVIO MENDOZA GONZÁLEZ	11 de junio al 27 de agosto de 1923
LÁZARO CÁRDENAS DEL RÍO	28 de agosto al 15 de octubre de 1931
MANUEL C. TÉLLEZ	16 de octubre de 1931 al 20 de enero de 1932
JUAN JOSÉ RÍOS	21 de enero al 3 de septiembre de 1932
RELACIONES EXTERIORES	
GENARO ESTRADA	5 de febrero de 1930 al 20 de enero de 1932
MANUEL C. TÉLLEZ	21 de enero al 3 de septiembre de 1932
GUERRA Y MARINA	
JOAQUÍN AMARO	5 de febrero de 1930 al 14 de octubre de 1931
PLUTARCO ELÍAS CALLES	15 de octubre de 1931 al 31 de julio de 1932
ABELARDO L. RODRÍGUEZ	1 de agosto al 3 de septiembre de 1932
HACIENDA Y CRÉDITO PÚBLICO	
LUIS MONTES DE OCA	5 de febrero de 1930 al 20 de enero de 1932
ALBERTO J. PANI	21 de enero al 3 de septiembre de 1932
AGRICULTURA Y FOMENTO	
MANUEL PÉREZ TREVIÑO	5 de febrero de 1930 al 31 de agosto de 1931
SATURNINO CEDILLO	1 de septiembre al 20 de octubre de 1931
FRANCISCO S. ELÍAS	21 de octubre de 1931 al 3 de septiembre de 1932
INDUSTRIA, COMERCIO Y TRABAJO	
LUIS L. LEÓN	5 de febrero al 8 de octubre de 1930
AARÓN SÁENZ	9 de octubre de 1930 al 20 de enero de 1932
ABELARDO L. RODRIGUEZ	21 de enero al 31 de julio de 1932
PRIMO VILLA MICHEL	1 de agosto al 3 de septiembre de 1932
EDUCACIÓN PÚBLICA	
AARÓN SÁENZ	5 de febrero al 8 de octubre de 1930
CARLOS TREJO Y LERDO DE TEJADA	9 de octubre al 9 de diciembre de 1930
JOSÉ MANUEL PUIG CASAURANC	10 de diciembre de 1930 al 22 de sep. de 1931
ALEJANDRO CERISOLA	23 de septiembre al 20 de octubre de 1931
NARCISO BASSOLS	21 de octubre de 1931 al 3 de septiembre de 1932
COMUNICACIONES Y OBRAS PÚBLICAS	
JUAN ANDREW ALMAZÁN	5 de febrero de 1930 al 20 de octubre de 1931
GUSTAVO P. SERRANO	21 de octubre de 1931 al 20 de enero de 1932
MIGUEL M. ACOSTA	21 de enero al 3 de septiembre de 1932
DEPARTAMENTO DE SALUBRIDAD	
AQUILINO VILLANUEVA	5 al 7 de febrero de 1930
RAFAEL SILVA	8 de febrero de 1930 al 20 de enero de 1932
GASTÓN MELO	21 de enero al 3 de septiembre de 1932
DEPARTAMENTO DEL DISTRITO FEDERAL	
JOSÉ MANUEL PUIG CASAURANC	5 de febrero al 31 de mayo de 1930
CRISÓFORO IBÁÑEZ	1 de junio al 7 de octubre de 1930
LAMBERTO HERNÁNDEZ	8 de octubre de 1930 al 15 de octubre de 1932
ENRIQUE ROMERO COUTARTE	16 al 20 de octubre de 1931
LORENZO HERNÁNDEZ	21 de octubre de 1931 al 20 de enero de 1932
VICENTE ESTRADA CANIJAL	21 de enero al 25 de agosto de 1932
MANUEL PADILLA	26 de agosto al 3 de septiembre de 1932

escribió *Memorias de un penitente*. Una vez libre, se adhirió al constitucionalismo, en el que obtuvo el grado de coronel. Gobernador de Michoacán (1918-20). Durante su gestión, el Colegio de San Nicolás se convirtió en Universidad Michoacana de San Nicolás de Hidalgo. En 1920 se unió al Plan de Agua Prieta y fue secretario de Comunicaciones y Obras Públicas en los gabinetes de Adolfo de la Huerta y Álvaro Obregón, con quien sólo permaneció tres meses en el cargo. Se estableció en España. En 1925 Plutarco Elías Calles lo nombró representante mexicano en Alemania y, en 1926, embajador en Brasil. Fue candidato del Partido Nacional Revolucionario para las elecciones extraordinarias de 1929 y ocupó la Presidencia de la República el 5 de febrero de 1930. Ese mismo día fue herido en un atentado y regresó semanas después a sus actividades. Durante su gestión puso en servicio la carretera México-Laredo, promulgó la Ley Federal del Trabajo y dividió la península de Baja California en los territorios Norte y Sur, en tanto que el de Quintana Roo fue suprimido e incorporado a Campeche y Yucatán. Sujeto a las órdenes de Plutarco Elías, entonces llamado "Jefe Máximo de la Revolución", fue objeto de una persistente campaña de desprestigio, en el curso de la cual le pusieron apodos como *El Nopalito*. Renunció al cargo el 2 de septiembre de 1932 y se exilió en Estados Unidos, donde permaneció hasta 1935, cuando regresó a México. Después de la expropiación petrolera, Lázaro Cárdenas lo designó director de la empresa Petromex, antecesora de Pemex. Escribió, entre otros, los siguientes libros: *Apuntes geográficos del estado de Michoacán* (1917), *Historia de Michoacán* (1920), *La revolución de 1910. Apuntes históricos* (s.f.) y unas *Memorias* (1963).

ORTIZ SALINAS, ANTONIO ♦ n. en el DF (?). Licenciado en derecho por la UNAM, con estudios en el Programa Internacional de. Impuestos de la Universidad de Harvard. Ha sido consultor-investigador en la Universidad de las Naciones Unidas y director general del

Nacional Monte de Piedad. Asimismo fue oficial mayor y subsecretario de planeación de la Secretaría de Turismo y presidente de la Comisión Nacional de los Salarios Mínimos. Secretario de finanzas del gobierno del DF (1997-99). Fue becario del Centro de Estudios Monetarios Latinoamericanos.

Ortiz Santos, Leopoldino ◆ n. en San Luis Potosí, SLP (1929). Licenciado en derecho por la Universidad Autónoma de San Luis Potosí (1952). De 1950 a 1952 fue secretario de acción juvenil del Partido Revolucionario Institucional en San Luis Potosí. Ha sido agente del Ministerio Público (1951-52), secretario de finanzas del Sindicato de Trabajadores del Poder Judicial Federal (1963-65), secretario de acuerdos del Primer Tribunal Colegiado del Primer Circuito del Distrito Federal (1963-65), juez de distrito en Durango, Puebla y Quintana Roo (1965-70); profesor de derecho en la Universidad Juárez de Durango (1967-68), magistrado de circuito (1978), procurador fiscal del Distrito Federal (1978-82), diputado federal (1982-85), ministro de la Suprema Corte de Justicia de la Nación (1986-87) y gobernador sustituto de San Luis Potosí (1987-1991).

Ortiz Segura, Gonzalo ◆ n. en Oaxaca, Oax. (1920). Estudió artillería (1940-43) e ingeniería industrial (1947-53) en el Colegio Militar, donde fue profesor (1959-65). Ha sido asesor del jefe del Departamento de la Industria Militar (1953); jefe de Control de Calidad (1954), de Fabricación y Control de Calidad (1957) y subdirector; del Laboratorio Nacional de Medicinas (1958) subdirector de la Fábrica Nacional de Pólvora (1965), director de la Fábrica de Pólvoras y Explosivos (1970), jefe de la Sección Operativa (1978), subdirector (1978) y director general de Materiales de Guerra (1982-) de la Secretaría de la Defensa Nacional. Pertenece al Colegio de Ingenieros Militares.

Ortiz Tirado, Alfonso ◆ n. en Álamos, Son., y m. en el DF (1893- 1960). Médico cirujano por la Escuela Nacional de Medicina (1919), especializado en ortopedia en Denver, EUA. Trabajó en el Hospital General del DF. En 1922 se inició como tenor en la ópera *Manón*, de Massenet. En octubre de 1930, acompañado de su hermana Sarah, mezzosoprano, se presentó por primera vez en la radiodifusora XEW, donde después cobraría fama como intérprete de música popular. Fue director del Hospital de Morelos. Construyó, en 1938, un hospital, el cual llevaría su nombre. En 1933 comenzó el rodaje de la película *Su última canción*, también filmó *La última copa*. Escribió *Diario de viaje de un cantante*.

Ortiz Tirado, José María ◆ n. Álamos, Son., y m. en el DF (1894-1968). Licenciado en derecho por la Universidad Nacional de México. Fue dos veces ministro de la Suprema Corte de Justicia (1934-47 y 1953-56) y en 1956 presidente del pleno. Fue embajador en Colombia (1948-52) y subsecretario de Gobernación (1952). Presidió la Comisión Nacional de Energía Nuclear.

Ortiz de la Torre Monge, Manuel ◆ n. en Álamos, Son., y m. en la ciudad de México (?-¿1840?). Estudió en el Colegio de San Ildefonso, de la Real y Pontificia Universidad de México, de la que fue profesor de teología y consiliario (1809). Fue diputado por Álamos al primer Congreso Constituyente (1822-23) y a la Junta Instituyente designada por Iturbide (1823). Representó a las Californias en el Constituyente de 1823-24. Oficial mayor encargado del despacho de Relaciones Exteriores con el presidente Victoria (del 23 al 25 de enero de 1829), con el triunvirato de Vélez, Alamán y Quintanar que ejerció el Poder Ejecutivo (23 al 31 de diciembre de 1829) y con Anastasio Bustamante (primero al 7 de enero de 1830). Autor de *Discurso de un diputado sobre la introducción de efectos extranjeros* (1823).

Ortiz Walls, Eugenio ◆ n. en Oaxaca, Oax. (1932). Licenciado en derecho por la UNAM. Profesor de secundaria y de la Escuela de Periodismo Carlos Septién García. Ha desempeñado varios cargos directivos en el Partido Acción Nacional, en el cual milita desde 1952. Fue diputado federal en cuatro legislaturas (1973-76, 1979-82, 1988-91, 1994-97). Presidente del Comité de Bibliotecas de la Cámara de Diputados (1994-97).

Ortiz de Zárate, Francisco ◆ n. en Oaxaca, Oax; y m. en la ciudad de México (1799-1868). Ingresó al ejército en 1824. En 1840 fue ascendido a general. Fue diputado (1843), prefecto de la ciudad de México (septiembre a octubre de 1841, diciembre de 1844 a junio de 1845 y julio a agosto de 1845), gobernador de los estados de Oaxaca (junio a octubre de 1847), México (mayo a agosto de 1862), Chihuahua (julio a agosto de 1865) y Durango (enero a diciembre de 1867); y nuevamente diputado federal (1867-68). Durante su gestión en Durango fue erigido el municipio de Villa de Juárez, hoy Lerdo, en la región lagunera. Combatió las intervenciones estadounidense y francesa y se opuso al imperio de Maximiliano.

Ortuño Gurza, Teresa ◆ n. en Torreón, Coah. (1957). Estudió economía en la Universidad Autónoma de Coahuila (1973-78) y tomó un curso de filosofía en la Universidad Autónoma de Puebla (1980-81). Ha sido profesora de la Universidad Popular Autónoma de Puebla, en el Instituto de Ciencia y Tecnología de Gómez Palacio, Durango, y en el Instituto Tecnológico y de Estudios Superiores de Monterrey, Unidad Laguna. Pertenece al Partido (de) Acción Nacional. Ha sido diputada en dos ocasiones (1982-85 y 1988- 91).

Orvañanos, Raúl ◆ n. en el DF (1947). Jugó futbol en la reserva profesional del equipo América (1963-66), se inició en la primera división con el club Atlante (1966-72), fue seleccionado nacional en 1967, pasó al Zacatepec en 1972 y estuvo los dos años siguientes en el Atlético Español. Comentarista deportivo de los Canales 7 y 13 de televisión (1973-91), de radio (1979-), de Cablevisión (1991), empresa de la que fue director de Eventos Especiales, y de Televisa. En 1985 dirigió con Carlos Albert el programa *Sobre el terreno de juego*, en Canal 7. Director del semana-

Alfonso Ortiz Tirado

Luis Gonzaga Osollo

Foto: Lourdes Almeida

Jorge Federico Osorio

rio *Once* (1991-92). Ha sido cronista en diversas competencias internacionales, entre otras las copas del mundo de Argentina (1978), España (1982), México (1986), Italia (1990), Estados Unidos (1994) y Francia (1998); así como de los Juegos Olímpicos de Montreal (1976), Moscú (1980), Los Ángeles (1984), Seúl (1988), Barcelona (1992) y Atlanta (1996). En Televisa conduce el programa *En la jugada*.

Orvañanos Zúñiga, Julio ◆ n. en Torreón, Coah. (1924). Licenciado en administración de empresas por la UNAM (1946). De 1944 a 1948 fue jugador profesional de futbol y, de 1965 a 1973, presidente del equipo Necaxa. Fundó, en 1950, la agencia de publicidad Camacho y Orvañanos. En dos ocasiones ha sido presidente de la Asociación Mexicana de Agencias de Publicidad (1968-69 y 1973-74). Fue vicepresidente del Consejo Nacional de la Publicidad (1975) y de la Confederación de Cámaras Nacionales de Comercio (1977-79), asesor de comunicaciones del Fondo Nacional para Actividades Sociales y representante de la Concanaco ante el Congreso Empresarial Mexicano.

Osante López, Manuel ◆ n. y m. en el DF (1937-1990). Licenciado en derecho por la UNAM (1958), donde fue profesor. Fue asesor técnico de la Secretaría Privada de la Presidencia de la República (1964-70), subdelegado en Venustiano Carranza, DF (1976-81), secretario de Divulgación Ideológica del Comité Ejecutivo Nacional del PRI (1981-82) y diputado federal (1982-85). Es autor del libro *La opinión pública en el derecho administrativo*.

O'Shaughnessy, Edith Louise ◆ n. y m. en EUA (?-1939). En 1901 se casó con Nelson O'Shaughnessy, diplomático estadounidense a quien acompañó cuando éste estuvo en México, primero como segundo secretario de la embajada estadounidense y, de julio de 1913 hasta abril de 1914, como encargado de negocios. Vació sus observaciones sobre el país y su gente en varias obras. Autora de *Diplomatic's Days* (1917), *Intimate Pages of Mexican History* (1920) y *A Diplomat's Wife in Mexico*, aparecido en inglés en 1916 y traducido, prologado y anotado por Eugenia Meyer para la edición mexicana de 1971 como *Huerta y La revolución vistos por la esposa de un diplomático en México*. Cartas desde la embajada norteamericana en México que se refieren al dramático periodo comprendido entre el 8 de octubre de 1913 y el rompimiento de relaciones que tuvo lugar el 23 de abril de 1914, junto con un resumen sobre la ocupación de Veracruz.

Oso, del ◆ Sierra de Durango. Forma parte de la Sierra Madre Occidental. Se encuentra en la parte norte del estado, entre las sierras de las Canoas y de los Guajolotes, al oeste-noroeste de Gómez Palacio.

Osollo, Luis Gonzaga ◆ n. en la ciudad de México y m. en San Luis Potosí, SLP (1828-1858). Estudió en el Colegio Militar. Combatió la invasión estadounidense de 1847. Sirvió a Antonio López de Santa Anna. Al triunfo de la revolución de Ayutla se exilió en Estados Unidos. De vuelta en México se sumó al levantamiento conservador contra la Constitución de 1857. En el gobierno de Félix Zuloaga fue jefe del ejército y como tal combatió a las fuerzas liberales, derrotándolas en el centro y occidente del país. Al entrar en Guadalajara, el 22 de marzo de 1858, asumió plenos poderes y convocó a una Junta de Notables que tuvo por función elegir gobernador de Jalisco. Poco después haber tomado San Luis Potosí, murió de tifo.

Osores de Sotomayor, Félix ◆ n. en Tulancingo, Hgo., y m. en la ciudad de México (?-1851). Licenciado (1802) y doctor en teología (1803) por la Real y Pontificia Universidad de México. Fue profesor del Colegio de San Juan de Letrán. Durante veinte años (1829-1849) desempeñó cargos en el arzobispado de México (1829- 1849). Fue representante por Querétaro a las Cortes de España (1814 y 1820), diputado al primer Congreso mexicano (1822-23), al General Constituyente (1923-24), al Constituyente del Estado de México (1825-27) y, por la misma entidad, al Congreso General (1825-26). Es autor de *Serie de los curas de Tezicapán desde 1590 hasta 1805*, *Reglamento interior del Congreso Mexicano* (1823) y *Noticia de algunos alumnos o colegiales de San Pedro y San Pablo y San Ildefonso, insignes por su piedad, literatura y empleos* e *Historia de todos los colegios de la ciudad de México desde la conquista hasta 1780*.

Osorio, Jorge Federico ◆ n. en el DF (1951). Pianista. Estudió en los conservatorios Nacional de Música de México, en el de París y en el Tchaikowski, de Moscú. Ha sido discípulo de Bernard Flavigny, Monique Haas, Jacob Milstein, Nadia Reisenberg y Wilhelm Kempff. Se ha presentado como solista con las orquestas Estatal de Moscú, Filarmónica de Israel, del Concertgebouw de Amsterdam, de la Radio Televisión Española, la Filarmónica de Varsovia, la Camerata Académica de Salzburgo, la Nacional de Canadá, Sinfónica de Dallas, Royal Philarmonic de Londres, la Sinfónica Nacional de México, la Sinfónica de Xalapa y la Filarmónica de la Ciudad de la Ciudad de México. Con varios de estos conjuntos ha grabado discos. Entre las distinciones que ha obtenido se cuentan el Gina Bachauer Memorial Award (EUA), el Premio Alex de Vries (Bélgica) y el Primer Premio en la Rhode Island International Master Pianist Competition.

Osorio, Lilia ◆ n. en el DF (1936). Es maestra en letras clásicas por la UNAM, donde ejerce la docencia desde 1976. Hace traducciones del portugués y el inglés. Ha colaborado en *Revista de la Universidad, Diálogos, Los Universitarios, La Cultura en México, México en la Cultura, Excélsior* y *unomásuno*. Autora de "Poesía occidental", incluido en *Las Humanidades en el siglo XX* (1978), *Palimpsesto* (cuentos, 1981) y una *Antología de María Luisa Bombal* (1983).

Osorio, Ramiro ◆ n. en Colombia (1951). Estudió actuación y dirección con Sergio Magaña. En 1974 fundó los grupos de teatro de la Casa de la Cultura, y en 1977 El Ropero, en León, Guanajuato. Fue jefe de producción de la Universidad de Guanajuato (1976-

77), jefe de extensión teatral del INBA (1984), director de Teatro y Danza de la UNAM (1984-85). Asesoró al Instituto de Cultura del gobierno de Nuevo León (1987). Coordinó la primera muestra de teatro español en México (1988). Fue fundador del Festival Ciudad de México. Posteriormente, regresó a su país natal para desempeñar diversas tareas administrativas, entre ellas, la de ministro de Cultura. En 1993 fue embajador de Colombia en México, cargo que desempeñó hasta 1994.

Osorio, Trinidad ♦ n. en el DF (1930). Estudió en la Escuela Nacional de Artes Plásticas de la UNAM (1942-49), de la que ha sido profesor desde 1954 y director interino en 1985. Estuvo becado en Estados Unidos (1956). Es profesor de dibujo y grabado en la ENAP. En México suman más de 30 sus exposiciones individuales. Ha expuesto en Argentina, Brasil, Costa Rica, Cuba, Checoslovaquia, China, España, Estados Unidos, Francia, Haití, Honduras, Japón, Panamá y Perú.

Osorio Benítez, Miguel Ángel ♦ n. en Colombia y m. en el DF (1883-1942). Es conocido como Porfirio Barba Jacob, aunque también utilizó los pseudónimos de Ricardo Arenales, Juan Azteca, Emigdio S. Paniagua y Main Ximénez. En Colombia estudió derecho, pero abandonó la carrera para dedicarse a la poesía y al periodismo. Después de servir en el ejército, fue profesor en la provincia de Antioquia y empezó a publicar poemas en diarios de Bogotá. Viajó a Cuba y más tarde a México. Se estableció en Monterrey y editó, en 1909, la *Revista Contemporánea*. Al año siguiente publicó el periódico *El Espectador*. A la caída de Porfirio Díaz se exilió en Estados Unidos y posteriormente se trasladó a varios países de Centroamérica y el Caribe. En 1913 volvió a México. Un año más tarde fundó la revista *Churubusco* y colaboró en *El Imparcial*. Viajó por El Salvador y Guatemala, países de los que fue expulsado. Regresó a Monterrey y en los años veinte fundó *El Porvenir*. Colaboró en el meridiano *Últimas Noticias*, del Distrito Federal. Se trasladó a Perú y ahí dirigió el cotidiano *La Prensa*. Volvió a México en 1933. Es autor de *El combate de la Ciudadela, narrado por un extranjero* (1913), *Canciones y elegías* (1932), *Flores negras* (1933), *Canción de la vida profunda y otros poemas* (1937) y *Poemas intemporales* (1957). En 1987 se publicó su *Obra poética*, reunida por Guillermo Rousset y prologada por Elías Nandino.

Osorio Bolio de Saldívar, Elisa ♦ n. en Pachuca, Hgo. (1906). Pianista. Ha colaborado con su esposo, Gabriel Saldívar y Silva, en diversas obras de musicología. Por su parte, es autora de *En el valle del Mezquital* (1944), *Técnica de cantos y juegos para el jardín de niños* (1952), *Diez personalidades del jardín de niños mexicanos* (1975) y *Ritmos, cantos y juegos* (1976).

Osorio y Carvajal, Ramón ♦ n. en Valladolid, Yuc., y m. en el DF (1914-1988). Médico cirujano por la Universidad del Sureste. Hizo cursos de posgrado en el extranjero. Fue director de la Facultad de Medicina (1943-44) y rector de la Universidad de Yucatán (1943). Miembro del PRI. Fue coordinador del Departamento de Turismo (1964-67), senador de la República (1967-70), delegado del DDF en Cuajimalpa (1971-76), presidente de la Junta Federal de Mejoras Materiales en Nuevo Laredo, Tamaulipas (1977-78), director de Estancias Migratorias de la Secretaría de Gobernación (1979), delegado del Registro Nacional de Electores (1979-82) y director de Asistencia del Instituto Nacional de la Senectud (1982-88). Director-fundador de la *Revista Yucateca de Ginecología y Obstetricia* (1947-52), del periódico *Presencia* (1954) y otras publicaciones. Colaboró en programas de la radiodifusora XEW y en *Jueves de Excélsior*. Autor de poesía: *Versos de hoy y de ayer* (1952); de novela: *Destinos diferentes* (1983); obras históricas: *Historia de la medicina en Yucatán* (1943), *Yucatán en las luchas libertarias* (1972) y *La conjura de Martín Cortés y otros sucesos de la época colonial* (1973); semblanzas: *Martí, calidad humana* (1953), *Andrés Quintana Roo, patricio excelso* (1967), *Juárez, restaurador de la República* (1972) y ensayo: *Problemas de la angustia* (1971), *La política mexicana nacional e internacional* (1974), *México en el arte, la ciencia y la política* (1975), así como obras epistolares: *Epístolas a un médico* (1947), *Cartas a un político* (1988) y cuatro tomos de *Cartas a mis hijos*. Académico emérito de la Academia Mexicana de Cirugía.

Osorio de Escobar y Llamas, Diego ♦ n. en España y m. en Puebla, Pue. (?-1673). Comenzó su carrera eclesiástica en Toledo y más tarde se trasladó a América. Entre junio y octubre de 1644 fue virrey de la Nueva España. Arzobispo de Puebla (1656-73). Rechazó el nombramiento de arzobispo de México.

Diego Osorio de Escober y Llamas

Osorio Marbán, Félix Miguel ♦ n. en Chaucingo, municipio de Huitzuco, Gro. (1936). Profesor normalista por la Escuela Nacional de Maestros (1953) y licenciado en derecho por la UNAM (1960). Profesor en diversas instituciones de enseñanza superior. En el Partido Revolucionario Institucional ha sido director nacional juvenil (1959-64), delegado del comité ejecutivo nacional en Morelos y Nayarit, representante ante la Comisión Federal Electoral, secretario particular del presidente del CEN (1966-1968), presidente de la comisión conmemorativa del cincuentario de esa formación política (1978-79) y secretario adjunto a la presidencia del CEN (1989). En el sector público fue gerente general de La Forestal (1968), subsecretario de Asuntos Agrarios (1976-78) y encargado del despacho (1978) de la Secretaría de la Reforma Agraria; y director general de Almacenes Nacionales de Depósito (1979). Diputado federal (1964-67, 1985-88 y 1991-94). Colaborador de los periódicos *El Nacional, Excélsior, Organización Editorial Mexicana, Jueves* de *Excélsior* y la revista *Impacto*. Autor de *El partido de la revolución mexicana, Revolución y política, La nueva generación militante, Lo que vi en China, Una mirada al África, La administración pública y el deber educativo del Estado, Partidos y organizaciones políticas* (2 t.,

1987), *El poder* (ensayo, 1989) y *Anecdotario político mexicano* (2 ed., 1998). Distinguido con las medallas por 30, 35, 40 y 45 años de militancia y lealtad al PRI, así como con la presea Lázaro Cárdenas.

Osorio Mondragón, José Luis ♦ n. en Texcoco, Estado de Méx., y m. en el DF (1885-1944). Se graduó como ingeniero en el Colegio Militar y en 1912 se incorporó a la División del Norte para combatir la rebelión orozquista. Se dio de baja en el ejército con el grado de mayor y se dedicó a la docencia y a la investigación. Fue profesor del Colegio Militar, de la Escuela Bancaria del Banco de México y de la Escuela Nacional Preparatoria y fungió como director de esta última. Escribió *Algunas rectificaciones importantes a la geografía de la República Mexicana y la división regional de su territorio* (1925) y *Breves apuntes de geografía humana, en sus ramas social y económica* (1927).

Osorio y Nieto, César Augusto ♦ n. en el DF (1939). Licenciado en derecho por la UNAM (1960-66). Profesor de las universidades Femenina de México (1968-69), Panamericana (1976-80) y Autónoma del Estado de México (1982). Ha sido jefe de la Sección Jurídica del Departamento de Utilidades de la Secretaría de Hacienda y Crédito Público (1971), jefe del Departamento de Averiguaciones Previas en las delegaciones Álvaro Obregón (1974) y Gustavo A. Madero (1975); subdirector general jurídico y consultivo (1976-80), agente del Ministerio Público (1976), subdirector de Mesas de Trámites (1980-84) y subdirector del Instituto Técnico de Formación Profesional (1984) de la Procuraduría de Justicia del Distrito Federal; agente del Ministerio Público Federal (1984), subdirector técnico jurídico (1984) y, desde 1985, director de Averiguaciones Previas de la Procuraduría General de la República. Autor de *La averiguación previa* (1981), *El niño maltratado* (1981) y *Síntesis de derecho penal* (1984). Pertenece a la National Geographic Society.

Osorio Palacios, Juan José ♦ n. y m. en el DF (1920-1997). Estudió en el Conservatorio Nacional de Música (1946). Cofundador de la CTM (1936), en la que fue secretario adjunto de organización y propaganda (1950), de organización (1956), secretario adjunto de promoción y organización sindical (1962), secretario de acción social (1974) y secretario de finanzas y administración (1979) de la CTM. cofundador y secretario general del Sindicato Nacional de Trabajadores de la Música de la República Mexicana (1946, 1948, 1949, 1960). Fundó la Federación Interamericana de Trabajadores del Espectáculo (1961). Fue secretario de la comisión de asuntos políticos del Congreso del Trabajo (1978); diputado federal en cinco ocasiones (1952-55, 1958-61, 1976-79, 1982- 85, 1988-91 y 1994-97) y presidente de la Gran Comisión de la Cámara de Diputados (1996-97). Miembro de la Asamblea de Representantes del DF y líder de la mayoría (1991-94). Director general del Fonacot (1997).

Osorio Romero, Ignacio Fernando ♦ n. en Temascalcingo, Edo. de Méx., y m. en el DF (1941-1991). Licenciado (1967), maestro (1978) y doctor (1989) en letras por la UNAM, de la que fue profesor, investigador, secretario de redacción del *Boletín de la Biblioteca Nacional de México* (1965-72), jefe de la carrera de letras clásicas (1977), director general de Publicaciones (1989-90) y director del Instituto de Investigaciones Bibliográficas y de la Biblioteca Nacional (1990-91). Miembro del consejo de redacción de *Nova Tellus* (1983-91) e investigador nacional desde 1986. Fue colaborador de *Historia Nueva*, *Revista de Bellas Artes*, *Libros de México*, *Omnia*, *Studi Latini e Italiani*, *Revista Mexicana de Cultura*, *Sábado* y *La Cultura en México*. Coautor de *Bibliografía general de don Justo Sierra* (1969), *Aproximaciones al mundo clásico* (1979), *Cultura clásica y cultura mexicana* (1983), *En torno a la formación de la conciencia mexicana en Nueva España* (1989), *Ensayos heterodoxos* (1989) y *Lenguaje y tradición en México* (1989). Autor de *Tópicos sobre Cicerón en México* (1976), *Colegios y profesores jesuitas que enseñaron latín en Nueva España (1572-1767)* (1979), *Floresta de gramática, poética y retórica en Nueva España 1521-1767* (1980), *Jano o la literatura neolatina de México. Visión retrospectiva* (1981), *Juan Montalvo. Textos. Una antología general* (1982), *Historia de las bibliotecas novohispanas. I* (1987), *Historia de las bibliotecas en el estado de Puebla* (1988), *Antonio Rubio en la filosofía novohispana* (1989), *Conquistar el eco. La paradoja de la conciencia criolla* (1989), *La enseñanza del latín a los indios* y *El sueño criollo. José de Villerías y Roelas (1695-1728)*.

Osorio Tafall, Bibiano ♦ n. en España (1903). Estudió biología en España y Alemania. En la República Española fue secretario de Gobernación, secretario general de la Izquierda Republicana y secretario de Defensa. Llegó en 1940 y se naturalizó mexicano. Ha sido profesor de la UNAM, del Politécnico y de El Colegio de México. Director del Centro de Estudios Económicos y Sociales del Tercer Mundo (1981-82). Funcionario de la ONU desde 1948, desempeñó los siguientes cargos: director de la oficina de la FAO para América Latina, jefe de la operación de las Naciones Unidas para el Congo (1964-67) y representante especial del secretario general de la organización en Chipre. Autor de *El mar de Cortés* (1942), *Rotíferos planctónicos de México* (1942), *La plataforma continental y la incorporación de sus riquezas naturales al patrimonio nacional* (1946), *Un capítulo de la geografía económica de México: la pesca* (1947), *Mares e islas mexicanas del Pacífico* (1948), *La planeación del aprovechamiento de los recursos naturales renovables para la industrialización de México* (1950), *Asistencia técnica de las Naciones Unidas para el desarrollo económico; Rebelión y violencia en la sociedad opulenta* (1968) y *El mundo en 1980* (1968).

Osornio Camarena, Enrique ♦ n. en Querétaro, Qro., y m. en el DF (1868-1946). Se graduó como médico en la Universidad de Querétaro. En 1913 se incorporó a la revolución en las filas constitucionalistas. Fue el encargado de amputarle el brazo a Álvaro Obregón en 1915. Tras el triunfo de la rebelión de Agua Prieta (1920), fue jefe del Cuerpo Médico Militar y jefe del Departamento de Unidad Militar de la Secretaría de Guerra. Gobernador del estado de Aguascalientes (1932-36).

OSORNO, JOSÉ FRANCISCO ◆ n. en la provincia de Puebla y m. en la hacienda de Tecoyuca, Pue. (¿1769?-1824). Insurgente. En 1811 se levantó en armas y tomó Zacatlán, que durante seis años sería su cuartel general. Operó en los actuales estados de Hidalgo, México, Puebla y Veracruz. Durante ese tiempo ocupó varias veces Apan, Pachuca, San Juan Teotihuacán, Texcoco y Tulancingo, entre otras plazas. En 1817 pidió y obtuvo el indulto, luego de lo cual se retiró a su hacienda.

OSTIÓN, LAGUNA DEL ◆ Estero de Veracruz. Se encuentra en el extremo noroccidental del istmo de Tehuantepec, al norte-noroeste de Minatitlán y al oeste de Coatzacoalcos. Se comunica con el golfo de México.

OSTIONES ◆ Barra de Tamaulipas que es atravesada por el trópico de Cáncer. Se encuentra al sur de Soto la Marina y al norte de Tampico.

OSTOS MORA, JAVIER ◆ n. en el DF (1917). Licenciado en derecho por la UNAM (1938). Ha sido presidente de la Federación Mexicana de Natación (1950-68 y 80-1981), presidente (1968-72 y 1976-80) y, desde 1981, miembro del buró de la Federación Internacional de Natación Amateur y vicepresidente del Comité Olímpico Mexicano (1976-80).

OSTROSKY, JENNIE ◆ n. en la ciudad de México (1955). Periodista, narradora, guionista y productora de programas de radio y televisión. Estudió ciencias y técnicas de la información en UIA. Obtuvo la maestría en letras en la UNAM, estudió dirección escénica en el Centro Universitario de Teatro. Fue jefa del Departamento de Publicaciones Infantiles del CNCA y secretaria académica del Centro Universitario de Teatro. Colaboró para *Excélsior*. Autora de cuento: *Los desentierros del agua* (1990) y *Giraluna* (1992); novela: *El abecedario, la ciudad y los días* (1981); y poesía: *Para una vigilia y otros poemas* (1980) y *Ritos de fuga* (1995).

OSTUACÁN ◆ Municipio de Chiapas situado en el noroeste de la entidad, al nor-noroeste de Tuxtla Gutiérrez y en los límites con Veracruz y Tabasco. Superficie: 946.4 km². Habitantes: 13,795, de los cuales 4,007 forman la población económicamente activa. Hablan alguna lengua indígena 277 personas mayores de cinco años (zoque 265).

OSTUTA ◆ Río de Oaxaca. Nace en la vertiente sur de la sierra Atravesada, en el istmo de Tehuantepec, al noreste de Juchitán de Zaragoza. Corre hacia el sur hasta desembocar en la laguna Oriental.

OSUMACINTA ◆ Municipio de Chiapas contiguo a Tuxtla Gutiérrez. Superficie: 221.1 km². Habitantes: 3,029, de los cuales 625 forman la población económicamente activa. Hablan alguna lengua indígena 209 personas mayores de cinco años (tzotzil 205).

OSUNA ◆ Códice escrito en náhuatl y en español que data de la séptima década del siglo XVI. De carácter judicial (contiene el sumario de un juicio), es también también un recuento de agravios sufridos por los indios. Una parte, que consta de 80 páginas, fue hallada en España en 1878. En 1945 se encontraron otras 400 páginas.

Ilustración del Códice de Osuna

OSUNA, CARLOS ◆ n. en Ciudad Mier, Tams. (?-1923). En enero de 1911 se levantó en armas a las órdenes de Pablo González. Combatió la rebelión orozquista y, bajo el mando del general Murguía, a la División del Norte. Entre abril de 1916 y junio de 1917 fue gobernador del estado de Durango.

OSUNA, RAFAEL *PELÓN* ◆ n. en el DF y m. en Monterrey, NL (1939-1969). Tenista. Estudió administración de empresas en la Southern University de California, EUA. Comenzó a destacar en el tenis cuando, en 1958, ganó una partido de Copa Davis contra Finlandia. En 1960 fue campeón de dobles en el torneo de Wimbledon, Gran Bretaña, haciendo pareja con el norteamericano Dennis Ralston. Tres años más tarde volvió a ser campeón de dobles, esa vez al lado del mexicano Antonio Palafox. También ganó la competencia de individuales en el torneo de Forest Hills. Murió en un accidente de aviación.

FOTO: REFORMA

Rafael *Pelón* Osuna

OSUNA HINOJOSA, ANDRÉS ◆ n. en Ciudad Mier, Tamps., y m. en el DF (1872-1957). Se graduó en la Escuela Normal Nocturna de Monterrey. Durante la revolución combatió al gobierno de Victoriano Huerta. Fue gobernador de Tamaulipas (1917-19), director de Educación Pública del Distrito Federal y de Nuevo León. Profesor de la Escuela Normal de Saltillo. Colaboró en diversos periódicos del país y escribió *Elementos de psicología educativa* y *Alcoholismo*.

OSUNA HINOJOSA, GREGORIO ◆ n. en Ciudad Mier, Tams., y m. en Ciudad Valles, SLP (1873-1941). Durante la presidencia de Francisco I. Madero fue gobernador del Distrito Sur de Baja California. Al producirse el golpe de Estado de Victoriano Huerta tomó las armas y comandó el regimiento de rurales Carabineros de Coahuila. Más tarde se incorporó al Ejército del Noroeste. En 1917 fue presidente municipal de la ciudad de México y, después de la revolución, senador de la República.

OSWALDO ◆ ☛ *Sagástegui, Oswaldo.*

OTÁEZ ◆ Municipio de Durango situado en el occidente de la entidad, al noroeste de la capital del estado y contiguo a Santiago Papasquiaro. Superficie: 906.5 km². Habitantes: 5,518, de los cuales 781 forman la población económicamente activa. La cabecera municipal es Santa María de Otáez.

OTAOLA, SIMÓN ◆ n. en España y m. en el DF (1907-1980). Fue comisionado

Mariano Otero

político en los frentes de Aragón y Lérida, durante la guerra civil española (1836-1939). Se refugió en México tras la derrota de la República. Colaboró en la revista *Las Españas* y en *Umbral*. Fue publicista de Películas Nacionales. Autor de *Unos hombres* (1950), *La librería de Arana* (1953), *Los tordos en el Pirul* (1953), *El lugar ese* (1957), *El cortejo* (1963) y *Tiempo de recordar* (1978).

Otates ◆ Río de Oaxaca que nace en la vertiente norte de la sierra de Miahuatlán, al noreste de Puerto Ángel y al este de Salina Cruz. Corre paralelo a la sierra, hacia el noreste, hasta que se une con el río Virgen para formar el Tequisistlán, que desemboca en la presa Benito Juárez.

Otatitlán ◆ Municipio de Veracruz situado al oeste de San Andrés Tuxtla, contiguo a Cosamaloapan y Tlacotalpan, en los límites con Oaxaca. Superficie: 53.46 km². Habitantes: 5,459, de los cuales 1,668 forman la población económicamente activa. Hablan alguna lengua indígena cien personas mayores de cinco años (mazateco 41).

Foto: Fondo Editorial Grupo Azabache

Templo del santuario de Otatitlán, Veracruz

Oteapan ◆ Municipio de Veracruz situado al oeste de Minatitlán y al suroeste del puerto de Coatzacoalcos. Superficie: 27.97 km². Habitantes: 12,190, de los cuales 2,360 forman la población económicamente activa. Hablan alguna lengua indígena 927 personas mayores de cinco años (náhuatl 883).

Oteiza y Vértiz, Juan José de ◆ n. y m. en la ciudad de México (1777-1810). Estudió en el Colegio de Minería. Colaboró con Alejandro de Humboldt. Escribió un estudio sobre las pirámides de Teotihuacán y el opúsculo *En defensa del proyecto de bomba del director Fausto de Elhúyar, contra el dictamen formulado por el capitán de navío Joaquín Zarauz*, asi como varios artículos, algunos de los cuales fueron publicados en el *Diario de México*.

Clementina Otero en *Carlota de México*, de Miguel N. Lira (1943)

Otero, Clementina ◆ n. y m. en la ciudad de México (1912-1996). Actriz de formación autodidacta. Fue profesora de la Escuela de Teatro del Instituto Nacional de Bellas Artes. Se inició en *Peregrino*, de Charles Vildrac, con traducción de Gilberto Owen y dirección de Celestino Gorostiza, pieza que constituyó la cuarta puesta en escena del Teatro de Úlises (1928). Fue promotora y participante del teatro Orientación, que también dirigió Gorostiza. Perteneció a varias compañías profesionales. Con el teatro de México encabezó el reparto en más de 15 obras, de las cuales se recuerdan: *Carlota de México*, de Miguel N. Lira; *Hedda Gabler*, de Henrik Ibsen, y *La voz humana*, de Jean Cocteau.

Otero, José Tiburcio ◆ n. en Mineral de Baroyeca y m. en Hatabampo, Son. (1834-1900). Combatió en las filas liberales durante la guerra de los Tres Años. Luchó contra la intervención francesa y el imperio. En 1879 fue elegido vicegobernador de Sonora. Desde septiembre de ese año, hasta enero de 1880, fue gubernador sustituto. Más tarde fue comandante del ejército en Sonora (1885), senador de la República (1886-90) y jefe de la I Zona Militar (1892-93).

Otero, Mariano ◆ n. en Guadalajara, Jal., y m. en la ciudad de México (1817-1850). Se tituló como abogado en Guadalajara (1835). En 1842 se le eligió diputado por Jalisco al Congreso Constituyente y se trasladó a la ciudad de México, donde formó parte de la Comisión de Constitución. Ésta elaboró un proyecto de Carta Magna sostenido por la mayoría, en tanto que Otero, Juan José Espinosa de los Monteros y Octaviano Muñoz Ledo propusieron que a la expresión "república popular representativa" se le agregara la palabra "federal", lo que fue objeto de un fuerte debate en la asamblea, que, finalmente, resolvió regresar el documento a la comisión, la que el 3 de noviembre presentó un nuevo texto, notoriamente influido por Otero, al que se opusieron los conservadores, pues terminaba con el monopolio de la religión católica al permitir, implícitamente, la práctica privada de otros cultos y declarar "libre" la enseñanza particular. Asimismo, el proyecto constitucional establecía la libertad de imprenta, por lo que Tornel, ministro de la guerra, lo describió como "un código de anarquía" y el gobierno de Nicolás Bravo desconoció al Congreso. En 1846, Otero fue elegido nuevamente diputado al Congreso Nacional Extraordinario con funciones de Constituyente, en el que encabezó el grupo que al año siguiente elaboró el *Acta Constitutiva y de Reformas*, que fue la fórmula para conciliar a los bandos en un momento en que el país estaba ocupado por una potencia extranjera. Fue uno de los cuatro diputados que se opusieron a los tratados de Guadalupe Hidalgo y votaron por continuar la guerra contra los invasores estadounidenses. Durante la presidencia de José Joaquín de Herrera fue secretario de Relaciones Exteriores (junio a noviembre de 1848). Colaboró en *El Siglo XIX* y otras publicaciones. Autor del *Ensayo sobre el verdadero estado de la cuestión social y política que se agita en la República*

Mexicana (1842), *Indicaciones sobre la importancia de y necesidad de la reforma de las leyes penales* (1844) y *Exposición interesante. Al Supremo Congreso Nacional, que dirige el Supremo Gobierno del Estado, sobre la guerra que sostiene la República contra los Estados Unidos del Norte* (1847), entre otras obras. El papa le impuso la Gran Cruz de la Orden de Piana.

OTERO, LISANDRO ♦ n. en La Habana (1932). Escritor y periodista. Realizó estudios de literatura en la Soborna, de filosofía en la Universidad de La Habana y se graduó de periodista en la escuela Manuel Márquez Sterling. Ha colaborado en periódicos de Europa, Estados Unidos y América Latina. En Cuba desempeñó cargos gubernamentales y diplomáticos. Fue presidente de la Unión de Escritores y Artistas de Cuba. En 1998 se naturalizó mexicano. Aquí es jefe editorial de *Excélsior* y director de *Arena*, suplemento del mismo diario. Entre sus muchos libros se cuentan las novelas *Temporada de ángeles*, primera finalista en el Premio Rómulo Gallegos en 1987; *Bolero* (1987); *La situación*, Premio Casa de las Américas 1963; y el ensayo periodístico *La utopía cubana desde adentro*. Su novela más reciente es *La travesía* (1995). También ha publicado un volumen de memorias, *Llover sobre mojado* (1999). Es miembro correspondiente de la Real Academia Española y de la Academia Norteamericana de la Lengua Española. Recibió el Premio Nacional de Periodismo de México en 1997.

OTERO FERNÁNDEZ, ALEJANDRO ♦ n. en España y m. en el DF (1888-1953). Se tituló como médico en la Universidad de Santiago de Compostela (1910). Especializado en ginecología y obstetricia, fue profesor de la Universidad de Granada, de donde llegó a ser rector (1932). Fungió como vicepresidente del Partido Socialista Español y diputado en las Cortes que en 1931 establecieron la segunda República Española. En 1936, al poco tiempo de iniciada al guerra civil, fue nombrado subsecretario de Armamento. Al triunfo del fascismo en España se exilió en México, donde trabajó en la sala de maternidad del Sanatorio Español de la ciudad de México. Fue secretario general del Partido Socialista Español.

OTERO SILICEO, ENRIQUE ALFONSO ♦ n. en el DF (1942). Médico cirujano por la UNAM especializado en neurología en el Instituto Nacional de Neurología y Neurocirugía. Hizo estudios de maestría en bioquímica en la UNAM. Jefe de la División de Neurología del Instituto Nacional de Neurología y Neurocirugía. Presidente del Capítulo Mexicano de la Liga Contra la Epilepsia (1985-87), presidente de la Sociedad Mexicana de Análisis de Decisiones y Computación en Medicina (1986-88) y vicepresidente y presidente de ciencias neurológicas de la Sociedad Mexicana de Neurología y Psiquiatría.

OTEYZA Y BARINAGA, JOSÉ ANDRÉS DE ♦ n. en España y m. en el DF (¿1865?-1953). Estudió agronomía. Más tarde desempeñó algunos cargos en el gobierno español. En 1939 llegó a México. Colaboró con la Junta de Ayuda a los Republicanos Españoles. Se dedicó a la escultura.

OTEYZA FERNÁNDEZ, JOSÉ ANDRÉS DE ♦ n. en el DF (1942). Licenciado en economía por la UNAM (1965) y maestro por la Universidad de Cambridge, Inglaterra (1968). Profesor en la Escuela Nacional de Economía de la UNAM (1968-1970). Miembro del PRI en el que fue coordinador del IEPES (1975-76). Ha sido subdirector de Análisis del Departamento de Control de Empresas del Estado (1970-71) y director general de Estudios y Proyectos de la Secretaría del Patrimonio Nacional (1972-74); director general de Nafinsa (1974-75); secretario de Patrimonio y Fomento Industrial (1976-82), embajador en Canadá (1982-87) y director general de Aeropuertos y Servicios Auxiliares (1988-94).

OTEYZA Y DE LA LOMA, JOSÉ ANDRÉS DE ♦ n. en España y m. en el DF (1897-1960). Estudió agronomía. En 1939 llegó a México, tras la derrota de la República española. Fue profesor de la Universidad de Chapingo y construyó varios jardines públicos.

Manuel José Othón

OTHÓN, MANUEL JOSÉ ♦ n. y m. en San Luis Potosí, SLP (1858-1906). Escritor. Estudió en el Instituto Científico y Literario de San Luis, donde se tituló como abogado (1881). Colaboró en diversas publicaciones potosinas y en *El Mundo Ilustrado* y la *Revista Azul*, de la ciudad de México. Fue agente del Ministerio Público, juez en distintas poblaciones del centro y norte del país y diputado federal. Es autor de *Poesías* (1880), *Poesías. Nuevas poesías* (1883), *Últimas poesías* (1888), *Himno de los bosques* (1893), *Montañas épicas* (1899) y *Poemas rústicos* (ilustrados por Julio Ruelas, 1902). Después de su muerte se editaron *Noche rústica de Walpurgis* (1907), *Poemas escogidos* (selección de Agustín Loera y Chávez, 1917), *Obras* (1928), *Breve antología lírica* (prólogo y selección de Jesús Zavala, 1943), *Paisaje* (prólogo y selección de Manuel Calvillo, 1943), *Obras completas. Poesía, prosa, teatro* (edición y prólogo de Jesús Zavala con apéndices de Alfonso Reyes, Luis G. Urbina y Victoriano Agüeros, 1945), *Poemas y cuentos* (selección de Miguel Bustos Cerecedo, 1945), *Epistolario* (1946), *Ensayos poéticos inéditos* (edición y prólogo de Joaquín Antonio Peñalosa, 1947), *En el desierto. Idilio salvaje* (1952), *Poesía, prosa, teatro, epistolario* (edición, prólogo y notas de Jesús Zavala, 1954) y *Poesías y cuentos* (prólogo, selección y notas de Antonio Castro Leal, 1963). Sus obras teatrales son *Herida en el corazón* (1877), *Viniendo de picos pardos* (1879), *Después de la muerte* (1883), *Lo que hay detrás de la dicha* (1886), *El último capítulo* (1905), *La sombra del hogar, La cadena de flores, Sendas de amor* y *Con el alma y con la espada*.

Poemario de Manuel José Othón

OTHÓN P. BLANCO ♦ Municipio de Quintana Roo que ocupa la porción sur del estado, en la costa del mar Caribe. Limita con Guatemala, Belice y Campeche. Superficie: 17,189.75 km². Habitantes: 202,046, de los cuales 52,632 forman la población económicamente

Foto: Fondo Editorial Grupo Azabache

Chetumal, cabecera municipal de Othón P. Blanco, Quintana Roo

activa. Hablan alguna lengua indígena 25,885 personas mayores de cinco años (maya 20,933, mame 1,613 y kanjobal 1,146). La cabecera municipal es Chetumal, que es también capital del estado. En la jurisdicción, que cuenta con variados atractivos turísticos. Setenta kilómetros al este de Chetumal se halla la zona arqueológica de Kohunlich, que guarda los restos de una gran ciudad maya del siglo V, de dos kilómetros cuadrados de extensión, la que estaba deshabitada al llegar los españoles. En 1968 se descubrió en ella una pirámide con seis mascarones de estuco. En la jurisdicción existen numerosos atractivos turísticos y en 1988 se decretó la creación del primer santuario para proteger a los manatíes.

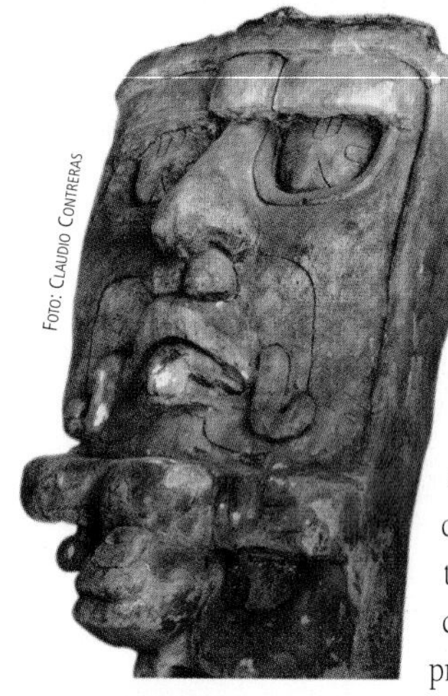

Foto: Claudio Contreras

Zona arqueológica de Kohunlich, en Othón P. Blanco, Quintana Roo

OTOMÍES ◆ Indios que habitan principalmente en el centro de Hidalgo y en el noroeste del Estado de México, así como en pequeñas zonas de Guanajuato, Michoacán, Morelos, Querétaro, Puebla, Tlaxcala y Veracruz. En 1980, 306,190 personas mayores de cinco años hablaban otomí, de las cuales 24 por ciento eran monolingües. En Hidalgo vivían 115,356, y en el Estado de México 98,115. Su lengua forma parte del grupo otomangue. La estructura de las casas habitación varía entre las diversas regiones y el único elemento común es el temazcal o baño de vapor. La indumentaria tradicional es conservada sólo por las mujeres: consiste en blusa de manta bordada, falda o enredo y quezquémetl. Por su parte, los hombres usan prendas de vestir de producción industrial. La actividad más importante es la agricultura de temporal, aunque en algunas zonas del Estado de México se ha introducido el riego. Los productos principales son maíz, frijol, calabaza y chile. La familia nuclear es la estructura básica de los agrupamientos otomíes. Normalmente, el novio se integra a la familia de la novia antes del casamiento para ayudar en las labores del campo. Su religión es la católica, la que practican mezclada con ritos de origen prehispánico. Los curanderos y los brujos tienen una importante presencia dentro de la comunidad. Los otomíes se establecieron en el noroeste del valle de México procedentes, al parecer, de Tula, y es posible que hayan dominado un territorio mayor al que ocupaban a la llegada de los españoles. Durante el siglo XIII el imperio de Xaltocan alcanzó su apogeo. Después de la conquista, los españoles los ubicaron en congregaciones que, a la vez que facilitaban la explotación de los indios, constituían puntos de defensa contra los grupos más septentrionales, los que todavía conservaban su independencia. Rechazan que se les adjudique la palabra otomí, que significa "agresivo", y prefieren llamarse *ñahñú*, "gente de aquí".

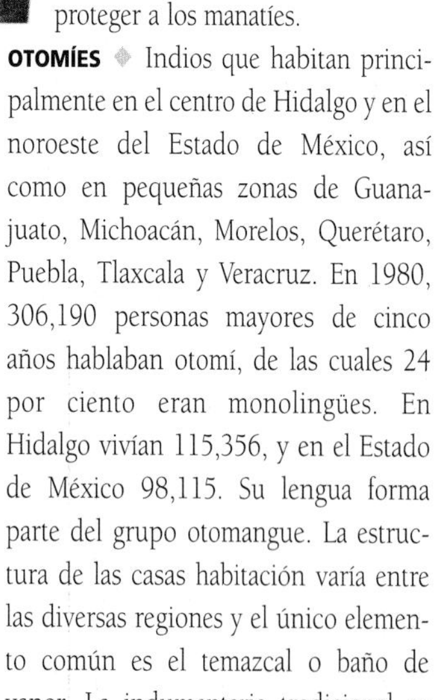

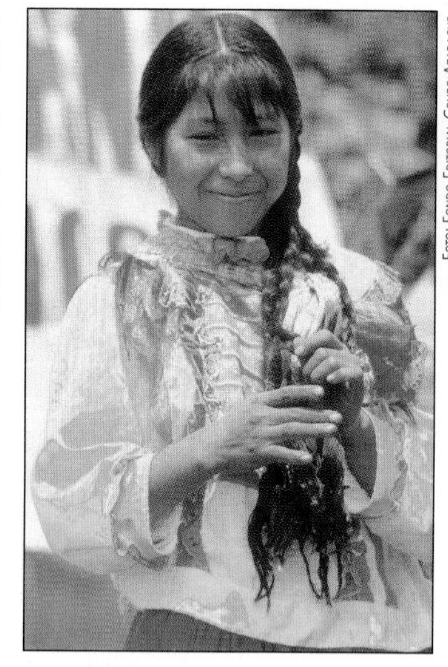

Foto: Fondo Editorial Grupo Azabache

Niña otomí del Estado de México

OTUMBA ◆ Municipio del Estado de México situado en el nororiente de la entidad, al noreste de Texcoco y al este de San Martín de las Pirámides, en los límites con Tlaxcala e Hidalgo. Superficie: 204.88 km². Habitantes: 25,415, de los cuales 6,608 forman la población económicamente activa. Hablan alguna lengua indígena 15 personas mayores de cinco años. La cabecera municipal es Otumba de Gómez Farías. Los primeros asentamientos en el territorio del actual municipio se produjeron hacia el siglo XI, durante la etapa de disgregación de los toltecas de Tula. En el siglo XIII los otomíes de Xaltocan fundaron un pueblo. A principios del siglo XVI, se

Foto: Lourdes Almeida

Familia de artesanos otomíes de Pahuatlán, Puebla

Foto: Fondo Editorial Grupo Azabache

Casa de la Cultura de Otumba, Estado de México

refugió en Otumba un pretendiente al trono del señorío de Texcoco, sometido por las fuerzas de Hernán Cortés en 1519. En julio de 1520 se produjo una de las batallas más importantes de la conquista, cuando los tenochcas dieron alcance a las fugitivas fuerzas de Cortés, entre las que se contaban tlaxcaltecas y huejotzincas. Los europeos y sus aliados sólo se salvaron de una derrota que hubiera sido decisiva por la muerte del comandante mexica, a manos de Cortés, según los hispanófilos, o víctima de una traición, según otros historiadores. Este hecho permitió la retirada de los invasores hasta Tlaxcala. Durante la Colonia, Otumba fue el lugar donde se encontraban el virrey saliente y el virrey entrante de la Nueva España. Desde 1965 se celebra, a fines de abril y principios de mayo, una feria regional que incluye un carnaval de burros, en el que desfilan jumentos decorados y vestidos como personajes de actualidad.

Otzoloapan ◆ Municipio del Estado de México situado en el suroccidente de la entidad, al suroeste de Valle de Bravo, en los límites con Michoacán. Superficie: 74.96 km². Habitantes: 4,687, de los cuales 886 forman la población económicamente activa. Hablan alguna lengua indígena 11 personas.

Otzolotepec ◆ Municipio del Estado de México situado al oeste de Naucalpan y al noreste de Toluca. Superficie: 77.45 km². Habitantes: 49,264, de los cuales 10,060 forman la población económicamente activa. Hablan alguna lengua indígena 5,658 personas mayores de cinco años (otomí 6,653). Indígenas monolingües: 82. La cabecera es Villa Cuauhtémoc.

Oumansky, Constantin Alexandrovitch ◆ n. en la Unión Soviética y m. en el DF (1902-1945). Después de trabajar en la agencia de noticias TASS, en 1931 ingresó al servicio exterior soviético. Fue embajador en Washington (1939-43) y en México (1943-45), al reanudarse las relaciones con Moscú, después del rompimiento en 1927. Durante su gestión hizo amistad con políticos e intectuales mexicanos y logró que siete naciones latinoamericanas establecieran relaciones con su país. Murió cuando, al despegar, se incendió y estrelló el avión en el que pretendía viajar a Costa Rica.

Ovaciones ◆ Diario publicado en el Distrito Federal. Fue fundado el 23 de enero de 1947 por Luciano Contreras. La edición matutina es fundamentalmente deportiva y cuenta con una sección de información general y espectáculos. La edición vespertina, de información general, aparece de lunes a sábado desde 1962 y llegó a tirar más de 300,000 ejemplares. Su principal atractivo es la página tres, integrada con gráficas de mujeres bellas y pies humorísticos. Se caracteriza también por lo ingenioso de sus titulares y el tono satírico de las columnas de espectáculos y comentarios policiacos, a cargo respectivamente de Héctor Pérez Verduzco y Jesús Munguía *Lirilón*. Han sido sus directores generales Fernando González Díaz Lombardo, Fernando González Parra y, después de adquirirlo el consorcio Televisa, Jacobo Zabludovsky y Fernando Alcalá. Desde 1999, la edición matutina publica el suplemento cultural dominical *Ovaciones en la Cultura*, dirigido por José María Espinasa.

Periódico *Ovaciones* del 28 de octubre de 1999

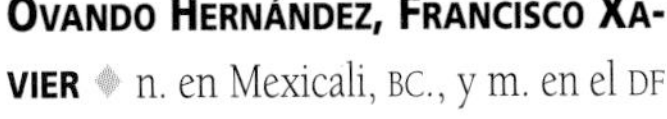

Ovalle Fernández, Ignacio ◆ n. en el DF (1946). Licenciado en derecho por la UNAM (1968). Es miembro del PRI. Ha sido jefe de la oficina de Vendedores Ambulantes del DDF (1967), secretario auxiliar y particular del secretario de Gobernación (1969-70), secretario particular del presidente Luis Echeverría (1970-72), subsecretario (1972-75) y secretario de la Presidencia de la República (1975-76); presidente del consejo de administración de la Empresa Naviera Multinacional del Caribe (1976), coordinador general del Plan Nacional de Zonas Deprimidas y Grupos Marginados, Coplamar (1976-82), director general del Instituto Nacional Indigenista (1976-82), embajador en Argentina (1982-87), embajador en Cuba (1987-88) y director general de Conasupo (1988-91). Pertenece a las asociaciones Nacional de Abogados y Mexicana de Planificación y al Instituto Nacional de Administración Pública.

Ovando Hernández, Francisco Xavier ◆ n. en Mexicali, BC., y m. en el DF (1947-1988). Licenciado en derecho por la Universidad Michoacana de San Nicolás de Hidalgo (1973), donde es profesor, y maestro en economía política por la UNAM (1979). Fue miembro del PRI hasta 1987, cuando salió de ese partido para incorporarse al Frente Democrático Nacional. Fue asesor jurídico de la Gerencia General de Nafinsa en

Lázaro Cárdenas, Michoacán (1973-75), secretario particular de Cuauhtémoc Cárdenas (1976), jefe del Departamento Jurídico Forestal y de la Fauna en la Secretaría de Agricultura y Recursos Hidráulicos (1977-79), procurador general de Justicia de Michoacán (1980-81), presidente del Comité Directivo Estatal del PRI en el mismo estado (1981-83) y diputado federal (1982-85). Era parte del equipo electoral de Cuauhtémoc Cárdenas cuando fue asesinado.

OVILLA MANDUJANO, MANUEL DE JESÚS ♦ n. en Tuxtla Gutiérrez, Chis., y m. en el DF (1945-1995). Licenciado en derecho por la UNAM. Fue militante de la Juventud Comunista en los años sesenta. Se desempeñó en Chiapas como presidente del Consejo Estatal Electoral. También trabajó con el gobierno estatal en la preparación de las iniciativas de ley para la pacificación en Chiapas, ante el alzamiento armado del Ejército Zapatista de Liberación Nacional (1994).

OWEN, ALBERT K. ♦ n. y m. en EUA (1840-1916). Según José C. Valadés murió en Guaymas, Sonora. Ingeniero topógrafo y urbanista. Vivió en la colonia New Harmony fundada en Estados Unidos por el utopista Robert Owen, de quien no era pariente. Realizó varios viajes por México y en 1872 escogió la bahía en la que posteriormente fundó la colonia socialista de Topolobampo, en el actual municipio de Ahome, Sinaloa. En 1880 publicó el ensayo *El oriente y el occidente* en el diario capitalino *La Libertad*, dirigido por Justo Sierra. Presentó un proyecto a Porfirio Díaz para construir el canal de Texcoco a Huehuetoca, que finalmente se encargó a empresarios ingleses. Para dar publicidad a su plan de colonización editó en Londres el folleto *A Dream of Ideal City*. El 13 de junio de 1881 obtuvo la concesión del presidente mexicano Manuel González para para fundar Ciudad González y tender la vía férrea que comunicaría a la colonia con Austin, para lo cual creó la empresa Texas, Topolobampo and Pacific Railroad Company. Obtenido el permiso publicó el folleto *Topolobampo*. En 1883 se asoció con los generales Buttler y Ulises Grant para constituir la firma The Credit Forcier of Sinaloa, que debía impulsar el asentamiento de población y monopolizaría la comercialización de los productos generados en la colonia. Confirmada la concesión por Porfirio Díaz en 1886, los colonos comenzaron a llegar a la que para entoces se llamó Ciudad de la Paz, aunque el puerto conservó el nombre de Topolobampo. En febrero de 1889, según el propio Owen, eran más de 5,200 personas las inscritas para poblar "metrópoli socialista de occidente", como llamó a la comunidad que imaginaba. Sin embargo, en 1891 sólo habían llegado unos 400 colonos hasta las costas de Sinaloa. La falta de organización y las duras condiciones climatológicas hicieron que a fines de 1893 la colonia desapareciera, después de lo cual Owen vivió en Mazatlán y en Guaymas. Expuso sus teorías sociales en *The Problem of the Hour* (1885) y *La cooperación íntegra* (1886). Valadés le atribuye la autoría del folleto *¿Fracasó la colonia anarquista de Topolobampo* (1904).

OWEN, GILBERTO ♦ n. en El Rosario, Sin., y m. en EUA (1904-1952). Estudió en la Escuela Nacional Preparatoria. Colaboró en las revistas *Ulises* (1926-28) y *Contemporáneos* (1828-31). Miembro del servicio exterior mexicano, vivió en Colombia, Ecuador, Estados Unidos y Perú. En este último país, colaboró con la Alianza Popular Revolucionaria Americana (APRA), en ese momento en la clandestinidad, por lo que el gobierno mexicano lo obligó a volver al pais. Autor de poesía: *Desvelo* (1925), *Línea* (1930), *Libro de Ruth* (1944) y *Perseo vencido* (1948), *Primeros versos* (1957) y *El infierno perdido* (1978); y prosa: *La llama fría* (relato, 1925), *Novela como nube* (1928) y *Examen de pausas* (1953). Trabajos de varios géneros están en las recopilaciones de Josefina Procopio *Poesía y y prosa* (1953) y en *Obras* (1979). Algunos de sus textos fueron leídos por Claudio Obregón y Óscar Chávez para un disco que grabó, con presentación de Alí Chumacero, la colección Voz Viva de México, de la UNAM (1968). En 1986 se publicaron sus *Cartas a Clementina Otero*.

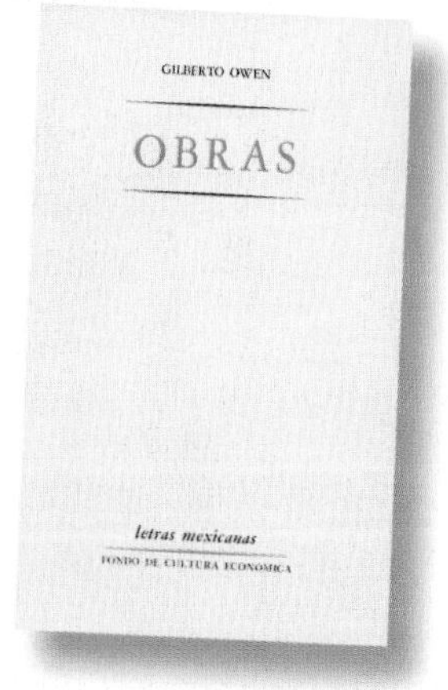

Obras de Gilberto Owen

OXCHUC ♦ Municipio de Chiapas situado en el centro del estado, al noreste de San Cristóbal de Las Casas y al este de Tuxtla Gutiérrez. Superficie: 72 km².

FOTO: GOBIERNO DEL ESTADO DE SINALOA
Biblioteca Gilberto Owen en el complejo cultural DIFOCUR, en Culiacán, Sinaloa

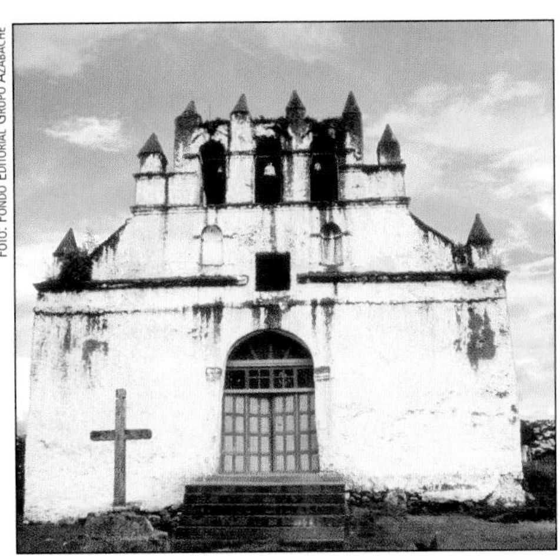
FOTO: FONDO EDITORIAL GRUPO AZABACHE

Iglesia de San Martín Abasolo en Oxchuc, Chiapas

Habitantes: 36,897, de los cuales 8,542 forman la población económicamente activa. Hablan alguna lengua indígena 27,796 personas mayores de cinco años (tzeltal 27,792). Indígenas monolingües: 8,613. El 21 de diciembre se celebra la fiesta de Santo Tomás Apóstol, la más importante de la cabecera.

OXKUTZCAB ◆ Municipio de Yucatán situado al sur de Mérida, al sureste de Ticul y al noroeste de Tekax. Superficie: 512.23 km². Habitantes: 24,005, de los cuales 6,110 forman la población económicamente activa. Hablan alguna lengua indígena 15,812 personas mayores de cinco años (maya 15,805). Indígenas monolingües: 1,224. Al suroeste de la cabecera se halla la zona arqueológica de Labná, formada por dos grandes conjuntos a los que une una calzada. Entre las construcciones destacan el Mirador, templo levantado sobre un basamento de 14 metros de altura, el Arco, edificación de estilo Puuc, y un edificio de dos pisos con cuartos que, se supone, alojaban a la aristocracia. La población, que alcanzó su esplendor hacia el siglo VIII, era la capital de un señorío vasallo de Uxmal.

OYARZÁBAL, JUAN DE ◆ n. en España y m. en el DF (1913-1977). Al iniciarse la guerra civil española se incorporó a la marina republicana. En 1939 estuvo tres meses detenido en un campo de concentración francés del Sájara. Vino en 1941 y se naturalizó mexicano. Estudió física y matemáticas en la Facultad de Ciencias de la UNAM, donde fue durante seis años jefe de la Sección de Física. Autor de varios libros de texto de su especialidad. Escribió poesía en esperanto y un libro llamado *El Naval* (1936).

OZTUMA ◆ Zona arqueológica de Guerrero situada en el municipio de General Canuto A. Neri, al oeste-noroeste de Iguala. Cuenta con fortificaciones construidas por los chontales a finales del siglo XV, para defenderse del avance de los tarascos. La mayor parte de los restos son murallas edificadas con lajas sin argamasa. En el cerro de La Malinche se encuentra un fuerte de base triangular, con muros de 1.90 metros de altura.

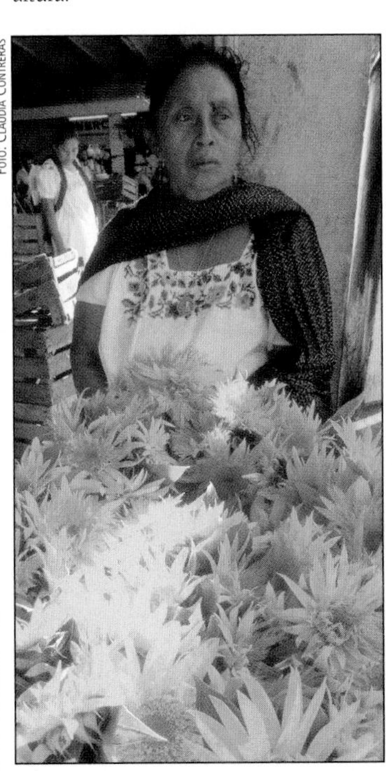
FOTO: CLAUDIA CONTRERAS

Vendedora de flores en Oxkutzcab, Yucatán

OZULUAMA ◆ Municipio costero de Veracruz situado en el norte del estado, al sur de Tampico y al norte de Tuxpan. Superficie: 2,357.39 km². Habitantes: 25,978, de los cuales 7,908 forman la población económicamente activa. Hablan alguna lengua indígena 202 personas mayores de cinco años (náhuatl 120, huasteco 42 y totonaco 33). En la jurisdicción se encuentra gran parte de la laguna de Tamiahua. La cabecera es Ozuluama de Mascareñas.

FOTO: BORIS DE SWAN

Celebración del 12 de diciembre en Ozuluama, Veracrúz

OZUMATLÁN ◆ Sierra de Michoacán. Forma parte del Eje Volcánico. Se halla al sur de Morelia, con cuyo valle limita al norte. Al noroeste se une con la sierra de Mil Cumbres. De sus laderas descienden, por el noroeste, varios arroyos que forman el río Cutzamala. Su extremo suroriental está al oeste de Pátzcuaro.

OZUMBA ◆ Municipio del Estado de México situado en el sureste del estado, contiguo a Amecameca y en los límites con Morelos. Superficie: 52.47 km². Habitantes: 21,424, de los cuales 4,647 forman la población económicamente activa. Hablan alguna lengua indígena 24 personas mayores de cinco años (náhuatl 21). La cabecera municipal es Ozumba de Alzate. En ella se encuentra un templo dominico de la época virreinal donde hay un retablo churrigueresco.

Fresco del convento de Ozumba, Estado de México

FOTO: FONDO EDITORIAL GRUPO AZABACHE

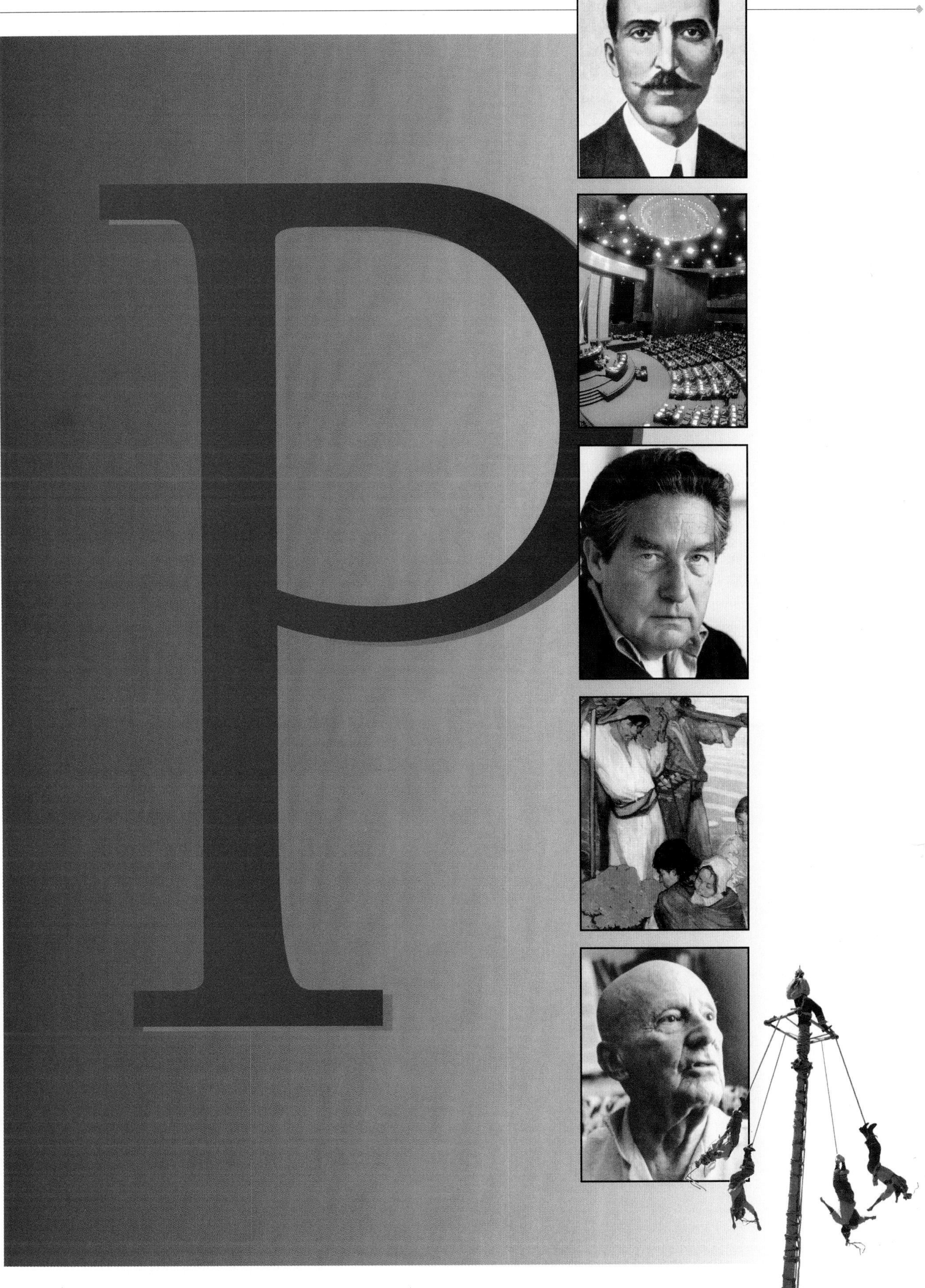

En esta casa Juan Pablos instaló la primera imprenta

PAALEN, WOLFGANG ◆ n. en Austria y m. en el DF (1905-1959). Pintor. Estudió en la escuela Hans Hofman de Munich. Entre 1929 y 1932 participó en diversas exposiciones colectivas en Berlín y París, con Paul Klee y Basili Kandinsky. Su primera muestra individual se montó en la galería Vignon de París (1934). En 1936 expuso con Pablo Picasso, May Ray y Alberto Giacometti y a partir de entonces participó en casi todas las exposiciones surrealistas de Europa. Inventó una técnica de pintura automática llamada *fumage*. En Canadá, donde vivió algún tiempo, estudió el arte totémico de ese país. Llegó a México en septiembre de 1939, luego de una breve estancia en Estados Unidos, y aquí desarrolló la mayor parte de su obra. En 1940 organizó, con André Breton y César Moro, la Exposición Internacional de Surrealismo. Participó en la fundación de la Revista *Dyn y Dynaton*. Entre 1949 y 1954 vivió nuevamente en Estados Unidos y en Europa. Regresó a México en 1954 y se suicidó cinco años después. Sus obras están en los museos de arte moderno de San Francisco, Nueva York, Tel Aviv y México, así como en las colecciones particulares de Isabel Marín de Paalen, Lefebvre Foinet, André Breton, Urvater Salomon y Peggy Guggenheim. Entre sus pinturas figuran *Bañistas*, *Amanecer*, *Composición de colores*, *Así es la vida* y *Migración de Yucatán*. Autor de los libros *El arte totémico* (1943), *Form and sense* (1945) y *Metaplastic* (1951).

Composición de colores, obra de Wolfgang Paalen

PABELLÓN, DEL ◆ Ensenada de Sinaloa situada en el golfo de California, entre la tierra firme y la península de Lucernilla. En el extremo sureste de la rada se encuentra Robalar, puerto dedicado al comercio de maderas. La entrada a la ensenada y a la bahía de Altata es por la boca de Tonina.

PABELLÓN DE ARTEAGA ◆ Municipio de Aguascalientes situado en el centro del estado, al noroeste de capital. Superficie: 310.80 km^2. Habitantes: 31,650, de los cuales 7,224 forman la población económicamente activa. Hablan alguna lengua indígena seis personas mayores de cinco años.

PABLILLO ◆ Río de Nuevo León, también llamado Linares, situado al sureste de Montemorelos, cerca de los límites con Tamaulipas. Nace en la sierra Madre Oriental, recibe al río Hualahuises y se une al Potosí para formar el Conchos.

PABLO SERNA, LUIS ANTONIO DE ◆ n. en el DF (1942). Licenciado en derecho por la UNAM (1960-64), maestro en economía por El Colegio de México (1965-67) y maestro en desarrollo económico y ciencia política por el Williams College de EUA (1969-70). Profesor de la UNAM (1967-75) y del Instituto de Capacitación Política del PRI (1971-75), partido al que pertenece. Ha sido director general de la Coordinación de Programación Económica y Social de la Secretaría de la Presidencia (1975-76), subdirector general de Promoción Fiscal de la Secretaría de Hacienda (1976-79), director general de Promoción Regional de la Secretaría de Programación (1979-82), director general de la Comisión de Fomento Minero (1982-88) y representante de México ante la Comunidad Económica Europea (1989-91) y Suiza (1991-94), director de Ferronales (1994-98), director de Infonavit (1998-). Autor de *Planeación* (1975). Pertenece a la Barra de Abogados, al Colegio de Economistas, a la Sociedad Mexicana de Planificación y a la Liga de Economistas Revolucionarios.

PABLOS, JUAN ◆ n. en Italia y m. en la ciudad de México (?-1561). Impresor cuyo verdadero nombre era Giovanni Paoli. En 1539 fue contratado por el alemán Juan Cromberger para dirigir la primera imprenta americana. Ese mismo año imprimió un libro que algunos autores consideran que fue la *Escala espiritual para llegar al cielo*, de San Juan Clímaco. Existe certeza en que la *Breve y más compendiosa doctrina cristiana en lengua mexicana y castellana*, de fray Juan de Zumárraga, es la obra conocida más antigua salida de ese taller. En 1548, una vez terminado su contrato con Cromberger, fue autorizado por el virrey Antonio de Mendoza para ser el único impresor de la Nueva España, monopolio del que gozó formalmente hasta 1560. Entre 1539 y 1547, realizó 14 obras bajo el nombre de la imprenta de Cromberger. De 1548 a 1559 imprimió 23 más, con su propio nombre. En su establecimiento se adiestraron otros impresores que trabajaron en el último tercio del siglo XVI.

PACÍFICO OCÉANO ◆ Mar que baña el este de la República Mexicana. Se encuentra al sur del océano Glacial Ártico, al oeste de América, al norte del océano Glacial Antártico, al noreste de Oceanía y al este de Asia. Superficie: 126,900,000 km^2, de los cuales 2,175,325 forman parte de la zona económica exclusiva de México. La mayor depresión es la Fosa de las Marianas, que tiene 9,600 metros de profundidad. Los estados mexicanos que tienen costas en el Pacífico son, de norte a sur, Baja California, Baja California Sur, Sinaloa, Nayarit, Jalisco, Colima, Michoacán, Guerrero, Oaxaca y Chiapas. Frente a estos dos últimos, se encuentra la Fosa de México, en el límite de la placa de Cocos, una depresión del relieve submarino cuyos movimientos son la principal causa de los temblores en México. El litoral continental, esto es sin considerar la península de Baja California (3,364 km), mide 3,974 km, pero incluye la costa de Sonora. Durante el periodo preclásico, una migración olmeca venida del sur de América desembarcó en Zacatula, en la desembocadura del río Balsas, y pobló la costa michoacana y guerrerense. Posteriores migraciones, también venidas de la actual costa peruana, ocuparon extensas zonas de Jalisco, Colima, Nayarit y Michoacán (☛), y crearon la cultura de Chupícuaro (los purépechas, que fueron conquistados por los españoles, aunque también descendían de los quechuas llegaron a Mesoamérica por la península de Yucatán). A pesar de que no existen pruebas definitivas, los restos de construcciones quechuas en la costa occidental de El Salvador y Panamá, así como la tradición oral de los purépechas, podría indicar la existencia de una ruta comercial establecida entre la región andina y el actual territorio de Michoacán, Nayarit y Jalisco. Una leyenda colimense, que cuenta que uno de los reyes de Colimán se entrevistó en la bahía de Manzanillo con un mandarín chino, también podría suponer que, antes de la conquista, los pueblos americanos sostuvieron contactos frecuentes con los asiáticos. Los primeros españoles que llegaron al Pacífico mexicano fueron tres enviados de Hernán Cortés, Juan Rodríguez de Villafuerte, Alonso de Ávalos y Juan Álvarez *Chico*, quienes, en 1522, fundaron el puerto de Zacatula, sobre el original asentamiento indígena. El puerto de Acapulco (☛), por su parte, ya funcionaba en 1528; en ese año, otro enviado de Cortés, Álvaro Saavedra, exploró el litoral. En 1532, Diego Hurtado de Mendoza salió de Acapulco para explorar la parte norte de la costa; quizá llegó hasta el golfo de California y, cuando regresaba, su tripulación fue diezmada por los tororame y por los españoles de Nuño Beltrán de Guzmán, y él desapareció. Al año siguiente, en una expedición organizada para buscarlo, que partió del puerto de Santiago de la Buena Esperanza (hoy Manzanillo), Hernando de Grijalva encontró el archipiélago de las Revillagigedo (☛). En 1535, el propio Cortés se embarcó para Baja California (☛). Durante 1542 y 1543, Juan Rodríguez Cabrillo exploró la costa norte del continente y descubrió la bahía de San Francisco. Al mando de una flota creada para la conquista de Filipinas (☛), que salió del puerto de Navidad, Andrés de Urdaneta, Miguel López de Legazpi y Felipe de Salcedo completaron, entre 1564 y 1565, el primer viaje de ida y vuelta entre Asia y América. Además del comercio de especias (clavo de las islas Molucas, nuez de Banda, sándalo de Timor, alcanfor de Borneo, canela de Ceilán y jengibre de Malabar), los barcos que hacían el viaje de Manila a Acapulco transportaban esclavos, aunque en menor cantidad que los negreros del Atlántico. Esto se debió, por una parte, a la mayor dificultad de los viajes en este océano, pero, sobre todo, a la oposición de los traficantes del Atlántico, deseosos de conservar el monopolio de la trata de esclavos. Aunque en 1608 Felipe II prohibió todo comercio humano entre Filipinas y la Nueva España, el auge del contrabando obligó al gobierno español, en 1620, a limitar el tráfico a un esclavo por pasajero. Estos esclavos provenían sobre todo de lo que ahora es China, Japón, Indonesia y Kampuchea. A mediados del siglo XVI, entre 1538 y 1578 aproximadamente, además del comercio asiático del que Acapulco tuvo el monopolio hasta la instauración de las reformas borbónicas de la segunda mitad del siglo XVII, la actividad comercial novohispana estuvo enfocada al tráfico con Perú a través de puerto de Huatulco, debido sobre todo a su cercanía con las ciudades de Antequera y Guatemala. Sin embargo, las enormes ganancias de los viajes asiáticos, así como el desarrollo de la costa peruana, que permitieron sustituir las importaciones de alimentos, cueros y especies que se hacían desde la Nueva España, ocasionaron que en el último cuarto de esa centuria Huatulco quedara reducido a una pequeña aldea de pescadores. La piratería, holandesa e inglesa principalmente, se concentró alrededor de Acapulco. Ya desde mediados del siglo XVI la Corona española organizaba expediciones para combatir a los corsarios, aunque la mayor parte de ellas no pudieron impedir su acción. En 1587, por ejemplo, Thomas Cavendish tomó Huatulco y Mazatlán; en 1614, Boris van Spillbergen estuvo a punto de ocupar Acapulco y lo mismo sucedió en 1624, cuando otra flota holandesa fue rechazada; en 1685, el inglés Thomas Peche ocupó Ixtapa; y, en 1687, un grupo de corsarios que se habían instalado en las islas Marías saqueó Mazatlán. Sin embargo, no sólo la presencia de piratas complicaba el comercio interoceánico. En el siglo XVII, los barcos tardaban más de tres meses en cruzar la distancia entre Manila y Acapulco, y no era extraño, dadas las condiciones sanitarias y climatológicas, que ocurrieran sucesos como el narrado por Fernand Braudel: "en mayo de 1657 llega a Acapulco un galeón de Manila sin una sola persona a bordo, pero todas las riquezas de su carga están completas y el barco fantasma llega por sí mismo al puerto." Quizá por eso, en cuanto se suponía la llegada de la *nao de China*, cuyas primeras noticias venían muchas veces del cabo San Lucas, el primer sitio americano que tocaban las naves, en el puerto de Acapulco se realizaban frecuentes peregrinaciones y misas especiales en los templos. Aunque los españoles habían navegado por las aguas septentrionales del océano desde fines del siglo XVI, sólo hasta fines del siglo XVIII, luego del descenso de la actividad comercial de Acapulco y en vista del avance ruso, francés e inglés por la zona, intentaron instalarse al norte de la bahía de San Francisco. Para solucionar los problemas de abastecimiento de estas expediciones, el gobierno virreinal fundó, hacia 1767, el puerto de San Blas (☛), en la costa nayarita; y entre 1774 y 1790 los españoles se apoderaron de la isla de Nutka, en el actual territorio de Canadá

(☛). Durante la guerra de Independencia, con la interrupción del tránsito entre Acapulco y México y la ocupación del puerto, en 1813, por las tropas de José María Morelos, San Blas se convirtió en el principal puerto mexicano del Pacífico. Como consecuencia de ese auge, entre 1822 y 1838 funcionó en Tepic una escuela naval dirigida por José Cardoso. En 1829, el presidente Vicente Guerrero (☛) fue capturado en el puerto de Acapulco y trasladado a Huatulco, donde fue entregado a sus asesinos. En enero de 1846, al inicio de la guerra contra Estados Unidos (☛), los invasores tomaron los puertos de Mazatlán y Acapulco y poco después bloquearon todos los demás. Acapulco volvió a activarse poco tiempo después debido al paso frecuente de viajeros que se dirigían a San Francisco, EUA, con la esperanza de enriquecerse durante la llamada *fiebre del oro*. Un gran número de estos viajeros, principalmente chilenos, se asentaron en la costa guerrerense (☛ *Chile*). En 1858, durante la guerra de los Tres Años, el presidente Benito Juárez se vió obligado a viajar de Manzanillo a Panamá (☛ *Reforma*). En 1894, durante el gobierno de Porfirio Díaz, se inauguró el ferrocarril de Tehuantepec, que permitió el comercio istmeño. A fines de 1942, luego del hundimiento de los barcos *Potrero del llano* y *Faja de oro* en aguas del golfo de México, el gobierno mexicano organizó dos grandes zonas militares, del Atlántico y del Pacífico; al mando de ésta quedó el ex presidente Lázaro Cárdenas. Dos años más tarde, en 1944, el Escuadrón 201 partió con la misión de combatir en Filipinas (☛ *Guerras mundiales*). En los años ochenta se discutió si el porvenir de México estaba en su integración económica con las naciones de la cuenca del Pacífico.

Pacto de la Embajada ◆ Convenio llamado también Pacto de la Ciudadela. Fue firmado el 18 de febrero de 1913 en la embajada de Estados Unidos en la ciudad de México, por Félix Díaz y Victoriano Huerta, a instancias del representante de Washington, Henry Lane Wilson, tras la detención del presidente Francisco I. Madero y el vicepresidente José María Pino Suárez, quienes fueron desconocidos y asesinados. Mediante este pacto se entregó el Poder Ejecutivo a Pedro Lascuráin, quien 45 minutos después lo cedió a Huerta, y se nombró un nuevo gabinete para la Presidencia provisional, integrado por Francisco León de la Barra (secretario de Relaciones Exteriores), Alberto García Granados (Gobernación), Manuel Mondragón (Guerra y Marina), Toribio Esquivel Obregón (Hacienda), Alberto Robles Gil (Fomento), Rodolfo Reyes (Justicia), Manuel Garza Aldape (Agricultura), Jorge Vera Estañol (Instrucción Pública) y David de la Fuente (Comunicaciones).

Pacto de la Empacadora ◆ Plan proclamado en la Casa Empacadora de la ciudad de Chihuahua, el 6 de marzo de 1911, por un grupo de militares encabezado por Pascual Orozco, quienes, con ese acto, anunciaron que se levantaban en armas contra el gobierno del presidente Francisco I. Madero y se comprometían a "luchar por el triunfo de los ideales del Plan de San Luis, reformado de Tacubaya, de conformidad con con la parte relativa del Plan de Ayala". El documento calificaba al presidente Madero como "el más ambicioso, inepto y miserable de los hombres, el fariseo de la Democracia, el Iscariote de la Patria". Lo acusaba de haber traicionado los propósitos del Plan de San Luis, de haber "usurpado el poder con la ayuda de nuestros expoliadores" en las elecciones de octubre de 1911 y de haber entregado el país a Estados Unidos, por lo que su régimen no era más "que una dependencia del gobierno de Washington." Por lo tanto, los alzados desconocían al gobierno maderista y a los poderes Legislativo y Judicial, pero al mismo tiempo daban por descontada la adhesión del Congreso de la Unión al levantamiento y reconocían como "legítimos representantes del pueblo a los actuales miembros de ambas Cámaras, cuyo periodo de mandato se declara prorrogado." En esos momentos, la mayoría de los diputados y senadores eran porfiristas. Luego de la caída del gobierno, los revolucionarios eligirían un presidente interino para gobernar durante un año. Los firmantes prometían la reconstitución de la Guardia Nacional, el respeto a la independencia de los ayuntamientos, la desaparición del cargo de jefe político, la erección de los estados de Nayarit y Baja California, la restitución del territorio de Quintana Roo a Yucatán, la paulatina nacionalización de los ferrocarriles, la supresión de las tiendas de raya, la prohibición del trabajo de menores de 10 años, la expropiación de las grandes haciendas improductivas y la entrega a sus legítimos propietarios de los terrenos usurpados.

Pacto de Xochimilco ◆ Nombre con que se conoce al acuerdo tomado por Francisco Villa y Emiliano Zapata el 4 de diciembre de 1914, poco antes de la ocupación de la ciudad de México por la División del Norte y el Ejército Libertador del Sur. El convenio, que para Paulino Martínez representaba "el primer día del primer año de la redención del pueblo mexicano" y para Roque González Garza significaba más que el Abrazo de Acatempan, llamaba a los jefes revolucionarios a que "no defrauden las esperanzas del pueblo", establecía que las fuerzas villistas debían secundar el Plan de Ayala (☛) y que "el general Zapata en el sur está obligado a garantizar el triunfo de la revolución en el Sur, y vos, señor general Villa, estáis obligado a garantizar el triunfo de la revolución en el Norte." La Soberana Convención Revolucionaria sería la encargada de gobernar el país mientras se realizaban elecciones, a cuyos resultados quedaban sometidos desde entonces los líderes campesinos. Sin embargo, unos meses después comenzaron las diferencias en la conducción del gobierno de la Convención. Además, las tropas zapatistas no recibieron todo el apoyo logístico de los villistas, quienes, por su parte fueron derrotados por el cuerpo de ejército del noroeste, comandado por Álvaro Obregón.

PACULA ◆ Municipio de Hidalgo situado en la porción noroccidental del estado, al nor-noroeste de Ixmiquilpan, en los límites con Querétaro. Superficie: 133.6 km². Habitantes: 6,142, de los cuales 1,296 forman la población económicamente activa. Hablan alguna lengua indígena 70 personas mayores de cinco años (otomí 69). El actual territorio del municipio, erigido como tal en 1870, fue evangelizado por los agustinos desde 1686. A comienzos del siglo XVIII numerosas rebeliones indígenas acabaron con las misiones levantadas por los frailes. Los franciscanos volvieron a la región una vez que, en 1715, el ejército la había pacificado. En 1811, durante la guerra de Independencia, un combate entre realistas e insurgentes, ocurrido en la actual cabecera municipal, Tezontepec, provocó un incendio que la destruyó casi por completo.

PACHECO, DE ◆ Grutas de Morelos situadas en las faldas del cerro de la Corona, donde se encuentran también las grutas de Cacahuamilpa. En las de Pacheco, llamadas así como homenaje al ex gobernador morelense Carlos Pacheco, existen los salones de los Pebeteros, de la Dama Blanca, del Monje, del Pabellón y de la Silla.

PACHECO, CRISTINA ◆ n. en San Felipe Torresmochas, Gto. (1941). Nombre profesional de Cristina Romo Hernández. Periodista. Estudió la licenciatura en letras españolas en la UNAM. Inició su carrera periodística en 1960, en los diarios *El Popular* y *Novedades*, y desde entonces ha colaborado en las revistas *Sucesos* (1963, con el seudónimo de Juan Ángel Real) y *Siempre!* (con una entrevista semanal durante casi 20 años); en los periódicos *El Sol de México* (1976-77), *El Día* (1977-85, donde, entre 1983 y 1985, publicó la sección "El Cuadrante de la Soledad") y *La Jornada* (desde 1986, donde aparece su sección "Mar de Historias"); y en *Sábado*, suplemento del cotidiano *unomásuno* (1981-86). Fue directora de las revistas *La Familia* y *La Mujer de Hoy*; y jefa de redacción de la *Revista de la Universidad*. Desde 1979 conduce el programa de televisión *Aquí nos tocó vivir*, que se transmite semanalmente por el Canal 11. Autora de *Para vivir aquí* (1983), *Orozco. Iconografía personal* (1983), *Sopita de fideo* (1984), *Testimonios y conversaciones* (1984), *Zona de desastre* (1986), *Cuarto de azotea* (1986), *La última noche del tigre* (1987), *La luz de México* (entrevistas, 1989), *Los dueños de la noche* (1990), *La rueda de la fortuna* (1993) y *Los trabajos perdidos* (1998). En 1989 se editaron sus volúmenes de relatos *El corazón de la noche* y *Para mirar a lo lejos*. Ha recibido el Premio Nacional de Periodismo en el género de entrevista (1975 y 1985) y por el mejor programa de servicios a la comunidad por televisión (1986), el premio de la Asociación Nacional de Periodistas, por *Aquí nos tocó vivir* (1986), el premio Teponaxtli de Malinalco por su labor en la televisión y el Premio de Periodismo Manuel Buendía (1992). Consejera de la Comisión de Derechos Humanos del DF (1996-).

PACHECO, FRANCISCO V. ◆ n. en Huitzilac y m. en Miacatlán, Mor. (¿1888?-1916). Militar. Se levantó en armas en 1911 y se incorporó al Ejército Libertador del Sur, donde obtuvo el grado de general de división. Combatió en el norte de Morelos y sur del Distrito Federal. En 1914 instaló su cuartel general en Huitzilac. Fue secretario de Guerra y Marina en los gobiernos de Roque González Garza (del 24 de mayo al 10 de junio de 1915) y Francisco Lagos Cházaro (del 14 de junio al 10 de octubre de 1915). Disuelta la Convención, volvió a Morelos y en marzo de 1916 fue acusado de dar paso franco a las fuerzas del carrancista Pablo González a Huitzilac; Emiliano Zapata ordenó su captura y su fusilamiento, cosa que llevó a cabo, en abril, una patrulla de Genovevo de la O.

PACHECO, JOSÉ EMILIO ◆ n. en el DF (1939). Escritor y periodista. Su apellido materno es Berny. Realizó estudios de derecho y letras en la UNAM. Trabajó en Difusión Cultural de la UNAM (1959-65), donde fue jefe de redacción de la *Revista Universidad de México* (1962). Codirigió el suplemento *Ramas Nuevas*, de la revista *Estaciones* (1963-79). Ha colaborado en revistas y suplementos culturales. Publica la columna "Inventario" en *Proceso* (1976-). Fue redactor del noticiero *Cine-verdad* (1967) y director de la colección Biblioteca del Estudiante Universitario. Asistió al Festival de Dos Mundos en Spoleto, Italia (1967). En 1976 grabó un disco en la serie Voz Viva de México, de la UNAM. Ha preparado antologías como *La poesía mexicana del siglo XIX*. Autor de poesía: *El castillo en la aguja* (1962), *Los elementos de la noche* (1963), *El reposo del fuego* (1966), *No me preguntes cómo pasa el tiempo* (1969, Premio Nacional de Poesía Aguascalientes), *Irás y no volverás* (1974), *Islas a la deriva* (1976), *Ayer es nunca jamás* (recopilación, 1978), *Tarde o temprano* (recopilación, 1980), *Desde entonces* (1980), *Los trabajos del mar* (1983), *Fin de siglo y otros poemas* (1984), *Aproximaciones* (traducción y versiones, 1984), *Alta traición* (recopilación, 1985), *Álbum de zoología* (1985), *Miro la tierra* (1986), *Ciudad de la memoria* (1989) y *El silencio de la luna* (1994); cuento: *La sangre de Medusa* (1959), *El*

Cristina Pacheco

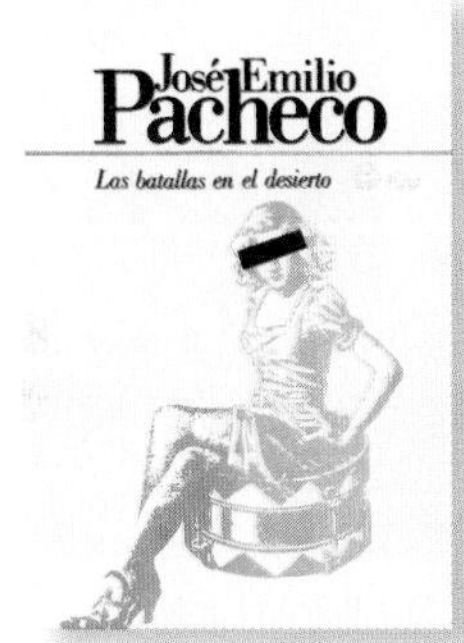

Novela corta de José Emilio Pacheco

José Emilio Pacheco

Foto: Rogelio Cuéllar

viento distante (1963), *El principio del placer* (1972, Premio Xavier Villaurrutia 1973) y *Latitudes* (1977); novela: *Morirás lejos* (1967, Premio Magda Donato 1968) y *Las batallas en el desierto* (1981); y teatro: *El pasado lo guardan las arañas*. En 1973 compartió con Arturo Ripstein los *Arieles* a la mejor historia original y a la mejor adaptación cinematográfica por la película *El castillo de la pureza*. Becario del Centro Mexicano de Escritores (1969-70) y de la Fundación Guggenheim (1970). Ha recibido los premios Nacional de Periodismo (1980), Malcolm Lowry (1991), Nacional de Letras (1992) y José Asunción Silva (Colombia, 1996). Miembro de El Colegio Nacional y creador emérito del SNCA.

José Ramón Pacheco

PACHECO, JOSÉ RAMÓN ◆ n. en Guadalajara, Jal., y m. en la ciudad. de México (1805-1865). Abogado. Fue secretario de Justicia en el gobierno de Mariano Salas (del 27 de agosto al 13 de octubre de 1846) y de Relaciones Interiores y Exteriores, durante la guerra contra Estados Unidos, en uno de los gabinetes de Antonio López de Santa Anna (del 7 de julio al 16 de septiembre de 1847). En 1953 recibió la designación de ministro plenipotenciario de México ante Napoleón III (1853-1862). Fungió como agente confidencial ante los gobiernos de Francia e Inglaterra (1862). Autor de *Cuestión del día o nuestros males y sus remedios* (1834), *Exposición sumaria del sistema frenológico del Dr. Gall* (1835) y *Descripción de la solemnidad fúnebre con que se honraron las cenizas del héroe de Iguala, dn. Agustín de Iturbide, en octubre de 1838* (1849).

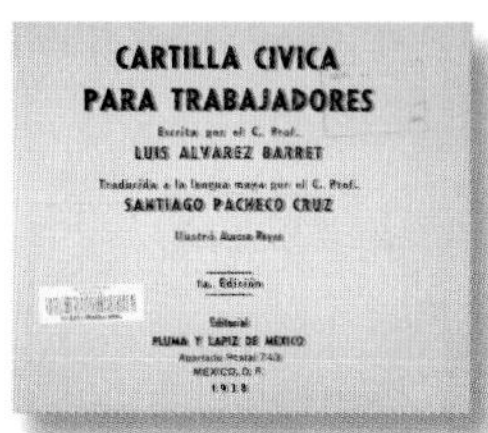

Obra de Santiago Pacheco Cruz

PACHECO, MÁXIMO ◆ n. en Huichapan, Hgo., y m. en el DF (1905-1992). Muralista. Su apellido materno era Miranda. Estudió en la Academia de San Carlos. Fue ayudante de Fermín Revueltas en los murales de la Escuela Nacional Preparatoria. En diciembre de 1922 participó en la fundación del Sindicato de Obreros Técnicos Pintores y Escultores, y al año siguiente se unió al equipo de asistentes de Diego Rivera, con quien colaboró en los murales de la Secretaría de Educación y de la Escuela Nacional de Agricultura de Chapingo. Militó en la Liga de Escritores y Artistas Revolucionarios y, con otros miembros, ejecutó los murales *Los trabajadores contra la guerra y el fascismo*, en los Talleres Gráficos de la Nación; y *Temas revolucionarios*, en la Confederación Revolucionaria de Michocacán. Coautor, con Jesús Guerrero Galván, Santos Balmori, Juan Manuel Anaya y Roberto Reyes Pérez, de los murales *La eduación socialista*, en la escuela Carlos A. Carrillo; *La Revolución mexicana en la educación*, en el IPN (1935); y *Retratos de líderes agrarios: Morelos, Zapata, Domingo Arenas y Ursulo Galván*, en la Confederación Campesina Emiliano Zapata de Puebla (1937). Autor de los murales *La fogata* (1933), en el Centro para Obreros Plutarco Elías Calles, en Atzacapozalco; *El lazo* (1934), en la Escuela Primaria Plutarco Elías Calles, en la colonia Portales; y uno en el Centro Nocturno para Obreros Vasco de Quiroga (1934), todos en el DF; y uno en la Escuela Industrial de Jiquilpan, Michoacán (1934). Dejó el muralismo en la década de los cuarenta y se dedicó a la pintura de caballete.

PACHECO ÁLVAREZ, ENRIQUE ◆ n. en Oaxaca, Oax. (1931). Licenciado en derecho por el Instituto de Ciencias y Artes de Oaxaca (1950-54). Profesor de la Universidad Benito Juárez de Oaxaca (1955-56) y de la UNAM (1967-70). Miembro del PRI desde 1950. Ha sido juez segundo en materia penal (1955) y tercero en materia civil (1956) en Oaxaca, diputado local (1956- 59) y federal (1961-64), subdirector general de Servicios Migratorios de la Secretaría de Gobernación (1979-80), coordinador nacional del Cuerpo Consultivo de la SRA (1980-81), director general de la Unidad Coordinadora de la Administración Pública Federal (1983) y director general de Enlace y Coordinación de la SEP (1984-85); y director general de Normas e Insumos de Vivienda de la Sedue (1985-88).

PACHECO CRUZ, SANTIAGO ◆ n. en Tinum, Camp., y m. en Mérida, Yuc. (1885-1970). Filólogo. Fue maestro estatal, inspector y director federal de Educación en Yucatán y Quintana Roo. Colaboró en la *Revista de Yucatán* y en el *Diario de Yucatán*. Tradujo al maya diversas leyes y documentos oficiales. Autor de *Compendio del idioma maya*, *Diccionario de etimologías toponímicas mayas*, *Usos, costumbres, religión y supersticiones de los mayas*, *Antropología cultural maya*, *Diccionario de la fauna yucateca*, *Verdadero diccionario maya* y *Geografía general del Territorio de Quintana Roo*; y de las obras teatrales *Amor de madre*, *Qué triste es amar sin ser amado*, *Mariblanca*, *Basta de majaderías*, *Los caprichos tontos*, *Los chicos se divierten*, *El amor es dulce*, *Matrimonios relámpago*, *Sotelito de mis ojos*, *El cabo abanderado*, *El cepo*, *Yolanda, o ¿Quiere usted su chocolatito?*, *La mujer moderna*, *La voz del amo*, *Leonel y Berenguela*, *Los apuros de un maestro* y *Yo no quiero ser maestra*. Por 50 años de labor docente recibió la medalla Ignacio Manuel Altamirano.

PACHECO MORENO, BULMARO ANDRÉS ◆ n. en Huatabampo, Son. (1954). Licenciado en ciencias políticas por la UNAM (1973-77). En el PRI, partido al que pertenece desde 1972, fue asesor del CEPES (1976) y subsecretario de Organización (1977) y de Finanzas (1978), secretario general adjunto (1984) y secretario general del PRI de Sonora (1987). Ha sido subdirector de Obras Públicas (1976) y oficial mayor y secretario del Ayuntamiento de Guaymas (1977-78); secretario auxiliar del secretario de Educación, Fernando Solana (1978- 82), y secretario técnico del siguiente titular, Jesús Reyes Heroles (1982-85); secretario de Fomento Educativo de la CNC en Sonora (1985), diputado federal (1985-88) y delegado del ISSSTE en Sonora (1999-).

PACHECO DE OSORIO, RODRIGO ◆ n. y m. en España (?-?). Tenía el título de marqués de Cerralvo. Fue comandante militar y gobernador de Galicia. Llegó a la Nueva España en 1624 y el 3 de noviembre de ese año tomó posesión como virrey (el decimoquinto de la colonia). Desempeñó el cargo hasta el 16 de septiembre de 1635. Durante su gobierno se abrió al culto la parte terminada de la nueva Catedral y demolió la vieja (1626- 27). Protegió al traficante de esclavos Manuel Solís y reinstauró el sistema de alcabalas (1626). En 1629, por la obstrucción del túnel de desagüe de Nochistongo, se inundó la ciudad de México. A consecuencia de la catástrofe murieron 30,000 personas y las aguas tardaron dos años en retirarse. Se propuso entonces trasladar la capital a Tacubaya, pero el proyecto se abandonó pues su costo se estimó en 50 millones de pesos (☛ *México*).

Pacheco Villalobos, Carlos ◆ n. en San Nicolás del Terreno, hoy de Pacheco, Chih., y m. en Orizaba, Ver. (1839-1891). En 1858 se incorporó a la Guardia Nacional de Chihuahua para combatir a los conservadores, luego de haber estado en prisión por oponerse al Plan de Tacubaya. Luchó contra la intervención francesa, fue hecho prisionero en 1864 y se reincorporó al ejército republicano en 1866, luego de ser canjeado. Perdió un brazo y una pierna en la batalla del 2 de abril de 1867, en Puebla. Diputado federal por Cholula a la IV Legislatura (1867-69) y administrador del Timbre en Puebla (1867-70). En 1876 se unió a la revuelta tuxtepecana y ascendió a coronel luego del derrocamiento del presidente Sebastián Lerdo de Tejada. Fue gobernador de Morelos (de diciembre de 1876 y 20 de abril al 4 de mayo de 1877) y de Puebla (1878), secretario de Guerra y Marina (del 15 de noviembre de 1879 al 30 de noviembre de 1880), en el primer gobierno de Porfirio Díaz; gobernador del Distrito Federal (1880-81), secretario de Fomento (del 27 de junio de 1881 al 30 de noviembre de 1884) en el gabinete de Manuel González y senador de la República (1882), aunque no ocupó su escaño. En agosto de 1884 fue elegido gobernador de Morelos y en octubre de Chihuahua, pero prefirió encargarse nuevamente de la Secretaría de Fomento, en el gabinete de Díaz (1 de diciembre de 1884 al 21 de marzo de 1891). Fue condecorado por el gobierno de Venezuela.

Pachuca ◆ Municipio de Hidalgo situado en la porción suroriental del estado, al sur de Atotonilco y al oeste de Tulancingo. Superficie: 195.3 km^2. Habitantes: 220,488, de los cuales 60,143 forman la población económicamente activa. Hablan alguna lengua indígena 5,114 personas mayores de cinco años (náhuatl 3,672 y otomí 1,105). La cabecera municipal, Pachuca de Soto, es también la capital del estado; fue llamada así en memoria de Manuel Fernando Soto, uno de los impulsores de la erección del estado de Hidalgo. Los restos más antiguos de asentamientos humanos datan del año 4,000 a.n.e. Hacia el año 200 a.n.e., los teotihuacanos se instalaron en el fondo de una cañada situada al sur del futuro Mineral del Chico, en lo que ahora es el barrio de San Bartolo. Cuatro siglos más tarde los sustituyeron los toltecas y durante su estancia se inició la extracción de metales. Luego de la destrucción de Tula, en el siglo XI, los otomíes ocuparon la cañada y llamaron a su ciudad Njunthé. Poco después, sin embargo, grupos chichimecas desalojaron a los otomíes y ocuparon el poblado. En el siglo XII, los texcocanos ocuparon la ciudad y a partir de 1182 fue dominio de Atzcapozalco, con el nombre de Pachoacan, que en náhuatl quiere decir estrechez. En 1431, la población quedó dentro de los límites del imperio mexica. Aunque la fecha de la fundación del poblado español no es precisa, es posible que desde 1524 hubiera conquistadores instalados en el lugar. En 1528, Francisco Téllez dominó la zona. A raíz del descubrimiento del proceso de beneficio de metales por amalgamación, realizado hacia 1555 por Bartolomé de Medina (☛), los europeos comenzaron a explotar extensivamente las minas situadas al norte de la ciudad y desde entonces la minería se convirtió en la principal actividad económica. El templo de la Asunción, el primero de la ciudad, se terminó de construir en 1553; fue demolido en 1647. En 1596, se inició la construcción del convento de San Francisco. Un siglo más tarde, en las cercanías del templo de la Asunción, se construyeron las Cajas Reales, donde se concentraba la plata extraída de las minas. La fama de la plata de la ciudad se extendió por Europa y el Medio Oriente al punto de que, según Agustín de Betancurt, los comerciantes de Jerusalén no aceptaban otra plata que no fuera la producida en Pachuca. En 1660 se terminó la construcción de un templo dieguino que posteriormente fue utilizado como cuartel militar y cárcel preventiva. A mediados del siglo XVIII, la población pachuqueña era de alrededor de 5,000 habitantes, más 1,000 indios, concentrados en la población de Pachuquilla; poco después se fundó el primer Banco de Avío. En 1770 se estableció el primer sistema de correo entre Pachuca y la ciudad de México y en 1787 se creó la provincia de Pachuca, dependiente de la Intendencia de México. En 1803, Alexander von Humboldt visitó el lugar. En octubre de 1811, un grupo insurgente al mando de Miguel Serrano intentó tomar la ciudad, pero fue rechazado por la guarnición española. En abril del año siguiente, sin embargo, el mismo Serrano la ocupó, luego de una larga batalla, en el curso de la cual se perdió la mayor parte de los archivos de las Cajas Reales. Las tropas coloniales recuperaron la plaza en agosto y desde entonces permaneció bajo su dominio, a pesar de los frecuentes ataques de las tropas de Manuel Fernando Osorno. Cinco años después, en junio de 1817, fray Servando Teresa de Mier estuvo preso en la cárcel pachuqueña, durante su traslado de Soto la Marina a la ciudad de México. También camino de la capital del virreinato, en plan victorioso, pasaron las tropas insurgentes de Guadalupe Victoria y Nicolás Bravo, quienes, en mayo de 1821, proclamaron la independencia. Al constituirse la República Federal en 1824, Pachuca quedó bajo la jurisdicción civil del Estado de México y la religiosa de la diócesis de Tulancingo. Ese mismo año se formó la primera

Carlos Pacheco Villalobos

María de los Dolores Padierna Luna

Ezequiel Padilla

empresa británica de explotación minera: la Compañía de los Caballeros Aventureros de las Minas del Real del Monte. La siguiente empresa inglesa fue la Compañía del Real del Monte y Pachuca, creada en 1849, propiedad de estadounidenses desde 1906, quienes en 1947 la vendieron al gobierno mexicano. Alrededor de 6,000 personas vivían en Pachuca a mediados del siglo XIX. En 1860 se instaló la primera imprenta de la ciudad. Luego de la guerra de los Tres Años, el enorme convento de San Francisco fue expropiado y en ese terreno se construyeron el parque Hidalgo, un rastro y el cementerio de San Rafael; el claustro propiamente dicho fue ocupado por la Escuela Práctica de Ingenieros de Minas y, desde 1976, por el Archivo Casasola, hoy Museo de la Fotografía del INAH. En julio de 1863, el ayuntamiento pachuqueño aceptó la intervención francesa y, en agosto de 1865, Maximiliano de Habsburgo visitó la ciudad: se hospedó en las Cajas Reales, fue agasajado por los británicos dueños de las minas y bajó a los socavones. Al año siguiente, los mineros atacaron a la guarnición francesa y, con el apoyo de los guerrilleros de José María Pérez, tomaron la ciudad. En 1869, al erigirse el estado de Hidalgo, la ciudad fue designada capital de la entidad. A partir de entonces, en sus alrededores se generalizaron los alzamientos campesinos, como el de Pedro Fabregat y Manuel Domínguez, *El Comunista*, quienes ocuparon Pachuca el 8 de marzo de 1870. Dos años más tarde se inauguró un acueducto situado en la parte norte de la ciudad, que llevaba agua desde la población de Los Leones. En septiembre de 1876, un grupo de rebeldes tuxtepecanos al mando de Rafael Cravioto y Manuel González, tomaron la capital del estado. El servicio de tranvías tirados por mulas se instaló en 1878 y cuatro años después, en 1882, se inauguró la primera línea ferroviaria, entre Pachuca y Venta de la Cruz. En los últimos años del siglo XIX, se instaló el alumbrado eléctrico y se pavimentaron las calles. El 15 de septiembre de 1910 se inauguró el reloj monumental, que se encuentra en la plaza de la Independencia. Unos meses antes, en enero, se había formado el primer club antirreeleccionista de la ciudad. En mayo de 1911, tropas maderistas al mando de Gabriel Hernández tomaron la población. Tres años después, en agosto de 1914, Álvaro Obregón pasó por Pachuca. Durante la lucha de facciones, la ciudad permaneció ocupada por los constitucionalistas. En 1923, las fuerzas delahuertistas intentaron tomar Pachuca, pero fueron rechazadas.

PACHUCA, DE ◆ Sierra de Hidalgo que forma parte del Eje Volcánico Transversal. Se une por el oriente con la sierra de Zacualtipán. En esta cordillera están las vetas de los principales distritos mineros de la entidad. En su vertiente oriental se encuentra el volcán Tecajete.

PADIERNA LUNA, MARÍA DE LOS DOLORES ◆ n. en el DF (1958). Profesora normalista. Fue dirigente de la Unión Popular Nueva Tenochtitlan. Cofundadora del PRD (1989). Representante en la ARDF (1994-97) donde coordinó al grupo parlamentario de su partido. Diputada federal (1997-2000), es vicecoordinadora de su grupo parlamentario. Secretaria general del Comité Capitalino del PRD (1999-).

PADILLA ◆ Municipio de Tamaulipas situado al norte de Ciudad Victoria y contiguo a Hidalgo, San Carlos, Jiménez, Casas y Güemes. Superficie: 1,351.26 km². Habitantes: 14,430, de los cuales 4,053 forman la población económicamente activa. Hablan alguna lengua indígena 20 personas mayores de cinco años (náhuatl 7). La cabecera municipal fue fundada en 1749 por José de Escandón; el 5 de julio de 1824 fue declarada capital del estado de Tamaulipas y en ella se instaló el primer Congreso Constituyente local. En ese mismo año, cuando Agustín de Iturbide regresó a México, se le aprehendió en Soto la Marina y se le condujo a Padilla, donde fue juzgado y fusilado. En 1825 Padilla dejó de ser la capital estatal. Fue evacuada en 1970 e inundada por el agua de la presa Las Adjuntas. La actual cabecera, Nueva Villa de Padilla, se localiza a 16 kilómetros de la antigua.

PADILLA, ÁNGEL ◆ n. en Morelia, Mich., y m. en la ciudad de México (1837-1905). Se tituló de abogado en el Colegio de San Nicolás. Fue miembro del Tribunal de Justicia de Michoacán (1867) y diputado federal. Aunque inicialmente se opuso a la rebelión tuxtepecana, después se reconcilió con Porfirio Díaz y fue gobernador de Michoacán en 1889. Más tarde volvió a ocupar una curul en la Cámara de Diputados.

PADILLA, EZEQUIEL ◆ n. en Coyuca de Catalán, Gro., y m. en el DF (1892-1971). Su apellido materno era Peñaloza. Alumno fundador y egresado de la

Foto: Fondo Editorial Grupo Azabache

Lago Guerrero en Padilla, Tamaulipas

Escuela Libre de Derecho. Hizo estudios de posgrado en las universidades de París y de Columbia, con una beca del gobierno de Victoriano Huerta. Profesor de la Escuela Nacional de Jurisprudencia. Fue presidente de la Junta de Beneficencia Privada durante el gobierno de Álvaro Obregón, tres veces diputado federal (1922-24, 1924-26 y 1932-34), procurador general de la República; secretario de Educación Pública (del 30 de noviembre de 1928 al 5 de febrero de 1930) en el gobierno de Emilio Portes Gil, fiscal en el proceso a José de León Toral (1928), enviado extraordinario y ministro plenipotenciario de México en Italia y Hungría (1930), senador por Guerrero (1934-40 y 1964-70) y secretario de Relaciones Exteriores (del 1 de diciembre de 1940 al 10 de julio de 1945) en el gobierno de Manuel Ávila Camacho. Presidió la Conferencia Internacional de Chapultepec y asistió a la de San Francisco, de la que surgió la ONU (1945). Fue candidato a la Presidencia de la República en 1946, por el Partido Democrático Mexicano. Autor de *En la tribuna de la revolución*, *La educación del pueblo*, *El escritor mexicano*, *Los nuevos ideales de Tamaulipas*, *El hombre libre de América* y *En el frente de las democracias*. Perteneció a la Academia Mexicana de Derecho Internacional, que presidió; a la Barra Mexicana-Colegio de Abogados, al Instituto Americano de Derecho y Legislación Comparada y a la Sociedad de Legislación Comparada, de París. La Universidad de Columbia le otorgó un doctorado *honoris causa*.

PADILLA, GERARDO ◆ n. en el DF (1959). Judoka. Estudió ingeniería en la Universidad de California en San José. Ha obtenido medalla de oro en los Juegos Panamericanos de Caracas (1976), medalla de plata en los Juegos Centroamericanos y del Caribe de Medellín, (1978), medalla de bronce en los Juegos Panamericanos de San Juan de Puerto Rico (1979) y medalla de oro en la Copa Canadá de Judo (1979). En 1979 ganó el campeonato nacional de Judo de Estados Unidos.

PADILLA, IGNACIO ◆ n. en el DF (1968). Licenciado en comunicación por la UIA. Ha sido colaborador del diario *unomásuno*, del semanario *Punto* y de la revista *Tierra Adentro*. Director editorial de *Playboy* México. Autor de *Subterráneos* (1989, premio de cuento de Ediciones Castillo, de Monterrey), *Los papeles del dragón típico*, *Trenes bajo la alfombra* (1990). Becario del Instituto Nacional de Bellas Artes (1989-90) y del Consejo Nacional para la Cultura y las Artes (1991-92). Premio Nacional de la Juventud Alfonso Reyes (1989, con *Subterráneos*). Premio "Kalpa" de Ciencia Ficción (1983, con *El año de los gatos amurallados*). Premio Juan Rulfo para Primera Novela (1994, con *La catedral de los ahogados*). Premio de Cuento Infantil Juan de la Cabada (1994, por *Las tormentas del mar embotellado*).

PADILLA, ISMAEL ◆ n. y m. en Sonora. (?-1913). Se levantó en armas en 1880, en apoyo de Manuel Márquez de León, pero fue derrotado, por lo que se exilió en Estados Unidos. Volvió a México poco después y se dedicó al comercio. En 1910 se adhirió al Plan de San Luis y al triunfo de la insurrección maderista fue secretario de Gobierno de Sonora, durante la gestión de José María Maytorena, a quien sustituyó en la gubernatura de la entidad (del 2 de diciembre de 1912 al 1 de febrero de 1913). Luego del golpe de Estado de Victoriano Huerta, éste lo envió a Coahuila. Después de entrevistarse con Venustiano Carranza, declaró que éste había reconocido al gobierno de Huerta. En marzo de ese año fue detenido por los constitucionalistas sonorenses y fusilado.

PADILLA, JAVIER ◆ n. en Múzquiz, Coah. (1948). Escultor y pintor. Estudió en la Escuela de Pintura y Escultura La Esmeralda (1963-66). Expuso por primera vez en 1966. Hizo viñetas para *El Gallo Ilustrado*, suplemento del diario *El Día*. En 1976, expuso en Guatemala (1976). En 1966, obtuvo el Primer Premio de Escultura de Nuevos Valores del INBA. Primer lugar del concurso nacional de Conasupo (1987). Ha recorrido todas las técnicas de pintura, desde el óleo hasta la serigrafía, pasando por el acrílico, tintas y técnicas mixtas. Ha participado en numerosas exposiciones en la república y el extranjero.

PADILLA, MANUEL ◆ n. en Morelia, Mich., y m. en el DF (1880-¿1951?). Se tituló de abogado en la Escuela de Jurisprudencia de Michoacán (1904). Fue diputado federal (1908-10), magistrado del Tribunal Supremo del Distrito Federal, secretario de Hacienda (del 10 de marzo al 10 de junio de 1915) en el gobierno de Roque González Garza, nuevamente diputado federal (1920-22 y 1922-24), magistrado (1924) y presidente de la Suprema Corte de Justicia (1925-26); jefe del Departamento Central del Distrito Federal (del 26 de agosto al 2 de septiembre de 1932), ministro de la Suprema Corte y jefe del Departamento Jurídico de la Beneficencia Pública (1934-38).

PADILLA AGUILAR, JAIME LUIS ◆ n. en Toluca, Edo. de Méx. (1954). Ingeniero industrial por la UIA. Miembro del PRI desde 1970. Ha sido coordinador del Registro Civil de la SG (1981-83), director de Coordinación del Servicio Nacional de Empleo (1983-84), director de planeación (1984-85) y director general de Capacitación y Productividad de la Secretaría del Trabajo y Previsión Social (1985-94).

PADILLA AGUILAR, JUAN CARLOS ◆ n. en Toluca, Edo. de Méx. (1946). Actuario titulado en la UNAM (1964-67), posgraduado en la Universidad de Michigan (1969); maestro en ciencias por la Universidad Estatal de Iowa (1969-71), posgraduado en administración pública en la Universidad del Sur de California (1972-73). Profesor de la UAEM. Desde 1973 es miembro del PRI. En el Estado de México fue subdirector del Centro de Cómputo (1971-72), director del Instituto de Desarrollo Urbano y Regional (1973-75) y secretario de Desarrollo Urbano y Obras Públicas (1989-93). Ha sido director general de Informática de Ingresos de la Secretaría de Hacienda (1976-78) y, en la Secretaría de Gobernación, subdirector de Análisis, de la Dirección General de Investigaciones Políticas y Sociales (1980), director general del Registro Nacional de la Población e Identificación Personal (1980-82), coordinador general del Sistema Nacional de Protección Civil (1986-88), director general del Cenapred (1988) y secretario general del CISEN (1988-89). Fue presidente del Colegio Nacional de Actuarios (1983-85).

PADILLA ARAGÓN, ENRIQUE ♦ n. en Cacalotán, Sin., y m. en el DF (1917-1984). Profesor egresado de la Escuela Normal Superior (1936) y licenciado en economía por la UNAM (1948), donde fue profesor desde 1944, secretario de la Escuela Nacional de Economía (1953-71), investigador del Instituto de Investigaciones Sociales (1969) y director del Centro de Economía Aplicada (1977). Fue miembro de la representación mexicana ante la Comisión Económica para América Latina (1950) y director de Promoción y Desarrollo Económico del gobierno de Sinaloa (1963). Durante el gobierno de Luis Echeverría, perteneció al Consejo Técnico de Economistas del PRI. Colaborador del periódico *El Día* desde 1971 y de *unomásuno* (1977-). Coautor de *Nuestro proteccionismo industrial* (1969), *Los calendarios de México* (1969), *Participación popular en el cambio social* (1969) y *Comentario económico al gobierno de Díaz Ordaz* (1969). Autor de *Características económicas y necesidades de crédito del noroeste de México* (1958), *Tratados sobre ciclos económicos* (1959), *Integración económica del noroeste. El puerto de Topolobampo* (1963), *Ensayos sobre desarrollo económico y fluctuaciones cíclicas en México* (1966), *Ciclos económicos y política de estabilización* (1967), *México: desarrollo con pobreza* (1970) y *Pobreza para muchos, riqueza para pocos* (1982).

PADILLA COUTTOLENC, EZEQUIEL ♦ n. en el DF (1942). Licenciado en economía por la UNAM (1960-65) y maestro en administración pública (1965-66), especializado en relaciones financieras y comerciales, por la Universidad de Harvard (1966-67). Profesor de la Escuela Nacional de Economía de la UNAM (1970-75). Fue presidente de la comisión de informática (1973) y director del Centro de Informática del IEPES del PRI (1974-75), partido al que pertenece desde 1961. Ha sido economista del BID (1966), asesor del director del FMI (1967), técnico del Banco Mundial (1967-68), asesor de la dirección adjunta (1968) y subgerente de Transacciones Internacionales de Nacional Financiera (1970), subdirector de Crédito de Finaciera Nacional Azucarera (1970-72), director (1976-79) y vicepresidente de Comunicación Social de Televisa (1979-83) y director general de Banca Confia (1983-88). Subdirector de Promoción y Fomento de la Secretaría de Turismo (1988-89). Embajador de México en los Países Bajos (1989), Suiza (1995) y Canadá (1998-). Autor de *El Plan Horowitz en el financiamiento del desarrollo de América Latina* (1965), *El financiamiento del desarrollo en América Latina* (1966), *Un modelo para el desarrollo de México* (1966) y *Crecimiento económico y estabilidad. El caso de México* (1967).

PADILLA Y ESTRADA, JOSÉ IGNACIO ♦ n. en la ciudad de México y m. en Mérida, Yuc. (1696-1760). Sacerdote. Estudió en la Real y Pontificia Universidad de México, de la que fue profesor. Ordenado en 1720, fue procurador general de la Orden de San Agustín en Roma y Madrid y arzobispo de Santo Domingo (1750-53). Declinó la diócesis de Guatemala y, en 1753, aceptó ser obispo de Yucatán.

PADILLA FITCH, ÓSCAR ♦ n. en el DF (1951). Ingeniero químico egresado del ITESM con maestría en la Universidad de San Diego y diplomado en Alta Dirección de Empresas. Director general de Relaciones Públicas del gobierno de Baja California en el gabinete de Ernesto Ruffo Appel (1989-91).

PADILLA GUTIÉRREZ, AARÓN ♦ n. en el DF (1942). Futbolista apodado *el Gansito*. Se desempeñó en la posición de extremo izquierdo. Jugó en diversos equipos de aficionados del Distrito Federal desde 1958 hasta ganar, en 1961, un campeonato regional con el conjunto de la Preparatoria 5 de la UNAM. En 1962 viajó a Panamá con una selección no profesional, para participar en el torneo de la Confederación Centroamericana y del Caribe de Futbol; en esa oportunidad ganó el campeonato de goleo individual. Ese mismo año se incorporó al futbol profesional, en el equipo Universidad, con el que jugó hasta 1972. En 1964 fue llamado por primera vez a la selección nacional. Participó en las Copas del Mundo de Inglaterra (1966) y México (1970). En 1972 fue contratado por el club Atlante y luego de volver al Universidad en 1973, se retiró del futbol profesional (1974). De gran habilidad en el manejo de la pelota, solía eludir a la defensa contraria con la suerte conocida como "la bicicleta". Ha sido comentarista de televisión.

PADILLA GUTIÉRREZ, LEONEL ♦ n. en Guadalajara, Jal. (1935-1982). Escultor. Estudió en la Escuela de Artes y Letras de la Universidad de Guadalajara (1954-58). Perteneció al Frente Neorrealista de Jalisco, al Frente de Escultores y al Taller de Gráfica Popular. Fundador del Taller José Clemente Orozco y profesor de la Escuela Nacional de Artes Plásticas. Es autor de una cabeza de Lázaro Cárdenas que se encuentra en Tehuantepec y de un busto de Ernesto *Che* Guevara, colocado en la Casa de las Américas, en La Habana.

PADILLA LONGORIA, JOSÉ ANTONIO ♦ n. en el DF (1948). Ingeniero en comunicación electrónica (1966-69) y maestro en ciencias administrativas por el IPN (1971-72) y licenciado en derecho por la UNAM (1978-82). Profesor de la UNAM y del Centro Nacional de Enseñanza Técnica Industrial. Ha sido analista (1971), jefe del Departamento de Ingeniería Económica y Proyectos (1972-74) y jefe del Departamento de Evaluación de Tecnología de Nacional Financiera (1975), director administrativo de la planta electrometalúrgica de Veracruz (1976), y, en la SCT, subdirector general de Permisos y Asuntos

Internacionales (1976-82), director general de Concesiones y Permisos de Telecomunicaciones (1983-86) y director general de Normatividad y Control de Comunicaciones (1986-88). Fue presidente de la Conferencia Interamericana de Telecomunicaciones (1983-87).

PADILLA LÓPEZ, RAÚL ◆ n. en Guadalajara, Jal. (1954). Licenciado en historia por la Universidad de Guadalajara (1977), de la que ha sido profesor, director de Intercambio Académico (1979-84), director del Departamento de Investigación Científica y Superación Académica (1984-89) y rector, electo para el periodo (1990-95), por lo que es la persona más joven que ha ocupado ese cargo. Fue presidente de la Federación de Estudiantes de Guadalajara (1977-79) y presidente de la Confederación de Jóvenes Mexicanos (1978-80). Promovió la creación de la Feria Internacional del Libro de Guadalajara.

PADILLA LOZANO, JOSÉ GUADALUPE ◆ n. en San Miguel el Alto, Jal. (1920). Sacerdote ordenado en 1946. Profesor del Seminario de San Juan de los Lagos. Ha sido maestro de ceremonias de la basílica de San Juan de los Lagos, capellán del cabildo de la catedral de Guadalajara y obispo de Veracruz (1964-).

PADILLA NERVO, LUIS ◆ n. en Zamora, Mich., y m. en el DF (1898-1985). Diplomático. Sobrino de Amado Nervo. Se tituló de abogado en la Escuela Nacional de Jurisprudencia. Estudió también en las universidades de Buenos Aires, en la George Washington de San Luis Missouri y en la de Londres. Inició su carrera diplomática en 1920, como ayudante de protocolo. Fue secretario de legación y encargado de negocios en Buenos Aires, Washington, Londres y Madrid (1920-33); enviado extraordinario y ministro plenipotenciario en Estados Unidos, El Salvador, Costa Rica, Panamá, Uruguay, los Países Bajos, Dinamarca y Cuba (1933- 45); delegado ante la Asamblea de la Sociedad de Naciones (1938), miembro del Comité Ejecutivo de la Comisión Preparatoria de las Naciones Unidas (1945), embajador permanente ante la ONU (1945-52 y 1958-63), secretario de Relaciones Exteriores en el gobierno de Adolfo Ruiz Cortines (del 1 de diciembre de 1952 al 30 de noviembre de 1958) y juez de la Corte Internacional de Justicia de La Haya (1963-73). Coautor de *Testimonios. 40 años de presencia de México en las Naciones Unidas* (1985). Designado embajador emérito, en 1980 recibió la medalla Belisario Domínguez, otorgada por el Senado de la República. *Doctor honoris causa* por la Universidad de Tolosa. Recibió condecoraciones de 24 países.

PADILLA PADILLA, JOSÉ DE JESÚS ◆ n. en San Juan de los Lagos, Jal. (1943). Industrial. Director general de Relaciones Públicas de la empresa zapatera "3 Hermanos". Fue secretario de la Cámara de la Industria del Calzado de Guanajuato (1977) y presidente del consejo de administración de Procesos Modernos de León. Ha sido secretario de Relaciones Públicas (1977-79) y de Finanzas (1982-84) y presidente de Despensas Populares del comité municipal del PRI en León, Gto., partido al que pertenece desde 1964; secretario de Finanzas de la CNOP en Jalisco (1980), presidente la Comisión Nacional de la Pequeña y Mediana Industria de la CNOP; diputado federal (1985-88; 1994-97) y coordinador de la Comisión Nacional de Núcleos Urbanos no Incorporados. Es miembro de la Asociación de Industriales de Guanajuato. Senador (1988-1994 y 1997-2000).

PADILLA RAMÍREZ, PABLO ◆ n. en Italia (1937). Licenciado en economía por el Instituto Tecnológico y de Estudios Superiores, de Monterrey, donde fue profesor (1974-77). Ha sido jefe del Departamento de Estudios Económicos de la Junta de Gobierno (1959-64) y subdirector de Control y Vigilancia (1964-66) de la dirección de Organismos Descentralizados y Empresas de Participación Estatal Mayoritaria de la Secretaría de Patrimonio Nacional; subdirector general de la fábrica de vidrio Negromex (1966-67), director financiero del Complejo Industrial de Ciudad Sahagún (1967-71), embajador mexicano en India e Indonesia (1971-72), director general de Azufrera Mexicana (1972-80), director general de la Compañía Exploradora del Istmo (1972-80) y director general del Grupo Industrial NKS (1980-).

PADILLA SEGURA, JOSÉ ANTONIO ◆ n. en San Luis Potosí, SLP (1922). Ingeniero electricista titulado en el IPN (1938-41), del que fue profesor (1945-64). También ejerció la docencia en la UNAM. Cofundador del Centro Nacional de Cálculo y del Planetario Luis Enrique Erro del Instituto Politécnico Nacional. Ha sido director general del IPN (1962-64), gerente de las empresas Fabricaciones y Ensambles y Consultores Industriales en Ingeniería (1946-57), presidente del Centro Nacional de Enseñanza Técnica Industrial (1964), secretario de Comunicaciones y Transportes en el gobierno de Gustavo Díaz Ordaz (del 1 de diciembre de 1964 al 30 de noviembre de 1970), director de Altos Hornos de México (1970-78), director general del Conalep (1979-82), senador de la República (1982-88) y miembro de la Asamblea de Representantes del DF (1988-91). Autor de *Ingeniería mecánica de ferrocarriles* (1952), *D'Lambert. Su vida y su obra* (1963). *La política siderúrgica de México* (1976) y *La industria siderúrgica mexicana en el contexto del desarrollo mundial* (1976). En 1974 recibió el Premio Nacional de Ingeniería. Es miembro de la Sociedad Mexicana de Geografía y Estadística, de la Academia Nacional de Ingeniería, de la Asociación Mexicana de Ingenieros y Arquitectos, de la Sociedad Mexicana de Física y de la Sociedad Mexicana de Ingenieros. *Doctor honoris causa* de las universidades de Yucatán y Sinaloa.

PADRÉS, MANUEL O. ◆ m. en el DF (1906-1976). Colaborador de Vicente Lombardo Toledano. Participó en la fundación de la Universidad Obrera y del periódico *El Popular*, en el que fungió como administrador. Fue jefe de la Oficina de Pesca de San Diego, EUA, y

Raúl Padilla López

Luis Padilla Nervo

director de Impuestos Exteriores de las secretarías de Industria y Comercio y de Hacienda. Se desempeñó también como director de producción del diario *El Sol de México*.

PADRÓN GONZÁLEZ, JOEL ◆ n. en Guanajuato (1938). Sacerdote. Se ordenó en el Seminario Conciliar de León (1955-1965). Licenciado en derecho eclesiástico por El Vaticano (1966-68). Ha sido párroco de Comitán y Simojovel. En 1991 fue a la cárcel, acusado de "alentar la invasión ilegal de tierras" en Simojovel y sus alrededores. Unas semanas más tarde salió de prisión por falta de pruebas.

PÁEZ, BRAULIO ◆ n. en San Juan del Río, Dgo., y m. en Chihuahua, Chih. (?-1917). Constitucionalista desde 1913, a fines de ese año se incorporó a la División del Norte y debido a su participación en la toma de Torreón, se incorporó al grupo de los Dorados. Desde fines de 1916, comisionado por los villistas, instaló dos cantinas en Chihuahua, donde solían emborracharse los soldados carrancistas, quienes, cuando agotaban su paga, obtenían licor a cambio de armas que Páez remitía inmediatamente a sus compañeros. Una vez descubierto, fue fusilado.

ARCHIVO JAVIER ESPARZA

Joaquín Arcadio Pagaza en retrato de Julio Ruelas

PÁEZ, JORGE *MAROMERO* ◆ n. en Mexicali, BC (1965). Boxeador. Desde la infancia comenzó a trabajar en un circo, propiedad de su abuela, pero aprendió a pelear para defenderse y en la adolescencia optó por dedicarse al boxeo como aficionado. En 1985 pasó al profesionalismo y se hizo famoso por su vestimenta y peinados estrafalarios y, particularmente, por hacer piruetas, rutinas de circo y payasadas antes y después de sus combates. En 1988 ganó el título de campeón mundial de peso pluma de la Federación Internacional de Boxeo, el que perdió en 1990. Se retiró en 1999.

Antología poética, de Joaquín Arcadio Pagaza

PÁEZ, JOSÉ DE ◆ n. en la ciudad de México (1720-?). Pintor. Es autor de *Mapa del Valle de México* (1753), *Cristo, los doctores y los sacramentos* (1758), que se encuentra en la catedral de San Luis Potosí; y *Vida de San Francisco Solano* (1764), que está en el convento de Zapopan. Entre sus obras sin fechar se hallan: *Muerte de Santa Rosalía*, en San Ildefonso; *Jesucristo según San Anselmo, San Cristóbal, Santa Gertrudis, San Antonio, Cristo conforme escribió San Anselmo*, en la Catedral de Guadalajara; *Conversión de David, de San Bruno* y *San Javier* y *Tránsito de San José*, en el templo de la Profesa; una *Piedad* en el Nacional Monte de Piedad y los cuatro arcángeles del coro de Santo Domingo, en Oaxaca. Hay un retrato suyo de Pedro de Betancourt en Guatemala y otro en Cajamarca, Perú. Varias de sus obras se hallan en España.

PÁEZ BROTCHIE, LUIS ◆ n. y m. en Guadalajara, Jal. (1893-1968). Fue archivista del Supremo Tribunal de Justicia (1916-28), paleógrafo del Archivo de Instrumentos Públicos de Guadalajara (1958-64) y Cronista de Guadalajara (1942-68). Colaboró en el diario *El Informador* de esa ciudad y en el *Boletín de la Sociedad Mexicana de Geografía y Estadística*. Coautor de *El teatro Degollado* (1964) y autor de *Historia mínima de Jalisco* (1940), *La Nueva Galicia a través de su archivo judicial* (1940), *Guadalajara novogalaica* (1942), *Guadalajara, Jalisco, México. Su crecimiento, división y nomenclatura durante la época colonial. 1542-1821* (1951), *Guadalajara de Indias* (1957) y *Guadalajara capitalina* (1961). En 1951 recibió el Premio Jalisco.

PAGAZA, JOAQUÍN ARCADIO ◆ n. en San Francisco del Valle de Temascaltepec, hoy Valle de Bravo, Edo. de Méx., y m. en Jalapa, Ver. (1839-1918). Escritor. Ingresó en el Seminario Conciliar de México en 1856 y fue ordenado sacerdote en 1862. Fue cura de Taxco, Cuernavaca y Tenango del Valle, párroco del Sagrario Metropolitano (1882), canónigo de la Catedral de México (1887), rector del Seminario de México (1891) y obispo de Veracruz (1895-1918). Como miembro del grupo literario la Arcadia Mexicana, utilizó el seudónimo de *Clearco Meonio*. Autor de *Murmurios de la selva. Ensayos poéticos* (1887), *Corona literaria* (1889), *María* (1890), *Algunas trovas últimas* (1893), *Horacio. Versión parafrástica de sus Odas* (1905), *Virgilio. Traducción parafrástica de las Geórgicas, Dos églogas* (1907) y *Obras completas de Publio Virgilio Marón vertidas al castellano* (1913). Después de su muerte, se publicaron la antología histórica *Selva y mármoles* (1940) y *Siluetas contemporáneas* (1944). En 1969 el Estado de México editó una *Antología poética*, con notas de Porfirio Martínez Peñaloza, y en 1989 aparecieron en edición aparte, con prólogo de Sergio López Mena, los 32 sonetos que forman *Los sitios poéticos del Valle de Bravo*, publicados originalmente en *Algunas trovas últimas*. Perteneció a la Academia Mexicana (de la Lengua).

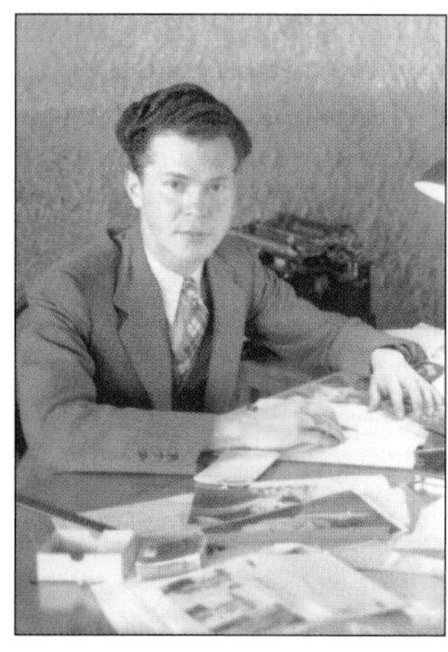

José Pagés Llergo

PAGÉS LLERGO, JOSÉ ◆ n. en Villahermosa, Tab., y m. en el DF (1910-1989). Periodista. Llegó a la ciudad de México en 1923. Fue mensajero de *El Demócrata* (1924) y compaginador de *El Heraldo de México*. Viajó a Los Ángeles en 1928 y desde 1929 trabajó en el diario *La Opinión*, donde fue corrector de pruebas, reportero, redactor, jefe de información y jefe de redacción. En 1930 era, simultáneamente, reportero de *The Daily News*. Volvió a México en 1937 y fundó la revista *Hoy* con Regino Hernández Llergo, dirigió *Todo* y fundó *Cine* y *Rotofoto* (1938), de la que sólo aparecieron 11 números, pues varios políticos, Vicente Lombardo Toledano entre ellos, promovieron una huelga y estimularon el asalto e incendio de sus instalaciones. En 1939 viajó a Europa, entrevistó a Adolfo Hitler, al presidente checoslovaco Emil Hacha, a Benito Mussolini y al papa Pío XII. En 1941 prosiguió su trabajo en Japón y China, fue recibido por el emperador Hirohito y entrevistó al príncipe Fuminaro Konoye, a Hideki Tojo, a Toyama Mitsuru (jefe de la sociedad secreta del Dragón Negro) y a Sadao Araki, que había dirigido la invasión japonesa en Manchuria. Señalado como simpatizante de las potencias del Eje, fue despedido de la revista. Director de *El Occidental*, de Guadalajara (1942). Volvió a la ciudad de México y fue jefe de redacción de *Mañana*, que fundó con Hernández Llergo. En 1948 fue nombrado director general de *Hoy*. En 1953 se vio obligado a renunciar por la publicación de una foto, captada en un cabaret de París, donde la hija de un ex presidente mexicano miraba severamente a su esposo, que a su vez contemplaba a una bella mujer semidesnuda (1953). Con él renunciaron sus colaboradores y un mes después fundó con ellos y dirigió desde entonces la revista *Siempre!* (☛). En 1986 recibió el Premio Francisco Martínez de la Vega, otorgado por la Unión de Periodistas Democráticos, y la Medalla José María Pino Suárez, del gobierno de Tabasco.

Pagés Rebollar, Beatriz ◆ n. en Guadalajara, Jal. (1954). Hija del anterior. Estudió ciencias de la comunicación en la Universidad Anáhuac, donde fue profesora. Ha sido reportera de la revista *Gente* (1976-77), de los diarios *Novedades* (1977-78), *unomásuno* (1979-80) y *Esto* (1983- 87), así como del suplemento cultural de *El Sol de México* (1983-87). Entre 1980 y 1986 fue conductora del noticiero *Enlace*, del Canal 11 de televisión. Desde 1987 es colaboradora y gerente administrativa de la revista *Siempre!*, revista que dirige a partir de 1989. Conductora del programa *Entrevistas* del Canal MAS de Multivisión (1998-99). En 1980 y 1985 obtuvo el Calendario Azteca de Oro a la mejor

Beatriz Pagés Rebollar

conductora de televisión. Autora de *Fidel Castro, presente y futuro de Cuba* (1991).

Pagés Rebollar, José ◆ n. en Guadalajara, Jal. (1948). Hijo de José Pagés Llergo. Hizo estudios en París. Fundó y dirigió la revista *Presagio* (1968). Fue comentarista político del noticiario matutino de televisión *Hoy Mismo*. En el semanario *Siempre!* coordinó la sección *Tribuna de la Juventud* (1972-74) y ha sido subdirector (1973-86) y director (1986-89) de la revista, en la que escribe desde 1972. Autor de *El conejo de la luna llena y otros relatos* (1974), *Los machos de los toreros* (1978) y *Anoné* (1980).

Pagliai, Bruno ◆ n. en Italia y m. en EUA (1902-1983). Empresario. Llegó a México en 1941 y obtuvo la nacionalidad mexicana. Constructor y administrador del Hipódromo de las Américas. Promovió la fundación de las empresas Tubos de Acero de México, Metalver, TF de México, Industrias Polifil, Industrias de Baleros Intercontinentales, Compañía de Seguros La Oceánica, Adamex y Fábrica de Papeles Especiales, entre otras. Logró la fusión de las dos compañías telefónicas que funcionaban en el país y controló el principal paquete de acciones de la American Smelting, que se convirtió en Industrial Minera de México. Fue también presidente de la Organización Editorial Novaro y consejero de Industrial Minera de México, Mexicana de Cobre y Capital National Bank. Miembro del patronato del Museo de San Carlos.

Pagola, José María ◆ n. en Salvatierra, Gto., y m. en Huetamo, Mich. (?-1818). En 1815 pertenecía a una junta subalterna del Congreso insurgente, establecida en Valladolid. Fue intendente de Guanajuato y el último presidente de la Junta de Jaujilla, en 1818. Ese mismo año fue apresado en Cantarranas, por el realista Tomás Díaz, y fusilado.

Pahtécatl ◆ También llamado Pantécatl. Una de las divinidades nahuas que protegen la elaboración del pulque y que se considera también dios de la medicina. Domina asimismo las plantas productoras de estupefacientes, como el peyote y el toloache.

Pahuatlán ◆ Municipio de Puebla situado en el norte del estado, al norte de Huauchinango, en los límites con Hidalgo. Superficie: 80.37 km². Habitantes: 17,783, de los cuales 4,289 forman la población económicamente activa. Hablan alguna lengua indígena 7,381 personas mayores de cinco años (náhuatl 4,254, otomí 3,115 y totonaco ocho). Indígenas monolingües: 2,161. La región donde se halla el municipio fue habitada por grupos otomíes hacia el año 500 antes de nuestra era y después por los nahuas. Hay una zona arqueológica aún sin explorar. Después de la independencia se introdujo el cultivo del café que, en la actualidad, es el más importante del lugar. El 28 de enero de 1865, durante la intervención francesa, la guarnición republicana de Pahuatlán presentó batalla a las tropas imperialistas y detuvo su avance. En la cabecera, Pahuatlán de Valle, llamada así en honor de Leandro Valle, hay una iglesia agustina construida entre 1532 y 1652. Durante la Semana Santa tiene lugar un festival cultural, con bailes populares, conciertos y exposiciones.

Painalton ◆ Deidad nahua también llamada Painalli (corredor veloz). Era el sustituto del dios de la guerra, Huitzilopochtli, o uno de sus lugartenientes. Estaba encargado de excitar a la matanza en los combates. Manuel Orozco y

Berra dice que era hermano menor de Huitzilopochtli pero otros autores creen que fue antecedente o precursor de éste. Fue venerado en Tenochtitlán y Tlaxcala.

PAI-PAI ◆ Indios que habitan en el norte de la península de Baja California, en el valle de la Trinidad, en el ejido de San Isidoro, en los terrenos de Arroyo de León y en la población de Santa Catarina, todos en el municipio de Ensenada. Emparentados lingüísticamente con los indios que vivían en el centro de Estados Unidos, los pai-pai quizá habitaron en el territorio de California, pero debido a las continuas guerras con otros grupos nómadas, se establecieron en la península. Fueron evangelizados por los jesuitas hacia 1767 y posteriormente por los franciscanos y los dominicos. Los pai-pai se dedican a la ganadería y a la agricultura de subsistencia. No se casan religiosamente sino que basta el mutuo consentimiento de los cónyuges y la construcción de una casa. Rinden culto a los fenómenos naturales y los curanderos fungen como mediadores. Sin embargo, sus dos fiestas más importantes son el día de San Francisco (4 de octubre) y la Navidad (25 de diciembre). En 1995 había 219 hablantes de su lengua.

PAÍS, EL ◆ Periódico católico de la ciudad de México fundado por Trinidad Sánchez Santos. Empezó a publicarse el 1 de enero de 1899. Al ser adquirido por la Compañía Editorial Católica, Sánchez Santos fue reemplazado en la dirección por León Sánchez y éste, por José Elguero. Su último director fue Antonio Enríquez. Durante el gobierno de Francisco I. Madero destacó por sus ataques al presidente y otros funcionarios, lo que motivó el encarcelamiento de su director en mayo de 1912. Introdujo innovaciones técnicas en el campo periodístico, como fue la denominada "prensa a colores" (*La prensa, pasado y presente de México*). Según sus editores, llegó a tirar 250 mil ejemplares. Desapareció al caer la dictadura de Victoriano Huerta, en 1914.

PAÍSES BAJOS, REINO DE LOS ◆ Estado de Europa situado en la costa del mar del Norte. Limita al este con Alemania y al sur con Bélgica. Superficie: 41,526 km², 38 por ciento de los cuales se encuentran bajo el nivel del mar. Habitantes: 15,619,000 (estimación de 1997), de los que 718,119 forman la población de Amsterdam, capital constitucional. La Haya, sede del gobierno, cuenta con 442,105 habitantes. Otras ciudades de importancia son Rotterdam (592,745 habitantes en 1996), Utrecht (234,254) y Eindhoven (197,374). El idioma oficial es el neerlandés. El Estado es una monarquía constitucional. El Poder Legislativo está formado por dos cámaras que constituyen los estados generales o parlamento. El Poder Ejecutivo lo ejerce el Consejo de Ministros y responde ante los estados generales. Cada provincia es administrada por un gobernador nombrado y un consejo elegido. Los Países Bajos cuentan aún con una colonia en el mar Caribe: las Antillas Neerlandesas, al noreste de Puerto Rico. *Historia:* la denominación de Países Bajos data del siglo XV, pero el nombre oficial se adoptó en el siglo XVI, cuando el gobierno de Carlos V llamó así a los terrenos de escasa elevación donde existían 17 provincias que, junto con el Franco Condado, formaban el círculo de Borgoña y comprendían lo que ahora está dividido en Holanda, Bélgica y parte de Francia. El territorio de los Países Bajos estuvo originalmente ocupado por los bátavos, celtas y frisones. En el siglo I de nuestra era fue conquistado por los romanos y en el siglo IV se establecieron allí los francos, frisones y sajones; en el siglo V, el territorio fue evangelizado por los santos Willibrord y Bonifacio. A fines del siglo XIV, los duques de Borgoña se hicieron del trono holandés y, en 1477, el poder quedó en manos de los Habsburgo. Hasta esa época, Holanda había estado dividida en ciudades-Estado carentes de unidad política, pero que lograron desarrollarse económicamente. En 1531 la parte norte empezó a convertirse al anabaptismo. El sentimiento antiespañol comenzó a generalizarse a mediados del siglo XVI y en 1566 se iniciaron los primeros levantamientos. Dos años después, Guillermo de Orange se levan-

Billetes de los Países bajos

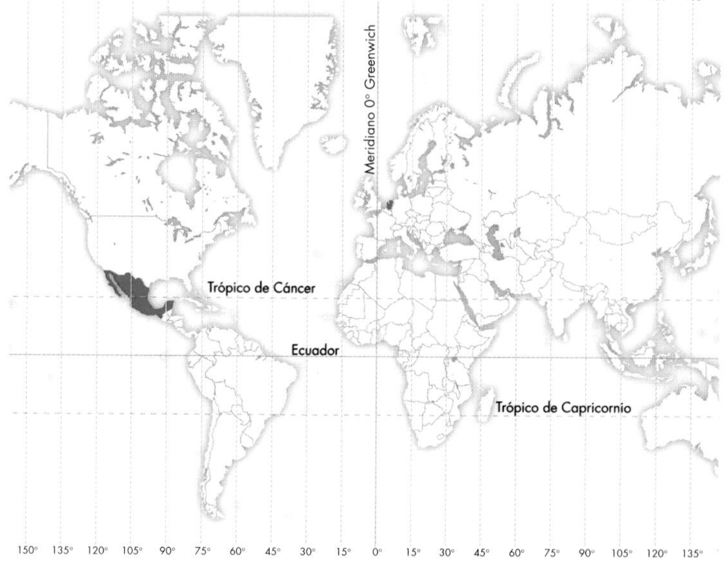

Reino de los Países Bajos

tó en armas. El país adoptó el nombre de República de las Siete Provincias del Norte y más tarde el de República de los Países Bajos Unidos. Durante toda la primera mitad del siglo XVII los holandeses intentaron independizarse de España y sólo lo consiguieron cabalmente hasta 1648, cuando el gobierno español firmó el Tratado de Münster. Durante esos años, los holandeses intentaron ampliar su presencia en América, fundamentalmente mediante dos acciones: la colonización en el Caribe y la acción de corsarios. En 1614, una pequeña flota holandesa, encabezada por Boris van Spillbergen, atacó el puerto de Acapulco e intentó provocar una sublevación de los esclavos negros de la costa. Una década más tarde, una flota al mando del príncipe de Nassau, bajo la misma bandera, bloqueó nuevamente Acapulco. La presencia de las fuerzas holandesas difirió por un momento la conclusión del enfrentamiento entre el arzobispo Juan Pérez de la Serna y el virrey Diego Carrillo de Mendoza y Pimentel, marqués de Gelves (☛ *México*). Sin embargo, apenas instalado en la ciudad de México el nuevo virrey, Rodrigo Pacheco y Osorio (1624), movilizó una gran cantidad de tropas que rompieron el bloqueo holandés. En 1633 el puerto de Campeche fue tomado y saqueado por piratas holandeses. Uno de sus capitanes era llamado *Pie de Palo*. Durante el resto del siglo, los corsarios de esa nacionalidad continuaron hostigando las costas novohispanas y del Caribe. De hecho, fueron los piratas más peligrosos para la corona española. Por ejemplo, sólo en la primavera de 1637, la Compañía Holandesa de Indias Occidentales (creada en 1602) se apoderó de 14 barcos mercantes de la Nueva España. Durante el siglo XVIII, la economía holandesa logró recuperarse un poco de la depresión de la segunda mitad del siglo XVII, pero no pudo alcanzar la prosperidad del siglo XVI. Aunque formalmente no existió comunicación entre el Reino de los Países Bajos y la Nueva España, debido en buena medida a los continuos enfrentamientos de los holandeses contra España en Europa, en 1729 llegó a México el botánico Guillermo Housto, quien se dedicó al estudio de las plantas locales durante cuatro años. En 1795, una revuelta antimonárquica apoyada por tropas revolucionarias francesas estableció la República Bátava. Sin embargo, luego del Congreso de Viena (1815) se restauró la monarquía y Holanda, nación protestante, quedó unida a Bélgica, con mayoría católica. En 1830 Bélgica se separó, pero Holanda no reconoció la independencia belga sino hasta 1839. En la época de la reina Guillermina, Luxemburgo se separó del reino. Los Países Bajos permanecieron neutrales en la primera guerra mundial y en la segunda fueron invadidos por el ejército alemán. Cerca de 100,000 holandeses murieron en los campos de concentración nazis. En 1949 el gobierno holandés concedió la independencia a la mayoría de sus colonias asiáticas. En 1954, la misión diplomática holandesa en México fue elevada al rango de embajada. Desde 1980 el país es gobernado por la reina Beatriz, como jefa del Ejecutivo, al frente de una coalición de la Convocatoria Demócrata Cristiana y el Partido Popular por la Libertad y la Democracia. El príncipe Bernardo de Holanda visitó México en 1959, 1963 y 1967; y la reina Juliana y los príncipes Bernardo y Beatriz, en 1964. El presidente López Mateos visitó los Países Bajos en 1963. Fue en Maastricht, ciudad holandesa, donde en 1992 los 12 miembros de la Comunidad Europea firmaron el tratado que dio pie a la creación de la Unión Europea, en 1998.

PAJACUARÁN ◆ Municipio de Michoacán situado al noroeste de Zamora, cerca de los límites con Jalisco. Superficie: 168.12 km². Habitantes: 20,390, de los cuales 4,297 forman la población económicamente activa. Hablan alguna lengua indígena 14 personas mayores de cinco años.

PAJAPAN ◆ Municipio de Veracruz situado en el sur del estado, al oeste de Coatzacoalcos, en la costa del golfo de México. Superficie: 305.98 km². Habitantes: 13,073, de los cuales 2,298 forman la población económicamente activa. Hablan alguna lengua indígena 7,777 personas mayores de cinco años (náhuatl 7,740). Indígenas monolingües: 53.

Timbre de los Paises Bajos

PAJARITA DE PAPEL ◆ Publicación del PEN Club de México. Eran hojas sueltas, plegadas, con un texto inédito de un escritor contemporáneo y una viñeta. Entre 1924 y 1925 aparecieron 28 números con trabajos de Xavier Villaurrutia, Jaime Torres Bodet, *Dr. Atl*, Alfonso Reyes, Luis Quintanilla (luego llamado Kintaniya), Xavier Icaza, Genaro Estrada, Alfonso Cravioto, Francisco Monterde, Carlos Barrera, Alejandro Quijano, José Juan Tablada, Manuel Toussaint, José Castellot Jr., Daniel Cosío Villegas, Alfonso Junco, Eduardo Villaseñor, Carlos Pellicer, el Marqués de San Francisco, Manuel Horta, Antonio Castro Leal, Martín Gómez Palacio, Julio Torri, Joaquín Ramírez Cabañas, Enrique González Rojo, Ricardo Parada León, Armando C. Amador y Carlos Gutiérrez Cruz. En 1965 Antonio Acevedo reeditó la colección en un solo volumen, con prólogo de Francisco Monterde, quien dice que *La pajarita* tuvo una segunda época, de 1941 a 1945. Hubo una tercera época de 1968 a 1969, cuando José Luis Martínez presidió el PEN Club.

PAJARITO, DEL ◆ Sierra de Sonora que forma parte de la sierra Madre Occidental. Se extiende de noroeste a sureste a lo largo de la frontera con Estados Unidos. Sus picos más altos son los cerros de Cibuta y Huacama.

PAJARITOS, DE ◆ Sierra de Guerrero y Oaxaca. Se extiende de norte a sur entre ambos estados. En su ladera sur nacen algunos de los afluentes del río Ometepec.

PAJARITOS, DE ◆ Sierra de Jalisco y Nayarit que forma parte del eje volcánico. Se extiende de este a oeste desde las lagunas de La Magdalena hasta la con-

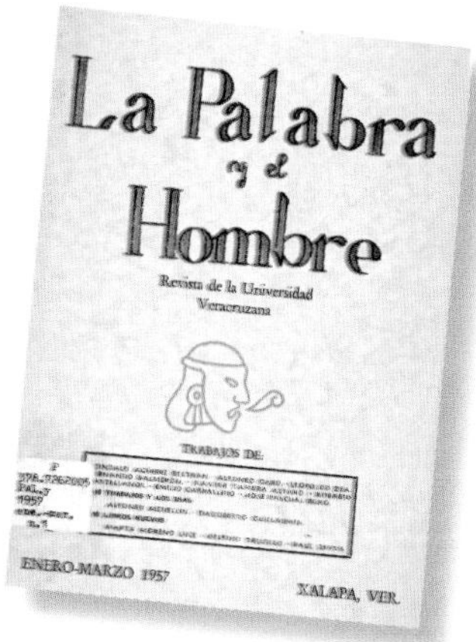

La Palabra y el Hombre

fluencia de los ríos Ahuacatlán y Ameca.

Palabra y el Hombre, La ◆ Revista trimestral editada por la Universidad Veracruzana. Fue fundada en enero de 1957 por Sergio Galindo, Adolfo García Díaz, Dagoberto Guillaumin, Alfonso Medellín Zenil, José Pascual Buxó, Ramón Rodríguez, Fernando Salmerón, Xavier Tavera Alfaro y Luis Ximénez Caballero. En su primer editorial, la revista se definió como "un órgano de investigaciones libres en el que todas la opiniones tienen cabida", que "quiere prestar servicios de información y de crítica y orientar al lector sobre una gran variedad de temas vivos para la inteligencia mexicana". Ha sido dirigida por Sergio Galindo, César González Chicharro, Sergio Pitol, Rosa María Phillips, Roberto Bravo Garzón, nuevamente Sergio Galindo, Jaime Augusto Shelley, Mario Muñoz, Juan Vicente Melo, Luis Arturo Ramos y Raúl Hernández Viveros, a lo largo de sus tres primeras épocas: 1957-62, 1963-71 y 1972-82. Algunos de sus colaboradores han sido, además de los nombres citados, Gonzalo Aguirre Beltrán, Homero Aridjis, Max Aub, Leopoldo Ayala, Agustí Bartra, Huberto Batis, Juan de la Cabada, Enoch Cancino, Emilio Carballido, Ernesto Cardenal, Germán Carrera Damas, Leonora Carrington, Ulises Carreón, Alfonso Caso, Rosario Castellanos, Dolores Castro, José de la Colina, Juan Comas, Jorge Juan Crespo de la Serna, Rosa Chacel, Alberto Dallal, Clementina Díaz y de Ovando, Oswaldo Dragún, Guadalupe Dueñas, Sergio Fernández, Enrique Florescano, José Gáos, Elena Garro, Santiago Genovés, José Agustín Goytisolo, Juan Goytisolo, Calixta Guiteras Holmes, Olga Harmony, Luisa Josefina Hernández, Aureliano Hernández Palacios, Jorge Ibargüengoitia, Carlos Isla, Raúl Leiva, Miguel León-Portilla, Jorge López Páez, Jorge Alberto Manrique, Joaquín McGregor, Porfirio Martínez Peñaloza, Manuel Michel, María del Carmen Millán, Carlos Monsiváis, Alejandra Moreno Toscano, Marco Antonio Montero, Augusto Monterroso, Elías Nandino, Salvador Novo, José Emilio Pacheco, Fernando del Paso, Octavio Paz, Javier Peñaloza, Elena Poniatowska, Ricardo Pozas, Raúl Prieto, Alfonso Rangel Guerra, José Revueltas, Alfonso Reyes, Salvador Reyes Nevares, Alejandro Rossi, Miguel Sabido, Jaime Sabines, Rafael Segovia Canosa, Tomás Segovia, Jaime Torres Bodet, Wonfilio Trejo, Emilio Uraga, Carlos Valdés, Tita Valencia, Josefina Zoraida Vázquez, Luis Villoro, Roberto Williams García, Paul Westheim, Ramón Xirau, María Zambrano, Eraclio Zepeda y José Benigno Zilli.

Anuncio de El Palacio De Hierro publicado en el *Mundo Ilustrado* el 11 de noviembre de 1987

Archivo Javier Esparza

Palacio, Adolfo ◆ n. en Guaymas, Son., y m. en La Reforma, Chih. (1835-1869). Militar. Se incorporó a la Guardia Nacional de Colima durante la guerra de los Tres Años y durante la intervención francesa comandó una columna guerrillera. Peleó en Sonora y Sinaloa. En 1867 asistió al sitio de Querétaro y al triunfo de la República fue jefe político y militar de Culiacán. En marzo de 1869 se levantó en armas contra el gobernador de Sinaloa, Domingo Rubí, pero fue capturado por tropas federales y fusilado.

Palacio, Jaime del ◆ n. en Durango, Dgo. (1943). Su nombre completo es José Jaime del Palacio Montiel. Licenciado en letras hispánicas por la UNAM (1965) y doctor en lingüística y literatura por El Colegio de México (1965). Miembro del PRI desde 1984. Profesor de las universidades de Michigan (1965) y Toulouse (1967-71). Ha sido secretario del titular de Educación Pública, Víctor Bravo Ahúja (1971-73), agregado cultural de la embajada mexicana en Argentina (1973-74), asesor del oficial mayor de la SOP (1974-78), del contralor de la CFE (1978-80), del director general de Aeropuertos y Servicios Auxiliares (1984-85) y del director general de Ferrocarriles Nacionales de México (1986-88); y coordinador de asesores del titular de la SCT (1988-). Fue responsable de la *Revista de Administración Pública* (1974-78), director de Publicaciones de El Colegio de México (1980-84) y director adjunto de la revista *Diálogos* (1981-85). Autor de las novelas *Parejas* (1981) y *Mitad de la vida* (1985). Por la primera recibió los premios Xavier Villaurrutia y Nacional de Narrativa de Colima.

Palacio, Lucas de ◆ n. y m. en el DF (1883-1958). Licenciado en derecho por la Escuela Nacional de Leyes, se especializó en las universidades de Génova, Bolonia y París. En 1900 ingresó en el cuerpo diplomático y desempeñó diversos cargos en Génova (1901), Filadelfia (1906) y Washington (1910-12). Fue segundo secretario de la legación en París (1913), gerente del Hotel Regis de la ciudad de México, presidente de la Asociación Mexicana de Turismo (1939) y gerente del Club de Banqueros de México. Autor de *Mesones y ventas de la Nueva España*, *Hoteles de México*, *De genealogía y heráldica*, *Manual de administración hotelera*, *El origen del cocktail*, *Usos y costumbres*, *La doctrina Monroe* y *La casa de palacio*.

Palacio, Ricardo ◆ n. en Guadalajara, Jal., y m. en Manzanillo, Col. (18-07-1880). Se desempeñó como administrador de la aduana de Guaymas, secretario de gobierno de Sonora y diputado federal (1846-47). En octubre de 1855 representó a Sonora en la Junta de Cuernavaca, donde se nombró presidente a Juan Álvarez. A la caída del gobierno de Antonio López de Santa Anna fue administrador de la aduana de Manzanillo, dos veces diputado local y dos veces gobernador interino de Colima. Llegó a ese estado con las fuerzas de Ignacio Comonfort en 1855. Fue el tercer gobernador constitucional de Colima (de enero a agosto de 1858). En este cargo le correspondió recibir al presidente Benito Juárez y a su gabinete, cuando se dirigían a Manzanillo para embarcarse. Combatió la intervención francesa y fue secretario de Gobierno de Sinaloa, durante la gestión de Antonio Rosales (1864-65).

PALACIO Y BASAVE, LUIS DEL REFUGIO DE ♦ n. y m. en Guadalajara, Jal. (1868-1941). Franciscano ordenado en 1894. Estudió en el Seminario Conciliar de Guadalajara. Fue misionero en Jalisco, Colima, Zacatecas, Durango y California y miembro de la Junta Auxiliar Jalisciense de la Sociedad Mexicana de Geografía y Estadística. Autor de una *Historia breve de la milagrosa imagen de nuestra señora de Zapopan* (1916).

PALACIO DE BELLAS ARTES ♦ ☛ *Bellas Artes, Palacio de.*

PALACIO DE HIERRO, EL ♦ Empresa comercial que en 1868 inició sus actividades bajo la razón social de Gassier y Reynaud. En 1898 se transformó en El Palacio de Hierro, S.A. El grupo francés que controlaba la empresa la cedió en 1963 al consorcio encabezado por Raúl Bailleres.

PALACIO LEGISLATIVO ♦ ☛ *Poder Legislativo.*

PALACIO Y MAGAROLA, LUCAS DE ♦ n. en Veracruz, Ver., y m. en la ciudad de México (1812-1874). Fue meritorio en la Secretaría de Relaciones Exteriores (1831), secretario de la Comisión México-Americana en Washington (1840-42) y oficial mayor de Relaciones Exteriores, encargado del despacho durante el gobierno de Ignacio Comonfort (del 11 al 12 de diciembre de 1855, del 25 de diciembre de 1856 al 7 de enero de 1857, del 1 al 24 de mayo de 1857, del 17 de septiembre al 19 de octubre de 1857 y del 17 de diciembre de 1857 al 18 de enero de 1858). Después del motín de Tacubaya se unió a Benito Juárez, quien lo designó titular de la misma cartera en dos ocasiones: del 12 al 17 de mayo de 1861 y del 18 de junio al 12 de julio de 1861. Fue recluido en San Juan de Ulúa en 1863, por no aceptar el Imperio, y liberado poco después.

PALACIO NACIONAL ♦ Edificio situado en el costado oriental de la Plaza de la Constitución. Está limitado por las calles de Moneda, al norte; Correo Mayor, al oeste; y Corregidora, al sur. Es la sede del Poder Ejecutivo Federal y aloja oficinas de la Secretaría de Hacienda y Crédito Público, la Presidencia de la República y la Procuraduría General de Justicia, así como el Museo Nacional de las Culturas y el Recinto de Juárez.

FOTO: BORIS DE SWAN

Fachada de Palacio Nacional

FOTO: CARLOS HAHN

Mural de Diego Rivera en Palacio Nacional

Se comenzó a construir en 1529, en el mismo sitio y con los mismos materiales que formaban las *casas nuevas* de Moctezuma Xocoyotzin, por órdenes de Hernán Cortés, dueño del solar. En 1562 la Corona española se lo compró a Martín Cortés, el hijo del conquistador, por 34,000 monedas de oro, y desde entonces fue sede del gobierno colonial. El primer virrey en ocuparlo fue Luis de Velasco, quien se mudó en 1563. En el ala norte se instaló la Casa de Moneda y en la sur la cárcel de la corte. Durante la insurrección popular de 1692, el edificio fue quemado casi en su totalidad. La reconstrucción, concluida en 1694, estuvo dirigida por el fraile agustino Diego del Valverde, quien diseñó las tres puertas con las que cuenta en la actualidad; las del sur y del centro fueron realizadas a principios del siglo XVIII y la del norte, llamada Mariana, se construyó en 1851, durante el gobierno de Mariano Arista. En 1812 la casa de Moneda fue sustituida por un jardín botánico. El Acta de Independencia se firmó en uno de los salones del palacio virreinal. Entre 1824 y 1860, todos los presidentes mexicanos, salvo Vicente Guerrero, habitaron en las habitaciones de los virreyes, situadas en el sur del palacio. En 1860, el presidente Juárez acondicionó el sector norte como residencia del Ejecutivo. De los 30 presidentes que vivieron en el inmueble, sólo dos murieron en él: Miguel Barragán en 1836 y Juárez en 1872. Maximiliano de Habsburgo residió ahí antes de trasladarse al Castillo de Chapultepec. La Cámara de Diputados se instaló en el edificio hacia 1845, en una construcción realizada por Alfonso Zápari, y funcionó ahí hasta 1872, cuando un incendio destruyó el local (☛ *Poder Legislativo*); un siglo después fue restaurado y convertido en museo. En septiembre de 1896, el gobierno de Porfirio Díaz instaló la campana de la iglesia de Dolores sobre el balcón central del edificio, en el mismo sitio donde, durante la colonia, habían estado un reloj y una campana sin badajo. A partir de entonces se acostumbra que el presidente de la República celebre la ceremonia de *el grito*, desde ese balcón, para conmemorar la independencia nacional, y que lo haga la noche del 15 de septiembre, aniversario de Porfirio Díaz, y no el 16. En 1927, Plutarco Elías Calles ordenó añadir un piso, con lo que el inmueble quedó como hoy se le conoce. Esta obra fue realizada por Augusto Petricioli, quien también dispuso que se cubrieran las paredes con tezontle para darle un aspecto "neocolonial". Diego Rivera ejecutó varios murales en su interior en 1929-35 y en 1941-52. En el ala norte se halla el Recinto de Homenaje a Benito Juárez.

Vista interior de Palacio Nacional

Foto: Carlos Hahn

Palacios, Adela ♦ n. en la ciudad de México (1910). Profesora titulada en la Escuela Nacional de Maestros (1928). Estudió corrección tipográfica en la Escuela de Artes del Libro. Fue redactora de la Comisión Popular de Educación Pública. Autora de *Cuadros escolares* (1935), *El angelito* (1949), *Adrián Rubí* (1950), *Mi amado Pablo* (1953), *Nacidos para pelear* (1953), *Muchachos* (1954), *Dulce y huraño* (1956), *El hombre* (1956), *Normalista* (1957), *Ricardo Flores Magón* (1960), *Yo soy tus alas* (1960), *Nuestro Samuel Ramos* (1960), *Viaje* (1961), *México* (1962), *Corrido biográfico de Leona Vicario* (1963), *Autorretrato de cincuenta años* (1964), *La isla de las mariposas* (1964), *El viaje de los niños del libro en la mano* (1964), *Lustros de Eva* (1968), *Colo tuituit* (1969), *Ancla del trino* (1974), *Tangente* (1974), *Zaguán cerrado* (1980), *Ilse Azar* (1981), *Como caña de azúcar* (1982), *El que un día.* (1984), *Mirta Lemus* (1985), *Fermi Chaquira* (1985), *Los palacios de Adela. Apuntes autobiográficos* (1986) y *Cazaul* (1988) y *Escritora* (1997). Pertenece a la Academia Mexicana de la Educación. En 1958 obtuvo el premio de cuento infantil del Comité Angloamericano Pro ONU y en 1968 el premio de Novela Corta de la revista *Hoy*.

Palacios, Emmanuel ♦ n. en Tolimán, Jal., y m. en el DF (1906-1987). Médico titulado en la Universidad de Guadalajara. Fue diputado a la Legislatura de Jalisco y funcionario de la Secretaría de Educación Pública. Colaboró en las revistas *Et Caetera*, *Bandera de Provincias*, *Contemporáneos*, *Fábula*, *Taller*, *Taller Poético* y *Cuadernos Americanos*. Dirigió la publicación *Alcance*. Autor de *Vida a muerte* (poesía, 1937) y *Mariano Azuela. Un testimonio literario* (ensayo, 1952).

Palacios, Feliciano ♦ n. en Villa de Ayala y m. en la hacienda de Chinameca (?-1919). Se incorporó al Ejército Libertador del Sur en 1913 y combatió a las órdenes directas de Emiliano Zapata, de quien fue secretario particular. Murió asesinado en la misma emboscada en que cayó Zapata.

Palacios, Irma ♦ n. en Iguala, Gro. (1943). Pintora. Estudió en la Escuela de Pintura y Escultura La Esmeralda. Expuso por primera vez en 1980. Sus obras se han presentado en exposiciones individuales en México, Chile y Estados Unidos. En 1982 fue premiada en la primera Bienal Rufino Tamayo, en 1984 obtuvo el segundo premio en pintura de la Feria de la Plata de Taxco, Gro., y en 1985 obtuvo el premio de adquisición del Salón Nacional de las Artes Plásticas. En 1986 fue becaria de la Fundación Guggenheim. Obra suya se encuentra en los principales museos de México y en los Estados Unidos.

Palacios, Jesús ♦ n. en el DF (1913). Compositor y cantante. Autor de las canciones *A la Virgen del Tepeyac*, *Detente corazón*, *Copitas de mezcal*, *El bravero*, *Flora*, *¡Ya para qué!*, *Ya lo viste, mujer* y *Amor quedito*, entre otros.

Palacios, Jesús María ♦ n. y m. en Chihuahua, Chih. (1824-1871). Se tituló como abogado en la ciudad de México (1845). Fue fiscal de la Junta Protectora de la Libertad de Imprenta al restablecerse la federación (1846), oficial mayor encargado de la Secretaría de Gobierno de Chihuahua, magistrado del Supremo Tribunal de Justicia del estado (1849), diputado local y federal (1852), vocal del Consejo del Estado al triunfo de la revolución de Ayutla (1855) y gobernador militar de Chihuahua (del 10 de febrero al 2 de noviembre de 1856). Durante su gestión restableció la Junta de Guerra para combatir a los indios, aunque luego pactó con los apaches mezcaleros que se asentaron en el municipio de Ojinaga. Luego de dejar la gubernatura, fue varias veces diputado local y federal. En 1866 se opuso a la reelección de Benito Juárez. Apoyó la candidatura de Porfirio Díaz y fundó el semanario *El Imparcial*.

PALACIOS, MANUEL ANTONIO ◆ n. en San Andrés Tuxtla y m. en Veracruz, Ver. (1834-1914). Combatió la intervención francesa. Fue hecho prisionero por los invasores y enviado a Francia. Volvió a México al triunfo de la República y fue profesor de literatura y francés en la Escuela Naval de Veracruz. Autor de las novelas *Crimen y castigo* y *Los hijos de los porteros*.

PALACIOS, MIGUEL ◆ n. en ciudad García y m. en Zacatecas, Zac. (1838-1886). Combatió a las órdenes de Ignacio Zaragoza y Jesús González Ortega contra la intervención francesa y el imperio. En 1867 Mariano Escobedo lo nombró custodio de Maximiliano, cuando éste fue hecho prisionero en Querétaro.

PALACIOS, TATIANA ◆ ☛ *Tatiana*.

PALACIOS AGUILERA, ELISEO ◆ n. en la Finca Don Ventura, municipio de San Fernando, y m. en Tuxtla Gutiérrez, Chis. (1896-1944). Realizó estudios en las escuelas Industrial Militar, Nacional de Agricultura y Nacional de Medicina. Profesor normalista desde 1935, fue inspector de la VI Delegación Federal de Salubridad y secretario de la Dirección de Educación Pública de Chiapas. Fundó el Museo de Historia Natural (que dirigió) y el Zoológico de Tuxtla Gutiérrez, con Miguel Álvarez del Toro. Fue miembro de la Sociedad Botánica de México.

PALACIOS ALCOCER, MARIANO ◆ n. en Querétaro, Qro. (1952). Licenciado en derecho por la Universidad Autónoma de Querétaro (1976) y maestro en derecho público por la Universidad Autónoma del Estado de México (1978-80). Ha sido profesor (1972-), director de la Facultad de Derecho (1979) y rector (1979-82) de la Universidad Autónoma de Querétaro. En el PRI, partido al que pertenece desde 1970, fue secretario general del Comité Directivo Estatal en Guerrero (1974-76), secretario general del Movimiento Nacional de la Juventud Revolucionaria (1975-76), secretario de Capacitación Política del CEN (1982) y presidente del Comité Ejecutivo Nacional (1997-99).

Mariano Palacios Alcocer

Fue diputado al Congreso local queretano (1973-76), delegado del Instituto Nacional de la Juventud Mexicana en Querétaro (1975-77), presidente municipal de Querétaro (1976-79), senador de la República a las LII-LIII Legislaturas (1982-88), gobernador constitucional de Querétaro elegido para el periodo 1985-1991 y diputado federal (1997-99). Secretario del Trabajo y Previsión Social (1999-).

PALACIOS BALBUENA, JOSÉ GUADALUPE ◆ n. en Mexicaltzingo, Edo. de Méx. (1958). Médico cirujano por la UAEM (1976-82) y licenciado en administración pública por El Colegio de México (1984-89). Miembro del PRI desde 1975. Ha sido encargado de la Biblioteca Pública (1980-86) y del Archivo Municipal (1980-), presidente municipal suplente (1985-87), cronista municipal (1983-) y secretario del ayuntamiento de Mexicaltzingo (1991-92); jefe del Centro de Documentación (1989-91) y subdirector del Centro de Información Municipal del Centro Nacional de Desarrollo Municipal de la Secretaría de Gobernación. Coautor de *Gobierno y administración municipal en México* (1993) y *El municipio mexicano* (1994), y autor de *Monografía municipal de Mexicaltzingo* (1986) y *Mexicaltzingo: monografía municipal* (1998). Es presidente de la Asociación Mexiquense de Cronistas Municipales.

PALACIOS LAGUNA, HUGO SERGIO ◆ n. en Tonalá, Chis. (1942). Topógrafo por el Instituto de Ingeniería y Arte (1957-59). Ha ejercido su profesión en empresas privadas y para Pémex, la SRA y el gobierno de Chiapas. Afiliado al PAN desde 1979, ha sido secretario de Acción Política en Chiapas (1985-91) y diputado federal (1988-94).

PALACIOS DE LA LAMA, RAFAEL ◆ n. en el DF (1944). Estudió medicina en la UNAM en donde obtuvo la maestría y el doctorado en bioquímica. Realizó un posdoctorado en la Universidad de Stanford. Ha sido instructor de histología (1963-64), instructor de bioquímica (1964-66), ayudante de profesor, profesor adjunto y de la maestría y el doctorado en bioquímica en la División de Estudios Superiores de la Facultad de Química e investigador de tiempo completo en el Departamento de Biología Molecular del Instituto de Investigaciones Biomédicas de la UNAM. Director del Centro de Investigación sobre Fijación del Nitrógeno, en

Movimiento del viento, obra de Irma Palacios, 1990

Cuernavaca, Morelos, desde su creación en 1981. Ha dictado numerosas conferencias en universidades e institutos nacionales y extranjeras. Hasta 1994 se tenían documentadas 2,260 referencias a sus trabajos dentro de la literatura científica. Ha recibido los premios de Ciencias Naturales de la Academia de la Investigación Científica (1979), Universidad Nacional (1986) y Nacional de Ciencias y Artes (1994). Designado Divisional Lecturer de la American Society of Microbiology (1992). Se le rindió un Simposio-Homenaje en 1994 para conmemorar sus 25 años de actividad profesional.

Palacios Macedo, José ◆ n. en Tulancingo, Hgo., y m. en el DF (1896-1965). Médico cirujano titulado en la Universidad Nacional de México (1919) y doctor en ciencias biológicas por la UNAM (1933), donde fue profesor y director de la Facultad de Medicina (1934-38). Ejerció la docencia en la Escuela Médico Militar. Se desempeñó como director de los Servicios Médicos de Ferrocarriles Nacionales de México y fue miembro del Comité de Higiene de la Sociedad de Naciones. Autor de *Fisiología patológica*.

Palacios Martínez, Isaac ◆ n. en Iguala, Gro., y m. en el DF (1911-1998). Profesor de escuela primaria, especializado en literatura, por la Escuela Normal Superior. Colaboró en los periódicos *Excélsior*, *El Nacional*, *El Siglo*, *El Porvenir*, *Diario de Yucatán*, *El Dictamen*, *Ecos del Sur* y, señaladamente, en *El Universal*, en el que desde 1945, y por más de 50 años, publicó una columna sobre gramática y dudas de lenguaje.

Palacios Mendoza, Enrique Juan ◆ n. y m. en el DF (1881-1953). Profesor de las escuelas Normal Superior (1902), Nacional Preparatoria (1906) y de la Universidad Nacional (1927-32). Fue arqueólogo de la Secretaría de Agricultura y Fomento (1925), inspector de monumentos prehispánicos (1927), jefe de arqueólogos de la Secretaría de Educación (1928-32) y director de Monumentos Prehispánicos del Instituto Nacional de Antropología e Historia (1933-36 y 1944-46). Logró la identificación del glifo maya en forma de cabeza que representa el numeral dos e hizo descubrimientos arqueológicos en Chiapas, Veracruz y Campeche. Fue colaborador de los diarios *Excélsior* y *El Universal*, así como de la *Revista de la Universidad de México*. Autor de *El puente de Dios* (1908), *Paisajes de México* (1917), *El templo de Quetzalcóatl en Teotihuacan* (1920), *What the Hieroglyphics of the Great Monument of Xochicalco Say* (1920), *Quetzalcóatl y la irradiación de su cultura* (1921), *Interpretaciones de la piedra del calendario* (1924), *¿De dónde viene el nombre de México?* (1925), *Yohualichan y el Tajín* (1926), *La piedra del escudo nacional* (1927), *En los confines de la selva lacandona* (1928) *Huaxtepec y sus reliquias arqueológicas* (1929), *La orientación de la pirámide de Tenayuca y el comienzo del año y del siglo* (1930), *Cómo se leen los jeroglíficos cronográficos mayas. Sinopsis preliminar* (1932), *La ciudad arqueológica del Tajín. Sus revelaciones* (1932), *Maya-christian Synchronology on Calendrial Correlation* (1933), *El calendario y los jeroglíficos cronográficos mayas* (1934), *Guía arqueológica de Chichén Itzá* (1936) y *El totonacapan y sus culturas precolombinas* (1941).

Palacios Real, Juan de ◆ n. en España (1642-?). Llegó a la Nueva España en 1658 y ejerció la docencia en el Colegio de Mérida (1671-81), del que fue rector en 1684. Más tarde dirigió los colegios de Guadalajara (1687) y Veracruz (1690-93). Fue provincial de 1696 a 1699 y prefecto de estudios del Colegio Máximo en 1708.

Palacios Roji Lara, Joaquín ◆ n. y m. en el DF (1891-1962). En 1910 fue enviado a Estados Unidos donde trabajó como sastre. Volvió a México hacia 1920 y se dedicó a la construcción y a la compraventa de bienes raíces. En 1928 fundó la empresa editora de la *Guía Roji*, que desde entonces se dedica a la publicación de planos, mapas y guías turísticas.

Palacios Sierra, Manuel ◆ n. y m. en el DF (1922-1977). Conocido como *Manolín*. Inició su carrera a los 17 años como cantante de la XEX. Adquirió popularidad al formar un dueto cómico con Estanislao Shilinsky. La pareja protagonizó, entre otras, las películas *Ahí vienen los gorrones*, *Las nenas del siete*, *Dos de la vida airada* (1947), *¡Fíjate que suave!* (1947), *Pobres pero sinvergüenzas* (1948), *Nosotros los rateros* (1949), *Vivillo desde chiquillo* (1950), *Pepito y los robachicos* (1957), *El robachicos* y *Autopsia de un fantasma*.

Palacios Treviño, Jorge ◆ n. en Burgos, Tams. (1931). Diplomático. Licenciado en derecho por la UNAM (1950-54), maestro en filosofía por la UIA (1954-56), donde fue profesor; y doctor en derecho (1960-62). Ingresó al Servicio Exterior Mexicano en 1955. En la Secretaría de Relaciones Exteriores ha sido jefe de los departamentos de Tratados (1957-59) y Transporte Aéreo Internacional (1959-66); subdirector adjunto (1967-69), subdirector general (1969-71) y director general (1979-80) del Servicio Exterior; delegado alterno ante los organismos internacionales de Ginebra (1971-73), subdirector y director general de Organismos Internacionales (1973-79), director general de Tratados (1980-83) y embajador mexicano en Egipto (1982-). Autor de *Tratados: legislación y práctica en México* (1982). Pertenece a la Academia de Derecho Aéreo y del Espacio.

Palacios Vargas, José Ramón ◆ n. en Puebla, Pue. (1916). Licenciado en derecho por la Universidad de Puebla (1938), de la que fue profesor (1938-48). También ejerció la docencia en la UNAM (1949-51), en la Universidad de Nuevo León (1954-69) y en la Universidad de Querétaro (1958). Fue agente del Ministerio Público en Tepeaca y Puebla (1941-43), magistrado del Tribunal Superior de Justicia del estado de Puebla (1951-57), magistrado de Circuito en Querétaro y Monterrey (1958-69) y ministro de la Suprema Corte de Justicia de la Nación (1970-85). Autor de *La tentativa* (1951), *La cosa juzgada* (1953) *La correlación entre acción y sentencia* (1955), *La Suprema*

Corte y las leyes inconstitucionales (1957), *Instituciones de amparo* (1963), *Estudios jurídicos* (1969) y *Los delitos del homicidio y lesiones* (1981). Es miembro de número de la Academia de Ciencias Penales desde 1947. Pertenece, además, a la Asociación Internacional de Derecho Penal, al Instituto Dante Alighieri y al Instituto de Derecho Procesal.

Palafox, Bernardo A. Z. ◆ n. en Orizaba, Ver., y m. en la ciudad de México (1857-1927). Militar. Fue subdirector del Colegio Militar (1896) y director del Cuerpo de Ingenieros en varios estados. Victoriano Huerta le impuso como gobernador provisional de Chiapas (del 19 de julio de 1913 al 13 de agosto de 1914).

Palafox, Manuel ◆ n. en Puebla, Pue., y m. en el estado de Morelos (¿1886?-?). Algunas fuentes ubican su nacimiento en 1876, en Morelos. Realizó estudios de ingeniería. En octubre de 1911, cuando era empleado de la hacienda de Santa Clara, propiedad de Luis García Pimentel, trató de sobornar a Emiliano Zapata en nombre de su patrón y fue hecho prisionero por los revolucionarios. Paulatinamente, sin embargo, se ganó la confianza de Zapata y debido a la escasez de alfabetizados entre las tropas campesinas, se encargó de la administración del Ejército Libertador del Sur, en el que fue apodado *Ave Negra*, por su habilidad para la intriga. En 1912 se le comisionó para negociar con Emilio Vázquez Gómez, quien estaba exiliado en Texas. El éxito que tuvo en esta misión lo convirtió en hombre de confianza de Zapata. Fue secretario de Agricultura y Colonización en los gobiernos de la Eulalio Gutiérrez (del 1 de enero de 1914 al 16 de enero de 1915), Roque González Garza (del 16 de enero al 27 de marzo de 1915) y Francisco Lagos Cházaro (del 14 de junio al 10 de octubre de 1915). Durante su gestión fundó el Banco Nacional de Crédito Rural (1915), escuelas regionales de agricultura, la Fábrica Nacional de Implementos Agrícolas y una oficina encargada del reparto de tierras; confiscó todos los ingenios y destilerías de alcohol de Morelos, las que puso bajo la administración de jefes revolucionarios; y el 28 de octubre de 1915 promulgó una ley agraria, redactada por él mismo. Formó parte de los consejos de guerra que condenaron a muerte a los generales Luis G. Cartón (1914) y Otilio Montaño (1917). En 1918 fue destituido de sus cargos en el zapatismo y en octubre lanzó una proclama, que sólo fue secundada por Victoriano Bárcenas, en la que incitaba a desconocer a Zapata. Algunos autores afirman que Zapata quiso fusilarlo al enterarse de que era homosexual. Se le aprehendió cuando trataba de huir a Guatemala. Escapó al año siguiente y redactó, con el general Everardo González, una nueva versión del Plan de Ayala. Ciertas fuentes indican que en 1920 se sumó a la revuelta de Agua Prieta y que se incorporó al ejército federal, en el que permaneció hasta su muerte, aunque no especifican la fecha de ésta; otros dicen que en 1919 fue aprehendido nuevamente por los zapatistas y fusilado.

Palafox y Mendoza, Juan de ◆ n. y m. en España (1600-1659). Estudió en las universidades de Alcalá de Henares y de Salamanca. Combatió en Flandes contra las Provincias Unidas y fue fiscal del Consejo de Indias. En 1626 fue diputado a las Cortes de Aragón, en la corte de Madrid trabajó en la Fiscalía del Consejo de Guerra y fue fiscal y luego miembro del Consejo de Indias. Ordenado sacerdote hacia 1629, fue nombrado capellán y limosnero mayor de la reina. Felipe IV, por influencia de su principal ministro, el conde-duque de Olivares, lo designó visitador especial de sus posesiones europeas y en 1639 lo presentó para obispo de Puebla. Fue consagrado en Madrid y antes de embarcarse recibió el nombramiento de visitador general de la Nueva España, a donde llegó en junio de 1640. Entre octubre y diciembre estuvo en la capital del virreinato, donde encabezó un centenar de juicios por corrupción y abuso de poder, lo que afectaba la posición de la burocracia colonial y produjo su enemistad con el virrey Diego López Pachecho, marqués de Villena. Regresó en diciembre a Puebla, donde las parroquias indígenas estaban confiadas a las órdenes mendicantes, en tanto que la mayoría de los 600 miembros del clero secular vivían en extrema pobreza. En diciembre dispuso, bajo amenaza de destitución, que los titulares de los curatos se sometieran a examen moral y lingüístico. Como no se cumpliera con lo anterior, Palafox ordenó a una fuerza armada ocupar 36 parroquias de indios en Tlaxcala, las que dejó en manos de sacerdotes seculares. De esta manera entró en conflicto con las órdenes, especialmente con los franciscanos, quienes se llevaron a sus conventos imágenes veneradas por la feligresía, empleando para ello, como en Cholula, palos y cuchillos. Uno y otro bando indicaron a los fieles que no eran válidos los sacramentos impartidos por sus contrarios. Como otros obispos empezaran a imitar a Palafox, el virrey decidió intervenir: prohibió que se transfirieran parroquias de las órdenes al clero diocesano y, contra la opinión de Palafox, autorizó a los corregidores para que dieran nuevamente indios a los conventos para el servicio de los frailes. El altercado entre el virrey y el visitador concluyó a partir de que Portugal se independizó de España. Como el marqués de Cadereyta era pariente de Juan IV, quien se convirtió en monarca portugués, esa circunstancia lo hizo sospechoso y Palafox, de acuerdo con la Audiencia, en acatamiento de unas cédulas secretas llegadas de Madrid, lo destituyó el 9 de junio de 1642 y asumió el gobierno. De esta manera reunió en su persona los cargos de virrey, visitador real, obispo de Puebla y arzobispo electo de México, designación esta última que se le comunicó en las referidas cédulas. Con todo ese poder expresó más acentuadamente

Archivo General de la Nación

Retrato y firma de Juan de Palafox y Mendoza

su puritanismo y continuó a la ofensiva contra sus enemigos: destituyó funcionarios e hizo detener o expulsar a los portugueses; abogó por una vestimenta femenina más pudorosa, no permitió que se empleara a mulatas en las pulquerías, retiró a las prostitutas de lugares públicos y abrió una casa de regeneración para ellas, llamada de La Magdalena; por temor al culto pagano, retiró de la Plaza Mayor las esculturas aztecas que se habían instalado ahí como trofeos de la conquista y prohibió los bailes de negros frente a la Catedral por juzgarlos licenciosos; suspendió a tres oidores, dio a la Audiencia reglamentos y a la Universidad unas *Constituciones* que no llegaron a aplicarse; estimuló el peonaje por deudas en perjuicio de los indios y, con el apoyo entusiasta de la Inquisición, desató una amplia persecución contra reales o supuestos judíos, lo que ocasionó la detención de unas 150 personas en lo que se llamó la "complicidad grande", que dio inicio a largos procesos que culminaron con autos de fe entre 1646 y 1649. El 23 de noviembre dejó la silla virreinal y volvió a su sede poblana, dos veces más rica que la arquidiócesis de México, a la que renunció. En Puebla reanudó la construcción de la catedral, cuyas obras se habían suspendido en 1618; fundó el convento de Santa Inés, hizo reparar más de 50 iglesias, estableció un colegio para huérfanas, dio ordenanzas al hospital de San Pedro y erigió el Real Colegio de San Pedro y San Pablo, para el que donó la biblioteca que hoy se conoce como Palafoxiana. Las instituciones educativas que creó entraron en competencia con las administradas por jesuitas, que estaban en litigio con el obispado por un asunto de diezmos. Entre 1644 y 1646 se amplió el abanico de enemigos de Palafox, en el que estaban el virrey García Sarmiento, la burocracia colonial, la Inquisición, varias órdenes religiosas y el arzobispo de México, Juan de Mañozca. En 1647 se recrudeció la disputa con los jesuitas, cuando Juan de Merlo, vicario de la diócesis poblana, exigió que mostraran los documentos que los autorizaban a predicar. Como la Compañía no acatara la disposición de la mitra palafoxiana, ésta prohibió a sus miembros no sólo predicar sino también fungir como sacerdotes y dar absoluciones, en tanto que a los fieles se les amenazó con excomunión si se confesaban con jesuitas y se ordenó a los estudiantes poblanos no tenerlos por maestros. En 1647 se nombró a dos frailes dominicos como "jueces conservadores" para dictaminar sobre el litigio y como el resultado fuera desfavorable a Palafox, éste excomulgó a los jueces y ellos, con el apoyo del Santo Oficio, hicieron lo mismo con el visitador. La sociedad poblana se dividió en dos bandos que se lanzaban insultos, hacían circular panfletos y pintaban lemas ofensivos en los muros. El 14 de junio Palafox se ocultó en la sierra por el rumbo de Tepeaca, después de que se produjera en su sede la más grande manifestación de apoyo a su causa. A la desaparición del visitador siguió la ostentosa entrada de sus enemigos en Puebla y varios días de banquetes ofrecidos por sus enemigos, así como fiestas, con bailes de mulatas, para agasajo de los dignatarios antipalafoxianos. Con la ciudad bajo patrullaje militar, ocupados los colegios fundados por el obispo y el palacio episcopal saqueado, el clero leal a su jerarca fue objeto de sistemática hostilidad. Los principales adversarios de Palafox eran peninsulares y el pueblo, receloso, suspendió la música y dejó de celebrar los bailes y juegos de los domingos. Los miembros del cabildo diocesano, puestos en prisión, fueron obligados a declarar vacante la sede episcopal, mientras que otros palafoxianos distinguidos eran enviados a la cárcel o sobornados. El 21 de julio los jesuitas organizaron un desfile en el que hicieron participar a estudiantes, esclavos y gente contratada para la ocasión. En la procesión iba un carro triunfal con la imagen de San Ignacio de Loyola y hombres con máscaras y atuendos que ridiculizaban a Palafox y sus principales seguidores, con "instrumentos indecentes" que usaban para hacer señas obscenas a las mujeres que veían el espectáculo. En septiembre hubo cuatro días de manifestaciones populares en las que se gritaba "¡Viva Palafox virrey!" y se llamaba a los jesuitas "perros herejes luteranos". La situación dio un vuelco en octubre, cuando por orden del soberano español debía trasladarse el virrey García Sarmiento a Perú y en su lugar nombraba a Marcos Torres y Rueda, obispo de Yucatán. Palafox regresó secretamente a Puebla y el 25 de noviembre, enterada la feligresía de su presencia, celebró grandes fiestas en su honor. Como García Sarmiento retrasara la entrega del poder virreinal a su sucesor, nuevas órdenes de Madrid llegadas en mayo exigían la inmediata cesión del gobierno a Torres y Rueda, disponían el cese de toda actividad de los jueces conservadores, reconvenían al arzobispo Mañozca y a los provinciales jesuita y dominico por su conducta durante la crisis de los meses anteriores, en tanto que a Palafox se le requería no interferir en el trabajo educativo de la Compañía. Torres y Rueda, contraviniendo las órdenes reales, procedió a sustituir a gran número de funcionarios. En la capital se produjeron nuevamente manifestaciones de uno y otro bando y los jesuitas, pese a que por bula del papa Inocencio X debían sujetarse a la autoridad de Palafox en la diócesis poblana, optaron por hacer caso omiso y alegaron que debía ser ratificada por el Consejo de Indias. El obispo respondió con una carta al pontífice en la que señalaba que la Compañía, de hecho, no pertenecía al clero secular ni al regular, pues usurpaba el ministerio del clero diocesano y, a la vez, eludía las mortificaciones de la vida conventual. En el aspecto educativo, según Palafox, los jesuitas minaban la fe y la moral de la juventud y sus doctrinas resultaban sumamente peligrosas y perjudiciales para la comunidad cristiana. La conclusión del dignatario era que la orden de Loyola debía desaparecer. La carta motivó una contraofensiva de la Compañía en Europa, donde debieron influir en la Corona española, pues en el otoño de 1648 se retiró a Palafox el nombramiento de visitador y se le ordenó volver a España en la flota del año siguiente, lo que hizo después de consagrar la catedral de su diócesis. Al llegar a Madrid entregó 4,000 "reales de a ocho" al monarca, quien en 1653 lo nombró obispo de Osma, España, cuando todavía se especulaba en México con su regreso y se veneraba su imagen en las iglesias, al extremo de que fue necesario que desde Madrid se ordenara quitar su retrato y se prohibiera su reproducción. Fue beatificado el 12 de septiembre de 1767 y, pese al empeño de Carlos II en su santificación, en favor de la cual amenazó al Vaticano con un cisma de la Iglesia española, la oposición de los jesuitas impidió que continuara el proceso. Escribió poesía, biografías, pastorales, relaciones, un tratado de ortografía, textos teológicos, políticos, históricos, de derecho canónico y civil, así como ensayos como *De la naturaleza del indio* (1650). En 1668 se publicaron en México sus *Constituciones de la Universidad de México*. En 1762 los carmelitas descalzos hicieron una edición de sus obras en 15 tomos.

Palafox Vázquez, Carlos Adolfo ♦ n. en Puebla, Pue. (1940). Profesor titulado en la Escuela Normal de Puebla (1956-58) y licenciado en derecho por la Universidad de Puebla (1959-63), donde ejerció la docencia (1964-68). Ha sido secretario del Juzgado Tercero de Defensa Nacional en Puebla (1965), secretario particular del gobernador de la entidad (1969-72), delegado del Infonavit (1973-80), diputado federal (1985-88) y presidente del Comité Directivo Estatal del PRI (1984-85), partido al que ingresó en 1962. Autor de *Derecho subjetivo* (1964).

Palau, Marta ♦ n. en España (1939). Pintora y escultora. Fue traída a México en 1940, a la caída de la República española. Estudió en la Escuela de Pintura y Escultura La Esmeralda (1955-65) y en San Diego. Ha sido coordinadora de Arte del Centro de Arte Contemporáneo de Guadalajara (1972-74) y asesora del Instituto Allende de San Miguel Allende (1977-78). Se ha dedicado principalmente a la elaboración de tapices. Expuso por primera vez en 1961, en la Galería Jacobo Glantz de la ciudad de México. Sus obras se han presentado en Colombia, Cuba, Chile, Ecuador, España, Estados Unidos, Japón, Polonia, Portugal, Puerto Rico, Suiza y Venezuela. Una de sus esculturas se encuentra en el bosque de Chapultepec y otra en la unidad Xochimilco de la Universidad Autónoma Metropolitana, ambas en la ciudad de México. Es autora de un mural que se encuentra en el Centro de Arte Contemporáneo de Guadalajara. En 1985 el gobierno de Michoacán editó el libro *Marta Palau*.

Palavicini, Félix Fulgencio ♦ n. en Teapa, Tab., y m. en el DF (1881-1952). Ingeniero topógrafo egresado del Instituto Juárez de San Juan Bautista, hoy Villahermosa (1901). En Tabasco fundó y dirigió el periódico *El Precursor*. En 1903 se trasladó a la ciudad de México y se tituló en la Escuela Normal de Profesores (1906). Estudió en el Conservatorio de Artes y Oficios de París (1906-07). Al volver fundó el periódico *Tabasco* (1907) *El Partido Republicano (1908)*. Con Filomeno Mata, en 1909 organizó el Centro Antirreeleccionista y dirigió *El Antirreeleccionista* (1910). Fue director de la Escuela Industrial de Huérfanos (1911), diputado por Tabasco a la XXVI Legislatura (1911-13). Al producirse el cuartelazo de Victoriano Huerta fue encarcelado (1913-14). Con Carranza fue subsecretario encargado del despacho de la SEP (25 de agosto de 1914 al 26 de septiembre de 1916). Fundó *El Universal* (1916), *El Globo*, *El Día* y la revista *Todo*. Fue diputado al Congreso Constituyente de 1916-17, diputado federal (1917-19), embajador extraordinario ante los gobiernos de Inglaterra, Francia, Bélgica, Italia, España (1920) y Argentina (1938-1942), y gerente general de PIPSA. Autor de *Pro-patria. Apuntes de sociología mexicana* (1905), *Las escuelas técnicas*, *Los diputados* (1913), *Construcción económica de escuelas técnicas*, *El primer jefe*, *Diez civiles notables de nuestra historia*, *La enseñanza técnica*, *Problemas de la educación*, *La democracia victoriosa*, *El arte de amar y ser amado*, *La Patria por la escuela*, *Palabras y acciones*, *Grandes de México*, *Lo que yo vi*, *Epistolario del amor*, *Libertad y demagogia*, *Democracias mestizas*, *La estética de la tragedia mexicana*, *Parábolas esotéricas*, *Historia de la Constitución de 1917*, *México, historia de su evolución constructiva*, *Los irredentos* (1923), *¡Castigo!* (1926) y *Mi vida revolucionaria* (1937).

Félix Fulgencio Palavicini

Palazuelos Léycegui, Leopoldo H. ♦ n. en Veracruz, Ver., y m. en el DF (1893-1969). Fue armador de barcos de cabotaje, tuvo negocios de importación y exportación, comisiones y consignaciones, ganado y operaciones bancarias. En 1936 era presidente de la Confederación Patronal de la República Mexicana y en 1937, presidente de la Confederación de Cámaras Nacionales de Comercio.

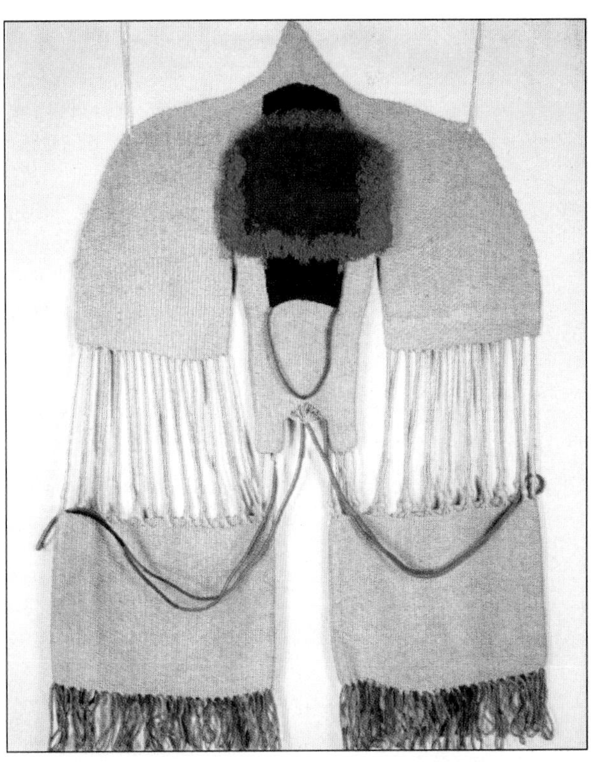

Macromóvil yuté, escultura tejida móvil de Marta Palau

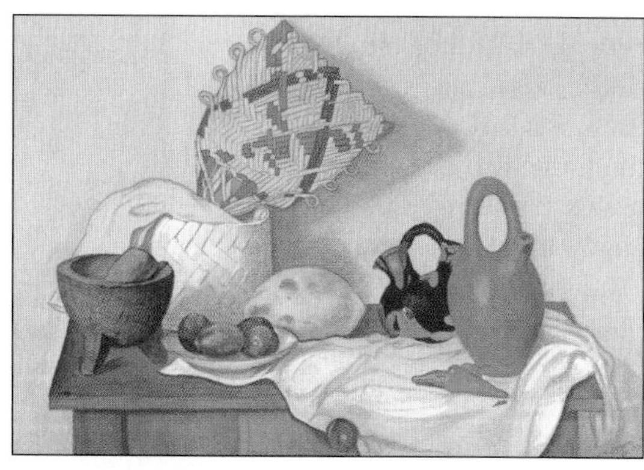

Naturaleza Muerta, obra de Ceferino Palencia

Juan Francisco Palencia Hernández

PALENCIA, CEFERINO ◆ n. en España y m. en el DF (1882-1963). Pintor y crítico de artes plásticas. Licenciado en derecho por la Universidad Central de Madrid. En España fue gobernador de las provincias de Almería, Guadalajara, Teruel y Zamora (1930-33), ministro plenipotenciario en los Países Bálticos y secretario del Museo de Arte Moderno de Madrid. Llegó a México en 1939, luego de la derrota de la República española, y se naturalizó mexicano en 1942. Colaboró en la revista *Las Españas* y, durante más de 30 años, en el periódico *Novedades*, donde participó en la creación del suplemento *México en la Cultura*. Profesor de historia del arte en la Academia de San Carlos y en la Escuela de Pintura y Escultura La Esmeralda. Fue vicepresidente del Ateneo Español de México. En 1934, tradujo y adaptó para teatro *El fantasma de Canterville*, de Oscar Wilde. Autor de *El romanticismo español* (1929), *Los fabliaux franceses* (1932), *Leonardo Alenza, pintor español* (1934), *Biografía de Pablo Picasso* (1942), *El arte en Tamayo* (1950), *El arte contemporáneo en México* (1951), *España vista por los españoles* (1952) y *México inspirador* (1963). En España ganó los premios nacionales de Pintura (1920), Grabado (1924) y Literatura (1930).

Ruinas de Palenque, Chiapas

Foto: Carlos Hahn

PALENCIA HERNÁNDEZ, JUAN FRANCISCO ◆ n. en el DF (1973). Futbolista. Como delantero, ha jugado en el equipo Cruz Azul. Seleccionado nacional, ha participado en los Juegos Olímpicos de 1996, la Copa América 1997 y el Campeonato Mundial 1998.

PALENCIA O., CEFERINO ◆ n. en España (1910). Médico. Estudió en la Universidad Central de Madrid, en la Escuela de Medicina de San Carlos y en la Academia de Sanidad Militar de Madrid, donde se tituló (1935). Durante la guerra civil alcanzó el grado de teniente coronel de Sanidad Militar en el ejército republicano. Al triunfo del fascismo vino como exiliado y se naturalizó mexicano en 1940. Profesor de la Universidad Michoacana de San Nicolás de Hidalgo (1944-46). En el Hospital General de México fue investigador del Departamento de Investigaciones Médicas (1940-47) y jefe de clínica en el Pabellón 28 (1943-44). Ha sido jefe del Departamento de Bacteriología de Laboratorios de México, director médico de los laboratorios André Bigaux (1952-60), Waltz y Abbat (1960-64) y Hormofarma-Riker (1964-70); y director médico de la Beneficencia Española (1975-77). Colaborador del periódico *Novedades* desde 1970, y de las revistas *Médico Moderno* y *R/m*, de la que es consejero editorial. Es miembro de las sociedades de Historia Natural de México, de Historia de la Medicina en México, de Farmacología y Terapéutica de México y de Bacteriología y Microbiología de México; y de la National Geographic Society.

Códice Maya

PALENQUE ◆ Municipio de Chiapas situado al noreste de San Cristóbal de Las Casas, en los límites con Tabasco y Guatemala. Superficie: 1,122.8 km². Habitantes: 77,998, de los cuales 16,433 forman la población económicamente activa. Hablan alguna lengua indígena 24,843 personas mayores de cinco años (chol 16,145 y tzeltal 8,229). Indígenas monolingües: 5,392. En el municipio se encuentra una de las zonas arqueológicas más importantes del país, constituida por las ruinas de la antigua ciudad de Otulum, que floreció entre los años 600 y 900 de nuestra era. Los principales monumentos descubiertos en ella son: el Palacio, el juego de pelota y los templos de las Inscripciones, del Bello Relieve, del Sol, de Cruz Foliada, de la Cruz, del León y del Conde. Hay un museo que guarda placas con jeroglíficos mayas, adornos de jade, esculturas y cerámicas. El 8 de diciembre de 1987, el conjunto arqueológico fue declarado patrimonio cultural de la humanidad por la UNESCO.

PALERM VICH, ÁNGEL ◆ n. en España y m. en el DF (1917-1980). Licenciado en historia por la UNAM (1949), maestro en etnología por la ENAH (1952), de la que fue profesor; y doctor en ciencias sociales por el Instituto de Planificación Regional de Washington (1962). Participó en la guerra civil española como miembro de la Federación Anarquista Ibérica; alcanzó el grado de comandante de infantería y recibió la medalla al valor. Llegó a México en 1939. Funcionario de la OEA en la capital de Estados Unidos (1953-65), ahí codirigió la revista *Ciencias sociales*. Volvió a México en 1965. Fue profesor e investigador de la Universidad Iberoamericana, donde fundó y dirigió la carrera de antropología social y el Instituto de Ciencias Sociales. Fue fundador y director del Centro de Investigaciones Superiores del INAH (1975-80). Colaboró en la revista *Comunidad*. Autor de *Studies in Human Ecology* (1957), *La agricultura y el desarrollo de la civilización en Mesoamérica* (1961), *Introducción a la teoría etnológica* (1967), *La base agrícola de la civilización urbana en Mesoamérica* (1968), *Planificación de la educación en México*, (1968), *Una defensa del modo asiático de producción según Marx y Wittfogel* (1970), *Manual de campo del antropólogo* (1971), *Agricultura y sociedad en Mesoamérica* (1974), *Modos de producción y formaciones socioeconómicas* (1976), *Historia de la etnología: los evolucionistas* (1976), *Historia de la etnología: Tylor y los profesionales británicos* (1977) y *Antropología y marxismo*, (1981).

PALESTINA ◆ Estado del medio oriente constituido el 15 de noviembre de 1988 por el Consejo Nacional Palestino, órgano parlamentario en el exilio. De acuerdo con las resoluciones de la ONU de noviembre de 1947, que fueron reconocidas por la dirigencia palestina, el Estado árabe ocuparía tres zonas del antiguo mandato británico: la porción occidental de Galilea, al norte; la margen occidental del río Jordán, también llamada Cisjordanía, al este; y la franja de Gaza, al noreste de la península del Sinaí, casi hasta Tel Aviv. Se calcula que hay en el mundo 5,300,000 palestinos, de los cuales 2.9 millones viven en la margen occidental del río Jordán y en la Franja de Gaza, territorios bajo la Autoridad Nacional Palestina. Los otros dos millones cuatrocientos mil palestinos viven en su mayoría en los países árebes vecinos, sobre todo en Jordania. Los primeros asentamientos en el territorio palestino e israelí datan de 4,000 años a.n.e. Hacia el siglo X a.n.e., los judíos crearon un reino independiente, que poco después se dividió en Judá e Israel. Los asirios conquistaron el territorio en el siglo VIII a.n.e., y en el siglo IV a.n.e. éste quedó en poder de Alejandro de Macedonia. A mediados del siglo I a.n.e., se creó un nuevo reino judío, encabezado por Judas Macabeo, que fue sometido por las tropas romanas en los primeros años de nuestra era. En el año 135, tras la rebelión judía de Bar Koljba, los romanos expulsaron a los judíos del territorio palestino y le dieron ese nombre, oficialmente, a toda la antigua Judea; en ese tiempo, Jerusalén fue destruida y reconstruida con el nombre de Aelia Capitolina. Hasta principios del siglo VI, Palestina estuvo dominada por el imperio bizantino, que la dividió en tres provincias para propósitos administrativos. En 635, los árabes conquistaron el territorio y lo controlaron totalmente hasta fines del primer milenio, cuando, a consecuencia de las cruzadas, surgieron algunos principados cristianos. En 1516 la zona cayó en poder de los turcos. A fines del siglo XVII, según Agustín de Betancurt, los comerciantes turcos de Jerusalén apreciaban tanto la plata producida en Pachuca, que se negaban a recibir lingotes que no tuvieran el sello de la ahora capital hidalguense. Los turcos mantuvieron el control de Palestina hasta el fin de la primera guerra mundial. A fines del siglo XIX llegaron a México los primeros palestinos, a quienes por su pasaporte otomano se llamaba turcos. Hacia 1920 surgieron los líderes palestinos Musa al-Hosari y Amin al Husaini, quienes fomentaban el rechazo hacia los inmigrantes judíos. En 1922 el gobierno británico obtuvo de la Sociedad de Naciones un mandato sobre la zona. En 1947, la ONU acordó la partición del territorio para constituir dos Estados, uno árabe y otro judío. En la parte asignada a la nación árabe, vivían 749,000 palestinos, y 497,000 en la destinada a Israel (☛). Luego de la derrota de los ejércitos árabes en la guerra de 1948-49, Israel ocupó la porción palestina de Galilea, la mitad suroriental de la franja de Gaza y un corredor entre su territorio y Jerusalén, que quedó dividida en dos partes; Jordania se hizo cargo de Cisjordania, y Egipto del resto de la franja de Gaza. Con el apoyo de uno u otro gobierno árabe, surgieron numerosas organizaciones palestinas, la mayoría de vida efímera. En mayo de 1964, promovido por los gobiernos de los países árabes, se creó el Consejo Nacional Palestino, del que nació la Organización para la Liberación de Palestina, que tuvo como primer dirigente a Ahmed al Choukairi. Al año siguiente, varios grupos guerrilleros independientes de la OLP iniciaron sus acciones en territorio israelí. En la guerra de junio de 1967, el ejército israelí derrotó a las fuerzas de Jordania, Siria y Egipto y ocupó la totalidad del territorio destinado por la ONU a Palestina, así como la península egipcia del Sinaí. Poco después de terminada la guerra, los grupos guerrilleros se unieron a la OLP y en 1969 Yasser Arafat fue elegido para asumir la dirección. Desde cuatro años antes, Arafat había encabezado al principal grupo político militar de los palestinos, Al-Fatah, frente amplio de nasseristas, panarabistas, socialistas y radicales musulmanes, fundado en 1959 por un grupo de estudiantes de la Universidad de El Cairo, los que se planteaban erigir un Estado palestino que diera cabida a musulmanes, cristianos y judíos, pero se oponían a la

Yasser Arafat

Hacia el siglo VI, los árabes llevaron el islam a Palestina

Habitantes palestinos

existencia del Estado judío. La segunda fuerza dentro de la OLP, sobre todo por el número y reconocimiento de los intelectuales que ahí militan, es el Frente Popular para la Liberación de Palestina, marxista-leninista, dirigido por el cristiano George Habache. Dentro del FPLP existe la tendencia "comandancia general" apoyada por Libia. Una escición del FPLP es el Frente Democrático para la Liberación de Palestina, tercera fuerza dentro de la OLP, marxista-leninista también, pero situado a la izquierda del FPLP, que proclama la unidad de los oprimidos tanto árabes y judíos para enfrentar a los conservadores árabes, el sionismo y el imperialismo. Otros grupos de menos importancia, como el prosirio Al Saika, dice el escritor Musa Muti, "recibe órdenes desde Damasco". Existe otro Frente de Liberación de tendencia proiraquí y la agrupación Jamás (Hamas), coalición de partidos religiosos que tuvo una activa participación en la *intifada*. La creciente independencia de la OLP irritó a los gobiernos árabes, especialmente a aquellos que deseaban manejarla con fines propios. En septiembre de 1970, por ejemplo, el ejército jordano realizó una matanza de miles de palestinos, conocida como "septiembre negro", lo que obligó a la OLP a trasladar su cuartel general de Amman a Beirut. Durante la primera mitad de la década de 1970, la OLP combinó la esporádica acción guerrillera dentro de Israel con una activa política exterior, que consiguió sus primeros triunfos cuando, en 1974, la ONU reconoció a la organización como la legítima representante de los palestinos y le otorgó un lugar de observador en la Asamblea General. Unos meses antes, el gobierno jordano había renunciado a sus "derechos" sobre Cisjordanía, si bien mantuvo lazos políticos y administrativos con la población de esa zona. Al año siguiente, el presidente mexicano Luis Echeverría se entrevistó con Yasser Arafat en Egipto y al año siguiente autorizó la apertura de una oficina en el Distrito Federal. En 1980, los gobiernos mexicano y francés demandaron al de Tel Aviv la desocupación de los territorios palestinos. En ese mismo año, el gobierno israelí tomó la mitad oriental de Jerusalén e inició un plan de colonización de las zonas invadidas. Dos años después, en 1982, el ejército de Israel invadió el sur de Líbano, zona donde se encontraban grandes campamentos de refugiados palestinos. La dirección de la OLP se trasladó a Túnez y poco después, azuzado por jefes militares israelíes, un grupo ultraderechista libanés asesinó a casi toda la población de los campos de Sabra y Chatila. Desde entonces, la OLP intensificó sus esfuerzos diplomáticos: abandonó la idea de la desaparición de Israel y en 1988 aceptó su existencia, pero exigió al gobierno israelí reconocer el derecho de los palestinos a la formación de un Estado propio. En febrero de 1986 el rey Hussein de Jordania rompió con Arafat, al que acusó de "mala fe" por no aprobar sus arreglos con Estados Unidos. Al año siguiente, el mismo Hussein renunció formalmente a toda pretensión sobre los territorios ocupados por Israel, junto a lo cual retiró la ayuda económica a los palestinos. El 8 de diciembre de 1987 se inició un levantamiento popular en los territorios ocupados, conocido por su nombre en árabe, *intifada*, durante el cual los palestinos sólo usaron piedras contra el ejército de ocupación, declararon una huelga de impuestos y el boicoteo comercial a los productos israelíes. El gobierno de Israel respondió con deportaciones, cárcel y persecución contra los presuntos líderes y represión militar de la población civil, lo que causó cientos de muertos y miles de mutilados entre hombres, mujeres y niños palestinos. Asimismo, fue intervenido el sistema educativo árabe-palestino por el gobierno israelí. En diciembre de 1988, un mes después de la proclamación del Estado Palestino, la Camara de Diputados de México se manifestó unánimente por su reconocimiento oficial, lo que hasta marzo de 1989 habían hecho 95 países. En abril del mismo año, Yasser Arafat fue elegido presidente del gobierno provisional de Palestina. México fue uno de los 105 países que votaron aprobatoriamente en las Naciones Unidas la constitución del Estado palestino. En 1998, de acuerdo con la Oficina Central Palestina de Estadísticas, dependiente de la Autoridad Nacional Palestina, la población del país era de 2.9 millones, de los cuales 1.9 millones vivían en la margen occidental del Jordán y el resto en la Franja de Gaza. Las estadísticas mostraban también que, a pesar de rezagos materiales y educativos (sólo la tercera parte de las casas tenía drenaje; el porcentaje de analfabetismo era de 11.6 y sólo 4.3 por ciento de la población había hecho estudios superiores), Palestina tenía expectativas de desarrollo mayores que las de otras naciones del mundo árabe. La comunidad mexicana de origen palestino es de unas 20,000 personas, las que viven principalmente en Monterrey y otras localidades de Nuevo León.

Paleta, Martín ◆ m. en Puebla, Pue. (?-1925). Obrero. Miembro del Partido Comunista. Era secretario general de la Confederación Sindicalista del Estado de Puebla cuando fue asesinado por la policía en la sede de la organización que dirigía una huelga en Puebla y Tlaxcala.

Paleta, Zbigniew ◆ n. en Polonia (1944). Músico. Hizo estudios de violín y viola en su país natal y obtuvo un posgrado en música por la Universidad de Cracovia. Llegó a México en 1978. Ha sido violinista de la Filarmónica de la Ciudad de México y de la Filarmónica de la UNAM. Ha participado en grabaciones y conciertos del grupo de *rock* El Tri, así como en ensambles de *jazz* y experimentales. Fue director musical de la película *Blanco*, de Krzystztof Kieslowski.

Paliza, Ruperto ◆ n. en la ciudad de México y m. en Hermosillo, Son. (1857-1939). En Culiacán reorganizó el colegio Rosales, del que fue profesor y director, fundó la Sociedad de Beneficencia y la Casa-asilo y fue director del Hospital Civil, regidor, diputado a dos legislaturas locales, magistrado supernumerario del Tribunal Superior de Justicia y gobernador interino de Sinaloa en 1911 y 1912. Recibió las Palmas Académicas de Francia.

PALIZADA ◆ Municipio de Campeche situado en el extremo suroeste del estado, en los límites con Tabasco. Superficie: 2,071.7 km^2. Habitantes: 7,903, de los cuales 1,979 forman la población económicamente activa. Hablan alguna lengua indígena 44 personas mayores de cinco años (maya 22). Parte de la laguna de Términos se encuentra dentro de su jurisdicción. Hacia 1672, varios grupos de piratas franceses e ingleses se instalaron en el territorio del municipio. Para desalojarlos, cuatro años después se organizó, desde Villahermosa, una expedición armada que fracasó. Los españoles lo recuperaron a principios del siglo XVIII. La cabecera municipal fue fundada en 1792.

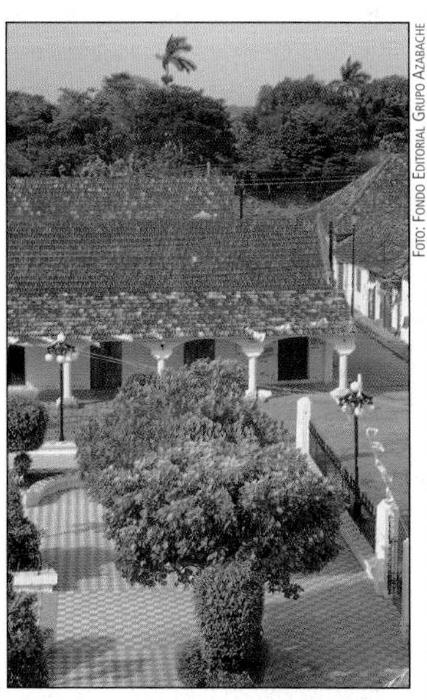
Foto: Fondo Editorial Grupo Azabache

Palizada, municipio de Campeche

PALIZADA ◆ Río de Campeche, uno de los brazos que se desprenden del Usumacinta. Tiene 60 kilómetros de longitud y desemboca en la laguna del Este.

PALMA, ANDREA ◆ n. en Durango, Dgo., y m. en el DF (1903-1987). Nombre profesional de la actriz Guadalupe Bracho Gavilán. Actuó en las obras de teatro *Maya, Santa, La casa de Bernarda Alba, Los derechos de la mujer, Medio tono* y *La dama de las camelias*, entre otras. Inició su carrera cinematográfica en Hollywood, hacia 1927, cuando apareció como extra en varias películas. Su primer papel principal fue en el filme

Foto: Fondo Editorial Grupo Azabache

Palizada, río de Campeche

mexicano *La mujer del Puerto* (1933), de Arcady Boytler. Posteriormente participó en cintas como *El primo Basilio* (1934), *Sor Juana Inés de la Cruz* (1935), *Amapola del camino* (1937), *Inmaculada* (1938), *Distinto amanecer* (1943), *Bel Amí (el buen mozo)* (1946), *Tarzán y las sirenas* (1947), *Aventurera* (1949), *Sensualidad* (1950), *Deseada* (1950), *El dinero no es la vida* (1951), *Mujeres sin mañana* (1951), *La ausente* (1951), *Eugenia Grandet* (1951), *Mujeres que trabajan* (1952), *Los hijos de nadie* (1952), *Lágrimas robadas* (1953), *Ángeles de la calle* (1953), *Padre nuestro* (1953), *Ensayo de un crimen* (1955), *A dónde van nuestros hijos* (1956), *Miércoles de ceniza* (1958), *Ama a tu prójimo* (1958), *La hermana blanca* (1960), *El cielo y la tierra* (1962), *México de mis recuerdos* (1963), *Historia de un canalla* (1963), *Andante* (1967) y *En busca de un muro* (1975), entre otras. Participó también en numerosas telenovelas. En 1955 y 1983 le fue impuesta por la Asociación Nacional de Actores la Medalla Eduardo Arozamena.

Foto: Época

Andrea Palma

PALMA, JUAN DE DIOS ◆ n. en Cantón de los Tuxtla y m. en San Andrés Tuxtla, Chis. (1874-1930). Profesor. Estudió en la Escuela Normal de Jalapa. En 1914 fundó un grupo liberal. Incorporado al carrancismo, fue diputado al Congreso Constituyente de 1916-17.

PALMA, MARÍA LUISA ◆ n. el DF (1947). Escultora. Estudió la licenciatura en artes plásticas en la Escuela de Artes Plásticas La Esmeralda. Ha presentado su obra, que comprende esculturas e instalaciones que reciclan materiales de desecho, en exposiciones individuales y colectivas en México, Estados Unidos y Europa.

PALMA, ÓSCAR EDMUNDO ◆ n. en Guatemala (1930). Periodista. Se inició profesionalmente hacia 1950. En su país de origen fue reportero de diversos diarios y escribió en la *Revista de Guatemala* que dirigía Luis Cardoza y Aragón. En Cuba fue editor de la agencia Prensa Latina y redactor de la revista *Cuba Socialista*. Vive en México desde 1970. Fue articulista y editor de *El Día* y jefe de la sección internacional de *unomásuno*. Autor de los libros *Guatemala, El maestro de la libertad* y *Periodismo en crisis*.

PALMA ARGÜELLES, ALEJANDRO ◆ n. en el DF (1935). Licenciado en derecho por la UNAM (1952-56), con estudios bancarios en EUA (1964). Fue director general del Canal 13, del Banco de la Ciudad de México y subdirector de la División de Promoción Industrial de Banamex (1970-75). Al ser nacionalizada la banca privada, en 1982, continuó su carrera en esa institución. Ha sido director general de la Casa de Bolsa Banamex (1983-84) y director general adjunto de Banamex (1984-).

PALMA MORENO, GUILLERMO ◆ n. en Guaymas, Son. y m. en el DF (1886-

1961). Se levantó en armas en 1911 y combatió en las fuerzas carrancistas desde 1913. Comandó el primer batallón de la división Supremos Poderes. En 1920 se unió a la rebelión de Agua Prieta y al triunfo de los sonorenses fue jefe del sector militar de Jalapa (1924), inspector general de la policía del DF (1933), director de intendencia de ejército (1934) y oficial mayor de la Secretaría de la Defensa Nacional (1935- 36).

PALMA Y PALMA, EULOGIO ◆ n. en Motul y m. en Mérida, Yuc. (1851-1914). Colaboró en diversas publicaciones regionales, como *La Revista de Mérida* y *El Eco del Comercio*, en las que siempre firmó con el seudónimo de *Nemo*. Fue diputado local y regidor de Motul. Escribió *La hija de Tutul Xiu* (1864), *Aventuras de un derrotado* (1886) y *Los mayas* (1901).

PALMAR DE BRAVO ◆ Municipio de Puebla situado al norte de Tehuacán, contiguo a Tecamachalco y cerca de los límites con Veracruz. Superficie: 341.88 km^2. Habitantes: 31,583, de los cuales 6,318 forman la población económicamente activa. Hablan alguna lengua indígena 27 personas mayores de cinco años. Lleva ese nombre porque en esta localidad, en 1812, Nicolás Bravo, auxiliado por Pablo Galeana, derrotó al realista Juan Labaqui. En 1813 hubo otra acción bélica en el mismo lugar, en la que Mariano Matamoros derrotó al realista Manuel Martínez.

PALMAS, DE LAS ◆ Río de Baja California que nace en la sierra de Juárez, situada en el extremo norte de la península. En el valle de Tijuana recibe al río Tecate y desemboca en el océano Pacífico. Surte la presa Rodríguez, que abastece de agua a la población de Tijuana.

Ricardo Palmerín

PALMERÍN, RICARDO ◆ n. en Tekax, Yuc. y m. en el DF (¿1887?-1944). Músico. Algunos autores aseguran que nació en 1883, 1884, 1888 o 1889. Su apellido materno era Pavía. Vivió en Mérida hasta mediados de los años veinte. Durante los gobiernos de Salvador Alvarado (1915-18) y Felipe Carrillo Puerto (1922-24) compuso lo más importante de su obra, como la canción *Peregrina* (1923), escrita sobre un poema de Luis Rosado Vega a petición del propio Carrillo Puerto, quien se la dedicó a la periodista estadounidense Alma Reed. Ambos asistieron a la casa de Palmerín a los ensayos. Poco después del asesinato de Carrillo Puerto se trasladó a la ciudad de México, donde vivió hasta su muerte. De entre las más de 400 canciones que escribió, destacan *El rosal enfermo*, *La flor del xhanlol*, *Semejanza*, *Entre las almas y entre las rosas*, *Novia envidiada*, *Rosalinda*, *Las turbias olas*, *Hube*, *Clarito de luna*, *Voluble mariposa*, *Mi tierra* y *Flores de mayo*.

PALMILLAS ◆ Municipio de Tamaulipas situado al suroeste de Ciudad Victoria y al noroeste de Ciudad Mante, cerca de los límites con Nuevo León y San Luis Potosí. Superficie: 764.67 km^2. Habitantes: 1,862, de los cuales 518 forman la población económicamente activa.

Calle en Palmillas, Tamaulipas

Foto: Fondo Editorial Grupo Azabache

PALMITO DEL VERDE ◆ Isla de la costa sur de Sinaloa, situada al sureste del puerto de Mazatlán. Es un cordón litoral que limita por el oeste con la laguna del Lagarto. Se extiende de noroeste a sureste entre la desembocadura del río del Baluarte y la boca de la laguna de Teacapan.

PALO ALTO ◆ Cabecera del municipio aguascalentense de El Llano (☛).

PALOMAR, JOSÉ ◆ n. en Santa María y m. en Guadalajara, Jal. (1807-1873). Fundador de la fábrica de hilados y tejidos de Atemajac y de la papelera del Batán. Colaboró en el establecimiento de la Compañía Telegráfica de Jalisco y participó en la fundación del Monte de Piedad, de la Escuela de Artes y de la Junta de Caridad de ese estado. Intervino en la reconstrucción del Hospital de Belén, el Hospicio y la Casa de Caridad de San Felipe. Fue diputado al Congreso local (1851) y gobernador interino de Jalisco (1853).

PALOMAR ARIAS, CARLOS ◆ n. en Guadalajara, Jal. y m. en el DF (1893-1972). Médico graduado en Bélgica. Al inicio de la primera guerra mundial regresó a México, donde fue músico e hizo investigaciones musicológicas. Durante 30 años ejerció la crítica musical en el diario *Excélsior*, con el pseudónimo de *Junius*. Fue jefe de traductores de la Secretaría de Relaciones Exteriores. Autor de *Ensayos*, *Alegro moderatto* y *Música clásica*.

PALOMAR DE MIGUEL, JUAN ◆ n. en España (?). Reside en México desde 1957. Estudió humanidades en España y en Inglaterra. Autor del *Diccionario de México*, 4 t. (1991).

PALOMAR Y VIZCARRA, MIGUEL ◆ n. en Guadalajara, Jal. y m. en el DF (1880-1968). Abogado. Profesor de la Escuela Libre de Derecho de Guadalajara (1906-14), del Liceo de Varones y de la Escuela Oficial de Derecho. Fue magistrado suplente del Supremo Tribunal de Justicia de Jalisco, fundador del Partido Católico Nacional (1911) y diputado local. En 1920 participó en la campaña presidencial de Alfredo Robles Domínguez. En 1926 intervino en la fundación de la Liga Nacional Defensora de la Libertad Religiosa, de la que fue vicepresidente. Autor de *Carlos Pereyra, el venerable episcopado y el derecho de los padres de familia* (1949) y de *Hacia la cumbre de la cristiandad*.

PALOMAS, DE ◆ Laguna de Chihuahua y Durango situada al sur de las sierras Mojada y del Diablo. En ella desemboca el río de la Cadena.

PALOMAS, DE LAS ◆ Sierra que forma parte de las estribaciones sudoccidentales de las sierras de Zacatecas. En su extremo noreste enlaza con el norte de la sierra Fría.

PALOMAS ◆ ☛ *Santiago Papasquiaro*.

PALOMEQUE SOLÍS, MANUEL ◆ n. en Mérida, Yuc. (1842-1867). Autor de un poema que, musicalizado por José Jacinto Cuevas, fue declarado himno yucateco.

PALOMERA, LUPITA ◆ n. en Guadalajara, Jal. (?). Cantante. Inició su carrera profesional en 1934, en la estación XEB de Guadalajara. Algunas de las canciones que ha interpretado son *Incertidumbre, Vereda tropical, Mi pensamiento, Frenesí, Hay que saber perder, Mis ojos me denuncian, Perfidia, Mi pensamiento* y *Tiempo aquel*.

PALOMERA LÓPEZ, JESÚS ◆ n. en Talpa de Allende, Jal. y m. en el DF (1888-1929). Se unió a la revolución constitucionalista en 1913. Fue jefe de la gendarmería montada del Distrito Federal. En 1929 se adhirió a la rebelión escobarista. Fue hecho prisionero y fusilado.

PALOMERA QUIROZ, ESTEBAN JULIO ◆ n. en Guadalajara, Jal. y m. en el DF (1914-1997). Ingresó en la Compañía de Jesús en 1929. Estudió el noviciado jesuita en El Paso, Texas, y en el Instituto de Ciencias de Guadalajara, del que posteriormente fue director. Maestro en teología y filosofía. Maestro y doctor en historia por la UNAM. Fue rector del Instituto Oriente de Puebla, investigador del Departamento de Historia de la UIA, presidente de la Federación de Escuelas Particulares de Puebla y la Confederación Nacional de Escuelas Particulares, y vicepresidente de la Confederación Interamericana de Educación Católica. Fue responsable de la sexta edición (1995) del *Diccionario Porrúa de Historia, Biografía y Geografía de México*. Coautor de una traducción de la *Rethorica Christiana* de Diego Valadés (☛). Autor de *Fray Diego Valadés. El hombre y su época* (1962), *La obra de fray Diego Valadés: la* Rethorica Christiana (1963), *La obra educativa de los jesuitas en Tampico (1962-1987)* (1987), *La labor educativa de los jesuitas en Puebla* y *La labor educativa de los jesuitas en Guadalajara (1586-1986)* (1996). Fue nombrado miembro de número de la Academia Mexicana de la Lengua en 1996.

PALOMINO, CARLOS ◆ n. en San Luis Potosí, SLP (1949). Boxeador. Fue campeón mundial de peso welter del Consejo Mundial de Boxeo, entre 1976 y 1980, cuando perdió por decisión ante Rodolfo González.

PALOMINO, GUILLERMO ◆ n. en Veracruz, Ver. y m. en Mérida, Yuc. (1834-1889). Fue comandante militar de Yucatán (1873-77 y 1880-81), gobernador provisional del mismo estado (del 14 de julio de 1876 al 13 de enero de 1877), senador de la República y gobernador constitucional de Yucatán (del 1 de febrero de 1886 al 9 de mayo de 1889).

PALOMINO Y OBREGÓN, MARÍA AMPARO ◆ n. en el DF (1947). Estudió arte y literatura (1972-77) y administración educativa (1977-81) en la Universidad Anáhuac. Profesora de educación primaria (1975-79) y de la Universidad Anáhuac (1979-81). Desde 1970 pertenece al PRI, en el que formó parte del consejo consultivo del IEPES. Ha sido presidenta del consejo de la empresa Malpasa (1981-84), subjefa de Servicios de Capacitación y Adiestramiento del Instituto Mexicano del Seguro Social (1983), directora de Capacitación y Adiestramiento (1983-85) y directora general de Capacitación y Productividad (1985-88) de la Secretaría del Trabajo y Previsión Social (1985-88).

PALOMINO TOPETE, JUAN FERNANDO ◆ n. en Aguascalientes, Ags. (1955). Licenciado en derecho por la UNAM, con diploma en administración y empresa pública por el CIDE Afiliado al PRI desde 1976, ha sido coordinador de Análisis Temático y secretario técnico del Consejo Consultivo del IEPES, secretario general y presidente del CDE del PRI en Aguascalientes, coordinador general del CDE del PRI en el estado de Colima; coordinador del Registro Civil en el DF, procurador nacional de Orientación y Apoyo a la Juventud y subdirector general del Crea, director general de Turismo del ISSSTE, delegado del Infonavit en Aguascalientes y senador de la República (1994-2000).

PALOMO ◆ n. en Chile (1943). Nombre profesional del caricaturista José Palomo Fuentes. Estudió dibujo. Comenzó su carrera en 1960. Llegó a México en 1973, luego del derrocamiento del presidente Salvador Allende. Trabajó en el diario *El Día* y más tarde en *unomásuno*, donde creó la tira *El cuarto reich*, recopilada en varios volúmenes. Colaborador de *La Jornada, Reforma* y otras publicaciones. Autor de *Matías y el pastel de fresas* (1986) y *Literatos* (1990). Primer lugar en el concurso internacional de caricatura *Encuentro de dos mundos* (1992), organizado por la Sociedad Mexicana de Caricaturistas y el gobierno de Veracruz.

FOTO: CATALINA HERRERA

Palomo

PALOU, PEDRO ÁNGEL ◆ n. en Puebla, Pue. (1966). Escritor. Licenciado en lingüística y literatura hispánicas y maestro en ciencias del lenguaje en la UDLA-Puebla (1991), en la que ha sido profesor de tiempo completo. Doctor en ciencias sociales por El Colegio de Michoacán (1998). Ha sido director de la Escuela de Escritores de la Sogem en Puebla y Secretario de Cultura del gobierno de Puebla. Autor de relato: *Pequeño museo de la melancolía* (1977); cuento: *Música del adiós* y *Amores enormes* (Premio Jorge Ibargüengoitia de narrativa satírica 1991); novela: *Como quien se desangra* (1991), *En la alcoba de un mundo* (1992), *Memoria de los días* (1996), *Bolero* (1997) y *El último campeo-*

nato mundial (1997); y ensayo: *La ciudad crítica* (1999, segundo lugar en el Premio Latinoamericano de Ensayo Las Imágenes de América Latina, convocado por la Universidad Pontificia Simón Bolívar de Medellín, Colombia). Premio Nacional de Investigación Histórica Francisco Xavier Clavijero por el libro *La casa del silencio, una aproximación en tres tiempos a Contemporáneos*. Ha sido becario del Fonca (1990-91). Miembro del SNI.

PALLARES, JACINTO ◆ n. en la hacienda de Los Remedios, municipio de Indaparapeo, Mich. y m. en la ciudad de México (1843-1904). Se tituló de abogado en el Colegio Primitivo de San Nicolás de Hidalgo (1863). Fue profesor de la Escuela Nacional de Jurisprudencia. Autor de *El Poder Judicial* (1874), *Inteligencia del artículo 16 de la Constitución de 1857* (1882), *Curso completo de derecho mexicano, Derecho mercantil mexicano, Código de beneficencia privada para el estado de Chiapas, Derecho mercantil mexicano, La filosofía y la ciencia* (1887), *La enseñanza oficial en sus relaciones con la religión, Prolegómenos del derecho civil mexicano, Personas morales* y *La pena de muerte*.

PALLARES, MANUEL ◆ n. el DF (1933). Periodista. Emigrado a Celaya, Gto., con su familia, se dedicó a numerosos trabajos eventuales en su infancia y adolescencia. Posteriormente hizo estudios inconclusos de teología y contaduría y fue locutor y reportero en emisoras y diarios locales. Regresó al DF y ha sido reportero, jefe de la sección de espectáculos y columnista del diario *El Sol de México* (1965-1991) y colaborador de *El Universal Gráfico* (1992-94) y *Reforma* (1994-). Al mismo tiempo ha sido locutor y conductor de varios programas de radio en las emisoras XEW, XEX, Radio Red, XEDF, y ha participado en programas televisivos de la empresa Televisa.

PALLEY, JULIAN ◆ n. en Estados Unidos (1925). Escritor. Se ha dedicado a la crítica literaria y ha residido en México. Autor de poesía: *Bestiario* (1987) y *Cuadros en una exhibición* (1989), y de varios volúmenes sobre literatura hispanoamericana.

PÁMANES ESCOBEDO, FERNANDO ◆ n. en Ojocaliente, Zac. (1909). Estudió en el Colegio Militar (1925) y en la Escuela Superior de Guerra, de donde egresó como oficial diplomado de Estado Mayor (1936). Participó en la guerra cristera hasta 1931. Entre 1938 y 1940 combatió en Guanajuato contra algunos grupos de alzados. Fue miembro del Estado Mayor Presidencial de Manuel Ávila Camacho (1942- 46), director de las revistas *Del Ejército* y *Del Soldado*, director de la Sección de Defensa Civil durante la segunda Guerra Mundial (1943), agregado militar de la embajada mexicana en China (1944-46), comandante de la primera División de Infantería de Voluntarios (1949-53), diputado federal (1955-58), delegado del PRI en Coahuila (1958), oficial mayor de la Secretaría de la Defensa Nacional (1958-65), embajador en Cuba (febrero a septiembre de 1967) y en Indonesia (1967-69), comandante de la V Zona Militar (1971-73), gobernador de Zacatecas (1974-80) y presidente de la Sociedad Mexicana de Geografía y Estadística (1981-83).

PAMES ◆ Indios del grupo otomangue que habitan zonas áridas y desérticas en el centro y sur de San Luis Potosí y en la zona de Querétaro que linda con aquel estado. En 1980 había 4,670 hablantes de pame en San Luis Potosí y 48 en Querétaro, aunque ambos grupos usan variantes dialectales de la misma lengua, lo que impide su comunicación. Debido al bajo rendimiento agrícola de sus tierras, los pames se ven obligados a emigrar temporalmente en busca de trabajos asalariados. Su unidad social básica es la familia nuclear. En su organización interior conservan el cargo de gobernador, que desempeña un hombre que haya cumplido con las mayordomías y que sea elegido por todos los miembros de la comunidad, aunque la mayoría de sus costumbres han sido desplazadas. La vestimenta tradicional pame ha sido sustituida por la ropa occidental. Practican la religión católica con elementos de su antigua religión.

FOTO: LOURDES ALMEIDA

Indios pames

PAMORANTES, DE ◆ Sierra de Tamaulipas situada al noreste de la de San Carlos, de la que está separada por el río Conchos o San Fernando, cerca de los límites con Nuevo León, al norte de la población de Méndez. Sus picos más altos son los cerros de la Botella y Venaditos.

PAN ◆ ☛ *Partido Acción Nacional.*

PANABÁ ◆ Municipio de Yucatán situado en la porción nororiental del estado y contiguo a Tizimín, Río Lagartos, San Felipe y Buctzotz. Superficie: 788.15 km². Habitantes: 7,432, de los cuales 2,053 forman la población económicamente activa. Hablan alguna lengua indígena 2,333 personas mayores de cinco años (maya 2,329).

PANABIÉRE, LOUIS ◆ n. y m. en Francia (1935-1995). Escritor y diplomático. Residió durante muchos años en México, y durante ese tiempo fue agregado cultural de la embajada francesa y director del IFAL. Fue también investigador del Centro de Estudios Americanos de la Unviersidad de Perpignan, Francia. Autor de la biografía *Itinerario de una disidencia. Jorge Cuesta 1903-1942* (1983) y numerosos ensayos y estudios literarios. Premio Jorge Cuesta 1992.

Panamá, República de ◆ Nación situada en el extremo sur del istmo Centroamericano. Tiene costas en el mar Caribe, al norte, y en el océano Pacífico, al sur. Limita al este con Colombia y al oeste con Costa Rica. Cuenta con 1,023 islas, islotes y cayos en el Caribe y 1,518 en el Pacífico, entre los que sobresalen los archipiélagos de Las Mulatas, de Bocas del Toro, de Coiba y del Rey y el grupo de Las Perlas. Superficie: 77,082 km². (incluida la Zona del Canal, que divide al país en su porción central). Habitantes: 2,767,000 (1998). La ciudad de Panamá es su capital y en 1994 tenía 445,902 habitantes. *Historia:* a la llegada de los conquistadores españoles el actual territorio panameño estaba poblado por chibchas, caribes y chocoes. En 1501, Rodrigo de Bastidas *descubrió* el istmo y al año siguiente Cristóbal Colón desembarcó en Portobelo. Ocho años después, en 1510, Vasco Núñez de Balboa fundó Santa María la Antigua de Darién. En 1519, Pedro Arias fundó la vieja ciudad de Panamá, desde donde partieron las expediciones de conquista a Colombia, Ecuador y Perú. La Audiencia de Panamá se creó en 1538. Durante los siglos XVI y XVII, los puertos panameños en ambos océanos sufrieron los ataques de los piratas, sin que el gobierno español pudiera combatirlos eficazmente. En 1718 fue disuelta la Real Audiencia y el istmo quedó bajó la jurisdicción del virreinato de Perú, hasta 1751, cuando pasó a depender del de Nueva Granada. En 1821, sin lucha armada, Panamá obtuvo la independencia y se integró a la República de la Gran Colombia, con el nombre de Departamento del Istmo. Cinco años más tarde, en 1826, a iniciativa de Simón Bolívar se reunió en Panamá el Congreso de Anfictionía, que fue el primero de carácter internacional celebrado en América, al cual asistieron los ministros plenipotenciarios de Perú, México, la Gran Colombia y las Provincias Unidas de Centroamérica; Brasil y Chile se limitaron a enviar mensajes de adhesión, otros países americanos no asistieron y Estados Unidos nombró una delegación de última hora, que no llegó a tiempo para participar; Gran Bretaña envió también un representante. Como resultado de este congreso se firmó un tratado de Unión, Liga y Confederación por medio del cual los países firmantes (Gran Colombia, Centroamérica, México y Perú) formaron una alianza militar para mantener su soberanía e independencia contra agresiones externas y acordaron establecer una asamblea general de plenipotenciarios que se reuniría periódicamente para regular las relaciones entre los miembros de la misma y garantizar la integridad de sus territorios. Se estipuló que el tratado se ratificaría en Tacubaya, en la ciudad de México, en un plazo máximo de ocho meses, lo que no ocurrió por la oposición del Congreso mexicano. En 1830 desapareció la Gran Colombia y Panamá se mantuvo como parte de Nueva Granada (hoy Colombia). Con el inicio de la "fiebre del oro" en California, en 1848, el tránsito a través del istmo se intensificó, pues era el camino más corto para pasar de uno a otro océano. Un grupo de empresarios estadounidenses tendió entre ambas costas una línea ferroviaria terminada en 1855. Varios liberales mexicanos que estaban exiliados en Nueva Orleans, entre ellos Benito Juárez, volvieron al país por la ruta del istmo y cruzaron el territorio panameño a bordo del recién inaugurado ferrocarril para dirigirse al puerto de Acapulco, donde se incorporaron a la revolución de Ayutla. En 1858, el presidente Juárez volvió a atravesar Panamá, en esa ocasión en sentido contrario, cuando se dirigía a Veracruz, durante la guerra de los Tres Años. En 1882 los franceses iniciaron la construcción de un canal interoceánico, pero un fraude bursátil hizo fracasar la empresa. La tarea, entonces, quedó en manos estadounidenses. En 1903, luego de que el Senado colombiano rechazó la construcción del canal, el gobierno de Washington promovió un levantamiento separatista, que triunfó gracias a la ayuda de los infantes de marina estadounidenses. Los rebeldes crearon la República de Panamá y firmaron con el gobierno estadounidense un tratado por el cual éste terminó de construir el canal y obtuvo a perpetuidad una franja de ocho kilómetros de ancho a cada lado del mismo, territorio que constituye la Zona del Canal, en posesión del gobierno de Washington desde entonces. En 1904 se promulgó la primera Constitución del país. En ese año, el presidente Porfirio Díaz reconoció a la nueva república. En 1922 se suspendieron las visas entre México y Panamá. A partir de 1936 Panamá inició una política de revisión del tratado del canal y en 1947 fue rechazado el convenio Filós-Hine, que cedería 14 bases militares a Estados Unidos. México fue uno de los países que suscribió el convenio que, en 1944, creó la Universidad Panamericana, con sede en Panamá. En 1955 se firmó el tratado Remón-Eisenhower, que revisaba aspectos conflictivos del tratado Hay-Buneau Varilla. Ese mismo año fue asesinado el presidente José Antonio Remón. En 1956 se celebró una conferencia internacional de presidentes latinoamericanos en la capital panameña, a la que asistió el presidente Adolfo Ruiz Cortines, en lo que fue el primer viaje de un presidente mexicano en funciones a otro país distinto de Estados Unidos, desde el viaje que, precisamente a Panamá, realizó el presidente Juárez en 1858. En 1962 los presidentes Roberto Chiari y John F. Kennedy formalizaron un acuerdo, por el cual la bandera panameña se izaría junto a la estadounidense en la Zona del Canal. Dos años después, sin embargo, soldados esta-

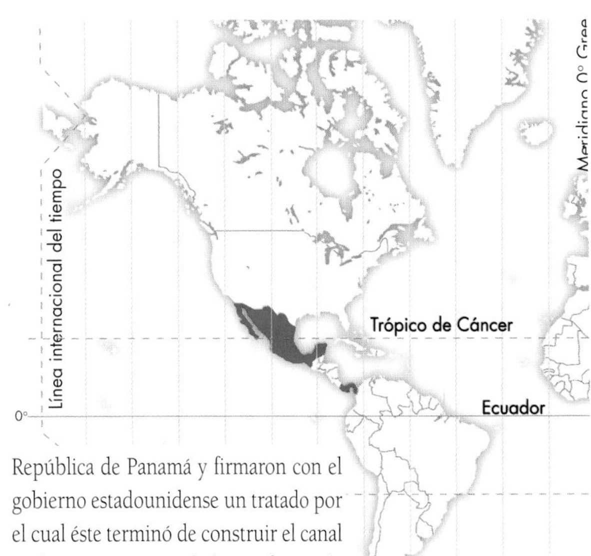

República de Panamá

Timbres de la República de Panamá

Monedas de Panamá

dounidenses balearon a un grupo de estudiantes panameños que pretendían izar su bandera en la Zona. Panamá rompió relaciones diplomáticas con Estados Unidos, las que se restablecieron tras la intervención de la OEA. El presidente Gustavo Díaz Ordaz visitó Panamá en 1966. Dos años después, en 1968, el general Omar Torrijos encabezó un golpe de Estado y se convirtió en el hombre fuerte del país. Desde esa posición, impulsó nuevas negociaciones con Estados Unidos, que incluyeron, en 1974, la declaración Tack-Kissinger, mediante la cual quedó abolido el tratado de 1903 y los estadounidenses se comprometieron a compartir la responsabilidad de operación, protección y defensa del canal. Tres años antes, en 1971, el presidente panameño Demetrio B. Lakas se había reunido con su homólogo mexicano Luis Echeverría, en Villahermosa, y acordaron formar grupos de trabajo que abordarían asuntos comerciales y de seguridad social. En 1975 Luis Echeverría recibió en Tuxtla Gutiérrez a Omar Torrijos. El convenio constitutivo del Sistema Económico Latinoamericano se firmó en 1975 en la capital panameña. Al año siguiente se produjeron nuevos motines estudiantiles contra la permanencia estadounidense. En 1977 Torrijos y el mandatario estadounidense James Carter firmaron los nuevos tratados del canal, que entraron en vigor en 1979 y prevén la nacionalización completa del mismo en el año 2000. Durante ese año, el presidente mexicano José López Portillo y el general Torrijos se encontraron en dos ocasiones, una en México y otra en Panamá. Al año siguiente, López Portillo volvió a Panamá y en 1979 se entrevistó con el presidente panameño, Arístides Royo, quien, a su vez, visitó la capital mexicana en 1981, año en el que Torrijos murió en un accidente de aviación. En 1982, el presidente Ricardo de la Espriella se entrevistó en México con López Portillo y al año siguiente con Miguel de la Madrid. También en 1983, los cancilleres de Colombia, México, Panamá y Venezuela se reunieron en la

Alberto J. Pani

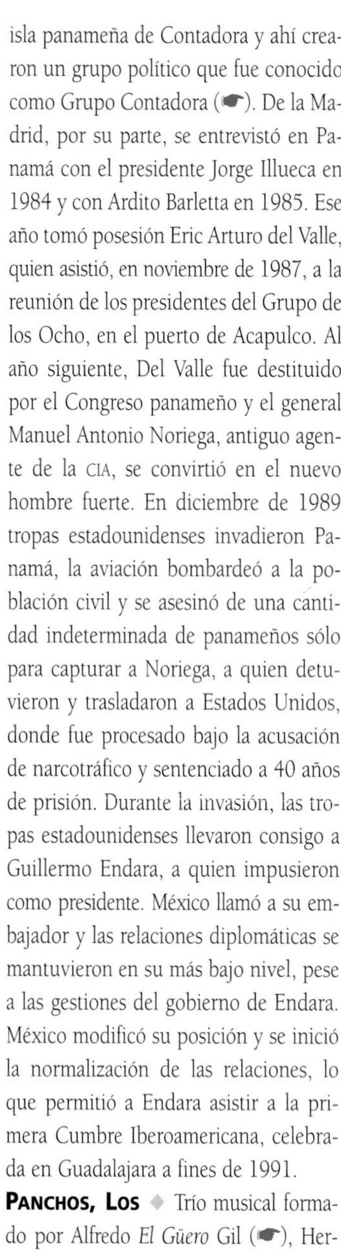

isla panameña de Contadora y ahí crearon un grupo político que fue conocido como Grupo Contadora (☛). De la Madrid, por su parte, se entrevistó en Panamá con el presidente Jorge Illueca en 1984 y con Ardito Barletta en 1985. Ese año tomó posesión Eric Arturo del Valle, quien asistió, en noviembre de 1987, a la reunión de los presidentes del Grupo de los Ocho, en el puerto de Acapulco. Al año siguiente, Del Valle fue destituido por el Congreso panameño y el general Manuel Antonio Noriega, antiguo agente de la CIA, se convirtió en el nuevo hombre fuerte. En diciembre de 1989 tropas estadounidenses invadieron Panamá, la aviación bombardeó a la población civil y se asesinó de una cantidad indeterminada de panameños sólo para capturar a Noriega, a quien detuvieron y trasladaron a Estados Unidos, donde fue procesado bajo la acusación de narcotráfico y sentenciado a 40 años de prisión. Durante la invasión, las tropas estadounidenses llevaron consigo a Guillermo Endara, a quien impusieron como presidente. México llamó a su embajador y las relaciones diplomáticas se mantuvieron en su más bajo nivel, pese a las gestiones del gobierno de Endara. México modificó su posición y se inició la normalización de las relaciones, lo que permitió a Endara asistir a la primera Cumbre Iberoamericana, celebrada en Guadalajara a fines de 1991.

PANCHOS, LOS ◆ Trío musical formado por Alfredo *El Güero* Gil (☛), Hernando Avilés (☛) y Jesús Navarro (☛), que se presentó por primera vez el 28 de diciembre de 1944. Durante más de 40 años hicieron giras internacionales y grabaron numerosos discos de larga duración. En 1987 lo integraban, junto con Navarro, Gabriel Vargas y Rafael Basurto, pero el trío se disolvió definitivamente tras la muerte de Navarro (1993). Algunas de las canciones más populares del trío son *Una copa más*, *Un siglo de ausencia*, *Rayito de luna*, *Mi último fracaso*, *Me voy pa'l pueblo* y *Hasta mañana*.

PANDO PENDÁS, ELÍAS ◆ n. en España y m. en el DF (1895-1998). Empresario. Llegó a México en 1910. Fun-

Los Panchos

dó el grupo Industrias Pando. Medalla de Honor Canaco al mérito empresarial (1991).

PANDOS, DE LOS ◆ Sierra de Chihuahua que forma parte de la cresta principal de la sierra Madre Occidental, conocida en ese tramo como sierra Tarahumara.

PANECATL O PANÉCATL ◆ Deidad nahua, una de las 400 de los borrachos. Algunos estudiosos hacen a este dios esposo de Mayahuel, la diosa del pulque.

PÁNFILO NATERA ◆ ☛ *General Pánfilo Natera.*

PANI, ALBERTO J. ◆ n. en Aguascalientes, Ags. y m. en el DF (1878-1955). Se tituló en la Escuela Nacional de Ingenieros (1902), de la que fue profesor. Fue miembro de la comisión encargada de construir el Palacio Legislativo Federal y de la Comisión Técnica de las Obras de Provisión de Aguas Potables para la ciudad de México. Realizó el proyecto del edificio para la planta de bombas en Nativitas y construyó el de la colonia Condesa. Antirreeleccionista en 1910, fue subsecretario de Instrucción Pública y Bellas Artes de Francisco I. Madero (1911) y director general de Obras Públicas del Distrito Federal (1912-13). Durante la Decena Trágica (febrero de 1913) redactó la hoja *Honor Nacional*. Al producirse el golpe de Estado de Victoriano Huerta se incorporó al constitucionalismo y fue delegado a las conferencias de New London y Atlantic City.

Secretario de Industria y Comercio con Carranza (primero de mayo de 1917 al 21 de enero de 1919) y ministro de México en París (1918); secretario de Relaciones Exteriores en el gabinete de Álvaro Obregón (del 27 de enero de 1921 al 23 de septiembre de 1923) y secretario de Hacienda y Crédito Público en el periodo presidencial de Plutarco Elías Calles (del 1 de diciembre de 1924 al 12 de febrero de 1927). En este último cargo promovió la unificación arquitectónica de la Plaza de la Constitución, lo que incluyó la construcción del tercer piso del Palacio Nacional. Fue por segunda vez ministro de México en París y primer embajador ante la República Española (1931). Nuevamente secretario de Hacienda en los gobiernos de Pascual Ortiz Rubio (del 15 de febrero al 2 de septiembre de 1932) y Abelardo L. Rodríguez (del 5 de septiembre de 1932 al 28 de septiembre de 1933), creó la Dirección de Pensiones Civiles de Retiro, el Banco Nacional de Crédito Agrícola, la Comisión Nacional de Caminos, la de Irrigación y el Banco de México. Dirigió las obras para terminar la construcción del Palacio de Bellas Artes. Autor de *La higiene en México* (1916), *La cuestión internacional mexicano-americana durante el gobierno del Gral. D. Álvaro Obregón* (1925), *La política hacendaria y la revolución* (1926), *Mi contribución al nuevo régimen (1910-1933)* (1933), *Tres monografías* (1941) y *Apuntes autobiográficos* (1951).

Pani, Arturo ◆ n. en Aguascalientes, Ags. y m. en el DF (1879-1962). Se tituló en la Escuela Nacional de Ingenieros (1915), en la que ejerció la docencia. Fue miembro de la Dirección Técnica de Provisión de Aguas Potables para la ciudad de México (1904-11), jefe del Departamento de Obras Públicas de la Secretaría de Comunicaciones, jefe del Departamento de Bosques de la Secretaría de Agricultura y Fomento, consultor de la Secretaría de Gobernación, miembro de la Comisión Nacional Agraria; cónsul general en Amberes (1918), Génova (1919-23), Milán (1923) y Francia (1924) y representante de México ante la Sociedad de Naciones. En 1938 fundó, con su hijo Mario Pani, la revista *Arquitectura/México*. Autor de *Messico* (con el pseudónimo de *Mario D'Arpi*), *Jesús Terán (ensayo biográfico)* (1949), *Una vida* (1949), *Ayer* (1954), *Un curioso testamento. La fundación Carsellini de Faenza* (1957) y *Alberto J. Pani, ensayo biográfico* (1961).

Pani, Mario ◆ n. y m. en el DF (1911-1993). Arquitecto. Se tituló en 1934 en la Escuela de Bellas Artes de París. Fue profesor de la UNAM, fundador y director de la revista *Arquitectura/México* (1938-78), de los comités de construcción del Centro Médico de la ciudad de México (1943-47) y del Programa Federal de Escuelas (1944-47); vicepresidente del Banco Internacional Inmobiliario (1948-69), codirector general, con Enrique del Moral, del Proyecto de Conjunto de las Obras de la Ciudad Universitaria (1950-52) y, con Del Moral y Salvador Ortega, del proyecto y construcción de la Torre de Rectoría (1950). Entre sus principales obras se cuentan los hoteles Reforma (1935-36), Alameda de Morelia (1942) y Plaza (1945); el estadio de Ciudad Victoria (1938), la Escuela Nacional de Maestros (1945), el Conservatorio Nacional de Música (1946), el Conjunto Urbano Presidente Miguel Alemán (1948), la Unidad Habitacional Modelo, en Iztapalapa (1948) y la segunda colonia del Periodista (1949). De sus obras en colaboración destacan el multifamiliar Juárez, del DF (1950), el Club de Yates de Acapulco (1955), el Banco Popular de Monterrey (1958), la Unidad Habitacional Santa Fe del IMSS (1953), el Centro Comercial Satélite (1958), la torre de Banobras (1962), y el Conjunto Urbano Nonoalco-Tlatelolco (1960-64); la Unidad Habitacional Tlalnepantla del IMSS (1955), la Unidad Kennedy, en el DF (1963) y el hotel Condesa del Mar, en Acapulco (1969-72); y el Club de Golf México (1951). Coautor de *Construcción de la Ciudad Universitaria* (1979) y autor de *Los multifamiliares de Pensiones* (1953). Miembro fundador del Colegio de Arquitectos de México (1946), de las academias de Artes y Nacional de Arquitectura (que presidió en 1977). En 1986 recibió el Premio Nacional de Ciencias y Artes.

Foto: Pablo González de Alba

Hotel Plaza, obra del arquitecto Mario Pani

Paniagua, Carolina ◆ n. en Tuxpan, Ver. (1946). Pintora. Estudió dibujo publicitario en los Estudios Orozco del DF (1963-64), psicología (1965-70) y artes visuales (1973-76) en la UNAM, donde participó en el movimiento estudiantil de 1968. Tomó un curso de car-

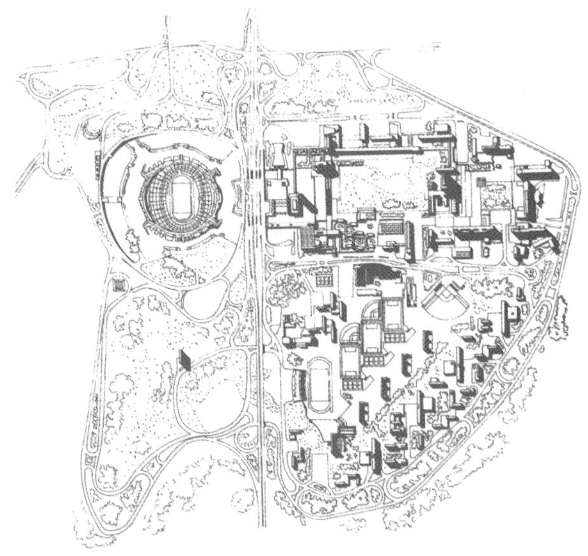

Plano de Ciudad Universitaria

Obra de Carolina Paniagua

tel con Wiktor Gorka en la ENAP (1974-75) y otro de grabado en el taller de Stanley W. Hayter, en París (1977). Fue psicóloga del Banco de México (1969-70). Es profesora del Centro Activo Freire (1971-). Militó en el Partido Comunista Mexicano (1977-81) y en la Corriente Democrática (1988). Cofundadora del Partido de la Revolución Democrática. Ha diseñado portadas de libros y revistas, la primera plana de *El Gallo Ilustrado* (1977-78) y carteles para la Facultad de Economía de la UNAM (1978-79). A partir de 1974 participa en exposiciones colectivas de pintura y desde 1980 ha presentado muestras individuales de su obra en México, Alemania, Australia, Yugoslavia, Corea del Sur, Dinamarca, Ecuador, Estados Unidos, Filipinas, Indonesia, Japón, Polonia, Rumania y Tailandia. Ejecutó murales en la unidad habitacional Soldominio, del DF (1970) y en la librería Corrupio, de San Salvador, Brasil (1984). Pertenece a la Somart y al grupo Acción Inmediata de Rescate Ecológico. En 1975 obtuvo el primer lugar en el concurso de viñeta de la revista *Punto de Partida*.

Paniagua, Flavio Antonio ◆ n. y m. en San Cristóbal de Las Casas, Chis. (1844- 1911). Se tituló de abogado en el Seminario Conciliar de San Cristóbal (1866). Fue procurador de Justicia de Chiapas. Autor de *Catecismo elemental de historia y estadística de Chiapas* (1876) y de *Documentos y datos para un Diccionario Etimológico, Histórico y Geográfico de Chiapas* (1911), así como de las novelas *Una rosa y dos espinas. Memorias del Imperio en Chiapas* (1870), *Lágrimas del corazón. Ensayo de novela histórica* (1873), *Florinda* (1889), *La cruz de San Andrés* (1890) y *Salvador Guzmán* (1891).

Paniagua, Ricardo A. ◆ n. en Motozintla y m. en Tuxtla Gutiérrez, Chis. (1896-1927). Líder obrero. Fue fundador de la Confederación Socialista de Chiapas. Combatió la rebelión delahuertista en 1923. Murió asesinado.

Paniagua, Trinidad ◆ n. en Real del Monte, Hgo. y m. en Huachinantla, Pue. (?-1916). Incorporado al Ejército Libertador del Sur en 1914, participó en las tomas de Chilapa, Chilpancingo, Zacatepec y Cuernavaca. En 1915 fue nombrado director de las fábricas de municiones que los zapatistas tenían en Oacalco y Atlihuayan. Uno de sus asistentes lo mató en forma accidental.

Paniagua Cortés, Amado ◆ n. en San Francisco Yaltepec, Hgo. y m. en Veracruz (1898-1918). Aviador. También se dice que nació en Real del Monte. Estudió en la Escuela de Artes y Oficios de Tulancingo. En 1915 ingresó al cuerpo de artillería del ejército carrancista y durante los dos años siguientes estudió aviación. Se graduó en julio de 1918 y poco después se incorporó a la Flotilla Aérea de Exploradores. Murió en un accidente.

Paniagua Vázquez, Cenobio ◆ n. en Tlalpujahua, Mich. y m. en Córdoba, Ver. (1812-1882). Músico. Estudió violín en Tlalpujahua y en la academia de Agustín Caballero y Joaquín Beristáin. Está considerado el primer mexicano autor de ópera. Fundó la Academia de Armonía y Composición, donde estudiaron Melesio Morales, Mateo Torres Serratos, Miguel Planas y Carlos J. Meneses. Fue profesor de Ángela Peralta. Compuso la opera *Catalina de Guisa* (1859), que fue estrenada para celebrar un cumpleaños del presidente conservador Miguel Miramón. Entre 1862 y 1863 participó en diversos conciertos organizados por un grupo de mujeres liberales encabezado por Margarita Maza de Juárez. En 1863 compuso *Pietro d'Abano* obra en la cual festejaba la derrota del ejército francés en Puebla en mayo del año anterior. Dos años después, ya durante el gobierno de Maximiliano de Habsburgo, intentó viajar a Cuba, pero luego de tres años de espera, en 1868 se trasladó a Córdoba, donde vivió hasta su muerte. Compuso además la ópera *El paria*, el oratorio *Tobías*, la pieza *Una niña de aguadores* y un *Réquiem*. En 1996, gran parte de su archivo fue descubierto en Córdoba.

Panindícuaro ◆ Municipio de Michoacán situado en el norte del estado, al sureste de La Piedad, al este de Zamora y al noroeste de Morelia. Superficie: 254.77 km^2. Habitantes: 18,538, de los cuales 4,851 forman la población económicamente activa. Hablan alguna lengua indígena seis personas mayores de cinco años.

Pankhurst, Eduardo G. ◆ n. en Zacatecas, Zac. y m. en la ciudad de México (1840-1908). A mediados de 1858 estudiaba en el Seminario de Guadalajara, cuando, luego de la sublevación de Antonio Landa, se incorporó al ejército liberal y combatió a los conservadores durante el resto de la guerra de los Tres Años. En 1861 se tituló como abogado en la ciudad de México, antes de volver a Zacatecas, donde fue redactor del *Periódico Oficial* y más tarde fue síndico procurador del ayuntamiento, regidor, catedrático, secretario de Gobierno y diputado local y federal. En 1864, poco después de la ocupación de Zacatecas por los invasores franceses, editó los periódicos *El Álbum Zacatecano* y *El Porvenir*, ambos de tendencia republicana, por lo que fue encarcelado. Al triunfo de la República se desempeñó como profesor en el Instituto de Ciencias (1867-75) y fue nuevamente diputado federal en 1875. En ese año se adhirió al Plan de Tuxtepec. Fue profesor de la Escuela Nacional de Jurisprudencia, magistrado del Tribunal Superior de Justicia del Distrito Federal, secretario de Gobernación (del 9 de abril de 1879 al 20 de enero de 1880) en el gabinete de Porfirio Díaz, y gobernador interino (del 4 de febrero al 16 de septiembre de 1904) y constitucional de Zacatecas (del 17 de septiembre de 1904 al 22 de junio de 1908).

Panotla ◆ Municipio de Tlaxcala contiguo a la capital del estado. Superficie: 57.8 km². Habitantes: 20,776, de los cuales 4,634 forman la población económicamente activa. Hablan alguna lengua indígena 170 personas mayores de cinco años (náhuatl 103).

Pantelhó ◆ Municipio de Chiapas situado al noreste de Tuxtla Gutiérrez y al norte de San Cristóbal de Las Casas. Superficie: 136.6 km². Habitantes: 14,073, de los cuales 3,374 forman la población económicamente activa. Hablan alguna lengua indígena 8,470 personas mayores de cinco años (tzotzil 4,615 y tzeltal 3,851). Indígenas monolingües: 4,060.

Panteón de Dolores ◆☛ *Dolores.*

Panteón de San Fernando ◆ Fundado en la ciudad de México en el siglo XVIII, perteneció a los sacerdotes del convento anexo. A raíz de la epidemia de cólera de 1835 fue declarado cementerio público. Ahí fueron enterrados, entre otros, Vicente Guerrero y Benito Juárez, así como Miguel Miramón, cuyos restos fueron exhumados en 1895.

Panteón de Santa Paula ◆ Creado por el arzobispo Haro y Peralta para el Hospital de San Andrés, se destinaba a quienes morían sin deudos. Empezó a operar en 1784 en terrenos de la parroquia de Santa María la Redonda. En 1836 se declaró cementerio general y se

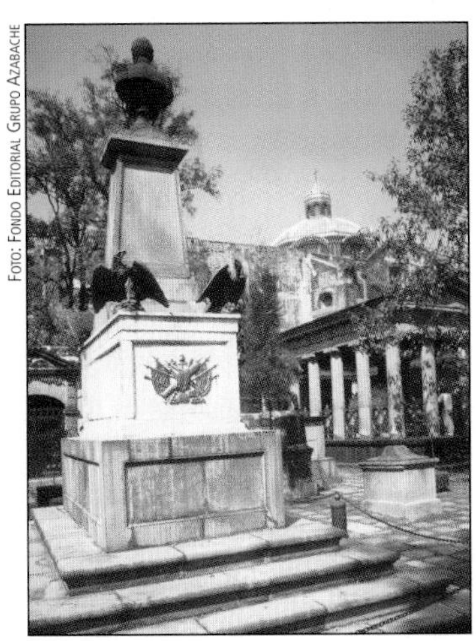

Foto: Fondo Editorial Grupo Azabache

Tumba de Benito Juárez en el Panteón de San Fernando en la ciudad de México

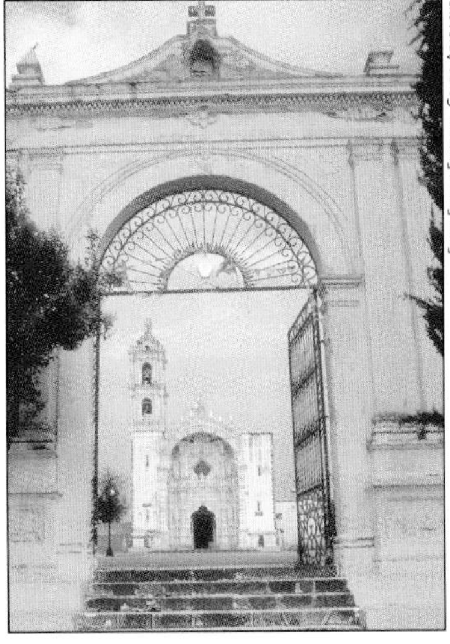

Foto: Fondo Editorial Grupo Azabache

Iglesia de San Nicolás de Neri en Panotla, Tlaxcala

amplió. En él fue sepultada con gran pompa la pierna de Antonio López de Santa Anna, la que en 1844 fue desenterrada por una multitud que la arrastró por toda la ciudad. El panteón fue clausurado al inaugurarse el panteón de Dolores, en 1875. Sus últimos vestigios, en las calles de Riva Palacio y Moctezuma, desaparecieron al ampliarse el Paseo de la Reforma, en 1964.

Pantepec ◆ Municipio de Chiapas situado al norte de Tuxtla Gutiérrez y al noroeste de San Cristóbal de Las Casas. Superficie: 47.2 km². Habitantes: 7,061, de los cuales 1,894 forman la población económicamente activa. Hablan alguna lengua indígena 3,040 personas mayores de cinco años (zoque 2,913 y tzotzil 115).

Pantepec ◆ Municipio de Puebla situado en el norte del estado, al noreste de Huauchinango, en los límites con Hidalgo y Veracruz. Superficie: 216.88 km². Habitantes: 17,387, de los cuales 4,159 forman la población económicamente activa. Hablan alguna lengua indígena 6,848 personas mayores de cinco años (totonaco 4,747, otomí 1,924). Indígenas monolingües: 913.

Pantepec ◆ Río de Hidalgo, Puebla y Veracruz. Nace en la sierra Madre Oriental, en los límites entre esos tres estados; baja a la llanura del golfo y se une al río Vinazco para formar el Tuxpan.

Pánuco ◆ Río de Hidalgo, Querétaro, San Luis Potosí, Tamulipas y Veracruz. Nace como río Tula, en Hidalgo; en Querétaro se une al de San Juan y forma el Moctezuma; recibe al Extorax y en San Luis Potosí al Amajaque; al unirse con el Tempoal recibe el nombre de Pánuco y más adelante le tributa el Tamuín. Se une al Tamesí diez kilómetros antes de desembocar en el golfo de México, entre Tampico y Ciudad Madero, donde separa los estados de Tamaulipas y Veracruz. Su cuenca, de 85,000 km², es la principal de la vertiente del golfo de México y la tercera en el país. Por su escurrimiento medio anual, de 11,800 millones de metros cúbicos, es el sexto entre los ríos más caudalosos de México. Su longitud aproximada es de 510 kilómetros.

Pánuco ◆ Municipio de Veracruz situado en el extremo norte del estado, en los límites con Tamaulipas y San Luis Potosí. Superficie: 3,277.81 km². Habitantes: 93,414, de los cuales 25,012 forman la población económicamente activa. Hablan alguna lengua indígena 1,355 personas mayores de cinco años (náhuatl 855 y huasteco 371). Al año siguiente de la llegada de los conquistadores a Veracruz, el gobernador español de la isla de Jamaica, Francisco de Garay, envió dos expediciones a la desembocadura del río Pánuco, las que fueron vencidas por los indios. En 1520, el propio Garay desembarcó en el Pánuco; para contrarrestarlo, Cortés envió a Gonzálo de Sandoval, quien fundó la villa de San Esteban del Puerto. Poco después, los indios se sublevaron y Cortés tuvo que enviar un fuerza de 100 españoles y 8,000 tlaxcaltecas para someterlos. En 1528 se le concedió el gobierno de la provincia a Nuño de Guzmán. De Pánuco partieron las expediciones que poblaron el actual territorio de Tamulipas. El petróleo se comenzó a explotar industrialmente a fines del siglo XIX y la

Foto: Michael Calderwood

Río Pánuco, en Tampico

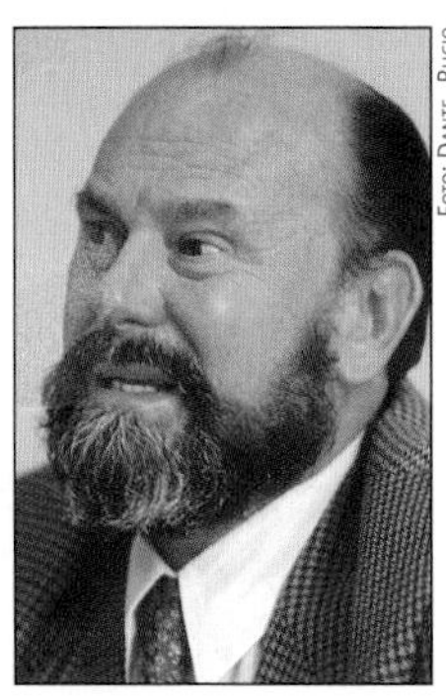
Foto: Dante Bucio

Francisco José Paoli Bolio

extracción indiscriminada provocó que, a mediados de los años ochenta del siglo XX, las propias autoridades tuvieran que reconocer que los daños ecológicos en las lagunas de Chairel y Chila, situadas al noreste del municipio, eran irreversibles.

PÁNUCO ◆ Municipio de Zacatecas situado al noreste de la capital de la entidad y contiguo a Fresnillo. Superficie: 336.5 km². Habitantes: 13,645, de los cuales 3,029 forman la población económicamente activa.

PÁNUCO ◆ Territorio independiente que fue gobernado por Nuño de Guzmán a partir de 1528 y que en 1533 se convirtió en provincia de la Nueva España. Ésta tuvo autoridad sobre numerosos corregimientos. A fines del siglo XVI, la parte occidental de la misma se convirtió en provincia de Valles y su región montañosa, en el sur, pasó a otra jurisdicción. En 1787 fue subdelegación de la intendencia de Veracruz.

PÁNUCO DE CORONADO ◆ Municipio de Durango situado en el centro de la entidad, al noreste de la capital del estado. Superficie: 1,059.9 km². Habitantes: 14,520, de los cuales 3,133 forman la población económicamente activa. Hablan alguna lengua indígena cinco personas mayores de cinco años. Su cabecera es Francisco I. Madero.

Foto: Fondo Editorial Grupo Azabache

Parroquia de San Esteban en Pánuco, Veracruz

PANZÓN PANSECO ◆ n. en Monterrey, NL, y m. en el DF (1910-1971). Nombre profesional del actor Arturo Ernesto Manrique Elizondo. Estudió en la Escuela de Ingeniería de San Luis Missouri (1930). En esa ciudad actuó ocasionalmente en la estación radiofónonica KMOK. Ya en la capital mexicana, trabajó sucesivamente en las emisoras XEB, XEQ y XEW, en las que destacó en papeles cómicos. Durante más de diez años formó pareja con el locutor Ramiro Gamboa. En la televisión apareció en varios programas, entre ellos: *El estudio de Pedro Vargas* y *El yate del Prado*. También se presentó en la televisión regiomontana. Se inició en el cine en 1933 con *La mujer del puerto*, de Arcady Boytler, y siguió con *¿Quién mató a Eva?*, *Jalisco nunca pierde* (1937), *Abnegación* (1937), *Los millones de Chaflán* (1938), *Canto a mi tierra* (1938), *El hijo de Cruz Diablo* (1941) y otras.

Foto: Héctor Herrera

Panzón Panseco

PAOLI BOLIO, FRANCISCO JOSÉ ◆ n. en Mérida, Yuc. (1941). Licenciado en derecho por la UIA (1960-64), maestro en sociología por la Universidad de Nueva York (1975) y doctor en ciencias sociales por la UIA (1982), en la que fue profesor (1968-78) y director de Sociología (1973-78). En la UAM ha sido profesor (1978-), director de Ciencias Sociales (1978-82), rector del plantel Xochimilco (1982-86) y abogado general (1988-). Miembro fundador del PMT (1974), mismo que abandonó en 1981, cuando esa organización se negó a fusionarse en el PSUM. Fue funcionario de la SCT (1965-67) y subcomisionado de Orientación Empresarial y Obrera del IMSS (1967-68). Ingresó al PAN en 1993. Ha sido miembro de la Asamblea de Representantes del Distrito Federal (1994-97) y dos veces diputado federal (1991-94 y 1997-2000). Colaborador de *Últimas Noticias* (1974-76), *Proceso* (1976-82), *La Jornada* (1985-) y otras publicaciones. Coautor de *¿Por qué un nuevo partido?* (1975) y *El socialismo olvidado de Yucatán* (1977). Autor de ensayo: *Las ciencias sociales* (1976), *Durkheim* (1980), *El cambio de presidente* (1981), *Ensayos de sociología y política* (1982), *Yucatán y los orígenes del nuevo Estado mexicano* (1984), *El modelo orgánico y el modelo Xochimilco* (1984), *Estado y sociedad en México 1917- 1984* (1985), *Salvador Alvarado* (1985) y *Memorial del futuro* (1996); novela: *Madrugando amanece* (1987); y poesía: *Amor disperso* (1968) y *Vuelta de sexenio, poemas políticos a la mexicana* (1975). Premio Latinoamericano de Ensayo en Ciencias Sociales, de editorial Siglo XXI (1978).

PAPÁ NABOR ◆ n. en Coalcomán de Vázquez Pallares, Mich. (1910). Su nombre verdadero es Nabor Cárdenas Mejorada. Fue ordenado sacerdote en 1935 y asignado a la parroquia de Carácuaro. En 1967 fue transferido a Puruarán, en la región de Tierra Caliente. Tras asistir a un seminario en Zamora acerca de las reformas del Concilio Vaticano II en 1973, abjuró de ellas. Al regresar a su parroquia, una campesina de nombre Gabina Romero aseguró que había tenido visiones de la Virgen del Rosario y que en ellas afirmaba que Cárdenas había de fundar una comunidad donde se le adorase, condenando las reformas del Vaticano y oficiando la misa en Latín. Desde entonces dirige la comunidad de La Nueva Jerusalén (☛), en Michoacán.

PAPAGAYO ◆ Río de Guerrero. Nace cerca del valle de Chilpancingo y desemboca en el Pacífico, luego de recibir los caudales de los ríos San Cristóbal, Coyuca y Omitlán. Abastece de agua potable al puerto de Acapulco.

PAPAGAYO ◆ ☛ *Tres Palos, laguna de.*

PAPAGAYOS, DE ◆ Sierra de Nuevo León. Forma parte de la sierra Madre Oriental. Está situada al este de Mon-

Foto: Michael Calderwood

Puente sobre el río Papagayo, Guerrero

terrey y al suroeste y sur de Cerralvo. Prolonga hacia el sureste la sierra de Picachos. La limita por el sur el río Pesquería.

PÁPAGOS ◆ Indios que habitan en los municipios de Puerto Peñasco, Altar, Caborca y Saric, en el noroeste de Sonora, y en las zonas desérticas de Arizona. Los grupos pápagos, aun divididos por la frontera, siguen manteniendo relaciones y conservan cierta unidad. En 1995, en el lado mexicano se registraron 132 hablantes de pápago, idioma que pertenece al grupo nahua-cuitlateco, tronco yutonahua, familia pimacora; la mayoría de los jóvenes pápagos hablan su lengua, inglés y español; han abandonado las vestimentas tradicionales y utilizan ropa de manufactura comercial, generalmente comprada en Estados Unidos. Se dan a sí mismos el nombre de *tono-ooh'tam*, que en su idioma significa "gente del desierto". Durante el estiaje, los pápagos emigran a poblaciones cercanas, donde se emplean como choferes, vaqueros, carpinteros o albañiles, labores que desempeñan tanto en poblaciones mexicanas como estadounidenses, aunque prefieren los empleos que consiguen del otro lado de la frontera por el pago en dólares. Las mujeres elaboran objetos de barro, de madera tallada, de chaquira y *coritas* o cestos de torote y ocotillo, que venden en la zona fronteriza. La unidad básica de su sociedad es la familia nuclear. El matrimonio es acordado por ambos contrayentes y la ceremonia se realiza dentro de la religión católica, que es la mayoritaria entre los miembros de esta etnia, que conserva también algunas de sus antiguas creencias, como la veneración de una deidad llamada "el hermano mayor", que rige la lluvia, el viento y los rayos. Los pápagos creen en brujos capaces de provocar el mal y en curanderos que son la contraparte de esos brujos. Cada una de sus seis comunidades tiene un representante que consulta a los demás para tomar decisiones, así como un gobernador y su suplente, que fungen como intermediarios entre el grupo y las autoridades municipales.

PAPALOAPAN ◆ Río de Puebla, Oaxaca y Veracruz. Tiene 540 kilómetros de longitud. Mide 200 metros en su parte más ancha. Se forma con dos corrientes: la primera nace en la sierra Juárez con el nombre de río Grande, al que afluyen los de las Vueltas, Apoala, San Pedro y Tomellín; la segunda se origina en el valle de Tehuacán y recibe a los ríos Zapotitlán, Hondo y Jiquila. Ambas corrientes se unen antes de cruzar la sierra Madre de Oaxaca y toman el nombre de Quiotepec; este río recibe al Usila y al del Valle Nacional y se convierte en el Papaloapan, que se alimenta con el Tonto y el San Juan antes de desembocar en el golfo de México. Su cuenca abarca 46,500 km^2. Tiene un escurrimiento medio anual de 47,000 millones de metros cúbicos, que lo hacen el segundo río más caudaloso del país.

PAPALOTLA ◆ Municipio del Estado de México que limita con Texcoco, Chiautla y Tepetlaoxtoc. Superficie: 8.74 km^2. Habitantes: 2,998, de los cuales 673 forman la población económicamente activa.

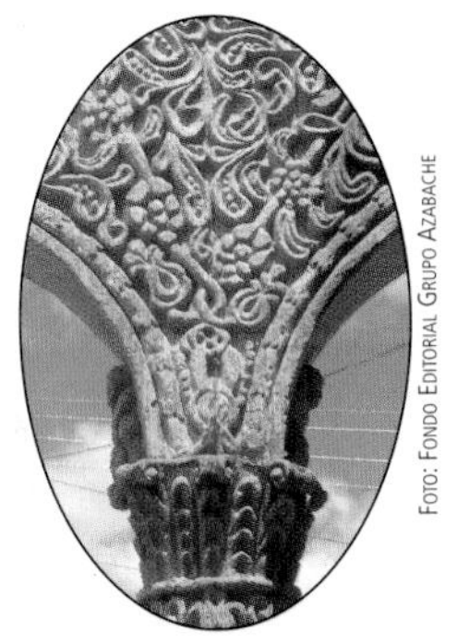

Foto: Fondo Editorial Grupo Azabache

Arcadas reales del siglo XVIII, en Papalotla, Estado de México

PAPALOTLA DE XICOHTÉNCATL ◆ Cabecera del municipio Xicohténcatl (☛).

PAPANOA ◆ Morro o saliente acantilada de Guerrero, formada por las estribaciones meridionales de la sierra Madre del Sur. Cierra por el sur la bahía de Tequepa.

PAPANTLA ◆ Municipio costero de Veracruz situado al sur de Tuxpan, en los límites con Puebla, y contiguo a Poza Rica, Gutiérrez Zamora y Teco-

Foto: Boris de Swan

Río Papaloapan, en Veracruz

Voladores de Papantla, en Veracruz

lutla. Superficie: 1,199.26 km². Habitantes: 171,167, de los cuales 42,449 forman la población económicamente activa. Hablan alguna lengua indígena 39,292 personas mayores de cinco años (totonaco 38,408, náhuatl 653 y otomí 127). Indígenas monolingües: 958. El municipio se halla en una zona de extracción de hidrocarburos y cuenta con campos petroleros como el Presidente Alemán y El Escollín. Destaca por su producción de vainilla, que se exporta casi en su totalidad. La fiesta más importante es la de Corpus Christhi, que se celebra a fines de mayo y principios de junio. El atractivo principal de la fiesta, es el baile de los "voladores". En la jurisdicción se halla la zona arqueológica del Tajín, en la zona llamada Totonacapan Septentrional. Las ruinas fueron descubiertas en 1785 y su exploración, todavía inconclusa, se inició en 1935 dirigida por Agustín García Vega. Lo conocido hasta ahora revela construcciones monumentales posiblemente de la cultura totonaca. Se estima que la ciudad del Tajín, con elementos arquitectónicos similares a los mayas y mexicas, data de los siglos IX y XIII. Los monumentos más importantes son: la pirámide de Tajín (nombre de la deidad totonaca de la lluvia, el trueno y el rayo) o pirámide de los Nichos (que tiene 365 de ellos), tres juegos de pelota decorados con bajorrelieves, la Plaza del Arroyo, diversas bóvedas y el edificio de las Columnas. La fundación de Papantla data del siglo XIII y fue obra de dos grupos de totonacos, procedentes unos de El Tajín y otros de la sierra de Puebla, acosados por los chichimecas. Se incluyó en la confederación de pueblos del Totonacapan, dependió de Tuzapan y fue tributaria del imperio mexica. Durante la colonia, la ciudad fue capital de la provincia de Papantla, que ocupaba la parte central de Veracruz (dependiente de la provincia de Hueytlalpan). Hacia 1600 se hizo independiente y en 1787 se convirtió en subdelegación de la intendencia de Veracruz. En 1910, la cabecera municipal, entonces villa, fue llamada Papantla de Hidalgo y en 1935 adoptó el nombre de Papantla de Olarte, en honor de Serafín Olarte, héroe local de la insurgencia. La cabecera municipal es también sede de la diócesis católica de Papantla, erigida en 1922 por Pío XI.

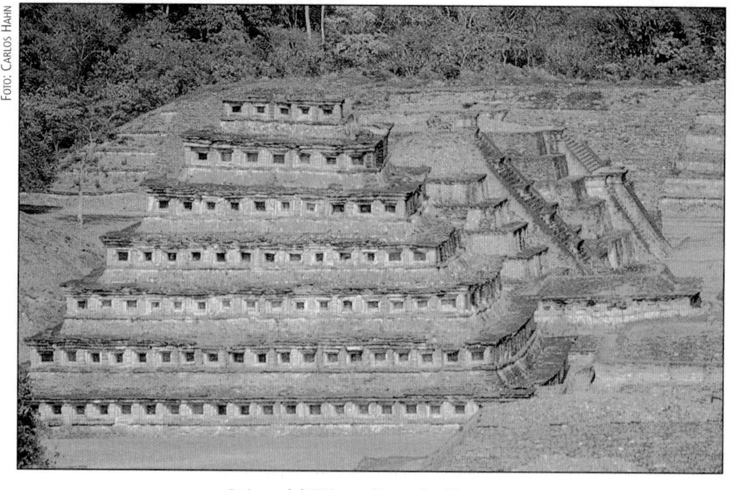

Ruinas del Tajín en Papantla, Veracruz

PAPASQUIARO ◆ ☛ *Santiago Papasquiaro.*

PAPAZTAC ◆ Deidad nahua, uno de los 400 dioses de los borrachos. Fue uno de los seis inventores del pulque, en el lugar de Tamoanchan.

PAPE, SUZANNE LOU ◆ n. en Francia y m. en Monclova, Coah. (1897-1988). Trabajó en su juventud como diseñadora de modas. En 1931, a la muerte de su primer esposo, el piloto Paul André Chiconeau, obtuvo una licencia de piloto y realizó el primer vuelo tripulado por una mujer de París a Casablanca. En 1934 se casó con el ingeniero Harold R. Pape, a quien se le encargó viajar a México para supervisar la construcción de la planta de Altos Hornos de México en Monclova. Ya establecidos allí, los Pape fundaron en 1942 un hospital infantil e hicieron numerosas obras de beneficencia a lo largo de casi 40 años; algunas de las más importantes, como el Museo Pape (1977) o el Parque Xochipilli (1988), fueron emprendidas después de la muerte de Harold Pape en 1972. Pintora, Suzanne Lou Pape expuso su obra plástica en Monclova y otras ciudades de México.

PAPEL ◆ Hacia el siglo XXV a.n.e., los egipcios iniciaron el procesamiento de fibras vegetales para producir papiro, un material del que podían hacerse hojas delgadas, ligeras y resistentes para escribir sobre ellas. El uso del papiro, palabra de la que se deriva el término papel, pasó a Europa durante la conquista de Egipto por los romanos. Al escasear la planta (*Cyperos papyrus*) que se procesaba para obtener ese primitivo papel, se empezó a usar el pergamino, que se elaboraba con pieles de ganado caprino y bovino. Entre los siglos X y XI los chinos iniciaron la producción de papel propiamente dicho mediante el desfibrado de materias celulósicas como la morera alba y el bambú. Gracias a los árabes, el procedimiento chino para elaborar papel fue conocido en Europa, inicialmente en España, entre los siglos

XI y XII. Los antiguos habitantes de Mesoamérica elaboraban papel a partir de fibras de agave y de la corteza de la higuera silvestre o amate, árbol del género *Ficus*, del que existen en México diversas variedades. Para obtener el amate (de *amatl*, papel en náhuatl), todavía en uso para la elaboración de pinturas *naïves* en Hidalgo, Puebla y Veracruz, se sigue un procedimiento semejante al empleado en la época prehispánica: la corteza se humedece y machaca hasta convertirla en una pasta, a la que se agrega algún tipo de goma que le da suficiente consistencia y permite laminarla. En algunas regiones se usan diversas sustancias para blanquear la pasta. Las hojas o láminas, una vez empleadas para la escritura, se doblaban en forma de biombo hasta formar libros que los conquistadores llamaron códices. Produjeron estos libros los mixteco-zapotecas, toltecas, nahuas, totonacas, huastecos y mayas. La fabricación de papel era una industria importante entre los nahuas: según el códice Mendocino, los señores mexicanos recibían anualmente, sólo de Amacoztitlán e Itzamatitlán, un tributo equivalente a 480,000 hojas tamaño doble folio. A lo anterior deben agregarse distintas cantidades procedentes de las tierras cálidas. Hans Lenz señala que la Matrícula de Tributos menciona que "16 pueblos daban cada seis meses 8,000 atados de papel, y que otros 26 pueblos tenían que proporcionar ocho mil rollos del mismo artículo por año". Los principales usos eran religiosos, decorativos, para ornamento de personas, objetos y casas, así como para elaborar algunas prendas de vestir. Se cree que su utilización para la escritura fue escasa en el México antiguo, pero esta apreciación puede deberse a mero desconocimiento, pues el interés de los frailes por imponer la nueva religión motivó la destrucción de templos, imágenes y documentos de las culturas precolombinas. Ante la falta de papel europeo, los evangelizadores debieron echar mano del amate para sus vocabularios, catecismos, imágenes religiosas y algunos

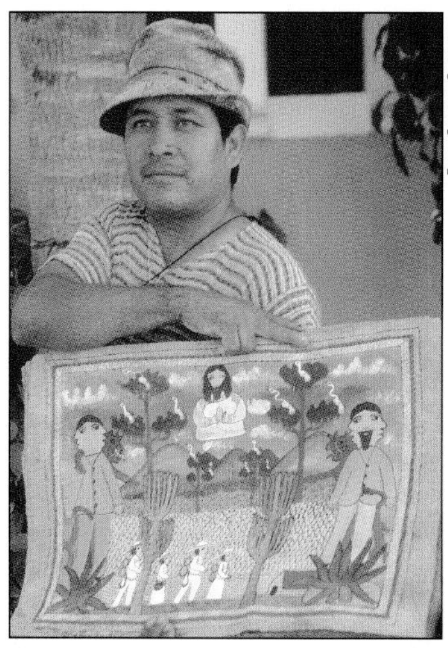

FOTO: CLAUDIO CONTRERAS

Vendedor de papel amate en Puerto Escondido, Oaxaca

manuscritos. Poco adecuado para la escritura alfabética, era en cambio muy útil para dibujar sobre él, de ahí que numerosos códices poscortesianos se hayan trabajado en papel de amate y ocasionalmente en papel de maguey. Sin embargo, como el papel europeo seguía siendo indispensable para las comunicaciones oficiales y otros oficios, en su primer viaje a España (1532-34) fray Juan de Zumárraga solicitó al Consejo de Indias que se permitiera su elaboración en Nueva España, reino para el que pidió también una imprenta. La llegada de ésta, en 1539 según la fecha oficial, incrementó la demanda de papel, producto que se importaba de la metrópoli. En 1580 fue instalada en Culhuacán la primera planta productora de papel europeo, con instrumentos traídos de España para fabricarlo mediante el viejo procedimiento chino. En 1630 existía un molino papelero en las márgenes del río Magdalena, al sur de la ciudad de México. Esta factoría se mantuvo en funcionamiento hasta el segundo tercio del siglo XVIII, pero muy probablemente producía sólo textiles. La tecnología de los batanes o plantas textileras era básicamente la misma que se requería para fabricar papel. No es descabellado suponer que de ahí salían las resmas necesarias para alimentar la nunca decaída elaboración clandestina de naipes. Henry Lepidus señala que "en las misiones jesuitas en México y en el resto de la América española se estableció un amplio y clandestino sistema de imprenta", para lo cual se trajeron de Alemania sacerdotes expertos en artes gráficas, los que seguramente se encargaron de producir el papel para alimentar sus prensas, al extremo, dice el mismo autor, de que "en el primer cuarto del siglo XVIII esta industria se hallaba en condiciones florecientes". Con procedimientos indígenas, hasta bien entrado el siglo XIX se mantuvo la producción artesanal de papel de envoltura. Las prohibiciones, la excesiva reglamentación y el nunca disimulado favoritismo por los productos que importaban los grandes comerciantes desde Sevilla, impidieron el desarrollo de una industria papelera en la Nueva

FOTO: FONDO EDITORIAL GRUPO AZABACHE

Fábrica de papel San Rafael

FOTO: JORGE CONTRERAS CHACEL

Altar de papel picado, obra de Humberto Spíndola

España. Por todo esto, a lo largo del virreinato el papel fue escaso y de alto precio, problema que se agudizaba cuando las flotas llegaban con mayor retardo. En el siglo XVIII se acentuó la escasez y el precio se elevó desproporcionadamente. La *Gaceta* de Francisco Sahagún de Arévalo, en su número de diciembre de 1739, anunciaba que suspendería su publicación porque "cortó la afilada tixera de la carestía del papel el hilo de las noticias". La falta de papel y el control burocrático sobre su utilización contribuyeron a que la imprenta no se extendiera por el país. Hasta el último cuarto del siglo XVIII, la actividad tipográfica se concentró en la capital novohispana. En 1812, José Joaquín Fernández de Lizardi denunciaba que entre las múltiples prohibiciones impuestas por la Corona española estaba la de fabricar papel. A mediados de 1823, José Manuel Zozaya Bermúdez, quien se había desempeñado como representante del imperio de Iturbide en Washington, regresó a la capital mexicana e inició los trabajos para instalar una papelera en Tizapán, también junto al río Magdalena, para lo cual trajo técnicos y maquinaria de Estados Unidos. A lo largo del siglo XIX se fundaron en el país varias factorías, casi todas con maquinaria estadounidense, las que producían papeles para envoltura, impresión y escritorio. En 1840 había cuatro en el Distrito Federal (Belén, Loreto, Santa Teresa y Peña Pobre), dos en Puebla, una en Orizaba (Cocolapan) y dos en Jalisco: una en Tapalpa y otra, El Batán, en Zapopan. Los batanes tomaron su nombre de las máquinas, generalmente movidas por fuerza hidráulica, empleadas para machacar la materia prima y reordenar la fibra a modo de producir paños. En tales instalaciones era relativamente fácil elaborar papel mediante el mismo procedimiento que se seguía en la fabricación de telas. Hacia 1870 se abrió la fábrica de la hacienda de La Huerta, en Michoacán; más tarde surgieron otras en Tlaxcala y Querétaro. Todas ellas trabajaban en pequeña escala y aprovechaban papel viejo, desperdicio de las empresas textiles y trapo, que obtenían de las traperías, establecimientos de los cuales había, hacia 1880, una veintena en la ciudad de México, que entonces contaba con 12 fábricas. La mala calidad del papel mexicano hizo que, entre 1875 y 1878, se debatiera en el Congreso la conveniencia o no de importarlo libremente. Al término de la discusión se mantuvo el gravamen al producto extranjero. En 1878 se produjeron 2,000 toneladas de papel y para 1886 ese volumen llegó a 5,750. La primera empresa que dejó de usar el trapo como insumo principal fue la de San Rafael, inaugurada en 1892 en los bosques del Iztaccíhuatl, cuya madera servía para obtener la pulpa. En 1905, el alemán Alberto Lenz compró el antiguo molino de Loreto y montó la fábrica más moderna del país en ese tiempo. En 1924, el mismo Lenz compró las instalaciones de Peña Pobre y en 1929 fusionó ambas firmas, con el nombre de Fábricas de Papel de Loreto y Peña Pobre. En la misma época se puso en servicio la fábrica La Aurora (1925), en el estado de México, que en 1956 pasó a ser propiedad de la firma estadounidense Kimberly Clark, que se convirtió en Kimberly Clark de México en 1959. Esta empresa instaló otra fábrica en Orizaba, en 1968. En 1934, el diario capitalino *Excélsior* y luego también *La Prensa* y *El Universal* entraron en conflicto con la empresa San Rafael, tradicionalmente encargada de suministrar el papel para las rotativas. Los editores de esos cotidianos señalaban que "el alto precio era la causa del lento e inarmónico crecimiento del periodismo nacional, de la retrogradación de la industria librera, del estancamiento de las artes gráficas y constituía un estorbo a la propagación de la cultura". Por todo esto, pedían al gobierno que le permitiera importar libremente papel, lo que no concedieron las autoridades. En cambio, el 21 de agosto de 1935, el presidente Lázaro Cárdenas acordó la creación de la empresa de participación estatal mayoritaria a la que se llamó Productora e Importadora de Papel, Sociedad Anónima (PIPSA), que tendría la finalidad de garantizar el abastecimiento de papel periódico a precios estables, función reguladora que ejercería durante 30 años. Contó con un subsidio cuyo monto era igual a la cantidad de divisas que exigía la importación del producto. El 11 de septiembre de ese año quedó constituida la empresa. Entre los miembros del primer Consejo de Administración figuraron Jesús Silva Herzog, Gustavo Espinosa Mireles (primer gerente de la empresa), Froylán Manjarrez, Rodrigo de Llano y Francisco Sayrols, quienes representaban al gobierno federal y a los editores. PIPSA ejerce el monopolio de la producción, importación y suministro del principal insumo de los periódicos y libros de texto gratuitos. Las empresas productoras de otros tipos de papel se hallan afiliadas a la Cámara Nacional de la Industria de la Celulosa y el Papel. En 1952, la firma estadounidense Scott Paper instaló una sucursal mexicana en Ecatepec: la Compañía Industrial de San Cristóbal. En 1965, a petición de la Cámara Nacional de Industria Editorial, el presidente Gustavo Díaz Ordaz acordó prorrogar 30 años más la duración de la sociedad anónima que era PIPSA. Sin embargo, ante las acusaciones de la Sociedad Interamericana de Prensa, de que su carácter de monopolio atentaba contra la libertad de expresión, el presidente Gustavo Díaz Ordaz decretó su liquidación, proceso que se inició el 1 de abril. Nuevamente, los editores de diarios y la Cámara de la Industria Editorial pidieron al Ejecutivo Federal que reconsiderara su decisión, lo que lograron en abril de 1970. En 1969 había en el país 45 fábricas y se producían 400 variedades de papel y cartón. En cuanto al papel periódico, en ese año la producción sólo satisfacía 15 por ciento de la demanda. Como apoyo a la industria papelera, desde 1952 se han instalado diversas plantas de fabricación de celulosa, como Celulosa de Chihuahua, aunque en 1968 aún se importaba más de 12 por ciento de ella. Una crisis mundial de la industria del papel elevó considerablemente los precios en 1973. A partir de entonces se ha procurado la autosuficiencia de México en este ramo. En 1980, PIPSA contabilizó activos totales por 2,859.4 millones de pesos y ventas por 4,088 millones. Al año siguiente, el Distrito Federal consumía 82.58 del papel periódico, Nuevo León 5.14 por ciento, Jalisco 2.31, Coahuila 1.93, Chihuahua 1.54, Yucatán 1.29 y Tamaulipas 1.28 por ciento. A finales de los años setenta se inició una serie de alzas en el precio del papel periódico: en mayo de 1979 aumentó 25 por ciento, en julio de 1980 otro 25 por ciento y en abril de 1981, 85 por ciento. En 1983 la industria papelera ocupaba a 32 mil personas, pero importaba 145,675 toneladas métricas de papeles diversos, en tanto que la producción interna total fue de 2,061,791 toneladas métricas, de las cuales correspondieron a periódicos y libros de texto 197 mil toneladas métricas. En el mismo año, la producción nacional de celulosa fue de 759,480 toneladas y se importaron 480,000 toneladas de materiales fibrosos. Las tres entidades con mayor producción de celulosa fueron, también en 1983, el Estado de México, con 21.4 por ciento del total nacional; Veracruz, con 18.4 por ciento; y Chihuahua, con 14.9 por ciento. En 1984 existía capacidad instalada para producir 3,194,000 toneladas métricas de papel y el consumo per cápita era de 36 kilos anuales. En ese año el director de PIPSA anunció que México era autosuficiente en papel periódico y que sólo se importaba una mínima parte para impresión en rotograbado y el destinado a directorios telefónicos (45 mil toneladas entre ambos). En 1984 había en el país 69 plantas productoras de celulosa y papel, de las cuales el Estado de México contaba con 25, el Distrito Federal con 11, Veracruz con cinco, Jalisco, Nuevo León y Tlaxcala con cuatro cada uno; Chihuahua, Michoacán, Oaxaca, Puebla, Querétaro y San Luis Potosí con dos; Baja California Norte, Durango, Guerrero y Morelos con una. Tres de estas fábricas, todas de PIPSA, producían papel periódico: Productora Nacional de Papel Destintado, en Villa de Reyes, San Luis Potosí, que recicla periódico viejo, en su mayoría importado; Fábricas de Papel Tuxtepec, en Tuxtepec, Oaxaca; y Mexicana de Papel Periódico, en Tres Valles, Veracruz, que emplea bagazo de caña como materia prima. En 1990, el gobierno mexicano anunció su intención de deshacerse de PIPSA, pero a petición de los editores, nuevamente se dio marcha atrás y se autorizó a los diarios que así lo requerían importar directamente su papel. En 1988 el consumo per cápita de papel en México fue de 30.0 kilos. En 1998, por acuerdo de la SHCP, se autorizó la desincorporación de PIPSA, la cual paso a manos del Grupo Industrial Durango.

PAPEL SELLADO ◆ Por cédula real del 28 de diciembre de 1638, se estableció su uso en México a partir del 1 de enero de 1640. Es el antecedente de los timbres fiscales y era obligatorio en los documentos que señalaban las ordenanzas, especialmente en contratos, escrituras de propiedad y certificados de transferencia de bienes. Durante la colonia era enviado de España. En el México independiente, el 6 de octubre de 1823, se reglamentó su empleo y por ley del 4 de agosto de 1824 se consignó su administración a los estados, que debían normar su utilización. El 3 de octubre de 1835 volvió esta renta al gobierno central, que el 23 de noviembre de 1836 emitió reglas para su administración y manejo. A principios del siglo XX se había suprimido su empleo en todo el país.

PAPIGOCHIC ◆ ☛ *Aros*.

PAPIROLAS ◆ n. en Tapachula, Chis. (1917). Su verdadero nombre es Juan de Dios Villegas Escobar. Fue miembro de los "camisas rojas" de Tomás Garrido Canabal. Emigrado a la ciudad de México, desempeñó varios oficios y se dedicó a trabajar el *origami* (figuras elaboradas con papel doblado) a las que ha llamado *papirolas*, de ahí su apodo. Se ha presentado en televisión y una firma refresquera lo llevó a Japón. Ha visitado Brasil, Venezuela y 19 veces Nueva York. Los domingos suele presentarse en la Casa del Lago del bosque de Chapultepec.

PAPOROV, YURI ◆ n. en la URSS (1925). Escritor y Diplomático. Causó baja en el Ejército Rojo después de la segunda guerra mundial. Viajó en 1949 a Argentina, donde trabajó en la embajada soviética y destacó como volibolista *amateur*, hasta el punto de que Eva Perón le propuso desertar para que jugara en la selección nacional de ese deporte. Al conocerse este hecho, se le envió a México, donde fue agregado cultural de la embajada soviética (1953-56). De vuelta en la URSS, se dedicó al periodismo y fue director de la revista *Novedades de Moscú* (1961-64). Enviado a Cuba como director de la agencia

FOTO: CARLOS HAHN

Papel picado

Novosti, cayó en desgracia al creérsele amigo del poeta disidente Heberto Padilla y fue devuelto, una vez más, a la URSS. Emigró a México en 1990. Autor de la ópera *Adelita* y de los libros *Hemingway en Cuba*, *Confesiones de Diego Rivera y David Alfaro Siqueiros*, *Trotsky leyendo a Descartes* y *Frida nació dos veces*, escritos en español.

PAPÚA-NUEVA GUINEA, ESTADO INDEPENDIENTE DE ◆ Estado de Oceanía situado al norte de Australia. Comprende la mitad oriental de la isla de Nueva Guinea, el archipiélago Bismarck, las islas del Almirantazgo, Trobriand y D'Entrecasteaux, el archipiélago de las Luisíadas y las más septentrionales de las islas Salomón. Tiene costas al norte y al este en el océano Pacífico, y al sur en el mar del Coral y el estrecho de Torres. Limita al oeste con Indonesia. Superficie: 462,840 km². Habitantes: 4,600,000 (1998), 193,242 de los cuales vivían en la capital, Port Moresby. Del total de la población sólo 40,000 personas son de origen europeo; el resto pertenecen a los grupos originales del país: papúes, micronesios, polinesios y negritos. El idioma oficial es el inglés, aunque sobreviven más de 700 lenguas locales y se emplea corrientemente una variante dialectal del inglés. *Historia:* en 1526 el portugués Jorge de Meneses llegó accidentalmente a la isla y la llamó Papúa, por la palabra malaya que describe el peinado de los isleños. En 1537, Juan de Grijalva fue derrotado por los papúes. En 1545, el español Íñigo Ortiz de Rétez la bautizó Nueva Guinea, pues encontró cierto parecido de los isleños con los pobladores de Guinea, en África. En 1884 Alemania declaró su protectorado sobre el sector noreste de Nueva Guinea, en tanto que Inglaterra hizo lo propio con la porción sureste; en 1886, el Reino Unido se anexó el sector que era su protectorado; en 1899, Alemania asumió el control directo sobre su protectorado, que llamó Nueva Guinea Alemana. Siete años más tarde, en 1906 la Nueva Guinea Británica pasó a depender de Australia, con el nombre de Territorio de Papúa. En 1914, al inicio de la primera guerra mundial, los australianos ocuparon la Nueva Guinea Alemana, seis años después Australia recibió de la Sociedad de Naciones la ex colonia alemana, en calidad de mandato. Durante la segunda guerra mundial, el ejército japonés ocupó casi la totalidad de la isla. En 1949, Australia obtuvo el derecho para la administración de ambos territorios y dos años después se instituyó un régimen autónomo para el territorio de Papúa-Nueva Guinea. En 1963 el Consejo Legislativo fue sustituido por la asamblea. En 1973 Papúa-Nueva Guinea obtuvo la autonomía interna total, pero Australia conservó el control sobre la defensa y las relaciones internacionales. Tres años después, en 1975, el país consiguió la independencia completa, dentro de la Comunidad Británica, y la asamblea se convirtió en el Parlamento Nacional. En 1976, los gobiernos de México y Papúa-Nueva Guinea establecieron relaciones diplomáticas, elevadas a rango de embajadas al año siguiente. Sus embajadores en Washington son concurrentes en México y los representantes mexicanos en Australia se encargan de los asuntos en aquella nación.

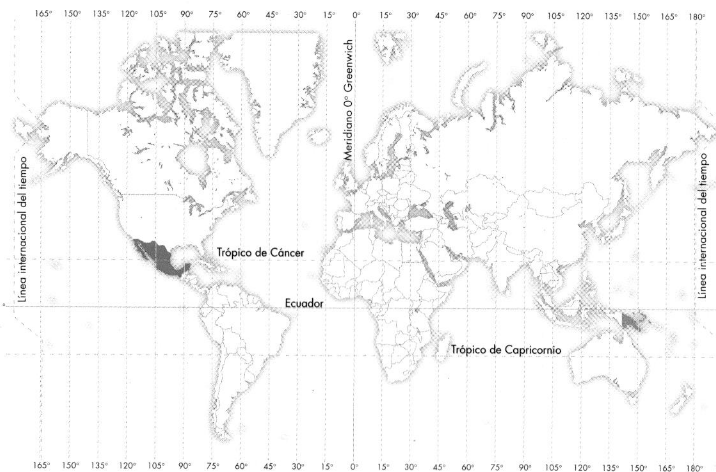

Estado Independiente de Papúa-Nueva Guinea

PAQUISTÁN, REPÚBLICA ISLÁMICA DEL ◆ Nación situada en la parte central de Asia. Limita con Afganistán, China, India e Irán. Tiene costas en el mar Arábigo. Superficie: 803.943 km². (sin incluir Jammu y Cachemira, en disputa con el gobierno indio). Habitantes: 148,166,000 en 1998. Su capital es Islamabad (204,364 habitantes en 1981). El idioma oficial es el urdú, aun-

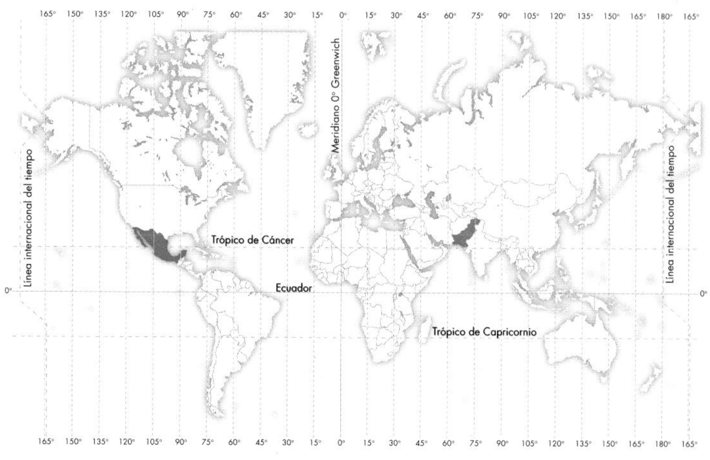

República Islámica de Paquistán

que también se hablan inglés, pendjabi, sindhi, pushtu y beluchi. *Historia:* en el siglo XIX la Compañía Británica de India Oriental se apoderó de los emiratos de Sind, Hyderabad y Khairpur y en 1857 fueron sometidos a la soberanía británica los territorios del noroeste. En 1895, sin embargo, los patanos iniciaron contra los colonialistas una guerra a la que llamaron *santa*. En 1906, a raíz de la partición de Bengala, se formó la Liga Musulmana que desde 1934, al mando de Mohammed Alí Jinnah, se propuso conseguir la autonomía de las regiones hindúes con mayoría islámica. Con la independencia de la India, el problema religioso se agudizó, a pesar de que, en 1947, Bengala y Pendjab se separaron del nuevo Estado indio y formaron Paquistán, que formaba de hecho dos entidades distintas, a ambos extremos de la península del Indostán. La definición de las fronteras, sobre todo la partición del Pendjab, provocó luchas entre musulmanes, hindúes y sijs. En 1948 se produjeron choques indio-paquistaníes en Cachemira, luego de que el rey de esa región decidió la incorporación de su territorio a la India. En 1955, México fue invitado por la ONU para formar parte de la Comisión de Tregua entre la India y Paquistán. En el mismo año se establecieron relaciones diplomáticas entre este país y México. En 1956, las provincias de Sind, Pendjab, Beluchistán y los territorios de la frontera del noroeste formaron Paquistán Occidental, mientras en Bengala, al noreste de la India, se formó Paquistán Oriental. Una nueva Constitución estableció la República Islámica incorporada a la Comunidad Británica de Naciones. Los ejércitos indio y paquistaní volvieron a enfrentarse entre 1965 y 1966, por la posesión de los territorios de Rann of Kutch y Cachemira. En 1970, Islamabad se convirtió en la capital de Paquistán Occidental. Al año siguiente, la India invadió Paquistán Oriental y derrotó a las tropas paquistaníes. Poco después, Paquistán Oriental proclamó la independencia y se convirtió en Bangladesh (☛). La porción occidental del Estado abandonó la Comunidad Británica y en 1972 promulgó una nueva Constitución que establece la República Federal. En 1974 fueron nacionalizados los bancos y la industria pesada, a la vez que se restablecieron el comercio y las comunicaciones con India. La independencia de Bangladesh fue reconocida por Paquistán en 1975. En 1979, luego de ser depuesto por un cuartelazo, el presidente Zulfiqar Alí Bhutto fue ejecutado. Desde entonces se estableció una dictadura ultraderechista, que islamizó toda la vida paquistaní y sirvió de base de operaciones a las fuerzas de la resistencia afgana. En 1988, el dictador Muhammad Zia ul-Haq murió en un accidente de aviación y en ese año se realizaron elecciones, en las que triunfó Benazir Bhutto, hija de Zulfiqar Alí. En 1995 fue asesinado a tiros Iqbal Masih, adolescente que criticó constante y duramente la explotación de la mano de obra infantil en Paquistán.

PAQUITA LA DEL BARRIO ◆ n. en Alto Lucero, Ver. (1947). Nombre profesional de la cantante Francisca Viveros Barradas. Llegó al DF en 1970 y con su media hermana, Viola Dorantes, formó el dueto Las Costeñitas, llamado posteriormente Las Golondrinas, que se disolvió en 1976 al serle ofrecido a Viola un contrato para cantar en Sudamérica. A partir de entonces *Paquita* se dedicó a cantar sola. En 1977 inauguró Casa Paquita, un pequeño restaurante en la colonia Guerrero en el que cantaba para los clientes. Allí fue "descubierta" en 1986 por Guillermo Ochoa, quien la presentó en el programa televisivo *Hoy Mismo*. Famosa por la gran emoción y agresividad de sus interpretaciones, se ha presentado en numerosos foros de América y Europa, además de continuar en su propio local, y ha grabado varios discos. Gusta de interpretar canciones en contra del machismo y ha popularizado la frase: "¿Me estás oyendo, inútil?".

FOTO: DANTE BUCIO

Paquita la del Barrio

PARACHO ◆ Municipio de Michoacán situado al sureste de Zamora, al este de Pátzcuaro y contiguo a Uruapan. Superficie: 278.05 km². Habitantes: 30,747, de los cuales 7,800 forman la población económicamente activa. Hablan alguna lengua indígena 10,465 personas mayores de cinco años (purépecha, 10,448). Indígenas monolingües: 481. La localidad es conocida por su producción de guitarras, que a mediados de los años ochenta era la principal fuente de traba-

FOTO: BORIS DE SWAN

Fabricantes de guitarras de Paracho, Michoacán

jo de 1,200 familias. La cabecera municipal es Paracho de Verduzco.

PARÁCUARO ◆ Municipio de Michoacán contiguo a Uruapan y Apatzingán. Superficie: 369.88 km². Habitantes: 23,237, de los cuales 5,205 forman la población económicamente activa. Hablan alguna lengua indígena 43 personas mayores de cinco años (purépecha 37). Su cabecera es Parácuaro de Morelos. El municipio destaca por su producción artesanal. En 1913 se emitió en esta localidad el Plan de Parácuaro, firmado por Cenobio Moreno, Daniel Pacheco, Carlos León, Rafael Garibay y Nicasio Villaseñor, entre otros, por medio del cual se condenaba el asesinato del presidente Francisco I. Madero y del vicepresidente José María Pino Suárez, se desconocía a Victoriano Huerta y se apoyaba el movimiento iniciado por Venustiano Carranza.

PARÁCUARO ◆ Población del municipio de Acámbaro, Guanajuato.

PARADA ARIAS, BONIFACIO EFRÉN ◆ n. en el DF (1943). Ingeniero bioquímico (1965) y maestro en ciencias por el IPN (1975) y doctor en tecnología de alimentos por la Universidad Politécnica de Valencia, España (1991). Ha sido subdirector de Investigación Tecnológica del Conacyt (1980-83), coordinador internacional del subprograma de Tratamiento y Conservación de Alimentos (1983-98) y secretario adjunto del Programa Iberoamericano de Ciencia y Tecnología para el Desarrollo (1998-). En el IPN fue jefe del Departamento de Graduados e Investigación en Alimentos (1972-77), director de la Escuela Nacional de Ciencias Biológicas (1977-80), director fundador de la Unidad Profesional Interdisciplinaria de Biotecnología (1987-93) y subdirector de apoyo del Instituto (1995). Fue jurado del Premio Nacional de Ciencias y Artes (1988 y 1993). Autor de 145 publicaciones en revistas especializadas del país y el extranjero. Consultor del Programa de las Naciones Unidas para el Desarrollo, el BID, los consejos nacionales de Ciencia y Tecnología de México y Ecuador, el Consejo Superior de Ciencia de Chile y la Secretaría de Ciencia y Técnica de Argentina. Presidente adjunto del International Life Sciences Institute, México. Premio Nacional al Mérito en Ciencia y Tecnología de Alimentos 1987. Premio Dr. Guillermo Soberón Acevedo al Mérito Ciudadano en Investigación Científica (1998). Miembro del SNI.

PARADA LEÓN, RICARDO ◆ n. en Lagos de Moreno, Jal., y m. en el DF (1902-1972). Dramaturgo. En 1923 se estrenó por primera vez una obra suya: *La agonía*. Fundador de la Unión de Autores Dramáticos y miembro del grupo de los Pirandellos. Fue director artístico de la Comedia Mexicana (1930) y subdirector de la Escuela de Teatro del Instituto Nacional de Bellas Artes (1947). Autor de *La esclava, El porvenir del doctor Gallardo, Vidas ajenas, Una noche de otoño, Sin alas, Camino real, Los culpables, Hacia la meta, La noche de agosto* y *El dolor de los demás*.

República de Paraguay

PARAGUAY, REPÚBLICA DE ◆ País situado en Sudamérica. Limita con Bolivia, Brasil y Argentina. Superficie: 406,752 km². Habitantes: 5,222,000 (1998) de los cuales la mayor parte son mestizos y cinco por ciento guaraníes. Su capital es Asunción, con una población estimada en 1992 de 502,426 habitantes (1,107,000 en el área metropolitana). El idioma oficial es el español, pero aún hay hablantes de guaraní. La moneda es el guaraní. *Historia:* el actual territorio paraguayo estuvo poblado, por lo menos desde del siglo XVI, por diversas tribus nómadas del grupo tupí-guaraní, especialmente carios y chiriguanos, que fueron llamados guaraníes a la llegada de los europeos. En 1525, un explorador español que buscaba un camino hacia los Andes, Alejo García, entró en contacto con los guaraníes, pero murió poco después sin haber penetrado en el territorio. Durante los 10 años siguientes, los conquistadores realizaron algunas expediciones por los ríos Paraná y Paraguay, pero no consiguieron asentarse. En 1537, Domingo Martínez de Irala y Pedro de Mendoza fundaron el fuerte de Nuestra Señora de la Asunción, a orillas del río Paraguay, y desde ahí iniciaron la conquista del territorio. Álvar Núñez Cabeza de Vaca, quien había alcanzado fama y poder gracias a su viaje por el norte de la Nueva España, encabezó en 1542 uno de los intentos más importantes por alcanzar la mítica sierra de la Plata. Luego de su explicable fracaso, gobernó la provincia del Paraguay (1542-44). Después de medio siglo de bonanza, debida a su situación geográfica que la colocaba a medio camino entre Perú y el Atlántico, a fines del siglo XVI la actividad comercial de Asunción decayó, y su posición fue ocupada por el puerto de Buenos Aires. Desde los primeros años del siglo XVII, la Compañía de Jesús formó en el norte y el este de la provincia de Guaranía (creada en 1617), una serie de misiones de indios de carácter colectivista, que a principios del siglo XVIII agrupaban a cerca de 200,000. Las primeras de estas misiones tuvieron que enfrentarse a las invasiones de los portugueses, que durante todo el siglo XVII intentaron apoderarse del norte del actual Paraguay. En agosto de 1737, la *Gazeta de México* informaba que "en la missión de los Chiriguanos, a 16 de mayo del año pasado, estando diciendo Missa el P. Julián Lisardi, jesuita (...), le assaltaron los Indios Infieles de Ingre, y aviéndole preso y maniatado (después de aver cortado la Cabeza á la Milagrosa Imagen de Nuestra Señora de Tariquea, y reducido la Iglesia a cenizas) le assaetearon cruelmente con treinta y dos flechas". Más graves que el acoso de los indios insumisos fueron los repetidos intentos de los encomenderos por apoderarse de indios de las misiones, lo que finalmente consiguieron al decretarse la expulsión de los jesuitas de España y sus posesiones. En 1777, la gobernación de Paraguay pasó a depender del virreinato del Río de la Plata. En 1810, el gobernador Velazco encabezó un movimiento independentista contra España y contra Buenos Aires. Dos años después, Argentina reconoció la independencia paraguaya y en 1813 se constituyó la República, gobernada por dos cónsules: José Gaspar Rodríguez de Francia y Fulgencio Yegros. Rodríguez, más conocido como *el Doctor Francia*, gobernó despóticamente de 1814 a 1840, lapso en el que se opuso a la penetración de los capitales británicos, realizó una reforma agraria y prácticamente erradicó el analfabetismo. Cuatro años después de la muerte de Rodríguez de Francia, el poder quedó en manos de Carlos Antonio López (1844-62), quien inició un proceso de industrialización, también sin participación inglesa. En 1865, tres años después de la subida al poder de Francisco Solano López (1862-70), los ingleses consiguieron agrupar a los gobiernos de Argentina, Brasil y Uruguay en la Triple Alianza. En ese año, los tres países sudamericanos le declararon la guerra a Paraguay y, pese a la tenaz resistencia de la nación agredida, el poder militar y económico de la Triple Alianza se impuso en 1870. La invasión le costó al país más de 700,000 víctimas y casi toda la población masculina. Desde ese año, las inversiones inglesas y argentinas proliferaron. A pesar de que los gobiernos paraguayos posteriores a la guerra fueron impuestos por los vencedores, en septiembre de 1871 el presidente Benito Juárez le envió una carta al presidente Salvador Jovellanos, en la que afirmaba que el pueblo y el gobierno de México, "que conocen los esfuerzos del patriotismo paraguayo par darse un gobierno popular (...) celebran justamente la regeneración del Paraguay". Durante los últimos treinta años del siglo XIX y los primeros treinta del siglo XX, Paraguay vivió una época de inestabilidad política, en la que sobresalió la acción de los nuevos partidos políticos, el Liberal y el Colorado. A principios de los años treinta, el descubrimiento de petróleo en la región del Chaco hizo que se exacerbara la competencia entre la empresa angloholandesa Royal Dutch Shell, que controlaba los pozos paraguayos, y la estadounidense Standard Oil, que poseía los bolivianos. Por eso, instigados por ambas firmas, los gobiernos de Paraguay y Bolivia se enfrentaron en la guerra del Chaco (1932-35), que costó al país más de 50,000 habitantes. El gobierno de Lázaro Cárdenas participó en la Comisión de Conciliación que puso fin a la guerra. En 1936, mediante la Revolución de Febrero, Rafael Franco llegó a la Presidencia y desde ahí intentó realizar una reforma agraria. Sin embargo, un golpe militar lo derrocó al año siguiente. En 1940 se promulgó una Constitución centralista y de esa fecha hasta 1948 gobernó Higinio Morínigo, quien en 1943 visitó México. En 1954, Alfredo Stroessner encabezó un golpe de Estado, instauró un régimen autoritario y dio asilo a gran número de criminales de guerra nazis. En 1966, el presidente Gustavo Díaz Ordaz estableció un procedimiento de crédito recíproco con Paraguay. A partir de 1969, los conflictos entre la Iglesia católica y el gobierno de Stroessner se agudizaron, debido en parte a los reclamos de la jerarquía en favor del respeto a los derechos humanos. En 1971, el arzobispo de Asunción abandonó el asiento que le correspondía en el Consejo de Estado. La dictadura ocasionó que cerca de 200,000 paraguayos marcharan al exilio por razones políticas. De éstos, unos 800 vivían en México hacia 1974. En 1975, Stroessner hizo una visita oficial al presidente mexicano Luis Echeverría. Cuatro años más tarde, después del triunfo de la revolución sandinista en Nicaragua, el dictador Anastasio Somoza se refugió en Asunción, donde vivió hasta 1980, cuando fue ejecutado. A principios de 1989, Stroessner fue derrocado por un golpe militar y se refugió en Brasil. En 1993 fue elegido presidente Juan Carlos Wasmosy en el primer proceso democrático y pacífico de Paraguay.

Paraíso ♦ Municipio costero de Tabasco situado al noroeste de Villahermosa. Superficie: 577.55 km². Habitantes: 65,266, de los cuales 15,287 forman la población económicamente activa. Hablan alguna lengua indígena 101 personas mayores de cinco años (zapoteco 43).

Páramo, Roberto ♦ n. en Álamos, Son. (1944). Escritor. Suspendió la carrera de arquitectura para obtener la licenciatura en filosofía y letras de la

Foto: Fondo Editorial Grupo Azabache

Municipio de Paraíso, Tabasco

UNAM. Formó parte del taller literario de Juan José Arreola y dirigió la revista *Mester*. Fundó la revista *Retablo*, de la que fue secretario de redacción. Ha colaborado en *Espejo*, *Cuadernos del Viento*, *Revista de Bellas Artes* y *Letras potosinas*; y en los suplementos *El Heraldo Cultural*, del diario *El Heraldo de México*; y *La Cultura en México*, de la revista *Siempre!* Autor de los relatos: *La condición de los héroes* (1971), *El sol hace brillar las hojas*; y la novela: *El corazón en la mesa* (1981). Fue becario del Centro Mexicano de Escritores (1967-68).

Foto : Época

Juan José Páramo Díaz

PÁRAMO DÍAZ, JUAN JOSÉ ◆ n. en el DF (1935). Licenciado en derecho por la UNAM, de la que fue profesor (1967-68). Pertenece desde 1964 al PRI. Ha sido asesor del director general de Conasupo (1971-76); secretario técnico del Programa Nacional de Alimentación (1973-74), asesor del director general de Crédito (1974-77) y tesorero de la Federación en la Secretaría de Hacienda (1976-82); subsecretario de Programación y Presupuesto de Desarrollo Industrial y de Servicios de la SSP (1982-88), director general de Nafinsa (1988-91) y de la Aseguradora Hidalgo (1991-97).

PARANGARICUTIRO ◆ Población de Michoacán que en 1943 quedó sepultada por la lava y las cenizas del volcán Paricutín. Era cabecera del municipio del mismo nombre (☛ *Nuevo Parangaricutiro*).

Foto: Michael Calderwood

Parangaricutiro, Michoacán

Foto : Época

Joaquín Pardavé

PARÁS ◆ Municipio de Nuevo León situado al noreste de Monterrey, en los límites con Tamaulipas. Superficie: 992 km². Habitantes: 1,087, de los cuales 309 forman la población económicamente activa. Se impuso nombre al municipio en honor de José María Parás, primer gobernador constitucional del estado. A 30 kilómetros de la cabecera se encuentran las pinturas rupestres del Frontón de Piedras Pintas.

PARÁS, JOSÉ MARÍA ◆ n. en valle del Pilón, municipio de Montemorelos, y m. en Monterrey, NL (1794-1851). Diputado al primer Congreso Constituyente de Nuevo León (1825) y primer gobernador constitucional del estado (1825-27). Durante su gestión estableció la imprenta del gobierno donde se publicó la *Gazeta Constitucional*, primer periódico neoleonés; donde se organizaron las milicias locales, se habilitó el Seminario Conciliar de Monterrey como universidad y se dictó una Ley de Instrucción Pública que hacía gratuita y obligatoria la enseñanza primaria. Posteriormente fue diputado federal (1829-30), vicegobernador de su estado (1831) y varias veces alcalde de Montemorelos. En 1847 luchó contra la invasión estadounidense y luego de firmarse la paz con Estados Unidos, volvió a ocupar la gubernatura (1848-51).

PARCERO LÓPEZ, JOSÉ ◆ n. en el DF (1940). Arquitecto titulado en la UNAM (1965), donde fue profesor (1965-68). Ha sido subjefe del Plano Regulador de la Ciudad de México (1965), director general de la Habitación Popular del DDF (1973), coordinador en el valle de México del Infonavit (1977), director general de Tierras y Aguas (1978) y de Procedimientos Agrarios de la Secretaría de la Reforma Agraria (1980), coordinador general de la agrupación Colonos e Inquilinos del DF, de la Confederación Nacional de Organizaciones Populares del PRI (1981-82); diputado federal (1982-85), director de Renovación Habitacional Popular (1985-86) y titular de la Delegación Gustavo A. Madero (1994-96). En 1986 fue nombrado coordinador general del Programa para la Reorganización Inmobiliaria del Departamento del Distrito Federal. Autor de *La vivienda popular en México*, *Plan nacional agrario* e *Historia del desarrollo urbano en México*. Pertenece al Colegio de Arquitectos. En 1965 obtuvo el tercer lugar del Premio Anual de Arquitectura.

PARDAVÉ, JOAQUÍN ◆ n. en Pénjamo, Gto., y m. en el DF (1900-1955). Compositor, actor y director cinematográfico. Se inició en el teatro en 1917 con la obra *La banda de las trompetas* y en el cine en la película muda *Viaje redondo* (1919). Hizo pareja con Roberto Soto en el Teatro Lírico. En la revista musical *Tradiciones que perduran*, creó al personaje *Don Susanito Peñafiel y Somellera*, que se hizo popular con la película

México de mis recuerdos (1943). Actuó en cintas como *Águilas frente al sol* (1932), *Jalisco nunca pierde* (1937), *Cada loco con su tema* (1938), *Los millones de Chaflán* (1938), *La tía de las muchachas* (1938), *En tiempos de don Porfirio* (1939), *Al son de la marimba* (1940), *El jefe máximo* (1940), *Cuando los hijos se van* (1941), *¡Ay que tiempos, señor don Simón!* (1941), *Yo bailé con don Porfirio* (1942), *El sombrero de tres picos* (1943), *La reina de la opereta* (1945), *Una gallega en México* (1949), *Esos de Pénjamo* (1952) y *La virtud desnuda* (1955). Fue actor y libretista de *El ropavejero* (1946). Dirigió *Lágrimas de sangre* (1946), *Soy charro de rancho grande* (1947), *La barca de oro* (1947), *Sangre torera* (1949). *Amor vendido* (1950), *Arrabalera* (1950), *Magdalena* (1954), *Dios nos manda vivir* (1954) y *Secreto profesional* (1954). Dirigió y actuó en *El baisano Jalil* (1942), *Los hijos de don Venancio* (1944), *Los nietos de don Venancio* (1945), *El barchante Naguib* (1945), *Los viejos somos así* (1948), *Dos pesos dejada* (1949), *Primero soy mexicano* (1950), *El gendarme de la esquina* (1950), *Doña Mariquita de mi corazón* (1952) y *El casto Susano* (1952). Reapareció en el teatro con la opereta *Orfeo de los infiernos*. Entre sus canciones se cuentan *La Panchita*, *No hagas llorar a esa mujer*, *Falsa*, *Aburrido me voy*, *Caminito de la sierra*, *Ventanita morada*, *Negra consentida*, *Carmen* y *Varita de nardo*.

A lo mejor en silencio, óleo sobre masonite de Silvia Pardo

PARDO, EDMÉE ◆ n. en el DF (1965). Escritora. Su segundo apellido es Murray. Licenciada en sociología por la ENEP Acatlán (1988). Diplomada de la Escuela de Escritores de la SOGEM (1991). Ha sido colaboradora de *Sábado*, suplemento del diario *unomásuno* (1992-99), así como de *Estilo*, *Escala*, *Quehacer de maestras* y otras publicaciones. Fue fundadora de Ediciones Brujas (1992) y gerente de la editorial Tava (1993-95). Ha impartido talleres literarios y conducido programas de radio. Trabajos suyos se encuentran en las antologías *Periferia de Eros* (1991), *La luna del miel según Eva* (1996), *Dispersión multitudinaria* (1997) y *Antología de letras y dramaturgia. Jóvenes Creadores* (1998). Autora de cuento: *Pasajes* (1993) y *Lotería* (1995); novela: *Espiral* (1994), *El primo Javier* (1996) y *El sueño de los gatos* (1998); y el libro de varia invención *Rondas de cama y la madera de las cosas* (1999). Premio Nacional de Cuento Benemérito de América de la UABJO (1999). Ha sido becaria del Fonca (1995-96 y 1997-98).

PARDO, EMILIO ◆ n. en ¿Pachuca, Hgo.?, y m. en la ciudad de México (1850-1911). Licenciado en derecho por la Escuela Nacional de Jurisprudencia (1870), de la que fue profesor. Fue diputado federal (1878), ministro plenipotenciario de México en los Países Bajos (1902) y senador de la República (1911). Colaboró en *La Abeja* y coeditó *Foro*. Coautor, con Pablo Mercado, de un *Diccionario de derecho y administración*.

PARDO, REGINA ◆ n. en Veracruz, Ver. (1904). Pintora. Estudió en la Academia de San Alejandro de La Habana, en el City Park Art Museum de Nueva Orleans (1926-28) y en la Academia de San Carlos. Expuso por primera vez en 1945 en la ciudad de México. Ha sido profesora del Instituto Nacional de Bellas Artes e investigadora del Museo Nacional de Antropología.

PARDO, SILVIA ◆ n. en el DF (1941). Pintora. Estudió con José Suárez Olvera (1953-55), José Bardasano (1955-57) y con Arturo Rosenblueth (1962-67), así como en la Universidad Iberoamericana (1957). Ha expuesto en Estados Unidos. En 1953 obtuvo el tercer premio de un concurso convocado por la ONU. Ejecutó un mural en el vestíbulo del Senado de la República.

PARDO ASPE, EMILIO ◆ n. y m. en el DF (1889-1963). Estudió derecho en Bélgica, Francia y México. Fue director de la Escuela de Jurisprudencia de la UNAM (1935-38), donde modificó el plan de estudios. Ministro de la Suprema Corte de Justicia (1941-47), de la que se separó por razones de salud. Colaboró en la revista *Criminalia*. Autor de *Homenaje*, estudio dedicado a Eugenio Florián.

PARDO GARCÍA, GERMÁN ◆ n. en Colombia y m. en el DF (1902-1991). Poeta. Estudió en el Seminario de Nuestra Señora del Rosario de Bogotá. Vivió en México desde 1931. En 1959 fundó la revista literaria *Nivel*, que dirigió hasta su muerte. Autor de *Voluntad* (1930), *Los júbilos ilesos* (1933), *Los cánticos* (1935), *Sonetos del convite* (1935), *Poderíos* (1937), *Presencia* (1938), *Claro abismo* (1940), *Sacrificio* (1943), *Antología poética* (1944), *Las voces naturales* (1945), *Los sueños corpóreos* (1947), *Poemas contemporáneos* (1949), *Lucero sin orillas* (1952), *Acto poético* (1953), *U. Z. llama al espacio* (1954), *Eternidad del ruiseñor* (1956), *Hay piedras como lágrimas* (1957), *Centauro al sol* (1959), *La cruz del sur* (1960), *Osiris preludial* (1960), *Los ángeles de vidrio* (1962), *El cosmonauta* (1962), *El defensor* (1964), *Los relámpagos* (1965), *Labios nocturnos* (1965), *Elegía italiana* (1966), *Mural de España* (1966), *Himnos del hierofante* (1969), *Apolo Thermidor* (1971), *Escándalo* (1972), *Desnudez* (1973), *Iris pagano* (1973), *Mi perro y las estrellas* (1974), *Génesis* (1974), *El héroe* (1975), *Himnos de la noche* (1975), *Tempestad* (1980), *Apolo Pankrator* (obra reunida, 1985) y *Últimas odas* (1986). En 1974 recibió del gobierno colombiano la condecoración M. A. Caro al mérito cultural.

ARCHIVO GENERAL DE LA NACIÓN

Retrato y firma de Mariano Paredes y Arrillaga

PARDO SEGURA, PÁVEL ◆ n. en Guadalajara, Jal. (1976). Futbolista. Jugó como defensa lateral en el equipo Atlas de la Primera División, y en la misma posición con el América. Con la selección juvenil participó en los Juegos Olímpicos de Atlanta 1996 y con la selección nacional en las copas América de 1997 y 1999, el Mundial de Futbol de Francia de 1998 y la Copa Confederaciones.

PARDO SEMO, ANNIE ◆ n. en el DF (1940). Licenciada en biología (1960), maestra (1973) y doctora en bioquímica por la UNAM (1976). Profesora de la Facultad de Ciencias de la UNAM (1961-) y de la Universidad Washington de San Luis Misouri (1984). Ha sido investigadora del Instituto Nacional de la Investigación Científica (1965-67) y del Laboratorio de Microbiología de la Escuela Nacional de Ciencias Biológicas del IPN (1967-68); e investigadora del Instituto de Investigaciones Biomédicas (1974-76) y jefa de la División de Estudios de Posgrado de la Facultad de Ciencias (1986-) de la UNAM. Ha colaborado en publicaciones especializadas. Pertenece al Sistema Nacional de Investigadores desde 1984.

PARDO VILLA, FAUSTINO ◆ n. en España y m. en el DF (1925-1986). Sacerdote ordenado en 1952, en Roma. Perteneció a la orden de los legionarios de Cristo. Llegó a México en 1952 y dos años después abrió el Instituto Cumbres. En 1964 fundó la Universidad Anáhuac. También creó la Universidad del Mayab, en Mérida.

PARÉ QUELLET, LUISA ◆ n. en Quebec, Canadá (1943). Se tituló como etnóloga en la ENAH (1968). Autora del libro *Los pescadores de Chapala y la defensa de su lago* (1989). Ha colaborado en *El Machete, La Jornada Semanal* y otras publicaciones.

PAREDES, ALBERTO ◆ n. en Pachuca, Hgo. (1956). Poeta y crítico literario. Licenciado (1980), maestro (1987) y doctor en letras por la UNAM (1991), donde ejerce la docencia. Profesor visitante extranjero en la Universidad de São Paulo, Brasil (1995-97). Fue jefe de publicaciones y fundador de la editorial del gobierno de Querétaro (1986-87). Colaboró en el *Diccionario de mexicanismos* de la Academia Mexicana. Fue asistente editorial de *México en el Arte*. Ha colaborado en *Páginas, México Indígena, Vuelta, Proceso, Revista de la Universidad, Anuario de Letras, La Jornada* y *unomásuno*. Miembro del SNI. Editor-compilador de *Notas sin música* de Juan Vicente Melo (1990) y *Personajes, celebraciones y lugares de la Huasteca hidalguense* (1995). Autor de ensayo: *Manual de técnicas narrativas. Las voces del relato* (1987 y 1993), *Abismos de papel: los cuentos de Julio Cortázar* (1988), *Figuras de la letra. Fichero personal sobre narradores mexicanos* (1990), *Una historia de imágenes: XIV estaciones para llegar a Paradiso* (coordinador y coautor, 1995), *Haz de palabras (ocho poetas mexicanos recientes)* (coordinador y coautor, 1999), *La poesía de cada día: un viaje al modernismo brasileño* (en prensa) y *Una semana en São Paulo*; poesía: *Derelictos* (1986 y 1992); y prosa *La edad de la mirada. Autorretratos* (en prensa).

PAREDES Y ARRILLAGA, MARIANO ◆ n. y m. en la ciudad de México (1797-1849). Militar. Ingresó en el ejército realista en 1812 y combatió a los insurgentes. Es posible que sea el Mariano Paredes y Arrillaga juzgado en 1809 en la ciudad de México por criticar a Fernando VII y condenado al destierro en España; este rastro se pierde en Perote, donde esperaba ser trasladado a Europa. En 1821 se unió al Ejército Trigarante. En 1823 se adhirió al Plan de Casa Mata y participó en la sublevación que derrocó al emperador Agustín de Iturbide. En diciembre de 1829, cuando era comandante militar de Guadalajara, apoyó el golpe de Estado de Anastasio Bustamante y combatió a las fuerzas del presidente Vicente Guerrero. Fue ascendido a general de brigada en 1832. En 1839 reprimió un levantamiento liberal en Jalisco. En Guadalajara, en agosto de 1841, proclamó el Plan de Progreso, en el que reclamaba al presidente Bustamante no haber intentado la reconquista de Texas; al triunfo de la rebelión (luego de la sublevación de Antonio López de Santa Anna en Veracruz) se encargó del gobierno de Jalisco (del 3 de noviembre de 1841 al 28 de enero de 1843). En noviembre 1844 acaudilló el alzamiento de la guarnición de Guadalajara contra Santa Anna y en favor de una reforma a las Bases Orgánicas. Derrotó a las fuerzas del gobierno e impuso en la Presidencia de la República a José Joaquín de Herrera. Dos años más tarde se le encargó el mando de una de las dos divisiones del ejército encargadas de contener el avance de las tropas estadounidenses en el norte del país, pero el 14 de diciembre de 1845 proclamó, en San Luis Potosí, un plan que desconocía al presidente Herrera. Marchó sobre la ciudad de México, con lo que el norte del país quedó desprotegido, y nombró una Junta de Notables que el 4 de enero de 1846 lo designó presidente interino de la República. Durante su gobierno, el presidente estadounidense James Polk declaró la guerra a México (11 de mayo) y las tropas mexicanas fueron derrotadas en Matamoros (18 de mayo). Convencido de que una monarquía regida por un soberano español era la mejor forma de enfrentar la agresión estadounidense, intentó llevar a la práctica esta idea, pero sus intenciones se vieron frustradas por una sublevación liberal en Guadalajara y, sobre todo, por el levantamiento de Mariano Salas en la capital de la República. Derrocado el 28 de julio, se exilió en Francia. Volvió a México en 1848 y en junio, dos meses después de la ratificación de los tratados de Guadalupe-Hidalgo, se unió a la sublevación de Celedonio Domeco de Jarauta y Manuel Doblado, con quienes se negó a reconocer los tratados y se manifestó por la continuación de la guerra. En julio intentó tomar Guanajuato y luego de ser derrotado, nuevamente se exilió. Regresó al año siguiente.

PAREDES COLÍN, JOAQUÍN ◆ n. y m. en Tehuacán, Pue. (1860-1928). Educador e historiador. En 1898 fundó la primera biblioteca pública de Tehuacán, que ahora lleva su nombre, y en 1909 el taller de tipografía El Refugio, que reprodujo el Plan de San Luis (1910) y editó *El Centinela*, primer diario de la localidad (1923). Fue diputado federal (1916) y varias veces presidente municipal de Tehuacán. Autor de *Apuntes históricos de la ciudad de Tehuacán* (1910) y *El distrito de Tehuacán. Breve relación de su historia, censo, monumentos arqueológicos, datos estadísticos, geográficos, etnográficos y otros* (1921). En 1918 ingresó en la Sociedad Mexicana de Geografía y Estadística.

Paredes Limón, Mariano ◆ n. en Veracruz, Ver., y m. en el DF (1912-1979). Pintor y grabador. Estudió en la Academia de San Carlos (1922-33), donde fue alumno de José Clemente Orozco, Armando García Núñez y Fernando Leal. Perteneció a la Liga de Escritores y Artistas Revolucionarios (1934-37), en la que se encargó de la sección de artes plásticas de su órgano mensual, *Frente a frente*. Miembro fundador del Taller de Gráfica Popular (1937) y uno de sus primeros administradores. Participó en las misiones culturales (1945) y fue profesor de artes plásticas en escuelas públicas. Fue miembro de la Sociedad Mexicana de Grabadores, cofundador de la Sociedad para el Impulso de las Artes Gráficas (1948) y fundó el Centro Popular de Artes Plásticas al Aire Libre en la Casa del Lago. De las más de 300 exposiciones en que participó, destacan las de Cuba (1943) y Haití (1950). Fue premiado en la primera Bienal Interamericana de Pintura y Grabado celebrada en el Palacio de Bellas Artes. En 1972, el Museo de Arte Moderno realizó una exposición retrospectiva de su obra, con motivo del cuadragésimo aniversario del inicio de su producción. Realizó más de 2,500 grabados.

Paredes Pérez, Trinidad ◆ n. en Actopan, Hgo., y m. en el DF (1875-1951). Ingeniero de minas titulado en el Instituto Científico y Literario de Hidalgo (1903). Profesor de las escuelas nacionales de Agricultura de San Jacinto y de Ingeniería. Fue consultor de las compañías mineras de Real del Monte (1915-17), director del Departamento

Monaguillo, carboncillo sobre papel de Mariano Paredes Limón

de Minas de la Secretaría de Industria (1917-20), director de la Comisión Siderúrgica de la Secretaría de Guerra (1920) y subjefe (1924) y jefe (1924) de la Comisión de Petróleo de la Secretaría de Industria.

Paredes Rangel, Beatriz Elena ◆ n. en San Esteban Tizatlán, Tlax. (1953). Licenciada en sociología por la UNAM. Desde 1973 pertenece al PRI, en el que fue secretaria de Acción Indigenista (1973) y presidenta del consejo estatal en Tlaxcala del Movimiento Nacional de la Juventud Revolucionaria (1975-77); y directora de Promoción y Gestoría de la Comunidad del Comité Ejecutivo Nacional (1981-82). En la Confederación Nacional Campesina se desempeño como secretaria de Acción Femenil del Comité de Huamantla (1977-79), secretaria de la Liga de Comunidades Agrarias y Sindicatos Campesinos de Tlaxcala (1977-79) y, dentro del Comité Ejecutivo Nacional de la propia Confederación, ocupó los cargos de secretaria de Planeación Familiar (1977-80), secretaria de Acción Educativa (1980-83) y secretaria general (1992-1993). Ha sido diputada federal (1979-82), subsecretaria de Organización Agraria de la Secretaría de la Reforma Agraria (1982-86), gobernadora constitucional del estado de Tlaxcala (1987-1992), subsecretaria de Gobierno de la SG (1993), embajadora en Cuba (1993-94), subsecretaria de Desarrollo Político de la SG (1994) y senadora de la República (1994-2000). Ha formado parte de las delegaciones mexicanas enviadas a varios encuentros internacionales. Premio "Mujer que hace la diferencia" del Foro Internacional de la Mujer (1994).

Paredes y Serna, Pedro ◆ n. en Nuevo Santander, ahora Tamaulipas (¿1780?-¿1840?). Fue diputado al Congreso Constituyente de 1823-24 y dos veces senador de la República (1825-26 y 1827-28).

Pareja, Pedro ◆ n. en España y m. en el DF (1891-1967). Profesor. Estudió en la Escuela Superior del Magisterio y se especializó en puericultura. En España fue director del Centro Escolar Luis Bello y director provincial de Primera Enseñanza en Madrid. Llegó a México en 1939, luego de la derrota de la República española. Participó en la fundación del Instituto Luis Vives (1940) y lo dirigió hasta su muerte.

Parés, Nuria ◆ n. en España (1925). Poeta. Llegó a México al fin de la guerra civil española (1939). Es autora de *Romances de la voz sola* (1951) y *Canto llano* (1959).

Parés Guillén, Carlos ◆ n. en España y m. en el DF (1907-1970). Médico graduado en Barcelona en 1933, se doctoró en urología en Madrid y estudió

Archivo General de la Nación

Beatriz Paredes

en Estados Unidos, Francia, Alemania, Italia, Suiza y Bélgica. Llegó a México luego de la derrota de la República Española. Aquí trabajó en el Cuerpo de Médicos del American British Cowdray Hospital (hoy Hospital Inglés), en el Hospital General de México y en el Centro de Cooperación Científica para América Latina de la UNESCO. Fue miembro del Ateneo Español de México y de la Sociedad Mexicana de Urología.

PARGA, PEDRO ◆ n. en Aguascalientes, Ags., y m. en Guadalajara, Jal. (1792-1873). Insurgente. Participó en la toma de la Alhóndiga de Granaditas y en la batalla del Puente de Calderón. Tras la derrota de Acatita de Baján se incorporó a las tropas de Ignacio López Rayón y José María Morelos. A la muerte de éste, continuó la lucha en el sur de Nueva Galicia. Poco después de la independencia colaboró con el gobernador de Jalisco, Prisciliano Sánchez.

PARIÁN ◆ Mercado de la ciudad de México que estuvo en la Plaza Mayor, frente al Palacio del Ayuntamiento. Se construyó en donde habían estado los cajones (tiendas) de ropa incendiados durante la insurrección de los capitalinos en 1692. La iniciativa provino de los locatarios afectados, así como del *gremio de los chinos* o *los filipinos*, comerciantes que distribuían las mercancías llegadas en la Nao de la China. El nombre de Parián se lo pusieron estos mismos comerciantes, pues así se llamaba el mercado correspondiente de Manila, que vendía los productos americanos y europeos. Tenía dos pisos (el superior para almacenes y el inferior para venta). Contaba con dos hileras de tiendas en la parte oriente y otras dos en la poniente; una en el norte y otra en el sur. En 1696, cuando fue terminado, los pequeños vendedores del Baratillo que estaba en el centro del actual Zócalo fueron obligados, "so pena de la vida" a trasladarse a la plaza del Volador y sólo se permitió que se comerciara "en casas y tiendas". A mediados del siglo XVIII se construyeron nuevas filas de tiendas en los costados norte y sur, en tanto que se sustituyó por una edificación de mampostería el conjunto de puestos de madera que se hallaban en el centro, en la parte llamada el Baratillo Grande, mercado de objetos usados y otros artículos. El Parián era propiedad del Ayuntamiento capitalino y ocupaba una superficie de 162,000 metros cuadrados. El 4 de diciembre de 1828, el mercado fue asaltado e incendiado por los pobladores de los barrios pobres, durante la insurrección de la Acordada, y desde entonces quedó vacío. En 1843, el presidente Antonio López de Santa Anna ordenó destruirlo.

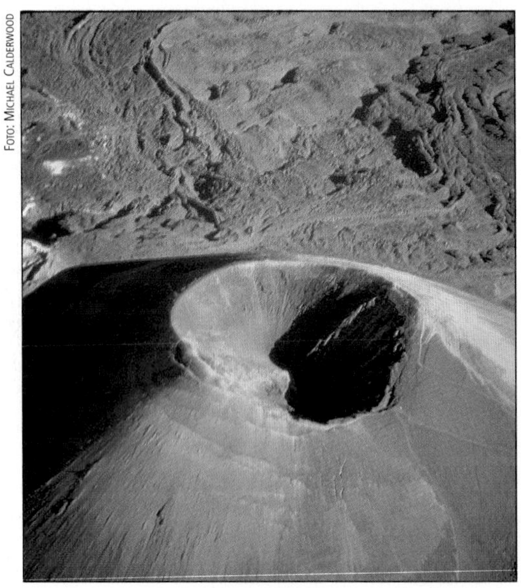

FOTO: MICHAEL CALDERWOOD

Volcán Paricutín

Ángeles, tríptico de Carmen Parra

PARICUTÍN ◆ Volcán de Michoacán surgido en 1942 en la parte norte de la base del Pico de Tancítaro, en el Eje Volcánico. La lava brotó principalmente de un cráter llamado Zapicho y sepultó el pueblo de Parangaricutiro (☛).

PARM ◆ ☛ *Partido Auténtico de la Revolución Mexicana.*

PARNASO, DEL ◆ Sierra de Jalisco situada en extremo occidental de la de Cacoma, al sur de la de Mascota y al este de la del Desmoronado.

PARODI DE MONTAÑO, ENRIQUETA ◆ n. en Cumpas, Son., y m. en el DF (1899-1976). Maestra normalista. En 1914 comenzó a colaborar en el diario *El Paso del Norte*, de San Antonio, Texas. En 1954 fundó la revista *Cauce*. Autora de *Reloj de arena* (1933), *Cuarto de hora* (1936), *Madre prosa* (1936), *Luis es un don Juan* (1937), *Sonora* (1941), *Cuentos y leyendas* (1944), *Alcancía madre* (1945), *Ventana al interior* (1948), *Abelardo L. Rodríguez, un devoto de la educación* (1951), *Abelardo L. Rodríguez, estadista y benefactor* (1957), *Mineros* (1959), *Alfonso Ortiz Tirado: su vida en la ciencia y en el arte* (1964) y *El estado de Sonora* (1969).

PARRA, CARMEN ◆ n. en el DF (1944). Pintora y escultora. Estudió en la Escuela Nacional de Antropología e Historia (1961-64). Tomó cursos de música en la Academia Villalobos, de Río de Janeiro, Brasil. Su aprendizaje formal de pintura y escultura lo hizo en la Academia de Bellas Artes de Roma (1963-64), en la Escuela de Pintura y Escultura La Esmeralda (1967), en el Royal College of Arts de Londres (1970) y con Robin Bond. Expuso por primera vez en 1963, en la Casa del Lago del DF. Su obra se ha expuesto en México (1967), Brasil (1970), Francia (1975, 1976 y 1986) y en la República Federal de Alemania (1979). Creó los vestuarios y escenografías para las obras *La paz*, de Aristófanes (1965), *Les fiancés de la Tour Eiffel*, de Jean Cocteau; el *Retablillo de Cristóbal* (1969) y *Ser o no ser*.

PARRA, FÉLIX ◆ n. en Morelia, Mich.,

y m. en la ciudad de México (1845-1919). Pintor. Estudió en el Colegio de San Nicolás y en la Academia de San Carlos. Fue discípulo de Octaviano Herrera, Pelegrín Clavé, Santiago Rebull y José Salomé Pina. Estuvo becado en Europa entre 1878 y 1892. Regresó a México y hasta 1915 se dedicó a la docencia en San Carlos, donde uno de sus alumnos fue Diego Rivera. Autor de un mural que se encuentra en la Sala de Cabildos del Ayuntamiento de México (1890) y de los cuadros *El cazador* (1871), *Autorretrato* (1871), expuestos permanentemente en el Museo de Morelia; *Fray Bartolomé de las Casas* (1876), *Una escena de la conquista* (1877), *Matanza de Cholula* (1877), *Galileo en la escuela de Padua* (1878) y *Jura del Patronato de 1737*, de la Basílica de Guadalupe.

Parra, Francisco de la ◆ (?-?). Sacerdote dominico. Estudió en la Universidad de Guadalajara. En septiembre de 1810, poco después de la entrada del ejército de Miguel Hidalgo a Guadalajara, recomendó la utilización de la imprenta de José Fructo Romero (la única de la ciudad), para la impresión de los primeros números de *El Despertador Americano*. En diciembre de ese año, Hidalgo lo nombró general y le encargó llevar la insurrección a las provincias internas de Occidente. Combatió en Nayarit y Sonora. Cayó preso a fines de 1811 y fue juzgado y condenado a muerte. Salvado por el sacerdote Francisco Madueño, se le envió a Durango, de donde escapó. Regresó a Guadalajara y hacia 1814 volvió a ser procesado por sus relaciones con los insurgentes. Recluido en un convento cerca de tres años, a fines de mayo de 1817 se escapó, se presentó ante las tropas coloniales estacionadas en Tequila y aceptó el indulto. Otros autores, sin embargo, afirman que permaneció recluido hasta después de la consumación de la independencia (1821) y que en 1824 obtuvo una recomendación de la Junta de Premios, para que el gobierno lo hiciera canónigo.

Parra, Gilberto ◆ n. en San Pedro Tesistán, municipio de Zapopan, Jal. (1913). Músico. Realizó estudios en la Escuela de Ingeniería de la Universidad de Guadalajara y más tarde pasó al Conservatorio de la misma ciudad. Fue miembro de la Orquesta del Estado Mayor del gobierno de Jalisco. Se trasladó a la ciudad de México y ahí formó un mariachi que acompañó a Pedro Infante, Lucha Reyes, Dora María y Luis Pérez Meza. Trabajó en la estación radiofónica XEQ, donde dió a conocer el corrido *El barzón*, de Miguel Muñiz Ávila. Compuso las canciones *La barca-Jalisco*, *No quiero esperar tanto*, *Sublime inspiración*, *Dos corazones*, *Por un amor* y *Amor de los dos*.

Parra, Gonzalo de la ◆ n. en Villa Escobedo, Chih., y m. en el DF (1892-1953). Periodista. Constitucionalista desde 1915, fue reportero de *El Imparcial*, fundador de los diarios *El Nacional* (1915), *El Heraldo* (1921) y *El Popular* (1930), así como de la revista *Continente* (1938). Dirigió el periódico *La Prensa*, órgano de la campaña presidencial de Juan Andrew Almazán (1940). Sustituyó a Carlos Noriega Hope como gerente y director de *El Universal Ilustrado*. Colaboró en el cotidiano *El Universal* y en la revista *Todo*. Autor de *Cómo se hizo revolucionario un hombre de buena fe* (1915), *La lepra nacional* (1923) y *Medias palabras* (1936).

Parra, Manuel de la ◆ n. en Sombrerete, Zac., y m. en el DF (1878-1930). Poeta. Trabajó en la Biblioteca Nacional y en el Museo Nacional de Arqueología. Perteneció al Ateneo de la Juventud. Colaborador de las revistas *Savia Moderna*, *Nosotros*, *México*, *La Nave*, *Revista Moderna*, *Revista de Revistas*, *Argos*, *El Mundo Ilustrado*, *Vida Moderna* y *El Nacional*. Autor de los poemarios *Visiones lejanas* (1914) y *Momentos musicales*, así como de la novela *En las ruinas* (1922).

Parra, Porfirio ◆ n. en Chihuahua, Chih., y m. en la ciudad de México (1854-1912). Médico cirujano titulado en 1878. En la Escuela Nacional de Medicina, donde fue profesor desde antes de terminar la carrera, tuvo entre sus maestros a Gabino Barreda y lo sustituyó en la cátedra de Lógica. Trabajó como médico del Hospital Juárez, del hospital de San Andrés y del Conservatorio. También ejerció la docencia en la Escuela Nacional de Agricultura y fungió como director de la Escuela Nacional Preparatoria. A partir de 1872 fue varias veces diputado federal por Chihuahua y Durango. Senador de la República en 1910. Fundó los periódicos *El Método* y *El Positivismo*; y colaboró en *La Libertad*, *Revista de la Instrucción Pública Mexicana*, *Revista de Chihuahua* y *Revista Positiva*, así como en el periódico *El Universal*. Se le ha considerado el maestro de la segunda generación de positivistas mexicanos. Redactó la parte correspondiente a "La ciencia en México", de *México, su evolución social*, de Justo Sierra (1901). Autor de *Lutero* (1886), *Oda a las matemáticas* (1887), *Estudios filosóficos* (1896), *Juicio crítico de la clasificación médico-legal de la heridas* (1896), *La colaboración intelectual de Barreda en la obra de Juárez* (1897), *Pacotillas* (1900), *Nuevo sistema de lógica inductiva y deductiva* (1903), *Juárez* (1906), *Estudio histórico-sociológico de la Reforma en México* (1906), *Ventajas e inconvenientes de la profesión médica* (1907), *Discursos* (1907), *La Escuela Nacional Preparatoria y las críticas del sr. dn. Francisco Vázquez Gómez* (1908), *Discursos y poesías* (1908) y *Plan de una historia de Chihuahua* (1911). Fue socio de número de la Academia Nacional de Medicina y miembro de la Academia Mexicana (de la Lengua).

Parra, Tomás ◆ n. en el DF (1937). Pintor y escultor. Estudió en la Escuela de Pintura y Escultura La Esmeralda (1949-56). Profesor de la Escuela Nacional de Artes Plásticas y del Taller de Experimentación de Pintura. Miembro del taller de Juan Soriano (1955). En 1959 colaboró con Carlos Pellicer en la realización del Museo Anahuacalli. Fue co-

Obra de Gonzalo de la Parra

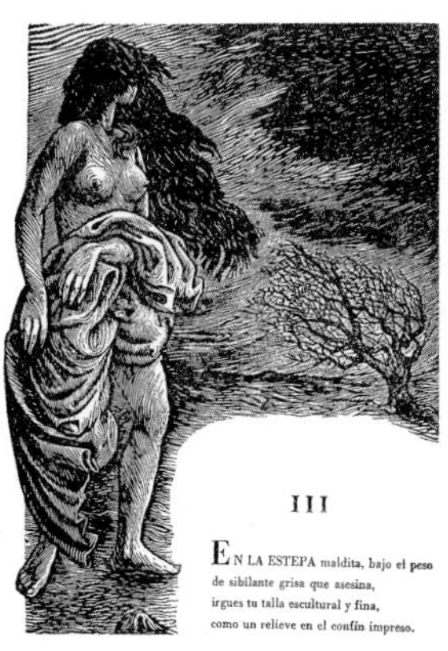

III
EN LA ESTEPA maldita, bajo el peso
de sibilante grisa que asesina,
irgues tu talla escultural y fina,
como un relieve en el confín impreso.

Obra de Manuel de la Parra

Tomás Parra

fundador y director (1978-80) del Foro de Arte Contemporáneo y coordinador académico del Centro de Investigación y Experimentación Individual. Ha expuesto en Brasil, Cuba, Chile, Holanda y Perú.

PARRA, VÍCTOR ♦ n. en Tula, Hgo., y m. en el DF (1920-1994). Actor. Se inició en el cine en la película *La sombra de Chucho el Roto* (1944). Participó, entre otras, en *Juan Charrasqueado* (1947), *Cuatro contra el mundo* (1949), *El suavecito* (1950), *La duda* (1953), *Reportaje* (1953), *Los tres Villalobos* (1954), *La venganza de los tres Villalobos* (1954), *La sospechosa* (1954), *Sombra verde* (1954) y *El túnel seis* (1955). En televisión actuó en la telenovela *El bastardo*. Ocupó diversos cargos en la Asociación Nacional de Actores y en los Estudios América. Fue director del Consejo Consultivo de la Cámara Nacional de la Industria Cinematográfica (1972-78). Recibió el Ariel por la mejor coactuación masculina por *El muchacho alegre* (1949) y por *Ángeles del Arrabal* (1950); así como a la mejor actuación masculina de 1955, por *Los Fernández de Peralvillo*.

PARRA DE ALANÍS, CARMEN ♦ n. en Casas Grandes, Chih. (1885-1941). Se levantó en armas en 1910 y participó en la toma de Ciudad Juárez (1911). Fue conocida como *La coronela Alanís*. Formó parte de la División del Norte y sirvió como correo a los gobiernos de la Convención. Apresada en Veracruz por los carrancistas, se incorporó a las tropas de Cándido Aguilar, de las que pasó a las de Manuel Murguía en Chihuahua (1916-18), donde se dedicó a tramitar indultos para exiliados y más tarde para sus ex compañeros.

PARRA GUTIÉRREZ, MANUEL GERMÁN ♦ m. en el DF (1917-1986). Profesor normalista y licenciado en economía y doctor en filosofía. Ejerció la docencia en la UNAM. Fue asesor de los presidentes Lázaro Cárdenas, Manuel Ávila Camacho, Adolfo Ruiz Cortines y Adolfo López Mateos. Como subsecretario de Economía, en el sexenio de Miguel Alemán, se opuso al ingreso de México al GATT y le tocó cancelar las concesiones que tenían empresas extranjeras para explotar los yacimientos de hierro de Las Truchas. Colaboró en *Hoy, Mañana, Siempre!, Tiempo, Excélsior* y *Novedades*.

PARRA PRADO, MANUEL GERMÁN ♦ n. en el DF (1938). Hijo del anterior. Licenciado en ciencias políticas por la UNAM (1957-61). Profesor de la UIA (1985). Ha sido investigador de Nacional Financiera (1962-64), jefe de la oficina de Venta de Maíz (1964-65) y ayudante ejecutivo del director general de Conasupo (1965-67); secretario general del Sindicato de Trabajadores de la Conasupo (1971-74), diputado federal (1979-82 y 1985- 88), director del Instituto Nacional de Capacitación Política, Sindical y Administrativa (1978) y secretario general de la Federación Nacional de Sindicatos de Trabajadores al Servicio del Estado (1983-86); y en 1981 vicepresidente de la Comisión de Trabajo y Previsión Social del IEPES del PRI, partido al que pertenece desde 1964. En 1988 fue nombrado coordinador general de Delegaciones del ISSSTE. Autor de *Esquema histórico de los trabajadores al servicio del Estado* (1978), *Historia del movimiento sindical de los trabajadores al servicio del Estado* (1982) y *Testimonios históricos* (1982).

PARRA VARGAS, MANELICK DE LA ♦ n. en el DF (1952). Licenciado en letras por la Universidad de París y maestro en dirección cinematográfica por el American Film Institute, Los Ángeles, California, Estados Unidos. Ha sido director de Editorial Argumentos (1976-79), Hotelera Kristal (1977-79) y Grupo Vid (1978-79); presidente de Grupo Vértice (1985), Fotonovelas (1993-94) y Grupo Editorial Vid (1992-). Ha colaborado en *Novedades, Proceso, El Nacional, Sábado* de *unomásuno* y *el Sol de México*. Autor de *Los vuelos del deseo* (1987), *La verdadera leyenda de Joaquín Murrieta* (Premio del Concurso de Guiones Cinematográficos organizado por la Sogem, RTC y la Dirección General del Derecho de Autor, SEP, 1985) y *Lorenza Torralba* (1999, en prensa). Premio al Mérito de la Presidencia de la República y el Consejo Nacional de la Publicidad (1977).

PARRAGUIRRE, MARÍA LUISA ♦ Grabadora. Estudió en la Escuela de Pintura y Escultura La Esmeralda (1965-72). Fue miembro del Taller de Grabado del Molino de Santo Domingo (1972-75) y becaria del periódico *El Nacional* en París (1976-77). Expuso por primera vez en 1971. Sus obras se han presentado en Checoslovaquia, Polonia, Suiza y Venezuela.

PARRAL, DEL ♦ Río de Chihuahua, afluente del Florido. Es una de las corrientes que bajan por la vertiente nororiental de la sierra de Santa Bárbara, cruza la ciudad de Parral y corre hacia el noreste hasta unirse al río Florido, al sureste de Ciudad Camargo.

PARRAS ♦ Municipio de Coahuila situado en el sur del estado, en los límites con Zacatecas, y contiguo a Viesca y Saltillo. Superficie: 9,271.7 km^2. Habitantes: 43,303, de los cuales 11,709 forman la población económicamente activa. Hablan alguna lengua indígena 15 personas mayores de cinco años. La cabecera es Parras de la Fuente. El municipio ha destacado por su producción vitivinícola.

PARRAS, DE ♦ Sierra de Coahuila que se extiende al norte de los límites con Zacatecas. Prolonga hacia el oeste-noroeste la sierra de la Concordia.

PARRÉS, JOAQUÍN ♦ n. en Silao, Gto., y m. en la ciudad de México (1793-1838). Inició su carrera militar en el ejército realista. En 1821 se adhirió al Plan de Iguala. En 1832 se levantó en armas contra el gobierno golpista de Anastasio Bustamante y a fines de ese año participó en la redacción de los Convenios de Zavaleta, que llevaron a la presidencia a Manuel Gómez Pedraza, en cuyo gabinete fue secretario de Guerra y Marina en (del 31 de enero al 20 de abril de 1833). Más tarde fue diputado local en Guanajuato.

PARRÉS ARIAS, JOSÉ ♦ n. en Mazamitla y m. en Guadalajara, Jal. (1913-1973). Cofundador de la Federación de Estudiantes Socialistas de Occidente y de la Confederación de Jóvenes Mexicanos. Fue director del Instituto

Jalisciense de Antropología e Historia, diputado local, secretario y síndico del ayuntamiento de Guadalajara, director de la penitenciaría estatal, jefe del Departamento de Trabajo y Previsión Social, director de la Escuela Preparatoria de Jalisco (1938-39 y 1966-71) y rector de la Universidad de Guadalajara (1971).

Parrés Guerrero, José G. ◆ n. en Real del Monte, Hgo., y m. en el DF (1888-1949). Estudió en el Instituto Científico y Literario de Hidalgo y en la Escuela Nacional de Medicina. Perteneció a la Cruz Blanca Neutral y en 1914 se incorporó al Ejército Libertador del Sur. Destinado a la zona de Cuautla, en esa ciudad fundó un hospital de sangre. Permaneció fiel a Emiliano Zapata luego de su rompimiento con Venustiano Carranza y al triunfo del Plan de Agua Prieta, en 1920, apoyó al grupo sonorense. Fue gobernador provisional de Morelos (del 10 de julio de 1920 al 12 de diciembre de 1923), candidato al gobierno de Hidalgo (1928), oficial mayor técnico (1924-27), subsecretario (1933-37) y, durante el gobierno del presidente Lázaro Cárdenas, secretario de Agricultura y Fomento (del 16 de agosto de 1937 al 30 de noviembre de 1940); cofundador (1940) y secretario general, del Frente Zapatista, miembro del Patronato del Nacional Monte de Piedad y director de las Escuelas Rurales de Agricultura.

Parrodi, Anastasio ◆ n. en Cuba y m. en la ciudad de México (1805-1867). Era comandante militar de Tamaulipas en 1846, cuando el presidente Antonio López de Santa Anna le ordenó evacuar la plaza ante el hostigamiento de las tropas estadounidenses. Al año siguiente participó en la batalla de Padierna. En 1854 se unió al Plan de Ayutla y luego del triunfo liberal sometió al gobernador de Jalisco, Ignacio Herrera y Cairo y, el 26 de julio de 1856, lo sucedió en el cargo. En agosto abandonó la gubernatura para combatir la sublevación conservadora de Luis G. Osollo, en San Luis Potosí. Nuevamente gobernador de Jalisco (del 28 de marzo de 1857 al 18 de enero de 1858), en diciembre de 1857, luego del golpe de Estado del presidente Ignacio Comonfort, formó una coalición militar con los gobiernos liberales de Colima, Zacatecas, Aguascalientes, Guanajuato, Querétaro, Guerrero y Veracruz. El 10 de marzo de 1858 fue derrotado en Salamanca por la tropas de Miguel Miramón y, unos días más tarde, el 22, entregó Guadalajara a los conservadores. Terminada la guerra de los Tres Años, fue gobernador del Distrito Federal (del 8 de enero al 23 de abril de 1862 y del 1 al 21 de mayo de 1862). Más tarde reconoció al gobierno de Maximiliano de Habsburgo.

Parrondo, Guadalupe ◆ n. en Perú (1948). Pianista. Estudió en la Academia Sas Rosay de Lima y en la Escuela Normal Superior de Música de París (1966-68). Se ha presentado en Checoslovaquia, Francia, Suiza y la Unión Soviética. En 1969, obtuvo el premio Albert Léveque a la mejor interpretación de Bach; en 1970, el Premio María Canal de Barcelona; en 1972, el premio del Concurso de Ejecución Musical de Ginebra; y en 1974 el premio del Primer Concurso Internacional Teresa Carreño de Caracas.

Partida ◆ Isla del golfo de California situada al sureste de la del Ángel de la Guarda, al norte de isla Rasa, al este de la punta Las Ánimas y al oeste de la isla de Tiburón. Reserva ecológica desde 1978, es el único criadero del ave llamada petrel pequeño.

Partida, Eugenio ◆ n. en Ahualulco de Mercado, Jal. (1964). Escritor. Estudió cine en la Universidad de Guadalajara. Autor de novela: *La ballesta de Dios*, y de cuento: *En los mapas del cielo* (1991, finalista del Premio Gilberto Owen 1990). Obtuvo el premio de cuento Juan Rulfo, convocado en Sayula, Jal., en 1987 y 1988.

Partido Acción Nacional ◆ Organización política fundada en la ciudad de México el 16 de septiembre de 1939, por iniciativa de Manuel Gómez Morín, con el apoyo de antiguos miembros de la Unión de Estudiantes Católicos. A la reunión constitutiva asistieron, entre otros, Miguel Estrada Iturbide, Ezequiel A. Chávez, Jesús Guiza y Acevedo, Manuel Bonilla, Enrique Loaeza, Carlos Ramírez Zetina, Efraín González Luna, Juan Landerreche Obregón, Roberto Cossío e Isaac Guzmán Valdivia. Unos días más tarde, el 17 de septiembre, se realizó una asamblea donde se aprobaron los estatutos. Gómez Morín fue el primer presidente del partido (1939-49). De acuerdo con sus documentos básicos, la doctrina del PAN establece que el interés nacional es preeminente, que no pueden subsistir ni perfeccionarse los valores humanos si se agota la colectividad, que ésta debe garantizar a la persona las libertades y medios para cumplir su destino; que la lucha contra la ignorancia y la miseria es deber, pero no monopolio, del Estado, y es responsabilidad y derecho de todos los miembros de la nación; que el Estado no tiene ni puede tener dominio sobre las conciencias, ni proscribir ni tratar de imponer convicciones religiosas; que la libertad de investigación y de opinión científica o filosófica no puede ser limitada por el Estado y que es su deber procurar a todos los miembros de la comunidad iguales oportunidades de educación; que el Estado debe garantizar el libre ejercicio del derecho al trabajo; que el Estado debe promover y garantizar el desarro-

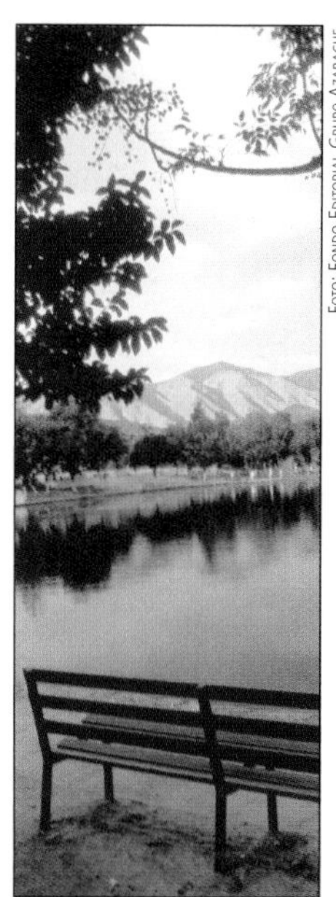
Foto: Fondo Editorial Grupo Azabache

Estanque de la Luz, en Parras, Coahuila

Manuel Gómez Morín, fundador del Partido Acción Nacional

Archivo General de la Nación

llo de la iniciativa privada; que la propiedad privada es el medio adecuado para asegurar la producción nacional y constituye el apoyo y la garantía de la dignidad de la persona; que el problema del campo exige que cada familia campesina, incluso la del ejidatario, obtenga en plena propiedad la tierra que sea capaz de hacer producir; que el Estado tiene autoridad, no propiedad, sobre la economía y que debe evitar la consideración del hombre como instrumento de la actividad económica; que el gobierno municipal ha de ser autónomo, sujeto a la voluntad y vigilancia de sus gobernados; y que la realización de la justicia es atribución primaria del Estado. "Por una patria generosa y ordenada" es su lema. Publica la revista *La Nación* (☛). En su segunda convención nacional, celebrada en 1940, el PAN perfiló un programa mínimo de acción política que señalaba, entre otras, las siguientes tareas: evitar el aislamiento económico o cultural de los grupos de población que están alejados de la vida nacional; reincorporar a los mexicanos

Logotipo del Partido Acción Nacional

emigrados o protegerlos en sus sitios de residencia; procurar una corriente inmigratoria que sea étnica y culturalmente asimilable en nuestro país; establecer relaciones diplomáticas con España; orientar la política exterior mexicana hacia la unidad de los países hispánicos; rechazar todos los textos legales y actos concretos vejatorios de la libertad de pensamiento, de conciencia, de opinión o de enseñanza; reformar la Ley de Expropiación; luchar contra las prácticas anticonceptivas, el aborto, la prostitución y la pornografía; moralizar a los gobiernos municipales; pugnar por la implantación del voto secreto en las elecciones sindicales y acabar con el desorden jurídico y económico de la propiedad rural. El PAN no presentó candidato presidencial en 1940, aunque de manera extraoficial apoyó a Juan Andrew Almazán. Tres años después presentó candidatos a diputados, pero todos fueron derrotados. Para las elecciones generales de 1946, el partido tampoco presentó candidato a la Presidencia de la República, aunque también apoyó, de manera extraoficial, a Ezequiel Padilla. Sin embargo, varios de sus candidatos a diputados ingresaron al Congreso. El partido obtuvo su registro legal en 1948 y al año siguiente cuatro panistas ingresaron en la Cámara de Diputados. También en 1949, Juan Gutiérrez Lascuráin asumió la presidencia del partido, en la que se mantuvo hasta 1956. Para la campaña de su primer candidato presidencial, Efraín González Luna (1952), el partido formuló una plataforma política y social en la que, luego de identificar a México como miembro de la "comunidad de naciones cristianas de Occidente", demandaba restaurar el equilibrio de la economía interna y solucionar los problemas del campo, además de exigir un sistema electoral imparcial. En las elecciones obtuvo el equivalente al 7.82 por ciento de los votos y cinco curules. González Luna venció al candidato del Partido Popular, Vicente Lombardo Toledano, y fue derrotado por Adolfo Ruiz Cortines y por Miguel Henríquez Guzmán. En las elecciones de 1955 el PAN ganó seis diputaciones. Alfonso Ituarte Servín presidió el partido de 1956 a 1958. Lo sucedió José González Torres (1958-62). La votación de Luis H. Álvarez, candidato presidencial en 1958, fue equivalente al 9.42 por ciento del total nacional. El PAN impugó el resultado e instruyó a sus seis diputados electos para que no ingresaran en la Cámara. Dos de ellos, sin embargo, desobedecieron la orden y se unieron a los diputados priistas. A raíz de este incidente fue reformada la ley electoral, para castigar a los partidos que optaran por esa forma de lucha. Durante los años cincuenta creció la presencia panista en provincia. En 1959, su candidato a la gubernatura de Baja California, Salvador Rosas Magallón, ofreció una de las primeras candidaturas poderosas frente al PRI. A principios de los años sesenta, un grupo de panistas trató de convertir al organismo político en una agrupación democristiana, intento que acabó con la salida de los miembros de esa corriente, que no pudieron vencer la oposición de Adolfo Christlieb Ibarrola, presidente del partido de 1962 a 1968. Cinco diputados panistas pertenecieron a la XLV Legislatura (1961-64). Para las elecciones de 1964, el PAN presentó como candidato a la presidencia a José González Torres y demandó, en su plataforma electoral, la instauración de un Estado representativo y democrático, la facilidad de acceso a la enseñanza superior y la derogación del delito de disolución social. González Torres obtuvo más de un millón de votos, equivalentes a 11.5 por ciento de los sufragios. En esos comicios, el PAN ganó dos diputaciones por mayoría y 18 de la nueva fórmula de elección, los diputados de partido. En 1967 logró más de un millón 225,000 votos (12.37 por ciento del total), lo que le dio un diputado de mayoría y 19 de partido. Para entonces, Acción Nacional había desarrollado un importante trabajo en Sonora, Baja California y Yucatán, que eran sus principales bastiones. Ignacio Limón M. ocupó la presidencia del partido en 1968-69 y fue sucedido por Manuel González Hinojosa (1969-72). En 1970, el candidato presidencial fue Efraín González Morfín (hijo de Efraín González Luna), quien exigió la independencia del Congreso de la Unión respecto del Poder Ejecutivo, la aplicación de reformas legales para que los trabajadores tuvieran acceso a la propiedad de las empresas y el establecimiento de un gobierno democrático en el Distrito Federal. Con esta plataforma, González Morfín le dio a su partido alrededor de un millón 800,000 votos (el 19 por ciento del total) y el PAN consiguió 20 diputados de partido. En las elecciones legislativas de 1973, el partido obtuvo algo más de un millón 200 1,000 votos, dos diputados de mayoría y 25 de partido. Dos años después, en lo que se ha considerado la primera manifestación de vida del *neopanismo*, José Ángel Conchello, quien encabezó a la organización entre 1972 y 1975, propuso que el candidato presidencial fuera Pablo Emilio Madero, a lo que se opusieron otros dirigentes y un amplio sector de la base partidaria. Conchello fue destituido como coordinador de la bancada panista en la Cámara de Diputados (sería expulsado del partido en 1978) y un año más tarde, en 1976, durante la convención nacional, el enfrentamiento entre las corrientes representadas por Conchello y Efraín González Morfín, presidente en ese momento del partido, impidió que alguno de los precandidatos, Madero, Rosas Magallón y David Alarcón Zaragoza, consiguiera el 80 por ciento de los votos de los delegados, mínimo indispensable para su nominación. Para evitar una escisión, González Morfín renunció a la presidencia de la organización, a la que volvió Manuel González Hinojosa (1975-78). En las elecciones de julio de ese año, el PAN obtuvo más de un millón 300,000 votos, lo que le significó 20 diputados de partido. La delegación panista que participó en las audiencias públicas de 1977, integrada por Fernando Estrada Sámano, Manuel González Hinojosa, Juan Landreche Obregón, Gerardo Medina y Abel Vicencio Tovar, se opuso a la reforma política y votó contra la iniciativa que dio origen a la Ley Federal de Organizaciones Políticas y Procesos Electorales. El mismo Vicencio Tovar ocupó la presidencia del partido de 1978 a 1984. En las elecciones legislativas de 1979, los resultados del PAN fueron los siguientes: diputados de mayoría relativa, 1,471,417 votos (10.59 por ciento) y diputados de representación proporcional, 1,525,111 (11.06 por ciento). Durante la segunda mitad de los años setenta aumentó la influencia panista en los sectores medios de la sociedad, especialmente en los estados del norte del país. El estallido de la crisis económica en 1981 y la nacionalización bancaria de 1982, denunciada como un atentado a la propiedad, dio mayor fuerza dentro del partido a la corriente *neopanista*, más beligerante en su oposición al gobierno y a las nacionalizaciones, más enérgica en sus denuncias de la corrupción y las irregularidades electorales. Algunos analistas políticos señalan que el *neopanismo* ha abandonado el aliento hispanista de los fundadores y se orienta decididamente a un modelo de sociedad como la estadounidense. Su preocupación central, más que educar cívicamente a los mexicanos, como querían los militantes de viejo cuño, es arribar al poder tan pronto como sea posible. En 1982, la convención nacional del partido eligió como candidato presidencial a Pablo Emilio Madero, considerado como representante del neopanismo, quien en los comicios de julio obtuvo 3,700,045 votos (15.68 por ciento del total) y mantuvo a su partido como segunda fuerza electoral del país. Ese mismo año, el partido obtuvo 3,678,096 votos en la fórmula 1 para elección de senadores y 3,564,721 en la fórmula 2 (16.40 y 17.77 por ciento, respectivamente), en tanto que en la votación para diputados de mayoría relativa computó 3,631,660 votos y 3,786,348 para los diputados de representación proporcional, 17.53 y 16.55 por ciento de los totales, respectivamente. Madero ocupó la presidencia del partido de 1984 a 1987. En 1986, el partido presentó fuertes candidatos a los gobiernos de Sinaloa (Manuel J. Clouthier), Sonora (Adalberto *el Pelón* Rosas), Chihuahua (Francisco Barrio) y Nuevo León (Fernando Canales Clariond). Todos los resultados oficiales favorecieron al PRI y todos, igualmente, fueron impugnados por el PAN, que organizó amplias movilizaciones contra lo que consideró fraudes electorales. La protesta cobró especial relevancia en Chihuahua, donde incluyó marchas (inusuales para los panistas), actos de *desobediencia civil* y una huelga de hambre, a fines de ese año, protagonizada por el candidato del PAN a la alcaldía de Chihuahua, Luis H. Álvarez, la que fue apoyada por varios militantes de izquierda y destacados intelectuales mexicanos, quienes propusieron anular los comicios. Con Luis H. Álvarez a la cabeza del partido (1987-93), Clouthier fue el candidato presidencial del PAN en las elecciones de 1988. Según las cifras oficiales obtuvo 3,267,159 votos (17.07 por ciento del total), resultado que su partido consideró fraudulento. El Frente Democrático Nacional, que desplazó del segundo al tercer lugar al candidato panista, de acuerdo con su propio cómputo, dijo que Clouthier había obtenido 23 por ciento de los sufragios. El PAN consiguió 101 diputados en la LIV Legislatura de la Cámara de Diputados. Ahí apoyó las iniciativas promovidas por el Ejecutivo, como las que implicaron la reprivatización de la banca, los cambios al artículo 27 Constitucional que modificaron el régimen ejidal y permitieron legalmente la enajenación de parcelas; y las reformas que dieron personalidad jurídica a las iglesias y derechos limitados a los ministros religiosos. En 1989 el PAN ganó su primera gubernatura, la de Baja California, con Ernesto Ruffo Apel como candidato. En febrero de 1990, tras cuatro rondas de votación, Luis Héctor Álvarez fue reelegido como presidente nacional del PAN, a despecho de quienes en marzo constituyeron el Foro Doctrinario y Democrático, los que reprochaban al grupo de Álvarez haber abierto las puertas del partido a los empresarios

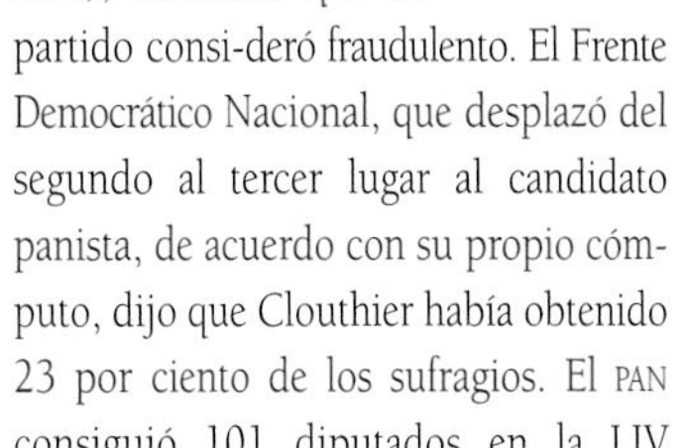

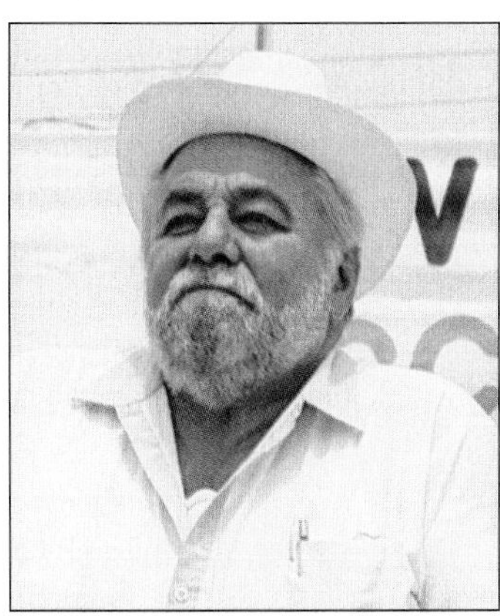

Manuel J. Clouthier, candidato presidencial del PAN en 1988

Foto: Imagen Latina

Ernesto Ruffo Apel, primer gobernador panista

Diego Fernández de Cevallos, candidato presidencial del PAN en 1994

veinte años atrás, la colaboración con el presidente de la República, la negociación de resultados electorales y, en suma, haber abandonado los principios rectores de la organización. En ese año, Carlos Castillo Peraza escribió: "Asistimos en el México de hoy a una victoria de Acción Nacional. No sólo política, por cierto, sino sobre todo cultural". Señalaba que los acontecimientos recientes demostraban que su partido había conseguido "incorporar a la cultura política de millones de mexicanos" una serie de conceptos y expresiones que formaban parte del legado ideológico e histórico de esa organización. Según Soledad Loaeza, autora de *El Partido Acción Nacional: la larga marcha 1939-1994*, "La idea de la victoria cultural era más que figura retórica. Sugería que los programas del partido eran política de gobierno y que Acción Nacional estaba en el poder, sin ambivalencias de ninguna especie (.) La idea de la victoria cultural panista servía a dos objetivos: (.) proyectar en la imaginación pública la creencia de que Acción Nacional era tan poderoso que, además de representar a un sector mayoritario de la población que había optado por la vía electoral, desde la oposición dictaba las políticas de gobierno; en segundo lugar, que el poder que ostentaba el partido había sido la culminación de su tarea educativa, de la formación de ciudadanos que se había propuesto medio siglo antes". En las elecciones federales de 1991 la votación del PAN bajó al 18 por ciento del total y con ello obtuvo 89 curules en la Cámara de Diputados — 80 plurinominales y nueve de mayoría — y dos escaños senatoriales. En el mismo año hubo elección de gobernador en Guanajuato y San Luis Potosí y en ambos casos Acción Nacional denunció la comisión de un fraude e impugnó los resultados. En San Luis Potosí se produjo una fuerte movilización encabezada por el Frente Cívico Potosino y su candidato Salvador Nava Martínez, al que apoyó el PAN. La culminación de ese proceso fue la renuncia de Fausto Zapata, presunto candidato triunfante, a quien sustituyó en la gubernatura el también priista Gonzalo Martínez Corbalá. En Guanajuato el resultado oficial reconocía 53 por ciento de los votos al candidato del PRI, Ramón Aguirre Velázquez, y 36 por ciento al candidato del PAN, Vicente Fox Quesada. Fox se declaró triunfador y el 20 de agosto Acción Nacional inició una movilización estatal y protestas en foros nacionales e internacionales para que se modificaran los resultados. El 29 de agosto Ramón Aguirre fue declarado gobernador electo, recibió su constancia de mayoría de manos del Consejo Estatal Electoral y el mismo día renunció. Pero Fox no fue declarado ganador, sino que el Congreso local nombró gobernador al también panista Carlos Medina Plascencia, diputado local y ex alcalde de León, lo que la opinión pública consideró resultado de un arreglo, o "concertacesión", como se dijo entonces, entre la dirigencia nacional del PAN y el gobierno federal. En 1992, Acción Nacional obtuvo en Chihuahua su tercera gubernatura con Francisco Barrio como candidato. El 7 de octubre de ese año renunciaron los principales miembros del Foro Doctrinario y Democrático, entre ellos, José González Torres, Pablo Emilio Madero, Jesús González Schmall, Bernardo Bátiz, Jorge Eugenio Ortiz Gallegos, Arturo Campos Villalobos, Alfonso Méndez Ramírez y Abel Martínez. En la carta común de renuncia, los foristas impugnaban al grupo diriegente del PAN su "relación simbiótica con el sistema" y su pragmatismo, "su apoyo abierto a la política estatal", la injerencia empresarial en la vida partidista, el voto a favor de las reformas electorales y la reprivatización de la banca y el acuerdo en Guanajuato. El 6 de marzo de 1993 fue elegido Carlos Castillo Peraza como presidente del partido después de tres rondas de votación. En noviembre siguiente, el entonces jefe del grupo parlamentario del partido en la Cámara de Diputados, Diego Fernández de Cevallos, fue designado como candidato de Acción Nacional a la presidencia de la República para las elecciones de 1994. El 21 de agosto de 1994, fecha en que se verificaron las eleccciones, de acuerdo con los resultados oficiales, el PRI obtuvo 50 por ciento del total de los sufragios, Acción Nacional recuperó su sitio de segundo lugar en elecciones presidenciales con el 27 por ciento de los votos, y el PRD quedó en tercero con 17 por ciento de los sufragios. Con esa votación, los panistas consiguieron 119 curules en la Cámara de Diputados y 25 escaños en el Senado de la República. En el mismo año, el partido se incorporó a la Internacional Demócrata Cristiana (☛) en calidad de observador. En 1995, Acción Nacional ganó la gubernatura de Jalisco, con el ex alcalde de Ciudad Guzmán, Alberto Cárdenas Jiménez, como candidato y referendó su aceptación en Baja California, con el triunfo de Héctor Terán en la elección de gobernador. En 1996 el partido Acción Nacional tuvo otro avance electoral importante, ganando 16 de los 18 municipios mexiquenses de la zona metropolitana del valle de México, entre ellos Naucalpan, Tlalnepantla, Cuautitlán, Cuautitlán Izcalli, Atizapan y Coacalco. Ese mismo año fue elegido presidente nacional del partido Felipe Calderón Hinojosa. En las elecciones federales intermedias de 1997, el PAN obtuvo el 26.61 por ciento de los votos, con lo que se adjudicó 122 curules en la Cámara de Diputados y aumentó a 31 sus escaños senatoriales, pero en el Distrito Federal sufrió una estrepitosa derrota al obtener apenas 15 por ciento de los votos y perder la jefatura de Gobierno de la capital del país. Como resultado de ese fracaso, Carlos Castillo Peraza, quien había sido candidato a la jefatura de gobierno del DF renunció al partido. Durante la LVII Legislatura que se inició en 1997, el grupo parlamentario del PAN en la Cámara de Diputados votó junto con el PRI para convertir en deuda pública las cuentas no cobradas por la banca a sus clientes, mismas que estaban en el llamado Fondo Bancario de Protección al Ahorro (Fobaproa), que entonces cambió su nombre a Instituto de Protección al Ahorro Bancario (IPAB) y absorbió lo que de otra manera hubieran sido pérdidas de los banqueros. El mismo año de 1997 Acción Nacional ganó la gubernatura de Nuevo León, con Fernando Canales Clariond como candidato y la de Querétaro, con Ignacio Loyola Vera. En 1998 sufrió un revés electoral al perder la gubernatura de Chihuahua, que recuperó el PRI tras seis años de gobierno panista, pero ganó la de Aguascalientes, con Felipe González González como candidato. Para ese año Acción Nacional contaba con seis gobernadores, 286 diputados locales y 287 alcaldes, muchos de los cuales cobraron relevancia nacional por sus actos de censura contra espectáculos y actividades artísticas. También en 1988, la fracción panista del Congreso de Guanajuato propuso incluir en el Código Penal de la entidad el delito de *embronicidio*, "para proteger los derechos de los no nacidos". La iniciativa fracasó. De acuerdo con datos de la organización, el PAN contaba a finales de 1998 con 150,000 miembros activos y 250,000 adherentes. En ese año el partido fue aceptado como miembro con derechos plenos en la Internacional Demócrata Cristiana y Felipe Calderón Hinojosa se convirtió en uno de los cuatro vicepresidentes de la organización. En 1999 fue elegido como presidente nacional del PAN Luis Felipe Bravo Mena. El 4 de julio, Antonio Echevarría ganó la gubernatura de Nayarit como candidato de la coalición opositora formada por el PRD, el PAN, PT y el PMS. Semanas después, un experimento similar fracasó en Coahuila. A los pocos días, las negociaciones que mantenía el PAN para integrar una coalición con el PRD y otros partidos acabó en fracaso en medio de recriminaciones mutuas. En septiembre fue elegido Vicente Fox Quesada como candidato panista a la presidencia de la República para las elecciones del año 2000.

PARTIDO ALIANZA SOCIAL ◆ Organización constituida el 29 de marzo de 1998 en la ciudad de México por ex militantes del Partido Demócrata Mexicano (☛), así como del PAN y del Partido del Foro Doctrinario y Democrático, aunque se asume como heredero directo de la tradición sinarquista. En su primer consejo nacional están Pablo Emilio Madero, Adalberto Rosas, Ignacio González Gollaz, Roberto Calderón, Víctor Atilano Gómez, Baltazar Ignacio Valadez Montoya y José Antonio Calderón Cardoso. En junio de 1999 obtuvo su registro ante el IFE.

PARTIDO ANTIRREELECCIONISTA ◆ Organización política surgida en 1927 para lanzar la candidatura presidencial del general Arnulfo R. Gómez y oponerse a la reelección de Álvaro Obregón. El 20 de junio de ese año celebró su convención constitutiva en el Tívoli del Elíseo de la ciudad de México, lugar donde, dieciocho años antes, Francisco I. Madero había sido elegido candidato del primer Partido Antirreeleccionista. Como en 1909, la convención de 1927 fue presidida por Juan Sánchez Azcona, pero en la segunda, los secretarios fueron Calixto Maldonado y Enrique Bordes Mangel. La campaña de Gómez fue dirigida por Francisco J. Santamaría.

PARTIDO ANTIRREELECCIONISTA ◆ ☛ *Partido Nacional Antirreeleccionista.*

PARTIDO AUTÉNTICO DE LA REVOLUCIÓN MEXICANA ◆ Organización política creada en 1954 por Jacinto B. Treviño, gracias al apoyo del presidente Adolfo Ruiz Cortines. Su antecedente principal es la Asociación Política y Social Revolucionaria de Hombres de la Revolución, agrupación fundada en 1951 por el propio Treviño y José Gonzalo Escobar, Emilio y Raúl Madero, Alfredo Breceda, Samuel N. Santos, Fernando Vázquez Ávila, Félix Rioja, Juan Barragán Rodríguez, Rafael Izaguirre y Francisco J. Aguilar, para aglutinar a ex combatientes carrancistas y villistas, luego de la desaparición del sector militar del Partido de la Revolución Mexicana (☛). Su declaración de principios establece que la base de su ideología son los postulados de la revolución y demanda la estricta observancia del derecho del pueblo para regirse a sí mismo, para dirigir la educación pública y para coordinar el esfuerzo del desarrollo económico nacional, sin abandonar el respeto y estímulo a la libre iniciativa. De acuerdo con sus documentos, el partido luchará por erradicar del medio obrero toda clase de *ismos* exóticos y contrarios a la nacionalidad, y pugnará por establecer el justicialismo en materia de relaciones obrero-patronales; declara como base de la existencia del pueblo la propiedad privada y aboga por la propiedad y posesión del territorio nacional por parte de los ciudadanos; las comunidades agrarias y la pequeña propiedad agrícola en explotación son las únicas formas lícitas de la tenencia de la tierra y reivindica el municipio libre como base de la organización política nacional. El partido obtuvo su registro en 1957. Aseguró contar entonces con 65,000 militantes, distribuidos en 19 estados y el Distrito Federal. Entre 1958 y 1982 apoyó a los candidatos presidenciales del PRI y sus resultados electorales fueron los siguientes: en 1964, 64,409 votos (0.71 por ciento del total) y colocó a cinco diputa-

Vicente Fox, candidato presidencial del PAN para el año 2000

FOTO: GUILLERMO AGUILERA

Porfirio Muñoz Ledo, candidato del PARM para las elecciones presidenciales del año 2000

Logotipo del Partido Auténtico de la Revolución Mexicana

dos de partido; en 1967, 149,313, (1.42 por ciento) y consiguió un diputado de mayoría y cinco de partido; en 1970, 111,883 (0.8 por ciento) y tuvo cinco diputados de partido; en 1973, 272,339 (1.82 por ciento), un diputado de mayoría y cinco de partido; y en 1976: 405,757 (2.53 por ciento), un diputado de mayoría y cinco de partido; en 1979, 249,106 votos en la fórmula para diputados de mayoría relativa (1.79 por ciento del total), y 298,184 en la de diputados de representación proporcional (2.16 por ciento); y en 1982, 153,495 votos en la fórmula 1 para elección de senadores (0.69 por ciento), 137,621 para la fórmula 2 (0.69 por ciento), 282,229 para diputados de mayoría relativa (1.36 por ciento) y 282,004 para diputados de representación proporcional (1.23 por ciento). Al no obtener el 1.5 por ciento requerido, el partido perdió su registro, mismo que inexplicablemente recuperó en 1984. En el libro *La grilla. Los Sótanos de la política*, Mario Guerra Leal, quien fuera secretario general del PARM en la década de los setenta, describe la relación de este partido con el gobierno. Según Guerra Leal mantuvieron férreo control sobre la dirigencia del PARM los secretarios de Gobernación Gustavo Díaz Ordaz, Luis Echeverría, Mario Moya Palencia y el director general de Gobierno y luego secretario de Gobernación Manuel Bartlett Díaz, así como el secretario de la Presidencia Emilio Martínez Manatou. Guerra Leal confiesa que él mismo redactó, por órdenes de Martínez Manatou, una "carta abierta" publicada en los diarios, pidiendo la detención de los líderes del movimiento médico de 1964, la represión del grupo de Víctor Rico Galán en 1966 y reseña los servicios prestados al gobierno en 1968, distribuyendo propaganda "para dividir a los estudiantes", firmada por un apócrifo Frente Estudiantil Revolucionario. En 1987 el partido admitió en su seno a los miembros de la Corriente Democratizadora del PRI y designó como su candidato presidencial para los comicios federales de 1988 a Cuauhtémoc Cárdenas Solórzano, obteniendo un 1,209,710 votos, que le dieron 22 curules en la Cámara de Diputados. No obstante, en los comicios federales de 1991 volvió a perder el registro al obtener menos del 1.5 por ciento de la votación. En total, este partido ha perdido en cuatro ocasiones su registro. A principios de 1992 surgió al interior del partido una Corriente Democratizadora, encabezada por el ex diputado federal Óscar Mauro Ramírez Ayala, advirtiendo sobre el declive parmista tras la caída en la captación de voto en las elecciones federales del año anterior, reivindicaba los "postulados que le dieron origen" al PARM y proponía fortalecer la democracia dentro de la organización, acusando al dirigente Carlos Cantú Rosas de ser el principal dique para ello, por lo que amenazó con formar un nuevo partido que se denominaría de Alianza Revolucionaria, lo que no ocurrió. En 1994 el PARM tuvo como candidato a la presidencia a Álvaro Pérez Treviño, quien obtuvo una pobre votación. En junio de 1999 recuperó el registro y lanzó como candidato presidencial para las elecciones del 2000, a Porfirio Muñoz Ledo, quien poco después dejó el PRD.

Foto: Dante Bucio

Manuel Camacho Solís, cofundador del Partido del Centro Democrático y candidato presidencial para el año 2000

Partido Cardenista ◆ Nombre que adoptó el Partido del Frente Cardenista de Reconstrucción Nacional para recuperar su registro y prerrogativas electorales en 1996. Su presidente fue Rafael Aguilar Talamantes. En las elecciones de 1997 tuvo como candidato al gobierno del Distrito Federal a Pedro Ferriz Santacruz, quien quedó en los últimos lugares de votación. En 1999 ya no obtuvo el registro de ley.

Partido Católico Nacional ◆ Organización fundada en 1911 en la ciudad de México por Gabriel Fernández Somellera, Emmanuel Amor, Luis García Pimentel, Manuel F. de la Hoz, José González Rubio, Miguel Palomar y Vizcarra, Carlos Díez de Sollano y Rafael Martínez del Campo. Otros de sus dirigentes fueron Francisco Pascual García y Eduardo Tamariz. Su lema era "Dios, patria y libertad". En su programa aceptaba la separación Estado-Iglesia, defendía las libertades democráticas de enseñanza y asociación, se sumaba a las demandas de sufragio efectivo y no reelección; pedía leyes basadas en la doctrina socialcatólica y la creación de instituciones de crédito para la industria y la agricultura. Afirmó contar con casi medio millón de afiliados. En las elecciones de 1911, el grupo apoyó la candidatura de Francisco I. Madero y propuso a Francisco León de la Barra como candidato a vicepresidente. En junio de 1912 obtuvo algunos triunfos electorales, sobre todo en Zacatecas y Jalisco, y logró influir en la legislación jalisciense. En las elecciones convocadas por Victoriano Huerta en marzo de 1913, el partido lanzó como candidatos a la Presidencia y la Vicepresidencia al escritor Federico Gamboa y a Eugenio Rascón, respectivamente. Consiguió 31 diputados. Desapareció al triunfo del constitucionalismo.

Partido Centralista ◆ ☛ *Centralismo*.

Partido del Centro Democrático ◆ Organización creada el 17 de enero de 1999 en una Asamblea Nacional Constitutiva celebrada en la ciudad de México. Entre sus fundadores están Manuel Camacho Solís, Marcelo Ebrard Casaubón y Alejandro Rojas Díaz-Durán, los tres ex priistas. Su proyecto político se resume en 17 puntos programáticos: "Una nueva Constitución que fortalezca los derechos ciudadanos y reconstituya la autoridad política; cons-truir el estado de derecho, establecer un sistema democrático de gobierno que funcione, reorganización del sistema federal y nuevo pacto, reformar la justicia y la seguridad, pactar la paz en Chiapas e iniciar la reconciliación; crecimiento económico sostenido e incluyente, educación como prioridad nacional, política social incluyente; revertir el abandono del campo mexicano, igualdad y respeto a la mujer, abrirle paso a los jóvenes, promover un nuevo pacto con las comunidades indígenas; programa de población y migración; protección de la biodiversidad y el medio ambiente; mantener la soberanía sobre el petróleo; y defender los intereses y el prestigio de México". Obtuvo su registro ante el IFE en junio de 1999. El lema del PCD es "A forjar el futuro".

PARTIDO CIENTÍFICO ♦ Aunque no se trataba de un partido en el sentido moderno del término, éste fue el nombre que recibió un grupo de secretarios de Estado que adquirieron una influencia determinante en el gobierno de Porfirio Díaz. Es posible que el origen del término se encuentre en una sentencia de Justo Sierra, según la cual, el gobierno debía estar formado por hombres de ciencia. El grupo, que también fue conocido como "partido de los tlaxcaltecas", fue descrito por Francisco Bulnes como "un coche completo que sólo tiene cuatro asientos que ocupan José Ives Limantour, D. Roberto Núñez, D. Miguel Macedo y D. Joaquín D. Casasús; y cuando la tarde se encuentra despejada, se llevan a D. Rosendo Pineda en el pescante". Aun cuando muchos autores niegan que el Partido Científico haya existido como tal, Andrés Molina Enríquez, en su libro *La revolución agraria en México*, lo da por cierto y remonta su origen a la época en que Manuel Romero Rubio llegó a la Secretaría de Gobernación. Por su parte, Limantour afirma en sus *Apuntes* que el grupo motejado como "los científicos" era una reminiscencia de la Unión Liberal (☛), agrupación surgida en 1892 a iniciativa de algunos amigos de Romero Rubio, Mariano Escobedo y Guillermo Prieto entre ellos, para dotar de una nueva plataforma política a Porfirio Díaz.

PARTIDO COMUNISTA BOLCHEVIQUE ♦ Grupo político formado en 1963 como consecuencia de una escisión del comité del Distrito Federal del Partido Comunista Mexicano (☛). Sus miembros más destacados eran Guillermo Rousset y Santiago González, quienes en 1964 formaron el Partido Revolucionario del Proletariado (☛). Algunos de sus documentos aparecen firmados como Partido Comunista Mexicano (Bolchevique).

PARTIDO COMUNISTA MEXICANO ♦ Organización marxista fundada el 24 de noviembre de 1919, en una reunión en la que participaron el bengalí Manabendra Nath Roy, los estadounidenses Frank Seaman y Evelyn Roy y los mexicanos José Allen, Eduardo Camacho, Vicente Ferrer Aldana y Leonardo Hernández, todos ellos miembros del Partido Nacional Socialista (☛), constituido semanas antes. La transformación del PNS en un partido similar al bolchevique fue impulsada por el ruso Mijail Borodin, representante de la Internacional Comunista (☛), quien no asistió a esa junta que se denominó formalmente "asamblea del comité nacional", aunque sólo asistieron seis de los 22 integrantes de ese órgano. Allen quedó como secretario general del naciente partido y el 29 de noviembre firmó la solicitud de afiliación a la Internacional. En diciembre desapareció el órgano comunista *El Soviet*, heredado del PNS, para dejar su lugar al semanario *El Comunista*, que fue prohibido por Carranza en abril de 1920. El 8 de agosto de 1920 apareció el primer número de *Boletín Comunista*. El día 22 de ese mes, por iniciativa del suizo Alfredo Stirner, dos docenas de militantes del grupo Juventud Igualitaria, entre otros José C. Valadés y Rosendo Gómez Lorenzo, fundaron la Federación de Jóvenes Comunistas, en la que figuró también Rafael Carrillo Azpeitia. El órgano de esta agrupación fue *Vida Nueva*. En febrero de 1921, anarquistas y comunistas fundaron la Confederación General de Trabajadores (☛). En el mismo mes, Allen pasó a formar parte de un secretariado colectivo con Valadés y Manuel Díaz Ramírez, quien fue nombrado primer secretario. En abril de 1921 vino a México al japonés Sen Katayama para dirimir la disputa entre el Partido Comunista de México (☛), el Partido Socialista Mexicano (☛) y el Partido Comunista Mexicano por la representación ante la Internacional. El japonés intentó sin éxito la unificación del y el PCM. El primero de estos partidos se disolvió, en tanto que la dirección del PC quedó en manos de Valadés, pues Díaz Ramírez se encontraba en Moscú. Tras la celebración de su primer Congreso Nacional Ordinario (del 25 al 31 de diciembre de 1921), el partido ratificó el acuerdo tomado en su fundación que lo obligaba a no participar en política electoral, planteamiento típicamente anarquista que chocaba con las concepciones marxistas; apoyó la colectivización de la tierra y la organización de los trabajadores agrícolas en sindicatos; se manifestó contra los movimientos militares, aprobó realizar una campaña contra el alza en los alquileres de las viviendas y adoptó el nombre de Partido Comunista de México como Sección Mexicana de la Internacional Comunista, para significar así que los comunistas de todo el mundo eran parte de un solo partido que, por razones prácticas, se dividía en secciones nacionales. En el segundo Congreso Nacional, realizado el 10 de abril de 1923, se acordó abandonar el abstencionismo electoral y se eligió un Comité Nacional Ejecutivo, integrado por Rosendo Gómez Lorenzo, Úrsulo Galván, Diego Rivera, Manuel Díaz Ramírez y Carlos Palacios. Tres meses después, Gómez Lorenzo era secretario nacional, Rivera secretario político, Díaz Ramírez secretario internacional, Allen secretario de Finanzas y Rafael Mallén secretario de Organización y Propaganda. Díaz Ramírez reasumió la secretaría general en noviembre. También en abril se incorporó al partido el senador Luis G. Monzón, que fue, de hecho, el primer legislador comunista de México. El 25 de agosto de 1923, el comité central se manifestó en favor de la candidatura presidencial de Plutarco Elías Calles, con quien se entrevistó para proponerle un programa que incluía la reglamentación del artículo 123 constitucional y la aplicación efectiva de la reforma agraria. Al estallar la rebelión delahuertista (☛ *Huerta, Adolfo de la*), en diciembre de 1923, el Consejo Nacional del PC organizó batallones de obreros, los que se unieron a las tropas federales en Gua-

José Ives Limantour, miembro del Partido Científico

Vicente Lombardo Toledano, integrante del Partido Comunista Mexicano

najuato, Guerrero, Puebla y Veracruz para combatir a los rebeldes. En 1920 Primo Tapia había iniciado los trabajos para organizar la Liga de Comunidades Agrarias de Michoacán, lo que fructificó en diciembre en 1922. Sin embargo, sería a partir de 1923 cuando los comunistas desplegarían la más intensa actividad en el agro, con Úrsulo Galván como presidente de la Liga de Veracruz. El 25 de abril 1924, durante la Conferencia Nacional del PC, Rafael Carrillo Azpeitia fue elegido secretario general de la organización, en lugar de Díaz Ramírez. Para entonces, además de Diego Rivera, habían ingresado al partido numerosos artistas, entre otros David Alfaro Siqueiros, Xavier Guerrero, Fermín Revueltas, Germán Cueto, Amado de la Cueva, Máximo Pacheco y el crítico Jorge Juan Crespo de la Serna. Entre el 7 y el 12 de abril de 1925, durante el III Congreso, el partido acordó presentar candidatos propios en las elecciones de 1926, realizar trabajo político dentro de la CROM y organizar una central campesina nacional. El 14 de septiembre de 1925 fue asesinado en Jalapa, Francisco J. Moreno, diputado comunista al Congreso de Veracruz. En noviembre de 1925, el periódico *El Machete* (☛) se convirtió en el órgano oficial del partido. En ese año, según datos de Frank Seaman, el PCM tenía 191 miembros, quienes dirigían varios sindicatos obreros y organizaciones campesinas que en total agrupaban a cerca de 40,000 personas. En 1926, durante su IV Congreso (del 21 al 27 de mayo), el partido decidió organizar a sus militantes en "células", es decir, en pequeños grupos bajo la dirección de los comités locales, que a su vez dependían del comité central; además, definió a México, de acuerdo con la idea de la Internacional, como "semicolonia"; consideró que el gobierno callista intentaba crear una burguesía nacional y que, por lo tanto, no era un "simple lacayo" del imperialismo; y ratificó su apoyo a la creación de una central agrarista, la que se fundó en noviembre de 1926 (☛ *Liga Nacional Campesina*). El PC contaba entonces con cerca de 600 miembros. En julio de 1927, el pleno del comité central consideró que "ante los esfuerzos de la reacción y el clero para derrumbar el gobierno de la pequeña burguesía, es un deber de la clase proletaria apoyar la candidatura de la burguesía y pequeña burguesía nacionales, o sea la candidatura del general Obregón". En abril de 1928 se celebró la V Conferencia Nacional del partido, que contaba con unos 1,500 militantes, y ahí se acordó aceptar a Valentín Campa y a Miguel Ángel Velasco en el comité central. También se resolvió, de acuerdo con lo dispuesto por la Komintern, expulsar a los simpatizantes de León Trotsky. De junio a septiembre de ese año, el cubano Julio Antonio Mella actuó como secretario general interino del partido. En las elecciones de julio, el dirigente ferrocarrilero Hernán Laborde fue elegido diputado federal, calidad que conservó hasta mayo de 1929, cuando fue desaforado. Luego del rompimiento entre el gobierno de Emilio Portes Gil y el grupo dominante de la CROM, encabezado por Luis N. Morones (☛), a fines de 1928, el partido determinó defender a esa central y paralelamente fundar otra organización obrera, el Comité de Defensa Proletaria (15 de diciembre). El 10 de enero de 1929 fue asesinado Julio Antonio Mella por pistoleros del dictador cubano Gerardo Machado. A fines de ese mes, impulsada por los comunistas, se constituyó en el DF la Confederación Sindical Unitaria de México, con Siqueiros como secretario general. En febrero, el PC participó en la fundación del Bloque Obrero y Campesino Nacional, una coalición electoral que eligió al general Pedro V. Rodríguez Triana como su candidato presidencial para los comicios de noviembre de 1929. Dos días después de iniciada la rebelión escobarista (☛ *Escobar, José Gonzalo*), el 5 de marzo de 1929, el partido lanzó un manifiesto en el que tachaba la asonada de reaccionaria, llamaba a los comunistas y a los obreros a formar grupos independientes para enfrentarse a los alzados, exigía al gobierno la entrega de armamento para estos cuerpos y demandaba la realización de una reforma agraria efectiva. Los batallones comunistas actuaron sobre todo en el norte y en el oriente del país, casi siempre con la oposición gubernamental. Al mismo tiempo, las autoridades hicieron circular el rumor de que los comunistas intentaban aprovechar la situación para derrocar al presidente Portes Gil. A fines de marzo se desató la represión gubernamental, que costó la vida a decenas de comunistas. A mediados de mayo fueron fusilados por fuerzas federales, sin formación de causa, el líder campesino J. Guadalupe Rodríguez y otros militantes de Durango, en tanto que en Acayucan, en julio, fue asesinado el general Hipólito Landero, dirigente local del Socorro Rojo Internacional. Las autoridades clausuraron las oficinas del PCM y destruyeron la imprenta de *El Machete*, que continuó apareciendo en forma clandestina hasta 1934. En julio de 1929, acusado de trotskista, fue expulsado Diego Rivera y el PCM adoptó una posición que se resume en la consigna de "Soviets para México". En diciembre Laborde sustituyó a Carrillo en la dirección nacional. El 23 de enero de 1930 fue deportada a Europa la fotógrafa Tina Modotti, quien había ingresado en el PCM en 1927. En el mismo barco salieron de México el italiano Vittorio Vidali y el ruso Julio Gómez-Rosovski, ambos comunistas. En 1930 el gobierno se negó a registrar a los candidatos del partido. En ese ambiente represivo, los dirigentes del PCM censuraban acremente a quienes se acercaban al gobierno, como era el caso de Augusto César Sandino, quien por buscar para su causa el apoyo del callismo fue acusado de "aliarse al gobierno contrarrevolucionario mexicano". El mismo Sandino, poco antes, había escrito que era del Partido Comunista Mexicano, "parte de la vanguardia del antiimperialismo mundial", de quien "más apoyo hemos recibido para nuestra lucha antiimperialista en Nicaragua". A fines de marzo Siqueiros fue expulsado del PCM. El 29 de junio, a manos de policías y guardias blancas, se produjo la mayor matanza de comunistas: 17 militantes cayeron en Matamoros Laguna, y Coahuila. Entre octubre y noviembre fueron detenidos decenas de militantes, entre otros Carrillo, José Revueltas y Dionisio Encina, quien fue torturado en Torreón. El 7 de noviembre, por el aniversario de la revolución rusa, un grupo de miembros del PCM izó en una torre de Catedral, la bandera roja con la hoz y el martillo. A principios de enero de 1931, fue secuestrado por la policía Valentín Campa, quien logró comunicarse con sus compañeros y tuvo que ser liberado dos meses después. El 23 de julio la policía atentó contra la vida de Hernán Laborde y resultó muerto su camarada Benjamín Jiménez. El 5 de noviembre de 1931, un grupo dirigido por Gómez Lorenzo tomó la radiodifusora XEW y emitió un mensaje por el XIV aniversario de la revolución rusa. En 1932 se informó que existían varias células de policías en la capital del país y que el periódico *El Máuser* circulaba en los cuarteles. El 10 de julio de ese año, *El Machete* informó que habían sido enviados a las islas Marías más de 30 militantes, entre ellos Velasco, Evelio Vadillo, Gómez Lorenzo y Revueltas, los que regresaron a la capital del país en el mismo año. Germán Rodríguez, quien se dirigió a Jalapa, fue asesinado el 22 de diciembre. En 1933 menudearon las aprehensiones de comunistas, entre otros, Consuelo Uranga, Benita Galeana, Carlos Sánchez Cárdenas, Juan de la Cabada, Andrés García Salgado y el cubano Juan Marinello. En noviembre, por sostener posiciones feministas, fue expulsada del PCM la cantante y compositora Concha Michel. A fines de ese año, Juan de la Cabada y otros comunistas promovieron la creación de la Liga de Escritores y Artistas Revolucionarios (☛). El 10 de enero de 1934, el PCM decía contar con 1,400 miembros. En marzo fue expulsado un grupo señalado como trotskista. En las elecciones del 1 de julio, Hernán Laborde, candidato del Bloque Obrero y Campesino a la presidencia de la República, obtuvo, según cifras oficiales, 6,406 votos. Lázaro Cárdenas asumió la presidencia de la República el 1 de diciembre y ordenó liberar a los comunistas presos. El 2 de marzo de 1935, en la plaza de Santo Domingo, el grupo de choque *Los Dorados*, de la organización pro nazi Acción Revolucionaria Mexicanista (☛), atacó un mitin de los comunistas. El 15 de junio se constituyó el Comité Nacional de Defensa Proletaria, promovido por el PCM, con lo que se inició una etapa de colaboración con Vicente Lombardo Toledano, hasta ese momento calificado de gobiernista. En el conflicto entre Plutarco Elías Calles y el presidente Cárdenas, el PCM manifiestó: "Ni con Calles ni con Cárdenas. Con las masas cardenistas sí". En julio la Internacional lanzó la consigna de formar frentes populares, lo que se reflejó en un viraje político del PCM. En noviembre, el comité central declaró: "no podemos lanzar como consigna de acción inmediata —dice—, la de 'gobierno popular revolucionario', porque esto sería contraponer tal consigna al gobierno de Cárdenas, cuando la situación de hoy día exige sostenerlo". El día 20 del mismo mes se produjo un nuevo enfrentamiento de *Los Dorados* contra los comunistas y éstos fueron apoyados por los choferes de taxis. Hubo muertos de ambos bandos. En febrero de 1936, las organizaciones sindicales dirigidas o influidas por los comunistas participaron en la fundación de la CTM. Lombardo Toledano fue elegido secretario general. Pese a que contaba con el apoyo de la mayoría de los delegados, el comunista Miguel Ángel Velasco retiró su candidatura a la secretaría de organización, segundo puesto en importancia, en favor de Fidel Velázquez, quien amenazaba con una escisión de no concedérsele ese cargo. El 10 de abril de 1936 *Los Dorados* asesinaron al general Ismael Díaz González, militante comunista. En junio, Laborde informó que el PCM tenía 5,000 miembros. Con el impulso de los comunistas, en agosto se fundó la Federación Nacional de Trabajadores al Servicio del Estado y en octubre Cárdenas expropió y repartió tierras de La Laguna. El 12 de diciembre, la CTM y el PCM protestaron por la concesión de asilo a León Trotsky, contra el que iniciaron una campaña que culminó con su asesinato a manos de Ramón Mercader del Río (☛). El 21 de enero de 1937 se adoptó la denominación de Partido Comunista Mexicano y se informó que contaba con 10,000 miembros; se calificó de "nacional reformista" y apegada a la Constitución la política de Cárdenas, a quien se ofreció "apoyo condicional", pues su posición era "punto de partida del pueblo para la acción revolucionaria y su liberación completa". En febrero el PCM firmó con el Partido Nacional Revolucionario, la CTM y Confederación Campesina Mexicana el llamado Pacto del Frente Electoral Popular, pero días después el PNR se negó a apoyar la candidatura de Laborde para diputado, quien en junio se retiró en nombre de "la unidad del pueblo". El 26 de abril se creó el Fondo de Cultura Popular, firma editorial del partido. Como protesta por las maniobras de Lombardo y Fidel Velázquez, en el IV Consejo Nacional de la CTM las organizaciones influidas por los comunistas y otros agrupamientos obreros, como los sindicatos de ferrocarrileros y electricistas, abandonaron la central. Por presiones de la Internacional se adoptó la política de "unidad a toda costa" y, en junio, el PCM planteó el regreso a la CTM de los escindidos. En esos días la dirección nacional del partido resolvió suprimir la organización de los comunistas en los sindicatos. En agosto, salvo los electricistas, todas las agrupaciones volvieron a la CTM y los comunistas, como muestra de buena voluntad, renunciaron a sus puestos en la dirección de esa central, que sería la encargada exclusiva de organizar el Frente Popular. El 26 de octubre se publicó el documento del líder del PC de Francia, Maurice Thorez, *Católicos y comunistas unidos ante el fachismo*. En diciembre, el comité central resolvió que "todos los comunistas deben adherirse

Valentín Campa, miembro del Partido Comunista Mexicano

Frida Kahlo, militante del Partido Comunista Mexicano, en dibujo de Monroy

individualmente al PNR". En marzo de 1938, decretada ya la nacionalización petrolera con el apoyo activo de los comunistas, al transformarse el PNR en Partido de la Revolución Mexicana, el PCM envió una delegación fraternal que declaró: "Queremos que se nos permita arrimar el hombro y poner el pecho en la obra y en la lucha común. Que se nos señale el sitio y las condiciones en que dentro del gran Partido de la Revolución Mexicana podamos cumplir con nuestro deber". El 10 de junio se informa que el PCM tenía 17,756 militantes, la tercera parte obreros y sólo 1,509 mujeres. En julio celebró su convención la Juventud Socialista Unificada, en la que se fusionó la Juventud Comunista. El 15 de septiembre, *El Machete*, diario desde el 26 de mayo, se transformó en *La Voz de México*. En octubre, el PC propuso sustituir la administración obrera, vigente en Ferrocarriles Nacionales, por la administración del Estado bajo control obrero. A fines de enero de 1939, en su séptimo congreso, el PCM dijo contar con 30,125 miembros y 2,776 células. Anunció, asimismo, que apoyaría a quien resultara candidato del PRM a la Presidencia de la República. Los dirigentes del PCM se opusieron al asesinato de Trotsky por considerarlo un "grave error". El 15 de abril se fundó la Confederación de Jóvenes Mexicanos, con la participación de los comunistas. Al ser destapado Manuel Ávila Camacho como candidato del partido oficial, el PCM le dio todo su apoyo y condenó a sus opositores. El 23 de agosto de 1939, los cancilleres de Hitler y Stalin firmaron un pacto de no agresión y el PCM adoptó una política neutralista. En diciembre se reunió el comité central con la asistencia de Vittorio Codovilla y otros representantes de la Internacional. Como resultado, se formó una "comisión depuradora", Laborde y Campa fueron expulsados y Dionisio Encina arribó a la dirección del PCM, con lo que se inició un periodo de *purgas*. En marzo de 1940 se readoptó el nombre de Partido Comunista de México. El 24 de mayo, Siqueiros, presuntamente fuera del PCM desde fines de los años veinte, encabezó un asalto armado a la casa de Trotsky. En mayo, el comunista Rafael Ortega Morales fue asesinado por los *Dorados*. El penúltimo día del sexenio de Cárdenas fue asaltado el local del PCM y resultaron detenidos 51 militantes. El 23 de diciembre se expulsó a Rafael Carrillo Azpeitia. El 11 de enero de 1941, el gobierno de Manuel Ávila Camacho encarceló a 42 comunistas. El 22 de junio de 1941, al producirse la agresión nazi a la URSS, el partido abandonó todo neutralismo y pidió que México declarara la guerra a los países del eje Roma-Berlín-Tokio, lo que sucedió el 22 de mayo siguiente; se declaró contra las huelgas y en favor de la unidad nacional "en la guerra y en la posguerra". La Tercera Internacional fue disuelta en 1943, lo que aprobó el PCM. En ese año fueron expulsados Miguel Ángel Velasco, Ángel Olivo Solís, Enrique Ramírez y Ramírez, José Revueltas, Genaro Carnero Checa y Luis Torres Ordóñez. El primero por abogar en favor de Laborde y Campa; Olivo por excederse en su demanda de apoyo al gobierno y el resto por su insistencia en fusionar al PCM con el grupo de Lombardo, al que Ramírez y Ramírez llamó "el jefe legítimo de los marxistas mexicanos". En ese año, el partido ya sólo contaba con 1,800 miembros. En mayo de 1944 volvió a tomar el nombre de Partido Comunista Mexicano y, en su afán de ser admitido dentro del PRM, bajo la tutela teórica del comunista estadounidense Earl Browder, resolvió suprimir las células de fábrica y las fracciones comunistas dentro de los sindicatos y agrupaciones campesinas, lo que a fines de 1946 se rectificaría, cuando ya había sido desmontada la red de organizaciones de base. Con el PCM centrado en sus ataques a los comunistas expulsados de sus filas y al trotskismo, en 1946 Lombardo invitó al propio PC y otras organizaciones y personajes de izquierda para formar una sola organización de la izquierda. Con ese fin convocó a la Mesa Redonda de los Marxistas (☛), celebrada en enero de 1947. En octubre de ese año, la dirección de la CTM, en manos de Fidel Velázquez desde 1941, resolvió que todos los miembros de esa central debían ser del PRI, con lo que quedaron formalmente excluidos los comunistas. En noviembre de 1947, el gobierno de Miguel Alemán fue calificado por Encina como "gobierno de la burguesía progresista", por lo que "nuestro partido no es de oposición". En marzo de 1948, Alberto Lumbreras, Carlos Sánchez Cárdenas, Alexandro Martínez Camberos, Miguel Aroche Parra y otros expulsados del PC se agruparon en el Movimiento Reivindicador del Partido Comunista. En el mismo año, con apoyo comunista, se fundó el Partido Popular. En mayo, dos grupos de expulsados, Acción Socialista Unificada y el Movimiento Reivindicador, invitaron a la dirección del PCM a

Archivo General de la Nación

Marcha de militantes del Partido Comunista Mexicano en apoyo a Miguel Alemán fusionarse en un solo partido. Encina respondió que "contra los renegados" y los "reivindicadores" no caben "concesiones ni apaciguamientos, sólo la lucha sin cuartel". En enero de 1950, una conferencia nacional acordó trabajar para la organización de la Juventud Comunista de México. A fines de ese mes, el PCM condenó a la dirección de los comunistas yugoslavos por "revisionista". En julio, los comunistas expulsados formaron el Partido Obrero Campesino de México (☛), que ratificó la invitación al PCM para unirse en una sola organización. En septiembre se caracterizó al gobierno de Miguel Alemán como "fiel representante" de "la política de las clases dominantes", que proceden a una "entrega cada vez mayor de nuestro país al imperialismo yanqui" y hacen retroceder la Revolución Mexicana. Se denunciaron las "constantes agresiones a la democracia sindical, a la independencia del movimiento obrero, al derecho de huelga, etc." Un año después se advirtió que "cada día se acentúa la política reaccionaria del gobierno" de Alemán. El 1 de mayo de 1952 el grupo paramilitar *Los Dorados*, con apoyo de la policía y fuerzas militares, atacó una manifes-tación de trabajadores en la que se participaban miembros del PCM y el POCM. Resultó muerto el joven comunista politécnico Luis Morales, en tanto que Mario H. Rivera, Díaz Ramírez y Sánchez Cárdenas fueron detenidos y procesados por el delito de disolución social. En las elecciones de 1952, el PCM apoyó la candidatura presidencial de Vicente Lombardo Toledano. Después de los comicios, consideró triunfador a Miguel Henríquez Guzmán. El 16 de noviembre, después de presentar su "autoconfesión", Diego Rivera fue readmitido en el PCM, donde ya militaba su compañera Frida Kahlo. En 1953 murió José Stalin, pero el PCM siguió ostentándose como "marxista-leninista-estalinista". En 1954 la policía detuvo a Encina y asaltó los talleres de *La Voz de México*, periódico quincenal que se convirtió en diario al año siguiente. En diciembre de 1956 fue readmitido José Revueltas. En abril de 1957 se realizó el congreso constituyente de la Juventud Comunista de México. En agosto, el comité del DF suspendió en sus cargos a Alejo Méndez, Edmundo Raya y Mónica Rodríguez. Al mes siguiente, la conferencia de los comunistas del DF se manifestó en contra de la sanción, con lo que se inició un movimiento contra la dirección nacional encabezada por Encina. Por acuerdo del comité central, al que en los hechos se opuso Encina, el 16 de octubre una delegación del PCM visitó a la dirección del POCM para invitar a este partido a una convención de las fuerzas populares, en busca de candidato a la Presidencia de la República y plataforma electoral común, lo que desembocó en 1958 con la candidatura, sin registro electoral, de Miguel Mendoza López Schwertfeger. El 20 de mayo, en medio de las grandes movilizaciones magisteriales en las que participaban los comunistas, Encina irritó a sus camaradas al declarar que "los maestros deben llegar a un acuerdo con el SNTE y presentar sus demandas a la Secretaría de Educación o en caso necesario al presidente". Militantes del PCM, el POCM y el PP participaron coordinadamente en la dirección del movimiento ferrocarrilero. El 23 de agosto la policía asaltó las oficinas del PCM y de *La Voz de México*. La conferencia de los comunistas del DF se opuso a las sanciones dictadas por el comité central contra Gerardo Unzueta, Manuel Terrazas y José Montejano; reprobó los "métodos de coacción que amenazan a la base del partido" y señaló que "la crisis del PCM" es resultado "de la política oportunista de derecha a la que fue arrastrado en los años de 1937 a 1939 por la vieja dirección", con lo cual "la ideología burguesa penetró a fondo en las filas del partido". En enero de 1959, PP, PCM y POCM manifiestaron su solidaridad con la revolución cubana. El 28 de marzo, el gobierno de Adolfo López Mateos ordenó detener a miles de ferrocarrileros y a los principales líderes del gremio, entre ellos varios comunistas, quienes fueron procesados. En agosto, el comité central, en reunión rigurosamente clandestina, acordó suprimir el puesto de secretario general y eligió un secretariado de tres miembros: el propio Encina, Manuel Terrazas y Arnoldo Martínez Verdugo. La misma reunión, que terminó en septiembre, insistió en la autocrítica, reprobó la política de "unidad a toda costa" y la complacencia con los gobiernos de Cárdenas, Ávila Camacho y Alemán, así como las alianzas con "los dirigentes sindicales corrompidos y traidores". En ese mes la policía torturó y asesinó en Monterrey al líder ferrocarrilero local Román Guerra Montemayor, miembro del PCM. El 2 de septiembre fue encarcelado Dionisio Encina y el 17 de mayo de 1960 se detuvo a Valentín Campa, quien junto con Demetrio Vallejo, del POCM, saldría de prisión en 1969. En abril de 1960 José Revueltas y una docena de militantes pasaron del PCM al POCM. Al mes siguiente se realizó el XIII Congreso del PCM, el que anuló la expulsión de Campa (Laborde ya había muerto) y resolvió proponer al POCM la fusión de ambos partidos. En octubre el Partido Popular agregó a su nombre la palabra Socialista, a lo que respondió el PCM que ya existía en México el "partido político de la clase obrera", el propio PC. En agosto fue detenido Siqueiros, quien per-

Foto: Héctor García

David Alfaro Siqueiros, militante del Partido Comunista Mexicano

FOTO: HÉCTOR GARCÍA

Demetrio Vallejo, integrante del Partido Comunista Mexicano

maneció en prisión hasta el 14 de julio de 1964. En febrero de 1961 apareció *Nueva Época*, órgano teórico del comité central. En julio se publicó un ataque de la dirección del PCM contra José Revueltas y su "grupo revisionista y liquidador". Al mes siguiente se constituyó el Movimiento de Liberación Nacional (☛), con la participación de los comunistas, quienes por esos días, en Puebla, hacían frente a la persecución y los atentados del gobierno y otros sectores de la derecha, especialmente en la Universidad. A fin de año, el comité central acordó disolver el comité del DF. En 1962, el PCM manifestó su apoyo a la posición del gobierno de López Mateos de no romper relaciones con Cuba. El 20 de abril, acusado de "izquierdismo", fue expulsado un grupo de militantes del DF entre los que se hallaban Guillermo Rousset, Mario Rivera, Martín Reyes y Carlos Félix. Al mes siguiente fue asesinado Rubén Jaramillo, miembro del PCM. En 1963 Martínez Verdugo fue elegido primer secretario, cargo que se transformaría en el de secretario general y que conservaría hasta la desaparición del PCM. En ese año, con la participación de los comunistas, se constituyeron la Central Campesina Independiente y el Frente Electoral del Pueblo, en tanto que en mayo, en Morelia, se realizaba el Congreso Nacional de Estudiantes Democráticos. En noviembre el FEP nombró candidato a la Presidencia de la República a Ramón Danzós Palomino, líder agrario comunista. En diciembre de 1964, Arnoldo Martínez Verdugo formó parte de un grupo de dirigentes de 10 "partidos hermanos" de Latinoamérica que se entrevistó en Moscú y Pekín, respectivamente, con Leonid Briezhnev y Mao Tse-tung (Mao Zedong), a quienes pidieron, infructuosamente, poner fin a la disputa chino-soviética. El 6 de abril fue reprimida una manifestación de solidaridad con Vietnam, en la que participaron miembros de la JCM. Una semana después, la policía asaltó las oficinas del partido y detuvo a decenas de militantes. A fines del año anterior se habia iniciado el movimiento médico, en el que intervinieron profesionales de la medicina militantes del PC. Reprimido este movimiento, la actividad comunista se redujo prácticamente al medio estudiantil. Los miembros del PCM intervinieron en las huelgas de 1966 en la UNAM, la Escuela Nacional de Maestros, la Normal Superior y la Universidad Nicolaíta. En abril de ese año se constituyó la Central Nacional de Estudiantes Democráticos (☛). En esos meses, el PCM declaró que en México hacía "falta una nueva revolución" y lanzó críticas cada vez más severas al Partido Comunista de China, enfrascado en una dura polémica con los soviéticos. En 1967 se negó registró electoral a la coalición del PCM y un grupo escindido del PPS. En mayo, el profesor Lucio Cabañas, hasta entonces miembro del PCM, amenazado de muerte se ocultó en la sierra de Guerrero con un núcleo de autodefensa armada. En febrero de 1968 fue detenida por el ejército, en Celaya, una marcha del DF a Morelia, organizada por la CNED para exigir la libertad de los presos políticos. Una decena de dirigentes comunistas fueron detenidos. Poco después se produjo una escisión en la Juventud Comunista de la UNAM. El 26 de julio se inició el movimiento estudiantil de 1968 (☛). Esa misma noche fueron allanados por la policía los locales del PCM y la JC. Decenas de militantes fueron a la cárcel. En agosto ocurrió el primer distanciamiento de Moscú, cuando el PCM condenó la entrada de las fuerzas del Pacto de Varsovia en Checoslovaquia. En México, el PCM fue la organización con mayor número de presos políticos por su actuación en el movimiento estudiantil. En febrero de 1969, el comité central se manifiestó contra el monolitismo en el movimiento comunista internacional y señaló que era un hecho "la diversidad de puntos de vista". En junio, en la Conferencia Internacional de Partidos Comunistas y Obreros celebrada en Moscú, Martínez Verdugo acusó al go-bierno de Gustavo Díaz Ordaz de haber ejecutado "a sangre fría la matanza del 2 de octubre, en la que murieron más de cien personas" y denunció que Demetrio Vallejo y Valentín Campa tenían más de 10 años en prisión "por el 'delito' de dirigir las huelgas ferrocarrileras". En la misma reunión, declaró que era "imposible e innecesaria en la actualidad la existencia de cualquier forma de centro dirigente, mundial o regional, del movimiento comunista". El 2 de octubre fue secuestrado por efectivos militares Antonio Becerra Gaytán, líder comunista de Chihuahua. En ese mes, el comité central llamó a la "abstención activa" de los ciudadanos ante las elecciones. En abril de 1970 apareció el primer número del nuevo órgano comunista, *Oposición*, en tanto que *La Voz de México* se convertía en órgano interno. En agosto, Martínez Verdugo dijo que la cuestión "de las relaciones entre las Iglesia y el Estado ha madurado ya para una revisión de fondo". En septiembre, en el número 31, desapareció *Nueva Época*. El 10 de diciembre, los comunistas encarcelados participaron, con otros presos políticos, en una huelga de hambre que terminó ante el violento ataque de los reos comunes dirigidos por las autoridades. También en diciembre se celebró en Monterrey el tercer Congreso de la Juventud Comunista, que terminó con la salida de cientos de militantes, muchos de los cuales decidieron formar grupos guerrilleros. Con Luis Echeverría en la Presidencia de la República, el 10 de junio de 1971 fue agredida una manifestación estudiantil por grupos paramilitares. El PCM, con su militancia reducida a unos 200 miembros, llamó a luchar por el "derrocamiento de la oligarquía en el poder y su reemplazo por un gobierno de amplia coalición". En el curso de 1971 fueron liberados los presos del 68, lo que incluyó a todos los comunistas. En junio, por sus posiciones gobiernistas, David Alfaro Siqueiros fue excluido del comité central. En 1972, los dirigentes del sindicato de la UNAM ingresaron al PCM y con ellos cientos de trabajadores. Por la actividad de los ex jóvenes comunistas, el gobierno acusó al PCM de promover actos guerrilleros. El 15 de abril fueron detenidos tres dirigentes del partido. El 27 de mayo fue expulsado Arturo Orona, líder campesino que se había ligado al gobierno. En ese año fueron asesinados Joel Arriaga y Enrique Cabrera, dirigentes del PCM en Puebla. En 1973 se llamó nuevamente a la abstención electoral. Manuel Terrazas y Fernando Granados Cortés encabezaron la llamada Asamblea Permanente del PCM, grupo de acentuado prosovietismo, por lo que fueron expulsados durante el XIV Congreso del partido, celebrado en octubre, en el cual se ratificó el acuerdo de disolver la Juventud Comunista, adoptado por esta organización el mes anterior. El 24 de marzo se resolvió suprimir *La Voz de México*, en el número 2,007. Con este congreso se inició un proceso de auge del PCM, cuyos militantes se hicieron presentes en las más importantes movilizaciones sociales. Ante el secuestro de Rubén Figueroa por la guerrilla de Lucio Cabañas, la dirección del PCM declaró que esperaba que éste "garantizará su vida y la de quienes le acompañan" si el gobierno respetaba los compromisos adquiridos por el propio Figueroa. Del rescate pagado por Figueroa, Lucio Cabañas entregó una suma al PCM, la que se destinó a financiar las actividades de esta organización. En agosto, la dirección jalisciense del partido condenó el secuestro de J. Guadalupe Zuno. En noviembre, el pintor comunista José Chávez Morado recibió el Premio Nacional de Artes. En enero de 1975 fue asesinado el profesor comunista Hilario Moreno Aguirre en los *separos* de la Jefatura de Policía del DF. En abril se constituyó la Unión de Periodistas Democráticos, impulsada principalmente por los comunistas que trabajaban en la prensa. Apareció en ese año *Socialismo*, órgano teórico del que se publicarían siete números. En las elecciones de 1976, el PCM, sin registro, tuvo como candidato a la Presidencia de la República a Valentín Campa. *Oposición* calculó que había obtenido más de un millón de votos. En 1977 se iniciaron conversaciones con la Tendencia Democrática de los electricistas, el Partido Mexicano Socialista y otros grupos, con los que se discutió la fusión en un solo partido. En abril se celebró el primer Festival de *Oposición* en el Auditorio Nacional. En junio de 1977, el PCM compareció ante la Comisión Federal Electoral, donde demandó su registro electoral y abogó por conceder derechos políticos plenos a militares y ministros de los cultos. Paralelamente, realizó una campaña para afiliar a 100,000 nuevos miembros. En 1978 el PCM recibió el registro condicionado al resultado de los comicios de 1979, en los que obtuvo 675,677 votos (4.87 por ciento) en la elección de diputados de mayoría relativa y 703,038 (5.1 por ciento) en los de representación proporcional; en consecuencia, obtuvo el registro definitivo. Antes del XIX Congreso, en los medios partidarios y en la prensa comercial se desplegó la más amplia e intensa polémica entre los propios comunistas, la que inusitadamente no terminó con la exclusión de los disidentes. En su XX congreso (noviembre de 1981), el PCM se disolvió como tal para fusionarse en el Partido Socialista Unificado de México (☛). La misma asamblea ratificó la expulsión, acordada por el congreso estatal de Puebla, de Alfonso Vélez Pliego, Daniel Cazés Menache, Pascual Urbano Carreto, Humberto Sotelo y José Doger.

Partido Comunista de México ◆ Grupo político creado el 7 de septiembre de 1919 luego de una escisión del Partido Nacional Socialista (☛). Estaba integrado, entre otros, por Linn A. Gale, Fulgencio G. Luna, Geo Barreda, Enrique H. Arce, José Estrada, Enrique H. Rodríguez, C.F. Tabler, J.C. Parker. Varios de ellos eran estadounidenses que se habían trasladado a México para escapar al reclutamiento militar en su país. Su órgano extraoficial era el *Gale's Magazine*. Este partido intentó que la Internacional Comunista lo reconociera como representante de los comunistas mexicanos. El grupo se disolvió el 19 de mayo de 1921, luego de que el gobierno de Álvaro Obregón expulsara de México a varios de sus integrantes.

Partido Comunista Revolucionario Mexicano ◆ Organización fundada el 1 de marzo de 1921 por Nicolás Cano, quien fue su primer secretario general, Diego Aguillón, Teódulo Loman y otros. Abogaba por la participación electoral de los trabajadores desde una posición marxista. Participó en actividades sindicales y se opuso a la "acción directa" que proponían los anarquistas. Consideró que la Confederación Regional Obrera Mexicana y los partidos Laborista, Socialista de Yucatán y Nacional Agrarista estaban "al servicio de la burguesía". Particularmente activo en Guanajuato, el grupo participó en varias elecciones estatales. Mantuvo relaciones amistosas con el Partido Comunista Mexicano hasta que, noviembre de 1924, se incorporó a éste. Su órgano era la revista *Rebeldía*.

Partido Constitucional Progresista ◆ Agrupación creada por Francisco I. Madero el 17 de julio de 1911, tras retirarse del Partido Nacional Antirreeleccionista (☛), con la idea de marginar a Francisco Vázquez Gómez de la candidatura a la Vicepresidencia de la República en las elecciones de octubre de 1911. Esta agrupación presentó a Madero como candidato a la Presidencia, junto con el mismo Partido Nacional Antirreeleccionista y el Partido Católico Nacional (☛). El candidato a la vicepresidencia fue José María Pino Suárez, quien derrotó en la elección interna a Fernando Iglesias Calderón, que formalmente encabezaba el Partido Liberal (☛).

Partido Democracia Social ◆ Organización constituida el seis de mayo de 1998, encabezada por Gilberto Rincón Gallardo (☛) y que se ubica como un partido de centro que privilegia "el diálogo y el consenso". En 1999 obtuvo su registro como partido político nacional ante el IFE.

Partido Demócrata Mexicano ◆ Organización política fundada en 1971 por Ignacio González Gollaz, Baltasar Ignacio Valadés, Juan Aguilera Azpeitia

Foto: Dante Bucio

Gilberto Rincón Gallardo, presidente del Partido Democracia Social

Logotipo del Partido Democracia Social

Logotipo del Partido Demócrata Mexicano

Logotipo del Partido del Frente Cardenista de Reconstrucción Nacional

Luis N. Morones fundó el Partido Laborista Mexicano

y Leonardo Durán Juárez, integrantes de la Unión Nacional Sinarquista. Su antecedente fue el Partido Fuerza Popular (☛). El lema del PDM era "Democracia, independencia y revolución". Su asamblea constitutiva se realizó formalmente en junio de 1975 y González Gollaz fue nombrado presidente del comité nacional. De acuerdo con su declaración de principios, la religión debe estar por encima de cualquier actividad política, reivindica la propiedad privada como cimiento de la actividad económica y declara al Estado como la más perfecta de las sociedades humanas. Su programa contempla una sociedad plural en la que el individuo sea promovido de una clase social a otra. González Gollaz fue su delegado a las audiencias públicas de 1977, de las que surgiría la reforma política. En mayo de 1978 consiguió el registro condicionado a los comicios de 1979, en los que obtuvo 283,232 votos para la elección de diputados de mayoría relativa (2.04 por ciento del total) y 293,495 para los diputados de representación proporcional (2.13 por ciento), por lo que obtuvo su registro definitivo. En la contienda electoral por la Presidencia de la República, en 1982, el PDM tuvo como su candidato a González Gollaz, que obtuvo 433,886 votos (1.85 por ciento del total); en la fórmula 1 para la elección de senadores ganó 438,471 votos (1.96 por ciento) y 376,939 (1.88 por ciento) para la fórmula 2. En la elección de diputados de mayoría relativa tuvo 473,362 votos (2.28 por ciento) y 534,122 (2.33 por ciento) en la de diputados de representación proporcional. En 1987 el partido designó como su candidato presidencial para los comicios federales de 1988 a Gumersindo Magaña Negrete. En ese año, el número de sufragios recibidos fue inferior a 1.5 por ciento, por lo que perdió el registro. Recuperó el registro y en 1994 llevó como candidato a la Presidencia de México al ex panista y ex miembro del Partido de Foro Doctrinario y Democrático, Pablo Emilio Madero, quien obtuvo pocos votos. En la elección de jefe de gobierno del Distrito Federal de 1997, propuso a Baltazar Ignacio Valadez Montoya, quien quedó en último sitio en la votación. La organización fue disuelta el 29 de marzo de 1998. Algunos de sus militantes se integraron al Partido Alianza Social (☛).

Partido Democrático ◆ Organización creada a fines de 1908 y consolidada en enero de 1909. Sus fundadores eran porfiristas no afiliados a la corriente de los científicos. Su dirección estuvo formada por Benito Juárez Maza, Manuel Calero, José Peón del Valle, Jesús Urreta, Diódoro Batalla, Rafael Zurbarán Capmany, Carlos Trejo de Tejada, Abraham Castellanos, Manuel Castelazo y Fuentes, José G. Ortiz, Carlos Basave y del Castillo Negrete y Mauricio Gómez. Su manifiesto declaraba que el único problema político nacional era el de la educación, rechazaba la violencia y exigía el cumplimiento de las leyes de Reforma. Su órgano de difusión fue el periódico *México Nuevo*, que más tarde se convirtió también en foro de reyistas y antirreeleccionistas.

Partido del Frente Cardenista de Reconstrucción Nacional ◆ Nombre que adoptó el Partido Socialista de los Trabajadores (☛) en octubre de 1987. Casi dos meses más tarde, el 22 de noviembre, la asamblea nacional electoral ratificó el acuerdo. El partido adoptó el lema "El cardenismo es la vía constitucional al socialismo en México" y el ideario del ex presidente Lázaro Cárdenas como programa. El 4 de octubre de ese año, el presidente del PFCRN, Rafael Aguilar Talamantes, comunicó la decisión partidaria de invitar a Cuauhtémoc Cárdenas a que fuera su candidato a la presidencia, lo que sucedió a fines de ese año. En esa ocasión el partido obtuvo 10 por ciento de los votos y 33 curules en la Cámara de Diputados. En 1988 su dirección estaba integrada por Pedro Etienne, secretario general; César del Ángel, secretario de organización; Jorge Amador Amador, secretario del Frente de Trabajadores Agrícolas; Israel Galán Baños, secretario de Trabajdores Intelectuales; Roberto Jaramillo, secretario de Relaciones; y Rubén Venadero, secretario de Educación Política. En 1989 el secretario general era Fernando Pineda Ménez y en el mismo año fue sustituido por Roberto Jaramillo. En las eleciones intermedias de 1991 la votación que alcanzó le permitió tener 20 curules en la Cámara de Diputados. En las elecciones de 1994 fue su candidato Aguilar Talamantes, quien no alcanzó el 1.5 por ciento de los votos reglamentarios y perdió el registro. En 1996 se transformó en Partido Cardenista (☛).

Partido Fuerza Popular ◆ Brazo político de la Unión Nacional Sinarquista (☛). Fue fundado en León, Guanajuato, por Antonio Madrigal Urbizo, Gustavo Arizmendi, Ignacio Martínez Aguayo, Luis Hernández Espinosa y Enrique Morfín González. Obtuvo su registro en mayo de 1946 y lo perdió en enero de 1949, a petición del PRI, el Congreso de la Unión y diversas organizaciones obreras y campesinas, debido a que este partido realizó un mitin, en diciembre de 1948, en el que la estatua de Benito Juárez fue cubierta con una capucha. El PFP aseguraba tener relaciones con la Falange Española.

Partido Laborista Mexicano ◆ Organización fundada el 29 de diciembre de 1919 por Luis N. Morones y Samuel Yúdico, como expresión política de la Confederación Regional Obrera Mexicana. Su antecedente fue el Partido Socialista Obrero (☛), que el mismo Morones creó en 1917. El Partido Laborista planteaba en su programa dar impulso a la educación, sobre todo en beneficio de los trabajadores; el mejoramiento de la seguridad social y el crédito a los campesinos. Junto con los partidos Liberal Cooperatista y Nacional Agrarista apoyó, en 1920, la candidatura de Álvaro Obregón. En 1922 formó con otras organizaciones obregonistas una coalición electoral, la Confederación Nacional Revolucionaria, destinada a restar influencia al Partido

Liberal Cooperatista, que se había distanciado del caudillo sonorense. Más tarde apoyó la candidatura de Plutarco Elías Calles (1924), quien ya al frente del Poder Ejecutivo Federal ordenó que a los empleados públicos se les descontaran cuotas en favor del PLM. En mayo de 1926 participó en la Alianza de Partidos Socialistas, frente de agrupaciones políticas gobiernistas, y en julio contendió en las elecciones como parte del Bloque Nacionalista. En ese año el partido contaba con un secretario de Estado, dos jefes de departamento, 40 diputados, once senadores y dos gobernadores. Sus miembros controlaban varios congresos locales y numerosos ayuntamientos. Asimismo, en ellos recaían las designaciones presidenciales de "agregados obreros" en las embajadas mexicanas. En 1928 tuvo nuevamente como candidato presidencial a Obregón, pero en el curso de la campaña tuvo serias discrepancias con el general. Cuando éste fue asesinado (17 de julio de 1928), los obregonistas señalaron como responsables a Morones y otros dirigentes laboristas, quienes tuvieron que renunciar a sus cargos en el gobierno. El partido perdió más fuerza cuando Emilio Portes Gil, viejo adversario de la CROM, asumió la Presidencia (septiembre de 1928) y poco después dispuso que no se descontaran a los empleados públicos las cuotas para el PLM. Al iniciarse los trabajos orientados a constituir el Partido Nacional Revolucionario, los laboristas participaron por disciplina hacia Calles, pero después éste optó por marginar al PLM del naciente partido oficial. Simultáneamente hubo una escisión en la CROM y el propio PLM, del que se desprendió un grupo que se llamó Partido Laborista Independiente y se incorporó al PNR, junto con los partidos Laborista de Jalisco, del Trabajo de San Luis Potosí y del Trabajo del Estado de Puebla, todos ellos cromianos. En un teatro capitalino se presentaba una obra llamada *El desmoronamiento de Morones*, ilustrativa del declive en que habían entrado el PLM y su líder, quien se mantuvo cercano a Calles hasta el final político de éste.

PARTIDO LIBERAL ◆ En agosto de 1911, los moderados que se habían separado del Partido Liberal Mexicano entre 1905 y 1910 fundaron en la ciudad de México un periódico llamado, al igual que el magonista, *Regeneración*. Fue dirigido por Juan Sarabia y Antonio I. Villarreal y aparecía como órgano de la Junta Iniciadora de la Reorganización del Partido Liberal, en el que también estaban Camilo Arriaga, Antonio Díaz Soto y Gama, Jesús Flores Magón y Santiago R. de la Vega. El presidente era Fernando Iglesias Calderón y el primer vocal Eduardo Hay. El grupo, que pronto empezó a llamarse simplemente Partido Liberal, consideraba que el viejo ejército porfiriano era una garantía de paz y no le escatimaron elogios. El 13 de agosto, Sarabia, Villarreal y Jesús Flores Magón enviaron una carta a los zapatistas y magonistas invitándolos a deponer las armas. Días después, Victoriano Huerta lanzó un ataque sobre un grupo de zapatistas inermes. Éste y otros hechos los hicieron modificar su visión del viejo ejército y desde el *Diario del Hogar*, periódico también dirigido por Sarabia, se llegó a decir "no hay zapatismo sino problema agrario" (19 de noviembre). Como varios integrantes de este Partido Liberal pertenecían también al Partido Constitucional Progresista (☛) de Francisco I. Madero, participaron en sus actividades, trataron de influir en su orientación y lanzaron como precandidato a la Viceprencia de la República a Iglesias Calderón, quien fue derrotado por Pino Suárez en la convención del PCP de agosto-septiembre de 1911, en la cual Camilo Arriaga es designado presidente del comité electoral (director de campaña), con lo que se convirtió en un personaje muy cercano a Madero, pero cada vez más lejos de sus compañeros del Partido Liberal. El 18 de octubre se fusionó con el Partido Democrático, en el que también militaba Villarreal, junto a personajes como Carlos Trejo Lerdo de Tejada. Poco después se hizo público que Luis Cabrera pertenecía al partido. El Partido Liberal prestó un apoyo activo a Madero y un personaje prominente de la organización, Jesús Flores Magón, fue miembro del gabinete maderista. Algunos de sus miembros, como Sarabia y Díaz Soto y Gama, ejercieron contra el gobierno una crítica de centro-izquierda, se opusieron a la represión del zapatismo lo mismo que a los movimientos antimaderistas. En la convención partidaria de abril de 1912, el ala derecha, con el apoyo de Villarreal, ocupó los principales puestos. En esa ocasión se acusó a Sarabia de recibir dinero de Pascual Orozco. Poco después Sarabia resultó elegido diputado por San Luis Potosí y formó con Soto y Gama "la extrema izquierda del Partido Liberal". Soto y Gama se concentró en el trabajo de la Casa del Obrero Mundial (☛) y se ligó al zapatismo, al que se incorporó después del golpe de Estado de Victoriano Huerta, en tanto que Jesús Flores Magón y Carlos Trejo Lerdo de Tejada apoyaron al nuevo dictador. Arriaga, ya distanciado del partido, se exilió en Estados Unidos.

PARTIDO LIBERAL CONSTITUCIONALISTA ◆ Agrupación fundada en 1916 en el Jockey Club de la ciudad de México, con el apoyo de Álvaro Obregón, Pablo González y Benjamín Hill. Entre sus miembros se contaban Pastor Rouaix, Jesús Acuña, José Inés Novelo, Rafael Zurbarán Capmany (ex integrante del Partido Democrático), Rafael Martínez de Escobar, Eduardo Neri y Manuel García Vigil. Defendía los principios de la revolución maderista y presentó como candidato presidencial a Venustiano Carranza. En 1920 apoyó la candidatura de Álvaro Obregón. De las elecciones de ese año emergió como el partido más importante, con mayoría en la Cámara de Diputados y varios de sus miembros en puestos importantes dentro del Poder Ejecutivo. En 1922 hubo un distanciamiento entre Obregón y el PLC, que se dividió en dos alas, una que integraban los incondicionales del presidente y otra alineada con Adolfo de la Huerta, la que se disolvió al ser derrotada la rebelión militar de 1923.

FOTO: ARCHIVO CASASOLA

Antonio Díaz Soto y Gama, fundador del Partido Liberal Mexicano

FOTO: ARCHIVO CASASOLA

Jesús Flores Magón, militante del Partido Liberal Mexicano

PARTIDO LIBERAL MEXICANO ◆ Por iniciativa de Camilo Arriaga, en agosto de 1900 se formuló una *Invitación al Partido Liberal*, firmada por 126 personas, en la que se convocaba a la creación de clubes liberales, los que celebrarían un congreso el 5 de febrero de 1901, en San Luis Potosí. El congreso se efectuó con la participación de representantes de 50 de esos clubes, entre ellos Ricardo Flores Magón, delegado del periódico *Regeneración*, y los miembros del Club Liberal Ponciano Arriaga de San Luis Potosí: Camilo Arriaga, Antonio Díaz Soto y Gama, José María Facha, Blas C. Rodríguez, Moisés García y Genaro L. Zapata, quienes habían hecho la invitación. En la reunión fueron aprobadas 51 resoluciones, entre las que destacan: defender la educación liberal, postular como principio el respeto a las leyes, instruir a los obreros acerca de sus derechos y luchar por la autonomía municipal y la libertad de elección. Como la reunión estuviera marcada por un acentuado anticlericalismo, el obispo potosino Ignacio Montes de Oca y Obregón excomulgó a todos los asistentes, lo que no impidió la creación de nuevos núcleos, que en octubre sumaban por lo menos 150. Ante ese crecimiento de la oposición, el gobierno de Porfirio Díaz clausuró clubes, cerró periódicos opositores y encarceló a los principales líderes, lo que impidió realizar el segundo congreso, que debía ser el 5 de febrero de 1902. En febrero de 1903 salió Arriaga de la cárcel y, en la ciudad de México, reorganizó el Club Ponciano Arriaga con Soto y Gama, los hermanos Sarabia y los Flores Magón, Santiago de la Hoz, Juana B. Gutiérrez de Mendoza, Alfonso Cravioto y otros luchadores, a los que se unieron Librado Rivera y Santiago R. de la Vega. En junio de 1903 Arriaga y Soto y Gama, sintiéndose amenazados de muerte por el general Bernardo Reyes, se vieron obligados a exiliarse en Estados Unidos. Un ala del grupo participó simultáneamente en el antirreeleccionista Club Redención (1903-04). *El Hijo del Ahuizote*, periódico que se había convertido en órgano del club desde noviembre de 1902, fue clausurado por Díaz el 16 de abril de 1903. En esa ocasión fueron detenidos los Sarabia, Enrique y Ricardo Flores Magón, Librado Rivera, De la Vega y Cravioto, entre otros que pasarían varios meses en prisión. A fines de ese año, la mayoría de ellos se trasladó a Laredo, Texas, en tanto que Cravioto y un pequeño grupo se quedó en la ciudad de México, donde publicaron *El Colmillo Público*. En marzo de 1904 los liberales se dividieron en dos grupos. En el primero, que marchó a San Antonio con Arriaga como dirigente principal, se alinearon Soto y Gama, De la Vega, Juana B. Gutiérrez de Mendoza y Elisa Acuña y Rosete. Por otra parte, con los Flores Magón quedaron Sarabia y Rivera. La ruptura todavía no era definitiva, pues Arriaga ayudó económicamente para que los Flores Magón pudieran editar *Regeneración*, para el que escribió algunos artículos y hasta consiguió una importante préstamo de Francisco I. Madero. En mayo de 1904 el núcleo de Laredo se trasladó a San Antonio, Texas, pero ante la hostilidad de las autoridades locales y la amenaza de pistoleros enviados por Porfirio Díaz, en febrero de 1905 pasó a San Luis Misuri, donde se acentuó su radicalismo y ahondó su distanciamiento con Arriaga, quien todavía en septiembre participó en la constitutución de la Junta Organizadora del Partido Liberal Mexicano, con Ricardo Flores Magón como presidente. Éste, al mes siguiente, rompió abiertamente con Arriaga, en un artículo aparecido en *El Colmillo Público*, donde lo acusaba de traidor y agente de la dictadura. Otros miembros de la Junta eran Juan Sarabia (vicepresidente), Enrique Flores Magón, Librado Rivera, Manuel Sarabia, Antonio I. Villarreal y Rosalío Bustamante. Pese a las diferencias entre los dirigentes, el tiraje de *Regeneración*, órgano oficial del partido, aumentó hasta 20,000 ejemplares en septiembre y a 30,000 en 1906. Era distribuido en México mediante los trabajadores ferroviarios y llegaba al citado Madero, a Salvador Alvarado, Adolfo de la Huerta, Eulalio Gutiérrez, Plutarco Elías Calles, Francisco J. Mújica y otros futuros líderes revolucionarios. En septiembre de 1905 se publicaron las *Bases para la Unificación del Partido Liberal Mexicano*, que establecían las "formación de células secretas" en México y la mayor confidencialidad en los manejos de la organización. En el mismo mes, los editores del periódico fueron procesados bajo el cargo de difamación y salieron de la cárcel hasta mediados de diciembre, cuando mediante una amplia campaña de solidaridad se reunió dinero suficiente para pagar su fianza. El 4 de octubre de 1905 miembros del PLM participaron en la huelga de la fábrica de tabacos El Valle Nacional, de Orizaba, Veracruz, donde sus 500 obreros triunfaron después de dos meses. En ese lapso se formó la Gran Liga de Torcedores de Tabaco. En marzo de 1906, Juan Sarabia y los Flores Magón, en riesgo de ser extraditados, se refugiaron en Canadá, hasta donde los siguieron los detectives de la agencia estadounidense Pinkerton, estimulados por la recompensa de 20,000 dólares que ofreció la dictadura porfiriana por cada uno. Rivera, Villarreal y Manuel Sarabia se quedaron en San Luis Misuri al frente del periódico. En julio de 1906 la Junta publicó el

PLAN LIBERAL

JUNTA ORGANIZADORA DEL PARTIDO LIBERAL MEXICANO

PROGRAMA DEL PARTIDO LIBERAL Y MANIFIESTO A LA NACION

MEXICANOS:

PROGRAMA DEL PARTIDO LIBERAL

EXPOSICION

PAGINA 71

Primera página del *Programa del Partido Liberal*

Huelga de Cananea, mural de Siqueiros, que ilustra el movimiento laboral en que tomó parte el Partido Liberal Mexicano

Manifiesto y programa del Partido Liberal Mexicano, que comprendía 52 puntos bajo el lema "Reforma, libertad y justicia". El documento, del que se hicieron 250,000 ejemplares, sentaba las bases de un sistema democrático y pedía el respeto a las leyes; consideraba ilegales las reformas a la Constitución de 1857 y se proponía reducir el periodo presidencial a cuatro años sin posibilidad de reelección; exigía libertad de pensamiento y expresión; demandaba la supresión de los tribunales militares especiales y de la leva; supresión de las escuelas del clero; separación efectiva entre Estado e Iglesia; nacionalización de los bienes eclesiásticos; jornada laboral de ocho horas, salario mínimo con descanso dominical y prohibición del trabajo infantil; demandaba, asimismo, la creación de un banco agrícola y un reparto agrario justo. En junio de 1906, dirigida por militantes del PLM, estalló la huelga de Cananea (☛), aplastada por el gobierno con ayuda de un grupo de *rangers* estadounidenses. Pese a la represión, este movimiento repercutió en nuevas adhesiones al partido, sobre todo de obreros. En diciembre se produjeron huelgas de obreros textiles en Puebla, Tlaxcala, Jalisco, Querétaro, el Distrito Federal y, especialmente, en Río Blanco (☛), Veracruz, lugares todos donde los militantes liberales dirigían la protesta laboral, como sucedió durante la huelga ferrocarrilera de San Luis Potosí, en julio y agosto del mismo año. Ricardo Flores Magón y Juan Sarabia llegaron a El Paso, Texas, el 2 de septiembre, con el fin de preparar una insurrección "en legítima defensa de las libertades holladas". Este alzamiento representó una ruptura con Madero, quien se negó a proporcionar ayuda a los rebeldes. El plan consistía en tomar Ciudad Juárez al mismo tiempo que se producían levantamientos en diversos puntos del país, para lo cual contaban con 42 grupos armados. El 26 los revolucionarios ocuparon Ciudad Jiménez, pero al día siguiente fueron derrotados por los federales; el levantamiento en Ciudad Juárez no se realizó, los grupos de otros puntos del país fallaron y sólo los clubes del sur de Veracruz lograron algún éxito, pues tomaron el Palacio Municipal de Acayucan, pero se frustraron los ataques sobre Minatitlán y Puerto México y el 4 de octubre fueron derrotados en Catemaco. En ese mes eran miles los liberales detenidos y la recompensa que ofrecía la dictadura por Flores Magón aumentó a 25,000 dólares. Después de la derrota, Flores Magón y Villarreal publicaron un "Balance" de lo sucedido en el que reafirmaban la necesidad de una revolución "anticapitalista" y "antiimperialista". En junio de 1907, en Los Ángeles, Rivera, Villarreal, Práxides G. Guerrero y Lázaro Gutiérrez de Lara, veterano de Cananea, empezaron a publicar *Revolución*, donde aparecieron textos de Pedro Kropotkin y en el que Ricardo Flores Magón, ya en tono abiertamente anarquista, abogaba por una "sociedad nueva, igualitaria y feliz", a la vez que llamaba a la ocupación de tierras y condenaba el parlamentarismo. En agosto, Flores Magón, Rivera y Villarreal fueron aprehendidos en Los Ángeles. En octubre, bajo la influencia ideológica de los liberales, más de tres mil ferrocarrileros de San Luis Potosí protagonizaron una huelga para igualar sus derechos con los que tenían los empleados extranjeros. En la primavera de 1908, la Gran Liga de Empleados del Ferrocarril dirigió una huelga nacional de seis días. Durante los primeros meses de ese año, dentro del partido se produjo el marginamiento de Villarreal y Manuel Sarabia, quienes no compartían las tesis anarquistas. En junio las autoridades estadounidenses efectuaron allanamientos y redadas contra los miembros del PLM y dieron información al gobierno porfirista para hacer lo mismo al otro lado de la frontera, con el fin de evitar otra rebelión liberal, esta vez de carácter francamente anticapitalista, la que se produjo el día 24 de ese mes, cuando Viesca, Coahuila, fue tomada por los rebeldes, que lograron sostenerse durante dos días. En Las Vacas, Chihuahua, el día 26 fue atacada infructuosamente la guarnición militar y en Palomas se combatió el 30 de junio y el 1 de julio hasta que los liberales emprendieron la retirada a través del desierto. Algo similar ocurrió en Los Hornos, Coahuila, y en la sierra de Jimulco, en Coahuila. Relativamente exitoso fue el ataque sobre Mexicali, desde donde los rebeldes se desplazaron a otros puntos cercanos. Como consecuencia, Flores Magón, Rivera y Villarreal, que permanecían prisioneros en Los Ángeles, fueron incomunicados. La derrota de este levantamiento no acabó con la actividad de los opositores a la dictadura, pues los gobiernos de México y Estados Unidos re-

FOTO: ARCHIVO CASASOLA

Camilo Arriaga, fundador del Partido Liberal Mexicano

forzaron las guarniciones de la frontera texana, donde se movían numerosos "socialistas". En la capital mexicana, en una entrevista concedida al periodista estadounidense James Creelman, Porfirio Díaz admitió la posibilidad de permitir elecciones libres, alentó a la oposición y a los políticos porfiristas que veían cercana la desaparición física del dictador. Surgió entonces el Partido Demócrata, con el general y cacique neoleonés Bernardo Reyes como caudillo, y después el Nacional Antirreeleccionista, encabezado por Francisco I. Madero, quien había roto sus relaciones con el PLM desde 1906. En las serranías de Coahuila y en el sur de Veracruz se mantuvieron en actividad sendos focos guerrilleros que hacían circular propaganda del PLM. A la guerrilla veracruzana se unió, en julio de 1910, el líder agrarista Santanón (☛). Como respuesta a la fe de Madero en el voto, el 3 de septiembre de 1910, *Regeneración* contestaba: "Nuestras boletas electorales van a ser las balas que disparen nuestros fusiles". Poco después insistía en que el país estaba sumido en una "guerra de clases" y que "el mal que aflige al pueblo mexicano no se cura con quitar a Díaz y poner en su lugar a otro hombre". Durante varios años el PLM había sido el principal partido de oposición, disponía de una extendida red de clubes que funcionaban en la clandestinidad y sus cuadros contaban con experiencia en la propaganda, la dirección de huelgas, la organización y la lucha armada. Cuando se abrió la posibilidad de proseguir el combate por vías legales y públicas, muchos miembros del partido abandonaron la estrechez del apoliticismo ácrata y se incorporaron a los sectores sociales que ya seguían a Madero. En consecuencia, la dirección del partido, a los problemas propios de la lejanía geográfica, sumó el exilio de sus concepciones políticas, aisladas de un movimiento que buscó el cambio pacífico. Al frente del PLM seguían los Flores Magón, Rivera, Guerrero y formalmente Villarreal, quien se hallaba al margen de las decisiones. Cuando Madero fue víctima de fraude electoral y optó por llamar a todos los ciudadanos para que tomaran las armas el 20 de noviembre de 1910, la dirección del PLM exhortó a sus miembros a unirse a la revuelta, sin olvidar que el "movimiento personalista" de Madero representaba al "partido conservador". La lucha, decía el núcleo magonista, debía convertirse en "revolución económica" y dirigirse contra los "explotadores capitalistas". Junto a los éxitos de Pascual Orozco, los triunfos más resonantes en la primera fase del levantamiento fueron los obtenidos por los miembros del PLM, quienes ocuparon Mexicali el 29 de enero de 1911, en tanto que en Chihuahua y parte de Sonora, en colaboración con Orozco, se distinguieron Luis A. García, José de la Luz Soto, Lázaro Alanís, Benjamín y Prisciliano G. Silva, Jesús M. Ángel, José Inés Salazar, Alfredo Lugo, Benjamín Aranda y José C. Parra. Como corriera el rumor de que al triunfo de la insurrección Madero sería presidente y Ricardo Flores Magón ocuparía la vicepresidencia, numerosos magonistas abandonaron toda reserva sobre el primero, pese a que en *Regeneración* se publicó que Ricardo no tenía la intención de ocupar cargo alguno, pues "los gobiernos son los guardianes de los intereses de las clases ricas". La aclaración no llegó a muchos miembros del PLM, pues la circulación de su periódico se había dificultado por la guerra civil. Paradójicamente, la siempre anhelada revolución acabó de aislar al núcleo dirigente, que poco podía hacer para coordinar a sus partidarios desde el exilio. En febrero, el ala no magonista del PLM se cobró la marginación de que la hicieron objeto los anarquistas: Lázaro Gutiérrez de Lara, con su contingente, se puso a las órdenes de Madero y días después Villarreal se dirigió a la frontera con el mismo fin. Lo que precipitó el rompimiento total entre los magonistas y Madero fueron las disposiciones de éste contra quienes no se sujetaban a sus órdenes. Hizo aprehender a Prisciliano Silva por indisciplina y posteriormente a Luis A. García y otros oficiales por izar la bandera roja, lo que juzgó el "presidente provisional" como un "acto de rebeldía". Flores Magón respondió en un artículo titulado "Francisco I. Madero es un traidor a la causa de la libertad". Al triunfo de la insurrección, los que habían sido miembros del ala moderada del PLM se colocaron a la izquierda de Madero, pero a la derecha del magonismo. Exigían el cumplimiento de las promesas agrarias, pero llamaban a deponer las armas. El 13 de junio de 1911, enviados por Madero, Sarabia y Jesús Flores Magón se reunieron con los hermanos de éste, Ricardo y Enrique, a quienes pidieron, sin éxito, abandonar la lucha armada que proseguían sus partidarios, el impulso a las huelgas y las tomas de tierras. Como al día siguiente Rivera, Anselmo L. Figueroa, Ricardo y Enrique Flores Magón fueran detenidos, Ricardo supuso que habían sido delatados por Sarabia, a quien llamó "Judas", lo que inició entre radicales y moderados una polémica en la que abundaron las acusaciones gratuitas y hasta los chismes de alcoba. Poco después los moderados formaron en la ciudad de México el Partido Liberal (☛), mientras que numerosos grupos armados dirigidos por miembros del PLM se incorporaron a la revuelta de Pascual Orozco, cuyo Plan de la Empacadora estaba fuertemente influido por el programa del Partido Liberal Mexicano de 1906. Al producirse el golpe de Estado de Victoriano Huerta, los miembros del PLM se dispersaron: unos se incorporaron a las fuerzas campesinas de Zapata, otros al Constitucionalismo y los demás a la División del Norte. Librado Rivera y Ricardo Flores Magón estuvieron en prisión de 1911 a 1914. Para este año, dice Juan Gómez Quiñones, "el PLM se había contraído tanto que sólo consistía en el círculo inmediato que rodeaba a Flores Magón". Volvió a aparecer *Regeneración*, pero con escaso tiraje, sin franquicia postal y sujeto a una vigilancia especial de las autoridades. Los magonistas alquilaron una granja, en Edendale, California, donde fundaron una comuna con sus familias.

Ricardo se dedicó a escribir ensayos y la obra de teatro *Tierra y libertad*, que se representó en Los Ángeles en diciembre de 1915. Ocasionalmente participaba en mítines de la Unión Obrera Revolucionaria, nombre que había adoptado su grupo. También en 1915, algunos miembros y ex miembros del PLM participaron en la insurrección del Plan de San Diego, que pretendía establecer una república chicana en los territorios conquistados por Estados Unidos durante la guerra de 1847. Ricardo mantuvo ciertas reservas sobre este levantamiento, pero envió dinero para armas a Aniceto Pizaña, colaborador de *Regeneración*, quien se embolsó esos fondos. En 1916 Ricardo y Enrique fueron nuevamente a prisión. Para sacarlos de ahí, la anarquista Emma Goldman encabezó una campaña que culminó con el pago de las fianzas necesarias para ponerlos en libertad. En junio de 1917 escribió Ricardo que su hermano "Enrique y algunos otros se han separado del Grupo Regeneración". En marzo de 1918, en el último número del periódico, Ricardo y Librado Rivera aparecían como firmantes de un "Manifiesto de la Junta Organizadora del Partido Liberal Mexicano a los miembros del partido, a los anarquistas de todo el mundo y a los trabajadores en general". Era un documento contra la guerra mundial y en favor de la revolución anarquista. Por su contenido, en agosto de 1918 Ricardo y Librado volvieron a la cárcel, en la que Rivera permaneció hasta 1923 y de la que no salió vivo Flores Magón. Fue el último texto del PLM, organización que pese a su influencia en el periodo 1906-1910 y a la proyección de sus ideas en el Congreso Constituyente de 1917, estuvo lejos de ser un partido en el sentido moderno y hasta el final fue sólo una "junta organizadora", la que coordinó en su mejor época decenas y quizá centenares de clubes distribuidos en toda la República mexicana y el suroeste de Estados Unidos. El líder del PLM, pese a la repulsa que experimentaba por toda adulación, heredó su nombre a numerosos sindicatos, ejidos, salones, calles, células comunistas y grupos políticos gobiernistas. Su producción escrita nutrió por décadas la retórica oficial y sus móviles utópicos quedaron en la intuición, en la memoria incierta de los mexicanos.

Venustiano Carranza apoyó la formación de Partido Liberal Yucateco

PARTIDO LIBERAL YUCATECO ◆ Grupo político creado en octubre de 1916 por un grupo de yucatecos avecindados en la capital de la República, con el apoyo de Venustiano Carranza. En ese mismo mes, el partido designó a Bernardino Mena Brito como su candidato a gobernador de Yucatán en las elecciones locales de mayo de 1917. La organización se opuso primero a Salvador Alvarado y más tarde a Carlos Castro Morales. En 1920, el partido apoyó la candidatura presidencial de Ignacio Bonillas. Un año más tarde, en 1921, volvió a presentar a Mena Brito como su candidato a la gubernatura, quien en las elecciones del 6 de noviembre de ese año, sumó 2,888 votos y volvió a perder.

PARTIDO MAYORITARIO ◆ Fue creado por Rosendo Salazar en 1922, para hacer campaña en favor de la candidatura de Adolfo de la Huerta. Desapareció al ser derrotada la rebelión delahuertista, en 1924.

PARTIDO MEXICANO DEL PROLETARIADO ◆ Grupo marxista de tendencia maoísta fundado en 1966, a partir de una escisión de la Asociación Revolucionaria Espartaco. A su vez, en 1968 sufrió una importante división, pues la mayor parte de sus miembros se incorporaron al movimiento estudiantil de ese año. Actuó entre algunos sectores universitarios del Distrito Federal hasta principios de los años setenta.

PARTIDO MEXICANO SOCIALISTA ◆ Organización surgida de la fusión del Movimiento Revolucionario del Pueblo, el grupo Unidad de Izquierda Comunista y los partidos Socialista Unificado de México, Mexicano de los Trabajadores y Patriótico Revolucionario, según el acuerdo tomado en marzo de 1987. Sus documentos definen al PMS como un partido revolucionario de masas, de carácter socialista, patriótico, antiimperialista y democrático. Su objetivo principal es convertirse en una fuerza alternativa de poder fundamentada en la lucha por la democracia, por las reivindicaciones de los sectores trabajadores y por la independencia de México. Obtuvo su registro ante la Comisión Federal Electoral el 26 de junio de 1987. Del 26 al 29 de noviembre del mismo año efectuó su primer congreso nacional. Previamente, mediante un sitema de elecciones primarias que se utilizó por primera vez en México, Heberto Castillo Martínez resultó su candidato a la presidencia de la República, para los comicios federales de 1988. El congreso eligió como secretario general del partido a Gilberto Rincón Gallardo. En junio de 1988, Castillo declinó su candidatura en favor de Cuauhtémoc Cárdenas, candidato del Frente Democrático Nacional. De acuerdo con las cifras oficiales, el PMS obtuvo 2.11 por ciento de la votación total. Después de las elecciones, los dirigentes anunciaron su interés en fusionar al partido con otras organizaciones del citado frente, principalmente con la Corriente Democratizadora integrada por expriistas. En abril de 1989 la mayoría de sus militantes se integraron al PRD (☛).

Heberto Castillo, fundador del PMS y del PMT

PARTIDO MEXICANO DE LOS TRABAJADORES ◆ Organización surgida entre el 5 y el 8 de septiembre de 1974, durante el último congreso del Comité Nacional de Auscultación y Organización (CNAO). Éste se había formado en noviembre de 1973 a partir del Comité

Logotipo del Partido Mexicano de los Trabajadores

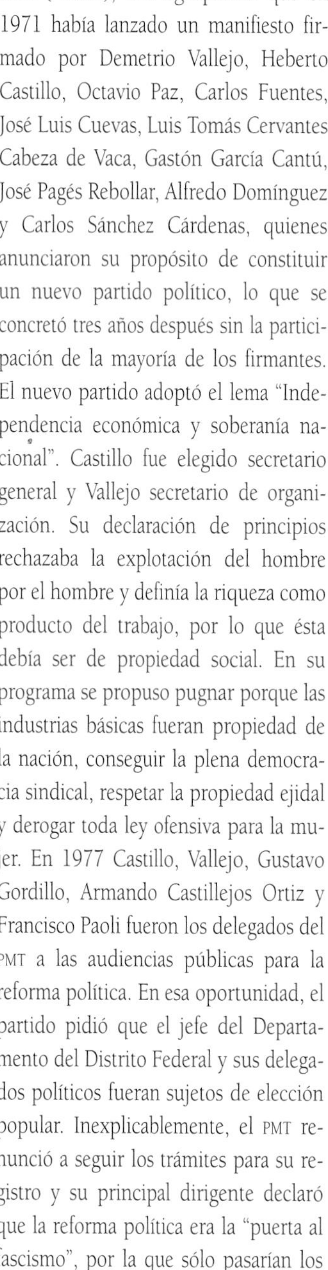

Nacional de Auscultación y Coordinación (CNAO), una agrupación que en 1971 había lanzado un manifiesto firmado por Demetrio Vallejo, Heberto Castillo, Octavio Paz, Carlos Fuentes, José Luis Cuevas, Luis Tomás Cervantes Cabeza de Vaca, Gastón García Cantú, José Pagés Rebollar, Alfredo Domínguez y Carlos Sánchez Cárdenas, quienes anunciaron su propósito de constituir un nuevo partido político, lo que se concretó tres años después sin la participación de la mayoría de los firmantes. El nuevo partido adoptó el lema "Independencia económica y soberanía nacional". Castillo fue elegido secretario general y Vallejo secretario de organización. Su declaración de principios rechazaba la explotación del hombre por el hombre y definía la riqueza como producto del trabajo, por lo que ésta debía ser de propiedad social. En su programa se propuso pugnar porque las industrias básicas fueran propiedad de la nación, conseguir la plena democracia sindical, respetar la propiedad ejidal y derogar toda ley ofensiva para la mujer. En 1977 Castillo, Vallejo, Gustavo Gordillo, Armando Castillejos Ortiz y Francisco Paoli fueron los delegados del PMT a las audiencias públicas para la reforma política. En esa oportunidad, el partido pidió que el jefe del Departamento del Distrito Federal y sus delegados políticos fueran sujetos de elección popular. Inexplicablemente, el PMT renunció a seguir los trámites para su registro y su principal dirigente declaró que la reforma política era la "puerta al fascismo", por la que sólo pasarían los que se agacharan lo suficiente. En 1981, Castillo propuso al PCM, el PPM y otras organizaciones fusionarse en un solo partido, lo que fue aceptado. Cuando se discutían los documentos básicos de la nueva formación política, el PMT se retiró del proceso, aparentemente porque no se aceptaron las propuestas de Castillo sobre los símbolos y la estructura interna. En 1983 fue expulsado Demetrio Vallejo. Para entonces ya habían abandonado el partido Gustavo Gordillo y Francisco Paoli, entre otros militantes. En 1984 solicitó y obtuvo su registro condicionado al resultado de las elecciones de 1985, donde obtuvo la votación suficiente para tener registro definitivo. En marzo de 1987 el PMT decidió fundirse con otros agrupamientos en el Partido Mexicano Socialista (☛). Su órgano de difusión fue *Insurgencia Popular*.

Filomeno Mata, miembro del Partido Nacional Antirreeleccionista

PARTIDO NACIONAL AGRARISTA ◆ Organización fundada el 13 de junio de 1920 por Antonio Díaz Soto y Gama, Rodrigo Gómez, Felipe Santibáñez y Octavio Paz Solórzano. En 1922, con el apoyo de Álvaro Obregón, el partido se alió con el Partido Laborista para formar la Confederación Nacional Revolucionaria, que obtuvo mayoría en el Congreso. En 1925 el PNA tuvo algunas discrepancias con Plutarco Elías Calles y empezó a declinar. En 1929 se integró al Partido Nacional Revolucionario.

PARTIDO NACIONAL ANTICOMUNISTA ◆ Grupo formado en la ciudad de México, el 18 de marzo de 1960. En su Comité Ejecutivo Nacional estaban Mario Guerra Leal, presidente; Roberto Cañedo, secretario de Acción Cinematográfica; Mateo Cruz Lara, secretario de Acción Obrera; y María Guerra Tejeda, secretaria de Acción Magisterial. Su principal actividad fue la publicación de desplegados periodísticos durante los meses en que se supo de su existencia.

PARTIDO NACIONAL ANTIRREELECCIONISTA ◆ Agrupación creada en 1909, en la ciudad de México, con el nombre de Centro Antirreeleccionista, para sostener las tesis expuestas por Francisco I. Madero en *La sucesión presidencial de 1910*. Su primer presidente fue Emilio Vázquez Gómez, quien estuvo auxiliado por el propio Madero, así como por Filomeno Mata, Luis Cabrera, Toribio Esquivel Obregón y José Vasconcelos. El centro promovió la creación de clubes similares en provincia, los cuales adoptaron el lema de la organización capitalina: "Sufragio efectivo, no reelección". Los principios básicos del antirreeleccionismo fueron la no reelección en los cargos públicos, el respeto a la Constitución, al voto y a las garantías individuales, así como la libertad municipal. Éstos se publicaron en 1910, en un folleto llamado *El Partido Nacional Antirreeleccionista y la próxima lucha electoral*. En su convención de 1910, el partido postuló a Madero y a Vázquez Gómez como candidatos a la presidencia y a la vicepresidencia, respectivamente. El partido editaba el periódico *El Antirreeleccionista*. Un año más tarde, el 9 de julio de 1911, Madero encabezó una importante escisión, de la que surgió el Partido Constitucional Progresista (☛). Con sus fuerzas notoriamente disminuidas, el partido, en el que permanecieron Vázquez Gómez, Rafael Martínez, Pedro Galicia, entre otros, participó en las elecciones de ese año, con Madero como candidato a la presidencia y Vázquez Gómez a la Vicepresidencia de la República.

PARTIDO NACIONAL COOPERATISTA ◆ Agrupación fundada en agosto de 1917 por Jorge Prieto Laurens, Otilio González, Rafael Pérez Taylor, Fernando Saldaña Galván y Gabriel García Rojas, entre otros, con el apoyo de Manuel Aguirre Berlanga, secretario de Gobernación de Venustiano Carranza. Su primer presidente fue Jacinto B. Treviño. Su programa tendía, entre otras cosas, a fortalecer el cooperativismo entre las clases populares y pugnaba por la nacionalización de la tierra y de las grandes empresas. Desde 1920 participó activamente en procesos electorales y obtuvo diversas diputaciones, gubernaturas y ayuntamientos (entre ellos el del Distrito Federal). Logró la mayoría de las curules en la XXIX Legislatura (1922). El PNC desapareció en 1923, luego de que sus dirigentes apoyaron el movimiento delahuertista.

Partido Nacional Reeleccionista ◆ Organismo fundado en 1909 por decisión de Porfirio Díaz para apoyar su candidatura a la presidencia de la República y la de Ramón Corral a la Vicepresidencia en las elecciones de 1910, últimas en las que el caudillo se adjudicó el triunfo.

Partido Nacional Revolucionario ◆ El 1 de septiembre de 1928, en su cuarto y último informe de gobierno, el presidente Plutarco Elías Calles propuso la formación de "reales partidos nacionales orgánicos" que permitieran "pasar de un sistema más o menos velado de gobierno de caudillos a un más franco régimen de instituciones". Con ese fin y para acabar con "la desunión de la familia revolucionaria", de manera informal se iniciaron los trabajos encaminados a constituir un partido de dicha "familia". Por iniciativa del mandatario se convocó a una junta celebrada el 22 de noviembre del mismo año en el número 156 de la calle de Londres, domicilio de Luis L. León, a la que asistieron 22 personas, entre las cuales había allegados al Ejecutivo lo mismo que políticos con influencia regional. El mismo día que Calles dejó la presidencia de la República, el 1 de diciembre, se dio a conocer el Comité Organizador del Partido Nacional Revolucionario, encabezado por el caudillo sonorense e integrado por Luis L. León, secretario general; Aarón Sáenz, secretario de Organización; Manuel Pérez Treviño, tesorero y segundo secretario de Organización; Basilio Vadillo, secretario del Interior; Manlio Fabio Altamirano, secretario de Propaganda y Publicidad; David C. Orozco, tercer secretario de Organización; y Bartolomé Gacía Correa, cuarto secretario de Organización. El Comité expidió el mismo día un manifiesto, dirigido "a todos los revolucionarios", en el que convocaba a una convención constituyente del PNR en la que se discutirían los estatutos y el programa del nuevo partido, se eligiría candidato a la presidencia de la República y se nombraría comité directivo. El 8 de diciembre Calles y Sáenz se retiraron del comité. El primero para dirigir efectivamente los trabajos, sin exponerse a los inevitables roces que implicaba su participación en un órgano semejante. Sáenz, por su parte, quedaba libre para preparar su campaña como aspirante a la candidatura presidencial por el PNR. Pérez Treviño pasó a encabezar el comité, que tenía su sede en avenida del Palacio Legislativo número 2, esquina con Paseo de la Reforma, local que el 10 de febrero de 1929 sufrió un atentado de origen desconocido. La convocatoria formal para la convención constituyente se emitió el 5 de febrero de 1929 y daba cinco días de plazo a "todos los partidos y agrupaciones revolucionarias" para afiliarse al comité. Los delegados a la asamblea serían elegidos en proporción de uno por cada 10,000 habitantes. El proyecto de Declaración de Principios señalaba que el PNR se comprometía a luchar por "la libertad del sufragio y el triunfo de las mayorías en los comicios", así como a lograr el pleno cumplimiento de los artículos 27 y 123 de la Constitución, pues consideraba que los obreros y campesinos eran "el factor social más importante de la colectividad mexicana". Establecía como fundamental "la lucha de clases" y el "cumplimiento de las leyes" como "garantía de los derechos del proletariado". El programa comprendía cinco capítulos: Educación, Industria, Agricultura, Comunicación y Hacienda. Señalaba que la enseñanza debía "fortalecer la conciencia de la nacionalidad a partir de factores étnicos e históricos", ponía a la colectividad por encima de "los intereses privados o individuales"; se proponía favorecer "las industrias basadas en los capitales mexicanos o extranjeros que se encontrasen en su totalidad en México" y, asimismo, "organizar a los pequeños industriales para colocarlos en posición de defensa frente a la competencia de la gran industria"; se hacía una defensa del ejido y se llamaba a repartir las grandes propiedades; se planteaba la necesidad de mejorar la red ferroviaria y construir caminos, así como "restablecer y mantener orden en la economía y en la hacienda nacionales a través de la coordinación de las actividades de producción, de circulación y de consumo". El proyecto de estatutos, elaborado principalmente por Basilio Vadillo, proponía una estructura vertical con comités municipales y estatales; un Comité Directivo Nacional, con un representante de cada partido local, que a su vez eligiría al Comité Ejecutivo Nacional. Paralelamente, tendría carácter confederado, pues subsistirían los partidos municipales, regionales y nacionales afiliados. El lema sería "Instituciones y reforma social". Hubo resistencias en algunos sectores oficialistas a incorporarse al nuevo partido. Adalberto Tejeda se marginó de los trabajos preparatorios; el Partido Nacional Agrarista, bastión del obregonismo, sufrió una escisión y sólo una parte llegó a la asamblea constitutiva; la CROM y el Partido Laborista, primero desairados por Calles y luego divididos, no llegaron a la Convención de Querétaro, a la que sólo asistieron delegaciones de partidos locales afiliados o del Partido Laborista Independiente, que agrupó a los antimoronistas. También se negaron a incorporarse los miembros del Partido Nacional Antirreeleccionista y los seguidores de Vasconcelos, así como los partidarios de Gilberto Valenzuela, Antonio I. Villarreal y Pedro Rodríguez Triana, aspirantes a la presidencia de la República. El 1 de marzo se inauguró la convención en el Teatro de la República, de Querétaro. Como no se concediera acreditación a numerosos delegados favorables a Sáenz, éste anunció que no asistiría y declaró que la asamblea no era "más que una farsa", con lo que dejó libre el camino a su contrincante, Pascual Ortiz Rubio. A las cuatro de la tarde, con 874 delegados presentes, se estableció que había *quórum* y dio inicio la reunión, que presidió Filiberto Gómez. El segundo día aumentó el número de delegados a 950. A la sesión del día 3 no se presentaron las representaciones de Guanajuato y Jalisco. Por la tarde se supo que ese día se habían levantado en armas los generales José Gonzalo Escobar, Francisco R.

Plutarco Elías Calles, fundador del Partido Nacional Revolucionario

Manzo y Jesús M. Aguirre. Calles, que se encontraba en la ciudad de México, urgió a Pérez Treviño a acelerar los trabajos ante la amenaza que representaba la asonada. En el cuarto día de sesiones se aprobaron los documentos fundamentales y los 148 partidos locales o regionales ahí representados, provenientes de 28 entidades, se comprometieron a adaptar sus estatutos a los del PNR. Se eligió a los integrantes del Comité Ejecutivo Nacional: Pérez Treviño, presidente; Luis L. León, secretario general; Bartolomé García Correa, secretario de Actas; Melchor Ortega, secretario de Prensa; David C. Orozco, tesorero; Gonzalo N. Santos, secretario del Distrito Federal; y, como secretario del Exterior, Filiberto Gómez, quien a las 12 horas con 20 minutos, declaró "formal y legalmente constituido" el Partido Nacional Revolucionario. Según otro acuerdo, su órgano oficial sería un diario denominado *Revolución*, que finalmente se llamó *El Nacional Revolucionario* (☛). También se propuso crear un Instituto de Ciencias Sociales. El delegado zacatecano Manuel Reyes propuso como candidato a la presidencia de la República a Pascual Ortiz Rubio, lo que se aprobó por aclamación. Acto seguido, éste rindió su protesta y pronunció un discurso, antes de que se diera por terminada la reunión. Entre las organizaciones que estuvieron representadas en Querétaro se cuentan el Partido Socialista del Sureste, el Partido Socialista Fronterizo, el Partido Liberal Independiente, el Partido Socialista Agrario de Campeche, el Partido Socialista Michoacano, el Partido Liberal Jalisciense, la Confederación de Partidos Guanajuatenses, el Partido Laborista del Estado de México, el Partido Laborista de Jalisco, el Partido Socialista del Trabajo de Veracruz, el Partido del Trabajo de San Luis Potosí y el Partido del Trabajo del Estado de Puebla. El 11 de mayo la Secretaría de Gobernación extendió al PNR su registro electoral y en los comicios federales de ese año Ortiz Rubio, de acuerdo con los datos oficiales, derrotó a José Vasconcelos, del Partido Antirreeleccionista, y a Pedro Rodríguez Triana, del PCM. Para fortalecer a la dirección nacional, se reconoció la autoridad de los principales partidos de cada entidad, los que acabaron por absorver a las otras organizaciones. De este modo cobraron preeminencia los líderes de agrupaciones como el Partido Socialista de Tlaxcala, el Partido Social-Demócrata de Nuevo León, la Confederación de Partidos Socialistas de Oaxaca o el Gran Partido Revolucionario de Jalisco, de Margarito Ramírez. Lo mismo sucedió con las organizaciones creadas en 1929, como el PNR del Centro de San Luis Potosí, de Saturnino Cedillo. En enero de 1930, Emilio Portes Gil dispuso que, en los meses de 31 días, se descontara a los empleados públicos un día de salario para entregarlo al partido. En este año dejó su cargo Manuel Pérez Treviño, el que pasó a ocupar un puesto en el gabinete presidencial. Le sucedió Basilio Vadillo, quien incapaz de acabar con la disputa interna entre "rojos" y "blancos", renunció el 22 de abril. Como ambos grupos se dijeran callistas, convirtieron en árbitro a Plutarco Elías Calles y de ese modo reforzaron su poder, que ya era notorio por las lealtades con que contaba en el ejército y la burocracia política. El día 28 Emilio Portes Gil, un "rojo", asumió la presidencia del partido, lo que debilitó la de por sí precaria situación del presidente Ortiz Rubio, a quien se identificaba como "blanco". El nuevo líder partidario procuró romper el cerco de lo puramente electoral, negó que la organización fuera a "ser un gestor de empleos para sus miembros", a quienes demandó ganar y organizar "a las colectividades" y anunció que impulsaría un programa social, lo que incluyó la adquisición de la radiodifusora XEFO y la apertura de una Universidad Obrera y Campesina, organizada por Jesús Silva Herzog y dirigida inicialmente por Miguel Othón de Mendizábal. Para disminuir tensiones, definió al PNR como un "órgano de agitación y defensa del gobierno". Sin embargo, para las elecciones legislativas de ese año fueron escogidos mayoritariamente candidatos "rojos", lo que incrementó las pugnas internas. Como subsistieran las disputas por la representación del partido en los estados, el 29 de mayo de 1930, la Secretaría de Gobernación hizo saber a los gobernadores qué partidos locales podían usar el emblema del PNR, lo que sólo favoreció a seis organizaciones: el Partido Socialista del Estado de México, la Confederación de Partidos Socialistas de Oaxaca, el Partido Socialista de Quintana Roo, el Partido Socialista Radical de Tabasco y el Partido Socialista del Sureste. De este modo, implícitamente fueron suprimidos los demás partidos afiliados. Portes Gil debió afrontar el ataque sistemático de la Alianza Revolucionaria Nacionalista que integraron el Partido Laborista Me-

Camión del Partido Nacional Revolucionario

xicano, de Morones, el Partido Nacional Agrarista y el Partido Socialista Mexicano. Para apaciguar a la oposición, Ortiz Rubio anunció que enviaría al Congreso una iniciativa de ley electoral para establecer la representación proporcional, pero se encontró con la repulsa de su partido, que se tradujo en una virtual paralización del aparato estatal. Como la situación se tornaba peligrosa para el conjunto de la "familia revolucionaria", Calles dio su respaldo a Ortiz Rubio y Portes Gil renunció en octubre de 1930. Para sucederlo, la prensa mencionaba a Melchor Ortega, Agustín Arroyo Ch. y Matías Rodríguez, pero Calles se inclinó por Lázaro Cárdenas, quien se rodeó de un equipo de colaboradores ajeno a las dos tendencias en pugna: Silvestre Guerrero, secretario general; Elías Campos, tesorero; Valentín Aguilar, secretario del Exterior y de Acción Obrera; Manuel Mijares V., secretario de Sesiones y de Acción Agraria; Manuel Jasso, secretario de Prensa y Propaganda; y José Pérez Gil y Ortiz, secretario del Distrito Federal. Cárdenas se propuso cohesionar y disciplinar al partido, al que entendía como armónico colaborador del gobierno, al que correspondía organizar a los diversos sectores sociales, asesorar a los trabajadores y ser canal de gestión. Para contener las presiones caciquiles en los estados, dijo que los gobernadores debían encontrar "una solidaridad íntegra en el mismo

EXCELSIOR
EL PERIODICO DE LA VIDA NACIONAL

LAZARO CARDENAS ES SECRETARIO DE GOBERNACION Y PEREZ TREVIÑO JEFE DEL P. NAL. REVOLUCIONARIO

ENTRO EN VIGOR LA LEY FEDERAL DEL TRABAJO Y SUS PRECEPTOS RIGEN PARA TODA LA NACION

TRABAJANDO BAJO LAS AGUAS Y LAS NIEVES DEL POLO

Excélsior anuncia el nombramiento de Manuel Pérez Treviño como presidente nacional del PNR en 1931

partido", siempre que respetaran el programa penerrista. Por la importancia que concedía a las instituciones, apoyó al presidente Ortiz Rubio e incluso, por faltar al "espíritu de partido", expulsó del PNR a un grupo de senadores que había criticado las negociaciones sobre la deuda del secretario de Hacienda, Luis Montes de Oca. Cárdenas promovió las actividades deportivas, dirigió una campaña antialcohólica y, en enero de 1931, cuando un sismo destruyó varias poblaciones de Oaxaca, encabezó una brigada de auxilio. Durante su gestión fue suprimida la Universidad Obrera y Campesina y se eliminó la palabra *Revolucionario* de la cabeza de *El Nacional* (15 de mayo de 1931). El problema más grave que afrontó don Lázaro fue el choque entre "rojos" y "blancos" en Jalisco, que produjo dos balaceras en el Congreso local. Los primeros intentaban destituir al gobernador Ignacio de la Mora, a lo que se opuso el hombre de Jiquilpan. Por iniciativa del partido, en agosto de 1931 se crearon sendos bancos ejidales en Oaxaca y Guerrero. Después de haber atenuado los conflictos dentro del partido, aunque sin resolverlos, Cárdenas renunció el 28 de agosto de 1931 y pasó a ocupar la Secretaría de Gobernación en el gabinete de Ortiz Rubio. El día 29 volvió al cargo Pérez Treviño. El comité quedó integrado con Gonzalo N. Santos, secretario general; Matías Rodríguez, secretario de Actas y de Acción Agraria; Manlio Fabio Altamirano, secretario del Exterior y de Acción Obrera; Rafael E. Melgar, secretario de Prensa y Publicidad; José Santos Alonso, secretario del Distrito Federal; Juan de Dios Bátiz, tesorero; y Lamberto Ortega, oficial mayor. Sin Cárdenas al frente del partido, se produjo la destitución del gobernador de Jalisco (9 de septiembre de 1931). El 14 de octubre de 1931 Calles ocupó la Secretaría de Guerra y Marina, lo que acentuó su papel de hombre fuerte del régimen en detrimento del escaso poder del presidente de la República. Dos días después, para expresar su desacuerdo con Ortiz Rubio y su respeto por Calles, Pérez Treviño promovió la dimisión del comité penerrista en pleno, lo que ocurrió el 16 de octubre. Sin embargo, sólo se aceptó la renuncia de los cuatro que podían ser identificados como "rojos": Gonzalo N. Santos, Altamirano, Melgar y Santos Alonso. Fernando Moctezuma ocupó la Secretaría General, Enrique Soto Reyes se convirtió en secretario del Distrito Federal, el coronel Juan N. Delgado, secretario de Prensa y Publicidad; y el coronel Francisco R. Mayer, secretario del Exterior y de Acción Obrera. Los dirigentes del partido hicieron ostensible su sumisión a Calles y *El Nacional*, con Luis L. León como director, lo empezó a llamar "jefe máximo de la revolución" y a señalar que su autoridad era indiscutible. En enero de 1932, el PNR realizó un Congreso Nacional de Legislaturas, con representantes de las cámaras locales y federales, en el que fueron derrotados los que abogaban por el voto femenino y la no reelección en

FOTO: ARCHIVO CASASOLA

Pascual Ortiz Rubio y Emilio Portes Gil observan una manifestación política del PNR

cargos legislativos. Esto último ocasionó el retiro de ocho delegaciones, por lo que el Comité Ejecutivo, para lograr su regreso, suspendió temporalmente a Gonzalo N. Santos, quien había actuado con lujo de violencia, y el mismo Pérez Treviño reconoció el derecho de los partidos locales a oponerse a la reelección, lo que fue apoyado por los gobernadores de los estados. Para integrar las planillas de candidatos a legisladores, el grupo de Pérez Treviño empezó por renovar los comités estatales, con gente ligada a la dirección nacional, lo que motivó la expulsión de cuatro diputados en Guanajuato, entre ellos Luis I. Rodríguez; la protesta de Cárdenas porque en Michoacán los "rojos" actuaban inescrupulosamente, y el retiro del PNR de Emilio Portes Gil, quien no había logrado obtener la candidatura de su partido para el gobierno de Tamaulipas. El 3 de julio de 1932 se realizaron las elecciones legislativas en medio de numerosas acusaciones de fraude provenientes de todos los sectores de la oposición. Calles dejó la Secretaría de Guerra y Marina y en su lugar quedó Abelardo L. Rodríguez. Con el partido cada vez más distanciado del gobierno, Ortiz Rubio renunció a la presidencia de la República el 2 de septiembre. Calles reunió a los principales dirigentes políticos e impuso como sucesor en el Poder Ejecutivo al mismo Rodríguez, quien fue formalmente designado por el Congreso como presidente sustituto constitucional. A fines de octubre se celebró en Aguascalientes la convención nacional extraordinaria del PNR para discutir sobre la no reelección de los legisladores, lo que se aprobó, así como la ampliación del periodo de diputados y senadores, de dos a tres y de cuatro a seis años respectivamente. La reunión fue presidida por el coronel Carlos Riva Palacio, con Aarón Sáenz y José Manuel Puig Casauranc como vicepresidentes y Vicente Estrada Cajigal, Melchor Ortega, Gonzalo N. Santos y Luis L. León como secretarios. Entre los 825 delegados empezaron a circular los nombres de los probables sucesores de Abelardo L. Rodríguez en la presidencia del país: Riva Palacio, Pérez Treviño, Cárdenas y Adalberto Tejeda. A fines de 1932, en Puebla, el gobernador Leónidas Andrew Almazán, de acuerdo con el Partido Laborista, trató de imponer sucesor en el Poder Ejecutivo local. El día de los comicios se impidió la entrada a las casillas y comités electorales a los representantes del PNR y, cuando estaba a punto de proclamarse el triunfo del candidato laborista, fuerzas federales ocuparon la sede del congreso, desalojaron a la policía y a los grupos de choque del PL y poco después se anunció el triunfo del candidato del PNR. En diciembre de 1932, el Congreso acordó la no reelección absoluta del presidente de la República y limitó la de gobernadores y legisladores, con lo que se ampliaron las posibilidades de ascenso de nuevos cuadros políticos. El 15 de mayo de 1933 Cárdenas renunció a la Secretaría de Guerra y Marina en la que había continuado durante la presidencia de Abelardo L. Rodríguez. Tres días antes, Pérez Treviño hizo lo mismo en la presidencia del PNR. De este modo, ambos resultaron habilitados para aspirar a la candidatura por su partido, al frente del cual quedó Melchor Ortega. Se ratificó en sus cargos dentro del CEN Fernando Moctezuma, secretario general; Lamberto Ortega, oficial mayor; y Luis L. León, director del periódico *El Nacional*. Fueron designados Guillermo Flores Muñoz, tesorero; Riva Palacio, secretario de Prensa y Publicidad; Matías Rodríguez, secretario de Actas y Acción Agraria; Julio Bustillos, secretario del Exterior y Acción Obrera; José Morales Hesse, secretario del Distrito Federal. En la contienda por la candidatura presidencial, Riva Palacio, de posiciones semejantes a las de Pérez Treviño, quedó descartado cuando Calles aparentó que apoyaría al segundo. Por su parte, Adalberto Tejeda contaba con el apoyo de las ligas agrarias más radicales, del Partido Socialista de las Izquierdas, formado por políticos veracruzanos como él, y de algunos sectores del PNR. Como los planteamientos socializantes le habían permitido a Tejeda ampliar su base popular y aun su autonomía frente al callismo, el CEN del PNR expulsó a todos los tejedistas el 28 de abril de 1933 y las autoridades se dedicaron a obstaculizar sus labores. En torno a Cárdenas se había formado una amplia coalición que comprendía al Partido Agrarista de Jalisco y la Liga de Comunidades Agrarias de Tamaulipas, que se unió a las de Michoacán, San Luis Potosí, Tlaxcala y Chihuahua para anunciar que se constituiría la Confederación Campesina Mexicana, que tenía entre sus promotores a Graciano Sánchez, Enrique Flores Magón y Emilio Portes Gil. Otro organismo cardenista fue el llamado Gran Partido Revolucionario Institucional. *El Nacional*, aunque controlado por pereztreviñistas, prometió absoluta neutralidad y todos los días daba a conocer las adhesiones que recibían los aspirantes. A principios de junio, Calles manifestó su simpatía por Cárdenas ante un grupo de allegados, después de los cual, connotados callistas hicieron pública su adhesión al hombre de Jiquilpan, que aceptó formalmente la precandidatura el 5 de junio de 1933. El 7 de junio, Pérez Treviño renunció a sus aspiraciones presidenciales y dos días después volvió a la presidencia del PNR, en tanto que Melchor Ortega reasumió la gubernatura de Guanajuato. Además de Pérez Treviño, en el Comité Ejecutivo del partido quedaron Bartolomé Vargas Lugo, secretario general; Guillermo Flores Muñoz, tesorero; Alejandro Lacy Jr., secretario de Prensa y publicidad; José Morales Hesse, secretario del Distrito Federal; Matías Rodríguez, secretario de Actas y Acción Agraria; y Julián Garza Tijerina, secretario del Exterior y de Acción Obrera. Se encomendó entonces al Instituto de Estudios Sociales, Políticos y Económicos del partido la elaboración de un programa de gobierno que se conocería como el "Plan Sexenal", que según Calles debía estar "basado en el cálculo, en la estadística (y) en las lecciones de la experiencia". Como el puro nombre hacía recordar el plan quinquenal de la Unión Soviética, el propio pre-

FOTO: ARCHIVO CASASOLA

Comité Ejecutivo Nacional del PNR en 1932

sidente Rodríguez reiteró que la empresa privada tendría garantías y que había "diferencias esenciales entre la revolución mexicana y la revolución rusa". La comisión del programa de gobierno la formaron Juan de Dios Bátiz, Enrique Romero Courtade, Gabino Vázquez, José Santos Alonso, Guillermo Zárraga, Juan de Dios Robledo, Gonzalo Bautista y Genaro Vázquez, presididos por Pérez Treviño. El gobierno federal decidió, a su vez, integrar una comisión de colaboración técnica para facilitar la elaboración del plan. Este organismo tuvo como miembros a cinco secretarios de Estado: Alberto J. Pani, presidente de la comisión; Primo Villa Michel, Miguel N. Acosta, Narciso Bassols y Juan de Dios Bojórquez. Como la división dentro del partido continuara, Calles hizo renunciar a Pérez Treviño a la presidencia del CEN y, simultáneamente, decidió suprimir los bloques cardenistas en el Congreso e hizo cerrar el Centro Director Cardenista. Para ocupar la presidencia del partido se mencionaron tres nombres: Aarón Sáenz, visto con simpatía por los empresarios; Francisco J. Múgica, del ala cardenista; y Riva Palacio, hombre de Calles por quien se decidió finalmente el "jefe máximo". El CEN quedó integrado por Federico Medrano V., secretario general; Guillermo Flores Muñoz, tesorero; Julián Garza Tijerina, secretario del DF; Alejandro Lacy, *Jr.*, secretario de Prensa y Publicidad; José Morales Hesse, secretario del exterior y acción obrera; y Matías Rodríguez, secretario de actas y acción agraria. El 28 de septiembre de 1933 Calles se convirtió en secretario de Hacienda en el gabinete de Abelardo L. Rodríguez. En ese puesto le correspondió sustituir a Pani en la presidencia de la Comisión de Colaboración Técnica, a la que convocó para dar redacción definitiva al proyecto de Plan Sexenal, lo que sucedió en la primera semana de octubre de 1933, pese a que formalmente correspondía a la comisión de programa del propio PNR. El documento fue presentado al presidente Rodríguez y éste, después de hacerle algunas observaciones, lo envió al partido, donde se reelaboró en la comisión respectiva, dividida en dos alas. La derecha, debido al jacobinismo callista, proponía el establecimiento de la educación socialista, pero tenía una visión por completo conservadora en torno a los problemas sociales y económicos; los cardenistas coincidían en lo referente a la transformación de la enseñanza, pero demandaban el reinicio de la reforma agraria, garantías para los trabajadores y una mayor intervención del Estado en la economía. En el proyecto definitivo, presentado el primero de diciembre, se recogieron parcialmente los planteamientos de los segundos. Del 3 al 6 de diciembre de 1933 se reunió en Querétaro la segunda Convención Nacional del PNR, con 1,772 delegados cuyos debates presidió Sebastián Allende, auxiliado por Melchor Ortega y Gonzalo Vázquez Vela, vicepresidentes; Ramón Ramos, Francisco López Cortés, Gabino Vázquez y Gonzalo N. Santos, secretarios. Los asistentes aprobaron el Plan Sexenal y la candidatura presidencial de Cárdenas, así como la supresión de los partidos locales y los que se ostentaban como nacionales adheridos al PNR, cuya dirección asumió "la organización y el control de todos los elementos revolucionarios del país unificándolos en una sola organización política". Para asegurar el cumplimiento de este último acuerdo, se daba a los miembros de los partidos adherentes un plazo de seis meses para reafiliarse individualmente al PNR. También se aprobó que el Comité Directivo Nacional continuara integrado por un representante de cada estado con la inclusión de un delegado por cada cámara del Congreso de la Unión. En el Comité Ejecutivo fue suprimida la secretaría del Distrito Federal y se crearon dos: la de Organización y Estadística y la de Acción Educativa, Deportiva y de Salubridad. La convención aprobó pugnar por la creación de un Departamento Autónomo Agrario, para atender los más urgentes problemas del campo. Antes de tres semanas, el presidente Rodríguez envió al Congreso la iniciativa de ley respectiva. El Ejecutivo se negó a aplicar la educación socialista, como había acordado la convención, porque la Constitución establecía la enseñanza laica. En diciembre, la Cámara de Diputados aprobó una partida del presupuesto federal para financiar las actividades del IESPE. El 29 de diciembre, el CEN quedó integrado con Riva Palacio en la presidencia, Gabino Vázquez como secretario general, Enrique Romero Courtade, secretario de Organización y Estadística; Froylán C. Manjarrez, secretario de Prensa y Propaganda; Gilberto Fabila, secretario de Acción Agraria, Fomento y Organización Agrícola; Guillermo Flores Muñoz, secretario de Acción Obrera y Organización Industrial; Federico Medrano V., secretario de Acción Educativa, Deportiva y de Salud; y Francisco

Trejo, secretario de Acción Económica y Tesorero. Luis L. León fue confirmado como director y gerente de *El Nacional*. El 28 de mayo de 1934 se anunció que el partido contaba con 865,000 miembros con credencial. La campaña de Cárdenas se realizó bajo el lema "Trabajadores de México, uníos". En mayo, en Tres Palos, Guerrero, declaró: "entregaré a los campesinos el máuser con el que hicieron la revolución para que la defiendan, para que defiendan al ejido y a su escuela". De acuerdo con los datos oficiales, Cárdenas, con dos millones y cuarto de votos, triunfó holgadamente sobre sus adversarios: Antonio I. Villarreal obtuvo 24,395 sufragios, Adalberto Tejeda 16,037 y Hernán Laborde 539. Después de los comicios, Calles pronunció un discurso en Guadalajara en el que aseguró que "las conciencias de la niñez y la juventud" pertenecían a la revolución. Cárdenas tomó posesión de la Presidencia de la República el 1 de diciembre de 1934 y unos días después el Congreso reformó la Constitución para implantar la "educación socialista", lo que fue ratificado por las legislaturas estatales. El 10 de diciembre, los *camisas rojas*, grupo de choque del Partido Socialista Radical de Tabasco, afiliado al PNR y dirigido por el cacique Tomás Garrido Canabal, realizaron una matanza de católicos en Coyoacán, lo que fue condenado por Cárdenas y el propio partido. El 14 de diciembre Carlos Riva Palacio renunció a la presidencia del CEN del partido y su lugar lo ocupó el general Matías Ramos Santos, quien quedó al frente de un comité integrado por Antonio I. Villalobos, secretario general; Manuel F. Ochoa, secretario de Organización y Estadística; Ausencio C. Cruz, secretario de Prensa y Propaganda; Gustavo Segura, secretario de Acción Educativa; Ángel Pozada, secretario de Acción Agraria; Guillermo Flores Muñoz, secretario de Acción Obrera; Máximo Othón, secretario de Acción Económica y Tesorería; Froylán C. Manjarrez, director-gerente de *El Nacional*, y Julián Garza Tijerina, presidente del IESPE. Villalobos fue reemplazado por José María Dávila el 5 de abril de 1935. En mayo, el CEN nombró candidato a gobernador de Guanajuato a Jesús Yáñez Maya, pero un grupo de senadores apoyó a Federico Medrano, ex secretario general del PNR. El CEN lo consideró un acto de indisciplina y expulsó a Medrano, pero, a fin de evitar que se le señalara como imposicionista, tuvo que retirar la candidatura de Yáñez para designar en su lugar a Enrique Fernández Martínez. Durante los primeros meses de su gestión, Cárdenas procedió a repartir tierras y respetó las huelgas y manifestaciones populares, pese a la resistencia de los principales personajes de su partido, el ala derecha del Congreso y la burocracia callista. Por su parte, el presidente se había ganado el apoyo de numerosas organizaciones campesinas y la simpatía de importantes núcleos obreros. En la Cámara de Diputados se había formado un "bloque cardenista", opuesto a los legisladores más dóciles al "jefe máximo", quien regresó el 3 de mayo de 1935 de Los Ángeles, donde había permanecido hospitalizado. Cárdenas fue a recibirlo al aeropuerto. El 11 de junio, Calles condenó a quienes, a su juicio, pretendían "sabotear la unidad del PNR, dividiéndolo entre callistas y cardenistas". Asimismo, censuró las huelgas, "a menudo injustificadas", que habían llevado al país a un "maratón de radicalismo". Las declaraciones del caudillo contaron con la inmediata adhesión personal o mediante desplegados periodísticos de sus seguidores, las cámaras empresariales y los laboristas. Cárdenas respondió de inmediato. Pidió la renuncia de Matías Ramos a la presidencia del CEN y sustituyó con militares leales a los jefes que le eran adversos y tenían tropas a su mando. El presidente de la República recibió telegramas de las organizaciones obreras y campesinas que le manifestaban su respaldo. Los sindicatos no callistas, que formaban la inmensa mayoría de la fuerza laboral organizada, se unieron en el Comité Nacional de Defensa Proletaria; las organizaciones agraristas se prepararon para resistir y el ala izquierda del Congreso rechazó que fuera un factor divisionista dentro del partido. Un sector callista guardó silencio, pues consideraba útil una política de reformas como la que representaba Cárdenas, quien rechazó el cargo de "divisionismo" que le hacían sus enemigos y declaró que las huelgas eran "la consecuencia del acomodamiento de los intereses representados por los dos factores de la producción". El día 14 pidió la renuncia de su gabinete, con lo que eliminó a los callistas más beligerantes, cuando en todo el país grandes manifestaciones pedían la salida de Calles del país. El 16, el que había sido hasta entonces el "jefe máximo" tomó un avión para dirigirse a Estados Unidos. El 17 de junio, al frente del PNR quedó nuevamente Emilio Portes Gil. Gobernadores y jefes mili-

FOTO: ARCHIVO CASASOLA

Mitin de apoyo a Lázaro Cárdenas, candidato del Partido Nacional Revolucionario en 1934 tares manifestaron su apoyo a Cárdenas y en el Congreso se fortaleció el ala cardenista con la adhesión de los que poco antes estaban indecisos y aun con el arribo de algunos tránsfugas del bando contrario. Cárdenas emergió de esta crisis como el líder indiscutible de las fuerzas revolucionarias, de dentro y fuera del PNR. El partido, encabezado formalmente por Portes Gil, tuvo un Comité Ejecutivo integrado plenamente por cardenistas: Ignacio García Téllez, secretario general; J. Ignacio García, secretario de Organización y Estadística; Roque Estrada, secretario de Prensa y Propaganda; Ernesto Soto Reyes, secretario de Acción Agraria, Fomento y Organización Agrícola; Gustavo A. Talamantes, secretario de Acción Obrera y Organización Idustrial; David Ayala, secretario de Acción Educativa, Deportiva y de Salubridad; y Rodolfo T. Loaiza, secretario de Acción Económica y Tesorería. Con esta dirección, el PNR apoyó cabalmente las decisiones de Cárdenas, por ejemplo, al ser destituidos ciertos gobernadores. Asimismo, cuando la designación de candidatos en algunas entidades favoreció a los callistas, el CEN anuló los nombramientos. El partido, de acuerdo con lo señalado por Cárdenas, se convirtió en organizador y gestor social: se prestó asesoría a demandantes de tierras y se orientó a los trabajadores en asuntos laborales; el CEN hizo donativos de libros y material didáctico a las escuelas y las ceremonias cívicas cobraron nuevo contenido al relacionarse, con una retórica socializante, los hechos históricos con la situación del momento y las demandas obreras y campesinas. *El Nacional* se ocupó con asiduidad de los problemas nacionales y populares, lo mismo que la radiodifusora XEFO, se creó la revista *Así Es* y se anunciaron emisiones de televisión que se quedaron en proyecto. En terrenos donados por el gobierno, se empezó a construir la nueva sede partidaria y el IESPE, encabezado por Lucio Mendieta y Núñez, editó la revista *Política Social*. Pese a todo, las principales organizaciones de trabajadores urbanos y rurales seguían al margen del PNR, de ahí que, por iniciativa de Cárdenas, el 20 de julio de 1935 se formara el Comité de Unificación Campesina, presidido por Portes Gil y con Gabino Vázquez, jefe del Departamento Agrario, como vicepresidente. Otros integrantes del comité fueron Ignacio García Téllez, Efraín Gutiérrez, Graciano Sánchez, Vicente Salgado Páez y Ernesto Soto Reyes. Se procedió entonces a organizar a los campesinos de manera que sólo hubiera una liga en cada estado. Los trabajos de organización contaron con patrocinio del gobierno "para facilitar la unificación de la clase campesina, dándole las facilidades necesarias para el transporte y gastos de las delegaciones", según declaró Cárdenas. Mientras avanzaban estas actividades, los callistas se reagruparon. Los generales José María Tapia y Melchor Ortega llamaban a los jefes militares a rebelarse contra el gobierno y el 11 de septiembre se produjo una balacera en la Cámara de Diputados en la que resultaron muertos dos legisladores cardenistas, Manuel Martínez Valadés y Luis Méndez. Al día siguiente, 17 diputados callistas fueron desaforados y expulsados del partido. El 13 de diciembre Calles regresó a México y, para apoyarlo, grupos fascistas, algunos sindicatos cromianos y otras organizaciones de derecha realizaron un "paro de trabajo anticomunista". Las organizaciones obreras y campesinas favorables a Cárdenas, con amplias movilizaciones en todo el país, dieron una formidable respuesta. El presidente, por su parte, removió a varios jefes militares, especialmente a Manuel Medinaveytia, comandante de la plaza del DF, y a Joaquín Amaro, director de Educación Militar. El general José María Tapia fue sometido a proceso por soborno y en el Congreso fueron desaforados cinco senadores, entre ellos Riva Palacio, y desaparecidos los poderes en cuatro entidades gobernadas por callistas: Guanajuato, Durango, Sinaloa y Sonora. Los sindicatos y las organizaciones campesinas advirtieron entonces que irían a la huelga si Calles no abandonaba el país. Los callistas crearon el periódico vespertino *El Instante*, donde se publicó un manifiesto que anunciaba la fundación del Partido Constitucional Revolucionario, lo que era una escisión formal del PNR. Entre los firmantes figuraban Luis L. León, Melchor Ortega, Francisco Javier Gaxiola y otros prominentes políticos cercanos al ex "jefe máximo". Al día siguiente, el PNR, por "traición al programa de la revolución y por conspirar contra las autoridades", expulsó de sus filas a los firmantes y con ellos a Bartolomé Vargas Lugo, Fernando Torreblanca, José María Tapia, Manuel Riva Palacio y otros políticos entre los que se contaba el propio Calles. El 22 de diciembre, en apoyo a Cárdenas, se realizó un desfile multitudinario encabezado por Vicente Lombardo Toledano, Fidel Velázquez, Fernando Amilpa y el comunista Valentín Campa, lo que representó la unidad de las fuerzas gobiernistas y de izquierda en torno a Lázaro Cárdenas, quien el 10 de abril expulsó del país, por sus "actividades delictivas", a Calles, Morones, Ortega y Luis L. León, los que al día siguiente fueron conducidos hasta el avión por un fuerte contingente militar. El presidente se había propuesto la unificación de "las clases laboriosas de la República", pero vigiló que tal unificación se diera por separado. En febrero de 1936 se constituyó al margen del PNR la Confederación de Trabajadores de México, con Lombardo como líder, pero las organizaciones campesinas continuaron trabajando por su lado. Como los cetemistas se empeñaran en incorporar a los campesinos a su central, el presidente les advirtió que la tarea de organizar a los trabajadores del agro la tenía encomendada el PNR y que si otra agrupación intervenía en ese proceso podía "incubar gérmenes de disolución". Las diferencias con la CTM, y el hecho de que ésta no fuera formalmente del partido, no impidieron que el CEN reconociera las credenciales expedidas por esa central como si fueran del PNR. En el curso de 1936, diversas organizaciones femeninas, pese a la acusación de "comunistas" que les lanzaba el grupo de Portes Gil, se incorporaron al trabajo del partido, que creó una Oficina de Acción Femenina mediante la cual las mujeres desplegaron una intensa actividad asistencial y de orientación laboral y jurídica. Refugio García, Esther Chapa y Thais García, las tres principales lideresas, actuaron políticamente y promovieron desde las páginas de *El Nacional* las actividades del sector que dirigían. Se dio especial impulso a los encuentros deportivos y otras tareas que atraían a los jóvenes. Se hicieron grandes tirajes de folletos y se fundó el semanario *Los Doce*. A partir de febrero de 1936, en la selección de candidatos pudieron participar, con iguales derechos que los miembros del partido, todos los obreros y campesinos que dijeran aceptar la Declaración de Principios del PNR, con lo que se pretendía una mayor participación popular dentro de la política que se llamó de "puerta abierta". Sin embargo, la respuesta de la CTM y de la Confederación Campesina Mexicana fue tibia, pues consideraban la presencia de Portes Gil como un obstáculo para la democracia. Ernesto Soto Reyes, secretario de acción agraria, en el Senado y en el partido inició una abierta campaña contra Portes Gil, a lo que éste respondió con otra campaña propagandística en su favor. *El Nacional*, ya bajo la dirección de José Ángel Ceniceros, dejó de publicar textos contrarios al portesgilismo. A fines de junio se reunió la asamblea del partido, convocada por Portes Gil para fortalecer su posición. Sin embargo, la ausencia del presidente Cárdenas y de varios miembros del CEN hizo evidente que el supuesto líder del partido se hallaba aislado. El conflicto se agravó cuando el "ala izquierda" del Congreso anunció que se opondría a la dirección del partido, a la que se había acusado de incurrir en prácticas callistas. En agosto, la Comisión Permanente del Congreso rechazó la elección de senadores en Campeche, Chiapas, Coahuila, Tamaulipas y Nuevo León, con lo que se desautorizó a los candidatos del PNR impuestos por Portes Gil, quien se vio obligado a renunciar el día 20. Silvano Barba González ocupó la presidencia del partido y el CEN quedó integrado con Esteban García de Alba, secretario general; Wenceslao Labra, secretario de Organización y Estadística; Antonio Mayés Navarro, secretario de Acción Agraria; Guillermo Flores Muñoz, secretario de Acción Educativa y Deportiva; Julián Aguilar G., secretario de Acción Económica y Tesorería; Gilberto Bosques, secretario de Prensa y Propaganda; y Arnulfo Pérez H., secretario de Acción Obrera. Manjarrez volvió a la dirección de *El Nacional* y Enrique Calderón fue designado director del IESPE. La nueva dirección partidaria ratificó, sin entusiasmar a las organizaciones sociales, la política de "puerta abierta" y consideró que quienes pertenecieran "a un sindicato de resistencia o a un centro de población ejidal" cumplían con los requisitos para ser miembros del PNR. Por otra parte, el uso de un lenguaje radical y socializante estimuló las campañas anticardenistas en el extranjero, por lo que el PNR inició la edición de libros y folletos en inglés, a fin de presentarse como un partido moderado. El 9 de febrero de 1937, el CEN anunció que la selección de candidatos se haría por los "sectores" agrario, obrero y militar. De los tres precandidatos que en cada caso resultarían de este proceso, el Comité Ejecutivo Nacional seleccionaría uno para representar al partido. El 21 de febrero de 1937, el PNR se comprometió con la CTM, la Confederación Campesina Mexicana y el Partido Comunista a constituir el Frente Popular Mexicano. Seis días después, con participación de oradores de las cuatro agrupaciones, se realizó un mitin en apoyo de la República Española, el que, según se anunció, había sido organizado por el Frente, que nunca llegó a tener existencia formal. En los hechos, el PNR no permitió que los comunistas, por tener "estatutos, ideología y tendencias muy diferentes", intervinieran en la selección de sus candidatos, que en 1937 motivó también severas críticas de la CTM y de legisladores penerrianos, quienes incluso pidieron la desaparición del partido, por considerar que se mantenían en pie los procedimientos antidemocráticos instaurados durante el callismo. El 29 de junio, el CEN expulsó del partido a numerosos miembros que se habían inscrito como candidatos independientes a las diputaciones, de los cuales sólo uno llegó a ocupar una curul por el DF. Después de las elecciones, la CTM contó con 30 diputados, pero las manifestaciones de inconformidad aparecían en todos los rincones del espectro político, pues pese a su aplastante triunfo, el PNR, con sus métodos y su estructura, no satisfacía las necesidades de participación de los sectores sociales organizados ni podía coordinar el apoyo a las reformas cardenistas. El 19 de octubre de 1937, los empleados públicos exigieron que no se les descontaran cuotas para PNR, a lo que accedió Cárdenas en diciembre, quien dijo que la organización partidaria "debió haber sido sostenida por todos". El 14 de diciembre de ese año, Cárdenas anunció a un reducido grupo de políticos su intención de transformar al PNR en un partido formado estatutariamente por cuatro sectores: obrero, campesino, militar y popular, lo que confirmó cinco días después en un manifiesto en el que apoyaba el propósito de formar un "Partido Nacional de Trabajadores y Soldados", con "hegemonía de las agrupaciones sociales", que permitiera a "los distintos gremios laborantes" y al "sector femenino" obtener una "representación proporcional" en todos los puestos de elección popular y en los cargos directivos dentro del propio partido. Para elaborar los documentos de la futura organización, el CEN comisionó a Luis I. Rodríguez, Esteban García de Alba, Alfonso Sánchez Madariaga, de la CTM; León García, representante de las Ligas Agrarias; y al general Edmundo M. Sánchez Cano, representante de la Secretaría de la Defensa Nacional. Cárdenas sostuvo frecuentes reuniones con los miembros de dicha comisión, que acabó por presentar un anteproyecto en el que hacía referencia al Partido Socialista Mexicano, nombre que fue desechado para adoptar el de Partido de la Revolución Mexicana (☛). (*Cfr.*: Luis Javier Garrido. *El partido de la revolución institucionalizada.*)

Partido Nacional de Salvación Pública ◆ Agrupación pronazi creada en febrero de 1939 por Adolfo León Ossorio, Francisco Coss, Bernardino Mena Brito y Luis del Toro. El PNSP demandaba destituir al presidente de la República o a los gobernadores de los estados cuando éstos sostuvieran a cualquier organización política; planteaba también la inconveniencia de permitir la sindicalización de los empleados públicos, la eliminación de los comunistas de los puestos oficiales y la expulsión del país de los judíos. En un banquete celebrado por este partido en Chapultepec, fueron oradores el general Pablo González y Manuel Pérez Treviño, ex presidente del PNR. En enero de 1939 el PNSP promovió el ataque contra negociaciones de judíos, por lo que sus dirigentes fueron detenidos brevemente. Cuando Almazán anunció su candidatura a la presidencia de la República, Mena Brito y otros miembros lo acusaron de simular su oposición a Lázaro Cárdenas y abandonaron el partido. Más tarde se retiró León Ossorio, quien luego acusó a Almazán de haberse "vendido al dinero judío". El partido desapareció tras la derrota de su candidato a la presidencia.

Partido Nacionalista Democrático ◆ Organización fundada en 1909 para apoyar la candidatura de Bernardo Reyes a la vicepresidencia de la República y la de Porfirio Díaz a la presidencia. Tuvo como origen los clubes reyistas que surgieron en diversos puntos del país a partir de 1908. En marzo de 1909, Reyes ofreció su apoyo a la candidatura de Ramón Corral y poco después abandonó a sus seguidores y se marchó a Europa. Aliado al Partido Nacional Antirreeleccionista, en 1910 dio su respaldo a la fórmula Madero-Vázquez Gómez. En 1911, el partido apoyó a Cándido Navarro como aspirante a la gubernatura de Guanajuato.

Partido Obrero-Campesino Mexicano ◆ Organización fundada en julio de 1950, al fusionarse el Movimiento Reivindicador del Partido Comunista Mexicano (☛) y el grupo Acción Socialista Unificada (☛), en el curso del segundo periodo de sesiones del Congreso de Unidad Marxista, realizado del 18 al 22 de julio de ese año. Sus principales líderes fueron Hernán Laborde, Valentín Campa, Miguel Aroche Parra, Miguel Ángel Velasco y Carlos Sánchez Cárdenas, quienes habían sido expulsados en diferentes momentos del Partido Comunista, pese a lo cual, el POCM mantuvo siempre la propuesta de unificar a "todos los comunistas de México en un potente organismo que recoja las mejores tradiciones de la lucha revolucionaria del pueblo mexicano, que se sustente con inquebrantable firmeza en la invencible teoría del marxismo-leninismo-estalinismo". En diciembre de 1950, el partido censuró al presidente Miguel Alemán por el envío de carne enlatada a Corea del sur (☛) y protestó porque "ningún funcionario del gobierno mexicano haya tratado de impedir que nuestra juventud esté siendo enrolada en la embajada norteamericana en nuestra patria para ir a servir (en Corea) como carne de cañón al servicio del imperialismo". El 29 de agosto de 1951, el partido exigió que el gobierno dejara de controlar los procesos electorales y propuso que todos los partidos políticos, en plan de igualdad, organizaran los comicios. También se manifestó por eliminar de la ley las referencias a las relaciones internacionales de los partidos y calificó de inconstitucional mantener sin derecho de voto a las mujeres. El 20 de enero de 1952, el POCM firmó un "pacto de acción conjunta" con el Partido Popular y apoyó la candidatura presidencial de Vicente Lombardo Toledano. El primero de mayo, la policía y *Los Dorados* agredieron una manifestación obrera y fueron detenidos varios militantes, entre otros Carlos Sánchez Cárdenas, quien fue procesado por el delito de disolución social. En septiembre de 1954, la dirección del partido denunció la persecución contra *Noviembre*, su órgano oficial. A fines de ese año, convocó al Partido Popular a convertir "en norma nacional la muy positiva línea seguida en el estado de Guerrero, donde el PP y el POCM han formado un solo frente para luchar en las elecciones". Asimismo, declaró: "el Partido Comunista es querido y respetado por nosotros". En abril de 1955 propuso al PP y al PCM participar unidos en las elecciones de ese año. El primero de mayo murió Hernán Laborde, miembro de la dirección partidaria. Un año después, el POCM llamó a luchar por la derogación del artículo 145 del Código Penal (sobre el delito de disolución social) y por la libertad sindical. En septiembre de 1956 reprobó el asalto militar a las instalaciones del Instituto Politécnico Nacional, "que tiene el objetivo de acabar con la educación técnica popular". El día 30 propuso al PCM discutir sobre la crisis del movimiento comunista mexicano, actuar en un solo frente y "realizar la unidad orgánica de nuestros partidos". El 16 de octubre, una delegación del PCM visitó las oficinas del POCM, lo que constituyó el primer acercamiento entre ambas organizaciones. En las elecciones de 1958 apoyó con el PCM la candidatura presidencial de Miguel Mendoza López. Los militantes del POCM participaron en las huelgas magisteriales de la segunda mitad de los años cincuenta. En el movimiento ferrocarrilero de 1958-59, el POCM, el PCM y el PPS coordinaron sus actividades. El 28 de marzo la fuerza pública rompió la huelga de los ferroviarios y miles de obreros fueron detenidos. Demetrio Vallejo, miembro del POCM y secretario general del sindicato fue procesado y lo mismo sucedió con Valentín Campa un año después. Ambos permanecerían en prisión hasta 1969. El 18 de septiembre de 1959, PCM y POCM anunciaron su propósito de unificarse. En 1960, un grupo encabezado por José Revueltas salió del PCM e ingresó al POCM, en tanto que varios militantes de este partido, entre ellos Eduardo Montes, Rosa Puig, Hugo Ponce de León, Wigberto Sandoval, Consuelo Uranga, Jaime Perches y Valentín Campa, entonces preso político, ingresaron al PCM. En el mismo año Revueltas abandonó el POCM para fundar la Liga Leninista Espartaco (☛). El primero de junio de 1963 se disolvió la organización, encabezada entonces por Sánchez Cárdenas y Velasco, y los militantes, incluidos Aroche Parra y Alberto Lumbreras que se encontraban presos, se incorporaron al Partido Popular Socialista.

PARTIDO OBRERO INTERNACIONALISTA ◆ Nombre que adoptó la Liga Comunista Internacionalista (☛) en septiembre de 1939. De filiación trotskista, su órgano de difusión era *Lucha Obrera*. En 1944, una fracción encabezada por Octavio Fernández se separó y formó el Grupo Socialista Obrero. El POI quedó bajo la dirección de Luciano Galicia, pero se disolvió en 1947 y sus miembros se dedicaron exclusivamente a la actividad sindical entre electricistas, telefonistas, profesores y ferrocarrileros. En 1951, algunos de esos militantes apoyaron la candidatura de Rubén Jaramillo a la gubernatura de Morelos.

PARTIDO OBRERO REVOLUCIONARIO ◆ Organización marxista fundada a principios de 1959. Su sigla era POR(t). La letra entre paréntesis indicaba su filiación trotskista. Sus primeros dirigentes fueron Felipe Galván, Vidal Solís y Francisco Moraga, a los que se sumaron poco después Eurice Campirán, David Águilar Mora, Fernando López Limón y Alfonso Lizárraga. El grupo apoyó al argentino J. Posadas cuando éste se separó de la Cuarta Internacional y formó el Buró Latinoamericano de la Cuarta Internacional, al que quedó afiliado como sección mexicana el POR(t). En 1966, el partido recibió a un grupo de militantes trotskistas de la guerrilla guatemalteca, entre ellos Adolfo Gilly, quienes días después fueron aprehendidos, torturados y procesados. Su órgano de difusión era *Voz Obrera*. Con presencia en los medios universitarios, por su participación en el movimiento estudiantil de 1968, varios de sus miembros, entre ellos Francisco Colmenares César, fueron a la cárcel. Los dos grupos de presos políticos abandonaron la prisión entre 1971 y 1972. Gilly fue expulsado del país y en 1974 se retiró del partido junto con varios militantes de México. En 1976, J. Posadas se opuso a que al POR(t) apoyara la candidatura presidencial de Valentín Campa, miembro del Partido Comunista Mexicano, porque esta organización, decía, "no es un partido de clase" y carece de "fuerza en las masas, en la clase obrera. Es un movimiento reformista". Para J. Posadas, "quien determina el curso de la lucha antiimperialista es el PRI y los sindicatos: allí está la fuerza". Basado en tales premisas, el dirigente indicó: "Nuestro partido a quien tiene que apoyar es al cadidato del gobierno, en forma condicional darle apoyo crítico. Un apoyo crítico significa un apoyo en base a que va a estimular la lucha antiimperialista". Este partido se extinguió a fines de los años setenta.(*Cfr.*: *Voz Obrera*, no. 255, abril de 1976, p. 3.)

ARCHIVO GENERAL DE LA NACIÓN

Mitin del Partido Popular

PARTIDO OBRERO SOCIALISTA ◆ Organización fundada en Guadalajara, en 1904, por Miguel Mendoza López Schwertfeger, Roque Estrada, Ramón Morales y J. M. Kerr. Sus concepciones políticas era una mezcla de anarquismo, liberalismo y elementos de diversas corrientes utópicas. El POS realizó una manifestación el 21 de marzo de ese año, en el aniversario del nacimiento de Benito Juárez. Morales, que llevaba un estandarte rojo, tuvo que huir de Jalisco ante la persecución policiaca. El mismo Morales inició, el 21 de marzo de 1906, la publicación de *El Obrero Socialista*.

PARTIDO DE LOS POBRES ◆ Nombre adoptado hacia 1975 o 1976 como expresión política de la guerrilla dirigida por Lucio Cabañas (☛), la que a su vez se presentó desde entonces como "Brigada de Ajusticiamiento del Partido de los Pobres". El 30 de marzo de 1977, la revista *Por Qué?* publicó que este partido se proponía "derrocar a la clase rica" para formar "un gobierno de campesinos y obreros, técnicos y profesionistas y otros trabajadores revolucionarios". De acuerdo con versiones gubernamentales, desde 1980 actuaba conjuntamente con el PROCUP (☛ *Partido Revolucionario Obrero Clandestino Unión del Pueblo*). En 1985, una presunta Brigada de Ajusticiamiento del mismo partido secuestró al líder comunista Arnoldo Martínez Verdugo, amenazó a otros militantes de izquierda y asesinó a antiguos miembros de la guerrilla.

PARTIDO POPULAR ◆ Organización fundada en junio de 1948 por Vicente Lombardo Toledano, Narciso Bassols, Víctor Manuel Villaseñor, y Antonio Betancourt Pérez, Enrique Ramírez y Ramírez, Diego Rivera, Alejandro Gómez Arias, Eulalia Guzmán, Jorge Cruickshank García, Indalecio Sáyago Herrera y otros políticos e intelectuales. Su principal antecedente fue la Mesa Redonda de los Marxistas (☛), celebrada en enero de 1947, donde Lombardo expuso su concepción del nuevo partido. A fines de marzo de ese año, durante su cuarto Congreso Nacional Ordinario, la Confederación de Trabajadores de México acordó respaldar la propuesta de Lombardo de crear un nuevo partido. El 29 de septiembre se constituyó el Comité Nacional Coordinador del Partido Popular, pero una semana después, el 2 de octubre, el XXXIII Consejo Nacional de la CTM decidió la afiliación forzosa de sus miembros al PRI. Finalmente, sin embargo, el nuevo partido se constituyó del 19 al 21 de junio de 1948. El primer Comité Directivo lo integraron, además del propio Lombardo como presidente, los vicepresidentes Bassols, Constantino Hernández, Antonio Mayés Navarro, Octavio Véjar Vázquez y Víctor M. Villaseñor. En el mismo año obtuvo su registro electoral. Este partido se propuso luchar contra el imperialismo y en favor de una política de nacionalizaciones, por la igualdad del hombre y la mujer y la educación popular. Su declaración de principios establecía que es necesario impulsar los valores de la revolución mexicana, a través de una sociedad socialista, en cuyo gobierno participen trabajadores, campesinos, intelectuales y burgueses nacionalistas, dirigidos por la clase obrera. Tres años más tarde, el 15 de diciembre de 1951, el partido celebró su primera Asamblea Nacional, en la que Lombardo fue elegido candidato a la presidencia. El 20 de enero de 1952, el Partido Popular firmó un Pacto de Acción Conjunta con el Partido Obrero Campesino Mexicano, mediante el cual, el POCM apoyó la candidatura de Lombardo. Bajo el cargo de "estar en servicio activo" en las fuerzas armadas, el 14 de abril de ese año fue detenido Véjar Vázquez, que había sustituido a Lombardo en la presidencia del PP. En noviembre de 1957, la segunda Asamblea Nacional Extraordinaria del partido declaró que "no obstante que el Partido Popular no postula al ciudadano Adolfo López Mateos como su candidato a la presidencia de la República, y pese a la resistencia del propio candidato y del PRI a cualquier tipo de alianza partidaria, el PP "recomienda a sus miembros votar por él, como primer paso obligado en la lucha por la integración del Frente Patriótico Nacional". Al año siguiente, el PP apoyó al movimiento ferrocarrilero (☛) y formó, con el POCM y el PCM, una comisión coordinadora de los militantes de las tres organizaciones que participaban en dicho movimiento, varios de los cuales fueron detenidos cuando se desató la represión gubernamental. Trinidad Estrada, miembro de la organización, fue preso político durante varios años. En 1959 se manifestó en favor de la revolución cubana. Dos años después, adoptó el nombre de Partido Popular Socialista (☛).

PARTIDO POPULAR MEXICANO ◆ Agrupación surgida en 1927 para apoyar la candidatura presidencial del general Francisco Serrano. La asamblea que lo nombró, reunida en el Teatro Arbeu de la ciudad de México, la presidió Javier Eroza. Integrado a la Confederación de Partidos Nacionales, desapareció luego del asesinato de Serrano.

Logotipo del Partido Popular Socialista

PARTIDO POPULAR SOCIALISTA ◆ Nombre que adoptó el Partido Popular (☛) el 16 de octubre de 1960, fecha en la que advirtió que continuaba basándose en los principios del materialismo dialéctico. En junio de 1963 los militantes del Partido Obrero-Campesino Mexicano se incorporaron al PPS. En 1964 apoyó al candidato presidencial del PRI, Gustavo Díaz Ordaz. A fines de ese año, la fracción parlamentaria pepesocialista presentó una iniciativa para permitir la reelección inmediata de los diputados, lo que aprobó la Cámara de éstos pero no el Senado. En 1965, un comando guerrillero integrado por ex militantes del PPS y de la Juventud Popular asaltó el cuartel militar de Madera, Chihuahua, ante lo cual la dirección partidaria negó toda responsabilidad. En 1966 se separó de la organización un grupo dirigido por el líder de la Unión General de Obreros y Campesinos de México, Jacinto López, y otro que encabezó el diputado Rafael Estrada Villa. Lombardo calificó como "de derecha" la primera escisión y como "de izquierda" la segunda. En 1968 murió Lombardo Toledano, quien había condenado el movimiento estudiantil de ese año, y fue sucedido en la dirección nacional por Jorge Cruickshank García. En 1970 el PPS apoyo a Luis Echeverría Alvarez, candidato del PRI a la presidencia de la República. En ese año se separó del PPS una corriente en la que estaban Carlos Sánchez Cárdenas, Miguel Ángel Velasco, Alberto Lumbreras, Miguel Aroche Parra y Alexandro Martínez Camberos. En noviembre de 1975 Alejandro Gascón Mercado, declarado oficialmente perdedor de las elecciones para el gobierno de Nayarit, se dijo víctima de un fraude. Al año siguiente, Gascón y 22 candidatos a diputados se retiraron del PPS, luego de que Cruickshank aceptó una alianza con el PRI, mediante la cual se convirtió en senador de la República, en los mismos comicios en que su partido apoyó a José López Portillo, candidato del PRI a la presidencia de la República. En 1977, el PPS comisionó a Cruickshank, Francisco Ortiz Mendoza y Ezequiel Rodríguez Arcos para asistir a las audiencias públicas sobre la reforma política, de la Comisión Federal Electoral, en la que Lázaro Rubio Félix integró la subcomisión relatora. El PPS se manifestó por que el jefe del Departamento del Distrito Federal y sus delegados políticos fuesen sujetos de elección popular. En las elecciones de 1979, el PPS obtuvo 354,072 votos para los diputados de mayoría re-

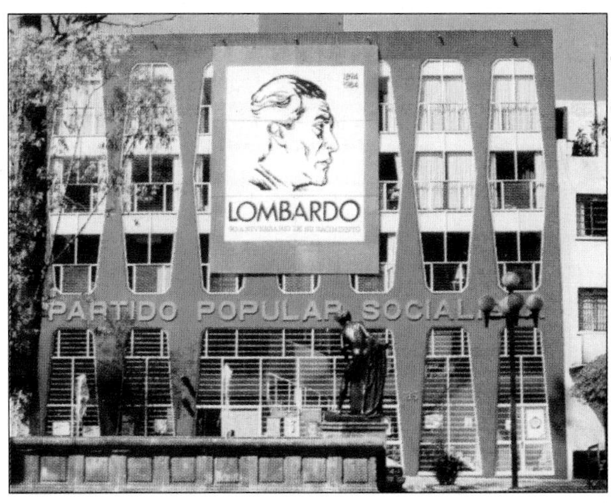

FOTO: EDUARDO GONZÁLEZ

Edificio del Partido Popular Socialista en 1984

lativa y 389,590 para los de representación proporcional (2.55 y 2.82 por ciento, respectivamente). En las elecciones de 1982, el partido apoyó a Miguel de la Madrid, candidato del PRI a la presidencia de la República, y obtuvo los siguientes resultados: en la fórmula 1 para la elección de diputados obtuvo 375,059 votos (1.67 por ciento) y 360,535 (1.8 por ciento) para la fórmula 2; para diputados de mayoría relativa, 393,227 votos (1.9 por ciento) y 459,303 (2 por ciento) para la elección de diputados de representación proporcional. A fines de 1987, el PPS se adhirió a la candidatura presidencial de Cuauhtémoc Cárdenas y se integró al Frente Democrático Nacional. En 1989 murió Jorge Cruickshank y fue sucedido en la secretaría general del partido por Indalecio Sáyago Herrera (1989-). En 1994 tuvo como candidata a la presidencia de México a Marcela Lombardo, quien no consiguió ni el uno por ciento de la votación. En 1997 postuló candidatos a diputados federales, obteniendo una votación global de .34 por ciento. En 1999 no pudo recuperar el registro como partido político nacional.

Partido del Pueblo Mexicano ◆ Organización fundada el 18 de septiembre de 1977 con el nombre de Partido Popular Socialista Mayoritario, y transformado poco después en Partido del Pueblo Mexicano, por un grupo de militantes del Partido Popular Socialista que en 1976 abandonó ese partido, luego que la dirección nacional del PPS aceptó el resultado de las elecciones para gobernador de Nayarit de 1975, aparentemente ganadas por Alejandro Gascón Mercado y estableció una alianza entre el PRI y el PPS, que hizo senador a Jorge Cruickshank. En su fundación participaron, entre otros, el constituyente Cándido Avilés, Alfredo Pantoja, Álvaro Ramírez Ladewig y el propio Gascón Mercado, quien fue elegido secretario general. Su declaración de principios establecía la lucha por la socialización de los medios de producción y por la construcción del socialismo, con base en el materialismo dialéctico. En las elecciones de 1979, aliado con el Partido Comunista Mexicano, consiguió cinco diputados, los que formaron parte de la Coalición de Izquierda. En 1981 desapareció al fusionarse con otras organizaciones en el Partido Socialista Unificado de México.

Partido de la Revolución Democrática ◆ Organización política constituida el 6 de mayo de 1989. Los trabajos encaminados a su formación se iniciaron el 16 de julio de 1988, días después de las elecciones en las que Cuauhtémoc Cárdenas Solórzano fue el candidato a la presidencia de la República por el Frente Democrático Nacional, coalición de centro-izquierda formada por cuatro partidos registrados y numerosas organizaciones políticas y sociales. De esos partidos, sólo el Mexicano Socialista se incorporó a los trabajos preparatorios del nuevo agrupamiento, que en octubre emitió la convocatoria para constituir lo que desde entonces se llamó Partido de la Revolución Democrática. El 5 de febrero se celebró una asamblea en la que se presentaron y discutieron los proyectos de documentos básicos. El 6 de mayo se constituyó el partido y solicitó su registro electoral. El día 14, el Partido Mexicano Socialista adoptó como propios los documentos básicos del PRD y, de acuerdo con éste, notificó a la Comisión Federal Electoral que adoptaba el nombre de Partido de la Revolución Democrática. El viernes 26 de mayo la citada comisión dio por registrada la nueva denominación del antiguo PMS, pero no aceptó los colores de su emblema (verde, blanco y rojo) por ser iguales a los de otro partido registrado con anterioridad, el PRI. En la constitución del PRD participaron, además del PMS, la Organización Revolucionaria Punto Crítico, la Organización de Izquierda Revolucionaria Línea de Masas, el Movimiento al Socialismo, el Partido Verde, el Partido Liberal, el Partido de Fuerzas Progresistas, el Consejo Nacional Obrero y Campesino de México, el Grupo Polifórum, la Asamblea de Barrios, la Asociación Cívica Nacional Revolucionaria, el Consejo Nacional Cardenista, Convergencia Democrática y otros grupos políticos y sociales, de los cuales la corriente separada del PRI en 1987 decía contar con la mayoría de los miembros del PRD y tener mayoría absoluta en los puestos de dirección. Cuahtémoc Cárdenas era el presidente del partido y Porfirio Muñoz Ledo el secretario general. Entre sus militantes más conocidos figuraban los ex candidatos presidenciales Cuauhtémoc Cárdenas, Heberto Castillo y Arnoldo Martínez Verdugo, los senadores Porfirio Muñoz Ledo, Ifigenia Martínez Hernández, Cristóbal Arias y Roberto Robles Garnica; un centenar de diputados federales y otros políticos, entre los cuales estaban Adolfo Gilly, Guadalupe Rivera Marín, Ricardo Valero, Celia Torres, Manuel López Obrador, Manuel Moreno Sánchez, Pablo Gómez, Gilberto Rincón Gallardo, Pedro Peñaloza, Ricardo Pascoe, Valentín Campa, Othón Salazar, Ramón Danzós Palomino, Antonio Tenorio, José Woldenberg y Graco Ramírez. De acuerdo con sus documentos básicos, se propone rescatar los aspectos positivos de la Revolución Mexicana. En enero de 1990 el PRD denunció ante la Secretaría de Gobernación que desde julio de 1988, 56 de sus militantes habían sido asesinados por motivos políticos. En noviembre de ese año se efctuó el Primer Congreso Nacional del PRD, de donde resultó electo Cuauhtémoc Cárdenas Solórzano como presidente del Comité Ejecutivo Nacional. En las elecciones

Logotipo del Partido de la Revolución Democrática

federales intermedias de 1991, de acuerdo con los resultados oficiales, el PRD alcanzó el ocho por ciento de la votación nacional, con lo que obtuvo 41 diputados federales. Roberto Robles Garnica asumió la presidencia del partido en calidad de interino de febrero a mayo de 1993, para conducir la elección interna en la que contendieron Porfirio Muñoz Ledo, Mario Saucedo, Heberto Castillo y Pablo Gómez. En julio de ese año se realizó el segundo Congreso Nacional del PRD, en el cual participaron 1,400 delegados de todo el país para elegir, con el 46.5 por ciento de los sufragios, a Porfirio Muñoz Ledo como presidente. La Secretaría General recayó en Mario Saucedo Pérez. Los derrotados Pablo Gómez y Heberto Castillo señalaron en tono acusatorio "el funcionamiento vertical de la estructura del PRD". En 1994 Cuauhtémoc Cárdenas fue elegido candidato del partido a la presidencia de la República y quedó en el tercer lugar de la votación con 16.31 por ciento de los sufragios. En la Cámara de Diputados el partido consiguió 70 curules plurinominales y una uninominal. Al final del gobierno de Carlos Salinas de Gortari (1988-94) el PRD denunció el asesinato de 300 de sus militantes en ese sexenio. A lo largo de ese mismo periodo ese partido alegó fraude electoral en las elecciones para gobenador de Michoacán y Guerrero, así como en diferentes comicios municipales. El tercer Congreso Nacional del PRD se efectuó en agosto de 1995 y en sus conclusiones señaló la necesidad de "una política de alianzas para obligar al pacto a la transición política democrática al gobierno" (*sic*). El 14 de julio de 1996 el partido eligió a su presidente nacional mediante el voto directo, universal y secreto, en un proceso abierto a todos los ciudadanos interesados. Contendieron Andrés Manuel López Obrador, Amalia García Medina, Heberto Castillo y Jesús Ortega, para lo cual se instalaron 3,424 casillas de las cuales fueron impugnadas 131, según registro del Comité General del Servicio Electoral, fundamentalmente en Tabasco, Guerrero y Oaxaca. Fue declarado como nuevo presidente Andrés Manuel López Obrador, quien obtuvo el 72 por ciento de la votación. En 1996 el PRD obtuvo un avance electoral importante al conquistar 27 municipios en las elecciones de ayuntamientos del Estado de México, entre ellos Nezahualcóyotl y Valle de Chalco. Asimismo, obtuvo triunfos en municipios importantes del estado de Guerrero. En las elecciones federales intermedias de 1997 Cuauhtémoc Cárdenas fue el candidato a la jefatura de gobierno del Distrito Federal, la que ganó por amplia mayoría. Además, en esos comicios el PRD se adjudicó 39 de las 40 curules uninominales de la Asamblea Legislativa del DF; 74 curules uninominales y 54 plurinominales en la Cámara de Diputados; y llegó a 16 escaños en el Senado de la República. Alegó fraude en Campeche, donde se realizó elección de gobernador en la misma fecha. En 1998 el PRD obtuvo el triunfo en la elección de gobernador del estado de Zacatecas, con el ex priista Ricardo Monrreal Ávila como candidato, Ganó también en Baja California Sur, con Leonel Cota Montaño como candidato; y apoyó la candidatura de la alianza formada por el PT, el PVEM y el PCD de Alfonso Sánchez Anaya, a la gubernatura de Tlaxcala, que igualmente ganó. Todos sus candidatos eran ex priistas. En marzo de 1999 se efectuaron elecciones para presidente nacional del partido mediante voto directo, universal y secreto. Contendieron Jesús Ortega, Amalia García, Félix Salgado Macedonio, Carlos Bracho, Mario Saucedo Pérez, Rosalbina Garavito Elías y Raúl Álvarez Garín. El Consejo General del Servicio Electoral del PRD registró impugnaciones en prácticamente todas las entidades del país, anuló 28.14 por ciento de las casillas, declaró un "empate técnico" entre los candidatos Jesús Ortega y Amalia García, cuyos representantes presentaron el mayor número de impugnaciones, y anuló la elección. El Consejo Nacional designó como presidente interino a Pablo Gómez Álvarez, que fungió como tal de abril a julio, cuando nuevamente se efectuaron elecciones. Resultó triunfadora Amalia García Medina. El 4 de julio de 1999 ganó la gubernatura de Nayarit Antonio Echevarría Domínguez, apoyado por una alianza opositora en la que participó activamente el PRD. El 29 de mayo, aun siendo jefe de gobierno de la ciudad de México, Cuauhtémoc Cárdenas tomó protesta como candidato a la presidencia de México por el Partido del Trabajo, en un acto realizado en Monterrey, Nuevo León, y en el mes de septiembre renunció a su cargo para "buscar la candidatura del PRD a la Presidencia de la República" por tercera ocasión. A principios de año, el ex presidente nacional del partido, Porfirio Muñoz Ledo, presentó la corriente Nueva República y renunció a la dirigencia del grupo parlamentario del PRD en la Cámara de Diputados para contender por la candidatura de su partido a la Presidencia de México. En el mes de septiembre tomó protesta como candidato del PARM a la Presidencia de la República y días después renunció al PRD. El lema del partido es "Democracia ya, patria para todos".

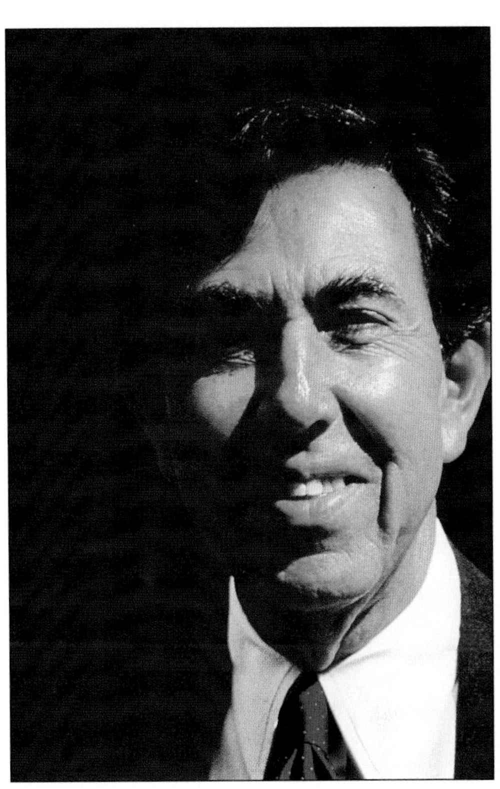

Cuauhtémoc Cárdenas, candidato del PRD para las elecciones presidenciales del año 2000

Logotipo del Partido de la Revolución Mexicana

Partido de la Revolución Mexicana ◆ Nombre que adoptó el Partido Nacional Revolucionario (☛) en su tercera Asamblea Nacional Ordinaria, celebrada en el Palacio de Bellas Artes del 30 de marzo al 1 de abril de 1938. Fue dirigida por el presidente del Comité Ejecutivo Nacional del PNR, Silvano Barba González, quien estuvo auxiliado en la mesa de debates por Heriberto Jara, vicepresidente; Alfonso Corona del Rosal, secretario por el Sector Militar; Alfonso Sánchez Madariaga, secretario por el Sector Obrero; Luis Padilla, secretario por el Sector Agrario; y Esteban García de Alba, secretario por el Sector Popular. En la asamblea participaron 96 representantes de las ligas de comunidades agrarias y sindicatos campesinos, quienes conformaban el Sector Agrario; 100 delegados del Sector Obrero, formado por la Confederación de Trabajadores de México, la Confederación Regional Obrera Mexicana, la Confederación General de Trabajadores, los sindicatos de minero-metalúrgicos y de electricistas; 101 representantes de las zonas navales y militares, de la Secretaría de la Defensa Nacional y del titular de esta dependencia, quienes integraban el Sector Militar; y 96 delegados del Sector Popular. La declaración formal de constitución se hizo a las 15:30 horas del 30 de marzo. Ese día, Hernán Laborde, secretario general del Partido Comunista Mexicano, intervino como "delegado fraternal" y pidió al PRM, en nombre de los militantes de su organización: "Queremos que se nos señale el sitio y las condiciones en que dentro del gran Partido de la Revolución Mexicana podamos cumplir con nuestro deber". La respuesta, nunca explícita, fue aceptar a los comunistas dentro del partido, pero individualmente y en calidad de perremistas. El lema aprobado fue "Por una democracia de trabajadores". El emblema, semejante al de su antecesor, estaba constituido por un círculo dividido en tres franjas con los colores de la bandera nacional. Carlos A. Madrazo leyó el informe sobre declaración de principios y programa de acción, donde se subrayaba que el partido aceptaba "la existencia de la lucha de clases, como fenómeno inherente al régimen capitalista de producción" y se recalcó "el derecho que los trabajadores tienen de contender por el poder político". El PRM, según sus documentos fundacionales, asumía como tarea central "la preparación del pueblo para la implantación de una democracia de trabajadores y para llegar al régimen socialista", lo que implicaba luchar, entre otros puntos, "por la progresiva nacionalización de la gran industria". Exigía la rectificación inmediata de la situación que propiciaba la discriminación de la mujer. Pugnaba por la explotación colectiva de la tierra, la intervención del Estado en la economía, el respeto a los derechos laborales, el establecimiento del seguro social y el impulso a programas de habitación popular. En materia internacional, el partido se manifestó enemigo "del fascismo y de cualesquiera otras formas de opresión" que adoptara "la clase privilegiada de la sociedad, con perjuicio de las libertades de la clase trabajadora". Se creó, como máxima autoridad partidaria, un Consejo Nacional formado por 32 miembros, seis por cada sector, un diputado y un senador, así como los seis integrantes del Comité Central Ejecutivo, órgano de dirección permanente constituido por un presidente y una secretaria de Acción Femenil, ambos elegidos por la asamblea nacional, y secretarios de Acción Obrera, Campesina, Militar y Popular designados cada uno por su respectivo sector. En cada estado debía existir un consejo y un comité formados sobre los mismos principios de representación. El general Juan José Ríos fue presentado por tres sectores como candidato a la presidencia del CCE, en tanto que Luis I. Rodríguez era el aspirante apoyado por el Sector obrero y también por Lázaro Cárdenas, quien hizo valer su influencia para que fuera retirada la otra candidatura y quedara Rodríguez al frente del partido. Otros miembros del Comité Central fueron Esteban García de Alba, secretario general; León García, secretario de Acción Agraria; Alfonso Sánchez Madariaga, secretario de Acción Obrera; el general Edmundo M. Sánchez Cano, secretario de Acción Social Militar; y Leopoldo Hernández, secretario de Acción Popular y Cultural. No se eligió secretaria de Acción Femenil porque las mujeres no estaban organizadas. Otros cargos fueron ocupados por Antonio Vargas MacDonald, jefe de Prensa y Propaganda; Ramón V. Santoyo, jefe del departamento de Organización y Estadística; Alejandro Carrillo Marcor, director del IESPE; y Raúl Noriega, director-gerente de *El Nacional*. En su primer mes de vida, el CCE pidió a las organizaciones sindicales afiliadas no recurrir a la huelga, pues la situación económica del país se hallaba amenazada por el boicoteo de las potencias, que respondieron de esa manera a la expropiación petrolera. En mayo se produjo la rebelión cedillista y el PRM organizó en San Luis Potosí una gigantesca concentración de apoyo a Cárdenas. El 23 de julio, tres senadores fueron expulsados por su adhesión al Frente Constitucional Demócrata Mexicano, formado por políticos callistas. El 28 de agosto se inauguró la asamblea en la que quedó constituida la Confederación Nacional Campesina, que a su vez se convirtió en el sector campesino del PRM, pues las agrupaciones agrarias que se negaron a incorporarse a la CNC no fueron reconocidas por el gobierno ni, en consecuencia, por el partido. En octubre, Luis I. Rodríguez calificó a los sindicatos blancos de Monterrey como avanzada del fascismo, lo que molestó a los dirigentes de la CGT, quienes decidieron retirar a su organización del partido. En diciembre de 1938 nació la Federación de Sindicatos de Trabajadores al Servicio del Estado, que se convirtió en la principal fuerza del sector popular. Las mujeres desplegaron una intensa actividad y, a tono con la declaración del principios del PRM, Cárdenas envió al Congreso una iniciativa para darles el voto, pero el asunto quedó congelado en la Cámara de Diputados, ante la oposición de influyentes personajes del partido, quienes argumentaban que el sufragio femenino favorecería a la oposición, especialmente a las fuerzas conservadoras. Como complemento de lo anterior, no llegó a elegirse a la secretaria de Acción Femenil ni el CCE convocó al congreso de mujeres a que lo obligaban los estatutos. En los últimos meses de 1938, Francisco J. Mújica, Rafael Sánchez Tapia y Manuel Ávila Camacho eran mencionados insistentemente como posibles sucesores de Cárdenas en la Presidencia de la República. El 17 de noviembre se constituyó en el Senado un "bloque avilacamachista", lo que fue calificado de "agitación prematura" por el líder del PRM y censurado por el propio Cárdenas, pese a lo cual continuaron manifestándose simpatías por uno u otro precandidato, especialmente por Ávila Camacho, secretario de la Defensa Nacional al que sus seguidores elogiaban por su moderación política, la que contrastaba con el radicalismo verbal de la dirección del partido. El 29 de noviembre Cárdenas pidió a los tres aspirantes renunciar a sus cargos en el gobierno, con el fin de que se dedicaran libremente a las actividades preelectorales. Como los dirigentes de los sectores popular y militar no ocultaran sus simpatías por Ávila Camacho, la CNC y la CTM condenaron "la agitación" y advirtieron que el candidato sería elegido por el conjunto de los sectores. El Comité Central amenazó con imponer medidas disciplinarias, lo que no impidió a los avilacamachistas continuar su campaña, al extremo de que el 29 de diciembre constituyeron un "comité central de orientación", el que una semana después se transformó en "centro preelectoral pro-Ávila Camacho". El 12 de enero la mayoría de los senadores expresaron su apoyo al militar poblano y el día 18 se formó el Grupo Nacional pro-Ávila Camacho. Los diputados obreros y campesinos, en su mayoría simpatizantes de Múgica, protestaron contra el abierto despliegue de sus adversarios, pero el CCE les respondió que debían esperar a las convenciones de sus respectivas centrales para manifestarse. En su mayoría, los mugiquistas acataron la orden mientras crecía la campaña por la candidatura de Ávila Camacho y sus partidarios ignoraban a la dirección del PNR. A principios de febrero se formó un bloque con la mayoría de los gobernadores para respaldar al político poblano. Luis I. Rodríguez no ocultó su irritación y declaró que la convocatoria a la Asamblea Nacional del partido no se publicaría antes del 15 de junio. El 27 de enero, la dirección de la CNC convocó a una reunión para elegir a su candidato, lo que señalaron los mugiquistas como violatorio de los estatutos del partido. La denuncia fue inútil, pues Lázaro Cárdenas declaró que la convocatoria era legal y Rodríguez se vio obligado a aceptarla, por lo que fue acusado de "favorecer de manera desleal" a Ávila Camacho. El Comité Central respondió entonces con amenazas de expulsión, por lo que el 16 de enero Múgica acusó a la dirección partidaria de traicionar "los ideales democráticos" de Cárdenas, calificó a funcionarios públicos y líderes de las centrales de maniobreros y señaló que legisladores y gobernadores avilacamachistas violaban los estatutos del PRM. El 20 de febrero se reunió el consejo nacional extraordinario de la CTM, el que aprobó un nuevo Plan Sexenal que se canjearía por el apoyo a Ávila Camacho que ahí mismo anunció Lombardo. Pese a las maniobras de Graciano Sánchez y otros líderes campesinos, los avilacamachistas tenían el temor de que la convención de la CNC no les fuera favorable y pidieron posponerla. Sin embargo, ésta se realizó y el 23 de febrero, por apretada mayoría, se resolvió apoyar al general poblano. Múgica denunció el "carácter antidemocrático" de ambas convenciones, en tanto que Sánchez Tapia, el otro precandidato, renunció al PNR, al que tachó de "burda máquina imposicionista" que usaba los procedimientos del viejo PNR. La CGT y la CROM antimoronista se unieron a la causa de Ávila Camacho, pero el sindicato ferrocarrilero se negó, al igual que Sindicato de Trabajadores de la Enseñanza, que se vio sometido a fuertes presiones hasta que una parte acató la consigna de los líderes sectoriales. Por fuera del partido había crecido la fuerza de Juan Andrew Almazán, quien contaba con el apoyo de un amplio abanico de fuerzas que incluía de manera preponderante a los grupos derechistas. Cárdenas y luego Luis I. Rodríguez invitaron a Almazán a luchar dentro del PRM, pero éste se negó e hizo saber que consideraba a ese partido como "totalitario" y a su líder como "demagogo" y "comunista". El 12 de abril se constituyó, encabezado por Miguel Alemán, el Comité Nacional Directivo de la campa-

Lázaro Cárdenas del Río, fundador del PRM

ña de Ávila Camacho, en el que estaban Adolfo Ruiz Cortines, Gabriel Leyva Velázquez, Ángel M. Corzo, Jesús González Gallo, Francisco Preciado, Adán Ramírez López, Gonzalo N. Santos, Eduardo Vidal Cruz y José María Dávila. El 16 de abril se realizó un mitin en el Toreo, donde los cuatro sectores del partido hicieron público su apoyo a la candidatura del general Manuel Ávila Camacho, quien ahí mismo se manifestó contra "la participación de los militares en la política" y consideró necesario "dar más garantías a los inversionistas". El 18 de abril de 1939 se constituyó la Confederación de Jóvenes Mexicanos, que quedó integrada al partido. La FSTSE hizo público su respaldo a Ávila Camacho hasta el 6 de mayo, pues antes debió vencer las resistencias de varios sindicatos afiliados. A mediados de ese mes renunciaron al partido tres senadores inconformes. En medio de las críticas de izquierda y derecha, Luis I. Rodríguez dejó la jefatura del PRM el 28 de mayo. Se desató entonces una enconada lucha interna por sucederlo y fue hasta el 19 de junio cuando se designó al general Heriberto Jara como presidente del Comité Central Ejecutivo, el cual quedó integrado con Esteban García de Alba, secretario general; César Martino, secretario de Acción Agraria; Alfonso Sánchez Madariaga; secretario de Acción Obrera; Edmundo M. Sánchez Cano, secretario de Acción Social y Militar; y Leopoldo Hernández, secretario de Acción Popular y Cultural. El 14 de julio renunció Múgica a su precandidatura. En octubre se publicó el anteproyecto de Plan Sexenal de la CTM, reformado por el comité ejecutivo del partido, que retiró demandas como las referentes a la explotación colectiva de los ejidos, la escala móvil de salarios y el control de inversiones. La primera asamblea nacional ordinaria del PRM se reunió del 1 al 3 de noviembre. La mesa de debates fue presidida por Heriberto Jara, a quien acompañaron Othón León Lobato, Lombardo, Graciano Sánchez y Leopoldo Hernández, representantes de los

ARCHIVO GENERAL DE LA NACIÓN

Actividad de comités locales del Partido de la Revolución Mexicana

sectores Militar, con 103 delegados; Obrero, con 351 delegados; campesino, 714 delegados; y Popular, 310 delegados. En la redacción final del Plan, Víctor Manuel Villaseñor y Ricardo J. Zevada, delegados cetemistas, tuvieron que ceder ante Jesús González Gallo y Octavio Véjar Vázquez, representantes de Ávila Camacho. Se eliminaron planteamientos que pudieran parecer radicales, se suprimió el adjetivo "socialista" que acompañaba a la palabra educación y se incluyó la promesa de dar seguridades a la pequeña propiedad y a la empresa privada. En el último día de sesiones se aprobó el plan sexenal y, por 1,217 votos en favor y 261 en contra, Manuel Ávila Camacho fue elegido formalmente como candidato del partido. Después de la asamblea, Jara continuó al frente del Comité Central, que se integró con Gustavo Cárdenas Huerta, secretario general; Sacramento Joffre, secretario de Acción Agraria; José Maximino Molina, secretario de Acción Obrera; Sánchez Cano continuó como secretario de Acción Social Militar y Eduardo Vidal Cruz fue secretario de Acción Popular y Cultural. En el curso de la campaña electoral, el candidato perremista hizo declaraciones que tendían a limitar lo asentado en el Plan Sexenal e incluso a contradecirlo. El 24 de noviembre, el propio CCE declaró que faltaba "aprobarlo en definitiva" y que se hallaba "todavía en estudio", con lo que rectificaba uno de los principales acuerdos de la Asamblea Nacional. Como había crecido la fuerza de Almazán, candidato de la derecha que contaba con la simpatía de algunos núcleos de obreros y campesinos del PRM, la dirección cetemista amenazó con sancionar a aquellos de sus agremiados que mostraran simpatías por la oposición y hasta las actitudes apolíticas. El PNR inició una amplia campaña publicitaria en la que Almazán aparecía como el "candidato millonario" de "la reacción" y un "traidor a la revolución". El Comité Central Ejecutivo llegó a decir que 98 por ciento de los votos serían para Ávila Camacho. Los partidos que apoyaban a Almazán contestaron que se preparaba un "fraude electoral" e insistieron en señalar al candidato del PRM como continuador de la política "comunista" de Cárdenas. El 3 de julio, la dirección perremista expulsó a todos los que se dijeran simpatizantes de Almazán, mientras los partidarios de éste denunciaban que grupos de choque del partido oficial se aprestaban a tomar las casillas por asalto, lo que en realidad hacían los seguidores de ambos candidatos, pues de acuerdo con la Ley Electoral, el recuento lo hacían los primeros ciudadanos en presentarse a votar. El día de las elecciones la mayoría de las casillas fueron ocupadas por gente del PRM, especialmente de la CTM. Esa misma noche el partido proclamó la victoria de su candidato, pero al día siguiente los almazanistas incluyeron en su lista de denuncias las presiones ilegales sobre los sufragantes, grupos que votaban en varias casillas, robo de urnas y choques violentos que produjeron decenas de muertos. Según las cifras oficiales, Ávila Camacho obtuvo 2,476,641 votos, contra 151,101 de Almazán, candidato del PRUN, y 9,840 de Sánchez Tapia, que mantuvo hasta el final su candidatura independiente. Antes de tomar posesión de la presidencia de la República, Ávila Camacho aclaró que no era socialista sino demócrata y manifestó, en referencia a sus sentimientos religiosos: "soy creyente". Lo anterior, muy explicable en un país católico, chocaba dentro del partido con el anticlericalismo tradicional, que con frecuencia se disfrazaba de "socialismo". El 1 de diciembre, al asumir el Poder Ejecutivo, Ávila Camacho anunció la desaparición del sector militar del PRM. Días después liberó a los oposicionistas presos con motivo de las elecciones y llamó a varios almazanistas a ocupar cargos públicos. Tres connotados callistas fueron designados secretarios de Estado: Ezequiel Padilla, Marte R. Gómez y Francisco Javier Gaxiola. Términos como "proletariado", "socialismo" y "lucha de clases" fueron sustituidos en el vocabulario oficial y partidista por "concordia", "conciliación" y "unidad nacional". El cambio de lenguaje halló cierta legitimidad no sólo por la adhesión de ciertos sectores sociales sino, sobre todo, por la amenazante situación internacional, pues la segunda guerra mundial ya se había iniciado. Para adaptar el partido a los nuevos tiempos, el 2 de diciembre fue designado presidente del CCE Antonio Villalobos Mayor. El 10 de diciembre, el jefe del Ejecutivo dio instrucciones a la Secretaría de la Defensa Nacional para que ordenara el retiro del PRM de los militares en servicio, lo que fue apoyado por Alfonso Corona del Rosal, secretario de Acción Social Militar del CCE y ratificado por el Consejo Nacional del partido, pese a que las facultades para resolver sobre un caso semejante correspondían a la asamblea nacional. El día 18, 13 diputados militares se incorporaron al sector popular, en tanto que otros se afiliaron a otros sectores o quedaron sin ubicación precisa. Varios perremistas de origen castrense se incorporaron a puestos de dirección alta e intermedia, pero como miembros de diversos sectores. Una consecuencia de estos hechos fue que disminuyó drásticamente el número de candidatos militares a puestos de representación popular. Con Villalobos, continuaron en el CCE Sacramento Joffre, Maximino Molina y Eduardo Vidal Cruz; Florencio Padilla fue el secretario general y Corona del Rosal el secretario de Acción Social Militar, cargo que desapareció al ser suprimido al sector castrense. El 1 de enero de 1941, por decreto del presidente, el periódico *El Nacional* dejó de pertenecer al partido y se convirtió en "órgano de Estado, dependiendo de la Secretaría de Gobernación". Las emisiones de las radiodifusoras XEFO y XEUZ, ambas del PRM, adoptaron una programación de corte comercial. Se anunció entonces que el partido, fuera de los periodos electorales, se dedicaría "especialmente a una labor social" y no política, lo que se confirmó, entre otras cosas, porque durante todo ese sexenio no se reeditaron sus documentos básicos y los planteamientos del plan sexenal fueron olvidados, por ejemplo en lo referente a las mujeres, que siguieron sin derecho al voto, pese a que Amalia Caballero de Castillo Ledón trabajaba para organizarlas dentro del partido. La revista *Trayectoria*, nuevo órgano perremista, era de escaso tiraje y circulación. El 17 de enero Vidal fue sustituido como secretario de Acción Popular del CCE por el mayor José Escudero, a quien reemplazó el también mayor Antonio Nava Castillo en diciembre de 1941. Pese al abandono de su plataforma izquierdizante, en los primeros años cuarenta el PRM fue el único partido con fuerza real. Las organizaciones almazanistas, que habían cobrado alguna significación por su anticardenismo militante, perdieron sus principales argumentos ideológicos con el viraje avilacamachista. Por la izquierda, el Partido Comunista vivía el periodo de las grandes purgas y, a pesar del anticomunismo de las esferas oficiales, estaba empeñado en que se le admitiera en el PRM, por lo que no escatimaba elogios para el nuevo gobierno. El PAN, fundado dos años antes, se hallaba en periodo de formación y ensayaba apenas sus armas verbales contra el oficialismo. La Unión Nacional Sinarquista, con verdadera fuerza de masas, atravesaba por un periodo de pugnas internas que le restaban eficacia política. Por instrucciones presidenciales, el CCE se empeñó en centralizar la selección de candidatos, lo que consideró necesario "en virtud de la postura imposicionista de algunos gobernadores", convertidos en "grandes electores" que pretendían "dejar como sucesores suyos

Cartel del PRM que promovía la unidad interna

en el Ejecutivo y como diputados en las legislaturas, a determinadas personas, burlando el voto de las mayorías populares". Las dificultades de la dirección partidaria no fueron únicamente con "algunos gobernadores". En el Senado y en la Cámara de Diputados se formaron sendos bloques: por una parte se agruparon los legisladores de derecha, favorables a la política de Ávila Camacho, y por otra los de izquierda, minoría proveniente sobre todo de la CTM y de la CNC, quienes pugnaban por la aplicación del plan sexenal. La CTM había sido hasta entonces la fuerza más organizada del partido y la que, siempre que fue necesario, demostró mayor capacidad de movilización. Asimismo, esta central, colocada en el ala izquierda del partido, permitía cierto equilibrio interno al PRM. Esta situación se alteró a partir del 1 de marzo de 1941, cuando Lombardo fue sustituido en la secretaría general de la CTM por Fidel Velázquez, quien inició una campaña para eliminar a lombardistas y comunistas de los puestos clave, con lo que también los descalificaba como aspirantes a cargos de elección popular. La actitud de Velázquez y sus allegados, a quienes llamaban "Los Cinco Lobitos", costó la salida de varios sindicatos de la central, los que repudiaban los métodos de la nueva dirección cetemista, pero siguieron dentro del partido cuando se integraron en la Confederación Proletaria Nacional, lo que favorecía el proyecto de dividir y debilitar al sector obrero, como se observó poco después, cuando Ávila Camacho ordenó suspender el descuento que se hacía a los profesores de cuotas destinadas a la CTM y al PRM, lo que perjudicaba principalmente a la central, lo mismo que las modificaciones a la legislación laboral que limitaban los derechos obreros. Los dirigentes cetemistas optaron por una actitud de conciliación y comenzaron a actuar, dice Luis Javier Garrido, "más como agentes del Estado que como representantes de los trabajadores". A fines de 1941 y principios de 1942 se produjo un tironeo por el control de los estratos sociales medios. Ramón G. Bonfil, Lauro Ortega, Carlos A. Madrazo y César Cervantes constituyeron la Comisión Coordinadora de Organizaciones Populares, pero fueron desautorizados por el partido cuando se anunció que el CCE sería el encargado de reorganizar el sector popular, hasta entonces el menos cohesionado, y decidieron adoptar el modesto nombre de Federación de Organizaciones Populares del Distrito Federal. Por los mismos días, en el Congreso menudeaban las críticas de izquierda y derecha contra la dirección perremista. El CCE inició formalmente, a mediados de diciembre, los trabajos de reestructuración nacional del sector popular, que debía "equipararse a los sectores obrero y campesino". El 1 de enero, el propio Ávila Camacho llamó a "la clase media" a organizarse y, a fines de ese mes, se integró el comité ejecutivo encargado de dirigir este trabajo, con Villalobos como presidente; Antonio Nava Castillo, presidente ejecutivo; Rafael Rangel, Manuel Bernardo Aguirre, Juan Gil Preciado, Andrés Manning, Carlos A. Madrazo, César Cervantes y Reynaldo Lecuona, este último como representante de la FSTSE. El 22 de mayo, el mismo día que el gobierno declaró la guerra a las potencias del Eje, el PRM organizó el "comité nacional de lucha contra el nazifascismo", que agrupó a las organizaciones del partido y a otras ajenas a él. En mayo, Fidel Velázquez anunció que, por el estado de guerra, la CTM no iba a recurrir a la huelga, lo que fue ratificado por otras organizaciones el 2 de junio, al firmarse el Pacto de Unidad Obrera, del que nació el Consejo Obrero Nacional. Los problemas derivados del estado de guerra reforzaron la política de unidad nacional, por lo que el PNR pudo olvidarse del plan sexenal y de toda concesión a las organizaciones de masas. A fines de diciembre, la CNC celebró su primera convención nacional ordinaria de la que salió como secretario general el divisionario Gabriel Leyva Velázquez, quien procedió a eliminar toda disidencia, a proteger la propiedad privada de la tierra y a centralizar las tareas de gestoría agraria. El 29 de enero de 1942, Fernando Amilpa sustituyó a Maximino Molina en la secretaría de Acción Obrera del CCE. En la convención nacional del sector popular, celebrada en Guadalajara los días 26, 27 y 28 de febrero de 1943, se creó la Confederación Nacional de Organizaciones Populares, cuyo primer presidente fue el mayor Antonio Nava Castillo. En junio, para participar en la muy breve campaña electoral de ese año, los problemas para conciliar intereses fueron de tal magnitud que el PRM sólo presentó 144 candidatos a diputados para los 147 distritos. De ellos 21 eran de la CTM, 43 de la CNC, 56 de la CNOP y el resto de otras organizaciones partidarias. Algunos líderes agrarios a quienes no se invistió como candidatos por su partido, se pre-

CRED No. 421.
SECTOR POPULAR
VERACRUZ
El C. [illegible]
es miembro activo de este Sector Popular del Partido de la Revolución Mexicana.
H. Veracruz, a 23 de Junio, de 19[illegible].
EL SRIO. GRAL. EL PRESIDENTE

Foto: Archivo General de la Nación

Credencial de un militante del Partido de la Revolución Mexicana sentaron a los comicios en forma independiente. Una treintena de ellos se agrupó en el Frente Electoral Revolucionario Nacional Campesino. Dionisio Encina, secretario general del Partido Comunista, ganó las elecciones internas del PRM en un distrito de Coahuila, pero no le fue reconocido ese triunfo y optó por presentar su candidatura independiente. Ante lo que parecía una desbandada, en los primeros días de julio el partido oficial repondió con la expulsión de 76 miembros, incluido Encina, quien consideraba que el PRM era la forma autóctona del frente popular recetado por Stalin. El CCE había integrado su planilla de candidatos con una clara mayoría de miembros del sector popular, que era minoritario en el partido, en detrimento de los sectores obrero y agrario, lo que originó nuevas tensiones al discutirse cada caso en el Colegio Electoral, donde el candidato campesino Jorge Meixueiro se suicidó en plena tribuna al negársele el triunfo. Finalmente, de los 147 diputados, 75 fueron del sector popular, 46 del agrario y 23 del obrero, en tanto que los otros tres habían participado en los comicios en forma independiente, pero como se trataba de perremistas disidentes, se plegaron sin problemas a la disciplina partidaria. En abril de 1944, durante el XXIII Consejo Nacional de la CTM, Lombardo Toledano criticó los procedimientos internos del PRM y la pasividad de la dirección partidaria ante la beligerancia de la derecha. Al mes siguiente, Villalobos asistió al IX Congreso del PCM, organización que, según dijo, se había identificado "plenamente con el régimen revolucionario". Ese y otros contactos con los comunistas estimularon la campaña de la derecha y, dentro del mismo PRM surgieron críticas como la del general Cándido Aguilar, quien declaró que la revolución estaba "maleada desde la copa hasta la raíz" y calificó de "organización totalitaria" a su partido, que lo expulsó el 9 de junio de 1944. En agosto se anunció un proyecto de reformas, elaborado por un connotado miembro del ala derecha, que hasta el nombre cambiaría al PRM para convertirlo en Partido Democrático Nacional, lo que suscitó una protesta extrañamente severa de la CTM, que juzgó como "inexistente" la democracia interna y declaró que las normas electorales internas eran ineficaces y que por lo mismo el país no se encaminaba hacia una "democracia de trabajadores", como se planteaba en sus documentos fundacionales. Sin embargo, los líderes cetemistas defendían la existencia del PRM desde el título mismo de su alegato: *¡Mejorar, no demoler al Partido de la Revolución Mexicana!* De mayor resonancia fue la crítica que hizo al partido el diputado Herminio Ahumada, al responder al IV informe presidencial. Ahumada señaló que las prácticas internas favorecían a los sectores derechistas del partido, que las "conquistas sociales" que proclamaban los líderes eran "engañosa promesa" y que era necesaria "una radical reforma" de la organización. Agregó que "mientras no sea un hecho entre nosotros el voto ciudadano, mientras no se depure la función electoral, mientras sigan siendo en ella factores decisivos la actuación de un solo partido y la falta de respeto a la opinión pública, la democracia no podrá realizarse en México". En la misma sesión, sus colegas impugnaron violentamente a Ahumada, quien fue excluido del bloque perremista. En ese día, el CCE lo expulsó del partido y, convocada por la CNC, la CTM y la CNOP, se reunió del 4 al 6 una "asamblea nacional de los sectores revolucionarios de México", la que, sin ser formalmente una reunión de partido, sirvió para ratificar el apoyo a Ávila Camacho, así como la oposición a que desapareciera o se modificara el PRM, lo que demandaban los críticos de la oposición y un sector de derecha del propio PRM. La asamblea fue presidida por Villalobos, Nava Castillo, Gabriel Leyva Velázquez, Fidel Velázquez y Lombardo Toledano, secretario general de la Confederación de Trabajadores de América Latina. A principios de 1945 se barajaban cuatro nombres para la sucesión presidencial: Miguel Alemán, secretario de Gobernación, a quien se presentaba como continuador de la política avilacamachista; Ezequiel Padilla, canciller y hombre ligado a los medios financieros estadounidenses; Javier Rojo Gómez, jefe del Departamento del Distrito Federal al que apoyaban notorios cardenistas; y Maximino Ávila Camacho, quien murió súbitamente el 28 de febrero y quedó fuera de la competencia. Padilla no contaba con suficientes adeptos para darle peso a su precandidatura y el debate se produjo en torno a Alemán y Rojo Gómez. Tres diputados simpatizantes de éste, Carlos A. Madrazo, Sacramento Joffre y Pedro Téllez Vargas fueron encarcelados, pese a que gozaban de fuero, acusados de traficar con tarjetas de contratación de braceros. A fines de abril surgió otro precandidato, el general Miguel Henríquez Guzmán, quien contaba con el respaldo de algunos círculos militares y campesinos en los que se acusaba de corruptos a los funcionarios públicos y se tachaba de derechista la política de Ávila Camacho, lo que quitaba viabilidad a Henríquez, pues los líderes del partido no iban a apoyar a alguien abiertamente contrario al presidente de la República. La división se mantuvo entre alemanistas y rojogomistas. Ambas fuerzas, por diferentes razones, proponían realizar cambios en el partido, por lo que el 19 de marzo se anunció que el PRM se sometería a "una reforma sustancial en su estructura, funcionamiento y técnica en materia electoral". El 5 de junio, la CTM hizo público su apoyo a Miguel Alemán, quien al día siguiente fue llamado por Lombardo "hijo de la revolución" y "cachorro de Lázaro Cárdenas y Manuel Ávila Camacho". El día 9 Rojo Gómez retiró su precandidatura y lo mismo hizo Henríquez el 12 de junio. Un día antes la FSTSE había anunciado su respaldo a Alemán y lo mismo hizo la CNOP el 28 de ese mes, lo que le valió la felicitación de la CNC, la FSTSE, el PCM y la CTM. El 4 de julio renunció Alemán a la Secretaría de Gobernación y tres días después la CNC le manifestó su apoyo. En diciembre de 1945, el Ejecutivo

Murió el PRM pero nació su sucesor PRI

Ya de retirada, Villalobos recomienda rectificar errores y habló contra los "prevaricadores".—Hoy escogen a Alemán

Programa del nuevo partido

Diferencias del PRI respecto del anterior PRM

PRELIMINARES

Noticia periodística sobre el nacimiento del Partido Revolucionario Institucional

envió al Congreso de la Unión una iniciativa de reforma al artículo tercero constitucional, la que fue aprobada por los legisladores del PRM que así eliminaron el concepto de "educación socialista". El 19 de de enero de 1946, el periódico *El Universal* publicó una nota titulada "El Partido de la Revolución murió ayer con el beneplácito nacional; Antonio Villalobos fue su enterrador". Durante su segunda asamblea nacional, a las 14 horas del 18 de enero de 1946, el PRM se transformó en Partido Revolucionario Institucional (☛). (*Cfr.*: Luis Javier Garrido, *El partido de la revolución institucionalizada.*)

PARTIDO DE LA REVOLUCIÓN SOCIALISTA ◆ Organismo fundado el 15 de diciembre de 1985 por un grupo que abandonó el Partido Socialista Unificado de México en febrero de ese año. El PRS se manifestó "en favor de la unidad de la izquierda, en contra del reformismo" y "dispuesto a hacer la revolución socialista con quien quiera" y a "combatir el capitalismo y las formas actuales del Estado Mexicano". Alejandro Gascón Mercado, su principal impulsor, fue elegido secretario general.

PARTIDO REVOLUCIONARIO ANTI-COMUNISTA ◆ Grupo constituido en enero de 1939 por políticos callistas entre los cuales destacaban Manuel Pérez Treviño, Melchor Ortega y Joaquín Amaro. Se proponía defender a la Constitución "de las doctrinas importadas a que ha sido sometida bajo el régimen actual", evitar la participación del Estado en la economía y en los conflictos obrero patronales, así como entregar en propiedad la tierra a los ejidatarios. Poco después de su fundación, el PRAC se fusionó con el grupo Vanguardia Nacionalista Mexicana y los partidos Social Demócrata y Nacionalista, en el comité organizador de la Convención Nacional Independiente, que en julio de 1939 se convirtió en Confederación Nacional de Partidos Independientes, y tuvo como candidato presidencial a Juan Andrew Almazán en las elecciones de 1940.

PARTIDO REVOLUCIONARIO INSTITUCIONAL ◆ Organización creada en enero de 1946, al término de la segunda asamblea nacional del Partido de la Revolución Mexicana (☛), que se convirtió en constitutiva del Revolucionario Institucional. Éste agrupó a los sectores obrero, campesino y popular, bajo el lema "Democracia y justicia social". En su declaración de principios y programa de acción, el PRI pugna por continuar la reforma agraria, lograr la igualdad del hombre y la mujer y mantener la preeminencia económica del Estado. Rafael Pascasio Gamboa fue elegido presidente del primer Comité Ejecutivo Nacional. El candidato a la presidencia de la República para las elecciones de ese año fue Miguel Alemán Valdés, quien triunfó en las elecciones con 2,178,690 votos sobre Ezequiel Padilla, quien al no lograr la candidatura por el PRM se presentó como candidato independiente.

Logotipo del Partido Revolucionario Institucional

En el mismo año, Rodolfo Sánchez Taboada sustituyó a Pascasio Gamboa al frente del CEN. En 1947, Vicente Lombardo Toledano y otros políticos iniciaron los trabajos para constituir un partido "popular" y de corte antiimperialista. En marzo, el IV Congreso Nacional Ordinario de la CTM acordó apoyar esos trabajos y el 18 de agosto Lombardo llamó a los trabajadores mexicanos a formar comités del futuro partido, del que se constituyó el Comité Nacional Coordinador el 18 de agosto. El 2 de octubre, el XXXII consejo de la CTM retiró su apoyo a Vicente Lombardo Toledano y acordó la militancia obligatoria de todos sus miembros en el PRI. En enero, la central expulsó a Lombardo, quien el 21 de junio de 1948 fundó el Partido Popular (☛), del que fue elegido presidente. En la mesa directiva de la nueva formación política figuraron connotados ex miembros del partido oficial, como Narciso Bassols, Antonio Mayés Navarro, Octavio Véjar Vázquez y Víctor Manuel Villaseñor. En febrero de 1950, el CEN del PRI convocó a la primera Asamblea Nacional, la que reformó la declaración de principios, el programa de acción y los estatutos. En 1951, dos grupos de lo que Plutarco Elías Calles llamó "la familia revolucionaria", desplazados de las posiciones de poder, decidieron constituir sendas organiza-

Asamblea Nacional del PRI en 1950

FOTO: ARCHIVO GENERAL DE LA NACIÓN

Marcha de las bases populares de apoyo del Partido Revolucionario Institucional en los años cincuenta

ciones: un grupo de militares acaudillado por Jacinto B. Treviño constituyó la Asociación Política y Social Revolucionaria Hombres de la Revolución, antecedente del Partido Auténtico de la Revolución Mexicana. El otro núcleo, dirigido por el general Miguel Henríquez Guzmán, marginado del proceso de selección interna del PRI, formó una agrupación propia llamada Partido del Pueblo Mexicano (☛) que, después de lograr la adhesión de otras agrupaciones de disidentes priistas, se convertiría en Federación de Partidos del Pueblo Mexicano, la que en 1952 tuvo como candidato presidencial al propio Henríquez. El PRI tuvo como candidato a la Presidencia de la República a Adolfo Ruiz Cortines, quien según datos oficiales recibió en las elecciones 2,713,745 votos (equivalentes a 74.31 por ciento del total de sufragios), con lo que derrotó a Efraín González Luna, candidato del PAN al que se le reconocieron 285,555 votos, y a los otros dos contendientes, Henríquez y Lombardo, ambos ex miembros del partido oficial, que recibieron 579,745 y 72,482 sufragios, respectivamente. En diciembre de 1952, Sánchez Taboada fue designado secretario de Marina y dejó la presidencia del CEN a Gabriel Leyva Velázquez, quien al año siguiente convocó a la segunda Asamblea Nacional, en la que se reformaron nuevamente el programa de acción y los estatutos. Agustín Olachea Avilés sucedió a Leyva Velázquez en la presidencia del partido en 1956. En las elecciones celebradas dos años después, el candidato presidencial priista fue Adolfo López Mateos y, de acuerdo con las cifras gubernamentales, fue el vencedor al obtener 6,767,754 votos. En ese año, Alfonso Corona del Rosal ocupó la presidencia del CEN y como tal fue el encargado de convocar, en marzo de 1960, a la III Asamblea Nacional, que reformó la declaración de principios, el programa y los estatutos. En marzo de 1963, bajo la presidencia nacional de Corona del Rosal, se llevó a cabo la asamblea nacional de programación. Medio año después se realizó la II Asamblea Nacional Extraordinaria, que reformó nuevamente los estatutos y la declaración de principios. Según estos documentos, bajo los principios de la Revolución Mexicana, el partido lucha por lograr la participación del pueblo en el gobierno, el dominio nacional sobre los recursos naturales y por mantener la preeminencia económica del Estado, dentro de los marcos de la Constitución de 1917. En 1964, el candidato priista Gustavo Díaz Ordaz, según datos oficiales, resultó vencedor en la elección presidencial con 8,368,446 votos. En abril de 1965, bajo la dirección nacional de Carlos Alberto Madrazo, se efectuó la IV Asamblea Nacional en la que se volvieron a reformar los estatutos y se estableció un mecanismo de selección interna para los candidatos a las presidencias municipales. Durante esos años, Madrazo encabezó un intento de renovación del PRI, lo que produjo tensiones internas que ocasionaron su salida de la presidencia del CEN. Corría el rumor de que estaba organizando un nuevo partido cuando murió, en 1969, en un accidente de aviación. Lauro Ortega fue presidente del PRI de 1965 a 1968. Le correspondió convocar a la V Asamblea Nacional, en febrero de 1968, en la que se reformaron nuevamente los estatutos. Entre 1968 y 1970 fue Alfonso Martínez Domínguez el presidente del CEN y le tocó dirigir la campaña del candidato presidencial Luis Echeverría Álvarez, quien en 1970, según cifras oficiales, ganó las elecciones con 11,923,743 votos. En diciembre de 1970 pasó a encabezar el CEN Manuel Sánchez Vite, quien dos años después dejó el puesto, aparentemente distanciado de Echeverría. Le sucedió Jesús Reyes Heroles, quien promovió un amplio programa editorial e impuso disciplina en casos espinosos, como la selección de candidato a gobernador de Veracruz, donde fue *destapado* uno de los aspirantes sin consentimiento de la dirección nacional (1974). La VII Asamblea Nacional reformó en octubre de 1972 la declaración de principios, el programa de acción y los estatutos. En esa oportunidad se estableció como prioridad luchar por la igualdad educacional y cultural para todos los mexicanos, por el derecho al trabajo, por la libertad y el pluralismo políticos. Por primera vez se habló de la rectoría económica del Estado como coordinador de la iniciativa privada y de los sectores estatal y social de la producción. Durante 1975 trabajaron numerosas comisiones partidarias en la elaboración del Plan Básico de Gobierno que, según se anunció, debía darse a conocer antes de la selección de candidato presidencial, a fin de escoger al hombre más adecuado para asegurar su aplicación. Sin embargo, antes de que el plan estuviera con-

Carlos A. Madrazo intentó democratizar al PRI en los años sesenta

cluido, fue *destapado* José López Portillo y Reyes Heroles se retiró de la dirección del PRI. Porfirio Muñoz Ledo se convirtió en presidente del CEN y Augusto Gómez Villanueva en secretario general. Con ellos en la dirección prosiguió la tarea editorial iniciada por Reyes Heroles y se dieron a conocer los cien puntos del *Plan básico de gobierno*, que incluía la lucha por el desarrollo económico y la independencia nacional, ofrecía garantizar el empleo para todos los mexicanos y pugnar por el mejoramiento del nivel de vida en el país. De los tres partidos de oposición con registro electoral, el PPS y el PARM dieron su apoyo al representante priista, en tanto que el PAN, en medio de una grave crisis interna, no tuvo candidato. El Partido Comunista y otros grupos privados de derechos electorales hicieron campaña en favor de Valentín Campa, candidato independiente. Sin contendiente registrado, López Portillo, de acuerdo con datos oficiales, resultó vencedor en los comicios de 1976 con 15,437,795 votos. A fines de ese año, la presidencia del CEN fue ocupada por Carlos Sansores Pérez. En 1977, en el marco de las audiencias públicas para la reforma política, el PRI nombró una comisión integrada por el propio Sansores, Blas Chumacero y Enrique Ramírez y Ramírez. Luis Dantón Rodríguez fue miembro de la subcomisión relatora de la Comisión Federal Electoral. En esa ocasión, el PRI se manifestó contrario a que se efectuaran actividades partidistas y políticas en las universidades y rechazó la presencia de la oposición en los sindicatos. La IX Asamblea Ordinaria, celebrada en agosto de 1978, modificó los estatutos, la declaración de principios y el programa de acción. Con ese motivo, se anunció que el PRI se convertía en un "partido de trabajadores". En las elecciones federales de 1979, según los resultados oficiales, el PRI ganó 9,515,173 votos en la elección de diputados de mayoría relativa (68.51 por ciento del total) y 9,418,178 (68.35 por ciento) para los diputados de representación proporcional. En ese año, Sansores fue sustituido en la presidencia del CEN por Gustavo Carvajal Moreno, quien se mantuvo en el cargo hasta 1981, cuando Javier García Paniagua llegó a la dirección del partido, donde se mantuvo hasta el *destape* del candidato presidencial Miguel de la Madrid Hurtado. García Paniagua renunció y fue sustituido por Pedro Ojeda Paullada. En las elecciones de 1982, el candidato del PRI obtuvo 16,748,006 votos (70.99 por ciento del total); en la fórmula 1 para la elección de senadores, ganó con 14,574,114 votos (65 por ciento) y, con 14,104,695 (70.34 por ciento) en la fórmula 2; en la elección de diputados de mayoría relativa obtuvo 14,350,021 votos (69.27 por ciento) y para los de representación proporcional, 14,289,793 (62.49 por ciento). A fines de ese año, Adolfo Lugo Verduzco ocupó la presidencia del Comité Ejecutivo Nacional, de la que salió en 1986 para ocupar la gubernatura de Hidalgo. Jorge de la Vega Domínguez asumió el liderazgo de la organización en ese año, cuando se gestó dentro del PRI la Corriente Democratizadora, encabezada por Cuauhtémoc Cárdenas Solórzano y Porfirio Muñoz Ledo. Este grupo criticó la organización y la orientación del gobierno y del partido, a las que calificó de antipopulares y antidemocráticas. A mediados de 1987, la Corriente sostenía como precandidato presidencial a Cárdenas, pero la dirección partidaria lo marginó al presentar a seis "distinguidos priistas" como "aspirantes a la precandidatura", todo ellos miembros del gabinete de Miguel de la Madrid. A fines de ese año, una vez que Carlos Salinas de Gortari había sido nombrado candidato del PRI a la Presidencia de la República, la mayoría de los miembros de la Corriente abandonó el partido y formó el Frente Democrático Nacional, que se constituyó en una amplia coalición de izquierda que tuvo como candidato al mismo Cárdenas. Los disidentes que se quedaron en el PRI formaron entonces la Corriente Crítica, en la que destacan Rodolfo González Guevara y Federico Reyes Heroles. De acuerdo con las cifras oficiales, Salinas fue el vencedor en los comicios presidenciales de 1988 con poco más del 50 por ciento de la votación, en tanto que en las elecciones legislativas perdió cuatro escaños en el Senado y se quedó con 260 de las 500 curules de la Cámara de Diputados. El candidato presidencial, al anunciar su triunfo, dijo que el país pasaba de un régimen de partido prácticamente único a un régimen pluripartidista de componente mayoritario. En septiembre, la secretaría general del partido fue ocupada por Manuel Camacho Solís, quien asumió de hecho el liderazgo de la organización. En diciembre hubo un nuevo cambio en los mandos partidistas, cuando Jorge de la Vega Domínguez pasó a ocupar la Secretaría de Agricultura y Luis Donaldo Colosio Murrieta se convirtió en presidente del Comité Ejecutivo Nacional; Colosio convocó a la XIV Asamblea Nacional del PRI, celebrada en los tres primeros días de septiembre de 1990, donde se realizaron distintas reformas a los estatutos, entre las que destacó la introducción para elegir a candidatos a presidentes municipales a través del voto universal y secreto, a manera de ensayo para elegir de candidatos a puestos de mayor importancia. En abril de 1992 Luis Donaldo Colosio fue nombrado secretario de Desarrollo Social y por dos

Francisco Labastida Ochoa, candidato del PRI a las elecciones presidenciales del 2000

meses la dirigencia nacional del PRI quedó a cargo de Roberto Rodríguez Barrera, quien dio paso a Genaro Borrego Estrada en la presidencia partidista. Éste convocó a la XV Asamblea Nacional, donde se echaron atrás las reformas colosistas. En marzo de 1993 fue sustituido por Fernando Ortiz Arana, quien se desempeñó en el puesto hasta abril de 1994. Luis Donaldo Colosio Murrieta fue *destapado* candidato a la Presidencia de la República el 28 de noviembre de 1993 y rindió protesta el 8 de diciembre de 1993, ocasión en que propuso una "reforma del poder". El partido entró en una fuerte crisis por las diferencias que manifestó Manuel Camacho Solís, en ese momento jefe del Departamento del Distrito Federal y ex secretario general del partido. La insurrección del EZLN en Chiapas el 1 de enero de 1994 aumentó la tensión entre los priistas y empezaron a correr rumores en torno a una eventual renuncia o sustitución del candidato. Colosio inició formalmente su campaña el día 10 de enero. El mismo día, Manuel Camacho Solís fue relevado de la cancillería y fue nombrado Comisionado para la Paz y la Reconciliación en Chiapas, ganando la atención de los medios de comunicación por encima del lanzamiento de la campaña presidencial de Colosio. La coincidencia generó suspicacias y crecieron los rumores sobre la posible sustitución del candidato. El 27 de enero el presidente de México, Carlos Salinas, reunió a los priístas de más alta jerarquía en la residencia oficial de Los Pinos para reiterarles: "El candidato es Colosio. No se hagan bolas". El seis de marzo siguiente, en un mitin en la Plaza de la República de la ciudad de México, Colosio volvió sobre su tesis de la "reforma del poder" en un discurso considerado como sumamente crítico del sistema. El 23 de marzo de 1994, en una concentración proselitista en la colonia Lomas Taurinas de la ciudad de Tijuana, Baja California, Colosio fue asesinado. Al quedar acéfala la candidatura presidencial, por primera vez se movieron diferentes grupos al margen de la voluntad del llamado "primer priista", el presidente de la República. Fernando Ortiz Arana, presidente del Comité Ejecutivo Nacional, recibió el apoyo de numerosos legisladores federales y de algunos gobernadores para ser el nuevo candidato. No obstante, la designación presidencial recayó en el hasta entonces coordinador general de la campaña de Colosio, Ernesto Zedillo Ponce de León, quien adoptó el lema "Bienestar para la familia". En abril fue relevado Fernando Ortiz Arana, e Ignacio Pichardo Pagaza fue nombrado presidente nacional del partido. De acuerdo con datos oficiales, el candidato del PRI ganó la elección con 50 por ciento de la votación, dejando en segundo lugar al PAN, que alcanzó 27 por ciento de los sufragios y en tercer sitio al PRD, que obtuvo 17 por ciento. El 28 de septiembre de 1994 fue asesinado frente al edificio del sector popular del partido, en la ciudad de México, el diputado electo y virtual coordinador del grupo parlamentario del PRI en la Cámara de Diputados, José Francisco Ruiz Massieu, secretario general de partido, lo que acentuó la crisis política en la esfera oficial y partidista. De acuerdo con la versión oficial, el crimen fue organizado por Raúl Salinas, hermano del ex presidente Carlos Salinas, a través del diputado Manuel Muñoz Rocha, de quien nunca más se supo el paradero. En diciembre del mismo año Pichardo Pagaza fue relevado y María de los Ángeles Moreno fue nombrada presidenta del PRI —siendo la primera mujer en el cargo—, en donde permaneció hasta agosto de 1995. Fue sucedida por Santiago Oñate Laborde quien concluyó su periodo en diciembre de 1996. Entre diciembre de ese año y septiembre de 1997 presidió la organización Humberto Roque Villanueva. En las elecciones federales intermedias de 1997 el PRI obtuvo una votación de 39.09 por ciento, con lo que por primera vez en su historia no tuvo la mayoría absoluta en la Cámara de Diputados, pues obtuvo 239 de las 500 curules en disputa. En el Senado conservó la mayoría con 76 de los 128 escaños. En septiembre de 1997 asumió la dirigencia Mariano Palacios Alcocer, quien se mantuvo en el cargo hasta abril de 1999, cuando fue sustituido por José Antonio González Fernández. En ese año se abrió el proceso para elegir por primera vez al candidato presidencial mediante el voto directo y secreto de todos los ciudadanos interesados en los 300 distritos del país. Se inscribieron como aspirantes a la candidatura Manuel Bartlett Díaz, Roberto Madrazo Pintado, Humberto Roque Villanueva y Francisco Labastida Ochoa, quien fue señalado por sus contrincantes como el favorito del poder. En la década de 1989 a 1999, el PRI pasó de gobernar 31 estados del país a sólo 22, perdió el control de la capital, la mayoría en nueve congresos locales y la presidencia municipal de 15 capitales estatales.

Partido Revolucionario Obrero y Campesino ◆ Grupo de vida efímera fundado a principios de 1939 por Diego Rivera, luego de su rompimiento con León Trotsky. En varias de sus declaraciones, el partido sostuvo que el gobierno del presidente Lázaro Cárdenas era "bonapartista". En 1940 apoyó la candidatura de Juan Andrew Almazán.

Partido Revolucionario Obrero Clandestino Unión del Pueblo ◆ Agrupación que se propone "la guerra popular prolongada basada en los fundamentos científicos del marxismo-leninismo para alcanzar el poder político y emancipar al pueblo de la burguesía y del imperialismo norteamericano". Sus militantes "deben cumplir las medidas de disciplina y clandestinidad, elevar constantemente su capacidad político-militar integral y garantizar la seguridad del partido por encima de la seguridad personal". El grupo antecesor del PROCUP fue fundado hacia 1964 por Héctor Eladio Hernández Castillo, quien estuvo encarcelado durante varios años, fue amnistiado y, en 1978, asesinado. En 1972 el grupo recogió los planteamientos de la agrupación armada Unión del Pueblo y se transformó en PROCUP. Se dedicó entonces a realizar "expropiaciones" bajo la dirección de Eleazar Campos Gómez, Lidia González Luján, Antonio Montaño Torres y Cristóbal Domínguez Román. Hacia 1977 Felipe Martínez Soriano, ex rector de la Universidad Autónoma Benito Juárez de Oaxaca, se convirtió en el presunto dirigente del PROCUP, según la versión gubernamental. En 1978, luego de una serie de ejecuciones de ex presos políticos y luchadores de izquierda, el Frente Nacional Contra la Represión (dirigido por Martínez Soriano) identificaba como líderes del PROCUP a Gabriel y Tiburcio González Sánchez, Guillermo Velasco Muñoz, Alejandro Elodia, Alberto Canseco Ruiz, Ana María, Rosa Elena y Gilberto Guerrero Parada, Esmeralda y Maribel Martínez Martínez y Victoria Urbieta Morales. Su labor, que se había circunscrito a Oaxaca, se amplió al ámbito nacional en 1985 cuando apoyó el secuestro de Arnoldo Martínez Verdugo realizado por el Partido de los Pobres, al que se ligó ideológicamente. Desde entonces usa las siglas PROCUP-PDLP. El 8 de noviembre de 1986 la agrupación realizó una marcha en la ciudad de México de la Plaza de las Tres Culturas al Zócalo. En abril de 1990 un "comando" del PROCUP-PDLP asesinó a dos vigilantes del periódico *La Jornada*. Esta agrupación edita el boletín *Proletario*.

Rosario Ibarra de Piedra, candidata del PRT a la presidencia de la República en 1988

PARTIDO REVOLUCIONARIO DEL PROLETARIADO ♦ Grupo marxista creado en 1964 por Guillermo Rousset y Santiago González, ambos expulsados del Partido Comunista Mexicano. A fines de ese año se fusionó con la Liga Leninista Espartaco para formar la Asociación Revolucionaria Espartaco.

PARTIDO REVOLUCIONARIO DE LOS TRABAJADORES ♦ Organización trotskista que constituía la sección mexicana de la Cuarta Internacional. Se fundó el 18 de septiembre de 1976, mediante la fusión de la Liga Comunista Internacionalista y la Tendencia Militante de la Liga Socialista. Los principales objetivos del partido eran la lucha contra la opresión de los trabajadores del campo y de la ciudad y por el establecimiento de un gobierno obrero y campesino. En 1977, el PRT designó a Lucinda Nava como su representante en las audiencias públicas para la reforma política. En esa oportunidad, el partido propuso que la jefatura del Departamento del Distrito Federal y sus delegaciones políticas fueran puestos de elección popular. En ese año se incorporaron al partido los miembros de las fracciones Bolchevique Leninista y Trotskista Leninista de la Liga Obrera Marxista. Al año siguiente, el 28 de noviembre de 1978, el partido, con el nombre de Movimiento por el Partido Revolucionario de los Trabajadores, fue reconocido como asociación política nacional y durante la campaña electoral de 1979 apoyó a diversos candidatos a diputados de otras organizaciones de izquierda. Ese mismo año, el PRT sufrió dos divisiones: un grupo de ex miembros de la Liga Socialista, encabezados por Ricardo Hernández, se adhirieron al Partido Comunista Mexicano. Otro núcleo, la Tendencia Bolchevique, que acusó al gobierno sandinista de burgués y contrarrevolucionario, se separó para adoptar más tarde el nombre de Partido Obrero Socialista, que a su vez sufrió en 1982 la escisión de militantes que dos años después volvieron al PRT. Con el registro condicionado obtenido el 11 de junio de 1981, el PRT integró a su alrededor la coalición llamada Unidad Obrera Campesina Popular y participó en los comicios generales de 1982. De acuerdo con las cifras oficiales, en la elección presidencial su candidata, Rosario Ibarra de Piedra, recibió 416,448 votos (1.76 por ciento del total), con lo que el partido obtuvo su registro definitivo. En las elecciones para senadores, fórmulas 1 y 2, tuvo 221,421 votos (0.99 por ciento) y 162,247 (0.81), respectivamente; en la de diputados de mayoría relativa, 264,153 (1.27 por ciento), y 308,099 en la de diputados de representación proporcional (1.34 por ciento), por lo que no tuvo acceso al Congreso de la Unión. El partido participó en los paros cívicos nacionales realizados en 1983 y 1984. En las elecciones de 1985 se alió con 14 organizaciones nacionales y regionales y, al obtener el 1.58 por ciento de los votos de representación proporcional, logró seis diputaciones federales. En 1986 realizó infructosas negociaciones para fusionarse con la Liga Obrera Marxista, el Partido Mexicano de los Trabajadores y la Organización de Izquierda Revolucionaria Línea de Masas. En 1987 tuvo nuevamente como candidata presidencial a Rosario Ibarra de Piedra y rechazó la alianza electoral propuesta, primero, por el Partido Mexicano Socialista y luego por el Frente Democrático Nacional. Esto provocó la separación de un gran número de militantes, incluidos 22 integrantes del comité central, entre ellos Ricardo Pascoe, Pedro Peñaloza (entonces diputados federales) y Adolfo Gilly, quienes participaron en la fundación del Movimiento al Socialismo (☛). En las elecciones de julio de 1988, el partido perdió el registro legal al recibir oficialmente menos de 1.5 por ciento de la votación total. En 1991 participó con registro condicionado y obtuvo otra vez menos del 1.5 por ciento y no pudo obtener el registro definitivo. Sus órganos máximos de dirección eran el comité central, de 54 miembros, y el comité político, de 18 integrantes. Publicaba el periódico *Bandera Socialista* y su órgano teórico era *La Batalla*. En los años noventa esta organización política se extinguió.

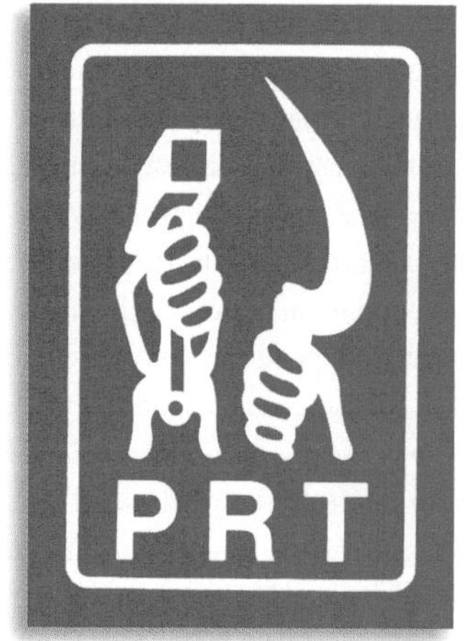

Logotipo del Partido Revolucionario de los Trabajadores

PARTIDO SOCIAL DEMOCRÁTICO ◆ Grupo fundado en julio de 1939 para apoyar, junto con varias organizaciones anticomunistas, la candidatura presidencial del general Juan Andrew Almazán. Unos días después se incorporó a la Confederación Nacional de Partidos Independientes, donde se concentraron los almazanistas. Fue dirigido por Gilberto Valenzuela.

PARTIDO SOCIALDEMÓCRATA ◆ Nombre que adoptó el grupo Acción Comunitaria, organización fundada el 13 de abril de 1967, que fue registrada como asociación política nacional el 28 de noviembre de 1978. Ya como Partido Socialdemócrata (PSD), obtuvo el 11 de junio de 1981 registro condicionado al resultado de los comicios federales del año siguiente. De acuerdo con sus documentos fundamentales, su filosofía es la de la Revolución Mexicana y su ideología la del socialismo democrático. Según su declaración de principios, México debe llegar a la economía participada, que no excluye a la iniciativa privada de la producción. El partido perdió el registro en las elecciones generales de 1982, al no obtener el equivalente al 1.5 por ciento de la votación nacional. En esa ocasión, su candidato a la presidencia fue Manuel Moreno Sánchez, que obtuvo 48,413 votos (0.2 por ciento del total); en las fórmulas 1 y 2 para la elección de senadores, el partido obtuvo 2,966 y 318 votos (0.01 y 0 por ciento, respectivamente); en la elección de diputados de mayoría relativa su votación alcanzó 38,994 y 53,306 para los diputados de representación proporcional, lo que equivalió a 0.19 y 0.23 por ciento, respectivamente. Para las elecciones de 1988, el PSD se incorporó al Frente Democrático Nacional y apoyó la candidatura presidencial de Cuauhtémoc Cárdenas. Su primer presidente fue Luis Sánchez Aguilar, a quien sucedió en el cargo Ernesto Sánchez Aguilar.

PARTIDO SOCIALISTA MEXICANO ◆ Organización constituida en la ciudad de Puebla el 4 de julio de 1878. Su mesa directiva fue integrada por Alberto Santa Fe (presidente), F. Urgell (vicepresidente), Manuel Serdán (primer secretario) y Jesús A. Laguna (segundo secretario). Su órgano fue *La Revolución Social*, en cuyo prospecto declaraban: "Los socialistas mexicanos, al constituirse en partido, resuelven: luchar por organizar a todos los elementos simpatizantes, con el fin de, a la mayor brevedad posible, conquistar, por la vía legal, el poder político de la República e implantar la Ley del Pueblo, bien por los miembros del partido o bien porque el gobierno federal la adopte por necesidad". Declaran también que se llamarán comunistas "a fin de distinguirse de los que no aceptan que el proletariado se constituya en partido de clase". En noviembre contaba con 17 centros político-socialistas en el país, sobre todo en Puebla y Veracruz. Santa Fe, junto con Laguna y Gabino López Olivera, dirigió insurrección agraria de San Martín Texmelucan, en abril de 1879, y fue aprehendido y encarcelado en la prisión de Santiago Tlatelolco. En enero de 1880, el PSM asistió al Segundo Congreso Obrero de la República Mexicana, pero el 20 de enero se retiró, al manifestarse la asamblea en favor de la candidatura presidencial de Trinidad García de la Cadena.

PARTIDO SOCIALISTA OBRERO ◆ Organismo político fundado el 20 de agosto de 1911 en el número 92 de la calle Francisco Pimentel, en la ciudad de México. Se atribuye la iniciativa al afinador de pianos Pablo Zierold y a Juan Humblot o Humbold, ambos alemanes. Otros fundadores, mencionados por Gastón García Cantú, fueron Adolfo Santibáñez, José R. Rojo, Fredesvindo Elvira Alonso, Enrique Erding, Jesús M. González, Emilio V. Rojo, Luis A. Rojo, Alberto Galván, Enrique Quintanar y Zenaido Cárdenas; también menciona al sastre Ciro Esquivel y afirma que Aquiles Serdán y Serapio Rendón participaron en algunas reuniones. Otros miembros, según Jacinto Huitrón, fueron Lázaro Gutiérrez de Lara, Isidro Rodríguez, Jesús González Monroy, Leonardo Cárdenas, Prudencio Casals, Moisés Mejía, O. C. Tello, Luis Méndez, J. Trinidad Juárez, Pioquinto Roldán y J. D. Rojas. El 22 de junio de 1912 Luis Méndez, Ciro Z. Esquivel y Pioquinto Roldán figuraron en la constitución del grupo anarquista Luz. El PSO parece haberse disuelto en ese tiempo o bajo la dictadura de Huerta. Resurgió como Partido Socialista Mexicano a fines de 1917, animado por Adolfo Santibáñez y Francisco Cervantes López. Está considerado como el primer partido marxista de México, pese a que la mayoría de sus miembros fueron anarquistas. Los marxistas eran de tendencia socialdemócrata. Su periódico fue *El Socialista*, órgano dirigido en algún tiempo por Manuel Sarabia.

PARTIDO SOCIALISTA OBRERO ◆ Organización fundada el 2 de junio de 1916 en la plaza de la Independencia de la ciudad de Mérida, por obreros que habían pertenecido a la Casa del Obrero Mundial y que apoyaban al gobierno de Salvador Álvarado, a quien algunos autores le atribuyen la creación del partido. Su primer comité estuvo integrado por el peluquero Rafael Gamboa *Rovachol* (presidente), el ferrocarrilero Gonzalo Lewis Heredia (secretario) y el profesor normalista Ramón Espadas y Aguilar (tesorero); vocales fueron el periodista Álvaro Rivera, el farmaceútico José Catalá, el ferrocarrilero Ignacio Solís y el profesor José J. Peniche López. Tres meses después, en septiembre, el partido ganó las elecciones para renovar el ayuntamiento de Mérida. Desde diciembre de 1916, apoyó la candidatura de Alvarado al gobierno constitucional de Yucatán. Luego de la declinación de éste, a fines de febrero de 1917, debido al requisito de residencia que había establecido en la ley, el grupo se transformó en el Partido Socialista de Yucatán (☛).

PARTIDO SOCIALISTA OBRERO ◆ Nombre adoptado para fines electorales por el grupo de Luis N. Morones. Surgió en la ciudad de México en febrero de 1917. Presentó algunos candidatos a diputados federales en los comicios de ese año. Su fracaso electoral determinó la desaparición, de hecho, del PSO.

Partido Socialista Revolucionario ♦ Nombre que en 1978 adoptó el Movimiento de Organización Socialista, grupo fundado en 1975, por Roberto Jaramillo Flores, quien en 1974 había salido del Partido Socialista de los Trabajadores. En su declaración de principios señalaba la necesidad de suprimir la explotación humana y que esto se conseguiría con la desaparición de las clases sociales, luego de lo cual se instauraría la dictadura del proletariado, que daría carácter social a la propiedad de los medios de producción. En 1976 apoyó la candidatura presidencial de Valentín Campa, del Partido Comunista Mexicano. Desde 1977 se vinculó a la lucha de la Tendencia Democrática del Sindicato Único de Trabajadores Electricistas de la República Mexicana y ese mismo año participó en las audiencias públicas para la reforma política, con una delegación integrada por Roberto Jaramillo y Arturo Salcido. Participó en las elecciones de 1979, bajo el emblema del PCM, y logró tres diputados, los que formaron parte de la Coalición de Izquierda. Uno de ellos, Salcido, se retiró del PSR por diferencias con Jaramillo. Fue registrado como asociación política nacional el 17 de abril de 1980. En 1981 se fusionó con otras organizaciones en el Partido Socialista Unificado de México. Sin embargo, no renunció a su registro ante la Comisión Federal Electoral y en 1984, luego de abandonar el PSUM, se volvió a constituir, de nuevo con Jaramillo como máximo dirigente.

Partido Socialista del Sureste ♦ Denominación que tomó el Partido Socialista de Yucatán (☛) a principios de 1921. La adopción del nuevo nombre fue un proceso que abarcó por lo menos la primera mitad de ese año, pues si bien en abril, en el comunicado en que se expulsaba a los simpatizantes del ex gobernador Salvador Alvarado, la organización se nombraba a sí misma Partido Socialista del Sureste, en la convocatoria al congreso obrero de Izamal, lanzada unos meses después, el partido continuaba llamándose Partido Socialista de Yucatán. En febrero de ese año, el secretario de la organización, Manuel Berzunza, había sido nombrado gobernador interino de Yucatán. En abril, en una convención realizada en Mérida, el PSS eligió a Felipe Carrillo Puerto como su candidato a la gubernatura y cuatro meses después organizó el Segundo Congreso Obrero, en Izamal, que se realizó del 15 al 20 de agosto de 1921, con la unión del Partido Socialista Agrario de Campeche. Durante el congreso, se aprobó la estructura organizativa del partido, que ratificó la autoridad del núcleo dirigente radicado en Mérida de la Liga Central de Resistencia y subordinó a ella, aunque de manera indirecta, las ligas de resistencia de Campeche y Quintana Roo. El congreso se manifestó también por luchar por "la expropiación de la tierra sin indemnización de ninguna "especie" por la expropiación sin rescate de los elementos de la producción industrial en beneficio del Estado proletario" y por "la desaparición del intermediario entre el productor y el consumidor, llamado comerciante, el cual será sustituido por el intercambio que existirá entre los productores". Aunque se manifestó por apoyar las resoluciones de la Internacional Comunista (☛), se decidió por no incorporarse a ella, luego de considerar que el movimiento comunista internacional era más amplio que la revolución rusa; es probable también que algunos líderes de la Confederación Regional Obrera Mexicana que asistieron al congreso, sobre todo Samuel Yúdico, hayan presionado para impedir la afiliación del PSS a la Komintern. En octubre de ese año comenzó a aparecer el periódico *El Popular*, que se convirtió en el órgano casi oficial de la campaña de Carrillo Puerto. En las elecciones, celebradas el 6 de noviembre de 1921, Carrillo Puerto obtuvo 62,801 votos. Dos años después, los miembros del partido sumaban cerca de 90,000 miembros que pagaban mensualmente 50 centavos y un peso por afiliación (hasta antes del congreso la cuota de incorporación era de dos pesos, mientras que la colaboración mensual era de 1.50 pesos). Según el *El Popular*, durante el gobierno de Carrillo Puerto (☛ *Yucatán*), en Mérida, a las asambleas semanales de la Liga de Resistencia asistían en promedio más de 800 personas. De hecho, el partido controló casi todas las actividades, incluida la educación y los servicios de salud. Abogó por el amor libre y organizó "bautizos socialistas" y "bodas societarias". En lo económico, promovió la organización de cooperativas y la protección del trabajador. Después del asesinato de Carrillo Puerto, en enero de 1924, la fuerza del partido disminuyó notablemente, pero sus militantes continuaron activos y, a pesar de que en 1929 el PSS se incorporó al Partido Nacional Revolucionario, muchos se negaron a desprenderse de sus "tarjetas rojas" de afiliación.

Partido Socialista de los Trabajadores ♦ Organización política creada en septiembre de 1973 por un grupo de ex miembros del Comité Nacional de Auscultación y Organización, entre los cuales figuraban Rafael Aguilar Talamantes, Jorge Abaroa, Graco Ramírez, Rafael Fernández, Juan I. del Valle, Teresa Beckman, José Pérez y Amparo Castro. Su declaración de principios establecía que los trabajadores deben ser dueños de las riquezas nacionales y que a la clase obrera corresponde transformar la realidad, basada en los principios marxista-leninistas. En 1977, en el marco de las audiencias públicas para la reforma política, el PST envió una delegación formada por Rafael Aguilar Talamantes, Graco Ramírez, Jorge Amador, Roberto Esperón y Primitivo Rodríguez. En 1978 consiguió su registro condicionado. Según datos oficiales, en las elecciones para diputados de mayoría relativa, en 1979, el PST obtuvo 280,573 votos (2.02 por ciento) y 311,556 para los de representación proporcional (2.26 por ciento), lo que le proporcionó el registro definitivo. En las elecciones de 1982, el candidato presidencial del PST fue Cándido Díaz Cerecedo, quien recibió 342,005 votos (1.45 por ciento del total); en las fórmulas 1 y 2 para la elección de senadores, ganó 320,672 y 328,706 votos (1.43 y 1.64 por ciento, respectivamente); en la elección de diputados, de mayoría relativa y de representación proporcional, obtuvo 370,244 y 428,153 votos (1.79 y 1.87 por ciento). Aguilar Talamantes fue secretario general del partido desde su fundación. En 1987, el PST cambió de nombre y adoptó el de Partido del Frente Cardenista de Reconstrucción Nacional (☛).

Partido Socialista Unificado de México ◆ Organización fundada en 1981, mediante la fusión de los partidos Comunista Mexicano, del Pueblo Mexicano y Socialista Revolucionario, así como de los movimientos de Acción y Unidad Socialista y de Acción Popular, además de otros núcleos de militantes de diverso origen y varias agrupaciones regionales. El PSUM participó en las elecciones presidenciales de 1982 con Arnoldo Martínez Verdugo como candidato presidencial, quien oficialmente recibió 821,995 votos (3.48 por ciento); en la elección de senadores, fórmulas 1 y 2, obtuvo 866,301 votos (3.86 por ciento) y 846,805 (4.22 por ciento); para diputados de mayoría relativa y de representación proporcional el PSUM ganó 905,058 y 932,214 votos (4.37 y 4.07 por ciento, respectivamente). En 1984 se escindió un grupo que reconstituyó el Partido Socialista Revolucionario y, al año siguiente, otro sector encabezado por Alejandro Gascón Mercado que dio lugar al Partido de la Revolución Socialista. En 1987, el PSUM se fusionó con otras organizaciones para crear el Partido Mexicano Socialista (☛). Su secretario general fue Pablo Gómez Álvarez.

Partido Socialista de Yucatán ◆ Nombre que adoptó el Partido Socialista Obrero (☛) a principios de marzo de 1917, poco después de que, debido a una norma constitucional, el gobernador provisional de Yucatán, Salvador Alvarado, renunció a su candidatura al gobierno del estado. El 16 de marzo se eligió el primer Comité Directivo del partido, integrado por Felipe Carrillo Puerto (☛), presidente; Felipe Valencia López, vocal secretario; Ceferino Gamboa, vocal tesorero; y José J. Peniche, José E. Ancona, Carlos Pacheco y Álvaro Rivera, vocales. Dos meses después, en mayo, decidió organizarse a partir de una estructura llamada "liga de resistencia", que según escribía Carrillo Puerto en 1924, "es más que un partido político; es más que una institución educativa; es más que un instrumento para gobernar. Es todo esto combinado". En noviembre de 1917, el candidato del PSY, Carlos Castro Morales, fue elegido gobernador de Yucatán. En febrero de 1918, la Legislatura yucatanense, dominada por los socialistas, aprobó un decreto que prohibía a los hacendados cultivar tierra que hubiera pertenecido a los pueblos. El primer Congreso Socialista de Yucatán, celebrado en en Motul entre el 29 y el 31 de marzo de 1918, marcó el inicio del viraje partidario hacia hacia posiciones marxistas, abandonando las tesis de cooperación entre hacendados y obreros y campesinos, que habían sido impulsadas por el gobierno de Alvarado. Durante el congreso, el partido instituyó su órgano más importante, la Liga Central; resolvió impulsar la creación de cooperativas y se manifestó por un tipo nuevo de escuela, la escuela "racionalista", que educara "no por medio de los libros sino del trabajo". En los primeros meses de 1918, alrededor de 30,000 personas militaban en el partido. En abril, el Congreso local, donde los socialistas conservaban la mayoría, le confirió a las ligas de resistencia personalidad jurídica para resolver conflictos. Durante el resto del año, el enfrentamiento entre socialistas y hacendados aumentó, hasta que en abril de 1919, el gobierno de Venustiano Carranza detuvo el reparto agrario iniciado por Carrillo Puerto, entonces gobernador provisional. Con vistas a las elecciones generales de noviembre, el partido apoyó la candidatura presidencial de Álvaro Obregón, pero en junio de 1919, el ejército estacionado en Yucatán comenzó una campaña represiva, que incluyó el envío de tropas para, según el propio Carranza, "no permitir que se me amenace con 72,000 socialistas". En noviembre, los federales asaltaron e incendiaron la sede de la liga central y expulsaron del estado a casi todos los dirigentes del partido. Al triunfo de la rebelión de Agua Prieta, el partido se reorganizó y, en agosto de 1920, sus candidatos a diputados federales, Felipe Carrillo Puerto y Edmundo G. Cantón, obtuvieron el triunfo en los dos distritos del estado. En noviembre se realizaron elecciones para el Congreso local y para los ayuntamientos. El PSY publicó un programa, el que incluía la municipalización de los servicios públicos y la formación de milicias obreras y campesinas, y ganó por muy amplio margen. A principios de 1921, la organización adoptó el nombre de Partido Socialista del Sureste (☛).

Partido Sociedad Nacionalista ◆ (☛ *Sociedad Nacionalista*).

Partido del Trabajo ◆ Organización constituida el 8 de diciembre de 1990 en asamblea realizada en el auditorio del centro deportivo Plan Sexenal de la ciudad de México. De acuerdo con su plataforma política registrada ante el IFE, lucha "por una sociedad socialista, plural, democrática y humana; por la construcción de instancias de poder popular independientes, que asuman tareas generales, dando cauce a la inicitaiva del pueblo para administrar y gobernar, hasta que todo el poder sea del pueblo organizado". El PT se formó a partir de la confluencia de varias organizaciones, tales como los Comités de Defensa Popular de Chihuahua y Durango, el Frente Popular de Lucha de Zacatecas, el Frente Popular Tierra y Libertad de Monterrey, así como de mili-

Logotipo del Partido del Trabajo

tantes de la Unión Nacional de Trabajadores Agrícolas, de la Coordinadora Nacional Plan de Ayala y del movimiento magisterial. En las elecciones federales intermedias de 1991 sólo obtuvo 270,000 votos, por lo que perdió su registro condicionado. En 1993 obtuvo su registro definitivo. El 13 de enero de 1994 obtuvo nuevamente registro. En las elecciones federales del 21 de agosto de ese año, con Cecilia Soto González como candidata presidencial, obtuvo un millón de sufragios, resultado que le permitió contar con diez diputaciones federales. En las elecciones federales de 1997 el PT obtuvo una votación que le dio siete curules plurinominales, pero a la mitad de LVI Legislatura su grupo parlamentario ya estaba conformado por 11 diputados, pues se le sumaron cuatro procedentes del PRD, PAN y el PVEN. También obtuvieron un escaño senatorial, ocupado por el único líder que ha tenido el PT desde su fundación, Alberto Anaya. Ese mismo año postuló como candidato a jefe de gobierno del Distrito Federal a Francisco González, quien luego de denunciar la falta de recursos para su campaña y la ausencia de apoyo del partido, renunció a la organización y a la candidatura. El PT improvisó entonces la candidatura de la cantante Viola Trigo. En 1999 contaba con alrededor de 300 militantes en cargos de elección popular conseguidos bajo su emblema: gobernaba la capital de Durango y Ciudad Nombre de Dios, en el mismo estado; así como tres municipios de Veracruz y uno de Hidalgo. Contaban con dos representantes a la ALDF. El 29 de mayo de 1999 eligió a Cuauhtémoc Cárdenas Solórzano como su candidato presidencial.

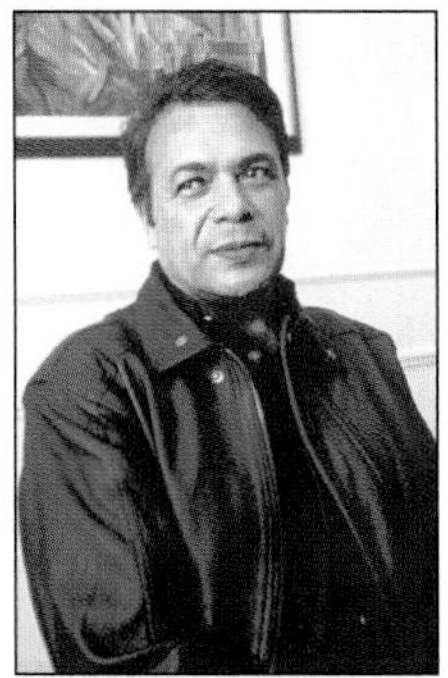

Alberto Anaya, presidente nacional fundador del PT

Jorge González Torres, candidato del PVEM para las elecciones presidenciales del año 2000

Partido Unificador de la Juventud Mexicana ◆ Organización que se constituyó el 31 de diciembre de 1938 para apoyar la precandidatura presidencial de Manuel Ávila Camacho. Tuvo una vida efímera.

Partido Verde Ecologista de México ◆ Organización constituida el 14 de mayo de 1993, interesada fundamentalmente "en el cuidado y la conservación de la naturaleza y del medio ambiente", según señala su declaración de principios. También pretende "la recuperación y afianzamiento de los auténticos valores culturales de México. En especial, de la tradición y conocimientos autóctonos, que son profundamente respetuosos de los seres vivientes, humanos, animales y vegetales, así como de los elementos naturales". Sus orígenes se remontan a la década de los setenta, cuando surgió una organización denominada Brigada de Trabajo y Democracia Social. En 1980 esta organización se transformó en la Alianza Ecologista Nacional, que se ocupó de realizar trabajos de denuncia de acciones que afectaban el entorno natural, destacando en la lucha contra la instalación de la nucleoeléctrica de Laguna Verde, Veracruz. En 1986 se constituyó como Partido Verde Mexicano, con la intención de participar en los comicios federales de 1988, objetivo que no cumplió por no haber obtenido el registro ante los órganos electorales. Se integró al Frente Democrático Nacional (☛) PRD para apoyar la candidatura de Cuauhtémoc Cárdenas, del que se separó al concluir el proceso electoral. En 1990 solicitó nuevamente registro ante el IFE, bajo el nombre de Partido Verde Ecologista Mexicano, pero fue rechazado. En sus dictamen, el IFE señalaba: "De las constancias aportadas se advierte que la organización de que se trata ha realizado una labor constante en defensa de la ecología, del medio ambiente, de la flora y la fauna (.) A juicio del Consejo General estas actividades no se consideran políticas en el espíritu del artículo 41 Constitucional y de lo dispuesto en el Cofipe". La organización impugnó la decisión ante el Tribunal Federal Electoral, que falló en su favor el 9 de febrero de 1991, otorgándole el registro condicionado como partido político nacional. El IFE condicionó el mismo a que la organización cambiara el nombre y el emblema, por lo que se denominó Partido Ecologista de México (PEM), Tras las elecciones federal de 1991, el PEM perdió su registro por haber obtenido sólamente el 1.44 por ciento de la votación nacional, mientras que la legislación determina que el registro se conservará con el 1.5 por ciento. No obstante, los dirigentes consideraron que la supresión del registro condicionado era ilegal, con base en el artículo 35 del Cofipe que establece: "un partido político con registro condicionado obtendrá el registro definitivo cuando haya logrado el 1.5 por ciento en alguna de las elecciones en que participe", y el PEM había obtenido 1.41 en la elección de senadores y 1.44 en la de diputados, pero 4.72 en la de asambleístas. El 13 de enero de 1993 recuperó el registro, que en 1994 refrendó con los resultados de los comicios federales. El 14 de mayo de 1993, en asamblea nacional, la organización determinó cambiar su nombre a Partido Verde Ecologista de México. Su dirigente nacional y fundador es Jorge González Torres, quien fue elegido candidato a la Presidencia de la República en dos ocasiones (1994 y 1999), y una a la jefatura de gobierno del Distrito Federal. El primer Comité Nacional del partido estuvo integrado, además, por Natalia Escudero, secretaria general; José Luis Atilano, secretario de Organización; Jorge Valencia, secretario de Finanzas; María Eugenia Ortega, secretaria de Relaciones Exteriores; Esveida Bravo, secretaria de Gobierno; y Carlos Ortiz, secretario de Acción Electoral. A partir de 1994 el PVEM comenzó a tener presencia en

Logotipo del Partido Verde Ecologista de México

diferentes ámbitos de representación popular y de gobierno. Ese año ganó dos curules de la Asamblea de Representantes del Distrito Federal. En 1999 contaba con presencia en nueve estados donde tenía regidores, alcaldes, diputados locales y federales.

PARTIDO YORKINO ◆ (☛) *Federalismo.*

PASAJES, JOSÉ LUIS ◆ n. en España y m. en el DF (1917-1987). Pintor. Fue copista del Museo del Prado de Madrid (1934-36). Al comenzar la guerra civil española se exilió en México. Pintó un mural en el Sanatorio Español. En 1932 fue condecorado por la Real Academia de Bellas Artes de España y en 1944 recibió un premio de la ciudad de Barcelona.

PASCAL, GABRIEL ◆ n. en el DF (1951). Escenógrafo. Estudió en el Centro Universitario de Estudios Cinematográficos. Fue asistente y más tarde director de escenografía del Taller Coreográfico de la UNAM (1973-75). Pasó al Ballet Nacional de México y luego fue asistente de Alejandro Luna. Es coordinador técnico del Teatro de la UNAM. Algunas obras para las cuales ha realizado escenografías son: *La cabeza del dragón*, dirigida por Beatriz Campos (1981), *El estupendo consuelo*, dirigida por Ignacio Retes, *De película* y *De la calle*, dirigidas por Julio Castillo; *Del día que murió el señor Bernal dejándonos desamparados* y *La pasión de Pentesilea*, dirigidas por Luis de Tavira; *Final de viernes*, de Carlos Olmos; *Palinuro en la escalera*, de Fernando del Paso; *La puerta del fondo*, de David Olguín, y *El rehén* de Juan Tovar. En 1993 participó en el proyecto de la construcción del Teatro El Milagro.

PASCASIO GAMBOA, RAFAEL ◆ n. en Tuxtla Gutiérrez, Chis. (1900-1979). Médico cirujano por la Universidad Nacional de México (1923). Se desempeñó como diputado federal (1937-38 y 1973-76), secretario general (1939) y gobernador de Chiapas (1940-44). Durante su gestión fundó la biblioteca del estado y el Museo de Historia Natural. En 1945 fue nombrado director de Pensiones Civiles. Fue el primer presidente del Partido Revolucionario Institucional (enero a diciembre de 1946) y secretario de Salubridad y Asistencia en el gabinete de Miguel Alemán (del 1 de diciembre de 1946 al 30 de noviembre de 1952).

PASCOE PIERCE, RICARDO ANDRÉS ◆ n. en el DF (1949). Licenciado en filosofía por la Universidad de Nueva York (1967-71), maestro en sociología por la Facultad Latinoamericana de Ciencias Sociales (1972) y licenciado (1974-75) y doctor (1978) en economía por la London School of Economics and Political Science. Profesor e investigador de la UAM-X (1977-82), donde fue jefe de Relaciones Públicas y secretario de Asuntos Académicos (1978- 79), así como secretario general del SITUAM (1979-81). De 1976 a 1987 militó en el Partido Revolucionario de los Trabajadores, de cuyos comités central (1979-87) y político (1981- 87). Diputado federal a la LIII Legislatura (1985-88). En 1987 se separó del PRT para apoyar la candidatura presidencial de Cuauhtémoc Cárdenas Solórzano y posteriormente formar el Movimiento al Socialismo (1988). En 1989 participó en los trabajos de organización del PRD, de cuyo CEN fue secretario de Comunicación (1989-93) y secretario de Relaciones Internacionales (1996). Ha sido vicepresidente ejecutivo de la Fundación para la Democracia Alternativa (1995), coordinador de análisis de la campaña de Cuauhtémoc Cárdenas (1997), colaborador de *El Universal* y *La Crónica*, comentarista en el programa de radio *Tertulia* (1997) y delegado del gobierno del DF en Benito Juárez (1997-). Coautor de *Salarios reales de la clase obrera (1939-75)*(1977). Autor de *Los resultados electorales en la transición democrática* (1978), *La oposición frente a la sucesión presidencial* (1988) y *Mexican Presidential Election* (1990).

PASCUA Y MARTÍNEZ, LADISLAO ◆ n. y m. en la ciudad de México (1815-1891). Médico graduado en 1837. Profesor de física en la Escuela de Medicina y en el Colegio de San Ildefonso. Perteneció a la primera Academia de Medicina (1840). En 1847 creó el grupo profesional antecesor del cuerpo médico militar. Ordenado sacerdote en 1854, fue cura de Tacubaya (1857) y de la Santa Veracruz (1866) y canónigo del cabildo de Guadalupe (1872). Autor de *Introducción a la física*.

Mercedes Pascual

PASCUAL, MERCEDES ◆ n. en España (1930). Actriz. Llegó a México a la caída de la República española (1939). Estudió danza con Nina Sestokova, teatro con Seki Sano y actuación cinematográfica con Andrés Soler. Becaria del gobierno de Francia (1960) y del INBA (1970) para estudiar teatro en París y Londres, respectivamente. Ha formado parte de la Compañía de Teatro del IMSS (1961-66), del Ballet Folklórico de Amalia Hernández, de la Academia Mexicana de la Danza y, desde 1978, de la Compañía Nacional de Teatro. En cine, participó en las cintas *El esqueleto de la señora Morales* (1959) y *Los años verdes* (1966). En 1968 fue premiada por su actuación en *Medusa*, de Emilio Carballido; en 1971, por *Como tú me deseas*, de Pirandello; y en 1979, por *Las mujeres sabias*, de Moliére.

Ricardo Pascoe

PASCUAL BUXÓ, JOSÉ ◆ n. en España (1931). Poeta y ensayista. Llegó a México en 1939, a la caída de la República española. Licenciado en letras españolas por la UNAM, de la que fue profesor (1953-59) e investigador (1958-59). Becario de El Colegio de México. Director de la Escuela de Letras de la Universidad Veracruzana (1957-58) y director de la Escuela de Humanidades de la Universidad de Zulia, Venezuela (1963-66 y 1968). Fue director de la revista *Ideas de México* (1953-55). Cola-

Fernando del Paso

borador de *México en la Cultura, Revista Mexicana de Cultura, La Palabra y el Hombre* (de la que es cofundador), *Revista de la Universidad de México* y *Revista de Bellas Artes*. Realizó las antologías *La generación del 98* (1956), *Arco y certamen de la poesía mexicana colonial. Siglo* XVII (1959), *Vida de Santa María Epigracia, libro de los tres reyes de oriente* (1961) y *Obras de Luis de Sandoval y Zapata* (1986). Coautor de *Apuntes para una bibliografía crítica de la literatura hispanoamericana* (Italia, 1973). Autor de ensayo: *Góngora en la poesía novohispana* (1960), *En torno a la muerte y al desengaño en la poesía novohispana* (1962), *Las jarchyas. Primitiva lírica hispánica* (1962), *Ungaretti, traductor de Góngora* (1968), *Muerte y desengaño en la poesía novohispana (siglos XVI y XVII)* (1975), *Teatro novohispano* (1975), *Ungaretti y Góngora. Ensayo de literatura comparada* (1978), *Introducción a la poética de Roman Jakobson* (1978), *La imaginación del Nuevo Mundo* (1988) y *El oráculo de los preguntones atribuido a Sor Juana Inés de la Cruz* (1991); y poesía: *Tiempo de soledad* (1954), *Elegías* (1955), *Memoria y deseo* (1963), *Boca del solitario* (1964), *Materia de la muerte* (1966) y *Lugar del tiempo* (1974).

Pascual Leone, Álvaro ◆ n. en España y m. en el DF (1894-1953). Se tituló como abogado en la Universidad de Valencia. Fue concejal del ayuntamiento de Valencia, diputado a Cortes (1931, 1933 y 1936), director general de Administración Local y magistrado del Tribunal Supremo de Justicia. En España colaboró en los diarios *La Voz* y *El Pueblo, El Luchador* y *La Libertad*. Llegó exiliado a México en 1939. Director de *España con honra* y secretario de la Diputación Permanente de la República española, trabajó hasta su muerte en el Departamento Jurídico del IMSS. Colaboró en los diarios mexicanos *Excélsior* y *El Nacional*. Autor de *Intenciones, Transformación del concepto de poder público en el siglo XVIII, Pedro Osuna, Raza y nacionalidad, La República Española existe* y *México y la seguridad social*.

Pascual Moncayo, Pablo José ◆ n. en San Pedro de las Colonias, Coah., y m. en el DF (1944-1997). Licenciado en economía por la UNAM (1961-66). Profesor del IPN (1969-70), de la UNAM (1969-) y de la Universidad Anáhuac (1972). Fue miembro de los comités ejecutivos de los sindicatos de Personal Académico de la UNAM (1974-77), de Trabajadores de la UNAM (1977-81) y Único Nacional de Trabajadores Universitarios (1981-84). Miembro de la dirección nacional del Movimiento de Acción Popular (1981) y de la comisión política del Partido Socialista Unificado de México (1981-87). Militante del Partido Mexicano Socialista. Diputado federal a la LIII Legislatura (1985-88). Coordinó la edición del libro *Las elecciones de 1994* (1995).

Pascual del Roncal, Federico ◆ n. en España y m. en el DF (1903-1958). Psiquiatra. Fue jefe del Departamento de Psiquiatría y Salud Mental del Ministerio de Salud de España e investigador del Instituto del Cerebro de Moscú. Llegó a México en 1939, luego de la derrota de la República Española. Trabajó en El Colegio de México. Profesor de la UNAM (1940-58). Fue jefe del servicio psiquiátrico del Instituto Médico Pedagógico de México y subdirector de la Clínica Neuropsiquiátrica Falcón (1943). Colaboró en *Cuadernos Americanos*. Autor de *Manual de neuropsiquiatría infantil* (1940), *El ruido en los medios urbanos, Teoría y práctica del psicodiagnóstico de Roscharch* (1944) y *Psicología del anciano*.

Pasión, de la ◆ Río de Jalisco y Michoacán. Nace en el norte de la sierra de las Bufas, atraviesa la de Tizapán y termina en el lago de Chapala. Su cauce sirve de límite a los dos estados.

Pasión, de la ◆ (☛) *Clipperton*.

Paso, Fernando del ◆ n. en el DF (1935). Escritor y pintor. Bisnieto de Francisco del Paso y Troncoso. Su segundo apellido es Morante. Hizo estudios de economía y literatura en la UNAM. Fue locutor de la BBC de Londres y de Radio Francia Internacional. En 1986 se le designó agregado cultural de la embajada mexicana en París. Director de la Biblioteca Iberoamericana Octavio Paz en la Universidad de Guadalajara, Jalisco. Expuso sus obras de creación plástica por primera vez en Londres (1973), y desde entonces sus trabajos se han presentado en España (1980), Estados Unidos (1981 y 1983), Francia (1989) y México. Ha colaborado en las principales publicaciones literarias de México. Autor de poesía: *Sonetos de lo diario* (1958), libros infantiles *De la A a la Z por un poeta* (1990) y *Paleta de diez colores* (1992, ilustrado por Vicente Rojo); novela: *José Trigo* (1966, Premio Xavier Villaurrutia), *Palinuro de México* (1977, ganadora de los premios México 1975; Rómulo Gallegos, Venezuela, 1982; Casa de las Américas, Cuba, 1985; y Médicis a la mejor novela extranjera editada en Francia, 1985-86), *Noticias del imperio* (1987, Premio Mazatlán de Literatura) y *Linda 67* (1995); y teatro: *La loca de Miramar* (1988), *Palinuro en la escalera* (1992) y *La muerte se va a Granada* (1998). Becario del Centro Mexicano de Escritores (1964-65) y de la Fundación Guggenheim (1970-71 y 1981-82). En 1986 le otorgaron el Premio Internacional Madrid de radiodifusión por su programa *Carta a Juan Rulfo*, transmitido por

Radio Francia. Premio Nacional de Ciencias y Artes 1991. Creador emérito del SNCA (1993-). Miembro de El Colegio Nacional (1996). En 1997 inauguró una muestra, *Destrucción del orden*, de su obra plástica.

Paso del Macho ◆ Municipio de Veracruz situado en el centro del estado, al este y noreste de Córdoba y al suroeste de Veracruz. Superficie: 323.26 km². Habitantes: 25,245, de los cuales 7,091 forman la población económicamente activa. Hablan alguna lengua indígena 24 personas mayores de cinco años (náhuatl 12).

Paso de Ovejas ◆ Municipio de Veracruz situado en el centro del estado, al noroeste del puerto de Veracruz. Superficie: 384.95 km². Habitantes: 30,453, de los cuales 8,140 forman la población económicamente activa. Hablan alguna lengua indígena trece personas mayores de cinco años.

Paso y Troncoso, Francisco del ◆ n. en Veracruz, Ver., y m. en Italia (1842-1916). Su nombre completo era Francisco de Borja del Paso y Troncoso Medina. Comerciante en su juventud, en 1867 pasó a la ciudad de México y estudió en las escuelas nacionales Preparatoria (con Gabino Barreda) y de Medicina. Fue profesor de náhuatl en la Escuela Nacional Preparatoria (1886-89), de historia de México en la Escuela Normal de Profesores de Instrucción Primaria y de náhuatl en el Museo Nacional de Historia, que dirigió en 1889. Traductor de italiano, inglés y náhuatl. Comentó algunos códices, entre ellos el Borgia (1899) y el Kingsborough. Director de la Comisión Científica de Cempoala (1890). Determinó la primera ubicación de la Villa Rica de la Vera Cruz, descubrió monumentos arqueológicos en Cempoala, reconoció el terreno entre Papantla y Cotaxtla e hizo excavaciones en Nautla, Soledad y Medellín. En 1892 se le nombró integrante de la Junta Colombina, que preparó los festejos del cuarto centenario del viaje de Cristóbal Colón y fue a España a coordinar los trabajos de la Exposición Histórica Americana de Madrid. Permaneció en aquel país como "director del Museo Nacional de Historia en misión en Europa" y desde 1895 vivió en Florencia. Colaborador de los *Anales del Museo Nacional de Arqueología* desde 1883, publicó la serie de documentos *Papeles de la Nueva España*, que recogió las relaciones de Felipe II. Recopiló las cartas de algunos personajes de la Colonia en *Epistolario de la Nueva España*; publicó una parte del *Códice Florentino* y un facsímil de los *Manuscritos matritenses*, de Bernardino de Sahagún; la *Crónica de la Nueva España*, de Francisco Cervantes de Salazar; el *Arte para aprender la lengua mexicana*, de Andrés de Olmos (1885), el *Arte de la lengua mexicana y castellana* de Alonso de Molina; *El arte mexicano*, de Diego de Galdo Guzmán; y la *Historia de los mexicanos*, de Cristóbal del Castillo, entre otras obras. Tradujo también piezas teatrales escritas en náhuatl, como *La invención de la santa cruz* y *El sacrificio de Isaac*, y los libros *Due monumenti di architettura messicana*, de Pedro José Márquez, y *Los libros del Chilam Balam*, de Daniel G. Brinton. Autor de *Los libros de Anáhuac* y *División territorial de Nueva España en el año de 1636*. Perteneció a las reales academias Española (de la Lengua) y de la Historia, y a las sociedades Mexicana de Geografía y Estadística y Científica Antonio Alzate.

Paso y Troncoso, Pedro del ◆ n. y m. en Veracruz (1780-1857). Fue prior del Consulado en 1819. Consejero de Agustín de Iturbide desde 1822, ese mismo año negoció un préstamo con Diego Barry. Al año siguiente habilitó la fragata *Rawlings*, en la que el emperador huyó de México. Luego de la proclamación de la República negoció otro empréstito con la casa B. A. Goldsmith y Compañía, de Londres. En 1853 era jefe del Departamento de Veracruz (1853).

Pasquel, Jorge ◆ n. en Veracruz, Ver., y m. cerca de Ciudad Valles, SLP (1907-1955). Fundador de los equipos de beisbol profesional *Azules* de Veracruz (1940) y *Diablos rojos* de México. Reorganizó la Liga Mexicana de Beisbol. Fue dueño del Parque Delta y copropietario del periódico *Novedades*. Murió en un accidente de aviación.

Pasquel, Leonardo ◆ n. y m. en Jalapa, Ver. (1910-1990). Licenciado en derecho por la UNAM (1940), donde estudió dos años de la maestría en Historia y ejerció la docencia a partir de 1949. Profesor en escuelas de la SEP desde 1947. Presidente de la Cooperativa de Empleados (1935) y secretario general del Sindicato de Trabajadores de la Lotería Nacional (1937); jefe de ventas de esa institución (1956); oficial mayor (1946) y secretario del Consejo Superior de Salubridad en la SSA; jefe del Departamento de Tránsito Federal (1948) y miembro de la Comisión Nacional de Tarifas de la SCT; magistrado del Tribunal Superior de Justicia del Distrito y Territorios Federales y asesor económico del gobierno de Tlaxcala. En 1958, fundó la editorial Citlaltépetl. Colaborador de *Vínculo*, *Ilustración*, *Veracruz*, *Hoy* y *Revista Jarocha*. Autor de varios libros entre los que destacan *Perfiles de Xalapa* (1948), *Discurso a Orizaba. Interpretación sociológica del mito de Quetzalcóatl-Citlaltépetl* (1965), *Díaz Mirón, orador* (1966), *Bibliografía diazmironiana* (1966), *Biografía integral de la ciudad de Veracruz* (1969), *Juárez en el baluarte de la Reforma* (1973), *Biografía de la cuenca del Papaloapan* (1975), *Biografía de Xalapa* (1976) y *El conflicto obrero de Río Blanco en 1907* (1976). Fue presidente de la Asociación de Estudios Históricos Clavijero.

Pasteles, guerra de los ◆ (☛) *Francia*.

Pastor, Julián ◆ n. en el DF (1943). Cineasta. Su apellido materno es Llaneza. Estudió dibujo y pintura con Robin Bond (1956-61), ingeniería (1960-61) y arquitectura (1961-64) en la UNAM, cine en la Universidad del Sur de California (1964) y actuación con Seki Sano, Héctor Mendoza y Juan José Gurrola. Fue asistente de dirección y coargumentista de José Estrada en las películas *Siempre hay una primera vez* (1967) y *Para servir a usted* (1968); y asistente de Manuel Wallerstein en *Las*

Julián Pastor

Novela de Federico Patán

reglas del juego (1967). Escribió y dirigió un espectáculo de sátira política que se presentó durante diez años en el bar Guau (1978-88) y que a partir de 1989 se escenifica en el restaurante El Refugio del Viejo Conde, ambos en el DF. En abril de 1986 fue elegido secretario general de la sección de directores del Sindicato de Trabajadores de la Producción Cinematográfica. Como actor ha participado en 46 películas, entre otras: *En este pueblo no hay ladrones* (1964), *Los recuerdos del porvenir* (1968), *Santa* (1968), *El jardín de la tía Isabel* (1971), *El hombre y la bestia* (1972), *Aquellos años* (1972), *Actas de Marusia* (1977) y *El lugar sin límites* (1977). Director de la telenovela *Ardiente deseo* (1978); de los mediometrajes *Noche de muertos* (1969) y *Mujeres de México* (1974); de los largometrajes *La justicia tiene doce años* (1970), *La venida del rey Olmos* (1974), *El esperado amor desesperado* (1975), *La casta divina* (1976), *Los pequeños privilegios* (1977), *El vuelo de la cigüeña* (1977), *Estas ruinas que ves* (1978), *Morir de madrugada* (1979), *El héroe desconocido* (1981), *Orinoco* (1984), *Coqueluche* (1986), *Los machos y las hembras* (1987), *Chiquita pero picosa* y *Lambada Night Club* (1990); y del videofilme *Pasa en las mejores familias* (1987). En 1988 dirigió la obra de teatro *Raptóla, violóla y matóla*, de Alejandro Licona. Se le consideró el mejor actor del I Concurso de Cine Experimental (1965). En 1976 ganó el primer premio del Festival Internacional de Panamá y en 1980 obtuvo un premio en el II Festival del Cine Latinoamericano, en La Habana.

Pastor Ortiz ◆ Cabecera del municipio michoacano de José Sixto Verduzco (☛).

Archivo Xavier Esparza

Manuel E. Pastrana

Pastrana, Manuel E. ◆ n. en Veracruz, Ver. (1852-?). Astrónomo titulado en la Escuela de Ingenieros de Minas de México (1878). Fue comisionado para los estudios de límites entre México y Guatemala (1884-99). Se desempeñó como director del Observatorio Meteorológico y profesor de astronomía y geodesia del Colegio Militar. Publicó diversas obras de su especialidad.

Pastrana Castro, Gonzalo ◆ n. en Tepocoacuilco, Gro., y m. en el DF (1920-1991). Líder de obreros. Ha sido secretario general de la sección 72 del Sindicato Nacional Azucarero (1951-52), miembro del consejo de administración del ingenio Emiliano Zapata de Zacatepec (1953-55), secretario general de la Federación de Trabajadores del Estado de Morelos (1958-75 y 1978-), senador suplente (1958-64), presidente en Morelos del PRI (1964), partido al que pertenece desde 1960; diputado federal (1964-67 y 1979- 82), director general del Registro Agrario Nacional de la SRA (1977-78) y senador por Morelos (1982- 88).

Pastrana Jaimes, David ◆ n. en Manlayar, municipio de Tepecuacuilco, Gro., y m. en el DF (1883-1953). Estudió en el Colegio de San Nicolás de Hidalgo. Se tituló como abogado en 1908. Fue secretario de la Comisión de Reformas del Código de Procedimientos Civiles del Estado de Michoacán (1907), juez en Chilpancingo (1910), agente del Ministerio Público Federal (1911), secretario del Juzgado de Instrucción Criminal de la ciudad de México (1912), secretario particular de Manuel Escudero y Verdugo, cuando éste era secretario de Justicia de Venustiano Carranza (1914); miembro de la Comisión Agraria de Puebla (1915), oficial mayor del Departamento de Justicia, juez en Puebla (1916), diputado al Congreso Constituyente de 1916-17, miembro de la Comisión Nacional Agraria (1918), oficial mayor de la III Sección de la Suprema Corte de Justicia (1919), diputado federal (1920-22), secretario general de Gobierno en Morelos (1924), juez en Baja California, Morelos, Puebla y Nuevo León; y magistrado de la IV Sala del Tribunal Fiscal de la Federación. Autor de *El problema agrario* (1913), *Justicia Social* (1919), *Regímenes de servicios públicos* (1935) y *Mujeres sin oídos* (1945).

Patamban ◆ Sierra de Michoacán que forma parte del Eje Volcánico. Se extiende al sur de la ciudad de Zamora. Es la prolongación, hacia el norte, de la sierra de Apatzingán.

Patamban ◆ Volcán de Michoacán que forma parte del eje volcánico, situado en el norte de la sierra del mismo nombre.

Patán, Federico ◆ n. en España (1937). Escritor. Licenciado y maestro en letras inglesas por la UNAM. Profesor de la Facultad de Filosofía y Letras de la UNAM desde 1969. Ha colaborado en la revista *México en el Arte*, *México en la Cultura*, *Ovaciones*, *La Palabra y el Hombre* y *Sábado*, suplemento de *unomásuno*. Realizó las antologías *El señor de los dínamos y otros cuantos ingleses* (1985), *Cuento norteamericano del siglo XX* (1987), *Poesía norteamericana del siglo XX* (1987), *Dos veces el mismo río* (1987) y *El paseo y otros acontecimientos* (1993), las dos últimas de su propia obra. Coautor de *Calderón, apóstol y hereje* (1982). Autor de cuento: *En esta casa* (1987); ensayo: *Calas menores* (1978), *Literatura e inseguridad* (1982) y *Contrapuntos* (1991); novela: *Último exilio* (1986) y *Puertas antiguas* (1989); poesía: *Del oscuro canto* (1965), *Los caminos del alba* (1968), *A orillas del silencio* (1977), *Del tiempo y la soledad* (1983), *Fuego lleno de semillas* (1980), *Imágenes* (1986) y *Umbrales* (1992); relato; *Diez novelas y un relato* (1983) y *Nena, me llamo Walter* (1985); y la autobiografía *De cuerpo entero* (1991). En 1986 ganó el Premio Xavier Villaurrutia.

Patiño, Bruno ◆ n. y m. en Morelia, Mich. (1831-1882). Abogado liberal. Fue diputado local y federal y gobernador de Michoacán (1877- 78).

Patiño, José Gregorio ◆ n. y m. en Morelia, Mich. (1825-1917). Combatió contra los invasores estadounidenses en 1847. En 1854 se adhirió al Plan de Ayutla y formó parte de los ejércitos liberales durante la guerra de los Tres Años. Durante la invasión francesa, como general, participó en la defensa de Puebla (1863), donde fue hecho prisionero, deportado a Europa y liberado tras la caída de Maximiliano.

Patiño, Maricruz ◆ n. en el DF (1950). Poeta. Realizó estudios de filosofía en la UNAM y más tarde asistió al taller de poesía de Juan Bañuelos y Humberto Batis. Ha sido maestra de primaria, guionista de radio y televisión, cantante de *rock* y actriz. Colaboradora de la *Revista de la Universidad* y *Casa del Tiempo*, del diario *unomásuno* y de *La cultura en México*, suplemento de la revista *Siempre!* Autora de *La circunstancia pesa* (1979), *Voces* (1984) y *Desorden armónico*. Poemas suyos figuran en varias antologías.

PATIÑO CAMARENA, ERNESTO JAVIER ◆ n. en el DF (1943). Licenciado en derecho por la UNAM (1969), con estudios de posgrado en técnicas legislativas en la Universidad de Austin (1969), y doctor en derecho por la Universidad de Montepellier (1971). Profesor de la UNAM (1971-). Pertenece al PRI. Ha sido miembro de la Comisión Intersecretarial para el Estudio del Problema Migratorio (1974-76), subdirector de Documentación y Asuntos Internacionales (1974-77), subdirector de Información y Difusión (1977) y director general de Asuntos Jurídicos de la STPS (1983-85); jefe del Centro de Documentación de la Secretaría General del IMSS (1977-83) y director general de Asuntos Jurídicos del INEA (1986-88). Director de las revistas *Reseña Laboral* y *Reseña Documental de la Seguridad Social*. Colaborador de *El Día* (1977-83). Coautor del *Diccionario Jurídico Mexicano* y *Las elecciones en México* (1988). Autor de varios libros entre los que destacan *Decisiones fundamentales en materia laboral* (1976), *Dinámica de la duración del trabajo* (1976), *Análisis de la reforma política* (1982), *Tránsito del constitucionalismo individualista y liberal al constitucionalismo social* (1985) y *La hazaña petrolera, perspectiva de la regulación jurídica del petróleo en el derecho mexicano* (1988).

PATIÑO Y GALLARDO, PEDRO ◆ n. en Celaya, Gto., y m. en Mazatlán, Sin. (1797-1836). Insurgente. Tomó parte en la conspiración de Querétaro. Fue detenido en septiembre de 1810, días después del inicio de la guerra de Independencia. Liberado en 1815, se unió a las fuerzas de Ignacio López Rayón (1815-17) y más tarde a las de Francisco Javier Mina (1817), a quien acompañó, luego del fallido intento por tomar Guanajuato, al rancho El Venadito, donde logró escapar del ataque realista del 27 de octubre de 1817, en el que Mina cayó prisionero. Huyó hacia Querétaro, pero antes de llegar fue capturado y condenado a muerte. Consiguió escapar y se estableció en la ciudad de México, donde trabajó en la Secretaría del Virreinato. En 1821 abandonó la capital y se incorporó al Ejército Trigarante, con el que regresó a la capital en septiembre de ese año.

PATIÑO GÓMEZ, ALFONSO ◆ n. en el DF (1910-1977). Fundador de la revista *Cine Gráfico*. En 1935 inició su carrera de director y productor de cine; dirigió la Alianza Cinematográfica y fue fundador del Sindicato de Trabajadores de la Industria Cinematográfica. Realizó, entre otras películas, *Carne de cabaret*, *Adiós Mariquita linda*, *Albur de amor* y *Viajera*.

PATIÑO GUERRERO, GUSTAVO ◆ n. en Cuernavaca, Mor. (1933). Contador público titulado en el Instituto Tecnológico Autónomo de México (1953-57). Ha sido subauditor general de la Unión Nacional de Productores de Azúcar (1957-59), contador general del Banco Nacional de Crédito Agrícola (1959-60), contador general del Banco Ejidal (1960-65), director general de Presupuesto de la Secretaría de Obras Públicas (1965-76), subcontralor general de la Comisión Federal de Electricidad (1976-77), director general de Administración y Finanzas de Covitur (1983-86) y oficial mayor (1983-86) y subsecretario de Transporte de la SCT (1986-94).

PATIÑO IXTOLINQUE, PEDRO ◆ n. en San Pedro Acatzingo, Pue., y m. en la ciudad de Méx. (1774-1835). Escultor, pintor y arquitecto. En 1778, con una de las dos pensiones para indios puros que otorgaba el gobierno virreinal, ingresó a estudiar pintura en la Academia de San Carlos, donde fue alumno de Rafael Ximeno y Planes, Andrés Ginés de Aguirre y Manuel Tolsá. Algunos autores afirman que en 1815 hizo una mascarilla fúnebre de José María Morelos, y que en 1817 se incorporó a las fuerzas insurgentes de Vicente Guerrero. Fue regidor del Ayuntamiento de México (1825) y tercer director de la Academia de San Carlos (1826-?). Es autor del retablo mayor del Sagrario de la Catedral de México (1827).

PATIÑO LEAL, FRANCISCO JORGE ◆ n. en Monterrey, NL (1947). Licenciado en economía por la UANL (1964-69); estudió la maestría en la Universidad de Columbia (1969-71). Profesor de la Universidad Labastida de Monterrey (1968-69) y profesor e investigador del Centro de Investigaciones Económicas de la UANL. Ha sido coordinador de Planes de Operación de la Cervecería Cuauhtémoc (1971-72), economista de la Secretaría de la Presidencia (1974-76), gerente de Estudios Económicos del Grupo Alfa (1977-78), asesor del secretario de Hacienda, David Ibarra Muñoz (1978), subdirector y director general de Planeación Hacendaria de la Secretaría de Hacienda (1978-79), director general del Banco Mercantil de Monterrey (1983-85) y director general del Banco Mercantil del Norte (1985-).

PATIÑO NAVARRETE, JESÚS ◆ n. en Tlalpujahua, Mich., y m. en el DF (1911-1970). Egresado de la Escuela Nacional de Agricultura de Chapingo, misma que lo condecoró dos veces como el agrónomo más distinguido del país. Trabajó en el Banco Nacional de Comercio Exterior y en la Comisión Nacional del Maíz. Fue subgerente del Banco Nacional de Crédito Ejidal, subsecretario de Agricultura y Ganadería en el sexenio de Adolfo López Mateos (1958-64) y subdirector del ramo agropecuario en el Banco Nacional de México.

PATIÑO VELÁZQUEZ, MIGUEL ◆ n. en La Piedad, Mich. (1938). Sacerdote ordenado en 1963. Profesor del Seminario de la Congregación de Misioneros de la Sagrada Familia. Fue párroco en diversos curatos de Chiapas y Michoacán. En 1981 fue preconizado obispo de Apatzingán.

PATONI, CARLOS ◆ n. en el Mineral de Guanaceví, Dgo., y m. en Tehuacán, Pue. (1853-1918). Ingeniero y botánico. Hijo de José María Patoni. En 1868 viajó a Estados Unidos para estudiar ingeniería y matemáticas. Volvió a México a fines del siglo XIX y se estableció en la Comarca Lagunera, donde se dedicó a la topografía. En 1905 levantó, con Pastor Rouaix, una carta geográfica de Durango, la que se publicó en 1917. En septiembre de 1912 tomó posesión como gobernador de Durango, cargo al que renunció en enero de 1913. Se exilió en Estados Unidos y a su regreso fue nombrado secretario de Fomento del presidente convencionista Roque González Garza, pero no ocupó el cargo. La administración de Venustiano Carranza lo nombró director de un campo experimental en Tehuacán. Publicó diversas monografías sobre la flora duranguense.

Jan Patula Dobek

PATONI, JOSÉ MARÍA ◆ n. en el Mineral de Guanaceví y m. en Durango, Dgo. (1828-1868). Hijo de Juan B. Patoni, italiano que llegó a México en la expedición de Alexander von Humbolt. Su apellido materno era Sánchez. Militar. Combatió contra los estadounidenses en la guerra de 1847. A principios de 1858 se incorporó a las fuerzas liberales en Durango y en julio de ese año participó en la toma de la capital del estado. Gobernador interino de la misma entidad de noviembre de 1858 a febrero de 1860, cuando fue derrotado por el conservador Domingo Cajén. En noviembre de ese año, luego de recibir ayuda de Santiago Vidaurri, derrotó a Cajén y volvió a la gubernatura. Dejó ese puesto a principios de 1862 para combatir la intervención francesa. Encargado del Fuerte de Ingenieros durante el sitio de Puebla (1863), fue capturado por los invasores. Junto con la mayor parte de los jefes prisioneros escapó en Orizaba. Se encontró con el presidente Benito Juárez en San Luis Potosí y reasumió la gubernatura duranguense. En marzo de 1864 abandonó el estado para combatir a Vidaurri, que había aceptado la intervención unos meses antes, y más tarde peleó en Chihuahua y Sinaloa. Comisionado para servir a las órdenes de Jesús González Ortega, en 1864 apoyó a éste en su intento por desplazar a Juárez de la Presidencia y debió exiliarse en Estados Unidos. Volvió a México en 1867 y fue aprehendido en Zacatecas. Liberado al año siguiente, viajó a Durango. Benigno Canto, comandante militar del estado, lo capturó y, sin formación de causa, lo fusiló.

PATOS, DE LOS ◆ Laguna de Chihuahua situada en una cuenca baja del norte de la altiplanicie mexicana. Recibe por el sur al río del Carmen. Se encuentra en peligro de desecación.

PATRIA, LA ◆ Periódico fundado en 1877 por Ireneo Paz, quien lo dirigió hasta 1912. Enemigo del periódico *La Libertad*, dirigido por Santiago Sierra Méndez, las diferencias que sostenían ambas publicaciones se resolvieron con un duelo armado entre sus directores en el que Paz mató a Sierra Méndez. Pese a recibir subsidio del gobierno, en 1910 el periódico se opuso a la reelección del presidente Porfirio Díaz.

Caricatura de Patricio publicada en El Chamuco

PATRICIO ◆ n. en el DF (1965). Pseudónimo de Patricio Ortiz González. Estudió dos años en el taller de caricatura e historia de *el Fisgón*, y en la Escuela Nacional de Artes Plásticas. Empezó a publicar en la revista *Los Universitarios* en 1984. Ha publicado en diferentes periódicos, como en *La Jornada, El Universal* y *El Día*, así como en innumerables revistas. Colaboró y codirigió la revista *El Chahuistle* y es codirector de la revista *El Chamuco*. Ha publicado los libros *El sexenio de los miserables*, *El verdulier, pequeño diccionario del verdulero* y *Pequeño Vulgarousse Ilustrado*. Es creador de personajes de historieta como *Los miserables*, *Don Chepino*, *Don Quijotillo Quitamanchas y Ancho Panza* y *Hombre Man, el hombre hombre*.

PATULA DOBEK, JAN ◆ n. en Polonia y m. en el DF (1944-1996). Historiador. Licenciado (1966) y maestro (1968) en historia por la Universidad de Jagellona, en Cracovia; posgraduado en ciencia política en la Universidad de Estrasburgo (1972) y en historia y literatura de los países de lengua alema na en la Universidad de Viena (1977). Se naturalizó mexicano en 1975. Profesor de la UNAM (1973-80) y de la Universidad Autónoma Metropolitana (1980-96). Fue coordinador de la licenciatura de historia (1980-82), director interino del área de historia (1982) y coordinador del programa de posgrado de historia de la UAM. Fue fundador del Comité de Apoyo al Sindicato Solidaridad (1982) de su país natal Colaborador del diario *Excélsior* y de las revistas *Dialéctica*, *Dí*, *Crítica Política*, *Casa de Tiempo* y *Teoría y Política*. Tradujo *Reflexiones sobre la historia* (1984), de W. Kula y *La forma pura en el teatro* (1983), de S. I. Witkewicz. Coautor de *La praxis religiosa en Polonia* (1983). Autor de *Revolución y contrarrevolución en Polonia* (1984). Fue miembro del Sistema Nacional de Investigadores desde 1984 y del PEN Club de México desde 1980.

PÁTZCUARO ◆ Lago de Michoacán situado en el centro del estado, al suroeste de Morelia y al este-noreste de Uruapan del Progreso, en la parte baja de una cuenca cerrada del Eje Volcánico. Lo alimentan diversas corrientes, entre ellas los ríos Guaní y Chapultepec. En sus orillas están las poblaciones de Pátzcuaro, Erongarícuaro, Quiroga, Tzintzuntzan, Pareo y Zirándaro. Tiene cinco islas, de las que están habitadas

Janitzio, Pacanda y Jarácuaro. Esta última se halla unida a tierra. En Janitzio hay un monumento a José María Morelos. En sus aguas se practica la pesca. En sus riberas se inició la cultura purépecha.

Pátzcuaro ◆ Municipio de Michoacán situado en el centro del estado, al sur de Quiroga y al suroeste de Morelia. Superficie: 261.25 km². Habitantes: 75,264, de los cuales 17,341 forman la población económicamente activa. Hablan alguna lengua indígena 4,773 personas mayores de cinco años (purépecha 4,720). Hacia el siglo XIII, los purépechas fundaron, en la ribera sur del lago, la población de Tzacapu Amúcutin Pátzcuaro, pero fue en la segunda mitad del siglo XIV cuando se instalaron definitivamente ahí y la convirtieron en su capital. Un siglo después, cuando el poder se había trasladado hacia Tzintzuntzan, Pátzcuaro se convirtió en el principal centro religioso de los purépechas. La ciudad española fue fundada en diciembre de 1531. Dos años después, Vasco de Quiroga llegó por primera vez al lugar y, cuando fue nombrado obispo michoacano, en 1538, convirtió la población en sede de la diócesis. Para mantener allí la sede del obispado, Quiroga proyectó la construcción de una catedral con cinco naves separadas, dispuestas como radios alrededor de una cúpula central, pero el edificio nunca fue completado. A mediados del siglo XVI, alrededor de 150 europeos y cerca de 30,000 indios vivían en la ciudad. Las autoridades purépechas de Pátzcuaro fueron mantenidas en sus puestos por los conquistadores, hasta que a fines del siglo XVI los europeos se hicieron cargo del gobierno de modo directo. Quiroga mandó construir el edificio del Colegio de San Nicolás y una catedral que habría tenido cinco naves, de las que sólo se construyó una, que actualmente es el templo de Nuestra Señora de la Salud. El obispo también hizo edificar el templo de El Salvador, donde instaló la oficina del obispado (que se mudó a Morelia en 1580). La conquista espiritual corrió a cargo de los franciscanos desde 1540, los jesuitas desde 1570 y los agustinos a partir de 1573. En 1767, a causa de la expulsión de la Compañía de Jesús de la Nueva España, los indios de la ciudad se sublevaron. Durante la guerra de Independencia la ciudad no fue ocupada, pero en los alrededores, y sobre todo en las riberas del lago, actuaron numerosos grupos de insurgentes. En 1867, Pátzcuaro fue escenario de una batalla en la que el republicano Nicolás de Régules derrotó al imperialista Magdaleno del Río, en la llamada Toma de Pátzcuaro. En 1913, Joaquín Amaro derrotó a las fuerzas huertistas en la llamada Batalla de Pátzcuaro. El municipio cuenta con diversos atractivos históricos y turísticos: el lago de Pátzcuaro, el cerro del Estribo, el antiguo Colegio de San Nicolás y las fiestas religiosas de la isla de Janitzio. El general Lázaro Cárdenas donó la Quinta Eréndira para alojar el Centro Regional de Educación Fundamental para América Latina, de la UNESCO.

Foto: Carlos Hahn

Pátzcuaro, Michoacán

Paulsen, Ernesto ◆ n. en Guadalajara, Jal. (1935). Escultor y joyero. Cofundador, con Gabriel Chávez de la Mora, del taller de arte sacro del monasterio benedictino de Cuernavaca. El proyecto había sido impulsado por el prior del convento, Gregorio Lemercier. En 1960 fundó la Galería Paulsen. Expuso sus esculturas por primera vez en 1964, en el pabellón mexicano de la Feria Mundial de Nueva York. Obras suyas se encuentran en la Torre de las Orquídeas, de Cancún; y, en la ciudad de México, en el Jardín del Arte, en la Plaza Comonfort, en la fachada del Paseo de la Reforma del Hotel Presidente Chapultepec, en la Plaza Andrés Bello y en las estaciones del metro La Villa e Instituto del Petróleo, entre otros edificios y espacios públicos de México y otros países. Realizó la llave y la chapa de la Basílica de Guadalupe (1979). En el Congreso Mundial de la Plata, en 1974, su obra fue considerada una de las 10 mejores del mundo. En 1991 se hizo una exposición retrospectiva de su obra en la ciudad de Guadalajara.

Pavía, Lázaro ◆ n. en Sabán, Yuc., y m. en el DF (1844-1933). Estudió en el Colegio de San Ildefonso de Mérida, donde vivió desde su niñez. En 1888 se tituló como abogado. En 1861 se inició como maestro de geografía. Combatió contra la intervención francesa. Fue director del Liceo del Centro, periodista, dos veces diputado local, oficial mayor del Congreso de Tabasco, subdirector de la Academia de Música de Tabasco, jefe político de Temax y diputado federal (1910-11). Fue administrador de la *Revista Azul* (1894-96). Colaboró en los periódicos *La Actualidad*, *La Voz Liberal*, *El Sonámbulo*, *Las Noticias*, *El Correo de las Doce*, *El Diario del Hogar*, *El Estado de Yucatán*, *Los Estados* y *El Combate*. Autor de *Los héroes de la independencia nacio-*

Foto: Carlos Hahn

Artesanía de palma de Pátzcuaro, Michoacán

nal. Breves bosquejos biográficos (1888), *La educación y el pueblo* (1888), *Los ingleses en México o sea el origen y fundación de las colonias británicas en el seno mexicano* (1888), *Los estados y sus gobernantes* (1890), *Ligeros apuntes biográficos de los jefes de los partidos de los estados de la República Mexicana* (1891), *Cromos* (1896), *Nociones elementales de economía* (1897), *El imperio en la península yucateca. Apuntes para la historia 1861-1867* (1897), *Estudios generales de educación e instrucción* (1903), *Nueva guía del profesor o nuevo manual del maestro* (1904), *El ejército y la política* (1909) *Caligrafía técnica, El clero mexicano* e *Historia del telégrafo*.

Pavón, Alfredo ◆ n. en Achotal, Ver. (1954). Ensayista. Licenciado y maestro en letras españolas por la UV. Ha sido becario e investigador del Centro de Investigación Lingüístico-Literaria de la UV (1976-78), maestro e investigador del área de humanidades (1980-86) y jefe del departamento de literatura de la Universidad Autónoma de Chiapas (1983-86), donde fundó las colecciones Maciel y Poesía no eres tú; maestro del departamento de filosofía y letras de la Universidad Autónoma de Tlaxcala, donde fundó la serie Destino Arbitrario; profesor invitado de la maestría en letras de la UV (1991-) e investigador del Centro de Ciencias del Lenguaje de la UAP (1986-), cuya revista, *Escritos*, dirigió (1989-91). Editó la compilación *El cuento está en no creérselo* (1985) y *Paquete: Cuento* (1990). Coautor de *Teoría y práctica del cuento* (1988) y *Te lo cuento otra vez: la ficción en México* (1991). Autor de ensayo: *El universo del relato literario (el sentido narrativo de* Polvos de arroz*)* (1984), *El presente insoportable (soliloquio de una solterona)* (1990), *Cuento de nunca acabar (la ficción en México)* (1991), *Cuento contigo (la ficción en México)* (1993) y *De mujeres y hombrecitos* (1993).

Pavón, Blanca Estela ◆ n. en Minatitlán, Ver., y m. en el Estado de México (1926-1949). Actriz. Comenzó su carrera en un programa radiofónico infantil; posteriormente fue actriz de doblaje para Metro Goldwyn Mayer. En el cine, debutó en la película *La liga de las canciones* (1941), pero destacó, sobre todo, a partir de su primer coestelar en *Cuando lloran los valientes* (1945, Ariel a la mejor actriz en 1948), al lado de Pedro Infante. También con Infante, formó una de las parejas míticas del cine nacional en la cintas *Nosotros los pobres* (1947), *Los tres huastecos* (1948) y *Ustedes los ricos* (1948), todas de Ismael Rodríguez. Además, participó en *El niño de las monjas* (1944), *Vuelven los García* (1946), *Cortesana* (1947), *En cada puerto un amor* (1948), *No me quieras tanto* (1949), *La ladronzuela* (1949), *Las puertas del presidio* (1949) y *La mujer que yo perdí* (1949). Murió en un accidente de aviación cerca del volcán Popocatépetl.

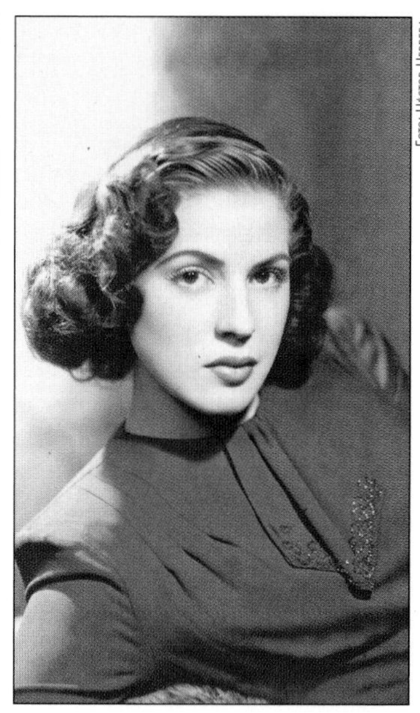
Foto: Héctor Herrera

Blanca Estela Pavón

Pavón, Desiderio ◆ n. y m. en Pánuco, Ver. (1820-1890). Militar. En 1854 se adhirió al Plan de Ayutla y formó parte del ejército liberal que derrocó a Antonio López de Santa Anna. Combatió a los conservadores durante la guerra de los Tres Años. Operó siempre en la Huasteca veracruzana. En enero de 1863 desalojó a los franceses de Tampico, pero en agosto de ese año fue desalojado por las tropas invasoras y formó una fuerza guerrillera que dirigió hasta fines de 1865, cuando por falta de elementos suspendió la lucha. A principios de 1866 volvió a las armas. En agosto recuperó Tampico y en septiembre Tuxpan. Al triunfo de la República fue gobernador interino y comandante militar del Distrito Sur de Tamaulipas (del 3 de abril al 5 de julio de 1867), gobernador y comandante militar de los distritos Centro y Sur de Tamaulipas (del 5 de julio al 27 de agosto de 1867) y gobernador interino de Tamaulipas (del 27 de agosto de 1867 al 16 de abril de 1868). En octubre de 1871 se levantó en armas contra el gobierno del presidente Benito Juárez y fue rápidamente derrotado.

Pavón, Herminia ◆ n. en el DF (?). Pintora. Estudió decoración de interiores en la Universidad Motolinía y artes plásticas en la Universidad Iberoamericana y fue discípula de Aguirre Tinoco y Guati Rojo. Ha expuesto acuarelas en México, Dallas, San Antonio, Galveston y Nueva York. Miembro de la Sociedad Mexicana de Acuarelistas y de la Agrupación de Acuarelistas de Cataluña.

Pavón, José Ignacio ◆ n. en Veracruz, Ver., y m. en la ciudad de México (1791-1866). Estudió en el Colegio de San Ildefonso. Fue regidor honorario del ayuntamiento de la ciudad de México (1818), secretario de la Junta de Censura (1820), oficial mayor de la Secretaría de Hacienda (1823), jefe político de Tabasco (1824), oficial mayor de la Secretaría de Relaciones (1825), ministro de la Suprema Corte de Justicia (1841-45) y magistrado del Tribunal Superior de Justicia del Departamento de México (1845-51). Se jubiló en 1851. Dos años después, Antonio López de Santa Anna lo nombró ministro suplente de la Corte y más tarde presidente del Tribunal Superior de Justicia. En diciembre de 1857 quedó como presidente de la Suprema Corte de Justicia del gobierno conservador. Tres años más tarde, en 1860, por renuncia del presidente conservador Miguel Miramón, asumió el Poder Ejecutivo el 13 de agosto. Al día siguiente reunió a una "Junta de Representantes de los Departamentos" que designó presidente interino a Miramón y entregó el poder el día

15. El 18 de junio de 1863, la Asamblea de Notables integrada por los invasores franceses lo nombró miembro de la Junta Superior de Gobierno, en la que formó parte de la comisión de Hacienda, y el 24 ésta lo hizo miembro suplente del Poder Ejecutivo imperialista, transformado en Regencia a los pocos días, y magistrado del Supremo Tribunal. Fue destituido por desobedecer a la Regencia.

PAVÓN, YEKINA ◆ n. en Tabasco (1957). Cantante. Comenzó su carrera en su infancia, en programas para niños. En 1970 obtuvo el segundo lugar en el concurso *Baladista del 70*. En 1984 comenzó a cantar en bares y pequeños foros culturales. Ha participado en los programas televisivos *Música y algo más*, *En vivo* y *Para gente grande*, entre otros, así como en el Festival Internacional Cervantino.

PAVÓN FLORES, MARIO ◆ n. en Coatzacoalcos, Ver. (1909). También se dice que nació en 1905. Licenciado en derecho por la Universidad Veracruzana. Militante del PCM, en octubre de 1940 fue expulsado del buró político y del comité central. Perteneció al grupo literario Noviembre y fue expulsado del estado de Veracruz por sus posiciones políticas. Fue director de la biblioteca de la SEP. Perteneció al comité de redacción de la revista *Ruta* (1938-39). Autor de *Los gusanos rojos* (cuentos, 1943). Algunos de sus textos fueron incluidos por Lorenzo Turrent Rozas en *Hacia una literatura proletaria* (1932).

PAVÓN JARAMILLO, LAURA ◆ n. en San Miguel Amatepec, Edo. de Méx. (1944). Profesora titulada en la Escuela Normal de Profesores (1961) y licenciada en derecho por la UAEM (1972). Ejerció la docencia de 1962 a 1965. Desde 1961 pertenece al PRI, en el que fue secretaria general de la Anfer (1974-79), integrante del Consejo Político Nacional y representante ante el consejo de la Internacional Socialista y la Women International Socialist Organization (1997-). Ha sido jefa del Departamento de Alfabetización del gobierno mexiquense (1975), diputada a la Legislatura del Estado de México (1975-77), secretaria particular del secretario del Trabajo del gobierno local (1981), dos veces diputada federal (1985-88 y 91-94), presidenta municipal de Toluca (1988-90) y senadora de la República (1994-2000). Miembro del Consejo Consultivo del Programa Nacional de la Mujer. Representante de la Comisión de la Mujer en el Parlamento Latinoamericano. Representante del Senado en la Conferencia Interparlamentaria de las Américas (1998-) y la Conferencia de la Unión Interparlamentaria Mundial (1998).

PAVÓN VASCONCELOS, FRANCISCO ◆ n. en Acayucan, Ver. (1920). Licenciado (1942) y doctor (1954) en derecho por la UNAM, donde ejerció la docencia (1958-70). Ha sido agente del Ministerio Público Federal (1949-51), jefe de la oficina de Averiguaciones Previas (1951-53) y auxiliar del titular de la PGR (1954-58); juez de distrito en Zacatecas (1961-62), Michoacán (1962-65) y el Distrito Federal (1965-68); magistrado de distrito en Monterrey, Puebla y el DF (1968-76); y ministro de la Suprema Corte de Justicia de la Nación (1976-). Autor de *Nociones de derecho penal* (2 t., 1961-62), *Los delitos de peligro para la vida y la integridad corporal* (1973), *La tentativa* (1974), *El concurso aparente de normas* (1975), *Lecciones de derecho penal* (1981), *Los delitos del peligro* (1981), *Comentarios de derecho penal* (1982), *Código penal comentado de Michoacán* (1982), *Derecho penal mexicano. Parte especial* (1982), *La causalidad en el delito* (1983), *Imputabilidad e inimputabilidad* (1983). Es miembro de la Academia de Ciencias Penales.

PAWLING, ALBERTO J. ◆ n. en Campeche, Camp., y m. en el DF (1888-1955). Ingeniero graduado en la Escuela Naval de Veracruz. Fue capitán de altura (1913), gerente de Henequeneros de Yucatán, jefe de Puertos, Faros y Marina; y secretario de Marina (del 21 de octubre de 1949 al 7 de febrero de 1952) en el gobierno de Miguel Alemán.

PAYÁN, LEOPOLDO ◆ n. en Tlaxiaco y m. en Oaxaca, Oax. (1872-1950). Simpatizante del Partido Liberal Mexicano desde 1906, en 1909 fue secretario del Club Liberal de Oaxaca y fundador del Partido Antirreeleccionista de la misma entidad. Combatió la dictadura de Victoriano Huerta. Estuvo prisionero del gobierno *soberanista* oaxaqueño hasta 1916. Fue diputado al Congreso Constituyente de 1916-17. Participó en la fundación del Partido Constitucionalista y de la Unión de Veteranos de la Revolución.

GABINETE DEL PRESIDENTE JOSE IGNACIO PAVÓN 8 al 14 de agosto de 1860
SECRETARÍA DE RELACIONES EXTERIORES:
JOSÉ MIGUEL ARROYO, OMED[1]
SECRETARÍA DE GOBERNACIÓN:
JOSÉ IGNACIO DE ANIEVAS, OMED
SECRETARÍA DE JUSTICIA Y NEGOCIOS ECLESIÁSTICOS:
JOSÉ MARÍA DURÁN, OMED
SECRETARÍA DE GUERRA Y MARINA:
JUAN DE DIOS PEZA, OMED
SECRETARÍA DE HACIENDA:
FRANCISCO JAVIER REIGADAS, ED
OMED= Oficial Mayor Encargado del Despacho ED= Encargado del Despacho

PAYÁN CERVERA, ANA ROSA ◆ n. en Campeche, Camp. (1951). Estudió en la Escuela de Economía y Administración de la Universidad de Yucatán. Afiliada al PAN desde 1983, ha sido miembro de Promoción Política para la Mujer (1986-87), secretaria de Actas y Acuerdos (1985-87), consejera estatal y nacional (1987-), diputada federal (1988-90), presidenta municipal de Mérida (1991-93), candidata a la gubernatura de Yucatán (1993), presidenta del Comité del Distrito Electoral (1994-97), senadora de la República (1994-2000), diputada local (1995-97) y miembro del CEN (1996-99). También ha sido dirigente del Movimiento de Cursillos de Cristiandad (1981-84), presidenta y tesorera del Asilo de Niñas Huérfanas de Chuminópolis (1982-85) y presidenta de la Comunidad de Profesionales Católicos (1985-88).

PAYÁN VELVER, CARLOS ◆ n. en el DF (1929). Hizo estudios de derecho en la UNAM (1952). Fue subdirector de Fomento Cooperativo de la SIC (1962-64) y director de Crédito del Infonavit (1972-76). Fue coordinador de publicaciones de la Comisión Nacional Editorial del PRI (1975-76). Subdirector de *unomásuno* (1977-83) y director general de *La Jornada* (1984-96). Consejero de la CNDH (1990-), senador por el PRD (1994-2000) y accionista de la empresa Argos. Ha recibido tres premios del

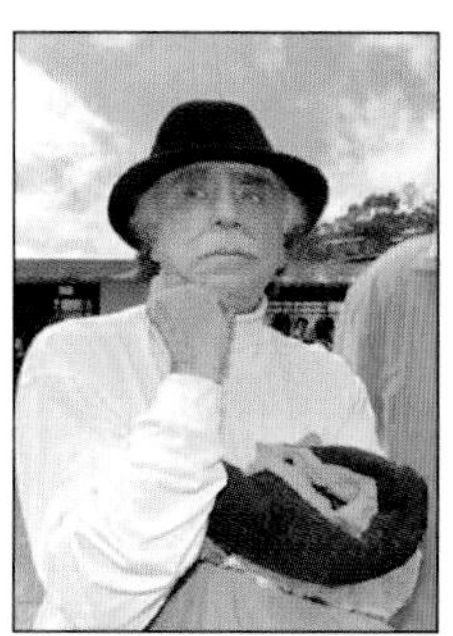

Carlos Payán Velver

Club de Periodistas (1993, 94 y 95). Miembro de la Comisión Nacional de Garantías y Vigilancia del PRD.

Payén, José Encarnación ◆ n. en la ciudad de México y m. en Morelia, Mich. (1844-1919). Músico. Cornetista y director de bandas musicales (1856-85). En 1884, en gira por Estados Unidos, participó en la ceremonia de toma de posesión del presidente Stephen Grover Cleveland. Fue profesor del Conservatorio Nacional (1887). Participó en la exposición de Minneapolis (1891) y en Madrid concurrió a las celebraciones del cuarto centenario del viaje de Cristóbal Colón (1892), donde fue condecorado por la reina María Cristina de Austria. Volvió a México en 1893 y se encargó de la dirección de la Academia de Música y de la Escuela de Artes y Oficios de Morelia. Su banda, la del Octavo Regimiento, se convirtió en 1893 en la Banda del Estado Mayor, con sede en la ciudad de México. Fue director de la Academia de Música del Estado de Aguascalientes (1902). En 1914, Francisco Villa lo nombró mayor inspector de bandas de la División del Norte.

Payeras, Mario ◆ n. en Guatemala (1940). Maestro de primaria, estudió también filosofía en la UNAM (1962) y en la Universidad Karl Marx de la RDA (1968). Miembro de la Juventud Comunista a fines de los años cincuenta, después de más de una década de viajes por América y Europa regresó a Guatemala en 1971 y al año siguiente formó parte de la guerrilla del Ejército Guerrillero del Pueblo (EGP); en 1974 fue electo miembro de su Dirección Nacional, para la que redactó su *Línea militar*, y en 1980-81 fue comandante urbano y combatió contra fuerzas gubernamentales. En 1984 rompió con el EGP por motivos políticos y fundó el movimiento Octubre Revolucionario. Ha sido traducido al inglés, alemán e italiano. Autor de *Poemas de la Zona Reina* (1972-78), *Los días de la selva* (1979), *El trueno en la ciudad* (1987), *El mundo como flor y como invento* (1987), *Lentitud de la flor y el granizo* (1988) y *Los fusilados de octubre* (1991). Premio Casa de las Américas 1981.

Retrato y firma de Manuel Payno

Payno, Manuel ◆ n. y m. en la ciudad de México (1820-1894). Fue contador de la aduana marítima de Matamoros, secretario de Mariano Arista (1840), administrador de rentas del estanco de tabaco, jefe de sección en la Secretaría de Guerra y secretario de la legación mexicana en Sudamérica (1842). Viajó a Estados Unidos para estudiar los sistemas penitenciarios de Nueva York y Filadelfia. Combatió la invasión estadounidense de 1847 en la zona de Puebla y estableció un correo secreto entre México y Veracruz. Secretario de Hacienda en los gobiernos de José Joaquín de Herrera (del 4 de julio de 1849 al 13 de enero de 1851) y Mariano Arista (del 16 al 28 de enero de 1851). Fue perseguido por Santa Anna y se exilió en Estados Unidos. Volvió al triunfo de la revolución de Ayutla y se encargó de la Secretaría de Hacienda (del 14 de diciembre de 1855 al 5 de mayo de 1856 y del 20 de octubre al 11 de diciembre de 1857) en el gabinete de Ignacio Comonfort, a quien apoyó en el golpe de Estado de diciembre de 1857. En enero de 1858 se adhirió al Plan de Tacubaya de Félix Zuloaga. En 1861, luego del triunfo liberal, fue juzgado y marginado de la actividad política. Aunque partidario de la intervención, en 1863 la Regencia del imperio lo acusó de conspiración y fue encarcelado. Derrotado el imperio volvió a la vida política y fue diputado en tres ocasiones consecutivas (1867-75). Fundó, con Ignacio Manuel Altamirano, el periódico *El Federalista*. Fue profesor de historia en la Escuela Preparatoria, senador de la República (1880-84), enviado a París por el presidente Manuel González para atraer inmigrantes (1882); cónsul en Santander (1886), cónsul general en España y nuevamente senador (1892). Colaboró en *El Museo Mexicano, El Ateneo Mexicano, El Año Nuevo, Don Simplicio, El Siglo XIX*, el *Boletín de la Sociedad de Geografía y Estadística* y la *Revista Científica y Literaria de México*, que editó con Guillermo Prieto. En 1865 publicó las memorias de Servando Teresa de Mier con el nombre de *Vida, aventuras, escritos y viajes del dr. d. Servando Teresa de Mier*. Coautor de *Apuntes para la historia de la guerra entre México y los Estados Unidos* (1848) y *El libro rojo* (1871). Autor de ensayo y crónica: *Memorias e impresiones de un viaje a Inglaterra y Escocia* (1853), *Contestación de los agentes de la convención inglesa* (1855), *La convención española* (1857), *México. 1845-1846* (1859), *Memoria sobre la revolución de diciembre de 1857 y enero de 1858* (1860), *México y sus cuestiones financieras con la Inglaterra, la España y la Francia* (1862), *Memoria sobre el maguey mexicano y sus diversos productos* (1864), *La deuda interior de México* (1865), *Cuentas, gastos, acreedores y otros asuntos del tiempo de la intervención y el imperio* (1868), *Compendio de la historia de México para el uso de los establecimientos de enseñanza primaria* (1870) y *Barcelona y México en 1888 y 1889* (1889); y novela: *El fistol del diablo* (1845-46), *El hombre de la situación* (1861), *Tardes nubladas* (1871) y *Los bandidos de Río Frío* (1889). En 1901, con el título *Obras de don Manuel Payno*, se publicaron 17 de sus novelas cortas: *María, Un doctor, El mineral de Plateros, La víspera y el día de la boda, El monte virgen, ¡Loca!, Alberto y Teresa, La esposa del insurgente, Pepita, La lámpara, Trinidad de Juárez, Aventura de un veterano, El lucero de Málaga, El castillo del barón d'Artal, Amor secreto, El rosario de concha nácar* y *El cura y la ópera*. En 1945 apareció un volumen en la Biblioteca del Estudiante Universitario con sus *Artículos y narraciones*.

Payo del Rosario, El ◆ ☛ *Villavicencio, Pablo de.*

Payró Armengol, Gregorio ◆ n. en Teapa, Tab., y m. en EUA (1818-1890). Médico titulado en La Habana en 1847. Como gobernador constitucional de Tabasco (del 5 de diciembre de 1850 al 30 de mayo de 1851), encabezó a las tropas tabasqueñas durante la guerra de la Otra Banda, en 1851, contra el gobierno de Chiapas. Fue diputado al Congreso Constituyente de 1856-57. Se exilió en Estados Unidos durante la guerra de los Tres Años.

Paz, de la ◆ Bahía de Baja California Sur situada en el litoral del golfo de California, al sur del paralelo 25. La cierran las islas Partida y Espíritu Santo. En el extremo meridional se halla el puerto de La Paz.

Paz, de la ◆ Llano de Baja California Sur. Está limitado al norte por la bahía de la Paz y las primeras estribaciones de la sierra de la Giganta; al este por las sierras de la Paz y Novillos y al sur por las cordilleras del extremo meridional de la península de Baja California.

Paz, La ◆ Municipio de Baja California Sur situado en el extremo meridional de la península. Tiene costas en el golfo de California y en el océano Pacífico. Superficie: 20,275 km^2. Habitantes: 182,418, de los cuales 54,086 forman la población económicamente activa. Hablan alguna lengua indígena 1,402 personas mayores de cinco años (mixteco 1,051 y zapoteco 109). La cabecera municipal, del mismo nombre, es también la capital del estado. En 1535, Hernán Cortés llamó Santa Cruz a la población y en 1596 adoptó su nombre actual. En 1829 fue cabecera de la jefatura política del Partido Sur del Territorio de la Baja California y en 1931 capital del territorio de Baja California, que en 1974 se transformó en el estado de Baja California Sur. En esta ciudad se hizo el Pronunciamiento de la Paz, por el cual, en 1865, Clodomiro Cota, enviado por Benito Juárez, desconoció a Félix Gibert, jefe político del territorio. La cabecera municipal, que fue sede de la prefectura apostólica del mismo nombre desde 1957, se convirtió en diócesis sufragánea de la de Hermosillo en 1988.

Paz, La ◆ Municipio del Estado de México situado en la porción oriente del estado, al noroeste de Chalco y al suroeste de Texcoco, en los límites con el Distrito Federal. Superficie: 36.65 km^2. Habitantes: 178,538, de los cuales 40,758 forman la población económicamente activa. Hablan alguna lengua indígena 1,020 personas mayores de cinco años (náhuatl 595 y mixteco 425). Su cabecera es Los Reyes Acaquilpan.

Paz, de la ◆ Teatro construido por el arquitecto José Noriega en la ciudad de San Luis Potosí, en el terreno que ocupaba el convento del Carmen. Le costó 350,000 pesos al gobierno de Carlos Díez Gutiérrez. Su edificación se inició en 1889 y concluyó en 1894. Se estrenó con la ópera *Lucrecia Borgia*, de Donizetti.

Paz, Francisco ◆ n. en Jalapa, Ver., y m. en Francia (1825-1888). Militar. Combatió a los invasores estadounidenses en 1847 y luchó en el bando liberal durante la guerra de los Tres Años. Ascendió a general de brigada en 1861. Defendió Puebla en el sitio de 1863. Fue aprehendido por los invasores y deportado a Francia. Volvió a México al triunfo de la República. Fue gobernador del Distrito Federal (1871) y gobernador interino de Tlaxcala (1872). Más tarde regresó a Francia, comisionado para estudiar artillería.

Paz, Helena ◆ n. en el DF (1948). Hija de Octavio Paz y Elena Garro. Vivió en Francia, Suiza, Estados Unidos, México, India, Singapur y Sri Lanka. Posteriormente se estableció con su madre en Cuernavaca, Mor. Ha escrito en español y francés. Autora de poesía: *Criaturas de la noche* (España, 1992), *Ónix* (Francia, 1994) y *La rueda de la fortuna* (Francia, 1997).

Paz, Ireneo ◆ n. en Guadalajara, Jal., y m. en Mixcoac, DF (1836-1924). Escritor y periodista. Su apellido materno era Flores. Estudió en el Seminario Conciliar de Guadalajara. Abogado titulado en la Escuela Nacional de Jurisprudencia (1861). En Guadalajara fundó, redactó y dirigió el periódico *El Payaso*, desde donde apoyó a los liberales en la guerra de los Tres Años. Combatió la intervención francesa y obtuvo el grado de coronel. Secretario de gobierno de Sinaloa, en 1871 apoyó la asonada del Plan de la Noria, por lo que fue encarcelado. Participó en la redacción del Plan de Tuxtepec y a principios de 1876 se levantó en armas contra el gobierno constitucional de Sebastían Lerdo de Tejada. Al triunfo del alzamiento fue secretario de gobierno de Jalisco, juez, magistrado y secretario de gobierno de Colima, donde fundó el periódico *El Padre Cobos*; diputado federal, presidente de la Prensa Asociada de México, fundador de la revista *La Patria Ilustrada* y fundador (1877) y director (1877-12) del periódico *La Patria*, cuyos continuos ataques al periódico *La Libertad*, dirigido por Santiago Sierra Méndez, desembocaron en un duelo en el que mató a Sierra. Coautor de *Los hombres promi-*

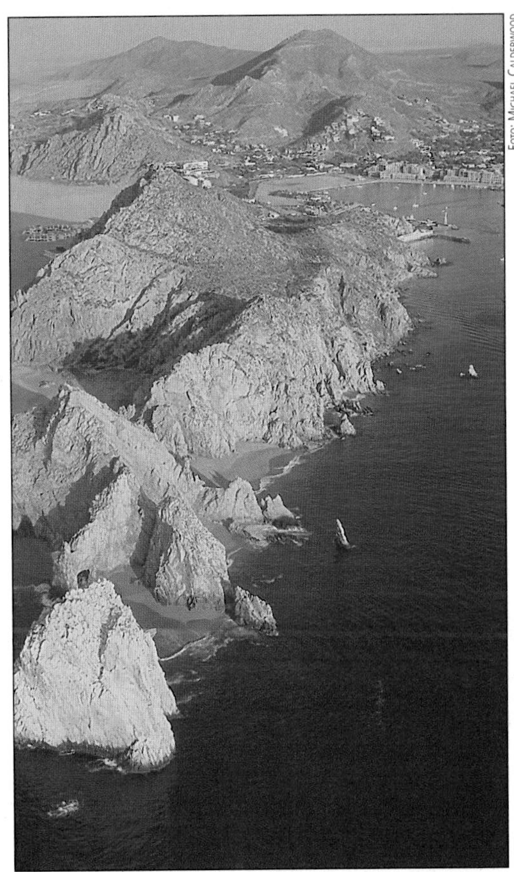

Foto: Michael Calderwood

La Paz, Baja California Sur

Foto: Rogelio Cuéllar

Octavio Paz

Libro de poemas de Octavio Paz

nentes de México (1888). Autor de biografías y obras históricas: *Datos biográficos del general de división Porfirio Díaz* (1884), *Leyendas históricas de la independencia* (primera serie, 1886-94), *Leyendas históricas* (segunda serie, 1894-1914), *Algunas campañas* (1884-85), *México actual, galería de contemporáneos* (1898), *Vida y aventuras de Joaquín Murrieta, famoso bandolero mexicano* (4a. edición de 1908) y *Porfirio Díaz* (1911); novela: *La piedra del sacrificio* (1871), *Amor y suplicio* (1873), *Amor de viejo* (1874), *Guadalupe* (1874), *Doña Marina* (1883) y *Las dos Antonias* (1883); poesía y teatro: *Cardos y violetas (1859-1878)* (1982); y teatro: *La bolsa o la vida* (1863), *Los héroes del día siguiente* (1871) y *La manzana de la discordia* (1871). Se le atribuyen también las obras escénicas *Canas verdes, El poeta y la lugareña, Llueven ingleses, El don de errar, El mártir del deber* y *Al borde del abismo*.

Paz, Octavio ◆ n. y m. en el DF (1883-1936). Abogado. Hijo del anterior. Su nombre completo era Octavio Irineo Paz Solórzano. Estudió en la Escuela Nacional Preparatoria, en el Instituto Científico y Literario del estado de Hidalgo y en la Escuela Nacional de Jurisprudencia (1905-11), donde se tituló como abogado. Reyista en 1909 y antirreeleccionista desde 1910. Fungió como gerente del periódico *La Patria* (1911). A la caída de Porfirio Díaz fue consultor de jueces menores de Ensenada (1912) y más tarde desempeñó funciones judiciales bajo el gobierno de Victoriano Huerta. En julio de 1914 se incorporó a las tropas del Ejército Libertador del Sur. Fue secretario de Emiliano Zapata, editor de *El Nacional* (1914) y de *El Monitor* (1915), colaborador de *El Clarín*, representante zapatista en Estados Unidos (1916-20), diputado federal por el Partido Nacional Agrarista (1920-22), asistente al Congreso Nacional Agrarista (1923), secretario de Gobierno de Morelos (1924), gobernador provisional de Morelos (8 de septiembre al 10 de octubre de 1924), colaborador de *El Magazine para Todos*, suplemento del diario *El Universal* (1929-33) y de la revista *Crisol* (1930-31). Coautor, con Arturo Paz, de *Álbum a Juárez* (1931). Autor de *Novísimo manual del elector* (1911) e *Historia del periodismo en México* (1932). Algunos de sus artículos, así como testimonios de sus contemporáneos y de su hijo, Octavio Paz Lozano, fueron recopilados por Felipe Gálvez en *Hoguera que fue* (1986).

Paz, Octavio ◆ n. y m. en el DF (1914-1998). Poeta y ensayista. Hijo del anterior. Su apellido materno era Lozano. Estudió en las facultades de Derecho y Filosofía y Letras de la UNAM. Colaboró en las revistas *Barandal* (1931-32), *Alcancía* (1933), *Cuadernos del Valle de México* (1933-34), *Taller Poético* (1936-38), *Poesía* (1938), *Ruta* (1938), *Tierra Nueva* (1941), *América, Estaciones* (1958), *Revista Mexicana de Literatura* y otras publicaciones. En 1937 asistió al antifascista Segundo Congreso Internacional de Escritores, celebrado en Valencia, durante la guerra civil española. Volvió a México al año siguiente y dirigió la revista *Taller* (1938-41), perteneció a la redacción del diario *El Popular* (1939) y participó en la creación de *El Hijo Pródigo* (1940), a cuya redacción perteneció (1943-46). En 1944 obtuvo una beca de la Fundación Guggenheim y al año siguiente ingresó en el servicio exterior mexicano, para el cual desempeñó misiones en Estados Unidos (1944-46) y Francia (1946-52). Durante su estancia en París se relacionó con los miembros del movimiento surrealista. A su regreso colaboró en *Hoy, Letras de México, Revista de la Universidad, La Palabra y el Hombre* y *México en la Cultura*, suplemento de *Novedades*. Tomó parte en la fundación del grupo Poesía en Voz Alta (1955). Fue director de Organismos Internacionales de la Secretaría de Relaciones Exteriores (1956) y embajador mexicano en la India (1962-68). En 1968 abandonó la embajada, en protesta por la matanza del 2 de octubre de ese año, en Tlatelolco. Entre 1970 y 1972 fue profesor de la Universidad de Cambridge. Fundó y dirigió los primeros 58 números de la revista *Plural*, del diario *Excélsior*, hasta su renuncia en 1976. Al año siguiente encabezó la fundación de la revista *Vuelta*, que dirigió hasta su muerte. También escribió para los suplementos *La Cultura en México*, de la revista *Siempre!*, y *Sábado*, del cotidiano *unomásuno*; así como en los diarios *Excélsior* (1972-76 y 1989), *El Universal, Novedades* y *La Jornada*. Realizó las antologías *Anthologie de la poésie mexicaine* (1952), *Anthology of Mexican Poetry* (1958), *Antología de Fernando Pessoa* (1962), *Cuatro poetas contemporáneos de Suecia* (1963), *New Poetry of Mexico* (1970) y *Poemas de William Carlos Williams*. Coautor del ensayo *Magia de la risa* (1962), la antología *Poesía en movimiento* (1969, con José Emilio Pacheco, Homero Aridjis y Alí Chumacero), *Las cosas en su sitio* (1971, con Juan Marichal), y los poemas *Renga* (1971, con Jacques Roubaud, Edoardo

Sanguinetti y Charles Tomlinson), e *Hijos del aire* (traducciones mutuas con Charles Tomlinson, 1989). Autor de poesía: *Luna silvestre* (1933), *¡No pasarán!* (1936), *Raíz del hombre* (1937), *Bajo tu clara sombra y otros poemas sobre España* (1937), *Voces de España* (1938), *Entre la piedra y la flor* (1941), *A la orilla del mundo* (1942), *Libertad bajo palabra* (1949), *¿Águila o sol?* (1951), *Semillas para un himno* (1954), *Piedra de sol* (1957), *La estación violenta* (1958), *Agua y viento* (1959), *Libertad bajo palabra* (obra poética 1935-58, 1960), *Dos y uno tres* (1961), *Salamandra* (1962), *El día de Udiapur* (1963), *Vindrabam Madurai* (1965), *Viento entero* (1965), *Blanco* (1967), *Discos visuales* (1968), *Ladera este* (1969), *La centena* (1969), *Topoemas* (1971), *Solo a dos voces* (1973, antología y una entrevista con Julián Ríos), *El mono gramático* (1974), *Pasado en claro* (1975), *Poemas* (antología, 1975), *Vuelta* (1976), *Hijos del aire* (1979), *In mediaciones* (1979), *Poemas* (1979), *Kostas* (1979), *Carta de creencia* (1987), *Árbol adentro* (1987), *Obra poética. 1935-1988* (antología, 1989) y *El fuego de cada día. Lo mejor de Octavio Paz* (selección, prólogo y notas del autor, 1989); ensayo: *El laberinto de la soledad* (1950), *El arco y la lira* (1956), *Las peras del olmo* (1957), *Rufino Tamayo* (1959), *Cuadrivio* (1965), *Los signos de rotación* (1965), *Horas situadas de Jorge Guillén* (1966), *Puertas al campo* (1966), *Corriente alterna* (1967), *Claude Levi-Strauss o el nuevo festín de Esopo* (1967), *Marcel Duchamp o el castillo de la pureza* (1968, reeditado como *Apariencia desnuda. La obra de Marcel Duchamp*, 1973), *Conjunciones y disyunciones* (1969), *México, la última década* (1969), *Posdata* (1970), *Traducción: literatura y literalidad* (1971), *Los signos en rotación y otros ensayos* (1971, selección de Carlos Fuentes), *El signo y el garabato* (1973), *Los hijos del limo* (1974), *La búsqueda del comienzo* (1974), *Xavier Villaurrutia en persona y en obra* (1978), *El ogro filantrópico* (1979), *México en la obra de Octavio Paz* (1979, edición y prólogo de Luis Mario Schneider), *Tiempo nublado* (1980), *Sor Juana Inés de la Cruz o las trampas de la fe* (1982), *Sombras de obras* (1983), *Lectura y contemplación* (1985), *Pasión crítica* (1985), *Hombres en su siglo* (1986), *Primeras letras* (antología, 1988), *Poesía, mito, revolución* (1989), *Pequeña crónica de grandes días* (1990), *La otra voz. Poesía y fin de siglo* (1990), *Convergencias* (1991), *Al paso* (1992), *La llama doble. Amor y erotismo* (1993). *Un más allá erótico: Sade* (1993), *Estrella de tres puntas: el surrealismo* (1995) y *Vislumbres de la India* (1996); y teatro: *La hija de Rapaccini*, poema dramático basado en el cuento *Rapaccini's Daugther*, de Nathaniel Hawthorne (1844), que fue representado en 1956 bajo la dirección de Héctor Mendoza por el grupo Poesía en Voz Alta (la escenografía fue de Leonora Carrington y la música de Joaquín Gutiérrez Heras) e inspiró una ópera de Daniel Catán (1994). Asimismo, su obra poética y sus cuentos han inspirado numerosos espectáculos teatrales, y un libro-*collage* de sus textos, *Teatro de signos* (1974) de Julián Ríos. En 1994 comenzó la publicación de sus *Obras completas*, editadas por él mismo, y de las que hasta 1999 habían aparecido 12 tomos. Recibió, entre otras, las siguientes distinciones: Premio Xavier Villaurrutia (1956), Gran Premio Internacional de la Maison Internationale de la Poésie, de Bruselas (1963); Premio del Festival de Poesía de Flandes, otorgado a los mejores poetas de los últimos 20 años (lo compartió con Jorge Guillén, Saint-John Perse, Leopoldo Sega y Giullia Yllyes); Premio Jerusalén de la Paz, del gobierno de Israel (1977); Premio de la Crítica Española, en Barcelona (1977); Premio Nacional de Ciencias y Artes, de México (1977), Premio de la Crítica de Editores de España (1977), Premio Tel Aviv (1978), Águila Dorada del Festival Internacional de París (1979), Gran Águila de Oro del Festival Internacional del Libro, en Niza (1979), Premio Ollin Yoliztli (1980); Premio Miguel de Cervantes Saavedra, de España (1981); Premio Neustadt, de la Universidad de Oklahoma (1982); Premio de la Paz, de editores y libreros de Frankfurt (1984); Premio Oslo de Poesía (1985), Premio Mazatlán de Poesía (1985), Premio Internacional Alfonso Reyes (1986), Premio Internacional Menéndez Pelayo, de Santander (1987); Medalla Picasso, de la UNESCO (1987); Premio Enciclopedia Británica (1988), Premio Alexis de Toqueville, del Instituto de Francia (1988) y Premio Nobel de Literatura (1990), que le fue otorgado "por una escritura apasionada y de amplios horizontes, caracterizada por su inteligencia sensual y su integridad humanística"; posteriormente se le concedió la Orden Nacional del Mérito, con grado de Gran Cruz, del gobierno de Ecuador (1991), el Premio Mariano de Cavia (1995) y el Premio Blanquerna de Cataluña (1996). *Doctor honoris causa* por las universidades de Boston (1973), Nacional Autónoma de México (1979), Harvard (1980) y de Nueva York (1984). En 1984 y 1989 se organizaron sendos homenajes nacionales por sus 70 y 75 años de edad. Miembro de El Colegio Nacional (1967), de la American Academy of Arts and Letters (1972) de la Academia Mexicana (1981) y del Consejo de Crónica de la Ciudad de México (1988). Fue miembro emérito del SNCA.

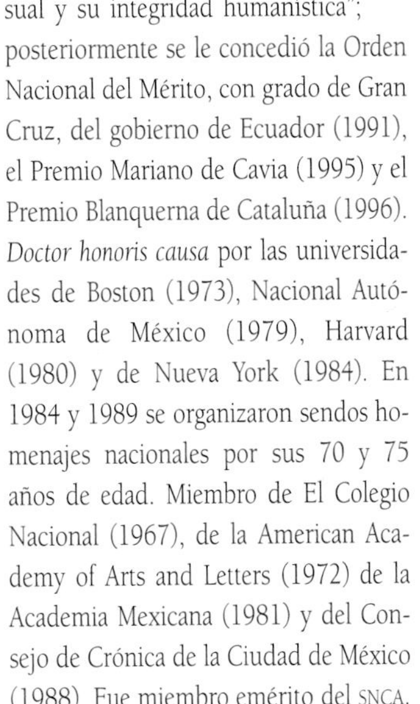

Vuelta, revista fundada y dirigida por Octavio Paz

Paz Guerra, Antonio de la ◆ n. y m. en Monterrey, NL (1882-1916). Abogado. En 1904 fundó, con Santiago Roel, la revista literaria *Renacimiento*, que desapareció en 1910. Fue contrincante político de Bernardo Reyes, secretario general de Gobierno en Nuevo León con Antonio I. Villarreal (1913-15), gobernador interino del mismo estado (1914) y secretario particular de Pablo González. En 1904 escribió, con Roel, *Juárez*, libro que firmaron con el seudónimo de *Un estudiante* y que era refutación de *El verdadero Juárez*, de Francisco Bulnes.

Octavio Paz, en su juventud, dibujado por José Moreno Villa

Paz Horta, René ◆ n. en el DF (1947). Licenciado en derecho por la UNAM (1966-70). Ha sido agente de Mi-

Margarita Paz Paredes

Luis Pazos

nisterio Público (1973-75), secretario del presidente del Tribunal Superior de Justicia del Distrito Federal (1975-78), asesor del Instituto Nacional de Ciencias Jurídicas (1976-81), juez penal (1978-82) y primer subprocurador general de justicia del DF (1982-86). También dirigió el Instituto Nacional para el Combate a las Drogas. Pertenece a la Federación Mexicana de Abogados.

Paz Paredes, Margarita ◆ n. en San Felipe Torres Mochas, Gto., y m. en el DF (1922-1980). Nombre profesional de la escritora Margarita Camacho Baquedano. Estudió periodismo en la Universidad Obrera y literatura en la UNAM. Autora de poesía: *Sonaja* (1942), *Oda a Constantin Oumansky* (1945), *Voz de la tierra* (1946), *El anhelo plural* (1948), *Retorno* (1948), *Génesis transido* (1949), *Elegía a Gabriel Ramos Millán* (1949), *Andamios de sombras* (1949), *Canto a México* (1952), *Dimensión del silencio* (1953), *Presagio en el viento* (1955), *Casa en la niebla* (1956), *Coloquio de amor* (1957), *Cristal adentro* (1957), *Los animales y el sueño* (1960), *Rebelión de ceniza* (1960), *Elegía a César Garizurieta* (1961), *La imagen y su espejo* (1962), *El rostro imposible* (1963), *Adán en sombra y la noche final y siete oraciones* (1964), *El rostro imposible* (1965), *Lumbre cautiva* (1968), *Señales* (1972), *Otra vez la muerte* (1976), *La terrestre esperanza* (1977), *Puerta de luz líquida* (1978), *Litoral del tiempo* (antología de su obra, 1978), *Segundo litoral del tiempo* (1978) y *Memorias de hospital y presagio* (1979); y prosa: *Viaje a la China popular* (1966). En 1986 apareció una edición de *Litoral del tiempo* aumentada con poemas inéditos.

Paz Paredes, Yamilé ◆ n. en el DF (1946). Poeta. Licenciada en letras hispánicas y maestra en literatura latinoamericana por la UNAM. Profesora de la UNAM y la Universidad Autónoma Metropolitana. Ha colaborado en las revistas *Plural*, *Los Universitarios* y *La Brújula en el Bolsillo*, así como en los suplementos *Sábado*, de *unomásuno*, y *Revista Mexicana de Cultura*, de *El Nacional*. Autora de *Fuego sordo* (1977) y "Alquimista de inmenso", incluido en *Cinco botellas al mar* (1985).

Paz Paredes Camacho, Sigfrido ◆ n. en el DF (1938). Técnico en operaciones aeronáuticas titulado en el Centro Internacional de Adiestramiento de Aviación Civil. Ha sido jefe de aeropuerto de la empresa Aeroméxico, jefe de Operaciones de Aeronaves Civiles de la Dirección General de Aeronáutica Civil (1969), subdirector de Infraestructura turística del Banco de México (1971-75), director adjunto de Desarrollo del Fondo Nacional del Fomento al Turismo (1971-75), director general del Fideicomiso Acapulco (1975-76), director general de Aeroméxico (1976-79 y 1982-85) y gerente general de Operaciones de Aeropuertos y Servicios Auxiliares (1979-82), asesor de Fonatur (1988-89), coordinador de Asesores del secretario de Turismo (1990-94). Es autor de *Operaciones aeronáuticas*, *Operaciones aeronáuticas, fase física*, *Operaciones aeronáuticas, fase práctica de desarrollo* y *Operaciones areronáuticas, instrucción programada para piloto privado*. Fue presidente de la Asociación Mexicana de Despachadores de Vuelo.

Paz y Puente Mosse, Manuel ◆ n. y m. en Puebla, Pue. (1892-1910). Obrero. Se afilió al movimiento maderista y trabajó al lado de Aquiles Serdán. El 18 de noviembre de 1910, al ser atacada por la policía la casa de la familia Serdán, intentó ayudar a los sitiados, pero murió en el intento.

Paz Sánchez, Fernando ◆ n. en Huichapan, Hgo. (1932). Licenciado en economía por la UNAM (1954-58), donde ejerció la docencia (1961-69). Ha sido subjefe y jefe del Departamento de Economía Agraria de la hoy Universidad Autónoma de Chapingo (1962-65), donde fue profesor (1960-64); subdirector general de inversiones públicas de la Secretaría de la Presidencia (1966-76), subdirector general de Planificación Hacendaria de la Secretaría de Hacienda (1977), asesor técnico de la Subsecretaría de Minas y Energía, de la Sepanal (1978-80); asesor del director general de Pemex (1981-82), director general de Programas Especiales de la SPP (1981-82), director de Proyectos del Banco Mexicano Somex (1982-85), secretario de Desarrollo Económico del gobierno de Hidalgo (1985-87) y oficial mayor de la SEMIP (1988). Colaboró en la revista *Política*. En 1969 recibió un diploma del Banco Mundial. Pertenece al Colegio Nacional de Economistas, al Instituto Nacional de Administración y a la Liga de Economistas Revolucionarios de la República Mexicana.

Pazos, Luis ◆ n. en Veracruz, Ver. (1947). Obtuvo el título de abogado en la Escuela Libre de Derecho. Hizo estudios de economía y administración en el ITESM y de administración pública en la Universidad de York. Cursó maestría y doctorado en la especialidad de finanzas públicas en la UNAM. Es profesor de la Escuela Libre de Derecho y de la Facultad de Derecho de la UNAM y director del Instituto de Integración Iberoamericana y del Centro de Investigaciones sobre la Libre Empresa. Colabora en más de 20 periódicos mexicanos y latinoamericanos. Es editorialista de *Visión* y ha escrito para el *Wall Street Journal*. Autor de *Ciencia y teoría económica*, *Devaluación en México*, *Futuro económico de México*, *¿Dónde vivir mejor?*, *Mitos y realidades del petróleo mexicano*, *El gobierno y la inflación*, *La estatización de la banca*, *El socialismo, ¿la solución?*, *Marxismo básico*, *Democracia a la mexicana*, *Cómo proteger mi dinero de la inflación*, *Radiografía de un gobierno* (1981), *El rey populachero* (1985), *El pacto, ¿otro engaño más?* (1988), *Hacia dónde va Salinas* (1989), *Los límites de los impuestos* (1990), *Libre comercio México-EUA. Mitos y hechos* (1991), *La disputa por el ejido* (1991), *Lo que le falta a Zedillo* (1994) y *La globalización, riesgos y ventajas* (1998), entre otros títulos.

PCD ◆ ☛ *Partido del Centro Democrático.*

PCM ◆ ☛ *Partido Comunista Mexicano.*

PCN ◆ ☛ *Partido Católico Nacional.*

PDM ◆ ☛ Partido Demócrata Mexicano.

PDS ◆ ☛ *Partido Democracia Social.*

Pe, La ◆ Municipio de Oaxaca situado en el distrito judicial de Ejutla, al sur de la capital del estado y contiguo a

Ejutla de Crespo. Superficie: 26.79 km^2. Habitantes: 1,747, de los cuales 510 forman la población económicamente activa.

PEARSON, FREDERICK STARK ◆ n. en EUA y m. en el océano Atlántico (1861-1915). Ingeniero, doctorado en ciencias en 1900. Introdujo los tranvías eléctricos en Estados Unidos y la electricidad para el regadío, los transportes y el alumbrado en Brasil. Durante el gobierno de Porfirio Díaz fue presidente de las compañías Mexican North Western Railway y de los Ferrocarriles Nacionales; director de la Mexican Land Navegation Railway, la Mexican Light and Power y la Veracruz Railways; y gerente de la Compañía de Tranvías de la ciudad de México. Proyectó y realizó la presa de Necaxa, inaugurada en 1905. Murió cuando fue torpedeado el barco *Lusitania*.

PEARSON, WEETMAN ◆ n. y m. en Inglaterra (1867-1927). Ingeniero. Durante el gobierno del presidente Porfirio Díaz construyó el gran canal del desagüe de la ciudad de México, el hospital Inglés, diversas obras en el puerto de Veracruz y el Ferrocarril de Tehuantepec. En 1906, el gobierno le otorgó una amplia concesión para explotación petrolera; en 1908 fundó la Compañía Petrolera El Águila, pero ese mismo año se vio obligado a salir del país, debido a la presión de la la empresa estadounidense Standard Oil. Era miembro del parlamento inglés, pero sus frecuentes ausencias hicieron que se le llamara *member for Mexico* (representante por México).

PECANINS, BETSY ◆ n. en EUA (1954). Cantante. Llegó a México con su madre en 1967. Viajó a España para estudiar pintura, pero optó por dedicarse a la canción. Regresó a México en 1977, donde reside desde entonces. Ha grabado cerca de una decena de discos, incluyendo uno de música catalana, uno de *blues*, otro de *rock*, uno colectivo, *Mujeres* (1988), de canciones compuestas por Federico Álvarez del Toro, y uno de *blues* con Guillermo Briseño: *Nada que perder* (1995). En 1987 cantó con la Orquesta Filarmónica de la Ciudad de México en un homenaje a George Gershwin. En 1993 participó en el espectáculo colectivo *Babel* y grabó canciones para la película *La reina de la noche* (1996), de Arturo Ripstein.

PECH, AH NAKUK ◆ Cacique de Chac Xulub Chen. Pertenecía a la nobleza maya aunque descendía de los nahuas conquistadores de Uxmal. A la llegada de los españoles fue bautizado como Pablo Pech y probablemente fue discípulo del fraile Juan de Herrera. Era hijo del cacique de Zulkum Cheel, Ah Kom Pech, bautizado Mantón Pech, y hermano del cacique de Yakukul, Ah Macan Pech. Hacia 1553 escribió una *Crónica* de su región, que fue traducida en 1860 por Manuel Encarnación Ávila y en 1936 por Héctor Pérez Martínez, quien la publicó como *Historia y crónica de Chac-Xulub-Chen*.

PECIME ◆ ☛ *Periodistas Cinematográficos Mexicanos*.

PECONI, ANTONIO ◆ n. en Italia (1922). Licenciado en letras españolas por el Instituto Universitario Oriental de Nápoles, del que fue profesor adjunto. Durante 13 años fue profesor en el Instituto Cultural Español de Nápoles. Fue becario de las universidades de Santander, Barcelona y Salamanca. Dos veces agregado del Instituto Italiano de Cultura en México (1968-75 y 1979-88). En 1970 colaboró en la traducción al italiano de *Al filo del agua*, de Agustín Yáñez. Autor de *Cartas de un italiano a Benito Juárez* (1972), *Dos ilustres mexicanos en la Italia del siglo* XIX(1975), *El maestro Justo Sierra e Italia* (México, 1976), *Libros e impresores italianos en la Nueva España en el siglo XVI* (1979) y *La presencia de Italia en México en los siglos XVI y XVII* (1981).

PEDRAJA MUÑOZ, DANIEL JULIO DE LA ◆ n. y m. en el DF (1943-1996). Licenciado en relaciones internacionales por la UNAM y doctor en la misma especialidad por el Instituto de Altos Estudios Internacionales de Ginebra. Profesor de la UNAM. En la SRA fue jefe del Departamento de Programación (1971-73), adscrito a las embajadas mexicanas en China (1973-75) y Cuba (1975), subdirector general adjunto del Servicio Diplomático (1976-77), adscrito a la delegación mexicana ante la ONU (1977-79) y a la embajada en España (1979-83); y director general para Europa Occidental (1983-86), para África, Asia y Oceanía (1986-88) y para el Pacífico (1989-). Coautor y coordinador de *La cuenca del Pacífico. Perspectivas para México* (1988). Autor de *El comercio de México con África* (1967), *Control constitucional de la política exterior en América Latina* (1973), *La política exterior de China* (1976), *Terminología usual en las relaciones internacionales* (1980), *Manual de derecho internacional para oficiales de la Armada de México* (1983), *Condicionantes de la historia de las relaciones entre España y México* (1983) y *México y España, transición y cambio* (1983).

PEDRAZA, JOSÉ ◆ n. en La Mojonera, Mich., y m. en el DF (1937-1998). Marchista. Estudió en la Escuela Militar de Transmisiones. A mediados de los años sesenta empezó a practicar la caminata, en la especialidad de 20 kilómetros. Obtuvo 18 primeros lugares en competencias en el extranjero, la medalla de plata en los Juegos Panamericanos de Winniweg (1967) y también la medalla de plata en los Juegos Olímpicos de México (1968), que le valió su ascenso a subteniente del Ejército Mexicano. Fue seis veces campeón nacional de los 20 kilómetros de caminata. En 1977, cuando tenía el grado de teniente, fue director de la Escuela de Atletismo del Distrito Federal.

PEDRAZA, JOSÉ FRANCISCO ◆ n. en Villa de Xilitla, SLP (1914). Licenciado en derecho por la Universidad Autónoma de San Luis Potosí (1942), de la que es profesor. Desempeñó diversos cargos judiciales en Tampico, Nuevo Laredo, Reynosa y Matamoros. Colaborador de *Archivos de Historia Potosina*. Coautor de *Bibliografía histórica y geográfica del estado de San Luis Potosí* (1941); y autor de *Juárez en San Luis Potosí, 1853-1867* (1972) y *Estudio jurídico de la primera Constitución política del estado de San Luis Potosí* (1975). Perte-

FOTO: ANA LOURDES HERRERA

Betsy Pecanins

FOTO: ÉPOCA

José Pedraza

nece a la Asociación Mexicana de Historia Regional y a la Academia de Historia Potosina.

PEDRAZA SALINAS, JORGE ◆ n. en Monterrey, NL (1943). Licenciado en derecho por la UANL y maestro en Lengua y Literatura Españolas por la ENSE. Ha publicado en *El Porvenir*, *El Norte*, *Universidad*, *Armas y Letras* y *El Heraldo*. Ha sido director de Difusión de la UANL, secretario ejecutivo del Instituto de Cultura de Nuevo León y subdirector de Cultura de Monterrey. Autor de *La huella de Alfonso Reyes* y *Juárez en Monterrey*. Recibió el Premio Nacional Alfonso Reyes en 1974.

PEDRERO CÓRDOVA, JOAQUÍN ◆ n. en Teapa, Tabasco, y m. en el DF (1878-1943). Se tituló en la Escuela Nacional de Ingenieros (1906). En 1908, fue el encargado de la construcción del primer puente colgante en el país, destinado a facilitar el cruce del río Grijalva a la ciudad de Tuxtla Gutiérrez, Chiapas. En 1912 organizó el Partido del Sur contra Porfirio Díaz. Fue senador y gerente del periódico *El Heraldo de México* (1918). Fue jefe de la Comisión Internacional de Límites y Aguas entre México y los Estados Unidos, encargada de estudiar el regreso del Chamizal y la rectificación del río Bravo (1920 y 1938). En 1922 construyó la primera casa en las Lomas de Chapultepec. En 1923 fue subsecretario de Agricultura y Fomento, y en este cargo inauguró el Zoológico de Chapultepec. Posteriormente fue secretario de Agricultura. En 1930, nombrado representante del gobierno ante la Junta de Henequeneros de Yucatán, alentó la creación de una Junta de Mejoras Materiales de Yucatán para contrarrestar los efectos de la crisis henequenera y propuso la construcción de una carretera Coatzacoalcos-Campeche. También se encargó del trazo del Ferrocarril del Sureste. En 1939 patentó un puente desmontable cuyas estructuras no requieren remaches, tuercas ni tornillos.

Vista panorámica de Ixcapuzalco, cabecera municipal de Pedro Ascencio Alquisiras, Guerrero

ILUSTRACIÓN: JOSÉ DE SANTIAGO

PEDRERO FÓSIL, NAPOLEÓN ◆ n. en San Juan Bautista, hoy Villahermosa, y m. cerca de Sarlat, Tab. (1906-1937). Poeta. Autor de *Tu risa*, *Peregrino*, *El cóndor ciego* y *Corazón, corazón*. Uno de sus poemas, *Adelante*, fue musicalizado por Domingo Díaz y Soto y se convirtió en el himno de los Camisas Rojas de Tomás Garrido Canabal. Participó en la fundación del Bloque de Jóvenes Revolucionarios y de las revistas *La Provincia* y *Frente Rojo*. Fue asesinado mientras realizaba su campaña propagandística como candidato a diputado federal.

PEDRERO PRIEGO, HOMERO ◆ n. en Teapa, Tab. (1922). Político. En el PRI, partido al que pertenece desde 1961, fue secretario de Organización (1968) y de Acción Política (1969-70), secretario general (1974) y oficial mayor (1985) del PRI de Tabasco. Ha sido inspector general de Trabajo (1943-48), secretario del ayuntamiento de Centla (1950-52), delegado del Departamento de Prestaciones Sociales del IMSS en Tabasco (1956-58), gerente de tiendas populares del gobierno de Tabasco (1963-65), secretario del ayuntamiento de Centro (1965-69), diputado a la Legislatura de Tabasco (1968-70), presidente municipal de Centla (1971-73), receptor de rentas del municipio de Centro (1984), director de educación obrera de la CTM tabasqueña (1985-87) y diputado federal (1985-88). Autor de *Estas cosas* (1981).

PEDRETTI, HUMBERTO ◆ n. en Italia y m. en EUA (1879-1937). Pintor y escultor naturalizado mexicano. Llegó a México en 1902 y se instaló en Guadalajara. Colaboró en la academia de Félix Bernardelli y ejecutó bustos de Benito Juárez, Francisco I. Madero, José María Morelos y Amado Nervo que se hallan en Guadalajara.

PEDRO ASCENCIO ALQUISIRAS ◆ Municipio de Guerrero situado en el norte del estado, al noroeste de Ixcateopan, en los límites con el Estado de México. Superficie: 510.1 km². Habitantes: 7,284, de los cuales 1,329 forman la población económicamente activa. Hablan alguna lengua indígena siete personas mayores de cinco años. Su cabecera es Ixcapuzalco.

PEDRO ESCOBEDO ◆ Municipio de Querétaro situado en el centro del estado, entre las ciudades de Querétaro y San Juan del Río. Superficie: 290.9 km². Habitantes: 46,270, de los cuales 10,162 forman la población económicamente activa. Hablan alguna lengua indígena 38 personas mayores de cinco años (otomí 19 y náhuatl 13).

PEDROSO, MANUEL ◆ n. en Cuba y m. en el DF (1883-1956). Su nombre completo era Manuel Martínez Aguilar y de Pedroso. Doctor en derecho por la Universidad Central de Madrid (1910). Vivió y estudió en Alemania, salvo breves intervalos, entre 1905 y 1914. Colaborador del periódico argentino *La Nación* (1914-27). Fue profesor (1927), decano de la Facultad de Derecho y vicerrector de la Universidad de Sevilla, delegado de España en la Conferencia de Desarme y en el Consejo de la Sociedad de Naciones (1931-33) y miembro de la comisión jurídica que redactó la Constitución republicana española de 1931. Diputado a Cortes en 1936, durante la guerra civil efectuó labores diplomáticas en Tánger, Varsovia y Moscú. Llegó exiliado a México en 1939. Fue profesor de la Casa de España, hoy El Colegio de México; catedrático de la UNAM, donde fundó el primer seminario sobre teoría del Estado y derecho internacional; y asesor de la Secretaría de Relaciones Exteriores. Colaborador de la *Revista de la Universidad de México*. Tradujo al español *El capital*, de Karl Marx (1946), *La monarquía española en los siglos XVI y XVII*, de Leopold von Ranke (1946), y *Discurso sobre la historia de la revolución en Inglaterra*, de Francois Guizot (1946). Realizó una *Antología de ideas políticas*. Autor de *La perversión de* *la guerra* (1943) y *La aventura del hombre natural y civil* (1946). Dejó inéditos dos libros: *Teoría del Estado* y *Soberanía y derecho internacional*.

PEGASO ◆ Revista con "páginas de palpitante actualidad" y secciones de creación y crítica literarias. Fue fundada en 1917 por Enrique González Martínez, Efrén Rebolledo y Ramón López Velarde. Publicó 15 números. En los tres últimos, su director y gerente fue Jesús B. González. Publicó textos de los citados, así como de Rubén M. Campos, Antonio Caso, Abraham Castellanos, Antonio Castro Leal, Alfonso Cravioto, Rubén Darío, Genaro Estrada, Enrique Fernández Ledesma, Genaro Fernández MacGregor, José D. Frías, Joaquín Gallo, Francisco González León, Enrique González Martínez jr., Luis González Obregón, Carlos González Peña, Xavier Icaza, José López Portillo y Rojas, Salvador de Madariaga, Amado Nervo, Manuel de la Parra, Carlos Pellicer Cámara, Eca de Queiroz, Alejandro Quijano, Alfonso Reyes, José Enrique Rodó, Mariano Silva y Aceves, Alfonso Toro, Jaime Torres Bodet, Julio Torri, Manuel Toussaint, Manuel Ugarte y Luis G. Urbina, entre otros autores.

Pegaso

PEHUAME ◆ Diosa purépecha de las parturientas, esposa del sol poniente e identificada con la luna; variante de Cuerauáperi y correspondiente a la Toci de la religión náhuatl. Su nombre significa "mujer que da a luz".

PEIMBERT SIERRA, MANUEL ◆ n. en el DF (1941). Bisnieto de Justo Sierra. Se tituló como físico en la UNAM (1962). Es maestro (1965) y doctor (1967) en astronomía por la Universidad de California en Berkeley, donde fue profesor asociado (1967-68). En la UNAM ha sido profesor e investigador desde 1968, consejero universitario (1979-83) y presidente del Colegio de Profesores del Instituto de Astronomía (1982-83). Fue investigador huésped del Kitt Peak National Observatory, de Tucson, EUA (1975-76), del Department of Physics and Astronomy del University College de Londres (1976) y del Observatorio de Radioastronomía de Nobeyama, de la Universidad de Tokio (1986). Durante el movimiento estudiantil de 1968 fue delegado de la Facultad de Ciencias a la Coalición de Profesores pro Libertades Democráticas. Miembro fundador del Sindicato de Profesores de la UNAM (1974-77) y del Sindicato de Trabajadores de la UNAM (1977-). Cofundador y miembro del Consejo Nacional del PRD (1989-). Es autor de más de 100 investigaciones aparecidas en revistas especializadas. Ha sido citado más de 5,000 veces en otros trabajos científicos. Sus ensayos están incluidos en libros como *Physical Processes in Red Giants* (1981), *Gas in the Interstellar Medium* (1981), *Star Forming Dwarf Galaxies and Related Objects* (1986), *Star Forming Regions* (1987), *Interstellar Processes* (1987) y *Planetary and Protoplanetary Nebulae From IRAS to ISO* (1987). Miembro del Consejo Editorial de *Geofísica International* (1970-80), del Comité Editorial de la *Memoria de la Sociedad Astrofísica Italiana* (1976-80), del Consejo Editorial de *Astronomy Express*, revista de la Universidad de Cambridge (1984-85); y editor asociado de *Fundamentals of Cosmic Physics*, de Nueva York y Londres (1986-). Pertenece a corporaciones académicas de México y otros países. Fue vicepresidente de la Unión Astronómica Internacional (1982-88). Ha recibido el Premio de la Academia de la Investigación Científica (1971), la Medalla Guillaume Budé del College de France (1974), el Premio Nacional de Ciencias y Artes (1981) y el Premio Universidad Nacional en Ciencias Exactas (1988). Es miembro de El Colegio Nacional desde 1993.

PEIMBERT SIERRA, MARGARITA ◆ n. en el DF (1940). Hermana del anterior. Milita en el PRI. Licenciada (1961) y doctora (1963-65) en derecho por la UNAM. Ejerció la abogacía en el despacho Peimbert Sierra Abogados (1970-76) y ha sido directora de Asuntos Jurídicos del Conacyt (1976-82), directora general de Promoción y Fomento del Banco de Promoción y Fomento (1983-85), directora general de Banca de Servicios Financieros Especializados de Banca Cremi (1985-88) y delegada del DDF en Cuajimalpa (1988-1994).

Foto: Época

Manuel Peimbert Sierra

PEINADO ALTABLE, JOSÉ ◆ n. en España (1909). Pedagogo. Llegó a México en 1942. Ha sido profesor de la Universidad Michoacana de San Nicolás de Hidalgo (1942-43) y de la Escuela Normal de Especialización (1944). Fue psicoanalista de la Clínica de Higiene Mental de la Dirección General de Asistencia Infantil (1944). Colaborador de las revistas *América Indígena* y *Educación*. Autor de *Pedagogía de los trastornos de la palabra* (1945), *Paidología* (1977) y *Psicología clínica* (1978).

PEINADOR CHECA, RAMÓN ◆ n. en España y m. en el DF (1904-1964). Pintor. Expuso en España, Francia y Alemania. Formó parte del grupo de dibujantes de la revista *Prensa Gráfica* de Madrid. Llegó exiliado a México en 1939 y aquí montó ocho exposiciones.

PELÁEZ, ANTONIO ◆ n. en España y m. en el DF (1921-1994). Pintor. Llegó en 1936 y se naturalizó mexicano al año siguiente. Estudió en la Escuela de Pintura y Escultura La Esmeralda. Expuso por primera vez en 1952, apoyado por Frida Kahlo. Participó en muestras colectivas en París (1964), Montreal (1967) y San Antonio (1968). En 1973 representó a México en la primera Bienal de Pintura de Sidney, y participó en la X Bienal de São Paulo, Brasil. Algunas de sus obras están expuestas en los museos de arte moderno de Madrid, Tel

La compuerta, óleo sobre tela de Antonio Peláez (1979)

Foto: Ana Lourdes Herrera

Alejandro Pelayo

Aviv y México. Otras se han presentado en Estados Unidos, Francia y Puerto Rico. Fue colaborador de *México en la Cultura*, suplemento del diario *Novedades*, y de las revistas *Hoy*, *Cuadernos Americanos*, *Revista de Bellas Artes*, *Tiempo*, *Prisme des Arts*, *Cahiers du Museé de Poche*, *Índice* y *The Arts Review*. Autor de *21 dibujos de mujeres de México* (1956).

PELÁEZ, RICARDO ◆ n. en el DF (1964). Futbolista. Como delantero ha jugado en los equipos Necaxa (con el que permaneció ocho temporadas), América y Guadalajara. Seleccionado nacional, participó en el campeonato mundial de 1998.

PELÁEZ, SILVIA ◆ n. en Cuernavaca, Morelos (1959). Obtuvo la maestría en comunicación social en la UNAM. Traductora e intérprete. Estudió actuación en el Instituto Regional del INBA de Cuernavaca, con José Luis Ibáñez y Soledad Ruiz y asistió al taller de dramaturgia de Gerardo Velázquez. Ha sido coordinadora editorial en el Instituto Nacional de Estudios Históricos de la Revolución Mexicana. Autora de teatro: *La espera* (1989, Premio de los Juegos Florales de Acapulco, Guerrero), *La bolivariada* (1989), *Velorio* (1990, Premio del Concurso Nacional de Dramaturgos de la Universidad Autónoma de Nuevo León), *El Hechicero*, *Las hermanas* y *Luna de sangre* (1992), *El vampiro de Londres* (1994), *El guayabo peludo* (1995), *Morir de risa* (1995), *Suicidio a dos manos* y *El detective Linares* (1996), y *Susurros de inmortalidad* (1997). Becaria del Centro Mexicano de Escritores (1989-90).

PELÁEZ GOROCHOTEGUI, MANUEL ◆ n. en Tuxpan, Ver. (?-?). Ganadero. A principios del siglo XX tenía rentadas la mayor parte de sus propiedades a las empresas petroleras estadounidenses y británicas del norte de Veracruz, las cuales lo hicieron contratista, hacia 1910. Dos años después fue elegido presidente municipal de Temapache. Opositor al gobierno de Francisco I. Madero, simpatizó primero con el felicismo y luego con el huertismo. Al caer el gobierno de Victoriano Huerta (1914) salió al exilio, pero volvió al año siguiente. Con el apoyo de las compañías petroleras, organizó una fuerza militar que controló el norte veracruzano y el sur tamaulipeco entre 1916 y 1917, con lo que los capitalistas anglosajones estuvieron a salvo de la política de Venustiano Carranza. En 1920 apoyó la rebelión de Agua Prieta y poco después fue comisionado al extranjero.

PELÁEZ RAMOS, GERARDO ◆ n. en Huajintepec, municipio de Ometepec, Gro. (1946). Estudió en la Escuela Nacional de Maestros. Miembro fundador del Movimiento de Izquierda Revolucionaria Estudiantil, a fines de 1967 presidió el primer Congreso Nacional de Estudiantes Revolucionarios. Fue detenido en ese año, acusado de dinamitar la estatua del ex presidente Miguel Alemán que se encontraba en la Ciudad Universitaria y de colocar una bomba en la embajada boliviana en México, como protesta por la muerte de Ernesto *Che* Guevara (☛). Permaneció en prisión hasta 1973. Al año siguiente se afilió al Partido Comunista Mexicano, en el que fue miembro del consejo de redacción del órgano *Oposición* (1975-77). Director de la Escuela de Capacitación Sindical del STUNAM (1980). Cofundador del Partido Socialista Unificado de México y miembro del consejo de redacción del periódico de esa organización *Así Es* (1982). Pertenece a la coordinación del Centro de Estudios del Movimiento Obrero y Socialista y al Centro de Investigaciones Históricas sobre el Sindicalismo Universitario. Ha colaborado en *unomásuno*, *El Periódico de México* y la revista *Siempre!* Coautor de *Historia del comunismo en México* (1985) y de *Sindicatos nacionales. Educación y telefonistas* (1989). Autor de *1974. El movimiento obrero y sindical* (1975), *Situación actual y perspectivas del movimiento sindical en México* (1978), *Insurgencia magisterial* (1980), *Partido Comunista Mexicano. 60 años de historia* (2 t., 1980), *1975. Cronología obrera y sindical* (1981), *Historia del Sindicato Nacional de Trabajadores de la Educación* (1984) y *Las luchas magisteriales de 1956-60* (1984).

PELAYO, ALEJANDRO ◆ n. en el DF (1945). Cineasta. Su segundo apellido es Rangel. Hizo estudios en el CUEC y en la Escuela de Cine de Londres. Desempeñó actividades relacionadas con el cine en diversas instituciones y, posteriormente, trabajó con varios directores de la empresa Directores Asociados, S. A. Su primer largometraje, *La víspera* (1982, ganador de cuatro Arieles), lo reveló como un director interesado en el cine político y en mostrar los mecanismos del poder en México, como lo confirmaron *Días difíciles* (1987, producida por la Cooperativa José Revueltas, de la que él fue cofundador) y *Morir en el Golfo* (1989). Posteriormente realizó *Miroslava* (1992). Ha sido director general de la Cineteca Nacional.

PELAYO, LUIS MANUEL ◆ n. y m. en el DF (1922-1989). Actor, su segundo apellido era Ortega. Dejó inconclusos sus estudios de medicina. Comenzó como compositor e intérprete en Radio Universidad; pasó luego como locutor y actor cómico a las radiodifusoras XELA, XEQ y XEW; en esta última participó en más de mil radionovelas. En la emisora RCN interpretó el papel de *Kalimán* en la radioserie del mismo nombre. Debutó en teatro en 1946 en la obra *Don Quijote*, perteneció a la compañía de las hermanas Blanch y actuó, entre otras, en las obras *La vedette y el cardenal*, *Otra viuda alegre*, *Buena para todo*, *La pícara Coco*, *La dama del Maxims*, *La hora soñada*, *Me enamoré de una bruja*, *El desperfecto* y *Fuera complejos*. Pionero de la televisión mexicana, donde participó en telenovelas y programas cómicos y de variedades, entre ellos *Casos y cosas de casa* (donde popularizó al personaje *Félix Amargo*) y *Luis de Alba presenta.* Hizo doblaje de series estadounidenses. Durante varios años condujo los programas de concurso *Juan Pirulero* y *Sube Pelayo, sube*. Actuó también en cine.

PELEGRÍ, ALFONSO SIMÓN ◆ n. en España (1926). Escritor radicado en México desde los años cincuenta. Profesor de literatura de la Escuela Normal Superior y de la Universidad Autónoma de Puebla. Autor de poesía: *Hombre dado a la voz* (1964), *Acta de contricción* (1969), *Arquitectura de soledad* (1969), *Cero en retórica* (1972) y *Poemas convocando el imposible hombre* (1978); novela: *Población de barro*; y cuento: *La isla azul de terminarse el mundo* (1991).

PELLICER, ANA ◆ n. en el DF (1949). Escultora. Estudió artes plásticas en la Art Students League de Nueva York (1965) y dibujo y escultura en la New York Social Resarch (1967); joyería con James Wilson, grabado en el Taller Libre de Grabado, pintura con Luis Orozco Romero, Artemio Sepúlveda y Lucas Johnson; y técnicas metalúrgicas de escultura con James Metcalf. En 1968, con la colaboración de Metcafl y artesanos de Santa Clara del Cobre, realizó el pebetero que fue utilizado en los XIX Juegos Olímpicos en la ciudad de México. Una obra suya se encuentra en el Museo de Arte Moderno. En 1980 expuso en París.

Prendedor etrusco-cuajense, obra de Ana Pellicer (1981)

PELLICER, CARLOS ◆ n. en Villahermosa, Tab., y m. en el DF (1897-1977). Poeta. Su apellido materno era Cámara. Estudió en la Escuela Nacional Preparatoria y en Colombia, a donde fue enviado por el gobierno de Venustiano Carranza. Cofundador de la revista *San-Ev-Ank* (1918) y de un nuevo Ateneo de la Juventud (1919). Fue secretario privado de José Vasconcelos. En agosto de 1921, junto con Vicente Lombardo Toledano, Diego Rivera, José Clemente Orozco y Xavier Guerrero, entre otros, fundó el Grupo Solidario del Movimiento Obrero. Colaboró en las revistas *Falange* (1922-23), *Ulises* (1927-28) y *Contemporáneos* (1928-31). Fue profesor de poesía moderna en la UNAM y director del Departamento de Bellas Artes. Organizó los museos Frida Kahlo, el de La Venta y el Anahuacalli. En 1976 fue elegido senador de la República por el PRI. Coautor de *El trato con escritores* (1961). Autor de *Colores en el mar y otros poemas* (1921), *Piedra de sacrificios* (1924), *Seis, siete poemas* (1924), *Oda de junio* (1924), *Hora y 20* (1927), *Camino* (1929), *Cinco poemas* (1931), *Esquemas para una oda tropical* (1933), *Estrofas al mar marino* (1934), *Hora de junio (1929-1936)* (1937), *Ara virginum* (1940), *Recinto y otras imágenes* (1941), *Exágonos* (1941), *Discurso por las flores* (1946), *Subordinaciones* (1949), *Sonetos* (1950), *Práctica de vuelo* (1956), *Material poético 1918-1961* (1962), *Dos poemas* (1962), *Con palabras y fuego* (1963), *Teotihuacan y 13 de agosto: ruina de Tenochtitlan* (1965), *Bolívar, ensayo de biografía popular* (1966), *Noticias sobre Netzahuacóyotl y algunos sentimientos* (1972) y *Cuerdas, percusión y alientos* (1976). Luego de su muerte han aparecido *Reincidencias* (1978), *Cosillas para el nacimiento* (1978), *Cartas desde Italia* (1985) y *Cuaderno de viaje* (1987). En 1997 se publicó *Era mi corazón piedra de río*, antología de sus poemas amorosos. Miembro de la Academia Mexicana (de la Lengua) desde 1953. En 1964 recibió el Premio Nacional de Ciencias y Artes. En 1981, Luis Mario Schneider realizó la edición de sus *Obras (poesías)*. Sus restos están en la Rotonda de los Hombres Ilustres.

FOTO: ROGELIO CUÉLLAR

Carlos Pellicer

Celebración del centenario de Carlos Pellicer

PELLICER, PILAR ◆ n. en el DF (?). Actriz. Estudió teatro en la UNAM; danza en el INBA, actuación con Seki Sano y, becada en Francia, arte dramático. En París trabajó con la Compañía Nacional de Teatro Clásico. Formó parte del grupo Poesía en Voz Alta. Ha actuado en telenovelas y en teatro. Empezó su carrera cinematográfica en 1958 en el filme *Nazarín* de Luis Buñuel, a la que le siguieron *El vendedor de muñecas* (1958), *Los ambiciosos* (1959), *Tajimaroa* (1965), *Pedro Páramo* (1966), *Los bandidos* (1966), *Las visitaciones del diablo* (1967), *Andante (vértigo de amor en la oscuridad)* (1967), *La trinchera* (1968), *Los amigos* (1968), *Una mujer honesta* (1969), *El mexicano* (1976), *Tres mujeres en la hoguera* (1977) y *Rigo es amor* (1980). En 1974 recibió la Diosa de Plata y el Ariel a la mejor actriz por *La Choca*.

FOTO: DANTE BUCIO

Pilar Pellicer

PELLICER, PINA ◆ n. y m. en el DF (1938-1964). Nombre profesional de la actriz Josefina Yolanda Pellicer de Llergo. Formó parte del grupo Poesía en Voz Alta. Participó en las películas *El rostro impasible*, *Macario* (1959), *Días de otoño* (1962) y *El gran pescador*. En 1963 recibió la Diosa de Plata a la mejor actriz por *Tiburoneros*.

FOTO: COLECCIÓN PECIME

Pina Pellicer en *Macario*, película de Roberto Gavaldón

PELLICER CÁMARA, JUAN ◆ n. y m. en el DF (1910-1970). Abogado. Hermano del poeta Carlos Pellicer. Cuando era estudiante participó en el movimiento vasconcelista. Desde los años cuarenta fue juez de las plazas de toros México y El Toreo. Perteneció al Consejo Técnico del Departamento de Espectáculos de la ciudad de México. Cronista taurino en los periódicos *La Prensa*, *Últimas No-*

ticias, Atisbos, Tiempo y *Esto*. En este último firmaba con el seudónimo de *Juan de Marchena*. Fue gerente de la compañía Cinematográfica Grovas y produjo *Las señoritas Vivanco*, entre otras películas; subdirector (1953) y director de Cinematografía de la Secretaría de Gobernación, gerente de Inmuebles y Equipo (1961) y gerente general de la Operadora de Teatros (1963); gerente de la Cadena de Oro y de Inversiones Reforma (1963).

Pellicer López, Carlos ◆ n. en el DF (1948). Pintor. Estudió en la Escuela Nacional de Artes Plásticas. Expuso por primera vez de manera individual en 1974. Ha contribuido a difundir la obra del poeta Carlos Pellicer, de quien es sobrino.

Pellicer Silva, Olga ◆ n. en el DF (1935). Licenciada en relaciones internacionales por la UNAM (1953), posgraduada en el Instituto de Altos Estudios Internacionales de la Universidad de París (1959-61) y diplomada de la Escuela de Altos Estudios Internacionales. Profesora e investigadora de El Colegio de México, de la Facultad de Ciencias Políticas y Sociales de la UNAM, del Instituto Matías Romero y del ITAM, entre otras. Investigadora visitante en el Saint Anthony College y la Queen Elizabeth House de la Universidad de Oxford. Ha sido directora de la Comisión Consultiva de Política Exterior (1980-84), embajadora mexicana en Grecia (1984-88), embajadora alterna de México ante la ONU (1988-1992), asesora y directora general del Sistema para las Naciones Unidas (1992-94) y directora del Instituto Matías Romero de la SRE (1994-1999). Coautora de *Las empresas trasnacionales en México* (1976), *El afianzamiento de la estabilidad: vida política en México 1957-60* (1978) y *El entendimiento con los Estados Unidos y la gestación del desarrollo estabilizador* (1978). Autora de *México y la revolución cubana* (1973) y *La política exterior de México*. Pertenece a la Academia de la Investigación Científica y al SNI (1996).

Ana Luisa Peluffo

Pellón Riveroll, Alfredo ◆ n. en el DF (1923). Licenciado en derecho por la UNAM (1947), donde fue consejero (1947-48) y profesor (1960-66). Ha sido secretario de Trabajo del Sindicato Nacional de Trabajadores de la Secretaría de Bienes Nacionales e Inspección Administrativa (1948-49), jefe de los departamentos de las Juntas Federales de Mejoras Materiales (1950-54) y de Personal (1956-58) de la Secretaría de Obras Públicas; jefe del Departamento de Personal de la SCT (1958-64), presidente de la Cámara Nacional de la Industria Avícola (1963-65), director general de Personal (1965-66) y de Administración (1967-70) de la SEP; director administrativo de los Servicios Coordinados de Salud Pública de la SSA (1977-80) y director general de Recursos Humanos de la SRA (1980-88).

Peluffo, Ana Luisa ◆ n. en Querétaro, Qro. (1929). Nombre profesional de la actriz Ana Luisa Quintanar. Dirigió el ballet acuático del Club Deportivo Chapultepec. Inició su carrera cinematográfica a principios de los cincuenta como extra en la cinta *Tarzán y las sirenas*, con Johnny Weismuller. Ha trabajado en más de 180 cintas en México, Panamá, Inglaterra, Francia, Italia, Brasil, Argentina, Puerto Rico, Uruguay, España y Checoslovaquia, entre ellas, *La fuerza del deseo* (1955, en su primer papel protagónico), *El seductor* (1955), *La ilegítima* (1955), *Camino del mal* (1956), *La adúltera* (1956), *Esclavas de Cartago* (1956), *La Diana Cazadora* (1957), *Sed de amor* (1957), *La mujer marcada* (1957), *El vestido de novia* (1958), *La mujer y la bestia* (1958), *Socios para la aventura* (1958), *Nacida para amar* (1958), *Las señoritas Vivanco* (1958), *Ama a tu prójimo* (1958), *Orquídeas para mi esposa*, *Lágrimas de amor* (1958), *¡Yo sabía demasiado!* (1959), *El fantasma de la opereta* (1959), *La venenosa* (1959), *Cada quien su vida* (1959), *El gángster* (1964), *Réquiem por un canalla* (1966), *El último pistolero* (1968), *Vagabundo en la lluvia* (1968), *Ángeles y querubines* (1971), *Triángulo* (1971), *Vals sin fin* (1971), *La muerte de Pancho Villa* (1973), *El valle de los miserables* (1974), *El reventón* (1975), *Pafnucio santo* (1976), *Flores de papel* (1977), *Bandera rota* (1977), *Deseos* (1977), *Perro callejero* (1979), *Arriba Michoacán* (1986) y *Reportero* (1987). Ha actuado también en teatro, televisión y centro nocturno. En 1975 recibió la Diosa de Plata a la Mejor Actriz, por *La venida del rey Olmos* (1974) y en 1977 por *La casta divina* (1976). Recibió otra Diosa de Plata por su trayectoria en 1996.

Pen Club de México ◆ Sección local del PEN Club Internacional, organización de escritores fundada en Londres en 1920 por George Bernard Shaw, Anatole France y Thomas Mann, entre otros. La palabra *pen* significa en inglés "pluma". Se dice que el nombre se forma con las iniciales de "poetas, ensayistas y narradores", aunque la agrupación reúne también a dramaturgos y editores. El PEN, que estimuló la constitución de Amnistía Internacional (☛), denuncia sistemáticamente las amenazas a la libre expresión y demanda la libertad para los escritores presos. La filial mexicana se fundó en 1922 y llegó a contar con unos 150 miembros hacia 1925. En su primera época estuvo presidida, entre otros, por Genaro Estrada (1922-24), Francisco Monterde, Alejandro Quijano, Juan de Dios Bojórquez, Francisco Orozco Muñoz y Francisco

Rojas González. "Tras algunas inevitables pausas —dijo Monterde—, nuestro PEN Club se extinguió, con el último de los mencionados, lamentablemente desaparecido en 1951". Publicó en sus primeros años *La Pajarita de Papel* (☛). En esa etapa inicial realizó cenas en las que algún miembro leía sus textos. En la segunda mitad de los años sesenta se reconstituyó la agrupación, que fue presidida inicialmente por José Luis Martínez, quien hizo editar nuevamente *La Pajarita*. A partir de 1968, cuando José Revueltas fue encarcelado por el gobierno de Gustavo Díaz Ordaz, el PEN Club Internacional abogó reiteradamente por su libertad y denunció el atentado de que él y otros presos políticos fueron víctimas el 1 de enero de 1970. En 1979 el PEN mexicano editó un *Boletín* bajo la dirección de Julieta Campos. Posteriormente han sido presidentes Ramón Xirau, Eduardo Lizalde y Víctor Manuel Mendiola (1998-).

PENATES ◆ Dioses domésticos de los nahuas. Eran representados con estatuillas y la costumbre establecía que los señores debían poseer al menos seis de ellos; los nobles cuatro y los plebeyos dos. También se colocaban en los caminos.

PENICHE, MANUEL ◆ n. en Mérida, Yuc., y m. en Veracruz, Ver. (1834-1889). Abogado y agrimensor. Fue regidor del ayuntamiento de Mérida, diputado federal y representante en México de las sociedades bancarias y ferrocarrileras de Yucatán; senador de la República por Yucatán y por Campeche. Colaboró en los periódicos *El Pueblo*, *La Burla* y *El Eco de los Estados*. Autor de *Historia de las relaciones de España y México con Inglaterra sobre el establecimiento de Belice*.

PENICHE BLANCO, ALBERTO ◆ n. en Puebla, Pue., y m. en el DF (1920-1990). Periodista. Inició su carrera en 1942. Fundó, entre otros, los diarios *El Sol de Puebla* y *El Sol de Tlaxcala*. Fue secretario de Francisco Martínez de la Vega (1958-64) cuando éste fue gobernador de San Luis Potosí. Se desempeñó como gerente general del diario *El Heraldo de México* (1965-76). En el sector público fue director de los Talleres Gráficos de la Nación (1976), director de Relaciones Públicas de la Presidencia de la República (1976-79), director de Información de la Secretaría de Gobernación (1979-82), jefe del Departamento de Prensa y Difusión del Instituto Mexicano del Seguro Social (1983-84), director general de Información de la Secretaría de Gobernación (1984-88) y director general de Información y Relaciones Públicas de la Secretaría de Educación (1988-90). Fue condecorado por los gobiernos de Bulgaria, China y España.

PENICHE CEREZO, ALBERTO ◆ n. en Puebla, Pue. (1944). Hijo del anterior. Contador público titulado en la Universidad del Valle de México (1962-67). En la Conasupo ha sido subgerente de Administración y Finanzas de los Almacenes de Ropa (1973-74), subgerente de Finanzas de Diconsa en el área metropolitana de la ciudad de México (1974-76), gerente de Finanzas (1976-82), director de Comercialización Agropecuaria (1982-85) y director de Empresas Industriales y Comerciales (1985-).

PENICHE LÉGER, MARIA ELENA ◆ n. y m. en el DF (1938-1988). Maestra en lengua y literatura españolas por la UNAM. En el IPN fue jefa del departamento de literatura e idiomas de la Preparatoria Técnica Piloto, coordinadora del Taller de Lectura y Redacción y subdirectora de la *Revista IPN: Ciencia, Arte, Cultura*. Autora del libro de poesía *Díaz sin tiempo* (1989).

PENICHE LÓPEZ, VICENTE ◆ n. en Espita de Peniche, Yuc., y m. en el DF (1888-1952). Abogado. En Yucatán se desempeñó como juez militar, síndico del ayuntamiento de Mérida (1914), director del *Diario Oficial* (1915) y juez de distrito del estado (1917-19). En la UNAM fue profesor de la Escuela Nacional de Jurisprudencia (1925-52) y profesor de la Escuela de Comercio y Administración (1921-28); así como director de la Escuela Nacional de Derecho y Ciencias Sociales de la UNAM (1941-50). Autor de *De la investigación de la paternidad* (1920), *Curso de garantías y amparo*, *El artículo 14 constitucional* y *Rejón y el juicio de amparo*.

PENJAMILLO ◆ Municipio de Michoacán situado en el norte del estado, al noreste de Zamora, en los límites con Guanajuato. Superficie: 212.11 km². Habitantes: 21,034, de los cuales 5,415 forman la población económicamente activa. Hablan purépecha 10 personas mayores de cinco años. La cabecera municipal es Penjamillo de Degollado.

Foto: Época

Alberto Peniche Blanco

PÉNJAMO ◆ Municipio de Guanajuato situado en el extremo suroeste del estado, en los límites con Michoacán y Jalisco. Superficie: 1,774.8 km². Habitantes: 141,135, de los cuales 28,121 forman la población económicamente activa. Hablan alguna lengua indígena 70 personas mayores de cinco años (purépecha 28). En purépecha, Pénjamo significa "lugar de sabinos". En el pueblo de Corralejo, dentro del municipio, están las ruinas de la casa en la que nació Miguel Hidalgo y hay un monumento a su memoria.

Foto: Fondo Editorial Grupo Azabache

Pénjamo, Guanajuato

PÉNJAMO ◆ Sierra volcánica de Guanajuato. En el oeste enlaza con la sierra de Arandas. Sus laderas este y sur forman parte del límite occidental del Bajío.

PENSADOR MEXICANO, EL ◆ Periódico fundado y redactado por José Joaquín Fernández de Lizardi tras establecerse en Nueva España la libertad de imprenta, al entrar en vigor la Carta de Cádiz. El primer número apareció el 9 de octubre de 1812. Salió regularmente cada jueves. Se publicó sin censura hasta el número 9, en el cual Lizardi prevenía al virrey Venegas contra los aduladores y le recordaba que estaba sujeto "al engaño, a la preocupación y a las pasiones". El elogio más sincero, decía *el Pensador*, será el que reciban los príncipes después de

Núm. 8. Pag. 59.

EL PENSADOR MEXICANO.

Execucion de justicia.

En el núm. 5. de este periódico á fox. 34. se lee: *¿es verdad, Galvez?* y debe leerse, *¿es verdad Galve?* como se debió haber puesto, y asi, borrese la *z*, pues ni debemos, ni queremos que pase ningun descuido que sea capáz de confundir el mérito.

El Excmo. Sr. *D. Bernardo de Galvez*, Cónde de Galvez, fué Virrey de México, y amó mucho á los Americanos: su coche quando salia al paséo, era conducido, como en triunfo entre vivas y aclamaciones que inspiraba la gratitud: hacia repetidas y públicas limosnas, como lo saben todos, oía al pobre con la mayor apacibilidad, en un año de una escacés espantosa de maíz, fabricó ese Alcázar de *Chapultepec*, en cuya obra gastó muchos pesos, y libró de la hambre devoradora á muchos infelices, y por último, manifestó su piedad y religion quitando del suplicio á tres reos que iban á ser ajusticiados (juzgo) que en un dia privilegiado.

Estas virtudes le grangearon el título recomendable de *humano*, que los soberbios fanfarrónes volvieron en el de *popular*. El general sentimiento de los Mexicanos en su muerte hace su completo panegiris.

Del otro Cónde de *Galve*, que es de quien allí hablamos, podemos asegurar que no debió su gobierno de ser muy suave á esta Ciudad, pues el dia 8. de Junio del año de 1692. con motivo de haber faltado el maíz, hubo un tumulto sangriento: quemaron parte de Palacio, de las casas capitulares &c., el Virrey estaba por fortuna en el Convento de S. Francisco con su muger Doña Elvira de Toledo, donde se quedó, te-

El Pensador Mexicano

muertos, cuando ya no sean "capaces de infundir temor ni de prodigar mercedes". Le recordaba al virrey que al llegar a México ignoraba todo sobre el país, le pedía revocar un bando que sometía a los sacerdotes a la justicia militar y alegaba que "el oficial más relumbroso" no era más digno de consideración que "el sacerdote más despilfarrado". Por lo anterior, Lizardi fue encarcelado du-rante siete meses y su periódico sometido a censura. Ese fue el pretexto para quitar el filo a la publicación, que en números anteriores había señalado la libertad de imprenta como freno a "la arbitrariedad de los que nos gobiernan". Criticó "el lujo, la imitación de las costumbres galicanas, las excesivas contribuciones, la falta de economía en el comercio, las manos muertas, los empeños, las aduanas, el descuido en la agricultura, la permisión de extranjeros en la monarquía, la colocación de éstos en el gabinete, la desatención de los nacionales de mérito, los infinitos empleos, los escandalosos sueldos, las Américas mal gobernadas" y otros asuntos. Dijo claramente que la reina María Luisa de Parma había obtenido de su esposo, Carlos IV, el cargo de primer ministro para Manuel Godoy por sus amoríos con éste. "Vosotros los déspotas y el mal gobierno habéis inventado la insurrección presente", acusaba en el número 5, en el que advertía: "si hubiéramos tenido siempre un gobierno protector, unos ministros sabios, políticos y amantes de la humanidad, que no hubieran atado las manos a los americanos, sino franqueádoles los arbitrios de la industria y la naturaleza para que adquiriesen con menos embarazo su subsistencia; si a los indios se hubiera tratado como lo que son y no como lo que quisieron que fueran; si se les hubieran concedido los privilegios de hombres, quitándoles exenciones de neófitos, exenciones que les han sido terriblemente perjudiciales; si hubiéramos gozado, por último, los generales beneficios de la libertad, no digo Hidalgo, ni el mismo Lucifer hubiera sido capaz de reunir tan en breve las numerosas gavillas con que vimos comenzar la insurrección, ni ésta hubiera tomado cuerpo ni los pueblos se hubieran obstinado". En el número 7 propone algunas medidas para pacificar la Nueva España: "hágase un armisticio, ínterin se averigua la causa con razones; callen los cañones mientras hablan las leyes; descansen las bayonetas mientras trabajan las plumas; consúltese a España; veamos lo que reprueba y lo que admite; entre tanto no se derrama nuestra sangre, no se talan nuestros campos, no se entorpece nuestro comercio y, lo que es más, no fermenta el odio hasta lo sumo". A partir del número 10, bajo la censura de José Mariano Beristáin de Souza, moderó el tono y tocó temas menos espinosos. El 10 de enero de 1813, en el número 13, indicó a los suscriptores, a los que había dado también cinco *extras* a los que llamó "pensamientos extraordinarios", que había cumplido con ellos: "Suspendo ahora mi efímero periódico, porque el papel me ha costado y está costando muy caro, de modo que no me ofrece cuenta proseguir; si abaratare se continuará".

PENTATHLÓN ◆ Organización cuyo nombre completo es Pentathlón Deportivo Militarizado Universitario. Fundada en 1939, se propuso formar a jóvenes mexicanos en una disciplina militarizada con énfasis en los deportes y "lo espiritual" como "necesarios para el desarrollo integral". La agrupación ha sido apoyada por benefactores como Gustavo Baz Prada, Luis Enrique Bracamontes, Walter C. Buchanan y Rodolfo Sánchez Taboada, a los que se rinden homenajes anuales. El Pentathlón cuenta con internados en los que viven y estudian muchachos reclutados en provincia y en los que se procuraba imbuir una "mentalidad de trabajar en beneficio de la patria".

PENTECOSTALES ◆ Miembros de diversas agrupaciones religiosas estadounidenses que se escindieron del baptismo a fines del siglo XIX para formar un movimiento, no organizado, en el que el bautismo del Espíritu Santo es el elemento principal. Éste consiste en manifestaciones extáticas como la glosolalia ("hablar en lenguas"), la creencia en la sanidad divina de la oración y una expectativa milenarista por el regreso de Jesucristo al mundo. Los pentecostales son el grupo religioso cristiano no católico más grande en México; agrupan alrededor de 70 por ciento de los protestantes mexicanos. Esta doctrina se difundió por la acción de braceros mexicanos repatriados a principios del siglo XX. El primer grupo pentecostal fue la Iglesia Apostólica de la Fe en Cristo Jesús, fundada en Chihuahua en 1914, que durante la década de 1920 amplió su influencia hacia el occidente y noroccidente del país. La autoridad máxima de esta Iglesia es la Convención General de Pastores, que ha dividido el territorio mexicano en 15 distritos. Afirma contar con 100,000 miembros; y publica la revista trimestral *El Expositor Bíblico Cristiano* y la mensual *Hechos de los apóstoles*. En 1921 se crearon las Asambleas de Dios, de organización religiosa similar a la Iglesia Apostólica, pero más descentralizada. Otros grupos pentecostales son la Iglesia de Jesucristo Interdenominacional (fundada en 1940), la Iglesia de Dios en la República Mexicana, la Iglesia Cristiana Bethel, la Comunidad de Iglesias Pentecostales Libres, la Iglesia Evangélica Independiente, la Unión de Iglesias Independientes, las Iglesias Apostólicas Pentecostales Independientes, el Movimiento Libre Pentecostés, la Iglesia Evangélica Cuadrangular, la Iglesia Berea del Pentecostés, la Iglesia de Dios Independiente, las Iglesias Pentecostales de Dios y la Iglesia Cristiana Gedeón. Todos estos grupos se han unido, con las Asambleas de Dios, en la Asociación Fraternal de Iglesias Pentecostales. Han organizado diversos actos masivos de oración en estadios y parques, como la oración en el estadio Azteca de agosto de 1999. En años recientes, grupos denominados neopentecostales, escindidos de otros ya establecidos, se han inclinado más aún por las manifestaciones extáticas y han reaccionado fuertemente contra la teología y las doctrinas escritas.

PEÑA, ALFONSO X. ◆ n. en Ciudad Victoria, Tams., y m. en el DF (1903-1964). Pintor. Cuando vivía en Nueva York, a fines de la década de 1930, formó parte de un grupo de artistas integrado por Rufino Tamayo, José Juan Tablada, Matías Santoyo, Adolfo Best Maugard y Miguel Covarrubias. En 1957 asistió a la Exposición Internacional de París, donde obtuvo una medalla de oro como muralista. Permaneció en Francia con una beca de la Secretaría de Relaciones Exteriores. Se inició como caricaturista de *El Mundo*, de Tampico. Colaboró en el periódico *El Universal* de la ciudad de México, y en varias publicaciones de Latinoamérica. Pintó murales en París, Caracas, Los Ángeles, Mazatlán y Cuernavaca. Expuso en España, Estados Unidos, Francia e Italia. En 1950 recibió la Medalla José Clemente Orozco.

PEÑA, CARLOS HÉCTOR DE LA ◆ n. en Saltillo, Coah. (1922). Escritor. Miembro de la Compañía de Jesús. Estudió letras en la UNAM. Investigador del Instituto de Investigaciones Filológicas de la UNAM. Colaboró en la revista *Ábside*. Realizó una *Antología de la literatura universal* (1960). Autor de *Flor de martirio: María de la Luz Camacho, primera mártir de la Acción Católica* (1940), *La novela moderna, su sentido y su mensaje* (1944), *Diez y seis años* (1944), *Hernando Santaren, el domador de indios* (1944), *Historia de la literatura universal* (1945), *Nosotros los muertos* (1951), *El hipócrita* (1959), *Historia de la literatura universal* (1961) y *Don Francisco Monterde* (1979).

PEÑA, ERNESTO DE LA ◆ n. en el DF (1927). Escritor. Licenciado en letras clásicas por la UNAM, donde también hizo estudios de idiomas y otras materias literarias. Ha traducido al español numerosos textos clásicos y contemporáneos y ha sido traductor del griego y el latín para la Bibliotheca Scriptorum Graecorum et Romanorum, colección de textos clásicos de la UNAM; perito traductor oficial de la SRE, comentarista y conductor de televisión, locutor de la estación radiofónica XEW y colaborador en programas del Instituto Mexicano de la Radio. Ha colaborado en los diarios *El Sol de México* y *Excélsior*, así como en las revistas *Siempre!*, *Vuelta* y *Milenio* y en la italiana *Enciclopedia Dantesca*. Autor de cuento: *Las estratagemas de dios* (1988, Premio Xavier Villaurrutia) y *Las máquinas espirituales* (1991); novela: *El indeleble caso de Borelli* (1992); y poesía: *Mineralogía para intrusos* (1993). En 1993 ingresó en la Academia Mexicana de la Lengua y desde 1994 pertenece al Sistema Nacional de Creadores de Arte.

Foto: Rogelio Cuéllar

Ernesto de la Peña

PEÑA, FELICIANO ◆ n. en Silao, Gto., y m. en el DF (1915-1982). Pintor y grabador. Estudió en la Academia de San Carlos y en la Escuela de Pintura al Aire Libre de Tlalpan (1928-32). Maestro en grabado, diplomado en la Escuela de Artes del Libro (1942). Expuso por primera vez en 1933, en la Secretaría de Educación. Profesor de Escuela de Pintura y Escultura La Esmeralda y de la Escuela Nacional de Artes Gráficas (1942-66). Fue fundador de la Sociedad Mexicana de Grabadores y del Salón de la Plástica Mexicana. Expuso en Estados Unidos, Francia, Gran Bretaña, Japón, Noruega, Perú, Suecia y Suiza. En 1944 recibió el Premio del Salón Libre 20 de Noviembre y, en 1957 y 1975, el premio de adquisición del Salón Anual de Pintura del Salón de la Plástica Mexicana. Autor de un mural que representó a México en la Exposición Internacional de Bruselas (1958) y del álbum *Estampas mexicanas*.

PEÑA, JOSÉ ◆ n. en Ciudad Juárez, Chih. (1942). Beisbolista. Lanzador derecho. Entre 1969 y 1972 jugó en las grandes ligas de Estados Unidos, en los equipos *Rojos* de Cinccinnati y *Dodgers* de Los Ángeles.

PEÑA, JOSÉ ENRIQUE DE LA ◆ n. en el estado de Jalisco y ¿m. en Guadalajara, Jal.? (1807-¿1842?). Militar. En 1825 se enroló en la corbeta *Libertad*, como aspirante a la Marina, y se dio de baja en 1827. En julio de ese año participó en la campaña contra Isidro Barradas, en Tampico. Condiscípulo y amigo de Miguel Miramón y Rómulo Díaz de la Vega durante su estancia en el Colegio Militar (1831), en 1835 fue nombrado agregado de la legación mexicana en Francia, pero renunció para participar en la campaña de Texas: combatió en la batalla de El Álamo y en 1836 testificó contra Vicente Filisola, por su retirada después del desastre de San Jacinto. En 1837 se sumó al pronunciamiento de José de Urrea en Arizpe, contra el gobierno de Anastasio Bustamante, y fue derrotado en Mazatlán por las fuerzas de Mariano Paredes y Arrillaga. Fue aprehendido y purgó una larga condena en Guadalajara. Colaboró en los periódicos *El Sol*, el *Correo de la Federación* y *El Mosquito Mexicano*. Autor de una *Reseña y diario de la campaña de Texas*, cuya publicación estuvo prohibida. En 1955, Jesús Sánchez Garza la editó como *La rebelión de Texas. Manuscrito inédito de 1836 por un oficial de Santa Anna*.

Foto: Pablo González de Alba

El Centro Comercial Galerías de la ciudad de México, obra arquitectónica de Julio de la Peña

PEÑA, JULIO DE LA ◆ n. en Guadalajara, Jal. (1917). Arquitecto. Estudió en la Universidad Autónoma de Guadalajara (1935-39) y en la UNAM (1939-41). Cofundador (1947) y secretario de la Escuela de Arquitectura de la Universidad de Guadalajara (1947-49) y cofundador de las empresas Módulo Industrial y Modistral. Recibió la medalla José Clemente Orozco, del estado de Jalisco, y el premio de Cementos Guadalajara, para la mejor obra en concreto. Proyectó diversas edificaciones en Gua-

FOTO: ÉPOCA

Margarita Peña

dalajara, entre otras: El Palacio de Hierro, Sears Roebuck (1948), Plaza de la Reforma (1957), la Glorieta Guadalajara (1958), la Biblioteca y Casa de la Cultura (1959), la Plaza Juárez (1960), la Plaza de la República (1962), la avenida Chapultepec (1965) y el Auditorio del Estado (1968); también tiene obras en el Distrito Federal, como la cubierta colgante del Auditorio Nacional y el centro comercial Galerías (1978-88); el estadio Neza, de Ciudad Nezahualcóyotl, y otras construcciones en diversas ciudades de México y del extranjero. Autor de *Cincuenta años de arquitectura en Guadalajara* (1957) y *Arquitectura contemporánea tapatía* (1992). Ha recibido el Premio de Arquitectura Clemente Orozco 1965, el Premio Anual de Arquitectura 1989, el Gran Premio de la Academia 1992 y el Premio de Arquitectura Jalisco 1994. Es académico emérito de la Academia Nacional de Arquitectura y miembro honorario del Colegio de Arquitectos de Jalisco.

PEÑA, MARGARITA ◆ n. en el DF (1937). Maestra en letras hispánicas por la UNAM, donde es profesora, con estudios de doctorado en El Colegio de México. Ha hecho trabajos de investigación literaria en la Biblioteca Nacional de París, el Instituto de Cooperación Iberoamericana de Madrid (1982-83), el Archivo General de la Nación (1984), la Universidad de Indiana (1985) y el Instituto Iberoamericano de Berlín (1986). Fue secretaria de Extensión Académica de la UNAM. Condujo el programa *Academia Literaria* en Radio UNAM. Colaboradora de *Fem, Diálogos, Revista Universidad de México, Los Universitarios* y *unomásuno*. Autora de *Una de cal y otra de arena* (reseñas literarias, 1969), *Alegoría y auto sacramental* (ensayo, 1975), *Vivir de nuevo* (crónica, 1980) y *Entre líneas* (ensayos, 1983). Hizo la edición crítica de *Flores de baria poesía* (1980) y de *Mofarandel de los oráculos de Apolo* (1986).

PEÑA, MARGARITA DE LA ◆ n. en Guadalajara, Jal. (1957). Pintora. Estudió pintura en la Escuela de Artes Plásticas de la Universidad de Guadalajara. Tuvo su primera exposición individual en el Teatro Degollado de su ciudad natal (1978). Ha expuesto en varias ciudades del país. Radica en San Cristóbal de Las Casas, Chis., desde 1991. Allí abandonó la pintura figurativa de sus comienzos en favor de un estilo abstracto. Premio de adquisición en el quinto Festival de Artes Plásticas de Chiapas (1997).

PEÑA, MOISÉS T. DE LA ◆ n. en Iturbide, NL (1899- ?). Economista egresado de la UNAM. Profesor de la UNAM y director del Banco Nacional Agrícola y Granadero. Autor de *El problema agrícola nacional* (1935), *Planeación del crédito ganadero* (1938), *El servicio de autobuses en el Distrito Federal* (1943), *La mexicanización del indio: problema nacional* (1945), *Veracruz económico* (1946), *Guerrero económico* (1949), *Chiapas económico* (1949), *Problemas sociales y económicos de las Mixtecas* (1960), *El pueblo y su tierra. Mito y realidad de la reforma agraria en México* (1964) y *La industria textil del algodón* (1983).

PEÑA, RAFAEL ÁNGEL DE LA ◆ n. y m. en la ciudad de México (1837-1906). Lingüista. Estudió en el Seminario Conciliar de México. Profesor del Colegio de San Juan de Letrán y de la Escuela Nacional preparatoria. Como José María Vigil, pretendió que la metafísica se incluyera como materia en el plan de estudios de la preparatoria. Autor de *Apéndice a la sintaxis latina* (1867), *Discurso sobre los elementos constantes y variables del lenguaje castellano* (1876), *Sobre los oficios lógicos y gramaticales del verbo* (1878), *Estudio sobre los oficios lógicos y gramaticales del artículo* (1881), *Estudio filológico y fonológico de algunas letras* (1884), *Discurso sobre las antinomias y deficiencias del positivismo* (1885), *Tratado del gerundio* (1889), *Gramática teórica y práctica de la lengua castellana* (1898), *Influencia de los métodos lógicos en los progresos de las ciencias* y *Tratado de sintáxis latina*. En 1875 ingresó en la Academia Mexicana (de la Lengua) y fue su secretario perpetuo desde 1883. Perteneció al Liceo Hidalgo.

PEÑA, RAÚL DE LA ◆ n. en el DF (¿1960?). Waterpolista. Delantero del equipo de water polo de la UNAM (1977-87) y hombre-boya del equipo berlinés Spandau 04 (1987-), equipo con el que ha ganado dos veces la Copa Europea y una vez el Campeonato Europeo. Fue subcampeón goleador de la Liga Alemana de Water Polo y se le calificó como mejor hombre-boya de Europa en 1987. En 1990 jugó de nuevo con el equipo de la UNAM, con el que ganó el Campeonato Nacional y el título de goleo.

PEÑA, ROBERTO ◆ n. en San Luis Potosí, SLP (1943). Licenciado en economía por la UNAM (1967) y maestro en economía por El Colegio de México (1968). Profesor de la UNAM y de la preparatoria de Ciudad Sahagún. Fue gerente de Relaciones Industriales de la Constructora Nacional de Carros de Ferrocarril (1979), gerente de Sistemas y Procedimientos de Siderúrgica Nacional (1980), subdirector de Integración y Análisis del Presupuesto Energético e Industrial de la SPP (1981); director de Administración (1984-86) y director general de Ruta 100 (1986-88). En los años noventa se convirtió en sacerdote de la Iglesia Ortodoxa.

PEÑA, RODOLFO F. ◆ n. en Ciudad Victoria, Tams., y m. en el DF (1939-1999). Periodista, hermano del anterior. Su nombre completo era Rodolfo Fernando Peña Villanueva. Fue contador público por la Escuela Bancaria y Comercial. Hizo la carrera de letras hispanoamericanas en la UNAM. Perteneció al grupo Acción Democrática Electricista y a la Tendencia Democrática del SUTERM. Fue asesor de los directores generales de Conacine (1970-76) e Imcine (1984-85) y subdirector de Promoción del Instituto Nacional del Consumidor (1985-89). Escribió los guiones de las películas *Evasión, El encuentro de un hombre solo, Cambio de vía* y *Alguien que vino de lejos*. Fue director de las revistas *Solidaridad* (1969-73) y *Transición* (1973-75), subdirector editorial de *unomásuno* (1979-81) y director del suplemento *Página Uno* (1980-83) de ese diario, así como director del suplemento *La Jornada de los Trabajadores*, de *La Jornada*. Fue colaborador de *Revista de* *la Universidad*, *El Día* (1964-68), *Siempre!* (1968-75), *El Sol de México* (1975-76), *unomásuno* (1977-83) y *La Jornada* (1984-98). Coautor de *Aún tiembla* (1987) y *La sucesión presidencial en 1988* (1987). Autor de *La mujer en nuestro mundo* (ensayo, 1975) y *Crónicas bajo protesta* (artículos periodísticos, 1982).

Peña, Sergio de la ◆ n. en Saltillo, Coah., y m. en el DF (1931-1998). Ingeniero civil egresado de la UNAM (1956), con estudios en economía y planificación en el Institute of Social Studies, de Holanda (1958-59). Trabajó para la Secretaría de la Presidencia (1959-63) y para la CEPAL (1964-72). Fue profesor e investigador del Instituto de Investigaciones Económicas y miembro del Consejo Universitario de la UNAM (1970-73). También se dedicó a la fotografía. Colaboró en *Historia y Sociedad*, *Oposición*, *El Machete*, *unomásuno* y *Excélsior*. Coautor de *¿Crecimiento o desarrollo económico? Presente y futuro de la sociedad mexicana* (1971), *El perfil de México en 1980* (1972), *En torno al capitalismo latinoamericano* (1975), *La devaluación en México* (1977), *Seis aspectos del México real* (1979), *Polémica sobre las clases sociales en el campo mexicano* (1979), *Economía y política en el México actual* (1980), *La sucesión presidencial en 1988* (1987) y *El agrarismo y la industrialización de México, 1940-1950* (1989). Autor de *Introducción a la planeación regional* (1959), *El antidesarrollo en América Latina* (1971), *La formación del capitalismo en México* (1975), *El modo de producción capitalista* (1978), *Capitalismo en cuatro comunidades rurales* (1981) y *Trabajadores y sociedad en México en el siglo XIX* (1984). Fue miembro del PCM y del PSUM.

Peña Díaz, Antonio ◆ n. en Metates, Dgo. (1936). Obtuvo el título de médico cirujano y se doctoró en bioquímica en la UNAM, donde es profesor e investigador de tiempo completo desde 1960 y ha sido coordinador del posgrado en bioquímica (1978-79) y en investigación biomédica básica (1987-89), director del Centro y el Instituto de Fisiología Celular y director del Instituto de Ciencias del Mar y Limnnología. Realizó un posdoctorado en el Albert Einstein College of Medicine de Nueva York (1964-65). Profesor visitante en las Universidades de Rochester (1969-70) y de Indiana (1975-76). Autor, editor o coeditor de 10 libros especializados. Ha escrito más de 70 artículos de divulgación y docencia y dictado ponencias en 140 congresos nacionales e internacionales Su línea de investigación es la de los mecanismos de transporte y efectos de iones sobre el metabolismo, empleando la levadura como sujeto experimental; diseñó un método para medir el pH interno de ésta, más confiable que los existentes. Miembro de la Sociedad Mexicana de Bioquímica, de la Academia de Ciencias de América Latina, de la Academia de Ciencias del Tercer Mundo, de la American Society for Biochemistry and Molecular Biology, de la American Society for Microbiology y de la Biophysical Society. Investigador emérito de la UNAM (1994). Presidente de la Academia de la Investigación Científica (1992-93).

Peña y Llerena, Rosario de la ◆ n. y m. en la ciudad de México (1847-1924). En su casa paterna se efectuaban tertulias a las que llegaron a asistir, entre otros, José Martí, Guillermo Prieto, Gabino Barreda, Francisco Sosa, Justo Sierra, José Peón Contreras, Ignacio Manuel Altamirano, Vicente Riva Palacio, Juan de Dios Peza, Ángel de Campo y Luis G. Urbina. Fue pretendida por Manuel M. Flores y por Manuel Acuña, quien escribió *Nocturno a Rosario* antes de suicidarse.

Peña López, Francisco ◆ n. en Santa María del Río y m. en San Luis Potosí, SLP (1821-1903). Historiador. Estudió en el Colegio Guadalupano Josefino y en el Convento de San Francisco de la capital potosina. Ordenado sacerdote en 1856, salió del país durante la guerra de los Tres Años. Apoyó la intervención francesa y el gobierno de Maximiliano de Habsburgo. Fue canónigo de la catedral de San Luis (1873-1900) y arcediano y vicario general de esa diócesis (1900-1903). Colaborador de la revista *El Estandarte*. Publicó unos *Documentos para la historia del obispado de San Luis Potosí* (1870). Autor de *Persecución contra el ilmo. sr. obispo de San Luis Potosí, dr. d. Pedro Barajas* (1858) y *Estudio histórico sobre San Luis Potosí* (1894).

Peña Navarro, Everardo ◆ n. en Ixtlán del Río, y m. en Tepic, Nay. (1887-1970). Historiador. En 1911 se unió a la insurrección maderista. Fue jefe de los departamentos de Turismo y Publicaciones y de Antropología e Historia del estado de Nayarit, visitador de Gobernación y Hacienda, oficial mayor del gobierno nayarita, prefecto político en San Blas, diputado federal, presidente municipal de Tepic, gobernador interino de Nayarit (1925) y director del Museo Regional. Autor de *Estudio histórico del estado de Nayarit* (1946), *Recopilación de datos históricos de la guerra de la Independencia en Nayarit*, *Misioneros y colonizadores* (1949), *Conquista en el alma. Estado de Nayarit* (1963), *La creación del Territorio de Tepic y su posterior elevación a rango de estado*, *Cuentos y leyendas nayaritas*, *Del amor y del dolor* (poemas) y *Estudios históricos sobre el general Eulogio Parra y el comandante Trinidad Ramírez*. Fue miembro del Seminario de Cultura Mexicana.

Peña y Navarro, José Antonio de la ◆ n. en Zamora y m. en Tarécuato, municipio de Tangamandapio, Mich. (1799-1877). Estudió en el Seminario de Morelia y se ordenó sacerdote en Puebla (1827). Fue prebendado y canónigo de la Catedral de Morelia en 1848 y en 1857 era gobernador de la mitra. En 1862 fue nombrado obispo *in partibus*, auxiliar de Clemente de Jesús Munguía, y en 1863 primer obispo de Zamora, diócesis que gobernó hasta su muerte.

Peña Palacios, Felipe ◆ n. y m. en Tonalá, Chis. (1899-1967). Músico. Promotor del folklor chiapaneco y director del conjunto Hermanos Peña Ríos. Entre sus composiciones figuran: *Linda tierra chiapaneca*, *Primavera*, *Tres preguntas*, *Zanatenco*, *Tonalá*, *Lindas tonaltecas*, *Sarabua*, *Noche de amor*, *Himno a Juárez* y *Minatitlán*.

Gabinetes del presidente Manuel de la Peña y Peña[1]

16 de septiembre al 13 de noviembre de 1847

Ministerio de Relaciones Interiores y Exteriores	
José María Ortiz Monasterio, ED[2]	16 al 26 de septiembre de 1847
Luis de la Rosa	27 de septiembre al 11 de nov. de 1847
Ministerio de Justicia	
Luis de la Rosa	26 de septiembre al 13 de nov. de 1847
Ministerio de Guerra y Marina	
Luis de la Rosa	26 de septiembre al 13 de nov. de 1847
Ministerio de Hacienda	
Luis de la Rosa	27 de septiembre al 13 de nov. de 1847

[1] Al ocupar los invasores estadounidenses la capital mexicana, Santa Anna huyó y por ministerio de ley correspondió a Peña y Peña, presidente de la Suprema Corte de Justicia, ejercer el Poder Ejecutivo. Éste se trasladó a Toluca y el país quedó, de hecho, sin gobierno interior hasta que se procedió al nombramiento de ministros. Formalmente, sólo se despacharon los asuntos de la Cancillería, debido a los mecanismos de sustitución automática que rigen en esa cartera

[2] ED= Encargado del Despacho

8 de enero al 3 de junio de 1848

Secretaría de Relaciones Interiores y Exteriores	
Luis de la Rosa	9 de enero al 3 de junio de 1848
Secretaría de Justicia	
José María Durán	8 de enero al 3 de junio de 1848
Secretaría de Guerra y Marina	
Pedro María Anaya	9 de enero al 3 de junio de 1848
Secretaría de Hacienda	
Luis de la Rosa	8 de enero al 3 de junio de 1848

Archivo General de la Nación

Retrato y firma de Manuel de la Peña y Peña

Peña y Peña, Manuel de la ◆ n. y m. en la ciudad de México (1789-1850). Se tituló de abogado en 1811. Fue síndico del Ayuntamiento de la ciudad de México (1813), promotor fiscal de la Capitanía General, auditor de guerra y ministro suplente de la Audiencia de Guadalajara. En 1820 la Corona española lo designó oidor de Quito, pero a la proclamación del Plan de Iguala (1821) prefirió quedarse en México. Fue magistrado de la Audiencia territorial durante la regencia y, en el imperio de Agustín de Iturbide, consejero de Estado, encargado de las fiscalías de Hacienda y del Crimen y ministro plenipotenciario en Colombia (la caída del gobierno dejó sin efecto la designación). En 1824 era ministro de la Suprema Corte de Justicia de la Nación. Ministro del Interior (del 27 de abril al 24 de octubre de 1837), en el gobierno de Anastasio Bustamante. En noviembre de 1838 pasó a formar parte del Supremo Poder Conservador. Cinco años más tarde, en 1843, redactó un código civil y, como miembro de la Junta Nacional Legislativa, participó en la elaboración de las Bases Orgánicas (1843). Profesor de la Universidad, presidente de la Academia de Jurisprudencia y rector del Colegio de Abogados, fue consejero honorario de Gobierno (1843), senador de la República, ministro de Relaciones Interiores y Exteriores (del 14 de agosto al 13 de diciembre de 1845) en el gobierno de José Joaquín de Herrera y ministro plenipotenciario en Roma (1845). Al inicio de la guerra contra Estados Unidos era presidente de la Suprema Corte de Justicia. El 26 septiembre de 1847, luego de las derrotas de Churubusco, Molino del Rey y Chapultepec, la ocupación de la ciudad de México y la huida del presidente Antonio López de Santa Anna hacia Puebla, ocupó la Presidencia de la República. Trasladó la capital a Toluca y el 13 de noviembre entregó el poder a Pedro María Anaya, en cuyo gabinete fue ministro de Relaciones (del 14 de noviembre de 1847 al 8 de enero de 1848). Para acelerar las negociaciones de paz con los invasores, el 8 de enero de 1848 volvió a ocuparse del Poder Ejecutivo. Durante su gobierno se ratificó el tratado de rendición (☛ *Tratado de Guadalupe-Hidalgo*), el 2 de febrero. Dejó el poder el 3 de junio de 1848 y al año siguiente fue elegido gobernador del Estado de México (del 22 de marzo al 10 de mayo de 1849). Perteneció a la Academia de San Carlos, a la Sociedad Médica y a la Sociedad de Amigos del País. Autor de *Lecciones de práctica forense mexicana*.

Peña y Ramírez, Manuel ◆ n. en Alfajayucan, hoy en el estado de Hgo., y m. en Querétaro, Qro. (?-1867). Se tituló como abogado en la Escuela Nacional de Jurisprudencia. Fue diputado al Congreso Constituyente de 1856-57 y diputado federal a la III Legislatura (1861-63). Durante la guerra contra los invasores franceses y el imperio de Maximiliano, se encargó de la Secretaría de Gobierno y de la Comandancia Política y Militar del Segundo Distrito Militar del Estado de México (el actual estado de Hidalgo) y, en 1867 asistió al sitio de Querétaro, donde murió en combate.

Peña y Reyes, Antonio de la ◆ n. y m. en la ciudad de México (1869-1928). Abogado. Hijo de Rafael Ángel de la Peña y discípulo de Ignacio Manuel Altamirano. Fue director de la revista *La Reelección* (1908-10), diputado federal, secretario particular del presidente Francisco León de la Barra, ministro plenipotenciario y subsecretario de Relaciones Exteriores, encargado del despacho, en el gobierno de Victoriano Huerta (del 25 al 30 de septiembre de 1913). Al triunfo del constitucionalismo se exilió en Cuba, donde fundó *El Escolar Urbano*. A su regreso a México, redactó 21 volúmenes del *Archivo histórico diplomático mexicano*, dirigido por Genaro Estrada. Colaborador de los periódicos *El Nacional*, *El Siglo* XIX, *El Renacimiento*, *La República* y *El Partido Liberal*. Autor de *Algunos poetas* (1889), *Cartilla popular de ortografía* (1915), *Vidas y tiempos* (1915), *Antología moral* (1920), *La diplomacia mexicana* (1923), *Vivos y muertos* y *Artículos y discursos*. Fue miembro de la Academia Mexicana (de la Lengua).

Peña Reyes, Humberto ◆ n. en San Agustín del Palmar, municipio de Tezonapa, Ver. (1947). Licenciado en economía por la Universidad Veracruzana (1966-70). Ha sido secretario de Comercialización (1977-80) y secretario general (1980-) de la Unión Nacional de Productores de Hule, secretario de comercialización de la Liga de Comunidades Agrarias y Sindicatos Campesinos de Veracruz y diputado federal (1988-91).

Peña Terán, Joaquín de la ◆ n. en San Juan del Río, Qro., y m. en el DF (1892-1959). Militar e industrial. Estudió en el Colegio Militar hasta 1912. Al año siguiente se incorporó a las fuerzas de Guillermo Rubio Navarrete y más tarde pasó a la División del Norte. Comandó las tropas villistas de Querétaro en 1915 y luego de las derrotas de Francisco Villa en el Bajío se rindió al ejército obregonista. Fue gobernador interino de Querétaro (del 15 de diciembre de 1923 al 25 de agosto de 1924), diputado federal y oficial mayor del Departamento Central del Distrito Federal. Se retiró del ejército en 1935 y se dedicó a atender sus negocios, como la empacadora de alimentos Ibero-Mex. Presidió la Financiera de las Industrias de Transformación y la Cámara Nacional de la Industria de Transformación.

Peñafiel, Antonio ◆ n. en Atotonilco el Grande, Hgo., y m. en la ciudad de México (1830-1922). Médico e historiador. Su apellido materno era Barranco. Estudió en el Instituto Científico y Literario del Estado de Hidalgo y en la Escuela Nacional de Medicina. Interrumpió la carrera en 1862 y se incorporó a las fuerzas de Ignacio Zaragoza para combatir al ejército francés. Participó en la defensa de Puebla. Al triunfo de la República se graduó y fue profesor en el Hospital Militar de San Lucas, subinspector del cuerpo médico militar (1870) y fundador de la Sociedad de Historia Natural, durante el gobierno de Lerdo de Tejada fue diputado federal por Hidalgo (1873-75); presentó algunas iniciativas para legislar en materia de minería, agricultura y ganadería. Fue director general de Estadística y en 1895 dirigió el censo de la República. En 1899 fue comisionado a la Exposición de París, junto con Antonio M. Anza. Promovió la edición de numerosas obras relativas a la historia antigua de México, como el Códice Fernández Leal, el *Arte mexicano* de Antonio del Rincón, los *Cuatro libros de la naturaleza* de Francisco Ximénez, el *Diccionario tarasco* de Maturnino Gilberti y el *Arte de la lengua tarasca* de Diego Basalenque. Autor de *Monumentos del arte mexicano*, *Memoria sobre las aguas potables en la ciudad de México* (1884), *Nomenclatura geográfica, etimológica y jeroglífica*, *Teotihuacan, estudio histórico y arqueológico*; *Indumentaria antigua mexicana*, *Fábulas de Esopo, traducidas al mexicano*; *Cerámica mexicana y loza de Talavera de Puebla*, *Nombres geográficos de México*, *Época colonial y moderna*, *Alfabetos adornados aztecas*, *Cuadro sinóptico y estadístico de la República Mexicana* y *Ciudades coloniales y capitales de la República Mexicana* (1911). Perteneció al Instituto Internacional de Estadística y a las sociedades Mexicana de Geografía y Estadística, Científica Antonio Alzate, de Economía Política de París y de Filología Americana.

Peñaflor Gutiérrez, David ◆ n. en Irapuato y m. en la hacienda La Ordeña, Gto. (1888-1917). En su juventud fue ferrocarrilero y petrolero: trabajó en la Compañía El Águila de Tampico. Se incorporó al constitucionalismo en 1913 en el Ejército del Noreste y combatió en Tamaulipas, San Luis Potosí y Guanajuato. Participó en la ofensiva obregonista contra la División del Norte en el Bajío (1915), pero fue apresado por los villistas. Escapó en Aguascalientes y se reincorporó a las fuerzas carrancistas. Fue comandante militar de Guanajuato (1916) y diputado al Congreso Constituyente de 1916-17. Volvió al ejército luego de proclamada la nueva Constitución. Murió en una emboscada.

Peñalosa, Javier ◆ n. y m. en el DF (1921-1977). Periodista y poeta de formación autodidacta. Profesor de la Escuela de Periodismo Carlos Septién García y del Colegio de Ciencias y Humanidades. Fue director del taller de periodismo de la Universidad Iberoamericana, director del Centro Nacional de Documentación e Información Educativa y del Museo Pedagógico de la Secretaría de Educación Pública. En *México en la Cultura*, suplemento de *Novedades*, escribió la columna "Nombres, títulos y hechos". Colaboró en los diarios *Excélsior* y *Novedades*; en las revistas *Ábside*, *La Palabra y el Hombre*, *Tiras de Colores*, *Nivel*, *Rueca*, *América*, *Acento*, *Poesía de América* y *Proceso*, en cuya fundación participó (1976-77). Redactó el prólogo de *Los miserables*, de Víctor Hugo, para la Editorial Porrúa. Coautor de *Ocho poetas mexicanos*. Autor de *Preludio en sombra* (1946), *La noche nueva* (1960) y *Paso de la memoria* (1965). Ganó flores naturales en concursos literarios de Culiacán y Aguascalientes. Fue secretario de la Asociación Continental de Intelectuales de América.

Peñalosa, Joaquín Antonio ◆ n. en San Luis Potosí, SLP (1922). Estudió en el Seminario de San Luis Potosí. Fue ordenado sacerdote en 1947. Doctor en letras por la UIA (1955). Profesor de la UASLP y del Instituto Tecnológico Regional de esa entidad (1969-). Es fundador de la la revista *Estilo*. Colaborador de *Señal*, *Ábside*, *Familia Cristiana* y *Letras Potosinas*. Autor de *Pájaros de la tarde* (poesía, 1948), *Canciones litúrgicas* (1948), *Ejercicios para las bestezuelas de Dios* (poesía, 1951), *Francisco González Bocanegra. Su vida y obra* (1954), *Diego José Abad, poeta castellano* (1955), *Luis de Mendizábal, fabulista de la independencia* (1956), *Siete poemas* (1959), *Toros, box y moral católica* (1960), *Escenarios del amor* (1960), *Canciones para entretener la Nochebuena* (1961), *Sonetos desde la esperanza* (1962), *Vocabulario y refranero religioso de México* (1965), *La práctica religiosa en México, siglo XVI; asedios de sociología religiosa* (1969), *El mexicano y los siete pecados capitales* (1972), *Pasión y muerte de un mexicano* (1973), *Cien mexicanos y Dios* (1975), *Humor con agua bendita* (1977), *Flor y canto de poesía guadalupana. Siglo XX* (1984), *Flor y canto de poesía guadalupana. Siglo XIX* (1985), *Flor y canto de poesía guadalupana. Siglo XVIII* (1987) y *Flor y canto de poesía guadalupana. Siglo XVII* y *Vida, pasión y muerte del mexicano*, entre otras obras. Pertenece a la Academia Mexicana (de la Lengua), a la Sociedad Folklórica de México y al Seminario de Cultura Mexicana.

Peñalosa Castro, Javier ◆ n. en DF (1955). Editor y periodista. Egresado de la Escuela de Periodismo Carlos Septién García, en la que ha sido profesor de historia de la literatura. También ha impartido clases de redacción periodística y trabajo editorial y de imprenta en la ENEP Acatlán, de la UNAM. Ha sido subdirector de noticieros de Imevisión (1983-85), subdirector de

Estudios y Promoción de Servicios de Telecomunicaciones de México (1989-90), subdirector de Difusión de la Dirección General de Autotransporte Urbano (1992), colaborador y coordinador de redacción del diario *El Economista* (1993-96), director creativo asociado en la empresa Imagen y Comunicación Organizacional y editor del periódico *El asesor comercial* (1997-98), subdirector (1998-99) y director de Información del Gobierno del Distrito Federal (1999-).

Peñaloza, Pedro José ◆ n. en el DF (1953). Licenciado en economía por la UNAM (1971-75). Militó en la Juventud Marxista Revolucionaria y en la Liga Socialista, organización que en 1977 se incorporó al Partido Revolucionario de los Trabajadores, en el que fue miembro del Comité Central (1979-87) y del Comité Político (1980-87), representante del partido a la fundación del Frente Nacional Contra la Represión, coordinador electoral (1981) y vocero de su partido. Diputado federal a la LIII Legislatura (1985-88) y coordinador de la fracción parlamentaria del PRT (1985-87), organización de la que se separó en 1987. Al año siguiente participó en la fundación del Movimiento al Socialismo y fue fundador del PRD. Fue miembro de la ARDF (1994-97) y coordinador de Participación Ciudadana para la Prevención del Delito del gobierno de la ciudad de México (1997-). Ha colaborado en *Siempre!*, *El Universal*, *Excélsior*, *Época* y *El Nacional*. Autor de *Génesis y crisis de la prostitución en México* y *Crisis económica y seguridad pública en México*.

Pedro Peñaloza

Foto: Michael Calderwood

Peñasco, Sonora

Foto: Michael Calderwood

Peñasco, Sonora

Peñaloza Martínez, Faustino ◆ n. en el DF (1940). Escultor. Licenciado (1969) y maestro en artes plásticas por la UNAM (1982). Profesor de la Academia de San Carlos, de la Escuela de Pintura y Escultura La Esmeralda y del Colegio de Ciencias y Humanidades. Fue coordinador del área de Escultura del INBA (1984) y secretario académico de La Esmeralda (1984). Expuso por primera vez en 1962. Ha participado en las bienales del Museo de Arte Moderno. En 1969 obtuvo el primer lugar en el Certamen Nacional de Proyectos de Escultura Monumental a los Niños Héroes de Chapultepec, organizado en Culiacán.

Peñamiller ◆ Municipio de Querétaro situado en el norte del estado, al norte de Cadereyta, en los límites con Guanajuato. Superficie: 795 km^2. Habitantes: 17,748, de los cuales 3,506 forman la población económicamente activa. Hablan alguna lengua indígena 20 personas mayores de cinco años (otomí 15).

Peñas Alarnes, José de las ◆ n. en España (1921). Vitralista. Estudió en la Escuela de Bellas Artes de San Fernando, en España (1934-36) y en Alemania. Vive en México desde 1952. Es autor de los vitrales de la iglesia de San Agustín, en Polanco (1958), de los hoteles María Isabel Sheraton de la ciudad de México (1962) y Hilton de Acapulco (1964), del templo de Nuestra Señora de la Paz de Guadalajara (1968) y de la Biblioteca Central de la UNAM (1969). Ha realizado obras similares en Japón, Estados Unidos y Arabia Saudita.

Peñasco ◆ Punta de Sonora, saliente del litoral del golfo de California, que señala el límite noroeste de la bahía de San Jorge. Al oeste se abre la bahía de Punta Peñasco. Es un centro turístico y la población ahí establecida cuenta con una planta para la destilación de agua marina.

Peñitas ◆ Presa construida sobre el río Grijalva, en el municipio chiapaneco de Ostuacán, en los límites con Tabasco. Su cortina mide 50 metros de altura. Alimenta una planta hidroeléctrica capaz de producir 420,000 kiliovatios-hora. El embalse tiene una superficie aproximada de 65 km^2. Comenzó a producir energía a fines de 1986.

Peñoles ◆ Empresa minera fundada en 1887 en Mapimí, Durango, por el español José M. Bermejillo y los estadounidenses Charles Reidt y Jacobo Langeloth. Pasó después a manos de un consorcio alemán y en la actualidad pertenece al grupo Bailleres. Extrae una gran variedad de metales de sus minas situadas en diversos puntos del país.

Peñón ◆ Sierra de San Luis Potosí y Zacatecas. Es una de las estribaciones septentrionales de la sierra de Zacatecas. Se extiende de oeste-suroeste a este-noreste, a lo largo del límite entre ambos estados. Su punta más alta es el cerro del Peñón Blanco.

Peñón de los Baños ◆ Cerro de origen volcánico situado en el centro de la cuenca de México, al suroeste del vaso de Texcoco. En la parte sur de su base hay manatiales de aguas sulfurosas a las que se atribuyen propiedades terapéuticas. Según la mitología náhuatl, en el cerro se refugió Copil, sobrino de Huitzilopochtli, cuando intentó expulsar a los mexicas de la cuenca de México. Guiados por una orden de Huitzilopochtli, los sacerdotes aztecas asesinaron a Copil y arrojaron su corazón a un cañaveral; en ese sitio nació el tunal que fue la señal del dios para la fundación de la capital mexica. Otra versión supone que del corazón de Copil nacieron las aguas termales.

PEÑÓN BLANCO ◆ Municipio de Durango situado al suroeste de Gómez Palacio y al noreste de la capital del estado. Superficie: 1,827 km². Habitantes: 11,272, de los cuales 2,456 forman la población económicamente activa. Hablan alguna lengua indígena 14 personas mayores de cinco años. En la jurisdicción se encuentra el balneario La Concha.

PEÑÓN DEL MARQUÉS ◆ Cerro del Distrito Federal situado al noreste del cerro de la Estrella y al sureste del Peñon de los Baños. En tiempos prehispánicos fue un islote del lago de Texcoco, llamado Tepepolco. Moctezuma Xocoyotzin lo utilizó como lugar de descanso. En la Colonia cambió de nombre, debido a que en 1521, durante el sitio de Tenochtitlan, Hernán Cortés, futuro marqués del valle de Oaxaca, instaló ahí su cuartel general antes de dirigirse a Coyoacán. En el presente siglo se la ha conocido también como el cerro del Peñón Viejo. En la década de los años setenta quedó dentro de la mancha urbana.

PEÓN, RAMÓN ◆ n. en Cuba y m. en Puerto Rico (1897-1970). Director de cine. Llegó a México a principios de los años treinta, luego de haber realizado varias películas en Cuba. Aquí dirigió *La Llorona* (1933), *Sagrario* (1933), *Tiburón* (1933), *Mujeres sin alma* (1934), *Oro y plata* (1934), *Tierra, amor y dolor* (1934), *Todo un hombre* (1935), *Sor Juana Inés de la Cruz* (1935), *Silencio sublime* (1935), *Más allá de la muerte* (1935), *¿Qué hago con la criatura?* (1935), *Mujeres de hoy* (1936), *Los chicos de la prensa* (1936), *El bastardo* (1937), *La llaga* (1937), *No basta ser madre* (1937), *Mujer mexicana* (1937), *Entre hermanos* (1944), *Flor de un día* (1945), *Papá Lebonard* (1945), *Espinas de una flor* (1945), *Usted tiene ojos de mujer fatal* (1945), *El cocinero de mi mujer* (1946), *Rocambole* (1946), *Ahí vienen los Mendoza* (1948), *Opio* (1949), *Festín de buitres* (1949), *Nunca debieron amarse* (1951), *Pueblo quieto* (1954), *Música, amor y espuelas* (1954), *El Águila Negra* (1954), *El tesoro de la muerte* (1954), *El vengador de la muerte* (1954), *La ley de los fuertes* (1956), *Los enmascarados de la muerte* (1956) y *Los diablos de la pradera* (1956). En su película *La madrina del diablo* (1937) se inició como actor cinematográfico Jorge Negrete.

PEÓN Y CANO, MANUEL ALBINO ◆ n. en Mérida, Yuc., y m. en Italia (1811-1878). Fue comisario imperial de Puebla durante el gobierno de Maximiliano de Habsburgo (1865-66) y prefecto imperial de Orizaba. Huyó de México al triunfo de la República.

PEÓN CONTRERAS, JOSÉ ◆ n. en Mérida, Yuc., y m. en la ciudad de México (1843-1907). Médico y escritor. Se graduó en 1862, en el Instituto de Ciencias y Literatura de Mérida. Al año siguiente se trasladó a la ciudad de México, donde trabajó en el Hospital de Jesús (1863-65) y dirigió el Hospital de Dementes de San Hipólito (1867-?). Profesor de la Escuela Nacional de Medicina y de la Escuela de Medicina de Mérida. Fue varias veces diputado y senador por Yucatán y Nuevo León. En 1871 apoyó la reelección del presidente Benito Juárez. Autor de poesía: *Poesías* (1868), *Romances históricos mexicanos* (1871) y *Trovas colombinas* (1881); novelas: *Taide* (1885) y *La veleidosa* (1891); y de obras dramáticas: *El Castigo de Dios* (1861-62), *El conde Santiesteban* (1861-62), *María la loca* (1861-62), *¡Hasta el cielo!* (1876), *El sacrificio de la vida* (1876), *Luchas de honra y amor* (1876), *La hija del rey* (1876), *Gil González de Ávila* (1876), *Un amor de Hernán Cortés* (1876), *Antón de Alaminos* (1876), *Juan de Villalpando* (1876), *Esperanza* (1876), *El conde de Peñalva* (1877), *La ermita de Santa Fe* (1877), *Entre mi tío y mi tía* (1878), *Doña Leonor de Sarabia* (1878), *Por el joyel del sombrero* (1878), *El capitán Pedreñales* (1879), *Vivo o muerto* (1879), *Impulsos del corazón* (1879), *El umbral de la dicha* (1885), *La cruz del perdón*, *El bardo* (1886), *Gabriela* (1888), *La cabeza de Uconor* (1890), *Soledad* (1892), *Laureana* (1893), *Una tormenta en el mar* (1893) y *¡Por la patria!* (1894), que fueron reunidas en *Obras dramáticas en verso y prosa* (1879) y *Obras de José Peón y Contreras* (1896). También fue compositor e hizo populares algunas de sus canciones, como *La despedida*, *La mestiza* y *Aquí estoy*. Perteneció a la Academia Mexicana (de la Lengua).

FOTO: CLAUDIO CONTRERAS

Busto de José Peón Contreras en el teatro que lleva su nombre, en Mérida, Yucatán.

PEÓN DEL VALLE, JOSÉ ◆ n. en Orizaba, Ver., y m. en EUA (1866-1924). Abogado y escritor. Hijo de José Peón Contreras. Se graduó en 1893 en la Escuela Nacional de Jurisprudencia. Fue agente del Ministerio Público, juez cuarto de lo criminal, diputado a la Legislatura veracruzana (1904-06), vicepresidente del Partido Democrático, que en 1808 apoyó la candidatura de Bernardo Reyes, y nuevamente diputado local (1910-11). Renunció al triunfo de la insurrección maderista. Deportado a Cuba en 1916, en 1920 se instaló en Nueva York. Colaboró en los periódicos cubanos *La Nación*, *Universal*, *Cuba y América* y *Diario de la Marina*. Autor de *Vibraciones y cadencias* (1886), *Poemas y versos* (1903), *Tierra nihilista. Recuerdos de Rusia* (1907), *Brumas del norte (leyendas y tradiciones)* (1907) y *Cuba victrix (romancero de las guerras de independencia)* (1918).

PERAL, MIGUEL ÁNGEL ◆ n. en Chiautla, Pue. (1900-?). Participó en la revolución. Estudió periodismo en la Universidad Interamericana de Nueva York. Dirigió diversos periódicos en Estados Unidos: *El dictamen*, en Brownsville; *Anáhuac*, en El Paso; *El Nacional*, en Chicago; y *La Patria*, en Detroit. En México dirigió *Evolución* y *Política y políticos*. Autor de *México, sus detractores y defensores* (1936), *Diccionario biográfi-*

Ángela Peralta

co mexicano (1944), *El pelelismo en México* (1951), *Miguel Alemán, presidente de México* (1952) y *Diccionario histórico, biográfico, geográfico e industrial de la República Mexicana* (1960), además de novelas y obras teatrales como *Por qué se pierden ellas* (1933), *La mujer de todos y de nadie* (1934) y *Amémonos hoy y olvidémonos mañana* (1938).

Alejo Peralta

Carlos Peralta

Elda Peralta

PERALTA, ALEJO ◆ n. en Puebla, Pue., y m. en el DF (1916-1997). Su nombre completo era Alejo Peralta y Díaz Ceballos. Ingeniero mecánico electricista titulado en 1935 por la ESIME del IPN. Era director del Instituto Politécnico Nacional, en 1956, cuando la fuerza pública invadió y clausuró el internado de la institución. Propietario y fundador de los equipos de beisbol profesional *Aztecas* (1953) y *Tigres* (1955). En 1957 se inició como proveedor de materiales eléctricos del gobierno federal. Era dueño de más de 60 empresas, agrupadas en el consorcio Industrias Unidas, S.A. (IUSA), uno de los más poderosos del país.

PERALTA, ÁNGELA ◆ n. en la ciudad de México y m. en Mazatlán, Sin. (1845-1883). Cantante de ópera y compositora. Su apellido materno era Castera. En el Conservatorio Nacional de Música estudió solfeo con Manuel Barragán, piano con Agustín Balderas y piano y composición con Cenobio Paniagua. Se inició profesionalmente en 1860, en el Teatro Nacional, en el papel de Leonora de *El trovador*, de Guiseppe Verdi. Entre 1861 y 1865 vivió en Italia, donde estudió con Pietro Lampertti y se presentó en la Scala de Milán (1862). Actuó en Cuba, España, Estados Unidos, Grecia, Portugal y Rusia. En Europa fue conocida como *el Ruiseñor Mexicano*. A su regreso a México, cantó para el gobierno de Maximiliano de Habsburgo y formó su propia compañía. Tocaba piano y arpa. Compuso los valses, danzas, fantasías, mazurcas y chotises *Né m'oublie pas, Pensando en ti, Absence, Nostalgia, Io t'ameró, Eugenio, Margarita, Un recuerdo a mi patria, Adiós a México, El deseo, Sara, México, Ilusión, María, Retour*, y *Lejos de ti*. Murió de cólera durante una gira.

PERALTA, ANTONIO ◆ n. en Zumpango de la Laguna, Edo. de Méx., y m. en Pátzcuaro, Mich. (1668-1736). Teólogo jesuita. Profesor de filosofía y teología en Puebla y México. Fue provincial de la Compañía. Autor de *Dissertationes Scholasticae de sma. Virgine Maria, Dissertationes Scholasticae de Divina Scientia Media, De Divinis Decretis* y *Dissertationes Scholasticae de Sancto Josepho*.

PERALTA, BRAULIO ◆ n. en Tuxpan, Ver. (1953). Licenciado en periodismo y literatura dramática y teatro por la UNAM. Ha trabajó como periodista desde 1976 en Radio Educación y los periódicos *El Día, unomásuno* y *La Jornada*, donde fue coordinador de la sección de cultura (1993-1997) y corresponsal en España (1988-93 y 1997-98). Director y fundador de la revista *Equis* (1998-). Coautor de *Creatur Principium*, coordinador de *Tres generaciones (la visión plástica de Francisco Toledo, Julio Galán y Rodolfo Morales)* y autor de *De un mundo raro* (crónica y entrevista, 1997), *El poeta en su tierra: Diálogos con Octavio Paz* (entrevista, 1997). Premio El Gallo Pitagórico otorgado por los reporteros del Festival Internacional Cervantino.

PERALTA, CARLOS ◆ n. el DF (1953). Empresario. Hijo de Alejo Peralta (☛). Al morir su padre, heredó el control del grupo IUSA, pero ya antes había participado en su expansión y era presidente de Iusacell, subsidiaria dedicada a ofrecer servicios de telefonía celular. Ha sido fundador de la Asociación Mexicana de Concesionarios de Telefonía Celular y miembro del grupo financiero Asemex-Banpaís, el Grupo Mexicano de Video y Cambridge Lee.

PERALTA, ELDA ◆ n. en Hermosillo, Son. (1932). Actriz y escritora. Colaboró en *El Heraldo Cultural*. Coautora de *Las mujeres de la torre* (1996) y *Veneno que fascina* (1997). Autora de ensayo: *La época de oro sin nostalgia. Luis Spota en el cine 1949-59* (1988); biografía: *Luis Spota. Las sustancias de la tierra. Una biografía íntima* (1990); novela: *Nocturno mar sin espuma* (1998); y cuento: *Remedios para olvidar* (1999).

PERALTA, GASTÓN DE ◆ n. en Francia y m. en España (¿1510?-1587). Tercer virrey de la Nueva España (1566-67). Llegó a Veracruz en septiembre de 1566. Durante su gobierno enfrentó la agitación provocada por los procesos y ejecuciones generados por la conspiración de Martín Cortés y suspendió la ejecución de Luis y Martín Cortés, hijos del conquistador. La Audiencia pidió su remoción y regresó a España en 1568. Durante su gobierno, abrió un hospital para viejos, inválidos, convalecientes y locos. Tenía el título de marqués de Falces.

PERALTA, JAIME ◆ n. en Cuernavaca, Mor. (1954). Caricaturista. Comenzó a trabajar en *El Diario del Sur*. Su trabajos han aparecido en *Los Universitarios, Cine Mundial* y *La Garrapata*.

PERALTA, MIGUEL ÁNGEL ◆ n. en Chilpancingo, Gro., y m. en Huitzilac, Mor. (1889-1927). Militar. Estudió en el Seminario Teológico Presbiteriano de Coyoacán, donde fue ordenado ministro evangelista. Se levantó en armas en 1913 y combatió en las filas constitucionalistas. Fue diputado federal, jefe del Estado Mayor de Benjamín Hill y oficial mayor de la Secretaría de Guerra y Marina en 1919. En ese año mató al general Juan Banderas, *el Agachado*, en una riña a las puertas de la pastelería El Globo, de la ciudad de México. Fue procesado y absuelto. Representante de México en Perú (1922) y director del

Colegio Militar (1923-25). En 1927, ya como general de brigada, se unió al grupo promotor de la candidatura de Francisco Serrano y fue asesinado con éste en Huitzilac.

PERALTA LÓPEZ, JOSÉ MARÍA ◆ n. y m. en Villahermosa, Tab. (1928-1995). Licenciado en derecho por el Instituto Juárez de Tabasco (1952). Fue profesor y director de la Escuela de Derecho de la Universidad Juárez Autónoma de Tabasco. Fue agente del Ministerio Público, procurador general del Justicia de la entidad (1977-82), presidente del Tribunal Superior de Justicia (1983-85), secretario general de gobierno (1985-87) y gobernador sustituto de Tabasco (1987-88).

PERALTA RODRÍGUEZ, ALBERTO ◆ n. en Hermosillo, Son., y m. en el DF (1890-1950). En 1909 se integró al Club Antirreeleccionista de Guaymas. En 1913 se levantó en armas contra la dictadura de Victoriano Huerta. Combatió a las órdenes de Benjamín Hill y Plutarco Elías Calles. En 1914 era administrador general de bienes ausentes en Sonora. Fue diputado por Morelia al Congreso Constituyente de 1916-17, diputado federal, comandante militar de Guanajuato, oficial mayor de la Contraloría General de la República y presidente de la Comisión Reorganizadora de Secretarías y Departamentos de Estado en el gobierno de Álvaro Obregón; gerente liquidador del Ferrocarril Nacional de Tehuantepec y subjefe y jefe provisional de la policía del Distrito Federal y jefe del Departamento de Licencias e Inspección del Departamento Central, durante la presidencia de Pascual Ortiz Rubio. También se dedicó a la invención de instrumentos científicos.

PERAZA Y CÁRDENAS, MARTÍN FRANCISCO ◆ n. y m. en Mérida, Yuc. (1804-1872). Militar. Ingresó al ejército colonial en 1816. En 1823 era comandante del puerto yucateco de Sisal. En 1832 se levantó en armas contra el gobierno de Anastasio Bustamante. Al triunfo de la rebelión fue nombrado comandante militar del puerto de Tampico. En 1835, se vinculó con Valentín Gómez Farías, Lorenzo de Zavala y José Antonio Mejía; estuvo con ellos en Nueva Orleans, en la conspiración de la Junta Anfictiónica. Acompañó a Zavala a Texas y fue aprehendido en El Álamo. Estuvo preso un año en Galveston. Regresó a Yucatán en 1840, se unió al movimiento separatista y fue designado secretario de Guerra y Marina de Yucatán, en el gobierno de Gregorio Méndez. En esa condición, al año siguiente se embarcó para adquirir armamento y firmó una alianza militar con Mirabeau B. Lamar, presidente de la República de Texas. Fue diputado local (1846) y federal (1852-53) y gobernador de Yucatán (del 10 de diciembre de 1857 al 3 de octubre de 1858) hasta que lo derrocó el alzamiento de Liborio Irigoyen y Cárdenas. En 1863 reconoció al imperio, pero más tarde se incorporó a las filas republicanas. Desde 1869 fue presidente de la Junta Auxiliar en Mérida de la Sociedad Mexicana de Geografía y Estadística.

PERAZA MEDINA, FERNANDO ◆ n. en Yucatán (1908). Licenciado en derecho por la Universidad de Yucatán (1942). Ha sido fundador y secretario de Acción Educativa de las Juventudes Socialistas de México (1935-42), militante (1935-43) y miembro del buró político del Comité Estatal de Yucatán del Partido Comunista Mexicano (1936-42); regidor del ayuntamiento de Mérida (1938), fundador y militante de los partidos Popular (1948-61) y Popular Socialista (1961-71), diputado federal (1967-70), miembro del Comité Central del PPS (1968-71), candidato a la gubernatura de Yucatán (1969), fundador, miembro del Comité Central y miembro de la Comisión Ejecutiva del Partido del Pueblo Mexicano (1977-81); nuevamente diputado federal (1979-82) y cofundador y miembro del Comité Central del Partido Socialista Unificado de México.

PERAZA OJEDA, HUMBERTO ◆ n. en Mérida, Yuc. (1925). Escultor. Licenciado y maestro en artes plásticas por la UNAM (1955), donde es profesor. En 1945 colaboró con Alfred Just en la decoración de la Plaza de Toros México. Expuso por primera vez en 1952. Se ha especializado en figuras taurinas de bronce. Son obra suya las estatuas de Balderas (1954) y Juan Silveti (1960) que se encuentran en el Toreo de Cuatro Caminos; la ecuestre del general Joaquín Amaro, en el Campo Marte (1958); las de Rodolfo Gaona (1960) y Carmen Anaya (1962), el conjunto *El encierro y el Monumento a la tauromaquia* en la plaza de toros de Tijuana (1961); *La fuente de los niños*, en Hermosillo (1963); un toro de bronce (1965) y el Lorenzo Garza de la plaza de San Luis Potosí (1977); una estatua dedicada al ballet, en Cuernavaca; una Virgen del Carmen, en Tampico (1967); *La sirena y el tritón*, en el Parque Industrial de Naucalpan (1968); el Carlos Arruza (1969) y el Fermín Espinosa *Armillita* de la plaza México (1973); las estatuas de Agustín Lara (1972), Tata Nacho (1973) y Mario Talavera de la SACM (1973); la de Javier Rojo Gómez, en Hidalgo (1972); la de *Cri-Crí*, en Orizaba (1972); Benito Juárez en Irapuato (1973) y Ecatepec (1973); Felipe Carrilo Puerto en Mérida y la ciudad de México (1973); Federico García Lorca, en San Luis Potosí (1973); el Pedro Infante, de Garibaldi, DF (1973); los bustos de Manuel Ramos Arizpe, Crescencio Rejón, Mariano Otero, Ignacio Vallarta, José María Morelos y Emilio Rabasa de la Biblioteca del Congreso de la Unión (1973); *Los Patos*, en Teapa (1973); el Agustín Lara de Veracruz (1974); el *Pegaso* del patio central del Palacio Nacional (1975); un busto de Hank González en Toluca (1978) y otro de Ricardo Flores Magón frente al Congreso del Trabajo, del DF (1978); la escultura monumental de Nezahualcóyotl, en la carretera Texcoco-Pirámides (1978); las estatuas de Eloy Cavazos en Villa de Guadalupe, Monterrey (1979), y de Silverio Pérez, en la plaza de Texcoco (1980); el busto de Jorge Jiménez Cantú, en Toluca (1980); y una estatua de Antonio Dehesa Ulloa en Chihuahua (1980).

Gastón de Peralta

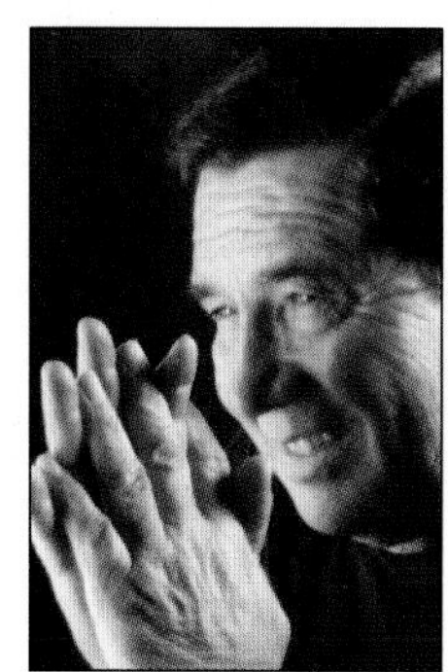

Humberto Peraza Ojeda

PERCHES ENRÍQUEZ, JOSÉ ◆ n. en Chihuahua, Chih., y m. en EUA (1882-1939). Músico. Hijo del también músico José Perches Porrás. En 1898 llegó a la ciudad de México y realizó estudios en el Conservatorio Nacional de Música. Salió de México en 1910, al iniciarse la insurrección maderista. Es autor de los valses *Secreto eterno*, *Caprichoso*, *Alicia* y *Danza Toño*.

PERCHES PORRÁS, JOSÉ ◆ n. y m. en Chihuahua, Chih. (1853-1913). Músico. Estudió en el Conservatorio Nacional, donde se graduó como maestro de piano y director de orquesta. Es obra suya el vals *El poder de tu mirada*.

PERDIGÓN, LETICIA ◆ n. en el DF (1956). Actriz. Inició su carrera profesional en 1972, en la película *Eva y Darío*. Ha trabajado en las cintas *La otra virginidad* (1974) *Presagio* (1974), *Longitud de guerra* (1975), *Coronación* (1975), *Lagunilla mi barrio* (1980), *Lagunilla 2* (1981), *Día de difuntos* (1988), *Anoche soñé contigo* (1991) y *La asesinadita* (1993). También actúa en televisión, teatro, doblaje y radionovelas.

PEREA, HÉCTOR ◆ n. en el DF (1953). Escritor. Licenciado en periodismo por la UNAM, donde es investigador, y doctor por la Universidad Complutense de Madrid. Fue profesor de los talleres de cine y fotografía de la Universidad La Salle. Ha colaborado en publicaciones periódicas de México y España. Realizó la presentación y notas de *Cartas echadas. Correspondencia Alfonso Reyes-Victoria Ocampo 1927-1959* (1983) y *Correspondencia Proust-Straus* (1984), así como la selección y prólogo de *Homenaje a Martín Luis Guzmán* (1987), *Cuento español del siglo XX* (1988) y *Alfonso Reyes y el cine. La caricia de las formas* (1988) y la recopilación y notas de *España en la obra de Alfonso Reyes* (1990). Autor de cuento: *Imágenes rotas y otras cosas* (1980), *Aboli bibelot dinanité sonore* (1982), *A contraluz* (1989) y *Aguas vivas* (1998); ensayo: *Por entregas. El ensayo periodístico y sus derivados* (1988), *La caricia de las formas (Alfonso Reyes y el cine)* (1988), *El viento en fuga* (1990), *Encuentro con el Himalaya. La aventura de Carlos y Elsa Carsolio* (1990), *La obra de Jesús R. Jáuregui* (1991), *La flecha y el boomerang* (1996), *La rueda del tiempo (mexicanos en España)* (1996, Premio José Revueltas 1994) y *Océano de colores* (1996); y antología: *El cuento español del siglo XX* (1987), *Homenaje a Martín Luis Guzmán en su centenario* (1987), *España en la obra de Alfonso Reyes* (1991), *De surcos como trazos, como letras. Antología del cuento mexicano finisecular* (1992). Becario del Centro Mexicano de Escritores (1980-81) y del INBA-Fonapas (1982-83). Premio Nacional de Periodismo Cultural (1989). Pertenece al Sistema Nacional de Creadores (1993-).

Nuestas naves, obra de Héctor Perea

PEREA, JESÚS ◆ n. en San Juan de Guadalupe y m. en Durango, Dgo. (?-1914). Abogado. Durante el gobierno del presidente Porfirio Díaz fue jefe político de los partidos de San Juan de Guadalupe y de Lerdo. En 1913 asumió interinamente la gubernatura de Durango, por renuncia de Carlos Patoni.

PEREA SÁNCHEZ, EZEQUIEL ◆ n. y m. en San Luis Potosí, SLP (1911-1986). Sacerdote ordenado en 1936. Estudió en la Universidad Gregoriana de Roma. Profesor del Seminario de San Luis Potosí. Fue asistente de la Acción Católica, vicario capitular (1959-67) y general (1972-73) y obispo de San Luis Potosí (1973-86).

PEREDA, JUAN NEPOMUCENO DE ◆ n. en España y m. en la ciudad de México (1802-1883). En 1821 estaba en México, dedicado al comercio, y apoyó el Plan de Iguala. Afectado por las leyes de expulsión de 1827, vivió en el extranjero entre 1828 y 1832. Fue cónsul de Venezuela en México (1837-42) y en 1844, el presidente Antonio López de Santa Anna le otorgó algunas concesiones para suministrar armamento al ejército. Encarcelado en 1846 por el gobierno de Mariano Paredes y Arrillaga, fue liberado y, al regreso de Santa Anna al poder, se le designó miembro de la Junta de Colonización. En octubre de ese año, el nuevo presidente, José Mariano Salas, le encomendó una misión diplomática secreta en Europa y las Antillas, consistente en formar una escuadrilla de corsarios que atacaran barcos estadounidenses. Fracasó y estuvo en Europa como encargado de negocios de la legación mexicana en Bruselas (1846-48). Fue ministro plenipotenciario en Guatemala (1853-58), miembro de la Junta de Notables que instauró la monarquía (junio de 1863) y subsecretario interino del Ministerio de Negocios Extranjeros, encargado del despacho (del 25 de septiembre de 1866 al 16 de enero de 1867), en el gobierno de Maximiliano de Habsburgo. Al triunfo de la República se exilió en Cuba. Volvió a México en 1871.

PEREDA, RAMÓN ◆ n. en España y m. en el DF (1897-1986). Actor y director cinematográfico. Llegó a México en 1909. Viajó a Estados Unidos a mediados de los años veinte y hacia 1927, impulsado por John Carradine, se incorporó como actor al cine "hispano". En ese país actuó en más de 15 cintas, entre ellas. *El cuerpo del delito* (1930), *Amor audaz* (1930), *Cascarrabias* (1930), *Carne de cabaret* (1931) y *Hombres de mi vida* (1932). Volvió a Mexico en 1932. Unos años antes había participado en *Conspiración* (1928) y *Contrabando* (1931). Actuó en *El vuelo de la muerte* (1933), *La noche del pecado* (1933), *El héroe de Nacozari* (1933), *El primo Basilio* (1934), *Cruz Diablo* (1934), *No matarás* (1934), *El baúl macabro* (1936), *Irma la mala* (1936), *Mujeres de hoy* (1936), *Malditas sean las mujeres* (1936), *Ahí está el detalle* (1940), *La torre de los suplicios* (1940), *La isla de la pasión* (1941), *Los tres mosqueteros* (1942), *Cinco fueron escogidos* (1942), *El médico de las locas* (1943), *El gran calavera* (1949), *Nazarín* (1958), *El Ángel exterminador* (1962) y *Simón del desierto* (1965). Dirigió *Canto a las Américas* (1942). Dirigió y actuó *Las cuatro milpas* (1937 y 1958), *México lindo* (1938), *Los olvidados de Dios* (1939), *El gavilán* (1939), *El capitán Centella* (1941), *El herrero* (1943), *El pecado de una madre* (1943), *Bienaventurados los que creen* (1945), *Arsenio Lupín* (1945), *Nuestras vidas* (1949), *La reina del* *mambo* (1950), *El ciclón del Caribe* (1950), *María Cristina* (1951), *La niña popoff* (1951), *Casa de perdición* (1954), *Flor de canela* (1957), *Sucedió en México* (1957) y *Acapulqueña* (1958).

Peredo, Luis G. ◆ n. en Zacatecas, Zac., y m. en el DF (1891-¿1975?). Periodista y director cinematográfico. Su apellido materno era Reyes. Fue profesor del Conservatorio Nacional de Música. Se inició como reportero en el diario *El Demócrata*; más tarde fue director de *México al Día*. En 1919 realizó la primera versión de *Santa*, con Elena Sánchez Valenzuela y Ricardo Beltri. Más tarde dirigió *La llaga* (1937), protagonizada por David Silva.

Peredo, Manuel ◆ n. y m. en la ciudad de México (1830-1890). Dramaturgo. Estudió en el Seminario Conciliar de México. Se tituló como médico en 1859. Participó en la fundación del Conservatorio Nacional de Música. Fue profesor de la Escuela Normal de Señoritas y del Colegio de las Vizcaínas. Colaboró en *El Semanario Ilustrado*, *El Correo de México*, *El Siglo XIX*, *Boletín de la Sociedad Mexicana de Geografía y Estadística*, *El Renacimiento* y *El Domingo*, donde se publicó su columna de crítica "Revista teatral". Tradujo obras de Dante Alighieri, Benedetto Ferrari, Pietro Metastasio, Victorien Sardou y de Gustav Gostkowski. Autor de *El que todo lo quiere* (1869), *Gramática italiana* (1873), *Discurso en elogio de don Juan Ruiz de Alarcón* (1876), *Breve reseña de la formación, progresos y perfeccionamiento de la lengua castellana* (1879) y *Curso elemental de arte, métrica y poética* (1883). Perteneció a la Academia Mexicana (de la Lengua).

Peredo, Melchor ◆ n. en el DF (1927). Pintor. Estudió en Escuela de Pintura y Escultura La Esmeralda, donde montó su primera exposición, en 1948. Se interesó en el muralismo y fue asistente de Pablo O'Higgins. Trabajó con José Gutiérrez en el mural del que fuera estadio del Instituto Politécnico Nacional; con Tomás Otero, en el club Siroco de Acapulco (1950) y con Luis Arenal en los murales del palacio de gobierno de Chilpancingo (1951). En 1953 fue representante en Europa del Frente Nacional de Artes Plásticas. Ha expuesto en Chicago (1961), Toronto (1963) y en el Museo de Arte Moderno de Nueva York, que adquirió dos de sus cuadros. Profesor del Taller de Arte de Toronto, coordinador de la obra mural en el Museo Nacional de Antropología (1965) y coordinador del taller de pintura y dibujo (1977) y del Taller Libre de Pintura Mural (1988) de la Universidad Veracruzana. Entre sus obras se cuentan murales en la Maternidad Guadalupe de Los Reyes (1959), en la Saint Christopher House de Toronto (1964), en el Colegio Larue (1969), en la Biblioteca Alfonso G. Alarcón, de Acapulco (1973). En el Tribunal Superior de Justicia de Jalapa: *Resistencia heroica del pueblo mexicano ante las invasiones* (1979).

Peredo y Pereira, Francisco Antonio de ◆ n. en Actopan, en el actual estado de Hgo., y ¿m. en Zacatlán, Puebla? (¿1775-1814?). Sacerdote. En 1809, procesado por herejía y vida disipada, huyó del país. En Portugal se hizo pasar por obispo; en Cuba y Estados Unidos se dedicó a investigar, para el gobierno español, las actividades del imperio napoleónico en las colonias americanas. Regresó a México a principios de 1810, con el encargo de informar al virrey de su labor de espionaje, pero éste lo envió a España para que comunicara sus noticias ante la corte. En el camino hacia Veracruz fue aprehendido por órdenes de la Inquisición, que lo procesó por "apóstata y partidario de la independencia" y lo condenó a seis años de prisión. En enero de 1813 se fugó de su reclusión en el convento de San Diego y se reunió en Tlalpujahua con Ignacio López Rayón, quien en abril lo nombró coronel y representante insurgente en Estados Unidos, encargado de obtener ayuda para los rebeldes y establecer relaciones con la Gran Bretaña. Luego de combatir en Guerrero y Oaxaca, a fines de 1813 estuvo en Filadelfia, aunque se ignora qué resultados obtuvo de su gestión. Algunos autores señalan que fue aprehendido y ejecutado por los realistas en la toma de Zacatlán, en 1814. Otros dicen que en 1816 acompañó a José Manuel de Herrera a Estados Unidos, pero una tercera versión señala que en 1817 combatía en Palmillas.

Peredo y Navarrete, Diego Bernardo ◆ n. en León, Gto., y m. en San Juan Bautista, hoy Villahermosa, Tab. (1696-1774). Estudió en el Seminario de Valladolid y en el Colegio de San Ildefonso de la ciudad de México. Fue canónigo, arcediano y deán de la catedral de Valladolid, obispo de Cartagena de Indias (1767-72) y obispo de Yucatán (1773-74).

Peregrino, María Antonia ◆ ☛ *Toña la Negra.*

Peresiano ◆ Códice llamado también de París o Peresianus. Pertenece a la cultura maya, es de carácter cronométrico y astronómico. Se encuentra en la Biblioteca Nacional de París. Fue publicado por primera vez en Francia (1887).

Benjamín Peret

Peret, Benjamín ◆ n. y m. en Francia (1899-1959). Poeta. Trabajó como reportero de policía para el diario *Petit Parisien*. En la capital francesa participó en los movimientos dadaísta (-1924) y surrealista (1924-). Codirigió la revista *Revolución Surrealista*. En Brasil convivió con grupos anarquistas y en la guerra civil española combatió en la Brigada Durruti. Con su compañera Remedios Varo, vino a México en 1942. Aquí se dedicó a difundir el surrealismo. Interesado en el periodo indígena mexicano, coeditó, con Manuel Álvarez Bravo, *Los tesoros del Museo Nacional de México. Escultura azteca*, donde escribió que "la totalidad de la nación azteca participaba en la creación artística, mientras que hoy día los públicos civilizados carecen fundamentalmente de la capacidad para sentir el arte". Volvió a Francia en 1947. En México escribió *Les Deshonneur des Poètes* (1945), *Dernier Malheur, Dernière Chance* (1945) y *Feu Central* (1947); y sobre México, el poema *Air Mexican*, el que, con litografías de Rufino Tamayo, publicó por primera vez en 1952; apareció en español por primera vez en

1975, en la revista *Plural*, traducido por José de la Colina. Redactó el prólogo a la primera edición francesa del *Chilam Balam* en 1959; realizó la *Anthologie des Mythes, Légendes et Contes Populaires d'Amérique*.

PERETE, RICARDO ◆ n. en Celaya, Gto. (1934). Nombre profesional del periodista Ricardo Pérez Gutiérrez. Estudió ciencias políticas en la UNAM. Se inició en el periodismo en 1954 en *Ultimas Noticias*, como colaborador de *Lumiere*, quien firmaba la columna "Cámara". En 1956 ingresó en la cooperativa Excélsior, donde ha sido reportero de espectáculos de los diarios de esa casa. En el matutino *Excélsior* escribe la columna *Corte!* y dirige la primera edición de *Ultimas Noticias*. Fue presidente de la Asociación Mexicana de Periodistas de Radio y Televisión; en 1989 fue elegido presidente de la Asociación de Periódicos Diarios de la República Mexicana. En 1983 recibió los premios Antonio Alzate y Fernández de Lizardi, del Club de Periodistas de México, por reportaje y artículo de fondo, respectivamente.

Sally de Perete

PERETE, SALLY DE ◆ n. en el DF (?). Nombre profesional de Celia López de Pérez, esposa del anterior. Estudió actuación en el Instituto Andrés Soler, literatura en el Instituto Doncella de Orleans y periodismo en el taller de Francois Baguer. Ha sido jefa de información de los noticiarios *Síntesis* y *Minutero*, del Canal 4 (1968-73); corresponsal en México de *Buenhogar* (1968-74) y de *Radio Hit* de Nueva York; condujo, con Luis G. Basurto, los programas de televisión *Club del espectador* y *Marquesina* (1973) y con Pedro Ferriz *El Gran Premio del Millón* (1985). Pertenece desde 1971 al grupo "20 mujeres y un hombre". Fue jefa del departamento de Promociones Sociales de la Secretaría del Trabajo (1971-76), redactora del periódico *Tribuna del Año Internacional de la Mujer* (1975); asesora del Consejo Nacional de Cultura y Recreación de los Trabajadores, jefa de la Unidad de Actividades Artísticas, Culturales y Turísticas de la delegación Benito Juárez (1984) y subdirectora de Eventos Especiales de Socicultur. Produjo la película *Nosotros somos Dios* (Guatemala, 1973) y la obra teatral *Casa de mujeres*. Condujo el programa de radio *Estrella de la semana* (1985); en televisión, *Tribuna Pública*, *Ocio y cultura*, *Primera fila*, *Cine Mexicano* y *México, Distrito Federal*. Ha recibido 48 premios.

PEREYNS, SIMÓN ◆ n. en Flandes (¿1530?-?). Pintor. En España trabajó en la corte de Felipe II. Llegó a la Nueva España en 1566, con el virrey Gastón de Peralta, y ejecutó varios murales en el palacio virreinal. Se le conocía por la versión castellanizada de su apellido: Perines. Poco tiempo después de su llegada, la Inquisición lo acusó de luterano, lo procesó y torturó, pero en 1668 lo dejó en libertad. Se dedicó a pintar retablos en numerosas iglesias del país. Sólo se conserva el de Huejotzingo, fechado en 1586. Se sabe que entre 1585 y 1588, como penitencia impuesta por el Santo Oficio, ejecutó retablos en la Catedral Metropolitana. Hizo también los retablos de los templos de Mixquic, Tepeaca, Malinalco, Teposcolula, Ocuilan, Tula, Cuernavaca y Cuautitlán. En la colección de San Carlos hay tres cuadros que son probablemente suyos. Algunos de sus lienzos se conservan en la Pinacoteca Virreinal.

FOTO: ROGELIO CUÉLLAR

Carlos Pereyra

PEREYRA, CARLOS ◆ n. en Saltillo, Coah., y m. en España (1871-1942). Historiador. Se tituló como abogado en la Escuela Nacional de Jurisprudencia. En 1892 fundó el periódico *El Pueblo Coahuilense* y luego el *El Pendón Coahuilense*. En 1897 dirigía en Monterrey *El Espectador*. Colaboró en los diarios *El Imparcial* y *El Mundo Ilustrado* de la ciudad de México. Fue profesor de la Escuela Nacional Preparatoria, primer secretario de la Legación mexicana en La Habana (1910), diputado federal (1910), primer secretario (del 7 de enero al 22 de diciembre de 1911), encargado interinamente de la embajada mexicana en Estados Unidos (del 27 de marzo al 7 de abril de 1911 y del 16 de junio al 16 de julio de 1911); subsecretario encargado del despacho de Relaciones Exteriores durante la dictadura de Victoriano Huerta (del 8 al 27 de julio de 1913), quien lo designó ministro plenipotenciario en Bélgica y los Países Bajos (1913-1914). En 1914 se estableció en España. Autor de *De Barradas a Baudin* (1904), *Juárez, discutido como dictador estadista* (1904), *Correspondencia secreta de los principales intervencionistas mejicanos* (1905), *Historia del pueblo mejicano* (1906), *Lecturas históricas mexicanas. La conquista del Anáhuac* (1906), *Hernán Cortés y la epopeya del Anáhuac* (1916), *Tejas. La primera desmembración de Méjico* (1917), *La Constitución de los Estados Unidos como elemento plutocrático* (1919), *La obra de España en América* (1920), *Historia de la América española* (1920-26), *Las huellas de los conquistadores* (1920) y *Hernán Cortés* (1931), así como de *Los Estados Unidos y las desmembraciones territoriales de Méjico*, *La vida temeraria de Hernán Cortés* y *Humboldt en América*, entre otras obras.

PEREYRA, ORESTES ◆ n. en Santa María del Oro, Dgo., y m. en Sin. (1861-1915). Obrero. Se afilió al Partido Antirreeleccionista en 1910. En ese año se unió a la insurrección maderista en Gómez Palacio, en 1911 tomó Durango y Torreón. Combatió al orozquismo en 1912; al año siguiente luchó contra el gobierno de Victoriano Huerta. Al lado de Francisco Villa, como general brigadier, participó en la toma de Torreón. Fue gobernador provisional de Coahuila (del 20 de junio al 4 de septiembre de 1915). Combatió al carrancismo junto con Juan Banderas. Fue ejecutado por los constitucionalistas en Sinaloa.

PEREYRA BOLDRINI, CARLOS ◆ n. y m. en el DF (1940-1988). Politólogo. Licenciado en economía y licenciado y maestro en filosofía por la UNAM. Militó en las Juventudes Comunistas de México, en la Liga Comunista Espartaco, en el Movimiento de Acción Popular (1981), en el Partido Socialista Unificado de México (1981-87), a cuyo Comité Central perteneció, y en el Partido Mexicano Socialista (1987-88). En la UNAM fue profesor, coordinador del Colegio de Filosofía (1983-86) y coordinador del Centro de Apoyo a la Investigación de la Facultad de Filosofía y Letras; investigador y miembro de la Comisión Dictaminadora del Instituto de Investigaciones Filosóficas; Consejero universitario. Colaboró en *Novedades* (1973-75), *Cuadernos Políticos* (1974-), *Excélsior* (1975-76), *Proceso* (1976-78), *Nexos* (1977-88), *unomásuno* (1978-82), *Así Es* (1982-83), *Punto* (1983-84), *La Jornada* (1985-88) y *Revista de la Universidad*. Coautor de *México hoy*, *Historia, ¿para qué?*, *La desigualdad en México*, *El Estado en México*, *México, presente y futuro* (1985), *La crisis en México* y *México 83: a la mitad del túnel* (1983); autor de *Política y violencia* (1974), *Configuraciones: teoría e historia* (1979) y *El sujeto de la historia* (1974). Recibió el doctorado *honoris causa post mortem* de la UAM (1988).

Pereyra Saldrat, Fernando A. ◆ n. en Acayucan y m. en Veracruz, Ver. (1882-1965). Telegrafista desde 1897. En 1910 era jefe de Telégrafos en Veracruz. Tres años más tarde se levantó en armas y se incorporó al ejército constitucionalista. Fue miembro del Estado Mayor de Jesús Carranza, jefe de Telégrafos en Sonora, en la Costa Chica y la Costa Grande de Guerrero; jefe de la Sección de Líneas de la República, diputado al Congreso Constituyente de 1916-17 y oficial segundo de Telecomunicaciones. Se retiró en 1940.

Pérez, Absalón ◆ n. en Cuba y m. en el DF (1900-1972). Músico. Llegó a México en 1934, con la orquesta de Ernesto Lecuona. Aquí formó su propia agrupación musical, con la que actuó en las estaciones radiofónicas XEW, XEB y XEQ. Destacó como pianista y arreglista de música afroantillana.

Pérez, Amador ◆ n. en Zaachila, Oax., y m. en el DF (1902-1976). Compositor y trombonista. Perteneció a las bandas militares del Estado Mayor (1920-24) y de Policía (1924-32). Fue fundador y director de la Danzonera América y de la Danzonera Prieto y Dimas. Se desempeñó como presidente municipal de Zaachila. Es autor del danzón *Nereidas*. Compuso también *Mi amigo Eloy*, *El que siembra su maíz* y *Adela*.

Pérez, Antonio ◆ ☛ *Zapata, Mario*.

Pérez, Arnulfo G. ◆ n. en Tepeji del Río, Hgo. (1884-?). Periodista. Fue obrero textil y empleado en la fábrica de Río Blanco. A fines de 1906 participó en la huelga que se produjo en esa empresa. Durante la insurrección maderista combatió a las órdenes de Matías Rodríguez. Escribió para los periódicos *El Sacristán*, *La Sotana*, *La Patria*, *El Hijo de la Patria*, *El Libre Pensador*, *El Faro* y *Acción Libertaria*. En 1966 era editor del diario *La Voz de Juárez*.

Pérez, Carmelo ◆ n. en Texcoco, Edo. de Méx., y m. en España (1908-1931). Torero. Hermano mayor de Silverio Pérez. Su apellido materno era Gutiérrez. Lidió por primera vez en 1929, en el Toreo del DF. Recibió la alternativa ese mismo año, pero se retiró a causa de una cornada. Reapareció en 1931 en la Plaza México y se presentó después en España, donde sólo pudo lidiar una vez. Murió a consecuencia de las heridas que recibió en México.

Pérez, Eleuterio ◆ n. en Astapa, municipio de Jalpa, Tab. (1823-1903). Agricultor en su juventud. Intentó sin éxito, estudiar en La Habana. Combatió la intervención francesa desde 1863. En 1864 fue elegido diputado local y más tarde se reincorporó a las tropas republicanas y participó en la toma de la última posesión de los imperialistas en Tabasco (1866). Autor de *Tratado de moral práctica*, *Cartas a mis hijos* y *Cartas a mi nieto Arquímedes*.

Pérez, Francisco ◆ n. en Guadalajara, Jal., y m. en el DF (1883-1959). Periodista. Colaboró en *El Imparcial* de la ciudad de México, en 1920 escribió un reportaje sobre el asesinato del presidente Venustiano Carranza. Dirigió el departamento de cables del periódico *Novedades*. En Estados Unidos trabajó para la agencia United Press, a su regreso a México estuvo en *Excélsior* y más tarde volvió a *Novedades*.

Pérez, Gustavo ◆ n. en el DF (1950). Ceramista. Estudió ingeniería, matemáticas y filosofía en la UNAM. Fue alumno de Enrique Rangel, Felipe Bárcenas y Martín Lima en la Escuela de Diseño y Artesanías, donde fue profesor (1973-74). Estuvo becado en la Sint Joost Akademie, de Breda, Holanda (1980-82). Trabajó como invitado en la Sint Paulus Abdij de Oosterhout, Holanda (1982-83). En Jalapa, Veracruz, instaló su propio taller, El Tomate, donde trabajó ocho años (1984-92). A partir de 1976 y hasta 1999 ha presentado 36 exposiciones individuales y participado en medio centenar de muestras colectivas.

Pérez, Jesús C. ◆ n. y m. en San Luis Potosí, SLP (1903-1970). Escritor. Fue jefe de redacción de la revista *Letras Potosinas*. Colaboró en la revista *Bohemia*. Autor de *Cuentos y ensayos* (1943), *Cuentos del viejo San Luis* (1959), *La muerte del poeta* (1961) y *Los platillos voladores* (1969).

Pérez, Lázaro ◆ n. y m. en Zapotlán, hoy Ciudad Guzmán, Jal. (1817-1900). Farmacéutico graduado en 1845 en la Universidad de Guadalajara. Fue profesor del Liceo de Varones de esa ciudad, donde financió la instalación de los laboratorios. Fundó el primer observatorio astronómico de la capital tapatía y, al parecer, introdujo la primera máquina eléctrica a Jalisco. Publicó algunos textos sobre química.

Pérez, Luis *Pichojos* ◆ n. en Guadalajara, Jal., y m. en el DF (1908-1964). Futbolista. Padre del también futbolista Mario *Pichojos* Pérez. Su segundo apellido era González. Llegó a la ciudad de México en 1928 con la Selección Jalisco y se quedó en el club Germania, del que pasó al Necaxa, que en su tiempo era conocido como *los once hermanos*. Ocupó la posición de extremo izquierdo y se caracterizaba por jugar siempre con una boina blanca. Perteneció a la selección nacional que actuó en la primera Copa del Mundo, en Uruguay (1930). Participó también como seleccionado nacional en los Juegos Deportivos Centroamericanos de El Salvador (1935) y Panamá (1938). Se retiró en 1943.

PÉREZ, MARCOS ◆ n. y m. en San Pedro Teococuilco, hoy de Marcos Pérez, Oax. (1805-1861). Se tituló como abogado en 1838, en el Instituto de Ciencias y Artes de Oaxaca, que dirigió en 1856. Fue presidente del Tribunal Superior de Justicia (1847) y gobernador de Oaxaca tras la destitución de Francisco Ortiz de Zárate y antes del nombramiento de Benito Juárez (del 23 al 29 de octubre de 1847). Detenido en 1853, durante la revolución de Ayutla, se le expulsó del estado (1855). Perteneció a la Junta Provisional de Gobierno, que en agosto de 1855 derrocó al gobierno santanista. Combatió contra los conservadores en la guerra de los Tres Años y se hizo cargo del gobierno oaxaqueño del 24 de enero al 8 de noviembre de 1860, cuando fue obligado a renunciar por un grupo de liberales disidentes. Su nombre fue añadido al de su lugar de nacimiento en 1936.

PÉREZ, MARTÍN ◆ n. en San Martín, Jal., y m. en Sin. (1590-1623). Ingresó en la Compañía de Jesús en 1577 y fue ordenado sacerdote en 1585. Cinco años más tarde pasó a la provincia de Nueva Vizcaya, con el primer grupo de jesuitas. Escribió una *Cronología* sobre la vida de los indios del actual estado de Sinaloa.

PÉREZ, PASCUAL ◆ n. y m. en Puebla, Pue. (?-1721). Pintor. Pintó *Los misterios del rosario* que se hallan en la Universidad de Puebla; *La crucifixión* y *El descendimiento*, del vestíbulo de la parroquia de San José; *El juicio final*, de la iglesia de San Andrés, Cholula; *Escenas de la vida de San Cayetano*, del templo de la Concordia; y la *Santa Margarita de Pazzi* que se encuentra en la iglesia del Carmen.

PÉREZ, PEDRO ◆ n. en Puebla, Pue., y m. en el DF (1940-1978). Caricaturista. En Guanajuato colaboró en *El Sol de León* y más tarde se trasladó a la ciudad de México. Trabajó en *El Sol de México* hasta su muerte.

PÉREZ, *POCHO* ◆ n. en Uruguay y m. en el DF (1927-1990). Arreglista y director de orquesta, su nombre era Rubén Alfredo Pérez Izzi. Estudió piano desde los seis años de edad y a los 18 se incorporó a una orquesta de tango en Montevideo. Vivió luego en Argentina y Brasil. Fue arreglista de Emmanuel, Vicky Carr, Denis de Kalafe, Pedro Vargas, Julio Iglesias y José José, entre otros. Llegó a México en 1970 como director artístico de una compañía discográfica. Ganó varios premios internacionales, entre ellos el OTI y el del Festival Latinoamericano.

PÉREZ, SILVERIO ◆ n. en Texcoco, Edo. de Méx. (1915). Matador de toros. Su apellido materno es Gutiérrez. Se dice que se dedicó a la tauromaquia a causa de la muerte de su hermano Carmelo. Toreó por primera vez en 1933, como novillero. Se presentó en España en 1935. Fue *sobresaliente* de la cuadrilla de Fermín Espinosa *Armillita*, de quién recibió la alternativa en 1938, en la plaza de toros de Puebla. Lidió en plazas de Colombia, Ecuador, España, Portugal y Venezuela. Se retiró en 1953. Ha sido tres veces presidente municipal de Texcoco y diputado federal.

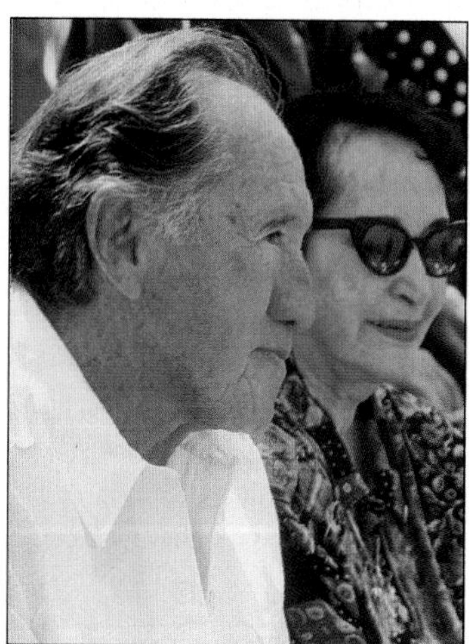

Silverio Pérez y señora

PÉREZ, VALERIANO ◆ n. en Guerrero, Coah. (1877-?). Opositor al régimen de Porfirio Díaz desde 1909. Fue delegado por Piedras Negras a la Convención Antirreeleccionista de la ciudad de México, que en 1910 eligió a Francisco I. Madero candidato a la Presidencia. A fines de ese año se levantó en armas. Durante el gobierno de Madero combatió la rebelión orozquista (1912). En 1913, al producirse el golpe de Estado de Victoriano Huerta, se incorporó al constitucionalismo. Trabajó como empleado aduanero hasta 1923.

PÉREZ ABREU, HERMINIO ◆ n. en Campeche, Camp. (?-1931). Elegido diputado al Congreso Constituyente de 1916-17, fue nombrado por Venustiano Carranza ministro mexicano en Centroamérica, por lo que no participó en la redacción del texto constitucional. En 1921 presidió el ayuntamiento de la ciudad de México (1921). Promovió la publicación de una iconografía de los gobernantes de la Nueva España.

PÉREZ ABREU DE LA TORRE, JUAN ◆ n. en Campeche, Camp., y m. en el DF (1886-1975). Abogado y sociólogo. Por su militancia maderista, en 1910 fue expulsado del país. Se refugió en Cuba y obtuvo el grado de doctor en derecho en la Universidad de La Habana. En 1929 fundó los Grupos Infantiles José Martí. Durante la dictadura de Gerardo Machado, ayudó a quienes huían de la persecución política. Regresó a México en 1933 y fue profesor de psicología y sociología de la educación en las escuelas nacionales Preparatoria, de Jurisprudencia y de Economía y en la Facultad de Filosofía de la UNAM. A la caída de la dictadura machadista, el gobierno cubano le ofreció el cargo de magistrado en la Sala Civil del Tribunal Supremo, pero lo rechazó. En 1946 era director de profesiones de la Escuela Nacional de Maestros, en 1949 director de Enseñanza Normal. Profesor de la Facultad de Derecho de la UNAM hasta su jubilación en 1965.

PÉREZ ACOSTA, ERNESTO ◆ n. en Tijuana, BC (1946). Golfista. Inició su carrera profesional en 1970. Ha ganado los torneos Abierto Mexicano (1970), de Maestros de México y de Profesores de Golf Asociado (1975), así como varias competencias en Estados Unidos.

PÉREZ-ARCE IBARRA, FRANCISCO ◆ n. en Tepic, Nay. (1948). Licenciado en economía por la UNAM, donde fue profesor. Es investigador del Instituto Nacional de Antropología e Historia. Participó en un taller literario, coordinado por José Emilio Pacheco. Perteneció a la redacción de la revista *Nexos*. Colaboró en *La Cultura en México*, suplemento de la revista *Siempre!* En 1988 realizó la compilación *A muchas voces. Testimonios de la lucha magisterial*. Autor de novela: *La blanca* (1988) y *Dios nunca muere* (1992).

Pérez Arreola, Evaristo ◆ n. en Ciudad Acuña, Coah. (1940). Líder sindical. Licenciado en derecho por la UNAM. Fue boxeador, agente del Ministerio Público y empleado de la rectoría de la UNAM. Militó en el PCM y más tarde organizó su propio grupo político, Unidad Democrática, que dirige desde su fundación. Ha sido secretario general del Sindicato de Trabajadores y Empleados de la UNAM (1971-77) y del Sindicato de Trabajadores de la UNAM (1977-89); diputado federal por el PCM (1979-82), diputado por el PARM a la Legislatura de Coahuila para el trienio 1989-92 y asesor del presidente Carlos Salinas de Gortari (1989-94). Autor de *La concertación democrática, una propuesta mexicana* (1987).

Pérez de Bocanegra, Hernán ◆ n. y m. en España (¿1504?-1567). Llegó a la Nueva España en 1526. Alguacil mayor de México en 1527, formó parte del poblamiento de Granada (Michoacán) y participó en la conquista de Nueva Granada. Se hizo cargo de la capitanía general del virreinato cuando Antonio de Mendoza hizo la campaña de Jalisco. Fue alcalde ordinario de la capital en 1537 y 1543. Tuvo la encomienda de Acámbaro y volvió a ser capitán general del virreinato (1551-52), cuando Luis de Velasco inició la conquista de los territorios chichimecas. Acusado de complicidad en la conjura de Martín Cortés, se le desterró.

Pérez y Bourás, Jorge ◆ n. en el DF y m. en Canadá (1918-1997). Ingeniero aeronáutico titulado en el Instituto Politécnico Nacional (1938-40) y posgraduado en el Instituto Chrysler de Ingeniería y en la Wayne State University, EUA (1962). Profesor del IPN (1942-55) y de la Universidad Anáhuac (1975-79). Fue gerente de Aluminio Industrial Mexicano (1946-49), director de la Escuela Superior de Ingeniería Mecánica y Eléctrica del IPN (1950-55), gerente de producción y superintendente de la empresa Studebaker Packard de México (1951-59), director general de Aeroméxico (1959-71), director de la Escuela de Ingeniería de la Universidad Anáhuac (1975-79) y representante permanente de México ante la Organización de Aviación Civil Internacional (1983-97). Perteneció a la Academia Mexicana de Ingeniería, a la Asociación de Transporte Aérero Internacional (que presidió en 1966-67), a la Asociación Mexicana de Ingenieros en Aeronáutica y a la Cámara Nacional de Aerotransportes (que fundó y presidió, en 1964-68). Fue condecorado por los gobiernos de Bélgica, Italia y Suecia.

Pérez Blas, Alberto ◆ n. el DF (1952). Licenciado en economía por el IPN. Diplomado en políticas públicas y administración estatal y municipal por el Instituto Nacional de Administración Pública. Afiliado al PRI. Ha sido director general del Servicios Educativos para el Estado de México de la SEP; subdirector general de Turismo Sociocultural en la Secretaría de Turismo; director general regional en la Coordinación General de Delegaciones de Sedesol; coordinador de asesores de la Subsecretaría de Población y Servicios Migratorios de la SG; comisionado nacional del Instituto Nacional de Migración, contralor general y director de Comunicación Social de la SSA.

Pérez Botello, Adolfo *Negro* ◆ n. en el DF y m. en Irapuato, Gto. (1922-1999). Manejador, entrenador y promotor de boxeo. En su juventud fue futbolista y llegó a las reservas del equipo Atlante. En 1938 pasó al boxeo como ayudante del *manager* Pepe Hernández; eventualmente tuvo a sus propios peleadores, entre los que destacan los ex campeones mundiales Raúl *Ratón* Macías y Vicente Saldívar. Fue entrenador de la selección mexicana de boxeo que asistió a los Juegos Centroamericanos y del Caribe de 1969.

Pérez Budar, José Joaquín ◆ n. en Huajuapan de León, Oax., y m. en el DF (1851-1931). En 1872 se adhirió al Plan de la Noria y combatió al gobierno de Benito Juárez. Enviudó dos años más tarde, y en 1881 fue ordenado sacedote, aunque pertenecía a la logia masónica Los Amigos de la Luz. Estuvo encarcelado dos años en Puebla por conspirar contra el gobierno, lo que provocó su expulsión de la Iglesia. Fue liberado gracias a la intervención del presidente Porfirio Díaz y se reincorporó al ejército. En 1912 volvió a ser aceptado en la Iglesia y fue párroco en Iztapalapa y Tepetlaoxtoc. En 1925, cuando era cura de Santa María la Redonda, con Manuel Monje y con el apoyo del presidente Plutarco Elías Calles, fundó la Iglesia Católica Apostólica Mexicana, consiguió ser nombrado obispo en Estados Unidos y se autonombró patriarca de los cismáticos. Al año siguiente, en Chicago, fue nombrado Primado de los Viejos Cristianos para América del Norte, grupo que reivindicaba a Benito Juárez. A pesar de su postura contra la jerarquía, poco antes de morir se reconcilió con la Iglesia Católica Apostólica Romana (☛).

Alberto Pérez Blas

Pérez Caballero, Francisco ◆ n. y m. en Tulancingo, Hgo., (1810-1864). Militar. Combatió la invasión de Isidro Barradas en 1829. Durante la guerra contra Estados Unidos participó en las batallas de la Angostura, Padierna y Churubusco (1847). Fue gobernador interino de Puebla (1853), general de división desde 1855 y gobernador del Departamento de México (1856). En la guerra de los Tres Años se mantuvo en el bando conservador y ocupó interinamente la gubernatura de Puebla en dos ocasiones (del 12 de julio al 21 de diciembre de 1858 y del 25 de diciembre de 1858 al 26 de julio de 1859); volvió a ser gobernador del departamento del Valle de México (de mayo de 1860 a enero de 1861). Durante la intervención francesa se incorporó al ejército republicano y fue comandante militar de Tulancingo.

Pérez Cámara, Carlos ◆ n. en Campeche, Camp. (1922). Licenciado en derecho por la Universidad del Sureste (1938-42), donde ha sido profesor. Desde 1940 pertenece al PRI (antes PRM), en el que fue delegado del CEN en Nayarit (1972) y Puebla (1976), así como secretario de Acción Electral en el DF (1985). En la Confederación de Organizaciones Populares se ha desempeñado como secretario de Acción Política (1970), delegado en Veracruz (1970) y en Tabasco (1973) y secretario de Acción Ideológica (1973). Ha sido secretario de gobierno (1961-64), tesorero general del estado (1970-73) y gobernador interino de Campeche (1973); diputado federal (1964-67), senador de la República (1970-76), presidente municipal de Campeche (1977-79) y director general de gobierno del Distrito Federal (1986-88).

PÉREZ CÁMARA, EFRAÍN ♦ n. en Mérida, Yuc. (1892-?). Músico. Estudió composición con Julián Carrillo (1910-13). Profesor de la Escuela de Música de Yucatán (1915). Miembro de las orquestas Sinfónica Beethoven y Americana, ambas dirigidas por Carrillo. Fue director de las bandas de Música de Yucatán (1918-20), de Música del Quinto Regimiento (1926) y de la Presidencial de El Salvador (1927-29); director de Enseñanza Musical de Baja California Sur. Autor de la opereta *Un sueño de verano* (1917), de los poemas coreográficos *Siete puertos del Mayab,* (1938) y *El Mayab*, y de la ópera *Zaantzontli* (1940).

PÉREZ CAMPUZANO, SYLVIA ♦ n. en el DF (1943). Licenciada en psicología por la UIA (1961-64), donde fue profesora (1966-69). Ejerció la docencia en la Universidad de Buenos Aires (1971-76) y la UAEM. Ha sido jefa de selección de la empresa General Electric de México (1964-68), subgerente de Desarrollo de la aerolínea argentina Austral (1970-75), subgerente de Personal de Aerolíneas Argentinas (1976-81), asesora del gobernador del Estado de México (1981-84), directora de Desarrollo y Administración en la misma entidad (1984-86) y directora general de Servicios Administrativos de la SEMIP (1986-88). Pertenece al PRI desde 1981.

PÉREZ CÁRDENAS, MANUEL ♦ n. en Tepic, Nay. (1953). Licenciado en economía por la UNAM (1971-75), donde ha sido profesor de la Escuela Nacional Preparatoria y de la Facultad de Ciencias Políticas y Sociales e investigador del Instituto de Investigaciones Económicas y del Proyecto Mundial de Investigación, de la ONU-OIT. Ha sido subdirector general de la Coordinación Técnica de la Industria Paraestatal, de la Secretaría de Patrimonio (1980-82), director general de Programación Financiera de la Secretaría de Energía (1982-83); coordinador de asesores del secretario de Gobernación (1984) y director general de Normatividad y Control Paraestatal de la Secretaría de Agricultura (1984-1988). Dirige la Fundación Colosio, en Nayarit.

PÉREZ CORONA, FELIPE ♦ n. en Tonaya y m. en Guadalajara, Jal. (1884-1965). Médico graduado en 1910. Sirvió como médico militar en Sonora y Jalisco y dirigió el Hospital Militar de Colima. Más tarde ejerció en Guanajuato y el Distrito Federal y dirigió el Hospital Militar de Monterrey. Fue diputado federal. Autor de *Filosofía, Génesis y evolución de las religiones, Monografías y escritos diversos, Bocetos biográficos de tres guerrilleros jaliscienses* y *Monografía de Tonaya.*

PÉREZ CORONADO, MANUEL ♦ n. en Uruapan, Mich., y m. en el estado de Guanajuato (1929-1970). Estudió grabado en la Escuela Nacional de Artes Plásticas, donde fue discípulo de Alfredo Zalce (1948). Participó, en 1950, en el Taller de Gráfica Popular. Fue director de la sección de artes plásticas de la Escuela de Bellas Artes, de la Universidad Michoacana de San Nicolás de Hidalgo. En 1951 dirigió un taller de ilustración de carteles en el Centro Regional de Educación Fundamental para América Latina. Hacia 1952, difundió un método de grabado de su invención. Participó en el primer Congreso Latinoamericano de las Juventudes, en La Habana (1960). Fundó y dirigió el Taller de Gráfica Popular de Uruapan. En 1967 lanzó un manifiesto contra la corriente proimperialista en las artes plásticas. Murió en un accidente automovilístico.

PÉREZ CORREA, CLEMENTE ♦ n. en Torreón, Coah. (1940). Ingeniero titulado en el IPN (1952). En la Secretaría de Comunicaciones y Transportes ha sido coordinador general de Telecomunicaciones durante los XIX Juegos Olímpicos (1968), coordinador general de la Secretaría durante la Copa del Mundo de 1970, subdirector general de servicios, coordinador de la Secretaría durante los Juegos Panamericanos de 1975 y director general de Telecomunicaciones.

PÉREZ CORREA FERNÁNDEZ DEL CASTILLO, FERNANDO ♦ n. en el DF (1942). Licenciado en derecho por la UNAM. En Francia se graduó como licenciado (1967) y doctor en ciencias políticas (1971). Profesor de la Escuela Bancaria y Comercial (1961-64), de la UNAM (1970-82), de El Colegio de México (1971-77) y de la Universidad de Harvard, EUA. Coordinador del Centro de Estudios Políticos, coordinador del Colegio de Ciencias y Humanidades y coordinador de Humanidades de la UNAM. Desde 1972 pertenece al PRI. En la Secretaría de Gobernación fue coordinador general de Estudios y Proyectos (1982-84) y subsecretario (1984-88). Director general del Instituto Nacional para la Educación de los Adultos (1988-1994).

Emiliano Pérez Cruz

PÉREZ CRUZ, EMILIANO ♦ n. en el DF (1955). Pasó su infancia y adolescencia en Ciudad Nezahualcóyotl, Edo. de Méx. Estudió periodismo en la UNAM. Ha sido coordinador de la revista *La Semana de Bellas Artes* (1977-81), cronista de Ciudad Nezahualcóyotl, jefe de Publicaciones del Crea y de la Universidad de Sonora. Colaborador del diario *unomásuno*, del semanario *Punto* y de las revistas *Pie de Página, La Onda, Revista de la Universidad, Su Otro Yo, Encuentro, La Orquesta, Territorios, La Cultura en México, Comala* y *La Garrapata*, entre otras. Coautor de *Los siete pecados capitales* (1989). Autor de crónica: *Borracho no vale* (1988) y *Aventuras de pata de perro* (1992); y cuento: *Tres de ajo* (1983), *Si camino voy como los ciegos* (1987) *Me matan si no trabajo y si trabajo me matan* (1998); y novela: *Reencuentro* (1993). En 1977 obtuvo la Beca Salvador Novo, en 1980 la del

INBA-Fonapas. Fue primer lugar en el concurso de cuento convocado por los 25 años de la Facultad de Ciencias Políticas y Sociales de la UNAM (1976). Obtuvo mención honorífica en el Concurso Nacional de Cuento del INBA-Casa de la Cultura, de Aguascalientes (1978), mención honorífica del Concurso Latinoamericano de Cuento (1980). Becario del Fondo para la Cultura y las Artes del Estado de México (1994-95).

PÉREZ DÍAZ, LUIS ◆ n. en San Martín Texmelucan, Pue. (1931). Líder de obreros. Miembro del PRI. Perteneció al Movimiento Juvenil Revolucionario. Ha sido secretario del Interior del Sindicato de Trabajadores Tahoneros, secretario de Acción Juvenil (1971-73) y del Interior (1976-79) de la Confederación Regional Obrera Mexicana; secretario de Organización y Propaganda de la Federación de Agrupaciones Obreras del Estado de México (1984), y diputado federal (1985-88, 1991-94).

PÉREZ DUARTE, CONSTANTINO ◆ n. en Pachuca, Hgo., y m. en el DF (1886-1956). Ingeniero de minas titulado en la Escuela Nacional de Ingenieros (1911). Fue uno de los redactores de las leyes mineras mexicanas. Representó a México en las conferencias económicas de Londres (1931) y Montevideo (1934). Organizó algunas compañías mineras en Nayarit y Baja California y trabajó en Real del Monte. Ocupó la presidencia de la Comisión de Fomento Minero y reabrió las minas de Angangueo. Fue consejero de Altos Hornos de México, de los Ferrocarriles Nacionales y de la Camara Minera. Al momento de morir era subsecretario de Economía.

PÉREZ ESCAMILLA, AGUSTÍN ◆ n. en el DF (1914). Fotógrafo. De formación autodidacta, comenzó su carrera en 1933 en *El Universal Gráfico*. Pasó a *La Prensa*, en la que trabajó para todas las secciones y permaneció hasta 1965. Tras una breve temporada en el ISSSTE, pasó al PRI. Adscrito a la fuente de la Presidencia, ha fotografiado a todos los presidentes de México, desde Lázaro Cárdenas, y numerosos acontecimientos relevantes en las fuentes de deportes. Obtuvo el Premio Nacional de Periodismo en 1994.

PÉREZ GALLARDO, REYNALDO ◆ n. en Rioverde, SLP (1896-?). Militar y escritor. Estudió ingeniería en el Colegio Militar. Combatió durante la revolución. Elegido gobernador de San Luis Potosí en 1939, fue destituido en 1942. Fundó *El Momento*, *Gaceta Militar*, *Huasteca* y *Abekas*. Colaboró en los periódicos *Excélsior*, *El Occidental*. *El Nacional*, *El Heraldo Michoacano* y el *Diario del Sureste*. Autor de *Abrojos del camino* (1918), *Guillermina o el herido 390. Novela de la revolución constitucionalista* (1933), *A la luz de la fogata* (1935), *Mi amigo loco* (1935), *El general Rafael Cházaro Pérez* (1935), *Noches de insomnio* (1937), *Rudimentos de apicultura* (1937), *¿Dónde surgió la primera chispa de la revolución,* (1938), *Flores de perdición* (1941), *Bahía Magdalena. Un aporte para la historia contemporánea* (1943), *La voz de la tormenta* (1944), *Sangre mexicana en el Pacífico. Fuerza Aérea Mexicana. Escuadrón 201* (1945), *Al trotar de la vida* (1946), *La chamaca* (1952), *Primeros pasos en apicultura* (1957), *Michoacán y sus leyendas* (1957), *El teniente general Mariano Matamoros* (1965), *Tierra sin esperanza* (1966), *Cuando brama el huracán* (1968), *La sangre de los vencidos*, *Está lloviendo en la sierra*, *Al morir la tarde*, *Corazón vencido*, *Fantasmas y aparecidos*, *La rebelión de las palomas* y *Desde el Bravo hasta el Suchiate*.

PÉREZ GARCÍA, ANTONIO ◆ ☛ *Zapata, Mario*.

PÉREZ GARCÍA, CARLOS ◆ n. en San Luis Potosí, SLP (1946). Licenciado en economía por la UNAM (1965-69) y maestro por la Universidad de Manchester (1971-73). Profesor de la UNAM (1969-79), del CIDE (1975-77) y de El Colegio de México (1980). Ha sido responsable de asuntos editoriales del Cemla (1969-71), economista de la Sección de Fabricantes de Alimentos Balanceados de la Canacintra (1971), jefe del Departamento de Empresas Públicas de la Sepanal (1974), coordinador del sector externo de la Oficina de los asesores del presidente de la República (1977-80), jefe del Servicio de Planeación del IMSS (1980-82), director general del Instituto del Trabajo (1983) y coordinador general de Políticas, Estudios y Estadísticas del Trabajo de la Secretaría del Trabajo (1983- 88),; subdirector de Protección al Salario del ISSSTE (1988-93) y oficial mayor de la SEMIP (1993-94). Es miembro del Colegio Nacional de Economistas.

PÉREZ GASGA, ALFONSO ◆ n. en Pinotepa Nacional, Oax., y m. en el DF (1890-1964). Abogado. Se graduó en el Instituto de Ciencias y Artes de Oaxaca, que más tarde dirigió. Fue defensor de oficio en Veracruz (1915-18), oficial mayor del Tribunal Superior de Justicia, subjefe del Departamento de Justicia Militar, profesor de jurisprudencia militar en la Academia del Estado Mayor y secretario auxiliar de la Comisión de Reclamaciones de Daños de la Revolución (1918-23). Obtuvo el grado de general. Miembro de la Comisión Recopiladora de Rentas de Hacienda, juez federal (1931), diputado federal, ministro de la Suprema Corte de Justicia de la Nación (1933-38), miembro de la delegación mexicana en la formación de la Organización de las Naciones Unidas, senador de la República (1952-56) y gobernador de Oaxaca (del 1 de diciembre de 1956 al 30 de noviembre de 1962).

PÉREZ GASGA, FLAVIO ◆ n. en Pinotepa Nacional, Oax., y m. en el DF (1887-?). Abogado. Estudió en el Instituto de Ciencias y Artes de Oaxaca. Asesoró al general revolucionario Juan José Baños y consiguió que Venustiano Carranza pertrechara a los rebeldes de Pinotepa. Fue diputado federal (1917-18), enviado mexicano en Argentina, secretario general de gobierno y gobernador interino de Oaxaca (1923).

PÉREZ GAVILÁN Y ECHEVERRÍA, NICOLÁS ◆ n. en Durango, Dgo., y m. en Chihuahua, Chih. (1856-1919). Estudió en el Seminario Conciliar de Durango, que más tarde dirigió. Ordenado sacerdote en 1880, fue prebendado del cabildo de la catedral (1891-95), canónigo (1895-97), chantre de la diócesis de Durango (1897-1902) y obispo de Chihuahua (1902-19).

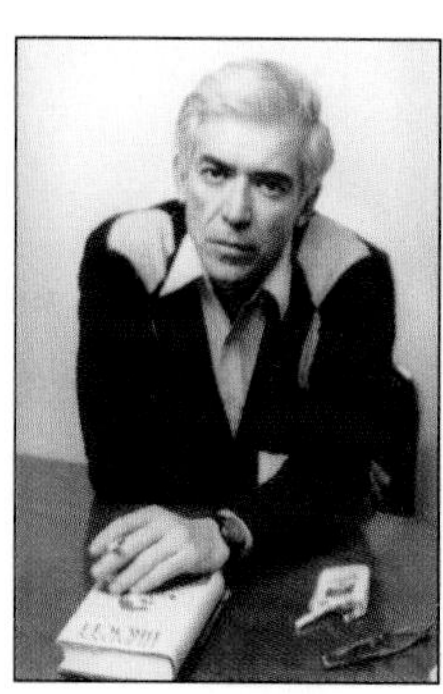
José María Pérez Gay

Dionisio Pérez Jácome

PÉREZ GAY, JOSÉ MARÍA ◆ n. en el DF (1944). Licenciado en ciencias y técnicas de la información por la Universidad Iberoamericana (1964) y doctor en sociología por la Universidad Libre de Berlín (1964-71). Becario del CNCA (1989-90). Ingresó al Servicio Exterior Mexicano en 1969. Ha estado adscrito a las embajadas mexicanas en Bonn, Viena y París. Profesor de la Facultad de Ciencias Políticas y Sociales de la UNAM, coordinador del suplemento *La Jornada, Libros* del diario *La Jornada*, miembro del consejo de redacción de la revista *Nexos* y director del Canal 22 (1992-). Ha traducido obras de Thomas Mann, Franz Kafka, Robert Musil, Elías Canetti y Ludwig Wittgenstein. Autor de *La difícil costumbre de estar lejos* (novela, 1984) y *El imperio perdido o las claves del siglo* (ensayo, 1991). Recibió del Estado alemán la medalla Goethe en 1995.

PÉREZ GAY, RAFAEL ◆ n. en el DF (1957). Estudió letras francesas en la UNAM. Ha sido gerente editorial de Nueva Imagen, coordinador editorial de *La Cultura en México*, suplemento de la revista *Siempre!*, corresponsable de la edición de la revista *Nexos* y director editorial de Cal y Arena. Colaborador de los diarios *unomásuno* y *La Jornada*. Director del suplemento dominical de *Crónica*. Autor de ensayo: *La vida por entregas, Historia crítica de la literatura mexicana*; cuento: *Me perderé contigo* (1988) y *Llamadas nocturnas* (1993); y novela: *Esta vez para siempre* (1990).

PÉREZ GAYTÁN, JOSÉ ENCARNACIÓN ◆ n. en Monterrey, NL (1922). Profesor normalista. Ingresó al PCM en 1939 y durante 35 años perteneció a su Comité Central. Participó en el movimiento magisterial de 1956-60. Al desatarse la represión gubernamental contra los trabajadores ferrocarrileros fue detenido y estuvo en prisión de 1959 a 1965. Cofundador y miembro del comité central del PSUM (1981-87). Cofundador del PMS y del PRD. Fue diputado federal a la LI Legislatura (1979-82). Colaborador de las revistas *Política* y *Tribuna*. Autor de *De la lucha comunista pasada y presente por la democracia*.

PÉREZ-GIL GONZÁLEZ, MANUEL ◆ n. en Morelia, Mich. y m. en Tlalnepantla, Edo. de Méx. (1920-1996). Sacerdote ordenado en 1943. Estudió en los seminarios Conciliar de Morelia y Nacional de Montezuma, EUA. Profesor del Seminario Mayor de Morelia (1943-66). Fue obispo en las diócesis de Mexicali (1966-84), Tepic y Tlalnepantla (1984-1989); al convertirse la última en arzobispado, fue su primer arzobispo, cargo en el que permaneció hasta su muerte. En 1968 y 1979 asistió a la conferencias episcopales latinoamericanas realizadas en Medellín y Puebla. Fue presidente de la Comisión Especial para la Liturgia, la Música y el Arte Sacro (1980-85), secretario general (hasta 1988) y vicepresidente (1993-96) de la Conferencia del Episcopado Mexicano.

PÉREZ Y GONZÁLEZ, RAIMUNDO ◆ n. en Bacalar y m. en Mérida, Yuc. (1768-1832). Sacerdote. Fue párroco de Tepatitán, Tabasco, y diputado a las Cortes Españolas, que se reunieron en Cádiz en 1812.

PÉREZ GUERRERO, CARLOS ◆ n. en Oaxaca, Oax. (1888-?). Se incorporó al Ejército Revolucionario del Sur en 1913 y llegó a coronel en 1916. Cuando el gobierno de Zapata se instaló en Tlaltizapán (1917), fue nombrado secretario de Instrucción Pública. En 1920 fue director de Educación Primaria en el estado de Morelos. Miguel Ángel Peral, en su *Diccionario biográfico mexicano*, señala que Pérez Guerrero es el autor de *Zapata y el agrarismo en México*, libro firmado por Gildardo Magaña.

PÉREZ DE LAS HERAS, JOAQUÍN ◆ n. en el DF (1940). Caballista. Participó en los Juegos Olímpicos de México (1968) y Moscú (1980), donde obtuvo la medalla de bronce en la prueba de salto de obstáculos.

PÉREZ HERNÁNDEZ, ESTANISLAO ◆ n. en Cruillas, Tams. (1952). Contador privado por la Escuela Comercial de Hidalgo. Miembro del PARM desde 1976. Fue diputado federal del PARM (1991-94).

PÉREZ HERNÁNDEZ, JOSÉ MARÍA ◆ n. en Cuba y m. en la ciudad de México (1820-1879). Militar. En México se unió al Plan de Ayutla y combatió al lado de Juan Álvarez. Alcanzó el grado de general en 1857. Preparó un *Diccionario geográfico, estadístico, biográfico, de industria y comercio de la República Mexicana*, en colaboración con Manuel Orozco y Berra y Alfredo Chavero. Escribió una biografía de Juan Álvarez.

PÉREZ JÁCOME, DIONISIO ◆ n. en Coatepec, Ver. (1936). Licenciado en derecho (1959) y contador público y auditor (1965) titulado en la UV. Profesor de la UNAM, la UV y el IPN. Miembro del PRI, en el que ha sido secretario de Prensa y Propaganda (1986) y presidente de la Comisión de Acción Electoral del CEN (1999-). Ha sido agente del Ministerio Público (1960-61), jefe del departamento de la Unión Nacional Agrícola de Cafeteros (1961-62), director general de Enseñanza Superior de la Universidad Veracruzana (1966-67), jefe del Grupo de Sistematización, subgerente y subdirector de Operaciones y gerente de Control de Conasupo (1970-76); subdirector general de Administración Fiscal Regional, de la Secretaría de Hacienda; secretario particular del secretario (1977-79) y subsecretario (1979-82) de Comercio, diputado federal (1988-91, 1994-97), subsecretario de Protección Civil de la Secretaría de Gobernación (1991-93) y senador de la República a la LVII Legislatura (1997-2000).

PÉREZ JIMÉNEZ, LÁZARO ◆ n. en Tizimín, Yuc. (1943). Sacerdote. Hizo estudios en el Seminario Conciliar de Nuestra Señora del Rosario y San Ildefonso y en la Pontificia Universidad Gregoriana de Roma. Licenciado en Teología por el Pontificio Colegio Pío Latinoamericano. Ha sido obispo de la diócesis de Autlán, Jal. (1991-).

PÉREZ MARTÍNEZ, ANTONIO JOAQUÍN ◆ n. y m. en Puebla, Pue. (1763-1829). Sacerdote. Estudió en el Colegio Carolino de Puebla, donde fue profesor de filosofía y teología. Cura de varias parroquias y del Sagrario poblano y canónigo de la catedral de esa ciudad. Fue diputado a las Cortes españolas (1810-14), donde se vinculó con el grupo absolutista de *los persas*. Volvió a

México en 1815 y a partir del año siguiente fue obispo de la diócesis poblana (1816-29). En 1821 estuvo a punto de ser procesado por las nuevas Cortes españolas. Firmó el acta de independencia e integró la primera Junta Provisional Gubernativa. Fue presidente de la Regencia y capellán mayor de la corte del imperio mexicano. A principios de 1829, formó parte de una junta de notables opuesta al gobierno de Guadalupe Victoria, órgano constituido durante el alzamiento de Melchor Múzquiz y que desapareció cuando José Joaquín de Herrera tomó la capital poblana.

Pérez Martínez, Héctor ♦ n. en Campeche, Camp., y m. en Mocambo, Ver. (1906-1948). Periodista y escritor. Odontólogo egresado de la Universidad Nacional en 1928. Fue colaborador, redactor (1930) y subdirector (1936-38) del diario *El Nacional* de la ciudad de México, diputado federal (1938-40), gobernador de Campeche (1941-45) y oficial mayor (1946); secretario de Gobernación (del 1 de diciembre de 1946 al 12 de febrero de 1948) en el gabinete de Miguel Alemán. Perteneció al grupo *Agorista*. Sostuvo una famosa polémica epistolar con Alfonso Reyes, sobre la oposición entre el arte nacionalista y el cosmopolita, que se editó en 1988 con el título *A vuelta de correo. Una polémica sobre literatura nacional*. Editó un *Catálogo de documentos para la historia de Yucatán y Campeche* (1943), la *Crónica* de Ah Nakuk Pech (1936), la *Relación de las cosas de Yucatán*, de Diego de Landa (1938), y el *Diario de nuestro viaje a los Estados Unidos*, de Justo Sierra O'Reilly (1958). Coautor, con José Elguero, de *Una polémica en torno a frailes y encomenderos* (1938) y, con Juan de Dios Pérez Galaz, de una *Bibliografía del estado de Campeche* (1943). Autor de *A la sombra del patio*, (1927), *Dante Alighieri. Sonetórpidos* (1927), *Un rebelde* (1930), *Imagen de nadie* (1932), *Juárez, el impasible* (1934), *Facundo en su laberinto* (1934), *Trayectoria del corrido* (1935), *Se dice de amor en cinco sonetos* (1936), *Atraco de Lorencillo a Campeche* (1937), *Piratería en Campeche* (1937), *Por los caminos de Campeche* (1939), *Introducción de la imprenta en Campeche* (1943) y *Cuauhtémoc. Vida y muerte de una cultura* (1944).

Pérez Meza, Luis ♦ n. en La Rastra y m. en Guasave, Sin. (1917-1981). Cantante conocido como el *Trovador del campo*. En su juventud se dedicó al boxeo. A raíz de su triunfo en un concurso de aficionados, en la radiodifusora XESA de Culiacán, se dedicó profesionalmente a la música. Perteneció al grupo Los Párragos, al trío Los Hermanos Pérez (1937-44) y al Cuarteto Metropolitano (1944-45), antes de iniciar su carrera como solista. Trabajó, entre otras, en las películas *Juan Charrasqueado* (1947), *La casa colorada* (1947) y *Allá en el rancho grande* (versión de 1948). Fueron muy exitosas sus interpretaciones de *El sinaloense*, *El barzón*, *Las Isabeles*, *Al morir la tarde*, *¿Me estás oyendo, Chucha?*, *El carro del sol*, *Heraclio Bernal*, *Ojitos aceitunados*, *La piedrecita*, *Valentín de la sierra*, *Clavelito, clavelito*, *Acuérdate de mí*, *El sauce y la palma* y *El huizache*.

Pérez de Mezquía, Pedro ♦ n. en España y m. en la ciudad de México (1688-1764). Fraile franciscano. Llegó a la Nueva España en 1715 y al año siguiente viajó a Texas con la misión de contener el avance francés por el litoral del golfo de México. Fue en dos ocasiones guardián y prelado del Colegio Misionero de Santa Cruz de Querétaro. Viajó dos veces a España para organizar sendas expediciones de misioneros a Sierra Gorda (1742 y 1749). En la segunda de éstas vino fray Junípero Serra.

Pérez Montfort, Ricardo ♦ n. en en DF (1954). Licenciado (1981) y maestro (1988) en historia por la UNAM; realizó estudios en el Centro de Capacitación Cinematográfica (1980-83). Profesor de la UNAM (1979-) y del Centro de Arte Mexicano (1983-84). Ha sido programador musical (1979-) y jefe del Departamento de Información (1983) de Radio Educación; e investigador del Centro de Investigaciones y Estudios Superiores en Antropología Social (1981-). En televisión dirigió las series *Siglo XX, la vida en México* (1985) y *Apuntes de música popular mexicana* (1986-87), ambas producidas por la Unidad de Televisión Educativa y Cultural. Participó como cantante en la grabación el disco *Cancionero de la intervención francesa* (1974). Con Enrique Florescano compiló Historiadores de México en el siglo XX (1995). Coautor de *Qué onda con la música popular mexicana* (1982), *Morelos, cinco siglos de historia regional* (1985) y *La revolución y los presidentes*. Autor de *El fondo documental Genaro Amezcua* (1981), *Por la patria y por la raza* (1982), *Fascismo y antifascismo en América Latina* (1984), *Los empresarios alemanes, el Tercer Reich y la oposición a Cárdenas* (1982-88), "La irrupción de la cultura popular" en *Así fue la revolución mexicana* (8 t., 1985), *Cárceles y campo* (poesía, 1986), *Trova de agua* (poesía, 1991) y *Estampas de nacionalismo popular mexicano* (1994). En 1989 recibió el Premio Marcos y Celia Mauss a la mejor tesis de la maestría en historia, de la UNAM.

Pérez Moreno, José ♦ n. en Lagos de Moreno, Jal., y m. en el DF (1900-1985). Periodista y escritor. Estudió contaduría en la UNAM. Profesor de geografía y fundador del Instituto Técnico de la Policía y de la Escuela de Periodismo Carlos Septién García. Inició su carrera periodística en 1916, en *El Pueblo*, y más tarde trabajó en *El Demócrata* y en *El Universal*. En 1923 participó en la fundación del Sindicato Nacional de Redactores de Prensa. Durante la segunda guerra mundial fungió como corresponsal de guerra. Fue oficial mayor de la Secretaría de Agricultura, diputado federal (1959-61) y cónsul general en Milán. Colaborador de los periódicos *El Mexicano*, *México Nuevo*, *El Demócrata*, *El Universal* y *La prensa*; y de las revistas *El Universal Ilustrado*, *Todo*, *Hoy*, *Mañana*, *Imaginación de México* y *Siempre!* Uno de sus cuentos, *La mulata de Córdoba*, fue llevada a la pantalla. Autor de la novela *El tercer canto del gallo* (1955), que en 1956 obtuvo el Premio Ciudad de México.

Dámaso Pérez Prado

PÉREZ ORTIZ, FRANCISCO ◆ n. en Pénjamo, Gto., y m. en el DF (1883-1959). Periodista. Fue redactor de *Revista de Revistas*. En 1917 participó en la fundación del diario capitalino *Excélsior*. Entre 1925 y 1943 trabajó en Estados Unidos.

PÉREZ PALACIOS, AUGUSTO ◆ n. en el DF (1909). Arquitecto titulado en la UNAM (1933). Profesor de la UNAM (1934-) y del IPN. Ha sido jefe de Proyectos en la Dirección de Pensiones (1935), supervisor de las obras del Hotel del Prado y director de la construcción de la fábrica Fibracel, en Ciudad Valles (1948). Coautor del proyecto del Estadio Olímpico universitario (1950) y autor del proyecto del edificio de la Secretaría de Comunicaciones y Obras Públicas (1953), que resultó dañado a raíz de los temblores de septiembre de 1985.

PÉREZ PÉREZ, CELESTINO ◆ n. en Tlacolula de Matamoros, Oax., y m. en el DF (1894-1982). Abogado titulado en el Instituto de Ciencias y Artes de Oaxaca (1914). Profesor de los institutos de ciencias y artes de San Luis Potosí y Oaxaca. Militó en el Partido Antirreeleccionista y estuvo preso durante la dictadura de Victoriano Huerta. Fue diputado por Oaxaca al Congreso Constituyente de 1916-17, agente del Ministerio Público, juez en Baja California, el Distrito Federal, Puebla, San Luis Potosí, Tabasco, Tamaulipas y Zacatecas; presidente de la Junta Central de Conciliación y Arbitraje de Mexicali, fundador del Sindicato Único de Trabajadores Petroleros de la República Mexicana, subdirector del Departamento Jurídico de la Secretaría del Patrimonio Nacional y senador de la República (1970-76).

El Estadio Olímpico de Ciudad Universitaria, proyecto de Augusto Pérez Palacios

PÉREZ PEÑAFIEL, JUVENTINO ◆ n. en San Agustín Metzquititlán, Hgo. (1923). Profesor titulado en la Escuela Rural Campesina de El Mexe y licenciado en derecho por la UNAM. Ha sido secretario particular del gobernador de hidalgo, Oswaldo Cravioto (1958-60); diputado local (1960-63), profesor y rector (1963-70) de la Universidad Autónoma de Hidalgo, magistrado (1970) y presidente (1971-73) del Tribunal Superior de Justicia del mismo estado; asesor jurídico (1973-79) y jefe del Departamento de Defensoría de Oficio del Departamento del Distrito Federal (1979).

PÉREZ PLAZOLA, HÉCTOR ◆ n. en Guadalajara, Jal. (1933). Estudió derecho y administración en la Universidad de Guadalajara. Profesor del Instituto de Capacitación Cooperativa Conducción Regional de las Instituciones de Ahorro. Militante del Partido Acción Nacional desde 1951, ha sido diputado a la Legislatura de Jalisco (1980-83), regidor del ayuntamiento de Guadalajara (1983-85) y dos veces diputado federal, la segunda ocasión, plurinominal (1985-88 y 1991-94).

PÉREZ PORRÚA, JOSÉ ANTONIO ◆ n. en España y m. en el DF (1907-1996). Editor. Fue presidente y director general de la Librería de Porrúa Hermanos, S.A. y de Editorial Porrúa, S.A., que fundó en 1944. Recibió la Orden del Águila Azteca (1968), la Orden de Doña Isabel en grado de Comendador, otorgada por el gobierno español (1990), y el Premio Nacional Juan Pablos al mérito editorial (1994).

PÉREZ PORRÚA, FRANCISCO ◆ n. y m. en España (1903-1987). Librero y editor. Llegó a México en 1918. Desde entonces trabajó en la empresa de sus tíos, la Librería Porrúa. En 1933, al retirarse José Porrúa, pasó a formar parte de la sociedad mercantil. Creó la colección *Sepan cuantos.* (1950) y la *Biblioteca histórica Porrúa*. Promovió que, en 1964, José María Garibay realizara el primer *Diccionario Porrúa de historia, biografía y geografía de México*. En 1969 recibió la Orden del Águila Azteca.

PÉREZ PRADO, DÁMASO ◆ n. en Cuba y m. en el DF (1916-1989). Músico. Estudió piano en la ciudad de Matanzas, Cuba. Llamado *el Rey del Mambo*, por haber sido creador de ese ritmo, y *Cara de Foca* por su fisonomía. En Cuba formó varios conjuntos musicales y trabajó como arreglista del cantante Orlando Guerra, *Cascarita*. Llegó a México en 1949 y formó una orquesta con ejecutantes mexicanos. Se presentó en teatro y televisión. Participó, entre otras, en las películas *Perdida* (1949), *Al son del mambo* (1950), *Serenata en acapulco* (1950), *Sindicato de telemirones* (1954), *Locura musical* (1956), *Locos por la tele* (1956), *Música y dinero* (1956), *El dengue del amor* (1965) y *A fuego lento* (1977). Compositor de unos 300 mambos y dengues, entre ellos, *¡Qué rico mambo!*, *El pachuco bailarín*, *Mambo a la Kenton*, *Mambo número 5*, *Lupita*, *Rebeca*, *Norma la de Guadalajara*, *Mambo a Sasha Montenegro*, *Caballo negro*, *Mambo del Politécnico*, *Mambo universitario*, *Mambo número 8*, *El ruletero*, *El suby*, *Rico, caliente y sabroso*, *Mambo del taconazo*, *Mambo en sax*, *Tomando café*, *Al compás del mambo*, *Mambo negro*, *Patricia* (usada por Federico Fellini para sonorizar la cinta *La dolce vita*), *Mambo del Politécnico* y arreglos, entre los cuales destaca *Cerezo rosa*. Grabó más de 100 discos de larga duración. Se ha escrito una biografía suya: *Pérez Prado y el mambo* (1995).

Pérez Rayón, Reinaldo ◆ n. en el DF (1918). Arquitecto titulado en el IPN (1945). Ha sido jefe del Plano Regulador de la ciudad de México (1950-56) y asesor de arquitectura y urbanismo de la Secretaría de Comunicaciones y Transportes (1965-70) y, en el Instituto Politécnico Nacional, jefe del proyecto de la Unidad Profesional de Zacatenco (1957-65), jefe del Centro de Investigación y Estudios Avanzados (1961), jefe del Centro Nacional de Enseñanza Técnica Industrial (1962-64), director del Planetario Luis Enrique Erro, presidente del Patronato de Obras e Instalaciones (1967-70) y jefe de la Unidad de Ciencias Básicas de la Escuela Superior de Ingeniería Mecánica y Eléctrica (1972-73) y de la ciudad de la Ciencia y la Tecnología. Fue miembro de la Junta Directiva de la UAM (1980-87) y es miembro del Consejo Consultivo de Ciencia de la Presidencia de la República (1989-). Articulista y conferenciante, es autor de *Ideas y obras* (1991). Premio Fundidora Monterrey (1967) y Premio Nacional de Ciencias y Artes (1976); ha recibido también el diploma de la Unión Internacional de Arquitectos. Académico de número y consejero de la Academia Mexicana de Arquitectura; académico emérito de la Academia Nacional de Arquitectura de la Sociedad de Arquitectos Mexicanos.

Pérez Ríos, Francisco ◆ n. en Temascaltepec, Edo. de Méx., y m. en el DF (1908-1975). Líder obrero. Fue fundador y secretario general del Sindicato Nacional de Electricistas Federales, magistrado del Tribunal de Arbitraje, secretario general del Sindicato Nacional de Electricistas y Conexos de la República Mexicana (1942-72), secretario general del Sindicato Único de Trabajadores Electricistas de la República Mexicana (1972-75), tres veces diputado federal y senador (1970-75). Perteneció al Partido Revolucionario Institucional y al Jockey Club.

Pérez de Rivas, Andrés ◆ n. en España y m. en la ciudad de México (1575-1655). Sacerdote. Ingresó en la Compañía de Jesús en 1602. En ese mismo año llegó a la Nueva España y en 1604, luego de cumplir su noviciado en Puebla, fue enviado como misionero a Sinaloa para evangelizar a los ahomes. En 1617, con Tomás Basipio, fundó una misión en territorio yaqui. Fue rector (1620-22) y presidente (1626-32) del Colegio Máximo de Tepozotlán, provincial de los jesuitas (1636-41), procurador de la provincia mexicana de los jesuitas en Europa (1643-47) y prepósito de la Casa Profesa de México (1648). Durante 16 años evangelizó a los ahomes, zuaques y yaquis. Autor de *Historia de los triunphos de nuestra santa fe* (1645), *Historia de Sinaloa* y *Crónica e historia religiosa de la Compañía de Jesús en la Nueva España*.

Pérez Rivera, Antonio ◆ n. y m. en Jalapa, Ver. (1860-1933). Hacendado. Durante el porfiriato fungió como jefe político de Jalapa. En 1910 se adhirió al Plan de San Luis Potosí. Fue gobernador de Veracruz (de diciembre de 1912 a febrero de 1913); tras el asesinato del presidente Francisco I. Madero se exilió en Estados Unidos.

Pérez Rivero, José Antonio ◆ n. y m. Puebla, Pue. (1913-1988). Hizo estudios de abogacía en el Colegio del Estado. Catedrático de la Universidad de Puebla, en la que intervino en las negociaciones para lograr la autonomía universitaria (1956); miembro del Consejo de Honor y fundó la Escuela de Administración de Empresas. Fue presidente del Centro Patronal de Puebla y Tlaxcala (1941-76) y la Cámara de la Industria de la Transformación de Puebla y Tlaxcala (1942-78).

Pérez Rojas, Óscar ◆ n. en el DF (1973). Futbolista. Su apodo es *Conejo*. Ha sido portero del equipo Cruz Azul. Como seleccionado nacional participó en la Copa América 1995, y en el Campeonato Mundial 1998.

Pérez Saavedra, Francisco Leonardo ◆ n. en Oaxaca, Oax. (1940). Profesor por la Escuela Normal Rural Federalizada (1965-67) y licenciado en economía por la UNAM (1972-76). Militante del PPS desde 1968. Director de escuela rural de la SEP (1968-70), profesor de primaria (1968-69), de la ENEP-Aragón (1976) y de la UPN (1979-89). En el SNTE ha sido secretario general delegacional (1982-84), secretario de Fomento Cultural (1983-86) y de Actas y Acuerdos de la sección X (1986-89) y, secretario general del Frente Revolucionario Unidad Magisterial (1989-). Representante plurinominal a la primera Asamblea del Distrito Federal (1988-91). Autor de *Estructura social y económica de México* (1978).

Pérez Salazar y de Haro, Francisco ◆ n. en Puebla, Pue., y m. en el DF (1888-1941). Abogado e historiador. Se graduó en 1913 en la Escuela Nacional de Jurisprudencia. Colaboró en las revistas *Memorias*, *Revista de la Sociedad Científica Antonio Alzate*, *Ocotlán* y *Revista de Literatura Mexicana*. Autor de *Historia de la Puebla de los Ángeles* (1926), *Biografía de Carlos de Sigüenza y Góngora* (1928), *El grabado en la ciudad de Puebla de los Ángeles* (1933), *Impresores de Puebla en la época colonial* (1939), *Poesías* (1953) e *Historia de la pintura en Puebla*.

Pérez Salazar y Venegas, Manuel ◆ n. y m. en Puebla, Pue. (1816-1871). Escritor. Estudió en el Seminario Conciliar Palafoxiano. Fue diputado local y federal (1848) y rector del Colegio del Estado. Redactor del *Diccionario de historia y geografía* de Manuel Orozco y Berra. Tradujo obras de Víctor Hugo, Thomas Gray, Alejandro Manzoni y Giacomo Leopardi, entre otros. Luego de su muerte, apareció un volumen con sus *Poesías* (1876). Perteneció a la Arcadia Romana y a las sociedades Lancasteriana y Mexicana de Geografía y Estadística.

Pérez San Vicente, Guadalupe ◆ n. en el DF (1925). Licenciada en pedagogía, maestra y doctora en historia por la UNAM. Es fundadora de la carrera de archivonomía de la UNAM y de los colegios de Historia e Historia del Arte en la UIA. Ha participado en la creación de los

Juan Antonio Pérez Simón

archivos históricos de la Facultad de Medicina, la Universidad de Veracruz y el gobierno de Baja California. Fundó y dirigió el Archivo Histórico de la UNAM y el Departamento de Documentación de la Secretaría de la Presidencia. Ha colaborado en la revista *Artes de México* y en los *Anales del Museo Mexicano*. Realizó las compilaciones *Cedulario cortesiano* (1949) y *Cedulario metropolitano* (1960). Coautora de *Joaquín Ramírez Cabañas. Semblanza de un maestro* (1946) y *Juárez en el arte* (1972). Autora de *Diosas y mujeres aztecas* (1944) y *Obra histórica de Atanasio G. Saravia* (1976).

Pérez Sánchez, Aurelio ◆ n. en el DF (1924). En la empresa Televisa ha sido jefe de producción y gerente del Canal 4 de televisión, director de Eventos Especiales, gerente de Televisoras de Provincia y vicepresidente de Noticias. Fue vicepresidente de la Cámara Nacional de la Industria de Radiodifusión. Autor de *Historia de la plaza de toros de México* y *Orígenes de la fiesta brava*.

Pérez de la Serna, Juan ◆ n. y m. en España (¿1573?-1631). Estudió en el Colegio de Sigüenza, de Castilla la Vieja, y en el de la Santa Cruz de Valladolid. Fue ordenado sacerdote en 1595. Profesor de la Universidad de Durango y canónigo de la Catedral de Valladolid. En enero de 1613, Felipe III lo nombró arzobispo de México. Llegó a la Nueva España en ese mismo año y de inmediato trató de ganarse la voluntad de los criollos, bien con su impulso al culto guadalupano o mediante su aparición en actos públicos, incluso en representaciones de teatro, tachadas de inmorales en la época, lo que le valió una reprimenda de las autoridades madrileñas. Tuvo serias fricciones con el gobierno de la Audiencia, presidido por Pedro de Vergara Gabiria (1621). El 16 de junio de 1622, ante la corrupción reinante en las esferas gubernamentales escribió al Consejo de Indias que era más fácil conquistar otra vez la Nueva España "que reformarla en los abusos introducidos en ella y convertidos en naturaleza por la larga costumbre y disimulación de los ministros públicos". Pese a coincidir con el nuevo virrey, Diego Carrillo de Mendoza Pimentel, en su oposición a la venalidad de los funcionarios, éste ordenó clausurar, en 1621, una carnicería que tenía el obispo, lo que inició entre ellos una rivalidad que se acentuó al negarse el virrey a transferir al clero secular las parroquias de indios, controladas por los regulares. El conflicto estalló cuando el ex corregidor de Metepec, Melchor de Varáez, sometido a proceso por el virrey, escapó de la cárcel y se refugió en el convento dominico, donde las autoridades pusieron una guardia permanente para evitar una nueva fuga. Los frailes, en excelentes relaciones con el marqués de Gelves, no pusieron objeción, pero sí Pérez de la Serna, quien excomulgó a los guardianes y a otros funcionarios. El arzobispo envió la notificación a Gelves y éste decidió deportar al mensajero, a lo que respondió el prelado con la excomunión del mismo virrey, quien presionó para que el 11 de enero de 1624, la Audiencia ordenara la deportación a España del propio arzobispo, el que, en la tarde de ese día, inició su viaje. Sin embargo, poco después, la misma Audiencia le pidió que disminuyera su marcha todo lo posible, y el día 12 suspendió la sentencia, por lo que Gelves hizo aprehender a los oidores, lo que originó una manifestación de protesta frente al palacio virreinal. Se desataron así una serie de hechos que culminaron en una insurrección popular que derrocó al virrey, después de que éste había cancelado la orden de deportación. A la medianoche del 15 de enero de 1624 regresó el arzobispo a la ciudad de México en medio de una manifestación multitudinaria. En 1625, Pérez de la Serna fue llamado a España, donde se encargó de la diócesis de Zamora.

Pérez Serrano, Gustavo ◆ n. en Altar, Son., y m. en el DF (1885-1979). Fue diputado federal (1920-22), secretario de Comunicaciones y Obras Públicas (del 21 de octubre de 1931 al 20 de enero de 1932), en el gobierno de Ortiz Rubio; embajador de México en Guatemala (del 25 de septiembre de 1932 al 4 de junio de 1933), presidente de la Cámara Minera de México y de la Asociación Nacional de Minería y secretario de Economía (del 1 de julio de 1944 al 30 de noviembre de 1946), en el gabinete de Ávila Camacho.

Pérez Simón, Juan Antonio ◆ n. en el DF (1941). Contador público. Presidente del Consejo de Administración, presidente ejecutivo y director general de Sanborns Hermanos; presidente del consejo y del Comité Ejecutivo de Fábricas de Papel Loreto y Peña Pobre; Consejero Propietario y miembro del Comité Ejecutivo de Tabacalera Mexicana, Empresas Frisco y Seguros de México; consejero propietario de Artes Gráficas Unidas, Industrial Nacobre, Galas de México, Grupo Carso e Inversora Bursátil; director general de Teléfonos de México (1990-). Miembro de la Junta de Gobierno del Colegio de Contadores Públicos de México.

Pérez y Soto, Atenedoro ◆ n. en Acayucan, Ver., y m. en el DF (1883-1961). Caricaturista y pintor. Estudió en la Escuela Nacional de Bellas Artes. Comenzó su carrera en 1910, en la revista *Sucesos Ilustrados*, y luego colaboró en *Anáhuac*, *La Semana Ilustrada*, *El Látigo*, *La Sátira*, *Multicolor* y *El País*. Salió de México luego del asesinato del presidente Francisco I. Madero. En Cuba dirigió la revista *La Política Cómica* (1916-32). A su regreso a México hizo caricaturas para *El Duende de la Catedral* y *La Ráfaga*. Más tarde trabajó como ilustrador del Departamento de Divulgación de la Secretaría de Educación.

Pérez y Soto, Atenógenes ◆ n. en Acayucan, Ver., y m. en el DF (1886-1957). Profesor titulado en la Escuela Normal de Jalapa, de la que fue director al igual que del Colegio Preparatorio de esa ciudad. En el Distrito Federal ejerció la docencia en la Escuela Nacional Preparatoria y en el Colegio Militar. Regresó a Veracruz y fue director general de Educación del estado. Autor de *El instante de la poesía*, *Simulación filosófica de Antonio Caso*, *Por abril*, *Ellas tienen la culpa*, *Un cuento de navidad*, *Díaz Mirón*, *Iris* y *Cuentos psicológicos*.

PÉREZ DE SOTO, MELCHOR ◆ n. en Cholula, Pue., y m. en la ciudad de México (1606-1655). Bibliófilo y arquitecto. Fue amigo de Porter de Casanate, quien lo instruyó en la astrología y lo llevó como asesor en la expedición a Baja California en busca de bancos de perlas. A su regreso fue enviado por el virrey a inspeccionar el entonces deteriorado fuerte de San Juan de Ulúa, en Veracruz, y después unas minas de Tetela, Puebla. En 1654 era obrero mayor de las obras de la Catedral Metropolitana cuando fue aprehendido por la Inquisición, acusado de prácticas heréticas. Fue asesinado en las mazmorras del Santo Oficio. Su biblioteca, confiscada al momento de detención, contaba con más de 1,600 volúmenes que incluían obras de creación literaria, religión, historia, filosofía, medicina, matemáticas, estrategia militar, navegación, astrología, astronomía, agricultura, minería, equitación, capintería, arquitectura y otras disciplinas. Entre los autores de tales libros se contaban Homero, Virgilio, Torcuato Tasso, Dante, Petrarca, Ariosto, Camoes, Santa Teresa, San Juan de la Cruz, fray Luis de León, fray Luis de Granada, Alonso de Ercilla, Bernardo de Balbuena, Garcilaso de la Vega, Francisco de Quevedo, Kepler y Copérnico. Cuando los inquisidores devolvieron la mayor parte de la biblioteca a la viuda, Leonor de Montoya, ésta consiguió comprador para algunos ejemplares y anunció que el resto deseaba "venderlos como papel usado".

PÉREZ TAMAYO, RUY ◆ n. en Tampico, Tams. (1924). Médico cirujano titulado en la UNAM (1943-50) y doctor en inmunología por el IPN (1968-73); realizó estudios de posgrado en la Washington University, en San Louis Misouri (1950-52), con una beca de la Fundación W. K. Kellog; y del Instituto Nacional de Cardiología (1953-54). Es profesor de la UNAM desde 1954. Ha sido investigador en el Instituto Nacional de Cardiología (1949-50), patólogo del Hospital Español (1953-54), director de la Unidad de Patología de la UNAM (1954-67), jefe de la Unidad de Patología

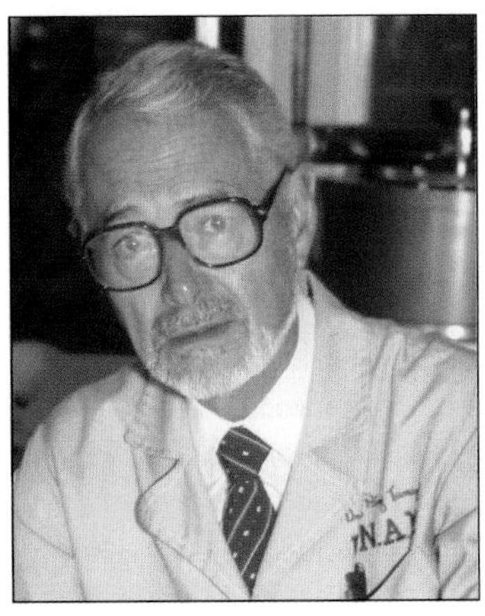

Ruy Pérez Tamayo

(1954-67) y jefe del Departamento de Enseñanza e Investigación Científica del Hospital General (1965-67); jefe del Departamento de Biología Celular del Instituto de Investigaciones Biomédicas de la UNAM (1967-74), jefe del Departamento de Patología del Instituto Nacional de Nutrición (1974-83), miembro de la Junta de Gobierno de la UNAM (1983-) y miembro del Patronato de la UAM (1984-). Escribe en *Excélsior*. Ha publicado más de 140 artículos científicos en revistas especializadas de México y el extranjero. Es coautor de una decena de libros y autor de *Principios de patología* (1959), *Mechanisms of Disease* (1961), *El viejo alquimista* (1974), *Tres variaciones sobre la muerte y otros ensayos biomédicos* (1974), *Patología molecular, subcelular y celular* (1975), *Introducción a la patología* (1976), *Serendipia. Ensayos sobre ciencia, medicina y otros sueños* (1979), *Temas de patología* (1980), *En defensa de la ciencia* (1980), *Tríptico* (1982), *La segunda vuelta* (1983), *Enfermedades viejas y nuevas* (1985), *Cómo acercarse a la ciencia* (1988), *El concepto de enfermedad. Su evolución a través de la historia* (1989), *Existe el método científico* (1990) y *Enfermedades viejas y enfermedades nuevas* (1998). Pertenece a la Academia Mexicana (de la Lengua), El Colegio Nacional, la Academia de la Investigación Científica y la Asociación Mexicana de Patólogos, de la que fue fundador (1954) y presidente (1957), entre otras corporaciones. Miembro emérito del Sistema Nacional de Investigadores. Becario Guggenheim. Premio Nacional de Ciencias y Artes (1974).

PÉREZ TAYLOR, RAFAEL ◆ n. y m. en el DF (1890-1936). Periodista. Militó en el Partido Liberal Constitucional Progresista, que apoyó la candidatura de Francisco I. Madero en 1911. En 1912 participó en la fundación de la Casa del Obrero Mundial. Fundador del periódico *El Universo*. Colaboró desde 1916 en *El Universal*, donde con el seudónimo de *Hipólito Seijas* publicó la columna "Por las pantallas", la primera de crítica cinematográfica en México. En agosto de 1917 participó en la fundación del Partido Nacional Cooperatista. Fue director del Museo Nacional, diputado federal y jefe de prensa de la Secretaría de Educación (1936). Colaboró en *Nueva Era*, *El Liberal* y *El Nacional*. Autor de teatro: *Un gesto* (1916), *Alma* (1918) y *Del hampa* (1935). Autor de *El socialismo en México*.

PÉREZ DE TEJEDA, JUAN JOSÉ ◆ m. en la Villa de Guadalupe, hoy en el DF (?-1817). Sacerdote. Su nombre completo era Juan José Pérez Tejeda Llera González Arratia. En 1766 era profesor de teología, en 1781 aparece como consiliario de la Real y Pontificia Universidad, de la que fue elegido rector en 1794, cuando era cura de Santa María, puesto en el que continuaba en octubre de 1810, cuando fue designado vicerrector y ocupó interinamente la rectoría por ausencia del titular, José Julio García Torres. En ese cargo, permitió que el virrey Venegas alojara tropas en la sede universitaria, la que sirvió como cuartel durante los años de la guerra de Independencia. Asimismo, presidió la reunión en que se excluyó de la nómina a Agustín Pomposo Fernández de San Salvador, por ocultar que era casado en las dos ocasiones que fue elegido rector. Apoyó la propuesta del virrey para reelegir a García Torres, pese a que se contravenían los estatutos, pero tuvo que ceder, al igual que Venegas, ante la disposición del claustro para defender la legalidad. En 1804 abogó, dentro del claustro universitario, por la reelección de su hermano Luis Agustín, elegido rector en 1803. Al morir era canónigo magistral de la Colegiata de Guadalupe.

PÉREZ DEL TORO, CARLOS ◆ n. en Jalapa, Ver., y m. en el DF (1920-1976). Contador. Profesor de las escuelas Nacional de Comercio y Administración de la UNAM y de Contaduría Pública de la Universidad Iberoamericana. Fue secretario (1957-62) y director (1965-69) de la Facultad de Contaduría y Administración de la UNAM; presidente del Colegio Mexicano de Contadores Públicos (1972-74). Presidió la Comisión de Vigilancia Administrativa del Consejo Universitario y de la Asociación de Facultades y Escuelas de Comercio, Contabilidad y Administración de la República Mexicana.

PÉREZ TORRES, MARIO ◆ n. en el DF (1928). Militar. Estudió en el Colegio Militar (1947-49). Es licenciado en administración militar por la Escuela Superior de Guerra (1962) y maestro en administración militar por el Colegio de Defensa. Ha sido comandante de la Sección de Fuegos del Cuerpo de Guardias Presidenciales (1950), comandante de batería y plana mayor (1961), jefe de la tercera sección (1966-68) y subjefe (1970-73) del Estado Mayor de la primera Zona Militar; comandante del segundo batallón de infantería (1973-74), jefe del Estado Mayor de la XXX (1974-76) y XXIX (1981-83) zonas militares; agregado militar y aéreo de la embajada mexicana en Perú (1978-81); comandante de la XIII Zona Militar (1984-85), subdirector de Seguridad Social Militar (1985-86) y director general de Archivo e Historia (1986-), de la Secretaría de la Defensa Nacional.

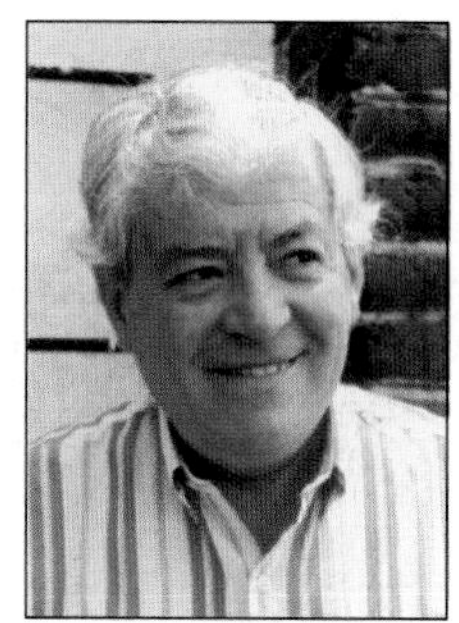
Tomás Pérez Turrent

PÉREZ TREJO, GUSTAVO A. ◆ n. en Siquisiva, Son., y m. en el DF (1910-1989). Realizó estudios de medicina (1932-39). Tomó cursos especiales en el FBI y trabajó en el Servicio Médico de la Policía (1935-47). Bibliotecario desde 1924, ha sido director de la Hemeroteca Nacional (1935-47) y la Biblioteca Miguel Lerdo de Tejada de la Secretaría de Hacienda (1962-). Es miembro de la Junta Dictaminadora del Instituto de Investigaciones Bibliográficas de la UNAM y asesor del *Diario Oficial de la Federación*. Editó una serie de *Documentos sobre Belice o Balice* (1958).

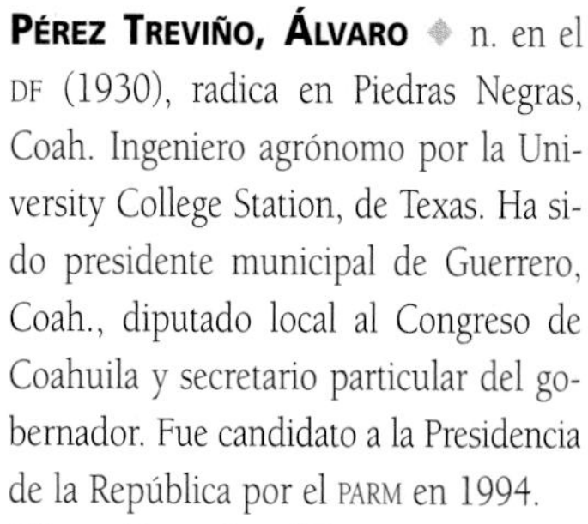

PÉREZ TREVIÑO, ÁLVARO ◆ n. en el DF (1930), radica en Piedras Negras, Coah. Ingeniero agrónomo por la University College Station, de Texas. Ha sido presidente municipal de Guerrero, Coah., diputado local al Congreso de Coahuila y secretario particular del gobernador. Fue candidato a la Presidencia de la República por el PARM en 1994.

PÉREZ TREVIÑO, MANUEL ◆ n. en Guerrero, Coah., y m. en el DF (1890-1945). Militar. Se afilió al constitucionalismo en 1913 y a la rebelión de Agua Prieta en 1920. Fue jefe del Estado Mayor de Álvaro Obregón, en cuya presidencia ocupó la Secretaría de Industria, Comercio y Trabajo (del 30 de octubre de 1923 al 30 de noviembre de 1924); general de brigada en 1924, gobernador de Coahuila (del 1 de diciembre de 1925 al 30 de noviembre de 1929), agregado militar en varias legaciones mexicanas en Sudamérica, miembro (del 1 al 8 de diciembre) y presidente del Comité Organizador del Partido Nacional Revolucionario (del 8 de diciembre de 1928 al 1 de marzo de 1929), primer presidente del PRN (del 4 de marzo de 1929 al 11 de febrero de 1930), secretario de Agricultura y Fomento del presidente Pascual Ortiz Rubio (del 5 de febrero de 1930 al 1 de septiembre de 1931), nuevamente líder del PRN (del 29 de agosto de 1931 al 12 de mayo de 1933), precandidato a la presidencia de la República (1933), por tercera vez presidente del CEN del PRN (del 9 de junio al 25 de agosto de 1933), embajador en España (1935-36) y fundador del Partido Revolucionario Anti-Comunista (1939).

PÉREZ TURRENT, TOMÁS ◆ n. San Andrés Tuxtla, Ver. (1931). Escritor y crítico de cine. En documentos oficiales aparece como nacido en el DF. Estudió filosofía en la UNAM (1960-62) y cine en París (1962-63). Ha sido profesor del Centro Universitario de Estudios Cinematográficos (1968-69 y 1976-77) y del Centro de Capacitación Cinematográfica (1975-82). Perteneció al grupo que editó la revista *Nuevo Cine* (1961-62). Trabajó en la Cinemateca Francesa (1963-67). Fue encargado de la Sección Cinematográfica de Telecadena Mexicana (1968), director de un programa de documentales y asesor de la Rectoría de la Universidad Veracruzana (1979-80), asesor de la Dirección de Difusión Cultural del IPN, donde dirigió la revista *Cine IPN* (1980-81), e investigador de la Filmoteca de la UNAM. Con José de la Colina y Fernando Gou, coordinó la sección de cine de *Oposición* (1970-72). Ha escrito en numerosas publicaciones mexicanas y extranjeras. Intervino en los programas de televisión *Tiempo de cine* (1971-73), *Cine corto, ideas largas* (1979-80), *Fábrica de sueños* (1981) y *Nueve Treinta* (1995-). Hizo los argumentos para las películas *Canoa* (1975), *Mina, viento de libertad* (1976), *Las Poquianchis* (1976), *El complot mongol* (1977), *Benjamín Argumedo, el rebelde* (1978), *Complot: petróleo* (adaptación de *La cabeza de la hidra*, de Carlos Fuentes, 1981), *Alsino y el cóndor* (1981), *Ulama* (en colaboración, 1986), *La furia de un dios* (1987), *Las inocentes* (1988), *Sandino* (1988) y *El último crimen* (en colaboración, 1989). Coautor, con José de la Colina, de *Prohibido asomarse al interior. Conversaciones con Luis Buñuel* (1985). Escribió dos anexos para la edición en español de la *Historia del cine mundial*, de Georges Sadoul (1972). Autor de *Buster Keaton* (1991), *La fábrica de los sueños, Luis Alcoriza* (1977) y *El futuro nos visita. El cine en el año 2000* (1981). En 1976 ganó la Diosa de Plata al mejor libreto de cine. Es miembro de la Academia Mexicana de Ciencias y Artes Cinematográficas. Obtuvo la medalla Salvador Toscano en 1999.

PÉREZ VALDELOMAR, BENITO ◆ n. en España y m. en Nueva Granada, hoy Colombia (1743-1813). En 1800 fue nombrado intendente de la Capitanía General de Yucatán. Llegó a Mérida a fines de ese año, luego de haber sido prisionero de un grupo de piratas ingleses. Durante su administración, el doctor Balmis introdujo en la península la vacuna antivariolosa, se abrió el puerto de Sisal al tráfico de altura (1811) y se enfrentó al proceso de Gustavo Nordingh de Witt, agente secreto de José Bonaparte. En 1811 dejó el país, designado virrey del Nuevo Reino de Granada.

PÉREZ VELASCO, GUILLERMO ◆ n. en Oaxaca, Oax. (1942). Licenciado en economía por la UNAM (1963-67) y maestro en derecho económico por la Universidad Autónoma Metropolitana (1980-81). Profesor de la UNAM (1970-71). Ha sido secretario técnico de la Cámara Nacional de la Industria Electrónica y de Comunicaciones Eléctricas (1967-68), coordinador de analistas de Organización y Métodos del Banco del Atlántico (1968-69), analista de las secretarías de la Presidencia (1969-70) y de Patrimonio Nacional (1971); director de Relaciones Humanas de la Comisión Coordinadora para el Desarrollo del Istmo de Tehuantepec (1972-74), subdirector de Bienestar de la Secretaría del Trabajo (1975-76), jefe de la editorial del ISSSTE (1977-78), jefe de Publicaciones de la Secretaría de Hacienda (1979-82), subdirector de Planeación de Radio Educación (1983-88), donde condujo el programa *El mundo en México*, y subgerente Internacional del FCE (1990-95). Ha colaborado en *Personas*, *La República* y otras publicaciones. Escribió el prólogo de *Semilla libertaria*, de Ricardo Flores Magón (1975). Es miembro del Colegio Nacional de Economistas y de la Liga de Economistas Revolucionarios del PRI.

PÉREZ VELÁZQUEZ, LONGINOS ◆ n. en el DF (1902). Atleta. Corredor aficionado desde su juventud. Ha participado en el Campeonato Mundial de Masters y en el Maratón Internacional de la Ciudad de México. En 1988, la UNESCO le otorgó el diploma Fair Play.

PÉREZ VERDÍA, ANTONIO ◆ n. y m. en Guadalajara, Jal. (1828-1875). Se tituló de abogado en el Instituto de Ciencias de Guadalajara (1856), donde ejerció la docencia. Fue asesor de la jefatura de Hacienda y director de la Biblioteca Pública de Jalisco, magistrado de circuito y del Supremo Tribunal de Justicia (1867), y secretario de Gobierno (1871-74), en el periodo de Ignacio L. Vallarta. Perteneció a la Falange de Estudio.

PÉREZ VERDÍA, BENITO XAVIER ◆ n. y m. en Guadalajara, Jal. (1892-1951). Se tituló como abogado en 1913. Fue secretario de la embajada mexicana en Guatemala, delegado de México a la cuarta Conferencia Interamericana realizada en Argentina (1910), secretario de la dirección de la Unión Panamericana (1911-16), regidor de la ciudad de México (1919-20) y delegado de México a la Sociedad de Naciones (1932). Colaboró en el diario *Excélsior* y fundó la revista *Ecos*. Autor de *La belleza* (1910), *Versos de juventud* (1922), *Frente al tinglado electoral* (1939) y *Cárdenas apóstol vs. Cárdenas estadista* (1939).

PÉREZ VERDÍA, ENRIQUE ◆ n. en Guadalajara, Jal., y m. en el DF (1909-1974). Licenciado en derecho (1933), posgraduado en la Universidad de Columbia (1934) y doctor en derecho por la UNAM (1963). Desde 1934 perteneció a la Barra Mexicana-Colegio de Abogados. Llevó cursos especializados en la Facultad Internacional para la Enseñanza del Derecho Comparado, en Estrasburgo. Fue director fundador de la Preparatoria 4 (1953-61).

PÉREZ VERDÍA, LUIS ◆ n. en Guadalajara, Jal., y m. en Guatemala (1857-1914). Abogado titulado en la Escuela de Jurisprudencia de Guadalajara (1877). Profesor, secretario (1877) y rector (1882) del Liceo de Varones de Guadalajara. Fue magistrado del Tribunal de Justicia (1884), diputado local (1889) y federal (1890-1912), director de la Junta Directiva de Estudios de Jalisco y ministro plenipotenciario de México en Guatemala (1913-15). Autor de *Biografía del exmo. sr. d. Prisciliano Sánchez, primer gobernador constitucional del estado de Jalisco* (1881), *Compendio de la historia de México desde sus primeros tiempos hasta la caída del segundo imperio* (1883), *Apuntes históricos sobre la guerra de independencia en Jalisco* (1886), *Remedo biográfico del señor licenciado don José Luis Verdía, deán de la catedral de Guadalajara* (1889), *Vida del ilmo. señor don fray Antonio Alcalde, "el fraile de la calavera"* (1892), *Cómo ha escrito el dr. Nicolás León su historia de México* (1902), *Tratado elemental de derecho internacional privado* (1908), *Estudio biográfico sobre el sr. licenciado d. Jesús López Portillo* (1908) e *Historia particular del estado de Jalisco* (1911).

PÉREZ VERDÍA Y FERNÁNDEZ, ANTONIO ◆ n. en Guadalajara, Jal., y m. en el DF (1876-1958). Abogado. Llegó a la ciudad de México en 1916. Fue el primer presidente de la Barra Mexicana-Colegio de Abogados. Autor de *Divagaciones de un devoto de la historia sobre cosas vistas o sabidas*. Perteneció a la Academia Mexicana de Jurisprudencia y Legislación. Recibió los premios al Mérito Forense y Peña y Peña, así como la medalla Ignacio L. Vallarta.

PÉREZ VERDUZCO, GUILLERMO ◆ n. en Toluca, Edo. de Méx., y m. en el DF (1931-1991). Periodista. Fundó la escuela Periodismo y Arte en Radio y Televisión, de la que era profesor. Se inició en la fuente de espectáculos en el semanario *El Redondel*. Reportero fundador del noticiero de televisión *24 Horas*, para el que fue corresponsal de guerra en El Salvador, las islas Malvinas e Irán.

PÉREZ ZARAGOZA, EVANGELINA ◆ n. en Vista Hermosa, Mich. (1950). Hizo la carrera de enfermería. Ha radicado desde 1963 en Atizapán de Zaragoza, Edo. de Méx. Militante del PAN desde 1988, ha sido candidata a diputada federal (1997), consejera del partido (1988-), responsable de capacitación en la Secretaría de Promoción Política de la Mujer en el PAN del Estado de México (1989-90), presidenta del voluntariado (1997), subdirectora de Desarrollo Social del DIF en Naucalpan de Juárez (1998-99), y senadora de la República (1997-2000).

PEREZCANO DE JIMÉNEZ ARRILLAGA, JOSEFINA ◆ n. ¿en el DF? (1913). Autora de *Destino sobre la guerra* (ensayo, 1939), *Mañana el sol será nuestro* (novela, 1940), *Al final del camino*, *El corazón del frasco verde* (ensayos, 1960), *México y la mexicanidad* (1978), *Historia crítica de la tecnología del valor* (1986), *Fenomenología de la evolución* (1986), *Mecánica de la evolución* (1986), *Lucha por la vida y selección natural* (1986).

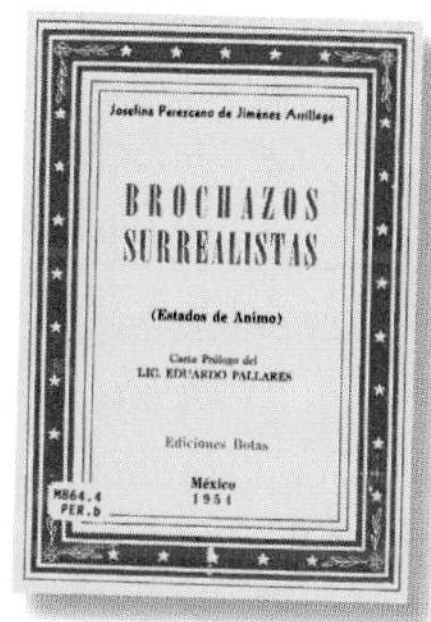

Obra de Josefin Perezcano de Jiménez Arrillaga

Tomás Perrín

PEREZNIETO CASTRO, FERNANDO ◆ n. en el DF (1938). Escultor y pintor. Estudió en la Escuela Nacional de Arquitectura en la UNAM, en la Academia de San Carlos y en Florencia. Autor del libro de dibujos *Apuntes*. En 1979 expuso su obra escultórica en la Galería Brod, de Londres. En 1986 ganó el primer premio Italia para Artes Visuales, sección de arte gráfico, de Florencia.

PEREZNIETO CASTRO, LEONEL ◆ n. en el DF (1943). Licenciado en derecho por la UNAM (1968) y doctor en derecho por la Universidad de París (1975). Profesor de la UNAM y de la Universidad Autónoma Metropolitana. Ha sido asesor del abogado general y coordinador de Humanidades de la UNAM. Es miembro de la Academia de la Investigación Científica y del Instituto Mexicano de Derecho Internacional Privado (del que es vicepresidente).

PEREZTEJADA, JUAN JOAQUÍN ◆ n. en Veracruz, Ver. (1962). Poeta. Licenciado en pedagogía por la Universidad Cristobal Colón. Ha sido auxiliar de la Coordinación Cultural del ayuntamiento de Veracruz, coordinador del taller de lectura del ISSSTE-Cultura y trabajó en publicaciones del Instituto Veracruzano de Cultura. Editor del suplemento *Ovaciones en la cultura* (1998-). Ha colaborado en *Tierra adentro, La Jornada Semanal, Galeón, Hipócrita lector, Literal, Pauta* y *Revista Mexicana de Cultura,* suplemento de *El Nacional*. Textos suyos aparecen en los volúmenes colectivos *De amares y de soles* (poesía, 1988), *Poetas de Tierra Adentro* (1992), *Poetas de Tierra Adentro III* (1997) y *La dama de la noche* (cuento, 1990). Autor de poesía: *Los refranes del jaranero* (1993) y *La casa de la pereza* (1996).

PERGAMINOS, LOS ◆ Grupo de amigos formado en la segunda década del siglo. Inicialmente las reuniones eran en el café *Los Monotes*, decorado por José Clemente Orozco y propiedad de un hermano suyo. Luego se hizo costumbre que cada uno de los amigos convocara a sesión en su casa, hábito que se conserva. Según Rafael Ruiz Villalpando, fueron sus iniciadores Luis Hidalgo, Miguel *el Chamaco* Covarrubias y Ernesto *el Chango* García Cabral, Adolfo Best Maugard y Xavier Sorondo. Posteriormente se sumaron Manuel Horta, Andrés Audiffred, Roberto Montenegro, Mario Talavera, Mario Moreno *Cantinflas*, Pedro Vargas, Carlos Arruza, el *Dr. Atl*, Silverio Pérez, Jesús Solórzano, Alfonso Quiroz Cuarón, Rafael Freyre, Francisco Liguori, Samuel Máynez Puente, Alfonso Noriega, Mariano Azuela, Agustín Arroyo Ch., Aquiles Elorduy, Raúl Horta, Emilio Portes Gil, Antonio Castro Leal, Hugo B. Margáin, Juan José Torres Landa, Justo F. Fernández, Rafael Corrales Ayala, Benito Coquet y Antonio Ariza. Xavier Olea Muñoz, quien renunció públicamente al grupo en agosto de 1990, dijo que eran 26 los "pergaminos en activo" en ese tiempo. Han sido patriarcas de la cofradía Manuel Horta y Pedro Vargas.

PERIBÁN ◆ Municipio de Michoacán situado al oeste de Uruapan y al norte de Apatzingán, en los límites con Jalisco. Superficie: 434.87 km². Habitantes: 18,955, de los cuales 4,283 forman la población económicamente activa. Hablan alguna lengua indígena 52 personas mayores de cinco años (purépecha 46). El nombre significa, en purépecha, "lugar donde hilan". La cabecera es Peribán de Ramos.

PERICOT GARCÍA, LUIS ◆ n. y m. en España (1899-1969). Historiador. Fue codirector de la revista *Paynae*. Autor de *Las razas de América* (1928), *La cueva de Parpalló* (1942), *La España primitiva* (1950 y *América indígena* (1962).

PERLA, LA ◆ Municipio de Veracruz situado en el centro del estado, en los límites con Puebla, al suroeste del puerto de Veracruz. Superficie: 199.88 km². Habitantes: 13,852, de los cuales 3,588 forman la población económicamente activa. Hablan náhuatl 17 personas mayores de cinco años.

PEROTE ◆ Municipio de Veracruz situado en el centro del estado, en los límites con Puebla, al oeste de Jalapa. Superficie: 735.35 km². Habitantes: 51,688, de los cuales 12,609 forman la población económicamente activa. Hablan alguna lengua indígena 206 personas mayores de cinco años (náhuatl 118). Durante el virreinato, el fuerte de Perote fue el principal cuartel de las tropas coloniales y, en el México independiente, de 1823 a 1828 tuvo ahí su sede el Colegio Militar.

PEROTE ◆ Sierra de Jalisco y Colima, que forma parte del eje volcánico. Por el noroeste se une a la sierra de Cacoma; su extremo sureste se conoce como sierra del Mamey.

PERRÍN, TOMÁS ◆ n. y m. en el DF (1924-1985). Locutor, actor y epigramista. Licenciado en derecho por la UNAM. En la radiodifusora XEW interpretó al detective Carlos Lacroix. Condujo el programa de televisión *Noticiero para niños y similares* y colaboró en *Metrópoli* y *Reina por un día* (1958-59). Actuó, entre otras, en las películas *Su adorable majadero* (1938), *Café Concordia* (1939), *El signo de la muerte* (1939), *Madre a la fuerza* (1939), *El rosario* (1943), *Tentación* (1943), *La hija del cielo* (1943), *El rey se divierte* (1944), *Amor de una vida* (1945), *El monje blanco* (1945) y *La sombra del caudillo* (1960); y actuó y escribió el argumento de *Cuando escuches este vals* (1944). Colaborador de la revista *Siempre!* y del diario *Excélsior*. Autor de *México epigramante*, y la obra teatral *Foro de México o el drama de una comedia*. En 1983 recibió un premio de periodismo.

PERRÍN, TOMÁS G. ◆ n. en España y m. en el DF (1881-1965). Médico titulado en 1907 en la Universidad Central de Madrid. Llegó a México en 1908. Profesor de la UNAM (1913-63) y de la Escuela Médico Militar. Fue embajador de Paraguay en México y jefe de Laboratorios de Química y Pruebas Funcionales del Instituto Nacional de Cardiología (1945). En el área de la investigación, desarrolló estudios sobre la transmisión de la sífilis y la triquinosis y descubrió la histoplasmosis. Autor de *Manual de histología normal humana* (1917) y de las obras de teatro *Lo mismo, Proteo, El cabo Noval* y *Trébol*. Fue miembro y presidente (1932) de la Academia Nacional de Medicina.

PERRY, MATHEW GALBRAITH ◆ n. en EUA (1794-1858). Marino. Ascendió a comodoro en 1843. En 1846, cuando se iniciaba la agresión estadounidense contra México, dirigió seis buques de esa nación que atacaron Frontera, en Tabasco, y varios puertos campechanos. Al año siguiente apoyó a Winfield Scott en la toma de Veracruz. Fondeado en ese puerto negoció con Justo Sierra O'Reilly, que llevaba la representación del gobierno de Yucatán, la disminución de inconvenientes para el tráfico comercial de la península, aunque no llegaron a ningún acuerdo. En 1856 firmó un tratado comercial con Japón, para que este país importara productos estadounidenses y europeos.

PERSHING, JOHN JOSEPH ◆ n. y m. en EUA (1860-1948). Militar. En Estados Unidos combatió a los indios apaches y siux (1886 y 1890-91). En 1898 participó en la intervención en Cuba. Reprimió un levantamiento independentista en Filipinas (1899-1904) y en marzo de 1916 se internó en territorio mexicano, al mando de la "expedición punitiva" enviada por Washington para capturar a Francisco Villa, que había atacado la población de Columbus en 1915. Sin embargo, luego de 11 meses de búsqueda infructuosa, abandonó el territorio nacional en febrero de 1917 y ese mismo año se puso al frente de las tropas estadounidenses que pelearon en la primera guerra mundial. Fue jefe del Estado Mayor del ejército de su país (1921-24). Autor de *My Experience in the World War* (1931).

PERÚ, REPÚBLICA DEL ◆ Estado latinoamericano situado en las costas del océano Pacífico. Limita al norte con Ecuador, al noreste con Colombia, al este con Brasil, al sureste con Bolivia y al sur con Chile. Superficie: 1.285.216 km^2. Habitantes: 24,797,000 (1998), de los cuales 6,022,213 (en 1995) poblaban Lima, la capital. Perú tiene dos idiomas oficiales: el quechua y el español. *Historia:* los restos arqueológicos más antiguos datan de hace 21,000 años. En el siglo XII, los quechuas, guiados por Manco Cápac, se instalaron en el actual territorio peruano y erigieron uno de los imperios más poderosos del continente, que tuvo relación con los pueblos mesoamericanos (☛ *Pacífico*). El primer europeo que estableció contacto con los quechuas fue el español Pascual de Andagoya, en 1522. Diez años más tarde, en 1531, Francisco Pizarro inició la conquista del imperio inca, al mando de una reducida tropa de 185 hombres. Ese mismo año, Pizarro se entrevistó por primera vez con el inca Atahualpa, uno de los dos herederos del imperio. En 1532, Pizarro fundó la ciudad de Piura y ahí capturó a Atahualpa, quien desde la prisión ordenó el asesinato de su hermano Huáscar, el otro heredero del imperio. Al año siguiente Pizarro asesinó a Atahualpa, ocupó la región del Cuzco, fundó la ciudad de Jauja, reconoció como soberano inca a Manco Cápac II, otro hermano de Atahualpa y, en 1535, fundó la Ciudad de los Reyes, hoy Lima. Un año más tarde, en 1536, Manco Cápac II se levantó en armas, reunió un gran ejército y sitió Lima durante diez meses, hasta que fue derrotado por los españoles. Ese mismo año, Hernán Cortés envió dos barcos al mando de Juan de Grijalva hacia la costa peruana, con lo que se inició el comercio marítimo entre la Nueva España y Perú, que durante el siglo XVI se realizó sobre todo entre el puerto peruano del El Callao y el mexicano de Huatulco. Desde 1537, varios grupos de conquistadores se disputaron por las armas el control del territorio peruano, hasta que en 1542 la Corona española creó el Virreinato y la Real Audiencia de Perú. Los conquistadores se negaron a someterse a la autoridad de los enviados reales, rechazaron la aplicación de las Leyes Nuevas (☛) y organizaron una rebelión, encabezada por Gonzalo Pizarro. Pizarro derrotó al primer virrey, Blasco Núñez de Vela, y los sublevados lograron que no desaparecieran las encomiendas. En 1545 se descubrieron las minas de plata del cerro de Potosí, situado en el actual territorio de Bolivia, y a partir de entonces el virreinato se dedicó casi exclusivamente a la explotación minera. Hacia 1550, el comercio con la Nueva España, consistente hasta entonces en alimentos, herramientas y caballos, comenzó a ser sustituido, debido a la instalación de huertas en la costa peruana, por el tráfico de ropa y enseres de ornato. Al igual que los puertos mexicanos del Pacífico, durante el siglo XVII los piratas ingleses hostigaron la navegación de los peruanos, sobre todo en las cercanías del Callao. En 1634, en los momentos en que la exportación de plata alcanzaba los mayores montos, el comercio entre la Nueva España y Perú fue interrumpido, y no se pudo reiniciar durante la colonia. En 1722 llegó a la Nueva España como virrey el marqués de Casa Fuerte, Juan de Acuña, quien había nacido en Perú. Entre 1780 y 1781, Túpac Amaru dirigió una gran rebelión indígena e independentista, que finalmente fue controlada por los españoles, quienes asesinaron al caudillo. Aunque desde 1813 se habían producido levantamientos, el gobierno virreinal se mantuvo en el poder e incluso

República del Perú

organizó expediciones militares para combatir a los insurgentes ecuatorianos. En 1821, tras la emancipación de Argentina y Chile, José de San Martín ocupó Lima y proclamó la independencia; los españoles se hicieron fuertes en los Andes y desde ahí iniciaron una guerra de reconquista, pero fueron vencidos por Simón Bolívar y José de Sucre. Dos años después, Bolívar fue nombrado presidente vitalicio de Perú. Fray Melchor de Talamantes, peruano, fue uno de los protagonistas del movimiento autonomista mexicano de 1808, por lo que fue aprehendido y enviado a San Juan de Ulúa, donde murió. En 1827 fue derrocado Bolívar y se instauró la República Independiente del Perú. Cuando, dos años después, la Corona española intentó la reconquista de México, el tercer presidente de la República, Agustín Gamarra, facilitó el regreso de los mexicanos que estaban avecindados en Perú y ofreció formar un ejército para combatir a los españoles. Al conocer la noticia del triunfo de las tropas de Antonio López de Santa Anna, el ministro de Relaciones Exteriores, José María Pando, declaró que si "el gabinete de Madrid se obstina en hacer atacar el territorio de los Estados Unidos Mexicanos, el Perú no trepidará en prestarle cuantos auxilios sean indispensables para defender una causa que es sagrada para todo buen americano y demostrar que se halla unido a los demás Estados del continente con lazos de la más tierna fraternalidad". En 1832, México y Perú firmaron su primer convenio bilateral: un tratado de amistad, comercio y navegación. En 1836, a iniciativa del presidente Andrés Santa Cruz, se creó la Confederación

Machu Picchu, en Perú

Bolivia-Perú. El intento unificador fracasó en 1839, al ser derrotada la Confederación por Chile. En 1854 fue abolida la esclavitud. En marzo de 1862, Manuel Nicolás Corpancho (☛) llegó a México como embajador del gobierno peruano; se opuso a la presencia de las tropas francesas, españolas y británicas en Veracruz y le ofreció al gobierno republicano, en nombre del presidente de su país, Ramón Castilla, el envió de 6,000 hombres para combatir la intervención. En marzo de ese año, en un informe para su gobierno, el embajador señalaba que la llegada del conde de Lorencez a Veracruz indicaba que las verdaderas intenciones de los franceses eran instaurar un nuevo gobierno en México. A fines de marzo, Corpancho se entrevistó con el presidente Juárez y unos días más tarde, el 9 de abril de 1862, propuso al gobierno republicano integrarse a una coalición a la que ya pertenecían, además de Perú, Ecuador y Chile. El gobierno mexicano aceptó y el 11 de junio de 1862 se firmó el tratado correspondiente, que promovía la integración entre los cuatro países (☛ *Unión Continental*). En agosto de 1863, luego de la ocupación de la ciudad de México, Corpancho fue expulsado por la Regencia del imperio. Uno de los peruanos que combatieron la intervención francesa y el imperio de Maximiliano de Habsburgo fue el coronel Estanislao Cañedo de la Cuesta (☛), perteneció al Estado Mayor de Ignacio Comonfort y que al triunfo de la República fue elegido diputado federal por Jalisco. En 1864 España ocupó unas islas peruanas, pero dos años más tarde las tropas españolas fueron derrotadas por una coalición integrada por Perú, Chile, Bolivia y Ecuador. Durante la primera mitad del siglo XIX, el principal producto de exportación eran el guano y el salitre. Este mineral, extraído de los desiertos del sur, fue la principal causa de la guerra del Pacífico (1879-84), en la que Perú y Bolivia fueron derrotados por Chile. Como indemnización, el gobierno peruano cedió al de Santiago las provincias sureñas, donde se explotaba el salitre. Hacia 1913 llegó a México el poeta peruano José Santos Chocano, quien tuvo una activa participación en la Casa del Obrero Mundial, presidió el mitin del primero de mayo de 1913, en el Hemiciclo a Juárez, después del cual fue aprehendido y deportado. Volvió al año siguiente y Venustiano Carranza lo designó representante del constitucionalismo en Estados Unidos, donde escribió varios folletos sobre la situación mexicana y los móviles de la revolución. Al desatarse la lucha de facciones pasó al villismo. En los años veinte colaboró en revistas literarias mexicanas, pole-

Moneda del Perú

mizó con José Vasconcelos y mató en Lima a un seguidor de éste. En 1918, el gobierno de José Pardo y Barreda reconoció al de Venustiano Carranza y al año siguiente ambos gobiernos celebraron un tratado de cambio de valijas diplomáticas. En mayo de 1924, un grupo de exiliados peruanos, encabezados por Víctor Raúl Haya de la Torre, fundaron en la ciudad de México la Alianza Popular Revolucionaria Americana, la cual, aunque inicialmente se definió como un partido marxista, incorporó a su plataforma política algunos planteamientos inspirados en la Revolución Mexicana. El hecho de que APRA hubiera nacido en México provocó la creciente hostilidad del gobierno peruano hacia el mexicano, hasta que en marzo de 1932, el dictador Luis Miguel Sánchez Cerro acusó de colaborar con APRA a Gilberto Owen, quien desempeñaba una misión diplomática en Lima, y al gobierno de Pascual Ortiz Rubio de estar vinculado con los autores de un atentado contra su vida, por lo que se rompieron las relaciones entre ambos países. Al año siguiente Óscar R. Benavides sustituyó a Sánchez Cerro en la presidencia peruana y se reanudaron los nexos diplomáticos. Cuatro años más tarde, en 1937, las representaciones de los dos países se elevaron a rango de embajadas. En 1938 llegó a México el poeta surrealista César Moro (☛), quien en 1940 organizó con Wolfgang Paalen y André Bretón la Exposición Internacional del Surrealismo, que se realizó en el Distrito Federal. Más tarde colaboró en las revistas *Letras de México* y *El Hijo Pródigo* y en 1948 volvió a Perú. En ese año, los apristas intentaron un levantamiento en El Callao, que fue cruelmente reprimido, después de lo cual se produjo un golpe militar. De 1951 a 1956, el comunista Gustavo Valcárcel, antiguo secretario de Haya de la Torre, se exilió en México; poeta, colaboró en la revista *Espacios* y publicó una novela: *La prisión*. En 1960, Adolfo López Mateos visitó Perú y firmó con el presidente Manuel Prado convenios de libre comercio e intercambio cultural. Dos años después, en las elecciones de 1962, Haya de la Torre obtuvo la mayoría de los votos, pero no los dos tercios del total necesarios para ser elegido. Se produjo un nuevo golpe de Estado y se instaló en el poder una junta militar. A mediados de los años sesenta surgió el Movimiento de Izquierda Revolucionaria, organización guerrillera compuesta por ex miembros de APRA y del Partido Comunista del Perú (que había sido fundado en 1928 por José Carlos Mariátegui). Uno de sus dirigentes, Luis de la Puente Uceda, se había asilado en México en los años cincuenta con Juan Pablo Chang Navarro, *El Chino,* miembro de la guerrilla boliviana del *Che* Guevara que murió en 1967. De la Puente, que estudió psicología en la Sorbona, trabajó en las agencias ANSA y AFP y perteneció al Ejército de Liberación Nacional del Perú, murió en combate en 1965. Fernando Belaúnde Terry, que había sido elegido presidente en 1963, fue derrocado en 1968 por un grupo de militares que instalaron en la Presidencia al general Juan Velasco Alvarado, quien aplicó una política nacionalista, expropió las industrias petrolera y minera y aplicó una amplia reforma agraria. En 1972, el presidente Luis Echeverría sostuvo en Lima una conversación informal con el presidente Velasco. Dos años después, Echeverría realizó una visita oficial, durante la que se firmaron varios convenios técnicos, comerciales y culturales. En 1975 Velasco fue derrocado por el también militar Francisco Morales Bermúdez, cuyo gobierno impulsó una política conservadora. En las elecciones de 1980, Belaúnde volvió a la Presidencia. A partir de 1981 se incrementó la actividad de Sendero Luminoso, organización guerrillera de tendencia maoísta que opera en la zona andina y tiene ramificaciones urbanas. En 1984, México exportó a Perú mercancías por 14,087,000 dólares e importó de ese país el equivalente a 6,481,000 dólares. En 1985, Alan García, candidato del Partido Aprista, ganó las elecciones. Al inicio de su gobierno se creó una nueva moneda, el inti, que sustituyó al sol, y el gobierno peruano redefinió los términos del pago de su deuda externa. Ese mismo año, García viajó a México. En 1986, el gobierno peruano constituyó, con el de Argentina, Brasil y Uruguay, el Grupo de Apoyo a Contadora. Al año siguiente, el presidente peruano visitó dos veces México; una en marzo, y la otra en noviembre, cuando asistió a la reunión del llamado Grupo de los Ocho, es decir, los presidentes de Argentina, Brasil, Colombia, México, Panamá, Perú, Uruguay y Venezuela. En 1990 un casi desconocido candidato presidencial, Alberto Fujimori, derrotó en las urnas al candidato de la derecha, quien aparecía como favorito, el escritor Mario Vargas Llosa. Desde entonces, Fujimori se ha perpetuado en la presidencia peruana. Durante sus años de gobierno Fujimori se adecuó al neoliberalismo económico, en boga en la mayor parte del mundo, y casi logró desmantelar al grupo guerrillero Sendero Luminoso, cuyos jefes están en prisión.

Billetes de la República del Perú

Perujo, Francisca ◆ n. en España (1934). Fue traída a México en 1939, a la caída de la República Española. Licenciada y doctora (1981) en letras hispánicas por la UNAM, ha sido investigadora del Instituto de Investigaciones Filológicas. En 1977 tradujo al italiano *Pedro Páramo*, de Juan Rulfo. Editó *Viaje a la Nueva España*, de Juan Francisco Gemelli Careri, y *Razonamientos de mi viaje alrededor del mundo*, de Francesco Carletti. Autora de *Pasar la líneas* (narrativa, 1977) y *Oriente en la cultura española del siglo XVI* (ensayo).

Pérula ◆ ☛ *Chamela, bahía de.*

Perus, Françoise ◆ n. en Francia (?). Licenciada en letras hispánicas por la Universidad de Clermont-Ferrand (1972). Desde 1974 es investigadora del Instituto de Investigaciones Sociales y desde 1975 profesora de la Facultad de Filosofía y Letras, ambos de la UNAM. Ha colaborado en la *Revista Mexicana de Sociología*. Autora de *Literatura y sociedad en América Latina: el modernismo* (1976).

Perusquía, Ernesto ◆ n. en San Juan del Río y m. en Tequisquiapan, Qro. (1877-1946). Fue director del Timbre en San Luis Potosí, diputado al Congreso Constituyente de 1916-17 y gobernador constitucional de Querétaro (del 30 de junio de 1917 al 12 de octubre de 1919): durante su gobierno se promulgó la constitución local del 9 de septiembre de 1917. Salió al exilio luego del asesinato del presidente Venustiano Carranza y volvió a México en 1923.

Perusquía, Mariano ◆ ¿n. en San Juan del Río, Qro.? (¿1771?-?). Escultor. Algunas fuentes señalan que era español. Estudió con Francisco Escobar y Manuel Tolsá en la Academia de San Carlos. Más tarde se trasladó a Querétaro, donde instaló un taller junto con Mariano Arce y Mariano Montenegro, que fue conocido como el de los *Tres Marianos*. En 1795 recibió un premio de la Real Academia de Nobles Artes de San Carlos. Entre sus obras figuran diversas esculturas religiosas para los conventos de San Antonio, de Carmelitas Descalzas, para la Cofradía del Santo Cristo de los Trabajos, para los templos de San Fernando y San Agustín, en la ciudad de México, y para numerosos templos en Querétaro, Zapotlán el Grande (hoy Ciudad Guzmán), Guadalajara y San Juan de los Lagos.

Perzabal Marcué, Carlos Manuel ◆ n. en el DF (1940). Licenciado (Universidad de La Habana), maestro y doctor (UNAM) en economía y maestro en filosofía por la Universidad Brunel de Inglaterra. Militante del PCM (1962-75), miembro del consejo nacional del PRD y asesor de su grupo parlamentario. Coordinador de Difusión Cultural de la Facultad de Economía, director de las revistas *Crítica Política* (1980-82) y *Rino* (1993-98). Ha colaborado en los periódicos *unomásuno* y *El Financiero* y en las revistas *Investigación Económica*, *Economía Informa*, *Crítica*, *Desarrollo Económico* (Cuba) e *Historia y Sociedad*. Autor de *Acumulación del capital dependiente y subordinado. El caso de México* (1978), *Acumulación e industrialización compleja* (1989) y *Los años de inflación: México* (1990).

Pesado de la Llave de Mier, Isabel ◆ m. en París (?-1913). Hija de José Joaquín Pesado Pérez. Con el legado que dejó, en 1917 se creó la Fundación Mier y Pesado en la ciudad de México. Esta institución tiene una casa de salud y asilo de ancianos en Tacubaya, un orfanatorio en Villa de Guadalupe y un hogar para ancianos en Orizaba, Veracruz. Su herencia se utilizó también para algunas obras de beneficencia en París. Publicó: *Apuntes de viaje de México a Europa en los años de 1870, 1871 y 1872* y *Dichas y penas*, ambos en 1910.

Pesado Pérez, José Joaquín ◆ n. en San Agustín del Palmar, Pue., y m. en la ciudad de México (1801-1861). Fue redactor del periódico *La Oposición* (1834), vicegobernador de Veracruz encargado del Poder Ejecutivo local en 1834, secretario del Interior (del 18 de octubre al 12 de diciembre de 1838) encargado del despacho de Relaciones Exteriores (del 13 de noviembre al 12 de diciembre de 1838), en el gobierno de Anastasio Bustamante; y ministro de Relaciones Interiores y Exteriores (del 1 al 4 de agosto de 1846) en el gabinete de Nicolás Bravo. Tradujo *La Jerusalem liberada*, de Torcuato Tasso, y algunas obras de Horacio. Colaboró en el periódico *La Cruz*. Coautor de *Los aztecas. Poesías tomadas de antiguos cantares mexicanos* (1854). Autor de *El amor frustrado* (novela, 1838), *El inquisidor de México* (novela, 1838) y *Poesías originales y traducidas* (1839). Después de su muerte aparecieron *Ensayo épico* (1856), *El liberador de México, don Agustín de Iturbide* (1872) y *El pescador negro* (1874). Perteneció a la Academia de Letrán y a la Real Academia Española.

José Joaquín Pesado Pérez

Pesado y Segura, Natal ◆ n. en Orizaba, Ver., y m. en la ciudad de México (1846-1920). Pintor. Hijo del anterior. Ingresó en la Escuela de Agricultura de San Jacinto, pero desertó para estudiar en la Academia de San Carlos (1870-78) y en la Real Academia de Bellas Artes de San Lucas, en Italia (1878). Fue profesor de pintura en el Colegio Hispano Romano de España y a su regreso a México, diputado federal suplente. En 1889 fundó una academia particular en Florencia y en 1894 otra en Orizaba. Aunque sus obras se encuentran principalmente en Europa, en el Salón de Embajadores del Palacio Nacional se halla su cuadro *Nicolás Bravo perdonando a los prisioneros* (1892).

Pesas y medidas ◆ ☛ *Sistema Internacional de Pesas y Medidas.*

Pescador, Felipe ◆ n. en Canatlán, Dgo., y m. en Cholula, Pue. (1879-1929). Ferrocarrilero desde su juventud, en 1904 era jefe de despachadores. Ese mismo año fundó, con Félix C. Vera, la Gran Liga Mexicana de Empleados de Ferrocarril. En 1908 encabezó un movimiento para eliminar de las estaciones a los despachadores extranjeros, para lo cual, y con el apoyo de José Yves Limantour, entrenó a técnicos mexicanos. Se adhirió al maderismo en 1910 y llegó a ser superintendente de la División de Durango en 1913. Al año siguiente se incorporó a las fuerzas de Venustiano Carranza, de cuyos ferrocarriles fue superintendente general. En el gobierno constitucionalista fue director de los Ferrocarriles Nacionales.

Pescador, Leonardo ◆ n. en Canatlán, Dgo. (1876-?). Ingeniero topógrafo. Fue reyista en su juventud, maderista en 1910 y constitucionalista desde 1913. En el gobierno de Venustiano Carranza organizó el Departamento de Pesca de la Secretaría de Agricultura y Ganadería y participó en la fundación de la Comisión Nacional Agraria. Fue senador de la República entre 1917 y 1920.

Pescador Osuna, José Ángel ◆ n. en Mazatlán, Sin. (1945). Se tituló como profesor en la Normal de Mazatlán (1964). Licenciado en economía por el ITAM (1970), donde fue profesor (1970-72), y maestro en economía y educación por la Universidad de Stanford (1978). Ha ejercido la docencia en la UAM (1974-78), la UNAM (1984-85) y el ITAM. En la Universidad Pedagógica Nacional fue jefe de Investigación (1978-79) y rector de la institución (1989). Miembro del PRI desde 1963. Fue secretario de Difusión del Sindicato de Trabajadores de la UAM (1975). Ha sido subdirector de Presupuesto de la Subsecretaría de Educación Superior (1977), director general del Instituto Nacional de Investigación Educativa (1978), director general adjunto de Educación para Adultos (1979-80), presidente del Consejo Nacional Técnico de la Educación (1980-83), subsecretario de Servicios Educativos para el DF (1992-94) y titular de la SEP (1994). Fue asesor del titular de la SEMIP (1983-85), diputado por el DF (1985-86), presidente municipal de Mazatlán (1987-89), cónsul general en Los Ángeles (1990-92) y subsecretario de Población de la Secretaría de Gobernación (1999-). Autor

José Ángel Pescador Osuna

de *La Revista del Instituto Nacional de Pedagogía* (1982), *América Latina y el proyecto principal de educación* (1982) y *Poder político y educación* (1983), *Innovaciones para mejorar la calidad de la educación en México* (1989), *Aportaciones para la modernización de la educación en México* (1989), *Modernidad educativa y desafíos tecnológicos* (1989). Es miembro del Colegio de Economistas.

Peschard Mariscal, Jacqueline ◆ n. en el DF (1947). Licenciada en sociología y maestra en ciencia política por la UNAM y doctora en ciencias sociales por El Colegio de Michoacán. Profesora de la UNAM (1979-98) y profesora investigadora de El Colegio de México (1992-96, en el Centro de Estudios

Jacqueline Peschard

Sociológicos). Ha sido articulista de *La Jornada*. También ha publicado en las revistas *Estudios Sociológicos* y *Perfiles Latinoamericanos*, así como en otras publicaciones. Consejera electoral del Consejo General del IFE (1996-). Coautora de *La voz de los votos: un análisis crítico de las elecciones de 1994* (1995), *El fin de siglo y los partidos políticos en América Latina* (1995), *Participación y democracia en la ciudad de México* (1997), *Representación política y democracia* (1998) y *Homenaje a Rafael Segovia* (1998). Autora de *La cultura política democrática* (1994). Pertenece al Sistema Nacional de Investigadores (1988-). Es miembro del consejo editorial de la revista *Nexos* y del Comité de Ciencias Sociales del Conacyt.

Peso ◆ Fue adoptado como moneda oficial por el Imperio Mexicano, que urgido de circulante hizo una emisión de billetes con fecha primero de enero de 1823 (☛ *Dinero*). Con Iturbide, la moneda se devaluó en 2.1 por ciento, al pasar de 95 a 97 centavos por dólar. A la caída del imperio fue retirado de la circulación el papel moneda, aunque el 11 de abril de 1823 el Congreso resolvió hacer una nueva emisión, la que se imprimió al reverso de un "Sumario de cuarta clase de indulto", ya vencido, en el que mediante el pago de dos reales de plata se permitía a los fieles comer carne, huevos y productos lácteos en los días de Cuaresma, con algunas excepciones. Pese a la devoción de los ciudadanos, los nuevos billetes no fueron aceptados por el público y durante más de cuarenta años no se emitió papel moneda. En 1825, la promesa de estabilidad que significó el ascenso de Guadalupe Victoria a la Presidencia de la República, influyó para una revaluación que puso la moneda en 95 y medio centavos de peso por dólar. En 1835, al instaurarse el centralismo, el tipo de cambio sería de 96 centavos de peso por dólar. Bajo el mismo régimen, con José Justo Corro como presidente, el 11 de marzo de 1837 se reprimió la manifestación de unas 11,000 personas que se reunieron en la Plaza de la Constitu-

Billete de 10 pesos (1914)

ción para protestar por la devaluación, no del peso sino de las "cuartillas", moneda fraccionaria de cobre de uso eminentemente popular. Durante la guerra de los Pasteles, las luchas fratricidas, la intervención estadounidense y la francesa, el peso mexicano mostró una fortaleza que algunos estudiosos adjudican a que las acuñaciones eran de metales preciosos, sobre todo de plata, por lo que en Estados Unidos fue más aceptado que el mismo dólar, que hacia 1843 contaba con 371.24 gramos de plata contra 374 de la moneda mexicana. El valor intrínseco de las monedas las hizo codiciadas en el extranjero. Se sabe que en 1864 Inglaterra y Francia importaron el peso "águila", que valía más de cinco francos en París y de cuatro chelines en Londres y era, asimismo, aceptado y hasta codiciado en lugares tan distantes como China o Palestina. La primera emisión de billetes en su forma moderna la hizo en México, en 1865, el Banco de Londres, México y Sudamérica. Hasta 1874, el peso rebasó en muy pocas ocasiones la barrera de los 96 centavos por dólar. En 1874, el descubrimiento de grandes yacimientos de plata en México y Estados Unidos hizo que el valor de ese metal descendiera en el mundo. Desde entonces, el peso mexicano inició su tendencia a la baja. En ese año, bajo la presidencia de Sebastián Lerdo de Tejada, el dólar pasó de 98 centavos mexicanos a 1.01 pesos. Hasta 1885 se mantuvo por debajo de 1.20 respecto del dólar, pero pronto sufrió algunos quebrantos, pues Manuel Gutiérrez Nájera escribió en 1886 que el peso "tiene gota". El mal se agravó durante el porfiriato, pues en 1900 el dólar valía 2.06 pesos y llegó a 2.38 en 1903. Una ley monetaria, en 1905, implantó el patrón oro con circulación de plata, para que las reservas nacionales pudieran darle estabilidad a la moneda. Así, cada peso de plata equivalía a 75 centigramos de oro puro, como unidad teórica, y se fijó una paridad del dólar de dos por uno, lo que más o menos funcionó, pues en 1910 la paridad era de 2.008 por dólar. Bajo el gobierno maderista la moneda pasó de 2.01 a 2.07 por dólar. De 1912 a 1917, los trastornos económicos del país provocaron nuevos cambios en la paridad: el dólar llegó a costar hasta 23.83 pesos en 1916. Un año después, al normalizarse la circulación de los pesos de plata, el valor del dólar bajó a 1.90 y a 1.80 en 1918, para empezar a subir de nuevo, paulatinamente, a partir de ese año. El decreto del 27 de octubre de 1919 estableció la ley de 0.720 de plata pura para las monedas de un peso, y en 1920 se regresó a la paridad del dos por uno. En 1921 se hizo la primera emisión de centenarios, que desde entonces cuentan con aceptación mundial. En la primera mitad de los años veinte, la paridad se mantuvo más o menos estable gracias a la amonedación de plata y la disminución del dinero en forma de billete. Éste, en 1925, representaba sólo 1.4 por ciento del circulante total. El precio de la plata en el mercado mundial volvió a ser un factor negativo para el peso mexicano: de 1925 a 1930 se produjo una lenta devaluación hasta llegar a 2.25 pesos por dólar. La ley monetaria de 1931 eliminó el bimetalismo, suprimió el talón oro y sacó de circulación las monedas de ese metal; se inició la formación de una reserva monetaria integrada por divisas extranjeras y oro y plata en monedas y lingotes; al mismo tiempo se inició la emisión de billetes del Banco de México. La cotización del dólar llegó a 2.55 y poco después a cuatro pesos, para bajar más adelante a 2.90. Con tales altibajos, de febrero de 1930 a septiembre de 1932, lapso en el que Pascual Ortiz Rubio ocupó la Presidencia de la República, el tipo de cambio pasó de 2.122 a 3.170 pesos por dólar. Una nueva ley monetaria, en 1932, mantuvo la cotización en alrededor de 2.50 pesos durante un año. La depresión económica, en 1933, marcó la nueva paridad en 3.60 pesos por dólar, que se mantuvo hasta 1938, cuando las empresas petroleras extranjeras retiraron sus fondos del país. El Banco de México se retiró del mercado cambiario y dejó que la ley de la oferta y la demanda marcara la nueva paridad, que llegó a ser de 5.99 pesos en 1939 y disminuyó a 5.40 al año siguiente. En 1941,

Moneda de dos pesos plata

Billete de 10 pesos (1975)

Monedas de 1,000 Pesos y de un nuevo peso

mediante un convenio con el gobierno estadounidense, la paridad se fijó en 4.85 pesos. En 1948 descendieron las reservas monetarias y el Banco de México volvió a retirarse del mercado cambiario. En 1949 la nueva paridad oficial era de 8.65 (aunque en el mercado libre llegó a costar diez pesos un dólar). En 1952 hubo nuevas fugas de capitales y en 1954, previo acuerdo con el Tesoro estadounidense y con el Fondo Monetario Internacional, se estableció la paridad con el dólar en 12.50 pesos, la que se mantuvo firme durante 22 años. En 1971 se produjo una crisis del sistema monetario internacional y Estados Unidos anunció que no pagaría, como hasta entonces, una onza troy de oro por cada dólar. La divisa estadounidense perdió valor en el mercado mundial y el peso la acompañó en su caída al mantenerse fija la paridad entre ambas monedas. El 31 de agosto de 1976, con Luis Echeverría como presidente, el peso, que tenía una sobrevaluación de 14 por ciento, fue puesto "en flotación" para que el mercado dictara el tipo de cambio. El 11 de septiembre el gobierno estableció la paridad en 19.70 pesos por cada dólar a la compra y 19.90 a la venta. El 26 de octubre el Banco de México se retiró nuevamente del mercado y el precio de cada dólar llegó a ser de 27.97 por dólar, para bajar a 19.95 al final del año. Con José López Portillo la moneda atravesó por un periodo de fluctuaciones que, el 17 de febrero de 1982, habían puesto el tipo de cambio en 26 pesos por dólar. Ese día se retiró el Banco de México del mercado cambiario y al siguiente el dólar se cotizaba a 48 pesos. El 15 de marzo, el presidente López Portillo, quien había prometido defender la economía y la moneda "como perro", se definió como un "presidente devaluado". El 2 de junio reingresó el Banco de México al mercado cambiario y la paridad se estableció en 47.62 pesos por dólar. El 5 de agosto se establecieron dos tipos de cambio para la moneda: uno preferencial, de 49.40 pesos por dólar, y otro libre, que hace pasar la cotización de 49 a 75 pesos por la divisa estadounidense. El 12 de agosto se anunció la suspensión temporal del mercado de cambios para proteger las reservas de la banca central. Al día siguiente, los dólares de las cuentas bancarias se transforman en *mexdólares*, para los cuales se fija un tipo de cambio de 69.5 pesos por cada uno, en tanto que en el mercado libre fue de hasta 150 pesos por cada dólar estadounidense. El 18 de agosto se establecen tres paridades: dólar preferencial, a 49.49 pesos; los *méxdólares* se mantienen en el precio anterior y el dólar general o libre se cotiza a 102 y 112 pesos para compra y venta respectivamente, a la vez que los bancos ponen un límite máximo de 200 dólares por cliente. El 1 de septiembre de 1982 fue nacionalizada la banca y establecido el control total de cambios, con lo que se prohíbe a los particulares negociar con divisas. El día 7 de septiembre se anuncia que el dólar preferencial costará 50 pesos y el ordinario, presuntamente para uso de particulares pero difícil de obtener, a 70 pesos. En el mercado negro, la divisa se cotizaba a fines de noviembre en 150 pesos por dólar. El 20 de diciembre de 1986, con Miguel de la Madrid en la Presidencia de la República, se establecen dos paridades: la del dólar controlado, en 70 pesos, y la del dólar libre, en 95 pesos. Además, se hace oficial una política de devaluación constante, pues se anuncia que el precio del dólar controlado se "deslizará" 13 centavos diarios y el libre 14 centavos. El 31 de diciembre, las paridades eran de 71.54 y 96.53 pesos por dólar. El 4 de febrero de 1987, el precio del dólar rebasó la barrera de los 1000 pesos. El 18 de mayo de 1989, el dólar controlado se cotizaba a 2,397 y 2,422 pesos a la compra y a la venta, respectivamente, en tanto que el libre tenía precios de compra y venta de 2,397 y 2,467 pesos en los bancos. En 1993, con Carlos Salinas de Gortari en la Presidencia, se introdujo el "nuevo peso", equivalente a 1000 pesos, cuyo propósito era fijar "de manera virtual" el tipo de cambio, al volver imperceptibles sus variaciones en operaciones por debajo de las decenas de miles de dólares. El dólar se mantuvo en alrededor de 3.50 nuevos pesos hasta el 28 de diciembre de 1994, cuando una súbita devaluación lo elevó a ocho nuevos pesos. Posteriormente, el valor del nuevo peso (cuyo nombre volvió a cambiar a "peso" en 1996) ha fluctuado notablemente en momentos de incertidumbre financiera o política. En 1996, el poder adquisitivo del peso era 80 por ciento menor que el que tenía en 1976. En octubre de 1999, el dólar se cotizaba a 9.75 pesos.

Pesqueira, Ignacio ◆ n. en Arizpe y m. en Bacanuchi, Son. (1820-1886). Militar. Estudió en España y Francia y volvió a México en 1839. En 1847 se alistó en la Guardia Nacional de Sonora para combatir a los invasores estadounidenses y posteriormente reprimió a los apaches. Fue diputado local (1851-53) y prefecto político y comandante militar de Ures (1854-55). En 1855 se adhirió al Plan de Ayutla. Al triunfo de los liberales fungió como presidente del Consejo de Estado y se le ascendió a coronel. En julio de 1855 se hizo cargo del Poder Ejecutivo de Sonora, luego de que Manuel María Gándara encarceló al gobernador constitucional, José de Aguilar. Combatió a los gandaristas y a los filibusteros de Henry A. Crabb, a quien fusiló en Caborca. En mayo de 1857 devolvió el poder al gobernador De Aguilar, pero en agosto lo reasumió y en diciembre de ese año se hizo cargo también del gobierno de Sinaloa. Combatió contra la intervención francesa y el imperio. Se opuso a las exigencias de los confederados de Estados Unidos. Hostigado por los franceses, se refugió en Ures, donde entregó el poder a Jesús García Morales. Enfermo, se exilió en Arizona y luego pasó a California en busca de recursos. Volvió a Sonora en marzo de 1866 y reasumió la gubernatura. Al triunfo de la República, emprendió una nueva campaña contra los yaquis. En 1872 combatió en Sinaloa a los partidarios de Porfirio Díaz y cuatro años más tarde, en marzo de 1876, fue derrocado.

PESQUEIRA, JOSÉ J. ◆ n. en Guaymas, Son. (1839-¿1895?). Luchó en las filas liberales en la guerra de los Tres Años. Combatió la intervención francesa y el imperio. En 1871 peleó contra los rebeldes de la Noria. Cuatro años más tarde, en 1875, recibió el Ejecutivo de Sonora de manos de su hermano Ignacio y lo entregó un año después al jefe federal de armas. Apoyó al presidente Sebastián Lerdo de Tejada, más tarde al presidente de la Suprema Corte, José María Iglesias, y finalmente quiso adherirse a la asonada del Plan de Tuxtepec, lo que no fue aceptado por los seguidores de Porfirio Díaz. A fines de 1875 fue expulsado de Sonora por el gobernador Vicente Mariscal.

PESQUEIRA D'ENDARA, MANUEL EDUARDO ◆ n. en Hermosillo, Son., y m. en el DF (1901-1987). Cirujano y urólogo graduado en 1927 en la Universidad Nacional. Profesor de la UNAM y del Instituto Nacional de Cardiología. Fue presidente de la Sociedad Mexicana de Urología (1946-48) y secretario de Salubridad y Asistencia (del 1 de diciembre de 1952 al 30 de noviembre de 1958) en el gobierno de Adolfo Ruiz Cortines (1952-58). Representó a México en diversos congresos internacionales y publicó trabajos relativos a su especialidad. Fue condecorado por los gobiernos de Francia y Venezuela.

PESQUEIRA MORALES, IGNACIO L. ◆ n. en Huépac, Son., y m. en Francia (1867-1940). Militar. Regidor de Cananea entre 1907 y 1908. En 1909 se unió al antirreeleccionismo y en 1911 fue elegido diputado local por Arizpe. El 26 de febrero de 1913, por licencia de José María Maytorena, asumió interinamente el gobierno de Sonora, se adhirió al Plan de Guadalupe y nombró a Álvaro Obregón jefe de las fuerzas del estado. El 4 de agosto de ese año entregó el poder a Maytorena y presidió el Supremo Tribunal de Justicia Militar. Fue subsecretario de Guerra y Marina, encargado del despacho (del 27 de septiembre de 1914 al 12 de marzo de 1916), en el gobierno de Venustiano Carranza; presidió de nuevo el Tribunal de Justicia Militar, fue diputado al Congreso Constituyente de 1916-17, gobernador interino de Sinaloa (marzo a junio de 1917) y jefe del Departamento de Establecimientos Fabriles Militares y de los Almacenes Generales de Artillería. En 1920, Carranza lo nombró gobernador de Sonora, pero la rebelión de Agua Prieta le impidió asumir el cargo. Se retiró de la actividad política luego del asesinato del presidente. En 1934, ya como general de división, volvió a presidir el Supremo Tribunal de Justicia Militar. Al morir desempeñaba una comisión del gobierno mexicano.

PESQUEIRA MORALES, ROBERTO V. ◆ n. en Arizpe, Son., y m. en el DF (1882-1966). En 1909 se adhirió al antirreeleccionismo y al año siguiente participó en la campaña presidencial de Francisco I. Madero. Diputado federal en 1912. En 1913, con Adolfo de la Huerta, representó al gobierno de su hermano Ignacio en la reunión de Monclova, en la que el gobierno sonorense reconoció a Venustiano Carranza como jefe del constitucionalismo, del que fungió como agente en Washington y Nueva York. A fines de 1914 acompañó a Carranza en su traslado del gobierno a Veracruz. Allí elaboró, con Ramón de Negri, la Ley Benito Juárez, antecedente del artículo 27 constitucional. Fue vocal del Consejo de la Beneficencia del Distrito Federal, representante en Estados Unidos de los gobiernos de Adolfo de la Huerta y Álvaro Obregón y funcionario de la Compañía Mexicana de Aviación.

PESQUEIRA OLEA, EDUARDO ◆ n. en el DF (1937). Hijo de Manuel Pesqueira D'Endara. Licenciado en derecho por la UNAM (1960). Estudió economía en la UNAM (1958-59), en la Universidad George Washington, de EUA (1977-78) y en la Universidad para Extranjeros de Perugia, Italia. En el PRI, partido al que pertenece desde 1962, fue miembro del Consejo Consultivo del IEPES (1981). En la Secretaría de Hacienda fue jefe del Departamento de Inversiones (1966-72), subdirector auxiliar de Crédito (1972-75) y director de Inversiones Extranjeras (1975-76). Ha sido director ejecutivo por México y otros países latinoamericanos y del Caribe del Banco Mundial (1977-78); director de Administración y Finanzas del Canal 13 de televisión (1978), coordinador general de Delegaciones de la Secretaría de Programación (1979-82), director general de Banrural (1982-84), secretario de Agricultura y Recursos Hidráulicos (del 18 de julio de 1984 al 30 de noviembre de 1984) en el gobierno de Miguel de la Madrid; y delegado permanente de México ante la FAO (1989-90).

PESQUERÍA ◆ Municipio de Nuevo León situado en el centro del estado, al noreste de Monterrey. Superficie: 307.5 km^2. Habitantes: 9,359, de los cuales 2,771 forman la población económicamente activa. Hablan alguna lengua indígena 13 personas mayores de cinco años (náhuatl 9).

PESQUERÍA ◆ Río de Coahuila y Nuevo León, afluente del San Juan que, a su vez, es tributario del Bravo. Nace en las laderas occidentales de la sierra Madre Oriental, corre hacia el norte y cruza la misma cordillera antes de recibir el caudal del Salinas Victoria y del arroyo Ayancual.

PETACALCO ◆ Bahía de Guerrero situada al este de las Bocas de Zacatula, en la desembocadura del río Balsas; en la parte oriental recibe al río de la Unión. Cuenta con manantiales de agua dulce, en donde se surten algunas embarcaciones.

PETATLÁN ◆ Bahía de Guerrero limitada en el noroeste por la punta Descanso, donde se encuentra el faro que alumbra la entrada a la bahía de Zihuatanejo. Al sureste tiene el morro de Petatlán y la desembocadura de la laguna de Potosí.

PETATLÁN ◆ Morro de Guerrero situado en el sureste de la bahía del mismo nombre.

PETATLÁN ◆ Municipio de Guerrero situado en la Costa Grande, al este de Zihuatanejo. Superficie: 2,071.7 km². Habitantes: 47,630, de los cuales 11,176 forman la población económicamente activa. Hablan alguna lengua indígena 134 personas mayores de cinco años (náhuatl 85).

PETATLÁN ◆ Río de Guerrero. Nace en la vertiente sudoccidental de las cumbres de la Tentación, en la cresta principal de la sierra Madre del Sur. Corre de noreste a suroeste y se une al río San Jeronimito. Ambos desembocan en el océano Pacífico por la laguna Colorada.

PETERSEN BIESTER, ALBERTO ◆ n. en Guadalajara, Jal. (1925). Estudió ingeniería civil. Militante del Partido Acción Nacional desde 1943, en ese partido ha sido secretario de Finanzas (1962-68) y tesorero regional (1968-76). Ha sido diputado federal (1979-82, 1991-94). Es fundador de la Sociedad Filatélica Mexicana y del Instituto Mexicano de Ingenieros Químicos.

PETERSEN BIESTER, CARLOS ◆ n. en Guadalajara, Jal. (1926). Ingeniero egresado de la Universidad de Guadalajara, en la que ha sido profesor y secretario de la Facultad de Ingeniería. Ha sido tesorero (1964) y vicepresidente de la Cámara Nacional de la Industria de la Construcción (1994-95), presidente estatal de la Unión Nacional de Padres de Familia (1968-69) y secretario de Desarrollo Urbano del gobierno de Jalisco (1995-). Es socio y administrador de la empresa constructora PRYS. Miembro del Colegio de Ingenieros del estado de Jalisco y socio de Ingenieros y Arquitectos, A.C.

PETLALCINGO ◆ Municipio de Puebla situado en el sur del estado, al sureste de Acatlán, en los límites con Oaxaca. Superficie: 155.63 km². Habitantes: 9,319, de los cuales 2,022 forman la población económicamente activa. Hablan alguna lengua indígena 482 personas mayores de cinco años (mixteco 474). El nombre significa en náhuatl "en donde está el petate".

PETO ◆ Municipio de Yucatán situado en el sureste del estado, al sur de Chichén-Itzá, en los límites con Quintana Roo. Superficie: 3,136.0 km². Habitantes: 21,112, de los cuales 4,785 forman la población económicamente activa. Hablan alguna lengua indígena 13,787 personas mayores de cinco años (maya 13,772). Indígenas monolingües: 1,302.

PETRICIOLI ITURBIDE, GUSTAVO ◆ n. y m. en el DF (1928-1998). Licenciado en economía por el Instituto Tecnológico Autónomo de México (1951) y maestro en economía por la Universidad de Yale (1956). Fue miembro del PRI desde 1952. En el Banco de México, donde comenzó a trabajar en 1948, fue jefe de la Oficina Técnica, ayudante del director general, asesor técnico del director general, gerente y subdirector. Fue director de Estudios Hacendarios (1967-70) y subsecretario de Ingresos (1970-74) de la Secretaría de Hacienda; Alto Comisionado del Futbol (1974-76), presidente de la Comisión Nacional de Valores (1976-82), director general de Multibanco Comermex (1982), coordinador general de la Banca Mexicana (1982-86), secretario de Hacienda y Crédito Público (del 17 de junio de 1986 al 30 de noviembre de 1988) en el gobierno de Miguel de la Madrid; y embajador en Estados Unidos (1988-93). También fue director general de CAPUFE (1993-94). Fue miembro del Colegio Nacional de Economistas y de la Liga de Economistas Revolucionarios del PRI. Fue nombrado "Mister Amigo" por la ciudad de Brownsville, Texas, en 1991, por su participación en las negociaciones del Tratado de Libre Comercio de América del Norte.

Gustavo Petricioli

ILUSTRACIÓN DE ANTONIO ESPARZA

Casa de la Cultura de Petatlán

PETRICH, BLANCHE ◆ n. en el DF (1953). Periodista egresada de la Escuela de Periodismo Carlos Septién García. Cursó una maestría en periodismo en la Universidad del Sur de California. Se inició profesionalmente en *El Correo de la Tarde*, de Mazatlán. Trabajó en el cotidiano *El Día* y ha sido reportera fun-

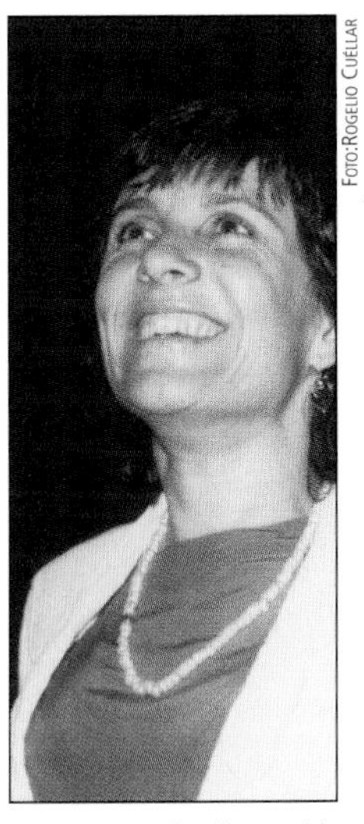

FOTO: ROGELIO CUÉLLAR

Blanche Petrich

dadora de los diarios capitalinos *unomásuno* y *La Jornada*. Fue corresponsal de *La Opinión*, de Los Ángeles, y de la televisión española. Coautora de *El Salvador, testigos de la guerra* (1991). Premio Nacional a la Trayectoria Periodística Manuel Buendía (1991). Es reportera del suplemento *Masiosare* de *La Jornada* (1998-).

PETRÓLEO ◆ Aceite natural producto de desechos fósiles animales y vegetales, abundante sobre todo en la costa del golfo de México y en la plataforma marina adyacente, aunque también existen yacimientos importantes en la costa de Chiapas. El nombre mexicano del petróleo, chapopote, proviene del náhuatl *chapopoctli*. Sobre el origen de este término no hay acuerdo: para algunos autores está formado de las palabras nahuas *chiautli*, grasa, y *poctli*, humo; mientras que para otros, proviene de las mayas *chaach*, mascar, y *pok*, limpiar. Entre los pueblos mesoamericanos, el petróleo se utilizó como sustituto del copal en las ceremonias religiosas, como droga adormecedora que se mezclaba con tabaco, como detergente dental cuando se masticaba, como medicina para padecimientos reumáticos, como fijador de colorantes y como pegamento y calafateante en la navegación. Este último fue el uso que le dieron los conquistadores españoles en 1521, cuando Hernán Cortés mandó construir 11 barcos, con los que realizó el sitio de México-Tenochtitlán. Durante la colonia, el petróleo comenzó a usarse como combustible y la Iglesia Católica mantuvo el empleo religioso que era tradicional entre los antiguos mexicanos. Se tiene noticia de que en el cerro del Tepeyac, en el siglo XVI, se descubrió un pozo de chapopote. Al aceite se le atribuían cualidades milagrosas y era vendido a los fieles, quienes alimentaban con él lámparas votivas. En el siglo XVII fue cegado el pozo al erigirse el santuario. En la Nueva España, el aprovechamiento petrolero fue regulado en mayo de 1783, cuando en el Código de Minería se incluyó a los "bitúmenes o jugos de la tierra" en el mismo régimen jurídico que los metales. Cuarenta años más tarde, en 1836, se firmó un tratado por medio del cual el gobierno español cedió al mexicano sus "derechos" sobre los campos chapopoteros mexicanos. En 1860 se constituyó una empresa para explorar el subsuelo de la Villa de Guadalupe del Distrito Federal y, dos años después, Antonio del Castillo perforó con fines exploratorios un pozo, situado en la calle de Aldama. Al llegar a los 60 metros de profundidad brotó agua mezclada con chapopote. Al año siguiente, el sacerdote Manuel Gil y Sáenz descubrió un yacimiento de petróleo en San Fernando, cerca de Tepatitlán, Tabasco, e inició la extracción y destilación de queroseno, que utilizó en el alumbrado de su parroquia y que más tarde intentó, sin éxito, comercializar en Estados Unidos. En 1865, Maximiliano de Habsburgo reformó la ley minera que databa de la colonia y en la nueva versión quedó contemplada, e incipientemente regulada, la extracción de petróleo. Basado en esta ley, el gobierno imperial autorizó a 38 particulares para explotar petróleo en diversas zonas del país. Sin embargo, el verdadero inicio de la industrialización petrolera ocurrió en 1869, dos años después del triunfo de la República, cuando Adolph Autrey, un estadounidense nacido en Irlanda, llegó a Papantla, se naturalizó mexicano, instaló un pequeño pozo y una rudimentaria refinería en 1875 y en 1881, gracias al descubrimiento de los yacimientos de La Constancia, comenzó a producir *aceite iluminante*. Un año antes, por su parte, un grupo de capitalistas británicos había instalado una pequena refinería en Tuxpan. En el sur del golfo de México, mientras tanto, Simón Sarlat Nova y Serapio Castillo fundaron en 1883 una empresa que reinició la explotación de los yacimientos de San Fernando, abandonados desde el fracaso de Gil y Sáenz. Aunque la exploración se vio favorecida con la promulgación, el 18 de marzo de 1884, de un Código de Minería que autorizaba a los particulares a buscar petróleo sin necesidad de informar al gobierno y les aseguraba la propiedad del subsuelo, la falta de mercado interno y lo costoso del proceso de extracción hicieron fracasar las primeras empresas. En 1890, por ejemplo, dejó de funcionar la refinería de Tuxpan y las propiedades de Autrey fueron adquiridas por la London Oil Trust Corporation, en la que participaba el británico Cecil Rhodes, fundador de la Mexican Oil Corporation. Estos dos consorcios, a su vez, quebraron al finalizar el siglo XIX, a pesar de que ya se conocía la existencia de algunos yaci-

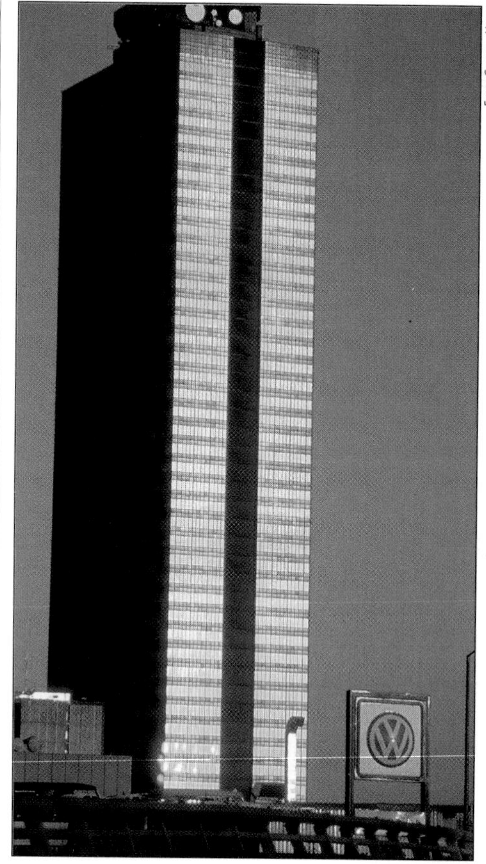

Foto: Carlos Hahn

Torre de Petróleos Mexicanos en el Distrito Federal

mientos en Veracruz, Chiapas y Tabasco. En 1899 continuaba en explotación el petróleo de la Villa de Guadalupe y había pozos en San Juan de Aragón, entonces suburbios de la ciudad de México. En ese mismo año, el Instituto Geológico Nacional publicó un informe redactado por Juan Villarelo, en el que se aseguraba que no existían grandes yacimientos de petróleo en México. No obstante, quizá con la intención de facilitar nuevas exploraciones, el gobierno porfirista expidió, en diciembre, una Ley del Petróleo redactada por los secretarios José Ives Limantour y Manuel Fernández Leal, que autorizaba a cualquier particular dedicarse a la explotación petrolera sin ninguna restricción, permitía la importación indiscriminada de materiales de exploración, la *expropiación* de cualquier terreno que a juicio del concesionario pudiera contener petróleo y la instalación de conductos en cualquier parte del país. Asimismo, eximía a las compañías petroleras del pago de casi todos los impuestos, excepto el del timbre. Con este apoyo, así como con la garantía de los mercados internacionales y la utilización de mejores técnicas de explotación, el estadounidense Edward L. Doheney y el británico Weetman D. Pearson se convirtieron en los principales explotadores del petróleo mexicano. Doheney, que había llegado de San Francisco, instaló el campamento de El Ébano, en terrenos pantanosos de la hacienda El Tulillo, San Luis Potosí, en los límites con Veracruz y Tamaulipas. Ahí perforó, en 1901, un pozo que arrojó 50 barriles diarios de crudo y fue el primero de la Mexican Petroleum Company. Durante los tres años siguiente, Doheney perforó algunos pozos más, pero todos resultaron muy pobres, por lo que estuvo a punto de quebrar. En 1904, sin embargo, uno de los empleados de la Mexican Petroleum, Ezequiel Ordóñez, descubrió el pozo llamado La Pez I, con una producción de 1,500 barriles diarios, el que permitió a Doheney fundar, en 1907, la Huasteca Petroleum Company. En 1901, a raíz de la expedición de la citada ley, Pearson aprovechó sus conocimientos sobre el istmo de Tehuantepec, los que había adquirido mientras construía el Ferrocarril de Tehuantepec a fines del siglo XIX, y formó una empresa exploradora y explotadora que operó en los alrededores de la desembocadura del río Coatzacoalcos. Cinco años más tarde, en febrero de 1906, el gobierno le otorgó una concesión para explotar petróleo en "el subsuelo de los lagos, lagunas y terrenos baldíos nacionales, ubicados en los estados de Veracruz, Tabasco, Chiapas, Campeche, San Luis Potosí y Tamaulipas". Gracias a la concesión, en 1908, con un capital de 100,000 pesos, Pearson fundó la Compañía Petrolera El Águila, misma que, entre 1910 y 1920, ganó 164 millones de pesos. En 1910, la producción petrolera era de 3,634,000 barriles, contra 502,000 en 1906 y sólo 10,000 en 1900. También en 1910, tres grandes consorcios controlaban la explotación: Mexican Eagle, Mexican Petroleum y Mexican Fuel Company. Dos años después de la insurrección maderista, en 1912, las compañías petroleras del norte de Veracruz y sur de Tamaulipas, desconfiadas de la presidencia de Francisco I. Madero, alentaron la formación de un ejército particular que al mando de Manuel Peláez controló la zona, primero con apoyo de los felicistas y más tarde con el de los huertistas, hasta que al triunfo del constitucionalismo, en 1914, Peláez huyó del país. Al año siguiente, el gobierno de Carranza creó una Comisión Técnica Petrolera, dependiente de la Secretaría de Obras Públicas, con la intención de controlar la explotación privada, por lo que las compañías hicieron regresar a Peláez, quien volvió a organizar su ejército privado, con el que dominó el norte veracruzano hasta 1918. Durante el Congreso Constituyente de 1916- 17, la participación de los diputados Francisco J. Múgica y Luis G. Monzón, entre otros, fue definitiva para la redacción del artículo 27 constitucional, que estableció lo siguiente: "Corresponde a la nación el dominio directo de todos los yacimientos minerales y orgánicos, los combustibles minerales sólidos, el petróleo y todos los carburos de hidrógenos sólidos, líquidos o gaseosos." En abril de 1917, dos meses después de promulgada la Constitución, el gobierno estableció el primer impuesto petrolero. Aunque las disposiciones afectaban las excesivas facilidades que les habían sido otorgadas dieciséis años antes, la empresas petroleras exportaron en 1917 poco más de 55 millones de barriles de petróleo, con lo que colocaron a México como tercer productor mundial. Más aún, como consecuencia de la primera

Depósito de petróleo

FOTO: CARLOS HAHN

guerra mundial, aumentó la extracción y en 1921 México se colocó como segundo productor mundial, con 193 millones de barriles de petróleo, 90 por ciento de los cuales provenían de la Huasteca, casi en su totalidad destinados a la exportación sin refinar. Como la Carta Constitucional dejaba abierta la posibilidad de la expropiación, las empresas maniobraron durante la primera mitad de 1921 y en agosto consiguieron que el Poder Judicial reconociera sus "derechos adquiridos" antes de 1917. En 1925, al mismo tiempo que se creaba la Administración Nacional del Petróleo, la primera empresa petrolera con participación estatal, el gobierno de Plutarco Elías Calles reiniciaba el otorgamiento de concesiones petroleras y reconocía la perpetuidad de las existentes. Dos años después, sin embargo, el gobierno redujo a 50 años la duración de las concesiones, pero en noviembre, la Suprema Corte de Justicia de la Nación determinó que el artículo 27 constitucional no era retroactivo y que, por lo tanto, la nación no poseía los recursos petroleros que hubieren sido concesionados antes de la promulgación de la Constitución. Finalmente, en los últimos años de esa década, el gobierno aumentó el monto de los impuestos petroleros. Por esos años, la explotación petrolera se limitaba a la costa del golfo de México, a pesar de varios intentos de exploración, como el de Juan Polhenz, quien en 1929 obtuvo una concesión para buscar el crudo en las municipalidades de Mixcoac, Tacubaya y San Ángel. Como consecuencia de la crisis económica iniciada en 1929, la producción petrolera disminuyó y en 1932 apenas se produjeron cerca de 33 millones de barriles. Un año más tarde, en 1933, se estableció una nueva empresa con participación gubernamental, llamada Petróleos Mexicanos S.A. En 1937 el gobierno creó la Administración General del Petróleo Nacional. A partir de la creación del Sindicato de Trabajadores del Petróleo de la República Mexicana, en agosto de 1935, los conflictos laborales se agudizaron, lo que el 18 de marzo de 1938 llevó al gobierno de Lázaro Cárdenas a declarar "expropiados por causa de utilidad pública y a favor de la Nación, la maquinaria, instalaciones, edificios, oleoductos, refinerías, tanques de almacenamiento, vías de comunicación, carros-tanque, estaciones de distribución, embarcaciones y todos los demás bienes muebles e inmuebles de propiedad de la Compañía Mexicana de Petróleo El Águila S.A., Compañía Naviera de San Cristóbal S.A., Compañía Naviera San Ricardo S.A., Huasteca Petroleum Company, Sinclair Pierce Oil Company, Mexican Sinclair Petroleum Corporation, Stanford y Compañía, Penn Mex Fuel Company, Richmond Petroleum Company de México, California Standard Oil Company of Mexico, Compañía Petrolera el Agwi S.A., Compañía de Gas y Combustible Imperio, Consolidated Oil Company of Mexico, Compañía Mexicana de Vapores San Antonio S.A., Sabalo Transportation Company, Clarita S.A., y Cacalilao S.A." (☛ *Expropiación petrolera*). Al día siguiente el gobierno creó el Consejo de Administración del Petróleo, el 31 de marzo se instituyó la Compañía Exportadora del Petróleo Nacional, encargada de exportar el hidrocarburo y así obtener fondos para indemnizar a las empresas expropiadas; y el 20 de julio empezaron a operar dos nuevos organismos: Distribuidora de Petróleos Nacionales y Petróleos Mexicanos. Al ser expropiadas, las empresas retiraron a sus técnicos, privaron de refacciones a la industria y realizaron una campaña para cerrarle mercados al crudo mexicano, todo lo cual ocasionó que la producción petrolera se desplomara hasta 38.5 millones de barriles. El 8 de agosto de 1940, todas las empresas del gobierno se fundieron en una sola, que se

FOTO: CARLOS HAHN

Industria petroquímica Tribasa en Tula, Hidalgo

Industria petroquímica Tribasa en Tula, Hidalgo

llamó Petróleos Mexicanos. Durante los primeros años posteriores a la expropiación, la falta de capital, los problemas laborales, los elevados costos de producción y el boicot internacional contra el crudo mexicano hicieron muy difícil la producción, así como su venta. Los trabajadores y técnicos mexicanos ocuparon los puestos dejados por los extranjeros y en muchos casos tuvieron que improvisar soluciones para los múltiples problemas que se les presentaban en una actividad tan compleja. En 1940 el Instituto Politécnico Nacional, creado por Lázaro Cárdenas en 1936, estableció la carrera de ingeniero petrolero, de la que han salido nueve de cada 10 técnicos empleados en la actividad petrolera. Para solucionar el problema de los mercados, México exportó hidrocarburos a la Unión Soviética y la República española y Lázaro Cárdenas se vio obligado a autorizar el comercio de crudo con la Alemania nazi y la Italia fascista. El intercambio con estas dos naciones se interrumpió en 1942, luego del hundimiento de los petroleros *Faja de oro*, *Potrero del llano*, *Tuxpan*, *Choapas* y *Amatlán*, lo que ocasionó la entrada de México en la segunda guerra mundial (☛ *guerras mundiales*). Durante el conflicto bélico se levantó el boicot de las potencias industriales contra Pemex y la industria nacional reinició su crecimiento. En 1949 se descubrió el primer campo de explotación de Tabasco. Dos años después, en 1951, dejó de operar en el país la Mexican Gulf Oil Company, última empresa extranjera en retirarse de México. Hasta entonces, Pemex le compraba el petróleo para refinarlo. El último pago de la indemnización a las compañías expropiadas se efectuó en agosto de 1962. Tres años después, con la idea de producir tecnología nacional e impulsar la investigación, se creó el Instituto Mexicano del Petróleo. En 1969-70, la producción llegó a medio millón de barriles diarios, esto es, cerca de 170 millones de barriles anuales, insuficientes para cubrir la demanda nacional, por lo que se tenía que importar crudo. En 1972 se iniciaron tareas de explotación en el campo de La Reforma, en Chiapas. Las reservas probadas pasaron de 5,400 millones de barriles en 1973 a 11,000 millones de barriles en 1976, cuando se anunció que la producción era suficiente para satisfacer las necesidades del mercado interno. En 1977 se inició la explotación de la sonda de Campeche, yacimiento descubierto en 1975 y que es uno de los más importantes del mundo. La capacidad productora de Pemex creció hasta alcanzar, en 1980, 2 millones de barriles diarios. Al año siguiente, México se colocó en el cuarto lugar mundial de los productores de petróleo.

PETTERSSON, ALINE ◆ n. en el DF (1938). Escritora. Estudió letras hispánicas en la UNAM. Profesora de creación literaria en la Escuela de Escritores de la SOGEM. Ha trabajado en Publicaciones del Conacyt y de la SEP. Colaboradora de *El Gallo Ilustrado*, *Sábado*, *Revista de Bellas Artes*, *Revista de la Universidad*, *Diálogos*, *El unomásuno*, *El Universal* y *Novedades*. Coautora de la novela *El hombre equivocado* (1988). Autora de relatos: *El papalote y el nopal* (1985), *Clara y el cangrejo* (1990), *Piratas de Veracruz* (1990, cuento infantil), *Más allá de la mirada* (1992), *Ontario, la mariposa viajera* (1993, cuento infantil), "Cuando el sol se ocultó en el cielo" (1996, en *La luna de miel según Eva*) y *Fer y la princesa* (1997); novela: *Círculos* (1976), *Casi en silencio* (1980), *Proyecto de muerte* (1983), *Los colores ocultos* (1986), *Sombra ella misma* (1986), *Piedra que rueda* (1990), *Querida familia* (1991), *La noche de las hormigas* (1997) y *Colores y sombras. Tres novelas* (1998, reunión de *Círculos*, *Los colores ocultos* y *Sombra ella misma*); ensayo: *Charla a tres voces* y *Las historias de mis personajes no son noticia de ocho columnas*; escritos autobiográficos: *De cuerpo entero* (1990) y *Mi familia y sus sagas* (1997); y poesía: *Tres poemas* (1985), *Cautiva estoy de mí* (1988) y *Mistificaciones* (1996). Ha sido becaria del Centro Mexicano de Escritores (1977-78) y del Programa Internacional de la Universidad de Iowa (1984). Nombrada Creadora Artística por el SNCA (1994). Recibió el Premio Gabriela Mistral 1998, otorgado por la editorial francesa Coté-Femmes al conjunto de su obra.

Aline Pettersson

PEYOTES ◆ Lomerío de Coahuila que forma parte de las sierras frontales de la sierra Madre Oriental.

PEYRÍ MACIÁ, ANTONI ◆ n. en España (1924). Arquitecto y pintor. Llegó en 1941, luego de la derrota de la República Española. En ese año se naturalizó mexicano. Arquitecto titulado en la UNAM (1950). Profesor de la UNAM (1951-81) y la UIA (1962-66). Ha sido jefe del Departamento de Diseño Arquitectónico de la División de Estudios Superiores de la Escuela Nacional de Arquitectura (1968-75) y delegado de esa escuela al Congreso Latinoamericano de Escuelas y Facultades de Arquitectura, celebrado en Argentina. Colaboró con Mario Pani en el plano urbanístico de Acapulco. Entre sus trabajos arquitectónicos se cuentan el edificio estacionamiento de Sears Roebuck y el Palacio de los Deportes (en colaboración), ambos en la ciudad de México. Pintor autodidacta, expuso por primera vez en la galería Proteo (1961). Sus obras se han presentado en España, Estados Unidos y Japón. En 1968 obtuvo el premio Kreimerman del Concurso Nacional de Pintura convocado por el INBA y al año siguiente participó en la elaboración de un mural del pabellón mexicano en Osaka.

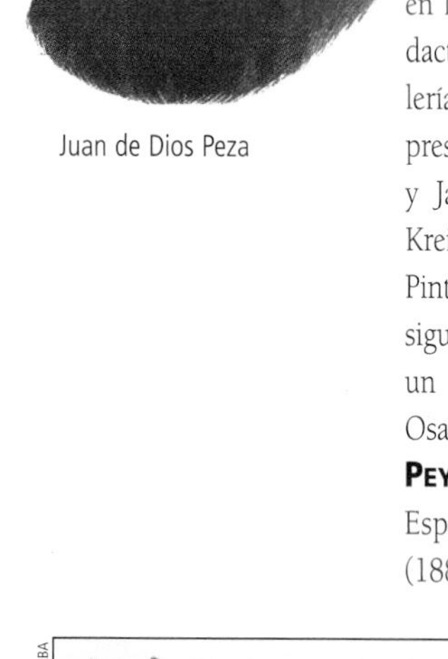

Juan de Dios Peza

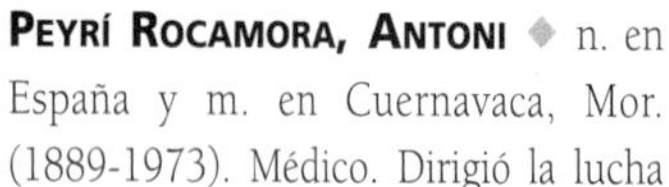

PEYRÍ ROCAMORA, ANTONI ◆ n. en España y m. en Cuernavaca, Mor. (1889-1973). Médico. Dirigió la lucha antivenérea en Cataluña y en 1939, a la derrota de la República Española, se encargó del leprosario de la Isla de Providencia, en Venezuela. Vino a México en 1941 y en ese año se naturalizó mexicano. Profesor de la Universidad de Nuevo León (1941). Fue jefe del servicio dermatológico del Hospital Civil de Monterrey y jefe de dermosifilografía del IMSS (1942-70). Fue fundador y colaborador de la *Revista Médica de Barcelona*. Autor de *Dermatología* (1943) y *El poder político* (1972).

Vicisitudes de una agonía, tinta litográfica sobre tela de Antoni Peyrí Maciá (1977)

PEZA, JUAN DE DIOS ◆ n. y m. en la ciudad de México (1852-1910). Poeta. Estudió en la Escuela Nacional Preparatoria, donde fue alumno de *el Nigromante* y de Ignacio Manuel Altamirano. Colaborador del periódico *El Siglo XIX*, editor de *El Búcaro* (1873) y director de *El Mundo Literario* (1873). Segundo secretario de la legación mexicana en España (1878-1900), donde colaboró en *La Ilustración Española y Americana*. Volvió a México en 1900. Fue diputado federal, director de la Beneficencia Pública del Distrito Federal y profesor del Conservatorio Nacional de Música. Al morir era diputado federal. Realizó las antologías *Poetas y escritores mexicanos* (1877), y *La lira mexicana* (1879). Coautor de *Tradiciones y leyendas mexicanas* (1900). Autor de textos históricos, ensayo, biografía, memorias y narrativa: *Biografía de Ignacio M. Altamirano* (1878), *La beneficencia en México* (1881), *Leyendas históricas, tradicionales y fantásticas de las calles de México* (1898), *De la gaveta íntima* (1900), *Epopeyas de mi patria. Benito Juárez. La reforma. La intervención francesa. El imperio. El triunfo de la República* (1904), *Recuerdos de España* (1904), *Recuerdos de mi vida* (1907) y *Diálogos históricos* (1910); poesía: *Poesías* (1873), *Un epílogo de amor* (1875), *Horas de pasión* (1876), *Canto a la patria* (1876), *Cantos del hogar* (1884), *Algunos versos inéditos* (1885), *Poesías completas* (1886), *Dos reales de versos festivos* (1888), *Horas de pasión. Versos del alma* (1888), *La musa de viaje* (1889), *La lira de la patria* (1890), *El arpa del amor* (1891), *Honor y patria* (1891) y *Recuerdos y esperanzas* (1892); y teatro: *Granaditas*, *Una fiesta en Santa Anita*, *Vísperas de la boda*, *La ciencia del hogar* (1874), *Últimos días de Colón* (1874), *Un epílogo de amor* (1875), *Capitán Miguel* (1887), *¡Ora Ponciano!* (1887), *El grito de dolores* (1909), *Diálogos históricos* (1910), *Las dos muñecas* (1909) y *Un duelo en el mar*. Póstumamente apareció el *Devocionario*

FOTO: PABLO GONZÁLEZ DE ALBA

El Palacio de los Deportes, obra en la que colaboró Antoni Peyrí Maciá

ARCHIVO XAVIER ESPARZA

EN LA MUERTE
DE LA
SEÑORITA PAZ ALGARA Y TERREROS

Llena de juventud, de gracia llena,
Tesoro de virtud y de ternura,
Te miré descollar fragante y pura
Como en un campo virgen la azucena.

En tu mirada límpida y serena
No sorprendí tristezas ni amargura,
Eras una alborada en hermosura
Que en silencio admiré por dulce y buena.

¿Quién ¡ay! sobre esa flor deslumbradora
La furia desató del cierzo impío?
¡La muerte, la implacable segadora!

Y tornó tu beldad en mármol frío,
Y en tinieblas los rayos de la aurora,
Y en lágrimas las gotas de rocío!

JUAN DE DIOS PEZA

México, 21 de Diciembre de 1897

Poema de Juan de Dios Peza publicado en *El Mundo Ilustrado* el 21 de diciembre de 1897

de mis nietos (prosa, 1930). Fundó la primera Sociedad de Autores Mexicanos y perteneció a la Academia Mexicana (de la Lengua).

PEZA Y FERNÁNDEZ DE CÓRDOBA, JUAN DE DIOS ◆ n. y m. en la ciudad de México (1815-1884). Militar. Padre del anterior. Fue oficial mayor de la Secretaría de Guerra y Marina, encargado del despacho en los gobiernos de Miguel Miramón (del 3 al 14 de febrero de 1859), José Ignacio Pavón (del 13 al 15 de agosto de 1860) y en el segundo de Miramón (del 15 al 18 de agosto de 1860); y ministro de Guerra en el gabinete de Maximiliano de Habsburgo (del 13 de junio de 1864 al 3 de marzo de 1866). Al triunfo de la República fue condenado a muerte, pena que se le conmutó por el destierro en Francia, de donde volvió tiempo después.

PFCRN ◆ ☛ *Partido del Frente Cardenista de Reconstrucción Nacional.*

PGR ◆ ☛ *Procuraduría General de la República.*

PHILIBERT MENDOZA, EDUARDO ◆ n. en el DF (1929). Contador público titulado (1946-51) y maestro en contaduría graduado (1965-66) en el IPN. Profesor del IPN (1955-68) y de la UNAM (1960-67). Ha sido jefe de Servicios de Personal (1967), delegado en Jalisco y el Estado de México (1979-80) y subdirector general administrativo (1982-85) del IMSS; director de Organización y Métodos de la Secretaría de Programación (1978), director del Fideicomiso Puerto Vallarta (1986) y contralor interno de la Sedue (1987-88); y contralor general (1988-92) y coordinador general del Transporte del DDF (1992-93).

PHILLIPS, ALEX ◆ n. en Canadá y ¿m. en el DF? (1900-1977). Nombre profesional del fotógrafo cinematográfico Alexander Pelepiock. Hijo de padres nacidos en Rusia, donde vivió hasta la primera guerra mundial, cuando se alistó en la armada canadiense. Fue herido en combate. En 1919 viajó a Estados Unidos. Impulsado por Mary Pickford se inició en el cine como ayudante de cámara en la Christy Comedies; pasó a la Metro Goldwyn Meyer, donde trabajó con Greg Toland. Vino a finales de los años veinte y en 1931 fotografió la primera película sonora de México: *Santa*, a la que siguieron, entre otras, *Águilas frente al sol* (1932), *El compadre Mendoza* (1933), *La familia Dressel* (1935), *El tesoro de Pancho Villa* (1935), *Celos* (1935), *Pepita Jiménez* (1945), *El pecado de ser pobre*, *La sin ventura* (1947), *La bien pagada* (1947), *Mi querido capitán* (1950), *Deseada* (1950), *Sensualidad* (1950), *Subida al cielo* (1951) y *Adán y Eva* (1956). Dirigió una sola película: *Hoy comienza la vida* (1935). En 1963 recibió la Diosa de Plata por la fotografía de *Viento Negro*; en 1967 volvió a ganar la Diosa de Plata, por *La Soldadera*; y en 1970, por *Zapata*; recibió Arieles en 1952, por *En la palma de tu mano*, y en 1955, por *Sombra verde*.

PHILLIPS, ALEX ◆ n. en el DF (1935). Hijo del anterior. Fotógrafo de cine. Estudió cine en Canadá y arquitectura en la UNAM. Profesor del CUEC y el Centro de Capacitación Cinematográfica. Se inició profesionalmente en 1960, en la película *Yanco*, a la que siguieron *El asesino de tontos* (1963), *Cabo blanco*, *Tráiganme la cabeza de Alfredo García* (1973), *El cumpleaños del perro* (1975), *Los albañiles* (1975), *Canoa* (1975), *Las Poquianchis* (1976), *El complot mongol* (1977), *Tate to Block* (1980), *Evita* (1980), *Trampa nocturna* (1982), *Anoche soñé contigo* (1991) y *La tarea prohibida* (1992), entre otras. En 1977 recibió un Ariel por su trabajo en *Fox trot*.

Alex Phillips

COLECCIÓN GUSTAVO GARCÍA

En *Las Poquianchis*, Alex Phillips, hijo, estuvo a cargo de la fotografía

PHILLIPS, HOWARD S. ◆ n. en Inglaterra y m. en el DF (?-1972). Cubrió la información en los frentes durante la primera guerra mundial. En 1923, con ciudadanía estadounidense, llegó a México como corresponsal de la agencia United Press International y se hizo cargo de la revista *The Pulse of Mexico*, que dejó en 1924 para fundar *Mexican Life*. En los años cincuenta se naturalizó mexicano. Colaboró en publicaciones nacionales y extranjeras.

PHILLIPS, RICHARD FRANCIS ◆ ☛ *Seaman, Frank.*

Alfredo Phillips Olmedo

PHILLIPS GREENE, ALFREDO ◆ n. en el DF (1961). Actuario por la Universidad Anáhuac y maestro en administración pública por la Universidad de Harvard. Ha sido asesor del secretario de Comunicaciones y Transportes, participó en la negociación del Programa de Modernización de las Telecomunicaciones y en la privatización de Teléfonos de México; subgerente de coinversiones en Nacional Financiera encargado de la administración de los Fondos y Convenios de Coinversiones Institucionales; funcionario asesor experto encargado de la Subdirección de Estudios Económicos y Estadística del Programa de Apoyo Integral a la Pequeña y Mediana Industria; asesor de la Dirección Adjunta de Promoción y Financiamiento de Nacional Financiera y director adjunto de Asuntos Internacionales del Conacyt.

PHILLIPS OLMEDO, ALFREDO ◆ n. en Matamoros, Tams. (1935). Hijo de Howard S. Phillips. Hizo la licenciatura en economía en las universidades de Londres y Cambridge (1956-60) y obtuvo la maestría en la Universidad George Washington, de EUA (1965-66). Profesor de la UIA (1961-63). Ha sido jefe del Departamento de Programación Económica y Fiscal (1962-64) y subjefe del Departamento de Bancos, Monedas e Inversiones de la Secretaría de Hacienda (1964-65); oficial de Préstamos del BID (1965-66), director ejecutivo del FMI (1966-70); gerente de Asuntos Económicos Internacionales (1971-75) y subdirector de Asuntos Internacionales del Banco de México (1975-82); director general del Banco de Comercio Exterior (1982-88) y embajador de México en Canadá (1989-91) y en Japón (1991-92); subsecretario de Vivienda y Bienes Inmuebles (1992- 1994) . Coautor de *50 años de banca central* (1981) y *El comercio exterior de México* (1981). Es miembro del PRI desde 1961, donde ha sido coordinador de la Comisión de Relaciones Internacionales (1994-96). Diputado federal (1997-2000).

PHILLIPS OLMEDO, EDUARDO ◆ n. en Matamoros, Tams. (1940). Ingeniero en electrónica titulado en Estados Unidos; es maestro en sistemas por la UIA. En la Secretaría de Hacienda ha sido coordinador de Sistemas de la Dirección General de Impuestos Interiores (1966-68), coordinador de Procesamiento de Datos (1972-73) y director del Centro de Cómputo de la Oficialía Mayor (1974-75); director de Informática de la Subsecretaría de Ingresos (1975-76), director general de Informática de Ingresos (1978-79 y 1983-87), subdirector general de Recaudación (1980-83) y administrador fiscal regional norte del Distrito Federal (1987-). Además, fue gerente de la División de Procesamiento de Datos de Kodak Mexicana (1968-72) y subdirector de Informática del Combinado Industrial Sahagún (1976-78). Pertenece a la Academia Mexicana de Informática, de la que fue presidente en 1982.

PI OROZO, LUIS ERNESTO ◆ n. en el DF (1953). Licenciado en lengua y literatura hispánicas por la Facultad de Filosofía y Letras de la UNAM (1972-1976). Realizó la tesis *El recurso del método y la novela del dictador latinoamericano* (1985); tomó el curso de actualización *La nueva Ley Electoral y los partidos políticos* en la UIA (1990); becario de la Agencia de Cooperación Internacional del Japón (JICA) en el Broadcasting Executives Seminar, Tokio, Japón (1992). Miembro del PRI. Ha sido coordinador de Actividades Cívicas y Ediciones de la Dirección de Servicios Sociales del DDF (1970-1978); subjefe del Departamento de Análisis del Centro de Documentación y Publicaciones (1979-1980), jefe de departamento de la Dirección de Televisión de RTC (1981-1982), director de Radio de RTC de la Secretaría de Gobernación (1988-1989); coordinador general de Comunicación Ciudadana del Consejo Consultivo de la Ciudad de México (1991) y director general de Radio Educación (1991-). Compilador del libro *Texto básico de capacitación política* (1986). Fue redactor de la *Revista Latinoamericana: Hora Cero* (1987-1988) y ha colaborado en *El Día* (1978-88) y *El Financiero* (1988-1990).

PI SUNYER, AUGUSTO ◆ n. en España y m. en el DF (1879-1965). Licenciado en medicina por la Universidad de Barcelona (1899) y doctor en medicina por la Universidad Central de Madrid (1900). Profesor de las universidades de Sevilla y Barcelona (1902-16). Fue diputado a Cortes (1916-23), director del Instituto de Fisiología de la Universidad de Barcelona (1920), presidente de la Academia de Medicina (1920-39) y miembro del Consejo de Cultura General de Cataluña (1932-39). A la derrota de la República española se asiló en Francia (1939). Profesor de la Universidad de Tolosa y de la Universidad Central de Caracas, Venezuela, donde fundó y dirigió el Instituto de Medicina Experimental. Llegó a México en 1962. Autor de *Tratado de fisiología general* (1909), *La unidad funcional* (1918), *Los mecanismos de correlación fisiológica* (1920), *Les Distrófies per Retard* (1933), *Equilibrio neurovegetativo* (1936), *Las anomalías del metabolismo de los glúcidos* (1939), *La sensibilidad trófica* (1939), *Principio y término de la biología* (1941), *Los fundamentos de la biología* (1943), *La novela del Besavi* (1943), *Dispersa y conjunta* (1945), *El sistema neurovegetativo* (1947), *La vida profunda* (1948), *Sueño y realidad en ciencia* (1950), *The Bridge of Life* (1951), *Classics of Biology* (1955), *Sunyer Metges, pare i fill* (1957) y *Fisiología humana* (1962). Póstumamente aparecieron *Poesías* (1970) y *Contacto con oriente* (1980). En 1948 recibió el Premio Pourat del Instituto de Francia y en 1955 el Premio Kalinga, de la UNESCO.

PI SUNYER BAYO, CÉSAR ◆ n. en España y m. en el DF (1905-1997). Farmacéutico titulado en la Universidad de Barcelona (1927) con estudios de posgrado en el KW. Institut F. Biochemie (1929) y en el Pathol Institut (1930), ambos de Berlín. Doctor en farmacia por la Universidad Central de Madrid (1932). En España fue investigador (1927) y jefe del Departamento de Bioquímica (1931-39) del Instituto de Fisiología de Barcelona, director químico del Laboratorio Chemirosa de Barcelona (1932-39) y, durante la guerra civil española, jefe de laboratorio del Hospital Militar de Barcelona (1937-39). Llegó como refugiado en 1939 y dos años después se naturalizó mexicano. Aquí ha sido director gerente de los Laboratorios Químicos (1939-54) y director gerente del laboratorio Syntorgam (1955-). Presidió el Orfeó Catalá de México (1971-74) y es presidente, desde 1975, del Institut Catalá de Cultura. Autor de *Metabolismo intermediario de los hidratos de carbono* (1932), *El complexe vitaminc B* (1933), *La bioquímica dels hidrats de carboni* (1966) y *Homenaje de los catalanes de México al general Lázaro Cárdenas* (1971).

Piani, Guillermo ◆ n. en Italia y m. en Cuernavaca, Mor. (1875-1956). Sacerdote. Estudió en la Universidad Gregoriana de Roma. Fungió como inspector general de las casas salesianas de México (1910-20). En 1921 fue nombrado obispo auxiliar de la arquidiócesis de Puebla, pero no aceptó el cargo. Fungió como delegado apostólico en Filipinas (1922-48). En México fue visitador de El Vaticano (1934 y 1948) y delegado apostólico (1951-55).

Piaxtla ◆ Municipio de Puebla situado en el sur del estado, al suroeste de Acatlán. Superficie: 275.55 km^2. Habitantes: 5,301, de los cuales 1,046 forman la población económicamente activa. Hablan alguna lengua indígena cinco personas mayores de cinco años. Su nombre significa en náhuatl "Tierra larga".

Piaxtla ◆ Río de Durango y Sinaloa. Nace de la confluencia de los arroyos Santa Rita y Piedra Parada, en la parte occidental de la sierra de Tepehuanes. Corre de este a oeste por el norte de la sierra del Espinazo del Diablo. Recoge el caudal de los ríos Dimas y Verde y desemboca en el océano Pacífico por la boca de Piaxtla.

Piazza, Luis Guillermo ◆ n. en Argentina (1922). Escritor. Doctor en derecho y ciencias sociales por la Universidad Central de Córdoba, donde fue profesor. Becario del Instituto de Educación Interamericana de Nueva York (1947-49). En 1952 llegó a México, empleado por la OEA, para la cual trabajaba desde 1949. Profesor de la Escuela de Verano y de la Facultad de Ciencias Políticas de la UNAM. Es cofundador del programa de televisión *Para gente grande* (1980), del Canal 2. Colaborador de los periódicos *Excélsior* y *Novedades*, de la estación Radio Universidad, y de las revistas *Cuadernos del Viento*, *Revista de la Universidad de México*, *Caballero* y *S. Nob.* Coautor de *Crónicas bastante extrañas* (1965). Autor de ensayo: *La Constitución argentina y su reforma de 1949* (1950), *El derecho de autor en las Américas* (1951), *Tendencias actuales en la literatura jurídica latinoamericana* (1951), *El país más viejo del mundo* (1964) y *El horror inútil. Tragedia y farsa del periodismo en América Latina* (1988); novela: *La siesta* (1956), *Los hombres y las cosas sólo querían jugar* (1963), *La mafia* (1967), *Temporada de excusas* (1981) y *Los cómplices* (1985); poesía: *Antifábulas* (1969) y *Fantasmas y desagravios* (1981); y teatro: *El tuerto de oro* (1963) y *Los locos* (1968). En 1988 fue nombrado Cronista de la Zona Rosa del Distrito Federal.

Picachos ◆ Sierra de Nuevo León que es una de las frontales de la sierra Madre Oriental. Su cima más alta es el cerro Sombreretillo, con una altura de 1,463 metros.

Picaluga, Francisco ◆ n. en Italia (1792-?). Pagado por el gobierno de Anastasio Bustamante, en 1831 invitó a su buque, anclado en Acapulco, al depuesto presidente Vicente Guerrero, al que secuestró. Lo llevó a Huatulco y ahí lo entregó a Miguel González, quien pasó por las armas al ex presidente. Por esa acción recibió 50,000 pesos de oro, dinero que debía repartir entre sus cómplices, pero los burló y llegó a Génova, su ciudad natal, donde fue detenido por el Real Consejo del Almirantazgo en 1832. Más tarde, sin embargo, huyó de la cárcel y desapareció. Algunas versiones indican que vivió en Esmirna, otras señalan que en Mazatlán y que se suicidió. En ausencia, en 1836 las autoridades de Génova lo sentenciaron a pagar indemnización a los herederos de Guerrero y, declarado enemigo de la patria y del Estado, fue condenado a muerte.

Píccolo, Francisco María ◆ n. en Italia y m. en Loreto, BC (1654-1729). Sacerdote. Ingresó en la Compañía de Jesús en 1673. Llegó a la Nueva España en 1684, destinado a las misiones del norte. Estuvo en la sierra Tarahumara en 1689 y en 1697 pasó a Baja California y Sonora, donde fue segundo de la orden, después de Eusebio Francisco Kino. Autor de *Informe del estado de la nueva cristiandad de California* (1702), el primer documento sobre California.

Pichanagobeche ◆ Dios mayor de los zapotecas de Chichicapan. Según la mitología, esta deidad aleja las enfermedades. Se le hacían ofrendas de sangre humana.

Pichanto ◆ Deidad de los zapotecas de Chichicapan, intermediario entre los hombres y Pichanagobeche; como a aquél, a Pichanto se le hacían ofrendas de sangre humana.

Pichardo, Ángel ◆ n. y m. en el DF (1929-1978). Pintor. Estudió en la Escuela Nacional de Artes Plásticas. Profesor del Instituto Potosino de Bellas Artes (1955-63) y de la Escuela de Diseño y Artesanías del INBA (1964-78). Expuso por primera vez en 1951. Coautor del mural *Libertadores de América* (1963), que se encuentra en el museo de Loreto, en Puebla. Sus obras se han presentado en Argentina, Canadá, Chile, Ecuador, Estados Unidos, Guatemala, Japón y Nicaragua. En 1955 obtuvo el Premio Nuevos Valores del Salón de la Plástica Mexicana y en 1967 el Premio de los Maestros de Enseñanza Artística del INBA.

Pichardo, José Antonio ◆ n. en Cuernavaca, hoy en el estado de Mor., y m. en la ciudad de México (¿1748?-1812). Historiador. Estudió en el Colegio de San Juan de Letrán, donde más tarde impartió las cátedras de filosofía y latín. Fue capellán del Hospicio de Pobres y presbítero del Oratorio de San Felipe Neri. Autor de *Elogio de San Felipe Neri*, *Historia de Nuestra Señora de los Remedios*, *Vida y martirio del protomártir mexicano San Felipe de Jesús de las Casas* y *Límites de Luisiana y Texas* (1812).

Luis Guillermo Piazza

Juan Josafat Pichardo Cruz

José Ignacio Pichardo Pagaza

PICHARDO CRUZ, JUAN JOSAFAT ◆ n. en Toluca, Edo. de Méx. (1912). Estudió en las escuelas nacionales de Maestros y de Jurisprudencia. Fue profesor y rector (1956-62) de la Universidad Autónoma del Estado de México, y magistrado del Tribunal Superior de Justicia de la misma entidad (1969-71).

PICHARDO PAGAZA, JOSÉ IGNACIO ◆ n. en Toluca, Edo. de Méx. (1935). Licenciado en derecho por la UNAM (1958), posgraduado en administración en la Escuela de Ciencias Económicas y Políticas de Londres. Desde 1958 pertenece al PRI, del que fue presidente del Comité Ejecutivo Nacional (de abril a septiembre de 1994). Ha sido asesor técnico de la CNOP (1965-66), miembro del Consejo Consultivo de la CNC (1966-), diputado federal (1967-69), director general de Hacienda (1969-70) y secretario general de Gobierno del Estado de México (1971-75); subsecretario de Ingresos de la Secretaría de Hacienda (1976-78), nuevamente diputado federal (1979-82); subsecretario A (1973-87) y secretario de la Contraloría General de la Federación (1987-88); procurador federal del Consumidor (1988-89), gobernador sustituto del Estado de México (1989-93), embajador en España (1994), titular de la SEMIP (1994-1995) y embajador en los Paises Bajos (1996-). Autor de *Diez años de planificación y administración pública en México* (1970), *Política fiscal de México* (1971), *Introducción a la administración pública mexicana* (1984) y *Administración pública y desarrollo urbano*. Pertenece a la Sociedad Mexicana de Planificación y al Instituto Nacional de Administración Pública.

PICHETA ◆ ☛ *Gahona, Gabriel Vicente.*

PICHILINGUE ◆ Bahía de Baja California Sur, situada cerca de La Paz. En 1861 el jefe político de Baja California autorizó a la armada estadounidense a establecer ahí una estación carbonera. Esta autorización fue confirmada por el gobierno nacional en 1867 y refrendada en 1900. La concesión fue retirada en 1924.

PICHUCALCO ◆ Municipio de Chiapas situado en el noroeste del estado, al norte de Tuxtla Gutiérrez, en los límites con Tabasco y Veracruz. Superficie: 1,078.1 km². Habitantes: 25,987, de los cuales 7,787 forman la población económicamente activa. Hablan alguna lengua indígena 292 personas mayores de cinco años (zoque 222). Su nombre en náhuatl significa "población de los jabalíes". Cuenta con el balneario El Azufre como atractivo turístico.

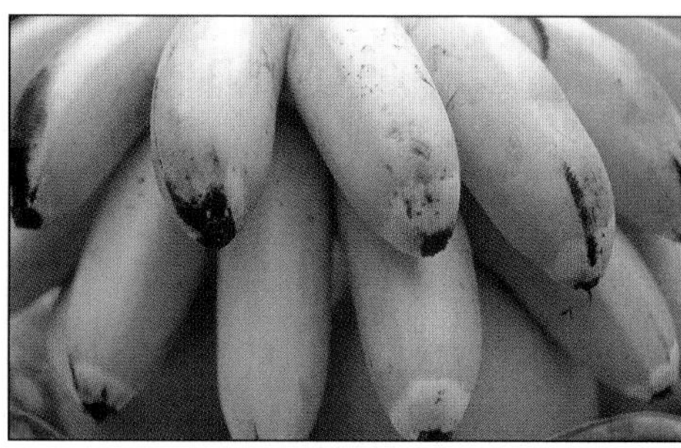

Producción platanera en Pichucalco, Chiapas

PICHUCALCO ◆ Río de Chiapas y Tabasco, también conocido como río Blanquillo. Nace cerca de Chapultenango, corre hacia el norte y se une al Grijalva, al sur de Villahermosa, Tabasco. Es navegable desde Paso de Cosayupa hasta su confluencia con el Grijalva.

PICILA, DE ◆ Sierra de Colima que se extiende de norte a sur y limita por el sureste al valle de Colima.

PICKERING, CARLOS ◆ n. en el DF y m. en Guadalajara Jal. (1918-1995). Locutor. Su segundo apellido era Jurado. Se inició profesionalmente en 1938, cuando la XEQ transmitió su primer programa. Participó en emisiones con gran arraigo en el público, como *El Doctor Canario, EXQ paga la diferencia, Boletín radiofónico de las Américas, Quiero trabajar, La Tómbola del saber, Tómelo y déjelo, y el Cochinito*, entre otros. Fue una de las principales figuras de la época de oro de la radio. Se le otorgó la primera licencia otorgada por la Secretaría de Comunicaciones y Obras Públicas como locutor (1942); más tarde recibió la de narrador y comentarista. Fue socio fundador de la Asociación Nacional de Locutores. Le correspondió narrar el retorno del Escuadrón 201 de la segunda guerra mundial; también comentó la Primera Carrera Panamericana de automóviles. Descolló más tarde como modernizador auténtico de los equipós de televisión, pues al término de su carrera profesional, en 1968, fue nombrado director del Canal 4, en Guadalajara, en donde siguió trabajando hasta 1984, cuando se retiró.

FOTO: MICHAEL CALDERWOOD

Panorámica de la bahía Pichilingue, BCS

PICO, JOSÉ LUCAS ◆ n. en el Mineral de Baroyeca y m. en Arizpe, Son. (1794-1859). Profesor. Dirigió una escuela primaria en Arizpe. Fue diputado al primer Congreso Constituyente de Sonora (1831), gobernador de ese estado en cuatro ocasiones (enero de 1833; 13 de agosto al 26 de noviembre de 1839; 26 de noviembre de 1840 al 5 de febrero de 1841, y 5 de noviembre de 1841 al 16 de abril de 1842); fundador del periódico oficial *El Mortero*; diputado federal, tesorero del gobierno de la entidad (1852); juez de primera instancia y prefecto político de Álamos. Colaboró en el *Boletín de la Sociedad Mexicana de Geografía y Estadística.*

PICO DE ORIZABA ◆ ☛ *Citlaltépetl o Pico de Orizaba.*

PIE DE PÁGINA ◆ Revista bimestral especializada en bibliografía, publicada en la ciudad de México entre octubre de

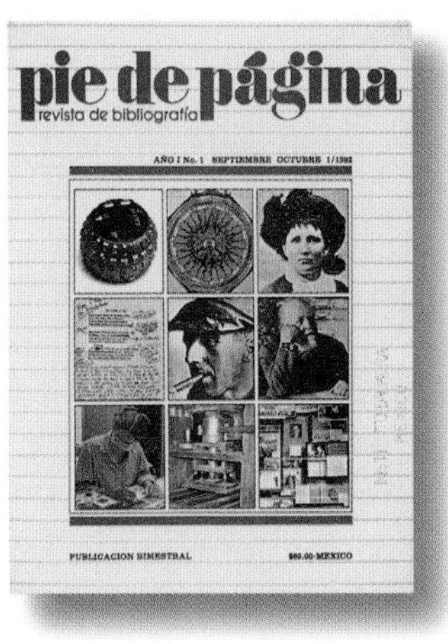

Revista *Pie de página*

1982 y mayo de 1984 (12 números). Dirigida por José Luis Morales Baltazar, la publicación se hizo con el apoyo de un equipo de periodistas jóvenes. Cada número incluía de 300 a 400 fichas comentadas de los libros publicados en México hasta la fecha de cierre, así como entrevistas con autores y editores nacionales o extranjeros, y periodistas como Manuel Buendía, de quien el reportero Tomás Tenorio obtuvo las últimas declaraciones que concediera. En su nómina de colaboradores figuraron, entre otros, José Agustín, Carlos Ramírez, Gustavo García, Arturo Trejo Villafuerte, Guillermo Schavelzon, Ignacio Trejo Fuentes, Martha Aurora Espinosa, Sandro Cohen, Guillermo Tovar y de Teresa, José Buil, Andrés de Luna e Ignacio Rodríguez Reyna. Insuficiencias económicas determinaron el cierre de la revista.

PIEDAD, LA ◆ Municipio de Michoacán situado en el norte del estado, al noreste de Zamora, en los límites con Jalisco y Guanajuato. Superficie: 271.59 km². Habitantes: 88,581, de los cuales 23,293 forman la población económicamente activa. Hablan alguna lengua indígena 130 personas mayores de cinco años (purépecha 61 y mazahua 37). Su cabecera municipal es La Piedad de Cabadas.

PIEDAD, DE LA ◆ Valle de Guanajuato y Michoacán; se conoce con ese nombre al extremo suroccidental de la región del Bajío. Está limitado al oeste por unas colinas que lo separan de la ciénaga de Chapala.

PIEDRA, EPIGMENIO DE LA ◆ n. en Taxco, Gro., y m. en la ciudad de México (1792-1873). Sacerdote. En 1821, comisionado por Agustín de Iturbide para hacer llegar una copia del Plan de Iguala al virrey Juan Ruiz de Apodaca, fue detenido por los realistas y encarcelado en el convento de San Fernando, de donde huyó disfrazado de mujer. Se reunió con Iturbide en Huetamo y entró a la ciudad de México con el Ejército Trigarante, en septiembre de ese año. Fue diputado al Congreso Constituyente de 1823-24 y era secretario de la asamblea al firmarse la Constitución. Formó parte del primero y segundo congresos constituyentes del Estado de México. En febrero de 1834 proclamó el fallido Plan de la Monarquía Indígena, también llamado Plan de Chicontla, en el que, para derrocar al gobierno de Gómez Farías, proponía que el Congreso eligiera "doce jóvenes célibes" que hubiesen "acreditado completamente ser descendientes inmediatos del emperador Moctezuma, de los cuales se sacará por suerte al que la Providencia destine para ser emperador de México". En 1861 era cura de Tenancingo y estuvo a punto de ser fusilado por el general Tomás O'Horan, por sus discrepancias con el mariscal Aquiles Bazaine, quien lo obligó a salir de esa plaza. En 1873, el arzobispo Pelagio Antonio de Labastida lo nombró canónigo de la Catedral de México.

PIEDRA RODANTE ◆ Revista que trataba de *rock*, drogas, sexo, arte y otros temas considerados como propios de la *contracultura*. Se fundó en 1971 y desapareció a principios de 1972. Colaboraron en ella José Agustín, Parménides García Saldaña, Juan Tovar, Jesús Luis Benítez y Óscar Sarquiz. Tenía un tiraje de 20,000 ejemplares se convirtió en el órgano central de la *contracultura* mexicana. Sin inhibición, vergüenza, pudor o recato, escribía sobre política, drogas, sexo, *rock*, arte. Fue clausurada a principios de 1972.

PIEDRAS, DE LAS ◆ Estero de Sinaloa situado en el litoral del golfo de California, al norte del estero de Lechuguilla, del que está separado por una lengua de tierra. En su parte norte desagua el río del Fuerte.

PIEDRAS NEGRAS ◆ Municipio de Coahuila situado en el noreste del estado, en la frontera con Estados Unidos. Superficie: 914.2 km². Habitantes: 116,148, de los cuales 32,906 forman la población económicamente activa. Hablan alguna lengua indígena 115 personas mayores de cinco años. La cabecera municipal, del mismo nombre, se llamó Porfirio Díaz.

Foto: Fondo Editorial Grupo Azabache

Arquitectura tradicional en Piedras Negras, Coahuila

PIÉLAGO, MANUEL ◆ m. en Guadalajara, Jal. (?-1858). Militar. Coronel del ejército conservador durante la guerra de los Tres Años, en 1858 ordenó el fusilamiento del ex gobernador liberal de Jalisco, Ignacio Herrera y Cairo. Cuando los liberales ocuparon la capital jalisciense, fue juzgado y ahorcado.

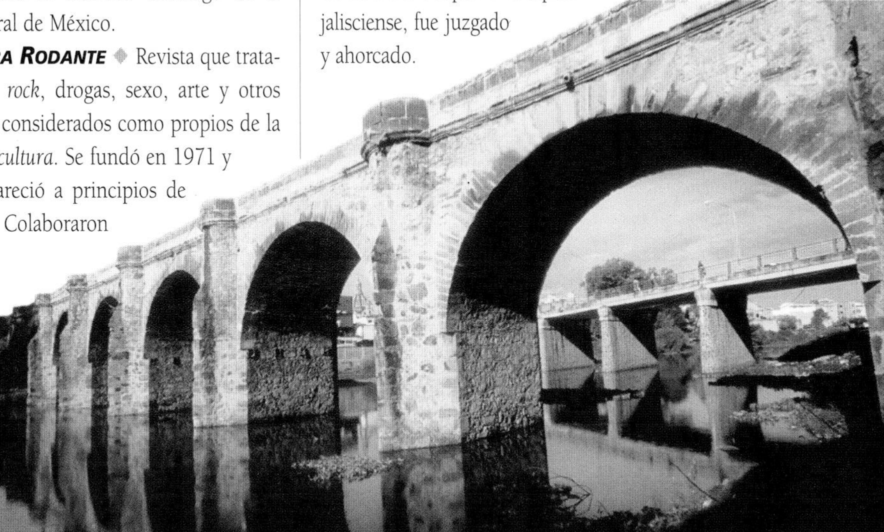

Foto: Carlos Hahn

Puente Cabadas en La Piedad, Michoacán

Pierre-Charles, Gérard ◆ n. en Haití (1936). Licenciado en ciencias sociales por la Universidad de Haití, posgraduado en estudios latinoamericanos. Profesor de la UNAM. Autor de *Haití, radiografía de una dictadura* (1960), *Sociología de la opresión* (1973) y *El Caribe a la hora de Cuba*.

Pierson, José Eduardo ◆ n. en la hacienda El Molino, Son., y m. en el DF (1861-1957). Músico. Estudió en el Ramsgate College de Inglaterra, en la Universidad de Santa Clara en Estados Unidos, con Enrico Testa en la ciudad de México, y con Vittorio de Vidal en Milán. En España, con el pseudónimo de *Mario Lorta*, fue cantante y declamador. Ahí formó una compañía de teatro con Carmen Coteña. Volvió a México en 1900, formó una compañía de ópera y fue profesor de canto. Algunos de sus alumnos fueron Juan Arvizu, Pedro Vargas, Jorge Negrete, José Mojica, Dolores del Río, Hugo Avendaño y Alfonso Ortiz Tirado.

Pieyre de Mandiargues, André ◆ ☛ *Mandiargues, André Pieyre de.*

Pihuamo ◆ Municipio de Jalisco situado en el extremo sur del estado, en los límites con Colima y Michoacán. Superficie: 1,007.85 km². Habitantes: 15,217, de los cuales 4,145 forman la población económicamente activa. Hablan alguna lengua indígena 14 personas.

Pijijiapan ◆ Municipio de Chiapas situado en el suroeste del estado, en la costa del Pacífico, al sureste de Tonalá. Superficie: 2,223.3 km². Habitantes: 47,616, de los cuales 11,672 forman la población económicamente activa. Hablan alguna lengua indígena 194 personas mayores de cinco años (tzeltal 130). Indígenas monolingües: 54. Entre sus atractivos turísticos cuenta con playas y esteros.

Ilustración de Antonio Esparza

Plaza principal de la cabecera municipal de Pilcaya, Guerrero

Pilcaya ◆ Municipio de Guerrero situado en el norte del estado, al norte de Taxco, en los límites con los estados de México y Morelos. Superficie: 62.1 km². Habitantes: 10,408, de los cuales 2,430 forman la población económicamente activa. Hablan alguna lengua indígena siete personas mayores de cinco años.

Pilliod, Charles J. ◆ n. en EUA (1919). Empresario. Estudió en la Universidad Estatal de Kent (1939- 41). Durante la segunda guerra mundial perteneció a la fuerza aérea de su país (1942-45). Desde 1945 trabajó para la compañía hulera estadounidense Goodyear, en la que fue gerente de la filial de Panamá (1947-50), gerente de ventas de la filial de Perú (1951-54), director de ventas de la filial de Colombia (1954-56), director gerente de la filial en Brasil (1956-63), director gerente y director de ventas de la filial en Gran Bretaña (1963), director de Operaciones Internacionales (1963-70), presidente (1970-83) y miembro de la junta directiva (1983-86). Fue embajador de Estados Unidos en México de 1986 a 1989.

Pilón ◆ Río de Nuevo León, también llamado Morelos. Nace en la vertiente este de la sierra Madre Oriental. Corre de suroeste a noreste, pasa por Montemorelos y se une al río San Juan.

Pilón ◆ Río de Tamaulipas. Nace entre la sierras Madre Oriental y de San Carlos. Corre de noroeste a sureste, recibe al río Baratillo y desemboca en el Purificación.

Piltzintecutli ◆ Dios nahua hijo de Oxomoco y Cipactonal y, por lo tanto, el primer hombre. Era protector de los niños nacidos dentro del matrimonio. Entre los pobladores de Jalisco, era el dios niño, o niño dios, que afirmaba la existencia de un sólo creador. Se le atribuía la invención del arco y la flecha y el control de los temporales.

Pimas ◆ Indios que viven en algunas zonas de la sierra Madre Occidental, en el este de Sonora y suroeste de Chihuahua, sobre todo en torno a Maycoba, municipio de Yécora, Sonora, y en Yepáchic y Mesa Blanca, en los municipios chihuahuenses de Temosachic y Madera. La región que habitaban los pimas en Sonora, Chihuahua y Arizona se designaba Pimería y se dividía en alta y baja. Los conquistadores españoles, que ubicaron en la Pimería Alta (norte de Sonora y sur de Arizona) la mítica región de El Dorado, realizaron desde mediados del siglo XVI una larga búsqueda de las ciudades de oro de Cíbola, Quivira y Teguayo. Con ese fin, destacaron las expediciones de Alvar Núñez Cabeza de Vaca y Andrés Dorantes (1530-36), Francisco Vázquez de Coronado (1540) y Vicente de Zaldívar (1618). La Pimería fue evangelizada por los misioneros jesuitas (entre ellos el padre Kino) y luego de su expulsión en 1767, por los franciscanos, aunque los indios se opusieron a la dominación española hasta finales del siglo XVII. En 1686, al mando de José Romo, alias *el Canito*, se levantaron en armas, pero fueron derrotados por las fuerzas del alcalde mayor de Sonora, Antonio de Barba Figueroa. El nombre de pimas se aplicaba tanto a los pápagos como a los habitantes de las Pimerías alta y baja, quienes se autodesignaban *o'otam* (gente) y hacían la diferencia entre la gente del desierto (pápagos) y la del río (pimas). Los pápagos occidentales fueron llamados *papawi o'otam* (gente del frijol), nombre que después se extendió a todos los habitantes del desierto. La división entre pimas altos y bajos ocurrió cuando se establecieron las fronteras culturales y militares. Los pimas bajos se subdividieron (según la región de su asentamiento) en los grupos yécora, nebome y ure, sibubapas (o zuaques), nures, híos, basioras, tehatas, sisibotaris y aibinos. En cuanto a los pimas altos, se subdividieron en los grupos piatos, sobaipuris, hímeris, sobas, potlapiguas, papalotas, papahotas, pápagos, opas, cocomaricopas, yumas, cuhanes y quiquimas. A partir de la conquista, los pápagos se alejaron del grupo pima, hasta conformar uno autónomo. En octubre de 1737, la *Gazeta* de Sahagún informaba que un indio guaíma llamado Agustín Ascubul difundió entre su pueblo y los pimas bajos "la engañosa voz de haverse aparecido el *Dios Moctezuma*, y que por ministerio suyo (.) era el Mayordomo *Arescibi*, ó *Propheta* de dicho *Moctezuma*; les ofrecía muchos dones, y citaba para ázia las vertientes del Mar del Sur, donde tenía su adoratorio, y que en él y su Trono los recibiría bajo de su obediencia; añadiendo que á la Pimería Alta havían ido ya los *Tlatoles* ó *Recados* sobre lo proprio, intimándoles al mismo tiempo, que a los que no le obedeciessen impondría rigorosíssimos castigos. Persuadida de las promesas o atemorizada con las amenazas la no bien firme creencia de estos Naturales, la noche del día 8 de Mayo, á una misma hora empezaron casi con generalidad á desamparar sus Xacales, Poblaciones y Rancherías de toda la circunferencia de la situación de dichas dos Naciones, que comprehende cien leguas de box, y cargando en Tlapeztles enfermos y viejos, creyendo sanaría a los unos y remozaría a los otros, y conduciendo por delante sus Cavallos, Mulas, Bacas, Cabras, y Ovejas, se encaminaron Hombres, Mugeres, y Muchachos, para el paraje y lugar donde se les havía convocado. Llegados, pues, que fueron á él, encontraron á las márgenes del Mar una Choza o Casilla fabricada de Esteras o Petates, y dentro de ella por Idolo una ridícula Figura vestida de negro, y encima un liezo blanco, a manera de Sobrepelliz, cubierta la cabeza con Bonete o Mitra". Dijo *Arescibi* "que cualquiera Persona humana ó Animal que entrasse en dicha Casa havía de morir (.) y sólo permitió morassen y detuviesse allí a servir en las inmediaciones del Idolo, seis Indizuelas muchachas de catorze a diez y seis años, solteras del mejor rostro y más agraciadas de toda la concurrencia. Congregáronse como cinco mil almas de una y otra Nación, y levantando de rato en rato la antepuerta exponía y manifestaba a todos, como haziendo mysterio, el mentido simulacro, para que a los reflejos de la Luna le fuessen divisando, prohibiendo que de día pudiesen verle. Festejábanle con Instrumentos músicos de Arpas, Guitarras, Violines y Canciones, y á tiempos le saludaban con Cohetes. Hízoles creer que comía el Idolo, con el engaño de enterrar en un hoyo los comistrajos y potages que aquellos miserables le ministraban; y al toque de una campanilla postrados, y arrodillados ofrecían sus Rosarios, Medallas, y todo lo demás conque se hallaban de algún precio y valor; y como por primicias de su veneración le sacrificaban sus Bacas y Ganado menor. El mencionado *Arscibi*, fraguador de semejantes quimeras, les refería, fingiendo ser su Intérprete, cómo aquel su Dios (mentido) havía criado el Cielo, la Tierra, el Agua y todas las demás cosas: que el mundo estaba tan delgado como un papel, que en breve se acavaría, y que en el mundo que havía de formar, resucitarían los muertos, volviéndose los Indios Españoles y los Españoles Indios para servirles a ellos: Que los manjares y vestidos que les havía de dar serían olorosos. Que no temiessen a los Soldados Españoles, aunque les amenazassen, puestos estos serían castigados y destruidos y con ellos se convertirían en piedra cuantos no le creyessen". Cuando el capitán Juan Bautista de Anza "llegó a entender la generalidad de esta conmoción y sus motivos", marchó al pueblo de San José de los Guaímas, donde aprehendió e hizo colgar al Arescibi, lo que sucedió el 1 de junio en el mismo pueblo. El mismo capitán español hizo reunir en Tecoripa a los principales seguidores de Ascubul, quienes, dice la *Gazeta*, "generalmente ofrecieron todos de su voluntad la espalda, para recibir en ella el castigo de azotes que se les impuso, confessando que á tan enorme culpa correspondían mucho más severas correcciones". En 1825 el yaqui Juan Banderas reunió a su pueblo con mayos, ópatas y pimas, los que formaron una Confederación Indiana, la que bajo un estandarte de la Virgen de Guadalupe protagonizó una de las primeras rebeliones indígenas del México independiente, insurrección que demandaba respeto del nuevo gobierno nacional a la *comunila*, organización cívica, religiosa y militar formada durante la evangelización de los jesuitas. Después de 1847, los subgrupos pimas quedaron separados por la frontera entre México y Estados Unidos. De acuerdo con el Conteo General de Población, en 1995 había en México 821 hablantes de la lengua pima, que pertenece al grupo nahuacuitlateco, tronco yutonahua, familia pima-cora. Tiene variantes dialectales que imposibilitan la comunicación entre las distintas comunidades. Los pimas han abandonado sus vestimentas tradicionales, excepto por los *teguas* o mocasines que utilizan los hombres y los sombreros tejidos de palma real que usan los ancianos. Cultivan la tierra sólo para autoconsumo y cada familia tiene dos o tres cabezas de ganado mayor. Los hombres emigran en busca de trabajo asalariado y las mujeres elaboran cerámica y cestería para la venta. Su base social es la familia nuclear; los matrimonios se celebran, previo acuerdo de los novios y las familias, después de un rapto tradicional. Practican la religión católica y su patrono es San Francisco de Asís. Algunas comunidades pimas designan a sus dirigentes (un gobernador, su suplente y un general), quienes solucionan los problemas internos y son intermediarios ante las autoridades municipales.

FOTO: LOURDES ALMEIDA

Familia de campesinos pimas de Kipor, Sonora

José Salomé Pina

PIMENTEL, EMILIO ◆ n. en Tlaxiaco, Oax., y m. Veracruz, Ver. (?-1926). Abogado y político porfirista. Fue secretario de Gobierno de Oaxaca (1886-87) en el periodo de Luis Mier y Terán; diputado federal, ministro de México en Argentina, regidor del Ayuntamiento de la ciudad de México y gobernador de Oaxaca (del 1 de diciembre de 1902 al 4 de mayo de 1911), reelecto en 1906 y 1910. Se retiró de la política en 1911, luego del triunfo de la insurrección maderista; radicó en la ciudad de México, donde fue miembro del Consejo de Administración del Banco de Londres y México.

PIMENTEL, FRANCISCO ◆ n. en Aguascalientes, Ags., y m. en la ciudad de México (1832-1893). Filólogo. Tenía los títulos nobiliarios de conde de Heras y vizconde de Queréndaro. Fue regidor y secretario del Ayuntamiento de la ciudad de México (1863-65), prefecto político de la capital durante el imperio de Maximiliano de Habsburgo (1864-65) y presidente del Liceo Hidalgo. Para el *Diccionario Universal de Historia y de Geografía* (1856) de Manuel Orozco y Berra, realizó las entradas de Michoacán, Texcoco y Toltecas y sostuvo que los chichimecas no pertenecieron a la familia nahua. Colaboró en el periódico *El Renacimiento*. Autor de *Cuadro descriptivo y comparativo de las lenguas indígenas de México o tratado de filología mexicana* (1862), *Memoria sobre las causas que han originado la situación actual de la raza indígena de México y medios de remediarla* (1864), *Economía política aplicada a la propiedad territorial en México* (1866), *Safo* (1872), *Algunas observaciones contra el espiritismo, hechas verbalmente en el Liceo Hidalgo* (1875) e *Historia crítica de la poesía en México* (1883). Las *Obras completas de don Francisco Pimentel* aparecieron entre 1903 y 1904. En 1875 participó en la fundación de la Academia Mexicana (de la Lengua).

PIMENTEL, RAFAEL ◆ n. en Oaxaca, Oax., y m. en el DF (1855-1929). Abogado. Fue asesor militar de los estados de Guerrero y Jalisco, diputado federal (1885-87) y, en Chihuahua, oficial mayor (1870), secretario de Gobierno y seis veces gobernador interino (1890, 1891 y 1892). Encargado de reprimir a los indios de Tomochic, luego de esta acción fue magistrado de la Suprema Corte de Justicia Militar (1892-94), asesor militar en Guerrero (1895), secretario general de Gobierno en Oaxaca (1895-96), gobernador constitucional de Chiapas (1899-05), diputado local en Oaxaca y senador por Colima (1906-10). En 1913, junto con otros miembros del Congreso, pidió la renuncia del presidente Francisco I. Madero. En febrero de ese año apoyó el golpe de Estado de Victoriano Huerta, quien lo nombró senador por Oaxaca.

PIMENTEL, RAFAEL S. ◆ n. y m. en Colima, Col. (1909-1954). Profesor en Nayarit y Guanajuato. Viajó a la ciudad de México e ingresó en la Alianza de Camioneros, misma que dirigió años después. Fue diputado federal (1949-52), presidente de la Comisión Nacional de Transporte en la campaña presidencial de Adolfo Ruiz Cortines (1952) y senador de la República por Colima (1952-54).

PIMENTEL Y FAGOAGA, FERNANDO ◆ n. y m. en el DF (1851-1929). Empresario. Hijo del filólogo Francisco Pimentel. Fue gerente y vicepresidente del Banco Central Mexicano, presidió el consejo del Banco Agrícola e Hipotecario de México, los Almacenes Generales de Depósito de México y Veracruz, la Aseguradora La Mexicana, la Compañía Bancaria de Obras y Bienes Raíces y la Harinera y Manufacturera Nacional. Fue vicepresidente de la Fundidora de Fierro y Acero de Monterrey; consultor de los bancos Yucateco y de Guanajuato, Michoacán y Morelos, entre otros; y presidente municipal de la ciudad de México (1903-10). Al inicio de la revolución se exilió en España, donde fundó diversas compañías pavimentadoras y de bienes raíces en Madrid y Barcelona.

PINA, FRANCISCO ◆ n. en España y m. en el DF (1900-1970). Escritor y crítico de cine. En España colaboró en el periódico *El Pueblo*, de Valencia. Al finalizar la guerra civil española estuvo en un campo de concentración en Francia. Llegó a México en 1940. Colaboró en *El Popular*, en los suplementos culturales de los diarios *Novedades*, *El Nacional*; y en las revistas *Las Españas*, *Revista de la Universidad de México*, *Siempre!* y *Nuevo Cine*, órgano del grupo del mismo nombre del que fue fundador (1961). Autor de *Escritores y pueblo* (1927), *Pío Baroja* (1929), *Charles Chaplin, genio de la desventura y la ironía* (1952), *El cine japonés* (1965), *El Valle-Inclán que yo conocí y otros ensayos* (1969) y *Praxinoscopio* (1970).

PINA, JOSÉ SALOMÉ ◆ n. y m. en la ciudad de México (1830-1909). Pintor. Estudió en la Academia de San Carlos, donde fue alumno de Pelegrín Clavé. En 1854, con una beca obtenida gracias a su cuadro *San Carlos Borromeo en la peste de Roma*, se trasladó a Europa, donde estudió con Gleyre en la Academia de París, expuso en el Salón de París (1859), vivió en Roma (1860-67) y estudió en Madrid (1867-69). Por encargo de Maximiliano de Habsburgo, dibujó un boceto de la visita de Carlota de Bélgica a Pío IX en 1866. Volvió a México en 1869. Fue profesor y director (1869-?) de la Academia de San Carlos y decorador de la Colegiata de Guadalupe (1889). Autor de los retratos de José María Velasco (1874), Juan Oreja y del arquitecto Labastida, propiedad del Instituto Nacional de Bellas Artes; y de los cuadros *Salida de Agar para el desierto* (1852) *Sansón y Dalila* (1853), *Abraham e Isaac*, *Agar e Ismael*, *Isaac y Abraham*, *La resurrección*, *La Virgen del Refugio*, *Dante y Virgilio*, *Santa Brígida*, *Santa Catalina*, *La Piedad* (premiado en París en 1859) y *Santa Ana*.

PINA MILÁN, RAFAEL DE ◆ n. en España y m. en el DF (1888-1966). Licenciado en derecho por la Universidad de Valladolid y doctor en derecho por la Universidad Central de Madrid. Profesor de las universidades de La Laguna, Islas Canarias (1929) y Sevilla. Fue diputado a Cortes y gobernador de la provincia de Santa Cruz de Tenerife (1939). En 1939, a la derrota de la República española, se exilió en México. Profesor de la Facultad de Derecho de la

UNAM y director del *Semanario de Aplicación Jurídica* (1949-62). Coautor de *Procedimientos judiciales* (1930) e *Instituciones de derecho procesal* (1946). Autor de *Los funcionarios públicos y el derecho a la huelga* (1927), *Programa de derecho procesal* (1929), *El juez no profesional en la justicia penal*, *Manual de derecho procesal penal* (1934), *Manual de derecho procesal civil* (1936), *Principios de derecho procesal civil* (1940), *La publicidad en el periodo de formación de sentencia* (1940), *Tratado de las pruebas civiles* (1942), *Tratado de derecho procesal* (1942), *Código penal para el Distrito y Territorios federales* (1944) y *Diccionario de derecho* (1965).

Pina Vara, Rafael de ◆ n. en España (1926). Licenciado (1951) y doctor (1956) en derecho por la UNAM. A la derrota de la República española, en 1939, se refugió en México. Profesor de la UNAM, de la Universidad de Guadalajara y del Instituto Luis Vives (1973-74). Ha sido subjefe (1950-66) y jefe (1966-73) del Departamento Jurídico de la CFE, gerente auxiliar de la empresa Industrial Eléctrica Mexicana (1966-71), jefe del Departamento Jurídico, apoderado y secretario del Consejo de Administración de la Compañía de Luz y Fuerza del Centro (1970-73), director general de Invenciones y Marcas de la Secretaría de Industria y Comercio (1974-76) y subdirector jurídico del Infonavit (1976-80). Autor de *Aumento de capital por revaloración del activo en las sociedades anónimas* (1951), *Elementos de derecho mercantil mexicano* (1958), *Teoría y práctica del cheque* (1960), *El Estado y la banca* (1961), *Régimen legal e institucional de la industria eléctrica en América Latina* (1961) y *La prima de antigüedad en la nueva Ley Federal del Trabajo* (1970). Es miembro de la Barra Mexicana-Colegio de Abogados y de la Academia Mexicana de Derecho del Trabajo y Previsión Social.

Pinabete, de ◆ Sierra de Jalisco y Nayarit, también llamada de Buenavista. Forma parte de las estribaciones sudoccidentales de la sierra de Zacatecas. Sus cimas más altas son el cerro de Zapopan (2,171 metros sobre el nivel del mar) y la Providencia de Pajaritos.

Foto: Michael Calderwood

Pico del Pinacate, en Sonora

Pinacate, Pico del ◆ Volcán extinguido de Sonora situado en el desierto de Altar. Tiene 1,390 metros sobre el nivel del mar y se localiza al norte de Punta Peñasco.

Pinal, Silvia ◆ n. en Guaymas, Son. (1931). Actriz. Se inició en el teatro en la compañía de Rafael Banquells con la escenificación de *Un sueño de cristal*. Ha participado, entre otras, en las obras *Ring, ring, llama el amor*, *Divorciémonos* y *Mame*. Ha trabajado, entre otras, en las películas *Bamba* (1948), *El pecado de Laura* (1948), *Mujer de media noche* (1949), *Puerta, joven* (1949), *La mujer que yo perdí* (1949), *El rey del barrio* (1949), *La marca del Zorrillo* (1950), *Recién casados, no molestar* (1950), *El amor no es ciego* (1950), *Ahora soy rico* (1951), *La estatua de carne* (1951), *Por ellas aunque mal paguen* (1952), *El casto Susano* (1952), *Me traes de un ala* (1952), *Doña Mariquita de mi corazón* (1952), *Las cariñosas* (1953), *Las tres viudas alegres* (1953), *La sospechosa* (1954), *Amor en cuatro tiempos* (1954), *El vendedor de muñecas* (1954), *Historia de una abrigo de mink* (1954), *La sospechosa* (1954), *Un extraño en la escalera* (1954), *Cabo de hornos* (1955), *El inocente* (1955), *Dios no lo quiera* (1956), *Viva el amor* (1956), *Mi desconocida esposa* (1956), *Una cita de amor* (1956), *Préstame tu cuerpo* (1957), *Desnúdate Lucrecia* (1957), *Una golfa* (1957), *Las locuras de Bárbara* (1958), *Charleston* (1958), *El hombre que me gusta* (1958), *Juego peligroso* (1966), *María Isabel* (1967), *Los novios* (1969), *La mujer de oro* (1969), *¡Cómo hay gente sinvergüenza!* (1971) y *Las mariposas disecadas* (1977). De más de medio centenar de cintas en la que ha participado, destacan los tres filmes en que fue dirigida por Luis Buñuel: *Viridiana* (1961), *El ángel exterminador* (1962) y *Simón del desierto* (1965). En 1956 ganó el Ariel por *Locura pasional* (1955) y en 1957 por *La dulce enemiga* (1956). Milita en el PRI desde 1987. Presidió la Asociación Nacional de Intérpretes (1988-94). Ha sido diputada federal (1991-94), representante a la ALDF (1991-94) y senadora (1998-99). También ha actuado en tele-

Foto: Armando Herrera

Silvia Pinal

visión, y ha fungido, desde 1988, como productora de la serie de televisión *Mujer, casos de la vida real*. Ha recibido dos Diosas de Plata: una en 1965 por *Los cuervos están de luto* (1964) y otra en 1977 por *Divinas palabras* (1976). Es productora teatral.

Pinal de Amoles ◆ Municipio de Querétaro situado al noreste de Querétaro y al sur de Arrollo Seco, en los límites con Guanajuato. Superficie: 611.9. Habitantes: 26,864, de los cuales 6,181 forman la población económicamente activa. Hablan alguna lengua indígena 15 personas mayores de cinco años (otomí 11).

Pinal de Amoles ◆ Sierra de Querétaro que forma parte de las estribaciones orientales de la sierra Gorda. Su parte noreste es conocida como sierra de Concá. Sus picos más elevados son el cerro de Jasso y el de la Calentura, que sobrepasan los 2,500 metros sobre el nivel del mar.

Pinal del Zamorano ◆ Sierra de Querétaro. Es parte de las estribaciones meridionales de la sierra Gorda, en los límites con el estado de Guanajuato. Su cumbre más elevada es el picacho del Carmen, con 3,718 metros sobre el nivel del mar.

Foto: Fondo Editorial Grupo Azabache

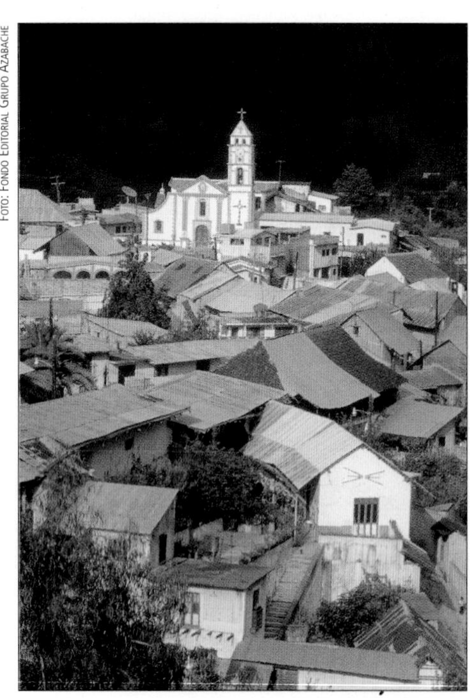

Panorámica de Pinal de Amoles, Querétaro

Pineda, Eloy ◆ n. en el DF (1957). Licenciado en lengua y literatura hispánicas por la UNAM. Asistió al taller literario de Miguel Donoso Pareja. Trabajó para el Instituto Nacional de Bellas Artes y el Correo del Libro. Ha sido corrector de *El Heraldo de México*, redactor de la revista *Selecciones* y jefe de redacción de *Caballero*. Es coautor del volumen de narrativa *Tiene que haber olvido* (1979). Autor de cuento: *Espejismos* (1981), *Vuelo de bailarina satín* (1982), *Cuentos con abuelo, niños, paisajes y un solo y enorme deseo* (Premio de Cuento para Niños Juan de la Cabada 1983), *El mago, las monarcas, el jazzista y la estrella* (1984), *Dos historias para un sueño* (Premio Juan de la Cabada 1985) y *La ballena* (1985).

Pineda, Emeterio ◆ n. y m. en San Cristóbal de Las Casas, Chis. (1795-1855). Estudió en la Universidad de San Carlos de Guatemala. Licenciado en derecho por la Universidad Nacional de México. Se le considera el primer geógrafo de Chiapas. Fue profesor, botánico empleado por el gobierno federal para realizar una investigación en el istmo de Tehuantepec (1824), magistrado y presidente del Tribunal Supremo de Justicia de Chiapas, consejero del gobierno, asesor de justicia, gobernador interino de esa entidad (de septiembre a octubre de 1832) y presidente de la comisión para formar la Estadística General de Chiapas (1842). Autor de *Descripción geográfica del departamento de Chiapas y Soconusco* (1845).

Pineda, Juan Claudio de ◆ n. en España y m. en la ciudad de México (1710-1772). Militar. Ingresó al ejército español en 1731. En 1760 fue ascendido a teniente coronel. Llegó a la Nueva España en 1763, con el nombramiento de gobernador y capitán general de Sonora y Sinaloa. En ese cargo, ofreció tres pesos por cada indio seri prisionero o muerto y 300 pesos por la cabeza del cacique principal de la tribu; además estableció la pena de muerte para quien protegiera a los indios rebeldes. En 1767 inició una campaña en Sonora para combatir a los indios insumisos. Se encargó de expulsar a los miembros de la Compañía de Jesús. Entregó el mando de la campaña al general Elizondo y lo acompañó en sus ataques a los seris y pimas. Ascendió a coronel en 1769. En 1770 enfermó y entregó el gobierno a Pedro Corbalán.

Pineda Ménez, Fernando ◆ n. en Zirándaro, Gro. (1939). Periodista. Profesor egresado de la Escuela Normal Superior (1971). Estudió sociología en las universidades de París y Patricio Lumumba de Moscú (1974-75). Profesor de la Universidad Autónoma de Guerrero, donde figuró entre los fundadores del sindicato de esa casa de estudios (1966-73). Ha ejercido la docencia en la Universidad Tecnológica de México, donde fue director de Extensión Universitaria (1987-). Ingresó en la Juventud Comunista en 1967, pero al año siguiente se separó de ella y se unió al grupo guerrillero de Genaro Vázquez Rojas. Entre 1970 y 1971 perteneció al Comité Nacional de Auscultación y Organización, del que dirigió la sección guerrerense. A fines de 1971 se incorporó al Partido Comunista Mexicano y fue miembro de su comisión organizadora en Guerrero, así como redactor (1974-79) y jefe de Información y Redacción del órgano *Oposición* (1980-81). Cofundador del PSUM, en el que desempeñó la jefatura de redacción del órgano *Así Es*. En 1988 ingresó en el PFCRN, del que fue secretario general (1988-89) y dirigente de la organización en el Estado de México (1989-94). Cofundador y dirigente del Partido del Pueblo Mexiquense (1995-). Ha colaborado en *El Día* e *Impacto*. Miembro fundador de la Unión de Periodistas Democráticos (1975-). Pertenece al secretariado de la Federación Latinoamericana de Periodistas.

Pineda Ogarrio, Alberto ◆ n. en San Cristóbal de Las Casas (1871-?). Militar. Combatió en Chiapas desde 1911, al frente de las tropas de San Cristóbal de Las Casas contra las fuerzas de Tuxtla. Partidario de Félix Díaz, hasta 1918 combatió a las tropas de Venustiano Carranza. Dos años después apoyó la rebelión del Plan de la Noria. Durante la presidencia de Adolfo de la Huerta fue comandante del ejército nacional.

Pineda Serino, Javier ◆ n. en el DF (1932). Abogado, músico y líder sindical. Ha sido director de la Orquesta de Ingeniería (1955), miembro del Comité Ejecutivo de la Comisión Coordinadora de la Juventud Revolucionaria del PRI (1964); jefe de Personal y administrador general (1968), auxiliar de la Secretaría General (1967) y secretario de Trabajo y Conflictos de la CTM (1980 y 1983); secretario general del Sindicato Nacional de Trabajadores de la Industria Láctea, Similares y Conexos de la República Mexicana (1979), diputado federal (1985-88 y 1994-97) y representante obrero ante la Comisión Nacional de Salarios Mínimos y subprocurador federal del Consumidor (1991-94).

Pingarrón, Gabriel ◆ n. en Cuernavaca, Mor. (1946). Actor, dramaturgo y director. Egresado de la EAT del INBA. Hizo su debut como actor en *La Escuela de bufones* (1966), después le siguieron: *Los argonautas* (1967), *Así que pasen cinco años* (1969), *El mundo que tú heredas* (1970), *Los insectos* (1974), *Arlequín, servidor de dos patrones* (1978), *De la calle* (1987) y *Visita conyugal* (1990). Escribió y dirigió *El lanzamiento o alguien vendrá que de tu casa te echará* (1991) y *El pacto o tres en el baño* (1993). Tiene inéditas: *Nunca me casaré con mi madre, Fredie Roma, Esperando al director y Las buenas familias*. En 1994 publicó su primer libro de poesía titulado *El cuidador de mares*.

Pinilla Pérez, Ángel ◆ n. en España (?-?). Desde 1804, en que recibió el nombramiento de letrado asesor de Nueva Vizcaya, desempeñó en varias ocasiones el cargo de gobernador intendente, como sustituto de Bernardo Bonavía. En 1811 se encargó de procesar a los compañeros de Miguel Hidalgo, quienes fueron ejecutados. De 1814 a 1815 fue asesor y auditor de guerra de la Comandancia General.

Pinitos, De ◆ Sierra de Sonora que es una de las estribaciones de la sierra Madre Occidental. Se extiende de noroeste a sureste paralelamente a la frontera con Estados Unidos. Al pie de su ladera noroccidental se halla Nogales.

Pino, Cerro del ◆ Volcán del Estado de México, al norte de Chalco y al sureste del lago de Texcoco. En la parte sur de su base se encuentra el pueblo de Ayotla.

Pino Desandoval, Hylda ◆ n. en Guayaquil, Ecuador (1893). Escritora, poeta y periodista. Se ha dedicado al periodismo por más de 40 años. En 1967 fundó la agrupación de periodistas Veinte Mujeres y un Hombre. Fue la primera mujer que firmó la nota principal en el periódico *Excélsior*, en 1963, cuando en una entrevista con el presidente Adolfo López Mateos, éste se autodescartó para obtener el Premio Nobel de la Paz, señalando que lo merecían más Kennedy y Jrúschof. Ha escrito 12 libros, en cuatro recopila las entrevistas que han concurrido a la mesa de trabajo de Veinte Mujeres y un Hombre.

Pino Suárez, José María ◆ n. en Tenosique, Tab., y m. en la ciudad de México (1869-1913). Abogado. Ejerció su profesión en Yucatán, donde también fundó y dirigió el vespertino liberal *El Peninsular* (1904). En 1905 vendió el periódico a la compañía de Alfredo Cámara Vales, después de fundar en su local la Asociación de la Prensa Yucateca. Se afilió al Partido Nacional Antirreeleccionista y participó en la campaña de Francisco I. Madero en Tabasco y Yucatán. Fue el encargado de mantener informado a Madero cuando éste fue detenido en 1910, en San Luis Potosí. A fines de ese año viajó a Guatemala para comprar armas. Participó en las negociaciones que concluyeron con la firma de los Tratados de Ciudad Juárez y fue secretario de Justicia en el gobierno provisional de Madero (del 10 al 21 de mayo de 1911). Encargado del gobierno de Yucatán del 5 de junio al 8 de agosto de 1911, en octubre fue elegido gobernador del estado, pero abandonó el puesto luego de que el Partido Constitucional Progresista (☛) lo hizo candidato a la vicepresidencia. Durante el gobierno de Madero combinó su papel de vicepresidente (del 6 de noviembre de 1911 al 18 de febrero de 1913) con el de secretario de Instrucción Pública y Bellas Artes (del 26 de febrero de 1912 al 18 de febrero de 1913). Detenido con el presidente el 19 de febrero de 1913 y obligado a renunciar al día siguiente, fue asesinado en las cercanías de la Penitenciaría de Lecumberri. Colaborador de la revista *Pimienta y mostaza*. En 1904 escribió el prólogo de las *Memorias de un alférez*, de Eligio Ancona. Autor de poesía: *Melancolías* (1896) y *Procelarias* (1908).

ARCHIVO: XAVIER ESPARZA

José María Pino Suárez

Pinos ◆ Municipio de Zacatecas situado en el sureste del estado, en los límites con San Luis Potosí y con Jalisco. Superficie: 2,645.43 km². Habitantes: 63,549, de los cuales 13,092 forman la población económicamente activa. Hablan alguna lengua indígena 10 personas mayores de cinco años. En este municipio se produjo la llamada Toma del Real de Pinos, cuando en junio de 1817 las fuerzas de Francisco Javier Mina desalojaron, sin derramamiento de sangre, a los colonialistas ahí fortificados.

Pinos, De ◆ Sierra de Zacatecas que enlaza en el sur con la de Comanja. Su porción norte es conocida como sierra del Peñón.

Pinos, Los ◆ Residencia oficial del Presidente de México, situada en las avenidas Molino del Rey y Constituyentes, en el Distrito Federal, en terrenos de lo que fue la hacienda de La Hormiga. Aun cuando el gobierno federal compró este predio a la familia Martínez del Río en 1923, no fue sino hasta 1934 cuando Lázaro Cárdenas convirtió a Los Pinos en la residencia presidencial.

PINOTEPA DE DON LUIS ◆ Municipio de Oaxaca situado en el suroeste del estado y contiguo a Santiago Pinotepa Nacional. Superficie: 51.03 km^2. Habitantes: 5,841, de los cuales 1,433 forman la población económicamente activa. Hablan alguna lengua indígena 4,337 personas mayores de cinco años (mixteco 4,334). Indígenas monolingües: 1,133. La primera parte de su nombre significa en náhuatl "Palacio del pinole"; la segunda se adoptó porque el municipio se halla en parte del territorio de las encomiendas de Luis de Castilla, uno de los protegidos de Hernán Cortés, quien por su éxito como minero llegó a ser el hombre más rico de la Nueva España.

PINOTEPA NACIONAL ◆ ☛ *Santiago Pinotepa Nacional.*

PINTADA ◆ Sierra de Baja California Sur situada en la parte media de la península, cerca del límite con Baja California. La cordillera se extiende de noroeste a sureste, entre la Punta Eugenia, que cierra por el sur la bahía de Vizcaíno, y el llano del Berrendo.

PINTADO, JOSÉ MANUEL ◆ n. en el DF (1948). Poeta. Su segundo apellido es De Wit. Estudió en la UNAM. Ha sido becario del Instituto Nacional de Bellas Artes (1975-76), coordinador del taller literario del centro cultural El Nigromante de San Miguel Allende y director del Centro de Creación Literaria de la Universidad Autónoma Metropolitana. Fue funcionario de la Unidad de Televisión Educativa de la Secretaría de Educación Pública. Produce y dirige programas culturales de televisión. Coautor de *El cuello de la botella* (1979) y *La rosa de los vientos* (1979). Autor de los poemarios *Batemares* (1979), *Cartas de navegación* (1980) y *Conversatorio de Yaxilán* (1991), del volumen de cuento infantil *Kayum* (1985) y del libro de crónicas *Los pueblos del viento*. En 1976 obtuvo el primer lugar en el Premio de Poesía Joven Francisco González de León, de Lagos de Moreno, Jalisco.

Los elementos, obra de Lorraine Pinto

PINTADO NIETO, JOSÉ MANUEL ◆ n. en Villahermosa, Tab. (1922). Contador público titulado en la UNAM (1942). Profesor de la UNAM (1964-70) y de la Universidad de Coahuila (1960). Ha sido contador general de la Compañía Genelectric Rayos X (1946-47), contralor de la Cervecería Tecate (1977), contador general de la Metro Goldwyn Meyer de México (1947-54) y subdirector técnico de Gossler Navarro, Ceniceros y Compañía (1960-67), contralor interno de la Secretaría de Gobernación (1985-1988). Coautor de *La contaduría pública* (1983) y autor de *Problemas fiscales del arrendamiento financiero* (1970), *Tres décadas y apenas el comienzo* (1980). Pertenece a la Academia de Estudios Fiscales de la Contaduría Pública (que presidió en 1969-71), al Colegio de Contadores Públicos de México (que presidió en 1964-66), al Instituto Mexicano de Contadores Públicos y al Instituto Nacional de Contadores Públicos al Servicio del Estado.

PINTADO SÁNCHEZ, ISMAEL ◆ n. en Zimapán, Hgo., y m. en el DF (1889-1939). Abogado. Participó en la revolución desde 1910. Fue juez V de la ciudad de México (1915), diputado al Congreso Constituyente de 1916-17, juez de instrucción militar en la capital de la República, diputado a la Legislatura de Hidalgo, procurador general de Justicia de Tamaulipas, agente del Ministerio Público Federal en Tampico y Juchitán y diputado federal (1926-28).

PINTO, JAMES ◆ n. en Yugoslavia, entonces Austria-Hungría y m. ¿en el DF? (1907-1987). Pintor y escultor. Estudió en Bosnia hasta 1939, cuando pasó a América. Se naturalizó estadounidense y estudió en el Instituto Chouinard de Arte, de Los Ángeles (1945-48). Llegó a México en 1948. Ese mismo año expuso por primera vez, en Los Ángeles. Sus obras se presentaron en Estados Unidos y Yugoslavia. Autor de un mural que se encuentra en el Instituto Allende de San Miguel Allende (1951). En 1957 obtuvo el primer premio de la First Exhibit of Unitarian Churches, de Los Ángeles, y en 1962 recibió el Premio Instituto Allende, de San Miguel Allende.

PINTO, LORRAINE ◆ n. en EUA (1931). Escultora y grabadora. En Estados Unidos estudió con John Hovannes y William Zorach. Llegó a México en 1953 y aquí estudió en la Universidad de las Américas. Profesora de diseño de la Facultad de Arquitectura de la UNAM (1970-75). Creó un laboratorio de arte cinético. Expuso por primera vez en 1959 en Nueva York. Obras suyas se han presentado o se encuentran en Canadá, Estados Unidos e Israel. En el edificio central del Instituto Mexicano del Seguro Social, en el Distrito Federal, se encuentra una obra suya: *El puente de Londres*. En 1964 obtuvo mención honorífica en la Segunda Bienal Nacional de Escultura, en 1968 el Premio Elías Sourasky y en 1968 el Premio Nacional de Escultura de la Exposición Solar, organizada por el INBA.

PINTO MAZAL, JORGE ◆ n. en el DF (1945). Licenciado en derecho por la UNAM, maestro en transacciones económicas internacionales por la Universidad de Nueva York y doctor en desarrollo económico por la Universidad de París. Subdirector de Finanzas de Conasupo, asesor del director general del IMSS (1970-76), investigador, profesor y secretario de la Rectoría de la UNAM, miembro de los consejos de administración del Canal 13, de la Comisión Nacional de Puertos y de la Comisión Promotora del Libro, secretario particular del secretario de Gobernación (1976-

79), representante de Nafinsa para Europa (1980-82). Ingresó al SEM en 1984. Ministro de la embajada en Estados Unidos (1984-88), asesor del titular de la SRE (1990-91), embajador en Suecia (1991-94) y cónsul general en Nueva York (1995-) Autor de *Los partidos políticos en México*, *La autonomía universitaria*, *Régimen legal de los medios de comunicación* y *George Sorel: antología*.

PINTOR, GUADALUPE *LUPE* ◆ n. en el DF (1955). Boxeador. Se inició como aficionado en 1971 y tres años más tarde se presentó como profesional. En junio de 1979 obtuvo el campeonato mundial de peso gallo del Consejo Mundial de Boxeo, al derrotar en Las Vegas al también mexicano Carlos Zárate. Más tarde fue campeón mundial de peso supergallo. Se retiró en 1985.

PINTURA ◆ En diversos puntos del país existen pinturas rupestres, sobre todo en el noroeste. La península de Baja California posee una gran riqueza de esta manifestación plástica, que se asocia a los pueblos nómadas, los que dejaban huellas de su paso en rocas y cavernas. En éstas, las imágenes de color fueron protegidas de los elementos y de la destrucción humana. Las grandes culturas prehispánicas cultivaban el arte de la pintura principalmente de tres maneras: mediante la elaboración de códices, donde el arte se subordinaba a la escritura; en la ejecución de murales trabajados con la técnica del fresco; y, por último, en la coloración de cerámica, esculturas y superficies arquitectónicas. Los códices, producidos por los *tlacuilos*, se realizaban sobre diversos materiales, especialmente piel o amate. La pintura mural fue una labor especializada que, pese a estar "sujeta al tiránico simbolismo religioso", según dijo José Juan Tablada, permitía expresar las capacidades artísticas de los ejecutantes, como se demuestra, por ejemplo, en las obras de Bonampak y Teotihuacán. En esta misma ciudad, lo mismo que en Tula, Monte Albán o en la zona arqueológica del Templo Mayor de la capital del país, se conservan rastros de la pintura que cubría amplias superficies. Raúl Flores Guerrero dice que "la grandiosa ciudad de piedra que ahora se admira en Teotihuacán fue en su tiempo una ciudad llena de color. Todos los edificios, desde la Pirámide del Sol hasta el más humilde templete estuvieron cubiertos de estuco coloreado. En ocasiones el color era uniforme, de preferencia rojo, pero casi siempre se emplearon combinaciones cromáticas. Las pirámides y los templos, los palacios y las residencias sacerdotales estaban cubiertos, por dentro y por fuera, de un terso aplanado pintado al temple o al fresco. Inclusive los relieves y las esculturas —los dioses con mayor razón— ostentaban una capa policromada que definía sus atributos mágicos". *Periodo colonial:* A la violencia, el pillaje y la destrucción que significó la conquista, siguió el establecimiento del nuevo orden y, con él, la tarea de reforzar la sumisión mediante la conquista espiritual. Para Manuel Toussaint, "la pintura nace en México por la necesidad de decorar los templos y conventos", como sucedió hacia 1530 en Cholula y hacia 1539 en Tlaxcala, según relata Motolinía. La ornamentación consistía en frisos y fajas, medallones, nichos y figuras de santos. Subsisten los decorados de numerosos edificios religiosos de los primeros años de la Colonia, como en Huejotzingo, Tlalmanalco, Ocuituco, Acolman, Atlatlauhcan, Yecapixtla, Tlayacapan, Oaxtepec, Totolapan, Malinalco, Actopan, Culhuacán, Yanhuitlán, Yuririapúndaro, Tepoztlán, el convento franciscano de Cuernavaca y el templo de Zacualpan de Amilpas, donde un trabajo de retoque ejecutado en el siglo XIX modificó radicalmente su aspecto. Los frailes europeos transmitieron a los indios los rudimentos del arte europeo. Fray Pedro de Gante fundó en la capital novohispana la Escuela de Artes y Oficios, donde se formó un considerable número de copistas y de pintores capaces de convertir los grabados de impor-

FOTO: FONDO EDITORIAL GRUPO AZABACHE

Pintura rupestre en la Sierra de San Francisco, Baja California Sur

Códice Borgia, obra pictórica hecha sobre piel, cultura mixteca

Pinturas rupestres en San Borjita, península de Baja California

Pintura mural en Bonampak, Chiapas

tación en obras pictóricas. El primer artista cuyo nombre se conserva es Diego de Valadés. A mediados de siglo, cuatro pintores de apellidos indígenas, Pedro Quauhtli, Miguel Toxoxhícuic, Luis Xochitótotl y Miguel Yohualahuach, ejecutaron una obra que representaba a los *Señores que habían gobernado el país azteca*. A Marcos Cípac, también llamado Marcos de Aquino, se le atribuye el *Retablo* de la capilla de San José de los Indios, del convento de San Francisco. Cípac tuvo como ayudantes a Pedro Chachalaca, Francisco Xinmámal y Pedro de San Nicolás. Poco después, Fernando Colli y Pedro Xóchmitl hicieron *Catorce Obras de Misericordia*, para la cárcel de la ciudad de México. Para Toussaint, "el Renacimiento aparece en la pintura colonial de México ya desde algunas decoraciones conventuales", como las de la escalera monumental del monasterio agustino de Actopan y el claustro del convento de la misma orden en Epazoyucan, donde el mismo autor advierte "las tres influencias que se dejan sentir en la pintura mexicana de esa época": la flamenca, la italiana y la de los primitivos españoles. De influencia renacentista son las pinturas de la iglesia franciscana de Tecamachalco, Puebla, atribuidas a Juan Gersón. Las *Ordenanzas* del gremio de pintores, publicadas en 1557, los dividen en "imagineros", la categoría más alta; doradores, pintores al fresco y sargueros. Éstos eran los que pintaban telas sin bastidor que se usaban como tapices. Algunos "veedores del gremio", como les llama Toussaint, fueron Juan de Illescas, Bartolomé Sánchez, Pedro Rodríguez, Pedro de Robles, Nicolás de Tejeda, Nuño Vázquez, Francisco de los Reyes, Gaspar Pérez de Rivera y el ya citado Juan Gersón. En 1566 llegó a México el flamenco Simón Pereyns, aquí conocido como Perines. Torturado por la Inquisición, fue sentenciado a pintar a su costa el retablo de la Virgen de la Merced, que se supone es el mismo del Altar del Perdón de la Catedral Metropolitana. En la misma iglesia se halla un *San Cristóbal* del mismo autor, que también ejecutó el retablo de Huejotzingo. En torno a Pereyns trabajaron su cuñado, el mexicano Juan de Arrúe, y los españoles Francisco de Morales, Francisco de Zumaya y Andrés de la Concha, a quien se debe el retablo de Yanhuitlán y el retablo y dorado de la nave central de la Catedral de México.

Fresco de la capilla abierta del ex convento de San Nicolás, en Actopan, Hidalgo

Foto: Fondo Editorial Grupo Azabache

Foto: Fondo Editorial Grupo Azabache

Santa Cecilia, óleo sobre madera de Andrés de Concha

De Zumaya es el *San Sebastián* de la misma catedral. A Juan de Arrúe se le debe el retablo del templo franciscano de Cuauhtinchan y el retablo de San Jerónimo del convento dominico de Tlacochayahua. De la obra de Morales poco se sabe, pues explotó el talento de Pereyns. Alonso de Villasana decoró la iglesia de Los Remedios a fines del siglo XIV. El español Baltazar de Echave Orio, llamado *el Viejo*, parece haber sido discípulo de Zumaya. Empezó a pintar hacia 1585, pero sus trabajos de importancia los realizó a partir de 1596. Son obra suya o se le atribuyen el *Retablo de Santiago Tlatelolco*, desaparecido en el siglo XIX, la *Visitación* y la *Ponciúncula* de San Carlos, una *Gloria de San Ignacio* que estuvo en la Profesa y que probablemente desapareció durante la expulsión de los jesuitas; el *Martirio de San Aproniano*, también de la Profesa (1612) y, entre otros cuadros, *La Flagelación*, de la catedral. El arte de Echave *el Viejo*, dice Toussaint, "alcanza verdaderamente excelsitudes de Siglo de Oro. Es un pintor renacentista, pero dotado aún de una ingenuidad extraordinaria". Su hijo, Baltazar de Echave Ibía, es autor de *Retrato de una*

Foto: Fondo Editorial Grupo Azabache

Fresco de la iglesia de San Miguel Arcángel, en Ixmiquilpan, Hidalgo

Foto: Fondo Editorial Grupo Azabache

Retrato de dama, óleo sobre tela de Baltazar de Echave Ibía

Foto: Fondo Editorial Grupo Azabache

Adoración de los pastores, óleo sobre madera de Baltazar Echave Orio

dama, un *San Juan Evangelista*, un *San Juan Bautista* y numerosas obras religiosas. Contemporáneo de éste y discípulo también del Echave *el Viejo*, es Luis Juárez, quien pintó la *Santa Teresa* del Museo de Guadalajara. En la misma generación hay tres Alonsos: Vázquez, López de Herrera y Franco. El español Alonso Vázquez ejecutó el *Martirio de Santa Margarita* para la capilla del Palacio Virreinal y el retablo, dedicado a Santa Catalina, de la capilla de la Real y Pontificia Universidad de México. Se le atribuyen, asimismo, el *Retrato de un niño* y un *San Miguel*. De López de Herrera, llamado *el Divino*, es un retrato del arzobispo-virrey García Guerra, el *Santo Domingo de Guzmán* del templo de Churubusco, un *Divino Rostro* que hizo para la catedral y otras obras. A Franco, artista celebrado por Bernardo de Balbuena, pertenece la autoría de un retrato del escritor Arias de Villalobos. Otros pintores de esa época son Tomás de Prado, Vicente Requena, Martín de Zumaya. En el primer cuarto del mismo siglo destacó en Puebla Luis Lagarto, cabeza de la dinastía de ese apellido, quien dejó miniaturas muy apreciadas por la crítica de hoy. El obispo poblano Juan de Palafox y Mendoza trajó a nueva España a Pedro García Ferrer, autor de varios cuadros de la Catedral de Puebla y al que se atribuyen, sin certeza, los retratos que mandó hacer Palafox de sus antecesores. En la misma ciudad y época floreció el flamenco Diego de Borgraf, quien dejó obras en Cholula, Tlaxcala y la propia capital poblana. Hacia 1640 llegó a la Nueva España el sevillano Sebastián López de Arteaga, quien pintó los retratos de 16 inquisidores, el del arzobispo Manzo y Zúñiga, un *San Francisco* que se halla en la Basílica de Guadalupe, el *San Ildefonso reciendo la casulla* del templo de Santo Domingo, *Los desposorios de la Virgen* y la *Incredulidad de Santo Tomás*. López de Arteaga influyó en los artistas de la primera generación del periodo barroco, como José Juárez, hijo de Luis del mismo apellido, a quien se debe una *Sagrada Familia* de 1655 que se halla en Puebla, la *Adoración de los Reyes*, el *San Ildefonso recibiendo la casulla de manos de la Virgen*, que perteneció al templo de Santo Domingo, la *Aparición de la Virgen a San Francisco*, el *San Lorenzo* de la colección de San Carlos, el *Calvario* de la Profesa, la *Adoración de los pastores* de la Academia de Puebla y, entre muchas otras obras, los santos *Justo y Pastor*, su obra maestra. De Pedro Ramírez, "el tipo perfecto del pintor barroco", según Toussaint, son las pinturas que forman parte del retablo de la capilla catedralicia de la Soledad, el retrato del obispo Juan Bohórquez, de 1653; un Cristo atado a una columna que se encuentra en el Museo de Guadalajara, el *Jesús atendido por los ángeles* del templo capitalino de San Miguel y su obra maestra: *Lágrimas de San Pedro*. Baltazar de Echave y Rioja, cuyo "barroquismo llega al exceso", de acuerdo con el citado crítico, empezó a pintar en 1666, cuando realizó el *Martirio de San Pedro Arbúes*, copia de un Murillo. Hizo después el *Entierro de Cristo* (1668), cinco lienzos con *Escenas de la vida de Santa Teresa* para la Catedral de México y dos copias de Rubens para la Catedral de Puebla: el *Triunfo de la religión* y el *Triunfo de la Iglesia*. Otros pintores del siglo XVII fueron Antonio de Alvarado, José Rodríguez de Carnero, Francisco y Nicolás de Angulo, Diego, Juan y Nicolás Becerra, José del Castillo, Tomás Conrado, Juan de Herrera, Sebastián López Dávalos y el prolífico Antonio Rodríguez, de quien existen obras en la parroquia de Coyoacán, en el templo de Churubusco, la Profesa y otros lugares. Su arte, dice Toussaint, "representa la transición entre la pintura de los grandes maestros y el comienzo del siglo XVIII, en que el arte se ve supeditado a distintas influencias y necesidades y va perdiendo poco a poco su decoro hasta llegar a ser completamente de-

Foto: Fondo Editorial Grupo Azabache

Cristo en la cruz, obra pictórica de Luis Juárez

FOTO: FONDO EDITORIAL GRUPO AZABACHE

San Juan Bautista, obra pictórica de Alonso López de Herrera

leznable". Rodríguez de Carnero dejó la mayor parte de su obra en Puebla, sobre todo en la Capilla del Rosario y el templo de la Concordia. En 1687 se publicaron las *Ordenanzas del arte de la pintura*, que ya no dividía a los ejecutantes en categorías. En el último tercio del siglo XVII florecieron Juan Correa y Cristóbal de Villalpando, de obra amplísima y dispareja según los críticos. De Correa son la *Visión de la mujer apocalíptica*, el *Arcángel San Miguel* y la *Entrada de Jesús en Jerusalem* (1691), que se hallan en la sacristía de la Catedral Metropolitana, y una *Virgen Apocalíptica*, del ex Colegio de Tepotzotlán. Villalpando es un pintor que, según Pedro Rojas, manifiesta su barroquismo "en los pronunciados encurvamientos con que aflige a las figuras, especialmente el de *ese* para las de pie, y en el frecuente zigzagueo que impone a las telas de los vestidos". Ejecutó la *Iglesia militante* y la *Iglesia triunfante* para la sacristía de la Catedral de México, 15 telas sobre la vida de San Francisco que se hallan en Guatemala, 22 acerca de San Ignacio de Loyola para el seminario jesuita de Tepotzotlán, las obras del retablo de Santa Teresa, de Azcapotzalco, *Desposorios, Anunciación, Adoración de los pastores* y *Huida a Egipto* del museo de la Catedral; *Oración del huerto, Flagelación* y *Ecce homo* del Museo del Carmen. Posteriores a Correa y Villalpando son Nicolás y Juan Rodríguez Juárez, hijos de Antonio Rodríguez, nietos de José Juárez y bisnietos de Luis Juárez. Al primero corresponde la autoría del *Profeta Isaías* (1690) de la Profesa, los retratos del arzobispo Vizarrón, Benedicto VIII, los virreyes Montañez y Alburquerque, el marqués de Santa Cruz y Pedro Rodríguez de Pisa; una *Magdalena Penitente*, un *San Cristobalón* que se halla en el Colegio de Guadalupe, cerca de Zacatecas; y una *Santa Teresa*, entre numerosas obras que se hallan en diversos puntos de la República. De Juan Rodríguez Juárez, "el último gran pintor de la Colonia" según Toussaint, son las series sobre la *Vida de la Virgen*, del convento de Tepotzotlán; sobre las de San Francisco y San Antonio de Padua, en el templo de San Francisco, en Querétaro, y, en la iglesia de la Congregación de esa misma ciudad la colección sobre la vida de San Pedro. Es suyo el retrato del arzobispo Lanciego y Eguiluz de la Catedral Metropolitana, la *Educación de la Virgen*, del Museo de Guadalajara; la *Transfiguración* y *Tempestad en la barca*, de la Profesa. De la misma época son Juan Aguilera, Pedro Calderón, Miguel de Herrera, Francisco de León, Francisco Martínez, José de la Mora, José de la Mota y Antonio de Torres. En el siglo XVIII, cuando el churrigueresco predomina en las artes plásticas, surge José de Ibarra, cuyo trabajo califica Toussaint de "teatral, grandilocuente, forzado". Él y otros pintores "tratan de estar a tono con el churrigueresco, pero carecen de genio para igualar la audacia y la fantasía de este arte". Ibarra, apoyado en los operarios de su obraje, produjo una cuantiosa obra en la que destacan *Mujeres del Evangelio*, así como las series *Vida de la Virgen* y *Pasajes de la Sagrada Escritura*. La figura mayor de la pintura dieciochesca fue el oaxaqueño Miguel Cabrera, de quien se admiran los retratos que ejecutó, como el de Sor Juana Inés de la Cruz, copiado de otro de autor desconocido. Sus obras para la iglesia de Santa Prisca, de Taxco, son lo más apreciado por los críticos, lo mismo que ciertos cuadros como su *San Anselmo*. Artistas contemporáneos de Cabrera e influidos por éste son Manuel de Ossorio, Juan Patricio Morlete Ruiz, Francisco Antonio Vallejo, José de Alcíbar, José Ventura Arnáez, José de Páez y Antonio Pérez de Aguilar, varios de los cuales prolongaron la vida del desfalleciente barroco, hasta toparse con el neoclásico y sus intentos por someter a un rígido racionalismo toda la creación artística. A tono con el absolutismo de las monarquías europeas, el nuevo culto estético tuvo como sede la Academia de San Carlos, fundada en 1781, de donde salían instrucciones de acatamiento obligatorio para quienes cultivaban los diversos géneros de la

La astronomía, óleo sobre tela de Juan Correa

FOTO: FONDO EDITORIAL GRUPO AZABACHE

Los desposorios, pintura de Luis Lagarto

plástica. De España vinieron, para encargarse de la sección de pintura, Ginés Andrés de Aguirre y Cosme de Acuña, quienes años después fueron sustituidos por el también peninsular Rafael Jimeno y Planes. Para Toussaint, la pintura neoclásica, "superior en calidad y técnica a la de los barrocos inmediatamente anteriores, no tiene ni su frescura ni su ingenuidad. Comparada con la de los siglos de oro resulta fría y de receta". De ahí que no aparezca "ninguna obra maestra en este periodo". De

El arcángel San Miguel, óleo sobre tela de Cristóbal de Villalpando

los maestros citados, quien fue más trascendente fue Jimeno y Planes, autor de un dibujo de la Plaza Mayor, y de retratos de Tolsá, Jerónimo Antonio Gil y otros personajes, lo mismo que imaginería religiosa. De mayor aliento se considera su obra muralística, realizada al temple, en la capilla del Palacio de Minería, las cúpulas de la Catedral de México y del Señor de Santa Teresa, esta última desaparecida. El insurgente José Luis Rodríguez de Alconedo, para Toussaint "el último gran pintor de la colonia", además de trabajos de orfebrería, dejó varios retratos y cuadros religiosos de mérito, así como un *Autorretrato* que es "una completa obra maestra". Otros pintores neoclásicos fueron José María Guerrero, José María Vásquez o Vázquez, Augusto Cerezo, Manuel García, José Antonio Castro, Juan de Sáenz, Atanasio Echeverría —dibujante en la expedición a Nutka de Sessé y Mociño—, los italianos Felipe Fabris —autor de un retrato de Revillagigedo— y José Perovani, el también periodista Francisco Ibar y José María de Uriarte. En este apartado cabe mencionar a los arquitectos Francisco Eduardo Tresguerras, quien incursionó en la pintura y dejó entre otras obras un *Autorretrato* (1794) y a Ignacio Paz, que pintó en 1823 una adulona *Alegoría de la coronación de Agustín de Iturbide* (*Cfr*.: Manuel Toussaint, *Arte colonial en México*). *Siglo XIX*: Durante el imperio de Iturbide, José María Vázquez hizo varias obras por encargo, entre ellas un retrato del mismo emperador. El francés Octaviano D'Alvimar trató infructuosamente de ganar el favor de la corte y acabó expulsado del país en 1823, después de estampar escenas de la vida cotidiana en la Plaza Mayor. Johan Moritz Rugendas, quien estuvo en México entre 1831 y 1834, además de numerosos bocetos y litografías, ejecutó varias pinturas que recogen los tipos y costumbres de la época, especialmente en Veracruz. En 1843 se expidió el decreto para reabrir la Academia de San Carlos, virtualmente cerrada desde la guerra de Independencia. Por las dificultades de la época, la apertura se produjo cuatro años después, con el catalán Pelegrín Clavé como director de la sección de pintura. Éste introdujo el dibujo ana tómico y el trabajo con modelos vivos, clases de perspectiva y de paisaje natural. La institución celebró una exposición anual de lo producido por los alumnos, junto a la obra de sus maestros y de algunos extranjeros. La planta docente de la Academia se enriqueció en 1855 con el arribo del italiano Eugenio Landesio, profesor de paisaje de quien se habían exhibido algunos cuadros en la exposición de 1853. Clavé, dominador de las técnicas académicas, fue muy apreciado como ejecutante de retratos, entre los que destacan los de Andrés Quintana Roo y el arquitecto Lorenzo de la Hidalga. Entre sus discípulos figuraron Santiago Rebull, José Salomé Pina, Felipe Gutiérrez, Joaquín Ramírez, Rafael Flores y Juan Urruchi. Después de una estancia en Roma, gracias a una beca, en 1853 regresó a México Juan Cordero, quien de inmediato entró en competencia con Clavé por el puesto de éste. El presidente de la Junta Directiva de San Carlos, José Bernardo Couto, le ofreció la subdirección de pintura, a lo que respondió Cordero: "no sacrifiqué los mejores años de mi vida en otros países, ni recibí los favores de la Academia, para venir a mi patria a ser dirigido por el señor Clavé". Rechazadas sus aspiraciones en ese centro de enseñanza, emprendió la decoración de la cúpula de Santa Teresa (1855-

Retrato de la monja, óleo sobre tela de Miguel Cabrera

La virgen del Apocalipsis, óleo sobre lámina de José de Ibarra

Doña María Luisa Gonzaga, óleo sobre tela de José María Vázquez

57) y continuó como muralista en San Fernando (1858-59). Clavé no quiso ser menos y se dio a pintar al óleo *Los siete sacramentos* en la cúpula de la Profesa, con la ayuda de sus discípulos Ramón Sagredo, Petronilo Monroy, Joaquín Ramírez, Rafael Flores y Felipe Castro. La obra, iniciada en 1861, fue suspendida cinco años y sólo pudo ser terminada en 1867, para que al año siguiente, después de recibir críticas adversas, Clavé regresara a Europa. De sus discípulos, Joaquín Ramírez realizó grandes lienzos con temas bíblicos, como *El arca de Noé, Los hebreos cautivos en Babilonia* y *Moisés en Raphidin*; de la antigüedad religiosa y pagana sacó Ramón Sagredo los motivos para sus telas: *Jesús en Emaús* o *La muerte de Sócrates*; en igual sentido se movió el pincel de Luis Monroy, autor de *La muerte de Atala* y *La Caridad romana*; Rafael Flores recibió sugerencias del *Nuevo Testamento* para ejecutar su *Jesús festejado por los ángeles* o *La sagrada familia*. José Obregón no despreció los temas hebraicos, como en *Agar e Ismael en el desierto*, pero incursionó en otros asuntos: *Giotto y Cimabué* o *El descubrimiento del pulque*, con lo que abrió espacio para el indigenismo en el mundo académico; Rodrigo Gutiérrez colaboró en esa tarea, pues a él se debe *El Senado de Tlaxcala*; y Petronilo Monroy realizó un *Isaac* ceñido a lo académico y se ganó un sitio como retratista al fijar en tela la figura de Eduardo M. Gallo. Los alumnos más destacados del maestro catalán fueron Salomé Pina, Santiago Rebull y Felipe S. Gutiérrez. El primero salió de San Carlos hacia a Europa en viaje de perfeccionamiento que se prolongó 15 años. Considerado mejor estudiante y profesor que artista, antes de partir dio muestras de su aplicación con la *Salida de Agar para el desierto* (1852), *Sansón y Dalila* (1853) y un *San Carlos Borromeo* (1854). Otras obras suyas son *Abraham e Isaac, La Piedad* y los grandes cuadros que ejecutó para la Colegiata de Guadalupe en 1889. Rebull, contemporáneo de Pina, destacó por su dominio del desnudo. En esta especialidad realizó el único *Cristo* académico del siglo XIX y *La muerte de Abel* (1852). En Italia pintó *El sacrificio de Isaac*, considerada por Justino Fernández "algo así como la culminación de la escuela clásica mexicana, o tan mexicana como era posible que fuese". Favorecido por Maximiliano, dejó inconcluso el retrato de Carlota cuando ésta se negó a posar, pero la imagen que pintó del Habsburgo le valió una condecoración imperial. A pedido del austriaco, para decorar el Castillo de Chapultepec hizo seis tableros de estilo pompeyano en los que, según Fernández, "el romanticismo de la época encuentra una de sus clásicas expresiones". Sus servicios al imperio no obstaron para que al triunfo de la República hiciera sendos retratos de Juárez y Porfirio Díaz. Obra muy comentada en su tiempo fue *La muerte de*

Panzacola, óleo sobre tela de Eugenio Landesio

La señorita Echeverría, retratada por Pelegrín Clavé

Autorretrato, de Juan Cordero

Marat, expuesta en 1875. Felipe Gutiérrez, viajero y escritor, pintó un *San Jerónimo* y un *San Bartolomé* que, dice Raquel Tibol, "nada tienen que ver con las criaturas maquilladas de los cuadros a la moda; son pinturas fuertes, en ellas el dibujo perfecto y la disposición académica no han molestado la severa expresión psicológica de los personajes. Son obras de alguien que tenía la necesaria madurez y la suficiente autocrítica como para evitar cualquier cursilería". Al mismo artista se debe el primer desnudo femenino integral de la pintura mexicana: *La amazona de los Andes*. Más popular que cualquiera de los discípulos de Clavé resultó ser Cordero, quien en Roma, en su época de estudiante, había pintado el *Retrato de los escultores Pérez y Valero*, "una de las obras maestras de la pintura mexicana" para Raquel Tibol. En Italia realizó una amplia producción de caballete y en 1850 ejecutó su obra *Colón ante los Reyes Católicos*, que "pese al clima general de falsedad" del cuadro, "consagró a Cordero en México", según la misma crítica, quien considera el *Retrato de Dolores Tosta*, mujer de Antonio López de Santa Anna, "un ejemplo extraordinario del arte de Cordero". En 1874 ejecutó un mural laico, esta vez en la escalera principal de la Escuela Nacional Preparatoria: *Triunfos de la ciencia y el trabajo sobre la envidia y la ignorancia*. La obra, inspirada por el positivismo en boga, desapareció en 1900. Para Raquel Tibol fue "uno de los grandes pintores del siglo XIX" y "punto culminante de una corriente", pues expresó "la crisis del clasicismo en la pintura mexicana", cuando "la realidad pujaba ya por salir a la superficie, resquebrajando la aureola de idealización que envolvía las creaturas plásticas". El paisajismo tuvo numerosos cultivadores formados a lo largo de tres lustros por Eugenio Landesio, quien pintó haciendas, *Chimalistac* y la *Arquería de Matlala*. Entre sus discípulos se contaron Luis Coto, autor de la *Fundación de México*, la *Colegiata de Guadalupe*, la *Hacienda de la Teja* y otras obras; José Jiménez, quien dejó una vista del *Patio interior del convento de San Francisco*; Javier Álvarez, quien recogió paisajes urbanos como la *Casa de la Hidalga*; Gregorio Dumaine, quien pintó *La hacienda de los Morales* y sus alrededores; Salvador Murillo, que tuvo a los árboles por tema; y, por encima de los anteriores, José María Velasco, quien para Justino Fernández adaptó la preceptiva de Landesio "con espíritu propio, con gran capacidad de artista, y con visión de poeta introdujo la vida del país, le dio expresión estética a la realidad social". Forman parte de su numerosa producción una *Vista de la Alameda de México* (1863), *Un paseo en los alrededores de México* (1866), *Ahuehuetes de Chapultepec* (1872), la serie *Lomas de Tacubaya* (1871- 73), el *Canal de Nochistongo*, dos versiones de *Rocas del Tepeyac* (1877 y 1897), *El valle de México visto desde Guadalupe* (1873), *Los volcanes* (1878), el *Citlaltépetl* (1875 y 1897), *El Valle de México* (1875), *Pirámides del Sol y de la Luna* (1878) y el *Puente de Metlac* (1881). Al margen de la Academia florecieron algunos artistas, entre los cuales destacan el guadalajareño José María Estrada, el duranguense Mariano Silva Vandeira, el moreliano Mariano de Jesús Torres y, principalmente, Hermenegildo Bustos, nativo de Purísima del Rincón, Guanajuato, quien se dedicó a múltiples oficios y ejerció la

Hacienda de Chimalpa, obra pictórica de José María Velasco

Xochimilco, de Joaquín Clausell

La ofrenda, de Saturnino Herrán

Caballo, óleo sobre tela de Roberto Montenegro

profesión de pintor. Realizó obras religiosas, pero la crítica aprecia más sus bodegones y sobre todo sus retratos, género en el que también destacó Estrada. Bustos, de acuerdo con Justino Fernández, "dejó una obra de esas que contribuyen al prestigio de la gran pintura". A una segunda generación académica corresponden los nombres de Manuel Ocaranza, José Ibarrarán y Ponce, Gonzalo Carrasco, Félix Parra, autor de un multirreproducido *Bartolomé de las Casas* (1876) y Leandro Izaguirre, quien pintó un *Suplicio de Cuauhtémoc* en 1892 y después de algunos años dedicado a la enseñanza se fue a Europa, donde ingresó en la pintura del siglo XX sin aclimatarse del todo. Lo mismo sucedió con otros artistas como Germán Gedovius, discípulo de Pina, que después de estudiar en Alemania regresó a ejecutar dos de sus obras mayores: un *Autorretrato* y un desnudo considerado entre lo más representativo del romanticismo agonizante. También con estudios en Alemania, Julio Ruelas, romántico y conocedor del impresionismo, se diferenció por la carga subjetiva de sus trabajos, liberados del puritanismo en el que había navegado el arte decimonónico. Lo más difundido de su producción corresponde a las ilustraciones que hizo para la *Revista Moderna*, en las que se aprecia su proclividad a mezclar lo picaresco con lo macabro. En dibujos, grabados y pinturas mezcló realismo y fantasía, puso lo que hoy se llamaría angustia existencial junto a un morboso gusto por el erotismo, por la vida. Otro artista, quizá el más influyente de la centuria por venir, recurriría también a la mixtura de elementos picarescos y macabros. A diferencia de Ruelas, no trabajaría para un público culto. Él se dirigía a los espectadores plebeyos, que eran también los protagonistas de su arte: José Guadalupe Posada. (*Cfr.*: Justino Fernández. *El arte del siglo XIX en México*; y Raquel Tibol. *Historia general del arte mexicano*, t. III, *Época moderna y contemporánea*). *Siglo XX*: Puente entre Velasco y el paisajismo contemporáneo es la obra de Joaquín Clausell, quien relativamente tarde, cerca de los 40 años, decidió combinar su profesión de abogado con el ejercicio de la pintura, en la que forjó un impresionismo propio, único. Llevó a la tela numerosas estampas campiranas y fue el primero en trabajar con asiduidad las marinas. Algunas paredes del actual Museo de la Ciudad de México guardan bocetos y pequeños cuadros que trabajaba directamente sobre los muros del viejo palacio de los condes de Calimaya, que fue su domicilio particular. Otros impresionistas fueron el michoacano Gilberto Chávez y el guerrerense Francisco Romano Guillemín, quien hasta su muerte en 1950 cultivó el puntillismo. En 1903, contratado por Justo Sierra, vino a México Antonio Fabrés, quien tendría entre sus discípulos a Saturnino Herrán, Roberto Montenegro, Diego Rivera y, en menor medida, José Clemente Orozco. En los tres años que permaneció en el país, Fabrés transformó la técnica de enseñanza, pero sus fines eran meramente académicos. De cualquier modo, los citados aprovecharían ampliamente lo aprendido y cada uno le daría un uso particular. Herrán, dice Tibol, tomó "de

Paisaje, obra de *Dr. Atl*

Detalle de *Sueño de una tarde dominical en la Alameda Central*, mural de Diego Rivera

La trinchera, mural de José Clemente Orozco

Fabrés el decorativismo académico", en tanto que de Izaguirre y Gedovius, que también fueron sus maestros, recibió el indigenismo y el interés por las cosas sencillas. Privado en ocasiones de óleos por su precariedad económica, encontró una forma creativa de combinar lápices y acuarelas. El resultado, a primera vista, fue un indigenismo representado con formas europeas, pero en el cual, por sus personajes, temas y tratamiento había destellos de una veta nacional que se desplegaría en los años veinte, lo que ya no vería Herrán, quien murió a los 31 años, en 1918. Otra figura precursora del llamado renacimiento mexicano fue Gerardo Murillo, el *Dr. Atl*. Nacido en 1875, inició su formación en Guadalajara y luego marchó a Europa, donde hizo estudios de filosofía y derecho, y volvió a México en 1903. Él impulsó la conversión de Clausell en pintor, inventó unos crayones de resina y cera, participó en polémicas artísticas y políticas y, en 1910, al enterarse de que el centenario de la independencia mexicana se celebraría con una exposición de pintura española, organizó una protesta con sus colegas y logró que el gobierno patrocinara una muestra de creadores mexicanos, a los que agrupó en el Centro Artístico, sociedad que pidió a las autoridades los muros del anfiteatro Bolívar para decorarlos. La solicitud fue respondida afirmativamente, pero el estallido de la revolución y las pugnas dentro de la sociedad de pintores impidieron iniciar el trabajo. *Atl* regresó a Europa, pero al año siguiente estalló una huelga en la Academia de San Carlos con tres demandas: la reforma de la enseñanza, la salida de los profesores extranjeros y la renuncia del director, el arquitecto Antonio Rivas Mercado. En lugar de éste entró Alfredo Ramos Martínez, admirador de los impresionistas franceses, quien propuso a los alumnos fundar en Santa Anita la primera de las Escuelas de Pintura al Aire Libre (☛). Después del golpe de Estado de Victoriano Huerta, el *Dr. Atl* volvió al país y se incorporó a las fuerzas de Carranza y dirigió el periódico *La Vanguardia*, del que Orozco fue caricaturista. Otros artistas participaron en la revolución, como David Alfaro Siqueiros, quien formó parte del Estado Mayor del general Manuel M. Diéguez, o Francisco Goitia, que militó en las filas comandadas por Felipe Ángeles. Es Goitia, según Raquel Tibol, el primero en tomar la guerra civil como tema en sus cuadros *Baile de la revolución* (1916) y *El ahorcado* (1917). Orozco, en la ciudad de México, presentó su primera exposición individual en 1916, con obras muy lejanas al formalismo académico. Por esa época, en Guadalajara, Xavier Guerrero ejecutó varios murales. En 1920, el *Dr. Atl* presentó una exposición en el ex convento de la Merced con cuadros que son, según Raquel Tibol, "la versión más áspera, austera y hombruna que se haya dado del paisaje mexicano", lo que podría definir toda su obra posterior. En 1921 retornó a México Diego Rivera, al término de una década en París, donde figuró en el movimiento cubista. Al llegar participó con otros artistas, escritores y políticos en el Grupo Solidario del Movimiento Obrero. Bajo la presidencia de Álvaro Obregón, el secretario de Educación Pública, José Vasconcelos, promovió el inicio del más trascendente movimiento pictórico mexicano y, según algunos estudiosos, el único de proyección universal que aquí se haya gestado. Vasconcelos ofreció a los artistas los muros de la Preparatoria y su anexo, el Colegio de San Pedro y San Pablo. En éste pintaron *Atl* y Roberto Montenegro; el anfiteatro de la Preparatoria fue decorado por Fernando Leal y Diego Rivera en

Madre campesina, óleo sobre tela de David Alfaro Siqueiros

Detalle de mural de Fermín Revueltas

El hombre con pipa, óleo sobre tela de Rufino Tamayo

El veterano, óleo sobre tela de Jorge González Camarena

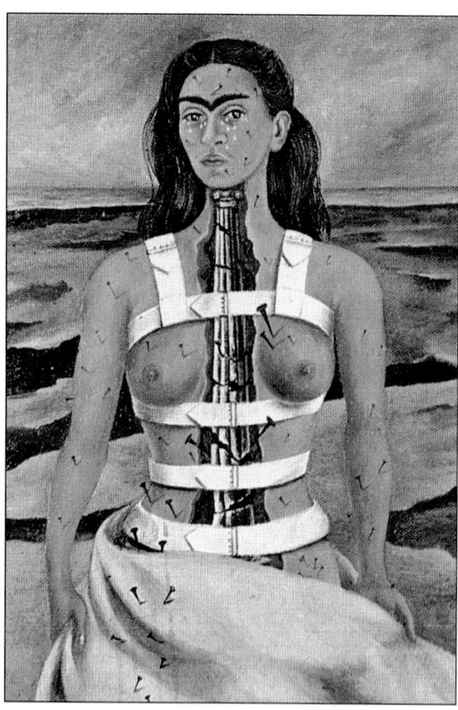

La columna rota, óleo sobre tela de Frida Kahlo

tanto que en torno a los patios trabajaron Orozco, Ramón Alva de la Canal, Jean Charlot, el mismo Leal, Fermín Revueltas y David Alfaro Siqueiros. En 1923 Vasconcelos encomendó a Rivera la decoración de la Secretaría de Educación Pública, quien se auxilió con Jean Charlot y Amado de la Cueva, que dejaron su obra personal en algunas áreas. A Montenegro se le encargaron los vitrales y la obra mural de la Biblioteca Iberoamericana, anexa al edificio. La fiebre estética afectó también a los particulares y Francisco Sergio Iturbe pidió a Orozco que pintara en el cubo de la escalera de Sanborn's, en la Casa de los Azulejos, lo que el artista hizo en 1925, año en el que Siqueiros y Amado de la Cueva trabajaban en Guadalajara, donde Carlos Orozco Romero pintó tres murales en esa época. Para entonces ya se había creado el Sindicato de Obreros Técnicos Pintores y Escultores (☛) y la mayoría de sus miembros pertenecían al Partido Comunista. El sindicato repudiaba el individualismo y rechazaba la pintura de caballete; se proponía socializar el arte, produciendo con ese fin obras monumentales, de carácter público, con un mensaje que impulsara la lucha popular contra la burguesía. Es dudoso que se hayan cumplido las finalidades políticas del muralismo, pero a su impulso se gestó un afán de monumentalidad que perdura hasta la fecha. Tampoco se abandonó la pintura de caballete, si bien abundaron los artistas que buscaron sus raíces en lo indígena, en lo popular, como Jesús Reyes Ferreira y Francisco Goitia. Montenegro hizo lo mismo, al margen de consideraciones políticas. El guatemalteco Carlos Mérida concilió sus simpatías hacia el movimiento mexicano con un peculiar geometrismo, del que fue maestro. Ángel Zárraga también participó en el muralismo y se empeñó en ser moderno, pero era un pintor de otro tiempo. Rufino Tamayo realizó murales en el Museo Nacional de Arqueología (1930), en el antiguo Conservatorio Nacional de Música (1933), en el Palacio de Bellas Artes (1952-53) y el restaurante Sanborn's de Lafragua (1954). La enorme diferencia entre los primeros y los ejecutados 20 años después permiten apreciar la transformación profunda de su pintura. En Bellas Artes ya habían hecho obra monumental Orozco (1934), Diego (1934) y Siqueiros (1945 y 1950). El formidable arranque del muralismo se produjo en los años veinte, pero su impulso se prolongó durante varios lustros: en los años treinta, en la ciudad de México, Alfredo Zalce y José Chávez Morado se iniciaron en el muralismo, al que darían sus mejores frutos en Michoacán y Guanajuato, respectivamente. Entre 1929-35 y 1941-51 trabajó Rivera su obra del Palacio Nacional; en 1931 Jesús Guerrero Galván pintó *Fecundidad*, en Guadalajara; en 1932, Fermín Revueltas decoró el edificio del periódico *El Nacional*, al año siguiente el Banco Nacional Hipotecario y en 1934 hizo los vitrales del Centro Escolar Revolución, donde en 1936-37 pintarían Raúl Anguiano, Gonzalo de la Paz Pérez, Ignacio Gómez Jaramillo, Antonio Gutiérrez, Everardo Ramírez y Aurora Reyes. Entre 1934 y 1936 se ejecutaron los murales del mercado Abelardo L. Rodríguez y el anexo Teatro del Pueblo, donde pintaron Ramón Alva

Opera de Pekín, óleo sobre tela de Juan Soriano

Paisaje de Papantla, óleo sobre masonite de Gunther Gerzso

El cantar de los cantares, óleo sobre tela de Pedro Coronel

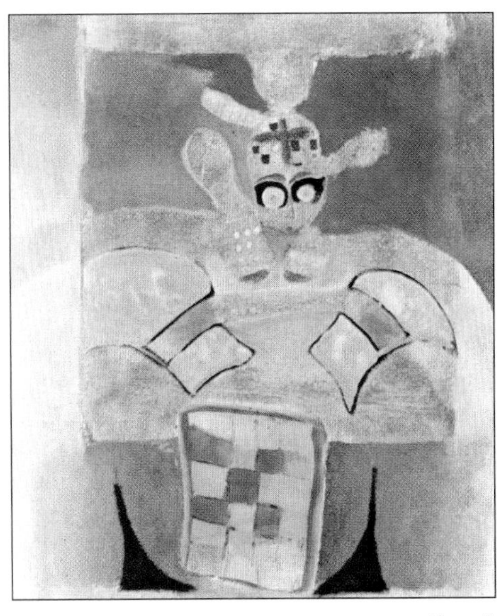

El conejo, óleo sobre tela de Francisco Toledo

Guadarrama, Ángel Bracho, Raúl Gamboa, Antonio Pujol, Pedro Rendón y Miguel Tzab y los estadounidenses Pablo O'Higgins, Marion y Grace Greenwood, así como su paisano de origen japonés Isamu Noguchi, quien dejó un escultomural de tema antifascista. En 1933 Julio Castellanos realizó el mural *La manteada* en la escuela Melchor Ocampo, de Coyoacán. Diego Rivera hizo en 1936 unos paneles transportables para el hotel Reforma, los que alteró y después ordenó retirar Alberto J. Pani, quien los vendió a un particular, del que pasaron a Bellas Artes. Orozco continuó su obra mural en la Universidad de Guadalajara, en el Palacio de Gobierno y el Hospicio Cabañas de la capital jalisciense (1936-39). En la misma época, Juan O'Gorman, quien ya había decorado una pulquería en 1925, ejecutó su obra del viejo aeropuerto del Distrito Federal. Miguel Covarrubias firmó en 1937 el mural *Xochimilco*, en el hotel Ritz, en tanto que Siqueiros, a su regreso de la guerra civil española, con Antonio Pujol, José Renau y Luis Arenal como ayudantes, pintó el cubo de la escalera del Sindicato Mexicano de Electricistas. Orozco decoró la Suprema Corte de Justicia (1941), el hospital de Jesús (1942-44), la Escuela Nacional de Maestros (1947-48), la sala de la Reforma del Castillo de Chapultepec (1948) y la Cámara de Diputados de Jalisco (1948-49), en tanto que dejó sin terminar sus trabajos del Conservatorio Nacional y el Multifamiliar Juárez del Distrito Federal. Manuel Rodríguez Lozano hizo un mural para una casa particular en 1933 y al comienzo de los años cuarenta realizó dos más: uno en la cárcel de Lecumberri, trasladado posteriormente a Bellas Artes, y *Holocausto* (1942), en la vieja casona de los condes de Miravalle, en Isabel la Católica 30; Fernando Castro Pacheco se inició como muralista en esta década y en Yucatán realizaría lo más cuantioso de su obra; Jorge González Camarena trabajó en el Banco Mercantil (1945) y el estadounidense George Biddle en la Suprema Corte (1945); Covarrubias, con varios ayudantes, entre los cuales estaba el futuro líder comunista Arnoldo Martínez Verdugo, hizo dos mapas en el desaparecido Hotel del Prado (1947); ahí mismo, Diego Rivera realizó su mural *Sueño de una tarde dominical en la Alameda* (1947). Antes había elaborado una obra en el Instituto de Cardiología (1943-44) y después, en 1951, trabajaría con volúmenes en la fuente exterior del Cárcamo del Lerma, en cuyo interior empleó un material plástico que no ha resistido la humedad; al año siguiente inició los relieves del estadio de la Ciudad Universitaria y en 1953 decoró con mosaicos el exterior del Teatro de los Insurgentes. A partir de 1947, O'Gorman, arquitecto de profesión, proyectó y construyó el edificio de la biblioteca Central de la UNAM, cuyos enormes ex-

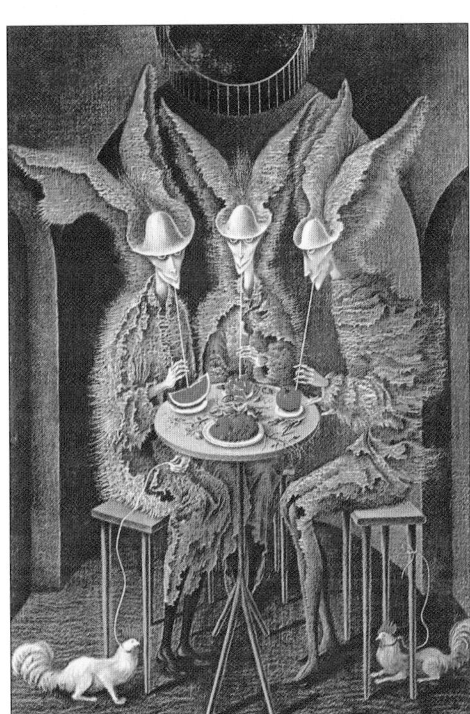

Vampiros vegetarianos, óleo sobre tela de Remedios Varo

Variedad, dibujo a tinta de José Luis Cuevas

teriores están decorados con piedras de colores. Para Nacional Financiera, Leopoldo Méndez ejecutó sobre plástico el grabado-mural transportable *Jugando con luces*; Federico Cantú pintó *Los informantes de Sahagún* en la actual Pinacoteca Virreinal; en 1951 Covarrubias realizó un *Mapa del arte popular mexicano* en el Museo de Artes e Industrias Populares que tiene por sede la ex iglesia de Corpus Christi; Chávez Morado trabajó con piedras de colores los murales experiores de la antigua SCOP (1953); Desiderio Hernández Xochitiotzin inició su labor como muralista en Tlaxcala; y Siqueiros, por su parte, en 1952 pintó *El hombre amo y no esclavo de la técnica*, en el Instituto Politécnico Nacional, y después, en el hospital de la Raza, *Por una seguridad completa para todos los mexicanos* (1952-54), donde, al igual que en la torre de la Rectoría de la Ciudad Universitaria, mostró su cabal dominio de las superficies irregulares. Muralistas de las décadas posteriores son, entre muchos otros, Benito Messeguer, Rina Lazo, Fanny Rabel, Mario Orozco Rivera, Arturo Estrada, Adolfo Mexiac, Jesús Álvarez Amaya, José Hernández Delgadillo, Arnold Belkin y Vlady, a quien se debe la decoración de la Biblioteca Lerdo de Tejada, una de las superficies mayores trabajadas por un artista de México. Este incompleto catálogo, al que deberían agregarse cientos de obras realizadas en México y en el extranjero, es una muestra del vuelo que levantó el arte monumental mexicano, con sus muy marcadas diferencias de calidad, de tendencia formal y hasta de inspiración política. Entre los citados se menciona a varios extranjeros, algunos de ellos aclimatados definitivamente en México, otros sólo aves de paso, pero todos atraídos por la proyección del muralismo, movimiento engarzado con la propia realidad del país. Todos los muralistas mencionados hicieron también una considerable obra de caballete. Junto o contra ellos, como parte de la llamada generación de la Ruptura o en movimientos posteriores, que han acercado la gráfica y la pintura a los llamados arte conceptual y arte objeto, otros artistas se limitaron al reducido espacio de la tela y han intentado otro tipo de búsquedas. Contemporáneos de la primera época del muralismo, pero con intereses diversos son Abraham Ángel, muerto muy joven; Frida Kahlo, elevada internacionalmente a los altares del mito en los años ochenta; María Izquierdo, Antonio Ruiz, Jesús Reyes Ferreira, Ricardo Martínez, Agustín Lazo, Julio Castellanos, Angelina Beloff o Belova, Guillermo Meza, José García Narezo, Olga Costa, José Reyes Meza, Regina Raull, Gerardo Cantú, Francisco Icaza, Lilia Carrillo, Leonardo Nierman y Waldemar Sjölander. Con obra de caballete que deja ver su formación de grabadores están Francisco Dosamantes, Isidoro Ocampo, Feliciano Peña, José Julio Rodríguez, Héctor Cruz, Mariano Paredes o Abelardo Ávila. Han destacado como acuarelistas Helen O'Gorman, Ignacio Beteta y Guati Rojo. De importante producción tanto en la pintura como la escultura son Juan Soriano, Mathias Goeritz, Pedro Coronel, Luis Nishizawa, Federico Silva, Feliciano Béjar o Marysole Worner Baz. Al témino de la guerra civil española vino un ejército de artistas entre los que se cuentan Vicente Gandía, Miguel Prieto, Alberto Gironella, Lucinda Urrusti, Monferrer, Remedios Varo, Ceferino Palencia, Alice Rahon, Arturo Souto, Antonio Peláez, Elvira Gascón, Enrique Climent, José María Giménez Botey y Vicente Rojo, inicialmente discípulo de Prieto, pero formado totalmente en México. Protagonistas de los movimientos adversos a la escuela mexicana, aun sin proponérselo, fueron algunos de los citados, así como Rafael Coronel, Manuel Felguérez, Gilberto Aceves Navarro, Pedro Friedeberg, Felipe Ehrenberg, Fernando García Ponce, Gunther Gerszo y José Luis Cuevas, quien fue el más activo en aquella polémica a la que contribuyó con declaraciones, ensayos y sobre todo con su obra, que dio al dibujo una categoría de gran arte que hasta entonces se le regateaba. En la gran corriente renovadora y frecuentemente al margen de ella ha realizado su obra Francisco Toledo, quien ha usado como

FOTO: MUSEO DE ARTE DE SINALOA

La señal, obra de Vicente Rojo

materia prima las leyendas de su natal Juchitán y ha creado formas que hoy cuentan con numerosos seguidores.

PINZÓN, LUIS ◆ n. en Acapulco y m. en Corral Falso, Gro. (1792-1863). En 1810 se incorporó a la insurgencia en el Regimiento de Nuestra Señora de Guadalupe. Peleó en las filas de José María Morelos y en 1814 ascendió a capitán; combatió junto con Vicente Guerrero, Julián Ávila y Hermenegildo Galeana y llegó a coronel en 1820. Al año siguiente se unió al ejército trigarante. Fue el segundo jefe del Ejército Mexicano que combatió contra los invasores estadounidenses en la batalla de Cerro Gordo (1847). Se desempeñó como comandante militar de Huajuapan de León.

PIÑA, HORACIO ◆ n. en Matamoros de la Luna, Coah. (1935). Beisbolista. Lanzador derecho. Inició su carrera en 1965, con los *Mineros* de Zacatecas de la Liga Central. En 1969 pasó a las ligas mayores, donde jugó para los *Indios* de Cleveland, los *Senadores* de Washington (1970-72), los *Atléticos* de Oakland (1973), con quienes ganó la Serie Mundial de 1973; los *Cachorros* de Chicago (1974-75) y los *Filis* de Filadelfia (1978). Volvió a México en 1978 y se incorporó a los *Rieleros* de Aguascalientes. Dos años después, en julio de 1980, lanzó uno de los dos únicos juegos perfectos que se han registrado en la Liga Mexicana de Beisbol. Se retiró en ese mismo año, debido a una lesión en el brazo derecho.

PIÑA, MIGUEL ◆ n. y m. en Ures, Son. (?-1931). Militar. En 1913 era capitán de las fuerzas constitucionalistas que combatían a las órdenes de Ramón V. Sosa. Fue pagador general del Ejército del Noroeste (1914-15); secretario de gobierno de Sonora (1918), encargado del Ejecutivo estatal en sustitución del gobernador Elías Calles (del 8 de mayo al 7 de junio de 1919), firmante del Plan de Agua Prieta (1920), oficial mayor del secretario de Guerra y Marina (1920), nuevamente gobernador de Sonora (del 1 de enero al 28 de febrero y del 23 de marzo al 19 de mayo de 1921) y subsecretario de Guerra y Marina durante el periodo presidencial de Plutarco Elías Calles (1926-28).

Román Piña Chan

PIÑA Y CUEVAS, MANUEL ◆ m. en la ciudad de México (1804-1877). Se tituló como abogado en 1833. Fue secretario de Hacienda en los gobiernos de José Joaquín de Herrera (del 11 de septiembre de 1848 al 22 de marzo de 1849) y de Mariano Arista (del 26 de mayo al 1 de septiembre de 1851). Presentó una iniciativa para la fundación de un banco nacional. En 1863 fue nombrado miembro de la Junta de Notables que apoyó al imperio de Maximiliano de Habsburgo. Al triunfo de la República se retiró de la política.

PIÑA CHAN, ROMÁN ◆ n. en Campeche, Camp. (1920). Arqueólogo titulado en la ENAH y doctor en antropología por la UNAM. Profesor de la Normal Superior, de la UNAM, la UIA y otras instituciones. Ha sido jefe de Investigaciones Arqueológicas, subdirector y director del Departamento de Monumentos Prehispánicos del INAH; conservador del Museo Nacional de Antropología, miembro del Consejo de Arqueología del INAH y miembro de la Comisión de Antropología de la UNAM. Entre 1945 y 1960 trabajó en los sitios arqueológicos de Chalcatzingo y Atlihuayán, Morelos; Tlapacoya, Edo. de México; Comalcalco y La Venta, Tabasco; estuvo después en Mulchic y Chichén-Itzá, Yucatán; Jaina, Campeche; Teotihuacán, Edo. de México y Cuicuilco, DF. Dirigió los proyectos Tenango (1971-75) y Huamango (1976-77), en el Estado de México, y Tingambato (1978- 79), en Michoacán. Instaló los museos de Dzibilchaltún, Campeche, Santiago Tuxtla, Cuicuilco, Ocoyoacac y Teotenango. A partir de 1984 se ha dedicado a descifrar jeroglíficos zapotecas. Autor de *Breve estudio sobre la funeraria de Jaina* (1948), *El horizonte preclásico del valle de México* (1951), *Las culturas preclásicas de la cuenca de México* (1955), *Bonampak* (1961), *Ciudades arqueológicas de México* (1963), *Los olmecas* (1964), *Una visión del México prehispánico* (1967), *Jaina, la casa en el agua*, *El problema de los olmecas* (1968), *Los olmecas en el centro de México* (1968), *A Guide to Mexican Archeology* (1969), *Arqueología y tradición histórica: un testimonio de los informantes de Sahagún* (1970), *Campeche antes de la conquista* (1970), *Historia, arqueología y arte prehispánico* (1972), *Culturas y ciudades del México prehispánico* (1973), *Ciencia y tecnología en el México prehispánico* (1973), *La región de Chalco en tiempos prehispánicos* (1975), *El Estado de México antes de la conquista* (1975), *Un modelo de evolución social y cultural del México prehispánico* (1976), *Los olmecas* (1980), *Selva y mar* (1982), *Quetzalcóatl, serpiente emplumada* (1985) y *Cultura y ciudades mayas de Campeche* (1986). Investigador emérito del INAH. Premio Nacional de Historia, Ciencias Sociales y Filosofía (1994).

PIÑA Y MAZO, LUIS DE ◆ n. en España y m. en Mérida, Yuc. (1723-1795). Fraile benedictino. Fue ordenado sacerdote en 1747. Llegó a la Nueva España en 1780, como obispo de Yucatán. Restableció el colegio de San Pedro y lo anexó al Seminario de San Ildefonso, con lo que sentó las bases de una futura universidad. Suprimió las estancias que eran propiedad de las cofradías y se distinguió por sus constantes fricciones con los distintos gobernadores de la provincia y con las autoridades eclesiásticas y militares. Gobernó la diócesis yucateca hasta su muerte.

PIÑA OLAYA, MARIANO ◆ n. en Champusco, Pue. (1933). Licenciado en derecho por la UNAM (1956), de la que es profesor desde 1958. Ha sido juez menor del Distrito Federal (1958-60), presidente de la Junta Local de Conciliación y Arbitraje en la capital de la República (1971), director general de la Cámara Nacional de las Industrias Azucarera y Alcoholera (1972-73), gerente general administrativo de la Comisión Federal de Electricidad (1974-76), director administrativo de Aeroméxico (1977-80), representante del gobierno de Puebla en el DF (1981) y diputado federal (1982-85). En 1986 fue elegido gobernador de Puebla para el periodo 1987-93. Elaboró un *Índice temático de la Revista Mexicana de Derecho del Trabajo*. Autor de *La naturaleza jurídica de la relación entre la Universidad y sus servidores*, *El derecho laboral en la industria de la aviación* y *La situación jurídica de la mujer*. Pertenece a la Barra Mexicana-Colegio de Abogados, a las academias Mexicana de Derecho Procesal del Trabajo y Mexicana del Derecho del Trabajo, a la Interamerican Bar Association, al Instituto Iberoamericano de Derecho Aeronáutico y a otras corporaciones.

Piña Rojas, José Antonio ◆ n. en el DF (1954). Estudió relaciones internacionales en la UNAM. Ingresó al servicio exterior en mayo de 1974 y alcanzó el grado de embajador en 1980. Ha sido analista en la dirección general de Organismos Internacionales (1974-77), asesor del Director General de Organismos Internacionles (1977-78), asesor del director en jefe de Asuntos Especiales (1978-79), asesor del coordinador de Asuntos Especiales Internacionales (1979-81), jefe del Departamento de Agregados Culturales (1981), secretario particular del subsecretario de Asuntos Culturales (81-83), director de la Unidad de Comunicaciones al Exterior (83-86), consejero de la embajada en Austria (1986-89), secretario particular del oficial Mayor (1989), director interino de Personal (1989); director general del SEM y de Personal (1990-94) y embajador en El Salvador (1995-).

Piña Soria, Rodolfo ◆ n. en Celaya, Gto., y m. en EUA (1904- 1944). Ferrocarrilero desde 1919, se distinguió en la actividad sindical. En 1927 era miembro de la Confederación de Transportes y Comunicaciones y participó en la huelga de mecánicos de ese año. En 1933 pertenecía al consejo directivo de la Confederación General de Obreros y Campesinos de México y en 1936 era presidente de la comisión de asuntos internacionales de la Confederación de Trabajadores de México. Ese mismo año fue delegado obrero por México ante la Organización Internacional del Trabajo y más tarde representó a los trabajadores mexicanos en Alemania, Austria, Bélgica, Argentina y Canadá. En 1939 asistió al Congreso Internacional de Montevideo, de donde surgió la Confederación de Trabajadores de la América Latina. Al morir era secretario general de ajustes de la CTM.

Piña Soria, Santiago ◆ n. en Celaya, Gto., y m. en el DF (1901-1971). Militar. Se incorporó a la revolución en las fuerzas constitucionalistas y llegó a ser general de división. Ocupó diversos cargos en las secretarías de Guerra y Marina y de la Defensa Nacional, donde fue comandante de algunas zonas militares. Obtuvo la Cruz de Guerra de Primera Clase y fue jefe del Estado Mayor Presidencial de Miguel Alemán.

Piñeiro López, Genaro José ◆ n. en el DF (1954). Licenciado en derecho (1976) y en filosofía (1974) por la UAP. Militante del PST desde 1974, fue responsable del Frente Estudiantil Nacional (1979-81 y 1986-), miembro del Comité Central (1980-), secretario de finanzas (1980) y de delegados centrales (1981-82) y subsecretario de la Comisión Nacional de Asuntos Electorales (1982). Miembro del PFCRN (1988-). Secretario de la Unión Nacional de Trabajadores Agrícolas (1982-83), fundador y asesor de la Comisión Nacional de Defensa del Pescador (1983-85), diputado federal (1985-88) y miembro de la Asamblea de Representantes del Distrito Federal (1988-91).

Piñera Rueda, Carlos Mario ◆ n. en Huimanguillo, Tab. (1919). Licenciado y doctor en derecho por la UNAM. Miembro del PRI. Ha sido jefe del Departamento Jurídico de la Dirección General de Policía y Tránsito, procurador general de Defensa del Trabajo, en el Distrito Federal; subdirector del penal de Santa Marta Acatitla, director general de Relaciones Públicas y Difusión de la UNAM, subdirector de Aduanas, director general del Trabajo de la Secretaría del Trabajo y diputado federal (1979-82).

Piñó Sandoval, Jorge ◆ n. en San Luis Potosí, SLP, y m. en el DF (1902-1976). En 1924 se inició como periodista en *El Machete*, órgano del Partido Comunista Mexicano. A causa de su militancia estuvo preso en 1930. Redactor de las columnas "Cosmópolis" (1939) y "A mañana, tarde y noche", que publicaba en el diario *Excélsior* (1940). Fue fundador del *Noticiero Cinematográfico Clasa-Excélsior* (1938), corresponsal de guerra de ese periódico; cofundador, con Álvaro Gálvez y Fuentes, del noticiero *Diario Relámpago del Aire* en la radiodifusora XEW; corresponsal de la Organización de las Naciones Unidas en Washington, fundador de las ediciones vespertina y nocturna del cotidiano *Últimas Noticias* (1942), fundador del periódico satírico *Don Timorato* (1946) y director de la revista *Presente* (1949), cuyas críticas al presidente Miguel Alemán motivaron la hostilidad de ciertas autoridades, por lo que se exilió en Argentina. Volvió a México en 1957 y colaboró en *La República*, órgano del PRI. Fue director del Departamento Editorial de la Presidencia de la República (1964-70) y de la Secretaría del Patrimonio Nacional (1971-75). Impulsó las publicaciones *Caminos del Aire*, *La Prensa del Mediodía* y *C M Amigos*, entre otras. Colaborador de *El 130*, *El Bonete*, *Novedades*, *Espartaco*, *Hoy*, *Todo* y *El Universal Ilustrado*. Autor de *Perote. Fortaleza violada* (1947) y *Ángela celeste. Picaresca mexicana* (1952). Miembro fundador de la Asociación Mexicana de Periodistas.

***Pípila*, el Juan José de los Reyes Martínez** ◆ n. y m. en San Miguel el Grande, hoy San Miguel de Allende, Gto. (1782-1863). Minero. Se unió a las fuerzas de Hidalgo en septiembre de 1810. El día 28 de ese mes, durante el ataque

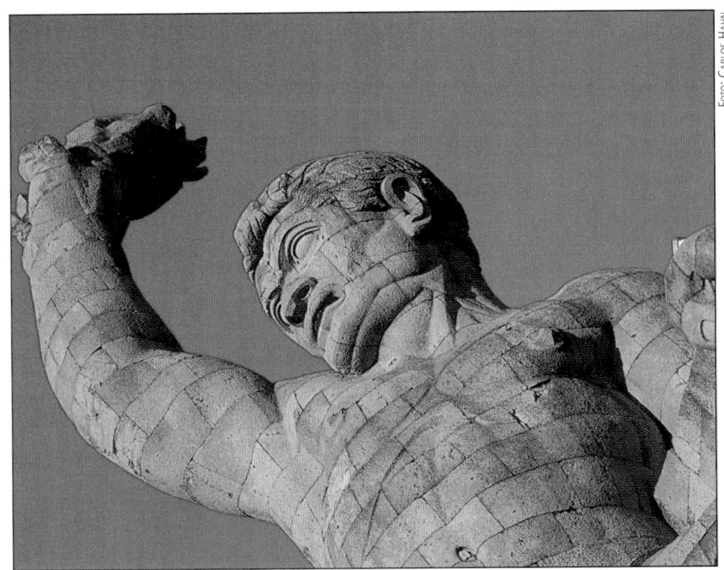

Monumento al *Pípila*, en Guanajuato

insurgente a Guanajuato, se arrastró desde las posiciones de los atacantes hasta la alhóndiga de Granaditas, cubriéndose la espalda con una losa y llevando una antorcha en la mano, con la que prendió fuego a la puerta del edificio, lo que precipitó la derrota de los colonialistas. Concluida la guerra de Independencia, *el Pípila* regresó a su ciudad natal y volvió a dedicarse a la minería. Existen varias versiones en torno a este personaje: algunos autores ponen en duda su existencia, otros señalan que su nombre era Mariano Martínez y que murió en la batalla del Monte de las Cruces y otros más lo llaman José María Barajas.

***Piporro*, Eulalio González Ramírez** ◆ n. en Los Herrera, NL (1921). Cantante, compositor y cómico cinematográfico. Fue contador, periodista y estenógrafo. A mediados de los años cuarenta comenzó a imitar cantantes en la estación radiofónica XEMR, de Monterrey. Más tarde se trasladó a la ciudad de México. Se inició en el cine en 1951, en la cinta *Ahí viene Martín Corona*, donde hizo el papel de *el Piporro*, apelativo que adoptó como nombre artístico desde entonces. Ha actuado en las películas *El mariachi desconocido* (1953), *Tres desgraciados con suerte* (1957), *Mujeres encantadoras* (1957), *¡Ay Calipso, no te rajes!* (1957), *Los mujeriegos* (1957), *Acapulqueña* (1958), *Calibre 44* (1959), *La nave de los monstruos* (1959), *El rey del tomate* (1962), *El terror de la frontera* (1962), *El bracero del año* (1963) y *Los tales por cuales* (1964), entre otras. En 1969 dirigió y actuó la cinta *El pocho*. Es autor de las canciones *Chulas fronteras*, *El taconazo*, *Melitón el abusón*, *El terror de la frontera* y *Genaro soltero*. Autor de *Autobiograjúa! y anecdotaconario* (1999). Recibió la Diosa de Plata *Cantinflas* de Periodistas Cinematográficos de México (1970).

Pisaflores ◆ Municipio de Hidalgo situado en el norte del estado, en los límites con San Luis Potosí y Querétaro. Superficie: 159.3 km^2. Habitantes: 15,789, de los cuales 3,957 forman la

Eulalio González *Piporro*

población económicamente activa. Hablan alguna lengua indígena 16 personas mayores de cinco años (náhuatl 14).

Pishmish, Paris ◆ n. en Turquía y m. en el DF (1901-1999). Astrónoma. Fue la segunda mujer turca que se dedicó a las ciencias físicas. Se doctoró en la Universidad de Estambul donde fue discípula de Edwin Freundlich. Vino a México en 1942 procedente de Harvard, recién casada con el matemático Félix Resillas. Trabajó en el Observatorio de Tonantzintla en Puebla. Fue profesora de la UNAM en la entonces recién fundada carrera de astrofísica. Autora de la autobiografía *Reminiscences in the Life of Paris Pishmis: a Woman Astronomer.* Premio Universidad Nacional 1989. Desde principios de 1999, el auditorio del Instituto de Astrofísica de la UNAM lleva su nombre.

Piso Joo, Silvia ◆ n. en el DF (1944). Licenciada en economía por la UNAM (1966) y maestra en estudios latinoamericanos por la Universidad de Stanford (1969). En la UNAM fue investigadora del Instituto de Investigaciones Económicas (1965-66) y profesora de la Escuela Nacional de Economía (1966). Trabajó para el Banco Mundial (1971-72) y Grupo ICA (1973-76). Ha sido subdirectora de Programación (1977-79) y directora de Programación de Servicios (1979-82) de la Secretaría de Programación y Presupuesto; así como directora general de la Industria Paraestatal del Azúcar de la Secretaría de Energía. Pertenece a la Sociedad Mexicana de Planificación.

Pita, Joaquín ◆ n. en el estado de Puebla y m. en el DF (1862-1950). Fundador y director de los diarios poblanos *La Luz* y el *Boletín Municipal*; fundador de la Sociedad Pulquera de Puebla y México. Estableció la primera embotelladora de aguas minerales de Tehuacán (1899). Impulsó la producción de cerámica de Talavera. En Puebla fue secretario del Ayuntamiento, diputado, visitador de jefaturas políticas, director general de Estadística y jefe político (1893-11), bajo el gobierno de Mucio P. Martínez. En 1910 auxilió a los

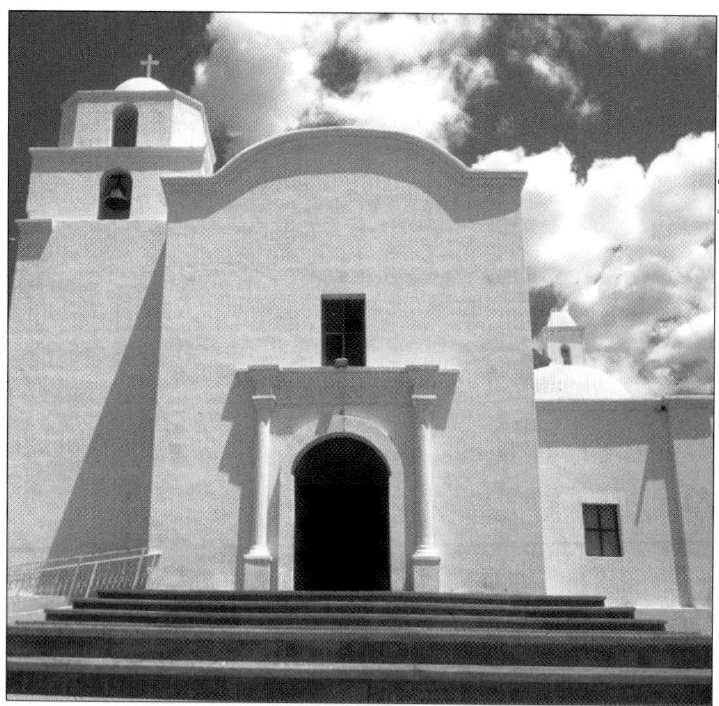

Iglesia de San Diego Pitiquito en Pitiquito, Sonora

familiares de Aquiles Serdán que se hallaban presos. Fue inspector de policía del Distrito Federal en 1913 y se negó a apresar a Jesús Urueta, Félix F. Palavicini y 10 diputados más, por lo que renunció a su cargo y se le hizo jefe político de Mazatlán. A la caída del gobierno de Victoriano Huerta fue encarcelado un año por Benjamín Hill. Autor de unas *Memorias*.

Pitiquito ◆ Municipio de Sonora situado en la costa del golfo de California. Limita al sur con Hermosillo y al norte con Caborca. Superficie: 11,979.96 km^2. Habitantes: 8,957, de los cuales 2,558 forman la población económicamente activa. Hablan alguna lengua indígena 206 personas mayores de cinco años (seri 114). El municipio Pitiquito se encuentra en el ex distrito de Altar.

Vicente Riva Palacio escribía en *El Pito Real*

Pito Real, El ◆ Periódico liberal y satírico escrito por el general Vicente Riva Palacio durante la segunda mitad de 1866, en Huetamo, Uruapan y Zitácuaro. Se anunciaba como un "libelo que se reparte gratis, pero cada número vale una cuartilla". En forma burlesca, como responsable de la publicación aparecía Pelagio Antonio de Labastida y Dávalos, el arzobispo de México. En

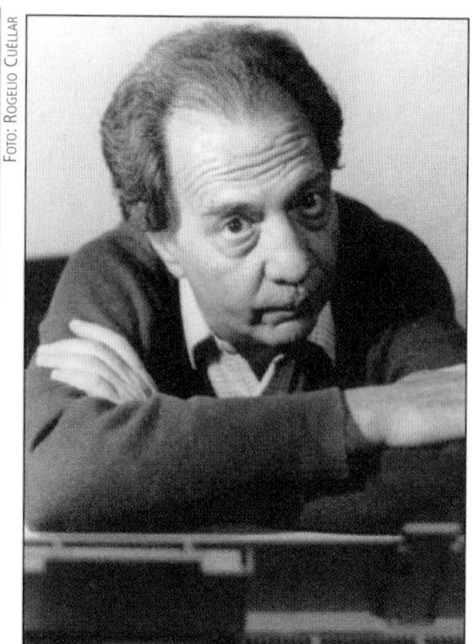

Sergio Pitol

julio se publicó en sus páginas la composición, del propio Riva Palacio, *Adiós mamá Carlota*, que se convirtió en canto de guerra de los republicanos. Se distribuía en las zonas controladas por los republicanos y circulaba clandestinamente en la parte ocupada por los franceses.

Pitol, Sergio ◆ n. en Puebla, Pue. (1933). Escritor. Su apellido materno es Deméneghi. Licenciado en derecho por la UNAM (1955). Realizó estudios en la Facultad de Filosofía y Letras de esa universidad. Profesor de la UNAM, de la Universidad Veracruzana (1966-77) y de la Universidad de Bristol (1971-72). Miembro del servicio exterior desde 1960, ha sido consejero cultural de las embajadas mexicanas en Francia, Hungría, Polonia y la Unión Soviética (1975-80), director de Asuntos Culturales de la Secretaría de Relaciones Exteriores (1981), director de Asuntos Internacionales del Instituto Nacional de Bellas Artes (1982) y embajador en Checoslovaquia (1982-87). Ha trabajado para las editoriales Novaro, Oasis (1955-60) y Tusquets (1969-70). Colaborador de *Revista de la Universidad, Estaciones, Revista de Bellas Artes, La Palabra y El Hombre* (de la que fue director) y *Letras Libres*, entre otras; de los suplementos *México en la Cultura, La Cultura en México, Sábado* y *La Jornada Semanal*; y del diario *Ovaciones*. Tradujo *Las puertas del paraíso*, de Jerzy Morzejweski (1965), y *Las excentricidades del cardenal Pirelli*, de Roland Firbank (1985). Compiló las antologías *Antología del cuento polaco contemporáneo* (1967), *Asimetría* (1980) y *Cuerpo presente* (1990). Autor de cuento: *Victorio Ferri cuenta un cuento* (1958), *Infierno de todos* (1964), *Los climas* (1966), *No hay tal lugar* (1966), *Del encuentro nupcial* (1970), *Nocturno de Bujara* (1981, Premio Xavier Villaurrutia), *Cementerio de tordos* (1982, Premio Latinoamericano de Narrativa Colima para obra publicada), *El asedio del fuego* (1984) y *Vals de Mefisto* (1984); ensayo: *De Jane Austen a Virginia Woolf* (1975), *La casa de la tribu* (1989), *Luis García Guerrero* (1993), *El arte de la fuga* (1996, Premio Mazatlán de Literatura) y *Pasión por la trama* (1999); novela: *El tañido de una flauta* (1972), *Juegos florales* (1982), *El desfile del amor* (1984, Premio Herralde de Novela), *Domar a la divina garza* (1989), *La vida conyugal* (1991) y *Tríptico del carnaval* (1999); también escribió *Tiempo cercano* (1959) y la autobiografía *Sergio Pitol* (1966). En 1973 recibió el Premio Nacional de Novela del INBA, en 1987 el Gran Premio de la Asociación de Cultura Europea, de Polonia, en 1993 el Premio

Nacional de Literatura y Lingüística y en 1999 el Premio de Literatura Latinoamericana y el Caribe Juan Rulfo. Ha sido condecorado por el gobierno de Polonia. Fue becario del Fonca (1992-1993) e ingresó al SNCA como creador emérito en 1994.

Pittaluga, Gustavo ◆ n. y m. en España (1906-1975). Músico. Realizó estudios incompletos de derecho. Fue discípulo del músico Óscar Esplá y miembro del Grupo de los Ocho (Escuela de Madrid). Durante la guerra civil española perteneció a la Alianza de Intelectuales Contra el Fascismo y musicalizó el documental *Canciones de Madrid*. Se exilió en Cuba al triunfo del franquismo y en 1948 se instaló en México, donde dirigió la Orquesta Sinfónica Nacional. Musicalizó la película de Luis Buñuel *Subida al cielo* (1951). Autor de *Llanto por Federico García Lorca*, *La romería de los cornudos*, *Homenaje a Mateo Albéniz*, *Elegía*, *Seis danzas españolas en suite* y *Homenaje a la tumba de Manuel de Falla*.

Pizá, Damián ◆ n. ¿en el DF? (1926). Nadador. En 1946, ganó una medalla de oro en los juegos Centroamericanos y del Caribe celebrados en Barranquilla. En 1953, en 15 horas, atravesó a nado el canal de la Mancha. En 1955 redujo su marca en dos horas. Se retiró al año siguiente y se dedicó a la enseñanza.

Piza Martínez, Pedro ◆ n. en Villahermosa, Tab. (1887-?). Militar. Combatió en el Ejército Libertador de Sur hasta 1914, cuando se incorporó a las tropas de Venustiano Carranza, a quien sirvió hasta 1920, cuando abandonó la comitiva que acompañaba al presidente a Veracruz y se unió a las tropas obregonistas. Se retiró brevemente del ejército, pero en 1923 combatió la rebelión delahuertista. Perteneció al Estado Mayor del presidente Lázaro Cárdenas. En 1940 fue ascendido a general de brigada.

Pizano y Saucedo, Carlos ◆ n. en Colima, Col. (1924). Periodista. Inició su carrera en 1942, en el periódico *Ecos de la costa*. Ha sido director de *El Heraldo de Colima*, *El Regional*, *El Heraldo de Manzanillo* y *El Demócrata Colimense*; corresponsal de publicaciones del DF y de la agencia *Associated Press*; redactor del periódico jalisciense *El Informador* (1945-49), colaborador de *Siempre!* y de los diarios de Guadalajara *El Occidental* (1958-83) y *Ocho Columnas*. En Colima fue secretario del gobernador Jesús González Lugo, director de la imprenta del estado y jefe de la Oficina de Prensa (1949-52). Delegado federal y director de Turismo (1953-59) y jefe de Prensa del gobierno de Jalisco (1959-65); director del Instituto Jalisciense de Bellas Artes (1965-71), jefe de Relaciones Públicas del Ayuntamiento de Guadalajara (1971-73) y jefe de Prensa y Relaciones Públicas de la CFE (1976-). Colaboró en la *Enciclopedia de México*. Autor de *El rey de Coliman* (1955), *Historia cronológica del periodismo colimense* (1955), *Platería. Siglo XX* (1961), *Jalisco en la conquista de las Filipinas* (1964) y *Fundación de la villa de Colima* (1973).

Pizarro, Nicolás ◆ n. y m. en la ciudad de México (1830-1895). Escritor. Simpatizante de los liberales, colaboró en *El Semanario Ilustrado*. Autor de *El monedero* (1861), *La coqueta* (1861), *Catecismo político constitucional* (1861), *Catecismo de moral* (1868), *La zahorí* (1868), *Compendio de gramática de la lengua española según se habla en México, escrito en verso con explicaciones en prosa* (1868) y *Leyendas y fábulas para los niños* (1872).

Pla Brugat, Dolores ◆ n. en España (1954). Licenciada en historia (1983) con estudios de posgrado en la UNAM (1986) y en el Instituto Nacional de Antropología e Historia (1978-79). Ha impartido cursos en la ENEP Acatlán (1979), la UIA (1983) y la Universidad Veracruzana (1988). Es investigadora del INAH (1982-), donde coordina el proyecto de historia oral "Refugiados españoles en México". Pertenece al consejo de redacción de la revista *Historias* (1985-) y a la Comisión Editorial de la Dirección de Estudios Históricos del INAH (1989-). Autora de *Los niños de Morelia* (1985).

Placencia, Alfredo R. ◆ n. en Jalostotitlán y m. en Guadalajara, Jal. (1875-1930). Poeta. Estudió en el Seminario de Guadalajara. Fue ordenado sacerdote en 1899. En 1922 era canónigo penitenciario en Guadalajara. Fue desterrado a Estados Unidos en 1923 y a El Salvador en 1924. Volvió a México en 1929. Autor de *El paso del dolor* (1924), *Del cuartel y del claustro* (1924) y *El libro de Dios* (1924, reeditado en 1990). En 1959 apareció una recopilación de sus *Poesías*, realizada por Luis Vázquez Correa.

Placencia y Moreira, Ignacio ◆ n. en Zapopan, Jal., y m. en Zacatecas, Zac. (1867-1951). Sacerdote. Estudió en el Seminario Conciliar de Guadalajara. Fue vicerrector del Seminario de Guadalajara, prosecretario de la Mitra, prebendado de la catedral y obispo de Tehuantepec (1908-22). Durante la guerra cristera fue expulsado dos veces del país. Volvió a México en 1935.

Plan de Acapulco ◆ Manifiesto lanzado por la guarnición militar de Acapulco el 11 de marzo de 1854, luego de una lectura del Plan de Ayutla (☛) organizada por el comandante militar del puerto, Rafael Solís, quien pese a que consideraba que el levantamiento de Ayutla "sacaría pronto a la Nación del estado de esclavitud y abatimiento a que por grados la había ido conduciendo el poder arbitrario y despótico del excmo. sr. gral. don Antonio López de Santa Anna", prefirió poner a consideración de la oficialidad la decisión de apoyar el levantamiento. Los militares decidieron sumarse a la revuelta y más aún, propusieron como comandante de la insurrección en Acapulco a Ignacio Comonfort. Como la proclamación del Plan de Ayutla, las acciones de la guarnición acapulqueña fueron planeadas por el grupo al que pertenecían el propio Comonfort, Juan Álvarez y Tomás Moreno. Finalmente, y a propuesta de Comonfort, la asamblea militar introdujo algunas reformas al Plan de Ayutla que consistieron, además de los añadidos formales, en proponer la reinstauración de la República Federal, el establecimiento de nuevos aranceles

Firmantes del Plan de Agua Prieta

para el comercio internacional y en establecer que cuatro meses después de la publicación de la convocatoria comenzaría a funcionar el Congreso extraordinario. Además, los firmantes reiteraron la oferta de mando a Nicolás Bravo, quien se negó a participar; y a Álvarez y Moreno, que se incorporaron como jefes del Ejército Restaurador de la Libertad, el 13 de marzo.

Plan de Agua Prieta ◆ Nombre con que se conoce el Plan Orgánico del Movimiento Reivindicador de la Democracia y de la Ley. Este documento fue firmado el 23 de abril de 1920, en la población sonorense de Agua Prieta, por legisladores y militares obregonistas encabezados por el gobernador de Sonora, Adolfo de la Huerta, para oponerse al intento del presidente Venustiano Carranza por imponer como su sucesor a Ignacio Bonillas. El plan desconocía a Carranza como presidente de la República, anulaba las elecciones locales del Distrito Federal, Guanajuato, San Luis Potosí, Querétaro, Nuevo León y Tamaulipas; declaraba gobernador constitucional de Nayarit a José Santos Godínez y nombraba jefe supremo del Ejército Liberal Constitucionalista al propio de la Huerta. Los alzados prometían designar un presidente provisional y convocar a nuevas elecciones presidenciales. La insurrección se propagó rápidamente debido a la participación de por lo menos la mitad del viejo ejército constitucionalista y, a fines de mayo, luego del asesinato del presidente en Tlaxcalantongo, los obregonistas triunfaron. Un mes después, el 28 de julio, los restos de la División del Norte pactaron la aceptación del nuevo gobierno, como lo habían hecho los principales jefes zapatistas.

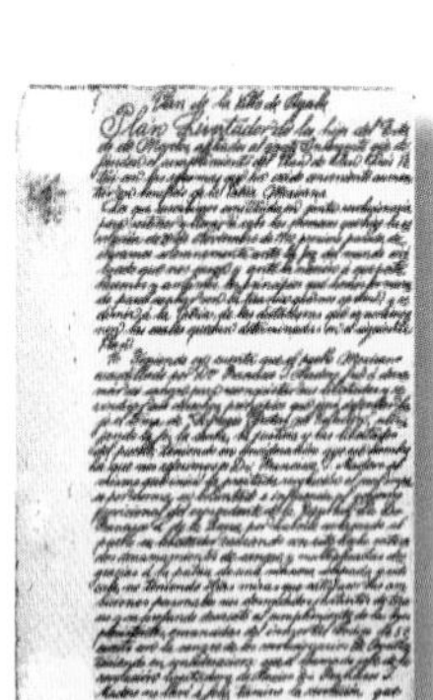

Página del Plan de Ayala

Plan de Ayala ◆ Programa revolucionario redactado en noviembre de 1911 por Otilio Montaño a partir de las ideas de Emiliano Zapata. El plan fue proclamado el día 28 en la población de Ayoxustla, situada en Puebla, en las estribaciones de la sierra Nevada, por una junta revolucionaria que encabezaba el propio Zapata. El "Plan libertador de los hijos de Estado de Morelos", que tal era su nombre, reformaba el de San Luis (☛) y acusaba al presidente Madero de haber "violado los sagrados principios que juró defender bajo el lema de 'Sufragio Efectivo. No Reelección', ultrajando la fe, la causa, la justicia y las libertades del pueblo"; de buscar la satisfacción de sus ambiciones personales, de haber impuesto en la vicepresidencia a José María Pino Suárez, de violar "el inmortal Código del 57" y de haber intentado establecer una dictadura "más oprobiosa que la de Porfirio Díaz". Más adelante se desconocía a Madero como jefe de la revolución y se proclamaba como sustituto a Pascual Orozco o, en su ausencia, a Emiliano Zapata. De los 15 artículos del documento, el sexto, el séptimo y el octavo se han considerado la base del agrarismo mexicano y, por lo tanto, los más importantes. En ellos, los zapatistas establecían que de los "terrenos, montes y aguas usurpados por los hacendados, científicos o caciques a la sombra de la tiranía y la justicia venal entrarán en posesión los pueblos y ciudadanos que tengan sus títulos correspondientes". En el caso de tierras adquiridas legalmente por los hacendados, se establecía el derecho a expropiarlas, "previa indemnización de la tercera parte de esos monopolios", con el fin "de que los pueblos y ciudadanos de México obtengan ejidos, colonias, fundos legales para pueblos o campos de sembradura o de labor, y se mejore en todo y para todo la falta de prosperidad y bienestar de los mexicanos". A los hacendados que se opusieran a la revolución, se les amenazaba con la nacionalización total de sus bienes. El documento concluía con una exhortación al "Pueblo mexicano", en la que se le llamaba a "apoyar con las armas en

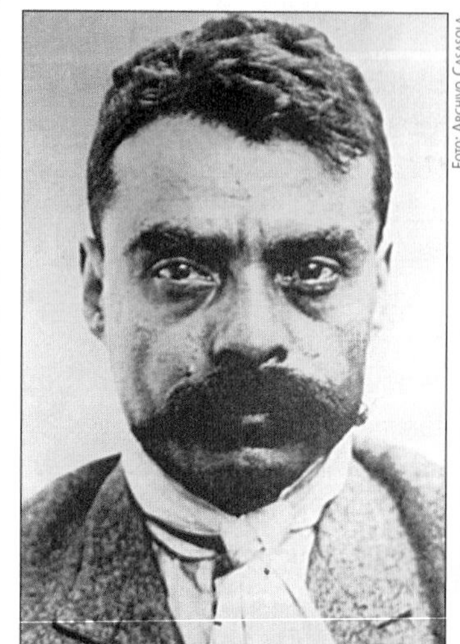

Foto: Archivo Casasola

Emiliano Zapata, autor del Plan de Ayala

la mano este plan", ya que así se lograría "la prosperidad y bienestar de la Patria". El plan fue reformado el 30 de mayo de 1913, tras el asesinato del presidente Madero, para desconocer tanto al gobierno de Victoriano Huerta como a Pascual Orozco y para designar como único jefe del movimiento a Emiliano Zapata. El documento fue ratificado en San Pablo Oxtotepec el 19 de junio de 1914 bajo el lema de "Reforma, libertad, justicia y ley". En esta ocasión, los firmantes impugnaban el despotismo de Huerta hacia el pueblo y, en especial, los trabajadores. El documento volvió a ser reformado por Genovevo de la O y Gildardo Magaña, entre otros, mediante el Plan de Milpa Alta, el 6 de agosto de 1919, tres meses después del asesinato de Zapata por los carrancistas.

PLAN DE AYUTLA ◆ Documento aprobado el 1 de marzo de 1854 por el destacamento militar de la población guerrerense de Ayutla, que estaba al mando del coronel Florencio Villarreal. El manifiesto había sido redactado unos días antes en la Hacienda de la Providencia, situada en los alrededores de Texca, por Juan Álvarez, Ignacio Comonfort, Trinidad Gómez, Rafael Benavides, Eligio Romero y Diego Álvarez, quienes, con Tomás Moreno y otros, formaban un grupo de liberales opuestos al gobierno de Antonio López de Santa Anna desde fines de 1853 y cuyas fuerzas se habían enfrentado con efectivos gubernamentales en los últimos días de febrero de 1854. El texto señalaba que la "permanencia en el poder de Santa Anna es un amago constante para las libertades públicas", debido a que había traicionado los principios republicanos que en 1853 le facilitaron la vuelta al poder; alertaba a los mexicanos por el "inminente peligro de ser subyugados por la fuerza de un poder absoluto" y condenaba el sacrificio "de nuestros hermanos de la frontera del norte", los habitantes del recién vendido territorio de La Mesilla, "que en adelante serán extrajeros en su propia Patria". Se desconocía al gobierno de Santa Anna, así como a todas las autoridades que lo apoyaran, y se prometía que una vez triunfante el levantamiento, los jefes militares que hubieran derrocado al gobierno eligirían un presidente interino, que a su vez quedaba comprometido a convocar, "15 días después de haber entrado en sus funciones", a un Congreso extraordinario, "el cual se ocupe exclusivamente de constituir a la Nación bajo la forma de República representativa popular". Finalmente, para aparentar una total independencia del grupo liberal, los sublevados de Ayutla llamaban a dirigir el movimiento a Nicolás Bravo, Juan Álvarez y Tomás Moreno. Ese mismo día, Villarreal remitió una copia del documento a la guarnición militar de Acapulco, la cual, con el apoyo del propio Comonfort, añadió algunas modificaciones y el 11 de marzo proclamó el Plan de Acapulco (☛). El movimiento iniciado por este plan desembocó en la Constitución de 1857.

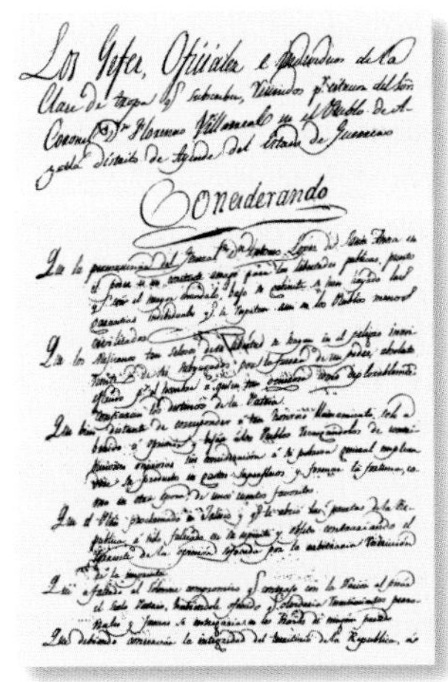
Considerando

Página del Plan de Ayutla

PLAN DE CASA MATA ◆ Nombre con el que comúnmente se conoce el Acta de Casa Mata, documento firmado en la población veracruzana de Casa Mata el 1 de febrero de 1823, por José Antonio Echávarri, Luis Cortazar, José María Lobato, Antonio López de Santa Anna, Guadalupe Victoria, Vicente Guerrero y Nicolás Bravo, entre otros, luego de la defección de los generales imperialistas Echávarri, Lobato y Cortazar, quienes habían sido comisionados por Agustín de Iturbide para combatir el movimiento iniciado en diciembre del año anterior, con la proclamación del Plan de Veracruz (☛). En el Acta se demandaba la reinstalación del Congreso Constituyente de 1822, que había sido disuelto por Iturbide, pero se aseguraba que el "ejército nunca atentará contra la persona del emperador".

PLAN DE LA CIUDADELA ◆ Manifiesto lanzado por Mariano Salas, entonces comandante militar de la ciudad de México, el 4 de agosto de 1846, contra el gobierno del presidente Mariano Paredes y Arrillaga, a quien Salas había ayudado a alcanzar la presidencia en diciembre de 1845. El documento consideraba que "desde que dejó de existir la Constitución (de 1824) que libre y espontáneamente se dio la República (.), las que posteriormente se han formado no han sido conformes con las exigencias y deseos de la gran mayoría de la nación", lo que había provocado "las continuas oscilaciones que han afligido al país, al extremo de que (.) se han creído autorizados algunos espurios mexicanos para quererlo someter al más vergonzoso vasallaje, pretendiendo llamar un príncipe extranjero que los gobierne con el título de monarca". Estos "espurios mexicanos" eran los políticos influidos por Lucas Alamán, entre ellos los miembros del Congreso que había formado Paredes un mes antes, por lo que los sublevados desconocían cualquier acuerdo de esas Cámaras y proclamaban la necesidad de reunir un nuevo Congreso, elegido de acuerdo a la Constitución de 1824, "el cual se encargará (.) de constituir a la nación adoptando la forma de gobierno que le parezca conforme a la voluntad nacional, como también de todo lo relativo a la guerra con los Estados Unidos". Todos los ciudadanos mexicanos eran llamados a sumarse a la defensa nacional, "especialmente" el "excmo. sr. general benemérito de la patria don Antonio López de Santa Anna", quien sería reconocido "desde luego como general en jefe de todas las fuerzas comprometidas y resueltas a combatir porque la nación recobre sus derechos, asegure su libertad y se gobierne por sí misma".

Mariano Paredes y Arrillaga

Panorámica de Cuernavaca a mediados del siglo XIX

PLAN DE CUERNAVACA ◆ Documento firmado el 25 de mayo de 1834 en la capital de Morelos por Ignacio Echeverría y otros militares leales a Antonio López de Santa Anna y muy probablemente instigados por él, quien buscaba legitimar sus ataques contra las reformas de 1833. Tras considerar que la República se hallaba "sumergida (.) en el caos más espantoso de confusión y desorden", debido a las reformas liberales que había impulsado el gobierno de Valentín Gómez Farías, "la villa de Cuernavaca, animada de las más sanas intenciones y con el deseo de abrir una nueva era" para el país, manifestaba "abierta repugnancia con las leyes y decretos (.) que se han dictado sobre reformas religiosas". El plan desconocía toda la tarea legislativa de la llamada Primera Reforma. Los sublevados demandaban "respetuosamente la protección" del "excmo. sr. presidente de la República don Antonio López de Santa Anna".

PLAN DE GUADALUPE ◆ Proclama firmada en la hacienda de Guadalupe, Coahuila, el 26 de marzo de 1913, por Jacinto B. Treviño, Lucio Blanco y Francisco Sánchez, quienes repudiaban al gobierno golpista de Victoriano Huerta, acusado en el documento de haber cometido "el delito de traición" contra el presidente Francisco I. Madero. Se desconocía a los tres poderes federales y a los poderes locales que no aceptaran el plan. Los sublevados nombraron "Primer Jefe del Ejército que se denominará 'Constitucionalista' al ciudadano

FOTO: FONDO EDITORIAL GRUPO AZABACHE

Hacienda de Guadalupe, Coahuila, en la cual se promulgó el plan del mismo nombre en marzo de 1913

Firmantes del Plan de Guadalupe

Venustiano Carranza". El texto establecía que, al entrar a la capital del país, Carranza o quien lo hubiese sustituido en el mando del ejército se encargaría del Poder Ejecutivo el tiempo necesario para convocar a elecciones. Este plan sufrió algunas reformas, entre ellas la del 12 de diciembre de 1914, en Veracruz, que establecía como obligación para el presidente interino lanzar la convocatoria a celebrar un Congreso Constituyente.

PLAN DE IGUALA ◆ Manifiesto redactado por Agustín de Iturbide y proclamado por él mismo el 24 de febrero de 1821 en Iguala, hoy estado de Guerrero. En la proclama introductoria, Iturbide decía que la independencia era un suceso semejante al del "padre de familia, que en su ancianidad mira separarse de su casa a los hijos y los nietos por estar ya en edad de formar otras y fijarse por sí"; aseguraba que España había educado y engrandecido a "la América Septentrional" y que había formado "esas provincias y reinos dilatados que en la historia del universo van a ocupar lugar muy distinguido", pero que por "los daños que origina la distancia del centro de su unidad (.) la opinión pública y general de todos los pueblos es la independencia absoluta de la España y de toda otra nación". Señalaba que las "tantas desgracias" que la revolución iniciada en Dolores en 1810 había ocasionado "al bello país de las delicias, por el desorden y otra multitud de vicios (.), fijó la opinión pública de que la unión general entre europeos y americanos, indios e indígenas, es la única base sólida en la que puede descansar nuestra común felicidad". Tal unión se basaba, entre otras cosas, en la "religión católica, apostólica, romana, sin tolerancia de otra alguna"; en un "gobierno monárquico templado por una Constitución

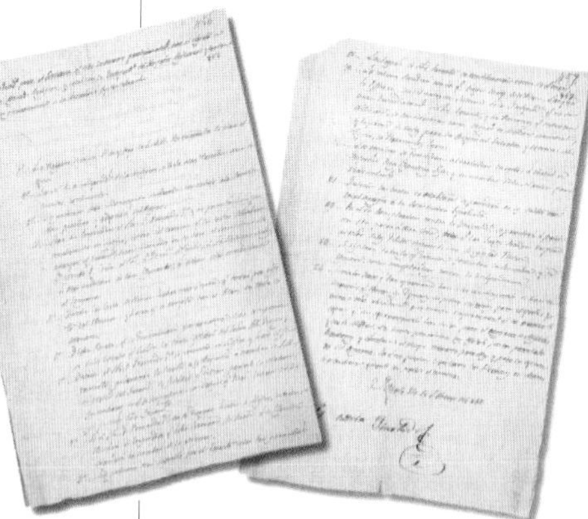

Páginas del Plan de Iguala

análoga al país", que sería regido por "Fernando VII y en sus casos los de su dinastía o de otra reinante (.) para hallarnos con un monarca ya hecho"; y en el "ejército de las Tres Garantías". El Plan contemplaba respetar "personas y propiedades" y los "fueros y propiedades" de la Iglesia. Finalmente, Iturbide resumía el proyecto independentista en "unión, fraternidad, orden, quietud interior, vigilancia y horror a cualquier movimiento turbulento".

PLAN DE LA NORIA ◆ Documento redactado y publicado por Porfirio

Firmantes del Plan de la Noria caricaturizados por Villasana en *La Orquesta* en 1871

Díaz, en los primeros días de noviembre de 1871, en su hacienda de La Noria, en Oaxaca, después de que el Congreso de la Unión hubiera declarado presidente de la República, por tercera ocasión consecutiva, a Benito Juárez, a quien este plan acusaba de haber convertido al Congreso "en una cámara cortesana, obsequiosa y resuelta siempre a seguir los impulsos del Ejecutivo"; de someter a los gobiernos locales al poder presidencial; y de haber "abajado y envilecido" al ejército, "obligándolo a servir de instrumento de odiososas violencias contra la libertad de sufragio". Para Díaz, las dificultades económicas del gobierno juarista se debían a "la ineptitud de unos, el favoritismo de otros y la corrupción de todos" los miembros del equipo gobernante, pues según el texto, las "rentas federales (.) deberían haber bastado para el pago de las obligaciones contraídas en la última guerra, así como para fundar el crédito de la Nación cubriendo el rédito de la deuda interior y exterior legítimamente reconocida". Por tales motivos, así como por la intolerancia gubernamental para con los antiguos conservadores e imperialistas, era que Díaz, "requerido (.) instado, exigido por numerosos y acreditados patriotas de todos los Estados", se lanzaba a la lucha armada. Poco después, afirmaba que combatiría "por la causa del pueblo, y el pueblo será el único dueño de su victoria. 'Constitución de 57 y libertad electoral' será nuestra bandera; 'menos gobierno y más libertades' nuestro programa". En la parte final del documento, Díaz se manifestaba por la elección directa de presidente de la República, en contra de la injerencia del Congreso en la designación de funcionarios del Ejecutivo, por el funcionamiento de jurados populares, por la libertad de los ayuntamientos y por la desaparición de las alcabalas. "Que ningún ciudadano se perpetúe en el ejercicio del poder, y ésta será la última revolución", concluía el plan.

PLAN DE SAN LUIS POTOSÍ ◆ Programa lanzado por Francisco I. Madero el 5 de octubre de 1910 en la capital de San Luis Potosí, ciudad a la que el gobierno de Porfirio Díaz lo había confinado desde junio de ese año, unos días antes de las elecciones generales. En el documento, Madero se mostraba convencido de que el pueblo mexicano se hallaba en uno de esos momentos en que era necesario "realizar los mayores sacrificios", pues la tiranía del presidente Díaz, "tiranía a la que no estamos acostumbrados los mexicanos (.) ha llegado a ser insoportable". Para Madero, no importaba que Díaz se vanagloriara de haber conseguido un largo periodo de paz, porque ésta "no tiene por base el derecho, sino la fuerza; porque no tiene por objeto el engrandecimiento y prosperidad de la Patria, sino enriquecer a un pequeño grupo", al que se debía que "la división de poderes, la soberanía de los Estados, la libertad de los Ayuntamientos y los derechos del ciudadano" sólo existieran "escritos en nuestra Carta Magna". En realidad, señalaba el texto, "en México casi puede decirse que reina constantemente la Ley Marcial", lo que permitió a Díaz, quien "ha demostrado que el principal móvil que lo guía es mantenerse en el poder y a toda costa", controlar durante un tercio de siglo la creciente oposición que se le enfrentaba, pero cuando intentó imponer a Ramón Corral como su sucesor, un gran número de personas "nos lanzamos a la lucha, intentando reconquistar la soberanía del pueblo". A continuación, Madero relataba la formación del Partido Nacional Antirreeleccionista, la campaña presidencial de 1909-10, su detención, la votación general de julio de 1910, el fraude electoral y la solicitud de anulación de los comicios. "El poder público no puede tener otro origen ni otra base que la voluntad nacional" y, decía Madero, "si se hubieran respetado" los "derechos electorales, hubiese sido yo electo para la Presidencia de la República". Por eso mismo, "con la virilidad del patriota resuelto a sacrificarse", declaraba nulas las elecciones, asumía provisionalmente el gobierno y, "para arrojar del poder a los audaces usurpadores", anunciaba que "el día 20 de noviembre, desde las seis de la tarde en adelante, todos los ciudadanos de la República tomarán las armas para arrojar del poder a las autoridades que actualmente gobiernan". Para conseguir la adhesión de los campesinos, en el artículo tercero del plan decía que "siendo de toda justicia restituir a sus antiguos poseedores los terrenos de que se les despojó" de modo arbitrario, "se declaran sujetas a revisión" las disposiciones amparadas en la ley de terrenos baldíos.

MANIFIESTO A LA NACION

Sufragio Efectivo. No-Reelección.

Facsímil del Plan de San Luis

PLAN DE TACUBAYA ◆ Pronunciamiento formulado por Félix Zuloaga el 17 de diciembre de 1857 en el municipio de Tacubaya, Distrito Federal, en nombre de la guarnición militar de la ciudad de México. El escueto manifiesto aseguraba que "la mayoría de los pueblos no ha quedado satisfecha con la Carta fundamental que le dieran sus mandatarios, porque ella no ha sabido hermanar el progreso con el orden y la libertad (.) Que la República necesita de instituciones análogas a sus usos y costumbres" y que "la fuerza armada no debe sostener lo que la Nación no quiere, y sí ser la defensa y apoyo de la voluntad pública", por lo que los sublevados determinaban que a partir de ese momento "cesará de regir en la República la Constitución de 1857". El documento reconocía que la elección de Ignacio Comonfort había "expresado" el "voto unánime de los pueblos", y disponían que siguiera encargado del Poder Ejecutivo, ahora con "facultades omnímodas" y con la misión de convocar a un "Congreso Extraordinario sin más objeto que el de formar una Constitución que sea conforme con la voluntad nacional y garantice los verdaderos intereses de los pueblos". Ese mismo día el presidente Comonfort se adhirió al documento y poco después se unieron los gobiernos de Puebla, Tlaxcala, Veracruz, México, Chiapas, Tabasco y San Luis Potosí y las guarniciones de Cuernavaca, Mazatlán y Tampico. A juicio de los alzados, Comonfort "adoptó un sistema de vacilación que ha puesto en alarma a cuantos lo secundaron, haciendo desconfiar de las promesas que hizo", por lo cual el 11 de enero de 1858, el plan fue modificado, "eliminando al Excmo. Sr. Comonfort del mando supremo de la Nación y proclamando como general en jefe del Ejército regenerador al Sr. general D. Félix Zuloaga, quien está decidido a salvar a la patria, conservando su religión, la incoluminidad del ejército y las garantías de los mexicanos". Bajo la firma del general J. de la Parra, se prometía que "restablecido el orden, se procederá desde luego a la organización del Poder Ejecutivo, nombrándose un presidente interino de la República por una junta compuesta de un representante por cada Departamento, nombrada por el expresado general en jefe".

La villa de Tacubaya a principios del siglo xx

PLAN DE TANTOYUCA ☛ *Tantoyuca.*

PLAN DE TUXTEPEC Documento redactado a fines de 1875 o principios de 1876 por los porfiristas Vicente Riva Palacio, Ireneo Paz y Protasio Tagle. Para los redactores, en el gobierno de Sebastián Lerdo de Tejada "el sufragio político se ha convertido en un farsa (.), la soberanía de los Estados es vulnerada repetidas veces (.), el tesoro público es dilapidado en gastos de placer (.), la administración de justicia se encuentra en la mayor prostitución (.), el poder municipal ha desaparecido completamente" y "la educación pública se encuentra abandonada". Los autores del texto acusaban al presidente Lerdo de haberse "rodeado de presidiarios y asesinos" y lo criticaban por haber segregado al cantón de Tepic del estado de Jalisco, por retirar a los estados fronterizos la "subvención que les servía para defensa de los indios bárbaros", por entregar el país a los ingleses "con la concesión del Ferrocarril de Veracruz y el escandaloso convenio de las tarifas", por pactar "el reconocimiento de la enorme deuda inglesa" y haber "acordado vender tal deuda a los Estados Unidos, lo cual equivale a vender el país a la nación vecina". Ante esto, decían los secuaces de Porfirio Díaz, "levantamos el estandarte de guerra". Asimismo, declaraban nula la elección presidencial de Lerdo. La parte final del documento

El Plan de Tuxtepec según *El Ahuizote*, en 1876

se ocupaba en establecer que "Son Leyes Supremas de la República la Constitución de 1857, el Acta de Reformas promulgada el 25 de septiembre de 1873 y la ley de 1874"; que el principio de no reelección también tendría el carácter de "Ley Suprema". Anunciaban que Porfirio Díaz sería el comandante en jefe de las fuerzas implicadas en el movimiento golpista, a las que ponían el nombre de "Ejército Regenerador". Prometían que, una vez triunfante la insurrección, la Presidencia de la República recaería en la persona elegida por una convención de gobernadores sublevados. El documento fue proclamado el 10 de enero de 1876 en la Villa de Ojitlán, municipio de San Lucas Ojitlán, distrito de Tuxtepec, Oaxaca, por un grupo de militares encabezados por el coronel Hermenegildo Sarmiento. Sin embargo, existe otra versión del plan que está firmada por el propio Díaz y fechada en diciembre de 1875, que no incluye tres de los artículos del otro, de los cuales el más importante es el nombramiento de Díaz como jefe de la insurrección. En marzo de 1876, cuando el alzamiento antilerdista comenzaba a propagarse, Díaz anunció una reforma al documento, consistente en establecer que a la caída del gobierno, el "Poder Ejecutivo, sin más atribuciones que las administrativas, se depositará, mientras se hacen elecciones, en el presidente de la Suprema Corte de Justicia (.), siempre que (.) acepte en todas sus partes el presente plan", pero que de no aceptar tal funcionario judicial, se "investirá al jefe de las armas con el carácter de jefe del Ejecutivo". Estas modificaciones a la primera versión del escrito, así como una proclama redactada por Díaz, fueron publicadas por los rebeldes el 21 de marzo de 1876 en la población de Palo Alto, Tamaulipas, y se conocen como Plan de Palo Alto.

PLAN DE VERACRUZ Proclama que lanzaron el 6 de diciembre de 1822 Guadalupe Victoria y Antonio López de Santa Anna, poco después de que éste fuera destituido como comandante militar de Veracruz. El plan era complemento de una proclama y de un manifiesto que los mismos firmantes habían publicado en los primeros días de diciembre. El colombiano Miguel de Santa María redactó los tres documentos. Los citados generales acusaban de tirano al emperador Agustín de Iturbide por la disolución del Congreso Constituyente y aseguraban que el "voto general de la Nación (estaba) por el sistema de República". Los pronunciados aseguraban que respetarían los fueros militar y eclesiástico, promoverían la "unión" entre españoles y mexicanos y, para efectos de gobierno mientras se promulgara una constitución, utilizarían la Constitución de Cádiz. En los primeros días de enero de 1823, los dos principales veteranos de la insurgencia, Vicente Guerrero y Nicolás Bravo, se sumaron a la insurrección, pero a fines de ese mes fueron derrotados por los generales imperialistas Luis Cortázar, José Antonio Echávarri y José María Lobato, con lo que los republicanos quedaron reducidos al puerto de Veracruz. Sin embargo, los enviados de Iturbide desertaron el 24 de enero y el 1 de febrero de 1823 firmaron con Santa Anna el Acta de Casa Mata, más conocido como Plan de Casa Mata (☛).

PLANCARTE Y NAVARRETE, FRANCISCO ◆ n. en Zamora, Mich., y m. en Monterrey, NL (1856-1920). Sacerdote ordenado en 1880. Doctor en filosofía, teología y derecho canónico en la Universidad Gregoriana de Roma. Fue delegado de la Sección Arqueológica a la Exposición de Madrid (1892), obispo de Campeche (1896-98) y Cuernavaca (1899-11) y arzobispo de Monterrey (1912-20). Autor de *Apuntes para la geografía del estado de Morelos* (1909) y *Temoanchan* (1911). Póstumamente apareció su *Prehistoria de México* (1923).

PLANCK HINOJOSA, CARLOS ◆ n. en el DF (1942). Licenciado en derecho por la UNAM (1966) y maestro en ciencias por la Universidad de Cornell (1970); realizó estudios en la Facultad de Filosofía y Letras de la UNAM (1962 y 1969), en la McGill University de Canadá (1964), en el Centro Interamericano de Estudios de Seguridad Social (1968) y en la Universidad de California en Berkeley (1970). Profesor del Instituto Matías Romero de Estudios Internacionales, de El Colegio de México y de la Universidad Anáhuac. Miembro del PRI. Ha sido jefe de Relaciones Laborales del IMSS (1965-69), jefe del Departamento de Relaciones Internacionales de la Secretaría del Trabajo (1971-72), secretario particular del director general de la Siderúrgica Lázaro Cárdenas (1972-75), subdirector general de Documentación e Informe Presidencial de la Secretaría de la Presidencia (1975-77), director general de Organismos Económicos Internacionales de la Secretaría de Hacienda (1977-81), director de Relaciones Internacionales del INBA (1981-82), cónsul general en Barcelona (1983-86) y embajador mexicano en Panamá (1986-88).

PLANK, CARLOS ◆ n. en Baroyeca, Son. (1876-1927). Comerciante en su juventud, en 1910 se afilió al Partido Nacional Antirreeleccionista y fue diputado local en 1911. Carrancista desde 1913, combatió contra José María Maytorena al lado de Plutarco Elías Calles y, a las órdenes de Álvaro Obregón, contra la División del Norte, en 1915. Fue director de la penitenciaría del Distrito Federal, jefe de la gendarmería fiscal de Sonora, diputado federal (1917-19), senador de la República (1919-22) y uno de los firmantes del Plan de Agua Prieta (1920).

PLATA, MANUEL M. ◆ n. en Toluca, Edo. de Méx., y m. en el DF (1855-1926). Egresado del Colegio Militar como teniente (1872-76), combatió a los rebeldes tuxtepecanos en Puebla, Morelos y Tlaxcala. Fue miembro del Cuerpo de Ingenieros del Distrito Federal (1877-78) y de la Comisión Geográfica Exploradora (1881-85); subdirector del Colegio Militar (1885), diputado federal (1897-99), brigadier desde 1891, jefe militar de Puebla, León y Chihuahua; y subsecretario de Guerra y Marina en el gabinete de Francisco I. Madero (1911-13). En 1912 fue ascendido a divisionario. Al producirse el golpe de Estado de Victoriano Huerta se retiró a la vida privada.

PLATAS, FERNANDO ◆ n. en el DF (1973). Clavadista. Ha hecho estudios de administración de empresas. Especializado en trampolín de tres metros y plataforma, ha obtenido la medalla de oro en plataforma de 10 metros y la medalla de bronce en saltos sincronizados en el Campeonato Mundial, y el tercer lugar en el Grand Prix de Sidney, Australia.

FOTO: EIKON

Fernando Platas

PLATÓN SÁNCHEZ ◆ Municipio de Veracruz situado en el noroeste del estado, al noroeste de Tuxpan, en los límites con Hidalgo. Superficie: 227.84 km^2. Habitantes: 18,229, de los cuales 4,322 forman la población económicamente activa. Hablan alguna lengua indígena 5,808 personas mayores de cinco años (náhuatl 5,800). Indígenas monolingües: 295.

PLAYA COLORADA ◆ Bahía de Sinaloa situada entre la península de Perihuete y las islas Garrapata y Saliaca. Se comunica con la bahía de Santa María y el estero de Altamura por el canal de Perihuete.

PLAYA VICENTE ◆ Municipio de Veracruz situado en el sur del estado, al suroeste de Coatzacoalcos, en los límites con Oaxaca. Superficie: 2,122.14 km^2. Habitantes: 52,754, de los cuales 12,843 forman la población económicamente activa. Hablan alguna lengua indígena 16,759 personas mayores de cinco años (zapoteco 8,214, mazateco 4,557, chinanteco 2,084 y mixteco 1,225). Indígenas monolingües: 512.

PLAYAS DEL ROSARITO ◆ Municipio de Baja California ubicado entre Tijuana y Ensenada, en el litoral del océano Pacífico. Habitantes: 46,596. Hablan alguna lengua indígena 519 personas mayores de cinco años (purépecha 230).

PLAZA, ANTONIO ◆ n. en San Juan del Llano, Gto., y m. en la ciudad de México (1833-1882). Militar. Combatió contra los conservadores durante la guerra de los Tres Años. Luchó contra la intervención francesa y el imperio. En 1862 fue ascendido a teniente coronel. Autor de poesía: *A María, la del cielo,*

Amor ideal, Es, Dos entierros, Amistad, La voz del inválido y *Álbum del corazón.*

Plaza de la Constitución ◆ ☛ *Zócalo.*

Plaza Mayor ◆ ☛ *Zócalo.*

Pliego Arenas, Humberto ◆ n. en Nogales, Ver. (1932). Profesor por la Escuela Nacional de Maestros (1954), profesor de biología por la Escuela Normal Superior (1961) y licenciado en filosofía por la UNAM (1963). Miembro del PPS desde 1958, a cuyo Comité Directivo y Central pertenece. Profesor de primaria (1955-61), secundaria (1961-72) y normal (1963-72). En el SNTE ha sido secretario auxiliar en la sección IX (1962), secretario de educación sindical en la sección X (1974) y secretario de relaciones internacionales del CEN (1977-81). Diputado federal (1979-82) y representante plurinominal a la primera Asamblea del Distrito Federal (1988-91). Vicepresidente de la Federación Internacional Sindical de Educadores (1979-81).

Foto: Reforma

Salvador Pliego

Pliego Montes, Salvador ◆ n. en Morelia, Mich., y m. en el DF (1920-1994). Licenciado en derecho por la UNAM (1944). Profesor de la Escuela de Policía (1939-40). Perteneció al PRI. Dedicado desde 1944 a la abogacía, fue director general de Asuntos Jurídicos de la Secretaría de Industria y Comercio (1970-76), titular de la Procuraduría Federal del Consumidor (1976-88) y procurador social del Departamento del Distrito Federal (1989-90). Fue miembro de la Barra Mexicana de Abogados.

PLM ◆ ☛ *Partido Liberal Mexicano.*

Plongeon, Augustus le ◆ n. en Inglaterra y m. en EUA (?-¿1908?). Arqueólogo. En 1849 construyó la población californiana de Marysville. Hizo dos viajes de exploración a Yucatán (1873 y 1875), en el primero de los cuales descubrió el Chac Mool de Chichen Itzá, que dejó en la ciudad maya. En 1877 entabló un juicio contra el gobierno mexicano para obtener el monolito, que había sido donado al Museo Nacional de México por el gobierno yucateco, pero los tribunales fallaron en su contra. Autor de *Archaeological Communication on Yucatán* (1878), *Ensayo sobre la antigüedad de la lengua maya* (1880), *Vestiges of the Mayas* (1881) y *Mayapan and Maya Inscriptions* (1881). Su esposa, Alice Dixson de le Plongeon, quien lo acompañó en sus exploraciones, publicó *Notes on Yucatán* (1878) y *Here and There in Yucatán* (1889).

Pluma Hidalgo ◆ Municipio de Oaxaca situado en el sur del estado, al norte de Puerto Ángel. Superficie: 179.89 km^2. Habitantes: 3,442, de los cuales 1,232 forman la población económicamente activa. Hablan alguna lengua indígena 157 personas mayores de cinco años (zapoteco 106). El municipio pertenece al distrito judicial de Pochutla.

Plumb, Edward L. ◆ n. en EUA (1826-?). Llegó a México en 1854 como agente de la Mexican Pacific Coal & Iron Mining and Land Company. En 1860 fue a Veracruz, como agente de un banco neoyorquino, para arreglar el pago a México convenido por el Tratado McLane-Ocampo. Trabajó en la legación estadounidense en México y durante la intervención francesa y el imperio fue agente del gobierno de Benito Juárez en Estados Unidos. Al triunfo de la República fue encargado de negocios de su país en México (1867-68). En 1882 era director y vicepresidente de la Mexican International Railroad.

Plural ◆ Revista mensual de letras y artes publicada en el Distrito Federal por la casa Excélsior. El primer número apareció en octubre de 1971, bajo la dirección de Octavio Paz. Éste y los colaboradores dejaron la revista el 8 de julio de 1976 y fundaron *Vuelta* (☛). Entre los colaboradores de la primera época se contaron José de la Colina, Salvador Elizondo, Alejandro Rossi, Juan García Ponce, Tomás Segovia, Jorge Alberto Manrique, Gabriel Zaid, Elena Poniatowska y Carlos Fuentes. En diciembre de 1976 se reanudó la aparición de este órgano con Jaime Labastida como director. En la segunda época han colaborado, entre otros, los escritores mexicanos Eraclio Zepeda, Elva Macías, Juan Bañuelos, Jaime Augusto Shelley, Óscar Oliva, René Avilés Fabila y José Agustín, así como numerosos autores de diversos países latinoamericanos.

Revista *Plural*

PMS ◆ ☛ *Partido Mexicano Socialista.*

PMT ◆ ☛ *Partido Mexicano de los Trabajadores.*

PNR ◆ ☛ *Partido Nacional Revolucionario.*

Poanas ◆ Municipio de Durango situado en el oriente del estado, en los límites con Zacatecas, al este de la capital estatal. Superficie: 1,841 km^2. Habitantes: 26,414, de los cuales 6,193 forman la población económicamente activa. Hablan alguna lengua indígena siete personas mayores de cinco años. La cabecera municipal es Villa Unión.

Poanas ◆ Río de Durango. Nace en la sierra de Santa María, entra al valle de Poanas y recibe a los ríos Súchil y Graceros. Se une al Tunal para formar el San Pedro o Mezquital.

Población ◆ Hacia 1521, el actual territorio mexicano estaba ocupado por más de 600 grupos indígenas que comprendían desde los grupos de cazadores y recolectores nómadas hasta las grandes culturas, entre las cuales sobresalían los Estados azteca y tarasco, pues para entonces los mayas se habían disgregado en pequeños señoríos. A la llegada de los españoles, se calcula que en el México central había 25 millones de habitantes. Como efecto de la violencia, las epidemias, el hambre y la sobreexplotación, para 1548, la población indígena se había reducido a 6,300,000 y en 1605 a sólo 1,075,000 personas. Cortés llegó con 1,500 europeos a Tenochtitlan y en 1546 la población blanca y mestiza era de 125,000 personas. En 1560 había en México 20,211 españoles y 16,147 esclavos de origen africano. A mediados del siglo XVII, negros y mulatos oficialmente eran ya 135,000, pero los datos son poco confiables porque para entonces existían núcleos de cimarrones en varias partes del país, sobre todo en Veracruz y Guerrero. Pese a la rígida división racial, que llegó al extremo de poner en los juzgados pinturas en las que se mostraba a las diversas castas, el mestizaje se intensificó hasta diluir totalmente la sangre negra en la población mexicana. De acuerdo con el historiador Enrique Semo, "la proporción total de europeos, criollos, mestizos y castas dentro de la población total era en 1570 de 0.7 por ciento, en 1646 de 18 por ciento (y) en 1742 de 27 por ciento". El primer censo más o menos confiable fue el ordenado por el virrey Revillagigedo, que para 1793 arrojó como resultado una población de 4,483,529 habitantes, cifra que Humboldt, por diversas consideraciones, elevó a 5,200,000 para 1794, en tanto que estimó la población total de 1803 en seis millones y medio de habitantes. De acuerdo con el Tribunal del Consulado, en 1803 el número de pobladores de México era de 5,764,731 y, según la *Memoria sobre la población del Reino de Nueva España*, en 1810 había 6,122,354 personas. Para 1820 existía una estimación, sin Colima ni California, que arrojaba la cifra de 6,204,000, lo que mostraba la tendencia estacionaria de los años de guerra civil. En 1827, Henry George Ward estimó en 8,000,000 el número total de habitantes de la República, aunque otros cálculos no llegaron a esa cifra en varias décadas. Orozco y Berra consideró que en 1854 la población era de 7,853,395, cifra muy próxima a la realidad, pues de acuerdo con datos censales, en 1856 México tenía 7,859,564 habitantes. Para 1861, García Cubas calculó la población del país en 8,174,400. De acuerdo con el mismo estudioso, en 1870 había 8,782,198 mexicanos, cifra que ajustó dos años después, basado en datos oficiales, para dejarla en 9,141,661. Estimaciones de extranjeros para los años de 1880 y 1882 ponían el total de población en nueve y 10 millones de habitantes, respectivamente. Más confiable fue la *Memoria* de la Secretaría de Fomento, que fijó en 10,879,398 el número de mexicanos en 1885. La siguiente cifra oficial, para 1893, estableció que el país estaba poblado por 11,994,347 individuos. Los datos censales dan los siguientes resultados: los habitantes de México eran 12,632,427 en 1895; 13,607,272 en 1900; 15,160,369 en 1910; 14,334,780 en 1921; 16,552,722 en 1930; 19,653,552 en 1940; 25,791,017 en 1950;

POBLACIÓN DE MÉXICO

AÑO	HABITANTES	AÑO	HABITANTES
1518	25,000,000	1845	7,263,246
1519	18,000,000	1855	7,515,538
1532	16,800,000	1865	8,105,443
1548	6,300,000	1875	8,183,705
1568	2,650,000	1885	9,568,408
1580	1,900,000	1895	11,347,625
1605	1,075,000	1900	13,607,259
1646	1,712,615	1910	15,160,369
1742	2,477,277	1921	14,334,780
1790	4,636,074	1930	16,552,722
1793	3,799,561	1940	19,653,552
1795	5,200,000	1950	25,791,017
1803	5,837,100	1960	34,923,129
1808	6,000,000	1970	48,225,238
1810	6,122,354	1980	66,846,833
1820	6,204,000	1990	81,249,645
1825	6,218,343	1995	91,158,290
1835	6,174,875	1997	93,716,332

GRUPO ETARIO	1990			1997		
	MUJERES	VARONES	TOTAL	MUJERES	VARONES	TOTAL
0 a 4	5,035,176	5,160,002	10,195,178	5,268,568	5,441,320	10,709,888
5 a 9	5,223,949	5,338,285	10,562,234	5,506,274	5,612,499	11,118,773
10 a 14	5,158,434	5,230,658	10,389,092	5,374,249	5,466,368	10,840,617
15 a 19	4,904,511	4,759,892	9,664,403	5,067,327	4,970,642	10,037,969
20 a 24	4,091,035	3,738,128	7,829,163	4,784,169	4,445,492	9,229,661
25 a 29	3,353,917	3,050,595	6,404,512	4,094,930	3,628,950	7,723,880
30 a 34	2,808,883	2,578,736	5,387,619	3,527,631	3,082,686	6,610,317
35 a 39	2,368,551	2,210,565	4,579,116	3,140,781	2,862,994	6,003,775
40 a 44	1,792,757	1,705,013	3,497,770	2,517,816	2,274,305	4,792,121
45 a 49	1,519,287	1,452,573	2,971,860	2,048,721	1,873,527	3,922,248
50 a 54	1,231,916	1,161,875	2,393,791	1,602,584	1,542,584	3,145,168
55 a 59	975,620	918,864	1,894,484	1,400,036	1,230,713	2,630,749
60 a 64	841,400	769,917	1,611,317	1,221,724	1,065,835	2,287,559
>65	1,798,033	1,578,808	3,376,841	2,469,004	2,164,118	4,633,122
NO ESPECIFICADO	252,207	240,058	492,265	8,527	21,958	30,485
Total	41,355,676	39,893,969	81,249,645	48,032,341	45,683,991	93,716,332

Fuente: INEGI

34,923,129 en 1960; 48,225,238 en 1970 y 66,846,833 en 1980. La población total de México en 1990 se estimaba en 86,154,000 habitantes y en 1995 se calculó en 91,158,290 personas y en 1997, en 93,716,332. En 1997 había en México 48,032,341 mujeres y 45,683,991 hombres.

POCHUTLA ◆ ☛ *San Pedro Pochutla.*

POCM ◆ ☛ *Partido Obrero Campesino Mexicano.*

PODER EJECUTIVO ◆ El Plan de Iguala establecía que "ínterin se reúnen las Cortes que hagan efectivo este plan", habría una junta en la que recaería la autoridad. Ésta, de acuerdo con los Tratados de Córdoba, se llamaría Junta Provisional Gubernativa y estaría encargada de nombrar "una regencia compuesta de tres personas, de su seno o fuera de él, en quien resida el Poder Ejecutivo y que gobierne en nombre del monarca hasta que éste empuñe el cetro del imperio". El Poder Legislativo, en tanto se reunían las Cortes (Congreso), sería ejercido por la Junta, "para que ambos (poderes) no recaigan en una misma autoridad". El Congreso, una vez en funciones, ratificó que "interinamente" el Ejecutivo recaería en la regencia. Según el *Reglamento Provisional Político del Imperio Mexicano*, "El poder ejecutivo reside exclusivamente en el Emperador, como jefe supremo del Estado" y "sólo sus ministros son responsables de los actos de su gobierno". En 1823, luego de la abdicación de Iturbide, el Congreso encargó el Poder Ejecutivo a un triunvirato formado por Nicolás Bravo, Guadalupe Victoria y Pedro Celestino Negrete. La Constitución de 1824 estableció el "Supremo Poder Ejecutivo", que se depositaría "en un solo individuo que se denominará Presidente de los Estados Unidos Mexicanos"; creó el cargo de vicepresidente y estableció que sería de cuatro años el periodo presidencial, con posibilidad de reelección "al cuarto año de haber cesado en sus funciones". Para ser presidente o vicepresidente se requería ser mexicano por nacimiento, de 35 años cumplidos al tiempo de la elección y residente en el país. Para la elección, cada uno de los congresos locales escogería, "a mayoría de votos", a dos ciudadanos, uno de los cuales no debía ser vecino de la entidad de que se tratara. Las legislaturas enviarían sus resultados al consejo de gobierno (hoy comisión permanente) del Congreso de la Unión, el que efectuaría el escrutinio. "El que reuniere la mayoría absoluta de los votos de las legislaturas será el presidente". En caso de muerte, renuncia o ausencia del presidente, el vicepresidente debería asumir el Ejecutivo. Una semana después de promulgada la Constitución de 1824, Guadalupe Victoria asumió el Poder Ejecutivo. En 1828 el Congreso declaró presidente a Manuel Gómez Pedraza, pero el Plan de Perote impugnó esta elección y logró que el Congreso nombrara a Vicente Guerrero, quien asumió el Poder Ejecutivo en 1829. Ese año Guerrero salió a combatir a Anastasio Bustamante y José María Bocanegra fue presidente interino. La rebelión del Plan de Jalapa destituyó a Bocanegra y entregó el Ejecutivo a un triunvirato formado por Pedro Vélez, Lucas Alamán y Luis Quintanar, quienes en 1830 entregaron el poder al vicepresidente Anastasio Bustamante. En 1832 Bustamante salió a combatir a Antonio López de Santa Anna y el Ejecutivo quedó en manos de Melchor Múzquiz; la sublevación de Santa Anna llevó a Gómez Pedraza a la presidencia, en la que se mantuvo hasta 1833. Para el siguiente periodo fueron elegidos Santa Anna como presidente y Valentín Gómez Farías como vicepresidente. Se alternaron en la presidencia cuatro veces cada uno hasta que en 1835 el Congreso destituyó a Gómez Farías y nombró a Miguel Barragán, quien murió en ese año y fue sustituido por José Justo Corro, el que publicó las *Bases Constitucionales* de 1835, las que establecían que "el ejercicio del Poder Ejecutivo residirá en un presidente de elección popular indirecta y periódica, mexicano por nacimiento". Las *Siete Leyes* de 1836 crearon el "Supremo Poder Conservador", encargado de sostener "el equilibrio constitucional entre los poderes sociales, manteniendo o restableciendo el orden constitucional en los casos en que fuere turbado". La cuarta ley del mismo ordenamiento centralista, señalaba que "El ejercicio del Poder Ejecutivo se deposita en un supremo magistrado, que se denominará *Presidente de la República*; durará ocho años". El presidente "en junta del Consejo y ministros", el Senado y la alta Corte de Justicia eliegirían "cada uno una terna de individuos" que debían pasar el mismo día a la Cámara de Diputados, la que escogería tres de los incluidos en dichas ternas "y remitirá la terna resultante a todas las juntas departamentales", cada una de las cuales seleccionaría a uno de los ciudadanos incluidos. El nombre del escogido debía ser enviado a la Cámara de Diputados que, en sesión conjunta con el Senado,

Vicente Guerrero, presidente en 1829

Valentín Gómez Farías, presidente en 1833

"declarará presidente al que hubiera obtenido mayor número de votos, y en caso de igualdad al que designe la suerte, verificándose el sorteo y todo lo demás en la misma sesión". Las *Siete Leyes* permitían la reelección, sujeta a condiciones que aseguraran una amplia mayoría. Como fuera suprimido el cargo de vicepresidente, "En las faltas temporales del Presidente de la República, gobernarará el Presidente del Consejo". Este órgano se componía de 13 individuos, "dos de los cuales serán eclesiásticos, dos militares y el resto de las demás clases de la sociedad". Los miembros del consejo de gobierno

Antonio López de Santa Anna ocupó nueve veces el poder ejecutivo

serían elegidos por el Presidente de la República de una lista de 39 ciudadanos presentada por el Congreso. En 1837, Anastasio Bustamante fue elegido presidente. En 1839, por licencia de Bustamante, Santa Anna y Nicolás Bravo se encargaron interinamente del Ejecutivo; Bustamante volvió ese año a la presidencia, en la que permaneció hasta 1841, cuando fue sustituido por Javier Echeverría. Ese año el Congreso nombró presidente a Santa Anna quien entregó el poder a Nicolás Bravo, para retomarlo en 1843. Durante su gestión sancionó las *Bases Orgánicas*, que en su artículo 83 establecían que "El Supremo Poder Ejecutivo se deposita en un magistrado, que se denominará Presidente de la República. Este magistrado durará

Ignacio Comonfort, presidente de 1855 a 1858

cinco años en sus funciones". Para ocupar ese cargo se requería ser mexicano por nacimiento, "ciudadano en ejercicio de sus derechos, mayor de cuarenta años y residir en el territorio de la República al tiempo de la elección", así como pertenecer al estado secular. Cada asamblea departamental elegiría a una persona y enviaría el resultado a la Cámara de Diputados, la que en sesión conjunta con el Senado declararía presidente de la República a quien hubiera reunido mayoría absoluta de sufragios de los emitidos por las juntas. Si ninguno reuniera mayoría absoluta, se elegiría de entre los dos con mayor número de votos. En caso de empate se haría nueva votación de los congresistas y, de repetirse el caso, se procedería sacar al ganador por sorteo. Santa Anna entregó el Ejecutivo a Valentín Canalizo y un año después ocupó y abandonó de nuevo la presidencia; fue suplido por José Joaquín de Herrera y Valentín Canalizo; este último fue desconocido por el Congreso (al igual que Santa Anna) y Herrera se encargó otra vez del Ejecutivo. A fines de 1845 Mariano Paredes y Arrillaga dio un golpe de Estado y asumió la presidencia en enero de 1846. En ese año lo sustituyó Nicolás Bravo, en su calidad de vicepresidente; éste fue derrocado por José Mariano Salas, quien asumió la presidencia y decretó el restablecimiento de la Constitución de 1824. Asimismo, convocó a un Congreso con facultades constituyentes y legislativas, órgano que sancionó el *Acta Constitutiva y de Reformas* a la Norma de 1824. El *Acta* derogaba el cargo de vicepresidente, hacía responsable directo al Presidente de los delitos comunes que cometiera y "de los de oficio" siempre que el "acto en el cual consisten" no estuviera firmado por el secretario del ramo. Se preveía la reglamentación de los procesos comiciales de acuerdo con la Constitución, "pudiendo adoptarse la elección directa". Reunido el Congreso, designó a Santa Anna y a Gómez Farías presidente y vicepresidente, respectivamente. Como de costumbre, el primero se ausentó y dejó el poder a Gómez Farías. Un año después, Gómez Farías entregó el Ejecutivo a Santa Anna, quien lo abandonó poco después. El Congreso desconoció al vicepresidente y encargó la jefatura del Estado a Pedro María Anaya. El mismo año regresó Santa Anna a la presidencia, pero la derrota frente al ejército estadounidense lo obligó a dimitir. Con Querétaro como sede de los poderes federales, el Ejecutivo recayó en Manuel de la Peña y Peña, presidente de la Suprema Corte, quien lo entregó al

Benito Juárez, presidente de México (1858-1872)

Miguel Miramón, ocupó el poder ejecutivo en 1859

presidente sustituto nombrado por el Congreso: Anaya. En 1848 Peña y Peña volvió a asumir la presidencia y, con el país ocupado por los invasores estadounidenses, reunió al Congreso para que ratificara el Tratado de Guadalupe, lo que logró después de acalorados debates. Ese año fue electo presidente José Joaquín de Herrera, quien trasladó la sede a la ciudad de México. En 1851 lo relevó Mariano Arista, quien renunció el 5 de enero de 1853. Lo sustituyó Juan Bautista Ceballos, presidente de la Suprema Corte, quien disolvió el Congreso. Desplazado Ceballos del Ejecutivo por la asonada del Plan del Hospicio, una junta militar, el 7 de febrero de 1853, nombró presidente interino al general Manuel María Lombardini. Representantes de las principales fuerzas políticas llamaron a Santa Anna, a quien las legislaturas locales eligieron presidente el 17 de marzo. El 20 de abril asumió el Poder Ejecutivo el hombre de Manga de Clavo, quien tres días después puso en vigor unas *Bases para la administración de la República*, redactadas por Lucas Alamán, mediante las cuales Santa Anna se autoinvistió de plenos poderes, suspendida como estaba la Constitución y en espera de que, en 12 meses, un Congreso expidiera el nuevo ordenamiento que habría de constituir al país. Los estados fueron convertidos en departamentos, se suprimieron las legislaturas locales y se centralizó tanto el poder político como la administración pública. Por orden del presidente, el Ministerio de Gobernación dispuso que, en cada departamento, el 1 de diciembre de 1854 se celebrara una "junta popular", encabezada por el gobernador respectivo y con asistencia de los comandantes generales y otras autoridades, con el fin de que los ciudadanos dijeran si deseaban que Santa Anna continuase en el poder "con las mismas amplias facultades". Como tales reuniones se efectuaron bajo riguroso control gubernamental, el gobierno anunció que se habían prorrogado indefinidamente los poderes dictatoriales y constitucionales de Santa Anna, quien ocho meses después, el 9 de agosto de 1855, fue derrocado por la rebelión del Plan de Ayutla. La guarnición de la capital se adhirió a última hora al Plan de Ayutla y el comandante en jefe, Rómulo Díaz de la Vega, designó a los integrantes de una junta con supuestos representantes de los departamentos y territorios, la cual nombró presidente a Martín Carrera, quien ocupó el cargo del 15 de agosto al 13 de septiembre e integró su gabinete con destacados santanistas. Desplazado Carrera por la oficialidad que se hallaba en la capital, ésta eligió a Rómulo Díaz de la Vega como general en jefe de la ciudad de México y en esa calidad se encargó del Poder Ejecutivo de la Nación, para lo cual aclaró en una proclama que lo hacía para imponer el orden en la capital mientras arribaban los caudillos de la insurrección de Ayutla, el principal de los cuales, Juan Álvarez, llegó a Cuernavaca el 1 de octubre y ahí designó una junta de representantes, quienes el 4 de octubre por mayoría de votos lo eligieron presidente interino de la República. Álvarez empezó a despachar en Cuernavaca, pero el 14 de noviembre pasó a la ciudad de México, nombró presidente sustituto a Ignacio Comonfort y le cedió el Poder Ejecutivo el 11 de diciembre. La Constitución de 1857 redujo el periodo presidencial a cuatro años y no prohibió la reelección; además, introdujo la elección popular "indirecta en primer grado y por escrutinio secreto", para lo cual se dividió al país en distritos electorales de 40,000 habitantes y cada distrito en secciones de 500 habitantes; cada sección nombraba un elector en elecciones primarias y éstos hacían la elección final en elecciones secundarias; se estableció también que la ausencia del jefe del Ejecutivo sería cubierta por el presidente de la Suprema Corte de Justicia de la Nación. De acuerdo con el nuevo ordenamiento, en 1857 Comonfort fue elegido presidente constitucional. El 17 de diciembre el mismo Comonfort se unió a la asonada conservadora conocida como Plan de Tacubaya (☛), que dio

Sebastián Lerdo de Tejada, presidente de México (1872-1876)

Porfirio Díaz, presidente de México (1871-1880 y 1884-1911)

Francisco I. Madero, gobernó el país de 1911 a 1913

inicio a la guerra de los Tres Años, y desconoció la Constitución. Ese mismo día renunciaron varios miembros de su gabinete y Benito Juárez, presidente de la Suprema Corte de Justicia, fue encarcelado. El 11 de enero, los alzados modificaron el segundo artículo de dicho plan, "eliminando al Excmo. Sr. Comonfort del mando supremo de la Nación y proclamando como general en jefe del Ejército regenerador al Sr. general Félix Zuloaga", con la promesa de que "restablecido el orden" se nombraría "un presidente interino de la República por una junta compuesta de un representante de cada Departamento, nombrada por el expresado general en jefe". Juá-

Venustiano Carranza, presidente de México (1917-1920)

rez, a quien constitucionalmente correspondía ocupar la Presidencia de la República al haberse colocado Comonfort en la ilegalidad, fue liberado el mismo 11 de enero y se dirigió a Guanajuato, donde con el reconocimiento de nueve estados integró su gabinete y el 19 de enero expidió un manifiesto en el que anunciaba el restablecimiento del gobierno de la República y decía: "he reasumido el mando supremo luego que he tenido libertad para verificarlo. Llamado a este difícil puesto por un precepto constitucional, y no por el favor de las facciones (.), entretanto se reúne el Congreso de la Unión a continuar sus importantes tareas, dictaré las medidas que las circunstancias demanden para expeditar la marcha de la

Álvaro Obregón, presidente de México (1920-1924)

administración en sus distintos ramos y para restablecer la paz". De hecho, el gobierno de Comonfort terminó en la mañana del día 21, cuando acompañado de una pequeña escolta salió de la ciudad de México. Ese mismo día se integró una junta de notables que al día siguiente eligió como presidente provisional del gobierno conservador a Zuloaga, quien fue depuesto el 23 de diciembre de 1858 por una junta de militares que se negaron a reconocer su autoridad y nombraron en su lugar al general Manuel Robles Pezuela, quien fue relevado por el también general José Mariano Salas el 21 de enero de 1859. El 2 de febrero asumió el gobierno conservador Miguel Miramón, quien un mes antes había sido designado presidente sustituto por una junta electoral de sus correligionarios. Miramón cargó el título de presidente sustituto en sus campañas militares, hasta el 13 de agosto de 1860, cuando renunció y el Consejo de Estado nombró en su lugar a José Ignacio Pavón, quien dos días después entregó el poder nuevamente a Miramón, quien había sido nombrado presidente interino por el mismo consejo. El 22 de diciembre de ese año fue derrotado el ejército conservador en la batalla de Calpulalpan y así terminó el gobierno anticonstitucional. Juárez, sometido al asedio de los conservadores, de Guanajuato había ido a Guadalajara y de esta ciudad al puerto de Manzanillo, donde el 11 de abril se embarcó con rumbo al sur, tocó Acapulco y siguió hasta Panamá, atravesó el istmo y fue a La Habana, luego a Nueva Orleans y de ahí volvió a territorio mexicano el 4 de mayo de 1859. Instaló su gobierno en Veracruz, donde obtuvo el reconocimiento de Washington, expidió las Leyes de Reforma (☛ *Reforma*) y, urgido por la necesidad de fondos, su secretario de Relaciones, Melchor Ocampo, firmó el tratado MacLane-Ocampo, mediante el cual se daba a Estados Unidos derecho de paso, a perpetuidad, por el istmo de Tehuantepec y hacía otras concesiones gravosas para la soberanía nacional, a cambio de la entrega de dos millones de dólares y créditos por una cantidad igual. Juárez dejó el puerto de Veracruz el 5 de enero de 1861 y entró en la ciudad de México seis días después. El 11 de junio, Juárez fue elegido presidente constitucional. En marzo de 1862, en Orizaba, ciudad ocupada por los franceses, el conservador Juan Nepomuceno Almonte se proclamó presidente interino, pero no fue reconocido por su partido ni por los invasores. Ante el avance de los intervencionistas, el 31 de mayo Juárez salió del Distrito Federal hacia San Luis Potosí, donde instaló la sede de los poderes. El 10 de junio entraron los invasores en la ciudad de México y Elías Federico Forey, comandante de las fuerzas de ocupación, designó el día 18

Plutarco Elías Calles, presidente de México (1924-1928)

a 35 personas que serían integrantes de la Junta Superior de Gobierno. Ésta se instaló el 20 y dos días después, para ejercer el Poder Ejecutivo, eligió un triunvirato formado por el citado Almonte, el ex presidente Mariano Salas y el arzobispo Antonio Pelagio de Labastida y Dávalos, con el obispo Juan Ormaechea y Antonio Pavón como suplentes. El mismo día 22, el triunvirato recibió simbólicamente el poder de manos del general francés, quien les hizo entrega del Palacio Nacional. El 2 de julio, los triunviros designaron a 215 "notables", quienes con los 35 miembros de la junta integrarían el Poder Legislativo. El día 10, este órgano resolvió que el país adoptaba la "monarquía moderada hereditaria, con un príncipe católico" y que la corona se ofrecía a Maximiliano de Habsburgo, lo que estaba arreglado desde 1861. Asimismo, acordó cambiar el nombre del Ejecutivo por Regencia del Imperio. El 10 de abril de 1864, previa aprobación de Napoleón III, emperador francés, Maximiliano cumplió el formulismo de aceptar la corona y en la misma fecha disolvió la Regencia y extendió diversos nombramientos. Acosado por los intervencionistas, el gobierno republicano encabezado por Juárez había salido el 22 de diciembre de 1863 de San Luis Potosí hacia Saltillo, donde permaneció del 9 de enero al 3 de abril, para pasar luego a Monterrey, donde el presidente de la República despachó hasta el 15 de agosto. Maximiliano había llegado el 28 de mayo a Veracruz y a la ciudad de México el 12 de junio. Juárez se vio obligado a dejar Monterrey y viajó por el norte hasta llegar a Chihuahua, donde se estableció del 12 de octubre de 1864 hasta fines de 1866, El avance del enemigo lo obligó a replegarse al Paso del Norte (hoy Ciudad Juárez) en varias ocasiones. En enero salieron de México las legiones austriaca y belga y en marzo concluyó el retiro de las tropas francesas. Conforme iban los invasores y avanzaban las fuerzas republicanas hacia el centro del país, Juárez trasladaba la sede del Poder Ejecutivo. En enero de 1867 despachaba en Durango, el día 22 en Zacatecas, luego en Fresnillo y, a partir del 11 de marzo, nuevamente en San Luis Potosí, donde recibió la noticia del triunfo republicano en Querétaro, donde el 19 de junio de 1867 fueron fusilados dos generales colaboracionistas y Maximiliano de Habsburgo, quien se rindió el 15 de mayo de 1867. Juárez volvió a la ciudad de México el 15 de julio y en el mismo año convocó a elecciones en las que fue ratificado en su cargo. Mediante nuevos comicios fue reelegido en 1871. Juárez murió en 1872 y Sebastián Lerdo de Tejada, presidente de la Suprema Corte, asumió la Presidencia para completar el periodo de Juárez. El 26 de octubre de 1876, Lerdo fue elegido presidente constitucional por el Congreso, pero fue desconocido por los participantes en la rebelión del Plan de Tuxtepec, proclamado por Porfirio Díaz desde el 10 de enero. Igualmente, el presidente de la Suprema Corte de Justicia, José María Iglesias, negó validez al proceso electoral y el 31 de octubre declaró que asumía la Presidencia e instaló su gobierno en Querétaro. Lerdo abandonó la ciudad de México el 18 de noviembre y marchó a Estados Unidos. El día 20 entró Porfirio Díaz en la capital, pero no asumió la Presidencia sino hasta el 28, después de proponer infructuosamente a Iglesias que se adhiriera al Plan de Tuxtepec. El 6 de diciembre, Díaz entregó la Presidencia al general Juan N. Méndez, mientras él perseguía las fuerzas adictas a Iglesias, quien inició una retirada que lo llevó hasta Manzanillo. Ahí se embarcó el 23 de enero de 1877 hacia Mazatlán, donde permaneció algunas semanas, hasta que en marzo salió del país. El 17 de febrero Díaz asumió nuevamente el Poder Ejecutivo, el que ocupó hasta el 30 de noviembre de 1880. En 1878 quedó prohibida la reelección para periodos seguidos. A Díaz le sucedió su compadre Manuel González, del 1 de diciembre de 1880 al 30 de noviembre de 1884. A González le correspondió publicar la enmienda constitucional que permitía la reelección para el periodo inmediato y el decreto mediante el cual se establecía que en ausencia temporal o absoluta del presidente de la República, el Poder Ejecutivo lo ocuparía el presidente o vicepresidente del Senado y, de estar este órgano en receso, por el presidente de la comisión permanente del Congreso de la Unión. Díaz volvió en 1884 al poder, en el que se hizo reelegir sucesivamente en 1888, 1892, 1896, 1900, 1904 y 1910. Un decreto de 1896 señalaba que en las faltas absolutas del presidente correspondía encargarse del Ejecutivo al secretario de Relaciones Exteriores y, de no haberlo, al secretario de Gobernación, en tanto el Congreso convocaba a elecciones. En caso de que el presidente solicitase licencia, a él correspondía designar sustituto. En 1904, el periodo presidencial se amplió a seis años y se estipuló que el vicepresidente

Lázaro Cárdenas, presidente de México (1934-1940)

Manuel Ávila Camacho, presidente de México (1940-1946)

Miguel Alemán Valdés, presidente de México (1946-1952)

sería el encargado de suplir las ausencias del jefe del Ejecutivo. La reelección de 1910, fue fraudulenta según la oposición. El 5 de octubre de ese año, Francisco I. Madero lanzó el Plan de San Luis, en el cual declaraba nulas las elecciones y, en tal virtud, consideraba que la República había quedado sin gobernantes legítimos, por lo que se autodesignaba presidente provisional y llamaba a tomar las armas para deponer a los que llamaba "usurpadores". En febrero de 1911, Madero, quien había permanecido en Estados Unidos, volvió a territorio nacional, después de haber nombrado comisionados en función de secretarios de Estado, y el día 15, en la población de Guadalupe, empezó a despachar como presidente. El 10 de mayo, al tomar Ciudad Juárez, designó a los miembros de su gabinete, entre los cuales había algunos de los comisionados que nombró en febrero. El 21 de mayo, en la misma ciudad, se firmaron los tratados que obligaban a renunciar a Porfirio Díaz y a Ramón Corral, presidente y vicepresidente de la República, y en los cuales se acordaba que Francisco León de la Barra ocuparía interinamente el Poder Ejecutivo. A la firma del documento, Maderó cesó como presidente provisional y Díaz dejó formalmente el Poder Ejecutivo el 25 de mayo. León de la Barra convocó a elecciones y el 6 de noviembre entregó la Presidencia a Madero, vencedor en los comicios junto con José María Pino Suárez, elegido vicepresidente. A fines de ese año el Congreso prohibió la reelección. En 1912 se estableció el sistema de voto directo y universal para los puestos de elección. El 18 de febrero de 1913, el presidente y el vicepresidente fueron aprehendidos por militares golpistas, cuyos líderes firmaron ese mismo día, en la embajada de Estados Unidos, un pacto mediante el cual se acordaba imponer como presidente a Victoriano Huerta. Al día siguiente, los alzados obligaron a renunciar a Madero y Pino Suárez. Pedro Lascuráin, secretario de Relaciones Exteriores, ocupó la Presidencia durante 45 minutos, los que sirvieron únicamente para que nombrara secretario de Gobernación al general Victoriano Huerta y luego renunciara, a fin de que éste asumiera el Poder Ejecutivo con un barniz de supuesta legalidad. El mismo día 19, la Legislatura de Coahuila desconoció al gobierno de Huerta e invistió de facultades extraordinarias al gobernador de la entidad, Venustiano Carranza, para que formara un ejército que restaurara el orden constitucional. El 27 de marzo se firmó el Plan de Guadalupe, que designaba primer jefe del Ejército Constitucionalista a Carranza y establecía que al ocupar las fuerzas revolucionarias la ciudad de México, el mismo primer jefe asumiría el Poder Ejecutivo y convocaría a elecciones. En realidad, desde el principio Carranza asumió funciones de presidente provisional, situación que se formalizó el 20 de agosto de 1914, al entrar en la capital. Huerta abandonó la Presidencia el 14 de julio de 1914 y dejó al frente del Poder Ejecutivo a Francisco S. Carvajal, cuyos representantes firmaron el 13 de agosto los convenios de Teoloyucan, en los cuales se acordaba la disolución del viejo ejército federal. Carvajal cesó en sus funciones y Carranza se trasladó a la capital, donde convocó a la Convención de Generales y Gobernadores, que instaló el 1 de octubre en la ciudad de México. Como villistas y zapatistas condicionaron su participación al cambio de sede, el día 6 la Convención acordó trasladarse a Aguascalientes, donde reanudó sus trabajos el día 10. Los convencionistas desconocieron a Carranza y el 6 de noviembre eligieron presidente a Eulalio Gutiérrez. Se desataron las hostilidades entre las facciones y, el 23 de noviembre, Carranza fijó la sede de su gobierno a Veracruz, en tanto que Gutiérrez entró en la ciudad de México el 3 de diciembre. El presidente convencionista entró en conflicto con Francisco Villa y Emiliano Zapata, huyó de la capital y sólo aceptó renunciar el 2 junio. Desde el 16 de enero de 1915, al frente del gobierno convencionista quedó Roque González Garza, quien entre el 26 y el 28 de enero trasladó la sede del Ejecutivo a Cuernavaca. El 10 de marzo, después de que los ejércitos convencionistas recuperaron la ciudad de México, volvió a instalarse en ella González Garza, quien el 10 de junio fue destituido por la Convención, que nombró en su lugar a Francisco Lagos Cházaro, quien permaneció en el Distrito Federal hasta el 10 de julio. El gobierno convencionista pasó a Toluca y después de un breve regreso a la ciudad de México, salió definitivamente el 1 de

Foto: Héctor Herrera

Adolfo Ruiz Cortines, presidente de México (1952-1958)

Adolfo López Mateos, presidente de México (1958-1964)

Foto: Héctor Herrera

Gustavo Díaz Ordaz, presidente de México (1964-1970)

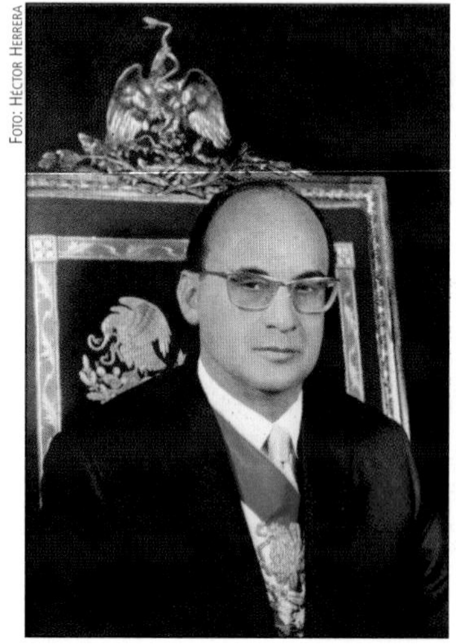
Foto: Héctor Herrera

Luis Echeverría Álvarez, presidente de México (1970-1976)

agosto para volver a Toluca, donde el 10 de octubre entraron los carrancistas. Lagos Cházaro pudo huir, pero su gobierno se extinguió. Venustiano Carranza volvió a la ciudad de México en agosto e inició una gira por varios estados del norte y el centro del país. El 5 de enero de 1916 tomó a Querétaro como sede de su gobierno, pero el 14 de abril la mudó nuevamente al Distrito Federal. El 16 de septiembre convocó al Congreso Constituyente, las elecciones de diputados se celebraron el 22 de octubre y el 1 de diciembre, en Querétaro, quedó instalada la asamblea, cuyos trabajos abrió el propio Carranza ese día. El 31 de enero fueron clausurados los trabajos de los constituyentes y el 5 de febrero de 1917 se promulgó la nueva Constitución, en la que se redujo el periodo presidencial a cuatro años y quedó establecido que, en caso de renuncia, muerte o ausencia del presidente de la República en los dos primeros años de su mandato, el Congreso designará a un presidente interino que deberá convocar a elecciones; si la ausencia del jefe del Ejecutivo se produce después de los dos primeros años de su administración, el Congreso nombrará a un presidente sustituto, que terminará el periodo de su antecesor. El 6 de febrero Carranza convocó a elecciones federales en las que se presentó como candidato a presidente de la República. El 11 de marzo se celebraron los comicios en los que resultó triunfador, por lo que el 1 de mayo de 1917 asumió el cargo de presidente Constitucional. En abril de 1920 se inició la rebelión del Plan de Agua Prieta, firmado por generales adictos a Álvaro Obregón. Según el documento, cesaba "en el ejercicio del Poder Ejecutivo de la Federación el C. Venustiano Carranza" y se designaba a Adolfo de la Huerta como "Jefe Supremo del Ejército, con todas las facultades necesarias para la organización militar, política y administrativa de este movimiento". La asonada se extendió por todo el país y el 7 de mayo Carranza decidió el traslado de los poderes a Veracruz. En la estación de Algibes debió abandonar el ferrocarril en que iba y se internó en la sierra de Puebla, donde el 21 de mayo de 1920 fue asesinado. Tres días después el Congreso nombró presidente sustituto a Adolfo de la Huerta, quien llegó al Distrito Federal el 1 de junio y asumió hasta entonces el cargo. Convocó a elecciones en las que apareció como vencedor Álvaro Obregón, quien ocupó la Presidencia de la República del 1 de diciembre de 1920 al 30 de noviembre de 1924. Plutarco Elías Calles le sucedió al frente del Poder Ejecutivo el 1 de diciembre de 1924. En 1926 reformó la legislación para permitir la reelección para periodos no consecutivos. El 13 de octubre de 1927 se estableció que el periodo presidencial fuese de seis años. En1928 se realizaron los comicios en los que Obregón resultó reelegido, pero el 17 de Julio fue asesinado por José de León Toral. El 1

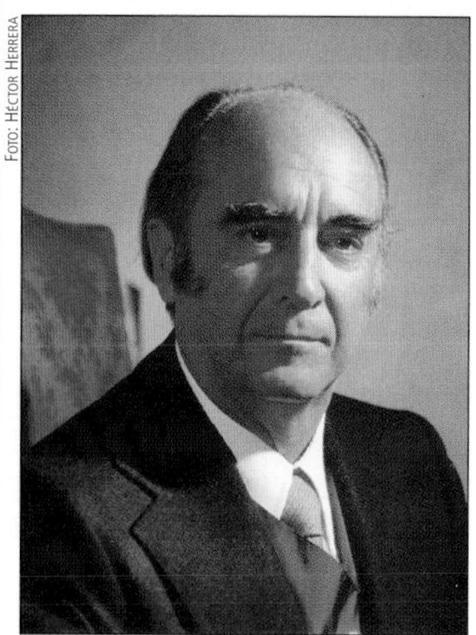
Foto: Héctor Herrera

José López Portillo, presidente de México (1976-1982)

Foto: Héctor Herrera

Miguel de la Madrid, presidente de México (1982-1988)

de diciembre, Calles entregó el cargo a Portes Gil, presidente interino designado por el Congreso. Como éste careciera de suficiente fuerza propia, Calles retuvo el poder real, pues era amplio su ascendiente sobre los caudillos y las organizaciones llamadas revolucionarias, a los que hizo formar parte del Partido Nacional Revolucionario (1929), y poco después empezaron a llamarlo "Jefe Máximo", lo que significaba que en sus manos estaban las principales decisiones de Estado. El gobierno de 400 días de Portes Gil terminó el 5 de febrero de 1930, cuando entregó la Presidencia a Pascual Ortiz Rubio, quien según la información oficial resultó vencedor en los comicios del 17 de noviembre de 1929. Ortiz Rubio debía completar el periodo para el que fue reelecto Álvaro Obregón, pero la imponente presencia de Calles le imposibilitó gobernar y, el 2 de septiembre de 1932, optó por presentar su renuncia, por el "desacuerdo" existente "entre el Ejecutivo y los demás órganos políticos o de gobierno". El 4 de septiembre el Congreso designó al general Abelardo L. Rodríguez como presidente sustituto constitucional, encargado de ocupar el Poder Ejecutivo Federal hasta el 30 de noviembre de 1934, cuando terminaba el sexenio que hubiera cubierto la segunda gestión obregonista. Con Rodríguez, el poder extrainstitucional del "Jefe Máximo de la Revolución", Plutarco Elías Calles, fue prácticamente absoluto. El 1 de diciembre ocupó la Presidencia de la República el general Lázaro Cárdenas, quien respetó los derechos laborales y dio un impulso sin precedentes al reparto agrario, lo que motivó la oposición de los grupos conservadores con los que había llegado a identificarse Calles, quien el 11 de junio censuró en declaraciones a la prensa el "maratón de radicalismo" que vivía el país: "Hace seis meses que la nación está sacudida por huelgas constantes, muchas de ellas injustificadas. Las organizaciones obreras están ofreciendo en numerosos casos ejemplos de ingratitud (.) Están provocando y jugando con la vida económica del país". Las palabras de Calles ponían en entredicho la autoridad del presidente y su acierto para conducir al país. Cárdenas contestó con el reemplazo de los jefes militares callistas, el cambio de dirigentes

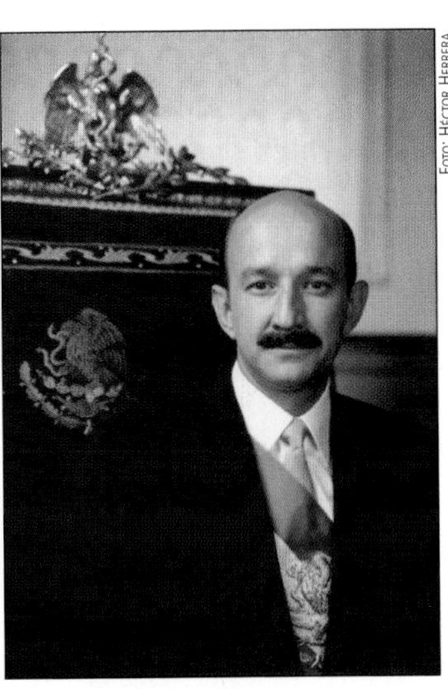

Carlos Salinas de Gortari, presidente de México (1988-1994)

en el Partido Nacional Revolucionario y, a su demanda, con la renuncia de los miembros del gabinete, varios de los cuales acataban las decisiones del llamado "Jefe Máximo". La mayoría de los gobernadores expresaron su adhesión al presidente y el ala izquierda del Congreso hizo frente a las presiones del callismo. Las organizaciones obreras constituyeron el Comité Nacional de Defensa Proletaria, claramente anticallista, y las principales agrupaciones campesinas se movilizaron en defensa de la política cardenista. En estas condiciones, el presidente respondió que las huelgas eran "la consecuencia del acomodamiento de los intereses representados por los dos factores de la producción" y que su "correcta solución trae como consecuencia un mayor bienestar para los trabajadores". Días después señaló los "procedimientos reprobables de deslealtad y traición" de sus críticos, los callistas, mientras manifestaciones multitudinarias pedían que se expulsara del país al hasta entonces "Jefe Máximo", quien el 19 de junio tomó un avión rumbo a Sonora y luego pasó a Estados Unidos. En los días siguientes fueron expulsados varios miembros del Congreso y algunos gobernadores resultaron depuestos. En su informe de gobierno del 1 de septiembre, Cárdenas dejó claro que él era el único responsable "de la marcha política y social de la nación". A partir de ese día los callistas iniciaron una nueva campaña para restarle poder al presidente en favor del "maximato". Mientras generales como Melchor Ortega y José María Tapia incitaban abiertamente a la rebelión, el 11 de septiembre fueron asesinados en la Cámara de Diputados dos legisladores cardenistas. La respuesta en el Congreso fue desaforar al día siguiente a 17 diputados callistas involucrados en el crimen. En las semanas siguientes se anunció profusamente que Calles regresaría a México. La CROM y otras agrupaciones sindicales dominadas por callistas y filonazis formaron la Alianza Nacional de Trabajadores Unificados, que llamó a realizar un "paro de trabajo anticomunista" el 13 de diciembre de 1935, precisamente el día en que volvía a México el ex "Jefe Máximo". Las organizaciones obreras, campesinas y de otros sectores anticallistas desplegaron una amplia movilización en defensa de la política de Cárdenas. El día 14 el Congreso desaforó a cinco senadores y el presidente de la República cesó al jefe de Educación Militar, Joaquín Amaro, y al comandante de la ciudad de México, Manuel Medinaveytia. El general Tapia

Ernesto Zedillo Ponce de Léon, presidente de México (1994-2000)

fue procesado bajo la acusación de soborno y la Cámara de Diputados declaró la desaparición de poderes en Guanajuato, Durango, Sinaloa y Sonora, entidades hasta ese momento gobernadas por callistas. El 17 de diciembre el propio Calles y sus principales colaboradores fueron expulsados del Partido Nacional Revolucionario (☛). El día 22 se realizó una manifestación de 100,000 personas que exigían echar del país al ex "Jefe Máximo", quien ese día fue calificado por Cárdenas de "tránsfuga de la revolución". El 9 de abril de 1936 se le llamó "traidor" en la Cámara de Senadores y dos días después, bajo fuerte escolta militar, fue llevado al aeropuerto y expulsado del país. De esta manera se resolvió la dualidad de poderes creada por el maximato y para todos quedó claro que el ejercicio del Poder Ejecutivo Federal correspondía en exclusiva al presidente de la República. Después de Lázaro Cárdenas han sido presidentes Manuel Ávila Camacho (1940-46), Miguel Alemán Valdés (1946-52), Adolfo Ruiz Cortines (1952-58), Adolfo López Mateos (1958-64), Gustavo Díaz Ordaz (1964-70), Luis Echeverría Álvarez (1970-76), José López Portillo (1976-82), Miguel de la Madrid Hurtado (1982-88), Carlos Salinas de Gortari (1988-94) y Ernesto Zedillo Ponce de León (1994-2000).

Representantes del Poder Ejecutivo

Emperador Agustín de Iturbide	23 de mayo de 1822 al 19 de marzo de 1823
Supremo Poder Ejecutivo[1]	31 de marzo de 1823 al 10 de octubre de 1824

Presidentes de la primera República Federal (1824-1835)

Guadalupe Victoria	10 de octubre de 1824 al 31 de marzo de 1828
Vicente Guerrero	1 de abril al 17 de diciembre de 1829
José María Bocanegra	18 al 22 de diciembre de 1829
Poder Ejecutivo de la Nación[2]	23 de diciembre al 31 de diciembre de 1829
Anastasio Bustamante	1 de enero de 1830 al 13 de agosto de 1832
Melchor Múzquiz	14 de agosto al 23 de diciembre de 1832
Manuel Gómez Pedraza	24 de diciembre de 1832 al 31 de marzo de 1833
Valentín Gómez Farías	1 de abril al 16 de mayo de 1833
Antonio López de Santa Anna	16 de mayo al 3 de junio de 1833
Valentín Gómez Farías	3 al 18 de junio de 1833
Antonio López de Santa Anna	18 de junio al 3 de julio de 1833
Valentín Gómez Farías	3 de julio al 27 de octubre de 1833
Antonio López de Santa Anna	27 de octubre al 15 de diciembre de 1833
Valentín Gómez Farías	15 de diciembre de 1833 al 23 de abril de 1834
Antonio López de Santa Anna	24 de abril de 1834 al 27 de enero de 1835
Miguel Barragán	28 de enero al 15 de diciembre de 1835

Presidentes de la República Centralista (1835-1846)

Miguel Barragán	15 de diciembre de 1835 al 27 de febrero de 1836
José Justo Corro	27 de febrero de 1836 al 19 de abril de 1837
Anastasio Bustamante	19 de abril de 1837 al 20 de marzo de 1839
Antonio López de Santa Anna	20 de marzo al 10 de julio de 1839
Nicolás Bravo	11 al 19 de julio de 1839
Anastasio Bustamante	19 de julio de 1839 al 21 de septiembre de 1841
Javier Echeverría	22 de septiembre al 10 de Octubre de 1841
Antonio López de Santa Anna	10 de octubre de 1841 al 25 de octubre de 1842
Nicolás Bravo	26 de octubre de 1842 al 4 de marzo de 1843
Antonio López de Santa Anna	5 de marzo al 4 de octubre de 1843
Valentín Canalizo	4 de octubre de 1843 al 4 de junio de 1844
Antonio López de Santa Anna	4 de junio al 12 de septiembre de 1844
José Joaquín de Herrera	12 de septiembre de 1844 al 21 de septiembre de 1844
Valentín Canalizo	21 de septiembre al 6 de diciembre de 1844
José Joaquín de Herrera	6 de diciembre de 1844 al 30 de diciembre de 1845
Mariano Paredes y Arrillaga	4 de enero al 28 de junio de 1846
Nicolás Bravo	29 de junio al 4 de agosto de 1846
Mariano Salas	6 al 22 de agosto de 1846

Presidentes de la segunda República Federal (1846-1872)

Mariano Salas	22 de agosto al 23 de diciembre de 1846
Valentín Gómez Farías	24 de diciembre de 1846 al 20 de marzo de 1847
Antonio López de Santa Anna	21 de marzo al 1 de abril de 1847
Pedro María Anaya	2 de abril al 20 de mayo de 1847
Antonio López de Santa Anna	20 de mayo al 16 de septiembre de 1847
Manuel de la Peña y Peña	16 de septiembre al 11 de noviembre de 1847
Pedro María Anaya	12 de noviembre de 1847 al 8 de enero de 1848
Manuel de la Peña y Peña	8 de enero al 2 de junio de 1848
José Manuel de Herrera	3 de junio de 1848 al 12 de enero de 1851
Mariano Arista	15 de enero de 1851 al 6 de enero de 1853
Juan Bautista Ceballos	7 de enero al 6 de febrero de 1853
Manuel María Lombardini	7 de febrero al 19 de abril de 1853
Antonio López de Santa Anna	20 de abril de 1853 al 8 de agosto de 1855
Martín Carrera	14 de agosto al 12 de septiembre de 1855
Rómulo Díaz de la Vega	12 de septiembre al 3 de octubre de 1855
Juan Álvarez	4 de octubre al 10 de diciembre de 1855
Ignacio Comonfort	11 de diciembre al 18 de enero de 1858
Benito Juárez	19 de enero de 1858 al 18 de julio de 1872
Sebastián Lerdo de Tejada	19 de julio al 20 de noviembre de 1876

Presidentes del gobierno conservador (paralelo) (1858-1860)

Félix Zuloaga	22 de enero al 22 de diciembre de 1858
Manuel Robles Pezuela	23 de diciembre de 1858 al 21 de enero de 1859
Mariano Salas	21 al 23 de enero de 1859
Félix Zuloaga	24 al 31 de enero de 1859
Miguel Miramón	1 de febrero de 1859 al 7 de agosto de 1860
José Ignacio Pavón	8 al 14 de agosto de 1860
Miguel Miramón	14 de agosto al 24 de diciembre de 1860

Representantes del Poder Ejecutivo
(continuación)

Bajo la ocupación francesa

Elías Federico Forey	10 al 22 de junio de 1863
Regencia del triunvirato de Juan N. Almonte, Mariano Salas y Antonio Pelagio de Labastida y Dávalos	22 de junio de 1983 al 10 de abril de 1864
Maximiliano de Habsburgo	10 de abril de 1864 al 15 de mayo de 1867

La república restaurada

Sebastián Lerdo de Tejada	18 de julio de 1872 al 20 de noviembre de 1876
José María Iglesias[3]	31 de octubre de 1876 al 15 de marzo de 1877
Porfirio Díaz[4]	23 de noviembre al 5 de diciembre de 1876
Juan N. Méndez	6 de diciembre de 1876 al 15 de febrero de 1877
Porfirio Díaz	16 de febrero de 1877 al 30 de noviembre de 1880
Manuel González	1 de diciembre de 1880 al 30 de noviembre de 1884
Porfirio Díaz	1 de diciembre de 1884 al 25 de mayo de 1911
Francisco I. Madero[5]	10 de marzo al 21 de mayo de 1911
Francisco León de la Barra	25 de mayo al 6 de noviembre de 1911
Francisco I. Madero	6 de noviembre de 1911 al 18 de febrero de 1913
Pedro Lascuráin	19 de febrero de 1913
Victoriano Huerta	19 de febrero de 1913 al 14 de julio de 1914
Venustiano Carranza[6]	18 de octubre de 1913 al 30 de abril de 1917

Presidentes de la Convención Revolucionaria

Francisco S. Carvajal[7]	14 de julio de 1914 al 13 de agosto de 1914
Eulalio Gutiérrez	1 de noviembre de 1914 al 16 de enero de 1915
Roque González Garza	16 de enero al 9 de junio de 1915
Francisco Lagos Cházaro	10 de junio al 11 de agosto de 1915

Presidentes constitucionalistas

Venustiano Carranza	1 de mayo de 1917 al 21 de mayo de 1920
Adolfo de la Huerta	24 de mayo al 30 de noviembre de 1920
Álvaro Obregón	1 de diciembre de 1920 al 30 de noviembre de 1924
Plutarco Elías Calles	1 de diciembre de 1924 al 30 de noviembre de 1928
Emilio Portes Gil	1 de diciembre de 1928 al 4 de febrero de 1930
Pascual Ortiz Rubio	5 de febrero de 1930 al 3 de septiembre de 1932
Abelardo L. Rodríguez	4 de septiembre de 1932 al 30 de noviembre de 1934
Lázaro Cárdenas	1 de diciembre de 1934 al 30 de noviembre de 1940
Manuel Ávila Camacho	1 de diciembre de 1940 al 30 de noviembre de 1946
Miguel Alemán Valdés	1 de diciembre de 1946 al 30 de noviembre de 1952
Adolfo Ruiz Cortines	1 de diciembre de 1952 al 30 de noviembre de 1958
Adolfo López Mateos	1 de diciembre de 1958 al 30 de noviembre de 1964
Gustavo Díaz Ordaz	1 de diciembre de 1964 al 30 de noviembre de 1970
Luis Echeverría Álvarez	1 de diciembre de 1970 al 30 de noviembre de 1976
José López Portillo	1 de diciembre de 1976 al 30 de noviembre de 1982
Miguel de la Madrid	1 de diciembre de 1982 al 30 de noviembre de 1988
Carlos Salinas de Gortari	1 de diciembre de 1988 al 30 de noviembre de 1994
Ernesto Zedillo Ponce de León	1 de diciembre de 1994 al 30 de noviembre del 2000

1 Triunvirato integrado por Nicolás Bravo, Pedro Celestino Negrete y Guadalupe Victoria

2 Triunvirato integrado por Lucas Alamán, Luis Quintanar y Pedro Vélez

3 Presidente de la Suprema Corte de Justicia que desconoció a su antecesor y se encargó del Poder Ejecutivo

4 Desconoció a sus dos inmediatos antecesores y se convirtió en presidente de facto de acuerdo con el Plan de Tuxtepec

5 Gobierno provisional en Ciudad Juárez

6 Primer jefe del Ejército Constitucionalista encargado del Poder Ejecutivo

7 Asumió el Poder Ejecutivo sólo para entregar la capital a los constitucionalistas

PODER JUDICIAL ◆ La Constitución de Apatzingán, sancionada el 22 de octubre de 1814, llegó a tener relativa vigencia en los territorios controlados por las fuerzas insurgentes de José María Morelos. Ese ordenamiento, sin hacer referencia a los poderes como hoy se conocen, dedicaba un capítulo a "las supremas autoridades", el que decía: "Permanecerá el cuerpo representativo de la soberanía del pueblo con el nombre de *Supremo Congreso Mexicano*. Se crearán, además, dos corporaciones, la una con el título de *Supremo Gobierno*, y la otra con el de *Supremo Tribunal de Justicia*", que correspondería al actual Poder Legislativo. Este tribunal contaba con 20 días para exponer al Congreso sus objeciones a cada nueva ley, las que el Legislativo estaba obligado a examinar con toda formalidad. Si por mayoría de votos las objeciones se consideraban bien fundadas, la ley se suprimía y quedaba prohibido ponerla nuevamente a discusión en un plazo mínimo de seis meses. El Supremo Tribunal se compondría de cinco ministros, elegidos por el Congreso, a quienes se exigían los mismos requisitos que a los diputados: "ser ciudadano en ejercicio de sus derechos, la edad de treinta años, buena reputación, patriotismo acreditado con servicios positivos, y tener luces no vulgares para desempeñar las augustas funciones de este empleo". La presidencia del tribunal se turnaba cada tres meses, los ministros se renovarían cada tres años, dos en el primero, dos en el segundo y uno en el tercero. El fiscal o fiscales, lo mismo que los secretarios, permanecerían cuatro años en su función. Quedaba prohibida la reelección para el periodo inmediato y un diputado sólo podía ser ministro dos años después, y no antes, de concluir su representación. Lo mismo se disponía para los funcionarios del Supremo Gobierno. El citado tribunal estaba facultado para conocer de las causas formadas a generales de división, secretarios de Estado, miembros del propio tribunal, del intendente general de Hacienda y en las de residencia de todo empleado público; "de los recursos de fuerza de los tribunales eclesiásticos y de las competencias que se susciten entre los jueces subalternos". Asimismo, este órgano debía ser tribunal de última instancia, salvo en el caso de prisioneros de guerra y delincuentes de Estado. El Supremo Gobierno nombraría a los jueces eclesiásticos y a los de partido y éstos, a su vez, a los tenientes de justicia. Para tomar posesión de su cargo, los ministros debían responder afirmativamente a las siguientes preguntas: "¿Juráis defender a costa de vuestra sangre la religión católica, apostólica, romana?, ¿Juráis sostener constantemente la causa de nuestra independencia contra nuestros injustos agresores?, ¿Juráis observar y hacer cumplir el decreto constitucional en todas y cada una de sus partes? ¿Juráis desempeñar con celo y fidelidad el empleo que os ha conferido la nación, trabajando incesantemente por el bien y prosperidad de la nación misma?". El Plan de Iguala, fechado el 24 de febrero de 1821, señalaba que "Todos los ramos del Estado y empleados públicos subsistirán como en el día, y sólo serán removidos los que se opongan a este plan". Asimismo, establecía que "Interin se reúnen las Cortes (el Congreso), se procederá en los delitos con total arreglo a la Constitución española" (es decir, regía la administración de Justicia el Reglamento de las Audiencias y Juzgados de Primera Instancia dictado por las Cortes de Cádiz), salvo en el de conspiración contra la independencia, que merecería prisión inmediata hasta en tanto las Cortes "dicten la pena correspondiente al mayor de los delitos, después del de Lesa Majestad divina". El 24 de febrero de 1822, una vez reunido el Congreso Constituyente, éste órgano emitió unas Bases Constitucionales, las que decían: "No conviniendo queden reunidos el poder Legislativo, Ejecutivo y el Judiciario, declara el Congreso que se reserva el ejercicio del poder Legislativo en toda su extensión, delegando interinamente el poder Ejecutivo en las personas que componen la actual regencia, y el Judiciario en los tribunales que actualmente existen, o que se nombrarán en adelante". Disuelto el Congreso por Iturbide, éste designó a los miembros de una Junta Nacional Instituyente, la que aprobó en febrero de 1823, por 21 votos contra 17, el Reglamento Político Provisional del Imperio. Este ordenamiento, que sustituía a la Carta de Cádiz, señalaba en su artículo 23 que "El sistema de gobierno político del imperio mexicano se compone de los poderes Legislativo, Ejecutivo y Judicial, que son incompatibles en una misma persona o corporación". La sección quinta, llamada "Del Poder Judicial", declaraba subsistentes los juzgados y fueros militares y eclesiásticos, excepto en los delitos "de lesa majestad humana, conjuración contra la patria, ó forma de gobierno establecido"; daba al consulado (☛) facultades conciliadoras y, a petición de las partes, arbitrales; y establecía que "En todo pleito por grande que sea su interés, habrá tres instancias no más, y tres sentencias definitivas. Dos sentencias conformes de toda conformidad causan ejecutoria. Cuando la segunda revoca ó altera la primera, ha lugar a suplicación que se interpondrá en el mismo tribunal". El ordenamiento decía que "La justicia se administrará en nombre del Emperador", a quien debían jurar fidelidad "Todos los jueces y magistrados". El artículo 76 prohibía la tortura, la confiscación absoluta de bienes y la pena "de infamia transmisible a la posteridad ó familia del que la mereció". Quedaba como facultad del gobierno nombrar "jueces de letras" y establecer "dos o tres audiencias nuevas". El segundo capítulo de la misma sección estaba dedicado al "Supremo Tribunal de Justicia", que tendría "la capital del imperio" por residencia y se compondría por nueve ministros a los que debía darse trato de excelencia. Cada uno de ellos recibiría 6,000 pesos anuales. El tribunal, decía el Reglamento, "Dirimirá todas las competencias de las audiencias", "juzgará a los secretarios de Estado y del despacho, cuando por queja de parte se declare haber lugar á exigir responsabilidad.",

"Conocerá de todas las causas de suspensión y separación de los consejeros de Estado y de los magistrados de las audiencias", "Juzgará las criminales de los secretarios de Estado y del despacho, de los consejeros de Estado, y de los magistrados de las audiencias", conocerá de todas las causas criminales y civiles de los individuos del cuerpo legislativo", "Conocerá de la residencia de todo funcionario público sujeto á ella por las leyes; de todos los asuntos contenciosos del patronato imperial, y de todos los recursos de fuerza de los tribunales eclesiásticos superiores de la corte", "De los de nulidad que se interpongan contra sentencias pronunciadas en última instancia, para el preciso efecto de reponer el proceso, devolviéndolo, y de hacer efectiva la responsabilidad de los magistrados que la pronunciaron", "Oirá las dudas de los demás tribunales sobre la genuina inteligencia de alguna ley, consultando al Emperador con los fundamentos de que nazcan, para que provoque la conveniente declaración del poder legislativo", "Examinará las listas que le deben remitir las audiencias para promover la pronta administración de justicia, pasando copia de ellas al gobierno con las observaciones que estime convenientes, y disponiendo su publicación por la imprenta", "Cuando de orden del Emperador se proceda al arresto de alguno (.) y no se suelte ni entregue á tribunal competente en los quince días (.), podrá el arrestado ocurrir á este tribunal, que si calificare justo y conveniente tal arresto por el interés del estado, pronunciará el siguiente decreto: Queda a esta parte salvo el segundo recurso en el término de la ley; y el arrestado podrá usar de él ante el mismo tribunal, si pasados quince días no se ha hecho la consignación a su juez respectivo"; "En este caso, ó cuando en virtud del primer ocurso, el tribunal estime que la salud pública no exige la prisión, oficiará al ministro que comunicó la orden de arresto invitándole á la libertad ó consignación del arrestado. Si el ministro no ejecuta uno u otro dentro de quince días, ni expone motivos justos de la demora, el tribunal dará segundo decreto en esta forma: Hay vehemente presunción de detención arbitraria contra el ministro N. por la prisión de N.; y desde este acto seguirá el propio tribunal en el conocimiento de la causa de responsabilidad por los trámites señalados en las leyes, oyendo al ministro, á la parte y al fiscal, y determinando lo más conforme en justicia"; y "En caso de acusación ó queja criminal contra individuos de este tribunal, se ocurrirá al emperador, que dará orden de que se reúna luego otro tribunal compuesto del letrado de más edad que hubiere en el cuerpo legislativo: del consejero de estado, también letrado más antiguo: del regente ó decano de la audiencia de esta corte: del rector del colegio de abogados, y del letrado de más edad que hubiere en la diputación provincial. Si no hay alguno, del catedrático jubilado ó profesor de derecho más antiguo de la universidad de esta corte que no sea eclesiástico". A la caída de Iturbide se instaló un nuevo Congreso Constituyente, el que aprobó el 24 de enero de 1823 el *Acta Constitutiva de la Federación Mexicana*, publicada el día 31 del mismo mes. Al igual que el *Reglamento* anterior, establecía la división de poderes, pero ahora dentro de una "república representativa popular federal". Para administrar "pronta, completa e imparcialmente justicia", se depositaba "el ejercicio del Poder Judicial en una Corte Suprema de Justicia, y en los tribunales que se establecerán en cada estado, reservándose demarcar en la Constitución las facultades de esta Suprema Corte". De acuerdo con el *Acta*, los juicios debían efectuarse por tribunales establecidos y sobre leyes vigentes antes de cometerse el acto objeto del juicio. La Constitución de 1824 establecía que "El Poder Judicial de la Federación residirá en una Corte Suprema de Justicia, en los tribunales de circuito y en los juzgados de distrito". La Corte estaría compuesta de 11 ministros distribuidos en tres salas y un fiscal y fue instalada en 1825 y su primer ley orgánica dictada en 1826. Correspondía al Congreso aumentar o disminuir su número. Para ser ministro se requería "estar instruido en la ciencia del derecho a juicio de las legislaturas de los estados; tener la edad de treinta y cinco años cumplidos; ser ciudadano natural de la República o nacido en cualquiera parte de la América que antes de 1810 dependía de la España, y que se han separado de ella, con tal de que tenga la vecindad de cinco años cumplidos en el territorio de la República". Los ministros lo serían "perpetuos en este destino y sólo podrán ser removidos conforme a las leyes". La elección de los ministros y el fiscal era facultad de los congresos locales. La Cámara de Diputados federal calificaría la elección e informaría del resultado. Si un senador o diputado era elegido para ministro o fiscal "preferirá la elección que se haga para estos destinos". Los elegidos, para entrar en funciones, debían prestar el siguiente juramento: "Juráis a Dios vuestro Señor haberos fiel y lealmente en el desempeño de las obligaciones que os confía la nación? Si así lo hiciéreis, Dios os lo premie, y si no, os lo demande". Entre las atribuciones de la Corte se hallaba conocer de las diferencias entre los estados de la federación, "terminar las disputas que se susciten sobre contratos o

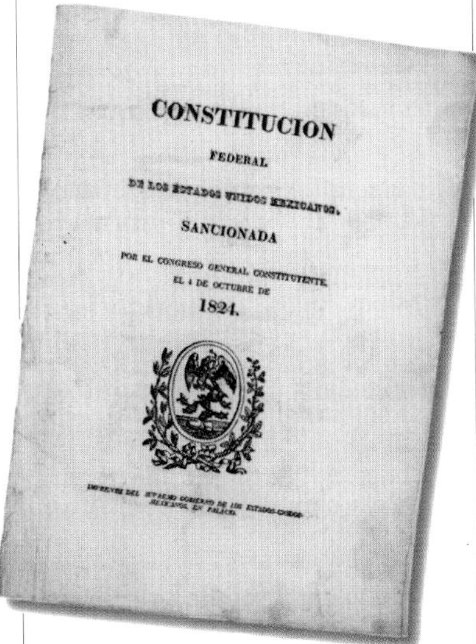

La Constitución de 1824 establecía que el Poder Judicial residiría "en una Corte Suprema de Justicia, en los tribunales de circuito y en los juzgados de distrito".

negociaciones celebrados con el gobierno supremo o sus agentes", consultar "sobre paso o retención de bulas pontificias, breves y rescriptos expedidos en asuntos contenciosos", dirimir las competencias que se susciten entre los tribunales de la federación, y entre éstos y los de los estados, y las que se muevan entre los de un estado y los de otro"; conocer "de las causas que se muevan al presidente y vicepresidente", después de que la Cámara de Diputados, erigida en gran jurado, hubiera decidido que hay lugar a formación de causa; de "las causas criminales de los diputados y senadores" una vez desaforados; "de las de los gobernadores" y secretarios del despacho en igual caso; "De los negocios civiles y criminales de los empleados diplomáticos y cónsules de la República"; "De las causas del almirantazgo", contrabandos, crímenes cometidos en alta mar, ofensas contra la nación, de los empleados de hacienda y justicia de la Federación y "de las infracciones de la Constitución y leyes generales". Los individuos de la Suprema Corte serían juzgados por un tribunal formado por el Congreso con juristas de semejantes "cualidades que los ministros de dicha Corte". Los tribunales de circuito"se compondrán de un juez letrado (y) un promotor fiscal" no menores de 30 años. Para resolver casos en primera instancia se establecían los juzgados de distrito, atendidos por un juez de letras no menor de 25 años nombrado de manera igual que los magistrados de circuito. La Constitución respetó los fueros militar y eclesiástico, ratificó que quedaban prohibidas la tortura, la aplicación retroactiva de las leyes, los jucios por comisión y la confiscación de bienes. El término de una detención "por indicios" sería como máximo de 60 horas. Al implantarse el centralismo, las Bases Constitucionales de 1835 ratificaban la separación de los tres poderes y decían que "El ejercicio del poder judicial residirá en una corte suprema de justicia, y en los tribunales y jueces que establecerá la ley constitucional". Ésta no fue otra que las llamadas *Siete Leyes*, promulgadas entre diciembre de 1835 y abril de 1836, según las cuales, "El Poder Judicial de la República se ejercerá por una Corte Suprema de Justicia, por los tribunales superiores de los departamentos, por los de Hacienda que establecerá la ley de la materia y por los juzgados de primera instancia". La Corte estaría compuesta por 11 ministros y un fiscal, que serían letrados mexicanos, no menores de 40 años, sin antecedentes penales y con 10 años como mínimo en el ejercicio de la abogacía. "La elección de los individuos de la Corte Suprema, en las vacantes que hubiere en lo sucesivo, se hará de la misma manera y en la propia forma que la del presidente de la República. Cada dos años, en los primeros seis días de enero, a propuesta del Ejecutivo, el Senado y la propia Corte, los suplentes de los ministros serían elegidos por la Cámara de Diputados. Las facultades de la Corte Suprema eran semejantes a las que establecía la Constitución de 1824. Tenía también la atribución de "Conocer de los recursos de protección y de fuerza que se interpongan de los muy RR. arzobispos y RR. obispos de la República", iniciar leyes sobre administración de justicia, dictaminar sobre iniciativas de los otros poderes en el mismo ramo, promover ante la Cámara de Diputados aclaraciones sobre leyes que ofrecieran dudas, confirmar el nombramiento de jueces de primera instancia hecho por los tribunales superiores y nombrar a los ministros y fiscales de estos órganos, tomando como base las listas elaboradas por los propios tribunales, las que debían ser aprobadas por los gobernadores y el Ejecutivo; y "Apoyar o contradecir las peticiones de indultos". Asociada con "oficiales generales" de división o de brigada, la Corte "se erigirá en marcial para conocer de todos los negocios y causas del fuero de guerra", pero en las causas criminales castrenses sólo correspondía decidir a los ministros militares, en tanto que en los negocios civiles decidirían los ministros letrados. Las causas mixtas serían conocidas y decididas conjuntamente.

Las Bases Orgánicas de 1843, también de carácter centralista, "El Poder Judicial se deposita en una Suprema Corte de Justicia, en los tribunales superiores y jueces inferiores de los Departamentos, y en los demás que establezcan las leyes. Subsistirán los tribunales especiales de hacienda, comercio y minería mientras no se disponga otra cosa por las leyes". La Corte estaría compuesta de 11 ministros y un fiscal, mexicanos, mayores de 40 años, sin antecedentes penales y abogados recibidos con 10 años de ejercicio en la judicatura "ó quince en el foro con estudio abierto". Sus atribuciones eran semejantes a las que señalaba la anterior Constitución centralista y se precisaba que estaba facultada para "Oír las dudas de los tribunales sobre la inteligencia de alguna ley, y juzgándolas fundadas, iniciar la declaración correspondiente". Podía hacer los nombramientos de "los dependientes y subalternos de la misma Corte, á los que expedirá sus despachos el presidente de la República". Los asuntos militares se atenderían en una Corte Marcial. El Congreso era el encargado de juzgar a los ministros mediante un tribunal especial. Por decreto del presidente Mariano Salas, el 22 de agosto de 1946 fue restablecida la Constitución de 1824 y el 22 de mayo del año siguiente fue publicada el *Acta de Reformas* a la propia Constitución, mediante la cual intervenía la Corte en el nombramiento de la mitad del Senado, recibía los casos de funcionarios sujetos a proceso y privados de fuero por el Congreso, sometía al examen de las legislaturas locales las leyes reclamadas como inconstitucionales y publicaría el resultado, "quedando anulada la ley si así lo resolviere la mayoría de las Legislaturas". El 23 de abril de 1853, con Santa Anna en la Presidencia, se promulgaron las Bases para la administración de la República, que decían: "Para que los intereses nacionales sean convenientemente atendidos en los negocios contenciosos que se versen sobre ellos (.), promover cuanto convenga á la Hacienda Pública y que se proceda en todos los ramos con los conocimientos necesarios en puntos de derecho, se nombrará *un procurador general de la nación*, con sueldo de 4,000 pesos, honores y condecoración de ministro de la Corte Suprema de Justicia, en la cual y en todos los tribunales será recibido como parte por la nación, y en los inferiores cuando lo disponga así el respectivo ministerio". El 23 de mayo de 1856, al triunfo de la Revolución de Ayutla, se expidió el decreto que contenía el Estatuto Orgánico Provisional de la República Mexicana, en el que se eliminaba implícitamente el fuero eclesiástico y se daba al Ejecutivo la facultad de visitar los tribunales, incluida la Suprema Corte, aunque el artículo 96 establecía que "El Poder Judicial es independiente en el ejercicio de sus funciones, las que desempeñará con arreglo a las leyes". Dicho poder sería "desempeñado por la Suprema Corte de Justicia y los tribunales de circuito y juzgados de distrito". Las atribuciones de la Corte eran semejantes a las que tenía, pero nuevamente se le privaba de "hacer reglamento alguno, ni aun sobre materias pertenecientes a la administración de justicia, ni dictar providencias que contengan disposiciones generales que alteren o aclaren las leyes". El artículo 101 ordenaba que "todos los negocios que comiencen en los juzgados inferiores de un estado, terminarán dentro de él en todas instancias". Los gobiernos de los estados tenían la atribución de nombrar empleados judiciales y proponer ternas al presidente de la República para la designación de magistrados superiores. La Constitución de 1857 estableció que "nadie puede ser juzgado por leyes privativas ni por tribunales especiales. Ninguna persona ni corporación puede tener fueros, ni gozar emolumentos que no sean compensación de un servicio público, y estén fijados por la ley. Subsiste el fuero de guerra solamente para los delitos y faltas que tengan esacta conecsión con la disciplina militar. La ley fijará con toda claridad los casos de esta escepción". La Norma Fundamental ampliaba

Caricatura sobre los poderes Legislativo, Ejecutivo y Judicial en 1875

los derechos ciudadanos y reglamentaba la administración de justicia, la que debía ser gratuita, "quedando en consecuencia abolidas las costas judiciales". El artículo 79 decía: "En las faltas temporales del presidente de la República, y en la absoluta mientras se presenta el nuevamente electo, entrará a ejercer el poder el presidente de la Suprema Corte de Justicia". De acuerdo con el artículo 90, "Se deposita el ejercicio del poder judicial de la federación en una Corte Suprema de Justicia y en los tribunales de Distrito y de Circuito". La Corte estaría compuesta por 11 ministros propietarios, cuatro supernumerarios, un fiscal y un procurador general, quienes durarían en su cargo seis años "y su elección será indirecta en primer grado en los términos que disponga la ley electoral". El aspirante debía ser "instruido en la ciencia del derecho, á juicio de los electores, ser mayor de 35 años y ciudadano mexicano por nacimiento en ejercicio de sus derechos". El juramento para tomar posesión fue muy diferente a los antes usados, pues debían responder afirmativamente a la pregunta "¿Juráis desempeñar leal y patrióticamente el cargo de magistrado de la Suprema Corte de Justicia que os ha conferido el pueblo, conforme a la Constitución, y mirando en todo por el bien y prosperidad de la Unión?". A la Corte sólo correspondía conocer "desde la primera instancia" de las controversias entre los estados "y de aquellas en que la Unión fuera parte", dirimir "las competencias que se susciten entre los tribunales de la federación, entre éstos y los de los estados, ó entre los de un estado y los de otro". En los demás casos, sería "tribunal de apelación, ó bien de última instancia, conforme a la graduación que haga la ley de las atribuciones de los tribunales de Circuito y de Distrito". En el caso de delitos oficiales cometidos por funcionarios de los poderes, una vez que tales funcionarios fueran desaforados, la Corte sería "juzgado de sentencia". Si los delitos fueran comunes, separado de su encargo el funcionario, quedaría sujeto a los tribunales ordinarios. El presidente de esta primera Suprema Corte de Justicia emanada de una norma constitucional fue Benito Juárez. Según el Estatuto Provisional del imperio de Maximiliano, "El Emperador presenta la Soberanía Nacional y, mientras cosa no se decrete en la organización definitiva del Imperio, la ejerce en todos sus ramos, por sí o por medio de las autoridades y funcionarios públicos". El título IV, "De los Tribunales", decía: "La justicia será administrada por los tribunales que determina la ley orgánica", "Los magistrados y jueces que se nombraren con el carácter de inamovibles, no podrán ser destituidos sino en los términos que disponga la ley

Foto: Archivo Casasola

Magistrados de la Suprema Corte de Justicia de la Nación en 1928

orgánica" y "gozarán de absoluta independencia". A los tribunales les quedaba vedado elaborar reglamentos o "suspender la ejecución de las leyes". Ningún juicio podía tener más de dos instancias. Al triunfo de los republicanos, Benito Juárez expidió una Convocatoria para la elección de los Supremos Poderes, que comprendían la de presidente y magistrados de la Suprema Corte, un fiscal y un procurador general. En noviembre de 1874 se adicionó y reformó la Constitución y pasó a ser facultad del Congreso calificar y decidir sobre las renuncias de magistrados de la Suprema Corte. En 1882 se introdujo otra reforma, mediante la cual en ausencia temporal o absoluta, el presidente de la República sería sustituido por el "presidente o vicepresidente del Senado, o de la Comisión Permanente" del Congreso en los periodos de receso. En 1896 quedó como facultad exclusiva de la Cámara de Diputados "Calificar y decidir" sobre las renuncias de los magistrados de la Corte. Una reforma constitucional de 1900 establecía que "La Suprema Corte de Justicia se compondrá de quince Ministros y funcionará en Tribunal Pleno o en Salas, de la manera que establezca la ley", misma que "establecerá y organizará los Tribunales de Circuito, los Juzgados de Distrito y el Ministerio Público de la Federación". El Ejecutivo nombraría a los "funcionarios del Ministerio Público y al Procurador General de la Federación". El Plan de San Luis, emitido por Francisco I. Madero el 5 de octubre de 1910, declaraba nulas las elecciones de ese año, que incluyeron las de magistrados de la Suprema Corte, y desconocía a todas las autoridades "cuyo poder debe dimanar del voto popular". En 1916, al iniciarse las sesiones de Congreso Constituyente, Venustiano Carranza emitió un mensaje en el que señalaba que el recurso de amparo, por el abuso que de él se hacía, se había convertido en "un medio apropiado para acabar con la soberanía de los estados", "pues de hecho quedaron sujetos a la revisión de la Suprema Corte hasta los actos más insignificantes de las autoridades de aquéllos" y "como ese alto tribunal, por la forma en que se designaban sus miembros, estaba completamente a disposición del jefe del Poder Ejecutivo", éste podía intervenir en la vida de las entidades federativas. Carranza se refirió también a "la acción arbitraria y despótica de los jueces", a sus "prácticas verdaderamente inquisitoriales", a las "muchas vacilaciones" de la Corte y a cómo "procuró abrir tantas brechas" en la reforma al juicio de amparo, "que en poco tiempo la dejó enteramente inútil". La Constitución de 1917 establece que "El Supremo Poder de la Federación se divide, para su ejercicio, en Legislativo, Ejecutivo y Judicial". El artículo 94 dice: "Se deposita el ejercicio del Poder Judicial de la Federación en una Suprema Corte de Justicia y en Tribunales de Circuito y de Distrito cuyo número y atribuciones fijará la ley. La Suprema Corte de Justicia de la Nación se compondrá de 11 ministros y funcionará siempre en tribunal pleno, siendo sus audiencias públicas, excepción hecha de los casos en que la moral o el interés público así lo exigieren". "Cada uno de los ministros de la Suprema Corte designados para integrar ese poder en las próximas elecciones, durará en su encargo dos años; los que fueren electos al terminar este primer periodo durarán cuatro años y a partir del año de 1923, los ministros de la Corte, los magistrados de Circuito y los jueces de Distrito sólo podrán ser removidos cuando observen mala conducta y previo el juicio de responsabilidad respectivo, a menos que los magistrados y los jueces sean promovidos a grado superior". Para ser ministro era necesario ser mexicano por nacimiento, en pleno ejercicio de sus derechos, tener 35 años cumplidos el día de la elección, haber residido en el país los últimos cinco años, poseer título de abogado, "gozar de buena reputación y no haber sido condenado por delito que amerite pena corporal de más de un año de prisión; pero si se tratare de robo, fraude, falsificación, abuso de confianza u otro que lastime seriamente la buena fama en el concepto público, inhabilitará para tal cargo, cualquiera que haya sido la pena". El artículo 96 decía que los miembros de la Corte "serán electos por el Congreso de la Unión en funciones de Colegio Electoral, siendo indispensable que concurran cuando menos las dos terceras partes del número total de diputados y senadores. La elección se hará en escrutinio secreto y por mayoría absoluta de votos. Los candidatos serán previamente propuestos, uno por cada Legislatura de los Estados". "Los magistrados de Circuito y los jueces de Distrito serán nombrados por la Suprema Corte de Justicia de la Nación. Tendrán los requisitos que exija la ley, durarán cuatro años en el ejercicio de su encargo y no podrán ser removidos de éste, sin previo juicio de responsabilidad o por incapacidad para desempeñarlo". La misma Corte, decía la Constitución, "nombrará alguno o algunos de sus miembros o algún juez de Distrito o magistrado de Circuito, o designará uno o varios comisionados especiales, cuando así lo juzgue conveniente o lo pidiere el Ejecutivo Federal, o alguna de las Cámaras de la Unión, o el gobernador de algún estado, únicamente para que averigüe la conducta de algún juez o magistrado federal o algún hecho o hechos que constituyan la violación de alguna garantía individual, o la violación del voto público o algún otro delito castigado por la ley federal". "La Suprema Corte cada año designará a uno de sus miembros como presidente, pudiendo éste ser reelecto". Cada ministro, al asumir su cargo, debía responder afirmativamente ante el Congreso de la Unión o, en sus recesos, ante la Comisión Permanente, la siguiente pregunta: "¿Protestáis desempeñar leal y patrióticamente el cargo de Ministro de la Suprema Corte de Justicia de la Nación que se os ha conferido, y guardar y hacer guardar la Constitución Política de los Estados Unidos Mexicanos, y las leyes que de ella emanen, mirando en todo por el bien y prosperidad de la Unión?" Los ministros, en caso de ausencia no mayor de un mes, no serían suplidos si la Corte "tuviere *quorum* para sus sesiones; pero si no lo hubiere, el Congreso de la Unión o en su receso la Comisión Permanente, nombrará por el tiempo que dure la falta, un suplente de entre los candidatos presentados por los Estados" que no hubieren sido electos. Si la falta fuere menor de dos meses, el Congreso o en sus recesos la Comisión Permanente, "nombrará libremente un ministro provisional". "Si faltare un ministro por defunción, renuncia o incapacidad, el Congreso de la Unión hará nueva elección en los términos prescriptos por el artículo 96". El cargo de ministro "sólo es renunciable por causa grave, calificada por el Congreso de la Unión, ante el que se presentará la renuncia" o, en sus recesos, ante la Comisión Permanente. Las licencias por menos de un mes las concedía la propia Corte y, cuando eran por más tiempo, el Congreso. "Los Ministros de la Suprema Corte de Justicia, los magistrados de Circuito, los jueces de Distrito y los respectivos secretarios, no podrán, en ningún caso, aceptar y desempeñar empleo o encargo de la Federación, de los Estados o de particulares, salvo los cargos honoríficos en asociaciones científicas, literarias o de beneficencia. La infracción de esta disposición será castigada con la pérdida del cargo". En el mismo capítulo dedicado al Poder Judicial, se incluye lo referente al Ministerio Público y al procurador general de la República, dependencias del Poder Ejecutivo. En 1928, mediante una reforma constitucional, se elevó el número de ministros a 16 y se permitió el funcionamiento en Pleno o en tres Salas. En 1934 el número de ministros subió a 21 y las salas a cuatro. Una reforma de 1944 dejó incierto el número de salas. En 1928 se facultó al presidente de la República para proponer ministros provisionales al Senado o, si estuviere en receso, a la Comisión Permanente. De igual manera se dispuso el procedimiento para nombrar nuevos ministros por defunción, renuncia o incapacidad. En el mismo paquete de reformas constitucionales se aprobó que las renuncias de los ministros "solamente procederán por causas graves; serán sometidas al Ejecutivo, y si éste las acepta, serán enviadas para su aprobación al Senado, y en su receso a la Comisión Permanente". Las licencias de los ministros por menos de un mes las concederá la propia Corte. Si exceden ese lapso "las concederá el Presidente de la República, con aprobación del Senado, o, en sus recesos, por la Comisión Permanente". En 1935 entró en vigor la Ley Orgánica del Poder Judicial (vigente, con modificaciones). En 1951 se abrieron cinco puestos más en la Suprema Corte, con la denominación de ministros supermumerarios (había un rezago de 38,000 asuntos pendientes). En 1968 se otorgó a los Tribunales Colegiados de Circuito la facultad de emitir jurisprudencia (interpretación de las dispocisiones legales de tribunales colegiados). En 1987 la Suprema Corte recibe facultades exclusivas para emitir resoluciones sobre la constitucionalidad en los litigios generados en el país y los Tribunales Colegiados de Circuito deliberen sobre asuntos de casación. En 1989, el Poder Judicial se depositó en "una Suprema Corte de Justicia, en Tribunales de Circuito, Colegiados en materia de amparo y unitarios en materia de apelación y en juzgados de Distrito". En ningún caso "los Ministros supernumerarios integrarán el Pleno". Para ser ministro se adicionaron algunos requisitos, como

Integrantes de la Suprema Corte de Justicia en 1999

"No tener más de 65 años de edad, ni menos de treinta y cinco, el día de la elección", y que el título de abogado haya sido expedido por lo menos cinco años antes. Los magistrados de Circuito y los jueces de distrito son designados por la Corte. El presidente de la Suprema Corte puede ser reelegido. En 1994 se impulsó la reforma para crear el Consejo de la Judicatura Federal (instalada el 2 de febrero de 1995) y reducir de 26 a 11 el número de ministros de la Suprema Corte de Justicia de la Nación. De acuerdo con esta reforma, el Ejecutivo propuso a 18 candidatos para los 11 puestos de ministros de la SCJN y el Senado aprobó a cada uno de los once con tres cuartas partes de la votación como mínimo. Además se reforzó a la SCJN como tribunal constitucional, al ampliarse sus facultades para conocer las controversias entre la Federación, los estados y los municipios, entre el Ejecutivo y el Congreso, entre los poderes de las entidades federativas o entre los órganos del Distrito Federal. Se propuso la carrera judicial y su reglamentación quedó pendiente. Actualmente la sede de la Suprema Corte de Justicia de la Nación se ubica en el DF, en la calle de Pino Suárez, a un lado de la Plaza de la Constitución y en terrenos donde se ubicó la antigua plaza El Volador. Desde 1997 se han producido roces entre algunos ministros de la SCJN y el Consejo de la Judicatura.

PODER LEGISLATIVO ◆ Entre las fuerzas insurgentes, el primer Congreso fue convocado por José María Morelos, quien buscaba dar a ese órgano carácter sólo constituyente, aunque ya reunido asumió otras funciones, como la designación de autoridades políticas y militares. El propio Morelos designó diputados por las provincias en poder de los realistas y sólo en Tecpan, hoy Guerrero, y Oaxaca fueron elegidos, respectivamente, José Manuel de Herrera y José María Murguía. El principal logro de esta asamblea fue la redacción de la Constitución de Apatzingán (☛ *Decreto Constitucional para la Libertad de la América Mexicana*). A la consumación de la Independencia, de acuerdo con lo dispuesto en el Plan de Iguala, Agustín de Iturbide nombró a los integrantes de la Junta Provisional de Gobierno, a la que correspondía designar los cinco integrantes de la regencia del Imperio Mexicano, legislar en casos de urgencia de acuerdo con ésta y convocar al Congreso Constituyente. La Junta hizo la convocatoria para elecciones indirectas de representantes al Congreso, órgano que debía dividirse en dos cámaras. Instalado el 24 de febrero de 1822, en solemne ceremonia realizada en la Catedral Metropolitana, se trasladó al ex templo jesuita de San Pedro y San Pablo, en las actuales calles de El Carmen y Venezuela. Además de asumir sus facultades de constituyente, la asamblea "se reservó el ejercicio del Poder Legislativo en toda su extensión" y no se dividió como estaba previsto, todo lo cual agudizó los choques con Iturbide, ya coronado emperador, quien lo disolvió el 31 de octubre de 1822 y en su lugar estableció la Junta Nacional Instituyente, donde incluyó a presuntos representantes de las provincias. Esta Junta acordó sustituir la Carta de Cádiz, porque "es un código peculiar de la nación de que nos hemos emancipado", y el 18 de diciembre de 1822 aprobó el Reglamento Provisional Político del Imperio Mexicano. En diciembre se levantó en armas Antonio López de Santa Anna (☛ *Plan de Veracruz*), quien lanzó un plan que proclamaba la República y exigía la reinstalación del Congreso, pues la nación, decía, "se halla al presente en estado natural", esto es, no constituida. Iturbide se vio obligado a reinstalar el Congreso (6 de marzo), ante el que abdicó el 19 de marzo. Sin embargo, la asamblea resolvió el 8 de abril que no cabía discutir la abdicación, pues declaró nula la coronación y por tanto la sucesión hereditaria, consideró ilegales todos los actos del emperador e insubsistente la forma de gobierno anterior, "quedando la Nación en absoluta libertad para constituirse como le acomode". El Congreso depositó el ejecutivo en una junta de tres miembros y en octubre de 1823 convocó a nuevas elecciones, pues las provincias no le reconocían facultades de constituyente. Pese a lo anterior, aprobó la forma de República Federada y un Plan de la Constitución Política de la Nación Mexicana, en el que se establecía que "la nación ejerce sus derechos por medio: 1o., de los ciudadanos que eligen a los individuos del cuerpo legislativo; 2o., del cuerpo legislativo que decreta las leyes; 3o., del ejecutivo que las hace cumplir a sus ciudadanos: 4o., de los jueces que las aplican en las causas civiles y criminales; (y) 5o., de los senadores que las hacen respetar a los primeros funcionarios". El 5 de noviembre se reunió el nuevo Constituyente, que el 31 de enero de 1824 aprobó el Acta Constitutiva de la Federación Mexicana, especie de Constitución provisional en la que se asentaba que "la base para nombrar a los diputados será la población" y que "cada estado nombrará dos senadores". El 4 de octubre fue sancionada y decretada la Constitución Federal de los Estados Unidos Mexicanos, la que establecía que "La nación mexicana adopta para su gobierno la forma de república representativa popular federal", en la que "se divide el supremo poder de la federación para su ejercicio, en legislativo, ejecutivo y judicial" y depositaba "el poder legislativo en un congreso general" dividido en dos cámaras, "una de diputados y otra de senadores". La primera se compondría "de representantes elegidos en su totalidad cada dos años, por los ciudadanos de los estados", mediante un proceso que reglamentarían las legislaturas de los estados. "La base general para el nombramiento de diputados será la población. Por cada mil almas se nombrará un diputado, o por una fracción que pase de cuarenta mil. El estado que no tuviere esa población, nombrará sin embargo un diputado". El mismo código indicaba que "el territorio que tenga más de cuarenta mil habitantes nombrará un diputado" con voz y voto, en tanto que si tuviere menos población de la indicaba podía nombrar un representante que sólo tendría derecho a voz. Los candidatos debían tener 25 años cumplidos al tiempo de la elección, haber nacido en el estado que elige o tener en él dos años de vecindad. Los no nacidos en el territorio nacional tenían como obligación acreditar ocho años de vecindad, 8,000 pesos en bienes raíces en la República "o una industria que produzca mil pesos cada año". Se exceptuaba de los requisitos por extranjería a los "nacidos en cualquiera otra parte de la América que en 1810 dependía de la España", así como a aquellos que, nacidos en cualquier parte fuera del país, "con las armas sostuvieron la independencia del país, a quienes bastará tener la vecindad de ocho años". No podían ser legisladores los funcionarios de los poderes ejecutivo y judicial, los gobernadores ni los miembros de la jerarquía eclesiástica, a menos que seis meses antes hubieran "cesado absolutamente en sus destinos". La Constitución señalaba que "El senado se compondrá de dos senadores por cada estado, elegidos a mayoría absoluta de votos por sus legislaturas, y renovados por mitad de dos en dos años". La edad mínima para ingresar en esta cámara era de 30 años cumplidos y se establecía que "no pueden ser senadores los que no puedan ser diputados". Se aclaraba que "cuando un mismo individuo sea elegido para senador y diputado, preferirá la elección primera en tiempo". La elección de senadores sería el 1 de septiembre "próximo a la renovación por mitad de aquellos", en tanto que las de diputados se celebrarían el primer domingo de octubre "próximo anterior" a la renovación del Congreso. Como la Constitución no incluía al Distrito Federal entre "las partes de la Federación", los habitantes del Distrito Federal no estuvieron representados en la primera Legislatura (1825-27). Senadores por la capital no hubo durante la primera República Federal (1824-35). El recinto de la diputación, acondicionado por el arquitecto Ignacio Paz, del partido escocés, se derrumbó a mediados de 1827. El 1 de enero de 1829 la Cámara de Diputados se instaló en el Palacio Nacional, en una sala debidamente acondicionada. De enero a marzo de 1833 Santa Anna suspendió la actividad del Congreso, con el afán de impedir lo que ya era inminente: la primera Reforma. Ésta se echó a andar con Valentín Gómez Farías en la Presidencia y un Poder Legislativo de mayoría federalista. El 15 de mayo de 1834, desplazado Gómez Farías del gobierno, Santa Anna instó al Congreso para que revocara varias de las leyes reformistas. Diputados y senadores, para eludir las presiones santanistas, decidieron suspender el periodo de sesiones. Santa Anna respondió emitiendo una nueva convocatoria para que se reunieran las cámaras, pero tan pocos representantes acudieron que no había quórum. La prensa federalista exhortó a los legisladores a reunirse para no abandonar a sus representados, lo que tuvo éxito, pues el 31 de mayo diputados y senadores se presentaron a sus respectivas sedes, pero se encontraron con guardias armados que les cerraban el paso, lo que significaba que Santa Anna había clausurado el Congreso. En julio, mientras echaba abajo las principales disposiciones de la primera reforma y los federalistas eran sometidos a implacable persecución, convocó a elecciones para diputados y senadores, quienes se reunieron, ya con mayoría centralista, el 4 de enero de 1835. En el mismo año, en un segundo periodo de sesiones, apoyado en varios pronunciamientos militares, el Congreso se declaró facultado "para considerar las manifestaciones públicas sobre el cambio de la actual forma de gobierno" y el 9 de septiembre se autodisolvió y volvió a constituirse cinco días después como cámara única para aprobar, el 3 de octubre, una ley que establecía el sistema centralista, disolvía las legislaturas de los estados y ponía el poder de las entidades federativas bajo control directo del gobierno central. El 23 de octubre se publicaron las bases de una nueva Constitución y el 29 de diciembre de 1836 fue sustituida la Constitución de 1824 por las Siete Leyes, que determinaban que el ejercicio del poder legislativo quedaba depositado "en el congreso general de la nación, el cual se compondrá de dos cámaras", la de diputados y la senadores. La primera se integraría con un diputado por cada 150,000 habitantes o fracción mayor de 80,000. Los departamentos (ya no había estados) que tuvieran una población menor elegirían un diputado. La cámara se renovaría "por mitad cada dos años". Las elecciones se realizarían el primer domingo de octubre y el Senado se encargaría de calificarlas. Los requisitos para los candidatos eran tener 30 años de edad el día de los comicios, ser nacidos en México o en la América antes española y tener una renta de por lo menos 1,500 pesos anuales, lo que imposibilitaba a la mayoría de los mexicanos. Los ciudadanos capaces de elegir debían tener una renta anual de por lo menos 100 pesos anuales, no ser sirvientes domésticos, desempleados ni analfabetos (a partir de 1846), todo lo cual limitaba el ejercicio de los derechos electorales a una minoría. El Senado tendría 24 integrantes, mayores de 35 años y con rentas anuales de 2,500 pesos como mínimo, elegidos mediante un complicado procedimiento: "En cada caso de elección, la cámara de diputados, el gobierno en junta de ministros y la Suprema Corte de Justicia elegirán, cada uno a pluralidad absoluta de votos, un número de individuos igual al que debe ser de nuevos senadores. Las tres listas que resultarán serán autorizadas por los respectivos secretarios y remitidas a las juntas departamentales (y) cada una de éstas elegirá, precisamente de los comprendidos en las listas, el número que se debe nombrar de senadores, y remitirá la lista especificativa de su elección al supremo poder conservador. Éste las examinará, calificará las elecciones. y declarará senadores a los que hayan reunido la mayoría de votos de las juntas, por el orden de la esa mayoría, y decidiendo la suerte en los números iguales". El Senado debía renovarse "por terceras partes cada dos años". Como la ciudad de México se había convertido en capital del departamento de México, los antiguos distritofederalenses estuvieron entonces representados en ambas cámaras. Se establecía la celebración de dos periodos de sesiones cada año. El 11 de noviembre de 1840, durante el segundo gobierno de Anastasio Bustamante, el Supremo Poder Conservador dio al Congreso facultades de Constituyente, función que no pudo cumplir por la inestabilidad política del país. El 28 de septiembre de 1841 varios generales alzados firmaron las Bases de Tacubaya, mediante las cuales cesaban los poderes supremos, con excepción del judicial, se convocaba a una junta de notables para elegir presidente y se anunciaba la convocatoria a un nuevo congreso que, "facultado ampliamente, se encargará de constituir a la nación". Sin embargo, como el resultado de las elecciones favoreciera a los liberales, Santa Anna condicionó la instalación del Congreso a que sus integrantes juraran acatamiento a las Bases de Tacubaya, a lo que procedieron los elegidos en la inteligencia de que sólo quedaban comprometidos ceñirse a su función constituyente. Como el proyecto a discusión disgustara a los centralistas, Nicolás Bravo, entonces presidente, desconoció al Congreso el 19 de diciembre de 1842. Clausurado el salón de sesiones, los constituyentes se reunieron en un domicilio particular y ahí formularon una enérgica protesta que no tuvo mayor efecto, pues Bravo, el día 23, designó a 80 notables que integraron lo que se llamó Junta Nacional Legislativa, encargada también de elaborar una constitución, las Bases de Organización Política de la República Mexicana, más conocidas como Bases Orgánicas, ordenamiento centralista que Santa Anna, por enésima vez en la Presidencia, sancionó el 12 de junio de 1843. Las *Bases*, que determinaban de modo semejante a las Siete Leyes las condiciones que debían satisfacerse para tener ciudadanía, establecían que el Poder Legislativo quedaba depositado en un Congreso dividido en dos cámaras, una de diputados y otra de senadores, "y en el Presidente de la República por lo que respecta a la sanción de las leyes". La primera se compondría de representantes elegidos indirectamente, por colegios electorales departamentales elegidos a su vez por los representantes de cada 500 ciudadanos. La Cámara de Diputados se integraría en razón de uno por cada 70,000 habitantes, más uno por cada departamento que tuviera una población menor. El candidato debía tener 30 años al momento de la elección y una renta anual efectiva de 1,200 pesos. La Cámara de Diputados se renovaría por mitad cada dos años. Habría dos periodos de sesiones al año, de tres meses cada uno, en los que se daría curso a los asuntos corrientes, al mismo tiempo que a la función de jurado y colegio electoral cuando fuera necesario. El Senado se compondría de 63 individuos, de los que dos tercios serían elegidos por las asambleas departamentales y otro tercio por la Cámara de Diputados, el presidente de la República y la Suprema Corte de Justicia. Cada una de estas autoridades elegiría 21 candidatos y las listas respectivas se enviarían "a la Cámara de Senadores o a la Diputación Permanente", para que ahí se invistiera formalmente a los que contaran con mayoría de votos. En 1843 exclusivamente el presidente de la República elegiría a los 21, que debían ser "sujetos que se hayan distinguido por sus servicios y méritos en la carrera civil, militar y eclesiástica". Los senadores elegidos por las asambleas departamentales debían representar a las clases propietarias. El 22 de agosto de 1846, tras una larga sucesión de golpes de Estado, el general Mariano Salas expidió un decreto que restablecía la Constitución de 1824 (☛ *Plan de la Ciudadela*), en tanto que el Congreso que estaba por reunirse elaboraba un nuevo ordenamiento. Este Congreso, constituyente y ordinario a la vez, se reunió el 6 de diciembre con una mayoría de liberales moderados. En medio de asonadas, medidas reformistas de Gómez Farías, el motín de los polkos y el regreso de Santa Anna a la Presidencia, en lugar de un nuevo ordenamiento, el 22 de mayo de 1847 fue aprobada un Acta de Reformas a la Constitución de 1824. Tal documento daba la ciudadanía a los varones mayores de 20 años, anunciaba las reglamentación de las inviolables garantías de "libertad, seguridad, propiedad e igualdad"; suprimía la vicepresidencia de la República, creaba el estado de Guerrero (☛), previo consentimiento de las legislaturas de México, Michoacán y Puebla; establecía que habría un diputado al Congreso general, mayor de 25 años al momento de la elección, "por cada cincuenta mil almas, ó por una fracción que pase de veinticinco mil". En el Senado, además de los dos representantes por entidad federativa, "habrá un número igual al número de los estados, electo a propuesta de la Cámara de Diputados, votando por diputaciones, del Senado y del Ejecutivo. Las personas que reunieren estos tres sufragios, quedarán electas, y la Cámara de Diputados, votando por personas, nombrará los que falten". Era facultad de la diputación erigirse en gran jurado para determinar si había lugar a una formación de causa contra altos funcionarios con fuero. El artículo 13 señalaba que para la elección de funcionarios, salvo el tercio de senadores antes señalado, podía "adoptarse la elección directa". En el mismo año, durante la ocupación estadounidense, el Congreso se trasladó a Querétaro, donde se le acondicionó la Academia de Bellas Artes para las sesiones en las que aprobó la cesión de la mitad del territorio nacional a los invasores. Una vez que las tropas extranjeras se habían retirado, los poderes volvieron a la ciudad de México, a principios de junio de 1848. El 21 de mayo de 1852 el Congreso negó al presidente Mariano Arista las facultades extraordinarias que había solicitado. Se produjeron varios alzamientos militares y el 5 de enero siguiente renunció Arista. Lo sustituyó Juan B. Ceballos, presidente de la Suprema

Corte, quien disolvió el Congreso y poco después renunció. Llamado por las principales facciones, Antonio López de Santa Anna volvió al poder en 1853, facultado para gobernar durante un año sin Constitución, en espera de que la elaborara un Congreso Constituyente al que debía convocar. Mientras tanto, los ministros del nuevo gobierno conservador expidieron el 23 de abril unas *Bases para la administración de la República hasta la promulgación de la Constitución*, las que fueron acompañadas de diversos decretos que abolieron en la práctica el sistema federal. Santa Anna, en uso de plenos poderes, se convirtió en un dictador que se hacía llamar "alteza serenísima" y, por supuesto, no convocó al Congreso. Estalló la revolución de Ayutla, que una vez triunfante, con Juan Álvarez en la Presidencia de la República, convocó al Congreso Constituyente el 16 de octubre de 1855. La asamblea se reunió en la ciudad de México el 17 de febrero de 1856 y un año después clausuraba sus sesiones, después de jurar, el 5 de febrero, la nueva norma fundamental. En ésta, el "Supremo poder de la federación se divide para su ejercicio en legislativo, ejecutivo y judicial". El Senado desaparecía y el Poder Legislativo quedaba depositado "en una asamblea, que se denominará Congreso de la Unión", compuesto de representantes elegidos en su totalidad cada dos años, con un diputado por cada 40,000 habitantes o fracción mayor de 20,000. "El territorio en que la población sea menor de la que se fija en este artículo, nombrará sin embargo un diputado. La elección sería indirecta en primer grado. Los candidatos debían tener 25 años al momento de la elección, ser vecinos del estado o territorio que hace la elección y no pertenecer al estado eclesiástico. Habría dos periodos de sesiones, del 1 de abril al 30 de mayo y del 16 de septiembre al 15 de diciembre. El Congreso tenía facultades para admitir otros estados, dar este carácter a territorios o formar nuevos dentro de los ya existentes "siempre que lo pida una población de

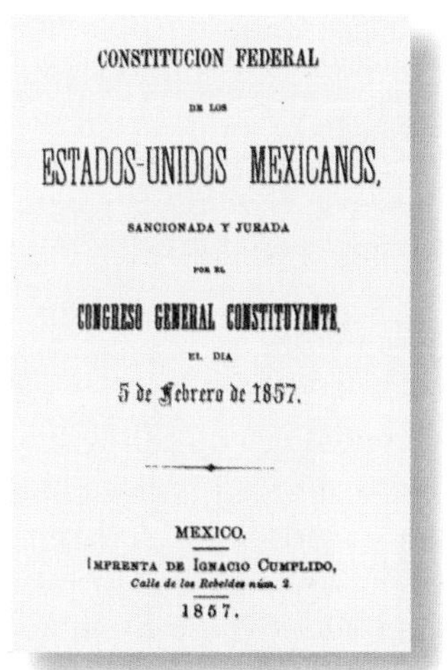

CONSTITUCION FEDERAL

DE LOS

ESTADOS-UNIDOS MEXICANOS,

SANCIONADA Y JURADA

POR EL

CONGRESO GENERAL CONSTITUYENTE,

EL DIA

5 de Febrero de 1857.

MEXICO.

IMPRENTA DE IGNACIO CUMPLIDO,

Calle de los Rebeldes núm. 2.

1857.

La Constitución de 1857 estableció la desaparición del Senado

ochenta mil habitantes, justificando tener los elementos necesarios para proveer a su ecsistencia política", siempre que el acuerdo lo ratificara la mayoría de las legislaturas locales. Constitucionalmente, la cámara única tenía la función de "ratificar los nombramientos que haga el Ejecutivo de los ministros, agentes diplomáticos y cónsules, de los empleados superiores de Hacienda, de los coroneles y demás oficiales superiores del ejército y armada nacional". Otras facultades eran "levantar y sostener el ejército y la armada", expedir reglamentos "con el objeto de organizar, armar y disciplinar la guardia nacional, reservando a los ciudadanos que la formen, el nombramiento respectivo de gefes y oficiales"; autorizar el establecimiento de "casas de moneda, fijar las condiciones que ésta deba tener, determinar el valor de la extranjera y adoptar un sistema generalizado de pesas y medidas"; "conceder amnistías", y prorrogar hasta por 30 días su primer periodo de sesiones. En diciembre de ese año, el presidente Ignacio Comonfort desconoció la Constitución y disolvió el Congreso, con lo que se inició la guerra de los Tres años. Al triunfo de los liberales y restablecido el orden constitucional, se convocó a elecciones y el 9 de mayo de 1861 se instaló la Diputación que recibió el nombre de Segundo Congreso Constituyente. En el discurso de apertura, el presidente Benito Juárez informó que su gobierno, desde que se instaló en Guanajuato (1858), "procuró la reunión del Congreso sin poderla lograr por circunstancias superiores a la voluntad de los representantes". En tal situación, "no pudo sacrificar la sustancia a la forma y se determinó a ejercer la facultad legislativa en cuantas materias era necesario". Juárez se refería a las Leyes de Reforma (☛ *Reforma*). En su respuesta, José María Aguirre, presidente del Congreso, dijo que el pueblo "proclamó principios que, nulificando el poder de sus enemigos, dejaron muy atrás a la Constitución misma de la República. Esos principios que son lo que comprenden las Leyes de Reforma, fueron desde entonces el estandarte a cuyo derredor se agruparon los defensores de la democracia, para conquistarlos con su sangre y sancionarlos con el poder de la victoria. No será, pues, el Congreso Nacional el que deje de reconocerlos. Ésta es la exigencia más grande de la revolución". En la misma fecha, celebradas las elecciones presidenciales, pero todavía en espera de los resultados, Francisco Zarco, Ignacio Zaragoza e Ignacio Ramírez renunciaron a sus puestos en el gabinete por "adhesión a los principios constitucionales", pues sus cargos no habían sido ratificados por la diputación, como establecía el ordenamiento de 1857. Zarco dijo a Juárez: "creo indispensable que el Jefe del Estado forme un gabinete parlamentario para evitar todo antagonismo entre los poderes". El Congreso dio curso al primer periodo de sesiones hasta el 31 de mayo, en que constitucionalmente llegaba a su término y cuando los invasores franceses se preparaban para tomar la ciudad de México. En esa ocasión, Juárez habló ante los diputados y reconoció que, "no obstante la violencia y lo peligroso de la situación", ellos habían cumplido su labor, lo que era "una prueba más del imperio sereno y seguro que conservan nuestras instituciones a la vista del enemigo extranjero", cuya influencia "no alcanza más allá del terreno que ocupa". El diputado Sebastián Lerdo de Tejada respondió, en

FOTO: FONDO EDITORIAL GRUPO AZABACHE

Antigua Cámara de Diputados, hoy Asamblea de Representantes de DF

nombre de la asamblea, que "mientras algunos de los representantes del pueblo han estado defendiendo con las armas el honor y la independencia nacional, otros vinieron de los estados más remotos para que el Congreso no dejara de reunirse". En el mismo discurso, informó que se ratificaban al presidente los poderes extraordinarios de que estaba investido por esa representación. Dos días antes, ante el avance de las fuerzas de ocupación, Juárez emitió un decreto en el cual decía que "los poderes de la Federación se trasladarán por ahora a la ciudad de San Luis Potosí". El 10 de junio de 1863 entraron los invasores en la capital del país y Elías Federico Forey, comandante de las fuerzas de ocupación, designó el día 18 a 35 personas que serían integrantes de la Junta Superior de Gobierno. Ésta se instaló el 20 y dos días después, para ejercer el Poder Ejecutivo, eligió un triunvirato formado por el citado Almonte, el ex presidente Mariano Salas y el arzobispo Antonio Pelagio de Labastida y Dávalos, con el obispo Juan Ormaechea y Antonio Pavón como suplentes. El mismo día 22, el triunvirato recibió simbólicamente el poder de manos del general francés, quien les hizo entrega del Palacio Nacional. El 2 de julio, los triunviros designaron a 215 "notables", quienes con los 35 miembros de la junta integrarían el Poder Legislativo. El día 10, este órgano resolvió que el país adoptaba la "monarquía moderada hereditaria, con un príncipe católico" y que la corona se ofrecía a Maximiliano de Habsburgo, lo que estaba arreglado desde 1961. Asimismo, acordó cambiar el nombre del Ejecutivo por Regencia del Imperio. El 10 de abril de 1864, previa aprobación de Napoleón III, emperador francés, Maximiliano cumplió el formulismo de aceptar la corona y en la misma fecha disolvió la Regencia y extendió diversos nombramientos. En el bando de los patriotas, con la ciudad de San Luis Potosí erigida en capital de la República, el Congreso tuvo como sede el edificio llamado de las Antiguas Cajas Reales, donde despachó la diputación permanente y la Junta Preparatoria del Congreso desempeñó sus funciones. Un fuerte incidente surgió entre el Poder Legislativo y el Ejecutivo, cuando Manuel Doblado, secretario de Relaciones Exteriores y Gobernación, dictó orden de expulsión del estado y del país contra los representantes populares Manuel María Zamacona y Francisco Zarco, quien además presidía la Comisión Permanente. Una comisión de 10 miembros de la Junta Preparatoria se entrevistó con Juárez, quien dijo desconocer el asunto, ofreció seguridades a los diputados y pidió a la comisión considerar el caso como no sucedido, con el fin de no hacer pública división alguna en el campo republicano. Los comisionados aceptaron y Zarco acudió a la oficina de Doblado a petición de éste, quien lejos de obrar con ánimo conciliatorio amenazó con emplear la fuerza para echarlo del país. El líder de los congresistas escribió a Juárez una carta de tono muy enérgico, en la que expresa que está en San Luis Potosí no por su voluntad, "sino por el estrecho deber" de cumplir su mandato. Poco después, el funcionario renunció y fue enviado a Guanajuato. La Permanente convocó al periodo ordinario de sesiones para principios de septiembre, pero la situación misma del país impidió la concurrencia de la mayoría de los diputados. En esa circunstancia, los 64 diputados que se habían reunido en San Luis firmaron un Manifiesto del Congreso de la Unión a sus Comitentes, el 27 de noviembre de 1863. En ese documento, llaman a resistir a los invasores, para lo cual "dos Congresos han facultado ampliamente al Ejecutivo para que emplee todos los recursos de la nación en salvarla", en la inteligencia de que "no podrá el Gobierno admitir ninguna clase de intervención, ni obligación alguna que afecte la integridad del territorio, el cambio de sus instituciones o sus Leyes de Reforma. cualesquiera que sea la posición en que los coloquen las vicisitudes de la presente contienda". De esta manera, los legisladores trataban de evitar que se repitiera la experiencia de 1848, en que después de una guerra injusta hubo quienes accedieron a firmar los Tratados de Guadalupe, que legalizaban el despojo. El 22 de diciembre, Juárez se vio obligado a salir de San Luis Potosí e instaló los poderes en Saltillo del 9 de enero al 3 de abril de 1864. En esta ciudad, la Diputación Permanente tuvo su sede en el ex Colegio Católico de la Paz, luego residencia obispal. Los poderes pasaron a Monterrey, de donde volvieron poco después a Saltillo. Ahí, el 31 de marzo, en nombre de la Diputación Permanente, Ignacio Pombo y José Díaz Covarrubias comunicaron al Poder Ejecutivo que, de acuerdo con la Constitución, debía iniciarse el periodo de sesiones en el mes de abril inmediato, por lo que debía comunicarse lo anterior a los gobernadores para que "éstos exciten respectivamente a los ciudadanos diputados" para que se presentaran en Saltillo. Como era obvio, la situación no permitió que el Congreso se reuniera. Tampoco la Diputación Permanente pudo mantenerse reunida en el continuo peregrinar del gobierno republicano. En noviembre de 1865, cuando estaba por concluir su periodo presidencial, Juárez lo prorrogó, basado en los poderes extraordinarios que le había conferido el Congreso, pero no hubo legisladores que pudieran ratificar o reprobar la medida. En carta a los gobernadores, en la que explica los motivos de la prórroga, Lerdo de Tejada señalaba que resolver sobre las dudas del caso "sólo correspondería al Poder Legislativo nacional, que ejerce ahora el ciudadano presidente de la República por habérselo delegado el Congreso con facultades omnímodas, para disponer cuanto juzgase conveniente en las circunstancia de la guerra". Al triunfo de la República, un mes después de haber entrado en la ciudad de México, Juárez lanzó la convocatoria para elegir diputados, presidente de la República, presidente y magistrados de la Suprema Corte y procurador general. Esta convocatoria incluía un plebiscito para autorizar la discusión, y aprobación en su caso, sobre adiciones y reformas constitucionales, especialmente las referentes a la división del Legislativo en dos cámaras, dar derecho de veto al Ejecutivo sobre las primeras resoluciones del Congreso, facultar al presidente para informar por escrito y no verbalmente a los legisladores y limitar la facultad de la Permanente para convocar a periodo extraordinario de sesiones. Todas las propuestas de Juárez sometidas a plebiscito tenían la finalidad de restar fuerza al Poder Legislativo y dar mayores poderes al presidente de la República. Lerdo de Tejada, en la *Circular* anexa a la Convocatoria, en términos evidentemente exagerados, argüía que "la marcha normal de la administración exige, que no sea todo el Poder Legislativo y que ante él no carezca de un poder propio el Ejecutivo. El despotismo de una convención puede ser tan malo, o más, que el despotismo de un dictador". Estas pretensiones de Juárez desataron una intensa polémica en la prensa, pues se advertían los peligros de reducir el papel del Congreso en favor de la Presidencia de la República. La oposición a las reformas llegó al extremo de que su convocatoria se publicara bajo protesta en varios estados y que en Guanajuato apareciera mutilada, sin la parte plebiscitaria, lo que ocasionó la destitución del gobernador León Guzmán. Asimismo, el colegio electoral del sexto distrito capitalino protestó formalmente "contra las reformas propuestas por el Ejecutivo" y contra el hecho "de dirigir sus iniciativas directamente al pueblo, porque este hecho contraviene el artículo 127 de la Constitución", mismo que impedía tales reformas. Las elecciones se realizaron a principios de octubre y Juárez resultó triunfador. El 13 de diciembre, cuando la diputación sesionó en el local del circo de Chiarini, envió la correspondiente iniciativa de reformas y adiciones a la Constitución, misma que la asamblea legislativa turnó a comisiones para su estudio. En 1870, Juárez insistió en la necesidad de crear el Senado, esta vez mediante una carta enviada a cada gobernador, "como amigo y haciendo abstracción completa de un carácter oficial", en la cual pedía que los mandatarios locales intercedieran en favor de su proyecto. En mayo, Juárez solicitó al Congreso un periodo extraordinario de sesiones para tratar exclusivamente las reformas constitucionales, lo que rechazaron los legisladores señalando que "no hay motivo ninguno para apresurar violentamente su expedición". En 1871, como ninguno de los candidatos presidenciales obtuviera mayoría absoluta, correspondió al Congreso declarar a Benito Juárez, quien tenía mayoría relativa, como presidente constitucional. En julio de 1872 se incendió la sede de la diputación en Palacio Nacional, por lo que el Congreso pasó al Salón de Embajadores, en el mismo edificio, y de ahí al Teatro Iturbide, en las calles de Donceles y Allende, donde estuvo el *baratillo* de la Cruz del Factor hasta 1851, año en que se empezó a construir el citado coso, de Francisco Abreu, que ofreció espectáculos artísticos entre 1856 y 1872. Fue hasta el 9 de abril de 1874 cuando concluyó la votación de los artículos referentes al Senado y, después de reunir la aprobación de las legislaturas estatales, el Congreso declaró aprobada la reforma, que comenzaría "a regir el día 16 de septiembre de 1875", fecha en la que el nuevo Con-

La Cámara de Diputados en grabado de Pedro Gualdi

greso, compuesto por dos cámaras, inició sus trabajos, después de ocho años de discusión sobre el asunto. La ex Capilla de la Emperatriz Carlota, en el Palacio Nacional, fue el recinto del Senado. Durante el porfiriato, si bien no se concedieron facultades extraordinarias a Porfirio Díaz, éste gobernó como si las tuviera. La reelección no fue exclusiva del dictador sino que se extendió a los diputados y senadores que le eran afines. Entre éstos no eran pocos los representantes de estados donde no habían nacido, no tenían vecindad y en ocasiones ni siquiera conocimiento físico de la entidad. Pese a la inutilidad de diputadores y senadores, Díaz ordenó convocar a un concurso para edificar un Palacio Legislativo. Adamo Boari fue el ganador del certamen, pero los amigos del dictador maniobraron para favorecer a otro arquitecto, con la idea de levantar una construcción semejante al Capitolio de Washington, de la cual sólo se erigió la cúpula principal, transformada en los años treinta del siglo XX en monumento a la Revolución. En marzo de 1908 se incendió la sede de los llamados representantes populares y éstos tuvieron que trasladarse al Palacio de Minería, en tanto que el arquitecto Mauricio de Maria y Campos, sobre un proyecto de Emilio Dondé Preciat, levantaba en la misma esquina de Donceles y Allende un nuevo edificio. En las elecciones de 1910, el gobierno anunció el triunfo de Díaz, candidato a la Presidencia, y de Ramón Corral, a la vicepresidencia. El Partido Nacional Antirreeleccionista solicitó al Congreso que se anularan los comicios, debido a una larga lista de irregularidades y violaciones a la Constitución y a la legislación electoral. La asamblea legislativa, dominada por los porfiristas, desestimó la petición y Francisco I. Madero, candidato supuestamente derrotado, desconoció el resultado oficial de las elecciones y llamó a los ciudadanos a alzarse en armas el 20 de noviembre del mismo año, a las seis de la tarde (☛ *Plan de San Luis Potosí*). Pocos respondieron a la hora establecida por la agenda maderista, pero en diversos puntos del país hubo grupos que antes y después de la fecha citada se levantaron contra la dictadura (☛ *Revolución mexicana*). El 21 de mayo se firmaron los Tratados de Ciudad Juárez que ponían término a la guerra civil. Díaz renunció ante el Congreso a la Presidencia de la República y su sucesor, Francisco León de la Barra, en acatamiento del mismo convenio, envió a las cámaras una iniciativa de reformas constitucionales para prohibir la reelección y convocó a elecciones. Madero y José María Pino Suárez resultaron vencedores y se instaló la XXVI Legislatura. Al desatarse los acontecimientos de la Decena Trágica (febrero de 1913), un grupo de senadores se entrevistó en la Ciudadela con los militares rebeldes, quienes se prestaron a solicitar a Madero su renuncia, lo que rechazó el mandatario. Después del arresto de Madero y Pino Suárez (18 de febrero), el día 19 por la tarde, la Cámara de Diputados, reunida apresuradamente y sin *quorum*, designó presidente a Pedro Lascuráin, quien 45 minutos más tarde cedió el poder a Victoriano Huerta, reconocido por la Suprema Corte de Justicia esa misma tarde, en tanto que León de la Barra, convertido en ministro del gobierno de facto, fue recibido por el Congreso para exponer "el programa que el nuevo gobierno legalmente constituido se propone desarrollar". Los senadores aprobaron "tan excelente programa" y dieron su apoyo a Huerta. Pese a que numerosos representantes se hallaban perseguidos por las autoridades militares, al ocurrir el asesinato de Madero y Pino Suárez sesionó la Cámara de Diputados. Ahí, Alfonso Cravioto hizo el elogio fúnebre de Madero, a lo que su colega José María Lozano respondió que la demostración de luto debía ser no sólo por el presidente y vicepresidente asesinados, sino por todas las víctimas de las luchas civiles, lo que respaldó Querido Moheno con la propuesta, que se aprobó, de que se enlutara la

FOTO: FONDO EDITORIAL GRUPO AZABACHE

El Palacio de Minería, en la ciudad de México, sirvió como sede del poder legislativo en 1908 fachada de la Cámara "por todas las víctimas", lo que ponía en igual circunstancia a los verdugos y a los ejecutados. Lozano y Querido Moheno formaban, con Nemesio García Naranjo y Francisco M. Olaguíbel, el "Cuadrilátero", grupo que se distinguió por su capacidad para el insulto contra Madero y que acabó incorporado al gabinete huertista. Entre los senadores que no aceptaron la imposición destacó Belisario Domínguez, finalmente asesinado por pistoleros de la dictadura. Entre los diputados hubo opositores a Huerta, como Eduardo Neri y Serapio Rendón, en tanto que otros, como Luis Cabrera, Eduardo Hay y Roque González Garza, se unieron a la revolución constitucionalista. Los miembros del Partido Nacional Católico, los partidarios de Félix Díaz y los llamados independientes dieron su aprobación al golpe. En la oposición se mantuvieron algunos antirreeleccionistas, a los que se unieron en junio los felicistas, cuando su líder fue desterrado con cargo diplomático a Japón. Mediante esta alianza fue posible rechazar la solicitud del Ejecutivo de un periodo extraordinario de sesiones y aun el nombramiento de un secretario de Estado. Huerta acabó por disolver la Cámara de Diputados mediante un decreto emitido el 10 de octubre de 1913; hizo arrestar a 84 legisladores y retiró el fuero de diputados y senadores, tras de lo cual el Senado acordó disolverse. El gobierno convocó a nuevas elecciones de presidente, diputados y senadores para el 26 de octubre. En medio del terror gubernamental, pocos ciudadanos se presentaron a votar, lo que no impidió que Huerta instalara el 20 de noviembre la llamada "segunda XXVI Legislatura", la que, por supuesto, se mostró dócil a los deseos del dictador. A esta pseudorrepresentación le correspondió aceptar la renuncia de Huerta a la Presidencia, en 1914, por mayoría de 121 votos contra 17 de sus más incondicionales servidores. Derrotada la dictadura, en acatamiento a las reformas al Plan de Guadalupe, Venustiano Carranza, en su calidad de Primer Jefe del Ejército Constitucionalista, convocó el 4 de septiembre de 1914 a la Convención de Generales y Gobernadores (☛), en la cual deberían estar representadas todas las facciones revolucionarias. La asamblea se inició el 1 de octubre de la ciudad de México sin la asistencia de villistas ni zapatistas. Con el fin de que estas fuerzas participaran, la reunión se trasladó a Aguascalientes, considerado lugar neutral, donde los delegados acordaron llamarla Soberana Convención Revolucionaria. El rompimiento de Carranza con Francisco Villa y Emiliano Zapata desató nuevamente la guerra civil y esta asamblea, con delegados de los dos últimos jefes, sólo pudo nombrar sucesivamente a tres presidentes que, al no tener control sobre las fuerzas militares, carecieron de poder real. La Convención se extinguió en octubre de 1915. Al decidirse la lucha de facciones en favor del carrancismo, el Primer Jefe expidió un decreto, el 14 de septiembre de 1916, en el cual convocaba a elecciones para integrar el Congreso Constituyente. Los requisitos para ser diputado eran los señalados en la Constitución de 1857, pero no eran elegibles "los que hubieren ayudado con las armas o servido empleos públicos en los gobiernos o facciones hostiles a la causa constitucionalista". La asamblea se reunió en el teatro Iturbide de Querétaro, donde se iniciaron las juntas preparatorias el 21 de noviembre. Ahí, Álvaro Obregón, el general victorioso, trató de impedir la acreditación de los diputados que habían pertenecido al bloque maderista en la XXVI Legislatura, a los que acusó de colaborar con Huerta. Carranza se dirigió a la asamblea en defensa de esos legisladores, los que una vez aceptados se alinearon en el ala derecha del Congreso. El día 30 se eligió la mesa directiva y el primero de diciembre Carranza entregó su proyecto de Constitución Reformada, con la intención de que la asamblea se limitara a hacer algunos cambios y agregados al ordenamiento de 1857. Integraron la Comisión de Constitución Enrique R. Colunga, Francisco J. Múgica, Luis G. Monzón, Enrique Recio y Alberto Román; el 23 de diciembre se formó una comisión paralela, integrada por Paulino Machorro, Hilario Medina, Arturo Méndez, Heriberto Jara y Agustín Garza González. El resultado de

Foto: Archivo Casasola

Sesión del Congreso de la Unión en 1921

Integrantes del Congreso de la Unión en 1924

los trabajos fue una Norma Fundamental mucho más avanzada que la anterior en los aspectos educativo, agrario y laboral, así como un artículo 130 que quedó marcado por el jacobinismo que imperó en las sesiones. Sin embargo, el documento que firmaron los diputados el 31 de enero se 1917 se llamó *Constitución Política de los Estados Unidos Mexicanos, que reforma la del 5 de febrero de 1857*. El artículo 49 de este ordenamiento, establece que "El Supremo Poder de la Federación se divide, para su ejercicio, en Legislativo, Ejecutivo y Judicial", dos o más de los cuales no podrán reunirse "en una sola persona o corporación, ni depositarse el Legislativo en un individuo, salvo el caso de facultades extraordinarias al Ejecutivo de la Unión conforme a los previsto en el artículo 29", que señala los casos de invasión extranjera, perturbación grave de la paz pública o cualquier otro que ponga a la sociedad en grande peligro o conflicto. El Legislativo quedó dividido en dos cámaras, la de diputados y la de senadores. La primera la componen representantes de la población electos cada tres años y los segundos duran en su encargo seis años. En 1930 el Senado abandonó su vieja sede, a punto de derrumbarse, y ocupó por breve tiempo el Salón Verde de la Cámara de Diputados, hasta el 17 de agosto de 1831, cuando fueron concluidas las adaptaciones al edificio de Donceles y Xicoténcatl, templo y convento de San Andrés construido por los jesuitas entre 1626 y 1643, donde a fines del siglo XVIII se instaló el hospital de San Andrés, en el que se depositó el cadáver de Maximiliano antes de ser enviado a Austria (1867). El 29 de abril de 1933 se amplió la duración del periodo legislativo, de dos a tres años (al mismo tiempo que el presidencial, que pasó de 4 a 6). El 11 de septiembre de 1935 la Cámara de Diputados fue escenario de un tiroteo, generado por una discusión entre los diputados Juan Benet y Román Campos Viveros; en ese tiroteo murió el legislador jalisiense Manuel Martínez Valdez. Todavía durante el gobierno de Lázaro Cárdenas, el Congreso mantuvo su independencia, pero a partir del sexenio de Manuel Ávila Camacho de hecho se convirtió en un apéndice del Ejecutivo. El 22 de junio de 1963, durante el gobierno de Adolfo López Mateos, se autorizó a los partidos políticos nacionales a acreditar de entre 5 y 20 diputados de entre sus candidatos perdedores (uno por cada medio punto porcentual), siempre y cuando la votación total del partido representara el 2.5 por ciento de la votación nacional y sus candidatos no hubieran triunfado en más de 20 distritos. La Cámara de Senadores no se benefició con la reforma y en su seno participaron sólo miembros del Partido Revolucionario Institucional. En 1976, el Partido Popular Socialista, en coalición con el partido gobernante, logró que su presidente, Jorge Cruickshank, fuera elegido senador por Oaxaca. El 4 de octubre de 1977, con la Ley Federal de Organizaciones Políticas y Procesos Electorales, se amplió el número de diputados a 300, de los cuales 200 serían electos por el principio de mayoría relativa y los 100 restantes por el de representación proporcional, para lo cual, se dividió al país en cinco circunscripciones plurinominales; ahí, en las elecciones legislativas de 1979, contendieron los partidos mediante listas regionales y en el recuento, se le adjudicaron di-

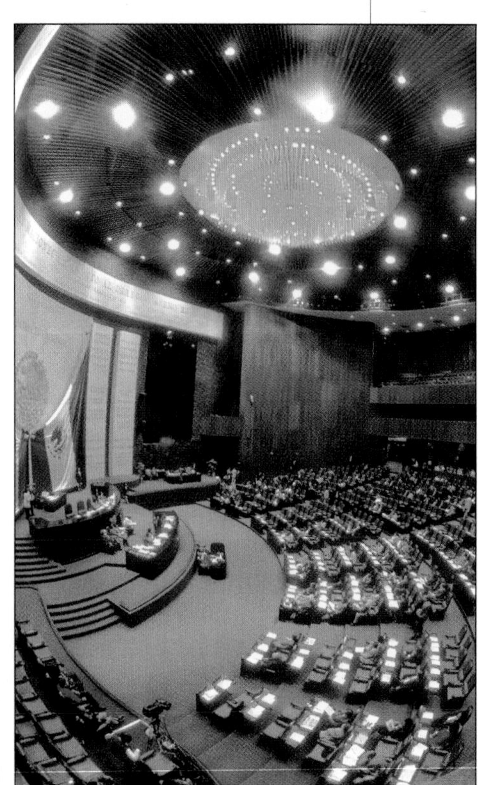

Cámara de Diputados

putados de acuerdo al porcentaje de su votación. Entre 1979 y 1981, los arquitectos Pedro Ramírez Vázquez, Jorge Campuzano y David Suárez se dieron a construir la sede del Congreso de la Unión en terrenos de la antigua estación de ferrocarriles de San Lázaro. Sin embargo, la crisis económica impidió concluir el inmueble y el senado se quedó en su viejo edificio del centro de la ciudad. El 31 de agosto de 1981, la Cámara de Diputados dejó el recinto de Donceles y Allende y se trasladó al Palacio Legislativo del barrio de San Lázaro. En 1987 se aprobó el Código Federal Electoral, por lo que el número de diputados creció hasta 500, siendo 300 de mayoría y de 200 de representación proporcional. En las elecciones de 1988, por primera vez en medio siglo, ingresaron al Congreso senadores de oposición (por Michoacán y el Distrito Federal). En 1989 un incendio "causado por un corto circuito" consumió el vestíbulo, el salón de plenos y otras instalaciones del Palacio Legislativo de San Lázaro, por lo que la Unidad de Congresos del Centro Médico Nacional fue habilitada como recinto de la Cámara de Diputados. En 1991 terminó la reparación del Palacio Legislativo y los diputados volvieron a su sede. De acuerdo con una reforma de la legislación electoral, el Senado se renovó por mitad cada tres años a partir de 1988 y en 1991, 1994 y 1997. La reforma de 1996 del Código Federal de Instituciones y Procedimientos Electorales estableció que en las elecciones federales de 1997 se elegirían por última ocasión senadores de tres años, para emparejar la renovación total del Senado en el año 2000. Asimismo, en 1997 se introdujo el sistema de representación proporcional a la elección del Senado, con lo que la Cámara pasó de 64 a 128 miembros: 64 de mayoría, 32 resultantes de la asignación a la primera minoría en cada entidad (uno por entidad) y 32 de representación proporcional. Así, por primera vez en el siglo, el Senado tuvo por primera vez 51 miembros no provenientes del mismo partido que el Ejecutivo, si bien en la legislatura inmediata anterior había contado con 34 de oposición. En esas mismas elecciones la Cámara de Diputados modificó sustancialmente su composición, pues, de 500 miembros, 262 fueron de filiación distinta al PRI. Su número permitió a los diputados de oposición, conforme a la disposición constitucional, instalar la LVII Legislatura, ante la renuencia del grupo parlamentario del PRI, con mayoría, pero con menos del 50 por ciento más uno de los votos. Los priistas rindieron protesta horas después de que lo había hecho la mayoría. De entrada, el llamado "bloque opositor", como se le llamó a la alianza de las minorías, modificó la Ley Orgánica para desaparecer la Gran Comisión, el órgano de gobierno de la Cámara que existía desde 1938, y en su lugar se instituyó la Comisión de Régimen Interno y Concertación Política (CRICP), con presidencia rotatoria y en la que están representados todos los grupos parlamentarios. En 1998 los diputados emprendieron una "modernización" de la Cámara, habilitaron alas del inmueble hasta entonces inconclusas o sin uso, invitaron a los integrantes del Senado a integrarse al conjunto de San Lázaro —lo que no aceptaron los senadores— y automatizaron el salón de sesiones, esto es, establecieron un sistema de acceso al salón de plenos a través de un identificador dactilar y clave de acceso en el vestíbulo, así como un sistema de votación mediante el cual cada diputado puede emitir su voto desde la curul, mismo que aparece en un tablero electrónico ubicado en un muro del salón de sesiones con los resultados de cada votación. En cada curul se instaló una consola con los controles para emitir el voto y solicitar el uso de la palabra, así como un micrófono para que cada legislador pueda ser oído al hablar desde su lugar. La modernización incluyó la cancelación del acceso de periodistas a los pasillos del salón de plenos y se les reservó un espacio en el mismo salón, en donde cuentan con terminales de computadora.

Foto: Dante Bucio

Cámara de Senadores

Poesía en Voz Alta ◆ Grupo creado en 1956 en la Casa del Lago de la UNAM. Presentó cuatro temporadas. Sus principales impulsores fueron Juan José Arreola, Emmanuel Carballo, Jaime García Terrés y Octavio Paz. Se desempeñaron como directores escénicos José Luis Ibáñez y Héctor Mendoza; Leonora Carrington, Héctor Xavier y Juan Soriano hicieron escenografías; y Juan José Arreola, Nancy Cárdenas, Carlos Castaño, María Luisa Elío, Carlos Fernández, Héctor Godoy, Juan José Gurrola, Ana María Hernández, Juan Ibáñez, Eduardo McGregor, Héctor Mendoza, Rosenda Monteros, Argentina Morales, Ana Ofelia Murguía, Tara Parra, Pina Pellicer, José Luis Pomar, Manola Saavedra, Rosa María Saviñón y Enrique Stopen figuraron como actores.

FOTO: BRAULIO TENORIO

Enrique González Rojo, representante del poeticismo

POETICISMO ◆ Tendencia literaria en la que actuaron, a fines de los años cuarenta y principios de los cincuenta, Enrique González Rojo, Eduardo Lizalde, Marco Antonio Montes de Oca, Arturo González Cosío, David Orozco Romo, Graciela y Rosa María Phillips. González Rojo dice que el poeticismo, juzgado como "una forma ya consabida de letrismo" por Octavio Paz, pretendía llegar a "la unidad en un todo del poeta y el crítico, del lírico consciente y el esteta", basada en "la originalidad, la complejidad y la claridad". Señala también que "no era sólo una teoría poética, sino que iba acompañado de una práctica existencial, un modus vivendi". Para Lizalde, "más que un proyecto ignorante y estúpido, (era) un proyecto equivocado" que partía "de una idea en el fondo mecánica y conceptual de la creación literaria", pues "pretendía la inteligibilidad, la 'univocidad' (.) de lo poéticamente expresado, para combatir la facilidad, la vaguedad significativa, la imprecisión verbal y conceptual de la poesía que imaginábamos en boga". A esta concepción literaria pertenecen *Martirio de Narciso*, poema publicado por Lizalde en *El Nacional* (1950), *Dimensión imaginaria*, de González Rojo (1952), y en menor medida *La mala hora*, libro del primero (1956).

POINSETT ◆ Códice formado por siete fragmentos de amate desprendidos de la Matrícula de Tributos (☛). Hacia 1820, el embajador estadounidense en México, Joel R. Poinsett, se apoderó de esas hojas y las donó a la Sociedad Filosófica Americana, de Filadelfia. Fueron devueltos en 1942, al inaugurarse la Biblioteca Benjamín Franklin en el Distrito Federal. En la actualidad se encuentran en la Biblioteca del Museo Nacional de Antropología e Historia. Las hojas de este códice corresponden a los fragmentos 7 a 13 de la colección de Alexander von Humboldt, que tratan de las provincias de Tlatelolco, Petlacalco, Tlatlauhquitepec, Tuchpa, Hueypuchtla, Atotonilco y Huaxtepec.

Joel Roberts Poinsett

POINSETT, JOEL ROBERTS ◆ n. y m. en EUA (1779-1851). Diplomático. Estudió medicina en la Universidad de Edimburgo. Entre junio de 1810 y mayo de 1815, viajó por Sudamérica para informar al gobierno estadounidense sobre los movimientos independentistas latinoamericanos: estuvo en Lima, Buenos Aires y Santiago de Chile, donde participó en la redacción de la primera Constitución chilena. Llegó a México en octubre de 1822, para informar al presidente James Monroe sobre el imperio de Agustín de Iturbide. Aquí se entrevistó con el emperador, con Antonio López de Santa Anna y con José Manuel de Herrera, a quienes propuso que México cediera a su país los territorios de Texas, Nuevo México y las Californias. En diciembre volvió a Washington y en 1825 el presidente John Quincy Adams lo nombró enviado extraordinario y ministro plenipotenciario de Estados Unidos en México, al que regresó en ese año. Insistió, ahora ante el presidente Guadalupe Victoria, sobre la cesión de territorios fronterizos y llegó a ofrecer 5 millones de dólares por Texas. Promovió la creación de logias masónicas del rito de York, lo que le permitió ejercer su influencia sobre los principales líderes del partido popular, como se llamaba a los yorkinos. Los rivales de éstos, los escoceses, demandaron con insistencia su destitución. La hostilidad contra su persona aumentó durante el gobierno de Vicente Guerrero, quien solicitó a la Casa Blanca su retiro en julio de 1829. Relevado en diciembre de ese año, volvió a su país en enero de 1830. En Estados Unidos fue líder del Partido Unionista en Carolina del Norte y secretario de Guerra en el gobierno de Martin van Buren (1837-41). Durante la guerra de 1847 asesoró al gobierno de Texas. Difundió en Norteamérica la flor mexicana de Nochebuena (*Euphobia pulcherrima*), que ahí se conoce como *Poinsettia pulcherrima*. Autor de *Notas sobre México* (1822).

POLA MORENO, ÁNGEL ◆ n. en Chiapa de Corzo, Chis., y m. en el DF (1861-1948). Periodista y editor. Estudió en el Instituto de Ciencias y Artes de la ciudad de Oaxaca, donde inició su carrera en el *Diario de Oaxaca*. Pasó a la ciudad de México en 1883 y poco después se incorporó a la redacción de *El Socialista*, donde empezó a usar el pseudónimo de *Lucretius T. Carus*. En 1894 fundó, y desde entonces dirigió, el diario *El Noticioso* de la ciudad de México, que costaba un centavo y llegó a tirar 30,000 ejemplares. Fue colaborador de los periódicos *El Siglo XIX*, *El Monitor Republicano*, *El Partido Liberal*, *El Monitor del Pueblo*, *El Porvenir Nacional*, *El Diario del Hogar*, *La Prensa*, *El Imparcial* y otros órganos. Se le considera el iniciador en México del género de entrevista y Gastón García Cantú, estudioso de su obra, ha hecho el elogio de sus reportajes "por su brevedad y concisión, no superados hasta la fecha". Con otros directores de diarios creó, en 1898, el primer dormitorio para voceadores. Fue dos veces diputado federal, la segunda durante el periodo presidencial de Francisco I. Madero. Fundador de la Editorial Reformista, publicó las *Obras* de Juárez (4 t.), las de Melchor Ocampo (3 t.), las poesías de Jorge Isaacs y los 15 tomos de la *Biblioteca reformista*. Retirado del periodismo, se dedicó a la atención de su librería, en Cuba 99, de la ciudad de México. Coautor, con Luis González Obregón, Enrique M. de los Ríos, Aurelio Garay y Francisco Gómez Flores, de *Liberales ilustres mexicanos de la reforma y la intervención*. Fue declarado Hijo Predilecto de Chiapas (1937) y el presidente Manuel Ávila Camacho lo condecoró en 1944, al inaugurarse la Hemeroteca Nacional, como decano de los periodistas mexicanos.

POLANCO ARAUJO, FELICIANO ◆ n. en Tlayacapan y m. en Cuernavaca, Mor. (?-1943). En mayo de 1911 se incorporó a las tropas de Lucio Moreno. Dos años después, al inicio del gobierno de Victoriano Huerta, fue hecho prisionero por elementos del gobierno, incorporado al ejército federal y enviado a combatir a los constitucionalistas, pero en el primer combate desertó y se unió a las fuerzas de la División del

Norte. Perteneció a la brigada de Maclovio Herrera y más tarde se incorporó al Ejército Libertador del Sur. En 1920 se adhirió al Plan de Agua Prieta. Fue jefe de las Fuerzas Auxiliares de Morelos (1927-29).

POLANCO ZAPATA, JORGE ◆ n. en Xcalac, QR (1952). Analista de sistemas. En Quintana Roo ha sido secretario de los ayuntamientos de Othón P. Blanco y Benito Juárez, director regional de Fonatur, director de Finanzas de la Secretaría de Desarrollo Económico, director de Organización y Control de Gestión de la Secretaría de Obras Públicas y director de Promoción Social del Instituto de Vivienda del gobierno del estado. Fue elegido senador de la República para el periodo 1997-2000. Renunció al PRI en 1999.

POLÍTICA ◆ Revista editada en el Distrito Federal, a partir de mayo de 1960, con el subtítulo de *Quince Días de México y del Mundo*. Fue fundada por su director general, Manuel Marcué Pardiñas (☛). La publicación, de tendencia izquierdista, declaraba tener un "compromiso revolucionario" con "las mejores causas del pueblo mexicano", de ahí que difundiera con amplitud la lucha por la libertad de los presos políticos, los movimientos laborales, agrarios, estudiantiles y de otros sectores opuestos al gobierno de Adolfo López Mateos y, sobre todo, al de Gustavo Díaz Ordaz, cuyo retrato apareció en una portada con la leyenda: "No será presidente". Asimismo, se consideraba "acaso el único órgano periodístico indemne ante el soborno oficial y, por eso, independiente". En sus páginas se informó con amplitud sobre el proceso revolucionario de Cuba, la guerrilla latinoamericana y los procesos de liberación nacional de diversas partes del mundo. La sección cultural hizo el seguimiento y la crítica de las principales actividades de la década de los sesenta. Caracterizó a la revista la reproducción de documentos políticos de México y del extranjero, destacadamente los discursos del líder cubano Fidel Castro. Jorge Carrión era director, Antonio Pérez Elías, subdirector; y Rosendo Gómez Lorenzo, jefe de redacción. En la lista de redactores de los primeros números figuraban Ermilo Abreu Gómez, Alonso Aguilar, David Alfaro Siqueiros, Pita Amor, Narciso Bassols Batalla, Fernando Benítez, Enrique Cabrera, Fernando Carmona, Fausto Castillo, Rosa Castro, José de la Colina, Lin Durán, Víctor Flores Olea, Carlos Fuentes, Alejandro Gómez Arias, Enrique González Pedrero, Eli de Gortari, Carlos Lagunas, Renato Leduc, Germán List Arzubide, Vicente Lombardo Toledano, Francisco López Cámara, Salvador Novo, Carlos Pacheco Reyes, Raúl Prieto, Víctor Rico Galán, Eduardo del Río, *Rius*, Antonio Rodríguez, José Santos Valdés y Emilio Uranga. En julio de 1967 habían desaparecido del directorio varios de los nombres citados y estaban los de Juan Duch, Roberto Escudero, Gerardo Unzueta, Gerardo Dávila, Enrique Semo, Nancy Cárdenas, José Antonio Alcaraz, Mario Soto, Raquel Tibol, Alberto Híjar, Jaime Labastida y Alberto Domingo. En el directorio, después de Marcué, sólo aparecía el nombre de Boris Rosen, jefe de redacción. Otros colaboradores fueron Lorenzo Carrasco, León Roberto García, Felipe Pardiñas, Valentín Campa y Demetrio Vallejo. Tenía servicios fotográficos de Prensa Latina, los Hermanos Mayo, Enrique Bordes Mangel, Rodrigo Moya, José Luis Múgica y *UPI*. Acosada por la hostilidad gubernamental y un permanente déficit en sus finanzas, la revista, ya sin periodicidad, se extinguió a principios de 1968.

POLÍTICA POPULAR ◆ Organización surgida en 1968 apartir del movimiento de masas de ese año, bajo la influencia de la revolución cultural proletaria china y de la revolución vietnamita. Su filosofía rectora consistía en "integrarse con el pueblo para que haga su propia política y establezca su propia organización", en la idea de que la revolución era una lucha prolongada. Su cabeza visible era Adolfo Orive Bellinger. Entre 1971 y 1972, efectuó trabajo político sobre todo en Sonora, Nayarit, Durango, la Comarca Lagunera, Monterrey y Tlaxcala. De 1973 a 1975 cosolidó los movimientos de su organización en las colonias populares de Monterrey, la Comarca Lagunera y Durango, integrando a brigadistas de base en organizaciones populares. En 1977, en Monterrey, se escindió una parte de los militantes y se produjo una represión a sus miembros en la Comarca Lagunera. En el mismo periodo empezó el trabajo conjunto con el sector no guerrillero de Unión del Pueblo (UP) en Chiapas y Oaxaca, con la participación de sus cuadros en el movimiento obrero, como en el caso de la sección 147 del sindicato minero. La organización creció fundamentalmente en el sindicato minero metalúrgico y estableció contactos e influencia en el movimiento magisterial, el sindicalismo universitario y el sindicato de telefonistas. En esos años surgió, como iniciativa de Política Popular y para su fortalecimiento, la Organización Ideológica Dirigente, una suerte de partido político centralizador de línea proletaria; y la Unión Nacional de Organizaciones Regionales Campesinas Autónomas (UNORCA). A inicios de los ochenta se estableció una alianza con la Unión Obrera Independiente (UOI) y se inició un distanciamiento de los organismos gremiales con que se había vinculado. Política Popular se disolvió en 1985.

POLK, JAMES KNOX ◆ n. y m. en EUA (1795-1849). Abogado. Diputado y presidente de la Cámara de Representantes (1835-39) y gobernador de Tennessee (1839-41), fue elegido presidente de Estados Unidos en 1845 y gobernó su país hasta 1849. Defensor de la política expansionista estadounidense, en 1845, ante el conflicto en Texas, ordenó al general Zachary Taylor que iniciara las agresiones contra México, al que declaró la guerra el 11 de mayo de 1846 (☛ *Estados Unidos*).

POLKOS ◆ Nombre coloquial que recibieron los miembros del batallón "Victoria" y del regimiento "Independencia" de la Guardia Nacional del

Distrito Federal, los cuales se levantaron en armas el 27 de febrero de 1847 en la ciudad de México, para impedir la aplicación de la ley de intervención de bienes eclesiásticos promulgada el 11 de enero por el vicepresidente interino encargado del Poder Ejecutivo, Valentín Gómez Farías. Ambos cuerpos armados estaban constituidos principalmente por "médicos, abogados, comerciantes, almacenistas y personas de cierta posición social", y por eso es probable que el apelativo que recibieron los pronunciados haya nacido de comprobar que la aristocracia y la burguesía citadinas eran particularmente afectas a bailar polkas en sus fiestas, aunque también es posible que el apodo provenga del hecho de que los "cívicos" de la Guardia Nacional le prestaron un importante servicio al presidente estadounidense James K. Polk, cuyas tropas habían invadido México. Por su composición social y afinidad con la jerarquía eclesiástica, situaciones que los convertían automáticamente en sospechosos de deslealtad al gobierno liberal, en los últimos días de febrero de 1847, el gobierno de Gómez Farías dispuso que los batallones de *polkos* fueran enviados a Veracruz para defender el puerto y así alejarlos del centro de la ciudad de México, donde hubieran podido ser peligrosos: el "Independencia" tenía su cuartel a un lado del Palacio Nacional y el "Victoria" en la casa de La Profesa. Sin embargo, apenas sabida la decisión gubernamental, los *polkos* se sublevaron, eligieron general en jefe de la asonada a Matías de la Peña Barragán y publicaron unas *Bases del plan para la restauración de los verdaderos principios federativos*, en las que, luego de anunciar su determinación de respetar la constitución de 1824 y reconocer como "general en jefe del ejército mexicano" a Santa Anna, demandaban la destitución de los poderes Ejecutivo y Legislativo "por haber desmerecido la confianza nacional" y determinaban que "No surtirán efecto los decretos relativos a la ocupación de los bienes de manos muertas". Ese mismo día se levantó en armas el regimiento "Hidalgo", y los rebeldes iniciaron una serie de ataques contra el centro de la ciudad y particularmente contra el Palacio Nacional, que duraron hasta fines de marzo, cuando convencieron a Santa Anna de que reasumiera la Presidencia, hecho que ocurrió el 23 de marzo.

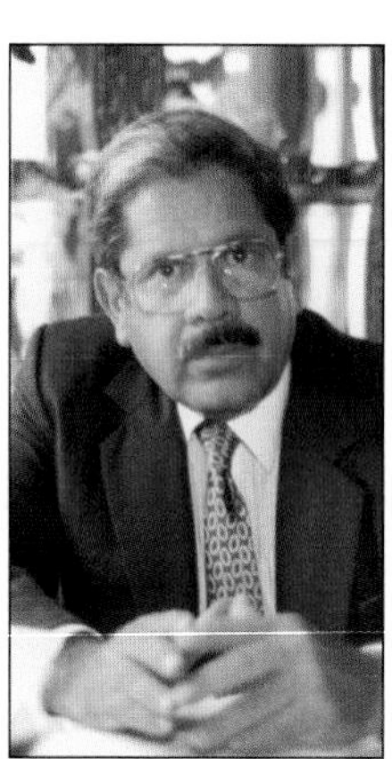
Abraham Polo Uscanga

POLO BERNAL, EFRAÍN ◆ n. en el DF (1941). Licenciado (1966) y maestro (1971) en derecho por la UNAM especializado en finanzas públicas (1971). Profesor de la UNAM (1968-82), de la UIA (1969-71) y del Instituto de Especialización del Poder Judicial Federal (1982-83). Ha sido juez séptimo de distrito en materia penal (1970), abogado en el Seminario Judicial de la Federación (1974), secretario de estudio y cuenta de la Suprema Corte de Justicia (1974-80) y juez cuarto de distrito en materia administrativa (1980-85). En 1982 concedió a unos particulares el amparo contra el decreto que implantó el control de cambios. Tres años después, en 1985, fue destituido por la Suprema Corte, acusado de haber trabajado para el IMSS entre 1980 y 1983, lo que contravenía las disposiciones constitucionales. Autor de *Juventud humana, reserva de México* (1958), *El recurso de inconformidad* (1970), *El seguro social y su problemática* (1976), *Tratado de derecho aduanero* (1976), *Ley de valorización aduanera* (1977) y *El valor de la aduana* (1977).

POLO DÍAZ DE LA VEGA, JOSÉ RAFAEL ◆ n. en San Nicolás de los Cerritos, hoy en el Estado de México, y m. en Los Mogotes, Mich. (1781-1814). Insurgente. En 1811, con sus hermanos Manuel y José Trinidad, armó un cuerpo de caballería que se unió a las fuerzas de Ignacio López Rayón. Participó en la defensa de Zitácuaro y mantuvo activas las guerrillas del Estado de México.

POLO USCANGA, ABRAHAM ANTONIO ◆ n. en Soledad de Doblado, Ver. y m. en el DF (1935-1994). Licenciado en derecho por la UNAM (1960) y por la Escuela Libre de Derecho (1970). En la Procuraduría General de Justicia del Distrito Federal fue jefe del Departamento de Averiguaciones Previas (1975-78), subdirector (1978-81) y director general (1981-88) de Averiguaciones Previas; y subprocurador de Averiguaciones Previas (1988). Magistrado del Tribunal Superior de Justicia del DF. Murió asesinado.

POLONIA, REPÚBLICA DE ◆ Nación de Europa situada en la porción noreste del continente. Limita al norte con Lituania, al noreste con Bielorrusia, al este con Ucrania, al sur con Eslovaquia, al

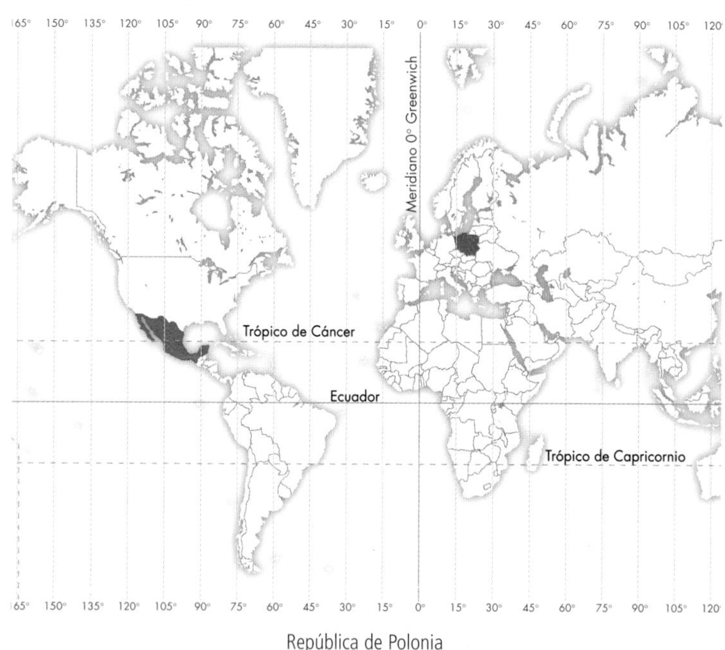

República de Polonia

suroeste con la República Checa y al oeste con Alemania. Tiene costas, al norte, en el mar Báltico. Superficie: 312,677 km². Habitantes: 38,718,000 en 1998. Su idioma oficial es el polaco y su capital es Varsovia (con 1,638,300 habitantes, en 1996). *Historia:* los eslavos se instalaron en el actual territorio polaco a partir del siglo V. En 875, el imperio de la Gran Moravia absorbió a los pequeños Estados polacos originales e introdujo el cristianismo. Un siglo más tarde, en 960, subió al poder Miezko I, que instauró la dinastía Plast, conquistó Silesia, creó el primer arzobispado, en Poznán; pero se sometió al gobierno germánico de la Marca del Norte. En el año 1,000, el rey Boleslao I *el Valiente*, consiguío la independencia, conquistó Moravia, Bohemia y Ucrania, y en 1025 fue coronado rey de Polonia. Sin embargo, para fines del siglo los checos y los rusos habían recuperado sus territorios, lo que provocó una serie de revueltas internas; éstas finalizaron en la primera mitad del siglo XII, durante el gobierno de Boleslao III. En 1194, Casimiro II *el Justo* introdujo en el país la monarquía electiva. En 1225, el gobierno polaco, atacado por prusianos, mongoles y lituanos, solicitó ayuda a la Orden de Caballeros Teutónicos, quienes luego de defender el país, se instalaron en el norte y crearon un gobierno independendiente. A partir de entonces se generalizó la inmigración de alemanes. En 1384, con el matrimonio entre la princesa heredera polaca y el gran duque de Lituania, ambos países se unieron y se fundó la dinastía de los Jagellones. Luego de conquistar Moldavia, Besarabia y Valaquia, el nuevo Estado se convirtió en el más importante de Europa oriental, pues se extendía desde el mar Báltico hasta el mar Negro. Mediante una serie de enlaces familiares, a fines del siglo XV los Jagellones gobernaban Polonia-Lituania, Bohemia y Hungría. En 1444, los turcos conquistaron los territorios del mar Negro. En 1515, la constitución de Radom formalizó la unión de Lituania y Polonia y creó la Dieta Nacional, elegida por los nobles polacos, encargada del poder legislativo. La dinastía de los Jagellones desapareció en 1572, con Segismundo II; dos años después, la nobleza eligió rey a Enrique de Valois, pero puso limitaciones a su poder. La reforma protestante, que se expandió en Polonia a mediados del siglo XVI, se vio relegada a partir de 1587, cuando Segismundo III Vasa fue elegido rey. Éste se alió con los obispos y con los aristócratas católicos, encabezó la contrarreforma en Suecia, donde también reinaba, e intentó conquistar Rusia, aunque fracasó en estas dos últimas empresas. En 1634, Ladislao VII firmó la paz con Rusia y con Suecia, y se negó a participar en la guerra de los Treinta Años. En 1702 el país fue invadido por el ejército sueco. En 1733, tras la muerte de Augusto II, se desató una guerra de sucesión en la que intervinieron Francia, Austria y Rusia. En 1772, durante el reinado de Estanislao II Poniatowski, último monarca polaco, Austria, Prusia y Rusia conquistaron Polonia y se repartieron el territorio. Dieciséis años más tarde, Prusia y Rusia volvieron a repartirse el territorio polaco. En 1795, luego de una rebelión popular, los ocupantes del país eliminaron la denominación de Polonia. A partir de 1797, los polacos refugiados en Francia fueron organizados en legiones del ejército francés. En 1807, después de vencer a Prusia, Napoleón Bonaparte formó un nuevo Estado polaco. En 1815, vencido Napoleón, el zar ruso Alejandro I logró en el Congreso de Viena un nuevo reparto del país e hizo de una parte de Polonia un reino adscrito a su imperio. Los alzamientos independentistas se iniciaron en 1830. Un gran número de polacos se exilió en Francia y en otros países europeos. El doctor Seweryn Galezowsky o Galezowsky, que vivió en México hacia 1834, quizá haya sido de estos exiliados. Otro de los polacos que vivieron en México en el siglo XIX fue Gustav Gostkowsky (☛), quien fue una destacada figura del periodismo y la cultura mexicana de la República restaurada. En su columna "Humoradas Dominicales" publicó una serie de artículos sobre literatura polaca, traducidos por Manuel Peredo. Durante la intervención francesa, Maximiliano de Habsburgo obtuvo que el gobierno de su hermano Francisco José le enviara a cientos de presos polacos para colonizar México. Se dice que, una vez aquí, los polacos se incorporaron al ejército republicano. A fines del siglo XIX se fundó el Partido Socialista Polaco, que en 1904 intentó un levantamiento en Varsovia. Durante la primera guerra mundial el territorio polaco fue invadido por los ejércitos alemán y austrohúngaro; en 1917 fue reconocido un gobierno en el exilio y al año siguiente, luego de la desaparición del imperio zarista, se creó la República de Polonia. Ese mismo año llegó a México el pianista y crítico musical Salomón Kahan (☛). El nuevo gobierno polaco aprovechó la guerra civil soviética y ocupó el territorio de Lituania, pero en 1920 se firmó un nuevo tratado de paz y límites entre la Unión Soviética y Polonia. Seis años después, en 1926, Joseph Pilsudski derrocó al gobierno socialista de Ignacy Daszynski e implantó una férrea dictadura. En 1930, México y Polonia establecierón relaciones diplomáticas. En 1935, luego de la muerte de Pilsudsky, Edward Smigly-Rydz se encargó del gobierno; al año siguiente reprimió un movimiento comunista y en 1937 una serie de huelgas campesinas. En septiembre de 1939 el país fue invadido por los ejércitos de

Timbre de Polonia

Timbre de Polonia

Glifo del municipio de Polotitlán

la Alemania nazi, lo que dio inicio a la segunda guerra mundial. México fue el primer país en condenar la agresión. El gobierno polaco se instaló en Francia y organizó un ejército que formó parte de las fuerzas aliadas. En 1941, por gestiones del violinista Henryk Szeryng, quien residió largas temporadas aquí, el gobierno mexicano dio asilo a más de 4,000 polacos y al año siguiente a 3,500 más. Estos últimos, en su mayoría niños huérfanos, mujeres y ancianos, fundaron en 1943 la colonia de Santa Rosa, cerca de León, gracias a un acuerdo entre el presidente Manuel Ávila Camacho y el presidente del gobierno polaco en el exilio, el general Sikorsky. Poco después, cien de las mujeres polacas de Santa Rosa organizaron una brigada que marchó a combatir al fascismo en Europa. La colonia existió hasta 1952. Numerosos colonos se instalaron entonces en Tlalpan, DF. En 1944, los soviéticos apoyaron la formación de un Comité de Liberación Nacional. Al año siguiente, las tropas del Ejército Rojo entraron en Polonia. La guerra costó al país más de la quinta parte de la población total: alrededor de seis millones de personas, la mitad de ellos judíos. En 1945, en la Conferencia de Yalta, los gobiernos soviético, estadounidense y británico fijaron las nuevas fronteras polacas y crearon un gobierno de unión nacional que fue dirigido por Wladyslaw Gomulka, secretario general del comunista Partido Obrero Polaco (que poco después se convirtió en Partido Obrero Unificado Polaco). En 1947 se promulgó la nueva Constitución. Durante esa década, un grupo de inmigrantes polacos encabezados por un sacerdote católico apellidado Jarzebowski había intentado establecer una colonia en la península de Yucatán, pero el proyecto fracasó a causa de las enfermedades y los animales ponzoñosos. En 1952 se promulgó otra Constitución, ésta de carácter socialista. En 1956 se produjo un movimiento popular contra la influencia soviética, que consiguió la liberación del cardenal católico Stefan Wyszynski, preso desde 1953. En esa década llegaron a México más familias polacas, entre otras la del director de teatro Ludwik Margules. En 1962 se produjeron visitas recíprocas de los jefes de Estado de México y Polonia. En 1966 llegó a México un grupo de entrenadores polacos, quienes han preparado a la mayoría de los medallistas olímpicos mexicanos: Cazimiro Marzek, en boxeo; Jerzy Hausleber, en caminata; Vladimir Puzio, en atletismo; Jorge Buczak, en esgrima; Tadeuz Kempa, en carreras de fondo; Jorge Jokiel, en gimnasia; y Edmundo Portzebowsky, en carreras de medio fondo. En 1970, una nueva movilización popular derrocó al gobierno de Gomulka, quien fue sustituido por Edward Gierek. En 1979, el presidente Henryk Jablonski realizó una visita oficial a nuestro país. Al año siguiente, en 1980, una serie de huelgas y protestas obreras, dirigidas por el sindicato independiente Solidaridad, obligó a renunciar a Gierek, que fue sustituido por Stanislaw Kania. Sin embargo, las protestas obreras continuaron durante 1981, y el 13 de diciembre, el general Wojciech Jaruzelski se hizo cargo del gobierno, implantó el estado de sitio, declaró ilegal a Solidaridad y arrestó a los principales dirigentes obreros. Diez días más tarde, la cancillería mexicana emitió un comunicado en el que consideraba "trágica" la situación, "porque el establecimiento del estado de sitio y la toma de medidas de fuerza por el ejército afecta seriamente a la población civil". Los partidos de la izquierda mexicana no trotskista aprobaron el golpe de Estado. Sin embargo, unos 200 miembros del Partido Socialista Unificado de México, ex militantes del desaparecido Partido Comunista Mexicano, reprobaron tajantemente el golpe militar y la agresión contra los trabajadores. La comunidad polaca en México también reprobó los hechos y formó el comité "Solidaridad con Solidaridad", el sindicato independiente. En 1983 Lech Walesa, secretario general de esa organización, recibió el premio Nobel de la Paz. Ese mismo año se levantó la ley marcial, se disolvió el Consejo Nacional Militar de Salvación y se decretó una amnistía general. En 1990 renunció Jaruzelski y Walesa ganó las elecciones presidenciales. Bajo la presidencia de Walesa, Polonia se alejó de la influencia soviética y se inscribió en el modelo neoliberal. En Varsovia existe una escuela llamada Benito Juárez.

Polotitlán ◆ Municipio del Estado de México situado en el extremo norte de la entidad, al norte de Aculco, en los límites con Querétaro e Hidalgo. Superficie: 189.89 km^2. Habitantes: 10,525, de los cuales 2,877 forman la población económicamente activa. Hablan alguna lengua indígena 12 personas mayores de cinco años (otomí 11). Su cabecera es Polotitlán de la Ilustración.

Pomar, José ◆ n. y m. en el DF (1880-1961). Músico. Estudió con Guadalupe Velázquez, Carlos J. Meneses, Tomás Alarcón y Gustavo Campa. Fue profesor de la Escuela Nacional de Maestros (1902-04) y del Instituto Científico y Literario de Pachuca (1909-15). En esa ciudad formó el Sexteto Pomar. En 1915 se incorporó a las tropas de Pablo González. En Guanajuato formó un conjunto sinfónico y en León una Orquesta Sinfónica. Miembro fundador de la Liga de Escritores y Artistas Revolucionarios. Profesor de la Escuela Nacional de Música y de la Escuela Superior Nocturna de Música. Fue director del conjunto musical de la Universidad Obrera de México y subdirector de la Escuela Superior de Música. Fundó la revista *Música*. Compuso un *Huapango* anterior al de Moncayo y la obra *Ocho horas*, en la que integró un silbato, un látigo, percusiones de madera y metal para reproducir el ambiente fabril. Compuso también un *Himno mutualista*, *El envite*, *Canción samaritana*, *La cajita de música*, *Segunda mazurka*, *Cómo es la muñeca*, *Concierto para piano*, *Cake-walk del gato*, *Mazurca, vals y danza*, *Preludio y fuga rítmicos*, *Al fin dormidos*, *El juglar*, *Dos puros lirios*, *Sonata para dos violines y piano*, *Tres interludios*, *Postludio*, *Tres preludios*, *La quimera*, *Oblación*, *Cuatro mazurkas*,

Sonatina, Trece arreglos, Sinfonía América, Balada de Navidad, Sonata, Concierto para piano y orquesta, México-España, Cuarto cuadro de la historia de México y *La murga*.

POMAR, JUAN BAUTISTA ◆ n. y m. en Texcoco, en el hoy Estado de México. (1540-1600). Nieto del rey Nezahualpilli. Escribió una *Información*, en la que reclamaba sus derechos sobre el señorío de Texcoco, y una *Relación de las antigüedades políticas y religiosas de las Indias* (1582), obra que en los últimos cien años se ha publicado tres veces con el título de *Relación de Texcoco*.

POMAR JIMÉNEZ, JULIO ◆ n. en el DF (1937). Periodista. Ingeniero mecánico titulado en el IPN (1955-58). Desde 1965 pertenece al PRI. Entre 1962 y 1976 trabajó en el diario *El Día*. Ha sido miembro del Comité Nacional de la Federación Nacional de Estudiantes Técnicos (1956-60), jefe de la Oficina de Planeación Social del DDF (1968), jefe de Divulgación del Programa de Inversiones para el Desarrollo Económico Rural Jalisco-sur (1976), director de Difusión Cultural (1977) y subdirector general de Información y Relaciones Públicas de la SEP (1984-85); coordinador de Difusión en Desarrollo Regional (1978-79) y director general de Comunicación Social de la SPP (1985-88); director de Información de la UAM (1979-82) y subdirector general de Comunicación de la Secretaría de Hacienda (1982-84). Coautor de *Historia y futuro de la economía latinoamericana* (1967). Pertenece al Club Primera Plana.

POMARES MONLEÓN, MANUEL ◆ n. en España y m. en el DF (1904-1972). Abogado titulado en la Universidad Central de Madrid. Fue gobernador de las provincias españolas de Teruel, Huesca y Alicante (1931-36) y magistrado de la Audiencia de Alicante. A la derrota de la República Española se exilió en México (1939). En el puerto de Veracruz, poco después de su llegada, fundó el primer grupo de teatro experimental de la ciudad, La Farándula. Profesor de literatura y fundador y director del grupo de teatro de la Universidad Veracruzana. Colaborador de los periódicos *El Dictamen, El Diario de Xalapa, Atisbos* y *Tele-guía*. En *Últimas Noticias* y luego en *El Sol de México*, publicó la columna política "Tronera", después llamada "Trinchera", que en su desmesurado anticomunismo tildaba de "rojas" a las organizaciones socialdemócratas y democristianas. Autor de *El pensamiento de Séneca* (1943), y *El preclaro ingenio y el ingenioso hidalgo*. En 1946 recibió un Premio Internacional de Novela por *Ya no existe luz en esa estrella*.

POMPA Y POMPA, ANTONIO ◆ n. en Guanajuato, Gto., y m. en el DF (1904-1994). Historiador. Estudió en la Universidad Pontifica Mexicana y en la ENAH. Fundó en Guanajuato el periódico anticallista *Cronos*, por lo que fue enviado sin juicio al penal de las Islas Marías, de donde lo rescató la Cruz Roja. Continuó sus críticas con distintos seudónimos, entre ellos *Fausto Vidrio, Sansón Barriga, Próspero Miró* y *Procopio Magueyales*. Organizó varios congresos de Historia de la República. Fue director de la Biblioteca Nacional de Antropología e Historia. Editó los diez primeros volúmenes del *Catálogo* de la biblioteca (1942). Profesor del Claustro de Sor Juana. En 1976, publicó una *Antología ideológica de Salvador Alvarado*. Autor de *Álbum del IV centenario guadalupano* (1938), *Homenaje al dr. Alfonso Caso* (1951), *El pensamiento político de Hidalgo* (1953), *Pinturas rupestres del norte de México* (1956), *La reforma liberal en México* (1956), *Sobre asuntos de Texas* (1959), *Proceso inquisitorial y militar seguido a don Miguel Hidalgo y Costilla* (1960), *Estudios históricos de Sinaloa* (1960), *Venezuela en la emancipación de América* (1966), *El humanismo de Las Casas* (1967), *Orígenes de la independencia mexicana* (1970), *La pintura rupestre pre y proto histórica en México* (1974), *El cronista Las Casas, humanista y político* (1975) y *450 años de la imprenta tipográfica en México* (1988). Fue secretario perpetuo de la Sociedad Mexicana de Geografía y Estadística. Fue miembro de la Academia Nacional de Historia y Geografía, del Institute International of American Ideal (1947), de la Academia de Historia Guadalupana y de la Sociedad Mexicana de Historia.

***POMPÍN* IGLESIAS** ◆ Nombre profesional del actor Alfonso Iglesias Soto (☛).

PONCE, ANÍBAL ◆ n. en Argentina y m. en el DF (1898-1938). En Buenos Aires fue colaborador de José Ingenieros (1920-25). Escribió para las revistas *Renovación* y *Revista de Filosofía*, órganos de la Unión Latinoamericana. Viajó a Europa y vivió en la Unión Soviética. Al regresar a Argentina constituyó la Asociación de Intelectuales, Artistas, Periodistas y Escritores y fundó la revista *Dialéctica*. En noviembre de 1936 fue expulsado de su cátedra de psicología en el Instituto Nacional del Profesorado Secundario. Llegó en 1937 a México, donde participó en la vida intelectual de la época. Murió a consecuencia de un accidente automovilístico ocurrido entre Morelia y Zitácuaro. Autor de *La vejez de Sarmiento* (1927) y *Educación y lucha de clases* (1936).

Relaciones de texcoco, de Juan Bautista Pomar

PONCE, FRANCISCO ◆ n. en el DF (1944). Periodista. Su apellido materno es Padilla. Estudió periodismo en la UNAM, donde fue profesor. Se inició profesionalmente en el diario *Excélsior*, en en que fue reportero, columnista deportivo y colaborador de *Revista de Revistas* (1973-76). En julio de 1976 abandonó esa casa editorial y participó en la creación de la revista *Proceso*, donde trabaja desde entonces como coordinador de la sección deportiva y escribe la columna "Marcador". Autor de la biografía de Filiberto Vigueras Lázaro, *De la sierra al senado. Crónica de una vida sindical* (1984).

PONCE, JESÚS ◆ n. en Zapotlán el Grande, Jal., y m. en Colima, Col. (1846-1893). Militar. Combatió a los invasores franceses en las batallas de Acutzingo (1862), Puebla (1862) y a las tropas imperialistas en el sitio de Puebla de 1867. Fue subprefecto de Ixtlahuacán y de Comala y administrador del Hospital Civil de Colima.

Foto: Época

Manuel M. Ponce

Ponce, Manuel ◆ n. en Tanguato, Mich. (1913). Poeta. Su segundo apellido es Zavala. Sacerdote ordenado en 1936. Estudió en el Seminario Tridentino de Morelia, Mich. Ha sido profesor de literatura, director de la revista *Trento* (1943-68) y presidente de la Comisión Nacional de Arte Sacro de la Conferencia Episcopal Mexicana (1969-). Fundador de la Academia de Historia Eclesiástica y de la Casa de Poesía (1986). Promovió el I Simposio Internacional de Arte Sacro en el DF (1992). Consultor de la Comisión Pontificia para la Guarda y Fomento del Arte y de la Historia (1991-96) y capellán del papa Juan Pablo II (1992-). Colaborador de las revistas *El Hijo Pródigo*, *Letras de México*, *Viñetas de Literatura Michoacana*, *Ábside*, *América* y *Cuadernos de Literatura Michoacana*. Autor de *Álbum Jubilar Monográfico, Diego José Abad, estudio literario, Panegíricos y Sermones del Excelentísimo Luis Altamirano y Bulnes, Antología de la Poesía Religiosa en México, Ciclo de vírgenes* (1940), *Cuadragenario y segunda pasión* (1942), *Misterios para cantar bajo los álamos* (1947), *El jardín increíble* (1950), *Cristo y María* (1955), *Elegías y teofanías* (1968), *Antología poética* (selección y prólogo de Gabriel Zaid, 1980 y 1991) y *Poesías 1940-84* (1988). Miembro de la Academia Mexicana (de la Lengua) desde 1977. Socio fundador del Comité Conmemorativo Vasco de Quiroga.

Ponce, Manuel M. ◆ n. en el Mineral de Fresnillo, Zac., y m. en el DF (1882-1948). Músico. En Aguascalientes inició su aprendizaje musical con su hermana Josefina (1888), estudió piano con Cipriano Ávila (1890) y fue ayudante (1895) y organista del templo de San Diego (1897). Prosiguió en el Conservatorio Nacional de Música (1901-02), del que fue profesor (1909-) y director (1933-34). En 1904 ofreció algunos conciertos en Estados Unidos y viajó a Italia, donde estudió en el Liceo Musical de Bolonia con Luigi Torchi (1904-06) y en el Liszt-Verein y en el Stern'sches Konservatorium de Berlín (1906-08) con Edwin Kioscher y Martin Krauze. Vivió en Cuba de 1915 a 1917. A su regreso dirigió la Orquesta Sinfónica de México (1917-20). En París (1925-33) estudió con Paul Dukas, fundó y dirigió la *Gaceta Musical* (1928-29) y evolucionó hacia el modernismo impresionista. En la Escuela Nacional de Música, que también dirigió (1945-46), estableció la cátedra de folclor. Dirigió la revista *Cultura Musical* (1936-37). Creó la Orquesta Sinfónica Mexicana (1947). Colaborador de *Excélsior*. En su obra destacan el *Concierto para piano* (1911), el *Concierto del sur para guitarra y orquesta* (escrito para Andrés Segovia, 1941), el *Concierto para violín y orquesta* (estrenado por Henryk Szeryng, 1943), música sinfónica: *Instantáneas mexicanas*, *Ferial* y *Chapultepec*; música instrumental: *Suite en estilo antiguo*, *Suite para violín, viola y cello*, *Bagatelas*, *Instantáneas mexicanas*, *Trío para piano, violín y cello*; música para piano: *Rapsodias mexicanas*, *Rapsodias cubanas* y *Malgré tout, danza para la mano izquierda*; la ópera *El jardín florido*; y las canciones populares *Marchita el alma*, *A la orilla de un palmar*, *Alevántate*, *Qué lejos ando*, *Serenata mexicana*, *Lejos de ti*, *Trigueña hermosa*, *La barca del marino*, *Estrellita* y *La pajarera*. Autor de: *Escritos y composiciones musicales* (1917) y *Nuevas composiciones musicales* (1949). Miembro del Seminario de Cultura Mexicana (1954). Premio Nacional de Ciencias y Artes (1947).

Ponce Cámara, Arturo ◆ n. y m. en Mérida, Yuc. (1877-1935). Periodista. Se desempeñó como gerente de la empresa comercial J. M. Ponce y Compañía y de la Cervecería Yucateca, fundadas por su padre. Fue jefe político de su ciudad natal y uno de los fundadores de la Cooperativa Henequeneros de Yucatán, de la que fue gerente ejecutivo y gerente director; fundó también el Banco y los Almacenes Generales de Depósito de Yucatán, y presidió la casa editora del *Diario de Yucatán*.

Ponce de León, Francisco ◆ n. en San Luis Potosí, SLP, y m. en la ciudad de México (1795-1861). Militar. Teniente de las tropas coloniales desde 1813. En 1821 se sumó al Ejército Trigarante, a las órdenes de Anastasio Bustamante. Dos años después, cuando era teniente coronel, se adhirió al Plan de Casa Mata y en 1829 combatió en Tampico contra la invasión de Isidro Barradas. Jefe de la guarnición militar de Chiapas, en 1830 se sublevó contra el gobierno de Vicente Guerrero y al triunfo de la rebelión fue colaborador del vicepresidente Bustamante. Combatió la revuelta liberal de 1832-33. Fue comandante general de Veracruz (1838), Michoacán (1841), Querétaro (1843) y Sinaloa (1843) y gobernador de Sinaloa (1843-44) y de Sonora (1844): durante su gobierno se fundó la primera escuela primaria en la región del Yaqui. Retirado del ejército en 1845, administró la aduana marítima de San Blas y combatió contra los invasores estadounidenses en 1847. Durante el gobierno de Antonio López de Santa Anna, quien lo nombró general de brigada en 1853, fue jefe militar de Sayula y jefe político y militar de Colima (1854-55): su gobierno expidió la primera ley del trabajo y prohibió el comercio de mariguana. Al triunfo del Plan de Ayutla se le confinó en Colima. En agosto de 1857 dirigió un motín contra el gobernador Manuel Álvarez, tras el cual fue desterrado. A principios de 1858 reconoció al gobierno de Félix Zuloaga y luchó contra los liberales en Guadalajara, durante la guerra de los Tres Años.

PONCE DE LEÓN, GREGORIO ◆ n. en Morelia, Mich., y m. en el DF (1885-1950). Periodista. Realizó estudios de derecho en el Colegio de San Nicolás de Hidalgo. Fundador del periódico *La Voz de la Juventud* (1903), fue apresado en varias ocasiones por su oposición al gobernador Aristeo Mercado. Director de *Política de los Estados* y *Juan Panadero* y colaborador de *El Imparcial* y *La Patria*. Autor de *Porfirio Díaz y el 2 de abril de 1867* (1913), *La paz y sus colaboradores* (1914) y *El interinato presidencial de 1915* (1921).

PONCE DE LEÓN, HUGO ◆ n. en Guanajuato, Gto., y m. en el DF (1929-1971). Periodista. Estudió en la UNAM. Fue uno de los dirigentes de la huelga universitaria de 1948, administrador de la Escuela Nacional de Ciencias Políticas y Sociales (1955) y editor y director del semanario *Futuro* (1956-58). En 1958 se hizo cargo de la redacción de *Unificación*, órgano del Sindicato de Trabajadores Ferrocarrileros de la República Mexicana, luego de la elección de Demetrio Vallejo como secretario general. Fue detenido el 28 de marzo de 1959, durante el asalto policiaco a las instalaciones sindicales, y estuvo preso más de cinco años en la penitenciaría de Lecumberri (☛ *Movimiento ferrocarrilero de 1958-59*). En 1960, cuando estaba encarcelado, ingresó al PCM, del que, al quedar en libertad, fue miembro del presidium del Comité Central, director de *La Voz de México* (1964-69) y jefe de redacción de *Oposición* (1970-71), órganos de ese partido.

PONCE DE LEÓN, LUIS ◆ n. en España y m. en la ciudad de México (?-1526). Llegó a la ciudad de México el 2 de julio de 1526, como visitador de la Nueva España y encargado de gobernar el virreinato mientras durara el juicio de residencia contra Hernán Cortés. Falleció el 20 de julio de ese año, antes de que el proceso finalizara, y su muerte se le atribuyó al propio Cortés.

PONCE DE LEÓN, PEDRO ◆ n. en la ciudad de México y ¿m. en Zampahuacán, Estado de México? (1546-¿1626?). Licenciado en teología por la Real y Pontificia Universidad de México. Fue cura de Zampahuacán (1571-1626). Escribió un libro que constituye la segunda parte del *Códice Chimalpopoca* o *Anales de Cuauhtitlán*, que se dio a conocer en 1892.

PONCE DE LEÓN ANDRADE, XAVIER ◆ n. en Morelia, Mich. (1941). Licenciado en administración por el ITAM (1962-66), especializado en información en la Universidad de Columbia (1968). Desde 1959 pertenece al PRI. Ha sido subdirector de Estudios Administrativos de la Secretaría de la Presidencia (1971-73), director adjunto del Conacyt (1973-75), director general de Administración, Organización y Presupuesto de la Secretaría de Hacienda (1976-82); oficial mayor (1983-87) y coordinador del Programa de Simplificación Administrativa (1987-88) de la Secretaría de la Contraloría General de la Federación, director adjunto de Administración y Asuntos Jurídicos Nafin (1988-1991) y subdelegado en Cuauhtémoc (1996-97). Es el representante gubernamental ante el Centro Latinoamericano de Administración para el Desarrollo.

PONCE DE LEÓN SALMÓN, JOSÉ MARÍA ◆ n. en Mineral de Uruáchic y m. en Chihuahua, Chih. (1878-1924). Historiador y periodista. Estudió en el Instituto Científico y Literario de Chihuahua. Se dedicó al periodismo. Colaboró en *La Idea Libre*, *El Siglo XIX*, *El Norte* y *El Correo de Chihuahua*. Fue editor de los anuarios estadísticos del gobierno local (1905-10), oficial mayor del Gobierno en Chihuahua (1905, 1913 y 1919) y director de la *Revista de Chihuahua* (1909-11). Autor de *Datos geográficos y estadísticos de Chihuahua* (1902). Perteneció a la Sociedad Mexicana de Geografía y Estadística.

PONCE REYES, TOMÁS ◆ n. en Cuba y m. en el DF (¿1896?-1972). Músico. Fue discípulo de Julián Carrillo en el Conservatorio Nacional. Participó en la fundación de la Sociedad de Autores y Compositores de Música. Hizo arreglos de canciones mexicanas antiguas como *Adolorido*, *La chancla*, *La rancherita*, *El venadito* y otras.

PONCE ROMERO, LUIS ◆ n. en Acaxochitlán y m. en Tulancingo, Hgo. (1839-1875). Estudió en la Escuela Nacional de Medicina. Se tituló en 1861. Al año siguiente se incorporó al Cuerpo Médico Militar y participó en la batalla de Puebla del 5 de mayo de 1862. En 1863 fundó en Tulancingo el periódico *El Tábano*. Colaboró en *El Renacimiento* y *La Orquesta* de la ciudad de México. Fue coeditor de la revista *El Ensayo*. Su creación literaria se publicó en 1889, en el volumen *Poemas y composiciones diversas*, prologado por Juan de Dios Peza.

PONCE SOTELO, FAUSTO *EL BRUJO* ◆ n. en Campeche, Camp. (1915). Periodista y softbolista. En su adolescencia practicó deportes de pista y campo, impuso marca nacional en salto largo y llegó a participar en torneos internacionales como especialista en salto triple. Como jugador de softbol participó en varios campeonatos mundiales y editó el periódico *Softbol*; fue después entrenador de ese deporte y finalmente reportero de la sección deportiva del diario *Excélsior*. En 1989 ingresó en el Salón de la Fama del Softbol y en 1993 recibió un homenaje por sus 50 años como periodista por parte de la Confederación Deportiva Mexicana.

PONCITLÁN ◆ Municipio de Jalisco, situado en el este del estado, al sureste de Guadalajara, y en los límites con Michoacán. Superficie: 672.31 km². Habitantes: 36,893, de los cuales 8,371 forman la población económicamente activa. Hablan alguna lengua indígena 24 personas mayores de cinco años.

PONIATOWSKA, ELENA ◆ n. en Francia (1933). Escritora. Su apellido materno es Amor. Se naturalizó mexicana en 1969. Estudió en Francia, Estados Unidos y México, donde vive desde 1942. Dirige el taller literario El Grupo. Realizadora de cortometrajes sobre Sor Juana Inés de la Cruz y José Clemente

Libro de Elena Poniatowska

Elena Poniatowska

Orozco, entre otros. Se inició en el periodismo en 1953. Ha escrito en las principales publicaciones de México. Coautora de *Gaby Brimmer* (1979) y *EZLN. Documentos y comunicados* (1994, con Carlos Monsiváis). Autora de cuento: *Lilus Kikus* (1954), *De noche vienes* (1979) y *Métase mi prieta entre el durmiente y el silbatazo* (1982); ensayo: *Melés y Teleo* (1956) y *El último guajolote* (1982); entrevista: *Palabras cruzadas* (1961), *Todo empezó el domingo* (1963), *Domingo 7* (1982), *Todo México I* (1990), *Todo México II* (1994), *Octavio Paz. Las palabras del árbol* (1997) y *Juan Soriano. Niño de mil años* (1998); novela: *Hasta no verte Jesús mío* (1969, Premio Mazatlán de Literatura 1970), *Querido Diego, te abraza Quiela* (1978), *Moletiques y pasiones* (1987), *¡Ay vida, no me mereces!* (1986), *La flor de lis* (1988), *Tinísima* (1992, Premio Mazatlán de Literatura 1993) y *Paseo de la Reforma* (1996); testimonio: *La noche de Tlatelolco* (1971), *Fuerte es el silencio* (1980), *Nada, nadie, las voces del temblor* (1988), *Tlacotalpan* (1988), *Juchitán de las mujeres* (1989, fotos de Graciela Iturbide) y *Todo empezó el domingo* (1997); y poesía *La primavera de los banqueros y otros poemas* (1957). Algunos de sus poemas se encuentran en la antología italiana *Rojo de vida y negro de muerte*. Becaria del Centro Mexicano de Escritores (1957-58) y de la Fundación Guggenheim (1994). Ha recibido los premios de periodismo (1965 y 1973), Xavier VIllaurrutia (1970, por *La noche de Tlatelolco*, que rechazó), Nacional de Periodismo (1978, primera mujer en recibirlo), del diario *El Porvenir* de Monterrey (1986), Manuel Buendía (1987), Coatlicue (1990) y Nacional Juchitán (1993). Creadora emérita del SNCA (1993-). Doctora *honoris causa* por la Columbia University of New York (1994) y por la Florida Atlantic University (1995). Recibió la Medalla Gabriela Mistral en 1995.

PONS, MARIA ANTONIETA ◆ n. en Cuba (1922). Actriz y bailarina. Dirigida por Juan Orol, protagonizó las cintas *Cruel destino* (1943), *Los misterios del hampa* (1944), *Pasiones tormentosas* (1945) y *Embrujo antillano* (1945). Además, trabajó en *Noches de ronda* (1942), *La última aventura de Chaflán* (1942), *Mi reino por un torero* (1943), *Viva mi desgracia* (1943), *Bajalú* (1943), *Konga roja* (1943), *Rosalinda* (1944), *Toda una vida* (1944), *La vida íntima de Marco Antonio y Cleopatra* (1946), *La insaciable* (1946), *La bien pagada* (1947), *La sin ventura* (1947), *Nuestras vidas* (1949), *La mujer del puerto* (versión de 1949), *La hija del penal* (1949), *El ciclón del Caribe* (1950), *La reina del mambo* (1950), *La niña popoff* (1951), *María Cristina* (1951), *Casa de perdición* (1954), *La gaviota* (1954), *¡Qué bravas son las costeñas!* (1954), *Sucedió en México* (1957), *Flor de canela* (1957), *Acapulqueña* (1958), *Ferias de México* (1958) y *Las cuatro milpas* (1958).

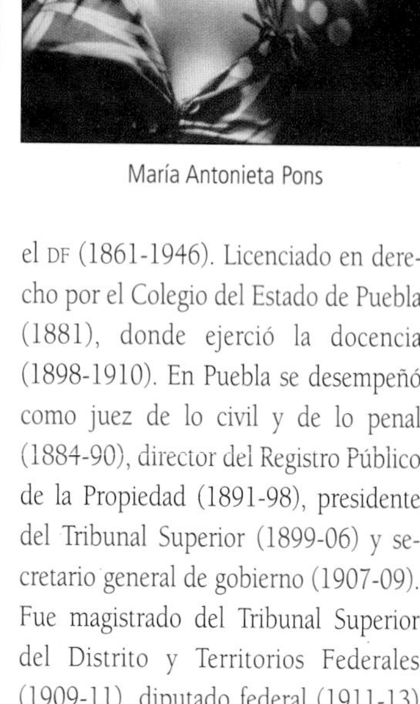
María Antonieta Pons

PONTÓN, JOSÉ MARIANO ◆ n. en Puebla, Pue., y m. en el DF (1861-1946). Licenciado en derecho por el Colegio del Estado de Puebla (1881), donde ejerció la docencia (1898-1910). En Puebla se desempeñó como juez de lo civil y de lo penal (1884-90), director del Registro Público de la Propiedad (1891-98), presidente del Tribunal Superior (1899-06) y secretario general de gobierno (1907-09). Fue magistrado del Tribunal Superior del Distrito y Territorios Federales (1909-11), diputado federal (1911-13) y secretario de estudio de la Suprema Corte de Justicia de la Nación (1924-46). Profesor de las escuelas nacionales Preparatoria y de Jurisprudencia (1924-35). Autor de *La organización de la Suprema Corte de Justicia y el juicio de amparo* (1921), *Apuntes sobre legislación y política agraria* (1922), *Derecho público* (1930), *Derecho romano* (1930), *Las razas indígenas de México* (1933), *Síntesis histórica de Puebla*

Escultura de Octavio Ponzanelli Conti

(1935) y *El seguro social obligatorio* (1944). Perteneció a las sociedades Científica Antonio Alzate y Mexicana de Geografía y Estadística.

Ponz y Ardil, Manuel ◆ n. y m. en Villahermosa, Tab. (1813-1865). Estudió farmacología. Elegido vicegobernador (1850-52), fue gobernador interino de Tabasco del 9 de agosto al 23 de septiembre de 1852.

Ponzanelli, Adolfo Octavio ◆ n. y m. en Italia (1879-1952). Escultor. Estudió con Augusto Rodin. Llegó a México en 1906 y trabajó con Adamo Boari en la construcción del Palacio de Bellas Artes. Dirigió una marmolería en la ciudad de México y fue codueño de las canteras de Torreón y Dinamita. Realizó los revestimientos interiores del Palacio de Bellas Artes (1932-34), de la Basílica de Guadalupe y de los monumentos a los Niños Héroes, a la Revolución y a Obregón. Junto con su hijo, Octavio Ponzanelli Conti, esculpió la Virgen de Guadalupe y el Juan Diego para la Ciudad del Vaticano, obra por la que recibió la Cruz de San Lázaro.

Ponzanelli, Gabriel ◆ n. en el DF (1942). Escultor. Hijo de Octavio Ponzanelli Conti. Estudió en la Universidad de Nueva York. Expuso por primera vez en 1960. Sus obras se han presentado en Argentina y Canadá (1967). Autor del busto de Albert Einstein que se encuentra en la Facultad de Ciencias de la UNAM, de un altorrelieve de la batalla de Pansacola, en el bosque de Chapultepec; 15 bustos de poetas que se hallan en el Polyforum Cultural Siqueiros; los coyotes del jardín Hidalgo, la estatua de Frida Kahlo y de Ricardo Flores Magón, y la serie de desnudos en la avenida Miguel Ángel de Quevedo en Coyoacán; dos bustos de Fidel Velázquez, en Sinaloa; y las estatuas de Ignacio Zaragoza, Ignacio Ramírez *El Nigromante*, Benito Juárez, Francisco I. Madero y Venustiano Carranza, en el Palacio de Gobierno de Culiacán. Esculturas suyas se encuentran en museos de Hawai y Nueva York en EUA; Londres, Inglaterra; París, Francia; Ontario y en las Cataratas del Niágara, *Las razas*, en Canadá.

Ponzanelli Conti, Octavio ◆ n. y m. en el DF (1918-1986). Escultor. Hijo de Adolfo Octavio Ponzanelli. Estudió en la Real Academia de Bellas Artes de Florencia. Fue director fundador de la Academia de Bellas Artes de la isla Margarita, Venezuela (1961). Sus obras se expusieron en Argentina, Brasil, Chile, Italia y Paraguay. Es autor de los bustos de Gonzalo Curiel, María Greever, Agustín Lara, Juventino Rosas y Silvestre Revueltas que se encuentran en la Calzada de los Compositores del Bosque de Chapultepec; tres monumentos a Rubén Darío, en el DF, Guadalajara y Jalapa; la estatua de Agustín Lara que está en la Casa de Cultura de Tlacotalpan; la estatua de Gregorio Torres Quintero de la plaza principal de Colima; la estatua de Francisco I. Madero, de Parras de la Fuente, Coahuila; el monumento a Lázaro Cárdenas, de Los Mochis; una estatua de Benito Juárez, que se halla en Zacatecas; el *Monumento a la Familia* de Naucalpan; y el monumento a Miguel Hidalgo de la delegación Magdalena Contreras, DF. Recibió la Cruz de San Lázaro del Santo Sepulcro, en Italia.

Popocatépetl ◆ Volcán situado en la confluencia de los estados de México, Morelos y Puebla, en el extremo sur de la sierra Nevada, al sur del volcán Iztaccíhuatl. Su nombre náhuatl significa "Cerro que humea". Se eleva 5,452 metros sobre el nivel del mar y tiene nieves perpetuas a partir de los 4,300 metros, las que en invierno se inician a los 4,100 metros. Es el segundo volcán más alto de México, después del Citlaltépetl o Pico de Orizaba. Sus dos cimas son el Espinazo del Diablo y el Pico Mayor. Su cráter tiene un diámetro de 850 metros y una profundidad de 300; en su extremo sureste hay una pequeña laguna. De los tres glaciares importantes que existían, sólo uno pequeño (1,000 metros de longitud por 600 de ancho), situado en la ladera norte del volcán, ha sobrevivido. Formado sobre un volcán primitivo llamado Nexpayantla, hace aproximadamente 300,000 años, el Popocatépetl es un volcán activo que permanentemente arroja humo. Desde

Popocatépetl

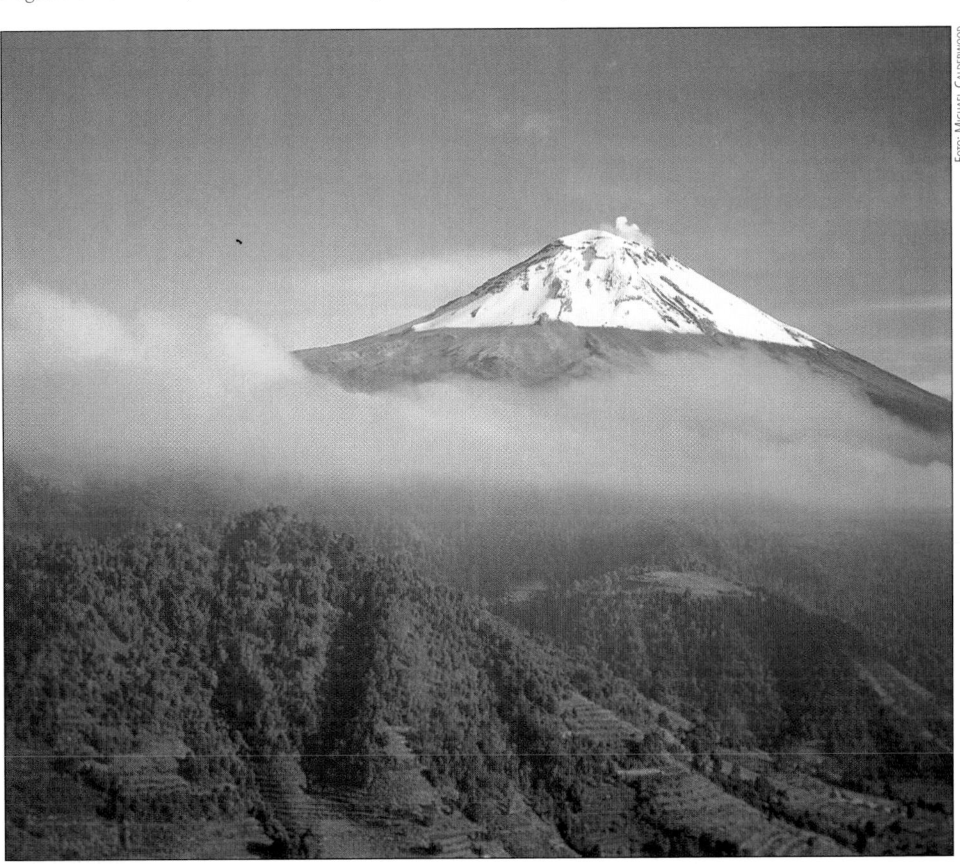

Foto: Michael Calderwood

que se instalaron en su ladera occidental, hacia el siglo XII, los pueblos nahuas consideraron al volcán una divinidad, cónyuge del Iztaccíhuatl, y destinaban un mes, el *teotleco*, a reverenciarlo. Frente a sus casas colocaban varios pequeños cerros de masa de amaranto y uno de ellos más grande, que representaba al volcán; sobre los montículos pequeños dibujaban rostros humanos. Durante dos días alimentaban los cerritos, considerados representaciones de los *tepeme* o dioses de los montes; y luego los cortaban, les extraían el centro y se lo comían. En los lugares más poblados, los sacerdotes hacían la masa de amaranto y con ella recubrían ramas torcidas, que se convertían en los *tepeme*; posteriormente repartían la masa entre los minusválidos. Según Juan de Torquemada, el final de la fiesta consistía en el sacrificio de cuatro doncellas. En la otra ladera, la que ocupa el estado de Puebla, una forma similar de relación entre el Popocatépetl y la población indígena todavía se practicaba a mediados de los años ochenta del siglo XX, en las comunidades poblanas de Nealtican, San Mateo Ozolco, San Nicolás de los Ranchos y Santiago Xalitzintla, situadas en los alrededores del Paso de Cortés. En cada uno de los pueblos había un mago encargado de comunicarse con los volcanes, llamado *quiampero*, que había sido invitado por el propio volcán para ser interlocutor entre él y su pueblo. Esta invitación ocurría cuando una persona era tocada por un rayo y lograba sobrevivir. Entonces el elegido era entrenado por los *quiamperos* más viejos y adquiría el derecho de hablar con el Popocatépetl, al cual llamaba *Don Gregorio*, y con el Iztaccíhuatl, que se convertía en *Doña Manuela*. La función principal de los *quiamperos* era encabezar, cada 3 de mayo, una peregrinación de los cuatro pueblos a un cueva natural situada en la ladera del volcán, donde se encontraban una pequeña cascada y cuatro grandes piedras que representaban los cuatro pueblos. Ahí los *quiamperos* interpretaban las formas del agua de la cascada, y de acuerdo con ellas pronosticaban el régimen de lluvias para cada una de las comunidades. Mientras los peregrinos hacían ofrendas de mole y tamales salados y rezaban en silencio, los *quiamperos* conversaban con *Don Gregorio* y lo urgían para que permitiera la abundancia de las cosechas. Estos ruegos no siempre resultaban efectivos, pues en ocasiones el Demonio enviaba granizo para dañar los cultivos. Cada vez que se anunciaba la granizada, mientras las campanas de los templos se hacían sonar para llamar a los campesinos que se encontraban en sus parcelas, los *quiamperos* se vestían de manta, se anudaban un paliacate rojo en la frente y se lanzaban, espada en mano, hacia el volcán, a combatir al granizo-Diablo. En su combate eran ayudados por los campesinos, quienes desde las torres de las iglesias lanzaban cohetes contra el granizo. Aunque casi todos los *quiamperos* han sido hombres, se sabe de la existencia de una mujer *quiampera*. Según relatan los habitantes de Santiago Xalitzintla, esta muchacha rubia de 15 años, fue tocada por un rayo en el bosque ejidal del Popocatépetl y se convirtió en interlocutora entre el volcán y la gente de su pueblo. Fue una *quiampera* un poco extraña, pues además de que perdió el cabello rubio y de que su piel se oscureció, tenía la capacidad de predecir las granizadas por medio de visiones a las que sucedían ataques convulsivos. Sin embargo, la tradición de los *quiamperos* se encontraba hacia 1985 en un momento de crisis, pues de los cuatro *quiamperos* existentes, sólo vivía el de San Mateo Ozolco, a lo que se atribuyeron las malas cosechas de 1987, pues *Don Gregorio* no tenía con quien hablar. En la época prehispánica, el Popocatépetl hizo erupción por lo menos en cuatro ocasiones: en 1347, 1354, 1363 y 1509. En agosto de 1519, después de la matanza de Cholula, Hernán Cortés envió a diez de sus hombres, al mando de Diego de Ordaz, a explorar el cráter, pero las bajas temperaturas y los fuertes vientos frustraron el intento. Unos días después, los españoles cruzaron la sierra Nevada entre ambos volcanes, por lo que hoy se conoce como Paso de Cortés. En 1520, mientras las tropas conquistadoras se reponían en Tlaxcala de su derrota en México-Tenochtitlan, Cortés envió al cráter a Francisco Montaño y Francisco de Meza, artilleros ambos. Montaño descendió y extrajo el azufre necesario para la elaboración de la pólvora que fue utilizada por los conquistadores en el ataque final a la capital mexica en 1521. A mediados del siglo XVI, los frailes agustinos construyeron un convento en Ocuituco, población de Morelos situada en la ladera suroccidental del volcán. En 1545, el franciscano Bernardino de Sahagún realizó una ascención al volcán, aunque no llegó al cráter. Durante el siglo XVI, el Popocatépetl entró en actividad en siete ocasiones: 1519, 1530-39, 1540, 1542-43, 1548, 1571, 1592 y seis veces en el siglo XVII: 1642,

Los volcanes Iztaccíhuatl y Popocatépetl

FOTO: DANTE BUCIO

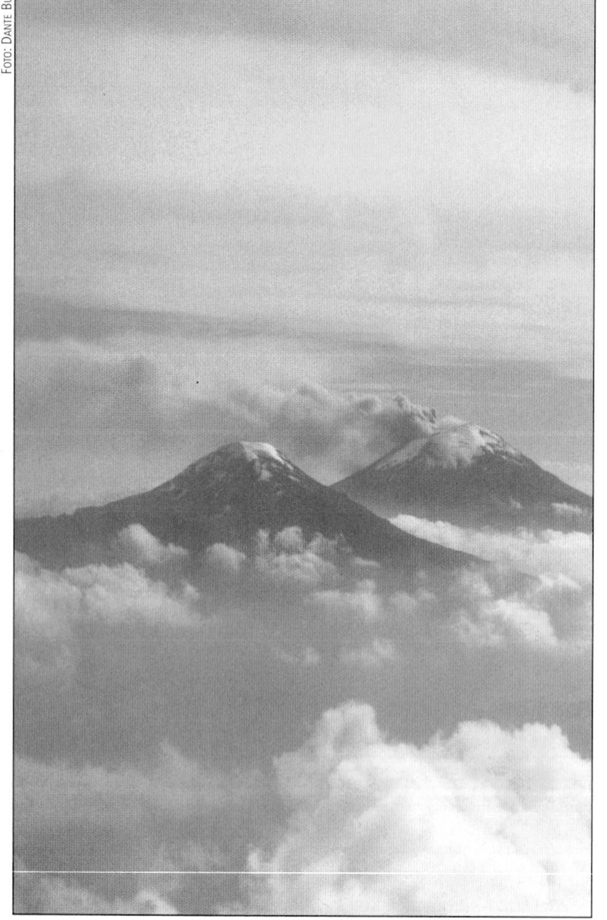

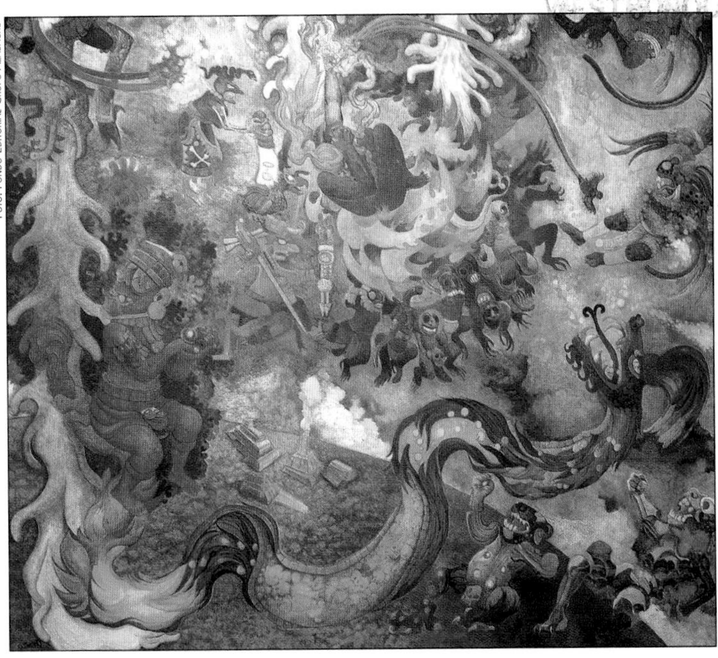
FOTO: FONDO EDITORIAL GRUPO AZABACHE

Mural en el Hotel Cencali, en Tabasco, obra de Daniel Ponce Montuy, que narra la historia de la creación según el *Popol Vuh*

1663, 1664, 1665-66, 1667 y 1697. Uno de los primeros extranjeros en intentar la ascención fue el minerólogo alemán Fiedrich Sonneschmidt, quien exploró el volcán en 1772. Durante ese siglo el volcán entró en actividad en 1720 y en 1790. En 1803, Alexander von Humboldt calculó la altura del volcán. Al año siguiente el Popocatépetl volvió a hacer erupción. En 1827 William y Frederic Gleinne y Berbek ascendieron al cráter; en 1834, el barón de Gros y Federico von Geroldt; y en 1857, Laverrière y Sontag, quienes fueron los primeros en descender profundamente al cráter. En 1918 se inició la explotación del azufre del cráter; al año siguiente se hizo estallar dinamita en el interior del cráter, lo que provocó una erupción que duró hasta 1922. El Popocatépetl volvió a hacer erupción en 1926. A partir de 1994 el volcán está activo nuevamente, ha tenido erupciones pequeñas y levantado humaredas de hasta seis kilómetros de altura.

POPOL VUH ◆ Conocido también como *Libro nacional de los antiguos votánides*, *Popol buj*, *Popol buh*, *Popol vuj*, *Manuscrito de Chichicastenango*, *Libro nacional de los quichés*, *Libro del común* o *Libro del consejo*. Recoge la mitología y parte de la historia de los mayas de la región del Quiché. El manuscrito original, hoy desaparecido, estaba escrito en quiché y fue traducido y publicado por Francisco Ximénez entre 1701 y 1703. Esta traducción permaneció hasta mediados del siglo XIX en la Biblioteca Nacional de Guatemala, cuando fue obtenida por el estadounidense Clement Ayer. Más tarde pasó a manos de la Biblioteca Newberry de Estados Unidos, donde se encuentra hasta la fecha.

POPOLOCAS ◆ Indios que habitan en algunas regiones del sur de Puebla y del norte de Oaxaca, distribuidos en tres áreas geográficas principales: la zona alta del Valle de Tehuacán y las zonas semidesérticas de las mixtecas Alta y Oaxaqueña. Los hablantes de popoloca no aparecen en el censo nacional de 1980. En el censo de 1970 fueron contados 27,818, de los cuales 23,060 hablaban también español, y en el de 1980 no aparecieron, pero según el Conteo Nacional de Población, en 1995 había 14,390 hablantes de la lengua popoloca, que pertenece al grupo otomangue, tronco savizaa, familia mazateco-popoloca. En cada una de las tres regiones se hablan variantes dialectales, lo que imposibilita la comunicación entre los diferentes grupos. Los jóvenes, en su mayoría, han abandonado las vestimentas tradicionales y emigran a las ciudades cercanas, en busca de trabajo asalariado. La organización básica es la familia nuclear, aunque también hay familias extensas; el compadrazgo (principalmente el de bautizo) es un vínculo sólido. El matrimonio lo pacta un intermediario que visita la casa de la novia, con una serie de regalos equivalentes a la dote. Practican la religión católica, aunque tienen en sus comunidades especialistas en cuestiones sobrenaturales, brujos y curanderos, quienes se encargan de curar el "mal aire, el espanto" y "la pérdida del alma". En algunos pueblos existe una junta auxiliar, integrada por siete regidores que han desempeñado diversos cargos, que se encarga de resolver los problemas internos, designa a los sacristanes, fiscales y topiles y sirve como intermediaria entre la comunidad y las autoridades municipales. Las comunidades popolocas sobreviven de la agricultura temporalera de maíz y frijol negro; ocasionalmente cultivan aguacate, naranja, limón y papaya. Las mujeres elaboran algunas artesanías de barro, palma y cuero, destinadas al comercio.

POPOLUCAS ◆ Indios que viven en la región tropical del sureste de Veracruz. Según el Conteo Nacional de Población de 1995 había en el país 34,684 hablantes de popoluca, idioma del grupo maya-totonaco, tronco mixeano, familia mixeana, subfamilia mixe-popoluca. El idioma tiene variantes dialectales que impiden la comunicación entre individuos de distintos pueblos. Han abandonado las vestimentas tradicionales. Se dedican a la agricultura de temporal para el autoconsumo y la venta; algunos popolucas de la zona costera cazan y pescan y todos practican la recolección. Algunas familias poseen ganado y las mujeres elaboran artesanías de barro y palma, destinadas al comercio. La base de su organización social es la familia nuclear, con tendencia a la familia extensa. El matrimonio lo concierta un intermediario que visita

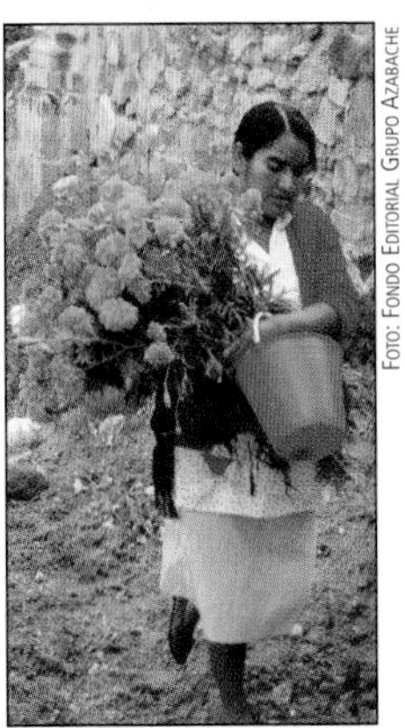
FOTO: FONDO EDITORIAL GRUPO AZABACHE

Mujeres popolocas de la región norte de Oaxaca

repetidamente la casa de la novia, llevando presentes de diversa índole; la "entrega de la novia" queda pactada con una última remesa de regalos. Tiene gran arraigo la institución del compadrazgo. Los popolucas son católicos, aunque conservan algunas de sus antiguas creencias, como el culto a la deidad del maíz, *Homshuk*, y a los *chanecos* o *chaneques*, espíritus protectores de los animales que propician la caza.

POPULAR, EL ◆ Diario aparecido en 1938 que inicialmente fue órgano de la Confederación de Trabajadores de México. Vicente Lombardo Toledano fue su primer director, Fidel Velázquez era el gerente general, Rodolfo Piña Soria el subdirector y Mario Rojas Avendaño el jefe de redacción. Tenía sus oficinas de dirección, redacción y talleres en Basilio Vadillo 9 en el DF. Contaba con 16 páginas y se vendía a 5 centavos. Otros directores fueron Alejandro Carrillo Marcor y Enrique Ramírez y Ramírez. El periódico desapareció a fines de los cincuenta.

POR ESTO! ◆ Revista editada en el Distrito Federal a partir de 2 de julio de 1981. El director es Mario Menéndez Rodríguez. De acuerdo con el editorial del primer número, la publicación se propone "informar con la verdad (.), cumplir con el compromiso de ser leales a los trabajadores, campesinos, estudiantes, profesionales, productores, al pueblo mexicano que labora por una Patria digna y justa para todos sus hijos" y oponerse a "quienes pretenden negarle su destino soberano e independiente". Por dificultades económicas se suspendió la publicación en el número 68, del 14 de octubre de 1982, y se reanudó el 28 de julio de 1983. Posteriormente mudó su sede a Yucatán, donde se convirtió en diario de circulación regional. Por sus páginas han pasado colaboradores como Roger Menéndez Rodríguez, Alberto Híjar, Raúl Ugalde, Horacio Espinosa Altamirano, Rafael Loret de Mola, Laura Bolaños, Oralba Castillo Nájera, Juan Gabriel Torres Landa, Juan Ortega Arenas y otros.

FOTO: LOURDES ALMEIDA

Familia de campesinos popolucas de Hueyapan, Veracruz

Códice Porfirio Díaz

POR QUÉ? ◆ Revista editada en el Distrito Federal a partir del 28 de febrero de 1968. En el editorial del primer número prometía enfocar "los problemas nacionales sin frases adulatorias para cómitres y sayones, sin vestiduras políticas que cubran mercenariamente la lepra de sectarismos interesados que traicionan el Bien Público, y sin olvidar, como dijo el clásico, que 'el dolor de los humildes está más cerca de Dios'. Sólo una brújula ha de guiar a *Por Qué?*: la Verdad; su bandera será la Justicia, y su anhelo más ferviente: el progreso constante de la Patria". Inicialmente de periodicidad catorcenal, a partir del número 15 se convirtió en semanario. Durante el movimiento estudiantil de 1968 editó un número extraordinario del que se tiró un millón de ejemplares. Desde entonces, los editores fueron hostilizados por el gobierno, que encarceló en 1970 a Mario Menéndez Rodríguez (☛), director de la publicación, quien fue desterrado a fines de 1971. Lo sustituyó en la dirección su hermano Roger Menéndez Rodríguez hasta septiembre de 1974, cuando los talleres fueron destruidos por la fuerza pública y detenidos y torturados los hermanos Roger y Hernán Menéndez y los colaboradores Horacio Espinosa Altamirano y Jorge Delgado Ramírez. Hasta el 8 de septiembre de 1974, cuando desapareció la publicación, aparecieron 324 número ordinarios y ocho *extras*.

PORCAYO, GERARDO HORACIO ◆ n. en Cuernavaca, Mor. (1966). Escritor. Licenciado en lingüística y literatura hispánica por la UAP, en la que ha hecho estudios de maestría y ha sido catedrático. Fundador y director de la revista electrónica *La langosta se ha posado*, pionera de las publicaciones mexicanas en ese medio. Textos suyos han aparecido en las antologías *Más allá de lo imaginado I* (1991), *Sin permiso de Colón* (1992), *Principios de incertidumbre* (1992), *Silicio en la memoria* (1997) y *Rock. Cuentos compactos* (1998). Autor de novela: *La primera calle de la soledad* (1991), *Ciudad espejo, ciudad niebla* (1996) y *Dolorosa* (1999); y cuento: *Sombras sin tiempo* (1999). Ha obtenido los premios Puebla (1993) y Kalpa (1993) de cuento de ciencia ficción, así como el premio internacional Axxón Primordial (1992).

PORCAYO URIBE, JUVENAL ◆ n. en Buenavista de Cuéllar, Gro., y m. en Tapachula, Chis. (1917-1983). Sacerdote ordenado en 1941. Estudió en el Seminario Conciliar de Chilapa. De 1976 a 1980 fue obispo de Tapachula.

PORFIRIO DÍAZ ◆ Códice posthispánico oaxaqueño realizado a fines del siglo XVI o principios del XVII. De contenido histórico y calendárico, tiene leyendas en zapoteco y numerosos jeroglíficos de lugar, como los de Comitán, Quetzaltenango, Juchitán, Acatlán y Tlaxiaco. Consta de 21 hojas de piel cosidas en una banda de más de cuatro metros y plegado en forma de biombo. Lo divulgó por primera vez Alfredo Chavero. Se encuentra en la Biblioteca Nacional de Antropología e Historia.

PORRAS BERMÚDEZ, RODOLFO ◆ n. en Tlaxcala, Tlax., y m. en el DF (1921-1973). Ingeniero. Uno de los precursores de la televisión mexicana. Trabajó para Telesistema Mexicano y en 1971 fue nombrado director del Canal 11. Murió en un accidente automovilístico.

PORRAS MUÑOZ, GUILLERMO ◆ n. en EUA y m. en el DF (1917-1988). Historiador. Estudió en la Escuela Libre de Derecho. Doctor en historia por la Universidad de Sevilla (1951) y doctor en derecho canónico por la Universidad de Navarra (1964). Profesor de la Universidad de la Rábida. Miembro del Opus Dei desde 1947. En 1951 se ordenó sacerdote y fue capellán de los estudiantes católicos de la Universidad de Harvard (1953-61). Volvió a México en 1965 y fue capellán de la Residencia Universitaria Panamericana de la ciudad de México (1966- 88), investigador del Instituto de Investigaciones Históricas de la UNAM (1982-88) y miembro del Sistema Nacional de Investigadores (1984-88). Colaborador de las revistas *Mi-Nos* y *Humanitas*. En 1945 editó el *Diario y derrotero de Pedro de Rivera*. Coautor de *Los vascos en México y su Colegio de las Vizcaínas*. Autor de *Iglesia y Estado en Nueva Vizcaya (1562-1821)* (1966), *La frontera con los indios de Nueva VIzcaya en el siglo XVII* (1980), *El gobierno de la ciudad de México en el siglo XVI* (1982) y *Refexiones sobre la traza de la ciudad de México* (1987). Perteneció a la Academia Mexicana de la Historia, a la Academia Nacional de Historia y Geografía, y a la Sociedad de Historia Eclesiástica. En 1982 recibió el Premio Ciudad de México; en 1986, el Premio Capitán Alonso de León, de la Sociedad Nuevoleonesa de Historia, Geografía y Estadística; en 1987, el Premio Tomás Valles Vivar, de Fomento Cultural Chihuahua; y en 1988, el Premio Banamex Atanasio G. Saravia de Historia Regional Mexicana.

Edificio de la Librería Porrúa, en Justo Sierra y Argentina, en la ciudad de México

PÓRREZ, PEDRO M. ◆ n. en Guanajuato, Gto., y m. en la ciudad de México (?-1877). Periodista. Fue condiscípulo de Manuel Acuña. Colaboró en varias organizaciones obreras y, con el pseudónimo de *Cromwell*, escribió para los periódicos *El Desheredado* y *El Socialista*. Conoció algunos textos de Marx y abogaba por la organización de los trabajadores para combatir a los capitalistas, sus "enemigos natos"; llamaba a la revolución social para construír "el imperio de la *Igualdad Universal*"; y demandaba superar el mutualismo para "aspirar a mayores conquistas". Fue delegado al Congreso Obrero de 1876 en representación de la Sociedad Protectora de Artes y Oficios de Veracruz.

PORRÚA ◆ Editorial y librería fundada en 1900 por los españoles Francisco, Indalecio y José Porrúa Estrada, con la razón social de Librería Porrúa Hermanos. Desde entonces se encuentra en la esquina de las calles de Argentina y Justo Sierra, en el Distrito Federal. En 1904, con la publicación de los primeros *Boletines bibliográficos*, se inició su labor editorial. Cuatro años más tarde, en su primer *Catálogo*, la editorial anunciaba ya ediciones propias, sobre todo de libros mexicanos antiguos. En 1913 aparecieron los primeros títulos de la colección *Obras de América*. Al retiro de José Porrúa, en 1933, la empresa cambió su razón social por Porrúa Hermanos y Compañía, a la que se integró José Antonio Pérez Porrúa. En 1944 se creó la Editorial Porrúa S.A., a la que se debe el *Diccionario Porrúa de historia, biografía y geografía de México* (1964). Bajo la dirección de Felipe Teixidor, en 1950 se inició la colección *Sepan Cuántos...*, que cuenta con más de medio millar de títulos de literatura, filosofía e historia. En 1978 la Asociación Nacional de Libreros le otorgó a la editorial el Premio Anual para Libreros Distinguidos.

Logotipo de Editorial Porrúa

PORRÚA ESTRADA, FRANCISCO ◆ n. en España y m. en el DF (1877-1968). Librero y editor. Llegó a México en 1890. Diez años después, en 1900, fundó, con sus hermanos Indalecio y José, la Librería Porrúa Hermanos, en la cual trabajó hasta su muerte.

PORRÚA ESTRADA, INDALECIO ◆ n. en España y m. en el DF (1875-1944). Librero y editor. Llegó a México en 1888. En 1900 fundó, con sus hermanos José y Francisco, la Librería Porrúa Hermanos. Además de ser el principal impulsor de la librería y luego editorial, se dedicó a la ganadería y fundó la empresa pasteurizadora El Perujo, en el estado de Hidalgo.

PORRÚA ESTRADA, JOSÉ ◆ n. en España y m. en el DF (1873-1941). Librero y editor. Llegó a México en 1886. Fundador, en 1900, de la Librería Porrúa Hermanos, al lado de sus hermanos Indalecio y Francisco. Se retiró de la empresa en 1933.

PORRÚA TURANZAS ◆ Códice que consta de nueve fragmentos de un manuscrito pictográfico de papel de amate que fueron encuadernados en el siglo XVI. Fue propiedad del librero José

Porrúa Turanzas. Se encuentra en la Biblioteca Nacional de Antropología e Historia.

PORRÚA TURANZAS, JOSÉ ◆ n. en la ciudad de México y m. en España (1909-1964). Hijo de José Porrúa Estrada, uno de los fundadores de la librería Porrúa Hermanos. Dirigió la antigua Librería de Robredo e inició la colección Biblioteca Histórica de Obras Inéditas, dirigida por Genaro Estrada. Editó diversos catálogos de obras mexicanas y, en Madrid, las coleciones Chimalistac y Tenanilla.

PORRÚA TURANZAS, RAFAEL ◆ n. y m. en el DF (?-1988). Hermano del anterior. Fue copropietario de la Librería de Robredo, desaparecida a fines de los años setenta, al derribarse las construcciones que ocultaban el Templo Mayor de Tenochtitlan. En esa negociación participó de la tertulia que animaban Francisco Gamoneda, Luis González Obregón, Artemio de Valle Arizpe, Manuel Toussaint, Genaro Estrada y, más tarde, Jesús Reyes Heroles, Francisco de la Maza, Andrés Henestrosa y José Rojas Garcidueñas.

PORRÚA VENERO, MIGUEL ÁNGEL ◆ n. en el DF (1951). Licenciado en estudios hispánicos por la Universidad de Madrid (1971), llevó un curso de bibliografía hispanoamericana en el Instituto de Cooperación Iberoamericana de Madrid (1969), donde fue asistente de librero en la Biblioteca América de esa institución (1970-71). Trabajó en la Librería Manuel Porrúa (1971-77) en la elaboración de proyectos editoriales y en el manejo y clasificación de libros antiguos. En 1978 estableció la Librería Miguel Ángel Porrúa, en 1980, el Grupo Editorial Miguel Ángel Porrúa, y en 1988, la Distribuidora de Libros Miguel Ángel Porrúa.

PORSET DUMAS, CLARA ◆ n. en Cuba y m. en el DF (?-1981). Estudió arte, arquitectura y diseño en diversos países. Se dedicó al diseño de mobiliario. En 1940 fijó su residencia en el DF. Fue profesora en la UNAM (1969-81) y colaboró en varios periódicos y revistas. Promovió la primera exposición latinoamericana de diseño industrial (México, 1952). Primer Premio Continental del Museo de Nueva York (1941) y medalla de plata en la Trienal de Milán (1957). Por disposición testamentaria, sus bienes se vendieron para crear un fideicomiso que otorga la beca Clara Porset y el Premio-beca Nacional de Diseño Industrial Clara Porset.

PORTE PETIT, CELESTINO ◆ n. en Córdoba, Ver. (1910). Licenciado en derecho por la UNAM (1934). Profesor de la Universidad Veracruzana. Ha sido agente del Ministerio Público y juez de primera instancia en Córdoba; agente auxiliar de la Procuraduría General del estado y magistrado del Tribunal Superior de Justicia de Veracruz y del Distrito y Territorios Federales. Fundador del Grupo Orientación, de Jalapa. Es editor de la *Revista de Jurisprudencia* y director de la *Revista Jurídica Veracruzana*. Autor de *La propiedad agraria mexicana como función social* (1934), *Código de procedimientos civiles del estado de Veracruz* (1940), *Tabla de concordancias del código civil de Veracruz* (1944), *El código penal mexicano del porvenir* (1944), *La reforma penal mexicana: el proyecto de 1949* (1951), *Evolución penal legislativa en México* (1965), *Dogmática sobre los delitos contra la vida y la salud personal* (1969), *Ensayo dogmático sobre el delito de violación* (1980), *Ensayo dogmático sobre el delito de rapto propio* (1984), *Robo simple* (1984), *Derecho penal mexicano*, *Ensayo dogmático sobre el delito de estupro*, *Un paso atrás en la trayectoria judicial veracruzana*, *La labor fecunda de José Agustín Martínez*, *Legislación penal mexicana comparada*, *Labor jurídica de Raúl Carrancá y Trujillo* y *Legislación y jurisprudencia*.

PORTE-PETIT MORENO, LUIS OCTAVIO ◆ n. en Córdoba, Ver. (1938). Licenciado en derecho por la UNAM (1961), donde fue profesor (1965-70). Hasido agente del Ministerio Público 63), subdirector general de Investigaciones de la Procuraduría de Justicia del Distrito Federal (1963-64), secretario particular del presidente del PRI (1965), partido al que pertenece desde 1957; director general de Averiguaciones Previas de la PJDF (1970-73), subgerente y gerente general de la Compañía Operadora de Teatros (1973-74), secretario de Gobierno de Veracruz (1974-77), director general de Control de Inmuebles y Zona Federal de la Secretaría de Asentamientos Humanos (1977-79), diputado federal (1979-82), representante de la Cámara de Diputados ante la Comisión Federal Electoral (1981), presidente de la Junta Federal de Conciliación y Arbitraje (1982), coordinador general de la Campaña Nacional contra el Narcotráfico (1982-85), segundo subprocurador (1982-85) y subprocurador jurídico de la Procuraduría General de la República (1986-91) y presidente del Tribunal Superior Agrario (1998-). Coautor de *México en las Naciones Unidas* (1986). Es miembro del Colegio de Abogados, de la Academia Mexicana de Finanzas Públicas y de la Federación Mexicana de Abogados.

PORTELA, MARIBEL ◆ n. en el DF (1960). Ceramista. Estudió en la Escuela Nacional de Artes Plásticas de la UNAM (1979-82). Ha expuesto individualmente en la Galería del Museo de los Constituyentes (1985), en la Galería de Fomento Cultural Banamex (1986), en La Casa del Lago de la UNAM (1987) y en la Galería Kahlo-Coronel (1988). En 1983 y 1987 participó en el Encuentro Nacional de Arte Joven en Aguascalientes y, en 1987, en la exposición Imágenes Guadalupanas del Centro Cultural Arte Contemporáneo.

PORTER, DAVID ◆ n. en EUA y m. en Turquía (1780-1843). Marino. Alcanzó el grado de comodoro en la armada estadounidense. Combatió contra Gran Bretaña y a los piratas del Caribe, en 1812. A sugerencia de Joel R. Poinsett, el presidente Guadalupe Victoria le encargó la formación de una armada mexicana, tarea que emprendió en 1825. Al frente de ésta, desde 1826 hizo frente a la marina española en aguas del Caribe. Renunció en 1829, cuando la Secretaría de Hacienda se negó a indemnizar a la familia de un sobrino su-

Emilio Portes Gil

yo que había muerto en 1828, cuando comandaba el barco mexicano *Guerrero*, frente a las costas de Cuba. Se unió al servicio exterior de su país y fue cónsul en Argel y embajador en Constantinopla.

Porter, Katherine Anne ◆ n. y m. en EUA (1894-1980). Escritora. Hacia 1920 conoció en Nueva York a Adolfo Best-Maugard y a *Tata Nacho*, quienes la convencieron de venir a México. En el Distrito Federal fundó una academia de baile y fue corresponsal de diversas publicaciones estadounidenses. Se dice que inspiró la canción *La norteña*, de Eduardo Vigil y J.F. Elizondo, y, en competencia con Alma Reed, *Peregrina*, de Ricardo Palmerín. En 1922, en colaboración con Best-Maugard, organizó la primera exposición de arte y artesanías mexicanos que se presentó en Estados Unidos; promovió a Diego Rivera, a quien satirizó en su cuento *The martyr* (1923), y recomendó a Miguel Covarrubias en la revista *Vanity Fair*. Entre 1931 y 1932 acompañó al cineasta soviético Serguei Eisenstein durante la filmación del episodio "Maguey" de *¡Qué viva México!*, y sobre esta experiencia elaboró el relato *Hacienda*. En México escribió su primer libro, *Flowering Judas* (1930), con cuatro relatos de tema mexicano. Becada por la Fundación Guggenheim se instaló en Europa y sólo volvió a México en 1964. Tradujó obras de Sor Juana Inés de la Cruz y de José Joaquín Fernández de Lizardi (*El Periquillo Sarniento*, 1941). Autora de *Pale Rider* (1939), *The Days Before* (1952) y *Ship of Fools* (1962); el primer capítulo de esta novela, traducida al español en 1962 con el nombre de *La nave del mal*, es una descripción "realista, zoológica y despectiva" de los mexicanos del puerto de Veracruz en 1931 (*Cfr*.: José Emilio Pacheco: "Inventario", en *Proceso* núm. 209; 3 de noviembre de 1980). En 1998 se publicó *Un país familiar*, libro que recoge textos sobre México y los mexicanos.

Porter Casanate, Pedro ◆ n. en España y m. en Chile (1610-1662). Marino. En 1638 solicitó un permiso para realizar una expedición a California y entre 1643 y 1649 exploró las costas del Pacífico. Más tarde fue gobernador de Sinaloa (1649-51) y gobernador de Chile.

Portes Gil, Emilio ◆ n. en Ciudad Victoria, Tamps., y m. en el DF (1890-1978). Se tituló como abogado de la Escuela Libre de Derecho (1915). Antirreeleccionista desde 1909, fue director del periódico *El Cauterio* (1912-13), empleado del Departamento de Justicia (1915), abogado consultor y miembro de la Comisión de Revisión de Leyes Militares de la Secretaría de Guerra y Marina; juez de primera instancia y magistrado del Supremo Tribunal de Justicia de Sonora, diputado federal (1917-18), director de *El Diario* (1918-20), firmante del Plan de Agua Prieta (1920), gobernador interino de Tamaulipas (del 8 de mayo al 8 de junio de 1920), dos veces diputado federal (1921-23 y 1923-25); abogado general de los Ferrocarriles Nacionales; gobernador constitucional de Tamaulipas (del 5 de febrero de 1925 al 4 de junio de 1928) y secretario de Gobernación en el gobierno de Elías Calles (del 18 de agosto al 30 de noviembre de 1928). Tras el asesinato de Álvaro Obregón, el Congreso lo nombró presidente provisional y tomó posesión el 1 de diciembre de 1928. Durante su go-

Gabinetes del presidente Emilio Portes Gil
1 de diciembre de 1928 al 5 de febrero de 1930

Gobernación:	
Felipe Canales	1 de diciembre de 1928 al 28 de abril de 1929
Carlos Riva Palacio	29 de abril de 1929 al 5 de febrero de 1930
Relaciones Exteriores:	
Genaro Estrada	lo. de diciembre de 1928 al 5 de febrero de 1930
Guerra y Marina:	
Joaquín Amaro	1 de diciembre de 1928 al 2 de marzo de 1929
Plutarco Elías Calles	2 de marzo al 18 de mayo de 1929
Joaquín Amaro	20 de mayo de 1929 al 5 de febrero de 1930
Hacienda y Crédito Público:	
Luis Montes de Oca	1 de diciembre de 1928 al 5 de febrero de 1930
Industria, Comercio y Trabajo:	
José Manuel Puig Casauranc	1 al 31 de diciembre de 1928
Ramón P. de Negri	1 de enero de 1929 al 5 de febrero de 1930
Agricultura y Fomento:	
Marte R. Gómez	1 de diciembre de 1928 al 5 de febrero de 1930
Educación Pública:	
Ezequiel Padilla	1 de diciembre de 1928 al 5 de febrero de 1930
Comunicaciones y Obras Públicas:	
Javier Sánchez Mejorada	1 de diciembre de 1928 al 5 de febrero de 1930
Departamento de Salubridad:	
Aquilino Villanueva	1 de diciembre de 1928 al 5 de febrero de 1930
Departamento Central:	
José Manuel Puig Casauranc	1 de enero de 1929 al 5 de febrero de 1930

bierno se rebeló el general José Gonzalo Escobar, se fundó el Partido Nacional Revolucionario (☛), fueron promulgados el Código Penal y la Ley Orgánica del Ministerio Público, se dio asilo a Augusto César Sandino (☛ *Nicaragua*), realizó una campaña antialcohólica, los estudiantes obtuvieron la autonomía de la Universidad Nacional (☛ *Huelga estudiantil de 1929*), concluyó el movimiento de los cristeros (☛), se creó el Comité Nacional de Protección a la Infancia e inauguró el Puerto Aéreo (1929). Su gobierno persiguió a los militantes del Partido Comunista Mexicano y rompió relaciones diplomáticas con la Unión Soviética. Dejó la Presidencia a Pascual Ortiz Rubio el 4 de febrero de 1930 y en el gabinete de éste ocupó la Secretaría de Gobernación (del 5 de febrero de 1930 al 28 de agosto de 1931). Fue presidente del Comité Ejecutivo del PNR (del 22 de abril al 14 de octubre de 1930), enviado plenipotenciario en Francia y primer representante de México ante la Liga de las Naciones (1932); procurador General de la República (1932-34), secretario de Relaciones Exteriores (del 1 de diciembre de 1934 al 15 de junio de 1935) en el gabinete de Lázaro Cárdenas, nuevamente presidente del PNR (del 15 de junio de 1935 al 19 de agosto de 1936), embajador en Ecuador (1946) y en la India (1951), presidente de la Comisión Nacional de Seguros (1959) y presidente del Comité Técnico Consultivo de la Comisión Nacional Bancaria y de Seguros (1971-78). Autor de *La lucha entre el poder civil y el clero* (1934), *Evolución política de la propiedad territorial de México, El Plan de Ayutla, la reforma y la constitución de 1857* y *Autobiografía de la revolución mexicana* (1964).

Portilla, Anselmo de la ◆ n. en España y m. en la ciudad de México (1816-1879). Periodista y escritor. Llegó a México en 1840. Colaboró en los periódicos *El Católico, El Eco del Comercio, El Universal, La Voz de la Religión* y *El Despertador Literario*. Fundó *El Español* (1850), *El Eco de España* y *La Cruz*. Exiliado en Nueva York durante la guerra de los Tres Años, en 1858 editó *El Occidente*. Volvió a México en 1862 y en Veracruz editó *El Eco de Europa*. Durante el gobierno de Maximiliano de Habsburgo dirigió el *Diario del Imperio* y al triunfo de la República fundó la revista *La Iberia* (1867-76), en la que difundió documentos de la historia mexicana, como la *Historia verdadera de la conquista de la Nueva España*, de Bernal Díaz del Castillo, y la *Conquista de México*, de Francisco López de Gómara. Colaborador de *El Espectador de México*. Participó en la redacción del *Diccionario universal de historia y geografía* (1853-56), de Manuel Orozco y Berra. Autor de ensayo: *Historia de la revolución de Méjico contra la dictadura del general SantaAnna. 1853-55* (1856), *Méjico en 1856 y 1857. Gobierno del general Comonfort* (1858), *Episodio histórico del gobierno dictatorial del señor don Ignacio Comonfort en la República Mejicana, Cartilla de geografía para niños* (1865) y *España en Méjico* (1871); y novela: *De Miramar a México, Virginia Steward* (1861) y *La revolución de Ayutla*. En 1875 participó en la fundación de la Academia Mexicana (de la Lengua).

Portilla, Jorge ◆ n. y m. en el DF (1918-1963). Licenciado en derecho por la UNAM (1942). Estudió filosofía en México, Francia, Bélgica y Alemania. Participó en el XIII Congreso Internacional de Filosofía y perteneció al grupo Hyperión. Autor del libro de ensayos *Fenomenología del relajo* (1966). Becario del Centro Mexicano de Escritores en dos ocasiones, categoría ensayo (1953-54 y 1955-56).

Portilla Longoria, José Casiano ◆ n. en Zaragoza, Coah. (1972). Fue llevado a Houston, EUA, por su familia a los seis años. Estudió la licenciatura en arte en la Universidad de Arizona donde jugó en su equipo de futbol americano. Juega desde 1998 en la Liga Nacional de Futbol de EUA como tacle ofensivo del equipo *Halcones* de Atlanta, con el que jugó el Súper Tazón XXXIII en 1999.

Portilla, Nicolás de la ◆ n. en Jalapa, Ver., y m. en la ciudad de México (1808-1873). Militar conservador. Luchó contra la invasión estadounidense de 1847. General de brigada en 1856, fue ministro de Guerra y Marina en el gabinete de Maximiliano de Habsburgo (del 11 de febrero al 15 de mayo de 1867). Se le desterró al triunfo de la República.

Portilla Livingston, Alfredo ◆ n. en el DF y m. en EUA (1948-1988). Cineasta. Hijo de Jorge Portilla. Estudió cine en Nueva York y en Boston, y con Nicholas Ray. Codirigió, con Alfredo Becerril, el documental *Peleas de tigres (una petición de lluvias nahua)* (1987). Murió atropellado en Nueva York.

Portilla Livingston, Jorge ◆ n. en el DF (1943). Escritor. Hermano del anterior. Ha sido corrector de estilo y traductor. Autor de *Los murmullos* (novela, 1975) y *Relatos y retratos* (cuentos, 1987) y *El coro en la luz* (novela, 1989).

Portilla Osio, Enrique ◆ n. y m. en el DF (1923-96). Maestro. Ingresó en la Compañía de Jesús en 1940. Estudió letras y humanidades en el Instituto Libre de Estudios Superiores (1946), del que fue maestro. Licenciado en filosofía por el Ysleta College de El Paso, Texas (1951), maestro en la misma especialidad por la Loyola University de Los Ángeles, California (1947-51), licenciado en teología por el Heythrop College de Inglaterra (1956) y maestro en literatura clásica y psicología educacional por la Fordham University de Nueva York (19 60). Fue ordenado sacerdote en 1955. Ingresó en la UIA como profesor de medio tiempo (1960-68) y como profesor en el Instituto Libre de Filosofía y ciencias, del que fue rector (1963-68). Posteriormente fue rector del Collegio S. Roberto Bellarmino de Roma (1968-1974) y director general del Centro de Estudios Educativos (1974-76). Director general de Relaciones Públicas (1976) y rector de la UIA (1976-80).

Portilla Quevedo, Manuel ◆ m. en la URSS (1942-1985). Estudió en la Universidad de Pekín. Ingeniero bioquímico titulado (1949-65), maestro en ciencias químicas por la Universidad

Patricio Lumumba (1965) y doctor en ciencias biológicas por la Universidad Lomonosov de Moscú (1972). Profesor de la UNAM. En el Instituto Politécnico Nacional fue profesor, jefe del Laboratorio Biofísico (1966), jefe de la Sección de Investigación del Departamento de Biofísica (1973-75) y jefe de la Sección de Instrumentación (1975-76) de la Escuela Nacional de Ciencias Biológicas. Fue consejero de la embajada mexicana de la Unión Soviética durante los gobiernos de José López Portillo y Miguel de la Madrid.

PORTILLO, AGUSTÍN ◆ n. en el DF (1960). Pintor. Desde 1983 expone individualmente en museos como el del Chopo y galerías como la Arvil y la Óscar Román en el país, además en EUA. Su obra forma parte del acervo de los museos Raly de Montevideo, Uruguay; Universitario del Chopo, del DF, y de Arte Contemporáneo de Monterrey, además de la Fundación Cultural Televisa. Becario de la Mid America Arts Alliance de EUA (1988) y del programa de intercambio de residencias artísticas (1994).

PORTILLO ACOSTA, GUILLERMO ◆ n. en Puebla, Pue. (1915). Locutor. En 1934 trabajó en la XEFO como cantante al lado de Emilio Tuero. Ingresó a la XEW en 1939 donde fue cantante, protagonizó distintas radionovelas y condujo los programas *La casa de los Pérez García, Dispara Margot, dispara, Apague la luz y escuche* y *El que la hace la paga.* Grabó discos con historias para niños (*La Bella Durmiente, Blanca Nieves* y *Cenicienta)* y con poemas de Amado Nervo, Pablo Neruda y Víctor Manuel Otero, entre otros, destacando sus versiones dramatizadas de *El brindis del bohemio, El milagro del Tepeyac* y *Las pasiones de Cristo.* Fue el locutor titular de *La Hora Nacional* durante 40 años.

PORTILLO Y TEJADA, BUENAVENTURA DEL PURÍSIMO CORAZÓN DE MARÍA ◆ n. en San Antonio Teocaltiche, Jal., y m. en Zacatecas, Zac. (1827-1899). Sacerdote ordenado en 1850. En la orden de los franciscanos se desempeñó como guardián del Convento de Zapopan

Foto: José Antonio Íñiguez

Agustín Portillo

(1862), definidor general (1870-72) y comisario general (1875-80). Fue el tercer vicario apostólico de la Baja California (1880-83), obispo de Chilapa (1883-89) y después obispo de Zacatecas (1889-99).

PORTOCARRERO Y LASSO DE LA VEGA, MELCHOR ◆ n. en España y m. en Perú (1636-1705). Militar. Tenía el título de conde de la Monclova y era apodado *Brazo de Plata* y *Brazo de Hierro* por la prótesis que usaba. En 1686 fue designado virrey de la Nueva España y llegó a la ciudad de México el 30 de noviembre de ese año. Durante su gobierno se expulsó a los franceses de Texas, se fundó en Coahuila el fuerte de la Monclova, llamado así en su honor, y se financió la construcción del acueducto de Chapultepec al Salto del Agua. Dejó el cargo en 1688 y al año siguiente se embarcó hacia Lima, con el cargo de virrey de Perú.

PORTOLÁ, GASPAR DE ◆ n. y m. en España (¿1723?-¿1784?). Militar. Combatió en Holanda y Portugal. En 1767, Carlos III lo nombró gobernador de la Baja California, con la misión de expulsar de ese territorio a los jesuitas y poner sus misiones en manos de los franciscanos. En 1769 se le encargó comandar una expedición hacia la Alta California, para frenar las incursiones rusas e inglesas. En esa expedición lo acompañó fray Junípero Serra, con quien fundó la misión de San Diego, antes de pasar por las bahías de Monterrey y San Francisco. En 1770 erigieron la misión y presidio de San Carlos, que sería después la capital misional y militar de la provincia. Portolá fue gobernador político y militar de Puebla en 1777 y permaneció en ese puesto por lo menos hasta 1779. Hacia 1784 regresó a España.

PORTUGAL ◆ ☛ *Portuguesa, República.*

PORTUGAL, JUAN CAYETANO ◆ ☛ *Gómez de Portugal y Solís, Juan Cayetano.*

PORTUGAL, ONOFRE ◆ m. en Chihuahua, Chih. (?-1811). Insurgente. En septiembre de 1810, en San Miguel el Grande, hoy de Allende, se unió al movimiento de independencia, a las órdenes de Ignacio Allende. Ese mismo año obtuvo el grado de general brigadier y se unió a las fuerzas de Mariano Jiménez, con quien participó en la batalla de Puerto del Carnero. Combatió en San Luis Potosí, Coahuila y Nuevo León. En 1811 los realistas lo aprehendieron en Acatita de Baján, junto con los caudillos insurgentes, y fue trasladado a Chihuahua, donde se le fusiló.

PORTUGAL Y SERRATO, JOSÉ MARÍA DE JESÚS ◆ n. en la ciudad de México y m. en Aguascalientes, Ags. (1838-1912). Ingresó en la Orden de Franciscanos Menores en 1853. Recibió las órdenes sacerdotales en Cuba (1861). Fue cura de Atoyac y de Asientos. Obispo de Sinaloa (1889-98), de Saltillo (1899-02) y de Aguascalientes (1902-12). Autor de *El amable Jesús, La santa voluntad de dios* y *El positivismo.*

PORTUGUESA, REPÚBLICA ◆ Estado de Europa occidental situado en la porción suroeste de la península Ibérica. Limita al norte y este con España y tiene costas al sur en el golfo de Cádiz y al oeste en el océano Atlántico. Superficie: 92,389 km²., que incluye el territorio insular de las islas Azores y Madeira. Habitantes: 9,943,000 (1997). Su capital es Lisboa (681,063 habitantes en 1991), su idioma oficial el portugués y su moneda el escudo. El catolicismo es la religión mayoritaria. *Historia:* los originales pobladores de Portugal fueron

Archivo Xavier Esparza

Buenaventura del Purísimo Corazón de María Portillo y Tejeda

Retrato y firma de Melchor Portocarrero y Lasso de la vega

Lisboa, capital de la República Portuguesa

Monedas de la República Portuguesa

los lusitanos, pueblo emparentado con los celtas, que habitaron la parte central del territorio. Hacia el siglo II a.n.e., los lusitanos fueron conquistados por Roma, luego de una gran resistencia, que concluyó totalmente hasta el año 94 a.n.e. A la caída del imperio romano el territorio fue ocupado por los visigodos y, en el siglo VIII, por los árabes. El primer rey de Portugal fue Alfonso I Henriques, coronado en 1139; en 1147 recuperó Lisboa y en 1263 los árabes abandonaron Portugal. En 1249, con la reconquista de Algarve por Alfonso III, quedaron delimitadas las fronteras portuguesas. Durante el gobierno del rey Diniz (1279-1325) se sentaron las bases de la marina portuguesa, se desamortizaron las tierras de la Iglesia y se fundaron las universidades de Coímbra y Lisboa. En 1335, la casa de Avis llegó al trono de Portugal y a partir de 1394, y hasta 1460, alentados por el rey Enrique *el Navegante*, se realizaron las expediciones portuguesas por la costa de África. Portugal inició así la conquista de territorios africanos, desde los cuales controló el tráfico de esclavos hacia América: los que llegaron a la Nueva España procedían en su mayoría de Angola. En 1500, Pedro Álvares Cabral inició la conquista de Brasil. En 1536, durante el reinado de Juan III, la Inquisición se instaló en territorio portugués. En 1580, a raíz de la muerte del rey Sebastián, Portugal pasó a depender de Felipe II de España. La unión permitió a los portugueses instalarse en varios lugares de las colonias españolas, sobre todo en la Nueva España. En 1619, alrededor de 170 portugueses vivían en la Colonia. Uno de ellos, que además era judío, fue Sebastián Váez de Acevedo, quien estuvo al mando de la Armada de Barlovento, la flota mercante que los españoles tenían en el océano Pacífico. Se sabe que en San Luis Potosí vivían entre 1620 y 1630 los dos mejores fabricantes de fuelles de la Colonia, los cuales eran portugueses. De 1629 a 1634, el provincial de los de Michoacán fue Pedro de Santa María, del mismo origen. No obstante, la presencia de los portugueses nunca fue bien vista por algunas de las autoridades y el clero virreinales. De los 200 criptojudíos procesados por la Inquisición entre 1620 1650, más de 100 eran portugueses. Durante su gobierno (1621-24), el virrey Diego Carrillo de Mendoza y Pimentel expulsó a los portugueses de San Luis Potosí y Zacatecas, prácticamente les impidió trabajar en Veracruz y Acapulco y encarceló a algunos en la ciudad de México. Como consecuencia, tuvieron una importante participación en el conflicto de 1624, entre el arzobispado capitalino y el virrey Carrillo, que desembocó en una insurrección popular y el derrocamiento del segundo. En abril de 1641, cuando se supo en la Nueva España del alzamiento encabezado por el duque de Braganza contra la dominación española, el virrey Diego López Pacheco y Bobadilla prohibió la entrada de portugueses a la Colonia, el uso de los puertos mexicanos por barcos de Portugal y ordenó interceptar la correspondencia de los comerciantes portugueses avecindados en el virreinato. A partir de ese momento, las relaciones entre españoles y portugueses se agriaron, en parte por los rumores de supuestas conspiraciones de lusitanos para independizarse de España, pero también porque según la opinión generalizada, un gran número de nuevos cristianos portugueses seguían practicando el judaísmo. Desde mediados de 1641 comenzaron los enfrentamientos entre el virrey López Pacheco y el arzobispo de México, Juan de Palafox y Mendoza. Éste acusaba al virrey de adoptar una actitud de negligencia respecto de los portugueses novohispanos y aducía dos casos particulares: uno, la permanencia al frente de la Armada de Barlovento de Váez de Acevedo y, el otro, el hecho de que en el puerto de Veracruz vivieran menos es-

Mapa y billete de la República Portuguesa

pañoles que portugueses. A pesar de que López Pacheco, que además estaba emparentado con el duque de Braganza, intensificó la persecución contra los portugueses, Palafox maniobró en la corte española y consiguió la destitución del virrey, en junio de 1642. El propio Palafox lo sustituyó, y durante su gobierno desató una campaña de persecución contra los portugueses, que incluyó el cese de los que ocupaban cargos públicos, salvo, paradójicamente, el propio Váez de Acevedo; la reubicación de los lusitanos que vivían en Veracruz y el procesamiento judicial de presuntos criptojudíos. En Europa, mientras tanto, la sublevación había triunfado, y el duque de Braganza ocupó el trono de Portugal con el nombre de Juan IV. Durante el periodo en que permanecieron unidos ambos Estados, el comercio de esclavos negros aumentó considerablemente bajo el monopolio de tratantes portugueses. Los vínculos entre la Nueva España y Portugal no pudieron desaparacer completamente en 1640 y todavía hacia 1648 el puerto de Veracruz era considerado un refugio seguro para los buques y comerciantes lusitanos. España reconoció la independencia de Portugal en 1668. Desde entonces, Portugal se hizo cada vez más dependiente de la Gran Bretaña y de Francia. En 1807 Francia y España pactaron la partición de Portugal y la familia real se refugió en Brasil. Al año siguiente ocurrió un levantamiento general que sentó las bases para la invasión británica de 1811 y la derrota de las tropas naepoleónicas. En 1821, el rey Juan VI regresó a Portugal. En 1851 México abrió un consulado en Lisboa y en 1857 otro en Oporto. En 1865 se instaló la primera legación diplomática portuguesa en nuestro país. En 1910, tras una época de movimientos políticos violentos, se proclamó la república, que un año más tarde fue reconocida por nuestro gobierno. En 1916 Alemania declaró la guerra a Portugal. En 1926, mediante un golpe de Estado, llegó a la presidencia el general Carmona, con Oliveira Salazar como primer ministro, quien ejerció el poder de 1932 a 1968. En 1933, una nueva Constitución dio carácter institucional a la dictadura de Oliveira Salazar. En 1949 Portugal ingresó en la Organización del Tratado del Atlántico Norte. Dos años después llegó a la presidencia Francisco H. Craveiro y en 1955 el país fue admitido en la Organización de las Naciones Unidas. En 1963 la Organización de la Unidad Africana acordó romper relaciones diplomáticas con Portugal, para obligarlo a conceder la independencia a sus colonias. En 1974, un golpe de Estado incruento dejó el poder en manos del Movimiento de las Fuerzas Armadas. Al año siguiente, luego de un intento fallido de contrarrevolución, se creó un Consejo Supremo Revolucionario. En ese año se concedió la independencia a todas las colonias, excepto a Macao. En 1978, tras una crisis política, llegó al gobierno Carlos Mota de Pinto. En 1980, el presidente Sá Carneiro murió en un accidente de aviación. En 1981 Francisco Pinto Balse-mao fue nombrado primer ministro. En 1983 el primer ministro era Mario Soares, quien intercambió visitas con el presidente mexicano Miguel de la Madrid.

Cabo da Roca, el punto más occidental de Europa, en Portugal

Portuondo, José Antonio ◆ n. y m. en Cuba (1911-1996). Se doctoró en filosofía y letras por la Universidad de La Habana. Vino a México a inicios de los años cuarenta, donde por dos años fue discípulo de Alfonso Reyes. Fue profesor de las universidades de Wisconsin, Columbia y Pennsylvania State en EUA (1940-50). Embajador de Cuba en México y el Vaticano. Autor, entre otras, de *El heroísmo intelectual* (1955), *La historia y las generaciones* (1958), *Estética y revolución* (1963) y *Astrolabio* (1973). Fue presidente del Instituto de Literatura y Lingüística de Cuba, vicepresidente de la Unión de Escritores y Artistas de Cuba y miembro de la Academia Cubana de la Lengua. Premio Nacional de Literatura de Cuba en 1987.

Ebowsky, Edmundo ◆ n. en Polonia (1927). Entrenador de atletismo. En su juventud practicó el futbol y el atletismo. Asistió a los Juegos Olímpicos de Helsinki, en 1952, donde participó en las competencias de medio fondo. Entre 1968 y 1973 fue entrenador del equipo cubano de medio fondo y, entre otros, preparó al campeón de 400 m Alberto Juantorena. Llegó a México en 1974 y desde entonces se dedicó a instruir a los equipos mexicanos de atletismo, así como al equipo de Copa Davis y a la selección nacional de futbol.

Porvenir, El ◆ Municipio de Chiapas situado en el sur del estado, al norte de Tapachula. Superficie: 121.7 km^2. Habitantes: 10,574, de los cuales 2,551 forman la población económicamente activa. Hablan alguna lengua indígena 792 personas mayores de cinco años (mame 775). Su cabecera es El Porvenir de Velazco Suárez.

Porvenir, El ◆ Diario editado en la ciudad de Monterrey, NL. Fue fundado en 1919 por Jesús Cantú Leal y el poeta colombiano Porfirio Barba Jacob (nombre profesional de Ricardo Arenales) y salió a la venta el 19 de enero de ese año con el objetivo de "contribuir al bienestar social". Rogelio Cantú Gómez, hijo de Jesús, fue director de 1950 a 1983, imponiéndole el lema de "El periódico de la frontera" y dotándolo de corres-

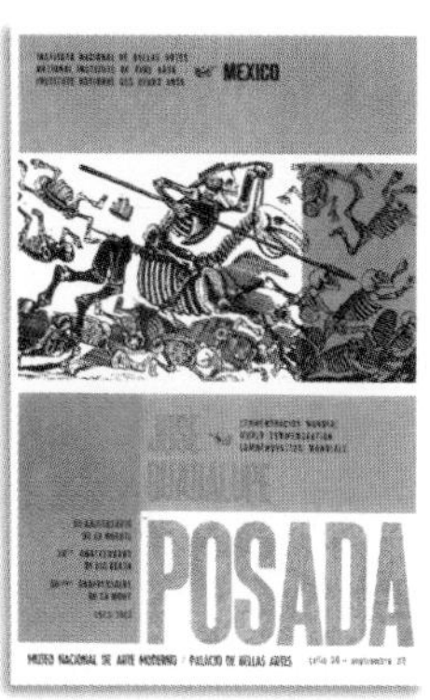

Conmemoración mundial del 50 aniversario de la muerte de José Guadalupe Posada

ponsales en 70 municipios de la región norte del país.

Posada, Ángel ◆ n. en Parral, Chih. (1890-1938). Ingeniero agrónomo titulado en Ciudad Juárez. Fue diputado local, oficial mayor de la Comisión Nacional Agraria (1933), oficial mayor del gobierno de su estado y jefe del Departamento Agrario (1934). Era senador y candidato a la gubernatura de Chihuahua cuando fue asesinado.

Posada, José Guadalupe ◆ n. en Aguascalientes, Ags., y m. en la ciudad de México (1852-1913). Grabador. Su apellido materno era Aguilar. Estudió en la Academia Municipal de Dibujo. En 1868 ingresó al taller de Trinidad Pedroso, donde colaboró en el periódico *El Jicote* (1870) y se dedicó a la litografía comercial y a la estampa religiosa (1872-76). Desde 1876 se hizo cargo del taller. Perseguido por las autoridades estatales, se trasladó a León (1883-87), donde fue profesor de dibujo en la Escuela Preparatoria y de litografía en la Escuela de Artes y Oficios. En la misma ciudad colaboró en los diarios *El Popular* y *El Amigo del Pueblo* y en la revista *La Patria Ilustrada*. En 1887 se trasladó a la ciudad de México y se empleó en la imprenta de Irineo Paz. Al año siguiente instaló su propio taller, donde comenzó a grabar con zinc. Asociado desde 1890 con Antonio Vanegas Arroyo, ilustró cancioneros, crónicas, sainetes costumbristas, oraciones y cuentos; fundó los periódicos *La Gaceta Literaria*, *El Centavo Perdido* y *La Casera*; y colaboró en *Revista de México*, *El Padre Cobos*, *El Teatro*, *Nuevo Siglo*, *El Boletín*, *El Argos*, *La Patria*, *El Ahuizote*, *El Hijo del Ahuizote*, *Don Chepito*, *Fray Gerundio* y *El Fandango*. Autor de unos 15 mil grabados. A partir de los años veinte se revaloró su obra, debido a un artículo de Jean Charlot, aparecido en *Revista de Revistas*, que despertó el interés por sus grabados y calaveras. En 1943 se efectuó, en el Palacio de Bellas Artes, una exposición-homenaje, que un año después se presentó en el Instituto de Arte de Chicago. Se ha hecho numerosas ediciones de sus obras, entre otras *Obras de José Guadalupe Posada, grabador mexicano* (1930, con introducción de Diego Rivera), *José Guadalupe Posada: 36 grabados* (1943), *Primicias litográficas del grabador J. Guadalupe Posada* (1952) y *La revolución mexicana vista por G. Posada* (1960).

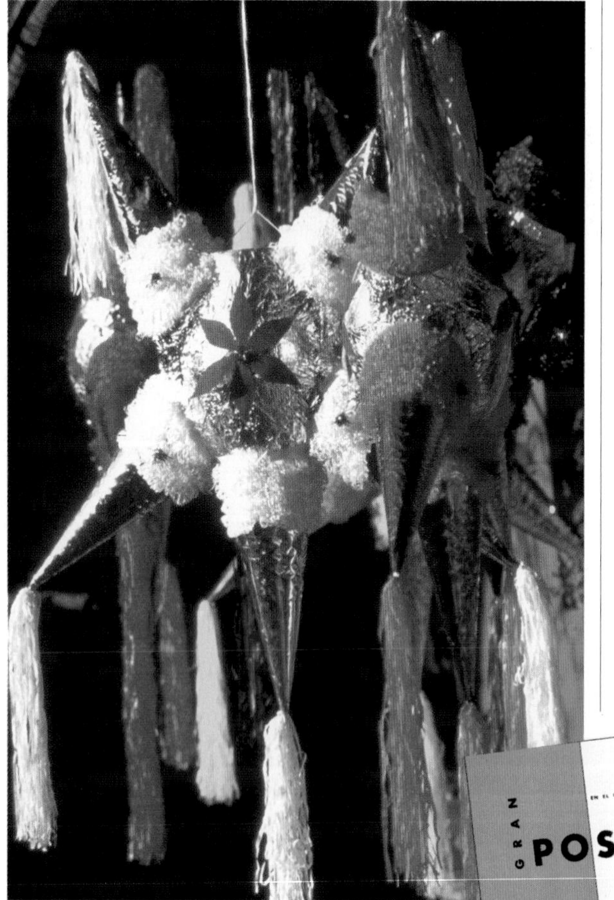

Anuncio de posada para el 19 de diciembre de 1953

Posada y Garduño, Manuel ◆ n. en la Villa de San Felipe del Obraje, hoy del Progreso, Estado de México, y m. en la ciudad de México (1780-1846). Sacerdote. Licenciado (1808) y doctor (1809) en cánones por la Real y Pontificia Universidad de México. Fue vicario general y gobernador de la mitra de Puebla. En diciembre de 1823 participó en un movimiento federalista poblano, del que resultó un efímero Estado Libre y Soberano de la Puebla de los Ángeles, que desapareció tres semanas antes de la erección del estado (☛ *Puebla*). Senador de la República en lugar de Luis Mendizábal (1824-26). En 1833, por la Ley de Caso, emitida por el gobierno de Valentín Gómez Farías, fue desterrado a Estados Unidos, pero volvió al año siguiente. Preconizado arzobispo de México en diciembre de 1839, se le consagró en la Catedral Metropolitana en mayo de 1840. Gobernó la arquidiócesis hasta 1846.

Grabado de José Guadalupe Posada

Posadas ◆ Los aztecas tenían por costumbre reunirse durante el Panquetzaliztli (del 7 al 26 de diciembre) para celebrar la llegada de la estación invernal y honrar el advenimiento de Huitzilopochtli (☛). Al notar los misioneros agustinos la coincidencia de estas fiestas con las que rememoran la peregrinación de José y María, del 16 al 24 de diciembre, unieron ambas. La celebración de las posadas se inició en el pueblo de San Agustín Acolman, tras la bula del papa Sixto V que fray Diego de Soria obtuviera en 1587 para celebrar en la Nueva España las misas de aguinaldo, las que se efectuaban en los atrios de las iglesias con representaciones dramatizadas de los pasajes del Nuevo Testamento en que se explicaba el adviento o espera, el misterio de la preñez de la Virgen María y los nueve días anteriores al nacimiento de Jesús, durante los cuales sus padres viajaron de Nazaret a Belén, buscando posada. Un ángel conducía a un pollino montado por María y seguido por José a pie, se rezaban novenarios y se cantaba la rogativa de "petición de posada": "En el nombre del cielo/ os pido posada/ pues no puede andar/ mi esposa amada", tras lo cual la feligresía regresaba a su hogar. La población se fue oponiendo gradualmente a efectuar estas representaciones en los atrios de iglesias y conventos, regresando a las costumbres prehispánicas de hacerlo en las casas, obsequiando a los invitados con abundante comida e idolillos comestibles confeccionados con una pasta llamada tzóatl. Tras la independencia mexicana, las posadas se convirtieron en un festejo secular y profano con resabios religiosos, en el que se rompen piñatas, ollas de barro adornadas con papeles de colores en cuyo interior se guardan confituras y frutas y que simbolizan, de acuerdo con Martha Eva Rocha, historiadora del INAH, "la lucha que debe sostener el hombre, valiéndose de la fe, para destruir las malas pasiones: la olla, a Satanás o el espíritu del mal que con su apariencia atrae a la humanidad; la colación que encierra, los placeres desconocidos que ofrece al hombre; la persona vendada es la fe que debe ser ciega y destruirá el espíritu maligno". Actualmente las posadas son bailes en que se escucha la música popular de moda, se ingieren bebidas alcohólicas y ponche (infusión de frutas) y comida tradicional.

Posadas, Claudia ◆ n. en el DF (1970). Periodista. Estudió letras en la UNAM y el diplomado de la Sogem. Colabora en el suplemento *Arena* de *Excélsior.* Autora de los poemarios *La memoria blanca de los muros* (1997) y *El oro en la ciudad profunda.* Primer lugar del concurso de poesía de *Punto de Partida* 1996.

Juan Jesús Posadas Ocampo

Posadas, Marcos Leonel ◆ n. en el DF (1938). Político. En 1957 ingresó en la Juventud Comunista de México, en la que ocupó la secretaría general (1965-69). En el Partido Comunista Mexicano fue director del periódico *Oposición*, responsable de asuntos internacionales, responsable de organización y miembro de la comisión política. Cofundador del Partido Socialista Unificado de México (1981) donde estuvo encargado de las áreas internacional y de organización y fue miembro del secretariado. Cofundador del Partido Mexicano Socialista (1987). Ha colaborado en *Últimas Noticias* y otras publicaciones. Autor de *La situación internacional. El problema de Afganistán* (1980).

Posadas Ocampo, Juan Jesús ◆ n. en Salvatierra, Gto. y m. en Guadalajara, Jal. (1926-1993). Sacerdote ordenado en 1950. Fue profesor y vicerrector del Seminario de Morelia. En la Conferencia Episcopal Mexicana ocupó la presidencia de la Comisión para las Migraciones y el Turismo (1976-79) y de la Comisión de la Doctrina de la Fe (1979-). Fue obispo de Tijuana (1970-83), obispo de Cuernavaca (1983-87) y arzobispo de Guadalajara (1987). En 1991 fue nombrado cardenal, el quinto en la historia de México. Era vicepresidente de la Conferencia del Episcopado Mexicano. Fue asesinado en 1993 en el aeropuerto de Guadalajara por narcotraficantes.

Poseilov, Hana ◆ n. en Israel (1946). Escultora. Estudió arquitectura en la escuela Ort, de Ramat Gan, y dibujo y pintura en la Escuela de Arte Betzalel-Jerusalem. Ha desarrollado una técnica escultopictórica. Expuso por primera vez en 1965. Llegó a México a fines de los años sesenta. Sus obras se han presentado en Estados Unidos e Israel.

Possani Postay, Lourival Domingos ◆ n. en Brasil (1939). Licenciado en historia natural (1965) y maestro en biofísica molecular por la Universidad Federal de Brasil, y doctor en biofísica molecular y diplomado de estudios avanzados en biofísica en la Facultad de Ciencias D'Orsay, en la Universidad de París (1970). Posdoctorado en la Universidad Rockefeller, EUA (1973). Adquirió la nacionalidad mexicana en 1976 y ha realizado en el país el 95 por ciento de su trabajo científico, centrado en desarrollar un antídoto o vacuna contra el veneno del alacrán. Autor de más de 100 artículos publicados en revistas internacionales y 18 capítulos de libros sobre el tema. Ocupó la Cátedra Patrimonial de Excelencia Nivel 1, del Conacyt (1994 y 1995). Premio UNAM (1993), Premio Jorge Rosenkranz, de Syntex (1994), y Premio Nacional de Ciencias y Artes en la categoría de Ciencias Físico-Matemáticas y Naturales (1995).

Potosí ◆ Laguna de Guerrero situada al noreste del morro de Petatlán. Se comunica por el oeste con la bahía de Petatlán.

Potosí ◆ Monte de Nuevo León, también llamado Grande, que pertenece a la sierra Madre Oriental. Su cumbre, siempre nevada, llega a los 3,800 metros sobre el nivel del mar.

Potosí ◆ Río de Nuevo León que nace en las laderas del monte Potosí o Grande. Corre de oeste a este y se une al río Linares o Pablillo para formar el Conchos.

Potrero del Llano ◆ Población del municipio de Temapache (☛).

Arcadio Poveda

Obra de Ricardo Pozas

POUS ORTIZ, RAÚL J. ◆ n. en Tlacotalpan, Ver., y m. en el DF (1900-1989). Licenciado en derecho. Estudió en las universidades Nacional de México y Michoacana. En la Escuela Nacional Preparatoria de la UNAM fue profesor (1930-62), subdirector del plantel número 2 (1923), director general (1953-62) y presidente de la Comisión de Festejos del Centenario de esa institución (1966-69). En la Secretaría de Educación Pública fue comisionado para fundar escuelas obreras en el estado de Veracruz (1922) y de 1966 a 1970 ocupó la Dirección General de Enseñanza Media. De 1962 a 1964 fue asesor jurídico del secretario de Obras Públicas, Javier Barros Sierra. Colaboró en *Foro de México* y en la *Revista de Filosofía*. Profesor emérito de la Facultad de Derecho de la UNAM, donde fue miembro de la Junta de Gobierno.

POVEDA, ARCADIO ◆ n. en Mérida, Yuc. (1930). Su segundo apellido es Ricalde. Matemático y físico titulado en la UNAM (1951) y doctor en astronomía por la Universidad de California en Berkeley (1956). Realizó estudios de posgrado en Holanda (1960) y Francia (1966). Profesor de la Facultad de Ciencias de la UNAM. Ha sido investigador (1980-) y director del Instituto de Astronomía de la UNAM (1968-80), director del Observatorio Astronómico Nacional (1975-80), coordinador de Investigación Científica de la UNAM y fundador y primer director del Programa Universitario de Investigación y Desarrollo Espacial (1990-91). Promovió en 1979 la creación del Observatorio Astronómico de San Pedro Mártir, en Baja California Norte, y del Centro Astronómico de Ensenada. Fue también investigador visitante del Institute d'Astrophysique de París (1963), en Columbia (1967), del Kitt Peak National Observatory, en Tucson (1981, 1982 y 1983-84) y del Center for Astrophysics and Space Science, en San Diego (1982-83). Ha publicado más de 50 artículos en revistas científicas internacionales y ha colaborado en *Ciencia y Desarrollo, Información Científica y Tecnológica, R&D de México* y *Naturaleza*. Autor de *El método Poveda para determinar las masas de las galaxias esféricas de los cúmulos de galaxias* (1958). Investigador emérito del Sistema Nacional de Investigadores y catedrático patrimonial del Conacyt. Ha obtenido el premio Dorothe Kumpe al mejor estudiante de astronomía de la Universidad de California (1952); el premio de la Academia de la Investigación Científica (1966); el Premio Nacional de Ciencias y Artes (1975); la Medalla Eligio Ancona del gobierno de Yucatán (1984) y el doctorado *honoris causa* de la Universidad Autónoma de Yucatán (1984). En 1989 ingresó en El Colegio Nacional.

POZA RICA DE HIDALGO ◆ Municipio de Veracruz situado al sur de Tuxpan, contiguo a Papantla y en los límites con Puebla. Superficie: 230.31 km^2. Habitantes: 154,586, de los cuales 45,932 forman la población económicamente activa. Hablan alguna lengua indígena 2,669 personas mayores de cinco años (totonaco 1,915 y náhuatl 513). En 1928, la compañía petrolera El Águila comenzó a explotar algunos pozos en el actual territorio del municipio. Éste se erigió el 13 de noviembre de 1951, en terrenos que pertenecían a Coatzintla. Siete días después se elevó a rango de ciudad la congregación de Poza Rica de Hidalgo, su cabecera, población fundada en 1872 y que 100 años después, por su número de habitantes, ocupaba el tercer lugar en la entidad. En la jurisdicción hay un campo petrolero cuyo primer pozo productivo (el Poza Rica 2) empezó a funcionar en julio de 1930. Tiene una planta de recuperación de azufre y una refinería, desde la que parten un gasoducto y dos oleoductos, uno de los cuales llega a la ciudad de México.

POZAS, RICARDO ◆ n. en Amealco, Qro. y m. en el DF (1912-1994). Antropólogo. Su apellido materno es Arciniega. Estudió en la Escuela Normal de San Juan del Río (1927), en la Escuela Nacional de Maestros (1936) y en la Escuela Nacional de Antropología (1939-44). Maestro en ciencias antropológicas (1957) posgraduado en sociología (1966-67) por la UNAM. Fue profesor rural en Querétaro (1929-30), profesor de la Escuela Secundaria para hijos de Trabajadores (1937), etnólogo del Museo Nacional de Antropología e Historia, investigador del Instituto de Alfabetización para Maestros de Indígenas Monolingües, de la Junta de Protección de las Razas Indígenas de Costa Rica y del Instituto Nacional Indigenista; y director del Centro Coordinador tzeltal-tzotzil (1953), del Centro Coordinador Indigenista del Papaloapan (1954-56) y del Programa de Investigación y Acción Autogestionaria en los Pueblos Indígenas (1984). Colaborador de *Anales del Instituto de Antropología e Historia, Memorias del Instituto Nacional Indigenista, La Palabra y el Hombre, Revista Mexicana de Ciencias Políticas, Artes de México, México Indígena* y *Revista Mexicana de Sociología*. Coautor, con Isabel Horcasitas, del ensayo *Los indios en las clases sociales de México* (1971). Autor de *Juan Pérez Jolote, biografía de un tzotzil* (1948), *Zis Ma Isa* (texto de alfabetización en lengua cabecar, 1948), *Los mazatecos* (1957) y *Chamula, un pueblo indio de los altos de Chiapas* (1959). Medallas Manuel Gamio y al Mérito Universitario (1982), premios Chiapas y Universidad Nacional (1985); y Premio Querétaro (1986).

POZO BALBÁS, AGAPITO ◆ n. y m. en Querétaro, Qro. (1899-1976). Abogado titulado en el Colegio Civil de Querétaro (1932). Fue agente del Ministerio Público en León (1924-26), secretario de Gobierno en Querétaro (1927-31), jefe de la oficina administrativa de la Jefatura de Policía y secretario particular del secretario de Gobierno del Distrito Federal; magistrado del Tribunal Superior de Justicia de Guanajuato (1933-35), nuevamente secretario de Gobierno en Querétaro (1935), jefe del Departamento Jurídico de la policía del DF, ministro del Tribunal Superior de

Justicia del Distrito y Territorios Federales (1941), gobernador de Querétaro (del 1 de octubre de 1943 al 9 de abril de 1949), presidente de la Suprema Corte de Justicia de la Nación (1949-69), rector de la Universidad Autónoma de Querétaro (1970-72) y presidente del Tribunal Superior de Justicia del Estado (1973-76).

Pozo Rangel, Efrén del ♦ n. en San Luis Potosí, SLP, y m. en el DF (1907-¿1978?). Médico graduado en 1933 en la Escuela Nacional de Medicina. Realizó estudios de posgrado en Inglaterra, Francia y Estados Unidos. Fue profesor (1928-30) y secretario general de la Universidad de San Luis Potosí; profesor de fisiología (1936-46) y director (1943-44) de la Escuela Nacional de Ciencias Biológicas; investigador de la UNAM y de la Universidad de Cambridge (1943-53); profesor de la Facultad de Medicina y del Instituto Nacional de Antropología (1946); jefe del laboratorio de Fisiología y Farmacología de la Secretaría de Salubridad y Asistencia, secretario general de la UNAM durante la rectoría de Nabor Carrillo y becario de las fundaciones Simon Guggenheim y de Investigación en Fisiología de la Harvard Medical School de Boston. Colaboró en *Electroencephalography and Clinical Neurophysiology*, *Gaceta Médica de México* y *American Journal of Physiology*.

PP ♦ ☛ *Partido Popular*.

PP ♦ ☛ *Política Popular*.

PPM ♦ ☛ *Partido del Pueblo Mexicano*.

PPS ♦ ☛ *Partido Popular Socialista*.

PRAC ♦ ☛ *Partido Revolucionario Anti-Comunista*.

Prada Oropeza, Renato ♦ n. en Bolivia (1937). Escritor. Estudió en la Escuela Normal Católica de Cochabamba. Ha sido profesor universitario. Reside en México, donde ha sido investigador del Centro de Investigaciones Lingüísticas y Literarias de la UV y director de la revista *Semiosis*. Autor de novela: *Argal* (1968), *Ya nadie espera al hombre* (1969), *Al borde del silencio* (1969), *Los fundadores del alba* (1969, Premio Casa de las Américas), *El último filo* (1975) y *Mientras cae la lluvia* (1988).

Lilia Prado

Pradeau Avilés, Alberto Francisco ♦ n. en Guaymas, Son., y m. en EUA (1894-1980). Doctor en ciencias por la Universidad del Sur de California (1923), donde fue profesor y recibió, en 1920, la medalla de oro del Colegio de Odontología. Fue dentista de algunos actores de Holywwod y formó una colección numismática. Miembro de la Real Academia de Historia de Madrid y de su correspondiente mexicana. Colaboró en las *Memorias de la Academia Mexicana de la Historia*. Autor de *Historia numismática de México* (1956), *Tlacos y pilones mexicanos; don Antonio de Mendoza y la Casa de Moneda en México en 1543*, *Expulsión de los jesuitas de Sonora, Ostimurí y Sinaloa* y *Misiones y misioneros jesuitas en Sonora*.

Prado, Lilia ♦ n. en Sahuayo, Mich. (1929). Actriz y cantante. Estudió actuación en la Escuela de Bellas Artes y en el taller de Celestino Gorostiza. Ganó el concurso Señoritas Noveles de la Pantalla. Ha trabajado, entre otras, en las películas *Dueña y señora* (1947), *La malagueña* (1947), *La barca de oro* (1947), *La pecadora* (1947), *Soy charro de Rancho Grande* (1947), *Han matado a Tongolele* (1948), *Un milagro de amor* (1949), *Novia a la medida* (1949), *Confidencias de un ruletero* (1949), *Si yo fuera una cualquiera* (1949), *Amor con amor se paga* (1949), *Crimen y castigo* (1950), *Las mujeres de mi general* (1950), *El desalmado* (1950), *Pata de palo* (1950), *El gavilán pollero* (1950), *Cuando acaba la noche* (1950), *Corazón de fiera* (1950), *El puerto de los siete vicios* (1951), *Subida al cielo* (1951), *Las tres alegres comadres* (1952), *El jugador* (1952), *Las interesadas* (1952), *Cuarto de hotel* (1952), *Rumba caliente* (1952), *Traigo mi 45* (1952), *Abismos de pasión* (1953), *La ilusión viaja en tranvía* (1953), *Los gavilanes* (1954), *La vida no vale nada* (1954), *Talpa* (1955), *Después de la tormenta* (1955), *Horas de agonía* (1956), *La locura del rock and roll* (1956), *A media luz los tres* (1957), *Ando volando bajo* (1957), *Mi esposa me comprende* (1957), *Quiero ser artista* (1957), *La reina del cielo* (1958), *Kermesse* (1958), *Mis secretarias privadas* (1958), *Dicen que soy hombre malo* (1958), *Vuelta al paraíso* (1959), *Dos maridos baratos* 1959), *Senda prohibida* (1959), *El analfabeto* (1960), *Cuánto vale tu hijo* (1961), *Pueblito* (1961), *La vida de Pedro Infante* (1963), *Audaz y bravero* (1964), *Los cuervos están de luto* (1965), *Lagunilla 3*, *Más buenas que el pan*, *Dos tipas de cuidado* y *Puerta negra* (1988). También ha actuado en televisión, entre otras, en la telenovela *Dulce desafío*. En 1973 obtuvo una Diosa de Plata de Pecime por su actuación en *El rincón de las vírgenes*(1972) en 1999 recibió un reconocimiento por su trayectoria, dentro del cine nacional.

Prado, Raúl ♦ n. en Lagos de Moreno, Jal., y m. en el DF (1914-1989). Cantante. Se le considera el creador del falsete. En 1937 formó con José Saldívar y Miguel Bermejo el trío Los Calaveras, que en ese año se presentó al público en el teatro Máximo de la capital del país. Los integrantes del conjunto trabajaron en 15 películas al lado de Jorge Negrete, hicieron presentaciones en México y en el extranjero, actuaron en radio y televisión y grabaron numerosos discos.

Prado Galán, Gilberto ♦ n. en Gómez Palacio, Dgo. (1960). Escritor.

Estudió la licenciatura en psicología. Ha sido profesor en la UIA y la Universidad Autónoma de la Laguna. Ha colaborado en *Revista de Coahuila*, *Plural*, *Historia de América*, *Sábado* y *Excélsior*. Coautor de *Homenaje a Malcolm Lowry* (1989). Autor de poesía: *Exhumación de la imagen* (1985) y *Fundación del deseo* (1988); y ensayo: *Acotaciones sobre la plástica de Rufino Tamayo* (1988, Premio Nacional de Crítica Luis Cardoza y Aragón), *Las máscaras de la serpiente* (1992, Premio Malcolm Lowry de Ensayo 1989), *Los comentarios reales: un asedio a la magia solar incaica* (1990) y *Huellas de la salamandra* (1993). Ha obtenido los premios internacionales Garcilaso de la Vega 1990, convocado por la revista *Plural*, y de Ensayo Literario Hispanoamericano Lya Kostakowsky 1993. Ha sido becario del Fonca (1992-93).

Emilio Prados

PRADO PAZ, MIGUEL ◆ n. en Tingüindín, Mich., y m. en San Miguel Allende, Gto. (1905-1987). Músico autodidacto. Llegó a la ciudad de México en 1921. Trabajó como pianista en la estación radiofónica XEB. En 1928 compuso su primera canción, *Culpable no eres tú*, que fue popularizada por Pedro Vargas. Perteneció a la orquesta El Escuadrón del Ritmo (1935). Fue fundador y dirigente de la Sociedad de Autores y Compositores de México. Puso música a poemas de Rubén C. Navarro, Luis Mora Tovar, Martín Galas jr., Gabriel Luna y José A. Zorrilla. Compuso alrededor de 150 canciones, entre otras *Duerme*, *Media noche*, *Me dices que te vas*, *Qué sabes tú*, *Cuéntame un cuento*, *Ramillete*, *Ofrenda*, *Te quiero así*, *Nieve*, *La vorágine*, *Fragilidad*, *Redención*, *En la intimidad*, *Vuelves a mí*, *Cita con el amor*, *Navidad guadalupana* y *Estival*. En 1969 recibió un homenaje en el Palacio de Bellas Artes.

PRADO POZO, MÁXIMO ◆ n. en Tuxtla Gutiérrez, Chis., y m. en el DF (1931-1963). Grabador y pintor. Trabajó para el Instituto Nacional Indigenista, el Centro Tarahumara de Chihuahua, el Centro Tzeltal-Tzotzil de San Cristóbal de Las Casas y en la Fundación Arqueológica Norteamericana Nuevo Mundo. Sus obras se presentaron en Japón, Alemania, Israel y varios países de América Latina. Perteneció al Grupo de Grabadores de Chiapas Franco L. Gómez y al Taller de Gráfica Popular. En 1957 recibió el Premio de Artes Plásticas de Chiapas.

PRADOS SUCH, EMILIO ◆ n. en España y m. en el DF (1899-1962). Poeta de la Generación del 27. Empezó a escribir influido por Federico García Lorca. Cursó dos años de la licenciatura en ciencias naturales en la Universidad Central de Madrid y estudió filosofía en Alemania. Volvió a España en 1922 y dos años después fundó, con Manuel Altolaguirre, la Imprenta Azul, de la que fue propietario y director (1924-30). Con el mismo Altoaguirre dirigió la revista *Litoral* (1927-29). Colaborador de la *Revista de Occidente*. En 1933 se incorporó a la Alianza de Intelectuales Antifascistas. Colaboró con las Misiones Culturales de la República Española y durante la guerra civil fue agregado a la Comandancia de las Brigadas Internacionales. Colaboró con *Hora de España* y en la edición del *Romancero general de la guerra española*. Tras la derrota de la República, en 1939, se exilió en México. Aquí fue empleado de la editorial Séneca, profesor del Instituto Luis Vives, editor de la tercera época de *Litoral* y colaborador de *Cuadernos Americanos*, *Revista de la Universidad de México*, *Presencia* e *Independencia*, todas de México; de *Papeles de Sons Armands*, *Ínsula*, *Poesía Andaluza* e *Índice*, de España; y de la revista estadounidense *The Texas Quaterly*. Con Juan Gil Albert, Xavier Villaurrutia y Octavio Paz, realizó la antología *Laurel* (1941). Autor de *Tiempo* (1925), *Canciones del farero* (1926), *Vuelta* (1927), *Llanto subterráneo* (1936), *Llanto de la sangre* (1937), *Cancionero menor para combatientes* (1938), *Memoria del olvido* (1940), *Penumbras* (1942), *Mínima muerte* (1942), *Jardín cerrado* (1946), *Antología 1929-1953* (1954), *Río natural* (1957), *Circuncisión del sueño* (1957), *Sonoro enigma* (1958), *La sombra abierta* (1961), *Aceptación de la palabra* (1961), *La piedra escrita* (1961), *Signos del ser* (1962), *Transparencias* (1962) y *Últimos poemas* (1965). En 1960, Carlos Blanco Aguinaga publicó *Emilio Prados. Vida y obra. Bibliografía. Antología*.

PRATS MEDINA, JOSÉ ENCARNACIÓN ◆ n. en Villahermosa y m. en Teapa, Tabasco (1807-1853). Vicegobernador (1847-48) y gobernador de Tabasco en tres ocasiones (del 11 de enero al 11 de mayo de 1848, de junio a octubre de 1848 y del 21 de noviembre al 15 de diciembre de 1850).

PRATTS, ALARDO ◆ n. en España y m. en el DF (1904-1984). Periodista. Vino al término de la guerra civil de España, donde había combatido en favor de la República. Obtuvo la nacionalidad mexicana. Dirigió las revistas *Hoy* y *América*. Autor de *El torbellino de Medio Oriente*, *Visión actual de Belice* y *La ruta de Humboldt*.

PRAXEDIS G. GUERRERO ◆ Municipio de Chihuahua situado en el norte del estado, al sureste de Ciudad Juárez, lo rodea Guadalupe y colinda con Estados Unidos. Superficie: 808.97 km². Habitantes: 8,986, de los cuales 2,655 forman la población económicamente activa. Hablan alguna lengua indígena 13 personas mayores de cinco años (maya ocho). El municipio comenzó a poblarse hacia 1849 con grupos de mexicanos que no quisieron permanecer en los territorios ocupados por los estadounidenses, después de la firma de los tratados de Guadalupe Hidalgo. Esos inmigrantes fundaron la población de San Ignacio. En 1859 se erigió el municipio. Sin embargo, perdió esa condición en el curso de la guerra contra los invasores franceses y sólo hasta 1922 fue rehabilitado como tal. Diez años después recibió, junto con la cabecera, su actual nombre, en honor del revolucionario anarquista.

PRECIADO, JESÚS H. ◆ n. en Guaymas, Son., y m. en Cuernavaca, Mor. (¿1832?-1894). Militar. Reprimió a los yaquis y combatió a los filibusteros de Raousset de Boulbon. Durante la guerra de los Tres Años, alistado en la Guardia Nacional de Sonora, peleó dentro del bando liberal. Más tarde luchó contra la intervención francesa y el imperio. En 1865 fue aprehendido luego de la derrota republicana en Oaxaca, pero consiguió escapar. Al triunfo de la República combatió la rebelión de los indios coras, así como diversos levantamientos en Oaxaca y Michoacán. Alcanzó el grado de general de brigada. Fue gobernador de Morelos (1887-94).

Preciado Hernández, Rafael ◆ n. en Guadalajara, Jal., y m. en el DF (1908-1991). Licenciado en derecho por la Universidad de Guadalajara. Fue profesor de la Escuela Libre de Derecho, de la UIA y de la UNAM, en la que fue director del Seminario de Filosofía del Derecho. Cofundador del PAN, del que fue presidente en el Distrito Federal (1946-49) y miembro del consejo nacional. Fue diputado federal (1967-70). Colaboró en *La Nación* (1946-63). Autor de *Lecciones de filosofía del derecho, Ensayos filosófico-jurídicos y políticos, Discursos parlamentarios, Tribuna parlamentaria* y *Discursos e iniciativas*. Fue nombrado profesor emérito de la UNAM.

Preciado de la Torre, Luis ◆ n. en Zapotlán el Grande, Jal., y m. en Tinajitas, Zac. (¿1895?-1920). Ingresó a la Escuela Militar de Aviación en 1916 y dos años después obtuvo el grado de teniente piloto aviador. Fue enviado a Sonora con la primera escuadrilla de la aviación nacional, comandada por Plutarco Elías Calles. Murió en un accidente aéreo.

Preliminares de La Soledad ◆ Acuerdo redactado y firmado el 19 de febrero de 1862, en la población veracruzana de La Soledad, por Manuel Doblado y Juan Prim y Prats, conde de Reus, secretario de Relaciones Exteriores de México y comandante de las fuerzas españolas situadas en Veracruz, respectivamente, con lo que concluyeron dos meses de negociaciones entre los representantes del gobierno de Benito Juárez y los de las tropas españolas, británicas y francesas, que habían ocupado el puerto de Veracruz en diciembre de 1861. El documento fue aprobado ese mismo día por los ingleses Charles Lennox Wyke y Hugh Dunlop, y los franceses E. Jurien de la Graviere y Alphonse Dubois de Saligny. De esta forma, los representantes de las tropas invasoras reconocían que "El Gobierno Constitucional que actualmente rige en la República Mexicana (.) tiene en sí mismo los elementos de fuerza y opinión para conservarse contra cualquier revuelta intestina" y aseguraban que "las potencias aliadas (.) nada intentan contra la independencia, soberanía e integridad del territorio de la República". Así, "los aliados entran (.) en el terreno de los tratados para formalizar todas las reclamaciones que tienen que hacer en nombre de sus respectivas naciones". Las negociaciones debían celebrarse en Orizaba. Mientras tanto, y debido a la insalubridad del puerto de Veracruz, "las fuerzas de las potencias aliadas ocuparán (.) Córdoba, Orizaba y Tehuacán", pero "Para que ni remotamente pueda creerse que los aliados han firmado estos Preliminares para procurarse el paso de las posiciones fortificadas que guarnece el ejército mexicano, se estipula que, en el evento desgraciado de que se rompiesen las negociaciones, las fuerzas de los aliados desocuparán las poblaciones antedichas y volverán a colocarse en la línea que está adelante de dichas fortificaciones, rumbo a Veracruz, designándose como puntos extremos principales el de Paso Ancho en el camino de Córdoba y Paso de Ovejas en el de Jalapa." Finalmente, en cuanto las tropas invasoras hubieran ocupado Córdoba, Orizaba y Tehuacán, "se enarbolará el pabellón mexicano en la ciudad de Veracruz y en el Castillo de San Juan de Ulúa".

Prendes Álvarez, Amador ◆ n. en España y m. en el DF (1904-1978). Gastrónomo. Llegó a México en 1928 y trabajó en el restaurante fundado por Manuel Prendes en 1892. Paulatinamente compró acciones del mismo, hasta adquirir por completo la negociación que dirigió hasta su muerte.

Prensa, La ◆ Diario del Distrito Federal fundado en 1928 por Pablo Langarica como una sociedad anónima, entre cuyos principales accionistas se contaba Luis Novaro. Su primer director fue José E. Campos. El primer número apareció el 29 de agosto de 1928. El 10 de julio de 1935, al término de un conflicto laboral que suspendió la publicación del periódico durante cinco meses, el periódico se transformó en una sociedad cooperativa encabezada por Geo W. Glass y el citado Novaro, quien dejó la publicación en 1955. Desde entonces quedó al frente Mario Santaella como director-gerente. Manuel Buendía dirigió este cotidiano entre 1960 y 1963. En 1993, la cooperativa La Prensa dejó de existir, al ser vendido el periódico a un grupo de empresarios encabezado por Mario Vázquez Raña.

Presbiterianos ◆ Miembros de la Iglesia oficial de Escocia, fundada por el calvinista John Knok a mediados del siglo XVI. De Escocia pasó a Estados Unidos, donde hay más de 4,000,000 de fieles. La presencia de los presbiterianos en México se remonta a 1854, cuando Melinda Rankin, misionera estadounidense, fundó en Brownsville una escuela para niños mexicanos. De ese trabajo misionero derivaron otros dos en el norte (1872) y sur (1873) de la República y posteriormente la Iglesia Nacional Presbiteriana, calvinista y nacionalista, que se ha dedicado a la obra social (construcción de hospitales, sanatorios y centros sociales), educativa y asistencial (hogares para estudiantes en Monterrey y la ciudad de México). Su templo principal es el Príncipe de la Paz, del Distrito Federal. Los presbiterianos han ganado prosélitos sobre todo en Tabasco, Yucatán, Oaxaca y Chiapas, donde han trabajado en la traducción parcial de la *Biblia* a lenguas indígenas, lo que les ha permitido, por ejemplo, la conversión de 6,000 choles y tzeltales. En los años cincuenta, los presbiterianos se dividieron en dos corrientes: una, vinculada a la Iglesia Presbiteriana del Sur de Estados Unidos, y la otra, más liberal, influida por la Iglesia Presbiteriana del Norte, también estadounidense. La Iglesia Nacional Presbite-

La Prensa

riana está organizada en tres sínodos (regiones), su cuerpo coordinador es el Sínodo General, formado en 1901. En 1925 contaban con 25,000 adeptos, los que para 1960 se habían multiplicado por cuatro: 60,000 practicantes y 40,000 simpatizantes. La Iglesia Presbiteriana Asociada Reformada fue fundada en 1878 y en 1984 tenía alrededor de 12,000 miembros, con presbíteros en Hidalgo, San Luis Potosí, Tamaulipas y Veracruz, así como un seminario en Tampico.

PRESCOTT, WILLIAM HICKLING ◆ n. y m. en EUA (1796-1859). Se tituló como abogado en la Universidad de Harvard. La ceguera, adquirida después de su graduación, le impidió dedicarse a las leyes y optó por la historia. Por medio del ministro de España en México, Ángel María Calderón de la Barca, se relacionó con intelectuales mexicanos como José Fernando Ramírez, Lucas Alamán y Joaquín García Icazbalceta. Editó *La vida en México*, de la condesa Calderón de la Barca. Su principal obra sobre México es la *History of the Conquest of Mexico* (1843). Es autor, además, de *Life of Charles Brokden* (1834), *The History of the Reign of Fernand and Isabella the Catholics* (1835), *Biographical and Critical Miscellanies* (1845), *History of de Conquest of Peru* (1847) e *History of the Reing of Phillip II* (1855-58).

Tonatiuh, tapiz de Pedro Preux

PRESIDENCIA DE LA REPÚBLICA ◆ ☛ *Poder Ejecutivo*.

PRESIDIO ◆ Río de Sinaloa, también llamado Mazatlán o Villa Unión. Nace de la confluencia de varios arroyos en el sur de la sierra del Espinazo del Diablo; corre de noreste a suroeste y la primera parte de su curso es conocido como río de las Ventanas. Recibe al río Verde y desemboca en el Pacífico, al sureste de Mazatlán.

PRESIDIOS ◆ Nombre que recibieron los fuertes españoles establecidos a fines del siglo XVI en los alrededores de Zacatecas, para impedir que los chichimecas bloquearan el comercio de plata. Las primeras guarniciones de este tipo se instalaron en Postezuelos y Ojuelos. La denominación de presidios se extendió a todos los cuarteles fronterizos que las autoridades virreinales dispusieron en el norte de la colonia, para proteger las poblaciones españolas. La mayor parte de ellos se encontraban en Durango, Sonora, Alta y Baja California, Nuevo León, San Luis Potosí, Nuevo México, Zacatecas y Yucatán. En 1786, el sistema de presidios agrupaba a cerca de 40,000 soldados.

PRETO Y NETO, FRANCISCO ◆ n. en España (?-?). Cónsul de España en Tampico (1840-42) y cónsul general de España en la ciudad de México (1842-?). En Tampico fundó la primera sociedad de beneficencia y en la ciudad de México en 1842, creó la Beneficencia Española, que subsiste hasta la actualidad.

PREUSS, KONRAD THEODOR ◆ n. y ¿m.? en Alemania (1869-1938). Antropólogo, discípulo de Eduardo Seler. Vino a México en 1905, en una expedición etnológica. Fue el primero en basar los estudios etnográficos en la historia de las religiones. Interpretó el Calendario Azteca. Autor de *Die Nayarit expedition I. Die religion der cora indianer* (1912), "El concepto de la estrella matutina según textos recogidos entre los mexicanos del estado de Durango, México", en *México antiguo VIII* (1955), y *Nahua-Texte aus San Pedro Jícora in Durango. Erster Teil: Mythen und Sagen* (1968), del que Mariana Frenk-Westheim tradujo una parte, aparecida en México como *Mitos y cuentos nahuas de la sierra Madre Occidental* (1982).

PREUX, PEDRO ◆ n. en Francia (1932). Pintor. Llegó a México en 1942 y expuso por primera vez en 1954. Estudió tapicería con Michel Tourliere y Jean Lurcat, en París (1961). Ha sido profesor de la Escuela Nacional de Artes Plásticas, de la UNAM; de la Universidad Iberoamericana y del Instituto Nacional de Bellas Artes, así como director del Taller Nacional de Tapiz (1973-). Ha expuesto linograbados y tapices de bajoliso en Colombia, Estados Unidos, Israel, Polonia y Puerto Rico.

PREUX, ROBERTO ◆ n. en Alemania y m. en el DF (1905-1992). Pintor y restaurador. Estudió con Otto Müller en academias de arte de Breslau y Berlín. De convicciones liberales, abandonó su país en 1932, acosado por el partido nazi. Vivió en Francia, Palestina y España, donde combatió dentro de las Brigadas Internacionales en defensa de la República. Posteriormente se naturalizó español y se incorporó al ejército regular. Debió huir tras la victoria de Franco, y fue recluido en el campo de concentración de Saint-Cyprien, Francia, del que escapó. En 1942 pasó a México, donde realizó una importante y vasta labor como restaurador de pinturas para coleccionistas particulares, galeristas y el INBA. Restauró la obra completa de José María Velasco (☛), así como cuadros de Rubens, Rembrandt, Van Dyck, Zurbarán, Murillo, Mondrian, Modigliani, Van Gogh, Degas, Gauguin, Rivera, Orozco, Siqueiros, Tamayo, Mérida y otros.

PREZA, VELINO M. ◆ n. en Durango, Dgo., y m. en el DF (1875-1946). Músico. Estudió en la Escuela de Santa Catarina de Durango y en el Conservatorio Nacional de Música (1889-94). Fue director de la Banda de Zapadores (1900-04) y director fundador de la Banda de Policía (1904-46).

Compuso alrededor de 400 obras, entre las que destacan *Adelante*, *Vals amoreux*, *Gardenias*, *Cuarto poder*, *23 de julio*, *Canto al pueblo*, *Chapultepec*, *Adelante*, *Viva México*, *Manuel Mondragón*, *Gaviota*, *Himno a la patria*, *Ramo de azahar*, *Lindas tapatías* y la zarzuela *La hija de Tetis*. En 1930 recibió la medalla al mérito civil y las Palmas Académicas francesas.

PRI ◆ ☛ *Partido Revolucionario Institucional*.

PRÍA, MELBA ◆ n. en el DF (1958). Hizo estudios de ciencias políticas y sociales (1979) y sociología en la UNAM (1985). Ha hecho estudios en el ITESM y en Inglaterra, la RDA y Estados Unidos (1972-73 y 1975-76). Pertenece al Servicio Exterior Mexicano. Ha sido asesora del secretario de Relaciones Exteriores y agregada de la Embajada de México en Tel Aviv, Israel (1979-81), editora y jefa de Promoción Cultural en el IMSS (1982-91), subdirectora de Desarrollo y Comunicación en la Compañía Mexicana de Aviación, directora de la Delegación Especial de la SEP en el estado de Chiapas (1994-98) y directora general del INI (1998-).

PRIANI, ALFONSO ◆ n. y m. en el DF (1888-1945). Odontólogo. Estudió en la Escuela de Odontología de México, que más tarde dirigió. Fue jefe del Departamento de Psicopedagogía de la Secretaría de Educación, presidente del patronato de la Fundación Rafael Dondé, secretario del Departamento Central del Distrito Federal, gerente de la Lotería Nacional y secretario de la Beneficencia Pública. Fundó la Cruz Roja de la Juventud y sirvió como voluntario en los pueblos cercanos al Paricutín. Murió a consecuencia de una enfermedad pulmonar provocada por los gases de ese volcán. Autor de *La Cruz Roja de la Juventud y su cooperación permanente en la protección a la infancia* y *La ciencia como factor de confraternidad entre los pueblos*.

PRIDA SANTACILIA, PABLO ◆ n. y m. en el DF (1886-1973). Escritor y periodista. Colaboró en los diarios *El Heraldo de Cuba* y *Excélsior*. Editó las revistas *Azulejos*, *El Tío del Gabán*, *El Mercurio*, *Thalia*, *Gaceta de Policía* y *La Tarántula*. Fue argumentista de radio, cine y televisión. Autor, entre otras obras de *La clínica del amor*, *El último impuesto*, *La tierra de los volcanes*, *La república del Bataclán*, *Colorines*, *Rebozo de bolita*, *El reino de Mercurio*, *Los cascos del mostrador*, *Las cuatro milpas*, *El golpe del coyote*, *De España vengo*, *La alegre España*, *El colmo de la revista*, *La elección de Calles*, *La flor de la Lagunilla*, *Trapitos al sol*, *Aquellos treinta y cinco años*, *SM el billete*, *Los efectos del vacilón*, *El país de los cartones*, *Parece que fue ayer*, *La ciudad de los camiones*, *Las fiestas del centenario*, *Hasta que llovió en Sayula*, *Corazón de obrero*, *Domingo siete*, *Frente al error*, *Recordar es vivir*, *La raza de bronce*, *Apuntes biográficos de Pedro Santacilia*, *Así fue Juárez, su vida en láminas*, *La flor de la Lagunilla*, *Las distracciones de don Luis Cabrera* y *Se levanta el telón, mi vida dentro del teatro*.

PRIDA SANTACILIA, RAMÓN ◆ n. y m. en el DF (1862-1937). Abogado. Se tituló en la Escuela Nacional de Jurisprudencia (1882). Fue empleado del Banco Mercantil, consejero del Banco Nacional de México, regidor del Ayuntamiento de la ciudad de México (1884), fundador de la cerillera La Latina (que más tarde se unió a La Central), profesor de la Escuela de Comercio (1892) y juez federal (1892). Juzgó a Salvador Díaz Mirón por el asesinato de Federico Wolter. Diputado federal suplente (1892-94) y propietario (1894-96). Fue dueño del periódico *El Universal*, que dirigió hasta 1897, cuando perseguido por el gobierno porfirista debió abandonar el país. A su regreso colaboró en el diario oposicionista *El Tercer Imperio*. Fue diputado federal por Tamaulipas (1906-10) y en 1910 presidía el Gran Jurado de la Cámara de Diputados: dictaminó sobre el caso Díaz Mirón-Chapital. Como presidente de la Comisión Electoral, convocó a las elecciones de mayo de 1911, luego de la renuncia de Porfirio Díaz. Encarcelado por el gobierno de Victoriano Huerta en 1913, al ser liberado se refugió en Estados Unidos, donde dirigió la edición en español de *El Paso Morning Times* y participó en la redacción de la sección en castellano de la revista neoyorquina *Dun*. Regresó a México en 1915 y fue encarcelado en Chihuahua. Donó a la Biblioteca Nacional los archivos de Pedro Santacilia (☛). Fue empresario teatral y promotor del jaialai. Colaboró en los periódicos *El Cable Submarino*, *La Verdad*, *Criminalia*, *Azulejos*, *Excélsior* y *El Heraldo de Cuba*, entre otros. Autor de *La ley del domicilio y la nacionalidad* (1899), *El arbitraje internacional en América* (1901), *La nueva ley electoral* (1912), *De la dictadura a la anarquía* (1914), *Procedimientos judiciales que existían en Anáhuac al llegar los conquistadores* (1921), *Datos y observaciones sobre los Estados Unidos* (1922) y *Conferencias de carácter histórico* (1935).

PRIESTLEY, HERBERT INGRAM ◆ n. y m. en EUA (1875-1944). Historiador. Doctor en filosofía por la Universidad de California en Berkeley (1917). Profesor de historia de México (1917-20) y director de la Biblioteca Brancroft de la Universidad de California. Pasó algunas temporadas en México. Fue miembro de la Sociedad Mexicana de Geografía y Estadística, de la Sociedad Antonio Alzate y de la Sociedad Chihuahuense de Estudios Históricos. Coautor de *Some Mexican Problems* (1926). Autor de *José de Gálvez, Visitor General of New Spain, 1765-71* (1916), *Modern Mexican History* (1920), *The Carranza Debacle* (1920), *Constitucional Interpretation in Mexico* (1923), *The Mexican Nation, a History* (1926), *The Luna Papers* (1928), *The Coming of the White Man* (1929), *Tristán de Luna, conquistador* (1936), *France Overseas Through the Old Regime* (1939) y "The Contemporary Program of Nationalization in Mexico" en *The Pacific Historical Review* (1939). En 1918 ganó el Premio Loubat. El Museo Nacional de México lo designó profesor honorario.

PRIETA ◆ Sierra de Sonora situada en el desierto de Altar, al este de la bahía de San Jorge.

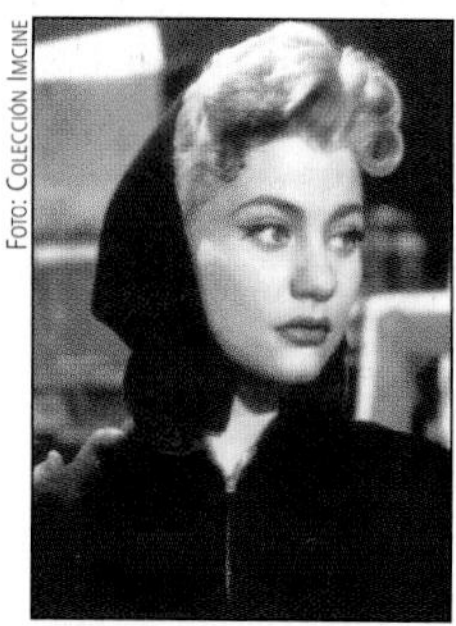

Chula Prieto en *Ultraje de amor*, película de Rafael Portillo

Francisco Prieto

Carlos Prieto

PRIETO, ADOLFO ◆ n. en España y m. en el DF (1867-1945). Estudió en la Universidad Central de Madrid. Llegó a la ciudad de México en 1890, donde trabajó en la casa bancaria de Antonio Basagoiti. Por iniciativa suya, en 1902, la fábrica de hilados y tejidos de lana La Victoria se trasladó fuera de la capital. Fundador (1900) y director (1907) de la Compañía Fundidora de Fierro y Acero de Monterrey; y fundador de Sociedad Agrícola Colonia Acero, la Estación Sericola Acero y la Maternidad María Josefa. Fue presidente de la Confederación Nacional de Cámaras Industriales y consejero del Banco de México.

PRIETO, ALEJANDRO ◆ n. en la hacienda de Chacoy y m. en Tampico, Tams. (1841-1921). Ingeniero topógrafo titulado en la Escuela de Agricultura de la ciudad de México. Combatió la intervención francesa hasta que fue capturado por la contraguerrilla de Aquiles Dupin; condenado a muerte, fue salvado por un mexicano imperialista y abandonó la lucha. Al triunfo de la República fue jefe político de Tampico, juez del Registro Civil, diputado federal, secretario de la legación mexicana en Guatemala, primer ingeniero de la Comisión del Ferrocarril de Tehuantepec, gobernador de Tamaulipas (1888-96) y senador de la República. Perteneció a la Sociedad Mexicana de Geografía y Estadística. Autor de *Historia geográfica y estadística de Tamaulipas, El ferrocarril de Guatemala, Los intereses del puerto de Tampico, La construcción del camino de Tampico a San Luis Potosí* y *El establecimiento de colonias agrícolas en Tehuantepec*.

PRIETO, CARLOS ◆ n. en España y m. en el DF (1898-1991). Su nombre completo era Carlos Prieto Fernández de la Llana. Se tituló como abogado en la Universidad de Oviedo (1919). Llegó a México en 1923. Fue empleado fundador (1923), consejero (1931), delegado (1934) y presidente del consejo de administración de la Compañía Fundidora de Fierro y Acero de Monterrey (1945-78). Naturalizado mexicano en 1942. Fundador del Instituto del Hierro y de Metales y del Instituto Latinoamericano del Hierro y del Acero (1950), con sede en Chile, del que fue presidente. Perteneció al cuerpo directivo de los bancos de México y Nacional de México y a los patronatos de la Orquesta Sinfónica Nacional, Orquesta Filarmónica de la UNAM, Instituto Tecnológico y de Estudios Superiores de Monterrey (al que donó en 1954 su biblioteca cervantina, con más de 1,000 volúmenes), Centro Mexicano de Escritores, Sociedad de Historia Natural de Nuevo León y del Instituto Nacional de Cardiología. En Tecolutla, Veracruz (ciudad que lo declaró "hijo adoptivo" en 1952), fundó un Museo Malacológico y el Jardín Botánico Tropical e introdujo el cultivo de cítricos. Miembro honorario de la Sociedad de Historia Natural de Nuevo León. Autor de *La minería del nuevo mundo* (1968, traducido al francés y portugués) y *El océano Pacífico, navegantes españoles del siglo XVI* (1972). Instituyó un premio anual para la mejor obra sobre Cervantes en castellano y perteneció al jurado del Premio Banamex de Economía.

PRIETO, CARLOS ◆ n. en el DF (1937). Violonchelista. Estudió música con Imre Hartam e ingeniería metalúrgica y economía en el Instituto Tecnológico de Massachusetts. Fue ejecutivo de la Fundidora Monterrey hasta 1970, cuando inició su carrera como concertista. Más tarde estudió con Leonard Rose en Nueva York y con Pierre Fourier en Ginebra (1979). Ha estrenado obras de Blas Galindo, Manuel Castillo, Tomás Marco, Robert X. Rodríguez, Manuel Enríquez, Joaquín Rodrigo, Mario Kuri-Aldana y Raúl Ladrón de Guevara, entre otros. Autor de *Cartas rusas* (1962), *Alrededor del mundo con el violonchelo* (1988), *De la URSS a Rusia* (1993) y *Las aventuras de un violonchelo* (1999). Presidente de la Fundación del Conservatorio las Rosas (1995-). En 1981 recibió el premio al mejor solista del año, de la Unión Mexicana de Cronistas de Música y Teatro. Premio Mozart 1991. Medalla Mozart, otorgada por el gobierno de Austria (1995). En 1999 fue nombrado Oficial de la Orden de las Artes y las Letras de Francia. Miembro del Consejo Consultivo del Departamento de Música y Artes Escénicas del Instituto Tecnológico de Massachusetts. Miembro titular del Seminario de Cultura Mexicana desde 1995.

PRIETO, *CHULA* ◆ n. y m. en el DF (1929-1960). Nombre profesional de la actriz María del Carmen Prieto Salido. Era nieta de Guillermo Prieto. En 1945, gracias a su triunfo en un concurso de belleza, se incorporó al cine estadounidense. En 1948 se inició en el teatro. Entre otras, participó en las películas *El amor abrió los ojos* (1946), *Quinto patio* (1950), *Retorno al quinto patio* (1951), *El dinero no es la vida* (1951), *Yo fui novio de Rosita Alvírez* (1954) y *El Rayo de Sinaloa* (1957). En teatro trabajó, entre otras obras, en *Siga mi ejemplo* y *Despedida de soltera*, que se mantuvo un año en cartelera.

PRIETO, EMA ◆ n. en EUA (1924). Estudió letras españolas en la UNAM. Pertenece a la generación que agrupó a Ernesto Cardenal, Ernesto Mejía Sánchez, Emilio Carballido, Sergio Fernández y Rosario Castellanos. Autora de *Los testigos* (1985).

PRIETO, FRANCISCO ◆ n. en Cuba (1942). Escritor. Vive en México desde su infancia. Licenciado en comunicación y maestro en filosofía por la Universidad Iberoamericana. Hizo estudios de antropología social. Ha sido director del Departamento de Comunicación de la Universidad Iberoamericana. Colaborador de las revistas *Comunidad, Proceso* y *Vuelta* y de los suplementos *Diorama de la Cultura*, de *Excélsior*, y *Sábado*, de *unomásuno;* y del diario *Reforma*. Autor de novela: *Caracoles* (1975), *Taller de marionetas* (1978), *Ruedo de incautos* (1983), *Si llegamos a diciembre* (1985), *La inclinación* (1986), *Deseo* (1989), *Ilusiones tardías* (1993) y *La francesa del Café de Tacuba* (1997); ensayo: *Cultura y comunicación* (1984) y *Comunicación y educación*; teatro: *Shakespeare y yo* (1964), *La expiación* (1987) y *Una comedia nacional*.

PRIETO, GUILLERMO ◆ n. y m. en la ciudad de México (1818-1897). Estudió en el Colegio de San Juan de Letrán. Fue secretario particular de Valentín Gómez Farías y de Anastasio Bustamante, inspector de tabacos en Zacatecas (1842) y profesor de historia y economía en el Colegio Militar. Combatió contra los estadounidenses en la guerra de 1847. En la guerra de los Tres Años estuvo al lado de Juárez, colaboró en la redacción de las leyes de Reforma y, según se dice, impidió que soldados conservadores fusilaran al presidente en Guadalajara, el 14 de marzo de 1858. Durante la resistencia contra los franceses se opuso a Juárez e intentó hacer presidente a González Ortega. Con el presidente José María Iglesias ocupó cinco carteras (1876-77). Desde 1848 hasta su muerte fue 18 veces diputado y constituyente en 1857. Secretario de Hacienda en siete ocasiones entre 1852 y 1876. Inició su carrera periodística como redactor de *El Cosmopolita* (1835-43) y del *Diario Oficial*; desde 1841 trabajó para *El Siglo XIX*, donde publicó la columna "San lunes", firmada como *Fidel*. Fundó *Don Simplicio* (1845), *El Tío Cualandas* (1858), *El Monarca* (1862) y *La Chinaca* (1862-63). En Paso del Norte dirigió el *Diario Oficial* (1865). Colaboró en *El Museo Mexicano* (1843-44), el *Semanario Ilustrado*, *El Ateneo Mexicano* (1844), *El Monitor Republicano* (1847 y 1873-85), *El Álbum Mexicano* (1849), *Las Cosquillas* (1852-1861), *La Orquesta*, *El Semanario Ilustrado*, *El Domingo* (1871-73), y *El Búcaro* (1873), *La Libertad* (1878-81), *El Eco de México* (1879), *El Republicano* (1879-81), *La República* (1880-82 y 1885), *El Federalista* (1883-87), *El Tiempo* (1884, 1890 y 1897) y *El Universal* (1890). En 1890, en una encuesta realizada por *La República*, se le nombró el poeta más popular del país. Colaboró en el *Diccionario Universal de Historia y Geografía*, de Manuel Orozco y Berra. Coautor de *Apuntes para la historia de la guerra entre México y los Estados Unidos* (1848). Es autor de *Lecciones elementales de economía política* (1871) y *Lecciones de historia patria escritas para los alumnos del Colegio Militar* (1886), *Compendio de historia universal* (1888) e *Iniciaciones a mis discípulos para sus recuerdos de la época colonial* (1888); crónica: *Memorias de mis tiempos* (1853), *Viajes de orden suprema* (1857), *Viaje a los Estados Unidos* (1877-78); teatro: *El alférez* (estrenada en 1840), *Alonso de Ávila* (1842), *El susto de Pinganillas* (1843), *A mi padre*, *Patria y honra*, *Alfonso de Ávila* y *La novia del erario*; y poesía: *Versos inéditos* (1879), *Musa callejera* (1883), *Romancero nacional* (1885) y *Colección de poesías escogidas, publicadas e inéditas* (1895), entre otras obras. Se le atribuye la marcha satírica *Los cangrejos*, himno de los liberales. Perteneció a la Academia de Letrán (1836) y al Ateneo Mexicano (1844).

Retrato y firma de Guillermo Prieto

PRIETO, INDALECIO ◆ n. en España y m. en el DF (1883-1962). Político y periodista. Militante de la Unión General de Trabajadores y del Partido Socialista Obrero Español desde 1899. Participó en la fundación de la Juventud Socialista de España. Fue colaborador (1901) y director del diario *El Liberal*, de Bilbao. Participó en el movimiento revolucionario catalán de 1917 y al año siguiente fue elegido diputado. Durante la República Española fue ministro de Hacienda (1931) y de Obras Públicas (1933). Durante la guerra civil fue ministro de Marina y Aviación (1936-37) y Defensa Nacional (1937-38). Llegó exiliado a México en 1939, como representante de la Junta de Auxilio a los Republicanos Españoles y fue el encargado de recibir el tesoro de la República, que llegó a Veracruz en el barco *El Vita*. Colaboró en los diarios *Excélsior* y *Novedades* y en las revistas *Hoy*, *Mañana* y *Siempre!* En 1948 fue elegido presidente del Partido Socialista Español. Autor de *Palabras de ayer y de hoy* (1938), *La tragedia de España* (1939), *Palabras al viento* (1942), *Discursos en América* (1944), *Trayectoria de una actitud* (1959) y *Cartas a un escultor* (1961). Póstumamente se editaron *De mi vida* (1965) y *Obras* (1968).

Obra de Indalecio Prieto

PRIETO, JULIO ◆ n. y m. en el DF (1912-1977). Escenógrafo, grabador y pintor. Estudió arquitectura en San Carlos. Fue subdirector de Bellas Artes (1945-48), fundador del Departamento de Producción Teatral y de la carrera de escenógrafo del INBA; profesor de la Academia de Arte Dramático de la ANDA, jefe del Departamento de Escenografía de Telesistema Mexicano (1952-58), gerente del Patronato para la Operación de Teatros del IMSS (1960-67), representante de la Federación Teatral en el Centro Mexicano de Teatro y director de espectáculos del Programa Cultural de los Juegos Olímpicos (1968). Entre sus aportaciones escenográficas destacan la introducción del escenario giratorio (1948), la eliminación de la concha del apuntador y la sustitución de las escenografías de papel por las de tela y madera. Diseñó las instalaciones de los teatros Insurgentes (1952), Jiménez Rueda (1960), Ferrocarrilero (1967) y Orientación (1967), así como del Centro de Convenciones de Acapulco (1973). Diseñó los dioramas de la Galería de Historia La Lucha del Pueblo Mexicano por su Libertad (1964) y de la Sala de Orientación del Museo Nacional de Antropología (1964), donde también se encargó de la iluminación. Autor de más de 500 diseños escenográficos. Como grabador, estudió aguafuerte con Francisco Díaz de León en la Escuela de Arte para Trabajadores (1937), trabajó diversos materiales, ilustró libros y en los sesenta montó un taller de litografía. Como pintor expuso en la capital del país y en Monterrey. *Novedades* lo premió como mejor escenógrafo por la obra *El emperador Jones*, de O'Neill (1947); y la Asociación Nacional de Críticos por la ópera *Mefistófeles*, de Arrigo Boito (1948), y por *La muñeca muerta* (1956). Premio Nacional de Ciencias y Artes (1976).

PRIETO, MANUEL M. ◆ n. en Camargo, Chih., y m. en el DF (1888-1950). Colaboró en la campaña presidencial del Francisco I. Madero en 1910. A la caída del gobierno porfirista trabajó en las aduanas de Ciudad Juárez

Obra de Isabel Prieto de Landázuri

y de Agua Prieta. Se opuso al gobierno de Victoriano Huerta y al triunfo del constitucionalismo presidió el ayuntamiento de Ciudad Juárez. Fue diputado federal al Congreso Constituyente de 1916-17, el único por Chihuahua; diputado federal (1917-19), administrador principal del timbre en Monterrey (1919), administrador de las aduanas de Progreso, Tampico y Piedras Negras, senador de la República (1924-28) y jefe de la oficina federal de Hacienda en Mérida.

Prieto, Miguel ♦ n. en España y m. en el DF (1907-1956). Pintor, escenógrafo y diseñador. Perteneció a la Alianza de Intelectuales Antifascistas, al Consejo Nacional de Teatro de la Dirección General de Bellas Artes y al teatro ambulante de Federico García Lorca. Durante la guerra civil española fundó el teatro guiñol La Tarumba. Se exilió en Francia al triunfo del franquismo y estuvo en el campo de concentración de Argelès Sur-mer. Llegó a México en 1939. Fue diseñador artístico de la revista *Romance*, director artístico de *México en la Cultura*, suplemento del diario *Novedades*; director artístico de las ediciones del Instituto Nacional de Bellas Artes y asesor de la *Revista de la Universidad de México*. Autor de un mural en el observatorio de Tonantzintla (1955). Ilustró diversas publicaciones y realizó la escenografía para varias obras de teatro.

Prieto, Rodrigo ♦ n. en el DF (1965). Fotógrafo de cine. Hizo estudios en el CCC. Ha fotografiado, entre otras, las películas *El sótano* (1988), *Objetos perdidos* (1991), *Un instante para morir* (1992), *Perfume efecto inmediato* (1993), *Un beso a esta tierra* (1994), *Sobrenatural* (1996), *Edipo alcalde* (1996), *Fibra óptica* (1996, Premio de fotografía del Festival de Cine Latino de Nueva York, 1998) y *Un embrujo* (1998). Premio de fotografía del Festival de Cartagena, Colombia, por las películas *Edipo alcalde* y *Sobrenatural* (1996).

Prieto, Valerio ♦ n. y m. en el DF (1882-1932). Dibujante, pintor y grabador. Alumno de Félix Parra en la Academia de San Carlos. Fue conservador de la Sala de Arte Colonial del Museo Nacional de Arqueología e Historia. Ilustró la mayoría de las ediciones de la Secretaría de Educación Pública hasta 1932. Entre sus obras están diversos paisajes de Puebla y Veracruz, acuarelas de Guanajuato y Querétaro, así como los mapas para la *Historia gráfica de Nueva España* (1928). Autor de *Abanicos y tabaqueras* (1925) y *Capitulares de libros de coro* (1935).

Prieto Argüelles, Carlos ♦ n. en el DF y m. en Cuernavaca, Mor. (1922-1998). Dramaturgo. Estudió en las facultades de Derecho y Filosofía y Letras de la UNAM, y en la Universidad de Notre Dame, EUA. Comenzó a publicar en la revista *Hoy*. Realizador de documentales gubernamentales y de la ONU (1961-62). Durante muchos años fue columnista del diario *Chicago Tribune*, del que fue fundador. Autor de *Atentado al pudor* (1952), *A medio camino* (1954), *Por el ojo de una aguja* (1955), *El lépero* (1956), *El gato encerrado* (1956), *Ashes for Bread* (1957), *El jugo de la tierra* (1957), *El pregón de las gallinas* (1962) y *La rebelión de los tepehuanes* (1963). En 1954 recibió el Premio del Festival Nacional de Teatro del INBA.

Prieto Calderón, Fernando Enrique ♦ n. en la ciudad de México (1927). Doctor en física por la UNAM (1957), institución en la que se ha desempeñado como profesor (1947-), investigador del Instituto de Física (1948-), director de la Facultad de Ciencias (1965-69) y miembro de la Junta de Gobierno.

Prieto Coogar, Irene ♦ n. en el DF (?). Poeta. Vive en Estados Unidos desde 1969. Doctora en letras hispánicas por la Universidad de Nueva York. Ha colaborado en *Mester*, *Parva* y *El Búho*, suplemento de *Excélsior*. Publicó una pieza teatral en la revista peruana *Hueso Húmero*. Autora de *Los poemas de Irene* (Chile, 1991).

Prieto Fortún, Guillermo ♦ n. en el DF (1935). Licenciado en economía por la UNAM (1953-57). Ha sido secretario particular del secretario de Industria y Comercio (1960-63), asesor de la Secretaría del Trabajo (1964-66), director general del Impuesto Sobre la Renta (1970-75), director general de la Administración Fiscal Central (1976-78) y subsecretario de Ingresos (1978-86) de la Secretaría de Hacienda; director general de Multibanco Comermex (1986-89), presidente de la Comisión Bancaria y de Valores (1989- 1995). Es miembro del Colegio Nacional de Economistas, del Centro Interamericano de Administradores Tributarios y de la International Fiscal Association. En 1961 recibió el Premio Anual de Economía.

Prieto González, Luis Jesús ♦ n. en Monterrey, NL (1926). Ingeniero industrial titulado en el Instituto Tecnológico y de Estudios Superiores de Monterrey (1944-48). Miembro del PAN, en el que ha formado parte del Consejo Nacional y del Consejo Regional de Nuevo León. Fue diputado federal a la LII Legislatura (1982-85). Ha sido presidente diocesano de Acción Católica de la Juventud Mexicana, presidente de la Confederación Mexicana de Asociaciones de Relaciones Industriales (1973), presidente de la Unión Cristiana Mexicana y fundador de la asociación Ejecutivos de Relaciones Industriales de Monterrey.

Prieto de Landázuri, Isabel ♦ n. en España y m. en Alemania (1833-1876). Poeta. Vivió en Guadalajara Jalisco desde su infancia y ahí desarrolló su producción literaria. Colaboró en *El Domingo* y en *El Renacimiento*. Tradujo obras de Lamartine, Schiller, Goethe, Shelley y Víctor Hugo, entre otros autores. Autora de las obras de teatro *Las dos flores*, *Los dos son peores*, *Un lirio entre las zarzas*, *Oro y oropel*, *La escuela de las cuñadas* y *¿Duende o serafín?*; y de los poemas *La plegaria*, *La madre y el niño*, *A mi hijo dando limosna* y *Bertha Sonnenborg*. En 1883 se publicó el volumen antológico *Obras poéticas*. Perteneció a la Sociedad Literaria La Concordia (1872-77) y a la Sociedad de Escritores Dramáticos Eduardo Gorostiza (1875-77).

PRIETO LAURENS, JORGE ◆ n. en San Luis Potosí, SLP, y m. en el DF (1895-1990). Militar. Estudió derecho en la Escuela Nacional de Jurisprudencia. Participó en la revolución. Fue regidor del Ayuntamiento de la ciudad de México, fundador del Partido Nacional Cooperatista (1917), diputado federal (1920-22 y 1922-23), gobernador interino de San Luis Potosí (1923) y presidente municipal de la ciudad de México (1923). Fue desterrado por su participación en la asonada delahuertista (1923-24). Dirigió *La Tribuna*, de Houston. Volvió a México en 1933 para fundar y encabezar el Partido Social-Demócrata. En 1935 dirigió la *Revista de Economía y Estadística*. En 1939 fusionó a su partido con otros núcleos pronazis para constituir el Partido Revolucionario Anti-Comunista, que apoyó la candidatura presidencial de Juan Andrew Almazán. Al término de la segunda guerra abandonó su germanofilia y se convirtió en activo propagandista de la política estadounidense. Organizó y presidió el Frente Popular Anticomunista y fue secretario de la Confederación Interamericana de Defensa del Continente. Colaboró en la revista *Impacto*. Coautor de *En defensa del ayuntamiento* (1919). Autor de *La república cooperativa* (1933), *Balance moral y político de la XXX Legislatura* (1935), *Primera exposición del Plan Sexenal. Mayo de 1937* (1937), *El problema de la Laguna. Antecedentes, soluciones* (1937), *Por los fueros de la verdad* (1938), *El libro negro del comunismo en Guatemala* (1954), *Cincuenta años de política mexicana. Memorias políticas* (1968), *Antonio Díaz Soto y Gama, precursor de la revolución, ideólogo del agrarismo* (1971) y *Anécdotas históricas* (1977).

PRIETO LUJÁN, GUILLERMO ◆ n. y m. en Chihuahua, Chih. (1933-1990). Hizo estudios de derecho y de historia en la UNAM. Ingresó en 1955 al PAN, en el que presidió el Comité Estatal de Chihuahua (1981-90). Fue diputado local al Congreso de Chihuahua.

PRIETO Y MADARIAGA, FRANCISCO ◆ n. y m. en Chihuahua, Chih. (1813-1898). Trabajó en el Supremo Tribunal de Justicia (1841) y en el Tribunal Mercantil (1842). En 1845 ingresó a la milicia. Fue oficial mayor de gobierno y miembro de la Junta de Notables que convocó en Chihuahua al general conservador Domingo Cajén. Fue juez del Registro Civil (1864-65), secretario de la prefectura imperial de Chihuahua, prefecto municipal y prefecto imperial de Chihuahua (1865-66). Al triunfo de la República fue desterrado. Durante la rebelión porfirista de La Noria fue nombrado jefe político del Cantón de Iturbide. Después fue administrador del timbre en Chihuahua.

PRIETO POSADA, ALEJANDRO ◆ n. en el DF (1924). Arquitecto titulado en la UNAM. Profesor del IPN (1952) y de la UNAM (1954-55). Ha sido subjefe del Departamento de Arquitectura del INBA (1947-51), director de programas del Instituto Nacional de la Vivienda (1954-58), jefe del Departamento de Inmuebles y Construcciones del IMSS (1958-64). Durante su gestión se construyeron las unidades Independencia, Cuauhtémoc y Padre Hidalgo y el Centro Vacacional Oaxtepec. Director general de la Compañía Constructora Industrial Irolo (1961) y presidente de la compañía Arquitectos Industriales (1988). Son obra suya los teatros Hidalgo (1950) e Insurgentes (1952) y las plantas de Ciba (1954), Cyanamid (1955), Avon (1964), el Tecnológico Regional de Tuxtla Gutiérrez (1972) y el Subcentro Coordinador Indigenista de Ocosingo (1972), entre otras construcciones. Fue presidente de El Colegio de Arquitectos (1964-65), de la Sociedad de Arquitectos (1964-65) y de la Federación de Colegios de Arquitectos (1966), así como vicepresidente de la Academia Mexicana de Arquitectura (1975).

PRIETO RIODELALOZA, RAÚL ◆ n. en la ciudad de México (1918). Lexicólogo, escritor y caricaturista. Usa los pseudónimos de *Nikito Nipongo* y *Nik Nip*. Ha hecho la crítica permanente, sistemática y total de la Real Academia Española y su correspondiente, la Academia Mexicana (de la Lengua), y de varias ediciones del *Diccionario de la lengua española*. Trabajó en la agencia informativa *Prensa Latina*. Ha colaborado en *Tiempo, La Prensa, Novedades, Siempre!, Ja-Já, Últimas Noticias, La Jornada, La Palabra y el Hombre, Revista de Revistas* y *Excélsior*, donde en 1949 empezó a aparecer su columna "Perlas Japonesas", en la que muestra, en forma satírica, las incorrecciones gramaticales. Cofundador de la revista *Proceso* (1976) y del diario *unomásuno* (1977). Fue subdirector de *El Fígaro* (1980-81). Autor de *Hueso y carne* (1956), *El diccionario* (1959), *La lotería* (1960), *Nueva lotería, Madre academia* (ilustrado por Alejo Vázquez Lira, 1977), *Perlas japonesas* (1979), *Pemex muere* (1981), *Nuevas y viejas perlas japonesas* (1985), *Vuelve la real madre academia* (1986), *Museo nacional de horrores* (con la colaboración de Ana Lilia Arias e ilustraciones de Alejo Vázquez Lira, 1986), *La virgen murió en Chichicateopan* (novela, 1988), *Álvaro Obregón resucita. De los tratados de Bucareli al Tratado de Libre Comercio* (1993) y *Desenróllame tu rollo* (1998).

PRIETO RODRÍGUEZ, SOTERO ◆ n. en Guadalajara, Jal., y m. en el DF (1884-1935). Matemático. Estudió en la Escuela Nacional de Ingeniería de la UNAM. Profesor de las escuelas nacionales Preparatoria y de Ingenieros. Fundador de la sección de matemáticas de la Sociedad Científica Antonio Alzate, misma que presidió (1932). Autor de *Enseñanza de las matemáticas, Convergencia de series, Geometría cinemática, Secciones cónicas* e *Historia de las matemáticas* (1991, editado por José Heras Gómez).

PRIGIONE, GIROLAMO ◆ n. en Italia (1921). Doctor en filosofía y letras y graduado en derecho canónico, hizo estudios en la Escuela de Diplomacia de El Vaticano. Ha sido arzobispo titular de Lauriaco, Austria; nuncio apostólico de El Vaticano en Guatemala y el Salvador y delegado apostólico en Ghana y Nigeria. Llegó a México como delegado apostólico en 1978. En 1988 fue el

Regina, escultura de Alejandro Prieto Posada

Girolamo Prigione

primer representante de El Vaticano invitado a la toma de posesión de un presidente mexicano (Carlos Salinas de Gortari) en el siglo XX. A raíz del restablecimiento de vínculos diplomáticos entre México y El Vaticano, en 1992, la delegación fue convertida en nunciatura, de la que Prigione fue titular. Fue retirado en 1996.

Prim y Prats, Juan ◆ n. y m. en España (1814-1870). Militar. Ingresó al ejército español en 1834 y participó en la primera guerra carlista. Diputado a Cortes en 1841, dos años más tarde combatió una rebelión centralista en Barcelona. Fue capitán general y gobernador de Puerto Rico (1847-48) y durante su gobierno reprimió varios levantamientos de esclavos. En 1858, cuando era senador, se opuso a cualquier intervención española en la guerra de los Tres Años. Combatió en Marruecos entre 1859 y 1860. El 21 de noviembre de 1861 fue nombrado jefe de la fuerza expedicionaria española que, con similares cuerpos de Francia y Gran Bretaña, ocupó el puerto de Veracruz en diciembre de ese año. Sin embargo, se opuso a la pretensión francesa de establecer una monarquía en México y, en Orizaba, se entrevistó con el enviado del gobierno de la República, Manuel Doblado, con quien firmó, el 19 febrero de 1862, los Preliminares de la Soledad (☛), y negoció con éste la retirada de las tropas españolas, que partieron hacia La Habana poco después. En 1865 fue nombrado senador vitalicio y tres años después encabezó la revolución liberal que derrocó a la monarquía y estableció un gobierno democrático, en el que primero fue ministro de Guerra y más tarde jefe de gobierno. Trabajó para restablecer la monarquía constitucional y fue asesinado antes de la coronación de Amadeo de Saboya.

Juan Prim y Prats

Primera Internacional ◆ ☛ *Internacional*.

Principal ◆ Teatro de la ciudad de Puebla que se comenzó a construir en 1742, luego de que el alcalde otorgara el permiso para construir un "corral de comedias". El recinto fue terminado hasta 1761. En 1902 se incendió. Fue reconstruido por Maximino Ávila Camacho y reinaugurado en 1940.

Principal ◆ Teatro de la ciudad de México llamado así desde 1826, cuando cambió de nombre el Coliseo Nuevo de la ciudad de México. En las primeras décadas del siglo XX se le conoció como la Catedral de las Tandas, cuando ese género estuvo en boga. En marzo de 1931 fue destruido por un incendio que se produjo durante una función.

Prisma ◆ n. en el DF (1948). Compositora y cantante, su nombre es Silvia Tapia Alcázar. Hija del músico español Simón Tapia Colman. Egresada del Conservatorio Nacional, donde estudió solfeo, piano, historia y composición con los maestros Eloísa de Baqueiro, Abel Eisenberg, Andrés Araiz y Rodolfo Halffter, entre otros. Fundó varios conjuntos estudiantiles, creó el conjunto vocal e instrumental Celanese y el Trío Juventud, de la Comisión Federal de Electricidad, con el que ganó el premio del año de la Unión Mexicana de Cronistas de Teatro y Música. Fue solista del Coro de la CFE. Ha compuesto e interpretado más de 300 canciones, entre ellas *Silencio*, *Con las alas rotas*, *Mamá*, *Se me cansó el corazón*, *La montaña de las gaviotas*, *Piel a piel*, *Sueños*, *De color de rosa* y *Calla*. En 1986 ganó el concurso nacional de la OTI y quedó en segundo lugar del certamen internacional de la misma organización.

PRM ◆ ☛ *Partido de la Revolución Mexicana*.

Pro Juárez, Miguel Agustín ◆ n. en Guadalupe, Zac., y m. en el DF (1891-1927). Sacerdote. Entre 1906 y 1910 trabajó en la Agencia Minera de Concepción del Oro, propiedad de su padre. En 1911 ingresó a la Compañía de Jesús, en el noviciado de El Llano, cerca de Zamora; más tarde estudió en seminarios de la orden en Estados Unidos (1914-15), España (1915-20 y 1922-24) y Bélgica (1924-25). Se dedicó a la docencia en una escuela rural cerca de Granada, Nicaragua (1920-22). Fue ordenado sacerdote en Bélgica, en 1925. Durante su estancia en ese país conoció el funcionamiento de organizaciones obreras socialistas, comunistas y, por supuesto, católicas. En mayo de 1925, en un artículo en el que comentaba las actividades de uno de estos grupos, la Juventud Obrera Católica, escribió: "Quiera Dios nuestro Señor inspirarnos para promover en México una obra semejante, adaptada a las circunstancias y cuyo fruto sea el mejoramiento religioso, económico y social de nuestros queridos obreros mexicanos". Volvió a México a mediados de 1926 y se incorporó a la Liga Nacional Defensora de la Libertad Religiosa (☛), para la que realizó trabajos de difusión y apoyo logístico a la lucha de los cristeros (☛). En diciembre

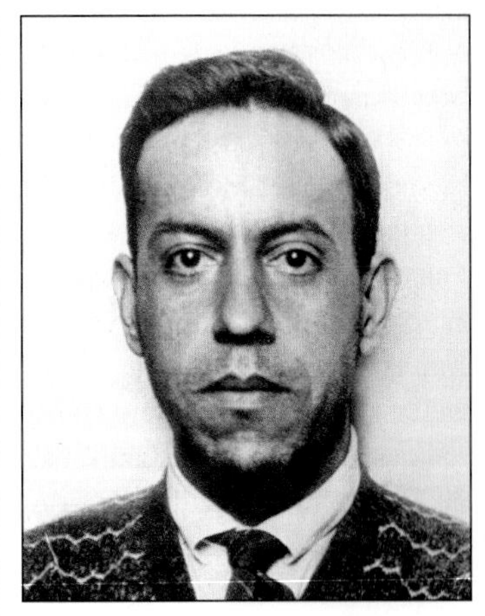

Miguel Agustín Pro Juárez

de ese año fue encarcelado por varios días en la prisión militar de Santiago Tlatelolco. Considerado por el gobierno como el autor intelectual del intento de asesinato del ex presidente Álvaro Obregón, cometido por la liga el 13 de noviembre de 1927, el 18 de noviembre fue detenido junto con su hermano Humberto y, el 23, fusilado sin juicio. Después de un proceso iniciado en 1935, El Vaticano lo beatificó en 1988.

Pro Vida ◆ Organización de católicos creada en 1978, en el Distrito Federal, cuyo nombre oficial es Comité Nacional Pro Vida. De acuerdo con sus dirigentes, que niegan toda vinculación del grupo con la jerarquía eclesiástica o con algún partido político, "la misión del comité es luchar contra todo aquello que dañe la vida humana y su dignidad, por ejemplo el aborto, la drogadicción, el alcoholismo, la vasectomía, la eutanasia, la fecundación *in vitro*, la homosexualidad y las relaciones sexuales pre o extraconyugales". Igualmente, se opone al funcionamiento de la planta nucleoeléctrica de Laguna Verde y al fraude electoral. Entre 1978 y 1982, el comité realizó una intensa campaña contra el proyecto de ley de despenalización del aborto, que había sido redactado por diversos grupos feministas; la movilización incluyó la elaboración de carteles con fotografías de fetos y de los diputados de la Coalición de Izquierda, a los que se acusaba de "asesinos" por impulsar el proyecto de ley. Una vez que la mayoría priista decidió archivar la iniciativa, la actividad del grupo se redujo a la organización de algunas peregrinaciones. A principios de 1988, Pro Vida realizó una manifestación en el Museo de Arte Moderno, en el Bosque de Chapultepec, con la exigencia de que se retiraran unos cuadros que se exhibían ahí y en la Galería del Auditorio Nacional, por juzgarlos ofensivos para "la religión y la patria". A consecuencia de la manifestación, los autores aceptaron retirar sus obras y el director del museo, Jorge Alberto Manrique, fue obligado a renunciar. El 28 de febrero de ese año, el grupo realizó una marcha que llamó de "desagravio" a la Virgen de Guadalupe, la que partió de la Plaza de la Constitución y concluyó en la Basílica de Guadalupe. Unos meses después, cuando la Secretaría de Salud inició una campaña de prevención del síndrome de inmunodeficiencia adquirida (Sida), la organización se opuso por considerar la información como pornográfica y contraria a los valores morales del pueblo mexicano, ya que, a su juicio, fomentaba la promiscuidad y el homosexualismo, sobre todo la sugerencia gubernamental de emplear el condón, palabra que también consideró ofensiva y corruptora. La difusión del Sida era, para el comité, "la consecuencia del desorden sexual que la sociedad misma ha provocado". Para remediarla, propuso limitar las relaciones íntimas a las heterosexuales y siempre dentro del matrimonio. El grupo admite afiliaciones individuales y colectivas, dice contar con 200,000 miembros divididos en "delegaciones especialmente formadas en los estados de Puebla, Querétaro, México, San Luis Potosí, Guanajuato y Nuevo León"; y asegura tener la adhesión de cerca de 150 organizaciones, entre ellas "los Caballeros de Colón, la Legión de María, el Centro Nacional Billings (que promueve el método del ritmo para el control de la natalidad), la Acción Católica, los Caballeros del Santo Sepulcro, las asociaciones de padres de familia, las Damas Voluntarias Vicentinas, las Damas Isabelinas, las Congregaciones Marianas, etc". Sus presidentes han sido Jaime Aviña (1978-81), Alfonso Bravo (1981-87) y Jorge Serrano Limón (1987-). (*Cfr*.: prensa diaria del DF y *Contenido* núm. 300, junio de 1988).

Proa ◆ Denominación usual de la Compañía Mexicana de Comedia, grupo de teatro fundado por José de Jesús Aceves, que funcionó entre 1941 y 1962. Fue patrocinado por el Sindicato de Telefonistas de la República Mexicana y la Secretaría de Educación Pública. Sus temporadas se realizaron, principalmente, en el Palacio de Bellas Artes y en el auditorio del Sindicato Mexicano de Electricistas. Los autores de las obras presentadas fueron María Luisa Algarra, Ermilo Abreu Gómez, José Attolini, Edmundo Báez, Luis G. Basurto, Wilberto Cantón, Sor Juana Inés de la Cruz, Antón Chéjov, Celestino Gorostiza, Benjamín Jarnés, Magdalena Mondragón, Eugene O'Neill, George Bernard Shaw, Clemente Soto Álvarez, Charles Vildrac y Xavier Villaurrutia. El elenco estable estuvo integrado por Luis Aceves Castillo, David N. Arce, Luis Beristáin, Enrique del Castillo, Mario Duncan, Emma Fink, Stella Inda, José Luis Jiménez, Héctor López Portillo, Julio Monterde, Francisco Müller, Diana Ochoa, Gabriela Peré, Rubén Rojo, Gustavo Rojo, Hortensia Santoveña, María Sierra, Rebeca Uribe y Esperanza Zambrano. Carlos Jiménez Mabarak se encargó de la parte musical y las escenografías fueron, entre otros, de Julio Castellanos, María Izquierdo, Agustín Lazo y José Julio Rodríguez.

Proal, Herón ◆ n. en Tulancingo, Hgo., y m. en Veracruz, Ver. (1881-1959). Algunas fuentes señalan que nació en Guatemala. Su apellido materno era Islas. Fue marino en su juventud; sirvió en la armada mexicana y algunos autores afirman que en Europa estudió con el educador ácrata Francisco Ferrer Guardia. Más tarde se instaló en el puerto de Veracruz, donde ejerció el oficio de sastre. Del 15 al 17 de marzo de ese año presidió el Congreso Nacional Obrero de Veracruz, donde se constituyó la Confederación del Trabajo de la Región Méxicana, de la que fue elegido secretario general. En 1919 participó en la fundación del grupo anarquista Antorcha Libertaria. En enero de 1922 fundó el Sindicato de Inquilinos de Veracruz y fue elegido secretario general de la Confederación de Trabajadores del estado. En diciembre asistió como delegado al primer Congreso del Partido Comunista (21 al 31 de diciembre). En marzo de 1922 encabezó una huelga de inquilinos en el puerto jarocho. A fines de ese mes, el 22, fue detenido y encarcelado, pero la movilización de los huelguistas lo liberó poco después. En mayo

Herón Proal

Revista *Proceso*

Logotipo de la Procuraduría Federal del Consumidor

de ese año volvió a caer preso y permaneció detenido hasta marzo de 1924 (☛ *Huelga inquilinaria de Veracruz*). Considerado guatemalteco, en 1925 fue expulsado del país. Se le ha llamado "el Lenin mexicano". Colaboró en los periódicos *La Guillotina*, *Frente Único* y *El Inquilino*.

Proal de la Isla, Arturo ◆ n. en Querétaro, Qro. (1953). Licenciado en derecho por la Universidad Autónoma de Querétaro, de la que ha sido maestro, consejero universitario e integrante del patronato. Hizo estudios de posgrado en la Universidad Complutense de Madrid. Ha sido secretario de acuerdos del Tribunal Fiscal de Querétaro (1976-77), abogado litigante (1979-85), secretario particular del gobernador de Chihuahua (1986-92), secretario de Educación de Querétaro (1992-97), notario público (1997-98) y secretario de Educación y Cultura del gobierno de Chihuahua (1998-). Es miembro del Colegio de Abogados Litigantes de Querétaro y del Consejo de Notarios del Estado de Querétaro.

Proceso ◆ Revista semanal publicada en el Distrito Federal por un grupo de periodistas encabezados por Julio Scherer García, quienes el 8 de julio de 1976 se vieron obligados a salir del diario *Excélsior*. Días después, con financiamiento de numerosos particulares, se creó la empresa Comunicación e Información, editora del semanario. El número uno apareció el 6 de noviembre de 1976, con el propio Scherer como director general y presidente de un consejo de administración en el que estaban: Hero Rodríguez Toro, vicepresidente; Samuel I. del Villar, tesorero; Jorge Barrera Graf, secretario; Adolfo Aguilar y Quevedo y Abel Quezada, vocales. El director-gerente era Miguel Ángel Granados Chapa; los editores, Vicente Leñero y Miguel López Azuara; coordinadores: María de Jesús García, Carlos Marín y Rafael Rodríguez Castañeda. La administración estuvo a cargo de Roberto Galindo y Enrique Sánchez España. El primer editorial decía: "proceso de los hechos, proceso a los hechos y a sus protagonistas; estas son las líneas básicas de acción de nuestro semanario". En enero de 1989, además de Scherer, figuraban en el directorio Vicente Leñero, subdirector; Enrique Sánchez España, gerente; Rafael Rodríguez Castañeda, jefe de redacción; Enrique Maza, jefe de información; Froylán López Narváez, coordinador editorial; y Carlos Marín, coordinador de producción. En 1996, Scherer, Leñero y Maza se retiraron de la revista, pero el primero conservó el control de la sociedad. Los sucedió un consejo directivo integrado por Rodríguez Castañeda, López Narváez, Marín, Gerardo Galarza, Carlos Puig y Enrique Sánchez España. Al año siguiente el consejo se desintegró y los tres primeros ejercieron una dirección colectiva. Posteriormente, López Narváez, Marín y un grupo de trabajadores de la revista renunciaron cuando el consejo de administración encabezado por Scherer impuso como director general a Rodríguez Castañeda.

Procuna, Luis ◆ n. en el DF y m. en El Salvador (1923-1995). Torero. Su apellido materno era Montes. Lidió por primera vez en Puebla en 1938. En 1942, en El Toreo de la ciudad de México, ganó la Oreja de Plata. Tomó la alternativa de manos de Carlos Arruza en Ciudad Juárez, en 1943, y la confirmó en El Toreo ese mismo año, apadrinado por Luis Castro *El Soldado*. Su padrino en Madrid fue Paquito Muñoz. Actuó en las películas de tema taurino *El niño de las monjas* (1944), de Carlos Villareal, *Sol y sombra* (1945), de Rafael E. Portas, y *Torero* (1956), de Carlos Velo, cinta premiada en Venecia, Berlín y Nueva York. Se retiró en 1974. Murió en un accidente aéreo.

Procuraduría Agraria ◆ Organismo descentralizado de la administración pública federal creado en 1992 para defender los derechos de los sujetos agrarios. Presta servicios de asesoría jurídica y coadyuva a la conciliación de intereses, "promueve el ordenamiento y regularización de la propiedad rural y propone medidas encaminadas al fortalecimiento de la seguridad jurídica en el campo". Su antecedente más antiguo se ubica en la época colonial, en la figura del "protector fiscal", funcionario virreinal responsable de pedir la nulidad de las "composiciones" de tierras que los españoles hubiesen adquirido a los indios, en contra de las cédulas reales u ordenanzas o con algún otro título viciado. En 1947, en San Luis Potosí, el Congreso local creó la Procuraduría de los Pobres, dependiente de la Comisión Nacional Agraria, "para patrocinar a los pueblos que lo desearen, gratuitamente, en sus gestiones de dotación o restitución de ejidos". En 1953, por decreto del presidente Adolfo Ruiz Cortines, se creó la Procuraduría de Asuntos Agrarios, con el objetivo de asesorar gratuitamente a los solicitantes de tierras y aguas. Años después se creó la Dirección General de Inspección, Procuración y Quejas, que en 1989 se tranformó en Dirección General de Procuración Social Agraria, la cual debía "atender las demandas planteadas por particulares y comuneros, provenientes de violaciones a la legislación agraria que lesionen los derechos de los promovientes; intervenir por la vía conciliatoria en la solución de controversias que se susciten entre ejidatarios, comuneros y pequeños propietarios; practicar las investigaciones y diligencias necesarias para comprobar los hechos relacionados con divisiones, fraccionamientos, transmisiones y acaparamiento de predios". Tras las reformas de 1992 al artículo 27 Constitucional y la promulgación de la Ley Agraria, se creó la Procuraduría Agraria, que cuenta con personalidad jurídica y patrimonio propios.

Procuraduría Federal del Consumidor ◆ Institución creada por decreto presidencial del 5 de febrero de 1976 para vigilar el cumplimiento de la Ley Federal de Protección al Consumidor. Representa los intereses de la población consumidora ante los organismos privados y las autoridades administrativas y judiciales; asesora gratuitamente a los consumidores y propone mecanismos para la defensa de sus derechos. Está facultada para imponer penas como multas, clausuras e incluso cárcel a quienes violen la legislación de su ramo. El 1 de enero de 1993 se le fusionó lo que fuera el Instituto del Consumidor.

Procuraduría General de la República ◆ La Constitución de Apatzingán preveía la existencia de "fiscal o fiscales" para la procuración de justicia, lo mismo que el Reglamento Político Provisional del Imperio, de 1823, que declaró subsistentes los juzgados coloniales y dejaba como facultad del gobierno establecer "dos o tres audiencias nuevas". Esta norma indicaba que el Supremo Tribunal de Justicia conocería de "todos los asuntos contenciosos del patronato imperial". El emperador o sus ministros podían encargarse de perseguir delitos y el Consejo de Estado contaba con juristas para asesorar al gobierno. De acuerdo con la Constitución de 1824, había un fiscal que formaba parte de la Suprema Corte de Justicia, el cual debía satisfacer los mismos requisitos que los ministros, como ser mexicano por nacimiento, de 35 años como mínimo y "estar instruido en la ciencia del derecho". El fiscal era elegido por las legislaturas locales y la Constitución consideraba preferible este cargo al de senador o diputado. La Constitución centralista conocida como las Siete Leyes (1835-36), señalaba que la Suprema Corte estaría compuesta por 11 ministros y un fiscal, los que serían letrados mexicanos no menores de 40 años, con por lo menos un decenio de ejercicio profesional de la abogacía. Todos ellos eran elegidos por las legislaturas locales. Las Bases Orgánicas de 1843 contenían disposiciones semejantes para el fiscal y señalaba que la Corte podía nombrar a "los dependientes y subalternos de la misma", a los que expediría "sus despachos el Presidente de la República". El 23 de abril de 1853, con Santa Anna en la Presidencia, se promulgaron las Bases para la administración de la República, que decían: "Para que los intereses nacionales sean convenientemente atendidos en los negocios contenciosos que se versen sobre ellos (esto es), promover cuanto convenga á la Hacienda Pública y que se proceda en todos los ramos con los conocimientos necesarios en puntos de derecho, se nombrará un procurador general de la nación, con sueldo de cuatro mil pesos, honores y condecoración de ministro de la Corte Suprema de Justicia, en la cual y en todos los tribunales será recibido como parte por la nación, y en los inferiores cuando lo disponga así el respectivo ministerio". De acuerdo con el artículo 90 de la Constitución de 1857, "Se deposita el ejercicio del poder judicial de la federación en una Corte Suprema de Justicia y en los tribunales de Distrito y de Circuito". La Corte estaría compuesta por 11 ministros propietarios, cuatro supernumerarios, un fiscal y un procurador general, quienes durarían en su cargo seis años "y su elección será indirecta en primer grado en los términos que disponga la ley electoral". El aspirante a cualquiera de esos cargos debía ser "instruido en la ciencia del derecho, á juicio de los electores, ser mayor de 35 años y ciudadano mexicano por nacimiento en ejercicio de sus derechos". El Código de Procedimientos Civiles y Federales de 1897 reglamentó las funciones de la Procuraduría General de la República y del Ministerio Público. Una reforma constitucional de 1900 establecía que "La Suprema Corte de Justicia se compondrá de 15 Ministros y funcionará en Tribunal Pleno o en Salas, de la manera que establezca la ley", misma que "establecerá y organizará los Tribunales de Circuito, los Juzgados de Distrito y el Ministerio Público de la Federación". El Ejecutivo nombraría a los "funcionarios del Ministerio Público y al Procurador General de la Federación". Las funciones del procurador y del Ministerio Público fueron reformadas en 1908 por la Ley de Organización del Ministerio Público, que entró en vigor el 5 de febrero de 1909. La Constitución de 1917 establece como facultad del presidente de la República "nombrar y remover libremente a los secretarios del Despacho (y) al procurador general de la República". El artículo 102 señalaba que "La ley organizará el Ministerio Público de la Federación, cuyos funcionarios serán nombrados y removidos libremente por el Ejecutivo, debiendo éstos estar presididos por un procurador general, el que deberá tener las mismas calidades requeridas para ser magistrado de la Suprema Corte" (☛ *Poder Legislativo*). "Estará a cargo del Ministerio Público de la Federación la persecución, ante los tribunales, de todos los delitos del orden federal; y, por lo mismo, a él le corresponderá solicitar las órdenes de aprehensión contra los reos; buscar y presentar pruebas que acrediten la responsabilidad de éstos; hacer que los juicios se sigan con toda regularidad para que la administración de justicia sea pronta y expedita; pedir la aplicación de las penas e intervenir en todos los negocios que la misma ley determine". El procurador "intervendrá personalmente en todos los negocios en que la Federación fuese parte; en los casos de los ministros, diplomáticos y cónsules generales, y en aquellos que se suscitaren entre dos o más Estados de la Unión, entre un Estado y la Federación o entre los poderes de un mismo Estado. En los demás casos en que deba intervenir el Ministerio Público de la Federación, el procurador general podrá intervenir por sí o por medio de alguno de sus agentes. El procurador general de la República será el consejero jurídico del Gobierno. Tanto él como sus agentes se someterán estrictamente a las disposiciones de la ley, siendo responsables de toda falta, omisión o violación en que incurran con motivo de sus funciones". Con variantes de redacción, se conservan las disposiciones constitucionales.

Logotipo de la Procuraduría General de la República

Productora e Importadora de Papel, S.A ◆ ☛ *Papel*.

Proenza Proenza, Teresa ◆ n. en Cuba y m. en el DF (1911-1989). Periodista y diplomática. Desde 1935 residió en México, donde ejerció el periodismo en los diarios *El Nacional, El Popular* y *El Día*. Trabajó como corresponsal de periódicos mexicanos y cubanos durante la guerra civil española. Fue agregada de prensa de la embajada de Cuba en México (1960-64).

PROFESOR ZOVEK ◆ ☛ *Zovek*.

PROGRESO ◆ Municipio de Coahuila en el este del estado, al noreste :lova, en los límites con Nuevo uperficie: 1,858.3 km². Habi- 3,613, de los cuales 1,125 for- oblación económicamente acti- blan alguna lengua indígena 23 rsonas mayores de cinco años náhuatl 21).

José María Luis Mora promovió el protestantismo a través de *El Observador de la República*

PROGRESO ◆ ☛ *San José del Progreso*, municipio de Oaxaca.

PROGRESO ◆ Municipio de Yucatán situado en el nor-noroeste do, en el litoral del golfo de México y contiguo a Mérida. Superficie: 270.8 km². Habitantes: 43,892, de los cuales 11,661 forman la población económicamente activa. Hablan alguna lengua indígena 3,577 personas mayores de cinco años (maya 3,533). El 25 de enero de 1856, el presidente Ignacio Comonfort extendió el permiso para establecer una población "en el lugar llamado Progreso, en la costa norte de Yucatán", que ya había sido explorado desde el siglo XVI y promovido, desde 1840, como sitio adecuado para un puerto por un grupo encabezado por Juan Manuel de Castro. En memoria de éste, la población fue llamada Progreso de Castro. En el siglo XX el lugar se convirtió en el principal centro de recreo para la población de Mérida. A cinco kilómetros de la población, que es también cabecera municipal, se construyó el puerto de Yukalpetén, para lo cual se aprovechó una laguna en la ciénega costera, donde se hicieron una dársena y un canal artificiales. Se inauguró el 1 de junio de 1968. Más tarde se amplió la dársena y el 15 de diciembre de 1969, por decreto presidencial, se le habilitó como puerto de altura y cabotaje. Con capacidad para embarcaciones hasta de tres metros y medio de calado, cuenta con dos muelles, de 300 metros de largo cada uno, destinados respectivamente a la pesca comercial y a la deportiva; tiene frigoríficos, edificios administrativos, hoteles y un club de yates.

Progreso, Yucatán

Foto: Claudio Contreras

PROGRESO DE OBREGÓN ◆ Municipio de Hidalgo situado al noroeste de Pachuca y al sur de Ixmiquilpan. Superficie: 106 km². Habitantes: 19,267, de los cuales 4,550 forman la población económicamente activa. Hablan alguna lengua indígena 513 personas mayores de cinco años (otomí 478). Su cabecera es Progreso.

PROTESTANTES ◆ Se considera que el primer protestante que llegó a México fue el joyero moravo Andrés Moral, quien fue aprehendido en 1536 por la Inquisición y desterrado en 1538. Pedro Ocharte, yerno del impresor Juan Pablos, fue acusado de editar libros con ideas luteranas, por ese motivo fue martirizado en 1572. Dos años después, el pirata John Hawkins tuvo que dejar en Tampico a varios de sus marineros, entre quienes estaban Marin Cornu y George Ribley, considerados los primeros mártires protestantes de México. Cornu trabajó como peluquero en Yucatán y en la ciudad de México, donde se le aprehendió, ahorcó y quemó "por hereje contumaz y luterano". Ribley se hizo minero en Guanajuato, donde lo detuvieron para trasladarlo a la ciudad de México, en la que fue ahorcado y quemado "por luterano". En 1569 circuló en la Nueva España una traducción al castellano de la *Biblia* que produjo el movimiento místico del Biblismo, al que se adscribieron los reformadores españoles. La traducción de Reyna-Valera era llamada la *Biblia del oso*, pues en su pasta tenía el dibujo de un oso tratando de alcanzar un panal, lo que constituía la contraseña de los protestantes españoles. En 1827 llegó a México Diego Thomson, un representante de la Sociedad Bíblica Británica, que aquí se convirtió en uno de los principales promotores del protestantismo, apoyado por José María Luis Mora, desde cuyo periódico, *El Observador de la República*, se recomendaba la lectura de la *Biblia* en español. En 1828 se fundó en Orizaba una Sociedad Bíblica Nacional, dirigida por José Joaquín Pesado, mientras en Puebla, con la ayuda del obispo, se tradujeron partes de la *Biblia* al náhuatl. Estos trabajos fueron base de las congregaciones protestantes que se formarían después. Hacia 1846, el ministro de Prusia solicitó al gobierno licencia para establecer una capilla protestante que funcionaría de manera privada. En 1852 la solicitud continuaba sin respuesta. El 31 de julio de 1856, en el Congreso Constituyente, José María Lafragua, secretario de Gobernación del presidente Comonfort, se opuso a la libertad de cultos, pues a su juicio no tenía caso establecerla por "50 a 100 protestantes" que había "en Temascaltepec, en Maravatío o en Tehuacán". Si bien la Constitución no estableció claramente la libertad de conciencia, dejó los asuntos de culto en manos del gobierno, lo que permitió que actuaran públicamente algunos núcleos de protestantes mexicanos, apoyados por las sociedades bíblicas Británica y Americana. Protestantes y liberales mexicanos coincidían en algunos planteamientos: la nacionalización de los bienes eclesiásticos, la libertad de cultos y la separación Estado-Iglesia. Antes de este año, la difusión del protestantismo había sido casi nula debido al monopolio de la Iglesia Católica como religión estatal. En 1857 se formó la Iglesia de Jesús, primera congregación protestante nacional, apoyada por Benito Juárez y Melchor Ocampo. En 1862 empezó la labor proselitista de los bautistas. En 1869 llegó la Iglesia Católica Apostólica

Anglicana (los episcopales o anglicanos). Entre 1869 y 1878, Román Castillo publicó en Zacatecas el periódico *La Antorcha Evangelista.* La Iglesia de los Amigos (cuáqueros) se estableció en México en 1871, pero se confinó en una comunidad reducida de Matehuala. En 1872 inició sus actividades en México la Iglesia Congregacional, calvinista. Sus fundadores, el estadounidense Stephens y el mexicano Islas, fundadores de la misma, fueron asesinados por unos fanáticos católicos. Esta rama del protestantismo ha sido una de las principales animadoras de la Convención Nacional Evangélica y del Concilio Evangélico (Federación de Iglesias Evangélicas). Los presbiterianos del sur empezaron su labor en 1872. En 1873 llegó a México Guillermo Butler, fundador de la Iglesia Metodista de la India, y formó la mexicana, como filial de la Iglesia Metodista del Norte, de Estados Unidos. Los presbiterianos del norte llegaron en 1874 y la Iglesia Presbiteriana Asociada Reformada, en 1878. En ese año circulaba en México *El Ramo de Olivo*, periódico protestante. Una característica de las instituciones protestantes desde esos tiempos sería su defensa de la Constitución y el culto cívico a Benito Juárez y los hombres de la Reforma. La Iglesia Bautista del Norte empezó a trabajar en nuestro país en 1883. Esta rama calvinista del protestantismo se difundió exitosamente en México, al grado de contar con varias escuelas, internados, hospitales y dos seminarios, uno de ellos considerado ejemplar para Latinoamérica. También en 1883 empezó a funcionar en México la Iglesia Metodista del Sur, animada por Juan C. Keener. En 1889 se inició formalmente la obra de la Iglesia Bautista del Sur, estadounidense, que se reivindica no como procedente de la reforma protestante sino de la corriente anabaptista de la iglesia primitiva. En 1891 llegan la Iglesia de los Hermanos y los Adventistas del Séptimo Día. En 1895 se inició la obra de la calvinista Iglesia Cristiana (de los discípulos) en Ciudad Juárez; ésta se ha extendido por Zacatecas, Aguascalientes y San Luis Potosí. En 1898 se creó en la ciudad de México el Seminario de San Andrés, de la Iglesia Episcopal de México, dedicado a la preparación de pastores protestantes. En la actualidad forma parte de la Comunidad Teológica o Instituto Internacional de Estudios Superiores. Los episcopales fundaron numerosas escuelas, mismas que han cerrado paulatinamente para evitar fricciones con el gobierno federal. La más famosa institución episcopal fue el Internado Hooker para niñas, que funcionó de 1885 a 1971; en 1975 tenían cuatro casas de este tipo en el país. En 1901 se instaló en México la Asociación Cristiana de Jóvenes, de la congregación presbiteriana. En 1902 llegó la Iglesia de la Ciencia Cristiana. En 1903 se creó la Convención Bautista Mexicana, que en 1965 estaba dividida en 13 distritos. En 1906, mediante un acuerdo con la Iglesia Anglicana de Estados Unidos, se constituyó la Iglesia Episcopal de México. En 1906 se instaló la Iglesia del Nazareno, metodista. Numerosos protestantes militaban entonces en el Partido Liberal Mexicano y otras organizaciones antiporfiristas. En 1905, el periódico *El Testigo* elogiaba la labor de las escuelas evangélicas, pues, decía, cumplen la tarea de "llevar el pan de la instrucción a todos los hijos del pueblo, sea cual fuere su posición o categoría" y buscan "a los pobres que, debido a su miseria, son vistos con indiferencia por las clases acomodadas". Protestantes eran José Rumbia y Andrés Mota, dos de los promotores de la huelga de Río Blanco; Esteban Baca Calderón, dirigente de la huelga de Cananea; Andrés R. Salas, líder obrero de Parral, José Valencia, dirigente de la oposición en Zaragoza, Chihuahua, todos ellos ligados al Partido Liberal Mexicano. El presbiteriano Moisés Sáenz fue, desde 1909, jefe de redacción del periódico de Francisco I. Madero, *El Anti-Reeleccionista.* De los protagonistas de la revolución, fueron protestantes Pascual Orozco y su padre, que pertenecían a la Iglesia Congregacional, lo mismo que Braulio Hernández, pastor y maestro de escuela que fue secretario general de Gobierno cuando Abraham González ocupó el Poder Ejecutivo en Chihuahua. Metodistas eran Benigno Zenteno, uno de los que alzaron en armas a Tlaxcala, y los zapatistas Otilio Montaño y José Trinidad Ruiz, redactores del Plan de Ayala. La mayoría de los protestantes revolucionarios tenían como único objetivo acabar con la antidemocracia porfirista. Sin embargo, algunos advertían que algo más que la situación política tenía que cambiar. *El Evangelista Mexicano*, en septiembre de 1912, ante la actitud vacilante de Madero, decía: "la revolución reciente, si cumple sus promesas, hará surgir una ley sabia y equitativa conducente a desapropiar a esos herederos del perico de los palotes de sus vastísimos terrenos que poseen improductivos para cederles a la gran masa de mexicanos que se mueren de hambre". Durante la dictadura de Victoriano Huerta la mayoría de los protestantes se incorporaron al constitucionalismo. Al desatarse la lucha de facciones la mayoría permaneció leal a Carranza, por identificación con sus ideas moderadas. El primer jefe designó al pastor metodista Gregorio Velázquez como director de la Oficina Central de Información y Propaganda Revolucionaria. Durante la dictadura de Huerta, Adolfo Abreu Salas, de la misma cofesión, coordinaba el espionaje carrancista en la capital. Benjamín Velasco encabezó al grupo de 100 maestros mexicanos enviado por Carranza a estudiar los sistemas de enseñanza normal en Estados Unidos. El director de Educación Pública del DF y territorios fue Andrés Osuna, quien cesó a los que cobraban sin trabajar. El presbiteriano Gustavo Espinosa Mireles fue gobernador de Coahuila. Salvador Alvarado, cuando fue gobernador de Yucatán, contó con amplio respaldo protestante para su gestión educativa. El citado Moisés Sáenz fue director de la Escuela Nacional Preparatoria con Carranza, oficial mayor durante la presidencia de Álvaro Obregón y subsecretario y secre-

Pascual Orozco, protestante congregacional en el periodo revolucionario

Moisés Sáenz, activo protestante de principios de siglo

tario de Educación con Plutarco Elías Calles. La Iglesia Apostólica de la Fe en Cristo Jesús nació en las congregaciones protestantes de los grupos minoritarios en Estados Unidos, sobre todo de negros y mexicanos; estos últimos la trajeron a México en 1914 y aquí, conocidos como pentecostales, han llegado a agrupar al 70 por ciento de los protestantes del país. Las congregaciones protestantes se organizaron de acuerdo con un plan de cooperación (Plan de Cincinnati) que empezaron a aplicar en 1919 y que dividía al país en ocho zonas, cada una de las cuales sería cubierta por una iglesia distinta. En 1920 iniciaron sus actividades la Iglesia Cristiana de los Discípulos y la Iglesia de los Peregrinos. En 1921 se instalaron las Asambleas de Dios. En 1922 arribaron a México los menonitas. A partir de 1917 el protestantismo conoció cierto auge gracias a que los gobiernos revolucionarios, principalmente los de Obregón y Calles, se apoyaron en él en su lucha contra la jerarquía católica. Dos iglesias episcopales de Estados Unidos enviaron a Obregón un telegrama en el que le comunicaban que "millones de americanos se solidarizan con usted y rezan por su lucha para librar a su gran país del grillete que la Iglesia católica romana le ha impuesto". En 1929, el Congreso Evangélico de La Habana felicitó al presidente Portes Gil por su campaña antialcóholica. Por motivos más terrenales, los inversionistas estadounidenses dieron su apoyo a los misioneros protestantes que operaban en México. El empresario Wallace Thomson escribió: "las compañías listas y ansiosas de servir, encuentran a través de las misiones un medio por el cual su dinero y la gran fuerza de su prestigio tendrán orientación eficaz", pues tales misiones, decía, "pueden mejorar la moralidad y la capacidad productiva de los cuales su negocio depende". Sin embargo, el saldo de ese periodo no fue del todo positivo para el protestantismo. William Cameron Townsend, el fundador del Instituto Lingüístico de Verano, publicó años más tarde un recuento de lo que sucedió al protestantismo de la época: "Las escrituras de propiedad de sus iglesias se habían transferido a favor del Estado; la mayoría de sus escuelas fueron cerradas, a sus ministros los obligaron a registrarse y en algunos casos a pagar impuestos especiales de clerecía; en cuanto a los ministros que no pertenecían al país, se les prohibió que ejercieran como pastores (.) La maquinaria de Calles dio manos libres a los furiosos dirigentes de su campaña antirreligiosa. En varios estados cerraron las iglesias protestantes y se expulsó a sus ministros; algunos niños fueron puestos en la escuela bajo influencias agnósticas; en ciertos casos, congregaciones enteras desaparecieron al renegar los creyentes débiles que tendieron a congraciarse con las autoridades. Pero la mayor parte de las iglesias protestantes continuó con su tarea y algunas aumentaron sus fieles. Por ejemplo en Tabasco, después de la enconada persecución emprendida por el gobernador Garrido Canabal, las fuerzas evangélicas se encontraron más fuertes". Otros autores se han expresado en idénticos términos de lo sucedido a los católicos. Notoriamente distintos fueron los términos empleados en un folleto de 1934, citado por Jean Pierre Bastian (*Protestantismo y sociedad en México*), texto en el que los protestantes se dicen herederos de "la tradición histórica de los indios conquistados, de las heroicas chusmas insurgentes y de los indómitos chinacos de la Reforma" y se presentan, lo que creen indiscutiblemente cierto, como precursores del "gran movimiento de educación campesina y de incorporación indígena que actualmente forma parte del programa de la Revolución". En ese tiempo el jacobinismo formaba parte de la ideología oficial, el partido en el poder había decidido implantar la educación socialista y grandes movilizaciones presagiaban un cambio hacia la izquierda. Entre los protestantes, ante el cambio que se advertía, se produjeron diversas tomas de posición. Un grupo en el que destacaba Gonzalo Báez-Camargo abrió el fuego contra todo lo que oliera a marxismo. En el otro extremo, el profesor Gumaro García, a partir de una rama del metodismo, creó el movimiento Unidad y Progreso, identificado con el agrarismo y la retórica socializante de la época. En 1930, la Iglesia Metodista del Sur se convirtió en Iglesia Metodista de México y absorbió a su similar del norte; asimismo, se declaró arminiana, por el calvinista holandés Arminio; a esta congregación perteneció el líder campesino Rubén Jaramillo, asesinado en 1962. Al iniciarse el sexenio de Lázaro Cárdenas, las iglesias protestantes decidieron reorientar su trabajo misionero hacia las zonas rurales indígenas, de acuerdo con los planteamientos del Congreso Evangélico de La Habana. En ese marco, el Instituto Lingüístico de Verano, que operaba en México por lo menos desde 1934, incrementó su actividad con el visto bueno del presidente de la República. Al irse apagando el fervor izquierdizante, ya con Manuel Ávila Camacho en el poder, las iglesias protestantes encontraron mejores condiciones para su actividad y pudieron aplicar los acuerdos del Congreso Evangélico Nacional de 1939, en el que se propusieron la colaboración con el gobierno y el combate al comunismo. Estas concepciones encontraron un campo propicio en el ambiente de la posguerra, cuando el gobierno mexicano se alineó junto a Estados Unidos durante la guerra fría. Pese a todo, dentro del protestantismo surgieron tendencias opuestas a ese acomodo, como la encabezada por el líder evangélico marxista Rubén Jaramillo, quien en los años cuarenta y cincuenta se mantuvo en pie de lucha por reivindicaciones agraristas y laborales. Al inicio de su sexenio, el presidente Adolfo López Mateos, mediante tres enviados de filiación protestante, le prometió resolver los problemas que habían motivado su rebeldía. Los asuntos siguieron pendientes, pero Jaramillo fue asesinado con todo y su familia en mayo de 1962. La colaboración con el gobierno y los empresarios favoreció la propagación de las congregaciones protestantes en el país, y de 1940 a 1950 crecieron 86 por ciento (de 177,954 a 330,111 fieles). En 1940 César Augusto Lazo, representante del Sínodo de Misuri, fundó en Monterrey la Iglesia Luterana y un año después la trasladó a la ciudad de México. Esta Iglesia fundó varias escuelas, reputadas por el buen nivel de su enseñanza. En 1956, en el Congreso de Iglesias Evangélicas celebrado en Guadalajara, el protestantismo mexicano renunció a sus tradicionales labores de tipo asistencial, sobre todo en la creación de escuelas y hospitales, y acordó concentrarse en el trabajo meramente espiritual. La Convención Evangélica Nacional de 1960, reunida en San Luis Potosí, ratificó lo anterior y declaró que su función en el mundo es "afirmar la doctrina escrituraria, buscar el avivamiento por el Espíritu Santo, promover la evangelización personal y la unidad en el Espíritu Santo". En la segunda Conferencia Evangélica Latinoamericana, reunida en Lima, Perú, en 1960, se demandó no rehuir "un enfrentamiento con los problemas sociales y políticos de nuestros días". Era un grito, dice Bastian, "al cual respondió el silencio de las iglesias mexicanas". En 1967, la congregación luterana sugirió a sus pastores que estudiasen marxismo. De 1950 a 1970 el protestantismo creció en 166 por ciento (de 550,000 a 879,241 fieles). También en 1940 se fundó en la ciudad de México la Iglesia de Jesucristo Interdenominacional, pentecostal, una de las más exitosas en su tarea de ganar adeptos. En 1950 iniciaron su trabajo en México la Asociación Cristiana de Estudiantes y la Unión Latinoamericana de Jóvenes Evangélicos, surgidas del ecumenismo postulado en Amsterdam en 1948. En 1970, los maestros y alumnos mexicanos de la Iglesia Bautista del Norte tomaron las instalaciones de la misma y expulsaron del país a los misioneros estadounidenses; a partir de entonces, la Iglesia Bautista del Norte forma parte de la Comunidad Teológica y trabaja en la redefinición del ecumenismo. La Sociedad Bíblica Mexicana distribuyó, en 1974, traducciones de la *Biblia* en más de 70 lenguas indígenas. Jean-Pierre Bastian concluye que el protestantismo mexicano lo integran "tres sectores: por un lado el protestantismo 'histórico' formado por las iglesias de origen misionero que penetraron a partir de la segunda mitad del siglo XIX; se relacionan todavía con las iglesias madres, las grandes denominaciones norteamericanas. Por otro lado encontramos las misiones de fe, organizadas por cristianos independientes a partir de los años 1920 como sociedades interdenominacionales, utilizando técnicas modernas de evangelización de masas o dirigiéndose a sectores particulares de la población como los indígenas o los estudiantes. Finalmente, el pentecostalismo reagrupa el conjunto de sociedades religiosas que acentúan las manifestaciones 'calientes' de su convivialidad y de su espiritualidad. El conjunto de estos protestantismos representa actualmente tres por ciento de la población total de México. Se dividen en un centenar de sociedades religiosas dominadas en sus tres cuartas partes por los pentecostalismos". Según el mismo autor, el protestantismo dejó de ser un fenómeno típico de los estados del norte, pues su influencia se ha desplazado "hacia el sur rural", como lo prueba el porcentaje de protestantes, respecto de la población total, en estados como Chiapas (9), Quintana Roo (9.01), Yucatán (5.32), Tabasco (12.59) y Campeche (10). El Distrito Federal y el Estado de México, presumiblemente en las zonas proletarias del área metropolitana del Valle de México, reúnen a la cuarta parte de los protestantes del país (9.01 y 15 por ciento, respectivamente). En las áreas rurales, sobre todo en las de población indígena, el culto protestante se mezcla frecuentemente con los ritos tradicionales, aun con los prehispánicos. El 2 de febrero de 1990, un grupo de evangélicos fue linchado en las cercanías del Ajusco, en el DF. Un mes más tarde, numerosas iglesias y denominaciones protestantes publicaron una "Declaración protestante al pueblo de México", en la que denunciaban "el clima de intolerancia religiosa que se está dando en nuestra sociedad". En ese año, según datos censales, el número de mexicanos evangélicos o protestantes eran 3,447,507. En 1999, según Benjamín Rivera, eran 15 millones los evangélicos de México, país donde de acuerdo con Adoniram Gaxiola, pastor y director de los Ministerios Apostólicos, existen 2,500 asociaciones evangélicas, las que tienen una tasa de crecimiento de 10 por ciento anual. De acuerdo con la Conferencia Episcopal Latinoamericana hay en México 400 denominaciones evangélicas (1999).

PROTOMEDICATO ♦ Tribunal colegiado creado en la ciudad de México en 1628, con las siguientes funciones: dirigir la enseñanza médica, impartir justicia en todos las ramas de la medicina, administrar los fondos provenientes de las licencias y multas, regular la actividad médica, quirúrgica y farmacéutica, y difundir el uso de las plantas medicinales. En la práctica perseguía curanderos, exigía a cirujanos y médicos la presentación de títulos, examinaba a los boticarios, supervisaba boticas y asesoraba en litigios judiciales. Tuvo como antecedentes la Fiscalía de Médicos y Cirujanos, instituida por Hernán Cortés, quien designó a Diego de Pedraza para ocuparla. En 1571 llegó a Veracruz Francisco Hernández, con el nombramiento de "Protomédico de Nueva España". En 1788 el Protomedicato absorbió otro tipo de funciones, como el cuidado del jardín botánico del Palacio Virreinal, pero diez años más tarde, en 1798, una cédula del rey de España redujo sus atribuciones. Al año siguiente fue suprimido; para sustituirlo se creó una Junta General de Médicos o Físicos de Cámara que a su vez desapareció en 1801. El protomedicato se restableció y funcionó con restricciones hasta 1831, cuando desapareció definitivamente. La responsabilidad sobre los profesionales del ramo quedó a cargo de una Facultad Médica del Distrito Fe-

Aarón Redekop, líder menonita en el territorio nacional

Enrique Provencio

deral, hasta 1841, y luego del Consejo de Salubridad.

Provencio, Enrique ◆ n. en Ciudad Obregón, Sonora (1956). Licenciado en economía por la Universidad de Sonora. Maestro en economía por la UNAM. Ha sido investigador de El Colegio de México, profesor e investigador de la UNAM, consultor externo en la Comisión Económica para América Latina y el Caribe y del Instituto Interamericano de Cooperación para la Agricultura, subdirector de Planeación del gobierno de Sonora, director general de Investigación y Desarrollo Tecnológico del Instituto Nacional de Ecología (1994), subsecretario de Planeación de la Secretaría del Medio Ambiente, Recursos Naturales y Pesca (1995-97), y presidente del Instituto Nacional de Ecología (1997-).

Provincias Internas ◆ Territorios delimitados en 1776 para dar gobierno y protección efectivos a las regiones norteñas de la Nueva España, amenazadas por el expansionismo de Rusia, Inglaterra y Francia, y por la resistencia de los indios. La Comandancia General de las Provincias Internas se creó ese mismo año. El comandante general de las provincias tenía facultades políticas y militares semejantes a las de un virrey sobre los territorios de la Nueva Vizcaya, Coahuila, Texas, Chihuahua y parte de Sonora. La Comandancia General de las Provincias Internas tuvo cinco diferentes estructuras: la primera, desde su creación, fue la de una comandancia única e independiente del virrey; la segunda, en 1785, como una comandancia triple, dependiente del virrey; la tercera, desde 1787, la de una comandancia doble, dependiente del virrey; la cuarta, en 1792, volvió a ser una comandancia única e independiente; su última etapa, en 1810, fue la de comandancia dependiente y subdividida en las Provincias Internas de Oriente (Coahuila, Texas, Nuevo León y Nueva Santander) y las de Occidente (Sinaloa, Sonora, California, Nueva Vizcaya y Nuevo México).

Provincias Mayores de Nueva España ◆ Antes de que el territorio nacional quedara dividido políticamente en intendencias, el Reino de la Nueva España estaba formada por las provincias de Tlaxcala, México, Puebla de los Ángeles, Antequera y el reino de Michoacán o provincia de Valladolid, en el reino de México; Xalisco o Nueva Galicia, Zacatecas y Colima, en el reino de Nueva Galicia; Durango o Guadiana y Chihuahua, en la gobernación de Nueva Vizcaya; y Yucatán, Campeche y Tabasco, en la gobernación de Yucatán. La otras provincias mayores eran Nuevo Reino de León, colonia del Nuevo Santander o provincia de Tamaulipas, provincia de los Tejas o Nueva Filipinas, Coahuila o Nueva Extremadura, Sinaloa, Sonora, San José de Nayarit o Nuevo Reino de Toledo, Vieja California, Nueva California y Nuevo México de Santa Fe.

Provincias Menores de Nueva España ◆ Se dio el nombre de provincias menores de Nueva España a una serie de unidades administrativas en una región que, de 1535 a 1787, abarcaba la parte actual del país hasta el istmo de Tehuantepec, hacia el sur, la costa del este y noreste del golfo de México hasta la desembocadura del Pánuco, la costa del Pacífico hasta el puerto de Navidad, al oeste, y San Luis Potosí, al norte. Las provincias se crearon en 1550 (también se les llamaba alcaldías mayores) como unidades dependientes del virrey. Desde su creación hasta 1570, el número de provincias varió pero siempre fue de alrededor de las 40. A fines del siglo XVI el número se acercó a 70 y hacia 1786 eran 116. Las provincias menores desaparecieron al crearse las intendencias.

PRT ◆ ☛ *Partido Revolucionario de los Trabajadores*.

Pruneda, Alfonso ◆ n. y m. en el DF (1879-1957). Médico cirujano titulado en 1902 en la Escuela Nacional de Medicina. Además de dedicarse a la docencia (1903-51), fue jefe de la Sección de Educación Secundaria, Preparatoria y Profesional (1905-10) y jefe de la Sección Universitaria (1910-12) de la Secretaría de Instrucción Pública, director de la Escuela de Altos Estudios de la Universidad Nacional de México (1912-13), rector de la Universidad Popular Mexicana (1913-22), rector de la Universidad Nacional (1924-28), director general de Acción Cívica del Departamento del Distrito Federal (1928-30), jefe del Departamento de Bellas Artes (1931), vocal de la Comisión Técnica Consultiva de la Secretaría de Educación (1932-51) y coordinador de Humanidades de la UNAM (1948-53). En 1923 ingresó a la Academia Nacional de Medicina, de la que fue secretario hasta 1950. *Doctor honoris causa* por la UNAM y la Universidad de Marburgo. Autor de *Higiene de los trabajadores* (1939), *La salud* (1940) y *El jardín de los niños*.

Pruneda, Álvaro ◆ n. y m. en la ciudad de México (1874-1916). Caricaturista y periodista. Estudió un año en la Escuela Nacional de Medicina y otro en la Escuela Nacional de Ingenieros. Realizó colaboraciones escritas y dibujadas, con el pseudónimo de *Pérez Brincos*, para los periódicos antiporfiristas *La Tarántula*, *El Alacrán*, *Tilín Tilín*, *El Diario*, *México Nuevo*, *Onofroff*, *El Hijo del Ahuizote* y *Frégoli*, y en la revista *Fin de Siglo*. Con Vicente E. Escobedo fundó el periódico *Ego*. Creó los billetes llamados infalsificables y en 1916 fue candidato a diputado al Congreso Constituyente. Autor de *Fin de siglo* (1900), con ilustraciones propias.

Pruneda, Margarita ◆ n. en el DF (1948). Cantante. Su nombre completo es Margarita Pruneda y López Negrete. Estudió letras clásicas en la UNAM. Gracias a su triunfo en el Primer Concurso de Canto, de la Sala Chopin, estudió becada en la Academia de Música de Detmold, Alemania. Más tarde estudió en Canadá. Pertenece a la Compañía Nacional de Opera. Se ha presentado en Alemania y Estados Unidos. En 1982, la Unión Mexicana de Cronistas de Teatro y Música la consideró la mejor soprano del año.

Pruneda, Salvador ◆ n. en Veracruz, Ver., y m. en el DF (1895-1985). Periodista y caricaturista. Inició su carrera en 1907, en el periódico *El*

Jacobino, y la continuó en *La Sátira, Política, Gil Blas, Tilín Tilín, Sangre y Arena, Motín, México Nuevo* y *La Madre Patria*, de Veracruz. En 1914 se incorporó a la revolución constitucionalista y obtuvo el grado de mayor. En 1916 colaboraba en *El Constituyente*, y al año siguiente participó en la fundación del diario *Excelsior*, de la ciudad de México, donde utilizó el pseudónimo de *Juan Lanas*. Más tarde escribió para la revista *Caricatos* (1919), y para los diarios *El Heraldo de México* (1920), *Cine Mundial* (1923) y *El Universal Gráfico* (1924). A mediados de los años veinte vivió en Estados Unidos, donde colaboró en los periódicos *The Times, Examiner* y *La Opinión*, y en las revistas *The Director, California Graphic, Sport and Vanitys*. De regreso a México colaboró en *Últimas Noticias*, donde hizo la tira cómica *Don Catarino y su familia* (1936), y *El Nacional*, donde, entre 1929 y 1970, aparecieron sus caricaturas; y en la *Revista Mexicana de Literatura*, suplemento de ese diario. También colaboró en *El Diario del Sureste*, de Mérida, y en el suplemento *México en la Cultura*, del diario *Novedades*. Director de los noticieros cinematográficos *Nacional* (1911), *Aztecart* (1924), *Clasa* (1933) y *Mexicano* (1940-43). En 1930, dirigió el largometraje *Abismos*, también conocido como *Naúfragos de la vida*. Autor de *Estampas* (1920), *Huellas* (1936), *La caricatura como arma política* (1958), *La caricatura* (1973) y *Periódicos y periodistas* (1975). En 1942 recibió un premio nacional de caricaturas, y en 1971 el Tlaticuilo de Oro. Miembro fundador del Sindicato Nacional de Redactores de Prensa (1922), del Club de Periodistas (1927) y de la Asociación de Fotógrafos de Prensa (1942).

PRUNEDA PADILLA, RAMÓN ◆ n. en el DF (1935). Arquitecto titulado en la UNAM (1958), donde fue profesor (1966-67). Ha sido jefe del Departamento de Análisis del Territorio Nacional (1965-71), subdirector de Planeación (1971-72) y coordinador adjunto de la Comisión de Desarrollo Urbano del País (1972-76) de la Secretaría de Obras Públicas; subdirector de Previsión de Programas de la SAHOP (1977), director de Planeación Económica Urbana del Fonatur (1978-82) y coordinador de asesores del subsecretario de Infraestructura (1983-84), director general de Planeación (1985-89) y coordinador de asesores del subsecretario de Infraestructura de la SCT (1989-94). Pertenece a la Sociedad de Arquitectos de México y al Colegio de Arquitectos de México.

PSD ◆ ☛ *Partido Socialdemócrata.*

PSICOLOGÍA ◆ En 1893 fue creada la cátedra de psicología en la Escuela Nacional Preparatoria. Ezequiel A. Chávez fue el encargado de impartirla y en 1904 tradujo los *Elementos de psicología*, de Edward Bradford Tichner, que sería libro de texto durante el siguiente cuarto de siglo. Al mismo Chávez se deben algunas aportaciones a la llamada psicología del mexicano. En 1902, Enrique O. Aragón había publicado *La psicología*. Durante el porfiriato, con base en el positivismo, dentro de esta disciplina se realizaron estudios sobre el crimen, la locura, el alcoholismo y la educación, en tanto que se hacían nuevas aportaciones a la psicología del mexicano. En 1906 se fundó la Sociedad Mexicana de Estudios Psicológicos, que estimuló la aparición de literatura de la especialidad. Como parte de las fiestas del centenario de la independencia, en 1910 se inauguró el Manicomio General de la Castañeda. En 1916, Enrique O. Aragón fundó el Laboratorio de Psicología de la Universidad Nacional de México, donde hacia 1925 trabajó Pablo Boder, un discípulo de Pavlov. Durante la gestión de José Vasconcelos en la Secretaría de Educación se aplicaron en forma masiva pruebas psicológicas a los escolares. En 1924 surgió, dentro del Departamento Escolar de la misma dependencia, una Sección de Psicología impulsada por el educador Lauro Aguirre. Esta sección se dedicó a elaborar y aplicar pruebas psicológicas individuales y colectivas en el nivel primario y lo mismo hace en el siguiente nivel la Dirección de Enseñanza Secundaria mediante la Oficina de Psicognosis, que hoy se llamaría de psicometría. En ese año se impartían tres cursos de psicología en la Escuela de Altos Estudios, que al dividirse dejó la formación psicológica en manos de la Facultad de Graduados y la Escuela Normal Superior. A principios de los años treinta, Samuel Ramos inició la publicación de su "Psicoanálisis del mexicano", como "resultado de una aplicación de las doctrinas de Alfredo Adler", el discípulo y disidente de Sigmund Freud. En 1932 se creó la Sección de Psicología dentro de la carrera de filosofía en la UNAM. El criterio predominante era el establecido por Pierre Janet en su *Psicología*, fuertemente influida por el espiritualismo de Henri Bergson. Janet era conocido por los maestros mexicanos, pues en 1925 había visitado el laboratorio que dirigía Aragón. En 1935 fue creado el Instituto Médico-Pedagógico para Niños Anormales Mentales Educables, que al año siguiente se transformaría en el Instituto Nacional de Psicopedagogía. En 1937 se estableció en la UNAM la carrera de maestro en psicología, de tres años de duración. En 1939 se incorporaron a la Facultad de Filosofía y Letras varios intelectuales del exilio español, quienes ampliaron los campos de estudio e intereses a los estudiantes. Destacó entre los maestros peninsulares Pascual del Roncal. En los años cuarenta, bajo la dirección de Oswaldo Robles, las con-

Salvador Pruneda por sí mismo

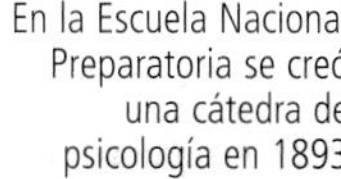

En la Escuela Nacional Preparatoria se creó una cátedra de psicología en 1893

cepciones bergsonianas fueron desplazadas por el neotomismo. En 1943 se fundó la Escuela Normal de Especialización, que tenía como fin la formación de profesores para atender niños ciegos, sordomudos, menores infractores, anormales físicos y mentales. Dos años después, la antigua Sección de Psicología de la Facultad de Filosofía y Letras de la UNAM se transformaría en Departamento bajo el impulso de Fernando Ocaranza. En 1951 se fundó la Sociedad Mexicana de Psicología, afiliada a la Sociedad Interamericana de Psicología. Un año antes había llegado a México Erich Fromm, quien pronto se rodeó de un grupo de seguidores como Raúl González Enríquez, Guillermo Dávila, Alfonso Millán y Ramón de la Fuente, quienes constituyeron en 1955 la Sociedad Mexicana de Psicoanálisis. La heterodoxia frommiana no satisfizo a estudiosos de Sigmund Freud, como Santiago Ramírez y Ramón Parres, quienes en 1952 formaron el Grupo Mexicano de Estudios Psicoanalíticos, que cinco años después se transformó en Asociación Psicoanalítica Mexicana. Ambos núcleos impartían cursos particulares y "restringieron el papel del psicólogo a aplicador de pruebas que les auxiliaran en el diagnóstico" (Valderrama Iturbe y Rivero del Pozo). A mediados de los años cincuenta los frommianos se concentraron en la Facultad de Medicina, en tanto que los freudianos se atrincheraron en el Departamento de Psicología. En 1959 se creó en la UNAM la licenciatura en psicología, con cuatro años de estudios. Cinco años después, en Jalapa, Veracruz, se abrió una escuela de psicología. En la década de los sesenta vinieron a impartir cursos especialistas extranjeros, sobre todo estadounidenses, y el grupo encabezado por Rogelio Díaz Guerrero promovió la psicología experimental, con el apoyo de viajes a Estados Unidos, la traducción de numerosos textos y la realización de congresos. En 1963 Rogelio Díaz Guerrero fundó, como dependencia del Centro de Cómputo de la UNAM, el Centro de Investigaciones en Ciencias del Comportamiento, que diez años después se separó de la Universidad y se convirtió en Instituto Nacional de Ciencias del Comportamiento y de la Actitud Pública. En 1966, como consecuencia de una prolongada huelga, se inició un proceso de cambio en los planes y programas de estudio de la UNAM, especialmente en las carreras del ala de humanidades, lo que en psicología llevó a implantar un currículum de cinco años de estudio. En 1967 existían 10 escuelas de psicología en el país, las que en total tenían 1,856 alumnos. A fines de la misma década ganaron espacio las concepciones conductistas de B. F. Skinner. En 1973, el Colegio de Psicología se separó de la Facultad de Filosofía y Letras para convertirse en Facultad de Psicología de la UNAM, bajo la dirección de Luis Lara Tapia. En 1974 ya eran 25 las escuelas de psicología y en 1977 su número se elevó a 40. En 1981 la licenciatura en psicología se impartía en 55 planteles y para 1983 se estimaba que eran 70 las escuelas de la especialidad, con unos 40,000 matriculados. (*Cfr.*: Rogelio Díaz Guerrero. "Momentos culminantes en la historia de la psicología en México", en *Enseñanza e Investigación en Psicología*, julio-diciembre de 1980; y Pablo Valderrama Iturbe y José Fermín Rivero del Pozo "El papel de las consideraciones históricas en la planificación de la enseñanza de la psicología" en *Foro Universitario*, diciembre de 1984).

PSM ◆ ☛ *Partido Socialista Mexicano.*

PSO ◆ ☛ *Partido Socialista Obrero.*

PSR ◆ ☛ *Partido Socialista Revolucionario.*

PST ◆ ☛ *Partido Socialista de los Trabajadores.*

PSSE ◆ ☛ *Partido Socialista del Sureste.*

PSUM ◆ ☛ *Partido Socialista Unificado de México.*

PSY ◆ ☛ *Partido Socialista de Yucatán.*

PUÁCUARO ◆ Lienzo michoacano del siglo XVI, pintado sobre cartoncillo de 84 por 75 cm. Contiene un dibujo del lago de Pátzcuaro, representaciones de templos indígenas y varias inscripciones en purépecha. Una copia, de 1892, se encuentra en la biblioteca del INAH.

PÚAS, EL ◆ ☛ *Olivares Rubén.*

PUCHE ÁLVAREZ, JOSÉ ◆ n. en España y m. en el DF (1895-1979). Médico. Estudió la licenciatura en la Universidad de Barcelona (1922) y el doctorado en la Universidad Central de Madrid (1929). Se especializó en Italia, Bélgica, Holanda y Suecia. Fue gobernador de Palencia (1931), rector de la Universidad de Valencia (1936-38), director del Instituto Nacional de Higiene de la Alimentación, consejero de Instrucción Pública (1937-39) y director de Sanidad de Guerra (1938-39). Exiliado en México desde 1939, se encargó del Comité Técnico de Ayuda a los republicanos españoles y fue director de Industrias Técnico Farmacéuticas, presidente del Ateneo Español de México (1949-), profesor de fisiología del IPN (1934-46) y de la UNAM (1945-65) e investigador de la UNAM (1967-79). Fundador y colaborador de la revista *Ciencia* y colaborador de los *Anales del Ateneo Ramón y Cajal*, *España Peregrina*, *Cuadernos Americanos*, *Boletín de la Unión de Intelectuales Españoles* y *Las Españas*. Autor de *Juan Luis Vives: comentarios acerca de un sabio corresponsal del siglo XVI* (1941) y numerosos artículos sobre su especialidad. Fue presidente de la Comisión Editorial de la Sociedad Mexicana de Ciencias Fisiológicas. Recibió el premio de la Academia de Ciencias Médicas de Cataluña por sus trabajos sobre electrocardiografía experimental y sobre los mecanismos cardiovasculares.

PUCHE PLANÁS, JOSÉ ◆ n. en Barcelona, España (1921). Ingeniero Químico por la UNAM. Llegó a México en 1939. Trabajó como jefe de producción en la fábrica de cemento y asbesto Techo Eureka. Posteriormente ocupo el mismo puesto en Aceros Esmaltados Acros (1953-1970). Formó parte de las Juventudes Socialistas Unificadas de España. Fundador y vicepresidente del Ateneo Español de México. Fue parte de la dirección de la revista *Las Españas.*

Melquiades Morales, gobernador constitucional del estado de Puebla

PUEBLA ◆ Estado de la República Mexicana situado en la porción centro-oriental del país, en la región sureste de la Altiplanicie Mexicana, donde queda gran parte de su territorio; una porción septentrional, sin embargo, alcanza la llanura costera del golfo de México. Limita al este y al norte con Veracruz, al sur con Oaxaca y Guerrero; y al oeste con Hidalgo, Tlaxcala, Morelos y el Estado de México. Superficie: 33,902 km² (equivalentes a 1.7 por ciento del total de la superficie del país), divididos en 217 municipios. El nombre de la capital del estado es Heroica Puebla de Zaragoza. Los principales sistemas montañosos de la entidad son: en el norte, la sierra norte de Puebla; en el oriente, las sierras de Quimixclán, Negra, de Zongolica y de Axuxco; en el occidente, la sierra Nevada; y en el sur, las formaciones de la Mixteca baja. Los ríos más importates son el Pantepec, el Vinazco, el Nautla, el San Marcos, el Necaxa y el Xoloco, en la vertiente del golfo de México; el Atoyac y el Zahuapan, en la vertiente del océano Pacífico; y el Tlapelmala, el Valiente, el Quetzolapa, el Capulines y el Atzala, en la vertiente interna. En la parte sur del estado se encuentran los manantiales minerales del valle de

Foto: Michael Calderwood

Tehuacán, Puebla

Tehuacán. Habitantes: 4,792.156 (1997; 5.1 por ciento de la población del país en 1995). Forman la población económicamente activa 56.3 por ciento de los mayores de 12 años. Contribuye con 3.26 por ciento al producto interno bruto total nacional (1996). Su tasa de alfabetismo es de 83.6 por ciento entre los mayores de 15 años (con un promedio de 6.43 grados escolares cursados) y 13.83 por ciento carecen de instrucción alguna. En 1995 hablaban alguna lengua indígena 527,559 personas mayores de cinco años (náhuatl 399,324, totonaco 86,392 y popoloca 13,252), de las cuales 69,956 no sabían español. *Historia:* los restos arqueológicos más antiguos fueron encontrados cerca de Valsequillo y datan de 22,000 años a.n.e. En los alrededores del valle de Tehuacán se han encontrado rastros que hacen suponer la presencia de una cultura que comenzó a desarrollarse 10,000 años a.n.e. y que hacia el año 6,000 a.n.e. inició la práctica de la agricultura. La influencia olmeca se dejó sentir en el actual territorio poblano a partir del año 1,000 a.n.e. Al inicio de nuestra era, la cultura teotihuacana estaba asentada en diversas regiones poblanas, principalmente en Cholula. En el norte, mientras tanto, había comunidades de lengua totonaca. Poco después del despoblamiento de Teotihuacán, los pipiles, hablantes de una forma arcaica de náhuatl, se instalaron en Cholula, pero en el siglo IX fueron desalojados por diversos grupos indígenas, sobre todo popolocas y mixtecos, llamados también olmecas-xicalancas u olmecas tardíos, quienes luego de tomar la ciudad, iniciaron su expansión hacia casi todo el actual territorio del estado. A mediados del siglo XII, un grupo exiliado de Tula, los toltecas-chichimecas, se instaló en la parte central del valle de Puebla y ocupó Cholula en 1168. En los últimos años del siglo, los olmecas-xicalancas intentaron reconquistar sus territorios centrales; los toltecas-chichimecas, que comenzaron a llamarse cholultecas por entonces, se aliaron con otros grupos chichimecas y nahuas y los derrotaron. Estos grupos aliados se establecieron dentro de los dominios cholultecas y formaron varios señoríos independientes, como Izúcar y Huejotzingo, que durante el siglo XIII combatieron contra los cholultecas. A partir de la segunda mitad del siglo XV, los mexicas se

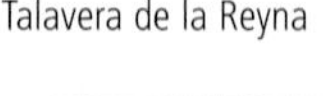

Talavera de la Reyna

Foto: Boris de Swan

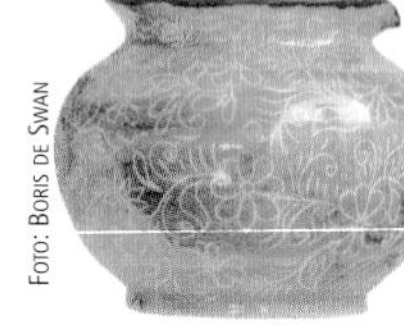

Foto: Michael Calderwood

Laguna Alchichica, Puebla

Foto: Michael Calderwood

Africam Safari, en Valsequillo, Puebla

establecieron en la zona y lograron conquistar todo el actual territorio poblano. Sólo dos de los antiguos señoríos, Cholula y Huejotzingo, consiguieron conservar su independencia, y con ellos, los mexicas establecieron una relación basada en las rituales guerras floridas (☛). Una parte del sur del estado, perteneciente al señorío de Toetitlán, también conservó su independencia. En octubre de 1519, camino de México-Tenochtitlán, las fuerzas de Hernán Cortés tomaron Huejotzingo y más tarde Cholula, donde asesinaron a gran parte de la población supuestamente para evitar una emboscada. Durante la segunda mitad de 1520, los españoles conquistaron Tepeaca, Tecamachalco, Tehuacán, Huaquechula, Izúcar, Xalacingo e Ixtacamaxtitlan. A fines de 1521, una vez derrotado el imperio azteca, los europeos reiniciaron la guerra en territorio poblano, y cayeron Zacatlán, Xuxupango y Chila, entre otros poblados. En 1524 se inició el reparto masivo de encomiendas entre los conquistadores. El 16 de abril de 1531, para establecer un punto medio entre la ciudad de México y el puerto de Veracruz, la segunda Audiencia de México fundó una ciudad que al año siguiente fue bautizada como Ciudad de los Ángeles, localidad a la que en 1539 se trasladó el obispado de Tlaxcala (llamado de Puebla desde 1640). En 1540 comenzó a funcionar en la entidad el consejo de la Mesta (☛), que controlaba la recién iniciada actividad ganadera. A mediados de siglo, en el suroeste se inició el cultivo de la caña de azucar; en el sureste, sobre todo alrededor de Tepeji, de seda; y en los alrededores de Atlixco, en la parte central del estado, se cultivaron vid y olivo. De acuerdo con la primera división política, el territorio poblano formó parte

Foto: Michael Calderwood

Catedral de Puebla

Foto: Michael Calderwood

Talavera de Puebla

Figurillas en ónix, de Puebla

Foto: Fondo editorial Grupo Azabache

FOTO: MICHAEL CALDERWOOD

Cholula, Puebla

FOTO: CARLOS HAHN

Ángel, símbolo de la ciudad de Puebla

de la provincia mayor de Puebla de los Ángeles, integrante del reino de México, cuyo territorio formaba una franja de tierra que se extendía desde las costas del golfo de México hasta las del océano Pacífico, incluyendo la porción suroriental de la huasteca y la costa chica (☛). Desde 1524, franciscanos se instalaron en Puebla, Huejotzingo y Cholula. Ese mismo año, los dominicos comenzaron la construcción de sus primeros conventos en Tepeji, Chila e Izúcar. Los agustinos, por su parte, ocuparon la sierra norte de Puebla, y desde 1542 se establecieron en Huauchinago. El primer convento de la Compañía de Jesús en territorio poblano fue el Colegio del Espíritu Santo, que se comenzó a construir en 1574 en la ciudad de Puebla. A principios del siglo XVII, 35 de las fabricas textileras más grandes de la Nueva España se encontraban en los alrededores de la ciudad de Puebla. La primera imprenta de Puebla se instaló en 1640. En ese año llegó como visitador general de Nueva España y obispo de Puebla Juan de Palafox y Mendoza (☛), preconizado dos años antes, quien entró en conflicto con las órdenes mendicantes en su afán de ocupar las parroquias con miembros del clero diocesano. Palafox fue virrey en 1642 y terminó la edificación de la catedral poblana en 1649. Veinte años más tarde, en 1670, se le confirió a Tehuacán la categoría de ciudad y se le dio el nombre de Ciudad de Indios de Nuestra Señora de la Concepción y Cueva. Para entonces, las poblaciones que habían sido erigidas ciudades eran Huejotzingo (1533), Cholula (1540) y Tepeaca (1559). La explotación y las enfermedades hicieron que la población indígena disminuyera drásticamente: Cholula, por ejemplo, en 1644 tenía cerca de 12,000 habitantes y en Huejotzingo, hacia 1669, vivían cerca de 9,000 personas. En 1706, las alcaldías de Atlixco, Tepeaca y Huauchinango fueron cedidas a José Sarmiento de Valladares, que se convirtió en marqués de Atlixco. En 1786, producto de las reformas de los nuevos reyes borbones, se creó la intendencia de Puebla, bajo cuya jurisdicción quedaron Cuautla y Tlaxcala, separadas nuevamente en 1793, y Tuxpan, que fue incorporada al estado de Veracruz en 1853. Las primeras acciones de la guerra de Independencia en el territorio poblano ocurrieron al este de Puebla, en el valle de Chalchico-

Mole poblano

Arco del triunfo en Puebla

mula, en abril de 1811. En mayo de ese año, en la sierra norte de Puebla, se levantó en armas José Francisco Osorno, quien a fines de agosto tomó Zacatlán y, con la ayuda de Mariano Aldama, extendió la sublevación a Huauchinango, Tecamachalco y Acatzingo. En diciembre, las fuerzas de José María Morelos penetraron en la parte suroccidental de la intendencia; tomaron Chiautla e Izúcar, donde se incorporó a la revolución el sacerdote Mariano Matamoros, y a principios de 1812 tomaron Atlixco. En febrero de 1812, los realistas al mando de Ciriaco del Llano intentaron tomar Atlixco, pero fueron rechazados. En mayo, José María Sánchez de la Vega conquistó Tehuacán. Mientras tanto, Del Llano avanzó hacia el norte, tomó Tepeaca y Tecamachalco, y obligó a Morelos a retirarse al sureste, quien se instaló en Tehuacán en agosto. Durante 1813, los principales grupos guerrilleros insurgentes fueron dirigidos por Vicente Guerrero, Miguel Bravo, Manuel Mier y Terán y Mariano Matamoros en el sur, y José Francisco Osorno en el norte. Al año siguiente, con el nombramiento de intendente de Puebla que había recibido del Congreso insurgente, Ignacio López Rayón comenzó a operar en la zona y desde mediados de 1814 se unió a las tropas de Osorno. A fines de 1815, el Congreso insurgente se instaló en Tehuacán, donde fue disuelto por una maniobra de Mier y Terán. Luego de la muerte de Morelos, la insurgencia se concentró en el sur de la intendencia (☛ *Guerrero*); en el sureste, encabezada por Mier Terán hasta enero de 1817; y en la sierra norte de Puebla, donde combatieron las tropas de Osorno hasta febrero de ese año. En 1820 apareció el primer periódico de la región, *La Abeja Poblana*. En abril del año siguiente, Tepeaca fue tomada por las tropas de José Joaquín de Herrera, uno de los militares realistas convertidos en insurgentes gracias al Plan de Iguala. Nicolás Bravo, por su parte, ocupó Izúcar y Huejotzingo. El 28 de julio de 1821, luego de un sitio a la que fue sometida por las tropas combinadas de Bravo, Mier y Terán, Herrera y Osorno, Del Llano entregó la ciudad de Puebla. A principios de agosto, Agustín de Iturbide entró en Puebla y proclamó la independencia. Dos años más tarde, poco después de la caída del gobierno imperial, en los alrededores de Tehuacán comenzó a operar el antiguo insurgente Vicente Gómez, quien al mando de un grupo llamado La Santa Liga apoyaba al mismo tiempo el regreso de Iturbide al poder y la expulsión de los españoles de México. En diciembre de 1823, un grupo de militares creó el Estado Libre de la Puebla de los Ángeles, al frente del que quedaron José María Calderón, Manuel Posada Garduño, José Antonio Echavarri y José María Morón. El gobierno nacional se opuso al intento federalista y envió a reprimir el levantamiento a Manuel Gómez Pedraza y Vicente Guerrero, quienes sitiaron Puebla y derrotaron a los soberanistas en los primeros días de 1824. Sin embargo, el Acta Constitutiva de la Federación, proclamada a fines de enero de ese año, contemplaba la erección del estado de Puebla de los Ángeles. El primer gobernador constitucional fue José María Tomás Calderón (1825-28). En 1825, el gobierno estatal reformó el Real Colegio Carolino del Espíritu Santo, San Jerónimo y San Ignacio (fundado en 1819), y lo convirtió en

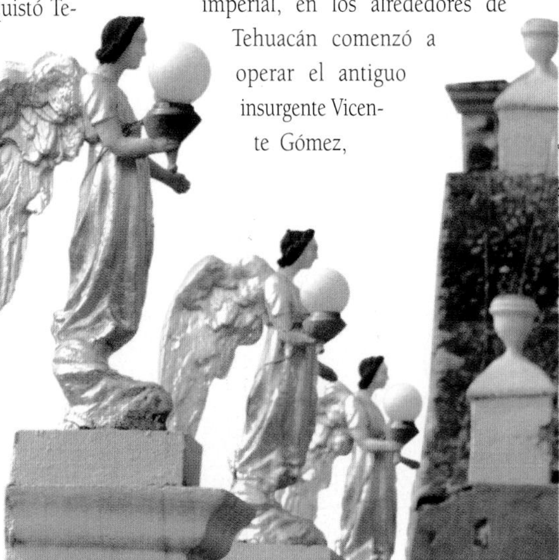

FOTO: MICHAEL CALDERWOOD

Detalle arquitectónico de Puebla de los Ángeles

FOTO: MICHAEL CALDERWOOD

Sierra de Tenzo, Puebla

Foto: Fondo Editorial Grupo Azabache

Laguna de Epatlán, en Puebla

Talavera de la ciudad de Puebla

Colegio del Estado. En diciembre de 1828, luego de la revolución de la Acordada (☛), dos de los principales jefes escoceses, Melchor Múzquiz y Vicente Filisola, desconocieron al gobierno de Victoria, organizaron tropas en Izúcar y Ometepec, y crearon una junta gubernativa encabezada por el gobernador Antonio de Haro y Tamariz y el obispo Antonio Pérez Martínez, pero a fines de diciembre las tropas gubernamentales mandadas por José Joaquín de Herrera recuperaron la ciudad. En diciembre de 1829, unos días después de la proclamación del Plan de Jalapa, las tropas del vicepresidente Anastasio Bustamante entraron en Puebla, recibieron el apoyo de los grupos escoceses, mayoritarios en la ciudad, y de ahí se dirigieron a la ciudad de México. En 1831 se instaló en las cercanías de la capital estatal la primera fábrica textil industrial. A fines de septiembre de 1832, los rebeldes liberales de Veracruz al mando de Antonio López de Santa Anna, tomaron la capital de Puebla, y en diciembre, luego de la derrota de las fuerzas gubernamentales en Cholula, Bustamante y Santa Anna se reunieron en la hacienda de Zavaleta, cerca de la capital estatal, y redactaron unos convenios por los que Manuel Gómez Pedraza se convirtió en presidente de la República. A principios de 1833 asumió la gubernatura Patricio Furlong, quien intentó aplicar en Puebla algunas de las reformas establecidas por el gobierno de Valentín Gómez Farías, pero se enfrentó con la oposición de la jerarquía eclesiástica. En mayo de 1834, la guarnición de la capital del estado se sublevó en contra del federalismo, pero fue rápidamente sometida. El presidente Santa Anna envió a Luis Quintanar a apoyar a los derrotados y en julio, luego de un sitio de dos meses, las tropas del gobierno tomaron la ciudad. Al instaurarse el régimen centralista, a fines de 1835, Puebla se convirtió en Departamento. En abril de 1839, en el curso de una sublevación antisantanista, José Urrea y José Antonio Mejía intentaron tomar la capital del estado. Tres años después, en 1842, Santa Anna proclamó el Plan de Huejotzingo, con el propósito de disolver el Congreso erigido en Constituyente, que intentaba realizar algunas reformas. En diciembre de 1844, las tropas de la capital del estado se sublevaron en favor del pronunciamiento de Mariano Paredes y Arrillaga (☛); Santa Anna marchó sobre la ciudad y la atacó en enero del año siguiente, pero se vio obligado a retirarse debido al ataque del propio Paredes. En enero de 1846, Manuel Arteaga y Domingo Ibarra intentaron reestablecer la república federal, pero fueron derrotados por el gobierno. Ese mismo año, el gobierno poblano formó un batallón especial, llamado "libre de Puebla", que participó en la guerra contra Estados Unidos. En mayo de 1847, dos meses después de la batalla de Cerro Gordo, Santa Anna, que estaba instalado en Puebla, ordenó el avance de sus tropas hacia Amozoc, supuestamente para impedir la caída de la ciudad. Sin embargo, sólo sostuvo una escaruza con las tropas estadounidenses y se retiró hacia la ciudad de México. Al día siguiente, el 15 de mayo, los invasores entraron en la capital del estado. Poco después comenzó a operar la guerrilla de Celedonio Domeco de Jarauta (☛), quien combatió a los invasores y a los grupos de contraguerrilla organizados con el beneplácito de la jerarquía católica. Luego de la caída de Puebla, el gobierno local se trasladó a Zacatlán, donde permaneció hasta el fin de la contienda. Con la erección del estado de Guerrero, en octubre de 1849, la región de la costa chica quedó fuera de la jurisdicción del estado. Cuatro años después, en diciembre de 1853, el Congreso autorizó la separación de los municipios de Tuxpan y Chichontepec, que se incorporaron al estado de Veracruz. A fines de 1854, una parte de la guarnición de la capital del estado se levantó en armas contra el gobierno de Santa Anna, pero fue derrotada a principios de 1855. El 19 de diciembre de ese año, aprovechando un levantamiento campesino que había comenzado poco antes, un grupo de sacerdotes y militares al mando de Luis

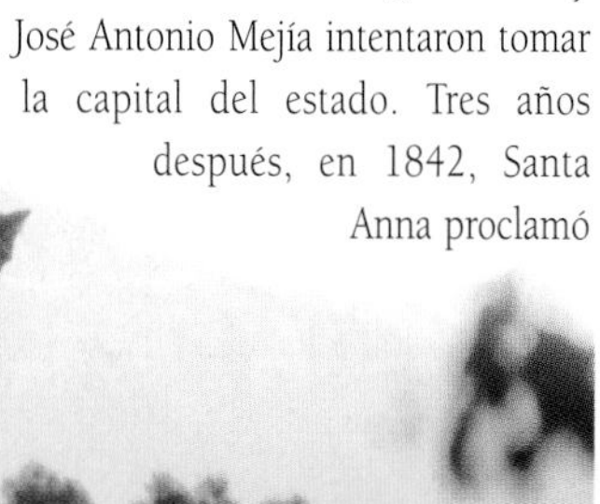

Foto: Fondo Editorial Grupo Azabache

Estatua ecuestre del general Ignacio Zaragoza en Puebla

G. Osollo, Juan de Olloqui y Francisco Ortega se levantó en armas en Zacapoaxtla, con la idea de derrocar al recién iniciado gobierno de Ignacio Comonfort y de volver a aplicar las Bases Constitucionales de 1843. Poco después, la plana mayor del santanismo se incorporó al movimiento: Antonio de Haro y Tamariz, que fue nombrado comandante en jefe; Severo del Castillo, Mariano Salas, Leonardo Márquez, Manuel Andrade, Joaquín Orihuela y Miguel Miramón entre otros. Los rebeldes se dirigieron hacia el sur y en enero de 1856 tomaron Puebla, donde recibieron apoyo material del obispo Pelagio Antonio de Labastida. El presidente Comonfort, por su parte, tomó Texmelucan, Ocotlán y, a fines de enero, la capital del estado. Apenas ocupada la ciudad, el gobierno desterró a Labastida, pero eso no impidió la acción de los conservadores, quienes, en octubre, ahora al mando de Orihuela y Miramón, volvieron a levantarse en armas y tomaron Puebla por segunda vez, aunque también por segunda vez fueron derrotados. Poco después de la promulgación de la nueva constitución, Marcelino Cobos se levantó en armas; tomó Izúcar y Atlixco, sitió Puebla y luego se retiró hacia Nopalucan, San Juan de los Llanos y Acatlán. En diciembre, Miguel Echegaray se adhirió al Plan de Tacubaya. A mediados de 1858, con el apoyo del clero católico, los conservadores había conquistado Puebla, Tehuacán, Atlixco, Izúcar y Huejotzingo. En el norte, mientras tanto, el gobernador liberal, Miguel Cástulo Alatriste, consiguió el apoyo del cacique norteño Juan N. Méndez, y a mediados del año tomó Zacatlán; avanzó hacia el sur y ocupó Acatlán, Huejotzingo y Cholula y en diciembre intentó apoderarse de Puebla, pero fue derrotado. Durante 1859 y 1860, los liberales se consolidaron en la sierra de Puebla, pero no pudieron apoderarse del sur del estado, y sólo lo consiguieron gracias al triunfo de Jesús González Ortega en Calpulalpan, en diciembre de 1860. A pesar de la derrota, los conservadores formaron varios grupos guerrilleros que durante 1861 operaron cerca de Izúcar, Tepeaca y Nopalucan, y que a mediados de año tomaron Tepeji y Acatlán, e Izúcar a principios de 1862. En marzo de ese año, una parte de las fuerzas invasoras francesas se instaló en Tehuacán, mientras el gobierno del presidente Benito Juárez negociaba con los representantes de la Triple Alianza. A fines de abril, procedente de Córdoba, el grueso del ejército francés comandado por el conde de Lorencez penetró en el estado, venció a los republicanos en Acultzingo y se dirigió hacia la ciudad de Puebla. Simultáneamente, una fuerza conservadora al mando de Félix Zuloaga y Leonardo Márquez tomó Atlixco, pero los republicanos de Tomás O'Horan lo recuperaron el 4 de mayo de 1862. Al día siguiente, los franceses intentaron tomar la capital del estado, pero fueron derrotados por las tropas del Ejército de Oriente dirigidas por Ignacio Zaragoza. Un año más tarde, ahora al mando de Ellie Federic Forey, los franceses marcharon sobre Puebla y en marzo le pusieron sitio. Dos meses después, en mayo, las fuerzas de Jesús González Ortega capitularon y entregaron la ciudad. Desde entonces, en el norte del estado comenzó a operar una fuerza guerrillera al mando de Méndez y Juan Francisco Lucas, que durante los tres años siguientes mantuvo el control de Zacapoaxtla y Teziutlán, pese al ataque de las tropas austriacas encargadas de someterla. Mientras tanto, el gobierno de Maximiliano de Habsburgo dispuso la desaparición del estado de Puebla; la

Foto: Fondo Editorial Grupo Azabache

Mixteca Baja, en Puebla

Foto: Fondo Editorial Grupo Azabache

Carnaval de Huejotzingo, Puebla

Foto: Fondo Editorial Grupo Azabache

Mural de la Batalla de Puebla

Foto: Fondo Editorial Grupo Azabache

Templo de San Francisco Acatepec, en Puebla

sierra norte de Puebla pasó a formar parte del Departamento de Tulancingo, la porción central del estado se convirtió en parte del Departamento de Tlaxcala, y la porción sur quedó bajo la jurisdicción del Departamento de Puebla. A fines de 1866, las tropas republicanas penetraron en el estado por el sur y conquistaron Izúcar y Acatlán, y en abril del año siguiente, luego de un mes de combates, los generales imperialistas Manuel Tevera y Hermenegildo Carrillo entregaron Puebla a Porfirio Díaz. Poco después del triunfo de la República, Méndez fue designado gobernador del estado, pero se le destituyó en septiembre de 1867 debido a su oposición al proyecto de reformas al poder legislativo (☛) impulsado por el presidente Juárez. Seis meses después, en marzo de 1868, con el apoyo de Díaz y de Miguel Negrete, Méndez se levantó en armas en Zacatlán. En febrero del año siguiente, por su parte, Negrete se sublevó en Puebla; marchó hacia Cholula y más tarde a Tepeji, donde fue derrotado por las tropas gubernamentales al mando de Ignacio Alatorre. En noviembre, sin embargo, un mes después de la inauguración del primer tramo del ferrocarril México-Puebla, Negrete consiguió que Lucas se sublevara en Zacapoaxtla; el gobierno envió a Rafael Cravioto y a Alatorre a combatir a los rebeldes y los vencieron a principios de 1870. En noviembre de 1871, poco después de la proclamación del Plan de la Noria, los porfiristas tomaron Atlixco, pero tuvieron que retirarse a Oaxaca. A principios de diciembre, mientras en el norte del estado se sublevaban Méndez y Lucas, las tropas de Porfirio Díaz tomaron Izúcar y luego de un rodeo por México y Tlaxcala, en los últimos días del año alcanzaron la sierra norte de Puebla y poco después volvieron a Oaxaca. Finalmente, a principios de 1872, las tropas de Méndez fueron derrotadas. Al año siguiente se puso en servicio la línea ferroviaria entre Puebla y Veracruz. En las primeros días de 1876, cuando Díaz volvió a insurreccionarse, Méndez se adhirió al Plan de Tuxtepec y ocupó todo el norte del estado. En Tecamachalco, por su parte, José María Coutolenc se levantó en armas, se unió a los rebeldes que marchaban hacia Puebla y con ellos fue derrotado en Epatlán, en enero de 1876; sin embargo, en noviembre de ese año, unos días después de su victoria en Teocac, las tropas de Díaz ocuparon la capital del estado. En 1879, encabezados por Alberto Santa Fe, los indios de San Martín Texmelucan se sublevaron contra el gobierno, pero fueron reprimidos violentamente por las fuerzas de José Ignacio Pavón, quien durante los 15 años anteriores se había encargado de reprimir a los campesinos poblanos. Al año siguiente, impulsados por el gobierno del presidente Díaz, comenzaron a llegar los primeros inmigrantes italianos al estado, que se establecieron sobre todo en los alrededores de Chipilo. También en 1880, en la capital del estado apareció la primera traducción al náhuatl de la Constitución de 1857. Durante los últimos 20 años del siglo, se inició el cultivo de café en la sierra norte de Puebla, y se industrializó la producción de azúcar en la parte meridional del estado, sobre todo cerca de Tehuacán, Izúcar, Chietla y Acatlán. Al mismo tiempo, en la zona de Puebla-Tlaxcala se instalaron numerosas fábricas textiles, que de 21 que había en 1877, pasaron a 40 en 1906. En 1906 se inauguró la presa de Necaxa. Paralelamente a la industrialización, los grupos metodistas comenzaron a hacer proselitismo entre la población, y participaron activamente

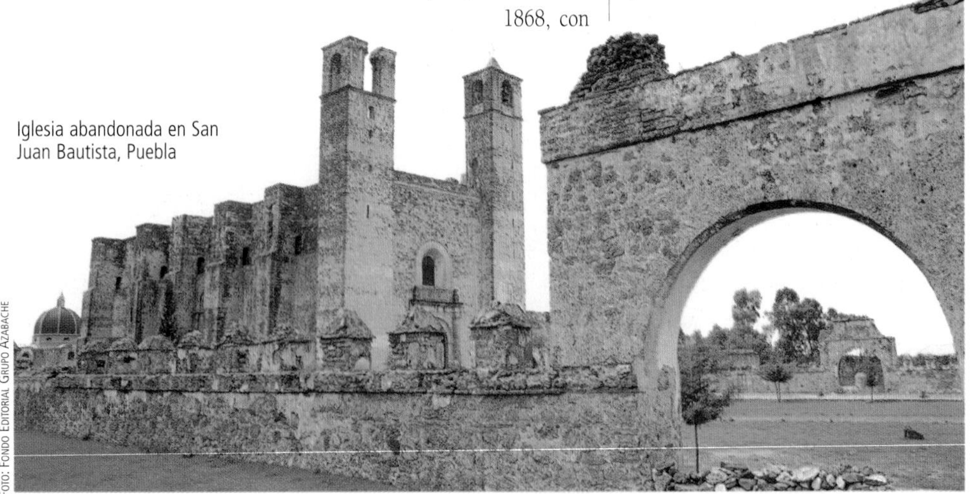

Foto: Fondo Editorial Grupo Azabache

Iglesia abandonada en San Juan Bautista, Puebla

FOTO: FONDO EDITORIAL GRUPO AZABACHE

Escena del Juicio Final tallada en cantera en una capilla en Calpan, Puebla

durante los movimientos huelguísticos que el Partido Liberal Mexicano organizó en los primeros años del siglo XX. En julio de 1909, Aquiles Serdán fundó el club antirreeleccionista Luz y Progreso, que encabezó la campaña presidencial de Francisco I. Madero al año siguiente. En noviembre de 1910, dos días antes del proyectado inicio de la rebelión antiporfirista, la familia Serdán fue sorprendida y asesinada por el ejército. Esta acción no impidió, naturalmente, la generalización del levantamiento maderista, y unos días más tarde se levantó en armas Juan Cuamatzi, quien combatió hasta principios del año siguiente, cuando fue fusilado. A fines de febrero de 1911 renunció el gobernador Muncio P. Martínez, que gobernaba el estado desde 1892. Durante los primeros meses de 1911 aparecieron varios grupos guerrilleros en el centro y norte del estado, y en abril, mientras los federales eran derrotados en Tecamachalco, las tropas de Emiliano Zapata penetraron en el territorio poblano al suroeste de Izúcar; tomaron Chiautla, Acatlán e Izúcar y volvieron a Morelos. En mayo de ese año, Metepec, Cholula y Tehuacán cayeron en manos de los maderistas. Dos meses después de la renuncia del presidente Díaz, uno de los principales jefes del ejército federal en Puebla, Aurelio Blanquet, organizó un motín en la capital del estado, que fue disuelto por las tropas revolucionarias. En noviembre de ese año, luego de romper con Madero, Zapata se retiró a la población de Ayoxustla, cerca de los límites con Morelos, y ahí, con la ayuda de Otilio Montaño, redactó y proclamó el Plan de Ayala (☛). En febrero del año siguiente, los zapatistas tomaron Chietla y Acatlán y se hicieron del control del sur del estado. En septiembre de 1913, las tropas constitucionalistas sitiaron a un importante contingente del ejército federal en Teziutlán y en junio de 1914 la población cayó en sus manos. En agosto de 1914, poco después del triunfo de las tropas de Venustiano Carranza, los huertistas Juan Andrew Almazán, Benjamín Argumedo e Higinio Aguilar entre otros se negaron a licenciar sus tropas y combatieron al gobierno carrancista hasta principios de 1916. Por su parte, a fines de 1914 las tropas del Ejército Libertador del Sur avanzaron hacia el norte y tomaron Puebla, pero en enero de 1915 fueron desalojados por Álvaro Obregón. A partir de entonces la fuerza del zapatismo en la entidad disminuyó sensiblemente, pese a lo cual, todavía hasta 1919 continuaron activos los ejércitos campesinos; en diciembre de 1915 tomaron Atlixco, en mayo de 1916 intentaron tomar la capital del estado, pero fueron derrotados; y en 1918 ocuparon San Martín Texmelucan, Huejotzingo y Cholula. Para 1919, sin embargo, las zonas dominadas por los zapatistas se reducían a algunos pueblos de la sierra Nevada. A principios de mayo de 1920, luego de que las tropas aguaprietistas de Ricardo Reyes Márquez habían tomado Puebla, el gobierno local se trasladó a Zacatlán y desconoció al de los rebeldes, medidas que no tuvieron ningún efecto, debido al asesinato del presidente Carranza, ocurrido en el pueblo de Tlaxcalaltongo a fines de ese mes. Dos años y medio más tarde, en diciembre de 1923, Antonio Villarreal y Cesáreo Castro se levantaron en armas para apoyar la insurreción de Adolfo de la Huerta y tomaron la capital estatal, aunque poco después las tropas de Máximo Rojas y Andrew Almazán recuperaron la plaza. El gobierno del presidente Obregón desconoció a la legislatura local, que era partidaria del levantamiento y persiguió a las fuerzas delahuertistas cuyas últimas posiciones, ubicadas en la parte oriental del estado, fueron vencidas en enero de 1924.

DISTRIBUCIÓN DE LA POBLACIÓN POR TAMAÑO DE LA LOCALIDAD, 1995

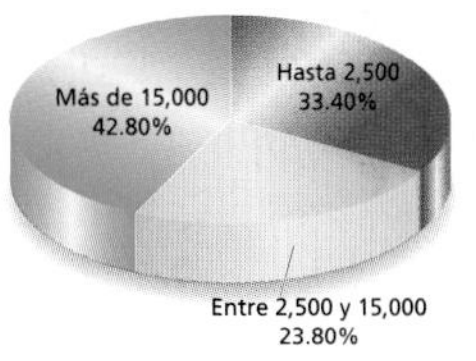

Más de 15,000 42.80%
Hasta 2,500 33.40%
Entre 2,500 y 15,000 23.80%

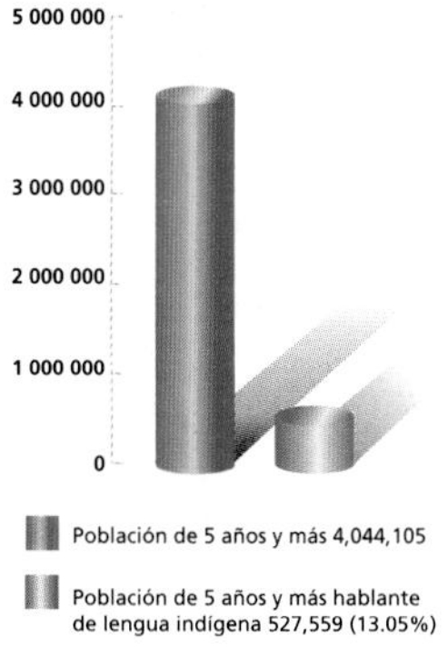

DISTRIBUCIÓN PORCENTUAL DE LA POBLACIÓN OCUPADA POR SECTOR DE ACTIVIDAD ECONÓMICA,1995

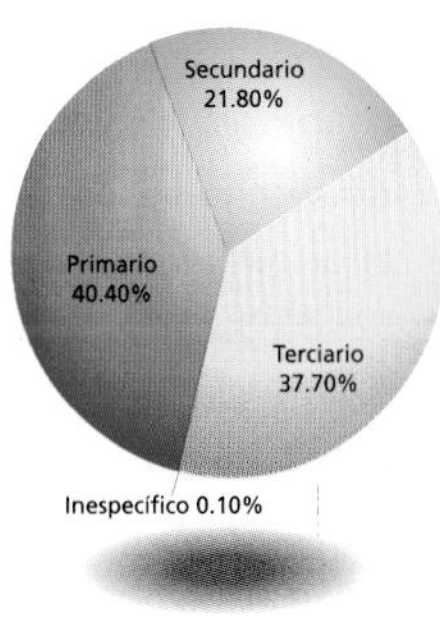

Secundario 21.80%
Primario 40.40%
Terciario 37.70%
Inespecífico 0.10%

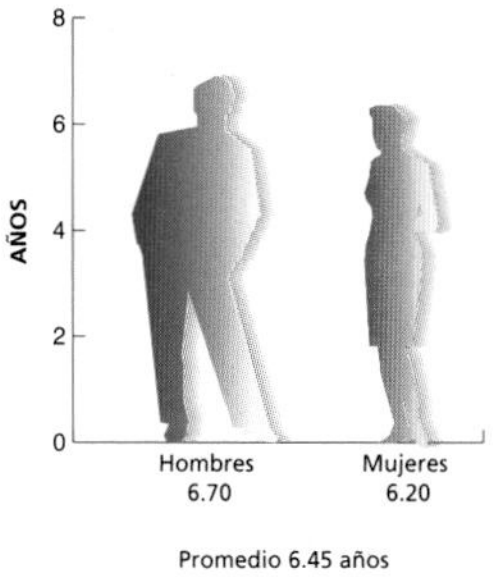

LONGITUD DE LA RED DE CARRETERAS POR SUPERFICIE DE RODAMIENTO, 1995

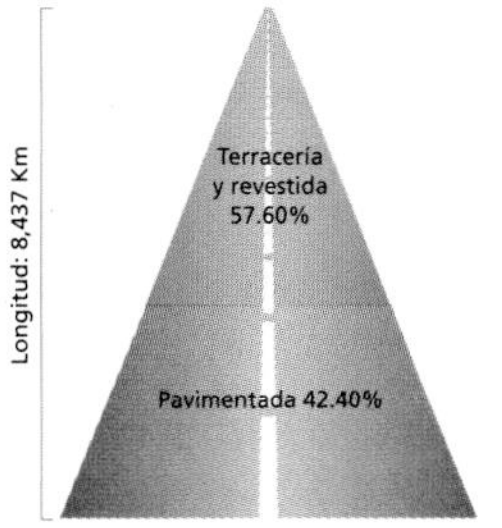

Longitud: 8,437 Km
Terracería y revestida 57.60%
Pavimentada 42.40%

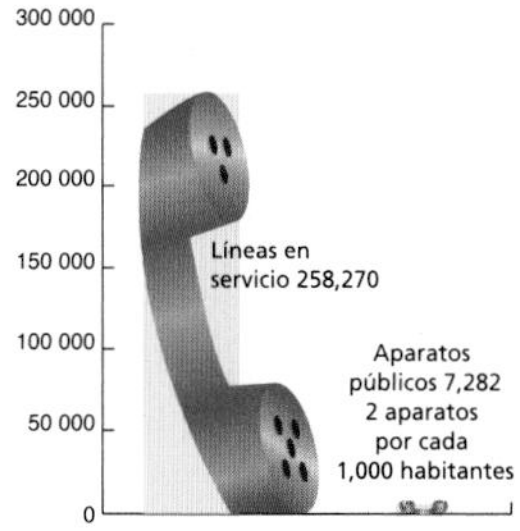

BIBLIOTECAS Y USUARIOS, 1993
Número de bibliotecas: 750

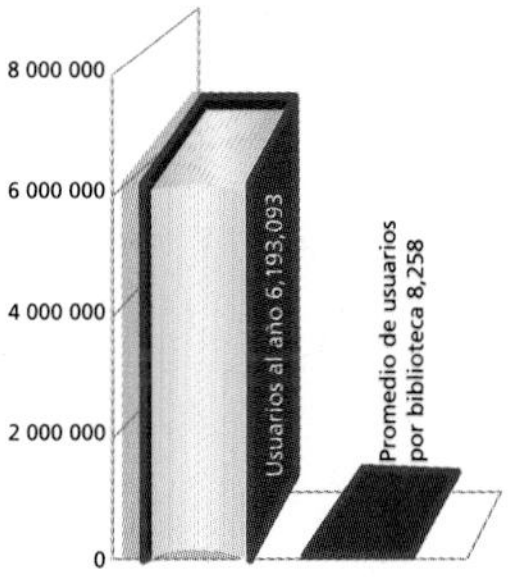

8 000 000
6 000 000
4 000 000
2 000 000
0
Usuarios al año 6,193,093
Promedio de usuarios por biblioteca 8,258

POBLACIÓN DE 5 AÑOS Y MÁS HABLANTE DE LENGUA INDÍGENA, 1995

5 000 000
4 000 000
3 000 000
2 000 000
1 000 000
0
Población de 5 años y más 4,044,105
Población de 5 años y más hablante de lengua indígena 527,559 (13.05%)

PROMEDIO DE ESCOLARIDAD DE LA POBLACIÓN DE 15 AÑOS Y MÁS, POR SEXO, 1995

AÑOS
8
6
4
2
0
Hombres 6.70
Mujeres 6.20
Promedio 6.45 años

LÍNEAS TELEFÓNICAS EN SERVICIO Y APARATOS PÚBLICOS, 1994

300 000
250 000
200 000
150 000
100 000
50 000
0
Líneas en servicio 258,270
Aparatos públicos 7,282
2 aparatos por cada 1,000 habitantes

PRODUCTO INTERNO BRUTO (PIB) A PRECIOS CORRIENTES

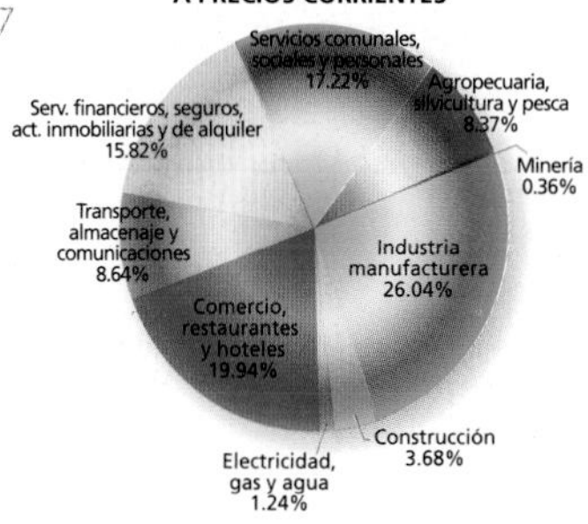

Servicios comunales, sociales y personales 17.22%
Agropecuaria, silvicultura y pesca 8.37%
Minería 0.36%
Industria manufacturera 26.04%
Construcción 3.68%
Electricidad, gas y agua 1.24%
Comercio, restaurantes y hoteles 19.94%
Transporte, almacenaje y comunicaciones 8.64%
Serv. financieros, seguros, act. inmobiliarias y de alquiler 15.82%

Foto: Michael Calderwood

Ciudad de Puebla

Puebla ◆ Municipio de Puebla situado en la porción centro occidental del estado. Limita al norte con Tlaxcala. Superficie: 524.31 km². Habitantes: 1,222,569, de los cuales 333,593 forman la población económicamente activa. Hablan alguna lengua indígena 34,665 personas mayores de cinco años (náhuatl 25,999, totonaco 3,348, mixteco, 1,965 y zapoteco 801). El municipio tiene diversos centros de atracción turística, como la catedral de la ciudad de Puebla, la capilla del Rosario, la iglesia de Santo Domingo, la Casa-Museo del Alfeñique, el Museo Bello; cuenta con cinco balnearios y dos parques nacionales: el de la Malinche y el estatal Africam Safari. Del 21 de abril al 15 de mayo se celebra una feria nacional con exposiciones artesanal, agrícola, ganadera y comercial; el 5 de mayo se conmemora la batalla de 1862 con un desfile militar, serenatas y fuegos artificiales. La cabecera municipal, que es también la capital estatal, se llama Heroica Puebla de Zaragoza; fue fundada en 1531 por Toribio de Benavente en el sitio llamado Cuextlaxcoapan, al pie de los cerros de Loreto y Guadalupe. La parte este de la ciudad es cruzada por los ríos Atoyac y San Francisco, que bajan del volcán de la Malinche. En 1534, vivían en la ciudad 234 españoles. El 8 de diciembre de 1987 la UNESCO declaró patrimonio cultural de la humanidad al centro histórico de la ciudad de Puebla.

Cascada de Apulco en la sierra de Puebla

Foto: Claudio Contreras

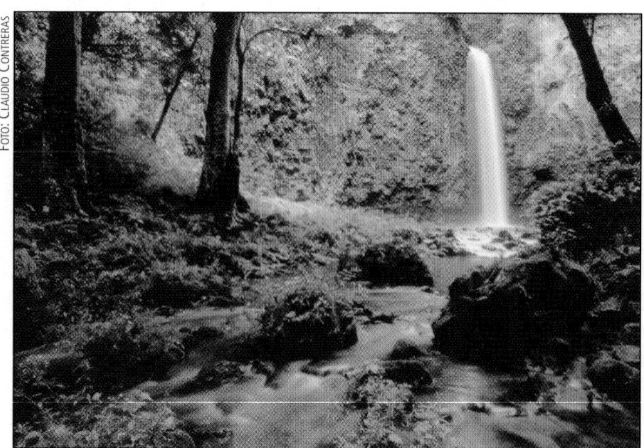

Puebla, de ◆ Sierra de Puebla, Tlaxcala e Hidalgo que forma parte de la sierra Madre Oriental; limita por el norte a los llanos de San Juan y al valle de Puebla, y por el oriente a los llanos de Apan.

Puebla ◆ Valle situado en el eje volcánico. Está limitada al oeste por la sierra Nevada, al norte por la de Puebla, al este por la de Acajete, al sureste por la de Tepeaca y al sur por la de Tentzo. Cuenta con una cantera de mármol de grano imperfecto en los cerros Tepenené y Totimehuacan.

Pueblo Nuevo ◆ Municipio de Durango situado en la porción sudoccidental del estado, al suroeste de su capital. Superficie: 6,178.3 km². Habitantes: 43,909, de los cuales 9,936 forman la población económicamente activa. Hablan alguna lengua indígena 2,306 personas mayores de cinco años (tepehuano 2,273). Indígenas monolingües: 77. En la cabecera municipal, El Salto, se encuentra la sede de la prelatura católica de El Salto, sufragánea de la diócesis de Durango.

Pueblo Nuevo ◆ Municipio de Guanajuato situado en la porción sudoccidental del estado, al sur de Irapuato. Superficie: 81.3 km². Habitantes: 10,524, de los cuales 2,057 forman la población económicamente activa. Hablan alguna lengua indígena 13 personas mayores de cinco años.

Pueblo Nuevo Comaltitlán ◆ ☛ *Villa Comaltitlán*, municipio costero de Chiapas.

Pueblo Nuevo San Juan Parangaricútiro ◆ Cabecera del municipio michoacano de Nuevo Parangaricútiro, situado 10 kilómetros al oeste de Uruapan. El poblado se creó en 1944 para reubicar a los habitantes de San Juan Parangaricútiro y Paricutín, pueblos destruidos por el nacimiento del volcán Paricutín en 1943.

Pueblo Nuevo Solistahuacán ◆ Municipio de Chiapas situado en la porción noroccidental del estado, al noreste de Tuxtla Gutiérrez. Superficie: 419.8 km². Habitantes: 20,819, de los cuales 4,583 forman la población económicamente activa. Hablan alguna lengua indígena 7,687 personas mayores de cinco años (tzotzil 7,657). Indígenas monolingües: 1,476.

Pueblo Viejo ◆ Municipio de Veracruz situado en la porción nororiccidental del estado, al noreste de Pánuco, en los límites con Tamaulipas. Tiene costas, al noreste, en el golfo de México. Superficie: 286.24 km². Habitantes: 48,054, de los cuales 13,085 forman la población económicamente activa. Hablan alguna lengua indígena 548 personas mayores de cinco años (náhuatl 383 y huasteco 111). La cabecera municipal es Villa Cuauhtémoc. Hace por lo menos 1,000 años a.n.e., los huastecos se instalaron en la desembocadura del río Pánuco y fundaron, en la ribera que actualmente pertenece al municipio, un poblado llamado Tampiko, "Lugar de nutrias" en español. Los huasecos, sin embargo, desalojaron la desembocadura del río y durante varios siglos permaneció deshabitada, hasta que hacia 1560 un grupo de españoles de Pánuco se instaló sobre el original asentamiento indígena y fundó el pueblo de San Luis de Tampico (☛ *Tampico*). Durante el siglo XVII, la población fue atacada frecuentemente por piratas, en especial por Lorencillo.

Puente, Ramón ◆ n. en Nieves, Zac., y m. en el DF (1879-1939). Médico. Miembro del Partido Nacional Antirreeleccionista desde 1909, al año siguiente se levantó en armas. Luego del asesinato del presidente Francisco I. Madero formó parte de las tropas carrancistas, pero desde 1914 militó en la División del Norte, con la que colaboró periodísticamente, por lo que tuvo que exiliarse en Estados Unidos (1915-35). En 1920, colaboró con el gobierno de Adolfo de la Huerta para conseguir la rendición de Francisco Villa. Autor de la novela *Juan Rivera* (1936), y de *Pascual Orozco y la revuelta de Chihuahua* (1912), *Villa en pie* (1916), *Vida de Francisco Villa contada por él mismo* (1919) y *La dictadura, la revolución y sus hombres* (1938).

Puente de Ixtla ◆ Municipio de Morelos situado en la porción sudoccidental del estado, al sur de Cuernavaca, en los límites con Guerrero. Superficie: 333.56 km². Habitantes: 51,099, de los cuales 11,853 forman la población económicamente activa. Hablan alguna lengua indígena 3,259 personas mayores de cinco años (náhuatl 3,211).

Puente Leyva, Jesús ◆ n. en el DF (1939). Licenciado en economía por la Universidad Autónoma de Nuevo León (1963), posgraduado en planeación en la oficina de la CEPAL, en Chile (1964); es maestro en teoría del desarrollo por el Williams College, EUA (1965-66). Profesor de la Universidad Autónoma de Nuevo León (1966-69) y de la UNAM (1969-72). Ha sido investigador de la Dirección de Planificación de la UANL (1966-69), asesor de la Secretaría de Obras Públicas (1971), director financiero de Nacional Financiera (1972-76), diputado federal (1976-79) y embajador mexicano en Venezuela (1981-86 y 1995-), Perú (1986-89) y Argentina (1989-94). Colaborador de *El Trimestre Económico*. Coautor de *El perfil de México en 1980* (1970) y autor de *Ocupación y salarios en Monterrey metropolitano* (1964), *El salario mínimo en Monterrey* (1965), *El índice de precios al consumidor en la ciudad de Monterrey* (1967), *El futuro urbano de Monterrey* (1968) y *Distribución del ingreso en un área urbana. El caso de Monterrey* (1969). En 1968 recibió el Premio Nacional de Economía.

Puente Nacional ◆ Municipio de Veracruz situado en la porción central del estado, al sureste de Jalapa. Superficie: 333.13 km². Habitantes: 19,341, de los cuales 5,545 forman la población económicamente activa. Hablan alguna lengua indígena 31 personas mayores de cinco años (zapoteco 14).

Puerto, Nicolás del ◆ n. en Santa Catarina de las Minas y m. cerca de Oaxaca, Oax. (¿1620?-1681). Su nombre completo era Nicolás Ortiz del Puerto y Colmenares Salgado. Se le llamó *el Cicerón mexicano*. Estudió en el Colegio de San Ildefonso y en el Colegio Mayor de Santa María de Todos Santos (1632). Fue profesor de ese colegio, cancelario y rector interino (agosto a noviembre de 1964) y propietario (noviembre de 1665 a noviembre de 1666 y noviembre de 1675 a noviembre de 1676) de la Real y Pontificia Universidad de México, canónigo doctoral de la catedral metropolitana, vicario general del arzobispado de México, comisario de la santa cruzada, consultor y juez ordinario de la Inquisición, presidente de la Real Audiencia de Guadalajara y obispo de Oaxaca (1679-81).

Puerto Ángel ◆ ☛ *San Pedro Pochutla.*

Puerto Escondido ◆ ☛ *San Pedro Mixtepec Juquila.*

Puerto Peñasco ◆ Municipio de Sonora situado en la porción noroccidental del estado, al sureste de San Luis Río Colorado, en los límites con Estados Unidos; tiene costas en el golfo de California. Superficie: 5,653.25 km². Habitantes: 27,169, de los cuales 7,868 forman la población económicamente activa. Hablan alguna lengua indígena 175 personas mayores de cinco años. En 1836 se descubrieron importantes yacimientos minerales en la comisaría de Sonoyta, de este municipio; Sonoyta era una villa pápaga, evangelizada en 1694 por los jesuitas. En 1701, Eusebio Kino estableció la misión de San Marcelo de Sonoydag; en 1736 esa misión se llamó San Miguel de Sonoydag; en noviembre de 1751, en ese sitio, el sacerdote Enrique Ruhen fue muerto por los seris. El municipio de Puerto Peñasco fue creado el 30 de mayo de 1952 con territorios de Caborca.

Puerto Rico ◆ Nación insular latinoamericana situada en el mar Caribe, al este de República Dominicana, al sur del océano Atlántico y al oeste de las Islas Vírgenes. Superficie: 8,897 km². Habitantes: 4,014,000 (1984), de los cuales 434,849 (1980) poblaban San Juan, la capital, situada en la costa septentrional. Otras ciudades importantes son Ponce, Bayamón y Caguas. Aunque la gran mayoría de la población habla español, el inglés es, debido a la ocupación estadounidense, uno de los dos idiomas oficiales en la isla. Por la misma situación de coloniaje, la moneda es el dólar estadounidense. *Historia:* los primeros pobladores de la isla fueron los banwari, taínos y araucanos, todos llegados del sur del continente. Estos últimos llamaron a su tierra Borinquen. Durante el siglo XV, los caribes realizaron numerosas incursiones sobre el territorio borincano. En 1493, Cristóbal Colón desembarcó en la isla y la llamó San Juan Bautista. En 1508, Juan Ponce de León fundó la villa de Caparra, que por orden de la Corona fue bautizada como San Juan de Puerto Rico, e inició la conquista. Tres años después, un levantamiento indígena fue violentamente reprimido por Ponce de León.

Puerto Peñasco, Sonora

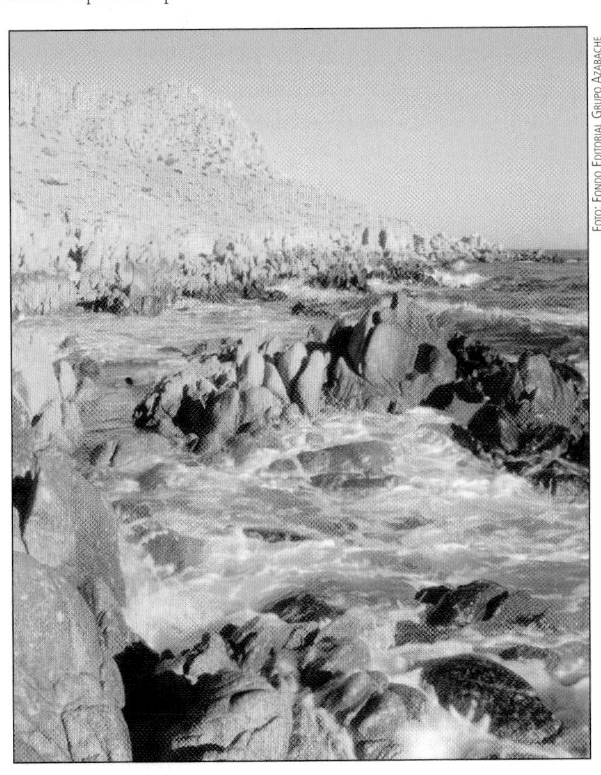

Foto: Fondo Editorial Grupo Azabache

Luego de acabar con la población nativa, los españoles iniciaron la importación de esclavos, sobre todo al introducirse el cultivo de la caña de azúcar, que se convirtió, con la trata de esclavos, en la principal actividad económica de la isla. Desde fines del siglo XVI, y durante el XVII y el XVIII, los piratas ingleses intentaron en varias ocasiones tomar el puerto de San Juan, debido a que ésta era la última escala de los barcos novohispanos y peruanos que viajaban hacia España. En 1619, Bernardo de Balbuena (☛), el autor de *Grandeza mexicana* (1604), fue nombrado obispo de Puerto Rico. En 1811 se creó la Intendencia de Puerto Rico. Cuatro años después, en 1815, para restarle importancia al comercio entre la isla y la Nueva España, el gobierno colonial liberalizó el comercio exterior puertorriqueño. Entre los acompañantes del virrey Juan de O'Donojú que se unieron a las tropas del Ejército Trigarante en 1821, se encontraba el puertorriqueño Antonio Valero, que dos años después participó en las conspiraciones masónicas que contribuyeron al derrocamiento de Agustín de Iturbide. En 1823 se formó en la ciudad de México la Legión del Águila Negra, organización integrada por cubanos y puertorriqueños independentistas. En 1824, México y Colombia acordaron promover la independencia de Cuba y Puerto Rico, pero la intervención del gobierno estadounidense frustró el proyecto. Entre 1847 y 1848, el gobernador y comandante de la isla, Juan Prim y Prats, reprimió un levantamiento de esclavos. Varios años después, en 1862, Prim negociaría con el gobierno de Benito Juárez el retiro de la flota española que se hallaba frente a Veracruz. En 1868, Ramón Emeterio Betances decretó la independencia de Puerto Rico, en un llamamiento conocido como Grito de Lares. Entre esos primeros insurgentes se encontraba el sacerdote mexicano Juan Montes de Oca. A pesar de que ese levantamiento fue rápidamente sofocado por el ejército colonial, la resistencia no pudo ser derrotada. En 1873 fue abolida la esclavitud y, en 1897, el gobierno español le concedió autonomía a la isla. Al año siguiente, en el curso de la guerra entre Estados Unidos y España, tropas estadounidenses ocuparon Puerto Rico y gobernaron militarmente el país hasta 1900, cuando el gobierno de Washington designó un presidente para la isla. Entre 1930 y 1935, el Partido Nacional (fundado en 1922) encabezó una rebelión independentista, que fue reprimida violentamente. Entre los patriotas puertorriqueños que se instalaron en México estuvieron el compositor Rafael Hernández (☛), llegado en 1935, a quien apodaron *el Jibarito*, y su principal intérprete, Daniel Santos. En 1940, el gobierno de Lázaro Cárdenas apoyó la independencia de Puerto Rico en el Congreso Mundial de la Paz y Contra el Fascismo. Tres años después, esa posición fue ratificada en la Conferencia de Uniones de Trabajadores de la América Latina. Durante la segunda guerra mundial, los estadounidenses instalaron siete bases militares en la isla. En 1948, durante la Conferencia Internacional Americana de Bogotá, el gobierno mexicano apoyó una resolución que exigía la independencia de la isla. No obstante, en ese mismo año, el país fue convertido en "Estado Libre Asociado" de Estados Unidos, eufemismo con el que se institucionalizó el coloniaje. El principal impulsor de esta fórmula fue Luis Muñoz Marín, que gobernó Puerto Rico entre 1948 y 1964. Nueve años antes se había formado, en la ciudad de México, el Comité de México Pro Independencia de Puerto Rico, dirigido por Mario Resendes. En 1959 se constituyó en la isla el Movimiento Pro Independencia. A finales de los años sesenta surgieron varias organizaciones guerrilleras, entre ellas los Voluntarios de la Revolución, las Fuerzas Armadas de Liberación Nacional (FALN) y el grupo Macheteros. Un gran número de puertorriqueños se han exiliado a México y en marzo de 1977, con varias organizaciones de izquierda, organizaron una Jornada Nacional por la Independencia de Puerto Rico. En mayo de 1983 fue detenido en Puebla uno de los dirigentes de las FALN, William Morales, un guerrillero que había escapado de Estados Unidos, donde había sido condenado a cadena perpetua por sus actividades revolucionarias. Durante los cuatro años siguientes, el gobierno estadounidense desató una campaña de presiones contra México, para conseguir la extradición de Morales, pero en 1988 el gobierno mexicano reconoció la condición de luchador social de Morales y negó la extradición. Ese mismo año fue enviado a Cuba. Desde 1953, los puertorriqueños han vivido en una especie de limbo jurídico y político. Son ciudadanos estadunidenses, pero, mientras vivan en la isla, no pueden elegir representantes al Congreso de Estados Unidos ni votar en la elección presidencial. Los puertorriqueños no pagan impuestos federales, pero tienen derecho a recibir ayuda del erario. Como nación, Puerto Rico tiene el ingreso per cápita más alto de América Latina, pero como parte de Estados Unidos es mucho más pobre que el estado más atrasado. En 1998 se llevó a debate el Proyecto Young, que busca realizar un plebiscito en el que los puertorriqueños votarían por una de tres opciones: permanecer como estado libre asociado; integrarse a Estados Unidos como entidad federativa o convertirse en país independiente. Esa iniciativa fue aprobada por la Cámara baja de EUA, con el apoyo expreso de Bill Clinton, pero todavía tendrá que ser aprobada por el Senado para convertirse en ley.

Puerto Rico

PUERTO VALLARTA ◆ Municipio de Jalisco situado al noroeste de Talpa, en los límites con Nayarit; tiene costas en el océano Pacífico. Superficie: 1,300.69 km^2. Habitantes: 149,876, de los cuales 39,659 forman la población económicamente activa. Hablan alguna lengua indígena 955 personas mayores de cinco años (huichol 523 y zapoteco 114). La cabecera municipal, del mismo nombre, es el principal puerto del estado y un centro turístico.

Puga, Jorge ◆ n. en Guadalajara, Jal. (1918-1953). Caricaturista. Estudió dibujo en la Academia de San Carlos. Colaboró en la revista *Don Timorato* y en el diario *Últimas Noticias*. Creó el personaje *Óscar*, que fue llevado al cine.

Puga, María Luisa ◆ n. en el DF (1944). Escritora. Estudió contaduría en Mazatlán. En Londres, donde residió tres años, trabajó en el periódico *The Economist*. Más tarde vivió en París, Madrid y Roma, donde trabajó para la FAO. Ha sido coordinadora de talleres literarios de la UNAM, del Instituto Nacional de Bellas Artes en Morelia y otros lugares, así como en El Molino, de Erongarícuaro, Michoacán. Vive en Zirahuén. Ha colaborado en *unomásuno*, *El Universal*, *La Jornada*, *Nexos*, *La Plaza*, *Revista de la Universidad* y *Revista de Bellas Artes*. Coautora de *Itinerario de palabras* (crónicas, 1987) y *Los siete pecados capitales* (cuento, 1989). Autora de novela: *Las posibilidades del odio* (1978), *Cuando el aire es azul* (1980), *Pánico o peligro* (1983, Premio Xavier Villaurrutia), *La forma del silencio* (1987), *Antonia* (1990), *Las razones del lago* (1991) y *La ceremonia de iniciación* (1994) e *Inventar ciudades* (1999); cuento: *Inmóvil sol secreto* (1979), *Accidentes* (1981), *El tornado* (1985), *Intentos* (1987); y ensayo: *Cuando rinde el horno. La cerámica de Hugo X. Velázquez* (1983) y *Lo que le pasa al lector* (1990).

Puga, Vasco de ◆ n. y m. en España (?-1576). Doctor en derecho por la Real y Pontificia Universidad de México. Llegó a la Nueva España en 1559 como oidor de la Real Audiencia de México. Desempeñó el puesto hasta 1566, cuando fue suspendido por el visitador Jerónimo Valderrama. Reasumió el cargo dos años después (1568-72), para destituir al juez Alonso de Muñoz, quien había torturado a Martín Cortés y asesinado a Cristóbal de Oñate. Por encargo de Felipe II, realizó una compilación de las *Provisiones, cédulas, instrucciones de su magestad: ordenanzas de difuntos y audiencia para la buena expedición de los negocios y administración de justicia: y governación desta Nueva España: y para el buen tratamiento y conservación de los indios, desde el año 1525 hasta el presente de 63* (1563), que se conoce como *Cedulario de Puga*.

Puga y Acal, Manuel ◆ n. en Guadalajara, Jal., y m. en el DF (1860-1930). Escritor y periodista. Estudió en México, Francia y Bélgica. Profesor de las escuelas de Altos Estudios y Nacional Preparatoria e investigador del Archivo General de la Nación. Fue diputado local y federal y colaborador de diversos periódicos de Guadalajara, San Luis Potosí y la ciudad de México, entre ellos *La Aurora Literaria* (1877), *El Pabellón Nacional*, *El Partido Liberal* y *Excélsior*. Tradujo al francés obras de Gustavo Adolfo Bécquer, y al español de Emile Olivier: *La intervención francesa y el imperio de Maximiliano en México* (1906); Charles Baudelaire, Alfred de Musset y Gregorio Silvestre. Las célebres polémicas que, con el seudónimo de *Brummel*, sostuvo con Salvador Díaz Mirón, Manuel Gutiérrez Nájera y Juan de Dios Peza, se editaron con el título de *Los poetas mexicanos contemporáneos* (1888). Usó también el pseudónimo de *Facistol*. Editó *90 documentos para la historia patria* (1898). Autor de *Después del beneficio* (1884), *Baladas lúgubres* (1892), *Verdad y Talamantes, primeros mártires de la independencia mexicana* (1908), *Fray Gregorio de la Concepción y su proceso de infidencia* (1911), *Fundamento de sus opiniones* (1916), *La fase diplomática de nuestra guerra de independencia* (1919), *Lirismos de antaño* (poesía, 1923) e *Intermezzo* (1927). En 1918 fue admitido como miembro correspondiente de la Academia Mexicana (de la Lengua), y en 1922, como numerario.

Puga Tovar, José de Jesús Rafael ◆ n. en Querétaro, Qro. (1958). Arquitecto titulado en el Instituto Tecnológico de Querétaro (1980-84). Pertenece al PAN desde 1970, donde ha sido miembro y secretario general el CDE de Querétaro (1983-91). En Querétaro ha sido regidor suplente (1982-85) y electo diputado local (1988-91) y diputado federal (1991-94).

Pugibet, Ernesto ◆ n. en Francia y m. en la ciudad de México (1855-1915). Empresario. En 1870 viajó a Cuba, donde aprendió a cultivar tabaco y a elaborar cigarros. Llegó a México en 1879 e instaló una fábirca cigarrera, que en 1884 se convirtió en la fábrica El Buen Tono, una de las primeras en usar el sistema de engargolado en la producción cigarrera. Además, introdujo nuevas formas publicitarias, como la utilización, en 1907, de un dirigible para anunciar los cigarros. En 1913, luego del asesinato del presidente Francisco I. Madero, lanzó al mercado los cigarros *Viva Huerta*, que en el frente tenían un retrato de Victoriano Huerta. Fue fundador de una sociedad financiera encargada de traer capitales franceses a México, codueño de la Cervecería Moctezuma, fundador de la Compañía Nacional Mexicana de Dinamita y Explosivos, y accionista y consejero del Banco Nacional de México, de la fábrica de tejidos San Ildefonso, del Ferrocarril de Monte Alto y de El Palacio de Hierro. También fue uno de los primeros que editaron historietas en México.

Pugwash, Conferencia de ◆ Proyecto que intenta promover, en el ámbito internacional, una cultura capaz de enfrentar los conflictos y encontrar soluciones no violentas apoyadas en la ciencia. Se originó en el manifiesto Russell-Einstein, publicado en 1953, en contra de la utilización de la energía atómica con fines bélicos y que organizó una primera Conferencia Mundial de Científicos por la Paz en Pugwash, Canadá, en 1957. En dichas conferencias han participado los científicos mexicanos Ana María Cetto, Raúl García, Octavio Miramontes y Omar Mancera. En junio de 1999, 4,800 personas de más de 60 países se habían adherido a él. Joseph Rotblat, su fundador y presidente, recibió el Premio Nobel de la Paz 1995.

Puerto Vallarta

Maria Luisa Puga

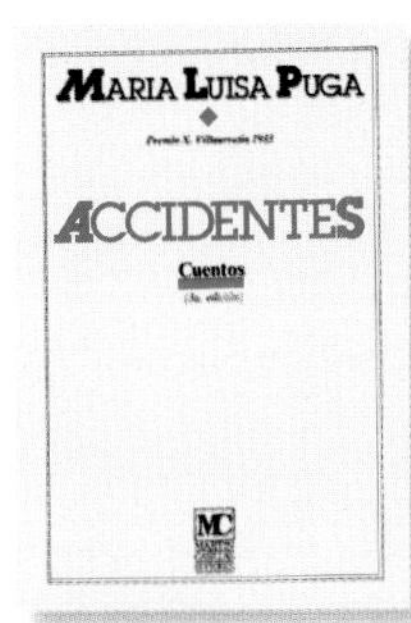

Libro de Maria Luisa Puga

Novela de Manuel Puig

José Manuel Puig Casauranc

PUIG, MANUEL ◆ n. en Argentina y m. en Cuernavaca, Mor. (1932-1990). Escritor. En 1989 llegó a México. Escribió varios libros, algunos de ellos llevados con éxito al cine. Entre sus obras figuran *El Beso de la Mujer Araña*, *La Traición de Rita Hayworth*, *Pubis Angelical* y *Maldición eterna a quien lea estas páginas*. En 1973 publicó *The Buenos Aires Affair*. Sus obras fueron traducidas a varios idiomas.

PUIG CASAURANC, JOSÉ MANUEL ◆ n. en Ciudad del Carmen, Camp., y m. en Cuba (1888-1939). Médico titulado en la Escuela Nacional de Medicina (1911). Colaborador de *El Imparcial*, redactor de *El Universal* y director de *El Demócrata* (1924), fue diputado por Veracruz (1911-13 y 1922-24), senador por Campeche (1924-28), secretario de Educación Pública (1 de diciembre de 1924 al 22 de agosto de 1928), secretario de Industria, Comercio y Trabajo con los presidentes Calles (del 1 de agosto al 30 de noviembre de 1928) y Portes Gil (del 30 de noviembre al 31 de diciembre de 1928); jefe del Departamento Central del Distrito Federal en los gabinetes de Portes Gil (del 1 de enero de 1929 al 5 de febrero de 1930) y Pascual Ortiz Rubio (del 5 de febrero al 31 de mayo de 1930), en cuyo gobierno volvió a ser secretario de Educación (del 9 de diciembre de 1930 al 22 de septiembre de 1931); embajador en EUA (1931), fundador de la editorial La Razón y de la revista *Resumen* (1931), presidente de la Comisión Reorganizadora de la Administración Pública (1931), jefe de la delegación mexicana y vicepresidente de la séptima Conferencia Internacional Americana (celebrada en Montevideo en diciembre de 1933), secretario de Relaciones Exteriores (del 1 de enero de 1933 al 30 de noviembre de 1934) con Abelardo L. Rodríguez; y embajador en Argentina (1935-38). Autor de un *Atlas general del Distrito Federal* (1930), y de cuento: *De la vida* (1922), *De otros días* (1926), *Su venganza* (1931) y *Mirando la vida* (1933); ensayo: *Páginas viejas con ideas actuales* (1925), *De nuestro México, cosas sociales y aspectos políticos* (1926), *Juárez, una interpretación humana* (1928), *La cosecha y la siembra* (1928), *La cuestión religiosa en relación con la educación primaria en México* (1928), *El esfuerzo educativo en México* (1928), *La obra integral de la revolución mexicana* (1929) *Memoria del ramo de educación pública* (1931), *La aspiración suprema de la revolución mexicana* (1933), *Una política socio-económica de aspiración socialista* (1933) y *El sentido social del proceso histórico de México* (1936); novela: *La hermana impura* (1927) y *Los Juan López Sánchez López y López Sánchez de López* (1933); poesía: *Poemas del espíritu y de la carne* (1925) y *Para las madres* (1925); y teatro: *Los errores de Satanás* (1937) y *Galatea rebelde a varios pigmaliones* (1938). En 1934 ingresó a la Academia Mexicana (de la Lengua).

PUJALTE, CARLOS ◆ n. en el DF (1953). Licenciado en Derecho por la UNAM, en la que ha sido profesor de licenciatura y posgrado. Maestro en Derecho Internacional por la Universidad de Nueva York y en Derecho Internacional y Comparado por las universidades Americana y de Georgetown. Hizo estudios en el Instituto Matías Romero de la SRE. Fue abogado litigante (1976-77) y trabajó en la Dirección de Asuntos Jurídicos de la UNAM. Es miembro de carrera del Servicio Exterior Mexicano desde 1980. Ha sido cónsul de México en Nueva York (1981-85), encargado de Asuntos Jurídicos en la embajada de México en Estados Unidos (1985-86), director de Asuntos Consulares (1989-90) y consultor jurídico adjunto de la SRE (1990-92), representante de México ante la OEA (1992-95) y director de Asuntos Jurídicos de la SRE (1995-).

PUJOL, ANTONIO ◆ n. en San Gregorio Cuautzingo, municipio de Chalco, Pue., y m. en el DF (1913-1995). Pintor. Militó en el Partido Comunista Mexicano. Fue miembro de la Liga de Escritores y Artistas Revolucionarios (1934-37) y del Taller de Gráfica Popular (1939-40 y 1961-62). Ejecutó un mural en el mercado Abelardo L. Rodríguez de la ciudad de México (1934) y participó con Siqueiros y Josep Renau en la decoración de la escalera del Sindicato Mexicano de Electricistas. Participó en el primer atentado contra León Trotsky. Después del asesinato del viejo bolchevique se exilió, primero en Estados Unidos, donde trabajó en el Experimental Workshop de Nueva York, y después en Montevideo, Uruguay, donde pasó 20 años. Regresó a México en 1961 y fue profesor de pintura y grabado en los centros comunitarios del IMSS.

PULIDO, BLANCA LUZ ◆ n. en Teoloyucan, Edo. de Mexico (1956). Editora y poeta. Estudió la licenciatura en lengua y literatura hispánicas en la UNAM. Ha sido editora en el FCE y en El Colegio de México. Ha colaborado en *Intermedios*, *Casa del Tiempo* y *El Nacional Dominical*. Es autora de los poemarios *Fundaciones* (1979), *Ensayo de un árbol* (1983), *Raíz de sombras* (1988) y *Estación del alba* (1992).

PULIDO, ESPERANZA ◆ n. en Zamora, Mich., y m. en el DF (1901-1991). Musicóloga y pianista. Estudió en el Conservatorio Nacional de Música, donde ejerció la docencia. Fue discípula de Mildred Dosst, Lazar Livy, André Shaeffner, Alfred Cortor y Claudio Arrau. Impartió cátedra en la New York School of Music de Nueva York y durante muchos años fue concertista. Al morir era investigadora del Centro Nacional de Investigación, Documentación e Información Musical del INBA. Ejerció la crítica musical en diarios y revistas de México y otros países. En 1968 fundó la revista especializada *Heterofonía*, misma que dirigió por el resto de su vida. Dejó inéditos los libros *La mujer en la música, desde la época prehispánica hasta nuestros días* y *Bernard Shaw, crítico musical*.

PULIDO, MARÍA EUGENIA ◆ n. en el DF (1952). Actriz y locutora. Estudió en la Facultad de Filosofía y Letras y en el Centro Universitario de Teatro de la UNAM, en el Teatro Núcleo Ferrara (1981-83) y en el laboratorio de Jerzy Grotowsky. Desde 1974 es locutora de Radio Educación, donde ha intervenido en *La causa de las mujeres* y muchos otros programas. Ha actuado en las películas *El muro* y *Ahorcados*.

PULIDO, ÓSCAR ◆ n. y m. en el DF (1906-1974). Actor cómico. Trabajó en radio, teatro, cine y televisión. *Primavera y otoño* fue la primera de las más de 180 películas en las que participó. En 1969 recibió la medalla Virginia Fábregas de la ANDA.

PULIDO ARANDA, ALBERTO ◆ n. en el DF (1950). Trabajador de la Escuela Nacional Preparatoria (1970-). Durante el movimiento estudiantil de 1968 fue encarcelado. Fue delegado sindical de la Preparatoria 7 (1972) y participó en la huelga del STEUNAM que consiguió la contratación colectiva. Fue jefe de redacción de los periódicos *Venceremos* (del STEUNAM), *Enlace* (de la FSTU) y del órgano del SUNTU. Fue secretario de Prensa y Propaganda del SUNTU y director de su semanario: *Unión*. Fue fundador del Centro de Investigaciones Históricas del Sindicalismo Universitario y coordinador de los Cuadernos de Comunicación Sindical del STUNAM, agrupación en la que es secretario de Organización Administrativa. Ha sido productor y guionista del programa *Ideas y rock*, de Radio Educación, y colaborador de *Excélsior*, *El Universal*, *unomásuno*, *La Jornada*, *A Propósito*, *Venceremos*, *Unión*, *Galera*, *Enlace*, *Oposición* y *Así Es*. Secretario de Prensa de la UPD y director de su órgano informativo: *Galera* (1986-88). Autor de *Cronología de 50 años de sindicalismo universitario (1929- 1979)* (1983), *Primeras luchas del sindicalismo en la UNAM (1929-1938)* (1986), *De algo un poco* (1988), *Cronología del sindicalismo universitario 1980* (1999) y *1968, la crónica de un año maravilloso* (1999).

PULIDO ISLAS, ALFONSO ◆ n. en Ixtlán del Río, Nay., y m. en EUA (1907-1981)). Profesor egresado de la Escuela Normal de Jalisco y licenciado en economía por la UNAM. Profesor y director (1942) de la Escuela Nacional de Economía, y director del Instituto de Investigaciones Sociales de la UNAM. Fue secretario general de la Confederación Obrera de Jalisco (1925-29), fundador del Partido Nacional Revolucionario (1929), dirigente del Consejo Técnico de Economistas (1963-80), consejero de la Secretaría de Hacienda (1965-81) y gerente de Cinematográfica Mexicana Exportadora. Autor de *La industria cinematográfica de México* (1938), *Las artes populares de México* (1940), *Las tribus indias cora y huichol* (1940) y *El crédito popular en México* (1943).

PULQUE ◆ Bebida fermentada de aguamiel de maguey llamada *Octli* en náhuatl y *seí* en otomí. Se comenzó a producir a mediados el siglo XI, en Tula. La mitología mexica tiene dos versiones sobre su origen. Una señala que la diosa Mayahuel descubrió el aguamiel, que Pachtécatl o Pantécatl, uno de los 400 dioses de los borrachos y probablemente su esposo, descubrió su proceso de fermentación y que más tarde, Tepoztécatl, Cuatlapanqui, Tlilhua y Papáztac perfeccionaron el "vino de la tierra". La segunda versión náhuatl indica que el aguamiel fue descubierto por un noble llamado Papatzin, quien se lo envió con su hija Xóchitl al rey de Tula, Tecpancaltzin. Éste se casó con Xóchitl, quien tuvo un hijo llamado Meconetzin (hijo del pulque) que murió de alcoholismo. Entre los pueblos nahuas, los centzontotochtin, o 400 conejos, hermanos de Mayahuel, eran también patrones del pulque. Los sacerdotes de Mayahuel eran sólo hombres mayores de 60 años y los únicos que podían beber pulque en todo tiempo y sin límite. Las mujeres, por su parte, sólo podían beberlo cuando estaban embarazadas o en estado de lactancia. Los guerreros consumían pulque mezclado con mariguana antes de entrar en combate. Cecilio Robelo dice que en las ceremonias religiosas se empleaba el *teooctli*, un pulque especial que quizá se elaboraba del jugo del *teometl*, maguey divino de los llanos de Apam. Entre los purépechas, Thares Upeme era la deidad del pulque y para los otomíes lo era Yudó. La palabra pulque no pertenece a ninguna de las lenguas indígenas mexicanas: algunos autores indican que su origen es antillano y otros dicen que es araucano. En 1529, la Corona española prohibió que los indios bebieran pulque en las fiestas. Durante la colonia existía un impuesto municipal sobre el pulque, que era de 12 reales por cada carga. Los reyes Carlos V y Felipe III trataron de eliminar de la Nueva España la industria pulquera; al no lograrlo, se le toleró y gravó en 1664, por cédula de Felipe IV, que permitía la existencia de 36 pulquerías en la ciudad de México (24 para hombres y 12 para mujeres). En 1692, el virrey Gaspar de la Cerda pidió su parecer a la Real y Pontifica Universidad sobre la prohibición de la bebida. El claustro universitario reunido en pleno discutió el asunto y los maestros y doctores "fueron dando sus pareceres fundándolos en lugares de la Sagrada Escriptura, textos de los derechos y, por lo que toca a la Facultad de Medicina, en aforismos, con toda erudición",

Españita Tlaxcala, afamada región pulquera

FOTO: MICHAEL CALDERWOOD

FOTO: FONDO EDITORIAL GRUPO AZABACHE

Joven purépecha en *El Mundo Ilustrado* de diciembre de 1897

después de lo cual se determinó informar al virrey acerca de "los grandes inconvenientes, pecados graves, ofensas a Dios Nuestro Señor y daños que se han recrecido y en lo de adelante pueden resultar en la permisión de la venta del pulque y que no solamente se debe prohibir el trajino sino el uso desta bebida, informando a Su Majestad, que Dios guarde, se prohíba totalmente, que se destruyan, arranquen y quiten los magueyes, para que en ninguna manera se pueda usar de tal bebida del pulque". En diciembre de 1772, José Ignacio Bartolache le dedicó al pulque tres números de su *Mercurio Volante*. En ellos, luego de describir el maguey y narrar el proceso de producción del pulque, aseguraba que entre los conocedores, el pulque que llegaba a la ciudad de México en invierno era el mejor de todos, y que el peor era el llamado pulque *criollo*, el que se fermentaba en verano en las pulquerías. En 1787, el tomar ciertas clases de pulque eran considerado delito por el Breve Compendio del Juicio Criminal. Durante el siglo XIX la hostilidad contra el pulque casi desapareció. Guillermo Prieto escribió sobre la bebida y la Marquesa Calderón de la Barca, que lo hallaba repulsivo a su llegada, se convirtió en una adicta al poco tiempo, al extremo de confesar a su partida que lo extrañaría. En octubre de 1874, el periódico *El Obrero Internacional* protestaba porque algunas pulquerías de la ciudad de México tenían nombres como *La ilustración del siglo XIX* o *La unión de los artesanos*, y porque "los especuladores del vicio" tenían en sus expendios retratos de Benito Juárez, Ignacio Zaragoza, Miguel Hidalgo y aun de Ángela Peralta. Tres años más tarde, en julio de 1877, otro periódico, *La Unión de los Obreros*, al comentar una disposición gubernamental que obligaba a las pulquerías a cerrar a las seis de la tarde, decía que "no somos partidarios de la embriaguez, pero sí de la libertad de comercio, máxime cuando por el abuso de unos cuantos individuos, a quienes puede corregir fácilmente la policía, se priva a los demás de un alimento necesario y acaso medicinal, y se protege así la especulación de las fondas y demás comercios donde se expende esa bebida". En agosto de 1877, la misma publicación decía, luego de constatar la inutilidad de la medida del ayuntamiento capitalino, que "inumerables accesorias se abren después de esa hora (las seis de la tarde) para expender a tambor batiente el blanco licor del maguey". En las zonas de Otumba y Tlaxcala se elabora el copaloctli o pulque de incienso, fermentado con semillas de pirú y al que se atribuyen facultades curativas, principalmente contra ciertas enfermedades venéreas. Las regiones de Apan y del Valle del Mezquital, Hidalgo, son grandes productoras de esta bebida. En 1986, según datos de las secretaría de Salud, en la zona metropolitana del valle de México existían 900 tinacales y 1,200 pulquerías. De éstas, sobresalen los siguientes nombres: El abrevadero de los dinosaurios, Al pasito pero llego, La ametralladora, Amores de Cupido, Aquí es donde le sacaron la muela al gallo, La bomba atómica, Bb y bt, Las buenas amistades, La canica, El cañón de largo alcance, La casa de todos, El circo Orrin, La conquista de roma por los aztecas, Changri-la, La Dama de noche, Las damas del triunfo, Un día de campo, Las duelistas, Los efectos de la batalla, El emperador de la china, La encantadora de los dioses, Éntrale enallunas (sic), Entre violetas, La estocada de la tarde, La del estribo, Fe y constancia revolucionaria, Los fifís, La fuente embriagadora, La gallina de los huevos de oro, El gorgeo de las aves, El gran atorón, La gran batalla de Otumba, El gran califa, La gran estocada, La gran mona, La hija de los apaches, La hija de Baco, La hija de la traviata, Los hombres sabios sin estudio, La jaladora, El judío errante, El jugo de maguey, El K Ch T, La liga de las naciones, El lucero de mis noches, Me estoy riendo, Me siento aviador, Mi vida es otra, Los mosqueteros de Dumas, Las mulas de don Cristóbal (antes Los Caballeros de Colón), Las mulas de siempre, Napoleón en Santa Elena, La nieta de Napoleón, El pajarillo barranqueño, El paso de Venus por el disco del Sol, Por ti hasta moderado soy, Las preocupaciones de Baco, El purgatorio, El quinto toro. El recreo de los de enfrente (situada frente a la antigua Cámara de Diputados), El recreo de mis placeres, Los recuerdos del porvenir, El relox de arena, El retoño del durazno, La rumba del Caribe, Salsipuedes, La sangre minera, El sueño de Xóchitl, La toma de Nueva York en el año dos mil por el ejército mexicano, El triunfo del bombardeo, El triunfo de la tambora sobre la divina providencia, Los triunfos de Gaona, Un viaje a la luna, Vayan entrando, vayan pidiendo, vayan pagando, vayan saliendo y El viento libre.

Plaza cívica de Ciudad Altamirano, cabecera municipal de Pungarabato, Guerrero

PUNGARABATO ◆ Municipio de Guerrero situado en la porción noroccidental del estado, al oeste de Teloloapan. Limita al oeste con Michoacán. Superficie: 212.3 km^2. Habitantes: 32,546, de los cuales 6,710 forman la población económicamente activa. Hablan alguna lengua indígena 84 personas mayores de cinco años. La cabecera municipal es Ciudad Altamirano.

PUNGUATO ◆ Volcán basáltico de Michoacán situado en el valle de Morelia. Forma parte del Eje Volcánico.

PUNTA, LA ◆ Rancho de ganado bravo. Está en Lagos de Moreno, Jalisco. Inicialmente fue adquirida por Ignacio Madrazo Corral, padre de Francisco y José Madrazo García Granados, quienes en 1918 la dedicaron a la crianza de reses bravas. La fundaron con 40 vacas de San Nicolás Peralta y dos sementales, uno de Parlade y otro del marqués de

Saltillo. En 1919 se agregaron 50 vacas y dos sementales de San Mateo, y en 1924 se presentó con éxito en El Toreo. Sin embargo, al año siguiente se renovó todo el ganado, para lo cual los dueños trajeron de España 10 vacas de dos toros padres de pura sagre y, en septiembre de 1995, compraron 42 vacas y cinco sementales de Campos Varela. De esta ganadería se derivaron otras, como Matancillas. En 1960 falleció Francisco Madrazo, heredando su parte de la ganadería a sus hijos Francisco y Carmen Madrazo Solórzano. Francisco se quedó con la totalidad en 1967, al adquirir la parte de su hermana y la de su tio José.

PUNTO DE PARTIDA ◆ Revista literaria, creada por la UNAM. Surgió en 1966, durante el gobierno universitario del rector Javier Barros Sierra. El título de la revista fue sugerido por Henrique González Casanova. La revista no se encerró en los muros de la universidad, sino que dio cabida a los estudiantes politécnicos y de otras instituciones. En ella se publicaron cuentos, obras dramáticas, poesía, viñetas, dibujos, fotografías. Quienes empezaron a escribir en la revista fueron: José Joaquín Blanco, Marco Antonio Campos, Manuel Capetillo, Víctor Manuel Toledo, David Capetillo, David Huerta, Gonzalo Celorio, Mónica Mansour, Jaime Goded, Luis de Tavira, Cesáreo Morales, Evodio Escalante, José de Jesús Samperio, Verónica Volkov, Ethel Krauze, Paco Ignacio Taibo II, entre otros.

PURÉPECHAS ◆ Indios que viven en las zonas lacustre y serrana del noreste michoacano. De acuerdo con el Conteo Nacional de Población, en 1995 había en el país 107,950 hablantes de purépecha, lengua del grupo maya-totonaco, con ligeras variantes dialectales que no impiden la comunicación entre las diversas comunidades. Los hablantes de esta lengua se dan a sí mismos el nombre de purépechas, pues el de tarascos (usado desde la época colonial) tiene una connotación despectiva. En la época prehispánica, los purépechas no habían sido sometidos por los mexicas y su influencia se extendía hasta los estados de México, Querétaro y Guanajuato (☛ *Michoacán*). Sólo las mujeres de este grupo conservan la indumentaria tradicional. Su actividad principal es la agricultura, complementada con la pesca en la zona lacustre, la explotación de maderas en la sierra, la elaboración de artesanías y la emigración temporal en busca de trabajo asalariado, sobre todo a Estados Unidos. Su organización social básica es la familia nuclear y el compadrazgo juega un papel importante. Practican la religión católica, pero con influencia de sus antiguas creencias; tienen rezanderos y la mayordomía empieza a decaer. Su organización política está supeditada a la municipal.

PURÉPERO ◆ Municipio de Michoacán situado en la porción centro-norte del estado, al sureste de Zamora. Superficie: 275.47 km². Habitantes: 15,453, de los cuales 3,601 forman la población económicamente activa. Hablan alguna lengua indígena 35 personas mayores de cinco años (purépecha 31).

PURIFICACIÓN ◆ Río de Jalisco que nace en el extremo sur de la sierra de Cacoma; corre hacia el suroeste y desemboca en el Pacífico, al norte de la bahía de Tenacatita.

PURIFICACIÓN ◆ Río de Tamaulipas que nace en la vertiente este de la sierra Madre Oriental por la confluencia de los ríos Blanco, Limón y San Antonio; corre hacia el este, recibe al Pilón y se une con el Corona para formar el Soto la Marina.

PURÍSIMA DEL RINCÓN ◆ Municipio de Guanajuato situado en el suroeste de León, en los límites con Jalisco. Superficie: 209.5 km². Habitantes: 34,779, de los cuales 8,277 forman la población económicamente activa. Hablan alguna lengua indígena 13 personas mayores de cinco años. Su cabecera es Purísima de Bustos.

PURUÁNDIRO ◆ Municipio de Michoacán situado en el norte del estado, al norte de Quiroga, en los límites con Guanajuato. Superficie: 722.48 km². Habitantes: 74,079, de los cuales 15,947 forman la población económicamente activa. Hablan alguna lengua indígena 73 personas mayores de cinco años (purépecha 45). Su cabecera es Ciudad de Calderón. En este municipio se efectuó un combate que fue la primera victoria de los constitucionalistas en el estado; el 25 de mayo de 1913, las fuerzas de Joaquín Amaro derrotaron en la hacienda de Ururuta a los federales comandados por el capitán Díaz Rivera.

FOTO: BORIS DE SWAN

Niñas purépechas

FOTO: LOURDES ALMEIDA

Familia de campesinos purépechas de Parangaricútiro, Michoacán

PURY-TOUMI, SYBILLE DE ◆ n. en Francia (1945). Nahuatlata. Estudió lingüística y letras modernas. Autor de *Le Paradis sur Terre, récit de la vie d'une femme à Xalitla Guerrero, De palabras y maravillas* y *Ensayo sobre la cultura y la lengua de los nahuas* (1997).

PUTLA ◆ Río de Oaxaca, también llamado Cuchara. Nace en la sierra de Tlaxiaco, corre de noroeste a sureste; recibe al río Zapote y se une al Sordo para formar el Yolotepec.

PUTLA VILLA DE GUERRERO ◆ Municipio de Oaxaca situado en la porción sudoccidental del estado, al suroeste de Tlaxiaco. Limita al oeste con Guerrero. Superficie: 884.15 km². Habitantes: 26,154, de los cuales 5,447 forman la población económicamente activa. Hablan alguna lengua indígena 7,084 personas mayores de cinco años (triqui 3,726 y mixteco 3,250). Indígenas monolingües: 1,124. Pertenece al distrito judicial de Putla y su nombre le fue impuesto en honor de Vicente Guerrero.

Iglesia en Putla Villa de Guerrero, Oaxaca

FOTO: FONDO EDITORIAL GRUPO AZABACHE

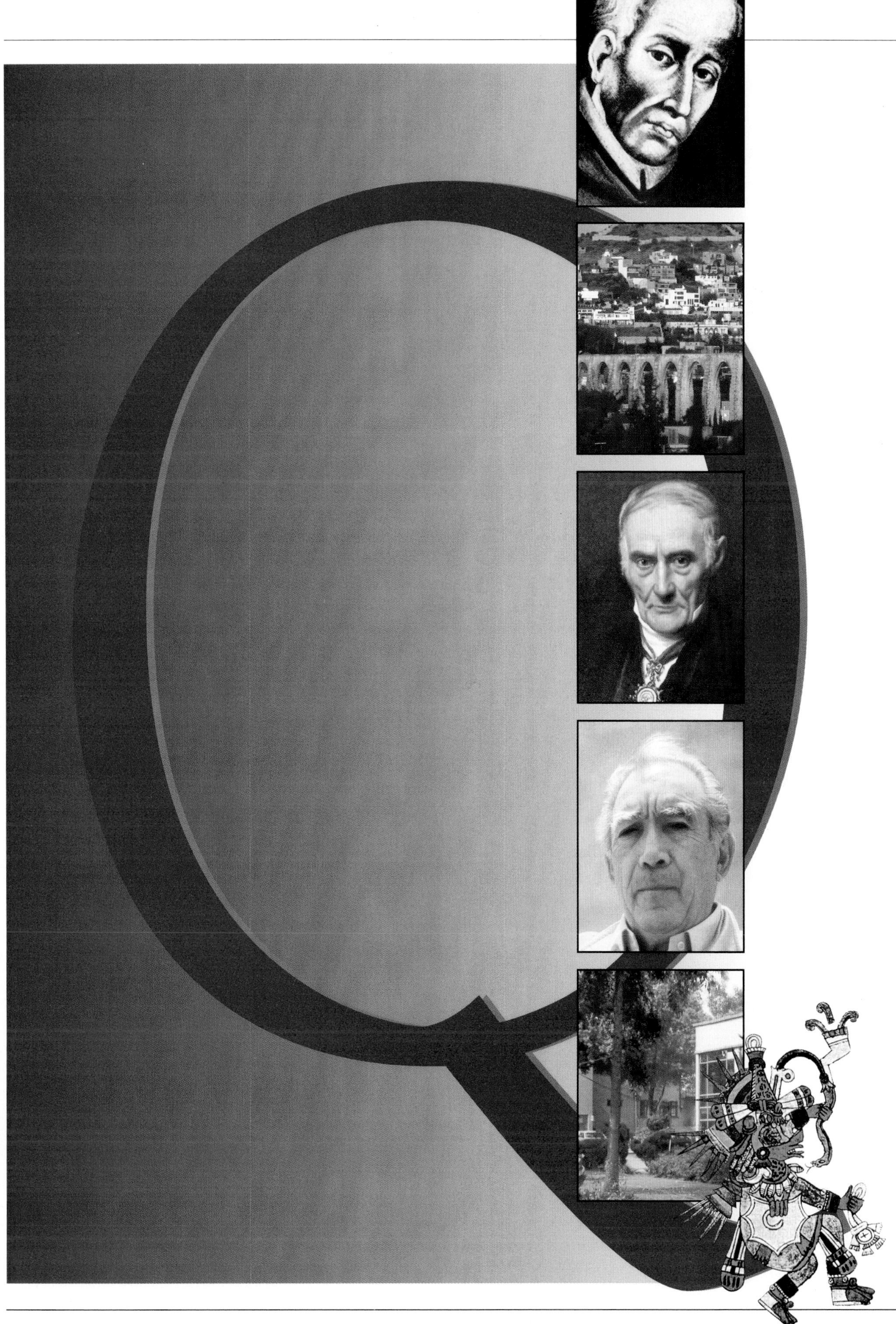

Gabriel Quadri de la Torre

Miguel Ángel Quemáin Sáenz

QATAR, ESTADO DE ◆ Emirato asiático que limita al norte y este con el golfo Pérsico, al sur con Arabia Saudita y los Emiratos Árabes Unidos y al oeste con el golfo de Bahrein. Se encuentra en la península de Qatar y casi la totalidad de su territorio es desértico. Superficie: 11,437 km². Habitantes: 579,000 (1998). Su capital es Doha (Al Dawhah), con 339,471 habitantes (1993). El idioma oficial es el árabe y su unidad monetaria, el riyal de Qatar. Se gobierna por una monarquía absoluta. La nación estuvo sucesivamente bajo las tutelas de Arabia Saudita (1803-69), el Reino Unido (1869-71), el imperio otomano (1871-1916) y, nuevamente el Reino Unido (1916). En 1949 se inició la explotación de los hidrocarburos, que aportan al país 95 por ciento de sus ingresos. En 1970 se proclamó una constitución provisional, que aún rige, y un año después, el emirato se independizó de la Gran Bretaña. En 1972 llegó al poder el emir Khalifa bin Hamad al-Thani. El 30 de junio de 1975 se establecieron las relaciones diplomáticas entre México y el emirato. En 1977 fue nacionalizado el petróleo. Mediante un golpe incruento, en 1995, Abdullah bin Khalifa al-Thani, príncipe heredero y ministro de Defensa, depuso a su padre, quien huyó del país. Un año más tarde padre e hijo se reconciliaron y el ex emir retornó a Qatar, pero sin mando alguno.

QUADRI DE LA TORRE, GABRIEL ◆ n. en el DF (1954). Ingeniero civil por la UIA, maestro y candidato a doctor en Economía por la Universidad de Texas en Austin. Ha sido analista (1977-79) y jefe de financiamiento externo en el Banco de México (1983-87), director de Planeación Ecológica en el DDF (1989-92), director general de Normatividad Ambiental (1994), presidente del INE (1994-97) y director general del Centro de Estudios del Sector Privado para el Desarrollo Sostenible (1997). Se ha dedicado a la docencia y ha escrito varios libros sobre temas relacionados con el medio ambiente y el desarrollo sustentable. Es articulista del periódico *La Crónica*.

Iglesia de la Merced, en Quecholac, Puebla

QUECHOLAC ◆ Municipio de Puebla situado en el centro del estado, al noreste de Tecamachalco. Superficie: 163.29 km². Población: 34,442 habitantes, de los cuales 7,195 forman la población económicamente activa. Hablan alguna lengua indígena 31 personas mayores de cinco años (náhuatl 20).

QUECHULTENANGO ◆ Municipio de Guerrero situado en el sureste del estado, al sureste de Chilpancingo. Superficie: 929.7 km². Población: 29,927 habitantes, de los cuales 5,199 forman la población económicamente activa. Hablan alguna lengua indígena 994 personas mayores de cinco años (náhuatl 458 y tlapaneco 441).

QUELITE, DEL ◆ Río de Sinaloa que nace en las montañas de La Silla; corre de noreste a suroeste y desemboca en el Pacífico. Su curso es de 100 kilómetros. Sus tributarios son los ríos Silla, Roble, Cañadas, Palmirito y Tasajera.

QUEMADA, LA ◆ Zona arqueológica de Zacatecas, también llamada Chicomoztoc, situada en la margen derecha del río Malpaso. La región fue descrita por Antonio Tello en 1650. Berghes visitó la zona en 1820 y levantó un plano. En 1947 se hicieron los primeros trabajos de exploración y reconstrucción, a cargo de Carlos Margáin y Hugo Moedano.

QUEMÁIN SÁENZ, MIGUEL ÁNGEL ◆ n. en el DF (1961). Periodista. Licencia-

Parroquia de Santiago Apóstol en Quechultenango, Guerrero

do en periodismo por la UNAM (1983). Guionista de los programas *Desde Temprano* y *Moviola*, de Canal 13 (1985). Reportero de *unomásuno* (1985). Reportero fundador (1985-89) y jefe de información (1987-89) del noticiero *Hoy en la cultura*. Ha colaborado en publicaciones literarias de México y otros países. Editor de cultura y encargado de anuarios y reportajes especiales en el semanario *Época* (1991-95). Dirigió la revista *Nitrato de Plata* (1994-95). Ha sido editor de teatro en Editores Mexicanos Unidos (1985-86), jefe del Departamento de Prensa del CNCA (1989-91), jefe de información del Festival de la Ciudad de México (1989-91), asesor en comunicación y promoción del Ballet Nacional de México (1991), director de Promoción y Difusión del Festival del Centro Histórico de la Ciudad de México (1991-95), del Festival Cultural de Tepoztlán, Mor. (1993), y responsable de difusión de la editorial Plaza y Janés. Corresponsal en México del programa *Los Libros* de TVE (1998-). Dirigió la *Revista Mexicana de Cultura*, suplemento del periódico *El Nacional* (1996-98). Director de Análisis, Síntesis y Monitoreo del gobierno del DF (1997-). Becario del INBA (1987-88) y del Fonca (1991-92). Autor de *Reverso de la palabra* (entrevista, 1996) y de *Voces cruzadas* (en prensa).

QUENAMICAN ◆ En la mitología nahua, el Quenamican o Quenonamican es el sitio "donde se existe de algún modo", es decir, la región en la que siguen viviendo los que han muerto y alguna vez habrán de regresar al mundo.

QUERÉNDARO ◆ Municipio de Michoacán situado en el noreste del estado, al este de Morelia. Superficie: 186.23 km^2. Población: 14,248 habitantes, de los cuales 2,950 forman la población económicamente activa. Hablan alguna lengua indígena siete personas mayores de cinco años.

QUERÉNDARO ◆ Río de Michoacán que nace en el norte de la sierra de Mil Cumbres; corre de sureste a noroeste y desemboca en el lago de Cuitzeo, tras recoger el caudal del río Zinapécuaro.

QUERÉTARO ◆ Municipio del estado de Querétaro situado en el extremo occidental de la entidad; limita al norte y oeste con Guanajuato. Superficie: 759.9 km^2. Población: 559,222 habitantes, de los cuales 143,819 forman la población económicamente activa. Hablan alguna lengua indígena 1,683 personas mayores de cinco años (otomí 552, náhuatl 464, zapoteco 102 y mazahua 101). La cabecera municipal, del mismo nombre, que también es la capital del estado, se encuentra a 300 kilómetros del Distrito Federal. Es el mayor centro agrícola de la región y eje de comunicaciones por donde pasa la mayoría del tránsito entre la capital del país, el valle de Toluca, el Bajío y la Altiplanicie. En épocas prehispánicas fue una comunidad otomí conquistada por los mexicas; en 1531 la ocuparon Fernando de Tapia y Nicolás de San Luis Montañez, cacique otomí de Xilotepec, y se le llamó Santiago de Querétaro. La traza original fue realizada por Juan Sánchez de Alanís. La ciudad formó parte, con San Juan del Río, de la provincia de Xilotepec. El 27 de octubre de 1537 fue erigida en pueblo y elevada a la categoría de villa en 1609; en 1655 fue hecha "muy noble y muy leal" ciudad. Por cédula real del 1 de octubre de 1671 se le otorgó el título de "tercera ciudad del reino". En 1790, su población era casi de 30,000 habitantes. Entre los monumentos coloniales de la ciudad de Querétaro están el acueducto, que empezó a construirse el 15 de enero de 1726 y fue concluido el 19 de octubre de 1739, patrocinado por Juan A. de Urrutia y Arana; la iglesia y el claustro de San Agustín, la Casa de los Perros, los templos de Santa Rosa, Santa Clara, del Carmen y de Teresitas; la fuente de Neptuno y la casa Cobián. En 1996, la zona de monumentos históricos de la ciudad fue declarada "Patrimonio de la Humanidad" por la UNESCO.

FOTO: MICHAEL CALDERWOOD

Ciudad de Querétaro, Querétaro

QUERÉTARO ◆ Río de Querétaro y Guanajuato que nace en las laderas meridionales de la sierra del Pinal del Zamorano; corre de noreste a suroeste, entra en el valle de Querétaro, recibe al río Pueblito y se transforma en el Apaseo.

Ignacio Loyola, gobernador de Querétaro

QUERÉTARO DE ARTEAGA ◆ Estado de la República Mexicana situado en el centro-oriente del país. Limita con San Luis Potosí, Hidalgo, el Estado de México, Michoacán y Guanajuato. Superficie: 11,449 km², equivalentes al 0.60 por ciento del territorio nacional, divididos en 18 municipios. El nombre proviene, probablemente, de la lengua tarasca, y es una corrupción de *Quereta-Parazicuyo* o *Ychahtzincuyo*, que significa "lugar del juego de pelota". Dos son los sistemas orográficos principales de la entidad: la sierra Gorda, al norte, y la Queretana, al sur. Su hidrografía pertenece a la cuenca del Pánuco y sus principales ríos son el San Juan, Santa María, Extórax y Moctezuma; tiene ocho grandes presas para riego y la laguna de Petzola. Población: 1,297,575 personas (1997; 1.4 por ciento del total nacional en 1995). La población económicamente activa es 54.5 por ciento de los mayores de 12 años. Aporta con 1.55 por ciento al producto interno bruto total (1996). Su índice de analfabetismo es de 12.27 por ciento de los mayores de 15 años. Hablan alguna lengua indígena 20,738 personas mayores de cinco años (otomí 18,889), de los cuales 1,156 no saben español. *Historia*: los primeros pueblos agricultores que poblaron el actual territorio queretano se establecieron, a mediados del último milenio antes de nuestra era, en los alrededores de San Juan del Río. En los primeros años de la época contemporánea se extendieron hacia el norte, hasta las estribaciones de la sierra Gorda. Estos grupos mantuvieron algún contacto con habitantes de Chupícuaro, pero, aproximadamente desde el año 400, la influencia teotihuacana fue la predominante. En la sierra Gorda, los habitantes de Toluquilla y Ranas desarrollaron un amplio comercio con Teotihuacan, la Huasteca y el Tajín. Hacia los siglos X y XI, los toltecas de Tula ocuparon la porción meridional del actual territorio del estado, y es posible que hayan sido ellos los introductores del juego de pelota en la región, práctica de la que proviene el nombre de Querétaro. Poco después de la destrucción de Tula, en el siglo XII, desaparecieron casi todos los grupos sedentarios y fueron sustituidos por núcleos nómadas de pames, que ocuparon toda la parte media y septentrional de la entidad. También en el siglo XII, los mexicas se establecieron momentáneamente en el sur de la región, camino del valle de México. A partir del siglo XIII, la porción meridional del actual territorio de Querétaro estuvo ocupada por el señorío otomí de Jilotepec, mientras que en el oeste se establecieron algunos grupos emparentados o relacionados con los purépechas. Es probable, además, que en el siglo XV las tropas mexicas de Moctezuma Ilhuicamina hubieran penetrado en el sur de Querétaro. Las primeras exploraciones españolas en el territorio fueron realizadas en 1522 por los otomíes Hernando de Tapia y Nicolás de

San Luis Montañez. Cuatro años más tarde, en 1526, Montañez fundó San Juan del Río; en julio de 1531 sus tropas otomíes derrotaron a las pames de Juan Bautista Criado. En el sitio de la batalla se fundó la ciudad de Querétaro, población que estuvo habitada, fundamentalmente, por otomíes y purépechas durante el siglo XVI. Desde 1532, los españoles ocuparon algunas zonas del sur queretano; y en 1540, el gobierno virreinal designó a Baltazar del Campo, Juan de Luna, Juan Ramírez y Miguel de la Paz como "fundadores y conquistadores" de la ciudad de Querétaro. Hacia 1550 se estableció el camino real entre México y Zacatecas, que pasaba por Querétaro, pero dos años después, los pames de la sierra Gorda y del actual San Luis Potosí, comenzaron a realizar saqueos en Jalpa y otros pueblos de otomíes católicos. Además de realizar varias expediciones, los españoles construyeron presidios (cuarteles) en Jalpan y Tolimán, lo que junto con la edificación de misiones religiosas permitió que, para 1600, la mayoría del actual territorio de la entidad hubiera sido pacificado. Hasta 1578, en que se creó la alcaldía mayor de Querétaro, el territorio, situado entre la actual capital del estado y San Juan del Río, dependió de la alcaldía mayor de Jilotepec. Desde fines del siglo XVI, los franciscanos se instalaron en la región. Hacia 1640 se desarrolló la agricultura en el sur del estado, entre Querétaro y Jilotepec, zona que contaba con unos 10,000 habitantes. En este tiempo, un gran número de esclavos negros fue traído de Mozambique por los portugueses; su presencia, y el desprecio que los españoles sentían por ellos, hizo que la palabra *mozambique* se convirtiera en un sinónimo local de *diablo*.

Estado de Queretaro

Foto: Michael Calderwood

Dalias de Querétaro

Desde mediados del siglo XVII, los agustinos intentaron evangelizar a los pames de la sierra Gorda, pero a raíz de una gran sublevación india que comenzó en 1704 y que fue derrotada en 1735, los franciscanos los sustituyeron y establecieron varias misiones en la región, de las cuales destacan las dirigidas por Junípero Serra. En 1787, debido a la implantación de las reformas borbónicas, el actual territorio del estado quedó bajo la jurisdicción de la intendencia de México. Durante el siglo XVIII, Querétaro se convirtió en uno de los centros textileros y comerciales más importantes de la Nueva España, por lo que, en 1794, la Real Audiencia de México dispuso que en vez de alcalde o subdelegado, la región tendría un corregidor, cargo casi similar al de intendente. En 1804, en la capital del corregimiento existían 18 obrajes y 327 trapiches textileros. Seis años más tarde, en agosto de 1810, José Mariano Galván denunció, ante la Audiencia de México, la existencia de una conspiración criolla de la que formaban parte, entre otros, el corregidor Miguel Domínguez, los abogados Francisco Araujo, Epigmenio González, Ignacio Gutiérrez y Emeterio González; los militares Ignacio Allende e Ignacio Aldama, y los sacerdotes Miguel Hidalgo y Mariano Matamoros. Y a pesar de que casi todos los conspiradores fueron detenidos en los días siguientes, poco pudieron hacer las autoridades coloniales, pues a mediados de septiembre, Hidalgo se levantó en armas. También en septiembre, las tropas virreinales de Manuel de Flon ocuparon Querétaro y, en noviembre de ese año, luego de la derrota de los insurgentes en Aculco, Félix María Calleja, comandante del ejército colonial, ocupó San Juan del Río y lanzó una proclama en la que ofrecía indulto a los sublevados. Poco después, sin embargo, el sacerdote Juan Manuel Corra se levantó en armas en el sur del corregimiento; en la sierra Gorda, mientras tanto, operaba Julián Villagrán. En 1811, una tropa insurgente al mando de Vicente Téllez tomó Tequisquiapan. En 1813, Manuel Toral organizó una fuerza de espionaje formada por sacerdotes, que en ese mismo año fue suprimida por la jerarquía. En 1814, la *Constitución de Apatzingán* consignó, por primera vez, la existencia de Querétaro como una entidad separada de la intendencia de México: una de las 17 provincias que constituían la América Mexicana. Durante el resto de la lucha insurgente, el territorio de Querétaro permaneció en poder de los realistas, aunque todavía en 1819 operaban las guerrillas de Miguel Borga y José Antonio Magos. El 24 de mayo de 1821, de la imprenta portátil de las fuerzas de Iturbide salió el primer periódico editado en territorio queretano: el *Ejército Imperial Mexicano de las Tres Garantías.*

Foto: Carlos Hahn

Panorámica de la ciudad de Querétaro

Foto: Fondo Editorial Grupo Azabache

Primer Colegio de Misiones de América

Foto: Fondo Editorial Grupo Azabache

Retablo de la virgen de Guadalupe en el Beaterío de Santa Rosa de Viterio

Al mes siguiente, el ejército Trigarante sitió y tomó la cabecera del corregimiento. Al expedirse la convocatoria al primer Congreso Constituyente, en noviembre de 1821, Querétaro fue considerado "provincia", con lo que de hecho se le separó de la intendencia de México. La confirmación de ese hecho ocurrió en enero de 1824, al ser proclamada el Acta Constitutiva de la Federación. En abril se eligió un Supremo Poder Ejecutivo Provisional del Estado. En agosto de 1825 se promulgó la primera Constitución local y se eligió el primer gobernador constitucional: José María Diez Marina (1825-29). Por entonces, la población del nuevo estado era de aproximadamente 100,000 personas. En junio de 1833, el gobernador José Rafael Canalizo se levantó en armas contra el gobierno de Valentín Gómez Farías y, aunque fue derrotado a fines de ese año, reasumió el poder tras la instauración de la República centralista, cuando el estado se convirtió en departamento de Querétaro. A fines de los años treinta comenzaron a circular los periódicos *El Pasatiempo*, *La Hoja Extraordinaria de la Otra Banda* y *La Revista Semanaria*. En 1844, el gobierno de Sabás Antonio Domínguez se opuso a la pretensión del presidente Antonio López de Santa Anna de establecer un impuesto extraordinario que, supuestamente, serviría para equipar a un ejército reconquistador de Texas, por lo que Santa Anna organizó una expedición contra Querétaro, destituyó a Domínguez y encarceló a la diputación queretana, pero, a causa de un pronunciamiento en la ciudad de México, se vio obligado a restaurar los poderes locales. A principios de 1847, luego de la promulgación de la ley de intervención de los bienes de manos muertas, varios miles de otomíes intentaron tomar el Palacio de Gobierno, pero fueron rechazados después de una larga batalla en el centro de la ciudad. En octubre de ese mismo año, ocupada la ciudad de México por los invasores estadounidenses, los poderes de la República se instalaron en la capital del estado, donde, después de un agitado debate, el Congreso aprobó, sin unanimidad, la firma de los tratados de Guadalupe-Hidalgo. En junio de ese año, Tomás Mejía lanzó en la sierra Gorda el Plan de San José de los Amoles, en el que se "desconoce al actual gobierno" y "se declara guerra sin tregua al invasor americano mientras pisa

FOTO: MICHAEL CALDERWOOD

Peña de Bernal, Querétaro

FOTO: BORIS DE SWAN

Detalle arquitectónico en Queretaro

FOTO: BORIS DE SWAN

Cerámica de Queretaro

nuestra tierra". Durante los dos meses siguientes, la insurrección campesina se extendió a Veracruz, Puebla, Hidalgo y San Luis Potosí, pero a partir de septiembre, casi todos los dirigentes agrarios aceptaron el indulto concedido por el gobierno de José Joaquín de Herrera. No obstante, a principios de 1849, los campesinos de la sierra Gorda se volvieron a levantar en armas, pero fueron derrotados por las fuerzas que comandaba Anastasio Bustamante. A principios de 1853, el gobernador, Ramón María Loreto Canal de Samaniego, intentó desobeceder una orden del gobierno de Santa Anna, por lo que el presidente envió a Querétaro una fuerza al mando de Pánfilo Barasorda, quien derrocó al gobierno local. El 1 de diciembre de ese año, el gobierno de Santa Anna creó el Territorio de Sierra Gorda, que comprendía, del lado queretano, los municipios de Espíritu Santo y Atarjea, es decir, toda la porción noroccidental del estado. El 2 de diciembre de 1855, con el apoyo de Mejía, José López Uraga se levantó en armas en Tolimán, en el centro del estado, con la idea de derrocar al nuevo gobierno de Ignacio Comonfort, pero en enero de 1856, las tropas de Luis Ghilardi ocuparon Tolimán; Mejía, por su parte, se dijo engañado por el movimiento y aseguró su lealtad al gobierno. El 13 de octubre, sin embargo, atacó y tomó la ciudad de Querétaro, donde al día siguiente publicó una proclama en la que acusaba a los liberales de aspirar "a la disolución, el desorden y la rapiña" y convocaba a que los queretanos se sumaran a la revuelta, en nombre de la religión católica. Los conservadores abandonaron la capital del estado a fines del mes, se retiraron a la sierra Gorda y en diciembre se unieron al levantamiento de Luis G. Osollo en San Luis Potosí. El gobierno movilizó a las tropas de Anastasio Parrodi, José María Arteaga, Miguel Negrete y Sóstenes Rocha, quienes en enero de 1857 lograron derrotar la sublevación. Durante el Congreso Constituyente de 1856-57 se consideró la posibilidad de instalar el Distrito Federal en Querétaro, pero, debido a la abstención de los diputados de esta entidad, el proyecto se desechó en diciembre de 1856. En febrero de 1857, al promulgarse la nueva Constitución, desapareció el departamento de Sierra Gorda. En noviembre de 1857, luego de reorganizar a sus fuerzas de la sierra Gorda, Mejía ocupó San Juan del Río y la ciudad de Querétaro, pero se retiró pocos días más tarde, ante el ataque de Manuel Doblado. A fines de diciembre, luego del golpe de Estado del presidente Comonfort, el gobernador Arteaga se unió a la coalición de gobiernos liberales organizada por Parrodi, entonces gobernador de Jalisco, pero eso no impidió que en febrero de 1858, las tropas de Mejía ocuparan, una vez más, la capital estatal e instalaran a Octaviano Muñoz Ledo en la gubernatura, cuya principal acción al frente del gobierno (de febrero a junio de 1858), fue la creación del primer cuerpo de guardias rurales del país. Un año más tarde, en marzo de 1859, las tropas combinadas de Santos Degollado, Leandro Valle e Ignacio Zaragoza, fueron derrotadas en la hacienda de Calamanda, pero en noviembre de 1860, los liberales recuperaron la capital de la entidad. Los conservadores se refugiaron en la sierra Gorda y, durante la primera mitad de 1861, formaron varias partidas, las que en mayo, al mando de Mejía, ocuparon brevemente Querétaro. Dos años después, en noviembre de 1863, las tropas de Mejía tomaron la capital del estado y unos días después la entregaron a las fuerzas invasoras de Fé-

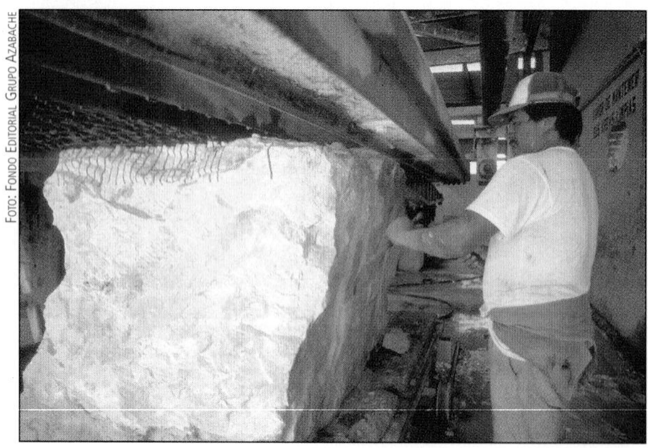
FOTO: FONDO EDITORIAL GRUPO AZABACHE

Mármol queretano

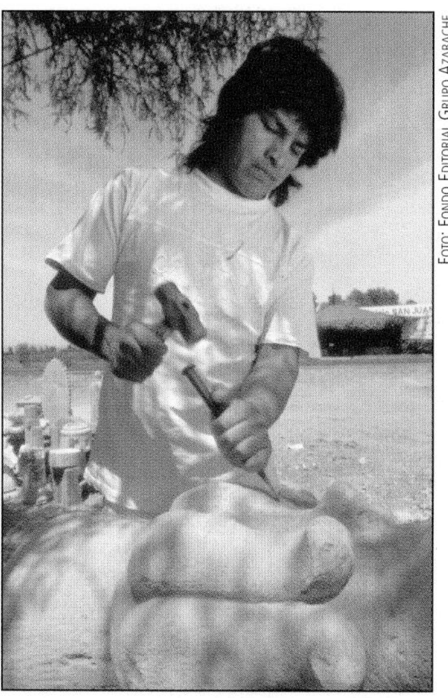
FOTO: FONDO EDITORIAL GRUPO AZABACHE

Tallador de cantera de San Juan del Río, Querétaro

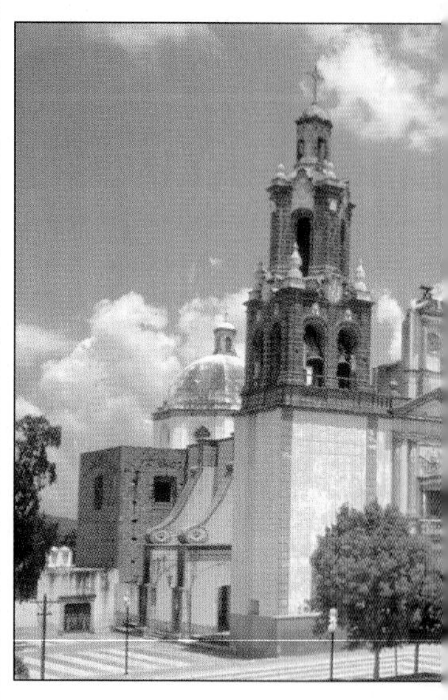

Foto: Michael Calderwood

Las margaritas se aprecian en la mayoría de las áreas verdes de Querétaro

Foto: Michael Calderwood

Jumiles de Querétaro

Foto: Pablo Cervantes

Cascada de Aculco

lix Douay. Durante el resto de la intervención, el territorio queretano, convertido en departamento por el gobierno de Maximiliano de Habsburgo en marzo de 1865, permaneció en poder de los franceses y más tarde de los imperialistas. En febrero de 1867, tras abandonar la ciudad de México, Maximiliano se instaló en Querétaro. En marzo, las tropas republicanas de Mariano Escobedo pusieron sitio a la ciudad y, dos meses después la ocuparon y detuvieron al Habsburgo y a los generales colaboracionistas Tomás Mejía y Miguel Miramón. Los tres fueron fusilados en junio de ese año, en el cerro de las Campanas. En 1868, el Congreso local acordó añadirle el apellido de José María Arteaga al nombre del estado. En noviembre de 1876, el gobernador Francisco Villaseñor se adhirió al Plan de Guanajuato, documento por el que se desconocía la reelección del presidente Sebastián Lerdo de Tejada, y que demandaba que

Foto: Fondo Editorial Grupo Azabache

Plaza principal de Cadereyta de Montes, Querétaro

Foto: Michael Calderwood

Colón, Querétaro

Ezequiel Montes, Querétaro

Convento de San Agustín, en Queretaro

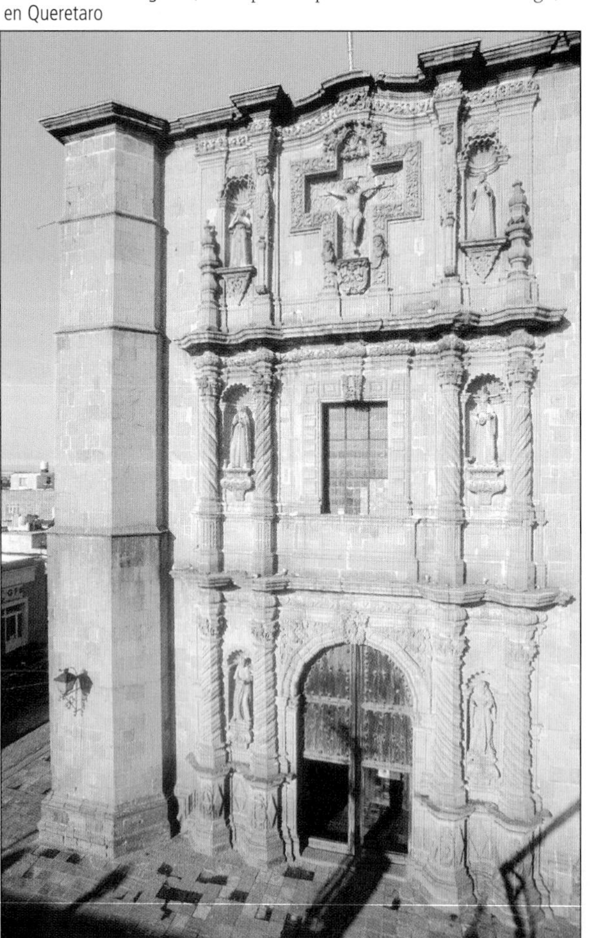

José María Iglesias ocupara el Poder Ejecutivo. Lerdo envió una fuerza militar al mando de Francisco A. Vélez, que ocupó la capital del estado. Sin embargo, el 20 de noviembre las tropas de Vélez se adhirieron al Plan de Tuxtepec y abandonaron Querétaro. Desde Guanajuato avanzaron los restos del gobierno *legalista* de Iglesias, tomaron Querétaro y, en los últimos días del año, el propio Iglesias se entrevistó con Porfirio Díaz en los suburbios de la capital. Díaz se negó a negociar su triunfo y los iglesistas abandonaron la ciudad. Tres años más tarde, en 1879, se proclamó el Plan de la Barranca, en el cual los campesinos guanajuatenses y queretanos de la sierra Gorda exponían una serie de postulados agraristas. A la rebelión se sumó Miguel Negrete, pero el movimiento fue derrotado en 1881. Un año antes, por otra parte, Francisco González de Cosío había asumido, por primera vez, la gubernatura estatal y salvo un breve periodo (1883-87), la ocuparía hasta marzo de 1911. En 1895, la población del estado era de 228,551 habitantes. En ese mismo año, los metodistas fundaron el Instituto Metodista de Querétaro, que fue una de las escuelas más importantes del porfiriato. En 1909, una huelga de los trabajadores del Ferrocarril Central Mexicano fue violentamente reprimida por el ejército. Por esos días, Francisco I. Madero creó el Partido Antirreeleccionista Queretano. A principios de 1911, a dos meses de iniciada la revuelta maderista, varios grupos se levantaron en armas en la sierra Gorda. En octubre fue elegido gobernador Carlos M. Loyola, quien en febrero de 1913 reconoció al gobierno golpista de Victoriano Huerta. En mayo, fuerzas ca-

Viñedos de la región de Tequisquiapan, Querétaro

rrancistas intentaron tomar Jalpan, en el norte del estado, pero fueron rechazadas. Finalmente, en octubre, los huertistas derrocaron al gobierno de Loyola. En julio del año siguiente, las tropas de Francisco Murguía ocuparon la capital del estado y en enero de 1916, al ser derrotada la División del Norte en el Bajío, el gobierno de Venustiano Carranza se instaló en la capital del estado. En septiembre de ese año, Carranza, ya en la ciudad de México, lanzó la convocatoria a un nuevo Congreso Constituyente, que se reunió en el Teatro Iturbide de la capital del estado, entre diciembre de 1916 y el 5 de febrero de 1917, cuando se promulgó la nueva Constitución. En 1920, las fuerzas del Plan de Agua Prieta ocuparon la capital del estado y el gobierno local se retiró a Tequisquiapan, pero al ser asesinado Carranza se disolvió. Al iniciarse la rebelión delahuertista, el presidente Álvaro Obregón destituyó al gobernador Francisco Ramírez, quien, se dijo, apoyaba el levantamiento. Durante la guerra cristera, prácticamente no hubo acciones armadas en Querétaro, aunque la Liga Nacional de Defensa de la Libertad Religiosa utilizó la capital del estado como centro de enlace entre los combatientes y la ciudad de México. Hacia finales de los años treinta se inició el reparto de tierras y el desarrollo industrial en la década de los cuarenta. El gobernador Octavio Mondragón fundó, durante su gestión (1949-55), la Universidad Autónoma de Querétaro. En 1997, el panista Ignacio Loyola se convirtió en el primer gobernador propuesto por un partido de oposición.

LONGITUD DE LA RED DE CARRETERAS POR SUPERFICIE DE RODAMIENTO, 1995

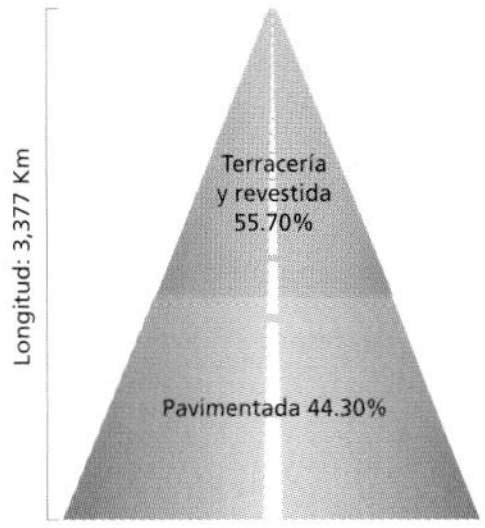

Longitud: 3,377 Km
Terracería y revestida 55.70%
Pavimentada 44.30%

BIBLIOTECAS Y USUARIOS, 1993
Número de bibliotecas: 133

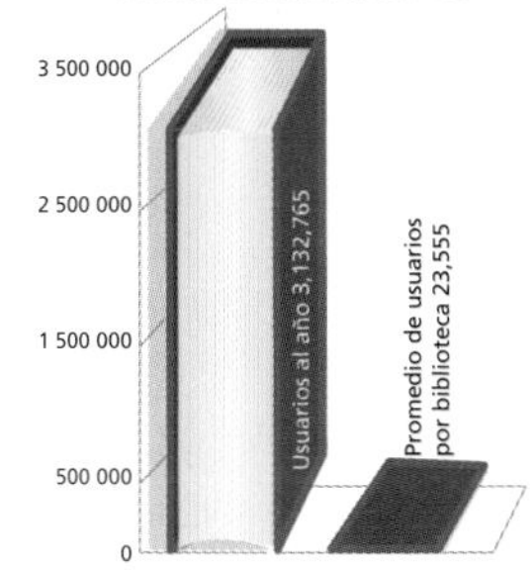

3 500 000
2 500 000
1 500 000
500 000
0
Usuarios al año 3,132,765
Promedio de usuarios por biblioteca 23,555

LÍNEAS TELEFÓNICAS EN SERVICIO Y APARATOS PÚBLICOS, 1994

100 000
80 000
60 000
40 000
20 000
0
Líneas en servicio 95,499
Aparatos públicos 1,774
Un aparato por cada 1,000 habitantes

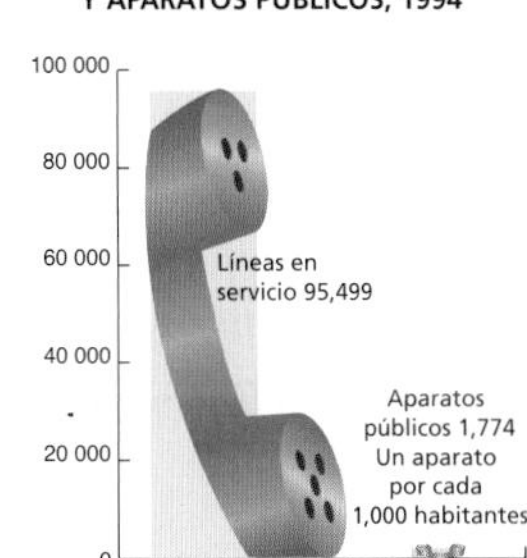

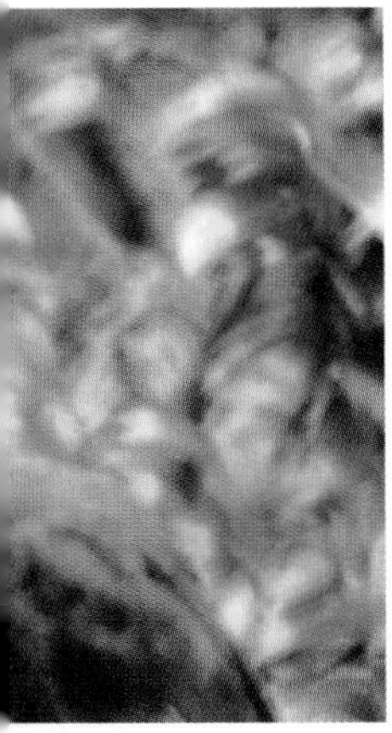

PRODUCTO INTERNO BRUTO (PIB) A PRECIOS CORRIENTES

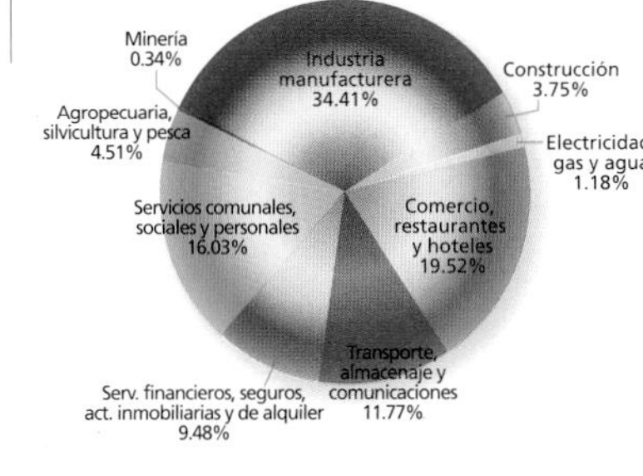

Minería 0.34%
Industria manufacturera 34.41%
Construcción 3.75%
Agropecuaria, silvicultura y pesca 4.51%
Electricidad, gas y agua 1.18%
Servicios comunales, sociales y personales 16.03%
Comercio, restaurantes y hoteles 19.52%
Transporte, almacenaje y comunicaciones 11.77%
Serv. financieros, seguros, act. inmobiliarias y de alquiler 9.48%

DISTRIBUCIÓN PORCENTUAL DE LA POBLACIÓN OCUPADA POR SECTOR DE ACTIVIDAD ECONÓMICA, 1995

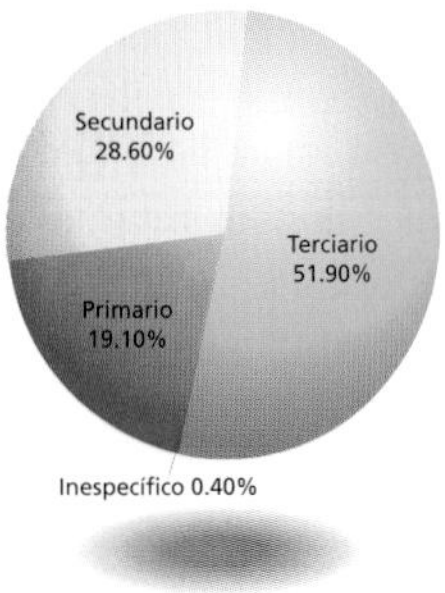

Secundario 28.60%
Terciario 51.90%
Primario 19.10%
Inespecífico 0.40%

PROMEDIO DE ESCOLARIDAD DE LA POBLACIÓN DE 15 AÑOS Y MÁS, POR SEXO, 1995

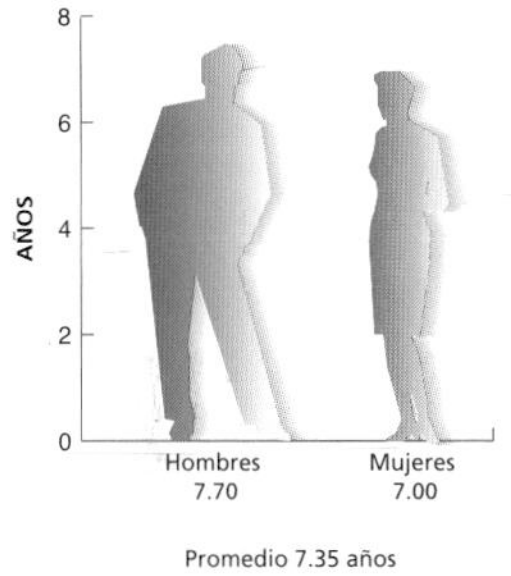

8
6
AÑOS
4
2
0
Hombres 7.70
Mujeres 7.00
Promedio 7.35 años

DISTRIBUCIÓN DE LA POBLACIÓN POR TAMAÑO DE LA LOCALIDAD, 1995

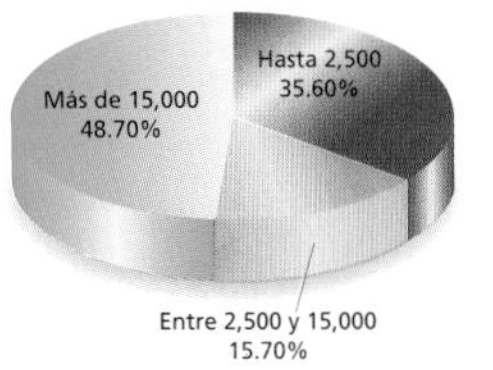

Más de 15,000 48.70%
Hasta 2,500 35.60%
Entre 2,500 y 15,000 15.70%

POBLACIÓN DE 5 AÑOS Y MÁS HABLANTE DE LENGUA INDÍGENA, 1995

1 200 000
1 000 000
800 000
600 000
400 000
200 000
0
Población de 5 años y más 1,088,599
Población de 5 años y más hablante de lengua indígena 20,738 (1.91%)

3

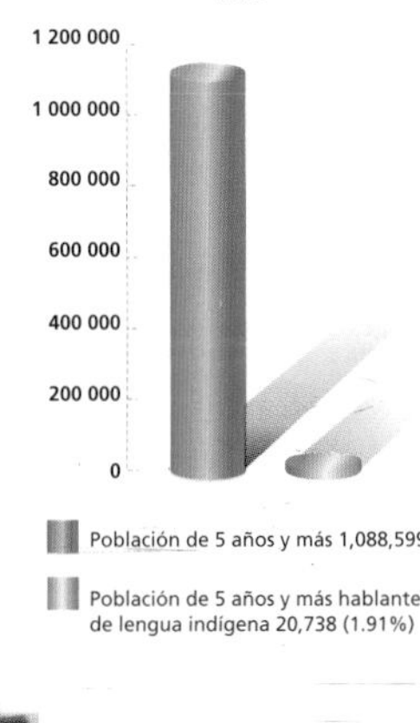

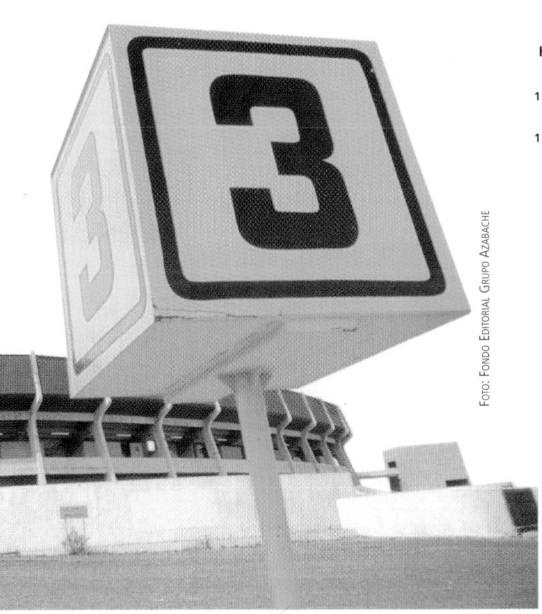

Estadio Corregidora, en Querétaro

FOTO: FONDO EDITORIAL GRUPO AZABACHE

QUETZALCÓATL ◆ Su nombre significa "Gemelo Precioso". Dios náhuatl creado por la pareja original Tonacatecuhtli y Tonacacíhuatl: era el Tezcatlipoca blanco y su lugar en el universo era el del sol poniente. Según la mitología, el día uno caña del año uno caña Quetzalcóatl se hizo hombre, encarnó como hijo del guerrero Mixcóatl y de Chimalma; mató a Tepotztécatl para vengar la muerte de su padre y le erigió un templo en el Citlaltépetl, a donde fueron a buscarlo los habitantes de Tollan para hacerlo su soberano. Gobernó esa ciudad hasta que fue embriagado por los sacerdotes de Yuyauhqui (el Tezcatlipoca negro) y rompió su voto de castidad. Huyó y se refugió en Cholula, donde derrotó a los mixteco-olmecas; siguió su viaje hacia la costa del golfo de México, donde se inmoló en una hoguera; bajó al reino de la muerte y nueve días después renació como la estrella matutina o vespertina (Venus). Otra versión señala que Quetzalcóatl siguió su camino hasta Yucatán, donde recibió el nombre maya de Kukulkán. Aparece como creador y sostenedor, patrono de la cultura y de las artes, dios que da vida. Está relacionado con Ehécatl, que probablemente sea una variante suya. También era dios de los caminantes y venerado con el nombre de Yacatecuhtli o "señor de los viajeros". La leyenda del Quetzalcóatl hombre fue tratada en diversos relatos de lengua náhuatl, recopilados en el *Manuscrito de Cuauhtitlán*, y recogida por Sahagún, en versiones orales de algunos indígenas.

Quetzalcóatl en detalle de las ruinas de Teotihuacán

Foto: Carlos Hahn

Quetzalcóatl representado en una página del códice Borbónico

QUEVEDO, DE ◆ Península de Sinaloa, también llamada de San José, situada al sur-sureste de Culiacán. Está formada por el cordón litoral que limita la bahía de Ceuta o de Quevedo. Su extremo norte limita con la boca de Tavalo o Navito, que da salida a las aguas de la bahía y a las del río San Lorenzo. Durante la temporada de lluvias, esta península se convierte en una isla.

QUEVEDO, MIGUEL ÁNGEL DE ◆ n. en Guadalajara, Jal., y m. en el DF (1859-1946). Ingeniero. Trabajó en el aprovechamiento del agua para la generación eléctrica y colaboró en las obras de Río Blanco, Veracruz, a fines del siglo XIX. Construyó la iglesia del Buen Tono y la sede del Banco de Londres y México en la ciudad de México. Durante varios años se desempeñó como jefe del Departamento Forestal de la Secretaría de Agricultura y se distinguió por su labor reforestadora en el país, por lo que fue llamado *el Apóstol del Árbol*. En Veracruz logró detener los médanos gracias a la plantación de casuarinas, especie que importó de Australia. Fue fundador de la Escuela y de la Sociedad Forestal. Cedió a la nación los Viveros de Coyoacán, que eran parte del rancho Panzacola, de su propiedad.

Foto: Pablo González de Alba

Viveros de Coyoacán, en el DF, cedidos por Miguel Ángel de Quevedo

QUEVEDO MORENO, RODRIGO M. ◆ n. en Casas Grandes, Chih., y m. en EUA (1889-1967). Militar. Se incorporó a la revolución maderista en Sonora, en 1910; luchó al lado de Francisco Miranda y Antonio Rojas. En 1911 se integró al Cuerpo Rural comandado por José de la Luz Blanco; y en 1912 participó en la rebelión orozquista a las órdenes de José Inés Salazar y Emilio P. Campa. En marzo de 1913 se rindió ante el gobierno de Victoriano Huerta, quien le reconoció el grado de mayor. Luchó contra la División del Norte, pero al vencer ésta, Quevedo se unió a las fuerzas villistas (1916). En 1918 se rindió ante el gobierno de Carranza; en 1919 se le nombró comandante militar de Jiménez e Hidalgo del Parral; se adhirió al Plan de Agua Prieta (1920). En 1929 combatió la rebelión escobarista. Alcanzó el grado de general de división. De 1932 a 1936 ocupó la gubernatura de Chihuahua. Fue también comandante de varias zonas militares y senador (1958- 64).

QUEVEDO Y ZUBIETA, SALVADOR ◆ n. en Guadalajara, Jal., y m. en el DF (1859-1935). Médico y abogado. Profesor en el Liceo de Varones de Guadalajara en 1879. Se graduó en leyes en 1880. En la ciudad de México colaboró en los periódicos *La Constitución*, *El Republicano* y *El Telégrafo* y fundó el semanario *El Lunes*, de oposición al presidente Manuel González, por lo que debió exiliarse en 1882. En España colaboró en *El Día* y *El Imparcial*. Fue corresponsal de prensa en Londres (1883). En Francia, donde vivió de 1885 a 1895, se doctoró en medicina (1894). Fue cónsul de México en Santander (1897) y en Saint-Nazaire (1908). Regresó a México y se incorporó al cuerpo médico militar. Autor de diversos libros de historia y literatura: *El carnaval de México en 1879*, *Recuerdos de un emigrado* (1883), *El general González y su gobierno en México* (2 t., 1884-85), *Un año en Londres* (1885), *Récits Mexicains, Suivi de Dialogues Parisiens* (1888), *L'etudiante, Notes d'un Carabin* (1888), *De l'hallaux Valgus* (1894), *El lépero* (1898), *Porfirio Díaz* (1906), *El caudillo* (1909), *La camada* (1912), *Campañas de prensa, los consulados mexicanos, socialismo* (1913), *Huerta* (1916), *Doña Pía o el contrachoque* (1919), *En tierra de sangre y broma* (1921), *México manicomio* (1927), *México marimacho* (1927), *Las ensabanadas* (1934) y *La ley de la sábana* (1935).

Quezada, Abel ◆ n. en Monterrey, NL, y m. en el DF (1920-1991). Caricaturista. Su segundo apellido era Calderón. Estudió ingeniería mecánica y eléctrica. Trabajó en Nueva York para la agencia Kennedy Associate (1946). Colaboró en numerosas publicaciones mexicanas, entre ellas *Ovaciones*, *Cine Mundial*, *Últimas Noticias*, *Excélsior* (1956-76 y 1989) y *Novedades* (1976-89). Fue colaborador eventual del diario *La Jornada* y de las revistas estadounidenses *The New Yorker* y *The New York Times Magazine*. Ilustró algunas publicaciones de la Secretaría de Obras Públicas, produjo el programa *Rayo veloz*, para el Canal 4, y durante seis días fue director del Canal 13 (diciembre 1976). En 1989 anunció su decisión de dejar el cartón político para dedicarse a la pintura; su despedida fue una serie

Caricatura de Abel Quezada publicada en 1975

de seis cartones políticos que se publicaron simultáneamente en todos los diarios mexicanos. Creó, entre otros, a los personajes *el Charro Matías* y *Gastón Billetes*. Expuso por primera vez sus pinturas, en 1985, en el Museo de Arte Moderno de la ciudad de México; algunos de sus cuadros se incluyeron en el volumen *La comedia del arte*. Autor de *El mejor de los mundos posibles*, *Nosotros los hombres verdes* (1985), *El cazador de musas* (Italia, 1990, prologado por Gabriel García Márquez), *Antes y después de Gardenia Davis* y *Petróleos Mexicanos. Una historia de dos murales* (1992), publicado póstumamente. En 1975 ganó el premio del Club de Periodistas y en 1980 el Nacional de Periodismo.

Quezada K., Armando ◆ n. en el DF (1937). Músico. Estudió en el Conservatorio de las Rosas, en Morelia; piano, en la Facultad de Música de la UNAM; becado, estudio composición con Walter Piston en la Universidad de Harvard, con Leonard Bernstein, en la de Brandaise, y tomó un curso de dirección de orquesta con Igor Markiewich. Regresó a México en 1956, impartió apreciación musical en la Escuela Médico Militar, donde formó un coro y escribió el himno de dicha escuela. Fue también profesor en la UIA. Compuso música sacra y sinfónica. En Brasil estudió música folclórica con Camargo Guarnieri. Fue a la selva amazónica, donde vive actualmente, para estudiar la música de los indios haribatzas.

Quezada Limón, Salvador ◆ n. en Yahualica, Jal. (1909). Sacerdote ordenado en 1933. Realizó estudios en el Seminario Mayor de Guadalajara y en la Pontificia Universidad Gregoriana de Roma. Obispo de Aguascalientes (1951-84), en 1967 creó el Consejo Presbiterial Diocesano; en 1968, la Fraterna Asistencia Sacerdotal, así como numerosos colegios. Participó en el Concilio Vaticano II y presidió la Conferencia Episcopal Mexicana.

Abel Quezada

Quezada Medrano, Armando ◆ n. en Chihuahua, Chih. (1905). Escultor. Estudió en San Carlos y, becado por el gobierno chihuahuense en La Grand Chaumiere, en París, donde también tomó un curso de historia del arte en la escuela del Museo del Louvre. Ha expuesto colectivamente en el Salón de Otoño, Salón de Francia y Salón de los Independientes, en París. Autor del relieve de la entrada y del águila del palco presidencial del Palacio de Bellas Artes, seis estatuas de bronce de los Niños Héroes en la balaustrada del castillo de Chapultepec, del frontispicio del Conservatorio Nacional de Música, figuras de los cines Chapultepec y Mariscala; de esculturas para el hotel Presidente, la Sala del Consejo de los Laboratorios Abott y el salón de baile del Casino Monterrey. Realizó la *Virgen del Mar* en la bahía de Acapulco y una cabeza monumental de Zapata para el ejido Emiliano Zapata.

Quichés ◆ Individuos de un pueblo emigrado de Tula y asentado en Guatemala que se fundió con los cakchiqueles; más tarde, ambos grupos se asimilaron a la cultura maya. Los quichés establecieron su capital en Utatlán, primero, y en Yximché alrededor del siglo XV, cuando entraron en guerra con los cakchiqueles, conflicto que se mantuvo hasta la llegada de los españoles. Herederos de ambos pueblos, subsisten hasta hoy y pertenecen a la familia lingüística maya-quiché.

Quijada, Diego de ◆ n. y m. en España (?-¿1571?). Se estableció en Guatemala en 1544; desempeñó varios cargos en diversas regiones de Cen-

Álvaro Quijano

troamérica y volvió a España. En 1560 se le nombró alcalde mayor de Yucatán, cargo que ejerció de 1561 a 1565.

Quijano, Alejandro ◆ n. en Mazatlán, Sin., y m. en el DF (1883-1957). Abogado graduado en 1907 en la Escuela Nacional de Jurisprudencia, de la que fue profesor y director (1920-22). Colaboró en *El Imparcial*, *Revista de Revistas*, *El Universal* y *El Libro y el Pueblo*. Fue profesor en la Facultad de Altos Estudios y en las escuelas nacionales de Maestros y Preparatoria, presidente de la Barra Mexicana Colegio de Abogados, de la Cruz Roja Mexicana (1932-57) y del Instituto Anglo-Mexicano de Cultura. Ocupó la vicepresidencia de la Cruz Roja Internacional. Dirigió el periódico *Novedades* de 1946 hasta su muerte. Autor de *Las letras en la educación* (1915), *La ortografía fonética* (1916), *En casa de nuestros primos* (1918), *En la tribuna* (1919), *La poesía castellana en sus cuatro primeros siglos* (1921), *Elogio del idioma español* (1933), *Don José de la Borda* (1933), *Cervantes y el Quijote en la Academia* (1935), *Mazatlán* (1939), *El Brasil y su cultura* (1944) y *Veracruz en la Academia de la Lengua* (1950). Miembro de la Academia Mexicana (de la Lengua) desde 1918, fue su director (1939-57) y presidió el primer Congreso de Academias de la Lengua Española en 1951.

Quijano, Álvaro ◆ n. en Hermosillo, Son., y m. en el DF (1955-1994). Escritor y periodista. Estudió Letras Hispánicas en la UNAM y Letras Inglesas en el Grant McQueen Community College en Edmonton, Canadá. Fue colaborador de *Revista de la Universidad*, *La Gaceta del Fondo de Cultura Económica* y *Memoria de papel* y de los suplementos *Sábado*, *La letra y la imagen*, *El semanario*, *La Jornada Semanal* y *El Ángel*. Impartió cursos y coordinó talleres de literatura, redacción y periodismo. Trabajó como redactor y corrector de estilo. Fue locutor de Radio Universidad de México. Autor de novela: *El libro de Tristán* (1991); y poesía: *La lucha con el ángel* (1985) y *Este jardín es una ruina* (1995).

Quijano, Benito ◆ n. en Yucatán y m. en EUA (1800-1865). Pertenecía al ejército realista cuando se adhirió al Plan de Iguala (1821). En 1823 participó en el levantamiento del Plan de Casa Mata. Estuvo en la defensa de Veracruz contra Isidro Barradas (1829). Fue comandante general de Tamaulipas, Veracruz y el Estado de México. En 1838 ocupó el ministerio de Guerra y Marina en el gabinete de Anastasio Bustamante. En 1848 se le comisionó para pactar la paz con Estados Unidos. Se adhirió al Plan de Ayutla, fue diputado constituyente (1856-57) y se negó a apoyar el Plan de Tacubaya. En 1860, como general de brigada, peleó contra Miramón en la batalla de Calpulalpan. Benito Juárez lo nombró gobernador de Yucatán en 1863 y lo comisionó para organizar fuerzas en el sureste y combatir a los imperialistas, misión que no pudo cumplir. Residió en Nueva York, donde organizó el Club Mexicano, del que fue presidente.

Quijano, Carlos ◆ n. en Uruguay y m. en el DF (1900-1984). Periodista desde 1917. Dirigió las publicaciones *Acción* y *Época* y el semanario *Marcha*, de orientación latinoamericanista, en el que difundió las letras mexicanas. En 1972 fundó el Frente Amplio de Uruguay. En 1975 llegó como asilado político a México, donde fundó y dirigió (1979-84) *Cuadernos de Marcha* y fue profesor de la UNAM. Publicó *Técnica sobre el control de cambios* (1980) y dejó inédito *Las leyes monetarias de México 1821-1983*. *Doctor honoris causa* por la Universidad de Montevideo (1972). En 1983 se le otorgó el premio literario Luchima de Chiapas.

Quijano, Jorge ◆ n. y m. en el DF (1893-1941). Ingeniero graduado en 1914. Fue profesor en varias facultades de la UNAM y dirigió la revista *Pitágoras*. Inventó un modelo de regla de cálculo. Publicó *Cálculo simplificado de estructuras de concreto armado* y *Aritmética y nociones de álgebra y geometría*.

Quijano, Yolanda ◆ n. en Mérida, Yuc. (1933). Pintora. Estudió en La Esmeralda (1961). Ha participado en exposiciones colectivas desde 1963 y presentado individualmente su trabajo desde 1966. Premio Nuevos Valores del Salón de la Plástica Mexicana (1963); primer premio en el Homenaje a José Guadalupe Posada del Injuve (1966); premio de pintura de la Secretaría de Marina (1967); medalla de oro de la Dirección de Educación Física de Yucatán (1973); diploma de la Sociedad Cultural Sor Juana Inés de la Cruz (1974); diploma al Mérito Artístico del Inmecafé (1975); medalla de plata en la exposición El Árbol en el Arte, del INBA (1976); y medalla de plata y diploma del Centro de Arte Contemporáneo de Acámbaro (1976). Es miembro del Salón de la Plástica. Hay obra suya en el Museo del Vaticano y en el Ateneo Cultural de Madrid.

Quijano Narezo, Manuel ◆ n. en San Luis Potosí, SLP (1919). Graduado en la Escuela de Medicina de la UNAM (1942), realizó estudios de posgrado en cirugía en el Hospital General y en el Hospital Saint Luke de la Clínica Lahey, en Estados Unidos. Entre 1948 y 1978 ejerció su profesión de manera independiente. Ha sido profesor de la UNAM (1956-78), director del Hospital General del Centro Médico del IMSS (1962-71), director general de Asuntos Internacionales de la Secretaría de Salud (1982-) y presidente del Consejo Ejecutivo de la Organización Mundial de la Salud durante 1988. Autor de *Principios fundamentales de la cirugía* (1981). Pertenece a la Academia Nacional de Medicina, a la Academia Mexicana de Cirugía, a la Academia Médica (que preside desde 1978), a la Academia de Cirugía de París (que presidió en 1971) y al Consejo Nacional de Cirugía General (del que es fundador). El gobierno francés le otorgó la Orden al Mérito.

Quijano Terán, Luis ◆ n. en Matehuala, SLP (1925). Agrónomo y contador graduado en la ciudad de Poughkeepsie, Estados Unidos. Uno de los iniciadores de la industria de los insecticidas en México, ha colaborado en los principales diarios de la ciudad de México; en 1972 fue designado director ejecutivo del Patronato del Instituto de Estudios Superiores del Estado de

México. Autor de unas *Novelas cortas*.

Quijano Terán, Margarita ◆ n. en Matehuala, SLP (1914). Maestra y doctora (1955) en letras por la UNAM. Estudió en Londres (1946) becada por el British Council, en la Universidad de Zaragoza (1947) y en las de Florencia y París (1948). En 1951 obtuvo una beca de Harvard y en 1956 la Rockefeller, con las que continuó en Europa el estudio de la obra de Shakespeare. Fue profesora de la Universidad Femenina (1944-) y de la UNAM (1954-). Autora de *Manuel M. Flores, su vida y su obra* (1946), *La Celestina y Otelo* (1957) y *Hamlet y sus críticos* (1962).

Quilá, de ◆ Sierra de Jalisco, también llamada Tetilla, que forma parte del eje volcánico. Se extiende al noroeste de la sierra de Tapalpa. Su ladera septentrional se inclina hacia el río Ameca y en la meridional nacen las corrientes que forman el río Armería.

Quilaztli ◆ Diosa madre de la mitología náhuatl, en su función de protectora de las plantas comestibles. Se le adoraba en Xochimilco, donde era identificada con Izpapalotl y Coahuatlicue. Algunos autores creen que Quilaztli era otro de los nombres de la Cihuacóatl; otros, que era una hechicera que acompañó a los mexicas en su peregrinación desde Aztlán y los inició en la costumbre de los sacrificios humanos.

Quilme, Pablo ◆ n. y m. en Bacerac, Son. (?-1696). Caudillo ópata que encabezó una rebelión contra la esclavitud a que eran sometidos hombres y niños en las minas. Fue ahorcado por los españoles.

Quimixtlán ◆ Municipio de Puebla situado al noreste de Tecamachalco, en los límites con Veracruz. Superficie: 114.81 km². Población: 18,211 habitantes, de los cuales 4,478 forman la población económicamente activa. Hablan alguna lengua indígena 415 personas mayores de cinco años (náhuatl 410).

Quinatzin ◆ m. en Texcoco (?-1357). Último rey chichimeca, señor de los colhuas. Subió al trono en 1298, a la muerte de su padre, Taltzin. Enfrentó y controló un levantamiento de algunos de sus guerreros, quienes quisieron hacer emperador a Tenancacaltzin. Quinatzin extendió su dominio hasta Azcapotzalco y trasladó definitivamente la capital colhua a Texcoco, en 1324.

Quinatzin, Mapa ◆ Códice elaborado en papel europeo, con técnica indígena. Proviene de la región texcocana. Se encuentra en la Biblioteca de París. Fue escrito en náhuatl, probablemente en 1550. Es de carácter histórico y abarca un periodo que inicia con el rey Quinatzin hasta Nezahualcóyotl (1472).

Quinn, Anthony ◆ n. en Chihuahua, Chih. (1915). Actor. Emigró a Estados Unidos en 1927 e ingresó en la industria cinematográfica. Ha actuado en más de 250 películas, entre las que destacan *Viva Zapata* (1952), *La strada* (1954), *Lust for Life* (1956), *El jorobado de Notre Dame* (1956), *Las sandalias del pescador* (1968), *Lawrence de Arabia* (1962), *Zorba el Griego* (1964), *Los hijos de Sánchez* (1978) y *Fiebre de selva* (1991). Ha recibido en dos ocasiones el Óscar como mejor actor. Se ha dedicado también a la escultura, la pintura y la literatura.

Quintana, Edison ◆ n. en Uruguay (1938). Pianista. Estudió con Hugo Balzo en Montevideo y Europa, becado por el gobierno de Rumania con Florica Musicescu y George Halmos, y por la Academia Chigiana de Siena, Italia, con Guido Agosti y Arturo Benedetti Michelangeli. Profesor visitante de la Universidad Católica de Washington (1999-). Vino en 1976 y se naturalizó mexicano. Ha tocado, prácticamente, con todas las orquestas del país, con la Camerata Punta del Este, y ha formado grupos de cámara con Irma González y Carlos Prieto. Becario del Fonca (1991 y 1996). Concertista del INBA y de la UNAM. También ha incursionado en el jazz y en la música tradicional latinoamericana. Ha grabado varios discos, entre los que destacan los arreglos para piano de Manuel de Elías, Ricardo Castro, Felipe Villanueva, Manuel M. Ponce y Rodolfo Halffter. Premiado en el Concurso Internacional de Leeds, Inglaterra (1966), primer premio del Concurso Internacional Beethoven en Mendoza, Argentina (1976), segundo premio del Concurso Internacional de Música Mexicana del INBA-Fonapas (1981).

Mapa Quinatzin

Quintana, José Matías ◆ n. en Mérida, Yuc., y m. en la ciudad de México (1767-1841). Político liberal. Padre de Andrés Quintana Roo. Militó con los *sanjuanistas*, que difundían las ideas constitucionalistas españolas. Publicó una hoja suelta en la que atacaba al virrey Calleja por violar la Constitución española de 1812. Editó uno de los primeros periódicos yucatecos, *Clamores de la fidelidad americana contra la opresión*, en 1814. Al abolirse la Constitución de 1812, fue aprehendido y recluido en San Juan de Ulúa, hasta 1817, junto con Lorenzo de Zavala y Francisco Bates. Regresó a Mérida y fue miembro de la Confederación Patriótica, que pedía la independencia yucateca. En 1821 fue colaborador del periódico *El Yucateco* o *El Amigo del Pueblo*. Fue más tarde diputado local (1822) y federal (1827). Autor de *El jacobinismo en México* y *Meditaciones*.

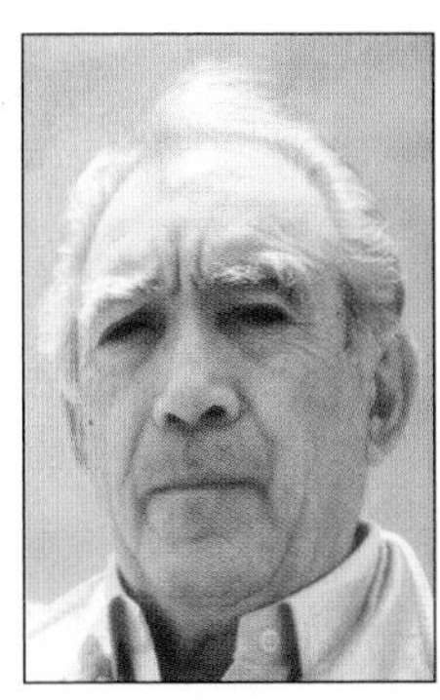

Anhony Quinn

Quintana, Miguel ◆ n. en Jerez, Zac., y m. en la ciudad de México (1840-1892). Militar. Se incorporó en 1862 a las fuerzas republicanas. Combatió a los invasores franceses en Durango, Chihuahua y Zacatecas. Desde abril de 1865 hasta agosto de 1866 hizo repetidos viajes a California para conseguir pertrechos de guerra. En 1867 asis-

Foto: Armando Herrera

Rosita Quintana

tió al sitio de Querétaro. Fue subdirector y director (1871-80) del Colegio Militar y autor del proyecto de la penitenciaría del DF.

Quintana, Miguel A. ◆ n. en Puebla, Pue., y m. en el DF (1877-1951). Economista e historiador. Fue gerente bancario hasta 1916, empresario, funcionario de la Secretaría de Hacienda, profesor de la UNAM (desde 1929) y colaborador de *El Nacional* (1939-46) y *El Popular* (1945-49). Autor de *El problema de la tierra* (1929), *El imperialismo de la mercancía americana y el establecimiento en México de The National City Bank of New York* (1930), *La nueva política americana con el exterior y sus efectos en la economía de México* (1930), *Los ensayos monetarios como consecuencia de la baja de la plata. El problema de la plata y el de la moneda de plata en el mundo y en México* (1931), *Curso de primer año de economía política* (1937), *Economía social (una introducción)* (1937), *Papel histórico de Puebla en el progreso industrial de la Nueva España* (1946) y *Esteban de Antuñano, fundador de la industria textil en Puebla* (1957).

Bernardo Quintana Arrioja

Quintana, Rosita ◆ n. en Argentina (1925). Actriz y cantante. Comenzó su carrera haciendo teatro de revista en su país natal. En México participó en películas como *Calabacitas tiernas* (1948), *Soy charro de levita* (1949), *Mala hembra* (1950), *Susana* (1950), *El hambre nuestra de cada día* (1952), *Melodías de amor* (1955), *El charro y la dama* (1958), *El hombre de la mandolina* (1982) y muchas otras. También participó en programas de televisión.

Elvira Quintana

Quintana Arrioja, Bernardo ◆ n. y m. en el DF (1919-1984). Ingeniero civil graduado en la UNAM (1943), donde participó en la creación del Instituto de Ingeniería. Cofundador de Ingenieros Civiles Asociados (1947). Fundador (1953) y primer presidente de la Cámara Nacional de la Industria de la Construcción. Presidió la Cámara Nacional del Cemento (1967-68) y la Asociación Mexicana de Caminos (1968). Presidió Cementos Tolteca (1971), Transmisiones y Equipos Mecánicos, Teleindustrias Ericsson y el Grupo Industria del Hierro de Querétaro. Fue vicepresidente de Fundidora Monterrey y miembro del consejo de Siderúrgica Lázaro Cárdenas-Las Truchas. Autor de *Estudio sobre la economía de las construcciones en México* (1956), *El problema del transporte en las grandes urbes: sus soluciones actuales* (1967), *Proyecciones de la ingeniería civil mexicana* (1971), *Las firmas de ingeniería y nuestro desarrollo económico y social* (1971), *La ciudad de México: su futuro* (1975), *La integración y el aprovechamiento de los recursos hidroeléctricos en América Latina* (1979), *El trópico: la nueva frontera de los asentamientos humanos en América Latina*, *Los ingenieros en el desarrollo de México* y *Los jóvenes y la industria de la construcción*. Cofundador del Colegio de Ingenieros Civiles de México (1945), de la Fundación Barros Sierra (1975) y de la Federación Interamericana de la Industria de la Construcción. Miembro de número de la Academia Mexicana de Ingeniería (1979). Doctor *honoris causa* por la Universidad Autónoma de Guadalajara (1970), Premio Nacional de Ingeniería (1976).

Quintana G., Valente ◆ n. en Matamoros, Tams., y m. en el DF (1889-1968). Detective. Fue policía desde 1918 y llegó a jefe de las Comisiones de Seguridad del Distrito Federal. Participó en la investigación sobre los asesinatos de Álvaro Obregón y Julio Antonio Mella. Se convirtió en investigador privado y abrió una escuela de detectives. Se hizo una película sobre su trabajo detectivesco.

Quintana Gómez-Daza, Carlos ◆ n. en Puebla, Pue., y m. en el DF (1912- 1987). Ingeniero mecánico electricista graduado en 1942 en el IPN, maestro en ciencias (1944) por la Universidad de Columbia, y en administración de empresas (1947) por la Harvard Graduate School of Business Administration, de Boston. Fue profesor del IPN (1935-42) y del Mexico City College (1943), gerente de producción de Ayotla Textil (1948-49); subdirector y director de la División de Desarrollo Industrial de la CEPAL, en Chile (1950-60), gerente de Programación Industrial de Nacional Financiera (1960-67), delegado del consejo directivo (1961-67) y asesor de la dirección general del Instituto Mexicano de Investigaciones Tecnológicas (1972-86), subsecretario general de la ONU a cargo de la Secretaría Ejecutiva de la CEPAL (1967-72), presidente del Centro Latinoamericano de Estadística, en Chile (1967-72); gerente general de Crédito (1974-76) y asesor de Nafinsa (1976-81). Coautor de *Formulating Industrial Development Programmes, with Special Reference to Asia and the Far East* (1961). Autor de *Productividad de la mano de obra en industria textil algodonera de cinco países latinoamericanos* (1951), *Posibilidades de desarrollo de la industria de papel y celulosa en América Latina* (1954), *Perspectivas de la industria de papel y celulosa en la América Latina* (1955), *Problemas de la industria siderúrgica y de transformación de hierro y acero en América Latina* (1957), *El desarrollo industrial del Perú* (1959) y *El desarrollo de la industria textil cubana* (1960).

Quintana, Elvira ◆ n. en España y m. en el DF (1935-1968). Actriz. Su segundo apellido era Molina. Llegó a México en 1952 y se inició como modelo antes de pasar al cine y la televisión. Estudió en el Instituto Cinematográfico Teatral y de Radiotelevisión de la Asociación Nacional de Actores. Participó en más de 30 películas, como *Pancho Pistolas* (1957), *Peligros de juventud* (1959), *El Siete de Copas* (1960) y *Se alquila marido* (1961). Incursionó también en el canto y escribió *Poesías de Elvira Quintana* (1971).

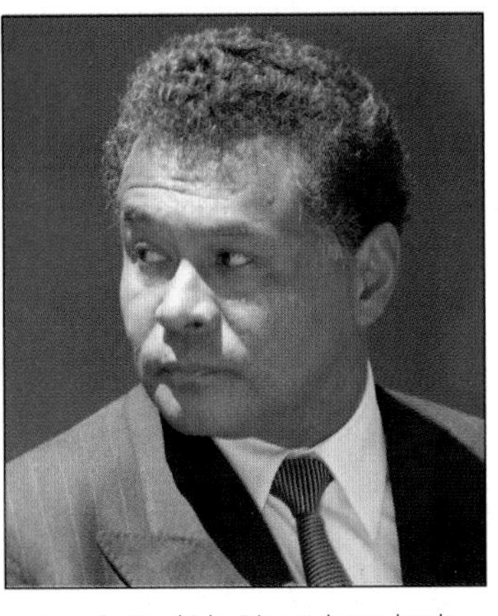

Joaquín Hendricks Díaz, gobernador de Quintana Roo

Quintana Roo ◆ Estado de la República Mexicana que se encuentra en el sureste del país, al oriente de la península de Yucatán, en la frontera con Belice y Guatemala. Limita con los estados de Campeche y Yucatán. Su costa este pertenece al mar Caribe y la norte, al oeste del cabo Catoche, al golfo de México. Parte de su territorio lo forman las islas Mujeres, Cozumel, Blanca, Contoy, Holbox y Cancún, ésta, unida a

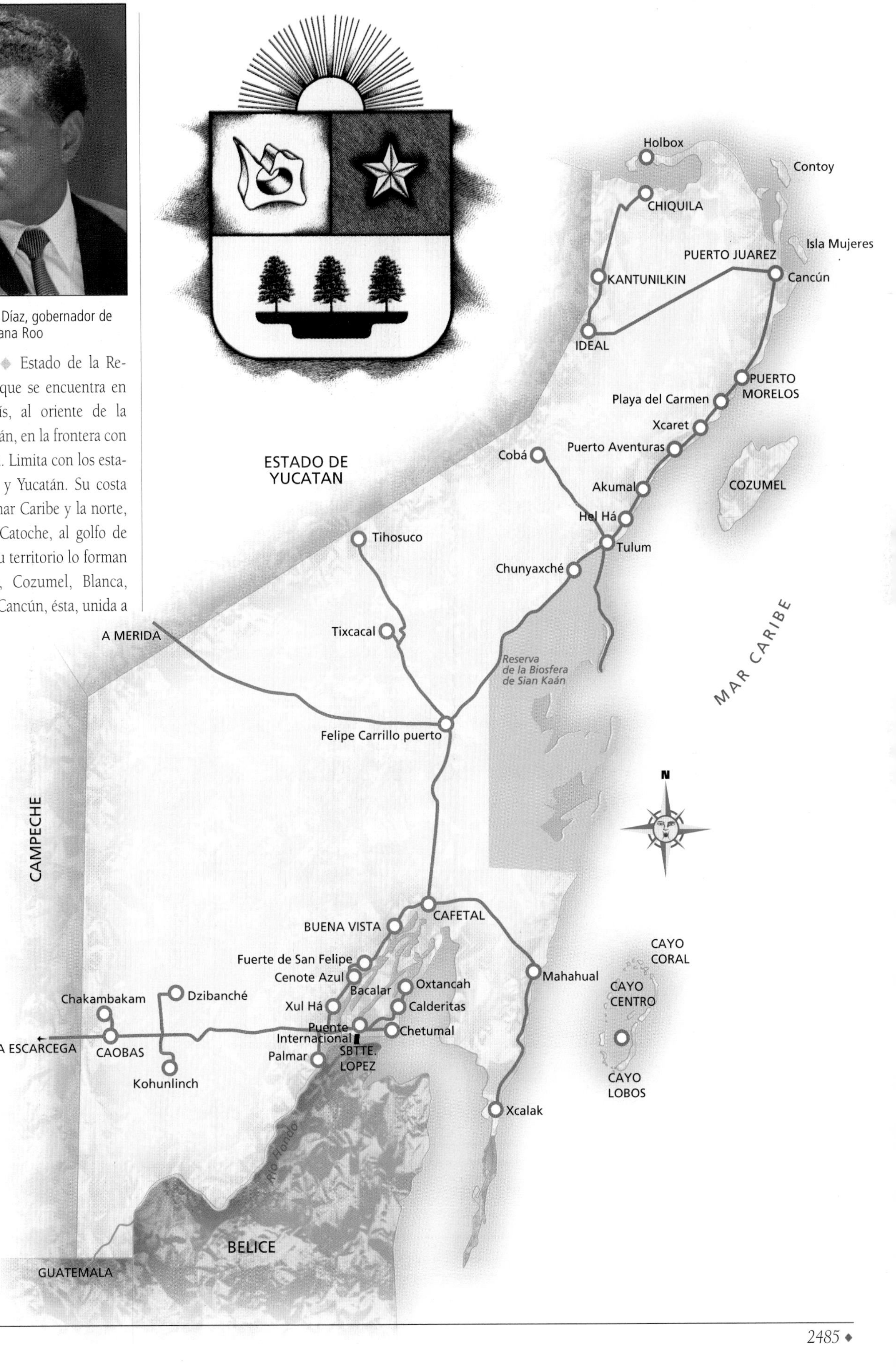

Foto: Pablo Cervantes

Coral y esponja en Quintana Roo

tierra por carretera. Superficie: 50.212 km² (es el decimonoveno por su extensión y representa el 2.56 por ciento del territorio nacional). Sólo dos de sus ríos llevan agua todo el año: el Hondo y el Azul. La entidad cuenta con numerosos cenotes, lagunas, esteros y bahías. La entidad está dividida en ocho municipios. En 1997 su población estimada era de 772,803 habitantes. De acuerdo con datos censales, en 1995 tenía 703,536 habitantes (la población urbana era de 564,753 y la urbana, 138,783), que representan el 0.8 por ciento de la población total del país. Es el estado con la mayor tasa de crecimiento promedio anual de población, con 6.48 por ciento, y la entidad con más alta inmigración, con 53.4 por ciento de su población. El producto interno del estado, en 1996, fue equivalente al 1.32 por ciento del total nacional. La población económicamente activa, en 1995, era 61 por ciento de los mayores de 12 años (la mayor en el país), y el analfabetismo era del 8.53

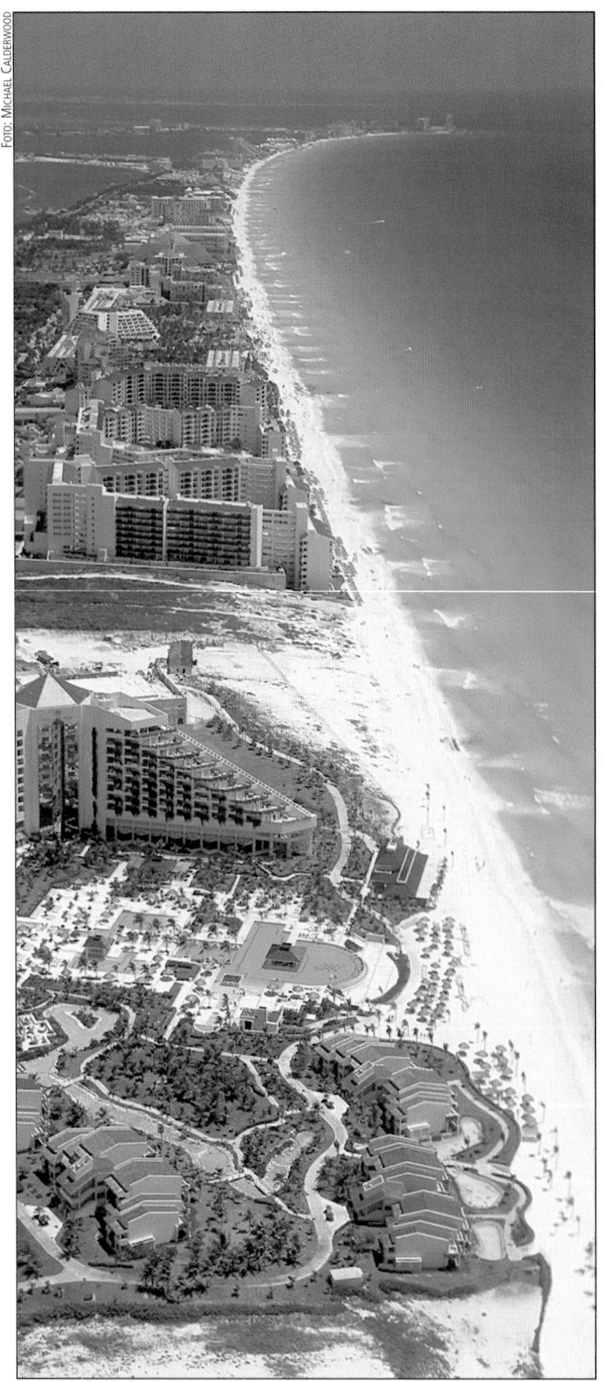

Foto: Michael Calderwood

Cancún, Quintana Roo

Foto: Claudio Contreras

Dzinbanché, Quintana Roo

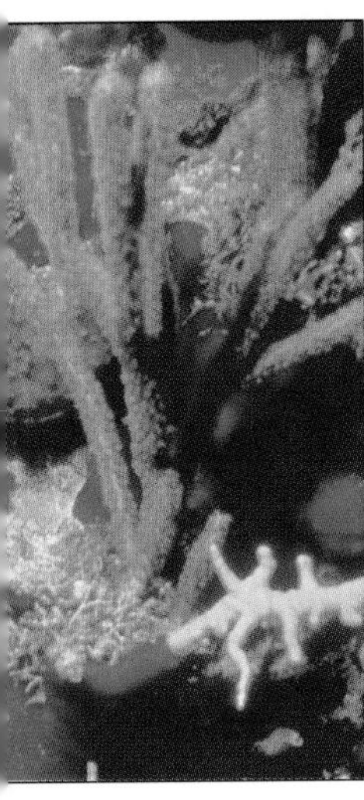

por ciento de la población mayor de 15 años. Hablan alguna lengua indígena 157,770 personas mayores de cinco años (maya 150,434, mame 1,627 y kanjobal 1,148), de las cuales 11,175 no dominan el español. Hace unos 5,000 años habitaban el territorio quintanarroense los hablantes de la lengua protomaya. A mediados del siglo X d.n.e. los itzáes del norte de Quintana Roo (fundadores de Chichén y de Champotón) participaron en la formación de las ligas y alianzas que se generaron después del inicio de la influencia cultural tolteca y chichimeca; así, Tulum y Cozumel se unieron a la Liga de Mayapán, que se mantuvo estable hasta el siglo XII. En 1194, los itzáes abandonaron Chichén y se establecieron en Petén, hostilizados por el jefe Hunacc Ceel, de la Liga de Mayapán. Los cocomes ejercieron la hegemonía en la Liga, entre 1441 y 1461 cuando fueron derrotados por los descendientes de los itzáes, auxiliados por los xius. En 1502 se produjo el primer contacto con los españoles, cuando algunos marineros de la última expedición de Cristóbal Colón avistaron unas embarcaciones en el Caribe, probablemente tripuladas por mayas. En 1511 se produjo el naufragio de los expedicionarios del Darién; algunos de ellos llegaron a la costa yucateca en donde fueron aprehendidos y sacrificados, excepto Gonzalo Guerrero y Jerónimo de Aguilar, quienes se asimilaron a la cultura maya de Xamancaan, cerca de Chetumal. Guerrero propició el primer mestizaje hispano-mexicano. En 1517, la expedición de Hernández de Córdoba llegó a Cabo Catoche, más tarde la de Juan de Grijalva arribó a Cozumel. En 1519, Hernán Cortés desembarcó en Chetumal, donde rescató a Jerónimo de Aguilar. En 1526, Francisco de Montejo propuso a Carlos V la conquista de la península de Yucatán, misma que inició en 1527 desde Cozumel y que concluyó en 1546 su hijo, Francisco Montejo y León, con la derrota de los cupules y chinchuncheles en el norte de la península. Durante los siglos XVI y XVII, las poblaciones costeras de Quintana Roo fueron atacadas repetidamente por los piratas que se refugiaban en las islas del Caribe. En 1652 la villa de Salamanca de Bacalar fue destruida por una incursión corsaria y quedó abandonada. En 1726, el gobernador de Yucatán, Antonio de Figueroa y Silva, dispuso la reocupación de Bacalar y su fortificación para evitar las incursiones inglesas desde Belice. La tarea evangelizadora y de conquista

Foto: Fondo Editorial Grupo Azabache

Parque ecológico de Chankanab, Quintana Roo

Foto: Michael Calderwood

Puerto Aventura, Quintana Roo

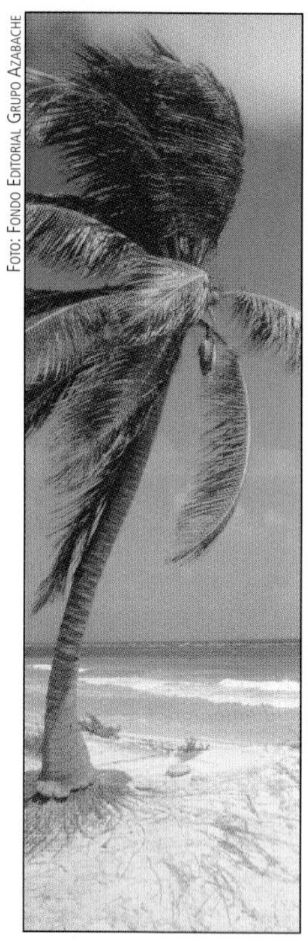
FOTO: FONDO EDITORIAL GRUPO AZABACHE

Reserva de la biosfera de Sian-Kaán, Quintana Roo

española no se extendió en Quintana Roo sino hasta el siglo XVIII, por lo que la población maya mantuvo su autonomía cultural a la consumación de la Independencia nacional. En 1823, Guatemala se anexó los 36.033 kilómetros cuadrados del distrito de Petén Itzá. En 1841, los latifundistas henequeneros que dominaban el Congreso local promulgaron un decreto que creaba la República Yucateca, misma que fracasó por la falta de reconocimiento internacional. En 1847 se inició la guerra de castas en Yucatán, estado al que pertenecía el actual territorio quintanarroense. El jefe Venancio Pec, controló diversas zonas de la península, Bacalar entre ellas. Esta área, prácticamente quedó fuera de la jurisdicción mexicana hasta finales del siglo XIX. Dado que por el sur del actual Quintana Roo, los ingleses de Belice seguían entrando en territorio mexicano, el gobierno nacional firmó con Gran Bretaña el Tratado de Límites Mariscal-Saint John, que establecía como frontera entre México y Belice el río Hondo. En 1899, Othón P. Blanco, fundó la población de Payo Obispo en el sitio donde se encontraba Chetumal. En 1901, Ignacio A. Bravo sometió a los últimos mayas rebeldes que se habían hecho fuertes en la población de Chan Santa Cruz, hoy Felipe Carrillo Puerto, donde adoraban a la "cruz que habla". En 1902, Quintana Roo, ya con ese nombre, se erigió como territorio federal y su capital fue Chan Santa Cruz, con el nuevo nombre de Santa Cruz de Bravo. En 1913, Venustiano Carranza reintegró Quintana Roo al estado de Yucatán, aunque, dos años más tarde, volvió a erigir el territorio federal. En 1931, Pascual Ortiz Rubio repartió el territorio de Quintana Roo entre los estados de Yucatán y Campeche. Lázaro Cárdenas volvió a decretar la creación del territorio quintanarroense y fijó su capital en Payo Obispo, ciudad que cambió su nombre por el de Chetumal. El 8 de octubre de 1974, Quintana Roo se convirtió en estado libre y soberano de la Federación. En los años setenta, grandes inversiones federales y privadas convirtieron a Cancún en uno de los cen-

FOTO: PABLO CERVANTES

Punta Laguna
Quintana Roo

FOTO: FONDO EDITORIAL GRUPO AZABACHE

Fuerte de San Felipe, en Quintana Roo

FOTO: CARLOS HAHN

Xcaret, zona turística de Quintana Roo

DISTRIBUCIÓN DE LA POBLACIÓN POR TAMAÑO DE LA LOCALIDAD, 1995

Más de 15,000
70.20%
Hasta 2,500
19.70%
Entre 2,500 y 15,000
10.10%

POBLACIÓN DE 5 AÑOS Y MÁS HABLANTE DE LENGUA INDÍGENA, 1995

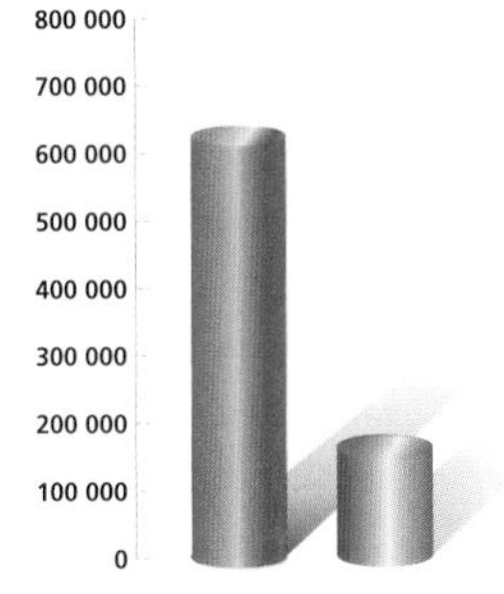

Población de 5 años y más 604,981

Población de 5 años y más hablante de lengua indígena 157,770 (26.08%)

PROMEDIO DE ESCOLARIDAD DE LA POBLACIÓN DE 15 AÑOS Y MÁS, POR SEXO, 1995

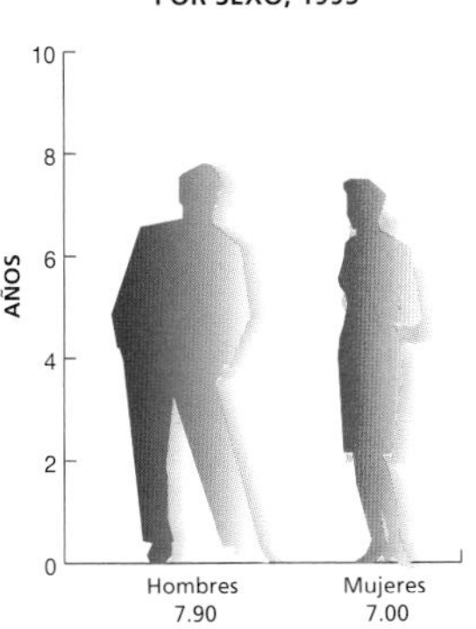

Promedio 7.45 años

PRODUCTO INTERNO BRUTO (PIB) A PRECIOS CORRIENTES

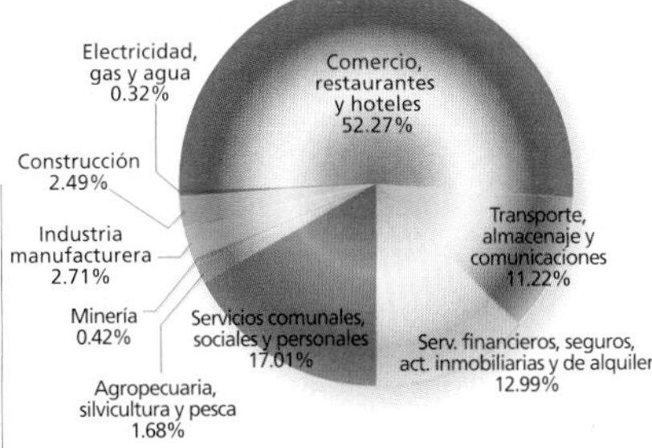

LONGITUD DE LA RED DE CARRETERAS POR SUPERFICIE DE RODAMIENTO, 1995

LÍNEAS TELEFÓNICAS EN SERVICIO Y APARATOS PÚBLICOS, 1994

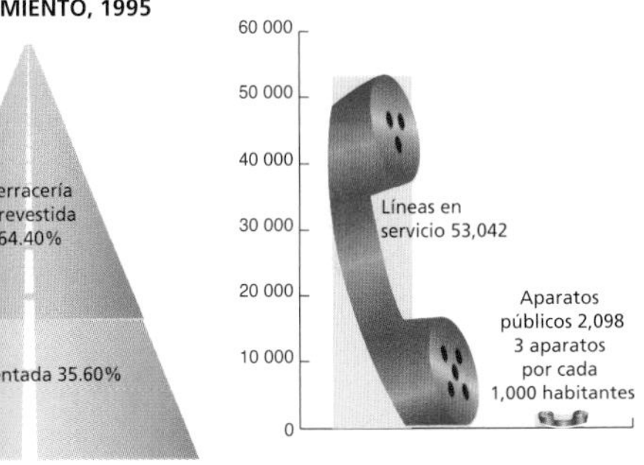

tros turísticos más importantes del mundo. En 1987, la UNESCO declaró la reserva ecológica de Sian Kaan como patrimonio natural de la humanidad. El Consejo Internacional de Monumentos y Sitios lo considera reserva de la biosfera, con especies de flora y fauna únicas en el mundo.

DISTRIBUCIÓN PORCENTUAL DE LA POBLACIÓN OCUPADA POR SECTOR DE ACTIVIDAD ECONÓMICA, 1995

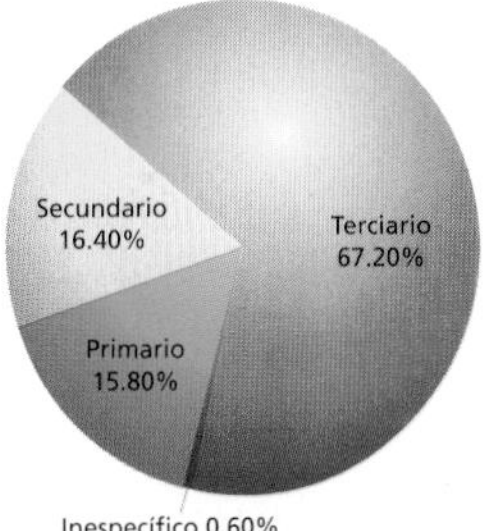

Foto: Pablo Cervantes

Coral y esponja en las playas de Quintana Roo

Foto: Fondo Editorial Grupo Azabache

Foto: Claudio Contreras

Xel-Há, en Quintana Roo

Zona arqueológica El Rey, Cancún

QUINTANA ROO ◆ Municipio de Yucatán situado al norte de Chichén Itzá. Superficie: 139.24 km². Población: 1,073 habitantes, de los cuales 254 forman la población económicamente activa. Hablan maya 522 personas mayores de cinco años.

QUINTANA ROO, ANDRÉS ◆ n. en Mérida, Yuc., y m. en la ciudad de México (1787-1851). Estudió leyes en la Real y Pontificia Universidad de México (1808-), publicó poesía en el *Diario de México* y trabajó en el despacho de Agustín Pomposo Fernández de San Salvador, con cuya sobrina, Leona Vicario, habría de casarse en Tlalpujahua, ya incorporados ambos a la insurgencia. Defendió la causa independentista desde los periódicos *Semanario Patriótico Americano* y *El Ilustrador Americano*, cuando militó en las filas de Ignacio López Rayón (1812). Presidió en Chilpancingo la Asamblea Nacional Constituyente que declaró la independencia en 1813 y eliminó el nombre de Fernando VII como soberano de México. Escribió el Manifiesto de 1813 y acompañó al Congreso en su huida por Coyuca, Uruapan, Apatzingán, Ario, Uruapan, Huetamo, Cutzamala, Tenan-

EL FEDERALISTA MEXICANO.

Quid deceat, quid non; quò virtus, quò ferat error.
Horat.

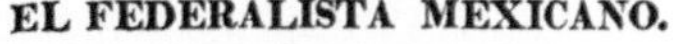

PROSPECTO.

Hace ya mas de un año que proclamado en Jalapa el imperio de la constitucion y de las leyes, se está repitiendo sin cesar que el gobierno sustituido por esta última revolucion al que nació de las turbulencias de la Acordada, no solo es el mas legítimo y puro, sino tambien el único que puede convenir á la nacion, ya porque los individuos que lo forman han identificado sus intereses con los de la clase mas importante de la sociedad, y ya porque las luces, el saber, la educacion y la esperiencia, son dotes que solo se encuentran en los que pertenecen al partido dominante.

Si este pudiera por un instante despojarse del carácter de tal, abjuraría un lenguaje tan injurioso á la inmensa mayoría de la nacion, y desmentido continuamente por los errores de la administracion: errores tanto mas funestos cuanto que erigidos en una especie de dogmas, cuya verdad no ha sido lícito poner en duda, han ejercido su perniciosa influencia en el saludable correctivo de la censura pública, enmudecida por tanto tiempo, ó sofocada en el instante que ha osado levantar la voz.

La época de la instalacion de las nuevas cámaras es la mas favorable para romper tan vergonzosas ataduras. Aunque entre los hombres ilustrados que las componen creemos que no faltarán algunos imbuidos en las preocupaciones del partido á que deben su eleccion, hacemos á la mayoría la justicia de suponer que adicta sinceramente á las instituciones que nos rigen, mirará su conservacion como el objeto mas importante de su mision, y que lejos de unirse á los designios liberticidas de los enemigos de la imprenta, removerá todos los obstáculos que hasta ahora han impedido la libertad de su ejercicio, adoptando al mismo tiempo las medidas convenientes para prevenir y contener los abusos.

En este concepto, hemos emprendido la obra periódica que hoy anunciamos: su objeto no es atacar al gobierno actual ni defender los intereses de la faccion contraria. Una inalterable imparcialidad dirigirá todos nuestros juicios. Con la misma severidad censuraremos, cuando se presente la ocasion, los desórdenes escandalosos de la Acordada, que las obscuras maquinaciones de la Ciudadela. Aplaudirémos del mismo modo los actos que lo merezcan del gobierno actual y las disposiciones que se hayan dictado por el anterior: las personas nada influirán en nuestros juicios: nos ocuparémos de las cosas, ora se trate de calificar la conducta de los gobernantes, ora de discurrir las ventajas ó inconvenientes de las leyes que se discutan ó promulguen.

En cuanto al poder judicial, que es la parte mas defectuosa de nuestro sistema, hablarémos tambien con la estension que requiere esta interesante materia; y sin aspirar al necio honor de la infalibilidad en nuestras opiniones, espondrémos modestamente las razones que en nuestro concepto las apoyen, dejando al recto discernimiento del público la libertad de apreciarlas en lo que valgan.

Por ahora solo publicarémos dos números cada semana en los dias de correo, porque el corto surtido de nuestra imprenta no permite dar mas amplitud á la empresa. Las suscriciones por los dos pliegos, se reciben en la calle de la estampa de San Andres, accesoria letra B, al precio de seis reales para dentro de la capital, y un peso para fuera, franco el porte, por el ciudadano Sabino Ortega, advirtiendo que los señores foraneos que gusten suscribirse deberán hacerlo por medio de sus encargados en ella, donde únicamente se admitirán abonados. El primer número se publicará el miércoles próximo.

Mexico enero 3 de 1831.— LOS EDITORES.

Andrés Quintana Roo editó *El Federalista Mexicano*

ARCHIVO GENERAL DE LA NACIÓN

Andrés Quintana Roo

go del Río, Santa Ana y Tehuacán. En 1814, él y Carlos María de Bustamante, entre otros, redactaron la Constitución de Apatzingán. Al ser dispersadas las fuerzas de Morelos, en 1815, Quintana Roo y Leona Vicario se refugiaron en el sur del país. Se acogieron al indulto en 1818 y vivieron en Toluca hasta 1820. En ese año regresó a la ciudad de México, terminó la carrera de leyes, se integró al Ilustre y Real Colegio de Abogados y fue designado diputado a Cortes. Luego de la consumación de la Independencia, fue diputado al primer Congreso General y subsecretario de Relaciones Interiores y Exteriores de Agustín de Iturbide (1822-23), pero su desacuerdo con el emperador hizo que se le destituyera y procesara. A la caída de Iturbide, Quintana Roo fue magistrado de la Suprema Corte de Justicia (1824-27 y 1835-), diputado por el Estado de México (1827, 1829-30 y 1833) y ministro plenipotenciario en Londres (1827-28). Participó en la negociación sobre límites fronterizos con Estados Unidos y frustró un intento separatista en Yucatán. Tras el asesinato de Vicente Guerrero, atacó al gobierno de Bustamante-Alamán desde su periódico, *El Federalista Mexicano*. Fue secretario de Justicia de Gómez Farías y de Santa Anna (1833-34); colaboró en *El Correo de la Federación*. Presidente de la Academia de Letrán (1836-). Fungió como protector de escritores hasta su muerte. Autor de *Justa memoria del heroísmo que en el sitio de Gerona manifestó el capitán don Felipe Peón Maldonado, hijo de la Ciudad de Mérida de Yucatán* (1810).

QUINTANAR, HÉCTOR ◆ n. en el DF (1936). Músico. Su segundo apellido es Prieto. Estudió en la Escuela Superior Nocturna de Música, el Conservatorio Nacional, el Taller de Composición de Carlos Chávez (1963), en la Universidad de Columbia (1964) y, becado por la SEP, estudió música electrónica en Nueva York (1964) y el Centro de Música Concreta de París (1967). Fue discípulo de Rodolfo Halffter, Carlos Jiménez Mabarak y Carlos Chávez, quien lo nombró su asistente en 1963. Trabajó en el Departamento de Música del INBA (1965-70) y fue asesor musical del Comité Organizador de los XIX Juegos Olímpicos (1967-68), director del Taller de Composición de Carlos Chávez, fundador y presidente de la Sociedad Méxicana de Música Contemporánea, jefe del Departamento de Música de Difusión Cultural de la UNAM, jefe del Departamento de Música de la Comisión de Radiodifusión, promotor y director (hasta 1977) del primer Laboratorio de Música Electrónica en México y director titular de la OFUNAM (1981-87), de la Sinfónica de Morelia (1987-1991) y de la Orquesta Sinfónica de la Universidad de Guanajuato (1992-1997). Cofundador de la SACM. Autor de *Sinfonía modal* (1961), *Sinfonía* (1961), *Sinfonía* (1962), poema sinfónico *El viejo y el mar* (1963), la cantata *Fábula* (1964), *Sinfonía* (1965), *Doble cuarteto* (1966), *Trío* (1966), *Aclamaciones* (1967), *Galaxias* (1968), *Sideral I* (1968), *Símbolos* (1969), *Sideral II* (1969), *Ilapso* (1970), *Sonidos* para piano (1970), *Opus I* (1971), *Sideral III* (1971), *Quinteto* (1972), *Diálogos* (1973), *Aries* (1974), *Fiesta* (1976), *Pequeña obertura* (1979), *Canto breve* (1981), *Himno* (1985), *Divertimento* (1989), *Trópico* (1992), *Paisaje* (para banda militar, 1986 y para orquesta, 1996). Recibió la beca Guggenheim en

1972 y la Lira de Oro del Sindicato Único de Trabajadores de la Música.

Luis Quintanar

QUINTANAR, LUIS ♦ n. en San Juan del Río, Qro., y m. en la ciudad de México (?-1837). Militar realista. Combatió a los insurgentes hasta 1821 cuando, con el grado de general de división, se sumó al Plan de Iguala. Apoyó la coronación de Iturbide, quien lo designó jefe político de Jalisco (1822-24). Secundó el Plan de Jalapa contra Vicente Guerrero. A la salida de éste de la capital, dirigió un cuartelazo (diciembre de 1829) y, con Pedro Vélez y Lucas Alamán, formó un triunvirato que se conoce como Supremo Poder Ejecutivo, el que entregó el mando al vicepresidente Anastasio Bustamante el primer día de 1830.

QUINTANILLA, PEDRO P. ♦ n. y m. en Monterrey, NL (1837-1906). Empresario. Inició en Nuevo León el cultivo de la morera y el negocio de la sericultura, fundó la cerillera La Constancia y una fábrica de pólvora, inició la producción del aceite de monilla e higuerilla, dirigió una factoría de productos derivados del maíz (1888-1901) y tuvo una fábrica de bonetería.

QUINTANILLA COFFIN, PEDRO F. ♦ n. en Monterrey, NL (1915). Licenciado en derecho por la UNAM (1940). Ha sido jefe del Departamento Jurídico (1949) y secretario del cuerpo consultivo de administración (1949-55) del gobierno neoleonés; diputado local (1961-63), secretario del ayuntamiento de Monterrey (1964-66), diputado federal (1967-69), presidente del comité municipal del PRI en Monterrey (1968), secretario de Acción Ideológica de la CNOP (1967), procurador general de justicia de Nuevo León (1979) y presidente municipal de Monterrey (1979-82). Ha sido colaborador del *Diario de Monterrey*.

QUINTANILLA MADERO, CARMEN ♦ n. en el DF (1958). Licenciada en derecho por la Escuela Libre de Derecho. Maestra en derecho por la Universidad de California en Los Ángeles. Diplomada en Administración Pública por la Escuela Nacional de Administración de Francia, y en Calidad Total y Mejora de Procesos por el ITAM. Ha impartido clases en este instituto y en la Escuela Libre de Derecho. Ha ejercido su profesión, y también ha sido procuradora auxiliar en la Procuraduría Federal de la Defensa del Trabajo de la STPS (1981-83), asesora del director general de Organización, Programación y Presupuesto de la Secofi (1983-85), directora de Legislación y Normatividad en la Dirección de Asuntos Jurídicos de la SPP (1989-91), coordinadora de asesores del oficial mayor de la PGR (1991), asesora del secretario (1991-92), directora general de Derechos de Autor de la SEP (1992-95), y directora general de Normas de la Secofi (1996-); en este cargo, encabezó el establecimiento de las normas internacionales de calidad ISO-9002 en la secretaría.

QUINTANILLA OCHOA, AGUSTÍN ♦ n. en el DF (1952). Licenciado en economía por el ITAM (1972-76), maestro en finanzas por la Northwestern University, de Estados Unidos (1978-80). Ha sido asesor de la Comisión Nacional de los Salarios Mínimos (1974-75), asesor de la Dirección General de Estudios Hacendarios Internacionales (1976) y de la Subdirección General de Promoción Fiscal (1980) de la Secretaría de Hacienda; profesor de la Universidad Anáhuac (1980), director de Apoyos Financieros y Presupuesto Regional de la Secretaría de Programación y Presupuesto (1982-86), jefe de la Unidad de Coordinación Sectorial (1986), director general de Recursos Financieros (1987-88) de la Secretaría de Desarrollo Urbano y Ecología y director general de Programación y Presupuesto del DDF (1988-93). Fue asesor del IEPES del PRI (1981-82).

QUINTANILLA DEL VALLE, LUIS ♦ n. en Francia y m. en el DF (1900-1970). Escritor y diplomático de nacionalidad mexicana. Licenciado en letras y doctor en filosofía y ciencia política, egresado de las universidades de París y Johns Hopkins. Fue profesor en diversas universidades de Estados Unidos (Harvard, Cambridge, George Washington) y en la UNAM. Ministro consejero y encargado de negocios en Washington (1939), delegado mexicano a la Conferencia de San Francisco, embajador de México en la Unión Soviética (1942-45), Colombia (1945), ante la ONU y la OEA (1945-58). Dirigió el Instituto Nacional de la Vivienda (1958-64) y fue presidente de la Academia Mexicana de Derecho Internacional. Como poeta participó activamente en el movimiento estridentista. Empleó los seudónimos de *Kintaniya, Kinta-niya, Cenizas* y *Cuele*. Colaboró en las revistas *Horizonte* y *Radiador*, así como en el diario *Novedades* (1964-80). Coautor de *The Caribbean, Contemporary Trends* y *The Control of Foreign Relations in Modern Nations*. Autor de *Murciélago, Avión, Radio, Estaciones, Bélicos, Nocturnos, Aguas fuertes, Íntimas, Democracia y panamericanismo, Bergsonismo y política, Teatro mexicano, La evolución del pensamiento democrático* (inédito) y *A Latin American Speaks* y *Obra poética* (1986).

QUINTERO ÁLVAREZ, ALBERTO ♦ n. en Acámbaro, Gto., y m. en el DF (1914-1944). Poeta. Perteneció a la generación de las revistas *Taller* y *Taller Poético*, en la que se contaban Efraín Huerta, Octavio Paz y Rafael Solana, entre otros. Fue argumentista y adaptador de cine, así como jefe de publicidad de una empresa productora. Publicó: *Saludo de alba* (1936), "Semblanza del llanto" en *Tres ensayos de amistad lírica para Garcilaso* (1936) y *Nuevos cantares y otros poemas* (1942).

Carlos Quintero Arce

QUINTERO ARCE, CARLOS ◆ n. en Etzatlán, Jal. (1920). Sacerdote ordenado en 1944. Ha sido vicario cooperador en la parroquia de Totatiche, Jalisco; profesor en el Seminario Auxiliar, prefecto de estudios en los seminarios Menor y Mayor de Guadalajara y director espiritual de aquél; obispo de Ciudad Valles (1961), arzobispo titular de Tixdro y coadjutor del de Hermosillo (1966), y arzobispo de Hermosillo (1968-95).

QUINTEROS, ADOLFO ◆ n. en Chihuahua, Chih., y m. en el DF (1928-1994). Grabador egresado de la ENAP en 1955. Perteneció al Taller de Gráfica Popular y al Salón de la Plástica Mexicana. Obtuvo el primer premio en el Cuarto Salón de Grabado, el Premio Nacional de Grabado en 1959 y la presea Al Mejor Grabador Latinoamericano (en Checoslovaquia, por su obra *Bahía de Cochinos*) en 1962; en 1965 recibió medalla de oro en la Exposición Internacional de Grabado en Leipzig. En 1982, en Moscú, ganó el primer premio del concurso de carteles La Lucha por la Paz Mundial.

Pescadores, grabado en linóleum de Adolfo Quinteros

En Teotihuacán, Nanahuatzin se sacrifica para la era del Quinto Sol

QUINTO SOL ◆ Según la mitología náhuatl, el mundo ha pasado por una serie de cataclismos, cada uno de los cuales ha destruido una era o sol cosmogónico. El quinto sol era el que se vivía en el altiplano mexicano a la llegada de los conquistadores españoles. Según la misma creencia, al terminar el cuarto sol (el sol 4-agua, que duró 676 años), la tierra quedó en tinieblas y los dioses esperaron al sol futuro; se ofrecieron para ello dos personajes, Nanahuatzin y Tecciztécatl o Tecuiciztécatl, quienes hicieron una penitencia ritual de cuatro días en Teotihuacan y después se inmolaron en una hoguera. El más decidido de los dos, Nanahuatzin, se arrojó sin titubeos a la pira y se transformó en sol, mientras que Tecciztécatl dudó antes de arrojarse y renació convertido en luna.

QUIÑONES, NIEVES ◆ n. en San Juan del Río y m. en El Rodeo, Dgo. (?-1918). Magonista. En 1908 participó en la acción armada de Las Vacas. Dos años después se unió a la revolución maderista en las fuerzas de Villa, de quien era pariente. En marzo de 1911 participó en el combate de Casas Grandes, Chihuahua, donde lo aprehendieron tropas de Samuel García Cuéllar. Fue pasado por las armas pero sobrevivió, lo que desde entonces le valió el mote de el *Muerto*. Reincorporado a la lucha revolucionaria, formó parte de la División del Norte de Villa. Murió en combate.

QUIÑONES HERNÁNDEZ, LUIS CARLOS ◆ n. en Durango, Dgo. (1958). Maestro normalista especializado en literatura hispanoamericana por la Escuela Normal del Estado de Durango, de cuyo Instituto de Investigaciones Educativas ha sido profesor e investigador. Ha colaborado en publicaciones de su estado y de la ciudad de México, fue editor de la revista *Tiempo de Educar*. Autor de poesía: *Cantos rodados* (1987) y *Resumen de nostalgia* (1993); novela: *La luna púrpura* (1991); y cuento: *Silvestre* (1992).

QUIOQUITANI ◆ ☛ *Santa Catarina Quioquitani*, municipio de Oaxaca.

QUIOTEPEC, GRANDE DE ◆ Río de Oaxaca que nace de la confluencia de los ríos Las Vueltas y Grande o de Ixtlán. Corre de sureste a noroeste, recibe los ríos Tomellín, Apoala y San Pedro; cerca de San Juan Quiotepec recibe al Salado para formar el Santo Domingo, que más adelante se convierte en el Papaloapan.

QUIRARTE, VICENTE ◆ n. en el DF (1954). Escritor. Licenciado en lengua y literatura hispánicas (1982), maestro (1990) y doctor en letras mexicanas por la UNAM (1998). Ha sido profesor e investigador en la UAM y la UNAM y profesor invitado en instituciones extranjeras. Participó en los talleres literarios de

Vicente Quirarte

Eduardo Lizalde, Óscar Oliva y Salvador Elizondo. Ha sido miembro de los consejos de redacción de *Sin Embargo* y *Vaso Comunicante* y colaborador de revistas y suplementos culturales. Fue secretario de redacción de la revista *Universidad de México*. Director de *Periódico de Poesía*. Autor de poesía: *Teatro sobre el viento armado* (1980), *Vencer a la blancura* (1982), *Fra Filippo Lippi. Cancionero de Lucrezia Buti* (1982), *Puerta del verano* (1982), *Bahía Magdalena* (1985), *Fragmentos del mismo discurso* (1986), *La luz no muere sola* (1987), *El cuaderno de Aníbal Egea* (1990), *El ángel es vampiro* (1991, Premio Xavier Villaurrutia), *The Child and the Wind* (1992), *Cicatrices de varias geografías* (Colombia, 1992), *Luz de mayo* (1994), *Viajes alrededor de la alcoba* (1994) *Some Poems* (1996), *Desde otra luz* (1996), *Material de lectura* (1998) y *El peatón es asunto de la lluvia* (1998); ensayo: *La poética del hombre dividido en la obra de Luis Cernuda* (1985), *Perderse para reencontrarse. Bitácora de Contemporáneos* (1985), *El azogue y la granada. Gilberto Owen en su discurso amoroso* (1990, Premio Nacional de Ensayo Literario José Revueltas), *Peces del aire altísimo. Poesía y poetas en México* (1993), *Enseres para sobrevivir en la ciudad* (1994), *Tras la huella del niño centenario* (1995), *Sintaxis del vampiro. Una aproximación a su historia natural* (1996) y *La ciudad como cuerpo* (1999); y narrativa: *Plenilunio de la muñeca* (1984) y *El amor que destruye lo que inventa* (1988). Premio Nacional de Poesía Joven Francisco González León (1979). Becario de poesía INBA-Fonapas. Miembro del Sistema Nacional de Creadores.

Quirarte Ruiz, Martín ◆ n. en Guadalajara, Jal., y m. en el DF (1923-1980). Maestro en historia por la UNAM (1952). Becado por el gobierno español estudió la obra de Carlos Pereyra; en 1954 estuvo becado en Francia. Fue profesor de la UIA, de la UNAM y de la Facultad de Filosofía y Letras de Israel, así como investigador del Instituto de Investigaciones Históricas de la UNAM y del Instituto Nacional de Antropología e Historia; subdirector del Archivo Histórico de la Secretaría de Relaciones Exteriores, organismo al que representó en 1968 en el Congreso de Historiadores Mexicano-Norteamericanos. Colaboró en *Diorama de la Cultura* (1961-67). Autor de *Carlos Pereyra, caballero andante de la historia* (1954), *Francisco Alonso de Bulnes* (1961), *Visión panorámica de la historia de México* (1965), *El problema religioso en México* (1965), *Gabino Barreda, Justo Sierra y el Ateneo de la Juventud* (1968), *Historiografía sobre el imperio de Maximiliano* (1970) y *Relaciones entre Juárez y el Congreso* (1973). En 1952 fue premiado en Cuba por su texto *Hernán Cortés en La Española, Cuba y México*.

Quiriego ◆ Municipio de Sonora situado en el sur del estado, al este de Ciudad Obregón. Superficie: 2,705.72 km^2. Población: 3,820 habitantes, de los cuales 1,012 forman la población económicamente activa. Hablan alguna lengua indígena 396 personas mayores de cinco años (guarijío 308).

Quirino Salas, Juan José ◆ n. en Río Grande, Zac. (1957). Licenciado en Economía por el IPN. Maestro en Economía por la UNAM y en Ciencias Sociales por el Centro de Investigaciones y Estudios Superiores en Antropología Social. Militante del PRD. En 1993 fundó El Barzón Zacatecano. Posteriormente ha sido presidente nacional de la sociedad de deudores de la banca El Barzón (1995-1998) y promotor de El Barzón Latinoamericano. Senador de la República por el PRD (1994-2000).

Quiroga ◆ Municipio de Michoacán situado en el centro-norte del estado, al oeste de Morelia, en la ribera del lago de Pátzcuaro. Superficie: 284.53 km^2. Población: 23,846 habitantes, de los cuales 6,503 forman la población económicamente activa. Hablan alguna lengua indígena 7,160 personas mayores de cinco años (purépecha 7,075). Indígenas monolingües: 169. En su cabecera, del mismo nombre, se comercializan ar-

Foto: Xavier Quirarte

Martín Quirarte Ruiz

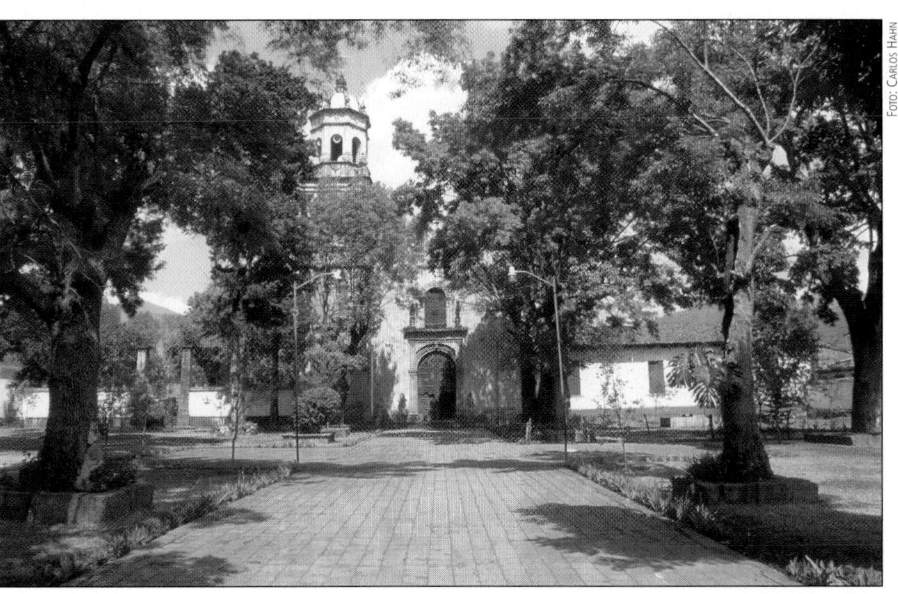
Foto: Carlos Hahn

Iglesia en Quiroga, Michoacán

tesanías de la región, como lacas de Uruapan, guitarras de Paracho, sombreros de Erongarícuaro, lana de Capácuaro, pieles y zapatos de Teremendo, alfarería de Tzintzuntzan, madera torneada, cerámica de Patamban y objetos de cobre de Santa Clara. La población se llamó Cocupao. El 3 de septiembre de 1852 se elevó al rango de villa y se le dio el nombre de Quiroga.

Quiroga, Julián ◆ n. en Ciénega de Flores y m. en Monterrey, NL (1827-1887). Militar. Combatiente liberal durante la revolución de Ayutla, apoyó en 1855 el Plan Restaurador de la Libertad, proclamado por Santiago Vidaurri. En 1858 apoyó a Vidaurri cuando dominó Nuevo León y Coahuila. En 1864 hizo salir de Monterrey a Benito Juárez, aunque se opuso a la entrada de tropas francesas en el estado; no obstante, dada la superioridad numérica de los extranjeros, recibió a Castagny el 26 de agosto de 1864. Apoyó al gobierno lerdista contra Porfirio Díaz en la batalla de Icamole. Luego del triunfo de la revolución de Tuxtepec, fue aprehendido, acusado de intento de rebelión y fusilado.

Retrato, firma y timbre postal de Vasco de Quiroga

Quiroga, Pablo ◆ n. en Ciénega de Flores, NL (1903-?). Abogado. En 1933 fue designado gobernador provisional de Nuevo León, por la renuncia de Francisco Cárdenas. Fue también agente del Ministerio Público, oficial mayor del gobierno estatal, magistrado del Tribunal de Justicia y presidente del Colegio de Notarios de Nuevo León. Se le señaló como responsable del asesinato de Manlio Fabio Altamirano, ocurrido el 25 de junio de 1936.

Quiroga, Vasco de ◆ n. en España y m. en Uruapan, Mich. (¿1470?-1565). Tenía el título de licenciado en cánones y supuestamente estudió jurisprudencia en Salamanca o Valladolid hacia 1515. Estuvo al servicio de la arquidiócesis de Granada, fue juez de residencia en Orán y representante diplomático en el norte de África. En 1528 acompañó a la corte española cuando pasó de Burgos a Madrid. Fue oidor de la segunda audiencia de la Nueva España, a donde llegó en enero de 1531. Compró algunos terrenos cerca de la ciudad de México y edificó en ellos su primer "pueblo-hospital", el de Santa Fe. En 1533, la audiencia lo envió a Tzintzuntzan, donde edificó el hospital de la Santa Fe de la Laguna, en las riberas del Lago de Pátzcuaro. Se ordenó sacerdote. En 1538, Juan de Zumárraga lo consagró obispo de Michoacán. Fundó el Colegio de San Nicolás, escuelas y hospitales, urbanizó numerosas poblaciones del estado y enseñó a los indios oficios artesanales. De 1547 a 1554 estuvo en España a su regreso, inició la construcción de la Catedral de Michoacán. Participó en el primer Concilio Provincial Mexicano (1555). Le llamaban *Tata Vasco*. Autor de *Manual de adultos* y *Tratado sobre la administración del bautismo*.

Quiroga Escamilla, Pablo ◆ n. en Ciénega de Flores, NL, y m. en el DF (1875-1948). Militar. En 1912 luchó contra el orozquismo y en 1913 se unió a las fuerzas de Manuel M. Diéguez para combatir a Victoriano Huerta. Al producirse la escisión revolucionaria, peleó contra Francisco Villa en el Bajío, a las órdenes de Álvaro Obregón (1915). Fue nombrado secretario general de gobierno en Nuevo León y jefe de operaciones en Chihuahua, en el valle de México y otras zonas militares. Se desempeñó como oficial mayor de la Secretaría de Guerra y Marina y jefe del Departamento de Establecimientos Fabriles, durante la presidencia de Pascual Ortiz Rubio. Alcanzó el grado de general de división en 1933 y fue titular de Guerra y Marina en los gabinetes de Abelardo L. Rodríguez (del 5 de septiembre al 31 de diciembre de 1932 y del 28 de junio de 1933 a 30 de noviembre de 1934), y de Lázaro Cárdenas (del 1 de diciembre de 1934 a 15 de junio de 1935). Gobernador de Nuevo León (1935-36).

Quiroz, Carlos ◆ n. en Apan, Hgo., y m. en el DF (?-1940). Periodista. Se inició en el semanario *Ratas y Mamarrachos*, que él mismo fundó y dirigió. Fue reportero parlamentario en *El Imparcial* y *El Universal*; como cronista taurino firmaba con el pseudónimo de *Monosabio*. En 1930 fue cofundador (con Alejandro Aguilar, *Fray Nano*) del periódico deportivo *La Afición*.

Quiroz, Eleuterio ◆ n. en San Luis Potosí, SLP, y m. en Querétaro, Qro. (1825-1849). Agrarista. En 1848 encabezó un levantamiento armado contra el gobernador Julián de los Reyes con campesinos de San Luis Potosí, Guanajuato y la sierra Gorda de Querétaro; la rebelión triunfó en la hacienda del Jabalí y Rioverde y Quiroz lanzó su plan político el 13 de marzo de 1849, con reivindicaciones agrarias. El encargado de combatir la rebelión era Anastasio Bustamante; éste recibió una copia del plan de Quiroz, la que fue enviada después al presidente José Joaquín Herrera, quien ordenó que se llegara a un acuerdo pacífico con los sublevados. Manuel Verástegui fue comisionado por los campesinos rebeldes para redactar un tratado, que no se firmó. Quiroz fue asesinado.

Quiroz, Juan Carlos ◆ n. en Aguascalientes, Ags. (1969). Licenciado en Letras Hispánicas por la Universidad de Aguascalientes. Coautor de *No había mar* (1996). Autor de poesía: *Tauromaquia* (1995), *Crónica de navegación (los demonios)* (1995) y *Versos para morir despacio* (1998).

Quiroz Cuarón, Alfonso ◆ n. en Jiménez, Chih., y m. en el DF (1910-1978). Perito en criminología por la UNAM (1939), donde ejerció la docencia. Fue jefe de la Sección Psicológica del Tribunal para Menores (1939), director de la Escuela Vocacional para Menores (1940), profesor del Instituto Técnico de Policía de la PJDF (1941), jefe del Departamento de Investigaciones Especiales del Banco de México (1941-65) y profesor de doctorado de la Universidad Veracruzana. En 1941 estableció la identidad del asesino de Trotsky, Ramón Mercader del Río, hasta entonces conocido como Jacques Mornard. En 1943 le correspondió efectuar el estudio de la personalidad de Gregorio *Goyo* Cárdenas Hernández, en 1952 el de Higinio *el Pelón* Sobera de la Flor. En 1948 estudió técnicas de asaltos a bancos en Venezuela; en 1948 resolvió el caso del falsificador Enrico Sampietro y, en ese mismo año, descubrió la identidad del escritor B. Traven. Coordinó los estudios sobre la autenticidad de los restos de Cuauhtémoc (1948-54). En 1965, luego de la invasión de Estados Unidos a la República Dominicana, fue enviado por la ONU para dictaminar acerca de los crímenes de guerra perpetrados por los *marines* estadounidenses; por iniciativa suya desapareció el penal de Lecumberri y se crearon los reclusorios Norte y Oriente de la ciudad de México; representó en México a la Interpol y fue secretario general de Prevención de la Delincuencia en la ONU. Trabajó también con las policías de Cuba, Turquía, Inglaterra, Holanda, Suiza y Dinamarca. Murió mientras daba una clase de medicina forense. Coautor de *Pescadores y campesinos tarascos* (1943), *Estudio biotipológico de los zapotecas* (1949), *Estudio de los otomíes* (1961); autor de *Tendencia y ritmo de la criminalidad en México* (1930), *Características biológicas de los escolares proletarios* (1937), *El examen somático y funcional del delincuente. Su técnica* (1939, tesis profesional), *Un estrangulador de mujeres* (1952), *Psicología del funcionario bancario* (1954), *La criminalidad en la República Mexicana* (1958), *La pena de muerte en México* (1962), *El asalto. Asaltos a bancos en Venezuela y en América* (1964), *Psicoanálisis del magnicidio* (1965), *El costo social del delito en México* (1970) y *Tratado de medicina forense* (1977).

Quiroz Gutiérrez, Fernando ◆ n. en Santa Cruz Ayotusco, Edo. de Méx., y m. en el DF (1889-1966). Médico graduado en el Hospital Militar de la ciudad de México, especializado en urología. Fue profesor de la Universidad Nacional (1911-66). Recibió la medalla Justo Sierra. En 1961, Adolfo López Mateos le entregó la insignia Andrés Vesalio. Fue organizador y presidente de la Sociedad Mexicana de Anatomía. Autor de *Patología médica y quirúrgica de la boca y anexos* y de *Anatomía humana* (1943), libro de texto en diversas universidades latinoamericanas.

Quiroz de la Vega, Samuel ◆ n. en Apizaco, Tlax. (1935). Licenciado en derecho por la Universidad Autónoma de Puebla (1959). Ha sido profesor de secundaria y de la UAP, asesor jurídico del Banco de Comercio, abogado postulante, asesor de la Federación de Trabajadores Poblanos, asesor del sindicato de la CROM en Puebla y Tlaxcala, asesor de sindicatos de la FROC-CROC, profesor y secretario académico de la Universidad Autónoma de Tlaxcala, visitador oficial mayor de gobierno, presidente del Tribunal de Arbitraje de Puebla, asesor jurídico del ayuntamiento de Apizaco, secretario general de gobierno de Tlaxcala, secretario y presidente del Tribunal Superior de Justicia del mismo estado, diputado federal (1985-88), asesor del titular del gobernador de Tlaxcala (1989-90), jefe de asesores de Pemex (1990), titular de los Servicios Coordinados de Educación Pública para Tlaxcala (1991-92) y gobernador sustituto de Tlaxcala (1992-1993). Pertenece al PRI, del que fue presidente del Comité Directivo Estatal en Tlaxcala. Autor de *Algunas consideraciones acerca de la personalidad en el derecho del trabajo.*

Quiroz Hernández, Alberto ◆ n. en León, Gto. (1907). En 1927 fundó en León el semanario *El Cóndor*, en 1932 fue cofundador de la Sociedad de Escritores y Artistas de la misma ciudad. Pasó al Distrito Federal en 1953 y fundó la Unidad Mexicana de Escritores. Dirigió, de 1954 a 1959, la revista *El Libro y el Pueblo* y escribió numerosos guiones cinematográficos. Autor de *Zigzag novelesco* (1929), *Esquema del heroísmo* (1931), *Situación de la literatura mexicana* (1934), *Carne y poesía* (1936), *Tu gloria, camarada* (1938), *El proyecto de Julia* (1938), *Nociones de estética cinematográfica* (1942), *Poesía y teatro infantil* y *Chifladuras de Sóstenes Irucha* (1945), *Una mujer decente* (1946), *Júbilo del río* (1947), *Los ladrones* y *Paraíso-Wesston* (1950), *Cristo Rey o la persecución* (1952), *El profesor Mentoláthum* (1954), *Magia silvestre* (1954), *Las Kúkaras* (1955), *Lupe fusiles* (1957), *Serpientes* (1959), *Odisea de la virgen morena. Historia política* (1961), *Biografía de Norteamérica. Retratos literarios de personajes y lugares de los Estados Unidos* (1963), *Historia para Óscar Lewis. El reverso de los hijos de Sánchez* (1966), *Diario mágico* (1966), *Un papa mexicano* (1969), *100 años de juventud* (1970), *Los magos de la revolución. Una historia para el señor presidente* (1972), *Diálogos frente al año 2000* (1976), *Los intelectuales* (1978), *Los magistrados* (1981) y *¡Tu gloria, Cárdenas!*

Fernando Quiroz Gutiérrez

Quitupan ◆ Municipio de Jalisco situado al este de Ciudad Guzmán, en los límites con Michoacán. Superficie: 616.19 km^2. Habitantes: 11,485, de los cuales 2,425 forman la población económicamente activa. Hablan alguna lengua indígena 43 personas.

Quitupan ◆ Río de Jalisco que nace en el valle de Juárez, sobre el eje volcánico; recibe las aguas que antes alimentaban la laguna de la Magdalena; se une al río Terécuato para formar el Tepalcatepec.

Quivira ◆ Reino legendario del que habló, por primera vez, Alvar Núñez Cabeza de Vaca, quien recorrió lo que ahora es el sur de Estados Unidos, en su viaje desde Florida hasta la ciudad de México. De acuerdo con la versión de Cabeza de Vaca, el reino de Quivira estaba formado por siete ciudades de oro y su capital era Cíbola. Volvió a referirse a este supuesto reino el explorador Marcos de Niza, lo que despertó la codicia española y generó una serie de expediciones al norte en busca de las siete ciudades, que nunca fueron encontradas. En su lugar se hallaron siete pueblos, entre los actuales condados de Socorro y Torrance, en Nuevo México. Francisco Vázquez de Coronado llegó en 1541 a lo que creyó era Quivira, en el pueblo indio de Piro; ahí se construyó una misión en 1629, llamada Gran Quivira, la que fue abandonada en 1670 y en su lugar fue construido un monumento nacional de Estados Unidos.

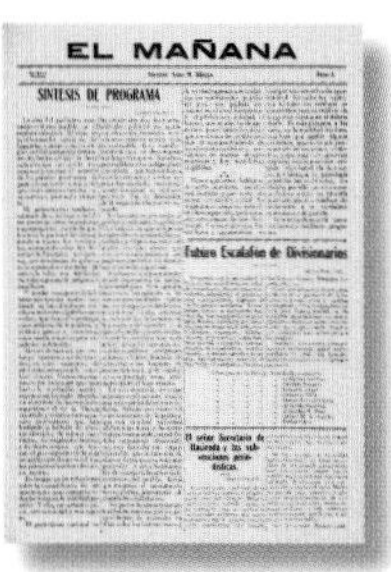
EL MAÑANA

Jesús María Rabago colaboró en *El Mañana*

Emilio O. Rabasa

FOTO: DANTE BUCIO

Emilio Rabasa Gamboa

RÁBAGO, JESÚS MARÍA ◆ n. en Zimapán, Hgo., y m. en el DF (1860-1939). Abogado y periodista. Con el pseudónimo de *Pablo de Góngora* colaboró en el semanario *Novedades* (1882) y en *El Universal* (1888-1901). Fundó y dirigió la revista *El Mañana*, de orientación antimaderista (1911), y publicó *Cronos* (1922). Autor de *Historia de un gran crimen* y *Consejo de ministros*.

RÁBAGO MALDONADO, ANTONIO ◆ n. en Celaya, Gto., y m. en Chihuahua, Chih. (1861-1915). Ingresó en el ejército en 1880. Era coronel en 1910, cuando lo enviaron a Chihuahua para combatir la insurrección maderista. Después de la firma de los tratados de Ciudad Juárez fue designado jefe de caballería de la Secretaría de Guerra. En 1912 peleó a las órdenes de Victoriano Huerta contra los orozquistas y se le designó jefe de la zona militar correspondiente a Chihuahua. Con ese puesto fue el encargado de apresar y ejecutar a Abraham González. Durante la dictadura huertista fungió como gobernador de Chihuahua (de febrero a mayo de 1913).

RÁBAGO PALAFOX, GABRIELA ◆ n. en San Juan Teotihuacán, Edo. de Méx., y m. en el DF (1950-1995). Profesora normalista. Comentarista y guionista de televisión. Colaboró en *La Onda*, *Geografía Universal*, *Él*, *Al Sur del Sur*, *Geo*, *El Cuento*, *Nonotza*, *La Semana de Bellas Artes*, *Política y Cultura*, *Natura*, *Nueva Vida*, *Tierra Adentro*, *El Universal*, *Excélsior*, *El Heraldo de México* y *El Día*. Participó en la redacción de *Secretos para hacer teatro* (1982) y *Teatro para principiantes* (1984). Coautora de *Los siete pecados capitales* (1989). Autora de cuento infantil: *Relatos de la ciudad sin dueño* (1981, Premio Nacional de Cuento Infantil Juan de la Cabada); relatos: *La señorita* (1982), *La voz de la sangre* (1990), *Ópera para dos voces y un lamento* (1996); novela: *Todo ángel es terrible* (1981), *Federico* (1983) y *La muerte alquila un cuarto* (1991); texto didáctico: *Taller de los títeres*; antología: *Teatro, obras cortas para representar* (1982), *Pequeño teatro* (1984) y *Estancias nocturnas* (1987); poesía: *Haikús* (1981); y teatro infantil: *La rata haragana* (1977) y *Godofrina* (1979, Premio Clementina Otero). En 1982 publicó *Testimonios: una solución para el alcoholismo*. Premio Puebla de Cuento de Ciencia Ficción (1988) y Premio José Martínez de la Vega (1994). Becaria del Centro Mexicano de Escritores (1979-80).

RÁBAGO PÉREZ, ANDRÉS ◆ ☛ *Russell, Andy*.

RABASA, EMILIO O. ◆ n. en la ciudad de México (1925). Licenciado (1948) y doctor (1956) en derecho por la UNAM. Ha sido jefe del Departamento de Escuelas Incorporadas (1948), secretario del doctorado de la Facultad de Derecho (1950-61) y profesor (1950-65 y 1976-80) de la UNAM; jefe del Departamento Jurídico del Banco Nacional de Crédito Ejidal y director general de la Afianzadora Mexicana y del Banco Nacional Cinematográfico (1965-70), asesor jurídico de las secretarías de Agricultura y Ganadería y de Salubridad y Asistencia, embajador en Estados Unidos (1970), secretario de Relaciones Exteriores (del 1 de diciembre de 1970 al 28 de diciembre de 1975) y profesor del Instituto Tecnológico Autónomo de México (1975). Es miembro del grupo mexicano de la Corte Permanente de Arbitraje de La Haya y del Comité Jurídico Interamericano de la OEA.

RABASA ESTEBANELL, EMILIO ◆ n. en Ocozocoautla, Chis., y m. en el DF (1856-1930). Licenciado en derecho por el Instituto de Ciencias y Artes de Oaxaca (1878). En Chiapas fue síndico del ayuntamiento de Tuxtla, diputado local (1881) y director del Instituto de Ciencias y Artes (1882). Juez de lo civil, secretario del gobernador Mier y Terán y diputado local en Oaxaca. En la ciudad de México fue defensor de oficio, agente del Ministerio Público, juez de lo penal y profesor en la Escuela de Comercio. En 1888 fundó, con Rafael Reyes Spíndola, el diario *El Universal*, que desapareció en 1901. Gobernador de Chiapas (1891-94) y senador por el mismo estado, ejerció la docencia en la Facultad de Leyes y en la Escuela Libre de Derecho, de la que fue director. El gobierno de Huerta lo nombró delegado a las Conferencias de Niagara Falls (del 20 de mayo al 15 de julio de 1914) para discutir la ocupación estadounidense de Veracruz. Al suspenderse las negociaciones por la caída de Huerta, decidió radicar en Nueva York (1914-21). Autor de poesía: *A Mercedes* (1884); ensayo: *El artículo 14* (1906), *La Constitución y la dictadura* (1912), *El juicio constitucional* (1919) y *La evolución histórica de México* (1920); y novelas, con el pseudónimo de *Sancho Polo*: *La bola* (1887), *Moneda falsa* (1888) y *La guerra de Tres Años* (1931), entre otras obras. Fue miembro de la Academia Mexicana (de la Lengua) y de la Academia Mexicana de Jurisprudencia.

RABASA GAMBOA, EMILIO ◆ n. en Tuxtla Gutiérrez, Chis. (1949). Licenciado en derecho por la UNAM (1973), con estudios de posgrado en la London School of Economics (1974-76). Ha sido abogado de la jefatura de Relaciones Laborales (1968-72) y asesor y secretario auxiliar de la Subdirección General Administrativa del IMSS (1972-73); profesor de la UNAM (1976-79), subdirector del Sistema de Evaluación de la Administración Pública de la Coordinación de Estudios Administrativos de la Presidencia (1977-78), abogado del bufete Rabasa (1978-81), asesor jurídico de la Oficialía Mayor del Registro Nacional de Electores (1979-81), subdirector y director de Gobierno (1981-82) y secretario técnico del Fondo Nacional de Solidaridad de la Secretaría de Gobernación (1982); director del Centro Interamericano de Estudios de Seguridad Social y jefe del Departamento de Asuntos Internacionales (1983-85), secretario general del Comité Permanente de Seguridad Social (1985), secretario general del IMSS (1985-88) y subsecretario de Protección Civil y de Prevención y Readaptación Social de la Secretaría de Gobernación (1988-90). Presidente de la Comisión de Concordia y Pacificación para Chiapas (1996-). Coautor de *Mexicano: ésta* *es tu Constitución, ¿Por qué la democracia?* y *De súbditos y ciudadanos, sentido y región de la participación política.*

RABEL, FANNY ◆ n. en Polonia (1924). Pintora, grabadora y escenógrafa. Llegó a México en 1938. Estudió en la Escuela Nocturna de Arte número 1 (1939), en La Esmeralda (1940-45) y en la Escuela de Artes del Libro (1945-48). Fue ayudante de Siqueiros (1939), Frida Kahlo (1943) y Diego Rivera (1948). Cofundadora del Salón de la Plástica Mexicana. Perteneció al Taller de Gráfica Popular (1950-62). En 1960 se incorporó como profesora al Taller de Grabado de la Ciudadela. Ha expuesto individualmente en Israel, Cuba, Estados Unidos y varias ciudades de México (desde 1951). Ha participado en las bienales internacionales de grabado de Liubliana, Yugoslavia (1955 y 57), de Sao Paulo y de Santiago de Chile. Hay cuadros suyos en museos de Nueva York, México, París, Washington, La Habana, Santiago de Chile, Buenos Aires, Copenhague y Tel Aviv. Son obra suya los murales de la Unidad de Lavaderos Públicos de Tepalcatitla (1945); *Alfabetización*, en Coyoacán (1952); *Sobrevivencia de un pueblo*, en el Centro Deportivo Israelita (1957); el Pabellón de la Revolución Mexicana en la cuarta Feria del Libro (1960); *Ronda del tiempo*, en el Museo de Antropología (1964); *Hacia la salud*, en el Hospital Infantil (1982), y *La familia mexicana* (1984), en el Registro Público de la Propiedad. Autora de *Niños de México* (1959) y *Réquiem por una ciudad. 40 obras* (1984). Obtuvo mención honorífica de grabado en la Casa de las Américas.

RABELL, MALKAH ◆ n. en Polonia (1921). Nombre profesional de la crítica Regina Rabinowitz. Hermana de la anterior. En su infancia vivió y estudió en Francia y en Bélgica, e hizo algunas incursiones en la actuación teatral. Llegó a México en 1937. Militó en la Juventud Comunista. Estudió en la UNAM e hizo la maestría en literatura francesa en Argentina, donde vivió desde 1943. Regresó a México en 1958 y se ha dedicado a la docencia y a la crítica teatral.

Silla retoñada, obra de Fanny Rabel

Ha colaborado en *México en la Cultura, Diorama de la Cultura, Los Universitarios, Escénica, El Día* y en las revistas de la UNAM, el IPN y el Conacyt. Tradujo *Sociología y destino del teatro*, de J. R. Bloch; *Vida y teatro*, de N. Evreinoff; *Demencia y muerte del teatro*, de R. Giraudon, y *Una ventana al infierno*, de Masha Greenbaum. Autora de *En el umbral de los ghettos* (novela, 1945), *Tormenta sobre el Plata* (novela, 1965), *Ensayos sobre el teatro judío moderno* (1965), *Por qué ríe la gente* (1967), *Luz y sombra del antiteatro* (1970) y *Decenio de teatro mexicano. 1975-1985* (1986).

RADIN, PAUL ◆ n. en Polonia y m. en Canadá (1883-1959). Doctor en filosofía por la Universidad de Nueva York (1911). Profesor de etnología en la Universidad Internacional de Arqueología y Etnología Americanas, de México (1912-13), y en universidades de Canadá y Estados Unidos. Entre sus textos referentes a México se hallan: "The Peyote Cult of the Winnebago" (1913), "The Folk Tales from Mexico" (1915), "Mixe Tests" (1933) y "The Nature and Problems of Mexican Indian Mytholo-gy" (1944), en *Journal of American Folklore*; "El folklore de Oaxaca" (1917), en *Anales de la Escuela Internacional de Arqueología y Etnología Americanas*; "The Relationship of Maya to Zoque-Huave" (1924) y "The Distribution and Pho-netics of the Zapotec Dialects" (1925), en *Journal de la Société des Américanistes de París*; "The Source and Authenticity of the History of Ancient Mexicans" (1920) y "Mexican Kinship Terms" (1931), en *Publications in American Archaeology and Ethnology. University of California*; "Maya, Nahuatl and Tarascan Kinship Terms" (1925), en *American Anthropologist*; y "Preliminary Sketch of the Zapotecan Language" (1930), en *Language*.

RADIO ◆ De acuerdo con el investigador Felipe Gálvez Cancino, la primera emisión radiofónica en México la llevó a cabo Adolfo Enrique Gómez Fernández en la ciudad de México, el 27 de septiembre de 1921, apenas un año después de que se realizara la primera transmisión radial en el mundo. Otros autores consideran que el iniciador de la radio fue Constantino de Tárnava, el 9 de octubre del mismo año, quien envió por este medio un mensaje de Monterrey a la ciudad de México, el que fue captado sólo por el gerente del Banco Regional de Monterrey en la capital de la República. En el mismo año, José R. de la Herrán y Fernando Ramírez, patrocinados por la Secretaría de Guerra, montaron la estación experimental JH, que se convertiría más adelante en la CYB (1923), de la cigarrera El Buen Tono, y en la XEB. El 6 de junio de 1922, los radioaficionados mexicanos se agruparon en la Liga Nacional de Radio, que más tarde se convirtió en Club Central de Radiotelefonía y, en 1923, en Liga Central Mexicana de Radio. En ese año empezaron a comercializarse en el país los llamados radios de galena, que costaban 12 pesos y se vendían en una empresa de Raúl y Luis Azcárraga. El 1 de junio de 1923, Álvaro Obregón dictó las primeras normas sobre la radiodifusión. El 14 de agosto de 1923 se inauguró la difusora del periódico *El Mundo*, de Martín Luis Guz-mán; ésta programó discursos y conferencias de José Vasconcelos, Antonio Caso, Carlos Pellicer, Manuel M. Ponce, y otros intelectuales y artistas. La emisora de *El Mundo* ofrecía, además, asistencia técnica a los radioaficionados. Se estima que en 1923 había en México unos 5,000 receptores de radio. El 15 de septiembre de ese año se inauguró formalmente la radiodifusora CYB, cuya transmisión inaugural fue la ceremonia del Grito de la Independencia, dado por Obregón. Para incrementar la cantidad de aparatos de radio en circulación, El Buen Tono los canjeaba por cierto número de cajetillas vacías de cigarros fabricados por dicha casa. El 18 de septiembre del mismo año, la empresa de los Azcárraga y *El Universal* inauguraron, con la primera transmisión de música sinfónica, la estación CYL, que emitía re-gularmente noticieros. El mis-mo día se efectuó la primera recepción radial del extranjero: la reseña de la pelea entre Jack Dempsey y Luis Ángel Firpo, transmitida por la estación WQL de Nueva York. En México, la pelea fue recibida por José Fernando Ramírez, técnico de la JH, quien traducía simultáneamente y retransmitía por conducto de la CYB; esta pelea fue escuchada en vivo en las ciudades de México, Guadalajara y Puebla, entre otras. El diario *Excélsior* y la casa comercial Parker inauguraron su estación de radio, la CYX, en marzo de 1924, cuando ya estaban en funcionamiento las transmisoras XIO, de Manuel Zetina González, y la oficial de la Secretaría de Guerra y Marina. En noviembre de ese año apareció la CYZ, de la SEP, dirigida por Joaquín Beristáin, y la CZE, que comenzó sus transmisiones con la toma de posesión del presidente Plutarco Elías Calles, pero que dejaría de transmitir a fines de la década. En 1925 operaban 11 estaciones en México, siete en la ciudad de México y cuatro en provincia. En 1925 se fundó la estación CYJ, utilizada por la empresa General Electric fundamentalmente para fines de propaganda comercial. El 1 de septiembre de 1928 la estación de la SEP se transformó en la XFX e inició las transmisiones de apoyo pedagógico para las escuelas del DF y los estados de México, Puebla, Morelos, Hidalgo y Tlaxcala. En 1928, Nuevo Laredo, Monterrey, Veracruz, Guadalajara, Ciudad Juárez, Tampico y San Luis Potosí tenían estaciones de radio; en 1929 había 17 estaciones comerciales y dos culturales en la onda larga del país. México suscribió los acuerdos de la Conferencia Internacional de Telecomunicaciones, por los que le fueron adjudicados los indicativos nominales XE y XF y en 1930 se inició el régimen de concesiones para las radiodifusoras, la primera de las cuales fue para la XEW. Esta emisora, llamada *La voz de la América Latina desde México*, fue fundada el 18 de septiembre de 1930 por Emilio Azcárraga, hermano de los propietarios de la CYL, que desapareció ese mismo año. La XEW fue una de las más importantes fuerzas unificadoras del México posrevolucionario, al alcanzar a un público muy amplio y comenzar a uniformar, poco a poco, sus gustos. En este proceso fueron muy importantes las numerosas estrellas de la canción que fueron lanzadas por la estación, particularmente en los cuarenta, así como cómicos, compositores, conjuntos y orquestas que convocaban a multitudes a los estudios de la radiodifusora. En 1930 surgieron también la XEFZ (con 250 vatios), la XEFO, del Partido Nacional Revolucionario, y *Radio Mundial*, antigua CYJ, que en ese año fue comprada por Félix F. Palavicini y que actualmente opera como XEN. También reapareció la antigua CZE, ahora como XEEP, Radio Educación, pero nuevamente volvería a cesar transmisiones en 1940. El 14 de junio de 1937 inició transmisiones XEXX, Radio UNAM, dirigida por Alejandro Gómez Arias, con sede en la antigua Escuela de Ciencias Químicas, en Popotla. En 1937 se creó la XEWW, filial de la XEW en la onda corta, con 10 kilociclos de potencia. El 27 de febrero surgió la Asociación de Estaciones Radiofónicas Comerciales, como una sección de la Cámara Nacional de Comunicaciones y Transportes. También en 1937 se inició la transmisión de *La Hora Nacional*, que encadena a todas las estaciones de radio del país. En ese año, la Secretaría de Educación Pública cedió su estación, XFX, al Departamento Autónomo de Prensa y Publicidad del Poder

Aparato radiofónico de la década de 1930

Pedro *El Mago* Septién en sus transmisiones radiofónicas de eventos deportivos

Foto: Archivo Fotográfico

La *XEW* en 1930

Ejecutivo, que la convirtió en la XEDP, con la filial XEXA en onda corta. Emilio Azcárraga, Enrique Contel y Emilio Balli fundaron la XEQ el 31 de octubre de 1938. XELA, *Radio Metropolitana*, entró en servicio el 5 de julio de 1940. Un año después, Azcárraga formó la cadena nacional Radio Programas de México, que llegó a tener 60 repetidoras y representaba en el país a las empresas National Broadcasting Company y National Broadcasting System. Radio Programas de México impulsó la creación de empresas auxiliares, como Programex (productora de radionovelas y radiominutos) y Audimex (importadora de equipos). En 1942 había 125 radiodifusoras en México, 34 de ellas en el DF. Existían entonces las estaciones XEDF, *Radio Gobernación*; XEQK, *Radio Exacta*; XEUZ, *Cadena Radio Nacional*; XEOY, *Radio Mil*; y XEQR (onda larga) y XERQ (onda corta) y *Cadena Radio Continental*, con 25 filiales en la República. El 12 de enero de ese año obtuvo su registro la Cámara de la Industria de la Radio y la Televisión (CIRT); un mes después, Manuel Ávila Camacho promulgó el Reglamento de las Estaciones Radiodifusoras Comerciales, Culturales, de Experimentación Científica y de Aficionados, que sustituía a la ley respectiva de 1936. En 1947, por iniciativa de Alonso Sordo Noriega, nació la XEX, *La Voz de México*, primera en transmitir en frecuencia modulada. *Radio Cadena Nacional* se constituyó el 1 de junio de 1948; y XEMX, *Radio Femenina*, el 14 de marzo de 1952, dirigida por Refugio Escobar de Perrín. En enero de 1956 surgió la Cadena Independiente de Radio, con 25 radiodifusoras situadas en diversos puntos del país, y en julio se creó la Red México, con tres emisoras en el DF (XEB, XEHP y XEMX). El 8 de enero de 1960 entró en vigor la Ley Federal de Radio y Televisión. En 1968 reapareció Radio Educación, que eventualmente se consolidaría como la radiodifusora cultural de más tradición en México. En 1971 inició labores la Comisión de Radiodifusión, encargada de aprovechar 12.5 por ciento del tiempo de transmisión que los concesionarios deben ceder al gobierno federal. El 19 de abril de 1973 entró en vigor el Reglamento de la Ley Federal de Radio y Televisión y se creó el Consejo Nacional de Radio y Televisión, organismo encargado de evaluar el nivel cultural, social y artístico de las radiodifusoras. En 1975, las principales empresas del ramo eran: Radiodifusoras Unidas Mexicanas (con 87 estaciones de amplitud modulada y nueve de frecuencia modulada), Red Radioprogramas de México (73 en AM y una en FM), Radio Ventas de Provincia (50 en AM y ocho en FM), Radiodifusoras Asociadas (44 en AM y una en FM), Grupo Acir (43 en AM y seis en FM), Radio Visión Activa (30 en AM y tres en FM), Radio Cadena Nacional (30 en AM y una en FM) y Corporación Mexicana de Radiodifusión (30 en amplitud modulada). En 1978, un decreto declaraba a Radio Educación organismo desconcentrado de la SEP. Durante esos años, y bajo el mando de Gerardo Estrada (quien llegó a la estación en 1977), la radiodifusora alcanzó su mayor auge, al ofrecer transmisiones que se convirtieron en una alternativa seria y variada a las emisoras comerciales. En 1987 había en México 11,441,693 aparatos receptores de radio, 70 radiodifusoras gubernamentales y 879 estaciones comerciales, reunidas en poco más de 20 grupos. Después de 1985, las emisoras entraron en una fuerte competencia noticiosa en la que destacó Radio Red, con el noticiero *Monitor*, el primero de larga duración, que se transmite desde 1974, inicialmente conducido por Mario Iván Martínez y luego por José Gutiérrez Vivó. La intensa competencia propició que se concentraran las frecuencias en poderosos grupos, los que generalmente tienen su sede y varias estaciones en la ciudad de México y numerosas repetidoras en los estados. Los grupos más importantes son la Organización Radio Centro, que cuenta en el DF con seis emisoras de amplitud modulada y seis de frecuencia modulada; el Grupo Acir, con tres frecuencias de AM y cuatro de FM; Radio Mil y Radiópolis con tres emisoras de AM y tres de FM cada uno; Radio Fórmula, con tres de AM y dos de FM; y MVS Radio que tiene una emisora de AM y cuatro de FM. El Estado dispone del Grupo Imer, con cuatro estaciones de AM y dos de FM, Radio Educación, de AM, y Radio UNAM, que transmite en AM y FM. A escala nacional la concentración ha sido mayor, pues en 1998 cuatro

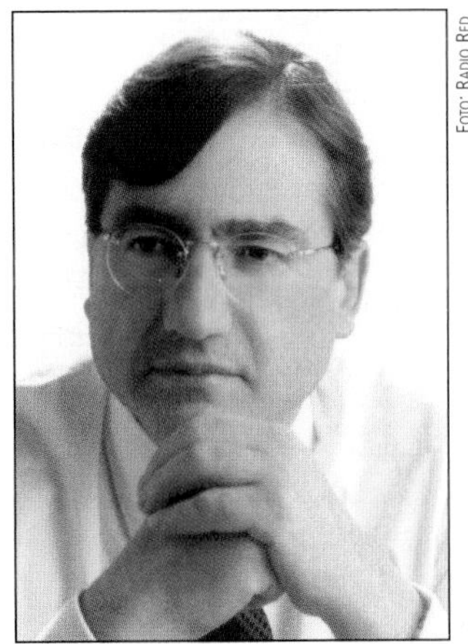
Foto: Radio Red

José Gutiérrez Vivó, conductor del programa radiofónico Monitor

Archivo General de la Nación

Grabación de radionovelas en la XEW en 1943

Logotipo de Grupo Radio Centro

Logotipo de Grupo Acir

Fernando Rafful Miguel

grupos controlaban casi la mitad de las frecuencias: Radiorama 161 emisoras, que representaban 13.93 por ciento del total; Acir, 147 emisoras y 12.72 por ciento del total; OIR/GRC 127 y 10.99 por ciento; y Cima Somer 120 emisoras y 10.38 por ciento.

RAFAEL DELGADO ◆ Municipio de Veracruz contiguo a Córdoba. Superficie: 39.48 km². Habitantes: 12,832, de los cuales 3,065 forman la población económicamente activa. Hablan alguna lengua indígena 7,149 personas mayores de cinco años (náhuatl 7,125). Indígenas monolingües: 274.

RAFAEL LARA GRAJALES ◆ Municipio de Puebla situado al noreste de la capital del estado. Superficie: 15.31 km². Habitantes: 13,398, de los cuales 2,879 forman la población económicamente activa. Hablan alguna lengua indígena 28 personas mayores de cinco años (náhuatl 22). El 25 de abril se celebra la fiesta de San Marcos, patrono de este municipio, antes llamado Xalixtlahuacan. La cabecera, del mismo nombre, se llamó San Marcos y San Marcos de Ocampo.

RAFAEL LUCIO ◆ Municipio de Veracruz situado al noroeste de Jalapa y contiguo a Banderilla. Superficie: 24.68 km². Habitantes: 4,657, de los cuales 1,180 forman la población económicamente activa. Hablan alguna lengua indígena 13 personas.

RAFAEL Y VILÁ, RAFAEL DE ◆ n. en España y m. en Cuba (1817-1882). Tipógrafo y grabador. En 1836 dirigió en Nueva York el periódico *El Eco de Ambos Mundos*. En 1837 aparecieron algunos de sus grabados en madera en *El Mosaico Mexicano*, aunque se sabe que no llegó a México sino hasta 1844. Trabajó en la imprenta de Ignacio Cumplido y en 1846 montó su propio taller, que cuidó especialmente los trabajos en color. Militó en el bando conservador y dirigió *El Universal* (1849), órgano del grupo encabezado por Lucas Alamán. En 1851 fue expulsado del país por inmiscuirse en los asuntos políticos nacionales. Viajó a Cuba, donde fundó los periódicos *La Constancia* y *La Voz de Cuba*. Autor de *La masonería pintada por sí misma*.

RAFELSON, MORLAND B. ◆ n. en EUA y m. en el DF (1900-1972). Comerciante llegado a México en 1931 como representante de algunas firmas estadounidenses. Fundó en 1940 la empresa Rafmex; se naturalizó mexicano y de 1946 a 1948 fue delegado político del Departamento del Distrito Federal en Cuajimalpa.

RAFFAELLO ◆ ☛ *Ilfara Fusi, Raffaello.*

RAFFUL MIGUEL, FERNANDO ◆ n. en Ciudad del Carmen, Camp. (1934). Licenciado en economía por la UNAM. Ha sido analista de la Dirección General de Estadística de la Secretaría de Industria y Comercio (1963), jefe del Departamento de Estudios Económicos de la Secretaría de Patrimonio Nacional (1965-66 y 1967-70). Director general de Control y Vigilancia de los Organismos Descentralizados y Empresas de Participación Estatal de (1970-73) y subsecretario del Patrimonio Nacional (1973-76), senador (1976), subsecretario de Pesca de la Secretaría de Industria y Comercio (1976), jefe del Departamento de Pesca (1977-82), en el gabinete de José López Portillo. Coordinador de la Maestría de Pesca de la UAM Xochimilco (septiempre de 1984 a junio de 1986), profesor de Política Económica y seminario de tesis en la maestría de Docencia Económica de los ciclos académicos, Colegio de Ciencias y Humanidades de la UNAM (mayo de 1984 a octubre de 1986). Asesor en cuestiones perqueras en la Secretaría de Pesca de 1988-1994. Coordinador de asesores de la SEMARNAP (diciembre de 1994 a enero de 1995), desde esta fecha es secretario de Gobierno del Estado de Campeche, hasta abril de 1997. Diputado local por el Distrito VIII de Campeche. Actualmente es representante de la Secretaría de Educación Pública en Campeche.

RAHON, ALICE ◆ n. en Francia y m. en el DF (1914-1987). Pintora. Estudió arte con su padre y con Wolfgang Paalen (☛), quien fue su esposo de 1931 a 1947. En 1936 se unió al movimiento surrealista. Viajó a la India y Canadá para estudiar el arte autóctono de esos países. Radicó en San Francisco y hacia 1939 llegó a México. Participó en la Exposición Internacional del Surrealismo (1940) y presentó su obra en diversas galerías de México, Francia y Estados Unidos. Autora de los poemarios *Sablier couché* (1936), *A meme la terre* (1939) y *Noir animal* (1941).

RAIGOSA, GENARO ◆ n. en Zacatecas, Zac., y m. en la ciudad de México (1847-1906). Se tituló como abogado en la Escuela Nacional de Jurisprudencia. Diputado local (1872) y federal (1875) por San Luis Potosí, senador por el mismo estado en varias ocasiones; desempeñó diversas labores diplomáticas en Alemania, Inglaterra y Estados Unidos (1899) y representó al país en la segunda Conferencia Panamericana (1901-02).

RAMBAL, ENRIQUE ◆ n. en España y m. en el DF (1923-1971). Actor. Se inició en 1943 en la compañía teatral de su padre, Enrique Rambal, en la obra *Drácula* (1943). Su primer papel estelar, al lado de su hermana Enriqueta, fue en *Rebeca* (1944). Llegó a México en una gira, en 1950, y decidió radicar en este país. *Bandera negra*, *Caviar y lentejas*, *Los grandes Sebastiani* y *Los prodigiosos* son algunas de las piezas que protago-

Enrique Rambal

nizó. Intervino en más de 50 películas, entre ellas: *El mártir del Calvario, El ángel exterminador* (de Luis Buñuel), *Las leandras, Secreto profesional, Tu hijo debe nacer, El cuerpazo del delito, Los hijos del divorcio* y *Cuna de valientes*. Actuó en las series de televisión *Los caudillos*, en la que personificó a Miguel Hidalgo, *Doña Macabra, Dos y su show* y *Arsenio Lupin*, así como en el programa de radio *Vale la pena vivir*. Grabó los discos *Cartas a mi hijo* y *Gustavo Adolfo Bécquer*.

RAMÍREZ, DE ◆ Sierra de Coahuila, Durango y Zacatecas que se extiende de este a oeste en los límites de estas entidades. Su pico más alto es el Frontón de Ahuichila, cuya cima es la confluencia de los tres estados. Tiene yacimientos de plata, cobre y hulla.

RAMÍREZ, AGUSTINA ◆ n. en Mocorito y m. en Mazatlán, Sin. (1813-?). Tuvo 13 hijos, 12 de los cuales murieron en la guerra contra la intervención francesa y el imperio. En 1868 el congreso de Sinaloa acordó otorgarle una pensión y más tarde hizo lo mismo el Congreso de la Unión, aunque esta última no se le entregó.

RAMÍREZ, AMBROSIO ◆ n. en Villa de Reyes y m. en San Luis Potosí, SLP (1859-1913). Licenciado en derecho por el Instituto Científico y Literario de San Luis Potosí. Fue secretario particular del gobernador de Morelos y juez en Ciudad del Maíz, Matehuala y Venado. En la ciudad de San Luis Potosí fue agente del Ministerio Público, defensor de oficio, secretario del Supremo Tribunal de Justicia y notario público. Diputado federal suplente (1911-13) por Santa María del Río, profesor del Seminario y colaborador de *El Estandarte* y *El Tiempo Ilustrado*. Autor de *Odas de Quinto Horacio Flaco* (1905), *Apuntes para la vida de Horacio, Colección de odas de Horacio traducidas por ingenios españoles, mexicanos y sudamericanos* (1911), *Cuestión de ejidos y linderos* (1912, con el pseudónimo de Romualdo Pérez), *Datos sobre el Tibur, Documentos relativos al derecho de tierras y aguas ejidales de Villa de Reyes* y *Disertación sobre la belleza*.

RAMÍREZ, ANDRÉS ◆ n. en Cuautla, Mor. (1972). Escritor y editor. Ha sido editor en jefe de la editorial Joaquín Mortiz. Autor de poesía: *Un canto para los navegantes* (1992) y *En nuestros ojos* (1998).

RAMÍREZ, ANTONIO ◆ n. en el DF (1926). Hizo estudios de pintura y dibujo en el Centro de Iniciación Plástica número 4 del INBA y en la ENAP. Fue profesor de pintura en el Centro Popular de Arte número 4 del INBA (1951-84) y de artes plásticas en los talleres Carlos Lazo (1952), la Escuela de Pintura y Escultura del INBA y de la ENAP (1951-86), de la que también fue rector (1974-78). Fue ayudante de Diego Rivera y José Chávez Morado. Autor de murales y numerosas obras de caballete. Berta Taracena y José de Santiago publicaron un estudio sobre su obra.

RAMÍREZ, ARMANDO ◆ n. en el DF (1952). Escritor autodidacto. Habitante del barrio capitalino de Tepito, participó en el grupo Arte Acá. Ha sido guionista de varios programas de televisión, comentarista de *Letras vivas*, conducido por José Agustín, y *Detrás de la noticia*, conducido por Ricardo Ochoa; director de *Hoy en la cultura* (1988). Autor del libro de crónicas *Tepito* (1983) y de las novelas *Chin Chin el teporocho* (1971), *Crónica de los chorrocientos mil días del barrio de Tepito* (1972), *El regreso de Chin Chin el teporocho en la venganza de los jinetes justicieros* (1978), *Violación en Polanco* (1980), *Noche de Califas* (1982), *Quinceañera* (1986) y *Me llaman la Chata Aguayo* (1994). Algunos de sus textos han sido llevados al cine.

RAMÍREZ, BENITO ◆ n. en Chicontepec, Ver., y m. en Puebla, Pue. (1891-1945). Profesor normalista titulado en la ciudad de México en 1914. Ese año se incorporó a la revolución constitucionalista en las fuerzas de Álvaro Obregón, con quien estuvo en las batallas de Celaya, Trinidad y León (1915). Diputado al Congreso Constituyente (1916-17) por el distrito de Tuxpan. Director general de Aduanas (1920-23) y director de Bienes Nacionales (1923). Secundó la rebelión delahuertista desde Tuxpan, Veracruz. Al fracasar ese movimiento se retiró a la vida privada. En 1941 fue jefe de las oficinas federales de Hacienda.

RAMÍREZ, CARLOS ◆ n. en Oaxaca, Oax. (1951). Estudió administración de empresas en la UIA (1971-72). Dedicado al periodismo, ha sido reportero de *El Heraldo de México* (1972-73), subjefe de la Sala de Prensa de la Dirección de Información y Relaciones Públicas de la Presidencia de la República (1974-75), reportero de asuntos especiales de *El Día* (1975-76), reportero de *Proceso*, encargado de asuntos económicos y financieros, subjefe de información y subdirector de la agencia CISA-Proceso (1977-83), profesor de la UNAM (1979-86), reportero de asuntos especiales económicos (1983-84) y columnista (1996-) de *El Universal;* reportero de asuntos especiales, columnista y coordinador de información económica de *El Financiero* (1984-95) y profesor de la UIA (1986). Dirige la revista *La Crisis*. Coautor de *Planes sin planificación* (1981), *Pemex: la caída de Díaz Serrano* (1981), *La devaluación de 1982* (1982), *La nacionalización de la banca* (1982), *La psicosis del dólar* (1985) y *Salinas de Gortari: candidato de la crisis* (1987). Autor de *El país de las maravillas* (1981) y *Operación Gavin: México en la diplomacia de Reagan* (1987) y *José Córdoba Montoya: el asesor incómodo* (1995). Miembro de la Unión de Periodistas Democráticos y de la Asociación de Periodistas y Economistas. En 1993 recibió el Premio de Periodismo Manuel Buendía.

RAMÍREZ, CIRILO ◆ n. y m. en Hermosillo, Son. (1818-1890). Fue comerciante, tesorero general de Sonora en 1856, secretario de gobierno de Ignacio Pesqueira (1856-57) y diputado local en 1861. Se negó a reconocer al imperio de Maximiliano. Redactor del periódico *La Estrella de Occidente*. En 1866 volvió a la secretaría de gobierno de su estado, mismo que gobernó interinamente varias ocasiones, por licencias o ausencias del titular. Fue administrador principal del timbre, vocal de la Junta de Instrucción Pública, magistrado del Tribunal Superior de Justicia

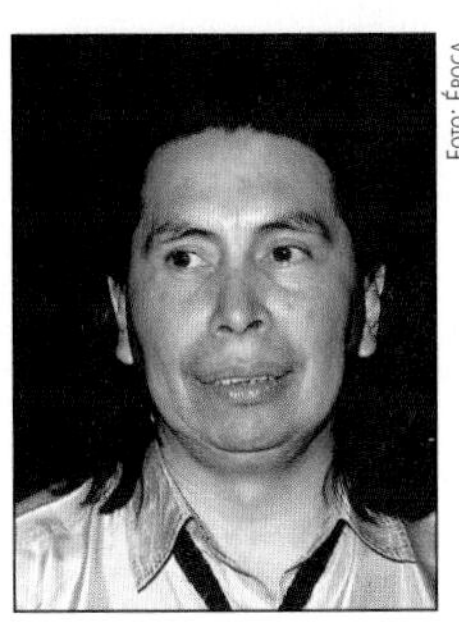
FOTO: ÉPOCA
Armando Ramírez

FOTO: EIKON
Carlos Ramírez

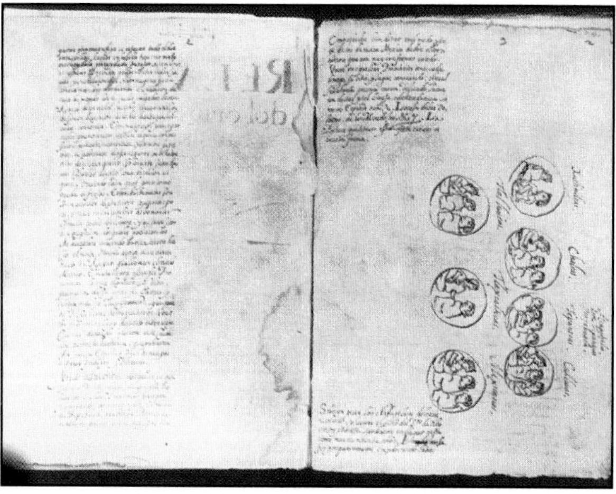

Códice Ramírez

(1875-77), prefecto político de Guaymas y nuevamente gobernador interino en 1882.

RAMÍREZ, CÓDICE ◆ Documento pictográfico nahua elaborado con técnica indígena en fecha posterior a la conquista. Recibió el nombre de José Fernando Ramírez, quien lo descubrió en 1856. Se divide en cuatro manuscritos que narran la historia de los mexicas, desde su peregrinación al valle de México hasta la caída de Tenochtitlán, y refieren algunos aspectos de la religión mexica. Se atribuye su versión castellana al fraile Diego Durán. El códice conservado en la Biblioteca Nacional de Antropología e Historia es una de las dos versiones manuscritas que se hicieron del mismo texto. El otro se halla en la Biblioteca John Carter Brown, de Rhode Island.

FONDO HISTÓRICO ALFONSO SÁNCHEZ GARCÍA

Ignacio Ramírez

RAMÍREZ, DAVID G. ◆ ☛ *Gram, Jorge.*

RAMÍREZ, EVERARDO ◆ n. en la ciudad de México (1906). Grabador. En 1930 empezó a trabajar en el Centro Popular de Pintura Santiago Rebull. Miembro fundador de la Liga de Escritores y Artistas Revolucionarios (1933) y del Taller de Gráfica Popular (1937). Autor del portafolios *Vida en mi barriada* (1948).

RAMÍREZ, FERNANDO ◆ n. en Veracruz, Ver. (1875-?). Profesor graduado en la Escuela Normal de Jalapa. Hizo también la carrera de ingeniería. En 1913 se unió a la revolución constitucionalista. Militó en la corporación Supremos Poderes y alcanzó el generalato. Dirigió el Cuerpo de Ingenieros Militares y fue jefe del Estado Mayor de la Secretaría de Guerra. Autor de *Implantación de estaciones radiomilitares para uso del ejército nacional en toda la República.*

RAMÍREZ, FRANCISCO M. ◆ n. en Ejutla, Oax., y m. en el DF (1867-1955). Estudió abogacía en el Colegio Católico de Oaxaca (1891). Fue juez de primera instancia, juez de lo civil, juez de hacienda, magistrado del Tribunal Superior de Justicia de Oaxaca, agente del Ministerio Público, síndico, diputado local y profesor del Instituto de Ciencias y Artes de Oaxaca, donde fue el primer profesor de práctica forense. Formó parte de la XXVI Legislatura federal, disuelta por Victoriano Huerta (1911-13). Ministro (1923-28) y presidente de la Suprema Corte de Justicia.

RAMÍREZ, GABRIEL ◆ n. en Mérida, Yuc. (1938). Pintor autodidacto y escritor. Llegó a la ciudad de México en 1956 y empezó a pintar en 1959. Colaboró en la revista *Nuevo Cine* con Emilio García Riera, con quien también editó *La semana en el cine* (1961-64). Su primera exposición individual fue en 1965. En 1968 fue miembro fundador del Salón Independiente. Desde 1970 sus obras han sido incluidas en muestras colectivas en Colombia, EUA, México, España e Italia. A fines de los ochenta regresó a Mérida, donde ha seguido su actividad como pintor y dirigido la revista *Camaleón* (1990-91). Participó en la cuarta Bienal de Jóvenes de París (1965). Ha ilustrado *La verdadera historia del flautista de Hammelin* (1982, de Álvaro Mutis) y *Con la música por dentro* (1982, de Jomi García Ascot). Es miembro del Consejo Consultivo de la enciclopedia *Yucatán en el tiempo*. Autor de la columna "La cosa cultural" en "Unicornio" de *Por Esto!* (1991-96). Autor de *El cine de Griffith* (1972), *El cine yucateco* (1980), la biografía *Lupe Vélez, la mexicana que escupía fuego* (1986), *Crónica del cine mudo mexicano* (1989), *Norman Foster y los otros* (1993) y *Miguel Contreras Torres* (1993). Becario del CNCA (1989-90). Ganó la Medalla Yucatán (1986) y el Premio Marco (1995).

RAMÍREZ, GUADALUPE I. ◆ n. y m. en el DF (1885-1948). Educadora, nieta de Ignacio Ramírez. Estudió farmacología y comercio en la Escuela de Artes y Oficios para Mujeres, de la que fue profesora, y trabajo social en Estados Unidos. Fundó la Comisión Voluntaria de Asistencia Infantil Juan María Rodríguez y en 1947 se le nombró delegada del Departamento del Distrito Federal en Xochimilco, donde hay una avenida con su nombre. Fue la primera mujer que ocupó ese cargo. Perteneció a la Comisión Técnica Feminista, la Alianza de Agrupaciones Femeninas Culturales y el Grupo Femenino de Acción Social de México.

RAMÍREZ, IGNACIO ◆ n. en San Miguel el Grande, Gto., y m. en la ciudad de México (1818-1879). Licenciado en derecho (1845). En 1845 fundó, con Guillermo Prieto y Vicente Segura, *Don Simplicio*, donde empleó el pseudónimo de *el Nigromante* y en 1846 formó el Club Popular. Secretario de Guerra y de Hacienda en el gobierno mexiquense de Olaguíbel (1846), combatió en Padierna contra los invasores estadounidenses. Jefe político de Tlaxcala (1848-49), vivió en Toluca hasta 1851, donde fundó el periódico *Themis y Deucalión*. Diputado federal por Sinaloa (1852). Por sus críticas a Santa Anna pasó 11 meses en prisión, la mayor parte del tiempo encadenado. Al triunfo de la revolución de Ayutla fue secretario de Comonfort y diputado por el Estado de México al Constituyente de 1856-57. En 1857 fundó con Alfredo Bablot *El Clamor Progresista*. Diputado a la primera Legislatura. Al producirse el golpe de Estado de los conservadores fue nuevamente a prisión. Preso hasta diciembre de 1858, se unió luego a las fuerzas liberales y participó en la elaboración de las Leyes de Reforma. Secretario de Justicia e Instrucción Pública (del 21 de enero al 9 de mayo de 1861) y de Fomento (del 19 de marzo al 3 de abril de 1861) en el gabinete de Juárez y presidente del ayuntamiento de la ciudad de

México (1861). Poco después fue nuevamente diputado. En 1864, en Sinaloa, escribió para *La Opinión* y la *Estrella de Occidente* hasta que fue desterrado a EUA. Regresó a México antes de la caída de Maximiliano y fue nuevamente encarcelado. En 1867 fundó con Altamirano, Prieto y otros liberales *El Correo de México*, financiado por Porfirio Díaz. Magistrado de la Suprema Corte de Justicia durante 12 años y secretario de Justicia de Porfirio Díaz en dos ocasiones (del 28 de noviembre al 6 de diciembre de 1876 y del 17 de febrero al 23 de mayo de 1877). Coautor de *Apuntes para la historia de la guerra entre México y los Estados Unidos* (1848). Autor de *Ensayo sobre las sensaciones* (1848), *Lecturas de historia política de México* (1871), *Observaciones de meteorología marina* y *Lecciones de literatura* (1884), entre otros libros. En 1984 se inició la publicación de sus *Obras completas*.

RAMÍREZ, JOAQUÍN ◆ n. y m. en la ciudad de México (1834-1866). Estudió dibujo y pintura en la Academia de San Carlos. Auxilió a Pelegrín Clavé en la decoración del templo de La Profesa (1859) y fue autor de cuadros como *El arca de Noé*, *Los hebreos cautivos en Babilonia*, *Moisés en Raphidín* y *La adoración de los pastores*. Por encargo de Maximiliano realizó un *Hidalgo* y copió el retrato del austriaco hecho por Rebull; el original del cuadro se envió a Miramar y la copia es la que se exhibe en el Museo Nacional de Historia.

RAMÍREZ, JOSÉ AGUSTÍN ◆ ☛ *José Agustín*.

RAMÍREZ, JOSÉ FERNANDO ◆ n. en Hidalgo del Parral, Chih., y m. en Alemania (1804-1871). Historiador. Abogado por el Colegio de San Luis Gonzaga, Zacatecas (1832). Fue fiscal del Tribunal Superior de Justicia de Chihuahua (1828-30), miembro del consejo de gobierno (1833), fiscal del Tribunal de Justicia (1833), diputado federal por Durango (1834), secretario de gobierno de Durango (1835), director del Instituto de Ciencias y Artes de Durango (1837), rector del Colegio de

José Fernando Ramírez

Abogados (1837-39 y 1856), presidente del Tribunal Mercantil (1841), de las juntas de Industria (1844) y de Fomento (1846) y ministro del Tribunal de Justicia (1848). Formó parte de la Junta de Notables (del 6 de enero al 12 de julio de 1843) que expidió las Bases Orgánicas. Director y conservador del Museo Nacional (1852), ministro de la Suprema Corte (1856), presidente de la Junta Directiva de la Academia de Bellas Artes (1856), dos veces senador (1845-46 y 1847-48) y secretario de Relaciones Interiores y Exteriores (del 24 de diciembre de 1846 al 27 de enero de 1847) de Gómez Farías, y de Relaciones Exteriores (11 de septiembre de 1851 a 3 de marzo de 1852) de Arista. Se adhirió al Plan de Ayutla (1854) y fue desterrado a Europa (1855-56). Regresó como ministro de la Suprema Corte (1856) y fue ministro de Maximiliano (del 21 de junio de 1864 al 3 de marzo de 1866). Descifró el Calendario Azteca. Autor de varias libros de historia.

RAMÍREZ, JOSÉ MARÍA ◆ m. en Irapuato, Gto. (?-1812). Sacerdote, era subdiácono de Yuriria. Alcanzó el grado de coronel durante la guerra de Independencia. En 1812, al pasar José María Liceaga por Yuriria, lo auxilió en la fundición de cañones, la fabricación de pólvora, la acuñación de moneda y la publicación de la *Gaceta del Gobierno Americano en el Departamento del Norte*. Al retirarse Liceaga de Yuriria lo dejó al frente de la plaza. El 31 de octubre del mismo año, Iturbide atacó la población, lo hizo prisionero y lo envió a Irapuato, donde fue ejecutado.

RAMÍREZ, JOSÉ MARÍA ◆ n. y m. en la ciudad de México (1834-¿1892?). También se dice que murió en 1891. Estudió en el Colegio de San Ildefonso y en el Seminario Palafoxiano. En 1852 se alistó en la Guardia Nacional para combatir la sublevación conservadora de Jalisco. Participó en la revolución de Ayutla y en 1857 se opuso al golpe de Estado de Comonfort. Combatió contra los conservadores en la guerra de los Tres Años, fue diputado federal (1861) y luchó contra la intervención francesa y el imperio. Cayó prisionero en Oaxaca, fue liberado en un canje de prisioneros y se incorporó a las fuerzas de Porfirio Díaz, con el grado de mayor, con quien permaneció hasta el triunfo de la República. Fue senador, subdirector del Departamento Administrativo de la Secretaría de Hacienda, administrador de mercados y recaudador de rentas. Colaboró en *El Crepúsculo*, *El Horóscopo*, *El Diario de Avisos* y *La Orquesta*. Autor de poesía: *Flores del retiro* (1858) y *Margaritas* (1868); y novelas: *Celeste* (1861), *Gabriela* (1862), *Ellas y nosotros* (1862), *Avelina* (1864), *Mi frac* (1868), *Una rosa y un harapo* (1868) y las desconocidas *Los pícaros*, *La rosa y la calavera*, *Herminia*, *El anillo y la flor blanca*, *María de las Angustias* y *El viejo y la bailarina*. Se le conocía con el sobrenombre de *el Viejo* y empleó el pseudónimo de *Joselín*.

RAMÍREZ, JUAN JOSÉ ◆ n. y m. en San Cristóbal de Las Casas, Chis. (1832-1913). Abogado y político liberal. Estudió literatura y jurisprudencia en Guatemala. Fue director del *Diario Oficial de Chiapas*, síndico del ayuntamiento de San Cristóbal de Las Casas, diputado suplente, fiscal del Tribunal Superior de Justicia del estado y secretario general del gobernador Juan Clímaco Corzo; diputado al Congreso Constituyente de 1857, profesor de la Escuela de Leyes de Chiapas y senador (1875).

RAMÍREZ, LINO ◆ n. en San Miguel de Allende, Gto. (?-1840). Padre de Ignacio Ramírez, *el Nigromante*. Participó en la masonería del rito yorkino. Fue vice-

Ramón Ramírez

Foto: Elena Ayala

Luis Enrique Ramírez

gobernador de Querétaro durante los gobiernos de José María Díez Marina y José Rafael Canalizo; gobernador interino (del 30 de junio al 24 de agosto de 1833) y constitucional del mismo estado (del 24 de agosto de 1833 al 8 de junio de 1834). Durante su gestión apoyó la primera Reforma de Valentín Gómez Farías y promulgó la segunda Constitución local; con el regreso de López de Santa Anna a la Presidencia y la vuelta al centralismo, defendió la soberanía del estado y promovió una coalición con Jalisco, Zacatecas, Guanajuato y San Luis Potosí, ante lo cual Santa Anna envió tropas que lo derrocaron.

Ramírez, Luis Enrique ◆ n. en Culiacán, Sin. (1963). Periodista egresado de la Escuela de Comunicación Social de Sinaloa. Ha sido reportero de *El Universal, El Financiero, La Jornada* y *Milenio* (1998-). Ha colaborado en las revistas *Viceversa, Cuartoscuro* y *Kiosco* y en el suplemento *El Ángel*, así como en el periódico sinaloense *Noroeste*. Autor de los libros de entrevistas *La muela del juicio* y *La ingobernable. Encuentros y desencuentros con Elena Garro* (1999). Obtuvo el Premio Sinaloa de periodismo y dos veces el Premio Pablo de Villavicencio por sus reportajes. También ha recibido el premio del Festival Cultural de Sinaloa y el Premio de Periodismo Juvenil José Pagés Llergo.

Ramírez, Martín ◆ n. en Jalisco y m. en EUA (1885-1960). En México fue lavandero. Cruzó la frontera hacia Estados Unidos y se desempeñó como peón ferrocarrilero hasta que, hacia 1930, después de presentar notorias manifestaciones de esquizofrenia, fue internado en un institución hospitalaria de Los Ángeles, donde le diagnosticaron catatonia. Fue pasado definitivamente a una clínica de Auburn en la que empezó a pintar. El doctor Tarmo Pasto, del Stanford Research Institute, se interesó en su caso y le proporcionó lápices de colores y otros materiales, con los que ejecutó una obra extraña, frecuentemente sobre envolturas y todo tipo de papel que en ocasiones pegaba sobre trabajos en ela-boración. Sus temas tienen reminiscencias de la cerámica, los juguetes populares y otros motivos mexicanos. Sus obras estuvieron en exhibición en la galería de la Universidad Estatal de Sacramento, California. En 1979 se mostró una selección de ellas en una exposición celebrada en Londres y en 1989 se presentó su más amplia exposición en el Centro Cultural Arte Contemporáneo de México.

Sin título, lápiz y técnica mixta sobre papel, obra de Martín Ramírez

Ramírez, Rafael ◆ n. en Las Vigas, Ver., y m. en el DF (1885-1959). Profesor graduado en 1905 en la Escuela Normal de Jalapa. Fue jefe de las misiones culturales de Hidalgo (1923) y Morelos (1924) y del Departamento de Escuelas Rurales de la Secretaría de Educación Pública (1935). Autor de *La enseñanza de la lectura, Curso de educación rural, Técnica de la enseñanza, La escuela de la acción dentro de la enseñanza rural* (1924), *Cómo dar a todo México un idioma* (1928), *La educación industrial* (1928), *La escuela proletaria* (1935), *Los nuevos rumbos de la didáctica, La educación normal y la formación de los maestros rurales que México necesita, Supervisión de la educación rural, La educación en los Estados Unidos, La visita a Chile, Libros de lectura para escuelas rurales, Plan sexenal para el ciclo inferior de las escuelas rurales* (1934), *Plan sexenal para el ciclo intermedio de las escuelas rurales* (1934), *Los grandes problemas nacionales y las tareas sociales, El interés mundial por la educación de los grupos sociales retrasados* (1935), *Corrientes educativas modernas* (1935), *Formación y capacidad de los maestros rurales para hacer eficaz la acción de la escuela en los pueblos indígenas* (1935), *Curso breve de psicología educativa para las escuelas regionales campesinas* (1937) y *El servicio de higiene mental escolar* (1937). Sus obras completas fueron editadas en 1966-68 por el gobierno veracruzano. Desde 1976 sus restos se hallan en la Rotonda de los Hombres Ilustres.

Ramírez, Ramón ◆ n. en Tepic, Nay. (1969). Futbolista. Ha sido mediocampista de los equipos Santos Laguna, Guadalajara, América y Tigres. Seleccionado nacional, ha participado dos veces en la Copa América (1993 y 1995), en los Campeonatos Mundiales de 1994 y 1998 y en la Copa Confederaciones 1999, en la que México fue campeón.

Ramírez, Raúl ◆ n. en Guadalajara, Jal. (1932). También se menciona el DF como su lugar de nacimiento. Hizo estudios de teatro en la Academia Andrés Soler. A su participación en numerosas obras teatrales se agrega su carrera cinematográfica, en la que comenzó como intérprete, pero en la que ha sido, también, argumentista, productor, director, editor y guionista. En su filmografía como actor destacan *Marejada* (1952), *La calle de los amores* (1953), *La sospechosa* (1954), *Donde el círculo termina* (1955), *Escuela de rateros* (1956) y *Cascabel* (1976). Ha dirigido *La cariñosa motorizada* (1975), *Rarotonga* (1977), *Mi querida vecindad* (1985) y *Vuelven los mecánicos ardientes* (1986). Actúa regularmente en televisión.

Ramírez, Rodolfo Rafael ◆ n. en Valle de Santiago, Gto., y m. en el DF (1874-1954). Se tituló como médico en el Colegio de Guanajuato, del que llegó a ser director. Se contó entre los discípulos del francés Alfredo Augusto Dugés. Fue diputado local (1914), director de la Escuela Normal de Guanajuato, senador (1924), director general de Educación Pública en su estado natal y en Querétaro, diputado local (1921) y jefe de la Biblioteca de la Suprema Corte hasta su muerte. Autor de *Ligeras con-*

sideraciones sobre la teoría atómica (1901).

RAMÍREZ, SANTIAGO ◆ n. y m. en el DF (1921-1989). Psicoanalista. Médico cirujano por la UNAM (1945), especializado en el Instituto Psicoanalítico de Buenos Aires (1952). En la UNAM fue profesor del Colegio de Psicología (1945-84), jefe de laboratorio en el Instituto de Orientación Profesional (1945-65), coordinador de psicología clínica (1966-84) y asesor (1971) de las facultades de Psicología y de Filosofía y Letras. Trabajó en el Departamento de Personal del Banco de México y fue el primero en aplicar pruebas proyectivas en el país. Fue uno de los iniciadores del movimiento psicoanalítico. Autor de *El mexicano. Psicología de sus motivaciones* (1953), *El mexicano. Educación, historia y personalidad* (1961), *Esterilidad y fruto* (1962), *El psicoanálisis. La técnica* (1965, en colaboración con Agustín Palacios y Gregorio Valner), *Antropología cultural* (1966), *El carácter y el teatro* (1967, con Víctor Aíza), *Infancia es destino* (1975, octava edición en 1985), *Ajuste de cuentas* (1979, en colaboración con Roberto Escudero y Santiago Ramírez Castañeda), *Un homosexual. Sus sueños* (1981) y *Obras escogidas* (1983). Miembro fundador de la Asociación de Neurocirugía y Psiquiatría (1946), del Grupo Mexicano de Estudios Psicoanalíticos (1952), de la Asociación Psicoanalítica Mexicana, de la Asociación Psicoanalítica de México (1960) y de la Asociación Mexicana de Sexología (1969). Miembro honorario de la Asociación Mexicana de Psicoterapia Psicoanalítica.

RAMÍREZ ACOSTA, ABEL ◆ n. en Molango, Hgo., y m. en el DF (1915-1979). Maestro rural por la Escuela Normal Regional de El Mexe (1934), profesor por la Escuela Nacional de Maestros y licenciado en derecho por la UNAM. Miembro del PRI, fue secretario de finanzas de ese partido (1970-72). Ejerció la docencia en Hidalgo (1934-37) y el Distrito Federal. En el SNTE fue secretario de Acción Obrera y Campesina de la Sección XV, secretario general de la Sección IX, y secretario de finanzas del Comité Ejecutivo Nacional. Miembro del Departamento Jurídico del sindicato ferrocarrilero, profesor de la Universidad Autónoma de Hidalgo, representante del gobierno hidalguense ante el federal, oficial mayor del gobierno de Hidalgo, diputado federal (1970-73), secretario general de gobierno (1972-75) y tesorero general de Hidalgo durante la gestión de Othoniel Miranda Andrade.

RAMÍREZ AGUILAR, ABEL ◆ n. en el DF (1943). Escultor. Estudió en la Escuela de Diseño y Artesanías (1963), en Rhode Island (1961); en La Esmeralda (1963, 68 y 69); y en la Real Academia de Bellas Artes de La Haya. Ha sido profesor de cerámica y metales en el Centro de Capacitación para el Trabajo Industrial Número 8, en Puebla, y en el Centro de Artes Plásticas y Artesanías Independencia del IMSS. Desarrolló una técnica para el trabajo en metales que llamó "de rechazo manual". Ha expuesto en diversas ciudades mexicanas, de Estados Unidos y Holanda. Participó en el primer Salón de Cerámica Moderna Mexicana (1967), la tercera Bienal Nacional de Escultura (1967), la primera Plenaria de Escultura (1971), el primer Salón Anual de Escultura (1971) y en la tercera Exposición del Espacio, en el IPN (1971). Primer lugar nacional de fotografía submarina, segundo lugar mundial y medalla de plata por equipos en el primer Gran Premio Mundial de Fotografía Submarina, en París. Mención honorífica en el concurso Nuevos Valores de la Plástica Mexicana (1976) y cuarto lugar nacional de Diseño en Cerámica (1976). Es fundador del Círculo de Escultores.

RAMÍREZ DE AGUILAR, ALBERTO ◆ n. y m. en el DF (1928-1970). Licenciado en derecho por la UNAM. Ingresó en 1947 en el diario *Últimas Noticias* y pasó después a *Excélsior*, donde destacó como reportero de policía y por su columna "Siguiendo pistas". Fue director de la segunda edición de *Últimas Noticias* (1965), subdirector (1968) y gerente general (1969) de *Excélsior*, guionista cinematográfico e iniciador de las entrevistas diarias en televisión, donde participó en el programa *Charlas de Café* con Alberto Cardeña Z., Fausto Castillo y Carlos Loret de Mola. Autor de las novelas *Camino a la nada*, *Noche de sábado* y *Falsos héroes*.

RAMÍREZ DE AGUILAR, FERNANDO ◆ n. en Oaxaca, Oax., y m. en el DF (1887-1953). Profesor normalista. Desde 1907 se dedicó al periodismo en *El Imparcial* y colaboró en *El País*, *El Universal Ilustrado*, *El Demócrata* y *El Independiente*. Durante la revolución fue corresponsal de varios periódicos. Radicado en la ciudad de México, ingresó en 1920 en el diario *El Universal*, en el que firmaba como Jacobo Dalevuelta y llegó a ser jefe de información. Miembro organizador del primer Congreso Nacional de Historia Patria (1933). Fue varias veces secretario general del Sindicato de Redactores de la Prensa y participó en el Teatro del Murciélago y en el Movimiento de Teatro de Masas. Autor de *Oaxaca. De sus historias y sus leyendas* (1922), *Las fiestas guadalupanas y otras crónicas* (1922), *Desde el tren amarillo* (1924), *La odisea de los restos de nuestros libertadores* (1925), *Supersticiones, antaño y hogaño, en algunas regiones de Oaxaca* (1925), *El canto de la victoria: escena chinaca en 1867* (1927), *El laborillo* (1929, en colaboración con Áurea Procel), *Nicolás Romero: un año de su vida, 1864-1865* (1929), *Visiones de la guerra de independencia* (1929, en colaboración con Manuel Becerra Acosta), *Estampas de México* (1930), *Don Vicente Guerrero, síntesis de su vida* (1931), *Los funerales de don Vicente Guerrero, hace un siglo* (1931), *El charro símbolo* (1932), *Monte Albán, mosaico oaxaqueño* (1933) y *Cariño a Oaxaca* (1938).

RAMÍREZ DE AGUILAR, RAMÓN ◆ n. en Oaxaca, Oax. (?-?). Abogado. En 1823 participó en la lucha por implantar el federalismo. Presidente del ayuntamiento de Oaxaca (1824) y vicegobernador del estado (1824) durante la administración de José Ignacio Morales. Fue tres veces gobernador interino de Oaxaca (del 28 de noviembre de 1827

Alberto Ramírez de Aguilar

al 15 de enero de 1828, del 28 de enero de 1829 al 1 de febrero de 1830 y del 29 de enero de 1833 al 4 de junio de 1834).

Ramírez Alonso, Alfonso ◆ n. en Aguascalientes, Ags. (1916). Torero llamado *El calesero*. Lidió por primera vez en 1930. Se presentó en 1933 en el Toreo de la Condesa, tomó la alternativa en 1939, de manos de Lorenzo Garza. Se presentó en Sevilla en 1946, donde Pepe Luis Vázquez le confirmó la alternativa. Se retiró en los años cincuenta.

Ramírez Altamirano, Alfonso ◆ n. en Acapulco, Gro., y m. en el DF (1906-1983). Profesor titulado en 1928 en la Escuela Nacional de Maestros. Fue profesor, director de varias escuelas, inspector y jefe de misión cultural; dirigió la Federación Mexicana de Trabajadores de la Enseñanza, el Sindicato Nacional de Trabajadores de la Educación y la Confederación Americana del Magisterio; fue rector de la Universidad Autónoma de Guerrero y, en la SEP, se desempeñó como presidente de la Comisión Nacional de Escalafón, director del Centro de Mejoramiento del Personal Administrativo (1974-78) y delegado en Guanajuato (1978) y Michoacán (1979-80). Fue coordinador del Sistema de Educación a Distancia de la Universidad Pedagógica Nacional (1980-82).

Ramírez Altamirano, José Agustín ◆ n. en Acapulco, Gro., y m. en el DF (1903-1957). Músico y profesor normalista. Fue pianista y organista en diversos cines e iglesias de la ciudad de México. En San Luis Potosí dirigió una escuela y más tarde la Normal y la Preparatoria de Guerrero. Desempeñó diversos cargos en la SEP. Estudió y divulgó el folklore guerrerense. Formó parte del grupo Trovadores Tamaulipecos, con Lorenzo Barcelata y Ernesto Cortázar, y fundó el Quinteto de Cancioneros Guerrerenses. De 1929 a 1930 organizó y dirigió los centros culturales para obreros del DF. Autor de las canciones *Acapulqueña*, *Vida plena*, *Himno a Monterrey*, *La milpa*, *Misa de once*, *Himno a la madre*, *Mi tesoro*, *Arroyito*, *Caleta*, *Himno a los centros culturales*, *La callejera*, *Playa de Hornos*, *Himno a Zapata*, *Canción de amores*, *Himno a los niños héroes*, *Ojos de almendra*, *Himno a la región lagunera*, *La chilena*, *Himno a los tres Juanes*, *Vida plena*, *Himno al hospital militar*, *El toro rabón*, *Diamante azul*, *Azoyú*, *Manos santas*, *Nochecita de octubre*, *Himno al agrarista*, *Al regresar a tus brazos*, *La sanmarqueña*, *Ometepec*, *Mañanita costeña*, *Mazorquita* y *La feria*. Recibió la medalla Adolfo Cienfuegos y Camus.

Ramírez Andrade, Antonio ◆ n. en el DF (1926). Artista plástico. Estudió en el Centro de Iniciación Plástica número 4 del INBA (1939) y en la ENAP (1941-48), que dirigió (1974-78). Becario del Taller de Integración Plástica (1950). Profesor en el Centro Popular de Arte (1951-84), en los talleres Carlos Lazo (1952), en la ENAP (1954-86) y en la Academia de San Carlos (1954-86). Ha expuesto individualmente desde 1954 en México y Estados Unidos. Participó en la exposición colectiva del Frente Nacional de Artes Plásticas en Checoslovaquia, Rumania, China y la Unión Soviética. Ha ganado el premio Vacaciones del Pintor (1943), mención honorífica en la Exposición del Gobierno Republicano (1952), premio Nuevos Valores del Salón de la Plástica Mexicana (1954), primer premio de la Feria de Saltillo (1958), premio Mención Plástica Mexicana (1962), premio-beca Maestros de Artes Plásticas del INBA (1966), primer premio Pintura Maestros de la ENAP (1969) y premio del Salón de la Plástica del INBA (1966).

Ramírez Anzaldúa, José Jesús ◆ n. en Matamoros, Tams. (1948). Licenciado en economía por la UASLP (1971) y maestro en administración pública por el Instituto de Estudios Superiores en Administración Pública (1980). Miembro del PRI. En San Luis Potosí fue promotor de comités de electrificación rural de la CFE (1970-71) e inspector de campo y analista de crédito del Banjidal (1971-72). En el Comité Nacional Mixto de Protección al Salario se ha desempeñado como jefe de la Unidad de Planeación y Análisis (1975-76), subdirector técnico (1976-78), subdirector de Planeación (1979-82), director técnico (1982-91) y director general (1991-). Ha sido, asimismo, asesor sectorial obrero ante la Comisión Nacional de Precios del Congreso del Trabajo (1977-78) y representante del Congreso del Trabajo ante la Comisión Nacional de Fomento Cooperativo de la Secretaría del Trabajo (1979-82).

Ramírez de Arellano, Domingo ◆ n y m. en la ciudad de México (1800-1858). Inició su carrera militar en el ejército realista. En 1821 se adhirió al Plan de Iguala y estuvo a las órdenes de Anastasio Bustamante. Combatió en 1831 algunas rebeliones centralistas en las Huastecas. En 1847 luchó contra la invasión estadounidense, como segundo general en jefe, en Churubusco, donde cayó prisionero. Fue gobernador de Sonora (1854-55).

Ramírez Arriaga, Manuel ◆ n. en San Luis Potosí, SLP, y m. en el DF (1900-1978). Bisnieto de Ponciano Arriaga. Licenciado en derecho por el Instituto de San Luis Potosí (1932), del que fue profesor y secretario. Debido a su filiación vasconcelista fue perseguido por el gobernador Saturnino Cedillo y se refugió en Michoacán (1928), donde ejerció la docencia y trabajó para el gobierno estatal. Radicado en la ciudad de México desde 1932, ejerció como abogado. Autor de *No resta decir nada*, *Sembradores*, *Las dos lanzas*, *Las manos*, *Las voces de Querétaro*, *Derecho burocrático*, *Génesis ideológica del doctor Mora*, *De la hermandad* (1918, poemario en colaboración), *El artículo 11 de la Constitución y el alcance de sus limitaciones ante el derecho internacional* (1932, tesis de licenciatura), *Ponciano Arriaga* (1937), *Ponciano Arriaga, las procuradurías de pobres* (1940), *Derecho burocrático* (1943), *Laudanza de Querétaro* (1948), *Ponciano Arriaga, exilio y retorno* (1950), *Literatura universal* (1950), *Espinas y espinelas de Dios* (1953), *Dos poemas al padre* (1954), *Canto a Bolívar* (1954), *La contribución potosina al Plan de Ayutla* (1955), *Venustiano Carranza* (1955), *El significado del Congreso Constituyente de*

1856 (1956), *Dos libros sobre México* (1965) y *Ponciano Arriaga, el desconocido* (1965). Fue presidente de la Sociedad Mexicana de Geografía y Estadística.

Ramírez Cabañas, Joaquín ◆ n. en Coatepec, Ver., y m. en el DF (1886-1945). Periodista que utilizó el pseudónimo de J. Pérez Lugo. Fue director de la revista *Tiempo*; fundador, con Francisco Gamoneda, de la librería Biblos; profesor de la Escuela Nacional Preparatoria y de la UNAM; auxiliar del Departamento de Publicaciones del Museo Nacional de Arqueología, Historia y Etnología e impulsor de la Sociedad de Bibliófilos Mexicanos. Colaboró en *Nosotros*, *Revista Moderna*, *Universidad de México*, *La Voz de la Revolución*, *El Demócrata*, *Contemporáneos*, *El Popular*, *El Universal Ilustrado*, *Filosofía y Letras*, *Cuadernos Americanos*, *Biblos*, *Revista de Revistas*, *El Heraldo* y *El Universal*, entre otras. En la SRE colaboró con Genaro Estrada en la redacción del *Archivo histórico diplomático mexicano*. Autor de *La sombra de los días* (1918), *La fruta del cercado ajeno* (1921), *Remanso de silencio* (1922), *Esparcimiento* (1925), *Las relaciones entre México y el Vaticano* (1928), *El empréstito de México a Colombia* (1930), *Un incidente diplomático. Altamirano y el barón de Wagner* (1932), *Cooperativismo* (1935), *Estudios históricos* (1935), *La sociedad cooperativa en México* (1936), *Gastón de Raousset, conquistador de Sonora* (1941), *La ciudad de Veracruz en el siglo XVI* (1943), *Comercio extranjero por el puerto de San Blas en los años 1812-1817* (1944) y *Mercedes y pensiones, limosnas y salarios en la Real Hacienda de la Nueva España* (1945).

Ramírez Calzada, Juan ◆ n. y m. en Puebla, Pue. (1838-1880). Militar liberal. Participó en la guerra de los Tres Años y luchó contra la intervención francesa y el imperio. Alcanzó el generalato en 1863. Gobernador y comandante militar de Tabasco (1876-77).

Ramírez Campos, Félix ◆ n. en Paracho, Mich. (1880-?). Historiador. Fue juez de primera instancia en Zamora y Uruapan. Luchó en las revoluciones maderista y constitucionalista y fue diputado local (1917). Autor de *Prehistoria de Michoacán*, *La verdad sobre la revolución mexicana*, *Ensayo de interpretación de la Relación de Michoacán*, *La pequeña propiedad*, *Cómo pensaban los indígenas de América*, *La pequeña industria*, *La religión y la ciencia de los primitivos michoacanos*, *Revisión de conceptos científicos y religiosos*, *Lenguas indoeuropeas de América*, *Semántica y mecanismos de construcción de la lengua phurhembe*, *Ireti khatape*, *Sentido secreto de las lenguas indoeuropeas*, *Comentarios a las gramáticas de Basalenque y Nájera* y *Cómo es la lengua phurhembe*.

Ramírez Campuzano, Javier ◆ n. en el DF (1944). Arquitecto y diseñador, hijo de Pedro Ramírez Vázquez ☛ Proyectó el monumento a Fray Bertino Montesinos en la República Dominicana. Tuvo a su cargo la restauración del Parque Recreativo Mexitlán, en Tijuana, y ha colaborado en los proyectos de los edificios del Comité Olímpico Internacional y del Museo Olímpico de Lausana. Como diseñador ha creado emblemas y mascotas para los equipos de futbol América, Guadalajara y Tigres, así como para la Expo Sevilla 1992 y los Juegos Olímpicos de Invierno de 1994 y 1998.

Ramírez Cárdenas, Leopoldo ◆ n. en Matehuala, SLP (1901). Estudió una carrera comercial. En 1918 empezó a publicar poemas en el semanario *Matehuala*. Radicado en Pachuca fundó el semanario *El Renacimiento*. Hacia 1922 pasó a la ciudad de México y se incorporó a *El Sol*. En Concepción del Oro, Zacatecas, fundó el semanario *Alma Obrera*. Participó en la rebelión escobarista como secretario del general Gutiérrez y tras la derrota de ese movimiento se exilió. Poco después fue amnistiado. En Saltillo fue redactor de *El Norte* y en Monterrey fundó *El Insurgente*. Trabajó después en *El Porvenir* y *El Sol*. Volvió a la ciudad de México en 1937 y se integró a *La Prensa*, diario del que fue director en 1958. Fundó el periódico *Medio Ambiente* (1973). Autor de *Cantos libertarios* (1937), *Los improvisados*, *Ante las alambradas*, *México. Viñetas de ayer* (1970), *Trayectorias*, *El trampas*, *Sinfonía de la Patria* y *La conquista de la tierra*.

Ramírez Cárdenas, Manuel ◆ n. en Matehuala, SLP, y m. en el DF (1898-1971). Hermano del anterior. Estudió una carrera comercial. Se inició en el periodismo como colaborador del semanario *Matehuala*. Hacia 1919 pasó a San Antonio, Texas, donde trabajó en *La Prensa*. Fue corresponsal de guerra de Obregón durante la rebelión delahuertista. En 1923, en la ciudad de México, ingresó en la redacción de *El Demócrata* y pasó después a *El Sol* y *El Universal*, diario que lo envió a Cuba para cubrir la información sobre el vuelo sin escalas México-La Habana de Roberto Fierro, de quien fue secretario durante su gestión al frente del gobierno de Chihuahua. Trabajó en la Escuela de Aviación Civil, en Monterrey, propiedad de Fierro. De nuevo en la ciudad de México ingresó en *La Prensa* como editorialista y fue director de Relaciones Públicas de la Compañía Mexicana de Aviación y de American Airlines.

Ramírez Cárdenas, Roberto ◆ n. en San Luis Potosí, SLP (1916). Periodista, hermano de los anteriores. Radicado en la ciudad de México desde 1933, se inició en el periódico *La Prensa*, del que fue director, así como de *Prensa Gráfica*. Colaboró en *Anáhuac*, *Vea*, *Estampas* y otras publicaciones.

Ramírez Cuecuecha, Anabel ◆ n. en Puebla, Pue. (¿1975?). Violista. Estudió música con su padre y con el soviético Garri Petrenko, en el Mozarteum de Salzburgo y en Florencia, con Carlo Chiarappa. Debutó a los seis años, dentro de la orquesta clásica La Belle Musique. Ha sido solista de las orquestas de cámara de la UAEM, la Sociedad Mexicana de Música y el Festival Musical de Texas, así como de la Orquesta Carlos Chávez y las orquestas sinfónicas de Aguascalientes, la Sociedad Filarmónica de Conciertos, la Escuela Nacional de Música.

Anabel Ramírez Cuecuecha

Primer lugar en los concursos de violín de la Escuela Nacional de Música de la UNAM (1988 y 1991), primer lugar en el concurso Alumnos Destacados de la Escuela Vida y Movimiento y premio especial Carlos Chávez (1992 y 1993). Medalla Cynthia Woods Mitchell Pavillion, otorgada en el Festival Musical de Texas (1992 y 1993).

Ramírez Cuéllar, Alfonso ◆ n. en Río Grande, Zac. (1959). Licenciado en antropología social por la ENAH. Militante del Partido Mexicano Socialista, fue su secretario general en el DF y perteneció a su Comité Ejecutivo Nacional. Militante del PRD desde 1989, donde ha sido miembro del Consejo Nacional y del Comité Ejecutivo. Dirigió la Organización Nacional de Estudiantes. Ha sido investigador en la Universidad Autónoma de Sinaloa y representante de la misma en el DF. Representante a la Asamblea Legislativa del DF (1991-94).

Ramírez Cuéllar, Héctor ◆ n. en Ciudad Juárez, Chih. (1947). Licenciado en ciencias políticas por la UNAM. Desde 1967 es militante del Partido Popular Socialista, en el que ha desempeñado los cargos de secretario general de la Juventud Popular Socialista (1969-74), miembro del comité central (1969), secretario de Educación Política de la Dirección Nacional (1976-90) y secretario general de la organización partidaria en el Distrito Federal (1990-). Ha sido profesor del IPN y de la Universidad Obrera de México; colaborador de los periódicos *El Día*, *El Nacional* y *La Jornada*; tres veces diputado federal (1976-79, 1982-85 y 91-94), miembro de la ARDF (1988-91).

Ramírez Favela, Eduardo Maurilio ◆ n. en Ciudad Lerdo, Dgo. (1938). Ingeniero civil graduado en la UNAM (1960). Profesor de las universidades Iberoamericana (1968-70), Anáhuac (1970-74) y Nacional Autónoma de México (1973-76). Ha sido jefe de departamento de estructuras de Zevaeert Ingeniero Consultor (1963-64), gerente técnico en el Grupo Industrial de la Construcción y Constructora Ocasa (1969-70 y 1979), jefe del Departamento de Conservación de Inmuebles de la SSA (1971-75), subjefe de Programación, subjefe de Organización y asesor de la Subdirección Administrativa del IMSS (1975-78), subdirector técnico de Tecnhogar (1980), director de administración y proyectos del Grupo Industrial Balder (1981-82), subjefe de Evaluación y jefe de la Unidad de Control y Seguimiento del IMSS (1983-84), presidente de la Comisión de Avalúos de Bienes Nacionales de la Sedue (1985-88) y director general de Diconsa (1993-95).

Ramírez de la Fuente, Beatriz ◆ ☛ *Fuente, Beatriz de la.*

Ramírez Gamero, José ◆ n. en Durango, Dgo. (1938). Licenciado en derecho por la Universidad Juárez de Durango, con estudios de posgrado en derecho laboral en la UNAM (1969-70) y de formación profesional en la OIT. Fue director del Departamento de Educación Física y profesor de la Escuela de Derecho de la Universidad Juárez de Durango (1964-76). Desde 1965 pertenece al PRI, en el que desempeñó los cargos de secretario de Acción Política y secretario de organización del comité estatal de Durango. En la CTM fue titular de la secretaría de acción política del CEN, jefe del Departamento Jurídico y miembro del comité estatal de esa organización obrera. Fue actuario notificador, abogado postulante, diputado federal (1976-79), presidente de la Subcomisión del Sector Social y de la Comisión del Trabajo y Justicia de la Secretaría del Trabajo y procurador federal de Organización Colectiva de la Profeco (1979-82). Dos veces senador de la República (1982-86 y 1994-2000). En Durango fue primer regidor del ayuntamiento de la capital, diputado local, jefe del Departamento Jurídico del Consejo de Planeación y Urbanización, jefe del Departamento Jurídico del ayuntamiento de Durango, jefe del Departamento Legal de la Tesorería General, procurador de la Defensa del Trabajo y gobernador (1986-1992).

Ramírez Garrido, Jaime ◆ n. en el DF (1970). Estudió la carrera de letras en la UNAM y tomó un curso impartido por Manuel Cruz en la Universidad Complutense de Madrid (1989). Ha sido miembro del consejo de redacción de las revistas *Cero a la Izquierda* y *Círculo Interior.* Coordinador de cultura de *Etcétera* y en *La Crónica de Hoy* (1999). Colaborador de: *México Indígena*, *Concertación*, *Revista de la Universidad*, *Nosotros* y *El Nacional*. Autor de los ensayos: *Dialéctica de lo terrenal. Ensayo sobre la obra de José Revueltas* (1991), *Delirio, zapatismo, entusiasmo en Chiapas. La guerra de las ideas* (1994), *De lo terrenal a lo divino* (1994, en *El naranjo en flor*), *Escenario de quimera* (1995, en *Antología de letras y dramaturgia de jóvenes creadores*) y *El gabinete del doctor Zedillo* (1995, en colaboración con Aymeé Campos). Becario del INBA (1991-92), del Fonca (1993-94) y del Centro Mexicano de Escritores (1995-96).

Ramírez Garrido, José Domingo ◆ n. en Macuspana, Tab., y m. en el DF (1888-1958). Militó en el Partido Liberal Mexicano. Colaboró en los periódicos *El Hijo del Ahuizote* y *Regeneración*. Se afilió al Partido Antirreeleccionista y trabajó en la campaña presidencial de Francisco I. Madero. Participó en la insurrección de 1910 y alcanzó el grado de general. Fue director de Educación en Yucatán durante el gobierno de Salvador Alvarado, subsecretario y secretario de gobierno en Tabasco, en la gestión de Francisco J. Múgica; inspector general de policía en la ciudad de México, dos veces diputado federal y director del Colegio Militar (1923). Se unió a la rebelión delahuertista, por lo que debió exiliarse tras la derrota de ese movimiento. Regresó a México en 1935 y fue jefe de las zonas militares de Tabasco y Campeche, así como director del Departamento de Archivo de Historia de la Secretaría de la Defensa. Autor de *Reos sin pena* (1910), *Vivir con honra o morir dignamente* (1911), *El porvenir de la América Latina. Esbozos críticos* (1912), *Al correr de la pluma* (1915), *La esclavitud en Tabasco* (1915), *El alma tabasqueña* (1915), *Desde la tribuna roja*

(1916), *Ardentia verba* (1918), *Al margen del feminismo* (1918), *El combate del cañón de Corona* (1923) y *El combate de Palo Verde. Reseña crítica* (1925).

Ramírez Garrido Abreu, Graco Luis ◆ n. ¿en Villahermosa, Tab.? (1949). Licenciado en derecho por la UNAM. Miembro fundador del Partido Socialista de los Trabajadores (1973), del que fue secretario general y de cuya fracción parlamentaria en la LIII Legislatura fue coordinador. Se retiró del PST y participó en la fundación del Partido Mexicano Socialista (1987). Al desaparecer esta organización pasó al Partido de la Revolución Democrática (1989). Ha sido dos veces diputado federal (1979-82 y 1985-88).

Ramírez Garrido Abreu, José Domingo ◆ n. en Villahermosa, Tab. (1938). Hermano del anterior. Egresado del Colegio Militar (1957), licenciado en derecho por la UAP (1961-63) y maestro en administración militar sobre seguridad pública y defensa nacional por el Colegio de Defensa Nacional (1981-82). Ha sido profesor de guerra irregular, táctica general, táctica de infantería e historia universal en el Colegio Militar; jefe de grupo de Acuerdos Presidenciales del secretario de la Defensa Nacional, miembro del comité de creación de la Fuerza de Tarea Cóndor y agregado militar adjunto de la embajada mexicana en Estados Unidos; director general de Operaciones (1984-86), miembro del Estado Mayor de la Secretaría de la Defensa y, con licencia, director general de Servicios y Autotransporte Público de la Dirección General de Policía y Tránsito (1983-84) en el DF. Fue secretario general de Protección y Vialidad del DDF (1986-88). Tiene el grado de general.

Ramírez Gómez, Ramón ◆ n. en España y m. en el DF (1913-1972). Era profesor normalista durante la guerra civil española, cuando fundó y presidió la Federación de Trabajadores de la Enseñanza. Llegó exiliado a México en 1940. Licenciado en economía por la UNAM (1947), donde fue profesor e investigador (1960-72). En la Escuela Nacional de Economía de la misma universidad, perteneció a la comisión mixta de profesores y estudiantes que modificó los planes y programas de estudio y fundó el seminario de *El Capital* (1970). Trabajó para el Banco de Obras y Servicios Públicos (1947-59). Colaboró en *Investigación Económica, Historia y Sociedad* y otras publicaciones. Autor de *El problema de la habitación: aspectos sociales, legales y económicos* (1948), *La posible revalorización del oro y sus efectos en la economía de México* (1961), *Principios para el desarrollo de una economía subdesarrollada* (1962), *El movimiento estudiantil de México* (2 t., 1971) y *La moneda, el crédito y la banca a través de la concepción marxista y de las teorías subjetivas* (1972).

Ramírez Granados, Esperanza ◆ n. y m. en el DF (1921-1991). Profesora egresada de la Escuela Nacional de Maestros (1938), donde se especializó en historia y se doctoró en pedagogía; realizó una especialización en educación en la Universidad de Houston. Dio clases en primarias y secundarias de la SEP, así como en la UNAM y la Escuela Normal Superior. Investigadora del Instituto Nacional de Pedagogía. Trabajó en el periódico *El Día* (1980-91) como responsable de las secciones "Educación y magisterio" y "Testimonios y documentos".

Ramírez Guerrero, Carlos ◆ n. en Molango, Hgo., y m. en el DF (1909-1983). Licenciado en derecho por la UNAM. Fue secretario general de gobierno durante la administración de José Lugo Guerrero y oficial mayor en el gobierno de Quintín Rueda Villagrán. Profesor y director del Instituto Científico y Literario y profesor de la Escuela Normal del Estado de Hidalgo. Diputado federal (1955-58), senador (1958-63) y gobernador de Hidalgo (del 1 de abril de 1963 al 31 de marzo de 1969), así como procurador de Justicia del Distrito y Territorios Federales (1970).

Ramírez Heredia, Rafael ◆ n. en Tampico, Tams. (1942). Escritor. Contador público titulado en 1964. Ha sido profesor de literatura en el IPN, jefe de redacción de las revistas *El Cuento, Semana Política, Economía Política* y *Activa*; miembro del consejo de redacción de *La Brújula en el Bolsillo* y *La Talacha* y colaborador de numerosos periódicos y revistas. Coautor de *El hombre equivocado* (1988, novela colectiva), *Ruiz Massieu: el mejor enemigo* (1995) y *Crónicas de una ciudad ganada* (1999). Autor de cuento: *El rayo Macoy y otros cuentos* (1984, Premio Internacional de Cuento Juan Rulfo), *Paloma negra* (1987), *Los territorios de la tarde* (1988), *De tacones y gabardina* (1996) y *Los rumbos del calor y otros cuentos* (1999); novela: *El ocaso* (1968), *En el lugar de los hechos* (1976, Premio del Club de Periodistas Primera Plana en 1978), *Trampa de metal* (1979), *Muerte en la carretera* (1985) y *Con M de Marilyn* (1997); teatro: *Final de domingo* (1976) y *Dentro de estos ocho muros* (1977), entre otras obras. Ha obtenido los premios Diana de Oro (1980), Nacional de Cuento Policiaco de *Ovaciones* y Aeroméxico (1983), Juan Ruiz de Alarcón (1990), Rafael Bernal (1993) y del IPN (1997), entre otros. Medallas Rafael Ramírez Castañeda (1997) y Juan de Dios Bátiz (1999), por 25 años al servicio del magisterio nacional y del IPN, respectivamente. Pertenece al SNCA y es miembro de la Asociación Internacional de Escritores Policiacos, la Sogem y la Asociación de Escritores de México.

Foto: Barry

Rafael Ramírez Heredia

Foto: Época

Graco Ramírez

Ramírez Juárez, Arturo ◆ n. en San Luis Potosí, SLP, y m. en el DF (1949-1988). Poeta y pintor. Estudió en Brasil (1969). En 1968 expuso individualmente por primera vez y se incorporó al programa Poetas Jóvenes. Autor de *Causas nocturnas*, *Las fuentes ocultas* (1984) y *Rituales* (1987).

Ramírez Laguna, Antonio ◆ n. y m. en el DF (1903-1966). Licenciado en filosofía por la UNAM, donde fue profesor. Fundador de la Unión Nacional de Exploradores de México y, en 1960, de la Escuela Preparatoria de Tula. Inventó el *bolon*, inspirado en el juego de pelota prehispánico. Colaboró en *Anales del Instituto de Biología*. Coautor de *Prácticas* *de biología*, *Prácticas de zoología* y *Prácticas de botánica*. Autor de *Plantas textiles de México* (1932), *Los agaves de México* (1932), *Una excursión científica a Ixtapan de la Sal* (1934) y *Manual de los exploradores mexicanos* (1950).

Ramírez Lavoignet, David ◆ n. en Misantla, Ver. (1916). Se tituló como profesor en la Escuela Normal Veracruzana. Ejerció la docencia en primarias y secundarias veracruzanas y del DF, así como en normales regionales. En Veracruz fue procurador general de Asuntos Indígenas, visitador especial de la Campaña Contra el Analfabetismo, jefe de la Misión Cultural de la SEP, inspector general de Educación, profesor y director de la Escuela de Historia e investigador y director del Seminario de Historia de la Universidad Veracruzana. Autor de *Relación de Misantla de Diego Pérez de Arteaga, de 1579* (1957), *Misantla* (1959), *Tlapacoyan. Monografía histórica* (1965), *La independencia en Misantla* (1967), *Manuel Joaquín Rincón y Calcáneo. Biografía* (1972), *Notas históricas de Tempoal* (1973), *Testimonios para una historia de Perote* (1973) y *Geografía del estado de Veracruz* (1974). Es cronista de la ciudad de Jalapa.

Heladio Ramírez López

Ramírez López, Heladio ◆ n. en Huajuapan de León, Oax. (1939). Licenciado en derecho por la UNAM, donde fue dirigente estudiantil y ejerció la docencia. Miembro fundador de la Tribuna de la Juventud. Desde 1959 pertenece al PRI, en el que fue dirigente juvenil en el DF, presidente del comité estatal de Oaxaca y delegado del CEN en Querétaro, Guanajuato y Baja California. Desempeñó los cargos de secretario general de la Federación de Jornaleros Agrícolas, secretario de Acción Sindical de la Confederación Nacional Campesina y delegado de la misma en Veracruz, Durango, Michoacán, Nuevo León y Chiapas. Ha sido director ejecutivo y delegado fiduciario de los fideicomisos Puerto Vallarta y Cumbres de Llano Largo, diputado federal (1976-79), senador (1982-86) y gobernador de Oaxaca (1986-92). En 1998 tomó posesión como secretario general de la Confederación Nacional Campesina, después de la primera elección abierta realizada en esa organización. Formó parte del Consejo Editorial de la *Revista del México Agrario*. Presidió la Asociación de Jóvenes del Sureste de la República Mexicana y es miembro de la Asociación Nacional de Abogados. Fue campeón nacional de oratoria en el concurso convocado por el Injuve.

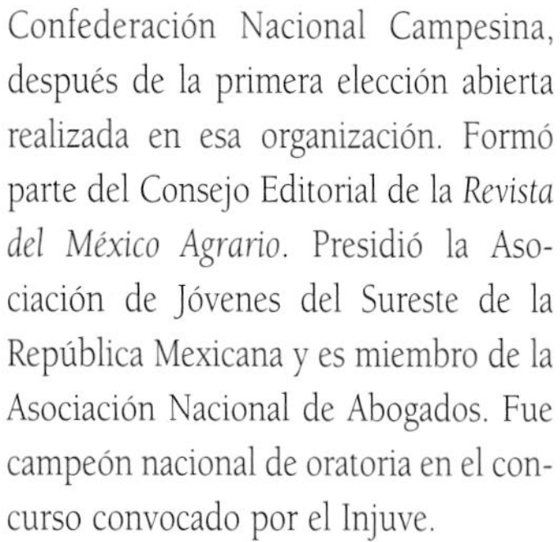

Ramírez López, Ignacio ◆ n. en San Felipe y m. en Salamanca, Gto. (1881-1965). Profesor normalista (1899). Ejerció la docencia en Guanajuato desde 1899 hasta su muerte. Participó en las revoluciones maderista y constitucionalista, fue uno de los creadores de la Escuela Rural Mexicana (1922), por lo que José Vasconcelos lo nombró jefe del departamento respectivo. Delegado de Educación Federal en Guanajuato (1923) y primer director general de Educación en la República (1925). Al morir dirigía un centro cultural en Salamanca. Autor de *El niño campesino*, *Geografía del estado de Guanajuato*, *Sociedades cooperativas en la escuela rural*, *Las misiones culturales*, *Papel social del maestro rural*, *La escuela rural* y *Tres biografías: Fray Pedro de Gante, Fray Alonso de la Veracruz y Fray Juan Bautista Moya*.

Ramírez Martínez, José Antonio ◆ n. en San Felipe de Jesús, Dgo., y m. en Monterrey, NL (1910-1996). Fue fundador del Partido Nacional Revolucionario y de la CTM, cuya dirigencia en Durango ocupó desde 1950 hasta su muerte. Fue cuatro veces diputado local, diputado federal, regidor del ayuntamiento de Durango, secretario de estadística del CEN de la CTM y fundador del Sindicato de Choferes de la CTM en Durango. Desde 1947 ocupaba, además, la secretaría de acción obrera del Comité Directivo Estatal del PRI.

Óscar Ramírez Mijares

Ramírez Mijares, Óscar ◆ n. en Torreón, Coah. (1922). Se tituló como profesor en la Normal de Saltillo (1942). Pertenece al PRI. En el comité del DF de ese partido fue secretario de organización, tesorero y secretario de Acción Agraria (1960-68); y entre 1966 y 1983 fue delegado del CEN en 11 entidades, secretario de Acción Agraria y presidente de la Comisión Coordinadora de Convenciones (1977-82). Ocupó la secretaría general del CEN de la CNC (1964-80). Ha sido profesor de enseñanza primaria (1942-43) y director de educación física municipal (1942-43) en Torreón, director de escuelas primarias (1943-74); cofundador, miembro de la dirección nacional y secretario de trabajo y conflictos de la sección IX del SNTE (1945-46); asesor técnico del Departamento de Asuntos Agrarios y Colonización, del Banjidal, del Banrural y de Banobras (1964-82), representante del sector campesino ante el consejo consultivo de la ciudad de México (1967) y director general de Abastos y Mercados del DDF (1970-73); en Banrural fue funcionario del Fideicomiso de Producción Perecedera (1970-77), miembro de los consejos de administración del propio banco y de organismos del sector agropecuario (1977-80). Ha sido tres veces diputado federal (1961-64, 1967-70 y 1982-85) y dos veces senador (1978-82 y 1988-94).

Ramírez Miranda, Margarito ◆ n. en Atotonilco el Alto y m. en Guadalajara, Jal. (1891-1979). Trabajador ferrocarrilero que en 1920 ayudó a Álvaro Obregón a escapar de la ciudad de México. Fue gobernador interino de Jalisco (1927-29), senador (1932-36), director del penal de las Islas Marías (1937-40), gerente de los Ferrocarriles Nacionales (1942), diputado federal y líder de la mayoría priista en la Cámara (1942-43) y gobernador del territorio de Quintana Roo (1944-59).

Ramírez Munguía, Miguel ◆ n. en Tacámbaro, Mich., y m. en el DF (1884-1951). Se tituló como abogado en la Universidad Michoacana. Miembro fundador del PAN (1939), integrante de su consejo nacional y primer diputado federal de esa organización (1946-49). Dirigió la Escuela Libre de Derecho de Michoacán y fue profesor en la institución similar del Distrito Federal.

Ramírez Osorio, Fernando ◆ n. en Puebla, Pue. (1922). Grabador egresado de la Academia Popular de Bellas Artes de Puebla. Fundó, con Ramón Pablo Loreto, el primer taller de grabado de Puebla y el primer Núcleo de Grabadores de Puebla (1947), del que surgieron el taller y la galería José Guadalupe Posada (1951). En 1953 retomó la tradición de elaborar estampas litográficas. Secretario general del Núcleo de Grabadores (1953-57). Profesor de grabado del Instituto de Artes Plásticas del Estado de Puebla. Dirige el Instituto de Artes Visuales de Puebla. Editó un álbum de 10 grabados en linóleo: *Carnaval de Huejotzingo* (1953). Mención honorífica en el Concurso Nacional de Grabado de la Secretaría de Recursos Hidráulicos (1952) y tercer lugar en grabado en el Concurso Nacional de los terceros Juegos Deportivos Nacionales y Eventos Culturales del Magisterio (1976).

Ramírez Palomares, Juan Manuel ◆ n. en León, Gto. (1957). Poeta. Estudió letras españolas en la Universidad de Guanajuato. Ha participado en numerosos encuentros y talleres literarios y ha dirigido el del ISSSTE (1985-88). Fue antologado en *Casa en interiores* (1989), antología de poetas jóvenes de Guanajuato. Coautor de *Asuntos de la lluvia* (1986). Autor de *La pesadumbre, el olor de la fruta* (1988) y *Aire en vendaval* (1991). Fue becario del INBA (1984-85).

Ramírez Plancarte, Francisco ◆ n. en Morelia, Mich., y m. en el DF (1886-1940). En 1912 fue uno de los fundadores de la Casa del Obrero Mundial. Formó parte de los Batallones Rojos dentro de las filas carrancistas. Autor de *La ciudad de México durante la revolución constitucionalista* (1940) y *La revolución mexicana: interpretación independiente* (1949).

Ramírez Pomar, Leonardo ◆ n. en el DF (1938). Periodista. Estudió química en el Instituto Politécnico Nacional. Ha sido profesor de periodismo en la Universidad Autónoma Metropolitana, la UNAM y la Universidad de Colima, donde se desempeñó como subjefe de Información. En la UAM fue director de Información y coordinador de Extensión Universitaria del plantel Azcapotzalco. Asesor del subsecretario de Ecología de la Sedue. Director general de Información de la UNAM (1989-1997) y director general de Comunicación Social de la Cámara de Diputados (1997-). Cofundador (1962) del cotidiano *El Día*, fundador y subdirector del vespertino *Crucero*, director de *El Comentario*, de Colima, Colima; subdirector y director del *Periódico del Consumidor* y director del diario *El Fígaro*. Fue codirector del semanario *Punto* y subdirector de *El Día* hasta finales de los noventa.

Ramírez de Prado y Ovando, Marcos ◆ n. en España y m. en Tacubaya (1592-1667). Fraile franciscano desde 1601. Estudió teología en la Universidad de Salamanca. Renunció a las mitras de Yucatán y Caracas. Fue obispo de Chiapas (1634-39) y de Michoacán (1639-66). En el gobierno de esta mitra tomó partido contra su colega poblano, Juan de Palafox y Mendoza, líder del clero diocesano en la disputa por las parroquias, mayoritariamente en manos de regulares. En el curso del conflicto, circuló un pasquín que en forma soez lo acusaba de mantener relaciones íntimas con la madre superiora de un convento de Valladolid. En 1660 colocó la primera piedra de la catedral de Morelia. Obispo electo de México, murió antes de tomar posesión.

Ramírez y Ramírez, Enrique ◆ n. en la ciudad de México y m. en Cocoyoc, Mor. (1915-1980). Militante del Partido Comunista Mexicano (1932-43) y miembro del Partido Popular, luego Partido Popular Socialista (1947-58) y del PRI (1964-80). Fue auxiliar y secretario político de Lombardo Toledano (1935-55), miembro fundador de la CTM (1936) y dirigente de la sección de periodistas del Sindicato Industrial de Trabajadores de las Artes Gráficas. Cofundador y miembro de la dirección de Juventudes Socialistas Unificadas de México (1937), primer secretario de organización de la Central Única de la Juventud Mexicana (1939), convertida meses después en Confederación de Jóvenes Mexicanos (1939). Intervino como representante de la Universidad Obrera de México en la Mesa Redonda de los Marxistas (☛). Fue secretario general del Centro Mexicano de Estudios Ricardo Flores Magón. En el PRI fue asesor del CEN (1967-70), profesor del Instituto de Capacitación Política (1971), miembro del consejo consultivo del IEPES y de la Comisión Nacional de Ideología (1972-80), así como presidente de la octava comisión para la elaboración del Plan Básico de Gobierno (1975). Dos veces diputado federal (1964-1967 y 1976-79). Periodista desde 1929, fundó *Cuadernos del Valle de México* con Octavio Paz, Salvador Toscano, José Alvarado y Rafael López Malo. Fue editorialista de *El Popular* (1938-46) y director de *El Día* (1962-80). Empleó el pseudónimo de *Carlos Hierro*. Autor de *Apuntes sobre la situación del movimiento revolucionario* (1957) y *Periodismo y política*.

Ramírez Sánchez, Hermenegildo ◆ n. en el DF (1929). Sacerdote ordenado en 1953. Ha sido secretario de la procura general de los josefinos en Roma, profesor del Estudiantado Mayor Josefino en México, rector del Juniorado, maestro de espíritu en México, vicepostulador en Roma de las causas de beatificación y canonización de José María Vilaseca, administrador apostólico *ad nutum Sancta Sedis* de la prelatura de Huautla y obispo de la misma desde 1975. Es miembro de la Comisión Episcopal para Indígenas.

Ramírez Terrazas, Ambrosio ◆ n. en Valle de San Francisco, hoy Villa de Reyes, y m. en San Luis Potosí, SLP (1857-1913). Se tituló como abogado en el Instituto Científico y Literario de San Luis Potosí (1894). Fue juez de primera instancia en Ciudad del Maíz, Venado y San Luis Potosí; agente del Ministerio Público y secretario del Tribunal Superior de Justicia del estado de San Luis Potosí. En 1885 fundó, con Primo Feliciano Vázquez, el bisemanario potosino *El Estandarte*, que en 1890 se convirtió en diario. Diputado local y

Pedro Ramírez Vázquez

secretario particular del gobernador de Morelos, Manuel Alarcón (1896-1912). Tradujo odas y sátiras de Horacio. Autor de *Oda al trabajo* (1884) y *Manuel José Othón, ensayo crítico de sus obras poéticas y de sus escritos en prosa*. Fue miembro de la Academia Mexicana (de la Lengua).

Ramírez Ulloa, Carlos ♦ n. en Guadalajara, Jal., y m. en el DF (1903-1980). Ingeniero civil por la Universidad Nacional (1924). Formó parte del grupo de iniciadores de la Comisión Nacional de Irrigación (1926-28 y 1929-34) y de la Dirección de Obras Hidráulicas de la Secretaría de Comunicaciones y Obras Públicas (1934-36). Fundador y organizador de la Comisión Federal de Electricidad (1937, por encargo de Lázaro Cárdenas), de la que fue vocal ejecutivo (1937-47) y director general (1952-59). Dirigió la nacionalización de las compañías eléctricas de Chapala, Morelia, Uruapan, Tlaxcala, Monclova y Occidental, y presidió sus consejos de administración. Fue fundador y primer gerente de Industria Eléctrica de México y director técnico de la constructora El Águila. En 1977 recibió la primera Medalla Lázaro Cárdenas y en 1978 el Premio Nacional de Ingeniería.

Ramírez Ulloa, Eliseo ♦ n. en Guadalajara, Jal., y m. en el DF (1888-1940). Doctor (1914) por la Escuela Nacional de Medicina, de la que fue jefe de clínica y cirugía. Profesor de la Universidad Nacional, interno del Hospital Juárez, profesor de la Escuela Médico Militar (1919-31), director de Sanidad en el Departamento de Salubridad Pública (1924-26) y director del Instituto de Higiene (1930). En 1935 promovió la campaña antivenérea y por su iniciativa fue abolida la prostitución reglamentada. Jefe del Laboratorio Central del Departamento de Salubridad Pública y director del Instituto de Enfermedades Tropicales (1939-40). Autor de *Elementos de patología general*. Miembro de las academias de Medicina y de Ciencias.

Ramírez Valle, Hermilo ♦ n. en el DF (1937). Escultor. Estudió en la Academia de San Carlos (1956-60). Fue ayudante de Augusto Escobedo e Ignacio Asúnsolo en sus cátedras en San Carlos. Ha sido profesor de dibujo en escuelas primarias y secundarias. Ha expuesto individualmente en Jalapa y colectivamente en México y Guadalajara. Entre sus obras están la Diana Cazadora, en bronce, de Tlalnepantla (1957-58), un busto en bronce de Obregón, en Chihuahua (1960), uno de Lázaro Cárdenas en Tamaulipas (1975), una Virgen en caoba en Huauchinango (1978) y la escultura de Cuitláhuac que se halla en Iztapalapa (1978).

Ramírez Vázquez, Manuel ♦ n. y m. en el DF (1905-1993). Licenciado en derecho por la Universidad Nacional de México (1924-29), de la que también fue profesor. Fue presidente del Tribunal Superior de Justicia de Veracruz (1937), miembro de la Junta de Conciliación y Arbitraje; subsecretario (1946-48) y secretario del Trabajo (1948-52).

Ramírez Vázquez, Mariano ♦ n. y m. en el DF (1903-1994). Hermano del anterior. Licenciado en derecho por la UNAM (1926), en cuya Escuela de Jurisprudencia fue profesor. Abogado defensor, juez civil en Cuernavaca, secretario del Tribunal en Materia Penal en el Distrito Federal, director del Departamento de Servicios Jurídicos del Departamento del Trabajo; secretario general de la Junta Federal de Conciliación y Arbitraje; secretario general del Departamento del Trabajo, subprocurador general de la República (1937-40), director del Instituto Nacional de la Juventud (1950-52) y ministro de la Suprema Corte de Justicia (1947-73).

Ramírez Vázquez, Pedro ♦ n. en la ciudad de México (1919). Hermano de los anteriores. Arquitecto graduado en la UNAM (1943), donde ejerció la docencia. Miembro del PRI, en el que ha tenido, entre otros cargos, los de asesor técnico del IEPES (1969-70) y secretario de prensa del CEN (1975-76). Se ha desempeñado, entre otras cosas, como gerente general del Comité Administrador del Programa Federal de Construcción de Escuelas (1958-64), director de la Unidad Artística y Cultural del Bosque (1953-65), director técnico del Centro Regional de Construcciones Escolares para América Latina de la UNESCO (1964-66), presidente del Comité Organizador de los XIX Juegos Olímpicos (1966-70), presidente del Comité Olímpico Mexicano (1971-74), rector general de la UAM (1974), secretario de Asentamientos Humanos y Obras Públicas en el sexenio de José López Portillo (del 1 de enero de 1977 al 30 de noviembre de 1982) y director del Instituto Nacional de Desarrollo Urbano y Ecología, de la Sedue (1988). Indivi-

Museo de Arte Moderno, en la ciudad de México, obra de Pedro Ramírez Vázquez, Rafael Mijares y Carlos Cásares

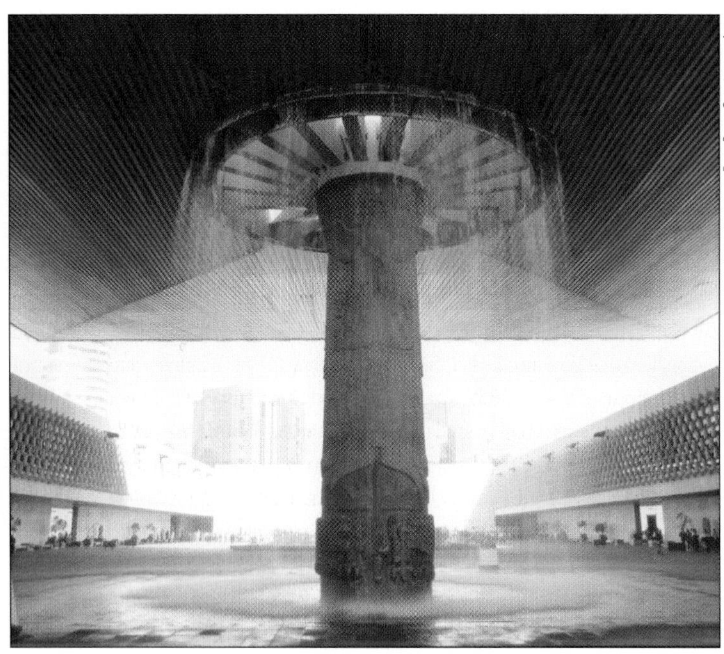
Foto: Pablo González de Alba

Museo Nacional de Antropología e Historia, en la ciudad de México, obra arquitectónica de Pedro Ramírez Vázquez, Jorge Campuzano y Rafael Mijares

dualmente o en equipo ha proyectado y dirigido la construcción o adaptación, entre otras obras, de la Escuela Nacional de Medicina (1953), la Secretaría del Trabajo (1954), el Instituto Nacional de Protección a la Infancia (1960), la Galería de Historia de Chapultepec (1960), las oficinas centrales del PRI (1961), el Museo de la Ciudad de México (1963), el Museo Nacional de Antropología (1963-64), la SRE (1965), el estadio Azteca (1965), el Museo de la Negritud, de Senegal (1972), la nueva Basílica de Guadalupe (1975-76), el Palacio Legislativo de San Lázaro (1980) y el Museo del Templo Mayor (1987). Dirigió la obra *Desarrollo urbano de México* (5 t., 1982). Autor de una veintena de libros y folletos sobre arquitectura. Pertenece, entre otras, a las siguientes corporaciones: Colegio Nacional de Arquitectos, Unión Internacional de Arquitectos, Academia de Artes, Industrial Designers Society of America y al Comité Olímpico Internacional.

Ramírez Velázquez, Josué ◆ n. en el DF (1963). Participó en los talleres literarios de Christopher Domínguez Michael, Javier Sicilia y Eduardo Vázquez Martín. Ha colaborado en *El Semanario*, suplemento de *Novedades*, y otras publicaciones. Ha sido secretario de redacción de la revista *Textual* (1989-91), encargado de publicaciones periódicas del Museo de Arte Carrillo Gil y secretario de redacción de la revista *Viceversa* (1993-94). Autor de los poemarios *Dirección inversa* (1988), *Rumor de arena* (1991) y *Tepozán* (1997). Mención honorífica en el segundo Concurso de Poesía y Cuento de Oaxaca (1998). Becario del Fonca (1990-91 y 1995-96).

Ramírez Villarreal, Francisco ◆ n. ¿en Monterrey, NL? (?-?). Abogado, fue jefe del Departamento de Gobernación de Nuevo León y diputado por ese estado al Congreso Constituyente de 1916-17. Fue oficial mayor (1934) y subsecretario (1935) de Gobernación.

Ramones, Los ◆ Municipio de Nuevo León, situado al este de Monterrey y contiguo a Cadereyta, Cerralvo y General Terán. Superficie: 1,378.8 km^2. Habitantes: 5,236, de los cuales 1,831 forman la población económicamente activa. Hablan alguna lengua indígena seis personas mayores de cinco años. La principal festividad del municipio es el 17 de agosto y se celebra con una feria popular. En la jurisdicción se halla la zona arqueológica de Paso del Indio.

Ramos, de ◆ Río de Durango. Nace de la confluencia del Santiago Papasquiaro y del Santa Catarina Tepehuanes, cerca de Atotonilco. Corre de suroeste a noreste por el cañón de Ramos, entre el norte de las sierras de la Magdalena y San Francisco y sur de la de Candela; recibe a los arroyos de la Casita, de Sardinas y Melchor y a los ríos Bueno y Mojitomé. Cerca de Rincón se une al río del Oro para formar el Nazas.

Ramos, de ◆ Sierra de San Luis Potosí. Enlaza por el norte con la sierra Herradura o del Gateado. Cuenta con yacimientos minerales.

Ramos, Agustín ◆ n. en Tulancingo, Hgo. (1952). Escritor. Estudió letras hispánicas en la UNAM. Ha sido coordinador de diversos talleres de narrativa, jefe de redacción de la *Revista Mexicana de Cultura*, colaborador de *Punto*, corrector de *unomásuno* y jefe de redacción de *Las Horas Extras* (1986). Autor de novela: *Al cielo por asalto* (1979), *La vida no vale nada* (1982), *Ahora que me acuerdo* (1985) y *Tú eres Pedro* (1996); y teatro: *La cadena (relaciones humanas)*, *La cruz no pesa, lo que cala son los filos* y *No importaba perderlo todo*.

Foto: Fernando Luna

Alejandro Ramos

Ramos, Alejandro ◆ n. en el DF (1947). Licenciado en ciencias de la comunicación por la UNAM. Estudió producción televisiva en la BBC de Londres. Ha sido redactor y reportero en el noticiero *Radionoticias el Heraldo* (1971), corresponsal en Londres y editor internacional de Notimex (1972-78), director periodístico de Informex (1979-80), director de información del Servicio de Información Financiera y Económica y colaborador de los periódicos *El Día*, *Journal of Commerce* (Estados Unidos), *Il Mondo Economico* (Italia) y *El Financiero*, del que ha sido subdirector de información y director. Ha sido catedrático de la UNAM y de la Escuela de Periodismo Carlos Septién García. Ha colaborado en los anuarios de la *Enciclopedia Británica*. Coautor de *La psicosis del dólar* (1985) y *Salinas de Gortari, candidato de la crisis* (1988). Autor de *Las arcas vacías* (1984) y *La guerra que viene* (1992). Coordinador de la edición de *La sucesión pactada* (1993).

Foto: Época

Agustín Ramos

RAMOS, GUILLERMO ◆ n. en Colima, Col., y m. en Chihuahua, Chih. (1869-1952). Compositor. Con sus hermanos fundó en Chihuahua la Casa Mexicana de Música, dedicada a la enseñanza. Autor de las piezas de teatro de revista *Las Estaciones* y *Allende el Bravo*, la canción *Desde que te vi venir* (que ganó un concurso en 1921) y la zarzuela *La muda*, entre otras obras.

Jorge Ramos

RAMOS, JORGE ◆ n. en el DF (1958). Periodista. Licenciado en ciencias de la comunicación por la UIA. Ha hecho estudios de periodismo y televisión en la Universidad de California, así como un posgrado en relaciones internacionales. Comenzó su carrera en 1978, en noticieros radiofónicos de las emisoras XEW y XEX. Después de un breve paso por la televisión mexicana, emigró en 1983 a Estados Unidos, donde ha sido reportero del Canal 34 de Los Ángeles y conductor de los noticieros *Mundo Latino* y *Noticiero Univisión*. Autor de *Detrás de la máscara* y *Lo que vi* (1999).

RAMOS, JOSÉ ◆ n. en San Luis Potosí, SLP, y m. en la ciudad de México (1859-1909). Se tituló como médico en la Universidad Nacional (1881). Fue profesor del Instituto Científico y Literario de Toluca (1881), miembro del Consejo de Salubridad y regidor del ayuntamiento de la capital mexiquense. En 1886 viajó a Francia para especializarse en oftalmología. A su regreso al país (1888), sustituyó en la cátedra a Rafael Lucio y Ricardo Vértiz. Fue senador y director del Instituto Médico Nacional. Autor de *Importancia de algunos fenómenos oculares en el diagnóstico del sistema nervioso*. En 1888 ingresó en la Academia de Medicina, que presidió en 1896; fundador y primer presidente (1893) de la Sociedad Oftalmológica Mexicana. *Doctor honoris causa* por la Universidad de Harvard.

RAMOS, JOSÉ MARÍA ◆ m. en Cointzio, Mich. (?-1818). Sacerdote insurgente. En 1811 unió sus fuerzas a las de Oropesa y Ochoa, con quienes expulsó a los realistas de Aguascalientes y recuperó la artillería perdida por Ignacio López Rayón en El Maguey. A fines de 1811 comandaba unos 2,000 hombres en La Barca, Jalisco, donde fue derrotado por Pedro Celestino Negrete. En 1818, al caer el fuerte de Jaujilla, fue aprehendido y conducido a Cointzio, donde se le ejecutó.

RAMOS, LEOPOLDO ◆ n. en El Triunfo, BC, y m. ¿en el DF? (1898-1957). Fue telegrafista de la División del Norte durante la revolución constitucionalista y el gobierno de la Convención. Inició su carrera periodística en *La Gaceta de Guaymas* y en la ciudad de México colaboró en *Excélsior* (con la columna "Plegaderas") y *Últimas Noticias*, entre otras publicaciones. Autor de los poemarios *Superación, Urbe, campiña y mar* (1932), *Presencias* (1934), *Un hombre en la calle* (1939), *Bauprés* (1942), *Sobretarde y un soneto a la luna* (1947) y *El mantel divino* (1950).

RAMOS, LUIS ARTURO ◆ n. en Minatitlán, Ver. (1947). Escritor. Licenciado en letras españolas por la Universidad Veracruzana, en la que ha sido profesor, director de la revista *La Palabra y el Hombre* y jefe de Publicaciones. Fue coordinador del taller literario del INBA en Orizaba, y colaborador de los suplementos culturales de los periódicos veracruzanos *La Nación* y *El Dictamen*. Profesor invitado de la Universidad de Missouri (1986-87). Ha sido coordinador de la maestría en creación literaria de la Universidad de Texas en El Paso. Autor de cuento: *Siete veces el sueño* (1974), *Del tiempo y otros lugares* (1979), *Los viejos asesinos* (1981) y *La señora de la fuente y otras parábolas de fin de siglo* (1996); narraciones infantiles: *Zili el unicornio* (1980, ilustrado por Leticia Tarragó), *La noche que desapareció la Luna* (1982), *La voz de Coatl* (1983, ilustrado por María Figueroa), *Cuentiario* y *Blanca-pluma* (1993); novela *Violeta-Perú* (1979, Premio Narrativa Colima-INBA), *Intramuros* (1982), *Domingo junto al paisaje* (1987), *Este era un gato* (1988) y *La casa del ahorcado* (1993); y ensayo: *Ángela de Hoyos: A Critical Look* (1980) y *Melomanías: la ritualización del universo. Una lectura de la obra de Juan Vicente Melo* (1989, Premio José Revueltas). Becario del Centro Mexicano de Escritores (1972-73) y del INBA (1976-77).

RAMOS, MANUEL *PULGARCITO* ◆ n. en Hermosillo, Son., y m. en el DF (1942-1999). Boxeador. Realizó gran parte de su carrera en cuadriláteros de Estados Unidos y otros países. Es reconocido como el mejor peleador de peso completo en México, aunque nunca pudo ganar un título mundial.

RAMOS, MARIANO ◆ n. en ¿el DF? (1953). Torero. En la infancia ya participaba en jaripeos haciendo suertes charras. Debutó como torero en 1971 en la Plaza México. Ese mismo año tomó la alternativa de Manolo Martínez, con Francisco Rivera *Paquirri* como testigo, y desde entonces fue uno de los más destacados matadores de la tauromaquia mexicana. En 1988 lidió su milésima corrida. Es famoso por no haber sido cornado nunca. Ha ganado tres veces el premio Estoque de Oro, además de tres escapularios, la Rosa Guadalupana y la Rosa de Mexicali.

RAMOS, RAMÓN ◆ n. en Villa de Chínipas y m. cerca de Chihuahua, Chih. (1894-1937). Estudió en la Escuela Nacional de Agricultura. Se estableció en Sonora desde 1918, donde fue diputado local (1924) y federal (1926-27), desaforado por oponerse a la reelección de Álvaro Obregón. Senador (1930-1934) y secretario de Gobierno de Sonora. En este cargo asumió el Poder Ejecutivo local en tres ocasiones (1931, 1932 y 1932) por ausencia del titular. Elegido gobernador constitucional de la entidad para el periodo 1935-39, ejerció el cargo hasta fines de 1935, cuando el Senado declaró la desaparición de los poderes locales. Murió en un accidente automovilístico.

RAMOS, RAYMUNDO ◆ n. en Piedras Negras, Coah. (1933). Licenciado en letras por la UNAM y maestro y doctor en filosofía por la UIA, de la que ha sido profesor, así como del IPN y de escuelas secundarias. Fue jefe del Departamento de Historia de la Educación en México en el Museo Pedagógico Nacional. Colabora en *unomásuno* y otras publicaciones de la ciudad de México y de Monterrey. Coautor de: *De tradición oral. Testimonios de una generación* (1968) y *Los desafíos del desarrollo social* (1989). Autor de narrativa: *Muerte amurallada* (1958, Premio Estaciones), *Enroque de verano* (1958) y *El campo del rencor* (1982); ensayo: *Antonio Caso, filósofo y educador* (1964), *Memorias y autobiografías de escritores mexicanos* (1967), *Centenario del Ateneo Fuente: 1867-1967* (1967), *Lizardi y la novela mexicana* (1978), *John Reed, soldado de la Revolución* (1980), *Vida del infortunado caballero Miguel de Cervantes* (1984); poesía: *Paloma de sur a polo* (1958), *Sonetos españoles* (1960), *Luz en las Segovias* (1963), *Marthin Luther King* (1963), *Homenajes* (1965), *Custodia de la palabra* (1967), *Mar erótica y otros estudios marinos* (1970), *De la primera herencia* (1976), *La calavera azul y otros poemas* (1977), *Him, el perro consentido del señor presidente* (1979), *Escorpión en invierno* (1980) y *La prisión y su forma* (1983). Becario del Centro Mexicano de Escritores (1956-57). Ha recibido los premios: Ulyses de Nueva York al poeta del año (1959) y de Ensayo Alfonso Reyes, del periódico *Ovaciones*.

RAMOS, ULTIMINIO ♦ n. en Cuba (1941). Boxeador apodado *Sugar*. En 1955 era bolero en Matanzas. Se inició en el pugilismo cuando su padre lo incluyó como peleador emergente en una función de box. En 1957 se presentó profesionalmente en La Habana, donde el 8 de noviembre de 1958 ganó por la vía rápida a su paisano José Blanco, quien murió a consecuencia de la pelea. Llegó a México en 1962. El 21 de marzo de 1963 derrotó en Los Ángeles al estadounidense Dave Moore (quien falleció como resultado del combate) y se coronó campeón mundial de peso pluma; defendió tres veces su campeonato y fue derrotado el 26 de septiembre de 1964 por el mexicano Vicente Saldívar. Tuvo 65 peleas profesionales. Retirado del deporte en 1972, se dedica desde entonces a la interpretación de música tropical y al manejo de peleadores.

RAMOS AGUIRRE, FRANCISCO ♦ n. en Saltillo, Coah. (1953). Realizó estudios en la Universidad Autónoma de Tamaulipas y en la Escuela Normal Superior. Editó en Veracruz la revista *Agrozoo* (1977). En Tamaulipas ha colaborado en *Arquitrabe*, suplemento del periódico *El Mercurio* (1982); fundó y dirigió el suplemento *El Tobogán* en el diario *El Tiempo* (1984), y trabajó en *Maratín*, suplemento del *Diario de Ciudad Victoria*. Jefe de Información del semanario *Cambio 21* (1990-). Autor de *Cambio de Vía* (1986), *Mujer de Arena y otros poemas* (1986). *Sin motivo aparente* (1987), *Corridos tamaulipecos* (antología, 1989), *Para hablar de Tamaulipas hay que cantar sus corridos* (1990), *Configuraciones de una tarde* (1990) y *Allá por el norte* (1990). Premio Estatal de Poesía (1989) y de Ensayo (1991) del Instituto Tamaulipeco de Cultura.

RAMOS ARCEO, JOSÉ ♦ n. en San Luis Potosí, SLP, y m. en el DF (1857-1909). Estudió humanidades y filosofía en el Seminario Conciliar y se graduó como médico en la Universidad Nacional (1881). Fue profesor y secretario del Instituto Científico y Literario de Toluca (1881-85), se especializó en oftalmología en Francia (1885-87) y fue profesor y médico en la ciudad de México. Senador de la República (1892-1902). Colaborador de la *Gaceta Médica*, *La Revista Médica*, *La Escuela de Medicina* y los *Anales de Oftalmología*. Autor de *Degeneración grasosa especial del hígado por el abuso del pulque* (1881), *Importancia de algunos fenómenos oculares en el diagnóstico de las afecciones del sistema nervioso* (1887), *La oftalmia purulante como causa de la ceguera en México*, *El tracoma en México* y *La ceguera nerviosa*.

RAMOS ARIZPE ♦ Municipio de Coahuila situado en los límites con Nuevo León y contiguo a Saltillo. Superficie: 5,306.6 km^2. Habitantes: 36,440, de los cuales 9,038 forman la población económicamente activa. Hablan alguna lengua indígena 38 personas mayores de cinco años. El Plan de Guadalupe se firmó en la hacienda del mismo nombre en este municipio, donde también se produjo, el 17 de mayo de 1914, el combate de Paredón, cuando 6,000 hombres de la División del Norte derrotaron a 15,000 soldados federales.

RAMOS ARIZPE, MIGUEL ♦ n. en Valle de Las Labores, actual Ramos Arizpe, Coah., y m. en Puebla, Pue. (1775-1843). Colegial fundador del Seminario de Monterrey y sacerdote ordenado en 1803. Fue promotor fiscal eclesiástico, defensor general de obras pías, profesor de derecho canónico y provisor, juez y canónigo doctoral de la catedral de Monterrey. Cura de Santa María de Aguayo y vicario de Güemes de Padilla (1805). Licenciado (1807) y doctor (1808) en cánones por la Universidad de Guadalajara, en la ciudad de México se recibió como abogado (1810) y la audiencia de Nueva España le otorgó el título de doctor en leyes. Era miembro del ayuntamiento de Saltillo cuando fue elegido diputado por Coahuila a las Cortes de Cádiz (1811), donde defendió ideas federalistas y precursoras del municipio libre. Al reocupar Fernando VII el trono español (1814), Ramos Arizpe fue encarcelado, acusado de ser jefe de las insurrecciones americanas. Desterrado en Valencia (1815-20), fue nuevamente elegido diputado a Cortes. Volvió a México en 1822 y fue diputado al Congreso General de 1823-24. Fue secretario de Justicia (del 30 de noviembre de 1825 al 7 de marzo de 1828 y del 26 de diciembre de 1832 al 1 de abril de 1833) en los gabinetes de Guadalupe Victoria y de Manuel Gómez Pedraza, y secretario de Hacienda de este último (del 5 de enero al 1 de febrero de 1833). El Congreso lo declaró Benemérito de la Patria.

RAMOS Y DUARTE, FÉLIX ♦ n. y m. en Cuba (1848-?). Educador. Llegó exiliado a México en 1868. Establecido en Yucatán, se graduó como profesor en el Instituto Literario de Mérida, en el que ejerció la docencia. Al consumarse la independencia cubana regresó a la isla, donde fue nombrado inspector de escuelas primarias. Coautor de *Actas del Congreso de Americanistas* (1897). Autor de *Diccionario de mexicanismos. Colección*

Miguel Ramos Arizpe

FOTO: FONDO EDITORIAL GRUPO AZABACHE

Casco de la ex Hacienda de Santa María en Ramos Arizpe, Coahuila

Alfredo Ramos Martínez

Gabriel Ramos Millán

de locuciones y frases viciosas (1895) y *Colección de curiosidades históricas* (1899).

RAMOS GURRIÓN, MANUEL ◆ n. en Coatzacoalcos, Ver. (1935). Licenciado en derecho por la UNAM (1962). Miembro del PRI, en el que ha sido secretario de Acción Política (1968), secretario de organización (1969), secretario general (1970) y presidente (1970) del Comité Directivo Estatal en Veracruz y delegado en diversas entidades del Comité Ejecutivo Nacional y secretario de Acción Electoral (1988). En la CNOP fue secretario de Organización del Comité Ejecutivo Nacional de la CNOP (1976). Ha sido secretario de Trabajo y Conflictos del Comité Ejecutivo Nacional del Sindicato de Trabajadores de la Secretaría de Obras Públicas (1960-63), subdirector de juntas de Mejoramiento Moral, Cívico y Material de Veracruz (1965), diputado local, dos veces diputado federal por Veracruz (1973-76 y 1979-82) y senador de la República (1982-88).

RAMOS MAGAÑA, SAMUEL ◆ n. en Zitácuaro, Mich., y m. en el DF (1897-1959). Doctor en filosofía por la Universidad Nacional (1944), especializado en Italia y Francia. Fue colaborador de la revista estudiantil *Flor de Loto*. Profesor de la Escuela Nacional de Maestros, jefe de Extensión Universitaria, director de Cooperación Intelectual y oficial mayor de la SEP. Profesor y director (1944-52) de la Facultad de Filosofía de la UNAM, donde promovió la corriente de la "filosofía del mexicano", y coordinador de Humanidades y Maestros de Carrera en la misma facultad. Autor de *Hipótesis* (1928), *El caso Stravinsky* (1929), *El perfil del hombre y la cultura en México* (1934), *Ensayo sobre Diego Rivera* (1935), *Más allá de la moral de Kant* (1938), *Hacia un nuevo humanismo* (1940), *Historia de la filosofía en México* (1943), *Filosofía de la vida artística* (1950), *Veinte años de educación en México* (1951), *El problema del a priori y la experiencia y las relaciones entre la filosofía y la ciencia* (1955) y *Nuevo ensayo sobre Diego Rivera* (1958). Fue miembro de El Colegio Nacional.

RAMOS MARTÍNEZ, ALFREDO ◆ n. en Monterrey, NL, y m. en EUA (¿1875?-1946). Pintor. Estudió en la Academia de San Carlos y en Francia (1900), pensionado por Phoebe Apperson. Expuso en Inglaterra en 1907 y regresó a México en 1910. Fue director de la Academia de San Carlos (1911-15 y 1920-28). En 1913 fundó en Santa Anita la primera de las Escuelas de Pintura al Aire Libre (☛), a la que se llamó Barbizón, por la presunta similitud que existía con los orígenes del impresionismo, del que era admirador confeso. Radicado en Estados Unidos (1929), se dedicó a pintar murales en residencias particulares de San Diego y San Francisco. Autor de *Viejo indio* (premiado en el Palacio de California y conservado en el Salón de la Legión de Honor de San Francisco), *La primavera* (1904), *El triunfo de la primavera* (primer premio en el Salón de París de 1906), los murales de las capillas de Santa Bárbara y La Joya, dos vitrales para la iglesia católica de San Juan, en California, y varios murales para el Colegio Scrips de Claramont. Su cuadro *Flores mexicanas*, premiado en Pomona, California, en 1932, fue adquirido por Emilio Portes Gil, quien lo regaló al aviador estadounidense Charles Lindbergh. Publicó *Escuelas de pintura al aire libre* (1926). En 1904 recibió una medalla de oro en el Salón Anual de Pintura.

Obra de Alfredo Ramos Martínez

RAMOS MARTÍNEZ, LEOBARDO ◆ n. en Guadalajara, Jal. (1916). Contador privado (1930) y profesor normalista (1936) por el Instituto del Estado de Nayarit. Miembro fundador de la CTM (1936), secretario de Organización de la Federación de Trabajadores de Nayarit (1940-46), secretario de Acción Obrera del Comité Directivo Estatal del PRM en Nayarit (1942-50), secretario de trabajo y conflictos de la Federación de Trabajadores de Nayarit (1946-58) e instructor sindical de la CTM (1968). Ha sido profesor de educación primaria, gerente general de la Sociedad Cooperativa de Transportes de Carga Mololoa (1936), quinto regidor de Tepic (1940), diputado local (1943-46 y 1949-52), senador por Nayarit (1964-70), inspector de campo y auxiliar del jefe de zona de Banjidal, delegado del Instituto Nacional del Consumidor en Nayarit, representante obrero ante la Junta Local de Conciliación y Arbitraje, la Comisión Reguladora de Salarios Mínimos y la Comisión de Planeación y Urbanización de Nayarit. Diputado federal (1985-88) y senador (1976-82).

RAMOS MILLÁN, GABRIEL ◆ n. en Ayapango, Edo. de Méx., y m. cerca del DF (1903-1949). Licenciado por la Escuela Libre de Derecho. Ejerció la abogacía en Pachuca. Fue funcionario público en Veracruz, durante el gobierno de Miguel Alemán; diputado federal (1943-46), senador (1946-52), presidente fundador de la Comisión Nacional del Maíz (1947), consejero de Guanos y Fertilizantes de México y de la Compañía Americana de Fianzas, presidente del Consejo de Administración de la Financiera de Construcciones y vicepresidente del Consejo de Administración de la Producción Agrícola. Fraccionó terrenos al oeste y al sur de la ciudad de México y, por iniciativa suya, el antiguo toreo se trasladó a la zona de Cuatro Caminos. Fue llamado *el Apóstol del Maíz*. Murió en un accidente de aviación.

Ramos Oliveira, Antonio ◆ n. en España y m. en el DF (1907-1973). Historiador. Dirigió un diario en Madrid, fue corresponsal de la prensa española en Alemania, Suiza e Inglaterra y agregado de prensa en la embajada de la República Española en Londres. Llegó en 1940 a México, donde se naturalizó. Fue director de la *Revista de Historia de América*, traductor y miembro del cuerpo técnico del Fondo de Cultura Económica y funcionario de la ONU comisionado en Chile, República Dominicana, Argentina, Estados Unidos y México. Tradujo a Heinz Woltereck, G. J. Whitrow, Albert Schweitzer y R. F. Harrod, entre otros. Autor de *A people's history of Germany*, *Historia social y económica de Alemania*, *Historia de España* (3 t.), *Politics, Economics and Men of Modern Spain*, *Hernán Cortés y sus parientes los Juárez* y *Los orígenes del cristianismo y de la Iglesia*.

Ramos Pedrueza, Rafael ◆ n. y m. en el DF (1897-1943). Profesor autodidacto. Realizó un viaje de estudio por varios países europeos, comisionado por la SEP. Fue diputado federal (1921), profesor de la UNAM y del Conservatorio Nacional. Autor de *Excelsitud del arte*, *Crímenes de los imperialismos*, *Estudios históricos, sociales y literarios*, *La estrella roja, 12 años de vida soviética* (traducido al ruso), *La lucha de clases a través de la historia de México* (2 t.), *Sugerencias revolucionarias para la enseñanza de la historia*, *Emiliano Zapata y el agrarismo nacional*, *José María Morelos y Pavón, precursor del socialismo en México* y *Javier Mina, representativo de la lucha clasista en Europa y América*.

Ramos Praslow, Ignacio ◆ n. en Culiacán, Sin., y m. en el DF (1885-1978). Estudió abogacía en Guadalajara. Participó en el movimiento antirreeleccionista. Al producirse el golpe de Estado de Victoriano Huerta se unió a las fuerzas constitucionalistas. Fue secretario particular de Venustiano Carranza y de Enrique Estrada. Diputado al Congreso Constituyente de 1916-17 y subsecretario de Justicia en el gabinete de Carranza. Se adhirió a la rebelión del Plan de Agua Prieta y fue gobernador interino de Jalisco (1920), administrador de la Junta de la Propiedad Extranjera, presidente de la Asociación de Diputados Constituyentes y director de la Aseguradora Hidalgo. Fue asesor de varios presidentes. Recibió las medallas Belisario Domínguez y Miguel Hidalgo.

Ramos Roa, Joaquín ◆ n. en Guanajuato, Gto., y m. en el DF (1875-1929). Abogado. Luchó en la revolución constitucionalista. Durante la lucha de facciones se adhirió a los gobiernos de la Convención de Aguascalientes. Fue oficial mayor de la Secretaría de Instrucción Pública y Bellas Artes, encargado del despacho en 1915 (en sustitución de Ramón López Velarde), en el gabinete de Roque González Garza.

Ramos Romero, Esteban ◆ n. en Oaxaca, Oax. (1934). Escultor egresado de la ENAP (1968). Hizo sus primeros trabajos en Monumentos Coloniales del Museo de Antropología y en el Palacio Nacional. En 1969 realizó trabajos para el Patrimonio Nacional y para la Casa de la Moneda. Ha expuesto individualmente en México, Oaxaca y San Antonio, Texas. Autor del *Águila* del Palacio Nacional (1962) y del estucado en relieve de las ruinas de Bonampak en el Museo Nacional de Antropología (1963). Trabajó en la restauración del templo de Tlatelolco (1963) y de la iglesia de la Soledad, en Oaxaca. Obtuvo mención honorífica en el concurso Nuevos Valores de la Galería Chapultepec (1967) y mención honorífica del Injuve (1968).

Ramos Sánchez, Pilar ◆ n. en San Antonio Encinas, Coah., y m. en el DF (1888-1950). Militar, en 1911 se unió a la insurrección maderista. Participó en los combates de Concepción del Oro, Zacatecas y Cuatro Ciénegas. En el constitucionalismo alcanzó el grado de general. Estuvo representado en la Convención de Aguascalientes por Alfredo M. Jaimes. Luego de la escisión revolucionaria permaneció fiel al carrancismo y combatió a Emiliano Zapata (1916-19). En 1920 acompañó a Carranza en su huida de la ciudad de México. Fue jefe de operaciones en Puebla, Tlaxcala y Oaxaca y jefe del Departamento de Caballería de la Sedena.

Ramos Santos, Matías ◆ n. en San Salvador, Zac., y m. en el DF (1891-1962). Presidente del Partido Nacional Revolucionario (1934). Se unió en 1911 a la insurrección maderista. Luchó contra el huertismo (1913-14), el villismo (1915), el delahuertismo (1923) y el escobarismo (1929). Fue jefe de operaciones militares en Zacatecas, Oaxaca, Nayarit y Tamaulipas, diputado federal (1918-20), general de división (1929), subsecretario de Guerra y Marina (1929), gobernador de Zacatecas (1932-36) y secretario de la Defensa Nacional (del 1 de diciembre de 1952 al 30 de noviembre de 1958) en el gabinete de Adolfo Ruiz Cortines.

Matías Ramos Santos

Ramos Smith, Maya ◆ n. en ¿el DF? (¿1962?). Bailarina, actriz y escritora. Estudió actuación en el Stella Adler Conservatory of Acting de Nueva York, y danza en la Academia de la Danza Mexicana del INBA, con posgrado en la Ecole Supérieure d'Etudes Chorégraphiques de París. Trabajó seis años con la Compañía Nacional de Danza y dos con el Ballet Independiente. Como actriz ha trabajado para el Teatro de la Nación, el Teatro de la UNAM y Televisa. Ha escrito artículos sobre teatro y danza para diversas publicaciones. Coautora de *Los mil grandes del diseño y la fotografía* (1982) y *Homenaje a Otón Arróniz* (1994). Autora de una introducción a *Teatro de Rodolfo Usigli* (1979) y de los libros *El mundo maravilloso del ballet* (1978), *La danza en México durante la época colonial* (1979, Premio Casa de las Américas de ensayo), *María de Jesús Moctezuma* (1987), *El ballet en México en el siglo XIX* (1991), *El actor en el siglo XVIII: entre el Coliseo y el Principal* (1994), *Teatro musical y danza en el México de la Belle Epoque* (1995) y *Censura y marginalidad en la Colonia*.

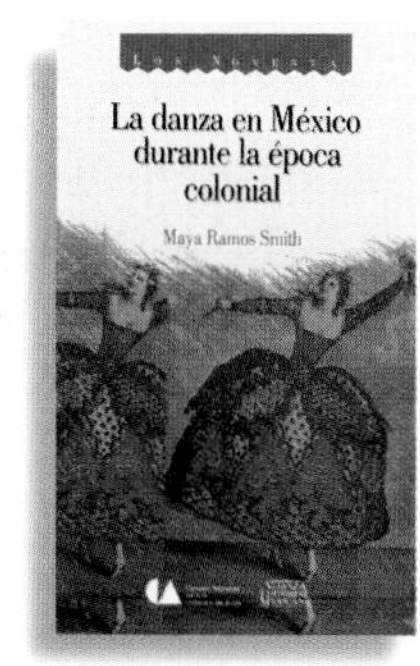

Libro de Maya Ramos Smith

José María Rangel reprimió la rebelión de Tomochic

RAMUSIO, GIOVANNI BATTISTA ♦ n. y m. en Italia (1485-1557). Fue secretario del Senado de Venecia (1515) y secretario del Consejo de los Diez (1533). Diplomático al servicio de la República de Venecia. Se interesó en la cartografía por su relación con Américo Vespucio, Sebastián Caboto y Gonzalo Fernández de Oviedo. Editó la colección *Delle navigationi e viaggi*, cuyo tercer tomo se refiere a América y en el que aparecen las únicas versiones originales conocidas de la relación *El conquistador anónimo*, sobre la conquista de México.

RANDALL, CARLOS E. ♦ n. en Guaymas, Son., y m. en EUA (1862-1929). Minero y comerciante en San Marcial, se afilió en 1910 al Partido Antirreeleccionista y fue vocal de la Junta Revolucionaria de Nogales. Gobernó interinamente Sonora (del 23 de julio al 1 de septiembre de 1911). En 1912 fue tesorero del estado y diputado federal. Combatió al huertismo y fue nuevamente gobernador interino de Sonora (de enero a marzo de 1914), en sustitución de Maytorena. Fue expulsado del estado, pero al regresar Maytorena a la gubernatura, Randall ocupó de nuevo la tesorería general. Del 1 de octubre al 26 de noviembre de 1915 volvió a gobernar interinamente el estado, nombrado por Francisco Villa.

RANDALL, MARGARET ♦ n. en EUA (1936). Escritora autodidacta. Vivió en México desde 1961 y se casó con un mexicano; en 1987 se naturalizó. Vivió en Cuba (1969-79) y en Nicaragua (1979-84). En 1984 volvió a Estados Unidos y en enero de 1989 el Servicio de Inmigración y Naturalización la expulsó "por sus tendencias comunistas y feministas".

RANGEL, JAIME ♦ n. en Tula, Hgo. (1940). Torero. Se presentó profesionalmente en 1956. En 1962 recibió la alternativa de manos del portugués Manolo dos Santos y se la confirmó en Madrid Joaquín Bernadó (1962). En la plaza México lidió un astado de 630 kilos. Fue tres veces secretario general de la Asociación Nacional de Toros y Novillos. Se retiró en 1985.

RANGEL, JOSÉ MARÍA ♦ n. en San Luis de la Paz, Gto., y m. en la ciudad de México (1836-1896). Militar. Con el grado de capitán participó con los republicanos en el sitio de Querétaro y fue el encargado de recibir al coronel imperialista Miguel López, quien facilitó la entrada de las tropas de Mariano Escobedo en la ciudad y la consecuente derrota de Maximiliano. Como coronel se le comisionó en Guaymas para sostener a los empleados de Hacienda separados por el gobernador Pesqueira. Fue declarado ciudadano sonorense en 1874, prefecto político y comandante militar de Guaymas en 1876. En 1887 combatió a los rebeldes Ramírez Terrón y Márquez de León. Con el grado de general se le nombró jefe político del territorio de Baja California y al ocurrir la partición de la península, Rangel mantuvo su cargo en Baja California Sur hasta 1889. Fue jefe de la segunda zona militar de Chihuahua y reprimió la rebelión indígena de Tomochic (1891).

RANGEL, MARIO ♦ n. en el DF (1938). Pintor. Estudió en el Taller Infantil de Artes Plásticas de Roberto Pérez Rangel (1952-54), en La Esmeralda y en la ENAP. Efectuó su primera exposición en 1954. En 1965 ingresó en el Taller Profesional de Grabado de La Esmeralda y se perfeccionó en Estados Unidos y Europa (1966-67). Ha hecho escenografías, dibujos y murales. Hizo el mural *Quema de códices* en la biblioteca Cervantes de la capital del país. Intervino en la elaboración del mural colectivo *Mesoamérica*, del Museo Nacional de Antropología. Trabajó grabado en el taller de Mario Reyes (1979) y en Italia desarrolló una técnica para el estampado a mano sobre seda natural.

RANGEL, NICOLÁS ♦ n. en León, Gto., y m. en Cuernavaca, Mor. (1864-1935). Historiador y escritor. Colaboró en la *Revista Moderna*. En 1910 se hizo cargo del *Boletín de la Biblioteca Nacional* y el mismo año colaboró con Pedro Henríquez Ureña y Luis G. Urbina en la *Antología del centenario*. Fue profesor en la Escuela Nacional Preparatoria (1916-34) y oficial de investigaciones históricas del Archivo General de la Nación (1920-35). Colaborador de *Crisol* y del *Boletín del Archivo General de la Nación*. Hizo la paleografía, prólogo y notas de la *Crónica de la Real y Pontificia Universidad de México*, de Cristóbal Bernardo de la Plaza y Jaén (1931). Autor de *Álbum histórico gráfico* (en colaboración con Luis González Obregón), *Los primeros evangelizadores de la Nueva España*, *Los estudios universitarios de don Juan Ruiz de Alarcón y Mendoza* (1913), *Noticias biográficas del dramaturgo mexicano don Juan Ruiz de Alarcón y Mendoza* (1915), *Churubusco-Huitzilopochco* (1921, en colaboración con Ramón Mena), *Primer centenario de la Constitución de 1824* (1924, en colaboración con Pedro de Alba), *Historia del toreo en México. Época colonial* (1924), *Documentos para la historia de la Independencia* (1926, en colaboración con Ramón Mena), *Bibliografía de Juan Ruiz de Alarcón* (1927), *Nuevos datos para la biografía de José Ma. de Heredia* (1930), *La vida colonial* (2 t., 1932), y *Los precursores ideológicos de la guerra de independencia, 1789-1798* (1932). Miembro fundador de la Academia Mexicana de la Historia.

RANGEL DOMENE, ERNESTO ♦ n. en Monterrey, NL (1936). Estudió la maestría en administración pública en la Universidad Autónoma de Nuevo León. Profesor de la facultad de Ciencias Políticas de la UNAM. Fundó la revista *Administración Municipal*, de Monterrey. Colaborador de diversas publicaciones del Distrito Federal, Nuevo León, Sonora y Yucatán. Autor de poesía: *Los ríos de polvo* (1960), *El suplicio del agua* (1962), *Balada de la cárcel del mundo* (1969), *Canción junto al abismo* (1970) y *Carta de amor silvestre y otros poemas* (1979). Becario del Centro Mexicano de Escritores (1965-66).

RANGEL FRÍAS, RAÚL ♦ n. y m. en Monterrey, NL (1913-1993). Licenciado en derecho por la UNAM (1938), donde fue profesor, así como de la Universidad de Nuevo León, en la que ocupó la jefatura del Departamento de Acción Social (1944), fundó y dirigió la Facultad de Filosofía y Letras, creó la Escuela de Verano, fue rector de la institución (1949-55), cargo desde el cual inició la construcción de la Ciudad Universitaria de Monterrey, y director general de Investigaciones Humanísticas (1975). En Nuevo León fue jefe del Departamento de Prensa, oficial mayor, gobernador (1955-61), delegado de la SEP (1980-86) y director general del Instituto de Cultura (1987). Dirigió el periódico *Rumbo* y las revistas *Armas y Letras* y *Universidad*. Autor de *Apuntes históricos del Colegio Civil* (1931), *Identidad de Estado y derecho en la teoría pura de Hans Kelsen* (1938), *Situación económica de las universidades* (1953), *Hidalgo y la patria mexicana* (1953), *Discursos universitarios* (1959), *Testimonios* (1961), *Discurso final* (1961), *Evocación de Alfonso Reyes* (1963), *Gerónimo Treviño. Héroes y epígonos* (1967), *Cosas nuestras* (1971), *El reino. Un libro de relatos* (1972), *José Alvarado en el recuerdo* (1975), *Óyeme, Pedro* (1979), *Versiones 2. Sierra Madre. El nagual* (1979), *Kato* (1981), *Alma mater* (1984), *Federico Cantú y su obra* (1986) y *Escritos* (1997). Fue miembro del Grupo Alfonso Reyes. *Doctor honoris causa* de la Universidad de Nuevo León (1984).

RANGEL GASPAR, ELISEO ◆ n. en Bimbaletes, Zac. (1928). Se tituló en la Escuela Nacional de Maestros (1950). Licenciado en derecho por la UNAM (1955), donde fue profesor (1959-73). Miembro del PRI, en el que ha sido presidente del comité directivo en Zacatecas (1974-80), miembro de la Comisión Nacional de Ideología y subdirector de educación política del CEN. Fue secretario general del comité municipal de la CNOP en Zacatecas (1957). En la CNC fungió como coordinador de educación política (1962), auxiliar del oficial mayor (1964) y oficial mayor (1983). Ha sido asesor jurídico de la Federación Estatal de Pequeños Propietarios (1956), agente del Ministerio Público (1956), juez de primera instancia en Zacatecas (1957), secretario del Juzgado Segundo en Materia Civil del DF (1960-66), jefe de Personal de la Secretaría de Salubridad (1966-70), subdirector de Trabajo y Previsión Social del DDF (1970-73), asesor del secretario de Obras Públicas (1973-74), diputado local (1974-77), diputado federal (1982-85) y senador (1988-94). Autor de *Jesús González Ortega, caudillo de la Reforma* (1960), *Hacia una teoría de la revolución mexicana* (1962), *Economía política* (1964), *Los principios de la no intervención y autodeterminación de los pueblos* (1966), *El PRI y la reforma política* (1976), *Francisco García Salinas, tata Pachito* (1984), *Veinte zacatecanos universales* (1989) y *De política y políticos* (1990), entre otras. Miembro de la Sociedad Mexicana de Geografía y Estadística.

RANGEL GUERRA, ALFONSO ◆ n. en Monterrey, NL (1928). Licenciado en derecho y en ciencias sociales por la Universidad de Nuevo León (1946-53), donde ha sido profesor, director de la Preparatoria 1 y de la Facultad de Filosofía y Letras, oficial mayor, secretario general y rector (1955-64). Estudió literatura francesa y literatura comparada en la Universidad de París (1958-59). Presidente del Instituto Internacional de Literatura Iberoamericana (1963-65), corresponsal en Monterrey del Seminario de Cultura Mexicana, secretario general ejecutivo de la ANUIES (1965-76), director general de Educación Superior de la SEP (1977-82), ministro para asuntos culturales de la embajada mexicana en España (1983-85) y secretario general de El Colegio de México. Colaborador de *Armas y Letras*, *Universidad*, *Khatarsis*, *Humanitas* y *Vida Universitaria*. Preparó y prologó la edición de *Páginas sobre Alfonso Reyes* (2 t., 1955-57) y *Crónicas y artículos sobre teatro*, de Manuel Gutiérrez Nájera (1974). Autor de *Imagen de la novela* (1964), *Historia de la literatura española* (1965), *Agustín Yáñez y su obra* (1969), *The Provincial Universities of Mexico. An Analysis of Growth and Development* (1971, traducida al español en 1972 como *Nueve universidades mexicanas*), *Systems of Higher Education: Mexico* (1978, traducida al español en 1979), *Las ideas literarias de Alfonso Reyes* (1989) y *Desde el cerro de la Silla* (1992).

RANGEL HIDALGO, ALEJANDRO ◆ n. en Colima, Col. (1923). Pintor. Fue ayudante de José Clemente Orozco en Guadalajara. En 1947 viajó a España para montar la escenografía de la ópera *Tata Vasco*, de Miguel Bernal Jiménez, y permaneció en aquel país para estudiar las pinturas rupestres de Altamira. Volvió a México en 1950. Radicado en Comala, Colima, en 1970 fundó una escuela de artesanías. Por encargo de la gobernadora Griselda Álvarez proyectó el remozamiento de Colima, Comala y Villa de Álvarez (1979-85). Cofundador de la Escuela de Arquitectura y el Ballet de la Universidad de Colima (1982). Ha hecho diseño, pintura, artesanías, arquitectura e ilustración.

RANGEL PERALES, TOMÁS ◆ n. en Gómez Palacio, Dgo. (1929). Estudió contaduría en el Colegio Pitman (1949-50) de Gómez Palacio. Miembro del PRI, en el que ha sido delegado general del Comité Ejecutivo Nacional en Aguascalientes, Zacatecas, Tlaxcala e Hidalgo (1977-82). En el Sindicato de Trabajadores Ferrocarrileros de la República Mexicana fue representante nacional de Fogoneros del Camino (1965-68), auxiliar del secretario nacional (1968-71), secretario nacional de organización (1971-74) y secretario nacional (1974-77). Ha sido miembro del Consejo de Administración de Ferrocarriles Nacionales (1971-77), vicepresidente (1974-77) y presidente interino (1976) del Congreso del Trabajo y senador (1976-82), así como auxiliar del director general (1982-83) y oficial mayor de los Ferrocarriles Nacionales de México (1984-88).

RANSOM, ROBERTO ◆ n. en el DF (1960). Escritor. Licenciado en literatura dramática y teatro por la UNAM. Ha realizado estudios de doctorado en la Universidad de Virginia. Ha coordinado talleres literarios. Autor de novela: *En esa otra tierra* (1991), *Historia de dos leones* (1994), *Chantarelle* (1997) y *La línea del agua* (1999); ensayo: *Por qué aterra Lecter* (1994); y relato: *Saludos a la fa-*

Obra de Roberto Ransom

milia (1995). Becario Fullbright-García Robles (1999).

RAOUSSET DE BOULBON, GASTÓN ◆ n. en Francia y m. en Guaymas, Son. (1817-1854). Filibustero. En 1850 viajó a California, para buscar oro. No pudo enriquecerse y buscó fortuna en México, donde formó la Compañía Restauradora de las Minas de Arizona y obtuvo, en 1852, una concesión para desembarcar en Guaymas al frente de 150 hombres armados con los que exploraría La Mesilla, Arizona, y tomaría posesión de las minas de ese territorio. Reclutó a 250 mercenarios franceses, desembarcó en Guaymas en junio de 1852 y avanzó a Hermosillo, donde el comandante militar de Sonora, Miguel Blanco, conminó a los extranjeros a renunciar a su nacionalidad. El 30 de septiembre de 1852, desde La Magdalena, Raousset persuadió a los jefes políticos de la región de que se opusieran a Blanco. José de Aguilar, socio del francés y gobernador de Sonora, le ordenó rendirse. El filibustero proclamó la independencia de Sonora y marchó a Hermosillo para combatir a Blanco, a quien derrotó. En octubre enfermó de disentería y huyó a San Francisco. En abril de 1853, Santa Anna volvió a la Presidencia y Raousset viajó para entrevistarse con él, quien le prometió una reparación de daños, mientras el francés se comprometía a exterminar a los indios del noroeste de México. Santa Anna incumplió su promesa y Raousset volvió a EUA, organizó otra expedición y en junio de 1854 desembarcó cerca de Guaymas. Los filibusteros fueron derrotados. Raousset fue fusilado el 12 de agosto.

Gastón Raousset de Boulbon

RASA I ◆ Isla del golfo de California, situada al noreste de la isla de Salsipuedes. Tiene una superficie aproximada de 62 hectáreas y es un criadero de gaviotas de cabeza blanca provenientes de Canadá y Estados Unidos (se calcula que anidan cerca de 50,000 de estas aves cada año). Los seris recolectan en Rasa los huevos de esta especie. En 1978 se le declaró "zona de reserva y refugio de aves marinas migratorias y de la fauna silvestre".

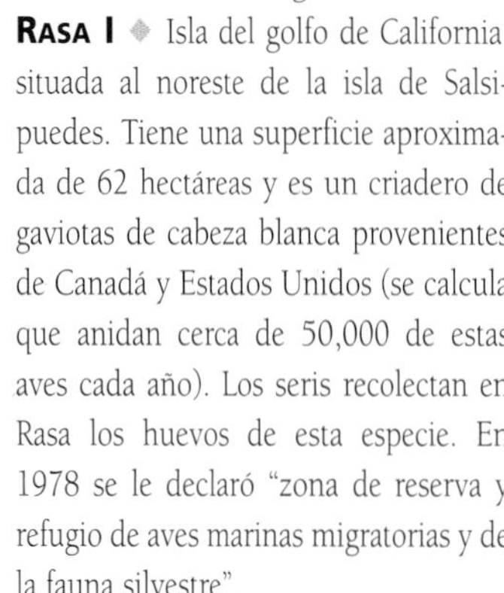

RASCÓN, ARMANDO ◆ n. en Chihuahua, Chih. (1934). Locutor. Llegó a México en 1949 con la intención de estudiar ingeniería, pero casi de inmediato comenzó a trabajar en la radiodifusora XESP. En 1952 fue el primer locutor de la emisora XEFR, en la que trabajó hasta 1954, y posteriormente ha sido locutor de las estaciones XEAI (1954-55), XESP (1955-57), XERPM (1957-58) y XENK (1958-99). Medalla Carlos Pickerin de la Asociación Nacional de Locutores por sus 50 años de carrera (1999).

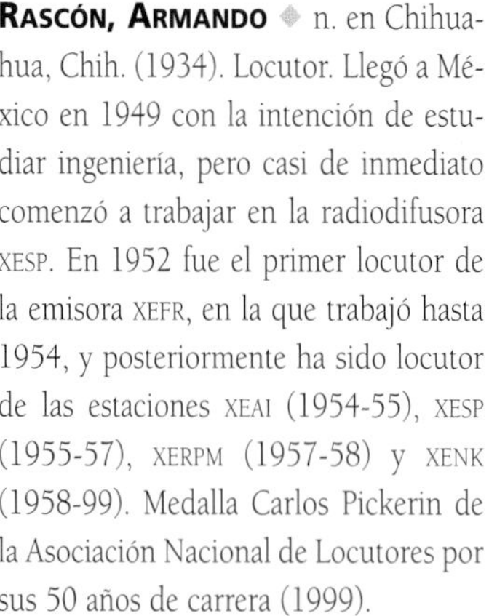

RASCÓN, EUGENIO ◆ n. y m. en el DF (1844-1922). Militar. Secretario de Guerra y Marina (del 26 de mayo al 15 de julio de 1911) en el gabinete de Francisco León de la Barra. Reconoció el gobierno golpista de Victoriano Huerta y éste lo designó gobernador interino de Yucatán (1913).

RASCÓN, MARCO ◆ n. en Naco, Son. (1952). Radicado en Chihuahua, militó en la Liga Comunista 23 de Septiembre, por lo que estuvo encarcelado (1972-75). En el DF ha sido colaborador de la revista *Punto Crítico* y, desde 1989, de *La Jornada*. Fundó en 1983 la Coordinadora de Cuartos de Azotea de Tlatelolco y el Comité de Lucha Inquilinaria del Centro. En 1985 participó en la Coordinadora Única de Damnificados y en 1987, en la fundación de la Asamblea de Barrios, de la que ha sido dirigente y para cuyas actividades creó a *Superbarrio* (☛). Miembro fundador del Frente Democrático Nacional (1988), al año siguiente fue miembro fundador del PRD, del que ha sido consejero estatal y nacional, miembro del CEN, presidente del partido en el DF (1993) y secretario de Divulgación Política y Propaganda (1994). Fue impulsor y creador de la Convención del Anáhuac (1989). Creó las emisoras de baja potencia Radio Verdad y Radio Pirata (1994), dedicadas a la difusión de programas de contenido social. Diputado federal (1994-97, adquirió notoriedad cuando se puso una máscara de cerdo durante un informe de Ernesto Zedillo) y asesor del gobierno del DF. En 1999 era precandidato del PRD a la jefatura del Gobierno del DF. Autor de *Memorias de un líder moderno* (1997).

RASCÓN, VERÓNICA ◆ n. en Naco, Son. (1946). Licenciada en ciencias de la comunicación por la UNAM (1967). Formó parte del grupo Mujeres en Acción Solidaria (1968-73). Dentro del PRI ha sido integrante del IEPES (1976) y subdirectora de difusión del CEPES del Distrito Federal (1987-88). Ha sido reportera de *El Fronterizo* de Ciudad Juárez (1963), *Últimas Noticias* (1965), Mexico Press Service (1966), *Kena*, *Cine-Avance* y *Deporte Ilustrado* (1967-68); productora y conductora de series periodísticas y revistas culturales del Canal 13 (1973-77); conductora titular de los noticieros *Cada hora en la hora* y de varios programas de opinión en el Canal 11 (1977-78), titular de los noticieros informativos general, científico y cultural y del programa *Testimonio Diario*, de Radio Educación (1977-80), directora de Difusión Cultural de la Subsecretaría de Cultura de la SEP (1980-82), conductora de la emisión radiofónica *Onda política*, del Crea (1980-82), y del programa de televisión *¿Cómo vivir mejor?* (1982-85); titular de la Coordinación Nacional de Promoción y Servicios Culturales y responsable del Fideicomiso de Teatros de la Nación, del IMSS (1982-85).

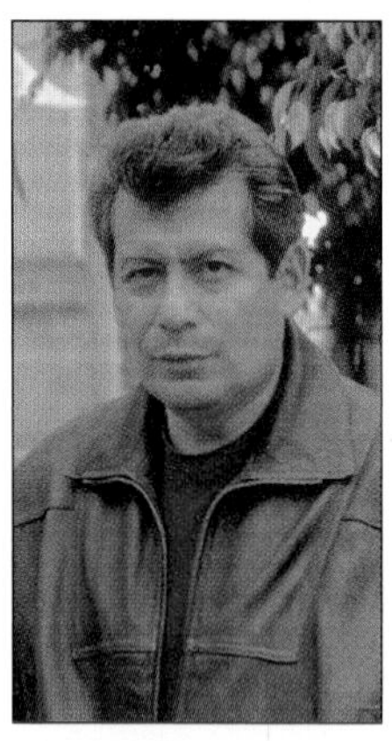

Víctor Hugo Rascón Banda

RASCÓN BANDA, VÍCTOR HUGO ◆ n. en Uruáchic, Chih. (1950). Dramaturgo. Licenciado y doctor en derecho por la UNAM, donde ha sido profesor. Ha sido miembro del proyecto Teatro Clandestino, presidente del Consejo Consultivo de Teatro del INBA y presidente de la Sogem (1999-). Escribió el guión de la película *Días difíciles*, de Alejandro Pelayo (1988), y el libreto de la serie de televisión *La isla de la pasión*, dirigida por Gonzalo Martínez (1988). Autor de teatro: *Nolens volens* (1974), *Las fuentes del derecho* (1974), *De lo que aconteció a Litigonio y a su esposa Prudencia con Fraudonio (siete casos de derecho romano)* (1976), *Voces en el umbral* (1979), *Los ilegales* (1979), *La maestra Teresa* (1979, Premio Nacional Ramón López Velarde), *Tina Modotti* (1981, Premio Nuestra

América, de las universidades de Puebla y Sinaloa), *Salón Plaza* (1981), *Las armas blancas* (1981), *El baile de los montañeses* (1982, Premio Ramón López Velarde), *Playa azul* (1984), *Manos arriba* (1984, premio Sor Juana Inés de la Cruz a la mejor obra de autor mexicano en 1986), *La fiera del Ajusco* (1984), *Máscara contra cabellera*, *¡Manos arriba!* (1986), *¡Ah, la ciencia!*, *Alucinada* (1987), *El machete* (1988), *Guerrero Negro* (1988), *Playa Azul*, *Puerto Escondido*, *¡Cierren las puertas!* (1988), *La banca* (1989), *Homicidio calificado*, *El criminal de Tacuba* y *La malinche*, entre otras; y novela: *Contrabando* (1991, Premio Juan Rulfo de Primera Novela) y *Volver a Santa Rosa* (1996).

Rasgado, Víctor ◆ n. en el DF (1959). Compositor. Comenzó sus estudios musicales con Rosa Cobo. Estudió en la Escuela Nacional de Música de la UNAM, el Centro de Investigación y Estudios Musicales Tlamatinime, la Royal Academy of Music de Londres, el Conservatorio Verdi de Milán (donde estudió composición y música electrónica con Franco Donatoni), la Academia Chigiana de Siena y la Academia de Alto Perfeccionamiento Lorenzo Perosi. Cofundador del Ensamble Sones Contemporáneos, ha sido organizador, coordinador académico y asistente de los cursos de Franco Donatoni en México. Ha escrito obras sinfónicas, de cámara, para coro y diversos instrumentos, además de música electrónica o electroacústica, partituras para cine y la ópera *Anacleto Morones* (1991), basada en textos de Juan Rulfo. Primer lugar en el IV Concurso Internacional de Composición Alfredo Casella de la Academia Chigiana (1993) y en el Concurso Internacional de Composición Olympia de la Radio Nacional de Grecia (1993). Becario del Fonca (1990-91), pertenece al SNCA.

Raull, Regina ◆ n. en España (1931). Reside en México desde 1935. Pintora egresada de la ENAP. En 1956, en una muestra colectiva en la Galería Metropolitana de Arte, se incluyeron algunas de sus obras. En 1967 expuso individualmente en Los Ángeles, donde recibió un diploma de honor. Autora de los murales *La educación en la época mexica*, en el Museo Nacional de Antropología, *Atención y rehabilitación*, en un hospital psiquiátrico infantil, *El origen de la vida*, en un local de la Secretaría de Salud, y las composiciones de luces realizadas en diciembre de 1971, como parte de la decoración navideña de la capital del país.

Ravizé, Manuel A. ◆ n. y m. en Tampico, Tams. (1904-1993). Hizo estudios en la Academia Militar de Georgia, EUA. Miembro del PRI, fue síndico del ayuntamiento de Tampico, senador suplente, jefe de la Junta Federal de Hacienda, director de la Junta de Materiales de Tampico y Madero y gobernador de Tamaulipas (1969-75).

Rayo del Campo, Ángel ◆ n. en España (1913). Estudió en la Escuela de Minas de Almadén y se especializó en siderurgia en Bilbao. Ingresó en el ejército y estudió en la Escuela de Oficiales de Complemento de Artillería. Era teniente cuando comenzó la guerra civil y se alineó en el bando republicano. Al término del conflicto fue miembro del Estado Mayor franco-español para organizar un campo de refugiados en Argeles Sur-Mer. Emigró a República Dominicana en 1940 y trabajó como ingeniero en Grenada Company (1940-45). Pasó a México, donde fue ingeniero en la empresa Equipos Mecánicos y jefe del departamento de maquinaria de Bunge México. Fue uno de los promotores de la instalación de una planta de coque en Monclova para obtener carbón de coque y sus derivados a partir de hulla, y fundador de su propia empresa, Industrial Técnica Rayo, que presidió hasta su retiro.

Rayón ◆ Municipio de Chiapas situado al noreste de Tuxtla Gutiérrez y al noroeste de San Cristóbal de Las Casas. Superficie: 94.4 km². Habitantes: 6,167, de los cuales 1,252 forman la población económicamente activa. Hablan alguna lengua indígena 2,091 personas mayores de cinco años (zoque 1,885).

Rayón ◆ Municipio del Estado de México situado al sureste de Toluca. Limita con Calimaya y Tenango del Valle. Superficie: 26.23 km². Habitantes: 8,300, de los cuales 1,955 forman la población económicamente activa. Hablan alguna lengua indígena 10 personas mayores de cinco años. Su cabecera es Santa María Rayón.

La suave brisa, óleo sobre tela de Regina Raull

Rayón ◆ Municipio de San Luis Potosí situado al oeste de Ciudad Valles y contiguo a Río Verde. Superficie: 809.5 km². Habitantes: 16,763, de los cuales 4,738 forman la población económicamente activa. Hablan alguna lengua indígena 842 personas mayores de cinco años (pame 805).

Rayón ◆ Municipio de Sonora situado al noreste de Hermosillo y contiguo a Ures. Superficie: 1,106.54 km². Habitantes: 1,695, de los cuales 578 forman la población económicamente activa.

Rayones ◆ Municipio de Nuevo León situado al sur de Monterrey y contiguo a Linares y Montemorelos, en los límites con Coahuila. Superficie: 905.2 km². Habitantes: 2,791, de los cuales 974 forman la población económicamente activa. Hablan alguna lengua indígena cinco personas mayores de cinco años.

FOTO: FONDO EDITORIAL GRUPO AZABACHE

Iglesia de San Miguel en Rayones, Nuevo León

Durante la segunda quincena de julio se celebran en el municipio corridas de toros, para festejar la temporada de la pizca y el 12 de diciembre se festeja a la Virgen de Guadalupe con la representación de pastorelas. Cuenta con los balnearios El Toro y Romualdo.

RAZ GUZMÁN, JUAN B. ◆ n. y m. en la ciudad de México (¿1780-1830?). Abogado. Fue uno de los firmantes del acta de independencia. Oficial mayor de la Secretaría de Relaciones Exteriores, encargado del despacho (1824-25), con el Supremo Poder Ejecutivo y en el gabinete de Guadalupe Victoria.

REAL FRANYUTI, CARLOS ◆ n. en Acayucan, Ver., y m. en el DF (1898-1985). Cofundador del Partido Nacional Revolucionario y oficial mayor del PRI (1946-49). Diputado local en Veracruz y cinco veces diputado federal. Fue desaforado en 1937 por su filiación callista.

REAL Y PONTIFICIA UNIVERSIDAD DE MÉXICO ◆ Se fundó por cédula real del 21 de septiembre de 1551. La inauguración formal la hizo el catedrático Francisco Cervantes de Salazar el 3 de junio de 1553 y las clases comenzaron el lunes 5 del mismo mes. Alonso de la Veracruz fue declarado decano. El 21 de julio, en las casas de la Audiencia, en presencia del virrey y los oidores, se eligió rector a Joan Negrete. Las escuelas o facultades eran teología, derecho, artes y medicina. El financiamiento de la Universidad provenía del alquiler de inmuebles y de la explotación de extensiones agrícolas, que eran cultivadas por indios sometidos obligatoriamente a ese trabajo. A partir de 1560 la elección de rector pasó a ser atribución del claustro, especie de consejo universitario donde tenían representación las escuelas. La elección era anual y la fecha límite era el 10 de noviembre. A falta de acuerdo en el claustro, el nombramiento de rector quedaba en manos del virrey. Para ocupar el cargo de rector se requería ser estudiante, aunque con frecuencia se argüía que no había estudiante que cumpliera con los requisitos estatutarios y se elegía a un profesor. La universidad cambió de estatutos en 1580, en que adoptó los redactados por Pedro Farfán y aprobados por la Audiencia; en 1586 los del visitador Pedro Moya de Contreras; en 1626 los elaborados por una comisión. Pese a lo anterior, Juan de Palafox y Mendoza encontró que "no había estatutos determinados, por el número grande que había de ellos, observándose unas veces los de Salamanca, otras los de Lima", los de Moya o los Farfán, de los que "resultaba grande confusión, y disposición a muchas dispensaciones, desórdenes, é inconvenientes". Revocó toda la legislación anterior y en octubre de 1645 se leyeron ante el claustro las *Constituciones* dictadas por el visitador. Sin embargo, en 1694 el virrey Lope de Armendáriz dispuso su actualización. La Universidad estuvo en las casas del hospital de Nuestra Señora que se derrumbaron en 1589. En 1584 la institución obtuvo un crédito de 12,000 pesos para levantar un inmueble atrás de donde hoy está la Suprema Corte, edificio que tardó varios lustros en levantarse y que sirvió de sede definitiva. En 1593 no se había terminado y se resolvió alojar provisionalmente las escuelas en los corredores. Por bula del papa Clemente VIII, de fecha 7 de octubre de 1597, la Real Universidad se convirtió en Pontificia y sus graduados obtuvieron el derecho de enseñar en todas partes. También en 1597 se expidió la real cédula que otorgaba a los universitarios mexicanos el fuero de que disfrutaban los miembros de las universidades españolas, por lo que desde 1616 era el rector quien juzgaba ciertos delitos y las penas de prisión debían cumplirse dentro de la cárcel de la propia universidad. En 1652, el también visitador Pedro de Gálvez hizo responsable al claustro porque la Universidad, todavía en construcción, se estaba cayendo, los profesores no asistían a sus clases y la matrícula había disminuido. En junio de 1696 el mismo año, fray Felipe Galindo, obispo de Guadalajara, pidió al rector Diego de la Veguellina Chávez que recomendara a la Corona la fundación de una universidad en la capital de Nueva Galicia, a lo que se opuso el claustro. En 1709 la Real y Pontificia casa de estudios se vio obligada a ceder los salones *generales* de cánones y medicina a la Real Audiencia, en tanto se le construía a ésta un local en Palacio, lo que implicó el ingreso de guardias armados al recinto académico. Hacia 1725, el rector Pedro Ramírez del Castillo hizo construir "una sala librería" en la Universidad, que en 1729 quedó a cargo del secretario de la casa de estudios, Juan de Ímaz Esquer, que sin sueldo ni nombramiento se convirtió en el primer bibliotecario de la Universidad de México. La biblioteca se terminó hasta 1761. En 1640 se adoptó a San Luis Gonzaga y San Juan Nepomuceno como patronos de la Universidad. En 1747, una cédula real autorizó al bachiller José Mateo de Ímaz para suceder a su padre como secretario de la Universidad, pese a que no tenía la edad mínima requerida. En estos años se sucedieron las quejas porque no

Estatutos y Constituciones de la Real y Pontificia Universidad de México

se hacía el número debido de anatomías, lo que perjudicaba a los estudiantes. En 1767 fueron expulsados los jesuitas de España y sus dominios. Tres años después, la Universidad solicitó se le dieran los libros de la Compañía de Jesús. En 1774 se le entregaron los de la Casa Profesa y el claustro acordó solicitar las bibliotecas de otros colegios jesuitas. En 1768, Antonio Rafael de Portillo, quien durante más de 25 años había dirigido en la Universidad una "capilla de música", con instrumentos y voces, pidió que se designara al conjunto "Real Capilla". El claustro estuvo conforme en gestionar la petición y en que Portillo continuara como maestro del grupo filarmónico. Por gestión del rector Valentín García Narro, en 1770 el virrey dispuso que los profesores de primeras letras se sujetaran a examen en la Universidad, institución que quedó encargada de aplicar el reglamento que sobre el particular elaboró el mismo García Narro y de vigilar por la "buena y sana educación de la juventud", con lo que la Universidad se convirtió en una especie de ministerio de educación del virreinato. El 26 de abril de 1775 y 1782 el claustro rechazó la erección de la Universidad de Guadalajara. En 1777, con el tono reverencial propio del caso, el claustro abordó un problema que estallaría en 1810. En una carta al monarca español le hace ver la discriminación de que eran objeto los nacidos americanos, a quienes se negaba capacidad para todo cargo público por mero capricho, "contra la constante experiencia de su aptitud y capacidad sobresalientes". En 1788 se abrió la Real Escuela de Cirugía, ajena a la universidad, y un Jardín Botánico adscrito a la Universidad, pero con cierta autonomía que resultó inaceptable para las autoridades universitarias. En 1792 se fundó el Real Colegio de Minería. Otro golpe al exclusivismo de la Universidad de México lo constituyó la apertura, en 1793, de la Universidad de Guadalajara, al amparo de una orden real. En 1808, cuando la invasión napoleónica de España y la abdicación de los monarcas españoles, Matías de Monteagudo, representante de la Universidad a las juntas celebradas en el Palacio Virreinal, se opuso al intento autonomista de Iturrigaray y participó en su derrocamiento. En la reunión del 17 de octubre, pese a la precariedad financiera de la institución, se resolvió aportar de inmediato 10,000 y mil más cada año, para acudir en auxilio de "la sagrada persona de nuestro Rey y Señor natural el señor Don Fernando Séptimo". En 1810, al estallar la guerra de independencia, el virrey Venegas dispuso convertir la Universidad en cuartel. El 9 de octubre de 1812 los universitarios, en la capilla de la propia Universidad, juraron la Constitución de la Monarquía Española o Carta de Cádiz. Este ordenamiento conservó los fueros eclesiástico y militar, pero suprimió los demás, incluido el universitario que desapareció definitivamente, pese a que semanas después fue suspendida la vigencia de su propia Constitución. A partir de este año, el puesto de rector, antes codiciado, se convirtió en una responsabilidad pesada y onerosa para su ocupante, pues los fondos universitarios, depositados en las Cajas Reales, fueron confiscados por el estado de guerra. En octubre de 1814 debió estar muy menguada la matrícula universitaria, pues se acordó concentrar las cátedras en el salón general mayor, el que se dividiría en capilla, antecapilla y sacristía. En 1816, a cambio de 500 pesos anuales que se entregaron al virrey, la tropa desalojó el edificio de la Universidad, pero ya se había iniciado la declinación de la casa de estudios que se prolongaría medio siglo. El 6 de marzo de 1822, cuando los universitarios juraron fidelidad a la independencia del Imperio Mexicano y obediencia a sus leyes, se menciona ya no a la Real sino a la Imperial y Pontificia Universidad de México. El 29 de octubre de 1824, al jurarse la Constitución de la República, el nombre de la institución se mudó por Nacional y Pontificia Universidad de México. En noviembre de 1832, una parte de la sede universitaria fue convertida nuevamente en cuartel. El 19 de octubre de 1833, Valentín Gómez Farías, al frente del Poder Ejecutivo Federal, expidió el decreto que suprimió la Universidad. Ésta fue restablecida el 31 de julio de 1834 por Antonio López de Santa Anna. La Ley del 18 de agosto de 1843, ya bajo las centralistas *Bases Constitucionales para la Organización de la República Mexicana*, abrogó la enseñanza en la Universidad, tarea que se limitó a los colegios. Durante la intervención estadounidense, otra vez la universidad sirvió de cuartel. En 1848 había un considerable número de cátedras vacantes, a consecuencia del "abatimiento y decadencia" en que se hallaba la institución, la que ya no buscaba sucesores para los catedráticos muertos. En 1851, avanzada la agonía de la Universidad, el rector Braulio Sagaceta se refirió a la disminución de profesores "que hoy es notable y a poco más será decisiva". Paradójicamente, en 1853, bajo el último gobierno de Santa Anna, cuando se hizo llamar Alteza Serenísima, la Secretaría de Justicia, Negocios Eclesiásticos e Instrucción Pública elaboró un plan educativo que proponía hacer de la universidad una institución civil, hacer un fondo común con los diversos ingresos universitarios y suprimir la rectoría y los claustros pleno y de hacienda, para dejar en su lugar un claustro por escuela o facultad, cada una de las cuales tendría dos representantes dentro de un Consejo que, a su vez, elegiría un presidente. Los claustros tendrían por sede los respectivos colegios: el de juristas estaría en San Ildefonso, el de teólogos en el

Escudo de la Real y Pontificia Universidad de México

Juan de Palafox y Mendoza reformó los estatutos de la Real y Pontificia Universidad de México

Seminario, el de filósofos en Minería y el de médicos en la facultad correspondiente. Los canonistas deberían elegir entre el colegio de teología o el de derecho civil. Los claustros otorgarían los grados de bachiller, licenciado, profesor y doctor. El 20 de septiembre de 1857 en la Sala de Claustros se dio lectura al decreto del gobierno de Ignacio Comonfort que suprimía "esta Nacional y Pontificia Universidad" y ordenaba entregar al conservador, del Museo Nacional, "edificio, oficinas y fondos" de la institución. El gobierno conservador de Félix Zuloaga decretó el 5 de marzo de 1858 su restablecimiento, pero al triunfo del partido liberal en la guerra de los Tres Años, Ignacio Ramírez, secretario de Justicia e Instrucción Pública, comunicó a Díez de Sollano que el presidente Benito Juárez había acordado que la Universidad volviera "al estado en que se encontraba antes de la interrupción del orden legal por efecto del Plan de Tacubaya" y que, en consecuencia, debía entregar "el local, con todo lo que le pertenece", al comisionado del gobierno, Fernando Ramírez. Disponía, asimismo, que José María Benítez quedará encargado de la biblioteca, cuyos empleados seguirían percibiendo sus sueldos, en tanto que los demás empleados de la Universidad quedaban cesados. Al amparo de los invasores franceses, los conservadores quisieron revivir la vieja Universidad, pero un decreto de Maximiliano, del 30 de noviembre de 1865, confirmó la supresión definitiva de la institución.

REALH DE LEÓN, ROBERTO ◆ n. en el DF (1950). Artista plástico. Estudió dibujo, pintura y modelado en el Estudio Internacional de Arte (1964-66), pintura en la Academia de San Carlos (1966-68) y en el taller de Antonio Rodríguez Luna (1968-70); y diseño gráfico, escenografía y vestuario en la Academia di Costume, de Roma (1973-74). Ha sido profesor de artes visuales de la Escuela Activa de Croly, de la UNAM y de la UAM, e ilustrador de libros de texto y de las revistas *Universidad de México*, *Diálogos* y *Vuelta*. Colaboró en la *Revista de Bellas Artes*. Presentó su obra por primera vez en San Antonio, Texas (1970) y ha montado muestras individuales de escultura y pintura en diversas ciudades de Japón y México. Ha participado en muestras colectivas en México y otros países. Hay obras suyas en el Club de Industriales, la Pinacoteca de la Casa de la Cultura de Aguascalientes, el Museo de Arte Moderno, el Palacio de Bellas Artes, el Centro de Arte Moderno de Guadalajara y el Museo de Bulgaria. Primer premio y mención honorífica en el tercer concurso Nacional para Estudiantes de Artes Plásticas, de Aguascalientes (1968), y premio de pintura del Salón Nacional de Artes Plásticas (1980).

Mastín mexica, acrílico y óleo sobre tela de Roberto Realh de León

REBOLLAR, RAFAEL ◆ n. y m. en la ciudad de México (1847-1915). Se tituló como abogado en 1871. Fue prefecto y profesor de la Escuela Nacional de Jurisprudencia, director del *Diario Oficial*, magistrado del Tribunal de Casación, juez de lo penal, oficial mayor, secretario de gobierno (1878-98) y gobernador del Distrito Federal (de agosto de 1896 a septiembre de 1899 y de noviembre de 1899 a octubre de 1900); procurador general de la República, director de la Deuda Pública, redactor de la Ley de Jurados y miembro de la Comisión Revisora del Código de Procedimientos Penales. Colaborador de *El Renacimiento*, *El Foro*, *Gaceta Médica* y *El Anáhuac*. Miembro fundador de la Sociedad Literaria Nezahualcóyotl, socio de la Real Academia de Jurisprudencia de Madrid y del Instituto de Coimbra, de Portugal. Representó a México, como delegado del Colegio de Abogados, en el Congreso Iberoamericano de Madrid, en 1892. Autor de *Abordajes y auxilios en alta mar, entre buques de distintas naciones*. *Legislación, competencia y procedimiento para hacer efectivas las consecuencias jurídicas de estos hechos* (1897). Recibió una condecoración del gobierno español.

REBOLLEDO, EFRÉN ◆ n. en Actopan, Hgo., y m. en España (1877-1929). Licenciado por la Escuela Nacional de Jurisprudencia. Fue secretario de la legación mexicana en Guatemala (1902) y Japón (1907-17), comisionado para estudiar el establecimiento de relaciones económicas con Noruega, consejero de la representación en Cuba y Chile, jefe de Protocolo de la SRE durante el huertismo, profesor de la Escuela Nacional Preparatoria y diputado federal (1917-18 y 1920-22). Colaborador de la *Revista Moderna* y cofundador de *Nosotros*. Al morir era consejero de la legación mexicana en España. Autor de *El enemigo* (1900), *Cuarzos* (1902), *Más allá de las nubes* (1903), *Hilo de corales* (1904), *Estela* (1907), *Joyeles* (1907, reunión de sus tres primeros poemarios), *Rimas japonesas* (1909), *Nikko* (1910), *Hojas de bambú* (1910), *El desencanto de Dulcinea* (1916), *El águila que cae* (obra de teatro, 1916), *Caro Victrix* (1916), *Libro de loco amor* (1916), *Salamandra* (1919), *La saga de Sigfrida la blonda* (1922), *El enemigo* (1922) y *Joyelero* (1922). Sus *Obras completas* se editaron en 1968.

REBOLLEDO, FRANCISCO ◆ n. en el DF (1950). Hizo estudios de química y filosofía en la UNAM. Autor de novela: *Rasero* (1993, reeditada en 1995, premio Pegaso de Literatura para Latinoamérica 1994) y *La ministra* (1999). También es autor de un volumen de cuentos: *Historias del abuelo* (1997).

ARCHIVO XAVIER ESPARZA

TIBI, BEATRIX.

Clamando á tu piedad en mi suplicio,
Como en un claustro vivo en mi amargura,
Y tu desdén tenaz, como un cilicio,
Mortifica mi alma y la tortura.
Tu sólo nombre mi aflicción modera,
Y cuando á tí suspiro y en tí pienso,
Perfuma mi aflicción, como si fuera
Tu nombre un grano de oloroso incienso.
¿Me verás con tus ojos soñadores
Y me darás tus manos bendecidas,
Cuando hayas descubierto mis dolores
Y cuando hayas tocado mis heridas?
Cuando hayas descubierto mis dolores
Y cuando hayas tocado mis heridas,
Me verás con tus ojos soñadores
Y me darás tus manos bendecidas.
Eres el agua que la sed apaga,
Eres sombra, eres bien, eres dulzura,
Y para el corazón que es una llaga,
Un óleo milagroso de ternura.
Mi amor fundir espera tus enojos,
Y ya mi amor ha visto á la esperanza
En el azul abismos de tus ojos
Relucir como el signo de la alianza.
Y quiere tu bondad mi sufrimiento,
Y ante tu solio mi pasión se inclina:
Oye mi voz, alivia mi tormento,
TURRIS EBURNEA, STELLA MATUTINA.

EFREN REBOLLEDO.

Poema de Efrén Rebolledo publicado en *El Mundo Ilustrado* el 12 de marzo de 1899

REBOLLEDO, MARIO G. ◆ n. en Jalapa, Ver., y m. en el DF (1914-1987). Licenciado en derecho por la Universidad Veracruzana (1935), de la que fue profesor (1945-50). En Veracruz fue agente del Ministerio Público, auxiliar de la Procuraduría de Justicia, juez de primera instancia, presidente de la Junta Local de Conciliación y Arbitraje, secretario del Tribunal Superior de Justicia, procurador general de Justicia y secretario general de gobierno, durante la gestión de Antonio M. Quirasco. Juez decimoquinto penal del DF, magistrado del Tribunal Superior de Justicia, ministro (1955-74) y presidente (1974-76 y 1979-82) de la Suprema Corte de Justicia.

REBOLLEDO, MIGUEL ◆ n. en Perote, Ver., y m. en el DF (1868-1962). Ingeniero naval especializado en Francia. Fue funcionario de la Secretaría de Guerra y Marina. En 1902 introdujo en México el concreto armado, en sociedad con Ángel Ortiz Monasterio, y con esa técnica construyó, entre otros edificios, el del periódico *Excélsior*.

REBOLLEDO GOUT, JUAN ◆ n. en Jalapa, Ver. (1950). Licenciado en derecho por la UNAM (1973), maestro en filosofía por la Universidad de Tulane, Estados Unidos (1977) y maestro y doctor en derecho por la Universidad de Harvard (1981). Profesor de las universidades de Harvard (1979-81) y Oklahoma (1981), secretario de Proyectos en la Coordinación de Humanidades (1982), profesor (1982-86), secretario académico del Proyecto Justo Sierra (1983) y jefe de Estudios de Posgrado de la Facultad de Ciencias Políticas y Sociales de la UNAM (1983-84), vocal ejecutivo del Instituto Nacional de Estudios Históricos de la Revolución Mexicana, coordinador de asesores de la Oficina de la Presidencia, subsecretario de asuntos bilaterales y subsecretario para América del Norte y Europa de la SRE (1998-). Pertenece a la Academia Mexicana de Filosofía del Derecho, de la que fue cofundador en 1972.

REBOLLEDO MORALES, ANTONIO MATÍAS ◆ n. y m. en Coatepec, Ver. (1832-1905). Impresor y editor. Fue profesor de la Escuela Municipal de Niñas, director de la Escuela de Varones de Coatepec, fundador de la primera imprenta y de la primera librería de Coatepec, donde organizó una Sociedad de Artesanos (1873). Fundó y dirigió los periódicos *El Faro* (1879) y *Antorcha de la Niñez* (1891). Diputado federal (1877), jefe político de Coatepec y visitador general de administración del cantón del mismo nombre (1901-05). En 1891 fue premiado por la labor de difusión de obras pedagógicas extranjeras.

RÉBORA, ROBERTO ◆ n. en Guadalajara, Jal. (1963). Pintor. Comenzó dibujando caricaturas para periódicos de su ciudad. Hizo estudios en Italia en el taller de grabado Il Bisonte, donde estudió grabado y litografía. Autor de *Si existieras, señor mecenas* (1983). Becario del Fonca (1990-91).

RÉBSAMEN, ENRIQUE CONRADO ◆ n. en Suiza y m. en Jalapa, Ver. (1857-1904). Se tituló como profesor en la Normal de Kreuzlingen (1876). Estudió francés, inglés, geología, paleontología y botánica en la Universidad de Lausana; y filosofía, letras francesas e inglesas, historia y pedagogía en la Universidad de Zurich. Era director de una escuela secundaria en Alemania, hacia 1878, cuando entabló amistad con el alemán Karl von Gagern, quien había participado en las guerras de Reforma y contra la intervención francesa en México. Hacia 1883, éste persuadió a Rébsamen para trasladarse a México. Ejerció la docencia en León y pasó a Orizaba para estudiar las nuevas técnicas pedagógicas que experimentaba el alemán Heinrich Laubscher. En 1886 fue nombrado director de la Escuela Normal de Jalapa, establecida en ese año, donde difundió las ideas de Pestalozzi, Herbart, Bencke, entre otros, y fundó y dirigió la revista *México Intelectual*. En 1889 representó a Veracruz en el Congreso Pedagógico Nacional, del que fue vicepresidente. Director general de Educación Pública (reorganizó la educación primaria y fundó las escuelas normales de Oaxaca, Jalisco y Guanajuato) y, en 1901, de Enseñanza Normal, nombrado por Porfirio Díaz. Autor de *Adaptación al Atlas de Volckmar* (1888), *Método de escritura y lectura en el primer año escolar* (1899), *Guía metodológica para la enseñanza de la historia* (1890) y *Guía metodológica para maestros y alumnos* (1901).

REBULL, SANTIAGO ◆ n. en alta mar y m. en la ciudad de México (1829-1902). Pintor. Discípulo de Pelegrín Clavé en la Academia de San Carlos, a la que ingresó en 1846. Debido a su cuadro *La muerte de Abel*, en 1852 obtuvo una beca para estudiar en Roma, donde fue alumno de Tomás Ponsoni. Regresó a México en 1859. Fue profesor (1859-60) y director (1860-63, nombrado por Benito Juárez) de la Academia de San Carlos. Renunció a la llegada de los invasores franceses; no obstante, fue contratado por Maximiliano para hacer los retratos de él y de Carlota. Autor de *Jesucristo en agonía* (1851), *El sacrificio de Abraham* (1852), *Moisés* (1852), *La muerte de Abel* (1852), *El sacrificio de Isaac* (1852), *Autorretrato*, *Retrato de Maximiliano* (conservado en Austria), *Retrato de Carlota*, *Retrato de Juárez*, *Retrato de Altamirano* y *La muerte de Marat* (1875).

Obra de Santiago Rebull

RECASÉNS SICHES, LUIS ◆ n. en Guatemala y m. en el DF (1903-1975). Estudió leyes, historia y filosofía en las universidades de Barcelona, Madrid, Roma, Berlín y Viena. Ejerció la docen-

Alma Reed

cia en las Universidades de Santiago de Compostela (1927-30), Salamanca (1930), Valladolid (1931-35) y La Habana (1938). Llegó a México en 1937. Fue investigador y profesor de la UNAM. Colaboró en *Dianoia* (1956-75). Autor de *La filosofía del derecho de Francisco Suárez* (1927), *Direcciones contemporáneas del pensamiento jurídico* (1929), *Los temas de la filosofía del derecho en perspectiva histórica y visión del futuro* (1934), *Estudios de filosofía del derecho* (1935), *Vida humana, sociedad y derecho, fundamentación de la filosofía del derecho* (1939), *La filosofía del derecho en el siglo XX* (1941), *Panorama del pensamiento jurídico en el siglo XX* (2 t., 1963), *Nueva filosofía de la interpretación del derecho* (1973), *Tratado general de sociología* (1978), *Tratado general de filosofía del derecho* e *Introducción al estudio del derecho*. Miembro de la Casa de España en México (1938-40), de la Sociedad Mexicana de Filosofía, de la Academia Mexicana de Jurisprudencia, de la Asociación Nacional de Abogados de México y de El Colegio de México.

Redo, Joaquín ◆ n. en Durango, Dgo., y m. ¿en Mazatlán, Sinaloa? (?-?). Empresario. Desde su juventud destacó entre los industriales y comerciantes de Sonora, Sinaloa y Durango. Estableció en Culiacán una planta textil que quebró al poco tiempo. En 1878 abrió una fundición de fierro y una fábrica de maquinaria. Produjo azúcar, aguardiente y alcohol. Tuvo haciendas ganaderas, arroceras y cañeras. Estableció una línea de vapores para el comercio de cabotaje entre Guaymas, Mazatlán, Altata y otros puertos, misma que acabó quebrada, aunque conservó un vapor para el servicio postal. En Sinaloa introdujo la fabricación de añil, zapatería y muebles con sistemas mecánicos. La mayoría de sus empresas aparentemente le reportaban más pérdidas que ganancias, pero obtenía su capital, sobre todo, de las acciones de la empresa minera Negociación del Pánuco. Fue senador por Sinaloa (1875).

Redo de la Vega, Diego ◆ n. en Mazatlán, Sin., y m. en el DF (1869-1963). Hijo del anterior. Diputado federal y gobernador de Sinaloa (1909-11). Fue secretario particular de Porfirio Díaz durante su exilio en Francia. Fundó un ingenio azucarero en España y regresó a México a trabajar en las empresas familiares (dos ingenios y una fábrica textil). Miembro fundador de las uniones nacionales de Productores de Azúcar y de Alcohol y consejero del Banco Nacional de México y de la Compañía General de Seguros.

Redondo, Luis ◆ n. en Altar y m. en Saric, Son. (?-1850). Fue visitador de misiones (1829), presidente municipal de Altar (1830), diputado federal (1831-32), juez de paz en Hermosillo (1837), diputado a la asamblea departamental (1846), diputado local (1847), gobernador interino de Sonora (1847) y vicegobernador (1848). Durante su gestión al frente del Poder Ejecutivo sonorense tuvo facultades extraordinarias para organizar la resistencia contra la invasión estadounidense.

Redondo, Patricio ◆ n. en España y m. en San Andrés Tuxtla, Ver. (1889-1967). Profesor por la Escuela Normal Superior de Madrid, ejerció la docencia en diversas aldeas españolas. Adscrito al movimiento de la Técnica Freinet creó una escuela basada en ésta. Llegó a México en 1940 con el último grupo de refugiados de la guerra civil española. Se estableció en San Andrés Tuxtla, donde fundó una escuela para los niños que no habían encontrado cupo en las primarias oficiales. Hacia 1950, ya con ayuda de la SEP y de la Comisión del Papaloapan, fundó la Escuela Experimental Freinet. En 1959 inició estudios en la Universidad Veracruzana, en la que se doctoró en pedagogía.

Reed, Alma ◆ n. en EUA y m. en el DF (1894-1966). Periodista. En California, donde era trabajadora social, defendió a un inmigrante mexicano condenado a muerte y lo salvó. A raíz de este caso, la legislatura californiana aprobó una ley contra la ejecución de menores de 18 años. Estudió historia y literatura en Italia y Grecia. Colaboró en el *New York Times*, periódico que la envió a Yucatán a hacer un reportaje sobre ruinas mayas. Conoció al gobernador Felipe Carrillo Puerto. Se interesó por el muralismo mexicano, que dio a conocer en su país. Volvió a Estados Unidos, fue editora del *San Francisco Call Bulletin*, directora cultural de la *Mobile Press Register* y fundadora de los estudios Delphic, que promovieron, entre otros, a José Clemente Orozco. En 1933 abrió en Chicago una galería de pintura mexicana y más tarde creó, en Alabama, la Sociedad Estadounidense de Amigos de México. Volvió a dedicarse al periodismo durante la segunda guerra mundial. En México publicó sus trabajos en *The News*, *Novedades* y *Mexican Life*. Autora de *Dedication* (1928), *Cumal* (1930), *José Clemente Orozco* (1932, traducido al español en 1955), *Mexican muralists* (1960), *Ten leading mexican mural painters* (1966) y *The ancient past of Mexico*. El gobierno mexicano le concedió el Águila Azteca (1961). Se hizo acreedora a la Orden del Santo Sepulcro, de la Iglesia Ortodoxa, y a la Medalla al Mérito del gobierno libanés. En 1923, a instancias de Carrillo Puerto, Luis Rosado Vega y Ricardo Palmerín compusieron en su honor la canción *Peregrina*.

Reed, John ◆ n. en EUA y m. en la URSS (1887-1920). Estudió en Harvard (1910). En sus años de estudiante fundó un club socialista. Trabajó en las redacciones de los periódicos *Saturday Evening Post*, *Collier's* y *Smart Set*, donde destacó por sus campañas de denuncia contra la Standard Oil y Rockefeller. Desde 1911 fue corresponsal en México del *Metropolitan Magazine* y presenció como reportero la revolución en el norte del país. Colaboró en la revista *The Masses* desde 1913, fue corresponsal en la primera guerra mundial y cubrió la información de la revolución rusa de 1917, cuando participó en la fundación del Partido Comunista de Estados Unidos. Se le abrió un proceso por sedición, en 1918, pero fue absuelto. Regresó a la URSS, trabajó en la oficina de propaganda y fue nombrado cónsul soviético en Nueva York, cargo que el gobierno estadounidense objetó. Murió de tifo y sus restos están sepultados en la Plaza Roja de Moscú. Autor de *Insurgent Mexico* (1914, traducido al español en 1954), *Ten Days that Shook the World* (1919) e *Hija de la revolución* (1931). Reed escribió además varios artículos y reportajes sobre la lucha armada en el norte de México, que fueron traducidos y publicados en 1983 por Jorge Ruffinelli en el volumen *Villa y la revolución mexicana*.

Reed Torres, Luis ◆ n. en el DF (1947). Historiador y periodista. Estudió historia en la UNAM. Ha publicado en *El Sol de México*, *Impacto*, *Jueves de Excélsior*, *Revista de Revistas* y *El Heraldo de México*, del que fue jefe de la sección internacional, así como en la revista *Negocios y Bancos*, de la que fue subdirector. Fue jefe de prensa de la Canaco y ha sido coordinador de asesores de la Coordinación General de Comunicación Social del ISSSTE. Coautor de *El periodismo en México: 500 años de historia* (1973, reeditado en 1981 y 1995). Autor de *El almirante de las mil nacionalidades* (1988), *El general Tomás Mejía frente a la doctrina Monroe* (1989) y *El panteón del Tepeyac y sus residentes* (1996).

Reforma ◆ Diario editado en la ciudad de México a partir del 20 de noviembre de 1993. Es filial de *El Norte*, de Monterrey. Su director es Alejandro Junco de la Vega y ha contado entre sus colaboradores a Jesús Silva-Herzog Márquez, Miguel Ángel Granados Chapa, Raymundo Riva Palacio, René Delgado, Adolfo Aguilar Zínser, Carlos

Carrera al cielo

REFORMA

Cae 36% cartera vencida

Se salva Bush Jr. de sufrir accidente

CALAVERAS '99

Reforma

Fuentes y Guadalupe Loaeza. Tiene un suplemento cultural, *El Ángel*, y otro político, *Enfoque*.

Reforma ◆ Municipio de Chiapas situado en el extremo norte del estado, al noroeste de San Cristóbal de Las Casas, al norte de Tuxtla Gutiérrez y en los límites con Tabasco. Superficie: 399.9 km². Habitantes: 32,283, de los cuales 7,838 forman la población económicamente activa. Hablan alguna lengua indígena 159 personas mayores de cinco años.

Reforma, La ◆ Municipio de Oaxaca situado al noreste de Santiago Pinotepa Nacional y contiguo a Putla de Guerrero. Superficie: 496.3 km². Habitantes: 3,338, de los cuales 692 forman la población económicamente activa. Hablan alguna lengua indígena 14 personas mayores de cinco años.

Reforma ◆ Proceso histórico del siglo pasado que expresó el conflicto económico, político, social y religioso que existía desde la consumación de la independencia. Se manifestó inicialmente en la pugna entre centralistas y federalistas, partidos que después se conocieron como conservadores y liberales o imperiales y republicanos. Ambas facciones deseaban el desarrollo de la economía de mercado. La primera mediante la alianza entre las clases propietarias, la aristocracia colonial, el ejército y la jerarquía eclesiástica, para lo cual debían respetarse los privilegios de estos sectores sociales y establecerse un gobierno fuertemente centralizado. El otro bando planteaba la necesidad de descentralizar el poder, abrir oportunidades económicas para todos, lo que implicaba eliminar monopolios y privilegios, y lanzar al mercado las propiedades de *manos muertas*, esto es, los bienes de los pueblos, la Iglesia y otras corporaciones, protegidos por un régimen de tenencia que hacía inenajenable la tierra y demás riquezas. En 1833-34, el vicepresidente Valentín Gómez Farías (☛) se alternó cuatro veces en la jefatura del Poder Ejecutivo con Antonio López de Santa Anna e inició la llamada Primera Reforma, programa reformista de gobierno tendiente a abolir los fueros e inmunidades del clero y los militares, a desamortizar la propiedad territorial de la Iglesia, romper su monopolio sobre la educación y a posibilitar la igualdad de oportunidades económicas y políticas. Gómez Farías fue destituido y Santa Anna suprimió todas las disposiciones reformistas de su antecesor. En 1847 Gómez Farías, de nuevo vicepresidente, para allegarse fondos que sirvieran en la lucha contra la agresión de Estados Unidos, decretó la ocupación de bienes de la Iglesia, lo que produjo la rebelión de los polkos y su caída. Después de la intervención estadounidense, Lucas Alamán empezó a promover el establecimiento de un régimen monárquico, idea que encontró fuerte oposición. La inestabilidad política facilitó en 1853 el regreso al poder de Santa Anna, quien declaró abolida la Constitución de 1824 y ejerció una dictadura con rasgos aristocratizantes que contó con el apoyo de los conservadores. El 1 de marzo de 1854 se proclamó el Plan de Ayutla, en la población guerrerense del mismo nombre, que proponía un programa político liberal. El alzamiento pronto se convirtió en un movimiento revolucionario de alcance nacional que tuvo como líder al viejo insurgente Juan Álvarez, quien recibió el apoyo, entre

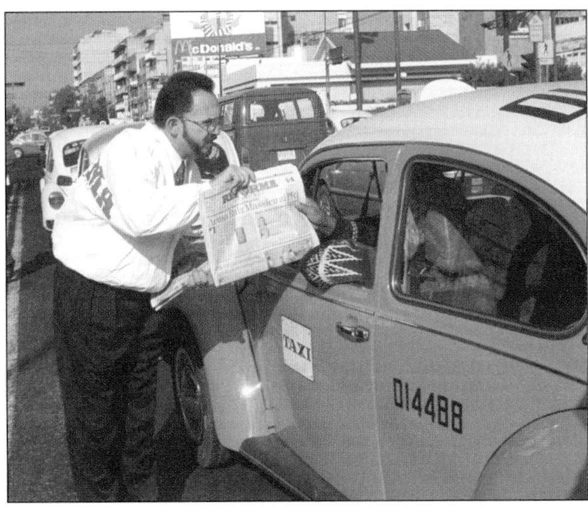

Alejandro Junco de la Vega

Juan Álvarez, jefe de la Revolución de Ayutla

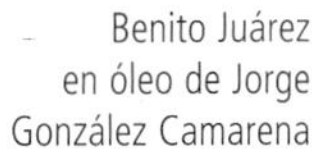

Benito Juárez en óleo de Jorge González Camarena

Benito Juárez, líder de la Reforma, en un detalle de *Sueño de una tarde dominical en la Alameda Central*, de Diego Rivera

otros, de Ignacio Comonfort, Epitacio Huerta, Santos Degollado, Ignacio de la Llave, Luis de la Rosa, José María Lafragua, Manuel Doblado, Benito Juárez, Melchor Ocampo, Guillermo Prieto, Ponciano Arriaga, Francisco Zarco y José María Mata. La revolución de Ayutla triunfó y Santa Anna abandonó el poder y el país en agosto de 1855. Juan Álvarez fue elegido presidente interino y convocó a un Congreso Constituyente. A fines del mismo año nombró presidente sustituto a Ignacio Comonfort y le entregó el poder. Entre tanto, el 23 de noviembre se expidió la Ley Juárez, que suprimió los tribunales militares y eclesiásticos y abolió los fueros de los representantes de ambas instituciones. El 28 de diciembre de 1855 se expidió la Ley Lafragua, en la que se consideraba abuso de la libertad de imprenta el ataque directo a la religión católica. El presidente Comonfort debió enfrentar varios pronunciamientos conservadores durante 1856. Antes de que terminaran los trabajos del Congreso Constituyente, Comonfort

Melchor Ocampo, uno de los redactores de las Leyes de Reforma

expidió el Estatuto Orgánico Provisional, que mezclaba las ideas reformistas con disposiciones que intentaban apaciguar a los conservadores. Comonfort confirmó la Ley Juárez, extinguió la Compañía de Jesús, redujo el número de efectivos militares y el 25 de junio expidió la Ley Lerdo, que desamortizaba los bienes del clero en todo el país. Asimismo, estableció el Registro Civil y disolvió la comunidad franciscana. Estas medidas, cuyo fin último era el de liberar a la economía de mercado de sus viejas ataduras, hicieron crecer la tensión entre la Iglesia y el Estado, lo que anunciaba la proximidad de una nueva guerra civil. La Constitución del 5 de febrero de 1857 dejó en manos del gobierno la autoridad sobre actos de culto externo, con lo que abrió la posibilidad de ejercer la libertad religiosa. El 11 de abril de 1857 fue dictada la Ley Iglesias, decreto federal que señalaba los aranceles parroquiales para el cobro de derechos y obvenciones. Esta legislación provocó protestas de los representantes eclesiásticos, entre ellos, las de Clemente de Jesús Munguía, obispo de Michoacán, y de Lázaro de la Garza y Ballesteros, arzobispo de México, y algunos levantamientos armados que sofocó el gobierno. La división de los liberales entre moderados y *puros* se hizo más notoria. Los primeros, encabezados por Comonfort, Lafragua y Manuel Doblado, temían que la reacción conservadora pusiera en peligro el orden y se inclinaban por hacer concesiones a sus adversarios, aun a costa de modificar radicalmente la Constitución en espera de mejores tiempos. Los *puros* o *rojos*, como también se les llamaba, defendían cabalmente la Constitución de 1857 y se oponían a toda medida que significara un retroceso. En esta facción se contaban Benito Juárez, Santos Degollado, Francisco Zarco, Guillermo Prieto e Ignacio Ramírez. El 17 de diciembre de 1857 se produjo el pronunciamiento del Plan de Tacubaya, encabezado por Félix María Zuloaga, al que se adhirió Ignacio Comonfort, con lo que el presidente desconoció la Constitución y encarceló a varios legisladores y a Benito Juárez, presidente de la Suprema Corte de Justicia. El Plan de Tacubaya fue modificado por el pronunciamiento de la Ciudadela (11 de enero de 1858), de José de la Parra, quien desconoció a Comonfort y nombró presidente a Zuloaga. Juárez, liberado poco antes, se trasladó a Guanajuato y, en su carácter de jefe del Poder Judicial, asumió por ministerio de ley la Presidencia de la República el 19 de enero de ese año. El país tuvo de esta manera dos presidentes, cada uno al frente de uno de los bandos en que se dividió el país, que en estos años vivió la guerra de los Tres Años o guerra de Reforma. Zuloaga expidió las Cinco Leyes, con las que anulaba las reformas liberales. Los conservadores contaban con destacados jefes, todos ellos militares profesionales: el propio Zuloaga, Tomás Mejía, Severo del Castillo, Joaquín Orihuela, Leonardo Marquez, Luis Gonzaga Osollo y, el más brillante de todos, Miguel Miramón. Los liberales estaban encabezados por

Miguel Miramón, líder de los conservadores

un civil, Benito Juárez, y tenían líderes militares salidos de las filas del pueblo, como Santos Degollado, Mariano Escobedo, Jesús González Ortega, Epitacio Huerta, Manuel Doblado, Ignacio Zaragoza, Juan Zuazua, Leandro Valle, Santiago Vidaurri y el guerrillero Antonio Rojas. El 10 de marzo de 1858, Osollo derrotó en Salamanca a los liberales. El gobierno juarista, establecido en Guadalajara en febrero del mismo año, debió enfrentar un motín de la guarnición militar durante el cual Guillermo Prieto salvó a Juárez de ser fusilado en el acto. Ante la presión militar de Osollo, Juárez y su gabinete huyeron hacia Colima y las fuerzas conservadoras ocuparon Guadalajara el 23 de marzo de 1858. El 7 de abril la comitiva juarista marchó al puerto de Manzanillo, donde se embarcó para cruzar el istmo de Panamá y dirigirse a La Habana, Nueva Orleans y, finalmente, Veracruz, a donde llegó el 4 de mayo e instaló su gobierno. Ahí, Juárez expidió las Leyes de Reforma, redactadas por Melchor Ocampo y Miguel Lerdo de Tejada: Ley de Nacionalización de los Bienes Eclesiásticos, Ley de Matrimonio Civil, Ley Orgánica del Registro Civil, Ley Sobre el Estado Civil de las Personas y la Ley sobre Libertad de Cultos, así como los decretos que cancelaban la intervención del clero en los cementerios y camposantos, establecían los días festivos y prohibían la asistencia oficial a las funciones de la Iglesia, secularizaban los hospitales y establecimientos de beneficencia y extinguían las comunidades religiosas. Antes de embarcarse en el Pacífico, Juárez nombró al secretario de Gobernación, Santos Degollado, general en jefe de las fuerzas liberales. El conservador Osollo murió, por enfermedad, el 18 de junio de 1858 y la jefatura del ejército conservador recayó en Miguel Miramón, quien se propuso destruir las fuerzas de Santos Degollado, objetivo que no consiguió pues, a pesar de sus numerosas derrotas, el liberal siempre se reorganizaba y mantenía el control en el sur de Jalisco, Michoacán y Colima. Miramón también enderezó sus ataques contra las fuerzas de Santiago Vidaurri, quien dominaba Nuevo León y Coahuila y amenazaba San Luis Potosí y Zacatecas, aunque tampoco tuvo éxito en esa empresa. Un tercer objetivo del jefe conservador fue la toma de Veracruz, que intentó infructuosamente en tres ocasiones: la primera vez, la ofensiva correría a cargo de Miguel María Echegaray, quien la frustró con su alzamiento de Ayotla, mediante el cual trataba de crear un tercer partido político que conciliase los intereses de liberales y conservadores. Los pronunciados de Ayotla destituyeron al presidente conservador Zuloaga y entregaron el poder a Miramón (enero de 1859), quien restituyó a Zuloaga como presidente interino para que éste designara presidente sustituto a Miramón (31 de enero de 1859). El segundo intento de tomar Veracruz se frustró por el ataque de Santos Degollado a la ciudad de México, acción en la que el liberal fue derrotado por Leonardo Márquez (en Tacubaya, el 11 de abril de 1859) con el concurso de Miramón. El tercer ataque a Veracruz, un sitio por tierra y mar, fracasó cuando las fragatas conservadoras *El Miramón* y *Marqués de La Habana*, declaradas piratas, fueron capturadas en cumplimiento de las leyes internacionales por la corbeta estadounidense *Saratoga*, el 6 de marzo de 1860. Entre tanto, las fuerzas liberales iniciaban el dominio del Bajío, Oaxaca y el noroeste de México. Los conservadores iniciaron su repliegue hasta ser definitivamente derrotados en la batalla de Calpulalpan, el 22 de diciembre de 1860. Las fuerzas liberales entraron triunfantes en la ciudad de México el 1 de enero de 1861 y 10 días después lo hizo Juárez, quien convocó a elecciones, resultó triunfador y tomó posesión como presidente constitucional en junio de ese año. La lucha entre conservadores y liberales no cesó con el triunfo de estos últimos. Hubo enfrentamientos y crisis que desembocaron en la intervención francesa y el imperio. Con la retirada de las tropas de Napoleón III y el fusilamiento de Maximiliano y sus dos principales colaboradores, se impuso definitivamente la legislación liberal. En 1873, durante la presidencia de Sebastián Lerdo de Tejada, las Leyes de Reforma fueron incorporadas a la Constitución.

Reforma de Pineda ◆ Municipio de Oaxaca situado en el istmo de Tehuantepec, al este de Juchitán de Zaragoza. Superficie: 193.92 km^2. Habitantes: 2,580, de los cuales 699 forman la población económicamente activa. Hablan alguna lengua indígena 81 personas mayores de cinco años.

Regato, José María del ◆ n. y m. en Durango, Dgo. (1800-1856). Ingeniero. Fue gobernador de Durango (1835), diputado al segundo Congreso Constituyente local, jefe político de San Dimas (1849) y nuevamente gobernador de Durango desde el 1 de enero de 1852. En diciembre del mismo año rechazó unirse al pronunciamiento contra el presidente Mariano Arista y abandonó la gubernatura. En 1855, al triunfo de la revolución de Ayutla, volvió a ser gobernador hasta 1856. Durante su gestión intentó sin éxito aplicar algunas leyes reformistas. Fue después primer director del Instituto Civil, miembro del Consejo de Gobierno y del Tribunal de Minería y senador.

Regazzoni, Ricardo ◆ n. en el DF (1942). Escultor. Arquitecto por la UNAM (1967), especializado en el Instituto de Urbanismo de París (1970-72) y en diversos museos de Estados Unidos (1978-80). Ha sido profesor de la UNAM (1967-75), jefe de

Palma, escultura en madera y hoja de oro de Ricardo Regazzoni

Diseño y Arquitectura del Departamento de Museos del INAH, jefe de diseño del Departamento de Ferias y Exposiciones del Instituto Mexicano de Comercio Exterior (1972-73) y diseñador del Museo Hirshhorn y del Jardín de Esculturas de Washington. Ha expuesto individualmente en México y Guadalajara, y colectivamente en México, Guadalajara, Buenos Aires, Barcelona y Cali.

REGENCIA, PRIMERA ◆ El 28 de septiembre de 1821, un día después de la entrada triunfal del ejército trigarante en la ciudad de México, se instaló este cuerpo, previsto por el Plan de Iguala, compuesto por Agustín de Iturbide, Manuel de la Bárcena, José Isidro Yáñez, Manuel Velázquez de León y Juan O'Donojú. Éste murió al mes siguiente y fue sustituido por Antonio Joaquín Pérez. Esta Regencia cesó en sus funciones el 11 de abril de 1822.

REGENCIA, SEGUNDA ◆ El 11 de abril de 1822, el Congreso Constituyente sustituyó a Manuel de la Bárcena, Antonio Joaquín Pérez y Manuel Velázquez de León (integrantes de la primera Regencia) por Nicolás Bravo, el conde de la Casa de Heras y Miguel Valentín, quienes formaron la segunda Regencia junto con Agustín de Iturbide y José Isidro Yáñez. El 18 de mayo de 1822 desapareció este cuerpo al proclamarse a Iturbide como emperador (☛ *Imperio Mexicano*).

REGENCIA DEL IMPERIO ◆ El 10 de julio de 1863, el llamado Poder Legislativo convirtió en Regencia del Imperio Mexicano al Supremo Poder Ejecutivo, triunvirato designado de acuerdo con las normas dictadas por el mariscal Forey, comandante de las fuerzas francesas de ocupación. La Regencia fue el cuerpo encargado de ofrecer a Maximiliano la Corona de México, asunto arreglado desde 1861. El 10 de abril 1864, cuando el austriaco hizo la aceptación formal del trono, disolvió la Regencia, órgano que integraron el arzobispo Antonio Pelagio de Labastida y Dávalos y los generales Juan Nepomuceno Almonte y Mariano Salas. El obispo Juan Ormaechea y el licenciado Antonio Pavón fungieron como suplentes (☛ *Imperio de Maximiliano*).

REGENERACIÓN ◆ Periódico político antiporfirista cuyo primer número apareció el 7 de agosto de 1900, en la ciudad de México, publicado por los hermanos Antonio Horcasitas, Jesús y Ricardo Flores Magón. Reprimidos sus editores el 21 de mayo de 1901, pasó a imprimirse en el taller del *Diario del Hogar*, hasta el 7 de octubre, cuando se suspendió la publicación, con los hermanos Flores Magón en la cárcel. En noviembre de 1904, en San Antonio, Texas, se inició la segunda época del periódico, con Ricardo Flores Magón como director, Juan Sarabia como jefe de redacción y Enrique Flores Magón a cargo de la administración. En enero de 1905 dejó de editarse. Reapareció al mes siguiente en San Luis Missouri. El 12 de octubre fue destruida su imprenta y se suspendió nuevamente la publicación. El 1 de febrero de 1906 se empezó a imprimir en otro taller y a partir del 20 de marzo, cuando los Flores Magón y Juan Sarabia tuvieron que huir hacia Canadá, quedaron como editores Librado Rivera y Manuel Sarabia. A fines de septiembre, la represión impidió otra vez que continuara publicándose este órgano. El 3 de septiembre de 1910, en Los Ángeles, California, dio principio la tercera época del periódico, editado por Anselmo L. Figueroa. Eran colaboradores los hermanos Flores Magón, Lázaro Gutiérrez de Lara, Antonio I. Villarreal y Alfred Sanftleben, quien se hacía cargo de la sección en inglés. Después de una oleada de detenciones, en junio de 1911, Enrique Flores Magón, libre bajo fianza, continuó publicando *Regeneración*. El periódico apareció muy irregularmente en 1912 y 1913, dirigido entonces por Blas Lara con Antonio P. Araujo como colaborador. En enero de 1914 salieron de la cárcel los hermanos Flores Magón, Librado Rivera y Anselmo L. Figueroa, quienes normalizaron la publicación. El 18 de febrero de 1916 vuelven a la cárcel los Flores Magón y su órgano es sacado de registro, lo que dificulta su circulación. Al salir de prisión se reincoporan al periódico. En marzo de 1918, Ricardo Flores Magón y Librado Rivera son encarcelados y *Regeneración* desaparece definitivamente. (*Cfr.*: Bartra, Armando. *Regeneración 1900-1918*).

Regeneración.
Semanal revolucionario.
La Revolucion en Mexico.
Cronica Pormenorizada de los Ultimos Acontecimientos

Regeneración

REGIL Y DE LA PUENTE, PEDRO MANUEL DE ◆ n. en España y m. en Campeche, Camp. (1774-1855). Comerciante en Veracruz y Campeche, en 1811 fue síndico procurador de esta ciudad y un año después fue elegido diputado por Yucatán a las Cortes de Cádiz, aunque no acudió a ellas por su mal estado de salud. El gobernador yucateco, Castro y Araos, se opuso a promulgar en la península la Constitución de Cádiz. Regil y otros diputados encabezaron un movimiento por el que ésta fue jurada en Campeche en 1820, lo que obligó a Castro a hacer lo propio en Mérida. Regil presidió, en 1823, la instalación del primer Congreso local yucateco. Autor de *Memoria instructiva sobre el comercio general de Yucatán, en particular de Campeche* (1812), *Instrucciones que la diputación provincial de Yucatán dio a los señores diputados que eligió para concurrir a las Cortes Generales y ordinarias de la monarquía española de los años de 1821-1822*.

REGIL RODRÍGUEZ, MATEO DE ◆ n. en Ahualulco, SLP (1923). Cirujano por la UNAM, con un posgrado en oftalmología por la Asociación para Evitar la Ceguera en México. Ha sido oftalmólogo del IMSS (1951), profesor en la UNAM, médico, jefe del servicio y jefe de clínica de la Asociación para Evitar la Ceguera en México, diputado federal por el Distrito Federal (1982-85) y presidente del Congreso del Trabajo. Pertenece a la Sociedad Mexicana de Oftalmología y a la Sociedad Oftalmológica Manuel Covarrubias.

Registro, del ◆ Sierra de Durango. Es una de las estribaciones orientales de la sierra Madre Occidental, que separa al valle de Guadiana o Durango del de Nombre de Dios.

Reglamento Provisional Político del Imperio Mexicano ◆ Cuerpo de leyes aprobado el 18 de diciembre de 1822 por la Junta Nacional Instituyente, organismo creado por Agustín de Iturbide luego de disolver el Congreso General. El Reglamento, puesto en vigor el 24 de febrero de 1823, fue formulado por Iturbide y es, de hecho, la primera Carta Magna mexicana. El artículo 90 de este Reglamento, dice Felipe Tena Ramírez, "se refirió al problema agrario por primera vez en los anales legislativos" del México independiente, pues ordenaba a las autoridades locales "enviar al gobierno supremo para su aprobación planes juiciosos, según los cuales, pueda hacerse efectivo en plena propiedad, entre los ciudadanos indígenas y entre los beneméritos e industriosos, el repartimiento de tierras comunes o realengas, salvo los ejidos precisos a cada población". El 19 de marzo de 1823 Iturbide abdicó, presionado por los pronunciados del Plan de Casa Mata, y el Congreso anuló todos sus actos el 8 de abril, con lo que el Reglamento fue abolido.

Regueiro, Luis ◆ n. en España y m. en el DF (1908-1995). Futbolista conocido como *el Corso*. Estudió la carrera de perito mercantil y se desempeñó como agente aduanal. Desde 1921 jugó en el equipo Real Unión Club de Irún, con el que ganó en 1924 la Copa de España, y se hizo profesional al incorporarse al Real Madrid (1932). Fue seleccionado español y participó en los Juegos Olímpicos de 1928 y en el Campeonato Mundial de 1934 en Italia; jugó también en la Selección Vasca, antifascista, formada en 1936. Con ese equipo llegó a México en 1937; decidió quedarse en este país y jugó en el equipo Asturias. Se retiró como jugador en 1940, fue entrenador del América y se dedicó después a la actividad comercial.

Régules ◆ Municipio de Michoacán situado en la ribera del lago de Chapala, en los límites con Jalisco, y contiguo a Sahuayo. Superficie: 387.98 km^2. Habitantes: 10,480, de los cuales 2,631 forman la población económicamente activa. Hablan alguna lengua indígena 32 personas mayores de cinco años. Su cabecera es Cojumatlán de Régules.

Régules, Nicolás de ◆ n. en España y m. en la ciudad de México (1826-1895). Militar liberal. Combatió a los carlistas en su país. Se exilió en Cuba y Estados Unidos antes de llegar a México, en 1846. Se integró en 1847 al Ejército Mexicano y peleó contra los invasores estadounidenses en la Angostura, Padierna, Molino del Rey y Chapultepec. En 1855 se adhirió a la revolución de Ayutla, a las órdenes de Epitacio Huerta, en Michoacán. Obtuvo el grado de general de brigada durante la guerra de los Tres Años. Al iniciarse la intervención de la Triple Alianza pidió su retiro para no luchar contra España, pero tomó las armas en Michoacán contra los invasores franceses y el imperio. En 1865 ascendió a general de división. Sustituyó al general Arteaga en el mando del Ejército del Centro; incorporado al Ejército de Occidente, participó en el sitio de Querétaro. Al triunfo de la República comandó la División del Centro. Durante la presidencia de Manuel González fue vicepresidente de la Suprema Corte de Justicia Militar.

Régulo ◆ n. y m. en el DF (1916-1987). Cómico de nombre Manuel Tamez Herrera. Inició su carrera profesional en las carpas. Hizo pareja con Francisco Fuentes, con quien formó el dúo *Faustis y Cornis*, que más tarde se convirtió en *Régulo y Madaleno*. Con este nombre se presentaron en la radio y en el teatro de revista. Con *Madaleno* actuó en las películas *Una gringa en México* (1950), *Retorno al quinto patio* (1951), *Ella y yo* (1952), *Del rancho a la televisión* (1952), *Yo soy mexicano de acá de este lado* (1953). En radio trabajó en el programa *El Risámetro*. En 1973 recibió la Medalla Virginia Fábregas de la ANDA.

Rehilete, El ◆ Revista literaria trimestral fundada por iniciativa de Beatriz Espejo y Margarita Peña. En su directorio estuvieron algunas integrantes del taller de narrativa de Juan José Arreola: Blanca Malo, Lourdes de la Garza, Thelma Nava, Guadalupe de León, Esther Ortega, Carmen Rosenzweig, Elsa de Llarena y Rosa María Galindo. Su primer número apareció en abril de 1961. En su nómina de colaboradores figuraron Elena Poniatowska, Froylán Ojeda, José Luis Cuevas, Jaime Augusto Shelley, Alfonso de Neuvillate, Federico Campbell, Angelina Muñiz, Juan Tovar, Fernando Macotela, Luis Mario Schneider, Edmundo Valadés, José Emilio Pacheco, José Luis Martínez, Agustín Yáñez, Tomás Segovia, Vicente Leñero, José Revueltas, Antonio Alatorre, Marco Antonio Montes de Oca, Alfonso Reyes, Juan Rejano, Miguel Donoso Pareja, Ernesto Cardenal, Ramón Xirau, Eduardo Lizalde, Salvador Elizondo, Efraín Huerta, Francisco Monterde, Ermilo Abreu Gómez, Rafael Gutiérrez Girardot, Guadalupe Dueñas, Leopoldo Chagoyán Beltrán, María Teresa Vieyra, Efrén Hernández, Carlos Pellicer, Julio Torri, Juan José Arreola, Francisco Arrabal, Rosario Castellanos, Manuel Alcalá, Sergio Fernández, Ernesto Mejía Sánchez y Rubén Bonifaz Nuño. En 1970 se incorporaron al consejo de redacción Mariano Flores Castro y Mario del Valle. Su último número fue el de enero de 1971.

Reiche, Karl Friedrich ◆ n. en Alemania y m. en el DF (1860-1932). Botánico. Fue profesor del Instituto Agronómico e investigador del Museo Nacional de Santiago de Chile. Llegó a México a principios de siglo. Se desempeñó como profesor en la Universidad Nacional y fue miembro del Instituto Médico Nacional. Autor de *Lecturas botánicas* (1918), *La vegetación de los alrededores de la capital de México* (1924), *Flora*

Nicolás de Régules

Manuel Crescencio Rejón

Carlos Reinoso

Juan Rejano según Moreno Villa

excursoria en el valle central de México. Claves analíticas y descripciones de las familias y géneros fanerogámicos (1926), *Lecturas biológicas* (1928), *Elementos de botánica para la enseñanza agrícola forestal* (1929) y *Kreuz und quer durch Mexiko* (1930).

Reichenbach, Francois ◆ n. y m. en Francia (1921-1993). Cineasta. Dirigió las películas *Un corazón así de grande, la América insólita* (1959), *la Douceur du Village* (Gran Premio del Festival de Cannes al mejor cortometraje, 1964) *México, México, El quinto sol* (1965), *Arthur Rubinstein, el amor de mi vida* (Óscar al mejor largometraje documental, 1970), *¿No oyes ladrar los perros?* (1975, basada en relatos de Juan Rulfo) y *Pelé* (1977), entre otras. Fue miembro del jurado del Festival de Cannes en 1965. La Academia Francesa lo premió por el conjunto de su obra en 1975. Fue nombrado Gran Oficial de la Orden Nacional del Mérito de Francia en 1991.

Reino Unido ◆ ☛ *Gran Bretaña e Irlanda del Norte, Reino Unido de.*

Reinoso, Carlos ◆ n. en Chile (1945). Futbolista. Seleccionado chileno desde los 17 años, jugó en el Campeonato Mundial de 1974. Llegó a México en 1970 para jugar con el equipo América. Ha sido director técnico de varios equipos, entre ellos América y León.

Rejano, Juan ◆ n. en España y m. en el DF (1903-1976). Poeta y periodista. Fue soldado en Marruecos y, en Madrid, uno de los integrantes de la editorial Cenit. Miembro del Partido Comunista Español, durante la guerra civil ejerció el periodismo. Salió de España en el barco *Sinaia*, a bordo del cual fundó con Manuel Andújar el primer diario de la emigración, el *Sinaia*. Llegó exiliado en 1939 y obtuvo la nacionalidad mexicana dos años después. Fundó y dirigió las revistas literarias *Ars*, *España*, *Paz*, *Litoral* (1944), *Romance* y *Ultramar* (1947), dirigió el suplemento *Revista Mexicana de Cultura* de *El Nacional* (1947-57 y 1969-75) y coordinó la página cultural del mismo diario, para el que colaboraba desde 1942 y donde publicaba la columna "Cuadernillo de señales". Fue profesor en la Universidad de Nuevo León (1952-1953). Autor de *El modernismo*, *Fidelidad del sueño* (1943), *El genil y los olivos* (1944), *El poeta y su pueblo* (1944), *La esfinge mestiza* (1945), *Víspera heroica* (1947), *El oscuro límite* (1948), *Noche adentro* (1949), *Oda española* (1949), *Constelación menor* (1950), *Canciones a la paz* (1955), *El río y la paloma* (1960), *El libro de los homenajes* (1961), *Elegía rota para un himno. En la muerte de Julián Grimau* (1963), *El jazmín y la llama* (1965) y *La tarde* (1976). En 1975 la UNAM reunió su obra en el volumen *Alas de tierra*.

Rejón, Manuel Crescencio ◆ n. en Bolonchenticul, Yuc., y m. en la ciudad de México (1799-1849). Creador del juicio de amparo. Diputado al Congreso General (1822-23), pidió la independencia de Tabasco con respecto a Yucatán y la abolición de pensiones y encomiendas a los descendientes de los conquistadores; defendió las ideas republicanas, liberales y federalistas y se opuso a Iturbide, por lo que fue encarcelado cuando éste disolvió el Congreso (1822). Una vez en libertad pasó a Puebla y se dedicó a imprimir folletos. Diputado al Congreso Constituyente (1823-24), como miembro de la Comisión de Constitución fue uno de los redactores de la Carta de 1824. Diputado federal (1827-28) y senador por Yucatán (1829-30, 1831-32 y 1833-34). Estuvo en la cárcel por su oposición al golpe de Estado de Anastasio Bustamante y luego se exilió en EUA. A su regreso apoyó la gestión reformista de Gómez Farías. Encabezó la comisión que redactó la Constitución de Yucatán (1841). Ministro plenipotenciario de México en Sudamérica. En 1843 formó parte del Consejo de Gobierno. Secretario de Relaciones Exteriores e Interiores (del 19 de agosto al 12 de septiembre, del 12 al 21 de septiembre y del 21 de septiembre al 6 de diciembre de 1844, y del 27 de agosto al 20 de octubre de 1846) en los gabinetes de Santa Anna, Herrera, Canalizo y Salas. Diputado federal (1846), se opuso a la firma del tratado que cedió la mitad del territorio mexicano a Estados Unidos (1848). Colaboró en el *Correo de la Federación*.

Relación de Michoacán

Rejón Peraza, Luis Alberto ◆ n. en Mérida, Yuc. (1945). Licenciado en derecho por la Universidad de Yucatán (1981). Afiliado al PAN, ha sido secretario de afiliación del comité de ese partido en Yucatán, miembro de su departamento jurídico, diputado local (1988 -90) y diputado federal (1991-94).

Reko Blas, Pablo ◆ n. en Austria y m. en Oaxaca, Oax. (1876-1953). Se tituló como médico en la Universidad de Viena (1901). Llegó a México en 1911. Ejerció su profesión en Guadalajara en 1922, en el Distrito Federal y en Monterrey (1923). Trabajó 15 años como médico de una compañía minera en Oaxaca, aunque su interés se centró en la numerología y en la herbolaria. Relacionó los nombres indígenas de las plantas medicinales con sus etimologías, luego éstas con la mitología y así llegó a la "astromitología". Colaboró en las revistas *American Anthropologist*, *Atlantis*, *Ethnos* y *México Antiguo*. Miembro fundador de la Sociedad Alemana Mexicanista y de su órgano de difusión, en cuyo primer número publicó una síntesis de su libro inédito *Sinonimia vulgar y científica de la flora oaxaqueña*, en la que sostiene que la sífilis ya existía en América antes de la llegada de los españoles. Clasificó diversas plantas medicinales mexicanas, entre ellas el hongo narcótico *paneolus campanulatus*, utilizado por los mazatecos, el peyote y el *teonanácatl*. Autor de *Mitolobotánica zapoteca* (1945).

RELACIÓN DE MICHOACÁN ◆ Documento que trata de asuntos históricos, religiosos, legales y de costumbres del pueblo purépecha, desde su llegada a Pátzcuaro hasta la caída del señorío del gran tariácuri Caltzontzin, derrotado por Nuño de Guzmán. Fue dictada en purépecha por "los viejos de la ciudad de Michoacán" y el original se conserva en El Escorial. Se ignora el nombre del compilador de la obra, pero algunos autores creen que fue Martín de Jesús o de la Coruña, y que se redactó en Tzintzuntzan alrededor de 1539.

RELIGIÓN Y FUEROS ◆ Lema y grito de guerra de varios levantamientos armados que se produjeron simultáneamente contra el presidente Valentín Gómez Farías cuando éste inició las reformas liberales de 1833. Entre los alzados, que fueron derrotados por falta de coordinación, se hallaban Ignacio Escalada en Michoacán, Gabriel Durán en Tlalpan, Mariano Arista en Amecameca, José Domínguez Manzo en Querétaro, Vicente Canalizo en Oaxaca, Ponce y José de Santa Anna en Puebla, Evaristo Sánchez en Tabasco y Guerra Manzanares en los Estados Internos de Oriente. En 1834 el Plan de Cuernavaca tomó nuevamente la misma consigna.

REMBAO, ALBERTO ◆ n. en Chihuahua, Chih., y m. en EUA (1895-1962). Predicador congregacionista. Estudió en las universidades de California en Berkeley (1920-24) y de Yale (1927-28). Radicó en Nueva York, donde editó la revista *La Nueva Democracia* y fue profesor en Estados Unidos, México y Cuba. Predicó en Sudamérica, Europa e India. Colaboró en *La Prensa* y en *La Opinión*, de Los Ángeles, así como en diversos periódicos mexicanos. Editó en Nueva York la revista *La Nueva Democracia* (1939-62). Autor de *Lupita* (novela, 1939; reeditada en 1941 con prólogo de John A. MacKay y epílogo de Carleton Beals), *Mensaje, movimiento y masa* (1939), *Meditaciones neoyorkinas* (1939), *Outlook in Mexico* (1942), *Democracia trascendente* (1945), *Flor de traslaciones* (1947), *Chihuahua de mis amores y otros despachos de mexicanidad neoyorquina* (1949), *Discurso a la nación evangélica* (1949), *Lecciones de filosofía de la religión* (1956) y *PNEUMA. Los fundamentos teológicos de la cultura* (1957). Miembro del Instituto Hispánico de la Universidad de Columbia.

REMBAO DE TREJO, SILVINA ◆ n. en el Mineral de Morelos y m. en Chihuahua, Chih. (1853-1940). Periodista y militante del Partido Liberal Mexicano. Adherida al magonismo, en 1906 participó en el levantamiento encabezado por Hilario C. Salas, en Acayucan, Veracruz. Organizó con su esposo el Centro Revolucionario de Chihuahua (1907-13), que desplegó actividades antirreeleccionistas y luego se opuso a la dictadura de Victoriano Huerta. Fue llamada *Matrona de la revolución*. Sus colaboraciones periodísticas atacaban a la oligarquía Terrazas-Creel, por lo que fue encarcelada varias veces.

REMESAL, ANTONIO DE ◆ n. y m. en España (¿1573?-1619). Fraile dominico. Llegó a Guatemala en 1613, de donde pasó a Oaxaca. Efectuó el registro de los archivos y bibliotecas de los conventos dominicos. Autor de *Historia general de las Indias Occidentales, y particular de la provincia de San Vicente de Chiapa y Guatemala, de la orden de nuestro glorioso padre Santo Domingo* (1619), obra objetada por las autoridades de su orden.

REMOLINA, MARÍA TERESA ◆ n. en Toluca, Edo. de Méx. (1930). Escritora. Se tituló como química-farmacéutica en la UNAM. Es doctora en ciencias por la Universidad de La Sorbona de París. Profesora del IPN. Participó en talleres literarios. Ha colaborado en *Páginas*. Coautora de *Sapos y espantajos* (1984), *Mi cuento de Navidad* (1986), *Día de muertos* (1987) y *Diversiones y pasatiempos mexicanos* (1987). Autora de *Siguiendo pistas* (1984), *Cinco plumas de colores y otros cuentos* (Premio de Cuento Infantil Juan de la Cabada 1984), *El ciempiés descalzo* (1985) y *En busca de la lluvia. Cuentos mexiquenses* (1986).

REMOLINA ROQUEÑÍ, MANUEL FELIPE ◆ n. en el DF (1942). Licenciado en derecho por la UNAM (1964). Fue secretario de la Comisión Nacional Editorial del PRI (1975-76). Ha sido investigador del Instituto de Investigaciones Jurídicas de la UNAM (1967). En la Junta Federal de Conciliación y Arbitraje se desempeñó como asesor de la Oficialía Mayor (1971), subdirector general de Previsión Social (1972) y secretario general de Control Procesal y Codificación (1974-76). Director general del Derecho de Autor de la SEP (1977), jefe de Documentación e Información (1978), de Servicios Sociales de Ingreso (1978-79) y secretario particular del director general del IMSS (1979-80). Fue asesor del subsecretario de Bienes Inmuebles de la Secretaría de Asentamientos Humanos y Obras Públicas (1981), asesor del subsecretario de Gobernación (1983) y director general de Asuntos Jurídicos de la SRE (1983-88). Coeditor de *La obra jurídica de Luis Cabrera* (1972). Autor de *Positividad y vigencia de la Constitución de Apatzingán* (1972), *Declaraciones de derechos sociales* (1974), *El Artículo 123* (1974), *Evolución de las instituciones y del derecho del trabajo en México* (1975) y *Prontuario de legislación federal del trabajo, 1910-1975* (1975).

RENACIMIENTO, EL ◆ Periódico literario semanal fundado en enero de 1869 por Ignacio Manuel Altamirano,

El Renacimiento

con el apoyo económico de Gonzalo A. Esteva, directores ambos de la publicación. En junio de ese año los impresores Francisco Díaz de León y Santiago White se hicieron cargo de la parte administrativa del semanario y Altamirano siguió como director hasta diciembre de 1869, cuando *El Renacimiento* desapareció, después de haberse significado en su intento de reunir a los escritores al margen de banderías políticas, con el fin de promover una literatura nacional. Entre la nómina de colaboradores estaban el propio Altamirano, Manuel Peredo, Francisco Pimentel, José M. Roa Bárcena, Manuel Orozco y Berra, Alfredo Chavero, Eduardo Ruiz, José T. Cuéllar, Gonzalo y Roberto A. Esteva, Santiago Sierra, Ramón Aldana, José Rosas Moreno, Gertrudis Tenorio Zavala, Rita Cetina Gutiérrez, Manuel Acuña, Manuel M. Flores, Isabel Prieto y Justo Sierra. El material gráfico consistía en litografías de Iriarte, Salazar, Lara y Debray.

Renán, Raúl ◆ n. en Mérida, Yuc. (1928). Escritor. Estudió letras en la UNAM. Publicó sus primeros poemas y cuentos en periódicos estudiantiles yucatecos, en la revista *Voces Verdes* y en *Letras Yucatecas*. Ha colaborado en *Estaciones, El Gallo Ilustrado, Sábado, La Jornada Semanal, El Ángel, La Cultura en México, Vuelta, México en el Arte, Casa del Tiempo* y *Alforja*. Ha sido coordinador de diversos talleres de poesía y subdirector de Publicaciones y Documentación del Centro Nacional de Información y Promoción de la Literatura del INBA. Autor de poesía: *Lámparas oscuras* (1981), *Catilinarias y sáficas* (1981), *De las queridas cosas* (1982), *Pan de tribulaciones*, *Los urbanos* (1988, con fotos de Arturo David Schmitter), *Viajero en sí mismo* (1992), *Henos aquí* (1993), *Los silencios de Homero* (1998), *El libro de las queridas cosas* (1998), *Rama de cóleras* (1998) y *Volver a las cosas* (1999); cuento: *Juan corta las flores* (1972), *Una mujer fatal... y otra* (1983), *Los niños de San Sebastián* (1986), *Comparsa* (1990), *Serán como soles* (1996) y *Ambulario* (1997); prosas: *Gramática fantástica* (1983); y ensayo: *Los "otros libros". Distintas opciones en el trabajo editorial* (1988) y *La sagrada familia Sabines* (1996). Creador artístico del SNCA (1999). Obtuvo la medalla Yucatán 1987 y el Premio Antonio Mediz Bolio 1992. En 1998 fue creado el Premio Nacional de Poesía Experimental Raúl Renán.

Renau Berenguer, José ◆ n. en España y m. en la RDA (1907-1982). Pintor egresado de la Escuela de Bellas Artes de San Carlos, de Valencia (1925), de la que fue profesor (1934-36). Militante del Partido Comunista Español (1931-39), fundador de la Unión de Escritores y Artistas Proletarios (1932) y director general de Bellas Artes (1936), donde creó las Milicias de la Cultura. En 1939 llegó como refugiado político a México y se dedicó a la pintura. Obtuvo la nacionalidad mexicana en 1940. En 1958 se estableció en la RDA y en 1976 volvió a España. Colaboró con Siqueiros en el mural del SME *Retrato de la burguesía* y se encargó de terminarlo (1939-40). Ejecutó los murales *España hacia América* (Casino de la Selva, Cuernavaca, 1944-50), *Evolución de la arquitectura* (en la Sociedad de Alumnos de la Escuela Nacional de Arquitectura, 1956), *La educación del niño en la época mexica* (Museo Nacional de Antropología, 1966) y *Protección y rehabilitación del niño* (1967). Escribió en las revistas *España Peregrina* (1940), *Romance* (1940-41), *Las Españas* (1941-46), *Nuestro Tiempo* (1949-53) y el *Boletín de Información de la Unión de Intelectuales Españoles* (1956-57). Autor de *Función social del cartel publicitario* (1937) y *Arte en peligro* (1978). Ganó el primer premio en el concurso internacional celebrado con motivo del Congreso de la Paz, de Viena, y el primer premio en el concurso para el timbre de la OIT.

Rendón, Alejandro César ◆ n. en el DF (1936). Escritor. Licenciado en ciencias humanas por el Colegio Universitario de Ciencias Humanas y en arte dramático por la UNAM. Ha sido guionista de radio y televisión. Escribió los textos de la versión del ballet *El lago de los cisnes*, representada en el Lago de Chapultepec desde 1976. Ha sido fundador y director de la Escuela de Teatro del Instituto de Ciencias Autónomo de Zacatecas, hoy UAZ (1963-65), maestro del Instituto Andrés Soler de la ANDA (1965-69 y 1979-86), subdirector académico del mismo (1984-86), coordinador de guionismo en el Colegio Universitario de Ciencias Humanas y fundador y director (1987-98) de la Escuela de Escritores de la Sogem, de la que es consejero (1998-). Ha escrito una veintena de obras de teatro, entre las que destacan *La botella* (1959), *Dio-*

Marina, óleo sobre masonite de José Renau

rama poético de México (1961), *Xiuhcóatl* (1963), *Lázaro, el perdón* (1967), *El hombre que detuvo el tiempo* (1969), *Madame de Stäel* (1981), *¡Güera!* (1982), *Pastorela de dos mundos* (1992) y *Las plazas* (1996-99). Premio al mejor teleteatro de difusión política en el Festival de Televisión de Sofía, Bulgaria, por *Tania la guerrillera* (1981), de la serie Teatro al Aire Libre.

Rendón, Julio ◆ n. y m. en Mérida, Yuc. (1864-1949). Ingeniero y abogado. Se dedicó al comercio y colaboró en la *Revista de Mérida*, que llegó a dirigir, y en el *Diario de Yucatán*. Fue diputado federal y local (se opuso en 1902 a la creación del territorio de Quintana Roo) y regidor del ayuntamiento de Mérida. Durante el gobierno de Salvador Alvarado fue director de la Comisión Reguladora del Mercado del Henequén y dos veces director de los Ferrocarriles Unidos de Yucatán.

Rendón, Serapio ◆ n. en Mérida, Yuc., y m. en Tlalnepantla, Edo. de Méx. (1867-1913). Abogado, hermano del anterior. Se afilió a los primeros movimientos antiporfiristas y apoyó la candidatura vicepresidencial de su amigo José María Pino Suárez. Fue diputado a la XXVI Legislatura (1912-14) y se erigió en defensor del gobierno maderista. Tras el asesinato de Madero y Pino Suárez, Rendón salió del país, pero regresó para oponerse desde la Cámara a Victoriano Huerta. Aurelio Urrutia, secretario de Gobernación de Huerta, ordenó la ejecución sumaria del legislador, que hizo efectiva Fortuño Miramón.

Rendón Ibáñez, Pedro ◆ n. y m. en el DF (¿1911?-1975). Se volvió famoso por su estampa, que pudo haber inspirado la del personaje *Avelino Pilongano* de Gabriel Vargas: desaseado, dicharachero, escritor de versos cómicos y grotescos que vendía para subsistir, frecuentaba diversos cafés de la ciudad. Varias tertulias se formaron a su alrededor, y durante décadas fue de los personajes urbanos más reconocidos y apreciados. En 1951, en el Café París, sus contertulios lanzaron en forma festiva su candidatura a la Presidencia de la República y a partir de entonces fue conocido como el "Próximo presidente de México por aclamación popular". Carlos Monsiváis lo llamó "Bohemio oficial de México". Pintó un mural en el mercado Abelardo L. Rodríguez (1934).

Rendón Lozano, Mario ◆ n. en el DF (1941). Escultor. Estudió en la Academia de San Carlos (1958-62) y tomó cursos de didáctica y talla en México, Italia y Estados Unidos. Ha sido profesor de La Esmeralda, escuela a la que representó en la undécima Conferencia Internacional de Escultura. Fue colaborador de Federico Canessi. Intervino en la realización de la escultura del Padre Kino en la línea divisoria entre Baja California y Baja California Sur (1981). Ha participado en la segunda Bienal Nacional de Escultura (1964), tercera Bienal Nacional de Escultura (1967), Exposición Solar del Museo de Arte Moderno (1968), exposición itinerante de Arte Nacional (Bogotá, Quito, Caracas, Lima, La Paz y Buenos Aires 1971-72) y en la Exposición Colectiva de Extranjeros, en el Instituto Profesional del Mármol, Italia (1979). Primer premio de escultura en el Concurso Nacional "La Revolución Mexicana, sus realizaciones" (1960), primer premio de escultura en las exposiciones anuales de la Escuela Nacional de Artes Plásticas (1962 y 63), primer lugar en escultura en el Concurso Anual de Aguascalientes (1965) y selección de la escultura *Suave patria* para la colección del Ministerio de Relaciones Exteriores de Italia (1979).

Rendón Muñoz, Alfonso ◆ n. y m. en Mérida, Yuc. (1905-1973). En 1910 inició estudios de piano que continuó en el Chicago Musical College, institución que le otorgó algunos premios. En 1920 pasó a Nueva York, donde tomó clases con Alberto Jonás y Paula Joutard. Estudió en Londres con Thobias Mathey y en París con Isidore Philip. Como recitalista de piano hizo giras por México, Cuba, Centroamérica y Estados Unidos. Fue huésped de varias orquestas sinfónicas. Ejerció la docencia en el Miami Conservatory of Music, la New York School of Music y la Cecilia Music School of New York City. En 1932 fundó una academia de piano en Mérida.

Rendón Peniche, José ◆ n. y m. en Mérida, Yuc. (1829-1887). Financió al Cuerpo de Caballería Voluntaria que combatió a los indígenas mayas durante la guerra de castas. En 1854, Santa Anna lo nombró administrador de rentas en la isla del Carmen. En Mérida se dedicó al comercio y fue designado miembro del Consejo del Estado, cargo al que renunció durante el imperio de Maximiliano, al que combatió en las fuerzas del general Cepeda Peraza. Al triunfo de la República fue jefe de Hacienda de Yucatán, diputado federal y presidente del ayuntamiento de Mérida. En 1874 se le otorgó la concesión para construir el ferrocarril Mérida-Progreso.

Renn, Ludwig ◆ n. en Alemania (1889-?). Escritor cuyo nombre era Arnold Vieth von Golsenau. Oficial del ejército durante la primera guerra mundial, se unió al movimiento revolucionario obrero alemán. Encarcelado por los nazis en 1933, tres años después escapó a Suiza, de donde pasó a España para incorporarse a las brigadas internacionales. Fue comandante del Batallón Thaelmann (1936-37) y jefe de la segunda Brigada Internacional. Viajó a Estados Unidos, Canadá y Cuba (1937-38) como propagandista de la República Española. De nuevo en la península ibérica dirigió una Escuela para Oficiales. Al triunfo franquista estuvo en Inglaterra y pasó a EUA, invitado por la League of American Writers. En 1939 llegó a México para colaborar con Alfons Goldschmidt en la Liga pro Cultura Alemana, de la que fue presidente. Entre 1940 y 1942 vivió en Morelia, donde fue profesor del Colegio de San Nicolás de Hidalgo. Volvió al DF como presidente del movimiento Alemania Libre. El 24 de mayo de 1942 pronunció en español un discurso en el acto que el presidente Ávila Camacho encabezó en el Zócalo, luego de declarar la guerra al eje Roma-Berlín-Tokio. Fundó

Pedro Rendón Ibáñez

la editorial El Libro Libre. En 1946 volvió a Alemania, donde presidió la Unión Cultural, en Dresde, y fue profesor de antropología en la Escuela Superior Técnica, así como director del Instituto de Ciencias de la Cultura. Colaborador de *Esquire*. Autor de *Krieg, Nachkrieg, Kriegsführung und Propaganda* (1939), *Warfare. The Relation of War to Society* (1939) y *Morelia, una ciudad universitaria en México* (1950).

Daniel Reséndiz Núñez

Rentería, Teodoro ◆ n. en el DF (1937). Licenciado en periodismo por la escuela Carlos Septién García (1955-58), de la que fue profesor (1978-80), así como de la UIA (1968-69). Miembro del PRI, fue coordinador de radio del CEN durante la campaña presidencial de Miguel de la Madrid (1981-82). Ha sido editor fundador y gerente de la revista *Libertas* (1956-57), reportero fundador de *Cada Hora en México*, de la estación XEDF (1956-58), reportero del sistema Radiópolis (1958-59), reportero fundador de la agencia Servicios Informáticos Mexicanos (1959-60) y de la agencia Informex (1960), donde también fue secretario del trabajo del sindicato (1961-64), jefe de información (1962) y de redacción (1963) y director periodístico y administrativo (1964-68); director y comentarista de noticiarios de Telesistema Mexicano (1968-69), gerente de noticias especiales y comentarista de Televisión Independiente de México (1969-71), director de la División de Noticias del Núcleo Radio Mil (1972-77), director de comunicación y noticiarios (1978-82) y miembro del consejo de administración (1981-82) del Grupo Acir; director de Divulgación de la Presidencia (1977), director de Radio de RTC (1982-83) y director general del Instituto Mexicano de la Radio (1983-88). Pertenece a la Asociación de Periodistas de Radio y Televisión y al Club Primera Plana.

Rentería Luviano, José ◆ n. en Huetamo, Mich., y m. en el DF (1883-1925). Militar. A principios de siglo se alistó en la segunda reserva del ejército, creada por Bernardo Reyes. Se unió a la revolución maderista, combatió al huertismo en las fuerzas de Gertrudis Sánchez, peleó contra Francisco Villa y, en Guanajuato y Michoacán, contra Inés Chávez García. En 1917 gobernó interinamente Michoacán. Se adhirió en 1920 el Plan de Agua Prieta y en 1923 apoyó la rebelión delahuertista. Fue acusado de conspirar contra el gobierno y se suicidó al saber que iba a ser aprehendido.

Represas, Carlos Eduardo ◆ n. en el DF (1945). Licenciado en economía por la UNAM (1965). Trabajó en la Secretaría de Hacienda (1965-68). En 1968 ingresó al Grupo Nestlé, donde ha sido especialista de productos en la Compañía Industrial y Comercial Brasileña de Productos Alimenticios, jefe de División Comercial de Grandes Consumidores, en Barcelona; gerente general de Inedeca, presidente de la Sociedad Anónima de Alimentos, en Quito; consejero del Centro Nestlé de Investigación y Desarrollo Tecnológico de Alimentos para América Latina y director general de Especialidades Alimenticias, en Caracas, y presidente y director general desde 1983. Es miembro del patronato del Hospital Infantil de México. El gobierno y la iniciativa privada venezolanos lo han condecorado con la Orden al Mérito en el Trabajo, primera clase; Orden de Francisco de Miranda, primera y segunda clases; título de Industrial del Año (1982) y Botón de Oro del Mérito Empresarial (1983).

República, La ◆ Órgano mensual de difusión del PRI. Su primer número apareció el 1 de mayo de 1949, cuando Rodolfo Sánchez Taboada era presidente del Comité Ejecutivo Nacional del partido. Su director fundador fue Moisés Ochoa Campos. En épocas más recientes se han contado entre sus directores Héctor Murillo Cruz, Salvador Reyes Nevares, Antonio Álvarez Lima y Raúl Moreno Wonchee. Han sido sus colaboradores Salvador Calvillo Madrigal, Antonio Magaña Esquivel, Agustín Yáñez y Salvador Pruneda. La revista ha dejado de aparecer durante largos periodos y ha cambiado de formato en repetidas ocasiones.

República Árabe Unida ◆ ☛ *Egipto.*

República Checa ◆ ☛ *Checa, República.*

República Democrática de Alemania ◆ ☛ *Alemania.*

República Dominicana ◆ ☛ *Dominicana, República.*

República Federal de Alemania ◆ ☛ *Alemania.*

Reséndiz, Rafael ◆ n. en el DF (1939). Licenciado en administración por la UNAM. Afiliado al PRI, fue secretario de Información y Propaganda del CEN de ese partido (1990-92). Director de Relaciones Públicas y asesor de Asuntos Especiales de la Presidencia (1976-80), subdirector (1980-82) y director de Comunicación Social de la Secretaría de Hacienda (1982-86), oficial mayor de la Secretaría de Desarrollo Social (1992-94) y vicepresidente de Información y Comunicación de Televisa (1994-).

Reséndiz Núñez, Daniel ◆ n. en Maravillas, Hgo. (1937). Ingeniero civil graduado en la UNAM (1959), con maestría (1960) y doctorado (1965) en la misma institución, después de haber hecho estudios de doctorado en Harvard (1963-64). Ha sido profesor (1958), investigador (1959) y director del Instituto de Ingeniería (1974-82) y de la Facultad de Ingeniería de la UNAM (1987-91); consultor de la Fundación Ford (1966), asesor técnico de la CFE (1969), consultor del DDF (1971), director técnico de Ingenieros Consultores (1971-74), secretario general del Conacyt (1982-87), subdirector técnico de la CFE y de la Comisión Nacional del Agua, presidente del Patronato de la UAM (1991-96) y subsecretario de Educación Superior e Investigación Científica (1996-). Miembro de las academias de la Investigación Científica y Nacional de Ingeniería, presidente del Fondo de Estudios e Investigación Ricardo J. Zebada, integrante del Comité Asesor de la ONU sobre Ciencia y Tecnología para el Desarrollo y miembro del Consejo Consultivo de Ciencias de la Presidencia. Investigador nacional y emérito de la UNAM, ha recibido los premios Javier Barros Sierra (1977), José A. Cuevas

(1978), Elías Sourasky (1978), Miguel A. Urquijo (1982) y Nacional de Ciencias y Artes (1990).

RESORTES ◆ n. en el DF (1916). Nombre profesional de Adalberto Martínez. En su juventud desempeñó diversos oficios antes de formar, en 1931, el dueto Los Espontáneos. Más tarde, como bailarín solista en el Salón Smirna y por su gran movilidad, se ganó el sobrenombre. Después de ganar fama como bailarín y cómico en numerosos escenarios del teatro frívolo (actividad en la que se mantuvo hasta 1977 y de la que se retiró, según sus palabras, por la vulgaridad imperante en el medio), pasó al cine, en el cual ha filmado más de 90 películas. Destacan sus interpretaciones de personajes populares, aderezadas casi siempre por números de baile. Entre las películas en las que ha participado destacan *Voces de primavera* (1946), *Yo dormí con un fantasma* (1947), *Confidencias de un ruletero* (1949), *El beisbolista fenómeno* (1951), *Soy un golfo* (1955), *El rey de México* (1955), *¡Viva la juventud!* (1955), *Asesinos, S.A.* (1956), *Quiero ser artista* (1957), *Del suelo no paso* (1958), *La chamaca* (1960), *Jóvenes y rebeldes* (1961), *El dengue del amor* (1965), *Los tres mosqueteros de Dios*, *Matar no es fácil* (1966), *Los albañiles* (1976, Diosa de Plata a la mejor coactuación masculina), *El futbolista fenómeno* (1978, en cuyo argumento colaboró) y *Día de difuntos* (1988). En 1987 el INBA le organizó un homenaje, en el que se le otorgó medalla y diploma. Obtuvo un Ariel de Oro por su trayectoria en 1994.

Resortes

RESTREPO FERNÁNDEZ, IVÁN ◆ n. en Colombia (1938). Licenciado en economía, especializado en tenencia de la tierra y desarrollo agrícola en Washington. Ha sido investigador en el Centro de Investigaciones Agrarias (1966-70), fundador de la Sección de Graduados y de la División de Estudios Superiores de la Escuela Superior de Economía del IPN y primer director de su maestría en economía industrial (1970-72), profesor en el posgrado de la Facultad de Ciencias Políticas y Sociales (1972-74) y fundador del Centro de Ecodesarrollo, que dirigió (1975-91), dicho centro fue cerrado por el gobierno debido a su posición crítica. Desde 1993 dirige el Centro de Ecología y Desarrollo. Obtuvo la nacionalidad mexicana en 1982. Ha colaborado en *Economía Política*, *Revista del México Agrario*, *La Cultura en México*, *El Día*, *unomásuno* y *La Jornada*, diario del que fue fundador (1984) y en el que sostiene, desde 1991, el suplemento *La Jornada Ecológica*. Coautor de *Estructura agraria y desarrollo agrícola en México* (1974, Premio Nacional de Economía en 1971). Autor de *El azúcar: problema de México* (1971), *¿Tiene límites el crecimiento?* (1977), *La basura: consumo y desperdicio en el Distrito Federal* (1982) y *El paraíso fraccionado* (1986) y *Los plaguicidas en México* (1986), entre otras obras. Miembro de número del Ateneo de Angangueo. ProHábitat lo nombró Personaje del Año en 1990. Obtuvo un reconocimiento especial del Consejo Consultivo de la Ciudad de México (1993), Ciudadano Distinguido de México (1997).

RETA MARTÍNEZ, CARLOS ◆ n. en el DF (1943). Ingeniero civil (1960-63), licenciado en ciencias políticas y administración pública (1970) y maestro y doctor en administración pública por la UNAM (1971-74), donde es profesor. Desde 1958 es miembro del PRI, en el que fue secretario de Organización (1960-61), subdirector (1965-66) y director nacional de la organización juvenil (1966-67); secretario auxiliar del CEN (1968-70), secretario de Prensa y Propaganda del comité del DF (1984-85) y presidente del Instituto Político Nacional de Administración Pública (1983-86); en la CNOP ocupó la secretaría y la presidencia nacional juvenil (1962-68). Ha sido supervisor de Obras, Estructuras y Cimentaciones de ICA (1962-63), secretario general del DDF (1970-71), director general de Establecimientos Turísticos (1973-76), director técnico de Consejeros y Asesores Asociados (1974), director general de Materiales Didácticos y Culturales de la SEP y director general del ILCE (1978-79), director general de Información y Relaciones Públicas de la SEP (1979-82), director de Difusión y Relaciones Públicas de Sidermex (1983), director general de Difusión y Relaciones Públicas del DDF (1985-88), director general de Comunicación Social de la SRE (1988-94), secretario general de gobierno del DDF (1994-97) y director general de RTC (1997-1999).

RETES, GABRIEL ◆ n. en el DF (1947). Actor y director de cine y teatro. Comenzó a actuar en teatro a los 12 años de edad. En formato de ocho milímetros realizó cortos, medios y largometrajes documentales y de ficción: *Sur* (1969), *El paletero* (1970), *Fragmento* (1971),

Foto: Armando Herrera

Resortes

Iván Restrepo

Gabriel Retes

Tribulaciones en el seno de una familia burguesa (1972), *El asunto* (1972), *Los años duros* (1973) y *Los bandidos* (1973). En 1972 participó en la fundación de la Cooperativa de Cine Marginal, patrocinada por la Tendencia Democrática del SUTERM. Fue cofundador y presidente del Consejo de Administración de la Cooperativa Río Mixcoac, secretario del trabajo del Sindicato de Autores Cinematográficos y miembro de la Comisión de Premiación de la Academia Mexicana de Ciencias y Artes Cinematográficas. Realizó 26 programas de la serie de televisión de la SEP *Niñas y niños* (1981) y coprodujo la serie de televisión *La rebelión de los colgados*, de Juan Luis Buñuel (1986). Entre 1989 y 1991 dirigió los *videohomes La mudanza de la muerte, La mujer fiel, Dispárenle a matar, El nacimiento de un guerrillero* y *La muerte de un paletero*. Ha dirigido las cintas *Chin Chin el teporocho* (1975, ganadora de un Ariel e invitada al Festival de Pesaro, Italia), *Nuevo mundo* (1976), *Flores de papel* (1977, participante en el Festival de Berlín), *Bandera rota* (1978), *Los náufragos del Liguria* (1983), *Los piratas* (1983), *Mujeres salvajes* (1984), *La ciudad al desnudo* (1988), *El bulto* (1991) y *Bienvenido/Welcome* (1993).

RETES, IGNACIO ◆ n. en la ciudad de México (1918). Padre del anterior. Fundador del Teatro Universitario en San Luis Potosí (1937), estudió arte dramático en la UNAM y con Rodolfo Usigli y Seki Sano. Ha sido guionista, director y actor de televisión, fundador y director del grupo teatral La Linterna Mágica (1946-49), director de los teatros del IMSS (1959-65), profesor y director de la Academia de la ANDA y profesor del Instituto Cinematográfico de México. Colaborador de *Letras de México*. Argumentista de *Albur de amor* (1946) y *Noches de angustia* (1948); director de las obras de teatro *El cuadrante de la soledad* (1950, de José Revueltas, con escenografía de Diego Rivera) y *La chunga* (1993, de Mario Vargas Llosa); guionista de *El fuego cautivo, Unos cuantos días* (premio de la Sociedad General de Escritores de México en 1977), *Flores de papel* (1978), *Bandera rota* (1979) y *La profecía*; director de *Los hijos de Sánchez* (1977, de Lewis y Leñero) y del documental *Nuevo amanecer*; coautor del segundo tomo de *El teatro en México* (1965) y autor de las obras de teatro *El día de mañana* (1945), *El aria de la locura* (1953), *Una ciudad para vivir* (1954), *Juan Pérez Jolote* (versión escénica de la obra de Ricardo Pozas, 1964), *Los hombres del cielo* (1965) y *Viento sur*. Como actor ha participado, entre otras, en la película *Bienvenido/Welcome* (1993) y en la puesta en escena *Madero, el otro* (1994) Premio Universidad Nacional (1998).

FOTO: ROGELIO CUÉLLAR

Ignacio Retes en *Perfecto cornudo*

RETES, PILAR ◆ ☛ *Campesino, Pilar*.

REUTER, JAS ◆ n. en España y m. en el DF (1934-1985). Obtuvo la nacionalidad mexicana en 1952. Licenciado (1959), maestro (1974) y doctor (1978) en filosofía por la UNAM, con estudios de posgrado en Heidelberg. Fue profesor e investigador de la UNAM, jefe de publicaciones del Fondo de Cultura Económica y de El Colegio de México, editor del Instituto Latinoamericano de Planificación Económica y Social de la ONU, consultor de la UNESCO y asesor de la Dirección General de Culturas Populares de la SEP. Cofundador de la Peña y del grupo Los Folkloristas (1964), en el que tocaba instrumentos de aliento. Editor y coautor del *Cancionero folklórico de México* (5 t., 1973-84). Autor de *Fausto, el hombre* (1965), *Los niños de Campeche cantan y juegan* (1978), *La música popular de México* (1980), *¡Salvemos lo nuestro!* (1979-82), *Instrumentos musicales de México* (1982), *Indigenismo, pueblo y cultura* (1983), *Lírica infantil de Perú* y *Coplas de amor y cancioneros* (coautor), así como del audiovisual *Una visita al pasado de Tabasco* (1978).

REUTER, WALTER ◆ n. en Alemania (1906). Fotógrafo. En 1930 comenzó su carrera periodística haciendo reportajes políticos para la publicación comunista alemana *Arbeiter-Illustrierte Zeitung*. Debido a un trabajo suyo contra Hitler fue perseguido por los nazis y huyó de su país en 1933. Pasó a España donde fue fotógrafo en Málaga y Gibraltar (1936) y, al estallar la guerra, fotorreportero para los republicanos y soldado de la Juventud Socialista Unificada. Exiliado en México colaboró en las revistas *Nosotros, Hoy, Siempre!* y *Mañana*, y fue corresponsal de la agencia Black Star. Desde 1972 ha sido fotógrafo de Sicartsa, la CFE, el Ejército Mexicano, el INI, el INBA, la revista *Memoranda/ISSSTE* y el Museo del Hombre, de París. Ha filmado los documentales *Historia de un río* (1950), *Tierra del chicle* (1952, Premio del Festival de Cine Rural, de México, y Espiga de Plata en el Festival Cinematográfico de Roma), *Descubrimiento de Bonampak* (1952, para el Museo del Hombre), *El hombre de la isla* (1957), *Tierra de esperanza* (1957), *El Botas* (1957), *La brecha* (1957) y *Voladores de Papantla* (1957); también ha filmado las películas argumentales *Raíces* (1953, Premio de la Crítica en el Festival de Cannes), *Tierra de los mayas* (1957), *Los pizcadores de algodón* (1957), *Norte* (1958), *La gran caída* (1958), *El brazo fuerte* (1958), *Los pequeños gigantes* (1959) y *La güera Xóchitl* (1963). Creador artístico del SNCA (1993-96). En 1999 recibió el Ariel de Oro.

Reveles, José ◆ n. en el DF (1944). Periodista egresado de la Escuela Carlos Septién García (1967). Ha impartido cursos en universidades (1970-80) y en el Conacyt (1982). Fue reportero de *La Prensa* (1967-68), *Novedades* (1968-70) y *Excélsior* (1970-76); cofundador y jefe de información de *Proceso* (1976-83); corresponsal de ANSA (1982-1988) y colaborador de *El Financiero* (1993-) y *Detrás de la noticia* (1996-1999), cuya emisión radifónica condujo. También condujo *La hora de la verdad*. En 1989 participó en el proyecto del diario *El Independiente*. Fundó la revista *Filo Rojo*, especializada en nota roja y derechos humanos. Coautor de *Irán: la religión en la revolución*, *Los escritores* (1980) y *La Quina: el lado oscuro del poder*. Autor de *Una cárcel mexicana en Buenos Aires* (1980). Miembro fundador de la Unión de Periodistas Democráticos, en la que fue secretario de Organización (1984-86) e integrante del consejo consultivo (1986-88). Premio de la Fraternidad de Reporteros de México por su trayectoria (1997).

Revilla, Manuel Gustavo ◆ n. y m. en la ciudad de México (1863-1924). Abogado. Fue profesor (1892-1902) y secretario (1902-05) de la Academia de San Carlos. En colaboración con José Salomé Pina formó el catálogo de pinturas de esa institución. Profesor de las escuelas Nacional Preparatoria y de Altos Estudios (1905-11) y cónsul en Centroamérica, Sudamérica y Europa. Autor de *De la división del poder público* (1887), *El arte en México en la época antigua y durante el gobierno virreinal* (1893), *Cánovas y las letras* (1898), *Las obras literarias de D. Joaquín Baranda* (1900), *Santiago Rebull* (1902), *Biografías de artistas mexicanos* (1908), *Hacia la paz por la justicia* (1911), *El paisajista D. José M. Velasco* (1912), *En pro del casticismo* (?), *Las urracas académicas y el bulbul modernista, o los deslices gramaticales de don Francisco Villaespesa* (1917) y *El lenguaje popular y el erudito* (1921). Miembro de la Academia Mexicana (de la Lengua).

Revilla Lugo, José Rafael ◆ n. en Valle de San Bartolomé, hoy de Allende, y m. en Chihuahua, Chih. (1800-1849). Comerciante. Fue depositario de los fondos de la Diputación Provincial de Chihuahua (1823-24), vocal del Tribunal de Cuentas (1826), fiscal de la Junta Protectora de la Libertad de Imprenta (1827), juez de primera instancia y alcalde segundo constitucional de la ciudad de Chihuahua (1828). En 1830 se unió al Plan de Jalapa, contra Vicente Guerrero, como miembro de la milicia cívica y se le hizo asesor judicial de los partidos del sur del estado. Fue nombrado vicegobernador constitucional de Chihuahua. Renunció en 1832 y marchó a Durango a concluir sus estudios de jurisprudencia. En 1833 volvió a nombrársele vicegobernador de Chihuahua, cargo al que renunció ese mismo año, después de ocupar interinamente la gubernatura. Ejerció la abogacía y desempeñó diversos cargos judiciales hasta 1837, cuando se le designó magistrado suplente del Tribunal de Justicia de Chihuahua. Fue magistrado propietario de 1840 a 1844 y de 1845 hasta su muerte.

Revilla Valenzuela, Bernardo ◆ n. en Valle de San Bartolomé, hoy Valle de Allende, y m. en Chihuahua, Chih. (1798-1879). Comerciante. Presenció en 1811 el fusilamiento de Miguel Hidalgo. Fue regidor (1826) y síndico (1830) del ayuntamiento de Chihuahua, diputado local (1830 y 1843) y vocal en las Juntas Departamentales (1837-43). Se alistó en el ejército para combatir la invasión estadounidense (1847). Financió numerosas campañas de exterminio contra los apaches. Colaboró en *La Colación*, *La Época* y *El Asperges*, desde donde apoyó el Plan de Ayutla (1855). Combatió al gobernador centralista Monterde. Fue gobernador de Chihuahua en dos ocasiones (1838). Como republicano, fue hostilizado por los imperialistas franceses. En 1957 se le declaró benemérito del estado de Chihuahua.

Walter Reuter

Celebración del Año Nuevo mazahua en fotografía de Walter Reuter

Revillagigedo ◆ Islas del océano Pacífico situadas frente a Colima y llamadas Socorro, San Benedicto, Santa o Clarión, Roca Partida y La Pasión. En 1533 llegó al archipiélago Hernando de Grijalva, pero fue hasta 1790 cuando el virrey Güemes, conde de Revillagigedo, envió una expedición que tomó posesión de las islas en nombre de la Corona española. En 1896 la isla Clarión fue ocupada por marinos ingleses, que explotaron los yacimientos carboníferos. Tradicionalmente abandonadas, el 10 de marzo de 1957 el presidente Adolfo Ruiz Cortines envió una expedición con 250 marinos y 12 periodistas. El viaje duró 12 días y culminó con el izamiento de la bandera nacional en la isla Socorro. Desde entonces se mantiene un destacamento de la Armada en ese lugar del territorio nacional.

Revillagigedo, virreyes ◆ ☛ *Güemes y Horcasitas, Juan Francisco de y Pacheco de Padilla y Horcasitas, Juan Vicente de.*

REVISTA AZUL

AL PIE DE LA ESCALERA

Revista Azul

REVISTA AZUL ◆ Publicación literaria semanal fundada por Manuel Gutiérrez Nájera y Carlos Díaz Dufoo. Fue editada por la empresa periodística de *El Partido Liberal*. Se publicaron 128 números. La primera entrega es del 6 de mayo de 1894 y la última del 11 de octubre de 1896. Se le considera el principal órgano del modernismo. Publicó entre otros, textos de los franceses Daudet, Prévost, Richepin, Loti, Lemaitre, Coppée, Bourget, Maupassant, Laforgue, Maizeroy, Béranger, Reynolds, Gauthier, Lahor y Verlaine; españoles: Rueda y Núñez de Arce; latinoamericanos: Martí, Darío, Santos Chocano, Jaimes Freyre, Gómez Carrillo, Blanco Fombona, Leopoldo Díaz y Darío Herrera; y mexicanos: Gutiérrez Nájera, Urbina, Díaz Dufoo, Urueta, Ángel de Campo *Micrós*, Amado Nervo, Díaz Mirón, Othón, Sierra, Valenzuela, Pagaza, Olaguíbel, Juan B. Delgado, Dávalos y Tablada.

REVISTA DE REVISTAS

EL CULTO DE LOS HEROES

Revista de Revistas

REVISTA MEXICANA DE LITERATURA ◆ Publicación bimestral fundada por Emmanuel Carballo y Carlos Fuentes, quienes la dirigieron en su primera época (1955-58). Durante 1958 la dirección corrió a cargo de Antonio Alatorre y Tomás Segovia. En su tercera época (1959-65) fue dirigida por Juan García Ponce, con el auxilio de Inés Arredondo, Huberto Batis, José de la Colina y Juan Vicente Melo, con Rita Murúa como administradora. Su primer número correspondió a septiembre-octubre de 1955 y el último, a mayo-junio de 1965. Entre sus colaboradores se contaron Inés Arredondo, Isabel Fraire, Jomi García Ascot, Jorge Ibargüengoitia y Federico Álvarez.

REVISTA MODERNA ◆ Publicación literaria quincenal fundada en 1898 por Bernardo Couto Castillo, quien sólo pudo editar el primer número de julio. Reapareció al mes siguiente dirigida por Jesús E. Valenzuela. Se mantuvo hasta 1903 con el apoyo económico de Jesús E. Luján y de ese año hasta 1911 fue dirigida conjuntamente por Valenzuela y Amado Nervo. Como *Revista Azul*, dio a conocer sobre todo a los autores modernistas, franceses y mexicanos, aunque no publicó sólo poesía y prosa de ficción, sino también ensayos, biografías y bibliografías. Dio cabida a textos de Manuel José Othón, Francisco M. de Olaguíbel, Alberto Leduc, Rafael Delgado, Federico Gamboa, Rubén C. Campos, Jesús Urueta, Ciro B. Ceballos, José Juan Tablada, Balbino Dávalos, Luis G. Urbina, Rafael López, Enrique González Martínez, José López Portillo y Rojas, Manuel Puga y Acal y de los franceses Lamartine, Heredia, Leconte de Lisle, Gautier, Lorrain, Lahor, Baudelaire, Lemaitre Mendès, Richepin, Clarétie, Chavette y Goncourt. Las ilustraciones de la revista eran obra de Julio Ruelas, Germán Gedovius y Lázaro Pavía.

REVISTA DE REVISTAS ◆ Publicación semanal fundada en la ciudad de México por Luis Manuel Rojas, su primer número apareció el 23 de enero de 1910. Entre los fundadores de la publicación estaban Manuel Horta, Rafael Alducin, Ernesto García Cabral, Roberto Montenegro, José Gómez Ugarte, Enrique Carrillo y José de Jesús Núñez y Domínguez. Sus directores han sido Luis Manuel Rojas (1910-12), Fernando R. Galván (1912-13), José Gómez Ugarte (1913-15), José de Jesús Núñez y Domínguez (1915-25), Manuel Horta (1925-29), Teodoro Torres (1929-32), Héctor D. Falcón (1932), Roque Armando Sosa Ferreiro (1932-39), Roberto Núñez y Domínguez (1940-49), Héctor D. Falcón (1949-51), Carlos Denegri (1951-63), Gustavo Durán de Huerta (1963-72), Vicente Leñero (1972-75), Patricia Torres Maya (1975-76), Magdalena Saldaña (1976-84) y Enrique Loubet Jr. (1984-).

REVISTA UNIVERSAL ◆ Fue fundada en agosto de 1867. En 1874 fue adquirida por José Vicente Villada, quien la utilizó en 1876 para apoyar la candidatura presidencial de Sebastián Lerdo de Tejada, por lo que al triunfar la revolución de Tuxtepec, en ese mismo año, la publicación desapareció. Entre sus colaboradores se contaban Javier Santa María, Juan de Dios Peza, Hilarión Frías y Soto, F. Gómez Palacio, Juan A. Mateos, José Peón Contreras, Agapito Silva, Rafael de Zayas Enríquez, Ignacio Ramírez, Guillermo Prieto, Eduardo Ruiz, Manuel Peniche, Francisco Hernández y Hernández, Alberto G. Bianchi y Gustavo Baz.

REVOLUCIÓN MEXICANA ◆ Aunque la Revolución Mexicana, como proceso social e histórico, cubre un amplio lapso, ha dado en llamarse así sólo al periodo de la lucha armada, que se desarrolló principalmente del 20 de noviembre de 1910, fecha del levantamiento convocado por Francisco I. Madero (☛), hasta el 5 de febrero de 1917, cuando se promulgó la Constitución. Entre los principales antecedentes están las actividades de oposición al gobierno de Porfirio Díaz, como los levantamientos armados y las huelgas obreras de Río Blanco y Cananea, organizados y dirigidos por el Partido Liberal Mexicano (☛). En 1908, durante una entrevista con el reportero estadounidense James Creelman, Porfirio Díaz declaró que no pensaba reelegirse una vez más y que vería con agrado la aparición de un partido opositor. Ésta fue la señal que aprovecharon varias personas, entre ellas Madero, quien en ese año publicó *La sucesión presidencial en 1910*, libro que constituyó un llamado a la conciencia cívica. Simultáneamente, Madero fundó el Partido Antirreeleccionista y recorrió el país como candidato a la Presidencia. En las elecciones de 1910 Porfirio Díaz se hizo reelegir fraudulentamente, lo que denunció Madero, quien después de huir de la ciudad de San Luis Potosí donde estaba confinado (5 de octubre), lanzó el Plan de San Luis Potosí (☛), se refugió en Estados Unidos y convocó a los antiporfiristas a tomar las armas a las seis de la tarde del 20 de noviembre de 1910. El 18 de noviembre de ese año, uno de los principales maderistas del país, Aquiles Serdán (☛), fue descubierto como conspirador, fuerzas del gobierno atacaron su casa en la ciudad de Puebla y resultaron asesinados él y algunos miembros de su familia. En las semanas siguientes se produjeron alzamientos en diversos puntos del país. En Chihuahua los principales jefes militares fueron Inés Salazar, Pascual Orozco (☛) y Francisco Villa (☛). La lucha cobró fuerza el 13 de febrero de 1911, cuando Madero ingresó de nuevo en el territorio nacional. En el sur del territorio nacional se produjo el levantamiento encabezado por Emiliano Zapata (☛), quien había iniciado años atrás una lucha local contra la dictadura. Cuando las tropas de Orozco y Villa tomaron Ciudad Juárez, el 8 de mayo de 1911, Madero, reconocido como el jefe de la revolución y presidente provisional, organizó un gobierno con Francisco Vázquez Gómez como secretario de Relaciones Exteriores, Federico González

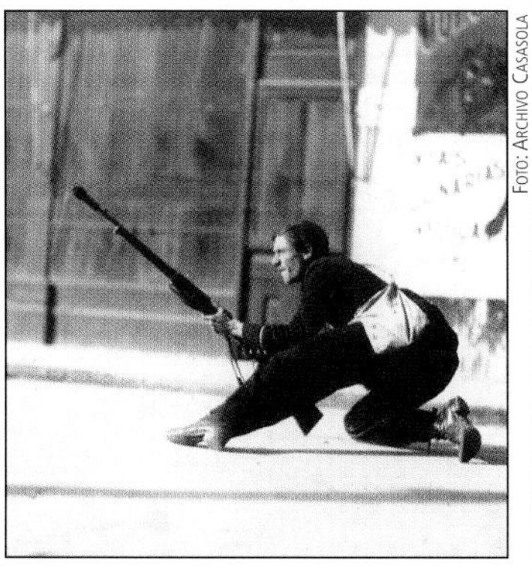

FOTO: ARCHIVO CASASOLA

Soldado maderista lanzando bombas en febrero de 1913 en la ciudad de México, durante la decena trágica

Garza en Gobernación, Gustavo A. Madero en Hacienda, Venustiano Carranza en la Secretaría de Guerra, José María Pino Suárez en la de Justicia y Manuel Bonilla en Comunicaciones. Este gabinete produjo algunas disensiones en las filas revolucionarias, pues quedó marginado el principal jefe militar de esa etapa, Pascual Orozco. El 21 de mayo de 1911, Porfirio Díaz envió un representante que firmó los Tratados de Ciudad Juárez y el 25 de mayo de 1911 renunció a la Presidencia. Madero hizo lo propio junto con su gabinete e interinamente ocupó el Poder Ejecutivo Francisco León de la Barra, quien lo ejerció hasta la toma de posesión de Madero como presidente constitucional, el 6 de noviembre de ese año. El hecho de haber llevado a José María Pino Suárez como candidato a la vicepresidencia también causó fisuras en las filas revolucionarias, donde un amplio sector se inclinaba por Francisco Vázquez Gómez, en tanto que los conservadores preferían a León de la Barra. Emiliano Zapata, quien había luchado contra las fuerzas enviadas primero por Díaz y luego por León de la Barra, ante el incumplimiento de las promesas agrarias de Madero lanzó el Plan de Ayala (☛) el 28 de noviembre de 1911 y continuó la lucha. Bernardo Reyes (☛) se pronunció contra Madero el 16 de diciembre de 1911, pero su rebelión fue sofocada. Pascual Orozco, aparentemente instigado por el terrateniente chihuahuense Terrazas, se rebeló también contra Madero el 3 de marzo de 1912 y su alzamiento cundió por Chihuahua, Coahuila y Sonora. El 3 de julio de ese año, Orozco fue derrotado por Victoriano Huerta en Bachimba y días después también fue derrotado en Sonora. Félix Díaz, sobrino de Porfirio, se levantó en armas en Veracruz, pero fue derrotado el 23 de octubre y encarcelado en la prisión militar de Santiago Tlatelolco, junto con Bernardo Reyes. Mientras tanto, las fuerzas conservadoras del país obstaculizaban la gestión presidencial de Madero, quien no pudo aplicar más que unas cuantas reformas. El 9 de febrero de 1913 se sublevaron los militares Manuel Mondragón, Bernardo Reyes y Félix Díaz, quienes habían sido liberados por sus correligionarios, dando inicio a la Decena Trágica (☛). Ese día Reyes murió cuando encabezaba el asalto al Palacio Nacional. El 11 de febrero fue designado jefe de la plaza Victoriano Huerta, quien el 18 de febrero abandonó la legalidad y a Madero y se unió a Mondragón y Félix Díaz, con quienes firmó el Pacto de la Embajada (☛), en combinación con el embajador estadounidense Henry Lane Wilson. El 19 de febrero el Congreso de la Unión aceptó las renuncias de Madero y Pino Suárez, firmadas bajo coacción, y nombró presidente interino a Pedro Lascuráin (☛), quien designó secretario de

FOTO: ARCHIVO CASASOLA

Francisco I. Madero con algunos miembros de su gabinete en 1912

Gobernación a Huerta y renunció 45 minutos después para que éste asumiera el Poder Ejecutivo y diera una apariencia de legalidad al golpe de Estado. El dictador fue reconocido por el Senado y la Cámara de Diputados, con excepciones como la representada por Belisario Domínguez, poco después asesinado. El 22 de febrero fueron ejecutados Madero y Pino Suárez, lo que provocó rebeliones antihuertistas en todo el país. En marzo, los gobiernos de Sonora y Coahuila desconocieron a Huerta y el 27 de ese mes Carranza promulgó el Plan de Guadalupe (☛) y se erigió en primer jefe del ejército constitucionalista. La lucha contra Huerta duró poco más de un año y en ella destacó Villa, quien resultó victorioso en las batallas de Torreón, Ojinaga, Tierra Blanca, Paredón, San Pedro de las Colonias, Zacatecas y otras, con lo que abatió al ejército federal y abrió el camino hacia la capital del país. Por el

Pareja de revolucionarios

FOTO: ARCHIVO CASASOLA

FOTO: ARCHIVO CASASOLA

Francisco Villa en la silla presidencial; a su izquierda, Emiliano Zapata, en 1914

noroeste avanzó el cuerpo de ejército de Álvaro Obregón y por el noreste el de Pablo González. Mientras tanto, Zapata siguió luchando en el sur. El 9 de abril de 1914 se produjo el incidente de Tampico, entre marinos estadounidenses y autoridades portuarias mexicanas, lo que empeoró las relaciones entre Huerta y Wilson. El 21 de abril de ese año, con el pretexto de impedir que el buque alemán *Ypiranga* descargara armas para las fuerzas federales, la marina de Estados Unidos ocupó el puerto de Veracruz y Huerta rompió las relaciones diplomáticas con Washington. El 23 de junio Francisco Villa tomó Zacatecas y los constitucionalistas iniciaron una serie de golpes contra el ejército huertista al ocupar las ciudades de Guadalajara, Colima, Aguascalientes y Guanajuato. El 24 de junio, los embajadores argentino, brasileño y chileno en Washington ofrecieron mediar en el conflicto diplomático entre México y Estados Unidos. Se aceptó la propuesta y estos diplomáticos se reunieron en Niagara Falls con los representantes de los países en conflicto. Huerta disolvió su gabinete el 10 de julio y el día 14 entregó el poder a Francisco S. Carvajal. El día 15 de agosto las fuerzas constitucionalistas entraron en la ciudad de México, tras haberse firmado los Convenios de Teoloyucan, en virtud de los cuales fue disuelto el viejo ejército. Carranza, para allanar las dificultades entre las facciones revolucionarias, convocó a la Convención de Generales y Gobernadores (☛), que iniciaría sus trabajos el 1 de octubre en la ciudad de México. Los jefes de los grupos villistas y zapatistas exigieron que la asamblea se trasladara a un punto neutral, que resultó ser Aguascalientes, donde continuaron las sesiones con representación de los principales líderes. La Convención desconoció a Carranza como jefe del Ejecutivo y se nombró presidente provisional a Eulalio Gutiérrez. Éste asumió el poder el 6 de noviembre, pero Carranza, a su vez, desconoció a la Convención y a sus autoridades y se mantuvo como primer jefe constitucionalista, para lo que estableció su gobierno en Veracruz con el apoyo de Obregón, González y otros jefes mi-litares. Se inició la lucha armada entre ambos grupos revolucionarios y exis-tieron paralelamente el gobierno convencionista y el carrancista. El 14 de noviembre de 1914, Carranza logró que las tropas estadounidenses salieran del país. El 3 de diciembre de 1914 las fuerzas de Villa y Zapata ocuparon la ciudad de México y ahí se instaló el presidente Gutiérrez. En enero de 1915, Gutiérrez retiró el mando de tropas a Zapata y Villa, por lo que fue obligado por éstos a dejar la Presidencia en manos de Roque González Garza, quien se vio forzado a trasladar la capital a Cuernavaca, ante el acoso de las tropas de Obregón. En abril de ese año las tropas obregonistas iniciaron una campaña contra Villa, en la que éste fue derrotado en casi todas las batallas y obligado a retroceder al norte. El 10 de junio, González Garza entregó el poder a Francisco Lagos Cházaro, quien lo ejercería hasta enero de 1916, cuando se disolvió el gobierno convencionista, con sede, entonces, en Toluca. Carranza volvió a la ciudad de México el 11 de octubre de 1915 y cuatro días después obtuvo el reconocimiento diplomático de Estados Unidos, Argentina, Bolivia, Chile, Brasil y Uruguay. A partir de entonces, varias naciones más reconocerían al gobierno carrancista. El 9 de marzo de 1916, Villa efectuó una incursión al poblado estadounidense de Columbus, lo que dio pretexto para que penetraran en México las fuerzas de la llamada expedición punitiva, comandada por John Joseph Pershing. Éste no tuvo éxito en su misión y fue constantemente hostilizado por las fuerzas villistas, dispersadas en guerrillas. Del 2 al 11 de mayo se celebraron varias reuniones en Ciudad Juárez, entre los representantes de los gobiernos de México y Estados Unidos, para pactar la salida de las tropas de Pershing, aunque antes de que abandonaran el país, se produjo un enfrentamiento entre las tropas mexicanas y las invasoras (20 de junio), favorable a las primeras. El 19 de septiembre de 1916, Carranza convocó a elecciones de diputados para integrar el Congreso Constituyente, cuya finalidad original era sólo reformar la Constitución de 1857. Las elecciones se llevaron a cabo el 22 de octubre y el 1 de diciembre se instaló el Congreso en la

FOTO: ARCHIVO CASASOLA

Gente del pueblo espera en una estación ferroviaria la llegada de provisiones, durante la Revolución (1915)

Tren militar empleado durante la Revolución Mexicana

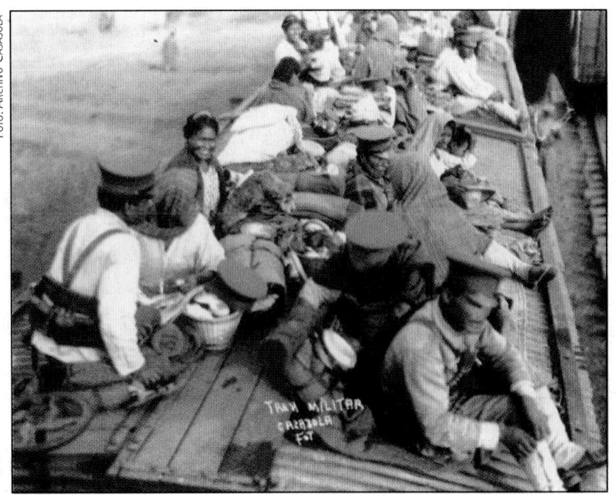

FOTO: ARCHIVO CASASOLA

Álvaro Obregón, Venustiano Carranza, Pablo González y otras personas en La Cañada, Querétaro, 1916

ciudad de Querétaro. El 5 de febrero de 1917 se promulgó la Constitución y un día después se convocó a elecciones presidenciales, mismas que ganó Carranza el 11 de marzo. El 1 de mayo de 1917, Carranza entró en la ciudad de México como presidente constitucional. A partir de entonces se agudizó el conflicto entre los propios constitucionalistas, el que desembocó en el pronunciamiento del Plan de Agua Prieta, el asesinato de Carranza (1920) y la llegada de Obregón a la presidencia. Emiliano Zapata, que no había depuesto las armas, fue traicionado y murió en una emboscada en 1919. Villa fue asesinado en 1923. Plutarco Elías Calles, sucesor de Obregón en la Presidencia de la República, inició desde este cargo las gestiones para constituir el Partido de la Revolución Mexicana, en el que aglutinó a los principales caudillos sobrevivientes del movimiento armado.

Revueltas, Andrea ◆ n. en el DF (1938). Hija de José Revueltas. Maestra en sociología urbana (1975) y doctora en ciencias políticas (1980) por la Universidad de París. Ha sido profesora de la UNAM y de las universidades de Varsovia (1981-82) y Barcelona (1985). Con Philippe Cheron preparó las obras completas de José Revueltas, publicadas en 25 tomos. Autora de *El campamento 2 de Octubre* (1976), *Los caminos de Sartre* (1980), *Ante la crisis. Analogías y diferencias entre el caso polaco y México* (1983), *Revueltas en la mira* (1984), *Clase política y élites políticas* (1987), *La novela política, expresión de la realidad* (1988, coautora), *Estado y modernidad* (1993).

Revueltas, Eugenia ◆ n. en el DF (1934). Maestra en letras hispánicas por la UNAM, donde es profesora, especializada en teoría y crítica literaria e historia de la cultura. Autora de los libros de ensayo: *Vida y poesía en la obra de Alfonso Reyes* (1979), *Vasos comunicantes* (1985), *Novela mexicana contemporánea I* (1985), *Cuento folclórico y sus ecotipos* (1985), *La novela policiaca en Latinoamérica* (1985), *Hermenéutica de Los Sueños de Quevedo* (1987), *José Revueltas en el banquillo de los acusados y otros ensayos* (1987), *Lexicón alarconiano. Eros y ethos: siete calas en el discurso de Juan Ruiz de Alarcón* (1991), *Breve panorama de la literatura mexicana* (1992).

Revueltas, Fermín ◆ n. en Santiago Papasquiaro, Dgo., y m. en el DF (1903-1935). Pintor, hermano de José y Silvestre Revueltas. Estudió en el Art Institute de Chicago (1913-19). Regresó a México (1920) y participó en el movimiento muralista. Se integró a la Escuela de Chimalistac, fundó la Escuela de Pintura al Aire Libre de Milpa Alta (1921) y dirigió la de la Villa de Guadalupe, dio clases en la Escuela Industrial Insurgentes y en el INBA. En 1922 fue cofundador del Sindicato de Obreros Técnicos Pintores y Escultores, organizado por Diego Rivera y David Alfaro Siqueiros. Militó en el Partido Comunista y participó en el movimiento estridentista. Fundó la Escuela de Pintura de Cholula. En 1929 se integró a las Misiones Culturales y realizó varias escenografías en Tabasco. Expuso en EUA, invitado por la Federación Americana de las Artes y The College Arts Association. Realizó los vitrales del Centro Escolar Revolución y de una organización campesina en Sonora. Hay pinturas suyas en el Museo de Arte Moderno, en la Cámara Agrícola de Cuernavaca y en la Biblioteca de la Escuela Eréndira de Pátzcuaro. Decoró los interiores del monumento a Obregón y del Instituto Técnico Industrial (1927). Ejecutó los murales *Alegoría de la Virgen de Guadalupe* (1922), *Símbolos del trabajo* (1932, en el edificio del periódico *El Nacional*) y *Alegoría de la producción*, para el Banco Nacional Hipotecario (1934, trasladado al Museo Nacional de Arte en 1977). Perteneció a la Liga de Escritores y Artistas Revolucionarios (1934-35).

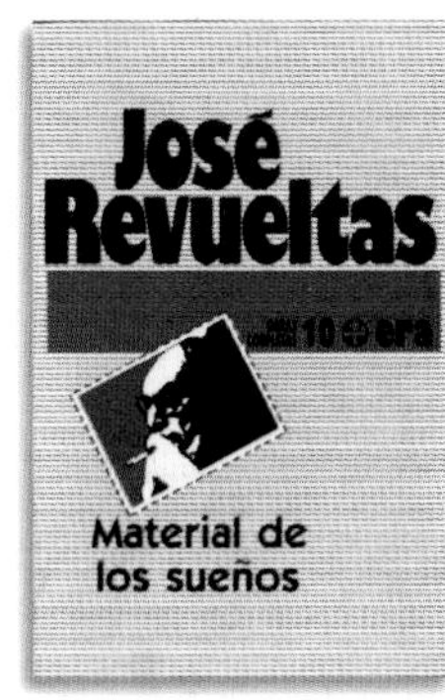

Portada de libro escrito por José Revueltas

Revueltas, José ◆ n. en Durango, Dgo., y m. en el DF (1914-1976). Hermano del anterior. Inició su militancia comunista hacia 1928 en el Socorro Rojo Internacional e ingresó en el Partido Comunista (1932), en el que trabajó en la reorganización de la Federación de Jóvenes Comunistas. Fue expulsado en 1943 y formó parte del Grupo Marxista El Insurgente, que se fusionó con otras organizaciones para fundar el Partido Popular (1947), en el que permaneció hasta mediados de los cincuenta. Volvió en 1956 al PCM, del que salió en 1959 e ingresó en el Partido Obrero Campesino Mexicano, que dejó al año siguiente para fundar la Liga

Dibujo de Fermín Revueltas para el cuento "Pax tecum"

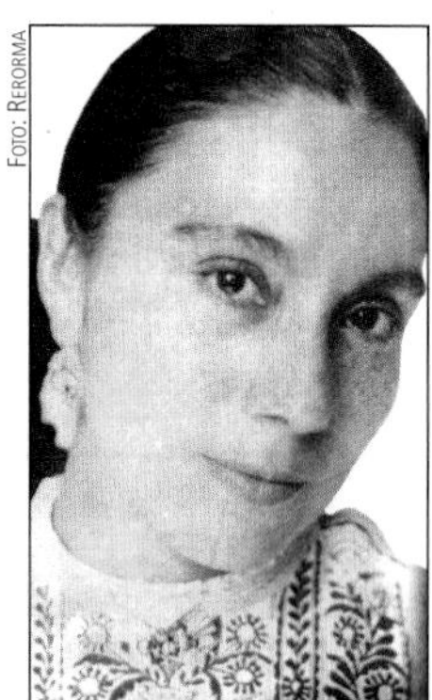

FOTO: REFORMA

Rosaura Revueltas

FOTO: ÉPOCA

Silvestre Revueltas

Román Revueltas Retes

FOTO: ROGELIO CUÉLLAR

José Revueltas

Leninista Espartaco, de la que fue expulsado en 1963. Cofundador del Grupo Comunista Internacionalista (1968). Fue secretario juvenil de la Confederación Sindical Unitaria de México (1929-35). Ocupó la secretaría del interior y la secretaría general (1949) de la Sección de Autores y Adaptadores del Sindicato de Trabajadores de la Producción Cinematográfica. Fue encarcelado numerosas veces, dos de ellas en las islas Marías: la primera a los 14 años de edad y la última, en la penitenciaría de Lecumberri, por su participación en el movimiento estudiantil de 1968. Quedó en libertad en 1971. Profesor del CUEC (1963-65), fue reportero de *El Popular* y *El Día*. Entre 1944 y 1960 fue argumentista y adaptador de varias películas, entre las que destacan *El rebozo de soledad* (1952) y *La ilusión viaja en tranvía* (1953). Autor de *Los muros de agua* (1941), *El luto humano* (1943, Premio Nacional de Literatura), *Dios en la tierra* (1944), *Los días terrenales* (1949), *El cuadrante de la soledad* (1950), *En algún valle de lágrimas* (1956), *Los motivos de Caín* (1957), *México: una democracia bárbara* (1958), *Tierra y libertad* (1960), *Dormir en tierra* (1960), *Ensayo sobre un proletariado sin cabeza* (1962), *Los errores* (1964), *Apuntes para una semblanza de Silvestre Revueltas* (1966), *El apando* (1969) y *Material de los sueños* (1974), entre otras muchas obras. De 1978 a 1984 se editaron sus *Obras completas* preparadas por Andrea Revueltas y Philippe Cheron. Miembro de la LEAR (1934-38) y de la Asociación de Escritores de México. Obtuvo un premio de la editorial Farrar and Reinhert de Nueva York y en 1951 rechazó un premio del gobierno franquista español. Recibió en 1968 el Premio Xavier Villaurrutia.

REVUELTAS, JULIO ◆ n. en el DF (1969). Músico. Nieto del anterior. Su primer apellido es Leal. Estudió en la Escuela Superior de Música y cursó la carrera de afinador de pianos. Guitarrista, trabajó en empleos eventuales hasta la grabación de su primer disco, *De cielo y tierra* (1995), producido por él mismo. Después grabó *Mi Santa María* (1998) y se ha presentado en foros del país y el extranjero.

REVUELTAS, ROSAURA ◆ n. en Ciudad Lerdo, Dgo., y m. en el DF (1920-1996). Bailarina y actriz. Hermana de José, Fermín y Silvestre Revueltas. Trabajó en Alemania en el Berliner Ensamble de Bertolt Brecht y dos años con el teatro cubano. También fue miliciana y oficial de postas en Cuba durante la invasión estadounidense a Playa Girón. Fue bailarina del ballet de Waldeen. En 1986 fue jurado en el Festival Cinematográfico de Berlín y en 1988, en el de Barcelona. Actuó en diversas películas, entre ellas: *Islas Marías* (1950), *Muchachas de uniforme* (1950), *El rebozo de Soledad* (1952, Ariel a la mejor actriz), *Morir para vivir* (1954), *La fuerza de los humildes* (1954) y *La sal de la tierra* (1955, premio a la mejor actriz en el Festival de Karlovy Vary); después de filmar ésta fue calificada de "comunista" por el gobierno de Washington y expulsada de Estados Unidos. Fue profesora de danza y de yoga. Editó *Silvestre Revueltas por él mismo* (1989). Autora de *Los Revueltas* (1979).

REVUELTAS, SILVESTRE ◆ n. en Santiago Papasquiaro, Dgo., y m. en el DF (1899-1940). Músico. Hermano de la anterior. Estudió violín en el Conservatorio Nacional (1913-16) y en el Saint Edward College de San Antonio, Texas (1917) y violín y composición en el Chicago Musical College (1918 y 1922). Con Carlos Chávez organizó un ciclo de conciertos para dar a conocer composiciones de contemporáneos (1924-25). En 1926 inició una gira por el país con Lupe Medina y Francisco Agea y después se desempeñó como violinista y director en varias orquestas del sur de Estados Unidos. A su regreso impartió la cátedra de composición en el Conservatorio Nacional y, llamado por Carlos Chávez, fue subdirector de la recién creada Orquesta Sinfónica Nacional (1929-35). En 1936 dirigió la Orquesta de Alumnos del Conservatorio y sustituyó a Carlos Chávez al frente de la Sinfónica Nacional. También en 1936 ocupó la secretaría general de la Liga de Escritores y Artistas Revolucionarios y un año después fue a España, donde ofreció conciertos en los frentes republicanos. Volvió a México, compuso numerosas obras de concierto y música para películas: *Cuauhnáhuac* (1930), *Esquinas* (1930), *Tres cuartetos de cuerda* (1931), *Ventanas* (1931), *Ranas* (1931), *El tecolote* (1931), *Dúo para pato y canario* (1931), *Tres piezas para violín y piano* (1932), *Feria* (1932), *Alcancías* (1932), *Tocata* (1933), *8 por radio* (1933), *Colorines* (1933), *Planos* (1934), *Redes* (1935), *Caminos* (1936), *Janitzio* (1936), *Homenaje a García Lorca* (1936), *Vámonos con Pancho Villa* (1936), *El renacuajo paseador* (1936), *Dos canciones* (1937), *Siete canciones* (1938), *Sensemayá* (1938), *El indio* (1938), *Ferrocarriles de Baja California* (1938), *La noche de los mayas* (1939), *Bajo el signo de la muerte* (1939), *La coronela* (1940, ballet finalizado por Blas Galindo y Candelario Huízar) y *Los de abajo* (1940). Su correspondencia fue editada por Rosaura Revueltas en el volumen *Silvestre Revueltas por él mismo* (1989). Para conmemorar su centenario, la Orquesta Sinfónica Nacional ofreció una serie de conciertos en 1999.

REVUELTAS RETES, ROMÁN ◆ n. en el DF (1952). Hijo de José Revueltas. Violinista. Inició su aprendizaje en 1960 con los profesores Vladimir Vulfman y José Smilovits. Estudió en la

Academia Rubin de la Universidad de Tel Aviv (1974), el Conservatorio Real de Lieja (1974, donde obtuvo el primer premio de violín en 1977 y el diploma superior en 1980) y la academia de Igor Ozim en Colonia. Se presentó en México en el décimo Festival Internacional Cervantino (1982) con la Orquesta Filarmónica de la UNAM. Ha ofrecido conciertos en varias ciudades de México y Europa. Ha sido solista de las principales orquestas mexicanas, primer concertino de la Filarmónica de la Ciudad de México (1982-86) y de la Orquesta Ciudad de Barcelona (1992-94), primer concertino invitado de la Sinfónica de Euzkadi (1995-96) y director de la Orquesta San Ángel. Fue asesor de cultura de la campaña de Carlos Castillo Peraza por el gobierno del DF (1997). Fue colaborador de *La Crónica de Hoy* (1996-97) y escribe en el *Diario de Monterrey* (1994-). Editor de cultura (1997-99) y de asuntos especiales de *Milenio* (1999-). Entre sus composiciones se cuentan *Camino cerrado* (1989), *19 de septiembre* (1990), *Cuarteto* (1990), *Fanfarria para la Filarmónica de la Ciudad de México* (1990), *Andante elegíaco* (1991), *Pasos perdidos* (1991) y *Presagio y luna* (1997).

REX, DOMINGO ◆ n. en España (1900-?). Escritor y diplomático. Fue agregado cultural del consulado general de la República Española en São Paulo, Brasil (1936-38). Llegó a México en 1939. Fue agregado cultural de la embajada de España en México, trabajó en la radiodifusión cultural y fundó ediciones Rex y la Editorial Clavileño. Editor de *Retrato Hispánico*. Autor de *A través de España* (1944), *Tierra y sangre de España* (1944) y *Galerías de España* (1945).

REY, BRUNO ◆ n. en Guadalajara, Jal., y m. en el DF (1939-1995). Actor. Nombre profesional de Eliseo Reynoso González. Comenzó su carrera en 1970, al unirse al taller de teatro de José de Jesús Aceves. Luego pasó al cine, donde destacó en papeles recios. En su filmografía descatan *El principio* (1972), *Longitud de guerra* (1975, Diosa de plata al mejor actor de reparto), *Pedro Páramo*, *El hombre de la Media Luna* (1976), *Las noches de Paloma* (1977) y *El jinete de la divina providencia* (1988). También hizo telenovelas (entre ellas, *Senda de gloria* y *El vuelo del águila*).

REY, CARMELA ◆ n. en Jalapa, Ver. (1931). Cantante. Fue alumna de Fanny Anitúa. José Sabre Marroquín la indujo a interpretar música popular y Agustín Lara la dio a conocer. En los años cincuenta cobró popularidad por sus presentaciones en la XEW, en teatro, televisión y cine. Con Rafael Vázquez, su esposo, formó el dueto Carmela y Rafael.

REY, VENUS ◆ n. en Ciudad Mendoza, Ver. (1916). Nombre profesional del músico Venustiano Reyes López. Trombonista y maestro de música por el Conservatorio Nacional, cuya sociedad de alumnos presidió. Se especializó en la Juilliard School of Music y en la Universidad Columbia de Nueva York. Regresó a México en 1946 y dirigió la Orquesta Sinfónica de Bellas Artes. Formó después una orquesta de música popular bailable. Ha sido profesor en la UNAM y en el Conservatorio Nacional, dos veces diputado federal (1976-79 y 1982-85), presidente de la Sociedad Mexicana de Ejecutantes de Música y secretario general del Sindicato Único de Trabajadores de la Música, cargo al que renunció en 1989 a raíz de un movimiento opositor dentro de la organización.

REYERO, MANUEL ◆ n. en el DF (1941). Arquitecto graduado en la UNAM, donde fue profesor (1964-66). Ha sido fundador de la empresa Synergetics de México (1964), asesor del proyecto de la Universidad de Chapingo (1965-66), coordinador y corresponsal de área en México para la World Design Science Decade (1965-75), asesor del presidente del Colegio Nacional de Arquitectos (1973), asesor de la presidencia de Televisa (1974-88), asesor del secretario de Relaciones Exteriores (1978-80). Autor de *Leonardo da Vinci* (1955), *Visión del México antiguo* (1956), *Visión de la antigua Mesopotamia* (1959), *Visión del antiguo Egipto* (1960), *World Comunications* (19-66), *The Information Environment* (19-66), *Expansión ecológica* (1967), *Crisis on World Energy* (1967), *Colección prehispánica* (1979, premiado en París con Le Grand Aigle d'Or al mejor libro de arte del mundo en 1979 y Le Cadrat d'Or a la mejor impresión de arte en 1980, y en Leipzig con el Schoenste Bücher aus Aller Welt al mejor diseño de libro de arte del mundo en 1980), *Recinto prehispánico* (1980), *Catálogo general. Colección del Museo Rufino Tamayo* (1981, premio a la mejor impresión del año de la New York Printers Association) y *Diego Rivera* (1983, diploma al mejor libro de arte de la Asociación Nacional de Artes Gráficas de México en 1984). Miembro de número de la World Futures Studies Federation (1967) y miembro fundador y presidente de la Fundación Cultural México 2000 (1977).

REYES, LOS ◆ Municipio de Michoacán situado al sur de Zamora y al noroeste de Uruapan, en los límites con Jalisco. Superficie: 523.77 km^2. Habitantes: 54,039, de los cuales 13,759 forman la población económicamente activa. Hablan alguna lengua indígena 7,831 personas mayores de cinco años (purépecha 7,792), de las cuales 1,001 no dominan el español. A 24 kilómetros de la cabecera, Los Reyes de Salgado, están las caídas de agua Chorros del Varal: cinco torrentes que salen de una montaña y caen en una barranca, donde forman el principal afluente del río Tepalcatepec.

REYES, LOS ◆ Municipio de Veracruz situado al sur de Orizaba y contiguo a Zongolica. Superficie: 33.72 km^2. Habitantes: 3,609, de los cuales 883 forman la población económicamente activa. Hablan náhuatl 2,964 personas mayores de cinco años. Indígenas monolingües: 1,088.

REYES, LOS ◆ ☛ *Paz, La*.

REYES, ALFONSO ◆ n. en Monterrey, NL, y m. en el DF (1889-1959). Escritor. Hijo de Bernardo Reyes. Licenciado en derecho por la Universidad Nacional

Carmela Rey

Foto: Época

Alicia Reyes

Alfonso Reyes

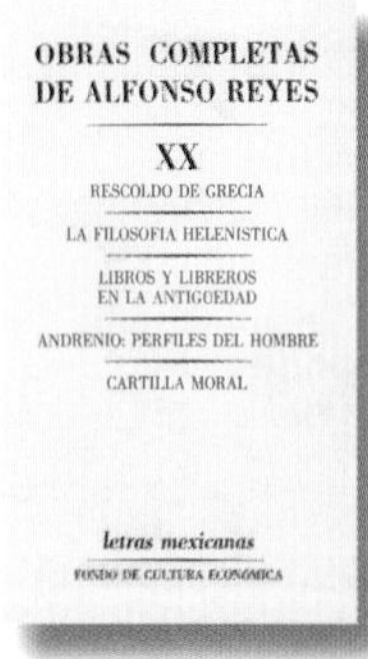

Tomo XX de las *Obras Completas de Alfonso Reyes* editadas por el Fondo de Cultura Económica

(1913). En 1909 fundó con José Vasconcelos, Pedro Henríquez Ureña y Antonio Caso, entre otros, el Ateneo de la Juventud. Fue secretario (1912-13) de la Escuela Nacional de Altos Estudios, donde fundó las cátedras de lengua y literatura españolas. Segundo secretario de la legación en Francia (1913-14), al triunfo del constitucionalismo fue destituido. Radicado en España se dedicó a la literatura y al periodismo. En 1920 fue nombrado segundo secretario de la legación en Madrid. Encargado de negocios plenipotenciario en España (1922-24), ministro en Francia (1924-27), embajador en Argentina (1927-30 y 36-37) y en Brasil (1930-36), donde inició la publicación de *Monterrey. Correo Literario de Alfonso Reyes*, periódico redactado casi íntegramente por él. Regresó a México en 1939 y fue presidente fundador de la Casa de España, antecedente de El Colegio de México. Colaboró en las principales publicaciones del país. Autor de un centenar de volúmenes de narrativa, ensayo, teatro y poesía, entre los que destacan *Cuestiones estéticas* (1910-11), *Visión de Anáhuac* (1917), *Ifigenia cruel* (1924), *Égloga de los ciegos* (1925), *Reloj de sol* (1926), *Cuestiones gongorinas* (1927), *Discurso por Virgilio* (1931), *Tren de ondas* (1932), *Cantata en la tumba de Federico García Lorca* (1937), *Última Tule* (1942), *Los trabajos y los días, 1934-1944* (1945), *Por mayo era, por mayo* (1946), *Mi idea de la historia* (1949), *La X en la frente* (1952), *Trayectoria de Goethe* (1954), *Estudios helénicos* (1957), *Crónica de Monterrey* (1960) y *Oración del 9 de febrero* (1963). En 1955 el Fondo de Cultura Económica inició la publicación de sus *Obras completas*. Fue miembro de número y presidente (1957-59) de la Academia Mexicana (de la Lengua) y miembro fundador de El Colegio Nacional. Recibió en 1945 el Premio Nacional de Ciencias y Artes (primer galardonado con el mismo). *Doctor honoris causa* por las universidades de Nuevo León (1933), Tulane y Harvard (1942), Michoacán, Berkeley y Princeton (1952), Nacional Autónoma de México (1953) y de La Habana (1955).

Retrato de Alfonso Reyes

Reyes, Alicia ◆ n. en el DF (1940). Nieta del anterior. Laboratorista médica graduada en la Universidad Femenina. Se especializó en el Instituto Pasteur y estudió letras francesas en la Universidad de París. Trabajó en el Instituto Nacional de Cardiología y simultáneamente estudió letras españolas. Ha colaborado en *Excélsior*, *Novedades*, *Diálogos*, *Revista de la Universidad*, *Historium* y *Nueva Era*. Ha sido profesora en la Alianza Francesa y dirige desde 1965 la Capilla Alfonsina, donde en 1973 creó los talleres literarios y, con Francisco Zendejas, instituyó el premio internacional Alfonso Reyes. Fundó la Sociedad Alfonsina Internacional y edita el *Boletín* de la capilla. Autora de *Poésies* (1965), *Poesías* (1965), *Y en la sombra viva* (1968), *Anecdotario de Alfonso Reyes* (1968), *Diario de Alfonso Reyes (1911-1930)* (1969), *Presencia de Alfonso Reyes* (1969), *A solas.* (1974), *Diario poético* (1974), *¿Qué pasó con las parcas?* (1976), *Genio y figura de Alfonso Reyes* (1976), *Ambartú* (1984), *Fetiche* (1984), *Cómo apreciar a Alfonso Reyes* (1990), *El almacén de Coyoacán* (1990), *Voces para un retrato* (1991) y *Alfonso Reyes en Madrid* (1992), entre otros. Administra el premio Xavier Villaurrutia y fue secretaria general de la Unión Femenina de Periodistas y Escritoras.

Reyes, Antonio de los ◆ n. en España y m. en Teposcolula, Oax. (?-1603). Estudió en la Universidad de Salamanca e ingresó en la orden de los dominicos. Llegó a la provincia de Santiago, actual Oaxaca, en 1555, como vicario del convento, cargo en el que permaneció hasta su muerte. Autor de *Arte en lengua mixteca* (1593).

Reyes, Aurora ◆ n. en Hidalgo del Parral, Chih., y m. en el DF (1908-1985). Nieta de Bernardo Reyes. Se tituló como profesora en la Normal de Chihuahua. Estudió pintura en la Academia de San Carlos, donde fue alumna de Fermín Revueltas y Emilio García Cahero. Fue la primera mujer mexicana que ejecutó un mural, el del Centro Escolar Revolución (*Atentado a las maestras rurales*, 1936). En 1936 ingresó en la LEAR. Expuso por primera vez en 1954. Ejerció la docencia y fue secretaria de acción femenil del SNTE. Son obra suya los cuatro murales del Auditorio 15 de Mayo, del SNTE, y el mural *El primer encuentro* (1977, en el cabildo de Coyoacán), así como los cuadros *Muchacho frente al mar* (premiado en 1940), *Dama de fin de siglo* (premiado en 1940), *Frida frente al espejo* (premiado en 1940), *Autorretrato*, *Mujer de guerra*, *Niña morena* y *Retrato de Krupskaya* (1930). Autora de *Hombre de México* (1947), *Economía dirigida de la vagancia en México* (1951), *Astro en camino* (1951), *Estancias en el desierto* (1952, poemario premiado en el Cincuentenario de la Fundación de Mexicali), *Humanos paisajes* (1953), *Madre nuestra la Tierra* (1958), *La máscara desnuda* (1970), *Poetisas mexicanas. Siglo XX* (1976) y *Espiral en retorno* (1981). En 1975 grabó el disco *Poemas de Aurora Reyes*. Acerca de ella se publicó el libro *La sangre dividida* (1990) de Leticia Ocharán y Roberto López Moreno.

Reyes, Benjamín *Cananea* ◆ n. en Churunababi y m. en Hermosillo, Son. (1937-1991). Beisbolista. Estudió medicina. En 1961 fue integrante de la selección amateur de beisbol que participó en el campeonato mundial de La Habana. Fue jardinero de *los Charros* de Jalisco (1965-67) y de *los Naranjeros* de Hermosillo (1966); jugó en la liga tabasqueña, donde impuso la marca de 43 bases robadas. Entrenador de *los Charros* de Jalisco (1967), de Fresnillo (1969) y de San Luis Potosí (1969), primer equipo al que hizo campeón; dirigió luego al equipo Puerto México (1970) y nuevamente a *los Charros* (1971-72); fue *coach* de *los Naranjeros* de Hermosillo (1972) y dirigió a *los Indios* de Ciudad Juárez (1973) y, simultáneamente, a *los Diablos Rojos* (1974-80); *coach* de los Marineros de Seattle (1980-82), equipo al que dirigió en tres partidos. Dirigió a *los Azules* de Coatzacoalcos (1982-83) y regresó a los *Diablos Rojos* en 1983. Dirigió también a *las Águilas* de Mexicali (1986). Se le conocía como *Supermánager* o *el pelón mágico*. Hizo campeones a varios de los equipos que dirigió. En 1988 fue el primer entrenador en ganar mil juegos en la Liga Mexicana y el único entrenador mexicano que ha ganado la Serie del Caribe.

REYES, BERNARDO ♦ n. en Guadalajara, Jal., y m. en la ciudad de México (1850-1913). Militar. En 1865 se alistó en el ejército republicano para combatir la intervención francesa y el imperio. Se opuso a la rebelión de Tuxtepec y, triunfante ésta, aceptó el gobierno de Díaz, quien lo ascendió a general en 1880 y cinco años más tarde lo nombró comandante de Nuevo León, estado que gobernó provisionalmente (1885-87), cuando reprimió los levantamientos agraristas de Mauricio Cruz y Juan Rodríguez. Volvió a gobernar Nuevo León (1889-1900) y fue secretario de Guerra y Marina (del 25 de enero de 1900 al 24 de diciembre de 1902). En 1903 fue reelegido gobernador de Nuevo León. Por su oposición al gabinete científico de Díaz, los promotores del Partido Democrático iniciaron una campaña con el fin de llevarlo como candidato a la vicepresidencia de la República, pero optó por abandonar a sus seguidores. En 1909 viajó a Europa en un destierro disfrazado de misión diplomática y regresó a México en 1911, durante la presidencia de Madero, contra quien encabezó en el norte del país un levantamiento prontamente sofocado. Fue encarcelado y en 1913, al inicio de la Decena Trágica, lo liberaron los pronunciados. Murió frente al Palacio Nacional en su intento de dar un golpe de Estado. Autor de *Ensayo sobre un nuevo sistema de reclutamiento* (1885), *El ejército mexicano* (1901), *El general Porfirio Díaz. Estudio biográfico* (1903) y *Conversaciones militares* (1907).

REYES, ESTEBAN *PAJARITO* ♦ n. en Contepec, Mich. (1914). Tenista. En 1932 ganó el Torneo Nacional Juvenil. En 1935 fue seleccionado nacional y jugó la serie contra el equipo de Estados Unidos en la Copa Davis, en la que obtuvo el primer punto hecho por un mexicano, al enfrentarse a Gene Mako. Desde 1942 se ha dedicado a la enseñanza en escuelas y centros deportivos de la ciudad de México.

REYES, GUADALUPE ♦ n. en El Refugio, Qro. (1931). Músico autodidacto. Aprendió a tocar guitarra sexta y fue discípulo de Melitón Orozco, quien le enseñó a hacer décimas. Ha competido numerosas veces con otros decimistas y ha logrado "tratados" de hasta 10 décimas continuadas sobre el mismo tema. Desde 1963 se acompaña con la guitarra quinta huapanguera. Ha grabado seis discos.

REYES, ISIDRO ♦ n. en Querétaro, Qro., y m. en Morelia, Mich. (1798-1848). Militar realista desde 1813. Se unió en 1821 al ejército trigarante y participó en la toma de Perote (1823). Ocupó la jefatura militar de Michoacán, México, San Luis Potosí y Monterrey. General de brigada en 1835. Fue comandante militar y gobernador de Puebla (1843) y secretario de Guerra y Marina (del 11 de junio al 12 de septiembre, del 12 al 21 de septiembre, y del 21 de septiembre al 23 de noviembre de 1844) en los gabinetes de Santa Anna, José Joaquín de Herrera y Valentín Canalizo. Al ser ocupada la ciudad de México por los invasores estadounidenses (1847), Manuel de la Peña y Peña lo nombró jefe del ejército.

REYES, JAIME ♦ n. y m. en el DF (1947-1999). Poeta. Estudió periodismo en la UNAM, donde fue coordinador de conferencias de la Casa del Lago y editor de cuadernos de lectura para los Colegios de Ciencias y Humanidades. Fue colaborador de *La Gaceta del* FCE, *Imaginaria, Plural, Crisis*, de Buenos Aires, *Sábado* y *La Cultura en México*. Autor de *Salgo de lo oscuro* (1970), *Isla de raíz amarga, Insomne raíz* (1976, Premio Xavier Villaurrutia), *La oración del ogro* (1984), *Al vuelo el espejo de un río* (1986) y *Un día, un río* (1999, publicado póstumamente). Premio Nacional de Poesía de la Universidad Autónoma de Zacatecas (1983).

FOTO:ARCHIVO XAVIER ESPARZA

Bernardo Reyes

REYES, JORGE ♦ n. en Uruapan, Mich. (1950). Músico. Hizo estudios en la Escuela Nacional de Música de la UNAM, estudió improvisación de jazz con Herb Heller en Hamburgo, y música tradicional en Turquía, Afganistán, Pakistán y Sri Lanka. Fue guitarrista y flautista de los grupos de rock Nuevo México y Chac Mool. Como solista se ha dedicado a crear "texturas sonoras", mezclar instrumentos prehispánicos con sintetizadores y muestreo digital. Ha grabado los discos de larga duración *Ek-tunkul* (1985), *A la izquierda del colibrí* (1986, con Antonio Zepeda; premio de la Academia de Ciencias de la URSS), *Comala* (1987), *Viento de navajas* (1988, banda sonora de la película *El ombligo de la Luna*, de Jorge Prior), *Niérika* (1990), *Crónica de castas* (1991, con Suso Sáiz), *Bajo el sol jaguar* (1991), *Suspended Memories, Forgotten Gods* (1992, con Suso Sáiz y Steve Roach) y *El costumbre* (1993). Durante el eclipse total de sol de 1991 ofreció un concierto en Teotihuacán con música compuesta *ex profeso*, y ha continuado ofreciendo conciertos en zonas arqueológicas y en el Espacio Escultórico de la UNAM, además de en numerosos festivales en el extranjero. También en 1991 organizó

FOTO:GUILLERMO AGUILERA

Jorge Reyes

FOTO: ÉPOCA

Lucha Reyes

el primer Encuentro Internacional de Músicas Visuales, que agrupó a músicos de cinco países.

REYES, JOSÉ JOAQUÍN ◆ n. y m. en Puebla, Pue. (1795-1862). Militar realista desde 1811, luchó contra los insurgentes hasta 1821, cuando se adhirió al Plan de Iguala. Fue ayudante y secretario de la comandancia militar de Oaxaca. General en 1841. En 1843 sustituyó a Isidro Reyes en la gubernatura de Puebla y ocupó el mismo cargo en 1846. Combatió a los invasores estadounidenses.

REYES, JUAN JOSÉ ◆ n. en el DF (1955). Estudió filosofía en la UNAM. Ha sido profesor del ITAM. Ha colaborado en *El Correo del Libro* (del que fue editor de 1978 a 1982), *Revista Mexicana de Cultura*, *El Día de los Jóvenes* (suplemento cultural de *El Día* y el Crea, que fundó y dirigió), *Casa del Tiempo*, *Universidad de México*, *La Letra y la Imagen*, *Nexos*, *Crónica*, y *El Semanario Cultural de Novedades*, del que fue jefe de redacción (1983-98). Fue fundador y director de la revista *Textual* del periódico *El Nacional* y jefe de redacción de la revista *Estudios*, del ITAM. Redactor de *Letras Libres* (1999-). Coautor de *Hambre de gol*. Autor de *Cuestión de suerte*.

REYES, JUDITH ◆ n. cerca de Tampico, Tams., y m. en el DF (¿1920?-1988). Cantante conocida como *la Tamaulipeca*. Empezó a actuar en el Teatro de los Alijadores de Tampico a los 14 años de edad. A los 18 años integró un dueto con su esposo y ambos realizaron una gira por EUA, donde vendió sus primeras cuatro canciones. Trabajó en la Rondalla de *Tata Nacho*, en la XEW. Fue reportera del diario chihuahuense *El Informador* y de *El Monitor*, de Parral, donde también tuvo un programa de radio. En 1960 empezó a componer e interpretar canciones de corte político. En la ciudad de Chihuahua fundó el periódico *Acción. Voz Revolucionaria del Pueblo* (1960-66) y fue corresponsal de *Política* (1964). En 1964, cuando era candidata del Frente Electoral del Pueblo a senadora por Chihuahua, fue encarcelada. Cofundadora de la Sociedad de Autores y Compositores de México. Vivió exiliada en varios países de Europa (1970-74). Autora de unas 300 canciones, entre las que se cuentan: *Los tupamaros*, *Tal como lo dijo Marx*, *Corrido de la represión estudiantil del 26 de julio*, *Corrido del desagravio*, *Corrido del incendio de Iztacalco (Campamento 2 de octubre)*, *Corrido de la huelga Peralvillo-Cozumel*, *Corrido del cuarto informe del gobierno de Díaz Ordaz*, *Corrido de la ocupación militar de la Universidad*, *Canción de la Universidad*, *Canción del Politécnico*, *Corrido de los combates de Zacatenco* y *Tlatelolco*. Autora de los libros *El corrido. Presencia del juglar en la historia de México*, *El cantar materialista de la historia* y *La otra cara de la patria* (1974).

REYES, LUCHA ◆ n. en Guadalajara, Jal., y m. en el DF (1906-1942). Cantante cuyo nombre era María de la Luz Flores Acevedo. Inició su carrera como cantante de corridos en 1918 en una carpa de la ciudad de México. Actuó después en otras carpas donde alternó con José Limón, Amelia Wilhelmy y los hermanos Acevedo. En 1920 realizó una gira por el sur de Estados Unidos y a su regreso fue contratada por los teatros Iris y Lírico. Formó parte, durante un breve lapso, del trío Reyes-Ascencio, del que se separó para continuar su carrera como solista en teatros y en la radio, ya con el pseudónimo que la hizo popular. Grabó numerosos discos. Actuó para la radio y participó en las películas *Canción del alma* (1937), *La tierra del mariachi* (1938), *Los dorados de Villa* (1939), *El zorro de Jalisco* (1940), *¡Ay Jalisco, no te rajes!* (1941) y *Flor silvestre* (1943).Compuso las piezas *La tequilera*, *La mujer ladina* y *El herradero*. Se suicidó. En años recientes su figura se ha convertido en parte del imaginario colectivo, como lo testimonia la película *La reina de la noche* (1993), de Arturo Ripstein, que se basa muy libremente en su biografía.

REYES, MARIANO ◆ n. y m. en Querétaro, Qro. (1815-1882). Militar conservador. Participó en 1836 en la guerra de Texas y más tarde en la sublevación de Paredes y Arrillaga. En 1846 se le envió a la frontera norte para efectuar obras de defensa, peleó contra los invasores estadounidenses en Palo Alto y Resaca de Guerrero, luego en Monterrey y volvió a la capital del país para preparar la defensa del valle de México. Combatió en Padierna, donde cayó prisionero. Al fin de la guerra fue nombrado jefe militar de San Luis Potosí y en 1854 combatió a los partidarios del Plan de Ayutla. En 1858, alineado con los golpistas del Plan de Tacubaya, se le nombró comandante general del territorio de Iturbide (Morelos) y recibió el grado de general dos años después. Apresado en Silao, González Ortega ordenó su liberación. Fue gobernador y comandante militar de Querétaro. Al triunfo de los liberales se retiró del ejército. En 1863, bajo la ocupación francesa, se le nombró ingeniero militar. Adherido al imperio, participó en la defensa de Querétaro (1867). Al triunfo de la República pasó siete años en la cárcel, despues de los cual se dedicó a la docencia. Era director del Colegio Civil de Querétaro cuando murió.

REYES, MARIO ◆ n. en el DF (1929). Estudió pintura y escultura en La Esmeralda (1950-56). Su primera exposición pictórica fue en 1953. Fundó en 1965 el Taller Libre de Grabado Mario Reyes, que él mismo dirige, donde ha editado libros y carpetas de Francisco Toledo, David Alfaro Siqueiros, Francisco Corzas, Vlady, Luis López Loza, Antonio Rodríguez Luna y Rodolfo Nieto. Profesor del Colegio Madrid, de la Escuela de Diseño y Artesanías y de la UIA. Ha participado en exposiciones colectivas en Sofía, México, Buenos Aires, Nueva York y Toronto. En 1970 ganó el Premio Nacional de Grabado del Salón de la Plástica Mexicana.

REYES, MIGUEL ◆ n. en La Manzanilla y m. en Guadalajara, Jal. (1914-1991). Músico. Fundó con sus hermanos el grupo Los Hermanos Reyes, que grabó 60 discos de larga duración, participó en 19 películas y tuvo éxito con las canciones *Pancho López*, *Río Colorado* y *La sirenita*, entre otras. Abrió un hotel en

Guadalajara, en el que actuó con sus hermanos hasta su muerte.

Reyes, Refugio ◆ n. en Sauceda, Zac., y m. en Aguascalientes, Ags. (1862-1945). Arquitecto autodidacto. Entre los 14 y los 19 de edad trabajó como peón en el tendido de vías férreas en Zacatecas, donde aprendió los rudimentos de la ingeniería. En Zacatecas construyó la torre del reloj de la iglesia de Guadalupe (1882), el mercado municipal (1888), los altares del templo de San Francisco (1890), el santuario de Guadalupe (1892), la capilla del Soyotal (1894) y la capilla de Río de Medina (1898-1901). En Aguascalientes proyectó y edificó el templo de San Antonio, considerado su obra maestra (1894-1908), el edificio del Banco Nacional de México (1905), el Banco de Zacatecas (1906), el hotel París (1914), el hotel Francia (1915) y numerosas casas particulares. Escribió unas *Notas de los años que llevo de vida*.

Reyes, Rodolfo ◆ n. en San Cristóbal de Las Casas, Chis. (1936). Bailarín y coreógrafo. Hizo estudios de escultura, pintura y danza en México, y de etnografía y etnocoreografía en Cuba y Chile. Ha fundado 18 compañías de danza, entre las que destacan el Teatro de la Danza de La Habana, el Ballet Contemporáneo de la Universidad Veracruzana, el Ballet de Danza Contemporánea de Nicaragua y el Conjunto Nacional de Danza Contemporánea de Chile. También ha practicado la docencia. Como promotor cultural, ha asesorado y participado en la organización de festivales culturales en México y el extranjero. Director del Conjunto Cultural Ollin Yoliztli (1998-).

Reyes, Salvador *Chava* ◆ n. en Guadalajara, Jal. (1936). Futbolista. Como aficionado, representó a Jalisco en los Juegos Juveniles de la Revolución (1952). Comenzó su carrera profesional, jugando como interior derecho, en 1953 en el Guadalajara, con el que fue siete veces campeón de liga y cinco de copa. Fue campeón individual de goleo en la temporada 1956-57 y seleccionado nacional (1955-56). Jugó nueve partidos en tres campeonatos del mundo (1958, 1962 y 1966). Terminó su carrera jugando en Estados Unidos.

Reyes, Víctor M. ◆ n. en Campeche, Camp., y m en el DF (1896-?). Pintor y escritor. Estudió en la Escuela de Bellas Artes de Mérida, en la Academia de San Carlos y en la Academia de Artes Decorativas, de París, donde fue ayudante de Santos Balmori. Decoró el pabellón de México en la Exposición Iberoamericana de Sevilla (1943). Fue profesor de dibujo en escuelas públicas. Representó a México en la Asociación Internacional para la Enseñanza del Arte. Organizó exposiciones de arte mexicano en varios países europeos y latinoamericanos. Dirigió la Escuela de Bellas Artes de San Miguel Allende (1951-). Fue jefe del Departamento Artes Plásticas de la Secretaría de Educación Pública (1953-56), subdirector general (1953-60) y subdirector técnico del Instituto Nacional de Bellas Artes (1961-88). Colaboró en *México en el Arte* y otras publicaciones. Autor de *Pedagogía del dibujo* (1943), *Breve ensayo sobre el pintor Francisco Goitia* y numerosos prólogos, presentaciones y monografías de artistas. En 1988 recibió un homenaje público organizado por la Universidad Autónoma Metropolitana.

Reyes Aurrecoechea, Alfonso ◆ n. en San Luis Potosí, SLP (1916). Radicado en Monterrey. Profesor por la Escuela Normal para Maestros (1938). Ha ejercido la docencia y colaborado en *El Porvenir*, *Tribuna*, *Armas y Letras*, *El Tiempo* y *Resurgimiento*. Fue director del mensuario *Nuevo León* y fundador y director de la Editorial Alfonso Reyes. Vicepresidente de la Sociedad Nuevoleonesa de Historia y director de su órgano, *Roel*. Autor de *Alfonso Reyes entre burlas y veras* (1960), *Francisco M. Zertuche. Homenaje en el X aniversario de su muerte* (1966) y *Orozco. Una voz mexicana de categoría* (1967).

Reyes Avilés, Salvador ◆ n. en Durango, Dgo., y m. en el DF (1893-1954). Se unió en 1913 al Ejército Libertador del Sur y formó parte del Estado Mayor de Emiliano Zapata, de quien fue secretario particular. Sobrevivió a la emboscada de Chinameca (1919) y redactó el parte oficial del asesinato de Zapata. Medio año más tarde se separó del ejército, con el grado de teniente coronel. Fue diputado federal (1924-25) y trabajó en la Comisión Nacional Agraria y en el Departamento Agrario, del que era director de organización al morir. Autor de *Cartones zapatistas* (1928) y *Biografía del general Emiliano Zapata y parte oficial de su muerte* (1934).

Chava Reyes

Reyes Etla ◆ Municipio de Oaxaca situado al noroeste de la capital estatal, en el centro de la entidad. Superficie: 24.24 km^2. Habitantes: 2,566, de los cuales 690 forman la población económicamente activa. Hablan alguna lengua indígena ocho personas mayores de cinco años.

Foto: Reforma

Chucho Reyes

Reyes Ferreira, Jesús *Chucho* ◆ n. en Guadalajara, Jal., y m. en el DF (1882-1977). Pintor autodidacto. Presentó su obra por primera vez en 1950, en la galería Arquitac, de Guadalajara. Participó en 1961 en la exposición internacional de Los Hartos, en la galería Antonio Souza, y su primera exposición individual tuvo lugar en 1967, en Bellas Artes. Expuso en Barcelona en 1972 y, en 1975, por última vez, en la Galería Pecanins. Se dedicó también al comercio de antigüedades. Entre sus obras destacan los cuadros *Ángel*, *El alquimista*, *Demonio*, *Pasa güero*, *San Francisco muerto*, *Virgen*, *Calavera*, *Payaso*, *Cristo negro*, *Diablo*, *Flores*, *Caballos*, *Tigre enjaulado* y sus famosos *Gallos*, realizados al óleo sobre papel de china.

Reyes Heroles, Federico ◆ n. en el DF (1955). Hijo de Jesús Reyes Heroles. Licenciado en ciencias políticas por la UNAM, donde ha sido asesor de la Secretaría General Académica (1977-78), profesor, coordinador y subdirector del Programa de Superación Académica (1981-82), investigador del Instituto de Investigaciones Jurídicas (1982-85) y coordinador de Humanidades (1985-86). Ha colaborado en *Cuadernos Políticos* (1980), *unomásuno* (1981-83),

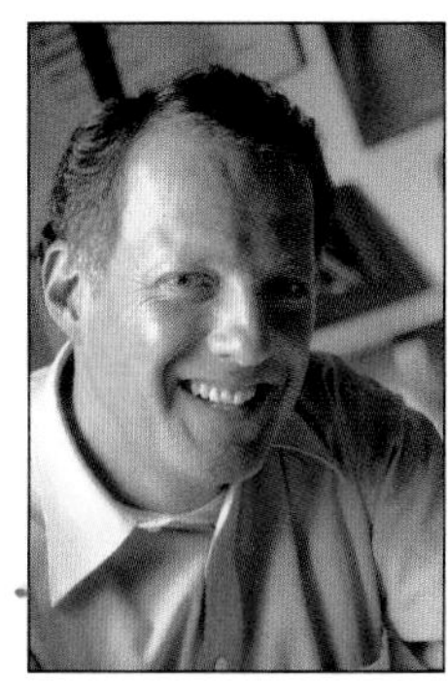

Federico Reyes Heroles

Jesús Reyes Heroles González Garza

Luis Reyes de la Maza

Nexos (1983-), *Los Universitarios*, *La Jornada* (periódico del que fue fundador en 1984 y en el que ocupó la presidencia del Consejo de Administración de 1987 a 1988) y *Reforma* (1993-). Dirigió La Revista de la *Universidad* (1985-86) y dirige *Este país* (1992-). Autor de *Ensayo sobre los fundamentos políticos del Estado contemporáneo* (1982), *Política y administración a través de la idea de vida* (1983), *Transfiguraciones políticas del Estado mexicano* (1987), *Contrahechuras mexicanas* (1988), *La democracia difícil* (1991), *Transfiguraciones y semblanzas* (1992); de la novela: *Ante los ojos de Desireé* (1983); y *Anclajes* (1985, artículos periodísticos). Editó el volumen de ensayos *Los partidos políticos mexicanos en 1991* (1991). Consejo de la CNDH desde 1998.

Reyes Heroles, Jesús ◆ n. en Tuxpan, Ver., y m. en EUA (1921-1985). Licenciado en derecho por la UNAM (1944), hizo estudios de posgrado en las universidades de Buenos Aires y de La Plata y en el Colegio Libre de Estudios Superiores de Buenos Aires (1945). En el PRI fue miembro del IEPES (1949) y de su consejo consultivo (1960), consejero del presidente (1952) y presidente (1972-75) del CEN. En la UNAM fue profesor (1944 y 1946-63) e investigador (1979-85). Vocal del Patronato para el Fomento de las Actividades de Alta Especialización Docente en el IPN (1964-67). Entre otros cargos en el gobierno, desempeñó los de jefe de Estudios Económicos de los Ferrocarriles Nacionales (1953-58), subdirector general técnico del IMSS (1958-64), diputado federal (1961-64), director general de Pemex (1964-70), de Diesel Nacional, Siderúrgica Nacional y Concarril (1970-72); presidente del Centro Interamericano de Estudios de Seguridad Social (1975), director general del IMSS (1975-76), secretario de Gobernación (del 1 de diciembre de 1976 al 16 de mayo de 1979) en el gabinete de José López Portillo, y de Educación Pública (del 10 de diciembre de 1982 al 19 de marzo de 1985) en el de Miguel de la Madrid. Autor de

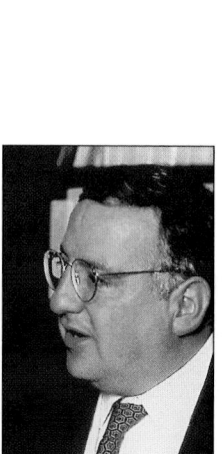

Jesús Reyes Heroles

Tendencias actuales del Estado (1945), *La idea del Estado de derecho* (1946), *Apunte sobre la idea de Estado de derecho* (1947), *La Carta de La Habana* (1948), *Bajo el signo de la inflación* (1951), *Restauración, revisión y tercer camino* (1952), *El liberalismo mexicano* (3 t., 1957-61), *La Iglesia y el Estado* (1960), *El liberalismo social de Ignacio Ramírez* (1961), *Las ideas democráticas en México* (1961), *Rosseau y el liberalismo mexicano* (1962), *México: historia y política* (1978), *Hacia un Estado social en derecho* (1980), *En busca de la razón de Estado* (1981) y *Educar para construir una sociedad mejor* (2 t., 1985), entre otras obras. Fue miembro de número de la Academia Mexicana de la Historia y miembro honorario de la Real Academia de Historia de Madrid. *Doctor honoris causa* por la Universidad de Alcalá de Henares (1981).

Reyes Heroles González Garza, Jesús ◆ n. en el DF (1952). Hijo del anterior. Licenciado en economía por el Instituto Tecnológico Autónomo de México y doctor en la misma especialidad por el Instituto Tecnológico de Massachusetts (1980). Hizo estudios de derecho en la UNAM. Fue profesor de la UIA (1974-75) y del ITAM (1975-76 y 1981-83). Trabajó para el Banco de México (1975-82) y ha sido director general de Planeación Hacendaria de la Secretaría de Hacienda (1983-88), coordinador de asesores del secretario de Relaciones Exteriores, director de Banobras (1995-96), secretario de Energía en el gabinete de Ernesto Zedillo (1996-97) y embajador de México en Estados Unidos desde 1997. Autor de *Política macroeconómica y bienestar en México* (1983). Premio Nacional de Economía Banamex (1976).

Reyes de Juárez, Los ◆ Municipio de Puebla situado al este de la capital del estado, al noroeste de Tehuacán y contiguo a Tecamachalco. Superficie: 30.62 km². Habitantes: 18,761, de los cuales 3,403 forman la población económicamente activa. Hablan alguna lengua indígena 14 personas mayores de cinco años (náhuatl 9).

Reyes Luján, Sergio ◆ n. en el DF (1941). Licenciado en física (1962) con estudios de doctorado en la UNAM (1967) especializado en la Universidad de Uppsala (1964). Miembro del PRI. En la UNAM ha sido profesor (1960-74), investigador (1968-71), secretario auxiliar de la Facultad de Ciencias (1969-71) y director fundador del Centro de Instrumentos (1972-74). En la UAM fue profesor (1974), secretario de la Unidad Iztapalapa (1974-76), secretario general (1976-79), secretario de la Unidad Xochimilco (1980-81) y rector general (1981-85). Ha sido técnico electricista de la Comisión Nacional de Energía Nuclear (1964-66), subsecretario de Ecología de la Secretaría de Desarrollo Urbano y Ecología (1986-92) y director general del Instituto Nacional de Ecología de la Sedesol (1992-94). Secretario adjunto y presidente de la Sociedad Mexicana de Física (1967-77), tesorero y secretario de la Academia de la Investigación Científica (1968-69 y 1973-74) y miembro del Consejo Ejecutivo de la Unión de Universidades de América Latina (1983-85).

Reyes Martínez, Alfonso ◆ n. en Monterrey, NL (1943). Arquitecto egresado de la UANL. Ha dirigido las revistas *Salamandra*, *Cathedra* y *Armas y Letras* y ha sido director artístico del suplemento cultural *Aquí Vamos* del periódico *El Porvenir*. Autor de *En el tiempo* (1964), *Péndulos rotos* (1966), *Litoral de sombra* (1974) y *Colección de poemas* (1976).

Reyes de la Maza, Luis ◆ n. en

San Luis Potosí, SLP (1932). Licenciado en letras españolas (1956) por la UNAM, donde ha sido investigador del Instituto de Investigaciones Estéticas. También ha sido profesor del Instituto Andrés Soler, consejero para la administración de los teatros del IMSS, fundador y director del Museo Teatral del INBA (1964-66), jefe del Departamento de Supervisión Literaria de Televisa (1972-80), director de Radio y Televisión de la Secretaría de Gobernación (1976-80), presidente de la Sogem (1997-99) y asesor literario de Televisión Azteca (1999-). Colaborador de *El Nacional, Excélsior, El Sol de México, Novedades, Anales del Instituto de Investigaciones Estéticas, Centro, Letras Potosinas* y *Cuadrante*. Autor de ensayo: *El teatro en 1857 y sus antecedentes (1855-1856)* (1956), *El teatro en México entre la reforma y el imperio (1858-1861)* (1958), *El teatro en México en la época de Juárez (1868-1872)* (1961), *El teatro en México durante el porfirismo* (3 t., 1964-68), *El teatro en México durante la Independencia (1810-1839)* (1969), *El teatro en México durante la época de Santa Anna* (2 t., 1972), *En el nombre de Dios hablo de teatros* (1983) y *Circo, maroma y teatro* (1985); de cuento: *El obispo y su hermana* (1968); de teatro: *Dalila. Peluquería* y *La hermana Carmela y su parentela*; y de novela: *Memorias de un pentonto* (1984) y *Juan Xóchitl I. El pontífice mexicano* (1999), entre otras obras.

Reyes Meza, José ◆ n. en Tampico, Tams. (1924). Estudió en la Academia Nacional de Artes Plásticas (1948) y en la ENAH, donde fundó el Teatro Estudiantil Autónomo y se inició como diseñador y escenógrafo, actividades que continuó en el ballet de la Academia de la Danza Mexicana (1952-56), Teatro Clásico de México (1952-60), Ballet de la UNAM (1954), Compañía Locura Sana (1955-59), Compañía Enrique Rambal (1958-66) y Teatro de Revista Can-Can (1958-68). Fue ilustrador de *El Día* (1963-73). Auxilió a Canessi en la elaboración del mural de la presa Nezahualcóyotl, en Malpaso (1964) y diseñó el escudo de la Universidad de Baja California (1967). Como pintor participó en las bienales panamericanas de 1958 y 1960 y ha ejecutado murales en el Casino de la Selva (1959-62), la fachada del Pan American National Bank de Los Ángeles (1956-66), el edificio administrativo de la Universidad de Tamaulipas (1967), el Museo Nacional de Historia (1968); el Registro Público de la Propiedad en el DF (1978), la Comisión Coordinadora para el Desarrollo Agrícola y Ganadero del Estado de México (1977-80) y la Casa de Cultura de Bejucos de Sánchez Colín (1980-81). Ganó el premio de la Agrupación de Críticos por el montaje de *Bodas de sangre* (1957). Preseas Estado de México (1989) y Cecilio Robelo del estado de Morelos (1991) y Premio de Cultura del estado de Tamaulipas (1993).

Reyes Nava, Manuel ◆ n. en Tlalpan, DF, y m. en Toluca, Estado de México (?-1927). En 1912 se unió al Ejército Libertador del Sur con el que hizo la campaña del Estado de México a las órdenes de su hermano Valentín. En 1920, al triunfo de plan de Agua Prieta se unió al ejército federal. Durante la rebelión cristera, combatió en el Distrito Federal y los estados de Morelos, Puebla y Michoacán. Fue aprehendido en Toluca y fusilado.

Reyes Nava, Valentín ◆ n. en Tlalpan, DF, y m. en Tlaltizapán, Mor. (?-1923). Hermano del anterior. En 1910 organizó una guerrilla que, adscrita en cierta forma a la revolución maderista, operó por su cuenta en la zona del Ajusco y partes del Estado de México. Al proclamarse el Plan de Ayala se unió al zapatismo a las órdenes de Genovevo de la O, quien en 1916 lo nombró su lugarteniente. En 1920 se sumó al Plan de Agua Prieta y en ese año, ya como militar federal, dirigió el rescate de Benjamín Hill en los Dinamos de Contreras. Tres años después fue fusilado por soldados a las órdenes de Rafael Pimienta, sin que se conozca la causa de la ejecución.

Reyes Nevares, Beatriz Pruneda de ◆ n. en el DF (1936). Periodista. Esposa del también periodista Salvador Reyes Nevares. Colaboradora de *México en la Cultura, La Cultura en México, Revista Mexicana de Cultura, El Nacional* y *El Día*. Autora de *Desnutrición del mexicano* (1974), *De médicos* (1975), *Trece directores del cine mexicano* (1974), *La historia de las prisiones en México* (1976), *Rosario Castellanos* (1976), *Ángela Peralta* (1976) y *Tierra adentro. Hablan catorce gobernadores* (entrevistas, 1989).

Reyes Nevares, Salvador ◆ n. en Durango, Dgo., y m. en el DF (1922-1993). Licenciado en derecho por la UNAM (1949). Miembro del PRI, en el que fue director de la revista *La República* (1976). Abogado del Departamento Agrario, profesor de la UNAM (1949), secretario general y fundador de la rama de escritores y periodistas de la CNOP (1951-53). Abogado de la Comisión Nacional de Seguros (1951-53), subgerente de la editorial Labor Mexicana (1953-73), presidente del Instituto Mexicano del Libro (1970-71), subdirector de prensa y relaciones públicas de la Secretaría del Trabajo (1973-75), fundador de la editorial Los Epígrafes, diputado federal por Durango (1976-79), director de la biblioteca del Congreso de la Unión (1976-82), presidente de la Asociación de Escritores de México (1978-79), asesor técnico de la dirección general de Pemex (1979-87), subdirector de Comunicación de Fomento Cultural de Somex y director del suplemento cultural del diario *El Nacional* (1982-86) y del Instituto Mexiquense de Cultura, en Toluca. Autor de *Relaciones entre el existencialismo y el derecho* (1950), *El amor en tres poetas* (1951), *El amor y la amistad del mexicano* (1952), *El estilete prodigioso* (1954), *Frontera indecisa* (1955), *Proyecciones del existencialismo en el derecho* (1959), *Historia de las ideas colonialistas* (1975) y *Tiempo arriba* (novela, 1987).

Reyes Ochoa, Rodolfo ◆ n. en Guadalajara, Jal., y m. en España (1878-1954). Abogado. Hijo de Bernardo y hermano de Alfonso Reyes. Desde su época estudiantil fue redactor del periódico *La Protesta*, que atacaba al grupo de los científicos, del gabinete de Porfirio Díaz. Fue profesor en la Escuela de Jurisprudencia. En 1910 se opuso a Francisco I. Madero y cuando éste llegó a la presidencia (1911), se exilió brevemente en Estados Unidos, desde donde fue uno de los promotores del cuartelazo huertista. Fue secretario de Justicia (del 19 de febrero al 11 de septiembre de 1913) de Victoriano Huerta y diputado federal. Al ser disuelto el Congreso estuvo encarcelado durante cuatro meses. En 1914 fue desterrado a España. Escribió *De mi vida* (2 t., 1929). Miembro de la Real Academia de Jurisprudencia de Madrid.

Patricia Reyes Spíndola

Reyes Osorio, Sergio ◆ n. en el DF (1934). Ingeniero agrónomo por la Escuela Nacional de Agricultura de Chapingo (1952-58) y maestro en ciencias económico-agrícolas por la Universidad de Wisconsin (1963-64). Profesor de Chapingo (1962, 1965-66 y 1968). Ha sido director del Centro de Investigaciones Agrarias (1965-70), secretario general de Organización y Fomento Ejidal del Departamento de Asuntos Agrarios y Colonización (1970-74); consultor de la OCDE, en Francia (1968); presidente del Instituto Nacional de Economía Agrícola (1969-72 y 1982-85); investigador asociado de El Colegio de México (1971); presidente de la Junta de Gobierno del Centro de Investigaciones Agrarias (1973-82); subsecretario de Organización y Desarrollo Agrario de la SRA (1974-76); secretario técnico del gabinete agropecuario (1977-82); coordinador general de la SARH (1982-83); asesor del secretario (1983-84), coordinador del Programa Nacional de Alimentación de la SPP (1983-86); coordinador general de delegaciones (1986-88) y subsecretario de Agricultura (1988-89), y director general del Instituto Nacional de Investigaciones Forestales y Agropecuarias de la SARH (1989-92). Premio Nacional de Economía Banamex (1970).

Reyes Retana y Rivero, Óscar ◆ n. en la ciudad de México (1922). Licenciado en derecho por la UNAM (1940-44). Ha sido pasante del Departamento Legal de Ferrocarriles Nacionales (1944), pasante, abogado, jefe de abogados, subgerente y gerente de personal de Pemex (1945-71), director general de Aduanas (1972-76) y subsecretario de Inspección Fiscal de la Secretaría de Hacienda (1976-79); asesor del director de Pemex (1979-84) y director general del Fondo Nacional para los Desarrollos Portuarios, de la Secretaría de Comunicaciones (1980-89).

Reyes Ruiz, Jesús ◆ n. y m. en Aguascalientes, Ags. (1908-1988). Licenciado en derecho por la UNAM. Fue profesor de la UNAM y de escuelas secundarias de la SEP, director de la Escuela de Iniciación Artística del INBA. Ingresó al servicio exterior en 1948 y fue embajador en Bolivia, Honduras, Ghana, Senegal y Guinea, representante en las reuniones México-Estados Unidos sobre los problemas de los trabajadores migratorios y delegado a la XII Conferencia General de la UNESCO. Colaboró en *Tierra Nueva* (1940). Autor de *Cuatro poemas* (1940), *Romance de Alfonso Ramírez "Calesero"* (1943), *Raíz y voz del libro* (1946), *Llanto en la nube* (1946), *Discurso para un héroe* (1947), *La época literaria de sor Juana Inés de la Cruz* (1951), *Tres epístolas para hablar de tu ausencia* (1953), *Casa en el recuerdo* (1955, Premio de Poesía Presidente Ruiz Cortines), *Trinidad del hombre* (1963), *El centauro* (Premio Olímpico de Poesía en 1968), *Árbol de soledad, El problema del derecho natural, su planteamiento en la filosofía de valores* y *Réquiem en silencio mayor* (1968), *Abel, eres Caín* (1972) y *El otro Cid* (1974). Miembro del Seminario de Cultura Mexicana, del que fue vicepresidente y secretario general, y de la Academia Mexicana de Historia y Geografía.

Reyes Spíndola, Patricia ◆ n. en el DF (1953). Actriz, productora y directora de teatro. Hizo estudios de actuación en México, España e Inglaterra. Ha actuado en películas como *Actas de Marusia* (1975, Heraldo a la revelación femenina y Ariel a la mejor actriz, 1975), *La casa del sur* (1976), *México Norte* (1977), *Los hijos de Sánchez* (1978), *Ahora sí tenemos que ganar* (1980 y Ariel a la mejor actriz,1986) *Los motivos de Luz* (1985 Ariel a la mejor actriz, 1986), *Goitia, un dios para sí mismo* (1988), *Nocturno a Rosario* (1991), *La mujer del puerto* (1992), *La reina de la noche* (1993, Ariel a la mejor actriz, 1996), *Mujeres insumisas* (1995, nominación al Ariel a la mejor actriz, 1996), *Profundo carmesí* (1996), *El evangelio de las maravillas* (1998) y *El coronel no tiene quien le escriba* (1999), entre otras. También ha actuado en telenovelas como *El Maleficio* (1985), *El extraño retorno de Diana Salazar* (1988), *Teresa* (1989), *El vuelo del águila* (1994) y *La antorcha encendida* (1997). En 1999 debutó como directora de la obra *Dos gardenias* (1999). También ha impartido cursos de actuación.

Reyes Spíndola, Rafael ◆ n. en Tlaxiaco, Oax., y m. en la ciudad de México (1860-1922). Se tituló como abogado en el Instituto de Ciencias y Artes de Oaxaca. Destacó también como pianista y compositor. En su época de estudiante editó el periódico *Don Manuel*. Ejerció su profesión y, en 1885, fue secretario particular del gobernador de Michoacán, Mariano Jiménez. Llegó a la ciudad de México en 1888 y fundó el diario *El Universal*, que poco después vendió a Ramón Prida, quien le prohibió abrir otro diario en la capital del país. En Puebla creó *El Mundo Ilustrado*, primer periódico que publicó fotografías noticiosas, y en 1896 regresó a la ciudad de México para fundar *El Imparcial* y su vespertino *El Mundo*, que en 1914 incautaron las tropas carrancistas por lo que Reyes Spíndola debió exiliarse hasta 1920. Está reputado como el creador del periodismo moderno en México. Autor de una *Geografía de Michoacán*.

Reyes Tayabas, Jorge ◆ n. en Orizaba, Ver. (1922). Licenciado (1942) y doctor (1958) en derecho por la UNAM. Ha sido secretario en las cortes penales de los juzgados undécimo, noveno y décimo (1944-46), agente del Ministerio Público en el DF (1947), agente del Ministerio Público Federal

(1948-51), profesor de la Universidad Militarizada Latinoamericana (1954-55), fundador y director del Bufete Reyes Tayabas (1959-78), secretario de estudio y cuenta de la Suprema Corte (1951-58) y juez de distrito en Querétaro (1979-81). En la PGJDF ha sido juez de distrito (1981-86), subprocurador de Procesos (1986-88), subprocurador (1988-1991) y director general de Asuntos Jurídicos (1991-94). Autor de *La excesiva onerosidad superviniente como motivo de revisión de los contratos* (1958), *Bases para el estudio del Estado* (1966) y *Los requisitos de procedibilidad en los delitos fiscales* (1985). Miembro de la Barra Mexicana-Colegio de Abogados y de la Asociación Nacional de Funcionarios. En 1971 el ayuntamiento de Córdoba le otorgó la medalla y el diploma Poeta Cordobés y, en 1985, la Distinción Treinta Caballeros.

Reyes Vayssade, Martín ◆ n. en Torreón, Coah. (1936). Licenciado en derecho por la UNAM (1963), también estudió periodismo. Militó en el PCM y en el espartaquismo (☛). Miembro del PRI. Ha sido profesor de la Universidad Femenina de México (1958-60), de la Normal Superior (1965-68) y de la UNAM (1966-68 y 1974-75). Editor del suplemento cultural de *La Opinión*, de Torreón (1954), jefe del Departamento de Publicaciones de Previsión Social de la Secretaría del Trabajo (1971-72), gerente de Relaciones Públicas del grupo ICA (1972-79), director de Producción de la Dirección General de Difusión, editor de la revista *Programa*, de la SPP (1979-81) y director general de los estudios Churubusco (1982-85). En la SEP fue secretario particular del director de Enseñanza Superior (1964-68), director de Publicaciones y Medios de la Subsecretaría de Cultura (1985-86) y subsecretario de Cultura (1986-88). Tradujo *El papel de la violencia en la historia*, de Engels. Recibió el Teponaxtli de Malinalco de la Asociación Nacional de la Publicidad, las Palmas de Oro del Círculo de Periodistas de Espectáculos, el Heraldo de la Publicidad y el Calendario Azteca de Oro de la AMPRYT, el Heraldo de Oro de Cine a la mejor película (como coproductor de *Nocaut*, 1983) y la Orden del Fénix del gobierno griego.

Reyes Zavala, Ventura ◆ n. en Atotonilco el Alto y m. en Guadalajara, Jal. (¿1837?-1911). Se tituló de abogado en la Universidad de Guadalajara (1862). Fue profesor del Liceo de Varones de Guadalajara (1867) y director del Liceo Católico de la misma ciudad (1879-89). Autor de *Las bellas letras en Jalisco* (1882) y *Apuntes para formar unos prolegómenos de la clase de historia* (1886).

Reyes Zurita, Antonio ◆ n. en Tierra Colorada, Tab., y m. en el DF (1940-1997). Fotógrafo. Fue reportero en *El Hijo del Garabato*, *Rumbo Nuevo*, *Momento*, *Diario de Tabasco* y *Presente*, periódicos locales de Tabasco, donde además fue director del semanario *Detective* y creador del programa radiofónico *Tele-reportaje*. Radicado en la ciudad de México, se dedicó a la fotografía. Fue subdirector de información gráfica de *Novedades* (1961-68) para el que tomó fotos de la matamza del 2 de octubre, y fotógrafo de *Excélsior* (1969-1997), enviado a Canadá y Alemania. En El Salvador, fotografió la matanza de 1980 en la catedral, lo que le valió el Premio Nacional de Periodismo, dos premios de la Stichting World Press Photo de Holanda y el Premio del Club de Periodistas de México. Estuvo en Cuba, la Unión Soviética, Colombia, Puerto Rico, Nicaragua, Egipto, Irak, Líbano y en Kuwait, fue el único mexicano que obtuvo fotos del cuartel general de Saddam Hussein durante la Guerra del golfo. Autor de *El poder del papel* (1997). Dos veces fue premiado por el gobierno de Tabasco y cuatro por el Club de Periodistas. Premio por la mejor crónica (1959) otorgado por Exportab, preseas internacionales en España, Argentina, Puerto Rico y Holanda, y un premio en el segundo Certamen de Periodismo José Pagés Llergo (1997).

Reygadas, Fermín ◆ n. en la ciudad de México (1916). Pintor y escultor. Odontólogo graduado en la UNAM. En 1964 realizó su primera exposición individual de pintura. Es el creador de la magnetoescultura (figuras de piedra, madera, barro o metal, que se mueven por su propia fuerza magnética) e inventó el sistema de autotraducción simultánea que se utilizó por primera vez en el Congreso Mundial de Filosofía de 1973, en Bulgaria. Fue director del Museo Tecnológico de la Comisión Federal de Electricidad.

Reygadas Barquín, Carlos ◆ n. en el DF (1943). Contador público por el ITAM (1963-69). Pertenece al PRI desde 1974; ha sido coordinador de Recursos Financieros y contralor general del Conacyt (1973-76), comisario en Asesoría Técnica (1974-76) y comisario en Mexicana de Tecnología (1975-76), miembro de la Comisión de Administración Financiera de la UIA (1977-78); director de Programación, Organización y Presupuesto de la subsecretaría de Cultura (1977-78), director de Auditoría del INBA (1979-82), coordinador de asesores del subsecretario de Cultura de la SEP (1983-86), secretario general del CIESAS (1986); director de Desarrollo, Planeación y Presupuesto del Centro de Obra y Equipamiento en la Salud (1986-88) de la Secretaría de Salud y director general de Administración del CNCA (1988-94). Pertenece al Colegio de Contadores Públicos de México y al Instituto Nacional de Contadores Públicos.

Reynés Berezaluce, Nicolás ◆ n. en Villahermosa, Tab., y m. en el DF (1929-1992). Licenciado en derecho por la UNAM (1947-51). Profesor de la Universidad Juárez Autónoma de Tabasco (1956-58) y de la UNAM (1966-70). Miembro del PRI, del que fue delegado del CEN en varias entidades y director jurídico (1971-73); miembro honorario de la Comisión Revisora de Documentos Básicos de la CNC (1986-88). Fue secretario auxiliar del subsecretario (1953) y jefe de la Oficina de Regularización de Extranjeros de la Secretaría de Gobernación (1954); secretario particular del gobernador de Tabasco (1955-58), agente del Minis-

Nicolás Reynés Berezaluce

Foto: Fondo Editorial Grupo Azabache

Reynosa, Tamaulipas

Foto: Rogelio Baeza

David Reynoso

Foto: Rogelio Baeza

Luis Reynoso Cervantes

terio Público, subdirector de averiguaciones Previas de la PGJDF (1959-64); delegado fiduciario y director general del Fideicomiso Hel-Ha y del Caribe de Nafinsa (1974-76); diputado federal (1985-88), dos veces senador (1976-82 y 1988-94) y delegado del DDF en Xochimilco (1982-85).

Reynosa ◆ Municipio de Tamaulipas situado en el norte del estado, al oeste de Matamoros, en los límites con Nuevo León y Estados Unidos. Superficie: 2,961.26 km^2. Habitantes: 337,053, de los cuales 93,249 forman la población económicamente activa. Hablan alguna lengua indígena 896 personas mayores de cinco años (náhuatl 281, totonaco 191 y huasteco 114). Su cabecera, del mismo nombre, está ubicada en la frontera y es un importante centro agrícola, petrolero y ganadero. Tiene destilerías y refinerías de crudo y cuenta con un gasoducto que llega a Monterrey. Antes de la conquista española, lo habitaron chichimecas coahuiltecas (nombre genérico de la etnia formada por las tribus katuhano, bobola, carrizos, borrados, comecrudos, pintos, tejones y sacatiles). La primera incursión española ocurrió en 1686, cuando Alonso de León *el Mozo* recorrió la margen derecha del río Bravo hasta su desembocadura, para evitar el asentamiento de franceses.

Reynoso, Antonio ◆ n. en Toluca, Edo. de Méx., y m. en en DF (1917-1996). Fotógrafo y pintor. Hizo estudios de medicina y arquitectura. Su obra fotográfica ha sido muy poco difundida, aunque varias veces presentó exposiciones en museos y salas de arte de Estados Unidos. La más conocida de sus fotos es *La gorda*, que retrata a una mujer obesa peinándose. Pasó a la pintura en los treinta y posteriormente se dedicó también al cine. Fue camarógrafo del cortometraje *Perfecto Luna* (1959) de Archibald Burns, que también produjo, y al año siguiente produjo e hizo su primera y única incursión en la dirección con *El despojo*, corto con guión de Juan Rulfo. Fotografió *La Sunamita* de Héctor Mendoza (1965), *Un alma pura* de Juan Ibáñez (1965), *Olimpiada en México* (1968) de Alberto Isaac, *La magia* (1972) de René Rebétez, *Fando y Lis* (1967) de Jodorowsky (en colaboración con Rafael Corkidi) y *Landrú* (1973) de Juan José Gurrola.

Reynoso, David ◆ n. en Aguascalientes, Ags., y m. en el DF (1926-1994). Actor. Comenzó su carrera en el teatro en 1949, después de dedicarse a la locución. Se hizo famoso a partir de su papel protagónico en la película *Viento negro* (1964), a partir de la que tomó como apodo el nombre de su personaje, *el Mayor*. Otras películas destacadas de su filmografía son *Los hermanos del hierro* (1961), *La sangre enemiga* (1969), *Maten al león* (1975), *Había una vez una estrella* (1989) y *Misa de cuerpo presente* (1992). También fue cantante y realizó giras por Centro y Sudamérica. Fue secretario general de la ANDA (1978-86); participó en obras de teatro y programas de televisión. Medalla Virginia Fábregas por 25 años de carrera.

Reynoso, José J. ◆ n. en Guanajuato, Gto., y m. en el DF (1868-1945). Ingeniero. Fue gobernador constitucionalista de Guanajuato (1913), subsecretario de Hacienda encargado del despacho (1914) en el gabinete de Venustiano Carranza, y gobernador sustituto de Guanajuato (1943).

Reynoso, Juan ◆ n. en Coyuca de Catalán, Gro. (1912). Violinista llamado *el Paganini de Tierra Caliente*. Destacó desde su infancia, por lo que se ganó un primer mote: *el Guache* (el chamaco, el niño). Ha tocado en fiestas durante toda su vida, y también, en temporadas, en la XEW y en presentaciones organizadas por la Universidad de Guerrero. Es el último intérprete de varias formas musicales tradicionales de su región, entre las que destacan los gustos, también llamados zapateados o chilenas, y el arrastre, que originalmente se ejecutaba con dos violines, guitarra panzona y tamborita. Premio Nacional de Ciencias y Artes 1997, en la categoría de Artes y Tradiciones Populares.

Reynoso, Leobardo ◆ n. y m. en Juchipila, Zac. (1902-1993). Fue diputado, senador y líder de ambas cámaras del Congreso. Gobernador de Zacatecas (1944-1950), embajador en Portugal (1959), Guatemala y Dinamarca. En *La democracia en México*, Pablo González Casanova escribió de él: "otros (caciques y caudillos regionales), como Leobardo Reynoso, un año después de los acontecimientos de San Luis Potosí en 1959 (motín contra Gonzalo N. Santos), se vieron expuestos a presiones políticas muy semejantes. Hoy ministro de México en Guatemala, Reynoso pierde paulatinamente su antiguo poder. Por estas fechas (1965) es quizá uno de los últimos sobrevivientes del viejo cacicazgo estatal."

Reynoso Cervantes, Luis ◆ n. en Azcapotzalco, DF (1926). Sacerdote ordenado en 1950. Ha sido capellán de religiosas, cofundador de la Parroquia Universitaria, rector de la iglesia de Santa María de los Apóstoles, profesor del Seminario Conciliar y de la UNAM, fundador y director del postseminario San Pío X, obispo auxiliar de Monterrey y obispo de Case Calane (1978-82), Ciudad Obregón (1982-87) y Cuernavaca (1987-).

Reynoso y del Corral, Maximino ◆ n. en Silao y m. en León, Gto. (1841-1910). Estudió leyes en el Colegio de San Ildefonso (1868). Sacerdote ordenado en 1878, año en el que fue nombrado vicario de Silao. Fue prebendado, juez hacedor de la Catedral, profesor del seminario de León, obispo de Tulancingo (1898-1902) y de Neo Cesórea (1903-08).

REYNOSO DÍAZ, LEOPOLDO ♦ n. en el Mineral de Zacualpan, Edo. de Méx., y m. en Cuernavaca, Mor. (1878-1957). En 1911 se unió a la revolución en las fuerzas del zapatista Lorenzo Vázquez. Con Díaz Soto y Gama, Palafox y los hermanos Magaña, fundó el Centro de Consulta para la Propaganda y la Unificación Revolucionaria (1916), en Tlaltizapán, Morelos. En 1919 fue capturado por las fuerzas carrancistas cerca de Huautla, y se le trasladó a Cuautla, donde Pablo González lo amnistió. Fue diputado federal (1920-23) y presidente del Partido Nacional Revolucionario en Morelos.

REYNOSO LÓPEZ, DANIEL P. ♦ n. en Temascalcingo, Edo. de Méx. (1911). Se tituló como profesor en la Normal de Toluca (1931), estudió tres años en la Escuela Libre de Derecho y se graduó como dibujante comercial en la Escuela de Arte y Publicidad (1941). Estudió estadigrafía en la Dirección General de Estadística (1956). Fue profesor en Toluca (1931-34), en el Colegio Francés La Salle de la ciudad de México (1934-36), en varias escuelas primarias (1936-38) y secundarias (1938-66) y en la Escuela Industrial Rafael Dondé (1938-42). Miembro del Departamento Técnico de la Dirección General de Educación Primaria de la SEP (1950). Creador del modelo de lista de asistencia que utilizan las escuelas de la SEP, inventor de la escuadra poligonal y del multiplicador automático. Colaborador de la revista *Todo*. Fue uno de los fundadores del Canal 4 de televisión. Autor de *Aritmética para el tercer grado de primaria* (1946), *Reglamento para el uso de la bandera mexicana y del himno nacional* (1956) y *Método de escritura*. Miembro fundador del SNTE.

REYNOSO RAMÍREZ, LORENZO ♦ n. en Jalostotitlán, Jal., y m. en el DF (1931-1991). Militante del PAN desde 1967, en ese partido se desempeñó como consejero regional (1986-91). En la Tesorería del Distrito Federal, fue delegado de su sindicato. Diputado federal (1973-76) y miembro de la primera Asamblea de Representantes del Distrito Federal (1988-91), en la que coordinó la fracción panista.

REZA DELÓN, RAÚL ♦ n. en Coyoacán, DF (1914). Ajedrecista. Ingeniero civil por el IPN. Fue ingeniero en los Ferrocarriles Nacionales, Cementos Anáhuac y el Comité Administrador del Programa Federal de Construcción de Escuelas. Formó parte del equipo mexicano que compitió en la XVI Olimpiada de Ajedrez en Tel Aviv (1964) y en el encuentro internacional Cuba-México en La Habana (1965). Colaborador de *El Sol de San Luis* y *El Heraldo*. Autor de *Programa de obras del* CAPFCE (1958), *Técnica ajedrecista* (1966), *Un meteoro mexicano en el ajedrez* y *Partidas de un ajedrecista*. Fue campeón nacional de ajedrez en 1955 y 1956.

RHODAKANATY, PLOTINO C. ♦ n. en Grecia (1828-?). Sastre. Estudió en Austria y Alemania (1848). Se cree que participó en la revolución húngara de 1848. En 1857 se estableció en París, donde estudió filosofía e idiomas. Vivió en España (1860) y supo de la invitación que Comonfort hacía a los extranjeros para trabajar en México, por lo que en 1861 llegó a Veracruz. Trató de crear un sistema socialista de colonias agrícolas. Hizo amistad con algunos estudiantes de San Ildefonso, con quienes fundó un grupo al que llamó Escuela de Filosofía Trascendental. Su primera colonia, en Chalco, no funcionó, por lo que decidió dedicarse a la docencia. Dio clases en una escuela establecida y fundó una propia, la Escuela de la Razón y el Socialismo (1866-68). De entre sus alumnos formó el Grupo de Estudiantes Socialistas (1865), que se reivindicaba rama mexicana del bakuninismo. En 1865, Rhodakanaty y sus alumnos participaron en la huelga de las fábricas de San Ildefonso y La Colmena, cuyos trabajadores pedían a Maximiliano la supresión de las tiendas de raya y una jornada laboral de 14 horas. En 1866 intentó fundar en Chalco un falansterio, pero fracasó también en esa ocasión, aunque estableció la Escuela Moderna y Libre. En 1869 trató de unirse a la insurrección encabezada por Julio Chávez, pero fue detenido en Huamantla. Meses después fue liberado y se refugió en Tierra Caliente. En 1870 impulsó la creación del Gran Círculo de Obreros de México. Fundó y dirigió *El Craneoscopio, Periódico Frenológico y Científico* (1874). Hacia 1879 se interesó en el mormonismo y alentó la entrada en México de esa iglesia, de la que fue primer sacerdote en el país. En 1880, en medio de un decaimiento general del movimiento obrero, fue a Chalco, don-de intentó restablecer la Escuela Moderna. Regresó a Europa en 1886. Escribió *De la naturaleza* (1860), *Cartilla socialista o sea el catecismo elemental de la escuela de Carlos Fourier. El Falansterio* (1861), *Neopanteísmo, consideraciones sobre el hombre y la naturaleza* (1864), *Apuntes biográficos de los más célebres comunistas franceses* (1872), *Las atracciones guardan proporción a los destinos, Fourier* (1879) y *Médula panteísta del sistema filosófico de Spinoza* (1885).

RIANCHO, JORGE ALBERTO ♦ n. en Mérida, Yuc., y m. en el DF (1943-1992). Locutor. Comenzó su carrera en 1969 y durante 15 años trabajó para Televisa, donde obtuvo reconocimiento como locutor de identificación del Canal 2 y presentador de programas. Llegó a ser socio-administrador de la ANDA, a la que ingresó en 1983.

RIAÑO Y BÁRCENA, JUAN ANTONIO DE ♦ n. en España y m. en Guanajuato, Gto. (1757-1810). Marino. De 1792 hasta su muerte fue corregidor, comandante y gobernador intendente de Guanajuato. Al estallar la guerra de Independencia fue encargado de defender la Alhóndiga de Granaditas, cuya construcción había ordenado. Murió al defender esa plaza del ataque insurgente.

FOTO: FONDO EDITORIAL GRUPO AZABACHE

Riaño y Bárcena fue el defensor de la Alhóndiga de Granaditas

RICALDE GAMBOA, GRACIANO ♦ n. en Hoctún y m. en Mérida, Yuc. (1873-1942). Profesor por la Escuela Normal de Mérida (1889), inició sus estudios profesionales a los 12 años de edad. Fue profesor de matemática razonada en el Internado Literario, colaborador de *L'Intermédiare des Mathematiecien* de París y profesor y director de la Escuela de Ingeniería. En 1910 realizó estudios y mediciones sobre el cometa Halley. En 1923 calculó el eclipse total de sol de ese año y formó parte de la Comisión Geodésica Mexicana que observó este fenómeno en Champotón. Destacó por haber resuelto la ecuación general de quinto grado por medio de funciones elípticas.

Víctor Rico Galán

Ricaut, Alfredo ◆ m. ¿en la ciudad de México? (?-1933). Hijo adoptivo de una hermana de Venustiano Carranza, quien apadrinó su carrera militar y política. Se unió a la revolución constitucionalista en 1913 en San Pedro, Coahuila, desde donde cortó las líneas de comunicación federal hacia Monterrey. Firmante del Plan de Guadalupe, se incorporó a las fuerzas de Pablo González con quien perdió y recuperó el estado de Coahuila. A fines de 1913 participó en el infructuoso ataque a Monterrey y en la toma de Montemorelos. Luchó contra el villismo en 1915 y en 1917 sustituyó a Pablo de la Garza como gobernador de Nuevo León. En 1918 Carranza lo hizo gobernador interino del estado de Tamaulipas. Alcanzó el grado de general de brigada.

Rice García, Humberto ◆ n. en Mazatlán, Sin. (1940). Licenciado en administración de negocios por el Tecnológico de Monterrey (1961). Desde 1982 es miembro del PAN, en el que ha ocupado la secretarías de acción política y de acción electoral (1983-87) y la secretaría ejecutiva del CEN (1987). Ha sido presidente de Fundiciones Rice (1965-75), gerente general de Distribuidora Rice (1965-85), presidente de Ventas y Mercadotecnia (1966), presidente de Vehículos y Accesorios del Pacífico (1967-78), tesorero del Centro Patronal (1970), consejero (1973) y presidente (1977-78) de la Cámara de Comercio de Mazatlán; coordinador de la Junta de Agua Potable y Alcantarillado de Mazatlán (1979), vicepresidente de Metalmex (1980-87), presidente del Grupo Industrial Mazatlán (1982-87) y diputado federal plurinominal (1985-88). Es decano de la Asociación Nacional de Licenciados en Administración.

Rico, Guillermina ◆ n. y m. en el DF (1934-1996). Llamada la *Reina del ambulantaje*, desde 1958 hasta su muerte fue lideresa de comerciantes ambulantes en la ciudad de México. Militó en el PRI, al que se afilió a los 12 años. Tradicionalmente ofreció a ese partido el apoyo de sus seguidores, aunque en 1988 lo dio al Frente Democrático Nacional.

Rico, Juan Felipe ◆ n. y m. en la ciudad de México (1890-?). Se graduó como subteniente de infantería en la Escuela Militar de Aspirantes. En 1912 combatió la rebelión orozquista desde el Batallón de Voluntarios de Xico, comandado por Alberto Braniff. Combatió en el norte a las órdenes de Victoriano Huerta y participó en la represión del levantamiento felicista en Veracruz. A la caída de la dictadura huertista se retiró a la vida privada. En 1920 se adhirió a la rebelión del Plan de Agua Prieta. Combatió las rebeliones delahuertista (1923) y escobarista (1929). Alcanzó el grado de general de división (1942).

Rico Arzate, Enrique ◆ n. en Apaseo el Alto, Gto. (1948). Ingeniero químico por el IPN (1972) y doctor en petroquímica por el Instituto de Tecnología de Moscú (1979). Fue profesor del IPN (1972) e investigador del Instituto Mexicano del Petróleo (1979-84). Secretario de la Academia de Catálisis (1988-90). Ha sido militante de los partidos Comunista Mexicano (1967-71), Socialista Unificado de México, Mexicano Socialista y de la Revolución Democrática (1989-), por el que ha sido presidente municipal de Apaseo el Alto (1989-91) y diputado federal (1991-94).

Rico Cano, Tomás ◆ n. en Uruapan y m. en Morelia, Mich. (1916-1993). Profesor normalista y licenciado en derecho por la Universidad Michoacana de San Nicolás de Hidalgo. Fue profesor de escuelas primarias, de la Escuela Normal Urbana y del Primitivo y Nacional Colegio de San Nicolás. Coordinador del taller de poesía de la Casa de la Cultura de Morelia y coeditor de las revistas *Pliego* y *Undani*. Colaborador de *Paideia*, *La Voz de Michoacán*, *El Centavo*, *Ímpetus*, *El Zumbido*, *Universidad Michoacana*, *Juventud*, *El Nacional*, *La Chispa*, *El Popular*, *Rebeldías*, *Diario de Michoacán*, *Clarinadas*, *El Sol de Michoacán* y *Voces*. Coautor de *Por la tierra y el alba* y *De madura pasión*. Prologuista de *Romances michoacanos* (1961) y *El poeta Sansón Flores, antología* (1961). Autor de *Esta niebla encendida* (1946), *De amor quince sonetos* (1948), *Diástole sin regreso* (1949), *Notas sobre el pensamiento político y jurídico de don José María Morelos y Pavón* (1950), *Amando a tres ciudades* (1952), *Un recado a mi madre* (1957), *Un canto a la revolución mexicana* (1960), *Algunos poemas* (1962), *Tres romances morelianos* (1964), *Un retablo purépecha* (1964), *Fervor de Uruapan* (1971) y *Año nuevo* (1973).

Rico Galán, Fernando ◆ n. en España y m. en el DF (1929-1987). Escritor. Llegó exiliado a México en 1940. Estudió lengua y literatura españolas en la UNAM. Fue colaborador de las revistas *Retorno* y *Clavileño* (1948), profesor del Colegio Israelita, de la Normal Superior y de la UNAM (1952-60), y trabajador de la imprenta universitaria (1960-66). En Cuba fue jefe de los departamentos de historia y de filosofía del Instituto Cubano del Libro (1966-72). De nuevo en México fue jefe de corrección de estilo del Centro de Nuevos Métodos de Enseñanza en la UNAM (1972-77), jefe del Departamento de Documentación y Publicaciones del Centro de Investigaciones y Servicios Educativos y editor de la revista *Perfiles Educativos*.

Rico Galán, Víctor ◆ n. en España y m. en el DF (1928-1974). Periodista. Hermano del anterior. Llegó exiliado a México en 1940. En España, en su infancia, sirvió como correo de las fuerzas republicanas en territorio franquista. Maestro en filosofía por la UNAM (1952). Colaborador de *Impacto*, *Sucesos*, *América*, *Política*, *Siempre!* y *Diario de México*. Hizo visitas profesionales a Cuba en 1962, 1963 y 1966 y realizó una serie de reportajes sobre Centroamérica en 1963. Miembro del Movimiento Revolucionario del Pueblo, en 1966 se le acusó de "incitación a la rebelión, conspiración y acopio de armas" y se le detuvo el 12 de agosto. El 19 de agosto fue consignado y estuvo preso hasta 1972 en la penitenciaría de Lecumberri, donde organizó grupos de estudio y militó en el Frente Socialista. Enseñó marxismo y filosofía y dirigió un seminario sobre *El capital* en la UNAM. Autor de *El Partido Obrero y el Frente Nacional Antiimperialista* (1974). Su obra poética permanece dispersa.

RICO GONZÁLEZ, VÍCTOR ♦ n. en España y m. en el DF (1900-?). Exiliado en México (1940), fue profesor de la UNAM (1940), de la Escuela Nacional de Bibliotecarios y Archivistas y de la Escuela Superior del Magisterio; crítico en el Conservatorio Nacional y secretario del Consejo Editorial de la UNAM (1944). Autor de *Filosofía del arte en España e Iberoamérica en el siglo XVI* (1945), *Orientación pedagógica en materia de arte* (1945), *La música aborigen mexicana vista desde el ángulo sociológico*, *Universalidad del pensamiento español*, *Historiadores mexicanos del siglo XVIII* (1949) y *La expulsión de los jesuitas de la Nueva España. Documentos sobre extrañamientos de los jesuitas y ocupación de sus temporalidades, 1772-1783* (1949).

RICO RODRÍGUEZ, ALFONSO ♦ n. en España (1930). Ingeniero civil (1950-54), maestro (1958) y doctor en mecánica de suelos por la UNAM (1962-64). Ha sido profesor de la UNAM (1953-56) y de la UIA (1956-70), jefe de sección (1959) y jefe del Departamento de Geotecnia de la SOP (1965-81); asesor de la Fundación Ford (1967), del BID (1968) y del Comité de Ciencias de la Tierra del Instituto Nacional de la Investigación Científica (1970); representante de México ante el Comité Permanente de los Congresos Mundiales de Carreteras (1974), subdirector de Geotecnia e Hidrología de la SAHOP (1981-82); director (1983-87) y director general del Instituto Mexicano del Transporte de la SCT (1987-88). Autor de *Mecánica de suelos* (3 t., 1963-69) y *La ingeniería de suelos en las vías terrestres* (2 t.). Presidente de la Sociedad Mexicana de Mecánica de Suelos (1971-72). Ha recibido los premios Nacional de Ciencia y Tecnología (1973) y Javier Barros Sierra (1980).

RICO Y SANTOYO, JESÚS MARÍA ♦ n. en Irapuato, Gto., y m. en Hermosillo, Son. (1831-1884). Sacerdote ordenado en 1854. Fue guardián del convento de Querétaro y fundador del Colegio Mariano Pío. En 1883 fue preconizado obispo de Sinaloa y gobernó simultáneamente la diócesis de Sonora y el vicariato de Baja California.

RIERA, SALVADOR ♦ n. en España (¿1812?-?). Se tituló como médico en las universidades de Madrid y de La Habana. Estudió homeopatía con el sistema del alemán Hahnemann y dio a conocer esta disciplina en Mérida, Yucatán, ciudad a la que llegó en 1851. La comunidad médica local se opuso a sus métodos terapéuticos y fue retado a duelo por su colega de origen estadounidense, José M. Tappam, quien resultó herido. En 1853 azotó a Yucatán una epidemia de cólera, enfermedad que resistieron mejor los pacientes de Riera, pese a lo cual, la oposición a sus métodos aumentó, hasta que decidió abandonar el país.

RIERA LLORCA, VICEN ♦ n. en España (1903). Periodista y escritor. Fue redactor de los diarios catalanes *L'Opinió* y *La Rambla*, secretario del Consejo de Agricultura de la Generalidad de Cataluña y voluntario del ejército republicano durante la guerra civil. Al triunfo franquista se exilió en Francia y en la República Dominicana, donde colaboró en el periódico *La Nación*. Llegó a México en 1942. Fue secretario de redacción de *La Nostra Revista* y fundador y director de *Pont Blau*. En 1944 y 1945 tradujo libros del francés y el inglés. Autor de *Giovanna i altres contes* (1945), *Tots tres surten per l'Ozama* (1945), *¡Oh, mala bestia!*, *Joc de xocs*, *¿Qué vols, Xavier*, *Cavi de via*, *Fes memoria* y *Roda de malcontensts*.

RIESGO, JUAN MIGUEL ♦ n. en San Miguel de Horcasitas, Son. (?-1834). Fue contador de azogues y visitador de aduanas. En 1811 participó en la conspiración que intentaba eliminar al virrey Venegas. Fue capturado y permaneció en prisión hasta 1813. Diputado al primer Congreso General (1822) y miembro de la Junta Nacional Instituyente creada por Agustín de Iturbide. Intendente de Hacienda en el noroeste del país. Fue fundador de las primeras logias masónicas del rito yorkino. Jefe político de Sinaloa (de abril a junio de 1824) y primer gobernador del estado de Occidente (del 12 de septiembre al 7 de octubre de 1824). Fue después comisario general, diputado local y presidente municipal de San Miguel de Horcasitas. Autor de *Memoria estadística del estado de Occidente* (1828, en colaboración con Antonio J. Valdez).

RIESTRA, ADOLFO ♦ n. en Tepic, Nay., y m. en el DF (1944-1989). Escultor y pintor. Estudió derecho en la Universidad de Guanajuato (1966) y pintura en el Taller de Jesús Gallardo. Radicado en San Francisco, California, trabajó con John Hamilton en el Potrero Hill Graphics Workshop. Después de vivir en Ajijic, Tepoztlán y la ciudad de México, fijó su residencia en Francia. Participó en las bienales de Pintura del INBA (1977 y 79), en la primera Bienal Iberoamericana (1978), la Bienal Iberoamericana de Dibujo (1980) y en la Trienal de Escultura del INBA (1980).

RIESTRA, GLORIA ♦ n. en Tampico, Tams. (1929). Estudió comercio, pero se ha dedicado profesionalmente al periodismo desde 1946. Trabajó para la cadena García Valseca. Colaboradora de *Ábside*, *Unión*, *Mundo Mejor*, *La Nación*, *Señal* y *La Prensa* de Nicaragua. Autora de los poemarios *La soledad sonora* (1950), *Celeste anhelo* (1952), *Al aire de su vuelo* (1954), *La noche sosegada* (1960), *Salmos de adoración* (1963), *Cena de amor* (1964), *Lagar. El libro del dolor* (1965), *El camino eterno* (1967); y los vo-

Manuel E. Rincón

FOTO: ÉPOCA

Gilberto Rincón Gallardo

Casa de Pedro Rincón Gallardo

ARCHIVO XAVIER ESPARZA

lúmenes en prosa *Según tu palabra* (1961), *Tormenta sobre la iglesia* (1971) y *Contra la tradición* (1976). Miembro de la Asociación Nacional de Periodistas, Escritores, Libreros y Editores Católicos.

RIGUAL, CARLOS ◆ n. en Cuba y m. en el DF (1920-1994). Músico. Adoptó la nacionalidad mexicana. Con sus hermanos Carlos y Pedro formó el trío Los Rigual y comenzó su carrera en la radiodifusora cubana CMQ. Se hizo de fama mundial con su canción *Cuando calienta el sol* (1961), de la que se han grabado más de 1,000 versiones, y en menor medida con *Corazón de melón*, *El pollo de Carlitos* y *La del vestido rojo*.

RIMOCH, ROSA ◆ n. en Veracruz, Ver. (¿1932?). Cantante. Hizo estudios en el Conservatorio Nacional de Música y en la Academia de Ópera del INBA. A partir de su primera función de ópera, un papel en *El pobre marinero*, de Darius Milhaud (1947), fue reconocida como una de las figuras más notables del canto en México. Ha actuado en todos los teatros líricos del país. Entre sus interpretaciones, destacan las de las óperas *Madam Butterfly*, *Tosca* y *Turandot* de Puccini, *Mefistófeles* de Boito, *Atzimba* de Ricardo Castro, *El teléfono* de Giancarlo Menotti y *Carlota* de Luis Sandi. También ha ofrecido numerosos recitales de *lied*, música folclórica y *spiritual* e interpretado obras de Orff, Poulenc, Berg, Mascagni, Verdi, Mahler, Galindo, Penderecki y muchos otros compositores, alternando temporadas en México y el extranjero. Ha obtenido el premio a la mejor cantante de la Unión de Cronistas de Teatro y Música (1954) y la Medalla Bellas Artes (1996).

RINCÓN, ANTONIO DEL ◆ n. en Texcoco, Estado de Méx., y m. cerca de Puebla, Pue. (1556-1601). Jesuita desde 1573, se dedicó a la docencia en la diócesis de Puebla y al estudio de la lengua náhuatl. Autor de *Arte mexicana* (1595) y *Vocabulario breve*.

RINCÓN, MANUEL E. ◆ n. en Perote, Ver., y m. en la ciudad de México (1784-1849). Militar realista. En 1821 se unió al Ejército Trigarante. No reconoció los convenios de Zavaleta por lo que causó baja (1823). Anastasio Bustamante lo readmitió en las fuerzas armadas y le encomendó la jefatura de operaciones contra la fortaleza de San Juan de Ulúa. Secretario de Guerra y Marina (del 10 de febrero al 3 de marzo de 1827) de Guadalupe Victoria, general de división (1837), fue segundo jefe del Ejército de Oriente y combatió a los invasores estadounidenses. Fue comandante general y gobernador de Puebla (1835), gobernador de Veracruz, presidente del Supremo Tribunal de Guerra y Marina y senador.

RINCÓN, MARIANO ◆ m. ¿en Papantla, Ver.? (?-1814). En 1811 formó parte de la junta secreta que reunió en Jalapa el sacerdote Cerdeña, en pro de la independencia. Detenido el prelado (1812), Rincón creó la Junta de Naolinco, con Tamariz y Ortiz y Fiayo. La junta fue descubierta y se trasladó a Misantla, donde se disolvió. Rincón se unió a las fuerzas de Nicolás Bravo, con quien concurrió al ataque de Jalapa. Morelos lo nombró comandante de Papantla, pero tuvo poca autoridad debido a las pugnas internas de las fuerzas insurgentes. Fue fusilado por órdenes de Serafín Olarte.

RINCÓN COUTIÑO, VALENTÍN ◆ n. en Tuxtla Gutiérrez, Chis., y m. en el DF (1901-1968). Licenciado en derecho por la UNAM, donde ejerció la docencia. Fue profesor de la Universidad de Jalapa. Fundó el Frente Socialista de Abogados. En Veracruz fue presidente del Tribunal Superior de Justicia y coautor del Código de Procedimientos Civiles. En el Distrito Federal se desempeñó como juez de primera instancia, presidente del Tribunal Supremo para el Distrito y Territorios Federales y diputado federal. Era gran maestro de la Gran Logia Valle de México y fue presidente de la Sociedad Mexicana de Geografía y Estadística (1966-67). Autor de *El raudal del potro*, *Ignacio Ramírez, el Nigromante*, *Chiapas, entre Guatemala y México, injusto motivo de discordia*, *La batalla del 21 de octubre*, *Ángel Albino Corzo* y *Cárdenas ante el pensamiento revolucionario*.

RINCÓN GALLARDO, GILBERTO ◆ n. en el DF (1939). Licenciado en derecho por la UNAM. Perteneció al PCM (1963-81), en el que fue miembro de la Comisión Ejecutiva del Comité Central. Estuvo en la cárcel de Lecumberri como preso político de 1968 a 1971. Miembro fundador del PSUM, fue secretario general de su comité en el DF, secretario de Relaciones Internacionales y miembro de la Comisión Política y del secretariado del Comité Central. Cofundador y miembro del PMS (1987-89); cofundador y miembro de la dirección del PRD (1989-97). Fundador y dirigente del Partido Democracia Social (1997-). Dos veces diputado federal (1979-82 y 1991-94).

RINCÓN GALLARDO, PEDRO ◆ n. en Ciénega de Mata, Jal., y m. en la ciudad de México (1836-1909). Militar. Financió un batallón con el cual combatió al imperio de Maximiliano. Fue regidor del ayuntamiento de la ciudad de México, organismo que presidió en tres ocasiones (1881, 82 y 85). Seis veces diputado federal (dos por Aguascalientes, dos por el Distrito Federal y dos por Jalisco), fue senador por San Luis Potosí y ministro de México en Rusia y Alemania. General en 1891 y gobernador del Distrito Federal (1891 y 1893-96).

Rincón Gallardo y Romero de Terreros, Carlos ◆ n. y m. en el DF (1874-1950). Militar. Secretario de Agricultura (del 10 al 14 de julio de 1914) en el gabinete de Victoriano Huerta. Aficionado y promotor de la charrería, fue juez honorario del International Jockey Club de México y presidente del Polo Club de México y del jurado de honor de la Sociedad Hípica Nacional, de la Comisión de Carreras y del *Stud Book* del Jockey Club de México. Autor de *El libro del charro mexicano*, *Diccionario ecuestre*, *Manganas y pialas* y *Comentario sobre algunas suertes ecuestres*.

Rincón Piña, Agapito ◆ n. y m. en el DF (1897-1973). Pintor y grabador. Estudió en la Academia de San Carlos y en la Escuela de Pintura al Aire Libre de Santa Anita. Profesor de escuelas de la SEP (1922), expuso por primera vez en 1924, en la Feria de la Flor, donde ganó el primer premio de pintura. Su obra está recopilada en el volumen *Mexican Graphic Art*. Miembro del Instituto de Arte de México y del Círculo Acuarelista. En 1952 ganó el primer premio de la Exposición Internacional de Arte de Florida y un año después el premio de grabado de la Biblioteca del Congreso, en Washington.

Rincón de Romos ◆ Municipio de Aguascalientes situado al noreste de San José de Gracia, en los límites con Zacatecas. Superficie: 399 km^2. Habitantes: 38,752, de los cuales 8,815 forman la población económicamente activa. Hablan alguna lengua indígena 13 personas mayores de cinco años.

Río, Andrés Manuel del ◆ n. en España y m. en la ciudad de México (1764-1849). Minerólogo graduado en 1782 en la Universidad de Alcalá de Henares. Becado por el gobierno español, se especializó en Alemania, donde fue alumno del geólogo Abraham Werner. Estudió también en Inglaterra y Francia, donde hizo amistad con Humboldt. En París, durante la revolución, estuvo a punto de ser guillotinado. Volvió a Madrid y se le designó catedrático del Colegio de Minería de la Nueva España. Llegó a la ciudad de México en 1794 y un año después inició el primer curso de minerología en el país. En 1801 descubrió lo que parecía ser un nuevo elemento, al que llamó eritronio. La comunidad científica mundial pensó que ese elemento era en realidad cromo y no dio importancia al hallazgo. Tres décadas después, el sueco Nils Gabriel Sefstrom descubrió el vanadio, que no era sino el eritronio descubierto por Del Río. Fundó la ferrería de Coalcomán, donde se produjo el primer hierro mexicano, en 1807. Fue diputado a las Cortes de Cádiz en 1820 y abogó por la independencia mexicana. Regresó a México en 1824 y cinco años después fue expulsado del país junto con sus compatriotas. Se refugió en Estados Unidos y volvió en 1835. Autor de *Tablas minerológicas de Karsten* y *Elementos de orictognosia* (1804).

Río, Dolores del ◆ n. en Durango, Dgo., y m. en EUA (1902-1983). Nombre profesional de la actriz Dolores Asúnsolo López Negrete. Sobrina de Francisco I. Madero. Vivió en EUA donde inició su carrera en 1925, cuando Edwing Carewe la incluyó en el reparto de la película *Joanna*. Alcanzó renombre en el cine sonoro de Hollywood. En los años cuarenta empezó a filmar en México, dirigida por Emilio Fernández y Gabriel Figueroa. En 1958 actuó por primera vez en teatro, en la obra *El abanico de lady Windermere*, de Wilde. Alternó su trabajo escénico con la filmación de películas en el DF, España y EUA. Participó en series estadounidenses de televisión. Sus últimos años los dedicó a patrocinar una guardería infantil y a encargarse de la Sociedad Defensora del Tesoro Artístico de México. Entre las películas que filmó destacan: *El precio de la gloria* (1926), *Resurrección* (1927), *Ramona* (1928), *El malo* (1930, su primer filme sonoro), *Acusada* (1936), *Flor Silvestre* (1943), *María Candelaria* (1943), *Bugambilia* (1944), *Historia de una mala mujer* (1948) y *La dama del alba* (1965). Actuó en las comedias musicales *Ave del paraíso*, *Volando a Río*, *Wonder bar*, *In caliente (Tijuana)* y *Vivo para amar*. En 1967 recibió un homenaje de la OEA. Fue galardonada en 1978 por el presidente estadounidense James Carter. Recibió numerosas distinciones de la ANDA. Por su labor en el cine mexicano recibió tres Arieles.

Río, Eduardo del ◆ ☛ *Rius*.

Río, Marcela del ◆ n. en el DF (1932). Licenciada en letras españolas por la UNAM. Estudió en las academias de Seki Sano y Cinematográfica de México y en la Escuela de Arte Teatral del INBA, donde fue profesora. Ha ejercido la docencia en instituciones superiores. Fue secretaria de redacción de *La Mujer de Hoy* (1963-64), conferencista y directora de la Sala de Arte del Organismo de Promoción Internacional de Cultura (1964-65), becaria del Centro Mexicano de Escritores (1965-66), agregada cultural en Checoslovaquia (1972-77) y Bélgica, coordinadora de talleres literarios y guionista de cine y televisión. Autora de *Fraude a la tierra* (1957), *Miraldina*. *El hijo de trapo*. *Claudia y Arnot* (1964, piezas teatrales), *La tercera cara de la luna* (1965), *Trece cielos* (1970, Premio Olímpico 1968 de poesía), *Cuentos arcaicos para el año 3000* (1972), *Antología de cuentos* (1972, premio León Felipe), *El pulpo (tragedia de los hermanos Kennedy)* (1973, Premio Juan Ruiz de Alarcón en 1970), *Proceso a Faubritten* (novela, 1976), *Opus 9* (1978), *De camino al concierto* (1984) y

Andrés Manuel del Río

Dolores del Río

Foto: Gabriel Figueroa

FOTO: FONDO EDITORIAL GRUPO AZABACHE

Río Bravo, Tamaulipas

Río Frío, Puebla

la obra teatral *Año nuevo, vida nueva* (1989), entre otras obras. A la fecha vive en Orlando, Florida, EUA.

RÍO, SALVADOR DEL ◆ n. en Salamanca, Gto. (1934). Periodista. Su segundo apellido es Ortiz. Profesor en la UNAM (1977-82). Se inició profesionalmente en 1954, en el diario *Zócalo*. Ha sido subdirector de Información de la Secretaría de Hacienda (1975-76), jefe de Prensa de la Comisión Nacional de la Industria Azucarera (1977-79), director de *Informex*, gerente de Información y Relaciones Públicas de Pemex (1982-87) y coordinador general de Comunicación Social del gobierno del Estado de México (1988-93). Director de *El Mundo*, de Tampico (1967-72); jefe de redacción de *El Día* (1972-75), jefe de las secciones cultural y financiera de *El Sol de México* y jefe de redacción de *Línea*, órgano teórico del PRI. Autor de *Los presidentes de México* (1982).

RÍO ALBERO, RICARDO DEL ◆ n. en España (1908). Interrumpió sus estudios de medicina para dedicarse al periodismo. Fue corresponsal en Madrid de algunos diarios de provincia y en 1927 ingresó en la agencia Noti-Sport. Fundó después la agencia ALPE y dirigió la agencia ZENA hasta el fin de la guerra civil, durante la cual formó parte de la Jefatura de Sanidad de Servicios Quirúrgicos. Colaboró en el periódico *Claridad* y fue subdirector de *El Diluvio*. Tras la derrota de la República pasó al campo de concentración de Argeles-sur-Mer, en Francia. En 1939 vino a México, donde se naturalizó. Colaboró en el diario *La Prensa* y más tarde ingresó como cronista deportivo en *Novedades*, del que fue nombrado subdirector en 1957.

RÍO HAZA, FERNANDO DEL ◆ n. en el DF (1940). Estudió física en la Facultad de Ciencias de la UNAM (1963) y se doctoró en la Universidad de California, en Berkeley (1969). Investigador del Instituto de Investigación en Materiales de la UNAM y del Instituto Mexicano del Petróleo. Miembro fundador de la revista *Naturaleza* y director de *Ciencia*. Fundó la termodinámica experimental en laboratorios de la UNAM, la UAM y el Instituto Mexicano del Petróleo. Su proyecto para la creación de un Instituto de Metrología y Mediciones Fundamentales (1978), culminó en lo que hoy es el Centro Nacional de Metrología. Desde 1984 es miembro del Sistema Nacional de Investigadores, nivel III. Fue presidente de la Academia de la Investigación Científica (1988-89). Autor de seis libros y más de 80 artículos especializados. Dirigió los primeros trabajos en el país sobre teoría de perturbaciones y ecuaciones integrales para plasmas y fluidos densos. Ha recibido los premios de Investigación de la UAM (1983) y la Medalla Académica de la Sociedad Mexicana de Física (1984).

RÍO BEC ◆ Zona arqueológica de Yucatán, localizada en el municipio de Hopelchén, 23 kilómetros al sur de Xpuhil. Su exploración la inició en 1908 Maurice de Perigny. En 1912 Merwin y Hay localizaron otras construcciones y en 1943 la Institución Carnegie catalogó cinco conjuntos de edificios. La zona arqueológica de Río Bec dio nombre a un estilo arquitectónico caracterizado por edificios de uno o dos pisos, combinaciones de crujías con cuartos paralelos, bancos adosados a las paredes interiores, torres ornamentales, mascarones en las puertas principales, columnas de mampostería y tumbas con techos de bóveda.

RÍO BLANCO ◆ Municipio de Veracruz situado al oeste de Orizaba, cerca de los límites con Puebla. Superficie: 24.68 km². Habitantes: 38,866, de los cuales 11,004 forman la población económicamente activa. Hablan alguna lengua indígena 466 personas mayores de cinco años (náhuatl 409). Su cabecera es Tenango de Río Blanco. En este municipio ocurrió la *Huelga de Río Blanco* (☛), como uno de los movimientos precursores de la revolución.

RÍO BLANCO ◆ Río de Veracruz que nace en las Cumbres de Acultzingo, en su recorrido, de 114 kilómetros, tributan en él los ríos Orizaba, Tlilapan y Escamela. Desemboca en la laguna de Alvarado. En su curso forma cuatro caídas de agua, una de las cuales, la de Rincón Grande, se aprovecha para dar energía a la Compañía Industrial de Orizaba.

RÍO BRAVO ◆ Municipio de Tamaulipas situado en el norte del estado, al oeste de Matamoros y contiguo a Reynosa, en los límites con Estados Unidos. Superficie: 2,140 km². Habitantes: 100,373, de los cuales 28,642 forman la población económicamente activa. Hablan alguna lengua indígena 289 personas mayores de cinco años (náhuatl 100, huasteco 69 y otomí 35).

RÍO CAÑEDO, FRANCISCO DEL ◆ n. en Veracruz, Ver., y m. en Italia (1897-1963). Se tituló como médico en la Universidad Nacional (1922). Presidente de la Federación de Estudiantes Universitarios (1921). Realizó cursos de especialización en Viena, Berlín, Londres y París e instaló una clínica en Texas. Ingresó en el servicio diplomático en 1940, como ministro plenipotenciario y embajador extraordinario en Uruguay. Fue embajador en Guatemala, Canadá, Chile, Francia, Yugoslavia, República Dominicana, Bélgica, Luxemburgo, Checoslovaquia e Italia. Entre 1950 y 1953 se desempeñó como director del Departamento de Turismo.

RÍO FRÍO ◆ Población del municipio de Ixtapaluca, situada a 63 km de la ciudad de México, en los límites con el estado de Puebla. En sus alrededores se encuentran el parque Sierra Tláloc-Telapon y el Parque Nacional Zoquiapan. A principios de los años treinta del siglo XIX fue base de operaciones de la banda de salteadores de caminos comandada por Juan Yáñez, que dio pie a la novela *Los bandidos de Río Frío*, de Manuel Payno.

Río Grande ◆ Municipio de Zacatecas situado al norte de la capital del estado, contiguo a Fresnillo y Sombrerete. Superficie: 2,805.91 km². Habitantes: 60,559, de los cuales 13,373 forman la población económicamente activa. Hablan alguna lengua indígena 33 personas mayores de cinco años.

Río Grande, República de ◆ Proyecto separatista, previo a una anexión estadounidense, impulsado por Antonio Canales y los militares José María González y Antonio Zapata, quienes se pronunciaron en Texas, en 1838, contra el centralismo de Anastasio Bustamante. Su plan pretendía formar una república independiente con parte del territorio norte de México. Fueron secundados por las fuerzas estadounidenses de S. W. Jordan y Rubén Ross. En 1839 Canales convocó a una convención de delegados para promulgar el nacimiento de la República de Río Grande e inició las acciones armadas contra el Ejército Mexicano. Ese mismo año fue derrotado en Coahuila por las fuerzas de Mariano Arista y fijó su cuartel general en San Patricio, Texas, donde recibió el apoyo militar de William S. Fischer. En 1840, sus tropas habían ocupado varias ciudades norteñas. Se produjo entonces una división entre las fuerzas mexicanas y las estadounidenses y estas últimas abandonaron el territorio mexicano, luego de lo cual Canales depuso las armas.

Río Lagartos ◆ Municipio de Yucatán situado en el extremo norte del estado y contiguo a Tizimín, en el litoral del golfo de México. Superficie: 249.09 km². Habitantes: 2,843, de los cuales 855 forman la población económicamente activa. Hablan maya 466 personas mayores de cinco años.

Río de la Loza, Leopoldo ◆ n. y m. en la ciudad de México (1807-1876). Estudió en la Escuela de Cirugía, de donde salió en 1827, y se tituló como médico y farmacéutico en la Facultad de Medicina (1833). Trabajó en el Hospital de San Lucas y simultáneamente administraba una farmacia, en la que experimentó la obtención de oxígeno, anhídrido carbónico y nitrógeno, primeros ensayos de esa naturaleza en México. Fue inspector de boticas y medicinas de la citada Facultad (1835), profesor del Establecimiento de Ciencias Médicas (1838) y de la Escuela de Medicina (1845), e inspector de establecimientos industriales (1845). Colaborador de la *Gaceta Médica de México* (1846). Tomó las armas en 1847 para combatir la invasión estadounidense. En 1851 promovió la creación de la segunda Academia de Medicina de México. Fue profesor del Colegio de San Gregorio y de las escuelas de Agricultura, de Bellas Artes, Nacional Preparatoria y de Medicina, que dirigió en 1873. Instaló en Tlaxcoaque la primera fábrica de ácidos que hubo en México. Fue miembro del Consejo Superior de Salubridad (1846). El 10 de enero de 1866 ingresó en la Academia Nacional de Medicina. En 1911 se publicaron los *Escritos de Leopoldo Río de la Loza*, recopilados por Juan Manuel Noriega.

Río de la Loza y Gordejuela, Rodrigo ◆ n. ¿en España? y m. cerca de Cuencamé, Dgo. (?-1604). Soldado del conquistador Francisco Ibarra. Descubrió en 1564 las vetas de Santa Bárbara, por lo que se le considera el primer minero del norte de la Nueva España. Fue gobernador de Nueva Vizcaya, donde se dedicó a la cría de ganado y al cultivo de viñedos.

Río Ortegón, Guillermo del ◆ n. en Campeche, Camp., y m. en el DF (1943-1999). En su estado fue diputado local en dos ocasiones, presidente del PRI y secretario general de la CNOP. Organizó las "marchas de las cacerolas" para protestar por el aumento en el precio de los productos básicos. En 1994 fue electo senador de la República por el PRD, del que se separó en 1997 para ingresar en el PT y ser candidato al gobierno de Campeche. Fue miembro de la Cocopa.

Leopoldo Río de la Loza

Río Ortiz, Gabriel del ◆ n. en el DF (1932). Periodista, actor y escritor. Estudió actuación en el INBA. Profesor en el Injuve, en preparatorias de la UNAM y en escuelas de iniciación artística del INBA, reportero de los periódicos *Novedades*, *El Sol de México* y *El Universal Gráfico*; subdirector de *El Mundo*, de Tampico, y director de *El Diario de Xalapa*. Ha ofrecido recitales de poesía en México y el extranjero y ha participado en numerosos programas de radio y televisión. Actuó en la cinta *Pueblito* (1960), de Emilio Fernández. Autor de ensayo: *La Guadalupana es española* y *México, país de tradiciones*; y tambien de poesía: *La rebelión de las flores* y *Universo cautivo*.

Gabriel del Río Ortiz

Río Reynaga, Julio del ◆ n. Zamora, Mich., y m. en el DF (?-1997). Fue profesor de la Facultad de Ciencias Políticas y Sociales de la UNAM y director de la misma (1975-79). Autor de *Teoría y práctica de los géneros periodísticos informativos*.

Río Rodríguez, Carlos Antonio del ◆ n. en el DF (1929). Doctor en derecho por la UNAM (1958). Ha sido abogado y jefe del Departamento de lo Contencioso en la Procuraduría Fiscal de la Federación, de la Secretaría de Hacienda (1954-63); profesor del Instituto de Ciencias Sociales, Económicas y Administrativas (1956) y de la Facultad de Derecho de la UNAM (1959-82); miembro de la comisión reformadora del Código Fiscal de la Federación y del Código Aduanero (1961); magistrado del Tribunal Fiscal de la Federación (1963), miembro de la comisión elaboradora del anteproyecto del Código Fiscal de la Federación y de la Ley Orgánica del citado tribunal (1966), ministro (1969-86) y presidente (1986-90) de la Suprema Corte de Justicia. Embajador en Portugal (1991-97). Pertenece a la Academia Mexicana de Derecho Fiscal.

Carlos Antonio del Río Rodríguez

FOTO: JORGE CONTRERAS CHACEL

Pilar Rioja

FOTO: ARMANDO HERRERA

Elvira Ríos

Lázaro Ríos

RIOJA, PILAR ◆ n. en Torreón, Coah. (1932). Estudió danza en México y España, y coreografía en el Carnegie Hall. Creó, con el musicólogo español Domingo José Samperio, el concepto concierto de danza con castañuelas. Su primer recital fue un homenaje a León Felipe. En 1965 recibió el premio de danza que otorga la Unión Mexicana de Cronistas de Teatro y Música. Se ha presentado en ciudades de México, Estados Unidos, Canadá, España, la Unión Soviética y decenas de países más. Fue declarada hija predilecta de la ciudad de Torreón.

RIOJA LO-BIANCO, ENRIQUE ◆ n. en España y m. en el DF (1895-1963). Doctor en biología por la Universidad Central de Madrid (1917). Fue profesor de escuelas de segunda enseñanza, de la Escuela de Estudios Superiores del Magisterio y de la Universidad Central de Madrid, donde también trabajó como investigador. Miembro del Consejo Nacional de Cultura (1931-33), vicepresidente (1936-39) y vocal del patronato de Misiones Pedagógicas y miembro de la junta directiva de la Sociedad Española de Historia Natural. Llegó exiliado a México en 1940 e ingresó como investigador en el Instituto de Biología y como profesor en la Facultad de Ciencias de la UNAM. Colaborador de *Ciencia*, *Romance* y *Las Españas*. Fue jefe del Departamento de Hidrobiología del IPN, donde también ejerció la docencia, y presidente de la Sociedad Mexicana de Hidrobiología. Autor de *La vida en el mar*, *Estudio de los poliquetos de la península Ibérica*, *El libro de la vida*, *El mar, acuario del mundo*, *Estudio crítico sobre las esponjas de Xochimilco*, *Contribución al conocimiento de los poliquetos de las costas mexicanas del Pacífico* y *Los crustáceos cavernícolas de México*.

RÍOS, ADOLFO ◆ n. en Uruapan, Mich. (1966). Futbolista. Ha sido portero de los equipos Uruapan, UNAM, Veracruz, Necaxa y América. Subcampeón de liga con la UNAM en la temporada 1987-88. Seleccionado nacional, jugó en la Copa América 1997, donde se obtuvo el tercer lugar.

Códice Ríos

RÍOS, CÓDICE ◆ Llamado también Códice Vaticano 3,738 Códice Vaticano A o *Codex Vaticanus*. Documento pictográfico posthispánico en 101 hojas de papel europeo, de 46 por 29 cm, elaborado con técnica indígena en el valle de México entre 1566 y 1589. Se halla en la Biblioteca Apostólica Vaticana. De acuerdo con Francisco del Paso y Troncoso, se trata de una copia del original comentado en italiano por el dominico Pedro de los Ríos, quien estuvo auxiliado en la reproducción por uno o más amanuenses, pues existen diferencias caligráficas. El documento contiene información sobre los pueblos recién descubiertos, como el ciclo adivinatorio de 260 días, tradiciones diversas, cómputos de los días, meses y años, indicaciones sobre fiestas, trajes y adornos mexicanos y unos anales históricos hasta 1563. La característica más importante de este manuscrito es que se refiere a una de las creencias de los antiguos mexicanos: la de que el mundo ha transitado a través de varias etapas (soles) con diferentes humanidades y fines catastróficos para cada una.

RÍOS, ELVIRA ◆ n. y m. en el DF (1913-1987). Nombre profesional de la cantante Elvira Gallegos, conocida como *La voz de humo* o *La emocional*. Fue una de las intérpretes más sobresalientes del elenco de la XEW en la década de los treinta. Realizó presentaciones en varios países de América y Europa, grabó unos 25 discos de larga duración y destacó como intérprete de Agustín Lara, María Greever y Vicente Garrido. Se retiró en 1977.

RÍOS, ERNESTO ◆ n. en Saltillo, Coah. (1890-?). En 1913 se unió a la revolución. Durante la lucha de facciones apoyó a los gobiernos de la Convención y militó en la División del Norte. Más tarde fue director de propaganda de la campaña presidencial callista (1924) y diputado federal por el Estado de México (1924-26).

RÍOS, JUAN JOSÉ ◆ n. en Fresnillo, Zac., y m. en el DF (1882-1958). Militar. Como dirigente de la huelga de Cananea, en 1906, fue encarcelado en San Juan de Ulúa, de donde lo liberaron las fuerzas maderistas en 1911. En 1913 se unió al constitucionalismo en el Cuerpo de Ejército del Noroeste. Gobernador y comandante militar de Colima (1914-15), participó en la campaña de Nayarit, a las órdenes de Álvaro Obregón, con quien estuvo también en la batalla de Celaya. Nuevamente gobernador de Colima (1915-17), durante su gestión implantó el salario mínimo y creó la Junta Central de Conciliación y Arbitraje. Secretario de Guerra y Marina (del 7 de abril de 1918 al 18 de febrero de 1920) en el gabinete de Venustiano Carranza, fue encargado de los Establecimientos Fabriles, jefe del Estado Mayor y secretario de Gobernación en el gobierno de Pascual Ortiz Rubio, (del 20 de enero al 2 de septiembre de 1932). General de división en 1938.

RÍOS, LÁZARO ◆ n. en Monterrey, NL (1957). Ingeniero industrial y maestro en sistemas de información para la administración por la Universidad Autónoma de Nuevo León (de la que ha sido profesor), y maestro en desarrollo organizacional por la Universidad de Monterrey. Trabajó en diversos puestos dentro de los grupos Vitro e Industrial Chihuahua. Pasó al periódico *El Norte*, en el que colaboró y del que fue director de Recursos Humanos. En 1993 fue designado director del proyecto del periódico *Reforma*, del que desde entonces es director editorial adjunto, así como de *El Norte* y *Palabra*. Miembro de Profesionales en Desarrollo Organizacional, World Future Society e Innovation International Media.

Ríos, Rafael L. de los ◆ n. y m. en el DF (1890-1948). Abogado. Fundador y secretario del Partido Liberal, del que se separó en 1909 para incorporarse al Partido Antirreeleccionista. Se opuso a la dictadura de Victoriano Huerta y se incorporó a las fuerzas de Venustiano Carranza, quien en 1914 lo nombró director interino de Minas y Petróleos. Diputado al Congreso Constituyente de 1916-1917 y regidor del ayuntamiento de México (1917). Trabajó en la Secretaría de Comunicaciones, de cuyo sindicato fue secretario general. Colaborador del *Diario del Hogar*, *México Nuevo* y *El Combate* (del que fue fundador). Vicepresidente de la Sociedad Manuel José Othón, socio del Ateneo de la Juventud, secretario del Primer Congreso de Escritores y Artistas y miembro fundador de la Liga de Escritores y Artistas Revolucionarios (1934-38).

Ríos Castillo, Tirso ◆ n. en el DF (1930). Ingeniero químico por la UNAM (1956), especializado en fitoquímica. Ha sido investigador titular de tiempo completo en el Instituto de Química de la UNAM y editor de la *Revista Mexicana de Química* (1970-72). Miembro del Sistema Nacional de Investigadores y de la Asociación Latinoamericana de Fitoquímica. Premio a la mejor tesis de licenciatura (1956) y Premio Nacional de Química (1987).

Ríos Elizondo, Roberto ◆ n. y m. en el DF (1918-1978). Licenciado (1944) y doctor (1975) en derecho por la UNAM. Fue profesor en las facultades de Derecho y de Comercio de la UNAM, y en la Escuela Superior de Comercio y Administración del IPN. Desempeñó diversos cargos públicos en la Secretaría de Obras Públicas, en el DDF y en el IMSS (1951-73) y fue ministro de la Suprema Corte de Justicia (1977-78). Miembro de la Barra Mexicana-Colegio de Abogados.

Ríos Ferrer, Luis Roberto ◆ n. en el DF (1949). Hijo del anterior. Licenciado (1974), maestro (1976) y doctor (1978) en derecho por la UNAM. Integrante del PRI desde 1970. Ha sido profesor de la UNAM (1975-76), secretario particular del director general (1977-78) y gerente general de Electrificación Rural (1978-80) de la CFE, director de Parques Industriales del Fondo Nacional para los Desarrollos Portuarios (1980-82); gerente general de Planeación (1983-84) y subdirector (1984-85) de Aeropuertos y Servicios Auxiliares; director general de Puertos (1985-88), vocal ejecutivo de Puertos Mexicanos (1989-92) y subsecretario de Comunicaciones y Desarrollo Tecnológico de la SCT (1992-94). Autor de *Exégesis de la Carta de Derechos y Deberes Económicos de los Estados* (1976).

Ríos Zertuche Díez, Francisco Guillermo ◆ n. en el DF (1948). Licenciado en derecho por la UNAM (1972), maestro en administración por la Universidad de Derby (1979) y en desarrollo por la Universidad de Cambridge, Inglaterra (1980). Miembro del PRI desde 1963. Ha sido gerente de Desarrollo de la Comunidad del Indeco (1974-76); director de Recursos Humanos (1980-82) y secretario del Consejo de Administración de Uranio Mexicano (1983); coordinador de Control del subsecretario (1983), secretario particular del subsecretario (1984-85), coordinador de asesores del subsecretario (1985-86) y director general de la Unidad de Apoyo Técnico de la SEMIP (1987); y asesor del director general de Astilleros Unidos (1987-88). En el DDF se desempeñó como subdelegado jurídico (1989-90) y delegado en Tlalpan (1990-94).

Rioverde ◆ Municipio de San Luis Potosí situado al este de la capital del estado y al oeste de Ciudad Valles, en los límites con Guanajuato. Superficie: 3,242.9 km². Habitantes: 88,922, de los cuales 21,948 forman la población económicamente activa. Hablan alguna lengua indígena 90 personas mayores de cinco años. La región de Rioverde estuvo habitada por los huastecos alrededor del año 650 de nuestra era. A la llegada de los conquistadores españoles, poblaban la zona las comunidades guachichiles y pames. El evangelizador Juan de San Miguel llegó a Rioverde hacia 1544, pero no tuvo éxito en su misión entre los guachichiles. Después de San Miguel llegó el sacerdote Bernardo Cossín, alrededor de 1551, quien impartió algunos bautismos pero supuestamente fue muerto por los indígenas. Juan de Cárdenas fue el siguiente misionero, quien logró fundar la cabecera de la custodia de Santa Catarina Virgen y Mártir del Río Verde. Aproximadamente en 1592 se formó en San Luis una expedición que viajó a Rioverde, atraída por las noticias de la riqueza de los recursos naturales de la región; esta primera expedición fue comandada por Miguel Caldera. Hubo otra en 1597, dirigida por Gabriel Ortiz de Fuenmayor. Ambas incursiones lograron someter a los guachichiles, aunque la conquista plena sólo se obtuvo a principios del siglo XVII, por la misión evangelizadora de Juan de Cárdenas y Juan Bautista Mollinedo. Durante la guerra de Independencia, Rioverde fue escenario, en 1827, de un combate entre el realista Piedras y el insurgente Francisco Javier Mina. El 23 de mayo de 1821, Juan José Zenón Fernández secundó en este municipio el Plan de Iguala y proclamó la independencia de México. En 1849 se produjo la rebelión de Eleuterio Quiroz, quien buscaba iniciar una revolución socialista de acuerdo con el "Plan Político y Eminentemente Social del Ejército Regenerador de Sierra Gorda", redactado por el rioverdense Manuel Verástegui. Bustamante y Tomás Mejía aplastaron esta rebelión el mismo año de su inicio, pero el directorio de Rioverde, fundado por Quiroz, se mantuvo activo y en 1852 declaró la guerra al gobernador potosino Julián de los Reyes, quien fue ejecutado. Durante la guerra de Reforma, el 17 de enero de 1861 se produjo en Rioverde un combate entre las tropas de Mariano Escobedo y las de Tomás Mejía; el triunfo correspondió a las fuerzas conservadoras.

Rippey, Carla ◆ n. en EUA (1950). Grabadora. Licenciada en artes liberales

Juan José Ríos

Foto: Braulio Tenorio

Tirso Ríos Castillo

Carla Rippey

Sin título, grabado a punta seca, de Carla Rippey

Foto: Rogelio Baeza

Carlos Riquelme

Foto: Época

Arturo Ripstein

por la Universidad de Nueva York, donde también estudió arte y comunicación. Ingresó en los talleres de grabado de la Universidad Católica de Chile (1972). Radicada en México desde 1973, trabaja en el taller de grabado de la Universidad Veracruzana. Ha expuesto, desde 1976, en diversas ciudades de México, Francia, Estados Unidos, Argentina, Puerto Rico y Colombia. Participó en la muestra Confrontación (1986) en el Palacio de Bellas Artes.

Ripstein, Arturo ◆ n. en el DF (1944). Cineasta. Dejó inconclusa la carrera de derecho. Fue ayudante de Buñuel en la filmación de *El ángel exterminador* (1962). Ha dirigido *Tiempo de morir* (1965), *Juego peligroso* (1967), *Los recuerdos del porvenir* (1968), *La hora de los niños* (1969), *El náufrago de la calle Providencia* (1970, en colaboración con Rafael Castanedo), *El castillo de la pureza* (1972), *El Santo Oficio* (1973), *Los otros niños* (1974), *Foxtrot* (1975), *Lecumberri* (1976), *El lugar sin límites* (1977, premio especial del jurado del Festival Internacional de Cine de San Sebastián en 1978), *La viuda negra* (1977), *Cadena perpetua* (1978), *La tía Alejandra* (1978), *La ilegal* (1979), *La seducción* (1979), *Rastro de muerte* (1981), *El imperio de la fortuna* (1986, exhibida en el Festival Internacional de Cine de San Sebastián del mismo año y ganadora de nueve Arieles), *Mentiras piadosas* (1987), *La mujer del puerto* (1991), *Principio y fin* (1993, Concha de Plata en el Festival de San Sebastián), *La reina de la noche* (1993), *Profundo Carmesí* (1996, tres premios del Festival de Venecia y Sol de Oro en el Festival de Biarritz), *El evangelio de las maravillas* (1998) y *El coronel no tiene quien le escriba* (selección oficial de Cannes, 1999), entre otras cintas. En 1999 dirigió una puesta en escena de la ópera *Salomé*, de Richard Strauss, presentada en el Palacio de Bellas Artes. Premios Nacional de Ciencias y Artes (1997) y Akira Kurosawa en el Festival de San Francisco (1999).

Riquelme, Carlos ◆ n. y m. en el DF (1913-1990). Actor. Se inició en 1934 con *La verdad sospechosa*, de Alarcón, puesta para inaugurar el Palacio de Bellas Artes. Durante 25 años formó parte de la compañía de comedia de Nadia Haro Oliva. Participó, entre otras, en las cintas *Su adorable mujeriego* (1934), *Murallas de pasión*, *Mexicanos al grito de guerra*, *Fuego en la carne*, *El ángel caído*, *Teatro Arbeu*, *Los amores de una viuda*, *La malquerida*, *Pancho Villa vuelve*, *Mujer de media noche*, *Una gallega en México*, *Yo quiero ser mala*, *Display*, *Los que no deben nacer*, *Una aventura en la noche* y *Una familia de tantas*. Hizo radio y telenovelas y actuó en películas extranjeras como *Viva María*, de Louis Malle, *Bajo el volcán*, de John Houston, y *El secreto de milagro*, de Robert Redford. Fue uno de los fundadores de la Asociación Nacional de Actores.

Rius ◆ n. en Zamora, Mich. (1934). Nombre profesional de caricaturista Eduardo del Río García. Se inició en la revista *Ja-Já* (1954), fue cartonista político de *Ovaciones*, donde sustituyó a Abel Quezada. Ha colaborado en las publicaciones *Sucesos para todos*, *Excélsior*, *Siempre!*, *Política*, *Proceso* y *La Jornada*. Fundó y dirigió las publicaciones *La Gallina*, *Marca Diablo*, *El Mitote*, *El Mitote Ilustrado* y *La Garrapata*, y es cofundador y codirector de *El Chahuistle* y *El Chamuco*. Creó las historietas *Los Supermachos* y *Los Agachados*. Autor de lo que llama "librocómics", por su formato de historieta: *Cuba para principiantes* (1964), *Pequeño Rius ilustrado*, *Cristo de carne y hueso*, *Manifiesto comunista ilustrado*, *Lenin para principiantes*, *Marx para principiantes* (1972), *A b che* (1978), *Historia rapidísima de España* (1980), *Manual del perfecto ateo* (1980), *El diablo se llama Trotsky* (1981), *La interminable conquista de México* (1983), *Hitler para masoquistas* (1983), *El amor en los tiempos del Sida* (1988), *Quetzalcóatl no era del* PRI (1989), *La perestroika según Rius* (1990), *La droga que refresca* (1990), *500 años fregados pero cristianos* (1992), *De aborto, sexo y*

El imperio de la fortuna, película dirigida por Arturo Ripstein

ARCHIVO: XAVIER ESPARZA

Los Supermachos de Rius

otros pecados (1993) y *El supermercado de las sectas* (1999), entre otros que suman cerca de un centenar. Premio de la Asociación Mexicana de Periodistas (1959), Gran Prix de Montreal (1968), Premio Nacional de Periodismo (1987) y Premio Forte del Marni de sátira política (1995). Ganó el Concurso Nacional de Cartel "Con nuestro ingenio invitemos a leer" (1991).

Rius, Luis ◆ n. en España y m. en el DF (1930-1984). Su segundo apellido era Azcoitia. Llegó a México en 1939. Maestro (1954) y doctor (1968) en letras españolas por la UNAM, donde fue profesor (1965-84); así como en las universidades de San Luis Potosí, Iberoamericana y de las Américas. Fue jefe del Departamento de Letras y secretario de la Facultad de Filosofía y Letras de la Universidad de Guanajuato. Profesor invitado del Mexico City College. Impartió cursos de literatura por radio y televisión. Fundó las revistas *Clavileño* (1948) y *Segrel* (1950). Colaboró en la *Revista Mexicana de Literatura, Las Españas, Anuario de Letras, México en la Cultura, Presencia, Diorama de la Cultura, El Nacional, La Cultura en México, El Heraldo de México, Ideas de México* y *Cuadernos Americanos*. Autor de poesía: *Canciones de vela* (1951, dibujos de Arturo Souto y epílogo de Julio Torri), *Canciones de ausencia* (1954), *Canciones de amor y sombra* (1965), *Canciones a Pilar Rioja* (1968, Premio Olimpiada Cultural), y *Cuestión de amor y otros poemas* (1984); ensayo: *El mundo amoroso de Cervantes y sus personajes* (1954, tesis de maestría), *Los grandes textos creativos de la literatura española. Siglos XI-XIII* (1966), y *La poesía* (1972); y biografía: *León Felipe, poeta de barco* (1968). En 1973 grabó un disco dentro de la colección Voz viva de México, de la UNAM. Fue becario del Centro Mexicano de Escritores (1956-57).

Rius Facius, Antonio ◆ n. en el DF (1918). Dirigente de la Asociación Católica de la Juventud Mejicana (1940), miembro del Comité Ejecutivo del PAN (1964), fundó la Asociación de Comerciantes del Centro de la Ciudad de México (1967) y la sección del centro de la Cámara Nacional de Comercio. Colaborador de *Ser, El Hogar, Lectura* y *Rutas*, de Monterrey, *Norte, La Voz de Chihuahua, Boletín de la Sociedad Chihuahuense de Estudios Históricos, Revista del Club España, Juventud Católica* (fundadas y dirigidas por él), *Excélsior, El Universal Gráfico, El Sol de México* y *La Nación*. Autor de *Ilusiones* (1938), *Los demoledores de la Iglesia en México. Historia de la ACJM 1910-1925* (1958), *El retrato de ovalito* (1959), *Horizontes interiores* (1959), *Historia de la ACJM 1925-1931. Méjico cristero* (1960), *La juventud católica y la revolución mexicana* (1963), *Palestra espiritual* (1965), *Con la prosa de la Nueva España* (1968), *Lanza en ristre frente a los ataques del progresismo marxista* (1968), *Bernardo Bergoend S. J. Guía y maestro de la juventud mexicana* (1972), *Un joven sin historia* (1973), *Caudal poético* (1977), *Una santa, católica y apostólica Iglesia* (1977), *Galería de pintores* (1981) y *En mi sillón de lecturas* (1988). Miembro fundador del Instituto Cultural Hispano Mexicano (1959) y editor de su órgano, *Acento*.

Rius de la Pola, Pilar ◆ n. en España (1928). Tras la derrota de la República Española pasó con su familia a Francia y llegó exiliada a México en 1939. Licenciada en química por la Universidad Femenina de México y maestra en química teórica por la UNAM. Ha sido directora de la Escuela de Ciencias de la Universidad Femenina, directora del bachillerato del Colegio Margarita de Escocia, coordinadora del área de química-física en la UNAM, jefa del Departamento de Materias Estructurales de la Facultad de Química de la UNAM, jefa del Departamento de Becas y profesora titular de esa Facultad, donde ha realizado trabajos de investigación sobre mecánica cuántica y dispersión múltiple. Ha hecho trabajos de cálculo teórico de intensidades de banda en el infrarrojo, en la Universidad John Hopkins y en la Universidad Complutense de Madrid. Autora de *Fundamentos teóricos de la espectroscopía de vibración* (1982).

Rius de la Pola de Riepen, Magdalena ◆ n. en Francia (1937). Hija de españoles, hermana de la anterior, llegó exiliada en 1939 y obtuvo la nacionalidad mexicana en 1950. Química farmacobióloga por la Universidad Femenina de México (1958). Becada por la UNAM realizó estudios de posgrado en Europa (1965-66) y se doctoró (1976) por la UNAM y el Institut Fur Physikalische Dhemie, de la República Federal de Alemania. Ha sido profesora de química en escuelas particulares (1958-64), profesora e investigadora de la UNAM (1958-) y asesora técnica de Química Knoll de México (1977-). En la UNAM inició la investigación para el desarrollo de la energía solar y estableció programas de colaboración científica con universidades de la RFA, Estados Unidos y España. Colaboradora de la *Revista de la Sociedad Química*.

Rius Zunón, Luis ◆ n. en España y m. en el DF (1901-1974). Abogado y escritor. Fue alcalde de Tarancón (1931), presidente de la Diputación Provincial de Cuenca y gobernador civil de las provincias de Soria y de Jaén durante la guerra civil. Llegó exiliado a México en 1939. Fue autor de la música y letra de numerosas canciones que se reunieron en dos discos llamados *Cancionero de Tarancón* (1972 y 74). Autor de *Romancero de Fernando Muñoz y la reina María Cristina* (1966), *El candil* (1969) y *Ni ná ni cosa* (1970).

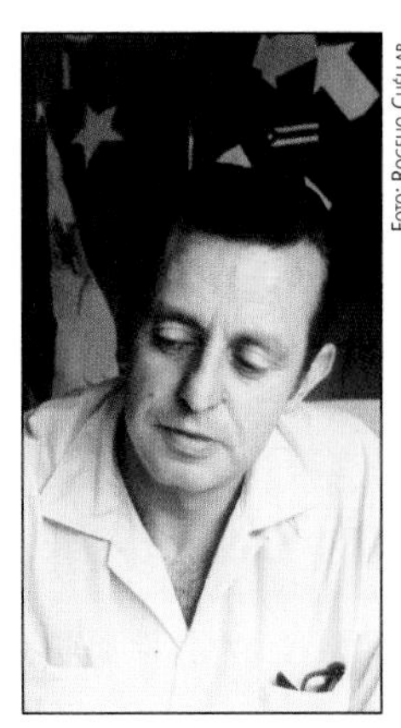

FOTO: ROGELIO CUÉLLAR

Rius

Foto: Ana Lourdes Herrera

Juan Antonio de la Riva

Carlos Riva Palacio

Foto: Rogelio Baeza

Carlos Riva Palacio

Foto: Rogelio Baeza

Mariano Riva Palacio

Riva, Juan Antonio de la ◆ n. en San Miguel de las Cruces, Dgo. (1953). Cineasta. En 1972 participó en la creación del Taller de Cine Independiente en Súper 8. Estudió dirección cinematográfica en el CCC (1975-78). Con su trabajo final para esta institución, el corto *Polvo vencedor del sol* (1979), obtuvo el premio principal de ficción en el Festival de Cortometraje y Documental de Lille, Francia, así como un Ariel. Realizó algunos trabajos para la televisión educativa y cultural. Ha dirigido las cintas *Vidas errantes* (1984), *Obdulia* (1985), *Pueblo de madera* (1990), *Soy libre* (1992), *Una maestra con ángel* (1993), *Monarca* (1994), *La última batalla* (1996) y *Elisa antes del fin del mundo* (1997). Dirigió también varios episodios de la serie televisiva *Hora marcada*.

Riva, Míriam de la ◆ n. en el DF (1940). Pintora. Hizo estudios en la Kent State University y en el taller de Carlos Orozco Romero. Ha presentado su obra en exposiciones individuales y colectivas en México y el extranjero. Ha creado murales fijos y transportables. Mención honorífica en el concurso Francisco Goitia (1992).

Riva Palacio ◆ Municipio de Chihuahua contiguo a la capital del estado. Superficie: 2,417.05 km². Habitantes: 9,300, de los cuales 2,818 forman la población económicamente activa. Hablan tarahumara 25 personas mayores de cinco años. En el siglo XVII los franciscanos evangelizaron en la actual juriscción del municipio, erigido en 1908. Su cabecera, San Andrés Riva Palacio, se llamó San Andrés de Osaguiqui (1696-1932).

Riva Palacio, Carlos ◆ n. en Toluca, Edo. de Méx., y m. en Costa Rica (1892-1936). Diputado federal, gobernador del Estado de México (1925-29) y secretario de Gobernación en el gabinete de Emilio Portes Gil (1929-30). Cofundador del PNR (1929), fue precandidato a la Presidencia de la República (1932-33), secretario de prensa y publicidad (1933) y presidente del Comité Ejecutivo Nacional (1933-34), antes de ser expulsado por su filiación callista en diciembre de 1935, cuando era senador. Participó en la fundación del Partido Constitucional Revolucionario (1935). Fue embajador en Chile. Fundó el *Boletín del Archivo General de la Nación*. Coautor de *La cuestión agraria mexicana* (1934).

Riva Palacio, Carlos ◆ n. en Texcoco, Edo. de Méx., y m. en el DF (1934-1997). También se dice que nació en el DF. Se tituló como médico en la UNAM (1959). Becado por la Organización Internacional del Trabajo estudió medicina del trabajo en la República Federal de Alemania. Perteneció al PRI y fue secretario general de la CNOP, del Sindicato Nacional de Trabajadores del ISSSTE y de la FSTSE. Diputado federal y director del ISSSTE (1979-82).

Riva Palacio, Mariano ◆ n. y m. en la ciudad de México (1803-1880). Abogado. Fue el primer regidor del ayuntamiento de México (1829) y figuró más de 12 veces en el Congreso de la Unión como diputado o senador. Secretario de Hacienda (del 3 de junio al 20 de agosto de 1848) de José Joaquín de Herrera, varias veces gobernador del Estado de México (en 1849, 1857 y 1871) y diputado al Congreso Constituyente (1856). En 1855 declinó pertenecer a los gabinetes de Martín Carrera y de Juan Álvarez y en 1856 pidió licencia al Congreso para formar parte de la Junta del Desagüe del Valle de México. En 1863 fue nombrado miembro de la Junta de Notables, puesto que también rechazó, lo mismo que la cartera de Gobernación, en 1864, ofrecida por Maximiliano, quien en 1867, preso, lo nombró uno de sus defensores, encargo que aceptó. En 1868 presidió de nuevo el ayuntamiento de México y fue electo presidente de la Cámara. El 16 de diciembre de 1871 la legislatura mexiquense lo declaró benemérito y en 1876 fue director del Nacional Monte de Piedad.

Riva Palacio, Raymundo ◆ n. en el DF (1954). Periodista. Cursó la carrera de periodismo en la Escuela Carlos Septién. Fue corresponsal en Washington de *El Sol de México* (1975-76), *Proceso* (1976-77), *unomásuno* (1978-80) y *Excélsior*, periódico del que cubrió también la corresponsalía en París y Madrid. En mayo de 1988, enviado por este diario a Colombia, fue secuestrado, junto con 17 periodistas, diplomáticos y políticos, por el comando Unión Camilista del Ejército de Liberación Nacional, organización que exigía al gobierno de aquel país una amplia investigación acerca de la violación de los derechos humanos, el cese de la guerra sucia y la nacionalización del petróleo. Su secuestro duró cinco días (del 5 al 9 de mayo). Director general de Notimex (1988), trabajó en los diarios *El Financiero* (1993 y 1998) y *Reforma* (1993-97) y fue colaborador de *La Crónica de Hoy* (1997). Cofundador de *Milenio* (1997), es director editorial del grupo Multimedios-Estrellas de Oro (1998-), empresa editora de ese semanario. Coautor de *Aún tiembla* y *La cultura de la colisión*. Autor de *Centroamérica: la guerra ya empezó* (1987), *Más allá de los límites*. Premio Nacional de Periodismo (1985) y premio del Club de Periodistas de México (1987).

Riva Palacio, Vicente ◆ n. en la ciudad de México y m. en España (1832-1896). Era hijo de Mariano Riva Palacio. Abogado graduado en 1854. Fue regidor (1855) y secretario del ayuntamiento de la ciudad de México (1856) y diputado federal (1861-62). Entre 1861 y 1862 escribió una decena de obras de teatro con Juan A. Mateos. Organizó una guerrilla y estuvo en el sitio de Puebla de 1863. Siguió al gobierno juarista a San Luis Potosí, donde fue designado gobernador del Estado de México. Reunió tropas y tomó Tulillo y Zitácuaro. En 1865 fue designado gobernador de Michoacán y general en jefe del Ejército del Centro. A principios de 1867, con una fuerza irregular sitió y tomó Toluca. Asistió al sitio de Querétaro. Durante la guerra editó periódicos satíricos como *El Monarca* (1863) y *El Pito Real*. Al triunfo de la República dirigió *La Orquesta* y fue magistrado de la Suprema Corte de Justicia (1868-

1870). Apoyó la rebelión de Tuxtepec. Fue secretario de Fomento con Porfirio Díaz y con Juan N. Méndez. (1876-80) y embajador en España y Portugal (1885-96). Coautor de *El libro rojo 1520-1867* (1870) y *Tradiciones y leyendas mexicanas* (1922). Autor de novela histórica: *Monja y casada, virgen y mártir* (1868), *Martín Garatuza* (1868), *Calvario y Tabor* (1868), *Las dos emparedadas* (1869), *Los piratas del golfo* (1869), *La vuelta de los muertos* (1870), *Memorias de un impostor, don Guillén de Lampart, rey de México* (1872) y *Un secreto que mata* (1917). Escribió también *Cuentos de un loco* (1874), *Flores del alma* (1875, poesía, con el pseudónimo de *Rosa Espino*), *Historia de la administración de don Sebastián Lerdo de Tejada* (1875), *Los ceros* (1882), *Páginas en verso* (1885), *Mis versos* (1893) *Cuentos del general* (1896) e *Historia de la guerra de intervención en Michoacán* (1896), Dirigió la elaboración de *México a través de los siglos* (1884-89), de cuyo volumen de historia colonial es autor.

Riva Palacio López, Antonio ◆ n. en Cuautla, Mor. (1928). Licenciado en derecho por la UNAM (1946-52), donde fue presidente de la Asociación de Estudiantes (1948). Miembro del PRI. Profesor (1964) y miembro del consejo técnico de la Escuela de Derecho y presidente de la Junta de Gobierno de la Universidad Autónoma de Morelos (1968, 1971, 1980 y 1981), entidad en la que ha sido presidente de la Junta Central de Conciliación y Arbitraje (1958-60), asesor legal de la Comisión de Planificación y Zonificación (1958-60), secretario general de Gobierno (1960-64), asesor de la Liga de Comunidades Agrarias y Sindicatos Campesinos (1976) y gobernador (1988-94). Fue diputado federal (1976-79) y senador por el mismo estado (1982-87), asesor de la Subsecretaría de Gobernación (1982) y embajador en Ecuador (1997-98). En 1974 obtuvo diploma como el postulante más relevante, otorgado por el Tribunal Superior de Justicia y el Colegio de Abogados de Morelos.

Riva Palacio Morales, Emilio ◆ n. en Jojutla y m. en Cuernavaca, Mor. (1910-1990). Fue gobernador de Morelos (1964-1970). Durante su gestión apoyó el establecimiento de la Universidad Autónoma de Morelos.

Rivas, Candelario ◆ n. en Fresnillo, Zac., y m. en Pachuca, Hgo. (1860-1916). En 1890 era subdirector de una banda militar en Puebla, con la que realizó una gira por España dos años después. Organizó la Banda de Rurales del estado de Hidalgo en 1900 y la dirigió hasta 1906. Dirigió la Banda del Parque Luna de la ciudad de México (1907) y obtuvo el primer lugar en un concurso que reunió a los mejores conjuntos musicales de su tipo en el país. En 1908 dirigió la banda de Zacatecas y en 1911 la del estado de Hidalgo. Autor de la polka *Risas y fuego* (por la que ganó una mención honorífica en 1888), *Fantasía heroica 1910* e *Himno a Hidalgo*.

Rivas, Carlos ◆ n. en Guaymas, Son., y m. en la ciudad de México (1834-1908). Abogado. Fue tres veces diputado federal por el cantón de Tepic y contribuyó a la erección del estado de Nayarit. En 1876, acusado de conspirar contra el gobierno de Lerdo de Tejada, fue expulsado de Tepic. En 1879 se sumó a las fuerzas de Manuel González que combatieron la insurrección de la sierra de Alica. Fue secretario particular del presidente Manuel González y en 1883 se le encomendó renegociar la deuda con Inglaterra. Volvió el mismo año a México y fue nuevamente secretario particular de Manuel González, diputado, gobernador del Distrito Federal (de mayo a diciembre de 1884) y senador.

Rivas, Enrique de ◆ n. en España (1931). Hijo de Cipriano Rivas Cherif. Poeta y ensayista. Al término de la guerra civil española pasó a Francia y llegó exiliado a México en 1939. Licenciado en letras por la UNAM, realizó estudios de posgrado en la Universidad de Puerto Rico y se doctoró en la de California en Berkeley. Ha sido profesor del Mexico City College, jefe del Departamento de Español de la Universidad de las Américas y funcionario de la FAO en Roma (1967-). Editó la obra *Retrato de un desconocido (Vida de don Manuel Azaña)*, escrito por su padre, así como la correspondencia que éste mantuvo con Azaña entre 1931 y 1937. Autor de *Primeros poemas* (1949), *En la herencia del día* (1966), *Tiempo ilícito* (1980), *Endimión en España* (1968) y *De estrellas y figuras de las cosas* (1969).

Rivas, José Luis ◆ n. en Tuxpan, Ver. (1950). Escritor. Estudió letras hispánicas y filosofía en la UNAM, donde trabajó en el Centro de Estudios Sociales. Dirigió el taller de poesía Tierra Adentro, del INBA. Fundador y miembro del consejo de redacción de *Caos* y coordinador de la *Gaceta del FCE*. Ha colaborado en *Pauta, Revista de la Universidad, Novedades* y *Sábado*. Se encargó de la selección, versión en español y prólogo de *Fuentes del viento*, de Pierre Reverdy (1987). Tradujo *El vuelo del vampiro*, de Michel Tournier (1987), *La era de Ezra Pound* (1987), *El niño y el río* (1987), la *Poesía completa de T. S. Elliot (1909-1962)* (1990, premio Xavier Villaurrutia), La *Poesía completa de St. John Perse* (1991), *Poetas metafísicos ingleses* (1990, premio de Traducción de Poesía INBA-FNCA) y *Omeros*, de Derek Walcott (1994). Autor de poesía: *Fresca de risa* (1981), *Tierra nativa* (Premio Carlos Pellicer, 1982), *Relámpago de muerte* (1985), *La balada del capitán* (1986), *La transparencia del deseo* (Premio Nacional de Poesía de Aguascalientes, 1986), *Brazos de mar* (1990, premio Xavier Villaurrutia), *Ras de marea* (1993) y *Río* (1998). Fue becario del CNCA (1989-90).

Rivas, Manuel ◆ n. en San Luis Potosí, SLP, y m. en El Salvador (?-?). Abogado. Luchó en las revoluciones maderista y constitucionalista. Fue gobernador de Sinaloa (1916) y ministro de México en El Salvador. Fue también periodista y escritor.

Rivas, Manuel *Wello* ◆ n. en Mérida, Yuc. y m. en el DF (1913-1990). Compositor. Estudió solfeo con Federico Méndez. Fue el intérprete más reconocido de Rafael *El Jibarito* Her-

Foto: Época

Raymundo Riva Palacio

Vicente Riva Palacio

Foto: Dante Bucio

Antonio Riva Palacio López

nández, y se hizo de fama en la XEW, con sus propias composiciones, en los cincuenta. Actuó en teatros de revista y centros nocturnos e hizo giras por México y otros países con su propia orquesta. Entre sus más de 1,500 canciones destacan *Llegaste tarde*, *Más y más*, *Quisiera ser golondrina*, *Con las alas rotas*, *Como golondrina* y *Cenizas*.

Lupe Rivas Cacho

RIVAS CACHO, LUPE ◆ n. y m. en el DF (1894-1975). A los 13 años de edad empezó a participar en zarzuelas y operetas. Trabajó en diversos teatros de Guadalajara, Monterrey y Mérida hasta llegar a primera figura en el teatro Lírico de la ciudad de México, donde fue iniciadora de la revista mexicana de sátira política. Formó después su propia compañía (1920), con la que recorrió diversos países del continente. Cofundadora del Grupo Solidario del Movimiento Obrero con Vicente Lombardo Toledano, Diego Rivera, José Clemente Orozco y Xavier Guerrero (31 de agosto de 1921). Incursionó en el cine con películas como *Comisario en turno*, *La culpa de los hombres* y *Mi canción eres tú*. Actuó en radio y televisión. En 1970, la Asociación Nacional de Actores le otorgó la medalla Eduardo Arozamena.

RIVAS CID, BENIGNO ◆ n. en Orizaba, Ver. (1907). Estudió pintura y escultura en la Academia de San Carlos (1927-32). En 1929 inauguró la Galería de Artes del Palacio de Bellas Artes con una exposición conjunta con Francisco Dosamantes. En 1930 organizó el Grupo de Pintores Independientes de México, que exponía en las Galerías Excélsior. En 1936 expuso en Bellas Artes con la estadounidense June Claire y formó parte del grupo Generación Revolucionaria Unificadora de Artistas.

Antonieta y Antonio Rivas Mercado

RIVAS CHERIF, CIPRIANO ◆ n. en España y m. en el DF (1891-1967). En los años veinte editó con Manuel Azaña, que sería su cuñado, las revistas literarias *España* y *La Pluma*. Fue crítico teatral en otras publicaciones y se dedicó a la dirección de compañías escénicas, además de dirigir el Conservatorio Nacional. Fue cónsul español en Ginebra (1936-38) y jefe de ceremonial del Ministerio de Estado (1939). Un año después fue detenido por los alemanes en Francia, enviado a España y condenado a muerte, pero su pena fue conmutada y estuvo encarcelado hasta 1947. Llegó a México en 1948 y se dedicó a la producción teatral, la crítica en diversas publicaciones y la docencia en las universidades Nacional Autónoma de México y de las Américas. Tradujo a diversos autores ingleses, franceses e italianos y en su trabajo periodístico usó el pseudónimo de *Tito Liviano*. Autor de *Versos de abril*, *Los cuernos de la luna*, *Un camarada más* y *Retrato de un desconocido*. En 1931 recibió el premio nacional de Literatura de España.

RIVAS CHERIF, MANUEL DE ◆ n. en España y m. en el DF (1894-1966). Hermano del anterior. Fue profesor y jefe de servicios del Departamento de Oftalmología de la Facultad de Medicina de Madrid y consejero de Sanidad de la República Española. Llegó exiliado a México en 1939 y ejerció su profesión en el IMSS y en el Departamento de Oftalmología del Hospital de la Raza, desde la fundación de este nosocomio. Fue jefe de servicio de la Asociación Mexicana para Evitar la Ceguera. Autor de *La fotografía de las membranas profundas del ojo*, *Higiene del cinematógrafo*, *La fotoftalmografía y la cámara de Notdenson*, *Agudeza visual fisiológica y profesional* y *Fotoftalmología sin reflejos*. Trabajó en El Colegio de México y fue presidente de la Asociación Mexicana de Oftalmología.

RIVAS GUILLÉN, GENOVEVO ◆ n. en Rayón y m. en Potrero de Pará, SLP (1886-1947). En 1910 se incorporó a la insurrección maderista en las fuerzas de Alberto Carrera Torres. Su padre, Francisco Rivas, fue asesinado por los huertistas en junio de 1913 y Genovevo se incorporó a las filas del constitucionalismo. Recibió la condecoración del valor heroico en la batalla de El Carrizal, donde se enfrentó a la expedición punitiva de Pershing (1916). Como comandante de la XIV Zona Militar, luchó contra los cristeros en Jalisco (1926-28). General de división en 1933. En 1938 combatió la rebelión cedillista en San Luis Potosí y gobernó interinamente ese estado. Fue comandante militar de Querétaro, Oaxaca y Sonora. Al retirarse se dedicó a la agricultura.

RIVAS MERCADO, ANTONIETA ◆ n. en la ciudad de México y m. en Francia (1900-1931). Hija del arquitecto Antonio Rivas Mercado. Estudió idiomas, música y filosofía en Europa (1923-25). Colaboró en la revista *Ulises* (1927), que ella financió; en *El Sol* de Madrid (1928) y en *Contemporáneos* (1929). Fue cofundadora y patrocinadora de la compañía Teatro de Ulises (1928) que representó en México las obras de Shaw, Cocteau, Yeats y Vildrac, entre otros. Financió la publicación de los libros *Dama de corazones*, de Villaurrutia, *Novela como nube*, de Gilberto Owen y *Los hombres que dispersó la danza*, de Andrés Henestrosa. Participó en el patronato para crear la Sinfónica Nacional y puso nombre a las calles de las Lomas de Chapultepec. Colaboró con José Vasconcelos en la campaña presidencial de 1929 y en septiembre de ese año se exilió en EUA, donde hizo amistad con Federico García Lorca y en diciembre se reencontró con Vasconcelos. Luego de una breve visita a México (1930), donde secuestró a su hijo, cuya tutoría había pasado al padre, huyó a Nueva Orleans, donde se embarcó a Francia para reunirse de nuevo con Vasconcelos. Se suicidó el 11 de febrero de 1931, en la catedral de Notre Dame, en París. Póstumamente aparecieron sus colaboraciones en la revista *La Antorcha* (1931-32) y Luis Mario Schneider los reunió en *La campaña de Vasconcelos* (1982). Otros textos formaron *Cartas a Manuel Rodríguez Lozano 1927-1930* (1975) y *87 cartas de amor y otros papeles* (1982). Sus *Obras completas*, con prólogo del mismo Schneider, aparecieron en 1987.

Rivas Mercado, Antonio ◆ n. en Tepic, en el actual Nayarit, y m. en el DF (1853-1927). Arquitecto por la Escuela de Bellas Artes de París e ingeniero por la Sorbona (1878). Dirigió la Academia de San Carlos (1903-12), puesto al que renunció presionado por una movilización estudiantil. Autor del proyecto de la fachada del ayuntamiento del Distrito Federal (1887), el teatro Juárez de Guanajuato (1892-1903), la aduana de Santiago Tlatelolco, de la fachada del Palacio Nacional (1899), el Palacio Municipal de Tlalpan (1900-1907), la Columna de la Independencia de la ciudad de México (1910) y el inmueble que actualmente alberga al Museo de Cera de la ciudad de México, en la colonia Juárez.

Rivas Muñoz, Oscar Luis ◆ n. en Chihuahua, Chih. (1945). Arquitecto por la Universidad Autónoma de Nuevo León (1964-69). Ha sido director de la Escuela de Arquitectura de la Universidad Autónoma de Ciudad Juárez, presidente diocesano del Movimiento Familiar Cristiano de Chihuahua y diputado federal plurinominal por el PAN (1985-88).

Rivas Ochoa, Beatriz ◆ n. en el DF (1965). Licenciada en ciencias y técnicas de la información por la Universidad del Nuevo Mundo (1988), con estudios de posgrado en la Universidad de París (1983), de derecho en la UNAM (1985) y maestría en letras modernas en la UIA (1995); hizo un diplomado de literatura mexicana en la UAM-Xochimilco (1993). Coordinadora de producción de *Perspectiva Internacional* (1985-88), coordinadora editorial del noticiero *Monitor* (1988-92), directora general de Infopress (1993-96), coordinadora de producción del Grupo Radiópolis (1994), directora de comunicación del Conjunto Calakmul (1996-97), editora ejecutiva del semanario *Milenio* (1997-99) y coordinadora ejecutiva del Grupo Editorial Multimedios (1999-). Colaboradora de *El Búho*, *Macrópolis*, *Etcétera* y del Canal 40. Cuentos suyos se incluyeron en los volúmenes colectivos *Las mujeres de la torre* (1996) y *Veneno que fascina* (1997). Autora del libro de cuentos *¿Y si Dios fuera uno de nosotros?* (1999). Presidenta de la Asociación Mundial de Mujeres Periodistas y Escritoras para el periodo 1998-2000.

Rivas Torres, Armando ◆ n. y m. en el DF (1919-1970). Se inició como productor en la radiodifusora XEB de la ciudad de México y fue reportero, entre otras, de las publicaciones *Hoy* y *Excélsior*, periódico en el que llegó a desempeñarse como jefe de información. Fue director de la agencia Informex y de los diarios *El Universal* y *El Universal Gráfico*, director general de Televisión Independiente de México y de la empresa periodística Francisco Lanz Duret y Asociados. Profesor de las universidades Iberoamericana y Femenina de México.

Rivera, Arturo ◆ n. en el DF (1945). Artista plástico. Estudió pintura y grabado en la Academia de San Carlos (1963-68) y serigrafía y fotoserigrafía en The City Lit Art School, de Londres (1973-74). Ha participado en exposiciones colectivas en México, Nueva York, Guatemala, San Juan de Puerto Rico, La Habana, Munich, Medellín, Estocolmo, Roma, Berlín, París, Tokio, Londres y varias ciudades de Polonia. Individualmente ha expuesto en México, Mazatlán, Chicago y Nueva York. Hay obra suya en los museos La Tertulia de Cali, del Banco Central de Quito, de Arte Moderno de México, Haus der Kunst de Munich, así como en el Instituto de Cultura Puertorriqueña y en la Casa de las Américas.

Rivera, Aureliano ◆ n. en Veracruz, Ver., y m. en la ciudad de México (1832-1904). Militar liberal. En la guerra de los Tres Años formó una guerrilla que acosó a los conservadores en los alrededores de la ciudad de México. El 7 de junio de 1861, ya con el grado de general de brigada, se le encomendó la persecución de Leonardo Márquez, luego del asesinato de Melchor Ocampo. Fue destacado a Cuautla y, al iniciarse la intervención francesa, dirigió una guerrilla que operó cerca de Veracruz. En marzo de 1863 participó en la defensa de Puebla, militó en las fuerzas de Juan José de la Garza y de Porfirio Díaz y fue gobernador del Distrito Federal. Durante la lucha contra el imperio hizo las campañas en Zacatecas y San Luis Potosí. En 1866 apoyó las pretensiones presidenciales de Jesús González Ortega. Participó en la rebelión del Plan de Tuxtepec.

Rivera, Columba ◆ n. en Mineral de Atotonilco el Chico, Hgo., y m. en el DF (1870-1943). Profesora por la Escuela Normal de Hidalgo (1887), cirujana y obstetra por la Escuela Nacional de Medicina (1894-1900). Fue la primera mujer hidalguense y la segunda mexicana que cursó la carrera de medicina. Fue profesora de escuelas primarias, miembro de la Junta de Vigilancia de escuelas oficiales de Pachuca y practi-

Foto: Herrera

Arturo Rivera

Santiago, obra de Arturo Rivera

cante en el Hospital de San Andrés. Dio consultas gratuitas en las zonas pobres de Pachuca. Comisionada por el gobierno federal para estudiar la organización de los departamentos antropométricos de Estados Unidos (1904). Promovió en México la aplicación de los mismos y logró establecer los servicios de inspección médica en las escuelas oficiales. Profesora de la Escuela Nacional de Medicina, de la Escuela de Enfermeras y de la Cruz Blanca; médica jefa de enfermeras visitadoras del Departamento de Salud Pública e inspectora médica y secretaria de la Sociedad Protectora de Mujeres. Fundó y dirigió la revista *La Mujer Mexicana* y colaboró en *El Mundo Ilustrado* donde publicó su columna "Junto a la cuna". Autora de los dramas *Cerebro y corazón* y *Sombra y luz*.

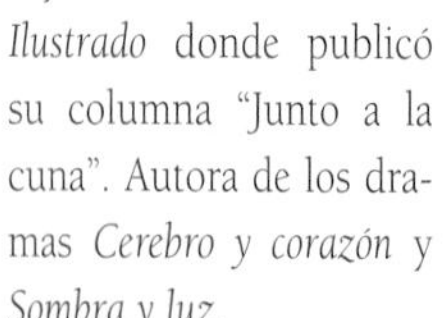

Autorretrato de Diego Rivera

RIVERA, *CURRO* ◆ n. en el DF (1951). Nombre profesional del torero Francisco Martín Rivera Agüero. Hijo de Fermín Rivera. Vivió desde niño en San Luis Potosí, donde se inició como novillero (1967). En 1968 Joselito Huerta le dio la alternativa en Torreón. Se ha presentado en México, España, Venezuela, Portugal, Francia, Colombia y Ecuador. En 1990 había toreado en 1,500 corridas. Ha ganado varias veces el trofeo Estoque de Oro. Tiene una ganadería de toros de lidia.

FOTO: HÉCTOR HERRERA

Curro Rivera

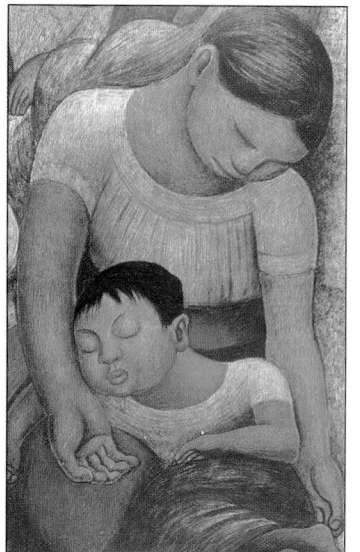

Detalle de un mural de Diego Rivera

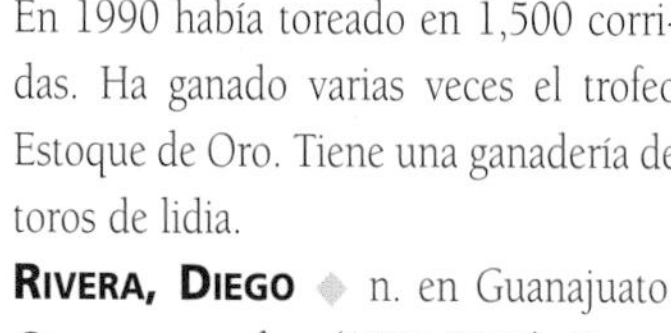

RIVERA, DIEGO ◆ n. en Guanajuato, Gto., y m. en el DF (1886-1957). Pintor. Estudió en la Academia de San Carlos y en la Academia de San Fernando de Madrid. Vivió 10 años en París, donde fue uno de los protagonistas del cubismo y expuso en el Salón de los Independientes. Volvió a México en 1921 e inició su labor como muralista en la Escuela Nacional Preparatoria (1922), ingresó en el Partido Comunista y formó el Sindicato de Obreros Técnicos Pintores y Escultores, junto con Siqueiros y Orozco (1923). Trotskista en los años treinta, en 1939 formó el Partido Revolucionario Obrero y Campesino y en 1947 figuró entre los fundadores del Partido Popular, del que se retiró en 1949 para reingresar al PCM en 1954. Autor de cientos de cuadros, entre otros *La era* (1902), *Iglesia de Leiquetic* (1907), *La puerta de Ávila* (1907), *Nuestra Señora de París* (1908), *La casa sobre el puente* (1908), *Vista de Toledo*, *El guerrillero* (1917), *Autorretrato a lápiz* (1918), *Retrato de Ruth Rivera*, *Retrato de Lupe Marín* (1938), *Bailarina en reposo* (1939), *Danza de la tierra* (1939); y de los murales *La creación* (1922), *La repartición de tierras*, *La celebración del primero de mayo*, *Mujeres de Tehuantepec*, *La liberación del peón*, *La maestra rural*, *La muerte que fecunda la vida*, *La semilla de la revolución*, *La evolución natural*, *La transformación social*, *La muerte*, *La fructificación*, *La trinidad positiva*, *El hombre y la naturaleza*, *La madre Tierra*, *La Tierra dormida*, *Las fuerzas del subsuelo*, *Las fuerzas espirituales internas*, *La germinación*, *La revolución*, *La floración*, que decora el cubo de la escalera del Palacio Nacional (1929-35). Pintó un mural en el Rockefeller Center de Nueva York (destruido en esa ciudad y reproducido más tarde en el Palacio de Bellas Artes). *Retrato de América*, para la New Worker's School (1933); decoró el primer piso del patio central del Palacio Nacional (1944-51). Realizó *Sueño de una tarde dominical en la Alameda Central* en el Hotel Del Prado (1947-48, trasladado a un local especial en 1987); el mural transportable *Sueño de paz y pesadilla de guerra* (1948); la decoración del Cárcamo de Dolores, la fuente de Tláloc (1951), la fachada del

El sol, obra de Diego Rivera

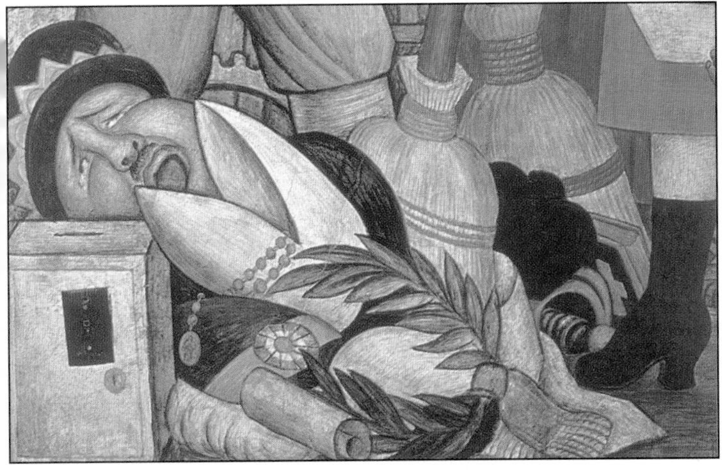

Detalle de un mural de Diego Rivera

Paisaje zapatista, óleo sobre tela de Diego Rivera

Teatro de los Insurgentes (1953) y pintó *Baño en el río* en la Casa de Cuernavaca (1954). Miembro fundador de El Colegio Nacional (1951). Premio Nacional de Ciencias y Artes en 1950.

Rivera, Felipe ◆ n. y m. en Zinapécuaro de Figueroa, Mich. (1852-1920). Abogado. Diputado local (1900-10) y federal (1911-13). Dedicado a la astronomía, descubrió una estrella, que lleva su nombre, en la constelación de Perseo. Perteneció a las sociedades astronómicas de París y de México. Autor de *Rasgos biográficos del Sr. Cura D. Juan Bautista Figueroa* (1905).

Rivera, Fermín ◆ n. en San Luis Potosí, SLP, y m. en Ojuelos, Jal. (1918-1991). Torero. Se inició como matador en 1933, en el antiguo Toreo, y tomó la alternativa dos años después, de manos de Fermín Espinosa *Armillita*. En 1941 ganó la oreja de oro y en ese año alternó en Portugal con Juan Belmonte hijo y en España con Luis Gómez *el Estudiante* y Manuel Rodríguez *Manolete*. En 1945 confirmó en España su alternativa de manos de Manuel Álvarez *el Andaluz*. Se retiró en 1957 para dedicarse a la ganadería.

Rivera, Francisco ◆ n. en España y m. en Valladolid, Mich. (1561-1637). Llegó a Nueva España (1607) como visitador general de los conventos mercedarios. A su regreso a la península se le nombró obispo de Guadalajara (1617) y tomó posesión de su sede en 1619. En 1630 fue trasladado a la diócesis de Michoacán.

Rivera, José ◆ n. en Huichapan y m. cerca de Pachuca, Hgo. (?-1933). Fue diputado federal (1928 y 1933), senador, director del Instituto Científico y Literario de Hidalgo y director del periódico *El Censor*. Murió en un accidente automovilístico.

Rivera, José Primitivo ◆ n. y m. en Veracruz, Ver. (1869-1916). Abandonó los estudios de medicina para dedicarse al periodismo. Militante del Partido Liberal Mexicano, colaboró en *El Monitor Republicano*, *El Diario del Hogar* y *La Opinión*. Profesor y director del Instituto Veracruzano y director de la Biblioteca del Pueblo. Coautor de *Liberales ilustres mexicanos* (1890) y *Antología de poetas hispanoamericanos* (2 t., 1893-95). Autor de *Cuentos de mi tierra*.

Rivera, Librado ◆ n. en Rayón, SLP, y m. en el DF (1864-1932). Profesor por la Normal de San Luis Potosí (1888), en la que ejerció la docencia (1895-1900). En 1901 se afilió al Club Liberal Ponciano Arriaga y participó en el Congreso del Partido Liberal. Colaboró en las publicaciones de oposición al régimen de Díaz (*Regeneración* y *El Hijo del Ahuizote*, entre ellas), por lo que en 1905 tuvo que refugiarse en EUA. Fue capturado en San Luis Misuri y luego en Los Ángeles, donde colaboró en el periódico *Revolución*. En 1911 fue confinado en la prisión de MacNeil y más tarde en la de Leavenworth, junto con Ricardo Flores Magón. Ambos firmaron el anarquista *Manifiesto a los trabajadores del mundo* (1918) y se les condenó a 15 años de prisión por delitos de prensa. En abril de 1923 el Congreso de San Luis Potosí autorizó una pensión de cinco pesos diarios para Rivera mientras permaneciera en prisión, misma que rehusó. En 1923 el Departamento de Estado de EUA le ofreció la libertad bajo palabra, pero se negó a aceptarla porque no se reconocía culpable de ningún delito. Le ofrecieron un indulto condicionado al reconocimiento del delito, a lo que nuevamente se negó. En octubre de ese año se conmutó su pena de 15 años por la deportación. Llegó a San Luis Potosí

Mural de Diego Rivera en el edificio de la SEP en el centro histórico

Fermín Rivera

Manuel Rivera

Foto: Rogelio Cuéllar

Silvia Tomasa Rivera

donde se relacionó con los círculos obreros, difundió el *Manifiesto a los trabajadores del mundo* y rechazó una curul, un escaño y una cátedra. En 1924 se unió al grupo anarquista Hermanos Rojos, que editaba el periódico *Sagitario*, y organizó el comité de defensa de los magonistas presos en Texas. En 1926 y 1927 participó en el movimiento pro Sacco y Vanzetti. En Monterrey surgió un periódico impulsado por él, *Avante*, que en febrero de 1928 se empezó a editar en Villa Cecilia con Rivera como director. En abril de 1930, en la ciudad de México, empezó a colaborar en *Verbo Rojo*, mientras sobrevivía como vendedor de grasa para zapatos. El 1 de mayo de 1931, aún en la ciudad de México, inició la publicación de *Paso!*, que en diciembre de 1931 se convirtió en órgano del grupo anarquista Ideas y Acción. En febrero de 1932 fue atropellado en San Ángel y llevado al Hospital de Fabriles y Militares de la Ciudadela, donde, por negligencia médica, contrajo tétanos y murió. Autor de *Persecución y asesinato de Ricardo Flores Magón* (1924, tomo V de *Ricardo Flores Magón. Vida y obra*).

Rivera, Manuel ◆ n. y m. en la ciudad de México (1859-1916). Estudió en el Colegio Militar (1879). En 1901 trazó el ferrocarril que se utilizó en una de las campañas contra los mayas. Pidió y obtuvo su retiro en 1902, pero en 1904 se reincorporó al ejército. Fue inspector de las obras militares en el Distrito Federal (1906) y jefe del Departamento de Caballería de la Secretaría de Guerra y Marina. General de brigada en 1909. Fue magistrado del Supremo Tribunal Militar (1911). Apoyó el golpe de Estado de Victoriano Huerta y éste lo designó gobernador de Campeche (1913-14).

Rivera, Silvia Tomasa ◆ n. en El Higo, Ver. (1956). Poeta. Fue integrante de los talleres de poesía de Raúl Renán y de Carlos Illescas. Ha colaborado en *La Cultura en México*, *Gilgamesh*, *Nexos*, *Revista Mexicana de Cultura* y *Sábado*. Coautora del volumen sobre *rock Crines* (1984) y del libro de poesía *¿Será esto el mar?* (1984). Autora de poesía: *Poemas al desconocido/Poemas a la desconocida* (1985), *Apuntes de abril* (1986), *El tiempo tiene miedo* (1987, Premio Paula de Allende de la Universidad Autónoma de Querétaro), *Duelo de espadas* (1988, antología), *Por el camino del mar. Camino de piedra* (1988, Premio Nacional de Poesía Jaime Sabines), *La rebelión de los solitarios/El sueño de Valquiria* y *Alta montaña* (1997, Premio Carlos Pellicer para obra publicada); y teatro: *Alex y los monstruos de la lomita* (1991, premio de Obra de Teatro para Niños 1991, INBA-Gobierno de Coahuila) y *Vuelo de sombras* (1994). Algunos de sus poemas han sido musicalizados e interpretados por Emilia Almazán. Becaria INBA-Fonapas en poesía (1982-83). Obtuvo una mención en el premio Poesía Joven de México (1983).

Rivera, Virgilio Ariel ◆ n. en San Luis Potosí, SLP (1939). Ha estudiado composición y teoría dramáticas con Luisa Josefina Hernández, Mercedes de la Cruz y Hugo Argüelles. Autor de las obras de teatro *Aquel domingo en el club*, *El enemigo está en casa*, *Fusiles y muñecas* y *La ronda de un niño emplumado*.

Rivera Cabrera, Crisóforo ◆ n. en Tehuantepec, Oax., y m. en el DF (?-1955). Estudió en el Instituto de Ciencias y Artes de Oaxaca. Antirreeleccionista, ejerció el periodismo desde muy joven. Fue delegado en Tehuantepec del Partido Nacional Antirreeleccionista. Diputado a la XXVI Legislatura (1911-13), formó parte del bloque renovador. En 1913 se unió a la revolución constitucionalista al levantarse en armas en el istmo de Tehuantepec. Formó parte del Estado Mayor de Jesús Carranza. Fue administrador de la aduana de Piedras Negras (1916), diputado al Congreso Constituyente de 1916-17, dos veces diputado federal (1917-18 y 1920-22), abogado auxiliar y presidente sustituto de la Junta Central de Conciliación y Arbitraje (1937-39).

Rivera Cambas, Manuel ◆ n. en Jalapa, Ver., y m. en la ciudad de México (1840-1917). Ingeniero de minas por la Escuela de Minería de la ciudad de México (1864), de la que fue profesor. Luchó contra la intervención francesa y el imperio. Fundador y director del periódico *El Combate* (1876-80), desde el que criticó los gobiernos de Sebastián Lerdo de Tejada, Manuel González y Porfirio Díaz. Se dedicó al estudio de la historia. Autor de *Memoria sobre el Mineral de Pachuca* (1864), *Historia antigua y moderna de Jalapa y de las revoluciones de Veracruz* (5 t., 1869-1871), *Los gobernantes de México* (2 t., 1873), *Historia de la intervención europea y norteamericana en México y del imperio de Maximiliano* (2 t., 1875), *Cartilla de historia de México* (1875), *Biografías de los jefes principales de la revolución de Tuxtepec* (1876), *Episodios de la guerra de reforma* (1880) y *México pintoresco, artístico y monumental* (3 t., 1880-1883).

Rivera del Campo, Manuel ◆ n. en Ciudad Valles, SLP (1940). Licenciado en ciencias de la comunicación por la Universidad de Hidalgo (1973). Afiliado al PAN desde 1957, ha sido secretario del Comité Estatal de SLP (1962-64) y secretario de Acción Electoral (1984-91), así como diputado federal (1979-82 y 1991-94), regidor del ayuntamiento de San Luis Potosí (1983-85) y diputado local (1987-90). Fue gerente de la Canaco (1970-73) y de la Canacintra (1976-79) en Ciudad Valles.

Rivera Carrera, Norberto ◆ n. en La Purísima, Dgo. (1942). Sacerdote. Cursó estudios de filosofía en el Seminario Diocesano de Durango y de teología en la Pontificia Universidad Gregoriana en Roma. Fue ordenado sacerdote en 1966. Tras desempeñar diversos cargos en las diócesis de Zacatecas y Durango, fue catedrático de la Pontificia Universidad de México y obispo de Tehuacán y presidente de la Comisión Pastoral Familiar del Episcopado Mexicano. En 1995 fue nombrado arzobispo primado de México. Desde 1998 es cardenal. Miembro del Comité del Pontificio Consejo para la Familia del Vaticano.

Rivera Flores, Fernando ◆ n. en Pachuca, Hgo. (1958). Estudió en la Facultad de Ciencias Políticas de la

UNAM, donde fundó el taller literario Tacreli. Miembro fundador del taller dirigido por Juan García Ponce. Fue redactor de *unomásuno* (1982) y jefe de la sección cultural del periódico *Cero*, en Pachuca. Autor de narrativa: *Cuentos pachuqueños* (1987); y novela: *Mi más sentido pésame* (1983), *Canto rodado* (1984), *Hasta que la muerte no-s-e-pare*, *Rico mineral* (1992) y *En torno de una mesa de cantina* (1997). Becario del Centro Mexicano de Escritores (1987-88) y del Fonca (1990-91).

RIVERA GARZA, CRISTINA ◆ n. en Matamoros, Tams. (1964). Escritora e investigadora. Licenciada en sociología por la UNAM, maestra y doctora en historia latinoamericana por la Universidad de Houston. Ha sido profesora asistente en la Universidad de San Diego. Apareció en la antología *Parte del horizonte. Antología de jóvenes narradores* (1982). Autora de cuento: *La guerra no importa* (1991, Premio Nacional de Cuento San Luis Potosí 1987); poesía: *La más mía* (1998); y novela: *Nadie me verá llorar* (1999, Premio Nacional de Novela José Rubén Romero 1997). Ha obtenido el Premio de Poesía de la revista *Punto de Partida* (1984) y las becas Salvador Novo (1984) y del Fonca (1994-95).

RIVERA MARÍN, GUADALUPE ◆ n. en la ciudad de México (1924). Hija de Diego Rivera. Licenciada (1947) y doctora (1952) en derecho por la UNAM. Integrante del PRI, fue subsecretaria de Asuntos Internacionales (1983-84). Ha desempeñado diversos cargos en las secretarías de Bienes Nacionales, Hacienda, Relaciones Exteriores y Gobernación, en Nacional Financiera, el DDF y la Presidencia de la República. Representó a México en la Conferencia Internacional del Trabajo, en Ginebra (1955). Ha sido profesora en la UNAM, diputada federal (1961-64 y 1979-82), senadora suplente para el periodo 1982-88 (en funciones en 1984-85). Ha sido directora de El Colegio del Bajío (1986-88), vocal ejecutiva del Instituto de Estudios Históricos de la Revolución Mexicana (1989-97) y delegada en Álvaro Obregón (1997-) en el gobierno perredista de la capital. Coautora de *Bases para la planificación de México* (1966), *Plan integral de desarrollo del área metropolitana de la ciudad de México* (1976) y *Plan de acción de México para integrar a la mujer al desarrollo* (1982). Autora de *El contrato de reaseguro en México* (1947), *El mercado de trabajo en México* (1955), *La propiedad territorial en México 1300-1800* (1983), *Un río, dos Riveras. Vida de Diego Rivera, 1886-1929* (1990) y *Las fiestas de Frida y Diego* (1994). Becaria de la Fundación Rockefeller (1993), fue la primera mujer en recibir el Premio Nacional de Economía (1956).

RIVERA MARÍN, RUTH ◆ n. y m. en el DF (1927-1969). Hermana de la anterior. Primera arquitecta del IPN. Trabajó en el Departamento de Arquitectura del INBA mientras se desempeñaba como ayudante de su padre, Diego Rivera, en sus trabajos murales y como colaboradora de Pedro Ramírez Vázquez en diversos proyectos arquitectónicos. Profesora de enseñanza secundaria de la SEP, del IPN, la Academia de San Carlos, la Escuela de Diseño y Artesanías y la Escuela Normal Superior. Fue directora del Departamento de Arquitectura (1959) y miembro del Consejo Técnico del INBA (1959); miembro del Consejo Intersecretarial para la Protección de la Pintura Mural del subcomité de museos de la UNESCO (1957) y secretaria general de la Unión Internationale des Femmes Architectes. Organizadora de la exposición El Objeto Cotidiano en el Arte, presentada en el Museo de Arte Moderno. Autora de *Meditaciones ante una crisis formal de la arquitectura*, *Treinta años de funcionalismo en la ESIA*, *Urbanismo y planificación en México*, *Anahuacalli* y *Arquitectura viva japonesa*. Perteneció al Colegio de Arquitectos, a la Sociedad de Arquitectos Mexicanos, a la Asociación Mexicana de Críticos de Arte, a la Unión Internacional Femenina de Arquitectos, que presidió, y Arquitectas Mexicanas, de la que fue vicepresidenta.

RIVERA Y MONCADA, FERNANDO DE ◆ n. en Compostela, en el actual estado de Nayarit, y m. en La Concepción, ahora en EUA (1725-1781). Capitán del presidio de Loreto, Baja California, en 1752. Participó en la fundación de las misiones jesuitas de Santa Gertrudis, San Borja y Santa María. En 1769 encabezó la primera expedición militar para la colonización de la Alta California y fue nombrado comandante militar y gobernador de esta provincia en 1774. Dos años después, durante su gobierno, se fundó San Francisco. En 1777 volvió a ser comandante militar de Loreto. Murió a manos de los indios yumas cuando dirigía a un grupo de colonos hacia Los Ángeles.

Foto: Rogelio Baeza

Norberto Rivera Carrera

RIVERA PÉREZ CAMPOS, JOSÉ ◆ n. en Celaya, Gto., y m. en el DF (1907-1989). Licenciado (1931) y doctor (1951) en derecho por la UNAM, institución de la que fue profesor (1929-48) y secretario general (1946). Fue director general de Estudios Superiores de Guanajuato (1936) y del Colegio de Guanajuato, profesor honorario de la Universidad de Texas, juez de paz, consultor legal en las secretarías de Agricultura y de Hacienda, magistrado del Supremo Tribunal de Guanajuato, oficial mayor del Departamento Autónomo de Prensa y Publicidad del Departamento del Trabajo, abogado general de los Ferrocarriles Nacionales de México y de Petróleos Mexicanos, secretario general del Departamento de Publicidad y Propaganda del gobierno federal, ministro

Guadalupe Rivera Marín

de la Suprema Corte y senador (1946-52 y 1970-76), así como director de asuntos legales (1977-79) y subsecretario de Gobernación (1979-82). Autor de *Justificación del Estado*, *La angustia por el derecho*, *Necesidad jurídica de la expropiación petrolera*, *La filosofía del marxismo*, *Publicidad turística de México*, *Manuel José Othón, clásico y estoico*, *La libertad, valor de lo político* y *Contra la simulación del revolucionarismo*. Colaboró en la redacción de los códigos civil, penal y de procedimientos penales del estado de Morelos.

Agustín Rivera y San Román

Rivera y Río, José ◆ m. en Tacubaya, DF (?-1891). Escritor liberal. Tomó las armas para combatir a la intervención francesa y el imperio. Fue aprehendido en Puebla. Cuando se le conducía a Francia, huyó hacia Estados Unidos. Regresó a México luego de radicar varios años en Nueva York. Autor de *Los misterios de San Cosme* (1851), *Facultad y providencia* (1861), *Mártires y verdugos* (1861), *Las tres aventureras* (1861), *Flores del destierro* (1868), *El hambre y el oro* (1869), *Luceros y nebulosas* (1869), *Esqueletos sociales* (1870), *La virgen del Niágara* (1871), *Memorias de unos náufragos* (1872), *Pobres y ricos de México* (1884) y *Los dramas de Nueva York*. González Obregón, Manuel Sánchez Mármol y Altamirano le atribuyen también la autoría de unas *Obras poéticas* y de las novelas *Alfredo o los remordimientos*, *Paula*, *La vida del corazón*, *Recuerdo y desencanto* y *La beldad de los sepulcros*.

Rivera Robles, José ◆ n. y m. en el DF (1902-1979). Fue presidente honorario y director de la Asociación Mexicana de Caminos, director del Comité de Caminos Vecinales, director administrativo de la Compañía de Luz, gerente general del Ferrocarril del Pacífico y fundador y presidente de la Asociación Mexicana Automovilística. Perteneció a la Cámara Nacional de Comercio y a la Confederación Nacional de Cámaras Industriales. Autor de *Los mitos de Darién*.

Rivera Rodríguez, Guillermo ◆ n. en el DF (1946). Licenciado en derecho por la UNAM (1963-68). Cursó la maestría en finanzas en la Universidad de París. Desde 1970 es miembro del PRI, donde fue subdirector (1976-77) y subcoordinador del IEPES (1987-88). Ha sido gerente de Finanzas de Finasa (1974-76), gerente de Captación y subdirector de Banrural (1977-82), director de Administración y Sistema de ANDSA (1982-88), director de Financiamiento del Desarrollo de Banobras (1988-90) y subsecretario de Desarrollo Urbano de la Sedue (1991-94).

Rivera y San Román, Agustín ◆ n. en Lagos, Jal., y m. en León, Gto. (1824-1916). Sacerdote ordenado en 1848 y doctor en derecho (1852). Fue profesor de disciplinas eclesiásticas y sacristán mayor en Lagos. Autor de *Anales mexicanos. La reforma y el segundo imperio*, *Viaje a las ruinas de Chicomoztoc*, *Viaje a las ruinas del Fuerte del Sombrero*, *Compendio de la historia antigua de México*, *Principios críticos sobre el virreinato de la Nueva España* y *Principios críticos sobre la revolución de independencia*. Doctor *honoris causa* por la Universidad Nacional (1910).

Rivera Terrazas, Luis ◆ n. en Sonora y m. en Puebla, Pue. (1913-1989). Astrónomo. Estudió en la Universidad de Chicago. Miembro del Partido Comunista Mexicano, cofundador del Partido Socialista Unificado de México y del Partido Mexicano Socialista. Fue candidato a la gubernatura de Puebla. Trabajó en el Instituto de Astrofísica de Tonatzintla. En la Universidad Autónoma de Puebla fue profesor, fundador de la Escuela de Físico-Matemáticas y del Instituto de Ciencias y rector (1975-81). Miembro de la Sociedad Mexicana de Física. Recibió un premio del Conacyt.

Rivera Torres Fernández, Paulino ◆ m. en el DF (?-1985). Empresario. Caballista, fue presidente de la Federación Nacional Ecuestre y miembro del Buró Internacional Ecuestre. Jugador de golf, poseía dos campos en su propiedad, en Cocoyoc. En 1948 fue cofundador de Impulsora Panamericana, empresa dedicada a la promoción deportiva. Director general del fraccionamiento Lomas de Cocoyoc y de Inmobiliaria Rincón del Pozo. Fraccionó terrenos urbanos y suburbanos, entre ellos el hotel Hacienda Cocoyoc y Lomas de Cocoyoc.

Rivera Velázquez, Mariano ◆ n. en el DF (1945). Pintor y escultor. Estudió arquitectura en la UIA (1962-67). Participó en el Congreso de L'Union Internationale d'Architects, en París (1965). Becado por el gobierno francés, estudió artes plásticas en París (1967) y artes gráficas en el Atelier Fritlander (1968). Participó en el primer Salón Independiente en la Biblioteca Isidro

La carta de Vasco de Quiroga, construcción en madera de fresno, obra de Mariano Rivera Velázquez

Fabela. Ha expuesto en Italia, México, India, Holanda y Estados Unidos.

RIVERA VENEGAS, ANTONIO ◆ n. en Orizaba, Ver., y m. en el DF (1885-?). Trabajador ferrocarrilero. Fue superintendente de los talleres del Ferrocarril Mexicano. En 1913 se incorporó a la revolución constitucionalista en la División de Oriente comandada por Agustín Millán, quien le encomendó el taller de reparación de armas. Al término del conflicto se dedicó a fabricar corcholatas para la cervecería Moctezuma y en 1935 fundó la empresa Embotelladora de México.

RIVERA *EL VIEJO* CARMEN ◆ Cabecera del municipio chiapaneco de Francisco León (☛).

RIVERA VILLALÓN, PEDRO DE ◆ n. en España y m. en la ciudad de México (?-1744). Fue gobernador interino del presidio de Veracruz (1711) y desalojó a los corsarios de la isla del Carmen (1713); gobernador de armas de Yucatán (1719) y gobernador de Tlaxcala (1724). Inspeccionó los presidios del norte de Nueva España (1724); su misión duró tres años y medio y durante ella levantó planos, fijó linderos entre las provincias, formó juicios a los comandantes militares, fue el primero en fijar las coordenadas geográficas de varias poblaciones e hizo un recuento de los grupos indígenas. Con el grado de mariscal de campo, se le designó gobernador de la ciudad y puerto de Veracruz (1731-32) y capitán general de Guatemala (1732-34). Autor de un *Diario* (1736).

RIVERA VILLASEÑOR, MIGUEL ÁNGEL ◆ n. en Reynosa, Tams. (1945). Licenciado en economía por el ITESM (1967), maestro en economía por El Colegio de México (1969) y maestro en administración pública por la Universidad de Harvard (1975). Ha sido subgerente de Comercio y Desarrollo del Banco de México (1975-77); subdirector general de industrias (1977-80), director general adjunto de industrias (1981) y director general de industrias de la Sepafin (1982); director general de la Industria Metalmecánica y de Bienes de Capital de la Secretaría de Comercio (1982-88) y coordinador ejecutivo de Programación y Control Financiero de Pemex (1989-94).

RIVERO, JORGE ◆ n. en el DF (1938). Actor. Su apellido paterno es Pous. Comenzó su carrera en los años sesenta y llegó a ser uno de los galanes más populares. Ha alternado la actuación en el cine (particularmente en películas de acción de bajo presupuesto) y en televisión. Vivió y trabajó en EUA en la década de los ochenta. Entre las películas en las que ha participado destacan *El mexicano* (1967), *Pedro Páramo* (1967), *Al rojo vivo* (1968), *Basuras humanas* (1972), *Bellas de noche* (1974), *El llanto de la tortuga* (1974), *Manaos* (1978) y *Dos camioneros con suerte* (1990). Produjo las cintas *Indio* (1971) y *El caballo del diablo* (1974).

FOTO: COLECCIÓN IMCINE

Jorge Rivero en *Operación 67*

RIVERO QUIJANO, JESÚS ◆ n. en España y m. en el DF (1888-1968). Estudió técnica textil en las universidades de Saint Mary, Harvard y Manchester. En las ciudades de Puebla y México fundó y dirigió numerosas empresas del ramo textil, una despepitadora de algodón, industrias de refrigeración, una productora de oxígeno así como una cadena de tiendas de telas. Formó parte de los consejos de administración de numerosas empresas bancarias, financieras y aseguradoras. Fue fundador y segundo presidente de la

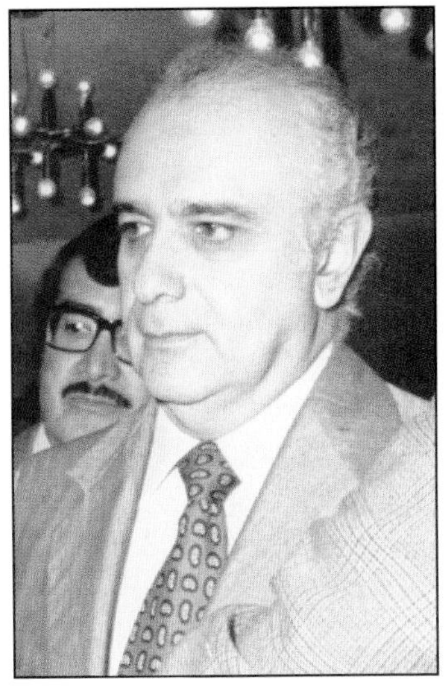

Octavio Rivero Serrano

Confederación de Cámaras Industriales, presidente de la Comisión de Derecho Obrero de la Convención Obrero Patronal de 1928. Participó en la redacción del Código de Trabajo. Fue vicepresidente de la Cámara Textil de México, fundador y director general del Centro Nacional de Productividad y vicepresidente de la Cámara Oficial Española de Comercio, Industria y Navegación. Autor de *La industria textil de algodón* y *El maquinismo*. Miembro de la Real Academia de la Historia de Madrid, de la de Buenas Letras de Sevilla y de la de Ciencias y Artes de Cádiz.

RIVERO SERRANO, OCTAVIO ◆ n. en Puebla, Pue. (1929). Médico cirujano por la UNAM (1952), donde ha sido profesor, director de la Facultad de Medicina (1977-81), rector (1981-84) y coordinador del Programa Universitario del Medio Ambiente. Fue profesor en el Hospital General (1953-54, 1962 y 1968-70) y en el IPN (1955-65) y médico en los hospitales General, de la Secretaría de Comunicaciones y San Fernando de los Ferrocarriles Nacionales. Presidente del Centro Internacional para la Medicina General Familiar (1981-83) y secretario del Fideicomiso para la Historia General de la Medicina en México (1985-86). Secretario del Consejo de Salubridad General (1995-). Fue embajador en Italia (1986-88). Autor de *Evaluación y marco de referencia*

José María Roa Bárcena

Foto: Dante Bucio

Sócrates Rizzo García

para los cambios académico-administrativos (1983), *Plan rector de desarrollo institucional* (1984), *Reforma universitaria* (1984) y *Contaminación atmosférica y enfermedades respiratorias* (1993). Miembro de la Junta Directiva del Consejo Nacional de Ciencia y Tecnología, del Consejo de Premiación de Ciencias y Artes, de la Junta Directiva de El Colegio Nacional y del Consejo Académico del Conalep (1981-84).

RIVET, PAUL ◆ n. y m. en Francia (1876-1958). Médico por la Ecole de la Sanité Militaire, de Lyon. De 1901 a 1907 vivió en Ecuador, donde decidió dedicarse a la antropología. Volvió a Francia y combatió en la primera guerra mundial. Le correspondió organizar los servicios médicos en el oriente de su país. Al finalizar el conflicto armado fundó el Museo del Hombre. Durante la segunda guerra mundial creó el primer periódico de la resistencia. Fue denunciado y se refugió en Bolivia, donde formó el Instituto de Etnología. Charles de Gaulle lo designó consejero cultural para América Latina. En la ciudad de México fundó el Instituto Francés de América Latina y la Librería Francesa. En 1945 regresó a París a dirigir el Museo del Hombre. Su libro más conocido es *Les Origines de l'Homme Américain* (1943). Sobre México publicó "Les Indies du Texas et les Expeditions Francais de 1720 et 1721. Baie de Saint Bernard", en *Journal de la Societé des Américanistes* (1918), "Etude sur l'Archeologie Mexicaine", en *Comptes Rendus de l'Académie des Inscriptions & Belles Lettres* (1921) y "Nouvelle sur la Métallurgie Mexicaine", en *L'Antropologie* (1923).

Foto: Héctor Herrera

Antonio Riviello Bazán

RIVIELLO BAZÁN, ANTONIO ◆ n. en la ciudad de México (1926). Estudió en el Colegio Militar (1944), del que fue subdirector (1965-68). Es licenciado en ad-ministración militar por la Escuela Superior de Guerra, donde ejerció la docencia (1965). Fue oficial del Estado Mayor Presidencial (1950-52). General brigadier en 1973. Ha sido subjefe del Estado Mayor de la XIX Zona Militar (1960-62), segundo comandante y jefe del Grupo de Comando del XLIII Batallón de Infantería (1962-65), comandante del IV Batallón de Infantería (1968-70), subjefe del Estado Mayor de la Defensa Nacional (1970-73), jefe del Estado Mayor de la II Zona Militar (1973-75), comandante de la III Zona Militar (1975-76), comandante de la XXI Zona Militar (1977-80), de la XXV Zona Militar (1980-82); inspector y contralor general del Ejército y Fuerza Aérea (1983-84), agregado militar y aéreo de la embajada en España (1985-86), inspector y contralor general del Ejército y Fuerza Aérea (1987-88), comandante del primer cuerpo de ejército (1988) y secretario de la Defensa Nacional (1988-94).

RIZZO GARCÍA, SÓCRATES CUAUHTÉMOC ◆ n. en Linares, NL (1945). Licenciado en economía por la UANL (1969), maestro por El Colegio de México (1971) y doctor por la Universidad de Chicago (1975). Fue profesor en instituciones de enseñanza superior. Militó en el PCM, en el espartaquismo (☛) y en el PRI, del que ha sido presidente del Comité Directivo en Nuevo León (1987-88). Fue jefe de asesores de la dirección general de Nafinsa (1978-79), director de Estudios de Política Hacendaria de la SHCP (1979-81), director de Análisis Macroeconómicos (1982), director general de Programación Económica y Social (1982-83) y director general de Política Económica y Social de la SPP (1983-85). Diputado federal por el DF (1985-88), presidente municipal de Monterrey (1989-91) y gobernador de Nuevo León (1991-96). Autor de *Opciones de política económica: 1977-1982* (1977), *Excedente petrolero y apertura externa: el caso de México* (1983) y *Generation and Allocation of Oil Economic Surplus* (1984).

ROA BÁRCENA, JOSÉ MARÍA ◆ n. en Jalapa, Ver., y m. en la ciudad de México (1827-1908). Escritor. Colaboró en los periódicos *El Universal* (1853-55), *La Cruz* y *El Tiempo* y dirigió *El Nuevo Mundo*, *El Eco Nacional* y *La Sociedad*. Formó parte de la Junta de Notables que votó por la monarquía (1863) y fue miembro de la Academia Imperial de Ciencias y Literatura que fundó Maximiliano (1865). Al triunfo de la República pasó algunos meses en prisión. Escribió con el pseudónimo de *Antenor* en *El Renacimiento* (1868). En 1875 figuró entre los fundadores de la Academia Mexicana (de la Lengua), de la que fue el primer tesorero (1875-78). Fue consejero del Banco Nacional de México. Autor de *Poesías líricas* (1859), *Catecismo elemental de geografía universal* (1861), *Leyendas mexicanas, cuentos y baladas del norte de Europa y algunos otros ensayos poéticos* (1862), *Ensayo de una historia anecdótica de México en los tiempos anteriores a la conquista* (1862), *Compendio de historia profana* (1870), *Novelas originales y traducidas* (1870), *Biografía de don José Joaquín Pesado* (1878), *Vasco Núñez de Balboa (1513-1517)* (1879), *Varios cuentos* (1883), *Recuerdos de la invasión norteamericana (1846-48)* (1883), *Acopio de sonetos castellanos con notas de un aficionado* (1887), *Ultimas poesías líricas* (1888), *Diana* (1892), *Antología de poetas mexicanos* (1894), *Novelas cortas* (1910) y *Obras poéticas* (1913), entre otras obras.

ROA BÁRCENA, RAFAEL ◆ n. en Jalapa y m. en Veracruz, Ver. (1832-1863). Abogado. Fue regidor y síndico del ayuntamiento de México (1858) y juez de primera instancia en Veracruz. Autor de *Manual razonado de práctica civil forense*, *Manual de práctica criminal* y médico-legal, *Manual teórico-práctico de obligaciones y contratos*, *Manual de testamento en México*, *Manual de derecho canónico mexicano*, *Cartas a Josefina* y *Reminiscencias del colegio*. Dejó inédito un *Curso de lógica*.

Robelo, Cecilio A. ◆ m. en Cuernavaca, Mor. (1839-1916). No hay certeza sobre el lugar donde nació. Estudió abogacía en el Real y Pontificio Seminario de la ciudad de México (1866). En 1869, al crearse el estado de Morelos, fue diputado local, juez y magistrado del Tribunal Superior de Justicia y gobernador interino. En 1913 se le nombró director del Museo Nacional de Arqueología, Historia y Etnografía. Autor de *Vocabulario etimológico de literatura* (1880), *Vocabulario comparativo castellano y náhuatl* (1889), *Efemérides de Cristóbal Colón* (1892), *Nombres geográficos indígenas del estado de Morelos* (1897), *El lagarto de San Antón* (1898), *Nombres geográficos indígenas del Estado de México* (1900), *México-Tenochtitlan y Tlatelolco* (1901), *Nombres geográficos indígenas del estado de Veracruz* (1902), *Diccionario de aztequismos* (1904), *Diccionario de mitología náhuatl* (1905), *Aztlán, cuna de los indios mexicanos, no se sabe dónde está* (1910), *Nociones del idioma náhuatl* (1912) y *Toponimia maya-hispano-nahua* (1913).

Robelo, Jorge ◆ n. en el DF (1957). Pintor egresado de la Academia de San Carlos. Ha expuesto en varias ciudades de México, Perú y España. Participó en la primera Bienal Internacional de Uruguay (1980), en el primer Encuentro Nacional de Arte Joven (Aguascalientes, 1981) y en el XXII Concurso de Dibujo Joan Miró (Barcelona, 1983). Tercer premio de dibujo en el Concurso Nacional de Artes Plásticas de Aguascalientes (1978).

Robert y Yarzábal, Bartolomé ◆ n. en Tampico, Tams., y m. en España (1842-1902). Vivió en Barcelona desde su juventud. Doctor en medicina (1867), fue diputado a Cortes por Cataluña y alcalde de Barcelona. Autor de *La aclimatación humana* (1870), *La antropología y la historia* (1881), *Prolegómenos clínicos* (1889) y *Patología médica* (1894). Presidió la Academia de Medicina de Barcelona y el Ateneo Barcelonés.

Robertson, Joseph Andrew ◆ n. y m. en EUA (1849-1939). Abogado. Veterano de la guerra de secesión, en los años setenta del siglo pasado llegó a Nuevo León, donde inició los cultivos de cítricos, con Arnulfo Berlanga y León Stuart, en la región de Montemorelos. Construyó el ferrocarril de Tampico a Monterrey y en esta ciudad fundó la primera fábrica de ladrillos y el diario *Monterrey News*, para la colonia estadounidense. Puso en servicio algunos tranvías y la línea eléctrica a Topo Chico.

Robertson, Thomas A. ◆ n. en Topolobampo, Sin., y m. en Ensenada, BC (1898-1980). Hijo de inmigrantes daneses que llegaron a México atraídos por el proyecto Utopía de Albert K. Owen (☛). Hizo estudios profesionales en Estados Unidos y radicó en Baja California, donde se dedicó a la preservación de las antiguas misiones dominicas. Autor de *A Southwestern Utopia, an American Colony in Mexico* (1964) y *Baja California and its Missions* (1978).

Robina Rothiot, Ricardo de ◆ n. en la ciudad de México (1919). Se tituló de arquitecto en la UNAM (1942) y estudió arqueología en la ENAH. Ha sido asesor del grupo ICA. Elaboró los proyectos del Centro Comercial Azteca, Centro de Compras Pedegral y varias tiendas Woolworth, numerosos hoteles, conjuntos habitacionales y centros industriales. Restauró el templo de San Lorenzo (1954), el Colegio de Niñas (1985) y el Colegio de las Vizcaínas (1985) en el DF. Dirigió la edición de *El mundo mágico de los mayas* (1968), *La arquitectura Puuc* (1981) y *La escultura de Palenque*. Coautor de *Cuatro mil años de arquitectura en México* (1952), *Esplendor del México antiguo* (1952), *40 siglos de plástica mexicana* (3 t., 1968) y *40 siglos de arte mexicano* (1969). Autor de *Estudio arquitectónico de las ruinas de Hochob* (1948), *Ruinas de Dzibilnocac* (1948), *Ruinas tabasqueñas* (1948) y *Encuesta sobre la significación de la arquitectura barroca en Hispanoamérica* (1965); los poemarios *Algo que nunca se volverá a repetir* y *Cuenta de oro*; el volumen de cuentos *Pronto retorno*; y la obra *El teatro de la vida*.

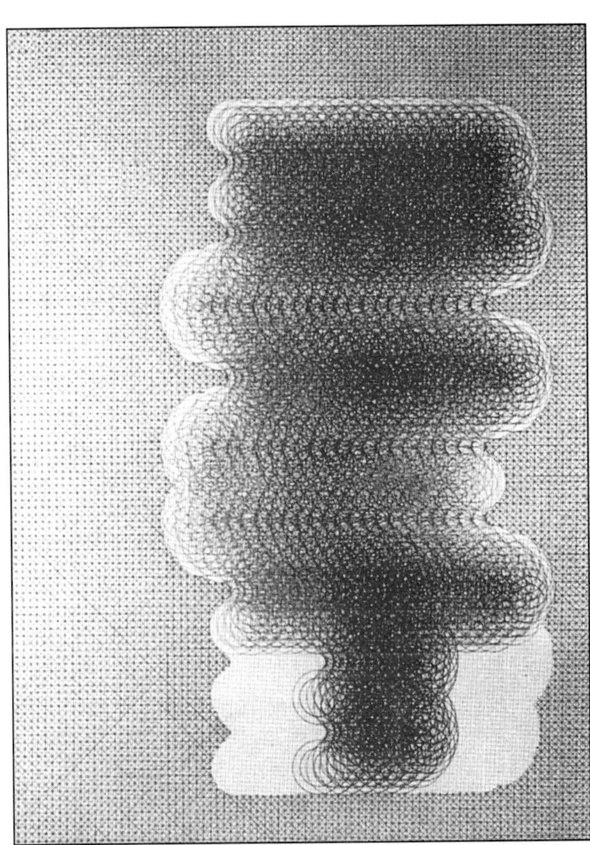

El jardín del mago, técnica mixta sobre papel, de Jorge Robelo

Robinson, William Davis ◆ n. y m. en EUA (1774-¿1830?). Comerciante. En 1815 publicó el folleto *A Cursory View of Spanish America*, en el que apoyaba la causa independentista mexicana. En 1816 fue comisionado por una casa comercial de Nueva York para vender fusiles a los insurgentes mexicanos; el mismo año, en Nueva Orleans, entró en contacto con los insurgentes y viajó a Puente del Rey para entrevistarse con Guadalupe Victoria, quien se negó a comprarle armas. Robinson viajó a Tehuacán donde se entrevistó con Mier y Terán, con quien cerró el trato de compra-venta. Asimismo, lo convenció de atacar Coatzacoalcos, aun sin el consentimiento de Victoria, para utilizar ese puerto como lugar de entrega del armamento, y le aseguró que había numerosos voluntarios estadounidenses dispuestos a pelear por la independencia mexicana.

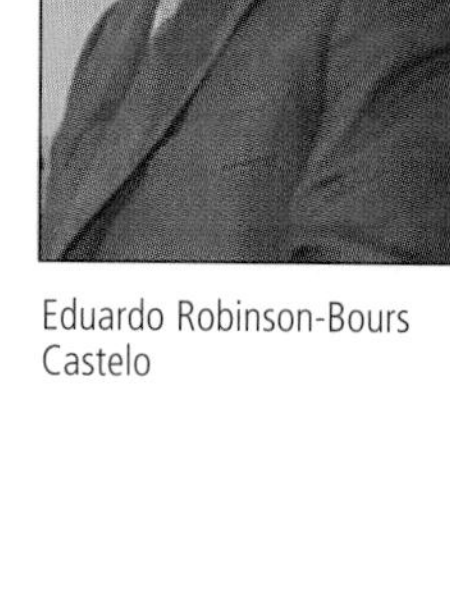
Foto: Eikon

Eduardo Robinson-Bours Castelo

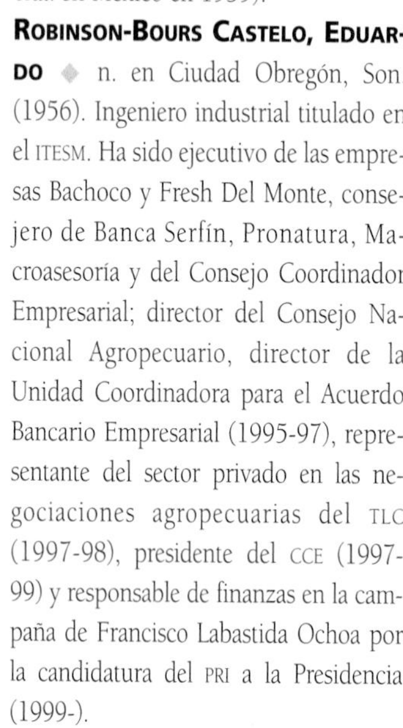

Mier y Terán, acompañado por Robinson, intentó el ataque, con muy pocas fuerzas; fue sorprendido y derrotado por los realistas y Robinson huyó. Poco después fue aprehendido y conducido a la ciudad de México. El virrey Apodaca ordenó que fuera encarcelado en San Juan de Ulúa en 1817. Un año después fue trasladado al Castillo del Morro, en La Habana, y en 1819 fue transportado a España. Escapó de su confinamiento en Cádiz y llegó a Gibraltar. Regresó a Estados Unidos en 1820. Autor de *Memoirs of the Mexican Revolution, Including a Narrative of the Expedition of General Xavier Mina* (Londres, 1821) y *Mis aventuras* (aparecida en México en 1939).

Robinson-Bours Castelo, Eduardo ◆ n. en Ciudad Obregón, Son. (1956). Ingeniero industrial titulado en el ITESM. Ha sido ejecutivo de las empresas Bachoco y Fresh Del Monte, consejero de Banca Serfín, Pronatura, Macroasesoría y del Consejo Coordinador Empresarial; director del Consejo Nacional Agropecuario, director de la Unidad Coordinadora para el Acuerdo Bancario Empresarial (1995-97), representante del sector privado en las negociaciones agropecuarias del TLC (1997-98), presidente del CCE (1997-99) y responsable de finanzas en la campaña de Francisco Labastida Ochoa por la candidatura del PRI a la Presidencia (1999-).

Robledo, Juan de Dios ◆ n. en Guadalajara, Jal. (1894-?). En 1913 abandonó los estudios de derecho para unirse a la revolución constitucionalista. Diputado al Congreso Constituyente de 1916-17, fue presidente municipal de Guadalajara, dos veces diputado federal (1917-18 y 1922-24), dos veces senador por Jalisco (1925 y 1928) y gobernador sustituto de ese estado (1931). Fundó el periódico tapatío *El Occidental*.

Robledo Cabello, Luis Francisco ◆ n. en Saltillo, Coah. (1935). Ingeniero civil (1962) y maestro en planeación de obras (1966) por la UNAM, donde ha sido profesor (1959-63 y

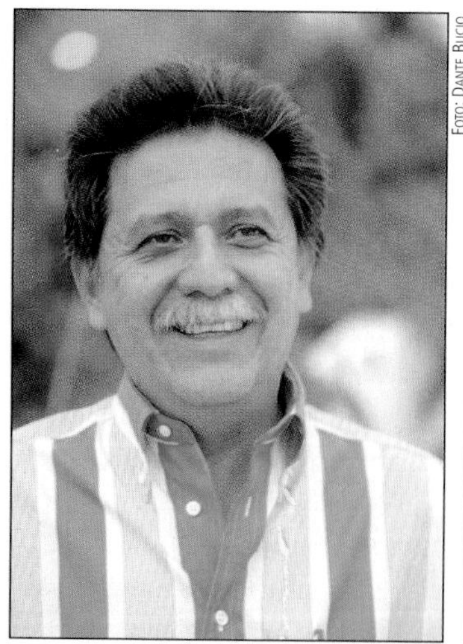
Foto: Dante Bucio

Eduardo Robledo Rincón

1965-66) y miembro del Grupo Consultivo de la División de Estudios de Posgrado de la Facultad de Ingenieria (1983). En el sector público se ha desempeñado como vocal ejecutivo de la Comisión de Aguas del Valle de México (1975-80 y 1981-82), presidente del Instituto de Fomento a la Planeación (1979), director general de Conducciones y Captaciones de Agua (1980-81) y subsecretario de Infraestructura de la SARH (1981-82); director general de Fertilizantes de la SEMIP (1983); director general de Obras Marítimas (1984-86) y vocal coordinador ejecutivo de la Comisión Nacional Coordinadora de Puertos de la SCT (1986-88). Es académico de número de la Academia Mexicana de Ingeniería.

Edgar Robledo Santiago

Robledo Rincón, Eduardo ◆ n. en Tuxtla Gutiérrez, Chis. (1947). Profesor por el Instituto Federal de Capacitación del Magisterio de Tuxtla Gutiérrez (1966-68) y licenciado en ciencias políticas por la UNAM (1974-78). Miembro del PRI, en el que ha sido secretario de Organización del CEN (1982), presidente del CDE de Chiapas (1983) y secretario general adjunto del CEN (1988-). En Chiapas fue secretario general del Consejo de Acción para el Desarrollo de la Sierra Madre (1972), subdirector del Centro Nacional de Capacitación de la Liga de Comunidades Agrarias (1975), secretario general de gobierno (1984) y gobernador (del 8 de diciembre de 1994 al 4 de febrero de 1995). Ha sido director de Promoción del Crea (1980), diputado federal por Chiapas (1985-88), embajador en Argentina (1995-98) y secretario de la Reforma Agraria (1999-). Autor del libro *Alfonso Reyes en Argentina* (1999).

Robledo Ruiz, Juan Ramiro ◆ n. en San Luis Potosí, SLP (1949). Licenciado y maestro en derecho por la UNAM. Afiliado desde 1971 al PRI, en el comité de ese partido en San Luis Potosí fue secretario de Capacitación Política (1979-81) y presidente (1991). Actuario del Tribunal de lo Contencioso Administrativo del DF (1971-72) y defensor de oficio (1972-73). En el gobierno de SLP ha sido síndico del ayuntamiento de San Luis Potosí (1977-79), subsecretario (1985) y secretario general de gobierno (1985-91). Secretario general de la Universidad Autónoma de San Luis Potosí (1986-88), diputado federal (1991-94) y senador (1997-2000).

Robledo Santiago, Edgar ◆ n. en Belisario Domínguez, Chis. (1917). Estudió en la Universidad Obrera de México. Maestro rural federal (1934), profesor del Instituto de Ciencias y Artes de Chiapas y de la Prevocacional Chiapas; inspector escolar federal, coordinador de actividades educativas y culturales de Banobras, diputado federal (1967-70), senador (1970-76), secretario de educación del gobierno chiapaneco y director general del ISSSTE. Fue secretario general del SNTE. Autor de *Epistolario social*, *El folklore y la educación*, *La escuela y la Constitución*, *Por la patria*, *En defensa del artículo tercero constitucional*, *Solidaridad*, *Apuntes de viajes*, *México, paz, libertad*, *Interpretación del SNTE*, *Panorama del SNTE*, *La revolución mexicana y la educación*, *Concepción ideológica del sindicalismo*, *Ideario juarista*, *La política educativa de la revolución mexicana*, *Ideario político y social*, *Tesis social y política de la FSTSE* (14 folletos), *Apuntes para la historia de la FSTSE*, *Unidad sindical*, *Revolución mexicana y seguridad social* y *Lecturas chiapanecas* (1980). Miembro del Ateneo de Ciencias y Artes de Chiapas y del Ateneo Torres Bodet. Premio Chiapas 1991.

Robledo Sicairos, Eleazar ◆ n. en Culiacán, Sin. (1944). Egresado de la Escuela Normal Superior, se especializó en Geografía. Integrante del PRI desde 1962. Ha sido secretario general del Comité de Vigilancia del SNTE, secretario de la FSTSE y secretario general de la CNOP en Sinaloa, así como director de Educación y Cultura y asesor en materia educativa del Congreso de ese estado. Diputado local y senador para el periodo 1994-2000.

Robles, Fernando ◆ n. en Guanajuato y m. en Silao, Gto. (1897-1974). Estudió filosofía en México, Francia e Inglaterra, arte en Italia y ciencias sociales en Estados Unidos. Fue editorialista de la *International Comunications Review*, de Nueva York, y colaborador de *La Nación* y *Crítica*, de Buenos Aires, y *Lectura*, de la ciudad de México. Autor de *A la sombra de Alá* (1925), *La virgen de los cristeros* (1934), *El santo que asesinó* (1934), *El amor es así* (1935), *Europa eterna* (1940), *Sucedió ayer* (1940), *Cuando llega tarde el amor* (1943), *Dos ensayos de drama* (1943), *Sangre al amanecer* (1943), *La Argentina también es México* (1951), *Cuando el águila perdió sus alas* (1951), *La estrella que no quiso vivir* (1957) y *Flor silvestre*.

Robles, Germán ◆ n. en España (1929). Actor y diseñador. Estudió en la Academia Aguirre, en la Academia

Germán Robles

España y en el Colegio Montera. Llegó a México en 1946, reclamado por su padre, el pintor Germán Horacio. Se inició en el espectáculo como bailarín profesional de danzas regionales españolas en California (1948). Fundó la casa de decoración D'Carvill y fue director artístico de la empresa publicitaria CAP (1951), de Litoarte y de Mosaicos Venecianos. En la la compañía teatral de Enrique Rambal hizo el papel de Cristo en *El mártir del calvario* (1951). Ha actuado en numerosos teleteatros y telenovelas desde los años cincuenta. Participó en el programa de televisión *Operación Convivencia* y diseñó el logotipo de la Fundación Cultural Televisa. Pertenece a la Compañía Nacional de Teatro desde 1977, año en el que participó en la puesta de *Luces de Bohemia*, de Valle-Inclán; y en 1979, en *Ricardo III*. En 1981, patrocinado por la SEP, el Fonapas y la UNAM, presentó el espectáculo *Imágenes para un hombre solo*. Ha trabajado, entre otras, en las películas *El vampiro* (1956), *La vida de Agustín Lara* (1957), *Viva la soldadera* (1958), *¿Dónde estás, corazón?* (1960), *Pueblo en armas* (1960, que le valió una medalla otorgada por la Unión Nacional de Veteranos de la Revolución), *El barón del terror* (1961), *En la vieja California* (1962), *El río de las ánimas* (1963), *El asesino de tontos* (1963), *El zurdo* (1964), *El proceso de Cristo* (1965) y *El cuarto chino* (1966). Ha recibido numerosos premios.

Robles, Gervasio Trinidad ◆ n. en el Edo. de Méx. (?-?). Pintor, Estudió en la Academia de San Carlos, donde participó en las exposiciones de 1871, 1875 y 1876. Entre sus obras está *El niño de la cervatana*, obra que pertenece a la colección del Museo José María Velasco.

Robles, José Isabel ◆ n. en Jalapa, Zac., y m. en Oaxaca, Oax. (¿1891?-1917). Se levantó en armas contra la dictadura de Victoriano Huerta. A mediados de 1913 participó en el frustrado ataque a Torreón y se incorporó a la División del Norte. En 1914 dirigió la ocupación de Saltillo, fue secretario de Guerra y Marina (del 6 de noviembre de 1914 al 16 de enero de 1915) en el primer gabinete de la Convención de Aguascalientes, siguió al presidente Eulalio Gutiérrez en su huída, pero se rindió en 1915. Volvió a militar en las fuerzas de Venustiano Carranza, pero se pronunció contra él en 1916. En 1917 fue capturado y fusilado.

Robles, Juvencio ◆ n. en Juchitán, Oax. (?-1920). En 1866 se alistó en la Guardia Nacional de Juchitán para combatir al imperio de Maximiliano. Participó en la batalla del 2 de abril de 1867 en Puebla. Durante el porfirismo reprimió las sublevaciones de Tlaxcala, Oaxaca, Veracruz y el Estado de México. En 1910 combatió la insurrección maderista. En 1912 dirigió la campaña contra las fuerzas de Zapata, en la que se distinguió por sus excesos. Fue comandante de la División del Sur federal durante el huertismo y gobernador de Guerrero (1913). Se retiró al firmarse los Tratados de Teoloyucan.

Robles, Martha ◆ n. en Guadalajara, Jal. (1949). Escritora. Licenciada en sociología (1973) y maestra en letras hispánicas por la UNAM, donde ha sido profesora (1976-84) e investigadora del Centro de Estudios Políticos y del Instituto de Investigaciones Filológicas (1985-89). Estudió literatura, filosofía y artes plásticas en las universidades de Nueva York, Columbia y de California en Berkeley. Es maestra en desarrollo social urbano por el Institute of Social Studies de La Haya, Holanda. Autora de los ensayos: *Educación y sociedad en la historia de México* (1976), *La sombra fugitiva. Escritoras en la cultura nacional* (1986), *Círculos del tiempo* (1988), *Primeros papeles* (1989), *La poesía de Margarita Michelena* (1991), *Espiral de voces* y *La metáfora del poder* (1993), *Memorias de la antigüedad* (1994), *Nosotras y el sistema* (1995), *Mujeres, mitos y diosas* (1996) y *Carlota: el esplendor de los cetros* (1999); las novelas: *Memorias de la libertad* (1979), *Los octubres del otoño* (1982), *Nostalgia de Odiseo* (1995), *Biografías clandestinas. La condena* (1996) y *Biografías clandestinas. La ley del padre* (1998); y los poemarios: *Inscripción de su presencia* (1985), *Tebas* (1986), *El signo* (1987), *El cielo de los deleites* (1989), *Evocación de goces* (1990) y *Deslumbramientos* (1991), entre otras obras. Recibió un premio del Club de Periodistas de México (1996). Becaria del Centro Mexicano de Escritores (1978-79). Ha sido miembro del SNI (1989-95) y del International Women's Forum.

Robles, Rosario ◆ n. en el DF (1956). Licenciada en economía y maestra en desarrollo rural, por la UNAM, donde ha sido profesora. Cofundadora del PRD (1989) y consejera nacional del mismo, ha sido también responsable de Movimientos Sociales (1993-94) y secretaria de Organización del Comité Ejecutivo Nacional (1996-97), así como coordinadora del programa Brigadas del Sol (1997). Diputada federal (1994-97). Secretaria general (1997-99) y jefa de Gobierno del DF (1999-2000). Es la primera mujer que gobierna la capital del país.

Robles, Sergio *Kalimán* ◆ n. en Magdalena de Kino, Son. (¿1952?). Beisbolista. Después de jugar en las Ligas Mayores de Estados Unidos con los *Orioles* de Baltimore (1972-73) y los *Dodgers* de Los Ángeles (1976), optó por regresar a México, donde jugó con los *Tigres* (1977), los *Naranjeros* de Hermosillo (con los que fue campeón de la Serie del Caribe en 1976) y los *Diablos Rojos* de México (1978-86). Se retiró en 1986, como jugador en activo de la Liga Mexicana del Pacífico.

Foto: Dante Bucio

Rosario Robles

Robles, Xavier ◆ n. en Teziutlán, Pue. (1949). Escritor. Autor de *Los robos más sensacionales de la historia* (1974, con el pseudónimo de *Aníbal Palacios*) y de los guiones de las cintas *La jaula de oro*, *Tres veces mojado*, *La puerta negra*, *Contagio de amor*, *Las poquianchis* (1976, con Tomás Pérez Turrent), *El tres de copas* (1978, con Humberto Robles), *¡Qué viva Tepito!* (1980, Premio Gran Torre de Panamá Viejo, Globo de Oro en Taiwán y varias Diosas de Plata), *Noche de carnaval* (1981), *Polvo de luz* (1982), *Bajo la metralla* (1984, ganadora de cuatro Arieles y 11 Diosas de Plata), *Astucia* (1984, premiada por RTC), *Los motivos de Luz* (1985, premio Concha de Plata en el Festival de San Sebastián), *Tierra viva* (1986), *Muelle rojo* (1987), *Zapata en Chinameca* (1987, con Guadalupe Ortega Vargas), *El jinete de la divina providencia* (1989, con Sergio Molina y Óscar Blancarte) y *Rojo amanecer* (1990, con Guadalupe Ortega Vargas; premiado en el Festival de San Sebastián). En 1991 adaptó *Rojo amanecer* al teatro. Fundador de las cooperativas cinematográficas Tlacaélel, Río Mixcoac y José Revueltas, es miembro vitalicio e integrante del comité ejecutivo de la Sección de Autores del Sindicato de Trabajadores de la Producción Cinematográfica.

Robles Arenas, Jorge Humberto ◆ n. y m. en el DF (1922-1984). Estudió contaduría en la Escuela Bancaria Comercial (1940) y artes dramáticas en el Mexico City College (1951). Fundó en Veracruz la Compañía Teatral Cómicos de la Legua. Autor de las obras de teatro *Trampa para dos marionetas*, *Manos de lumbre*, *Dos boletos para México* (1952), *Los desarraigados* (1953, traducida a varios idiomas y llevada al cine en 1956 y 1975), *Raíces muertas* (1954), *Esfera sin eje* (1955), *El forastero* (1960), *Muñeca de paja* (1963), *La voz de la tierra* (1976), *Romance de Epigmenio Zarzosa o del ladino timado por su propio desatino* (1980) y *Perfiles de ausencia (la mujer que venció al tiempo)* (1981); la telenovela *Los marginados* (1979) y el guión *Las primeras lluvias* (1981), con el que ganó el séptimo Concurso Nacional de Escritores de Cine. Trabajó en teatro, televisión y cine. Fue el protagonista de la película *Pafnucio Santo* (1976).

Robles Catalán, José Rubén ◆ n. en Atoyac de Álvarez, Gro. (1943). Licenciado en derecho por la Universidad Autónoma de Guerrero (1965). Miembro del PRI, del que ha sido presidente en Guerrero (1985). En ese estado se ha desempeñado como secretario de la quinta sala del Tribunal Superior de Justicia (1960), juez penal, oficial mayor de la Cámara de Diputados (1967-69), secretario general de la Federación de Organizaciones Populares (1970-72), diputado local (1970-72 y 1981-84), asesor jurídico (1972) y jefe de servicios (1973-79) de la delegación estatal del IMSS; director de gobernación del ayuntamiento (1979-81) y recaudador de rentas de Acapulco (1984), agente del Ministerio Público, diputado federal (1985-88) y procurador general de justicia de Guerrero (1988-93). Autor de *Antecedentes y desarrollo de la seguridad social en México*. Pertenece a la Sociedad Mexicana de Geografía y Estadística.

ROBLES COTA, ALFONSO HUMBERTO ◆ n. en Los Mochis, Sin. (1931). Sacerdote ordenado en 1953. Ha sido asistente de Acción Católica en Puebla, párroco de San Martín Texmelucan, obispo titular de Assavia y auxiliar del obispo de Texcoco (1973), administrador apostólico y obispo residencial de la misma diócesis (1978-81) y obispo de Tepic (1981-).

ROBLES DÍAZ, LUIS ◆ n. en El Grullo, Jal. (1938). Estudió en el Seminario de Guadalajara, donde se ordenó sacerdote en 1962, y en la Academia Eclesiástica de El Vaticano. Licenciado en derecho canónico por la Universidad Gregoriana de Italia. Comenzó su carrera diplomática para el Vaticano en 1967 y ha trabajado en las sedes pontificias de Honduras, África Meridional, Etiopía, Sri Lanka, Ecuador, Colombia, Sudán y Uganda. Nuncio apostólico en Cuba (1999-).

ROBLES DOMÍNGUEZ, ALFREDO ◆ n. en Guanajuato, Gto., y m. en el DF (1876-1928). Arquitecto e ingeniero graduado en Estados Unidos. En la ciudad de México construyó un edificio que sirvió sucesivamente como centro de reunión del Partido Democrático, del Club Reyista, del Partido Nacionalista Democrático y del Club Antirreeleccionista. Diseñó un avión que logró volar unos cuantos metros. Manifestó su antiporfirismo mediante una serie de artículos publicados en *México Nuevo* y fue uno de los dirigentes antirreeleccionistas en la ciudad de México. En 1910, con la representación del Partido Democrático Nacionalista, asistió a la Convención Antirreeleccionista, de la que fue nombrado vicepresidente. Al iniciarse la lucha armada de 1910, Madero lo nombró jefe del movimiento en el centro y sur del país, pero antes de que pudiera actuar, la policía porfirista lo encarceló. Salió de prisión en 1911 y fue uno de los precandidatos a la vicepresidencia. Se autoexilió en Europa. Regresó a México en 1913 y luchó contra Victoriano Huerta. Representó a Venustiano Carranza ante el gobierno provisional de Francisco Carvajal y fue uno de los firmantes de los Tratados de Teoloyucan. En 1914 fue gobernador del Distrito Federal y en 1915 director de Obras Públicas y jefe de la División del Sur. Diputado al Congreso Constituyente (1916-17), En 1918 Emiliano Zapata lo nombró su representante en la capital del país. En 1920 opuso su candidatura presidencial a la de Álvaro Obregón. Autor de un *Tratado sobre locomoción aérea*.

ROBLES DOMÍNGUEZ Y MAZARIEGOS, MARIANO ◆ n. en San Cristóbal de Las Casas, Chis., y m. en Puebla, Pue. (¿1792?-1830). Sacerdote. Estudió en el Seminario Conciliar de Chiapas. Fue secretario del obispado durante la gestión de Ambrosio Llano, provisor y deán de la iglesia de Chiapas, diputado a las Cortes de Cádiz (1812) y representante de Chiapas ante el Congreso General del Imperio Mexicano (1821-23).

ROBLES GARNICA, ROBERTO ◆ n. en EUA (1927). Médico cirujano graduado en el IPN (1950) con maestría en la Escuela de Salud Pública (1954). Integrante de la Corriente Democrática del PRI (1986), fue cofundador del PRD (1989) y su presidente interino (1993). Desempeñó diversos cargos relativos a su profesión en el IMSS. Ha sido coordinador de extensión universitaria de la ENEP-Zaragoza (1977), secretario de gobierno del estado de Michoacán (1980-82), presidente municipal de Morelia (1983-86), senador por Michoacán (1988-94), candidato a gobernador por el PRD y secretario de Salud del gobierno priista.

ROBLES GIL, ALBERTO ◆ n. y m. ¿en Guadalajara, Jal.? (1868-1936). Ingeniero. De filiación antimaderista, fue gobernador de Jalisco (1911-12). Ocupó la Secretaría de Fomento (del 19 de febrero al 8 de julio de 1913) en el gabinete de Victoriano Huerta.

ROBLES GIL, EMETERIO ◆ n. y m. en Guadalajara, Jal. (1831-1906). Abogado. Fue diputado al Congreso Constituyente de Jalisco (1857), a varias legislaturas locales y al Congreso de la Unión. Profesor en diversas escuelas de Guadalajara. En 1868 gobernó Jalisco. Colaborador de *La Alianza Literaria*. Autor de las comedias *Al mejor postor* (1856) y *Episodios conyugales* (1868).

ROBLES GONZÁLEZ, GUSTAVO ◆ n. en Aguascalientes, Ags. (1939). Licenciado en derecho por la UNAM (1962), donde ejerció la docencia (1976-80). Miembro del PRI, en el que ha sido subsecretario de Acción Social (1978-80) y de Organización (1980-81) del Comité Ejecutivo Nacional. Fue director de Acción Social y secretario de Organización de la Federación de Organizaciones Populares del DF y secretario de Colonos Urbanos y Asentamientos Humanos del Comité Ejecutivo Nacional de la CNOP. Ha sido agente del Ministerio Público, subdirector de Acción Social (1971-72) y delegado del DDF en Miguel Hidalgo (1972-76); subdirector general de Expropiaciones de la SRA (1977-80), subdirector general de la Comisión Reguladora de la Tenencia de la Tierra (1980-85) y diputado federal por el Estado de México (1985-88). Pertenece a la Federación Nacional de Abogados.

ROBLES JIMÉNEZ, JOSÉ ESAÚL ◆ n. en Jalpa, Zac., y m. en Zamora, Mich. (1925-1993). Sacerdote ordenado en 1949. Fue vicario cooperador en la parroquia de Guadalupe, juez prosinodal de la curia y prefecto general, vicerrector y rector del Seminario de la diócesis de Zacatecas, obispo de Tulancingo (1962-74) y de Zamora (1974-93), vicepresidente del Episcopado Mexicano

Roberto Robles Garnica

(1982-88) y vocal de la Comisión Permanente de la Presidencia de la Conferencia del Episcopado.

Robles Morales, Serafín Maximiliano ◆ n. en Jonacatepec, Mor., y m. en el DF (1883-1955). Trabajó en los ingenios de Tenango y Santa Clara. En 1912, en Puebla, se unió al Ejército Libertador del Sur en las fuerzas de Francisco Mendoza Palma. Pasó después a la escolta personal de Emiliano Zapata como auxiliar del despacho de la secretaría particular, en el cuartel general de Tlaltizapán. Fue jefe del Departamento de Guerra y alcanzó el grado de general brigadier. Por motivos de salud se retiró al campamento de San Marcos Acteopan, Puebla. En 1920, al triunfo del aguaprietismo, se incorporó al ejército federal, del que se dio de baja el mismo año. Fue después empleado de las secretarías de Agricultura y de Industria y Comercio. Cofundador del Frente Zapatista (1940), del que fue oficial mayor y secretario de Organización del Comité Directivo.

Robles Ochoa, Oswaldo ◆ n. en Monterrey, NL, y m. en el DF (1904-1969). Era vicepresidente de la Confederación de Estudiantes Católicos de México cuando se produjo la guerra cristera, por lo que se exilió en EUA. Médico por la Universidad de Nebraska (1928), doctor en filosofía (1936) y maestro en sicología (1958) por la UNAM, de la que fue profesor y funcionario (1936-44). Ejerció la docencia en el Centro de Cultura Católica de Buenos Aires, la Universidad Católica de Milán, la Universidad Central de Madrid, el Consejo Superior de Investigaciones Científicas de Madrid, la Universidad Nacional de Santo Domingo y la Universidad Nacional de Colombia (1949-54). Colaborador de la *Revista de Estudios Universitarios*, *Filosofía y Letras*, *The Modern Schoolman*, *Ábside* y la *Revista de Psicología*. Autor de *El alma y el cuerpo* (1936), *La teoría de la idea en Malebranche y la tradición filosófica* (1937), *Esquema de antropología filosófica* (1942), *Propedéutica filosófica* (1943), *The Main Problems of Philosophy* (1946), *Introducción a la psicología científica* (1948), *Filósofos mexicanos del siglo XVI* (1950), *Freud a distancia* (1955), *Símbolo y deseo* (1956) y *La doctrina jasperiana de la angustia* (1958). Miembro del Instituto de Psicosíntesis y Relaciones Humanas de la Universidad de los Andes, de la Sociedad Internacional para el Estudio de la Psicología de los Pueblos, de la Sociedad Peruana de Psicología, de la Unión Mundial de Filosofía de Friburgo y de la Sociedad Española de Filosofía. *Doctor honoris causa* por la Universidad Autónoma de Guadalajara (1954).

Robles Ortega, Francisco ◆ n. en Mascota, Jal. (1949). Estudió en los seminarios de Autlán, Guadalajara y Zamora. Fue ordenado sacerdote en 1976. Licenciado en teología por la Pontificia Universidad Gregoriana de Roma (1979). Ha sido vicario de la parroquia de Santa María de Guadalupe (1979) y rector del Seminario Menor de Autlán (1980-85); miembro de la Comisión Diocesana para la Doctrina de la Fe, vicario general de la diócesis de Autlán (1985-91), promotor diocesano para el arte sacro (1987), obispo titular de Bossa (1991-), obispo auxiliar (1991-96) y obispo titular de la diócesis de Toluca (1996-). Es presidente de la Comisión Episcopal de Educación y Cultura.

Francisco Robles Ortega

Robles Pezuela, Manuel ◆ n. en Guanajuato, Gto., y m. en San Andrés Chalchicomula, hoy Ciudad Serdán, Pue. (1817-1862). Ingeniero militar. Combatió la invasión estadounidense (1846-47) y fue secretario de Guerra y Marina (del 16 de enero de 1851 al 18 de junio de 1852) de Mariano Arista. Era comandante de la ciudad de México el 20 de diciembre de 1858, cuando se pronunció en Ayotla Miguel María de Echegaray, proponiendo la reunión de un Congreso que formara una nueva Constitución. Tres días después se sublevó en la capital el batallón de infantería que mandaba Manuel Gual, aunque no en apoyo del Plan de

Gabinete del presidente Manuel Robles Pezuela
23 de diciembre de 1858 al 21 de enero de 1859

Secretaría de Relaciones Exteriores	
Joaquín M. de Castillo y Lanzas	23 de diciembre de 1858 al 21 de enero de 1859
Secretaría de Gobernación	
Juan M. Fernández de Jáuregui	23 de diciembre de 1858 al 21 de enero de 1859
Secretaría de Justicia y Negocios Eclesiásticos	
Francisco Javier Miranda	23 de diciembre de 1858 al 21 de enero de 1859
Secretaría de Fomento	
José María Zaldívar	23 de diciembre de 1858 al 21 de enero de 1859
Secretaría de Guerra y Marina	
José María García	23 de diciembre de 1858 al 21 de enero de 1859
Secretaría de Hacienda	
Pedro Jorrín	23 de diciembre de 1858 al 21 de enero de 1859

Ayotla, sino para desconocer al gobierno de Zuloaga y dar a Robles y Echegaray la facultad de nombrar una junta de notables que eligiera presidente interino. Este movimiento fue inspirado por Robles Pezuela y secundado por las fuerzas de la Ciudadela. Fue presidente del 23 de diciembre de 1858 al 21 de enero de 1859, cuando lo sucedió José Mariano Salas. Durante su gestión mantuvo conversaciones con el presidente Buchanan, de Estados Unidos, quien deseaba comprar Sonora y Chihuahua. Al triunfo liberal se refugió en la legación francesa, amparado por el ministro Saligny; sin embargo, el gobierno de Juárez lo aprehendió y lo confinó en Sombrerete, Zacatecas. Al iniciarse la intervención francesa intentó unirse a las fuerzas de Almonte, pero fue capturado y fusilado por Ignacio Zaragoza.

Manuel Robles Pezuela

Robles Quintero, Salvador ◆ n. en San Miguel Zapotitlán, Sin., y m. en el DF (1934-1992). Licenciado en economía por el IPN (1954-59) y maestro en administración pública por la Universidad de Harvard (1964). Miembro del PRI, en el que fue integrante del Consejo Nacional (1963), subsecretario de Organización (1981) y subsecretario y secretario de Información y Propaganda (1982) del Comité Ejecutivo Nacional. Secretario auxiliar y miembro del Consejo Técnico Consultivo de la CNC (1965-67). Secretario del Comité Nacional de la CNOP (1973). Profesor y director de la maestría en economía industrial (1964-65) y secretario de apoyo del IPN (1980-82). Socio fundador de la cooperativa del periódico *El Día* (1962). Fue asesor técnico de los directores de Nafinsa (1966) y Conasupo (1969), gerente general del Banco Nacional Cinematográfico (1970-76), diputado federal por el DF (1973-76), director general de Organización y Métodos (1976-77), director general de servicios sociales y del Teatro de la Ciudad (1977-78) y secretario del Comité de Nomenclatura (1977-78) del DDF; subsecretario de Planeación e Infraestructura Agraria de la SRA (1982-85), diputado federal por Sinaloa (1985-88) y por el DF (1991-92). Presidente de la Liga de Economistas Revolucionarios (1973-74) y miembro del Colegio de Economistas. El IPN le otorgó la presea General Lázaro Cárdenas.

Robles Sasso, Daniel ◆ n. en Tuxtla Gutiérrez, Chis., y m. en el DF (1933-1971). Poeta. Licenciado por la Escuela de Derecho de San Cristóbal de Las Casas (1962) y por la Facultad de Derecho de la UNAM. Miembro del PRI. Profesor y rector del Instituto de Ciencias y Artes y secretario del patronato Pro-Universidad de Chiapas. Diputado federal por Pichucalco y jefe del Departamento Jurídico de Industrial de Abastos, en la ciudad de México. Fue colaborador de *Poesía de América* y los *Anuarios de Poesía Mexicana del INBA*. Coautor de *Antología de la oratoria chiapaneca* (1967) y autor de *Encuentro con Vallejo en la tierra del hombre* (1965) y *Viento al hombro* (1959). En 1957 ganó el Premio de Poesía del Ateneo de Chiapas.

Robles Segura, Raúl ◆ n. en el DF (1933). Contador público por la UNAM (1954). Profesor de la UIA y la UNAM. Miembro del PRI. Socio de los despachos de contadores Casas Alatriste (1963-66) y Manuel Resa (1967-76). Ha sido delegado mexicano ante el Comité de Normas Internacionales de Contabilidad e Información de la ONU, asesor de la CFE (1965-70), subcontralor general del DDF (1971-73), gerente de Contraloría de Nafinsa (1973-78), director general de Fiscalización de la Secretaría de Hacienda (1978-82), subsecretario de la Contraloría General de la Federación (1983-87), consejero y comisario de empresas paraestatales, miembro del Consejo Técnico Consultivo de Auditoría Gubernamental, y subdirector comercial (1987-90) y de Petroquímica y Gas de Pemex (1990-94). Miembro del Colegio de Contadores Públicos de México.

Robles Soler, Antonio ◆ ☛ *Antoniorrobles*.

Robredo Galguera, Pedro ◆ n. en España y m. en Puebla, Pue. (1884-1979). Librero, editor e impresor. Llegó a México hacia 1899. En 1903 empezó a trabajar en la librería Porrúa, de la capital del país, y en 1906 se le encomendó la dirección de la sucursal de esa casa en Isabel la Católica, donde permeneció hasta 1917, cuando fundó su propia librería. En 1936 fundó la editorial Pedro Robredo y en 1940, con sus hijos, la imprenta Aldina. Su biblioteca fue donada al Instituto Tecnológico de Monterrey.

Rocabruna, José ◆ n. en España y m. en el DF (1879-1957). Estudió en el Conservatorio del Liceo y en 1900 ocupó el puesto de violín concertino en el Teatro de la Ópera del Liceo. Actuó en conciertos sinfónicos dirigido por Camilo Saint-Saëns, Vicente D'Indy y Richard Strauss. Formó parte del Cuarteto Clásico de la Asociación de Música de Cámara y de los de Pablo Casals, M. Crickboom y Enrique Granados. Viajó a América como integrante del Octeto Español y tuvo éxito como violín concertino en la Metropolitan Opera House de Nueva York. Llegó a México en 1902 con el mismo conjunto y decidió fijar su residencia en este país. Formó un trío con el pianista Juan Roura y el chelista Guillermo Ferrer. Justo Sierra lo nombró profesor del Conservatorio Nacional en 1903, cargo que desempeñó hasta 1957. De 1926 a 1928 dirigió la Orquesta Sinfónica del Sindicato de Filarmónicos y la Orquesta Alemana.

En 1938 fundó y dirigió la Orquesta Sinfónica de la Universidad y fue director de la Escuela Nacional de Música.

ROCAFUERTE, VICENTE DE ◆ n. y m. en Ecuador (1783-1847). Diputado a las Cortes de Cádiz (1812), fue encarcelado al restaurarse el absolutismo. Escapó de España y vivió en Francia y Estados Unidos antes de llegar a México (1824), donde fue nombrado secretario de la legación en Londres. Por ausencia de Mariano Michelena, ministro plenipotenciario, quedó como encargado de negocios en Inglaterra hasta 1829. Volvió a México en 1830, colaboró en diversos periódicos y tres años después retornó a Ecuador, donde fue diputado y presidente de la República (1835-39). Autor de *Bosquejo ligerísimo de la revolución de Méjico desde el grito de Iguala hasta la proclamación imperial de Iturbide* (1822).

Mireille Roccatti

ROCCATTI, MIREILLE ◆ n. en Monterrey, NL (1948). Licenciada en derecho por la UAEM, maestra y doctora en derecho por la UNAM. Ha sido profesora en la UAEM (1987-88), juez segundo municipal en Atizapán de Zaragoza (1988-91), magistrada del Tribunal Superior de Justicia del Estado de México (1991-93), presidente de la Comisión de Derechos Humanos del Estado de México (1992-96) y de la Comisión Nacional de Derechos Humanos (1997-). Coautora de *Reflexiones sobre derechos humanos* (1995), *Justicia juvenil en el Estado de México* (1995), *Modernización y recursos municipales* (1996) y *Derechos humanos y sistemas comparados de justicia juvenil* (1996). Autora de *Los derechos humanos y las experiencias del Ombudsman en México* (1994). Es miembro fundador de la Federación Iberoamericana del Ombdusman, miembro del Colegio de Abogados del Estado de México y de la Academia Mexicana de Derecho Internacional.

Sóstenes Rocha

ROCES, WENCESLAO ◆ n. en España y m. en el DF (1897-1992). Doctor en derecho por la Universidad Central de Madrid. Se especializó en las de Berlín y Friburgo. Militante del Partido Comunista Español desde 1931. Catedrático de derecho romano en la Universidad de Salamanca (1923-29), de la que fue expulsado por solidarizarse con Miguel de Unamuno en su lucha contra la dictadura de Primo de Rivera. Fundó en 1931 la editorial Cenit, que publicó obras de Lenin, Engels y el primer tomo de *El Capital*, de Marx. En la República Española fue presidente de la Institución para el Fomento de las Artes. Durante un viaje de trabajo fue testigo de la rebelión minera de Asturias (1934), al término de la cual volvió a Madrid. Fue detenido y encarcelado en Oviedo, de donde salió libre en 1935. Viajó a la URSS y ahí trabajó en las ediciones castellanas de la Editorial Progreso. Volvió a España al llegar a la presidencia Largo Caballero. Fue subsecretario del Ministerio de Instrucción Pública (1936-38), creó los institutos para obreros y las milicias de la cultura. Exiliado tras el triunfo franquista, ejerció la docencia en las universidades de Santiago de Chile y La Habana. Vino a México y se incorporó al Fondo de Cultura Económica. Fue profesor de la UNAM (1944-77). En 1977 regresó a España como candidato a senador por Asturias, propuesto por una coalición de los partidos Comunista y Socialista; ganó las elecciones pero renunció poco después al escaño, por motivos de salud. Regresó a México hacia 1980. Tradujo del alemán, entre otras obras, *El capital* y *Teoría crítica de la plusvalía*, de Marx, el *Anti-Dühring*, de Engels, *Lecciones sobre el método de estudio académico*, de Schelling, *Paideia*, de Werner Jaeger, *Fenomenología del espíritu* y tres volúmenes de la *Historia de la Filosofía*, de Hegel; *El historiador y la historia antigua*, de Eduard Meyer, *El renacimiento en Italia*, de Symonds, *El asalto a la razón*, de Lukács, y los *Cuadernos filosóficos* de Lenin. Autor de *El derecho de superficie en la jurisprudencia romana* (tesis de doctorado), *La cultura de nuestro tiempo*, *El vicio del modernismo en la historia antigua* y *Los problemas de la universidad*. Maestro emérito de la UNAM (1969), *doctor honoris causa* por la Universidad Michoacana de San Nicolás de Hidalgo y Premio Universidad Nacional (1985). En 1980 le fue impuesta la Orden del Águila Azteca.

Enrique Rocha

ROCHA, ENRIQUE ◆ n. en Guanajuato, Gto. (1942). Actor. De formación teatral, desde mediados de los sesenta ha hecho carrera en el cine mexicano, con actuaciones en películas como *Un alma pura* (1964), *Tiempo de morir* (1965), *Damiana y los hombres* (1966), *El club de los suicidas* (1968), *El caudillo* (1968), *Santa* (1968), *Apolinar* (1971), *Historias violentas* (1984), *El otro crimen* (1988, nominación al Ariel como mejor actor en 1989), *Morir en el golfo* (1989, Diosa de Plata al mejor actor en 1990), *Ciudad de ciegos* (1991), *Kino* (1992) y *Mujeres insumisas* (1994). Ha participado en numerosas obras de teatro y telenovelas, entre las que destaca *Pasión y poder* (1990).

ROCHA, JUAN IGNACIO DE LA ◆ n. en España y m. en San Miguel el Grande, Gto. (1715-1782). Llegó a la Nueva España en 1730 como paje del arzobispo Vizarrón. Estudió en el Seminario de México, del que fue rector (1749-52) y en la Real y Pontificia Universidad de México, donde fue profesor de filosofía durante 20 años. En 1781 cedió a la propia Universidad los 300 pesos anuales que le correspondían por su jubilación, para que se destinaran a enriquecer el acervo de la biblioteca. Fue también rector del Colegio de San Ildefonso (1767) y obispo de Michoacán (1772-82).

ROCHA, RICARDO ◆ n. en el DF (1950). Periodista. Hizo estudios de ciencias sociales y administración de empresas. Trabajó para la radiodifusora XEX (1975-76). Incorporado a la empresa Televisa, fue reportero y titular de los noticiarios *Punto final*, *En punto* y *En contacto directo*, así como de los programas *Nuestras realidades* (1976), *Para gente grande*, *Reportaje*, *En vivo* (1983-87) y *Detrás de la noticia* (1996-99, del que había también una emisión radiofónica en la XEQ). Fue presidente del grupo Radiópolis y rector del Centro de Estudios Universitarios de Periodismo y Arte en Radio y Televisión (1992-99). En 1999 se incorporó a Radio Acir, donde dirige el noticiario *Detrás de la noticia*. Fue corresponsal de guerra en la revolución sandinista. Ha colaborado en la revista *Siempre!* y en otras publicaciones. Coautor de *Yo, corresponsal de guerra* (1982). En 1984 ganó el Premio Nacional de Periodismo en la especialidad de televisión y un año después fue designado Comunicador del Año. Premio de la Fraternidad de Periodistas (1998).

ROCHA, SÓSTENES ◆ n. en el Mineral de Marfil, Gto., y m. en la ciudad de México (1831-1897). Estudió en el Colegio Militar. Combatió la insurrección del Plan de Ayutla (1854-55). En 1858, después del pronunciamiento del Plan de Tacubaya, se adhirió a la causa de la legalidad que representaba Benito Juárez. Militó en el ejército liberal al inició de la guerra de los Tres Años. Se pasó a la facción conservadora y en 1860 cambió nuevamente de bando. Luchó contra los invasores franceses, quienes lo hicieron prisionero. Se escapó y logró reunirse con Juárez en San Luis Potosí, donde reorganizó el batallón de zapadores para luego continuar al lado del jefe republicano, a quien acompañó hasta Paso del Norte. Desde 1864 militó a las órdenes de Mariano Escobedo y asistió al sitio de Querétaro, donde obtuvo el grado de general de brigada. Se opuso a la rebelión del Plan de la Noria y llegó a general de división en 1871. Se adhirió al Plan de Tuxtepec (1876) y al triunfo de Porfirio Díaz, éste lo envió a estudiar en Europa. Fue director del Colegio Militar (1880-86). Dirigió el órgano liberal *El Combate*. Autor de *Ayuda de memoria del oficial mexicano en campaña*, *La ciencia de la guerra* y *Enquiridión para cabos y sargentos*.

ROCHA BANDALA, JUAN FRANCISCO ◆ n. en Tuxpan, Ver. (1925). Licenciado en derecho por la UNAM. Miembro del PRI. Ha sido profesor de la UNAM (1960-65), jefe de Relaciones Laborales del IMSS (1966-74), coordinador general jurídico del Banjidal, del Banco Nacional de Crédito Agrícola y del Banrural (1975), presidente de la Junta Federal de Conciliación y Arbitraje (1976-79), oficial mayor de la SARH (1980-82) y subdirector general jurídico del IMSS (1982-88). Autor de *La competencia en materia laboral* (1975) y *Habitación al trabajador. Obligación social solidaria* (1981). Pertenece a la Sociedad Mexicana de Geografía y Estadística.

ROCHA CORDERO, ANTONIO ◆ n. en San Luis Potosí, SLP, y m. en el DF (1912-1993). Licenciado en derecho por la Universidad de San Luis Potosí (1935). Fue procurador general (1943-45) y secretario general de Justicia (1947-48) de Tamaulipas, diputado federal (1949-52 y 1979-82), senador (1952-58), procurador general de la República (1964-67) y gobernador de San Luis Potosí (1967-73). Durante su periodo al frente del Ejecutivo potosino se suprimió la pena de muerte. Fue ministro de la Suprema Corte de Justicia (1974-82).

ROCHA DÍAZ, SALVADOR ◆ n. en San Miguel de Allende, Gto. (1937). Licenciado en derecho por la UNAM (1954-58), diplomado en derecho comparado por la Universidad de Estrasburgo (1963-65). Profesor de la UNAM (1964-82) y de la UIA (1967-74). Miembro del PRI desde 1961. Ha sido socio director de Rocha y Hegewish-Abogados (1959-82), diputado federal (1982-85) y secretario general del gobierno de Guanajuato (1984-85); director general de Asuntos Jurídicos de la Secretaría de Gobernación (1985-88), ministro de la Suprema Corte de Justicia (1988), secretario de gobierno del estado de Guanajuato (1988-94) y senador (1994-2000). Autor de *Los contratos aleatorios* (1968), *Municipio libre: autonomía fiscal y democracia* (1983) y *Las reformas constitucionales iniciadas por el Lic. Miguel de la Madrid Hurtado* (1983). Miembro del Consejo Directivo de la Barra Mexicana-Colegio de Abogados (1972-76), del Consejo Directivo de la Federación Interamericana de Abogados (1975-87) y del Consejo Asesor de Euroforum, Centro Europeo de Desarrollo de la Empresa (1976-87).

FOTO: EIKON

Salvador Rocha Díaz

FOTO: ÉPOCA

Ricardo Rocha

Lorenzo de Rodas

RODARTE, FERNANDO ◆ n. en Zacatecas, Zac., y m. ¿en el DF? (1886-?). Profesor por la Escuela Normal de Zacatecas. En 1910 se unió a la revolución maderista y en 1913, a la constitucionalista. Con la División del Norte participó en los combates de San Pedro de las Colonias, Torreón, Paredón y Zacatecas. Fue diputado federal, senador y gobernador de Zacatecas. Como integrante de la CROM formó parte de la comisión que elaboró el primer Código del Trabajo.

RODARTE ESQUIVEL, MARIO ◆ n. en el DF (1951). Ingeniero mecánico por la UNAM (1973), licenciado en economía por el ITAM (1977), maestro en economía por la Universidad de Rochester (1980) y doctor en economía por la Agriculture and Mechanics de Texas (1982). Ha sido profesor del ITAM (1983-84) y de las universidades La Salle (1984-87) y Anáhuac (1986). Jefe del Departamento de Estudios Especiales de la Secretaría de Hacienda (1978), director de Estadísticas de Corto Plazo (1983) y director técnico del INEGI (1985), asesor (1986), coordinador de asesores (1987) y director general del Sector Paraestatal (1987-88) de la Secretaría de Turismo. Coordinador de asesores (1989-90) y coordinador ejecutivo del INEGI (1991-94). Premio Nacional de Economía de Banamex (1981).

RODARTE RAMÓN, LEOPOLDO ◆ n. en Saltillo, Coah. (1940). Ingeniero civil por la UNAM (1965). Doctor en ciencias técnicas por el Instituto de Ingenieros Civiles de Moscú (1974). Ha sido consultor de la SARH, la UAM, la UNAM, la Comisión de Aguas de Valle de México, el DDF, la UANL, la compañía Minera de Cananea y otras. Desde 1962 ha impartido clases en la UNAM, el IPN, la UAM, la Universidad Autónoma de Yucatán, la UANL y varias empresas privadas. Director general de la Comisión de Aguas del DF (1998-). Autor de *Manual para evaluar recursos hidráulicos subterráneos* (1994) e *Hidrología subterránea* (1999), así como de una cincuentena de artículos publicados en revistas mexicanas y extranjeras.

RODAS, LORENZO DE ◆ n. en España (1930). Actor cuyo nombre es Lorenzo López de Rodas Martín. En 1942 llegó como exiliado y obtuvo la nacionalidad mexicana en 1947. Estudió pintura y arquitectura en la Academia de San Carlos. Se inició como actor teatral en 1949 con *Santa locura* y participó en un grupo de teatro experimental (1949-50). Es uno de los iniciadores de la televisión mexicana, donde ha trabajado como actor o director en numerosos teleteatros, telenovelas y otros programas. Participó en el Teatro Español de México, de Álvaro Custodio, y en 1964 creó el Teatro Popular Independiente con el que llevó a fábricas, cárceles y escuelas obras como *El principito* y *El juglarón*. Ha actuado o dirigido más de 1,000 obras de teatro, radionovelas, películas, teleteatros o telenovelas. Ha actuado, entre otras obras de teatro, en *¿Conoce usted la Vía Láctea?*, *La prostituta respetuosa*, *La Celestina* (1953), *Jazz* (1954), *La herida luminosa* (1956), *Morena clara* (1962), *Pablo y Carolina* (1958), *Los árboles mueren de pie* (1969), el espectáculo *Mística y erótica del barroco*, *La sonata de los espectros* (1986) y *El sueño de la razón* (1987); dirigió la puesta en escena de *El bosque petrificado* (1964, de Sherwood), *Locura de amor* (1969), *Un sombrero lleno de lluvia* (1970-74), *Fuenteovejuna* (1975), *El pagador de promesas* (1979), *Amor y sueños* (1981-82) y *El candidato de Dios* (1986). Entre las distinciones que ha obtenido está el premio al mejor actor de 1986 de la Asociación Mexicana de Críticos de Teatro, por su desempeño *Sonata de espectros*.

RODEO ◆ Municipio de Durango situado al norte de la capital estatal y contiguo a Comonfort. Superficie: 1,854.90 km^2. Habitantes: 13,547, de los cuales 3,137 forman la población económicamente activa. Hablan alguna lengua indígena siete personas mayores de cinco años.

RODILES, SAÚL ◆ n. en Atlixco, Pue., y m. en Guadalajara, Jal. (1884-1951). Estudió en la Escuela Normal de Jalapa. Fue profesor en la escuela de Tlacotepec, Puebla, regidor del ayuntamiento y presidente municipal de Puebla. Fundó el periódico antiporfirista *Últimas Noticias*, en Jalapa, y en 1910 se unió al movimiento maderista. Fue nombrado presidente del Consejo de Educación de Veracruz, diputado al Congreso Constituyente de 1916-17 por el distrito de Tantoyuca y director del Departamento de Trabajo de Puebla (1917-20). Tras el asesinato de Venustiano Carranza volvió a la docencia y en 1922 fijó su residencia en Guadalajara, donde fundó una escuela obrera, y en 1941 se le nombró director de la Escuela Normal de Jalisco.

RODRIGO, ANABEL ◆ n. en el DF (1960). Licenciada en filosofía por la Universidad Michoacana de San Nicolás de Hidalgo (1982), diplomada en literatura del siglo XX en el ITAM (1986), estudió también psicoanálisis. Becaria del Instituto Pro-Helvetia, vivió en Suiza en 1988. Ha sido directora de Ediciones de Editorial Esfinge (1988-89) y encargada del Departamento de Promoción y Edición de la Coordinación de Difusión Cultural de la UNAM (1989-). Algunos de sus poemas se incluyeron en la *Antología del Primer Festival Internacional de Poesía* (1982). Autora de los poemarios *Tribulaciones* (1981), *Los poemas de Hania* (1984). Cofundadora del feminista Colectivo Venseremos (1982), participó en la Red Nacional de Mujeres (1984-86) y otros grupos feministas. Primer lugar en el concurso de poesía de la revista *Punto de Partida* (1980) y primer lugar en el Concurso Nacional de Poesía Universitaria de la Universidad Autónoma de Querétaro (1981).

RODRÍGUEZ, ABEL S. ◆ n. y m. en Jalapa, Ver. (1880-1955). Profesor por la Escuela Normal de Jalapa. De 1895 a 1911 fue director de las Escuelas Filomáticas y director general de educación primaria en Chihuahua, nombrado por Abraham González; gobernó provisionalmente Chihuahua en dos ocasiones (1920 y 1927-28), fue dos veces senador por Chihuahua, gobernador del Distrito Federal (1923-24), gobernador provisional de Veracruz (1927-28) y senador por el mismo estado (1930-34).

RODRÍGUEZ, ABELARDO L. ◆ n. en San José de Guaymas, Son., y m. en EUA (1889-1967). Fue minero en Cananea. En 1913 se unió al Ejército Constitucionalista y de esa fecha a 1915 participó en la toma de Culiacán, en la campaña del Bajío, a las órdenes de Álvaro Obregón, en la segunda batalla de Celaya, en los combates de Aguascalientes y Saltillo, en la defensa de Agua Prieta y en la campaña de Benjamín Hill hacia la ciudad de México y contra las fuerzas zapatistas. Fue el encargado de reprimir el levantamiento yaqui en Sonora. En 1920 se adhirió al Plan de Agua Prieta (☛) y se le designó jefe de operaciones en Tehuantepec contra el pronunciamiento de Esteban Cortés. En 1923 fue nombrado comandante militar del territorio norte de Baja California, del que también fue gobernador hasta 1929. Durante su gestión impulsó una campaña contra la población china de la península, fomentó el sindicalismo, formó las juntas de Conciliación y estableció un salario mínimo. En 1928 obtuvo el grado de general de división. En 1929 viajó por varios países de Europa para estudiar las nuevas técnicas industriales. Subsecretario de Guerra y Marina (1931), secretario de Industria, Comercio y Trabajo (del 20 de enero al 2 de agosto de 1932) y secretario de Guerra y Marina (del 2 de agosto al 2 de septiembre de 1932), en el gabinete de Pascual Ortiz Rubio. Presidente de la República (del 4 de septiembre de 1932 al 30 de noviembre de 1934), fue nombrado por el Congreso tras la renuncia de Ortiz Rubio. Durante su gestión estableció los salarios mínimos, decretó la ampliación de las fronteras litorales en 50 kilómetros y creó la empresa estatal Petróleos México; modificó la Ley del Patrimonio Ejidal, creó el Banco Hipotecario y de Obras Públicas, expidió la Ley de Beneficencia Privada y una nueva Ley Orgánica de la UNAM; inició los trabajos para constituir Nacional Financiera, dictó una Ley sobre Monopolios e inauguró el Palacio de Bellas Artes. De 1943 a 1948 fue gobernador de Sonora, donde fundó la Universidad de ese estado. Al dejar los puestos públicos, fundó y presidió el Banco Mexicano, el Banco Mexicano de Occidente y Crédito Central Mexicano, así como numerosas empresas industriales y pesqueras, sobre todo en el norte de Baja California. En 1961 fue designado presidente del Consejo Consultivo de Pesca. Autor de *Notas de mi viaje a Rusia* (1938) y *Autobiografía* (1962).

Abelardo L. Rodríguez

GABINETE DEL PRESIDENTE ABELARDO L. RODRÍGUEZ
4 de septiembre de 1932 a 30 de noviembre de 1934

SECRETARÍA DE GOBERNACIÓN:	
EDUARDO VASCONCELOS	5 de sep. de 1932 al 9 de mayo de 1934
NARCISO BASSOLS	9 de mayo al 30 de septiembre de 1934
JUAN DE DIOS BOJÓRQUEZ	1 de octubre al 30 de noviembre de 1934
SECRETARÍA DE RELACIONES EXTERIORES:	
MANUEL C. TÉLLEZ	5 de septiembre al 31 de diciembre de 1932
JOSÉ MANUEL PUIG CASAURANC	1 de enero al 11 de octubre de 1933
	y 8 de nov. de 1933 al 30 de nov. de 1934
ENRÍQUE JIMÉNEZ DOMÍNGUEZ	12 de octubre al 7 de noviembre de 1933
SECRETARÍA DE HACIENDA Y CRÉDITO PÚBLICO:	
ALBERTO J. PANI	5 de sep. de 1932 al 28 de sep.de 1933
PLUTARCO ELÍAS CALLES	29 de septiembre al 31 de diciembre de 1933
MARTE R. GÓMEZ	1 de enero al 30 de noviembre de 1934
SECRETARÍA DE GUERRA Y MARINA:	
PABLO QUIROGA	5 de septiembre al 31 de diciembre de 1932
	y 28 de junio de 1933 al 30 de nov. de 1934
LÁZARO CÁRDENAS	1 de enero al 15 de junio de 1933
SECRETARÍA DE AGRICULTURA Y FOMENTO:	
FRANCISCO S. ELÍAS	5 de sep. de 1932 al 30 de nov. de 1934
SECRETARÍA DE COMUNICACIONES Y OBRAS PÚBLICAS:	
MIGUEL M. ACOSTA	5 de sep. de 1932 al 21 de nov. de 1934
MARIANO MOCTEZUMA	22 al 30 de noviembre de 1934
SECRETARÍA DE INDUSTRIA, COMERCIO Y TRABAJO:	
PRIMO VILLA MICHEL	5 de sep. de 1932 al 30 de nov. de 1934
SECRETARÍA DE EDUCACIÓN PÚBLICA:	
NARCISO BASSOLS	5 de sep. de 1932 al 9 de mayo de 1934
EDUARDO VASCONCELOS	9 de mayo al 30 de noviembre de l934
DEPARTAMENTO DE SALUBRIDAD:	
GASTÓN MELO	5 de sep. de 1932 al 26 de octubre de 1933
MANUEL F. MADRAZO	26 de octubre de 1933 al 30 de nov. de 1934
DEPARTAMENTO DEL DISTRITO FEDERAL:	
JUAN G. CABRAL	5 de septiembre al 15 de diciembre de 1932
AARÓN SÁENZ	16 de dic. de 1932 al 30 de nov. de 1934

RODRÍGUEZ, ANTONIO ◆ n. y m. en la ciudad de México (?-?). Pintor activo en el siglo XVII. Fue alumno de José Juárez. Son obra suya *Santo Tomás de Aquino* y *Santo Tomás de Villanueva* (1665, que se conservan en el Museo de San Carlos), *San Agustín* (en la Pinacoteca Virreinal de San Diego), *Ánimas del purgatorio* (en el ex convento de Churubusco) y *San Antonio* (en la parroquia de Coyoacán), entre otros cuadros.

RODRÍGUEZ, ANTONIO ◆ n. en Portugal y m. en el DF (1908-1993). Crítico de arte. Hizo estudios de historia del arte en la URSS. Fue periodista en Portugal, de donde lo expulsó el dictador Oliveira Salazar. Participó en el bando republicano durante la guerra civil española, al término de la cual pasó a Francia y de ahí a México, a donde llegó en abril de 1939. Dirigió el Departamento de Difusión Cultural del Politécnico y ahí fundó la revista *IPN: Ciencia, Arte, Cultura*. Fue director del Museo Tecnológico de la CFE. Escribió en *El Nacional, El Día, El Universal, El Diario de México, Hoy, Mañana, Siempre!* y *Excélsior*. Autor, entre otros, de los libros y folletos: *El Quijote, mensaje oportuno* (1947), *La revolución francesa, síntesis histórica* (1947), *Diego Rivera, pintor del pueblo mexicano* (1948), *La nube estéril, drama del Mezquital* (novela, 1952), *Declaración de amor a Praga* (1959), *El henequén, una planta calumniada* (1967), *Le Corbusier, paladín y profeta de los tiempos nuevos* (1967), *A History of Mural Painting* (1969), *Dr. Atl* (1969), *El hombre en llamas* (1970), *Siqueiros* (1974), *Saudade* (1979), *Crucifixión y resurrección en la pintura de Grunewald* (1983), *La pintura mural en la obra de Orozco* (1983), *Canto a la tierra. Los murales de Diego Rivera en Chapingo* (1986), *Diego Rivera. Los murales de la Secretaría de Educación Pública* (1986) y *Diego Rivera. Pintura mural* (1987). En 1979 ganó el Premio Nacional de Periodismo Cultural.

RODRÍGUEZ, ANTONIO L. ◆ n. y m. en Monterrey, NL (1899-1975). Trabajó en casas comerciales de Estados Unidos y fue cónsul mexicano en Nueva York y en Londres. En 1928 organizó el Departamento de Turismo del Banco de México. Volvió en 1930 a Monterrey, donde ocupó la gerencia de la Cámara de Comercio (1930-1936) y del Centro Patronal, así como de diversas empresas financieras. Fue uno de los fundadores del Partido Acción Nacional.

RODRÍGUEZ, ARTURO ◆ n. en Durango, Dgo., y m. cerca de Parral, Chih. (?-1916). Luchó al lado de Francisco Villa en la revolución maderista y combatió la rebelión de Pascual Orozco. Participó en las acciones de Las Escobas y Chihuahua. Formó parte de los Dorados. Murió en abril de 1916, en combate contra la expedición punitiva de J. Pershing.

RODRÍGUEZ, AURELIO ◆ n. en Cananea, Son. (1947). Beisbolista. Luego de participar en la Liga Central con el equipo de Fresnillo, fue contratado para la Liga Mexicana por el Jalisco. De allí pasó a las Grandes Ligas, donde se mantuvo 17 años (1967-1984), obtuvo un Guante de Oro (1976) y participó en la Serie Mundial de 1981 con los *Yanquis* de Nueva York. Regresó a México, jugó con los equipos *Tigres* y *Sultanes* de Monterrey y se retiró con los *Saraperos* de Saltillo. Ha sido entrenador de los *Acereros* de Monclova. Miembro del Salón de la Fama del Beisbol Mexicano.

RODRÍGUEZ, BLAS E. ◆ n. en La Labor, municipio de Cárdenas, SLP, y m. en Tampico, Tams. (1880-1949). Profesor (1897) y licenciado en derecho por el Instituto Científico y Literario de San Luis Potosí. Participó en la organización del Primer Congreso Liberal. Después de vivir en Estados Unidos, en 1915 fijó su residencia en Tampico, donde fue colaborador de la revista *Divulgación Histórica*. Autor de *Informe acusatorio presentado por el estudiante de jurisprudencia Blas E. Rodríguez, ante el juez de la primera instancia de Tancahuitz, en la vista de los procesos acumulados contra Salomón Morales y socios por el homicidio del señor don Francisco Morales* (1906), *Tampico. Datos para la historia de la Huasteca* (1932), *Nuestra bandera* (1942), *Una fiesta de Moctezuma* (1943) y *Culturas huaxteca y olmeca* (1945).

RODRÍGUEZ, DAGOBERTO ◆ n. en Aguascalientes, Ags., y m. en el DF (1916-1974). Actor. Inició su carrera como cantante en EUA. A su regreso a México trabajó en la televisión regiomontana y participó en numerosas películas, como *El Lobo Solitario* (1951), *El pozo, Juan sin miedo, Dos caballeros de espada, Tres hombres malos, La gaviota* y *El último mexicano*. Al morir era tesorero de la ANDA.

RODRÍGUEZ, DIEGO DE ◆ n. en Portugal y m. en Monterrey, NL (?-1624). Procurador de Saltillo (1591). En Monterrey fue alcalde de primer voto (1600 y 1616), mayordomo (1601), procurador (1605 y 1607) y justicia mayor (1621-24). Teniente gobernador interino (1611-13) y titular (1614-24) del Nuevo Reino de León. Murió durante un ataque de los huachichiles a la ciudad de Monterrey.

RODRÍGUEZ, DIEGO ◆ n. en Atitalaquia, en el actual Hidalgo, y m. en la ciudad de México (¿1596?-1668). Fraile mercedario. Profesó en 1613. Fue comendador del convento de la Veracruz (1623-27), profesor de teología en la provincia de la Visitación y, desde 1637, catedrático de matemáticas y astrología de la Real y Pontificia Universidad de México. Autor de *Geometría especulativa, De aritmética, Tratado de ecuaciones* y *Discurso etherológico sobre el cometa aparecido en México en 1652*.

RODRÍGUEZ, ESTEBAN ◆ n. en España (?-1567). Era piloto mayor de la nave *San Pedro* que en 1564 encabezó la expedición que descubriría las Filipinas. Una vez llegados a las islas, el comandante Miguel López de Legaspi ordenó a Rodríguez que regresara a la Nueva España, para fijar la ruta comercial de lo que sería la Nao de China. Murió en alta mar, tres años después. Autor de *Relación de la navegación que hizo la armada de S. M. a cargo del general Miguel López de Legaspi desde 21 de noviembre de 1564, que salió del puerto de Navidad hasta su llegada a la isla de Zebú, de las Filipinas, y de lo ocurrido en su conquista*.

RODRÍGUEZ, GUILLERMO HÉCTOR ◆ n. en Jalapa y m. en Veracruz, Ver.

(1910-1988). Licenciado en derecho y en filosofía por la UNAM, de la que fue profesor hasta jubilarse. Especialista en Kant, sostuvo polémicas con Antonio Caso, Samuel Ramos y Recasens Siches. Autor de *La fundamentación de la jurisprudencia como ciencia exacta* y *Ética y jurisprudencia*. Dejó inédita una obra en diez tomos sobre el platonismo.

Rodríguez, Horacio ◆ n. en Argentina (1946). Periodista. Llegó a México en 1976. Fue productor y coordinador de la Unidad de Noticieros de la Dirección de Radio de RTC, de la Secretaría de Gobernación. Ha colaborado en *Proceso, Melodía, El Día, La Jornada, Las Horas Extras, Revista de la Universidad, Ciencia y Desarrollo, Fin de Siglo, Vogue* y otras publicaciones de México; en el periódico *Toronto Star*, de Canadá, y en *Oasis*, de Italia. Trabaja en *Contenido* y en *De Polanco para Polanco*. Autor de *Entre el ruido y el swing* ("anticrítica de jazz", 1988).

Rodríguez, Ismael ◆ n. en el DF (1917). Cineasta. Comenzó como actor en las películas *Rosario* (1935), *No te engañes, corazón* (1936) y *Los chicos de la prensa* (1936); simultáneamente estudió sonorización en EUA, donde diseñó y construyó un equipo de sonido. Fue mozo, extra, cómico, microfonista, sonidista y guionista. Se inició como realizador en 1942 con la película *¡Qué lindo es Michoacán!* Sonorizó las cintas *Cinco noches de Adán* y *Cuando las estrellas viajan*. Ha dirigido *Amores de ayer* (1944), *Escándalo de estrellas* (1944), *Cuando lloran los valientes* (1945), *Ya tengo a mi hijo* (1946), *Los tres García* (1946), *Vuelven los tres García* (1946), *Chachita la de Triana* (1947), *Nosotros los pobres* (1947), *Los tres huastecos* (1948), *Ustedes los ricos* (1948), *La oveja negra* (1949), *No desearás la mujer de tu hijo* (1949), *Sobre las olas* (1950), *La mujeres de mi general* (1950), *ATM* (1951), *¿Qué te ha dado esa mujer?* (1951), *¡Mátenme porque me muero!* (1951), *Dos tipos de cuidado* (1952), *Pepe el Toro* (1952), *Del rancho a la televisión* (1952), *Maldita ciudad* (1954), *Los paquetes de Paquita* (1954), *Cupido pierde a Paquita* (1954), *Tizoc* (1956), *Tierra de hombres* (1956), *Así era Pancho Villa* (1957), *Pancho Villa y la Valentina* (1958), *Cuando ¡Viva Villa! es la muerte* (1958), *La Cucaracha* (1958), *Los hermanos del Hierro* (1961), *Ánimas Trujano* (1961), *El hombre de papel* (1963), *Así era Pedro Infante* (1963, documental), *El niño y el muro* (1964), *Autopsia de un fantasma* (1966), *Nosotros los feos* (1972), *Ratero* (1978), *Ratero II* (1981), *Burdel* (1981), *Yerba sangrienta* (1986) y *Reclusorio I, II y III* (1995), entre otras.

Rodríguez, Jesús ◆ n. en Chihuahua, Chih., y m. en el DF (1918-1991). Músico. Estudió en la Escuela Normal de Maestros en su ciudad natal, en la que participó en una orquesta de estudiantes, y en la Escuela Libre de Música. Se inició en 1942 en el Son Clave de Oro. Trabajó también en el Son Veracruz de Raúl de la Rosa. Fundó y dirigió el conjunto Chucho Rodríguez y sus Maravillas, que con el tiempo se convirtió en la Orquesta Latina, que fue semillero de cantantes y músicos en los años cuarenta y cincuenta. Fue director artístico de las disqueras Orfeón y RCA Víctor y miembro de la SACM. Grabó cerca de 500 canciones, entre las que destacan *Cosas del ayer, Esta noche corazón, Sin razón ni justicia, Bicho gordo, Besos de fuego, Chucho sacando candela* y *Qué más puedo pedirle a la vida*.

Rodríguez, Jesusa ◆ n. en el DF (1955). Estudió en el Centro Universitario de Teatro (1973). Formó parte del grupo Sombras Blancas que puso *Vacío*, dirigida por Julio Castillo. Hizo escenografías para *Arde Pinocho*, *Qué formidable burdel*, de Ionesco dirigida por Castillo, *Sueño de una noche de verano, Madre judía* y *Claudine va a la escena*. Ha dirigido y protagonizado *El concilio del amor* (1988), de Óscar Panizza, obra que presentó en varios países europeos, al igual que la ópera de Mozart *Don Giovanni* o *Donna Giovanna*, sólo con mujeres que no eran intérpretes de *bel canto*. Dirigió y actuó la pastorela *El reino de Interpelandia* (1988, de Jaime Avilés). Es dueña de un cabaret donde monta obras suyas y de otros autores. Premio Julio Bracho de la Unión de Críticos y Cronistas de Teatro por *Atracciones Fénix*, como la mejor obra de teatro de búsqueda en 1986. Obtuvo la Beca Guggenheim 1990-91.

Rodríguez, Joaquín María ◆ n. y m. en Jalapa, Ver. (1855-1912). Profesor por la Escuela Normal de Orizaba. Antirreeleccionista, se dedicó al periodismo y fue director de *El Gato Negro, El Eco Jalapeño* y *El Orden*. Dramaturgo, autor de *Apuntes sobre el cantón de Jalapa* (1895) y de varios textos escolares.

Ismael Rodríguez

Rodríguez, José ◆ n. en Satevó y m. en Madera, Chihuahua. (1892-1915). Tomó las armas en 1912 para combatir la rebelión de Pascual Orozco y en 1913 se unió a la revolución constitucionalista. Participó en la fundación de la División del Norte villista y en los combates de Torreón, Chihuahua, Ciudad Juárez, Tierra Blanca y Ojinaga. En 1914 fue nombrado comandante de la Brigada Villa, con la que participó en las tomas de Torreón, San Pedro de las Colonias y Paredón y en el ataque a Zacatecas. Al producirse la escisión revolucionaria permaneció en el villismo. En diciembre de 1914 derrotó a Jacinto B. Treviño. En 1915 combatió en Guadalajara y Cuesta de Sayula. Fue enviado al noreste y trató infructuosamente de tomar Matamoros. Se reincorporó a las fuerzas que Villa dirigía en Sonora y tomó Cananea, plaza de la que fue desalojado por Plutarco Elías Calles. Fue aprehendido y fusilado por Margarito Márquez, uno de sus ex soldados.

Jesusa Rodríguez

Rodríguez, José ◆ m. en Cuautla, Mor. (?-1926). En 1911 se unió al Ejército Libertador del Sur y combatió en Morelos, Guerrero y el Distrito Federal. El 10 de abril de 1919 fue comisionado por Emiliano Zapata para vigilar las inmediaciones de la hacienda de Chinameca. Luego del asesinato del jefe suriano, siguió la lucha hasta 1920, cuando se incorporó al ejército federal con el grado de general de brigada. Causó baja en el ejército pero se incorporó a la colonia militar establecida en Chinameca.

Ofrenda floral, fotografía de José Ángel Rodríguez

Rodríguez, José Ángel ◆ n. en Peñón Blanco, Dgo. (1957). Fotógrafo. Laboratorista de los talleres del Club Fotográfico de México, donde tomó un curso de capacitación básica con Alejandro Parodi (1971-74). Fotógrafo independiente (1975-76), trabajó con Manuel Álvarez Bravo en la impresión de portafolios de archivo (1977 y 79) y vivió en las zonas indígenas huichol, cora y tepehuán (1978). Colaboró con la SEP en la realización de libros de texto bilingües (1980). Colaboró en la documentación gráfica de la costa atlántica de Nicaragua con el Ministerio de Cultura de ese país (1980). Radicado en Chiapas desde 1981, ha fotografiado las comunidades de las selvas chiapanecas y los campamentos de refugiados (1982-85). Colaboró en la revista *Ámbar*. Desde 1974 ha expuesto en México y otros países.

Mi otro yo, grabado en madera de José Julio Rodríguez

Rodríguez, José Antonio ◆ n. en el DF (1961). Licenciado en ciencias de la comunicación por la UNAM. Estudió cine y conservación de fotografía. Fundó y coordinó el Archivo Histórico y Fotográfico de Tabasco (1984-87), ha sido investigador del proyecto Historia de la Fotografía en Querétaro (1987-89), subdirector del Museo Estudio Diego Rivera (1989-92), investigador y curador independiente especializado en fotografía mexicana (1992-) y editor de la revista *Alquimia* del Sistema Nacional de Fototecas del INAH (1997-). Colaborador, entre otras publicaciones, de *El Financiero* (1990-), *Luna Córnea* (1992-), *El Nacional Dominical*, *Memoria de Papel*, *Artes de México*, *Los Universitarios*, *Fotozoom*, *Anuario del Centro de Investigaciones Históricas de la Universidad Veracruzana* y de la *Enciclopedia de México*. Autor de *Martín Ortiz, fotógrafo. El último de los románticos* (1992), *Manuel Álvarez Bravo. Los años decisivos. 1925-1945* (1992), *Corazón de mi corazón. Trece años de fotografía polaroid de Lourdes Almeida* (1993), *Manuel Álvarez Bravo y la fotografía mexicana de medio siglo* (1996), *Juan Crisóstomo Méndez Ávalos, 1885-1902, fotógrafo de Puebla* (1996), *Bernice Kolko, fotógrafa* (1997) y *10 Mexican Photographers, A Select-End-of-Century Generation* (EUA, 1999).

Rodríguez, José Guadalupe ◆ n. y m. en el estado de Durango (?-1929). Miembro del comité central del Partido Comunista Mexicano y tesorero de la Liga Nacional Campesina. Maestro rural en Durango, hacia 1920 se convirtió en dirigente agrarista. Durante la rebelión escobarista formó grupos de campesinos que apoyaron a las fuerzas gubernamentales, pese a lo cual fue asesinado por Manuel Medinaveitia, jefe de operaciones en Durango. En su libro *Quince años de política mexicana*, Emilio Portes Gil dijo: "El general Manuel Medinaveitia, comandante militar en aquel estado, ordenó el fusilamiento, sin formación de causa, del jefe agrarista Guadalupe Rodríguez, a quien se acusaba de haber mandado herrar con la hoz y el martillo cierta partida de mulas propiedad de un rico hacendado. Existía la circunstancia de que ya la rebelión escobarista estaba totalmente vencida y no había razón alguna que justificara procedimiento tan riguroso."

Rodríguez, José Julio ◆ n. en San Miguel de Allende, Gto. (1912). Grabador. Estudió en la Academia de Bellas Artes de Querétaro y en la Escuela de Artes del Libro, de la ciudad de México, donde fue profesor de dibujo y grabado desde 1947. Realizó su primera exposición individual en 1940 y cinco años después fundó la Academia de Artes Plásticas de Guanajuato. En 1941 fundó una galería con el patrocinio del Sindicato Mexicano de Electricistas. Participó en el Salón Anual de Grabado (1941). Ha montado exposiciones en la República Federal de Alemania, México, Yugoslavia, Suiza, Italia y Estados Unidos. Autor de la monografía *Francisco Díaz de León como pintor, dibujante y artista gráfico*. Miembro fundador de la Sociedad Mexicana de Grabadores. Ganó en 1958 el premio nacional de Grabado del Salón de la Plástica Mexicana.

Rodríguez, José M. ◆ n. en Torreón, Coah., y m. ¿en el DF? (?-?). Médico cirujano. En 1913 se incorporó a la revolución constitucionalista, movimiento al que representó en San Antonio Texas. Fue presidente municipal de Torreón, diputado al Congreso Constituyente de 1916-17 y jefe del Departamento de Salubridad.

Rodríguez, Joselito ◆ n. y m. en el DF (1907-1985). Cineasta. Introductor del cine sonoro en México. Argumentista, editor, actor y director. Luego de un entrenamiento en Hollywood construyó un aparato de sonorización de películas que puso a prueba con el filme *Sangre mexicana*. Grabó el sonido de las cintas *Santa* (1931), *El anónimo*, *El prisionero número 13*, *Bajo el cielo de México*, *El Tigre de Yautepec*, *El fantasma del convento*, *Una vida con otra*, *Revolución* y *Sobre las olas*. Fue productor de cintas realizadas por él u otros directores, como *¡Ay Jalisco no te rajes!* (1941, ganadora de seis Arieles). Dirigió *El secreto del sacerdote* (1940), *Angelitos negros* (1948 y 1969) *¡Y murió por nosotros!* o *Jesús de Nazareth* (1951), *Huracán Ramírez* (1952), *Santo contra los hombres infernales* (1958) *Dos diablillo en apuros* y *Pepito, as del volante*.

Rodríguez, Juan Manuel ◆ n. en Álamos, Son., y m. en Pitorreal, Chih. (1780-1828). Vivió en el estado de Chihuahua donde se dedicó al comercio y la minería. En 1824 fue diputado al Congreso Constituyente del estado, desempeñó algunos puestos públicos y llegó a ser magistrado del Supremo Tribunal de Justicia. Electo gobernador constitucional de Chihuahua, murió antes de asumir el cargo.

Rodríguez, Lorenzo ◆ n. en España y m. en la ciudad de México (1704-1774). Aprendió arquitectura trabajando con su padre, maestro mayor de Reales Alcázares y Fábrica del Obispado de Guadix, en la construcción de las catedrales de Guadix y de Cádiz. Llegó a la Nueva España aproximadamente en 1731 y realizó las puertas de la Casa de Moneda. En 1740 se graduó como arquitecto y dos años más tarde construyó la Casa de los Virreyes, en Huehuetoca. Fue veedor de arquitectura (1744) y constructor del Sagrario Metropolitano (1749-68). Maestro mayor de la Catedral, del Real Palacio y de la Inquisición (1758), realizó las portadas de la Real y Pontificia Universidad (1760), hizo la casa del Conde de Xala, en la actual calle de Venustiano Carranza (1763), reedificó el Colegio de Niñas (1768) e hizo la portada exterior de la Capilla del Colegio de las Vizcaínas (1772). De él se ha dicho que "es el definidor del estípite y quien lo impone en la Nueva España". Probablemente también sean obra suya el edificio de la Acordada y la iglesia de San Felipe Neri (inmuebles ya desaparecidos), la portada lateral de la iglesia de San Francisco, la de Santa Catalina y la de la Santísima Trinidad, así como el templo de San Francisco, en San Miguel de Allende, y el de San Martín, en Tepozotlán.

Rodríguez, Luis Ángel ◆ n. en Toluca, Edo. de Méx. (1893-?). Licenciado en derecho por la Universidad Nacional (1919), especializado en derecho penal. Fue magistrado del Tribunal Superior de Justicia del Estado de México durante la gubernatura de Isidro Fabela. Autor de *Mosaicos, cuentos y crónicas de la guerra* (1923), *Mi pozo en el desierto* (poesía, 1928), *Jaulas y pájaros de amor. Veinticinco estampas del vicio en México* (1934), *Nakria. Mala vida de una mujer buena* (1936), *La monja alférez. Novela histórica americana. Su vida y hazañas* (1937), *Las grandes muertes de la historia* (1938), *Un viento de otoño* (1942), *Carlos III. El rey católico que decretó la expulsión de los jesuitas* (1944), *La ciencia médica de los aztecas* (1944) y *La agonía de un imperio* (novela, 1947).

Rodríguez, Luis I. ◆ n. en Silao, Gto., y m. en el DF (1905-1973). Licenciado en derecho por la Universidad de Guanajuato (1929), de la que fue profesor y rector. Fue el primer presidente del Partido de la Revolución Mexicana (1938-39). Diputado local (1930) y federal (1934-36) por Baja California Sur, secretario de gobierno en el territorio de Baja California (1933), secretario particular de Lázaro Cárdenas (1935-37) y coautor del Plan Sexenal, gobernador de Guanajuato (1937-38), embajador en Francia (1940), Chile (1942-46), Guatemala (1951), Canadá y Venezuela (1961-65) y senador (1952-58). Autor de *Veinte discursos, Francia, la del espolón quebrado, Refugiados sin refugio* y *Ballet de sangre* (ensayo, 1942).

Rodríguez, Marcelino ◆ n. en San Pablo Hidalgo, Mor., y m. en San Felipe Coapexco, Pue. (?-1917). En marzo de 1911 se unió a la insurrección maderista en las fuerzas de Francisco Mendoza, con quien participó en el asalto y toma de Cuautla. Fue parte de la escolta de Mendoza y más tarde comandó una guerrilla, con la que combatió sucesivamente a Madero, Huerta y Carranza. En 1914 Emiliano Zapata lo ascendió a general brigadier. Murió en combate contra las fuerzas de Fortunato Maycotte.

Foto: Imcine

Joselito y Roberto Rodríguez

Rodríguez, María Teresa ◆ n. en Pachuca, Hgo. (1923). Estudió música con Antonio Gómezanda (1930-38). Se inició profesionalmente en 1931, a los ocho años de edad, tocando en piano obras de Beethoven, Bach, Mozart, Chopin y Debussy. Se graduó como concertista a los 14 años (1937). De 1945 a 1948 se especializó en Estados Unidos con Alexandr Borovsky y en 1947 ganó un concurso en Boston, cuyo premio fue el ser solista de la sinfónica de esa ciudad, dirigida por Arthur Fiedler. Regresó a México y fue becada por Carlos Chávez, entonces director del INBA. Estudió en España y Estados Unidos (1952-54) y ofreció conciertos en Inglaterra, España, Holanda y Alemania. Regresó a México en 1954 y ofreció recitales con casi todas las orquestas del país. Ha sido profesora del Conservatorio de Querétaro (1941-60), solista de la Orquesta Filarmónica de la UNAM y profesora (1966) y directora (1988-91) del Conservatorio Nacional. En 1981 ganó la Lira de Oro del Sindicato Único de Trabajadores de la Música del DF y en 1986 la Universidad Veracruzana creó el Concurso de Piano María Teresa Rodríguez.

Foto: Fondo Histórico Alfonso Sánchez García

Luis Ángel Rodríguez

Luis I. Rodríguez

Pedro L. Rodríguez

Rodríguez, Matías ◆ n. en Tetepango y m. ¿en Pachuca, Hgo.? (1876-?). Antirreeleccionista, se unió a la revolución con las fuerzas de Nicolás Flores, en las que alcanzó el grado de coronel. Fue diputado al Congreso Constituyente de 1916-17, diputado federal (1918-20), senador por Hidalgo (1922-26) y gobernador de ese estado (1925-29). Durante su gestión fue inaugurada la carretera México-Pachuca (1926) y se inició la construcción de caminos estatales y de la presa La Estanzuela; combatió a los núcleos cristeros que operaban en la entidad, ocupó templos católicos, cerró escuelas religiosas, clausuró conventos y obligó a los ministros de culto a registrarse ante las autoridades.

Rodríguez, Nicolás ◆ n. en Chihuahua y m. en EUA (?-1940). Se unió a las fuerzas de Francisco Villa, en cuya División del Norte alcanzó el grado de general brigadier. Durante la presidencia de Álvaro Obregón acompañó a Enrique Estrada en su infructuosa campaña en Baja California. En marzo de 1934 fundó el grupo fascista Camisas Doradas (☛ *Acción Revolucionaria Mexicanista*). Al año siguiente de un enfrentamiento con el Partido Comunista, provocado por los Camisas Doradas el 20 de noviembre de 1935, Rodríguez fue expulsado del país. Se estableció en Mission, Texas, y desde ahí, en nombre de su grupo, a principios de 1938 lanzó un manifiesto dirigido "a la nación" en el que llamaba a la rebelión. Sus bandas armadas atacaron varios puntos fronterizos, pero fueron rechazadas por la población local. En mayo, al estallar la rebelión acaudillada por Saturnino Cedillo, a quien le había prometido apoyo, dejó Missión acompañado de su asesor principal, un coronel nazi de apellido Von Merck, trató de conseguir armamento en Estados Unidos e hizo lanzar volantes de propaganda hitleriana sobre la franja fronteriza, pero su muerte repentina disgregó sus fuerzas.

Rodríguez, Nicolás ◆ n. en España y m. en el DF (1914-1966). Llegó exiliado a México en 1943. Actor, inició su carrera cinematográfica en la película *La señorita de Trévelez* (1935), a la que siguieron *Sierra de Teruel*, *Miércoles de ceniza* (1958), *Mientras el cuerpo aguante* (1958), *Cuenta de una mujer* (1958), *Jugándose la vida* (1959), *Los jóvenes* (1960) y *Cri-Cri, el grillito cantor* (19-63). Actuó también en televisión.

Rodríguez, Óscar ◆ n. en el DF (1943). Estudió en la Escuela de Artes Decorativas (1961-62), La Esmeralda (1965-67), el Taller de Grabado de la Universidad Benito Juárez de Oaxaca (1972) y en el Pratt Graphic Center de Nueva York (1972). Participó en la fundación del Taller Libre de Artes Plásticas de la Universidad de Oaxaca. Ha hecho escenografías para cine y teatro y participó en el primer Salón de Tapiz (1970), la primera Bienal de Arte de Morelia (1974), primera Bienal Iberoamericana (1978) y en el primer Salón Mexicano de Arte Erótico (1979). Ha expuesto individual y colectivamente en México, Estados Unidos, España, Canadá y otros países. Miembro del Salón de la Plástica Mexicana. Premio Primera Etapa del Concurso Nacional de Escultura (1981), premio de adquisición del Salón Nacional de Artes Plásticas del INBA (1981) y premio del Salón de la Plástica Mexicana (1985).

Rodríguez, Pedro ◆ n. en el DF y m. en la RFA (1940-1971). Piloto de autos de carreras. Estudió en el Western Military College, de Alton, Estados Unidos. Fue campeón infantil de ciclismo (1951 y 52) y campeón nacional de motociclismo (1954 y 55). En 1955 se inició en las competencias automovilísticas, en el circuito de Avándaro. En 1961, él y su hermano Ricardo obtuvieron el segundo lugar en el Gran Premio de Canadá y participaron en las 24 horas de Le Mans en 1961 y 1962. Ganó las competencias de los 1,000 kilómetros de París y el Gran Premio de Sudáfrica (1967), las 24 horas de Le Mans (1968, donde impuso una marca de velocidad que no ha sido superada), el Gran Premio de Bélgica (donde también marcó un récord de velocidad que no ha sido roto), las 24 horas de Daytona (1967, 68, 69 y 70), los 1,000 kilómetros de Brands Hatch, las seis horas de Watkins Gleen y los 1,000 kilómetros de Monza (1970 y 71), de Francorchamp (1971) y de Austria (1971). Murió en la carrera de las 200 millas de Alemania.

Rodríguez, Pedro L. ◆ n. en Etla, Oax., y m. en la ciudad de México (1841-1918). Radicado en Hidalgo, construyó la línea telegráfica México-Pachuca (1871), fue diputado local, jefe de la Oficina de Telégrafos de Tulancingo y gobernador interino (1897-1901) y constitucional del estado (1901-05, 1905-09 y 1909-11).

Rodríguez, Ricardo ◆ n. y m. en el DF (1942-1962). Piloto de autos de carreras. Hermano del también corredor Pedro Rodríguez. Participó en competencias de ciclismo infantil. Fue campeón nacional de motociclismo (1956). En 1957, a los 15 años de edad, participó y triunfó en su primera carrera automovilística internacional, en California. Ganó las 24 Horas de Le Mans. Murió durante una práctica en el autódromo de la Magdalena Mixhuca, que ahora lleva el nombre de Hermanos Rodríguez.

Rodríguez, Roberto ◆ n. y m. en el DF (1909-1995). Cineasta. Hermano de Ismael y Joselito Rodríguez. Hizo estudios de fotografía y decoración en México. Emigró a EUA con sus hermanos al comenzar la guerra cristera y estudió en la Brooklyn High School. Vivió en Los Ángeles (1926-30), donde trabajó en la industria del cine de Hollywood y patentó, con su hermano Joselito, un sistema de sonido: el Rodríguez Sound Recording System, empleado por ellos en un filme experimental, *Sangre mexicana*, y, de vuelta en México, en *Santa* (1931), la primera película sonora mexicana. Después de trabajar como sonidista de numerosas películas, se inició como productor y director con *Viviré otra vez* (1939) y, siempre junto con sus hermanos, fundó la empresa Producciones Rodríguez, que ganó notoriedad al hacer varias de las películas más famosas protagonizadas por Pedro

Infante. Además de *La sonrisa de la virgen* (1957, Hoja de Roble en el Festival de Mar del Plata, San Teodoro de Oro en la Muestra de Venecia) y *El billetero* (1983, premio en el Festival de Moscú), destacan de su filmografía *¡Viva mi desgracia!* (1943), *La mujer que yo perdí* (1949), *El seminarista* (1949), *Mamá nos quita los novios* (1951), *Tres balas perdidas* (1960) y *Caperucita Roja y Pulgarcito contra los monstruos* (1960).

RODRÍGUEZ, TRINIDAD ◆ n. en Huejotitlán, Chih., y m. en Zacatecas, Zac. (1882-1914). En 1912 tomó las armas para combatir a Pascual Orozco y en 1913 se levantó en Chihuahua contra la usurpación huertista. Se integró a la División del Norte y participó en los principales combates villistas: Chihuahua, Ciudad Juárez, Tierra Blanca, San Pedro de las Colonias y Paredón. Murió durante la toma de Zacatecas.

RODRÍGUEZ ACEVES, GLORIA ◆ n. en el DF (1926). Profesora normalista. Ha sido secretaria de acción femenil en el comité de la Sierra Norte de Puebla (1961-63) y secretaria de asuntos obreros (1963), del PPS; fundadora de los Sindicatos de Autotransportes Teziutecos (1966), dirigente del Sindicato de Industrias Icas y diputada federal plurinominal (1988-91).

RODRÍGUEZ ADAME, JULIÁN ◆ n. en Pachuca, Hgo., y m. en el DF (1904-1989). Ingeniero agrónomo por la Escuela Nacional de Agricultura de Ciudad Juárez, se especializó en comercio internacional y legislación agraria. Fue integrante de las comisiones agrarias en Colima, Jalisco, Veracruz y Tlaxcala, director general de Agricultura (1934), director de la Escuela Central Agrícola, jefe del Departamento de Agronomía y jefe de crédito de la Secretaría de Agricultura y Ganadería; cofundador de la CNC (1938) y profesor de la UNAM (1939). Fue primer jefe del Departamento de Crédito y gerente general del Banco Nacional de Crédito Ejidal, secretario general del DAAC (1940-44). Exportador de algodón y director general de precios en la Secretaría de Economía Nacional (1951-52), diputado federal (1955-58), gerente de la Ceimsa (1957-58), senador (1958), secretario de Agricultura y Ganadería (del 1 de diciembre de 1958 al 30 de noviembre de 1964) de Adolfo López Mateos y embajador en Japón. Fue presidente de la ANIERM (1951-52) y presidente del Patronato del Instituto Mexicano de Recursos Naturales Renovables. Al morir era miembro del comité editorial de la revista *Comercio Exterior* y presidente del Patronato para el Fomento Académico del Colegio de Postgraduados de Chapingo.

RODRÍGUEZ AGUILAR, MANUEL ◆ n. en Culiacán, Sin., y m. en el DF (1910-1956). Ingeniero petrolero. Trabajó para la compañía El Águila y fue enviado después a Trinidad y Tobago y a la Royal Dutch, de Holanda. En 1938, al producirse la expropiación petrolera, acudió a la embajada mexicana en La Haya para ofrecer sus servicios; sin embargo, el embajador Padilla Nervo ignoró su oferta y Rodríguez volvió a su empleo en la Royal Dutch. En 1940 se le encomendó la jefatura de exploraciones de la empresa en las Indias Orientales Holandesas, a su paso por el continente americano en su viaje al oriente, recibió un telegrama de Pemex en el que se requerían sus servicios. Llegó a México y fundó, en 1943, el Departamento Central de Exploración y, más adelante, la Gerencia de Exploración de Pemex. Renunció después a la paraestatal mexicana y se desempeñó como consultor de diversos gobiernos hispanoamericanos. En 1949 se le designó delegado de México a la Asamblea Científica de las Naciones Unidas para el Estudio de la Conservación y Utilización de los Recursos Naturales.

RODRÍGUEZ ALCAINE, LEONARDO ◆ n. en Texcoco, Edo. de Méx. (1919). Líder obrero apodado *la Güera*. Miembro del PRI. Ha sido secretario general del Sindicato Único de Trabajadores Electricistas de la República Mexicana (1979-) y secretario general de la CTM (1997-). Fue presidente del Banco Obrero. Diputado por el Estado de México al Congreso de la Unión en tres ocasiones (1955-58, 1967-70, 1973-76) y dos veces senador (1976-82 y 1988-94).

RODRÍGUEZ ALCONEDO, JOSÉ LUIS ◆ n. en Puebla, Pue., y m. en Apan, en el actual Hidalgo (1762-1815). Maestro en platería en 1791, fue catedrático de la Academia de San Carlos. En 1794 cinceló los escudos de la Catedral, que fueron destruidos en 1823. En 1803 la Inquisición le abrió un proceso debido a sus simpatías hacia Francia. En 1808 habló de iniciar una revolución de independencia, fue delatado y encarcelado en España durante dos años. Regresó a México en 1810. Fue superintendente general de la casa de moneda y fundidor de arcabuces y cañones de los ejércitos de José María Morelos (de quien fue secretario particular) y de Ignacio López Rayón. Fue capturado en el asalto del realista Águila a Zacatlán y fusilado. En el Museo de Historia de Chapultepec se conserva un medallón de plata con la efigie de Carlos IV, realizado por él. Son obra suya los cuadros *San Pedro* y *Santa Teresa* (1801, con los que introdujo al país la técnica del pastel), *Autorretrato*, *Retrato de Fernando VII* y *Retrato de la señora Hernández Moro* (1809) y una serie, *Apostolado*, que se conserva en la ex hacienda de El Altillo. En 1799 recibió el título de académico de honor de la Academia de las Tres Nobles Artes de San Carlos.

RODRÍGUEZ ALEMÁN Y PEÑA, MANUEL ◆ n. en la ciudad de México y m. en Cuba (1783-1810). Sacerdote. Viajó a España en 1804. Al ocurrir la invasión napoleónica se puso al servicio de los franceses como empleado de la Secretaría de la Inspección General de los Ejércitos Franceses. Estuvo en Valencia a las órdenes de Moncey y con José Bonaparte en la campaña del Ebro, fue intérprete del príncipe de Newchatel y comisario de segunda clase. Acompañó a Bonaparte a Valladolid, donde fue ascendido a comisario de primera clase. Participó en las batallas de Talavera y Almonacid, fue herido en esta última y pidió su retiro, aunque Bonaparte lo

Julián Rodríguez Adame

Leonardo Rodríguez Alcaine

José Luis Rodríguez Alconedo

Fernando Rodríguez

Octavio Rodríguez Araujo

hizo comisario ordenador y lo envió a México como espía. Pasó a Inglaterra y Estados Unidos, antes de llegar a Cuba (1810), donde fue detenido como conspirador, juzgado y ejecutado.

Rodríguez Alonso, Ceferino ◆ n. en España y m. en el DF (1880-1956). Colaboró en las publicaciones *El Diario Universal*, *Madrid Cómico*, *El Imparcial*, *Nuevo Mundo*, *Blanco y Negro* y *ABC*, de su país. Al término de la guerra civil española pasó a Francia y de ahí vino a México, donde prosiguió su actividad periodística en *Excélsior* y otros órganos. Autor de *Los crepúsculos*, *Rincón de humildes*, *La sombra enmascarada*, *Noche de feria* y el drama *La condenada*.

Rodríguez Álvarez, Fernando ◆ n. en el DF (1957). Diseñador gráfico de la Comisión de Información y Propaganda del Partido Comunista (1979), de Ediciones de Cultura Popular y Discos Fotón (1980), de la Comisión de Impresos y Publicaciones del PSUM (1981) y de la Dirección de Publicaciones del IPN (1983), jefe de diseño de Tipografía, Diseño e Impresión (1984) y cofundador de Equipo Editor (1986). Ha diseñado las revistas *Ensayos*, *Notirsas*, *Confluencias*, *Informe Bibliográfico*, *Revista Internacional*, *El Economista Mexicano*, *Cero en Conducta*, *Zurda*, *Utopías*, *Socialismo*, *Tierra Nuestra*, *Kiosco*, *Epitafios*, *Dialéctica*, *El Séptimo Sueño* y *Memoria*; carteles para el PCM, PSUM, PMS, PRD, PRT, la UAM, las facultades de Economía y Filosofía y Letras, Movimiento Mexicano por la Paz, FDR-FMLN de El Salvador, Radio Venceremos, Sindicato de Trailmobile, Comité de la Nueva Canción, Unión de Vecinos y Damnificados 19 de Septiembre y la COCEI; y portadas, tipografía, logotipos e ilustraciones para libros en las editoriales del IPN, Ediciones de Cultura Popular, UNICEF, Anfión, Universidad Autónoma de Chapingo, INBA, Factor, Nuevomar, INI, Medios Útiles, Probosque, Claves Latinoamericanas y el Instituto de Cultura de Tabasco. Segundo premio del concurso de carteles conmemorativos del bicentenario de la revolución francesa (1989) y primera mención del concurso de cartel del XXIII Foro Internacional de la Cineteca (1990).

Rodríguez Arangoity, Emilio ◆ n. y m. en la ciudad de México (1833-1891). Ingeniero militar. Luchó al lado de los liberales en la guerra de los Tres Años y contra la intervención francesa y el imperio. Fue el encargado de fortificar los cerros de Guadalupe y Loreto para la batalla del 5 de mayo, durante la cual tuvo a su cargo la artillería republicana. En 1863 participó en el sitio de Puebla, fue aprehendido y conducido a Francia. Regresó a México en 1864 y se reincorporó al ejército republicano en 1866. Participó en el sitio de Perote y en la batalla del 2 de abril, así como en el sitio de la ciudad de México. Benito Juárez le extendió un diploma "por su acendrado patriotismo y sus buenos y leales servicios a la causa nacional de la guerra extranjera".

Rodríguez Arangoity, Juan María ◆ n. y m. en la ciudad de México (1828-1894). Hermano del anterior. Médico obstetra, trajo a México las técnicas de la tocología. Fue profesor en las escuelas nacionales Preparatoria y de Medicina. En 1867 se integró a la Academia Nacional de Medicina, que presidió hasta 1884. Colaboró en la *Gaceta Médica de México*. Autor de *Breves consideraciones sobre las condiciones higiénicas de las maternidades*, *Cuadro sinóptico de obstetricia* y *Manual del arte de los partos*.

Rodríguez Arangoity, Ramón ◆ n. y m. en la ciudad de México (1830-1882). Hermano de los anteriores. Arquitecto. Era alumno del Colegio Militar cuando participó en la batalla de Chapultepec de 1847. Se graduó como doctor en matemáticas en la Universidad de Roma (1855). Fue arquitecto imperial durante el gobierno de Maximiliano (1864-65) y tuvo a su cargo la remodelación del castillo de Chapultepec. Entre sus obras se cuentan el primer monumento a los Niños Héroes, en la ciudad de México (1882); la Catedral de Toluca y los edificios de los palacios Municipal, de Justicia y de Gobierno del Estado de México, que se construyeron en la década de 1880.

Rodríguez Araujo, Octavio ◆ n. en Puebla, Pue. (1941). Licenciado (1968) y doctor en ciencias políticas por la UNAM (1979), diplomado por la Universidad Victoria de Manchester (1970). En la UNAM ha sido profesor, investigador, asesor del rector (1985-88) y, dentro de la Facultad de Ciencias Políticas, coordinador del Centro de Investigaciones en Administración Pública (1977-78) y jefe de Posgrado (1979-84). Profesor de la UAEM (1974-78), del CIDE (1976-79) y del INAP (1980-84). Ha trabajado en Pemex (1969-74) y la SRE (1972-74). Escribe en *La Jornada*. Coautor de *El Partido Comunista Mexicano* (1973), *En el sexenio de Tlatelolco, 1964-1970*. *Acumulación de capital, Estado y clase obrera* (1984) y *Partidos y elecciones en México* (1986). Autor de *La reforma política y los partidos en México* (1979) y *Partidos políticos* (1986).

Rodríguez Arriaga, Manuel ◆ n. en Monterrey, NL (1949). Licenciado por la Escuela Libre de Derecho (1972), maestro en política por la Universidad de Essex (1975) y en administración pública por la Universidad de Warwick, Inglaterra (1976). Miembro del PRI. Ha sido director del Centro General de Documentación de la SEP (1976-77), subdirector de Relaciones Bilaterales y Organismos de Integración Económica de la Secretaría de Hacienda (1977-79), consejero para Asuntos Económicos en la misión de México ante la ONU (1979-81), consejero político de la embajada en EUA (1982), secretario particular (1983-85) y coordinador general de asesores del secretario de Relaciones Exteriores (1985-88), subsecretario de Cooperación Internacional de la SRE (1988-89) y embajador en Noruega (1989-1993), China (1993-) y Bélgica (1998-).

Rodríguez Baños, Roberto ◆ n. en Chiapas (1941). Se inició como periodista en *El Día* (1963). Ha trabajado en *Diario de México* (1965), *La República*, revista del PRI, y *La Prensa*. Fue jefe de información de la Agencia Mexicana de Noticias (Amex) y de la revista *Hoy* y colaborador de las agencias TASS, AFP, PL, IPS y APN, los diarios *Pravda*, *Izvestia*, *Rude Pravo* y *Granma* y las revistas *Marcha* y *Cuba Internacional*. Dirigió la revista *Plural* (1976-82) y el programa de televisión *Diorama*. Director del semanario *Excélsior and The New York Times Weekly Review*, el trimestral *Un Solo Mundo* y del programa *Enfoque Periodístico* (1982-91), del Canal 11, y su versión radiofónica (1987-91). Asesor editorial de la Presidencia (1973-76) y de la Secretaría del Trabajo y coordinador de información del INAH, la UNAM, la CNDH y otras instituciones. También ha sido miembro del consejo editorial de *Le Monde Diplomatique* (1982), colaborador de Notimex, de las revistas *Tiempo* e *Impacto* y de *El Nacional*, así como director adjunto a la presidencia de la Organización Editorial Mexicana (1992-94), coordinador de la colección Periodismo Cultural del CNCA, coordinador de comunicación social del Gobierno del DF (1998-99) y coordinador de edición de *unomásuno* (1999-).

RODRÍGUEZ BARRAGÁN, NEREO ◆ n. en Ciudad del Maíz y m. ¿en San Luis Potosí? SLP (1884-?). Fue director del *Periódico Oficial* de San Luis Potosí (1917-19) y de *El Heraldo* de la capital de ese estado (1919). Profesor del Instituto Científico y Literario potosino (1926-34). Trabajó en el Museo Nacional de Historia de la ciudad de México (1934-38) y fue director de la Biblioteca de la Universidad Potosina. Colaboró en *El Sol de San Luis*, *Acción*, *Estilo*, *Cuadrante* y *Letras Potosinas*. Autor de *Apuntes para la historia de la universidad en cien años de vida (1826-1926) con algunos datos históricos y estadísticos* (1936), *Relación de la revolución en San Luis Potosí formada por fray Luis Herrera, lego de San Juan de Dios, la noche del 10 al 11 de noviembre de 1810* (1944), *Apuntes para la historia y la geografía de la ciudad de Salinas en el estado de San Luis Potosí* (1947), *Síntesis biográfica del C. Juan Bustamante* (1951), *Dn. Pedro Barajas, primer obispo de San Luis Potosí* (1953), *Juárez y la princesa Salm-Salm* (1955), *Don Juan Bustamante, gobernador liberal de San Luis Potosí* (1956), *El canónigo Mauricio Zavala, apóstol del agrarismo en el valle del Maíz* (1958), *Mesa revuelta* (1961), *Rasgos biográficos del historiador potosino don Manuel Muro* (1965), *Juárez y Maximiliano* (1967), *Historia de San Luis Potosí* (1969) e *Historia y geografía del municipio de Rayón* (1972), entre otras obras.

RODRÍGUEZ BARRERA, RAFAEL ◆ n. en Campeche, Camp. (1937). Licenciado en derecho por la Universidad de Campeche (1958). Miembro del PRI, en el que ha sido presidente del Comité Directivo de Campeche (1962-64), representante ante la Comisión Federal Electoral (1971-72) y, en el CEN, secretario de Acción Política (1970-71), secretario de Organización (1971-72), secretario de Asuntos Internacionales (1974- 80), oficial mayor (1980-81) y secretario general (1988). En Campeche fue profesor del Instituto del estado (1956-61), notario, secretario auxiliar del Juzgado de lo Penal (1957-58), secretario del ayuntamiento (1959-61), profesor de la Universidad del Sudeste (1960), director de Tránsito y Seguridad Pública del gobierno de la entidad (1961-62), abogado asesor de la Cooperativa de Pulperos de la Sonda de Campeche (1961-63), diputado local (1962-64), abogado asesor de la Cámara Nacional de la Industria Pesquera (1964-66), asesor del Banco Nacional de Crédito Agrícola (1964-67), presidente del ayuntamiento (1965-66), gerente de la Cámara Pesquera (1966-67), secretario general de gobierno (1967-70) y gobernador (1973-79). Diputado federal (1970-73), subsecretario de Organización Agraria (1981-82), subsecretario de Asuntos Agrarios (1983-86), secretario de la Reforma Agraria (1986-88) y embajador en Israel (1988-91).

RODRÍGUEZ BARROSO, HUGO ◆ n. en el DF (1961). Nadador y alpinista. Licenciado en ciencias de la comunicación, en derecho y en economía, y maestro y doctor en administración. En las dos disciplinas deportivas que practica ha conquistado las máximas pruebas: cruzar el Canal de la Mancha (en 1986, fue el quinto mexicano en hacerlo, y en 1993) y llegar a la cima del Everest (1997). Rompió la marca mundial de distancia en nado de mariposa en alberca (20 kilómetros y medio en 1986) y en mar abierto, de Cozumel a Cancún (70 kilómetros en 1988); por estas dos pruebas ingresó en el libro *Guinnes*. También cruzó los 84 kilómetros del Canal de Yucatán en 1990. Como alpinista ha efectuado ascensos a las cumbres mexicanas del Iztaccíhuatl, el Popocatépetl y el Citlaltépetl, a varias cumbres en los Himalaya, al Mount Blanc, en Francia (1994), al Aconcagua, en Argentina (1995) y al Matterhorn, en Suiza (1995). Autor de *Everest: la voluntad a prueba* (1997). Premio Nacional del Deporte (1986).

Rafael Rodríguez Barrera

RODRÍGUEZ BELTRÁN, CAYETANO ◆ n. en Tlacotalpan y m. en Jalapa, Ver. (1866-1939). Fue profesor en las escuelas Juan Enríquez y Especial de Comercio, de Jalapa. Director de Educación Federal de Veracruz, inspector de la SEP y director de la Escuela secundaria y preparatoria de Jalapa. Colaborador de *El Correo de Sotavento*, *México Intelectual*, *El Mundo Ilustrado*, *Don Quijote*, *El Mundo* (de La Habana) y director de *La Idea Liberal*, órgano del Partido Gómez Farías. Utilizó los pseudónimos de *Licenciado Vidriera* y *Onateyac*. Autor de *Una docena de cuentos* (1900), *Atrevimientos ¿literarios?* (1901), *Perfiles del terruño* (1902), *Cuentos costeños* (1905), *Por mi heredad* (1906), *Pajarito* (1908), *Un ingenio* (1919) y *Cuentos y tipos callejeros* (1922). Fue miembro correspondiente en Veracruz, Veracruz, de la Academia Mexicana (de la Lengua).

Cayetano Rodríguez Beltrán

RODRÍGUEZ CABO, MATILDE ◆ n. en Ciudad de las Palmas, SLP, y m. en el DF (1902-1967). Esposa de Francisco J. Múgica. Estudió medicina en la UNAM (1929) y se especializó en psiquiatría en la Universidad de Berlín (1929-30). En Alemania se le comisionó para estudiar las guarderías de la URSS. A su regreso a México fue magistrada del Consejo

Supremo de Prevención Social, jefa del Departamento de Prevención Social, encargada de los niños con deficiencia mental del manicomio La Castañeda, promotora de los desayunos escolares gratuitos, directora de Asistencia a la Niñez, inspectora de las escuelas de enfermería de la UNAM y miembro del Frente Único pro Derechos de la Mujer. Colaboró en la revista *Criminalia*. Autora de *La organización soviética de protección a la madre y al niño* (1929), *Esquema de la protección a la madre y al niño en la Unión Soviética* (1929), *Los procedimientos de medición mental en su aplicación* (1935), *La eutanasia en los anormales* (1935), *Los tribunales para menores en el Distrito Federal y sus instituciones auxiliares* (1936), *Normas generales para la ejecución de sanciones* (1936), *El control de la natalidad* (1937), *La lucha contra la prostitución en la URSS* (1937), *La situación de las obreras en México* (1938), *La mujer trabajadora* (1938), *La prostitución en México* (1939), *Cómo debe ser la nueva cárcel* (1959) y *Breve informe sobre la situación actual de la mujer mexicana* (1959), entre otras obras.

Rodríguez Cabrera, Rufino ◆ n. en Ciudad Ixtepec, Oax. (1952). Licenciado en antropología social por la ENAH (1985). Integrante de la COCEI (1974-) y miembro fundador del PRD (1989-), es miembro de su Consejo Nacional (1990-). Ha sido profesor en la UABJO (1977-82) y diputado federal plurinominal (1991-94). Coautor de *Medio milenio* (1988).

Rodríguez Cabrillo, Juan ◆ n. en Portugal y m. en San Miguel, en el actual territorio de EUA (¿1495?-1543). Llegó a la Nueva España en 1520, con la expedición de Pánfilo de Narváez. Se unió a las fuerzas de Hernán Cortés, participó en la expedición de Orozco a Oaxaca e intervino en la conquista de Guatemala, dirigida por Pedro de Alvarado (1523). En 1542, por órdenes del virrey Antonio de Mendoza, encabezó una expedición que costeó Baja California, tomó posesión del puerto de San Quintín, descubrió la bahía de San Diego, las islas del Farallón y la de Santa Catalina, el canal de Santa Bárbara y la isla de San Miguel, donde Rodríguez Cabrillo se fracturó una pierna. La expedición continuó, alcanzó las montañas de Santa Lucía y el Punto Reyes y regresó hasta descubrir la bahía de Monterrey. Sin recuperarse de la fractura, Rodríguez Cabrillo desembarcó en San Miguel, donde murió.

Rodríguez Calderón, Carlos J. ◆ n. en Jalapa, Ver., y m. en EUA (1865-1912). Egresado de la Escuela Normal de Orizaba, fundó la Escuela Práctica anexa a la Normal Veracruzana de Jalapa. Fue director del Instituto Particular de Tulancingo. El gobierno lo pensionó para especializarse en pedagogía en Estados Unidos, donde fundó una escuela. Autor de un *Tratado de pedagogía*.

Rodríguez Calderón, Guillermo ◆ n. y m. en Jalapa, Ver. (1876-1944). Egresado de la Escuela Nacional de Jurisprudencia, en Veracruz se desempeñó como juez de primera instancia, agente del Ministerio Público, secretario del Tribunal Superior de Justicia del estado, juez instructor militar en Córdoba y procurador general de Justicia. Fue profesor de la Facultad de Leyes de Jalapa. Autor del drama *Blanco y negro*.

Rodríguez Calderón, Leopoldo C. ◆ n. en Jalapa, Ver., y m. en el DF (1870-1933). Profesor por la Escuela Normal Veracruzana. Con el pseudónimo de *Zenón Torres* colaboró en *La Opinión* de Veracruz. Fue profesor en diversas escuelas de Sonora, Coahuila y la ciudad de México, donde dirigió la Escuela Nacional de Maestros. Fundó las escuelas para niños anormales. Autor de *Principios sobre pedagogía* y *Tratado de psicología*.

Rodríguez Cano, Enrique ◆ n. en Balcázar, Ver., y m. en el DF (1912-1955). Fue presidente municipal de Tuxpan (1936), jefe de glosa del Congreso de Veracruz (1938-40), director de la Biblioteca del Congreso de la Unión (1940-42), diputado local (1944-45), secretario general de la Liga de Comunidades Agrarias (1946) y subsecretario de gobierno de Veracruz (1948); diputado federal (1949), oficial mayor de la Secretaría de Gobernación (1946-52) y secretario del presidente Adolfo Ruiz Cortines.

Rodríguez Caracalla, Francisco ◆ n. en Mascota, Jal. (1907). Pintor y escultor. Dejó la carrera de derecho para ingresar en la Escuela Libre de Pintura de Ixca Farías. Asistió al taller de José Vizcarra (1929-34). En 1934 se unió al grupo Pintores Jóvenes de Jalisco. En el Distrito Federal fue uno de los organizadores del taller Evolución, con Jorge Martínez, Ricardo Baeza y Juan Soriano. Fue ayudante de Orozco en la decoración del Hospicio Cabañas, del Palacio de Gobierno y de la Universidad de Guadalajara. Profesor de la Escuela de Bellas Artes de Guadalajara. Publicó en el periódico *Arte Nuevo* y en 1947 fue uno de los fundadores de la revista *Galerías* y de la Galería de Arte Moderno del DF. Decoró el Instituto Colón y dos hoteles de Guadalajara.

Rodríguez Carnero, José ◆ n. en la ciudad de México y m. en Puebla, Pue. (?-1725). Hijo del pintor Nicolás Rodríguez Carnero de Aguilar. En 1680 colaboró en la decoración del arco triunfal con que se recibió al virrey conde de Paredes, junto con Antonio de Alvarado. Solicitó en 1681 nuevas ordenanzas para los pintores, mismas que se promulgaron en 1687. La mayor parte de sus pinturas se conservan en la ciudad de Puebla. Son obra suya *Retrato del ilustrísimo señor don Manuel Fernández de Santa Cruz*, *Triunfo o apoteosis de la Compañía de Jesús*, *Santa Margarita* y *Santa Bárbara*, los cuadros de la capilla del Rosario (1690), los del templo de la Compañía de Jesús, de la Concordia (1693) y de la parroquia de Cholula.

Rodríguez Castañeda, Rafael ◆ n. en Pachuca, Hgo. (1940). Estudió en la Escuela Nacional de Maestros y en la Facultad de Derecho de la UNAM, antropología social en La Habana (1969) y planeación urbana en la Universidad de Edimburgo (1980). Ha sido reportero en Pachuca, maestro rural, investigador asistente en el Departamento de Antropología de la Universidad de Illinois (1966-67), coeditor del *Boletín ISSSTE* (1968), profesor en el Instituto de Humanidades de la UAEM (1972-73) y en la ENAP (1973-75), coordinador de ediciones de la UAM-Xochimilco (1975-76), consultor del Banco Interamericano de Desarrollo en Washington (1976-77), director de información del Sector de Asentamientos Humanos de la SPP (1977-80), y presidente del comité editorial (1987), así como profesor y jefe de actividades culturales de la UAM-X (1994-). Autor de cuento: *El descarrilado* (1979, Primer Premio en el Concurso de Cuento de la UNAM 1965); novela: *Viaje* (1991); y ensayo: *Cincuenta años del Cruz Azul 1931-1981* (1981) y *La Profesa. Patrimonio histórico y cultural* (1988). Fue becario del Centro Mexicano de Escritores (1964-65).

RODRÍGUEZ CASTAÑEDA, RAFAEL ◆ n. en el DF (1944). Licenciado en ciencias de la comunicación por la UNAM (1967). Ha sido reportero del semanario *Crucero* (1965), de la revista *Tiempo* (1966), redactor de la agencia Informac (1967), reportero y corrector de estilo de la revista *Mañana* (1967), corrector de estilo del periódico *El Día* (1968), redactor de la agencia Amex (1968-70); corrector de estilo y reportero (1970-74), corresponsal en Washington (1974-76) y coordinador de corresponsales extranjeros de *Excélsior* (1976). Profesor (1977-) y jefe del Área de Tecnología de la Información de la ENEP Acatlán, jefe de redacción de la edición vespertina del *Diario de México* (1976-77), secretario del consejo de administración de CISA-*Proceso*, cofundador y coordinador de información nacional (1976-79), jefe de redacción (1979-99) y director general de *Proceso* (1999-). Autor de *El asesinato de Orlando Letelier* (1979), *El viaje* (1991) y *¡Prensa vendida!* (1993).

RODRÍGUEZ CETINA, RAÚL ◆ n. en Mérida, Yuc. (1953). Escritor. Profesor normalista. Llegó en 1975 a la ciudad de México para estudiar cine, proyecto que abandonó para incorporarse al taller literario de Andrés González Pagés en el IPN. Fue jefe de redacción de la revista *Primera Plana*, de Mérida. Autor de las novelas *El desconocido* (1978), *Flash back* (1982), *Primer plano* (1984), *Alejamiento* (1987) y *Fallaste corazón* (1990).

RODRÍGUEZ CLAVERÍA, JOSÉ ◆ n. en Veracruz, Ver., y m. en el DF (1892-1958). En 1913 se unió a las fuerzas constitucionalistas de Salvador Alvarado, a quien acompañó a Yucatán cuando ocupó el gobierno de aquel estado y fue jefe de la policía meridana. En 1923 se unió a la rebelión delahuertista, por lo que tuvo que exiliarse en Estados Unidos. Fue director de Turismo en Veracruz y en el Distrito Federal, diputado federal y senador (1952-58).

RODRÍGUEZ COS, JOSÉ MARÍA ◆ n. en Tulancingo, en el actual Hidalgo, y m. en la ciudad de México (1823-1899). Profesor de la Escuela Normal y de la Escuela Nacional Preparatoria, así como profesor y director de un colegio de su propiedad. Participó en el Congreso Higiénico-Pedagógico (1882). Tradujo a Pablo Mantegazza. Autor de *Enciclopedia para la juventud*, *Elementos de aritmética* y *Elementos de gramática castellana*; de los poemarios *El Anáhuac* (1853) y *La Revolución francesa*; y del libreto de ópera *Cuauhtémoc*. Fue miembro de número de la Real Academia Española.

RODRÍGUEZ CHICHARRO, CÉSAR ◆ n. en España y m. en el DF (1930-1984). Fue traído en 1940 y se naturalizó mexicano. Licenciado y maestro en letras hispánicas por la UNAM (1959), de la que fue profesor, así como de las universidades de Guanajuato y Veracruzana, en México, y de Zulia, en Venezuela. En la Universidad Veracruzana fue director del Departamento Editorial y de la revista *La Palabra y el Hombre*. Autor de poesía: *Con una mano en el ancla* (1952), *Eternidad es barro* (1955), *La huella de tu nombre* (1955) y *Aguja de marear* (1973); antología: *Aventuras del miedo* (1962); y ensayo: *La novela indigenista mexicana* (1959), *Estudios literarios* (1963) y *Estudios de literatura mexicana* (1983). En 1963 recibió el segundo premio en el Concurso Cer- vantino del Instituto Tecnológico de Monterrey.

RODRÍGUEZ ELÍAS, JOSÉ ISABEL ◆ n. en Ciudad Cuauhtémoc, Zac., y m. en Morelia, Mich. (1917-1994). Fue presidente del PRI estatal, senador, gobernador de Zacatecas (1962-68), director del Banco de Crédito Ejidal y presidente nacional de la Vieja Guardia Agrarista.

RODRÍGUEZ FAMILIAR, RAMÓN ◆ n. en Querétaro, Qro., y m. en el DF (1898-1986). Militar. Entre 1914 y 1923 participó en 43 hechos de armas. En los años veinte fue secretario particular del gobernador de Baja California, Abelardo L. Rodríguez, quien al ocupar el Poder Ejecutivo Federal lo designó subjefe y jefe del Estado Mayor Presidencial (1932-34). Se desempeñó como director de Pensiones Militares, director general de Personal de la Secretaría de la Defensa Nacional, intendente general del Ejército, comandante de varias zonas militares y gobernador constitucional de Querétaro (1935-39). Durante su gestión permitió la reapertura de los templos, cerrados por su antecesor, Saturnino Osornio; volvió a funcionar el Colegio Civil (1936), puso en servicio un nuevo camino al Distrito Federal, reformó la impartición de justicia y repartió tierras, especialmente las del Plan de San Juan del Río, del Valle de Querétaro y el latifundio de Osornio, la hacienda de Tlacote. Al morir era general de división.

RODRÍGUEZ DE LA FUENTE, JESÚS ◆ n. en Nadadores, Coah., y m. en el DF (1894-1967). Licenciado en derecho por la Universidad Nacional (1916). En 1913 se unió al ejército constitucionalista, en el que fungió como oficial mayor del Cuerpo de Ejército de Oriente. Fue secretario general de gobierno en Puebla y Querétaro (1917) y jefe de la oficina jurídica del ayuntamiento del DF (1918). Diputado federal (1918-20), secretario general de gobierno del DF, oficial mayor de la Secretaría de Industria, Comercio y Trabajo, presidente

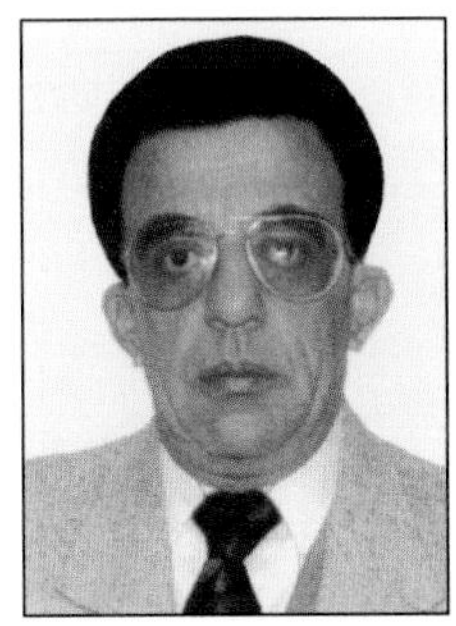

Rafael Rodríguez Castañeda

Novela de Raúl Rodríguez Cetina

municipal de Tacubaya (1923), nuevamente jefe de la oficina jurídica del DDF (1932-35), tesorero general de Nuevo León y secretario general de gobierno de Coahuila (1948).

Rodríguez de la Gala, Leandro ◆ n. y m. en Mérida, Yuc. (1814-1887). Doctor en teología por la Universidad de Yucatán (1855). Gobernador de la diócesis (1863-68) y obispo de Yucatán (1868). Promovió y consiguió la creación de la diócesis de Tabasco en 1880. En 1877 fue perseguido por violar las Leyes de Reforma y se le condenó a un mes de confinamiento fuera de Mérida.

OVACIONES

Francisco Rodríguez

Rodríguez Galván, Ignacio ◆ n. en Tizayuca, Hgo., y m. en Cuba (1816-1842). Escritor. Fue dependiente de la librería de su tío, Mariano Galván Rivera, editor del *Calendario de Galván*. De manera autodidáctica estudió latín y letras españolas, francesas e italianas. Colaboró en publicaciones literarias de Veracruz y en 1836 figuró entre los fundadores de la Academia de Letrán. Director del *Calendario de las señoritas megicanas* (1838). Con su hermano, Antonio Rodríguez Galván, fundó el periódico *Año Nuevo* y editó *El Recreo de las Familias*. José María Tornel, secretario de Guerra, le encomendó la redacción de la sección literaria del *Diario del Gobierno* (1841). Adscrito al cuerpo diplomático, fue enviado a Sudamérica; su primera escala fue en La Habana, donde murió de vómito negro. Tradujo autores franceses e italianos. Autor de novela y teatro: *La hija del oidor* (1836), *La capilla* (1837), *Manolito el pisaverde* (1838), *Muñoz, visitador de México* (1838), *La procesión* (1838), *Tras un mal nos vienen ciento* (1840), *El privado del virrey* (1842), *Bailad, bailad*, *El buitre* y *Nuño de Almazán*. De su poema *Adiós, oh, patria mía*, Vicente Riva Palacio hizo una paráfrasis que es la letra de la canción *Adiós mamá Carlota*.

La Iglesia triunfante, detalle del óleo sobre tela de Nicolás Rodríguez Juárez

Rodríguez García, Francisco ◆ n. en el DF (1953). Periodista. Estudió Ciencias de la Comunicación en la UNAM, de la que egresó en 1974. Columnista político de *El Heraldo de México* (1977-81), *Ovaciones* (1981-1987 y 1998-), *El Economista* (1987-88) y *El Sol de México* (1988-98). Director de la edición matutina de *Ovaciones* (1998-). Ha colaborado en *Impacto* (1979-85), *Siempre!* (1985-97) y *La Crisis*, del cual es codirector (1997-). Ha dirigido programas de Radio Chapultepec (1988), XEW Radio (1993-94) y ABC Radio (1993-94). Conductor del programa *Detrás de...* del Canal 13 de Imevisión (1985 y 1986).

Rodríguez García, Víctor Manuel ◆ n. en Puebla, Pue. (1933). Licenciado en relaciones internacionales por la UNAM (1955), con estudios de posgrado en El Colegio de México (1963-64). Ha sido canciller (1956-61) y vicecónsul (1961-62) en Sacramento, vicecónsul en Moscú (1964-65), tercer secretario de las embajadas en Ghana (1965-66) y Etiopía (1966-68), encargado interino de negocios de la embajada en Indonesia (1968-70), jefe del departamento y subdirector general de Servicios Diplomáticos (1971-76), embajador en Albania, Líbano, Chipre, Kuwait e Irak (1976-83), director general para Europa Oriental y la Unión Soviética (1983-85), director general del Servicio Exterior (1985-89), asesor del subsecretario A (1989-92), profesor del Instituto Matías Romero de Estudios Diplomáticos (1990-93), asesor del subsecretario B (1992-93) y coordinador de asesores de la Subsecretaría C (1993-) de la Secretaría de Relaciones Exteriores.

Rodríguez Jaime, Luis Dantón ◆ n. en Guanajuato, Gto. (1933). Licenciado en derecho por la UNAM (1958), con posgrados en el CEMLA de Venezuela (1962) y en la Escuela Bancaria Comercial (1962-63). Pertenece al PRI, del que ha sido coordinador en Guanajuato (1968), representante en San José de Costa Rica (1969), director general (1975-78) y miembro del consejo consultivo del IEPES (1979); subsecretario de acción política (1974) y secretario adjunto a la presidencia del CEN (1983). Miembro de los consejos técnicos de la CNC (1965) y de la CNOP (1970-82). Trabajó en la Secretaría de Hacienda (1959-63). Fue gerente regional del Banco Agropecuario del Centro (1967-71), gerente de crédito del Banco Nacional Agropecuario (1971-73), jefe de proyectos de Banrural (1973-79) y director general de gobierno de la Secretaría de Gobernación (1979-82). Cuatro veces diputado federal (1964-67, 1973-76, 1982-85 y 1991-94), fue presidente de la Cámara de Diputados (1966), secretario y presidente de la Gran Comisión del Congreso de la Unión (1973) y embajador en Italia (1988-91). Autor de *Obras y ensayos sobre la intervención del Estado en la economía* (1980).

Rodríguez Jorge, Luis Felipe ◆ n. en Mérida, Yuc. (1949). Astrónomo. Doctor en astronomía por la Universidad de Harvard (1978) e investigador titular del Instituto de Astronomía de la UNAM, del que fue director (1980-1986). Responsable de la unidad Morelia del Instituto de Radioastronomía de la UNAM. Además de ser el iniciador de la radioastronomía en México, es célebre por sus trabajos sobre la formación estelar, que lo han situado a la vanguardia de la investigación en la especialidad. Ha publicado muchos artículos científicos y obras de divulgación. Autor de *Un universo en expansión*. Ha ganado los premios Robert J. Tumpler, de la Sociedad Astronómica del Pacífico; Bruno Rossi, de la Sociedad Astronómica Americana; de Física de la Academia de Ciencias del Tercer Mundo, Universidad Nacional, Nacional de Ciencias y Ricardo J. Zevada (1999).

Rodríguez Juárez, Juan ◆ n. y m. en la ciudad de México (1675-1728). Se le llamaba el *Apeles mexicano*. Hay cuadros suyos en la Catedral Metropolitana, en el Museo Nacional de Historia, en la Pinacoteca Virreinal de San Diego, el Museo Nacional de Artes Plásticas, el Museo Regional de Guadalajara y en numerosas iglesias. Autor de los cuadros *Epifanía* (1693), *San Cristóbal* (1693), *Santa Gertrudis* (1693), *San Francisco Javier* (1693), *Virgen de San Juan* (1694), *Retrato de don Juan de Escalante* (1697), *Retrato del arzobispo Lanciego* (1714), *Retrato del virrey duque de Linares* (1717), *La educación de la Virgen* (1720), *Autorretrato* (1720), *Asun-*

ción (1720), *San José* (1724), *Retrato del virrey marqués de Casafuerte* (1726), *Adoración de los reyes* (1726), *San José* (1726) y *Santa Teresa* (1726).

Rodríguez Juárez, Nicolás ◆ n. y m. en la ciudad de México (1667-1734). Con su hermano Juan y el pintor Antonio de Torres, fue encargado de inspeccionar la tela original de la Virgen de Guadalupe (1721). La mayor parte de su obra se encuentra en diversos templos del país. Autor de los cuadros *Ángel* (1690), *El profeta Isaías* (1690), *Retrato del niño Fernández de Santa Cruz* (1695), *El triunfo de la iglesia* (1695), *Magdalena penitente* (1718) y un *San Cristobalón* (1722).

Rodríguez Lapuente, Manuel ◆ n. en el DF (1927). Graduado en la Escuela Libre de Derecho (1951) y doctor en derecho por la Universidad Complutense de Madrid (1953). Miembro de las juventudes del PAN y promotor de un movimiento democristiano en ese partido. En 1988 fue candidato a diputado por el Frente Democrático Nacional y al año siguiente cofundador del PRD, de cuyo comité estatal en Jalisco es presidente (1992-). Fundador (1963) y director (1963-65) del Instituto Técnico de Estudios Sindicales; y profesor en la Universidad de Querétaro (1965-67). En la Universidad de Guadalajara ha sido profesor, director del Seminario de Derecho Internacional (1972-80), del Instituto de Estudios Sociales (1976-83 y 1989-) y de la *Revista de la Universidad de Guadalajara* (1976-83), comentarista de Radio Universidad (1976-89) y director de la Facultad de Filosofía y Letras (1983-88). Presidente fundador de la Academia Jalisciense de Derechos Humanos (1990-). Colaborador de *uno**más**uno*, *El Universal* y *Tiempo de Jalisco*. Autor de *El ejido* (1956), *Historia de Iberoamérica* (1966), *La universidad y el Estado* (1971), *El campo* (1976), *Análisis judicial de la doctrina Monroe* (1978), *La revolución industrial* (1979), *Historia económica de América Latina* (1983) y *Breve historia gráfica de la revolución mexicana* (1987). Miembro del Consejo Mexicano de Ciencias Sociales y miembro de la Junta de Gobierno del Colegio de Jalisco (1982-).

Rodríguez Lascano, Sergio ◆ n. en Los Reyes, Edo. de Méx. (1950). Licenciado en economía por la UNAM (1974). Participó en el movimiento estudiantil de 1968. Se incorporó al Grupo Comunista Internacionalista (1971) y fue miembro del comité central y el buró político (1972). Fundador y dirigente del PRT (1976), formó parte del comité central, el comité político y el secretariado de organización. Fue miembro del comité ejecutivo de la IV Internacional (1979). Responsable de la Comisión Internacional del PRT y director de su órgano, *Bandera Socialista* (1985). Profesor de la UAP (1974-76).

Rodríguez León, Jorge ◆ n. en Aguascalientes, Ags. (1942). Líder sindical. Miembro del PRI desde 1963. Ha tenido diversos cargos en el SUTERM y en la CTM. Ha sido diputado local suplente, diputado local, senador suplente (1988-91) y senador (1991-94).

Rodríguez López, Daniel ◆ n. en Tizayuca, Hgo., y m. en San Juan de Casa Blanca, Edo. de Méx. (1875-1914). Médico cirujano por la Universidad Nacional (1909). Estableció un consultorio en Tizayuca, se unió al club antirreeleccionista Benito Juárez, de Pachuca, y en 1910 viajó a Chihuahua para unirse a las fuerzas de Pascual Orozco. Al triunfo de la revolución, Madero lo comisionó para combatir la epidemia de tifo en Ciudad Juárez. Ejerció la medicina en Tizayuca y, tras el cuartelazo huertista, reunió un grupo armado que puso a las órdenes del constitucionalista Nicolás Flores. Murió en combate.

Rodríguez Lozano, Amador ◆ n. en San Luis Potosí, SLP (1951). Licenciado en derecho por la UNAM (1981), de la que fue profesor, así como de la Universidad Intercontinental (1981). Afiliado al PRI desde 1973, donde ha sido secretario de capacitación política del CEN (1978-79), representante ante la Comisión Federal Electoral (1988-91) y consejero político nacional (1991). Secretario técnico de la Comisión Calificadora de Libros y Revistas Ilustradas y coordinador de asesores del subsecretario de Gobernación. Diputado federal (1991-94) y senador (1994-2000). Autor de *Partidos y elecciones: episodios de política contemporánea* (1992), *Lo claroscuro de la representación política* (1996) y *La reforma al Poder Legislativo en México* (1998). Fue becario del Instituto de Investigaciones Jurídicas de la UNAM.

Santa Ana muerta, técnica mixta sobre tela de Manuel Rodríguez Lozano

Rodríguez Lozano, Manuel ◆ n. y m. en el DF (1895-1971). Estudió pintura en la Academia de San Carlos y en 1914 viajó a Francia para especializarse. Inició su actividad artística y se vinculó con el grupo de Matisse, Braque y Picasso. Volvió a México en 1921, se casó con Magdalena Mondragón y en 1928 colaboró con Antonieta Rivas Mercado (☛) en el Teatro de Ulises. Fundó el Grupo de Intelectuales Contemporáneos (1930). En 1939 se le nombró director de la Escuela Nacional de Artes Plásticas y fundó la revista de este plantel. En 1941 fueron sustraídos de esta escuela tres grabados de Durero y uno de Guido Reni, de lo que se acusó a Rodríguez Lozano, quien estuvo encarcelado cuatro meses y medio en Lecumberri, donde pintó el mural *La Piedad en el desierto*, trasladado al Palacio de Bellas Artes en 1966, año en el que las obras robadas se entregaron a un periódico capitalino y devueltas a San Carlos. En 1948 realizó una exposición en el Museo de l'Orangerie, en Francia, patrocinada por Paul Rivet (☛) y por el rector de la Universidad de París. En 1968, durante la Olimpiada Cultural, presentó su última exposición. Apareció como personaje de la novela *Ensayo de un crimen*, de Rodolfo Usigli. Dejó un *Autorretrato* (1924) y los retratos de *Alfonso Reyes* (1915), *Andrés Henestrosa* (1924), *Salvador Novo* (1924), *Daniel Cosío Villegas* (1926) y *Rodolfo Usigli* (1953). Ejecutó un mural en la casa de Francisco I. Iturbe, hoy convertida en edificio de oficinas en la calle Isabel la Católica: *Holocausto* (1946).

Antonio Rodríguez Luna

Rodríguez Luna, Antonio ◆ n. y m. en España (1910-1985). Egresado de la Escuela de Bellas Artes de Sevilla (1923-26) y de la Academia de San Fernando de Madrid (1927-28), durante la guerra civil española colaboró en la Alianza de Intelectuales y en 1937 publicó, en Valencia, dibujos sobre el conflicto. Obtuvo el primer premio de dibujo en el concurso nacional de Barcelona. Al triunfo del franquismo se refugió en París y llegó exiliado a México en 1939. En 1941 fue becario de El Colegio de México y de la Fundación Guggenheim. Desde 1943 ejerció la docencia en la Escuela Nacional de Artes Plásticas. Expuso su pintura en México, España y Estados Unidos. De nuevo en España, en 1982 inauguró su propio museo en Montoro, su ciudad de origen. En México se han montado dos exposiciones homenaje a Rodríguez Luna, en 1959 y en 1986. Premio de Pintura del Salón de la Plástica Mexicana (1963).

Rodríguez Malpica, Hilario ◆ n. en Coatzacoalcos, Ver., y m. en Guaymas, Son. (1889-1914). Egresó en 1909 de la Escuela Naval de Veracruz. En 1911 fue ascendido a subteniente y se le asignó el buque *Tampico*. Teniente en 1913, un año después se unió a la revolución constitucionalista. El 16 de junio el *Tampico* fue derrotado por el *Guerrero* y Rodríguez se suicidó tras ordenar la inundación de su nave.

Rodríguez Martínez, José Guadalupe ◆ n. en el DF (1959). Ingeniero en comunicaciones y electrónica por la Universidad de Guadalajara (1984). Afiliado al PAN desde 1978, ha sido dirigente juvenil y presidente del Comité Estatal de Jalisco, así como diputado local (1989-91) y federal (1991-94).

Rodríguez Martínez, Tarcisio ◆ n. Guadalajara, Jal. (1959). Ingeniero en comunicaciones y electrónica por la Universidad de Guadalajara. Ha sido diputado federal y senador por el PAN, al que se afilió en 1978. También ha sido diputado local y ha tenido diversos cargos dentro de su partido, entre los que destaca el de secretario general del Comité Nacional.

Rodríguez Mata, Emilio ◆ n. en España (1903). Ingeniero mecánico electricista (1926). Estudió en Alemania, donde se tituló como ingeniero en electrónica (1927-30). Trabajó en los laboratorios de telefonía de las fábricas Siemens, construyó un oscilógrafo de rayos catódicos en el laboratorio del Instituto Nacional de Física y Química Rockefeller, de Madrid (1931), fue secretario de redacción de la revista *Ingeniería y Construcción* (1931-34) e ingeniero en la sección de Luminotecnia de la Geathom (1934-36). Llegó como refugiado político en 1939 y obtuvo la nacionalidad mexicana un año después. En el IPN fue profesor (1944-71), jefe del Departamento de Especialización del Patronato de Talleres, Laboratorios y Equipos (1961-63), vicepresidente del Patronato de Publicaciones (1964-67), coordinador de estudios de la ESIME (1967-71) y secretario de la sección editorial de la Comisión de Operación y Fomento de Actividades Académicas. Director del Instituto Mexicano de Iluminación (1946-48), director técnico de la *Revista Mexicana de Electricidad* (1942-63), asesor del Departamento de Investigaciones Industriales del Banco de México (1950-77), consultor de la Comisión de la Electrificación de México (1957) y consultor de la Secretaría de Comunicaciones (1964-70). Autor de varios libros sobre iluminación eléctrica. Miembro de la Asociación Mexicana de Ingenieros Mecánicos y Electricistas, del Colegio de Ingenieros Mecánicos y Electricistas y del Institut of Electrical and Electronics Engineers.

Rodríguez Mata, Ramón ◆ n. en España y ¿m. en el DF? (1896-?). Egresado de la Facultad de Medicina de Madrid (1919), obtuvo el doctorado en 1920. Fue teniente médico con servicio en Melilla (1920), profesor clínico en la Facultad de Medicina de Madrid (1922-24), jefe de clínica médica del Santo Hospital Civil de Bilbao (1921-37), comisario de Sanidad en Bilbao (1936), capitán médico, director de hospitales militares en Santander y Valencia (1937) y director del Hospital Base de San Gervasio, Barcelona (1938-39). Llegó exiliado a México en 1939. Médico adscrito al Servicio de Evacuación de Republicanos Españoles (1939), director de la Policlínica (1939-41), médico de la Beneficencia Española (1940), profesor de la Escuela Superior de Medicina del IPN (1941) y de la Academia Hispano-Mexicana (1942-44), asesor de los laboratorios Sanfer (1942-46), Merk Sharp & Dohme (1945) y Hormona (1947-50), redactor de la *Revista de Endocrinología* de los laboratorios Wyeth Vales (1951), asesor de los laboratorios Colliere (1951-60), director de la revista *Sinapsis* (1951-60), redactor del boletín *Asesores Médicos* de los laboratorios Squibb (1961-63), director médico de los laboratorios Reforma (1963-82), médico de la Benéfica Hispana (1948-73) e inspector médico en la Nueva Escuela (1959-82).

Rodríguez Melgarejo, Matías ◆ n. en Tetepango, Hgo., y m. en Acolman, Edo. de Méx. (1876-1954). Fue peón agrícola y contratista de obras en el DF. Preso político en 1911. Fundó en la ciudad de México el periódico *El Voto*, se unió a la insurrección maderista en Hidalgo, a las órdenes de Nicolás Flores. En 1913 militó en las fuerzas constitucionalistas de Antonio Medina y Teodoro Escalona, en las que ascendió a mayor. Diputado al Congreso Constituyente de 1916-17, cofundó en Querétaro, con Heriberto Jara y Vega Sánchez, el periódico *El Constituyente*. Diputado federal (1918-20 y 1922-24) y gobernador de Hidalgo (1925-29), se dedicó más tarde a la cría de toros de lidia. Murió en un accidente automovilístico.

Rodríguez Mendoza, Fernando ◆ n. en el DF (1938). Escritor. Ingeniero químico por la UIA (1961) y licenciado en filosofía por la Panamericana (1980). Ha sido colaborador de *La Opinión*, de Torreón, *La Brújula en el Bolsillo*, *Nivel*, *El Rehilete* y *Pájaro Cascabel*. Coeditor de *Zarza* (1960-63) y fundador de la editorial Cuadernos Cara a Cara (1981). Autor de poesía: *Doce poemas* (1961), *Equis city* (1962), *Cantos para un oficio de tinieblas* (1978), *A contratiempo* (1981), *Autobiografía de un desconocido* (1985) y *Memorial de este tiempo* (1985).

RODRÍGUEZ MIAJA, FERNANDO ◆ n. en España (1918). Ingeniero. Se alistó en las fuerzas republicanas durante la guerra civil y recibió el grado de teniente de ingenieros. Sirvió en el Cuartel General de Ejército del Centro, con sede en Madrid, y en el grupo de ejércitos de la Zona Centro-Sur. Fue secretario particular del jefe de ambas unidades, José Miaja. Llegó exiliado a México en 1939, fundó la Compañía Constructora del Centro (1957) y fue consejero y socio de honor de la Asociación Mexicana Automovilística, en la que fungió como secretario y tesorero; vocal y socio de honor del Centro Asturiano, consejero de la Cámara Nacional de la Industria de la Construcción y secretario del patronato de la Orquesta Sinfónica de México.

RODRÍGUEZ MORALES, MANUEL ◆ n. en Ciudad Victoria, Tams. (1953). Ingeniero civil por el ITESM (1973), maestro en ciencias por la Universidad de Texas (1976) y maestro por la École Nationale de Ponts et Chaussées, de Francia (1978). En la Secretaría de Comunicaciones ha sido superintendente de la Compañía Rodríguez Mejía (1976-77), jefe de la Oficina de Desarrollo de Proyectos (1979-80), jefe del Departamento de Previsión de Programas de la Dirección General de Análisis de Inversiones (1980-81); secretario particular del titular (1982-84), coordinador general sectorial (1985), coordinador de asesores (1985-86), coordinador general de Planeación y Control Sectorial (1987-88), director general del Centro SCT Tamaulipas (1989-92), director general del fideicomiso Conacal (1992-93), director general de carreteras federales (1993-94) y subsecretario de Infraestructura (1994-). Pertenece a la Asociación de Ingeniería de Vías Terrestres, al Colegio de Ingenieros Civiles de México, a la Sociedad Mexicana de Ingeniería y a la Sociedad Mexicana de Ingeniería de Costos.

RODRÍGUEZ OSORIO, ELSA ◆ n. en el DF (1938). Egresada de la Escuela de Periodismo Carlos Septién García. Trabajó en la sección de espectáculos de *Excélsior* (1962-65) y en el suplemento *Vida capitalina* de *Novedades* (1969-72). Colaboró en las revistas *Karma*, *Activa*, *Tele-Guía* y *Claudia*. Desde 1972 trabaja en la revista *Contenido*, de la que es jefa de redacción. Participó en el programa de televisión *La familia Tele-Guía* (1975-76). Sus trabajos han obtenido dos menciones del Club de Periodistas.

RODRÍGUEZ PALAFOX, RAMIRO ◆ n. en Santiago Papasquiaro, Dgo. (1912). Caballista, participó en los Juegos Olímpicos de Berlín (1936). Campeón mundial militar de equitación, en la competencia International Military Special Challenge Trophy, en el Madison Square Garden de Nueva York (1938), sitio en el que se le erigió una estatua. Campeón de equitación del Ejército Mexicano (1939), participó en torneos internacionales en La Habana, Washington, Nueva York y Toronto. Fue capitán del equipo de equitación en los Juegos Olímpicos de Tokio (1964). Fundó el Club Hípico Azteca (1949) del que es instructor. En 1982 ingresó en el Salón de la Fama de la Confederación Deportiva Mexicana. Alcanzó el generalato. La Secretaría de la Defensa le otorgó la condecoración al Mérito Deportivo Militar en primera clase con dos estrellas.

RODRÍGUEZ PÉREZ, FRANCISCO ◆ n. en Mazatlán, Sin. (1939). Licenciado en economía por la UNAM (1960-64), posgraduado en administración y control de inventarios y contraloría general por el Instituto de Especialización para Ejecutivos (1971-72). Miembro del PRI, en el que ha sido secretario de organización (1961-63) y secretario general (1965-67) de la sección 17 del Sindicato Nacional de Trabajadores de Hacienda, inspector fiscal de la Dirección de Impuestos de la Secretaría de Hacienda (1967-69), profesor y director de la Escuela de Economía de la Universidad Autónoma de Ciudad Juárez (1969-71); gerente de Adquisiciones (1970-71) y contralor general de Conasupo (1971-73); dos veces diputado federal (1973-76 y 1982-85) y representante del gobierno de Chihuahua en el DF (1980). Autor de *Acción legislativa* (1976). Pertenece al Colegio Nacional de Economistas.

RODRÍGUEZ PRAMPOLINI, IDA ◆ n. en Veracruz, Ver. (1925). Maestra en historia (1947) y doctora en letras con especialidad en historia por la UNAM (1948). Estudió historia del arte en la Universidad de Santander (1948-49) y en la Universidad McGill de Montreal (1952). En 1944 fue reina del carnaval de Veracruz. Ha sido profesora en diversas escuelas particulares (1946-47) y en la Universidad Femenina de México (1949-51), investigadora del Instituto de Investigaciones Estéticas de la UNAM (1957-64 y 1965-73), profesora de la Universidad de Morelos (1962), de la UNAM (1963-64 y 1966) y de la UIA (1963-64). Fue jurado de la IX Bienal de Sao Paulo (1967). Profesora fundadora del CCH de Tlayacapan (1973) y directora general del Instituto Veracruzano de Cultura (1987-93). Ha ejercido la crítica de arte en *México en la Cultura* (1960-61) y *La Cultura en México* (1962-63). Autora de *La crítica de arte en México en el siglo XIX* (3 t., 1964), *El arte contemporáneo, esplendor y agonía* (1964), *El surrealismo y el arte fantástico de México* (1969), *Una década de crítica de arte* (1973), *Herbert Bayer, un concepto total* (1973), *Dadá: documentos* (1977), *El geometrismo mexicano* (1977), *Juan O'Gorman: arquitecto y pintor* (1982), *Homenaje a O'Gorman* (1983) y *Ensayo sobre José Luis Cuevas y el dibujo* (1988), entre otras obras. Pertenece a la Academia de Artes y a la Academia Mexicana de la Historia.

Libro de Ida Rodríguez Prampolini

RODRÍGUEZ PRATS, JUAN JOSÉ ◆ n. en Pichucalco, Chis. (1946). Licenciado en derecho por la Universidad Veracruzana (1968). Afiliado al PRI desde 1965, ha sido presidente del Comité Estatal en Tabasco (1973-74), delegado en Chihuahua (1986) y Chiapas (1986) y delegado de la CNOP en Sonora; en el gobierno de Tabasco ha sido director de Ingresos (1971), subsecretario de Finanzas (1971-73) y secretario particular del gobernador (1974-76); en el DDF fue subdelegado en Tláhuac (1976-78) y Cuauhtémoc (1978-79), delegado en Venustiano Carranza (1979-82), director general de la Comisión de Desarrollo Urbano (1982-83) y director general de Regularización Territorial (1985); también ha sido gerente de Desarrollo Social de la CFE (1988-90), director del Instituto Mexicano del Café (1990-91) y dos veces diputado federal (1991-94 y 1997-2000). Compilador de *Oradores de Tabasco* (5 t., 1990). Autor de *La política del derecho en la crisis del sistema mexicano* (1986), *Que ellos decidan* (1989) y *Adolfo Ruiz Cortines* (1990).

RODRÍGUEZ PUEBLA, JUAN ◆ n. y m. en la ciudad de México (1798-1848). Abogado (1824). Fue diputado al Congreso Constituyente (1824), senador por Durango (1829-30) y diputado por el Distrito Federal (1833-34). En 1829 fue nombrado rector del Colegio de San Gregorio, en el que introdujo numerosas reformas. Fundador de la Academia de Profesores y de varios centros de enseñanza musical y literaria. Fue magistrado del Tribunal Superior de Justicia de Durango y ministro del Interior, del 13 al 16 de diciembre de 1838, en el gabinete de Anastasio Bustamante. Durante la invasión estadounidense, Rodríguez Puebla y sus alumnos se encargaron de los trabajos de fortificación y defensa del Peñón.

Ramón Rodríguez Rivera

RODRÍGUEZ QUEZADA, JOSÉ ANTONIO ◆ n. en el DF (1962). Estudió ciencias políticas y la maestría en sociología política en la UIA. Ha sido analista para la Gran Comisión de la Cámara de Diputados (1986-87), coordinador de analistas para la Dirección General de Investigaciones Políticas y Seguridad Nacional de la Secretaría de Gobernación (1987-89), coordinador de asesores en la delegación Gustavo A. Madero (1989) y en el SNTE (1990-92), asesor de la Secretaría General de Gobierno del DDF (1992-93), coordinador de estudios y proyectos Especiales del SNTE (1994-95) y del Instituto de Estudios Educativos y Sindicales de América (1995-96) y consultor independiente en temas de educación, sindicalismo, movimientos sociales, transición política y política social. Miembro del Colegio Nacional de Ciencias Políticas y Administración Pública.

RODRÍGUEZ RAMÍREZ, ELISEO ◆ n. en Pénjamo, Gto. (1925). Estudió en la Escuela Militar de Intendencia (1945). Es licenciado en derecho por la UNAM (1953). Miembro del PRI. Ha sido profesor del Colegio Militar (1951-57), de la Secretaría de la Defensa (1956) y de la UNAM (1959). Agente del Ministerio Público (1957), mayor intendente de la Secretaría de la Defensa (1959), agente del Ministerio Público auxiliar del procurador de Justicia del DF (1960), dos veces diputado federal por Guanajuato (1961-64 y 1985-88), senador por el mismo estado (1967-73), jefe de oficina de ANDSA (1971), oficial mayor de la Cámara de Senadores (1971), jefe de departamento en la Secretaría de la Defensa Nacional (1977), consejero del Cuerpo Consultivo Agrario (1977) y subdirector administrativo de Servicios Migratorios de la Secretaría de Gobernación (1980). Autor de *Vestuario y equipo del ejército mexicano* (1953). Presidió la Academia Mexicana de Administración Pública (1986-88) y la Asociación de Abogados (1949-53 y 1981-83).

RODRÍGUEZ REYNA, IGNACIO ◆ n. en el DF (1960). Periodista. Hizo estudios de comunicación en la UAM-Xochimilco y tomó un curso de periodismo de investigación en la Universidad del Sur de California en Los Ángeles (1993). Se inició profesionalmente en *La Jornada* (1984-90). Trabajó en *El Financiero*, donde creó y coordinó la Unidad de Asuntos Especiales (1991-93). Fue reportero y editor de reportajes especiales de *Reforma* (1995-97). Cofundador, coordinador editorial (1997-99) y editor asociado del semanario *Milenio* (1999-). Autor del libro *Ruiz Massieu, crímenes desde el poder* (1995). Pertenece al consejo directivo del Centro de Periodistas de Investigación.

RODRÍGUEZ DE RIVAS Y VELASCO, DIEGO ◆ n. en Ecuador y m. en Guadalajara, Jal. (¿1707?-1770). Doctor en derecho civil y en derecho canónico por la Universidad de Alcalá de Henares. Fue presbítero de Santa Cruz de Zarza (1730), maestrescuela, chantre, procurador de la diócesis de Guatemala en Madrid, arcediano, obispo de Comayagua, Honduras (1750-61), y de Guadalajara (1763-70).

RODRÍGUEZ RIVERA, RAMÓN ◆ n. y m. en Córdoba, Ver. (1850-1889). Alumno fundador de la Escuela Nacional Preparatoria. Se tituló en la Escuela Nacional de Medicina (1875). Fue colaborador de la *Revista Universal*, *El Domingo*, *El Eco de Ambos Mundos*, *El Liceo de la Juventud* y *La Esperanza*. Ejerció su especialidad en Córdoba (1882), donde fue síndico del ayuntamiento profesor del Colegio Preparatorio de Ciencias y Artes de Veracruz y de la Escuela de Enseñanza Superior de Niñas; varias veces diputado local y federal, secretario general de gobierno en Veracruz (1880-83), médico del Hospital de San Andrés y presidente del comité del Distrito Federal para la Exposición Universal de París (1888). Autor de *Versos* (1876, con prólogo de Ignacio Manuel Altamirano) y de un tratado sobre enfermedades hereditarias. Perteneció a la Sociedad de Historia Natural, la Sociedad Mexicana de Geografía y Estadística, a la Sociedad de Filoiátrica y al Liceo Hidalgo.

RODRÍGUEZ Y RODRÍGUEZ, JESÚS ◆ n. en el DF (1920). Licenciado en derecho por la UNAM (1937-41), donde fue profesor (1942-60). Miembro del PRI. En la Secretaría de Hacienda fue abogado de la Oficina de Deuda Pública

(1942), jefe de la Oficina de Seguros y Fianzas (1945-46), subdirector general de Crédito (1947-49) y subsecretario (1959-70). Ha sido secretario del Tribunal Fiscal de la Federación (1943-44), vicepresidente de la Comisión Nacional de Seguros (1949-51), secretario particular del director general del IMSS (1953-58), director ejecutivo por México en el BID (1971-78), director general del Instituto Nacional de Valores (1979-82) de Bancrecer (1982) y de la Lotería Nacional (1982-88). Senador por Morelos (1988-94). Autor de *Los monopolios en México* (1948) e *Impacto económico del turismo*. Pertenece a la Academia de Derecho Bursátil, a la Academia Mexicana de Derecho Burocrático, a la Asociación Nacional de Abogados, a la Federación Nacional de Abogados al Servicio del Estado y al Instituto Nacional de Administración Pública.

Rodríguez y Rodríguez, Joaquín ◆ n. en España y m. en el DF (1910-1949). Doctor en derecho por la Universidad Central de Madrid. Fue capitán del Cuerpo Jurídico Militar del Ejército Español. Llegó exiliado a México en 1939. Ejerció la docencia en la UNAM, la Escuela Libre de Derecho y el Instituto Tecnológico de Monterrey. Fue director del seminario de derecho privado (1940) y de la *Revista de la Escuela Nacional de Jurisprudencia* (1941-43). Autor de *Concepto de los agentes de comercio de derecho comparado, con especial consideración del derecho español y del mexicano* (1939), *Datos para un estudio de las adquisiciones de un no titular según el derecho mercantil español* (1939), *La empresa mercantil. Concepto, elementos y formas* (1941), *El problema del método en la ciencia jurídica mercantil* (1941), *Principio de la libre circulación de las acciones y sus restricciones* (1942), *Apuntes para una reforma del Código de Comercio mexicano* (1943), *Derecho bancario* (1945) y *La separación de bienes en la quiebra* (1948).

Rodríguez Roldán, Santiago ◆ n. en la ciudad de México (1922). Licenciado en derecho. Ha sido primer secretario de acuerdos del Juzgado Segundo de Distrito en Veracruz, juez de distrito en Tapachula y en Acapulco, magistrado de Circuito en Veracruz y en Toluca, magistrado unitario de circuito en el DF y ministro (1979-) de la Suprema Corte de Justicia.

Rodríguez Solís, Eduardo ◆ n. en el DF (1938). Escritor. Estudió ingeniería y literatura en la UNAM y teatro en el INBA. Fue jefe de redacción de *Mester* (1965-66), dio clases de teatro en Puerto Rico (1981-83) y en EUA (1983-85), fue fundador de la compañía escénica La Comedia Nuestra, en Texas, y jefe de Difusión Cultural de la UAM-X (1985), donde editó la revista *Hojas Sueltas*. Autor, entre otras obras, de teatro: *Banderitas de papel picado* (1964, obra premiada en el XI Festival Regional del DF del INBA), *Las ruedas ruedan* (1965, Trofeo de la Asociación de Críticos de Arte de Michoacán en 1967), *Sobre los orígenes del hombre* (Premio del Primer Festival de Primavera, 1967), *Black jack y otra farsa* (1968), *Entrar y entrar en la galería* (1972), *Helicóptero de miércoles* (1973), *Una relación cercana al éxtasis* (1974), *Las ondas de la catrina* (1978, puesta en Brodway en 1994), *069 reportándose* (1979), *Extrema libertad a los paquidermos* (1982), *El señor que vestía pulgas* (1985), *El nido de los amantes pobres* (1986, representada en Checoslovaquia), *Cógele bien el compás* (1991) y *Doncella vestida de blanco*; cuento: *La puerta de los clavos* (1966) y *Qué chévere, crónica puertorriqueña* (1992); novela: *No es la soledad* (1969) y *Primer curso ilustrado de amor* (1992); y los guiones cinematográficos: *Alucinado* (1975) y *Cocker Spaniel* (1977). Su cuento *San Simón de los Magueyes* fue llevado al cine en 1972. Fue becario del Centro Mexicano de Escritores (1964-1965).

Rodríguez Tagle, Simón ◆ n. en San Luis Potosí, SLP (1906). Estudió música con su padre, José Lucio Rodríguez, y con los profesores Flavio F. Carlos y Enrique Saloma, en San Luis Potosí; y con José Rocabruna, Aurelio Fuentes y Vladimir Vulman, en la ciudad de México. Fue integrante de las orquestas de San Luis Potosí, Aguascalientes, Puebla, México y Saltillo, dirigió el Cuarteto Clásico de la Universidad de San Luis Potosí y la Escuela de Música de Villa de Reyes (1968). Compuso el vals *Melancolía*. Autor de *Consideraciones sobre la técnica del violín* (1946), *Apuntes básicos para el estudio de la guitarra* (1976) y *Stradivarius, su vida y su obra*.

Rodríguez del Toro de Lazarín, Mariana ◆ n. en la ciudad de México (¿1775?-¿1821?). Esposa de Manuel Lazarín, alguacil mayor de guerra. Simpatizantes ambos con la causa independentista, proporcionaron informes y ayuda económica a los insurgentes guanajuatenses y fraguaron un plan para secuestrar al virrey Venegas en la ciudad de México. Fueron delatados el 29 de abril de 1811, capturados y encarcelados. Mariana Rodríguez permaneció diez años en un calabozo, sujeta con grilletes. Recobró la libertad en 1820.

La Güera Rodríguez

Rodríguez Triana, Pedro V. ◆ n. en San Pedro de las Colonias, Coah. (?-1960). Magonista, participó en el levantamiento de Las Vacas (1908) promovido por el Partido Liberal. Se unió a la insurrección maderista en las fuerzas de Pascual Orozco y en 1913 se incorporó a la División del Norte. Fue miembro del estado mayor de Benjamín Argumedo (1915) y luchó en Morelos con el Ejército Libertador del Sur. Se adhirió al Plan de Agua Prieta (☛) y en 1922 hizo la campaña en Durango contra Francisco Murguía. Miembro de la Liga Nacional Campesina, en 1929 fue candidato del Partido Comunista Mexicano y otras organizaciones a la Presidencia de la República, en oposición a Pascual Ortiz Rubio. Fue gobernador de Coahuila (1937-41).

Rodríguez de Velasco y Osorio Barba, María Ignacia ◆ n. y m. en la ciudad de México (1778-1850). Conocida como *la Güera Rodríguez*, fue colaboradora de la corriente insurgente de Ignacio Allende y Miguel Hidalgo. En 1811 fue juzgada por la Inquisición y desterrada a Querétaro. Se le atribu-

Gabriela Roel

Santiago Roel García

Rosamaría Roffiel

yen romances con Humboldt, Bolívar e Iturbide.

RODRÍGUEZ VELÁZQUEZ, ROSA ICELA ◆ n. en Xilitla, SLP (1960). Egresada de la Escuela de Periodismo Carlos Septién García (1987). Trabajó en la Secretaría de Comercio (1984-87) y en el Departamento de Difusión de la SEP (1986-87) y ha sido reportera de *La Afición* (1988-93) y de *La Jornada* (1993-97), corresponsal del periódico *Liberazione*, de Italia (1996), y directora general de Comunicación Social de la Asamblea Legislativa del Distrito Federal (1997-).

ROEDER, RALPH ◆ n. en EUA y m. en el DF (1890-1969). Escritor. De padre alemán. En su carácter de presidente del Comité de Salvación de Refugiados de la Liga de Escritores Americanos, hizo frecuentes viajes a México durante la segunda guerra mundial. Aquí coordinaba la ayuda a los alemanes antinazis perseguidos por Hitler. Se dedicó al estudio de la historia. Autor de *The Man of Renaissance, Four Lawgivers: Savonarola, Machiavelli, Castiglione, Arentino* (1933), *Juarez and his México, a Biographical History* (1947, traducida al español por él mismo en 1952). Dejó inédito *Hacia el México moderno*. Se suicidó. Recibió en 1965 la Orden del Águila Azteca.

ROEL, GABRIELA ◆ n. en Delicias, Chih. (1959). Actriz. Se llama Gabriela Guadalupe Reyes Roel. Estudió teatro en la Universidad de Chihuahua con Julio Castillo, así como en los talleres de teatro de la UNAM. En los ochenta incursionó en el cine y en televisión. Ha actuado en las películas *Viaje al paraíso* (1985), *Amor a la vuelta de la esquina* (1985, premio Ariel a la mejor actuación), *El tres de copas* (1986), *Historias de la ciudad* (1988), *Pueblo de madera* (1989), *Bandidos* (1990), *Ciudad de ciegos* (1991), *En medio de la nada* (1992), *Ámbar* (1993), *El jardín del Edén* (1993), *Gringo viejo* y *El dorado*, entre otras.

ROEL, SANTIAGO ◆ n. y m. en Monterrey, NL (1885-1957). Se tituló de abogado en la Escuela de Jurisprudencia de Monterrey (1907). En 1903 colaboró en el periódico estudiantil antirreyista *Redención* y en 1904 publicó artículos sobre historia en *Renacimiento*. Síndico del ayuntamiento de Monterrey (1912), diputado local constituyente (1917), diputado federal y senador suplente (1928). Colaborador del diario *El Porvenir*, donde se hizo cargo de la sección "Conozca Nuevo León". Autor de *El sufragio proporcional* (1913), *La representación proporcional en África del Sur, Alemania y Australia* (1919), *Correspondencia Juárez-Vidaurri* (1946), *Malinchismo nacional* (1955) y *Nuevo León. Apuntes históricos* (1957).

ROEL GARCÍA, SANTIAGO ◆ n. en Monterrey, NL (1919). Licenciado en derecho por la Universidad de Nuevo León (1943), de la que fue profesor. Ha sido director jurídico del gobierno de Nuevo León, senador suplente (1964-70), diputado federal (1970-73), asesor del secretario de Hacienda (1975- 76) y secretario de Relaciones Exteriores (del 1 de diciembre de 1976 al 16 de mayo de 1979) en el gabinete de José López Portillo. Autor de *Pedro Garfias, poeta* (1962), *La experiencia constitucional de México: de Zitácuaro a Querétaro 1811-1917* (1967), *El cura de Tamajón* (1967) e *Historia del Senado de la República Mexicana*. Presidente de la corresponsalía en Monterrey del Seminario de Cultura Mexicana (1956).

ROEL TREVIÑO, IGNACIO ◆ n. y m. en Monterrey, NL (1885-1962). Médico (1910). Llegó en 1914 a Baja California, cuando en la península se producían enfrentamientos constantes entre carrancistas, huertistas y villistas, para mediar entre las facciones. Diputado por el distrito norte de Baja California al Congreso Constituyente de 1916-17. En 1917 fundó en Mexicali el Club Benito Juárez y el periódico *La Vanguardia*. A partir de los años veinte se dedicó exclusivamente al ejercicio de su profesión en el Distrito Federal, en Coahuila y Nuevo León.

ROFFIEL, ROSAMARÍA ◆ n. en Veracruz, Ver. (1945). Periodista. Ha editado libros artesanales con textos de mujeres. Fue colaboradora de *Proceso*. En los noventa trabajó como guionista para la televisión estadounidense. Coautora de *Irán, la religión en la revolución*. Autora de *Todas mis amigas son poetas*, del poemario *Corramos libres ahora* (1986) y de la novela *Amora* (1989) y del libro de cuentos *El para siempre dura una noche* (1999).

ROFFIEL GUTIÉRREZ, OTHÓN ◆ n. en Veracruz, Ver., y m. en el DF (1918-1955). Se inició como cronista deportivo en el diario *El Dictamen*, del que fue más tarde redactor y autor de la columna "Bzzz". En la ciudad de México se integró a la redacción de *Excélsior* y fue jefe de información de *Últimas Noticias*, donde publicó la sección "Recortes".

ROGEL NAVA, CARLOS ◆ n. en Coatepec, Edo. de Méx., y m. ¿en el DF? (1924-1992). Sacerdote ordenado en 1949. Fue rector del Seminario Conciliar de México, vicerrector del Seminario Mexicano, en Roma, y canónigo de la Basílica de Guadalupe. Fundó la orden de los Misioneros de Santa Teresa de Jesús.

ROGOZINSKI SCHTULMAN, JACQUES ◆ n. en Francia (1950). Licenciado en administración de empresas por el ITAM (1974), maestro en economía (1977) y doctor en finanzas públicas por la Universidad de Colorado (1980). Miembro del PRI desde 1981. Ha sido gerente de Administración (1979-80) y subdirector de Administración y Sistemas del Instituto para el Depósito de Valores (1980-82); director de Administración y Programación (1983) y cordinador general de Administración de la Lotería Nacional (1983-88); asesor (1988) y coordinador de asesores del titular de la SPP (1988-89), coordinador general de la Unidad de Desincorporación de la de la Secretaría de Hacienda (1990-93) y director de Banobras (1993-95).

ROJANO PALACIOS, GABRIEL ◆ n. en Puebla, Pue., y m. en el DF (1888-1964). Antirreeleccionista. Colaboró con el grupo de Aquiles Serdán. Se levantó en armas en 1910 y disolvió sus tropas al firmarse los Tratados de Ciudad Juárez. En 1913 se unió a la revolución constitucionalista. Alcanzó el grado de coronel. Fue diputado por Huejotzingo al Congreso Constituyente de 1916-17 y en 1917 regresó al ejército, en el que se mantuvo hasta 1920. Trabajó después en las secretarías de Hacienda, de Comunicaciones y Obras Públicas y en la de Industria y Comercio.

Rojas, Antonio ◆ n. en Tepatitlán y m. en Potrerillos, Jal. (1818-1865). Campesino, formó una guerrilla (1858) con la que se puso a las órdenes del liberal Pedro Ogazón al inicio de la guerra de los Tres Años. Se incorporó a la Primera División en Zapotlán, participó en la toma de Guadalajara (1858) y dio muerte al general conservador José María Blancarte, por lo que Santos Degollado lo declaró fuera de la ley. Se separó del ejército federal pero mantuvo activa su guerrilla. Se reincorporó a las fuerzas de Ogazón (1859), participó en la campaña que avanzó hacia Aguascalientes y Zacatecas (1860) y tomó la plaza de Guadalajara (octubre de 1860). En 1861 hizo la campaña de Nayarit contra Manuel Lozada. Durante la guerra contra la intervención francesa y el imperio su guerrilla hostilizó a los invasores en Jalisco. Murió en combate contra las fuerzas de Berthelin.

Rojas, Antonio ◆ n. en Sahuaripa, Son., y m. en Huixquilucan, Edo. de Méx. (?-1914). Se unió en 1910 a la revolución maderista y operó en Chihuahua y Sonora hasta alcanzar el grado de coronel. A fines de 1911 se unió a la rebelión vazquista en Dolores, Chihuahua, aunque pronto fue aprehendido y encerrado en la capital chihuahuense, de donde escapó en 1912 aprovechando un motín de internos del penal. Se unió a la rebelión de Pascual Orozco, con quien tuvo problemas luego de asaltar, sin permiso, el Banco Nacional de Ciudad Juárez. Invadió Sonora, pero fue rechazado por los federales. Reconoció al régimen huertista y poco después se unió al zapatismo. Murió en combate.

Rojas, Luis Manuel ◆ n. en Ahualulco, Jal., y m. en el DF (1871-1949). Se tituló de abogado por la Escuela de Leyes de la ciudad de México (1897). Antirreleccionista (1909), fue diputado federal (1911-13) y uno de los cinco legisladores que se negaron a reconocer las renuncias de Francisco I. Madero y José María Pino Suárez y que atacaron desde la tribuna al embajador estadounidense Henry Lane Wilson, por lo que fue encarcelado. Apoyó la revolución constitucionalista y presidió el Congreso Constituyente de 1916-17. Fue director del Departamento Universitario y de Bellas Artes y de la Biblioteca Nacional (1917-20), profesor de la Universidad Nacional, ministro en Guatemala, miembro de la comisión de reclamaciones por daños causados por la revolución y magistrado del Tribunal Militar, con el grado de general de división. Fue uno de los fundadores de *Revista de Revistas* y de la *Gaceta de Guadalajara*. Dirigió los diarios *El Universal* y *El Siglo XX*. Autor de *México pide justicia. ¡Yo acuso al embajador Lane Wilson!* (1926) y *La culpa de Henry Lane Wilson en el gran desastre de México* (1928).

Rojas, Máximo ◆ n. en Tlaxcala, Tlax., y m. en San Juan de los Llanos, Pue. (1881-1924). En 1910 se unió a la revolución maderista en las filas de Juan Cuamatzi, primero, y de Francisco Gracia, después. Presidente municipal de Papalotla (1912), en 1913 se levantó en armas contra Victoriano Huerta. Fue gobernador de Tlaxcala (1914, 1915 y 1918-21). Murió en combate contra los pronunciados delahuertistas.

Rojas, Pedro ◆ n. y m. en el DF (1919-1984). Licenciado en derecho y maestro y doctor en filosofía con especialidad en historia del arte por la UNAM, donde fue profesor (1948-82), director y editor de los *Anuarios* (1953-60), investigador del Instituto de Investigaciones Estéticas (1953-70), coordinador de la Colección de Arte (1954-61), coordinador de los Servicios de Radio, Televisión y Grabaciones (1955-61) y director fundador de la *Gaceta* (1956). Fue profesor de la Escuela Nacional de Maestros, de la Normal Superior y de la UIA (1948-70); director de la *Historia del arte mexicano* de Editorial Hermes (1956-63), director de la serie de monografías *Monumentos y Paisajes de Latinoamérica* (1960-65), jefe del Departamento de Acción Social Educativa (1964-66) y director de Radio Educación (1968-70), en la SEP, y coordinador general de asambleas y conferencias de la Unión de Universidades de América Latina (1971). Colaborador de la *Revista de la Facultad de Filosofía y Letras*, *Anales del Instituto de Investigaciones Estéticas*, *México en la Cultura*, *Cuadernos Americanos*, *Artes de México*, *Dianoia*, *Revista de la Universidad de México* y *Diorama de la Cultura*. Autor de *Tonantzintla* (1956), *Historia del arte mexicano. Época colonial* (1963), *Acámbaro colonial. Estudio histórico, artístico e iconográfico* (1967) y *The Art and Architecture of Mexico. A Comprensive Survey* (1968). Miembro de la Academia de Artes, de la Asociación Internacional de Críticos de Arte y del Comité Internacional de Historia del Arte.

Luis Manuel Rojas

Rojas, Rafael R. ◆ n. en Cholula y m. en Atlixco, Pue. (1886-1926). Antirreeleccionista, fue tesorero de la primera junta revolucionaria constituida por Aquiles Serdán. Se unió a la revolución maderista (1910), combatió al zapatismo y alcanzó el grado de general brigadier. Fue dos veces diputado federal por Puebla (1917-20 y 1920) y gobernador suplente de ese estado (del 8 de mayo al 16 de julio 1920), asi como jefe de operaciones militares de Puebla y Tlaxcala (1921-22).

Rojas, Xavier ◆ n. en Puebla, Pue. (1921). Dramaturgo cuyo nombre es Xavier Moreno Monjaraz. Estudió en el IPN y en la ENAH. Fue fundador de los grupos Poliart (1941) y Teatro Estudiantil Autónomo del IPN (1946), y de los Teatros Círculo, con Pedro Ramírez Vázquez. Ha sido profesor del INBA y de la Academia Teatral de la ANDA, jefe del departamento cultural del Injuve y del Teatro para Obreros, y director del Instituto Andrés Soler. Ha dirigido, entre otras, las puestas en escena de *Los desarraigados*, *La zona intermedia*, *El*

Mario Rojas Avendaño

Francisco Rojas González

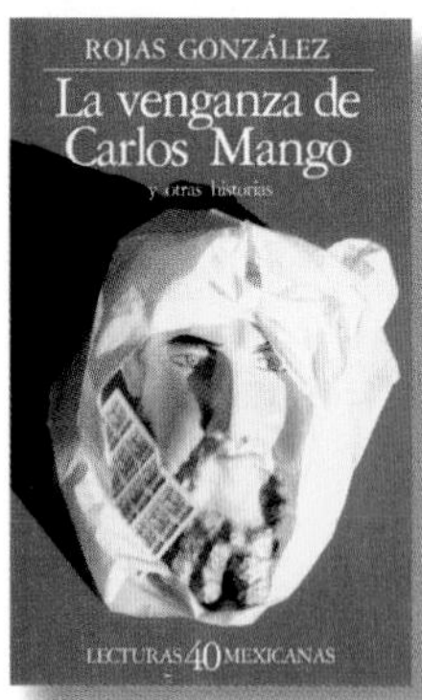

Obra de Francisco Rojas González

hombre que hacía llover, La carroza del Santísimo, Sandino debe nacer, Un sombrero lleno de lluvia, Bodas de sangre, Contradanza, ¿Quién le teme a Virginia Woolf?, Largo viaje de un día hacia la noche, El deseo bajo los olmos, Rencor al pasado, El vigilante, Una gota de miel, Los duendes, A caza del amor, La señorita Julia, El proceso Oppenheimer, Te juro Juana que tengo ganas., Las fascinadoras, El dulce pájaro de la juventud, Orfeo desciende, Voces de gesta, La verdad sospechosa, De acá, de este lado, La reina y los rebeldes, Pudo haber sucedido en Verona, Pandilleros y *El eclipse*. Autor de las obras de teatro *El despertar de un pueblo, Escándalos en el Olimpo, Cristóbal Colón ante la reina Isabel, Personaje Mario, Retorno* y *Faja de Oro*; y de la autobiografía *Medio siglo en escena: Xavier Rojas*. El INBA le rindió un homenaje por sus 50 años de carrera en 1996.

Rojas Avendaño, Mario ◆ n. en Tuxtla Gutiérrez, Chis., y m. en el DF (1897-1975). Se unió a la revolución en el Ejército Libertador del Sur y, más tarde se incorporó a las fuerzas de Venustiano Carranza. Ejerció el periodismo desde 1915 en *El Demócrata, El Demócrata Mexicano, El Universal, El Pueblo, El Mundo, Excélsior* y *El Popular*, del que fue fundador. Fue subjefe de la oficina de prensa de la Presidencia de la República (1958-64), profesor de la UNAM y la UIA, jefe de redacción de *Novedades*, productor de los primeros noticieros para televisión en el país, fundador del Club de Periodistas de México y del Club Primera Plana y presidente de la Asociación de Profesionales de la Comunicación. Autor de *Cincuenta años de la historia en Excélsior* (1967).

Rojas Bernal, Enrique ◆ n. en El Limón, Sin. (1942). Licenciado en derecho por la UNAM, donde formó parte de la dirección del primer Consejo Estudiantil Universitario (1966). Militó en la Juventud Comunista de México (1965-) y fue presidente de la Central Nacional de Estudiantes Democráticos (1966-). Formó parte del Frente Democrático Nacional (1988) e ingresó al PRD en 1990; en ese partido ha sido miembro del CEN, donde presidió la comisión Nacional de Garantías y Vigilancia, consejero en el DF (1999-) y consejero nacional (1999-). Notario Público 18 del DF desde 1973, ha sido diputado federal (1988-91) y subdelegado de Tlalpan (1997-). Autor de *La contrarreforma electoral de 1989-1990* (1992).

Rojas Cruz, Graciela ◆ n. en el DF (1950). Miembro del comité central del PST (1977-87), integrante del Consejo Nacional y del Comité Estatal Electoral en el DF del PMS (1987-89) y militante del PRD (1989-). Dirigente del Movimiento Vida Digna (1986-89). Representante plurinominal a la primera Asamblea del Distrito Federal (1988-91) y delegada en Tláhuac (1997-).

Rojas de Cuauhtémoc ◆ Municipio de Oaxaca situado al este de Zaachila y cercano a la capital del estado. Superficie: 25.52 km². Habitantes: 1,047, de los cuales 376 representan la población económicamente activa. Hablan alguna lengua indígena ocho personas mayores de cinco años (zapoteco 6).

Rojas Dávila, Efrén ◆ n. en Capultitlán, Edo. de Méx. (1953). Químico graduado en la UAEM (1974) y maestro en ciencias por la UNAM. Fue secretario general adjunto del comité del PRI en el estado de México. En la UAEM ha sido profesor (1972-93), secretario académico (1978-80) y director de la Escuela de Ciencias Químicas (1980-84), director de Control Escolar (1984-85), secretario académico (1985-89) y rector (1989-93). Secretario de Educación, Cultura y Bienestar Social del Estado de México (1993-99).

Rojas Díaz-Durán, Alejandro ◆ n. en el DF (1959). Hizo estudios de filosofía, ciencias políticas y periodismo en la UIA. Fue dirigente de las juventudes priistas; más tarde fundó y presidió la Corriente Democrática, la Corriente Crítica y el grupo Democracia 2000 dentro del PRI, al que renunció después de haber sido enlace entre la Presidencia y la Corriente Democrática. Fue miembro independiente de la Asamblea de Representantes del DF (1991-94), a la que ingresó por el Partido Verde; se afilió luego al PT y al Partido del Centro Democrático.

Rojas Garcidueñas, José ◆ n. en Salamanca, Gto., y m. en el DF (1912-1981). Licenciado en derecho (1938) y maestro en letras (1954) por la UNAM. Abogado del Departamento Jurídico de la Secretaría de Asistencia Pública (1938-39), gerente de la Orquesta Sinfónica de México (1944-47), jefe del Departamento de Investigación para el Extranjero de la SRE (1947-48), investigador del Instituto de Investigaciones Estéticas de la UNAM (1939-74), administrador del Instituto Tecnológico de México (1951-53), director de la Escuela de Filosofía y Letras de la Universidad de Guanajuato (1953-54) y abogado consultor de la Dirección General de Límites y Aguas Internacionales (1956-74). Autor de *El teatro de Nueva España en el siglo XVI* (1935), *El epistolario de Nueva España, México* (1941), *Fiestas de México 1578* (1942), *El heraldista* (1949), *Christmas-Nochebuena* (1950), *El erudito y el jardín* (1951), *Ejemplo de la vanidad* (1953), *Gilberto Owen y su obra* (1954), *Una aurora boreal* (1957), *Bernardo de Balbuena. La vida y la obra* (1958), *De historia mínima* (1959), *Relato de las islas Mistrocks* (1960), *In Terra Pax* (1961), *Genaro Fernández MacGregor, escritor e internacionalista* (1962), *Presencias de don Quijote en las artes de México* (1968), *Letras vivas* (1972) y *El Ateneo de la Juventud y la Revolución* (1979), entre otras obras. Perteneció a la Academia Mexicana (de la Lengua) y a la Association Internationale des Critiques d'Art.

Rojas González, Francisco ◆ n. y m. en Guadalajara, Jal. (¿1903?-1951). Estudió contaduría en la Escuela de Comercio y Administración, etnografía en el Museo Nacional y etnología y sociología en la UNAM, donde fue investigador del Instituto de Investigaciones Sociales (1935). Ingresó en el servicio diplomático en 1920, como cónsul en Guatemala y después en Salt Lake City, Denver y San Francisco. Fue director de Estadística y colaborador de *Crisol, Hoy,*

Tiras de Colores, México en el Arte, Novedades, Cuadernos Americanos, El Universal Ilustrado y *El Hijo Pródigo*. Coautor de *Carta etnográfica de México* (1939), *Cuatro cartas de geografía de las lenguas* (1957), *Estudios etnológicos del Valle del Mezquital* (1957), *Estudio etnológico de Ocoyoacac* (1957) y *Etnografía de México* (1957). Autor de *Historia de un frac* (1930), *Y otros cuentos* (1931), *El pajareador. Ocho cuentos* (1934), *Sed. Pequeñas novelas* (1937), *La negra Angustias* (1944), *Chirrín y la celda 18* (1944), *Cuentos de ayer y de hoy* (1946), *Lola Casanova* (1947), *La última aventura de Mona Lisa* (1949), *El diosero* (1952), *Antología del cuento americano contemporáneo* (1953) y *Cuentos completos* (1971). Miembro de las sociedades de Geografía y Estadística, Mexicana de Sociología, Mexicana de Antropología y Folklórica de México. Premio Nacional de Literatura (1944).

Rojas Gutiérrez, Carlos ◆ n. en el DF (1954). Ingeniero industrial por la UNAM (1977). Desde 1979 milita en el PRI, donde ha sido secretario general del Comité Ejecutivo Nacional (1998-99). Asesor de la Unión de Ejidos Adalberto Tejeda (1980) y consejero técnico consultivo de la CNC (1984). Ha sido investigador en la UNAM (1977-79), director del INI en Huayacocotla (1979-82) y, en la Secretaría de Programación y Presupuesto, director del Programa de Atención a Zonas Marginadas (1983), director de Operación Regional Sur (1984), coordinador de asesores del subsecretario de Desarrollo Regional (1985), secretario técnico del Programa de Descentralización (1986) y subsecretario de Desarrollo Regional. Coordinador del Programa Nacional de Solidaridad (1988-1994) y secretario de Desarrollo Social (1994-98). Autor de *Combate a la pobreza* (1990).

Rojas Gutiérrez, Francisco José ◆ n. en el DF (1944). Hermano del anterior. Contador público por la UNAM, especializado en planeación y presupuesto en Israel y en alta dirección de empresas en el IPADE. Miembro del PRI. Ha sido jefe de Control de Presupuestos y subdirector de la Contraloría del DDF (1971-72); coordinador de Control Presupuestal de Organismos Descentralizados, subdirector de Control Presupuestal, subdirector general de Egresos y jefe de asesores del subsecretario en la Secretaria de Hacienda (1973-79); coordinador de la Secretaría de Programación y Presupuesto ante la Comisión Gasto-Financiamiento del gobierno federal y coordinador general de Control de Gestión de la SPP (1979-82); secretario de la Contraloría General de la Federación (del 1 de diciembre de 1982 al 6 de febrero de 1987) y director general de Pemex (1987-88).

Rojas Mena, Luis ◆ n. en Jalapa de Cánovas, Gto. (1917). Sacerdote ordenado en 1945. Ha sido párroco y obispo auxiliar de Guadalajara (1968-69) y titular (1969-92) y emérito de Culiacán.

Rojas Soriano, Raúl ◆ n. en Tetecalita, Mor. (1948). Licenciado (1966) y doctor (1972) en sociología por la UNAM. Ha sido profesor y funcionario de la UNAM, funcionario del IMSS y presidente del Colegio de Sociólogos de México. Colaborador de *Excélsior*. Autor de *Investigación social. Teoría y praxis, Teoría e investigación militante, Guía para realizar investigaciones sociales* (1977), *El proceso de la investigación científica* (1979), *Capitalismo y enfermedad* (1982), *Métodos para la investigación social: una proposición dialéctica* (1983) y *Sociología médica* (1985).

Rojina Villegas, Rafael ◆ n. en Orizaba, Ver., y m. en Acapulco, Gro. (1908-1976). Doctor en derecho por la UNAM (1951), donde fue profesor desde 1934. Fue secretario de Estudio y Cuenta, magistrado del Tribunal Colegiado del Primer Circuito y ministro de la Suprema Corte de Justicia. Autor de *Los ámbitos del contrato como norma jurídica* (1957) y *Proyecto de reformas al Código Civil del Distrito y Territorios Federales* (1976).

Rojkind Matluk, Marcos ◆ n. en el DF (1935). Médico graduado en la UNAM (1960), obtuvo el doctorado en el Cinvestav (1971) después de haber realizado estudios de posgrado en el Departamento de Bioquímica del Colegio de Medicina Albert Einstein, de Nueva York (1962-65), en la UNAM (1966) y en el Instituto Nacional de la Nutrición (1966). Profesor de la UNAM (1961-67), trabajó en la Unidad de Patología del Hospital General de México (1961-67). Jefe del Departamento de Bioquímica del INN (1967-70), profesor en el Cinvestav (1970-75 y 1978), investigador visitante y profesor asociado de los departamentos de Medicina y Bioquímica del Colegio de Medicina Albert Einstein (1975-78) y profesor titular de medicina y patología en la misma institución (1978-). Ha escrito numerosos artículos para publicaciones especializadas. Autor de tres libros y de capítulos de 45 libros especializados. Miembro de la Asociación Mexicana de Hepatología, que presidió entre 1985 y 1986, y del Comité Consejero del Centro de Investigación en Hígado de la Universidad de Yale. Ha obtenido los premios en Investigación Médica (1971 y 1972), Elli Lilly (1974), de la Asociación Mexicana de Medicina Interna (1979), Sandoz Dr. Manuel Jiménez (1982) y Nacional de Ciencias y Artes (1985).

Rojo, Alba Cama de ◆ n. en España (1937). Esposa de Vicente Rojo desde 1957. Licenciada en historia por la UNAM. Fue profesora del Colegio Hebreo Sefaradí. Desde 1971 trabajó para el Fondo de Cultura Económica, en el que fue jefa de Relaciones Públicas (1982-84). Ha sido asesora del Departamento de Bellas Artes del gobierno de Jalisco (1972-76), asesora cultural de Pemex (1976), responsable de Relaciones Públicas de la revista *Nexos* (1977-79), asesora de El Colegio Nacional (1979-81) y de la Coordinación de Humanidades de la UNAM. Autora de la investigación sobre imágenes y textos de *José Moreno Villa. Iconografía* y de *Luis Buñuel. Iconografía personal* (1988, con textos de Octavio Paz, Jaime García Terrés y Luis Buñuel).

Rojo, Guadalupe ◆ n. en Culiacán, Sin., y m. en el DF (1856-1922). Viuda de Casimiro Alvarado, editor y director

Carlos Rojas Gutiérrez

Francisco Rojas Gutiérrez

Foto: Rafael Donis

Alba Rojo

María Rojo

Vicente Rojo

del periódico antiporfirista *Juan Panadero*. A la muerte de Alvarado, siguió publicando ese órgano y fue encarcelada en varias ocasiones. Tras la caída de Porfirio Díaz siguió ejerciendo el periodismo y fue pensionada por el gobierno de Venustiano Carranza.

Rojo, María ◆ n. en el DF (1943). Actriz de cine, teatro y televisión. Estudió actuación en la Universidad Veracruzana. En 1988 dio un curso en la Escuela de Cine de Cuba. A los ocho años de edad comenzó su trabajo en teatro, con la obra *La mala semilla*, y en televisión en el programa *Teatro Fantástico*, de Enrique Alonso. Ha actuado en las películas *Besos prohibidos* (1956), *Los recuerdos del porvenir* (1968), *Los cachorros*, *El castillo de la pureza* (1972), *El Apando* (1975), *Naufragio* (1977), *Las poquianchis* (1976), *María de mi corazón* (1980), *Bajo la metralla* (1983), *Lo que importa es vivir* (1987), *Rompe el alba* (1988), *Los confines* (1988), *Día de difuntos* (1988), *Rojo amanecer* (1991), *La tarea* (1991), *Danzón* (1991), *Tequila* (1991), *El callejón de los milagros* (1994), *Intimidades en un cuarto de baño* (1997) y *De noche vienes, Esmeralda* (1998), entre otras; y en obras teatrales como *Los hijos de Sánchez*, *La mudanza*, *La tarea* y *Cada quien su vida*. Ha participado en varias telenovelas. Entre otros premios, ha ganado dos veces la Diosa de Plata, un Ariel por coactuación en *Las poquianchis*, tres Arieles a la mejor actriz por *Naufragio*, *Lo que importa es vivir* y *Bajo la metralla*, premio a la mejor actriz en el Festival de Cine de Cartagena por *María de mi corazón* (1980) y *La Tarea* (1991) y premio a la mejor actriz en el Festival de Valladolid por *Danzón* (1991). En 1991 la Cineteca Nacional le rindió un ciclo-homenaje llamado "María Rojo. María de mi corazón". Diputada federal por el PRD (1997-2000), preside la comisión de Cultura.

Rojo, Rubén ◆ n. en España y m. en el DF (1925-1993). Actor. Estudió arte dramático en las universidades de La Habana y Viena. Vivió la mayor parte de su vida en México, cuya nacionalidad adoptó, y participó en más de 180 películas cono intérprete y productor. Entre ellas destacan *Imprudencia* (1944), *Adán, Eva y el Diablo* (1944), *El gran calavera* (1949), *Aventurera* (1949), La hija del engaño (1951), *El barón del terror* (1961), *Santo en el museo de cera* (1963), *Condenados a muerte* (1963) y *Yerba sangrienta* (1986). En 1964 escribió el argumento de la cinta *Mar rojo*. También participó en telenovelas. Premios de la Asociación de Críticos de México por mejor actor en las obras *La señorita de Tacna* y *Los empeños de una casa* (1992).

Rojo, Vicente ◆ n. en España (1932). Pintor, escultor y diseñador gráfico. Estudió escultura y cerámica en la Escuela Elemental del Trabajo de Barcelona. Vino en 1949 y en ese año le fue otorgada la nacionalidad mexicana. Estudió en La Esmeralda (1950) e inició su aprendizaje en el diseño gráfico con Miguel Prieto en el Departamento de Ediciones del INBA. Fue discípulo del pintor Arturo Souto (1953-54). Dirigió la oficina técnica de ediciones del INBA (1953-54). Fundador y director artístico de *Artes de México* (-1963). Fue diseñador tipográfico de la Dirección de Difusión Cultural de la UNAM (1954-56), jefe de anuncios para cine de la empresa Teleproducciones (1954-55), asistente (1950-56) y director artístico de *México en la Cultura* (1956-61). Cofundador, director artístico y miembro del consejo de Ediciones Era (1959-). Di-

Cartel diseñado por Germán Montalvo y Vicente Rojo para la exposición Cuarenta Años de Diseño Gráfico, de este último

Obra de Vicente rojo

señó el suplemento *La Cultura en México* y dirigió las ediciones de la Imprenta Madero. Hizo el diseño gráfico original de *Diálogos*, *Universidad de México*, *Plural* (con Kasuya Sakai) y el diario *La Jornada* (1984). Ha expuesto individual o colectivamente en México y en el extranjero. En 1989 el museo Carrillo Gil organizó en su honor la retrospectiva *Vicente Rojo, cuarenta años de diseño gráfico*. En 1978 obtuvo la beca Guggenheim. Ha ganado los premios Nacional de Ciencias y Artes (1991), México de Diseño (1991) y la medalla de Oro al Mérito del Estado Español (1993). Creador emérito del SNCA. Miembro de El Colegio Nacional desde 1994.

ROJO CAMA, VICENTE ◆ n. en el DF (1960). Hijo del anterior. Músico. Estudió electroacústica en el Conservatorio Superior de Música, de París (1979-81), con Pierre Shaeffer y Guy Reibel, y música por computadora en el Brooklyn College (1985). En 1987 recibió una beca para reiniciar estudios en París. Ha trabajado desde 1981 en el Centro Independiente de Investigación Musical y Multimedia. Coautor del disco *Música electroacústica mexicana* (1987, en colaboración con Antonio Russek, Roberto Morales y Raúl Pavón).

ROJO GÓMEZ, JAVIER ◆ n. en Bondojito, Hgo., y m. en el DF (1896-1970). Licenciado en derecho por la Universidad Nacional (1924). Fue secretario general de gobierno de Hidalgo, diputado local (1920) y federal (1925), juez de distrito en materia administrativa en la ciudad de México (1930), gobernador de Hidalgo (1937-40), jefe del DDF (1940-46), embajador en Japón e Indonesia (1952-58), fundador y secretario general de la Confederación Nacional Campesina (1958-61) y gobernador del territorio de Quintana Roo (1967-70).

ROJO LUGO, JORGE ◆ n. en Huichapan, Hgo. (1933). Licenciado en derecho por la UNAM. Miembro del PRI, ha sido secretario auxiliar de la presidencia del Comité Ejecutivo Nacional (1961-63) y delegado en Aguascalientes, Tabasco y Chiapas. Miembro del consejo consultivo de la CNC. Trabajó como abogado en la Secretaría de Recursos Hidráulicos (1959-60) y la Secretaría de Hacienda (1960-61). Ha sido diputado federal (1961-64), subdirector y director general del Banco Nacional Agropecuario, presidente del consejo de administración del Banco Provincial de Sinaloa y de la Financiera Promex, primer director del Banco Nacional de Crédito Rural (1975), gobernador de Hidalgo (1975-76 y 1978-81), secretario de la Reforma Agraria (del 1 de diciembre de 1976 al 1 de junio de 1978), coordinador regional del Programa Nacional para la Protección al Empleo de la Secretaría de Programación y Presupuesto (1981-87) y secretario ejecutivo de la Comisión Nacional para el Desarrollo Agropecuario (1987-88).

ROJO DEL RÍO LAFUENTE LUBIÁN Y VIEYRA, MANUEL ANTONIO ◆ n. en Tula, en el actual Hidalgo, y m. en las Filipinas (1708-1764). Algunos autores sostienen que nació en Huichapan, en la misma entidad. Sacerdote. Estudió en la Real y Pontificia Universidad de México, de la que fue consiliario (1729) y se doctoró en cánones en la Universidad de Salamanca. Regresó hacia 1739 y durante años pugnó infructuosamente por obtener el derecho a concursar por una cátedra. Fue abogado de la corte de España, consultor del tribunal de la Inquisición de la Nueva España, inquisidor ordinario para las diócesis de Yucatán, Filipinas y Nicaragua; racionero (1738), prebendado (1746) y canónigo (1756) de la Catedral Metropolitana; fundador del Ilustre Colegio de Abogados de México (1759), juez conservador de las regiones de San Francisco y La Merced, arzobispo de Manila (1758-64), gobernador de la diócesis de Nueva Segovia y gobernador y capitán general de las Filipinas. Autor de *La mejor devoción del fiel cristiano* (escrito en tagalo) y *Catecismo en lengua tagala*.

ROJO DE LA VEGA, JOSÉ ◆ n. en Culiacán, Sin., y m. en el DF (1891-1960). Médico. Fue miembro y jefe del Servicio Médico Legal, presidente del quinto Congreso de Cirujanos, jefe de cirugía del Sanatorio Español y cirujano de la plaza de toros durante 37 años. Perteceió a la Sociedad Mexicana de Cirugía.

Obra de Vicente Rojo

ROJO DE LA VEGA, JUAN B. ◆ n. en Culiacán, Sin., y m. en el DF (1889-1946). Licenciado en derecho por la Universidad Nacional, con posgrado en la Universidad George Washington. Fue profesor en la Escuela Nacional Preparatoria, secretario de la Comisión Mixta Mexicano-americana de Nueva Londres y Atlantic City (1916); primer secretario (1917), consejero (1917) y encargado de negocios (1918-19) de la embajada mexicana en Estados Unidos (fue declarado persona *non grata* por sus críticas al Departamento de Estado de ese país); miembro del Consejo de Gobierno de la Unión Panamericana y delegado de la segunda Conferencia Comercial Panamericana de Washington (1919); miembro del Consejo Directivo de los Ferrocarriles Nacionales, ministro plenipotenciario en Japón y ministro titular en China (1920); miembro del Comité Organizador de la Barra Internacional de Abogados en Tokio, jefe del Departamento de Gobernación de la Secretaría de Gobernación (1929), patrono de la Fundación Torres Adalid y magistrado del Tribunal Supremo de Justicia del Distrito Federal (1929).

Luis G. Roldán

José Rolón, según Ibarra

ROLDÁN, EMMA ◆ n. en San Luis Potosí, SLP, y m. en el DF (1893-1978). Se inició como actriz de teatro en la compañía de Amparo Romo. Pasó a las de Esperanza Iris, Virginia Fábregas y Alfredo del Diestro, su segundo esposo. Durante cinco años actuó, hizo doblajes y confeccionó vestuario en Hollywood. En Francia y Colombia estableció casas de modas. Volvió a México en 1931 y fundó otro negocio dedicado a la confección de vestuarios para teatro. Trabajó en más de 500 películas, entre otras: *Una vida por otra* (1931), *El prisionero 13* (1933), *Allá en el Rancho Grande* (1936), *La casa del ogro* (1939), *Vino el viento y nos alevantó* (1950), *Canasta de cuentos mexicanos* (1956), *La edad de la inocencia* (1963) y *La pasión según Berenice* (1977). Intervino en 15 telenovelas.

ROLDÁN, LUIS G. ◆ n. y m. en el DF (1908-1986). Cantante, estudió con María Greever. Se inició profesionalmente en 1931. Cantó en *La Hora Azul*, de la radiodifusora XEW, donde el locutor Pedro de Lille lo llamó *el Cancionero Romántico*. Ocupó diversos cargos en la ANDA. Actuó en la película *La vida de don Porfirio*. Grabó más de 500 discos. Interpretó, entre otras, las canciones *María Elena*, de Lorenzo Barcelata; *No hagas llorar a esa mujer*, de Joaquín Pardavé; *Temor*, de Gonzalo Curiel, y *Así*, de María Greever.

ROLDÁN MÁRQUEZ, ROBERTO ◆ n. en Pachuca, Hgo., y m. cerca de Puebla, Pue. (1921-1971). Estudió contaduría. Dedicado a la publicidad fue fundador, locutor, publicista y gerente de la radiodifusora XEPK, de Pachuca, locutor y funcionario de la XEW, de la ciudad de México, XET, de Monterrey y XEOA, de Oaxaca. Publicista de la agencia Walter Thompson de México, gerente de la Central de Grabaciones de la Organización Radio Centro, fundador del periódico *Labor* (1941), de Atotonilco el Grande, colaborador de *El Observador* y *Renovación*, de Pachuca; director de *Respetable Público*, subdirector de *Hidalgo Gráfico*, colaborador de *El Norte*, de Monterrey; *Oaxaca Gráfico* y *La Voz de Hidalgo*. Autor de *50 poemas de amor*, *Acuarelas provincianas*, *Por la senda prohibida* y *El sembrador*. Masón, fue venerable maestro del Taller Ramón M. Rosales. Murió en un accidente automovilístico.

ROLDÁN VERA, MANUEL ◆ n. en Jalapa, Ver. (1943). Estudió en la Facultad de Artes Plásticas y en el taller de escultura de Kiyoshi Takahashi, en la Universidad Veracruzana (1977), de la que es profesor. Miembro fundador de la Escuela de Artes Plásticas de la Universidad Veracruzana. Ha expuesto colectivamente en México, Jalapa y Aguascalientes. Segundo lugar del Concurso del Cartel del IMSS (1971). Una de sus obras fue seleccionada en el Concurso Nacional de Escultura Monumental para la carretera Transpeninsular de Baja California (1973) y primer lugar en la rama de escultura del Concurso Nacional para Estudiantes de Artes Plásticas, en Aguascalientes (1974).

ROLÓN, JOSÉ ◆ n. en Zapotlán el Grande (hoy Ciudad Guzmán), Jal., y m. en el DF (1876-1945). Músico. Estudió composición, órgano y piano en Guadalajara (1898); y armonía, formas musicales, alta teoría y pedagogía con Moritz Moskowsky y André Gédalde en París (1907). Fue fundador (1907) y director de la Escuela de Música de Guadalajara (1907-27), fundador de la Academia de Piano de la Escuela de Música de Guadalajara (1911), fundador del Cuarteto Clásico de Guadalajara (1911), fundador de la Orquesta Sinfónica de Jalisco (1916) y del Orfeón de Voces Mixtas (1923). Estudió contrapunto y armonía con Nadia Boulanger y orquestación y fuga con Paul Dukas en la Escuela Normal de Música de París (1930). De nuevo en México, fue profesor y director de la orquesta de alumnos del Conservatorio Nacional, jefe de la Sección de Música del Departamento de Bellas Artes (1931-38) y director del Conservatorio (1938). Autor de *Obertura de concierto* (1920, estrenada por Julián Carrillo), *Obertura melancólica* (1922), *Sinfonía en mi menor* (1923), *Cuarteto opus 16*, *El festín de los enanos* (1925, premiada en 1927), *Cuauhtémoc* (1930, estrenada por la Orquesta Filarmónica de Berlín, dirigida por Bruno Seidler), *Piezas para canto y piano* (1930), *Scherzo sinfónico* (1930), *Zapotlán* (1930, suite sinfónica), *Danzas jaliscienses* y *Concierto en mi menor para piano y orquesta* (1929). Sus escritos fueron recopilados por Ricardo Miranda en *El sonido de lo propio* (1995).

ROMÁN, GILBERTO ◆ n. en Mexicali, BC, y m. cerca de Chilpancingo, Gro. (1961-1990). Boxeador. Fue secretario de Fomento Deportivo del Frente Juvenil Revolucionario. Peleador aficionado desde 1974, participó en los Juegos Olímpicos de Moscú en 1980. Boxeador profesional desde 1981, se convirtió en campeón mundial de peso supermosca, versión del Consejo Mundial de Boxeo, al derrotar a Jiro Watanabe (1986). Perdió el campeonato en 1988 frente al argentino Santos Laciar; lo recuperó el mismo año, al derrotar al colombiano Jesús *Sugar Baby* Rojas, en Miami, y lo perdió definitivamente en 1989 ante el ghanés Nana Konadu. El CMB lo designó Peleador del Mes en septiembre de 1988. Murió en un accidente automovilístico cerca de Chilpancingo. Sostuvo 61 combates profesionales, de los cuales ganó 54.

ROMÁN CALVO, NORMA ◆ n. en la ciudad de México (1924). Escritora. Maestra en lengua y literatura españolas por la UNAM. Diplomada en teatro para adolescentes por el CUT. Fue profesora del Instituto Andrés Soler, del CADAC, de la UNAM, la Escuela de Teatro del INBA y la Escuela de Escritores de la Sogem. Autora de teatro: *Los mimos parlantes* (1952), *Ni tanto que queme al santo.* (1956), *Pollo, mitote y casorio* (1967), *Los compadres* (1968), *Los encantos del relajo* (1968), *Éste es el juego,* (1971), *Las patas de hilo* (1971), *¿Cómo te quedó el ojo, Lucifer?* (1974), *Retablos mexicanos* (1973), *Junípero, juglar* (1975), *Médico, poeta y loco* (1975), *Escándalo en el paraíso* (1984), *El desertor*, *Pero luego luego, que se me hace tarde*, *Las enaguas coloradas*, *El demontre atravesado*, *Las yuntas*, *Que me entierren con pompa*, *Retablos mexicanos*, *Un paciente impaciente*, *El secreto* (1988), *En un lugar de la*

Mancha (1989), *A partir de las once* (1989), *Vuelo de campanas* (1989, Premio de Plata TIAFT, otorgado en Japón), *Dónde vas, Román Castillo* (1991) y *Delgadina y la reina su madrina* (1994, primer lugar en el Concurso de Obra de Teatro de la Facultad de Filosofía y Letras de la UNAM); cuento: *Retablos mexicanos* (1979); y la antología *Teatro para adolescentes* (1963). Mención de honor en el Festival de Teatro del INBA, por *Retablos mexicanos* (1973). Segundo lugar en el Premio Salvador Novo por *Escándalo en el paraíso* (1984).

Román Celis, Carlos ◆ n. en Coyuca de Catalán, Gro., y m. en el DF (1922-1995). Hizo estudios de derecho en la UNAM. Colaboró en *Excélsior* y otras publicaciones. Fue diputado federal, senador y presidente de la Sociedad Mexicana de Geografía y Estadística y del Consejo Consultivo de la Ciudad de México. Autor de *Belisario Domínguez, legislador sin miedo, El alcoholismo en México, Esplendor y tragedia de Coyuca de Catalán, Fiesta de palabras, Señores y señoras* y *El pistolerismo, flagelo nacional*.

Román Cuevas, Alberto ◆ n. en Teloloapan, Gro., y m. en el DF (1872-1942). Cirujano por la Escuela Nacional de Medicina (1893). Acosado por la policía porfirista debido a sus ideas antirreeleccionistas, pasó a Torreón y luego a Huatusco, Veracruz, donde fijó su residencia. Viajó a Europa y a su regreso se afilió al Partido Liberal. A fines de 1910, al iniciarse la insurrección maderista, se encontraba en Cuernavaca y entró en contacto con las fuerzas de Emiliano Zapata. En 1914 volvió a Huatusco y se incorporó al carrancismo, como jefe de los servicios sanitarios a las órdenes de Agustín Millán. Diputado al Congreso Constituyente de 1916-17, formó parte de su ala radical. Fue diputado federal (1917 y 18) y pasó a Toluca para ejercer la medicina. En 1920 se adhirió a la rebelión de Agua Prieta y fue jefe de los Servicios Médicos de la Secretaría de Guerra en el gobierno de Obregón.

Román Lugo, Fernando ◆ n. en Chilpancingo, Gro., y m. en Xalapa, Ver. (1916-1995). Licenciado en derecho por la Universidad Veracruzana, de la que fue profesor. Fue secretario general de Gobierno de Veracruz (1944-48), magistrado del Tribunal Superior de Justicia de Veracruz (1952), director del Registro Federal de Electores (1952), oficial mayor de la Secretaría Gobernación (1952-53), subsecretario de Gobernación (1953-58) y procurador de Justicia del Distrito y Territorios Federales (1958-64). Fue uno los redactores del *Código Penal del Estado de Veracruz* (1948).

Román Palacios, Humberto ◆ n. en Mata Redonda, Ver. (1936). Licenciado en derecho por la UNAM. Como abogado ha tenido cargos en el STPRM, la PGJDF, el gobierno del estado de Guerrero y diversos tribunales del país. Ha ejercido la docencia en la UAG, la UNAM, la Universidad Anáhuac, el Instituto Técnico de la PGJDF, la Universidad Panamericana y el Instituto de Especialización Judicial de la SCJN. Ministro de la Suprema Corte de Justicia (1994-). Ha impartido conferencias sobre temas legales. Coautor de *Dinámica del procedimiento penal federal y el amparo penal directo e indirecto. Metodología para el control y seguimiento* (1994).

Romance ◆ Revista quincenal literaria fundada en 1940 y desaparecida en 1941. La dirigió Juan Rejano. Su comité de redacción estuvo integrado por el propio Rejano, Miguel Prieto, Lorenzo Varela, José Herrera Perete, Antonio Sánchez Barbudo y Adolfo Sánchez Vázquez. Entre sus colaboradores figuraron, entre otros, Enrique González Martínez, Martín Luis Guzmán, Enrique Díez-Canedo, Pablo Neruda, Pedro Henríquez Ureña, Rómulo Gallegos y Juan Marinello.

Romano y Govea, Diego de ◆ n. en España y m. en Puebla, Pue. (?-1606). Sacerdote, fue oidor, canónigo, vicario general e inquisidor de Granada, visitador de la Inquisición en Llerena y Barcelona y obispo de Puebla (1578-1606). Participó en el Tercer Concilio Mexicano (1585) y promovió la beatificación de Sebastián de Aparicio. Autor de *Constituciones y reglas para el cabildo y coro de la Santa Iglesia Catedral de la Puebla de los Ángeles*.

Romano Guillemín, Francisco ◆ n. en Tlapa, Gro., y m. en Cuautla, Mor. (1884-1950). Fue discípulo de los pintores José Arpa, Fabrés y Gedovious. Entre sus cuadros destacan *Campo de coles, El beso, Naturaleza muerta* y *Patrono del atrio de la iglesia de San Miguel de Analco,* que se hallan en el Palacio de Bellas Artes.

Romano Iglesias, Dolores ◆ n. y m. en el DF (?-1999). Galerista y promotora de arte. En su Galería Romano, abierta en 1945, expusieron más de 600 artistas plásticos, entre los que destacan Frida Kahlo, Diego Rivera y David Alfaro Siqueiros.

Romano Muñoz, José ◆ n. en Villa de Cos, Zac., y m. en el DF (1890-1967). Doctor en filosofía por la UNAM. Fue director de la Escuela Nacional de Música y Arte Teatral (1915-17). Como jefe de la Sección de Preparatoria de la UNAM (1924-30), en 1928 participó en la redacción del proyecto de ley sobre la reforma universitaria. Subdirector de Dibujo y Trabajos Manuales de la SEP (1925-27), fundador y jefe de la Comisión Investigadora de la Situación de la Mujer y de los Menores Trabajadores (1936-38), miembro de la Comisión Revisora y Coordinadora de Planes de Estudios y Textos Escolares (1944-48) y jefe del Departamento de Cooperación Intelecual de la SEP (1949-52). Dirigió las escuelas normales Superior y de Especialización y el Museo Pedagógico Nacional. Tuvo a su cargo el Archivo General de la Nación y fue director general de Enseñanza Superior e Investigación Científica de la SEP (1952-53). Autor de *Ética valorativa* (1933), *El secreto del bien y del mal* y *Hacia una filosofía existencial* (1948). Miembro de la Sociedad Mexicana de Filosofía.

Romeo Lozano, Aurelio ◆ n. en España y m. en Monterrey, NL (1880-1944). Médico. Estudió en la Universidad Central de Madrid (1902) y la Autónoma de Nuevo León, donde fue

Carlos Román Celis

Fernando Román Lugo

Félix Romero

Héctor Manuel Romero

profesor. Director del Instituto Municipal de Puericultura (1926-39) y presidente de la Cruz Roja Española (1936-39). Llegó exiliado a México en 1939 y trabajó en la Casa de España. En Monterrey fundó los *Archivos Médicos Mexicanos* (1943). Colaborador de los *Archivos Españoles de Pediatría* (que dirigió en 1917-39), la *Revista Clínica de Madrid* y *Anales de Obstetricia, Ginecología y Pediatría*.

ROMER, ERNST ◆ n. en Austria y m. en el DF (1904-1974). Músico. Estudió con Frank Schreker y Arnold Schönberg. Entre 1922 y 1933 trabajó en Berlín en el Grosses Schauspielhaus y en el Staatstheater. Fue director de Ópera Cómica. Perseguido por los nazis, a fines de los años treinta estableció su residencia en México, donde participó en actividades antifascistas: fue cofundador y vicepresidente del Club Heine (1941-44). Al frente de la Sinfónica Nacional, continuó la labor de difusión, iniciada en Europa, de las obras de Mahler y el citado Schönberg, prohibidas por el régimen hitleriano. Fue director musical de la *Ópera de tres centavos*, de Brecht, montada por los demócratas germanohablantes. Dirigió diversos conjuntos sinfónicos del país y ejerció la docencia en el Conservatorio Nacional, donde creó la Ópera de Cámara.

ROMERO, EPIFANIO ◆ n. en Morelia, Mich., y ¿m. en la ciudad de México? (1824-?). También se cree que murió en Estados Unidos. Llegó muy joven a la capital de la República. Aprendió el oficio de ebanista y el de sastre. Fundó una agrupación de artesanos llamada Sociedad Artístico-Industrial (1844). En 1847 combatió a los invasores estadounidenses. En 1853 participó en la creación de la Sociedad Particular de Socorros Mutuos y en la Sociedad Mutua del Ramo de Sastrería, de la que fue presidente. Fue detenido por el gobierno de Santa Anna y permaneció un año en prisión. Se fugó para incorporarse a la revolución de Ayutla. Aparentemente participó en la guerra de Reforma y luchó contra la intervención francesa y el imperio. A su regreso a la ciudad de México, hacia 1867, se halló con que la Sociedad Artístico-Industrial existía de nuevo y propuso a Santiago Villanueva, su principal animador, que nombrase a Juárez presidente honorario de la misma, a lo que aquél se negó. La radicalización de la sociedad lo llevó a retirarse para fundar, con Juan Cano (☛), el Conservatorio Artístico-Industrial. En septiembre de 1871 participó en la fundación del Gran Círculo de Obreros de México, del que fue vicepresidente (1871-73) y presidente (1873). Existe la hipótesis de que emigró a Estados Unidos y luego se estableció en California, donde un hijo o nieto suyo, llamado también Epifanio Romero, alcanzó renombre como boxeador con el pseudónimo de *Bert Colima*.

ROMERO, FÉLIX ◆ n. en Oaxaca, Oax., y m. en la ciudad de México (¿1828?-1912). Estudió abogacía en el Instituto de Ciencias y Artes de Oaxaca (1852), donde fue profesor y director (1867 y 1876). Editó el periódico *La Bandera Amarilla*, opositor al gobierno de Martínez Pinillos, lo que le valió ser encarcelado. Se unió a la revolución de Ayutla y, por instrucciones de Benito Juárez, publicó *El Azote de los Tiranos*, órgano antisantanista. Fue diputado al Congreso Constituyente de 1856-57 y también constituyente de Oaxaca (1857). En la guerra de los Tres Años y durante la intervención francesa y el imperio luchó en las filas liberales y republicanas. Fue secretario general de Gobierno en Oaxaca durante la gestión de Félix Díaz, regente de la Corte de Justicia, gobernador sustituto (del 9 de noviembre de 1871 al 8 de enero de 1872), diputado federal y ministro y presidente de la Suprema Corte de Justicia.

ROMERO, HÉCTOR MANUEL ◆ n. y m. en el DF (1923-1998). Estudió medicina en la UNAM y música en el Conservatorio Nacional. Trabajó para la British Broadcasting Corporation y para la radiodifusora XELA, y fue asesor de las emisiones latinoamericanas de Radio Netherland. Fundador de la primera Agencia Mexicana de Relaciones Públicas (1947), coordinador de Enseñanza Turística de la SEP (1971), creador de la licenciatura en la Escuela Superior de Turismo (1974), primer director de Capacitación de la Secretaría de Turismo (1978), creador del espectáculo "Luz y Sonido" de Uxmal. Promovió la construcción de una sala de conciertos en las grutas de Cacahuamilpa. Fedatario del Haber Histórico y Cultural de la delegación Cuauhtémoc del DDF (1981-98) y miembro del Consejo Consultivo de la Ciudad de México (1983-86). Director de la *Enciclopedia mexicana de turismo*. Autor de *Temática socioeconómica del turismo* (1973), *Dónde y cómo vive el capitalino* (1978), *El turismo en México y el eterno femenino* (1981), *Historia del transporte en la ciudad de México* (1985), *Cuauhtémoc, historia temática de la delegación* (1988), *Barrios y colonias de la delegación Cuauhtémoc* (1988), *La hotelería en la ciudad de México* (1989), *Del tianguis a la modernización del coabasto* (1991) y *Enciclopedia temática de la delegación Cuauhtémoc* (1994), entre otras obras. Recibió el Premio de Literatura Alejo Carpentier (1983). Cofundador de la Asociación Mexicana de Profesionales en Relaciones Públicas (1953) y de la Asociación Interamericana de Publicidad (1961). Vicepresidente honorario de la Asociación Interamericana de Productores de Radio y Televisión.

ROMERO, JAVIER ◆ n. en Champotón, Camp. (1923). Hizo estudios de medicina e historia en la UNAM. Militó en el Partido Popular (1950-56), del que fue candidato a diputado federal en 1952. Fue traductor de la revista *Paz*, órgano del Comité Mexicano por la Paz (1951-52). Colaboró en el diario *El Popular* (1958-61) y fue fundador de la Cooperativa Publicaciones Mexicanas (1961), que lanzó en 1962 el diario *El Día*, en el que dirigió el suplemento *El Gallo Ilustrado*; subdirector (1965-70 y 1976-81) y director de *Crucero*, vespertino del periódico (1970-76). Ha colaborado en *Excélsior*, *Jueves de Excélsior*, *Revista de Revistas*, *El Nacional*, Notimex y en el programa *Enfoque periodístico* del

Canal 11 (1982-86). Coautor de *Papeles y documentos públicos de Lázaro Cárdenas* (1978), *VII Jornadas de Historia de Occidente Francisco J. Múgica* (1984), *Conciencia mexicana en lucha* (1985). Fundador del Seminario de Estudios Marxistas de la Facultad de Filosofía y Letras de la UNAM (1950), Premio Nacional de Periodismo al mejor artículo de fondo (1979). Medalla Justo Sierra otorgada por el estado de Campeche (1996). Ha sido miembro de la Sociedad de Estudios Mexicanos (1951-52) y del Centro de Estudios para la Historia de Campeche (1954-55).

ROMERO, JESÚS C. ◆ n. y m. en el DF (1893-1958). Musicólogo. Se tituló de médico en la Escuela Nacional de Medicina (1917), especializado en obstetricia. Estudió armonía con Juan B. Fuentes. Fue secretario de la Unión Filarmónica y en 1921 participó en la organización de los conciertos de las Fiestas del Centenario. Fue investigador de historia de la música en la SEP y profesor de esa especialidad en la UNAM; director de la Escuela Nacional de Música, director del Museo Pedagógico Nacional de la SEP y colaborador de *El Universal*. Autor, entre otros, de los libros y folletos *Ensayo de una nueva nomenclatura obstétrica y su aprovechamiento en la clínica* (1924), *Instrucciones para antes y después del parto, con una serie de indicaciones para el cuidado y aseo del niño* (1926), *México carece de tintura oficial de yodo* (1928), *Compendio de historia universal* (1933), *Atlas de geografía histórica. El antiguo Oriente* (1937), *Músicos yucatecos distinguidos* (1943), *Historia de la música de Yucatán* (1944), *La ópera en Yucatán* (1945), *El folklore en México* (1946), *La ópera nacional en México y su génesis* (1947), *Durango en la evolución musical de México* (1949), *Chopin en México* (1950) y *La música en Zacatecas y los músicos zacatecanos* (1953). Fue secretario perpetuo de la Academia Mexicana de la Historia, miembro de honor de la Confederación Mexicana de Sociedades Mutualistas y miembro de la Sociedad Mexicana de Geografía y Estadística.

ROMERO, JOSÉ ANTONIO ◆ n. ¿en Guadalajara, Jal.?, y m. en la ciudad de México (?-1857). Fue diputado local, secretario de Gobierno en Jalisco y miembro de la comisión redactora del Código Civil de ese estado (1832). Se unió a los conservadores y, tras la promulgación del Plan de Cuernavaca, fue gobernador interino y constitucional de Jalisco (1834-36). Ocupó la Secretaría del Interior (del 25 de octubre de 1837 al 8 de marzo de 1838, del 18 de mayo al 10 de julio de 1839 y del 19 al 26 de julio de 1839) en dos gabinetes de Anastasio Bustamante y con Santa Anna. Fue magistrado de la Suprema Corte de Justicia y miembro del Colegio Nacional de Abogados.

ROMERO, JOSÉ GUADALUPE ◆ n. en Silao y m. en León, Gto. (1814-1866). Doctor en cánones por la Universidad de Guadalajara. Profesor, secretario y rector del Colegio de la Purísima Concepción, de Guanajuato, y del Seminario Tridentino de Morelia. Fue cura de Silao y de San Felipe y canónigo doctoral de Morelia. Miembro del cabildo eclesiástico y diputado local. Autor de *Noticias para formar la historia y la estadística del obispado de Michoacán* (1862), *Opúsculo sobre el distrito de Coalcomán* y *Mapa del estado de Michoacán*. Su biblioteca se conserva en el Colegio de San Nicolás de Hidalgo.

ROMERO, JOSÉ RUBÉN ◆ n. en Cotija de la Paz, Mich., y m. en el DF (1890-1952). Durante su adolescencia editó el periódico *Iris*, en Ario de Rosales, donde publicó sus primeros poemas. Fue empleado público en Sahuayo y Santa Clara del Cobre. En 1911 se unió a la insurrección maderista y fue ayudante del gobernador michoacano Miguel Silva González (1912). Encarcelado tras el cuartelazo huertista, huyó a la ciudad de México, pero regresó en 1914 a Michoacán, donde se dedicó al comercio. Al término del conflicto armado fue secretario particular de Pascual Ortiz Rubio, gobernador de Michoacán, y su representante en la ciudad de México. Inspector general de Comunicaciones (1920), jefe de los departamentos de Publicidad y Administrativo de la SRE (1921), cónsul general en Barcelona (1930-33 y 1935-37), director del Registro Civil (1933-35), embajador en Brasil (1937-39) y en Cuba (1939) y rector interino de la Universidad Michoacana (1943). Autor de *Fantasías* (1908, poesía), *Cuentos rurales* (1915), *Alma heroica* (1917), *Sentimental* (1919), *Tacámbaro* (1922), *Versos viejos* (1930), *Apuntes de un lugareño* (1932), *Desbandada* (1934), *La vida inútil de Pito Pérez* (1938), *Una vez fui rico* (1939), *Rostros* (1942), *Alusiones a la guerra* (1943), *Algunas cosillas de Pito Pérez que se me quedaron en el tintero* (1945) y *Mis andanzas académicas* (1950), entre otras obras. Perteneció a la LEAR (1934-38) y fue miembro correspondiente y de número de la Academia Mexicana (de la Lengua). En 1978 el INBA instituyó en su honor el Premio Nacional de Novela José Rubén Romero.

ROMERO, MATÍAS ◆ n. en Oaxaca, Oax., y m. en EUA (1837-1898). Abogado. Fue funcionario judicial y colaborador de Benito Juárez en la elaboración de la *Ley de Administración de Justicia Orgánica de los Tribunales de la Nación, del Distrito y Territorios*. Desde el inicio de la guerra de los Tres Años acompañó a Juárez hasta la instalación del gobierno liberal en Veracruz. En 1859 fue secretario de la legación mexicana en Washington y un año después quedó

Jesús C. Romero

ARCHIVO: XAVIER ESPARZA

Matías Romero

como encargado interino de negocios, hasta 1862. En 1863 tomó las armas contra la intervención francesa y el imperio como coronel y jefe del Estado Mayor de Porfirio Díaz. Volvió a Estados Unidos como ministro, cargo que ocupó hasta 1867. Secretario de Hacienda (del 16 de enero al 25 de mayo de 1868, del 8 de agosto al 20 de noviembre de 1868 y del 30 de septiembre de 1869 al 12 de junio de 1872) de Juárez, senador por Chiapas (1875), diputado local en Oaxaca (1876) y secretario de Hacienda (del 24 de mayo de 1877 al 4 de abril de 1879 y del 1 de enero de 1892 al 7 de mayo de 1893) de Díaz. En Estados Unidos inició la formación de una compañía para construir un ferrocarril de México a Guatemala, en asociación con Ulyses Grant, proyecto que luego desechó. Fue embajador extraordinario en Estados Unidos (1882-92 y 1893-98). Autor de *El estado de Oaxaca* (1886), *Cultivo del café en la costa meridional de Chiapas* (1893), *Mexico and the United States* y *Coffee and Indian Rubber Culture in Mexico* (1898).

Romero, Nicolás ♦ n. en Nopala (actual estado de Hidalgo), y m. en la ciudad de México (1827-1865). Obrero textil, se unió a la guerrilla liberal de

Archivo: Xavier Esparza

Capilla de Nicolás Romero en el Panteón de Dolores

Archivo: Xavier Esparza

Nicolás Romero

Aureliano Rivera (1858), con quien luchó durante la guerra de los Tres Años. Volvió a tomar las armas contra la intervención francesa y el imperio, organizó una guerrilla que operó principalmente en Michoacán, Guerrero y el Estado de México, muchas veces en combinación con las tropas irregulares de Vicente Riva Palacio. Se le conocía como *el León de las Montañas*. Fue aprehendido en Michoacán y fusilado.

Romero, Salvador ♦ n. en Dolores Hidalgo, Gto. (1936). Pintor y grabador. Estudió en el Instituto de Ciencias y Artes de Baja California, en la ENAP (1961) y en La Esmeralda (1962). En 1959 expuso individualmente por primera ocasión en la Universidad Obrera. Ingresó al Taller de Gráfica Popular (1968). En 1970 expuso en Berlín y ha participado en tres bienales de grabado en Puerto Rico (1972, 1974 y 1976). Coautor, con Francisco Luna, de *La educación en México*, serie de cinco murales para la Dirección de Educación Primaria en la ciudad de México.

Romero Alonso, Miguel ♦ n. en Yucatán (1887-?). Médico militar graduado en 1914. Fue jefe del Departamento de Salubridad Pública de Yucatán (1915), diputado al Congreso Constituyente de 1916-17, diputado federal en dos legislaturas (1917-20), regidor y alcalde de la ciudad de México (1922), presidente honorario del Consejo Cultural y Artístico de la ciudad de México y enviado extraordinario y ministro plenipotenciario en Japón y China (1923).

Romero Apis, José Elías ♦ n. en Toluca, Edo. de Méx. (1948). Licenciado en derecho por la UNAM y maestro en administración por el Instituto Panamericano de Alta Dirección de Empresas. Ingresó en 1982 a la PGR, donde ha sido subprocurador de la Zona Norte, subprocurador de Averiguaciones Previas y subdirector de Comunicación Social (1994-99). Escribe en el diario *Excélsior*.

Romero Armendáriz, Ventura ♦ n. en San Buenaventura, Chih. y m. en el DF (1913-1994). Estudió comercio, aviación, teneduría de libros, violín, guitarra y acordeón. En 1932 se inició como cantante en la radiodifusora XEFI de Chihuahua. En 1935 llegó a la ciudad de México y un año después ganó un concurso de canciones promovido por Pepe Guízar. En 1941 cantaba para la organización Radio Mil y más tarde, al frente de un grupo, llegó a la XEQ; perteneció al Cuarteto Metropolitano y al Trío Tamaulipeco. En 1949 tenía un programa propio en la XEW; se inició como actor de cine en la cinta *Norteña de mis amores*. Son obra suya las canciones *La burrita*, *Nueva claridad*, *Margarita*, *El gavilán pollero*, *Madrigal*, *Tu castigo*, *Allá en mi pueblito*, *El sapito*, *Me voy a casar*, *El panadero*, *Lupita mía*, *Soy infeliz*, *La vaca de Ventura*, *Los velices*, *Senderito de amor*, *El norteño* y *Peregrino*, entre otras. En 1994 recibió la Medalla General Ángel Trías como ciudadano distinguido de su estado.

Romero Arvizu, Manuel ♦ n. en Etzatlán, Jal. (1919). Sacerdote ordenado en 1945. Ha sido profesor de diversos seminarios franciscanos, párroco en Hebbronville, Texas, y Monterrey; guardián de los conventos de Guadalajara y Zapopan, obispo titular de Dusa y prelado del Nayar (1962-94).

Romero Castillo, Cecilia ♦ n. en el DF (1952). Secretaria bilingüe graduada en el Centro de Estudios Comerciales y Lingüísticos (1970), donde ejerció la docencia (1971-84), y profesora de inglés por el Instituto Anglo Mexicano de Cultura (1974-75). Desde 1970 pertenece al PAN, en el que ha sido miembro del CEN (1986) y consejera del Comité Distrital en el DF (1987). Presidenta de la Asociación Nacional Cívica Femenina (1973 y 1981-84), diputada federal plurinominal (1985-88) y diputada federal (1994-97).

Romero Deschamps, Carlos ◆ n. en Tampico, Tams. (1944). Hizo estudios de contaduría en su ciudad natal. Afiliado al PRI desde 1961, ha coordinado campañas electorales en su estado y ha sido miembro del Consejo Político Nacional de ese partido. Es miembro del Sindicato de Trabajadores Petroleros de la República Mexicana, de cuyo Comité Ejecutivo ha sido secretario, entre otros cargos. También ha sido primer secretario nacional sustituto de la CTM y secretario de la Comisión Ejecutiva del Congreso del Trabajo. Diputado federal (1979-82 y 1991-94), y senador para el periodo 1994-2000.

Romero Flores, Jesús ◆ n. en La Piedad de Cabadas, Mich., y m. en el DF (1885-1987). Profesor normalista en el Colegio de San Nicolás (1905), fundó el Colegio León XIII en La Piedad (1906-08), editó los semanarios *Don Quijote* (1906) y *El Distrito* (1907), dirigió el Instituto Hidalgo (1909) y la Escuela de Niños de Tangancícuaro (1910). Participó en la insurrección maderista, al término de ésta fue director de la Escuela Oficial de La Piedad (1911), inspector general de Escuelas Oficiales y Particulares de Michoacán (1913-15), director general de Instrucción Pública de Michoacán (1915) y diputado al Congreso Constituyente de 1916-17. En la ciudad de México presidió el Ateneo Nezahualcóyotl, dirigió una escuela primaria y el semanario *La Escuela del Trabajo*. Diputado local (1920) y federal (1924), director de la Escuela Normal de Michoacán (1926), director de Bibliotecas de Michoacán (1928), director de Educación Primaria de la SEP (1930), editor de la revista *Orientación*, jefe del Departamento de Historia del Museo Nacional (1935-36), rector de la Universidad de Michoacán (1943), senador (1964-70) y director de la Biblioteca del Senado (1977-80). Autor de más de 60 libros, entre los que destacan: *Don Vasco de Quiroga, su vida y sus obras* (1911), *Historia de la civilización mexicana* (1924), *Historia de la ciudad de Morelia* (1928), *Leyendas y cuentos michoacanos* (2 t., 1938), *Anales históricos de la Revolución Mexicana* (4 t., 1939), *Don Miguel Hidalgo, padre de la Independencia mexicana* (1945), *Historia de Michoacán* (2 t., 1946), *Chapultepec en la historia de México* (1947), *México. Historia de una gran ciudad* (3 t., 1948), *Diccionario biográfico mexicano* (1950), *Diccionario michoacano de historia y geografía* (1960), *Antología literaria de los diputados constituyentes* (1969) y *Lázaro Cárdenas, biografía de un gran mexicano* (1972). Recibió la Medalla Belisario Domínguez (1976). *Doctor honoris causa* por la Universidad de Michoacán (1951).

Romero González, Salvador ◆ n. en Dolores Hidalgo, Gto. (1936). Estudió pintura en el Instituto de Ciencias y Artes de Baja California y en la ENAP. En 1968 ingresó en el Taller de Gráfica Popular. Es director del Taller Infantil de Artes Plásticas Num. 4 del INBA. Ha presentado numerosas exposiciciones de grabado, individuales y colectivas, en México, la República Democrática de Alemania, Puerto Rico y la Unión Soviética. Premio de adquisición del Concurso Anual de Dibujo, Pintura, Escultura y Grabado de Maestros de Artes Plásticas del INBA (1973) y primer premio del mismo concurso en 1979, con la obra *Diurno a Augusto César Sandino*.

Romero Ixtlapale, Serafín ◆ n. en Tepeyanco, Tlax. (1944). Licenciado en derecho por la UAP. Integrante del PRI desde 1962. Ha sido oficial mayor del Instituto de Estudios Superiores de su estado, agente del Ministerio Público y presidente del Tribunal Superior de Justicia de Tlaxcala. Senador para el periodo 1994-2000 e integrante de la Gran Comisión del Senado. Es presidente de la Barra de Abogados del estado de Tlaxcala.

Romero Kolbeck, Gustavo ◆ n. en la ciudad de México (1923). Licenciado en economía por la UNAM (1946) con estudios de posgrado en análisis económico en la Universidad George Washington (1948). Profesor de la UNAM (1949-82) y de la UIA (1953-54). En la Presidencia ha sido director de la Comisión de Inversiones (1954-58) y director de Inversiones Públicas (1959-61). Director fundador del CEESP (1962-65), director general del boletín *Business Trends* y de la revista *Expansión* (1966-70), director de la Escuela de Economía de la Universidad Anáhuac (1967-70), embajador en Japón (1971-73), director general de Finasa (1973), presidente del Patronato de la UNAM (1974-82), director general de Nafinsa (1974-76), director general del Banco de México (1976-82), embajador en la Unión Soviética (1982-83) y director general del Banco Obrero (1983-90). Coautor de *México, 50 años de revolución* (1965) y *La exención fiscal como instrumento de atracción de industrias* (1970). Autor de *Tres etapas de la planeación del desarrollo económico*, *Estudio económico del estado de Baja California*, *Estudio económico del estado de San Luis Potosí*, *Estudio de evaluación económica de las obras de cuota* y *Planeación de industrias rurales*. Miembro de la American Economic Association y del Colegio de Economistas de México. *Doctor honoris causa* por la Universidad de las Américas (1978). En 1951 creó el Premio Anual de Economía del Banco Nacional de México.

Romero Llamas, Ángel *Zapopan* ◆ n. en Zapopan, Jal. (¿1933?). Comenzó en el ciclismo a los 16 años. Ganó varias vueltas ciclistas nacionales. Compitió en los Juegos Olímpicos de Helsinki (1952) y en el Campeonato Mundial de Ruta. Se retiró en 1955. Fue dos veces presidente municipal de Zapopan, diputado al congreso local, regidor de Guadalajara y encargado del Deporte en el gobierno de su estado. Fue presidente de la Federación Mexicana de Ciclismo (1978-82).

Carlos Romero Deschamps

Jesús Romero Flores

Gustavo Romero Kolbeck

Romero Ortega de Rayo, Carmen ◆ n. en España (1923). Licenciada en civilización francesa por la Universidad de París. Llegó exiliada a México al término de la guerra civil española. Tomó cursos de comercio en el Colegio Madrid y de administración, artesanía y restauración artística en la Dirección General de Educación de la SEP. Ha sido editora adjunta de la revista *Defensa Militar*, gerenta de producción de los laboratorios Thomé, subgerenta de Roberto Block, fundadora y administradora de la fábrica de tejidos de punto Darling, consejera de la empresa Industrial Técnica Rayo, promotora voluntaria del Desarrollo Integral de la Familia y vocal del Ateneo Español de México. Fundó el Centro de Desarrollo para la Comunidad República Española. Coautora del libro *Nuevas raíces*.

Pedro Romero de Terreros

Romero Pérez, Humberto ◆ n. en La Piedad, Mich. (1923). Licenciado en derecho por la UNAM (1951). Ha sido secretario general del procurador general de la República (1946-52), jefe de prensa de la Secretaría del Trabajo (1952-58), presidente sustituto de la Junta Federal de Conciliación y Arbitraje (1953), jefe de prensa de la Presidencia de la República (1953-58), secretario particular del presidente Adolfo López Mateos (1958-64), presidente del Instituto de Relaciones Culturales México-Argentina (1962), jefe de asesores de la sección general de gobierno A del DDF (1963), diputado federal (1979-82), diputado local en Michoacán y director general de Difusión y Relaciones Públicas del DDF (1982-85).

Manuel Romero Rubio

Romero Rubio, Manuel ◆ n. y m. en la ciudad de México (1828-1895). Abogado. Fue juez de Tulancingo y secretario de la Suprema Corte de Justicia. Apoyó la revolución de Ayutla. Diputado al Congreso Constituyente (1856-57) y secretario de Gobierno del Distrito Federal. En 1858 peleó en las fuerzas liberales en la guerra de los Tres Años. Fue representante del gobierno juarista en Veracruz, se le aprehendió y estuvo encarcelado ocho meses en la ciudad de México. Liberado, militó en los ejércitos de Santos Degollado, Zuazua y González Ortega, con quien organizó el gobierno del Distrito Federal al triunfo de los liberales. Diputado federal, al iniciarse la intervención francesa acompañó a Juárez a San Luis Potosí y volvió a la ciudad de México, donde se le aprehendió y desterró. Regresó al país después de un recorrido por Europa y fue nuevamente diputado federal y secretario de Relaciones Exteriores (del 31 de agosto al 20 de noviembre de 1876) de Sebastián Lerdo de Tejada. A la caída de éste se exilió en Panamá y Estados Unidos. Volvió a México como senador por Tabasco y fue secretario de Gobernación (del 1 de diciembre de 1884 al 3 de octubre de 1895) en el gobierno de Porfirio Díaz, quien en 1881 se convirtió en su yerno.

Romero Ruiz, Francisco ◆ n. en Contepec, Mich. (1946). Estudió escultura, pintura, grabado, dibujo y esmaltes en la Academia de San Carlos (1970). Ha sido profesor de escuelas preparatorias y en talleres de escultura y pintura. Formó parte del grupo de pintores y escultores que realizaron el Polyforum Cultural Siqueiros (1970). Autor de la escultura monumental de Morelos en San Bartolo Naucalpan (1973).

Romero Soto, Luis ◆ n. en San Juan del Río, Qro., y m. en el DF (1876-1964). Ingeniero, estudió en la Escuela Nacional de Bellas Artes (1894). Profesor de la Escuela de Maestros Constructores. Fue fundador de la empresa Jackson y Compañía (1894), que hizo la conversión de libras a kilogramos en las básculas. Fundó las primeras fábricas de tortillas (1900), de tortilladoras (1903), de harina de maíz (1912), de techos de cemento prefabricados (1914), de pan (1916), frituras (1928), estufas (1932) y láminas de fibrocemento (1938), así como un taller de herrería artística que hizo trabajos para la Cámara de Diputados, el Palacio Nacional, el Palacio de Bellas Artes, el Departamento Central, la Suprema Corte de Justicia, Pemex, el Banco de México, la Joyería La Esmeralda, el Orfanatorio Mier y Pesado, la Catedral Metropolitana y la Basílica de Guadalupe. Patentó 69 inventos, entre los cuales destacan un buzón que automáticamente cancelaba los timbres, foliaba las cartas y expedía recibos (1895), diversas máquinas tortilladoras (1899-1911), un filtro para agua (1907), un procedimiento para elaborar harina de maíz (1911), techos y vigas prefabricados de cemento armado (1914), un extractor de aguamiel (1929), una lavadora de ropa (1930), una estufa de gas butano comercializada con el nombre de *Llamazul* (1933), una freidora automática (1954) y una quesadillera automática (1960).

Manuel Romero de Terreros

Romero de Terreros, Manuel ◆ n. y m. en la ciudad de México (1819-1878). Fue miembro de diversas instituciones de beneficencia, senador (1847 y 1875), secretario de Hacienda del Estado de México y gobernador del DF (1862-63). Durante la intervención francesa militó a las órdenes de Zaragoza (1862). En 1964 estaba en Estados Unidos y en 1865 en París, donde en 1866 fue allanada su casa por la policía francesa que suponía, con razón, que ahí se reunían los mexicanos antiintervencionistas. Ayudó a la repatriación de los prisioneros mexicanos que se hallaban en Europa.

Romero de Terreros, Pedro ◆ n. en España y m. en San Miguel Regla, Hgo. (1710-1781). Llegó a la Nueva España en 1732, se dedicó a la arriería y accidentalmente descubrió una veta de plata, debido a la cual se enriqueció. En 1742 fue alcalde ordinario, alférez y alguacil mayor de Querétaro. En 1743 se asoció con José Alejandro Bustamante e inició la explotación de las minas de Real del Monte, donde en 1766 rebajó el salario de los trabajadores y estalló la huelga más importante del México colonial (☛*Huelga minera de 1766*). Destinó parte de sus cuantiosas ganancias económicas a diversas obras religiosas y filantrópicas, prestó dinero a los gobiernos virreinales de Croix y Bucareli y, entre otros regalos que hizo a la Corona española, se contó un buque de guerra que participó en la batalla de Trafalgar. Por su generosidad, Carlos III le otorgó el título de conde de Santa María de Regla (1769). En 1775 fundó el Monte Pío de Ánimas, actual Nacional Monte de Piedad.

Romero de Terreros y Vinent, Manuel ◆ n. y m. en el DF (1880-1968). Historiador y crítico de arte. Estudió en el Colegio de Stonyhurst y en las universidades de Cambridge y Oxford. Formó parte del grupo literario la Arcadia, con el nombre de *Gliconte Tirio*. Fue miembro y presidente del patronato del Nacional Monte de Piedad, profesor universitario, bibliotecario del Museo Nacional de Arqueología, Historia y Etnografía (1920), investigador del Instituto de Investigaciones Estéticas de la UNAM y curador del Museo Numismático del Banco de México (1955). Autor de medio centenar de libros, entre los que destacan: *Los condes de Regla* (1909), *Arte colonial. Apuntes* (3 t., 1916-21), *Residencias coloniales de la ciudad de México* (1918), *La casa de los azulejos* (1919), *Nociones de literatura castellana* (1920), *Don Pedro Romero de Terreros, primer conde de Regla, caballero de Calatrava y fundador del Monte de Piedad de Ánimas* (1933), *Paisajistas mexicanos del siglo XIX* (1943), *Acueductos de México en la historia y en el arte* (1949), *La puerta de bronce y otros cuentos* (1957), *Ayotzingo* (1959); y las obras de teatro *Intuición*, *La confesión*, *Luciferina*, *Paso macabro*, *Asmodelia*, *Comedia absurda*, *El rey sueña*, *Entre las flores*, *Fausto II*, *La mujer blanca*, *Casa de huéspedes* y *El juez*. En 1917 ingresó en las academias mexicanas de la Lengua y de la Historia. De ésta fue presidente (1962-68) y en ambas aparece como marqués de San Francisco.

Romero de Valle, Emilia ◆ n. en Perú y m. en el DF (1903-1968). En 1941 se casó con el escritor hondureño Rafael Heliodoro Valle y ambos fijaron su residencia en México. En 1949, Valle fue designado embajador de su país en Estados Unidos (cargo que desempeñó hasta 1959) y, en Washington, Emilia Romero ayudó a la formación del Ateneo Americano. Autora de *Corpancho, un amigo de México* (1949), *Recuerdo a Rafael Heliodoro Valle en los cincuenta años de su vida literaria* (1958), *Fray Melchor de Talamantes, precursor y protomártir* (1961), *Corona a la memoria de Rafael Heliodoro Valle* (1963), *México en la poesía y en la vida de Chocano* (1965) y *Un estudiante hondureño en el México de 1908 a 1911* (1966). Perteneció a la Sociedad Folklórica de México, a la Asociación Mexicana de Historiadores y a la Sociedad Mexicana de Historia de la Ciencia y la Tecnología. En su testamento donó sus libros y los de su esposo a la Biblioteca Nacional de México y legó un fondo de un millón de pesos para el establecimiento del premio bianual (de 100,000 pesos) y la beca Rafael Heliodoro Valle, para escritores latinoamericanos.

Romero Vargas, Ignacio ◆ n. en Acatzingo, Pue., y m. en la ciudad de México (1835-1895). En 1855 abandonó el seminario para formar una guerrilla liberal que resistió al sitio que Haro y Tamariz puso a la ciudad de Puebla. Se unió a las tropas de Ignacio de Llave. Fue diputado y presidente de la primera Legislatura Constitucional de Puebla. Luchó contra la intervención francesa y el imperio. Fue gobernador interino (1869-72) y constitucional (1876) de Puebla, varias veces diputado federal, senador durante la presidencia de Manuel González y ministro mexicano en Berlín.

Romero de Velasco, Flavio ◆ n. en Ameca, Jal. (1925). Licenciado en derecho por la UNAM. Miembro del PRI, en el que ha sido secretario general del comité del DF, delegado en varias entidades y director de la Comisión de Divulgación Ideológica (1957-58). Fue gerente general de La Forestal, tres veces diputado federal (1955-58, 1961-64 y 1973-76), director de Acción Social Educativa de la SEP, administrador de la aduana de Ciudad Juárez (1965-71) y gobernador de Jalisco (1977-83). En 1998 fue detenido bajo la acusación de lavado de dinero y asociación delictuosa.

Romita ◆ Municipio de Guanajuato situado al sur de León. Superficie: 493 km². Habitantes: 51,174, de los cuales 9,756 forman la población económicamente activa. Hablan alguna lengua indígena 12 personas mayores de cinco años.

Romo, Daniela ◆ n. en el DF (1959). Cantante y actriz. Se inició en la televisión como animadora de un programa de concursos de baile. Ha actuado en numerosas telenovelas. Empezó a cantar en 1978. Ha grabado cinco discos de larga duración; entre sus canciones más conocidas se encuentran *Mentiras*, *Celos* y *Mujer de todos, mujer de nadie* (1986).

Daniela Romo

Romo, José María ◆ n. en Guanajuato, Gto., y m. en el DF (1884-1955). Escritor. Se inició como periodista en la redacción del órgano antiporfirista *Juan Panadero*. Autor de las obras de teatro del género chico: *El último recurso* (1909), *El filón de oro* (1909), *La pepita de oro* (1910), *Los pichones* (1910) y *La séptima luna* (1910).

Romo, Vicente *Huevo* ◆ n. en Santa Rosalía, BCS (1943). Beisbolista. De 1968 a 1974 fue lanzador de grande ligas en los equipos *Dodgers* de Los Ángeles, *Indios* de Cleveland, *Medias Rojas* de Boston, *Medias Blancas* de Chicago y *Padres* de San Diego.

Romo Armería, Jesús ◆ n. en Aguascalientes, Ags., y m. en el DF

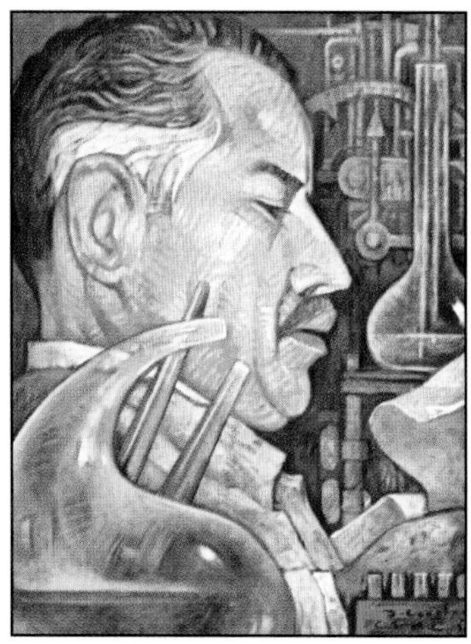

Jesús Romo Armería en retrato al óleo de Jorge González Camarena

Arturo Romo Gutiérrez

Humberto Roque Villanueva

(1922-1977). Químico farmacobiólogo (1945) y doctor en ciencias químicas por la UNAM (1949), institución en la que fue profesor, investigador (1945) y director del Instituto de Química (1971-75). Fue catedrático de la Universidad Motolinía y profesor honorario de la Universidad Autónoma de Guadalajara (1970). Investigador de los laboratorios Syntex (1947-57) y fundador de la *Revista Latinoamericana de Química*. Perteneció a la Academia de la Investigación Científica de México, a la Sociedad Americana de Química, al Comité de Química Orgánica de la Unión Internacional de Química Pura y Aplicada. En 1972 ingresó en El Colegio Nacional. Premio de Ciencias de la Academia de la Investigación Científica (1962), Medalla Andrés Manuel del Río (1966) de la Sociedad Química de México y Premio Nacional de Ciencias y Artes (1971).

Romo Estrada, Ramiro ◆ n. en San Juan de los Lagos, Jal. (1919). Pintor. Estudió en la Escuela Libre de Arte y Publicidad (1944) y en La Esmeralda (1947). Fue profesor de la Universidad Veracruzana (1956-57). Autor de los murales *La luz* (1947), *Triunfo del deportista* (1947, en el Centro Deportivo Chapultepec, ya destruido), *Geometría gráfica* (1948), *La enseñanza dentro del ejército* (1948), *Ciencia y técnica optométrica* (1948), *Pasado, presente y futuro del deporte en México* (1949, en el Centro Deportivo Chapultepec), *Capacidad creativa del pueblo de México* (1950, en Nuevo Laredo), *Cultivo y beneficio del café* (1956, en Jalapa), *El hombre y su técnica de cultivo cafetalera* (1957, en Nueva York), *Alimentos* (1958), *Evolución médica* (1959), *Flores y fauna* (1960), *Circo* (1960), *Niños jugando* (1960, en el Hospital Shriner), *Cultura teotihuacana* (1964), *Quetzalcóatl* (1964, en el Museo Nacional de Antropología), *Leyenda de la creación del sol y la luna* (1965, en el hotel Continental-Hilton, destruido), *Mural a todo mecate* (1965) y *Transformación del café en licor* (1965).

Romo Gutiérrez, Arturo ◆ n. en Fresnillo, Zac. (1942). Licenciado por la Escuela Libre de Derecho y por la UNAM (1972), posgraduado en economía en la Universidad de Georgetown (1969). Miembro del PRI, en el que ha sido secretario de Acción Política de la Dirección Nacional Juvenil, miembro del Consejo Consultivo del IEPES (1981-82), integrante de la Comisión Nacional de Acción Política (1981-82), colaborador de las revistas *Línea* y *La República* y presidente del Consejo Consultivo del IEPES (1988-94), así como secretario de Divulgación Ideológica (1981-82) y secretario adjunto de la presidencia del CEN (1982-88). En la CTM se ha desempeñado como secretario de Educación (1983-86), director del periódico *Ceteme* (1985-88) y secretario de Educación y Comunicación Social (1986-88). Ha sido asesor de agrupaciones de trabajadores, delegado general del Sindicato Industrial de la Construcción, secretario de Finanzas de la Federación Obrera de Organizaciones Juveniles, diputado federal suplente por el DF (1970-73), secretario de la Asociación Mexicana de Orientación e Información Obrera (1971), delegado especial del Injuve para la organización de las Casas de la Juventud (1972-73), subprocurador de Quejas y Organización Colectiva de la Profeco, dos veces diputado federal por Zacatecas (1973-76 y 1979-82), senador suplente (1976-82) y propietario por Zacatecas (1982-88), secretario general de la Federación de Trabajadores de Zacatecas y gobernador de Zacatecas (1992-98). Autor de *El banco de los trabajadores* (1969).

Rómulo, Teódulo ◆ n. en San Bartolomé Matlalocan, Tlax. (1943). Pintor egresado de La Esmeralda, estudió en Argentina y en 1963 fue becado por el gobierno de Francia. Creador de la técnica de la aquilografía. Expuso por primera vez en 1970, en la Galería Chapultepec. Ha expuesto en Alemania, Japón, Estados Unidos, Francia, Noruega, Argentina, Suiza, Bulgaria y España.

Ronquillo, Víctor ◆ n. en el DF (1957). Licenciado en lengua y literatura hispánicas por la UNAM. Fue reportero en la sección cultural de *El Nacional* y en la Dirección de Literatura del INBA, jefe de Información del programa televisivo *Expediente 13/22:30*, colaborador de *Diálogos*, *Encuentro*, *México en el Arte*, *Punto*, *El Universal* y *unomásuno*. Autor de la biografía *Miguel N. Lira: polígrafo* (1988); las crónicas: *La nota roja en México 1950-1960* (1995), *El caso Molinet* (1995, con Paco Ignacio Taibo II) y *La nota roja en México 1920-1929* (1996); el testimonio: *La muerte viste de rosa* (1994); y los reportajes: *La guerra oculta. Impunidad y violencia* (1996) y *Las muertas de Juárez* (1998). Becario del INBA (1984-85) y del Centro Mexicano de Escritores (1987-88).

Rooth, Laszlo ◆ n. en Rumania (1932). Director de orquesta. Estudió con Zoltan Kodaly y Ferencz Farkas. Viajó a México por primera vez en 1964 para dirigir la Temporada Internacional de Bellas Artes. En 1975 trabajó con la Orquesta de Cámara de Bellas Artes. Ha dirigido óperas y orquestas como la Sinfónica de Xalapa, la Sinfónica Nacional y conjuntos y orquestas de Estados Unidos, Europa y Asia.

Roque Villanueva, Humberto ◆ n. en Torreón, Coah. (1943). Licenciado en economía por la UNAM (1970), de la cual fue profesor (1971-74). Pertenece al PRI desde 1960, donde ha sido subsecretario de Organización (1984-86), presidente del CEN (1996-97) y precandidato a la presidencia de la república (1999). Coordinador de Estudios Técnicos (1971-73), secretario de Planeación (1974-77) y secretario de Comercialización de la CNC (1988-91), subjefe de Capacitación del Injuve (1968-70), subdirector de Finanzas de la Fonafe (1977), asesor del titular de la SARH (1978-92), diputado federal (1988-91), subsecretario de Organización y Administración de Sepesca (1991) y director de Aseguradora Hidalgo (1997-99). Autor de *Seis años para ganar un siglo* (1997).

Ros Sáez, Antonio ◆ n. en España (1899-?). Médico por la Universidad Central de Madrid. Fue jefe del Servicio Oftalmológico del Hospital de Ornealsville y profesor agregado del Hospital Oftalmológico Adolphe de Rothschild. Llegó exiliado a México en 1940. Jefe del Departamento de Oftalmología del Sanatorio Español. Autor de *El tracoma, rebelde y milenario, su historia y su terapéutica, su profilaxis* (1941), *Los ciegos de la Biblia* (1942), *Las sulfamidas en la práctica oftalmológica* (1944), *El tabaco, el café y el vino* (1963), *Un español en Egipto* (1946), *El ciego de Asís* (1959), *Evolución de la histopatología y el tratamiento del tracoma* (1961), *Evocación de la India* (1962), *Los gobiernos españoles desde la pérdida de las colonias hasta la caída de Alfonso XIII* (1981). Fue condecorado por Hindenburg en 1933 y por el presidente Masaryk, en 1934, con la Cruz del León Blanco.

Rosa, Juan Manuel de la ◆ n. en Sierra Hermosa, Zac. (1945). Estudió en el Taller de Artes Plásticas de la Universidad de Nuevo León (1964) y en La Esmeralda (1968). Participó en 1970 en la Bienal Interamericana de Santiago de Chile y es profesor fundador del Taller de Grabado José Guadalupe Posada. Primer Premio Nacional de Grabado del INBA (1969).

Rosa, María de Jesús de la ◆ n. en Parras, Coah., y m. en Nuevo Laredo, Tams. (?-1958). Conocida como *La Coronela*, se unió al Ejército Constitucionalista y participó en la batalla de Palo Alto (1913), se mantuvo como combatiente activa hasta 1918 y desde entonces adoptó la costumbre de portar siempre dos pistolas. Murió quemada al incendiarse su casa. Inspiró el corrido *Jesusita en Chihuahua* y el ballet *La coronela*, de Waldeen (1940).

Rosa, Raúl de la ◆ n. en San Luis Potosí, SLP (1950). Escultor. Estudió en el Taller de Artes Plásticas de la UANL y en La Esmeralda, vaciado en cera con Walter Weber, joyería y cera perdida en San Miguel de Allende. Trabajó en el Taller de Artesanía y Platería de México y ha sido profesor de la Casa de la Cultura de Gómez Palacio y de la Casa de la Cultura del estado de Nuevo León. Profesor de la Escuela de Artes e Idiomas de Monterrey. Ha participado en muestras colectivas en varias ciudades y ha expuesto individualmente en Ciudad Anáhuac, Garza García, Reynosa, Monterrey y Guanajuato.

Rosa López, María Alicia de la ◆ n. en Aguascalientes, Ags. (1963). Licenciada en derecho por la Universidad Autónoma de Aguascalientes. En ese estado ha sido directora del Registro Civil (1987-88), subsecretaria general de Gobierno (1989-91), presidenta suplente de la Comisión Estatal Electoral y presidenta municipal de Aguascalientes (1991-94).

Rosa Martínez, Rolando de la ◆ n. ¿en Guatemala? (1951). Pintor. Estudió en la Escuela Superior de Ingeniería y Arquitectura (1973) y en la Escuela Nacional de Pintura y Escultura (1980). Ha expuesto individualmente en Montreal (1975) y colectivamente en México y Montreal. En 1987 se incluyeron algunas de sus obras en una selección que se presentó en el Museo de Arte Moderno de México, en la que combinó en collages las imágenes de la Virgen de Guadalupe y Marilyn Monroe, lo que provocó una violenta reacción de grupos de ultraderecha, que lograron que la exposición fuese retirada y el director del museo, Jorge Alberto Manrique, cesado.

Rosa Oteiza, Luis de la ◆ n. en el Mineral de Pinos, Zac., y m. en la ciudad de México (1804-1856). Participó en el movimiento popular que derrocó a Santa Anna (1844). Fue secretario de Hacienda (del 28 de marzo al 10 de agosto de 1845) de José Joaquín de Herrera; de Justicia y Negocios Eclesiásticos (del 16 al 19 de mayo de 1847 y del 14 de noviembre de 1847 al 8 de enero de 1848) de Pedro María Anaya; de Todos los Ramos (del 26 de septiembre al 13 de noviembre de 1847) de Manuel de la Peña y Peña; y de Relaciones Interiores y Exteriores (del 9 de enero al 3 de junio de 1848) en el segundo gobierno de De la Peña. Intervino en la firma de los Tratados de Guadalupe-Hidalgo en 1848, año en que fue nombrado ministro ante el gobierno de EUA. En 1851 opuso su candidatura presidencial a la de Arista. En 1853, Santa Anna lo encarceló en La Acordada y más tarde lo confinó a Zacatecas. Al triunfo de la revolución de Ayutla fue gobernador de Puebla (1856). Dirigió el Colegio de Minería desde 1855 hasta su muerte. Fue secretario de Relaciones Exteriores de Comonfort (del 13 de diciembre de 1855 al 29 de agosto de 1856) y diputado al Constituyente de 1856 a 1857. Nombrado presidente de la Suprema Corte de Justicia, murió antes de ocupar el cargo. Autor de *Impresiones de un viaje de México a Washington en octubre y noviembre de 1848* (1848), *El porvenir de México, Cultivo del maíz en México* (1846) y *Miscelánea de estudios descriptivos* (1848).

Luis de la Rosa Oteiza

Rosado, Octavio ◆ n. en Sisal y m. en Mérida, Yuc. (1842-1893). Egresado del Colegio Militar (1857). Durante la guerra de los Tres Años militó en las filas liberales. Combatió la intervención francesa y el imperio. Defendió Puebla durante el sitio de 1863. Capturado por los invasores, escapó cuando lo trasladaban a Veracruz para deportarlo. En 1864 se reincorporó a las fuerzas de Degollado y en 1866 fue reaprehendido y condenado a muerte, aunque fue indultado por Maximiliano. Se reincorporó a la lucha y participó en el sitio y toma de Querétaro. General de brigada en 1879. Fue diputado federal (1880), comandante militar y gobernador de Yucatán (1882-86) y senador por ese estado.

Rosado González, Leandro ◆ n. en Orizaba, Ver. (1882-1958). En 1910 se unió a la insurrección maderista en las fuerzas de Benjamín Camacho y José María Morales. En 1914 se alistó en el Cuerpo de Ejército de Oriente y sirvió en el regimiento Servando Canales, comandado por Juan N. Vela. Estuvo después a las órdenes de Lucio Blanco. Al término del conflicto armado fue inspector de las Fuerzas de Caballería de la Secretaría de Guerra y Marina y presidente de la Unión Nacional de Militares Retirados (1937-39 y 1939-41). En 1939 fue ascendido a general.

Rosado Vega, Luis ◆ n. en Chemax y m. en Mérida, Yuc. (1873-1958). Dirigió el Museo Histórico y Arqueológico de Yucatán y el Ateneo de Ciencias y Artes de Tlaxcala. Colaborador de la *Revista de Mérida*, *El Peninsular*, *Arte* (de Mocorito), *Crónica de Guadalajara*, *Arte y Letras*, *Pimienta y Mostaza*, *Diario Yucateco*, *El Eco del Comercio*, *Revista de Yucatán*, *El Ateneo de Mérida*, *Revista de Revistas* y *Tlaxcala* (que dirigió). Por encargo de Felipe Carrillo Puerto escribió la letra de *Peregrina*, canción dedicada a Alma Reed y cuya música fue compuesta por Ricardo Palmerín. Autor de *Sensaciones* (1902), *Alma y sangre* (1906), *Libros de ensueño y de dolor* (1907), *La ofrenda a Venus* (1911), *María Clemencia* (1912), *Nicte-há* (1917), *Vaso espiritual* (1919), *Parnaso de México* (1919), *El desastre* (1919), *Payambé* (1928), *El sueño de Chichén* (1929), *Explotaciones cínicas. El falso intelectualismo y el caso típico de Luis de Oteyza* (1930), *Bartolomé García Correa. Cómo se hizo su campaña política* (1930), *El alma misteriosa del Mayab* (1934), *En los jardines que encantó la muerte* (1936), *Poema de la selva trágica* (1937), *Claudio Martín. Vida de un chiclero* (1938), *Amerindmaya* (1938), *Un pueblo y un hombre* (1940), *Lo que ya pasó y aún vive* (1947), *Entraña yucateca* (1947) y *Romancero yucateco* (1949).

Rosal Díaz, Amaro del ◆ n. y m. en España (1904-1991). Fue miembro de la Asociación de Empleados de Comercio, Industria y Banca (1926), presidente del Sindicato de Banca de Madrid y de la Federación Nacional de Banca (1930-39), miembro del Comité Nacional (1933), vocal de la Comisión Ejecutiva y secretario adjunto (1937-39) de la Unión General de Trabajadores y cofundador del periódico madrileño *Claridad*. Al término de la guerra civil española se refugió en Francia, Marruecos y México, donde fue director de la Constructora Nacional de Carros de Ferrocarril, de Siderúrgica Nacional y director adjunto de la Dirección General del Combinado Industrial de Ciudad Sahagún. Fue colaborador del diario *Excélsior*. Autor de *Problemas sindicales y de unidad* (1936), *Historia de la UGT* (3 t., 1940), *La violencia, enfermedad del anarquismo* (1975), *Los congresos obreros internacionales del siglo XX* (1975) y *Los congresos obreros internacionales del siglo XIX* (1975).

Foto: Archivo Xavier Esparza

Antonio Rosales

Foto: Fondo Editorial Grupo Azabache

Rosales, Chihuahua

Rosales ◆ Municipio de Chihuahua contiguo a Ciudad Delicias. Superficie: 1,716.6 km². Habitantes: 14,809, de los cuales 4,476 forman la población económicamente activa. Hablan alguna lengua indígena 121 personas mayores de cinco años (tarahumara 118). Los franciscanos llegaron a principios del siglo XVIII y en 1714 fundaron Santa Cruz de Tapacolmes, que cambió luego su nombre a Víctor Rosales. En 1820 fue erigido el municipio. Su cabecera es Santa Cruz de Rosales.

Rosales, Antonio ◆ n. en Juchipila, Zac., y m. en Álamos, Son. (1822-1865). En 1846 abandonó los estudios de jurisprudencia y se alistó en la Guardia Nacional para combatir a los invasores estadounidenses. Participó en los combates de Resaca y Palo Alto y en la defensa de Monterrey. Al terminar la guerra volvió a Guadalajara y en 1850 fundó y dirigió el periódico liberal *El Cantarito*, por lo que pasó un año encarcelado. Al triunfo de la revolución de Ayutla fue oficial mayor de la Corte de Justicia de Sinaloa, secretario particular del gobernador Pomposo Verdugo, redactor del *Diario Oficial* y secretario de gobierno (1856-57). Le correspondió jurar la Constitución de 1857. Fue designado jefe político del cantón de Tepic. Se opuso al pronunciamiento conservador de Tacubaya y se incorporó a las fuerzas liberales, con las que combatió en Jalisco y Sinaloa durante la guerra de los Tres Años. En 1861, Manuel Márquez lo nombró comandante militar de Culiacán y al iniciarse la invasión francesa volvió a filas, a las órdenes de Ramón Corona. En 1864 asumió los poderes de Sinaloa. Derrotó al francés Grazielle y al argelino Bel Kassam ben Mohamed, cerca de Culiacán, acción por la que llegó al generalato. En 1865 entregó el gobierno sinaloense, para retormarlo casi inmediatamente y renunciar a él poco después, en protesta porque no se castigó al rebelde Correa. Marchó a colaborar en la defensa de Álamos, donde murió combatiendo la intervención. La capital sinaloense se llama Culiacán de Rosales en su honor. Publicó poesía en el periódico *La Aurora Poética de Jalisco*.

ROSALES, ARIEL ◆ n. en el DF (1946). Editor. Licenciado en filosofía por la UNAM (1968). Colaboró en *La Cultura en México* y *Revista de la Universidad* (1966-74). Ha sido director editorial de Editorial Posada (1974-87), para la que además editó las revistas *Eros*, *Duda* y *Natura*, entre otras, y director editorial de Editorial Grijalbo (1988-).

ROSALES, DIEGO ◆ n. en Coyoacán, DF (1927). Pintor, egresado de La Esmeralda (1950), fue ayudante de Diego Rivera en la realización de los murales del Palacio Nacional, el Palacio de Bellas Artes y el Cárcamo de Dolores. Participó en la restauración de la obra de José Clemente Orozco en Michoacán, Veracruz y Jalisco. Es jefe del taller de dibujo y pintura del Centro Cultural de Belem de las Flores, fundador de los talleres plásticos de la Secretaría de Comunicaciones y Transportes (1972) y profesor de pintura de la Casa de Cultura de Coyoacán (1984-). Autor del mural sobre el tormento de Cuauhtémoc, en la delegación Coyoacán, y del mural de la Casa de Cultura Jesús Reyes Heroles (1987). Posee una importante colección de piezas arqueológicas.

ROSALES, FRANCISCO *PANCHO* ◆ n. y m. en el DF (1907-1993). Manejador de boxeo. Fue uno de los más famosos en la historia del pugilismo mexicano. Formó a centenares de boxeadores, entre los que destacan Raúl *Ratón* Macías, Arturo *Cuyo* Hernández, Rubén *Púas* Olivares, Ultiminio Ramos y Miguel Ángel González.

ROSALES, JOSÉ NATIVIDAD ◆ n. en Parras de la Fuente, Coah., y m. en el DF (1919-1976). Estudió teología y latín en el Seminario de Monterrey y militó en la Asociación Católica de la Juventud Mejicana. Fue profesor de dibujo en la Academia Luisiana. Periodista, fundó en Parras varias publicaciones y una Academia de Taquigrafía, Mecanografía e Inglés. Colaborador de *El Siglo de Torreón* y *El Popular*, de Parras. Trabajó en Publicidad Ferrer, fue columnista de *Claridades* y reportero de *Siempre!* Durante su carrera periodística publicó entrevistas con Mao Zedong, Fidel Castro, *el Che* Guevara y el papa Pío XII, la que inventó e hizo publicar con una foto del pontífice supuestamente dedicada a los lectores de *Siempre!* Mecanógrafo extraordinariamente rápido, solía escribir las entrevistas mientras hablaba su interlocutor. Fue, además, pintor, publicista, productor de programas de radio, contador y agente viajero. Autor de *Vida amorosa de Cristo*, *Los sin Dios y los indios*, *Sal sobre el rostro de México*, *El diccionario de la grosería*, *Madero y el espiritismo*, *¿Qué hizo el Che en México?*, *Dios no existe*, *¿Quién fue Lucio Cabañas?*, *La muerte de Lucio Cabañas*, *Misión secreta en El Vaticano*, *Tras las rejas de El Vaticano*, *Europa a golpe de huarache*, *Diario de viaje a China* y *El último Cristo*.

ROSALES, VÍCTOR ◆ n. en Zacatecas, Zac., y m. en Ario, Mich. (¿1776?-1817). Interrumpió sus estudios de jurisprudencia para dedicarse al comercio. El 29 de septiembre de 1810 se unió en Valladolid a las fuerzas insurgentes de Allende y en 1811 se incorporó a las tropas de Ignacio López Rayón, con quien luchó en Puerto de Piñones, el Maguey y Zacatecas y a quien acompañó en su marcha hacia el sur, hasta Guanajuato, desde donde fue a Michoacán a ponerse a las órdenes de Verduzco. Algunos autores aseguran que en 1811 era comandante insurgente de Zacatecas y que pidió y obtuvo el indulto. Sin embargo, combatió en Uruapan y participó en el fallido ataque a Valladolid en 1813. Formó un ejército de 3,000 efectivos con el que marchó a Zacatecas, participó en el ataque a Aguascalientes y, en 1815, con el grado de mariscal de campo, fue designado comandante general de Zacatecas y Michoacán. Los insurgentes Muñiz y Barragán se opusieron a su nombramiento y Rosales salió a batirlos. Murió en combate contra aquéllos en Ario, que en su honor lleva, desde 1853, el nombre de Rosales.

ROSALES ARAIZA, NABOR ◆ n. y m. en Copala, municipio de Venustiano Carranza, Jal. (1877-1940). Mariachi en su juventud, formó después una orquesta típica y se dedicó a la composición musical. Fue conocido como *el Gigante de los sones*. Son obra suya o se le atribuyen *La Negra*, *Camino real de Colima*, *Las coquetonas*, *Severiana*, *Maracumbé*, *La loba*, *Zacoalpaneca*, *La amapolita*, *El tildío*, *La margarita*, *La Pancha*, *La zamba*, *El cihuateco*, *El jabalí*, *Los arrieros*, *El huaco*, *El calero*, *El gavilancillo*, *El cangrejo* y *El tejero*.

ROSALES RODRÍGUEZ, RAMÓN M. ◆ n. en Pachuca, Hgo. (1872-1928). Ingresó en 1891 en la Escuela Nacional de Comercio y Administración. Estudió sociología y filosofía en el Instituto de Ciencias de Nueva York (1905). Estuvo encarcelado en Belén por sus ideas antiporfiristas (1892). Fue agente de la Secretaría de Fomento en los ramos de minería y tierras (1900-09) y fundador de la Corporación Patriótica Privada (1901), organización oposicionista. Fundador de un Club Antirreeleccionista (1910) y delegado a la Convención Nacional Antirreeleccionista. Organizó el inicio de la revolución maderista en Hidalgo y Veracruz. Fue gobernador interino (1911-12) y constitucional (1912-13) de Hidalgo. Masón de grado 33.

ROSAMORADA ◆ Municipio de Nayarit situado en el noroeste del estado, al norte de San Blas y al noroeste de Tepic. Superficie: 2,073.1 km^2. Habitantes: 35,007, de los cuales 10,023 forman la población económicamente activa. Hablan alguna lengua indígena 1,500 personas mayores de cinco años (cora 1,052 y huichol 377).

ROSARIO, DEL ◆ Bahía de Baja California Norte. Sus extremos norte y sur son, respectivamente, las puntas Baja y San Antonio. Cuenta con fondeaderos hasta de 100 metros de profundidad y mide unos 22 km de punta a punta.

ROSARIO ◆ Municipio de Chihuahua situado al sur de la capital estatal, cerca de los límites con Durango y contiguo a Parral. Superficie: 1,785.66 km^2. Habitantes: 3,130, de los cuales 4,476 forman la población económicamente activa. Hablan tarahumara 26 personas mayores de cinco años. A mediados del siglo XVII los jesuitas se asentaron en te-

Víctor Rosales

Matachín danzando en honor de la Virgen de la Candelaria en Matatán, El Rosario, Sinaloa

FOTO: GOBIERNO DEL ESTADO DE SINALOA

rritorio de este municipio, que en 1788 adquirió categoría de subdelegación real. Su cabecera, Valle del Rosario, fue fundada en 1640 por los jesuitas José Pascual y Nicolás Zepeda, con el nombre de Santa Cruz de Tarahumaras.

ROSARIO, EL ♦ Municipio de Sinaloa situado en el litoral del Pacífico y contiguo a Mazatlán, en los límites con Durango y Nayarit. Superficie: 2,723.28 km². Habitantes: 49,240, de los cuales 13,060 forman la población económicamente activa. Hablan alguna lengua indígena 35 personas mayores de cinco años (tepehuano 17).

FOTO: GOBIERNO DEL ESTADO DE SINALOA

Iglesia del Real de El Rosario, Sinaloa

ROSARIO ♦ Municipio de Sonora situado en los límites con Chihuahua y contiguo a Cajeme, Álamos y Navojoa. Superficie: 3,301.94 km². Habitantes: 5,962, de los cuales 1,631 forman la población económicamente activa. Hablan alguna lengua indígena 26 personas mayores de cinco años (guarijío 11).

ROSARIO, DEL ♦ Río de Baja California. Corre de la sierra de San Pedro Mártir al océano Pacífico, aunque durante la mayor parte del año su caudal se evapora o es absorbido por la arena. Su desembocadura está al norte de la bahía del Rosario.

ROSARIO, DEL ♦ Sierra de Durango que se extiende de noroeste a sureste, paralelamente a la sierra de Mapimí. Cuenta con numerosas cumbres que superan los 2,500 metros sobre el nivel del mar.

ROSARIO TORRES, GUSTAVO ♦ n. en Frontera, Tab. (1950). Licenciado en derecho por la Universidad Juárez Autónoma de Tabasco. Miembro del PRI desde 1970, fue secretario de Capacitación Política del Comité Directivo Estatal. Presidente del Congreso local y diputado federal (1988-91), coordinador general de delegaciones de la Sedue (1991-92) y coordinador de giras presidenciales de la Presidencia (1992-94).

ROSARITO ♦ Población de Baja California Norte, a 28 km de Tijuana. Es un centro turístico en la costa del océano Pacífico. Junto a la población hay una planta termoeléctrica de la Comisión Federal de Electricidad (con 307, 000 kilovatios de potencia) y desde 1969 funciona allí la desaladora de agua de mar más grande del mundo, capaz de potabilizar 28 millones de litros al día.

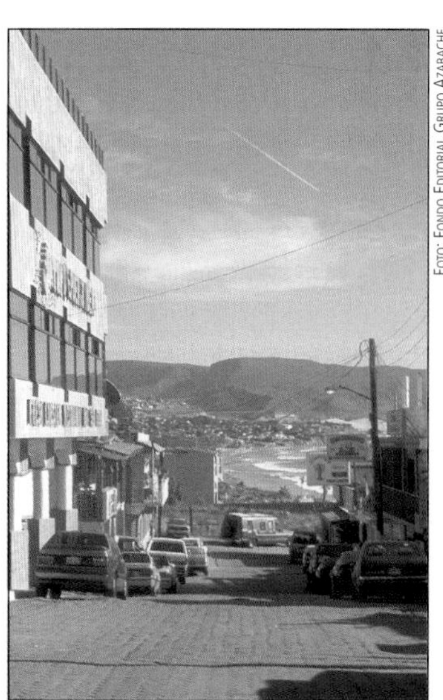

FOTO: FONDO EDITORIAL GRUPO AZABACHE

Rosarito, Baja California

ROSAS, LAS ♦ Municipio de Chiapas situado en la región central del estado y contiguo a Comitán. Superficie: 233.5 km². Habitantes: 19,503, de los cuales 4,954 forman la población económicamente activa. Hablan alguna lengua indígena 1,714 personas mayores de cinco años (tzeltal 1,564). Su cabecera, del mismo nombre, se llamó Pinola.

ROSAS, FERNANDO ♦ n. en el Mineral de Xichú, Gto., y m. en San Luis Potosí, SLP (1789-1815). Militar. Se hallaba en Guanajuato, en 1810, cuando fue delatado como conspirador y encarcelado. Quedó en libertad al iniciarse la guerra de Independencia y se unió a las fuerzas de Miguel Hidalgo, de quien fue secretario. Logró huir de la emboscada de Acatita de Baján, se incorporó a las fuerzas de Ignacio López Rayón y más tarde a las guerrillas de Albino García y de Tomás Baltierra, que accionaron en Guanajuato, Jalisco, Aguascalientes y Querétaro. En 1814 inició una campaña para batir a los cuatreros que se hacían pasar por insurgentes y fue secretario del doctor Cos. Como comandante militar de Guanajuato y San Luis Potosí, colaboró en la reorganización de las fuerzas de Pedro Moreno y de Encarnación Ortiz. En 1815 fue capturado por los realistas, conducido a San Luis Potosí y fusilado.

ROSAS, IGNACIO ♦ n. en Orizaba, Ver., y m. en el DF (1880-1950). Ingresó en la Academia de San Carlos en 1902. En 1905 ganó un concurso de pintura y obtuvo una beca para estudiar en Francia, donde fue condiscípulo de Diego Rivera. Volvió a México en 1911 y participó en la insurrección maderista, a las órdenes de Ignacio L. Pesqueira. En 1923 secundó la rebelión delahuertista. Fue director de la Academia de San Carlos. En 1925 marchó a Estados Unidos, donde se dedicó a pintar retratos. Autor de *La vuelta del soldado* (1905), diversas copias de lienzos de Rembrandt (que se hallan en el Palacio de Bellas Artes y en la Academia de San Carlos) y retratos de Santiago Rebull y *Nahui Ollin*.

ROSAS, JUVENTINO ♦ n. en Santa Cruz de Galeana, hoy de Juventino Rosas, Gto., y m. en Cuba (1868-1894). Con su padre y hermanos formó un conjunto que tocaba sones en las calles de la ciudad de México, hacia 1875. Fue sacristán y violinista de la iglesia de San Sebastián. Estudió en el Conservatorio Nacional. En 1883 acompañó a Ángela Peralta en la gira en que murió esta cantante. Cuando se presentaba en Cuba, murió de cirrosis. Compuso música de salón, danzas, valses, polkas y mazurkas, entre ellos: *Carmen* (vals dedicado a Carmen Romero Rubio), *Sueño de las flores*, *Cuauhtémoc* (1888, marcha guerrera), *Ensueño*, *Sobre las olas* (1888), *Ojos negros*, *La cantinera*, *Te volví a ver*, *Seductora*, *Dolores*, *Soledad*, *Josefina*, *Ilusiones juveniles*, *Ensueño seductor*, *Aurora*, *Dos pensamientos*, *Soñando*, *Amelia*, *Flores de margarita*, *Último adiós* y *Lejos de ti*. Desde 1939 está sepultado en la Rotonda de los Hombres Ilustres.

Rosas, Manuel José de ◆ n. y m. en San Cristóbal de Las Casas, Chis. (?-?). Fue jefe político (1821-22), diputado provincial (1823) y gobernador (1825-26) de Chiapas. Durante su gestión se expidió la primera Constitución local, luego de votarse la anexión a la República Mexicana.

Rosas, Pedro ◆ n. en Zacoalco y m. en Guadalajara, Jal. (¿1742?-1812). También se cree que nació en Cocula, Jalisco. Arriero, se encontraba en el poblado de Zacoalco cuando supo del levantamiento armado del insurgente José Antonio Torres, quien acababa de tomar Sayula. Se reunió con el caudillo y se incorporó a su guardia personal. Realizó algunas misiones de espionaje y fue ascendido a capitán. Asistió al combate de Zacoalco (noviembre de 1810) y marchó a Ahualulco, para cooptar al cura de esa parroquia, José Mercado. Éste levantó un pequeño ejército, que incluyó a Rosas, con el que tomó las plazas de Tepic y San Blas. Pasó después a las fuerzas de Zea y estuvo en la derrota de Mochiltiltic. Huyó a Sinaloa, donde volvió a dedicarse al comercio y a la arriería hasta que fue descubierto por las autoridades españolas y encarcelado. Liberado en 1811 viajó a Zacoalco y fue reaprehendido. Se le condujo a Guadalajara en 1812, donde fue ejecutado. Su cabeza fue expuesta en las afueras de Zacoalco.

Rosas Benítez, Alberto ◆ n. en Guadalajara, Jal. (1926). Licenciado en derecho por la Universidad de Guadalajara, institución en la que es profesor desde 1950. Ha sido paleógrafo y catalogador de la Biblioteca Pública de Jalisco, secretario del Instituto de Bibliotecas, director de una preparatoria, secretario general de la Universidad de Guadalajara, secretario del Supremo Tribunal de Justicia, secretario general de gobierno (1971-77) y notario público (1978-). Colabora en *El Informador*, de Guadalajara, con la columna "Perfiles del tiempo" (1982-). Autor de *Especialidad del derecho indiano* (1955), *Introducción a la historia del derecho* (1962), *Manual de historia del derecho* (1965), *Juárez en Jalisco* (1972), *Hojas sueltas* (1973) e *Historia del derecho. Teoría general y edad antigua* (1982). Ganó la Presea Fray Antonio Alcalde por 40 años de docencia (1986).

Rosas López, Adalberto *Pelón* ◆ n. en Ciudad Obregón, Son. (?). Militante del PAN desde 1973, fue presidente municipal de Cajeme (1979-81) y candidato a gobernador de su estado en 1985. Renunció al partido al serle negada una nueva candidatura a la gubernatura en 1997.

Rosas de la Luz, Concepción ◆ n. en Transfiguración, Edo. de Méx. (1934). Afiliado al PAN desde 1964, ha sido presidente del Comité Directivo Regional del Estado de México (1976-79), secretario de Organización del partido en el estado y diputado federal (1991-94). Fundador de la Asociación Civil Independiente, que presidió (1976-78).

Rosas Magallón, Salvador ◆ n. en Tepic, Nay., y m. en Tijuana, BC (1916-1996). Se tituló como abogado en el Distrito Federal. Fue juez y fiscal en Guerrero y Sinaloa. Se estableció en Tijuana en 1945 y estuvo entre los promotores de la conversión del territorio de Baja California en estado de la Federación, lo que se logró en 1953. Litigó en favor de los habitantes de las márgenes del río Tijuana, cuando éstos fueron desplazados por las obras de entubamiento, y se le llamó "el abogado de los pobres". En 1946 ingresó en el PAN, del que fue candidato a gobernador de Baja California en dos ocasiones (1959 y 1971) y precandidato a la Presidencia de la República.

Juventino Rosas

Rosas Monroy, Ezequiel ◆ n. en Atlacomulco, Edo. de Méx., y m. en el DF (1907-1966). Sacerdote ordenado en 1930. Fue vicario cooperador de varias parroquias del Estado de México, vicario fijo y ayudante de párroco en Santo Domingo de Mixcoac y cura en diversas parroquias del Estado de México y del DF. Autor de *Florilegio poético* (1955), *Ofrenda a María* (1955), *Pétalos del alma* (1956), *Testamento a María Santísima* (1961), *Padre, maestro, pastor* (1962), *Arpegios de mi laúd* (1963), *El trovador de la virgen* (1963) y *Poemas bucólicos* (1972).

Ezequiel Rosas Monroy

José Rosas Moreno

Rosas Moreno, José ◆ n. y m. en Lagos, ahora de Moreno, Jal. (1838-1883). Llamado *el Poeta de la niñez*. Siendo estudiante del Colegio de San Gregorio empezó a participar en actividades liberales, por lo que sufrió persecuciones. Después del triunfo republicano (1867) fue varias veces diputado federal. Fundó y dirigió los periódicos *El Tío Canillitas*, *La Madre Celestina*, *La Educación*, *El Álbum Literario*, *La Edad Infantil* y *Los Chiquitines*. Colaborador de *El Tiempo*. Autor de *Flores y espinas* (1861), *Nadie se muere de amor* (1862), *Una mentira inocente* (1863), *Poesías* (1864), *Un proyecto de divorcio* (1868), *Los parientes* (1872), *Fábulas* (1872), *Excursiones por el cielo y por la tierra* (1874), *Amor filial* (1874), *El año nuevo* (1874), *Una lección de geografía* (1874), *Sor Juana Inés de la Cruz* (1876), *Compendio de la historia de México* (1877), *Nuevo compendio de la historia de México* (1877), *Un viajero de diez años* (1881), *Un libro para mis hijos* (1881), *Ramo de violetas* (1891), *Libro de la infancia* (1893), *¡Pobre madre!* (1894), *Amigo de los niños*, *Nuevo amigo de los niños*, *Ciencia de la dicha*, *Libro de oro de las niñas*, *Manual de urbanidad*, *Recreaciones infantiles*, *Compendio de ortología*, *Devocionario poético de los niños*, *Nuevo libro segundo*, *La flor prisionera*, *Recuerdo de la infancia*, *El pan de cada día*, *El coronel Santibáñez*, *La mujer de César*, *Alrededor de la cuna*, *Nezahualcóyotl, el bardo de Acolhuacán*, *El premio de la virtud* y *La escuela del bello sexo*.

Rosas de Oquendo, Mateo ◆ n. en España (¿1559?-?). Militar. Viajó a la Nueva España y pasó a Argentina, aparentemente con el gobernador Juan Ramírez de Velasco. En la provincia de Tucumán, a finales del siglo XVI, se inició en la nigromancia. Cofundador de la ciudad de Rojas (1591) y encomendero en Camiquín y Canchanga (1593), fue criado del virrey de Perú y volvió a la Nueva España hacia 1598. Adoptó el nombre de *Juan Sánchez*. Se ignora el lugar de su muerte, aunque Alfonso Reyes afirma que fue Sevilla. Autor de *Memoria de las cosas notables y memorias que han sucedido en la ciudad de México en la Nueva España, desde el año de 1611 hasta hoy cinco del mes de mayo de 1612* y de los poemarios *Soneto a Lima del Perú*, *Romance en alabanza de la provincia de Yucatán en Campeche*, *Yndiano volcán famoso* y *Montañas de Guadalupe*.

Rosas y Reyes, Román ◆ n. y m. en el DF (1890-1966). Alcanzó el grado de teniente coronel durante la lucha revolucionaria. Fue diputado al Congreso Constituyente de 1916-17. A la caída de Venustiano Carranza se exilió durante dos años en España. Fue gerente del Ferrocarril del Sureste, secretario de la Dirección General de Correos, inspector, presidente del Comité de Apelación, jefe del Departamento de Auditoría de los Ferrocarriles Nacionales e inspector del Registro Civil (1958). Autor de *Las imposturas de Vicente Blasco Ibáñez* (1920, libro en el que refuta a este autor por la obra *El militarismo mejicano*).

Rosas Torres, Alfonso Joel ◆ n. en Durango, Dgo. (1952). Licenciado en derecho por la Universidad Juárez de Durango. Militante del PAN desde 1983, ha sido miembro de sus comisiones Política y Financiera. Fue presidente del Instituto Mexicano de Ejecutivos de Finanzas-Grupo Durango (1984), presidente de la Canacintra de Durango (1985) y diputado federal plurinominal (1985-88).

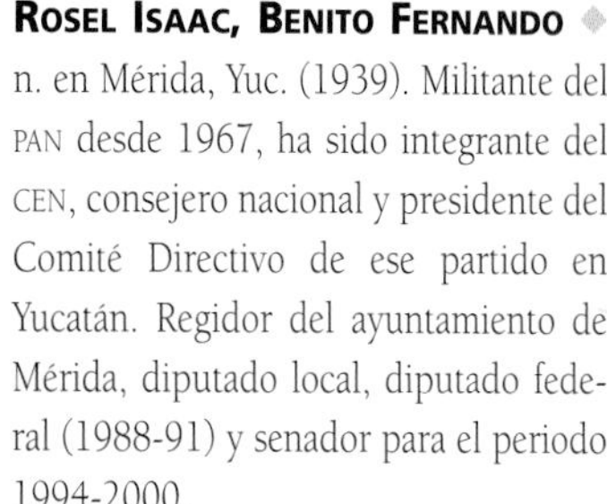

Rosel Isaac, Benito Fernando ◆ n. en Mérida, Yuc. (1939). Militante del PAN desde 1967, ha sido integrante del CEN, consejero nacional y presidente del Comité Directivo de ese partido en Yucatán. Regidor del ayuntamiento de Mérida, diputado local, diputado federal (1988-91) y senador para el periodo 1994-2000.

Rosell, Basilio *el Brujo* ◆ n. en Cuba y m. en el DF (1902-1994). Beisbolista. Se inició en 1917 en el equipo Aragua, de aficionados, que derrotó al equipo profesional Matanzas. Jugó profesionalmente en Cuba y Estados Unidos antes de llegar a México. Fue lanzador de los equipos *Águilas* de Veracruz y México, al que puso el sobrenombre de *Diablos Rojos*. Tras su retiro se dedicó a entrenar equipos de aficionados. Miembro del Salón de la Fama mexicano desde 1979.

Foto: Guillermo Aguilera

Hebe Rosell

Rosell, Hebe ◆ n. en Argentina (1943). Estudió flauta, piano y canto en los conservatorios Nacional de Argentina y Municipal de Buenos Aires. Licenciada en musicoterapia por la Universidad del Salvador, de Buenos Aires. Tomó cursos de pedagogía musical, psicología en Suiza, metodología, psicodrama y programación musical; de teatro y voz en Francia, de expresión total en Francia, de teatro de la situación en Canadá, de expresión corporal y danza en Argentina; y de creación literaria con David Huerta y Héctor Manjarrez (1987), en México. Formó parte del grupo musical Huerque Mapu con el que recorrió Argentina y dio conciertos en España, Holanda y Francia (1976-77). Llegó a México en 1978 y se integró al grupo Sanampay, con Guadalupe Pineda, Delfor Sombra y Carlos Díaz *Caíto*, entre otros. En 1979 se unió a los sucesivos grupos de *rock* de Guillermo Briseño (☛), con los que se ha presentado en ciudades de México y Cuba; grabó los discos *Viaje al espacio visceral* y *Está valiendo el corazón*, hizo los programas de televisión *Espectáculo de la ciudad* y *La lista negra* y presentó el espectáculo *Rocanrolario* (1985). Como solista ha montado *Reina por un día*

(1987) y *Hebestroika* (1988). Coordina talleres de *rock* para niños y adultos. Perteneció al Comité Mexicano de la Nueva Canción (1984-88).

Rosell Abitia, Mauricio Alejandro ◆ n. en el DF (1965). Hijo de Guillermo Rosell de la Lama. Doctor en derecho. Ha sido coordinador y asesor de la Subsecretaría de Promoción Industrial y Comercio Exterior y director de Promoción e Inversiones de Comercio Exterior de la Secretaría de Comercio. Preside la Fundación Colosio en Hidalgo. Colabora en *El Universal*. Diputado federal para el periodo 1997-2000. Fundador y dirigente del Grupo Reflexión, propuso un reglamento interno para el grupo parlamentario del PRI en la Cámara de Diputados.

Rosell de la Lama, Guillermo ◆ n. en Pachuca, Hgo. (1925). Se tituló como arquitecto por la UNAM (1949). Ha sido fundador y director de las revistas *San Carlos* y *Espacios* (1942 y 1949 respectivamente), director del Departamento de Turismo (1952) y de Desarrollo y Planeación de la Secretaría de Comunicaciones y Obras Públicas; director de los Consejos de Planeación Económica y Social de la campaña presidencial de Adolfo López Mateos (1958), oficial mayor (1958-59) y subsecretario de Patrimonio Nacional (1959-64); consejero del Instituto Nacional de la Vivienda, presidente de la Comisión Reglamentaria de las Ciudades Fronterizas México-norteamericanas, senador (1976), secretario de Turismo (del 1 de diciembre de 1976 al 13 de agosto de 1980), gobernador de Hidalgo (1981-87) y presidente de la Corporación de Planificación. Entre sus obras se encuentran el conjunto Chrysler, la Facultad de Ciencias Químicas de la UNAM, el plano regulador de Puerto Juárez, QR, la Unidad Administrativa Gubernamental del DF, la embajada de México en Tokio, el Tecnológico del Noroeste, el Liceo Franco-Mexicano, el Palacio Municipal de Nuevo Laredo, multifamiliares en La Habana, la ciudad industrial Alce Blanco en Naucalpan, el Polyforum Cultural Siqueiros, las sedes de la SARH y de la SRA, la delegación Iztacalco, la iglesia Ortodoxa, el Centro Social de la Comunidad Helénica; y los desarrollos turísticos de Caleta de Xel-Ha, Ixtapa-Zihuatanejo, Puerto Escondido, San José del Cabo y Loreto-Napló. Autor de *México, importantes retos en el siglo XXI* (1998).

Guillermo Rosell de la Lama

Foto: Pablo González de León

Polyforum Cultural Siqueiros, obra de Guillermo Rosell de la Lama

Rosell Ocampo, Lauro Elías ◆ n. y m. en el DF (1885-1973). Ejerció algunos puestos en la Secretaría de Comunicaciones y Transportes y en el Instituto Nacional de Antropología e Historia. Publicó en el diario *Excélsior* la columna "Hace 50 años". Autor de *México y la Guadalupana* (1931), *Catálogo de monumentos coloniales* (1939), *Fisonomía de una ciudad* (1945), *Iglesias y conventos coloniales de México* (1946) e *Historia de Tlaxcala de Muñoz Camargo. Cotejo de un manuscrito de Alfredo Chavero* (1947).

Rosen Jélomer, Boris ◆ n. en Ucrania (1917). Periodista, investigador y editor radicado en México desde 1929. Licenciado en derecho por la UNAM. Ha sido reportero del periódico *Der Weg* (1935), fundador de organizaciones juveniles y culturales de la comunidad judía en México (1933-53), director del periódico *Fraiwelt*, órgano semanal de la Liga Popular Israelita de México (1946-53), delegado del Movimiento Mexicano por la Paz al segundo Congreso Mundial de Partidarios de la Paz (Varsovia, 1950) y a la Conferencia de Paz de las Regiones de Asia y del Pacífico (Pekín, 1952), miembro de la redacción y del Consejo Editorial de la revista *Historia y Sociedad* (1965-81), jefe de redacción de la revista *Política* (1966-67), coordinador de investigación de la sección socioeconómica de *Panorámica socio-económica del Estado de México* (1976), coordinador de investigación para el *Atlas de la salud de la República Mexicana* (1973). Entre 1980 y 1990 fue investigador, compilador y editor de *Obras de Jorge L. Tamayo* (8 t.), *Pedro Santacilia. El hombre y su obra* (2 t.), *México y Cuba: dos pueblos unidos en la historia* (2 t.), *México y la paz. Testimonios 1810-1986* (3 t.), *Obras*

Boris Rosen Jélomer

completas de Ignacio Ramírez (8 t.), *Obras completas de Francisco Zarco* (30 t.) y *Obras completas de Guillermo Prieto* (34 t.).

ROSENBLUETH, ARTURO ◆ n. en Ciudad Guerrero, Chih., y m. en el DF (1900-1970). Doctor en medicina por la Universidad de París (1927), especializado en neurología y psiquiatría. Fue profesor de la UNAM (1927-30), profesor e investigador de la Universidad de Harvard (1930-43), jefe del Laboratorio de Fisiología del Instituto Nacional de Cardiología (1944-60), jefe del Departamento de Fisiología y director del Centro de Investigación Científica y Estudios Superiores del IPN (1960-70). Autor de *Fisiología del sistema nervioso autónomo* (1937, con Walter Cannon), *The Supersensitivity of Denervated Structures, a Law of Denervation* (1949), *Transmission of Nerve Impulses at Autonomic Neuro-juntions and Peripheral Synapses* (1950), *Mente y cerebro, una filosofía de la ciencia* (1970) y *El método científico* (1971, antología preparada por Juan García Ramos). Investigó el mecanismo químico de la transmisión de los impulsos nerviosos y elaboró la teoría de las dos simpatinas, que explica los fenómenos de inhibición de los efectos autónomos. Estudió los problemas del músculo cardiaco y las leyes que rigen el flútter y la fibrilación de la aurícula. Ingresó en 1947 en El Colegio Nacional. Recibió en 1966 el Premio Nacional de Ciencias y Artes, fue vocal del Instituto Nacional de la Investigación Científica y colaborador de varias revistas médicas. Sus restos están en la Rotonda de los Hombres Ilustres. En agosto de 1978 se iniciaron las labores de la Fundación Arturo Rosenblueth para el Avance de la Ciencia.

Arturo Rosenblueth

ROSENBLUETH, EMILIO ◆ n. en Ciudad Juárez, Chih., y m. ¿en el DF? (1896-1945). Pintor. Estudió en el Colegio Civil de Monterrey. Fue gerente de la Cervecería Modelo en el DF. Empezó a pintar en 1936. Hizo dibujos, unos 300 óleos y otros cuadros con diferentes técnicas. Expuso por primera vez en 1941. En 1988 el INBA montó una exposición-homenaje de su obra.

ROSENBLUETH DEUTSCH, EMILIO ◆ n. y m. en el DF (1926-1994). Se tituló como ingeniero civil en la UNAM (1948). Maestro en ciencias (1949) y doctor en ingeniería (1951) por la Universidad de Illinois en Urbana. En 1951 creó un método para estimar la respuesta estructural máxima, llamado "Regla de Rosenblueth", que es utilizada desde entonces por todos los ingenieros del mundo. Fue coordinador de Investigación Científica, investigador, profesor y especialista de ingeniería sísmica de la UNAM, presidente de la Academia de la Investigación Científica (1963-65), empleado de ICA y de la SARH; subsecretario de Educación (1978-82) y asesor del Centro de Investigación Sísmica. Miembro de El Colegio Nacional. Investigador emérito del Instituto de Ingeniería y *doctor honoris causa* por la UNAM (1985). Premio Nacional de Ciencias y Artes (1974), Premio Príncipe de Asturias en Investigación Científica (1985) y Medalla Nathan M. Newmark otorgada por la American Society of Civil Engineers (1988).

ROSENKRANZ, JORGE ◆ n. en Hungría (1916). Ingeniero químico y doctor en ciencias técnicas por el Instituto Politécnico Federal de Zurich (1939). Estudió psicología con Carl Jung. Fue ayudante de Leopoldo Ruzicka en la Universidad de Zurich y director técnico de los laboratorios Vieta Plasencia, en La Habana. Llegó a México en 1944. En la empresa Syntex se dedicó al procesamiento de hormonas sintéticas a partir del barbasco y fue director científico de la empresa. Promovió la fundación del Instituto Nacional de Química. Presidente honorario del Consejo de Administración de Syntex y miembro de los comités científicos del Instituto Weizman y de la Universidad de Tel Aviv. Socio honorario de la Academia Nacional de Medicina y *doctor honoris causa* por la Universidad de las Américas. En 1984, Syntex instituyó el Premio Anual de Investigación Médica Doctor Jorge Rosenkranz. Jugador de bridge, ha inventado un sistema total de remate y varias convenciones y ha representado a México en 10 campeonatos mundiales; ha ganado más de 50 títulos nacionales y 10 norteamericanos y ganó el título de Maestro Vitalicio; miembro honorario de la Liga Americana de Bridge (1990).

FOTO: MARGHARITA MONROY HERRERA / TIINASTRAL

Carmen Rosenzweig

ROSENZWEIG, CARMEN ◆ n. en Toluca, Edo. de Méx. (1925). Cursó una carrera comercial en la capital mexiquense. Becada, estudió letras francesas en la Universidad de París (1962). En 1961 fundó, con Beatriz Espejo, la revista femenina de literatura *El Rehilete*, que dirigió hasta 1971. Ha colaborado en los *Anuarios del Instituto Nacional de Bellas Artes*, *Revista Mexicana de Literatura*, *Nivel*, *Estaciones* y en los suplementos culturales de los diarios *Excélsior*, *El Universal*, *El Nacional* y *Novedades*. Autora de *El reloj* (1956), *Mi pueblo* (1958), *1956* (1958), *Recuento para el recuerdo* (1967), *Van Gogh y la juventud* (1970), *Esta cárdena vida* (1974), *Simone, el desierto, Simone el huerto* (1979) y *Volanteo* (1984). En 1996 apareció su *Obra reunida*.

Fondo Histórico Alfonso Sánchez García

Alfonso Rosenzweig Díaz

Rosenzweig Díaz, Alfonso ◆ n. en Toluca, Edo. de Méx., y m. en el DF (1886-1963). Abogado. Estudió en la Escuela Nacional de Jurisprudencia. En 1908 se incorporó al servicio exterior mexicano. Fue secretario de legación en China, Guatemala y Brasil; encargado de negocios interino en Brasil, cónsul general en Guatemala, consejero en Brasil, encargado de negocios en Colombia, los Países Bajos e Inglaterra; jefe de Protocolo de la SRE (1927), ministro en El Salvador, Suecia, Paraguay, Panamá y Venezuela (1931-43); embajador en Inglaterra, Francia y Yugoslavia; ministro ante los gobiernos de Polonia, Bélgica y Noruega, exiliados en Londres; promotor del primer Congreso Indigenista, celebrado en Pátzcuaro (1940); jefe de la Delegación de México ante la primera Asamblea de las Naciones Unidas, en Londres, y delegado ante la primera Reunión del Consejo de Seguridad de la ONU (1945); delegado a la Conferencia de la Paz, en París (1946), embajador en Nicaragua (1948) y en la Unión Soviética (1953-60). Se jubiló en 1960. Fundador de la *Revista México*, en Bolivia, y la *Gaceta del Xinantécatl*, en Nicaragua. Autor de *Mexicanidades de México* (3 t., 1955-59).

Rosenzweig Díaz Azmitia, Alfonso de ◆ n. en Brasil y m. en el DF (1921-1989). Diplomático mexicano. Hijo del anterior. Licenciado en derecho por la UNAM (1944). Fue funcionario de asuntos políticos del Departamento del Consejo de Seguridad de la Secretaría General de la ONU (1946-51). En la Secretaría de Relaciones Exteriores fue secretario particular del oficial mayor (1945-46), director general interino de Organismos Internacionales (1951-52), secretario particular del secretario (1952-55), embajador en la Unión Soviética (1955-58), director general de Asuntos Jurídicos (1959-61), director general del Servicio Diplomático (1961-64), director en jefe para Asuntos Bilaterales (1964-74), consultor jurídico (1975-76), subsecretario B (1976-79) y subsecretario de Relaciones Exteriores (1979-89), así como miembro del grupo de la Corte Permanente de Arbitraje Internacional de La Haya. Presidente de la Asociación del Servicio Exterior Mexicano (1974-76). Perteneció a la Academia Mexicana de Derecho Internacional Privado, la American Society of International Law, al Cuadro Permanente de Conciliadores Americanos y al Instituto Hispano-Luso-Americano de Derecho Internacional. Fue condecorado como Embajador Eminente por el gobierno mexicano, recibió una medalla por 25 años en el servicio exterior mexicano y numerosas condecoraciones de gobiernos extranjeros. Decano del servicio exterior mexicano y embajador emérito (1988).

Rosenzweig Díaz Azmitia, Roberto de ◆ n. en los Países Bajos (1924). Diplomático mexicano. Hermano del anterior. Licenciado en filosofía, ciencia política y economía por la Universidad de Oxford. En la Secretaría de Relaciones Exteriores ha sido secretario particular del director general de Servicios Diplomáticos, jefe del Departamento de Tratados, jefe del Departamento de Naciones Unidas y secretario particular del subsecretario de Relaciones Exteriores; embajador en El Salvador y Egipto, representante permanente ante la ONU en la República Federal de Alemania, Austria y los Países Bajos; asesor, suplente, delegado y jefe de delegación en diversas conferencias y organismos internacionales, adscrito a las embajadas en Suiza, Gran Bretaña, Brasil y Francia; embajador en Austria y representante permanente de la delegación de México ante el OIEA y la ONUDI (1981-86), embajador en Venezuela (1986-88) y en Uruguay (1988-90). Fue condecorado por 25 años en el servicio exterior mexicano.

Rosenzweig Hernández, Fernando ◆ n. en Toluca, Edo. de Méx., y m. en el DF (1922-1988). Estudió derecho y economía en la UNAM. Profesor de El Colegio Mexiquense, el ITAM y El Colegio de México, donde fue director de Investigaciones de Historia Económica (1958-62). Director de Investigaciones sobre Historia Económica del CIDE (1974-76). Ha sido redactor de temas económicos y jefe de redacción de la revista *Tiempo* (1943-52), jefe de redacción de *Problemas Agrícolas e Industriales de México* (1953-54), director de Economía de la Comisión del Papaloapan (1954-57), jefe de Proyecciones Agrícolas del Banco de México (1963-65), director general de Política de Ingresos de la SHCP (1976-78), coordinador general del Programa de Puertos Industriales (1978-82) y director general del INEA (1983-85). Colaborador de *Ciencias Políticas y Sociales*, *El Trimestre Económico* y *Comercio Exterior*. Coautor de *Historia moderna de México. El porfiriato. La vida económica* (1965) y *Breve historia del Estado de México* (1987).

Rosny, León de ◆ n. y m. en Francia (1837-1914). En 1880 dirigió la Escuela de Estudios Superiores de la Universidad de París, donde impartió un curso sobre las religiones del México antiguo. Dio a conocer el *Códice Peresiano* en 1883. Autor de *Archives Pa-*

léographiques de l'Orient et de l'Amérique (1869, con láminas del *Códice Peresiano*), *Les Écritures Figuratives et Hiéroglyphiques des Differents Peuples Anciens et Modernes* (1870), *Ensayo e interpretación de la escritura hierática de la América Central* (1881), *Vocabulaire de l'Écriture Hiératique Yucatèque* (1883) y *L'Amérique Precolombienne, Études d'Histoire de Linguistique et de Paléographie sur les Anciens Temps du Nouveau Monde* (1904). Socio fundador de la Sociedad de Etnografía Americana y Oriental.

Ross, Ramón ◆ n. en Álamos, Son., y m. en el DF (1864-1934). Fue presidente municipal de Huatabampo (1905) y diputado al Congreso Constituyente de 1916-17. Dirigió la Beneficencia Pública de la ciudad de México y fue gobernador del Distrito Federal en 1923. En ese año participó como delegado en las Conferencias de Bucareli. Ocupó la Secretaría de Comunicaciones y Obras Públicas (del 21 de junio de 1926 al 30 de noviembre de 1928) en el gabinete de Plutarco Elías Calles.

Stanley Ross

Ross, Stanley R. ◆ n. y m. en EUA (1921-1985). Maestro (1943) y doctor (1948) en historia por la Universidad de Columbia. Fue asistente y profesor en las universidades de Columbia y Nebraska, presidente del Departamento de Historia y decano del Colegio de Ciencias y Artes de la Universidad Estatal de Nueva York; director del Instituto de Estudios Latinoamericanos, decano interino preboste, vicepresidente y coordinador del Programa de Investigación de la Frontera y de la Oficina de Estudios sobre México, de la Universidad de Texas. Editor y coautor de *Historia documental de México* (1964, del Instituto de Investigaciones Históricas) y *Críticas constructivas del sistema político mexicano* (1973). Autor de *Fuentes de historia contemporánea de México: periódicos y revistas* (1965-69, obra por la que recibió del gobierno mexicano el Águila Azteca en 1982), *Francisco I. Madero, apóstol de la democracia mexicana* (1955), *¿Ha muerto la Revolución Mexicana?* (1965), *Latin American Intransition: Problems in Training and Research* (EUA, 1970) y *Views Across*

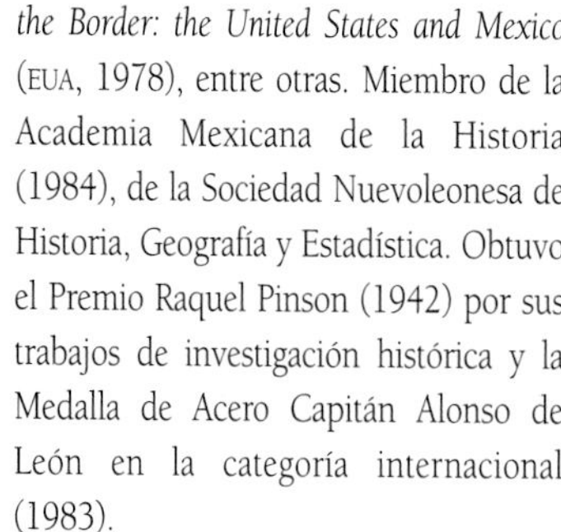

the Border: the United States and Mexico (EUA, 1978), entre otras. Miembro de la Academia Mexicana de la Historia (1984), de la Sociedad Nuevoleonesa de Historia, Geografía y Estadística. Obtuvo el Premio Raquel Pinson (1942) por sus trabajos de investigación histórica y la Medalla de Acero Capitán Alonso de León en la categoría internacional (1983).

Ross Landa, María Luisa ◆ n. en Tulancingo, Hgo., y m. en el DF (¿1885?-1945). Se tituló como profesora en la Escuela Nacional de Maestros. Hizo estudios en la Escuela de Altos Estudios y en el Conservatorio Nacional, instituciones de las que fue profesora. En 1903 se inició en el periodismo en *El Mundo Ilustrado* y continuó en *El Imparcial*, *El Universal*, *El Universal Ilustrado* (que dirigió) y *Revista de Revistas*. Dirigió la Biblioteca del Museo Nacional, fue fundadora de la Cruz Roja Mexicana, de la primera radiodifusora de la SEP y de la Unión Feminista Iberoamericana. Se dice que inspiró el libro *Metamorfosis*, de Luis G. Urbina. Coautora de *Diez civiles notables de la historia patria* (1914). Autora de *Cuentos sentimentales* (1916), *Rosas de amor* (1917), *Historia de una mujer*, *Así conquista España* (1923), *Lecturas instructivas y recreativas*, *Lecturas selectas*, *Memorias de una niña* y *El mundo de los niños*. Fue presidenta de la Sociedad de Autores Didácticos.

Rossains, Juan Nepomuceno ◆ n. en San Juan de los Llanos, Gto., y m. en Puebla, Pue. (1782-1830). Estudió abogacía en la Real y Pontificia Universidad de México (1808). Administraba la Hacienda La Rinconada, de Tehuacán, cuando se unió a la lucha independentista (1812). Mariano Matamoros lo comisionó para combatir a las bandas que no se sometían a la disciplina insurgente. Auditor de Guerra y secretario particular de Morelos, simultáneamente trabajó en la organización del Congreso de Chilpancingo, del que fue secretario, y se le atribuye la redacción de los *Sentimientos de la Nación*. Teniente general y segundo al mando, persuadió a Morelos de que renunciara al Poder Ejecutivo y dirigió la batalla de Chichihualco, en la que fue derrotado. El Congreso lo nombró comandante general en Puebla, Veracruz, Oaxaca y el norte del Estado de México. Se trasladó a Huamantla, donde fue desconocido por López Rayón. Pasó a Veracruz y fue mal recibido por Rincón. Derrotado en Puebla por Hevia, logró hacerse fuerte en Tehuacán. Después de perder algunas batallas trató de refugiarse en Veracruz, pero Guadalupe Victoria tampoco lo recibió. Finalmente fue detenido por Terán, quien lo envió prisionero al Congreso. Logró escapar y se acogió al indulto (1815). Viajó a México, proporcionó al virrey información sobre las posiciones insurgentes y se retiró a la vida privada. En 1821 ofreció sus servicios a Iturbide, pero fue rechazado. En 1823 la Junta de Recompensas le asignó una pensión. Senador por Puebla (1825-26 y 1827-28). En 1830 se unió a una conspiración contra el presidente Bustamante; fue capturado y fusilado. Autor de una *Relación de mi historia de insurgente*.

Rossas ◆ n. en Guadalajara, Jal. (1935). Nombre profesional del caricaturista Ramón Aguilar Rosas. Se inició como humorista en la revista *Ja-já* y ha sido después cartonista político del *Diario de México* y de *Novedades*. Premio del Club de Periodistas (1982).

Rossi, Alejandro ◆ n. en Italia (1932). Escritor. Maestro en filosofía por la UNAM (1955) con estudios de posgrado en Friburgo, Alemania (1957) y candidato a doctor por la Universidad de Oxford (1961) y la UNAM, donde ha sido investigador, director de Personal Académico y de la Imprenta Universitaria. Fundó y dirigió la revista *Crítica*, fue miembro del consejo de redacción de *Vuelta* y forma parte de los consejos editoriales de *Diánoia* y *Revista Latinoamericana de Filosofía*. Coautor de *Ortega y Gasset* (1984), *Philosophie und Rechtstheorie in Mexiko* (Alemania, 1989) y *Philosophical Analysis in Latin America*. Autor de ensayo: *Lenguaje y significado* (1968), *Manual del distraído* (1978) y *Cartas credenciales* (1999); y

Alejandro Rossi

relato: *Sueños de Occam* (1982) y *La fábula de las regiones* (1988). Editó la antología *José Gaos: Filosofía de la filosofía* (1989). Ha sido becario de El Colegio de México, la Fundación Rockefeller y la Guggenheim. Recibió la Orden del Águila Azteca en 1988. Es creador emérito del SNCA desde 1994, investigador emérito de la UNAM y miembro de El Colegio Nacional desde 1996. Premio Nacional de Artes y Ciencias 1999.

ROTARIO, CLUB ◆ Institución fundada en Chicago por Paul Harris en 1905, con la finalidad de agrupar a los profesionales y empresarios estadounidenses, aunque pronto el rotarismo se internacionalizó. Los miembros de este club consideran que su filosofía básica es "dar de sí antes de pensar en sí"; predican el conocimiento mutuo, la amistad, la ayuda y la buena fe como base de toda negociación; sostienen también que son neutrales en todas las cuestiones políticas y religiosas y realizan permanentemente obras de beneficencia. En México se fundó el primer club rotario en la capital del país, en 1921, con 30 socios (22 estadounidenses, un canadiense, tres ingleses y sólo cuatro mexicanos). Actualmente hay 300 clubes rotarios en la República, divididos en cuatro distritos, cada uno de ellos dirigido por un gobernador. En 1935, por primera vez se efectuó una convención internacional de rotarios en la capital mexicana. Desde entonces se han efectuado otras dos, en 1952 y 1968. En 1999 había más de 320 clubes en territorio nacional y sumaban más de 10,000 los rotarios mexicanos, de los cuales 1,200 estaban en el DF.

ROTBERG, DANA ◆ n. en el DF (1961). Cineasta. Estudió música en el Conservatorio Nacional y la Universidad Veracruzana y estudios latinoamericanos en la UNAM, en cuya filmoteca trabajó. En 1984 ingresó en el CCC, en el que asistió a Gustavo Montiel en el rodaje del documental *A Renato Leduc* (1984) y rodó, en colaboración con Ana Díez Díaz, *Elvira Luz Cruz: Pena máxima* (1985, Diosa de Plata al mejor documental). Posteriormente fue asistente de Felipe Cazals en varias películas y en la serie televisiva *Cuentos de madrugada*. Ha dirigido los largometrajes *Intimidad* (1989) y *Ángel de fuego* (1991, seleccionada para la Quincena de Realizadores del Festival de Cannes).

ROTH, MARTHA ◆ n. en Italia (1932). Actriz. Su apellido materno es Pizzo. Siendo niña, su familia la trajo a México. Ganadora de concursos escolares de belleza, debutó en el cine en 1948 en la película *Una familia de tantas* de Alejandro Galindo, por la que obtuvo un Ariel. Estudió actuación con Seki Sano. De su filmografía destacan *No me quieras tanto* (1948), *El abandonado* (1949), *Anillo de compromiso* (1951), *Una gringuita en México* (1951), *Sucedió en Acapulco* (1952), *Cuando se quiere se quiere* (1953), *A media luz los tres* (1957), *La madrecita* (1973), *Intriga contra México* (1988) y *Violencia a domicilio* (1989). Ha actuado en numerosas obras de teatro, teleteatros y telenovelas. También ha sido cantante y ha compuesto algunas canciones.

Rotofoto

ROTOFOTO ◆ Revista gráfica semanal editada en la ciudad de México por Regino Hernández Llergo y dirigida por José Pagés Llergo. El 22 de mayo de 1938 apareció el número 1 de esta publicación en la que el editorial, las entrevistas, los reportajes y todo el material era fotográfico. Publicó tomas del presidente Lázaro Cárdenas y sus secretarios en paños menores, del jefe de la Policía dormido y de un aspirante presidencial que roía un hueso. Sus fotógrafos fueron Ismael y Gustavo Casasola, Antonio Carrillo Jr., Luis Olivares, I. Sánchez Mendoza, Luis Zendejas, Enrique Delgado y Enrique Díaz, la estrella del equipo. Víctima de la hostilidad oficial sólo llegó al número 11, pues fuerzas de la CTM promovieron una huelga y estimularon el asalto e incendio de su local.

ROTONDA DE LOS HOMBRES ILUSTRES ◆ En 1823 el Congreso de la Unión planteó la necesidad de establecer un panteón nacional que recibiera los restos de los próceres patrios. A este efecto se dispuso que los cadáveres de los héroes insurgentes fuesen llevados a la Catedral Metropolitana, mientras se construía tal panteón nacional. La primera parte de la disposición del Congreso se cumplió, no así la segunda, debido a la inestabilidad económica y política que reinaba en aquellos tiempos. El proyecto fue retomado en 1874, cuando el gobierno de Sebastián Lerdo de Tejada otorgó a la empresa Benfield, Becker y Compañía la concesión para construir el Panteón de Dolores, con una cláusula que establecía que el lugar de honor del cementerio debería destinarse "a la erección de monumentos que guarden los restos o perpetúen la memoria de los hombres ilustres a

Logotipo del Club Rotario

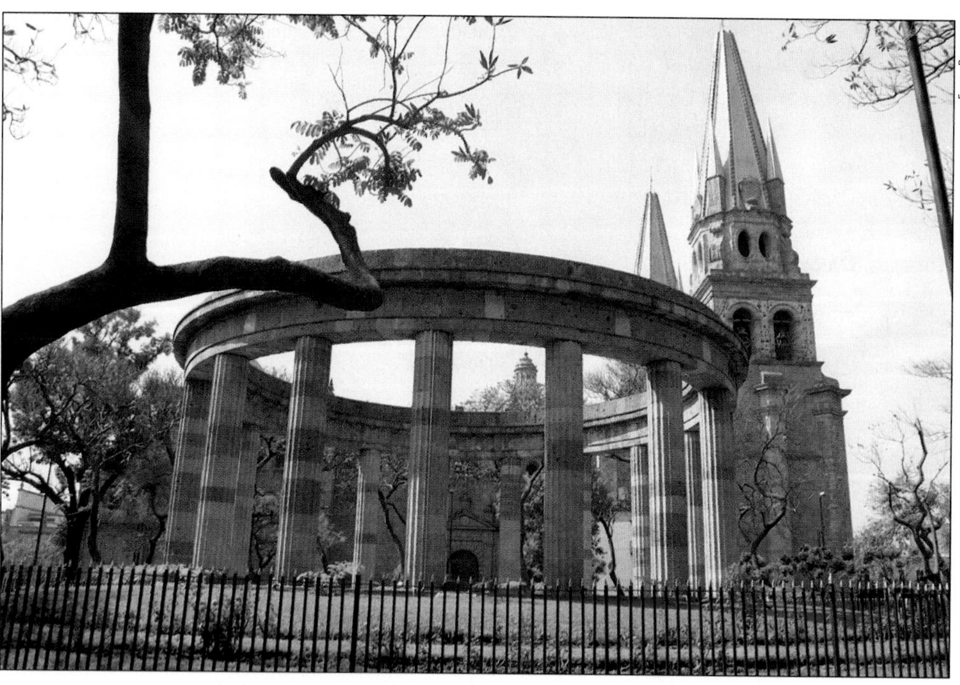

Rotonda de los Hombres Ilustres en el Panteón de Dolores de la ciudad de México

quienes se hubieren decretado o a quienes se decretaren en el futuro honores póstumos". Así, sobre unos 4 km^2 del citado necrosario se erigió la Rotonda de los Hombres Ilustres. Pedro Letechipía, coronel muerto en combate contra la rebelión del Plan de Tuxtepec, fue el primer personaje inhumado en la Rotonda, en 1876, por disposición del gobierno de Sebastián Lerdo de Tejada, aunque tal medida suscitó cierto rechazo, como el manifestado por Justo Sierra y Guillermo Prieto, quienes debían ser oradores en el sepelio. En 1903, Joaquín D. Casasús propuso nuevamente la construcción de un panteón nacional, del que incluso llegó a ponerse la primera piedra, cerca del templo y panteón de San Fernando. El proyecto de la obra, de Guillermo de Heredia, incluía una enorme cripta de granito, única pieza del panteón que quedó concluida, en 1912. Los restos de los héroes de la Independencia, que aguardaban en la Catedral la construcción de sus mausoleos, fueron finalmente trasladados a la Columna de la Independencia, del Paseo de la Reforma. La misma suerte corrieron, en 1942, los despojos mortales de los héroes de la revolución de 1910-17, los que fueron inhumados en el Monumento a la Revolución. Vicente Guerrero y Benito Juárez están en el Panteón de San Fernando y los Niños Héroes en el monumento que les fue erigido en Chapultepec. Por su parte, los diputados del Congreso Constituyente de 1916-17 cuentan con un lote especial en el mismo Panteón Civil de Dolores. El último intento por establecer un panteón nacional se produjo en 1949, cuando Alfonso Cravioto y la Academia de Historia y Geografía propusieron que el templo de Santa Teresa, en la ciudad de México, se destinase a esa causa. Tampoco esta iniciativa halló eco. La rotonda guarda los restos de David Alfaro Siqueiros, Ignacio Manuel Altamirano, Juan Álvarez, Eligio Ancona, Agustín Aragón y León, Mariano Arista, Ponciano Arriaga, Manuel de Aspiroz, Mariano Azuela, Basilio Badillo, Joaquín Baranda, Gabino Barreda, Felipe B. Berriozábal, Calixto Bravo, Emilio Carranza, Nabor Carrillo, Julián Carrillo, Alfonso Caso, Antonio Caso, Rosario Castellanos, Cesáreo Castro, José Ceballos, Francisco Javier Clavijero, Diódoro Corella, Carlos Chávez, Santos Degollado, Francisco Díaz Covarrubias, Salvador Díaz Mirón, Mariano Escobedo, Juan José Espinosa de los Monteros, Genaro Estrada, Virginia Fábregas, Ricardo Flores Magón, Juan José de la Garza, Valentín Gómez Farías, Manuel González, Francisco González Bocanegra, Ignacio González Guzmán, Enrique González Martínez, Jesús González Ortega, Donato Guerra, Agustín Lara, Sebastián Lerdo de Tejada, Pedro Letechipía, Ramón López Velarde, José María Mata, Juan A. Mateos, Ignacio Mejía, Juan N. Méndez, José Vicente Miñón, Francisco Montes de Oca, José María Luis Mora, Gerardo Murillo, Miguel Negrete, Amado Nervo, Jaime Nunó, Melchor Ocampo, Isaac Ochoterena, Pedro Ogazón y Rubio, Juan O'Gorman, José Clemente Orozco, Manuel José Othón, Carlos Pacheco, Carlos Pellicer, Manuel de la Peña y Peña, Ángela Peralta, Basilio Pérez Gallardo, Manuel M. Ponce, Guillermo Prieto, Andrés Quintana Roo, Ignacio Ramírez, Rafael Ramírez, Carlos Ramírez Ulloa, Miguel Ramos Arizpe, Silvestre Revueltas, Alfonso Reyes, Vicente Riva Palacio, Diego Rivera, Sóstenes Rocha, Antonio Rosales, Juventino Rosas, Arturo Rosenblueth, Carlos Rovirosa Pérez, Miguel Ruelas, Moisés Sáenz, Pedro Sainz de Baranda, Rosendo Salazar, Rosendo Salazar Álamo, Francisco Sarabia, Pablo Sidar, Justo Sierra Méndez, José Juan Tablada, Jaime Torres Bodet, Gregorio Torres Quintero, Luis G. Urbina, Jesús Urueta, Ignacio L. Vallarta, Leandro Valle, Leona Vicario, Felipe Villanueva y Agustín Yáñez.

Rouaix Méndez, Pastor ◆ n. en Tehuacán, Pue., y m. en el DF (1874-1949). Ingeniero topógrafo egresado de la Escuela Nacional de Ingeniería (1897). En 1911 fue jefe político de la ciudad de Durango, diputado local (1912) y jefe político en 1913. Renunció tras el cuartelazo de Huerta. Asumió provisionalmente la gubernatura de Durango (del 4 de julio de 1913 al 25 de agosto de 1914, como representante del constitucionalismo). Con la División del Norte participó en los combates de Gómez Palacio y de Lerdo y en la toma de Torreón (1914). Fue oficial mayor encargado del despacho de la

Secretaría de Fomento y Colonización (1914-15). Al producirse la escisión revolucionaria fue a Veracruz con Carranza, de quien fue secretario de Industria y Comercio (del 26 de agosto de 1914 al 1 de mayo de 1917). En 1915 promulgó la Ley Agraria del 6 de enero. Diputado al Constituyente de 1916-17, intervino decisivamente en la redacción de los artículos 27 y 123. Permaneció en el gabinete de Carranza hasta el asesinato de éste. Diputado federal (1924-25 y 1925-26), senador (1927) y secretario de Gobierno de Durango (1928-30). Entre septiembre de 1931 y septiembre de 1932 gobernó provisionalmente ese estado. De 1933 a 1935 fue presidente de la Junta Local de Caminos y más tarde jefe de la Dirección de Geografía, Meteorología e Hidrología de la Secretaría de Agricultura y Fomento. Autor de *Génesis de los artículos 27 y 123 de la Constitución política de 1917* (1923), *La influencia azteca en la República Mexicana* (1929) y *Diccionario geográfico, histórico y biográfico del estado de Durango* (1939), entre otras obras.

ROUMAGNAC, CARLOS ◆ n. y m. en el DF (¿1875?-1937). Traductor de M. Maeterlinck. Autor de *Elementos de policía científica* (1923). Autor, con Alberto Leduc y Luis Lara Pardo, del *Diccionario de geografía, historia y biografía mexicanas* (1910), en el que se encargó de elaborar los artículos geográficos. Fue miembro de la Sociedad Mexicana de Geografía y Estadística, de la Sociedad Antonio Alzate, de la Alianza Científica Universal y de la Sociedad Mexicana Sanitaria y Moral.

ROURA, VÍCTOR ◆ n. en Mérida, Yuc. (1955). Estudió comunicación gráfica en la UNAM. Desde 1972 ha escrito sobre temas musicales, principalmente *rock*, en las publicaciones *Dimensión*, *México Canta* (que dirigió en 1973-75), *Usted*, *El Zeppelin* (de cuyo editor fue asistente en 1976), *Sesión* (de la que fue editor en 1977) y *Melodía Diez Años Después* (que dirigió en 1978-80). En *unomásuno* fue colaborador (1977-80), reportero (1981-82) y jefe de Información Cultural (1982-84). En ese lapso colaboró en las publicaciones *La Garrapata*, *El Machete*, *Balletomanía*, *Punto*, *La Regla Rota*, *Pie de Página*, *Obús* y *El Buscón*. Ha sido fundador (1984), jefe de la sección cultural (1984-85) y colaborador (1984-86) del diario *La Jornada*. En 1986 fundó y dirigió el periódico cultural *Las Horas Extras* (1986-87). Dirigió el Departamento de Publicaciones de la ENEP Iztacala y fue jefe de redacción de la revista *Quimera* (1987). Desde 1988 dirige la sección cultural del diario *El Financiero*. Ha sido coordinador de talleres de periodismo y guionista del programa *Bellas Artes en Radio*. Coautor de *Crines. Lecturas de rock* (1984). Autor de *Reflexión tardía* (1977), *Negros del corazón* (1984), *Apuntes de rock* (1985), *El viejo vals de casa* (1985), la novela *Polvos de la urbe* (1987) y *Diaria escritura* (1988).

Víctor Roura

ROURA PARELLA, JUAN ◆ n. en España (1897-?). Filósofo y pedagogo. Ejerció la docencia en la Universidad de Barcelona. Llegó exiliado a México en 1939. Profesor de El Colegio de México y de la UNAM. Fue presidente del Patronato Cervantes y vocal de la Academia Hispano-Mexicana. En 1945 pasó a Estados Unidos, como profesor de la Universidad Wesleyan. Autor de *Educación y ciencia* (1940), *Eduardo Spranger y las ciencias del espíritu* (1944), *El mundo histórico social*, *Ensayo sobre la morfología de la cultura de Dilthey*, *La educación viva* y *Tema y variaciones de la personalidad*.

ROURE TORENT, J. ◆ n. en España (1902). Abogado y escritor. Llegó exiliado a México en 1942. Fue director de la revista *Nova Era*, órgano del Partido Socialista Catalán (1944-46), colaborador de *Pont Blau* y del *Diccionario Enciclopédico* UTEHA. Autor de una versión de *Las mil noches y una noche* (1945), *Contes d'Eivissa* (1945) y *L'alé de la Sirena i Altres Contes* (1956).

ROUSSET BANDA, GUILLERMO ◆ n. y m. en el DF (1926-1996). Escritor, traductor y editor. Separado del Partido Comunista Mexicano, del que había formado parte, fue miembro fundador de la Liga Comunista Espartaco y de la Asociación Revolucionaria Espartaco. Se autoexilió en Francia durante 11 años y participó en el movimiento de mayo de 1968 en París. Regresó a México para ser encarcelado en Lecumberri, de donde salió amnistiado tras siete años. Colaboró en la revista *Autogestión*. Su traducción de *Personae* de Ezra Pound obtuvo una mención en la entrega del Premio Xavier Villaurrutia (1978). Obtuvo el premio Juan Pablos por su edición y tipografía de *Las décadas del Chango García Cabral* (1979). Fue presidente del Premio Nacional de Traducción de Poesía y presidente fundador del Premio Alfonso X de Traducción Literaria. Fue profesor e investigador de El Colegio de México, el México City College, la UNAM y otras instituciones. Coordinó talleres literarios y fue catedrático de la ENAH. Dejó inédito el libro *Propios y extraños*, con traducciones y poemas originales.

ROUSSET DE JESÚS Y ROSAS, FRANCISCO ◆ n. en Cuba y m. en Imalá, en el actual estado de Sinaloa (1749-1814). Llegó a la Nueva España en su juventud para dedicarse al comercio. En 1775 profesó como fraile franciscano en Zacatecas y fue misionero en el noroeste del país. Fue enviado a la misión de la Tarahumara, de la que llegó a ser vicepresidente. Preconizado obispo de Sonora (1795), fue consagrado en Zacatecas (1798), tomó posesión en 1799 y gobernó la diócesis hasta su muerte.

Foto: Archivo Xavier Esparza

José Narciso Rovirosa

Foto: Archivo Xavier Esparza

Leandro Rovirosa Wade

Rovalo Azcué, José Pablo ◆ n. y m. en el DF (1925-1999). Sacerdote ordenado en 1951. Fue profesor del Seminario (1952-57), director espiritual (1957-59) y coordinador general (1964-68) del Colegio Franco Inglés, párroco de Nuestra Señora Reina de la Paz del DF (1959-64), asistente general de la Sociedad de María en Roma (1968-70), obispo de Zacatecas (1970-72), asesor nacional del Movimiento de Jornadas de Vida Cristiana, vicario episcopal de la tercera zona de pastoral de la arquidiócesis de México y presidente del Departamento de Pastoral Juvenil de la Comisión Episcopal para el Apostolado de los Laicos (1983-90) y obispo emérito de Zacatecas.

Rovirosa, José Narciso ◆ n. en Macuspana, Tab., y m. en la ciudad de México (1849-1901). Ingeniero topógrafo egresado del Instituto de Campeche (1871). Fue profesor e investigador en ciencias naturales. Comisionado por la Secretaría de Fomento, desde 1887 dirigió varias expediciones a Tabasco y Chiapas, en las que descubrió y clasificó diversas especies botánicas, realizó mediciones altimétricas y efectuó estudios antropológicos entre los zoques y los tzotziles. Colaborador de la revista *La Naturaleza* y autor de *Nombres geográficos del estado de Tabasco. Estudio etimológico* (1888), *Ensayo histórico sobre el río Grijalva* (1897) y *Pteridografía del sur de México* (1909).

Rovirosa Macías, José ◆ n. en ¿Veracruz, Ver.? y m. en el DF (1934-1997). Cineasta. Egresado del CUEC del que también fue catedrático. Dedicado al documental, fue autor de *El médico veterinario, Nuestro idioma, Ratigobicha 70, Ayautla, Restauración del Palacio de Minería, Herencia barroca de Fray Junípero Serra en la Sierra Gorda, Minería* (1977, nominado al Ariel como mejor cortometraje científico, educativo o de divulgación artística) y *Perdón..., investidura* (1991, Ariel al mejor cortometraje documental), entre otras. Autor de los libros *Miradas a la realidad I* y *II*. Obtuvo el primer premio del concurso de guiones de Televicine con *Cándidos avasalladores*. Fue creador artístico del SNCA y miembro de la Comisión de Premiación de la Academia Mexicana de Artes y Ciencias Cinematográficas (1981-84).

Rovirosa Pérez, Carlos ◆ n. en Villahermosa, Tab., y m. cerca de Costa Rica (1902-1930). Teniente piloto aviador egresado de la Escuela Militar de Aviación (1927). Participó en varias campañas militares contra los cristeros en Jalisco (1927) y combatió la rebelión escobarista (1929). En 1930 intentó con Pablo L. Sidar (☛) realizar un vuelo sin escalas México-Argentina; ambos murieron cuando su aparato fue abatido por una tormenta en el Caribe, cerca de Puerto Limón, Costa Rica.

Rovirosa Wade, Leandro ◆ n. en Villahermosa, Tab. (1918). Ingeniero civil titulado en la UNAM (1943). Ha sido jefe de Obras Públicas en Ensenada, supervisor de Obras Viales e Hidráulicas (1944), jefe de Planificación del Departamento del Distrito Federal (1951-52), director del Departamento de Construcción de la División de Obras Marítimas y de Obras Portuarias en la Secretaría de Marina (1952-56), presidente de la Cámara Nacional de la Industria de la Construcción, director de obras de la Presa Nezahualcóyotl, secretario de Recursos Hidráulicos en el gabinete de Luis Echeverría (del 1 de diciembre de 1970 al 21 de agosto de 1976) y gobernador de Tabasco (del 1 de enero de 1977 al 31 de diciembre de 1983).

Roy, Manabendra Nath ◆ n. y m. en la India (1887-1954). Su nombre era Marendranath Bhattacharjee. Militó desde los 14 años en el nacionalismo radical hindú. Viajó a Alemania en busca de ayuda para el movimiento independentista indio y en ese país lo sorprendió la primera guerra mundial. Una operación de compra de armas alemanas fue descubierta por los ingleses y Roy escapó a Batavia. Se embarcó a Shanghai y en alta mar abordó una lancha con la que llegó a Cantón. Pasó a Estados Unidos (1916) con intención de seguir su viaje a Alemania. En Stanford se casó con la estudiante Evelyn Trent y se vio involucrado en el juicio contra los nacionalistas indios, acusados de violar la neutralidad estadounidense. Adoptó el nombre de Manabendra Nath Roy y pasó a México (1917), donde reestableció contacto con los alemanes, quienes le proporcionaron fondos para la lucha india. En enero de 1919 fundó la Liga Internacional de Amigos de la India, que dirigió con su esposa. Se relacionó con Adolfo Santibáñez y otros miembros del Partido Socialista. Según él, se convirtió en director de *El Socialista*. Fundador del Partido Comunista Mexicano (1919). Salió hacia Moscú en 1920 y fue miembro destacado de la Internacional Comunista. Autor de *La voz de la India* (1918), *La India, su pasado, su presente y su porvenir* (1918) y *Memorias* (1964).

Rozental Gutman, Andrés ◆ n. en el DF (1945). Licenciado por la Universidad de las Américas (1965) y maestro en relaciones internacionales por la Universidad de Pennsylvania (1967). En la SRE ha sido jefe de departamento (1967-71), representante alterno de México en la OEA (1971-74), consejero de la embajada en Inglaterra (1974-76), subdirector adjunto de Cooperación Técnica Internacional (1976), asesor general del titular (1977-79), director general del Servicio Diplomático (1979), director general para Asuntos de América del Norte (1979-82), representante permanente ante los Organismos Internacionales con sede en Suiza (1982-83), embajador en Suecia (1983-88), subsecretario de Asuntos Multilaterales (1988-92), subsecretario de Relaciones Exteriores (1992-94) y embajador en Inglaterra (1994-). Ha sido director general de la empresa Rozental y Asociados. Pertenece a la Asociación de Derecho Internacional, al Instituto de Derecho del Mar, al Seminario de Derecho Internacional de las Naciones Unidas y al Seminario sobre Derecho del Mar *Pacem in Maribus*.

Rozo, Rómulo ◆ n. en Colombia y m. en Mérida, Yuc. (1899-1964). Escultor. Estudió en la Escuela Nacional de Bellas Artes y en el Instituto Técnico Central de Bogotá; en la Academia de San Fernando y en la Escuela de Arte, Artistas y Artesanos de Madrid (1925); en la Escuela de Bellas Artes y en las academias Julián Colarossi y de la Grand Chaumiére, de París (1928). Fue profesor de escultura y dibujo en Colombia (1921-23), dirigió la construcción y decoración del pabellón colombiano para la Exposición Iberoamericana de Sevilla (1928-29). Agregado de la embajada colombiana en México (1931), fijó su residencia en este país. Profesor de la ENAP (1933) y de la Escuela de Bellas Artes de Mérida (1946-64). Diseñó la ornamentación del Hospital Morelos, de la Escuela Belisario Domínguez y del Teatro al Aire Libre de Chetumal (1937-38), realizó en Mérida los monumentos a la Patria (1946-57) y a la Canción (1958); la maternidad del Monumento a la Revolución; y el monumento a las Leyes de Reforma en Veracruz (1959-60). Autor de la escultura de un campesino, ensarapado y cubierto por su sombrero en actitud de dormir, a la que supuestamente se considera representativa de los mexicanos. Objeto de plagios y variaciones, Rozo llamó a esta pieza *El Pensamiento* (1933). Compuso la canción *Reina de mi alma*. En 1999, el INBA y el Museo de Arte Moderno de Bogotá organizaron una exposición retrospectiva de su obra, con motivo de su centenario.

Ruanda ◆ Nación africana llamada oficialmente República Ruandesa. Limita al norte con Uganda, al este con Tanzania, al sur con Burundi y al oeste con Zaire, país con el que comparte el lago Kivu. Es el país más densamente poblado de África, pues en una superficie de 26,338 km² hay 6,604,000 habitantes (1998). Su capital es Kigali (con 237,782 habitantes en 1991) y otras ciudades importantes son Butaré, Ruhengeri y Gisenyi. La moneda es el franco ruandés y sus idiomas oficiales son el kinya-rwanda, inglés y francés, aunque también se utilizan en gran medida el suahili, el watusi y el inglés. *Historia*: los habitantes originales de Ruanda, los pigmeos o tuas y los hutus, empezaron a ser desplazados por los watusi o tutsi, procedentes de Etiopía, alrededor del siglo XV de la era contemporánea. La ocupación watusi se consolidó 500 años más tarde con el establecimiento de una monarquía feudal. El desarrollo de la vida ruandesa se vio interrumpido por la llegada de los colonialistas europeos: en 1897 Alemania estableció el protectorado sobre la nación y en 1916 los belgas desplazaron a los germanos. En 1919 la Sociedad de Naciones entregó a Bélgica el territorio de Ruanda-Urundi, como mandato, situación que cambió ligeramente en 1946, cuando la ONU convirtió ese mandato en un fideicomiso, administrado igualmente por Bélgica. En 1959 la lucha interna que existía desde antes de la llegada de los europeos resurgió: una rebelión hutu (dirigida por el Partido del Movimiento de Emancipación Hutu, Parmehutu), derrocó a la monarquía watusi. 120,000 tutsis se asilaron en Burundi y algunos otros países vecinos. El movimiento hutu se consolidó y en 1961 esta etnia ganó unas elecciones supervisadas por la ONU. Un referéndum hutu decidió establecer la república y separarse de Burundi. En 1962 la ONU reconoció la independencia de la nueva república y ésta promulgó una constitución. Un año después los watusi intentaron retomar el poder en Ruanda, pero su invasión fracasó y unos 12,000 de ellos murieron. En 1964 se canceló la asociación económica entre Ruanda y Burundi. Los watusi no se dieron por vencidos e intentaron repetidas veces reconquistar Ruanda. En 1973, en medio de otro enfrentamiento hutu-tutsi, el general Juvenal Habyarimana dio un golpe de Estado contra el presidente Gregoire Kayibanda, derogó la constitución y disolvió la Asamblea Nacional. Dos años después, Habyarimana formó el Movimiento Revolucionario Nacional para el Desarrollo, que se convirtió en el único partido político permitido. En 1978 un referéndum aprobó una nueva constitución, que preveía la devolución del poder a los civiles, y se eligió un Consejo de Desarrollo Nacional, integrado por 70 diputados. En 1982 Uganda expulsó de su territorio a numerosos refugiados ruandeses y Ruanda cerró su frontera con aquella nación. La República Ruandesa y México establecieron relaciones diplomáticas el 21 de enero de 1976. En 1990 cientos de refugiados tutsis invadieron Ruanda desde Uganda con lo que se desencadenó una cruenta guerra civil, la que fue detenida por una intervención armada franco-belga. En 1994 los presidentes de Burundi, Cyprien Ntaryamira, y de Ruanda, Juvenal Habyarimana, murieron al ser derribado, con fuego antiaéreo, el avión en que acababan de despegar de Kigali, lo que recrudeció la guerra civil que había estado latente varios años y que se manifestó, sobre todo, en la matanza de

FOTO: FONDO EDITORIAL GRUPO AZABACHE

Fachada del Hospital Morelos, obra de Rómulo Rozo

República de Ruanda

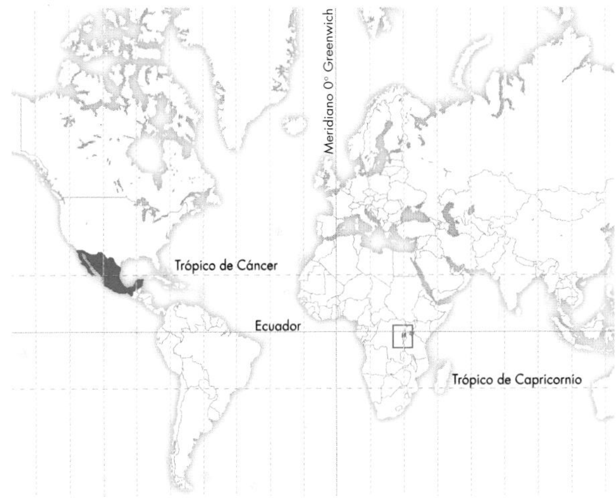

Luis Carlos Ruano Angulo

Obra de Ramón Rubín

más de medio millón de hutus y en el éxodo de más de un millón de refugiados a Zaire, Burundi y Tanzania.

Ruano Angulo, Luis Carlos ◆ n. en Veracruz, Ver. (1927). Almirante. Ingeniero geógrafo por la Escuela Naval Militar Antón Lizardo (1942-45) y por la Escuela Naval del Pacífico (1945-47); maestro en estado mayor por la Escuela Superior de Guerra (1956-57), maestro en manejo de personal y mercadotecnia por el Instituto Fayol (1965), maestro en estado mayor por el Colegio Interamericano de Defensa (EU, 1966-67) y por el Centro de Estudios Superiores Navales (1972). Profesor de la Escuela Superior de Guerra. En la Secretaría de Marina se ha desempeñado como agregado naval de la embajada en EU (1966-70), inspector general de Armas Navales (1970-72), comandante de la zona naval de Tampico (1972-73 y 86-88), del sector naval de Chetumal (1973-75) y de la Fuerza Naval del Golfo (75-77), presidente de la Comisión de Leyes y Reglamentos (1977-80), agregado naval de las embajadas en Francia e Inglaterra (1982-83), inspector general de la Armada (85-86), presidente de la junta de almirantes (1989), agregado naval en la embajada en Perú (1989-90) y secretario de Marina (1990-94). Presidente nacional de la Asociación Cívica Venustiano Carranza. Pertenece a la Asociación del H Colegio Militar, a la Junta Interamericana de Defensa y al United States Naval Institute Proceding.

Ruano Micó, Félix ◆ n. en España y m. en Saltillo, Coah. (1884-1959). Realizó estudios de derecho, música y contaduría. Fue contador general y subadministrador del Ministerio de Hacienda español. Era funcionario en un banco valenciano cuando decidió viajar a Francia, dirigir una orquesta y continuar sus estudios en el Conservatorio de París. Como director de orquesta realizó en 1907 una gira por Asia y América y decidió residir en México y dedicarse a dirigir orquestas, operetas y zarzuelas. Realizó diversas giras por Centroamérica y en 1918 fue a Estados Unidos, donde fundó el Conservatorio de Música Bach, en San Antonio, Texas. Colaboró en *La Prensa* de esa ciudad con la columna "Musicalerías". En 1925 obtuvo la nacionalidad mexicana y fijó su residencia en Saltillo, donde fue profesor de la Escuela Normal de Coahuila y de varias academias comerciales, fundó la Academia Mozart y la primera Orquesta Sinfónica de Saltillo. Perteneció al Club Rotario y fue secretario y oficial mayor de la Cruz Roja local. Autor de *Romance de la sulamita* y el "gran ballet azteca" *El fuego nuevo*.

Rubí Zazueta, Domingo ◆ n. en Las Flores y m. en Mazatlán, Sin. (1826-1896). Minero, en 1858 se unió al ejército liberal. Realizó la campaña de Sinaloa contra la intervención francesa y en 1866 alcanzó el grado de general de brigada. Fue gobernador de Sinaloa (1865, 66-71 y dos veces en 1872).

Rubiales Calvo, Francisco ◆ ☛ *Malgesto, Paco*.

Rubiell Lozano, Jesús ◆ n. y m. en el DF (1953-1993). Se graduó en antropología social (1977) y lingüística (1977) en la ENAH. Perteneció al PRI desde 1983, donde fue subsecretario de Programación y Gestoría del CEN (1987-88) y secretario técnico de la Comisión de Asuntos Indígenas del IEPES (1988). Fue jefe del área de capacitación de la CFE (1973-77), coordinador del Centro Coordinador Indigenista en Guelatao (1978), subdelegado del INI y la Coplamar en Veracruz (1978-79), jefe de Estudios Biosociales del Departamento de Pesca (1979), director de evaluación y seguimiento de la Secogef (1983-84), subdirector de Organización y Capacitación del INI (1984-86), director del secretariado técnico de descentralización de la SPP (19-86-87), director de operación y desarrollo del INI (1988-91) y director general de Organización Social de la Sedesol (1992-93).

Rubín, Ramón ◆ n. en Mazatlán, Sin. (1912). Fue educado en España. En su juventud recorrió gran parte del mundo a bordo de un barco mercante. En 1938 se unió a las brigadas internacionales que combatieron en favor de la república Española. Residió en Guadalajara, donde dirigió la revista *Creación* y fundó dos pequeñas fábricas de zapatos. Ha sido profesor de las universidades de Sinaloa y de Guadalajara. En 1972 regaló sus empresas, autorizó a una editorial chicana a publicar sus libros en forma de historietas y se retiró a vivir en Autlán. Autor, entre otras obras, de *Cuentos del medio rural mexicano* (1942), *Ese rifle sanitario* (1948), *Cuentos de México* (1948), *Diez burbujas en el mar. Sarta de cuentos salobres* (1949), *La loca* (1950), *Cuarto libro de cuentos mestizos* (1950), *La canoa perdida* (1951), *El canto de la grilla* (1952), *La bruma lo vuelve azul* (1954), *La sombra del techincuagüe* (1955), *En carne propia* (1956), *Cuentos de indios. Segundo libro* (1958), *Las cinco palabras* (1959), *Lago Cajititlán* (1960), *El hombre que ponía huevos* (1961), *El seno de la esperanza* (1964), *Los rezagados* (1983), *Navegante sin ruta* (1983), *La revolución sin mística. Pedro Zamora, historia de un violador* (1983), *Cuentos del mundo mestizo* (1985), *Casicuentos del agente viajero* (memorias, 1987) y *Cuentos de la ciudad* (1991). Premio de las Américas, otorgado por la Asociación de Libreros de Nuevo México (1994).

Rubín de la Borbolla, Daniel Fernando ◆ n. en Puebla, Pue., y m. en el DF (1907-1990). Antropólogo (1931). Profesor del Museo Nacional (1931-36), de la UNAM (1931-42), de la Escuela Nacional de Ciencias Biológicas del IPN (1937-42), del INAH y de El Colegio de México entre otras instituciones. Fue director del Museo Nacional de Antropología (1947-53), fudador y primer director de los museos Nacional de Artes e Industrias Populares (1948-67), consejero técnico del Comité Organizador de los XIX Juegos Olímpicos (1966-68), director general de Monumentos Históricos, Arqueológicos y Museos del estado de México (1970-76). Entre sus obras se encuentran *Las artes populares en el estado de México* (1957) y *José María Velasco* (1974).

RUBINSTEIN, BECKY ◆ n. en el DF (1948). Licenciada en lengua y literatura hispánicas y maestra en literatura española por la UNAM, donde es profesora de literatura medieval sefaradita. Estudió hebreo y psicología infantil en Israel. Colaboradora de *Ovaciones*, *El Universal*, *El Sol de México*, *Casa del Tiempo*, *Alejandría*, *Cocolitos*, *El Cocodrilo Poeta*, *Foro*, *Alejandría* y *Tiempo de Niños*. Autora de cuento: *La casamentera* (1983), *El circo* (1984), *Hechizos* (1985), *Invéntame un cuento. Inventos y algo más* (1989), *Del tianguis de Juan Juguetero* (1992) y *El único unicornio* (1993); poesía: *Los servidores públicos* (1985), *Máscaras para la luna* (1986), *Yo quiero un verso, yo quiero dos* (1987), *Senderos de cuatro licores* (1988), *De nubes* (1991), *Caballero de polvoso azul* (1993), *Vitrales* (1993) e *Hijas de la rueca* (1994); y novela: *El árbol gatológico* (1988, premio de cuento para niños Juan de la Cabada), entre otros títulos. Premios Gabino Barreda de la UNAM (1980) y de Cuento Brevísimo de la revista *El Cuento* (1986). Presea Sor Juana-Venera de Bronce en ensayo (1990), mención de honor del Premio Mundial de Literatura José Martí, de la Fundación Iberoamericana de Creación para Niños y Jóvenes José Martí (Costa Rica, 1997).

RUBIO, ARNULFO ◆ n. en Jalisquillo, Mich. (1953). Escritor y periodista. Egresado de la Facultad de Ciencias Políticas y Sociales de la UNAM. Comenzó su carrera colaborando en *Diorama de la Cultura*. Ha sido corrector en el periódico *La Jornada* y editor de cultura de *La Afición* y la revista *Tiempo*. Fundó las revistas *Letra* y *Rock You*. Autor de poesía: *Retrato de perro con artista joven* (1985), *Andan por ahí* (1986), *El corazón de la noche* (1986), *Canto del obseso* (1989), *Voces de piedra* (1993) y *Trece sonetos*; novela: *La sombra del viajero* y *Oniria*; y cuento: *El conductor y otros relatos* (1981) y *Cuatro relatos* (1984).

RUBIO, DARÍO ◆ n. en el Mineral de la Luz, Gto., y m. en el DF (1878-1952). Fundó el periódico local *El Correo de Guanajuato*, viajó a la ciudad de México y fue regidor y jefe del departamento administrativo del Ayuntamiento, así como director de varias sucursales del Nacional Monte de Piedad. Escribió con el pseudónimo de *Ricardo del Castillo*. Autor de *Ligeras reflexiones acerca de nuestro teatro nacional* (1912), *Los llamados mexicanismos de la Real Academia Española* (1917), *Nahuatlismos y barbarismos. Estudio lexicográfico* (1919), *La anarquía del lenguaje en la América Española* (1925), *El lenguaje popular mexicano. Discurso* (1927) y *Refranes, proverbios, dichos y dicharachos mexicanos* (1937). A partir de 1931 fue secretario perpetuo y desde 1934 también tesorero de la Academia Mexicana (de la Lengua), en la que ingresó como miembro correspondiente en 1918 y de número en 1925.

RUBIO, JOSÉ RAFAEL ◆ n. en Zamora, Mich., y m. en EUA (1880-1916). A fines del siglo XIX se inició en el periodismo, cuando residía en Guadalajara. A principios del siglo XX viajó a la ciudad de México, colaboró en diversas publicaciones con el pseudónimo de *Rejúpiter* y fundó y dirigió el periódico antihuertista *El Chubasco*, que le valió ser obligado a exiliarse en Estados Unidos. Autor del monólogo *Juan Soldado* y la obra lírica *El surco*.

RUBIO DONNADIEU, FRANCISCO ◆ n. en el DF (1932). Médico cirujano por la UNAM (1955), posgraduado en medicina interna y neurología en el Hospital de Enfermedades de la Nutrición (1958). Ha sido consultor titular de neurología del Instituto Nacional de la Nutrición (1961), neurólogo del IMSS (1961-62), profesor de la Facultad de Medicina de la UNAM (1962-66) y de su División de Estudios Superiores (1966-70). En el Instituto Nacional de Neurología y Neurocirugía ha sido jefe de la División de Neurología (1967-83), profesor (1970-), jefe de Enseñanza (1970-83) y director general (1983-). Miembro numerario de la Academia Nacional de Medicina. Pertenece a la Academia Mexicana de Neurología, a la American Academy of Neurology, la American Neurological Association, a la Sociedad Mexicana de Medicina Interna y a la Sociedad Mexicana de Neurología y Psicología. Fue presidente de la Epilepsy International, Capítulo Mexicano de la Liga contra la Epilepsia, presidente y fundador del Consejo Mexicano de Neurología.

RUBIO LARA, ENRIQUE ◆ n. en el DF (?). Licenciado en ciencias políticas por la UNAM. Ha sido coordinador ejecutivo de la Dirección General de Conasupo, director general del Instituto Nacional del Consumidor (1980-82), gerente de *unomásuno* (1983), cofundador de *La Jornada* (1984), director general de la empresa Consultores en Comunicación Social y director general de Radio, Televisión y Cinematografía de la Secretaría de Gobernación (1995-97).

RUBIO MAÑÉ, JORGE IGNACIO ◆ n. en Mérida, Yuc., y m. en el DF (1904-1988). Estudió historia en las universidades de Carnegie, de Loyola (en Nueva Orleans) y Harvard. En 1924 empezó a colaborar en publicaciones yucatecas, con artículos sobre historia. En 1933 se incorporó al equipo de investigadores de la institución Carnegie de Washington y hasta 1941 trabajó en diversos archivos de Yucatán, Campeche y el Distrito Federal. Estuvo becado en Harvard (1937). Desde 1944 fue investigador en el Archivo General de la Nación y profesor e investigador de la UNAM. Estuvo becado en los archivos de Madrid y el General de Indias de Sevilla (1946). Fue comisionado del Instituto Panamericano de Geografía e Historia para investigar en los archivos de París, Londres, Madrid, Sevilla, Génova, Turín, Roma, Nápoles y Palermo (1956-58). Fue director del Archivo General de la Nación y escribió en su *Boletín*. Autor de *Biografía sobre los Montejo*, *Monografía de los Montejo* (1930), *El separatismo de Yucatán* (1934), *Los piratas Lafitte* (1938), *Don Luis de Velasco, el virrey popular* (1946), *Movimiento marítimo entre Veracruz y Campeche, 1801-1810* (1954), *Introducción al estudio de los virreyes de Nueva España, 1535-1746* (4 t., 1955-60), *El virreinato* (1983), *Andrés Quintana Roo. Ilustre insurgente yucateco* (1987) y *Pedro Contreras Elizalde*

Becky Rubinstein

Darío Rubio

(1987), entre otras obras. Presidió la Fraternidad Iberoamericana y desde 1932 fue miembro de número de la Academia Mexicana de la Historia.

Rubio Monteverde, Horacio ◆ n. en el DF (1941). Médico cirujano por la UNAM (1958-63), posgraduado en neumología en el Hospital de Enfermedades Pulmonares (1966-68) y en otorrinolaringología en el Hospital General de México (1977-80). Ha sido jefe de enseñanza del Hospital de Enfermedades Pulmonares (1971-77), asesor de la Subdirección General Médica del IMSS (1974-77), profesor de la UNAM (1974-), miembro del Consejo Técnico del Instituto Nacional de Enfermedades Pulmonares (1972), asesor médico suplente y definitivo del Consejo Técnico y de la Comisión de Vigilancia del IMSS; tesorero, vicepresidente y presidente de la Sociedad Mexicana de Neumología y Cirugía del Tórax (1977-83); asesor del Programa de Reforma Administrativa en el Área de Salud (1981-82) y director general del Instituto Nacional de Enfermedades Respiratorias (1982-). Coautor de *Introducción a la neumología* (1981) y autor de *Producción, comercialización y consumo de medicamentos* (1976). Pertenece al American College of Chest Physicians, Asociación Médica Latinoamericana, Asociación de Médicos Mexicanos para la Prevención de la Guerra Nuclear, Consejo Nacional de Neumología, Sociedad Peruana de Fisiología, Neumología y Enfermedades del Tórax y a la Sociedad Venezolana de Neumología, entre otras agrupaciones profesionales.

Rubio Oca, Julio ◆ n. en el DF (1950). Licenciado, maestro y doctor en ciencias por la UNAM, realizó estudios de posdoctorado en la Universidad Estatal Stilwater de Oklahoma. En la unidad Iztapalapa de la Universidad Autónoma Metropolitana ha sido coordinador de Investigación y Posgrado y rector (1990-96).

Rubio Rubio, Filiberto ◆ n. en Jacala y m. en Pachuca, Hgo. (?-1948). Licenciado en derecho por la Universidad Nacional. Fue juez de Zacualtipán y Pachuca, dos veces gobernador interino de Hidalgo (1912-14 y 1921), secretario general de gobierno y presidente del Tribunal Superior de Justicia del Estado.

Rubio y Rubio, Horacio ◆ n. en Jacala, Hgo., y m. en el DF (1881-1964). Fue simultáneamente profesor y alumno del Instituto Científico y Literario de Hidalgo (1899-1900). Se tituló como médico cirujano en la Universidad Nacional (1907). Militó en el antirreeleccionismo y fue diputado local (1913-14). Profesor de la Escuela Normal de Maestras (1915), director del *Boletín del Consejo de Salubridad* de Hidalgo (1916-17), varias veces presidente de la Sociedad Mutualista Hidalguense, director de la Sociedad Española de Beneficencia (1928) y presidente del Ateneo Hidalguense Dr. Antonio Peñafiel (1939-42). Tradujo a Schiller, Christian Friedrich Henrich, Sargent y Cunnington. Autor de *Cuando Marcos volvió, Apuntes sobre la flora hidalguense, Vocabulario de la lengua náhuatl, ¿Sabe usted observar las aves?, Ensayo sobre literatura* y *El niño campesino, la huerta y la granja*. Fue miembro de la Sociedad de Medicina Interna, del Seminario de Cultura Mexicana, el Ateneo de Ciencias y Artes de México, la Academia de la Lengua Náhuatl y la Sociedad de Geografía e Historia de Honduras.

Rubio y Salinas, Manuel ◆ n. en España y m. en la ciudad de México (1703-1765). Estudió en la Universidad de Alcalá de Henares. Sacerdote. Fue capellán de Felipe V, fiscal de la real capilla, casa y corte, juez de las reales jornadas, vicario de Alcalá y abad de San Isidro de León. En 1748 fue presentado para el arzobispado de México y consagrado en Puebla en 1749.

Rublúo Islas, José Luis ◆ n. en el DF (1940). Licenciado en derecho (1963) y en historia (1968) por la UNAM. Hizo estudios de biblioteconomía y archivonomía en la SCT. Ha sido representante del Instituto Panamericano de Geografía e Historia de la OEA, bibliotecario e investigador de la Biblioteca Nacional de México y del Instituto de Investigaciones Bibliográficas de la UNAM. Autor de *Bibliografía mexicana sobre la Navidad* (1965), *Sahagún y los refranes de los antiguos mexicanos* (1966), *Estética de la Historia Verdadera de Bernal Díaz del Castillo* (1969), *La tarea del historiador* (1974), *Cronistas de la ciudad de México* (1975), *El sueño de un fauno* (crítica literaria, 1976), *Juego de palabras* (poesía, 1978), *La dimensión del mar* (poesía novelada, 1979), *México en sus artesanías* (ensayo, 1979), *El álbum de Rosario* (crítica literaria, 1981), *Historia de la revolución mexicana en el estado de Hidalgo* (2 t., 1983-85), *Historia de la banca mexicana* (1984), *Tradiciones y leyendas hidalguenses* (1986), *Los pintores del siglo de oro, Los alcaldes mayores del Real de Minas de Pachuca* y *Valle Arizpe y el arte de la historia*, entre otras obras.

Rudenko, Boris Timofiévich ◆ n. en la URSS (1917). Estudió en el Instituto de Ciencias Pedagógicas. Doctor en ciencias por la Universidad de Moscú. En 1941-45 estuvo en el Ejército Rojo y alcanzó el grado de coronel en la lucha contra la Alemania de Hitler. Se dedicó a estudiar la realidad mexicana desde 1937 y perteneció a la Sociedad URSS-México. Coautor de *México en la encrucijada de su historia*. Autor de *México en vísperas de la revolución, La estructura social de México antes de 1910-17* y otros ensayos históricos.

Rudomín Zevnovaty, Pablo ◆ n. en el DF (1934). Licenciado en biología (1956), maestro en ciencias (1963) y doctor en fisiología por el IPN (1965). En el Cinvestav del IPN se ha desempeñado como profesor (1961-68), jefe de la sección de Control Neural del Departamento de Farmacología y Toxicología (1972-74), jefe de la sección de Control Neural del Departamento de Fisiología (1974-84), director del Programa de Neurociencias (1984-92) y jefe de Fisiología, Biofísica y Neorociencias (1992-). Ha escrito más de 100 artículos para publicaciones científicas y ha formado parte del consejo editorial de las principales revistas internacionales de su especialidad. Ha disfrutado seis veces la beca de los

Institutos Nacionales de Salud de EUA, tres la de Conacyt, dos la Guggenheim, y una la Rockefeller. Vicepresidente (1979-81) y presidente (1981-83) de la Academia de la Investigación Científica; fundador de la Academia Latinoamericana de Ciencias (1982), presidente de la Comisión de Evaluación del Área de Ciencias Biológicas, Médicas y Químicas del Sistema Nacional de Investigadores (1984-88), asesor del Colegio Nacional (1993-), coordinador del Consejo Consultivo de Ciencias de la Presidencia (1995-97) y asesor del Conacyt. Pertenece al Sistema Nacional de Investigadores. Ha recibido, entre otros, los premios Alfonso Caso (1972), de la Academia de la Investigación Científica (1986), Nacional de Ciencias y Artes (1979) y Príncipe de Asturias (1987).

RUEDA ♦ n. en España (1924). Caricaturista llamado Ángel Rueda. Llegó exiliado a México en 1939. Naturalizado mexicano, fue cartonista político de *El Popular*, *Esto* y *El Día*.

RUEDA MEDINA, GUSTAVO ♦ n. en Aguascalientes, Ags., y m. en el DF (1905-1959). Egresado de la Escuela Naval de Veracruz, se especializó en la Escuela de Submarinos de Cartagena, España. Fue subjefe del Estado Mayor Naval, director de la Escuela Naval de Veracruz, comandante de la octava zona naval y diputado federal. Alcanzó el grado de contraalmirante. Autor de las novelas *¿Quién tiene un sacacorchos?* (1945) y *Las islas también son nuestras* (1946).

RUEDA QUIJANO, ALFREDO ♦ n. en San Luis Potosí, SLP, y m. en la ciudad de México (¿1890?-1927). Estudió en la Escuela Militar de Aspirantes. Se unió a la revolución constitucionalista en las fuerzas de Eugenio Martínez y Joaquín Amaro. En 1927 apoyó la campaña de Serrano, por lo que fue aprehendido en Texcoco y fusilado en la antigua Escuela de Tiro de la ciudad de México.

RUEDA RAMÍREZ, EMMA ♦ n. en Durango, Dgo. (1947). Escritora. Licenciada en arte dramático por la UNAM. Hizo estudios de Psicología y comunicación. Ha hecho programas de radio y televisión. Ha colaborado en *El Sol de Durango*, en la *Revista Mexicana de Cultura*, suplemento de *El Nacional*, en *Excélsior* y otras publicaciones. Autora de cuentos: *Lecturas de un ladrón improvisado* (1976); poesía: *Ilnamiqui* (1983), *Esto sé del beso* (1986) y *Piel de la paz* (1990); teatro: *El alcaraván* (1966), *Este cuatro* (1968), *Ellos* y *Cómo evitar el suicidio* (1981) y *La jirafa Teoltecáyotl* (Premio de Teatro Infantil de la SEP, 1982); y lírica testimonial: *Testimonia* (1980), *Palenque* (1980), *Madre Teotihuacán* (1981) y *Chollollan-Chulula* (1981).

RUEDAS DE LA SERNA, JORGE ♦ n. en el DF (1945). Escritor. Licenciado en lengua y literatura hispánicas y maestro en letras mexicanas por la UNAM; doctor en teoría literaria por la Universidad de São Paulo, Brasil. Profesor e investigador de la UNAM. Fue agregado cultural de la embajada mexicana en Brasil (1973-76). Ha colaborado en *Revista de la Universidad, Diorama de la Cultura*, de *Excélsior*, la Revista *Mexicana de Cultura*, suplemento de *El Nacional*, y otras publicaciones. Coautor de *La prosa de Ramón López Velarde* (Premio Internacional de Ensayo de la SEP, 1971) y *Antología de la prosa en lengua española. Siglos XVI y XVII* (1971). Autor de un antología de *Manuel González Prada* (1982).

RUELAS, ELIGIO ♦ m. en Tzompantenec, Tlax. (?-1894). Militar conservador. Alcanzó el generalato en 1856. Durante la guerra de los Tres Años fue gobernador interino de Puebla (1860).

RUELAS, ENRIQUE ♦ n. en Pachuca, Hgo., y m. en el DF (1913-1987). Licenciado en derecho por la Universidad de Guanajuato (1943), de la que fue profesor desde 1952. Ejerció la docencia en la UNAM, donde fundó el Teatro Preparatoriano y la carrera de literatura dramática (1976) y fungió como jefe del Departamento de Actividades Estéticas de la Preparatoria (1976). Fue representante del Departamento de Cooperación Intelectual de la SEP ante la UNESCO (1947-49), secretario del Centro Mexicano de Teatro (1949-63), subdirector del Instituto de Cultura Cinematográfica de la UIA (1957-60) y director del Teatro de la Televisión, de Telesistema Mexicano (1951). A partir de 1953 dio en representar entremeses de Miguel de Cervantes en plazas de la ciudad de Guanajuato, lo que dio origen al Festival Internacional Cervantino (1972). Dirigió las obras *Don Juan Tenorio* (1943), *Arsénico y encaje* (1952-53), *Cristóbal Colón* (de Fernando Benítez, 1954), *Pasos* (1955), *La soga* (1959), *El tiempo es un sueño* (1948 y 1950), *El emperador Jones* (1949-50), *Saber morir* (1951), *Retablillo jovial* (1958), *El caballero de Olmedo* (1962-68), *Yerma* (1963) y *Estampas del Quijote* (1972).

FOTO: ROGELIO CUÉLLAR

Enrique Ruelas

RUELAS, JUAN N. ♦ n. en Guadalcázar y m. en San Luis Potosí, SLP (1855-1930). Sacerdote y abogado. Fue profesor del Seminario y del Instituto Científico y Literario de San Luis Potosí. Ejerció el periodismo como opositor al régimen de Porfirio Díaz. Durante más de 25 años fue director del periódico *El Estandarte*, de la capital potosina.

RUELAS, JULIO ♦ n. en Zacatecas, Zac., y m. en Francia (1870-1907). Pintor. Estudió en el Colegio Militar, del que fue expulsado junto con José Juan Tablada por la publicación de un pasquín que él ilustró. Ingresó en la Academia de San Carlos, donde fue alumno de Rafael Flores. De 1891 a 1895 estudió en la Escuela de Arte de la Universidad de Karlsrühe. En México fue ilustrador de la *Revista Moderna* (☛) e hizo obra de caballete. Volvió a Europa en 1904, becado por el gobierno. Estudió grabado en Francia con J. María Cazin. Hay obras suyas en la Galería Nacional de Pintura y en la Secretaría de la Defensa Nacional. Ilustró, entre otros, los libros *El éxodo*, *Las flores del camino* y *Jardines interiores*, de Amado Nervo. Autor de óleos, pasteles y grabados al aguafuerte: *Ahuehuetes de Chapultepec* (1896), *Retrato de don Francisco de Alba* (1896), *El papelero* (1896), *El pordiosero* (1899), *Retrato de la señora de Larquet* (1899), *El caballero con sombrero de copa* (1899), *Estudio de un árbol* (1899), *Huerta de Durango*

FOTO: ARCHIVO XAVIER ESPARZA

Obra de Julio Ruelas

(1899), *Retrato de Manuel José Othón* (1900), *El general Rocha y su estado mayor* (1901), *Madre muerta* (1901), *Retrato de Rubén M. Campos* (1902), *El sátiro ahogado* (1904), *El duelo* (1904), *Paleta* (1904), *Entrada de don Jesús Luján a la Revista Moderna* (1904), *La escalera del dragón*, *La araña*, *La muerte*, *La esfinge*, *La caridad*, *Fuegos fatuos*, *La medusa*, *La meona*, *El suplicio de la reina mora*, *El murciélago* y el autorretrato *La crítica* (1906-07).

Ruffinelli, Jorge ◆ n. en Uruguay (1943). Jefe del Centro de Investigaciones Lingüístico-Literarias de la Universidad Veracruzana y director de *Texto Crítico*. Fue profesor en la Facultad de Letras de esa universidad. Autor de *José Revueltas* (1976), *Crítica en marcha* (1979), *El lugar de Rulfo y otros ensayos* (1980), *Las infamias de la inteligencia burguesa* (1980), *Literatura e ideología: el primer Mariano Azuela (1896-1918)* (1981), *Poesía y descolonización* (1985) y *La escritura invisible* (1986). Premio de Ensayo Literario José Revueltas (1980).

Ruffo Appel, Ernesto ◆ n. en EUA (1952). Político de nacionalidad mexicana. Es licenciado en administración de empresas por el ITESM (1975). Ha sido jefe de Personal y de Flota, gerente de Operaciones, gerente general y director general de Pesquera Zapata (1976-89). Fue sargento segundo del Servicio Militar Nacional (1970), presidente de la Asociación de Estudiantes Bajacalifornianos en Monterrey (1973-74); gerente administrativo (1975), consejero, secretario y presidente del Centro Empresarial de Ensenada (1978-82), consejero y secretario de la Cámara Pesquera de la misma ciudad (1980-85), presidente nacional de la Asociación de Productores de Harina y Aceite de Pescado (1984), consejero de la Cámara Nacional Pesquera (1985) y presidente del Consejo Coordinador Empresarial de Ensenada (1986). Desde 1985 pertenece al PAN, de cuyo Consejo Nacional ha sido miembro desde 1989. Fue presidente municipal de Ensenada (1986-88) y gobernador de Baja California (1989-95). Fue el primer gobernador de oposición desde 1929, cuando fue creado el partido oficial.

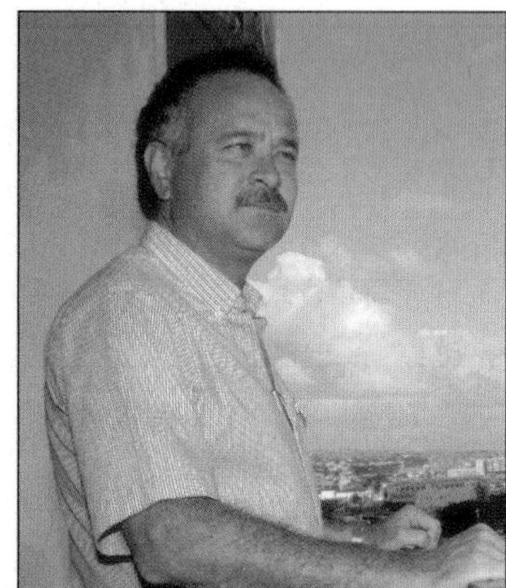

Ernesto Ruffo Appel

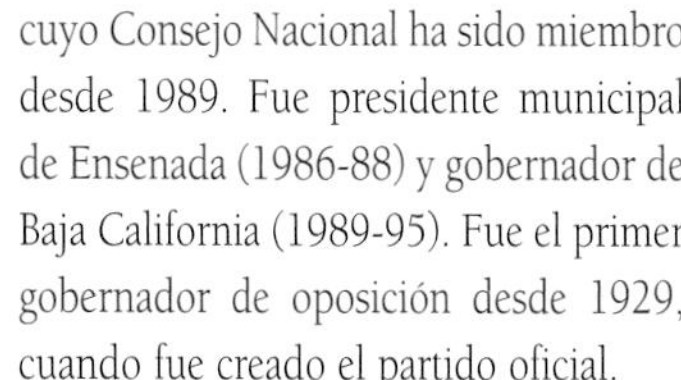

Rugendas, Johan Moritz ◆ n. y m. en Alemania (1802-1858). Estudió pintura en Augsburgo y Munich. En 1831 estuvo en Haití, de donde pasó a México. Aquí permaneció hasta 1834, recorriendo el país con el cartógrafo y estratega Eduard Harkort. Fue expulsado de México, después de estar encarcelado durante unos días, pues se le involucró en una conspiración contra el presidente Santa Anna. Entre 1834 y 1846 visitó Sudamérica. Hay obra suya en el Museo de Historia de Chapultepec, en la Galería Nacional de Arte de la República Federal de Alemania y en diversas colecciones y museos de Berlín y Munich. En el libro *Mexico. Landscapes and Popular Sketches* (1860), de Christian Sartorius, hay 18 grabados suyos. En 1959 se realizó en el Palacio de Bellas Artes una exposición de los cuadros que Rugendas pintó en México, y en 1986 se presentaron en la ciudad de México y Guadalajara 197 obras, algunas de las cuales nunca habían salido de Europa. Autor de *Retrato de doña Luisa C. de Jiménez*, *Salteador de diligencias*, *Poblanas*, *Tortilleras a la entrada de una casa*, *Interior de una casa en Jalapa*, *Entretenimiento musical*, *Trapiche de Tyzamapa*, *Alameda en México*, *Entrada a Jalapa con el Cofre de Perote*, *Bosque sagrado de Chapultepec* y *Barranca de Jamapa*.

Ruhland, Emilio ◆ ¿n. y m. en Alemania? (?-?). Llegó a México alrededor de 1880 y fundó el semanario *Deustche zeitung von Mexico* (1883). En 1885 Isidoro Epstein lo acusó de calumnia e inició un proceso contra él, por lo que el periódico dejó de aparecer hasta 1900. Autor de un *Directorio general de la República* (1890).

Ruisánchez Serra, José Ramón ◆ n. en el DF (1971). Licenciado en letras hispánicas por la UNAM. Estudió en la Escuela de Escritores de la Sogem y asistió al taller de Rafael Ramírez Heredia. Ha sido traductor y director de talleres literarios. Es profesor de tiempo completo del ITESM-ciudad de México. Miembro del consejo editorial de las revistas *Péndulo* y *Opinión*. Autor de relatos: *Mortal y biodegradable* (1996); novela: *Novelita de amor y poco piano* (1993, Premio Juan Rulfo para primera novela), *Y por qué no tenemos otro perro* (1997) y *Remedios infalibles contra el hipo* (1998); antología: *Memorial de las ciudades* (1995) y *La habitación de al lado* (1996, en colaboración); y poesía: *Catorce poemas para sordos* (1994). Becario del Centro Mexicano de Escritores (1994-95) y del Fonca (1998-99).

Ruiz ◆ Municipio de Nayarit situado al norte de San Blas y al noroeste de Tepic. Superficie: 900.1 km^2. Habitantes: 21,591, de los cuales 6,047 forman la población económicamente activa. Hablan alguna lengua indígena 1,866 personas mayores de cinco años (cora 1,119 y huichol 670). Indígenas monolingües: 57. Cuenta con yacimientos de metales preciosos.

Ruiz, Águeda ◆ n. en Uruapan, Mich. (1938). Licenciada en periodismo por la Escuela Carlos Septién García, especializada en el Instituto Latinoamericano de Comunicación Educativa. Hizo estudios de historia y de introducción a la ciencia pesquera en la UNAM y de arte dramático en el INBA. Trabajó en un programa de la FAO, fue editora científica, asesora del Departamento de Pesca (1977-81) y de la Secretaría de Pesca (1982); y jefa de publicaciones del Instituto Nacional de Pesca (1983-86). Ha colaborado en *Sucesos*, *América*, *Siempre!*, *Pájaro Cascabel*, *El Corno Emplumado*, *Letras de Ayer y Hoy* y otras publicaciones. Cofundadora de *Técnica Pesquera* (19-68-77) y de *Energía* (1978-83). Fue responsable de la secretaría técnica y jefa de reportajes especiales de *El Nacional* (1990-94). Autora de poesía: *Oficio de mujer* (1977) y *Tres tiempos del tiempo* (1982).

Ruiz, Andrés ◆ n. en el DF (1950). Periodista. Estudió sociología en la UNAM y ejerce el periodismo desde

1971. Trabajó en la mesa de redacción de los periódicos *unomásuno* y *La Jornada*, de la que fue fundador. Ha sido jefe de redacción de la revista *Fin de Siglo*, editor del boletín *El Correo del Libro* de la SEP, secretario de redacción de la revista *Memoria de Papel*, miembro de la redacción del suplemento cultural de las revistas *Siempre!* y *Proceso*, coordinador de la sección cultural de *El Universal*, editor de *El Ángel*, suplemento cultural del periódico *Reforma* (1993-95), coordinador de cultura y espectáculos del periódico *La Jornada* (1997-98) y director general del periódico *Liberación*, de Toluca (1998-99). Autor del libro *Catástrofes y compañía*, que reúne sus colaboraciones para el periódico *El Financiero*.

RUIZ, ANTONIO ◆ m. en San Felipe y Santiago de Sinaloa (¿1553?-¿1603?). Hacia 1565 acompañó a su padre, el soldado español Juan Ruiz, en una expedición a Paquimé dirigida por Francisco de Ibarra. En 1568, cuando estallaron varias insurrecciones indígenas, se alistó en el ejército colonial, que ante el empuje de los rebeldes se retiró a Culiacán, donde permaneció Ruiz hasta 1583, cuando se unió a las fuerzas de Pedro de Montoya, a quien acompañó como escribano en la fundación de la villa de San Felipe y Santiago de Carapoa, que poco después desapareció por los ataques indígenas. Ruiz, con otros españoles (Bartolomé de Mondragón, Tomás de Soberanes, Juan Martínez del Castillo y Juan Caballero, fundó más tarde la villa de San Felipe y Santiago de Sinaloa (hacia 1585). En 1590, cuando la villa estaba poblada por ocho españoles, Ruiz era el caudillo de la misma. Autor de una *Relación* que narra con detalle las conquistas en el norte, desde las de Francisco de Ibarra hasta las de Diego Martínez de Hurdaide.

RUIZ, ANTONIO ◆ n. en Texcoco y m. en el DF (1897-1964). Pintor. También se dice que nació en el DF. Lo llamaban *el Corcito*. Estudió en Morelia y en 1916 ingresó en la Academia de San Carlos. Profesor del IPN y la UNAM. Fue director de *La Esmeralda* (1942-54). Efectuó en Buenos Aires, en 1927, su primera exposición. Entre 1927 y 1929 estuvo en Hollywood, donde estudió escenografía y ejecutó cuatro murales portátiles para la Pacific House. Elaboró los decorados de las piezas teatrales *Diferente*, de Eugene O'Neill, y *El gesticulador* (1947) y otras obras de Rodolfo Usigli. Fue escenógrafo de *¡Vámonos con Pancho Villa!* y varias películas más, así como de las compañías de danza de Ana Sokolov y Nelly Campobello. Participó en la Exposición Internacional del Surrealismo, celebrada en la Galería de Arte Mexicano, en el DF (1940). Autor de un mural en la sede del Sindicato de Trabajadores de la Industria Cinematográfica (1935, destruido en 1943) y de otro en el edificio Souza. Hay obra suya en el Museo de Arte Moderno de Nueva York. En 1942 ingresó en el Seminario de Cultura Mexicana.

RUIZ, BERNARDO ◆ n. en el DF (1953). Escritor. Licenciado en letras hispánicas por la UNAM, de la que ha sido profesor e investigador. Fue director de Literatura del INBA. Ha ejercido la docencia en la UAM, donde fue jefe del Departamento Editorial y director de Difusión Cultural. Ha colaborado en *Revista de Bellas Artes, Excélsior, Casa del Tiempo, Revista de la Universidad* y otras publicaciones. Coautor de la novela policiaca *El hombre equivocado* (1988). Autor de cuento: *Viene la muerte* (1976), *La otra orilla* (1980), *Vals sin fin* (1982) y *Reina de sombras* (1996); poesía: *La noche y las horas* (1981), *El tuyo, el mismo* (1986) y *Controversia de sombras* (1990); cuento infantil: *La cofradía de las calacas* (1988); novela: *Olvidar tu nombre* (1982) y *Los caminos del hotel* (1991); la autobiografía *De cuerpo entero* (1990) y la antología *Antes y después de Drácula* (1998). Becario de narrativa INBA-Fonapas (1973-74).

RUIZ, CRISTÓBAL ◆ n. en España y m. en el DF (1881-?). Pintor. Fue profesor de la Academia de San Fernando en Madrid y uno de los firmantes del Manifiesto de los Artistas Ibéricos (1925). Hacia 1938 se instaló en Puerto Rico, donde fue profesor del Instituto Politécnico (1940-43) y profesor y pintor residente de la Universidad de Río Piedras (1943). Llegó a México en 1944. Expuso en la Universidad de Puerto Rico en 1938 y 1942, en Nueva York en 1939, en México en 1940 y en Cuba en 1945. Autor de un *Retrato de Antonio Machado*. Hay obras suyas en el Ateneo Español de México.

El autorretrato, obra de Antonio Ruiz

Foto: Rogelio Cuéllar

Bernardo Ruiz

RUIZ, DIEGO ◆ n. en Oacalco, Mor., y m. en Tula, Hgo. (?-1915). Se unió en 1911 a la insurrección maderista en las fuerzas del zapatista Amador Salazar, con el que participó en la toma de Metepec, Puebla, y el sitio y toma de Cuautla. A la caída del porfiriato volvió a la vida civil. Desatada la lucha de facciones se reincorporó al Ejército Libertador del Sur. Murió en combate contra los carrancistas.

RUIZ, EDUARDO ◆ n. en Uruapan, Mich., y ¿m. en la ciudad de México? (1840-1902). Abogado por el Colegio de San Nicolás de Hidalgo (1863), donde estudió becado por Melchor Ocampo. Combatió la intervención francesa y el imperio. Trabajó en el go-

Gabriel Ruiz

Foto: Héctor Herrera

José Carlos Ruiz

bierno de Berriozábal; a las órdenes de Vicente Riva Palacio fue oficial mayor de la Secretaría de Gobernación y se desempeñó como auditor general del Ejército del Centro, comandado por Nicolás de Régules. Al triunfo de la República se convirtió en secretario particular de Justo Mendoza, gobernador de Michoacán, y en director del *Periódico Oficial* del estado. Juez de letras en Uruapan (1872), diputado federal, procurador general de la República (1892) y ministro de la Suprema Corte de Justicia (1900). Colaborador de *El Siglo XIX*, *La Tribuna*, *La Revista Universal* y *La República*. Autor de *Biografía de Melchor Ocampo* (1882), *Curso de derecho constitucional y administrativo* (1888), *Michoacán. Paisajes, tradiciones y leyendas* (1891) e *Historia de la guerra de intervención en Michoacán* (1896), así como del drama *El despertar de un pueblo*.

Ruiz, Eduardo ◆ n. en Guaymas, Son., y m. en el DF (1879-1942). Participó en la insurrección maderista (1910-11) y en 1913 se incorporó al constitucionalismo, a las órdenes de Álvaro Obregón. En 1914 fue gobernador provisional de Colima. Suscribió el Plan de Agua Prieta (1920) y fue cónsul en San Francisco y ministro en Costa Rica.

Ruiz, Francisco H. ◆ n. en Jalisco y m. en el DF (1872-1958). Abogado. Fue magistrado y presidente del Tribunal Superior de Justicia de Jalisco, profesor de las escuelas Nacional Preparatoria y Nacional de Jurisprudencia. Miembro de la comisión revisora del Código Civil (1928), ministro de la Suprema Corte de Justicia (1928-40), secretario del Ayuntamiento de Guadalajara, secretario general de gobierno y gobernador interino de Jalisco.

Ruiz, Gabriel ◆ n. en Guadalajara, Jal., y m. en el DF (1908-1999). En 1931 abandonó los estudios de medicina. Se tituló como concertista en el Conservatorio Nacional. Fue profesor del INBA y desde 1935 dio a conocer sus canciones en la estación de radio XEW, generalmente en las voces de Gloria Luz y José Luis Caballero. También han sido sus intérpretes Amalia Mendoza, Alfonso Ortiz Tirado, Pedro Infante, Pedro Vargas, Hugo Avendaño y Salvador García, entre otros. En 1945 realizó en Hollywood la música para la película *Mexicana* y de ese año a 1947 estudió en el Conservatorio de París. Actuó en centros nocturnos y teatros al lado de *Cantinflas*, Roberto Soto, *Palillo* y Joaquín Pardavé. Escribió música para varias películas de Jorge Negrete, Pedro Infante y Luis Aguilar. Asistió a la Conferencia de la Confederación Internacional de Sociedades de Autores y Compositores, en Italia (1962), como representante de la Sociedad de Autores y Compositores de Música. En 1967 dirigió en bellas Artes la Sinfónica Nacional en la interpretación de sus canciones. Autor de *Noches de Mazatlán*, *Plenilunio*, *Jamás*, *Se fue*, *Despierta*, *Mar*, *La parranda*, *Desesperadamente*, *Noche*, *La noche es nuestra*, *Despierta*, *Un minuto*, *La cita* y *Condición*, entre otras. Medalla José Clemente Orozco del estado de Jalisco (1956), medalla de oro y diploma del Consejo Nacional de Turismo, Premio Jalisco (1986) y Premio Nacional de Ciencias y Artes (1989).

Ruiz, Gregorio ◆ n. en Perote, Ver., y m. en la ciudad de México (1847-1913). Estudió en el Colegio Militar. En 1864 era teniente de auxiliares del ejército. Luchó contra la intervención francesa y el imperio de Maximiliano (1862-67) y participó en las campañas de pacificación de Puebla y Oaxaca (1876) y en las de Tepic y Sinaloa (1877-78). En 1911, con más de 35 años de servicio, se dio de baja del ejército y en 1912 fue diputado federal por Monclova. Durante la Decena Trágica se asoció con los sublevados, lo que le valió ser fusilado el 9 de febrero de 1913 en el Palacio Nacional.

Ruiz, Guillermo ◆ n. en Real de Minas, SLP, y m. en el DF (1896-1965). Escultor. Estudió en la Escuela de Bellas Artes. En París trabajó bajo la dirección de José de Creeft y Mateo Hernández. Fundó la Escuela de Escultura y Talla Directa (1927), antecedente de La Esmeralda, que dirigió durante 17 años (1927-44). Fundó y dirigió la revista *Libertad*, en Uruapan (1950). Autor de la escultura monumental de Morelos en la isla de Janitzio (1933), Gertrudis Bocanegra en Pátzcuaro (1937), Morelos en Zacapu (1937), Juárez en Jiquilpan (1937), Tangaxoan (1937), Mariano Escobedo en Monterrey (1947) y *Congreso de Apatzingán* (1950, altorrelieve en bronce). Sus esculturas *Pureza* y *La madre* fueron premiadas.

Ruiz, Joaquín ◆ n. y m. en Puebla, Pue. (?-1888). Fue diputado al Congreso Constituyente de 1856. Secretario de Fomento (del 12 de junio al 12 de julio de 1861) de Benito Juárez y magistrado supernumerario interino de la Suprema Corte de Justicia. Fue dos veces procurador general de la República (1867 y 1877).

Ruiz, José Carlos ◆ n. en Jerez, Zac. (1938). Actor. Estudió actuación en el INBA con una beca de Celestino Gorostiza donde fue discípulo de André Moreau, Seki Sano, Salvador Novo, Fernando Wagner y Ana Mérida. Fue actor titular de la Compañía de Teatro del IMSS y actuó en teleteatros y telenovelas, entre las que destaca *El carruaje*, donde interpretó a Benito Juárez (1972). En su filmografía destacan *Viento negro* (1964), *El escapulario* (1966), *Los marcados* (1970), *Emiliano Zapata* (1970), *El apando* (1975), *Actas de Marusia* (1975, Diosa de Plata al mejor actor), *Los albañiles* (1976), *Cananea* (Diosa de Plata al mejor actor, 1976), *Cascabel* (1976), *La guerra santa (La cristiada)* (1977), *Noche de carnaval* (1981), *Fuego en el mar* (Ariel al mejor actor, 1979), *El milusos* (1981), *Bajo la metralla* (1983), *Toña Machetes* (1983, Ariel al mejor actor), *Vidas errantes* (Ariel al mejor actor, 1984), *Robachicos* (1985), *Goitia, un dios para sí mismo* (Ariel al mejor actor y nominación para el premio al mejor actor en el Festival de Tokio, 1989), *Pueblo de madera* (1989) y *Dos crímenes* (Ariel y Diosa de Plata al mejor actor, 1993).

Ruiz, José L. ◆ n. en Tehuacán, Pue. (1903). Escultor. Estudió en la Academia de San Carlos (1917). En Tehuacán instaló un taller donde continuó la tradición familiar de tallar imágenes de santos. Autor de las esculturas de Moisés Sáenz, en Nuevo León, y de Morelos en Veracruz.

Ruiz, José Trinidad ◆ m. en Texcoco, Edo. de Méx. (?-1915). Predicador protestante, en marzo de 1911 se unió a la revolución en el Ejército Libertador del Sur. Fue firmante del Plan de Ayala. En 1912 operó en el noroeste de Morelos y parte del Estado de México y un año después intentó negociar con Huerta, por lo que Francisco Mendoza lo expulsó del ejército zapatista, mismo al que volvió al producirse la escisión revolucionaria (1914). Murió en combate.

Ruiz, Juan ◆ m. cerca de León, Gto. (?-1915). En 1907 fue incorporado, mediante leva, al ejército porfirista para reprimir a los yaquis de Sonora. En las tropas federales conoció a Antonio Villa, hermano de Francisco Villa. En 1910 desertó del ejército federal y se incorporó a la insurrección maderista en Chihuahua. Durante la lucha contra Victoriano Huerta militó en la División del Norte y siguió a Villa después de la escisión revolucionaria. Formó parte de los Dorados. Murió en combate contra las fuerzas obregonistas.

Ruiz, Luis Bruno ◆ n. en Pachuca, Hgo., y m. en el DF (1911-1991). Hizo estudios de medicina y psicología. Fue colaborador de *Excélsior*, como crítico de danza, desde 1948 hasta su muerte. También colaboró en las revistas *Tiempo*, *Carnet musical*, *Ballet* (Perú) y *Sur les Pointes* (Francia). Autor de poesía: *Agua clara*, *Cantos de Ahora*, *Es necesario predicar en el desierto* y *Soneto de danza*; prosa: *Breve historia sobre la danza en México* y *Ocelotl, el profeta terrestre*; novela: *Desnuda tocó a la puerta*, *Fronteras del sueño*, *Del amor y la muerte*, *La Biblia y la danza* y *El complejo de Circe*; y teatro: *Fedra en la noche*, *La jaula*, *Marcela y la paloma* y *El cumpleaños de la muerte*. Fue secretario de la Asociación de Cronistas de Teatro y Música de México.

Ruiz, Manuel ◆ n. en Oaxaca, Oax., y m. en la ciudad de México (1822-1871). Se tituló de abogado en el Instituto de Ciencias y Artes de su estado natal (1845). Con Antonio León en el Poder Ejecutivo de Oaxaca, sustituyó a Benito Juárez en la Secretaría General de Gobierno, puesto que desempeñó con varios gobernadores liberales. Diputado en 1848, el gobierno de Santa Anna lo confinó en Atlixco. Al triunfo de la revolución de Ayutla fue secretario del Consejo de Gobierno. Diputado federal (1857), secretario de Justicia, Negocios Eclesiásticos e Instrucción Pública de Ignacio Comonfort (del 20 de septiembre al 16 de diciembre de 1857), ministro universal en el primer día de gobierno de Benito Juárez (del 19 al 20 de enero de 1858) y secretario de Justicia (del 20 de enero de 1858 al 20 de enero de 1861). Redactó dos de las Leyes de Reforma (la de nacionalización de los bienes de la iglesia y exclaustración de las órdenes religiosas y sobre el matrimonio civil). Después del triunfo liberal volvió a ser diputado y, más tarde, magistrado de la Suprema Corte de Justicia de la Nación. Durante la intervención francesa, en 1863, Juárez lo nombró gobernador de Tamaulipas, pero no ocupó el cargo pues fue aprehendido por Juan N. Cortina. Liberado más tarde, tomó las armas contra los invasores. Tomó partido por Jesús González Ortega en su conflicto con Juárez. Murió siendo director del Registro Público de la Propiedad.

Ruiz, Nicolás ◆ n. en San Cristóbal de Las Casas, Chis. (1806-1879). Dos veces gobernador interino (1847 y 1877) y jefe político de Chiapas (1877). Durante la guerra de los Tres Años luchó en el bando liberal (1858-60). Combatió la intervención francesa y el imperio.

Ruiz, Raúl G. ◆ n. en Huatusco, Ver. (1886-?). En 1913 se unió a la revolución constitucionalista en la División de Oriente, comandada por Cándido Aguilar. Pasó después al felicismo, en las fuerzas de Pedro Gabay, y en 1920 se adhirió al Plan de Agua Prieta. Alcanzó el grado de general de brigada. Delahuertista en 1923, tras el fracaso de ese movimiento se exilió.

Ruiz, Rafael ◆ n. en el DF (1969). Hizo estudios de huecograbado, dibujo y xilografía en la ENAP. Ha participado en exposiciones colectivas y tuvo su primera exposición individual, *Dibujo y grabado*, en 1995. Premio de adquisición en el Salón Nacional de la Miniestampa (1993). Seleccionado en el II Concurso Nacional José Guadalupe Posada (1994).

Ruiz, Roberto ◆ n. en España (1925). Escritor. Al término de la guerra civil española pasó a Francia (1939) y de ahí a México. Maestro en lengua y literatura españolas por la UNAM, en Estados Unidos fue profesor de su especialidad en diversos centros de estudio. Colaboró en la revista *Presencia* y dio clases en el Wheaton College. Autor de *Esquemas* (1954, grabados de Virgilio Ruiz), *Plazas sin muros* (1960), *El último oasis* (1964), *Los jueces implacables* (1970) y *Paraíso cerrado, cielo abierto* (1977).

Manuel Ruiz

Ruiz, Roberto ◆ n. en Miahuatlán, Oax. (1928). Artesano. Llegado al DF en 1943, trabajó con un pintor, quien le enseñó restauración de pinturas y retablos; de 1944 a 1967 surtió de moldes de madera a fábricas de juguetes y envases de plástico. Simultáneamente se dedicó a elaborar miniaturas de madera o cerámica, que vendía en tiendas de artesanías. En 1957 expuso sus miniaturas en el Museo de Artes e Industrias Populares del INI, institución que, a partir de 1967, le encarga trabajos específicos. Desde 1970 sus obras se exponen permanentemente en ese museo y han sido exhibidas en diversas ciudades de México, así como en Londres, París y Los Ángeles. En 1985 fundó una escuela de miniaturistas en Tabasco. Ha recibido los premios Nacional de Miniatura (1987) y Nacional de Ciencias y Artes (1988). En 1988 se publicó el libro *El arte de Roberto Ruiz*.

Ruiz, Rodolfo Diódoro ◆ n. en Mapimí, Dgo., y m. en San Luis Potosí, SLP (1896-1947). Abogado. Editó el periódico estudiantil *Juventud*. Dirigió la Academia Comercial Moderna, donde impartió clases de esperanto. Fue profesor de la Universidad Autónoma de San

Luis Potosí. Autor de *Canto a la mujer aliada* (1918), *Celajes de primavera* (1918), *Del lírico vergel potosino. Semblanzas y pergenios* (1919), *Algo sobre el hidrógeno* (1920), *Aromas de leyenda, Brumas de invierno, Camafeos. Semblanzas líricas, Cármenes líricos, De mi huerto íntimo, Del momento vivido, Deuda sagrada, Ensayos etimológicos, Heroísmo, Lámparas votivas, Lampos de otoño, Mosaicos, Nébulas de verano, Oblación, Tratado de literatura, Unción, Crepúsculo de ensueño, Panegírico de la mujer, Holocausto, Urna cordial* y *Cómo puede América pronto y fácilmente evitar para siempre las guerras. Plan pro-paz* (1925).

RUIZ, SAMUEL ◆ n. en Irapuato, Gto. (1924). Sacerdote ordenado en 1949, estudió en el Seminario Conciliar de León y en la Pontificia Universidad Gregoriana de Roma. Ha sido profesor (1952), prefecto de estudios (1952-54) y rector (1954-59) del Seminario de León, canónigo (1954), examinador prosinodal, censor de libros, confesor de religiosas, delegado para los procesos de beatificación de la diócesis de León y obispo de Chiapas (1960-), diócesis que cambió su nombre por el de San Cristóbal de Las Casas. Participó en el Concilio Vaticano II (1962-65) y en la segunda Conferencia General del Episcopado Latinoamericano (1968); fue presidente interino (1966) y titular (1967-69 y 1970-72) de la Comisión Episcopal para Indígenas de la Conferencia del Episcopado Mexicano y presidente del Departamento de Misiones del Consejo Episcopal Latinoamericano (1969, reelecto en 1972). En 1994, tras el levantamiento en Chiapas del Ejército Zapatista de Liberación Nacional, se convirtió en una figura central del conflicto al formar la Comisión Nacional de Intermediación (Conai), que se propuso mediar entre los zapatistas y el gobierno federal y funcionó hasta 1998. En noviembre de 1999 dejó el obispado al llegar al límite de edad. Autor del prólogo de la novela *Cosecha de 200 soles* de "Maus" (1998) y de *Teología bíblica de la liberación* (1974). Premio Óscar Arnulfo Romero por la Dignidad (1994). Doctor *honoris causa* por la Facultad de Teología Católica de la Universidad de Tübingen, Alemania (1994).

FOTO: ÉPOCA

Samuel Ruiz

RUIZ ACOSTA, JOSÉ ANTONIO ◆ n. en Querétaro, Qro., y m. en el DF (1914-1976). Profesor de la UNAM, fue secretario (1964-66) y director del plantel número siete de la Escuela Nacional Preparatoria (1966-67), elegido por los estudiantes, maestros y trabajadores del plantel. Colaboró en *El Nacional, Caballero* y otras publicaciones. Autor de *Manifiesto del águila y la serpiente* (1949), *Estética, Dialéctica mundial, La esencia del derecho* y *Pedagogía integral*. Dejó inédito el trabajo *Café Negro*, que recuerda los años cuarenta y cincuenta del Café París.

RUIZ DE ALARCÓN, JUAN ◆ n. en Taxco, en el actual estado de Guerrero y m. en España (¿1580?-1639). Algunos autores afirman que nació en la ciudad de México. Estudió derecho en la Universidad de Salamanca (1602). En marzo de 1609, como licenciado, "era tan pobre" que solicitó a la Real y Pontificia Universidad de México recibir sin pompa "el grado de doctor en la Facultad de Leyes", para evitarse el pago de propinas. El claustro aprobó la petición. Entre 1606 y 1608 ejerció la abogacía en Sevilla y desde 1609 lo hizo en la ciudad de México y en Veracruz. De 1614 hasta su muerte residió en Madrid. Nunca fue aceptado por los dramaturgos españoles, algunos de los cuales, Lope de Vega entre ellos, hacían burla de su contrahechura física y aun saboteaban sus estrenos en los corrales de comedia. En 1626 el Consejo de Indias lo nombró relator interino y en 1633 ocupó el cargo en propiedad. Autor de *Los favores del mundo, La industria y la suerte, Las paredes oyen, El semejante a sí mismo, La cueva de Salamanca, Mudarse por mejorarse, Todo es ventura, El desdichado en fingir, Los empeños de un engaño, El dueño de las estrellas, La amistad castigada, La manganilla de Melilla, Ganar amigos, El Anticristo, La verdad sospechosa, El tejedor de Segovia, Los pechos privilegiados, La prueba de las promesas, La crueldad por el honor* y *El examen de maridos* (Comedias, parte segunda, 1634). También se le atribuyen *La culpa busca la pena y el agravio la venganza, Quien mal anda mal acaba, No hay mal que por bien no venga, Quién engaña más a quién* y *Siempre ayuda la verdad*. Escribió, asimismo, las primeras escenas del segundo acto de *Algunas hazañas de las muchas de don García Hurtado de Mendoza, marqués de Cañete*.

Retrato y firma de Juan Ruiz de Alarcón

RUIZ DE ALARCÓN Y MENDOZA, HERNANDO ◆ n. en Taxco, en el actual estado de Guerrero (?-?). Hermano del anterior. Estudió en la Real y Pontificia Universidad de México. Fue cura de diversas parroquias, recogió en la zona de Guerrero lo que él llamó "conjuros" (himnos prehispánicos preservados por la tradición oral). Su manuscrito fue rescatado en 1892 por Francisco del Paso y Troncoso y publicado como *Tratado de las supersticiones de los naturales de esta Nueva España, escrito en 1629*.

RUIZ ALMADA, GILBERTO ◆ n. en Culiacán, Sin. (1926). Ingeniero civil por la UNAM (1950). Miembro del PRI. Ha sido topógrafo de la Comisión Agraria Mixta del gobierno sinaloense (1948-49), perito valuador de la Asociación Hipotecaria Mexicana (1955-57) y jefe el Departamento de Obras Públicas de Culiacán (1957-60). En la Secretaría de Gobernación ha sido visitador de los servicios de migración (1960-64), jefe del Departamento de Compras (1964-65), subdirector general de administración (1965-66), subdirector del Registro Nacional de Electores (1966-68), director general de Administración (1968-70) y director general de la Compañía Operadora de Teatros (1982-87). Director general de administración (1970-73) y oficial mayor (1973-74) de la Secretaría de la Presidencia, subsecretario de Investigación y Ejecución Fiscal de la Secretaría de Hacienda (1974-76), senador por Sinaloa (1976-82) y embajador en Nicaragua (1987-89).

Ruiz Anchondo, Patricia ◆ n. en Chihuahua, Chih. (1958). Licenciada en filosofía por la Universidad Autónoma de Chihuahua (1985). Afiliada al PRD desde 1989, ha sido miembro de su Consejo Nacional (1991) y diputada federal (1991-94). Fue profesora en la Escuela de Periodismo Carlos Septién García (1986-88) y del CIDE (1988-90). Ha sido dirigente de la Asamblea de Barrios (1985-), coordinadora de la Convención Nacional de Mujeres por la Democracia y el Movimiento Nacional Municipalista.

Ruiz de Apodaca, Juan ◆ n. y m. en España (1754-1835). Militar de carrera. Embajador de España en Londres. Gobernador de Cuba (1812-1815). Se le concedió el título de Conde del Venadito. Penúltimo virrey de Nueva España (1816-1821). Fue invitado a suscribir el Plan de Iguala y ponerse a la cabeza del movimiento por la independencia. Rechazó el ofrecimiento y un grupo de militares realistas lo destituyó y embarcó para España.

Ruiz Armengol, Mario ◆ n. en Veracruz, Ver. (1914). Estudió piano en el Conservatorio Nacional. En 1928 tocaba en los teatros y cines de la ciudad de México y se le encomendó dirigir el conjunto musical del teatro Lírico. La XEW lo contrató en 1931. Estrenó sus primeras canciones en el programa *La Hora Azul*. Fue compositor y arreglista y formó su propia orquesta, con la que acompañó, entre otros, a Jorge Negrete, Pedro Vargas y Luis G. Roldán. También ha sido interpretado por Emilio Tuero, Juan Arvizu, María Luisa Landín, Miguel Aceves Mejía y otros. Musicalizó varias películas. Autor de las canciones *Alma mía, Muchachita, Tengo miedo, Ausencia, Estoy enamorado, ¿Por qué llorar?, Aunque tú no me quieras* y *¿Por qué te vas?*, así como de danzas cubanas, estudios para piano, reflexiones, sonatas, valses, *scherzos* y muchas otras composiciones.

Ruiz y Ávila, Eleazar Benjamín ◆ n. en Puebla, Pue. (1951). Licenciado en relaciones internacionales por la UNAM y maestro en administración pública por el Instituto de Estudios Superiores de Administración Pública. Ha sido asesor de la Dirección de Asuntos Políticos Bilaterales de la SRE (1978-79), jefe del Departamento de Asia en la Dirección de África, Asia y Oceanía (1980-83), subdirector de Asuntos Bilaterales en la Dirección General para el Pacífico Oriental (1990-91), director de área para Derechos Humanos en la ONU (1991-93) y director de Derechos Humanos de la misma dependencia. También ha tenido diversos cargos en la CNDH y fue miembro de la delegación mexicana a las sesiones de la Comisión de Derechos Humanos de la ONU; en 1993, 1994 y 1995 colaboró en la presentación de informes al Grupo de Trabajo sobre Desapariciones Forzadas o Involuntarias de esa comisión. Ha sido catedrático de la UIA, la Escuela Superior de Guerra, el Instituto Matías Romero y el Instituto de Estudios Superiores de la Armada de México. Ha coordinado la elaboración de informes sobre violaciones a los derechos humanos de migrantes en las fronteras de México, así como de una *Guía sobre derechos, deberes y obligaciones de la familia* y el folleto *Principales derechos de las personas con discapacidad* (1996).

Ruiz de Bustamante Gutiérrez, José Antonio ◆ n. y m. en Chihuahua, Chih. (1788-1840). Estudió derecho en la Real y Pontificia Universidad de México. En 1818 fue alcalde del Ayuntamiento de Chihuahua, diputado federal (1825), magistrado del Tribunal de Justicia de Chihuahua (1825-26) y gobernador constitucional de ese estado (1826-27). En 1830 presidió el Tribunal de Justicia de Chihuahua y fue magistrado del mismo, cargo que ocupó hasta su muerte. Miembro del Colegio de Abogados de la ciudad de México.

Ruiz-Cabañas, Miguel ◆ n. en el DF (1957). Licenciado en relaciones internacionales por El Colegio de México. Maestro y doctor en ciencias políticas por la Universidad de Columbia. Diplomático de carrera del Servicio Exterior Mexicano. Ha publicado artículos sobre relaciones bilaterales México-Estados Unidos, y particularmente sobre el narcotráfico, en publicaciones de ambos países. Ha impartido clases en la UIA. Ha sido jefe del Departamento de Naciones Unidas (1979-81), secretario de la misión permanente ante la ONU (1981-86), director para Naciones Unidas II (1989-91), coordinador de asesores del subsecretario B (1991-92), coordinador de asesores del subsecretario A (1992-93), jefe de la Sección de Asuntos Sociales y Fronterizos de la Embajada en Estados Unidos (1993-95) y jefe de la Oficina de Asuntos Especiales de la SRE (1995-); en este cargo se ha dedicado a formular la política exterior mexicana en materia de combate al narcotráfico.

Ruiz Cabañas, Samuel ◆ n. y m. en el DF (1884-1967). Poeta. Participó en la revolución maderista de 1910. En 1922 se incorporó a la planta de redactores de *El Universal*. Colaboró en *El Universal Gráfico*, donde tuvo una sección que firmaba como Iván Zinco, *El Universal Ilustrado* y *Rotográfico*, del que fue director. Guionista cinematográfico.

Mario Ruiz Armengol

Retrato, escudo y firma de Juan Ruiz de Apodaca

Foto: Fondo Histórico Alfonso Sánchez García

Maximiliano Ruiz Castañeda

Recibió varias condecoraciones españolas y la medalla Dante Alighieri, de Italia. Autor de *Primicias líricas* (1904), *La vida se deshoja* (1906), *Cuentos del sábado* y *El cancionero de Pierrot*.

Ruiz de Cabañas y Crespo, Juan Cruz ◆ n. en España y m. en la Estancia de los Delgadillos, Zac. (1752-1824). Sacerdote. Doctor en teología por la Universidad de Alcalá. Fue canónigo en Burgos, obispo de Nicaragua (1794-96) y de Guadalajara (1796-1824). Fundador del Hospicio de Guadalajara (hoy Museo Cabañas). En 1821 apoyó económicamente al Ejército Trigarante.

Ruiz Camarillo, Leobardo ◆ n. en la hacienda de Santiago, Zac., y m. en el DF (1894-1965). En 1910 ingresó en el Colegio Militar y en 1914 se unió a la revolución constitucionalista. Fue comandante de artillería en el Ejército del Noroeste y tuvo un cargo directivo en los ferrocarriles constitucionalistas. Subjefe del Departamento de Caballería de la Secretaría de Guerra y Marina (1928), jefe del Departamento de Aeronáutica (1931), cónsul en Holanda y encargado de negocios en Francia (1935), director de Reclutamiento y Reservas del Ejército (1941), oficial mayor de la Secretaría de la Defensa (1946), agregado militar en Estados Unidos y Canadá, embajador en Perú (1952) y director del Colegio Militar (1953).

Ruiz Castañeda, María del Carmen ◆ n. en Tampico, Tams. (1926). Maestra en letras españolas (1950), con estudios de doctorado y pasante de la licenciatura en derecho por la UNAM. Ha sido profesora de la UIA y de la UNAM (1954-72), directora de la Hemeroteca Nacional (1973-78) y del Instituto de Investigaciones Bibliográficas (1978-) de la UNAM. Escribió en *Excélsior* las columnas "Ofertas sin demanda", con Luis Mario Schneider, (1964-65), y "Arcón del siglo XIX" (1965-76); y en *Últimas Noticias* la columna "Tijeretazos" (1964-76). Ha colaborado en *Revista de la Universidad*, *Revista Mexicana de Sociología*, *Estudios Sociológicos*, *Cuadernos de la Hemeroteca*, *Boletín del Instituto de Investigaciones Bibliográficas*, *Anglia*, *México en la Cultura*, *La Cultura en México*, *Deslinde*, *Revista de la Biblioteca José Martí*, de La Habana, *Los Universitarios* y *Comunidad Conacyt* (1977-81). Prologó *Clamores de la fidelidad americana contra la opresión o fragmentos para la historia futura de Mérida de Yucatán* (1985, de José María Quintana) y *El Iris. Periódico crítico y literario* (1986). Coautora de *El periodismo en México. 450 años* (1973), *Catálogo de seudónimos, anagramas, iniciales y otros alias de escritores mexicanos y extranjeros que han publicado en México* (1985). Autora de *Periodismo político de la reforma en la ciudad de México (1854-1861)* (1950) y *La prensa periódica en torno a la Constitución de 1857* (1959).

Ruiz Castañeda, Maximiliano ◆ n. en Acambay, Edo. de Méx. y m. en el DF (1896-1992). Médico por la Universidad Nacional (1923), posgraduado en la de París (1925). Becado por la Fundación Rockefeller desarrolló trabajos de investigación sobre el tifo (1927), cuya vacuna descubrió en 1937. Fue instructor de bacteriología e inmunología de la Universidad de Harvard (1930-36) y senador por el Estado de México (1958-64). Autor de *Brucelosis* (1942) y *Microbios. Eslabón entre la muerte y la vida* (1962). Miembro de las sociedades mexicanas de Medicina Tropical, Microbiología y de Médicos del Hospital General de México. Recibió los premios Gabino Barreda, Agustín Andrade y Nacional de Ciencias y Artes (1948).

Ruiz Colmenero, Juan ◆ n. en España y m. en Guadalajara, Jal. (¿1596?-1663). Doctor en teología y filosofía por la Universidad de Alcalá de Henares. Fue profesor en las universidades de Cuenca y Alcalá y canónigo magistral de las catedrales de Ciudad Rodrigo y Sigüenza. Fue propuesto obispo de Guadalajara en 1646, preconizado el mismo año y consagrado en 1647.

Ruiz Cortines, Adolfo ◆ n. y m. en Veracruz, Ver. (1890-1973). Fue ayudante de contador en la empresa comercial de Julián Aragón (1906-12). En 1913, en lucha contra la dictadura de Victoriano Huerta, Alfredo Robles Domínguez le encargó una misión propagandística entre las tropas federales de la ciudad de México. Al triunfo de la revolución constitucionalista formó parte del cuartel general de Robles Domínguez, permaneció con él como su ayudante, cuando fue gobernador del Distrito Federal (1914), y desempeñó el mismo puesto con Heriberto Jara. Volvió a Veracruz con éste, al salir del puerto las tropas estadounidenses (19-14). Al ser designado Robles Domínguez gobernador de Guerrero, fue nombrado oficial de órdenes en el cuartel general de la División del Sur. Participó en la batalla de El Ébano, San Luis Potosí, contra las fuerzas villistas, a las órdenes de Jacinto B. Treviño, de quien fue secretario particular. Fue pagador en la brigada Muriel. En 1920 se adhirió al Plan de Agua Prieta y al desaparecer el gobierno carrancista rescató y entregó el tesoro nacional al presidente Adolfo de la Huerta. Fue secretario particular de Treviño en la Secretaría de Industria y Comercio, desempeñó diversos puestos en el Departamento de Estadística (1921-35), fue oficial mayor del DDF (1935) y diputado local en Veracruz (1937). Se desempeñó también como tesorero de la campaña presidencial de Manuel Ávila Camacho y secretario general de gobierno en Veracruz (1939) durante la gestión de Miguel Alemán; oficial mayor de la Secretaría de Gobernación (1940), gobernador de Veracruz (1944-48), secretario de Gobernación de Miguel Alemán (del 30 de junio de 1948 al 13 de octubre de 1951) y presidente de la República (del 1 de diciembre de 1952 al 30 de noviembre de 1958). Durante su sexenio, en que llamó a México "al trabajo fecundo y creador", repartió 3.5 millones de hectáreas a los campesinos, entre ellas las tierras de los latifundios propiedad de extranjeros de Cananea, San José Cloete y Bavícora (en Sonora, Coahuila y Chihuahua); inauguró la Presa Falcón y se entrevistó, en esa ocasión, con el presidente estadounidense Dwight D. Eisenhower; se establecieron los precios de garantía en el campo y se estableció el seguro agrícola; se formuló un Programa de Progreso Marítimo conocido como "la Marcha al Mar", se impulsó la Campaña Nacional para la Erradicación del Paludismo, continuó la política de apoyo a la industria, se concedió el voto a la mujer, el peso se devaluó y cambió su paridad frente al dólar de 8.40 a 12.50 (1954) y se realizaron numerosas obras urbanas en la capital. En 1958 dejó la Presidencia de la República a Adolfo López Mateos y presidió después la Comisión Fideicomisaria de Metales no Ferrosos, para retirarse más tarde de la actividad pública.

Ruiz de Chávez, Jenaro ◆ n. en San Cristóbal de Las Casas, Chis., y m. en el DF (1892-1958). Abogado. Fue director del periódico antiporfirista *El Hijo del Pueblo*, oficial mayor de gobierno y magistrado del Tribunal Superior de Justicia de Chiapas; diputado federal, juez séptimo penal (1940), magistrado del Tribunal Superior de Justicia del DF, ministro de la Suprema Corte y profesor de la UNAM. Fue miembro de la Asociación Nacional de Funcionarios Judiciales y de Veteranos de la Revolución.

Ruiz de Chávez Robinson, Arturo ◆ n. en el DF (1937). Licenciado en derecho por la UNAM (1960). Miembro del PRI. Profesor de la UNAM (1964 y 1985) y del Instituto de Estudios del Trabajo de la UAM (1979-82). Inició su carrera en la administración pública en 1963. Ha sido subdirector general de Servicios Turísticos del Departamento de Turismo (1966-67), oficial mayor de la Cámara de Diputados (1967-73), director general de Asuntos Jurídicos de la Secretaría de Gobernación (1973-76), director general de Conciliación (1976-79), presidente de la Junta Federal de Conciliación y Arbitraje (1979-82) y subsecretario A de la Secretaría del Trabajo (1982); director corporativo de Relaciones Industriales de Sidermex (1982-86) y director general de Asuntos Jurídicos de la Secretaría de la Reforma Agraria. Fue presidente de la Asociación Iberoamericana del Derecho al Trabajo, Filial México (1990-92) y secretario general fundador del IFE, puesto en el que permaneció hasta 1993. Ha sido representante de México ante la OIT y fue delegado ante el Comité Permanente sobre Asuntos Laborales de la OEA. Autor de *El derecho colectivo del trabajo* (1979), *El derecho político y la revolución popular* y *El poder legislativo en el derecho electoral mexicano*.

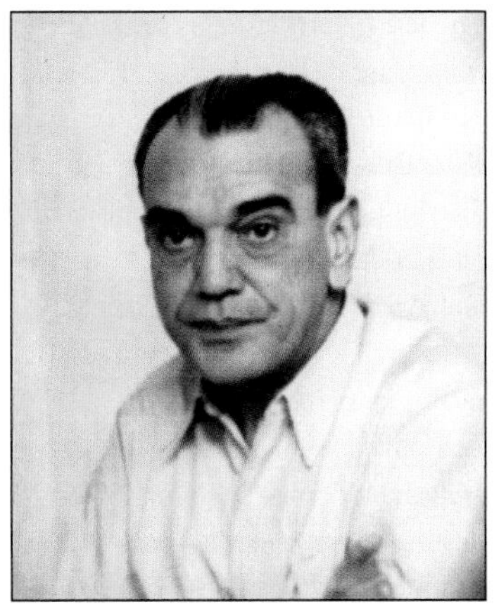

Adolfo Ruiz Cortines

Ruiz-Dana Zavala, Luis ◆ n. en España (1914). Militar. Participó en la

Gabinete del presidente Adolfo Ruiz Cortines
1 de diciembre de 1952 a 30 de noviembre de 1958

Secretaría de Gobernación:	
Ángel Carvajal	1 de diciembre de 1952 al 30 de noviembre de 1958
Secretaría de Relaciones Exteriores:	
Luis Padilla Nervo	1 de diciembre de 1952 al 30 de noviembre de 1958
Secretaría de Hacienda y Crédito Público:	
Antonio Carrillo Flores	1 de diciembre de 1952 al 30 de noviembre de 1958
Secretaría de la Defensa Nacional:	
Matías Ramos Santos	1 de diciembre de 1952 al 30 de noviembre de 1958
Socretaría de Agricultura y Ganadería:	
Gilberto Flores Muñoz	1 de diciembre de 1952 al 30 de noviembre de 1958
Secretaría de Comunicaciones y Obras Públicas:	
Carlos Lazo	1 de diciembre de 1952 al 5 de noviembre de 1955
Walter C. Buchanan	6 de noviembre de 1955 al 30 de noviembre de 1958
Secretaría de Economía Nacional:	
Gilberto Loyo	1 de diciembre de 1952 al 30 de noviembre de 1958
Secretaría de Educación Pública:	
José Ángel Ceniceros	1 de diciembre de 1952 al 30 de noviembre de 1958
Secretaría de Salubridad y Asistencia:	
Ignacio Morones Prieto	1 de diciembre de 1952 al 30 de noviembre de 1958
Secretaría de Marina:	
Rodolfo Sánchez Taboada	1 de diciembre de 1952 al 1 de mayo de 1955
Alfonso Poiré Ruelas	2 de mayo al 22 de diciembre de 1955
Roberto Gómez Maqueo	23 de diciembre de 1955 al 2 de abril de 1958
Héctor Meixueiro Alexander	7 de abril al 30 de noviembre de 1958
Secretaría del Trabajo y Previsión Social:	
Adolfo López Mateos	1 de diciembre de 1952 al 18 de noviembre de 1957
Salomón González Blanco	18 de noviembre de 1957 al 30 de noviembre de 1958
Secretaría de Recursos Hidráulicos:	
Eduardo Chávez	1 de diciembre de 1952 al 30 de noviembre de 1958
Secretaría de Bienes Nacionales:	
José López Lira	1 de diciembre de 1952 al 30 de noviembre de 1958
Departamento Agrario:	
Cástulo Villaseñor	1 de diciembre de 1952 al 30 de noviembre de 1958
Departamento del Distrito Federal:	
Ernesto P. Uruchurtu	1 de diciembre de 1952 al 30 de noviembre de 1958

Jorge Ruiz Dueñas

guerra civil española, en la que fue instructor de milicias del ejército republicano. Fue herido en combate en Toledo, se incorporó a la defensa de Madrid como instructor de lanza-bombas, participó en la batalla del Jarama, ascendió a mayor por méritos de guerra, combatió en el norte de España, fue herido de gravedad en la Cabeza de Puente de Balaguer y terminó la guerra al mando de los batallones de ametralladoras. Llegó exiliado en 1939 y obtuvo la nacionalidad mexicana en 1940. Fundó una empresa dedicada al comercio exterior (1942), la Agroindustria Conservas de Baja California (1971) y la Unión Olivarera (1966).

Ruiz Dueñas, Jorge ◆ n. en Guadalajara, Jal. (1946). Escritor. Pasó su niñez y adolescencia en La Paz, BCS. Licenciado en derecho y maestro en administración por la UNAM, hizo estudios en la Universidad de Oxford. Ha sido profesor-investigador y, entre otros cargos, secretario general de la UAM (1981-1985). En 1986 fue designado investigador nacional en el área de Ciencias Sociales y Humanidades. Ha sido también profesor de la UNAM, el ITAM, el Cinvestav, el INAP, El Colegio de México y la Fundación Getulio Vargas de Río de Janeiro. Ha ocupado diversos cargos en la administración pública, entre ellos: director técnico del CNCA (1989-92), director del IMER (1993-94), director general de Talleres Gráficos de México (1995) y gerente general del FCE (1995-). Autor de *Espigas abiertas* (1968), *Tierra final* (1980), *El pescador del sueño* (1981), *Tornaviaje* (1984), *Las noches de Salé* (1986), *Tiempo de ballenas* (1989), *Antologia pessoal* (1992), *El desierto jubiloso* (1995), *Guerrero negro* (1996), *Material de lectura* (1997), *Saravá* (1997) y *Habitaré tu nombre* (1997). Es autor del libreto de *Tierra final*, cantata de Daniel Catán, encargada en ocasión del 75 aniversario de la UNAM. Dirigió la revista *Tierra Adentro*, por la que recibió el Premio Nacional de Periodismo en Divulgación Cultural (1992). Obtuvo también el Premio Nacional de Poesía Manuel Torre Iglesias (1980) y el Premio Xavier Villaurrutia de Escritores para Escritores (1997).

Ruiz Durán, Clemente ◆ n. en el DF (1948). Licenciado en economía por la Universidad Anáhuac (1972), maestro en economía por la Universidad de Pittsburgh (1975) especializado en instituciones sociales en la Universidad de Uppsala (1971). Ha sido analista de la Bolsa Mexicana de Valores (1970-72), analista de proyectos de la Secretaría del Patrimonio Nacional (1972-73), analista del Banco Interamericano de Desarrollo (1975), analista del área internacional del Banco de México (1976), asesor del subsecretario de Ingresos de la SHCP (1976), asesor del secretario de Programación y Presupuesto (1976-78), profesor de la UNAM (1978-), asesor del director general de Financiera Nacional Azucarera (1978-82) y asesor técnico del director general del Banco de México (1982). Coautor de *México. Una economía en transición* (1984), *México ante la crisis* (1985), *Aún tiembla. Sociedad, política y cambio social: el terremoto del 19 de septiembre de 1985* (1986), *Latin American Political Economy, Financial Crisis and Political Change* (1986), *Crecimiento, equidad y financiamiento externo* (1989), *Debt and Transfiguration? Prospects for Latin America's Economic Revival* (1990) y *Crisis financiera y mecanismos de contención* (1990). Autor de *90 días de política monetaria y crediticia independiente* (1984, segunda edición en 1985) y *Changes in the Industrial Structure and the Role of Small and Medium Industries in Developing Countries: the Case of Mexico* (Tokio, 1991).

Ruiz Esparza, Gerardo ◆ n. en el DF (1949). Licenciado por la UNAM, (1973) y maestro en derecho por la Universidad de Michigan (1978). Miembro del PRI. Ha sido especialista jurídico del Banco de México (1969-77), subdirector jurídico (1977-78) y subdirector de Política Fiscal de la Secretaría de Hacienda (1978-81); secretario de Gabinete, subsecretario de gobierno (1981-87) y secretario general del gobierno del Estado de México (1987); profesor en la UAEM (1985-87), asesor especial del titular de la SEMIP (1987-88), coordinador de giras del presidente de la República (1988), coordinador del Infonavit en el DF (1989-91) y subdirector jurídico del IMSS (1991-94).

Ruiz y Esquivel, Adrián ◆ n. en el DF (1928). Graduado como subteniente del Colegio Militar y diplomado de estado mayor por la Escuela Superior de Guerra. Ocupó numerosas comisiones, que le valieron ascensos hasta el rango de general de división. Fue inspector general del ejército y oficial mayor de la Secretaría de la Defensa Nacional de 1994 hasta su retiro en 1997.

Ruiz Ferro, Julio César ◆ n. en Tapachula, Chis. (1949). Licenciado en economía por la UNAM (1972) y maestro en desarrollo económico por la Universidad de Leicester. Ha sido jefe de Ventas y Personal de Panificadora Conasupo (1968-70), jefe técnico y de servicios a la producción y comercialización y subgerente técnico de Bodegas Rurales Conasupo (1971-76), secretario técnico del Comité de Desarrollo en el estado de Chiapas (1976-77), coordinador de la Comisión del Inventario Nacional de Productos Básicos, subdirector de delegaciones (1978-79) y director general de Productos Básicos de la Secretaría de Comercio (1979-82); coordinador administrativo de la Subsecretaría de Desarrollo Industrial y de Servicios, encargado de la Dirección General de Pagos (1982-84); director general de Programación y Presupuesto de Servicios, director general de Programación y Presupuesto Energético Industrial de la SPP, gobernador sustituto de Chiapas (1994-97) y agregado de asuntos agrícolas en la embajada en Estados Unidos.

Ruiz y Flores, Leopoldo ◆ n. en Amealco, Qro., y m. en Morelia, Mich. (1865-1941). En 1888 fue ordenado sacerdote con dispensa de edad. Doctor en filosofía, teología y derecho canónico por el Pontificio Colegio Pío Latino Americano de Roma. Fue profesor del Seminario Arquidiocesano de México, cura de Tacubaya, canónigo penitenciario y abad de Guadalupe, obispo de León (1900-07) y de Monterrey (1907-11), arzobispo de Morelia (1912-41) y delegado apostólico (1929-37). Con este carácter negoció con el presidente Emilio Portes Gil el llamado *modus vivendi* que dio fin a la guerra cristera. Fue tres veces desterrado de Mexico: en 1914, 1926 y 1932-37.

Ruiz y Flores, Maximino ◆ n. en Atlacomulco, Edo. de Méx. (1875-1949). Recibió las órdenes sacerdotales en 1901. Doctor en teología sagrada por la Universidad Pontificia Mexicana, de la que fue profesor y secretario. Prefecto de estudios del Colegio Mayor, rector del seminario, oficial mayor de la curia (1907-09), prosecretario (1909-13) y canónigo penitenciario de Nuestra Señora de Guadalupe (1913). En 1913 fue designado obispo de Chiapas, diócesis a la que renunció en 1919 para aceptar el obispado titular de Derbe. Rector del Seminario Conciliar (1920-29), gobernador de la curia metropolitana (1927-28), vicario general, deán de la Iglesia Mexicana y director de Acción Católica de la arquidiócesis (1938).

Ruiz-Funes García, Mariano ◆ n. en España y m. en el DF (1889-1953). Licenciado (1909) y doctor en derecho (1912) por la Universidad Central de Madrid y doctor en criminología por la UNAM. Profesor (1919) y vicerrector de la Universidad de Murcia y catedrático del Instituto de Estudios Penales de Madrid (1932). Representó a Bilbao en las Cortes Constituyentes de la segunda República Española, de la que fue ministro de Agricultura y Justicia, encargado de negocios en Polonia y embajador en Bélgica. Llegó exiliado a México (1939). Fue profesor de la UNAM y El Colegio de México, así como consejero de la Unión de Profesores Universitarios en el Extranjero. Autor de *La criminalidad y las secreciones internas* (1927), *La criminalidad y la guerra* (1947), *Las ideas penales de Anatole France, La protección penal de la energía genésica, El suicidio y el homicidio en España, La protección penal de la electricidad, Notas sobre la celda, La pena de muerte en Italia, El derecho penal de los soviets, Delito y libertad, Tres experiencias democráticas de la legislación penal, Endocrinología y criminalidad, Progresión histórica de la pena de muerte en España* y *Actualidad de la venganza y evolución del delito político*. Premio Lombroso (1927) y Premio Afranio Peixoto (1947). Perteneció a la Academia Mexicana de Ciencias Penales y fue socio honorario de la Academia Argentina de Criminología.

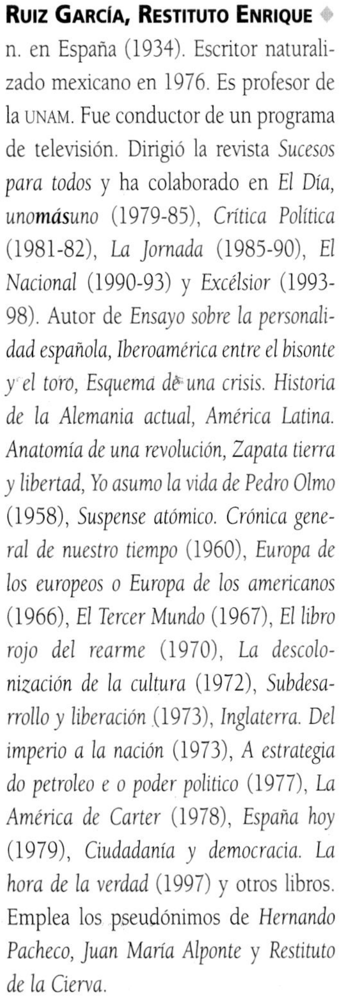

Ruiz-Funes Montesinos, Concepción ◆ n. en el DF (1941). Licenciada y maestra en letras hispánicas por la UNAM con posgrado en estudios de la mujer en la UAM-Xochimilco y doctorado en historia por la ENAH. Ha sido profesora en la Universidad de La Habana y en la UNAM. Investigadora del INAH, del Archivo del Ateneo Español de México y de la Asociación Guerra Civil y Exilio en España. Autora de *León Felipe. Poeta Español, Palabras del Exilio 2. Final y Comienzo: El Sinaia, Señas de identidad de las mujeres españolas exiliadas en México* y *La Unión de Mujeres Españolas Antifascistas en México*.

Ruiz Galindo, Antonio ◆ n. en Córdoba, Ver. (1897-1981). De 1913 a 1917 luchó en las filas del ejército constitucionalista. En 1923 se dedicó a la distribución de muebles extranjeros de acero, al fundar la empresa Distribuidora Mexicana, que en 1926 se transformó en fábrica con el nombre de DM Nacional. Fue presidente de la Asociación Mexicana de Hoteles y Moteles, presidente honorario vitalicio de la Asociación Interamericana de Hoteles y secretario de Economía Nacional (del 1 de diciembre de 1946 al 21 de octubre de 1948) en el gobierno de Miguel Alemán.

Ruiz Galindo, Antonio ◆ n. en la ciudad de México (1921). Hijo del anterior. Licenciado en administración de empresas por la Universidad del Noreste, en Chicago. Ha sido presidente de la Concamin (1958-59), vicepresidente ejecutivo de DM Nacional (1969-71), embajador de México en la RFA (1971-72), presidente del consejo de la Sociedad de Fomento Industrial Desc (1973-89), miembro de los consejos de Desc, Grupo Irsa, Novum, Spicer, Universal de Valores, The Mexico Fund, Banca Confía, Telmex, Dana Corporation (Ohio), International Advisory Board del Chemical Bank (Nueva York), Incorporación Industrial San Luis, Kimberley Clark de México y Grupo Industrial Minera México. Realizó diseños de muebles y el primero en México de un automóvil. Miembro académico de honor de la Academia Mexicana de Diseño, miembro honorario del Instituto Nacional de Diseñadores Industriales y Gráficos de México. Ganó el Premio México 1990 del Patronato Nacional de las Asociaciones de Diseño.

Leopoldo Ruiz y Flores

Ruiz García, Restituto Enrique ◆ n. en España (1934). Escritor naturalizado mexicano en 1976. Es profesor de la UNAM. Fue conductor de un programa de televisión. Dirigió la revista *Sucesos para todos* y ha colaborado en *El Día, unomásuno* (1979-85), *Crítica Política* (1981-82), *La Jornada* (1985-90), *El Nacional* (1990-93) y *Excélsior* (1993-98). Autor de *Ensayo sobre la personalidad española, Iberoamérica entre el bisonte y el toro, Esquema de una crisis. Historia de la Alemania actual, América Latina. Anatomía de una revolución, Zapata tierra y libertad, Yo asumo la vida de Pedro Olmo* (1958), *Suspense atómico. Crónica general de nuestro tiempo* (1960), *Europa de los europeos o Europa de los americanos* (1966), *El Tercer Mundo* (1967), *El libro rojo del rearme* (1970), *La descolonización de la cultura* (1972), *Subdesarrollo y liberación* (1973), *Inglaterra. Del imperio a la nación* (1973), *A estrategia do petroleo e o poder politico* (1977), *La América de Carter* (1978), *España hoy* (1979), *Ciudadanía y democracia. La hora de la verdad* (1997) y otros libros. Emplea los pseudónimos de *Hernando Pacheco, Juan María Alponte* y *Restituto de la Cierva*.

Antonio Ruiz Galindo

Ruiz Girón, Amón ◆ n. en España (1902). Perito agrícola graduado en Valladolid. Fue policía en Guipúzcoa. Durante la guerra civil tomó con 300 voluntarios el cuartel de la Guardia Civil de Eibar. Organizó y mandó fuerzas

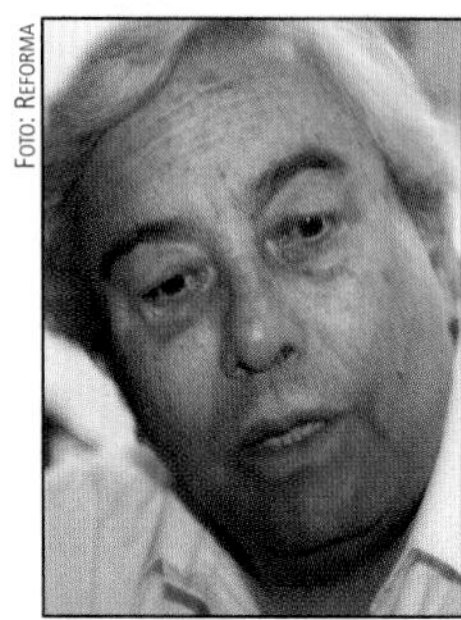

Foto: Reforma

Rafael Ruiz Harrell

en el norte de España y dirigió brigadas en el frente del Ebro y en Extremadura. Llegó exiliado a México en 1939. Colaboró con la Junta de Auxilio a los Refugiados Españoles. Trabajó en el Banco Nacional de Crédito Agrícola como supervisor de Planeación en Sonora, fue supervisor de fruticultura del Banrural, miembro de la Comisión Nacional del Olivo, asesor de forestación del Departamento Central, conferencista y director de prácticas para ingenieros de la Dirección General de Forestación y Manejo de Suelos Forestales de la Secretaría de Agricultura y fundador de una escuela de podadores y cultores de plantas, en Atlixco.

Ruiz González, Tomás ♦ n. en el DF (1963). Licenciado por la Escuela Libre de Derecho (1986) y maestro en economía política internacional por la Universidad de Columbia (1990). Profesor en la Escuela Libre de Derecho y en la UIA. En el Banco de México fue abogado (1985-87), subgerente de Operaciones Internacionales (1990-91), subgerente de Operaciones Cambiarias (1991-92) y gerente de Asuntos Jurídicos Internacionales (1992-93). Director general de Banca Múltiple (1993-98), presidente del Servicio de Administración Tributaria (1993-98) y subsecretario de Ingresos de la Secretaría de Hacienda (1998-).

Ruiz Granados, Fernando ♦ n. en el DF (1958). Escritor. Ingeniero y licenciado en letras españolas por la Universidad Veracruzana. Fundó la revista *Literal*, del ISSSTE, que también dirigió (1990-95). Autor de *El ritual del buitre* (cuento), *El árbol sagrado* (poesía) y *Poemas de Brindisi* (1990) y *Jardín de piedra* (1996). Ganador del Premio Nacional de Poesía Ramón López Velarde (1990), del Premier Prix de Poesía (1991), otorgado por el Club de Poésie de Veyrier du Lac de Francia, y del Premio de Poesía Plural 1992.

Ruiz Harrell, Rafael ♦ n. en el DF (1933). Licenciado en derecho y en letras por la UNAM, donde fue profesor y secretario ejecutivo de la Comisión Editorial. Fundador de las revistas *Ideas de México* y *Medio Siglo*. Condujo el programa *La Ciudad y el Crimen* en la estación de radio XEB. Colaborador de *Revista de la Universidad* y de los periódicos *El Universal* y *Reforma*. Autor de poesía: *Ocho cosas de papel* (1953) y *Te cantaron la muerte* (1962); de la novela *El secuestro de William Jenkins* (1992) y de los ensayos *Exaltación de ineptitudes* (1986, en el que criticó duramente al presidente Miguel de la Madrid) y *Criminalidad y mal gobierno* (1998). Ha obtenido dos primeros lugares por sus ensayos, otorgados por la Facultad de Derecho de la UNAM (1952 y 1955). Becario del Centro Mexicano de Escritores (1955-56 y 1956-57). La Sociedad Mexicana de Criminología le otorgó la Medalla al Mérito Criminológico Alfonso Quiroz (1998).

Ruiz de la Herrán, José ♦ ☛ *Herrán, José de la.*

Ruiz Herrera, José ♦ n. en el DF (1935). Químico bacteriólogo parasitólogo graduado en el IPN (1958), se doctoró en la Universidad Estatal de Rutgers (1963). Profesor y jefe del Departamento de Microbiología del IPN (1963-76), ha sido profesor invitado en diversas universidades de EUA y España. Jefe del Departamento de Genética y Biología Molecular del Cinvestav (1976-79). Participó en la fundación del Instituto de Investigación en Biología Experimental de la Universidad de Guanajuato (1981), donde creó y coordina la maestría en ciencias y el doctorado en biología experimental. Autor de más de cien publicaciones originales en revistas especializadas. Miembro del Consejo Consultivo de Ciencias. Ha recibido los premios de la Academia de la Investigación Científica (1974), Ruth Allen (1983) y Nacional de Ciencias y Artes (1984).

Ruiz Labastida, Leopoldo ♦ n. en Jiliapan y m. en Pozuelos, Hgo. (¿1882?-1924). Fue profesor de educación primaria en Pacula y Zimapán. Se unió a las fuerzas del constitucionalista Nicolás Flores, de quien fue secretario (1913). Con el grado de mayor fue delegado a la Convención de Aguascalientes, en sustitución de Flores. Carrancista, militó en las fuerzas de Otilio Villegas (1915), con quien participó en la defensa de Zimapán. Alcanzó el grado de coronel. Diputado al Congreso Constituyente de 1916-17. Se unió a la rebelión delahuertista, por lo que fue fusilado.

Ruiz Maldonado, Gerardo ♦ n. en Puebla, Pue. (1948). Escultor, pintor y diseñador gráfico. Estudió artes visuales en la Academia de San Carlos (1974). Fue seleccionado por el Comité Nacional Mexicano de la Asociación Internacional de Artes Plásticas para reunir la colección "Homenaje del pueblo y los artistas de México al pueblo y los artistas de Bulgaria". Ha participado en exposiciones colectivas en México y Jalapa. Autor de un mural transportable para el grupo Spicer (1977) y un mural transportable para la Canacintra (1978, en colaboración con Carlos Olachea). Miembro de la Asociación Mexicana de Artes Plásticas. Primer premio de diseño en el concurso Eduque Jugando, de la UNAM (1972) y mención honorífica de la Sección Trienal del INBA (1979).

Ruiz Malerva, Demetrio ♦ n. en Tuxpan y m. en Álamo, Ver. (1941-1986). Licenciado en derecho por la UNAM (1969). Miembro del PRI, en el que fue director de *La República* (1977-78), presidente del Comité Directivo Estatal en Veracruz (1980-81) y subsecretario de Organización del CEN (1981-82). Fue profesor en la UV, abogado consultor y oficial mayor de la legislatura de Veracruz, director general de Información de la Cámara de Diputados (1976-79), consejero cultural de México en Cuba, tres veces diputado federal, presidente de la Junta Municipal de Conciliación de Tuxpan y director general de Comunicación Social de la SPP (1982-86). Colaborador de *Siempre!*, *El Sol de México*, *El Día* y *El Universal*. Propietario de una estación de radio en Álamo, enlazada al sistema de noticieros de Radio Educación. Autor de *PRI: crítica, autocrítica y quintacolumnismo* (1983). Fue asesinado.

RUIZ MARISCAL, MARÍA DE LA LUZ ◆ n. en el DF (1958). Licenciada en derecho por la Universidad La Salle. Entre 1982 y 1992 desempeñó varios cargos en la SPP. Ha sido auditora general de la SEP (1992-94), contralora jurídico-financiera en la campaña presidencial del PRI (1994), y en la SCT, a la que ingresó en 1995, ha sido oficial mayor desde 1996. Miembro de los consejos de administración de Caminos y Puentes Federales de Ingresos y Servicios Conexos, Ferrocarriles Nacionales de México, ASA y Telecomunicaciones de México. Miembro de la junta directiva del Servicio Postal Mexicano.

RUIZ MASSIEU, ARMANDO ◆ n. en Acapulco, Gro. (1941). Médico cirujano por la UNAM (1964) especializado en traumatología y ortopedia en el IMSS (1969). Miembro del PRI. Ha sido subdirector de la Clínica Médica de la Villa Olímpica (1968), director del hospital de la delegación de la Cruz Roja en Acapulco (1974-75), director del hospital del Centro Médico Quirúrgico de Acapulco (1975), delegado en Guerrero de la Subsecretaría de Mejoramiento del Ambiente de la SSA (1980-82); subdelegado (1980-82) y delegado médico en Guerrero (1982-84), subdirector de los servicios médicos de los estados (1984-85) y coordinador general de delegaciones del ISSSTE (1985-88); y director general de Servicios de Salud Pública de la SSA en el DF (1988-90), coordinador general del hospital del DF (1990-91) y director general de la Unidad de Atención Primaria a la Salud de la SSA (1991-). Autor de *Gabinetes presidenciales de México* (1988) y de *Hacia una mística partidista del servicio público.*

RUIZ MASSIEU, JOSÉ FRANCISCO ◆ n. en Acapulco, Gro., y m. en el DF (1946-1994). Hermano del anterior. Licenciado en derecho por la UNAM (1969), donde ejerció la docencia (1970-86). Miembro del PRI, en el que era secretario general de CEN al ser asesinado. Fue jefe de Orientación y Servicios Jurídicos (1972-74), asesor del director general y secretario de la Asamblea General del Infonavit (1974-79); miembro del Grupo Consultivo Agrario (1979-80), secretario general de gobierno del estado de Guerrero (1981); oficial mayor (1982) y subsecretario de Planeación de la SSA (1982-86) y gobernador de Guerrero (1986-92). Colaborador de *La Jornada* (1984-86). Autor de *Régimen jurídico de las empresas multinacionales en América Latina* (1972), *Normación constitucional de los partidos políticos en América Latina* (1974), *Nueva administración pública federal* (1977), *Empresa pública* (1980), *Estudios jurídicos sobre la administración pública* (1981), *Estudios de derecho político de estados y municipios* (1986), *¿Nueva clase política o nueva política?* (1986) e *Ideas a tiempo. Las perspectivas de la democracia* (1990). En 1979 recibió el Premio Nacional de Administración Pública y un año después la Medalla Francisco Figueroa Mata otorgada por el estado de Guerrero.

RUIZ MASSIEU, MARIO ◆ n. en Acapulco, Gro., y m. en EUA (1950-1999). Hermano del anterior. Licenciado en derecho y maestro en historia de México por la UNAM, donde fue profesor, subdirector de Información, subdirector de Radio UNAM, investigador del Instituto de Investigaciones Jurídicas, director general de Planeación, secretario de la Facultad de Filosofía y Letras y secretario general auxiliar. Miembro del PRI desde 1971. Fue embajador en Dinamarca (1990-93); oficial mayor (1993-94) y subprocurador general de la PGR (1994-). En 1994, por petición propia, se encargó de la investigación del asesinato de su hermano, José Francisco Ruiz Massieu (☛); la abandonó poco después y renunció a su cargo y a su militancia en el PRI. En el mismo año fue aceptado en PRD. Acusado de obstrucción de la justicia por sus sucesores en la investigación, y de otros cargos en cortes de EUA, fue arrestado en 1995 en Nueva Jersey, donde permaneció bajo arresto domiciliario hasta que las autoridades de Estados Unidos dijeron que se había suicidado, aunque hay dudas sobre la veracidad de las causas de su muerte. Autor de *Elementos jurídico-históricos del municipio en México* (1979), *Temas de derecho agrario mexicano* (1981), *Derecho agrario revolucionario* (1987), *El cambio en la universidad* (1988), *Yo acuso* (1995) y *El dinosaurio vencido* (1997).

RUIZ MEJÍA, CARLOS ◆ m. en el DF (1939-1995). Doctor en física por la UNAM. Autor de novela: *La otra cara de la muerte* (1982, Premio de Novela Querétaro), *Falso retrato de Gerardo* (1985), *Ciudad en suspenso* (1986, Premio Nacional de Novela José Rubén Romero) e *Inesperadamente el verano* (1989).

RUIZ MEZA, VÍCTOR ◆ n. en Capulhuac, Edo. de Méx., y m. en el DF (1917-1969). Abandonó los estudios de derecho para dedicarse al comercio de libros y a la investigación bibliográfica. Trabajó para la SEP. Colaborador de *Excélsior*, *Revista de América*, *Personalidad* y del almanaque *Previsión y Seguridad*, de Monterrey. Colaboró con Mario Colín Sánchez en la edición de la *Biblioteca enciclopédica del estado de México.* Autor de *Los arrieros* (1946), *Apuntes para la historia de la litografía en Toluca en el siglo XIX* (1948), *La primera imprenta en Toluca* (1949) y *Altamirano (bocetos juveniles)* (1958). Obtuvo el primer premio de historia en los cuartos Juegos Florales de la ciudad de México (1948).

Obra de Víctor Ruiz Meza

José Francisco Ruiz Massieu

FOTO: UNIVERSIDAD AUTÓNOMA DEL ESTADO DE MÉXICO

Tomás Ruiz Pérez

Alfredo Ruiz del Río

RUIZ OROZCO, EUGENIO ◆ n. en Guadalajara, Jal. (1947). Egresado de la Escuela Normal de Jalisco y Licenciado en Derecho por la Universidad de Guadalajara (1968). Desde 1963 es miembro del PRI, del que fue candidato a gobernador del estado de Jalisco (1994-95). Ha sido regidor del Ayuntamiento de Guadalajara (1971-73), diputado en el Congreso del Estado de Jalisco (1974-77), presidente municipal de Guadalajara (1986-88) y senador de la República elegido para el periodo 1994-2000. En 1999 obtuvo licencia para asumir el cargo de vocal ejecutivo del Fovissste. Fue catedrático de la Universidad de Guadalajara (1967-70), miembro fundador del Instituto de Administración Pública de Jalisco y notario público.

RUIZ DE LA PEÑA Y URRUTIA, AGUSTÍN ◆ n. en Cunduacán y m. en la hacienda La Luz, Tab. (1790-1868). Fue el primer gobernador constitucional de Tabasco, nombrado por el Congreso Constituyente (1824). La designación provocó un enfrentamiento con el comandante militar, Rincón Calcáneo, quien lo hizo abandonar la capital estatal ese mismo año. El 6 de diciembre de 1824 fue aprehendido por el secretario de Guerra y Marina y sometido al gran jurado del Congreso General (1825). Dos veces gobernador constitucional (1825-27 y 1829-30) y gobernador provisional (1840) de Tabasco.

RUIZ PÉREZ, LEOBARDO CARLOS ◆ n. en el DF (1930). Se tituló en la Escuela Médico Militar (1950-56), tomó un curso en medicina física y rehabilitación en el Hospital Infantil de México (1959) e hizo su residencia en institutos y hospitales de Estados Unidos (1962). Profesor de la Escuela de Graduados del Servicio de Sanidad Militar (1973 y 1980), del Hospital General (1973), del Hospital Juárez (1975), de la Escuela Militar de Enfermeras (1980) y de la Escuela Médico Militar, de la que fue director (1977-79). Miembro del PRI. Fue jefe de residentes del Instituto de Medicina de Rehabilitación del Centro Médico de la Universidad de Nueva York (1960), jefe de residentes del Departamento de Medicina de Rehabilitación del Hospital Bellevue (1961) y subdirector técnico del Instituto Mexicano de Rehabilitación (1962-66). En el Hospital Central Militar ha sido jefe de Rehabilitación (1966-81) y subdirector de ese nosocomio (1979-81). Médico de la Clínica Primavera de Ortopedia (1966-76), director médico de la Asociación Pro Paralítico Cerebral (1969-75), jefe del Departamento de Medicina Física del Hospital General (1970-71), jefe del Departamento de Medicina de Rehabilitación del Hospital Mocel (1971-), director médico de la Asociación Camino Abierto (1975-82) y director general del DIF y médico del Presidente de la República (1982-88). Director general de sanidad militar (1988-94). Pertenece a corporaciones profesionales mexicanas y extranjeras.

RUIZ PÉREZ, TOMÁS ◆ n. en Teococuilco, Oax. (1947). Licenciado en derecho por la UAEM (1973) y maestro en derecho (1976) y doctor en derecho por la UNAM (1976-77). Ha sido profesor, director de la Facultad de Derecho (1979-83), director general Jurídico (1983-85) y rector de la UAEM (1985).

RUIZ PÉREZ, VIRGILIO SERGIO ◆ n. en Oaxaca, Oax. (1940). Profesor titulado en la Escuela Normal Mixta Federalizada del estado de Oaxaca (1957-59). Es licenciado en ciencias políticas por la UNAM (1967-71). Militante del PPS desde 1963, ha sido secretario de Relaciones Internacionales de la Juventud Popular Socialista (1967-69), oficial mayor del Comité Central (1971-72), oficial mayor (1982), miembro (1983) y secretario de Finanzas del Comité del DF. Ha sido profesor de educación primaria en escuelas federales (1960-72), secretario de Educación Sindical (1977-79) y de Relaciones Internacionales de la sección 9 del SNTE y diputado federal (1982-85).

RUIZ DEL RÍO, ALFREDO ◆ n. en Villamar, Mich. (1915). Estudió en la Escuela Nacional de Maestros y en el Conservatorio Nacional. Fue empleado de la Secretaría de Hacienda y líder de su sindicato. En 1933 se inició como declamador, actor y guitarrista de la radiodifusora XEB. Miembro fundador de la Asociación Mexicana de Periodistas de Radio y Televisión. Compuso las canciones *A tus ojos*, *Mírame*, *Gotita de amor*, *Amor de ayer*, *Lamento gaucho* (tango con música de Emilio Pulido Islas), *Clavel* y *Flor oriental*. Autor del poemario *Voces de vanguardia* (1937) y de *Apuntes para la historia de la radio y la TV en México* (1962).

RUIZ RIVERA, RAFAEL ◆ n. y m. en Jaral del Progreso, Gto. (1865-1932). Abandonó los estudios en el seminario y fundó los periódicos locales *La Voz del Jaral* y *Renacimiento*. Autor de *Romances históricos* (1921), *Piedras y bronces*, *Lirios y lágrimas*, *Matilde o la cruz solariega*, *Mi resumen epistolar*, *Rosas fúnebres*, *Hojas de tulipán* y *Las campanas de la Profesa*. Ganó un premio nacional de literatura en 1921, durante la conmemoración del primer centenario de la consumación de la independencia.

RUIZ SACRISTÁN, CARLOS ◆ n. en el DF (1949). Licenciado en administración de empresas por la Universidad Anáhuac y maestro en administración por la Northwestern University of Chicago. Tuvo diversos cargos en el banco de México (1988), entre ellos el de director del Fideicomiso de Cobertura de Riesgos Cambiarios. Fue director general .de Crédito Público de la Secretaría de Hacienda y subsecretario de Normatividad de la misma secretaría. Ha sido miembro de los consejos de administración de Aeropuertos y Servicios Auxiliares, Caminos y Puentes Federales de Ingresos y Servicios Conexos, Ferrocarriles Nacionales de México y la Constructora Nacional de Carros de Ferrocarril. Secretario de Comunicaciones y Transportes (1994-).

RUIZ SOBREDO, SANTIAGO ◆ n. en Teapa y m. en Villahermosa, Tab. (1885-1958). Luchó en la revolución constitucionalista en las fuerzas del general Green. Diputado al Constituyente local y firmante de la Constitución de Tabasco (1919). Tres veces gobernador interino de ese estado (1922, 24 y 26).

RUIZ SOLÓRZANO, FERNANDO ◆ n. en Pátzcuaro, Mich., y m. en alta mar (1903-1969). Egresado del Seminario Conciliar de Morelia, llegó a ser vicerrector del mismo. Sacerdote ordenado en 1928, dirigió el seminario hasta 1938. Prosecretario de la mitra, secretario de cámara y gobierno y canónigo de la catedral de Morelia. En 1944 se le consagró segundo arzobispo de Yucatán. Asistió al Concilio Vaticano II (1962-65).

RUIZ SUASNÁBAR, MARIANO N. ◆ n. en San Cristóbal de Las Casas y m. en Comitán, Chis. (1867-1945). Estudió teología, derecho canónico y filosofía en el Seminario Conciliar de San Cristóbal y odontología y relojería en el Colegio Jesuita de Nueva Orleans. Volvió a San Cristóbal de Las Casas (1884) donde fue profesor de inglés, latín, física y mecánica. Fundó una escuela industrial en Comitán (1897), realizó investigaciones odontológicas y aplicó la fluorina al tratamiento de la caries dental. Perteneció a la Sociedad Científica Antonio Alzate, la Societé Astronomique du France y a la Societé Botanique de Lyon. Creó un calendario perpetuo (1883) y un método analítico-sintético de lectura. Autor de una *Gramática*, *La dentadura natural y artificial* (1894), *Catecismo de economía política* (1920), *Errores económicos del socialismo* (1921), *Catecismo de instrucción cívica* (1923), *Catecismo geográfico de Chiapas* (1929) y *La afinación del piano por el método de las pulsaciones* (1930).

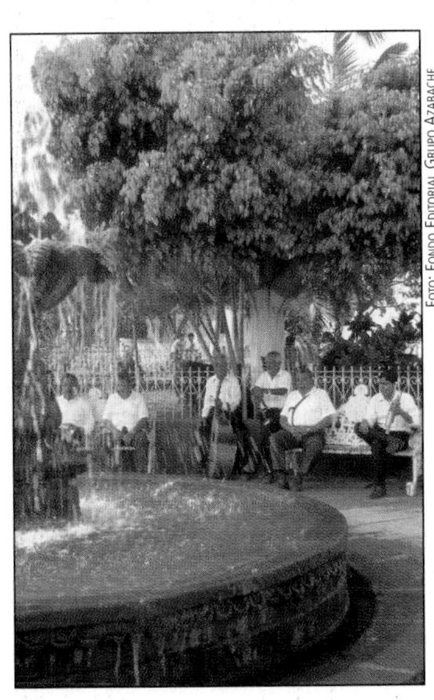

Foto: Fondo Editorial Grupo Azabache

Comala, municipio colimense donde se ambientó la novela *Pedro Páramo*, de Rulfo

Carlos Ruiz Sacristán

RUIZ VALERIO, FILIBERTO ◆ n. en Alvarado, Ver. (1935). Ingeniero mecánico naval por la Escuela Naval Militar de Veracruz (1954-58), posgraduado en informática en la UNAM (1960-61). Tomó un curso de desarrollo de funcionarios en la SPP. Miembro del PRI. Ha sido jefe del Departamento de Computación Electrónica de la Secretaría de Marina (1961-63), jefe de Análisis y Programación del Centro Nacional de Cálculo del IPN (1963-65), subjefe de Organización de la Contraloría General del DDF (1966-68), profesor en el IPN (1968) y en el ITAM (1968-70), subdirector técnico (1968-74) y subdirector general (1974-80) de la Dirección General de Procesos Electrónicos de la Secretaría de Hacienda; director de Procesos Electrónicos de la SPP (1980-82) y director general de Informática y Estadística de la Secretaría de Marina (1982-). Autor de *Introducción al lenguaje básico* (1981). Primer Premio del certamen convocado por la Fundación Arturo Rosenblueth, el Conacyt y la SEP.

RUIZ VELÁZQUEZ, ESTELA ◆ n. en Jalapa del Marqués, Oax. (1911). Maestra de educación física y danza folklórica. Trabajó para varios sindicatos enseñando danzas regionales. Entre 1938 y 1975 su retrato circuló en los billetes de 10 pesos. En 1993, la Lotería Nacional reprodujo el mismo grabado en sus billetes. Perteneció a la tertulia del café París y fue retratada por Aurora Reyes, Walter Pack y otros artistas. Le llamaban *la Tehuana*.

RUIZ VÉLEZ, TOMÁS *PEPE* ◆ n. en Nochistlán, Zac., y m. en el DF (1921-1991). Comenzó como actor, pero ganó reconocimiento como locutor en programas de la XEW, entre los que destacaron *La hora del cochinito* y *El risámetro*. También fue cantante y participó en películas como *Aventurera* (1949), *Doña Diabla* (1949), *Tacos, joven* (1950), *El beisbolista fenómeno* (1951) y *El bello durmiente* (1952). Miembro de la ANDA desde 1942.

RULFO, JUAN ◆ n. en Sayula, Jal., y m. en el DF (1918-1986). Escritor. Su nombre completo era Juan Nepomuceno Carlos Pérez Rulfo Vizcaíno. En 1935 llegó al DF y desempeñó diversos empleos hasta llegar a director del

Foto: Rogelio Cuéllar

Juan Rulfo

Departamento Editorial del Instituto Nacional Indigenista. Fue también aficionado a la fotografía. En los años cuarenta y cincuenta publicó cuentos en *Pan* y en *América. Revista Antológica*. Colaboró también en la *Revista Mexicana de Literatura* y *La Cultura en México*, que publicaron algunos de sus textos de creación. Autor de *El llano en llamas* (cuentos, 1953), la novela *Pedro Páramo* (1955), *Antología personal* (1978) y *El gallo de oro* (textos de cine). Grabó un disco para la colección Voz Viva de México de la UNAM. Varias de sus obras han sido llevadas al cine, se han hecho adaptaciones para radio y teatro y Víctor Rasgado compuso la ópera *Anacleto Morones* (1994). Fue becario del Centro Mexicano de Escritores (1952-53 y 1953-54) y posteriormente se desempeñó como asesor literario de esa institución (1967-83). Miembro de la Academia Mexicana (de la Lengua) desde 1980. Fue presidente honorario de la Sociedad General de Escritores de México. Recibió los premios Nacional de Ciencias y Artes (1970) y Príncipe de Asturias (1983). Doctor *honoris causa* por la UNAM (1985).

FOTO: GUILLERMO AGUILERA

Juan Carlos Rulfo

RULFO, JUAN CARLOS ◆ n. en el DF (1964). Cineasta. Hijo del anterior. Autor del corto *El abuelo Cheno y otras historias* (1998) y el largometraje *Del olvido al no me acuerdo* (1999, Premio a la mejor ópera prima del Festival de Biarritz).

FOTO: REFORMA

Pablo Rulfo

RULFO, PABLO ◆ n. en el DF (1955). Pintor. Hermano del anterior. Se inició en el diseño gráfico en el Grupo Madero, donde trabajó con Vicente Rojo. Hizo el diseño original del diario *unomásuno* (1977). Ha pasado largas temporadas en París. Ha expuesto en México y Francia. Participó en el XVII Festival Internacional de Pintura de Francia (1980).

Único volumen de cuentos y única novela de Juan Rulfo

RUMANIA ◆ Nación situada en el sureste de Europa, en el norte de la península de los Balcanes; limita al norte con Ucrania, al noreste con Moldavia, al este con Ucrania y el mar Negro, al sur con Bulgaria, al suroeste con Yugoslavia y al noroeste con Hungría. Tiene una superficie de 237,500 km² y 22,474,000 habitantes (1998). La capital es Bucarest (con 2,080,363 habitantes en 1994) y otras ciudades importantes son Constanza (348,575), Iasi (339,889), Timisoara (327,830) y Galati (326,728). El idioma oficial es el rumano (lengua romance), aunque también se hablan húngaro y alemán. La moneda es el leu. *Historia*: se han hallado pruebas arqueológicas de que hace un millón de años ya había pobladores en lo que hoy es territorio rumano. Los primeros habitantes de que se tiene noticia eran llamados tracios, getos (según los griegos) o dacios (según los latinos). En el siglo I a.n.e. se fundó un primitivo Estado dacio, cuyo primer rey fue Burebista. Su sucesor, Decebalo, está considerado como el consolidador de Estado dacio. En el año 106 de nuestra era, los romanos iniciaron su dominio en lo que ellos llamaban la Dacia; tal dominio se consolidó en el 271, con la victoria de Trajano. En el 275 los godos desplazaron a los romanos y se inició una era de invasiones germánicas, eslavas y turanias. Entre 375 y 453 los hunos dominaron el país, aun cuando la población tracia nunca abandonó su territorio. En el siglo VI dominaron los ávaros y de entonces al VII la dominación fue eslava. De los siglos VII a VIII se consolidó un gobierno búlgaro. En el siglo IX, los magiares o húngaros desplazaron a los búlgaros. De los siglos XI a XIII, los magiares se anexaron Transilvania en calidad de voivodato autónomo de Hungría. En el siglo XIV se fundaron los dos primeros estados rumanos: Muntenia o Valaquia (en 1310) y Moldavia (en 1359). En 1475, Esteban III *el Grande*, de Moldavia, venció a los turcos en Rahova, pero éstos se apoderaron de los principales enclaves costeros. En el siglo XVI, la caída de Belgrado (1521) y el desmembramiento de Hungría (1526) completaron el cerco otomano en torno a los príncipes rumanos. Valaquia y Moldavia, sin embargo, mantuvieron cierta autonomía interna, mientras que Transilvania se convirtió en principado autónomo del Imperio Otomano. Entre 1600 y 1601, el príncipe valaco Miguel *el Bravo* consiguió unir a los estados de Valaquia, Moldavia y Transilvania bajo su gobierno. En 1699 Austria se anexó Transilvania; 76 años después se anexó también Bucovina. En 1812, al terminar la guerra entre el imperio Otomano y la Rusia zarista, esta nación se anexó la región rumana de Besarabia. En 1848, una revolución que pretendía unir todos los principados (encabezada por Nicolae Balcescu), fracasó por la intervención ruso-turca. En 1859, los moldavos y valacos unificaron el gobierno y eligieron gobernador al príncipe Alejandro Ion Cuza (quien secularizó los bienes monásticos, implantó la reforma agraria, creó el ejército y orga-

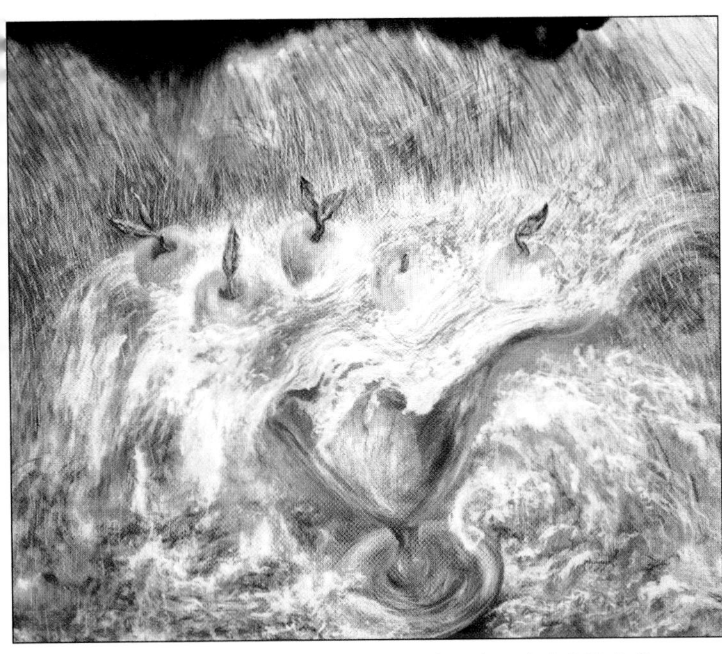

El diluvio (homenaje a Vicente Rojo), temple y óleo sobre tela de Pablo Rulfo

nizó la enseñanza). En 1861, el príncipe rumano Jorge Bibesco y su hermano Alejandro vinieron a México como integrantes del ejército invasor de Napoleón III, en virtud de que Jorge había estudiado en el Colegio Militar de Saint Cyr, en Francia. Este príncipe escribió varias obras sobre su actuación en nuestro país. En 1862, el Estado formado por Cuza adoptó el nombre de Rumania. En 1866 la nobleza (molesta a causa de las medidas tomadas por el gobernante) expulsó a Cuza, nombró como sustituto al extranjero Carol de Hohenzollern-Sigmaringen y estableció una monarquía constitucional (Carol consolidó las clases dominantes, constituyó los partidos políticos conservador y liberal e introdujo el sistema parlamentario). En 1877 Rumania proclamó su independencia del imperio otomano. En 1881, el príncipe Carol se convirtió en el primer rey rumano: Carol I. En 1916 Fernando I, hijo y sucesor de Carol I, intervino en la primera guerra mundial, en el bando aliado. En 1918 Besarabia, Alba Julia, Bucovina y Transilvania proclamaron su unión con Rumania. En 1927 Mihai I heredó el trono de su abuelo Fernando I. En 1930 el príncipe Carol, que había renunciado al trono, volvió al país y se coronó como Carol II; siete años después disolvió el Parlamento e instauró una dictadura opuesta a los fascistas de la Guardia de Hierro. En 1940, en el marco de la segunda guerra mundial y de acuerdo con lo establecido en el pacto de no agresión, firmado entre la Unión Soviética y Alemania, los soviéticos ocuparon Besarabia y Bucovina; la presion italoalemana obligó a Rumania a entregar a Hungría el norte de Transilvania y a Bulgaria el sur de Dobruja, lo que obligó a Carol II a abdicar en favor de su hijo. Carol salió del país y estuvo una temporada en México, acompañado de Magda Lupescu, con quien se convirtió en figura infaltable en las reuniones sociales. Bajo la monarquía de su sucesor, Mihai I, se formó un gabinete dirigido por el general Ion Antonescu quien, un año después, se alió con los nazis. La resistencia popular y el ejército rumano recuperaron Besarabia y Bucovina. En 1944 los soviéticos entraron en Rumania, derrocaron a Antonescu y Mihai I ordenó a sus tropas combatir contra las fuerzas del eje Berlín-Roma. Se estableció el armisticio con los aliados y Rumania entregó (como indemnización de guerra) Besarabia y el norte de Bucovina a la Unión Soviética y Dobruja a Bulgaria. En 1947 la Asamblea Nacional (de mayoría comunista) obligó a abdicar a Mihai I y proclamó la República Popular Rumana. En 1949 Rumania se integró al Consejo de Ayuda Mutua Económica. En 1952 el primer ministro Petru Groza fue reemplazado por Gheorghe Gheorghiu-Dej. En 1955 el Partido Rumano de los Trabajadores se convirtió en Partido Comunista Rumano y el país se unió al Pacto de Varsovia y a la Organización de las Naciones Unidas. En 1961 el presidium del Partido Comunista Rumano fue sustituido por un consejo de Estado, presidido por Gheorghiu-Dej. Éste murió en 1965 y la asamblea lo sustituyó con Chivu Stoica. En 1973 se reanudaron las relaciones diplomáticas entre México y Rumania, rotas desde el inicio de la segunda guerra mundial. En 1974 Nicolau Ceausescu llegó a la presidencia de Rumania; un año después realizó una visita oficial a México y se entrevistó con el presidente Luis Echeverría. En 1989, después de 15 años de ejercicio despótico del poder, Ceausescu fue derrocado por una insurrección popular para ser ejecutado en forma sumaria junto con su esposa. En ese mismo año, por razones económicas, el gobierno de México cerró su embajada en la ciudad de Bucarest. La embajada fue reabierta en 1995.

Rumbia Guzmán, José ◆ n. en Tlacolula, Oax., y m. en Tlaxcala, Tlax. (1865-1913). Pastor metodista, pres-

Rumania

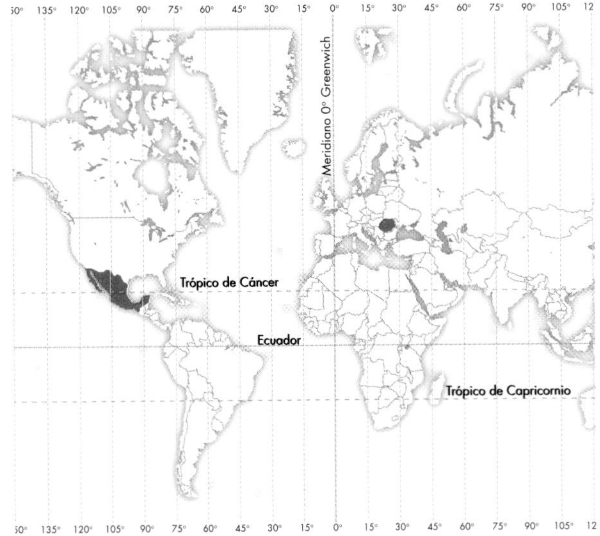

Carol II de Rumania (centro), con Magda Lupescu a su izquierda, en una reunión social en 1941 en México

bítero en 1896. Fue coordinador del distrito metodista de Orizaba y desde 1901 vivió en Río Blanco como pastor y profesor de la escuela primaria en Río Blanco y Orizaba. Colaboró en *La República*, de Tlaxcala, y *Revolución Social*, de Río Blanco. Fundó una primaria nocturna en la cárcel, de acuerdo con las autoridades municipales, y formó una congregación metodista. Organizó a los trabajadores y en 1906 participó en la fundación del Gran Círculo de Obreros Libres. Fue detenido en 1907, como uno de los cinco dirigentes de la huelga (☛ *Río Blanco*). Fue inspector general de escuelas en Guerrero y secretario particular del gobernador de Tlaxcala, Antonio Hidalgo (1912). Más tarde, su Iglesia lo desplazó a León y a Tlaxcala, donde fue asesinado por iniciar un movimiento antihuertista.

RUSIA, FEDERACIÓN DE ◆ Estado de Europa y Asia, con la mayor parte de su territorio en el segundo continente. Su nombre oficial es Federación de Rusia. Situado en las costas de los océanos Glacial Ártico y Pacífico, limita al noroeste con Noruega, Finlandia, el golfo de Finlandia, Estonia y Letonia, al oeste con Belarús y Ucrania, al suroeste con el mar Negro, Georgia, Azerbaiyán y el mar Caspio, al sur con Kazajstán y Mongolia y al sureste con China. La isla de Sajalín está separada de Japón por el estrecho de Perouse y el extremo nororiental de Rusia está separado de Alaska por el estrecho de Bering. Superficie: 17,075,400 km^2 que lo convierten en el país más grande del mundo. Habitantes: 147,434,000 en 1998. La capital es Moscú (8,400,200 habitantes en 1996) y otras ciudades importantes son San Petersburgo (4,200,000), Nizhny Novgorod (1,400,000), Novosibirsk (1,400,000) y Ekaterimburgo (1,300,000). El idioma oficial es el ruso y también se hablan tártaro, ucraniano y bashkir. La moneda es el rublo. *Historia*: entre los siglos X y IX a.n.e. partes de la actual Federación de Rusia fueron pobladas por los hombres de la edad del hierro: los finlandeses se establecieron en las regiones de Karma y Oka, los escitas en las estepas occidentales y los sármatas sostuvieron contactos con los pueblos helénicos, al este del río Don, en las riberas del mar Negro. A mediados del siglo II de nuestra era, los godos emigraron del Vístula y se establecieron en el litoral del mar Negro. En el año 375, los ostrogodos fundaron un reino en Ucrania, que más tarde fue arrasado por los hunos, una tribu mongólica procedente del norte de China. Entre los siglos V y VI, los búlgaros y los ávaros dominaron las estepas orientales de la parte europea del país, en tanto que los eslavos se movieron hacia el norte y el este y desplazaron a los finlandeses. En el siglo IX los vikingos incursionaron en el actual territorio ruso y siguieron el curso del Volga hasta el mar Negro y Constantinopla. En el año 862, el jefe vikingo Rurik erigió un reino con sede en Novgorod; sus sucesores trasladaron la capital a Kiev y extendieron el reino desde el golfo de Finlandia hasta el río Danubio y el mar Caspio. En el año 989, el rey Vladimiro *el Santo* aceptó la religión cristiana y ordenó el bautizo masivo de sus súbditos. En 1221, Gengis Kan realizó incursiones por el oriente ruso. En 1237, Ogodai Kan, hijo de Gengis Kan, invadió el país, conquistó Kiev y estableció el dominio mongol, que duró dos siglos. En 1425, Basilio II separó la Iglesia rusa del patriarcado de Constantinopla. En 1462, Iván III, el gran duque de Moscú, se proclamó zar (césar) y se independizó de los tártaros. En 1533, el zar Iván IV *el Terrible*, inició una lucha contra el poder de los señores feudales, con la idea de crear una monarquía centralizada. En 1613, la Asamblea Nacional reunida en Moscú designó zar a Miguel Romanov, hijo del patriarca Filareto, pues la línea masculina de Rurik se había extinguido. En 1672, Pedro I, *el Grande*, inició la occidentalización de Rusia y en 1703 fundó San Petersburgo, la nueva capital. En 1725, luego de una guerra contra Suecia, Pedro I prolongó las fronteras rusas hacia el oeste. Desde 1741, a raíz de los descubrimientos geográficos del danés Vitus Johansens Bering, los rusos emprendieron varias exploraciones por la costa americana del Pacífico y establecieron puestos de avanzada en la actual costa de Alaska y Canadá (☛), donde comerciaban pieles con los indios; ocuparon la isla de Vancuver y continuaron hacia el sur, pero se detuvieron ante el avance de los misioneros franciscanos, quienes en 1775 fundaron una misión que sería el origen de la ciudad de San Francisco. Durante los años ochenta, de la Nueva España salieron expediciones que fueron más al norte de San Francisco e incluso entraron en contacto con los comerciantes rusos de Unalaska y Kodiak, la principal población de la "América rusa". En mayo de 1789, los enviados novohispanos se establecieron en Nutka, isla de Vancuver donde construyeron un baluarte fortificado para impedir el avance ruso, francés e inglés. A partir de 1790, cuando España cedió

Federación de Rusia

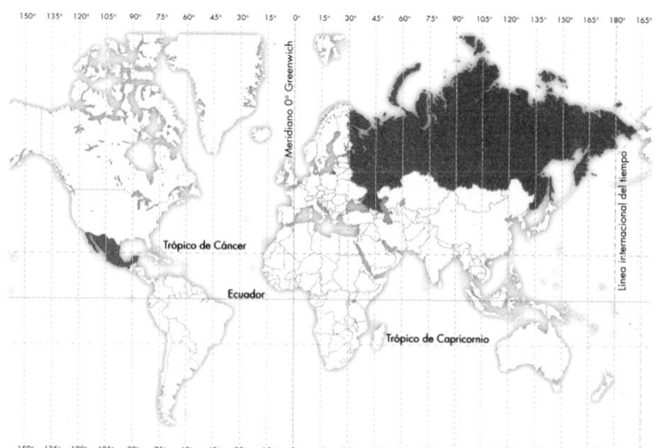

Iván IV, *el Terrible*, zar de Rusia en el siglo XVI

la isla a Gran Bretaña, los comerciantes rusos pudieron volver a comerciar con los indios de la costa del Pacífico y en 1804, el siberiano Grigori Chelekov creó la Compañía Rusoamericana, que controló el comercio de los rusos en América desde Stika, una población situada al suroeste de Juneau, la futura capital de Alaska. El clima de la región no era propicio para la agricultura y la ganadería y la importación de alimentos desde Siberia resultaba demasiado costosa para la Compañía, por lo que en 1806 su director, Nicolái Petrovich Rezanov, viajó a San Francisco y obtuvo de Luis Arrillaga, el gobernador de Californa, un permiso para comprar 290 toneladas de alimentos que llevó a Stika. Pero como el permiso era ilegal, pues los borbones habían monopolizado el comercio exterior de las colonias, Rezanov intentó negociar un acuerdo comercial con el virrey José de Iturrigaray (1807) y más tarde con Carlos IV (1808), pero fracasó a causa de la cautela del virrey, la invasión napoleónica y el inicio de la revolución de independencia. En Europa, mientras tanto, el zar Alejandro I se opuso a la política francesa desde 1801 y combatió al ejército de Napoleón de manera intermitente durante toda la década, hasta que en 1812 los franceses invadieron Rusia y tomaron Moscú, de donde poco después realizaron una costosa retirada. En 1812 Alejandro I había conquistado Finlandia y Besarabia. En ese mismo año, la Compañía Rusoamericana estableció un puesto a 12 leguas de San Francisco, que se llamó Fuerte Ross. Poco después, Iván Alexandróvich Kuskov se instaló en el puerto de Bodega con 100 de sus compatriotas y fundó una colonia dedicada a la pesca y al comercio de pieles. Uno de ellos, el siberiano Projor Yegorov, se incorporó más tarde a uno de los grupos de indios nómadas que se resistían a la dominación. Durante esa década, los asentamientos rusos al norte de San Francisco se generalizaron y para 1820 habían fundado, además de Bodega y Ross, las haciendas de Klebnilov, Tschernik y Kostranitinof. Su presencia despertó la inquietud del gobierno mexicano recién constituido y, en diciembre de 1821, la Soberana Junta Gubernativa del Imperio mexicano se interesó en firmar un acuerdo comercial y de límites con Rusia, para evitar la expansión de los europeos hacia California. A finales de los años veinte, un representante de México estableció contacto con el embajador del zar en Londres, pero el gobierno ruso consideró que el monto del comercio rusomexicano era demasiado pequeño para firmar un acuerdo. En octubre de 1834, el coronel José Figueroa intentó sin éxito que Fernando, el barón de Wrangel, comandante militar de la "Rusia americana", mediara entre los colonos texanos y el gobierno de México para resolver el conflicto que se iniciaba. Sin embargo, entre diciembre de 1835 y abril de 1836, Wrangel realizó un viaje por territorio mexicano y al parecer estableció algunos contactos diplomáticos y conoció a Antonio López de Santa Anna, a quien describió como "Un dictador sin escrúpulos, hombre deshonesto y fanfarrón, con mucho afán de poder y de dinero (.), el peor de los ladrones, fanfarrón, sinvergüenza, un hombre completamente inculto". Pero Wrangel también se dio cuenta de lo impráctico de las misiones rusas en California y desde entonces abogó por la retirada de la Compañía Rusoamericana, hecho que se realizó en 1842. Antes de irse, los rusos vendieron sus propiedades a John Sutter, el dueño del rancho donde siete años más tarde se descubriría la primera mina de oro californiana. En 1854 se inició la guerra por el dominio del mar Negro y la península de los Balcanes en la que Rusia fue derrotada. Varios regimientos franceses que participaron, entre otras, en la batalla de Sebastopol, formaron parte del cuerpo expedicionario francés que invadió México en los años sesenta. En marzo de 1861, apoyado en el decreto sobre inmigración publicado unos días antes, el secretario de Fomento del gobierno de Benito Juárez, Ignacio Ramírez, autorizó el establecimiento de una colonia rusa en el sur de Veracruz. En ese mismo año, mientras tanto, el zar Alejandro II emprendió una serie de reformas que liberaron a los

Estación de Metro, Rusia

Pedro I, *el Grande*, inició la occidentalización de Rusia a finales del siglo XVII

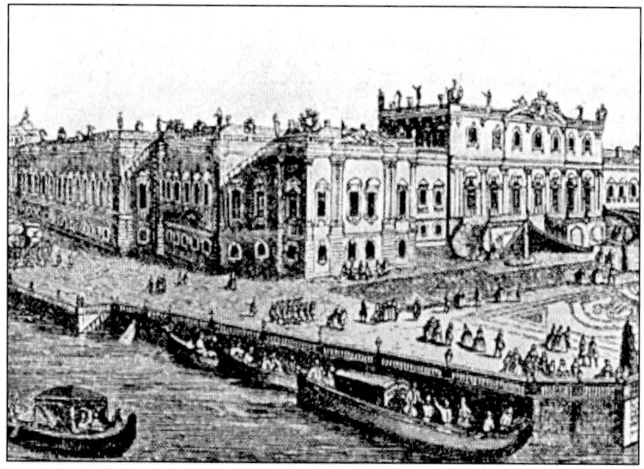

El antiguo palacio de Verano en los alrededores de San Petersburgo, ciudad de Rusia fundada en 1703

Matías Romero estableció contactos con el representante del zar de Rusia en Washington en la década de 1860.

campesinos de la servidumbre feudal. En septiembre de 1864, Francisco Serapio Mora, enviado especial de Maximiliano de Habsburgo, se acreditó en San Petersburgo como ministro plenipotenciario del "Imperio de México" y se entrevistó con el zar Alejandro. Los rusos, sin embargo, se negaron a enviar un representante a la ciudad de México y durante los dos años siguientes, Matías Romero, el embajador mexicano en Washington, sostuvo algunos contactos amistosos con Eduard Andréievich Stekl, el representante del zar en la capital estadounidense, quien, en octubre de 1866, recomendó al gobierno de Juárez alentar la enemistad entre Maximiliano y Napoleón III para que los franceses se retiraran y dejaran al gobierno imperial a merced del ejército de la república. La entrevista de Mora con Alejandro, así como una carta que el zar envió al ex archiduque de Austria a finales de 1865, hicieron que en marzo de 1867, cuando el triunfo republicano era inminente, el gobierno de Juárez incluyera a Rusia en la lista de países con los que México se negaba a tener relaciones diplomáticas. En ese mismo año, el zar vendió Alaska a Estados Unidos por 7,200,000 dólares, con lo que desaparecieron los dominios rusos en el continente. Los contactos diplomáticos entre Rusia y México se reanudaron a principios de los años ochenta, pero se limitaron a una solicitud de arbitrio por parte del embajador de México en Bruselas, Ángel Núñez Ortega, al embajador ruso en la capital belga, sobre el conflicto territorial entre Belice y Yucatán. A partir de entonces se estrecharon los contactos entre Núñez Ortega y el agregado militar ruso, Nicolái de Chichagov. En 1887 se iniciaron los preparativos para el establecimiento de relaciones diplomáticas. En marzo de 1890 el zar envió a México a Nicolái Romanóvich, el barón de Rosen, quien en enero de 1891 fue reconocido como enviado extraordinario y ministro plenipotenciario de Rusia en la República mexicana. También en enero, Pedro Rincón Gallardo fue nombrado embajador de México en San Petersburgo. A finales del siglo XIX se establecieron consulados rusos en Guadalajara, México, Monterrey y Veracruz, así como en la laguna del Carmen, donde debió existir una comunidad rusa. El gobierno de Porfirio Díaz, por su parte, abrió oficinas consulares en Helsinki, Moscú, Riga y San Petersburgo. En febrero de 1904 estalló la guerra entre Rusia y Japón, en la cual fue destruida la mayor parte de la flota del zar estacionada en el océano Pacífico. Luego de la derrota, la inquietud se generalizó por toda Rusia y resurgieron los grupos oposicionistas que habían sido destruidos por el zarismo. A partir de enero de 1905, luego de que una manifestación de los obreros de San Petersburgo fue reprimida por el ejército, se iniciaron varias sublevaciones. En la capital se creó un consejo de obreros llamado sóviet que se apoderó del control de la ciudad y obligó al zar Nicolás II a establecer un parlamento (duma) y a aceptar algunas reformas. En 1909 se firmó un tratado de comercio entre Rusia y México. Cinco años más tarde, en 1914, Rusia entró en la primera guerra mundial. La prolongación del conflicto ocasionó graves problemas económicos, malas cosechas y hambre, lo que aunado al reclutamiento masivo generó un sentimiento antibélico en la población. El descontento creció y volvieron a constituirse sóviets (consejos). Incapaz de ejercer la autoridad, el zar abdicó en marzo de 1917. En Petrogrado (que era el nombre de San Petersburgo desde 1914), la asamblea creó una inestable república, cuyos dirigentes se negaron a terminar la guerra. En noviembre, una nueva insurrección derrocó al gobierno de Alexánder Kerensky y dio el poder a los sóviets, que eran presididos por León Trotsky (☛). En los consejos la mayoría estaba formada por delegados bolcheviques, quienes eligieron un gobierno encabezado por Vladimir Ílich Lenin, quien prometió paz a los soldados, tierra a los campesinos y pan a los obreros. Al año siguiente, el nuevo gobierno firmó el tratado de Brest-Litovsk, que puso fin a la guerra con Alemania y Turquía. Como para entonces ya actuaban fuerzas contrarrevolucionarias en diversos lugares de Rusia, el gobierno organizó apresuradamente el Ejército Rojo, con Trotsky como comandante en jefe. Siguieron varios años de guerra civil y de intervención militar de más de 20 países, entre otros Alemania, Estados Unidos, Francia, Inglaterra, Hungría, Japón y Turquía. En octubre de 1918, cuando la guerra comenzaba a afectar a todo el país, Carlos L. Bauer, el cónsul mexicano en Moscú, salió de Rusia y en su lugar dejó a Basiliv Blidin, que intentó firmar un acuerdo comercial con los soviéticos para abastecer a Rusia de diversas mercancías, entonces muy escasas por la situación de guerra. Pero debido a que las comunicaciones entre

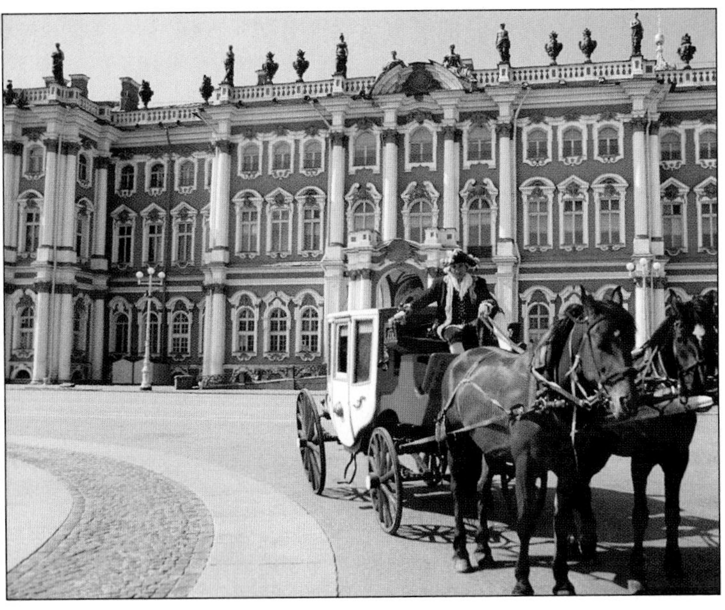

Palacio en San Petersburgo

Rusia y el resto del mundo estaban interrumpidas, Blidin comisionó en mayo de 1919 a uno de los empleados del consulado, Jorge Villardo de Zebrico, para que viajara a México y se entendiera directamente con el gobierno. El gobierno soviético aporovechó el viaje de Villardo y consiguió que lo acompañara Mijaíl Borodin (☛), quien además de representante del gobierno soviético era enviado de la Internacional Comunista (☛). Durante la segunda mitad de 1919, Borodin se entrevistó con el presidente Venustiano Carranza e impulsó la conversión del Partido Nacional Socialista en Partido Comunista Mexicano (☛), pero no pudo acreditarse oficialmente como embajador soviético. En 1922, un representante personal de Lenin asistió a la toma de posesión, como gobernador de Yucatán, de Felipe Carrillo Puerto (☛), líder del Partido Socialista del Sureste. El Partido Comunista Mexicano conmemoró por primera vez en 1921 el triunfo de la Revolución de Octubre, con un mitin celebrado en el Teatro Hidalgo al que asistieron 400 personas y en el que hablaron Genaro Gómez, del Sindicato de Obreros Panaderos del DF, y José C. Valadés. En 1922, el estado ruso se transformó en la Unión de Repúblicas Socialistas Soviéticas (☛), que se disgregaría tres cuartos de siglo después. Tras el colapso de la Unión Soviética, México estableció relaciones diplomáticas con la Federación de Rusia en 1992, cuando ya ésta pertenecía a la Confederación de Estados Independientes. Rusia se incorporó, en ese mismo año, al Banco Mundial y al Fondo Monetario Internacional, los dos instrumentos económicos más poderosos de su antiguo enemigo de la guerra fría. En enero de 1993 el presidente ruso, Boris Yeltsin, y el estadounidense, George Bush, firmaron en Moscú el segundo Tratado de Reducción de Armas Estratégicas, considerado el más amplio pacto de desarme de la historia. Poco después, el gobierno de Yeltsin resistió y derrotó con el apoyo de los mandatarios de la Comunidad de Estados Independientes un intento de golpe de Estado promovido por un sector de los viejos comunistas.

RUSSEK, ANTONIO ◆ n. en Torreón, Coah. (1954). Músico. Estudió piano con maestros particulares (1969-72). Radicado en México, desde 1976 se dedica a la composición de música electrónica. Construye parte del equipo que emplea, incluyendo sintetizadores. Viajó a París para trabajar en la computadora UPIC, diseñada por Iannis Xenakis (1978). Fue asesor de los cursos sobre música electroacústica impartidos por Jean Claude Eloy y Jean Etienne Marie (1981) y colaboró hasta 1985 con la Compañía de Repertorio Nuevo de la UNAM, bajo la dirección de Julio Estrada. Desde 1980 participa en espectáculos organizados por el Centro Nacional de Investigación, Documentación e Información Musical del INBA. Fundó el Centro Independiente de Investigaciones Musicales y Multimedia (1980). Dirige las ediciones de la Colección Hispanoamericana de Música Contemporánea. Premio Cuauhtémoc de las Artes (1988).

RUSSEK, JORGE ◆ n. en Guaymas, Son., y m. en el DF (1932-1998). Actor. Durante su infancia y adolescencia residió en Los Ángeles, California, en donde cursó estudios en una escuela militar. Comenzó su carrera cinematográfica en 1931 e intervino en cerca de 350 películas mexicanas y estadounidenses, en las que casi siempre interpretó papeles "de villano" y entre las que destacan *La vida de Agustín Lara* (1957), *El mal* (1966), *La batalla de San Sebastián* (1968), *Pat Garrett y Billy The Kid* (1973), *Todo o nada* (1973, Diosa de Plata como mejor actor de cuadro), *De todos modos Juan te llamas* (1975, Ariel como mejor actor), *La rebelión de los colgados*, *Valentín de la Sierra*, *El apando*, *Bandidos* (1990), *Gertrudis Bocanegra* (1992) y *Ámbar* (1997). Autor de la autobiografía *Una vida de película* (1977) y el libro de fotografía *Sonora*. También intervino en obras de teatro, series de televisión y numerosas telenovelas.

FOTO: REFORMA

Jorge Russek

RUSSEK BERMAN, MAURICIO ◆ n. en León, Gto., y m. en el DF (1931-1990). Biólogo graduado en el IPN (1954) y doctor en ciencias (1975) por la misma institución, en la que fue profesor (1958-84), jefe del Laboratorio de Fisiología de Mamíferos (1969-60) y del Departamento de Graduados de Fisiología y Biofísica (1979-88). Profesor invitado en las universidades de Lyon, de Pittsburgh, de California en Los Ángeles y Western Ontario. Fue asesor de la SSA (1974-77). Publicó 51 trabajos de investigación, capítulos de libros especializados y textos de divulgación científica. Profesor emérito de la Escuela Nacional de Ciencias Biológicas del IPN, misma que desde 1990 lleva su nombre. Fue investigador nacional nivel III (1984-90). Obtuvo el Premio de Ciencias de la Academia de la Investigación Científica (1970) y la medalla Claude Bernard de la Universidad de Lyon (1976).

Foto: Época

Eusebio Ruvalcaba

RUSSELL, ANDY ◆ n. y m. en EUA (1930-1991). Cantante y actor perteneciente a una familia de origen mexicano radicada en Los Ángeles. Su nombre original era Andrés Rábago Pérez. Fue cantante de la orquesta de Albino Rey y, como solista, grabó la canción *Bésame mucho* (1945). Cantó después *Amor amor*, *Mariquita linda* y *Tres palabras* (1946) y otras composiciones mexicanas y latinoamericanas. Estudió guitarra, piano, flauta y canto y se inició como compositor. Vivió en México de 1955 a 1970, actuó en cine y televisión e hizo giras por Centro y Sudamérica. Trabajó en las películas mexicanas *Qué bravas son las costeñas* (1954), *Mi canción eres tú* (1955), *Primavera en el corazón* (1955), *¡Viva la juventud!* (1955), *¡Vístete, Cristina!* (1958) y *Jóvenes y rebeldes* (1961). En Inglaterra filmó *El mago de Oz*.

Higinio Ruvalcaba Romero

RUTA ◆ Revista literaria mensual de la que aparecieron 12 números entre junio de 1938 y mayo de 1939. Tuvo como antecedentes las revistas *Noviembre* y *Ruta*. El editorial del primer número anunciaba que su propósito era dar "a conocer al mundo a los escritores mexicanos formados en esta hora en que México crea su destino histórico", teniendo como base "la defensa de la cultura" mediante la "lucha firme en contra de su más denodado enemigo: el fascismo internacional". El director fue José Mancisidor. Formaron el comité de redacción Ermilo Abreu Gómez, Mario Pavón Flores, Germán List Arzubide, Carlos Zapata Vela, Lorenzo Turrent Rozas, Miguel Bustos Cerecedo, Adolfo López Mateos, Gabriel Fernández Ledesma, Leopoldo Méndez y José Chávez Morado. Además de colaboraciones de los citados se publicaron textos de Louis Aragón, José Attolini, Neftalí Beltrán, Erskine Caldwell, Nelly Campobello, Luis Cardoza y Aragón, Verna Carleton de Millán, Alejandro Carrión, Jean Cassou, Alfonso Cuesta y Cuesta, William Fletcher, Jacobo Glantz, Pedro Geofroy Rivas, Martín Luis Guzmán, Andrés Henestrosa, Celestino Herrera Frimont, Efraín Huerta, José Iturriaga, James Joyce, Gastón Lafarga, León Felipe, Esperanza López Mateos, Gregorio López y Fuentes, Vladimir Maiakovsky, Ignacio Millán, Rafael F. Muñoz, Pablo Neruda, Nicolás Ostrovsky, Miguel Otero Silva, Carlos Pellicer, Héctor Pérez Martínez, José Revueltas, Alfonso Reyes, Romain Rolland, Upton Sinclair, Alfonso Teja Zabre, Loló de la Torriente, B. Traven, Tristan Tzara, Rodolfo Usigli, José Vázquez Amaral, Arqueles Vela, Agustín Yáñez y Solón Zabre, entre otros.

RUVALCABA, EUSEBIO ◆ n. en Guadalajara, Jal. (1951). Escritor. Hijo de Higinio Ruvalcaba Romero (☛). Licenciado en historia por la UNAM. Fue profesor de la UIA y coordinador de Cultura de Banamex. Escribe en *El Financiero* y otras publicaciones. Autor de poesía: *Atmósfera de fieras* (1977), *Homenaje a la mentira* (1982), *Gritos desde la negra oscuridad y otros poemas místicos I* (1993), *En la dulce lejanía del cuerpo* (1996), *Las jaulas colgantes* (1997), *El argumento de la espada* (1998), *Con olor a Mozart* (1998), *Gritos desde la negra oscuridad y otros poemas místicos II* (1998) y *Jugo de luz* (1998); teatro: *Las dulces compañías* (1984), *¡Ahí viene! ¡Ahí viene!*, *Bienvenido papá* (1979, Primer lugar en el concurso de teatro de la revista *Punto de Partida*), *¿Quién de ustedes ha recorrido el mundo?*, *La estrella de mar*, *La visita* y *Tiempo extra* (1984); divulgación para niños: *Me llamo Diego* (1988) y *Me llamo Mozart* (1991); cuento: *¿Nunca te amarraron las manos de chiquito?* (1990), *Jueves Santo* (1994, Premio de cuento San Luis Potosí 1992), *1994: Cuentos pétreos* (1995) *Clint Eastwood, hazme el amor* (1996) y *Las memorias de un liguero* (1997); novela: *Un hilito de sangre* (1992, Premio Agustín Yañez 1991, otorgado por la Secretaría de Educación y Cultura de Jalisco y la editorial Planeta), *Músico de cortesanas* (1993), *El portador de la fe* (1994), *Desde la tersa noche* (1994), *Lo que tú necesitas es tener una bicicleta* (1995), *En defensa propia* (1997), *El brindis* (1998) y *Desgajar la belleza* (1999); y ensayo: *Cájeme, un yaqui visionario* y *Primero la A* (1997) y *Las cuarentonas* (1998). Becario del INBA-Fonapas (1978-79 y 1979-80) y del Centro Mexicano de Escritores (1980-81). Premio de Cuento de *El Nacional* por "Antisonata" (1977).

RUVALCABA, GILBERTO ◆ n. en Autlán, Jal., y m. en el DF (1896- 1955). Se unió a la revolución zapatista. Fue redactor de *El Sol*, *El Demócrata*, *El Instante*, *El Diario* y *El Diario de Jalisco*. Figuró en el Comité Ejecutivo del Sindicato Nacional de Redactores de Prensa y fue colaborador de *El Nacional*. Autor de *Las alamedas del silencio* y *La revolución en China*.

RUVALCABA ROMERO, HIGINIO ◆ n. en Yahualica, Jal., y m. en el DF (1905-1976). Músico autodidacta que ofreció conciertos y recitales en México, Japón, varios países europeos y Estados Unidos. Fue concertino de la Orquesta Sinfónica de México y de la Filarmónica de la Ciudad de México, dirigida por Eric Kleiber; director titular de la Orquesta Sinfónica de Puebla y violinista del Cuarteto Lener, junto con Joseph Smilovitz, Sandor Roth e Imre Hartman. Casado con la pianista Carmen Castillo Betancourt, formó con ella un dueto musical. Hizo la transcripción para violín y piano de los 24 *Caprichos* de Paganini, escritos originalmente sólo para violín. Autor de obras sinfónicas y de cámara y de las canciones *Chapultepec*, *Juventud* y *Mi primer amor* (que compuso a los 12 años de edad).

RUVINSKIS, MIRIAM ◆ n. en el DF (1951). Escritora. Licenciada en letras hispanoamericanas por la UNAM. Fue guionista y coordinadora de noticieros del Canal 13 de televisión; directora editorial de *Cuadernos de Psicoanálisis* y directora del Instituto Cultural Mexicano-Israelí. Colaboró en el suplemento *Diorama de la Cultura* de *Excélsior*. Vive en Estados Unidos. Autora de ensayo: *Persecución judía en México* (1971); cuento: *La sala de partos verdes* (1971) , *La bóveda de los címbalos* (cuento y poesía, 1982), *El cuerpo del disfraz* (1983) y *El último pétalo* (1989); poesía: *Desde el polvo de un espejo* (1973); y novela: *El aullido crepitante de una dama nostálgica* (1985).

Ruvinskis, Wolf ◆ n. en Letonia (1921-1999). Vivió 25 años en Argentina. Fue campeón de lucha grecorromana (1938) y luchador profesional desde 1942. Jugó en los equipos de futbol Millonarios de Bogotá (1944) e Independiente de Santa Fe. Llegó a México en 1946 como luchador profesional, estudió actuación con Seki Sano y en 1948 se inició profesionalmente en la escena. Obtuvo la nacionalidad mexicana en 1952. Fue protagonista en la obra *Un tranvía llamado deseo* y actuó después en *La doma de la fiera, El estupendo cornudo, Ana Cristhy, Panorama desde el puente* y *Camino a Roma*. Para el cine hizo las películas *La isla de los hombres solos, La bestia magnífica, Pepe el Toro, El medallón del 13, Los tigres del ring, A media luz los tres* y *Los pistoleros famosos*, entre otras. Ha sido también cantante, prestidigitador y restaurantero. Medalla Virginia Fábregas de la ANDA por 25 años de actuación (1986). Premio como mejor actor de 1988 de la Unión de Críticos y Cronistas de Teatro.

Ruy Sánchez, Alberto ◆ n. en el DF (1951). Su segundo apellido es Lacy. Escritor. Licenciado en ciencias y técnicas de la información por la UIA: licenciado en filosofía, maestro en medios audiovisuales y doctor en ciencias de la información y documentación por la Universidad de París. Doctor en letras por la Escuela de Altos Estudios de Francia. Fue investigador en el área de cultura y poder bajo la dirección de Gilles Deleuze y Francois Chatelet. Asistió a los talleres literarios de Huberto Batis y Juan García Ponce. Ha escrito para publicaciones literarias. Fue secretario de redacción de *Vuelta* (1985-86) y dirige *Artes de México* (1988-). Autor de ensayo: *Mitología de un cine en crisis* (1981), *Al filo de las hojas* (1989), *Una introducción a Octavio Paz* (1990, premio José Fuentes Mares 1991), *Tristeza de la verdad. André Gide regresa de Rusia* (1991), *Con la literatura en el cuerpo* (1995), *Cuatro escritores rituales* (1996), *Diálogos con mis fantasmas* (1997) y *Aventuras de la mirada* (1999); novela: *Los nombres del aire* (1987, Premio Xavier Villaurrutia) y *En los labios del agua* (1996); autobiografía: *De cuerpo entero* (1992); poesía: *La inaccesible* (1990); y cuento: *Los demonios de la lengua* (1987) y *Cuentos de Mogador* (1994). Primer lugar en el concurso de cuento de la UIA con *La oca loca localizada* (1973). Ha sido becario de la Fundación Guggenheim (1988) y del CNCA (1990), así como miembro del SNCA (1993-).

Ruz Lhuillier, Alberto ◆ n. en Francia y m. en Canadá (1906-1979). Estudió en la Escuela Comercial de París (1921-23) y en la Universidad de La Habana (1933-34). Llegó a México en 1936. Se tituló como arqueólogo por la ENAH (1942). Maestro (1945) y doctor (1965) en arqueología por la UNAM. Fue jefe de la Zona Maya (1949-58), director de exploraciones arqueológicas en Campeche, Yucatán y Palenque (1943-58), arqueólogo del INAH, profesor y director del Centro de Estudios Mayas de la UNAM y director del Museo Nacional de Antropología (1977-79). En 1952 descubrió la tumba del Templo de las Inscripciones de Palenque, lo que revolucionó los conocimientos en torno a las pirámides americanas. Coautor de *Cuarenta siglos de plástica mexicana* (1969). Autor de *Campeche en la arqueología maya* (1945), *Guía arqueológica de Tula* (1945), *Guía oficial de Chichén- Itzá* (1955), *Guía oficial de Uxmal* (1956), *La civilización de los antiguos mayas* (1957), *Guía oficial de Palenque* (1959), *Guía oficial de Tulum* (1959), *Los mayas* (1964), *Costumbres funerales de los antiguos mayas* (1968), *La costa de Campeche en los tiempos prehispánicos* (1969), *El Templo de las Inscripciones. Palenque* (1973), *Los mayas de las tierras bajas* (1974) y *La tumba de Palenque* (1974). Hizo los guiones para los documentales *Palenque* (1972) y *Piedras serán la comida* (1973). Perteneció a la Sociedad Mexicana de Antropología, a la Societé des Américanistes y a la Society of American Archeology.

Ruz Menéndez, Rodolfo ◆ n. en Mérida, Yuc. (1928). Licenciado en derecho por la Universidad de Yucatán (1951). Ha sido jefe del Departamento de Bibliotecas de la Universidad de Yucatán y director de la Biblioteca Central Universitaria (1956-78). Fundador de las clases de métodos y técnicas de investigación socioeconómica (1964) y derecho obrero (1965) así como secretario fundador de los cursos de filología maya (1959) y de las escuelas de Antropología (1965) y Psicología (1971) de la Universidad de Yucatán. Colabora en publicaciones académicas. Autor de *Mérida, bosquejo biográfico de una ciudad* (1957, quinta edición en 1986), *En memoria de Wolfang Cordan* (1966), *Publicaciones periódicas yucatecas de la Hemeroteca Universitaria* (1966), *Aportaciones para el estudio de la historia del Instituto Literario de Yucatán* (1967), *La Facultad de Química de la Universidad de Yucatán* (1968), *La primera emigración cubana a Yucatán* (1969), *La emancipación de los esclavos en Yucatán* (1970), *El cervantismo en Yucatán* (1971), *Por los viejos caminos del Mayab* (1973), *Ensayos históricos y literarios* (1976), *Ensayos yucatanenses* (1976), *Verde teoría* (1977), *Trilogía de ensueño* (1978), *Sonetos de amor y desesperanza* (1983) y *Ultima punta y otros sonetos* (1987). Secretario perpetuo de la Academia Yucateca de Historia y Genealogía Francisco de Montejo (1966-), presidente de la Asociación Yucateca de Bibliotecarios y secretario fundador (1971) de la Corresponsalía del Seminario de Cultura Mexicana. Recibió la Medalla Yucatán (1973).

Colección Guillermo Vázquez Villalobos

Wolf Ruvinskis en *Caballero a la medida*, película de Miguel M. Delgado

Foto: Rogelio Cuéllar

Alberto Ruy Sánchez

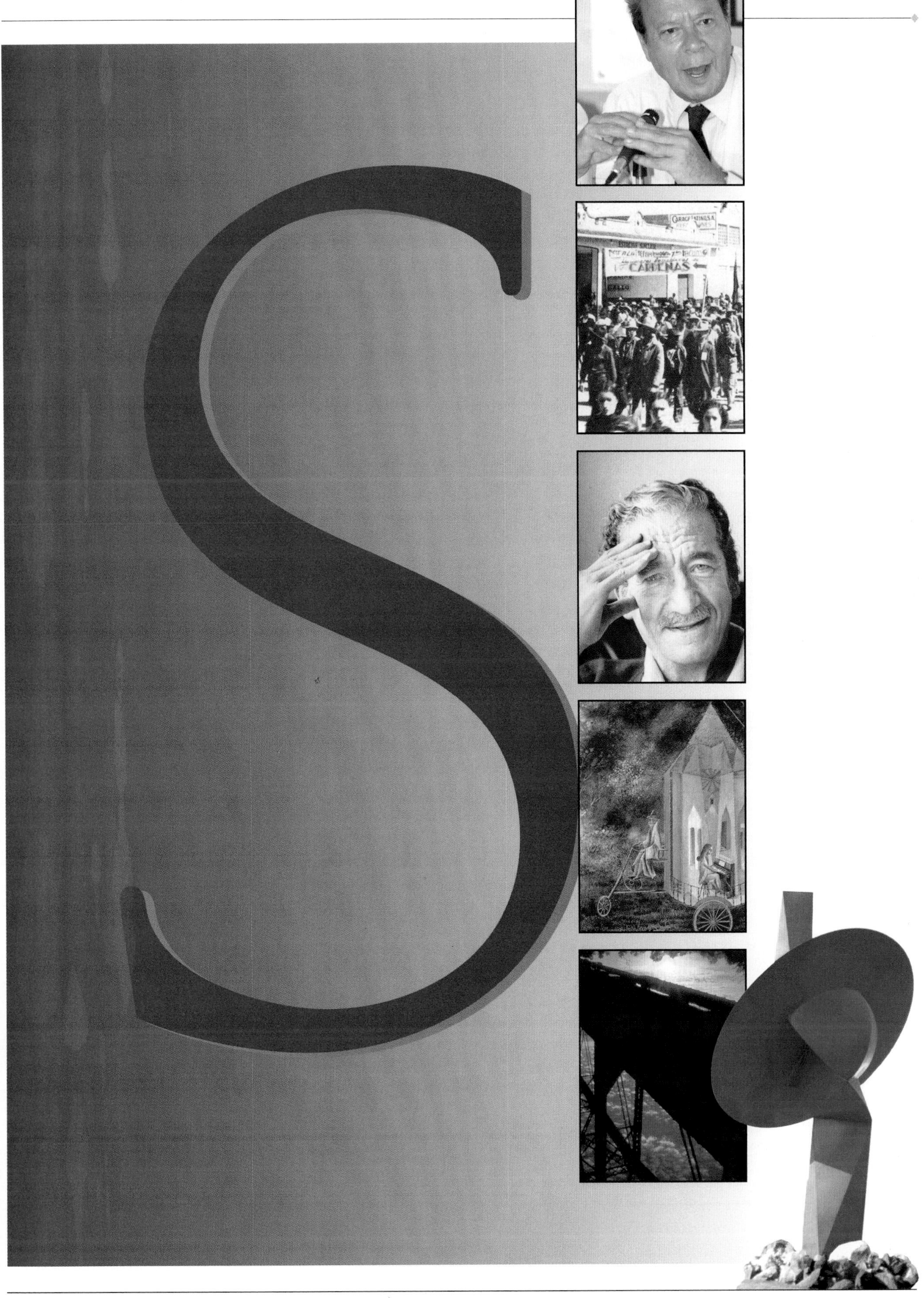

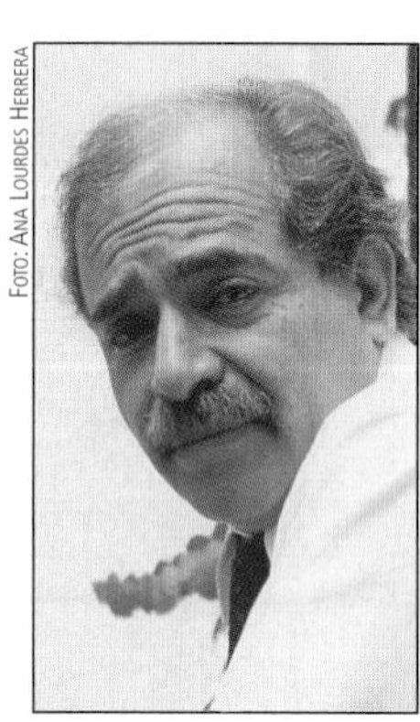
FOTO: ANA LOURDES HERRERA

Miguel Sabido

SAAL SCHIMRA, FRIDA ◆ n. en Argentina y m. en el DF (1935-1998). Psicóloga y escritora. Estudió en la Universidad de Buenos Aires. Se exilió en México en 1974. Se le conoció como *Talila*. De su aprendizaje sobre Jacques Lacan, en su país natal escribió *Psicología, ideología y ciencia* (1975). Autora de ensayos en las recopilaciones de los coloquios de la Fundación Mexicana de Psicoanálisis, de la cual fue fundadora (1980), así como del Centro de Investigaciones y Estudios Psicoanalíticos (1982). Colaboadora de *La Jornada*. Coautora de *El lenguaje y el inconsciente freudiano* (1982), *La re-flexión de los conceptos de Freud en la obra de Lacan* (1983), *Lecturas de Lacan* (1989), *La bella (in)diferencia* (1991), *Constancias del psicoanálisis* (1996), *El laberinto de las estructuras* (1997) y *Las suplencias del Nombre-del-Padre* (1998). Fue profesora en varias universidades. Algunos de sus escritos se antologaron en *Palabras de un analista* (1998).

SAAVEDRA, AURORA MARYA ◆ n. en el DF (1930). Escritora. Realizó estudios en la Universidad Femenina de México y en la de California en Los Ángeles. Ha sido directora de las secciones culturales de *El Universal Gráfico* (1968 y 74), *Negocios y Bancos* (1972) y *Crónica Ilustrada*, así como promotora de la primera Semana Internacional de Artes Plásticas auspiciada por la UNESCO (1977). Ha sido colaboradora de *Visión, Comunidad Conacyt, Cuadernos Americanos, Mundo, Art, Le Journal Francaise, Tribuna Israelita, Excélsior* (1967-69 y 80-86), *El Nacional* (1967-70) y *El Día* (1973-75), así como de la *Enciclopedia de México*. En 1988 tradujo *Lector de cenizas*, del poeta yugoslavo Aco Sopob. Autora de *Entrevista a Venus* (relatos, 1969), *Memoria de la SIAP en México* (1979), *Las rosas y los días* (1980, en colaboración), *Ni sin tiempo ni dolor* (poemas ilustrados por Juan Calderón, 1980), *Juegos de otoño* (poemas ilustrados por Froylán Ojeda, 1983), *El bengalí* (novela, 1985), *Antología de la poesía macedonia* (1986), *Cinco siglos de poesía en el valle de México* (1986), *Pan y sueño* (1988) y *Las divinas mutantes* (antología, 1996). Fue premiada en el XV Encuentro de Traductores Literarios de Tétovo, Yugoslavia (1987).

SAAVEDRA, HÉCTOR ◆ n. en el DF (1956). Músico. Estudió guitarra con el compositor Juan Helguera, en el Conservatorio Nacional y la Escuela Superior de Música. Tomó cursos de perfeccionamiento con Jesús Ortega en Cuba, Robert Guthrie en Estados Unidos, Javier Hinojosa en México y Óscar Ghiglia en Italia. Ha ofrecido conciertos en México y el extranjero y ha grabado varios programas de la serie *La guitarra en el mundo*, del Canal 11. En 1980 revisó parte de su repertorio con Narciso Yepes. En 1986 participó como miembro activo en el seminario de guitarra impartido por Leo Brouwer, en La Habana, durante el tercer Festival de Guitarra. Ganó el primer Concurso Nacional de Guitarra de la UAM y el Fonapas (1982).

SAAVEDRA, MANUEL ◆ n. en Sultepec, Edo. de Méx., y m. en la ciudad de México (?-1893). Diputado al Congreso Constituyente de 1856-57. Fue magistrado de la Suprema Corte de Justicia (1860-61 y 1871-93) y secretario de Gobernación (del 28 de octubre de 1869 al 9 de marzo de 1871) en el gabinete de Benito Juárez.

SAAVEDRA M., ALFREDO ◆ n. y m. en el DF (1893-1973). Médico. Profesor de instituciones de educación superior. Colaboró en *Medicina, Pasteur, Gaceta Médica de México* y *Eugenesia*. Autor de *Eugenesia y medicina social* (1934), *Apuntes de enfermería* (1938), *Nociones de biología* (1939), *Una lección de trabajo social* (1945), *Manual de trabajo social* (1958), *Ludoterapia* (1965), *Un siglo de lucha antivenérea* (1966), *Nuevo libro de trabajo social* (1967), *México en la educación sexual* (1967), *Historia de la puericultura* (1968), *Vocabulario de trabajo social* (1968) y *Servir, principios de trabajo social* (1970). Fundador de la Sociedad Mexicana de Eugenesia (1931).

SABANA, DE LA ◆ Río de Guerrero que nace en la sierra de la Providencia o de la Brea, en el sur del estado. Corre de norte a sur, recibe las aguas del río Coyuca al oeste de Xaltianguis y recorre 105 kilómetros hasta desembocar en la porción occidental de la laguna Papagayo, entre el puerto de Acapulco y la laguna Tres Palos.

SABANILLA ◆ Municipio de Chiapas situado en el norte del estado, en los límites con Tabasco, al norte de San Cristóbal de Las Casas y al suroeste de Palenque. Superficie: 171.4 km². Habitantes: 19,915, de los cuales 4,297 forman la población económicamente activa. Hablan alguna lengua indígena 11,675 personas mayores de cinco años (chol 10,110, tzotzil 1,565). Indígenas monolingües: 2,998.

SABIDO, MIGUEL ◆ n. en el DF (1937). Director, productor y adaptador de teatro y televisión. En la preparatoria participó en el Teatro de Coapa (1957). Estudió derecho y letras modernas en la UNAM. Tomó cursos con Salvador Novo y Luisa Josefina Hernández. Su primera puesta en escena fueron adaptaciones de cuentos de *El llano en llamas*, realizadas por el propio Juan Rulfo y presentadas en el teatro del Caballito. Fundó el Teatro Pedagógico, dependiente de la Subsecretaría de Asuntos Culturales de la UNESCO. Ha dirigido, además, las puestas en escena de *Las danzas de la muerte, El Sr. Arenque de Courtelinc, Don Juan de Figuereido* (1962), *El gran teatro del mundo* (1964), *La pastorela de Metepec* (1964), *Voces en el templo* (1965), *El divino Narciso* (1965), *Viento en la Pinacoteca virreinal* (1967), *Entremeses, La celestina* (1969, presentada en México y Colombia, en donde obtuvo el Premio Internacional Camilo Torres), *Los sueños* (1972) y *El avaro* (1976). Produjo *La pastorela* de Sor Juana (1980), *El carnaval de Huejotzingo* y *La pasión y muerte de Jesucristo* (1983). Ha dirigido series de televisión. Fue director del Canal 9 de Televisa y actualmente es vicepresidente del Departamento de Evaluación e Investigación de dicha empresa. Autor del poemario *Malas palabras* (1995); de los guiones de las telenovelas de corte histórico *La tormenta, Los caudillos, La Constitución* y *El carruaje*; así como de las obras de teatro *Falsa crónica de Juana la Loca* (1985, premio de la Agrupación de Periodistas Teatrales), *Pastorela de la fraternidad* (1985) y *Las mujeres de Troya* (1988). Fue premiado por la puesta de *Las tentaciones de María Egipciaca*. Presidente de la Asociación Teatro Popular Mexicano. Becario del Centro Mexicano de Escritores (1961-62).

Sabina, María ◆ ☛ *María Sabina.*

Sabinas ◆ Municipio de Coahuila situado en el noreste del estado, al este de Múzquiz y al norte de Monclova. Superficie: 2,345.2 km². Habitantes: 51,129, de los cuales 14,400 forman la población económicamente activa. Hablan alguna lengua indígena 67 personas mayores de cinco años (náhuatl 34). Tiene yacimientos de carbón, explotados sobre todo en las minas de Cloete y Agujitas. El 28 de julio de 1920 se firmaron aquí los Convenios de Sabinas, por los que Pancho Villa depuso definitivamente las armas.

Sabinas ◆ Río de Coahuila. Nace en la vertiente sudoriental de las serranías del Burro, en el noreste del estado. Corre de noroeste a sureste a través del lomerío de Peyotes, donde recibe numerosos afluentes; pasa por Nueva Rosita, Cloete y Sabinas y desagua en la presa Don Martín, cerca de los límites con Nuevo León, donde se une al río Salado de los Nadadores para formar el río Salado, de Nuevo León.

Sabinas Hidalgo ◆ Municipio de Nuevo León situado en el norte del estado, al norte de Monterrey y contiguo a Lampazos. Superficie: 1,661.6 km². Habitantes: 31,521, de los cuales 9,539 forman la población económicamente activa. Hablan alguna lengua indígena once personas mayores de cinco años. El 25 de junio se celebran bailes populares para conmemorar la fundación de la cabecera, Ciudad Sabinas Hidalgo; a cuatro kilómetros de ésta se encuentra el parque recreativo Ojo de Agua, laguna natural en la que se puede practicar la pesca. El templo de San José conserva el único retablo churrigueresco (tallado en madera en el siglo XVIII) del estado de Nuevo León.

Sabinas Hidalgo ◆ Río de Nuevo León. Nace al sur de la sierra de Lampazos, en el norte del estado, de la confluencia de los arroyos Huizache y Álamos. Corre de oeste a este, al sur de la sierra de las Iguanas, por el cañon de Sabinas; cruza la cabecera del municipio de Sabinas Hidalgo, tuerce al noreste y se prolonga como límite entre los estados de Nuevo León y Tamaulipas hasta desembocar en el río Salado.

Sabines, Jaime ◆ n. en Tuxtla Gutiérrez, Chis., y m. en el DF (1926-1999). Poeta. Cursó dos años de la carrera de medicina, la licenciatura en lengua y literatura españolas (1949) y estudios de posgrado en la UNAM. Se dedicó a la actividad comercial en Chiapas (1952-59). En 1965 formó parte del jurado del premio Casa de las Américas. Diputado federal por Chiapas (1976-79) y por el DF (1988-91), renunció al segundo cargo a la mitad del periodo. Autor de poesía: *Horal* (1950), *La señal* (1951), *Adán y Eva* (1952), *Tarumba* (1956), *Diario semanario y poemas en prosa* (1961), *Poemas sueltos* (1962), *Yuria* (1967), *Maltiempo* (1972), *Algo sobre la muerte del mayor Sabines* (1973), *Otros poemas sueltos* (1973-77), *Nuevo recuento de poemas* (1977), *Uno es el poeta. Sabines frente a sus críticos* (1986), *La poesía en el corazón del hombre, Jaime Sabines en sus sesenta años* (1987, material de homenaje UNAM/INBA), *Uno es el hombre* (1989, con ilustraciones de José Luis Cuevas y fotos de Daisy Asher) y *Nuevo recuento de poemas (1950-1991)* (1991). Grabó un disco para la serie Voz Viva de México, de la UNAM. Recibió los premios Chiapas (1959), Xavier Villaurrutia (1972), Elías Sourasky de Letras (1982), Nacional de Ciencias y Artes (1983), Mazatlán de Literatura (1996) y México de Literatura (1998); las preseas Juchimán de Plata en Letras y Artes (1986), Ciudad de México (1991) y la Medalla Belisario Domínguez (1994). Fue becario del Centro Mexicano de Escritores (1964-65). En 1993 fue nombrado creador emérito del SNCA.

Sabines Gutiérrez, Juan ◆ n. en el DF y m. en Tuxtla Gutiérrez, Chis. (1922-1987). Hermano del anterior. Tuvo varios negocios y ocupó la presidencia de la Cámara Nacional de Comercio de Tuxtla Gutiérrez. Miembro del PRI, del que fue presidente del Comité Directivo Estatal de Chiapas. Fue presidente municipal de Tuxtla Gutiérrez, tres veces diputado federal (1952-55, 1958-61 y 1976-79), senador de la República (1970-76) y gobernador sustituto de Chiapas (1979-82).

Foto: Rogelio Cuéllar

Jaime Sabines

Saborit, Antonio ◆ n. en Torreón, Coah. (1957). Estudió literatura e historia en la UNAM. Fue miembro del consejo de redacción de *La Cultura en México*. Ha colaborado en *Nexos, Sábado, La Jornada Semanal, Crónica* y otros medios impresos. Director de Estudios Históricos del INAH. Autor de *Los doblados de Tomochic* (1994) y *Una mujer sin país. Las cartas de Tina Modotti a Edward Weston (1921-31)*.

Sabre Marroquín, José ◆ n. en SLP y m. en el DF. (1910-1995). Músico. Escribió al menos 150 canciones populares, entre las que destacan *Así llegaste*, *Muchachita tropical*, *Vaivén*, *Gris*, *Así fue*. Compuso varias piezas de música de concierto. El violinista Henryk Syeryng divulgó sus composiciones por todo el mundo.

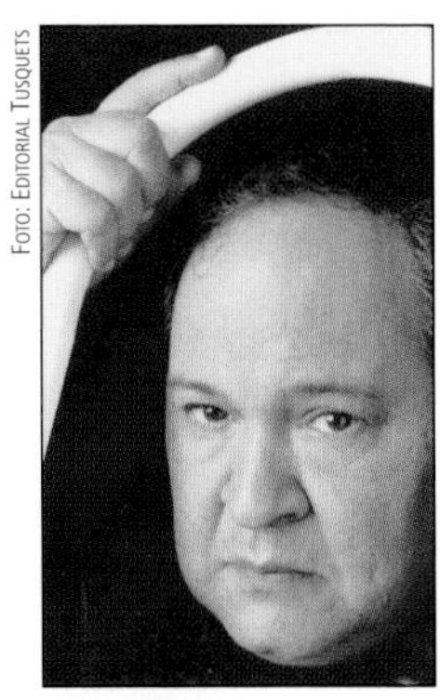

Foto: Editorial Tusquets

Daniel Sada

Sacalum ◆ Municipio de Yucatán situado al sur de Mérida y contiguo a Ticul. Superficie: 205.66 km². Habitantes: 4,009, de los cuales 838 forman la población económicamente activa. Hablan maya 2,790 personas mayores de cinco años. Indígenas monolingües: 84.

Sacramento ◆ Municipio de Coahuila situado en la región central del estado, al oeste de Monclova y contiguo a Cuatrociénegas. Superficie: 168.9 km². Habitantes: 1,995, de los cuales 613 forman la población económicamente activa.

Sacrificios ◆ Bahía de Oaxaca situada en el golfo de Tehuantepec, 16 kilómetros al noreste de Huatulco. Se halla rodeada de rocas, es estrecha y de difícil acceso; 26 kilómetros mar adentro hay una peña blanca que indica la entrada a la bahía, a la que sólo pueden acceder embarcaciones de poco calado.

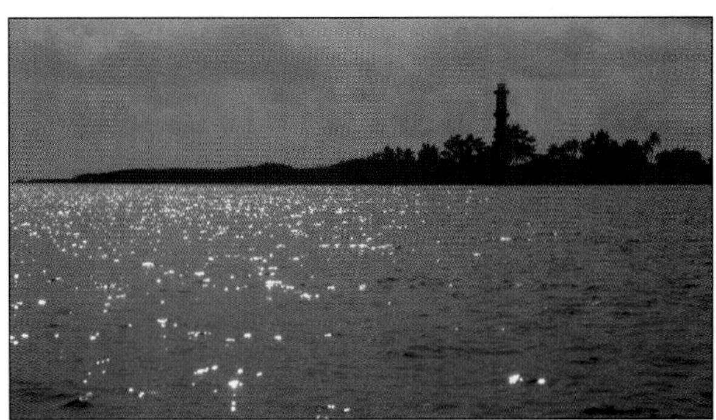

Isla Sacrificios

Sacrificios ◆ Isla de Veracruz situada cinco kilómetros al sureste del puerto jarocho. Hay en ella un faro y su fondeadero protege de los vientos dominantes.

Concepción Sada

Sacristán Colás, Antonio ◆ n. en España y m. en el DF (1902-1986). Doctor en derecho por la Universidad Central de Madrid, de la que fue profesor (1931), así como de la Universidad de Santiago de Compostela. En España fue diputado a las Cortes Constituyentes (1931), director general de Aduanas, director general de Obras Hidráulicas, secretario general del Consejo Nacional Bancario y secretario general del Partido Nacional Republicano. Durante la guerra civil fue director del Tesoro y subsecretario de Hacienda. Llegó a México en 1939 como refugiado político. Participó en la Comisión Redactora del Proyecto de Ley de Instituciones de Crédito, promulgada en 1941 y fue director fundador de la Sociedad Mexicana de Crédito Industrial (Somex), presidente del Centro de Investigación y Docencia Económica y profesor de la UNAM (1939-86), del IPN y de la Universidad Anáhuac. De 1977 hasta su muerte dirigió el Centro Interamericano de Documentación y Análisis de México. Colaborador de *El Heraldo* y *Excélsior*. Autor de *Principios esenciales del crecimiento económico* (1973), *Teoría monetaria* (1979), *Inflación, desempleo y desequilibrio comercial externo* (1982) y *Keynes ante la crisis mundial de los años ochenta* (1985). Maestro emérito de la UNAM.

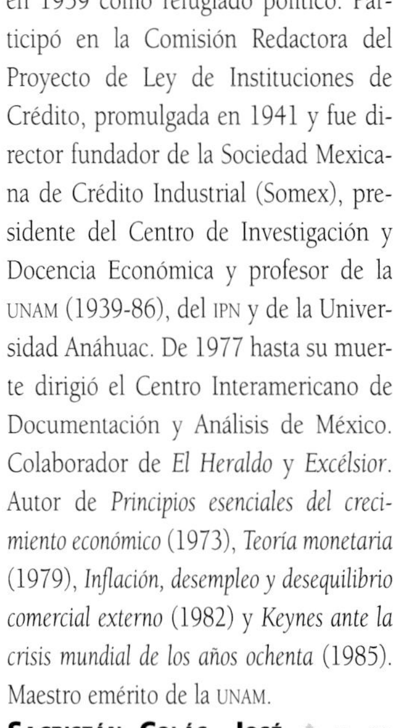

Sacristán Colás, José ◆ n. en España (1918). Economista por la UNAM. Participó en la guerra civil española de lado de la República y fue enviado a un campo de concentración en Francia. Llegó a México en 1939. Tuvo varios empleos antes de iniciar sus estudios superiores. Ha sido gerente general de Aceros Esmaltados S.A. (Acros), director general de Manufacturera Corpomex Kelvinator y tesorero de la misma empresa. Fue miembro de la Asociación de Jóvenes Patriotas Españoles en el Exilio.

Sacristán Roy, Antonio ◆ n. en Francia (1938). Hijo de Antonio Sacristán Colás. Maestro en ingeniería química por el Instituto Tecnológico de Massachusetts (19-61). Profesor del IPN (1963-67), del Instituto Tecnológico Regional de Ciudad Madero (1970-71) y de la UIA (1973-79). Ha sido ingeniero de proceso en Sosa Texcoco (1961-63), ingeniero en Du Pont (1963-79), director técnico de Empresas Lanzagorta (1979-81), director de la División Petroquímica de Fisomex (1981-83) y coordinador de marcadotecnia y planeación comercial e industrial de Pemex (1983-87). Miembro del American Institute of Chemical Engineers y presidente de la sección México-Centro del Instituto Mexicano de Ingenieros Químicos (1981-82).

Sada, Concepción ◆ n. en Saltillo, Coah., y m. en el DF (1899-1981). Escritora. Utilizó el pseudónimo de *Diana Compecson*. Participó en el movimiento de la Comedia Mexicana (1936), fue jefa de la sección de teatro de la Dirección General de Educación Extraescolar y Estética (1942) y fundadora de la Escuela de Arte Teatral del INBA. Organizadora del teatro infantil del INBA y traductora y adaptadora de varias obras de teatro para niños. Formó parte del Consejo Técnico y Cultural de Espectáculos de la Ciudad de México. Autora de las obras de teatro *El tercer personaje* (1935), *La hora del festín* (1936), *Un mundo para mí* (1937), *Como yo te soñaba* (1937), *En silencio* (1941), el guión de cine *Así era el amor* y las obras infantiles *Marujita* y *Cri-Crí, rey del bosque esmeralda*.

Sada, Daniel ◆ n. en el DF (1953). Escritor. Es licenciado en periodismo por la Escuela Carlos Septién García. Fue corrector de estilo en la UAM. Ha sido maestro de talleres literarios y cursos de literatura en diversas instituciones. Ha colaborado en *Diorama de la Cultura*, suplemento de *Excélsior*, *La Gaceta del FCE*, *Revista de la Universidad*, *La semana de Bellas Artes*, *El País*, *Proceso*, *Vuelta*, *Sábado*, suplemento de *unomásuno* y otras publicaciones. Coautor *de Los siete pecados capitales* (1989). Autor de poesía: *Los lugares* (1978); novela: *Lampa vida* (1980), *Albedrío* (1989), *Una de dos* (1994), *El límite* (1996) y *Porque parece mentira la verdad nunca se sabe* (1999); ensayo: *El cuento está en no creérselo* (1985) y cuento: *Un rato* (1984), *Juguete de nadie y otras historias* (1985), *Tres historias* (1990), *Registro de causantes* (1992, Premio Xavier Villaurrutia 1993) y *Antología presentida* (1993). Ha recibido las becas del Centro Mexicano de Escritores (1978-79), INBA-Fonapas (1980-81) y Fonca (1992-93). Miembro del SNCA desde 1994.

Sada y García, Luis G. ◆ n. en Saltillo, Coah., y m. en Monterrey, NL (1884-1941). Se graduó como maestro cervecero en Wall Hennius, EUA. Perteneció al consejo directivo de la Cervecería Cuauhtémoc, donde trabajó. Formó parte de los consejos de administración de las empresas Valores Industriales, Vidriera de Monterrey, Compañía General de Aceptaciones, Troqueles y Esmaltes, Banco Capitalizador de Monterrey, Seguros Monterrey y Técnica Industrial. Promotor y primer presidente de la Confederación Patronal de la República Mexicana (1929).

Sada y Muguerza, Francisco G. ◆ n. y m. en Monterrey, NL (1856-1945). Padre del anterior. Se dedicó a diversos negocios agrícolas y ganaderos en Tamaulipas, Chihuahua y Coahuila (1880-90). En 1894 fue nombrado gerente general de la Cervecería Cuauhtémoc.

Sada Treviño, Roberto G. ◆ n. en Monterrey, NL, y m. en Cancún, QR (1918-1972). Ingeniero en cerámica por la universidad de Texas A & M. En 1949 fue director general de Keramos y gerente general de Vidriera Monterrey. Presidente de las sociedades anónimas Vidrio Plano de Monterrey, Vidrio Plano de México y Fraccionadora las Flores. Fue ejecutivo y consejero de numerosas empresas financieras e industriales. Presidió la Cámara de la Industria de la Transformación de Nuevo León.

Saemisch, Ernesto ◆ n. en Alemania y m. ¿en el Estado de México? (1902-1984). Pintor y periodista radicado en México desde 1963. En su juventud fue campesino, marinero, amigo de Einstein y Dohr, y estudiante de la Bauhaus (bajo la tutela de Klee, Gropius y Feininger), en la cual se integró al expresionismo alemán. En sus últimos años trabajó con un grupo de artistas jóvenes de Tepito. Autor de más de 3,000 piezas, bocetos, dibujos, pinturas, grabados y *collages*, algunos de los cuales reunieron su viuda, Gertrudis Zenzes, y los pintores Arnold Belkin y Vlady, para exponerlos en México y Alemania (1985-86). Sus obras aún se exponen en muestras itinerantes como *El orden íntimo de las cosas*(1997-98) y pertenecen a museos, como La Casa del Lago y el Museo Carrillo Gil.

Sáenz, Josué ◆ n. en la ciudad de México (1915). Licenciado en economía por la UNAM (1940), de la que ha sido profesor (1941-66) así como del ITAM y del Centro de Estudios Monetarios Latinoamericanos (1948-60). Director general de Estadística (1942-46) y director general de Crédito de la SHCP (1946-47); director fundador de Bonos del Ahorro Nacional (1948-52); consejero económico del Banco de México; delegado a las reuniones constitutivas de la FAO, del Banco Mundial y de la Conferencia de las Naciones Unidas sobre Comercio y Desarrollo. Representó a México en las conferencias interamericanas de Chapultepec (1945) y Rio de Janeiro (1947). Fue el encargado de controlar el flujo legal de braceros hacia Estados Unidos durante la segunda guerra mundial. Ha colaborado en las revistas *Investigación Económica, El Trimestre Económico, Revista de Economía* y *Vuelta*. Autor de *La nueva ceguera* (1999). Presidente fundador de la Federación Mexicana de Tenis (1950-52) y del Núcleo Radio Mil (1952). Presidente del Comité Olímpico Mexicano (1966-68). Instaló una fábrica de radiorreceptores de frecuencia modulada y fundó la primera emisora que transmitió en esa frecuencia en el país. Miembro del Consejo Directivo de la Federación Internacional de Planificación Familiar y de su filial en México.

Sáenz, Juan de ◆ ¿n. y m. en México? (?-?). Pintor activo a fines del siglo XVIII y principios del XIX. Fue alumno de Jimeno y su colaborador en la decoración de la cúpula de la Catedral Metropolitana (1810). Hay obras suyas en el Museo de Pintura de Zacatecas, en el Templo de la Soledad de la ciudad de México, en el Santuario de Tepalcingo y en colecciones particulares.

Sáenz Arriaga, Joaquín ◆ n. en Morelia, Mich., y m. en el DF (1899-1976). Jesuita. Fue ordenado sacerdote en 1930. Doctor en filosofía, teología y derecho. Fue director de las Congregaciones Marianas. En 1952 fue expulsado de la Compañía de Jesús por objetar las normas del Concilio Vaticano II. Autor de *La nueva iglesia montiniana*, obra en la que criticó al líder espiritual de los católicos.

Sáenz Arroyo, José ◆ n. en Morelia, Mich., y m. en el DF (1917-1989). Licenciado por la Escuela Libre de Derecho (1940). Miembro del PRI. Fue abogado de la Junta de Administración y Vigilancia de Propiedad Extranjera (1943-48), jefe de la Oficina de Bienes del Enemigo (1948-52), jefe del Departamento de Bancos, Moneda e Inversiones (1951-58) y director general de Crédito de la SHCP (1959-65); director general del Banco Nacional Agropecuario (1965-70); presidente de la Comisión Nacional Bancaria y de Seguros (1970-76); asesor jurídico externo de diversas dependencias federales (1976-82) y director general de asuntos jurídicos de la Presidencia de la República (1982-88). Miembro de la Academia de Derecho Bursátil.

Sáenz de la Calzada, Carlos ◆ n. en España (1917). Llegó a México en 1939. Estudió geografía en la UNAM y fue uno de los fundadores de la rama de geografía médica en el país. Profesor de la UNAM y director técnico del Observatorio Meteorológico. Autor de "Educación y pedagogía", en *El exilio español de 1939; Los fundamentos de la geografía médica* (1956), *La geografía médica en México a través de la historia* (1958), *Ciencias y humanidades en la enseñanza media* (1963), *Si vis Pacem para Pacen. Sociología de la educación* (1964), *Balnearios de México* (1969), *La tierra, hogar del hombre* (1975), *Hidrología médica general y del estado de Michoacán* (1974) y *Geografía general* (1977).

Josué Sáenz

Sáenz de la Calzada Gorostiza, Arturo ◆ n. en España (1907). Estudió arquitectura en Madrid, vivió en la Residencia de Estudiantes y, durante la República, fue vocal de la Junta Constructora de la Ciudad Universitaria como representante de la Federación Universitaria Escolar. Presidente de la Unión Federal de Estudiantes Hispanos (1931-32), miembro fundador de "La Barraca", ganó en colaboración el primer premio en el Concurso Nacional de Arquitectura (1935). Llegó exiliado a México en 1939. Trabajó en la empresa constructora Vías y Obras, fundada por republicanos españoles, y construyó casas particulares, edificios de departamentos, laboratorios, la residencia del embajador de Suecia y la embajada de Noruega; colaboró en *Las Españas* y en la obra *El exilio español de 1939*, dirigida por José Luis Abellán, con el capítulo "La arquitectura en el exilio". Vivió en España desde 1975 hasta 1994 en que regresó a México.

Aarón Sáenz Garza

Sáenz Garza, Aarón ◆ n. en Monterrey, NL, y m. en el DF (1891-1983). Se tituló de abogado en la Escuela Nacional de Jurisprudencia. En 1913 se unió a la revolución constitucionalista y fue miembro del Estado Mayor de Álvaro Obregón, con quien hizo las campañas contra Huerta, Zapata, el convencionismo, Villa y Maytorena. Fue jefe del Estado Mayor de Manuel M. Diéguez y secretario particular de Obregón cuando éste fue secretario de Guerra y Marina (1916-17). General de división, diputado federal (1917-18), enviado extraordinario y ministro plenipotenciario en Brasil (1918), subsecretario y secretario de Relaciones Exteriores (del 14 al 26 de enero de 1921 y del 27 de septiembre de 1923 al 30 de noviembre de 1924); jefe de la segunda campaña presidencial de Obregón (1928) y gobernador de Nuevo León (1927-30). Miembro fundador e integrante del primer Comité Ejecutivo del Partido Nacional Revolucionario, del que fue el primer disidente al no obtener la candidatura presidencial de 1929. Poco después se *disciplinó* ante Calles y volvió al partido. Secretario de Educación Pública (del 5 de febrero al 8 de octubre de 1930) y de Industria, Comercio y Trabajo (del 8 de octubre de 1930 al 20 de enero de 1932), en el gabinete de Pascual Ortiz Rubio, así como jefe del Departamento del Distrito Federal (1932-35). En este cargo ordenó la pavimentación de numerosas calles de la capital del país. Empresario y socio de Plutarco Elías Calles en el ingenio El Mante. Como secretario de Industria, Comercio y Trabajo organizó a los dueños de ingenios (él mismo lo era) y constituyó con ellos Azúcar, S.A., que presidió. A partir de 1935, luego de que Lázaro Cárdenas expropiara el ingenio de El Mante para entregarlo a los cañeros, se retiró de la actividad política. Presidente de la Asociación Azucarera Nacional, del Banco Azucarero (del que fue fundador en 1932 y que en 1941 se convertiría en Banco de Industria y Comercio) y de la Asociación de Productores de Alcohol. En 1938 creó la Unión Nacional de Productores de Azúcar, que presidió aun después de que se convirtió en empresa del sector público. En el sexenio de Ávila Camacho estableció varios ingenios azucareros. Fundador de Finanzas Atlas (1936), Seguros Atlas (1941), Banco Inmobiliario Atlas (1944) y Financiera Atlas (1957). En 1977 se fusionaron varias de sus empresas en Banca Confía, cuyo consejo de administración presidió. Cofundador, asimismo, de la Compañía Mexicana de Aviación y de Aeronaves de México. Autor de *La política internacional del presidente Obregón* (1960) y *La política internacional de la Revolución* (1961).

Moisés Sáenz Garza

Sáenz Garza, Moisés ◆ n. en El Mezquital, municipio de Apodaca, NL, y m. en Perú (1888-1941). Hermano del anterior. Se tituló como profesor en la Escuela Normal de Jalapa. Doctor en ciencias y en filosofía por la Universidad de Columbia. Fue director de Educación en Guanajuato y en el Distrito Federal, dirigió la Escuela Nacional Preparatoria y la de Verano de la UNAM; fue profesor de la Escuela Nacional de Maestros, oficial mayor, subsecretario y secretario de Educación Pública (del 23 de agosto al 30 de noviembre de 1928) en el gabinete de Plutarco Elías Calles. En este cargo estableció bibliotecas ambulantes, creó el ciclo de secundaria, organizó las escuelas rurales y las misiones culturales. Como director de la Beneficencia Pública y del Instituto Indigenista Interamericano, creó un programa para la creación del Departamento de Asuntos Indígenas y para la protección legal del indio mexicano, presidio el Comité de Investigaciones Indígenas y organizó el primer Congreso Indigenista (1940, en Pátzcuaro). Ministro en Dinamarca y Ecuador y embajador en Perú. Autor de *Some Mexican Problems* (1926), *El sistema de escuelas rurales en México* (1927), *Sobre el indio peruano y su incorporación al medio nacional* (1933), *Sobre el indio ecuatoriano y su incorporación al medio nacional* (1933), *Carapan. Bosquejo de una experiencia* (1936), *México íntegro* (1939) y *Perú. Joyas, telas, cerámica* (1947).

Sáenz de Mañozca y Murillo, Juan de Santamaría ◆ n. en la ciudad de México y m. cerca de Puebla, Pue. (?-1675). Su nombre aparece también como Juan de Santo Matías. Estudió en el Colegio de San Ildefonso y obtuvo alguno de los "grados menores" (¿bachiller?) en la Real y Pontificia Universidad de México, donde en 1643 revalidó sus títulos de "licenciado y doctor" en cánones por la Universidad de San Marcos, en Lima. Desde ese año hasta 1661 fue inquisidor de la Nueva España. Obispo de Cuba (1661-67) y de Guatemala (1667-74), donde también se desempeñó como capitán general. Nombrado para gobernar la diócesis de Puebla, murió antes de asumir el cargo. Autor de *Estatutos y constituciones de la Universidad de San Carlos de Guatemala, erigida con autoridad apostólica a instancias del Católico Rey Felipe IV*.

Sáenz de Miera y Aguilar, Celeste ◆ n. en Michoacán (1965). Realizó estudios de música, historia del arte, piano, danza clásica del Medio Oriente, ballet, flamenco y folckore mexicano. Es autora de letra y música de más de 250 temas. En televisión, ha participado en programas en México, Estados Unidos, Europa y Medio Oriente. Publirrelacionista y periodista de diversos medios. Ha sido directora de Acción Femenil del Club de Periodistas, defensora de la sede del club, fundadora de *Voces del periodista* y de la Fundación Antonio Sáenz de Miera y Fieytal, la cual preside. Secretaria general del Club de Periodistas.

Sáenz de Miera y Fieytal, Antonio ◆ n. en Puebla y m. en el DF (1913-1999). Padre de la anterior. Periodista. Trabajó en las publicaciones *El diario de Puebla* (1934-38), *Bohemia* (1934-46), *Puro verso*, *Angelópolis*, *Puebla en marcha* (1938-40), *Diario ABC* (1941-42), *Hoy!* (1942-44), *Buró de Investigación Política* (1942-44), *Mexico City Herald* (1943-44), *Nosotros* (1944-46), *Crónica Ilustrada* (1946-82, director fundador), *Presente* (1947-49, fundador), *El Ciudadano* (1991-93), *Voces del Periodista* (1996, fundador). Creó la jefatura de Prensa de la SRH (la cual dirigió entre 1946 y 1958). Fue presidente de la Asociación Mexicana de Periodistas (1951-59), jefe de Prensa del Banjidal (1960-62), de la CFE (1974-76) y de la oficina de Información de la Presidencia (1976-82), asesor de Prensa del IMSS (1962-64), y de la Presidencia (1964-67), presidente del Club de Periodistas de México (1972-1999). Creó la Fundación que lleva su nombre (1996), impulsora de la Posada del Periodista y del Museo del Periodista.

Sáenz de Miera Santana, Luis Xavier ◆ n. en Puebla (¿?). Caricaturista. Firma como *Luis Xavier*. Comenzó a hacer cartones en *Excélsior* desde 1976. Ha participado en más de quince exposiciones colectivas e individuales en México y en el extranjero. Premio Ernesto García Cabral (1982). Mención Honorífica en el XVIII Certamen Nacional de Periodismo (1986). Premio Nacional de Periodismo (1987). En 1990 se inauguró la sala artística de la Asamblea de Representantes del DF con un montaje de sus caricaturas políticas.

Sáenz Ortiz, Liébano ◆ n. en Nuevo Casas Grandes, Chih. (1949). Licenciado en derecho por la UNAM, con estudios de posgrado en ciencias políticas y administración pública por la Universidad de Texas. Trabajó en el bufete jurídico de Arsenio Farell. Pertenece desde 1982 al PRI, en el que organizó reuniones del IEPES durante dos campañas presidenciales (1982 y 1988), fue secretario de información y propaganda del CEN (1993-94) y secretario particular del candidato a la Presidencia de la República Luis Donaldo Colosio (1994). Ha sido director de Azufrera Panamericana, director general del Patrimonio Inmobiliario Federal (1992 y oficial mayor de la Sedesol (1992-93). Secretario particular del presidente de la República (1994-).

Sagade Bugueiro, Mateo ◆ n. y m. en España (1605-1663). Doctor en cánones. Fue designado arzobispo de México en 1655, tomó posesión de la mitra el 8 de julio del año siguiente y fue consagrado por Pedro de Barrientos, obispo de Vizcaya, el día 25 del mismo mes. Muy pronto tuvo serios conflictos con el virrey Francisco Fernández de la Cueva, al que hacía sugerencias sobre la marcha de los negocios civiles y al que despectivamente llamaba "muchacho". El virrey, acusado a su vez de inmiscuirse en asuntos eclesiásticos, dijo de él, en una carta, que era en Nueva España "el hombre más duro, aferrado y firme en su dictamen." En 1659 los desaires entre la autoridad colonial y el dignatario eclesiástico fueron cada vez más notorios, hasta que sendas órdenes reales los obligaron a reprimir en público su mutua antipatía. En marzo de 1660 un soldado trató de asesinar al virrey dentro de la Catedral, y dos meses después, sin que aparentemente tuviera relación con lo anterior, llegó la orden de la Corona para que virrey y arzobispo volvieran a la península, lo que hizo Sagade en abril de 1661. En España fue presentado sucesivamente para las diócesis de Cádiz y León, que no llegó a ocupar, y en 1663 tomó posesión del obispado de Cartagena, días antes de morir. Sus restos se encuentran en la Catedral Metropolitana de la ciudad de México desde 1961.

Mateo Sagade Bugueiro

Foto: Rogelio Baeza

Liébano Sáenz Ortiz

Sagástegui, Marino ◆ n. en Perú (1938). Caricaturista. Firma como *Marino*. Estudió dibujo publicitario Ha sido caricaturista político de la revista *Extra* y de noticiarios televisivos en Perú (1958-62), así como fundador del periódico *Expreso*. Llegó a México en 1963. Ha sido caricaturista de *Caretas* y cartonista editorial de *Excélsior* (1963-). Sus trabajos han aparecido en *Saturday Evening Post*, *National Enquirer*, *National Review Saturday*, *Saturday*, *Evening Post*, *Asahi Shinbum*, *Look* y *Esquire*. Es coeditor de la revista *Rhumor*. Ilustró *La Constitución al alcance de los niños*. Autor de *El libro que faltaba*, *La política no sólo es cosa de risa*, *La caricatura no se devalúa ni se desliza*, *Caricaturas damnificadas*, *El tapado visto por Marino*, *La deuda e(x)terna* (1986), *El candidato de la crisis* (1988) y *La guerra, el humor y la paz* (1993). Miembro fundador de la So-

Marino Sagástegui

Cartón de Oswaldo Sagástegui publicado en *Excélsior* el 18 de noviembre de 1999

ciedad Mexicana de Caricaturistas. Premio Nacional de Periodismo (1975) y mención honorífica en el primer Salón del Humorismo, en Bordighera, Italia.

Sagástegui, Oswaldo ◆ n. en Perú (1936). Hermano del anterior. Caricaturista y pintor. Estudió en la Escuela de Bellas Artes de Lima. Vivió y trabajó en Francia, Italia y Estados Unidos. Llegó a México en 1968 y se incorporó a la casa *Excélsior* como cartonista. Está afiliado al Sindicato dé Cartonistas y Escritores de Nueva York, por lo que sus caricaturas políticas se distribuyen a diversas publicaciones del mundo. Premio Nacional de Periodismo (1984) y primer lugar en la Bienal de Dibujo del INBA (1986) con la obra *Amor a los animales*. En 1986 recibió un homenaje de la Sociedad de Cartonistas y Editorialistas de Estados Unidos y un año después montó una exposición en el Palacio Legislativo de San Lázaro.

Sagredo, Ramón ◆ n. en Real del Monte, Hgo., y m. en la ciudad de México (1834-1873). Pintor egresado de la Academia de San Carlos (1854-59), donde fue alumno de Pelegrín Clavé. Colaboró en la decoración de la cúpula de La Profesa. Al final de su vida se decepcionó de la pinturá e instaló un taller de fotografía. Se suicidó. Sus obras están en la Academia de San Carlos, el Museo Nacional de Artes Plásticas, el Museo de Querétaro y el Palacio Nacional. Autor de *El Bautista mostrando a dos apóstoles al Salvador* (1856), *Ismael en el desierto* (1857, segundo premio de una exposición en la Academia) *Los discípulos de Emaús* (1857), *La muerte de Sócrates* (1858), *Retrato de Vicente Guerrero* (1865, ejecutado por encargo de Maximiliano de Habsburgo y bajo la supervisión de Santiago Rebull) y los medallones del techo de las galerías de la antigua Academia de San Carlos.

Sahagún, Bernardino de ◆ n. en España y m. en la ciudad de México (¿1499?-1590). Cambió su apellido Ribeira por el nombre de la villa en la que nació. En 1516 interrumpió sus estudios en la Universidad de Salamanca para tomar el hábito de San Francisco. Llegó a la Nueva España en 1529. Residió en Tlalmanalco (1530-32), fue guardián del convento de Xochimilco y posiblemente su fundador (1535). Profesor del Colegio de Santa Cruz de Tlatelolco (1536-41) y lector en el convento anexo (1539). Recorrió como misionero el valle de Puebla (1540-45) y estuvo en los conventos de Tlatelolco (1545-50) y de Tula (1550-57). Fue definidor provincial (1552) y visitador de la custodia del Santo Evangelio, en Michoacán (1558). Se trasladó a Tepepulco (1558-60), nuevamente a Tlatelolco (1561-65), al convento Grande de San Francisco en la ciudad de México (1565-71), otra vez a Tlatelolco (1572-73) y a Tlalmanalco (1573-85). Fue por segunda vez definidor provincial (1585-89). Hacia 1547, mediante la aplicación de cuestionarios en náhuatl entre los ancianos de Tepepulco, Tlatelolco y la ciudad de México (llamados los *informantes de Sahagún*), empezó a recopilar, con el auxilio de los estudiantes del Colegio de la Santa Cruz de Tlatelolco, los materiales del libro *Historia general de las cosas de la Nueva España*, labor que interrumpió en 1570 por dificultades económicas, que lo obligaron a redactar una síntesis de la obra, misma que envió al Consejo de Indias, donde se perdió. Otro resumen, solicitado por el papa Pío V, se encuentra en El Vaticano con el nombre de *Breve compendio de los soles idolátricos que los indios desta Nueva España usaban en tiempos de su infidelidad*. Producto de su actividad son las *Fuentes de Sahagún*, colección de documentos en náhuatl que están parcialmente en en los códices Florentino y Matritense, así como en ediciones modernas e igualmente fragmentarias, como *Fr. Bernardino de Sahagún. Relación de los textos que no aprovechó en su obra* (1953), *Ritos, sacerdotes y atavíos de los dioses* (1957), *Veinte himnos sacros de los nahuas* (1958) y *Vida económica de Tenochtitlan* (1961). En 1577 Felipe II dispuso la confiscación del trabajo de Sahagún, ante el temor de que los indios tuvieran en esa obra un asidero para conservar sus antiguas tradiciones. En cumplimiento de esa disposición el fraile entregó al superior de su orden, Rodrigo de Sequera, una versión bilingüe náhuatl-castellana, la que se conserva como *Manuscrito de Sequera* (1580). Autor también de una *Salmodia cristiana* (1583).

Bernardino de Sahagún

Sahagún, Luis ◆ n. y m. en Sahuayo, Mich. (1900-1978). Pintor. Sus segundo apellido era Cortés. Sus primeros estudios los realizó en Guadalajara, con el maestro Ángel Vizcarra. En 1918 ingresó a la Escuela Libre de Bellas Artes. De 1922 a 1927 vivió en Italia y estudió en el Círculo Libre de Desnudo y en el Círculo de Bellas Artes de Florencia. Con una beca de la SEP viajó a Turquía y Egipto, a Palestina, Marruecos, y muchas otras ciudades (1930). Regresó a México en 1935. En 1937 Lázaro Cárdenas le encomendó la ejecución de los retratos de varios personajes michoacanos, así como paisajes de la entidad, cuadros que se encuentran en la Casa-museo Lázaro Cárdenas en Jiquilpan. En 1939 fundó el Círculo de Bellas Artes y fue maestro de Martha Chapa, Luis Nishizawa y Nicolás Moreno, entre otros. En 1940 instaló la primera galería de arte mexicano, en la colonia Juárez del DF. Durante 30 años enseñó en la Escuela Nacional de Artes Plásticas, de la que fue profesor emérito. Maestro emérito de la Academia de San Carlos. La mayoría de sus pinturas se recogieron en el volumen *Intimidad del paisaje* (1973). En 1998 se organizó un homenaje tras los 20 años de su fallecimiento. El Museo Alfredo Zalce de Morelia maneja parte de su acervo patrimonial y artístico.

Sahagún de Arévalo Ladrón de Guevara, Juan Francisco ◆ n. y m. en la ciudad de México (?-1761). Sacerdote y periodista. Estudió filosofía y teología en la Real y Pontificia Universidad de México. Fue presbítero domiciliario del arzobispado, penitenciario de Santa María de Guadalupe (1730), capellán de las franciscanas descalzas del monasterio de Corpus Christi y del Hospital de Jesús. Fue editor de la segunda *Gazeta de México*, de la que publicó 145 números mensuales entre enero de 1728 y diciembre de 1739. Hizo reaparecer su periódico, con el nombre de *Mercurio de México*, en enero de 1742. De éste sólo salieron 12 números, el último de ellos en diciembre del mismo año. Se le considera la primera publicación periódica que incluyó poesía, pues solía publicar décimas que contenían adivinanzas. A tono con el naciente nacionalismo criollo, exaltó los valores locales y el título de su órgano estaba decorado con el águila sobre un nopal devorando a la serpiente. El número 148 contiene el grabado de un cometa, por lo que esta *Gazeta* es también la primera ilustrada. A petición del ayuntamiento capitalino, el virrey Juan de Acuña lo designó en 1733 "Primer y general cronista e historiador de la ciudad de México".

Sahuaripa ◆ Municipio de Sonora situado en el oriente del estado, en los límites con Chihuahua, al sureste de Moctezuma y al este de Hermosillo. Superficie: 5,694.4 km². Habitantes: 7,222, de los cuales 1,889 forman la población económicamente activa. Hablan alguna lengua indígena doce personas mayores de cinco años (pima 10). El origen de Sahuaripa se remonta a 1641, cuando los jesuitas fundaron las misiones de Santa María de los Ángeles, San Mateo y Teopari. Del 9 al 12 de diciembre se celebra en el municipio la festividad de la Virgen de Guadalupe.

Sahuayo ◆ Municipio de Michoacán situado en el noroeste del estado, al oeste de Zamora y al suroeste de La Piedad. Superficie: 212.10 km². Habitantes: 60,034, de los cuales 16,230 forman la población económicamente activa. Hablan alguna lengua indígena 48 personas mayores de cinco años (purépecha 39). Su cabecera es Sahuayo de Morelos. La principal fiesta es el 12 de diciembre (día de la Virgen de Guadalupe) con feria, concursos literarios y espectáculos varios.

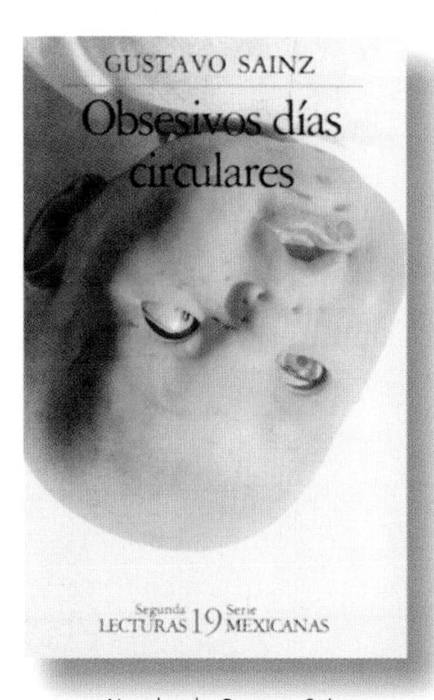

Novela de Gustavo Sainz

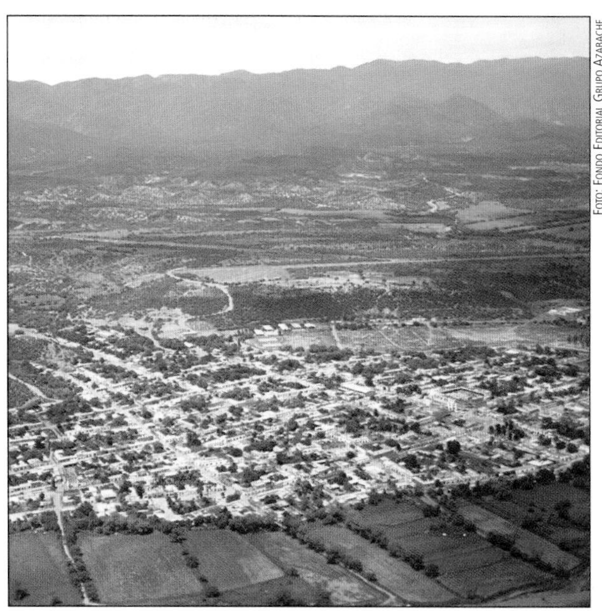
Foto: Fondo Editorial Grupo Azabache

Panorámica de Sahuaripa, Sonora

Sain Alto ◆ Municipio de Zacatecas situado al noroeste de la capital estatal y contiguo a Sombrerete. Superficie: 1,377.07 km². Habitantes: 21,779, de los cuales 4,863 forman la población económicamente activa. Hablan alguna lengua indígena siete personas mayores de cinco años.

Sainz, Gustavo ◆ n. en el DF (1940). Escritor. Hizo estudios de derecho y letras españolas en la UNAM, donde ha sido profesor (1972-77) y jefe del Departamento de Ciencias de la Comunicación (1975-77). Ha sido investigador y profesor de literatura española en la Universidad de Nuevo México (1982-) y director del Departamento de Literatura del INBA (1977-81). Cofundador de la colección Sep-Setentas (1972-77), conductor y director de programas de televisión (1975-77), director literario de la editorial Grijalbo (1975-81). Fue jefe de redacción de *Visión*, director de *Siete*, editor de *Caso Clínico* y director artístico de la *Revista de Bellas Artes*. Fundó *La Semana de Bellas Artes* y *Eclipse*. Dirigió las revistas *Claudia*, *Caballero* y *Audacia*. Ha colaborado en las principales publicaciones literarias de México. Autor de antologías, de *Gustavo Sainz. Autobiografía* (1996);

Foto: Rogelio Cuéllar

Gustavo Sainz

Foto: Rogelio Baeza

Sandalio Alfonso Sainz de la Maza

de las novelas: *Gazapo* (1965), *Obsesivos días circulares* (1969), *La princesa del Palacio de Hierro* (1974, Premio Xavier Villaurrutia), *Compadre lobo* (1976), *Fantasmas aztecas (un pre-texto)* (1982), *Paseo en trapecio* (1985), *Muchacho en llamas* (1987), *A la salud de la serpiente* (1991), *Retablo de inmoderaciones y heresiarcas* (1992), *La muchacha que tenía la culpa de todo* (1995), *Salto de tigre blanco* (1996) y *Quiero escribir pero me sale espuma* (1997); el ensayo *Autorretrato con amigos* (1967); los guiones cinematográficos: *Tramas de amor*, *La sorpresa* (1968) y *El quelite* (1970). Becario del Centro Mexicano de Escritores (1962-63), de las fundaciones Ford (1968), Guggenheim (1974) y Tinker (1981) y del National Endowment for the Arts (1983).

Sainz de Baranda y Borreiro, Pedro ◆ n. en Campeche, Camp., y m. en Mérida, Yuc. (1787-1845). Marino militar realista desde 1803. Participó en la batalla de Trafalgar, donde fue herido (1805). En 1808 volvió a Campeche. Al iniciarse la guerra entre Francia y España se le nombró comandante del pailebote *Antenor*. En 1815 estuvo a cargo de la fortificación de Campeche. En 1820 fue elegido diputado a Cortes, pero no concurrió a ellas. Diputado suplente por Yucatán al Congreso Constituyente de 1822, año en que fue ascendido a teniente de fragata y comandante de Marina de Veracruz y en el que comandó desde Alvarado un movimiento en defensa del imperio de Agustín de Iturbide contra la rebelión de Santa Anna. Comandante de las balandras *Chalco* y *Chapala* (1823), con las que estableció un apostadero en Campeche. Con las goletas *Tampico* y *Papaloapan* escoltó tropas de Veracruz a Campeche (1824). Comandante general del Departamento de Marina de Veracruz (1825), desalojó a los españoles fortificados en San Juan de Ulúa. En 1826 pidió y obtuvo su baja en la marina de guerra. Fue jefe político y comandante militar de Valladolid, Yucatán (1830-32), vicegobernador (1834-35) y gobernador de Yucatán (1835) y prefecto de Valladolid (1835-41), donde en 1833, asociado con el escocés John L. MacGregor, estableció una fábrica textil, la segunda en México con maquinaria de vapor.

Sainz de Baranda y Quijano, Pedro ◆ n. en Campeche y m. en Lerma, Camp. (1824-1891). Hijo del anterior. En 1848 combatió a los mayas durante la guerra de castas. Fue diputado al Congreso Constituyente de 1857, participó en la fundación del estado de Campeche y fue su primer comandante militar. Luchó contra la intervención francesa y el imperio. A la restauración de la República obtuvo el grado de general de brigada y ocupó una curul en tres diputaciones. Primer gobernador de Morelos (1869), senador por Campeche (1875 y 82), gobernador de Tabasco durante seis meses de 1876, senador por Morelos (1878) y jefe militar de Yucatán, Campeche y Tabasco (1882-91).

Sainz de la Maza Martínez, Sandalio Alfonso ◆ n. en el DF (1948). Profesor titulado en la Escuela Nacional de Educación Física (1966) y licenciado en periodismo por la escuela Carlos Septién García (1973). Miembro del PRI. Subdirector de los Juegos Campesinos Alfredo V. Bonfil y de los V Juegos Deportivos Nacionales de la Juventud Campesina (1977-81). Ha sido jefe de actividades deportivas de la delegación Benito Juárez (1971-75), coordinador de la Dirección General de Promoción Deportiva del DDF (1975-76), jefe del Departamento de Educación Física del Injuve (1976-77), coordinador nacional de Recreación (1977-81), asesor de la Dirección General de Educación Física (1981-82) y subdirector de Operación del Crea (1982); así como director general de Promoción Deportiva del DDF (1982-).

Sáizar Guerrero, Consuelo ◆ n. en Acaponeta, Nayarit (1961). Editora. Egresada de comunicación por la UIA (1983). Estudió ciencias políticas y administración pública en la UIA, y diplomados en contaduría, administración y finanzas en la UIA y en el ITAM. Realizó estudios sobre industria editorial en la Gran Bretaña. Jefa de Prensa de Fonapas Nayarit (1978-79). Gerente General de Editorial Jus (1983-90). Fundadora y directora general de Hoja Casa Editorial (1990). Colaboradora de *La Jornada* (1989-). Fue consejera electoral en el DF (1997). Es miembro del Consejo Asesor de Causa Ciudadana, APN.

Sáizar Manríquez, Martín ◆ n. en San Dimas, Dgo., y m. en Acaponeta, Nay. (1900-1970). Periodista. Dirigió hasta su deceso *El eco de Nayarit*, trisemanario fundado en 1917. En 1921 organizó el primer Sindicato de Obreros y Campesinos de Acaponeta y gestionó la instalación del Banco Ejidal del Norte de Nayarit.

Sakai, Kasuya ◆ n. en Argentina (1928). Estudió artes plásticas en Japón, Argentina y Estados Unidos

Genroku 99, obra de Kazuya Sakai

(1935-64). Profesor de la Universidad de Buenos Aires y de la Nacional de Tucumán. Llegó a México en 1965. Fue jefe de redacción y director artístico de *Plural* (1972-76) y profesor de la UNAM, del Centro de Estudios Orientales de El Colegio de México y de la Escuela de Artes Visuales. Tuvo un programa de *jazz* en Radio Universidad. Ha sido crítico de arte, diseñador gráfico, escritor y traductor de obras clásicas japonesas. Instalado en Estados Unidos desde 1977, ha sido profesor de las universidades de Iowa y Dallas. Expuso su pintura por primera vez en 1958. Hay obras suyas en los museos de Arte Moderno de Bahía, Rio de Janeiro, Buenos Aires, Tokio y México, así como en el Museo Nacional de Bellas Artes de Argentina, la Fundación Torcuato di Tella, de Buenos Aires, la colección Minetti de Buenos Aires, el Museo Juan Castagnino de Rosario, el Museo Universitario de Austin, los institutos de arte de Cleveland y Washington, el Centro de Arte Moderno de Guadalajara, la colección Lee Ault, de Nueva York, y en El Colegio de México. Ganó una medalla de oro en la Exposición Universal de Bruselas (1958) y el primer premio del Salón de la Pintura Actual de Buenos Aires (1961).

SALA, ATENOR ◆ n. en Tabasco y m. en el DF (1870-1936). Hacendado. Autor de *El problema agrario en la República Mexicana* (1912), obra en la que propone la colonización por extranjeros y la formación de la pequeña propiedad agrícola. Escribió también *Refundición de los proyectos de "Leyes Sala" y proyectos de ley para la creación del Banco Agrícola Nacional en la República Mexicana* (1914), *Sistema Sala para resolver el problema agrario en la República Mexicana* (1916) y *El sistema Sala y el Plan de Ayala. Correspondencia sostenida con el jefe suriano y su secretario Manuel Palafox* (1919).

SALADA ◆ Laguna de Baja California, también llamada Macuata. Se encuentra al suroeste de Mexicali, al oeste del delta del río Colorado y al este de las estribaciones de la sierra de Juárez; tiene una extensión variable debido a su poca profundidad. Durante las crecidas de los ríos Colorado y Hardy, las aguas se desbordan por el sur de la laguna.

Foto: Michael Calderwood

Laguna Salada, en Baja California

SALADO ◆ Río de Coahuila, Nuevo León y Tamaulipas, afluente del Bravo. Se forma por la confluencia de los ríos Salado de los Nadadores y Sabinas, que descargan sus aguas en la presa Don Martín, al sureste de Sabinas; corre de noroeste a sureste por la llanura costera del golfo, recibe los arroyos Jabalí y Ramos y los ríos de la Candela y Sabinas Hidalgo; desagua en la presa Falcón, al noroeste de Ciudad Camargo.

SALADO ◆ Río de Colima y Michoacán que nace en la ladera meridional del volcán de Colima, al este de la capital estatal; corre hacia el sureste y se une al Coahuayana en la base occidental de la sierra de Picila, ya en el estado de Michoacán.

SALADO ◆ Río de Puebla y Oaxaca que nace en el valle de San Andrés Chalchicomula, en las laderas occidentales del Pico de Orizaba; pasa por el valle de Tehuacán, recibe los arroyos Comulco, Coxcatlán, Tilapa y Teotitlán y los ríos Hondo o Capilla y Jiquila. El Salado se une, al suroeste de la Presa Miguel Alemán, con el Grande de Quiotepec para formar el Santo Domingo, cabeza del Papaloapan.

SALADO ÁLVAREZ, VICTORIANO ◆ n. en Teocaltiche, Jal., y m. en el DF (1867-1931). Licenciado por la Escuela de Leyes de Guadalajara (1890), ciudad donde dirigió El *Diario de Jalisco* y *La República Literaria*. Fue profesor de la Escuela Nacional Preparatoria, diputado federal, senador (1902-6), secretario de gobierno de Chihuahua (1906-08); primer secretario (1908-09) y encargado de negocios de la embajada en Washington (1909-11); secretario de Relaciones Exteriores (del 26 de mayo al 26 de junio de 1911) y ministro plenipotenciario en Guatemala, El Salvador y Brasil (1911-15). Colaboró en *El Imparcial*, *El Mundo Ilustrado*, *Excélsior*, *El Universal*, *El Informador* de Guadalajara, *El Diario de Yucatán*, *La Prensa* de Texas y *La Opinión* de Los Ángeles. Para algunos de sus trabajos utilizó el pseudónimo de *Don Querubín* de la Ronda. Coautor de *Nuevas orientaciones de la poesía femenina* (1924). Autor de *De mi cosecha* (1898), *De autos* (1901), *De Santa Anna a la Reforma* (3 t., 1902), *De la intervención al imperio* (4 t., 1903),

Victoriano Salado Álvarez

José Mariano Salas

Antonio Salanueva

La conjura de Aarón Burr y las primeras tentativas de conquista de Méjico por americanos del oeste (1908), *Breve noticia de algunos manuscritos de interés histórico para Méjico, que se encuentran en los archivos y bibliotecas de Washington* (1908), *Méjico peregrino* (1924), *Mejicanismos supervivientes en el inglés de Norte-América* (1924). Miembro de las academias Mexicana (de la Lengua) y de Historia. Su obra se ha recopilado en *La novela vivida del primer ministro de Méjico en los Estados Unidos* (1933), *La vida azarosa y romántica de Carlos María Bustamante* (1933), *Episodios nacionales* (1945), *Memorias* (2 t., 1946), *Minucias del lenguaje* (1957), *Rocalla de historia* (1958), *Epistolario* (correspondencia con personajes de su época, como Porfirio Díaz), *Estudio de la trascendencia sociológica de la enseñanza secundaria en México y datos para resolverlo* (facsímil), *Cuentos y narraciones*, *Minucias del lenguaje*, *Rocalla de historia*.

SALAMANCA ◆ Municipio de Guanajuato situado en el centro del estado y contiguo a Irapuato. Superficie: 774 km². Habitantes: 221,125, de los cuales 54,003 forman la población económicamente activa. Hablan alguna lengua indígena 174 personas mayores de cinco años (náhuatl 33, zapoteco 28, otomí 21 y mazahua 16). Los primeros habitantes del actual municipio fueron los otomíes, quienes fundaron la población de Xidóo, "Lugar de tepetates". Al inicio de la dominación española, Nicolás de San Luis Montañez se apoderó de la aldea y la llamó San Juan Bautista Xidóo. Oficialmente, la población adquirió el nombre de villa de Salamanca el primero de enero de 1603. El 10 de marzo de 1858 se produjo en ella la batalla con la que dio inicio la guerra de los Tres Años, cuando el conservador Luis G. Osollo derrotó a Anastasio Parrodi. La ciudad, cabecera del municipio, cuenta con la parroquia vieja y el convento anexo, construcciones del siglo XVI. Ahí se instalaron algunas de las primeras fábricas de loza y textiles del Bajío y durante muchos años albergó la planta de conservas La Fortaleza. En la jurisdicción se halla la refinería Antonio M. Amor, una de las más importantes del país, a la que un oleoducto lleva el crudo desde Poza Rica.

SALANUEVA, ANTONIO ◆ (1770-1835). Sacerdote franciscano que dio albergue a Benito Juárez entre 1819 y 1828, durante su niñez, en la ciudad de Oaxaca. Se dedicaba a encuadernar y empastar libros, fue padrino de Juárez e, infructuosamente, lo indujo a seguir la carrera eclesiástica.

SALAS, ADOLFO ◆ n. en Pedriceña, Dgo. (1923). Guitarrista. Vivió en Texas y reside en el Distrito Federal desde 1950. Autor de las canciones *Cita a las seis*, *Carta de Corea*, *Pobre del pobre*, *Esposa*, *Amor, no fumes en la cama*, *Adán y Eva*, *Instante de locura*, *El divorcio no es pecado*, *Cartas falsas*, *No vayas a negar*, *Declaración* y *La viuda Emilia Treviño*.

SALAS, HILARIO C. ◆ n. en Chazumba, Oax., y m. cerca de Ocosotepec, Ver. (1871- 1914). Desde principios de siglo se afilió al Partido Liberal Mexicano. En 1905 preparó y encabezó la rebelión agraria de Acayucan, Veracruz, reprimida en 1906; fue herido y se refugió en la sierra de Soteapan. Se unió en 1910 a la insurrección maderista, en la que alcanzó el grado de general. En 1913 combatió al huertismo. Murió en una emboscada.

SALAS, JOSÉ MARIANO ◆ n. y m. en la ciudad de México (1797-1867). Militar, se inició como cadete del regimiento de infantería de Puebla (1813) y combatió a los insurgentes en Jalapa y Veracruz a las órdenes de Santa Anna, aunque en 1821 se adhirió al Plan de Iguala. Se mantuvo fiel al gobierno al proclamarse el Plan de Montaño (1826) y combatió en Tampico la invasión de Isidro Barradas. Participó en los combates de El Álamo y Llano Perdido y protegió la retirada del Ejército Mexicano hasta Matamoros (1832). Jefe de la plana mayor del ejército (1844), en agosto de 1846 encabezó un pronunciamiento contra el vicepresidente en funciones, Nicolás Bravo; se posesionó del gobierno de la República y restableció la Constitución de 1824. Fue presidente del 5 de agosto al 23 de diciembre de 1846, cuando convocó a un nuevo Congreso y entregó el poder al vicepresidente Valentín Gómez Farías,

FOTO: JORGE PABLO DE AGUINACO
Detalle de la iglesia de San Agustín en Salamanca, Guanajuato

GABINETES DEL PRESIDENTE JOSÉ MARIANO SALAS	
5 de agosto al 23 de diciembre de 1846	
SECRETARÍA DE RELACIONES INTERIORES Y EXTERIORES:	
JOSÉ MARÍA ORTIZ MONASTERIO	5 al 26 de agosto de 1846
MANUEL CRESCENCIO REJÓN	27 de agosto al 20 de octubre de 1846
JOSÉ MARÍA LAFRAGUA	21 de octubre al 23 de diciembre de 1846
SECRETARÍA DE JUSTICIA:	
JOSÉ MARÍA DURÁN	5 al 26 de agosto de 1846
JOSÉ RAMÓN PACHECO	27 de agosto al 16 de octubre de 1846
JOSÉ MARÍA DURÁN	17 al 20 de octubre de 1846
JOAQUÍN LADRÓN DE GUEVARA	21 de octubre al 2l de diciembre de 1846
JOSÉ MARÍA DURÁN	22 al 23 de diciembre de 1846
SECRETARÍA DE GUERRA Y MARINA:	
IGNACIO DE MORA Y VILLAMIL	5 al 7 de agosto de 1846
MANUEL MARÍA SANDOVAL	8 al 27 de agosto de 1846
JUAN N. ALMONTE	28 de agosto al 23 de diciembre de 1846
SECRETARÍA DE HACIENDA:	
JOSÉ LUIS HUICI	5 al 27 de agosto de 1846
VALENTÍN GÓMEZ FARÍAS	28 de agosto al 21 de septiembre de 1846
JUAN N. ALMONTE	22 de septiembre de 1846
FRANCISCO MARÍA LOMBARDO	23 al 24 de septiembre de 1846
ANTONIO DE HARO Y TAMARIZ	25 de septiembre al 13 de noviembre de 1846
JOSÉ LÁZARO VILLAMIL	14 de noviembre al 10 de diciembre de 1846
JUAN N. ALMONTIO	11 al 22 de diciembre de 1846
MANUEL MARÍA SANDOVAL	23 de diciembre de 1846
21 de enero al 2 de febrero de 1859	
RELACIONES EXTERIORES:	
JOAQUÍN M. DE CASTILLO Y LANZAS	
JUAN M. FERNÁNDEZ DE JÁUREGUI	
JUSTICIA Y NEGOCIOS ECLESIÁSTICOS:	
FRANCISCO JAVIER MIRANDA	
FOMENTO:	
JOSÉ MARÍA SALDÍVAR	
GUERRA Y MARINA:	
JOSÉ MARÍA GARCÍA	
HACIENDA:	
PEDRO JORRÍN	

quien a su vez lo cedió a Santa Anna. General de división (1847), segundo jefe del Ejército del Norte en la guerra contra Estados Unidos, fue aprehendido en Padierna. Volvió a encargarse del Ejecutivo, en el gobierno conservador paralelo al de Benito Juárez, del 21 de enero al 2 de febrero de 1859, y se lo entregó a Miguel Miramón. Fue jefe militar de la ciudad de México (1863), miembro del Supremo Poder Ejecutivo y de la Regencia del Imperio Mexicano.

SALAS, LAURO ♦ n. y m. en Monterrey, NL (1927-1987). Boxeador, se inició profesionalmente en 1943. Antes de 1950 fue campeón de peso ligero de California, al derrotar a Rudy García. Primer boxeador mexicano que ganó el campeonato mundial de peso pluma, reconocido tanto por la National Boxing Association como por la Comisión Atlética de Nueva York, al derrotar en 1952 a James Carter en Los Ángeles. Ese mismo año, en Chicago, perdió el campeonato ante el mismo peleador. Se retiró del boxeo en 1961, luego de ser derrotado por Bunny Grant en Jamaica. Sostuvo cerca de 200 peleas profesionales.

SALAS ANZURES, MIGUEL ♦ n. en Puebla, Pue., y m. en el DF (1911-1965). Se tituló como profesor en el Instituto Normal del estado de Puebla (1934). Ejerció la docencia en Guerrero, Durango (1934) y Michoacán (1939). Fue inspector de educación pública en Yucatán y el Estado de México (1935-37), jefe de misiones culturales en La Laguna, Chiapas y Sinaloa (1937-39 y 1942-48), director de la Escuela Regional Campesina de San Ignacio, Baja California (1939) y de la Federal de Educación. Trabajó en diversas funciones para la Secretaría de Educación Pública (1948-54) y en 1954 ocupó la jefatura del Departamento de Artes Plásticas del Instituto Nacional de Bellas Artes. Sirvió también en el Instituto Federal de Capacitación del Magisterio (1961-65). Fundador del Museo de Arte Moderno y director fundador de la revista *Artes de México* (1953-65).

SALAS BARRAZA, JESÚS ♦ n. en El Oro, Dgo. (1888-1956). Durante la lucha de facciones fue carrancista y luchó contra Francisco Villa. Diputado local en Durango (1922). En 1923 participó, con Melitón Lozoya, en el atentado que acabó con la vida de Villa, por lo que fue procesado y condenado a 70 años de prisión. En 1924 recibió el indulto. Diputado federal y gobernador interino de Durango (1929), se unió a la rebelión escobarista, por lo que debió salir del país.

SALAS FERNÁNDEZ, MARIANO ♦ n. en Teapa, Tab., y m. en el DF (1852-1934). Opositor al gobierno de Manuel González, se exilió en Guatemala, donde hizo la carrera de abogado y conspiró contra la dictadura de Porfirio Díaz. Se afilió al antirreeleccionismo y en 1909, aún en Guatemala, representó a José María Pino Suárez. Participó en la insurrección maderista. Autor de *En defensa de México, la responsabilidad de la nación por los daños que causaron las insurrecciones* y *La inconstitucionalidad de las leyes expedidas por Venustiano Carranza*.

SALAS GARZA, EDMUNDO ♦ n. en Saltillo, Coah. (1953). Licenciado en economía por a UNAM (1976) y maestro

Gonzalo Salas Rodríguez

por el CIDE (1980). Fue profesor de la UAM (1976-82) y la UPN (1982-84). Miembro del PRI. En el INI ha sido subdirector de Desarrollo Económico e Infraestructura (1984-86) y delegado en Chiapas (1986-88). Director de Inspección y Vigilancia de la Dirección General de Servicios Migratorios de la SG (1988-93), director general de Financiamiento para el Desarrollo Urbano de la Sedesol (1993-94); director de Investigación del CISEN (1994), coordinador general de representaciones de la SEP en las entidades federativas (1995) y director general del Conafe (1995-). Autor de *Desarrollo económico de México. 1940-1970* y *Temas de economía*, libros de texto para la UPN.

SALAS PORTUGAL, ARMANDO ◆ n. en Monterrey, NL, y m. en el DF (1917-1995). Químico. Fotógrafo desde 1936. En 1944, montó su primera exposición. El *Dr Atl* lo catalogó como uno de los cinco mejores fotógrafos del mundo y Carlos Pellicer como "un extraordinario cantor y cronista del paisaje mexicano." Presentó cerca de 90 exposiciones en diversos países de América y Europa. Autor de más de 10 libros de fotografía, como *El universo en una barranca* (1986), *La arquitectura de Luis Barragán*, *La gran ciudad de México* y *Los pueblos de antes* (1991; edición restringida, de Chrysler de México). En el Centro Cultural Arte Contemporáneo montó *Los antiguos reinos de México* (1986-87) y *Las comarcas silvestres y el mundo campesino en el Distrito Federal* (1990). A su muerte se le consideraba como el último *"pictorialista"* mexicano.

El amor a los pájaros, fotografía de Armando Salas Portugal

Foto: Armando Salas Portugal

Fuente del Campanario, fotografía de Armando Salas Portugal

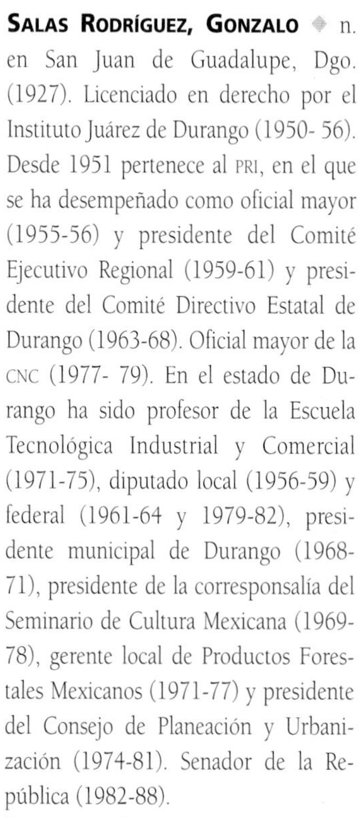

SALAS RODRÍGUEZ, GONZALO ◆ n. en San Juan de Guadalupe, Dgo. (1927). Licenciado en derecho por el Instituto Juárez de Durango (1950- 56). Desde 1951 pertenece al PRI, en el que se ha desempeñado como oficial mayor (1955-56) y presidente del Comité Ejecutivo Regional (1959-61) y presidente del Comité Directivo Estatal de Durango (1963-68). Oficial mayor de la CNC (1977- 79). En el estado de Durango ha sido profesor de la Escuela Tecnológica Industrial y Comercial (1971-75), diputado local (1956-59) y federal (1961-64 y 1979-82), presidente municipal de Durango (1968-71), presidente de la corresponsalía del Seminario de Cultura Mexicana (1969-78), gerente local de Productos Forestales Mexicanos (1971-77) y presidente del Consejo de Planeación y Urbanización (1974-81). Senador de la República (1982-88).

SALAZAR, ABEL ◆ n. en la cd. de México y m. en Cuernavaca, Mor. (1917-1995). Actor, director y productor de cine. Fue archivista de lo que sería después la SHCP y empleado de una mueblería. En cine, debutó en 1941 en la película *La casa del rencor*. Se reveló como guionista en *El conde de Montecristo* (1943) y se convirtió en guionista y director de cintas como *Tres hermanos*, *Me ha besado un hombre*, *Mi esposa busca novio* y *El pecado de Laura*. Actuó en cintas célebres, como *Los tres García* y *Vuelven los tres García*. Participó en más de 90 películas en todos los géneros, destacando las de aventuras como *El coyote*, *La justicia* y las de terror: *El vampiro*, *El ataúd del vampiro*, *La maldición de la llorona*, *El espejo de la bruja*, *El barón del terror* y *La cabeza viviente*. Dirigió también *Vuelva el sábado*, *Donde nacen los pobres*, *Los adolescentes*, *Paula*, *Rosas blancas*, *Para mi hermana la negra*, *Picardía mexicana*, *Lagunilla mi barrio II*, *Ya nunca más*, *Mentiras*. Participó en varias telenovelas, como *Mi segunda madre* y *Senda de gloria*.

SALAZAR, ADOLFO ◆ n. en España y m. en el DF (1890-1958). Estudió música en España con Manuel de Falla y Bartolomé Pérez Casas, y en Francia con Maurice Ravel. Fue jefe de redacción de la *Revista Musical Hispanoamericana* (1914-18), crítico musical en el diario *El Sol*, de Madrid (1918-36); agregado cultural de la embajada española en Washington y vicepresidente de la sección de música del Ateneo de Madrid (1938-39). A la caída de la República, vino como exiliado político (1939). Investigador de El Colegio de México, profesor del Conservatorio Nacional, fundador de la revista *Nuestra Música* (1946), crítico musical de *Novedades*, secretario de la sección musical del Ateneo Español en México y colaborador de *Las Españas*, *Romance*, *Cabalgata*, de Buenos Aires, y *Ultramar*. Autor de los libros *Música y músicos de hoy*, *El siglo romántico*, *La música actual en Europa y sus problemas*, *El problema de lo moderno*, *Música y sociedad en el siglo XX* (1939), *Las grandes estructuras de la música* (1940), *La rosa de los vientos en la música europea* (1940), *Los grandes periodos de la historia de la música* (1941), *La música en la sociedad europea* (1943), *La música moderna* (1945), *Síntesis de la historia de la música* (1945), *La danza y el ballet* (1949), *La música como proceso histórico de su invención* (1950), *La música en España* (1953) y *Teoría y práctica de la música a través de la historia* (1955). Dejó *Don Juan en los infiernos*, *Tres preludios para orquesta*, *Cuarteto para cuerdas*, *Sonata para violín y piano*, *Romancillo para guitarra* y *Cuatro letrillas de Cervantes*, entre otras composiciones.

SALAZAR, AMADOR ◆ n. en Cuernavaca y m. en Yautepec, Mor. (1868-1916). Su apellido materno era Jiménez. Primo de Emiliano Zapata. Fue peón en una de las haciendas de Pablo Escandón, contra quien hubo una movilización campesina en la que participó (1903-1905). Como castigo fue reclutado mediante leva y adscrito a la Escuela de Tiro de la ciudad de México. En 1911 se unió a la revolución maderista al frente de un grupo que operaba en el centro del estado de Morelos. Participó en el sitio y toma de Cuautla (mayo de 1911), fue uno de los firmantes del Plan de Ayala (28 de noviembre de 1911), combatió contra Madero (1912-13) y contra Huerta (1913-14). En abril de 1913 fue miembro de la Junta Revolucionaria del Centro y Sur de la República, encargada de reorganizar la lucha zapatista. En el Ejército Libertador del Sur alcanzó el grado de general de división. Secretario de Zapata, participó en la primera reunión entre el jefe suriano y Pancho Villa (4 de diciembre de 1914). A principios de 1915 el gobierno convencionista le encomendó la dirección del ingenio de Atlihuayán y en abril de ese año fue nombrado comandante de la guarnición de la ciudad de México, plaza de la que fue desalojado en julio por el ejercito carrancista.

SALAZAR, CARLOS ◆ n. en Matamoros, Tams., y m. en Uruapan, Mich. (1829-1865). Estudió en el Colegio Militar (1842-47), combatió la invasión estadounidense (1847), fue liberal en la revolución de Ayutla (1854) y en la guerra de los Tres Años (1858-60). Luchó contra la intervención francesa y el imperio. Participó en la batalla del 5 de mayo y estuvo a las órdenes de Jesús González Ortega en el sitio de Puebla; fue aprehendido en dicha plaza pero logró evadirse. Acompañó a Benito Juárez en su viaje hacia el norte. En 1863, ya con el grado de general, hizo campaña en Michoacán y fue dos veces gobernador provisional de ese estado (1864 y 1864-65). En 1865 fue derrotado por los imperialistas en Santa Ana Amatlán, capturado, llevado a Uruapan y fusilado.

SALAZAR, GONZALO ◆ n. en el DF (1959). Guitarrista. Recibió clases de su tío, Gonzalo López Codina. Ingresó en el Conservatorio Nacional, donde estudió con Guillermo Flores Méndez, composición con Salvador Contreras y teoría y técnicas de composición de música microinterválica con Julio Estrada. Ha tomado cursos de lectura e interpretación de tablaturas, música nueva de Europa e interpretación del repertorio latinoamericano con Wilhelm Bruck, Hopkinson Smith, Leo Brower, Roberto Aussel y Javier Hinojosa. Ha impartido cursos de especialización en varias ciudades de México y se ha presentado en los programas *La guitarra en el mundo* y *La hora de Bellas Artes*. Ha sido premiado en el primer Concurso Nacional (Michoacán, 1982), el segundo Premio Nacional de Guitarra (Monterrey, 1987) y en el décimo Concurso Internacional Casa de España (Puerto Rico, 1982). Obtuvo premio especial y mención y premio del jurado Gergely Sarkozi en los concursos internacionales de guitarra de La Habana (1984 y 1986). Miembro de la Asociación Mexicana Guitarra Nova.

SALAZAR, JOSÉ INÉS ◆ n. en Casas Grandes y m. en Janos, Chihuahua (¿1884?-1917). Militó en el Partido Liberal Mexicano (1906) y en junio de 1908 participó en el ataque magonista a Palomas, Chihuahua. En diciembre de 1910 formó parte del grupo magonista que, a las órdenes de Praxedis Guerrero, se incorporó al movimiento maderista en Chihuahua. Se unió a las fuerzas de Prisciliano Silva y participó en el ataque frustrado a Casas Grandes el 6 de marzo de 1911. En abril de ese año figuró entre los magonistas que incorporados a la revolución pidieron a Madero renunciar al mando, por lo que fue reducido a prisión. En febrero de 1912 se sublevó contra Madero y se convirtió en cabecilla del movimiento que poco después acaudillaría Pascual Orozco. En ese mes ocupó Ciudad Juárez y combatió a Francisco Villa en Boquilla de Conchos, Chihuahua; en marzo participó en el combate de Rellano, Chihuahua; a las órdenes de Orozco, derrotó a la columna gobiernista de José González Salas. Fue comisionado para avanzar sobre Coahuila, donde libró diversos combates. En julio de 1912 fue enviado a emprender la campaña orozquista en Sonora, donde sufrió continuas derrotas, por lo que regresó a Chihuahua en octubre y siguió luchando sin lograr triunfos significativos. En marzo de 1913 aceptó el indulto de Victoriano Huerta, quien le reconoció el grado de general brigadier y lo envió a Chihuahua para proteger la vía de ferrocarril entre Casas Grandes y Ciudad Juárez. En noviembre del mismo año participó en la defensa de la ciudad de Chihuahua, a las órdenes de Salvador R. Mercado, y se le ascendió a general de brigada. Combatió infructuosamente a las fuerzas villistas que ocuparon Ojinaga en enero de 1914. A causa de la derrota, Salazar y otros ocho generales cruzaron la frontera, pero fueron hechos prisioneros por las autoridades de Estados Unidos. El 6 de marzo de 1914 el gobierno huertista le confirió el grado de general de división. Desde Estados Unidos conspiró contra el gobierno de

Adolfo Salazar

Carranza: al salir de prisión organizó algunas fuerzas y se internó por Ciudad Juárez en territorio mexicano. Fracasó en su intento, fue hecho prisionero el 25 de mayo de 1916 y remitido a la penitenciaría de Chihuahua. Liberado por Villa se refugió en Estados Unidos, donde fue nuevamente aprehendido. En agosto de 1917 volvió a la lucha bajo la bandera villista, pero fue asesinado.

Salazar, Juan de ◆ n. en Querétaro, Qro., y m. en Monclova, Coah. (1768-1811). Fraile franciscano. Recibió las órdenes sacerdotales en 1792. En 1810 se adhirió al movimiento de independencia en Jerécuaro y más tarde se unió a las fuerzas de Miguel Hidalgo. Peleó en el Monte de las Cruces, combatió a las órdenes de Mariano Jiménez hasta llegar a Saltillo y desde allí acompañó a Ignacio Aldama. Fue aprehendido en Béjar y conducido a Monclova, donde se le fusiló.

Salazar, Lázaro ◆ n. en Cuba y m. en el DF (1911-1957). Beisbolista. En Cuba destacó como jugador y en 1938 llegó a México para dirigir equipos de la Liga Mayor. Llevó al campeonato nacional a los equipos Córdoba (1939), Veracruz (1941), Monterrey (1943, 47, 48 y 49) y *Diablos Rojos* (1956).

Salazar, Ricardo ◆ n. en Guadalajara, Jal. (1923). Fotógrafo. En su ciudad natal montó un estudio propio para efectos comerciales. En los inicios de los cincuenta llegó a la ciudad de México y con Emmanuel Carballo inició su carrera de fotógrafo de escritores mexicanos, la cual se ha extendido por más de cuatro décadas. En 1993 trabajaba para la Escuela Nacional Preparatoria.

Salazar, Rosendo ◆ n. en Zacapoaxtla, Pue., y m. en el DF (1888-1971). Era cajista y corrector de una imprenta en Puebla. En 1909 fue uno de los fundadores de la Unión Tipográfica Mexicana, que dirigió en 1912. En 1911 fundó y dirigió el periódico poblano *La Patria de Serdán* y en el DF fue uno de los fundadores de la Casa del Obrero Mundial (☛) y estuvo entre los firmantes del pacto que dio origen a los Batallones Rojos. Militó en el Círculo de Obreros Libres, la Confederación General de Trabajadores y la Confederación General de Obreros y Campesinos, de la que fue secretario general. Dirigió los periódicos *El Sindicalista*, *Revolución Obrera* y *Revolución Social*. En septiembre de 1928 pidió autorización a Calles para formar una central obrera independiente de la CROM y la CGT, a lo que éste respondió que no tenía "injerencia en el asunto". Pintor, expuso en 1930 en la Galería de Arte Moderno. Al final de su vida fue secretario general honorario de la Confederación de Trabajadores de México. Colaborador de *Arte y Letras* y *La Semana Ilustrada*. Autor de *Hacia el porvenir*, *Las pugnas de la gleba (los albores del movimiento obrero en México)* (1923), *Alma vibrante*, *Al rojo libertario*, *Dura Lex*, *Las masas mexicanas y sus poetas*, *El demagogo*, *Izquierda*, *México en pensamiento y acción* (1926), *Historia de las luchas proletarias de México* (1938), *Del militarismo al civilismo en nuestra Revolución* (1938), *Líderes y sindicatos*, *La carta de trabajo de la Revolución Mexicana* (1960), *La Casa del Obrero Mundial*, *Ricardo Flores Magón, el adalid*, *Los primeros de mayo en México*, *Samuel Gompers, presencia de un líder*, *Historia de la CTM*, *Cantos de combate* y *El maíz, la planta más humana*. Medalla Belisario Domínguez (1970).

Salazar, Severino ◆ n. en Tepetongo, Zac. (1947). Escritor. Estudió letras modernas en la UNAM y en la Swansea University. Participó en el taller de Juan José Arreola. Autor del volumen de cuentos *Las aguas derramadas*, *New Writing from México* (*Cuento mexicano de hoy*, 1991), *Zacatecas, cielo cruel, tierra colorada* (1968-1992; antología de poesía, ensayo y teatro), y de las novelas: *Donde deben estar las catedrales* (1984, premio Juan Rulfo para primera novela), *El mundo es un lugar extraño* (1989), *Llorar frente al espejo* (1989) y *La arquera loca* (1992). Tres de sus novelas se antologaron en *Tres noveletas de amor imposible* (1998; ahí se incluye *La provincia de los santos*). Profesor de la UAM.

Salazar y de Alarcón, Eugenio ◆ n. y m. en España (1530-1602). Licenciado en leyes por la Universidad de Sigüenza y doctor en derecho por la Real y Pontificia Universidad de México (1591), de la que fue rector (1592-93). Fue fiscal de la audiencia de Galicia, gobernador de Tenerife y Palma (1567-72), oidor en Santo Domingo (1573-89), fiscal y oidor de la audiencia de México (1589-98) y ministro del Consejo de Indias (1600-02) designado por Felipe III.

Salazar de la Cadena, Gonzalo de ◆ n. en España y ¿m. en Cuautitlán, Esstado de México? (?-1593). Fue alcalde ordinario de la ciudad de México (1564) y alcalde mayor de Cuautitlán (1592-93).

Salazar y Dávila, Gonzalo de ◆ n. en la ciudad de México y m. en Mérida, Yuc. (1559-1638). Hijo del anterior y nieto del conquistador Alonso Dávila. Ingresó en la orden de San Agustín en 1577. Fue predicador conventual, prior del convento de su orden en la ciudad de México, procurador en España y obispo de Yucatán (1609-36). Al frente de la diócesis yucateca, en su afán de evangelizar la península, destruyó 20,000 ídolos mayas, lo que le valió una felicitación del papa Paulo V.

Salazar Galindo, Juan ◆ n. y m. en Cuernavaca, Mor. (1877-1945). Campesino. En agosto de 1911 se incorporó a las fuerzas zapatistas de Amador Salazar. Ascendió a general de brigada en campaña contra los federales. Fue comandante militar en la Villa de Guadalupe (1914), se encargó de la defensa del Cerro Gordo (1915) y combatió a los carrancistas en Tlaltizapán (1916). En 1920 se adhirió al Plan de Agua Prieta, a las órdenes de Genovevo de la O, y se retiró pensionado en 1943.

Salazar Ilarregui, José ◆ n. en Hermosillo, Son., y m. en la ciudad de México (1823-1892). Ingeniero por el Colegio de Minería. Fue geómetra de la Comisión de Límites entre México y Estados Unidos (1850) y tomó parte en la operación de venta del territorio de La Mesilla. Jefe de la Comisión de Límites entre México y Guatemala, representó a Chihuahua en la Junta de Notables que ofreció la corona a Maximiliano. Subsecretario de Fomento durante la Regencia del Imperio (1863), encargado interino del Ministerio de Estado, ministro de Gobernación (del 4 de marzo al 14 de septiembre de 1866) en el gabinete del austriaco y comisario imperial de Yucatán (1867), donde inauguró la primera línea telegráfica de la península, entre Mérida y Sisal. Autor de *Datos de los trabajos astronómicos y topográficos dispuestos en forma de diario, practicados durante el año de 1849 y principios de 1850 por la Comisión de Límites en la línea que divide esta República de la de los Estados Unidos* (1850).

Salazar López, José ◆ n. en Ameca y m. en Guadalajara, Jal. (1910-1991). Ordenado sacerdote en 1934, fue profesor, prefecto de disciplina y de estudios, vicerrector (1944) y rector del Seminario Diocesano de Guadalajara (1950-60); obispo titular de Prusiade y coadjutor de la diócesis de Zamora (1961); obispo residencial de Zamora (1967-70) y arzobispo de Guadalajara (1970-87), cargo al que renunció por llegar al límite de edad. Presidente de la Conferencia Episcopal Mexicana (1973-82). Cardenal desde el 5 de marzo de 1973, participó en las elecciones de los papas Juan Pablo I y Juan Pablo II, ambas en 1978.

Salazar Mallén, Rubén ◆ n. en Coatzacoalcos, Ver., y m. en el DF (1905-1986). Licenciado en derecho por la UNAM (1934), donde fue profesor (1934-86). Militó en su juventud en el Partido Comunista Mexicano, del que se volvió un severo crítico. De 1930 a 1986 ejerció el periodismo en *El Universal, Claridades, Excélsior, Mañana, Jueves de Excélsior, Contemporáneos, Letras de México, Metáfora, Estaciones, Cuadernos del Viento* y *Sábado*, suplemento de *unomásuno*. En 1932, la publicación por entregas de su novela *Cariátide* en la revista *Examen* (☛) generó una amplia polémica. Autor de *El pensamiento político en América, Dos cuentos: ruta, orilla* (1932), *La dictadura del proletariado y el derecho* (1934, tesis de licenciatura), *Cariátide* (1934), *¿Por qué perdió el cóndor?* (1934), *Morelos* (1936), *La democracia y el comunismo* (1937), *Soledad* (1937), *Camino de perfección* (1937), *Páramo* (1944), *Tres temas de la literatura mexicana* (1947), *Ojo de agua* (1949), *Apuntes para una biografía de Sor Juana Inés de la Cruz* (1952), *Ejercicios* (1952), *Las ostras, o la literatura* (1955), *Ninón* (teatro, 1957), *Adela y yo* (1957), *Camaradas* (1959), *El sentido común* (1960), *Desarrollo histórico del pensamiento político* (2 t., 1962), *La polémica chino-soviética y la revolución proletaria* (1965), *El Hegel de Hegel y el Hegel de Marx* (1966), *La iniciación* (1966), *¡Viva México!* (1968), *Samuel Ramos* (1968), *La democracia y el comunismo* (1973), *El Estado corporativo fascista* (1977), *Las utopías del siglo XX* (1977), *La sangre vacía* (1982), *Alternativas del antiimperialismo latinoamericano* (1985) y *El paraíso podrido* (obra inconclusa, publicada póstumamente).

Obra de Rubén Salazar Mallén

Salazar Mendiguchía, Pablo ◆ n. en Soyaló, Chis. (1954). Licenciado en derecho por la Universidad Autónoma de Puebla. Profesor de la Escuela Normal Superior de Chiapas y de la Universidad Autónoma de Chiapas. Ha sido subprocurador general de Justicia, director jurídico de la Secretaría de Educación y Cultura de Chiapas, abogado de grupos indígenas desplazados, vocal ejecutivo del Instituto Federal Electoral en Chiapas y secretario general de Gobierno en ese estado. Senador por el PRI (1994-2000), partido al que renunció en 1998. Perteneció a la Comisión de Concordia y Pacificación de Chiapas.

Foto: Imagen Latina

Pablo Salazar Mendiguchía

Salazar Ramírez, Othón ◆ n. en Alcozauca, Gro. (1924). Profesor. Estudió en las escuelas Normal de Oaxtepec, Nacional de Maestros (en la que fue dirigente estudiantil) y Normal Superior. Militante del Partido Comunista Mexicano en el que fue miembro del Comité Central y de la Comisión Ejecutiva, así como responsable sindical (1958-81), cofundador y miembro de la dirección del PSUM (1981-87), cofundador del PMS (1987-89) y del PRD (1989-). En 1951 participó en actividades contra la reelección presidencial de Miguel Alemán. En la Normal Superior encabezó una huelga que consiguió la plaza de base de 12 horas. Dirigió el movimiento magisterial (1956-58) que obtuvo un importante aumento salarial después de un paro de labores y guardia permanente en la SEP que duró 38 días. Dirigente del Movimiento Revolucionario del Magisterio, en 1958 fue elegido secretario general de la sección nueve del SNTE, lo que no reconocieron las autoridades. Fue encarcelado el 6 de septiembre de 1958 y, desde prisión, ganó nuevamente las elecciones para la Secretaría General de la sección nueve por más de 12,000 votos contra 33. Por estar preso no pudo asumir su cargo. En 1960 el comité democrático de la sección nueve fue desconocido y el dirigente del MRM, todavía encarcelado, llamó a un paro de labores que fue reprimido (☛ *Movimiento magisterial de 1955-60*). En ese mismo año fue cesado como profesor. Una vez en libertad se unió a la campaña del candidato del Frente Electoral del Pueblo a la Presidencia de la República, Ramón Danzós Palomino (1964). Perteneció a la dirección del Frente Sindical Independiente. Candidato a diputado federal por Guerrero (1979), resultó triunfador, pero el Colegio Electoral anuló los comicios. Fue diputado federal plurinominal del PCM (1979-82) y presidente municipal de Alcozauca, Guerrero. Preso varias veces por su militancia comunista, ha organizado movimientos y luchas en defensa de los grupos étnicos en todo el país, así como la Alianza de Maestros y Padres de Familia. Diputado federal plurinominal perredista para el periodo 1991-94.

Salazar Sáenz, Francisco Xavier ◆ n. en el DF (1940). Ingeniero químico por la UNAM y la UIA. Maestro en administración por la Universidad Nacional de San Luis Potosí y candidato a doctor por La Salle. Pertenece al PAN, donde ha sido consejero estatal, consejero nacional, presidente del Comité Directivo Municipal de SLP, secretario general y presidente del Comité Estatal

FOTO: IMAGEN LATINA

Jesús Salazar Toledano

José Socorro Salcido Gómez

Celestino Salcedo Monteón

en SLP. Se desempeñó como secretario general del Sindicato Unión de Asociaciones del Personal Académico Universitario de la UASLP, secretario general de la Asociación Nacional de Sindicatos del Personal Académico Universitario y secretario general de la Confederación Nacional de Trabajadores Universitarios. Diputado federal (1991-94) y senador (1994-2000).

SALAZAR TOLEDANO, JESÚS ◆ n. en el DF (1940). Licenciado en derecho por la UNAM (1958-62). Miembro del PRI, en el que se ha desempeñado como coordinador de Acción Juvenil del DF (1960-61) y presidente del comité capitalino (1985-86). Oficial mayor (1970-71) y director de Acción Electoral de la CNC (1972). Secretario de colonos urbanos e inquilinos de la CNOP (1983). Ha sido director general de Acción Social (1966-70) y secretario de gobierno del DDF (1994-97), director general de Centros Conasupo de Capacitación Campesina (1973-76), gerente general de Electrificación Rural de la CFE (1976-77), director general de Coordinación Comercial de la Secretaría de Comercio (1977-78), subdirector de delegaciones Conasupo (1978-82), delegado del DDF en Tlalpan y Venustiano Carranza, diputado federal (1982-85), director general del Inmecafé (1989-) y subsecretario de Gobernación (1995-97). Recibió la Cruz al Mérito Legislativo de la Asociación Nacional de Abogados (1985). Secretario particular del gerente de relaciones públicas de Pemex y director corporativo de administración de Pemex (1997-).

SALCEDO, HUGO ◆ n. en Ciudad Guzmán, Jal. (1964). Su nombre es Hugo Octavio Salcedo Larios. Estudió letras en la Universidad de Guadalajara. Dramaturgo. Hizo su debut como autor y director con *En la oscuridad del laberinto* (1982). En su obra destacan, además, *San Juan de Dios* (Premio *Punto de Partida* 1986), *Cumbia (hasta las 3 de la mañana)* (Premio Nacional Mexicali 1987 del INBA), *Dos a uno* (Premio *Punto de Partida* 1987), *Si escuchas una rana croar* (1989, Premio Jornadas por la Paz en Sinaloa), *Juanete y Picadillo* (1989, Premio Torreón del INBA), *Arde el desierto con los vientos que llegan del sur* (1990), *Sinfonía en una botella* (1991), *El viaje de los cantores* (1991, premio Tirso de Molina, otorgado por el Instituto de Cooperación Iberoamericana, en 1990) y *Sobre las olas del mar* (1992), así como numerosas obras aún no representadas. Vive en Tijuana. Ha sido becario del Fonca (1989-90).

SALCEDO, JUAN DE ◆ n. y m. en la ciudad de México (1546- 1625). Profesor, fue vicerrector en tres ocasiones (1582, 1585 y 1586) y dos veces rector de la Real y Pontificia Universidad de México (1615-16 y 1621-22). Consultor de virreyes, de arzobispos y de la Inquisición. Autor de *Manual de administrar los sacramentos en las Indias* (1568) y *Concilio provincial mexicano de 1585* (1622).

SALCEDO AQUINO, ROBERTO ◆ n. en el DF (1943). Profesor por la Escuela Normal Superior, licenciado en ciencias políticas y administración pública y maestro en ciencias políticas por la UNAM, done ha sido consejero técnico de la ENEP Acatlán (1976-81), director de las carreras de ciencias políticas, administración pública y relaciones internacionales (1978-80) y profesor (1979-83). Desde 1965 es miembro del PRI, en el que se ha desempeñado como secretario auxiliar del CEN (1971-73), secretario técnico del Consejo Consultivo del IEPES (1982) y subdelegado general en Tabasco (1982-83). Ha sido subdirector de Producción de la Comisión Nacional de los Libros de Texto Gratuitos (1980-82), secretario técnico de la Comisión de Defensa del Idioma Español (1981-82), oficial mayor de la Sedue (1987-88), oficial mayor del DDF (1988) y subsecretario de desarrollo urbano y vivienda de la Sedesol (1998-).

SALCEDO MONTEÓN, CELESTINO ◆ n. en Ocotlán, Jal. (1936). Profesor normalista. Es ingeniero agrícola por la Escuela de Agricultura de Navojoa (1957) e ingeniero agrónomo por la Escuela Antonio Narro. Miembro del PRI. Ha sido secretario de la Liga de Comunidades Agrarias de Baja California (1960-70 y 1987-), comisionado ejidal en Mexicali (1963-66), director de Colonias, de Tierras Nacionales y del Programa Agrario Nacional del Departamento de Asuntos Agrarios y Colonización, secretario general de la Confederación Nacional Campesina (1974-76), dos veces diputado federal (1967-70 y 1973-76) y senador por Baja California (1976-82).

SALCIDO GÓMEZ, JOSÉ SOCORRO ◆ n. en Santa Bárbara, Chih. (1930). Licenciado en derecho por la UNAM (1951-56) con estudios de posgrado en turismo. Miembro del PRI desde 1951, en ese partido ha sido primer vocal de las juventudes ruizcortinistas, coordinador y coordinador general de la Comisión de Finanzas del Comité Directivo Estatal de Chihuahua (1980). Secretario general de la Liga Municipal de Organizaciones Populares de Parral (1963), secretario de Promoción Legislativa (1969) y secretario de Acción Profesional y Técnica de la CNOP (1975). Ha sido juez mixto de primera instancia en Ojinaga (1957-58), diputado federal suplente por Chihuahua (1964), diputado local (1968), primer vocal ejecutivo del Patronato de la Asistencia Social en Chihuahua (1981) y senador por la misma entidad (1982-88).

SALDAÑA, JORGE ◆ n. en Banderilla, Ver. (1931). Periodista. Hizo estudios de leyes en la Universidad Veracruzana, de derecho internacional en La Haya, de civilización francesa en la Universidad de París y de periodismo en Madrid. Durante su estancia en la capital francesa fue cantante en cafés. Ha sido reportero del *Diario de Xalapa* y de *El Dictamen* de Veracruz, locutor de las radiodifusoras XEKL, XEJJ y XEJA (1949-51), productor en la Radio Televisión Francesa (1954), locutor y comentarista en la sección de radio de la UNESCO (1955), narrador de radionovelas y asistente de Roberto Kenny (1959), empleado de Telesistema Mexicano (1962-73), productor artístico de radio y televisión del Comité Olímpico Mexicano (1968), colaborador del Canal 11

(1970-72) y, desde 1972, conductor de varios programas del Canal 13, como *Sábados culturales*, *Sábados con Saldaña*, *Desayunos del 13*, *Los 13 millones del 13*, *Sopa de letras*, *Nostalgia* y *Noticiero ecológico*. Algunos de sus programas han sido censurados, la última vez en 1997.

Saldaña, José Manuel ◆ n. en Puebla, Pue., y m. en Chiautempan, Tlax. (1805-1886). Estudió derecho en el Seminario de Puebla, del que fue profesor. Varias veces diputado federal por Puebla y Tlaxcala, así como gobernador interino de esta entidad (1858). Fue magistrado de la Suprema Corte.

Saldaña, Juan José ◆ n. en el DF (1944). Doctor en historia y filosofía de la ciencia por la Universidad de París. Ha sido profesor en la UNAM, director del Instituto Iberoamericano de Estudios sobre la Ciencia y la Tecnología y director fundador de *Quipu. Revista Latinoamericana de Historia de las Ciencias y la Tecnología*. Autor de *Introducción a la teoría de la historia de las ciencias*, *Nuevas tendencias en la historia de las ciencias*, *Cross Cultural Diffusion of Science: Latin America* y *El perfil de la ciencia en América*. Presidente fundador de la Sociedad Latinoamericana de Historia de las Ciencias y la Tecnología.

Saldaña, Mateo ◆ n. en Teocaltiche, Jal. (1875-1951). Pintor. Estudió en la Academia de San Carlos, donde fue alumno de Jesús F. Contreras, Santiago Rebull, Félix Parra y José María Velasco. Profesor de la Academia desde 1902. Sustituyó a Velasco como restaurador del Museo Nacional de Arqueología, Historia y Etnografía. Hay cuadros suyos en el Museo Nacional de Artes Plásticas.

Saldaña Espinosa, Judith ◆ n. en el DF (1939). Contadora pública (1963), maestra en administración (1978) y doctora por la UNAM (1984). Profesora del IPN (1967-71), de la UNAM (1971-83), del CIDE (1976-77) y del Centro Nacional de Productividad (1977-81). Pertenece desde 1963 al PRI, del que fue coordinadora femenil en el DF (1963). Ha sido auditora del Banco Nacional de Fomento Cooperativo (1962-63), supervisora de Auditoría Interna y de Sistemas y Procedimientos, jefa del Departamento de Programación y Organización (1964-80) y contralora general (1980-82) del Patronato del Ahorro Nacional; directora de Finanzas (1982-83) y subdirectora general de Pronósticos Deportivos (1983-). Autora de *Administración de la planificación familiar* (mención honorífica en el Premio Nacional de Administración, 1983).

Saldaña Oropesa, Román ◆ n. en Santa Ana Chiautempan, Tlax., y m. en el DF (1886-1955). Se tituló como profesor en el Instituto Científico y Literario de Tlaxcala. También estudió en la Escuela Nacional de Maestros y la Normal Superior. Durante la dictadura huertista fue perseguido por sus ideas políticas y se le prohibió ejercer la docencia. En 1919 se reincorporó a su profesión como maestro misionero. Profesor de enseñanza secundaria (1926-48) e inspector de escuelas primarias. Autor de *Primeras ordenanzas militares y civiles, ordenadas por el Cap. D. Hernán Cortés* (1950) e *Imágenes más antiguas y veneradas en Tlaxcala* (1952). Medalla Ignacio Manuel Altamirano (1952).

Saldívar, Vicente ◆ n. y m. en el DF (1943-1985). Boxeador conocido como *el Zurdo de Oro*. Peleó profesionalmente por primera vez en 1961, cuando derrotó en Oaxaca a *Babe* Palacios en el primer asalto. Campeón nacional (8 de febrero de 1964) y mundial (26 de octubre de 1964) de peso pluma, al derrotar a Ultiminio Ramos (☛) en la ciudad de México. En siete ocasiones defendió exitosamente su campeonato y anunció su retiro en 1967. Volvió a los cuadriláteros en 1969 y reconquistó el campeonato mundial pluma de la Comisión Mundial de Boxeo al vencer en Roma al australiano Famechon, el 9 de mayo de 1970. En ese año perdió su título en Tijuana, frente al japonés Kuniaki Shibata. En 1971 pasó a la categoría de peso gallo, en la que fue derrotado en su primer combate y decidió retirarse definitivamente.

Saldívar y Fernández del Valle, Jaime ◆ n. y m. en el DF (1926-1974). Estudió en la Academia de San Carlos y en La Esmeralda. Expuso en Perú (1961), México (1962, por primera ocasión) y España (1967). Es autor de la versión plástica de *La Suave Patria* que se halla en la residencia oficial de Los Pinos y de los cuadros *Retablos guadalupanos*, *Los arcángeles y querubines*, *Puebla de los Santos Angeles*, *Retablos de San Pascual Bailón*, *Las vírgenes*, *Las monjas y las aparecidas* y *Retablos de San Francisco y sus lamentos*.

Saldívar y Fernández del Valle, Pilar ◆ n. en la ciudad de México (1926). Tomó cursos para ingresar en el Servicio Exterior Mexicano (1967) y estudió historia de México y relaciones internacionales en El Colegio de México. En la SRE ha sido asesora del director general de Asuntos Culturales, subjefa del Departamento de Naciones Unidas, jefa de los departamentos de la UNESCO y del Sistema Interamericano; agregada cultural en Guatemala y Argentina; adscrita a la delegación de México ante la UNESCO; ministra consejera de la embajada en Austria y representante alterna ante organismos internacionales en Viena; miembro de las delegaciones de México en diversas conferencias internacionales, embajadora en Costa Rica (1977-83) y en la República Dominicana (1983-). Pertenece a la Asociación del Servicio Exterior Mexicano. Medalla por 25 años en el Servicio Exterior Mexicano y condecoraciones de varios países.

Saldívar y Silva, Gabriel ◆ n. en Jiménez, Tams., y m. en el DF (1909-1980). Abandonó la carrera de medicina para dedicarse a la investigación en historia y musicología. Fue editor del Archivo Histórico Diplomático Mexicano, historiador de la SRE, jefe de prensa de la Secretaría de Agricultura y Fomento y profesor de enseñanza superior. Jubilado en 1972, siguió dando clases particulares. Colaboró en los *Anales del Museo Nacional de Arqueología, Historia y Etnografía*, la *Enciclopedia de México* y en el *Boletín de la Sociedad Mexicana de Geografía y Estadística*. Editor de *Real*

Foto: Rogelio Baeza

Vicente Saldívar

Foto: Rogelio Baeza

Jorge Saldaña

Renato Sales Gasque

FOTO: DANTE BUCIO

Carlos Sales Gutiérrez

Cédula sobre los privilegios a los herederos de Cromberger, Vista de ojos a las tierras de doña María Moctezuma y Rosario de quince misterios a los dolores de la Virgen. Coautor de *Bibliografía agrícola y agraria de México* (1943). Autor de *La misión confidencial de don Jesús Terán en Europa, Un códice musical del siglo XVIII, Sor Juana Inés de la Cruz y la música de su tiempo, Biografía de Mariano Elízaga, Historia de la música en México* (1934), *La música en el valle del Mezquital* (1936), *Pintura mural otomí* (1936), *El jarabe, baile popular mexicano* (1937), *Mariano Elízaga y las canciones de la independencia* (1942), *Bibliografía de la Secretaría de Relaciones Exteriores* (1943), *La rebelión de Catarina Garza en la frontera de Tamaulipas y sur de Texas* (1944), *Historia compendiada de Tamaulipas* (1945), *Los indios de Tamaulipas* (1947), *Archivo de la historia de Tamaulipas* (10 t., 1947), *Bibliografía de musicología y musicografía mexicanas* (1952), *Refranero musical* (1983), *Códice Saldívar número 4* (1987) y *Musicología y musicografía mexicana, 1931-1980* (1988). Su biblioteca, con más de 18,000 y folletos sobre musicografía mexicana y partituras originales, fue donada al gobierno tamaulipeco. Medalla Pedro José Méndez del estado de Tamaulipas (1980).

SALES GASQUE, RENATO ◆ n. en Mérida, Yuc. y m. en Campeche, Camp. (1931-1995). Estudió en la Universidad del Sureste. Licenciado en derecho por la UNAM (1959-64). Profesor de las universidades de Campeche (1966-68), Autónoma de Hidalgo (1971-72), de Tabasco (1973-75) y Veracruzana (1976-77), así como del Instituto de Ciencias Penales (1977-80); y coordinador de la División de Estudios Superiores de la Universidad de Campeche (1980-82). Desde 1964 fue miembro del PRI. Fue juez mixto de primera instancia en las islas Marías (1962-63), secretario del Patronato para la Reincorporación Social por el Empleo en el DF de la Secretaría de Gobernación (1963), abogado consultor de la SEP (1963-65), actuario del Juzgado III penal (1964), secretario de acuerdos de la Segunda Corte Penal del Tribunal Superior de Justicia del DF (1964), secretario del Juzgado I de distrito en materia civil del DF (1965), primer secretario en el Juzgado de distrito de Campeche (1966-68), secretario de estudio y cuenta de la primera sala de la Suprema Corte (1968-69), juez de distrito en Chiapas, Puebla e Hidalgo y magistrado en los Tribunales Colegiados con sede en Tabasco, Veracruz y la ciudad de México (1969-80), presidente del Tribunal Superior de Justicia de Campeche (1980-82), senador (1982-85), procurador general de Justicia del DF (1985-88) y magistrado del Tribunal Colegiado del XIV distrito con sede en Mérida (1989-). Autor de *El presupuesto en el delito de abuso de confianza* (1964).

SALES GUTIÉRREZ, CARLOS ENRIQUE ◆ n. en el DF (1938). Licenciado en economía por el ITAM (1966). Profesor de la Universidad Anáhuac, del IPN y de la UNAM. Miembro del PRI. En la SHCP ha sido analista de comercio exterior (1956-58), investigador de la Sección de Indicadores Económicos (1958-61), jefe de la Sección de Ingresos (1961-65), jefe de la Sección de Deuda Pública (1965-66), asesor fiscal (1966-67) y jefe de la Oficina de Política Fiscal de la Dirección de Estudios Hacendarios (1967-68), jefe del Departamento de Estudios Económicos (1968-70), director general de Impuestos Interiores (1970-75), director general del Impuesto Sobre la Renta (1975-76), director general de Promoción Fiscal y Asuntos Internacionales (1976). Gerente general de Programación Financiera de Nafinsa (1977-79), subdirector general de Crédito Público (1979-82), director general de Crédito Público (1982), subsecretario de Banca Nacional (1983-86) y director general de Banobras (1986-88). Tesorero (1988-89) y secretario general de Planeación y Evaluación (1989), secretario general de Planeación y coordinador general de Coplade (1990-91). Senador (1991-97). Autor de *Apuntes de finanzas públicas* (1967), *Indemnización bancaria y evolución del sistema financiero* (1992) entre otras obras.

SALGADO, JESÚS H. ◆ n. en Los Sauces y m. cerca de Tecpan de Galeana, Gro. (1873-1919). Agricultor y comerciante, en 1911 se incorporó a la insurrección maderista. Reunió a 2,000 hombres con los que tomó Iguala. Al aparecer el Plan de Ayala (☛) se unió a las fuerzas de Emiliano Zapata; como general de división hizo campaña contra Victoriano Huerta, tomó Chilpancingo y Zapata lo nombró, en 1914, gobernador de Guerrero. Luchó contra el ejercito carrancista en las filas de la Convención de Aguascalientes. Murió en combate.

SALGADO, JOSÉ ◆ n. y ¿m.? en Los Reyes, ahora Los Reyes de Salgado, Mich. (?-?). Participó en la guerra de Independencia. Formó parte del Congreso Constituyente de Michoacán (1824-25). Miembro de la logia yorkina. Segundo gobernador constitucional del estado, fue desaforado en 1830 y se levantó en armas. En 1831 fue capturado y condenado a muerte, aunque logró escapar a tiempo para sumarse al pronunciamiento en favor de Gómez Pedraza y reasumir el Ejecutivo local el 18 de enero de 1832. El 27 de mayo del mismo año fue depuesto por Ignacio Estrada, uno de los sublevados bajo el lema de "Religión y fueros". Una vez sofocado este levantamiento, Salgado volvió a asumir el gobierno. En su primera gestión aplicó la ley de expulsión a los españoles.

SALGADO ALBARRÁN, JOSÉ TOMÁS ◆ n. en Valle de Santiago, Gto., y m. en la ciudad de México (1775-1834). Doctor en derecho por la Real y Pontificia Universidad de México (1806), de la que fue rector en dos ocasiones (1810-11 y 1814-15). Ejerció su profesión en la Audiencia, fue miembro del Colegio de San Juan de Letrán, teniente letrado de la Intendencia, juez de la Hacienda Pública (1824) y secretario del ramo (del 5 de marzo al 1 de noviembre de 1827) en el gabinete de Guadalupe Victoria. Diputado federal por Guanajuato (1827- 28), magistrado y vicepresidente de la Suprema Corte de Justicia de la Nación.

Salgado Brito, Juan ◆ n. en Temimilcingo, Mor. (1948). Licenciado en derecho por la Universidad Autónoma del Estado de Morelos (1973). Profesor de la Escuela Normal Maestro Rafael Ramírez (1972-75). Miembro del PRI desde 1964, en el que ha sido delegado del CEN en Guerrero (1977-78) y en Coahuila (1979), presidente y secretario general del Comité Directivo Estatal en Morelos (1980-81). Ha sido secretario particular del presidente mu-nicipal de Cuernavaca (1967-70), diputado federal titular (1973-76 y 1982-85) y suplente (1979-82); director del Instituto de Promoción Municipal en Morelos (1974-76). Delegado estatal del ISSSTE (1979-81) y director general de Concertación del DDF (1989-).

Salgado Cordero, Enrique Tomás ◆ n. en el DF (1937). Se graduó como subteniente en 1956. Licenciado en administración militar por la Escuela Superior de Guerra (1962-65) y maestro en seguridad nacional por el Colegio de la Defensa Nacional (1985-86). Ha sido profesor en el Colegio Militar (1965-70), subjefe operativo del Estado Mayor, agregado militar en Israel, comandante del 65 y 68 batallón de infantería, jefe del Estado Mayor de la XXI Zona Militar, comandante de la guarnición de la plaza en Ciudad Reynosa, jefe del Estado Mayor del 1er cuerpo del Ejército del Centro, director del colegio de Defensa Nacional, jefe del Estado Mayor de la Defensa Nacional, subdirector de la Dirección General de Policía y Tránsito del DDF (1974-76), secretario de Seguridad Pública del DDF (-1997) y director de Cartografía de la Sedena (1997-). Ha recibido las condecoraciones a la perseverancia de quinta a primera clases, al Mérito Docente y servicios distinguidos. Oficial honorario de la División Civil de la Orden del Imperio Británico.

Salgado Macedonio, José Félix ◆ n. en Ciudad Altamirano, Gro. (1957). Ingeniero agrónomo por la Universidad Autónoma de Guerrero. Fundador del PRD, donde ha sido miembro del Comité Directivo Estatal en Guerrero, consejero nacional, presidente del Comité Directivo Estatal de Guerrero y candidato a gobernador del mismo estado. Diputado federal (1988-91) y senador (1994-2000).

Salgó, Andrés ◆ n. en Hungría y m. en el DF (1909-1977). Pintor egresado de la Escuela Superior de Bellas Artes de París. Naturalizado mexicano en 1941, dos años más tarde expuso por primera vez en México. Expuso su obra de caballete en París (1932), Nueva York (1947) y en varias ciudades de Canadá (1958), Europa (1965 y 1967), África (1968) y Asia (1970). Hay cuadros suyos en el Museo de Angola, la Casa de la Cultura en Mozambique y en las colecciones privadas Dwight D. Eisenhower, Ahmed Sukarno, Pablo Casals y Felipe de Edimburgo. Realizó murales en el Seminario de Lille (1933), en la Casa del Alentejo, en Lisboa (1940); en la casa de gobierno de Puerto Rico (1961), en el edificio de la Montreal Trust Company (1963) y en la embajada de Indonesia en México (1973).

Salido, Felipe ◆ n. en Álamos, Son., y m. en el DF (1863-1939). Egresado del Colegio Militar. Se incorporó al Estado Mayor de la primera Zona Militar (1884), abrió una escuela primaria y secundaria en Álamos (1888) y en 1900 fue nombrado director del Colegio de Sonora e inspector de escuelas primarias, cargos que desempeñó hasta 1911, cuando se dedicó a ejerecer su profesión de ingeniero. Fue senador por Sonora (1920-24).

Salido, Martín ◆ n. y m. en Alamos, Son. (1815-1896). En 1843 era comandante militar de la subprefectura de Batopilas y del municipio de Chínipas. Fue varias veces jefe político del cantón de Matamoros, Chihuahua. En 1857, con ese cargo, le correspondió jurar la Constitución. Diputado federal en 1861. Combatió la intervención francesa y el imperio. Fue diputado local en cuatro legislaturas de Chihuahua y de 1880 hasta su muerte volvió a su oficio de minero.

Salido Beltrán, Roberto ◆ n. en Álamos, Son., y m. en el DF (1912-1988). Subteniente táctico de artillería egresado del Colegio Militar (1929-32), piloto aviador por la Escuela Militar de Aviación (1935-37) y diplomado de Estado Mayor Aéreo en la Escuela Superior de Guerra (1948-53). General de división en 1969. Participó en la campaña contra la rebelión cedillista (1939) y en la segunda guerra mundial como jefe de pilotos del Escuadrón 201. Al término de la guerra fue miembro del Comité de Planes de Defensa Conjunta México-Estados Unidos. Fue instructor de la Escuela Superior de Guerra (1941-43), donde fundó el curso de Estado Mayor Aéreo; profesor de la Escuela Militar de Mecánicos Especialistas de Aviación (1947), jefe de la sección pedagógica e instructor de la Escuela Superior de Guerra (1952), subjefe de la Fuerza Aérea Mexicana (1953-55), director de la Escuela Militar de Aviación (1959), director fundador del Colegio del Aire (1959- 64), agregado militar y aéreo en Washington (1964-69), jefe de la delegación mexicana y vicepresidente de la Junta Interamericana de Defensa (1969-71) y comandante en jefe de la Fuerza Aérea Mexicana (1971-76). Recibió la condecoración de la Legión de Honor, Cruz y Placa del Cuerpo de Defensores de la República, condecoración al Servicio en el Lejano Oriente, medalla del Teatro de Guerra del Sudoeste del Pacífico, medalla del Mérito Técnico Militar, medalla de la Liberación de Filipinas, medalla de la Victoria (otorgada por los aliados) y la Orden Nacional de Miguel Larraynaga (otorgada por el gobierno nicaragüense). Colaborador de las revistas *Defensa*, *Kukulcán*, *Aguilas* y *Ejército*. Autor de *Campaña de Morelos en 1812*.

Salina Cruz ◆ Bahía de Oaxaca situada en el litoral del golfo de Tehuantepec, entre los cerros de Salina y del Morro o Punta Ventosa. Bien dragada permite el acceso a naves de hasta ocho metros de calado, pese a estar expuesta a fuertes vientos meridionales.

Salina Cruz ◆ Municipio de Oaxaca situado en el litoral del golfo de Tehuantepec, al suroeste de Juchitán de

Foto: Imagen Latina

José Félix Salgado Macedonio

Enrique Salgado Cordero

Foto: Ana Lourdes Herrera

Jesús *Chucho* Salinas

Foto: Rogelio Baeza

Carmen Salinas

Zaragoza. Superficie: 113.55 km². Habitantes: 76,198, de los cuales 19,601 forman la población económicamente activa. Hablan alguna lengua indígena 4,499 personas mayores de cinco años (zapoteco 3,076, chontal de Oaxaca 735, huave 195, mixe 191 y mixteco 106). Cuenta con diversos sitios de interés turístico, como el faro de Cortés, que sirvió de guía a las primeras naves que viajaron al golfo de California y a Centroamérica; una zona arqueológica inexplorada en San José del Palmar y playas como La Ventosa, en la barra del río Tehuantepec. En su jurisdicción se hallan las salinas de El Fraile. Su cabecera, del mismo nombre, es aduana marítima, centro pesquero y comercial, astillero y puerto artificial construido entre 1901 y 1905. Hasta ahí llega un ramal del oleoducto de Minatitlán. Cuenta también con empacadoras de camarón gigante.

Salinas ◆ Municipio de San Luis Potosí situado en el oeste del estado, al suroeste de Matehuala y en los límites con Zacatecas. Superficie: 2,116 km². Habitantes: 23,960, de los cuales 4,193 forman la población económicamente activa. Hablan alguna lengua indígena cinco personas mayores de cinco años. Su cabecera es Salinas de Hidalgo.

Salinas, Carmen ◆ n. en Torreón, Coah. (1942). En la ciudad de México. Actriz, se inició como imitadora. Ha participado en más de 80 películas, como *La vida inútil del Pito Pérez* (1969), *Doña Macabra* (1971), *El rincón de las vírgenes* (1972), *Calzonzin inspector* (1973), *Tívoli* (1974), *El lugar sin límites* (1977), *Las noches del Blanquita* (1981), *Las glorias del gran Púas* (1982), *Masacre en el río Tula* (1985), *El camino largo a Tijuana* (1988), *Ciudad de ciegos* (1991), *Danzón* (1991). *¡Que viva Tepito!* (1980 Premio Diosa de Plata) y *Mexicano tú puedes* (1983). En televisión ha actuado en más de 12 telenovelas y programas cómicos. Premio *El Heraldo* (1966), Premio Calendario Azteca de Oro (1966) como mejor cómica del año, Premio Estrella de Plata, Comediante del año de la ACCT, entre otros. En teatro ha participado en *Cada quien su vida*, *Aventurera* y muchas otras obras.

Salinas, Emilio ◆ n. en Cuatro Ciénegas, Coah., y m. en EUA (?-1927). Cuñado de Venustiano Carranza y padre de Gustavo A. Salinas Camiña (☛). En 1893 figuró entre los opositores al gobernador José María Garza Galán y tomó las armas para evitar su reelección. Participó en actividades antirreeleccionistas y en 1911 se incorporó a la insurrección maderista. Combatió en 1912 a Pascual Orozco y en 1913 se unió al constitucionalismo. General brigadier en 1914. Cuando el gobierno carrancista fijó su sede en Querétaro, Salinas fue gobernador y comandante militar de ese estado. Jefe de los Establecimientos Fabriles, senador por Coahuila (1918), cónsul en San Antonio, Texas, y gobernador provisional de Chihuahua (1920). Fue derrocado por los aguaprietistas. Se exilió tras el asesinato de Carranza.

Salinas, Gilda ◆ n. en el DF (1949). Cuentista y dramaturga. Autora de *Malicia en el país de las maravillas* (1994), *Narraciones de terror y fervor* (1995), *Lotería de cuentos* (1995) y *Las sombras del Safari* (1998). Se han montado sus obras de teatro *Tan buena la ingenua como la adivina* (1995-96), *Crisálida* (1996), *La agonía de Manuela Sáenz* (1995), *Patriota y amante de usted* (1996-97). Ha colaborado en *Tramoya* (1995-97) y *Estilo y dramaturgia II*. Premio internacional Emilio Carballido 1995. Ha sido becaria del Fonca (1993-94).

Salinas, Jesús *Chucho* ◆ n. en la ciudad de México (1928). Actor cómico. Formó parte del Quinteto Salinas. Durante muchos años hizo pareja con Héctor lechuga. También ha sido guionista y comentarista radiofónico. En cine actuó en *México 2000* (1981).

Salinas Alanís, Miguel ◆ n. en Toluca, Edo. de Méx., y m. en el DF (1858-1938). Radicado en Morelos, fue director de escuelas en Tlaltizapán y Tlaquiltenango y fundó una escuela (1882) que mantuvo durante 30 años. En la ciudad de México fue secretario de la Escuela Nacional Preparatoria y del Museo Nacional de Antropología e Historia. Autor de *Gramática inductiva de la lengua castellana* (1902), *Ejercicios lexicológicos para el aprendizaje de la lengua española* (1912), *Historias y paisajes morelenses* (1924), *Datos para la historia de Toluca* (1927) y *Mis árboles* (1936). Fue miembro correspondiente de la Academia Mexicana (de la Lengua).

Salinas Arriaga, León ◆ n. en Cuernavaca, Mor., y m. en el DF (1885-1973). Estudió ingeniería civil en la Universidad Nacional (1905), donde fue alumno de Alberto J. Pani. Ejerció su profesión en la comarca lagunera y en la región del Bajío. Trabajó en Morelos (1908-14), donde tuvo a su cargo la construcción de la vía férrea entre Huichila y Chinameca, acondicionó el ingenio de esta última población e intervino en la ampliación de la zona de riego de las haciendas del Hospital y Zacatepec. En 1914 se unió a la lucha antihuertista y un año después fue nombrado ingeniero en jefe de los ferrocarriles constitucionalistas. Oficial mayor (1917) y subsecretario de Industria y Comercio (1917-20), encargado del despacho en dos ocasiones (del 22 de enero al 31 de mayo de 1919 y del 22 de febrero al 21 de mayo de 1920), en el gabinete de Venustiano Carranza. Presidente ejecutivo de los Ferrocarriles Nacionales, senador por Morelos, subsecretario de Hacienda y Crédito Público (1923), presidente de la Comisión Nacional de Caminos (1924-26), funcionario del Banco de México (1930-40) y presidente interino del mismo (1946). Cofundador, con Aarón Sáenz, de Azúcar, S.A., y gerente general de la misma (1933-57). Fue consejero del Banco Azucarero, del Banco del Sur (del que fue presidente), de Seguros Atlas, Fianzas Atlas, Banco Inmobiliario Atlas y Financiera Banamex.

Salinas Camiña, Gustavo ◆ n. y m. en Cuatro Ciénegas, Coah. (1893-1964). Sobrino de Venustiano Carranza. Piloto aviador por la Escuela Moissant de Aviación, de Nueva York (1912). Combatió la rebelión orozquista. En 1913 se unió a la revolución constitucionalista, a las órdenes de Álvaro Obregón, y fue el primer aviador mexicano en realizar un bombardeo aéreo (1914), lo que hizo contra el buque *Guerrero* en el golfo de California. Obregón lo nombró jefe de su artillería en la campaña contra Pancho Villa. Fue el primer general de división que tuvo la Fuerza Aérea Mexicana. Agregado militar en Francia, Inglaterra y Bélgica y director de la Fundición Nacional de Artillería. En 1929 se unió a la rebelión escobarista. Amnistiado, años después, fue director de Aeronáutica Civil y uno de los organizadores del Escuadrón 201. Campeón nacional de tiro con pistola y rifle, lo condecoraron los cuerpos de aviación de Francia, Perú y Estados Unidos.

Salinas Carranza, Alberto ◆ n. en Cuatro Ciénegas, Coah., y m. en el DF (1892-1970). Sobrino de Venustiano Carranza y primo del anterior. Mecánico egresado del Instituto Politécnico Renselaer, de Nueva York, y piloto graduado en la Escuela de Aviación Moissant (1912), donde se especializó por órdenes de Francisco I. Madero. Tras el cuartelazo huertista, Venustiano Carranza lo comisionó para organizar una escuadrilla aérea que, con tres aparatos, actuó en Puebla, Veracruz, Yucatán y San Luis Potosí. En 1915 dirigió la recién creada Aviación Militar Constitucionalista. Perteneció al Estado Mayor Presidencial, creó el Departamento de Aviación y una escuela de pilotos militares; organizó la Cooperativa Obrera de Vestuario y Equipo y dirigió la fábrica de cartuchos del Departamento de Establecimientos Fabriles. Luego del asesinato de Carranza se exilió en Estados Unidos y Perú, aunque más tarde volvió a México. Fue dos veces jefe de la Fuerza Aérea Mexicana y dirigió la Aviación Civil. Senador, general de brigada (1951), agregado militar en Estados Unidos, Francia, Italia y Yugoslavia, consejero de la Presidencia, presidente de los Veteranos de la Revolución al Servicio del Estado y miembro del Consejo de la Legión de Honor Mexicana. Autor de *La expedición punitiva* (1936).

Salinas Chávez, J. Carlos ◆ n. en Azcapotzalco, DF (1906). Fue aprendiz en el Departamento de Dibujo del diario capitalino *El Demócrata*. Trabajó en la misma especialidad en *El Nacional* (1929) y en 1930 se instaló por su cuenta. En 1951, al examinar una foto en colores del lienzo de la Virgen de la Guadalupe vio en sus ojos la silueta del busto de un hombre, lo que después ratificó al observar el original estampado en la tilma. Autor del libro *Juan Diego en los ojos de la Santísima Virgen de Guadalupe. A la época actual que sólo cree en la ciencia la Guadalupana le hace el regalo de una prueba científica de su estampamiento* (1974).

Salinas de Gortari, Carlos ◆ n. en el DF (1948). Hijo de Raúl Salinas Lozano. Licenciado en economía por la UNAM (1969), maestro en administración pública (1973) y en economía política y gobierno (1976) y doctor en economía política y gobierno por la Universidad de Harvard (1978). Pertenece desde 1966 al PRI, en el que ha sido profesor del Instituto de Capacitación Política (1971), analista de informes presidenciales (1973-79), subdirector de Estudios Económicos (1979-81) y director general del IEPES (1981-82). Profesor de la UNAM (1971-72), del ITAM (1976) y del Cemla (1978), así como investigador en la Universidad de Harvard (1974). En la Secretaría de Hacienda fue analista (1971), jefe del Departamento de Estudios Económicos de la Dirección General de Asuntos Hacendarios y Asuntos Internacionales (1974-76), secretario técnico del Grupo Interno (1974-77), subdirector (1976) y director de Estudios Económicos de la Dirección General de Planeación Hacendaria (1977), subdirector (1978) y director general de Planeación Hacendaria (1978-79). Como director general de Política Económica y Social de la SPP (1979-81) coordinó la preparación del Plan Global de Desarrollo y fue secretario técnico del gabinete económico de la Presidencia. Secretario de Programación y Presupuesto (del 1 de diciembre de 1982 al 4 de octubre de 1987), en el gabinete de Miguel de la Madrid; fue jefe de la delegación mexicana a la cuarta Conferencia de Ministros y Jefes de Planificación Económica de América Latina y el Caribe (Buenos Aires, 1983); presidente de la séptima reunión del Subcomité Técnico del Instituto Latinoamericano de Planificación Económica y Social (Brasilia, 1984); presidente de la quinta Conferencia de Ministros y Jefes de Planificación Económica de América Latina y El Caribe (México, 1985); presidente del XXI periodo ordinario de sesiones de la CEPAL (México, 1986); presidente de la Conferencia Extraordinaria de la Comisión Económica para América Latina y El Caribe (México, 1987); presidente de la delegación mexicana a la sexta Conferencia de Ministros y Jefes de Planeación de América Latina y el Caribe (La Habana, 1987) y presidente de México (1988-1994). Durante su gestión presidencial se continuó con la política de privatización de las empresas paraestatales (alentada por él mismo como secretario de Programación y Presupuesto), se consolidó la apertura comercial de México (sobre todo con el Tratado de Libre Comercio con Estados Unidos y Canadá, cuya negociación duró cuatro años y entró en vigor el primero de enero de 1994) y se reformó el artículo 27 constitucional para dar a los ejidatarios no sólo la tenencia, sino la propiedad de la tierra. Lo

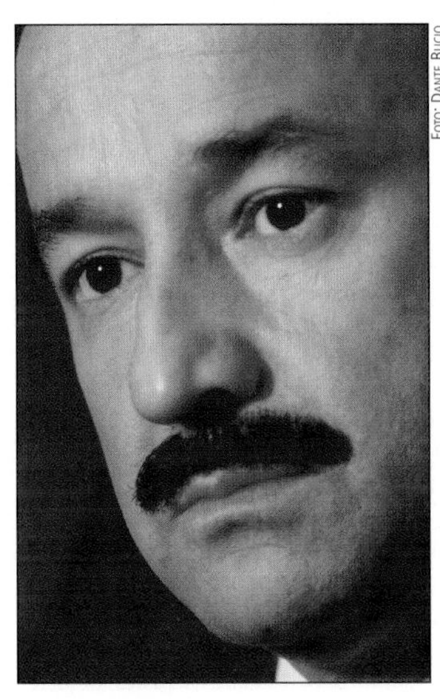
Foto: Dante Bucio

Carlos Salinas de Gortari

Gabinete del presidente Carlos Salinas de Gortari

1 de diciembre de 1988 a 1 de diciembre de 1994

Relaciones Exteriores:	
Fernando Solana Morales	1 de diciembre de 1988 a diciembre de 1993
Manuel Camacho Solís	diciembre de 1993 a 10 de enero de 1994
Manuel Tello Macías	10 de enero al 1 de diciembre de 1994
Gobernación:	
Fernando Gutiérrez Barrios	1 de diciembre de 1988 a 30 de diciembre de 1992
Patrocinio González Blanco Garrido	1 de enero de 1993 al 10 de enero de 1994
Jorge Carpizo McGregor	10 de enero a 1 de diciembre de 1994
Agricultura y Recursos Hidráulicos:	
Jorge de la Vega Domínguez	1 de diciembre de 1988 a diciembre de 1989
Carlos Hank González	4 de enero de 1990 a 1 de diciembre de 1994
Comunicaciones y Transportes:	
Andrés Caso Lombardo	enero de 1989 a 29 de marzo de 1993
Emilio Gamboa Patrón	1 de abril de 1993 a 1 de diciembre de 1994
Defensa Nacional:	
Antonio Riviello Bazán	1 de diciembre de 1988 a 1 de diciembre de 1994
Educación Pública:	
Manuel Bartlett Díaz	1 de diciembre de 1988 a 6 de enero de 1992
Ernesto Zedillo Ponce de León	7 de enero de 1992 a 30 de noviembre de 1993
Fernando Solana Morales	30 de noviembre de 1993 a mayo de 1994
José Ángel Pescador	mayo a 1 de diciembre de 1994
Hacienda y Crédito Público:	
Pedro Aspe Armella	1 de diciembre de 1988 a 1 de diciembre de 1994
Comercio y Fomento Industrial:	
Jaime Serra Puche	1 de diciembre de 1988 a 1 de diciembre de 1994
Secretaría de Programación y Presupuesto	
Ernesto Zedillo Ponce de Leon	1 de diciembre de 1998 al 7 de enero de 1992
Desarrollo Urbano y Ecología:	
Patricio Chirinos	1 de diciembre de 1988 a 7 de abril de 1992
Desarrollo Social, antes Desarrollo Urbano y Ecología:	
Luis Donaldo Colosio Murrieta	noviembre de 1992 a noviembre de 1993
Carlos Rojas Gutiérrez	noviembre de 1993 a 1 de diciembre de 1994
Marina:	
Mauricio Scheleske Sánchez	1 de diciembre de 1988 a 8 de julio de 1990
Luis Carlos Ruano Angulo	19 de julio de 1990 a 1 de diciembre de 1994
Energía, Minas e Industria Paraestatal:	
Fernando Hiriart Balderrama	1 de diciembre de 1988 a 1 de enero de 1993
Emilio Lozoya Thalmann	enero de 1993 a diciembre e 1994
Salud:	
Jesús Kumate Rodríguez	1 de diciembre de 1988 a 1 de diciembre de 1994
Trabajo y Previsión Social:	
Arsenio Farell Cubillas	1 de diciembre de 1988 a 26 de abril de 1994
Manuel Gómez Peralta	26 de abril a 1 de diciembre de 1994
Pesca:	
María de los Ángeles Moreno	1 de diciembre de 1989 a mayo de 1991
Guillermo Jiménez Morales	mayo de 1991 a 1 de diciembre de 1994
Contraloría General de la Federación:	
María Elena Vázquez Nava	1 de diciembre de 1988 a 1 de diciembre de 1994
Turismo:	
Carlos Hank González	1 de diciembre de 1988 a enero de 1990
Pedro Joaquín Coldwell	1 de enero de 1990 a 31 de diciembre de 1993
Jesús Silva Herzog	1 de enero a 1 de diciembre de 1994
Reforma Agraria:	
Víctor Cervera Pacheco	1 de diciembre de 1988 a 1 de diciembre de 1994
Procuraduría General de la República:	
Enrique Álvarez del Castillo	1 de diciembre de 1988 a 21 de mayo de 1991
Ignacio Morales Lechuga	22 de mayo de 1991 a diciembre de 1992
Jorge Carpizo McGregor	enero a diciembre de 1993
Diego Valadés Ríos	enero a abril de 1994
Humberto Benítez Treviño	mayo a noviembre de 1994
Departamento del Distrito Federal:	
Manuel Camacho Solís	1 diciembre de 1998 a diciembre de 1993
Manuel Aguilera Gómez	diciembre 1993 a 1 de diciembre de 1994

que les permitió venderla. Se promulgó una nueva Ley Agraria. Se modificó el artículo 130 de la Constitución para reconocer personalidad jurídica a las iglesias. Estableció relaciones diplomáticas con El Vaticano. Señalado como "neoliberal", dijo regirse por el "liberalismo social". Para paliar la pobreza, creó el Programa Nacional de Solidaridad (Pronasol). Renegoció la deuda externa, estimuló las exportaciones no petroleras, así como las inversiones extranjeras y la desregulación de la actividad económica. Fusionó la SPP con la SHCP y creó la Secretaría de Desarrollo Social (Sedesol), reprivatizó la banca, convirtió el monopolio estatal del servicio telefónico en un monopolio privado y vendió a particulares canales de televisión, estaciones de radio, estudios de cine y la empresa exhibidora Operadora de Teatros. Para mantener la inflación en límites manejables, instituyó el Pacto de Estabilidad, Competitividad y Empleo (PECE) que implicó un aumento controlado en los precios de bienes y servicios y la virtual congelación de los salarios. En 1990 creó la Comisión Nacional de Derechos Humanos. Creó la Comisión Nacional del Deporte (Conade), el Consejo Nacional para la Cultura y las Artes (Conaculta) y la Comisión Nacional del Agua (Conagua). Casi ocho millones de hectáreas de bosques y selvas pasaron al régimen de reservas de la biosfera y al de áreas naturales protegidas. Para combatir la contaminación en la ciudad de México se implantó el programa "Hoy No Circula" que impidió cada día la circulación de la quinta parte de los vehículos de particulares; se cerró la refinería de Azcapotzalco y Pemex puso en el mercado gasolina sin plomo. En 1989, en Baja California, por primera vez se reconoció el triunfo electoral de candidato a gobernador de un partido diferente al PRI y de ese modo el candidato del PAN se convirtió en gobernador de la entidad. Durante el sexenio se removió a varios gobernadores por conflictos postelectorales o por ser requeridos en la administración pública federal, al extremo de que en cierto momento sólo había en funciones 17 mandatarios estatales elegidos por voto popular. Se destacó el exceso de publicidad del gobierno y la falta de diálogo y entendimiento con la oposición, incluso el acoso a varios sectores políticos. El Partido de la Revolución Democrática tildó a Salinas de "usurpador" y de haber llegado a la Presidencia de la República por métodos fraudulentos, lo que también señalaron periodistas independientes del gobierno. El mismo partido tuvo más de 300 militantes asesinados en el sexenio. El 1 de enero de 1994, día que entraba en vigor el Tratado de Libre Comercio, hizo su aparición el Ejército Zapatista de Liberación Nacional, que atacó guarniciones militares de Chiapas y anunció su objetivo de llegar a la ciudad de México y derrocar al gobierno de Salinas. Éste ordenó el contrataque militar en Chiapas, pero la protesta nacional e internacional lo obligó a suspender las operaciones bélicas y a pactar una tregua. Las tensiones en el gabinete presidencial y entre las fuerzas priistas crecieron, pero la campaña presidencial del PRI se mantenía en un tono menor, lo que alentó los rumores sobre la eventual renuncia del candidato. Como crecieran las dudas, Salinas reunió a los dirigentes priistas y ratificó que el candidato era Luis Donaldo Colosio. Días después éste fue asesinado. En una asamblea priista realizada en la misma residencia oficial del Ejecutivo y encabezada por el presidente de la República, fue designado candidato sustituto el doctor Ernesto Zedillo Ponce de León. En medio de sospechas de todo tipo y con el descrédito en aumento, Salinas promovió la creación de la figura jurídica de los "consejeros ciudadanos" que habrían de ser mayoría en el Consejo General del Instituto Federal Electoral. Salvado el trámite de las elecciones, otra vez con el triunfo del PRI, el 28 de septiembre fue asesinado José Francisco Ruiz Massieu, secretario general del PRI y líder de la fracción parlamentaria de su partido en la Cámara de Diputados. Para hacer frente a los gastos extraordinarios de ese año, Salinas emitió deuda interna, en pesos, pero garantizando su pago contra cualquier fluctuación brusca del tipo de cambio, lo que fue equivalente a adquirir deuda en dólares, con el agravante de que su vencimiento era de muy corto plazo, lo que dio por resultado que, apenas 20 días despues de que dejara el poder, en diciembre, estallara la mayor crisis económica desde la revolución. Coautor de *Planeación para el desarrollo* (1981), *Aspectos jurídicos de la planeación en México* (1981) y *La Constitución mexicana: rectoría del Estado y economía mixta* (1985). Autor de *Tríptico de la dependencia* (1974) y *Producción y participación política en el campo* (1980). Fue miembro de la Asociación Nacional de Charros y está afiliado al Colegio Nacional de Economistas. Ganó una medalla de plata en equitación en los Juegos Panamericanos de Cali, Colombia (1971). Premio Tierra para el Liderazgo Ambiental y la Excelencia Humanitaria de la United Earth (1991). Doctor *Honoris causa* por la Universidad de Stanford, California (1991).

Salinas de Gortari, Raúl ♦ n. en Monterrey, NL (1946). Hermano del anterior. Ingeniero civil por la UNAM (1965-69), maestro en planeación del transporte por la École Nationale des Ponts et Chaussées (1972-73) y maestro en evaluación de proyectos de desarrollo industrial por la Universidad de París (1973-74). Profesor de la UNAM (1970-78) y director técnico del estudio *Caminos y Mano de Obra* de El Colegio de México (1975). Miembro del PRI, en el que formó parte del Comité Ejecutivo Nacional (1982). Ha sido auxiliar del Departamento de Planeación de ICA (1970-72), subpresidente general de Planeación en el Proyecto Hidroeléctrico Chicoasén (1975), director general de Obras a Mano de la SOP (1976), director general de Caminos Rurales de la SAHOP (1977-81), asesor del titular de la SPP (1982), gerente general (1982-86) y director general de Distribuidora e Impulsora Comercial Conasupo (1987-88) y director de Planeación de Conasupo (1988-94). En 1995 fue encarcelado como presunto autor intelectual del asesinato de Mario Ruiz Massieu (☛) y sentenciado primero a 50 años y luego a 25 años de prisión. También se le atribuyó malversación de fondos en Conasupo, sin que se comprobara. Coautor de *Por la soberanía alimentaria. Enfoques y perspectivas* (1984). Autor de *Camino y mano de obra* (1975), *Muerte calculada* (cuentos, 1980), *Evaluación de proyectos y selecciones de tecnología en los países subdesarrollados* (1982), *Tecnología, empleo y construcción en el desarrollo de México* (1983), *Diconsa en la modernización comercial y la regulación del abasto popular* (1987), *Agrarismo y agricultura en el México independiente y posrevolucionario* (1987) *El amante. Dos ventanas a la vida* (cuentos, 1989), *El secreto, un día* (1990) y *Lo que el juez ignoró para sentenciarme* (1999). Miembro de número de la Academia Mexicana de Ingeniería e integrante del Consejo Directivo del Colegio de Ingenieros Civiles (1979-80). Pertenece a la Sociedad de Exalumnos de la Facultad de Ingeniería, a la Asociación de Ingenieros y Arquitectos de México y al Colegio de Ingenieros Civiles de México.

Raúl Salinas de Gortari

Ricardo Salinas Pliego

SALINAS E INFANZÓN, JOSÉ VICENTE ◆ n. en Oaxaca, Oax., y m. en Durango, Dgo. (1819-1894). Recibió las órdenes sacerdotales en 1842. Se tituló de abogado en 1848. Ejerció diversos cargos eclesiásticos y fue diputado al Congreso local de Oaxaca. Fue designado obispo de Durango en 1868 y tomó posesión al año siguiente. En 1892, la antigua diócesis de Guadiana se elevó al rango de arquidiócesis, con lo que se convirtió en el primer arzobispo de Durango.

SALINAS LEAL, BONIFACIO ◆ n. en Gral. Bravo, NL (1900-1982). Se incorporó a la revolución constitucionalista en 1913 y participó en más de un centenar de hechos de armas. Llegó al generalato en 1929 y fue divisionario desde 1946. Gestionó el regreso de Plutarco Elías Calles a México, comisionado por Ávila Camacho. Fue gobernador constitucional de Nuevo León (1939-43) y de Baja California (1959-66). Senador de la República (1970-76).

SALINAS LOZANO, RAÚL ◆ n. en Monterrey, NL (1917). Licenciado en economía por la UNAM (1942), maestro en administración pública por la Universidad de Washington (1945) y maestro en economía por la de Harvard (1946). Profesor de la UNAM (1947-70) y de las universidades de San Salvador (1950) e Iberoamericana (1976). Ha sido jefe (1948-50) y director de Estudios Económicos de la Secretaría de Hacienda (1952-54), asesor fiscal del gobierno hondureño (1950-52), director de la Comisión de Inversiones de la Secretaría de la Presidencia (1954-58), secretario de Economía Nacional (del primero al 31 de diciembre de 1958) y de Industria y Comercio (1959-1964) en el gabinete de Adolfo López Mateos; director de la Comisión Nacional de Precios de la Secretaría de Comercio (1977), delegado de México ante el Fondo Monetario Internacional, director del Instituto Mexicano del Comercio Exterior (1978-79), presidente de los consejos de la Comisión Federal de Electricidad y de los bancos nacionales de Comercio Exterior y de Fomento Cooperativo. Senador de la República (1982-88). Colaborador la *Revista de Economía*, *El Trimestre Económico* y *Revista de Administración Pública*. Miembro del Colegio Nacional de Economistas, de la Fundación Javier Barros Sierra, del Instituto Nacional de Administración Pública (del que es presidente) y de la Liga de Economistas Revolucionarios. *Doctor honoris causa* por la Universidad de las Américas (1990).

SALINAS DEL PEÑÓN BLANCO ◆ Valle de San Luis Potosí. Lo limitan, al oriente, las sierras de Magdalena y de Charcas; al occidente, las de Ramos y del Gateado; y al sur, el estado de Zacatecas. Se explotan sus yacimientos de sal.

SALINAS PÉREZ, PABLO ◆ n. y m. en la ciudad de México (1926-1991). Dramaturgo. Fue profesor de teatro. Coescribió con Sergio Véjar el argumento de la película *Volantín* (1964), trabajo premiado por una asociación de escritores soviéticos. Autor de más de treinta obras (algunas para niños), como *Las urracas*, *Los guardianes del cielo*, *Resolución*, *Sueños de papel*, *Un día de milagros*, *Un día de paz*, *Verano en la muerte*, *La Godiva era una dama*, *A la sombra de una estrella*, *Cita en la soledad*, *El cordón de San Benito*, *Entre las piedras*, *Entre ratas*, *La estrella adolescente*, *La hora de las locas*, *La ira de dios*, *Tres días en la historia*, *Extraña relación erótica*, *Los hombrecillos de gris* (1958, obra premiada en el Festival de Primavera del INBA), *Tizoc emperador* (1965), *A caza del amor* (Premio Juan Ruiz de Alarcón de la Asociación de Críticos de Teatro, 1965), *Maxtla* (1969), *El cerro de los jumiles* (1970), *Sonata en miau menor para gato indiferente* (premiada en el Festival de Otoño 1970 del INBA), *Las bellas imágenes públicas* (1987, premios Sergio Magaña y María Tereza Montoya), *Las ladinas* (1988), *Mi querido Tomás* (1989) y *El asombro* (1989). Dejó inédita *Las adorables parejas*. Ganó 13 premios por sus obras de teatro.

SALINAS PLIEGO, RICARDO BENJAMÍN ◆ n. en el DF (1956). Se tituló como contador público en la Universidad de Tulane, EUA. Ha sido asesor financiero y desde 1982 presidente del Grupo Elektra, que en 1999 contaba con casi un millar de tiendas. Dirige también la cadena de tiendas Hecali y la empresa de telefonía Unefon. En julio de 1993, al frente de un grupo de inversionistas, adquirió los canales 7 y 13 de Imevisión, 19 estaciones locales y 250 repetidoras, así como los estudios cinematográficos América y los cines de la Operadora de Teatros. Días después de la adquisición transformó Imevisión en TV Azteca, firma que ha adquirido canales en varios países de Centro y Sudamérica.

SALINAS ROCHA, HUGO ◆ n. en Monterrey, NL (1907-¿?). Empresario. Egresado de Wharton School of Businness. Inició su carrera Monterrey, en la fábrica Camas de Metal, colaborando con su padre. En 1931 fue enviado al DF a clausurar la tienda SYR, pero decidió reubicarla y abrir lo que después sería Salinas y Rocha, en Avenida Juárez (1945). Extendió su red de tiendas en todo el país, con más de 100 establecimientos. Introdujo en México el concepto de ventas a la unión familiar. Anunciaba sus productos en la primera plana de los diarios. Se retiró en 1960. Fue impulsor de la mueblería Grupo Elektra (con más de 250 tiendas en el país). Se extendió a las áreas de bienes raíces. En 1980, con su hija Elisa, fundó zapaterías Manetti. En 1993 Grupo Elektra adquirió Imevisión, empresa que se transformó en Televisión Azteca.

SALINAS TORRE, ARMANDO ◆ n. en el DF (1965). Licenciado en derecho por la UNAM. Estudió posgrado en la Universidad Panamericana. Miembro del PAN desde 1985. Profesor del Centro Universitario Anglo-mexicano (1989-91) y la Universidad Panamericana (1992-93). Miembro de la barra de abogados (1992-) y diputado federal (1994-97). Secretario particular del procurador Antonio Lozano Gracia (1994-97). Legislador de la ALDF (1997-2000).

SALINAS VICTORIA ◆ Municipio de Nuevo León situado al norte de Monterrey y contiguo a Cerralvo y Sabinas. Superficie: 1,334.2 km². Habitantes: 15,925, de los cuales 3,280 componen la población económicamente activa. Hablan alguna lengua indígena 74 personas mayores de cinco años (náhuatl 59).

SALINAS VICTORIA ◆ Río de Coahuila y Nuevo León. Nace de la confluencia de los arroyos del Buey y del Mimbre, al noroeste de Monterrey y al sur de la sierra Espinazo de Ambrosio; corre de oeste a este, al sur de la sierra Minas Viejas, y es tributario del río Pesquería, al este de Ciénega de Flores y al nortenoreste de Monterrey.

SALM-SALM, PRINCESA DE ◆ m. en Francia (1840-1878). Su nombre real era Agnes Le Clerq. En 1862 se casó en Estados Unidos con Félix Constantino Alejandro, príncipe de Salm-Salm, a quien acompañó a México para ingresar en la corte de Maximiliano de Habsburgo. Durante el sitio de Querétaro, los príncipes de Salm-Salm intentaron convencer a Maximiliano de que abandonara la ciudad, sin conseguirlo; una vez aprehendido el Habsburgo, la princesa fue a San Luis Potosí para implorar a Benito Juárez el perdón para Maximiliano; se dice que incluso se arrodilló frente al presidente mexicano, a quien ofreció su cuerpo. Sin embargo, en sus memorias escribió que en esos momentos le hicieron falta cien mil pesos para comprar al ejército o al mismo Juárez, versión que ni los conservadores mexicanos dieron por cierta. Escribió un *Diario* (1868, incluido en el libro *Querétaro*, de su esposo) y *Querétaro. Apuntes del diario de la princesa de Salm-Salm* (1869).

SALMERÓN ROIZ, FERNANDO ◆ n. en Córdoba. Ver., y m. en el DF (1925-1997). Licenciado en derecho por la Universidad Veracruzana (1948), maestro (1955) y doctor en filosofía por la UNAM (1965), y la Universidad Albert Luvwing de Friburgo, Alemania. En la UNAM fue profesor, investigador (1964-) director del Instituto de Investigaciones Filosóficas (1966-78) y miembro de la Junta de Gobierno (1986-97). Fundador (1956), profesor (1956-63) y director (1956-58) de la Facultad de Filosofía y Letras de la Universidad Veracruzana, donde también fue secretario general (1957-58) y rector (1961-63). Director general de Enseñanza Superior e Investigación Científica de la SEP (1965-66), rector de la UAM-Iztapalapa (1978-79) y rector general de la UAM (1979-81). Editó las *Obras Completas* de José Gaos. Autor de *Las mocedades de Ortega y Gasset* (1959), *Cuestiones educativas y páginas sobre México* (1962), *La filosofía y las actitudes morales* (1971), *Ética y análisis* (1985), *Los filósofos mexicanos del siglo XX, Enseñanza y filosofía* (1991) *Ensayos filosoficos, Diversidad, cultural y tolerancia* (1998), *Perfiles y recuerdos, The Origins of Analityc Moral. Philosophy and Others Ensays* (1993); en 1999 están en prensa *Escritos sobre la Universidad, Ensayos sobre filosofía moderna y contemporánea, Ética analítica y derecho* y *Estudios sobre Gaos.* Miembro de El Colegio Nacional desde 1972 e integrante de su junta de gobierno desde 1986. Miembro de la Academia Mexicana (de la Lengua) (1994-1997). *Doctor honoris causa* de la Universidad Veracruzana (1980), Premio Universidad Nacional (1993) y Premio Nacional de Ciencias y Artes (1993).

SALMORÁN SALMORÁN, MARÍA CRISTINA ◆ n. en Oaxaca, Oax. (1918). Doctora en derecho por la UNAM (1953). Hizo estudios de posgrado de derecho laboral en la Organización Internacional del Trabajo, en Francia (1952). Profesora de la UNAM (1955-). Ha sido actuaria, secretaria de audiencias, secretaria de acuerdos, dictaminadora, auxiliar titular y presidenta sustituta de juntas especiales (1941-53) y presidenta de la Junta Federal de Conciliación y Arbitraje (1954-61), así como ministra de la Suprema Corte de Justicia (1961-85). Coautora de *El derecho laboral en Latinoamérica* (1974) y autora de *Breviario sobre material laboral* (1956). Miembro de la Alianza de Mujeres de México, de la Asociación Mexicana de Abogadas y de la Sociedad Mexicana de Geografía y Estadística.

SALOMA, ALICIA ◆ n. en Moroleón, Gto. (1924). Pintora. Becada por Ernesto García Cabral estudió en la ENAP (1940) y en La Esmeralda (1966), donde fue alumna de Fernando Castro Pacheco y Nicolás Moreno. En 1967 realizó su primera exposición individual en la Galería Chapultepec del INBA. Ha expuesto en Nueva York (1967 y 70), Niza (1969), Kansas y Pittsburgh (1972) y hay cuadros suyos en los museos de arte moderno de Santiago de Chile y de Morelia, así como en la colección del Banco Nacional del Pacífico, en California. Ha hecho también escultura. Ganó el primer premio de la Seventh Anual Art Exhibition Foreign Friends, de Acapulco.

SALOMA, LUIS G. ◆ n. en Huejotzingo, Pue., y m. en el DF (1866-1956). Violinista. Estudió en el Conservatorio Nacional (1892), del que también fue profesor. Se especializó en la Escuela de Música de Hoch, en Berlín (1904), becado por el gobierno. En 1896 fundó el Cuarteto Saloma, primer conjunto mexicano de música de cámara, que dio a conocer en México obras de Debussy, Ravel y Scriabine. Tocó como solista en el cuarteto de Bruselas e investigó el desarrollo de la música para violín desde 1693. Volvió a México y en 1906 se hizo cargo de la dirección de la orquesta de alumnos del Conservatorio. Fue fundador y director de la Orquesta

Iglesia de Nuestra Señora de Guadalupe en Salinas Victoria, Nuevo León

FOTO: FONDO EDITORIAL GRUPO AZABACHE

Bach-Beethoven-Brahms (1918), director de la primera Orquesta Sinfónica Nacional (1920), organizador de la Orquesta Femenina Haydn-Beethoven y director permanente de la Orquesta de Cámara de la UNAM. Autor de un *Cuarteto de cuerdas* que le valió un primer premio en Puebla (1900). Segundo premio del concurso anual de la Escuela de Música Hoch (1904) y medalla al Mérito Artístico por medio siglo de docencia musical (1956).

Carlos Salomón Cámara

Salomón, Moisés ◆ n. en Líbano y m. cerca de Cuautla, Mor. (?-1930). Exiliado de su país por los turcos llegó a México en 1906. Se dedicó al comercio ambulante. En Jojutla hizo amistad con Emiliano Zapata, de quien luego sería compadre. Se incorporó a la revolución como proveedor de tela para los uniformes del Ejército Libertador del Sur y por su conducto otros libaneses y sirios radicados en México prestaron diversos servicios a la lucha armada. Comerció después en Guerrero hasta establecerse en la ciudad de México (1919). Fundó la tienda El Puerto de Beirut. En 1921 se trasladó a los campos petroleros de Veracruz. Murió en un accidente automovilístico.

Salomón Cámara, Carlos ◆ n. en Tenosique, Tab. (1950). Licenciado en Economía por la UNAM (1970-75), con maestría en administración pública por la misma y en programación y planeación por el INAP. Profesor de economía en la UNAM (1972-81). Secretario particular en el SNTE (1989). Pertenece al PRI desde 1983, en el cual ha desempeñado diversos cargos. Ha sido consejero de la dirección comercial de Banrural (1979-82), gerente general de ventas de Fertimex (1979-82), jefe de asesores de la dirección de Ferronales (1982-83), contralor interno de las delegaciones Xochimilco (1983-84), Cuajimalpa (1984-85) y Magdalena Contreras (1985-88), subdelegado administrativo de la Gustavo A. Madero (1988), subdelegado de participación ciudadana en Venustiano Carranza (1990-91), secretario de Desarrollo Social en el DDF (1993), delegado en Coyoacán (1993-94), director general de Comunicación Social de la Presidencia (1994-95) y director de la Lotería Nacional (1995-). Autor de *El estancamiento económico en Brasil* (1972), *Dialéctica del proceso ganadero* (1975), *La industria de alimentos balanceados en Tabasco* (1976), *Elecciones 1898, parteaguas democrático en México* (1989) y *México: Estado y sociedad civil* (1990).

Salón de la Plástica Mexicana ◆ Institución fundada el 16 de noviembre de 1949 como una galería de ventas libres dependiente del Departamento de Artes Plásticas del INBA. Según sus documentos básicos, "proporciona a los artistas de México todas las facilidades para la exhibición y venta de su obra, sin descuento de comisión alguna por este servicio". Para el INBA es "parte esencial de su vasto programa de estímulo a la creación y divulgación del arte mexicano". Presta gratuitamente sus servicios al público en calidad de consejero artístico. Inicialmente tuvo su sede en Puebla 154. Su primera directora fue Susana Gamboa. Los fundadores son Ignacio Aguirre, David Alfaro Siqueiros, Raúl Anguiano, Luis Arenal, el *Dr. Atl*, Abelardo Ávila, Angelina Beloff, Alberto Beltrán, Ángel Bracho, Celia Calderón, Federico Cantú, Fernando Castro Pacheco, José Chávez Morado, Erasto Cortés, Olga Costa, Dolores Cueto, Germán Cueto, Gonzalo de la Paz Pérez, Francisco Dosamantes, Jesús Escobedo, Anturo García Bustos, Jorge González Camarena, Jesús Guerrero Galván, Xavier Guerrero, Frida Kahlo, Agustín Lazo, Amador Lugo, Leopoldo Méndez, Carlos Mérida, Guillermo Meza, Gustavo Montoya, Francisco Mora, Nicolás Moreno, Nefero, Luis Nishizawa, Juan O'Gorman, Pablo O'Higgins, Carlos Orozco Romero, Luis Ortiz Monasterio, Feliciano Peña, Fanny Ravinovitch (Fanny Rabel), Everardo Ramírez, Manuel Rodríguez Lozano, Diego Rivera, Antonio Ruiz, Juan Soriano, Cordelia Urueta, Héctor Xavier, Desiderio Hernández Xochitiotzin y Alfredo Zalce.

Salonio, Antonio María ◆ n. en Veracruz, Ver., y m. en la ciudad de México (¿1805?-1879). Abogado graduado en 1829 ante el Ministerio Superior de Justicia de Veracruz. Diputado local (1830), ministro del Tribunal Superior de Justicia (1837) y gobernador del Departamento de Veracruz (1838-41 y 1845-46). Fue dos veces diputado federal, en tres ocasiones senador y tres veces presidente del Tribunal Superior de Justicia de Veracruz. En 1847, al producirse la invasión estadounidense, era presidente del Congreso de la Unión. Contador mayor de Hacienda (1853) y magistrado de la Suprema Corte de Justicia hasta su muerte.

Salsipuedes ◆ Canal de Baja California situado en el mar de Cortés, entre tierra firme y las islas de Salsipuedes, Rasa y San Lorenzo, al sureste de la isla Ángel de la Guarda. En el extremo sur del canal está la bahía de San Rafael.

Saltabarranca ◆ Municipio de Veracruz situado al este de Tlacotalpan y al sureste de Alvarado. Superficie: 91.30 km^2. Habitantes: 6,289, de los cuales 1,641 forman la población económicamente activa. Hablan alguna lengua indígena cinco personas mayores de cinco años.

Saltiel Cohen, Jenny ◆ n. en el DF (1951). Licenciada en ciencias políticas y administración pública por la UNAM. Fue analista del Departamento Jurídico de la Cámara de Diputados, de la secretaría particular del candidato del PRI a la Presidencia de la República (1982) y en la Dirección de Quejas de la Presidencia de la República (1982-88). Investigadora del Programa de las Naciones Unidas para el Medio Ambiente (1988-1990), consultora de análisis político-electoral (1994-97), consejera electoral del Consejo Local del IFE en el DF (1994-97) y delegada del Gobierno del DF en Cuajimalpa (1998-).

Saltillo ◆ Municipio de Coahuila situado en el extremo sudoriental del estado, en los límites con Zacatecas y Nuevo León. Superficie: 6,837 km^2. Habitantes: 527,979, de los cuales 141,236 forman la población económicamente activa. Hablan alguna lengua indígena 613 personas mayores de cinco años (náhuatl 190, mayo 151, mazahua 91 y otomí 60). Es un centro industrial que cuenta con numerosas fábricas de hilados y tejidos, alimenticias, de vinos, jabones, aceites, enlatadoras y de maquinaria agrícola. El territorio del actual municipio fue frontera de los seminómadas huachichiles y coahuiltecos, de la nación chichimeca, grupos desaparecidos debido a las enfermedades traídas por los conquistadores españoles, quienes nunca pudieron derrotar a estas tribus con las armas. Su cabecera, del mismo nombre, es también capital de la entidad. Ésta, por encargo de Martín López de Ibarra, gobernador de Nueva Vizcaya, fue fundada en 1577 por Alberto del Canto, con el nombre de Villa de Santiago del Saltillo del Ojo de Agua, aunque en 1827, por un breve lapso, fue oficialmente llamada Leona Vicario y un año después fue elevada al rango de ciudad, con el nombre de Saltillo y en unión de la vecina villa de San Esteban de Nueva Tlaxcala, poblada desde el siglo XVI por familias tlaxcaltecas trasladadas hasta ahí por los conquistadores con dos finalidades: servir a los españoles en tareas defensa y enseñar a las etnias de la región los rudimentos de la agricultura y otras ocupaciones propias del sedentarismo. El principal edificio de la época virreinal es la catedral, que empezó a construirse en 1745 y se terminó alrededor de 1810. Existen también la capilla de Landín y varias casas, como muestra de la arquitectura colonial. Fue célebre la feria anual de Saltillo, celebrada de septiembre a octubre hasta 1814; a la misma concurrían, principalmente, los comerciantes de "tierra adentro" (lo que ahora son los estados de Sonora, Sinaloa, Chihuahua, Durango, Nuevo León, Tamaulipas, Nuevo México y Texas) para vender, comprar o trocar productos asiáticos, europeos o manufacturas de los indios del norte; se enviaban también los excedentes de otras dos ferias célebres, las de Acapulco y Xalapa. La diócesis de Saltillo fue erigida en 1891 por León XIII.

SALTO, EL ◆ Cabecera del municipio Pueblo Nuevo, Durango (☛).

SALTO, EL ◆ Municipio de Jalisco situado al sureste de Guadalajara y contiguo a Tlaquepaque. Superficie: 41.5 km². Habitantes: 70,085, de los cuales 10,964 forman la población económicamente activa. Hablan alguna lengua indígena 170 personas mayores de cinco años (purépecha 69). Debe su nombre a que, en su territorio, el río Santiago forma la cascada o salto de Juanacatlán.

SALTO, JOSÉ GUADALUPE ◆ m. en Valladolid, hoy Morelia, Mich. (?-1812). Cura de Teremendo. Se incorporó a la guerra de Independencia en 1810. En julio de 1811 participó en el ataque a Valladolid, donde fue aprehendido; se acogió al indulto y volvió a su curato, pero nuevamente se levantó en armas. Coronel en 1812, diezmó a las fuerzas del realista Linares, auxiliado por los indios de la región. Durante un combate en Teremendo fue herido de gravedad y capturado por los realistas. Murió poco después, a causa de sus heridas, pero su cadáver fue fusilado para cumplir la condena de muerte que se le había dictado.

SALTO DE AGUA ◆ Municipio de Chiapas situado en el norte del estado, en los límites con Tabasco, al suroeste de Palenque. Superficie: 1,289.2 km². Habitantes: 45,450, de los cuales 10,547 forman la población económicamente activa. Hablan alguna lengua indígena 31,438 personas mayores de cinco años (chol 28,233 y tzeltal 3,148). Indígenas monolingües: 11,416.

SALTO DE VALADEZ ◆ Sierra de Guerrero. Forma parte de la sierra Madre del Sur y se localiza al sur del valle de Chilpancingo, al norte de Tierra Colorada. Su cima más alta es el volcán Negro, a 2,470 metros sobre el nivel del mar.

SALVADOR, REPÚBLICA DE EL ◆ Estado centroamericano que limita al norte y este con Honduras, al sur con el océano Pacífico y al oeste con Guatemala. Es la más pequeña y más densamente poblada República de Centroamérica: tiene una superficie de 20,749 km² y en 1998 tenía una población de 6,100,000 habitantes. Su capital, San Salvador, tenía 422,570 habitantes en 1992 (1,522,126 en toda el área metropolitana). Otras ciudades de importancia son Soyapango (251,811 habitantes en 1992) y Santa Ana (202,337). Su idioma oficial es el español y se habla náhuatl en numerosas comunidades. La moneda es el colón. *Historia*: a mediados del siglo XI, cuando la cultura maya se extendía sobre la mayor parte de Centroamérica, llegaron al actual territorio salvadoreño los pipiles, llevados por Topilzin Acxitl, último señor de Tula, quien emigró en busca del presunto lugar de origen de los toltecas. A la llegada de los españoles, en el siglo XVI, dentro de las fronteras salvadoreñas de hoy vivían mayas, pipiles, lencas, chortis, ulúas, pocomanos, izalcos y panchos. El más importante asentamiento hu-

FOTO: FONDO EDITORIAL GRUPO AZABACHE

Museo de las Aves de México en Saltillo, Coahuila

Timbre de la República de El Salvador

República de El Salvador

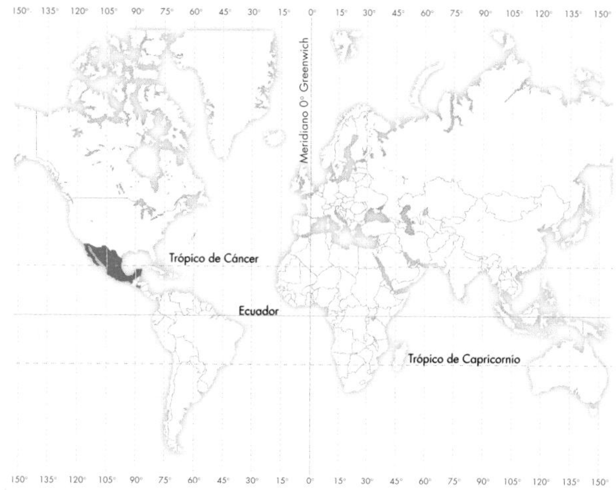

mano era Cuscatlán y el idioma predominante el náhuatl, por la influencia que había alcanzado el imperio mexica. En 1522, Andrés Niño bordeó la costa hasta el actual golfo de Fonseca, llamado así por este explorador. En 1524, tras someter a Guatemala, Pedro de Alvarado incursionó hasta Cuscatlán, asesinó al gobernante Atlácatl *el Viejo* y regresó a Guatemala. A principios de 1525 arribó Diego de Alvarado y fundó la villa de San Salvador, tras acabar con la resistencia encabezada por Atlácatl *el Joven*. En 1542, el territorio fue incorporado a la Real Audiencia de los Confines y más tarde a la Capitanía General de Guatemala (junto con Honduras, Chiapas, Costa Rica y Nicaragua). En 1786 se creó la Intendencia de San Salvador. En 1811 y 1814 fracasaron dos tentativas independentistas encabezadas por José Matías Delgado, Manuel José Arce y Manuel Rodríguez. En 1821 Guatemala proclamó su independencia de la Corona española, mediante un acta que firmó José Matías Delgado como representante de la entonces provincia de El Salvador. El 5 de enero del año siguiente, por medio del Acta de Unión, las provincias de Centroamérica pasaron a formar parte del imperio mexicano. En El Salvador surgió una fuerte oposición, encabezada por José Matías Delgado, e Iturbide envió un contingente militar, encabezado por Gabino Gaínza y Vicente Filisola, para someter a los rebeldes. En 1823, luego de la retirada de las tropas de Filisola, un grupo de soldados mexicanos decidieron fijar su residencia en la hacienda El Cipresal, colindante con la ciudad de San Salvador. En septiembre de 1828 estos soldados, ya casados con mujeres salvadoreñas, formaron un caserío al que llamaron Mejicanos, contiguo a la capital, que todavía existe con ese nombre. Al caer Iturbide se constituyó la Federación de las Provincias Unidas del Centro de América, y José Simeón Cañas decretó la abolición de la esclavitud. Previamente, aún en 1822, el Congreso General de la Provincia de El Salvador intentó integrarse a Estados Unidos, en calidad de miembro de la Unión Americana. En 1824 El Salvador promulgó su primera Constitución, primera también de Centroamérica. Un año después, Manuel José Arce fue elegido presidente de la República. En 1841 se separó de la Federación y en 1842 fracasó el intento de reunir en una sola república a El Salvador, Honduras y Nicaragua. En 1862 el gobierno salvadoreño condenó la idea de los conservadores de establecer una monarquía en México. El ministro Montúfar, representante salvadoreño en Washington, comunicó a Matías Romero la oposición de su país a una monarquía europea en México y a las intenciones del presidente guatemalteco Carrera de unirse al eventual imperio mexicano. Por la misma época, El Salvador, Honduras y Nicaragua tuvieron la intención de invadir Guatemala para derrocar a Carrera y establecer un gobierno liberal. La idea se desechó, pues hubiera podido provocar una intervención francesa en Centroamérica. En 1873 el venezolano Luis Pérez Gómez, quien en México había alcanzado el grado de general de brigada en las fuerzas conservadoras durante la guerra de los Tres Años, murió cuando era director del Colegio Militar de El Salvador. En 1880 se introdujo en el país el cultivo del café y se produjo una revuelta de los grupos dominantes, interesados en despojar a los campesinos de sus tierras. En 1917 murió en San Salvador el médico mexicano Rodolfo B. González, quien fuera jefe del servicio médico militar salvadoreño e impulsor de una campaña de vacunación. Luis Felipe Recinos representó en México a los obreros salvadoreños como delegado fraternal, al fundarse la Confederación General de Trabajadores. Recinos fue, asimismo, miembro del comité local del DF del Partido Comunista Mexicano (1920-21). En este partido militaron también los salvadoreños Farabundo Martí y Miguel Ángel Vázquez. En 1929 se inició una crisis económica y en 1932 estalló una insurrección que fue reprimida por la dictadura de Maximiliano Hernández, con un saldo de 12,000 a 20,000 muertos, entre ellos el líder comunista Farabundo Martí. La tiranía de Maximiliano Hernández se prolongó hasta 1944. En 1962 la Asamblea Legislativa Constituyente aprobó una nueva Constitución. En 1969 Honduras expulsó de su territorio a unos 11 mil salvadoreños (trabajadores migratorios), lo que dio inicio a la llamada "guerra del futbol", por haber comenzado luego de un encuentro deportivo entre las selecciones de ambos países. El Salvador invadió Honduras y la paz fue concertada tras una reunión de emergencia de la OEA. En 1970 el Partido de Conciliación Nacional obtuvo la mayoría de curules en las elecciones parlamentarias. En 1972 la Asamblea Nacional nombró presidente al coronel Arturo A. Molina, tras unas elecciones impugnadas por la Unión Nacional Opositora, de José Napoleón Duarte, quien fue expulsado del país. Un año después Molina se entrevistó con el presidente Luis Echeverría, en México. A mediados de los años setenta hubo un recrudecimiento de la violencia política y un aumento en la actividad guerrillera. En 1977, con el país en estado de sitio, llegó a la presidencia el militar Carlos Humberto Romero, quien desplegó una amplia actividad represiva contra las protestas populares. Como resultado de la violencia gubernamental hubo unos 7,000 muertos y el resurgimiento de la oposición izquierdista armada. En 1979 una junta cívico-militar derrocó a Romero y llevó a la presidencia al coronel Adolfo Arnoldo Majano, quien a su vez fue derrocado en 1980 y se asiló en México. En ese año fue nacionalizada la banca y el 24 de marzo bandas armadas y protegidas por el gobierno asesinaron al arzobispo Óscar Arnulfo Romero, durante una misa en la que estaba presente el arzobispo primado de México, cardenal Ernesto Corripio Ahumada. Duarte fue nombrado presidente y el país entró en un estado de guerra civil. En 1980 se constituyó el Frente Farabundo Martí para la Liberación Nacional (FMLN), que agrupaba a las organizaciones armadas:

Fuerzas Populares de Liberación Farabundo Martí, Partido Comunista de El Salvador, Fuerzas Armadas de la Resistencia Nacional, Ejército Revolucionario del Pueblo y Partido Revolucionario de los Trabajadores Centroamericanos. En ese mismo año fue asesinado por un francotirador el periodista mexicano Ignacio Rodríguez Terrazas, por lo que el embajador Héctor Pérez Gallardo fue retirado y el canciller mexicano, Jorge Castañeda, declaró: "en El Salvador hay una violación de los derechos humanos" y, por ende, las relaciones "son difíciles, no son normales". En 1981 Duarte anunció la creación de una Asamblea Nacional Constituyente y en agosto de ese año Francia y México reconocieron a la coalición FMLN-FDR como una fuerza representativa del pueblo salvadoreño. En 1982 se creó la asamblea y A. Magaña fue nombrado presidente, con el ultraderechista Roberto D'Aubuisson como líder legislativo. Mientras tanto, el FMLN-FDR dominó los departamentos de Chalatenango y Morazán. En 1983 fracasó una sublevación militar dirigida por Sigfrido Ochoa, se produjo una visita del papa Juan Pablo II y se promulgó una nueva Constitución. Un año más tarde, Duarte resultó triunfador en las elecciones presidenciales, decretó una amnistía para los presos políticos e inició conversaciones con el FMLN-FDR para llegar a la pacificación del país. Dichas conversaciones fueron interrumpidas por el propio Duarte. En 1985 el PDC ganó las elecciones legislativas, aun cuando la derecha impugnó el resultado de los comicios. En 1986 la Iglesia salvadoreña denunció que la guerra civil había causado, en seis años de guerra, 60,000 víctimas. En octubre de ese mismo año, un terremoto destruyó gran parte de la capital salvadoreña y dejó 20,000 damnificados. A principios de 1989 los representantes del gobierno y del FDR-FMLN se dieron cita en la ciudad de México para entablar pláticas tendientes a una solución pacífica de la guerra civil salvadoreña. Se celebraron nuevas elecciones presidenciales que fueron ganadas por Alfredo Cristiani, de la ultraderecha, que en entre otros candidatos derrotó a Guillermo Ungo, líder del FDR, distanciado para entonces del FMLN. En 1991 los gobiernos de México, Costa Rica, El Salvador, Guatemala, Honduras y Nicaragua acordaron integrar las economías de sus países en los siguientes seis años. En ese mismo año, bajo el auspicio de la ONU, comenzaron en la ciudad de México las negociaciones entre el gobierno salvadoreño y el FMLN, que decretó un cese indefinido de las hostilidades. El primer día de 1992, en una reunión en Nueva York, se acordó el fin de la guerra civil, que ya duraba 12 años, y 15 días después se formalizó la firma de la paz en una ceremonia en el Castillo de Chapultepec.

Salvador, El ◆ Municipio de Zacatecas situado en el extremo noreste de la entidad, en los límites con San Luis Potosí, Nuevo León y Coahuila. Superficie: 281.25 km². Habitantes: 3,798, de los cuales 798 forman la población económicamente activa.

Salvador Alvarado ◆ Municipio de Sinaloa situado en el norte del estado, al noroeste de Culiacán y contiguo a Guasave. Superficie: 1,195.5 km². Habitantes: 72,605, de los cuales 18,434 forman la población económicamente activa. Hablan alguna lengua indígena 48 personas mayores de cinco años. Es el municipio más pequeño del estado. Se constituyó en 1963 (con localidades segregadas al de Mocorito) y pertenece al circuito turístico Culiacán-Guamúchil-Mocorito. Cuenta con edificios coloniales, zonas arqueológicas y balnearios de aguas termales. La cabecera es Guamúchil.

Salvador Escalante ◆ Municipio de Michoacán situado en el centro del estado, al suroeste de Quiroga y al suroeste de Morelia. Superficie: 460.4 km². Habitantes: 38,236, de los cuales 7,148 forman la población económicamente activa. Hablan alguna lengua indígena 13 personas mayores de cinco años. Es conocida su Feria del Cobre, que se celebra del 10 al 17 de agosto. En ella se incluye una exposición de artesanías de cobre martillado que le han dado fama a la región. La cabecera (llamada oficialmente Villa Escalante, pero más conocida por su antiguo nombre de Santa Clara del Cobre) fue fundada en 1553; en ella, Vasco de Quiroga estableció una fundición de cobre que a fines del siglo XVIII se incendió y destruyó casi todo el poblado. En 1918 el pueblo fue incendiado nuevamente por las tropas revolucionarias de Ignacio Chávez y los habitantes de Itziparáchihco, donde habitaba una gran cantidad de cobreros, ocuparon las casonas coloniales abandonadas. Cuenta con el Museo del Cobre y con un kiosco recubierto con láminas de ese metal. Sirvió como escenario para la novela *La vida inútil de Pito Pérez*, de José Rubén Romero. Cuenta con 350 talleres donde laboran unos 1,500 artesanos.

Salvat Rodríguez, Agustín ◆ n. en Veracruz, Ver. (1909-). Licenciado en derecho por la UNAM. Miembro del PRI,

Aguas termales en Ciénega del Casal, Salvador Alvarado, Sinaloa

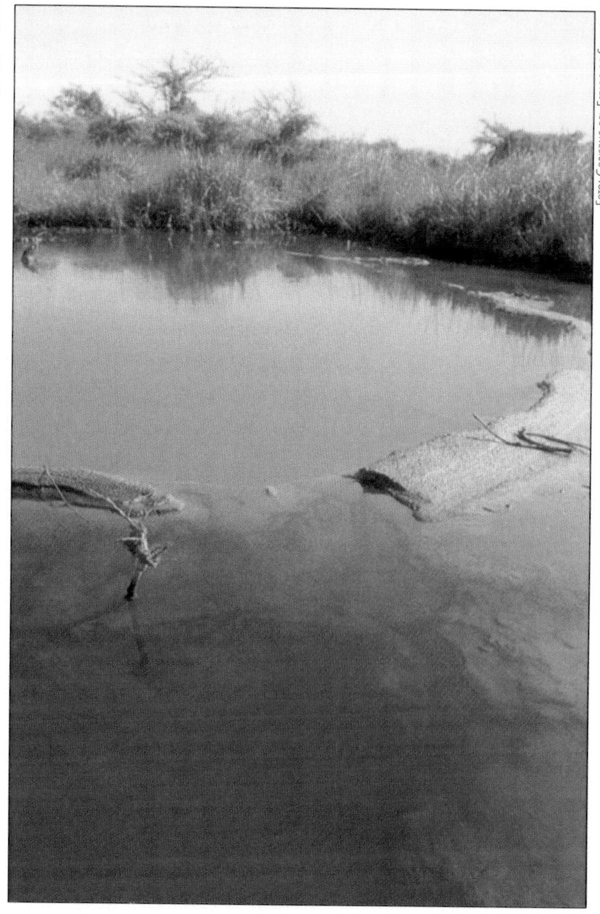

Foto: Gobierno del Estado de Sinaloa

del que fue tesorero en los periodos presidenciales de López Mateos y Ruiz Cortines. Fue empleado de la Compañía Mexicana de Luz y Fuerza Motriz (1924-39). Fue secretario del exterior del Sindicato Mexicano de Electricistas (1935). Jefe del Departamento de Turismo en el gobierno de Gustavo Díaz Ordaz (1964-70), representante de México ante la Organización Internacional de Turismo (1979-81) y embajador en Checoslovaquia (1981-82). Fue colaborador de *Excélsior*. Impulsó el sistema de desayunos escolares, centros de asistencia a la senectud y una villa de pescadores en Baja California Sur.

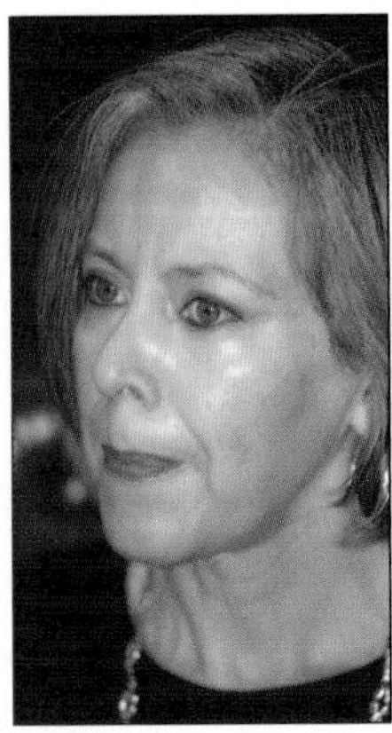

Norma Samaniego

Salvatierra ◆ Municipio de Guanajuato situado en el sur del estado, en los límites con Michoacán, al suroeste de Celaya. Superficie: 507.7 km². Habitantes: 97,822, de los cuales 21,642 forman la población económicamente activa. Hablan alguna lengua indígena 53 personas mayores de cinco años (mazahua 20). Entre sus atractivos turísticos, cuenta con la iglesia del Tercer Orden, el templo y convento del Carmen, los portales de Hidalgo y el paseo del Salto, la zona arqueológica de La Quemada con el templo a Ehécatl, lo que indica que la región era una avanzada del imperio tolteca. Su cabecera, del mismo nombre, fue fundada por Juan Bautista de Luyando y Bermeo, en 1643, en el sitio en que se hallaba la población purépecha de Huatzindeo.

Estatua de fray Andrés de San Miguel en Salvatierra, Guanajuato

Foto: Fondo Editorial Grupo Azabache

Salvatierra, de ◆ Valle de Guanajuato regado por el río Lerma. Está situado al sur-suroeste de Celaya. Tiene al oeste la laguna de Yuriria, al noroeste se encuentra el valle de Santiago (del que lo separa el cerro de Culiacán), al sureste el de Acámbaro y al suroeste el lago de Cuitzeo.

Salvatierra, Juan María de ◆ n. en Italia y m. en Guadalajara, Jal. (?-1717). Jesuita. Evangelizó en Chínipas, Chihuahua (1680-90). Fue visitador de las misiones en Sonora (1691), rector de los colegios de Guadalajara y Tepotzotlán y fundador de varias misiones en Baja California (1697-1704), donde vivió de 1707 a 1716. Autor de *Copia de cuatro cartas de el padre Juan María de Salvatierra de la Compañía de Jesús para solicitar medios para la empresa de California* (1698).

Sam López, Jesús Antonio ◆ n. en San Blas, Nay. (1935). Licenciado en derecho por la UNAM (1957), de la que fue profesor (1964-70). Ha sido jefe de la Oficina Jurídica (1962-64) y subdirector general de Prevención Social de la Secretaría de Gobernación (1964-70), director del penal de las Islas Marías (1966), director general de la Policía Judicial del Distrito y Territorios Federales (1970-75), procurador de Justicia de Nayarit (1976-81), jefe del Departamento de Estudios Especiales de Fertimex (1981-82) y director de Control de Estupefacientes y coordinador general de Operaciones de la Procuraduría General de la República (1982-85).

Samahil ◆ Municipio de Yucatán situado en el oeste del estado, al suroeste de Mérida y al noroeste de Ticul. Superficie: 185.22 km². Habitantes: 4,184, de los cuales 966 forman la población económicamente activa. Hablan alguna lengua indígena 2,417 personas mayores de cinco años (maya 2,415).

Samaniego Barriga, Manuel ◆ n. en Pangamacutiro, Mich. (1930). Sacerdote ordenado en 1953. Ha sido obispo titular de Passo Corese y auxiliar del obispo de Saltillo (1969), así como obispo de Ciudad Altamirano (1971-79) y de Cuautitlán (1979-).

Samaniego Breach, Norma ◆ n. en el DF (1944). Licenciada en economía por la UNAM (1962-66) con posgrado en planeación económica por el Instituto de Estudios Sociales, de Holanda (1969-70). Pertenece al PRI. Ha sido analista de la Dirección General de Planeación de la Secretaría de la Presidencia (1967-69), profesora e investigadora de la UNAM (1971), asesora en la Dirección Técnica de la Comisión Nacional para la Participación de los Trabajadores en las Utilidades de las Empresas (1974), subdirectora de Estudios de la Distribución del Ingreso y del Salario (1975) y directora adjunta de Investigación Económica de la Comisión Nacional de los Salarios Mínimos (1976), consultora externa del Programa de las Naciones Unidas para el Desarrollo (1977-78), asesora del subdirector general de Servicios Institucionales del IMSS (1978-82), directora técnica (1983-88) y presidenta (1988-91) de la Comisión Nacional de Salarios Mínimos, consultora externa de la Cepal (1987), subsecretaria del Trabajo y Previsión Social (1991-94), secretaria de la Contraloría (1994-95) y asesora de la Presidencia de la República (1995-). Autora de *Evaluation of the Impact of Minimum Wages on the Mexican Economy* (1984), *Los efectos de la crisis en las condiciones de vida de la población en México* (1986) y de *El empleo en México durante la crisis y perspectivas*. Pertenece al Colegio Nacional de Economistas y a la Liga de Economistas Revolucionarios.

Samaniego Delgado, Mariano ◆ n. en Bavispe, Son., y m. en Ciudad Juárez, Chih. (1831-1905). Médico cirujano graduado en Francia (1859). Ejerció su profesión en Ciudad Juárez. Ocupó diversos puestos públicos en Chihuahua, fue diputado federal (1867) y 10 veces diputado local. En 1872 luchó contra los pronunciados del Plan de la Noria y gobernó el estado (1876-77). Fue derrocado por la revuelta de

Tuxtepec. Volvió a ejercer el Ejecutivo estatal en 1881 y en 1882-83.

SAMANIEGO, FIDEL ◆ n. en el DF (1953). Periodista. Su nombre completo es Fidel Jesús Samaniego Reyes. Hizo estudios de derecho en la UNAM y en la Escuela Libre de Derecho, y de periodismo en la Escuela de Periodismo Carlos Septién García. Ha colaborado en *Señal* (1976-78), *El Universal* (1978-95) y *La Crónica de hoy* (1997-) y ha sido comentarista político en la emisora Radio 13 (1997-). Autor de *Las entrañas del poder* (1994). Premio Nacional de Periodismo en el género de crónica (1989). También recibió uno de los premios del Club de Periodistas de México (1995).

SÁMANO TORRES, ALFONSO T. ◆ m. en Tlaquiltenango, Mor. (¿1887?-1959). En 1912 se incorporó al Ejército Libertador del Sur. Fue senador y gobernador sustituto de Morelos en mayo de 1938. Fundador de la Liga de Comunidades Agrarias de Morelos y dirigente del Frente Zapatista.

SAMAYOA LEÓN, MARIANO ◆ n. en Chiapa de Corzo, Chis., y m. en el DF (1893-1960). Profesor normalista (1914). Fue dos veces diputado federal por el Partido Cooperatista, secretario de gobierno en Chiapas con Efraín Gutiérrez al frente de Ejecutivo local (1936-40), a quien sustituyó en la gubernatura en 1936. Fundador de la Confederación de Organizaciones Populares, director de Asuntos Indígenas (1946-52) y subdirector de Enseñanza Agrícola de la SEP. Se le otorgó el grado de mayor en el cuerpo de Veteranos de la Revolución.

SAMPEDRO, JOSÉ DE JESÚS ◆ n. en Zacatecas, Zac. (1950). Poeta. Estudió economía en la Universidad Autónoma de Zacatecas. Fue integrante del taller literario de José Donoso Pareja en San Luis Potosí y coordinador de un taller literario en La Laguna (1976-86). Militó en el Partido Comunista Mexicano. Es director de la revista *DosFilos*. Profesor de literatura, investigador, asesor editorial y director de la editorial DosFilos de la Universidad Autónoma de Zacatecas. Ha colaborado en *Crisis* (de Argentina), *Xilote, Los Universitarios, Punto y Aparte, Casa del Tiempo, Revista de la Universidad de México, El Gallo Ilustrado, Sábado, La Cultura en México, El Porvenir, El Sol de Zacatecas, Sicoseo* (de Ecuador), *Encuentro, El Buscón* y *Cambio*. Coautor del volumen de poesía *Crónicas de viaje* (1975) y del libro de *rock Crines* (1984). Autor de *Un (ejemplo) salto de gato pinto* (Premio Nacional de Poesía de Aguascalientes 1975), *Si entra él, yo entro* (1981), *La estrella, el tonto, los amantes* (ensayo, poesía y narrativa, 1985) y *Land Ho!* (1993).

SAMPEDRO, JUAN GERARDO ◆ n. en Zacatecas. Zac. (1955). Escritor. Hizo estudios de derecho en la Universidad Autónoma de Zacatecas. Licenciado en en psicología en la Universidad Autónoma de Puebla. Miembro de los talleres literarios de la Casa de la Cultura de Puebla y profesor en la Preparatoria de Tecamachalco. Ha colaborado en las revistas *Crítica, Paspartú, Arcano 17, El Pez Soluble* y *Dos Filos*, en la que formó parte del consejo editorial. Coautor de *Lo decisivo es ser fiel* (cuentos, 1982). Autor de los volúmenes de cuento *Lo terrible ya ha pasado* (1984) y *Tiempo de cambio* (1986).

SAMPER, BALTASAR ◆ n. en España y m. en el DF (1888-1966). Músico. Estudió en París con Eduardo Risler y antes, en Barcelona, con Enrique Granados y Felipe Pedrell. Autor de sardanas, composiciones para piano, obras corales, *Dos suites de canons i dances de la illa de Mallorca* para orquesta (1929), *L'estiu, cano trista, Joc de nins* para coro, *Balada, Variaciones, Danzas mallorquinas para piano y orquesta, Cantic Espiritual* para coro, orquesta y órgano, *Ritual de pagesia*, concierto para piano y orquesta, *Balada de luard* y *El marinero*. Colaborador del *Canconer popular de Catalunya* y crítico musical de *La Publicitat* de Barcelona. Llegó exiliado a México en 1942. Escribió música para cine, fue profesor del Conservatorio Nacional y se dedicó a la investigación folklórica. Dirigió el Archivo del Folklore Mexicano del Departamento de Música de la SEP. Tradujo la *Historia de la música* de Franco Abbiati (1958). Autor de los libros *Investigación folklórica en México* (1962) y *Folklore mexicano* (1945).

SAMPERIO, GUILLERMO ◆ n. en el DF (1948). Escritor. Ha coordinado talleres de creación. En la unidad Azcapotzalco de la UAM fue profesor (1979-80) y coordinador del grupo de radio (1980). Guionista y productor de Radio Educación para los programas *La literatura: hoy* y el noticiero cultural del INBA, coordinador de programas de la Dirección General de Publicaciones (1980-82), editor del *Boletín Enlace* de la Subsecretaría de Educación Superior (1980-82) y subdirector de la Comisión de Publicaciones del Consejo del Sistema Nacional de Educación Tecnológica (1983-85). coordinador del taller de narrativa del Instituto Tamaulipeco de Bellas Artes (1984), subdirector de Documentación Laboral de la Secretaría del Trabajo (1985-86), subdirector (1986-88) y director de Literatura del INBA (1986-90). Colabora en publicaciones literarias mexicanas y extranjeras. Coautor de la novela policiaca *El hombre equivocado* (1988). Autor de los volúmenes de cuento *Cuando el tacto toma la palabra* (1974), *Fuera del ring* (1975), *Cruz y cuernos* (1976), *Tomando vuelo y demás cuentos* (1976), *Miedo ambiente* (1977, Premio Casa de las Américas), *Lenin en el futbol* (1978), *Textos extraños* (1981), *Gente de la ciudad* (1986) y la recopilación *Cuando el tacto toma la palabra. Cuentos 1974-1999* (1999); de los relatos *Manifiesto de amor* (1980) y *Cuaderno imaginario* (1990); el poemario *De este lado y del otro* (1982), la colección de dibujos *Querida* (1985); la antología *Miedo ambiente y otros miedos* (1986); la novela *La señal oculta* (1996, con 42 fotos de Lázaro Blanco); y de *¿Por qué Colosio?* (1995).

Foto: Rogelio Cuéllar

Guillermo Samperio

SAMPERIO JÁUREGUI, DOMINGO JOSÉ ◆ n. y m. en España (1901-1968). Arquitecto y musicólogo. Fue profesor en la Escuela de Artes y Oficios y consejero de Hacienda en Santander, Palancín y Burgos (1931-39). Llegó

San Agustín de las Cuevas

exiliado a México en 1939. Trabajó en la empresa Bertran Cusiné y en un despacho de arquitectos; dio clases de danza flamenca y castañuelas adaptadas a la música clásica a Pilar Rioja y Lucerito Tena, entre otras.

San Agustín Amatengo ◆ Municipio de Oaxaca situado en la zona central del estado, al noroeste de Miahuatlán. Superficie: 58.69 km². Habitantes: 1,883, de los cuales 639 forman la población económicamente activa. Hablan zapoteco 12 personas mayores de cinco años.

San Agustín Atenango ◆ Municipio de Oaxaca situado en la zona noroccidental del estado, al suroeste de Huajuapan de León. Superficie: 82.93 km². Habitantes: 2,422, de los cuales 445 forman la población económicamente activa. Hablan alguna lengua indígena 1,115 personas mayores de cinco años (mixteco 1,108). Indígenas monolingües: 81.

San Agustín de las Cuevas ◆ Nombre de la población de Tlalpan durante el virreinato. Su designación actual y el rango de ciudad le fueron impuestos por el Congreso del Estado de México, al que pertenecía, el 27 de septiembre de 1827.

San Agustín Chayuco ◆ Municipio de Oaxaca situado en el suroeste del estado, al noreste de Santiago Pinotepa Nacional. Superficie: 107.17 km². Habitantes: 4,568, de los cuales 935 forman la población económicamente activa. Hablan alguna lengua indígena 1,739 personas mayores de cinco años (mixteco 1,732). Indígenas monolingües: 283.

San Agustín Etla ◆ Municipio de Oaxaca situado en el centro del estado, al norte de la capital de la entidad. Superficie: 81.65 km². Habitantes: 2,952, de los cuales 729 forman la población económicamente activa. Hablan alguna lengua indígena 48 personas mayores de cinco años (zapoteco 37).

San Agustín de las Juntas ◆ Municipio de Oaxaca situado en el centro del estado, al sur de la capital de la entidad. Superficie: 12.76 km². Habitantes: 3,898, de los cuales 683 forman la población económicamente activa. Hablan alguna lengua indígena 182 personas mayores de cinco años (zapoteco 85 y mixteco 44).

San Agustín Loxicha ◆ Municipio de Oaxaca situado en el sur del estado, al noroeste de Puerto Ángel. Superficie: 389.13 km². Habitantes: 18,839, de los cuales 4,798 forman la población económicamente activa. Hablan alguna lengua indígena 15,169 personas mayores de cinco años (zapoteco 15,154). Indígenas monolingües: 4,451.

San Agustín Metzquititlán ◆ Municipio de Hidalgo situado en el centro del estado, al noreste de Pachuca y en los límites con Veracruz. Superficie: 814.7 km². Habitantes: 21,595, de los cuales 2,210 forman la población económicamente activa. Hablan alguna lengua indígena 16 personas mayores de cinco años (náhuatl 12). Su cabecera es Metzititlán.

San Agustín Tlacotepec ◆ Municipio de Oaxaca situado en el centro-occidente del estado, al sureste de Tlaxiaco. Superficie: 79.10 km². Habitantes: 824, de los cuales 117 forman la población económicamente activa. Hablan alguna lengua indígena 668 personas mayores de cinco años (mixteco 665). Indígenas monolingües: 62.

San Agustín Tlaxiaca ◆ Municipio de Hidalgo situado en el sur del estado y al oeste de Pachuca. Superficie: 354.6 km². Habitantes: 21,571, de los cuales 5,249 forman la población económicamente activa. Hablan alguna lengua indígena 75 personas mayores de cinco años (otomí 49).

San Agustín Yatareni ◆ Municipio de Oaxaca situado en el centro del estado, al noreste de la capital de la entidad. Superficie: 33.17 km². Habitantes: 2,910, de los cuales 736 forman la población económicamente activa. Hablan alguna lengua indígena 438 personas mayores de cinco años (zapoteco 416).

San Andrés, de ◆ Albufera de Tamaulipas situada en el litoral del golfo de México, al norte de Ciudad Madero. Es alimentada por los ríos Barberena y Cachimbas o Tigre. Mide aproximadamente 45 km de largo por cuatro de ancho y está comunicada con el mar por la boca de Chavarría. En su extremo sur hay una planta de evaporación de agua de mar para la obtención de sal.

San Andrés, de ◆ Sierra del Estado de México, al sur de la laguna Huapango. Forma parte del eje volcánico. Está limitada al sur por el valle de Toluca y al sureste por la sierra de Monte Bajo. Su punta más alta es el cerro de Jocotitlán.

San Andrés Cabecera Nueva ◆ Municipio de Oaxaca situado en el centro-occidente del estado, al sureste de Putla de Guerrero. Superficie: 223.27 km². Habitantes: 3,266, de los cuales 642 forman la población económicamente activa. Hablan alguna lengua indígena 40 personas mayores de cinco años (mixteco 34).

San Andrés Calpan ◆ Cabecera del municipio de Calpan, Puebla (☛).

San Andrés Chalchicomula, de ◆ Valle de Puebla, situado al suroeste del Pico de Orizaba. Está limitado al oeste por la sierra del Monumento y al sureste por la sierra Negra. En él se encuentra ubicada Ciudad Serdán.

San Andrés Cholula ◆ Municipio de Puebla situado al oeste y contiguo a la capital de la entidad. Superficie: 68.89 km². Habitantes: 45,872, de los cuales 10,410 forman la población económicamente activa. Hablan alguna lengua indígena 2,270 personas mayores de cinco años (náhuatl 2,171).

San Andrés Dinicuiti ◆ Municipio de Oaxaca situado en el noroeste del estado, al sureste de Huajuapan de León. Superficie: 121.20 km². Habitantes:

2,156, de los cuales 332 forman la población económicamente activa. Hablan alguna lengua indígena 32 personas mayores de cinco años (mixteco 31).

San Andrés Huaxpaltepec ◆ Municipio de Oaxaca situado en el suroeste del estado, al este de Santiago Pinotepa Nacional. Superficie: 67.62 km^2. Habitantes: 5,354, de los cuales 1,170 forman la población económicamente activa. Hablan alguna lengua indígena 1,587 personas mayores de cinco años (mixteco 1,584). Indígenas monolingües: 116.

San Andrés Huayapan ◆ Municipio de Oaxaca situado en el centro del estado, al noreste de la capital de la entidad. Superficie: 14.03 km^2. Habitantes: 3,199, de los cuales 672 forman la población económicamente activa. Hablan alguna lengua indígena 379 personas mayores de cinco años (zapoteco 334). En la cabecera, del mismo nombre, hay una iglesia de cantera blanca con un retablo churrigueresco del siglo XVIII.

San Andrés Ixtlahuaca ◆ Municipio de Oaxaca situado en el centro del estado, al oeste de la capital de la entidad. Superficie: 33.17 km^2. Habitantes: 1,474, de los cuales 366 forman la población económicamente activa. Hablan alguna lengua indígena 260 personas mayores de cinco años (mixteco 245).

San Andrés Lagunas ◆ Municipio de Oaxaca situado en el noroeste del estado, al sureste de Huajuapan de León. Superficie: 100.79 km^2. Habitantes: 610, de los cuales 192 forman la población económicamente activa.

San Andrés Metla, Lienzo de ◆ Documento poshispánico localizado en la población de San Andrés Metla, cerca de Tlalmanalco, Edo. de México. Es copia de un documento fechado en 1674, hecha en el siglo XIX sobre tela de algodón, en la que se representan los límites de Metla con Tlalmanalco, Cocotitlán, Miraflores y Tematla. Aparecen también el señor Tlamatzin, como fundador del poblado, y la fecha 4-acatl. El lienzo fue descubierto, fotografiado y estudiado por los esposos Carmen Cook y Donald Leonard en 1952.

San Andrés Mixquic ◆ Pueblo constituido por cuatro barrios y una cabecera municipal, perteneciente a la delegación Tláhuac del Distrito Federal. Fundado en tiempos del posclásico, entre 1160 y 1168, en uno de los tres islotes del lago de Chalco, fue conquistado por los mexicas en 1430 y convertido en centro ceremonial donde se sacrificaba a los prisioneros capturados en los alrededores. Aparentemente su nombre significa "Lugar de mezquites". Durante la Conquista, Hernán Cortés y sus huestes pernoctaron en el lugar, aliándose con los chalcas y los xochimilcas. En 1537 se inició la construcción de su primera iglesia por frailes agustinos. La población adquirió fama al preservar el ritual náhuatl durante las festividades del Día de Muertos, mismas que, mezcladas con tradiciones del catolicismo, comienzan el 31 de octubre, cuando se coloca una estrella o cruz con una vela que permanece encendida durante una semana, se asean las casas y desde su zaguán hasta el altar familiar se hace un camino con flores de cempasúchil y en las tumbas se colocan ofrendas de flores, velas, incienso, comida y bebida para recibir las almas de los familiares fallecidos hasta la noche del 3 de noviembre. En años recientes la celebración, debido a la gran cantidad de turistas y curiosos que asisten, ha perdido algunos de sus valores originales.

San Andrés Nuxiño ◆ Municipio de Oaxaca situado al noroeste de la capital de la entidad. Superficie: 84.20 km^2. Habitantes: 2,168, de los cuales 437 forman la población económicamente activa. Hablan alguna lengua indígena 781 personas mayores de cinco años (mixteco 777).

San Andrés Paxtlán ◆ Municipio de Oaxaca situado al sureste de Miahuatlán. Superficie: 77.83 km^2. Habitantes: 2,884, de los cuales 779 forman la población económicamente activa. Hablan zapoteco 2,156 personas mayores de cinco años (monolingües 34).

San Andrés Sinaxtla ◆ Municipio de Oaxaca situado en el noroeste del estado, al noroeste de la capital de la entidad. Superficie: 34.45 km^2. Habitantes: 700, de los cuales 169 forman la población económicamente activa. Hablan alguna lengua indígena 17 personas mayores de cinco años (mixteco 16).

San Andrés Solaga ◆ Municipio de Oaxaca situado en el centro del estado, al noreste de la capital de la entidad. Superficie: 38.27 km^2. Habitantes: 1,869, de los cuales 521 forman la población económicamente activa. Hablan alguna lengua indígena 1,655 personas mayores de cinco años (zapoteco 1,654). Indígenas monolingües: 116.

San Andrés Tenejapan ◆ Municipio de Veracruz situado al sur de Orizaba. Superficie: 24.68 km^2. Habitantes: 1,777, de los cuales 474 forman la población económicamente activa. Hablan alguna lengua indígena 1,457 personas mayores de cinco años (náhuatl 1,435). Indígenas monolingües: 105.

San Andrés Teotilalpan ◆ Municipio de Oaxaca situado en el norte del estado, al sureste de Huautla de Jiménez. Superficie: 102.07 km^2. Habitantes: 4,070, de los cuales 962 forman la población económicamente activa. Hablan alguna lengua indígena 1,990 personas mayores de cinco años (cuicalteco 1,818 y chinanteco 117), de las cuales 149 son monolingües.

San Andrés Tepetlapa ◆ Municipio de Oaxaca situado en el noroeste del estado, en los límites con Guerrero, al sur-suroeste de Mariscala de Juárez. Superficie: 76.55 km^2. Habitantes: 352, de los cuales 50 forman la población económicamente activa.

San Andrés Tuxtla ◆ Municipio de Veracruz situado al sureste de Alvarado, en el litoral del golfo de México. Superficie: 918.77 km^2. Habitantes: 137,435, de los cuales 32,747 forman la población económicamente activa. Hablan alguna lengua indígena 328 personas mayores de cinco años (náhuatl 234). En su jurisdicción se halla la zona arqueológica de Matacapan. Su cabecera, del mismo nombre y anteriormente llamada

Los Tuxtlas, se ha convertido en el principal centro comercial de la región. La diócesis católica de San Andrés Tuxtla fue erigida el 23 de mayo de 1959 por Juan XXIII.

San Andrés Yaa ◆ Municipio de Oaxaca situado en el centro-norte del estado, al noreste de la capital de la entidad. Superficie: 33.17 km². Habitantes: 609, de los cuales 145 forman la población económicamente activa. Hablan zapoteco 541 personas mayores de cinco años (no dominan el español 140).

San Andrés Zabache ◆ Municipio de Oaxaca situado en el centro del estado, al noroeste de Miahuatlán. Superficie: 35.72 km². Habitantes: 1,051, de los cuales 219 forman la población económicamente activa. Hablan alguna lengua indígena 108 personas mayores de cinco años (zapoteco 102).

San Andrés Zautla ◆ Municipio de Oaxaca situado en el noroeste del estado, al noroeste de la capital de la entidad. Superficie: 21.69 km². Habitantes: 2,910, de los cuales 670 forman la población económicamente activa. Hablan alguna lengua indígena 59 personas mayores de cinco años (mixteco 39 y zapoteco 15).

San Antonino el Alto ◆ Municipio de Oaxaca situado en el centro del estado, al suroeste de la capital de la entidad. Superficie: 65.07 km². Habitantes: 1,866, de los cuales 482 forman la población económicamente activa. Hablan alguna lengua indígena 640 personas mayores de cinco años (zapoteco 631).

San Antonio Acutla, Oaxaca

San Antonino Castillo Velasco ◆ Municipio de Oaxaca situado en el centro del estado, al sur-sureste de la capital de la entidad. Superficie: 33.17 km². Habitantes: 4,739, de los cuales 1,465 forman la población económicamente activa. Hablan alguna lengua indígena 1,165 personas mayores de cinco años (zapoteco 1,135).

San Antonino Monte Verde ◆ Municipio de Oaxaca situado en el noroeste del estado, al sur de Huajuapan de León. Superficie: 178.62 km². Habitantes: 5,585, de los cuales 1,040 forman la población económicamente activa. Hablan alguna lengua indígena 4,580 personas mayores de cinco años (mixteco 4,572), de las que 41 no saben español.

San Antonio ◆ Municipio de San Luis Potosí situado en el sureste del estado, al sureste de Ciudad Valles y al sur de Tamuín. Superficie: 103.3 km². Habitantes: 8,525, de los cuales 1,957 forman la población económicamente activa. Hablan alguna lengua indígena 6,470 personas mayores de cinco años (huasteco 6,447 y náhuatl 21), de las que 425 son monolingües.

San Antonio Acutla ◆ Municipio de Oaxaca situado en el noroeste del estado, al este-sureste de Huajuapan de León. Superficie: 20.41 km². Habitantes: 331, de los cuales 58 forman la población económicamente activa.

San Antonio de la Cal ◆ Municipio de Oaxaca situado en el centro del estado, al sureste de la capital de la entidad. Superficie: 10.21 km². Habitantes: 11,214, de los cuales 2,075 forman la población económicamente activa. Hablan alguna lengua indígena 918 personas mayores de cinco años (zapoteco 653).

San Antonio Cañada ◆ Municipio de Puebla situado en el sureste del estado, al noreste y contiguo a Tehuacán. Superficie: 84.19 km². Habitantes: 3,833, de los cuales 782 forman la población económicamente activa. Hablan alguna lengua indígena 1,438 personas mayores de cinco años (náhuatl 1,437).

San Antonio Huitepec ◆ Municipio de Oaxaca situado en el centro-oriente del estado, al suroeste de la capital de la entidad. Superficie: 199.04 km². Habitantes: 4,346, de los cuales 1,159 forman la población económicamente activa. Hablan alguna lengua indígena 2,414 personas mayores de cinco años (mixteco 2,408), de las que 117 no dominan el español.

San Antonio la Isla ◆ Municipio del Estado de México situado en el centro de la entidad, al sureste de Toluca y al norte de Tenancingo. Superficie: 22.49 km². Habitantes: 9,118, de los cuales 1,931 forman la población económicamente activa. Hablan alguna lengua indígena 30 personas mayores de cinco años. El municipio fue erigido en 1847. Su cabecera es San Antonio de la Isla.

San Antonio Nanahuatipan ◆ Municipio de Oaxaca situado en el noroeste del estado, en los límites con Puebla, al este de Huautla de Jiménez. Superficie: 127.58 km². Habitantes: 1,266, de los cuales 327 forman la población económicamente activa. Hablan alguna lengua indígena 132 personas mayores de cinco años (náhuatl 123).

San Antonio Sinicahua ◆ Municipio de Oaxaca situado en el oeste del estado, al sureste de Tlaxiaco. Superficie: 48.48 km². Habitantes: 1,228, de los cuales 415 forman la población económicamente activa. Hablan alguna lengua indígena 1,050 personas mayores de cinco años (mixteco 1,048), de las que 167 no saben español.

San Antonio Tepetlapa ◆ Municipio de Oaxaca situado en el suroeste del estado, al norte de Santiago Pinotepa Nacional. Superficie: 65.07 km². Habitantes: 3,527, de los cuales 721 forman la población económicamente activa. Hablan alguna lengua indígena 2,651 personas mayores de cinco años (mixteco 2,645), de las que 461 no dominan el español.

San Baltasar Chichicapan ◆ Municipio de Oaxaca situado en el centro del estado, al sureste de la capital de la entidad. Superficie: 100.79 km². Habitantes: 2,953, de los cuales 885 forman la población económicamente activa. Hablan alguna lengua indígena 2,637 personas mayores de cinco años (zapoteco 2,631), de las cuales 152 no saben español. En la cabecera, del mismo nombre, hay una iglesia del siglo XVI.

San Baltasar Loxicha ◆ Municipio de Oaxaca situado en el sur del estado, al suroeste de Miahuatlán y al sur de la capital de la entidad. Superficie: 58.69 km². Habitantes: 2,662, de los cuales 622 forman la población económicamente activa. Hablan alguna lengua indígena 788 personas mayores de cinco años (zapoteco 785).

San Baltasar Yatzachi el Bajo ◆ Municipio de Oaxaca situado en el centro del estado, al este-noreste de la capital de la entidad. Superficie: 48.48 km². Habitantes: 780, de los cuales 165 forman la población económicamente activa. Hablan alguna lengua indígena 687 personas mayores de cinco años (zapoteco 675), de las que 98 son monolingües.

San Bartolo Coyotepec ◆ Municipio de Oaxaca situado en el centro del estado, al sur de la capital de la entidad. Superficie: 45.93 km². Habitantes: 4,083, de los cuales 1,116 forman la población económicamente activa. Hablan alguna lengua indígena 57 personas mayores de cinco años (zapoteco 32 y mixteco 12). En él se elaboran artesanías de barro negro. Su principal festividad, la del santo patrono, se celebra el 24 de agosto; durante ella, 16 campesinos ejecutan la *Danza de los jardineros*.

San Bartolo Morelos ◆ Cabecera del municipio de Morelos (☛), Estado de México.

San Bartolo Soyaltepec ◆ Municipio de Oaxaca situado en el noroeste del estado, al sureste de Huajuapan de León y al noroeste de la capital de la entidad. Superficie: 70.17 km². Habitantes: 895, de los cuales 217 forman la población económicamente activa. Hablan mixteco 242 personas mayores de cinco años.

San Bartolo Tutotepec ◆ Municipio de Hidalgo situado en el oriente del estado, en los límites con Veracruz, al noreste de Tulancingo y al noreste de Pachuca. Superficie: 305.8 km². Habitantes: 18,289, de los cuales 5,111 forman la población económicamente activa. Hablan alguna lengua indígena 7,327 personas mayores de cinco años (otomí 7,308). Indígenas monolingües: 574.

San Bartolo Yautepec ◆ Municipio de Oaxaca situado en el centro del estado, al sureste de la capital de la entidad y al este de Miahuatlán. Superficie: 196.48 km². Habitantes: 772, de los cuales 220 forman la población económicamente activa. Hablan alguna lengua indígena 276 personas mayores de cinco años (zapoteco 269).

San Bartolomé Ayautla ◆ Municipio de Oaxaca situado en el norte del estado, al sureste de Huautla de Jiménez y al oeste de Tuxtepec. Superficie: 118.65 km². Habitantes: 2,871, de los cuales 777 forman la población económicamente activa. Hablan alguna lengua indígena 2,415 personas mayores de cinco años (mazateco 2,405), de las cuales 966 no saben español. En 1972 se descubrieron en su jurisdicción ruinas de la civilización mazateca, consistentes en 12 edificaciones similares a las de Monte Albán.

San Bartolomé Loxicha ◆ Municipio de Oaxaca situado en el sur del estado, al sur-suroeste de Miahuatlán y al noroeste de Puerto Ángel. Superficie: 191.37 km². Habitantes: 2,275, de los cuales 638 forman la población económicamente activa. Hablan alguna lengua indígena 1,723 personas mayores de cinco años (zapoteco 1,722), de las que 295 no dominan el español.

San Bartolomé Quialana ◆ Municipio de Oaxaca situado en el centro del estado, al sur-sureste de la capital de la entidad. Superficie: 49.76 km². Habitantes: 2,534, de los cuales 383 forman la población económicamente activa. Hablan alguna lengua indígena 2,189 personas mayores de cinco años (zapoteco 2,179), de las cuales 123 son monolingües.

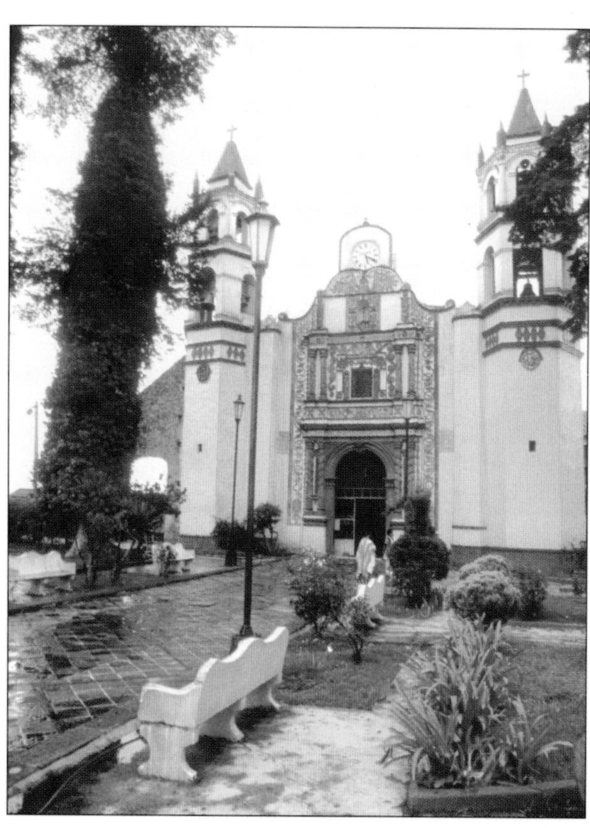

Foto: Fondo Editorial Grupo Azabache

Parroquia en San Antonio la Isla, Estado de México

San Bartolomé Yucuañe ◆ Municipio de Oaxaca situado en el oeste del estado, al sur-sureste de Huajuapan de León. Superficie: 65.07 km². Habitantes: 546, de los cuales 117 forman la población económicamente activa. Hablan mixteco 439 personas mayores de cinco años (monolingües 35).

San Bartolomé Zoogocho ◆ Municipio de Oaxaca situado en el centro del estado, al noreste de la capital de la entidad. Superficie: 22.96 km². Habitantes: 730, de los cuales 143 forman la población económicamente activa. Hablan alguna lengua indígena 678 personas mayores de cinco años (zapoteco 622), de las que 102 no saben español.

San Benedicto ◆ Isla de Colima. Es una de las cuatro que forman el archipiélago de las Revillagigedo.

San Benito ◆ Islas de Baja California en el océano Pacífico, al noroeste de la isla de Cedros.

San Bernardino ◆ Río de Sonora. Nace en Estados Unidos, corre hacia el sur por el valle de San Bernardino, recibe al río de Agua Prieta y continúa hacia el sur para unirse al Bavispe cerca

FOTO: MICHAEL CALDERWOOD

Bahía de San Blas, en Nayarit

de Batepito y formar el Yaqui. Alimenta a la presa de La Angostura.

SAN BERNARDO ◆ Municipio de Durango situado en el noroeste del estado, al norte de Tepehuanes y al noreste de la capital de la entidad. Superficie: 2,078 km². Habitantes: 4,883, de los cuales 1,595 forman la población económicamente activa. Hablan alguna lengua indígena 49 personas mayores de cinco años (tarahumara 33 y tepehuano 15).

SAN BERNARDO MIXTEPEC ◆ Municipio de Oaxaca situado en el centro del estado, al suroeste de la capital de la entidad. Superficie: 67.62 km². Habitantes: 3,028, de los cuales 506 forman la población económicamente activa. Hablan alguna lengua indígena 44 personas mayores de cinco años (zapoteco 26).

SAN BLAS, DE ◆ Bahía de Nayarit, al sur del puerto del mismo nombre y al sureste de la punta Camarón.

FOTO: MICHAEL CALDERWOOD

San Blas, Nayarit

SAN BLAS ◆ Municipio de Nayarit situado en el oeste del estado, en el litoral del océano Pacífico, al este de Tepic. Superficie: 823.6 km². Habitantes: 42,517, de los cuales 14,298 forman la población económicamente activa. Hablan alguna lengua indígena 338 personas mayores de cinco años (huichol 108, náhuatl 74, purépecha 31 y cora 28). Su cabecera, del mismo nombre, es el principal centro turístico de la entidad. En él se hallan el puerto y sus astilleros, existen esteros para practicar la pesca y sus salinas surten a todo el estado. En 1767, el virrey Carlos Francisco de Croix consideró conveniente fundar un puerto en las costas del Pacífico, desde el cual la Corona española enviara sus expediciones de conquista a California; se eligió la bahía de San Blas para erigir ese puerto, debido a sus buenas condiciones para el fondeo de naves de gran calado y por hallarse rodeada de bosques de maderas propias para la construcción de barcos. En 1768 el astillero de San Blas botó sus dos primeros paquebotes y sus dos primeras goletas. En el último tercio del siglo XVIII y principios del XIX se convirtió en puerto alternativo de Acapulco para la Nao de China, especialmente cuando había mal tiempo o surgía la amenaza de los piratas. Gran parte de su movimiento se debió al contrabando. Influyó decisivamente para que Tepic se convirtiera en una plaza comercial tan importante que llegó a ser sede de una feria regional y triplicó su población en el curso del siglo XVIII. En 1810 cayó en manos del cura insurgente José María Mercado. Cuando Morelos controló la ruta Acapulco-México (1811-15), el movimiento naviero se hizo por San Blas, en provecho de Nueva Galicia. Pese a la insalubridad del estero de Tobara, en 1818 se le erigió en partido. Hasta 1821 siguió utilizándose intensamente el puerto a causa de la actividad de Vicente Guerrero, cuyas fuerzas hacían intransitable el camino México-Acapulco. Después de la independencia decayó el puerto, al cesar el comercio con Filipinas, y fue utilizado principalmente para el contrabando, pero aun para este giro fue rebasado por Manzanillo, que ofrecía mejores comunicaciones con las grandes ciudades del occidente y el centro del país.

SAN BLAS ◆ Población del municipio de El Fuerte, Sinaloa (☛).

SAN BLAS ATEMPA ◆ Municipio de Oaxaca situado en el sur del estado, al norte de Salina Cruz y al sureste de Juchitán de Zaragoza. Superficie: 148 km². Habitantes: 14,453, de los cuales 3,367 forman la población económicamente activa. Hablan alguna lengua indígena 11,831 personas mayores de cinco años (zapoteco 11,794), de las cuales 2,856 no dominan el español. Se erigió en municipio en 1868, en territorio que antes pertenecía a Tehuantepec.

SAN BUENAVENTURA ◆ Municipio de Coahuila situado en el norte del estado, al noroeste de Monclova y contiguo a Múzquiz. Superficie: 3,527.8 km². Habitantes: 20,034, de los cuales 5,880 forman la población económicamente activa. Hablan alguna lengua indígena 30 personas mayores de cinco años.

SAN BUENAVENTURA, GABRIEL DE ◆ n. en Francia y m. en Cuba (?-?). Fraile franciscano del siglo XVII. En Yucatán fue cura doctrinero de la parroquia de Sisal y aprendió maya para predicar en ese idioma. Fue definidor de la provincia franciscana de San José y presidente y guardián del convento mayor de Mérida. Autor de *Arte de la lengua maya* (1684) y *Diccionario maya-hispano e hispano-maya, médico botánico regional.*

SAN BUENAVENTURA NEALTICAN ◆ Cabecera del municipio de Nealtican, Puebla (☛).

SAN CARLOS ◆ Municipio de Tamaulipas situado en el oeste del estado, en los límites con Nuevo León, al norte de Ciudad Victoria. Superficie: 2,692.04 km². Habitantes: 10,469, de los cuales 2,853 forman la población económicamente activa.

SAN CARLOS, DE ◆ Sierra de Tamaulipas en la llanura costera del golfo, entre los ríos San Fernando y Soto la Marina, al norte de la presa Las Adjuntas y al nor-noreste de Ciudad

Victoria. Sus principales cumbres son la Mesa del Diente y Santiago; cuenta con yacimientos de cobre, oro y plata.

SAN CARLOS YAUTEPEC ◆ Municipio de Oaxaca situado en el sureste del estado, al sureste de la capital de la entidad y al noreste de Miahuatlán. Superficie: 2,491.68 km². Habitantes: 10,988, de los cuales 2,354 forman la población económicamente activa. Hablan alguna lengua indígena 4,361 personas mayores de cinco años (zapoteco 2,908, chontal de Oaxaca 1,085 y mixe 365), de las que 129 no saben español.

SAN CIRO DE ACOSTA ◆ Municipio de San Luis Potosí ubicado al sur del estado, en los límites con Guanajuato y Querétaro, al sur de Rioverde. Superficie: 620 km². Habitantes: 10,824, de los cuales 2,230 forman la población económicamente activa. Hablan alguna lengua indígena ocho personas mayores de cinco años.

SAN CRISTÓBAL, DE ◆ Bahía de Baja California Sur en el litoral del océano Pacífico, localizada entre Morro Hermoso y San Pablo, al sur de la bahía Tortugas.

SAN CRISTÓBAL AMATLÁN ◆ Municipio de Oaxaca situado en el sur del estado, al este de Miahuatlán. Superficie: 96.96 km². Habitantes: 3,801, de los cuales 1,227 forman la población económicamente activa. Hablan alguna lengua indígena 2,862 personas mayores de cinco años (zapoteco 2,860), de las que son monolingües 382.

SAN CRISTÓBAL AMOLTEPEC ◆ Municipio de Oaxaca situado en el oeste del estado, al este de Tlaxiaco y al sursureste de Huajuapan de León. Superficie: 31.9 km². Habitantes: 1,101, de los cuales 213 forman la población económicamente activa. Hablan mixteco 824 personas mayores de cinco años (monolingües: 54).

SAN CRISTÓBAL DE LA BARRANCA ◆ Municipio de Jalisco situado en el norte del estado, en los límites con Zacatecas, al norte de Guadalajara. Superficie: 636.93 km². Habitantes: 4,638, de los cuales 758 forman la población económicamente activa.

SAN CRISTÓBAL DE LAS CASAS ◆ Municipio de Chiapas situado en el centro del estado, al este de Tuxtla Gutiérrez y al norte de Tapachula. Superficie: 484.4 km². Habitantes: 116,729, de los cuales 26,475 forman la población económicamente activa. Hablan alguna lengua indígena 35,045 personas mayores de cinco años (tzotzil 26,205, tzeltal 8,323 y chol 296). Indígenas monolingües: 5,489. Su cabecera, del mismo nombre, fue fundada en 1524 por el conquistador Diego de Mazariegos con el nombre de Chiapa de los Indios, que cuatro años después se convirtió en Villa Real de San Cristóbal. En 1531 se llamó Villa Viciosa y en el mismo año San Cristóbal de los Llanos. En 1536, Carlos I le otorgó la categoría de Ciudad Real y desde entonces fue capital de Chiapas. En 1829 adquirió su actual nombre, en honor de fray Bartolomé de las Casas. En 1892 dejó de ser capital chiapaneca, cuando Emilio Rabasa trasladó los poderes locales a Tuxtla Gutiérrez. Cuenta con atractivos turísticos como la catedral, la casa de la Sirena, las iglesias de San Nicolás y de La Merced, y los templos de San Francisco, Santo Domingo, de la Caridad y el del Carmen. El papa Paulo III erigió en 1539 la diócesis de Chiapas con sede en San Cristóbal, sufragánea de la arquidiócesis de Oaxaca. En 1964 la diócesis cambió su nombre por el de San Cristóbal de Las Casas. El 1 de enero de 1994, hizo su aparición en la ciudad el grupo guerrillero Frente Zapatista de Liberación Nacional, que derivó en el Ejército Zapatista de Liberación Nacional.

SAN CRISTÓBAL ECATEPEC ◆ ☛ *Ecatepec de Morelos.*

SAN CRISTÓBAL LACHIRIOAG ◆ Municipio de Oaxaca situado en el centro del estado, al noreste de la capital de la entidad. Superficie: 24.24 km². Habitantes: 1,264, de los cuales 404 forman la población económicamente activa. Hablan zapoteco 1,115 personas mayores de cinco años (monolingües 155).

SAN CRISTÓBAL Y NEVIS ◆ Estado del Caribe oriental. Está formado por las islas de Saint Kitts (nombre común de San Cristóbal) y Nevis. Superficie: 269.4 km². Habitantes: 42,300 (1998). El idioma oficial es el inglés y el hindi es una lengua no oficial importante. Su capital es el puerto de Basseterre (18,000 habitantes en 1995), fundada en 1627 en Saint Kitts; otra ciudad importante es el puerto de Charlestown (1,200 habitantes en 1990), situado en Nevis. La unidad monetaria en la zona es el dólar Caribe-Este. En 1999, la religión mayoritaria era el protestantismo (84.6%). El gobernador general, representante de la Corona de Inglaterra, gobierna junto con un primer ministro y una Asamblea

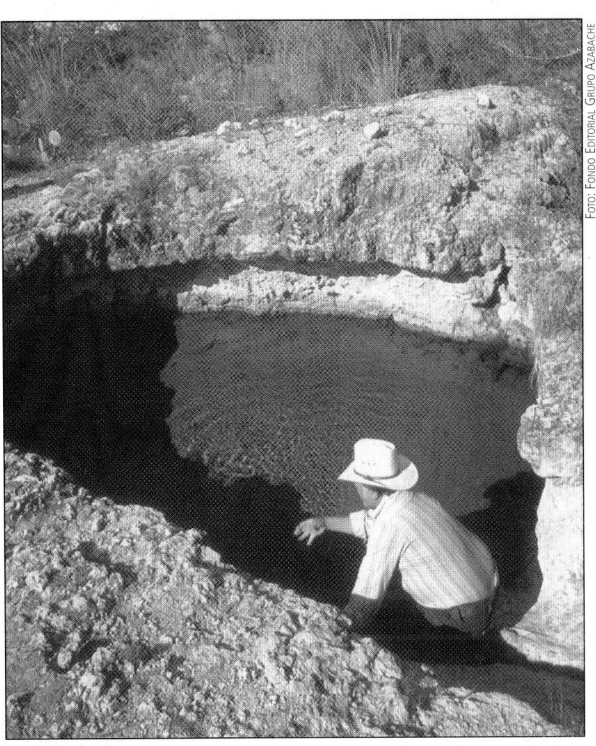

FOTO: FONDO EDITORIAL GRUPO AZABACHE

Manantial la Tacita en San Buenaventura, Coahuila

FOTO: FONDO EDITORIAL GRUPO AZABACHE

San Carlos cobijado por el cerro del Diente, Tamaulipas

General; en 1999, los dos primeros cargos eran ocupados, respectivamente, por Cuthbert Montraville Sebastian y Denzil Douglas. *Historia:* La isla de San Cristóbal fue descubierta por Cristóbal Colón en 1493; la bautizó, presumiblemente, en honor del santo y no de sí mismo. La isla se convirtió en el primer asentamiento colonial británico en las Indias Occidentales en 1623, después que los colonizadores exterminaran a sus pobladores originales. A pesar de haber sido disputadas constantemente con Francia y España, San Cristóbal y la cercana Nevis permanecieron bajo el dominio inglés durante los tres siglos siguientes y fueron hogar de una gran población de esclavos negros y una minoría de capataces blancos dedicados, al principio, a explotar plantaciones azucareras. En la cúspide de su poder, el Imperio Británico consideraba a Nevis una "joya de la Corona" y llamaba a San Cristóbal "Colonia Madre" y "cuna del Caribe". A mediados del siglo XIX, los precios del azúcar cayeron en todo el mundo y las islas perdieron su antigua importancia, pero no obtuvieron su independencia sino hasta el 19 de septiembre de 1983, cuando se convirtieron en una sola nación dentro de la comunidad británica de naciones. En julio de 1990 se establecieron relaciones diplomáticas con México.

San Cristóbal de Las Casas, Chiapas

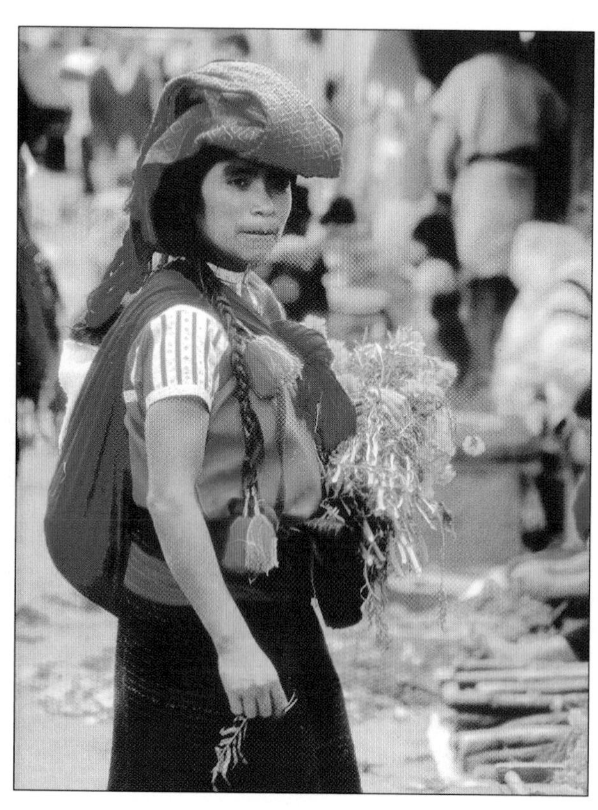

SAN CRISTÓBAL SUCHIXTLAHUACA ◆ Municipio de Oaxaca situado en el noroeste del estado, al este de Huajuapan de León. Superficie: 44.65 km^2. Habitantes: 328, de los cuales 82 forman la población económicamente activa. Hablan alguna lengua indígena 11 personas mayores de cinco años (chocho 10).

SAN DEMIÁN TEXOLOC ◆ Municipio de Tlaxcala erigido en 1995, contiguo a la capital del estado por el suroeste. Habitantes: 4,102. Hablan alguna lengua indígena 10 personas mayores de cinco años.

SAN DIEGO DE ALEJANDRÍA ◆ Municipio de Jalisco situado en el noreste del estado, en los límites con Guanajuato, al noreste de Guadalajara y al sur de Lagos de Moreno. Superficie: 361.24 km^2. Habitantes: 6,389, de los cuales 1,604 forman la población económicamente activa.

SAN DIEGO LA MESA TOCHIMILTZINGO ◆ Municipio de Puebla situado al suroeste de la capital de la entidad y al noreste de Izúcar de Matamoros. Superficie: 91.85 km^2. Habitantes: 1,214, de los cuales 288 forman la población económicamente activa.

SAN DIEGO DE LA UNIÓN ◆ Municipio de Guanajuato situado en el norte del estado, en los límites con San Luis Potosí, al norte de Dolores Hidalgo. Superficie: 1,035.3 km^2. Habitantes: 32,019, de los cuales 6,414 forman la población económicamente activa. Hablan alguna lengua indígena 10 personas mayores de cinco años.

SAN DIMAS ◆ Municipio de Durango situado en el suroeste del estado, en los límites con Sinaloa, al oeste de la capital de la entidad. Superficie: 5,620.5 km^2. Habitantes: 23,184, de los cuales 5,626 forman la población económicamente activa. Hablan alguna lengua indígena seis personas mayores de cinco años. Su cabecera es Tayoltita.

SAN DIONISIO DEL MAR ◆ Municipio de Oaxaca situado en la región del istmo de Tehuantepec, al sureste de Juchitán de Zaragoza, entre las lagunas Mayor y Menor del litoral del golfo de Tehuantepec. Superficie: 237.3 km^2. Habitantes: 4,438, de los cuales 1,131 forman la población económicamente activa. Hablan alguna lengua indígena 2,415 personas mayores de cinco años (huave 2,323 y zapoteco 88).

SAN DIONISIO OCOTEPEC ◆ Municipio de Oaxaca situado en el centro del estado, al sureste de la capital de la entidad. Superficie: 225.82 km^2. Habitantes: 9,004, de los cuales 1,940 forman la población económicamente activa. Hablan alguna lengua indígena 7,458 personas mayores de cinco años (zapoteco 7,452), de las cuales 1,227 son monolingües.

SAN DIONISIO OCOTLÁN ◆ Municipio de Oaxaca situado en el centro del estado, al sur-sureste de la capital de la entidad. Superficie: 20.41 km^2. Habitantes: 1,136, de los cuales 289 forman la población económicamente activa. Hablan zapoteco 10 personas mayores de cinco años.

SAN ESTEBAN ◆ Bahía de Sinaloa situada en el litoral del Pacífico entre tierra firme y un cordón de tierra llamado isla de Santa María. Se halla al este-sureste de Los Mochis, al noroeste de la bahía de San Ignacio.

SAN ESTEBAN ◆ Isla de Sonora en el golfo de California, al sureste de la isla Tiburón. De forma casi cuadrada, mide algo más de 6 km por lado.

SAN ESTEBAN ATATLAHUCA ◆ Municipio de Oaxaca situado en el oeste del estado, al sur de Tlaxiaco y al oeste de la capital de la entidad. Superficie: 61.24 km^2. Habitantes: 3,443, de los cuales 761 forman la población económicamente activa. Hablan alguna lengua indígena 2,834 personas mayores de cinco años (mixteco 2,829), de las cuales 132 no saben español.

SAN FELIPE ◆ Municipio de Guanajuato situado en el noroeste del estado, en los límites con San Luis Potosí y Jalisco, al norte de la capital de la entidad. Superficie: 2,691.9 km^2. Habitantes:

95,050, de los cuales 19,760 forman la población económicamente activa. Hablan alguna lengua indígena 28 personas mayores de cinco años. En su territorio hay yacimientos de estaño. Su cabecera se llamó Ciudad González y después Ciudad Doctor Hernández Álvarez.

San Felipe ◆ Municipio de Sonora situado en el norte del estado, al oeste de Moctezuma y al noreste de Hermosillo. Superficie: 152.85 km². Habitantes: 403, de los cuales 164 forman la población económicamente activa. Estuvo incorporado a las jurisdicciones de los municipios de Arizpe y Banámichi de diciembre de 1930 a mayo de 1931. Su cabecera es San Felipe de Jesús.

San Felipe ◆ Municipio de Yucatán situado en el noreste del estado, en el litoral del golfo de México, al noreste de Mérida y al noroeste de Valladolid. Superficie: 680.85 km². Habitantes: 1,641, de los cuales 467 forman la población económicamente activa. Hablan maya 217 personas mayores de cinco años.

San Felipe Ixtacuixtla ◆ Antiguo nombre de Villa Mariano Matamoros (☛), cabera municipal de Ixtacuixtla de Matamoros, Tlaxcala.

San Felipe Jalapa de Díaz ◆ Municipio de Oaxaca situado en el norte del estado, al sur de la presa Miguel Alemán y al sur-sureste de Huautla de Jiménez. Superficie: 154.38 km². Habitantes: 19,040, de los cuales 3,812 forman la población económicamente activa. Hablan alguna lengua indígena 15,221 personas mayores de cinco años (mazateco 14,693 y zapoteco 494), de las cuales 6,574 son monolingües.

San Felipe del Progreso ◆ Municipio del Estado de México situado en el noroeste de la entidad, en los límites con Michoacán, al noroeste de Toluca. Superficie: 797.03 km². Habitantes: 155,978, de los cuales 31,803 forman la población económicamente activa. Hablan alguna lengua indígena 44,693 personas mayores de cinco años (mazahua 44,633). Indígenas monolingües: 1,141. Su cabecera, del mismo nombre, fundada en 1700, se llamó originalmente San Felipe el Grande y después San Felipe del Obraje. En 1877 adquirió el rango de villa.

San Felipe Tejalapan ◆ Municipio de Oaxaca situado en el centro del estado, al noroeste y próximo a la capital de la entidad. Superficie: 76.55 km². Habitantes: 5,815, de los cuales 1,354 forman la población económicamente activa. Hablan alguna lengua indígena 43 personas mayores de cinco años (mixteco 25).

San Felipe Teotlalcingo ◆ Municipio de Puebla situado en el noroeste del estado, al noroeste de la capital de la entidad y al norte de Atlixco. Superficie: 54.85 km². Habitantes: 8,382, de los cuales 1,809 forman la población económicamente activa. Hablan alguna lengua indígena 117 personas mayores de cinco años (náhuatl 112).

San Felipe Tepatlán ◆ Municipio de Puebla situado en el norte del estado, al este de Huauchinango y al noroeste de Teziutlán. Superficie: 37 km². Habitantes: 4,353, de los cuales 1,380 forman la población económicamente activa. Hablan alguna lengua indígena 2,697 personas mayores de cinco años (totonaco 2,601 y náhuatl 94), de las que 216 son monolingües. Tiene yacimientos de plata y hierro sin explotar.

San Felipe Usila ◆ Municipio de Oaxaca situado en el norte del estado, al sur de la presa Miguel Alemán y al suroeste de Tuxtepec. Superficie: 255.17 km². Habitantes: 10,597, de los cuales 2,464 forman la población económicamente activa. Hablan alguna lengua indígena 8,759 personas mayores de cinco años (chinanteco 8,727), de las que 1,843 no dominan el español. En su jurisdicción hay ruinas arqueológicas de la civilización chinanteca.

San Felipe Orizatlán ◆ Municipio de Hidalgo situado en el extremo norte del estado, en los límites con San Luis Potosí y Veracruz. Superficie: 308.4 km². Habitantes: 38,020, de los cuales 8,451 forman la población económicamente activa. Hablan alguna lengua indígena 21,721 personas mayores de cinco años (náhuatl 21,708). Indígenas monolingües: 3,660. Su cabecera es Orizatlán, nombre anterior del municipio.

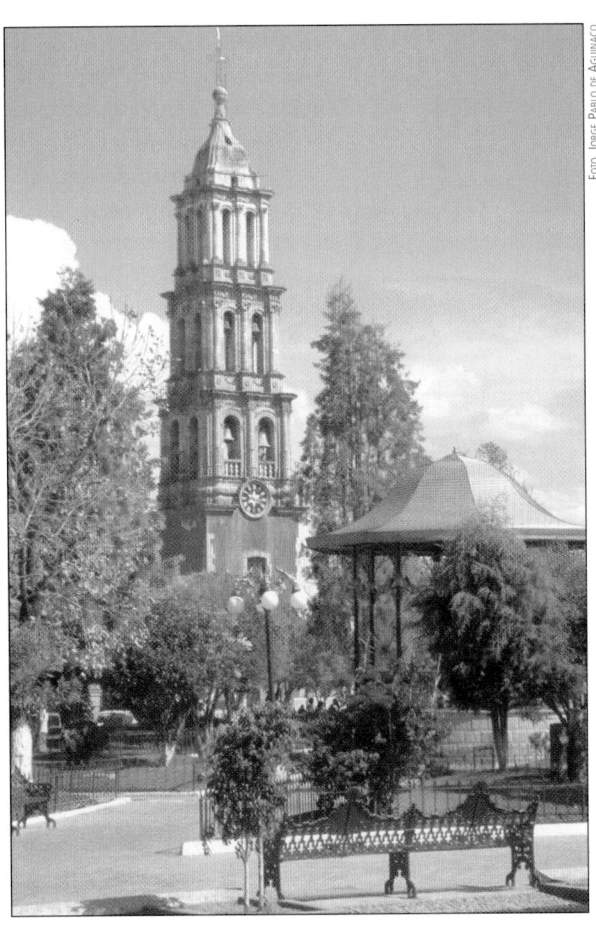

Foto. Jorge Pablo de Aguinaco

Templo parroquial de San Felipe, Guanajuato

San Fernando ◆ Municipio de Chiapas situado en el noroeste del estado y contiguo a Tuxtla Gutiérrez. Superficie: 258.3 km². Habitantes: 27,047, de los cuales 6,604 forman la población económicamente activa. Hablan alguna lengua indígena 102 personas mayores de cinco años (tzotzil 100). En su territorio se encuentra el cañón del Sumi-

Producción textil de San Felipe del Progreso, Estado de México

Foto: Fondo Editorial Grupo Azabache

dero, de 800 metros de profundidad, formado por el río Grijalva: en él hay cuatro miradores; el último, llamado de Los Chiapas, cuenta con una atalaya. 10 km adelante del mirador se localizan las grutas de Montecristo y Palmacristi. Su cabecera, del mismo nombre, se llamó Villa Allende.

San Fernando ◆ Municipio de Tamaulipas situado en el noreste del estado, en el litoral del golfo de México, al sur-sureste de Reynosa y al noroeste de Ciudad Victoria. Superficie: 6,096.38 km^2. Habitantes: 56,649, de los cuales 13,601 forman la población económicamente activa. Hablan alguna lengua indígena 163 personas mayores de cinco años (huasteco 44, náhuatl 42 y totonaco 37).

San Fernando ◆ Río de Tamaulipas. Nace al este de la ciudad de Méndez por la confluencia de los ríos Conchos (de Nuevo León) y San Lorenzo, en las estribaciones de la sierra Madre Oriental; recibe al río Burgos, pasa entre las sierras de San Carlos y Pamoranes y desagua en la laguna Madre, frente a la isla Los Bules. En tiempo de crecidas forma la laguna de la Resaca, a 15 km de su desembocadura.

San Francisco, Juan de ◆ n. en España y m. en la ciudad de México (?-1556). Fraile franciscano y sacerdote. Llegó a la Nueva España en 1529. En 1541 se le nombró obispo de Yucatán, cargo que rechazó. Autor de *Conferencias espirituales con ejemplos y doctrinas de santos, en lengua mexicana* y *Sermones morales y panegíricos en lengua mexicana*.

Panorámica de San Fernando, Chiapas

Foto: Fondo Editorial Grupo Azabache

San Francisco de Borja ◆ Municipio de Chihuahua situado al suroeste y próximo a la capital de la entidad. Superficie: 1,224.77 km^2. Habitantes: 2,635, de los cuales 956 forman la población económicamente activa. Hablan alguna lengua indígena 50 personas mayores de cinco años (tarahumara 47). Alrededor de 1742 se establecieron misiones jesuitas en el territorio del actual municipio, rango al que accedió en 1820. Su cabecera, del mismo nombre, fue fundada en 1645 en un punto llamado Dehualcachí.

San Francisco Cahuacuá ◆ Municipio de Oaxaca situado al oeste de la capital del estado y al sureste de Tlaxiaco. Superficie: 169.68 km^2. Habitantes: 2,998, de los cuales 614 forman la población económicamente activa. Hablan alguna lengua indígena 26 personas mayores de cinco años (mixteco 24).

San Francisco Cajonos ◆ Municipio de Oaxaca situado en el centro del estado, al este y próximo a la capital de la entidad. Superficie: 25.52 km^2. Habitantes: 733, de los cuales 157 forman la población económicamente activa. Hablan alguna lengua indígena 669 personas mayores de cinco años (zapoteco 668). En su cabecera se produjo en septiembre de 1700 el incidente de los llamados "mártires de Caxonos": los fiscales indígenas del pueblo, Juan Bautista y Jacinto de los Ángeles, delataron ante el cura Gaspar de los Reyes la celebración de un rito de la antigua religión local, efectuado por los indios de Cajonos; éstos, calificados de "idólatras", fueron sorprendidos y reprimidos de inmediato, lo que dio origen a un levantamiento durante el cual los vecinos de esta población y de otras aledañas asaltaron el convento en el que se habían refugiado seis sacerdotes españoles y los dos fiscales autores de la denuncia. La población insurrecta pidió y obtuvo que le fueran entregados los fiscales, a quienes se propuso volver a sus antiguas creencias; éstos se negaron y fueron ejecutados.

San Francisco de Conchos ◆ Municipio de Chihuahua situado en el sureste del estado, al oeste de Ciudad Camargo y al sureste de la capital de la entidad. Superficie: 1,169.06 km^2. Habitantes: 2,991, de los cuales 944 forman la población económicamente activa. En su jurisdicción se encuentra la presa de La Boquilla, del río Conchos. Colonizado por misioneros jesuitas, el territorio de San Francisco de Conchos obtuvo en 1820 el rango de municipio. La cabecera, del mismo nombre, fue fundada en 1604 por el jesuita Francisco Alonso de Oliva, con el nombre de San Francisco Coyamaus.

San Francisco Chapulapa ◆ Municipio de Oaxaca situado en el norte del estado, al suroeste de la presa Miguel Alemán y al sureste de Huautla de Jiménez. Superficie: 19.14 km^2. Habitantes: 1,967, de los cuales 491 forman la población económicamente activa. Hablan alguna lengua indígena 250 personas mayores de cinco años (cuicateco 185 y mixteco 61).

San Francisco Chindúa ◆ Municipio de Oaxaca situado en el noroeste del estado, al noroeste de la capital de la entidad y al sureste de Huajuapan de León. Superficie: 28.07 km^2. Habitantes: 735, de los cuales 146 forman la población económicamente activa. Hablan alguna lengua indígena cinco personas.

San Francisco Huehuetlán ◆ Municipio de Oaxaca situado en el norte del estado, en los límites con Puebla, al noroeste de Huautla de Jiménez y al este de la presa Miguel Alemán. Superficie: 15.31 km^2. Habitantes: 1,028, de los cuales 406 forman la población económicamente activa. Hablan alguna lengua indígena 868 personas mayores de cinco años (mazateco 854), de las que 141 no dominan el español.

San Francisco Ixhuatán ◆ Municipio de Oaxaca situado en el extremo sudoriental del estado, en los límites con Chiapas, al este-sureste de Juchitán de Zaragoza. Superficie: 406.99 km^2. Habitantes: 9,313, de los cuales 2,258 forman la población económicamente activa. Hablan alguna lengua indígena 1,308 personas mayores de cinco años (zapoteco 1,267).

San Francisco Jaltepetongo ◆ Municipio de Oaxaca situado en el noroeste del estado, al noroeste de la capital de la entidad y al noreste de Tlaxiaco. Superficie: 71.45 km². Habitantes: 1,256, de los cuales 324 forman la población económicamente activa. Hablan alguna lengua indígena 213 personas mayores de cinco años (mixteco 212).

San Francisco Lachigoló ◆ Municipio de Oaxaca situado en el centro del estado, al este y próximo a la capital de la entidad. Superficie: 31.9 km². Habitantes: 1,616, de los cuales 336 forman la población económicamente activa. Hablan alguna lengua indígena 406 personas mayores de cinco años (zapoteco 387).

San Francisco Logueche ◆ Municipio de Oaxaca situado en el sur del estado, al este de Miahuatlán. Superficie: 76.55 km². Habitantes: 1,722, de los cuales 106 forman la población económicamente activa. Hablan alguna lengua indígena 1,391 personas mayores de cinco años (zapoteco 1,366), de las que 243 son monolingües.

San Francisco del Mar ◆ Municipio de Oaxaca situado en la zona costera de la región del istmo de Tehuantepec, al sureste de Juchitán de Zaragoza. Superficie: 400.61 km². Habitantes: 4,850, de los cuales 1,126 forman la población económicamente activa. Hablan alguna lengua indígena 1,160 personas mayores de cinco años (huave 876 y zapoteco 267).

San Francisco del Mezquital ◆ Cabecera del municipio duranguense de Mezquital (☛).

San Francisco Nuxaño ◆ Municipio de Oaxaca situado en el noroeste del estado, al sureste de Huajuapan de León y al noroeste de la capital de la entidad. Superficie: 21.69 km². Habitantes: 424, de los cuales 122 forman la población económicamente activa. Hablan mixteco ocho personas mayores de cinco años.

San Francisco del Oro ◆ Municipio de Chihuahua situado en el sur del estado, en los límites con Durango, al noroeste de Santa Bárbara y al suroeste de Hidalgo del Parral. Superficie: 695.52 km². Habitantes: 6,918, de los cuales 2,597 forman la población económicamente activa. Hablan alguna lengua indígena 24 personas mayores de cinco años (tarahumara 21). En 1927 el territorio de San Francisco del Oro se separó del de Santa Bárbara y obtuvo el rango de municipio. Su cabecera, del mismo nombre, se fundó en 1658, al descubrir la primera mina el español Francisco Molina.

San Francisco Ozolotepec ◆ Municipio de Oaxaca situado en el sur del estado, al sureste de Miahuatlán y al oeste de Salina Cruz. Superficie: 251.34 km². Habitantes: 1,879, de los cuales 432 forman la población económicamente activa. Hablan zapoteco 1,412 personas mayores de cinco años (monolingües 72).

San Francisco del Rincón ◆ Municipio de Guanajuato situado en el occidente del estado, en los límites con Jalisco, al suroeste de León y al oeste de la capital de la entidad. Superficie: 517.7 km². Habitantes: 97,269, de los cuales 24,154 forman la población económicamente activa. Hablan alguna lengua indígena 43 personas mayores de cinco años. Cuenta con los balnearios de la Granja y los tanques de aguas termales que se hallan al pie del cerro del Palenque. Del 5 al 9 de diciembre se festeja el aniversario de la fundación de su cabecera, con peleas de gallos, corridas de toros, desfile de carros alegóricos y danzas regionales.

San Francisco de los Romo ◆ Municipio de Aguascalientes de reciente creación, situado en el centro del estado, al noroeste de la capital. Superficie: 399 km². Habitantes: 38,752, de los cuales 8,815 forman la población económicamente activa. Hablan alguna lengua indígena 15 personas mayores de cinco años. Su territorio formó parte del norte del municipio de Aguascalientes.

San Francisco Sola ◆ Municipio de Oaxaca situado en el centro del estado, al sur-suroeste de la capital de la entidad y al noroeste de Miahuatlán. Superficie: 71.45 km². Habitantes: 1,221, de los cuales 237 forman la población económicamente activa. Hablan alguna lengua indígena cinco personas mayores de cinco años.

San Francisco Telixtlahuaca ◆ Municipio de Oaxaca situado en el centro del estado, al noroeste de la capital de la entidad. Superficie: 79.1 km². Habitantes: 8,681, de los cuales 1,883 forman la población económicamente activa. Hablan alguna lengua indígena 50 personas mayores de cinco años (mixteco 18 y zapoteco 16).

San Francisco Teopan ◆ Municipio de Oaxaca situado en el noroeste del estado, al este de Huajuapan de León. Superficie: 45.93 km². Habitantes: 427, de los cuales 157 forman la población económicamente activa.

San Francisco Tetlanohcan ◆ Municipio de Tlaxcala erigido en 1995 y situado al sur de Chiautempan y al este de la capital del estado. Habitantes: 8,422. Hablan alguna lengua indígena 1,530 personas mayores de cinco años (náhuatl 1,505).

San Francisco de Borja, Chihuahua

Foto: Fondo Editorial Grupo Azabache

Foto: Museo de Arte de Sinaloa

Estero de San Ignacio, acuarela de Edgardo Coghlan

San Francisco Tlapancingo ◆ Municipio de Oaxaca situado en el noroeste del estado, en los límites con Guerrero, al suroeste de Huajuapan de León. Superficie: 114.82 km². Habitantes: 1,688, de los cuales 354 forman la población económicamente activa. Hablan alguna lengua indígena 759 personas mayores de cinco años (mixteco 755), de las cuales 187 son monolingües.

San Gabriel ◆ Municipio de Jalisco situado en el sur del estado, contiguo a Ciudad Guzmán, casi en los límites con Colima. Superficie: 449.01 km². Habitantes: 14,303, de los cuales 3,168 forman la población económicamente activa. Hablan alguna lengua indígena siete personas mayores de cinco años. Durante un periodo se le llamó Venustiano Carranza.

San Gabriel Chilac ◆ Municipio de Puebla situado en el sureste del estado, al sur de Tehuacán y al sureste de la capital de la entidad. Superficie: 104.61 km². Habitantes: 11,790, de los cuales 2,592 forman la población económicamente activa. Hablan alguna lengua indígena 7,160 personas mayores de cinco años (náhuatl 5,888 y popoloca 1,552). Indígenas monolingües: 498.

Sierra de los Frailes en el municipio de San Ignacio, Sinaloa

Foto: Gobierno del Estado de Sinaloa

San Gabriel Mixtepec ◆ Municipio de Oaxaca situado en el sur del estado, al norte de Puerto Escondido y al suroeste de Miahuatlán. Superficie: 482.26 km². Habitantes: 3,519, de los cuales 745 forman la población económicamente activa. Hablan alguna lengua indígena 105 personas mayores de cinco años (chatino 94 y zapoteco 10).

San Gregorio Atzompa ◆ Municipio de Puebla situado en el occidente del estado, al este y próximo a la capital de la entidad. Superficie: 15.31 km². Habitantes: 6,407, de los cuales 1,435 forman la población económicamente activa. Hablan alguna lengua indígena 41 personas mayores de cinco años (náhuatl 36).

San Hipólito ◆ Bahía de Baja California Sur situada en el litoral del océano Pacífico, entre la punta San Hipólito y el estero La Bocana, al sur del desierto de Vizcaíno.

San Ignacio ◆ Bahía de Sinaloa situada en el litoral del golfo de California, al sur de Topolobampo y al norte de la isla de San Ignacio.

San Ignacio ◆ Laguna de Baja California Sur situada en el litoral del océano Pacífico, al este de la bahía de las Ballenas y de la sierra de Santa Clara y al suroeste de la isla de Terranova. En sus costas abundan las aves marinas, caguamas, así como elefantes y lobos marinos.

San Ignacio ◆ Municipio de Sinaloa situado en el litoral del golfo de California, en los límites con Durango y contiguo a Mazatlán. Superficie: 4,650.97 km². Habitantes: 27,101, de los cuales 6,434 forman la población económicamente activa. Hablan alguna lengua indígena 10 personas mayores de cinco años.

San Ignacio Río Muerto ◆ Municipio de Sonora erigido el 26 de diciembre de 1996. Se ubica al suroeste del estado; colinda al sur con Guaymas, al este con Bácum y al oeste con el golfo de California. Habitantes: 16,798, de los cuales 1,767 forman la población económicamente activa. En los principales poblados (San Ignacio, Bahía de Lobos, La Democracia, Bachomobampo y San Isidro) se asienta gran parte de la población yaqui. Tiene litoral de 70 km.

San Ildefonso ◆ Fábrica textil de Tlalnepantla. Sus obreros y los de la factoría La Colmena, también de Tlalnepantla, crearon la Sociedad Mutualista del Ramo de Hilados y Tejidos del Valle de México el 15 de mayo de 1865. El 10 de junio se fueron a la huelga y al día siguiente, en solidaridad, los de La Colmena se les unieron. Fueron reprimidos por la gendarmería imperial, heridos varios y 50 encarcelados. El 2 de agosto de 1875 un grupo de obreros abandonó labores y el gobierno ordenó a la policía que los presentara en la fábrica. Ante ese acto de fuerza los demás obreros secundaron la huelga, a la que respondió la fuerza pública con la violencia para obligarlos a volver al trabajo. Los obreros se resistieron y la policía disparó sobre la multitud, hiriendo a varios tejedores y asesinando al obrero Doroteo Olvera.

San Ildefonso Amatlán ◆ Municipio de Oaxaca situado en el centro-sur del estado, al noreste y próximo a Miahuatlán. Superficie: 91.86 km². Habitantes: 1,980, de los cuales 443 forman la población económicamente activa. Hablan alguna lengua indígena 653 personas mayores de cinco años (zapoteco 625).

San Ildefonso Sola ◆ Municipio de Oaxaca situado en el sur del estado, al noroeste de Miahuatlán y al sur-suroeste de la capital de la entidad. Superficie: 52.31 km². Habitantes: 840, de los cuales 150 forman la población económicamente activa.

San Ildefonso Villa Alta ◆ Municipio de Oaxaca situado en el noreste del estado, al noreste de la capital de la entidad y al sur de Tuxtepec. Superficie: 136.52 km². Habitantes: 3,164, de los cuales 788 forman la población económicamente activa. Hablan alguna lengua indígena 2,017 personas mayores de cinco años (zapoteco 1,970), de las cuales 292 son monolingües.

SAN JACINTO AMILPAS ◆ Municipio de Oaxaca situado en el centro del estado y contiguo a la capital de la entidad. Superficie: 12.76 km². Habitantes: 3,834, de los cuales 683 forman la población económicamente activa. Hablan alguna lengua indígena 234 personas mayores de cinco años (zapoteco 107).

SAN JACINTO TLACOTEPEC ◆ Municipio de Oaxaca situado en el suroeste del estado, al este-noreste de Santiago Pinotepa Nacional y al oeste-noroeste de Miahuatlán. Superficie: 233.48 km². Habitantes: 2,108, de los cuales 362 forman la población económicamente activa. Hablan chatino 35 personas mayores de cinco años.

SAN JAVIER ◆ Municipio de Sonora situado al sureste de Hermosillo y al norte de Ciudad Obregón. Superficie: 793.27 km². Habitantes: 306, de los cuales 128 forman la población económicamente activa. En 1706, Antonio Becerra Nieto fundó la primera población española ubicada en el territorio que hoy ocupa el municipio; éste fue incorporado en 1930 al de Hermosillo, en 1931 al de Villa Pesqueira, en 1934 al de La Colorada y a finales de ese mismo año fue rehabilitado. Su población ha decrecido.

SAN JERONIMITO ◆ Río de Guerrero que nace de la confluencia del arroyo Murga con el río de las Cruces. Se une con el Petatlán antes de desembocar en la laguna Colorada, al sureste de Zihuatanejo.

SAN JERÓNIMO ◆ Río de los estados de México, Guerrero y Morelos, también llamado de Tenancingo. Nace en la vertiente sur de la sierra de Tenango, al sur del Nevado de Toluca; recibe los manantiales de Villa Guerrero o Tecualoya, por la cueva de Huitztemalco, penetra en las grutas de Cacahuamilpa. Tiene un curso subterráneo de unos 4 km, sale a la superficie y se une con el Chontalcuatlán para formar el Grande de Amacuzac, cerca del límite de los estados de México, Guerrero y Morelos.

SAN JERÓNIMO COATLÁN ◆ Municipio de Oaxaca situado en el sur del estado, al oeste-suroeste de Miahuatlán. Superficie: 338.1 km². Habitantes: 3,580, de los cuales 1,020 forman la población económicamente activa. Hablan alguna lengua indígena 34 personas mayores de cinco años (zapoteco 31).

SAN JERÓNIMO DE JUÁREZ ◆ Cabecera del municipio de Benito Juárez (☛), Guerrero.

SAN JERÓNIMO SILACAYOAPILLA ◆ Municipio de Oaxaca situado en el noroeste del estado, al oeste y cerca de Huajuapan de León. Superficie: 30.62 km². Habitantes: 1,901, de los cuales 419 forman la población económicamente activa.

SAN JERÓNIMO SOSOLA ◆ Municipio de Oaxaca situado en el centro del estado, al noroeste de la capital de la entidad. Superficie: 140.34 km². Habitantes: 2,620, de los cuales 817 forman la población económicamente activa. Hablan alguna lengua indígena nueve personas mayores de cinco años (mixteco 6).

SAN JERÓNIMO TAVICHE ◆ Municipio de Oaxaca situado en el centro del estado, al sur-sureste de la capital de la entidad. Superficie: 213.06 km². Habitantes: 1,491, de los cuales 298 forman la población económicamente activa. Hablan alguna lengua indígena 367 personas mayores de cinco años (zapoteco 366).

SAN JERÓNIMO TECOATL ◆ Municipio de Oaxaca situado en el norte del estado, al noroeste y próximo a Huautla de Jiménez. Superficie: 17.86 km². Habitantes: 1,542, de los cuales 418 forman la población económicamente activa. Hablan alguna lengua indígena 1,204 personas mayores de cinco años (mazateco 1,178), de los que 170 no dominan el español.

SAN JERÓNIMO TECUANIPAN ◆ Municipio de Puebla situado en el occidente del estado, al oeste de la capital de la entidad y al noroeste de Atlixco. Superficie: 30.62 km². Habitantes: 4,819, de los cuales 1,010 forman la población económicamente activa. Hablan alguna lengua indígena 94 personas mayores de cinco años (náhuatl 92).

Panorámica de la fábrica textil de San Ildefonso

SAN JERÓNIMO TLACOCHAHUAYA ◆ Municipio de Oaxaca situado al estesureste de la capital estatal, al sur de Ixtlán de Juárez y al nor-noreste de Ocotlán. Superficie: 47.2 km². Habitantes: 4,694, de los cuales 1,086 forman la población económicamente activa. Hablan alguna lengua indígena 2,607 personas mayores de cinco años (zapoteco 2,596). Hacia el año 5000 a.n.e., los zapotecas se instalaron en Danixiul, lugar ubicado en la actual jurisdicción, y posiblemente ahí establecieron su primera capital. En la cabecera hay un templo y un convento del siglo XVI. Se llamó Tlacochahuaya de Morelos.

SAN JERÓNIMO XAYACATLÁN ◆ Municipio de Puebla situado en el sur del estado, en los límites con Oaxaca, al este de Acatlán. Superficie: 229.62 km². Habitantes: 4,229, de los cuales 630 forman la población económicamente activa. Hablan alguna lengua indígena 2,328 personas mayores de cinco años (mixteco 128). Indígenas monolingües: 128.

SAN JERÓNIMO ZACUALPAN ◆ Municipio de Tlaxcala de reciente creación, situado al sur de la capital del estado. Habitantes: 3,196.

Foto: Michael Calderwood

Isla San José en el océano Pacífico

San Joaquín ◆ Municipio de Querétaro situado en el noreste del estado, al noreste de Cadereyta y de la capital de la entidad. Superficie: 499 km^2. Habitantes: 7,940, de los cuales 1,427 forman la población económicamente activa. Hablan alguna lengua indígena 13 personas mayores de cinco años.

San Jorge, de ◆ Bahía de Sonora, también llamada López Collado y anteriormente Adair, entre el estero La Pinta y Punta Salinas, en el litoral del golfo de California, al noroeste de Caborca, en la desembocadura del río Colorado.

San Jorge Nuchita ◆ Municipio de Oaxaca situado en el noroeste del estado, al suroeste de Huajuapan de León. Superficie: 67.62 km^2. Habitantes: 3,321, de los cuales 458 forman la población económicamente activa. Hablan alguna lengua indígena 2,050 personas mayores de cinco años (mixteco 2,017).

San José ◆ Isla del océano Pacífico situada frente a Baja California Sur, al nor-noroeste de La Paz y al norte de la bahía del mismo nombre. Tiene fuentes de agua potable y salinas en proceso de explotación. La isla estuvo habitada por los pericúes. Recibió su nombre actual en 1633, cuando llegó a ella el explorador Francisco de Ortega.

San José del Cabo, en Baja California Sur

Foto: Michael Calderwood

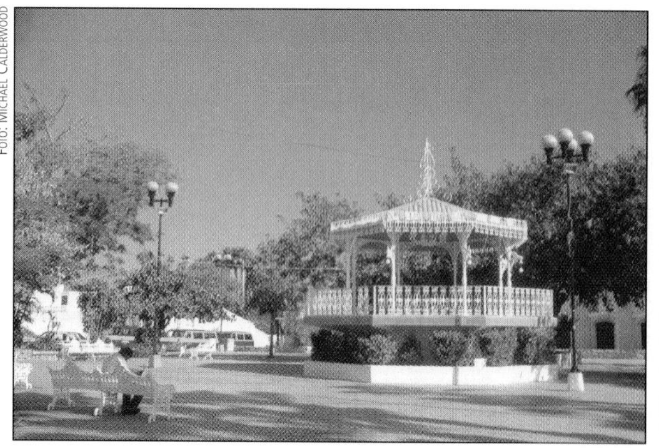

San José, de ◆ Sierra de Chihuahua, al sur-sureste de la capital. Forma parte de la sierra Madre Occidental; está limitada al norte por la sierra de Choreáchic y al oeste por el llano de los Gigantes, donde nace el río Papigochic.

San José Ayuquila ◆ Municipio de Oaxaca situado en el noroeste del estado, en los límites con Puebla, al noroeste de Huajuapan de León. Superficie: 35.72 km^2. Habitantes: 1,288, de los cuales 366 forman la población económicamente activa. En su jurisdicción se han hallado algunas pinturas rupestres, que guardan cierta similitud con las de la cueva de Altamira, en España.

San José del Cabo ◆ Bahía de Baja California Sur, situada en el extremo sur de la península, entre las puntas Gorda y Palmilla. En la bahía se halla el puerto de altura de San José.

San José del Cabo ◆ Cabecera del municipio de Los Cabos (☛), Baja California Sur.

San José Chiapa ◆ Municipio de Puebla situado en el centro del estado, en los límites con Tlaxcala, al norte de Tecamachalco. Superficie: 144.15 km^2. Habitantes: 6,259, de los cuales 1,344 forman la población económicamente activa. Hablan alguna lengua indígena cinco personas mayores de cinco años.

San José Chiltepec ◆ Municipio de Oaxaca situado en el norte del estado, al sur y próximo a Tuxtepec. Superficie: 204.3 km^2. Habitantes: 9,612, de los cuales 2,419 forman la población económicamente activa. Hablan alguna lengua indígena 3,343 personas mayores de cinco años (chinanteco 3,217), de las que 138 no saben español.

San José Estancia Grande ◆ Municipio de Oaxaca situado en el suroeste del estado, al este de Santiago Pinotepa Nacional. Superficie: 103.34 km^2. Habitantes: 877, de los cuales 184 forman la población económicamente activa. Hablan alguna lengua indígena 19 personas mayores de cinco años (mixteco 16).

San José de Gracia ◆ Antiguo nombre de la población de Ornelas, cabecera del municipio michoacano de Marcos Castellanos (☛).

San José de Gracia ◆ Municipio de Aguascalientes situado en el noroeste del estado, en los límites con Zacatecas, al oeste de Rincón de Romos. Superficie: 758.6 km^2. Habitantes: 7,170, de los cuales 1,509 forman la población económicamente activa. Se erigió en municipio en 1895, aunque durante un tiempo estuvo integrado al de Rincón de Romos. La fiesta popular de San José de Gracia se efectúa del 5 al 7 de enero y el Viernes Santo se lleva a cabo la peregrinación del silencio. Cuenta con el campo turístico ejidal del mismo nombre, que tiene un lienzo charro, hipódromo, un yate y lanchas para practicar deportes acuáticos. En las presas Plutarco Elías Calles y Jacóqui se puede practicar la pesca deportiva.

San José de Gracia ◆ Población de Baja California Sur.

San José de Gracia, Congregación de ◆ Población de Jiquilpan, Michoacán (☛).

San José Independencia ◆ Municipio de Oaxaca situado en el norte del estado, al sur de la presa Miguel Alemán y al suroeste de Tuxtepec. Superficie: 58.69 km^2. Habitantes: 4,100, de los cuales 955 forman la población económicamente activa. Hablan alguna lengua indígena 3,371 personas mayores de cinco años (mazateco 3,370), de las que 1,062 no saben español.

San José Iturbide ◆ Municipio de Guanajuato situado en el oriente del estado, en los límites con Querétaro, al noreste de San Miguel de Allende. Superficie: 517.7 km^2. Habitantes: 50,596, de los cuales 10,813 forman la población económicamente activa. Hablan alguna lengua indígena 16 personas mayores de cinco años (otomí 9). La cabecera, del mismo nombre, fue fundada por los españoles con el nombre de Los Llanos; se llamó después

San José Chiapa, Puebla

Casas Viejas y San José de Casas Viejas. En 1859, el gobernador Manuel Doblado le dio la categoría de villa y su actual nombre, en honor de Agustín de Iturbide. Durante un breve periodo, en los años sesenta, llevó el nombre de Ciudad Álvaro Obregón.

San José Lachiguirí ◆ Municipio de Oaxaca situado en el sur del estado, al este-noreste de Miahuatlán. Superficie: 132.69 km^2. Habitantes: 3,399, de los cuales 797 forman la población económicamente activa. Hablan alguna lengua indígena 2,854 personas mayores de cinco años (zapoteco 2,852), de las cuales 705 son monolingües.

San José Miahuatlán ◆ Municipio de Puebla situado en el sureste del estado, en los límites con Oaxaca, al sureste de Tehuacán. Superficie: 335.51 km^2. Habitantes: 10,285, de los cuales 2,359 forman la población económicamente activa. Hablan alguna lengua indígena 8,333 personas mayores de cinco años (náhuatl 8,303). Indígenas monolingües: 629.

San José del Peñasco ◆ Municipio de Oaxaca situado en el sur del estado, al este-sureste y próximo a Miahuatlán. Habitantes: 1,362, de los cuales 422 forman la población económicamente activa.

San José del Progreso ◆ Municipio de Oaxaca situado en el centro del estado, al sur de la ciudad de Oaxaca. Superficie: 66.34 km^2. Habitantes: 5,570, de los cuales 1,291 forman la población económicamente activa. Hablan alguna lengua indígena 412 personas mayores de cinco años (zapoteco 410). Pertenece al distrito judicial de Ocotlán.

San José Purúa ◆ Balneario del municipio de Jungapeo, Michoacán.

San José de las Rucias ◆ Sierra de Tamaulipas paralela al litoral del golfo de México y la sierra de Tamaulipas, entre los ríos Soto la Marina y Carrizal, al este de la barra Soto la Marina.

San José Teacalco ◆ Municipio de Tlaxcala erigido en 1995. Es contiguo a Huamantla por el noroeste. Tiene 4,600 habitantes distribuidos en ocho localidades.

San José Tenango ◆ Municipio de Oaxaca situado en el norte del estado, al este de Huautla y al oeste de la presa Miguel Alemán. Superficie: 144.17 km^2. Habitantes: 16,449, de los cuales 5,331 forman la población económicamente activa. Hablan alguna lengua indígena 14,019 personas mayores de cinco años (mazateco 14,013), de las que 5,732 no dominan el español.

San Juan ◆ Río de Durango que nace al suroeste de la sierra del Gamón, al noroeste de Francisco I. Madero; cruza por el valle de San Juan del Río, recibe a los arroyos de San Lucas y de Nogales y desemboca en el Nazas, al noreste de la sierra de Coneto.

San Juan ◆ Río de los estados de México y Querétaro. Nace de la confluencia del arroyo Zarco y el río Prieto, al noroeste de la presa de San Ildefonso. Pasa por el valle de San Juan del Río, al que riega, recibe el agua de los manantiales de Tequisquiapan y se une al río Tula, en la barranca del Infiernillo, para formar el Moctezuma.

San Juan ◆ Río de Nuevo León y Tamaulipas. Nace en las laderas orientales de la sierra Madre Oriental de la confluencia del río Monterrey y el arroyo Álamo, al sur-sureste de Monterrey; recibe al río Pilón, al arroyo Mohinas y al río Pesquería, forma la presa el Azúcar, al suroeste de Ciudad Camargo, y sigue su curso hasta desembocar en el Bravo, al norte de la misma ciudad.

San Juan, de ◆ Llanos de Puebla y Tlaxcala, situados al este-noreste del volcán de la Malinche. Están limitados al sureste por la sierra Madre Oriental, al norte por la de Puebla y al sur por la del Monumento. El suelo de los llanos está formado por las cenizas y arenas de las erupciones de las Derrumbadas y del Cofre de Perote. Cuenta con numerosos volcanes pequeños, como el Pico de Pizarro, las Derrumbadas, las Cumbres de Oyameles, los cerros de Torrecilla, Alchichica, Campana y Toluca.

San Juan, de ◆ Sierra de Nayarit situada al oeste de la sierra Madre Occidental, entre el valle de Tepic y el océano Pacífico, al este de San Blas.

San Juan, de ◆ Sierra de Sonora que forma parte de las estribaciones noroccidentales de la sierra Madre Occidental. Su extremo noreste se llama sierra de la Escondida, en la frontera con Estados Unidos, y su extremo sur tiene el nombre de sierra del Carrizal. Está al oeste-suroeste de Nogales.

San José Iturbide, Guanajuato

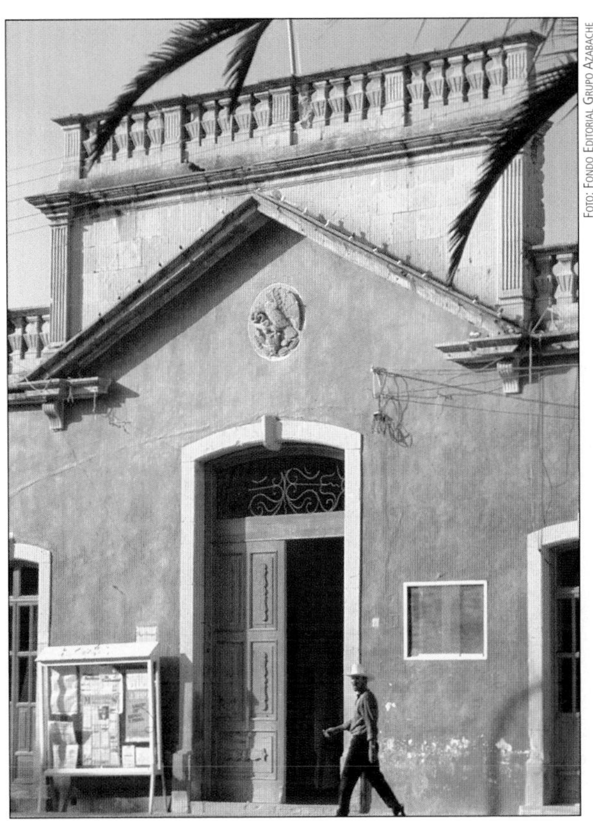

Foto: Fondo Editorial Grupo Azabache

San Juan, Catalina de ◆ ☛ *China poblana*.

San Juan Achiutla ◆ Municipio de Oaxaca situado en el oeste del estado, al sureste de Huajuapan de León y al oeste-noroeste de la capital de la entidad. Superficie: 49.76 km². Habitantes: 455, de los cuales 95 forman la población económicamente activa. Hablan mixteco cinco personas mayores de cinco años.

San Juan Atenco ◆ Municipio de Puebla situado al este de la capital de la entidad y al noreste de Tecamachalco, cercano a Veracruz. Superficie: 188.81 km². Habitantes: 3,715, de los cuales 872 forman la población económicamente activa. Hablan alguna lengua indígena cinco personas mayores de cinco años.

San Juan Atepec ◆ Municipio de Oaxaca situado en el centro del estado, al nor-noreste de la capital de la entidad. Superficie: 88.03 km². Habitantes: 1,678, de los cuales 432 forman la población económicamente activa. Hablan alguna lengua indígena 1,303 personas mayores de cinco años (zapoteco 1,302). En la jurisdicción hay pinturas rupestres y ruinas de la cultura zapoteca.

Foto: Fondo Editorial Grupo Azabache

Fachada del templo de San Juan Bautista, Oaxaca

San Juan Atzompa ◆ Municipio de Puebla situado en el centro del estado, al sureste de la capital de la entidad y al oeste de Tecamachalco. Superficie: 25.52 km². Habitantes: 616, de los cuales 185 forman la población económicamente activa. Hablan alguna lengua indígena cinco personas mayores de cinco años.

San Juan Bautista, de ◆ Llano de Sonora situado entre el litoral del golfo de California y la sierra Madre Occidental, al sur del desierto de Altar y del río Sonora, mismo que pierde sus aguas en este llano por evaporación e infiltración.

San Juan Bautista Ánimas Trujano ◆ ☛ *Ánimas Trujano*, municipio de Oaxaca.

San Juan Bautista Atatlahuaca ◆ Municipio de Oaxaca situado en el norte del estado, al nor-noroeste de la capital de la entidad. Superficie: 196.48 km². Habitantes: 1,680, de los cuales 429 forman la población económicamente activa. Hablan alguna lengua indígena 637 personas mayores de cinco años (chinanteco 628).

San Juan Bautista Coixtlahuaca ◆ Municipio de Oaxaca situado en el noroeste del estado, al este-sureste de Huajuapan de León. Superficie: 279.41 km². Habitantes: 3,398, de los cuales 795 forman la población económicamente activa. Hablan alguna lengua indígena 217 personas mayores de cinco años (chocho 209). En su territorio hay vestigios de la cultura zapoteca: en la loma de Inguiteria se encontraron monumentos y sepulcros con cerámica polícroma. Uno de los más importantes hallazgos fue la estatua de Ehécatl, que se conserva en el museo de Toluca. De ahí proviene también el códice ahora llamado de Coixtlahuaca. Su cabecera, del mismo nombre, tiene un templo y convento, de estilo renacentista, edificados en el siglo XVI, sobre un inmenso basamento indígena.

San Juan Bautista Cuicatlán ◆ Municipio de Oaxaca situado en el norte del estado, al este de Huajuapan de León. Superficie: 543.5 km². Habitantes: 9,226, de los cuales 2,557 forman la población económicamente activa. Hablan alguna lengua indígena 1,422 personas mayores de cinco años (cuicateco 860 y mixteco 491). En el cerro de las Juntas se halló una serie de fortificaciones de la cultura mixteca, de aproximadamente 3,000 años de antigüedad, con túmulos funerarios, estanques y restos de columnas similares a las de Chichén Itzá. Cuicatlán tiene una cascada de 200 metros de alto.

San Juan Bautista Guelache ◆ Municipio de Oaxaca situado en el centro del estado, al noroeste de la capital de la entidad. Superficie: 70.17 km². Habitantes: 3,131, de los cuales 913 forman la población económicamente activa. Hablan alguna lengua indígena 74 personas mayores de cinco años (zapoteco 52 y mixteco 16).

San Juan Bautista Jayacatlán ◆ Municipio de Oaxaca situado en el centro del estado, al norte-noreste de la capital de la entidad. Superficie: 173.51 km². Habitantes: 1,447, de los cuales 433 forman la población económicamente activa. Hablan alguna lengua indígena 10 personas mayores de cinco años (mixteco 6).

San Juan Bautista lo de Soto ◆ Municipio de Oaxaca situado en el suroeste del estado, en los límites con Guerrero, al noroeste de Santiago Pinotepa Nacional. Superficie: 63.79 km². Habitantes: 2,653, de los cuales 706 forman la población económicamente activa. Hablan alguna lengua indígena 67 personas mayores de cinco años (mixteco 53).

San Juan Bautista Suchitepec ◆ Municipio de Oaxaca situado en el noroeste del estado, al noreste de Huajuapan de León. Superficie: 38.28 km². Habitantes: 515, de los cuales 149 forman la población económicamente activa.

San Juan Bautista Tlacoatzintepec ◆ Municipio de Oaxaca situado en el norte del estado, al sur de la presa Miguel Alemán y al sureste de Huautla de Jiménez. Superficie: 183.72 km². Habitantes: 2,182, de los cuales 544 forman la población económicamente activa. Hablan alguna lengua indígena 1,827 personas mayores de cinco años (chinanteco 1,671 y ciucateco 138), de las que 531 no saben español.

San Juan Bautista Tlachichilco ◆ Municipio de Oaxaca situado en el noroeste del estado, en los límites con Guerrero, al suroeste de Huajuapan de León. Superficie: 116.1 km². Habitantes: 1,367, de los cuales 133 forman la población económicamente activa. Hablan alguna lengua indígena 129 personas mayores de cinco años (mixteco 127).

San Juan Bautista Tuxtepec ◆ Municipio de Oaxaca situado en el norte del estado, en los límites con Veracruz, al este-sureste de la presa Miguel Alemán. Superficie: 625.15 km². Habitantes: 127,707, de los cuales 33,525 forman la población económicamente activa. Hablan alguna lengua indígena 20,466 personas mayores de cinco años (chinanteco 15,453, mazateco 3,354 y zapoteco 766), de las cuales 344 son monolingües. Tiene yacimientos de carbón y cobre y cuenta con una de las mayores fábricas de papel del país. La diócesis de Tuxtepec fue erigida por el papa Juan Pablo II el 8 de enero de 1979.

San Juan Bautista Valle Nacional ◆ Municipio de Oaxaca situado en el norte del estado, al sur-suroeste de Tuxtepec y al sur-sureste de la presa Miguel Alemán. Superficie: 394.23 km². Habitantes: 22,276, de los cuales 5,467 forman la población económicamente activa. Hablan alguna lengua indígena 12,049 personas mayores de cinco años (chinanteco 11,825 y zapoteco 143), de los que 1,317 no dominan el español.

San Juan Cacahuatepec ◆ Municipio de Oaxaca situado en el suroeste del estado, en los límites con Guerrero, al nor-noroeste de Santiago Pinotepa Nacional. Superficie: 153.1 km². Habitantes: 7,812, de los cuales 1,719 forman la población económicamente activa. Hablan alguna lengua indígena 237 personas mayores de cinco años (mixteco 177 y amuzgo 52).

San Juan Cancuc ◆ Municipio de Chiapas situado al noreste de San Cristóbal de Las Casas, contiguo a Chenalhó y Ocosingo. Superficie: 163.08 km. Habitantes: 22,904, de los cuales 4,520 forman la población económicamente activa. Hablan alguna lengua indígena 16,647 personas mayores de cinco años, de las cuales 9,113 son monolingües. Fue erigido en 1990.

San Juan Cieneguilla ◆ Municipio de Oaxaca situado en el noroeste del estado, en los límites con Puebla, al oeste-noroeste de Huajuapan de León. Superficie: 167.3 km². Habitantes: 593, de los cuales 74 forman la población económicamente activa.

San Juan Coatzospan ◆ Municipio de Oaxaca situado en el norte del estado, al sureste de Huautla de Jiménez. Superficie: 63.79 km². Habitantes: 2,176, de los cuales 666 forman la población económicamente activa. Hablan alguna lengua indígena 1,839 personas mayores de cinco años (mixteco 1,810), de las cuales 331 no dominan el español.

San Juan Colorado ◆ Municipio de Oaxaca situado en el suroeste del estado, al norte y próximo a Santiago Pinotepa Nacional. Superficie: 85.48 km². Habitantes: 7,801, de los cuales 2,118 forman la población económicamente activa. Hablan alguna lengua indígena 4,587 personas mayores de cinco años (mixteco 4,584), de las que 1,167 no saben español.

San Juan Comaltepec ◆ Municipio de Oaxaca situado en el noreste del estado, al noreste de la capital y al sur-sureste de Tuxtepec. Superficie: 163.31 km². Habitantes: 1,937, de los cuales 419 forman la población económicamente activa. Hablan alguna lengua indígena 1,485 personas mayores de cinco años (zapoteco 896 y chinanteco 571).

San Juan Cotzocón ◆ Municipio de Oaxaca situado en el noreste del estado, al este-noreste de la capital de la entidad. Superficie: 945.39 km². Habitantes: 21,362, de los cuales 5,748 forman la población económicamente activa. Hablan alguna lengua indígena 9,419 personas mayores de cinco años (mixe 5,378, mazateco 2,166 y mixteco 1,378), de las cuales 714 no saben español.

San Juan Cuautlancingo ◆ Cabecera del municipio de Cuautlancingo (☛), Puebla.

San Juan los Cues ◆ Municipio de Oaxaca situado en el norte del estado, al suroeste de Huautla de Jiménez. Superficie: 116.1 km². Habitantes: 2,583, de los cuales 727 forman la población económicamente activa. Hablan alguna lengua indígena 973 personas mayores de cinco años (mazateco 940).

San Juan Chicomezúchil ◆ Municipio de Oaxaca situado en el centro del estado, al noreste de la capital de la entidad. Superficie: 76.55 km². Habitantes: 365, de los cuales 85 forman la población económicamente activa. Hablan zapoteco seis personas mayores de cinco años.

San Juan Chilateca ◆ Municipio de Oaxaca situado en el centro del estado, al sur de la capital de la entidad. Superficie: 31.9 km². Habitantes: 1,303, de los cuales 437 forman la población económicamente activa. Hablan alguna lengua indígena seis personas.

San Juan Diuxi ◆ Municipio de Oaxaca situado en el occidente del estado, al suroeste de Huajuapan de León y al oeste-noroeste de la capital de la entidad. Superficie: 96.96 km². Habitantes: 1,784, de los cuales 412 forman la población económicamente activa. Hablan mixteco 1,441 personas mayores de cinco años (monolingües 106).

San Juan del Estado ◆ Municipio de Oaxaca situado en el centro del estado, al norte de la capital de la entidad. Superficie: 94.42 km². Habitantes: 2,134, de los cuales 418 forman la población económicamente activa. Hablan alguna lengua indígena 20 personas mayores de cinco años (zapoteco 14).

San Juan Evangelista ◆ Municipio de Veracruz situado al sur de San Andrés Tuxtla y al oeste de Minatitlán, en los límites con Oaxaca. Superficie: 968.94 km². Habitantes: 33,580, de los cuales 8,859 forman la población económicamente activa. Hablan alguna lengua

Parroquia de San Juan Evangelista, Veracruz

indígena 321 personas mayores de cinco años (chinanteco 133 y náhuatl 61). El municipio y su cabecera llevaron el nombre de Santana Rodríguez.

San Juan Evangelista ◆ Río de Veracruz que nace de la confluencia de los ríos de la Lana y el de la Trinidad, al oeste de Acayucan, en la llanura costera del golfo. Corre entre las sierras Madre Oriental y San Martín Tuxtla, recibe al río Tuxtla Laurel, el desagüe del lago de Catemaco, el Santiago y el Hueyapan. El San Juan se bifurca y desemboca en el Papaloapan, cerca de Tlacotalpan. Es navegable para embarcaciones pequeñas.

San Juan Evangelista Analco ◆ Municipio de Oaxaca situado en el centro del estado, al nor-noreste de la capital de la entidad. Superficie: 33.17 km^2. Habitantes: 524, de los cuales 121 forman la población económicamente activa. Hablan zapoteco 235 personas mayores de cinco años. Los habitantes de este municipio son descendientes de los tlaxcaltecas que ayudaron a Cortés a conquistar Oaxaca. En el lugar se conserva un códice semejante al de Tlaxcala; este documento señala el origen de estos pobladores y la época de su asentamiento en la región zapoteca.

San Juan de Guadalupe ◆ Municipio de Durango situado en el extremo oriental del estado, en los límites con Coahuila y Zacatecas. Superficie: 2,343.1 km^2. Habitantes: 7.262, de los cuales 1,735 forman la población económicamente activa. Hablan alguna lengua indígena 13 personas mayores de cinco años.

San Juan Guelavía ◆ Municipio de Oaxaca situado en el centro del estado, al sureste de la capital de la entidad. Superficie: 17.86 km^2. Habitantes: 2,811, de los cuales 654 forman la población económicamente activa. Hablan alguna lengua indígena 2,110 personas mayores de cinco años (zapoteco 2,101), de las cuales 48 no saben español.

San Juan Guichicovi ◆ Municipio de Oaxaca situado en el este del estado, al norte de Juchitán de Zaragoza. Superficie: 563.91 km^2. Habitantes: 25,096, de los cuales 6,813 forman la población económicamente activa. Hablan alguna lengua indígena 18,309 personas mayores de cinco años (mixe 17,323, mixteco 284 y zapoteco 120), de las que 2,009 son monolingües.

San Juan Huactzinco ◆ Municipio de Tlaxcala erigido en 1995. Comprende la jurisdicción del mismo nombre que perteneció al municipio de Tepeyanco. Está situado al sur de la capital del estado. Tiene 5,510 habitantes.

San Juan Ihualtepec ◆ Municipio de Oaxaca situado en el noroeste del estado, en los límites con Puebla y Guerrero, al oeste de Huajuapan de León. Superficie: 146.72 km^2. Habitantes: 751, de los cuales 119 forman la población económicamente activa. Hablan mixteco 33 personas mayores de cinco años.

San Juan Ixcaquixtla ◆ Cabecera del municipio de Ixcaquixtla (☛), Puebla.

San Juan Juquila Mixes ◆ Municipio de Oaxaca situado en el centro del estado, al este-sureste de la capital de la entidad. Superficie: 227.1 km^2. Habitantes: 3,517, de los cuales 970 forman la población económicamente activa. Hablan alguna lengua indígena 2,879 personas mayores de cinco años (mixe 2,697 y zapoteco 180), de las cuales 1,181 no dominan el español.

San Juan Juquila Vijanos ◆ Municipio de Oaxaca situado en el centro del estado, al noreste de la capital de la entidad. Superficie: 37 km^2. Habitantes: 1,672, de los cuales 480 forman la población económicamente activa. Hablan zapoteco 1,366 personas mayores de cinco años (monolingües 196).

San Juan Lachao ◆ Municipio de Oaxaca situado en el sur del estado, al oeste de Miahuatlán y al este de Santiago Pinotepa Nacional. Superficie: 190.1 km^2. Habitantes: 3,340, de los cuales 845 forman la población económicamente activa. Hablan alguna lengua indígena 1,445 personas mayores de cinco años (chatino 1,420), de las cuales 120 son monolingües.

San Juan Lachigalla ◆ Municipio de Oaxaca situado en el sur del estado, al norte de Miahuatlán. Superficie: 136.51 km^2. Habitantes: 2,740, de los cuales 738 forman la población económicamente activa. Hablan alguna lengua indígena cinco personas mayores de cinco años.

San Juan de los Lagos ◆ Municipio de Jalisco situado al noreste de Guadalajara y al suroeste de Lagos de Moreno. Superficie: 832.15 km^2. Habitantes: 53,366, de los cuales 13,216 forman la población económicamente activa. Hablan alguna lengua indígena 18 personas mayores de cinco años. El santuario de San Juan de los Lagos tiene una imagen, al parecer llevada por el sacerdote Miguel de Bolonia en 1623. La veneración por esta Virgen se extendió hasta Centroamérica, desde donde se hacían peregrinaciones a pie, lo que motivó al obispo de Guadalajara, Leonel de Cervantes, a autorizar su culto. La Patrona de San Juan de los Lagos fue coronada en 1904 y su santuario elevado a la categoría de colegiata, en 1923, y de basílica menor, en 1947. A principios del siglo XVII la gran afluencia de devotos de la virgen convirtió la población en animado centro comercial y de diversiones. Su feria llegó a ser de las más importantes del país. En 1630 fueron 2,000 los visitantes; 3,000 en 1639, más de 8,000 en 1736 y 35,000 en 1792. Gracias a esa multitud de fieles y a los comerciantes que ponían sus puestos en el atrio durante la feria, se pudo construir el santuario entre 1732 y 1769. La reglamentación real para la feria la extendió Carlos IV el 20 de noviembre de 1792. Se iniciaba el 1 de diciembre y duraba de 15 a 18 días. Se suspendió en 1810, por la guerra de Independencia, y se reinició en 1822. Había juegos de azar, toros, teatro y circo. En 1870 era la más importante feria del país. Como era imposible albergar a todos los visitantes en la ciudad, los cerros se llenaban de tiendas y construcciones improvisadas. Manuel Payno retrató algunos aspectos de esta celebración en su novela *Los bandidos de Río Frío*. La diócesis de San Juan de los Lagos fue erigida por Paulo VI el 25 de marzo de 1972.

San Juan de los Lagos ◆ Río de Jalisco también llamado Lagos (☛).

San Juan Lajarcia ◆ Municipio de Oaxaca situado en el sureste del estado, al noreste de Miahuatlán. Superficie: 160.75 km^2. Habitantes: 737, de los cuales 176 forman la población económicamente activa. Hablan alguna lengua indígena 13 personas mayores de cinco años (zapoteco 12).

San Juan Lalana ◆ Municipio de Oaxaca situado en el noreste del estado, al sur-sureste de Tuxtepec y al noreste de la capital de la entidad. Superficie: 454.19 km^2. Habitantes: 15,321, de los cuales 3,210 forman la población económicamente activa. Hablan alguna lengua indígena 10,528 personas mayores de cinco años (chinanteco 9,491, mixe 610 y zapoteco 404), de las que 922 no dominan el español.

San Juan Mazatlán ◆ Municipio de Oaxaca situado en el oriente del estado, al noroeste de Juchitán de Zaragoza. Superficie: 1,990.28 km^2. Habitantes: 16,547, de los cuales 3,638 forman la población económicamente activa. Hablan alguna lengua indígena 8,568 personas mayores de cinco años (mixe 6,837, chinanteco 745 y mixteco 704), de las que 1,698 son monolingües.

San Juan Mixtepec-Juxtlahuaca ◆ Municipio de Oaxaca situado en el noroeste del estado, al sur de Huajuapan de León. Superficie: 209.24 km^2. Habitantes: 9,246, de los cuales 2,774 forman la población económicamente activa. Hablan alguna lengua indígena 7,994 personas mayores de cinco años (zapoteco 7,990), de las que 2,179 no dominan el español. Tiene minas de carbón bituminoso, explotadas en pequeña escala, y de oro, plata, fierro y antimonio.

San Juan Mixtepec-Miahuatlán ◆ Municipio de Oaxaca situado en el sur del estado, al este-sureste de Miahuatlán. Superficie: 53.59 km^2. Habitantes: 714, de los cuales 232 forman la población económicamente activa. Hablan mixteco 561 personas mayores de cinco años.

San Juan Nayotla, Lienzo de ◆ Documento poshispánico, también llamado Códice de Actopan, procedente del poblado veracruzano de San Juan Nayotla. Es una tela pintada al óleo en el siglo XVI en la que se representan iglesias, rostros, caminos, personajes indígenas, animales, inscripciones en náhuatl, jeroglíficos de lugares y la leyenda: "San Juan. Visorrey Don Antonio de Mendoza. Año 1534". La fecha de 1519 se repite varias veces. El original se conserva en la Biblioteca Nacional de Antropología e Historia y hay dos copias hechas en 1956 por Agustín Villagra Caleti.

San Juan Ñumí ◆ Municipio de Oaxaca situado en el occidente del estado, al sur de Huajuapan de León. Superficie: 43.38 km^2. Habitantes: 6,221, de los cuales 1,065 forman la población económicamente activa. Hablan alguna lengua indígena 5,256 personas mayores de cinco años (mixteco 5,247), de las cuales 422 no saben español.

San Juan Ozolotepec ◆ Municipio de Oaxaca situado en el centro-sur del estado, al sureste de Miahuatlán. Superficie: 117.38 km^2. Habitantes: 3,009, de los cuales 755 forman la población económicamente activa. Hablan zapoteco 1,727 personas mayores de cinco años.

San Juan Petlapa ◆ Municipio de Oaxaca situado en el noreste del estado, al noreste de la capital de la entidad y al sur de Tuxtepec. Superficie: 253.89 km^2. Habitantes: 2,091, de los cuales 666 forman la población económicamente activa. Hablan alguna lengua indígena 1,718 personas mayores de cinco años (chinanteco 1,716), de las cuales 625 no saben español.

San Juan Quiahije ◆ Municipio de Oaxaca situado en el suroeste del estado, al este de Santiago Pinotepa Nacional y al oeste de Miahuatlán. Superficie: 91.86 km^2. Habitantes: 3,570, de los cuales 637 forman la población económicamente activa. Hablan alguna lengua indígena 2,966 personas mayores de cinco años (chatino 2,964), de las que 1,336 son monolingües.

San Juan Quiotepec ◆ Municipio de Oaxaca situado en el norte del estado, al suroeste de Tuxtepec. Superficie: 325.34 km^2. Habitantes: 2,367, de los cuales 510 forman la población económicamente activa. Hablan alguna lengua indígena 1,814 personas mayores de cinco años (chinanteco 1,809), de las que son monolingües 162.

San Juan del Río ◆ Municipio de Durango situado en el centro del estado, al norte de la capital estatal y al este de Santiago Papasquiaro. Superficie: 1,297 km^2. Habitantes: 14,212, de los cuales 3,239 forman la población económicamente activa. Hablan alguna lengua indígena 20 personas mayores de cinco años. Su cabecera es San Juan del Río Centauro del Norte.

San Juan del Río ◆ Municipio de Oaxaca situado al sureste de la capital del estado. Superficie: 108.44 km^2. Habitantes: 1,227, de los cuales 415 forman la población económicamente activa. Hablan zapoteco 1,131 personas mayores de cinco años.

San Juan del Río ◆ Municipio de Querétaro situado en el sur del estado, en los límites con Hidalgo y el Estado de México. Superficie: 779.9 km^2. Habitantes: 154,922, de los cuales 36,928 forman la población económicamente activa. Hablan alguna lengua indígena 482 personas mayores de cinco años (otomí 175 y náhuatl 96).

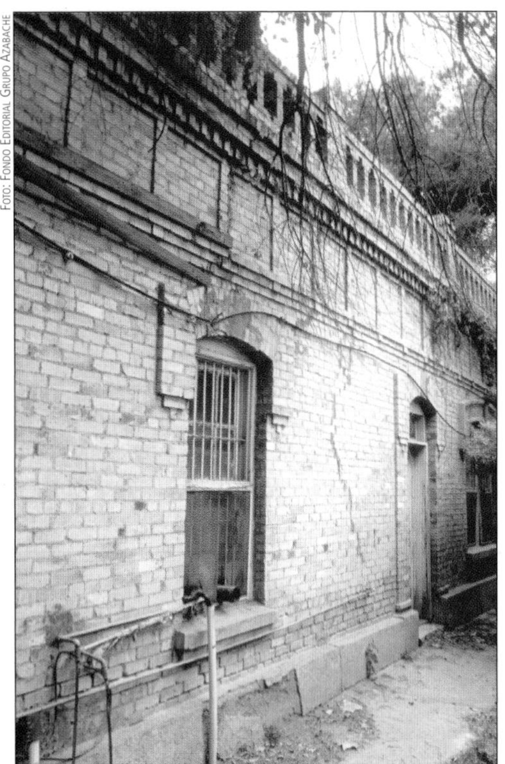

FOTO: FONDO EDITORIAL GRUPO AZABACHE

Casa de la Capitulación de Villa en San Juan de Sabinas, Coahuila

SAN JUAN DE SABINAS ◆ Municipio de Coahuila situado en el noreste del estado, cerca de Múzquiz y al noroeste de Saltillo. Superficie: 735.4 km². Habitantes: 40,731, de los cuales 12,314 forman la población económicamente activa. Hablan alguna lengua indígena 35 personas mayores de cinco años. En su jurisdicción se encuentra el mineral de Nueva Rosita, el mayor productor de hulla del país, que cuenta con una planta lavadora de carbón, hornos para fabricar coque y laboratorios donde se obtiene alquitrán, benzol, creosota, naftalina y otras materias primas para la industria.

SAN JUAN SAYULTEPEC ◆ Municipio de Oaxaca situado en el noroeste del estado, al noroeste de la capital de la entidad. Superficie: 16.59 km². Habitantes: 660, de los cuales 185 forman la población económicamente activa. Hablan alguna lengua indígena cinco personas mayores de cinco años (mixteco 4).

SAN JUAN TABAÁ ◆ Municipio de Oaxaca situado en el noreste del estado, al sur de Tuxtepec. Superficie: 26.79 km². Habitantes: 1,130, de los cuales 303 forman la población económicamente activa. Hablan zapoteco 970 personas mayores de cinco años (monolingües 73).

SAN JUAN TAMAZOLA ◆ Municipio de Oaxaca situado en el centro del estado, al noroeste de la capital de la entidad. Superficie: 156.93 km². Habitantes: 3,379, de los cuales 832 forman la población económicamente activa. Hablan alguna lengua indígena 1,654 personas mayores de cinco años (mixteco 1,648), de las que son monolingües 43.

SAN JUAN TEITA ◆ Municipio de Oaxaca situado en el occidente del estado, al oeste de la capital de la entidad y al sureste de Tlaxiaco. Superficie: 77.82 km². Habitantes: 455, de los cuales 136 forman la población económicamente activa. Hablan alguna lengua indígena 308 personas mayores de cinco años (mixteco 306).

SAN JUAN TEITIPAC ◆ Municipio de Oaxaca situado en el centro del estado, al sureste y cerca de la capital de la entidad. Superficie: 11.48 km². Habitantes: 2,945, de los cuales 724 forman la población económicamente activa. Hablan zapoteco 653 personas mayores de cinco años. En la cabecera, del mismo nombre, hay una iglesia y un convento del siglo XVI.

SAN JUAN TEOTIHUACÁN ◆ ☛ *Teotihuacán*.

SAN JUAN TEPEUXILA ◆ Municipio de Oaxaca situado en el centro-norte del estado, al sur de Huautla de Jiménez. Superficie: 366.16 km². Habitantes: 3,045, de los cuales 996 forman la población económicamente activa. Hablan alguna lengua indígena 1,842 personas mayores de cinco años (cuicateco 1,834).

SAN JUAN TEPOSCOLULA ◆ Municipio de Oaxaca situado en el noroeste del estado, al sureste de Huajuapan de León. Superficie: 57.41 km². Habitantes: 1,393, de los cuales 402 forman la población económicamente activa. Hablan mixteco 24 personas mayores de cinco años.

SAN JUAN XIUTETELCO ◆ Cabecera del municipio de Xiutetelco (☛), Puebla.

SAN JUAN YAÉ ◆ Municipio de Oaxaca situado en el noreste del estado, al noreste de la capital de la entidad y al sur-suroeste de Tuxtepec. Superficie: 93.14 km². Habitantes: 1,491, de los cuales 573 forman la población económicamente activa. Hablan alguna lengua indígena 1,328 personas mayores de cinco años (zapoteco 1,326) y son monolingües 183. En la jurisdicción se han encontrado algunas piezas arqueológicas de la cultura zapoteca; la más notable es una laja de 2 cm de espesor, con la figura de un conejo.

SAN JUAN YATZONA ◆ Municipio de Oaxaca situado en el noreste del estado, al noreste de la capital de la entidad y al sur de Tuxtepec. Superficie: 38.27 km². Habitantes: 504, de los cuales 127 forman la población económicamente activa. Hablan zapoteco 434 personas mayores de cinco años.

SAN JUAN YUCUITA ◆ Municipio de Oaxaca situado en el noroeste del estado, al noroeste de la capital de la entidad y al sureste de Huajuapan de León. Superficie: 75.27 km². Habitantes: 743, de los cuales 140 forman la población económicamente activa. Hablan mixteco nueve personas mayores de cinco años.

SAN JUANITO ◆ Isla de Nayarit que es la más pequeña de las Marías. Se halla situada al noroeste del archipiélago y al noroeste de la isla María Madre.

SAN JULIÁN ◆ Municipio de Jalisco situado en el noreste del estado, al sureste de San Juan de los Lagos, cercano a Guanajuato. Superficie: 268.44 km². Habitantes: 13,700, de los cuales 3,175 forman la población económicamente activa.

SAN LÁZARO ◆ Sierra de Baja California Sur que se extiende de norte a sur desde el este de la bahía de La Paz hasta el cabo San Lucas. Está separada de la sierra de la Trinidad por el valle y el río de San José. Se prolonga hacia el norte con la sierra de la Laguna y los minerales del Triunfo y Cacahuilas en las cercanías de La Paz.

SAN LORENZO ◆ Isla de Baja California situada en el extremo meridional del archipiélago que limita por el oriente al canal de Salsipuedes, en el golfo de California, al suroeste de la isla Tiburón.

San Lorenzo ◆ Municipio de Oaxaca situado en el suroeste del estado, al este y próximo a Santiago Pinotepa Nacional. Superficie: 89.31 km². Habitantes: 5,047, de los cuales 1,126 forman la población económicamente activa. Hablan alguna lengua indígena 3,272 personas mayores de cinco años (mixteco 3,261) y 956 son monolingües.

San Lorenzo ◆ Río de Durango y Sinaloa, también llamado Quilá. Nace de la confluencia de los arroyos que corren por las quebradas de las Vueltas y de los Fresnos, en la vertiente occidental de la sierra de Tepehuanes. En la primera parte de su curso es conocido como río de los Remedios. Otros nombres que recibe son Cihuatá, Vegas, Navito y Tavala. Desemboca en el golfo de California, al norte de la península de Quevedo, frente a la boca de Tavala. Recorre 700 Km y su cuenca es de 8,000 Km². En este río se construyó la presa derivadora de San Lorenzo, que riega unas 25,000 ha.

San Lorenzo Albarradas ◆ Municipio de Oaxaca situado en el centro del estado, al sureste de la capital de la entidad. Superficie: 61.24 km². Habitantes: 2,524, de los cuales 853 forman la población económicamente activa. Hablan alguna lengua indígena 438 personas mayores de cinco años (zapoteco 420). En la jurisdicción existen restos de los complejos sistemas de irrigación de las culturas prehispánicas. Cuenta también, como atractivo turístico, con las cascadas fosilizadas de carbonato de calcio, en la localidad de Hierve el Agua.

San Lorenzo Axocomanitla ◆ Municipio de Tlaxcala situado al norte de Zacatelco. Tiene 4,264 habitantes.

San Lorenzo Cacaotepec ◆ Municipio de Oaxaca situado en el centro del estado, al noroeste y próximo a la capital de la entidad. Superficie: 12.76 km². Habitantes: 8,341, de los cuales 1,922 forman la población económicamente activa. Hablan alguna lengua indígena 86 personas mayores de cinco años (zapoteco 41 y mixteco 21).

San Lorenzo Cuaunecuiltitla ◆ Municipio de Oaxaca situado en el norte del estado, en los límites con Puebla, al noroeste de Huautla de Jiménez. Superficie: 12.76 km². Habitantes: 598, de los cuales 173 forman la población económicamente activa. Hablan alguna lengua indígena 510 personas mayores de cinco años (mazateco 509) y 100 son monolingües.

San Lorenzo Chiautzingo ◆ Cabecera del municipio de Chiautzingo (☛), Puebla.

San Lorenzo Texmelucan ◆ Municipio de Oaxaca situado en el suroeste del estado, al noreste de Santiago Pinotepa Nacional y al suroeste de la capital de la entidad. Superficie: 303.65 km². Habitantes: 4,703, de los cuales 866 forman la población económicamente activa. Hablan alguna lengua indígena 3,830 personas mayores de cinco años (zapoteco 3,829), de las cuales 679 no dominan el español.

San Lorenzo Victoria ◆ Municipio de Oaxaca situado en el noroeste del estado, al suroeste de Huajuapan de León. Superficie: 30.62 km². Habitantes: 1,084, de los cuales 355 forman la población económicamente activa. Hablan mixteco ocho personas mayores de cinco años.

San Lucas ◆ Cabo de Baja California Sur situado en el extremo septentrional de la península. Marca el final de la sierra de San Lázaro. Limita por el oeste a la bahía de su nombre. Visible en alta mar desde unos 90 km, es uno de los puntos de escala de los transbordadores que viajan a Mazatlán y Puerto Vallarta.

San Lucas ◆ Municipio de Chiapas situado en el centro del estado, al este de Tuxtla Gutiérrez y contiguo a San Cristóbal de Las Casas. Superficie: 154 km². Habitantes: 4,723, de los cuales 1,102 forman la población económicamente activa. Hablan alguna lengua indígena 492 personas mayores de cinco años (tzotzil 491). Hasta el 3 de marzo de 1977 este municipio se llamó El Zapotal. En la cabecera se festeja del 6 al 8 de septiembre la Natividad de la Virgen.

San Lucas ◆ Municipio de Michoacán situado en el extremo sudoriental del estado, en los límites con Guerrero. Superficie: 775.96 km². Habitantes: 18,408, de los cuales 3,718 forman la población económicamente activa. Hablan alguna lengua indígena nueve personas mayores de cinco años.

San Lucas Camotlán ◆ Municipio de Oaxaca situado en el oriente del estado, al este de la capital de la entidad y al noroeste de Juchitán de Zaragoza. Superficie: 127.58 km². Habitantes: 2,568, de los cuales 742 forman la población económicamente activa. Hablan alguna lengua indígena 2,159 personas mayores de cinco años (mixe 2,158), de las que 489 no saben español.

San Lucas Ojitlán ◆ Municipio de Oaxaca situado en el norte del estado, al sur de la presa Miguel Alemán y al oeste de Tuxtepec. Superficie: 595.81 km². Habitantes: 18,449, de los cuales 3,949 forman la población económicamente activa. Hablan alguna lengua indígena 14,362 personas mayores de cinco años (chinanteco 14,297), de las que 2,156 son monolingües. En la cabecera, del mismo nombre, se proclamó el Plan de Tuxtepec (☛).

San Lucas Quiaviní ◆ Municipio de Oaxaca situado en el centro del estado, al sureste de la capital de la entidad. Superficie: 58.69 km². Habitantes: 2,088, de los cuales 581 forman la población económicamente activa. Hablan alguna lengua indígena 1,826 personas mayores de cinco años (zapoteco 1,819) y 211 no saben español.

San Lucas Tecopilco ◆ Municipio de Tlaxcala erigido en 1995, situado al norte de Xaltocan y al sur de Tlaxco. Tiene 2,820 habitantes, distribuidos en 10 localidades.

San Lucas Yatao, Lienzo de ◆ Documento pothispánico procedente del poblado oaxaqueño de San Lucas Yatao. Es una tela de 105 por 86 cm con dibujos de parejas de personajes, animales, ríos, cerros, la inscripción "San

Lucas Yatao" y la fecha de 1615. Se halla en la Biblioteca Nacional de Antropología e Historia.

San Lucas Zoquiapan ◆ Municipio de Oaxaca situado en el norte del estado, al suroeste y cerca de Huautla de Jiménez. Superficie: 38.27 km^2. Habitantes: 6,139, de los cuales 2,102 forman la población económicamente activa. Hablan alguna lengua indígena 5,147 personas mayores de cinco años (mazateco 5,143), de las cuales 1,464 no dominan el español.

San Luis ◆ Isla de Baja California situada 5 km al norte de la bahía de San Luis Gonzaga, en el golfo de California, al noroeste de la isla Ángel de la Guarda. Según decreto del 25 de julio de 1978 fue declarada zona de reserva y refugio de aves marinas y de la fauna silvestre.

San Luis ◆ Sierra de San Luis Potosí. Se extiende de norte a sur por el oeste del valle de San Luis Potosí. Se encuentra al norte de la sierra San Miguelito y al sur de la Moctezuma. Tiene yacimientos de plata y oro.

San Luis ◆ Valle de San Luis Potosí localizado entre las sierras de San Miguelito y de San Luis, que lo limitan por el oeste, y la de Juárez por el este; hacia el sur se prolonga en el valle de Santa María del Río. En él se encuentra la ciudad de San Luis Potosí.

San Luis Acatlán ◆ Municipio de Guerrero situado en el sureste del estado, al este de Acapulco y al noroeste de Ometepec. Superficie: 704.4 km^2. Habitantes: 31,308, de los cuales 5,373 forman la población económicamente activa. Hablan alguna lengua indígena 14,074 personas mayores de cinco años (mixteco 8,272 y tlapaneco 5,677). Indígenas monolingües: 2,844. Su cabecera es el más importante centro comercial de la región.

Foto: Carlos Hahn

Valle San Luis, en San Luis Potosí

Foto: Carlos Hahn

Sierra San Luis, en San Luis Potosí

San Luis Amatlán ◆ Municipio de Oaxaca situado en el sur del estado, al sur-sureste de la capital de la entidad. Superficie: 170.96 km^2. Habitantes: 3,771, de los cuales 877 forman la población económicamente activa. Hablan alguna lengua indígena 11 personas mayores de cinco años (zapoteco 5).

San Luis del Cordero ◆ Municipio de Durango situado en el noreste del estado, al norte de San Juan del Río y al norte de la capital de la entidad. Superficie: 543.9 km^2. Habitantes: 2,364, de los cuales 512 forman la población económicamente activa.

Ilustración de Antonio Esparza

Balneario natural Las Pilas, en San Luis Acatlán, Guerrero

San Luis Gonzaga ◆ Bahía de Baja California situada en el litoral del océano Pacífico, entre las puntas Willar y Final. Es un fondeadero que protege de los vientos del suroeste. En ella desemboca el arroyo de Calamajué.

San Luis de la Paz ◆ Municipio de Guanajuato situado en el noreste del estado, al noreste de Dolores Hidalgo, en los límites con San Luis Potosí. Superficie: 1,816.8 km^2. Habitantes: 90,441, de los cuales 17,296 forman la población económicamente activa. Hablan alguna lengua indígena 1,266 personas mayores de cinco años (chichimeca jonaz 1,244). Indígenas monolingües: 49. Región originalmente habitada por chichimecas de la sierra Gorda, el territorio de San Luis de la Paz, en 1552, era el corregimiento de Sichú y Puxinguía, sufragáneo de Michoacán; a fines del siglo XVI, con la expansión minera, se creó la región de minas de Sichú. A principios del siglo XVII, de acuerdo con un ajuste de límites, Palmar de la Vega y San Luis de la Paz pasaron a depender de la alcaldía mayor de Sichú. A fines del siglo XVII el alcalde mayor de Sichú trasladó su residencia a San Luis de la Paz, lo que dio su nuevo nombre a la provincia, que en 1787 se convirtió en subdelegación de la Intendencia de Guanajuato.

SAN LUIS POTOSÍ ◆ Estado de la República Mexicana situado en el centro-oriente del país. Limita con Nuevo León, Tamaulipas, Veracruz, Hidalgo, Querétaro, Guanajuato y Zacatecas. Tiene una superficie de 63,068 km^2 (es el decimoquinto estado en extensión y representa el 3.2 por ciento del total nacional). Entre sus ríos más importantes se hallan el Santa María y el Verde que se unen al entrar en la Huasteca para formar el Tampico, al que confluyen el Frío y el Valles, suma a su vez del Salto y el Mesilla; juntos originan el Tamuín y éste, al desembocar en el Moctezuma, cambia su nombre por el de Pánuco. El estado cuenta con 58 municipios. San Luis Potosí en 1997 tenía 2,247,042 habitantes. En 1995 la población urbana era de 1,271,852 personas y la rural, de 928,911. El porcentaje con que contribuye al producto interno bruto nacional es 1.73 (en 1996). La población económicamente activa la conforman 53.8 por ciento de los mayores de 12 años. La población analfabeta de mayores de 15 años en 1995 fue equivalente al 13.75 por ciento de la población estatal. Hablan alguna lengua indígena 213,717 personas mayores de cinco años (náhuatl 131,363, huasteco 74,026 y pame 7,162). *Historia*: Hace unos 12,000 años empezaron a poblar el actual territorio potosino grupos nómadas de recolectores y cazadores, cuyos primeros vestigios datan de los años 1300 a 1000 a.n.e. Poco antes de la llegada de los españoles ocupaban el territorio los chichimecas y huastecos. En octubre de 1522, Hernán Cortés inició la conquista de la Huasteca, misma que culminó con la fundación de Santiesteban del Puerto (actual Pánuco, Veracruz), a fines de ese año. En mayo de 1524, Nuño Beltrán de Guzmán tomó posesión como gobernador de la provincia y río de Pánuco y Victoria Garayana. Ahí se dedicó al secuestro de indios, de los que vendió miles como esclavos. Hacia 1539, los frailes Antonio de Roa y Juan de Sevilla evangelizaron la Huasteca y su obra de penetración religiosa fue continuada por los frailes Juan Estacio y Andrés de Olmos. El descubrimiento de las minas zacatecanas, hacia 1546, hizo que los españoles se desplazaran cada vez más al norte, hasta penetrar en territorio chichimeca, donde provocaron la reacción defensiva de los indios. La llamada guerra Chichimeca se produjo durante la segunda mitad del siglo XVI. En el valle de San Luis incursionó el franciscano Diego de la Magdalena, quien trató de congregar a los indígenas que se rendían ante los conquistadores y estableció el puesto de San Luis, con un hospicio. En 1583 el militar mestizo Miguel Caldera inició una política de pacificación para terminar con la guerra Chichimeca; no obstante, aún combatió durante varios años a los indios insumisos. El virrey Luis de Velasco determinó que 400 familias tlaxcaltecas cristianizadas fueran a convivir con los chichimecas, para servirles de ejemplo. Así, esas familias se establecieron, a partir de 1591, en Mexquitic, San Luis, Venado y otros sitios. En marzo de 1592, Caldera envió una partida exploradora hacia el oriente del valle de San Luis, enterado de que en los cerros de esa zona había metales preciosos. Pedro de Anda, miembro de la expedición, bautizó el sitio como Cerro del Señor San Pedro y Minas del Potosí. Este descubrimiento atrajo a numerosos mineros que se establecieron a unos 2 km al norte del puesto de San Luis y después, por un arreglo con los indios, intercambiaron los asentamientos. El 27 de agosto de 1592, el virrey nombró alcalde mayor de San Luis a Juan de Oñate y el 3 de noviembre de ese año se creó el pueblo de San Luis de Mexquitic, actual ciudad de San Luis Potosí. Hacia 1597, procedentes de Querétaro, llegaron otros españoles a poblar la zona de Rioverde. Éstos fundaron haciendas agrícolas y ganaderas que suminis-

Fernando Silva Nieto, gobernador de San Luis Potosí

Teatro de San Luis Potosí

traban alimentos a los pueblos mineros. A principios del siglo XVII el territorio del actual San Luis Potosí estaba conquistado. Políticamente, los ahora municipios de Ahualulco, Moctezuma, Venado, Ramos, Salinas, Santo Domingo, Charcas, Villa de Guadalupe, Catorce, Villa de la Paz, Matehuala, Vanegas y Cedral formaban parte de la Nueva Galicia, aunque el Nuevo Reino de León disputaba la jurisdicción de Matehuala, en tanto que las alcaldías mayores de Valles, Guadalcázar y San Luis Potosí estaban sujetas a la Nueva España. El 4 de diciembre de 1786 se promulgó la Ordenanza de Intendencias, de acuerdo con la cual, la de San Luis Potosí se formó con los pueblos de su antigua alcaldía mayor y el agregado de Guadalcázar, así como con los distritos de Charcas (que incluía Catorce, Matehuala y Venado), Ramos y Villa de los Valles, el Nuevo Reino de León, la colonia del Nuevo Santander y las provincias de Coahuila y Texas. Hacia 1805 empezó a funcionar la imprenta de "Alejo Infante en el Armadillo", hoy Armadillo de los Infante. El lego juanino Luis Herrera, después de servir como cirujano en las tropas de Miguel Hidalgo, fue a San Luis a propagar el movimiento insurgente, por lo que fue encarcelado sucesivamente en los conventos del Carmen y de San Juan de Dios. Se formó un foco revolucionario alrededor de éste y del carmelita Gregorio de la Concepción. El también juanino Juan Villerías ofreció sus servicios a Herrera y cooptó al militar Joaquín Sevilla y Olmedo, quien el 10 de noviembre de 1810 liberó a Herrera y Villerías y luego a los presos comunes, con los que se adueñó de la ciudad. El 14 de noviembre se les unió el cabo Leiton, que venía triunfante de Zacatecas, aunque cuatro días después aprehendió a los cabecillas potosinos y entregó la ciudad al saqueo. Villerías huyó rumbo a Guanajuato y Leiton se marchó llevándose a Herrera. Éste escapó y volvió a la ciudad de San Luis Potosí a mediados de febrero. A principios de marzo, ante la inminente llegada de Calleja, Herrera huyó, pero fue alcanzado y ejecutado por García Conde. Villerías se unió sucesivamente a Allende, Jiménez y López Rayón, pasó a Nuevo Santander y cuan-

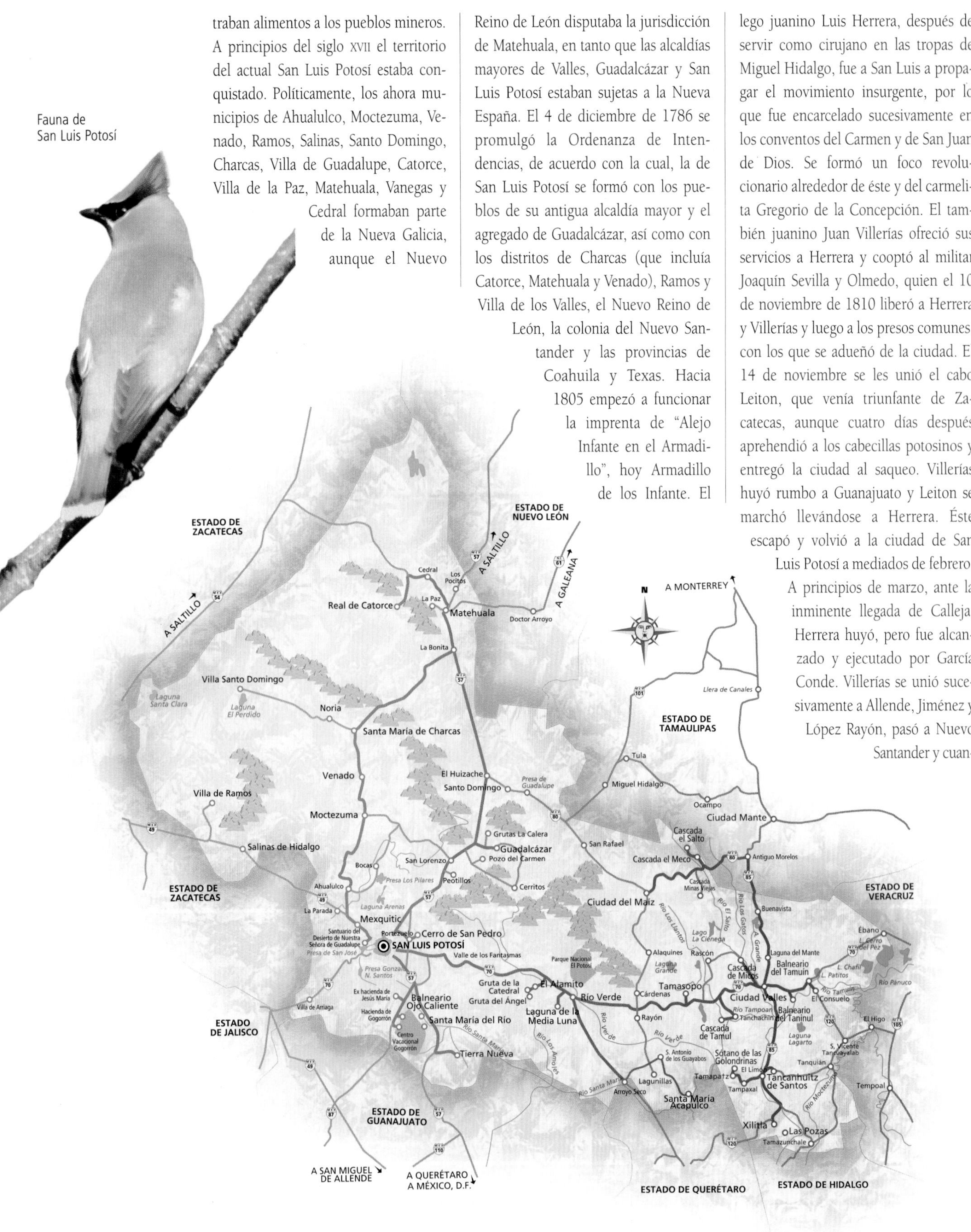

Fauna de San Luis Potosí

do se le separó Sevilla, para seguir a López Rayón, pasó a Matehuala, acosado por Arredondo; allí lo derrotó el sacerdote Semper y murió el 13 de mayo. Francisco Javier Mina inició su campaña derrotando a Villaseñor en Ciudad del Maíz, el 8 de junio de 1817; en Peotillos derrotó a Armiñán el 15 de junio, pasó luego a Moctezuma, Espíritu Santo y Pinos, en busca de los insurgentes que operaban en el interior, hasta unirse a Pedro Moreno en el fuerte del Sombrero, el 24 de ese mismo mes. En marzo de 1821 los militares Manuel Tovar, Nicolás Acosta y José Márquez se pronunciaron en favor del Plan de Iguala, se encaminaron al Bajío y se incorporaron a las fuerzas de Anastasio Bustamante. El 2 de julio ocupó la plaza Echávarri, nombrado comandante por Iturbide, y el día 3 se juró la Independencia. El 11 de diciembre siguiente, el intendente y la diputación provincial reconocieron a la Junta Provisional Gubernativa del Imperio Mexicano. El primero de octubre de 1822 empezó a circular el *Aparato para miselánea (sic) del Pensador de la Provincia del Potosí*, producido en la "Imprenta de D. Juan de Dios Rodríguez, que es a cargo de D. José Eusebio Salazar, en la ciudad de San Luis Potosí". Aunque parece haber quedado en el prospecto o, como se diría hoy, en número cero, está considerado como el primer periódico potosino. El 2 de marzo de 1823 la guarnición de la capital provincial se pronunció por el Plan de Casa Mata y destituyó al comandante Fernández. La proclamación de la República, el 5 de junio, hecha por Santa Anna en San Luis, concitó una fuerte oposición que produjo un alzamiento de civiles y parte de la guarnición. Próxima la brigada de Armijo, Santa Anna optó por retirarse. Con la abdicación de Iturbide y la implantación del sistema federal, la provincia de San Luis Potosí se convirtió en estado libre y soberano y se eligió a los integrantes del Congreso local, cuyo primer decreto, del 21 de abril de 1824, designó gobernador al jefe político, Ildefonso Díaz de León. El 26 de octubre de 1826 se juró la primera Constitución local. En 1828 apareció el primer periódico de publicación regular, *El Mexicano Libre Potosinense*, órgano de la logia yorkina del que salieron 85 números, el último en diciembre del mismo año. Once meses estuvo la entidad sin prensa, hasta la aparición, en noviembre de 1829, de *El Telégrafo Potosinense*. A partir de entonces no dejó de haber

FOTO: MICHAEL CALDERWOOD

Yucas y flor de Yuca de San Luis Potosí

Laguna de la media luna, San Luis Potosí

FOTO: PABLO CERVANTES

Peyote en flor de San Luis Potosí

FOTO: MICHAEL CALDERWOOD

Valle de los Fantasmas, en San Luis Potosí

por lo menos un periódico en el estado. En la guerra contra Estados Unidos, San Luis Potosí fue sitio de concentración para las tropas mexicanas y se construyeron dos fortificaciones en los puntos estratégicos de su capital. Ahí mismo, Ponciano Arriaga editó *El Estandarte de los Chinacates*, periódico que llamaba a resistir a los invasores. Al fin de la contienda, el gobernador Ramón Adame se pronunció contra el tratado de paz, pero fue derrocado por el comandante de la plaza, Valentín Amador, quien impuso a Julián de los Reyes, quien reprimió un levantamiento armado vinculado con Eleuterio Quiroz, primero en proclamar un plan agrario en San Luis Potosí y que fuera abatido el 6 de diciembre de 1849. Reelecto, De los Reyes murió el 8 de enero de 1853, ejecutado por uno de los revolucionarios quirocistas. En 1859 se fundó el Instituto Científico y Literario, en medio de la guerra de los Tres Años. Luego de la toma de Puebla por los franceses, Benito Juárez declaró la ciudad de San Luis Potosí en estado de sitio, nombró comandante de la región a Jesús González Ortega y estableció los poderes federales en la capital potosina del 9 de junio al 22 de diciembre de 1863. Abandonó la plaza ante la proximidad de Tomás Mejía, quien entró pacíficamente en ella el 24 de diciembre de 1863. El 4 de enero de 1864, San Luis Potosí firmó el acta de adhesión al imperio de Maximiliano. A fines de 1866 los invasores se retiraron de San Luis para concentrarse en Querétaro y los republicanos ocuparon aquella ciudad el 27 de diciembre. En 1879 el indio Juan Santiago se levantó en armas para obtener la restitución de tierras para las comunidades poseedoras de títulos antiguos; en agosto del mismo año el movimiento fue sofocado. Simultáneamente, otro movimiento fue promovido por el Directorio Socialista, que proponía la expedición de una ley agraria y la creación de una república socialista. A fines de 1880, Juan Santiago inició otra rebelión contra la prepotencia y la actitud criminal de los agentes del gobierno contra las poblaciones indígenas. En 1883, en Ciudad del Maíz, el sacerdote Mauricio Zavala inició otra revolución agraria que fue aplastada por fuerzas federales. Durante el porfiriato la minería resurgió en el Real de Catorce, por cuya influencia prosperaron las fundiciones de Matehuala y el comercio de Cedral. A principios del siglo XX se inició en la Huasteca la explotación de petróleo. Los precursores intelectuales de la revolución celebraron el Primer Congreso Liberal, inaugurado el 5 de febrero de 1901 en San Luis Potosí. Los movimientos agrarios del siglo XIX dieron pie al fraccionamiento de las tierras comunales en provecho de los hacendados. Por esos despojos, en 1905 los indígenas potosinos, capitaneados por Vicente Cedillo, protagonizaron otro levantamiento agrario, que también fue sofocado. Francisco I. Madero llegó preso a la ciudad de San Luis Potosí el 17 de julio de 1910, pero huyó semanas después y el 5 de octubre dio a conocer el Plan de San Luis, con el cual se inició la revolución. En San Luis Potosí se unieron a su movimiento Manuel Lárraga, Pedro Antonio de los Santos, Magdaleno, Cleofas y Saturnino Cedillo y Alberto Carrera Torres. En 1920, Rafael Nieto, ex secretario de Hacienda, llegó a la gubernatura potosina por su filiación aguaprietista. En enero de 1923, este mandatario promulgó el decreto que convirtió el Instituto Científico y Literario en Universidad Autónoma de San Luis Potosí (☛). Después de los gobiernos paralelos de Jorge Prieto Lau-

FOTO: MICHAEL CALDERWOOD

Río Naranjo en San Luis Potosí

rens y de Aurelio Manrique, así como del bienio de Abel Cano, en 1927 Saturnino Cedillo accedió a la gubernatura, desde donde impuso un prolongado cacicazgo. En 1926 había combatido a los cristeros en Jalisco, Guanajuato y el propio estado potosino, pero ya en la gubernatura se mostró moderado y evitó que la rebelión alcanzara en San Luis Potosí la magnitud sangrienta que tuvo en otras entidades, pese a la beligerencia del obispo local, Miguel de la Mora y Mora, quien se opuso al *modus vivendi* de 1929 y en marzo del año siguiente llamó a los fieles a unirse a la Liga Nacional Defensora de la Libertad Religiosa (☛) y apoyar sus actividades, que se centraban precisamente en la oposición armada. Cedillo dejó formalmente el cargo en 1931, pero mantuvo un estrecho control sobre sus sucesores. En mayo de 1938 se pronunció contra el gobierno de Lázaro Cárdenas, por divergencias en torno a la política de reformas y nacionalizaciones. Su levantamiento fue prontamente sofocado y él murió en campaña en enero de 1939. En 1943 se instituyó el cacicazgo de Gonzalo N. Santos, al que en 1958 le surgió una fuerza de oposición que acabaría por eliminarlo: el navismo, nombre tomado de su líder, el médico Salvador Nava, en ese año candidato a presidente del municipio de San Luis Potosí (☛). Como no se reconociera el triunfo electoral de Nava, las movilizaciones y enfrentamientos continuaron hasta que en 1959 el Senado decretó la desaparición de poderes en la entidad. Francisco Martínez de la Vega, enviado por el centro, se hizo cargo del Ejecutivo local y desplegó una política conciliatoria. En 1961, Nava se presentó como aspirante a gobernador y nuevamente se produjeron graves irregularidades en los comicios. Se organizó una amplia protesta social que fue reprimida de manera sangrienta por la fuerza pública. En ese año, Martínez de la Vega entregó el poder a Manuel López Dávila, quien como candidato del PRI fue declarado oficialmente triunfador en las elecciones. Durante el sexenio de José López Portillo fue expropiado el latifundio de El Gargaleote, propiedad de Gonzalo N. Santos, cuyo poder, ya muy menguado, se acabó en definitiva. En 1983, otra vez con Nava en la alcaldía de la capital potosina, se produjo un enfrentamiento popular contra el gobernador Carlos Jonguitud Barrios, quien mediante una amplia movilización fue obligado a entregar las partidas del presupuesto municipal que había retenido. En 1985 los navistas, agrupados en el Frente Cívico Potosino, denunciaron que en las elecciones de la capital del estado se había efectuado un nuevo fraude. El movimiento de protesta creció y el 1 de enero de 1986 la fuerza pública disparó contra la multitud y en medio de la balacera ardió el Palacio Municipal. Hubo un muerto y varios heridos. Como consecuencia de estos hechos, algunos funcionarios del gobierno estatal abandonaron sus puestos, inconformes con los métodos del Ejecutivo de la entidad. Lejos de aplacarse los ánimos, las medidas represivas avivaron la participación popular, que logró la renuncia del gobernador Florencio Salazar en mayo de 1987.

DISTRIBUCIÓN DE LA POBLACIÓN POR TAMAÑO DE LA LOCALIDAD, 1995

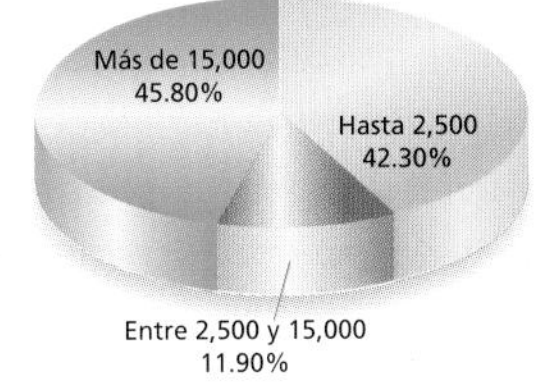

PRODUCTO INTERNO BRUTO (PIB) A PRECIOS CORRIENTES

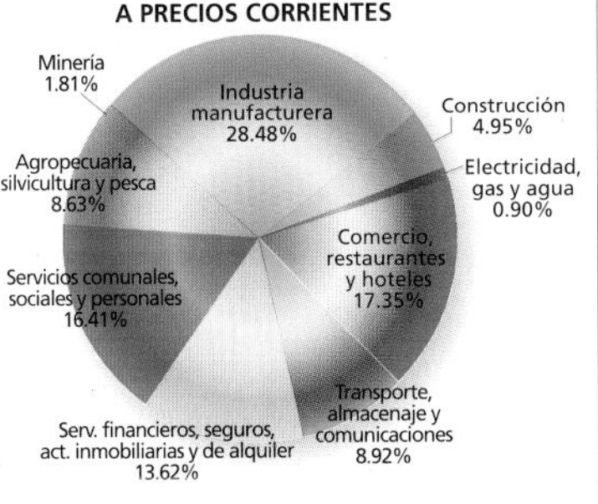

LÍNEAS TELEFÓNICAS EN SERVICIO Y APARATOS PÚBLICOS, 1994

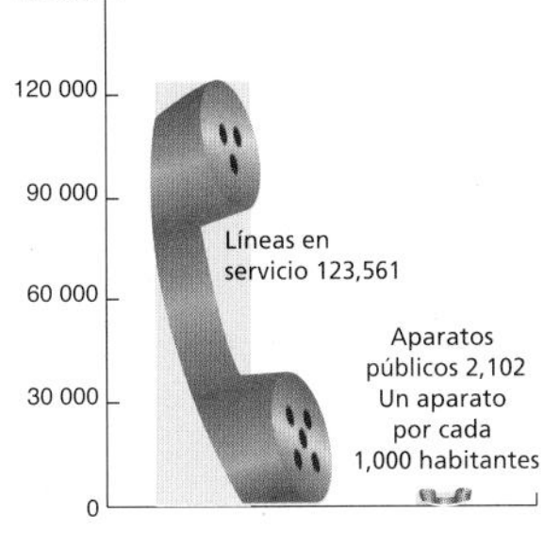

LONGITUD DE LA RED DE CARRETERAS POR SUPERFICIE DE RODAMIENTO, 1995

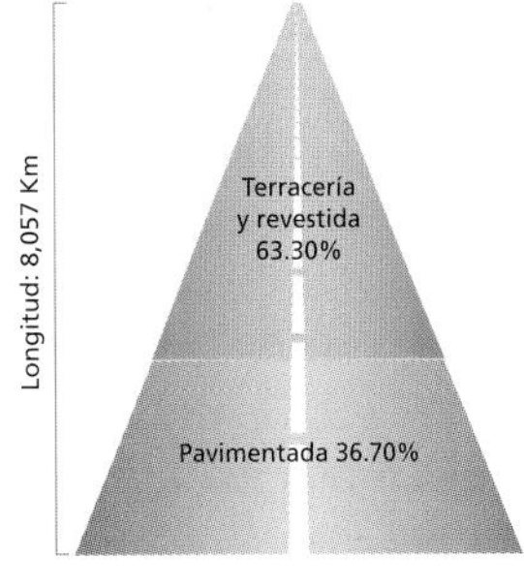

POBLACIÓN DE 5 AÑOS Y MÁS HABLANTE DE LENGUA INDÍGENA, 1995

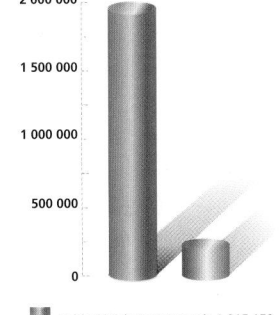

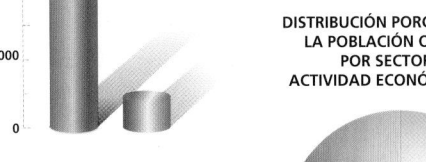

2 000 000
1 500 000
1 000 000
500 000
0

Población de 5 años y más 1,915,150

Población de 5 años y más hablante de lengua indígena 213,717 (11.16%)

BIBLIOTECAS Y USUARIOS, 1993
Número de bibliotecas: 201

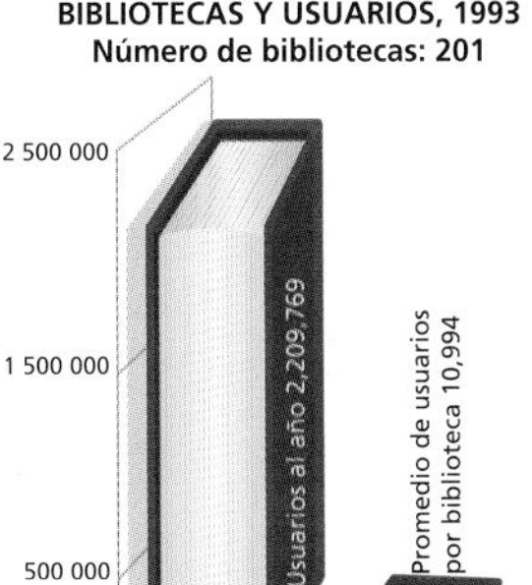

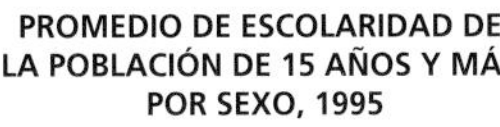

PROMEDIO DE ESCOLARIDAD DE LA POBLACIÓN DE 15 AÑOS Y MÁS, POR SEXO, 1995

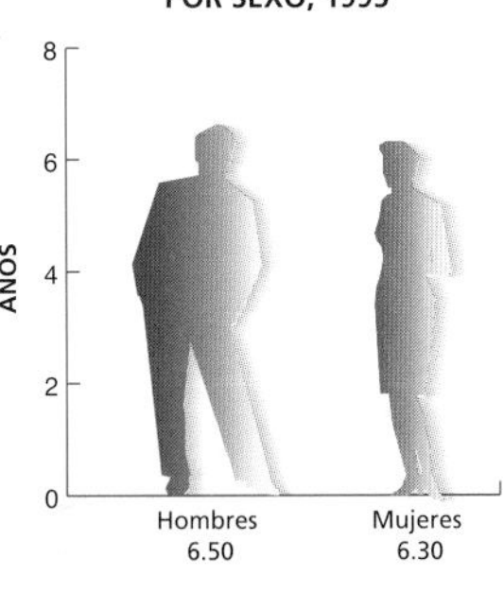

DISTRIBUCIÓN PORCENTUAL DE LA POBLACIÓN OCUPADA POR SECTOR DE ACTIVIDAD ECONÓMICA, 1995

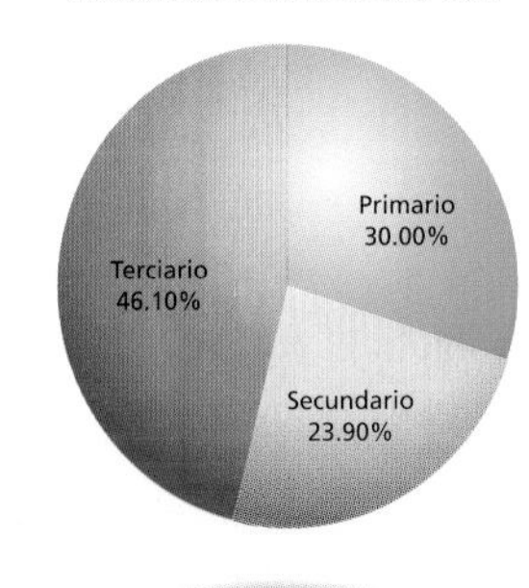

San Luis Potosí ◆ Municipio de San Luis Potosí situado en el suroeste de la entidad cerca de los límites con Zacatecas, Jalisco y Guanajuato. Superficie: 1,353.3 km². Habitantes: 625,466, de los cuales 168,011 forman la población económicamente activa. Hablan alguna lengua indígena 2,473 personas mayores de cinco años (náhuatl 1,308 y huasteco 627). La cabecera, del mismo nombre, es capital del estado. Es un importante centro minero, comercial, ganadero, industrial y ferrocarrilero. Cuenta con importantes obras arquitectónicas, como el convento de San Francisco (construido entre la segunda mitad del siglo XVII y 1707); la capilla de Aranzazú, churrigueresca, actualmente dentro del Museo Regional Potosino; el templo del Carmen, barroco, construido entre 1740 y 1760; la capilla de Loreto, la torre de San Agustín y el santuario de Guadalupe. El pueblo de San Luis Mexquitic fue fundado oficialmente el 3 de noviembre de 1592 y su primer alcalde fue Juan de Oñate. Hacia 1608 las minas de San Pedro empezaron a inundarse y para 1622 el mineral estaba casi desierto. La crisis económica pudo evitarse debido al comercio y a las haciendas ganaderas. A mediados del siglo XVI el pueblo de San Luis Minas del Potosí rehizo su economía por el descubrimiento de nuevos yacimientos minerales y el progreso de la ganadería y la agricultura. En 1631, San Luis era la tercera localidad en importancia en la Nueva España, después de México y Puebla. En 1637 nuevamente decayó la extracción de metales, lo que dio origen a una crisis económica que se manifestó en el cierre de negocios y una disminución del número de habitantes, pese a lo cual San Luis recibió el título de ciudad el 30 de mayo de 1656. Tal título fue confirmado por el rey Felipe IV el 17 de agosto de 1658. El 27 de mayo de 1767, influidos por las huelgas de sus colegas en Guanajuato y Real del Monte, los mineros de Cerro de San Pedro, molestos por las injustas exacciones, invadieron la ciudad, aunque fueron rechazados; apoyados por los mineros de San Nicolás y Soledad, volvieron el 6 de junio, obligaron al alcalde a vaciar la cárcel y saquearon la ciudad. La noche del 24 al 25 de junio del mismo año, luego del decreto de expulsión de la Compañía de Jesús, fueron aprehendidos en San Luis los nueve jesuitas que allí radicaban; la noticia se propagó y el pueblo potosino protagonizó uno de los mayores motines de la Nueva España: los mineros de Cerro de San Pedro se unieron a los de San Nicolás y a los peones de los ranchos y villas aledañas, rescataron a los jesuitas y los devolvieron a su colegio. Ese día y los siguientes destruyeron la cárcel y las Casas Reales, saquearon la residencia del alcalde y pidieron la expulsión de los españoles. El levantamiento fue sofocado por el visitador José de Gálvez, quien hizo efectiva la orden de expulsión de la Compañía de Jesús y enjuició a los amotinados, de los cuales 32 terminaron en la horca, 33 fueron desterrados y 269 recluidos en prisión con penas que iban de un año a cadena perpetua. A principios de junio de 1821 la ciudad se rindió a los militares adheridos al Plan de Iguala. Se pidió la renuncia del intendente Manuel Jacinto Acevedo, quien fue sustituido por Ignacio López Rayón. La diócesis de San Luis Potosí fue erigida el 31 de agosto de 1854 por Pío IX. Pedro Barajas Moreno fue el primer obispo. Luego de la retirada de los franceses Juárez volvió a establecer los poderes federales en San Luis Potosí (del 21 de febrero al 1 de julio de 1867), desde donde negó el indulto a Maximiliano, Miramón y Mejía. Al retirarse dejó como gobernador a Juan Bustamante, quien aplicó las Leyes de Reforma. Luego de las elecciones de 1910, Madero fue llevado preso a la ciudad de San Luis Potosí, aunque logró la libertad bajo fianza y logró escapar a San Antonio, Texas, donde dio a conocer el Plan de San Luis (5 de octubre de 1910), con lo que se inició la Revolución Mexicana. El 26 de mayo de 1911, Cándido Navarro, uno de los primeros insurrectos, entró en San Luis Potosí y al día siguiente renunció el gobernador José M. Espinosa y Cuevas. Lo remplazó Rafael Cepeda, quien gobernó hasta 1913, cuando fue encarcelado por órdenes de Victoriano Huerta. En 1958, el pueblo de la capital potosina apoyó masivamente la candidatura de Salvador Nava a la presidencia municipal y se expresó abiertamente contra el cacicazgo de Gonzalo N. Santos. Se organizaron manifestaciones, se suspendió el pago de impuestos y se cerraron comercios y fábricas. La protesta contó con el apoyo de un amplio abanico de fuerzas políticas que comprendía desde sinarquistas hasta comunistas, pasando por el Partido Acción Nacional y numerosos miembros del PRI. El desfile del 20 de noviembre de 1958 se convirtió en una expresión de rechazo al gobierno estatal y al cacique Gonzalo N. Santos. Finalmente, Nava triunfó en las elecciones y fue presidente municipal (1959-61). En 1961, Nava se presentó como candidato a la gubernatura del estado, lo que desató una prolongada campaña represiva contra él y sus partidarios, que culminó con

Foto: Michael Calderwood

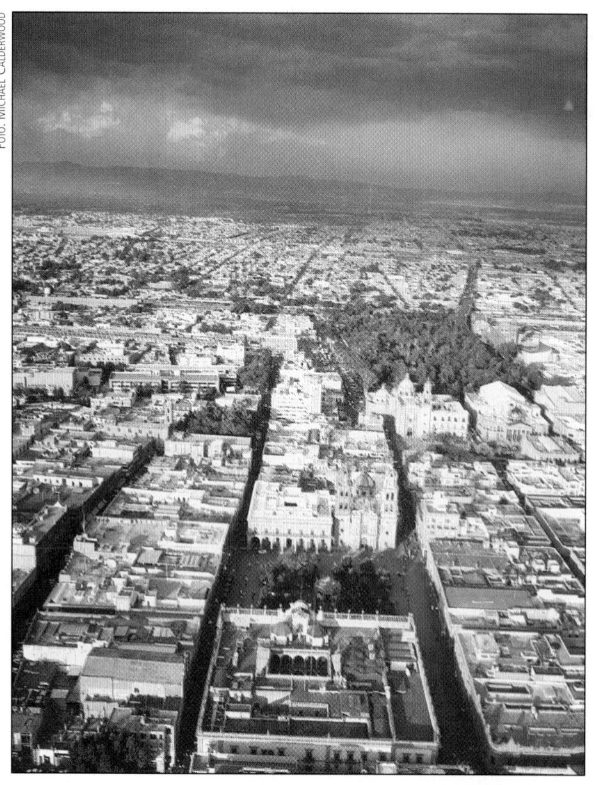

San Luis Potosí, ciudad capital del estado de San Luis Potosí

el incendio del diario *Tribuna*, la persecución masiva y la aprehensión y tortura de decenas y quizá cientos de sus seguidores. El propio Nava fue torturado por los cuerpos policiacos y el 15 de septiembre la fuerza pública ejecutó una matanza en la Plaza de Armas de la ciudad. En 1983, Nava volvió a ser elegido alcalde y sufrió la hostilidad del gobernador Carlos Jonguitud Barrios, quien retuvo las partidas que debía entregar al ayuntamiento. Por falta de pago, la Comisión Federal de Electricidad cortó el suministro de energía al Palacio Municipal, en marzo de 1983, lo que nuevamente desató una amplia movilización ciudadana y la Tesorería del estado se vio obligada a entregar al ayuntamiento los recursos que le adeudaba. A fines de 1985 el navista Frente Cívico Potosino apoyó la candidatura de Guillermo Pizzuto para la presidencia municipal. Oficialmente se declaró triunfador en las elecciones al candidato del PRI, Guillermo Medina de los Santos, pero los navistas denunciaron el fraude electoral ante la prensa y sus partidarios se lanzaron nuevamente a las calles en son de protesta por la imposición. El 1 de enero de 1986, la policía estatal disparó sobre los manifestantes y en medio de la balacera se incendió el Palacio Municipal sin que las autoridades trataran de controlar el siniestro. Luego de estos hechos se formó el Comité de Defensa de los Derechos del Pueblo Potosino con la participación del Frente Cívico Potosino y los partidos Acción Nacional, Demócrata Mexicano, Socialista Unificado de México, Revolucionario de los Trabajadores, Mexicano de los Trabajadores y Socialdemócrata. Las movilizaciones del comité obligaron al gobernador Florencio Salazar, el 26 de mayo de 1987, a pedir licencia para apartarse del cargo, con lo que virtualmente renunció al Ejecutivo local y fue sustituido por Leopoldino Ortiz Santos. En 1989 la diócesis fue elevada a arquidiócesis y Arturo Antonio Szymanski Ramírez, obispo desde 1986, se convirtió en su primer arzobispo.

San Luis Río Colorado ◆ Municipio de Sonora situado en el extremo noroccidental del estado, en los límites con Baja California y en la frontera con Estados Unidos. Superficie: 8,412.75 km^2. Habitantes: 133,140, de los cuales 35,628 forman la población económicamente activa. Hablan alguna lengua indígena 294 personas mayores de cinco años. Fue erigido el 14 de junio de 1939, en territorio que perteneció a Caborca. Se ha desarrollado debido a que es aduana de la frontera con Estados Unidos, al impulso agrícola que le brinda la presa Morelos, construida sobre el río Colorado.

San Marcial Ozolotepec ◆ Municipio de Oaxaca situado en el sur del estado, al sureste de Miahuatlán. Superficie: 53.58 km^2. Habitantes: 1,736, de los cuales 364 forman la población económicamente activa. Hablan zapoteco 1,487 personas mayores de cinco años (monolingües 107).

San Marcos ◆ Isla de Baja California Sur situada en el golfo de California, al sureste de Santa Rosalía y al sur de la ruta que siguen las embarcaciones entre esta población y Guaymas. Está separada de la península por el canal de Craig. Cuenta con yacimientos de yeso cristalizado, piedra pómez y talco. En sus alrededores hay ostras perlíferas.

San Marcos ◆ Municipio de Guerrero situado en el sureste del estado, en el litoral del océano Pacífico, al este de Acapulco. Superficie: 960.7 km^2. Habitantes: 46,800, de los cuales 8,618 forman la población económicamente activa. Hablan alguna lengua indígena 125 personas mayores de cinco años (amuzgo 57 y mixteco 48). Tiene numerosas salinas y canteras de mármol, así como yacimientos de hierro, que no se explotan. A sus mujeres está dedicada la canción *La sanmarqueña*.

Ilustración de Santiago Ortega

Fachada del palacio municipal de San Marcos, Guerrero

San Marcos ◆ Municipio de Jalisco situado en el occidente del estado, en los límites con Nayarit, al noreste de Guadalajara. Superficie: 292.85 km^2. Habitantes: 3,562, de los cuales 825 forman la población económicamente activa. Hablan alguna lengua indígena 11 personas mayores de cinco años (huichol 9).

San Marcos, de ◆ Laguna de Guerrero, también llamada Tecomate. Es una albufera del litoral del océano Pacífico, localizada al este-sureste de Acapulco. Cuenta con abundantes salinas.

Foto: Fondo Editorial Grupo Azabache

San Luis río Colorado

San Marcos Arteaga ◆ Municipio de Oaxaca situado en el noroeste del estado, al oeste de Huajuapan de León. Superficie: 133.96 km². Habitantes: 2,223, de los cuales 402 forman la población económicamente activa. Hablan alguna lengua indígena 52 personas mayores de cinco años (náhuatl 39 y mixteco 13).

San Martín ◆ Isla de Baja California situada en el litoral del océano Pacífico, al noroeste de la bahía de San Quintín y al sureste de la bahía Colnett. Fue descubierta por Juan Rodríguez Cabrillo, quien la bautizó como isla San Agustín en 1542. Tiene un faro y dos conos volcánicos; es refugio de leones marinos y focas. En sus aguas adyacentes abundan los delfines y en invierno pasan frente a ella las ballenas grises.

San Martín, de ◆ Sierra de Veracruz, también llamada Los Tuxtlas. Es una cadena volcánica situada en el sureste del estado, cercana a la costa del golfo de México, al sureste del puerto de Veracruz, al noroeste y próxima a Coatzacoalcos. Está separada de la cresta principal de la sierra Madre Oriental por las llanuras de los ríos Papaloapan y San Juan Evangelista. En el centro de la sierra se encuentra el lago de Catemaco. Su pico más alto es el volcán de San Martín.

San Martín de Bolaños ◆ Municipio de Jalisco situado en el norte del estado, en los límites con Nayarit y Zacatecas, noroeste de Guadalajara. Superficie: 991.99 km². Habitantes: 3,970, de los cuales 669 forman la población económicamente activa. Hablan alguna lengua indígena 59 personas mayores de cinco años (huichol 57).

San Martín de los Canseco ◆ Municipio de Oaxaca situado en el centro-sur del estado, al sur de la capital de la entidad. Superficie: 45.93 km². Habitantes: 828, de los cuales 231 forman la población económicamente activa. Hablan zapoteco siete personas mayores de cinco años.

San Martín Chalchicuautla ◆ Municipio de San Luis Potosí situado en el sureste del estado, en los límites con Veracruz, al sureste de Ciudad Valles. Superficie: 305.1 km². Habitantes: 22,968, de los cuales 5,467 forman la población económicamente activa. Hablan alguna lengua indígena 10,077 personas mayores de cinco años (náhuatl 10,065), de las que son monolingües 649.

San Martín Hidalgo ◆ Municipio de Jalisco situado en el centro del estado, al suroeste de Guadalajara y al oeste de Acatlán. Superficie: 324.57 km². Habitantes: 27,269, de los cuales 6,148 forman la población económicamente activa. Hablan alguna lengua indígena 13 personas mayores de cinco años.

San Martín Huamelulpan ◆ Municipio de Oaxaca situado en el noroeste del estado, al sureste de Huajuapan de León y al noreste de Tlaxiaco. Superficie: 29.34 km². Habitantes: 1,022, de los cuales 215 forman la población económicamente activa. Hablan mixteco 12 personas mayores de cinco años. En la región existen vestigios de construcciones, esculturas y jeroglíficos de las civilizaciones prehispánicas.

San Martín Itunyoso ◆ Municipio de Oaxaca situado en el noroeste del estado, al oeste-suroeste de Tlaxiaco y al suroeste de Huajuapan de León. Superficie: 82.93 km². Habitantes: 2,299, de los cuales 277 forman la población económicamente activa. Hablan alguna lengua indígena 1,887 personas mayores de cinco años (triqui 1,766), de las que 591 no dominan el español.

San Martín Lachila ◆ Municipio de Oaxaca situado en el centro-sur del estado, al sur-suroeste de la capital de la entidad. Superficie: 49.76 km². Habitantes: 1,288, de los cuales 351 forman la población económicamente activa. Hablan zapoteco 10 personas mayores de cinco años.

San Martín y Mondragón, Jesús ◆ n. en Chihuahua, Chih., y m. en Durango, Dgo. (1852-1927). Médico graduado en París (1877), donde trabajó al lado de Luis Pasteur. Radicado en Durango fue médico del Hospital Civil, de la penitenciaría y de la plaza de toros. Se dedicó también a la enseñanza del francés y a los estudios meteorológicos. Fue uno de los introductores del método antiséptico de Lister en México. Autor de *Plaies de séreuses traitées par le pansement de Lister* (tesis doctoral, 1877).

San Martín Peras ◆ Municipio de Oaxaca situado en el noroeste del estado, en los límites con Guerrero, al suroeste de Huajuapan de León. Superficie: 237.31 km². Habitantes: 7,742, de los cuales 1,204 forman la población económicamente activa. Hablan alguna lengua indígena 5,468 personas mayores de cinco años (mixteco 5,459), y de ellas, son monolingües 2,844. Tiene yacimientos de oro.

San Martín de las Pirámides ◆ Municipio del Estado de México situado en el noreste de la entidad, al norte de Texcoco, al este de Cuautitlán y contiguo a Teotihuacán. Superficie: 58.72 km². Habitantes: 16,881, de los cuales 4,047 forman la población económicamente activa. Hablan alguna lengua indígena 24 personas mayores de cinco años (otomí 21).

San Martín Texmelucan ◆ Municipio de Puebla situado en el occidente del estado, en los límites con Tlaxcala, al norte de Atlixco. Superficie: 71.45 km². Habitantes: 111,737, de los cuales 25,717 forman la población económicamente activa. Hablan alguna lengua indígena 383 personas mayores de cinco años (náhuatl 207 y totonaco 52). Su cabecera es San Martín Texmelucan de Labastida y a 3 km de ésta se halla lo que fue la laguna de Chiautla, hoy casi desecada.

San Martín Tilcajete ◆ Municipio de Oaxaca situado en el centro del estado, al sur-sureste y próximo a la capital de la entidad. Superficie: 26.79 km². Habitantes: 1,649, de los cuales 463 forman la población económicamente activa. Hablan alguna lengua indígena ocho personas mayores de cinco años (zapoteco siete).

San Martín Totoltepec ◆ Municipio de Puebla situado al noreste de Izúcar de Matamoros y al suroeste de la capital de la entidad. Superficie: 12.77 km². Habitantes: 898, de los cuales 139 forman la población económicamente activa. Hablan alguna lengua indígena 19 personas mayores de cinco años (náhuatl 16).

San Martín Toxpalan ◆ Municipio de Oaxaca situado en el norte del estado, al oeste de Huautla de Jiménez. Superficie: 62.52 km^2. Habitantes: 2,910, de los cuales 823 forman la población económicamente activa. Hablan alguna lengua indígena 1,246 personas mayores de cinco años (náhuatl 640 y mazateco 596), de las cuales 87 son monolingües.

San Martín Tuxtla ◆ Volcán de Veracruz situado al noroeste de Coatzacoalcos, en la porción noroccidental de la sierra de San Martín o Los Tuxtlas. Hizo erupción en 1664 y 1793.

San Martín Zacatepec ◆ Municipio de Oaxaca situado en el noroeste del estado, al oeste de Huajuapan de León y cerca de los límites con Puebla y Guerrero. Superficie: 76.55 km^2. Habitantes: 1,339, de los cuales 309 forman la población económicamente activa. Hablan mixteco 10 personas mayores de cinco años.

San Mateo Atenco ◆ Municipio del Edo. de México situado en el centro de la entidad, al este de Toluca y al suroeste del Distrito Federal. Superficie: 31.23 km^2. Habitantes: 54,089, de los cuales 11,570 forman la población económicamente activa. Hablan alguna lengua indígena 43 personas mayores de cinco años (otomí 28 y mazahua 15). Fue erigido el 1 de enero de 1872. Su cabecera cuenta con un convento franciscano fundado en 1653. Su ganadería de toros de lidia es la más antigua de México.

San Mateo Cajonos ◆ Municipio de Oaxaca situado en el centro-oriente del estado, al este de la capital de la entidad. Superficie: 25.52 km^2. Habitantes: 620, de los cuales 190 forman la población económicamente activa. Hablan alguna lengua indígena 544 personas mayores de cinco años (zapoteco 449).

San Mateo Calpulalpan ◆ Nombre anterior del municipio oaxaqueño Calpulalpan de Méndez (☛).

San Mateo Atenco

San Mateo Eloxochitlán ◆ ☛ *San Mateo Yoloxochitlán*, municipio de Oaxaca.

San Mateo Etlatongo ◆ Municipio de Oaxaca situado en el noroeste del estado, al sureste de Huajuapan de León y al noroeste de la capital de la entidad. Superficie: 24.24 km^2. Habitantes: 1,121, de los cuales 295 forman la población económicamente activa. Hablan alguna lengua indígena 13 personas mayores de cinco años (mixteco 12).

San Mateo del Mar ◆ Municipio de Oaxaca situado en el sureste del estado, en el litoral del golfo de Tehuantepec, al sur de Juchitán de Zaragoza. Superficie: 75.27 km^2. Habitantes: 9,522, de los cuales 2,267 forman la población económicamente activa. Hablan alguna lengua indígena 8,010 personas mayores de cinco años (huave 7,994) y 1,509 de ellas son monolingües. En su jurisdicción se encuentra parte de la laguna Superior, en la que se explotan varias salinas.

San Mateo Mexicaltzingo ◆ Cabecera del municipio mexiquense de Mexicaltzingo (☛).

San Mateo Nejapan ◆ Municipio de Oaxaca situado en el noroeste del estado, en los límites con Guerrero, al suroeste de Huajuapan de León. Superficie: 28.07 km^2. Habitantes: 1,147, de los cuales 48 forman la población económicamente activa. Hablan alguna lengua indígena 15 personas mayores de cinco años.

San Mateo Peñasco ◆ Municipio de Oaxaca situado en el occidente del estado, al sureste de Tlaxiaco y al sur-sureste de Huajuapan de León. Superficie: 155.65 km^2. Habitantes: 1,563, de los cuales 283 forman la población económicamente activa. Hablan mixteco 1,348 personas mayores de cinco años (son monolingües 225).

San Mateo Piñas ◆ Municipio de Oaxaca situado en el sur del estado, al noreste de Puerto Ángel y al sureste de Miahuatlán. Superficie: 211.79 km^2. Habitantes: 4,343, de los cuales 1,318 forman la población económicamente activa. Hablan alguna lengua indígena 453 personas mayores de cinco años (zapoteco 449). Tiene manantiales termales cerca del río Copalita.

San Mateo Río Hondo ◆ Municipio de Oaxaca situado en el sur del estado, al norte de Puerto Ángel y al sur-sureste de Miahuatlán. Superficie: 91.86 km^2. Habitantes: 3,642, de los cuales 1,012 forman la población económicamente activa. Hablan alguna lengua indígena 117 personas mayores de cinco años (zapoteco 116).

San Mateo Sindihui ◆ Municipio de Oaxaca situado en el centro-occidente del estado, al oeste de la capital de la entidad. Superficie: 181.17 km^2. Habitantes: 1,887, de los cuales 383 forman la población económicamente activa. Hablan mixteco 72 personas mayores de cinco años. En la jurisdicción se produjo, el 22 de diciembre de

1871, una acción de armas dentro del levantamiento del Plan de la Noria. Las fuerzas de los juaristas Venancio Leyva (que murió en la batalla) y Francisco Loaeza derrotaron a los porfiristas comandados por Luis Mier y Terán.

San Mateo Tlapiltepec ◆ Municipio de Oaxaca situado en el noroeste del estado, al este de Huajuapan de León. Superficie: 37 km². Habitantes: 278, de los cuales 43 forman la población económicamente activa.

San Mateo Yoloxochitlán ◆ Municipio de Oaxaca situado en el norte del estado, al norte y próximo a Huautla de Jiménez. Superficie: 15.31 km². Habitantes: 2,934, de los cuales 791 forman la población económicamente activa. Hablan alguna lengua indígena 2,255 personas mayores de cinco años (mazateco 2,249), de las que 293 no saben español. Se le refiere también como San Mateo Eloxochitlán.

San Matías Tlalancaleca ◆ Municipio de Puebla situado en el occidente del estado, en los límites con Tlaxcala, al noroeste de la capital de la entidad. Superficie: 52.3 km². Habitantes: 15,842, de los cuales 3,424 forman la población económicamente activa. Hablan alguna lengua indígena 14 personas mayores de cinco años.

San Melchor Betaza ◆ Municipio de Oaxaca situado en el centro-oriente del estado, al noreste de la capital de la entidad y al sur de Tuxtepec. Superficie: 37 km². Habitantes: 1,027, de los cuales 359 forman la población económicamente activa. Hablan alguna lengua indígena 901 personas mayores de cinco años (zapoteco 890); de ellas, 259 son monolingües.

San Miguel ◆ Río de Chiapas. Nace en la región montañosa del suroeste de Guatemala, con el nombre de Cuilco, entra en territorio mexicano al nor-noreste de Tapachula y suroeste de Ciudad Cuauhtémoc y se transforma en el San Miguel, que desemboca en la presa de la Angostura.

San Miguel ◆ Río de Sonora también llamado Horcasitas. Nace en la vertiente norte de la sierra de Santa Rosalía, al sureste de Nogales, corre de norte a sur, recibe al río Zanjón y se une al Sonora un poco antes de llegar, por el noreste, a Hermosillo. En la confluencia de ambos ríos se construyó la presa Abelardo Rodríguez.

San Miguel, Andrés de ◆ n. en España y m. en Salvatierra, Gto. (1577-1644). Nombre religioso de Andrés de Segura de la Alcuña. Arquitecto. En 1593 viajó por primera vez a la Nueva España, estuvo brevemente en Veracruz y emprendió el regreso a su país, pero la nave en que viajaba naufragó después de salir de Cuba. Juró hacer votos religiosos en caso de salvar su vida, lo que en efecto ocurrió. En 1595 viajó a España y en 1597 regresó a la Nueva España. Un año después llegó a Puebla y tomó el hábito de los carmelitas, con el nombre de Andrés de San Miguel, aunque no abandonó la práctica de la arquitectura. Entre 1606 y 1610 efectuó su primera obra: el convento del Desierto de los Leones; en 1615 construyó el convento de San Ángel, reputado como su obra maestra; en 1618 inició simultáneamente la construcción de los monasterios de México y de Querétaro; entre 1629 y 1632 construyó los de Puebla, Celaya y Morelia y finalmente edificó el de Salvatierra y el puente del río Lerma. Al final de su vida escribió un libro sobre arquitectura, astronomía, botánica, carpintería, matemáticas y ejercicios devotos, con una "prueba matemática del mérito de la Virgen María". Autor de *Qué cosa sea la arquitectura, De los cimientos de los edificios, Descripción del templo de Salomón, Fábrica de relojes horizontales, Algunos tratados de astronomía, Tratado de plantas y frutas de la huerta del Colegio de San Ángel, Chimalistac* e *Informe acerca del desagüe de México*.

San Miguel Achiutla ◆ Municipio de Oaxaca situado en el noroeste del estado, al sureste de Huajuapan de León y al noroeste de la capital de la entidad. Superficie: 59.97 km². Habitantes: 824, de los cuales 291 forman la población económicamente activa. Hablan mixteco 34 personas mayores de cinco años.

San Miguel Ahuehuetitlán ◆ Municipio de Oaxaca situado en el noroeste del estado, al oeste-suroeste de Huajuapan de León. Superficie: 94.41 km². Habitantes: 2,130, de los cuales 219 forman la población económicamente activa. Hablan alguna lengua indígena 1,128 personas mayores de cinco años (mixteco 1,116), de las cuales 242 no dominan el español.

San Miguel Aloapan ◆ Municipio de Oaxaca situado en el centro-norte del estado, al norte de la capital de la entidad. Superficie: 133.96 km². Habitantes: 2,461, de los cuales 317 forman la población económicamente activa. Hablan alguna lengua indígena 2,040 personas mayores de cinco años (zapoteco 2,012); de ellas, 245 no saben español.

San Miguel el Alto ◆ Municipio de Jalisco situado en el noreste del estado, al noreste de Guadalajara y al sur de Teocaltiche. Superficie: 507.59 km². Habitantes: 27,237, de los cuales 6,791 forman la población económicamente activa. Hablan alguna lengua indígena 19 personas mayores de cinco años.

San Miguel de Allende ◆ Cabecera del municipio de Allende (☛), Guanajuato. Se encuentra en la margen izquierda del río de la Laja, a 51.5 kilómetros de Celaya. Fue fundada el 2 de octubre de 1542, con el nombre de San Miguel el Grande, por el fraile Juan de San Miguel. Su población original fue la de los indígenas purépechas y

Foto: Michael Calderwood

San Miguel de Allende

FOTO: MICHAEL CALDERWOOD

San Miguel de Allende, Guanajuato

otomíes que habitaban el antiguo poblado de Itzcuinapan. A mediados del siglo XVI se creó la alcaldía mayor de la villa de San Miguel el Grande, sufragánea de Xilotepec hasta 1562, cuando se fundó la villa de San Felipe y ambas formaron la provincia de San Miguel, misma que en 1787 quedó dividida en dos subdelegaciones: San Miguel el Grande y Dolores. La ciudad es célebre porque en ella nacieron los caudillos insurgentes Ignacio Allende e Ignacio y Juan Aldama. Tiene yacimientos de estaño y es un importante centro turístico. Cuenta, entre otras construcciones virreinales, con el Palacio de la familia De la Canal (barroco), la casa del conde de Loja, la casa de los Perros, la casa en que nació Ignacio Allende (epónimo de la ciudad), la parroquia (del siglo XVII), la iglesia de San Francisco (churrigueresca), el colegio y templo del Oratorio (barrocos), la iglesia de la Salud, y la iglesia de la Concepción (copia Los Inválidos, de París).

SAN MIGUEL AMATITLÁN ◆ Municipio de Oaxaca situado en el noroeste del estado, al noroeste de Huajuapan de León. Superficie: 196.48 km². Habitantes: 6,139, de los cuales 909 forman la población económicamente activa. Hablan alguna lengua indígena 809 personas mayores de cinco años (náhuatl 471 y mixteco 335).

SAN MIGUEL AMATLÁN ◆ Municipio de Oaxaca situado en el centro-oriente del estado, al noreste de la capital de la entidad. Superficie: 15.31 km². Habitantes: 1,244, de los cuales 371 forman la población económicamente activa. Hablan alguna lengua indígena 97 personas mayores de cinco años (zapoteco 94).

SAN MIGUEL AMUCO ◆ Río de Guerrero. Nace en la vertiente norte de las cumbres de la Tentación, al noroeste de Atoyac de Álvarez, en la sierra Madre del Sur. Corre de sur a norte y se une al río Balsas, al sur de Coyuca de Catalán, en el noroeste del estado.

SAN MIGUEL CANOA ◆ Población del municipio de Puebla, Puebla. La noche del 14 de septiembre de 1968, cinco empleados de la Universidad Autónoma de Puebla —Jesús Carrillo Sánchez, Ramón Calvario Gutiérrez, Julián González Báez, Miguel Flores Cruz y Roberto Rojano Aguirre— llegaron a esta comunidad, distante 12 km de la ciudad de Puebla, en su camino al volcán La Malinche, que pretendían escalar. En esta población, sin embargo, fueron linchados por más de mil fanáticos armados con machetes, hachas, palos y escopetas, instigados por el párroco local, Enrique Meza Pérez, quien acusaba a los empleados universitarios de ser "estudiantes comunistas" que querían poner una bandera rojinegra en la iglesia, robar el ganado, llevarse a los niños, quemar al santo patrono y matarlo a él mismo. En el linchamiento, Jesús Carrillo y Ramón Calvario fueron asesinados junto con Lucas García García, quien los había asilado en su casa, y Odilón Sánchez Islas, trabajador de la Villa Olímpica de la ciudad de México, que se encontraba con ellos circunstancialmente. Julián González, Miguel Flores y Roberto Rojano fueron rescatados por un destacamento militar. El sacerdote Meza Pérez no fue procesado judicialmente y la jerarquía lo trasladó al curato de Santa Inés Ahuatempan, Puebla. El cineasta Felipe Cazals reconstruyó estos hechos en la película *Canoa* (1975).

SAN MIGUEL COATLÁN ◆ Municipio de Oaxaca situado en el sur del estado, al suroeste de Miahuatlán. Superficie: 165.86 km². Habitantes: 2,880, de los cuales 612 forman la población económicamente activa. Hablan zapoteco 353 personas mayores de cinco años.

SAN MIGUEL CHICAHUA ◆ Municipio de Oaxaca situado en el noroeste del estado, al sureste de Huajuapan de León y al suroeste de Huautla de Jiménez. Superficie: 94.41 km². Habitantes: 2,200, de los cuales 592 forman la población económicamente activa. Hablan alguna lengua indígena 1,574 personas mayores de cinco años (mixteco 1,588) y de ellas, son monolingües 64.

SAN MIGUEL CHIMALAPA ◆ Municipio de Oaxaca situado en el sureste del estado, en los límites con Chiapas, al noreste de Juchitán de Zaragoza. Superficie: 1,593.5 km². Habitantes: 6,013, de los cuales 1,490 forman la población económicamente activa. Hablan alguna lengua indígena 1,766 personas mayores de cinco años (zoque 1,627 y tzotzil 109).

SAN MIGUEL EJUTLA ◆ Municipio de Oaxaca situado en el centro-sur del estado, al sur de la capital de la entidad. Superficie: 40.83 km². Habitantes: 882, de los cuales 152 forman la población económicamente activa. Hablan zapoteco 29 personas mayores de cinco años.

SAN MIGUEL EL GRANDE ◆ Municipio de Oaxaca situado en el occidente del estado, al noreste de Santiago Pinotepa Nacional y al sur-sureste de Huajuapan de León. Superficie: 82.93 km². Habitantes: 4,128, de los cuales 723 forman la población económicamente activa. Hablan alguna lengua indígena 2,330 personas mayores de cinco años (mixteco 2,327); de ellas, son monolingües 194. Explota diversos yacimientos de yeso.

San Miguel de Horcasitas ◆ Municipio de Sonora situado en el centro del estado y contiguo a Hermosillo. Superficie: 1,768.45 km². Habitantes: 4,439, de los cuales 785 forman la población económicamente activa. Hablan alguna lengua indígena 215 personas mayores de cinco años. Estuvo incorporado al municipio de Ures entre diciembre de 1930 y octubre de 1934. Su cabecera, del mismo nombre, se fundó como presidio en 1749 y de ese año a 1777 fue la capital de la provincia de Sonora.

San Miguel Huautla ◆ Municipio de Oaxaca situado en el noroeste del estado, al suroeste de Huautla de Jiménez y al este-sureste de Huajuapan de León. Superficie: 111 km². Habitantes: 1,671, de los cuales 253 forman la población económicamente activa. Hablan alguna lengua indígena 502 personas mayores de cinco años (mixteco 495).

San Miguel Iglesias, Antonio de ◆ n. en España y m. en Valladolid, hoy Morelia, Mich. (1726-1804). Fraile de la orden de San Jerónimo (1741), de la que fue general (1768). Profesor en Sigüenza, Ávila y Salamanca. Fue obispo de Comayagua, Honduras (1776) y de Michoacán (1785-1804), donde promovió el empleo de la vacuna durante una epidemia de viruela e impulsó el establecimiento de fábricas de hilados y tejidos, auxiliado por Manuel Abad y Queipo, José María Morelos y Miguel Hidalgo, entre otros sacerdotes.

San Miguel Ixitlán ◆ Municipio de Puebla situado en el sur del estado, en los límites con Oaxaca, al suroeste de Tehuacán. Superficie: 25.52 km². Habitantes: 651, de los cuales 186 forman la población económicamente activa. Hablan alguna lengua indígena nueve personas mayores de cinco años.

San Miguel Mixtepec ◆ Municipio de Oaxaca situado en el centro del estado, al suroeste de la capital de la entidad. Superficie: 48.48 km². Habitantes: 2,168, de los cuales 595 forman la población económicamente activa. Hablan alguna lengua indígena 1,778 personas mayores de cinco años (mixteco 1,768), de las cuales 62 no saben español.

San Miguel Panixtlahuaca ◆ Municipio de Oaxaca situado en el suroeste del estado, al este de Santiago Pinotepa Nacional. Superficie: 264.1 km². Habitantes: 5,526, de los cuales 885 forman la población económicamente activa. Hablan alguna lengua indígena 4,340 personas mayores de cinco años (chatino 4,321); de ellas, 1,791 son monolingües.

San Miguel Peras ◆ Municipio de Oaxaca situado en el centro del estado, al oeste-suroeste de la capital de la entidad. Superficie: 121.2 km². Habitantes: 3,148, de los cuales 733 forman la población económicamente activa. Hablan alguna lengua indígena 607 personas mayores de cinco años (mixteco 501 y zapoteco 106). Durante una época fue célebre por la gran cantidad de oro que produjeron sus minas.

San Miguel Piedras ◆ Municipio de Oaxaca situado en el centro-occidente del estado, al oeste de la capital de la entidad. Superficie: 108.45 km². Habitantes: 1,358, de los cuales 307 forman la población económicamente activa. Hablan alguna lengua indígena 321 personas mayores de cinco años (mixteco 319).

San Miguel del Puerto ◆ Municipio de Oaxaca situado en el litoral del océano Pacífico, al suroeste de Juchitán de Zaragoza y al noreste de Puerto Ángel. Superficie: 488.64 km². Habitantes: 8,098, de los cuales 1,734 forman la población económicamente activa. Hablan alguna lengua indígena 425 personas mayores de cinco años (zapoteco 375).

San Miguel Quetzaltepec ◆ Municipio de Oaxaca situado en el oriente del estado, al este de la capital de la entidad y al noroeste de Juchitán de Zaragoza. Superficie: 199.03 km². Habitantes: 5,303, de los cuales 1,206 forman la población económicamente activa. Hablan alguna lengua indígena 4,544 personas mayores de cinco años (mixe 4,538), de las cuales 1,854 no dominan el español.

San Miguel del Río ◆ Municipio de Oaxaca situado en el centro del estado, al noreste de la capital de la entidad. Superficie: 40.83 km². Habitantes: 302, de los cuales 115 forman la población económicamente activa. Hablan alguna lengua indígena 132 personas mayores de cinco años (zapoteco 131).

San Miguel Santa Flor ◆ Municipio de Oaxaca situado en el norte del estado, al sureste de Huautla de Jiménez y al suroeste de la presa Miguel Alemán. Superficie: 38.27 km². Habitantes: 1,160, de los cuales 318 forman la población económicamente activa. Hablan alguna lengua indígena 677 personas mayores de cinco años (mixteco 664).

San Miguel Sola de Vega ◆ ☛ *Villa Sola de Vega*, municipio de Oaxaca.

San Miguel Soyaltepec ◆ Municipio de Oaxaca situado en el norte del estado, en la ribera sur de la presa Miguel Alemán y en los límites con Veracruz. Superficie: 579.22 km². Habitantes: 33,887, de los cuales 7,568 forman la población económicamente activa. Hablan alguna lengua indígena 21,145 personas mayores de cinco años (mazateco 20,683 y chinanteco 328), y de ellas, 3,692 son monolingües. La cabecera es Temascal.

San Miguel Suchixtepec ◆ Municipio de Oaxaca situado en el sur del estado, al norte de Puerto Ángel y al sur de Miahuatlán. Superficie: 107.17 km². Habitantes: 2,667, de los cuales 621 forman la población económicamente activa. Hablan alguna lengua indígena 1,881 personas mayores de cinco años (zapoteco 1,880).

San Miguel Talea de Castro ◆ ☛ *Villa Talea de Castro*, municipio de Oaxaca.

San Miguel Tecomatlán ◆ Municipio de Oaxaca situado en el centro-occidente del estado, al sureste de Huajuapan de León y al noroeste de la capital de la entidad. Superficie: 31.9 km². Habitantes: 262, de los cuales 44 forman la población económicamente activa. Hablan alguna lengua indígena seis personas.

San Miguel Tenango ◆ Municipio de Oaxaca situado en el sureste del estado, en el istmo de Tehuantepec, al oeste-suroeste de Juchitán de Zaragoza. Superficie: 326.61 km². Habitantes: 989, de los cuales 245 forman la población económicamente activa. Hablan chontal de Oaxaca 10 personas mayores de cinco años.

San Miguel Tequixtepec ◆ Municipio de Oaxaca situado en el noroeste del estado, al este de Huajuapan de León. Superficie: 146.72 km². Habitantes: 1,093, de los cuales 205 forman la población económicamente activa.

San Miguel Tilquiapan ◆ Municipio de Oaxaca situado en el centro-sur del estado, al sur-sureste de la capital de la entidad. Superficie: 39.55 km². Habitantes: 3,398, de los cuales 851 forman la población económicamente activa. Hablan alguna lengua indígena 2,892 personas mayores de cinco años (zapoteco 2,882); de ellas, 166 son monolingües.

San Miguel Tlacamana ◆ Municipio de Oaxaca situado en el suroeste del estado, al norte de Santiago Pinotepa Nacional. Superficie: 108.44 km². Habitantes: 2,860, de los cuales 613 forman la población económicamente activa. Hablan alguna lengua indígena 871 personas mayores de cinco años (mixteco 869).

San Miguel Tlacotepec ◆ Municipio de Oaxaca situado en el noroeste del estado, al sur de Huajuapan de León. Superficie: 112.27 km². Habitantes: 3,335, de los cuales 572 forman la población económicamente activa. Hablan alguna lengua indígena 501 personas mayores de cinco años (mixteco 499).

San Miguel Totolapan ◆ Municipio de Guerrero situado en el occidente del estado, al noroeste de Chilpancingo y al suroeste de Iguala. Superficie: 2,649.1 km². Habitantes: 26,830, de los cuales 3,861 forman la población económicamente activa. Hablan alguna lengua indígena 17 personas mayores de cinco años.

Ilustración de Javier Guadarrama

Traslado en balsas de madera sobre el río Balsas en San Miguel Totolapan, Guerrero

San Miguel Tulancingo ◆ Municipio de Oaxaca situado en el noroeste del estado, al este-sureste de Huajuapan de León. Superficie: 53.59 km². Habitantes: 490, de los cuales 151 forman la población económicamente activa. Hablan chocho 68 personas mayores de cinco años.

San Miguel Xoxtla ◆ Municipio de Puebla situado en el occidente del estado, en los límites con Tlaxcala, al norte de Atlixco. Superficie: 29.35 km². Habitantes: 8,589, de los cuales 1,769 forman la población económicamente activa. Hablan alguna lengua indígena 41 personas mayores de cinco años (náhuatl 30). Durante la Semana Santa, en la cabecera se representa la Pasión de Cristo.

San Miguel Yotao ◆ Municipio de Oaxaca situado en el centro-oriente del estado, al noreste de la capital de la entidad. Superficie: 58.69 km². Habitantes: 498, de los cuales 205 forman la población económicamente activa. Hablan zapoteco 423 personas mayores de cinco años (51 son monolingües).

San Miguel Zinacantepec ◆ Cabecera del municipio de Zinacantepec (☛), Estado de México.

San Miguelito, de ◆ Sierra de San Luis Potosí. Es una de las estribaciones orientales de la sierra de Zacatecas. Se extiende de norte a sur, al suroeste del valle y la ciudad de San Luis Potosí, al noroeste del valle de Santa María del Río y al norte de la sierra de Guanajuato. Se prolonga al oeste en la sierra de Canoas.

San Nicolás ◆ Municipio de Oaxaca situado en el sur del estado, al sur de la capital de la entidad y al norte de Miahuatlán. Superficie: 29.34 km². Habitantes: 1,248, de los cuales 382 forman la población económicamente activa.

San Nicolás ◆ Municipio de Tamaulipas situado al noreste de Ciudad Victoria y al suroeste de Reynosa. Superficie: 722.77 km². Habitantes: 1,030, de los cuales 193 forman la población económicamente activa.

San Nicolás ◆ Río de Jalisco de 103 km de curso. Nace en la vertiente suroccidental de la sierra de Cacoma, al

Foto: Fondo Editorial Grupo Azabache

Templo de San Nicolás, Tamaulipas

norte de Autlán de Navarro, de la confluencia de los arroyos Alpisahua y Alicante; corre a través de la llanura costera y desemboca en el Pacífico, al norte de la bahía de Chamela.

San Nicolás de Buenos Aires ◆ Municipio de Puebla situado al estenoreste y próximo a la capital de la entidad. Superficie: 195.19 km². Habitantes: 8,094, de los cuales 1,893 forman la población económicamente activa. La cabecera, del mismo nombre, se llamó Malpaís y San Nicolás de Malpaís.

San Nicolás de los Garza ◆ Municipio de Nuevo León contiguo a Monterrey. Superficie: 86.8 km². Habitantes: 487,924, de los cuales 147,410 forman la población económicamente activa. Hablan alguna lengua indígena 475 personas mayores de cinco años (náhuatl 200). En su territorio estuvo desde 1635 la estancia de Pedro de la Garza. Es el municipio más pequeño de la entidad y fue erigido el 16 de diciembre de 1830. En la actualidad forma parte del área metropolitana de Monterrey y en él se hallan el estadio deportivo y varios edificios de la Universidad Autónoma de Nueva León.

San Nicolás Hidalgo ◆ Municipio de Oaxaca situado en el noroeste del estado, al oeste de Huajuapan de León. Superficie: 56.14 km². Habitantes: 860, de los cuales 271 forman la población económicamente activa. Hablan alguna lengua indígena seis personas mayores de cinco años.

San Nicolás de los Ranchos ◆ Municipio de Puebla situado en el occidente de la entidad, en los límites con el Estado de México, al noreste de la cima del Popocatépetl. Superficie: 195.19 km². Habitantes: 10,173, de los cuales 2,346 forman la población económicamente activa. Hablan alguna lengua indígena 214 personas mayores de cinco años (náhuatl 211).

San Nicolás Tolentino ◆ Municipio de San Luis Potosí situado en el centro del estado, al este de la capital de la entidad y al noroeste de Río Verde. Superficie: 654.5 km². Habitantes: 7,433, de los cuales 1,719 forman la población económicamente activa. Hablan alguna lengua indígena cinco personas mayores de cinco años.

San Pablo Amicano ◆ Municipio de Puebla situado en el sur del estado, al suroeste de Tehuacán. Superficie: 81.64 km². Habitantes: 3,472, de los cuales 503 forman la población económicamente activa. Hablan alguna lengua indígena nueve personas mayores de cinco años.

San Pablo Coatlán ◆ Municipio de Oaxaca situado en el sur del estado, al suroeste de Miahuatlán. Superficie: 195.2 km². Habitantes: 3,862, de los cuales 829 forman la población económicamente activa. Hablan alguna lengua indígena 65 personas mayores de cinco años (zapoteco 64).

San Pablo Cuatro Venados ◆ Municipio de Oaxaca situado en el centro del estado, al oeste-suroeste de la capital de la entidad. Superficie: 59.96 km². Habitantes: 1,334, de los cuales 295 forman la población económicamente activa. Hablan alguna lengua indígena 39 personas mayores de cinco años (zapoteco 26).

San Pablo Etla ◆ Municipio de Oaxaca situado en el centro del estado, al nor-noroeste de la capital de la entidad. Superficie: 33.17 km². Habitantes: 4,670, de los cuales 1,276 forman la población económicamente activa. Hablan alguna lengua indígena 103 personas mayores de cinco años (zapoteco 48, mixteco 23 y mixe 19). En su jurisdicción se han encontrado tumbas prehispánicas. Su cabecera, del mismo nombre, tiene una iglesia del siglo XVI, peculiar por su techo de dos aguas.

San Pablo Huitzo ◆ Municipio de Oaxaca situado en el centro del estado, al noroeste de la capital de la entidad. Superficie: 63.79 km². Habitantes: 4,969, de los cuales 1,161 forman la población económicamente activa. Hablan alguna lengua indígena 103 personas mayores de cinco años (mixteco 91). Tiene yacimientos de mica.

San Pablo Huixtepec ◆ Municipio de Oaxaca situado en el centro del estado, al sur y contiguo a la capital de la entidad. Superficie: 17.86 km². Habitantes: 8,307, de los cuales 2,001 forman la población económicamente activa. Hablan alguna lengua indígena 115 personas mayores de cinco años (zapoteco 103).

San Pablo Macuiltianguis ◆ Municipio de Oaxaca situado en el norte del estado, al nor-noreste de la capital de la entidad. Superficie: 162.03 km². Habitantes: 1,265, de los cuales 330 forman la población económicamente activa. Hablan alguna lengua indígena 837 personas mayores de cinco años (zapoteco 768). En la cueva España y en San Juan Bautista Luvina, puntos de su jurisdicción, se han hallado pinturas rupestres.

San Pablo del Monte ◆ Municipio de Tlaxcala situado en el sur de la entidad, en los límites con Puebla, al sursureste de la capital del estado. Superficie: 58.1 km². Habitantes: 48,988, de los cuales 11,309 forman la población económicamente activa. Hablan alguna lengua indígena 6,802 personas mayores de cinco años (náhuatl 6,795), de las que son monolingües 714. Su cabecera es Villa Vicente Guerrero, un suburbio de la capital poblana.

San Pablo Tijaltepec ◆ Municipio de Oaxaca situado en el occidente del estado, al oeste de la capital de la entidad y al sureste de Tlaxiaco. Superficie: 63.79 km². Habitantes: 2,252, de los cuales 362 forman la población económicamente activa. Hablan alguna lengua indígena 1,743 personas mayores de cinco años (mixteco 1,741); de ellas, no saben español 325.

San Pablo Villa de Mitla ◆ Municipio de Oaxaca situado en el centrosur del estado, al sureste de la capital de la entidad. Superficie: 82.93 km². Habitantes: 10,642, de los cuales 3,040 forman la población económicamente activa. Hablan alguna lengua indígena 4,380 personas mayores de cinco años (zapoteco 4,284), y de ellas, 54 son monolingües. A 7 km de su cabecera se hallan las ruinas zapotecas de Mitla (nombre náhuatl que significa "donde abundan los muertos"), necrópolis, san-

San Pablo Villa de Mitla

San Pablo Villa de Mitla

tuario máximo de esa nación prehispánica y residencia del sumo sacerdote del culto. De las ruinas de Mitla destacan el grupo de columnas, los mosaicos en los muros, formados por miles de pequeñas piedras labradas, y las fortificaciones construidas sobre la cima de una roca. La principal festividad es el 25 de enero. La cabecera, del mismo nombre, cuenta con una iglesia del siglo XVI.

San Pablo Yaganiza ◆ Municipio de Oaxaca situado en el centro del estado, al este-noreste de la capital de la entidad. Superficie: 34.45 km². Habitantes: 1,080, de los cuales 323 forman la población económicamente activa. Hablan alguna lengua indígena 929 personas mayores de cinco años (zapoteco 925), de las cuales 115 no dominan el español.

San Patricio, Batallón de ◆ ☛ *Irlanda*.

San Pedro ◆ Municipio de Coahuila situado en el sureste del estado, al noroeste de Saltillo y al suroeste de Cuatro Ciénegas. Superficie: 9,942.4 km². Habitantes: 91,421, de los cuales 25,357 forman la población económicamente activa. Hablan alguna lengua indígena 18 personas mayores de cinco años.

San Pedro ◆ Río de Chihuahua que nace al suroeste de la capital, en la vertiente este de la sierra San José, al oriente de la sierra Madre Occidental; corre de este a oeste, recibe al río Satevó, al suroeste de Delicias, y desemboca en el Conchos, al norte de esta ciudad. Sobre este río se construyó la presa Francisco I. Madero, cuyas aguas riegan la región de Meoqui.

San Pedro ◆ Río de Tabasco. Nace en la región del Petén, en Guatemala, corre al noroeste y entra en México, donde recibe al Jotal. Tuerce al norte y al oeste. Es uno de los más caudalosos afluentes del Bajo Usumacinta, en el que desemboca al norte de Emiliano Zapata. Presenta numerosas caídas de agua, lo que dificulta la navegación en varios de sus tramos. En su nacimiento es navegable para embarcaciones de poco calado y 12 kilómetros antes de su encuentro con el Usumacinta permite la boga de pequeños vapores.

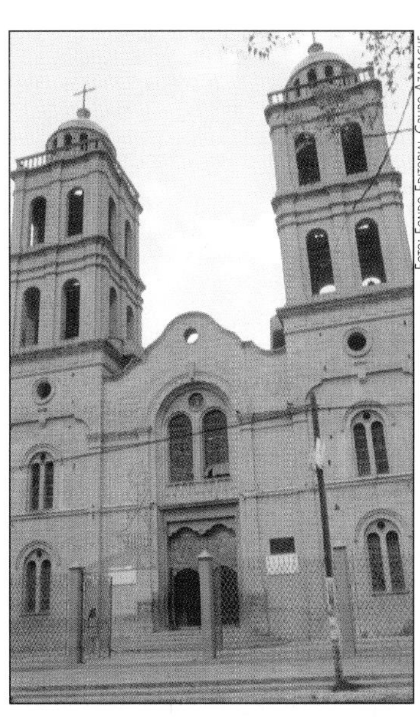
Foto: Fondo Editorial Grupo Azabache

Parroquia de San Pedro Apóstol, en San Pedro, Coahuila

San Pedro, de ◆ Sierra de Guanajuato situada al sur de los límites con San Luis Potosí. Es la prolongación nororiental de la sierra de Comanja. Se halla al noroeste del llano de San Felipe y al norte de la sierra de la Media Luna. Su porción sudoccidental se conoce como la Mesa del Tanque. Una de sus puntas más altas, el cerro del Fraile, tiene yacimientos de estaño y de mercurio.

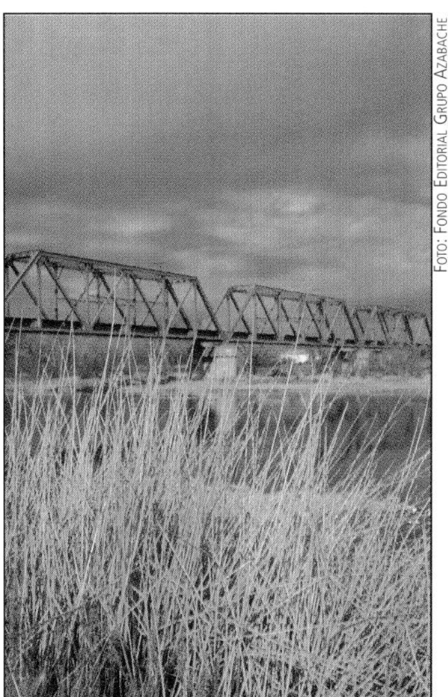
Foto: Fondo Editorial Grupo Azabache

San Pedro, río de Chihuahua

San Pedro, de ◆ Sierra de Nayarit que forma parte de la sierra Madre Occidental. Se halla en el extremo sur del estado. Va de noroeste a sureste, al norte del valle de Ixtlán y de la sierra Pajaritos. El río Grande de Santiago la separa de la sierra de Nayar. Su cima más alta es el cerro de Juanacate. El volcán Ceboruco se encuentra en su porción suroriental. Cuenta con yacimientos de plomo y metales preciosos.

San Pedro el Alto ◆ Municipio de Oaxaca situado en el sur del estado, al norte de Puerto Ángel. Superficie: 127.58 km^2. Habitantes: 3,570, de los cuales 784 forman la población económicamente activa. Hablan alguna lengua indígena 2,629 personas mayores de cinco años (zapoteco 2,627), de las cuales 346 no saben español.

San Pedro Amusgos ◆ Municipio de Oaxaca situado en el suroeste del estado, en los límites con Guerrero, al norte de Santiago Pinotepa Nacional. Superficie: 74 km^2. Habitantes: 4,949, de los cuales 1,199 forman la población económicamente activa. Hablan alguna lengua indígena 3,232 personas mayores de cinco años (amuzgo 3,190) y de ellas, 709 son monolingües.

San Pedro Apóstol ◆ Municipio de Oaxaca situado en el centro de la entidad, al sur de la capital del estado. Superficie: 22.97 km^2. Habitantes: 1,706, de los cuales 351 forman la población económicamente activa. Hablan alguna lengua indígena 86 personas mayores de cinco años (zapoteco 85).

San Pedro Atocpan ◆ Población de la delegación Milpa Alta, en el Distrito Federal, célebre por su Feria Nacional del Mole, especialidad gastrónomica de los lugareños que se celebra anualmente desde 1977. La localidad cuenta con un ex convento franciscano del siglo XVII.

San Pedro Atoyac ◆ Municipio de Oaxaca situado en el suroeste del estado, al nor-noreste de Santiago Pinotepa Nacional. Superficie: 94.41 km^2. Habitantes: 3,500, de los cuales 629 forman la población económicamente activa. Hablan alguna lengua indígena 2,198 personas mayores de cinco años (mixteco 2,197), de las cuales 686 no hablan español.

San Pedro Cajonos ◆ Municipio de Oaxaca situado en el centro de la entidad, al noreste de la capital del estado. Superficie: 76.55 km^2. Habitantes: 1,307, de los cuales 325 forman la población económicamente activa. Hablan alguna lengua indígena 1,137 personas mayores de cinco años (zapoteco 1,132), de ellas, no saben español 98.

San Pedro Cántaros ◆ Municipio de Oaxaca situado en el noroeste del estado, al noreste de Tlaxiaco y al sureste de Huajuapan de León. Superficie: 63.79 km^2. Habitantes: 1,077, de los cuales 284 forman la población económicamente activa. Hablan alguna lengua indígena 119 personas mayores de cinco años (mixteco 118). Su cabecera es San Pedro Coxcaltepec Cántaros.

San Pedro Comitancillo ◆ Municipio de Oaxaca situado al oeste y próximo a Juchitán de Zaragoza. Superficie: 165.86 km^2. Habitantes: 3,867, de los cuales 823 forman la población económicamente activa. Hablan alguna lengua indígena 2,063 personas mayores de cinco años (zapoteco 2,060).

San Pedro de la Cueva ◆ Municipio de Sonora situado al este de Hermosillo y al noreste de Guaymas. Superficie: 1,926.36 km^2. Habitantes: 1,890, de los cuales 562 forman la población económicamente activa. Su principal festividad se celebra el 28 de diciembre, día de los Santos Inocentes, con una feria regional, música, baile y juegos pirotécnicos.

San Pedro Cholula ◆ Municipio de Puebla situado en el centro-occidente del estado y contiguo a la capital de la entidad. Superficie: 51.03 km^2. Habitantes: 89,782, de los cuales 21,773 forman la población económicamente activa. Hablan alguna lengua indígena 823 personas mayores de cinco años (náhuatl 649 y totonaco 97). Sus principales festividades son la de la Candelaria, el 2 de febrero; la feria piloto regional, del 2 al 11 de septiembre; y la de Santa Bárbara, el 4 de diciembre. Sus mayores atractivos turísticos son la pirámide de Cholula con el museo que está en su base, así como el convento y 45 templos religiosos.

San Pedro del Gallo ◆ Municipio de Durango situado en el norte del estado, al norte de la capital de la entidad y al oeste de Gómez Palacio. Superficie: 2,008.3 km^2. Habitantes: 2,144, de los cuales 740 forman la población económicamente activa. En el municipio, que abarca casi la totalidad de la meseta de La Zarca, abundan los mantos carboníferos y las vetas de bromuros y yoduros de plata.

San Pedro del Gallo ◆ Sierra de Durango situada al oeste de la sierra del Rosario, en la porción nororiental del estado, al oeste de Torreón. Tiene mantos carboníferos y yacimientos de cobre, plata y oro.

San Pedro Garza García ◆ municipio de Nuevo León contiguo a Monterrey. Extensión: 69.4 km^2. Habitantes 120,913, de los cuales 41,248 forman la población económicamente activa. Hablan alguna lengua indígena 694 personas mayores de cinco años (náhuatl 506 y huasteco 74). En la cabecera municipal se halla el Centro Cultural Alfa que cuenta con un planetario, un multiteatro de pantalla hemisférica para películas programadas por computadora y exposiciones permanentes de astronomía y física elemental.

San Pedro Huamelula ◆ Municipio de Oaxaca situado en el sureste del estado, en la región del istmo de Tehuantepec, al suroeste de Juchitán de Zaragoza. Superficie: 505.23 km^2. Habitantes: 8,865, de los cuales 1,791 forman la población económicamente activa. Hablan alguna lengua indígena 784 personas mayores de cinco años (chontal de Oaxaca 741). La cabecera, del mismo nombre, cuenta con una iglesia del siglo XVIII.

San Pedro Huilotepec ◆ Municipio de Oaxaca situado en la región del istmo de Tehuantepec, al suroeste de Juchitán, en el litoral de la laguna Superior. Superficie: 102.06 km^2. Habitantes: 2,396, de los cuales 548 forman la población económicamente activa. Hablan alguna lengua indígena 1,445 personas mayores de cinco años (zapoteco 1,426).

San Pedro Ixcatlán ◆ Municipio de Oaxaca situado en el norte del estado, al oeste de Tuxtepec y al este de Huautla de Jiménez. El norte de su territorio está cubierto por la presa Miguel Alemán. Superficie: 373.82 km^2. Habitantes: 9,858, de los cuales 2,222 forman la población económicamente activa. Hablan alguna lengua indígena 7,852 personas mayores de cinco años (mazateco 7,849), de las que 2,284 no saben español.

SAN PEDRO IXTLAHUACA ◆ Municipio del estado de Oaxaca situado en el centro del estado y contiguo a la capital de la entidad. Superficie: 40.83 km². Habitantes: 3,174, de los cuales 783 forman la población económicamente activa. Hablan alguna lengua indígena 38 personas mayores de cinco años (mixteco 26).

SAN PEDRO JALTEPETONGO ◆ Municipio de Oaxaca situado en el noroeste del estado, al este-sureste de Huajuapan de León. Superficie: 44.66 km². Habitantes: 663, de los cuales 162 forman la población económicamente activa. Hablan alguna lengua indígena 570 personas mayores de cinco años (mixteco 568).

SAN PEDRO JICAYÁN ◆ Municipio de Oaxaca situado en el suroeste del estado, al norte y cerca de Santiago Pinotepa Nacional. Superficie: 65.07 km². Habitantes: 9,388, de los cuales 2,059 forman la población económicamente activa. Hablan alguna lengua indígena 7,111 personas mayores de cinco años (mixteco 7,103), de las que 1,859 no dominan el español.

SAN PEDRO JOCOTIPAC ◆ Municipio de Oaxaca situado en el suroeste del estado, al este de Huajuapan de León. Superficie: 40.83 km². Habitantes: 1,122, de los cuales 322 forman la población económicamente activa. Hablan alguna lengua indígena 565 personas mayores de cinco años (mixteco 563).

SAN PEDRO JUCHATENGO ◆ Municipio de Oaxaca situado en el suroeste del estado, al oeste y cerca de Miahuatlán. Superficie: 108.44 km². Habitantes: 1,590, de los cuales 284 forman la población económicamente activa. Hablan alguna lengua indígena 22 personas mayores de cinco años (zapoteco 20).

SAN PEDRO LAGUNILLAS ◆ Municipio de Nayarit situado en el sur del estado, al sureste de Tepic, en los límites con Jalisco. Superficie: 520.2 km². Habitantes: 7,787, de los cuales 2,117 forman la población económicamente activa. Hablan alguna lengua indígena doce personas mayores de cinco años. Tiene las lagunas de San Pedro Lagunillas y Detetiltic, al noroeste y sur, respectivamente, de la cabecera.

SAN PEDRO MÁRTIR ◆ Municipio de Oaxaca situado en el centro del estado, al sur de la capital de la entidad. Superficie: 14.03 km². Habitantes: 1,943, de los cuales 344 forman la población económicamente activa. Hablan alguna lengua indígena 1,145 personas mayores de cinco años (zapoteco 1,139).

SAN PEDRO MÁRTIR ◆ Sierra de Baja California situada en el norte del estado. Es la prolongación meridional de la sierra de Juárez. Los llanos de Buenos Aires la limitan por el sur. Su cima más elevada, la Encantada, es también la más alta de la península. Al suroeste de esta elevación, en la misma cordillera, se encuentra el Observatorio Meteorológico de San Pedro Mártir.

SAN PEDRO MÁRTIR QUIECHAPA ◆ Municipio de Oaxaca situado en el centro-sur del estado, al noreste de Miahuatlán. Superficie: 63.79 km². Habitantes: 776, de los cuales 187 forman la población económicamente activa. Hablan zapoteco 23 personas mayores de cinco años.

SAN PEDRO MÁRTIR YUCUXACO ◆ Municipio de Oaxaca situado en el noroeste del estado, al sureste de Huajuapan de León. Superficie: 51.03 km². Habitantes: 1,544, de los cuales 325 forman la población económicamente activa. Hablan alguna lengua indígena cinco personas mayores de cinco años.

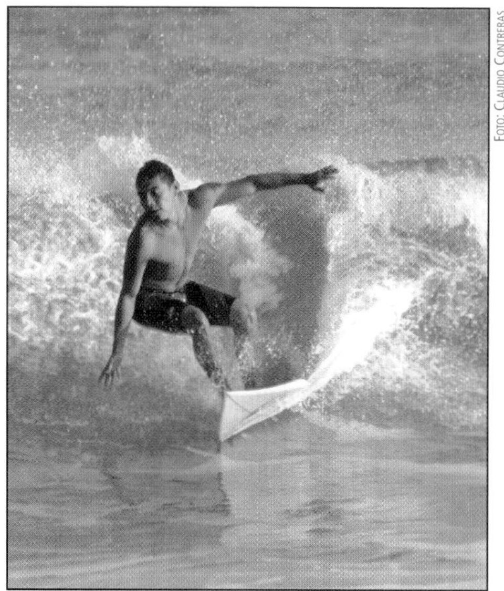

FOTO: CLAUDIO CONTRERAS

Deportes acuáticos en San Pedro Mixtepec Juquila, Oaxaca

SAN PEDRO MIXTEPEC JUQUILA ◆ Municipio de Oaxaca situado en el sur del estado, en el litoral del océano Pacífico, al oeste de Pochutla y al este-sureste de Pinotepa Nacional. Superficie: 331.71 km². Habitantes: 27,111, de los cuales 5,707 forman la población económicamente activa. Hablan alguna lengua indígena 668 personas mayores de cinco años (chatino 233 y zapoteco 233). Cuenta con un número conside-

FOTO: FONDO EDITORIAL GRUPO AZABACHE

Sierra de San Pedro Mártir, en Baja California

rable de pobladores cuyos antepasados fueron traídos de África. En la jurisdicción se halla Puerto Escondido, importante centro turístico que cuenta con numerosas playas y otros atractivos. Cerca de la cabecera, del mismo nombre, está la laguna de Manialtepec.

San Pedro Mixtepec Miahuatlán ◆ Municipio de Oaxaca situado en el sur del estado, al este de Miahuatlán. Superficie: 108.45 km². Habitantes: 1,227, de los cuales 254 forman la población económicamente activa. Hablan zapoteco 861 personas mayores de cinco años.

San Pedro Molinos ◆ Municipio de Oaxaca situado en el occidente del estado, al sureste de Tlaxiaco y al sur-sureste de Huajuapan de León. Superficie: 25.52 km². Habitantes: 768, de los cuales 134 forman la población económicamente activa. Hablan mixteco 522 personas mayores de cinco años (son monolingües 53).

San Pedro Nopala ◆ Municipio de Oaxaca situado en el noroeste del estado, al sureste de Huajuapan de León. Superficie: 20.41 km². Habitantes: 1,031, de los cuales 277 forman la población económicamente activa.

San Pedro Ocopetatillo ◆ Municipio de Oaxaca situado en el norte del estado, al noroeste de Huautla de Jiménez. Superficie: 11.48 km². Habitantes: 815, de los cuales 233 forman la población económicamente activa. Hablan alguna lengua indígena 704 personas mayores de cinco años (mazateco 703), de las cuales 174 no saben español.

San Pedro Ocotepec ◆ Municipio de Oaxaca situado en el oriente del estado, al este de la capital de la entidad. Superficie: 136.51 km². Habitantes: 1,807, de los cuales 410 forman la población económicamente activa. Hablan mixe 1,492 personas mayores de cinco años (605 son monolingües).

San Pedro Pochutla ◆ Municipio de Oaxaca situado en el extremo sur del estado, en el litoral del océano Pacífico, al sur de Miahuatlán, al este de Puerto Escondido y al oeste-suroeste de Salina Cruz. Superficie: 421.02 km². Habitantes: 30,911, de los cuales 6,577 forman la población económicamente activa. Hablan alguna lengua indígena 1,567 personas mayores de cinco años (zapoteco 1,068 y zapoteco de Ixtlán 286). Tiene yacimientos de cobre, fierro y manganeso. En la jurisdicción se halla el centro turístico de Puerto Ángel, bahía con una amplia infraestructura hotelera que forma parte del proyecto Bahías de Huatulco. En el extremo sur de la bahía hay un faro en funcionamiento para las instalaciones del puerto. Cerca de la pista aérea de la ciudad de Pochutla se han encontrado restos de cerámica mixteca: destaca una figura de jade de siete centímetros, que representa a un sujeto sedente con una máscara de tigre, similar a las representaciones de la Venta; algunos glifos inscritos en el reverso de esta figura, aún no descifrados del todo, parecen relacionarla con la primera fase de Monte Albán. En 1842, el naturalista danés Federico Miguel Liebmann, quien realizaba una expedición botánica, notó que algunos indios hablaban un danés arcaico. Liebmann, tras consultar a los ancianos pochutecas, supo que aproximadamente a fines del siglo XVI o principios del XVII un buque corsario danés fue atacado cerca de Huatulco y que numerosos piratas quedaron en tierra al huir su nave. Éstos se trasladaron a Pochutla, donde tuvieron descendencia a la que legaron su idioma, que todavía se escuchaba a fines del siglo XIX.

San Pedro Pochutla, Oaxaca

San Pedro Quiatoni ◆ Municipio de Oaxaca situado en el sureste del estado, al sureste de la capital de la entidad. Superficie: 537.2 km². Habitantes: 8,036, de los cuales 1,982 forman la población económicamente activa. Hablan zapoteco 6,642 personas mayores de cinco años (monolingües 1,380).

San Pedro y San Pablo ◆ Río del estado de Tabasco. Nace de un desprendimiento del Usumacinta, corre de sureste a noroeste y desemboca en el golfo de México en la barra de San Pedro y San Pablo, al noreste de Frontera. Tiene un curso de 20 km y es navegable. Su tramo final sirve de frontera a Tabasco y Campeche, al oeste de la laguna de Términos.

San Pedro y San Pablo Ayutla ◆ Municipio de Oaxaca situado en el centro-oriente del estado, al este de la capital de la entidad. Superficie: 108.45 km². Habitantes: 4,767, de los cuales 1,424 forman la población económicamente activa. Hablan alguna lengua indígena 4,007 personas mayores de cinco años (mixe 3,983), de las cuales 1,002 no saben español.

San Pedro y San Pablo Etla ◆ Nombre anterior del municipio oaxaqueño Villa de Etla (☛).

San Pedro y San Pablo Teposcolula ◆ Municipio de Oaxaca situado en el noroeste del estado, al sureste de Huajuapan de León. Superficie: 162.03 km². Habitantes: 3,454, de los cuales 869 forman la población económicamente activa. Hablan alguna lengua indígena 105 personas mayores de cinco años (mixteco 64). En la cabecera, del mismo nombre, se conservan restos del convento de San Pedro y San Pablo, construido en el siglo XVI; a un costado del templo adjunto está una capilla abierta, considerada la más bella del continente. El primer viernes de cada Cuaresma se lleva a cabo la feria agrícola y ganadera. En marzo de 1987, el gobierno de Oaxaca declaró a la cabecera de este municipio "zona de monumentos históricos", con el fin de preservarla.

San Pedro y San Pablo Tequixtepec ◆ Municipio de Oaxaca situado en el noroeste del estado, en los límites con Puebla, al noreste de Huajuapan de León. Superficie: 274.3 km². Habitantes: 2,529, de los cuales 582 forman la población económicamente activa. Hablan alguna lengua indígena 366 personas mayores de cinco años (mixteco 362). En el poblado de Mixquitlahuaca se encuentran las grutas del Obispo, con una caudalosa corriente subterránea.

San Pedro Sochiapan ◆ Municipio de Oaxaca situado en el norte del estado, al sureste de Huautla de Jiménez. Superficie: 193.93 km². Habitantes: 4,459, de los cuales 939 forman la población económicamente activa. Hablan alguna lengua indígena 3,564 personas mayores de cinco años (chinanteco 3,544); de ellas, 942 no dominan el español.

San Pedro Tapanatepec ◆ Municipio de Oaxaca situado en el extremo sudoriental del estado, en los límites con Chiapas, al este de Juchitán de Zaragoza. Superficie: 544.78 km². Habitantes: 14,203, de los cuales 2,852 forman la población económicamente activa. Hablan alguna lengua indígena 590 personas mayores de cinco años (zapoteco 439).

San Pedro Taviche ◆ Municipio de Oaxaca situado en el centro del estado, al norte de Miahuatlán y al sur-sureste de la capital de la entidad. Superficie: 75.27 km². Habitantes: 919, de los cuales 56 forman la población económicamente activa.

San Pedro Teozacoalco ◆ Municipio de Oaxaca situado en el centro-occidente del estado, al oeste de la capital de la entidad y al sureste de Tlaxiaco. Superficie: 108.45 km². Habitantes: 1,356, de los cuales 215 forman la población económicamente activa. Hablan alguna lengua indígena 11 personas mayores de cinco años (mixteco 9).

San Pedro Teutila ◆ Municipio de Oaxaca situado en el norte del estado, al sureste de Huautla de Jiménez. Superficie: 43.38 km². Habitantes: 3,591, de los cuales 1,007 forman la población económicamente activa. Hablan alguna lengua indígena 816 personas mayores de cinco años (mazateco 433, cuicateco 261 y chinanteco 80).

San Pedro Tidaá ◆ Municipio de Oaxaca situado en el noroeste del estado, al sureste de Huajuapan de León y al noroeste de la capital de la entidad. Superficie: 15.31 km². Habitantes: 926, de los cuales 253 forman la población económicamente activa. Hablan alguna lengua indígena 411 personas mayores de cinco años (mixteco 410).

San Pedro Topiltepec ◆ Municipio de Oaxaca situado en el noroeste del estado, al sureste de Huajuapan de León y al noroeste de la capital de la entidad. Superficie: 45.93 km². Habitantes: 452, de los cuales 148 forman la población económicamente activa.

San Pedro Totolapan ◆ Municipio de Oaxaca situado en el centro del estado, al sureste de la capital de la entidad y al noreste de Miahuatlán. Superficie: 391.68 km². Habitantes: 3,017, de los cuales 821 forman la población económicamente activa. Hablan alguna lengua indígena 186 personas mayores de cinco años (zapoteco 179).

San Pedro Tututepec ◆ ☛ *Villa de Tututepec de Melchor Ocampo*, municipio de Oaxaca.

San Pedro Xalostoc ◆ Población perteneciente al municipio de Ecatepec (☛), en el Estado de México.

San Pedro Yaneri ◆ Municipio de Oaxaca situado en el centro del estado, al noreste de la capital de la entidad. Superficie: 79.1 km². Habitantes: 930, de los cuales 260 forman la población económicamente activa. Hablan zapoteco 798 personas mayores de cinco años.

San Pedro Yeloixtlahuacán ◆ Municipio de Puebla situado en el sur del estado, en los límites con Oaxaca, al suroeste de Tehuacán. Superficie: 164.59 km². Habitantes: 3,490, de los cuales 673 forman la población económicamente activa.

San Pedro Yolox ◆ Municipio de Oaxaca situado en el centro-norte del estado, al sureste de Huautla de Jiménez y al suroeste de Tuxtepec. Superficie: 127.58 km². Habitantes: 2,572, de los cuales 430 forman la población económicamente activa. Hablan alguna lengua indígena 2,092 personas mayores de cinco años (chinanteco 2,066) y de ellas, 172 no dominan el español.

San Pedro Yucunama ◆ Municipio de Oaxaca situado en el noroeste del estado, al sureste de Huajuapan de León. Superficie: 30.62 km². Habitantes: 262, de los cuales 75 forman la población económicamente activa.

San Quintín ◆ Bahía de Baja California situada en el litoral del océano Pacífico, al norte del paralelo 30. La cierra por el sur el cabo San Quintín.

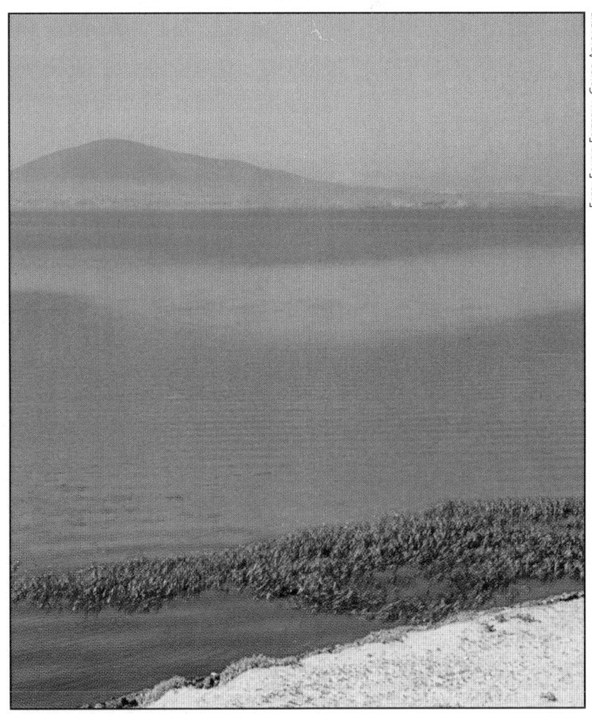

Foto: Fondo Editorial Grupo Azabache

Bahía de San Quintín, Baja California

SAN RAFAEL MATACHI ◆ Cabecera del municipio chihuahuense de Matachi o Matáchic (☛).

SAN RAYMUNDO JALPAN ◆ Municipio de Oaxaca situado en la zona central del estado, al sur-suroeste y próximo a la capital de la entidad. Superficie: 19.14 km². Habitantes: 1,555, de los cuales 358 forman la población económicamente activa. Hablan alguna lengua indígena 116 personas mayores de cinco años (zapoteco 105).

SAN ROMÁN, ÓSCAR ◆ n. en Querétaro (1970). Torero. Tomó la alternativa el 25 de diciembre de 1991 en Querétaro. Su confirmación fue en la Plaza México en 1992. Ha toreado en todo el país.

SAN SALVADOR ◆ Municipio de Hidalgo situado al oeste-noroeste de Pachuca y contiguo a Actopan. Superficie: 200.4 km². Habitantes: 28,799, de los cuales 5,930 forman la población económicamente activa. Hablan alguna lengua indígena 6,877 personas mayores de cinco años (otomí 6,840). Indígenas monolingües: 159.

SAN SALVADOR ATENCO ◆ Cabecera del municipio de Atenco (☛), Estado de México.

SAN SALVADOR HUIXCOLOTLA ◆ Municipio de Puebla situado al este de la capital de la entidad y al noreste de Tehuacán. Superficie: 33.18 km². Habitantes: 8,640, de los cuales 1,733 forman la población económicamente activa. Hablan alguna lengua indígena 19 personas mayores de cinco años (náhuatl 15).

SAN SALVADOR EL SECO ◆ Municipio de Puebla situado al este de la capital de la entidad, cerca de Tlaxcala. Superficie: 193.91 km². Habitantes: 23,294, de los cuales 5,258 forman la población económicamente activa. Hablan alguna lengua indígena 35 personas mayores de cinco años (náhuatl 15).

SAN SALVADOR EL VERDE ◆ Municipio de Puebla situado en el occidente de la entidad, en los límites con Tlaxcala y el Estado de México. Superficie: 150.53 km². Habitantes: 21,075, de los cuales 4,507 forman la población económicamente activa. Hablan alguna lengua indígena 53 personas mayores de cinco años (náhuatl 23).

SAN SEBASTIÁN EX IX CANTÓN ◆ Antiguo nombre del municipio jalisciense de Gómez Farías (☛).

SAN SEBASTIÁN EX X CANTÓN ◆ ☛ *San Sebastián del Oeste*.

SAN SEBASTIÁN ABASOLO ◆ Municipio de Oaxaca situado en el centro del estado, al sureste y próximo a la capital de la entidad. Superficie: 16.58 km². Habitantes: 2,032, de los cuales 381 forman la población económicamente activa. Hablan alguna lengua indígena 779 personas mayores de cinco años (zapoteco 777).

SAN SEBASTIÁN COATLÁN ◆ Municipio de Oaxaca situado en el sur del estado, al suroeste de Miahuatlán. Superficie: 177.34 km². Habitantes: 2,363, de los cuales 579 forman la población económicamente activa. Hablan zapoteco 22 personas mayores de cinco años.

SAN SEBASTIÁN IXCAPA ◆ Municipio de Oaxaca situado en el suroeste del estado, al noroeste de Santiago Pinotepa Nacional. Superficie: 104.62 km². Habitantes: 3,951, de los cuales 882 forman la población económicamente activa. Hablan alguna lengua indígena 246 personas mayores de cinco años (mixteco 227). Existe una comunidad de origen africano.

SAN SEBASTIÁN NICANANDUTA ◆ Municipio de Oaxaca situado en el noroeste del estado, al sur de Huajuapan de León. Superficie: 30.62 km². Habitantes: 1,582, de los cuales 491 forman la población económicamente activa. Hablan mixteco 679 personas mayores de cinco años.

SAN SEBASTIÁN RÍO HONDO ◆ Municipio de Oaxaca situado en el sur del estado, al sureste de Miahuatlán. Superficie: 81.65 km². Habitantes: 2,758, de los cuales 688 forman la población económicamente activa. Hablan zapoteco 206 personas mayores de cinco años.

SAN SEBASTIÁN DEL OESTE ◆ Municipio de Jalisco situado en el occidente del estado, en los límites con Nayarit, al noreste de Puerto Vallarta. Superficie: 1,195.76 km². Habitantes: 7,076, de los cuales 1,801 forman la población económicamente activa. Su cabecera es San Sebastián. Tiene yacimientos de cobre, oro, plata y plomo. Se llamó San Sebastián ex X Cantón.

SAN SEBASTIÁN TECOMAXTLAHUACA ◆ Municipio de Oaxaca situado en el noroeste del estado, al suroeste de Huajuapan de León. Superficie: 369.99 km². Habitantes: 8,861, de los cuales 1,683 forman la población económicamente activa. Hablan alguna lengua indígena 2,557 personas mayores de cinco años (mixteco 2,546); de ellas, 104 son monolingües.

SAN SEBASTIÁN TEITIPAC ◆ Municipio de Oaxaca situado en el centro del estado, al sureste de la capital de la entidad. Superficie: 30.62 km². Habitantes: 2,204, de los cuales 480 forman la población económicamente activa. Hablan alguna lengua indígena 799 personas mayores de cinco años (zapoteco 796).

SAN SEBASTIÁN TLACOTEPEC ◆ Municipio de Puebla situado en los límites con Oaxaca y Veracruz, al este de Tehuacán. Superficie: 241.11 km². Habitantes: 11,683, de los cuales 2,804 forman la población económicamente activa. Hablan alguna lengua indígena 9,431 personas mayores de cinco años (náhuatl 6,131 y mazateco 3,264). Indígenas monolingües: 2,126. Su cabecera es Tlacotepec de Díaz.

SAN SEBASTIÁN TUTLA ◆ Municipio de Oaxaca situado en el centro del estado, al sureste y próximo a la capital de la entidad. Superficie: 8.93 km². Habitantes: 12,293, de los cuales 1,438 forman la población económicamente activa,. Hablan alguna lengua indígena 647 personas mayores de cinco años (zapoteco 442).

SAN SEBASTIÁN ZINACATEPEC ◆ Cabecera del municipio de Zinacatepec (☛), Puebla.

SAN SIMÓN ALMOLONGAS ◆ Municipio de Oaxaca situado en el sur del estado, al noroeste de Miahuatlán. Superficie: 38.27 km². Habitantes: 3,021, de los cuales 588 forman la población económicamente activa.

San Simón de Guerrero ◆ Municipio del Estado de México situado en el sur de la entidad, al suroeste de Toluca y al sureste de Valle de Bravo. Superficie: 66.21 km². Habitantes: 4,504, de los cuales 794 forman la población económicamente activa. Hablan alguna lengua indígena cinco personas mayores de cinco años.

San Simón Zahuatlán ◆ Municipio de Oaxaca situado en el noroeste del estado, al oeste-noroeste de Huajuapan de León. Superficie: 35.72 km². Habitantes: 1,810, de los cuales 467 forman la población económicamente activa. Hablan mixteco 1,441 personas mayores de cinco años, de las cuales 370 son monolingües.

San Telmo ◆ Bahía de Michoacán y Colima, situada al oeste-suroeste de Coalcomán de Matamoros. Está limitada al norte por la Boca de Apiza, que es la desembocadura del río Coahuayana, y al sureste por la Punta Cabeza Negra. En ella sólo pueden penetrar barcos de poco calado.

San Vicente Coatlán ◆ Municipio de Oaxaca situado en el sur del estado, al noroeste de Miahuatlán. Superficie: 135.24 km². Habitantes: 3,587, de los cuales 751 forman la población económicamente activa. Hablan zapoteco 2,270 personas mayores de cinco años, de las cuales 570 no hablan español.

San Vicente y las Granadinas ◆ Estado del Caribe oriental. Está formado por las islas de Saint Vincent, Bequia, Mustique, Canouan, Mayrou y Union, así como un número de islotes cercanos. Superficie: 389 km². Habitantes: 113,000 (1998). El idioma oficial es el inglés y también se hablan hindi y *creole* (dialecto del inglés). Su capital es el puerto de Kingstown (15,908 habitantes en 1995). Otras ciudades importantes son Calliaqua (20,858 habitantes en 1995), Marriaqua (9,117 habitantes en 1995), Bridgetown (7,746 habitantes en 1995), Georgetown (7,511 habitantes en 1995) y Chateaubelair (6,217 habitantes en 1995). Un gobernador general, representante de la Corona de Inglaterra, gobierna junto con el primer ministro y una Asamblea General con seis senadores. *Historia*: se cree que las islas están habitadas desde el año 5000 a.n.e.; las poblaron los ciboney, un pueblo de cazadores-recolectores desplazado en los primeros años de n.e. por los arawaks, provenientes de la cuenca del Orinoco; éstos fueron a su vez desplazados por los caribes cerca del año 1000. Las islas fueron conquistadas, como otras del Caribe, por Inglaterra, que las empleó para establecer plantaciones azucareras, mantenidas por esclavos traídos de África hasta el siglo XIX (☛ *San Cristóbal y Nevis*). En los años ochenta, las islas obtuvieron su independencia del Reino Unido e ingresaron en la Commonwealth británica. En julio de 1990 se establecieron relaciones diplomáticas con México, que son manejadas de manera concurrente por la embajada en Trinidad y Tobago. En 1991, David Jack asumió el cargo de gobernador general. En 1995, James Fitz-Allen Mitchell tomó posesión como primer ministro.

San Vicente Lachixío ◆ Municipio de Oaxaca situado al suroeste de la capital de la entidad y al noroeste de Miahuatlán. Superficie: 93.13 km². Habitantes: 2,870, de los cuales 385 forman la población económicamente activa. Hablan alguna lengua indígena 2,292 personas mayores de cinco años (zapoteco 2,276); de ellas, no saben español 485.

San Vicente Nuñú ◆ Municipio de Oaxaca situado en el noroeste del estado, al sureste de Huajuapan de León y al noroeste de la capital de la entidad. Superficie: 100.79 km². Habitantes: 568, de los cuales 159 forman la población económicamente activa. Hablan alguna lengua indígena seis personas.

San Vicente Tancuayalab ◆ Municipio de San Luis Potosí situado en el oriente del estado, al sureste de Tamuín y al este de Ciudad Valles. Superficie: 425.7 km². Habitantes: 13,604, de los cuales 2,936 forman la población económicamente activa. Hablan alguna lengua indígena 2,498 personas mayores de cinco años (huasteco 2,365).

Sanahcat ◆ Municipio de Yucatán situado al sureste de Mérida y al sur de Motul. Superficie: 54.93 km². Habitantes: 1,482, de los cuales 391 forman la población económicamente activa. Hablan alguna lengua indígena 959 personas mayores de cinco años (maya 958).

Sanblancat, Ángel ◆ n. en España y m. en el DF (1885-1963). Escritor. Estudió abogacía. Como periodista fue uno de los fundadores de *Los Miserables*, en Barcelona, y director de *La Campana de Gracia*. Fue diputado a Cortes (1931) por el Partido Republicano Federal, del que fue cofundador, y magistrado en el Tribunal de Casación de Cataluña. Al término de la querra civil española se refugió en Francia (1939) y en 1942 llegó a México donde trabajó en el diario *El Nacional* y produjo gran parte de sus novelas. Autor de *Plumero salvaje*, *Cristo atado a la columna*, *Barro en las alas*, *Con el corazón extasiado*, *Caravana nazarena*, *Hubo una Francia*, *La ascensión de María Magdalena* y *La casa pálida*.

Sanborn, Frank ◆ n. en EUA y m. en el DF (1870-1956). Empresario radicado en México desde 1903. Con su hermano Walter Sanborn fundó la Sanborn's American Pharmacy, que se convertiría en una importante cadena de tiendas con restaurante anexo (☛ *cafeterías*). En 1946 se naturalizó mexicano y en ese año vendió la compañía a un grupo empresarial mexicano.

Sánchez, Aarón ◆ n. en el DF (1948). Fotógrafo de prensa. Se inició en 1967 en *Excélsior*. Es fundador (1977) y jefe de fotografía de *unomásuno*.

Sánchez, Carlos Cuauhtémoc ◆ n. en el DF (1964). Ingeniero industrial por el Instituto Tecnológico de Tlalnepantla (1984), especializado en alta dirección de empresas. Tras una breve incursión en la literatura con el libro de cuentos *Sheccid* (1984, Premio Nacional de la Juventud 1985), se ha dedicado a dar conferencias y escribir libros de "superación personal y familiar" en los que condena las relaciones sexuales extramaritales y promueve la preser-

Glifo de San Simón de Guerrero

Cuco Sánchez

vación de valores que llama "tradicionales". Fundador del Instituto para el Desarrollo de Niños con Alto Potencial y director del Instituto de Líderes Integrales. Autor de *Un grito desesperado* (1992), *Juventud en éxtasis* (1993), *La última oportunidad* (1994), *Volar sobre el pantano* (1995), *La fuerza de Sheccid* (1996), *Juventud en éxtasis 2* (1997), *Leyes eternas* (1998) y *Dirigentes del mundo futuro* (1999). Ha sido nombrado "El escritor del año" por el Círculo Literario Emma Godoy y obtenido el Premio Toastmaster a la expresión oral.

SÁNCHEZ, CUCO ◆ n. en Altamira, Tams. (1921). Compositor y cantante de música ranchera. Estrenó su primera pieza a los 13 años de edad. En 1940 fue contratado como artista exclusivo por la estación de radio XEW y le decían *El benjamín de los compositores*. Ha interpretado diversos papeles en películas y programas de televisión. Autor de más de 500 canciones (traducidas algunas a 12 idiomas), entre ellas *Mi chata* (1936), *Guitarras lloren guitarras, Grítenme piedras del campo, Que me lleve el diablo, Derecho a la vida, El charro chaparro, Anoche estuve llorando, No soy monedita de oro, Buenas noches, mi amor, Con la misma moneda, La cama de piedra, ¡Qué manera de perder!, Hasta luego, Fallaste, corazón, Bolero indio, Anillo de compromiso, Oígame, compadre, Yo también soy mexicano* y *¡Qué rechulo es querer!* Sus canciones se han empleado en filmes europeos. Ha compuesto música para las películas *Yo maté a Rosita Alvírez, Por qué peca esa mujer, Para que la cuña apriete, La vuelta del Charro Negro, Yo maté a Juan Charrasqueado, Guadalajara pues'n, El gallo giro* y *Los tres alegres compadres*, en algunas de las cuales actuó.

Retrato y firma de Delfín Sánchez

SÁNCHEZ, DELFÍN ◆ n. en España y m. ¿en la ciudad de México? (1828-1898). Empresario. Vivió en Cuba (1856-64), donde se dedicó al comercio. En 1864 se instaló en México, construyó los ferrocarriles Interoceánico, de Tehuantepec y el de Salina Cruz a Coatzacoalcos y editó el periódico *El Siglo* XIX. Fue yerno de Benito Juárez.

SÁNCHEZ, FRANCISCO ◆ n. en Ciudad Acuña, Coah. (1939). Guionista y crítico de cine. Su segundo apellido es Aguilar. Ha colaborado en *Revista Mexicana de Cultura* de *El Nacional* (1970-72) y en *Esto* (1972-80). Guionista desde 1973 con el largometraje *Los que viven donde sopla el viento suave* (premio a la mejor película en el Festival Internacional de Cine Documental de Bilbao 1974) y ha escrito libretos de más de 50 películas. Por sus guiones ha recibido el premio Heraldo 1977 (por *Las noches de Paloma*), premio Diosa de Plata por *Amor libre* (1978), Premio Ariel por *El tonto que hacía milagros* (1982) y premio Coral de La Habana por *Pueblo de Madera* (1991). Autor de *Todo Buñuel* (1978), *Hermosillo, pasión por la libertad* (1989), *Crónica antisolemne del cine mexicano* (1989), *La comezón del séptimo arte* (1998) y *Océano de películas* (1999). Prepara *Siglo Buñuel*. En el género de ficción ha escrito *Postales de los años de esplendor* (1994), *Tierra que fue mar* (1996), *Manuel Acuña protagonista* (1999). Premio Comala 1988 (por *La mujerte*). Escribió los guiones de las telenovelas *Teresa* (1989) y *Ramona* (1999).

SÁNCHEZ, GERTRUDIS G. ◆ n. en Saltillo, Coah., y m. en Huetamo, Mich. (1882-1915). Dejó los estudios normalistas para dedicarse a las actividades agrícolas, que en 1911 abandonó para incorporarse a la revolución, cooptado por los hermanos Francisco y Emilio Madero. Operó en el sur de Coahuila al lado de Andrés Vela, Andrés Saucedo, Luis y Eulalio Gutiérrez. En 1912 fue comisionado para combatir a Emiliano Zapata en Morelos y, más tarde, peleó cerca de Coyuca de Catalán contra los rebeldes salgadistas; combatió al huertismo en Michoacán junto con José Rentería Luviano, Cecilio García, Joaquín Amaro y otros caudillos locales. Fue villista hasta 1914, cuando se incorporó al carrancismo. Gobernador de Michoacán (1914-15), con el grado autoconferido de general de división. Fue herido cerca de Huetamo y capturado y fusilado por tropas de Alejo Mastache.

SÁNCHEZ, GRACIANO ◆ n. en San Luis Potosí, SLP, y m. en el DF (¿1890?-1957). Participó en la fundación de varias ligas agrarias en diversos estados de la República. Fue varias veces diputado local y federal, director fundador de la Confederación Campesina Mexicana (1933-38), que apoyó la campaña presidencial de Lázaro Cárdenas y que en 1938 se transformó en Confederación Nacional Campesina, dirigida por él. Fue jefe del Departamento de Asuntos Indígenas. Miembro del grupo Vieja Guardia Agrarista.

SÁNCHEZ, GUADALUPE ◆ n. en Teocelo y m. en Veracruz, Ver. (1890-?). En 1910 se incorporó a la insurrección maderista y tres años después al constitucionalismo. Luchó en la División de Oriente, a las órdenes de Cándido Aguilar. En 1914 fue delegado a la Convención de Aguascalientes, en representación de Antonio Portas. En las zonas del Cofre de Perote y del Pico de Orizaba combatió a Higinio Aguilar, Pedro Gabay y Constantino Galán (1914-15). Luchó contra el villismo en las fuerzas de Álvaro Obregón, con las que participó en las batallas de Celaya y Trinidad. Fue jefe de operaciones militares en Veracruz (1918) y en 1920, afiliado al aguaprietismo, hostilizó a la escolta de Venustiano Carranza, hasta derrotar a Francisco Murguía en la acción de Algibes. Delahuertista en 1923, el 8 de diciembre tomó Jalapa. Tras la derrota de ese movimiento vivió exiliado durante varios años.

SÁNCHEZ, HUGO ◆ n. en el DF (1958).

Su segundo apellido es Márquez. Futbolista. Le han llamado el *Niño de Oro* y *Hugol*. Hijo del también futbolista Héctor Sánchez Velázquez. Cirujano dentista por la UNAM (1981). Jugó en la selección nacional amateur, con la que ganó en el Torneo Mundial Juvenil de Cannes (1975) y participó en los Juegos Panamericanos (medalla de oro, 1975) y los Juegos Olímpicos de Montreal (1976). Se inició profesionalmente en 1976 en el equipo Universidad, en el que permaneció hasta 1981. Campeón de goleo con Universidad (1978-79), dos veces campeón de Liga (1976-77 y 1980-81), campeón de la Copa Interamericana (1980-81) y campeón de la Copa Concacaf (1980-81). Obtuvo dos premios Citlalli al mejor extremo (1977) y al mejor jugador (1978). Reforzó en dos ocasiones al San Diego Soccers (1979 y 1980). Como seleccionado nacional (en el periodo 1977-94) participó en los campeonatos mundiales de 1978, 1986 y 1994, en Argentina, México y Estados Unidos, y fue subcampeón en la Copa América (1993). Fue contratado por el club español Atlético de Madrid (1981-85) con el que ganó la Copa del Rey. Pasó al Real Madrid (1985-92), equipo con el que obtuvo cinco veces el campeonato ibérico, dos veces la Copa del Rey, dos Supercopas y ganó varios torneos continentales (como la Copa UEFA 1985-86). Participó en el partido de estrellas mundiales de la UNICEF contra el equipo Barcelona, entre otros. Ganó en cinco ocasiones el trofeo Pichichi, como campeón individual de goleo de la liga española, una con el Atlético y cuatro con el Real Madrid (1984-85, 1985-86, 1986-87, 1987-88 y 1989-90), y también recibió el Botín de Oro al mejor goleador de Europa (1989-90). En 1992 y 1993 jugó en el América y fue campeón de la Copa Concacaf 1993-94). Alineó también con Rayo Vallecano (1993-94), Atlante (1994-95), Linz (1995-96), Dallas Burn (1996) y Atlético Celaya (1997). Se retiró en 1997. Anotó 377 goles en campeonatos de Liga y 48 con la selección nacional. Es uno de los 25 mejores goleadores en la historia mundial del futbol. Es cronista deportivo de radio y televisión.

SÁNCHEZ, JOSÉ ◆ m. en el DF (?-1996). Impresor. Trabajó como docente durante 60 años en el Taller de la Gráfica Popular, del cual fue fundador. Imprimió obras de varias generaciones de miembros del taller, como Zalce, O'Higgins, Anguiano, Fany Rabel, Méndez, Arenal, Castro, Pacheco, Beltrán, Jean Charlot, Isidoro Ocampo, Jesús Escobedo, Everardo Ramírez, Andrea Gómez, Mariana Yampolsky, Mexiac, Castruita, Olivares, Salvador Romero, Luna, Siqueiros, Orozco, Tamayo, Leonora Carrington, Montenegro, Carlos Mérida, Fernández Ledesma y muchos otros artistas. Colaboró con Leopoldo Méndez en los inicios de la Editorial de la Plástica Mexicana (creada por Adolfo López Mateos). Imprimió *Mujeres de la revolución mexicana* y otros libros. A su muerte era el técnico mexicano más notable de la litografía, la calcografía y la xilografía.

SÁNCHEZ, LOURDES ◆ n. en Culiacán, Sin. (1950). Estudió en la Escuela Nacional de Maestros. Cursó la licenciatura en letras hispánicas en la UNAM, donde ha sido profesora de análisis retórico. Asistió a los talleres de poesía de Otto-Raúl González y Juan Bañuelos. Fue coordinadora de un programa cultural en zonas agropecuarias del DF, para el que dirigió el periódico mural *La Comunidad*, que recibió una mención de la FAO, y forma parte de la dirección colectiva de la editorial Factor (1985-), de la que es cofundadora. Coautora del poemario *Cinco botellas al mar* (1985). Autora de poesía: *La piel de las palabras* (1985), *Guardamar* (1987), *Juglarías* (1990), *Los ciegos paraísos* (1990), *La comparsa* (1991), *Levedades* (1995) y *Puertas terráqueas* (1998); ensayo: *Ley eterna en el cantar campesino del poeta Raúl Cervantes Ahumada* (1993), *La actitud literaria como perfil del habla sinaloense* (1994) y *El yo poético de las poetas mexicanas de 1900 a 1949* (1995); y cuento: *Inclínense, inclínense* (1995). Ha aparecido en antologías como *Poesía sinaloense contemporánea* (1993), *Sinaloa, lengua de tierra* (1995) y *Seeing the World Throught Women's Eyes* (Estados Unidos, 1996). En 1986 obtuvo Accésit Especial en el Concurso Nacional de Poesía de Granada, España. Encargada de la Comisión de Cultura y Educación del Movimiento Mexicano por la Paz y el Desarrollo.

FOTO: DANTE BUCIO

Hugo Sánchez

SÁNCHEZ, *LUPE* ◆ n. en San Felipe del Progreso, Edo. de Méx., y m. en el DF (1910-1990). Su nombre era José Guadalupe Sánchez Mejía. Fue boxeador profesional (1930-32) y auxiliar del entrenador Manuel el *Tío* Canseco (1933-41). Obtuvo licencia para manejar púgiles en 1942. Dirigió a 14 campeones nacionales y tres mundiales. Al morir era presidente de la Unión de Mánagers.

SÁNCHEZ, MARIANO ◆ n. en Tepoztlán y m. en Los Laureles, Mor. (?-1916). En 1911 se unió a la revolución zapatista a las órdenes de Amador Salazar. Participó en las tomas de Tepoztlán y Yautepec. Se mantuvo en el zapatismo, en lucha contra Madero, Huerta y Carranza. Murió a consecuencia de las heridas que recibió en el combate de Estación Cascada.

SÁNCHEZ, MATILDE ◆ ☛ *Torcacita, La.*

SÁNCHEZ, PEDRO ◆ n. en España y m. en la ciudad de México (1526-1609). Jesuita. Doctor por la Universidad de Alcalá, de la que fue profesor. Fue el primer provincial de la Compañía de Jesús en la Nueva España (1571-79), adonde llegó por orden de Francisco de Borja al frente de un grupo de 15 sacerdotes. Fundó el Colegio Máximo y los de Pátzcuaro, Oaxaca, Puebla y Valladolid (1572-80). Autor de *Libro del reino de Dios y del camino por do se alcanza* (Madrid, 1594).

Pedro Sánchez

SÁNCHEZ, PEDRO CELESTINO ◆ n. en San Nicolás Obispo, Dgo., y m. en el DF (1871-1956). Geógrafo e ingeniero en minas por la Escuela Nacional de Ingenieros. Fue profesor en el Colegio

Salvador Sánchez

Militar y en la Universidad Nacional; trabajó en el Instituto Geológico, en el Catastro y en la Comisión Geodésica, que dirigió. En 1915 organizó con Pastor Rouaix la Dirección de Estudios Geográficos y Climatológicos, fue director del Instituto Panamericano de Geografía e Historia (1930- 56), fundó la biblioteca José Toribio Medina y editó la *Revista de Historia de América* y el *Boletín Bibliográfico de Antropología Americana*. Autor de *Geografía física con aplicación a la República Mexicana* (1927), *Historia de la geodesia en México* (1928), *Estudio hidrológico de la República Mexicana* (1928), *Estudio orogénico de la República Mexicana* (1929), *Volcanismo* (1932), *Métodos geofísicos de prospección* (1933), *Importancia geográfica del Eje Volcánico* (1935), *La evolución de la geografía* (1935), *Enseñanzas fundamentales de la geografía humana* (1939), *Temblores de tierra o sismos y volcanes* (1939), *Figura y dimensiones de la Tierra* (1939) y *La geodesia a través de la historia y la geodesia en México* (1945).

SÁNCHEZ, PRISCILIANO ♦ n. en Ahuacatlán, en el actual Nayarit, y m. en Guadalajara, Jal. (1783-1826). Bachiller en derecho (1810). Fue comerciante en Compostela, donde más adelante se desempeñó como alcalde, regidor, síndico y director de anexos. Diputado al primer Congreso Nacional (1822), al Congreso General Constituyente (1823-24) y al Congreso Constituyente de Jalisco (1824). Se distinguió como federalista. En 1825 fue elegido primer gobernador constitucional de Jalisco. En este cargo reorganizó la división política del estado, reestructuró la enseñanza, fomentó el uso de cementerios seculares e impulsó la beneficencia pública. Autor de *Pacto federal de Anáhuac* (1823).

SÁNCHEZ, RAFAEL PLATÓN ♦ n. en Capadero, actual Platón Sánchez, Ver., y m. en Lobos, NL (1835-1867). Estudió en el Colegio Militar, de donde egresó como subteniente de artillería (1858). Combatió a la intervención francesa y el imperio, participó en la batalla del 5 de mayo y en el sitio de Puebla. Fue capturado por los invasores pero pudo escapar. Se unió en San Luis Potosí a la comitiva de Benito Juárez, a quien acompañó en su retirada hacia el norte. Combatió la intervención en Chihuahua, Saltillo, Monterrey, Matamoros y Temosáchic, donde volvió a ser aprehendido. Liberado en 1865, se reincorporó a la lucha. Alcanzó el grado de coronel en las fuerzas republicanas. En 1867 presidió el consejo de guerra que condenó a muerte a Maximiliano, Miramón y Mejía. En 1867 fue asesinado por unos soldados del ex regimiento de Carlota, que habían huido de Querétaro.

SÁNCHEZ, SALVADOR ♦ n. en Tehuacán, Pue. (1944). Actor de teatro, cine y televisión egresado del INBA. Comenzó su carrera teatral en los años sesenta con la obra *El señor Puntilla y su sirviente Matti*, de Bertolt Brecht. Ha actuado, entre otras, en las cintas *Canoa*, *Actas de Marusia* y *El apando*. Ha participado en las telenovelas *El pecado de Oyuki*, *La fuerza del amor* y *Senda de gloria* (en la que hizo el papel de Adolfo de la Huerta).

SÁNCHEZ, SALVADOR ♦ n. y m. en Santiago Tianguistenco, Edo. de Méx. (1958-1982). Boxeador amateur de peso gallo (1973). Ganó todas sus peleas por nocaut. Se inició profesionalmente en 1975 en la categoría de peso pluma, en la que ganó el campeonato americano (1978) y el del Consejo Mundial de Boxeo, al derrotar en Arizona a Danny *Coloradito* López (1980). Murió en un accidente automovilístico.

SÁNCHEZ, TIMOTEO ♦ n. en Santa Cruz, hoy Joaquín Caamaño, y m. en Tlacualpican, Mor. (?-1967). Se unió en 1911 a la revolución en el Ejército Libertador del Sur, en el que alcanzó el generalato. Con mando de tropas operó durante varios años en la zona de Yautepec y en los alrededores de Tepoztlán. En 1919 formó parte de la escolta de Emiliano Zapata que fue emboscada en Chinameca. Después del asesinato del jefe suriano, firmó el manifiesto de compromiso de continuación de la lucha armada. En 1920, al adherirse Genovevo de la O al Plan de Agua Prieta, se retiró a la vida privada.

SÁNCHEZ DE AGUILAR, PEDRO ♦ n. en Valladolid, Yuc., y m. en Perú (1555-?). Sacerdote. Doctor en derecho canónico (1602). Fue cura de Chancenote, Colotmul, Valladolid y del sagrario de la catedral de Mérida. Procurador de la diócesis durante el litigio entre ésta y los franciscanos por la posesión de varios curatos (1601-02, en Madrid). Autor de *Catecismo de doctrina cristiana*, *Memoria de los primeros conquistadores* (1598) y *De idolorum cultores* (1634).

SÁNCHEZ ANAYA, ALFONSO ABRAHAM ♦ n. en Apizaco, Tlax. (1941). Médico veterinario zootecnista por la UNAM, diplomado en extensionismo y sociología rural (UACH) y en control de gestión de empresas públicas (CIDE). Ingresó al PRI en 1958, en donde fue director del CEPES-Tlaxcala y presidente del Comité Directivo Estatal en la misma entidad (1988-89) y subsecretario de Acción Ganadera del CEN de la CNC. Ha sido director de Agricultura y Ganadería (1975), jefe del Programa Ganadero (1975-79) secretario de Desarrollo y Fomento Económico (1985) y secretario de Finanzas del gobierno estatal de Tlaxcala (1991-94); coordinador del Coplade en la misma entidad (1987-88), director de Ganadería de la Comisión Nacional para el Desarrollo Pecuario (1989-91); representante general en Tlaxcala (1979-81), subdirector de Producción de la Dirección General de Avicultura y Especies Menores (1981), secretario particular del subse-

FOTO: IMAGEN LATINA
Alfonso Abraham Sánchez Anaya

cretario de Ganadería (1981-82), subdirector general de Ganadería (1983-84), jefe de la unidad de seguimiento de programas en la subsecretaría de Organización Agraria (1984) y director general de Fomento Ganadero (1984-85) de la SARH. Fue presidente del Patronato de la Feria de Tlaxcala (1975, 1977, 1990) y diputado federal (1994-97). En 1998 renunció al PRI y como candidato de una coalición formada por el PRD, PT, PVEM y PCD, fue elegido gobernador del estado de Tlaxcala para el periodo 1998-2004. Promotor y miembro fundador de la Asociación Nacional de Gobernadores (1999). Fue director de la división agropecuaria de laboratorios Sintex. Miembro de la Asociación Mexicana de Especialistas en Cerdos.

Sánchez de Armas, Miguel Ángel ◆ n. en el DF (1949). Periodista. Hizo estudios de lengua y literatura hispánicas en la UNAM. Profesor de la UANL (1977-81) y de la UIA. Ha sido reportero de *Novedades* (1968-70), *El Día* (1971-72), *El Sol de México* (1972) y Notimex (1973). En Conacyt fue reportero (1974) y jefe de Prensa (1975-76). Gerente de Difusión y Relaciones Públicas del Grupo Fundidora de Monterrey (1977-81), jefe de Prensa del ININ (1981), coordinador técnico de la subdirección de información del IEPES (1982), subdirector de Análisis de la Dirección General de Comunicación Social de la SPP (1984), editor asociado de Ediciones Océano (1985), director de difusión en la Dirección General de Comunicación Social de la Presidencia (1986-1992), subdirector general de la Comisión Nacional de los Libros de Texto Gratuitos (1994-1995), presidente de PMC Consultores (1995-) y director general de Radiotelevisión de Veracruz (TV-MAS). Comentarista del programa *Detrás de*, del Canal 13 de televisión (1984-85), conductor de *Perfiles de la noticia* (1995) y director editorial del programa *Enfoque* de Radio Mil (1997-). Vicepresidente y presidente de la Fundación Manuel Buendía (1984-), en la que creó la *Revista Mexicana de Comunicación* (1988) y el *Mexican Journal of Communication*. Codirector de *Revista Iberoamericana de derecho de la información*. Coautor de *Los días de Manuel Buendía* y *De reporteros* (1996). Coordinó *Apuntes para una historia de la televisión mexicana* (2 t, 1998-99), *Comunicación y globalidad* (1998). Autor de *Estado de gracia, conversaciones con Edmundo Valadés* (1997).

Sánchez Azcona, Jorge ◆ n. en el DF (1941). Licenciado en derecho (1962) y doctor en ciencia política por la UNAM. Tomó cursos de sociología en la Universidad de California en Berkeley, donde fue investigador residente (1966). Ha sido profesor y director del Centro de Investigaciones y Servicios Educativos de la UNAM y del Instituto Técnico y Cultural. Director de la Coordinación de Apoyo y Servicios Educativos de la UNAM. Autor de *Introducción a la sociología de Max Weber* (1965, con prólogo de Luis Recaséns Siches; quinta edición, 1986), *Derecho, poder y marxismo* (1970), *Familia y sociedad* (1974), *Normatividad social. Ensayo de sociología jurídica* (1976), *Lectura de sociología y ciencia política* (1976), *Hacia dónde va la democracia* (1982) y *Reflexiones sobre el poder* (1990).

Sánchez Azcona, Juan ◆ n. en Campeche, Camp., y m. en Orizaba, Ver. (1843-1894). Alumno fundador del Instituto de Abogados de Campeche. Ahí se graduó y luego fue profesor. Ministro de México en Argentina, Brasil, Italia y Guatemala. Ocupó cargos en la magistratura durante los gobiernos de Benito Juárez y Porfirio Díaz. Era senador al morir.

Sánchez Azcona, Juan ◆ n. y m. en el DF (1876-1938). Hijo del anterior. Estudió en el Real Gymnasium de Stuttgart y en las universidades de Heidelberg y de París (1892), donde fue condiscípulo de Francisco I. Madero. Escribió en publicaciones periódicas y dirigió *El Diario, El Diario de la Tarde* y *México Nuevo* (1908). Diputado federal (1904-08). Fue directivo de la convención que hizo a Madero candidato presidencial (1910). Fue uno de los redactores del Plan de San Luis (☛) y agente confidencial de la revolución en Washington. En Chihuahua se unió a la lucha armada. Secretario particular del presidente Madero, diputado federal (1911-13), fundador y director de *Nueva Era*. Tras el cuartelazo huertista se exilió en Cuba y volvió a incorporarse al constitucionalismo. Fue secretario general de Gobierno en Sonora. Representante de la revolución constitucionalista en Europa (1914), regresó a México en 1916 para estudiar el anteproyecto de la Constitución. Ministro en España, Francia, Bélgica, Portugal e Italia (1916). Diputado federal (1917), secretario de Relaciones Exteriores (del 1 al 15 de junio de 1920) en el gabinete de Adolfo de la Huerta, embajador extraordinario en misión especial al frente de la legación en Madrid (1920) y consultor de la SRE (1921-24). En 1922 volvió a publicar *México Nuevo* y en 1923 *El Diario*. Fue colaborador de *El Universal* (1925) y vicepresidente del Partido Nacional Antirreeleccionista, que hizo candidato a la presidencia a Arnulfo R. Gómez; tras la derrota de éste se exilió en La Habana (1927-30), donde colaboró en *El País* y *El Heraldo de Cuba*. En 1932 inició la cuarta época de *México Nuevo*. Fue patrono secretario de la Fundación Rafael Dondé (1935-38).

Sánchez Baquero, Juan ◆ n. en España y m. en Oaxaca, Oax. (1548-1619). Ingresó en 1567 en la Compañía de Jesús y llegó a la Nueva España en 1574. Fue misionero en Guadalajara y Zacatecas y rector de varios colegios de su orden, entre ellos los de Valladolid y Oaxaca, que él fundó. En 1607 intervino en los proyectos de desagüe de la ciudad de México, por encargo del virrey Luis de Velasco, hijo. Fue el primero en ejecutar un mapa de las lagunas del valle de México. Autor de *Relación breve del principio y progreso de la provincia de la Nueva España de la Compañía de Jesús* y *La vida del padre Francisco Bazán de la Compañía de Jesús*.

Sánchez Barbudo, Antonio ◆ n. en España (1910). Periodista y escritor. Trabajó para el Ministerio de Instrucción Pública de la República Es-

Miguel Ángel Sánchez de Armas

Jorge Sánchez Azcona

Juan Sánchez Azcona

pañola (1931-36); fue colaborador de *El Sol* de Madrid, fundador de *Hoja Literaria* y cofundador de *Hora de España*. Llegó a México en 1939 como refugiado político. Escribió en *Romance*, *El Hijo Pródigo*, y *Taller*. Pasó a Estados Unidos, donde ejerció la docencia en las universidades de Texas (1945) y de Wisconsin. Autor de *Entre dos fuegos* (1938), *Sueños de grandeza* (1945), *Una pregunta sobre España* (1945), *Estudios sobre Galdós, Unamuno y Machado* (1959), *La segunda época de Juan Ramón Jiménez* (1962), *Cincuenta poemas comentados* (1963), *Los poemas de Antonio Machado* y *El sentimiento y la expresión*. Premio Nacional de Literatura de España (1938), compartido con Herrera Petere.

Carlos Sánchez Cárdenas

SÁNCHEZ DE LA BARQUERA, JUAN WENCESLAO ◆ ☛ *Barquera o Sánchez de la Barquera, Juan María Wenceslao.*

SÁNCHEZ BENÍTEZ, JOSÉ TRINIDAD ◆ n. en Ixtlahuacán, Jal. (1892-?). Abogado. Destacó en el desempeño en comisiones del ramo militar. Fue procurador de Justicia del Distrito y Territorios Federales (1932-34), magistrado de la octava sala del Tribunal Superior de Justicia del Distrito y Terrirorios Federales (1934-41), Juez de la cuarta corte penal del DF (1941-44), abogado de la oficina jurídica de la Dirección Feneral de Servicios Legales del DDF (1950-51).

Leopoldo Sánchez Celis

SÁNCHEZ CAMACHO, EDUARDO ◆ n. en Hermosillo, Son., y m. en Ciudad Victoria, Tams. (1838-1920). Sacerdote ordenado en 1862, doctorado en cánones por la Universidad Pontificia de Guadalajara. Fue el segundo obispo de Tamaulipas (1880-96) y celebró tres sínodos diocesanos (1882, 1883 y 1885) en los que planteó la necesidad de adaptarse a las Leyes de Reforma, lo que no fue aprobado por El Vaticano. Inscrito en la tradición antiaparicionista, en 1887 se opuso a la coronación de la Virgen de Guadalupe y publicó la carta de Joaquín García Icazbalceta en la que se refuta la autenticidad de la imagen del Tepeyac. En 1896 fue removido de su cargo.

SÁNCHEZ CÁRDENAS, CARLOS ◆ n. en Monclova, Coah., y m. en Crimea, URSS (1913-1982). Huérfano de padre a los tres años, emigró con su familia a la ciudad de México. Estudió en la Escuela Nacional Preparatoria y posteriormente hizo estudios de arquitectura y economía en la Universidad Nacional. En los primeros años de la década de los treinta formó parte de los grupos estudiantiles que buscaban la autonomía universitaria. Ingresó a las Juventudes Comunistas del PCM y comenzó a escribir artículos políticos en *El Machete* y *La Voz de México*, de los que fue director. En 1945 fue expulsado, por desacuerdos ideológicos, del PCM. En 1950 participó en la fundación del Partido Obrero Campesino Mexicano (☛), para el que dirigió el periódico *Noviembre*. Fue detenido por el delito de disolución social en 1951 y preso en Lecumberri, donde permaneció hasta 1953. Durante ese tiempo preparó su propia defensa, que publicó luego en su libro *Disolución social y seguridad nacional*, empleado como libro de texto en la Escuela Superior de Derecho. Tras la disolución del POCM en 1963, pasó con otros miembros de ese partido al PPS, por el que fue diputado federal, pero nuevas diferencias ideológicas llevaron a su expulsión, por lo que concluyó su periodo como diputado independiente. En 1971 participó en la fundación del Movimiento de Acción y Unidad Socialista (☛) y, en 1981, en la del Partido Socialista Unificado de México (☛), por el que fue de nuevo diputado hasta su muerte. En el Congreso de la Unión logró la abolición del delito de disolución social y luchó, constantemente, en favor del igualitarismo y contra la influencia de los Estados Unidos en México, que calificaba de "invasión silenciosa". Discursos e intervenciones suyos en la Cámara de Diputados se recogieron en el libro *Contra la corriente*. Fue colaborador de *El Universal*.

SÁNCHEZ CELIS, LEOPOLDO ◆ n. en Cosalá, Sin., y m. en Cuernavaca (1916-1989). Hizo estudios en la Universidad Obrera de México. Participó en la Confederación de Jóvenes Mexicanos. Fue miembro del Partido de la Revolución Mexicana y delegado del CEN en varios estados. Fue uno de los organizadores de la federación de Organizaciones Populares de Sinaloa (1942), con la cual apoyó las campañas presidenciales de Adolfo López Mateos y Adolfo Ruiz Cortines. Formó parte de la delegación mexicana al primer Congreso Mundial de la Juventud celebrado en Londres y a los congresos mundiales obreros de París y Praga. Cofundador del PRI, del que fue presidente del Comité Directivo Estatal en Sinaloa (1955) y secretario de Acción Política del CEN (1959). Diputado local en Sinaloa (1950), diputado federal (1955-58), senador de la República (1958-63) y gobernador constitucional de Sinaloa (1963-68). En este cargo impulsó las obras públicas, afectó latifundios (como El Dorado, de la Casa Redo Tetemache, perteneciente a la Sociedad Mercantil de Crédito Industrial), apoyó la formación de la Orquesta Sinfónica del Noroeste, promovió los trabajos exploratorios de ruinas arqueológicas de los indios guasaves o guasavos, se concedió la autonomía a la Universidad del estado, se instituyó el Premio Mazatlán de Literatura y promulgó una Ley de Bebidas Alcohólicas que por primera vez incluía a la cerveza en ese rubro, lo que motivó un prolongado litigio con las empresas del ramo que llegó a la Suprema Corte. Promovió la creación de la Unión de Ejidos Colectivos en el Valle de Culiacancito y el Valle del Carrizo.

SÁNCHEZ CONDOY DE GÓMEZ, PILAR ◆ n. en España (1925). Vino en 1939 y obtuvo la nacionalidad mexicana. Licenciada en economía por el Rockford College de Illinois y maestra en economía por el Mexico City College. Economista del Departamento de Estudios Económicos del Banco Nacional de Comercio Exterior (1948-52), colaboradora del despacho Economistas Asociados, fundadora y directora de la librería infantil Pigom (1968), representante y colaboradora del *Book Bird* y miembro activo del International Board of Books for Young Children.

Sánchez Cordero Dávila de García Villegas, Olga María del Carmen ◆ n. en el DF (1947). Licenciada en derecho por la UNAM. Cursó el posgrado en el University College of Swansea. Ha sido secretaria de Asuntos Escolares de la Facultad de Derecho de la UNAM (1976-79) y directora del Seminario de Sociología General y Jurídica de la Facultad de Derecho (1980-84). Fue la primera notaria en la historia del DF (1984). Ha impartido cátedra en diversas universidades. Magistrada numeraria de la Sexta Sala Civil del Tribunal Superior de Justicia (1993-93), es ministra de la Suprema Corte de Justicia de la Nación (1998-). Autora de *The Problem of Slums in Mexico City (Los problemas de los pobres en la ciudad de México)*, así como varios artículos en publicaciones especializadas en derecho; coautora de *Derecho notarial* (34 t., 1991). Pertenece a varias asociaciones, como la Internacional de Sociología, la Mexicana de Sociología, el Consejo de Profesores de Derecho Civil, el Colegio de Profesores de la Facultad de Derecho, la Barra Mexicana de Derecho Notarial, la Federación Mexicana de Mujeres Universitarias, entre otras.

Sánchez Flores, Ramón ◆ n. en Puebla, Pue. (1938). Licenciado en letras españolas por la UNAM (1956) y maestro en historia por la Universidad de California en Berkeley (1967). Fue investigador de tiempo completo en la Subsecretaría de Asuntos Culturales de la SEP, en el Archivo Histórico de Hacienda y en el Instituto Histórico del Petróleo, así como investigador y profesor huésped en varias universidades del país. Colaborador del suplemento cultural de *Novedades* (1959-62), *Revista Mexicana de Cultura* de *El Nacional* (1967-68), *El Heraldo* (1967), *Ovaciones* (1969-86) y *La opinión* (1978-81). Autor de *Historia de la tecnología y de la invención en México* (1980), *Tecnología minera en México S.S. XVI-XVIII*, *Tecnología de la acuñación en la Nueva España S.S. XVI-XVIII*, *Arqueología industrial en el valle de Atlixco*, *Historia de la comunicación esquemática en México*, *Escudo de armas de la ciudad de Puebla, relación histórica* (1981), *Zacapoaxtla, república de indios y villa de españoles* (1983-84), *José María Lafragua* (1985, premio del gobierno del estado de Puebla) y *Puebla de los rebeldes, movimiento de insurgencia 1808-1821*.

Sánchez Fogarty, Federico ◆ n. y m. en el DF (1901-1976). Fue jefe de relaciones públicas del grupo cementero Tolteca, presidente de la Cámara Nacional del Cemento, consejero de la Confederación de Cámaras Industriales, fundador y presidente de Publicidad Continental, de la Asociación Nacional de la Publicidad, de la Asociación Mexicana de Relaciones Públicas y de la Federación Interamericana de Asociaciones de Relaciones Públicas.

Sánchez Fuentes, Braulio ◆ n. en la ciudad de México (1922). Sacerdote ordenado en 1950. Ha sido superior de los colegios salesianos de Zamora, San Luis Potosí, Guadalajara, México, Tlahuiltoltepec y Ayutla, administrador apostólico de la Prelatura de Mixes (1966), obispo titular de Acque Nuove di Proconsolare y obispo prelado de Mixes (1970-).

Sánchez Gavito, Vicente ◆ n. y m. en el DF (1910-1977). Licenciado por la Escuela Libre de Derecho (1936). Fue consejero y abogado auxiliar de la Agencia General de Reclamaciones entre Estados Unidos y México, de la Secretaría de Relaciones Exteriores (1936-38) y abogado del Departamento Diplomático (1941). Participó en la firma del convenio sobre reclamaciones entre ambos países. Consejero jurídico (1943) y encargado de negocios en Washington en ausencia del embajador Antonio Espinosa de los Monteros (1945-47); representante de México en la Conferencia Interamericana para el Mantenimiento de la Paz (Río de Janeiro, 1947), director general del Servicio Diplomático (1948), enviado extraordinario y ministro plenipotenciario en Washington (1951), miembro de los tribunales de arbitraje de la ONU sobre Libia y Eritrea (1951-56), encargado de negocios *ad interim* en Washington (1958-59) y presidente del consejo de la OEA (1959 y 60). En 1963 colaboró con la Comisión Internacional de Límites y Aguas en El Paso, Texas. Fue embajador en Brasil, Gran Bretaña e Islandia.

Sánchez Gochicoa, Antonio ◆ n. en el DF (1950). Licenciado en economía por el ITAM (1974) y maestro en la misma especialidad por la Universidad de Cambridge (1977). Profesor (1978-83) y jefe de servicios académicos del ITAM (1974-75). Ha sido analista de la Secretaría del Patrimonio Nacional (1973-74), jefe de departamento en la Secretaría de Hacienda (1978-79), subdirector (1979-82) y director de área del INEGI (1983-85), coordinador de asesores de la Subsecretaría de Planeación y Control Presupuestal de la Secretaría de Programación y Presupuesto (1985-88) y oficial mayor de la Secretaría de Hacienda (1988-94). Diputado Federal (1994-97). Secretario de Desarrollo y Vivienda en Sedesol (1997-98). Director General Adjunto de BANOBRAS (1998-).

Sánchez González, Agustín ◆ n. en el DF (1956). Escritor. Licenciado y pasante de maestría en historia por la UNAM. Investigador del Cenidiap del INBA. Profesor de la UAM, el INI, el Instituto Nacional de Estudios Históricos de la Revolución Mexicana y del Cenart. Ha sido coordinador del programa *Domingo en el Chopo* (1985), jefe de prensa de la Subdirección de Acción Cultural del ISSSTE (1985-86), jefe de prensa del festival de cultura de Sinaloa (1986-88), vocal de prensa del Ateneo Español de México (1991-95), jefe de prensa del festival Días Mundiales de la Música (1993) y director de información cultural en el Instituto de Cultura de la Ciudad de México (1998-99). Colabora en publicaciones periódicas y fue coordinador cultural de *Así es*. Autor de *Por si cambias de opinión* (1985), *Fidel, una historia de poder* (1994), *El general en la bombilla* (1994), *Cuatro atentados presidenciales* (1994), *Los mejores chistes sobre presidentes* (1995), *La nota roja. 1910-1919* (1996), *José Guadalupe Posada, un artista en blanco y* *negro* (1996), *La nota roja. 1810-1854* (1997), *Los primeros cien años de Fidel Velázquez* (1997), *La banda del automóvil gris* (1997), *Diccionario biográfico mexicano de la caricatura mexicana* (1998), *Cri-Crí: historia de un señor que una vez fue grillo* (1999). Realizó la investigación documental de tres tomos de la *Historia documental de la* CNOP (1985), tomos IX y X de la *Historia documental del Partido de la Revolución* (1984). Coautor de *Jesús Reyes Heroles. Vida y obra* (1991).

SÁNCHEZ GONZÁLEZ, JOSÉ MARÍA ◆ n. en San Buenaventura, Coah., y m. en Chihuahua, Chih. (1850-1940). Durante la intervención francesa se alistó en la Guardia Nacional y combatió en Santa Gertrudis y Matamoros. Radicó en Chihuahua como socio de la Compañía Harinera de ese estado, fue regidor del ayuntamiento de Chihuahua (1880-81), organizó la Cámara Nacional de Comercio local y fue tesorero de la misma. Varias veces diputado local, tesorero general del gobierno del estado (1903-07), gobernador interino (1906, 1906-07, dos veces en 1908, 1909-10) y sustituto (1910), renunció al iniciarse la revolución maderista.

SÁNCHEZ GONZÁLEZ, ROGELIO ◆ n. en San José de Gracia, Mich. (1921). Sacerdote ordenado en 1944. Ha sido prefecto, profesor y vicerrector del Seminario Mayor de Zamora, rector del Seminario Menor de Zamora y obispo de Colima (1972-).

SÁNCHEZ HERNÁNDEZ, TOMÁS ◆ n. en León, Gto., y m. en el DF (1894-1980). Estudió en el Colegio Militar y se especializó como artillero en la Escuela Superior de Guerra de Francia. Desde 1920, de nuevo en México, desempeñó diversos cargos en el Colegio Militar. Fue director de la Fundación Nacional de Artillería (1935), director de la Escuela Superior de Guerra (1936), director técnico de la Secretaría de Guerra, agregado militar de la embajada mexicana en Estados Unidos (1942), jefe de estado mayor de la Secretaría de la Defensa Nacional, subsecretario de Educación Pública (1943-46) y director del Colegio Militar. General de división en 1952. Inspector general del ejército (1953), diputado federal (1973-74) y agregado militar de las embajadas en Francia y Polonia.

Alfonso Sánchez Madariaga

SÁNCHEZ JIMÉNEZ, JESÚS ◆ n. en Tampico, Tamps. (1940). Licenciado en economía por la UNAM. Economista de la Dirección General de Estudios Hacendarios de la Secretaría de Hacienda (1970-76), en la Secretaría de Comercio ha sido secretario particular del subsecretario de Comercio Exterior (1976-82), secretario particular del secretario (1982-85) y subsecretario de Comercio Interior (1985-88). Pertenece al Colegio Nacional de Economistas y a la Liga de Economistas Revolucionarios del PRI.

SÁNCHEZ LAMEGO, MIGUEL ÁNGEL ◆ n. y m. en el DF (1897-1988). Ingeniero militar (1923). En 1914 se unió a la revolución constitucionalista a las órdenes de Joaquín Amaro. Ingresó en la Academia del Estado Mayor como oficial de caballería (1919). En el Colegio Militar ejerció la docencia y fundó el curso de ingenieros constructores e industriales. Estudió becado en la École Militaire et d'Application du Genie, de Versalles. Diplomado de Estado Mayor en la Escuela Superior de Guerra. Fue director del Departamento Cartográfico Militar, elaboró cartas de la República y del valle de México con métodos aerofotogramétricos. Se retiró del ejército en 1969 con el grado de general de división. Fue colaborador de la *Enciclopedia de México.* Coautor de *Historia de una institución gloriosa: el Colegio Militar* (1972) e *Historia del H. Colegio Militar de México* (1973). Autor de *Historia del Batallón de Zapadores* (5 t.), *Historia de las murallas de Campeche* (1932), *El castillo de San Diego de Acapulco* (1937), *El castillo de San Carlos de Perote* (1938), *Origen de los ingenieros militares en el mundo y en México* (1943), *El castillo de San Juan de Ulúa* (1944), *Generales de ingenieros del ejército mexicano. 1812-1914* (1952), *El primer mapa general de México hecho por un mexicano* (1955), *Historia militar de la revolución constitucionalista* (5 t., 1956-57), *Historia del Batallón Activo Guarda Costa de San Blas* (1966), *La célebre acción de Arroyo Hondo: 30 contra 400* (1966), *El sitio de Querétaro* (1967), *The second mexican Texas war, 1841-1843* (1972), *La invasión española de 1829* (1972), *Historia militar de la revolución mexicana en la época maderista* (3 t., 1976-77) e *Historia militar de la revolución en la época de la Convención* (1983). Por hechos de armas ganó las condecoraciones Cruz de Guerra, Veterano de la Revolución y Legionario.

SÁNCHEZ LÓPEZ, HÉCTOR ◆ n. en Juchitán, Oax. (1950). Ingeniero electricista por la ESIME del IPN. Tomó el curso propedéutico de la maestría en matemáticas en la Universidad Autónoma de Guerrero. Profesor de secundaria en el DF, y en la Universidad Autónoma Benito Juárez de Oaxaca, el Instituto Regional del Istmo y la Universidad Autónoma de Guerrero. Fue consultor de Empresa Construcciones en Tijuana. Dirigente y fundador de la Coalición Obrera Campesina Estudiantil del Istmo. Fue presidente municipal de Juchitán (1974). Diputado federal (1982-85) y senador (1994-2000). Candidato a gobernador en Oaxaca por el Partido de la Revolución Democrática (1998).

SÁNCHEZ MACGREGOR, JOAQUÍN ◆ n. en Puebla (?). Doctor en filosofía por la UAM. Ha sido director fundador de la Escuela de Filosofía y Letras de la UAP (1965-69); profesor, director de Profesorado (hoy Personal Académico), secretario académico de la Coordinación de Humanidades (1978-80), jefe de la división de estudios de posgrado y catedrático de la Facultad de Filosofía y Letras (1986-) de la UNAM. Autor de *Acoso a Hiedegger, Claves dialécticas, Filosofía y sistema en la extensión universitaria, Rulfo y Barthes* y *Colón y Las Casas* (1992), entre otros.

SÁNCHEZ MADARIAGA, ALFONSO ◆ n. y m. en el DF (1904-1999). Sindicalista. Fundador, junto con su hermano y con Fidel Velázquez, de la Unión de Trabajadores de la Industria Lechera (1921), en la cual ingresó al Comité Ejecutivo en 1925. Su gremio estuvo afiliado a la Confederación Regional Obrera

Mexicana y se escindió de esta central para fundar la Federación Sindical de Trabajadores del Distrito Federal (1929), de la cual Sánchez Madariaga fue secretario de organización y propaganda. Fundador de la CTM (1936), de la cual fue secretario general (1945-47) y miembro del Comité Ejecutivo Nacional hasta su muerte. Ocupó la secretaría de asuntos internacionales de esa institución y promovió a la CTM ante la OIT, la ORIT, la CIOLS y la AFL-CIO. Fundador y secretario general del Comité Nacional del Partido Nacional Revolucionario (1937-38), fundador y secretario de acción obrera del Partido de la Revolución Mexicana (1938-40) y fundador y dos veces secretario de acción obrera del PRI. Ocupó diversos cargos en la Junta Federal de Conciliación y Arbitraje, fue diputado federal (1949-52 y 1955-58) y senador de la República (1940-46, 1970-76). Fue promotor de la Ley de Seguro Social y del IMSS (1941), en el cual fue miembro del comité de vigilancia y, hasta su muerte, miembro de su consejo técnico. A lo largo de su carrera recibió reconocimientos nacionales e internacionales.

SÁNCHEZ MÁRMOL, MANUEL ◆ n. en Cunduacán, Tab., y m. en la ciudad de México (1839-1912). Licenciado por la Escuela de Derecho de Chiapas (1865). En su época estudiantil fundó los periódicos *El Rayo* y *El Investigador*. Organizó en Mérida el Círculo Literario La Concordia, que editó el periódico *La Guirnalda*; fundó el periódico *La Burla*, con José Peón Contreras y Manuel Roque Castellano, y dirigió el semanario tabasqueño *El Águila Azteca*, opositor del imperio de Maximiliano. Fue asesor de guerra y secretario general de Gobierno en Tabasco. En la ciudad de México fundó el periódico *El Radical* (1867). Diputado federal (1871-76 y 1892). Fue secretario de Justicia e Instrucción Pública (del 4 de noviembre al 1 de diciembre de 1876) en el gabinete de José María Iglesias. En Tabasco dirigió el Instituto Juárez (1879) y formó parte del Tribunal Superior de Justicia del estado. Colaborador de *El Disidente*, *El Repertorio Pintoresco*, *El Clamor Público* y de *El Álbum Yucateco*. Coautor de *Poetas yucatecos y tabasqueños* (1861) y *México, su evolución social* (1902). Autor de *Pocahontas* (sátira política, 1882), *¡Ave patria!* (1889), *Juanita Souza* (novela, 1892), *Antón Pérez* (1903) y *Previvida* (1906). En 1906 ingresó en la Academia Mexicana (de la Lengua).

SÁNCHEZ MARROQUÍN, ALFREDO ◆ n. en Xicoténcatl, Tams. (1910). Realizó estudios profesionales en la Escuela Nacional de Ciencias Biológicas del IPN (1941), la maestría en microbiología y botánica en la Universidad de Illinois y el doctorado en microbiología en la UNAM, donde fue profesor. Ejerció la docencia en Chapingo y el Cinvestav. En el IPN fundó las materias de botánica criptogámica y ciencia del suelo y el laboratorio de microbiología experimental, en donde se realizaron los primeros trabajos de biotecnología en el país y fue subdirector técnico. En los laboratorios Sanyn desarrolló, con los investigadores Crespo y Lozano, la primera penicilina en Latinoamerica. Autor de los libros *Principios de microbiología industrial*, *Los agaves de México en la industria alimentaria* y *Potencialidad agroindustrial del amaranto*. Ha publicado más de 150 artículos en revistas especializadas. Recibió los premios Banamex (1972 y 1975), de Ciencia y Tecnología de Alimentos (otorgado por el Conacyt), Nacional de Investigación en Alimentos (entregado por la FAO) y Nacional de Ciencias y Artes 1995, en el área de Tecnología y Diseño. La UAM creó en 1994 una cátedra con su nombre.

SÁNCHEZ MAYANS, FERNANDO ◆ n. en Campeche, Camp. (1924). Estudió historia y letras españolas y francesas en la UNAM. Ha sido profesor de la UIA y del INBA, donde fue jefe de Literatura y Danza. Adscrito al servicio diplomático desde 1967, ha sido agregado cultural en Guatemala y Roma y cónsul general en Barcelona, Miami (1987) y San Juan de Puerto Rico (1988-). Autor de los poemarios *Decir lo de la primavera* (1955), *Soledades de la memoria*, *Poemas*, *Acto propicio* (1958), *Once sonetos* (1974), *18 pronunciamientos* (1976), *11 sonetos y 18 pronunciamientos* (reunión de las dos obras anteriores, 1980), *La palabra callada. Poesía 1951-1988* (1988, con prólogo de Hugo Gutiérrez Vega) y *La muerte de la rosa* (1991); de las obras teatrales *Las alas del pez* (1960; Premio Juan Ruiz de Alarcón, premio del diario *El Nacional* en 1959, Premio Nacional de Teatro en 1962, medalla de oro de la Asociación Nacional de Compositores de México en 1962, diploma de la Asociación de Críticos de México en 1963 y medalla de oro del Sindicato de Músicos en 1963), *Cuarteto deshonesto* (1962), *Un joven drama* (1966), *El pequeño juicio* (1968), *Un extraño laberinto* (1971), *La violenta visita* (1971), *Perdido en las estrellas* y *Los estudiantes* (1982); así como los ensayos *Historia del teatro en México* (1959), *Enrique González Martínez* (1961), *Cultura gastronómica en México* (1983) y *Rastros literarios* (1998); y la antología *Aguinaldo poético*. Premio Nacional de Poesía (1951) y Premio Nacional de Teatro (1962). Medalla Moliére de Francia (1969).

SÁNCHEZ MEDAL, LUIS ◆ n. en Morelia, Mich., y m. en el DF (1919-1997). Se tituló como médico cirujano en la UNAM (1943) y se especializó en el Instituto Simpson Memorial de la Universidad de Michigan (1945), en el Hospital Pratt de Diagnóstico, de Boston (1945), en la Universidad de Ohio (1945) y en la Clínica de Terapia Oncológica, de Boston (1951). Fue profesor en la UNAM, jefe de médicos residentes (1946-47), subjefe del Servicio Clínico y jefe del Laboratorio (1946-59) y del Departamento de Hematología del Hospital de Enfermedades de la Nutrición (1960). Dirigió la División de Enseñanza del Instituto Nacional de la Nutrición Salvador Zubirán (1965-97). Fundador de la Escuela Nacional de Hematología. Autor de *El alcoholismo en México* (1982). Presidió la Academia Nacional de Medicina (1969-70) y la Agrupación Mexicana para el Estudio de la Hematología (1959-60). Premio Nacional de Ciencias (1972).

Foto: Herrera

Juan Sánchez Navarro y Peón

Sánchez Mejorada, Carlos ◆ n. en Pachuca, Hgo. (1883-1952). Se tituló como abogado en la Escuela Nacional de Jurisprudencia (1904), de la que fue profesor. Coautor de *Algunas notas sobre la "propiedad minera" antes y después de la Constitución de 1917* (1947) y de *El contrato de explotación minera*. Autor del *Código de ética profesional de la Barra Mexicana de Abogados* y de *Evolución y tendencias del derecho mexicano*. Fue presidente de la Barra Mexicana-Colegio de Abogados (1943- 45).

Sánchez Mejorada, Javier ◆ n. en Pachuca, Hgo. (1886-1941). Fue presidente de los Ferrocarriles Nacionales de México, ministro plenipotenciario en Italia, Alemania e Inglaterra y secretario de Comunicaciones y Obras Públicas (del 30 de noviembre de 1928 al 5 de febrero de 1930), en el gabinete de Emilio Portes Gil. Autor de *El riego de las tierras, solución de varios problemas nacionales*.

Sánchez Mendoza, Cirila ◆ n. en Santa Cruz Pepenixtlahuaca, Oax. (1952). Maestra normalista. Profesora en educación bilingüe y técnico auxiliar en integración social. Pertenece al PRI, del que ha sido secretaria de asuntos indígenas en Oaxaca. Ha sido directora regional de Educación Indígena, directora del Centro Coordinador Indigenista Chatino, procuradora de la Defensa del Indígena, presidenta de la Unión de Pueblos Unidos en la Región Chatina-Costa Chica, presidenta del Consejo Supremo Chatino, diputada local, federal (1988-91) y senadora (1994-2000). Pertenece al Consejo Consultivo Ciudadano de la Secretaría de Desarrollo Social.

Sánchez Miguel, Juan ◆ n. en España (1901). Abogado, fue consejero del Consorcio de Industrias Militares de la República Española. Al triunfo del franquismo vino a México como refugiado político (1939). Fue jefe de la Sección de Divulgación Cultural y Acción Estética del gobierno de Veracruz y redactor de *Brotes*, de Jalapa. Autor de *Xalapa mística* (1940), *Xalapa racial y bella* (1943), *Del Xalapa secular* (1944), *Gráficos del gobierno del estado* (1945) y *La imprenta del gobierno del estado de Veracruz*.

Sánchez Montemayor, Jaime ◆ n. en Ciudad Victoria, Tams. (1947). Licenciado en derecho por la UNAM (1969), maestro por el Instituto Internacional de Administración Pública de París (1970- 72) y doctor en derecho administrativo por la Universidad de París (1970-72). Director corporativo de Banca del Interior de la zona sur del Banco Mexicano Somex (1980-82), en la Secretaría de Hacienda ha sido secretario particular del director de Crédito (1972-75), secretario particular del subsecretario de Hacienda y Crédito Público (1975-77), subdirector de Bancos, Seguros y Valores (1977-78), director de Regulación del Sistema Financiero de la SHOP (1978-80), asesor de la Dirección General del Banco BCH (1982) y director general de Multibanco Mercantil de México (1983-1992), en el cual se encargó de su fusión con Bancam SNC. Director general de Banpaís (1992-).

Sánchez Navarro, Carlos ◆ n. en Coahuila y m. en la ciudad de México (1816-1876). Heredero de un gran latifundio coahuilense, durante la guerra contra Estados Unidos vendió sus productos agrícolas y ganaderos tanto a las tropas mexicanas como a los invasores estadounidenses. Durante el último mes del imperio de Maximiliano fue ministro de la casa imperial.

Sánchez Navarro, José Ignacio ◆ n. en Saltillo, Coah., y m. en la ciudad de México (1781-1851). Sacerdote. Estuvo al frente de varias parroquias de Coahuila. Fue preconizado obispo de Linares en 1850, pero murió antes de su consagración.

Sánchez Navarro y Peón, Juan ◆ n. en la ciudad de México (1913). Empresario. Licenciado en derecho y filosofía por la Universidad Nacional. Doctor en filosofía y en derecho por la Universidad Central de Madrid. Ha sido catedrático de la UNAM, la Universidad Anáhuac, la UDLA y la Universidad Autónoma de Guadalajara, que le otorgó el doctorado *honoris causa* en 1996. Ha colaborado en diversas publicaciones. Ha sido miembro del Consejo Consultivo de la Ciudad de México y presidió Fomento de Investigación y Cultura Superior, el Centro de Estudios Económicos del Sector Privado, la Coparmex, el CEMAL, la Concanaco, la Concamin (fundador), el Consejo Nacional de Publicidad (fundador) y el Consejo Mexicano de Hombres de Negocios (fundador), el Consejo Coordinador Empresarial (fundador, 1975) y el Consejo Binacional México-España, entre otros organismos empresariales. Actualmente es líder de la Cámara de Comercio México-Alemania, vicepresidente del Grupo Modelo (y uno de los principales accionistas), consejero honorario vitalicio del Grupo Financiero Bital, miembro del consejo consultivo de una veintena de empresas y presidente de la Sociedad Mexicana de Bibliófilos (1997-98). Ex presidente de la Asociación de Industriales Latinoamericanos. Autor de ensayos sobre negocios, política y charrería. Alicia Ortiz Rivera escribió *Juan Sánchez Navarro. Biografía de un testigo del México del siglo XX* (1997).

Sánchez Novelo, Faulo Manuel ◆ n. en Motul, Yuc. (1953). Licenciado en antropología social por la Universidad de Yucatán. Fue director de Difusión, Prensa y Relaciones Públicas del gobierno de Yucatán (1976-82), director del *Diario del Sureste* y jefe de Relaciones Públicas del Banrural Peninsular (1983-86). Autor de *Yucatán bajo el segundo imperio* (2 t.), *La educación en Yucatán bajo el imperio* (1980) y *Yucatán durante la intervención francesa 1863-1867* (1983), *José María Iturralde Traconis "El Kanxoc"*, *Ideología y política en un régimen socialista yucateco* (1986).

Sánchez de Ocaña, Rafael ◆ n. en España y m. en el DF (1888-?). Escritor y periodista. Fue profesor ayudante de la Universidad Central de Madrid. Llegó exiliado a México tras la derrota de la República Española. Fue colaborador de *El Nacional* y *Romance* así como profesor de la UNAM. Autor de *Cartas irreverentes* (1937), *Enrique Heine y la cultura alemana* (1938), *Reflejos en el agua* (1940) y *Confesiones de un desvelado* (1945).

SÁNCHEZ OCHOA, GASPAR ◆ n. y m. en Guadalajara, Jal. (1837-1909). En 1854 se unió a la revolución de Ayutla, a las órdenes de Ignacio Comonfort. Al perpetrar éste su autogolpe de Estado, se unió a la lucha constitucionalista con Ignacio de la Llave. Combatió la intervención francesa y el imperio. A las órdenes de González Ortega estuvo en la defensa de Puebla (1863). Fue aprehendido por los invasores y conducido a Veracruz, pero escapó y se reincorporó a la lucha. Apoyó a González Ortega cuando éste pretendía desplazar de la Presidencia a Benito Juárez. Al triunfo de la República fue encarcelado en Tlatelolco. Se le rehabilitó en 1871 como general de brigada. Combatió la rebelión de la Noria. En el porfiriato fue jefe del Departamento de Ingenieros de la Secretaría de Guerra y magistrado de la Suprema Corte Militar (1897-1907).

SÁNCHEZ PAREDES, ENRIQUE ◆ n. en Amozoc y m. en Atlixco, Pue. (1876-1923). Sacerdote ordenado en 1903 en Roma. Fue profesor en el Seminario Palafoxiano, canónigo de Puebla, vicario capitular y arzobispo de Puebla (1919-23).

SÁNCHEZ PAREJA, JOSÉ MARÍA ◆ n. en Ameca, Nueva Galicia, y m. cerca de Culiacán, Sin. (1787-1851). En 1810 se unió a las fuerzas realistas y combatió a los insurgentes hasta 1816, cuando se retiró a la vida privada. Al consumarse la independencia desempeñó algunos puestos públicos. En 1827 se estableció en Chihuahua, volvió a ocupar cargos de gobierno y fue uno de los fundadores del rito yorquino en Chihuahua. Partidario de Vicente Guerrero, fue desterrado de Chihuahua en 1830, aunque se le reivindicó en 1833 como vicegobernador de la entidad, encargado del poder a fines de ese año. Presidió la primera Junta de Educación Pública, reprimió a los peones de las haciendas que se negaban a combatir a los indios y organizó milicias. Dejó el poder en 1834, aunque se mantuvo en la administración pública hasta 1846, cuando fue diputado federal y recaudó fondos para combatir la invasión estadounidense. Al ser ocupada la capital estatal por los invasores, fue designado gobernador provisional con sede en Guadalupe y Calvo. Entregó el poder en 1847 al gobernador constitucional, Laureano Muñoz. Fue senador en 1849.

SÁNCHEZ PÉREZ, CELERINO *COMANCHE* ◆ n. en El Guayabal, Veracruz, y m. en León, Gto. (1944-?). Beisbolista. Pelotero de la Liga Mexicana, se inició con *Tigres* (1964-74), luego estuvo con los *Cafeteros* de Córdoba, con los *Mineros* de Coahuila y los *Naranjeros* de Hermosillo. Participó en varias Series del Caribe. Jugó como titular de tercera base con los *Yanquis* de Nueva York en los 70, donde también fue jardinero y primera base.

SÁNCHEZ PIEDRAS, EMILIO ◆ n. en Tlaxcala, Tlax., y m. en el DF (1915-1981). Licenciado en derecho por la UNAM (1941). Militó en el movimiento Juventudes Revolucionarias y fue delegado general del PRI en Yucatán, Colima, Jalisco y Coahuila. Fue agente del Ministerio Público en la Procuraduría de Justicia del Distrito y Territorios Federales, abogado consultor del Departamento de Asuntos Indígenas (1941-44), secretario particular de los gobernadores de Tlaxcala Mauro Angulo y Rafael Ávila Bretón (1944-51), diputado local y director de Obras Públicas de Tlaxcala (1944-45), vocal ejecutivo de la Comisión del Desarrollo Industrial de Tlaxcala (1945-52), representante del gobierno tlaxcalteca en el DF (1952-55), dos veces diputado federal (1952-55 y 1958-61), presidente de la Gran Comisión del Congreso de la Unión y jefe de la delegación a la primera Reunión Interparlamentaria México-Estados Unidos; director del Departamento Jurídico de la Comisión Federal de Electricidad (1964) y gobernador de Tlaxcala (1975-81).

SÁNCHEZ PONTÓN, LUIS ◆ n. en Puebla, Pue., y m. en el DF (1895-1969). Estudió abogacía en el Colegio del Estado de Puebla (1910). En la UNAM fue profesor, cofundador de la Escuela Nacional de Economía y director de la Facultad de Derecho. Participó en el Congreso de Estudiantes que pidió la renuncia de Porfirio Díaz. Desde 1916 se integró al Partido Liberal Constitucionalista y se opuso a la permanencia en el poder de Venustiano Carranza. Se adhirió al Plan de Agua Prieta y fue gobernador interino de Puebla (1920-21), diputado federal (1937-40), senador, oficial mayor de la Secretaría de Hacienda y Crédito Público, secretario de Educación Pública (del 1 de diciembre de 1940 al 12 de septiembre de 1941) en el gabinete de Manuel Ávila Camacho; embajador en Ecuador, Suiza, Canadá, Uruguay y la URSS; consejero de la Presidencia de la República y senador. En 1952 militó en el henriquismo. Autor de *Hacia la escuela socialista*, *Las deudas públicas en el derecho internacional* y *Guerra y revolución*. Miembro de la Sociedad Mexicana de Geografía y Estadística, de la Barra Mexicana-Colegio de Abogados y de la Academia de Jurisprudencia.

SÁNCHEZ PONTÓN, MANUEL ◆ n. en Puebla, Pue. (1926). Se inició muy joven en el periodismo. Ha sido corresponsal de varios periódicos de la capital del país. Director de *La Opinión* de Puebla (1961-). Autor de *Nueva visita a la URSS* (crónica), *1988. La batalla por la libertad* (1987) y de las novelas *El golpe. Operación incruenta* (1983), *Estampida*, *El regreso del Mesías* y *El olor a tinta* (1985). Premio de periodismo de la Universidad de las Américas (1982).

SÁNCHEZ RAMÍREZ, EDGARD ◆ n. en Santa Rosalía, BCS (1949). Licenciado en historia por la UNAM (1974). Militante del Grupo Comunista Internacionalista (1969), en el que fue miembro del comité central (1970) y del buró político (1975). Cofundador del Partido Revolucionario de los Trabajadores (1976-), en el que forma parte de los comités central y político y del secretariado de organización del comité político; fue responsable de la Comisión Nacional Electoral 1982, director del órgano *Bandera Socialista* (1982-84) y representante ante la Comisión Federal Electoral (1985). Miembro del comité ejecutivo de la IV Internacional (1979-).

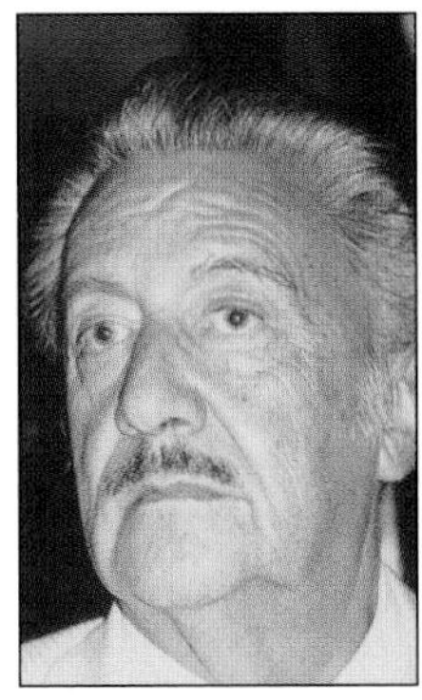

Emilio Sánchez Piedras

Retrato y firma de Gaspar Sánchez Ochoa

Sánchez Rebolledo, Adolfo ◆ n. en el DF (1942). Periodista. Realizó estudios de antropología en la ENAH (1965). Fue militante del PCM (1960-61), fundador del Movimiento de Acción Popular (1981), del PSUM (1981), en el que fue miembro del comité central, subdirector del órgano *Así Es* (1981-83); fundador del PMS (1987) y del PRD (1989). Miembro del Sindicato Único de Trabajadores de la Industria Nuclear (SUTIN). Cofundador del Instituto de Estudios de la Transición Democrática (1989) y miembro de la Junta de Gobierno. Cofundador del Instituto del Derecho de Asilo y las Libertades Públicas (Museo Casa de León Trotsky), A.C. (1991). Representante ante el Consejo General del IFE del partido Democracia Social (1999). Corresponsal de la agencia Inter Press Service, director general de la revista *Punto Crítico* (1971-77), coeditor de *Cuadernos Políticos* y director de *Solidaridad* (1983). Coordinador del programa televisivo *Nexos* (1989-99). Ha colaborado en *Nexos, La Cultura en México, Jueves de Excélsior, Etcétera* y *La Jornada*. Autor de *La revolución mexicana* (1967), *La revolución cubana* (1972) y *Secretos espejos* (1989).

Sánchez Rojas, José María ◆ n. en Chachapa, Pue., y m. en el DF (1890-1959). Luchó en el Ejército Libertador del Sur. Se pasó al carrancismo y estuvo a las órdenes de Álvaro Obregón. Fue diputado federal (1917-18), dos veces gobernador de Puebla (1921-22 y 1924) y senador (1928). Presidió el Partido Demócrata Socialista.

Sánchez Román, Felipe ◆ n. en España y m. en el DF (1893-1956). Licenciado y doctor en derecho por la Universidad Central de Madrid, de la que fue profesor. Presidente de la Comisión Jurídica Asesora del Gobierno de la República Española (1932), miembro del Consejo de Dirección del Instituto Internacional para la Unificación del Derecho Privado (1928), miembro del Tribunal Permanente de Arbitraje de La Haya (1931-39), abogado de la República Española en diversos litigios internacionales, miembro electo de la Academia de Ciencias Políticas y Sociales de España, vicepresidente primero de la Jurisprudencia y Legislación y diputado a las Cortes Constituyentes (1931-33). Llegó exiliado a México en 1939. Fue profesor de la UNAM, abogado consultor de la Presidencia de la República y fundador del Instituto de Derecho Comparado de la UNAM.

Sánchez Santos, Trinidad ◆ n. en San Bernardino, Tlax., y m. en la ciudad de México (1859-1912). Llegó a la ciudad de México en 1880 y se inició en el periodismo como colaborador de *La mosca, El amigo de la verdad, La voz de España, El centinela católico*, y *El Tiempo*, donde tuvo la sección "Guerrilla" (1883-87). Dirigió *El Nacional, El Heraldo* (1889-91), *La Voz de México* (1892-97) y *El País* (1899-1912). Autor de *Editoriales de El País en 1910, 1911 y 1912* (1923) y *Obras selectas* (2 t., 1962). Por su obra periodística fue censurado y encarcelado. En su honor, al municipio donde se ubica su pueblo natal se le nombró *Zitlaltepec de Trinidad Sánchez Santos*.

Sánchez Sarto, Manuel ◆ n. en España y m. en el DF (1897-1980). Licenciado en derecho y en historia por la Universidad de Zaragoza y doctor en derecho y en historia por la Central de Madrid. Estudió también en Alemania (1921-22). Llegó exiliado a México en 1939. Obtuvo la nacionalidad mexicana en 1951. Fue profesor de la UNAM, de la Universidad de Caracas (1946-48) y la de Asunción, Paraguay (1954); profesor y director de la Escuela Superior de Administración Pública para América Central de las Naciones Unidas en San José de Costa Rica (1954-56), técnico asesor de la Dirección de Estudios Hacendarios de la Secretaría de Hacienda, asesor economista del Banco de México (1949-53), economista asesor de la Corporación Venezolana de Fomento (1947-49), economista asesor de la CEPAL en México (1950), jefe de misión de la Administración de Asistencia Técnica de la ONU en Paraguay (1953-54) y en Costa Rica (1954-56) y colaborador en la comisión de la UNAM para la institución de la Universidad de La Laguna (1956). Autor de *La estadística en España, La banca pública en España, El contrato de edición* y *Economía y administración: métodos de investigación*. Profesor emérito de la UNAM (1971).

Sánchez Sesna, Francisco José ◆ n. en el DF (1950). Doctor en ingeniería, con especialidad en estructuras, por la UNAM (1979), donde ha sido profesor, investigador y miembro del Consejo Interno del Instituto de Ingeniería y del Comité Editorial de éste. Ha sido profesor visitante en la Universidad Pierre et Marie Curie en París, la Universidad del Sur de California, la Universidad de Kyoto en Japón, el Politécnico de Milán, la Universidad Joseph Fourier de Grenoble y en el Istituto di Ricerca sul Rischio Sísmico de Milán. Autor de numerosos artículos publicados en revistas especializadas o como capítulos de libros. Recibió la Medalla Gabino Barreda (1980) y los premios Miguel A. Urquijo (1988), otorgado por el Colegio de Ingenieros Civiles de México, Manuel Noriega Morales en el área de Aplicaciones de la Ciencia y la Tecnología (1988), otorgado por la OEA, y el Nacional de Ciencias y Artes, en Tecnología y Diseño (1994). Es miembro de los comités editoriales de las publicaciones *Soil Dynamics and Earthquake Engineering* y *Sismodinámica*.

Sánchez Sinencio, Feliciano ◆ n. en el DF (1938). Ingeniero en comunicaciones eléctricas y electrónicas por el IPN (1959), maestro en física por el Centro Brasileiro de Pesquisas Físicas (1966) y doctor en física por la Universidad de Sao Paulo (*Summa cum laude,* 1969). En el IPN ha sido profesor (1960-), jefe de la Sección de Graduados (1971-72), jefe del Departamento de Física de la ESFM (1970-72) y del Cinvestav (1988-90) y coordinador de Postgrado e Investigación (1998-). Profesor visitante del Centro Brasileiro de Pesquisas (1985 y 1986) y de las universidades de São Paulo (1976 y 1986), de Jerusalén (1973, 1975 y 1977), de Princeton (1967, 1981 y 1984). Descubrió un nuevo semiconductor (telurio de cadmio amorfo oxigenado) y otros materiales. Miembro de la American Physical Society, de la American Asociation for the Advancement of Science, de la Academia de la Investigación Científica y de las sociedades mexicana y brasileña de Física. Pertenece al SNI. Medalla al Mérito de la Academia de Ciencias de Cuba (1994). Premio al desarrollo de la física en México por la Sociedad Mexicana de la Física (1994). Premio Nacional de Ciencias y Artes 1997. Presea Lázaro Cárdenas 1998.

SÁNCHEZ SOLÍS, FELIPE ◆ n. en Zumpango de la Laguna, Edo. de Méx. (1816-?). Abogado, fue el primer director del Instituto Científico y Literario de Toluca (1846), diputado federal, secretario de la Suprema Corte, secretario de Fomento en Puebla, fundador de la Sociedad Artística Industrial para Artesanos, uno de los compiladores de los *Anales de Cuauhtitlán* y poseedor del Códice Zapoteco o Códice Waecker Gotter, que vendió al diplomático alemán y ahora se conserva en el Museo Etnológico de Berlín con el nombre de Códice Sánchez Solís.

SÁNCHEZ SOLÍS, JORGE MARIO ◆ n. en el DF (1955). Contador público por el IPN (1986). Miembro del PRI desde 1973. Profesor de secundaria (1985) y en el IPN (1985), jefe de oficina en la SEP (1987). En el SNTE ha sido representante ante la Comisión Mixta de Escalafón (1980-82), secretario general de la delegación III-18 (1982-84), secretario de asuntos profesionales (1982-85) y secretario general (1986-89) de la sección XI, así como secretario de organización del CEN (1989). Miembro de la primera Asamblea de Representantes del DF (1988-91). Obtuvo en 1988 la medalla al mérito sindical del SNTE.

SÁNCHEZ TABOADA, RODOLFO ◆ n. en Acatzingo, Pue., y m. en la ciudad de México (1895-1955). Estudió en el Colegio Militar. En 1913 se unió a la revolución constitucionalista, a las órdenes de Fortunato Maycotte. Durante la lucha de facciones combatió a los zapatistas en las filas de Jesús Guajardo. Gobernador del territorio de Baja California Norte (1937-44). En el PRI fue presidente del comité directivo del Distrito Federal (1946) y presidente del Comité Ejecutivo Nacional (1946-52). General de división en 1952. Dirigió la campaña presidencial de Adolfo Ruiz Cortines y fue secretario de Marina en su gabinete (del 1 de diciembre de 1952 al 1 de mayo de 1955).

SÁNCHEZ DE TAGLE, FRANCISCO MANUEL ◆ n. en Valladolid, hoy Morelia, Mich., y m. en la ciudad de México (1782-1847). Estudió en el Colegio de San Juan de Letrán, donde impartó la cátedra de filosofía. Fue consiliario bachiller de artes de la Real y Pontificia Universidad (1804). Regidor perpetuo y secretario del ayuntamiento; diputado (1815), vocal de la Junta de Arbitrios y censor (1820) de las Cortes Españolas. Fue uno de los firmantes del Acta de Independencia. Miembro de la Soberana Junta Provisional Gubernativa (1821), diputado al primer Congreso General (1822-23), vicegobernador del Estado de México, diputado federal por Michoacán (1827-28) y el Estado de México (1831-32). Abogó por los esclavos que cruzaban la frontera, en la idea de que servirían a México como soldados en una eventual guerra contra Estados Unidos. Secretario del Supremo Poder Conservador (1836). Era director del Nacional Monte de Piedad cuando murió, durante la ocupación estadounidense, días después de haber sido asaltado y herido por la soldadesca invasora. Perteneció al grupo literario la Arcadia, del que fue mayoral (1809). Escribió en el *Diario de México* (1805-1809) y en *El Observador de la República Mexicana*. Autor de *A la gloria inmortal de los valientes españoles* (1810), de una *Arenga cívica pronunciada en la Plaza Mayor de México, el 16 de septiembre de 1830* (1830) y de un *Discurso sobre la creación de un poder conservador* (1835). En 1833 quemó casi toda su obra lírica, aunque su hijo Agustín rescató una pequeña parte, publicada en 1852 en dos tomos de *Obras poéticas*. En 1802 obtuvo el primer premio en un certamen de poesía, con la obra *La lealtad americana*.

SÁNCHEZ DE TAGLE, MIGUEL ◆ n. y m. en el DF (1890-1950). Fue diplomático durante un breve lapso. Desde 1918 se dedicó al periodismo como editorialista y director de la sección financiera de *El Universal*. Fue profesor de economía en la Escuela de Comercio y Administración, consejero del Banco Nacional de México, donde dirigió la revista *Examen de la Situación Económica*; consejero del Banco de México, de Nacional Financiera y de la Bolsa de Valores. Dirigió la *Revista de Hacienda* y el *Boletín Financiero*.

SÁNCHEZ DE TAGLE, PEDRO ANSELMO ◆ n. en España y m. en Valladolid, hoy Morelia, Mich. (?- 1772). Egresado de la Universidad de Salamanca, llegó a la Nueva España como fiscal de la Inquisición. Fue obispo de Durango (1747-57) y de Michoacán (1757-72), donde erigió el Seminario Tridentino.

SÁNCHEZ TAPIA, RAFAEL ◆ n. en Aguililla, Mich., y m. en el DF (1887-1946). Se incorporó en 1911 a la revolución maderista. Fue prefecto de Jiquilpan y Coalcomán, gobernador sustituto de Michoacán (1934-35) y secretario de Economía Nacional (del 18 de junio de 1935 al 31 de diciembre de 1937) en el gabinete de Lázaro Cárdenas. General de división en 1938. En este año se le mencionó, junto a Francisco J. Múgica y Manuel Ávila Camacho, como precandidato a la Presidencia de la República por el Partido de la Revolución Mexicana (☛). A fines de noviembre, Cárdenas pidió su renuncia a los tres aspirantes. En febrero, Sánchez Tapia renunció al PRM, al que tachó de "burda máquina imposicionista", y prosiguió su campaña como candidato independiente. Oficialmente obtuvo 9,840 votos en las eleciones de julio de 1940. Recibió del gobierno la concesión para explotar los yacimientos de hierro de Las Truchas y la vendió a inversionistas extranjeros.

SÁNCHEZ TELLO, ALFONSO ◆ m. en EUA (?-1979). Se inició en la industria cinematográfica como actor y se convirtió después en productor. Gracias a sus gestiones, muchas películas de Hollywood se filmaron en México. Copropie-

Foto: Fondo Histórico Alfonso Sánchez García

Felipe Sánchez Solís

Francisco Manuel Sánchez de Tagle

tario de instalaciones cinematográcas en Baja California. Entre sus producciones se cuentan *Cabo Blanco*, *Allá en el rancho grande* y *La barraca*.

SÁNCHEZ TINOCO, ALFONSO ◆ n. en Tanhuato, Mich., y m. en Jalapa, Ver. (1918-1970). Sacerdote ordenado en 1942. Tercer obispo de Papantla (1959-70). Fue presidente de la Comisión Episcopal de Pastoral de Conjunto y asistió al Concilio Vaticano II (1963-65). Murió en un accidente automovilístico.

SÁNCHEZ DE TORRE, KATY ◆ n. en Cataluña, España (1926). Antropóloga y traductora. Exiliada en México desde 1939. Estudió antropología en la ENAH (1939-44) y en el Colegio Kalamazoo, de Michigan, con residencia en París. Trabajó como traductora de la Comisión Mexicana-Norteamericana para la Erradicación de la Fiebre Aftosa (1948-50), para la *Revista del Instituto Indigenista Interamericano*, el Fondo de Cultura Económica, las embajadas de Estados Unidos e Indonesia y, eventualmente, para la Presidencia de la República. Jefa de traductores y relatores de la Asociación de Personal Técnico para Conferencias Internacionales (1954-).

Julio Sánchez Vargas

SÁNCHEZ TREJO, ANTONIO ◆ n. en el DF (1940). Licenciado en economía por la UNAM (1966), donde ha sido catedrático. Profesor del CIDE, el Cemla y el Cenapro. Ingresó en el Banco de México como investigador y analista del Departamento de Estudios Económicos (1966-70), viajó a Guatemala para ser gerente general de la empresa Tintas y Productos Químicos (1970-71) y regresó a México para desempeñar diversos cargos en la CFE (1972-73 y 1974-76), la Secretaría de la Presidencia (1973) y el IMSS (1977-83). Posteriormente ha sido subdirector de Finanzas y Administración del Instituto Nacional del Consumidor (1983), delegado y comisario propietario de la Secogef (1983-87), coordinador general de Planeación del ISSSTE (1987-88), contralor general (1989-93) y director adjunto de Finanzas y Administración de Banrural (1993-95), auditor general de la Secretaría de Agricultura, Ganadería y Desarrollo Rural (1995), director de Administración y Finanzas de Caminos y Puentes Federales (1995-98) y oficial mayor de la Secretaría de la Contraloría y Desarrollo Administrativo (1998-).

FOTO: ROGELIO CUÉLLAR

Adolfo Sánchez Vázquez

SÁNCHEZ UNZUETA, HORACIO ◆ n. en San Luis Potosí, SLP (1949). Licenciado en derecho por la Universidad de Jurisprudencia de SLP (1972), maestro en práctica social y administrativa por la University College of Swansea (1977), maestro en desarrollo regional por el Institute of Social Studies de Holanda (1978) y maestro en desarrollo urbano por El Colegio de México (1979). Ha sido profesor de diversas instituciones. Desde 1972 pertenece al PRI, del que ha sido presidente del comité directivo estatal en SLP. Investigador del Archivo Histórico del Estado de SLP (1980-81), asesor del subsecretario de Programación y Presupuesto (1982-83), coordinador general de la Comisión Coordinadora del Servicio Social de Estudiantes de las Instituciones de Estudios Superiores SPP SEP (1983-85), secretario de Programación y Presupuesto del gobierno de SLP (1985-86), coordinador de asesores de la delegación Coyoacán en el DDF (1989-90), coordinador de asesores del oficial mayor de la Sedue (1990-91), diputado federal (1991-94), gobernador interino de de SLP (1993-97) y embajador en el Vaticano (1998-).

SÁNCHEZ VALENZUELA, ELENA ◆ n. y m. en el DF (?-1950). Fue la primera estrella mexicana del cine mudo, por su actuación en *Santa*, dirigida por Germán Camus (1918). Actuó también en el filme *En la hacienda*. Fue periodista y fundó la Filmoteca de la Secretaría de Educación Pública.

SÁNCHEZ VARGAS, JULIO ◆ n. en Omealca, Veracruz (1914). Egresado de la Escuela Libre de Derecho. Abogado en el departamento jurídico de la SRE (1936-37), abogado del Departamento Agrario de la Oficina de Resoluciones Presidenciales (1937-41), procurador de Justicia de SLP (1941), donde fue oficial mayor (1942-43) y secretario general de Gobierno. Secretario del jefe de la policía del DF (1944-46). Magistrado (1946-67) y presidente (1963-67) del Tribunal Superior de Justicia y Territorios Federales. Subprocurador (1967-68) y procurador general de la República (1968-71). Director general de la Sociedad Mexicana de Crédito Industrial (1971-76), consejero del secretario de Hacienda (1977-83), ministro de la Suprema Corte de Justicia de la Nación (1983), miembro de los Consejos de Administración del Banco Mexicano Somex, Banpaís, Comisión Nacional de Valores, Instituto de Depósitos de Valores y la Cruz Roja Mexicana. Director del Instituto Nacional de la Senectud (1990-).

SÁNCHEZ VÁZQUEZ, ADOLFO ◆ n. en España (1915). Estudió filosofía en la Universidad Central de Madrid. Llegó exiliado a México en 1939. Doctor en filosofía por la UNAM (1966). Ejerció la docencia en la Universidad Michoacana. En la UNAM se ha desempeñado como profesor, coordinador del Colegio de Filosofía e investigador del Instituto de Investigaciones Estéticas. Tradujo del ruso los siete tomos de la *Historia de la filosofía*, de M. A. Dynnik y ha escrito numerosos prólogos. Se le incluyó en la antología *Poetas libres de la España peregrina en América* (1947). Coautor de *Conciencia y autenticidad históricas* (1968), *Estructuralismo y marxismo* (1970), *La filosofía y las ciencias sociales* (1976), *¡Exilio!* (1977), *Las revoluciones y la filosofía* (1979) y *Transparences. Philosophical Essays in Honor of J. Ferrater Mora* (Nueva Jersey, 1981). Autor de *El pulso ardiendo* (poesía, 1942), *Las ideas estéticas de Marx* (1965), *Filosofía de la praxis* (1967), *Ética* (1969), *Rousseau en México* (1969), *Estética y marxismo* (2 t., 1970), *Del socialismo científico al socialismo utópico* (1975), *Ciencia y revolución: el marxismo de Althusser* (1978), *Ensayos marxistas sobre filosofía e ideología* (1983), *Ensayos marxistas sobre historia y política* (1985), *Del exilio en México, recuerdos y reflexiones* (1991) y *Cuestiones estéticas y artísticas contemporáneas* (1996). Premio de investigación de la UNAM (1985) y profesor emérito de la misma. *Doctor honoris causa* por la Universidad Autónoma de Puebla (1984), por la UNAM (1998) y Gran Cruz de Alfonso X *el Sabio*.

SÁNCHEZ VÁZQUEZ, SALVADOR ◆ n. en Tepic, Nay. (1940). Contador público. Miembro del PRI, ha sido delegado general del CEN en Zacatecas e Hidalgo, secretario de finanzas y presidente del comité directivo estatal en Nayarit. Secretario general del CEN de la FSTSE y del sindicato de trabajadores del Instituto Nacional de Protección a la Infancia. En el CEN de la CNOP fue secretario de acción burocrática y delegado general en Quintana Roo y Durango. Profesor de la UNAM, ha sido director general del ISSSTE, vocal propietario de la Comisión Ejecutiva del Fovissste, contralor de Caminos y Puentes Federales, miembro del consejo de administración de Tabamex, miembro de la Comisión Técnica del Fideicomiso Bahía de Banderas. Diputado federal (1988-91) y senador (1994-97). Colaborador de *El Día* y de la revista *Foro Político*.

SÁNCHEZ VILLAGRÁN, PABLO ◆ n. y m. en la ciudad de México (1797-1850). En 1810 se alistó en las fuerzas realistas y combatió a los insurgentes. En 1821 se adhirió al Plan de Iguala. Cerca de Querétaro confiscó una imprenta, en la que se imprimió *El Mejicano Independiente*. Sirvió en las guarniciones de Veracruz (1823) y México (1824-31) y a partir de 1830 se le encomendó la redacción del periódico semioficial *El Gladiador*, que apoyó al gobierno golpista de Anastasio Bustamante. Dirigió el primer periódico mexicano editado para militares: *La Aurora* (1836), fue vocal de la Escuela Normal del Ejército y secretario de la Comisión de Estadística Militar.

SÁNCHEZ VILLASEÑOR, JOSÉ ◆ n. en Morelia, Mich., y m. en el DF (1911-1961). Jesuita (1927). Doctor en filosofía por la UNAM (1941). Creó en la UIA las carreras de relaciones industriales y de administración de empresas. Autor de *El sistema filosófico de Vasconcelos* (1939), *Pensamiento y trayectoria de José Ortega y Gasset* (1943), *Gaos en Mascarones* (1945), *Introducción al pensamiento de Sartre* (1950) y *El drama de la metafísica*.

SÁNCHEZ VITE, MANUEL ◆ n. en Molango, Hgo., y m. en el DF (1915-1996). Maestro rural (1934). Se tituló como profesor en la Escuela Nacional de Maestros (1944). Licenciado en derecho por la UNAM (1951). Miembro del PRI, del que fue delegado en varias entidades y presidente del Comité Ejecutivo Nacional (1970-72). Secretario de acción juvenil de la CNOP. En el SNTE fue secretario general de la sección XXXI (1942-46), secretario general de la sección IX (1947-49), secretario de propaganda (1949-52), secretario general del CEN (1952-55) y presidente de la comisión política (1955). Representante de la FSTSE a la fundación del Sindicato de Trabajadores del ISSSTE (1962). Fue asesor jurídico del SNTE, del ISSSTE y del Sindicato de Trabajadores de Agricultura y Ganadería de la República Mexicana. Se desempeñó como profesor de educación primaria y secundaria, maestro rural y director de una escuela normal rural. Ha sido procurador general de Justicia de Hidalgo (1963), diputado federal, oficial mayor de la Contaduría de Hacienda, senador (1963-69) y gobernador de Hidalgo (1969-75).

SANCTÓRUM DE LÁZARO CÁRDENAS ◆ Municipio de Tlaxcala situado en la porción noroccidental de la entidad, al este de Calpulalpan y al noroeste de la capital del estado. Limita al norte con Hidalgo y al suroeste con Puebla. Superficie: 129.2 km². Habitantes: 6,690, de los cuales 2,486 forman la población económicamente activa. Hablan alguna lengua indígena 28 personas mayores de cinco años. La cabecera es Sanctórum. Se llamó sólo Lázaro Cárdenas.

SANDI MENESES, LUIS ◆ n. y m. en el DF (1905-1996). Estudió violín, composición y canto en el Conservatorio Nacional, del que fue profesor y secretario (1927). Fue jefe de la Sección de Música del Departamento de Bellas Artes (1929), fundador y director de los coros del Conservatorio y de Madrigalistas (1936), fundador de la LEAR (1933-38), jefe del Departamento de Música del INBA (1947), presidente de Juventudes Musicales de México (1948), presidente del Comité Nacional del Consejo Internacional de la Música, fundador de la Liga de Compositores de Música de Concierto (1981) y vicepresidente de la Fundación Morales Estévez (1948), director general de ópera del INBA (1959) y presidente del Consejo Interamericano de Música (1965). Dirigió las orquestas sinfónicas de México y Nacional. Creó los clubes corales y las orquestas rítmicas de las primarias y secundarias de la SEP. Fue coeditor de *Música. Revista Mexicana* (1930-31) y director de *Conservatorio y Arte*. En radio, colaboró en *Carnet musical*, *Boletín* XELA y *Conciertos comentarios*. Autor de *Bitácora de un viaje* (1968), *Introducción al estudio de la música* (texto de secundaria), *Do Re Mi*, *Canto por nota* y *De música y otras cosas*. Entre sus composiciones están *Danza del venado para orquesta mexicana* (1930), *Diez Hai Kais* (para canto y piano, 1931), *Norte* (1941) *Tema y variaciones* (1944), *Sexteto*, *Sonatina para violoncello y piano*, *Cuatro momentos* (cuarteto de cuerda), *Hoja de álbum para violoncello y piano*, *Aire antiguo para violín y piano*, *Canción exótica para violín y piano*, *Fátima* (suite para guitarra), *Invención*, *Cuarteto de cuerda*, *Sonata*, *La hoja de plata*, *Misa chamula para conjunto instrumental y coro*, *Carlota* (ópera, 1948-49), *La señora en su balcón*, *Rubayats* (para conjunto instrumental y voz), *Poemas del amor y de la muerte*, *Canción de la vida profunda*, *Canción obscura*, *Destino*, *Madrigal*, *Los cuatro coroneles de la reina*, *Cuatro canciones de amor*, *Cinco poemas de Salvador Novo*, *Cinco poemas de Tu Fu* (para voz y piano), *La vida pasa* (para dos voces y piano), *Tres madrigales*, *Silenciosamente*, *A la muerte de Madero*, *Cinco gacelas*, *La suave patria* (para coro y orquesta, 1947), *Mi corazón se amerita* (para coro mixto y dos pianos), *Gloria a los héroes* (para coro mixto, orquesta y banda), *Las troyanas* (para coro e instrumentos), *Cyrano*, *Norte*, el ballet *Día de difuntos*, *La Angostura*, *América* (poema sinfóni-

Foto: Dante Bucio

Manuel Sánchez Vite

Luis Sandi Meneses

Augusto César Sandino

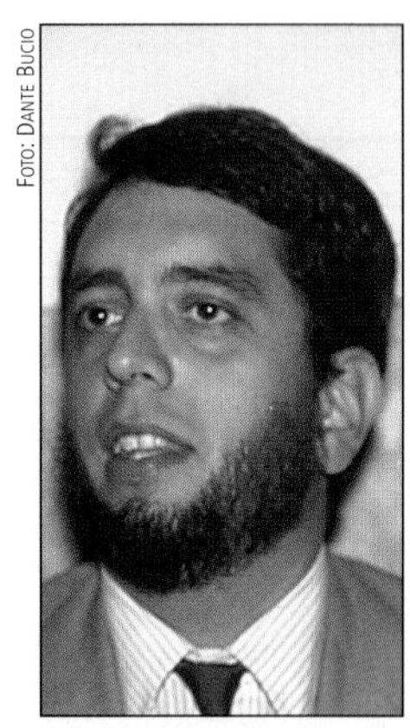

Alejandro Sandoval

Retato y firma de Gonzalo de Sandoval

co), *Segunda sinfonía*, *Bonampak* (ballet), *Esbozos sinfónicos*, *Cuatro miniaturas* y *Sonora, cántico a la creatura*, entre otras.

Sandino, Augusto César ◆ n. y m. en Nicaragua (1895-1934). En 1923 vino a México. En Veracruz y Tamaulipas fue mecánico de la Huasteca Petroleum Company, donde inició su militancia sindical y la práctica de la masonería y del espiritismo. En 1926 se produjo una intervención estadounidense en Nicaragua (☛) y Sandino regresó a su país para unirse a la resistencia. Formó el Ejército Defensor de la Soberanía de Nicaragua y se lanzó a la lucha en Las Segovias, con el propósito de expulsar a los invasores. En su estado mayor estaba el líder comunista salvadoreño Farabundo Martí (☛) y los mexicanos Andrés García Salgado y Manuel Chávarri. Escribió una carta a Emilio Portes Gil, el 6 de enero de 1929, en la que decía: "En la confianza de que es usted representante del heroico y viril pueblo mexicano, no vacilo en solicitar de su gobierno la protección necesaria para lograr y tener el alto honor de ser aceptado con mi Estado Mayor en el seno de su ejemplar pueblo". Desembarcó en Veracruz con la intención de viajar a la ciudad de México en busca de apoyo material. Entre sus acompañantes estaba el capitán mexicano José D. Paredes. Pese a que Portes Gil lo recibió con un abrazo y lo proclamó héroe de las Américas, el gobierno le impidió viajar a la ciudad de México; en cambio, se le rindieron honores de general de división. Invitado por el gobernador Tomás Garrido Canabal estuvo en Tabasco. Fue huésped de Yucatán entre julio de 1929 y abril de 1930. En ese estado contó con el apoyo del Partido Socialista del Sureste y fue colaborador del *Diario de Yucatán*. Por haber recurrido a Calles, los comunistas rompieron con él y el PCM lo tildó de "traidor" y lo llamó "instrumento del imperialismo yanqui". En 1930, sin haber conseguido ayuda del gobierno mexicano y después de depositar su archivo en la Gran Logia Masónica de Yucatán, volvió a Nicaragua. Reanudó la lucha armada hasta lograr, en 1933, que los invasores estadounidenses se retiraran del país. Las elecciones de ese año dieron el triunfo a Juan Bautista Sacasa, ante quien Sandino depuso las armas. Un año después fue asesinado.

Sandoiz, Alba ◆ ☛ *Izquierdo de Flores Muñoz, Asunción.*

Sandoval, Alejandro ◆ n. en Aguascalientes, Ags. (1957). Escritor. Licenciado en filología hispánica por la Universidad Central de Cuba (1980). Ha sido coordinador de Difusión del Museo de Arte Moderno (1981-82), editor de *El Correo del Libro* (1983), coordinador de Cultura de la delegación Álvaro Obregón (1984-85), director de la colección Premios Bellas Artes de Cultura (1984-85), director de Cultura de la delegación Cuauhtémoc (1985-88), coordinador de asuntos internacionales del Crea (1988-89), director de Cultura de Socicultur del DDF (1989-91), director del Programa Cultural para Jóvenes del CNCA (1992-93), director de Desarrollo Cultural del IMSS (1992-93) y director de Promoción Cultural de la Profeco (1998-). Autor de poesía: *Esquina de doble fondo* (1976), *Sobre el estado del tiempo* (1981), *Los héroes y los demás* (1982, Premio Nacional de Poesía de la UAZ), *Agua zarca* (1996) y *Playas del este* (1997); antología: *Poesía en Aguascalientes. Siglos XIX y XX* (1984) y *Ávidas mareas* (1988); novela: *La justa fatiga* (1984), *Piel de hormiga* (1992), *La tolvanera* (1996), *Un elefante sin circo* (1997) y *La travesía de los elefantes* (1998); la autobiografía *De cuerpo entero* (1992); el volumen de ensayos *Las fronteras iniciales* (1984) y la selección e introducción de *20 años de poesía en México. El Premio de Poesía de Aguascalientes 1968-88* (1988). Presidente de la Asociación de Escritores de México (1992-96) y directivo de la Sogem (1992-96). Premio Poesía Joven de México (1974), Premio Nacional de Poesía Ramón López Velarde (1983) y Premio El Barco de Vapor del CNCA (1997).

Sandoval, Gonzalo de ◆ n. y m. en España (1497-1528). Viajó a Cuba al servicio de Diego Velázquez y Hernán Cortés lo incluyó en su expedición hacia México. Estuvo a cargo de los bergantines que asediaron Tenochtitlan y, junto con García Holguín, fue quien capturó a Cuauhtémoc. En 1522 se le envió a someter a los indios de Colliman y fundó el pueblo de San Sebastián, actual ciudad de Colima. Acompañó a Cortés en la expedición a Las Hibueras y fue con él a España (1528).

Sandoval, José María ◆ n. en Valladolid, hoy Morelia, Mich., y m. en San Juan Bautista, hoy Villahermosa, Tab. (1799-¿1850?). Combatió a los insurgentes (1812). En 1821 se adhirió al Plan de Iguala. Fue oficial mayor de la Secretaría de Guerra y Marina y uno de los pronunciados contra Agustín de Iturbide. Gobernador de Chiapas (1837-40), decretó la amnistía para los federalistas, que la rechazaron. Combatió a los invasores estadounidenses durante la guerra de 1847.

Sandoval, Mauricio ◆ n. en Aguascalientes, Ags. (1960). Hijo de Víctor Sandoval. Pintor. Ha participado en exposiciones colectivas en Aguascalientes, Sao Paulo (1981), la ciudad de México, La Habana (1984), Houston (1987) y Monterrey. Individualmente ha expuesto en la Casa del Lago, en el Centro Cultural Guadalupe Posada, en el Centro de Artes Visuales, en la Casa de la Cultura de Aguascalientes, en la Galería Brent (Houston, 1986) y en el Museo Universitario del Chopo. Colaborador de *Plural*, *Voz Universitaria* (de la Universidad Autónoma de Aguascalientes), *Parota* y *El Sol de Aguascalientes*. Autor de la portada de *Yo no creo en la muerte* (1982, de Juan Domingo Argüelles). Ha ilustrado los libros *Sonetos a las cosas* (1983, de Víctor Manuel Mendiola), *Tríptico* (1984, de María Elena Aspíroz) y *La justa fatiga* (1984, de Alejandro Sandoval). Autor de la carpeta *Diario bestiaje* (1984). Hay obras suyas en la Casa de la Cultura de Aguascalientes, el Museo Nacional de Arte de Nicaragua, la Enron Corporation de Houston, la Casa del Lago y en el Museo Nacional de la Estampa, del INBA.

Premio de adquisición de la sección gráfica del Salón Nacional de Artes Plásticas (1981), premio de adquisición del Quinto Encuentro Nacional de Arte Joven (1985), premio de adquisición en la Bienal de Dibujo (1988) y premio de Estímulo de los Jóvenes del Crea y el INBA (1988).

SANDOVAL, VÍCTOR ◆ n. en Aguascalientes, Ags. (1929). Padre del anterior. Poeta. En Aguascalientes publicó la revista *Paralelo* y fundó la Casa de la Cultura, el Museo y Taller de Grabado José Guadalupe Posada, el Centro de Diseño Artesanal, la radiodifusora XENM, el Canal 10 de televisión, las bibliotecas públicas, el Centro de Artes Visuales, el Centro de Estudios Musicales Manuel M. Ponce y el Premio Nacional de Poesía Aguascalientes. En el INBA fue coordinador regional en Aguascalientes, creador de casas de cultura, institutos regionales de Bellas Artes y escuelas de iniciación artística; director fundador de la revista *Tierra Adentro* y de las ediciones Tierra Adentro; miembro del consejo editorial de *México en el Arte*, director de Promoción Nacional (1976-83), creador de diversos premios de carácter nacional e internacional, subdirector general (1983-88) y director general del propio Instituto (1988-91). Ministro de Asuntos Culturales de México en España (1991-94) y fundador del Instituto de México en Madrid (1992). En la SEP fue coordinador general del Programa de Animación Cultural en las Universidades (1994). Autor de *La poesía en México 1940-1990* (antología, 1994) y de los poemarios *Aire libre* (1957), *El viento norte* (1959), *Hombre de soledad* (1960), *Poemas a la juventud* (1964), *Poema del veterano de guerra*, *Retorno* (1967), *Che* (1969, en colaboración con Héctor Hugo Olivares y Desiderio Macías), *Para empezar el día* (1974), *Fraguas* (1980), *Agua de temporal* (1988), *Víctor Sandoval de bolsillo* (antología, 1989), *La poesía en México 1940-1990 (algunas aproximaciones)*, *Trovas de amor y desdenes* (1994) y *Coplas que mis oídos oyeron* (1998). Ha sido jurado del Premio Casa de las Américas (1980). Miembro del Seminario de Cultura Mexicana (1994), del que es vicepresidente (1995). Medalla General Lázaro Cárdenas del Río de la Universidad de Colima (1989) y Premio Aguascalientes (1990) por su trayectoria como promotor cultural.

SANDOVAL CASTARRICA, ENRIQUE ◆ n. y m. en el DF (1901-1976). En 1919 participó en la campaña contra Emiliano Zapata en el Estado de México y luchó contra diversos grupos rebeldes en Jalisco, Guanajuato y Michoacán. Se integró al Escuadrón 201, que combatió contra Japón en las Filipinas durante la segunda guerra mundial. Fue subdirector de la Escuela Superior de Guerra y del Colegio Militar y, en la Secretaría de la Defensa Nacional, subjefe del Estado Mayor (1954), director general de Transportes (1962) y subsecretario. General de división en 1968.

SANDOVAL ÍÑIGUEZ, JUAN ◆ n. en Yahualica, Jal. (1933). Arzobispo. Se ordenó como sacerdote en 1957. Licenciado en filosofía y doctor en teología por la Pontificia Universidad Gregoriana de Roma. Ha sido rector del Seminario Mayor y Menor de Guadalajara, dos veces presidente del Consejo Presbiterial, obispo coadjutor con derecho a sucesión (1988-92) y obispo de la diócesis de Ciudad Juárez (1992-94) y arzobispo de Guadalajara. Cardenal desde 1994, en Roma participó como relator en el Sínodo Especial para América (1997).

SANDOVAL LANDÁZURI, ALBERTO ◆ n. en la ciudad de México (1918). Realizó estudios profesionales en la Escuela Nacional de Ciencias Químicas (1940) y de posgrado en la Escuela de Graduados (1944) del Tecnológico de California, como alumno de Laszlo Zechmeister, y en la Facultad de Ciencias de la UNAM (1946-47) en donde obtuvo el grado de doctor. Fue investigador de carrera del Instituto de Química (1951-54), investigador de tiempo completo (1954-74) y director de dicho Instituto (1952-70). Miembro del Consejo Universitario y del Consejo de Ciencias de la UNAM en ese mismo periodo, dirigió

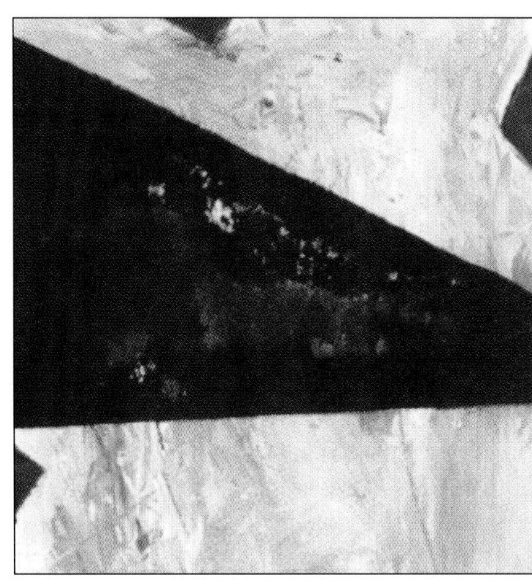

Ascensión, óleo sobre tela de Mauricio Sandoval

el *Boletín del Instituto de Química* de 1946 a 1970. Fue jefe de laboratorio de la Escuela Nacional de Ciencias Biológicas del IPN (1947), consejero del Instituto Mexicano del Petróleo (1966), presidente de la Academia de la Investigación Científica (1959-60), jefe del Departamento Químico-Biológico de Conacyt (1977), subdirector de investigación de la Subsecretaría de Educación Superior de la SEP (1978-82), subdirector de proyecto en la Semip (1982) y asesor del director general de la Comisión Federal de Electricidad (1987-1993). Ha sido invitado por la American Chemical Society y por la Fundación Rockefeller para visitar diversas universidades e impartir conferencias. Ha recibido las medallas Justo Sierra (1948) y de Oro, otorgada por el INIC (1971). Sus numerosos artículos científicos se han publicado en revistas internacionales.

Víctor Sandoval

SANDOVAL RAMÍREZ, PABLO ◆ n. en Tixtla, Gro. (1944). Político. Licenciado en derecho y doctor en ciencia política. Ha sido profesor de la UNAM y la UAG. En los sesenta intervino en la lucha por la autonomía universitaria de la UAG y el derrocamiento del gobernador Raúl Caballero Aburto; se salvó de la matanza del 30 de diciembre de 1960 en Chilpancingo y fue encarcelado. Participó en el MLN (1961-64) y en el Frente Electoral del Pueblo. Fue dirigente de la Central Nacional de Estudiantes Democráticos (CNED) y del Comité de Lucha de Derecho de la UNAM. Fue nuevamente en-

FOTO: DANTE BUCIO

Juan Sandoval Íñiguez

Manuel Sandoval Vallarta, retratado al óleo por Jorge González Camarena

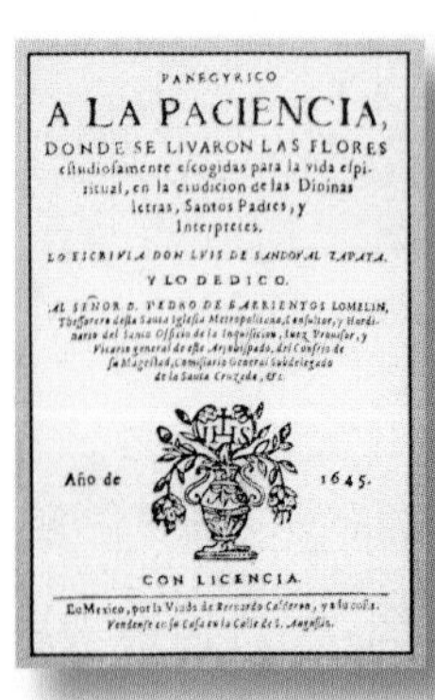

PANEGYRICO
A LA PACIENCIA,
DONDE SE LIVARON LAS FLORES
estudiosamente escogidas para la vida espiritual, en la erudicion de las Divinas letras, Santos Padres, y Interpretes.
LO ESCRIVIA DON LUIS DE SANDOVAL ZAPATA.
Y LO DEDICO.
AL SEÑOR D. PEDRO DE BARRIENTOS LOMELIN,
Año de 1645.
CON LICENCIA.

Obra de Luis de Sandoval Zapata

carcelado en Morelia en 1966. Participó en el movimiento estudiantil de 1968. Perteneció a la Organización Continental Latinoamericana de Estudiantes, la Unión Internacional de Estudiantes y la Federación Mundial de la Juventud Democrática. Fue encarcelado en Bogotá, Colombia, en 1969. Asistió a la manifestación del 10 de junio de 1971. Fue secretario general de la Unión Sindical de Catedráticos de la Universidad Autónoma de Guerrero y consejero universitario. Conformó el Frente de Defensa de los Derechos del Pueblo de Guerrero y sufrió persecución por el gobierno local de Rubén Figueroa. Dirigió el SUNTU en los ochenta y participó en la dirección del STUNAM. Encabezó la Mesa de Concertación Sindical. Fue miembro de la dirección del PCM, el PSUM y el PMS y participó en la fundación del Frente Democrático Nacional (1988) y del PRD (PRD), del cual es consejero nacional. Diputado federal (1997-2000).

Sandoval Vallarta, Manuel ◆ n. y m. en el DF (1899-1977). Doctor en ciencias especializado en física teórica por el Instituto Tecnológico de Massachusetts (1924). Becario de la Fundación Guggenheim (1927-28). Tomó cursos de física en Berlín y Leipzig con Einstein, Planck, Schrodinger, Heisenberg y Debye. Fue profesor asociado, adjunto y titular del Tecnológico de Massachusetts y profesor visitante de la Universidad de Lovaina (1923-46), donde dio clases a R. P. Feynman, futuro premio Nobel. Presidente y vocal de la Comisión Impulsora y Coordinadora de la Investigación Científica (1943-51; antecedente del Conacyt), presidente del Instituto Nacional de la Investigación Científica (1951-63), director del IPN (1944-47), miembro de la Junta de Gobierno de la UNAM (1946), subsecretario de Educación Pública (1953-58), vocal de la Comisión Nacional de Energía Nuclear (1956-72) y subdirector científico del Instituto Nacional de Energía Nuclear (1972-77). Realizó investigaciones de matemáticas, mecánica cuántica y relatividad general y destacó su trabajo en torno a los rayos cósmicos, tema acerca del cual creó la teoría Lemaître-Vallarta (1933), en colaboración con el belga Georges Lemaître, que explica la disminución de la potencia de los rayos cósmicos cerca del ecuador terrestre e, indirectamente, reforzó la teoría del *big bang*; desarrolló también la teoría de la radiación cósmica primaria y su aplicación a investigaciones sobre el campo magnético solar y los efectos de la rotación de la galaxia. Fundador del Instituto de Amistad e Intercambio Cultural México-URSS, miembro de El Colegio Nacional, de la Legión de Honor de Francia, la Academia Pontificia de Ciencias, Sociedad Filosófica Americana, la Sociedad Mexicana de Física (fundador, 1952), Academia Americana de Artes y Ciencias, Asociación Canadiense de Físicos y a la Sociedad de Física de Japón. Premio Nacional de Ciencias Exactas (1961). Se organizaron actos conmemorativos y reconocimientos en el centenario de su natalicio.

Sandoval Zapata, Luis de ◆ ¿n. y m. en la ciudad de México? (¿1618?-1671). De acuerdo con el investigador Ignacio Osorio Romero, es posible que haya nacido en Guadalajara. Escritor. En 1634 ingresó en el Real Colegio de San Ildefonso a estudiar filosofía y teología. Dejó la escuela en 1640. Autor de *Poesías varias a nuestra señora de Guadalupe* y *Panegírico a la paciencia* (1645). Dejó inéditas las obras *El gentil hombre de Dios* (auto sacramental), *Lo que es ser predestinado* (comedia prohibida por la Inquisición), *Relación fúnebre de la infeliz trágica muerte de dos caballeros*, *Misceláneas castellanas*, *El político Tiberio César*, *Elogio de la novedad*, *Panegírico de Orígenes*, *El epicteto cristiano*, *Quaestiones selectae*, *Examen veritatis*, *De magia* y *Doctrina gentium et haereticorum*.

Sangangüey ◆ Volcán de Nayarit, de 2,150 metros de altura, situado en el extremo septentrional de la sierra de San Pedro, al oeste de la de la Yesca y al este-sureste de la capital nayarita. De su cráter se eleva una aguja basáltica que destaca del perfil montañoso.

Sangri Aguilar, María Cristina ◆ n. en Chetumal, QR (1941). Hizo estudios de comercio en la Academia de Santa Catalina, en Belice (1959). Fue profesora de inglés. Pertenece al PRI, en el que ha sido coordinadora de Acción Política del Comité Femenil (1965-70), secretaria de Acción Social y secretaria de Acción Femenil del Comité Directivo Estatal de Quintana Roo (1971-73), así como representante de la Anfer en esa entidad (1973-81). Directora de Acción Femenil de la CNOP (1964- 65) y secretaria general de la Federación de Organizaciones Populares de Quintana Roo (1984-). Ha sido senadora suplente, diputada local a la primera Legislatura de Quintana Roo (1975), presidenta municipal de Othón P. Blanco (1981-84), diputada federal (1985-88), senadora (1988-91) y coordinadora del Programa Estatal de la Mujer (1993-99).

Sangri Namur, Enrique ◆ n. en Chetumal, QR (1931). Ingeniero geógrafo por la Escuela Naval Militar Antón Lizardo y maestro en administración militar por la Escuela Superior de Guerra Naval, de Perú (1983). Conferenciante del Centro de Estudios Superiores Navales (1983), de la Escuela Superior de Guerra (1983) y del Colegio de Defensa Nacional (1984-85). En la Secretaría de Marina ha sido comandante en diversos buques, comandante del sector naval de Coatzacoalcos, director de Armas Navales y Armamento Marinero, coordinador de asesores del jefe de Operaciones Navales (1983-85), comandante de la zona naval de Puerto Vallarta (1985-86) y coordinador general de Servicios Administrativos (1986-88). Vicealmirante diplomado de Estado Mayor Naval. Fue integrante de la delegación de México a la Conferencia de Armas Convencionales de la ONU (Ginebra, 1977-79) y jefe de la delegación mexicana a la Conferencia para el Rescate de la Vida Humana en el Mar, de la ONU (Hamburgo, 1979).

Sanjuán y Colmer, Alfredo de ◆ n. en Cataluña, España, y m. ¿en Monterrey, NL? (1892-?). Militar, fue director de la Escuela de Aplicación Táctica del Ejército y profesor de aeronáutica. Llegó exiliado a México en 1939.

Fue director de trabajos aerofotogramétricos en Chihuahua (1939-40) y profesor de la Escuela Militar de Aviación de Monterrey y de la Universidad de Nuevo León. Autor de *Manual de aviación* (1941) y *Cosmografía* (1945).

SANJUANISTAS ◆ Nombre que recibían los miembros de una agrupación que solía reunirse en la ermita de San Juan Bautista, en Mérida, Yucatán, bajo la guía del sacerdote Vicente María Velázquez, para discutir, sobre todo, acerca de los problemas de trato despótico que recibían los indios de la región. Se adhirieron al movimiento liberal constitucionalista de España y apoyaron la promulgación en Yucatán de la Constitución de Cádiz (1812). Entre los principales sanjuanistas se contaban Lorenzo y Agustín de Zavala, Manuel José Milanés, Pedro José Guzmán, José Matías Quintana, Pedro Almeida y José Francisco Bates. En 1813 se abocaron a defender la libertad de imprenta, a raíz de la llegada de la primera prensa a la península. En 1814, al suspender la vigencia de la Carta de Cádiz, Lorenzo de Zavala, Quintana y Bates fueron encarcelados en San Juan de Ulúa, de donde no salieron sino hasta 1817. Tras la independencia mexicana, los sanjuanistas se dividieron en diferentes corrientes políticas, una de ellas, la Confederación Patriótica, luchó por la independencia yucateca.

SANO, SEKI ◆ n. en China y m. en el DF (1905-1966). Vivió en Japón, país de origen de sus padres, donde incursionó en el teatro tradicional. Estudió dirección y actuación en la Unión Soviética y volvió a Japón. Ahí destacó como director y profesor de arte dramático. Se exilió en México en 1939 y continuó su labor docente (fue el introductor de la técnica de Stanislavski), primero auspiciado por el Sindicato Mexicano de Electricistas (ahí organizó el Teátro de las Artes y la primera obra que montó fue *La coronela*); escenificó obras en plazas y otros lugares públicos; fue fundador de la Asociación Mexicana de Teatros Experimentales; montó y organizó el grupo Teatro de la Reforma (1948), con el que presentó varias obras en el Palacio de Bellas Artes y en el teatro Esperanza Iris; dirigió el Grupo de los Trece, con el que presentó varias comedias francesas en el teatro Molière; fue profesor de la Escuela Teatral del INBA y militó en el Partido Comunista Mexicano. Dirigió *La fuerza bruta*, de Steinbeck, *La fierecilla domada* y *El rey Lear* (su último trabajo), de Shakespeare, *Un tranvía llamado deseo*, de Tennesse Williams, *La rebelión de los colgados*, de B. Traven, *Corona de sombra*, de Rodolfo Usigli, *La mandrágora*, de Maquiavelo, *Panorama desde el puente* y *Prueba de fuego*, de Arthur Miller, y *Ana Karenina*, de León Tolstoi, entre otras obras. Inauguró el Teatro Coyoacán. Recibió un homenaje nacional en 1996 organizado por el INBA.

Seki Sano

SANSÓN FLORES, JESÚS ◆ n. y m. en Morelia, Mich. (1909-1966). En los años veinte perteneció al grupo de poetas izquierdistas organizado por Carlos Gutiérrez Cruz. Colaboró en la aplicación del programa agrario de Lázaro Cárdenas. Fue primer secretario de la embajada mexicana en la República Española (1937). Dirigió los periódicos *Juventud* y *Redención* (órgano, este último, de la Confederación Michoacana de Trabajadores). Autor de los poemarios *¡Clarinadas!* (1928), *Puños en alto* (1932), *El niño proletario* (1936), *Canción del odio* (1938), *Bajo el sol de España* (1939), *Hampa* (1941) y *El camino perdido* (1954).

SANSORES PÉREZ, CARLOS ◆ n. en Champotón, Camp. (1918). Político. Licenciado en derecho por la Universidad de Campeche. Miembro fundador del PRI (1946). En el Comité Ejecutivo Nacional de este partido ha sido delegado en varias entidades, secretario auxiliar (1966), subsecretario general (1973-74) y presidente del Comité Ejecutivo Nacional (1976-79). En Campeche fue jefe de la Policía Judicial (1943-44), secretario general de Gobierno (1949-50) y gobernador constitucional (1967-73). Cuatro veces diputado federal (1946-49, 1955-58, 1961-64 y, como presidente de la Gran Comisión, 1973-76); senador de la República en dos ocasiones (1964-67 y 1976-79, presidente de la Gran Comisión en 1976); y director general del Instituto de Seguridad y Servicios Sociales de los Trabajadores del Estado (1979-80).

SANSORES PÉREZ, RAMIRO ◆ n. en Campeche, Camp., y m. en el DF (1929-1982). Se tituló como médico cirujano en la UNAM (1953), donde fue profesor (1953-82). Miembro del PRI, del que fue presidente del noveno comité distrital del DF (1964). En el sindicato de trabajadores del IMSS fue secretario de la Comisión Nacional de Fomento para la Vivienda, secretario de prensa del Comité Ejecutivo Nacional y presidente de la Comisión Nacional de Capacitación. Fundador y primer director del Instituto Médico Cultural. Jefe de sala y subdirector del Hospital de la Mujer y ginecoobstetra del Centro Médico Nacional. Director general del Servicio de Transportes Eléctricos del DF (1979-82).

SANSORES PREN, ROSARIO ◆ n. en Mérida, Yuc., y m. en el DF (1889-1972). Desde su juventud inició la publicación de poemas en diversos periódicos y revistas yucatecos. Fijó su residencia en Cuba y colaboró en el *Diario de la Marina* y *Bohemia*. Vivió en la capital mexicana desde 1932 e inició su participación en la crónica de sociales en *Hoy*, *Todo* y, desde 1937, en *Novedades*, donde publicó la sección "Rutas de emoción". Autora de los poemarios *La novia del sol*, *Cantaba el mar azul*, *Las horas pasadas*, *Fruta madura*, *Mi corazón y yo*, *Mientras se va la vida* y *El breviario de Eros*.

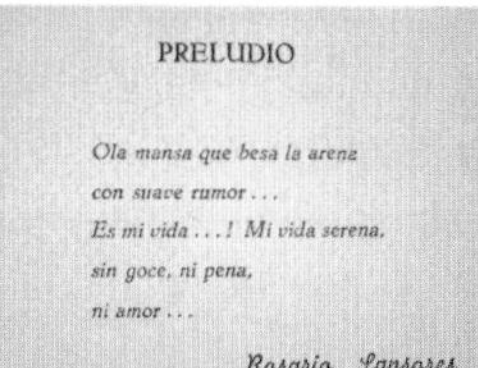
PRELUDIO

Ola mansa que besa la arena
con suave rumor...
Es mi vida...! Mi vida serena,
sin goce, ni pena,
ni amor...

Rosario Sansores

Poema de Rosario Sansores Pren

SANSORES SAN ROMÁN, LAYDA ELENA ◆ n. en el DF (1945). Hija de Carlos Sansores Pérez. Psicóloga por la UNAM. Maestra en psicología por la Universidad de Buenos Aires. Perteneció al PRI. Ha sido subdirectora y directora de política poblacional y subdelegada de desarrollo social en el DDF. Diputada federal (1991-94), senadora (1994-2000). En 1997 renunció al PRI y se integró al PRD. Es directora de promoción voluntaria del Comité Ejecutivo Nacional del PRD y coordinadora de administración del grupo parlamentario de ese partido en el Senado.

FOTO: IMAGEN LATINA

Layda Elena Sansores San Román

Santa Ana ◆ Municipio de Oaxaca situado en el centro-sur del estado, al oeste de Miahuatlán y al sur de la capital de la entidad. Superficie: 51.03 km^2. Habitantes: 1,596, de los cuales 445 forman la población económicamente activa. La cabecera fue hasta 1908 la hacienda de Miahuatlán.

Santa Ana ◆ Municipio de Sonora situado al norte de Hermosillo y al sur de Nogales. Superficie: 1,620.65 km^2. Habitantes: 13,374, de los cuales 3,829 forman la población económicamente activa. Hablan alguna lengua indígena 17 personas mayores de cinco años. En la jurisdicción se halla el parque nacional de El Pinacate. La cabecera, del mismo nombre, fue elevada al rango de ciudad el 16 de abril de 1943. La fiesta de Santa Ana se celebra el 26 de julio, con bailes, juegos pirotécnicos, música y una feria popular.

Santa Ana, Justo A. ◆ n. en Villahermosa, Tab., y m. en el DF (1890-1944). Antirreeleccionista. En 1910 participó en el Congreso de Estudiantes que pidió la renuncia de Porfirio Díaz. Se incorporó a la revolución en 1913, en las fuerzas constitucionalistas de Salvador Alvarado y Alberto Carrera Torres. Fue diputado local y federal. Presidió el segundo Congreso Nacional de Periodistas y fue secretario de prensa en la campaña presidencial de Plutarco Elías Calles. Autor de *El callismo de Tabasco*, *Mis maestros*, *Historia de Tabasco* y *Legislación revolucionaria de Yucatán*.

Santa Ana Alavez, Carlos ◆ n. en el DF (1941). Licenciado en comunicación por la UNAM. Colaborador de *El Nacional*, *El Universal*, *Últimas Noticias*, *Avance* y otras publicaciones, y de radio con *Ustedes y nosotros*. Pertenece a la Asociación Mexicana de Periodistas de Radio y Televisión, a la Asociación de Periodistas Críticos de Teatro y desde 1957 al Sindicato Nacional de Redactores de la Prensa y Trabajadores de Actividades Similares y Conexas, del que fue secretario general (1989-94). Director del diario capitalino *Cine mundial* (1985-).

Santa Ana Ateixtlahuaca ◆ Municipio de Oaxaca situado en el norte del estado, al noroeste y cerca de Huautla de Jiménez y al oeste de la presa Miguel Alemán, en los límites con Puebla. Superficie: 19.14 km^2. Habitantes: 559, de los cuales 156 forman la población económicamente activa. Hablan mazateco 481 personas mayores de cinco años (monolingües 112).

Santa Ana Cuauhtémoc ◆ Municipio de Oaxaca situado en el norte del estado, al sureste de Huautla de Jiménez y al suroeste de la presa Miguel Alemán. Superficie: 24.24 km^2. Habitantes: 948, de los cuales 269 forman la población económicamente activa. Hablan alguna lengua indígena 484 personas mayores de cinco años (mixteco 482). Su anterior nombre fue Santa Ana Chiquihuitlan.

Santa Ana Chávez, Armando ◆ n. en el DF (1951). Estudió lengua y literatura hispánicas en la UNAM. Escritor de relatos y escultor. Su pieza monumental *Dodecaedro solar* se encuentra en la ENEP-Iztacala. Efectuó trabajos escultóricos en los centros Steuben Glass y Corning Glass, gracias a la beca Fulbright que le otorgó la Universidad Estatal de Nueva York (1994). Muestras de su obra se exhiben en Universum, Museo de Ciencias de la UNAM. Fue becario del Centro Mexicano de Escritores (1972-73).

Santa Ana Jilotzingo ◆ Cabecera del municipio mexiquense de Jilotzingo (☛).

Santa Ana Nopaluca ◆ Municipio de Tlaxcala situado al oeste de la capital del estado. Tiene 5,302 habitantes, distribuidos en cuatro localidades.

Santa Ana Maya ◆ Municipio de Michoacán situado en el noreste del estado, en los límites con Guanajuato y al noreste de Morelia. Superficie: 117.69 km^2. Habitantes: 13,745, de los cuales 3,460 forman la población económicamente activa. Su cabecera, del mismo nombre, se encuentra en la ribera septentrional del lago de Cuitzeo.

Santa Ana Nextlalpan ◆ Cabecera del municipio mexiquense de Nextlalpan (☛).

Santa Ana Seuthe, Cuauhtémoc ◆ n. en Villa de Álvarez, Col. (1940). Licenciado en derecho por la UNAM (1960), posgraduado en la Universidad de Génova (1964). Desde 1957 es miembro del PRI, en el que ha sido presidente del Comité Directivo en el DF (1971-75). Ha sido secretario del oficial mayor (1965), secretario particular del subsecretario (1966-69) y subdirector general de Gobierno de la Secretaría de Gobernación; diputado federal (1970-73), delegado del DDF en Benito Juárez (1975-76) y en Cuauhtémoc (1977-79), secretario general de Obras y Servicios del DDF (1979-82), asesor (1983) y coordinador de asesores del secretario de la Contraloría General de la Federación (1984), coordinador del Programa de Simplificación Administrativa del Gobierno Federal (1984-87) y subdirector técnico administrativo de Pemex (1987-92). Fue presidente del Instituto Mexicano de Derecho Registral (1989-92).

Santa Ana Tavela ◆ Municipio de Oaxaca situado al sureste de la capital de la entidad y al oeste-noroeste de Juchitán de Zaragoza. Superficie: 81.65 km^2. Habitantes: 1,137, de los cuales 330 forman la población económicamente activa. Hablan alguna lengua indígena ocho personas mayores de cinco años.

Santa Ana Tlapacoyan ◆ Municipio de Oaxaca situado en el centro del estado, al sur-suroeste de la capital de la entidad y al nor-noroeste de Miahuatlán. Superficie: 116.1 km^2. Habitantes: 2,388, de los cuales 653 forman la población económicamente activa. Hablan alguna lengua indígena nueve personas.

Santa Ana del Valle ◆ Municipio de Oaxaca situado en el centro del estado, al este y próximo a la capital de la entidad. Superficie: 34.45 km^2. Habitantes: 2,147, de los cuales 579 forman la población económicamente activa. Hablan alguna lengua indígena 1,783 personas mayores de cinco años (zapoteco 1,776).

Santa Ana Yareni ◆ Municipio de Oaxaca situado en el centro-norte del estado, al nor-noreste de la capital de la entidad. Superficie: 43.38 km^2. Habitantes: 1,157, de los cuales 816 forman la población económicamente activa. Hablan alguna lengua indígena 965 personas mayores de cinco años (zapoteco 840 y zapoteco de Ixtlán 125); de ellas, 46 son monolingües.

SANTA ANA ZEGACHE ◆ Municipio de Oaxaca situado en el centro del estado, al sur de la capital de la entidad. Superficie: 26.79 km². Habitantes: 3,512, de los cuales 730 forman la población económicamente activa. Hablan alguna lengua indígena 1,165 personas mayores de cinco años (zapoteco 1,126).

SANTA ANNA, ANTONIO LÓPEZ DE ◆ ☛ *López de Santa Anna, Antonio.*

SANTA ANNA, JUSTO CECILIO ◆ n. en Macuspana, Tab., y m. en el DF (1861-1931). Se tituló de abogado en el Instituto Juárez de San Juan Bautista, del que fue profesor. Fue diputado local, profesor de la Facultad de Derecho de Mérida (1915), coautor de las leyes de Administración de Justicia y de Notariado de Yucatán y colaborador de la *Revista Ilustrada* de Nueva York, *Mundo Latino* de Madrid, *Revista Literaria* de Buenos Aires, y de *El Mundo Ilustrado*, de México. Autor de *Poetas mexicanos, estudios críticos* (1890), *Notas para la historia de Tabasco* (1893), *Tradiciones y leyendas tabasqueñas* (1894) y *Notas para la historia de la agricultura en Tabasco* (1909).

SANTA APOLONIA TEACALCO ◆ Municipio de Tlaxcala situado al sureste de la capital del estado, al norte de Papalotla de Xicohténcatl. Tiene 3,707 habitantes, distribuidos en seis localidades. Fue erigido el 8 de agosto de 1995 con terrenos que pertenecieron al municipio de Nativitas.

SANTA BÁRBARA ◆ Municipio de Chihuahua situado en el sur del estado, en los límites con Durango, al suroeste de Hidalgo del Parral. Superficie: 424.23 km². Habitantes: 12,699, de los cuales 4,103 forman la población económicamente activa. Hablan alguna lengua indígena 29 personas mayores de cinco años (tarahumara 27). Posee yacimientos de plomo, zinc, plata, cobre y oro.

SANTA BÁRBARA, DE ◆ Sierra de Chihuahua y Durango que sirve de límite a estos dos estados. Se extiende de noroeste a sureste; al oeste, suroeste y sur de Hidalgo del Parral y al noroeste de Santa María del Oro. Su cima más elevada es el Cerro Alto, con 2,700 metros sobre el nivel del mar. Cuenta con yacimientos minerales.

SANTA CATALINA ◆ Isla de Baja California Sur en el golfo de California, al este de la isla de Monserrate y al sureste de la del Carmen.

SANTA CATALINA QUIERI ◆ Municipio de Oaxaca situado en el sur del estado, al este de Miahuatlán y al noreste de Puerto Ángel. Superficie: 47.21 km². Habitantes: 875, de los cuales 319 forman la población económicamente activa. Hablan alguna lengua indígena 673 personas mayores de cinco años (zapoteco 671).

SANTA CATARINA ◆ Municipio de Guanajuato situado en el noreste del estado, en los límites con Querétaro, al noreste de la capital de la entidad. Superficie: 246.5 km². Habitantes: 4,284, de los cuales 655 forman la población económicamente activa. Hablan alguna lengua indígena 12 personas mayores de cinco años. Su principal festividad se celebra del 22 al 26 de noviembre.

SANTA CATARINA ◆ Municipio de Nuevo León situado en los límites con Coahuila y contiguo a Monterrey. Superficie: 984.5 km². Habitantes: 202,156, de los cuales 54,515 forman la población económicamente activa. Hablan alguna lengua indígena 309 personas mayores de cinco años (náhuatl 152). En su jurisdicción se encuentra la zona arqueológica llamada Guitarritas. Su celebración más importante es la fiesta de la Virgen de San Juan de los Lagos, del 10 al 15 de agosto, en la que hay procesiones, danzas y fuegos artificiales. Su cabecera es Ciudad Santa Catarina.

SANTA CATARINA ◆ Municipio de San Luis Potosí situado en el sureste del estado, en los límites con Querétaro, al suroeste de Ciudad Valles y al sureste de Río Verde. Superficie: 637.3 km². Habitantes: 10,642, de los cuales 2,160 forman la población económicamente activa. Hablan alguna lengua indígena 4,091 personas mayores de cinco años (pame 2,024). Indígenas monolingües: 1,001.

Sierra de Santa Bárbara, Chihuahua

FOTO: FONDO EDITORIAL GRUPO AZABACHE

SANTA CATARINA AYOMETLA ◆ Municipio de Tlaxcala situado al sur de la capital del estado y al este de Zacatelco. Tiene 6,998 habitantes. Fue erigido en 1995.

SANTA CATARINA CUIXTLA ◆ Municipio de Oaxaca situado en el sur del estado, al sureste y próximo a Miahuatlán. Superficie: 125.03 km². Habitantes: 1,719, de los cuales 488 forman la población económicamente activa. Hablan alguna lengua indígena 395 personas mayores de cinco años (zapoteco 394).

SANTA CATARINA IXTEPEJI ◆ Municipio de Oaxaca situado en el centro-norte del estado, al noreste de la capital de la entidad. Superficie: 196.48 km². Habitantes: 2,358, de los cuales 626 forman la población económicamente activa. Hablan alguna lengua indígena 169 personas mayores de cinco años (zapoteco 167). En el pueblo de San Pedro Nexicho, dentro de su jurisdicción, hay una pirámide, vestigio de la cultura zapoteca. En su cabecera, del mismo nombre, existe una iglesia construida en el siglo XVII.

SANTA CATARINA JUQUILA ◆ Municipio de Oaxaca situado en el suroeste

Artesania de Santa Clara del Cobre

del estado, al este-sureste de Santiago Pinotepa Nacional y al noroeste de Puerto Escondido. Superficie: 811.48 km². Habitantes: 12,560, de los cuales 3,036 forman la población económicamente activa. Hablan alguna lengua indígena 3,331 personas mayores de cinco años (chatino 3,307) y de ellas, 918 no saben español. Se festeja el 8 de diciembre a la Virgen de Juquila, con una feria y diversos actos religiosos. Esta imagen ha sido venerada desde 1633, cuando se rescató intacta de las ruinas de una casa quemada.

Santa Catarina Lachatao ◆ Municipio de Oaxaca situado en el centro del estado, al este de la capital de la entidad. Superficie: 276.85 km². Habitantes: 1,558, de los cuales 435 forman la población económicamente activa. Hablan zapoteco 652 personas mayores de cinco años.

Santa Catarina Loxicha ◆ Municipio de Oaxaca situado en el sur del estado, al sur de Miahuatlán. Superficie: 70.17 km². Habitantes: 3,375, de los cuales 1,005 forman la población económicamente activa. Hablan alguna lengua indígena 558 personas mayores de cinco años (zapoteco 556).

Santa Catarina Mechoacán ◆ Municipio de Oaxaca situado en el suroeste del estado, al este y próximo a Santiago Pinotepa Nacional. Superficie: 61.24 km². Habitantes: 3,997, de los cuales 898 forman la población económicamente activa. Hablan alguna lengua indígena 3,293 personas mayores de cinco años (zapoteco 3,286), de las cuales 709 son monolingües.

Santa Catarina Minas ◆ Municipio de Oaxaca situado en el centro del estado, al sur de la capital de la entidad. Superficie: 25.52 km². Habitantes: 1,594, de los cuales 418 forman la población económicamente activa. Hablan alguna lengua indígena siete personas mayores de cinco años.

Santa Catarina Quiane ◆ Municipio de Oaxaca situado en el centro del estado, al sur de la capital de la entidad. Superficie: 24.24 km². Habitantes: 1,791, de los cuales 392 forman la población económicamente activa.

Santa Catarina Quioquitani ◆ Municipio de Oaxaca situado al noreste de Miahuatlán. Superficie: 45.93 km². Población: 355 habitantes, de los cuales 180 forman la población económicamente activa. Hablan zapoteco 262 personas mayores de cinco años. Se le conoce sólo como Quioquitani.

Santa Catarina Tayata ◆ Municipio de Oaxaca situado en el noroeste del estado, al sureste de Huajuapan de León. Superficie: 47.2 km². Habitantes: 773, de los cuales 166 forman la población económicamente activa. Hablan zapoteco 56 personas mayores de cinco años.

Santa Catarina Ticuá ◆ Municipio de Oaxaca situado en el occidente del estado, al sur-sureste de Huajuapan de León y al nor-noreste de Santiago Pinotepa Nacional. Superficie: 15.31 km². Habitantes: 859, de los cuales 146 forman la población económicamente activa. Hablan alguna lengua indígena 534 personas mayores de cinco años (mixteco 533). Su cabecera, del mismo nombre, cuenta con una iglesia del siglo XVIII.

Santa Catarina Tlaltempan ◆ Municipio de Puebla situado en el centro del estado, al sur de la capital de la entidad y al este de Izúcar de Matamoros. Superficie: 42.11 km². Habitantes: 697, de los cuales 198 forman la población económicamente activa. Hablan mixteco 512 personas mayores de cinco años (monolingües: 75).

Santa Catarina Yosonotú ◆ Municipio de Oaxaca situado en el occidente del estado, al oeste de la capital de la entidad. Superficie: 71.45 km². Habitantes: 1,832, de los cuales 440 forman la población económicamente activa. Hablan mixteco 1,492 personas mayores de cinco años (110 son monolingües).

Santa Catarina Zapoquila ◆ Municipio de Oaxaca situado en el noroeste del estado, en los límites con Puebla, al noreste de Huajuapan de León. Superficie: 112.27 km². Habitantes: 703, de los cuales 152 forman la población económicamente activa. Hablan mixteco cinco personas mayores de cinco años.

Santa Clara ◆ Municipio de Durango situado en el oriente del estado, en los límites con Zacatecas, al sur de Gómez Palacio. Superficie: 1,004.2 km². Habitantes: 8,050, de los cuales 1,714 forman la población económicamente activa. Hablan alguna lengua indígena 15 personas mayores de cinco años.

Santa Clara, de ◆ Sierra de Baja California Sur situada al sureste del espolón que cierra por el sur la bahía de Sebastián Vizcaíno; se extiende al oeste de la sierra de Santa Lucía y al norte de la bahía de Ballenas.

Santa Clara Coatitla ◆ Poblado perteneciente al municipio de Ecatepec (☛), Estado de México.

Santa Clara del Cobre ◆ Nombre de la cabecera municipal del municipio michoacano Salvador Escalante (☛).

Santa Clara Ocoyucan ◆ Cabecera del municipio poblano de Ocoyucan (☛).

Santa Cruz ◆ Isla de Baja California Sur situada en el golfo de California. Se halla al nor-noroeste de la isla de San José y de la bahía de La Paz.

Santa Cruz ◆ Municipio de Sonora situado en el norte del estado, al este de Nogales, en la frontera con Estados Unidos. Superficie: 880.43 km². Habitantes: 1,407, de los cuales 475 forman la población económicamente activa.

Santa Cruz, de ◆ Sierra de Jalisco situada al noroeste de Guadalajara y al sur de la sierra de Bolaños. Su extremo septentrional llega al límite con Zacatecas.

Santa Cruz, Francisco ◆ n. en

Guaymas, Son., y m. en Colima, Col. (1836-1902). Fue prefecto político de Hermosillo (1867) y gobernador de Sonora (1869-71). Reelecto para el periodo siguiente, en 1872 fue obligado a renunciar por el movimiento en su contra que encabezó Filomeno Bravo. Volvió a ser gobernador de Sonora (1879-83) y dejó al estado en bancarrota. Fue diputado local, regidor y presidente del ayuntamiento de Colima, senador (1884-88) y gobernador de Colima desde 1891 hasta su muerte, en sucesivas reelecciones.

SANTA CRUZ ACATEPEC ◆ Municipio de Oaxaca situado en el norte del estado, al noroeste de Huautla de Jiménez. Superficie: 14.03 km^2. Habitantes: 986, de los cuales 300 forman la población económicamente activa. Hablan mazateco 810 personas mayores de cinco años, de las que 193 son monolingües.

SANTA CRUZ AMILPAS ◆ Municipio de Oaxaca situado en el centro del estado, al sureste y contiguo a la capital de la entidad. Superficie: 10.21 km^2. Habitantes: 5,737, de los cuales 1,461 forman la población económicamente activa. Hablan alguna lengua indígena 221 personas mayores de cinco años (zapoteco 168).

SANTA CRUZ DE BRAVO ◆ Municipio de Oaxaca situado en el noroeste del estado, en los límites con Guerrero, al suroeste de Huajuapan de León. Superficie: 112.27 km^2. Habitantes: 447, de los cuales 50 forman la población económicamente activa.

SANTA CRUZ ITUNDUJÍA ◆ Municipio de Oaxaca situado en el occidente del estado, al noreste de Santiago Pinotepa Nacional. Superficie: 211.78 km^2. Habitantes: 9,434, de los cuales 1,924 forman la población económicamente activa. Hablan alguna lengua indígena 848 personas mayores de cinco años (mixteco 834).

SANTA CRUZ DE JUVENTINO ROSAS ◆ Municipio de Guanajuato situado en el centro del estado, al sureste de la capital de la entidad y al este de Irapuato. Superficie: 394.4 km^2. Habitantes: 61,945, de los cuales 15,002 forman la población económicamente activa. Hablan alguna lengua indígena 21 personas mayores de cinco años.

SANTA CRUZ MIXTEPEC ◆ Municipio de Oaxaca situado en el centro del estado, al suroeste de la capital de la entidad. Superficie: 66.34 km^2. Habitantes: 3,284, de los cuales 1,117 forman la población económicamente activa. Hablan alguna lengua indígena 536 personas mayores de cinco años (zapoteco 533).

SANTA CRUZ NUNDACO ◆ Municipio de Oaxaca situado en el occidente del estado, al suroeste y próximo a Tlaxiaco. Superficie: 159.48 km^2. Habitantes: 2,525, de los cuales 458 forman la población económicamente activa. Hablan alguna lengua indígena 1,978 personas mayores de cinco años (mixteco 1,975); de ellas, 129 no saben español.

SANTA CRUZ PAPALUTLA ◆ Municipio de Oaxaca situado en el centro del estado, al sureste de la capital de la entidad. Superficie: 11.48 km^2. Habitantes: 1,699, de los cuales 457 forman la población económicamente activa. Hablan alguna lengua indígena 772 personas mayores de cinco años (zapoteco 769).

SANTA CRUZ QUILEHTLA ◆ Municipio de Tlaxcala erigido el 11 de agosto de 1995. Tiene 4,573 habitantes, distribuidos en dos localidades, Santa Cruz y Ayometitla, que pertenecieron a Acuamanala de Miguel Hidalgo y Costilla.

SANTA CRUZ TACACHE DE MINA ◆ Municipio de Oaxaca situado en el noroeste del estado, al oeste-noroeste de Huajuapan de León. Superficie: 33.17 km^2. Habitantes: 2,539, de los cuales 458 forman la población económicamente activa. Hablan alguna lengua indígena ocho personas.

SANTA CRUZ TACAHUA ◆ Municipio de Oaxaca situado en el occidente del estado, al sureste de Tlaxiaco y al noreste de Santiago Pinotepa Nacional. Superficie: 98.24 km^2. Habitantes: 1,336, de los cuales 282 forman la población económicamente activa. Hablan mixteco 599 personas mayores de cinco años (monolingües 45).

SANTA CRUZ TAYATA ◆ Municipio de Oaxaca situado en el noroeste del estado, al sureste de Huajuapan de León y al noreste de Tlaxiaco. Superficie: 42.1 km^2. Habitantes: 495, de los cuales 135 forman la población económicamente activa. Hablan mixteco cinco personas mayores de cinco años.

SANTA CRUZ TLAXCALA ◆ Municipio de Tlaxcala situado en el centro del estado, al noreste de la capital de la entidad. Superficie: 35.4 km^2. Habitantes: 11,688, de los cuales 2,889 forman la población económicamente activa. Hablan alguna lengua indígena 315 personas mayores de cinco años (náhuatl 300).

SANTA CRUZ XITLA ◆ Municipio de Oaxaca situado en el sur del estado, al oeste de Miahuatlán. Superficie: 38.27 km^2. Habitantes: 3,542, de los cuales 1,165 forman la población económicamente activa. Hablan zapoteco 2,417 personas mayores de cinco años.

SANTA CRUZ XOXOCOTLÁN ◆ Municipio de Oaxaca contiguo a la capital de la entidad. Superficie: 76.55 km^2. Habitantes: 40,815, de los cuales 8,990 forman la población económicamente activa. Hablan alguna lengua indígena 2,980 personas mayores de cinco años (zapoteco 1,564, mixteco 661, mixe 385 y chinanteco 103).

SANTA CRUZ ZENZONTEPEC ◆ Muni-

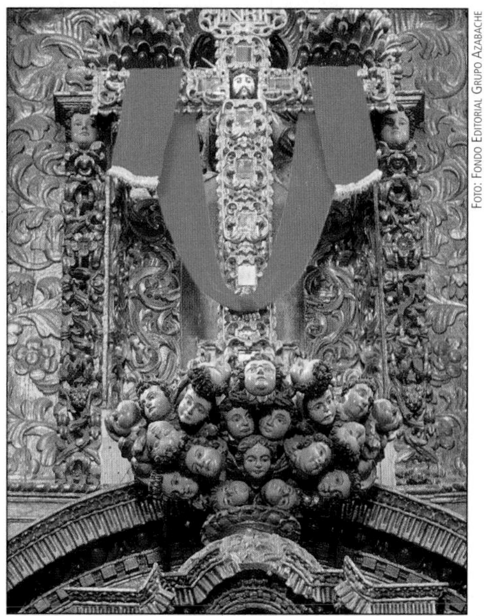
FOTO: FONDO EDITORIAL GRUPO AZABACHE

Cruz del altar mayor de la iglesia de Santa Cruz Tlaxcala, en Tlaxcala cipio de Oaxaca situado en el suroeste del estado, al noreste de Santiago Pinotepa Nacional. Superficie: 361.06 km². Habitantes: 13,978, de los cuales 2,903 forman la población económicamente activa. Hablan alguna lengua indígena 7,181 personas mayores de cinco años (chatino 7,165).

Santa Elena ◆ Municipio de Yucatán situado en el suroeste del estado, en los límites con Campeche, al sur de Mérida. Superficie: 694.9 km². Habitantes: 3,252, de los cuales 750 forman la población económicamente activa. Hablan maya 2,615 personas mayores de cinco años. Indígenas monolingües: 232.

Santa Gertrudis ◆ Municipio de Oaxaca situado en el centro del estado, al sur-suroeste de la capital de la entidad. Superficie: 21.69 km². Habitantes: 3,670, de los cuales 841 forman la población económicamente activa.

Santa Inés Ahuatempan ◆ Municipio de Puebla situado en el sur del estado, al sur de la capital de la entidad y al oeste de Tehuacán. Superficie: 289.58 km². Habitantes: 5,235, de los cuales 1,467 forman la población económicamente activa. Hablan alguna lengua indígena 536 personas mayores de cinco años (popoloca 449).

Santa Inés del Monte ◆ Municipio de Oaxaca situado en el centro del estado, al suroeste de la capital de la entidad. Superficie: 34.45 km². Habitantes: 2,209, de los cuales 397 forman la población económicamente activa.

Santa Inés Yatzeche ◆ Municipio de Oaxaca situado en el centro del estado, al sur-suroeste de la capital de la entidad. Superficie: 11.48 km². Habitantes: 1,332, de los cuales 299 forman la población económicamente activa. Hablan alguna lengua indígena 1,175 personas mayores de cinco años (zapoteco 1,174).

Santa Inés de Zaragoza ◆ Municipio de Oaxaca situado en el centro del estado, al noroeste de la capital estatal y al sureste de Huajuapan de León. Superficie: 61.24 km². Habitantes: 2,061, de los cuales 484 forman la población económicamente activa. Hablan alguna lengua indígena 876 personas mayores de cinco años (mixteco 875). La cabecera, del mismo nombre, se llamó Santa Inés del Río.

Santa Isabel ◆ Municipio de Chihuahua contiguo a la capital del estado. Extensión: 1,040.81 km². Habitantes: 5,289, de los cuales 1,431 forman la población económicamente activa. Hablan tarahumara siete personas mayores de cinco años. Su principal atractivo turístico es el lago artificial Jacales, que es un centro vacacional. La cabecera, del mismo nombre, la fundaron misioneros franciscanos en 1688 como Santa Isabel de Tarahumares. Al municipio se le refiere también con el nombre de General Trías.

Santa Isabel Cholula ◆ Municipio de Puebla situado en el occidente del estado, contiguo a Atlixco y cercano a la capital de la entidad. Superficie: 67.61 km². Habitantes: 8,188, de los cuales 1,886 forman la población económicamente activa. Hablan alguna lengua indígena 173 personas mayores de cinco años (náhuatl 160).

Santa Isabel Xiloxoxtla ◆ Municipio de Tlaxcala erigido en 1995 y contiguo por el sureste a la capital del estado. Tiene 3,171 habitantes.

Santa Lucía ◆ Estado insular americano en las Antillas Menores. Pertenece al grupo de las islas de Barlovento. Está situado al sur de la Martinica y al norte de San Vicente. Tiene una superficie de 619 km² y 150,000 habitantes (1998), en su mayoría mulatos, descendientes de esclavos africanos y colonizadores europeos. Su capital es Castries, con una población estimada en 1992 de 13,615 habitantes. Otra población de importancia es Vieux-Fort (13,617 habitantes). El idioma oficial es el inglés, aunque también se emplean el hindi y el *patois* (mezcla de francés y lenguas africanas). Es una monarquía constitucional, con la reina británica como jefa del Estado, representada por un gobernador general, designado por recomendación del primer ministro. *Historia.* Alrededor del año 200 de nuestra era la isla empezó a ser poblada por indios arauacos procedentes de Sudamérica. Un milenio después los caribes desalojaron del territorio a los arauacos. Cristóbal Colón arribó a Santa Lucía en 1502 y los ingleses hicieron en 1605 y en 1640 los primeros intentos de colonización, pero fueron muertos o desalojados por los caribes. En 1660, colonos franceses obligaron a los caribes a ceder sus reclamaciones sobre la isla, que en 1778 fue controlada por el imperio británico luego de una acción armada sobre las fuerzas francesas. En 1781 el conde francés De Grasse intentó recuperar el territorio, pero fue rechazado por las fuerzas inglesas. Un año más tarde De Grasse volvió a ser derrotado, aunque los tratados diplomáticos cedieron el dominio de Santa Lucía a Francia. En 1796 el inglés Ralph Abercrombie recuperó militarmente la isla, pero un nuevo tratado de paz devolvió a Francia los derechos sobre la misma. En 1803, en el marco de las guerras napoleónicas, las fuerzas británicas impusieron nuevamente su dominio. En 1814, con el Tratado de París, se legitimó esa cesión forzosa. En 1838 Santa Lucía fue incorporada a la colonia de las Islas de Barlovento y la esclavitud fue abolida. En 1940 Inglaterra cedió a Estados Unidos las bases navales de Santa Lucía para un periodo de 99 años, a cambio de armamento. En 1958 se integró a la Federación de las Antillas y dos años después se le designó un gobernador (británico) y el conjunto de la colonia de Barlovento recibió una Constitución, un administrador y un consejo legislativo. En 1962 se desintegró la Federación de las Antillas y cinco años más tarde, Santa Lucía adquirió el rango de Estado asociado, con autonomía interna. En 1971 suscribió la Declaración de Granada, tendiente a crear una nueva nación antillana. En 1979 adquirió plena independencia, se suscribió al Movimiento de Países no Alineados y firmó la Declaración de St. George's, que finca una colaboración más estrecha con Dominica y Granada. En ese mismo año se establecieron relaciones diplomáticas con México. En 1982, luego de una crisis política, el primer ministro laborista Winston Cenac fue sustituido por un gobierno provisional de unidad nacional y más tarde por el primer ministro John Compton. En 1983 un contingente de Santa Lucía participó en la invasión estadounidense a Granada.

SANTA LUCÍA DEL CAMINO ◆ Municipio de Oaxaca contiguo a la capital del estado. Superficie: 7.65 km². Habitantes: 35,631, de los cuales 9,633 forman la población económicamente activa. Hablan alguna lengua indígena 4,238 personas mayores de cinco años (zapoteco 2,729, mixe 665, mixteco 289 y chinanteco 169).

SANTA LUCÍA MIAHUATLÁN ◆ Municipio de Oaxaca situado en el sur del estado, al sureste y cerca de Miahuatlán. Superficie: 109.72 km². Habitantes: 2,406, de los cuales 669 forman la población económicamente activa. Hablan zapoteco 2,122 personas mayores de cinco años, de las cuales 430 son monolingües.

SANTA LUCÍA MONTEVERDE ◆ Municipio de Oaxaca situado en el occidente del estado, al sur de Tlaxiaco y noreste de Santiago Pinotepa Nacional. Superficie: 74 km². Habitantes: 6,979, de los cuales 1,320 forman la población económicamente activa. Hablan alguna lengua indígena 4,030 personas mayores de cinco años (mixteco 4,026); de ellas, 203 no saben español.

SANTA LUCÍA OCOTLÁN ◆ Municipio de Oaxaca situado en el centro del estado, al sur de la capital de la entidad. Superficie: 12.76 km². Habitantes: 3,183, de los cuales 637 forman la población económicamente activa. Hablan alguna lengua indígena 2,565 personas mayores de cinco años (zapoteco 2,563).

SANTA MAGDALENA JICOTLÁN ◆ Cabecera del municipio oaxaqueño Magdalena Jicotlán (☛).

SANTA MARGARITA ◆ Isla habitada de Baja California Sur. Está situada en el océano Pacífico. Es llamada también Margarita. Se encuentra al sureste de la isla Magdalena, sur de la bahía Magdalena y noroeste de la isla Creciente, frente a la bahía de las Almejas. En la costa oriental de la isla se encuentra la base naval de Puerto Cortés, lugar de concentración de los pescadores de langosta. Cuenta con yacimientos de magnetita.

SANTA MARGARITA, DE ◆ Sierra de Sonora. Es una de las estribaciones occidentales de la sierra Madre Occidental. Está situada al noreste de Hermosillo y este de la sierra de Aconchi. Su extremo sur lleva el nombre de sierra de Conejos y se prolonga hacia la de Batuc. Tiene yacimientos minerales.

SANTA MARÍA, DE ◆ Bahía de Sinaloa situada al sur de Guamúchil y este-noroeste de Culiacán. La cierran las islas Saliaca por el norte Altamura, por el oeste y Talchichiltle por el sur.

SANTA MARÍA, DE ◆ Laguna de Chihuahua en la que desemboca el río Santa María, al suroeste de Ciudad Juárez y noreste de Nuevo Casas Grandes. Está en proceso de desecación por la escasez de lluvia y la evaporación. En ella se explotan las salinas y el tequesquite.

SANTA MARÍA ◆ Río de Chihuahua también llamado Galeana o Guerrero. Nace con el nombre de Bachíniva en la vertiente noreste de la sierra Madre Occidental, al noroeste de la capital de la entidad. Sobre su curso se construyó la presa El Tintero, al oeste de la sierra de las Tunas. Tras 180 kilómetros de recorrido tributa en la laguna de Santa María, al suroeste de Ciudad Juárez.

SANTA MARÍA ◆ Río de Guanajuato, San Luis Potosí y Querétaro. Nace con el nombre de río Bravo en el extremo norte del estado de Guanajuato; entra en San Luis Potosí, pasa por el valle de Santa María del Río, donde recibe al Villela; entra de nuevo en Guanajuato, al norte de San Luis de la Paz; pasa a Querétaro, donde recibe al Jalpan; regresa a San Luis Potosí, al sur de Cárdenas, y recibe las aguas de los ríos Verde y Gallinas antes de unirse al Valles para formar el Tamuín.

SANTA MARÍA, DE ◆ Sierra de Durango y Zacatecas. Es una de las estribaciones noroccidentales de la sierra de Zacatecas. Se extiende de sureste a noroeste, al este y noreste de Victoria de Durango, y al sureste del valle de San Juan del Río.

SANTA MARÍA, CARLOS ◆ n. y m. en Durango, Dgo. (1834-1902). Cirujano por la Escuela Nacional de Medicina (1857). Liberal. Fue el encargado de comprar, en California, las armas con que los republicanos defendieron Puebla durante el sitio de los franceses en 1863. Fue profesor en diversos centros de enseñanza de la ciudad de Durango y diputado local y federal.

SANTA MARÍA, JAVIER ◆ n. y m. en la ciudad de México (1854-1910). Fue diputado local en Yucatán, visitador general de escuelas y jefe político de Progreso. Colaborador de la *Revista Universal*, *Pimienta y Mostaza*, *El Eco del Comercio*, *El Siglo XIX* y *El Eco de Ambos Mundos*. Fue director de la segunda época del periódico oficial *La Razón del Pueblo*, último director de *El Peninsular* y primero del *Diario Yucateco*. Autor de *Poesías escogidas* (1902).

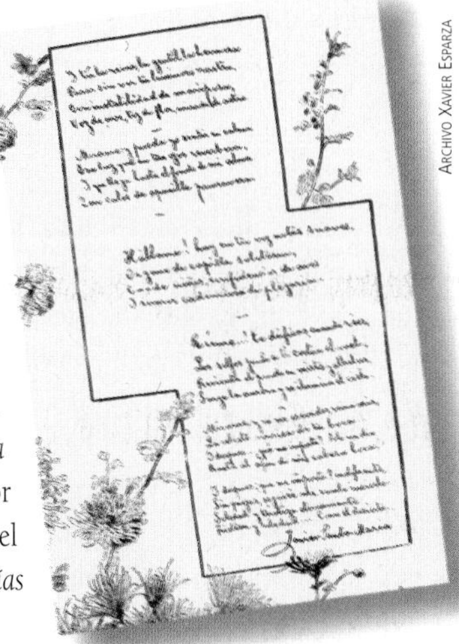

ARCHIVO XAVIER ESPARZA

Poema de Javier Santa María

SANTA MARÍA, JUAN ◆ n. en Durango, Dgo., y m. en el DF (¿1860?-1944). Se tituló de abogado en el Instituto Juárez de Durango (1882). Fue secretario de gobierno, gobernador interino (1898-1900) y gobernador constitucional de Durango (1900-04).

SANTA MARÍA, MANUEL ◆ n. en España y m. en Chihuahua, Chih. (?-1811). Llegó en su infancia a la Nueva España. En 1810 era gobernador del Nuevo Reino de León. Cuando el insurgente Mariano Jiménez se acercó a Monterrey, Santa María se adhirió al movimiento de independencia. Ignacio Allende le confirió el grado de mariscal. En 1811 fue capturado con la mayoría de los caudillos insurgentes en Acatita de Baján, llevado a Chihuahua y fusilado.

SANTA MARÍA, MIGUEL DE ◆ n. en Veracruz, Ver. (1789-1837). Abogado. Por negarse a servir en el ejército realista fue encarcelado. Huyó a Estados Unidos para no verse obligado a pelear contra los insurgentes. Desde aquel país ayudó económicamente a los expedicionarios de Francisco Javier Mina, con quien trató de reunirse en Veracruz, sin conseguirlo. Delatada su presencia, escapó hacia Jamaica, donde se unió a la expedición de Simón Bolívar, quien lo designó secretario del almirantazgo. Fue secretario del Congreso Constituyente en Cúcuta y ministro plenipotenciario de Colombia en México (1821). Expulsado de México por su oposición al imperio de Iturbide, en 1823; al instaurarse la República renunció a su puesto diplomático de Colombia y recuperó la ciudadanía mexicana. Viajó a París en 1829 y en 1835 fue encargado de la legación en Londres. Negoció el tratado de Santa María-Calatrava, por el que España reconoció la Independencia de México. Autor de *Informe secreto al pueblo soberano* y *El tratado de paz*.

Santa María, Vicente ◆ n. en Valladolid, hoy Morelia, Mich., y m. en Acapulco, en el actual estado de Guerrero (1775-1813). Fraile franciscano que desde 1808 apoyó la idea de la independencia mexicana. Fue uno de los conspiradores de Valladolid y teórico del movimiento, junto con los hermanos Michelena, Mariano Muñoz y Ruperto Mier. Fue denunciado, aprehendido a fines de 1809, recluido en el convento del Carmen, primero, y en otros claustros después. Huyó de su prisión, se unió a las fuerzas de José María Morelos y murió durante el asalto al fuerte de San Diego. Autor de *Relación histórica de la colonia del Nuevo Santander y costa del seno mexicano*.

Santa María Alotepec ◆ Municipio de Oaxaca situado en el oriente del estado, al este de la capital de la entidad y noroeste de Juchitán de Zaragoza. Superficie: 149.27 km². Habitantes: 2,610, de los cuales 710 forman la población económicamente activa. Hablan alguna lengua indígena 2,276 personas mayores de cinco años (mixe 2,270), de las cuales 601 no dominan el español.

Santa María de los Ángeles ◆ Municipio de Jalisco situado en el norte del estado, en los límites con Zacatecas, al noroeste de Teocaltiche. Superficie: 262.34 km². Habitantes: 4,184, de los cuales 1,014 forman la población económicamente activa. Hablan alguna lengua indígena seis personas mayores de cinco años.

Santa María Apasco ◆ Municipio de Oaxaca situado en el noroeste del estado, al suroeste de Huautla de Jiménez y sureste de Huajuapan de León. Superficie: 68.89 km². Habitantes: 2,422, de los cuales 585 forman la población económicamente activa. Hablan alguna lengua indígena 2,054 personas mayores de cinco años (mixteco 2,053), de las que 89 son monolingües. Su cabecera es Santa María Apaxco.

Santa María la Asunción ◆ Municipio de Oaxaca situado en el norte del estado, al sur y próximo a Huautla de Jiménez. Superficie: 33.17 km². Habitantes: 3,124, de los cuales 859 forman la población económicamente activa. Hablan alguna lengua indígena 2,622 personas mayores de cinco años (mazateco 2,617), de las cuales 1,800 son monolingües.

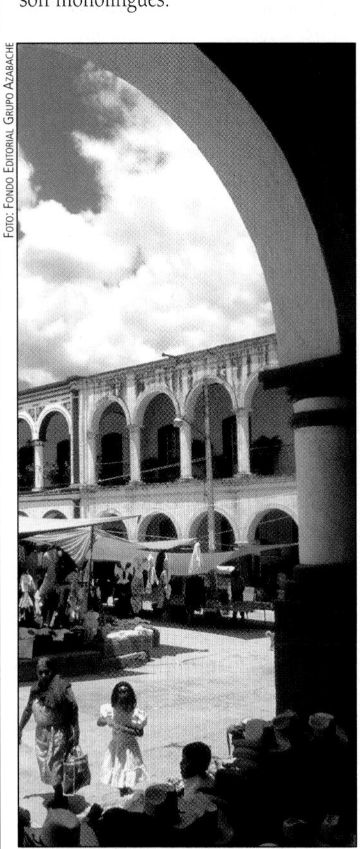
Foto: Fondo Editorial Grupo Azabache

Tianguis en Santa María la Asunción, en Oaxaca

Santa María Asunción Tlaxiaco ◆ Cabecera y antiguo nombre del municipio oaxaqueño de Heroica Ciudad de Tlaxiaco (☛).

Santa María Atzompa ◆ Municipio de Oaxaca situado en el centro del estado, al sureste y próximo a la capital de la entidad. Superficie: 22.96 km². Habitantes: 11,293, de los cuales 2,102 forman la población económicamente activa. Hablan alguna lengua indígena 988 personas mayores de cinco años (zapoteco 480, mixteco 246 y mixe 119). En un cerro localizado a dos kilómetros de su cabecera hay un cuerpo de construcciones, probablemente contemporáneas, de Monte Albán, de donde han sido extraídas varias piezas de cerámica.

Santa María Ayoquezco de Aldama ◆ ☛ *Ayoquezco de Aldama*, municipio de Oaxaca.

Santa María Camotlán ◆ Municipio de Oaxaca situado en el noroeste del estado, al noreste de Huajuapan de León. Superficie: 90.58 km². Habitantes: 1,507, de los cuales 269 forman la población económicamente activa.

Santa María Colotepec ◆ Municipio de Oaxaca situado en el litoral del océano Pacífico, al oeste de Puerto Ángel y al este de Puerto Escondido. Superficie: 663.43 km². Habitantes: 15,646, de los cuales 3,411 forman la población económicamente activa. Hablan alguna lengua indígena 821 personas mayores de cinco años (zapoteco 687).

Santa María Cortijo ◆ Municipio de Oaxaca situado en el suroeste del estado, en los límites con Guerrero, al noroeste de Santiago Pinotepa Nacional. Superficie: 88.03 km². Habitantes: 1,124, de los cuales 244 forman la población económicamente activa. Hablan alguna lengua indígena 79 personas mayores de cinco años (mixteco 76). La cabecera es Santa María Cortijos.

Santa María Coyotepec ◆ Municipio de Oaxaca situado en el centro del estado, al sur de la capital de la entidad. Superficie: 10.21 km². Habitantes: 1,550, de los cuales 252 forman la población económicamente activa. Hablan alguna lengua indígena 64 personas mayores de cinco años (zapoteco 48).

SANTA MARÍA CHACHOAPAN ◆ Municipio de Oaxaca situado en el noroeste del estado, al sureste de Huajuapan de León. Superficie: 25.52 km^2. Habitantes: 850, de los cuales 180 forman la población económicamente activa. Hablan alguna lengua indígena 11 personas mayores de cinco años (mixteco nueve).

SANTA MARÍA CHILAPA DE DÍAZ ◆ Cabecera municipal del municipio oaxaqueño Villa de Chilapa de Díaz (☛).

SANTA MARÍA CHILCHOTLA ◆ Municipio de Oaxaca situado en el norte del estado, en los límites con Puebla, al noreste de Huautla de Jiménez. Superficie: 347.02 km^2. Habitantes: 19,745, de los cuales 4,945 forman la población económicamente activa. Hablan alguna lengua indígena 15,570 personas mayores de cinco años (mazateco 15,558) y de ellas, 5,622 no saben español.

SANTA MARÍA CHIMALAPA ◆ Municipio de Oaxaca situado en el oriente del estado, en los límites con Veracruz y Chiapas. Superficie: 3,572.31 km^2. Habitantes: 7,080, de los cuales 1,463 forman la población económicamente activa. Hablan alguna lengua indígena 2,680 personas mayores de cinco años (zoque 1,724), de las cuales 317 son monolingües.

SANTA MARÍA ECATEPEC ◆ Municipio de Oaxaca situado en el sur del estado, al este-sureste de Miahuatlán. Superficie: 719.56 km^2. Habitantes: 3,608, de los cuales 776 forman la población económicamente activa. Hablan alguna lengua indígena 952 personas mayores de cinco años (chontal de Oaxaca 931).

SANTA MARÍA GUELACE ◆ Municipio de Oaxaca situado en el centro del estado, al este de la capital de la entidad. Superficie: 21.69 km^2. Habitantes: 729, de los cuales 176 forman la población económicamente activa. Hablan alguna lengua indígena 240 personas mayores de cinco años (zapoteco 238). Su cabecera es Santa María Guelaxe.

SANTA MARÍA GUIENAGATI ◆ Municipio de Oaxaca situado en el sureste del estado, al noroeste de Juchitán de Zaragoza. Superficie: 211.79 km^2. Habitantes: 2,794, de los cuales 573 forman la población económicamente activa. Hablan alguna lengua indígena 690 personas mayores de cinco años (zapoteco 547 y mixe 139).

SANTA MARÍA HUATULCO ◆ Municipio de Oaxaca situado en el sur del estado, en el litoral del océano Pacífico, al este de Puerto Ángel. Superficie: 579.22 km^2. Habitantes: 25,242, de los cuales 4,059 forman la población económicamente activa. Hablan alguna lengua indígena 816 personas mayores de cinco años (zapoteco 581). Tiene manantiales de aguas sulfurosas, a las que se atribuyen propiedades curativas. La región estuvo poblada desde el año 900 a.n.e. por zapotecas. Los conquistadores españoles crearon en 1550 la provincia de Huatulco, que en 1787 se convirtió en subdelegación de la intendencia de Oaxaca. Huatulco fue el principal puerto de la Nueva España en el Pacífico, antes del auge de Acapulco, para el comercio con Centroamérica y Perú y fue, también, objeto de ataques piratas, entre los cuales se cuentan los encabezados por Francis Drake (1579) y Tomás Cavendish (1587). Este último, durante su ataque al poblado, vio en la playa una gran cruz de madera venerada por los indios, quienes aseguraban que había sido colocada ahí por un "santo anciano" 15 siglos antes. Como el botín de Cavendish había sido exiguo, decidió vengarse destruyendo esa cruz, lo que, se dice, intentó hacer con hachas, serrotes y fuego sin que pudiera dañarla. Se propuso arrastrarla jalada por uno de sus barcos y tampoco lo consiguió. Esto hizo que la cruz de Huatulco fuese reverenciada con más fervor y que, en 1612, la iglesia Católica permitiera su adoración. Sus astillas circulaban como piezas milagrosas. En la actualidad, los viernes de Cuaresma se realiza en la ciudad de Oaxaca una ceremonia para honrar la reliquia. Durante la mayor parte del siglo XVII, el puerto quedó despoblado. Una de las bahias del lugar se llama La Entrega, pues en ese sitio, Picaluga entregó prisionero a Vicente Guerrero (1831). En 1987 se inició la construcción de infraestructura, como parte del proyecto turístico Bahías de Huatulco. Estos trabajos elevaron súbitamente la población flotante y fija del lugar, que se ha convertido en uno de los centros de mayor atractivo en la costa mexicana del Pacífico.

FOTO: CLAUDIO CONTRERAS

Santa María Huatulco, Oaxaca

SANTA MARÍA HUAZOLOTITLÁN ◆ Municipio de Oaxaca situado en el suroeste del estado, en el litoral del océano Pacífico, al sureste de Santiago Pinotepa Nacional. Superficie: 322.78 km^2. Habitantes: 9,895, de los cuales 2,366 forman la población económicamente activa. Hablan alguna lengua indígena 2,941 personas mayores de cinco años (mixteco 2,934); de ellas, 218 no hablan español.

SANTA MARÍA INCHÁURREGUI, ANTONIO ◆ n. y m. en Puebla, Pue. (?-?).

García Santa María Mendoza

Arquitecto graduado en la Academia de San Carlos (1796). Desarrolló su trabajo en la Nueva España en la segunda mitad del siglo XVIII y a principios del XIX. Fue el encargado de la reedificación de la iglesia de los Reyes en Cholula y del obelisco en honor de Carlos III, la decoración del Palacio Episcopal, el templo de la Compañía de Jesús, el Parián y la traza del paseo Bravo. Probablemente también hayan sido obra suya la Casa del Alfeñique y el Coliseo de Comedias (teatro Principal).

SANTA MARÍA IPALAPA ♦ Municipio de Oaxaca situado en el suroeste del estado, al nor-noreste de Santiago Pinotepa Nacional. Superficie: 109.72 km^2. Habitantes: 4,447, de los cuales 989 forman la población económicamente activa. Hablan alguna lengua indígena 1,029 personas mayores de cinco años (amuzgo 1,023).

SANTA MARÍA IXCATLÁN ♦ Municipio de Oaxaca situado en el norte del estado, al suroeste de Huautla de Jiménez. Superficie: 201.58 km^2. Habitantes: 686, de los cuales 195 forman la población económicamente activa. Hablan alguna lengua indígena 32 personas mayores de cinco años (ixcateco 31).

SANTA MARÍA JACATEPEC ♦ Municipio de Oaxaca situado en el norte del estado, al sureste de Tuxtepec. Superficie: 429.95 km^2. Habitantes: 9,242, de los cuales 1,986 forman la población económicamente activa. Hablan alguna lengua indígena 5,456 personas mayores de cinco años (chinanteco 3,628 y mazateco 1,584), de las cuales 257 son monolingües.

SANTA MARÍA JALAPA DEL MARQUÉS ♦ Municipio de Oaxaca situado en el sureste del estado, al oeste de Juchitán de Zaragoza y contiguo a Santo Domingo Tehuantepec. Superficie: 562.64 km^2. Habitantes: 11,242, de los cuales 2,333 forman la población económicamente activa. Hablan alguna lengua indígena 582 personas mayores de cinco años (zapoteco 427).

SANTA MARÍA JALTIANGUIS ♦ Municipio de Oaxaca situado en el centro-norte del estado, al norte de la capital de la entidad. Superficie: 45.93 km^2. Habitantes: 657, de los cuales 212 forman la población económicamente activa. Hablan alguna lengua indígena 327 personas mayores de cinco años (zapoteco 326).

SANTA MARÍA LACHIXÍO ♦ Municipio de Oaxaca situado en el centro-sur del estado, al suroeste de la capital de la entidad. Superficie: 113.55 km^2. Habitantes: 915, de los cuales 166 forman la población económicamente activa. Hablan zapoteco 689 personas mayores de cinco años, de las cuales 124 son monolingües.

SANTA MARÍA MENDOZA, GARCÍA ♦ n. en España y m. en la ciudad de México (¿?- 1606). Sacerdote ordenado en 1558 y fraile de la orden de San Jerónimo. Felipe III lo designó arzobispo de México en 1600, tras 15 años de ausencia de titular para el arzobispado. Su gestión se inició en 1601.

SANTA MARÍA MIXTEQUILLA ♦ Municipio de Oaxaca situado en el sureste del estado, al oeste de Juchitán de Zaragoza y contiguo a Santo Domingo Tehuantepec. Superficie: 186.27 km^2. Habitantes: 3,787, de los cuales 868 forman la población económicamente activa. Hablan alguna lengua indígena 30 personas mayores de cinco años (zapoteco 28).

SANTA MARÍA NATÍVITAS ♦ Municipio de Oaxaca situado en el noroeste del estado, al sureste de Huajuapan de León. Superficie: 127.58 km^2. Habitantes: 800, de los cuales 88 forman la población económicamente activa. Hablan alguna lengua indígena 239 personas mayores de cinco años (chocho 235).

SANTA MARÍA NDUAYACO ♦ Municipio de Oaxaca situado en el noroeste del estado, al noreste de Tlaxiaco. Superficie: 100.79 km^2. Habitantes: 660, de los cuales 211 forman la población económicamente activa. Hablan mixteco diez personas mayores de cinco años.

SANTA MARÍA DEL ORO ♦ Cabecera del municipio de El Oro (☛), Durango.

SANTA MARÍA DEL ORO ♦ Municipio de Nayarit situado en el sur del estado, al sureste y contiguo a Tepic. Superficie: 912.9 km^2. Habitantes: 20,714, de los cuales 4,384 forman la población económicamente activa. Hablan alguna lengua indígena 783 personas mayores de cinco años (huichol 777).

SANTA MARÍA OZOLOTEPEC ♦ Municipio de Oaxaca situado en el sur del estado, al sureste de Miahuatlán. Superficie: 95.69 km^2. Habitantes: 4,085, de los cuales 1,115 forman la población económicamente activa. Hablan alguna lengua indígena 1,113 personas mayores de cinco años (zapoteco 1,014).

SANTA MARÍA PÁPALO ♦ Municipio de Oaxaca situado en el norte del estado, al sur-sureste de Huautla de Jiménez. Superficie: 57.41 km^2. Habitantes: 1,958, de los cuales 448 forman la población económicamente activa. Hablan alguna lengua indígena 1,643 personas mayores de cinco años (cuicateco 1,611).

SANTA MARÍA PEÑOLES ♦ Municipio de Oaxaca situado en el centro del estado, al oeste de la capital de la entidad. Superficie: 181.17 km^2. Habitantes: 6,758, de los cuales 1,066 forman la población económicamente activa. Hablan alguna lengua indígena 5,358 personas mayores de cinco años (mixteco 5,345), de las cuales 1,322 son monolingües.

SANTA MARÍA PETAPA ♦ Municipio de Oaxaca situado en el oriente del estado, al nor-noroeste de Juchitán de Zaragoza y contiguo a Matías Romero. Superficie: 145.44 km^2. Habitantes: 13,037, de los cuales 2,851 forman la población económicamente activa. Hablan alguna lengua indígena 3,649 personas mayores de cinco años (zapoteco 2,637 y mixe 774).

SANTA MARÍA QUIEGOLANI ♦ Municipio de Oaxaca situado en el sur del estado, al este de Miahuatlán. Superficie: 122.48 km^2. Habitantes: 1,500, de los cuales 360 forman la población económicamente activa. Hablan alguna lengua indígena 1,195 personas mayores de cinco años (zapoteco 1,131), de las cuales 153 son monolingües.

SANTA MARÍA DEL RÍO ♦ Municipio de San Luis Potosí situado en el sur del estado, en los límites con Guanajuato, al sureste de la capital de la entidad. Superficie: 1,769.1 km^2. Habitantes: 37,448, de los cuales 7,703 forman la población económicamente activa. Hablan alguna lengua indígena 10 personas mayores de cinco años. Tiene numerosos manantiales de aguas termales, a los que se atribuyen propiedades terapéuticas, y yacimientos de estaño, plomo, cinabrio, calcita y plata, además de yeso, pizarra y canteras. La cabecera, del mismo nombre, es un importante centro de actividad económica, con un activo comercio, embotelladoras de aguas minerales y talleres de confección de rebozos de seda.

Santa María del Rosario ◆ Municipio de Oaxaca situado en el noroeste del estado, al noreste y próximo a Tlaxiaco. Superficie: 37 km^2. Habitantes: 430, de los cuales 98 forman la población económicamente activa. Hablan mixteco 40 personas mayores de cinco años.

Santa María Sola ◆ Municipio de Oaxaca situado en el centro-sur del estado, al noroeste de Miahuatlán. Superficie: 125.03 km^2. Habitantes: 1,741, de los cuales 344 forman la población económicamente activa. Hablan alguna lengua indígena siete personas.

Santa María Tataltepec ◆ Municipio de Oaxaca situado en el occidente del estado, al sureste de Tlaxiaco y oeste de la capital de la entidad. Superficie: 42.1 km^2. Habitantes: 293, de los cuales 85 forman la población económicamente activa. Hablan mixteco 54 personas mayores de cinco años.

Santa María Tecomavaca ◆ Municipio de Oaxaca situado en el norte del estado, al suroeste de Huautla de Jiménez. Superficie: 221.99 km^2. Habitantes: 1,888, de los cuales 475 forman la población económicamente activa. Hablan alguna lengua indígena 245 personas mayores de cinco años (mazateco 227).

Santa María Temaxcalapan ◆ Municipio de Oaxaca situado en el noreste del estado, al noreste de la capital de la entidad. Superficie: 28.07 km^2. Habitantes: 933, de los cuales 220 forman la población económicamente activa. Hablan alguna lengua indígena 815 personas mayores de cinco años (zapoteco 814), de las cuales 119 no saben español. En la jurisdicción se encontraron una pirámide y un patio (llamado Sala de los Danzantes), ruinas de una ciudad zapoteca.

Santa María Temaxcaltepec ◆ Municipio de Oaxaca situado en el suroeste del estado, al oeste-suroeste de Miahuatlán y al este-sureste de Santiago Pinotepa Nacional. Superficie: 86.76 km^2. Habitantes: 1,673, de los cuales 118 forman la población económicamente activa. Hablan chatino 1,311 personas mayores de cinco años.

Santa María Teopoxco ◆ Municipio de Oaxaca situado en el norte del estado, al oeste-noroeste de Huautla de Jiménez. Superficie: 25.52 km^2. Habitantes: 3,965, de los cuales 1,003 forman la población económicamente activa. Hablan alguna lengua indígena 3,323 personas mayores de cinco años (náhuatl 3,300), de ellas, 398 son monolingües.

Santa María Tepantlali ◆ Municipio de Oaxaca situado en el centro-oriente del estado, al este de la capital de la entidad. Superficie: 119.93 km^2. Habitantes: 2,453, de los cuales 648 forman la población económicamente activa. Hablan alguna lengua indígena 2,097 personas mayores de cinco años (mixe 2,096) y de ellas, no dominan el español 1,103.

Santa María Texcatitlán ◆ Municipio de Oaxaca situado en el norte del estado, al suroeste de Huautla de Jiménez. Superficie: 44.66 km^2. Habitantes: 1,122, de los cuales 532 forman la población económicamente activa. Hablan alguna lengua indígena 920 personas mayores de cinco años (mixteco 917), de las cuales 106 no saben español.

Santa María Tlahuitoltepec ◆ Municipio de Oaxaca situado en el centro-oriente del estado, al este de la capital de la entidad. Superficie: 75.27 km^2. Habitantes: 6,982, de los cuales 1,831 forman la población económicamente activa. Dominan alguna lengua indígena 5,966 personas mayores de cinco años (mixe 5,947), de las que 1,468 no hablan español. En la jurisdicción se han encontrado tumbas de la civilización mixe.

Santa María Tlalixtac ◆ Municipio de Oaxaca situado en el norte del estado, al sur de Huautla de Jiménez. Superficie: 63.79 km^2. Habitantes: 1,479, de los cuales 424 forman la población económicamente activa. Hablan alguna lengua indígena 762 personas mayores de cinco años (cuicateco 682); de ellas, 50 son monolingües.

Santa María Tonameca ◆ Municipio de Oaxaca situado en el sur del estado, en el litoral del océano Pacífico, al oeste de Puerto Escondido y contiguo a San Pedro Pochutla. Superficie: 454.19 km^2. Habitantes: 16,546, de los cuales 3,311 forman la población económicamente activa. Hablan alguna lengua indígena 4,888 personas mayores de cinco años (zapoteco 4,871), de las que 340 no saben español.

Santa María Totolapilla ◆ Municipio de Oaxaca situado en el sureste del estado, al oeste-noroeste de Juchitán de Zaragoza y contiguo a Santa María Jalapa del Marqués. Superficie: 267.92 km^2. Habitantes: 1,112, de los cuales 237 forman la población económicamente activa. Hablan alguna lengua indígena 507 personas mayores de cinco años (zapoteco 505).

Santa María del Tule ◆ Municipio de Oaxaca situado en el centro del estado, aproximadamente cinco kilómetros al este-sureste de la capital de la entidad. Superficie: 25.52 km^2. Habitantes: 7,182, de los cuales 2,218 forman la población económicamente activa. Hablan alguna lengua indígena 436 personas mayores de cinco años (zapoteco 343). En su jurisdicción se halla el Arbol del Tule, reputado como uno de los más grandes y viejos del mundo: es un sabino o ahuehuete de 40 metros de altura, con un diámetro en la copa de 51.88 metros, 705 metros cúbicos de volumen y un peso estimado en 549 toneladas, al que se le calculan 2,000 años de edad, aunque Alejandro de Hum-

Santa María del Tule, Oaxaca

boldt le atribuyó 4,000 y De Candolle, 6,000.

SANTA MARÍA XADANI ♦ Municipio de Oaxaca situado en el sureste del estado, en el litoral de la laguna Superior, al sureste de Juchitán de Zaragoza. Superficie: 89.31 km². Habitantes: 5,848, de los cuales 1,224 forman la población económicamente activa. Hablan alguna lengua indígena 4,905 personas mayores de cinco años (zapoteco 4,897), de las cuales 1,287 no dominan el español.

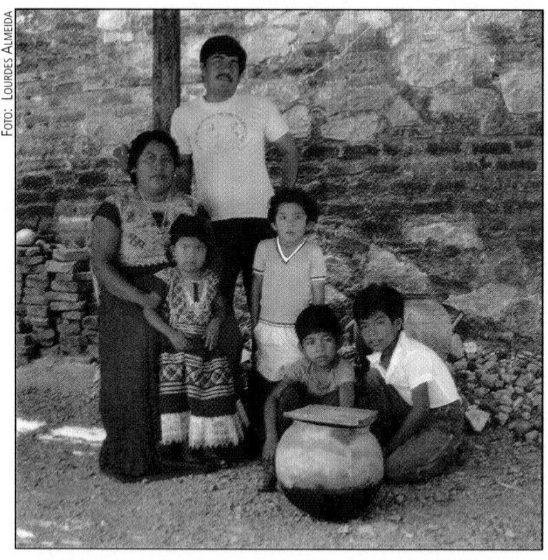

FOTO: LOURDES ALMEIDA

Familia de zapotecas de Santa María Xadani, Oaxaca

SANTA MARÍA YALINA ♦ Municipio de Oaxaca situado en el noreste del estado, al noreste de la capital de la entidad. Superficie: 40.83 km². Habitantes: 414, de los cuales 96 forman la población económicamente activa. Hablan alguna lengua indígena 345 personas mayores de cinco años (zapoteco 321).

SANTA MARÍA YAVESÍA ♦ Municipio de Oaxaca situado en el noreste del estado, al noreste de la capital de la entidad. Superficie: 38.27 km². Habitantes: 479, de los cuales 176 forman la población económicamente activa. Hablan alguna lengua indígena 118 personas mayores de cinco años (zapoteco 117). En su jurisdicción fueron halladas las ruinas de una pirámide de la cultura zapoteca.

SANTA MARÍA YOLOTEPEC ♦ Municipio de Oaxaca situado en el occidente del estado, al sur-sureste de Tlaxiaco. Superficie: 42.1 km². Habitantes: 575, de los cuales 119 forman la población económicamente activa. Hablan mixteco 115 personas mayores de cinco años.

SANTA MARÍA YOSOYÚA ♦ Municipio de Oaxaca situado en el occidente del estado, al sureste de Tlaxiaco. Superficie: 71.45 km². Habitantes: 1,371, de los cuales 269 forman la población económicamente activa. Hablan alguna lengua indígena 1,139 personas mayores de cinco años (mixteco 1,138), de las cuales 97 no saben español.

SANTA MARÍA YUCUHITI ♦ Municipio de Oaxaca situado en el occidente del estado, al suroeste de Tlaxiaco. Superficie: 72.72 km². Habitantes: 6,335, de los cuales 1,478 forman la población económicamente activa. Hablan alguna lengua indígena 5,411 personas mayores de cinco años (mixteco 5,380), de las cuales 319 son monolingües.

SANTA MARÍA ZACATEPEC ♦ Municipio de Oaxaca situado en el suroeste del estado, en los límites con Guerrero, al nor-noreste de Santiago Pinotepa Nacional. Superficie: 524.36 km². Habitantes: 14,822, de los cuales 2,868 forman la población económicamente activa. Hablan alguna lengua indígena 2,627 personas mayores de cinco años (tacuate 2,065 y mixteco 466), de las cuales 269 no saben español.

SANTA MARÍA ZANIZA ♦ Municipio de Oaxaca situado en el suroeste del estado, al noreste de Santiago Pinotepa Nacional. Superficie: 153.1 km². Habitantes: 1,296, de los cuales 263 forman la población económicamente activa. Hablan zapoteco 413 personas mayores de cinco años.

SANTA MARÍA ZOQUITLÁN ♦ Municipio de Oaxaca situado en el centro-sur del estado, al noreste de Miahuatlán. Superficie: 306.2 km². Habitantes: 4,086, de los cuales 1,134 forman la población económicamente activa. Hablan alguna lengua indígena 12 personas mayores de cinco años.

SANTA MARINA, JUAN ♦ n. en Durango, Dgo., y m. en el DF (1862-1944). Se tituló de abogado en el Instituto Juárez de Durango (1882). Fue secretario general de gobierno en Durango, durante la gestión de Leandro Fernández (1897-98), así como gobernador interino (1898-1900) y constitucional (1900-1904) de ese estado.

SANTA ROSA ♦ Sierra de Coahuila, también llamada Hermosa de Santa Rosa. Forma parte de la sierra Madre Oriental. Se extiende de noroeste a sureste, al sur de la sierra El Infante y suroeste de Piedras Negras. Tiene yacimientos minerales, entre otros los de Nueva Rosita y Múzquiz.

SANTA ROSALÍA ♦ Bahía de Baja California situada en el litoral del océano Pacífico, al noreste de la bahía Sebastián Vizcaíno. Está delimitada por las puntas Santa Rosalita y Rosarito, donde desemboca el río del mismo nombre.

Santa Rosalía ◆ Cabecera del municipio de Mulegé, Baja California Sur (☛).

Santacilia, Pedro ◆ n. en Cuba y m. en la ciudad de México (1826-1910). Viajó a España en 1836, acompañando a su padre, deportado por sus actividades políticas. En España concluyó su educación y se inició en la literatura. En 1845 volvió a Cuba, fundó la revista *Ensayos Literarios* y se dedicó a la lucha política en pro de la independencia de su patria, por lo que fue encarcelado y deportado a España (1852). Logró huir hacia Estados Unidos, desde donde compraba armas para los insurgentes cubanos. En Nueva Orleans conoció a los liberales mexicanos y, al volver a México, Benito Juárez lo designó su secretario particular. Santacilia se casó con Manuela Juárez, hija mayor del presidente. En México organizó diversos actos, como tertulias o veladas literarias, para reunir fondos y mandarlos a los independentistas cubanos. Al morir era presidente del Jockey Club de la ciudad de México. Autor de *El arpa del proscripto* (1856), *El genio del mal* (1861), *Apólogos* (1867), *Del movimiento literario en México* (1868) y *Juárez y César Cantú* (1885).

Santacruz, Lino ◆ n. en San Nicolás Panotla, Tlax. y m. en el DF (1888-1998). Director de escuela primaria en el DF, impulsó el Parque Álamos. Fundador de la CTM y líder de ésta en Tlaxcala (1944). Miembro del PRI. Fue cuatro veces diputado local.

Santajuliana, Celso ◆ n. en el DF (1960). Pseudónimo del escritor David Jorajuria. Hizo estudios de biología en la UAM y de administración de empresas en la Universidad Anáhuac. Asistió a talleres literarios con Elena Poniatowska, Rafael Ramírez Heredia, Alicia Trueba y Silvia Molina. Ha sido director de la editora Libros del Tapir y de las revistas *Surdesarrollo* y *Los alcances del rencor*. Ha impartido cursos y talleres literarios en el DF y otras ciudades del país, y ha sido jurado de concursos. Autor de cuento: *Ninguna noche especial* (1987), *Paulino Jerónimo* (1990), *Niantla* (1992), *Salón de usos múltiples* (1993, Premio Eraclio Zepeda 1992) y *El gato palomero* (infantil, 1998, premio de cuento de la Feria Internacional del Libro Infantil y Juvenil 1997); y novela: *Historia de Lorea* (1990, Premio Josefina Vicens) y *Palabras que sueñas como si vuelves* (1993, Premio Juan Rulfo de Primera Novela 1992). Premio Efraín Huerta 1992 por el cuento "La pena máxima" y segundo lugar en el mismo concurso en 1999. Becario de la Sogem (1992) y el CNCA (1993).

Santaló Pavorell, Miguel ◆ n. en España, y m. en Guadalajara, Jal. (1888-1962). Fue director de la Escuela Normal de Maestros y Maestras de Barcelona, miembro vitalicio de la Sociedad Española de Geografía, diputado a Cortes (1931, 33 y 36) y ministro de Comunicaciones (1934). Llegó exiliado a México en 1939. Colaborador de la Unión Tipográfica Editorial Hispanoamericana, ministro de Instrucción Pública del gobierno republicano en el exilio (1946) y consejero y presidente del Gobierno de la Generalidad de Cataluña (1962). Autor de *El materialismo histórico*, *La península ibérica*, *La enseñanza de la geografía en España* y *El gironés y Bañolas*.

Santaló Sors, Marcelo ◆ n. en España (1905). Astrónomo. Doctor en ciencias exactas por la Universidad Central de Madrid. Trabajó en el Observatorio Astronómico de Madrid y fue profesor del Instituto de Enseñanza Media en Ceuta y Gerona, profesor adjunto del Instituto Escuela de Madrid. En 1939 llegó exiliado a México a bordo del *Sinaia*. Profesor del Instituto Luis Vives, de la Academia Hispano-Mexicana, de la Escuela Nacional Preparatoria, del Colegio Madrid y de la Academia Militarizada México. Fue jefe de la Sección de Ciencia y Tecnología de la OEA en Estados Unidos (1957) y trabajó en la Dirección de Revalidación e Incorporación de Estudios de la UNAM. Colaborador especializado en matemáticas y astronomía del *Diccionario enciclopédico UTEHA* y colaborador de la *Enciclopedia Barsa*. Autor de *La constitución de la tierra* (1939), *El enigma lunar* (1939), *Los primeros conocimientos de aritmética y geometría*, *Planetas y satélites* (1946), *Guía para la observación del cielo de México*, así como de los libros de texto *Matemáticas* (para quinto año), *Geometría analítica* (para sexto año), *Cálculo diferencial integral* y *Geografía física* (en colaboración con Josefina Oliva de Coll).

Santamaría, Joaquín ◆ n. y m en Veracruz, Veracruz (1890-1975). Fotógrafo. Se inició en un laboratorio como ayudante y luego ingresó como reportero gráfico a *El Dictamen*, en el cual laboró más de 50 años. Destacó en su trabajo como retratista de la vida cotidiana del centro de su estado, así como de sus ciudades y paisajes, que lo llevaron a crear una de las colecciones más abundantes. En 1999 la Fototeca veracruzana expuso parte de su obra.

Santamaría, Francisco Javier ◆ n. en Cacaos, Tab., y m. en Veracruz, Ver. (1886-1963). Maestro normalista por el Instituto Juárez de Villahermosa, donde fue profesor de matemáticas. Se trasladó a la ciudad de México, donde ejerció la docencia y se tituló de abogado. Fue el único sobreviviente de la matanza de Huitzilac. Gobernador de Tabasco (1947-52). Según José Bulnes, al iniciar su periodo de gobierno exigió a cada uno de los diputados de la Legislatura local una cabeza de ganado para su finca Bayito. Autor de *Mi escapatoria célebre de la tragedia de Cuernavaca*, *El provincialismo tabasqueño* (1920), *Americanismo y barbarismo* (1921), *Glosa lexicográfica* (1926), *Bibliografía de Tabasco* (1930), *Las ruinas occidentales del viejo imperio maya. Notas de una excursión* (1933), *La poesía tabasqueña* (1940), *Ensayo de crítica del lenguaje* (1941, en colaboración), *Diccionario de americanismos* (1942), *El movimiento cultural en Tabasco* (1946) y *Diccionario de mexicanismos* (1959). Fue miembro de la Academia Mexicana (de la Lengua) desde 1948.

Santana, Carlos ◆ n. en Autlán, Jal. (1947). Músico y compositor. Su padre, integrante de un mariachi, le enseñó a tocar el violín. Radicado en Tijuana desde los años cincuenta, trabajó como guitarrista en bares de esa ciudad junto con Javier Bátiz. Pasó en 1963 a San Francisco, California, donde formó la *Santana Blues Band*. Con ese grupo se presentó en el Festival de Woodstock (1969). Ha hecho grabaciones con John Lee Hooker y el grupo mexicano El Tri, entre otros. Se unió a la corriente religiosa encabezada por el gurú Sri Chinmoy y se rebautizó como Devadip Carlos Santana. En 1988 fue promotor de un festival de *rock* cuyas ganancias se donaron a los salvadoreños afectados por la guerra civil. Entre los discos que ha grabado se cuentan: *Santana* (1969),

FOTO: DANTE BUCIO

Carlos Santana

Abraxas (1970), *Carlos Santana and Buddy Miles* (1971), *Carlos Santana and Buddy Miles Live* (1971), *Santana 3* (1972), *Caravanserai* (1972), *Welcome* (1973), *Love, Devotion, Surrender* (1973, con Mahavishnu John McLaughlin), *Illuminations* (1974, con Alice Coltrane), *Lotus* (1975), *Borboletta* (1975), *Amigos* (1976), *Festival* (1976), *Inner Secrets* (1978), *Zebop!* (1981), *Beyond Appearances* (1985), *Blues for Salvador* (1988), *Viva Santana!* (1989, antología con grabaciones inéditas), *Milagro* (1991), *Sacred Fire Live* (1993), *Brothers* (1995, con Jorge Santana y Carlos Hernández) y *Supernatural* (1999, este último fue el primero de su discografía en ocupar el primer lugar de popularidad en los Estados Unidos, de acuerdo con la revista *Billboard*).

SANTANA RODRÍGUEZ, JOSÉ ◆ n. en Acayucan, Ver. (1870-1910). Conocido como *Santanón*. Fue partidario de los hermanos Flores Magón y miembro del grupo antiporfirista dirigido por Cándido Donato Padua, en el que tomó las armas contra la dictadura antes del inicio de la insurrección maderista. Peleó hasta su muerte, después de haber sido aprehendido y alistado por leva.

SANTANDER, FELIPE ◆ n. en Monterrey, NL (1935). Actor, director teatral, guionista y dramaturgo. Ingeniero agrónomo por la Escuela de Agricultura Escobar Hermanos. Dramaturgo egresado de la Escuela de Teatro del INBA. Ha sido colaborador de *Por Esto!* Autor del guión cinematográfico *La casa del farol rojo* (1963) y de las obras de teatro *Luna de miel. para diez* (1959), *Las fascinadoras* (1961), *La orden* (1963, Premio de Teatro de la UNAM), *Una noche todas las noches* (1970), *El extensionista* (1978, premios Villaurrutia, sor Juana Inés de la Cruz, Juan Ruiz de Alarcón en 1978 y Casa de las Américas en 1980 y que, dirigida por el autor, superó las 3,200 representaciones en México, Ecuador, España, Cuba y Estados Unidos), *A propósito de Ramona* (1981), *Los dos hermanos* (1983, Premio Nacional de Teatro en 1982 y representada en México, Estados Unidos y Canadá), *Y el milagro* (1985, premio de la Asociación Mexicana de Críticos de Teatro en 1986) y *Dos hermanos*.

SANTANDER JIMÉNEZ ◆ Cabecera del municipio de Jiménez (☛), Tamaulipas.

SANTANÓN ◆ ☛ *Santana Rodríguez, José*.

SANTIAGO ◆ Municipio de Nuevo León situado al sur y próximo a Monterrey, en los límites con Coahuila. Superficie: 763.8 km². Habitantes: 34,187, de los cuales 9,916 forman la población económicamente activa. Hablan alguna lengua indígena 72 personas mayores de cinco años (náhuatl 30 y huasteco 20).

SANTIAGO ◆ ☛ *Lerma-Santiago*.

SANTIAGO, ABEL ◆ n. en Oaxaca (1936). Escritor. Autor de *El problema de ser joven* (1961), *Departamento vacío*, *Diario de un obrero mexicano*, *El avispero* (1975), *Cuentos del medio ambiente* (1978), *Morir, eso es todo* (1982) y *Los rezadores* (1994).

SANTIAGO, MARIO ◆ n. en el DF (1953). Poeta. Formó parte del movimiento infrarrealista. Trabajó como corrector en *El Financiero* y colaboró en numerosas publicaciones periódicas. Autor de *Beso eterno* y *Aullido de cisne* (1996), libro que firmó como Mario Santiago Papasquiaro.

SANTIAGO AMOLTEPEC ◆ Municipio de Oaxaca situado en el centro-sur del estado, al noreste de Santiago Pinotepa Nacional. Superficie: 142.89 km². Habitantes: 8,576, de los cuales 1,845 forman la población económicamente activa. Hablan alguna lengua indígena 5,112 personas mayores de cinco años (mixteco 5,101), y de ellas, 1,191 son monolingües.

SANTIAGO DE ANAYA ◆ Municipio de Hidalgo situado en el centro del estado, al noroeste de Pachuca. Superficie: 316.1 km². Habitantes: 13,605, de los cuales 3,087 forman la población económicamente activa. Hablan alguna lengua indígena 5,979 personas mayores de cinco años (otomí 5,965). Indígenas monolingües: 166.

SANTIAGO APOALA ◆ Municipio de Oaxaca situado en el noroeste del estado, al este-sureste de Huajuapan de León. Superficie: 57.41 km². Habitantes: 1,321, de los cuales 331 forman la población económicamente activa. Hablan mixteco 1,121 personas mayores de cinco años (monolingües 52). Las grutas de Apoala, dos galerías del cerro Xucutotondehui, tienen una laguna cuya profundidad no se ha establecido con precisión.

SANTIAGO APÓSTOL ◆ Municipio de Oaxaca situado en el centro del estado, al sur de la capital de la entidad. Superficie: 21.69 km². Habitantes: 4,761, de los cuales 1,052 forman la población económicamente activa. Hablan alguna lengua indígena 3,666 personas mayores de cinco años (zapoteco 3,623), de las cuales 40 son monolingües.

SANTIAGO ASTATA ◆ Municipio de Oaxaca situado en el sureste del estado, en el litoral del golfo de Tehuantepec, al suroeste de Juchitán de Zaragoza. Superficie: 446.54 km². Habitantes: 2,606, de los cuales 501 forman la población económicamente activa. Hablan alguna lengua indígena 290 personas mayores de cinco años (chontal de Oaxaca 276).

SANTIAGO ATITLÁN ◆ Municipio de Oaxaca situado en el oriente del estado, al este de la capital de la entidad. Superficie: 82.93 km². Habitantes: 2,475, de los cuales 540 forman la población económicamente activa. Hablan alguna lengua indígena 2,109 personas mayores de cinco años (mixe 2,106), de las cuales 803 son monolingües.

SANTIAGO AYUQUILILLA ◆ Municipio de Oaxaca situado en el noroeste del estado, al noroeste de Huajuapan de León. Superficie: 48.48 km². Habitantes: 2,242, de los cuales 496 forman la población económicamente activa.

SANTIAGO CACALOXTEPEC ◆ Municipio de Oaxaca situado en el noroeste del estado, al sur y próximo a Huajuapan de León. Superficie: 51.03 km². Habitantes: 1,275, de los cuales 234 forman la población económicamente activa. Hablan mixteco 547 personas mayores de cinco años.

SANTIAGO Y CALDERÓN, FRANCISCO ◆ n. en España y m. en Oaxaca, Oax. (1665-1736). Fraile mercedario. Fue electo obispo de Guatemala en 1728 y trasladado a Oaxaca en 1730.

SANTIAGO CAMOTLÁN ◆ Municipio de Oaxaca situado en el noreste del estado, al noreste de la capital de la entidad y sur de Tuxtepec. Superficie: 332.99 km². Habitantes: 3,019, de los cuales 843 forman la población económicamente activa. Hablan alguna lengua indígena 2,308 personas mayores de cinco años (zapoteco 2,295), de las cuales 407 no saben español.

SANTIAGO COMALTEPEC ◆ Municipio de Oaxaca situado en el norte del estado, al suroeste de Tuxtepec y al nornoreste de la capital de la entidad. Superficie: 65.07 km². Habitantes: 1,752, de los cuales 351 forman la población económicamente activa. Hablan alguna lengua indígena 1,410 personas mayores de cinco años (chinanteco 1,402), de las cuales 53 no saben español.

SANTIAGO CHAZUMBA ◆ Municipio de Oaxaca situado en el noroeste del estado, en los límites con Puebla, al nornoreste de Huajuapan de León. Superficie: 280.68 km². Habitantes: 4,600, de los cuales 1,109 forman la población económicamente activa. Hablan alguna lengua indígena 710 personas mayores de cinco años (mixteco 688).

Foto: Michael Calderwood

Santiago, Nuevo León

SANTIAGO CHOAPAN ◆ Municipio de Oaxaca situado en el noreste del estado, al noreste de la capital de la entidad. Superficie: 247.51 km². Habitantes: 4,241, de los cuales 1,154 forman la población económicamente activa. Hablan alguna lengua indígena 1,842 personas mayores de cinco años (chinanteco 1,402), y de ellas, 54 son monolingües.

SANTIAGO HUAJOLOTITLÁN ◆ Municipio de Oaxaca situado en el noroeste del estado, al este y próximo a Huajuapan de León. Superficie: 173.51 km². Habitantes: 4,555, de los cuales 1,127 forman la población económicamente activa. Hablan alguna lengua indígena 15 personas mayores de cinco años (zapoteco 13). En el pueblo de Atotonilco hay manantiales de aguas sulfurosas a las que se atribuyen propiedades terapéuticas. Cuenta además con la laguna Espejo y la bocabarra del río Verde, así como una zona arqueológica poco explorada.

SANTIAGO HUAUCLILLA ◆ Municipio de Oaxaca situado en el noroeste del estado, al noroeste de la capital de la entidad. Superficie: 89.31 km². Habitantes: 976, de los cuales 305 forman la población económicamente activa. Hablan alguna lengua indígena 40 personas mayores de cinco años (cuicateco 26).

SANTIAGO IHÜITLÁN PLUMAS ◆ Municipio de Oaxaca situado en el noroeste del estado, al este-noreste de Huajuapan de León, en los límites con Puebla. Superficie: 137.79 km². Habitantes: 625, de los cuales 133 forman la población económicamente activa.

SANTIAGO IXCUINTEPEC ◆ Municipio de Oaxaca situado en el oriente del estado, al noroeste de Juchitán de Zaragoza. Superficie: 102.07 km². Habitantes: 1,236, de los cuales 297 forman la población económicamente activa. Hablan alguna lengua indígena 1,027 personas mayores de cinco años (mixe 1,026), de las cuales 234 son monolingües.

SANTIAGO IXCUINTLA ◆ Municipio de Nayarit situado en el occidente del estado, en el litoral del océano Pacífico, al noroeste de Tepic y norte de San Blas. Superficie: 1,830.9 km². Habitantes: 95,385, de los cuales 30,313 forman la población económicamente activa. Hablan alguna lengua indígena 232 personas mayores de cinco años (huichol 155 y cora 36). En la jurisdicción están las lagunas de Chalpa, Toluca, Siete Cielos, Ávalos y Grande de Mezcaltitán. Esta última es una albufera que se extiende de noroeste a sureste, separada del océano Pacífico por un cordón litoral; por el norte se comunica con la laguna del Lagartero y al noroeste con el océano mediante la boca de Teacapan; En la parte sur hay numerosos islotes; de la isla de Mezcaltitán se dice que salió la peregrinación de los aztecas rumbo al valle de México. Esta laguna también goza de celebridad por la calidad de los camarones que ahí se capturan.

SANTIAGO IXTAYUTLA ◆ Municipio de Oaxaca situado en el suroeste del estado, al noreste de Santiago Pinotepa Nacional. Superficie: 367.44 km^2. Habitantes: 8,732, de los cuales 1,906 forman la población económicamente activa. Hablan alguna lengua indígena 5,259 personas mayores de cinco años (mixteco 4,862 y zapoteco 391).

SANTIAGO JAMILTEPEC ◆ Municipio de Oaxaca situado en el suroeste del estado, en el litoral del océano Pacífico, al sureste de Santiago Pinotepa Nacional. Superficie: 622.6 km^2. Habitantes: 17,794, de los cuales 4,062 forman la población económicamente activa. Hablan alguna lengua indígena 4,456 personas mayores de cinco años (mixteco 4,389). Desde 1983, cada 18 de octubre se lleva a cabo el Festival de la Chilena, único de su género en México: en él se recrean los versos, canciones y bailables que trajeron al país los inmigrantes chilenos, llegados en el siglo XVIII al puerto de El Minzo, actual Pinotepa Nacional.

SANTIAGO JOCOTEPEC ◆ Municipio de Oaxaca situado en el noreste del estado, al sur de Tuxtepec, en los límites con Veracruz. Superficie: 732.32 km^2. Habitantes: 11,331, de los cuales 2,353 forman la población económicamente activa. Hablan alguna lengua indígena 7,369 personas mayores de cinco años (chinanteco 7,062 y zapoteco 208), y de ellas, 1,062 no saben español. Su cabecera es Monte Negro.

SANTIAGO JUXTLAHUACA ◆ Municipio de Oaxaca situado en el occidente del estado, al suroeste de Huajuapan de León, en los límites con Guerrero. Superficie: 583.05 km^2. Habitantes: 29,416, de los cuales 5,934 forman la población económicamente activa. Hablan alguna lengua indígena 17,356 personas mayores de cinco años (mixteco 9,546 y triqui 7,674), de las cuales 4,327 son monolingües. Cuenta con mantos de yeso y se distingue por la calidad de su producción doméstica de tequila, mezcal e hilados y tejidos de lana. En el poblado de San Miguel Cuevas existen algunas grutas con pinturas rupestres; según los especialistas, dichas pinturas son las segundas más importantes del continente. La cabecera, del mismo nombre, tiene una iglesia construida en el siglo XVIII.

SANTIAGO LACHIGUIRÍ ◆ Municipio de Oaxaca situado en el sureste del estado, noroeste de Juchitán de Zaragoza y al nor-noroeste de Santo Domingo Tehuantepec. Superficie: 673.63 km^2. Habitantes: 5,873, de los cuales 1,971 forman la población económicamente activa. Hablan alguna lengua indígena 3,448 personas mayores de cinco años (zapoteco 2,353 y mixe 1,090).

SANTIAGO LALOPA ◆ Municipio de Oaxaca situado en el noreste del estado, al noreste de la capital de la entidad. Superficie: 112.27 km^2. Habitantes: 507, de los cuales 148 forman la población económicamente activa. Hablan zapoteco 427 personas mayores de cinco años (son monolingües 51).

SANTIAGO LAOLLAGA ◆ Municipio de Oaxaca situado en el sureste del estado, al noroeste de Juchitán de Zaragoza y contiguo a Ixtepec. Superficie: 506.5 km^2. Habitantes: 2,883, de los cuales 810 forman la población económicamente activa. Hablan alguna lengua indígena 208 personas mayores de cinco años (zapoteco 195). Tiene veneros de aguas minerales.

SANTIAGO LAXOPA ◆ Municipio de Oaxaca situado en el centro del estado, al noreste de la capital de la entidad. Superficie: 118.65 km^2. Habitantes: 1,519, de los cuales 386 forman la población económicamente activa. Hablan alguna lengua indígena 1,276 personas mayores de cinco años (zapoteco 1,270), de las cuales 46 son monolingües.

SANTIAGO LLANO GRANDE ◆ Municipio de Oaxaca situado en el suroeste del estado, al noroeste de Santiago Pinotepa Nacional. Superficie: 114.82 km^2. Habitantes: 3,449, de los cuales 658 forman la población económicamente activa. Hablan alguna lengua indígena 72 personas mayores de cinco años (zapoteco 35 y amuzgo 32).

SANTIAGO MARAVATÍO ◆ Municipio de Guanajuato situado en el sur del estado, contiguo a Yuriria y Salvatierra, cerca de los límites con Michoacán. Superficie: 81.3 km^2. Habitantes: 8,034, de los cuales 1,718 forman la población económicamente activa. Hablan alguna lengua indígena cinco personas mayores de cinco años.

SANTIAGO MATATLÁN ◆ Municipio de Oaxaca situado en el centro del estado, al sureste de la capital de la entidad. Superficie: 126.31 km^2. Habitantes: 7,993, de los cuales 1,818 forman la población económicamente activa. Hablan alguna lengua indígena 6,599 personas mayores de cinco años (zapoteco 6,598). En la jurisdicción hay una zona arqueológica de origen presumiblemente, similar a las de Yagul y Mitla. La cabecera, del mismo nombre, cuenta con una iglesia del siglo XVII.

SANTIAGO MIAHUATLÁN ◆ Municipio de Puebla situado en el sureste del estado, al sureste de la capital de la entidad y noroeste y próximo a Tehuacán. Superficie: 79.09 km^2. Habitantes: 11,708, de los cuales 2,663 forman la población económicamente activa. Hablan alguna lengua indígena 250 personas mayores de cinco años (náhuatl 162 y mazateco 54).

SANTIAGO MILTEPEC ◆ Municipio de Oaxaca situado en el noroeste del estado, al nor-noreste de Huajuapan de León, en los límites con Puebla. Superficie: 82.93 km^2. Habitantes: 424, de los cuales 92 forman la población económicamente activa.

SANTIAGO MINAS ◆ Municipio de Oaxaca situado en el suroeste del estado, al oeste-noroeste de Miahuatlán. Superficie: 389.13 km^2. Habitantes: 1,721, de los cuales 375 forman la población económicamente activa. Hablan alguna lengua indígena 47 personas mayores de cinco años (zapoteco 38).

SANTIAGO NACALTEPEC ◆ Municipio de Oaxaca situado en el norte del estado, al nor-noroeste de la capital de la entidad. Superficie: 213.06 km^2. Habitantes: 2,700, de los cuales 919 forman la población económicamente activa. Hablan alguna lengua indígena 49 personas mayores de cinco años (cuicateco 24).

SANTIAGO NEJAPILLA ◆ Municipio de Oaxaca situado en el noroeste del estado, al sureste de Huajuapan de León y noroeste de la capital de la entidad. Superficie: 38.27 km². Habitantes: 296, de los cuales 75 forman la población económicamente activa. Hablan mixteco ocho personas mayores de cinco años.

SANTIAGO NILTEPEC ◆ Municipio de Oaxaca situado en el istmo de Tehuantepec, al este de Juchitán de Zaragoza y contiguo a Reforma de Pineda. Superficie: 680.1 km². Habitantes: 5,693, de los cuales 1,431 forman la población económicamente activa. Hablan alguna lengua indígena 110 personas (zapoteco 89).

SANTIAGO NUNDICHE ◆ Municipio de Oaxaca situado en el noroeste del estado, al norte y próximo a Tlaxiaco. Superficie: 94.41 km². Habitantes: 1,038, de los cuales 265 forman la población económicamente activa. Hablan alguna lengua indígena 922 personas mayores de cinco años (otomí 921), de las cuales 65 son monolingües.

SANTIAGO NUYOO ◆ Municipio de Oaxaca situado en el occidente del estado, al suroeste de Tlaxiaco. Superficie: 48.48 km². Habitantes: 2,975, de los cuales 621 forman la población económicamente activa. Hablan alguna lengua indígena 2,216 personas mayores de cinco años (mixteco 2,199), de las cuales 300 no saben español.

SANTIAGO PAPASQUIARO ◆ Municipio de Durango situado en el occidente del estado, al noroeste de la capital de la entidad y oeste de San Juan del Río. Superficie: 7,238.4 km². Habitantes: 42,993, de los cuales 10,159 forman la población económicamente activa. Hablan alguna lengua indígena 80 personas mayores de cinco años (totonaco 29).

SANTIAGO PAPASQUIARO ◆ Río de Durango, también llamado Palomas. Nace al oeste de la capital estatal, en la vertiente norte de la sierra de Durango; corre hacia el norte, pasa por el valle de Otinapa con el nombre de Palomas, y por el de Santiago Papasquiaro, ya con ese nombre. Recibe los arroyos Acatita y Pachón y al sur de la sierra de la Candela se une al río Tepehuanes para formar el Ramos.

SANTIAGO PAPASQUIARO, MARIO ◆ ☛ *Santiago, Mario.*

SANTIAGO PINOTEPA NACIONAL ◆ Municipio de Oaxaca situado en el suroeste del estado, en el litoral del océano Pacífico. Superficie: 719.56 km². Habitantes: 42,116, de los cuales 9,710 forman la población económicamente activa. Hablan alguna lengua indígena 9,067 personas mayores de cinco años (mixteco 8,938), de las cuales 452 son monolingües. Cuenta con numerosas playas. En la cabecera, del mismo nombre pero más conocida como Pinotepa, destacan las reliquias arquitectónicas el antiguo Palacio Municipal y una iglesia construida en el siglo XVIII.

Palacio Municipal de Santiago Pinotepa Nacional, Oaxaca

FOTO: FONDO EDITORIAL GRUPO AZABACHE

SANTIAGO RAMÍREZ, CÉSAR AUGUSTO ◆ n. en San Cristóbal de Las Casas, Chis. (1943). Licenciado en derecho por la Universidad de Chiapas y maestro por la Harvard Law School. Miembro del PRI. Miembro del consejo consultivo del CEN de la CNC. Ha sido juez de primera instancia de lo penal en Tuxtla Gutiérrez, cónsul en Nueva Inglaterra (1974-76), subsecretario general de gobierno en Chiapas (1976-77), vocal ejecutivo de la Comisión de Programación y Presupuesto del gobierno chiapaneco (1976-78), secretario general de Gobierno de Chiapas (1978), tres veces diputado federal (1979-82, 1985-88 y 1991-94) e integrante de la primera Asamblea de Representantes del Distrito Federal (1988-91). Asesor del secretario de Comercio (1981), comisario A del Sector Forestal y comisario propietario de 48 organismos paraestatales en materia de bosques, selvas, zonas áridas, celulosa y papel de la Secretaría de la Contraloría; representante del PRI ante la Comisión Federal Electoral; director general de Desarrollo Político de la Secretaría de Gobernación (1993-97) y presidente de la Fundación Alternativa A.C. (1997). Pertenece a la Pan American Society of New England. Autor de *Polémica y partido* (1990).

SANTIAGO DEL RÍO ◆ Municipio de Oaxaca situado en el noroeste del estado, al noroeste de Tlaxiaco y suroeste de Huajuapan de León. Superficie: 82.93 km². Habitantes: 921, de los cuales 209 forman la población económicamente activa. Hablan mixteco 145 personas mayores de cinco años.

SANTIAGO SILVA, JOSÉ DE ◆ n. en Fresnillo, Zacatecas (1942). Licenciado en artes plásticas y maestro en artes visuales por la UNAM. Estudió Historia del Arte en Francia y en Italia (1966-67).

José de Santiago Silva

Desde 1964 imparte teoría e historia del arte en la ENAP. Ha estudiado las culturas de Centro, Sudamérica y África. Miembro de la comisión dictamindora del Instituto de Investigaciones Estéticas (1981-86), miembro del consejo interno del Centro Universitario de Teatro (1981-86), consejero técnico de la ENAP (1988-90), miembro del consejo asesor del CUT (1989-), coordinador del Departamento de Comunicación Gráfica (1977), jefe de la División de Estudios de Posgrado (1979-81 y 82-85), director de la ENAP (1990-94), coordinador de difusión cultural de la UNAM (1997-); subdirector del Museo Nacional de Historia (1974); director de la galería de historia del INAH y del Museo de Arte Moderno (1981-82). Curador de colecciones de pintura, escultura y grabado (1973-). Ha publicado más de 12 libros (*José Chávez Morado, vida, obra y circunstancia, Atotonilco, visión mística y literaria* y *Algunas consideraciones sobre las pinturas enconchadas*), múltiples artículos en libros, revistas y catálogos. Ha diseñado más de 70 escenografías en México y el extranjero, y realizado más de 80 exposiciones individuales y colectivas. Pertenece al SNCA. Por su labor artística ha recibido más de 15 premios: como el de mejor escenógrafo (1985), creador artístico (1994) y Premio Antonio López Mancera (1994 y 1995).

SANTIAGO SUCHILQUITONGO ◆ Municipio de Oaxaca situado en el centro del estado, al noroeste de la capital de la entidad. Superficie: 44.65 km². Habitantes: 6,828, de los cuales 1,572 forman la población económicamente activa. Hablan alguna lengua indígena 21 personas mayores de cinco años.

SANTIAGO TAMAZOLA ◆ Municipio de Oaxaca situado en el noroeste del estado, al oeste de Huajuapan de León, en los límites con Puebla. Superficie: 204.13 km². Habitantes: 3,185, de los cuales 473 forman la población económicamente activa. Hablan alguna lengua indígena 175 personas mayores de cinco años (mixteco 171).

SANTIAGO TAPEXTLA ◆ Municipio de Oaxaca situado en el extremo suroccidental del estado, en el litoral del océano Pacífico y en los límites con Guerrero. Superficie: 187.55 km². Habitantes: 3,473, de los cuales 707 forman la población económicamente activa. Hablan alguna lengua indígena ocho personas mayores de cinco años.

SANTIAGO TEJUPAM ◆ ☛ *Villa Tejupam de la Unión.*

SANTIAGO TENANGO ◆ Municipio de Oaxaca situado en el centro del estado, al nor-noroeste de la capital de la entidad. Superficie: 196.48 km². Habitantes: 1,672, de los cuales 421 forman la población económicamente activa. Hablan alguna lengua indígena seis personas. En la entonces hacienda de La Carbonera, el 7 de octubre de 1865 se libró una batalla en la que fuerzas republicanas al mando de Porfirio Díaz derrotaron a las imperialistas, que contaban con un destacamento de infantería austriaca.

SANTIAGO TEPETLAPA ◆ Municipio de Oaxaca situado en el noroeste del estado, al este de Huajuapan de León. Superficie: 24.24 km². Habitantes: 132, de los cuales 45 forman la población económicamente activa. Hablan alguna lengua indígena siete personas.

SANTIAGO TETEPEC ◆ Municipio de Oaxaca situado en el suroeste del estado, al este de Santiago Pinotepa Nacional. Superficie: 380.2 km². Habitantes: 4,825, de los cuales 1,090 forman la población económicamente activa. Hablan alguna lengua indígena 1,028 personas mayores de cinco años (mixteco 968 y chatino 59), de las que 194 son monolingües.

SANTIAGO TEXCALCINGO ◆ Municipio de Oaxaca situado en el norte del estado, al noroeste de Huautla de Jiménez, en los límites con Puebla. Superficie: 25.52 km². Habitantes: 2,480, de los cuales 572 forman la población económicamente activa. Hablan alguna lengua indígena 2,044 personas mayores de cinco años (náhuatl 2,038), de las cuales 351 no saben español.

SANTIAGO TEXTITLÁN ◆ Municipio de Oaxaca situado en el centro del estado, al suroeste de la capital de la entidad. Superficie: 192.65 km². Habitantes: 2,717, de los cuales 537 forman la población económicamente activa. Hablan alguna lengua indígena 347 personas mayores de cinco años (zapoteco 345).

SANTIAGO TILANTONGO ◆ Municipio de Oaxaca situado en el centro-norte del estado, al este de Tlaxiaco. Superficie: 116.1 km². Habitantes: 4,117, de los cuales 1,038 forman la población económicamente activa. Hablan alguna lengua indígena 1,990 personas mayores de cinco años (mixteco 1,986), de las cuales 61 son monolingües. En su jurisdicción se localiza la zona arqueológica de Monte Negro, ciudad probablemente fundada por zapotecas hacia el 700 a.n.e. Dicha zona, localizada en la cima de un cerro de aproximadamente 400 metros de altura, consta de una calle central de unos 170 metros que se extiende de este a oeste flanqueada por plataformas con edificios construidos en torno a patios cuadrados; en su extremo noreste hay cuatro templos con pequeños patios rodeados de columnas. La ciudad fue abandonada por sus constructores y poblada tiempo después por los mixtecos.

SANTIAGO TILLO ◆ Municipio de Oaxaca situado en el noroeste del estado, al noreste de Tlaxiaco. Superficie: 22.96 km². Habitantes: 512, de los cuales 124 forman la población económicamente activa. Hablan mixteco 17 personas mayores de cinco años.

SANTIAGO TLAZOYALTEPEC ◆ Municipio de Oaxaca situado en el centro del estado, al oeste de la capital de la entidad. Superficie: 93.3 km². Habitantes: 4,512, de los cuales 647 forman la población económicamente activa. Hablan alguna lengua indígena 3,724 personas mayores de cinco años (mixteco 3,719), de las cuales 1,241 no saben español.

SANTIAGO TULANTEPEC DE LUGO GUERRERO ◆ Municipio de Hidalgo situado en el sureste del estado, al sureste de Pachuca y sur de Tulancingo. Superficie: 89.9 km². Habitantes: 22,738, de los cuales 5,126 forman la población económicamente activa. Hablan alguna lengua indígena 205 personas mayores de cinco años (otomí 93 y náhuatl 87). Su cabecera es Santiago Tulantepec.

SANTIAGO TUXTLA ◆ Municipio de Veracruz situado al oeste de San Andrés Tuxtla y al sureste de Álvarado. Superficie: 621.84 km². Habitantes: 54,522, de los cuales 2,806 forman la población económicamente activa. Hablan alguna lengua indígena 283 personas mayores de cinco años (chinanteco 199 y tzotzil 40). En su jurisdicción se localiza la zona arqueológica de Tres Zapotes, cuya exploración se inició alrededor de 1940 y aún no se da por concluida. En ese sitio se han encontrado restos de cerámica, cabezas colosales similares a las de La Venta y El Trapiche, monumentos de piedra, cajas, pedestales y estelas que probablemente datan del siglo III a.n.e., muy similares a los de la cultura de Tlatilco. Posiblemente éste haya sido el asentamiento original de la cultura olmeca. De 1932 a 1936 tanto el municipio como su cabecera llevaron el nombre de Juan de la Luz Enríquez.

SANTIAGO XANICA ◆ Municipio de Oaxaca situado en el sur del estado, al sureste de Miahuatlán. Superficie: 187.55 km². Habitantes: 3,285, de los cuales 812 forman la población económicamente activa. Hablan alguna lengua indígena 1,403 personas mayores de cinco años (zapoteco 1,343) y de ellas, 47 son monolingües.

SANTIAGO XIACUI ◆ Municipio de Oaxaca situado en el norte del estado, al noreste de la capital de la entidad. Superficie: 67.62 km². Habitantes: 1,934, de los cuales 502 forman la población económicamente activa. Hablan alguna lengua indígena 206 personas mayores de cinco años (zapoteco 203).

SANTIAGO YAITEPEC ◆ Municipio de Oaxaca situado en el sur del estado, al oeste-suroeste de Miahuatlán. Superficie: 53.58 km². Habitantes: 3,242, de los cuales 361 forman la población económicamente activa. Hablan chatino 2,727 personas mayores de cinco años (monolingües 1,091).

SANTIAGO YAVEO ◆ Municipio de Oaxaca situado en el noreste del estado, al nor-noroeste de Juchitán de Zaragoza y al sureste de Tuxtepec, en los límites con Veracruz. Superficie: 1,315.37 km². Habitantes: 6,696, de los cuales 1,725 forman la población económicamente activa. Hablan alguna lengua indígena 2,095 personas mayores de cinco años (zapoteco 1,210 y mixe 425).

SANTIAGO YOLOMECATL ◆ Municipio de Oaxaca situado en el noroeste del estado, al sureste de Huajuapan de León y al nor-noreste de Tlaxiaco. Superficie: 63.79 km². Habitantes: 1,729, de los cuales 440 forman la población económicamente activa. Hablan alguna lengua indígena 62 personas mayores de cinco años (mixteco 57). La cabecera, del mismo nombre, cuenta con una iglesia del siglo XVIII.

SANTIAGO YOSONDÚA ◆ Municipio de Oaxaca situado en el occidente del estado, al sur-sureste de Tlaxiaco. Superficie: 215.61 km². Habitantes: 7,660, de los cuales 1,941 forman la población económicamente activa. Hablan alguna lengua indígena 2,376 personas mayores de cinco años (mixteco 2,367), de las cuales 51 no saben español. En su jurisdicción se hallan la cascada de Cabandihui, con una caída de 300 metros, y la gruta de Bequi (palabra que significa catrín) o del Diablo, cuyas formaciones rocosas semejan una jungla petrificada. La cabecera, del mismo nombre, tiene una iglesia del siglo XVII.

SANTIAGO YUCUYACHI ◆ Municipio de Oaxaca situado en el noroeste del estado, al sur de Mariscala de Juárez, suroeste de Huajuapan de León y noroeste de Tlaxiaco. Superficie: 90.58 km². Habitantes: 1,311, de los cuales 93 forman la población económicamente activa. Hablan alguna lengua indígena 234 personas mayores de cinco años (mixteco 229).

SANTIAGO ZACATEPEC ◆ Municipio de Oaxaca situado en el noreste del estado, al este-noreste de la capital de la entidad y sur-sureste de Tuxtepec. Superficie: 142.89 km². Habitantes: 5,136, de los cuales 1,459 forman la población económicamente activa. Hablan alguna lengua indígena 4,372 personas mayores de cinco años (mixe 4,354), de las cuales 1,488 no saben español. Cerca de la cabecera, del mismo nombre, hay una cueva con pinturas rupestres.

SANTIAGO ZOOCHILA ◆ Municipio de Oaxaca situado en el centro del estado, al noreste de la capital de la entidad y sur de Tuxtepec. Superficie: 24.24 km². Habitantes: 471, de los cuales 91 forman la población económicamente activa. Hablan zapoteco 401 personas mayores de cinco años. En la jurisdicción se encontró la llamada Piedra Labrada de Zoochila, de origen zapoteca.

SANTIAGO ZOQUIAPAN ◆ ☛ *Nuevo Zoquiapan*, municipio de Oaxaca.

SANTIBÁÑEZ, ALFONSO ◆ n. en Oaxaca, Oax. (?-1916). Se unió al ejército constitucionalista en las fuerzas de Jesús Carranza (1914), a quien secuestró y por quien pidió rescate. Venustiano Carranza se negó a pagar y Santibáñez fusiló a su rehén a fines de 1914 o principios de 1915. Fue capturado y fusilado por Eguía Lis.

SANTIBÁÑEZ, ENRIQUE ◆ n. en Oaxaca, Oax., y ¿m. en EUA? (1869-1931). Fue diputado federal (1896 y 1909) y cónsul en Praga y San Antonio, Texas. Autor de *La República Mexicana. Reseña geográfica y estadística* (1911), *Chiapas. Reseña geográfica y estadística* (1911), *El Ejecutivo y su labor política* (1916), *México y sus relaciones internacionales* (1917), *Historia de la América Latina desde sus tiempos más remotos hasta nuestros días* (1918), *Geografía comercial de las naciones latinoamericanas* (1919), *Geografía nacional de México* (1923) y *Ensayo acerca de la inmigración mexicana de los EUA* (1930). Fue miembro de la Academia Mexicana de Historia y de la Sociedad Mexicana de Geografía y Estadística.

SANTILLÁN, MARÍA TERESA ◆ n. y m. en el DF (1893-1965). Soprano egresada del Conservatorio Nacional de Música. Cantó al lado de Enrico Caruso, quien la llevó a la Opera de Chicago. Perteneció a la Compañía Impulsora de Opera y a la Orquesta Femenina de Cantantes. Se retiró hacia 1950.

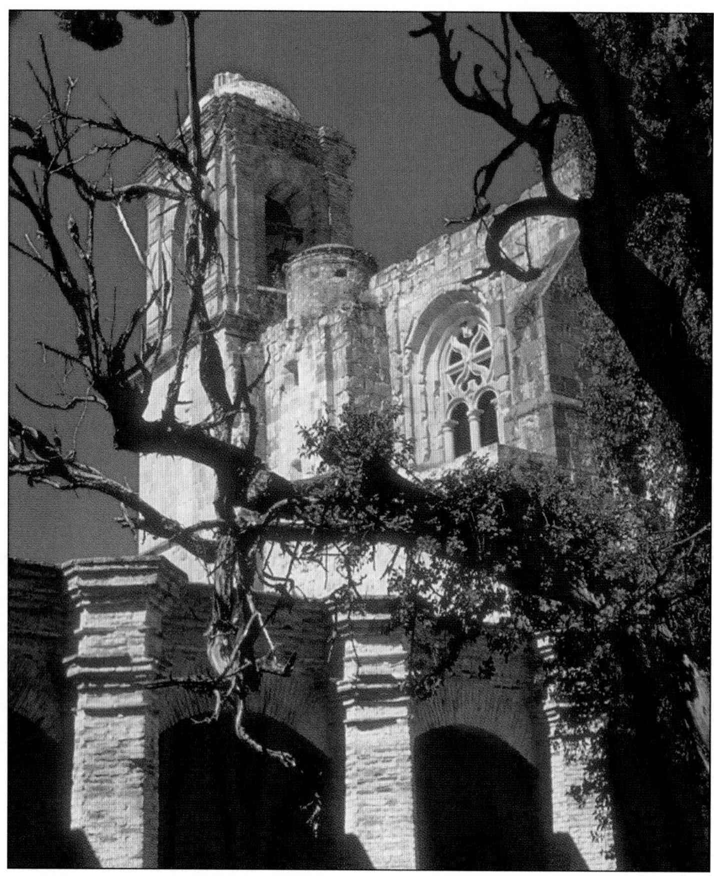

Santo Domingo, Oaxaca

Santo Domingo ◆ Antiguo nombre del municipio veracruzano de Filomeno Mata (☛).

Santo Domingo ◆ Municipio de Oaxaca situado en el oriente del estado, en el istmo de Tehuantepec, al noreste y próximo a Juchitán de Zaragoza. Superficie: 354.68 km². Habitantes: 8,091, de los cuales 1,819 forman la población económicamente activa. Hablan alguna lengua indígena 599 personas mayores de cinco años (zapoteco 537). Su cabecera es Santo Domingo Ingenio.

Santo Domingo ◆ Municipio de San Luis Potosí situado en el noroeste del estado, al oeste de Matehuala y noroeste de la capital de la entidad, en los límites con Zacatecas. Superficie: 6,266.8 km². Habitantes: 13,181, de los cuales 2,562 forman la población económicamente activa. Hablan alguna lengua indígena seis personas mayores de cinco años.

Santo Domingo ◆ Río de Chiapas también llamado Catarina la Grande. Nace en la sierra Madre de Chiapas, al noreste de Tonalá. Corre de suroeste a noreste, recibe a los ríos Escalera y Pando, se une al Suchiapa antes de desembocar en el Grande de Chiapa, al noreste de Chiapa de Corzo y sureste de Tuxtla Gutiérrez.

Santo Domingo ◆ Río de Oaxaca formado por el Salado y el Grande de Quiotepec. Nace al oeste del extremo septentrional de la sierra de Juárez, cruza la de Zongolica por el cañón de Santo Domingo y se une al río Tonto, junto a Tuxtepec, para formar el Papaloapan.

Santo Domingo Albarradas ◆ Municipio de Oaxaca situado en el centro del estado, al este de la capital de la entidad. Superficie: 140.34 km². Habitantes: 827, de los cuales 264 forman la población económicamente activa. Hablan alguna lengua indígena 698 personas mayores de cinco años (zapoteco 617), de las cuales 69 no saben español.

Santo Domingo Armenta ◆ Municipio de Oaxaca situado en el suroeste del estado, en el litoral del océano Pacífico, al oeste-suroeste de Santiago Pinotepa Nacional. Superficie: 125.03 km². Habitantes: 3,246, de los cuales 910 forman la población económicamente activa. Hablan alguna lengua indígena 22 personas mayores de cinco años (mixteco 19).

Santo Domingo Chihuitán ◆ Municipio de Oaxaca situado en el oriente del estado, en el istmo de Tehuantepec, al noroeste de Juchitán de Zaragoza y norte de Salina Cruz. Superficie: 67.62 km². Habitantes: 1,438, de los cuales 373 forman la población económicamente activa. Hablan alguna lengua indígena 99 personas mayores de cinco años (zapoteco 67 y mixe 27).

Santo Domingo Huehuetlán ◆ Cabecera y antiguo nombre del municipio poblano de Huehuetlán el Grande (☛).

Santo Domingo Ingenio ◆ Cabecera del municipio de Santo Domingo (☛).

Santo Domingo Ixcatlán ◆ Municipio de Oaxaca situado en el occidente del estado, al sur-sureste de Tlaxiaco. Superficie: 21.69 km². Habitantes: 857, de los cuales 174 forman la población económicamente activa. Hablan alguna lengua indígena 122 personas mayores de cinco años (mixteco 121).

Santo Domingo de Morelos ◆ Municipio de Oaxaca situado en el sur del estado, al norte y próximo a Puerto Ángel y al sur-sureste de Miahuatlán. Superficie: 107.17 km². Habitantes: 6,496, de los cuales 1,167 forman la población económicamente activa. Hablan alguna lengua indígena 4,770 personas mayores de cinco años (zapoteco 4,766), de las cuales 835 no saben español.

Santo Domingo Nuxaa ◆ Municipio de Oaxaca situado en el occidente del estado, al noroeste de la capital de la entidad. Superficie: 68.89 km². Habitantes: 3,141, de los cuales 590 forman la población económicamente activa. Hablan alguna lengua indígena 2,009 personas mayores de cinco años (mixteco 2,006), de las cuales 78 son monolingües.

Santo Domingo Ozolotepec ◆ Municipio de Oaxaca situado en el sur del estado, al sureste de Miahuatlán y al nor-noreste de Puerto Ángel. Superficie:

68.89 km^2. Habitantes: 1,114, de los cuales 220 forman la población económicamente activa. Hablan zapoteco 562 personas mayores de cinco años.

Santo Domingo Petapa ◆ Municipio de Oaxaca situado en el oriente del estado, en la zona del istmo de Tehuantepec, al nor-noroeste de Juchitán de Zaragoza. Superficie: 232.2 km^2. Habitantes: 7,786, de los cuales 1,836 forman la población económicamente activa. Hablan alguna lengua indígena 3,002 personas mayores de cinco años (zapoteco 2,328 y mixe 662).

Santo Domingo Roayaga ◆ Municipio de Oaxaca situado en el centro del estado, al noreste de la capital de la entidad y sur de Tuxtepec. Superficie: 74 km^2. Habitantes: 831, de los cuales 182 forman la población económicamente activa. Hablan alguna lengua indígena 706 personas mayores de cinco años (zapoteco 451 y mixe 255), de las cuales 104 no saben español.

Santo Domingo Tehuantepec ◆ Municipio de Oaxaca situado en el sureste del estado, en el litoral del océano Pacífico, al suroeste de Juchitán de Zaragoza y contiguo a Salina Cruz. Superficie: 965.8 km^2. Habitantes: 52,142, de los cuales 12,040 forman la población económicamente activa. Hablan alguna lengua indígena 6,045 personas mayores de cinco años (zapoteco 4,808, mixe 933 y chontal de Oaxaca 304), de las cuales 108 son monolingües. Es un importante polo turístico, pues cuenta con numerosas playas, balnearios, construcciones coloniales y fiestas tradicionales. Es también un activo centro de comercialización artesanal. En la jurisdicción se encuentran las ruinas de Guiengola, centro principal de la cultura zapoteca. Entre sus celebraciones se cuentan Las Velas, del 15 al 22 de enero; las fiestas en honor de San Juan, del 20 al 26 de junio; y la de la Asunción de la Virgen en el barrio de Santa María, el 15 de agosto. En la cabecera, del mismo nombre aunque conocida generalmente como Tehuantepec, hay diversas muestras de la arquitectura virreinal, como el convento de Santo Domingo, construido en el siglo XVIII, y la Catedral. Es sede de la diócesis de Tehuantepec, erigida por bula de León XIII del 23 de junio de 1891. El obispo es, desde 1971, Arturo Lona Reyes.

Santo Domingo Teojomulco ◆ Municipio de Oaxaca situado en el suroeste del estado, al noreste de Santiago Pinotepa Nacional y al noroeste de Puerto Escondido. Superficie: 145.44 km^2. Habitantes: 4,044, de los cuales 878 forman la población económicamente activa. Hablan alguna lengua indígena 22 personas mayores de cinco años (chatino 12).

Santo Domingo Tepuxtepec ◆ Municipio de Oaxaca situado en el centro del estado, al este de la capital de la entidad. Superficie: 66.34 km^2. Habitantes: 2,710, de los cuales 1,191 forman la población económicamente activa. Hablan mixe 2,312 personas mayores de cinco años (monolingües 925).

Santo Domingo Tlatayapan ◆ Municipio de Oaxaca situado en el noroeste del estado, noroeste de la capital de la entidad y al noreste de Tlaxiaco. Superficie: 12.76 km^2. Habitantes: 161, de los cuales 47 forman la población económicamente activa.

Santo Domingo Tomaltepec ◆ Municipio de Oaxaca situado en el centro del estado, al este y próximo a la capital de la entidad. Superficie: 49.76 km^2. Habitantes: 2,679, de los cuales 563 forman la población económicamente activa. Hablan alguna lengua indígena 655 personas mayores de cinco años (zapoteco 649).

Santo Domingo Tonalá ◆ Municipio de Oaxaca situado en el noroeste del estado, al suroeste y próximo a Huajuapan de León. Superficie: 126.31 km^2. Habitantes: 6,631, de los cuales 1,274 forman la población económicamente activa. Hablan alguna lengua indígena 1,832 personas mayores de cinco años (mixteco 1,818), de las cuales 302 son monolingües. En la cabecera, del mismo nombre, hay una iglesia construida en el siglo XVII.

Santo Domingo Tonaltepec ◆ Municipio de Oaxaca situado en el noroeste del estado, al sureste de Huajuapan de León y suroeste de Huautla de Jiménez. Superficie: 20.41 km^2. Habitantes: 347, de los cuales 51 forman la población económicamente activa. Hablan mixteco 63 personas mayores de cinco años.

Santo Domingo Xagacia ◆ Municipio de Oaxaca situado en el centro del estado, al este-noreste de la capital de la entidad. Superficie: 38.27 km^2. Habitantes: 1,027, de los cuales 298 forman la población económicamente activa. Hablan zapoteco 896 personas mayores de cinco años (monolingües 102).

Santo Domingo Yanhuitlán ◆ Municipio de Oaxaca situado en el noroeste del estado, al sureste de Huajuapan de León y noroeste de la capital

Palacio Municipal de Santo Domingo Tehuantepec, Oaxaca

Foto: Fondo Editorial Grupo Azabache

de la entidad. Superficie: 22.96 km². Habitantes: 1,630, de los cuales 481 forman la población económicamente activa. Hablan alguna lengua indígena 27 personas mayores de cinco años (mixteco 20). En la cabecera, del mismo nombre, se encuentran el templo y el convento de Yanhuitlán, construidos en 1541 y remozados en el siglo XVII. El primero es célebre por su retablo, obra de Andrés de Concha (☛).

Santo Domingo Yodohino ◆ Municipio de Oaxaca situado en el noroeste del estado, al sur-sureste y próximo a Huajuapan de León. Superficie: 56.14 km². Habitantes: 573, de los cuales 52 forman la población económicamente activa.

Santo Domingo Zanatepec ◆ Municipio de Oaxaca situado en el extremo oriental del estado, al este-noreste de Juchitán de Zaragoza, en los límites con Chiapas. Superficie: 1,024.49 km². Habitantes: 10,153, de los cuales 2,512 forman la población económicamente activa. Hablan alguna lengua indígena 196 personas mayores de cinco años (zapoteco 95 y zoque 86).

Santo, el Enmascarado de Plata ◆ n. en Tulancingo, Hgo., y m. en el DF (1917-1984). Nombre profesional del actor y luchador Rodolfo Guzmán Huerta. Hizo estudios de artes plásticas en la Academia de San Carlos. Se inició en la lucha libre en 1936, con el nombre de *Ruddy* Guzmán y tuvo los pseudónimos de *el Hombre Rojo y el Murciélago II*. En 1942 cambió su nombre a *Santo, el Enmascarado de Plata* y se cubría la cabeza con una máscara blanca hecha de cuero bovino. Como tal se convirtió en el protagonista de la historieta del mismo nombre y de películas de gran éxito económico. Actuó en 56 cintas, entre otras, *Santo contra el Cerebro del mal* (1952), *Santo contra las mujeres vampiro, El doctor Muerte, Las momias de Guanajuato, Las mujeres vampiro atacan de nuevo, Museo de cera, Chanoc y el hijo de el Santo contra los vampiros asesinos* y *Santo contra la furia de los karatecas* (1982). Inspirado en su influencia sobre el público se realizaron los filmes *Adiós, adiós, ídolo mío* y *La leyenda de una máscara*. Luchó en Centroamérica, Estados Unidos, Sudamérica y Cuba. Ostentó los campeonatos mundiales welter y medio y tres títulos nacionales (welter, medio y semicompleto). Se retiró de la lucha libre en 1982. Se presentó en televisión y murió cuando trabajaba en el teatro Blanquita. El grupo de rock Botellita de Jerez compuso una canción en su honor y la novela *Xanto, novelucha libre*, de José Luis Zárate, celebra su mito. Se le incluyó en el Salón de la Fama de la Comisión de Box y Lucha del Distrito Federal.

Santo, el Enmascarado de Plata en acción sobre el cuadrilatero

Santo Tomás ◆ Municipio del Estado de México situado en los límites con Michoacán y contiguo a Valle de Bravo. Superficie: 244.85 km². Habitantes: 8,257, de los cuales 1,565 forman la población económicamente activa. Hablan alguna lengua indígena siete personas mayores de cinco años. En su jurisdicción se encuentran la zona arqueológica de Malpaís, aún sin explorar, y una pintura rupestre (probablemente tolteca) en la barranca del Diablo, en Ixtapantongo. Malpaís tiene, asimismo, veneros de aguas termales y sulfurosas. El municipio fue erigido en 1863. Su cabecera es Nuevo Santo Tomás de los Plátanos.

Santo Tomás Hueyotlipan ◆ Municipio de Puebla situado al sureste de la capital del estado y contiguo a Tecali de Herrera. Superficie: 34.45 km². Habitantes: 6,582, de los cuales 1,304 forman la población económicamente activa. Hablan náhuatl 82 personas mayores de cinco años.

Santo Tomás Jalieza ◆ Municipio de Oaxaca situado en el centro del estado, al sur-sureste y próximo a la capital de la entidad. Superficie: 51.03 km². Habitantes: 2,822, de los cuales 683 forman la población económicamente activa. Hablan alguna lengua indígena 642 personas mayores de cinco años (zapoteco 637).

Santo Tomás Mazaltepec ◆ Municipio de Oaxaca situado en el centro del estado, al noroeste y próximo a la capital de la entidad. Superficie: 51.03 km². Habitantes: 2,021, de los cuales 599 forman la población económicamente activa. Hablan alguna lengua indígena 1,214 personas mayores de cinco años (zapoteco 1,204).

Santo Tomás Ocotepec ◆ Municipio de Oaxaca situado en el occidente del estado, al suroeste y próximo a Tlaxiaco. Superficie: 72.72 km². Habitantes: 3,939, de los cuales 1,098 forman la población económicamente activa. Hablan alguna lengua indígena 3,117 personas mayores de cinco años (mixteco 3,114), de las cuales 416 son monolingües.

Santo Tomás Tamazulapan ◆ Municipio de Oaxaca situado en el sur del estado y contiguo a Miahuatlán. Superficie: 66.34 km². Habitantes: 1,633, de los cuales 456 forman la población económicamente activa. Hablan alguna lengua indígena 59 personas mayores de cinco años (zapoteco 58).

Santos, Daniel ◆ n. en Puerto Rico y m. en EUA (1916-1992). Cantante conocido como *el Jefe* y autodefinido como "bolerista y guarachero". Se hizo cantante en Nueva York, donde vivió en su infancia y juventud, luego de la depresión de los años treinta y, según sus palabras, "por necesidad". En México se presentó en 1953, aunque algunas versiones relatan que ocurrió en los años cuarenta. Reconocido intérprete del compositor Pedro Flores. Fue solista de la Sonora Matancera, la mayor parte de su carrera la realizó en México. Reapareció en 1986. Grabó el disco *El telegrafista*, dedicado a Gabriel García Márquez. Hizo célebre la canción *Lamento borincano* y otras composiciones de Rafael Hernández, *El Jibarito*, en las que lamenta la situación colonial que vive su patria. Tuvieron gran éxito sus interpretaciones de *Dos gardenias* y *La despedida*, entre otras.

SANTOS, GONZALO N. ◆ n. en Villa Guerrero, SLP, y m. en el DF (1896-1979). En 1910 se unió a la revolución y en ella alcanzó el grado de general de división. Miembro fundador del Partido Nacional Revolucionario, del que fue secretario del Distrito Federal (1929) y secretario general del Comité Ejecutivo (1929). Cofundador del Partido de la Revolución Mexicana y el PRI. Fue cinco veces consecutivas diputado federal entre 1924 y 1934; senador (1934-40) y gobernador de San Luis Potosí (1943-49), donde implantó un cacicazgo que perdió fuerza durante el sexenio del presidente Adolfo López Mateos y terminó bajo la presidencia de José López Portillo, cuando fue afectado su latifundio El Gargaleote, el mayor de la entidad potosina y uno de los más grandes del país. Fue embajador en Bélgica (1940) y director de Pesca de la Secretaría de Industria y Comercio (1956-61). Autor de unas *Memorias* (1987).

SANTOS, JOSÉ E. ◆ n. en Bustamante, NL (1889-?). En 1910 se unió a la insurrección maderista en Coahuila, en las fuerzas de Alberto Guajardo. En 1913 secundó el movimiento constitucionalista, militó en las filas de Pablo González, obtuvo el generalato y fue jefe del Estado Mayor de Antonio I. Villarreal. Gobernador de Nuevo León (1919-20), participó en las rebeliones delahuertista (1923) y escobarista (1929).

Gonzalo N. Santos

SANTOS, LINA ◆ n. en Coahuila (1967). Actriz. Señorita Coahuila 1985 y tercer lugar en el certamen Señorita México. Segundo lugar en Miss Pacific. Primer Lugar en Miss Tanga 1986 en Puerto Rico. Ha actuado en cine, teatro y televisión y grabado discos.

SANTOS, NINFA ◆ n. en Costa Rica y m. en el DF (1914-1990). Escritora y militante comunista. Fundadora, en 1936, del Comité de Ayuda al Niño Español, el cual gestionó ante el presidente Lázaro Cárdenas el arribo a México de huérfanos de la guerra civil española, entre ellos los Niños de Morelia (☛). Pertenenció al servicio exterior mexicano. Autora de poesía: *Amor quiere que muera* (1938).

SANTOS, PEDRO ANTONIO DE LOS ◆ n. y m. en Tampamolón, SLP (1887-1913). Abogado. En 1909 participó como orador en la campaña antirreeleccionista de Francisco I. Madero. Perseguido por la policía porfirista pasó a Estados Unidos, donde permaneció hasta 1911. Diputado federal (1912) durante la decena trágica fue aprehendido junto con Madero y Pino Suárez, pero más tarde se le liberó. Se alistó en las fuerzas constitucionalistas de Jesús Agustín Castro y participó en la campaña de Tamaulipas. Fue capturado y fusilado por las tropas del dictador Victoriano Huerta.

SANTOS, SAMUEL M. ◆ n. en Tampamolón, SLP, y m. en el DF (1887-1959). En 1913 se unió a la revolución constitucionalista en San Luis Potosí. Fue diputado al Congreso Constituyente de 1916-17 y jefe de la Escuela de Práctica Militar en Guadalajara. En 1920 se adhirió a la rebelión del Plan de Agua Prieta y tres años después secundó la rebelión delahuertista. Al ser reivindicado, obtuvo el grado de general de división y fue miembro del consejo de administración de la Lotería Nacional.

SANTOS CHOCANO, JOSÉ ◆ n. en Perú y m. en Chile (1875-1934). Llegó a México en 1912, enviado por el presidente guatemalteco Manuel Estrada Cabrera, para establecer contacto con Francisco I. Madero. Participó en las actividades de la Casa del Obrero Mundial. Fue testigo de la decena trágica. Victoriano Huerta lo expulsó del país. En enero de 1914 volvió a México para unirse a la lucha de Venustiano Carranza, quien lo comisionó para representar en Estados Unidos a la revolución constitucionalista; al ocurrir la escisión revolucionaria manifestó su apego a la causa villista. En 1925 polemizó con José Vasconcelos y, a raíz de esta diferencia, mató en Perú al escritor Edwin Elmore Letts, vasconcelista. Santos Chocano, a su vez, fue asesinado por Martín Bruce Padilla, en la capital chilena. Autor, entre otros, de los poemas *Sinfonía heroica* (en honor de Madero) y *Última rebelión* (homenaje a Francisco Villa). Escribió también el drama *La princesa* (1906), de tema mexicano y estrenado en España, *Interpretación mexicana* (1915) y *El carácter agrario de la revolución mexicana*.

Ninfa Santos

SANTOS DE LA GARZA, LUIS SANTOS ◆ n. en Piedras Negras, Coah. (1922). Licenciado en derecho por la Universidad Autónoma de Nuevo León. Profesor del ITESM. Se especializó en derecho constitucional, mercantil, corporativo y electoral. Ha sido síndico en el municipio San Pedro Garza García (1973-76), diputado local en NL (1985-88), regidor del ayuntamiento de Monterrey (1992-94) y coordinador de los regidores del PAN. Senador (1997-2000). Ha ejercido en 12 países. Miembro de la Inter-American Bar Association, de la Barra Mexicana-Colegio de Abogados. Asesor legal del Congreso neoleonés (1996-), consejero y secretario del consejo de la Cámara de la Industria de Transformación, de la Coparmex, y el Centro Patronal de Nuevo León. Presidente de la Bolsa de Valores de Monterrey.

SANTOS GUAJARDO, VICENTE ◆ n. en Villa de Progreso, Coah., y m. en el DF (1895-1962). Se tituló de abogado en 1921, después de participar en la revolución. Fue diputado federal, profesor del Ateneo Fuente de Saltillo, jefe del Departamento Jurídico de la Secretaría de Agricultura y Ganadería, subsecretario de Gobernación, Trabajo y Relaciones Exteriores; subprocurador general de la República, magistrado del Tribunal Supremo de Justicia, ministro y presidente de la Suprema Corte de Justicia y director fundador del IMSS (del 19 de septiembre de 1943 al 1 de enero de 1944).

SANTOS DE HOYOS, ALBERTO ◆ n. en Monterrey, NL (1941). Licenciado en administración de empresas por el ITESM. Pertenece al PRI, donde ha sido miembro del CEPES y del Comité de Finanzas del Comité Directivo Estatal en Nuevo León. Diputado federal (1982-85) y senador (1994-2000). Ha sido presidente del Consejo de Empresas Santos, de Gamesa y de la Cámara de la Industria de Transformación. Es presidente de la Cámara de las Industrias Azucarera y Alcoholera (1998-).

SANTOS REYES NOPALA ◆ Municipio de Oaxaca situado en el suroeste del estado, al nor-noroeste de Puerto Escondido y suroeste de Miahuatlán. Superficie: 196.48 km^2. Habitantes: 11,403, de los cuales 2,690 forman la población económicamente activa. Hablan alguna lengua indígena 5,244 personas mayores de cinco años (chatino 5,212), de las cuales 888 son monolingües.

SANTOS REYES PÁPALO ◆ Municipio de Oaxaca situado en el noroeste del estado, al sur de Huautla de Jiménez. Superficie: 25.52 km^2. Habitantes: 2,300, de los cuales 598 forman la población económicamente activa. Hablan alguna lengua indígena 1,844 personas mayores de cinco años (cuicateco 1,837), de las cuales 117 no dominan al español. En el poblado de Cacalotepec se han encontrado pinturas rupestres.

SANTOS REYES TEPEJILLO ◆ Municipio de Oaxaca situado en el noroeste del estado, al sur de Huajuapan de León y noroeste de Tlaxiaco. Superficie: 89.31 km^2. Habitantes: 1,595, de los cuales 275 forman la población económicamente activa. Hablan alguna lengua indígena 1,414 personas mayores de cinco años (mixteco 1,413), de las cuales 188 no saben español.

SANTOS REYES YUCUNÁ ◆ Municipio de Oaxaca situado en el noroeste del estado, al oeste de Huajuapan de León. Superficie: 16.59 km^2. Habitantes: 1,345, de los cuales 188 forman la población económicamente activa. Hablan mixteco 1,058 personas mayores de cinco años (monolingües 257).

SANTOS ORDÓÑEZ, MELCHOR DE LOS ◆ n. en Torreón Coahuila (1950). Realizó estudios en el Instituto Tecnológico de Estudios Superiores de Monterrey, donde obtuvo el título de licenciado en economía. Pertenece al Partido Revolucionario Institucional desde 1982, donde se ha desempeñado como asesor del presidente y secretario de Coordinación Regional del Comité Ejecutivo Nacional. Fue asesor del subsecretario de Educación Superior en Investigación Científica de la Secretaría de Educación Pública, director de Programas Sociales en Fonapas, agregado en la representación de México ante la FAO, director de Programación Económica y Social de la Secretaría de Programación y Presupuesto, coordinador ejecutivo del INEGI y director de delegaciones de Banobras. Fue diputado federal (1991-94) y senador de la República (1994-2000).

SANTOSCOY, ALBERTO ◆ n. y m. en Guadalajara, Jal. (1857-1906). Dirigió la Biblioteca Pública de Jalisco, fue profesor en el Liceo de Varones de Guadalajara y jefe del Archivo Eclesiástico de la Mitra. Colaboró en el *Diario de Jalisco*. Autor de *Apuntamientos históricos y biográficos jalisciences* (1889), *Canon cronológico razonado de los gobernantes de Jalisco* (1890), *Biografía de D. Manuel López Cotilla* (1895), *Nayarit* (1899), *Báculo pastoral de la iglesia de Guadalajara* (1901) y *Los Cañedo. Apuntes heráldicos y biográficos de una prominente familia jalisciense* (1902).

SANTULLANO, LUIS A. ◆ n. en España y m. en el DF (1879-1952). Licenciado en derecho (1905) y profesor por la Escuela Normal de Oviedo. Vino a México en 1944 y fue oficial mayor de El Colegio de México hasta su muerte. Autor de *Carrocera, labrador* (1926), *La autonomía y la libertad en educación* (1927), *Los estudiantes* (1930), *Hacia una escuela mejor* (1930), *De la escuela a la universidad* (1930), *La escuela duplicada: sistemas de Gary y Detroit* (1931), *Piñón* (1931), *Paxarón, o la fatalidad* (1932), *Bartolo o la vocación* (1945), *Mirada al Caribe. Fricción de culturas en Puerto Rico* (1945), *Tres novelas asturianas* (1945), *Padres, hijos y maestros. Antipedagogía* (1945), *El pensamiento vivo de Cossío* (1946) y *Las mejores páginas del Quijote* (1948).

FOTO: ANA LOURDES HERRERA

Margarita Sanz

SANZ, MARGARITA ◆ n. en Guadalajara, Jal. (1954). Actriz egresada de la Escuela de Arte Teatral del INBA y del Centro Universitario de Teatro. Ha actuado en los programas de televisión *Los lunes, teatro; Canasta de cuentos mexicanos, Novelas semanales, Teleteatros, De la vida de las mujeres y Vida, cultura y magia*. En el cine participó en la cinta *Frida* (1983, de Paul Leduc). Ha sido premiada por su actuación en las obras de teatro *Crímenes del corazón* (1982) y *Amor a cuatro tiempos* (1985) y también ha destacado en *El destierro, Más laberinto* y *La señora Klein*. Premio Ariel por su actuación en *El callejón de los milagros* (1995). Participó en el Laboratorio del Teatro Campesino.

SANZ, PATRICIO ◆ n. y m. en la ciudad de México (¿1845?-1890). Heredero de numerosas propiedades, él mismo acrecentó el capital familiar al adquirir las haciendas de Mazaquiáhuac, Chimalpa, San Juan Ixquimalco, Mimiahuapan y Buena Vista, entre otras fincas de los estados de Hidalgo y Tlaxcala. Era dueño, asimismo, de la casa donde más tarde se instaló el restaurante la Bombilla, en San Ángel. En 1903, Ana María Llera viuda de Sanz instituyó la Fundación Asilo y el colegio Patricio Sanz.

SANZ, ROCÍO ◆ n. en Costa Rica y m. en el DF (1934-1993). Compositora. Estudió en el Conservatorio Nacional de Música, en el City College de Los

Ángeles. Llegó a México en 1954 e ingresó al Conservatorio Nacional de Música. También estudió en Rusia en el Vladimir Guiórguievich Feré. Se dedicó a la enseñanza y fue asesora musical de diversas compañías de danza, teatro y de la SEP. Compositora residente del Teatro de la Universidad Veracruzana, productora de programas de Radio UNAM y Radio Educación, dirigidos a los niños (desde 1976). Perteneció a la Liga de Compositores de Música de Concierto. Premio 150 años de la Independencia Centroamericana (Costa Rica, 1971) y premio único del Concurso Nacional (Costa Rica, 1976). Compuso obras para solos, dúos, cuartetos, quintetos, conjuntos instrumentales, piano, orquesta de cámara, coros, para ballet, para teatro, para niños, así como guiones teatrales, y el cuento *El cuento vacío*.

Sanz de Obregón, María Pilar ◆ n. en España (1912). Licenciada en ciencias físico-exactas por la Universidad Central de Madrid. Pertenecía a la dirección de la Asociación de Estudiantes de Ciencias de la Federación Universitaria Escolar, por lo que fue desterrada de Madrid; durante la dictadura de Primo de Rivera. Profesora del Instituto de Segunda Enseñanza Velázquez, de Madrid, durante la guerra civil fue subjefa de archivo del Servicio de Investigación Militar. Llegó exiliada a México en 1939. Contadora de varias empresas, voluntaria de la Cruz Roja Mexicana (1963-), fundadora del Comité Nacional de Donación Altruista de Sangre y cofundadora de la Unión de Mujeres Españolas.

Sanz Sainz, Julio ◆ n. y m en España (1913-1996). Periodista y editor. Durante la guerra civil fue corresponsal en varios frentes. Al triunfo del franquismo pasó a Francia y fue recluido en un campo de concentración. En 1940 pudo viajar a la República Dominicana, donde fue redactor de cables del diario *La Nación*. Estuvo en Cuba, donde trabajó para la radiodifusora CMQ y; en 1942 llegó a México. Colaborador y jefe de redacción de la revista *Tiempo* (1942-46), fundador de la Editorial Labor Mexicana, subgerente, gerente general y director de las sucursales en Hispanoamérica de la UTEHA, fundador de la Cámara Nacional de la Industria Editorial Mexicana, director general de ediciones en español de MacGraw-Hill (1969), organizador y presidente de la primera Exposición Editorial del Continente Americano y fundador de la librería Casa del Libro. Fundó Aconcagua Ediciones y Publicaciones (1972). Autor de *Los muertos no hacen ruido (novela de guerra para leer mientras dura la paz)* (1973). Medalla de bronce del Instituto Nacional del Libro Español (1972).

Sapiña, Juan ◆ n. en España y m. en el DF (1905-1973). Periodista. Fue profesor de lengua y literatura latinas en escuelas de segunda enseñanza, director del semanario *¡Adelante!* (1929-30), diputado socialista a las Cortes Constituyentes (1931), diputado a Cortes (1936) y director general de Minas y Combustibles de la República Española (1937-39). Llegó en 1940 y obtuvo la nacionalidad mexicana en 1942. Profesor del Colegio Franco-Español, traductor de latín en El Colegio de México, redactor de la editorial UTEHA y colaborador de *Juventud* y *Novedades*. Autor de *Prosas y versos*, *Iniciación en el estudio de la lengua latina* (2 t.), *Mexicanas* y *La última virgen* (1949).

Sarabia, Antonio ◆ n. en el DF (1944). Escritor. Estudió Ciencias de la Comunicación. Trabajó para la radio en Guadalajara. En esa ciudad fundó AS Publicidad. Radicó 16 años en París, donde comenzó a dar a conocer su obra literaria. Autor de *Tres pies al gato* (1978), *Los convidados del volcán* (1997) y *Amarillius* (1998), entre otras.

Sarabia, Antonio O. ◆ n. en Ciudad Lerdo, Dgo. (1885-?). Militante del Partido Liberal Mexicano. Participó en la insurrección maderista en Chihuahua (1910-11), como teniente del Cuerpo Mé-dico Militar. En 1913 se unió al constitucionalismo, fue miembro del Estado Mayor de Plutarco Elías Calles. Vi-cecónsul en Douglas y cónsul en No-gales, Arizona. Agente general de compras del constitucionalismo en Nueva York, administrador del Hospital Militar (1920), inspector del Timbre, visitador especial de Hacienda, jefe de procura-dores de pueblos (1924) y segundo jefe y luego jefe de las Comisiones de Seguridad (1925-32).

Sarabia, Francisco ◆ n. en Ciudad Lerdo, Dgo., y m. en EUA (1901-1939). Estudió ingeniería mecánica en Estados Unidos. Volvió a Ciudad Lerdo en 1919 e instaló un taller mecánico. En 1924 se inició como conductor de autos de competencia. Se tituló como piloto aviador en 1926. Fundó una aerolínea en Tabasco que se extendió a Chiapas y Yucatán en poco tiempo. Trabajó en el servicio postal aéreo de Estados Unidos. En 1929 fundó en Monterrey la primera escuela mexicana de aviación civil. En 1938 realizó un viaje sin escalas de los Ángeles a la ciudad de México, al año siguiente hizo un vuelo de 10 horas y 48 minutos entre la capital mexicana y Nueva York, en *El conquistador del cielo*. Cuando iniciaba el regreso, su avión falló y se desplomó en el río Potomac, en Washington.

Sarabia, Juan ◆ n. en San Luis Potosí, SLP, y m. en el DF (1882-1920). Abogado. Se opuso a la dictadura de Porfirio Díaz. En la ciudad de San Luis Potosí dirigió los periódicos *El Demócrata* (1899) y *El Porvenir* (1900), participó en el congreso de clubes liberales y fundó, con Camilo Arriaga y Librado Rivera, *El Demófilo (1902)*, cerrado por las autoridades. En la capital del país dirigió *El Hijo del Ahuizote* (1902) y colaboró en otros órganos. En San Antonio, Texas, y San Luis Missouri fue redactor en jefe de *Regeneración* (1904-1906) y cofundador de la Junta Organizadora del Partido Liberal Mexicano, de la que fue vicepresidente (1905-). En marzo de 1906, perseguido, huyó a Canadá. Firmó el *Manifiesto y Programa del Partido Liberal Mexicano*. Rompió con el ala anarquista de su partido. En 1908 fue capturado en Ciudad Juárez y recluido en San Juan de Ulúa (1908-11). En 1911, él y Jesús Flores Magón se entrevistaron en Estados Unidos con los hermanos de éste, Ricardo y Enrique, a quienes pidieron infructuosamente que

Julio Sanz Sainz

sus partidarios depusieran las armas y cesaran las huelgas y tomas de tierras. Al día siguiente, Ricardo y Enrique fueron detenidos y acusaron a Sarabia de haberlos delatado. Delegado a la convención electoral del maderista Partido Constitucional Progresista (1911) y cofundador de la Confederación Nacional de Trabajadores. En la ciudad de México, con Antonio I. Villarreal, publicó un nuevo periódico *Regeneración*, dirigió el *Diario del Hogar* y fundó un moderado Partido Liberal que se dividió en 1912. Con Arriaga y Soto y Gama estableció una efímera Escuela Socialista, pero se negó a ingresar en el Partido Socialista Mexicano. Fue diputado federal a la XXVI Legislatura, en la que presentó un proyecto de ley agraria. En 1913, Victoriano Huerta lo hizo encarcelar. Liberado en 1914, intentó, sin éxito, mediar entre carrancistas y zapatistas. En 1915 trabajó en la Biblioteca Nacional y dirigió la Escuela Industrial de Huérfanos. En 1917 fue candidato perdedor en las elecciones por la gubernatura de San Luis Potosí. Al morir era senador por el mismo estado.

Saravia y Aragón, Atanasio G. ◆ n. en Durango, Dgo., y m. en el DF (1888-1969). Desempeñó diversos puestos en el Banco Nacional de México, del que llegó a ser director y miembro del Consejo de Administración. Destacó como historiador y colaboró en numerosas publicaciones. Autor de *Las tribus primitivas del norte* (1916), *Los misioneros muertos en el norte de Nueva España* (1920), *Ensayos históricos* (1937), *El indio Rafael* (1938), *Apuntes para la historia de la Nueva Vizcaya* (2 t., 1938-41), *¡Viva Madero!* (1940), *La ciudad de Durango, 1563-1821* (1941), *La dominación* (1942), *Manual de historia de Durango* (1952) y *Cuatro siglos de la vida de una hacienda* (1959). Ingresó en 1920 en la Academia Mexicana de la Historia y fue su director vitalicio desde 1959.

Saravia González, Buenaventura ◆ n. en Nicaragua y m. ¿en Durango, Dgo.? (1828-1895). Político conservador. Radicado en Durango, adquirió en 1850 la nacionalidad mexicana. Durante la intervención francesa fue nombrado comisario imperial y prefecto político del Departamento de Durango, cargo en el que alternó con Juan de Dios Palacios (1864-66).

Sardá, José ◆ n. en España y m. en Colombia (?-1834). En España luchó contra la invasión francesa, pero fue aprehendido, llevado a Francia y obligado a servir al imperio napoleónico. Huyó a Inglaterra, donde conoció a Francisco Javier Mina, con quien vino a combatir por la independencia mexicana. Tras el desembarco de Mina en Soto la Marina (1817), fue nombrado comandante del fuerte que ahí se levantó. En 1818 fue derrotado por el realista Joaquín Arredondo, encarcelado en San Juan de Ulúa y llevado a España, donde se le confinó en la fortaleza de Ceuta; escapó de su prisión y llegó a Francia, desde donde viajó a Colombia para unirse a la lucha insurgente de Simón Bolívar. Éste lo nombró teniente coronel y gobernador de la región de Ríohacha (1821). Consumada la independencia colombiana conspiró (1833) contra el presidente Francisco de Paula Santander, sucesor de Bolívar. Fue delatado y encarcelado. Escapó de su prisión, luego de haber sido condenado a muerte, pero en 1834 fue recapturado y ejecutado.

Sardaneta, José Mariano ◆ n. y m. en Guanajuato, Gto. (1761-1835). Regidor perpetuo, alcalde ordinario, diputado de la territorial de Minería y administrador minero en Guanajuato. Fue apoderado del virrey Iturrigaray cuando éste fue depuesto. Diputado a Cortes en 1812, aunque el gobierno virreinal le negó los viáticos. Al ser aprehendido José María Morelos, se le encontraron algunos documentos que involucraban a Sardaneta, quien, a su vez, fue capturado y encarcelado en la prisión de la Ciudadela. Juzgado en 1816, se le condenó a la deportación a España, logró retrasar su traslado fingiendo en Veracruz una enfermedad, hasta que en 1820 se anuló su condena. En ese año, restablecida la Carta de Cádiz, fue miembro de la diputación provincial de Guanajuato y la Corte lo nombró miembro de la Junta de Censura de Libertad de Imprenta. En 1821 Agustín de Iturbide lo hizo miembro de la Junta Gubernativa del Imperio. Sardaneta firmó el acta de independencia con su título de marqués de San Juan de Rayas y fue diputado al primer Congreso Constituyente (1822-23). A la caída de Iturbide se alejó de la política. Al morir era síndico del convento de San Diego, en Guanajuato.

Sareli, Jorge *Che* ◆ n. en Coatzacoalcos, Ver (?). Cantante de tangos y pintor. Ganó en Orizaba el primer concurso de canto de la XEDF. Ha grabado más de 40 discos interpretando a Carlos Gardel y otros compositores de ese género. Autor de *El tango en México*, *El tango a través del tiempo* (1992) y *El libro mayor del tango*. Actuó en cine en *Pompeyo el conquistador* y otras películas. En la televisión grabó *Variedades del mediodía* y otros programas. Vivió 11 años en Argentina, donde lo bautizaron *El As del tango azteca* y donde obtuvo el premio del Festival de Tango de Buenos Aires en 1980. Como artista plástico es autor de más de 300 obras.

Sargento ◆ Punta de Sonora, situada al norte de la isla de Tiburón, en el extremo noroccidental de la bahía de Agua Dulce, al oeste-noroeste de Hermosillo.

Saric ◆ Municipio de Sonora, situado en el norte del estado, al noreste de Caborca y contiguo a Nogales, en la frontera con Estados Unidos. Superficie: 1,676.23 km^2. Habitantes: 2,287, de los cuales 617 forman la población económicamente activa. Hablan alguna lengua indígena seis personas mayores de cinco años. En 1931 el municipio fue incorporado al de Altar y se le rehabilitó en 1934. La cabecera, del mismo nombre, fue fundada en 1751 como misión jesuita. Un año después resultó destruida por un ataque indígena y la Compañía de Jesús la reconstruyó en 1756.

Sariñana y Cuenca, Isidro ◆ n. en la ciudad de México y m. en Oaxaca, Oax. (1631-1696). En 1662 ya era doctor en teología por la Real y Pontificia

Universidad de México, donde ejerció la docencia durante 17 años. Fue párroco y orador sagrado de la Santa Veracruz y del Sagrario; canónigo doctoral, chantre, arcediano y deán de la Catedral Metropolitana y obispo de Antequera, hoy Oaxaca, designado en 1682. Tomó posesión dos años después. Reprimió severamente las prácticas religiosas tradicionales de los indios. Autor de *Mitología sacra* (1652), *Noticia de la. dedicación del Templo Metropolitano de México* (1668), *Oración fúnebre de veintiún religiosos de S. Francisco que murieron a manos de los indios apóstatas de la Nueva México* (1681) y *Llanto del occidente en el ocaso del más claro sol de las Españas.*

Sariñana Márquez, Fernando ◆ n. en el DF (1958). Licenciado en comunicación social por la UAM (1980-85). Posteriormente (1986-1989) le otorgan la beca Fulbriht para estudiar la Maestría de Cine y Televisión en la Universidad de California (1986-89) y, en 1992, formó parte del Comité de Selección para becarios del Programa Fulbright, en México. De 1984 a 1990, en Los Ángeles, Cal., participó en los talleres de Dirección de Televisión con Ivan Cury; de Guion Cinematográfico con Syd Fiel; de Dirección de Cine con Paul Grey y de Dirección en Escena con Jersy Antzack. Como escritor, productor y director, en Los Ángeles, Cal., realizó el cortometraje *Roxanne* (1987) y la película para video *Big City* (1990). Como productor, en México, sus créditos incluyen los largometrajes: *Pruebas de amor* (1991) *Modelo antiguo* (1992) *y La vida conyugal,* (1993). En 1994 produjo y dirigió *Hasta morir*, con la que obtuvo el premio Sol en el Festival de Guadalajara .

Sarlat García Montero, Simón ◆ n. en Campeche, Camp., y m. en San Juan Bautista, hoy Villahermosa, Tab. (1810-1877). Médico y militar. En 1858, al enloquecer el gobernador tabasqueño Francisco Velázquez, Sarlat fue nombrado gobernador interino. Lo confirmó en el puesto el presidente conservador Félix Zuloaga. Médico mayor del Cuerpo de Sanidad Militar durante el imperio de Maximiliano.

Sarlat Nova, Simón ◆ n. en San Juan Bautista, hoy Villahermosa, Tab., y m. en la ciudad de México (1839-1906). Político porfirista. Hijo del anterior. Graduado en la Escuela de Medicina de la ciudad de México (1863). Fue vicegobernador, gobernador interino (1873-74) y constitucional de Tabasco (1877-80 y 1887-94). Al morir era senador por el Estado de México.

Sarmiento, Justino ◆ n. en Tlacotepec y m. en Veracruz, Ver. (1885-1937). Escritor. Se tituló como profesor en la Escuela Normal de Jalapa. Fue director de la escuela José Miguel Macías y colaborador de *El Dictamen* y *Revista de Revistas.* Autor de las novelas *Las perras* y *Bajo el sol veracruzano* y de los cuentos *Tierras patagónicas, Mi noche triste* y *El hijo del hombre.*

Sarmiento, Sergio ◆ n. en el DF (1953). Licenciado en filosofía por la Universidad York de Toronto, Canadá (1976). Comenzó su carrera periodística en 1970. Ha colaborado en *Siempre!*, *El Día*, *El Financiero* (del que fue colaborador fundador, columnista y coordinador editorial), *Reforma, Vuelta, Este País, The Wall Street Journal, Le Monde* y *Los Angeles Times*, entre otras publicaciones. En 1978 fue nombrado director editorial para América Latina de la *Encyclopaedia Britannica*, para la que realizó la *Enciclopedia Hispánica* y de la que es miembro del consejo editorial. Dirigió el semanario en lengua inglesa *El Financiero International Weekly Edition.* Ha sido comentarista en la emisora Radio Centro (1985-94), coordinador de noticias de la Independent Television News del Reino Unido para el Campeonato Mundial de futbol de 1986; comentarista (1993-95), vicepresidente de noticiarios y programas informativos (1995-98) y vicepresidente del comité editorial de TV Azteca (1998-), así como conductor del programa *La entrevista con Sarmiento* y colaborador del excelente noticiero *Hechos* en esta televisora. Premio Juan Pablos al mérito editorial, otorgado por la Cámara Nacional de la Industria Editorial.

Sarmiento de Hojacastro, Martín ◆ n. en España y m. en Puebla, Pue. (¿1505?-1557). Franciscano. Llegó a la Nueva España (1538) como evangelizador. En 1546 se le designó obispo de Tlaxcala. En 1555 participó en el Primer Concilio Mexicano y colaboró en la redacción de sus estatutos y conclusiones. Autor de *Constituciones del arzobispado y provincia de la muy insigne y muy leal ciudad de Tenoxtitlan México de la Nueva España.*

Sarmiento Pubillones, Leonor ◆ n. en España (1924). Al término de la guerra civil española se exilió con su familia en Francia (1939). Llegó a México el 20 de marzo de 1952 y obtuvo la nacionalidad mexicana. Desde 1977 pertenece a la Mesa Directiva de Ateneo Español de México. Forma parte del Comité Técnico del Instituto del Derecho de Asilo y las Libertades Públicos-Museo Casa de León Trotsky. Es miembro honorario del Grupo de Estudios Literarios de Exilio Español de la Universidad de Barcelona, España. Miembro activo en la Sociedad de Amigos de la Fundación Archivo de Indianos. En 1998 el rey de España le otorgó la Encomienda del Mérito Civil en reconocimiento a su labor en favor de los valores que representa el Ateneo Español de México.

Sarmiento de Sotomayor, García ◆ n. en España y m. en Perú (?-1659). Tenía los títulos de conde de Salvatierra y marqués de Sobroso. Virrey de la Nueva España (1642-48). Tuvo una conflictiva relación con el obispo de Puebla y visitador general, Juan de Palafox y Mendoza, pues mientras éste defendía las atribuciones del clero diocesano, Sarmiento tomó partido en favor de la burocracia virreinal, pese a la generalizada corrupción de los funcionarios. En 1647, al estallar el conflicto entre Palafox y las órdenes religiosas, se puso del lado de éstas e incluso envió a Puebla un fuerte contingente militar que impuso un virtual estado de sitio y tomó por cuartel los colegios de San Pedro y de San Juan. Las fuerzas del virrey allanaron domicilios, torturaron y ejercieron toda clase de

Foto: Imagen Latina

Sergio Sarmiento

Retrato y firma de García Sarmiento de Sotomayor

José Sarukhán Kermez

Retrato y firma de José Sarmiento y Valladares

presiones sobre los palafoxianos, hasta que la población poblana decidió protestar, lo que hizo ruidosamente en septiembre de 1647, durante cuatro días en los que se gritaba "Muera el gallego!", quien no era otro que el propio virrey. En octubre llegó la real cédula que ordenaba su traslado a Perú y la entrega del gobierno al obispo yucateco Marcos de Torres y Rueda. Sarmiento pospuso indefinidamente el traslado del poder, por lo que en mayo de 1648 Madrid dispuso que de inmediato pusiera el poder en manos del sucesor. Otros hechos ocurridos durante el gobierno de Sarmiento fueron la inundación de 1645 en la ciudad de México y la fundación de Salvatierra, Guanajuato, llamada así en su honor (1647). Asimismo, celebró dos autos de fe (1647 y 1648), en uno de los cuales fue penitenciado Martín Garatuza, según algunos autores.

Sarmiento y Valladares, José ◆ n. y m. en España (1643-1708). Se casó con María Jerónima Moctezuma Jofre, descendiente de Moctezuma Xocoyotzin, y adquirió así el título de conde de Moctezuma y Tula. Fue el trigésimo segundo virrey de la Nueva España (1696-1701). Durante su gestión salieron las expediciones de Salvatierra y Kino a las Californias, se crearon las rondas nocturnas en la ciudad de México y se produjo la hambruna de 1697.

Sarriá, Francisco Javier de ◆ n. en España (?-?). Viajó por primera vez a la Nueva España en 1767 y ese mismo año regresó a Europa a estudiar el funcionamiento de las loterías de Inglaterra y Holanda. Volvió a la Nueva España en 1769, año en el que el virrey Carlos Francisco de Croix lo comisionó para escoltar de Chilpancingo a Veracruz a los jesuitas expulsados del país. En 1770 presentó un proyecto para instalar una lotería en el virreinato y se convirtió en el primer director de la Real Lotería en Nueva España. Se jubiló en 1786, luego de haber sido encarcelado, acusado de fraude y más tarde reivindicado. Autor de *Ensayo de metalurgia.*

Sartorio, José Manuel ◆ n. y m. en la ciudad de México (1746-1829). Sacerdote. Estudió filosofía en el Colegio de San Ildefonso. Fue censor teatral del virreinato y censor religioso y político de libros y periódicos, cargo éste otorgado por la Mitra y la autoridad civil. Proclamado el Plan de Iguala, se negó a predicar contra la independencia. En 1821 fue vocal de la Junta Gubernativa y firmó el Acta de Independencia. Su amistad con Agustín de Iturbide estuvo a punto de provocar su expulsión del país en 1823. Autor de *Obras de elocuencia y poesía* (1791), *Gozo del Imperio Mexicano por su independencia y libertad* (1821), *Voto particular sobre el restablecimiento de las órdenes dispersas por las Cortes españolas* (1821) y *Poesías sagradas y profanas* (7 t., 1832). Su traducción de *Himnos del breviario romano y de algunas sagradas religiones* se publicó en 1832.

Sarukhán Kermez, José ◆ n. en el DF (1940). Biólogo por la UNAM (1964), maestro en ciencias agrícolas por la Universidad de Chapingo (1968), y doctor en ecología por la Universidad de Gales (1972). Profesor de Chapingo (1963-65), de la Organization for Tropical Studies, en Costa Rica (1965 y 1973-76), del University College of North Wales (1971). En la UNAM ha sido profesor desde 1973, investigador, consejero técnico, director del Instituto de Biología (1979-85), coordinador de Humanidades (1985-87), coordinador de la Investigación Científica (1987-88) y rector (1989-96). Ha prestado asesoría a organismos de México y otros países. Fue director de Ecología de Auris en el Estado de México (1974-75) y miembro del consejo directivo del ININ (1979-80). Se ha especializado en el estudio de ecología vegetal, botánica y darwinismo. Coautor, colaborador o editor de una veintena de libros sobre el tema. Autor de *Árboles tropicales de México* (1968), *Ecología de poblaciones* (1984) y *Las musas de Darwin* (1986). Hasta 1999 había recibido doctorados *honoris causa* por las universidades de Lima, Gales, Nueva York y Chapingo. Premio Nacional Forestal (1979, compartido con Miguel Franco B.), y Nacional de Ciencias Físico-Matemáticas y Naturales (1990); y Ciencias Naturales de la Academia de la Investigación Científica (1980). Miembro de El Colegio Nacional. Presidió la Academia de la Investigación Científica (1983-85).

Sasha ◆ n. en el DF (1970).Cantante y actriz. Nombre profesional de Sasha Mariana Díez-Barroso Cuillery. Se inició en los espectáculos con el grupo Timbiriche (1981-86). En 1987 inició su carrera como solista. En televisión ha trabajado en la serie *Tres generaciones* y en las telenovelas *Alcanzar una estrella* y *La vida en el espejo.* Recientemente ha adoptado el nombre artístico de Sasha Sokol.

Sastré, Arturo ◆ n. en el DF (1957). Director y dramaturgo. Su apellido materno es Blanco. Egresado del Foro Eón y alumno de Hugo Argüelles, fue asistente de dirección de Salvador Garcini y Juan José Gurrola. Debutó como director en 1988, con una adaptación de Víctor Hugo Rascón de *Querido Diego, te abraza Quiela* de Elena Poniatowska. Posteriormente ha dirigido, entre otras, *¿Quién es ese que anda ahí...?* (1989) y *Casa de comedias* (1991), de su autoría. Para escribir la segunda obtuvo, en 1990, una beca del Fonca.

Satevó ◆ Municipio de Chihuahua contiguo a la capital de la entidad. Superficie: 2,185.21 km². Habitantes: 5,907, de los cuales 1,852 forman la población económicamente activa. Hablan alguna lengua indígena 50 personas mayores de cinco años (tarahumara 47). La cabecera, del mismo nombre, fue fundada en 1640 por el jesuita José Pascual, con el nombre de San Francisco Javier de Satevó.

Satevó ◆ Río de Chihuahua que nace en la sierra de Cusihuiriachic, al sur de Ciudad Cuauhtémoc, en el oriente de la sierra Madre Occidental. Corre de noroeste a sureste, recibe al río Santa Isabel y desemboca en el San Pedro, al sur de la ciudad de Chihuahua.

Sauceda, de la ◆ Río de Durango que nace en la vertiente nororiental de la sierra de Cacaria. Corre de sur a norte, pasa por los llanos de la Sauceda y tuerce al sureste. Recibe al río de Pinos, sigue hacia el sur, recibe al arroyo Carpintero y entra en el valle de Durango. Ahí cambia su curso hacia el sur, cerca de ciudad Victoria de Durango, y se une al río Tunal para formar el San Pedro o Mezquital.

SAUCEDO, SALVADOR ◆ n. en Colima, Col., y m. en Guadalajara, Jal. (1890-1963). En 1909 era colaborador en el periódico *El Popular*, donde denunció el crimen de los indios tepames. Trabajó en *La Revancha* (1911), dirigió la imprenta del gobierno de Colima (1914) y fundó *Colima Libre* (1917). Fue tres veces diputado federal, funcionario de Hacienda y gobernador de Colima de 1931 y 1935, cuando, por su filiación callista se declaró la desaparición de los poderes en esa entidad, por acuerdo del Congreso de la Unión.

SAUCEDO PÉREZ, MARIO GILBERTO ◆ n. en el DF (1951). Licenciado en relaciones industriales por el ITESO de Guadalajara (1972), en el cual fue investigador y profesor (1972-77). Investigador analista de la SAHR (1978-79). Colaborador del Instituto Mexicano para el Desarrollo Comunitario (1970-71), fundador del Centro de Coordinación y Promoción Agropecuaria y asesor de asuntos agrarios e indígenas (1977-82); profesor (1980-81) y secretario general del Sindicato de Maestros y Trabajadores del Centro Regional de Enseñanza Técnica e Industrial (1980-81). Ejerció su profesión de forma individual entre 1982 y 1997. Militó en el PMT, en donde fungió como secretario de asuntos campesinos del comité del DF (1977-78); miembro fundador y dirigente de la Asociación Cívica Nacional Revolucionaria (1983-89). Miembro fundador del PRD (1989-), del que ha sido secretario general del CEN (1993-96). Senador de la República (1994-2000).

SAUCILLO ◆ Municipio de Chihuahua situado en el sureste de la entidad, contiguo a Ciudad Camargo y al sureste de la capital del estado. Superficie: 2,116.16 km². Habitantes: 31,048, de los cuales

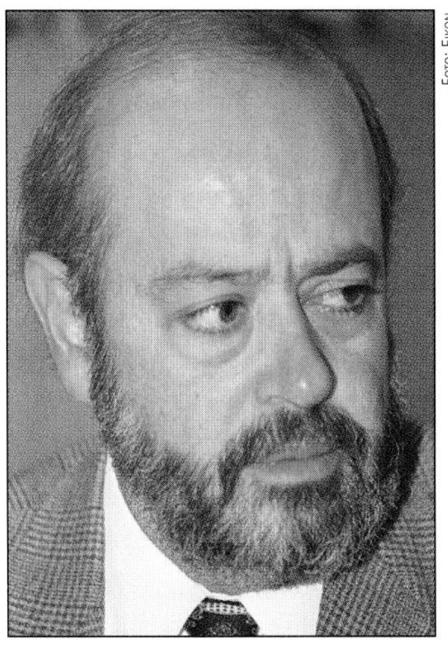
Foto: Eikon

Mario Saucedo

9,364 forman la población económicamente activa. Hablan alguna lengua indígena 42 personas mayores de cinco años (tarahumara 33). La cabecera, del mismo nombre, fue fundada en 1717 por Juan Antonio Trasviña y Retes, como hacienda de San Marcos. En 1907 fue elevada a la categoría de villa y en 1951 se le otorgó el rango de ciudad.

SAURET, NUNIK ◆ n. en el DF (?). Artista plástica. Estudió pintura en La Esmeralda (1967-79) y grabado en el taller del molino de Santo Domingo (1968). Ha participado en bienales de grabado y dibujo en países de Europa, Asia y América. Ha expuesto en galerías de México y otros países. Parte de su obra ha sido adquirida por museos como el Metropolitan Museum Art Center de Miami, el Museo de Arte Moderno de México, el Museo de la Estampa de México, entre otros. Ha participado en más de 20 exposiciones colectivas. Su obra ha sido editada en varios portafolios de arte. Ha obtenido premios y menciones honoríficas. Fue becaria del SNCA (1993-96).

SAURI RIANCHO, DULCE MARÍA ◆ n. en Mérida, Yuc. (1951). Licenciada en sociología por la UIA (1969-74). Desde 1981 pertenece al PRI, en el que ha sido directora del CEPES de Yucatán (1982), integrante del Comité de Estudios sobre Federalismo y Descentralización de la Vida Nacional (1982), presidenta del Comité Directivo Estatal de Yucatán (1983-87), secretaria de finanzas del CEN (1988) y secretaria general (1999). Profesora de las universidades de Guadalajara (1975-76) y Yucatán (1980-81). Ha sido investigadora de la Secretaría del Trabajo (1971-72), técnica del Departamento de Programación de la Secretaría de Programación y Presupuesto en Saltillo (1979), planificadora del desarrollo social en el Plan Lerma de Asistencia Técnica (1979), jefa del área de evaluación de la Unidad de Supervisión y Control (1979-80), jefa de la Unidad de Programación (1980-81) y delegada regional de la Secretaría de Programación y Presupuesto en Mérida (1981-82). Diputada local (1982) y federal (1982-85, 1994-97), senadora (1988-1991) y gobernadora interina de Yucatán a partir de 1991. Renunció en 1994. Primera presidenta del Programa Nacional para la Mujer (1996-1999). Presidenta de la Comisión Interamericana de Mujeres de la OEA (1998-2000).

SAUSSURE, ENRIQUE LUIS FEDERICO DE ◆ n. y ¿m.? en Suiza (1829-1905). Naturalista que en 1855 participó en una expedición en territorio mexicano, de la cual surgieron sus libros *Vistazo sobre la hidrología de México* (1862), *Carta de México representando el valle de Anáhuac y su vertiente oriental* (1862), *México y la expedición francesa* (1865), *Antigüedades mexicanas* (1891) y *Misión científica de México y de la América Central* (1891).

Foto: Imagen Latina

Dulce María Sauri Riancho

SAUZA MORA, FRANCISCO JAVIER ◆ n. en Tecolotlán y m. en Guadalajara, Jal. (1905-1990). Empresario tequilero. Fue pionero en la industria del tequila. Propietario fundador de Tequila Sauza, con la cual obtuvo reconocimiento internacional. Consejero de la empresa Pedro Domecq, a la cual vendió su fábrica. Dirigió en el Patronato de la Biblioteca Heladio Sauza, la sección internacional de buena vecindad. Patrocinó el programa de televisión *Noches tapatías*. Donó a la ciudad de Tequila varios monumentos y recibió reconocimientos y medallas por su labor empresarial y filantrópica.

SAVAGE, CARLOS ◆ n. en el DF (1919). Editor cinematográfico desde

1936. Ha participado en más de 500 películas, entre ellas: *Los olvidados* y *Robinson Crusoe* (ambas de Luis Buñuel); *Otra primavera y Campeón sin corona* (de Alejandro Galindo); *Con la rabia por dentro* (de Gilberto Gazcón); *La barraca* (1945, de Roberto Gavaldón); *La trampa* (de Rafael Baledón); *Veneno para las hadas* (1985, de Carlos Enrique Taboada); *El esqueleto de la señora Morales* (de Rogelio A. González); *Una familia de tantas* (de Alejandro Galindo); *Tiburoneros, Tarahumara, Ando volando bajo* y *El pequeño proscrito* (de los estudios Walt Disney); *Un mundo nuevo* (de René Cardona); *La guerra santa* y *Mecánica nacional* (de Luis Alcoriza); *Mariana, Mariana* (1987, de Alberto Isaac) y *El Imperio de la fortuna* (1987, de Arturo Ripstein). Ganó nueve veces el Ariel a la mejor edición. Ha recibido la medalla Salvador Toscano de la ANDA (1987), tres Ónix de la UIA, tres Diosas de Plata y más de 30 diplomas. Miembro de la Academia Mexicana de Artes y Ciencias Cinematográficas. Fue secretario general de la Sección de Técnicos y Manuales del Sindicato de Trabajadores de la Producción Cinematográfica.

Saval, Manolita ♦ n. en Francia (¿1920?). Actriz de teatro, televisión y cine. En el conservatorio de Valencia se graduó como pianista y estudió composición, canto, baile, guitarra y acordeón. Inició su carrera de actuación en la ópera *Don Gil de Alcalá* (1938),de la compañía de Perella, con la que hizo una gira por Latinoamérica. En Argentina conoció al cantante José Mojica, quien la invitó a México, donde fijó su residencia. Actuó en las películas *Don Gil de Alcalá* (con guión de Salvador Novo), *Virgen de medianoche, El capitán Malacara, Papacito lindo, La guerra de los pasteles* y *Adiós juventud*, entre otras. Ha actuado en las obras de teatro *Trampas para un amor, Curro Gallardo, Papaíto piernas largas, Tartufo o el impostor* y *Chao.*

Savariego, Morris ♦ n. en el DF (1949). Director teatral y diseñador. Ingeniero civil por la UNAM. Ha estudiado actuación, dirección, teoría y artes visuales. Asistente de Héctor Mendoza y Julio Castillo. Ha dirigido más de 20 obras, como *Terror y miserias del III reich* (1974), *El hombre que se convirtió en perro* (1975), *Concierto para guillotina* (1982), *La nueva arca de Noé* (1983), *Regina 52* (1985, de Leonor Azcárate), *La paz de la buena gente* (de Óscar Villegas), *Santísima nauyaca* (1986, de Tomás Espinoza), *Cupo limitado* (1988, de Tomás Urtusástegui; premio al mejor espectáculo independiente por la Unión de Críticos y Cronistas), *El señor y la señora*, de Óscar Villegas (1988; Premio Manolo Fábregas en el primer Festival de Teatro Independiente), *La checada* (1992, de Tomás Espinosa; premio al mejor espectáculo musical por la Unión de Críticos y Cronistas), *Cura y locura* (1992, premio al mejor director en el IV Festival de Teatro Independiente), *El loco amor viene* (1993) de Jorge Ibargüengoitia, y *Todos somos Marcos*, de Vicente Leñero. Ha dirigido lecturas dramatizadas de las piezas *Los niños prohibidos, El sueño de los peces, Voces en el umbral, Prometeo* y *Oulanem*, de Carlos Marx. Ha sido profesor de teatro en el CUC (1985-90), Televisa (1990), el Centro Israelita (1992), la Casa del Teatro (1995-), director fundador del Centro Teatral Doblespacio (1991-94). Ha colaborado en publicaciones periódicas. Como diseñador gráfico ganó tres veces el premio Heraldo de Plata (1981, 1982 y 1983). Ha sido becario del CNCA.

Savia Moderna ♦ Revista literaria mensual fundada y codirigida por Alfonso Cravioto y Luis Castillo Ledón. Roberto Argüelles Bringas fue jefe de redacción y José María Sierra y Pedro Henríquez Ureña secretarios de redacción. Aparecieron cinco números entre marzo y julio de 1906. Alfonso Reyes, "prologaba" la *Revista Moderna,* sin embargo, en el editorial del primer número los editores declaraban: "aspiramos al desarrollo de la personalidad propia, y gustamos más de las obras que de las doctrinas". De su grupo de colaboradores surgirían la Sociedad de Conferencias, el Ateneo de la Juventud y el Ateneo de México. Se publicaron textos, además de los citados, de Antonio Caso, Eduardo Colín, José F. Elizondo, José J. Gamboa, Álvaro Gamboa Ricalde, Ricardo Gómez Robelo, Carlos González Peña, Manuel Gutiérrez Nájera, Max Henríquez Ureña, Rafael López, Manuel José Othón, Manuel de la Parra, Edgar Allan Poe, José Enrique Rodó, Luis Rosado Vega, Justo Sierra, Enrique Uhthoff, Miguel de Unamuno, Luis G. Urbina, Jesús E. Valenzuela, Oscar Wilde y Ángel Zárraga, entre otros. La nómina de "Artistas" comprendía a Gonzalo Argüelles Bringas, Benjamín Coria, Jorge Enciso, Saturnino Herrán, Jesús Martínez Carrión, Roberto Montenegro, Diego Rivera y otros menos conocidos. La revista dio categoría de arte a la fotografía, en la que contaba con los servicios de José M. Lupercio, Kampfner y Casasola.

Saville, Marshall Howard ♦ n. y m. en EUA (1867-1935). Antropólogo y doctor en ciencias por la Universidad de Harvard (1894). Desde 1918 perteneció al servicio estadounidense de inteligencia. Realizó trabajos de exploración en Yucatán, en las ruinas de Copán (1890-92) y en Palenque (1897-98); efectuó cuatro expediciones a las ruinas de Mitla (1899-1904) y trabajó también en Perú, Ecuador, Colombia, Honduras y Guatemala. Fue profesor honorario del Museo Nacional de Arqueología de México (1933). Autor de *The Goldsmiths Art in Ancient Mexico* (1922), *Turquois Mosaic in Ancient Mexico* (1922), *The Woodcarrver's Art in Ancient Mexico* (1925), *Cruciform Structures of Mitla and Vicinity* (1929) y *Tizoc. Great Lord of the Aztecs 1481-1486* (1929).

Savín, Francisco ♦ n. en el DF (1929). Músico. Cursó la carrera de filosofía. Estudió música en la Academia José F. Velázquez con Rodolfo Halffter, Hermann Scherchen y Jean Giardino, y en la Academia de Altos Estudios Musicales de Praga. Ha sido subdirector de la Orquesta Sinfónica Nacional (1959-62), profesor de música en la Compañía Nacional de Danza, director de la Escuela Popular de Bellas Artes de la Universidad Michoacana de San Nicolás

Francisco Savín

de Hidalgo, profesor de la Universidad Veracruzana, director titular de la Orquesta Sinfónica de Xalapa (1963-67; ha repetido tres veces en el cargo, la última desde 1990), profesor y director del Conservatorio Nacional (1967-70), jefe del Departamento de Música del INBA (1971-72), director artístico de la OSN y de la Orquesta de Cámara de la UNAM (1972), director del Taller de Dirección Orquestal y de la Orquesta del Conservatorio Nacional (1975-79), director musical de la Compañía Nacional de Danza (1979), coordinador y director de la Escuela de Perfeccionamiento Vida y Movimiento (1983), director artístico de la Sinfónica de Xalapa (1984) y director titular de la OSN (1985-89). Dirigió las orquestas de la Radio Televisión Italiana y de la Televisión Francesa y participó en la Olimpiada Cultural de 1968. Autor de *Quetzalcóatl* (1957, interpretada por la Orquesta de la Radio de Praga, dirigida por Alois Klima), *Metamorfosis* (para orquesta, 1962, estrenada por la Sinfónica de Xalapa), *Tres líricas, Formas plásticas, Quinteto de alientos* (para mezzo y grupo instrumental, 1965), *Monología de las delicias* (para orquesta, 1969), *Concreción* (para orquesta, 1969), *Quasar* y *Quasar II* (para órgano electrónico, cinta magnetofónica y percusiones, 1970) y *Fragmentos de una liturgia de estío* (para orquesta, 1982). Primer Premio en el Concurso Nacional de Piano Rosita Renard (1955), premio al mejor compositor (1957), diploma de la Unión de Críticos de Música y Teatro al mejor director de orquesta (1961-78) y condecoración del gobierno de Italia por haber dirigido la Orquesta de la RAI de Roma (1968).

Saviñón, Luz ♦ n. en Puebla, Pue., y m. en la ciudad de México (1850-1902). Hija del industrial Gumersindo Saviñón y viuda de Bartolomé Saviñón y Rubín de Celis. Heredó una considerable fortuna, parte de la cual destinó a obras de beneficencia, como la creación de una escuela en Tacubaya y la fundación de un montepío en la capital de la República, instituciones que llevan su nombre. Murió tres meses antes de que Porfirio Díaz inaugurara su casa de empeño.

Sáyago, Bernardo ♦ n. en Naolinco y m. en Jalapa, Ver. (¿1800?-1885). En 1834 fue síndico de Jalapa y un año más tarde, presidente del Tribunal Mercantil de la misma ciudad. Dedicó parte de su capital a obras de beneficencia. En 1842 se le nombró miembro de la Junta Patriótica. Intervino en la revolución de Ayutla, como voluntario en el batallón Defensores Jalapeños de las Leyes, presidió el ayuntamiento de Jalapa (1847 y 49) y fue diputado al Congreso Constituyente de 1856-57.

Sáyago Herrera, Indalecio ♦ n. en Orizaba, Ver. (1910). Profesor normalista. Miembro fundador del PPS (1947), en el que ha sido secretario de Propaganda de la dirección nacional (1956-60), secretario de Finanzas del Comité Central (1960-89), coordinador de la fracción parlamentaria (1985-88) y secretario general (1988-). Se ha desempeñado como secretario de relaciones de la Unión de Oficios Varios (1931, fundador). En la CROM participó en el Sindicato de Maestros (1932-) y en el Sindicato de Obreros Intelectuales del Ramo Educativo (1936). Fue delegado al Congreso Constituyente del Sindicato de Trabajadores de la Enseñanza de la República Mexicana (1938), del que fue secretario de Relaciones Internacionales (1942); delegado al primer Congreso Nacional Ordinario de la CTM (1938); y secretario general de la Federación de Trabajadores de la Región de Orizaba, de la CTM (1939); vicepresidente del Comité Regional de Acción Antinazifascista de Orizaba (1942). En el SNTE ha sido secretario de la Comisión Nacional de Vigilancia (1947), presidente de la Comisión Nacional de Asuntos Técnicos (1958), secretario de Trabajo y Conflictos de la sección IX (1963), secretario de Educación Sindical de la sección IX (1965) y secretario de Relaciones Nacionales del CEN (1967). Diputado federal (1967-70 y 1985-88) y diputado local en Veracruz (1977). Recibió las medallas Rafael Ramírez (1964) e Ignacio Manuel Altamirano (1984) por 30 y 50 años de docencia, respectivamente.

Sayula ♦ Laguna de Jalisco situada en el sur del estado, al noroeste de Ciudad Guzmán y al suroeste del lago de Chapala. En sus riberas hay depósitos de carbón de piedra y sales de sodio y magnesio. Esta laguna tiende a desaparecer por desecación.

Sayula ♦ Municipio de Jalisco situado en el sur del estado, contiguo a Ciudad Guzmán. Superficie: 275.76 km^2. Habitantes: 30,844, de los cuales 7,975 forman la población económicamente activa. Hablan alguna lengua indígena 81 personas mayores de cinco años (mixteco 24). La cabecera, del mismo nombre, destaca por sus industrias lechera y jabonera.

Sayula de Alemán ♦ Municipio de Veracruz situado al sur de Acayucan y al suroeste de Minatitlán. Superficie: 640.76 km^2 . Habitantes: 29,624, de los cuales 6,339 forman la población económicamente activa. Hablan alguna lengua indígena 4,390 personas mayores de cinco años (popoluca de Veracruz 4,279).

Sbert Massanet, Antonio María ♦ n. en España y m. en el DF (1901-1980). En la segunda República Española fue dos veces diputado a Cortes (1931 y 36) y colaboró con la Generalidad de Cataluña como magistrado del Tribunal de Garantías

FOTO: ROGELIO BAEZA

Mauricio Scheleske Sánchez

Constitucionales, consejero de Gobernación y asesor de Sanidad y Asistencia Social. En 1939 se exilió en Francia, desde donde rescató a muchos de sus compatriotas de los campos de concentración y facilitó su traslado a México. Asimismo, fundó la *Revista de Cataluña*. Llegó a México en 1942, después de haber intervenido en la firma del Convenio Franco-Mexicano de 1940, entre los gobiernos de Lázaro Cárdenas y Pétain. Fue profesor en la UNAM y ejerció su profesión de ingeniero industrial. Fundó y dirigió (1945-55) el periódico *España Nueva* y colaboró en *Las Españas*.

SCAREÑO, VÍCTOR ◆ n. en el DF (1953). Artista plástico. Estudió en la Escuela de Artes Plásticas de Oaxaca (1974-76), la Academia de Bellas Artes de Florencia (1976-79) y otras escuelas italianas. En México e Italia ha impartido diversos cursos desde 1976 (como en el INBA y el ISSSTE, 1987-88); colaboró en el libro *Gesti Latinoamericani* (1977). Ha participado en más de 20 exposiciones colectivas y varias individuales en México e Italia.

SCOPELLI CASANOVA, ALEJANDRO *CONEJO* ◆ n. en Argentina y m. en el DF (1908-1987). Futbolista. Fue jugador del equipo Estudiantes de la Plata (1925-) y de la selección argentina, con la que participó en el Campeonato Mundial de 1930, en Uruguay. Como hijo de italianos, tuvo oportunidad de jugar en el Club Roma y en la selección italiana en el Campeonato Mundial de 1934. Volvió a Argentina para jugar en el *Racing Club* y nuevamente fue seleccionado nacional. Pasó a Francia y jugó en el *Red Star* de París (1937-39). En Portugal fue simultáneamente jugador y entrenador del Belenenses, en 1939, año en el que dejó de jugar para dedicarse sólo a la dirección técnica. Fue el inventor de la formación 4-3-3. Entrenador del Universidad de Chile, del Palestino y de la selección nacional de Chile; nuevamente del Belenenses y de la selección portuguesa (1947); del Celta de Vigo, la Coruña, Español de Barcelona y Granada, en España; y el *Sporting Club* de Portugal. Llegó a México en 1961 para preparar, junto con Ignacio Trelles, a la selección nacional que asistió al Campeonato Mundial de 1962, en Chile. Luego de una nueva estancia en Europa, en 1968 regresó a México y fue director técnico del América hasta 1971. Autor del libro *Hola, míster.* Asesor de la Federación Mexicana de Futbol (1970-87) y secretario general de la Asociación de Futbol Argentino.

Obra de Víctor Scareño

SCHARA, JULIO CÉSAR ◆ n. en el DF (1947). Doctor en ciencia política. Agregado cultural en Panamá, Costa Rica, Nicaragua y El Salvador. Ha sido profesor de la Facultad de Ciencias Políticas de la UNAM y coordinador de la serie de televisión *Introducción a la Universidad*. Es ma-estro de la Academia de San Carlos, catedrático de la UNAM y de la Universidad del Valle de México. Autor de los poemarios *Navegaciones* (1975), *Réquiem por Carlos Pellicer* (1977), *Abrirse paso* (1979), *Las palabras y los juegos* (1981), *Extremos poéticos* (1991) y *Summa poética* (1997).

SCHELE, LINDA ◆ n. en EUA y m. en México (1942-1998). Antropóloga y epigrafista. Estudió artes plásticas en EUA. Llegó a México en 1970 y desde entonces se dedicó a estudiar la epigrafía y la lingüística maya. Desarrolló un método de desciframiento basado inicialmente en el análisis fonético del ruso Yuri Knorosov, pero con el cual estableció marcadas diferencias, lo cual desató una prolongada polémica mundial. Participó en el Encuentro Vuelta que organizó Octavio Paz y en otras actividades culturales en México, como en las mesas redondas en Palenque, donde se dio nombre a las dinastías mayas (coordinadas por Merle Green). Autora de *The Bodega of Palenque* (1978), *Maya Glyphs: the Verbs* (1982), *The Mirror, the Rabbit, and the Bundle: Accesion's Expressions from the Classic Maya Inscriptions* (1983), *A forest of Kings: the Untold Story of the Ancient Maya* (1992), *The Blood of Kings: Dinasty and Ritual in Maya Art* (1992), *Maya Cosmos* (1995), *The Code of Kings: the Language of Seven Sacred Maya Temples and Tombs*.

SCHELESKE SÁNCHEZ, MAURICIO ◆ n. en Veracruz, Ver. (1926). Almirante diplomado de Estado Mayor Naval e ingeniero geógrafo por la Escuela Naval Militar Antón Lizardo (1942). Tomó un curso de mando y estado mayor en Estados Unidos. En la Secretaría de Marina ha sido ayudante del agregado naval en Washington, director general de servicios de la Armada de México, subjefe del Estado Mayor de la Armada de México, agregado naval de México en Washington, jefe del Estado Mayor de la Armada, director de la Escuela de Clases y Marinería, subdirector del Centro de Capacitación de la Armada y de la Escuela Naval Militar, jefe de Operaciones Navales (1986-88) y secretario de Marina (1988-91). Ha sido comandante de diversos buques, del sector naval de Matamoros, de la Fuerza Naval del Golfo y mar Caribe y de las segunda y cuarta Zonas Navales militares.

SCHERER GARCÍA, JULIO ◆ n. en el DF (1926). Periodista. Realizó estudios de filosofía y derecho. Ha sido profesor en la UNAM. Ingresó a *Excélsior* en 1946, del cual fue reportero de la fuente política, jefe de información, auxiliar de la dirección y director general (1968-76). Fundador de *Plural* (octubre 1971), revista que dirigió Octavio Paz, con quien tuvo, a partir de entonces, una relación ininterrumpida. En 1976, víctima de un golpe orquestado por el entonces presidente Luis Echeverría, fue obligado a dejar la dirección de *Excélsior* y abandonó el periódico en compañía de un numeroso grupo de reporteros y colaboradores. Al frente de muchos de ellos, el 6 de noviembre de ese año fundó la revista *Proceso*, de la que fue director general hasta el 6 de noviembre de 1996, y quedó como accionista principal y presidente del Consejo de Administración de Comunicación e Información, S.A., casa editora de la propia revista. Autor de *La piel y la entraña* (biografía de David Alfaro Siqueiros, 1965) y *Los presidentes* (1986), *El poder. Historias de familia* (1990), *Estos años* (1995), *Salinas y su imperio* (1997), *Cárceles* (1998). Coautor de *Parte de guerra* (1999). Premio María Moors Cabot (1971). Fue designado periodista del año por la *Atlas World Press Review* de Estados Unidos (1977). Premio Manuel Buendía (1986). Rechazó en 1998 el Premio Nacional de Periodismo.

Scherman Leaño, María Esther de Jesús ◆ n. en Guadalajara, Jal. (1957). Licenciada en derecho por la Universidad de Guadalajara, donde es profesora. Pertenece al PRI desde 1979. Secretaria de Acción Femenil de la Federación de Estudiantes de Guadalajara (1977-79) y de la Confederación de Jóvenes Mexicanos (1977-80), secretaria de Acción Social de la Federación de Estudiantes de Guadalajara (1979-80) y secretaria de Consulta Popular del CEN de la CNOP. Ha sido diputada local suplente al Congreso de Jalisco, diputada federal (1985-88 y 1991-94) y senadora de la República (1988-91). Oficial mayor de la secretaría de Energía (1994), delegada en Miguel Hidalgo, DDF (1994-97), y coordinadora general del Fideicomiso de la Tortilla desde 1997.

Schettino, Macario ◆ n. en Veracruz (1963). Ingeniero químico y de sistemas titulado en el ITESM (1985). Maestro en economía por el CIDE (1988). Doctor en administración por el ITESM y la Universidad de Texas (1993). Doctor en historia por la UIA. Ha sido articulista de diversas publicaciones, entre ellas *El Financiero* (1993-95) y *El Universal* (1995-). Comentarista en *Monitor* de Radio Red (1995-97) y *Detrás de la noticia* (1997-) con Ricardo Rocha. Profesor e investigador del ITESM (1990-94) e investigador del Colegio de México (1995); director general de Análisis y Prosprectiva Económica (1996-97); coordinador de Planeación y Desarrollo del Gobierno del Distrito Federal (1998-); asesor del PRD y de la Concamin (1997). Coautor de *Estrategia empresarial en una economía global* (1994). Autor de *Economía contemporánea* (1994), *TLC* (1994), *El costo del miedo* (1995), *Economía Internacional* (1995), *Para reconstruir México* (1996), *Propuestas para elegir un futuro* (1999).

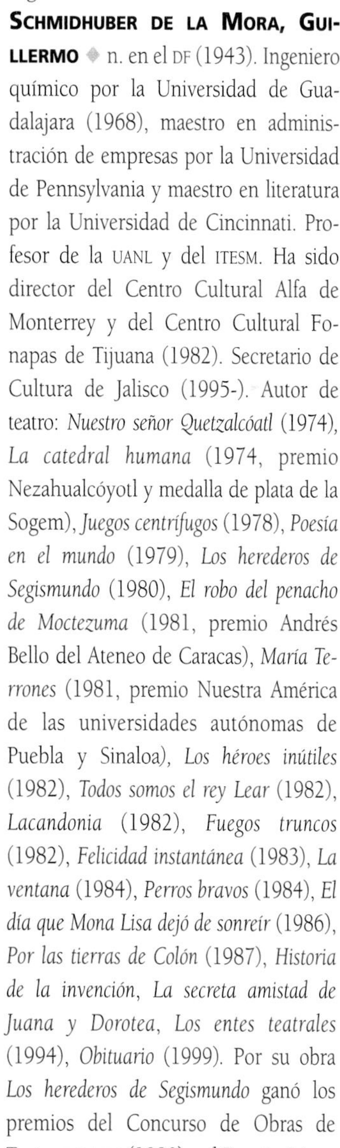

Schiaffino Izunza, Jorge Federico ◆ n. en el DF (1947). Licenciado en derecho por la Universidad Autónoma de Morelos. Pertenece al PRI desde 1964, donde ha sido secretario general del IEPES (1974-75), secretario de Organización y encargado del despacho de la CNOP (1979-1980); de Acción Social (1985) y de Promoción y Gestoría (1989) y secretario general del Sector Popular del DF (1997-). Secretario particular del gobernador de Morelos (1967), jefe de Archivo (1975) y subdirector de Servicios Sociales del ISSSTE (1979-1982), director de Operación, Servicio y Transportes Eléctricos del DDF (1985-86). Presidente de la Comisión de Hacienda (1978-1981) y de la Comisión Nacional de Divulgación Ideológica del CEN del sindicato del ISSSTE (1999); presidente de la Comisión Nacional de Asesoría (1986-89) y de la Comisión Nacional de Acción Política de la FSTSE. Diputado federal (1988-91).

Schiller, Fanny ◆ n. y m. en el DF (1901-1971). Actriz. Nuera de Virginia Fábregas y madre del actor Manolo Fábregas. Trabajó, entre otras, con Celia Montalván como tiplé de zarzuela. Se inició en el teatro dramático con *Tierra baja* y *El orgullo de Albacete* y perteneció a la compañía de Virgina Fábregas. Intervino en la película muda *El Cristo de oro* y en la sonora *Silencio sublime* (1935). Participó en 11 filmes en Estados Unidos. Entre las películas que protagonizó destacan *Alejandra, Santa, La corte del faraón, El abanico de lady Windermere, La monja Alférez, Ramona, Las tandas del Principal, Crimen y castigo, Cielo rojo, Los cuervos están de luto* y *Sor ye-yé*. Figuró entre los fundadores de la ANDA y estableció la tienda de esta organización.

Foto: Proceso

Julio Scherer García

Schmidhuber de la Mora, Guillermo ◆ n. en el DF (1943). Ingeniero químico por la Universidad de Guadalajara (1968), maestro en administración de empresas por la Universidad de Pennsylvania y maestro en literatura por la Universidad de Cincinnati. Profesor de la UANL y del ITESM. Ha sido director del Centro Cultural Alfa de Monterrey y del Centro Cultural Fonapas de Tijuana (1982). Secretario de Cultura de Jalisco (1995-). Autor de teatro: *Nuestro señor Quetzalcóatl* (1974), *La catedral humana* (1974, premio Nezahualcóyotl y medalla de plata de la Sogem), *Juegos centrífugos* (1978), *Poesía en el mundo* (1979), *Los herederos de Segismundo* (1980), *El robo del penacho de Moctezuma* (1981, premio Andrés Bello del Ateneo de Caracas), *María Terrones* (1981, premio Nuestra América de las universidades autónomas de Puebla y Sinaloa), *Los héroes inútiles* (1982), *Todos somos el rey Lear* (1982), *Lacandonia* (1982), *Fuegos truncos* (1982), *Felicidad instantánea* (1983), *La ventana* (1984), *Perros bravos* (1984), *El día que Mona Lisa dejó de sonreír* (1986), *Por las tierras de Colón* (1987), *Historia de la invención, La secreta amistad de Juana y Dorotea, Los entes teatrales* (1994), *Obituario* (1999). Por su obra *Los herederos de Segismundo* ganó los premios del Concurso de Obras de Teatro INBA-BC (1980) y el Ramón López

Foto: Época

Macario Schettino

Velarde (1980). Manuel Enríquez compuso la ópera *La encrucijada,* basada en su obra *Los héroes inútiles.*

Schmill Ordóñez, Ulises Sergio ◆ n. en el DF (1937). Licenciado (1958) y doctor (1962) en derecho por la UNAM.donde ha sido profesor (1961-73 y 1977-80) e investigador del Instituto de Investigaciones Jurídicas (1983-85). Ha sido secretario de Acuerdos del Tribunal Fiscal de la Federación (1960), secretario de Estudio y Cuenta de la Suprema Corte (1965), magistrado del Tribunal Fiscal de la Federación (1968), subdirector técnico de la Dirección del Impuesto Sobre la Renta de la Secretaría de Hacienda (1970), embajador en Austria, Hungría y la República Federal de Alemania (1973), coordinador general de la Dirección de Impuestos al Ingreso de la Secretaría de Hacienda (1977), socio de los despachos Bremer, Quintana, Vaca, Rocha, Obregón y Mancera (1977) y Schmill del Valle (1979). Ministro numerario desde 1985, y presidente de la SCJN (1991-96). Autor de *El sistema de la Constitución Mexicana* (1971), *La conducta del jabalí* (1983), *Pureza metódica y racionalidad en la teoría del derecho* (1984) y *Debate sobre Mitilene.*

Schneider, Luis Mario ◆ n. en Argentina y m. en el DF (1931-1999). Residió en México desde 1960. Licenciado en humanidades por la Universidad de Córdoba (1955), licenciado (1962) y doctor (1969) en letras por la UNAM, donde fue profesor e investigador (1985-). Director de la Escuela de Letras de la Universidad Veracruzana (1965). Autor de los poemarios: *El oído del tacto* (1962), *Valparaíso* (1963), *Memoria de la piel (1965)* y *Arponero del fuego* (1967); la novela *La resurrección de Clotilde Goñi* (1977, Premio Xavier Villaurrutia); y los ensayos, críticas y antologías: *Poesía y fábulas de José Joaquín Fernández de Lizardi* (1963), *Poemas y ensayos de Jorge Cuesta* (4 t., 1964), *Obras de Efrén Hernández* (1966, con prólogo de Alí Chumacero), *Obras de Xavier Villaurrutia* (1966, con prólogo de Alí Chumacero), *La literatura mexicana* (2 t., 1967), *Obras completas de Efrén Rebolledo* (1968), *El estridentismo o una literatura de la estrategia* (1970), *Ruptura y continuidad. La literatura mexicana en polémica* (1975), *México y el surrealismo. 1925-1950* (1978), *Inteligencia y guerra civil, 1937* (1978), *Obras de Gilberto Owen* (1979), *México en la obra de Octavio Paz* (1979), *El infierno perdido de Gilberto Owen* (1980), *Poesía completa de Carlos Pellicer* (1981), *Obras completas de Antonieta Rivas Mercado* (1981), *Los Contemporáneos* (1982), *Arte culinario mexicano. Siglo XIX* (1986), *El Iris* (2 t., 1987), *Diego Rivera y los escritores. Antología tributaria* (1987), *Jaime Torres Bodet: crítica cinematográfica* (1987), *López Velarde en La Nación* (1988), *Los otros contemporáneos* (1996) y *García Lorca y México* (1999).

Luis Mario Schneider

Schroeder, Anya ◆ ☛ *Herrera, Anya.*

Schulenburg, Guillermo ◆ n. en la ciudad de México (1916). Sacerdote. Estudió en el Seminario Conciliar de México, del que fue profesor (1946-63) y rector (1960-63). Estudió teología y derecho canónico en Roma (1937). En 1940 se ordenó sacerdote. Ejerció la docencia en el seminario de Temascalcingo (1943-45). Último abad de la Basílica de Guadalupe (1963-1996), donde coordinó la construcción del nuevo santuario (1970). Aunque su nombramiento como abad era de tipo vitalicio y dependiente del arzobispado de México, concedido por el papa Juan XXIII, el 23 de marzo de 1963, los conflictos originados por su escepticismo acerca de las apariciones de la Virgen de Guadalupe al indio Juan Diego ("es un símbolo, no una realidad", comentó a la revista *Ixtus* y luego a *30 Giorni*), lo llevaron a un conflicto con los jerarcas del clero mexicano y a su renuncia el 6 de septiembre de 1996. A su salida se suprimió la figura de abad en el santuario y se creó la de rector.

Foto: Dante Bucio

Guillermo Schulenburg

Schultz, Enrique E. ◆ n. y m. en el DF (1875-1938). Hijo de Miguel E. Schultz. Ingeniero en minas por la Universidad de México. Fue profesor del Instituto Científico y Literario de Toluca, del Colegio Militar y de las escuelas nacionales de Maestros, Preparatoria, de Comercio y Administración y de Agricultura. Fundó la Escuela de Ingeniería Municipal (1925). Elaboró una colección cartográfica de la República Mexicana y dirigió el plano regulador de la ciudad de México. Autor de *Geografía astronómica, Geografía política, Geografía económica* (libros de texto), *Biografía del general San Martín* y *El porvenir de México y sus relaciones con Estados Unidos* (1914). Miembro fundador de la Academia de Historia y Geografía.

Schultz, Miguel E. ◆ . n. y m. en la ciudad de México (1851-1922). Padre del anterior. Fue profesor (1882-1922) y director de la Escuela Nacional

Preparatoria, director de la Facultad de Altos Estudios, rector interino de la Universidad Nacional de México (1916-17) y profesor de las escuelas nacionales de Maestros y de Agricultura. Autor de *Curso general de geografía. Geografía general y especial, física, política, de las diversas naciones y países, con excepción de México* (1917). Miembro de la Academia Mexicana (de la Lengua) y *doctor honoris causa* de la Universidad Nacional de México.

Schultz Dávila, Miguel Ángel ◆ n. en Oaxaca, Oax. (1953). Periodista. Estudió teatro en la Universidad Benito Juárez de Oaxaca. Coordinador de la Federación Estudiantil Oxaqueña (1975-76). Ha militado en la COCEI, el MAP, el PSUM, el FDN y el PRD. Ha sido conductor y productor radiofónico en XUBJ y XEYN, corresponsal en Oaxaca de *Así es* (1982), *El Día* (1985), *Radio Educación* (1988), *La Jornada* (1989-94) y *Radio 13* (1999); reportero de *Noticias* de Oaxaca (1984-93); reportero del suplemento *Del campo y del campesino* (1986-87) y director del suplemento *El Agro al Día* (1997-98). Del periódico *El Día*. Coordinador general de Comunicación Social (1994-96) y director de la Casa de la Cultura del gobierno del estado de Oaxaca (1996-98).

Schumann, Simone ◆ n. en Alemania (1968). Pintora. Estudió en la Escuela Libre de Arte de Hamburgo (1989-90). Hizo estudios en países de Sudamérica (1989-90). Llegó a México en 1992, ingresó a la Academia de San Carlos y colaboró en diversos talleres. En este país ha participado en más de 10 exposiciones colectivas y cinco individuales. Coautora del mural *El Aguijón en el papel*, de la estación Copilco del Metro.

Schwartz, Perla ◆ n. en el DF (1956). Escritora. Licenciada en periodismo por la Escuela Carlos Septién García, de la que fue profesora (1983-86). Participó en el taller de poesía de Isabel Fraire. Asistió al seminario Historia y Literatura, impartido por Eduardo Galeano (Cuba, 1987). Ha sido reportera del INBA (1978), promotora sociocultural del Centro Deportivo Israelita (1979), encargada de información de la embajada de Israel en México (1980), guionista de Televisa (1981-82 y 1988) y jefa de Servicios Culturales de la Delegación Miguel Hidalgo del DDF (1989-). Colaboradora de la *Revista de la Universidad de México, El Heraldo Cultural, Novedades, Excélsior, Punto, El Sol de México, El Universal, Casa del Tiempo, Claudia* y *Plural*. Ha publicado poemas en *Fem, Sábado* y *El Búho*. Está incluida en el volumen de poesía *Las caligrafías de Ariadna* (1987) y en las antologías *Asamblea de poetas jóvenes de México* (1980), *Sonata a ocho voces* (1982), *La única respuesta* (1984) y *500 años de poesía en el valle de México* (1986). Autora de los poemarios: *Amanecer poético* (1976), *Vocación de vuelo* (incluye prosa; 1980), *Casa de lluvia* (1982), *Al tocar el viento* (1986) y *El trazo de la memoria* (1986); y de los ensayos: *Voces de la poesía hebrea contemporánea* (1981), *Rosario Castellanos, mujer que supo latín* (1984) y *El quebranto del silencio. Ensayos sobre mujeres poetas suicidas* (1989).

Schwarz, Mauricio-José ◆ n. en el DF (1955). Escritor. Ha colaborado en las publicaciones *Xilote* (1972), *El cuento* (1978), *Plural* (1985), entre otras. Autor de *Música para tus ojos* (1983, poemario), *La pequeña guerra* (1984, primer premio del Primer Concurso Nacional de Ciencia Ficción Puebla) *Álbum oscuro* (1987), *Sin partitura* (mención en el Primer Concurso Internacional de Novela Policiaca de Vanguardia, Nicaragua 1990), *El Tatuaje* (Premio *Plural* de cuento 1990), *Escenas de la realidad virtual* (1990, relatos), *Todos somos Superbarrio* (1994, crónica) y *Crónicas del desconcierto* (1995, crónica). Ha sido antologado en *Más allá de lo imaginado* (1991) y *Principios de incertidumbre* (1992). Fundador de *Estacosa, revista libre de especulación* (1991), de *Otracosa* (1992; primera revista literaria que se publica en disco flexible) y de la Asociación Mexicana de Ciencia Ficción y Fantasía (1992). Ha organizado convenciones sobre ciencia ficción. Director de la colección de relatos Hojas del tiempo: ciencia ficción y fantasía al borde del nuevo siglo. Mención honorífica en el Premio Nacional de Periodismo 1992. Ha impartido talleres de narrativa y publicado más de 70 cuentos y ensayos en América Latina. Colaboró en la *Science Fiction Enciclopedia* (1993).

Perla Schwartz

Schwebel, Leonardo ◆ n. en EUA (1959). Poeta y periodista. Desde los 14 años escribe poesía y cuento. Se naturalizó mexicano en 1980. Licenciado en periodismo por la ENEP Acatlán de la UNAM (1982). Ha dado cursos en el ITESM (1981-82), en la Carlos Septién (1984), en la ENEP Acatlán (1983-93) y en el Claustro de Sor Juana (1995). Ha escrito para periódicos capitalinos. Trabajó en el Instituto Nacional del Deporte (1978-90), Televisa (1980-90) y Radiópolis (1989-95). Autor de *Siento por ciento* (1993, poesía), *Querida Gloria* (1995, cuentos), *El secreto y otras historias imperdonables*, *Un buen amor* (1997), *La desgracia* (1997). Ha sido premiado por sus producciones en radio (mejor programa 1990 por *En confianza*) y televisión (por *En Vivo*), así como sus reportajes en EUA (*La fiesta de los jumiles*).

Schyfter Lepa, Guita ◆ n. en Costa Rica (1947). Licenciada en psicología por la UNAM (1969). Investigadora de la Comisión de Nuevos Métodos de Enseñanza y jefa de producción de programas para Telesecundaria de la SEP (1973-77). Becaria del Consejo Británico en tres ocasiones (1975, 1977 y 1988), por el cual hizo estudios de producción y dirección televisiva en la BBC de Londres. Filmó medio y cortometrajes para la UTEC, como *Rufino Tamayo* (1983), *Vicente Rojo* (1984), *Cavernario Galindo, el luchador rudo* (1984), *Héctor Mendoza* (1984) y *Archivo General de la Nación* (1984). *La fiesta y la sombra. Retrato de David Silveti* (1991), *Tamayo a los 91 años* (1991), *Xochimilco, la historia de un paisaje* (1991, Premio Ariel). Ha colaborado en la producción teatral con Hugo Hiriart. Ha filmado *Novia que te vea* (1992, premio del público en la VIII Muestra Internacional de Cine de Guadalajara) y *Sucesos distantes* (1994).

SEAMAN, FRANK ◆ n. en EUA (1892-?). Su verdadero nombre era Richard Francis Phillips. Estudió en la Universidad de Columbia, donde participó en la Liga de Estudiantes Contra la Guerra. Pasó a México en 1917 para evitar el llamado a filas. Dirigió la página en inglés de *El Heraldo de México*. Cofundador del Partido Nacional Socialista (1919), transformado a fines de ese año en Partido Comunista Mexicano (☛), de cuyo Comité Central formó parte. Realizó actividades en Cuba y Haití por órdenes de Mijáil Borodin (☛). En diciembre lo acompañó a Europa como su secretario, para lo cual adoptó el pseudónimo de *Jesús Ramírez* y tomó parte en la fundación del Partido Comunista Español. Representó al PCM en el segundo congreso de la Internacional Comunista, de la que se convirtió en militante profesional. Volvió a México a fines de 1920, con Louis Fraina y Sen Katayama, que habrían de fundar el Buró Latinoamericano de la Internacional Sindical Roja, y representó al PCM en la fundación de la CGT. Fundó *El Trabajador y el Obrero Comunista*, intervino en la huelga ferrocarrilera de febrero-marzo de 1921; en mayo fue deportado a Guatemala. Volvió clandestinamente a México, trabajó como periodista bajo el pseudónimo de *Manuel Díaz de la Peña*; regresó a Estados Unidos, donde militó en el Partido Comunista, fue secretario de la Liga Antiimperialista de las Américas (1925-29) y en 1928 representó al PCEU en el sexto congreso de la IC. En 1929 fue expulsado del partido, al que trató de reingresar, infructuosamente, durante la guerra civil española.

FOTO: ANA LOURDES HERRERA

Sebastián

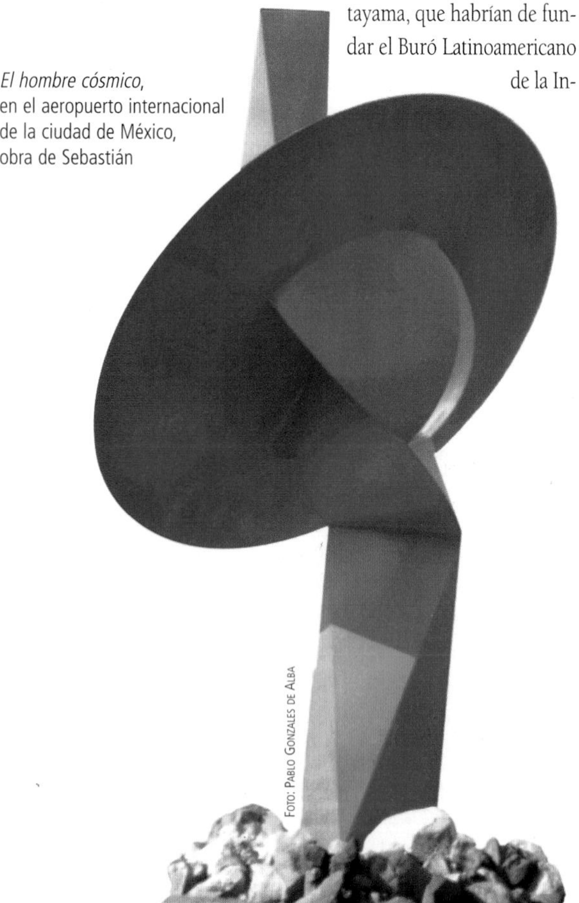
FOTO: PABLO GONZALES DE ALBA

El hombre cósmico, en el aeropuerto internacional de la ciudad de México, obra de Sebastián

SEBASTIÁN ◆ n. en Ciudad Camargo, Chih. (1947). Nombre profesional del escultor Enrique Carbajal González. Estudió en la ENAP (1967), de la que fue profesor (1970-78), así como de la Escuela Nacional de Arquitectura (1968-78) y de La Esmeralda (1970-78). Investigador de la UNAM (1978-), desde 1972 ha fundado o participado en una veintena de grupos de investigación plástica. Es uno de los autores del Centro del Espacio Escultórico, anexa al cual se encuentra *Tláloc*, una de sus obras monumentales. Autor de más de 100 esculturas urbanas, como *Glorieta* (1976, en Villahermosa), *Trono de Nezahualcóyotl* (1978, Canadá), *Casa abierta al tiempo* (1981, UAM-A), *Azcapotzalco* (1982, parque Tezozómoc) *La Puerta* (1985, en Monterrey), *La puerta de Chihuahua* (1988), *Variación Nuevo Mundo* (1989, EUA), *Arcos de Belice* (1991, Belice), *El caballito* (1992, Paseo de la Reforma del DF), *El hombre cósmico* (1993, aeropuerto internacional del DF), *Alegoría a la ficción* (1993, Japón), *Estela de la paz* (1995, Chile), entre otras. En el bosque de Chapultepec se hallan dos de sus piezas monumentales: una afuera del Museo de Arte Moderno y otra en la esquina con Chivatito. Miembro del Salón Independiente (1969-). Pertenece a la Academia de Artes (1985). Miembro fundador del World Arts Forum de Ginebra (1991). Premio del jurado en la Bienal Internacional de Noruega (1984), premio Tomás Valles Vivar (1985), Superior Prize en The Hakome Open Air Museum de Japón (1987), Premio Mainichi Broadcasting System de la Trienal Internacional de

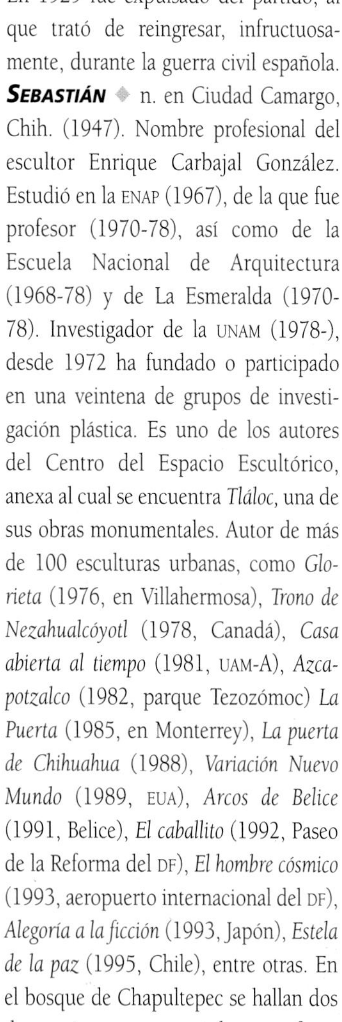

Araña roja, obra de *Sebastián*

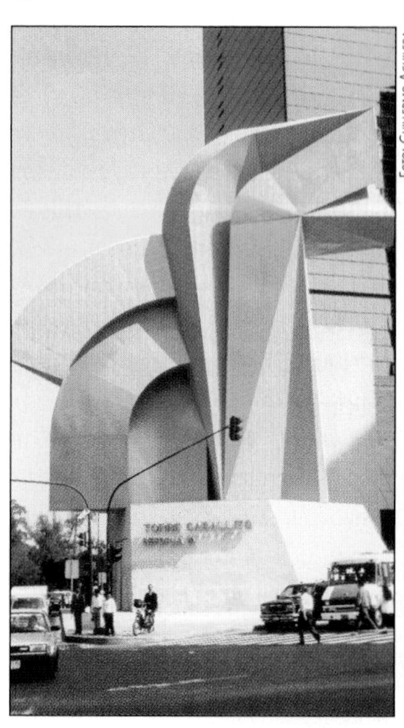
FOTO: GUILLERMO AGUILERA

El caballito

Pintura de Osaka (1993), Kinki Nippon Railway Price de la trienal de escultura de Osaka (1995 y 1998), entre otros. Becario del Sistema Nacional de Creadores (1994).

Sebastián Vizcaíno ◆ Bahía de Baja California Sur y Baja California, en el litoral del océano Pacífico. La cierra por el sur el espolón que se prolonga desde la parte media de la península hacia el oeste; los límites de la bahía son, por el suroeste, la punta Eugenia (extremo occidental del espolón, en territorio de Baja California Sur), y por el norte, la punta María, en Baja California. Al oeste se encuentra la isla Cedros. Contiene numerosas redes y fondeaderos y en ella se explotan salinas, la principal de las cuales es la de Guerrero Negro.

Seco ◆ Río de Sonora. Nace en la ladera oriental de la sierra del Humo, muy cerca de la frontera con Estados Unidos, al oeste de Nogales. Corre de norte a sur, recibe los ríos Consuelo y Altar y desemboca en la Magdalena al este de Caborca.

Seco ◆ Río de Tabasco, actualmente casi agotado. Era el primer brazo que el río Grijalva enviaba al mar. Pasaba por Cárdenas, Comalcalco y Paraíso para desembocar en el golfo de México por la barra de Dos Bocas, al oeste de la laguna Mecoacán y suroeste de Frontera.

Seco Mata, Rosa María ◆ n. en el DF (1947). Matemática. Estudió licenciatura en la UNAM y posgrado en Oxford, Inglaterra. Profesora e investigadora de la UNAM, donde ha sido coordinadora de la maestría en ciencias de la computación, secretaria general de los ciclos profesional y de posgrado del CCH, directora de Fomento Institucional de la Dirección General de Educación Superior de la SEP, secretaria técnica de la Coordinación de la Investigación Científica de la UNAM, coordinadora de asesores del rector de la UNAM (1989-96). Directora del Centro de Estudios e Investigaciones Estratégicas. Autora de *Futuros de la Universidad: UNAM 2025* y la novela *Complot presidencial*.

Sedeño, Livia ◆ n. en Cuba y m. en el DF (1945-1987). Escritora. Llegó en 1962 y obtuvo la nacionalidad mexicana. Fue maestra normalista. Estudió psicología clínica en la UNAM y literatura e historia del arte en la Universidad de La Habana. Obtuvo una maestría en antropología social en la UIA. Trabajó como investigadora de la Dirección General de Culturas Populares de la SEP y fue becaria del Programa Interdisciplinario de Estudios de la Mujer de El Colegio de México. Coautora de los ensayos: *Dos culturas y una infancia: psicoanálisis de una etnia en peligro* e *Idea del progreso y choque cultural* (1987). Autora de narrativa: *Los gnomos no tienen biblioteca* (1974) y *Pie de labio ausente* (1986); la novela: *En tiempo de marzo, en tiempo de abril* (1980, premio Juan Rulfo de primera novela); el poemario: *Matar la muerte* (1988). Ganó el Premio *Punto de Partida* (1975) y el Premio de la ONU por el programa de radio *María Teresa vestida de olvido*. Fue becaria de la Comunidad Latinoamericana de Escritores (1977), de El Colegio de México, y del Centro Mexicano de Escritores (1985-86).

Sefchovich, Sara ◆ n. en el DF (1949). Su segundo apellido es Wasongarz. Maestra en letras latinoamericanas. Licenciada, maestra y doctora en sociología por la UNAM, donde ha sido ayudante de investigación (1973-76) e investigadora (1980-). Ha colaborado en *El Universal, El Gallo Ilustrado, Sábado, Revista de la Universidad, unomásuno, Plural, La Jornada Semanal* y *Fem*, entre otras, y en programas de radio. Ha sido antologada en *Las piedras vivas* (1979), *Expresiones de los años cuarenta* y *En los cien años de Lukacs*. Coautora de *Literatura, ideología y lenguaje* (1977). Autora de antologías: *El discurso político, teoría y análisis* (1978), *América Latina, la mujer en lucha* (1980) y *Mujeres en el espejo. Narradoras latinoamericanas. Siglo XX* (2 t., 1983-85); ensayo: *La teoría de la literatura de Lukacs* (1979), *Las primeras damas* (1982), *Ideología y ficción en la obra de Luis Spota* (1985), *México: país de ideas, país de novelas* (1988), *Gabriela Mistral, en fuego y agua dibujada* (1997) y *La suerte de la consorte* (1999); y novela: *Demasiado amor*

Sara Sefchovich

(1991, Premio Agustín Yáñez de novela 1990) y *La señora de los sueños* (1993). Becaria de la UNAM (1970-71), el INBA (1980-81) y la Fundación Guggenheim (1989-90). Pertenece al Sistema Nacional de Investigadores (1985-). Medalla Gabino Barreda (1989), Premio *Plural* de ensayo (1989) y medalla Leona Gerard (1993).

Segale, Atenógenes ◆ n. en Zamora, Mich., y m. en Toluca, Edo. de Méx. (1868-1903). Fue ordenado sacerdote en 1892. Capellán y cura en diversas plazas y profesor en el Seminario Conciliar de México. Se encargó de la oración latina en los funerales de Pelagio Antonio de Labastida y Dávalos. Colaboró en *El Tiempo* y en *La Voz de México*, donde hizo traducciones de latín y griego y publicó trabajos propios con el pseudónimo de *Elio Turno de Zamora*. Autor de las novelas: *La estatua de Psiquis* (1892), *Recuerdos del Cairo, La negrita, Auras de abril* (1897), *Flor de durazno* (1897), *y Del campo contrario* (novelas cortas, 1987); las tragedias: *Aureliano, El príncipe de Viena* y *La púrpura del rey* y los poemarios: *Preludios, Sonetos* (1893), *Del fondo del alma* (1895), *Miniaturas* (1896), *Versos perdidos* (1897), *Marinas, Paisajes* (1898) y *A la madre santísima de la luz en la coronación de su célebre imagen* (1902).

Segarra Tomás, Enrique ◆ n. en España y m. en Veracruz, Ver. (1908-

1988). Arquitecto. Durante la guerra civil española fue dinamitero del ejército republicano. Pasó a Francia en 1939, donde estuvo en un campo de concentración y trabajó en una fábrica de pólvora. En 1940 llegó a Nueva York y de ahí pasó a México, donde se naturalizó en 1947. Trabajó con el arquitecto Carlos Contreras y fijó su residencia en el puerto de Veracruz. Músico, creó y dirigió una orquesta de cámara y compuso la suite sinfónica *Los árboles floridos de Veracruz* (1984). Fundador del Museo Veracruzano (1979).

Seghers, Anna ◆ n. y m. en Alemania (1900-1983). Escritora. Militante comunista. Al llegar al poder el Partido Nacional-Socialista se refugió en Francia. Pasó a México, donde fue presidenta del Club Enrique Heine (1941-46), asociación de intelectuales antinazis de lengua alemana. En enero de 1947 volvió a Europa y se estableció en la República Democrática Alemana. Autora de las novelas: *La séptima cruz* (escrita en inglés en 1942,en Estados Unidos vendió 600,000 ejemplares; publicada en alemán en 1943, llevada al cine ese año en Hollywood bajo la dirección de Fred Zinnemann; traducida al español por Wenceslao Roces y publicada en México en 1943), *Tránsito* (*Visado de tránsito* en su versión mexicana, terminada de escribir en México, 1944) y *Los muertos permanecen jóvenes* (escrita en México), así como del volumen de cuentos *La excursión de las muchachas muertas* (escrita en México y publicada en Nueva York, 1946). En su testamento dispuso la creación del premio que lleva su nombre y que se ha entregado a los mexicanos Carmen Boullosa y Hermann Bellinghausen.

Segovia, Antonio ◆ n. en España y m. en Guadalajara, en el actual estado de Jalisco (1485-1570). Fraile franciscano. Se le considera el primer evangelizador de la Nueva Galicia. Llegó en 1527 a la Nueva España y tres años después empezó su trabajo en territorio de los actuales Jalisco y Zacatecas. Atribuyó a una pequeña escultura de la Virgen, llamada desde entonces *la Pacificadora*, haber pacificado el Mixtón (1541). Donó a los indios de Zapopan la imagen que se adora en ese lugar.

Segovia, Francisco ◆ n. en el DF (1958). Poeta. Guionista, corrector y redactor de diversos medios. Fue investigador del *Diccionario del español de México*, de El Colegio de México. Escritor del grupo de teatro Atrezo. Ha traducido poesía y prosa de Pavese y Villiers de L'Isle Adam. Autor de los poemarios: *Dos extremos* (1977), *Alquimia de la luz* (1979), *El error* (1981), *Triga* (1983, en colaboración), *Fin de fiesta* (1994) y *Rellano* (1998), así como del volumen de ensayos *Ocho notas* (1984). Becario Salvador Novo de poesía (1976) y del SNCA (1999).

Foto: Dante Bucio

Francisco Segovia

Segovia, Rafael ◆ n. en España (1928). Al término de la guerra civil española fue traído a México (1940). Licenciado y maestro en filosofía por la UNAM y doctor por la Universidad de París (1962). Profesor del Liceo Franco Mexicano (1953-58), de la Universidad de Guanajuato (1954-55), el Mexico City College (1954-60), la UNAM (1963-66) y El Colegio de México (1962-), donde ha sido director del Centro de Estudios Internacionales (1972-) y de la revista *Foro Internacional* (1972-), coordinador general académico (1988-), profesor emérito (1995-) y miembro de la junta de gobierno (1996-). Ha colaborado en *Excélsior, Razones* (1980-82), *Línea* (1989) y *Reforma* (1993-). Coautor de *El maximato* (con Alejandra Lajous y Lorenzo Meyer, 1979) y *La vida política mexicana en la crisis* (con Soledad Loaeza, 1988). Autor de *Tres salvaciones del siglo XVIII español* (1960), *La politización del niño mexicano* (1969) y *El Estado contemporáneo. México 1940-1970* (1988), *Lapidaria política* (1996). El Colegio de México editó *Homenaje a Rafael Segovia* (1998). Ha sido becario de las fundaciones Rockefeller (1960-62) y Ford (1970-71). Comendador de Número de la Orden de Isabel la Católica (1978).

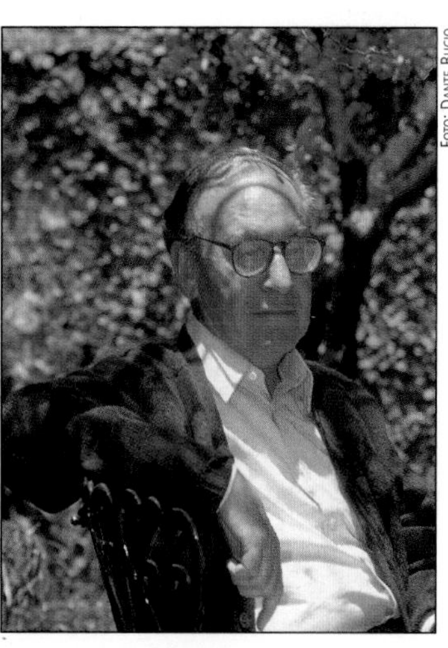
Foto: Dante Bucio

Rafael Segovia

Segovia, Tomás ◆ n. en España (1927). Vivió en México (1940-88). Estudió letras en la UNAM (1945-52) y en El Colegio de México (1953-54), del que fue investigador (1970-88). Cofundador de la revista *Presencia* (1946), editor de *Hoja Poética* (1948), jefe de redacción de *Claridades Literarias* (1955), codirector de la *Revista Mexicana de Literatura* (1958-63); director adjunto de *Mundo Nuevo* (París, 1966), secretario de redacción de *Plural* (1971-72), miembro del consejo de redacción de *Vuelta* (1976) y coordinador de la Casa del Lago. Autor de los poemarios: *La luz provisional* (1950), *Siete poemas (1955), Apariciones* (1957), *Luz de aquí* (1958), *El sol y su eco* (1960), *Anagnórisis* (1967), *Historias y poemas* (1968), *Terceto* (Premio Xavier Villaurrutia, 1972), *Cuaderno del nómada* (1978), *Figuras y secuencias* (1979), *Bisutería, juegos poéticos* (1981), *Partición* (1982), *Poesía 1943-1976* (1982), *Cantata a solas* (1985), *Lapso* (1987) y *Noticia natural* (1992); las obras en prosa: *Primavera muda* (1954), *Zamora bajo los astros* (1959), *Actitudes* (1970), *Contracorrientes* (1973), *Trizadero* (1974, Premio Magda Donato), *Personajes mirando una nube*

Tomás Segovia

(1981), *Poética y profética* (1986), *Cuadernos inoportunos* (1987), *Ensayos. Actitudes. Contracorrientes* (1988), *Sextante, Ensayos III* (1991) y *Páginas de ida y vuelta* (1993). Becario del Centro Mexicano de Escritores (1954-55 y 1955-56), de las fundaciones Farfield (1962) y Guggenheim (1968-69 y 1975-76). Tres veces Premio Nacional de Traducción Alfonso X (1982, 1983 y 1984). Nombrado Miembro del SNCA (1993-) y Creador Emérito (1997-). Vive en España.

SEGOVIA CABALLERO, JACINTO ◆ n. en España y m. en el DF (1892-1969). Licenciado en medicina y cirugía por la Universidad Central de Madrid (1915). Republicano, llegó exiliado a México en 1941. Se dedicó a la medicina privada y fue presidente del Centro Republicano Español. Autor de un *Tratado de operatoria general y especial* (6 t., 1951).

SEGRE, ENZO ◆ n. en Italia (1941). Antropólogo. Investigador de la Universidad de Florencia. En México ha sido profesor visitante de doctorado de antropología social en la UNAM (1976) y profesor de la ENAH (1976-78), así como corresponsal de la revista *Rinascita*, del Partido Comunista Italiano. Asimismo, realizó investigaciones acerca de la ideología indígena sobre el cuerpo humano. Entre 1978 y 1983, radicado en Italia, realizó numerosos viajes a México para estudiar el sincretismo religioso en Cuetzalan, Puebla (1984) y otros lugares (1986-88), trabajó sobre la historia del cuento en México y residió en Chinantla, Oaxaca. Autor de *Las máscaras de lo sagrado. Ensayos ítalo-mexicanos* (1987). Miembro de asuntos latinoamericanos del Centro de Estudios de Política Internacional de Roma.

SEGUNDA INTERNACIONAL ◆ ☛ *Internacional Socialdemócrata.*

SEGURA, VICENTE ◆ n. en Pachuca, Hgo., y m. en Cuernavaca, Mor. (1883-1953). Torero, recibió la alternativa en 1907, apadrinado por Antonio Fuentes, y la confirmó en España. Financió la construcción de una plaza de toros en Pachuca. En 1911 se unió a la revolución maderista, como proveedor de armas, mismas que transportaba en su barco desde Estados Unidos. Alcanzó el grado de general en las fuerzas de Venustiano Carranza, en las que organizó y financió la brigada Hidalgo, con la que realizó campañas en Morelos y Puebla contra el Ejército Libertador del Sur. En 1921 regresó a los ruedos.

SEGURA ARGÜELLES, VICENTE ◆ n. ¿en Córdoba, Ver.? y m. en la ciudad de México (?-1860). Algunos autores suponen que nació en la ciudad de México, en 1846. Fue uno de los fundadores del periódico satírico *Don Simplicio*, al lado de Ignacio Ramírez y Guillermo Prieto. Fue colaborador de *El Museo Mexicano* y editor de *El Ómnibus* (1855-56) y de *El Diario de Avisos* (1856-60). Estableció una imprenta en la entonces calle de Cadena. Murió asesinado.

SEGURA GUTIÉRREZ, JUAN ◆ n. y m. en el DF (1898-1989). Arquitecto. Estudió en la Academia de San Carlos (1917-21). Fue uno de los más importantes arquitectos de *art decó* mexicano (destacando su labor entre 1920 y 1945) y de la llamada arquitectura funcional. Fundador de la Sociedad de Construcciones Modernas (1925). Planeó los conjuntos urbanísticos de la colonia Santa María, en las calles de Sabino 190 (1927) y en Sadi Carnot 110 y 110-bis (1928 y 1930), así como el conjunto Isabel de Tacubaya, en Avenida Revolución 121 (los mismos años), y el conjunto Ermita (1929-1930, incluye el cine Hipódromo). Perteneció al Colegio de Arquitectos de México, a la Sociedad de Arquitectos Mexicanos y a la Academia Nacional de Arquitectura. Emérito de la Academia Nacional de Arquitectura.

SEGURA RIVERA, BERNARDO ◆ n. en San Mateo Atenco, Edo. de Mex. (1970). Licenciado en educación física por la ESEF. Atleta con especialidad en caminata. Fue el único mexicano medallista en los Juegos Olímpicos de Atlanta 96. Ha triunfado en diversas competencias internacionales, como los 20 kilómetros contra reloj en la Semana Internacional de la Caminata, especialidad en la que es recordista mundial. Fue presidente del Frente Juvenil Revolucionario de su localidad, asesor del Frente Estatal del Deporte (1996), coordinador de la Subdirección de Apoyo al Deporte del Instituto de la Juventud de su estado y secretario general de la Asociación Nacional de Atletas de Alto Rendimiento. Pertenece al PRD desde 1997. Diputado federal (1997-2000, impulsor de una nueva Ley del Deporte) y quinto regidor de su municipio.

SEGURA VILCHIS, LUIS ◆ n. en Piedras Negras, Coah., y m. en el DF (1903-1927). Ingeniero agrónomo graduado en la Universidad Nacional de México (1924), trabajó como técnico de la Compañía Mexicana de Luz y Fuerza Motriz. Perteneció al Círculo de Estudios Sociales Cardenal Mercier, que dirigido por Miguel Palomar y Vizcarra se incorporó en 1919 a la Asociación Católica de la Juventud Mejicana (ACJM). Participó en la manifestación del 8 de febrero de 1921, que fue agredida por la policía. Ante el temor de un atentado obregonista, formó parte de los grupos de defensa armada de la Basílica de Guadalupe. Perteneció al Centro de Estudiantes Católicos (1921) e intervino en un encuentro a balazos contra un grupo de obreros de la CGT que atacaron dicho centro. Fue miembro del Comité General de la ACJM (1923). Perteneció al Partido Popular Mexicano, creado para participar en las elecciones de 1924.

Bernardo Segura

Vicente Segura

Luis Segura Vilchis

Cofundador de la Liga Nacional Defensora de la Libertad Religiosa (1925), de la que fue jefe de Control Militar en el DF, encargado de suministrar armamento a los cristeros (☛). En 1927 dirigió en Chapultepec un atentado dinamitero contra el entonces presidente Álvaro Obregón, quien resultó ileso. No fue aprehendido y aun se fabricó una coartada presentándose de inmediato ante Obregón, como simpatizante suyo. Un día después del atentado, el 14 de noviembre, se entregó a la policía para evitar que la responsabilidad recayera en Miguel Agustín Pro Juárez. Fue fusilado.

Séjourne, Laurette ◆ n. en Francia (¿1915?). En 1950 se inició en la arqueología con Alfonso Caso, Ignacio Bernal y Alberto Cruz. Participó en exploraciones en Monte Albán y Palenque. Desde 1955 se dedicó al estudio de Teotihuacán, donde descubrió tres estructuras arquitectónicas completas. Autora de *Palenque, una ciudad maya, Un palacio en la ciudad de los dioses, La cerámica de Teotihuacán, El lenguaje de las formas en Teotihuacán, Arquitectura y pintura en Teotihuacán, Teotihuacán, Métropole de L'Amérique, Arqueología del valle de México, El pensamiento náhuatl cifrado y los calendarios, Supervivencias de un mundo mágico y El universo de Quetzalcóatl.*

Selden, Códice ◆ Documento conservado en la biblioteca Bodleiana de la Universidad de Oxford. Llamado así por haber pertenecido al abogado y anticuario inglés John Selden. Es una tira de piel de venado de 27.5 por 27.5 centímetros, con 20 hojas en forma de biombo, cada una con tres bandas de composición. Se trata de un palimpsesto genealógico, que abarca el periodo de entre 794 y 1556, acerca de alguna dinastía mixteca. Está pintado a la manera tradicional indígena, aunque se realizó a mediados del siglo XVI.

Selden II, Rollo ◆ Códice genealógico procedente de la Mixteca Alta, pintado en una tira de piel plegada en biombo, con 23 hojas de 29 centímetros. Como el códice anterior, lleva el nombre de su último poseedor, John

Una de las hojas del Códice Selden

Selden, quien lo donó a la biblioteca Bodleiana de la Universidad de Oxford. Refiere la genealogía de los señores mixtecos de Tilantongo y Teozacoalco, abarca el periodo de 920 a 1556 y sus primeras páginas parecen copia de otro documento.

Seler, Eduard Georg ◆ n. y m. en Alemania (1849-1922). Filólogo cuya tesis doctoral tituló *El sistema de conjugaciones de la lengua maya* (1887). En 1884 se inició en el estudio de los idiomas chibchas y en 1886 se abocó a la filología mayense. En 1887 viajó a México por primera vez, para efectuar algunas exploraciones etnográficas y arqueológicas. Estudió principalmente los códices mayas y mixtecos, fue director del Museo de Etnología de Berlín (1904), profesor del Instituto Internacional de Arqueología y Etnología (con sede en México) y de la Escuela de Antropología de México, que contribuyó a establecer. Se le considera el fundador de la escuela alemana de investigadores de la antigua cultura mexicana. Publicó *Gesammelte abbandlungen zur amerikanischen sprach und alterfums kunde* (5 t., 1902-15), obra en la que reunió sus estudios sobre mitología, religión, leyendas, costumbres, ceremonias, literatura, lenguaje e historia de las culturas mesoamericanas; en su obra describe las evidencias de la hasta entonces desconocida influencia tolteca en todas las culturas mesocamericanas. En México apareció, en 1910, su texto *Bases y fines de la investigación arqueológica en el territorio de la República Mexicana y países colindantes.* En 1908 recibió el premio Angrand, de París, por sus comentarios al Códice Borgia.

Seler-Sachs, Caecilie ◆ n. y m. en Alemania (1855-1935). Esposa del anterior. Arqueóloga y fotógrafa. En 1887 llegó a México e hizo sus primeras exploraciones en Xochicalco. Realizó recorridos por la huasteca y la mixteca alta, regiones aún inexploradas por los especialistas en esa época y en 1929 exploró Palenque. Coautora de *Reisebriefe aus Mexiko* (aunque sólo con la firma de Eduard Seler) y autora de *Auf alten wegen durch Mexiko und Guatemala.* Para complementar las investigaciones arqueológicas de su esposo, realizó estudios fotográficos de México y otros países de América. También elaboró materiales artísticos sobre el paisaje mexicano, su arquitectura y costumbres. Escribió ensayos sobre México para diversas publicaciones. Más de 2,500 fotografías suyas sobre México se encuentran en el Instituto Iberoamericano de Berlín. En 1998 se expuso parte de su obra en el Centro de la Imagen y en 1999 se hizo un coloquio internacional sobre la contribución del matrimonio Seler al conocimiento moderno de las culturas prehispánicas.

Seligson, Esther ◆ n. en el DF (1941). Estudió letras españolas y francesas en la UNAM y se especializó en estudios bíblicos, talmúdicos y de religiones comparadas en París y Jerusalén (1980-81). Ha sido profesora del INBA, la UIA y la UNAM. Coordinó el Taller de Arte Escénico Popular de la SEP (1977-81). Asesora del Consejo Consultivo de Teatro del INBA (1986-87). Ha escrito para publicaciones literarias. Autora de relato: *Tras la ventana un árbol* (1969), *Luz de dos* (1978, Premio Magda Donato), *De sueños, presagios y otras voces* (1978), *Indicios y quimeras* (1989) y *Hebras* (1996); prosas: *Diálogos con el cuerpo* (1981), *Sed de mar* (1986) e *Isomorfismos* (1998); novela: *Otros son los sueños* (1973, Premio Xavier Villaurrutia) y *La morada en el tiempo* (1981); poesía: *Tránsito del cuerpo* (1977); ensayo: *Las figuraciones como método de escritura* (1985). *La fugacidad como método de escritura* (1988) y *El teatro, festín efímero* (1990). En 1993 publicó *Tríptico*, reunión de *Otros son los sueños*, *Diálogos con el cuerpo* y *Sed de mar*. Textos suyos han aparecido en las antologías *Echad: An Anthology of Latin American Jewish Writers* (Estados Unidos, 1980), *Panorama de la poesía judía contemporánea* (Argentina, 1989), *A Necklace of Words* (Estados Unidos, 1996), *Passioni e scritura. Antología di narratrici messicane del sécolo XX* (Italia, 1998) y *El gran libro de la América judía* (Puerto Rico, 1998), entre otras. Becaria del Centro Mexicano de Escritores (1969-70).

Selser, Gregorio ◆ n. en Argentina y m. en el DF (1922-1991). Periodista radicado en México desde 1976. Fue director dos colecciones en Editorial Universitaria de Buenos Aires (1962-66), profesor de la Universidad Nacional de La Plata (1971-74), investigador de la Universidad Nacional de Buenos Aires (1974) e investigador del Instituto Latinoamericano de Estudios Trasnacionales (México, 1976-79). Escribió para *El Día* (1979-87), *La Jornada* (1987-), Inter Press Service y Prensa Latina. Autor, entre otras obras, de *Sandino, general de hombres libres* (1955), *El pequeño ejército loco. Operación México-Nicaragua* (1958), *El guatemalazo* (1961), *El rapto de Panamá. De cómo los Estados Unidos se apropiaron del canal* (1964), *¡Aquí, Santo Domingo! La tercera guerra sucia* (1966), *CIA, de Dulles a Raborn. Pifias y logros del contraespionaje* (1967), *La CIA en Bolivia* (1970), *Los cuatro viajes de Cristóbal Rockefeller* (1971), *El onganiato. La espada y el hisopo* (2 t., 1972), *Chile para recordar* (1974), *Los marines. Intervenciones norteamericanas en América Latina. Siglo XX* (1974), *El Pentágono y la política exterior norteamericana* (1975, en colaboración con Carlos Díaz), *De cómo Nixinger desestabilizó a Chile* (1975), *La batalla de Nicaragua* (volumen colectivo, 1979), *Trampas de la información y neocolonialismo. Las agencias de noticias frente a los países no alineados* (1979), *Apuntes sobre Nicaragua* (1981), *Reagan entre El Salvador y las Malvinas* (1982), *Honduras, república alquilada* (1983), *Nicaragua de Walker a Somoza* (1984), *Los días del presidente Allende* (1991, póstumo) y *Cronología de las intervenciones extranjeras en América Latina* (1995).

Foto: Rogelio Cuéllar

Esther Seligson

Gregorio Selser

Selser Ventura, Irene ◆ n. en Argentina (1955). Periodista y escritora. Hizo estudios en la Facultad de Filosofía y Letras de Buenos Aires. Llegó a México en 1976, huyendo de la dictadura militar en Argentina, y estudió ciencias políticas en la UNAM. Ha colaborado en periódicos, revistas y estaciones de radio y televisión de América Latina, así como en agencias internacionales de noticias. Fue corresponsal de prensa en Nicaragua (1982-92). Reside en México. Editora de la edición mexicana de *Le monde diplomatique*. Secretaria de la Fundación Latinoamericana Gregorio Selser. Autora de *Cardenal Obando, iglesia y revolución en Nicaragua* (1992) y *El arca de los sueños* (1997). Premio Latinoamericano de Periodismo José Martí (1991).

Selva y Escoto, Rogerio de la ◆ n. en Nicaragua y m. en el DF (1900-1967). Licenciado por la Escuela Libre de Derecho (1926). Llegó en 1921 y obtuvo la nacionalidad mexicana. Fue profesor de la UNAM, agente del Ministerio Público, secretario particular de Miguel Alemán (1938-65) y juez del fuero militar. Alcanzó el grado de general de brigada. Autor de *En torno a*

México (1951), *Un discurso de tres cartas* (1954), *Alegato mexicano* (1954) y *Lección académica* (1963).

Selva y Escoto, Salomón de la ◆ n. en Nicaragua y m. en Francia (1893-1959). En 1905 viajó becado a Estados Unidos, donde fue profesor en la Universidad de Cornell. Se alistó en el ejército británico y combatió en la primera guerra mundial. Vino a México y fue profesor de idiomas, matemáticas y literatura, así como uno de los fundadores de la revista *Tiempo*. Naturalizado mexicano, en 1950 fue agregado cultural de la embajada en Estados Unidos. Colaboró en *América, Letras de México* y otras revistas literarias. Autor de poesía: *Tropical Town and Other Poems* (1918), *A Soldier Sings* (1919), *Soldado desconocido* (1922), *Las hijas de Erectheo* (1933), *Romance que dice: ¡Qué abrileña que has llegado!* (1949), *Evocación de Horacio* (1949), *Tres poesías a la manera de Rubén Darío* (1951), *Canto a la independencia nacional de México* (1955), *Evocación de Píndaro* (1957) y *Acolmixtli Netzahualcóyotl* (1958); y de novela: *La vida de San Adefesio* (1932) y *La ilustre familia* (1950). Algunas obras las firmó como *Juan del Camino*. Miembro honorario de la Academia Mexicana (de la Lengua). Murió en Europa cuando desempeñaba una labor diplomática en representación del gobierno nicaragüense.

Seltzer Marseille, Elmar Harald ◆ n. en Yajalón, Chiapas, y m. en Monterrey, NL (1936-1998). Gobernador interino de Chiapas entre 1993 y 1994. Renunció al cargo en enero de ese año, tras el levantamiento armado del EZLN. En 1997 aseguró que el entonces presidente Carlos Salinas de Gortari sabía de la existencia de la guerrilla en el estado, pero calló para no afectar las negociaciones del Tratado de Libre Comercio con los Estados Unidos.

Semanario Patriótico Americano ◆ Periódico independentista publicado por Andrés Quintana Roo, en Sultepec y en Tlalpujahua, sucesivamente. Fue lo que se llamaría un órgano teórico y expresó las ideas más avanzadas de la insurgencia. Se conocen 27 números, de los cuales el primero probablemente apareció el 19 de agosto de 1812. El último salió con fecha del 17 de enero de 1813. En sus páginas se publicaron textos del propio Quintana Roo, José María Cos y fray Servando Teresa de Mier.

Seminario de Cultura Mexicana ◆ Institución creada por acuerdo presidencial del 28 de febrero de 1942 en la ciudad de México, cuando era secretario de Educación Pública Octavio Véjar Vázquez. Su Ley Orgánica, promulgada el 30 de diciembre de 1949, establece que es una institución dotada de personalidad jurídica y que sus finalidades son "estimular la producción científica, filosófica y artística; difundir la cultura en todas sus manifestaciones nacionales y universales; mantener activo intercambio cultural con los estados y con instituciones e individuos del extranjero interesados en la cultura mexicana; organizar trabajos de investigación y análisis en forma de seminario, ya sea con la colaboración unánime de sus miembros o por núcleos afines de los mismos; servir de órgano de consulta a la Secretaría de Educación Pública y colaborar con ella y con otras dependencias oficiales en actividades culturales". Está integrado por 25 miembros titulares, cuyo conjunto forma el Consejo, autoridad suprema. Miembros fundadores: Fanny Anitúa, Mariano Azuela, Carlos Bracho, Julián Carrillo, Luis Castillo Ledón, Esperanza Cruz, el arquitecto José Luis Cuevas, Francisco Díaz de León, Arnulfo Domínguez Bello, Aurelio Fuentes, Mathilde Gómez, Frida Kahlo, Alfredo Gómez de la Vega, Enrique González Martínez, Gregorio López y Fuentes, Maximino Martínez, Gabriel Méndez Plancarte, Manuel M. Ponce, Luis Ortiz Monasterio, Antonio Ruiz, Manuel Sandoval Vallarta, Fernando Soler y Ángel Zárraga. Ingresaron posteriormente Vito Alessio Robles (1943), Miguel Bernal Jiménez (1943), Amalia González Caballero de Castillo Ledón (1944), Antonio Castro Leal (1945), Carlos González Peña (1945), Francisco Orozco Muñoz (1945), Guillermina Llach (1947), Pedro Daniel Martínez (1947), Wigberto Jiménez (1947), Jesús Reyes Ruiz (1947), Juan D. Tercero (1948), Agustín Yáñez (1948), Carlos Graef Fernández (1949), Manuel Martínez Báez (1949), Eduardo García Maynes (1950), Dionisia Zamora (1950), Rodolfo Usigli (1951), Salvador Azuela (1951), Mauricio Magdaleno (1957), Enrique del Moral (1957), Salvador Aceves (1958), Francisco Monterde (1963), Antonio Acevedo Escobedo (1964), Jorge González Camarena (1965), Pablo Castellanos (1967), José Rojas Garcidueñas (1969), Ernesto De la Torre Villar (1969), Concepción Caso Muñoz (1973), Stella Contreras (1973), Manuel Enríquez (1979), Alberto Beltrán (1980) Raúl Cardiel Reyes (1980), Arturo Azuela (1986), Antonio

Integrantes del Seminario de Cultura Mexicana en 1999

Gómez Robledo (1986), Diego G. López Rosado (1986), Luis Ortiz Monasterio (1986), Elisa Vargaslugo (1986), Rafael Velasco Fernández (1987), Salvador Aceves (1988) y Luis Estrada Martínez (1988). Han sido sus presidentes Enrique González Martínez (1942-43), José Luis Cuevas (1943-44), Alfredo Gómez de la Vega (1944-45), Ángel Zárraga (1945-46), Antonio Castro Leal (1947-48), Gabriel Méndez Plancarte (1948-49), Agustín Yáñez (1949-52), Carlos Graef Fernández (1952-54), Pedro Daniel Martínez (1954-55), Salvador Azuela (1955-59), Wigberto Jiménez Moreno (1959-60), Mauricio Magdaleno (1960-62), Salvador Azuela (1962-67 y 1971-83) Enrique del Moral (1967-69), Luis Ortiz Monasterio (1969-71), Raúl Cardiel Reyes (1983-98) y Luis Estrada (1998-).

Semo, Enrique ◆ n. en Bulgaria (1930). Licenciado en economía por la Escuela Superior de Derecho de Tel Aviv, licenciado en historia por la UNAM (1965) y doctor por la Universidad Humboldt de Berlín (1971). Ha sido profesor e investigador de la UNAM y otras instituciones de enseñanza superior, director fundador del posgrado de la Facultad de Economía de la UNAM (1972-77), director del Centro de Estudios Contemporáneos de la UAP (1978-82) y creador de la maestría en historia regional de la UAS. Cofundador del MLN y militante del PCM (1961-81), en el que fue miembro del Comité Central (1963-81) y de la comisión política (1981). En 1967 sufrió un atentado por su militancia política. Cofundador y miembro del Comité Central del PSUM (1982-87). Fundador (1965) y dos veces director de la revista *Historia y Sociedad*. Colabora en *Proceso* y *El Universal*. Coordinador de *México, un pueblo en la historia* (4 t. 1981-83) e *Historia de la cuestión agraria mexicana* (4 t., en colaboración, 1988). Autor de *Historia del capitalismo en México. Los orígenes, 1521-1763* (1973), *La crisis actual del capitalismo* (1975), *Modos de producción en América Latina* (1977), *Historia mexicana. Economía y lucha de clases* (1978), *Viaje alrededor de la izquierda* (1987), *Entre crisis te veas* (1987), *Crónica de un derrumbe. Las revoluciones inconclusas del este* (1991) y *Dos obras de Francisco Pimentel* (1994). Becario del Social Science Research Council (1982) y de las fundaciones Mac Arthur y Guggenheim. Pertenece al Sistema Nacional de Investigadores (1984-). Maestro emérito de las universidades Autónoma de Ciudad Juárez (1992) y de Nuevo México (1997). *Doctor honoris causa* por la UAP (1998). Medalla Hegel por méritos en la investigación de la Universidad Humboldt (1971).

Semo, Ilán ◆ n. en Israel (1953). Hijo del anterior. Licenciado en física por la Humboldt Universitat (1973) y maestro en ciencias por la Akademie der Wissenschaften de Alemania (1974) y pasante de doctor en la UNAM (1987). Ha sido profesor en instituciones de enseñanza superior, investigador en la UAP (1978-82), el Cinvestav (1982-86), la Universidad de Illinois en Chicago (1987) y la Universidad de California en La Jolla (1988). Fue secretario de redacción de *Excélsior* (1985-86) y conductor del programa semanal *Historia de la Ciencia* de Radio Educación (1978-79). Director de las revistas *El Buscón* (1982-86) y *Fractal* (1996-). Escribe para *La Jornada*. Coautor de *La generación del fin de siglo* (1986) y *La sucesión presidencial* (1986), que coeditó. Coeditor de la *Revolución Mexicana en la escritura de su historia* (1995). Editor de *El corporativismo* (1988), *La transición interrumpida* (1992), *La rueda del azar* (1999) y *La nación: metáforas y rituales* (1999). Autor de *El ocaso de los mitos* (1982) y *Tierra de nadie* (1988). Miembro de los consejos editoriales de *Estudios Contemporáneos* (1980-82) y la serie de historia "Raíces y Razones" de Alianza Editorial.

Sen, Pilar ◆ n. en Colombia y m. en el DF (1918-1973). Llegó a México en 1939 y se inició como actriz radiofónica en la XEW. Pasó al teatro, donde desempeñó papeles menores en diversas compañías. Trabajó en las películas *Dos mexicanos en Sevilla*, *Jesús de Nazareth*, *La sangre manda*, *La bandida*, *En carne propia* y *El jardín de tía Isabel*. Fue una de las primeras actrices de la televisión mexicana y destacó su participación en las telenovelas *Lucía sombra* y *Hermanos coraje*.

Senado de la República ◆ ☛ *Poder Legislativo*.

Sendel, Virginia ◆ n. en el DF (1942). Periodista. Maestra en idiomas por la UNAM. Fue campeona nacional juvenil de tenis. Ha sido reportera del noticiero de televisión *24 Horas* (1971-79), conductora de *24 Horas del Sábado* (1975-79) y conductora de *La mujer ahora* (1979-80); reportera de *60 Minutos* (1979-80), conductora de *Introducción a la Universidad* (1978-80), directora y conductora de *Semanario* (1979-); coordinadora y conductora de *Increíble* (1980-) y directora de *Noche a noche*. Autora de *México mágico*. En 1979 fue declarada la mejor reportera de TV y en 1980 la Asociación Mexicana de Periodistas de Radio y Televisión la consideró como la mejor conductora de noticieros.

Virginia Sendel

Sender, Ramón J. ◆ n. en España y m. en EUA (1902-1982). Soldado y periodista republicano. En 1939 llegó a México como refugiado político. Cofundador de la editorial Quetzal. En 1942 viajó a Estados Unidos, donde fue profesor en el Colegio Amherst (1943-44), traductor para la Metro Goldwyn Mayer y profesor de la Universidad de Nuevo México, hasta su jubilación. Autor de *El problema religioso en Méjico* (1928), *Mister Witt en el cantón* (1935, Premio Nacional de Literatura en España), *El lugar del hombre* (1939), *Proverbio de la muerte* (1939), *Hernán Cortés, retablo en dos partes y once cuadros* (1940), *Mexicayotl* (1940, con viñetas de Darío Carmona), *Crónica del alba* (1942), *Epitalamio del prieto Trinidad* (1942), *El rey y la reina* (1947), *El verdugo amable* (1952), *Mosén Millán* (1953), *Los cinco libros de Ariadna* (1957), *Réquiem por un campesino español* (1960) y *En la vida de Ignacio Morell* (1969, Premio Planeta de España).

Libro de Enrique Semo

FOTO: ÉPOCA

Manuel Senderos Irigoyen

Fernando Senderos Mestre

SENDEROS IRIGOYEN, MANUEL ◆ n. en (1917). Empresario. Hijo de una familia de empresarios, desde 1937 se integró a Comercial Mexicana Seguros (hoy Seguros Comercial América), fundada por su padre un año antes (Liberto Senderos, cofundador del Banco de Comercio), de la cual se hizo director (1942). Formó la asociación Negromex (1967), petroquímica que produce la materia prima de las llantas. Después creó el Consorcio de Empresas Mexicanas (1969), antecedente de Desarrollo Económico (1973, con siglas Desc), uno de los diez grupos empresariales más grandes y diversificados del país. En 1973 impulsó el Decreto de las Sociedades de Fomento. Vendió Seguros La Comercial (1972) y se dedicó a ampliar su consorcio. En 1987 impulsó la Fundación Mexicana de Calidad Total y ese año se retiró de la posición ejecutiva como miembro del Comité de Dirección de Desc. Fundador del Instituto Panamericano de Alta Dirección de Empresas y del Instituto Tecnológico Autónomo de México. Miembro del Salón de Empresarios de México desde 1993.

SENDEROS MESTRE, FERNANDO ◆ n. en el DF (1950). Hijo del anterior. Hizo sus estudios superiores en 1968 en la Universidad Anáhuac, donde se graduó en la carrera de administración de empresas. Ingresó a Desc como miembro del Consejo de Administración y del Comité de Dirección en 1974. Fue nombrado presidente del Consejo Ejecutivo del Grupo Desc en 1989. Formó parte del equipo olímpico mexicano de equitación.

SENEGAL ◆ República del occidente africano, situado en la costa del océano Atlántico. Limita al norte con Mauritania, al este con Malí, al sur con Guinea y Guinea Bissau y al oeste con Gambia, cuyo territorio está completamente rodeado por el de Senegal. Tiene una superficie de 196,712 km² y 9,003,000 habitantes (1998). Su capital es Dakar, con 1,869,323 habitantes en 1994. Otras ciudades de importancia son Thies (216,381 habitantes), Kaolack (193,115) y Ziguinchor (161,680). El idioma oficial es el francés y la educación básica se imparte en inglés, lengua de la Confederación Senegambia. *Historia:* los primeros habitantes del actual territorio senegalés fueron los tocolores. En 1444 impusieron su dominio los portugueses, quienes en Cabo Verde controlaban el comercio de esclavos desde el río Senegal hasta Sierra Leona. En 1542, poco antes de su muerte, Hernán Cortés celebró un contrato con Leonardo Lomelín, a fin de traer 500 esclavos de Cabo Verde, la tercera parte "hembras", para sus haciendas mexicanas. Los negros debían ser de 15 y 26 años y se sabe que antes de año y medio había sido entregada la "mercancía". En 1561 se celebró otro contrato, éste firmado por Hernán Vázquez, para traer un millar de esclavos del mismo origen. Muchas otras licencias se concedieron para importar africanos, a lo que debe sumarse el número de esclavos traídos de contrabando en el siglo XVI, a lo largo del cual eran las islas de Cabo Verde y los llamados ríos de Guinea, nombre que en el siglo XV se daba a la actual Senegambia, de donde llegaron a México miembros de la etnia gelofe o wolof, sereres, conocidos aquí como berbesís; los ulof o diolas, llamados en Nueva España felupes; del pueblo denominado por los franceses bagnoul, esclavos a los que en México se decía bañoles y, ya en el siglo XVII, pañoles, vinieron también mandingas de los grupos saracolé y malinké, los fula, confundidos con mandingos, y los tucolor, aquí nombrados tucuxui, seres de facciones caucasoides, quienes para Gonzalo Aguirre Beltrán eran una mezcla de fulas y sereres. De la ribera sur del actual río Cazamancia llegaron los papeis o buramos y hubo negros de otras etnias a los que se llamó cazangas. Entre el siglo XV y el XVI los lusitanos fueron desplazados de la costa senegalesa por los franceses, quienes en el siglo XVII establecieron factorías en la costa, donde empezó a operar la Compañía del Senegal, constituida en Francia en 1696, que exportaba esclavos a sus bases en las Antillas, desde donde fueron introducidos en Nueva España. Era accionista de la empresa el monarca español Felipe IV, de la Casa de Borbón, "quien comprometió su fe y su palabra en la dicha Campaña, mirando la trata como su propio bien". El monarca hizo honor a su palabra y en 1704, dice Gonzalo Aguirre Beltrán, expidió una real cédula que prohibía "en forma terminante" a las autoridades coloniales cualquier entrometimiento en las "arribadas de negros". No obstante, como los franceses tenían el control de la firma, aprovechaban la licencia para el tráfico con seres humanos y con éstos disimulaban el contrabando de otras mercancías que les estaba prohibido introducir en las posesiones españolas. En 1707 llegó a Veracruz el buque *Alcyon* con 52 esclavos "que encubrían —dice Aguirre Beltrán— una importante cargazón de telas". Las autoridades autorizaron el desembarco de negros si antes se permitía la inspección del navío, a lo que se negó un mercader de apellido De la Bouyade, representante del puerto de la Compañía de Senegal, por lo que la embarcación tuvo que levar anclas. El 8 de junio de 1713 ocurrió algo parecido, cuando el barco *El Francés* llegó a Veracruz con 262 esclavos y 100 toneladas de diversos géneros de contrabando, que fue descubierto y confiscado. La Corona española ordenó a la Audiencia de México que se restituyera a los contrabandistas el valor de lo decomisado. La pésima administración acabó paulatinamente con la Compañía. Otros traficantes obtuvieron concesiones para mantener el flujo de sangre africana hacia América. En 1765, Miguel de Uriarte, mercader de Cádiz, se comprometió a entregar anualmente en Campeche 400 esclavos, a lo largo de una década, traídos de Senegal y lugares cercanos. En el siglo XVIII los franceses declararon abolida la trata de esclavos y se dedicaron al comercio de goma arábiga. En la segunda mitad del siglo XIX se intensificaron las luchas de los originales pobladores de Senegal en busca de su independencia. El líder musulmán Lat Dior mantuvo entre 1864 y 1885 una guerra de guerrillas que dificultó a los colonialistas el control del interior del país. La lucha fue continuada por Hamadú Lamine y Alburi N'Diaye hasta que las tropas francesas eliminaron toda resistencia en 1892. En 1958 Senegal se convirtió en una república autónoma dentro de la Comunidad Francesa. En 1959 se unió con el antiguo Sudán Francés para formar la Federación de Malí, aunque un año después Senegal se declaró independiente. En esa oportunidad, el presidente mexicano Adolfo López Mateos envió una delegación observadora. En 1962 el primer ministro Mamadou Día trató de derrocar al presidente Leopold Sédar Senghor (poeta, creador del concepto de la *negritud* y militante de la resistencia antinazi en Francia durante la segunda guerra mundial); falló en su intento y el cargo de primer ministro fue eliminado. En ese año se establecieron las relaciones diplomáticas entre Senegal y México. En 1964 fueron proscritos todos los partidos políticos excepto el Reunión Africana. En 1970 se restableció el cargo de primer ministro, que recayó en Abdou Diouf. En 1974 se legalizó el Partido Democrático Senegalés, como única opción opositora. En 1975 los presidentes mexicano y senegalés, Luis Echeverría y Senghor, se hicieron visitas oficiales recíprocas. En 1981, Diouf relevó a Senghor en la Presidencia de la República. El nuevo mandatario legalizó siete partidos políticos. Tropas senegalesas intervinieron en Gambia para evitar un golpe de Estado, después de lo cual se iniciaron conversaciones para fusionar a los dos países. En 1982 se estableció la Federación de Senegambia, en la que se fundan algunas de las instituciones de ambas naciones.

Senguio ◆ Municipio de Michoacán situado en el noreste del estado, al este de Morelia y al norte de Zitácuaro, en los límites con el Estado de México. Superficie: 292.28 km^2. Habitantes: 16,702, de los cuales 3,445 forman la población económicamente activa.

Sentíes Basal, Francisco de P. ◆ n. en Veracruz, Ver., y m. en el DF (1877-1953). Estudió en la Escuela Nacional de Agricultura. Periodista, fundó *La aurora del siglo XX* (1900), cofundó *El Entreacto* (1904) y fue colaborador de *El Diario del Hogar* y *La Patria,* donde publicó la columna "Cartas abiertas" con el pseudónimo de Félix Hernández. Fue redactor de *México Nuevo* y figuró entre los fundadores del Partido Democrático. Luego del triunfo maderista rechazó un puesto público, participó en la organización del Comité Cívico de la Defensa Nacional y se exilió en Texas, donde continuó su trabajo periodístico. Regresó a México en 1921, compró un rancho cerca de Texcoco y colaboró en los periódicos *Excélsior* y *El Dictamen.* Autor del folleto *La organización política de México* (1908).

Sentíes Echeverría, Yolanda Elisa ◆ n. en Toluca, Edo. de Méx. (1940). Hija de Octavio Sentíes Gómez. Química farmacéutica bióloga por la UNAM, licenciada en derecho y maestra en administración pública por la UAEM, donde ha sido profesora y secretaria técnica de la Facultad de Ciencias Químicas (1972-73). Desde 1961 pertenece al PRI, en el que fue secretaria general del CEN de la Anfer (1980-85). Organizadora y fundadora del Centro de Estudios sobre la Mujer (1974) y coordinadora ejecutiva del Comité Estatal del Año Internacional de la Mujer (1975). Ha sido presidenta del voluntariado del IMSS en el Estado de México (1970-73), presidenta del Comité Estatal del Instituto de Protección a la Familia del Estado de México (1972-73), diputada local (1972-75), presidenta municipal de Toluca (1976-78), diputada federal y coordinadora de la diputación mexiquense (1979-81), senadora (1982-88) y directora de Salud Materno Infantil de la SSA (1988-94). Mujer Destacada del Año (1981).

Sentíes Gómez, Octavio ◆ n. en Veracruz, Ver., y m. en el DF (1915-1996). Padre de la anterior. Licenciado en derecho por la UNAM (1942), donde fue profesor. Fue miembro del PNR y del PRM. Cofundador al PRI. Ejerció su profesión como abogado de transportistas (1942 y 1947-70). Fue secretario particular del gobernador del Estado de México Wenceslao Labra (1937-41), diputado federal (1943-46 y 1970-71, en esta ocasión fungió como presidente de la Gran Comisión) y jefe del Departamento del Distrito Federal (1971-76).

Sentmanat, Francisco ◆ n, en Cuba y m. en Jalpa, Tab. (1802-1844). Militar y político conservador. En 1840 Antonio López de Santa Anna lo designó gobernador y comandante militar de Tabasco. En 1843, al estallar el movimiento separatista de Yucatán, el gobierno central envió tropas al mando de Pedro Ampudia, y Sentmanat se opuso a que éstas pasasen por territorio tabasqueño. Ampudia atacó a Sentmanat, quien debió huir a Cuba, de donde pasó a Estados Unidos; desde ahí organizó una expedición filibustera y en 1844 desembarcó en Tabasco. Ampudia lo derrotó nuevamente, lo capturó y ordenó su fusilamiento.

Señal ◆ Revista semanal fundada en la ciudad de México en 1954 por José N. Chávez González, su primer director. Tuvo el apoyo de la agrupación religiosa Misioneros del Espíritu Santo, representada por el sacerdote Fernando de la Mora.

Septién Díaz, Alfonso María ◆ n. en Querétaro, Qro., y m. en el DF (1882-1969). Licenciado en derecho por la Escuela Nacional de Jurisprudencia (1906). Autor de *El régimen monetario de México y la baja de la moneda de plata, La deflación monetaria* y *el balance de México, La última reforma monetaria, La industrialización de México, La caída de los precios* y *La ciencia monetaria y nuestra agricultura.* Presidente de la Barra Mexicana-Colegio de Abogados (1939), de la que fue fundador, y miembro de número de la Academia de Jurisprudencia y Legislación.

Septién, Rafael ◆ n. en el DF (1954). A los 15 años fue campeón nacional de atletismo. Viajó a Estados Unidos, donde se enlistó en el equipo de futbol americano *Vaqueros* de Dallas, con el cual estableció en la década de los ochenta las marcas de más goles de campo en nueve

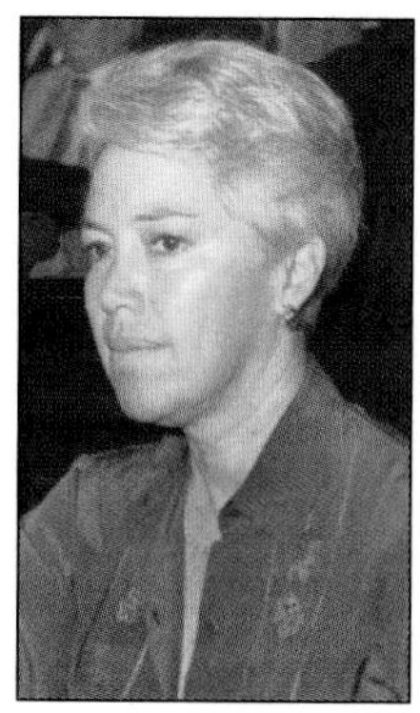

Yolanda Sentíes

Fondo Histórico Alfonso Sánchez García

Octavio Sentíes Gómez

Bernardo Sepúlveda Amor

Foto: Archivo General de la Nación

Guillermo *el Tigre* Sepúlveda

Escudo de la Escuela de Periodismo Carlos Septién García

años seguidos, más puntos extra y más distinciones en la historia de ese deporte para un mexicano. Después jugó con *Broncos* de Denver y *Raiders* de Los Ángeles.

Septién García, Carlos ◆ n. en Querétaro, Qro., y m. en la sierra Mamulique, NL (1915-1953). Destacó como deportista en su juventud. Licenciado en derecho por la UNAM (1940). Fundó dos periódicos estudiantiles: *El Chinto* (1927) y *El Escolapio* (1930) y en Querétaro editó las revistas *Provincia* y *Portal* y colaboró en *El Heraldo de Navidad*. Cofundador del PAN (1940) y fundador de su órgano, *La Nación* (1941). Fue candidato a diputado (1943 y 94). Desde 1944 escribió en *El Universal* crónicas taurinas con el pseudónimo de *Tío Carlos*, además de fundar el suplemento cultural de ese diario: *Revista de la Semana*. Dirigió la escuela de periodismo que lleva su nombre. Murió en un accidente de aviación cuando se dirigía a cubrir la información del encuentro entre los presidentes Ruiz Cortines y Eisenhower.

Carlos Septién García

Sepúlveda, Guillermo *el Tigre* ◆ n. en Guadalajara (1935). Futbolista. Participó en más de 500 juegos con las *Chivas* del Guadalajara y el Nuevo León en más de 20 años de jugador profesional. Fue campeón de Copa (62-63), de Liga (56-57, 58-59, 60-61, 61-62, 63-64 y 64-65), campeón de campeones (56-57, 58-59, 59-60, 60-61, 63-64 y 64-65), de Concacaf (1962 y 1963), seleccionado nacional en tres eliminatorias y el mundial de Chile 62. Ingresó a las *Chivas* en 1952 y permaneció ahí hasta 1966. En Nuevo León estuvo de 1966 a 1969. Su último equipo fue el Oro (1969-70).

Sepúlveda Amor, Bernardo ◆ n. en el DF (1941). Licenciado en derecho por la UNAM (1964) y maestro en derecho internacional por la Universidad de Cambridge (1966). Miembro del PRI, en el que fue secretario de asuntos internacionales del CEN (1981-82). Cofundador del Centro de Estudios sobre Estados Unidos del CIDE, profesor de El Colegio de México y director del seminario Problemas Jurídicos Internacionales de la Facultad de Ciencias Políticas de la UNAM (1971-75). En la Secretaría de Hacienda fue subdirector general de Asuntos Jurídicos de la Secretaría de Hacienda (1968-70), asesor (1971-75) y director general de Asuntos Internacionales (1976-81). Ha sido asesor para asuntos internacionales en la SPP (1981), embajador en Estados Unidos (1982), secretario de Relaciones Exteriores en el gobierno de Miguel de la Madrid (1982-88), y embajador en Gran Bretaña (1988-). Coautor de *La ONU: dilema de los veinticinco años* (1970). Autor de *La inversión extranjera en México* (1973) y *Las empresas transnacionales en México* (1974). Miembro del Instituto Hispano-Luso-Americano de Derecho Internacional. *Doctor honoris causa* por la Universidad de San Diego (1982). Director del Bufete Jurídico Sepúlveda y Asociados.

Sepúlveda Amor, Fernando ◆ n. en el DF (1940). Hermano del anterior. Se tituló como arquitecto en la UNAM (1962). Tomó cursos de planeación urbana en la Universidad Técnica de Sczcecin, Polonia (1966); de planeación de nuevas ciudades en el Consejo Británico (1966) y de urbanismo en el Ministerio de la Construcción de Francia (1967). Consejero técnico (1960-62) y profesor (1965-71) de la Escuela Nacional de Arquitectura de la UNAM. Desde 1963 es miembro del PRI. En el IMSS ha sido técnico en investigación de vivienda (1962), director de proyecto y construcción de hospitales en Chihuahua y Durango (1963-64) y director del proyecto sobre regeneración de vivienda (1964). Jefe de proyectos (1965-70), secretario técnico del grupo de trabajo de la vivienda de interés social (1967-68), asesor de la Dirección de Inversiones Públicas y secretario técnico de la Comisión del Área Metropolitana del Valle de México de la Presidencia de la República (1970-71). Director general de Planeación de la SSA (1972-77), secretario técnico de la Comisión de Conurbación del Centro del País de la SAHOP (1977-83) y director general de Planeación del Desarrollo del DDF (1983-85).

Sepúlveda Amor, Jaime ◆ n. en el DF (1954). Hermano de los anteriores. Se tituló como médico cirujano en la UNAM (1978). Es maestro en salud pública y medicina tropical (1981) y doctor en ciencias de la población por la Universidad de Harvard (1985). Ha sido profesor (1976), jefe de Laboratorios de Enseñanza de Fisiología (1977) y coordinador de investigación del Centro de Estudios en Atención Primaria a la Salud de la UNAM (1982-84 y 1983-85). Investigador en el Centro Médico Nacional (1977-78), jefe del Departamento de Estadísticas Vitales de la SPP (1978-79), coordinador adjunto de los Institutos Nacionales de Salud (1983-85) director general de Epidemiología (1985-91) y subsecretario de Organización y Desarrollo de la SSA (1991-). Miembro de la American Public Health Association. Fue vicepresidente de la Asociación Mexicana de Epidemiólogos (1986-87).

Sepúlveda Gutiérrez, Bernardo ◆ n. en Monterrey, NL, y m. en Cuernavaca, Mor. (1912-1985). Padre de los anteriores. Se tituló de médico cirujano en la UNAM (1935). Se especializó en gastroenterología y medicina experimental en la Clínica Mayo de Rochester y en universidades de Europa. Fue profesor, jefe de la División de Estudios

Superiores de la Facultad de Medicina (1958-67) y miembro de la Junta de Gobierno de la UNAM (1964-66). Cofundador del Instituto Nacional de la Nutrición y del Centro Médico Nacional. Médico del Hospital General de México (1935-46), jefe del departamento de Gastroenterología del Hospital del Enfermedades de la Nutrición (1946-62), asesor en investigación científica en el Hospital General del Centro Médico Nacional, jefe del Departamento de Planeación Técnica de los Servicios Médicos del IMSS, coordinador del Centro de Estudios sobre Amibiasis y secretario del Consejo de Salubridad General (1977-85) y vocal del Sistema Nacional de Investigadores (1984-85). Premio Nacional de Ciencias (1982) y *doctor honoris causa* por la UANL (1982). Miembro de El Colegio Nacional. Fue presidente de la Academia Nacional de Medicina (1957-58).

SEPÚLVEDA GUTIÉRREZ, CÉSAR ◆ n. y m. en el DF (1916-1994). Licenciado en derecho y maestro en historia por la UNAM, donde fue profesor (1943-66), director general de Servicios Escolares (1946), secretario de la Escuela Nacional Preparatoria (1947-48), director del Instituto de Derecho Comparado (1961) y director de la Facultad de Derecho (1962-66). Miembro del PRI. Fue asesor jurídico de la SRE (1946-50), director general de la propiedad industrial de la Secretaría de Economía (1950-59), profesor en El Colegio de México (1962), asesor del Consejo Nacional Técnico de la Educación (1971), director del Instituto Mexicano Matías Romero (1973-77), director del Centro Interamericano de Estudios de Seguridad Social del IMSS (1977-78), embajador en la RFA hasta 1987 y miembro de la Comisión de Derecho Internacional de la ONU hasta 1987. Autor de *La teoría y la práctica de reconocimiento de gobiernos* (1954), *El sistema mexicano de la propiedad industrial* (1955), *La frontera norte de México. Historia, conflictos* (1957), *Historia y problemas de los límites de México* (1958), *El sistema interamericano. Génesis, integración y decadencia* (1974), *México y el Club de Roma* (1974), *Las fuentes del derecho internacional americano* (1975), *Terminología usual en las relaciones internacionales* (1976), *Tres ensayos sobre la frontera septentrional de la Nueva España* (1977), *Curso de derecho internacional público* (1977), *El derecho internacional público* (1981) y *El sistema mexicano de la propiedad industrial* (1981), entre otras obras. Fundador de la Academia Mexicana de Derechos Humanos.

SEPÚLVEDA RUIZ VELASCO, JOSÉ TRINIDAD ◆ n. en Atotonilco el Alto, Jal. (1921). Sacerdote ordenado en 1948. Ha sido vicario cooperador de la parroquia de Talpa, prefecto de disciplina y profesor del Seminario de Guadalajara y obispo de Tuxtla Gutiérrez (1965-).

SERDÁN, AQUILES ◆ n. y m. en Puebla, Pue. (1876-1910). Abandonó los estudios para dedicarse al comercio, actividad que lo llevó a relacionarse con los obreros textiles de Puebla y Tlaxcala. Su militancia política se inició en 1908, en la revista *Partido Nacional Democrático*. Afiliado al Partido Nacional Antirreeleccionista desde 1909, realizó en la ciudad de Puebla una campaña de proselitismo en favor de Francisco I. Madero, fundó el periódico *No-reelección* y el club Luz y Progreso (ambos clandestinos), presidió la organización partidaria en Puebla y fue delegado a la Convención Nacional de 1910. Luego del fraude electoral de ese año huyó a Estados Unidos con su hermana, Carmen Serdán, y ambos se reunieron con Madero, quien les encomendó la organización de la lucha armada en Puebla. El 18 de noviembre de 1910, dos días antes del inicio de la revolución maderista, cuando la policía intentó allanar la casa de los Serdán, éstos y otros antiporfiristas lo impidieron. Por órdenes del gobernador poblano, Mucio P. Martínez, el inmueble fue sitiado por unos cien policías y más de mil soldados y rurales. La defensa de la casa se mantuvo hasta el día siguiente, cuando Aquiles Serdán fue sorprendido al salir por la puerta falsa de un sótano y acribillado.

Aquiles Serdán

SERDÁN, CARMEN ◆ n. y m. en Puebla, Pue. (1875-1948). Hermana del anterior. Adherida al antirreeleccionismo, colaboró en el periódico clandestino *No-reelección*, con el pseudónimo de Marcos Serrato. En 1910 acompañó a su hermano Aquiles a Estados Unidos. El 18 de noviembre de 1910 se encontró sitiada en su casa de Puebla e intervino en la defensa de la misma, acción en la que resultó herida. Fue aprehendida, junto con su cuñada, Filomena del Valle, y su madre, Carmen Alatriste; las tres fueron remitidas a la cárcel de La Merced y más tarde recluidas en el hospital municipal de San Pedro. Después del golpe de Estado de Victoriano Huerta participó en la revolución, mediante la Junta Revolucionaria en Puebla, y se incorporó como enfermera de las fuerzas combatientes. Al triunfo del constitucionalismo se retiró a la vida privada.

SERDÁN ÁLVAREZ, MARÍA ISABEL ◆ n. en Puebla, Pue. (1948). Química farmacobióloga por la Universidad Autónoma de Puebla (1970). Tomó un curso de manejo administrativo en Inglaterra (1972). Pertenece al PRI. Fue secretaria general de la Anfer en Puebla (1981-82) y secretaria femenil del CEN de la CNOP. Se desempeñó como secretaria de Acción Social de la Comisión del Río Grijalva. Ha sido profesora de la UAP, trabajadora del IMSS y diputada federal (1982-85). Autora de una *Biografía de Carmen Serdán*. Pertenece al Inter-

Bernardo Sepúlveda Gutiérrez

Carmen Serdán

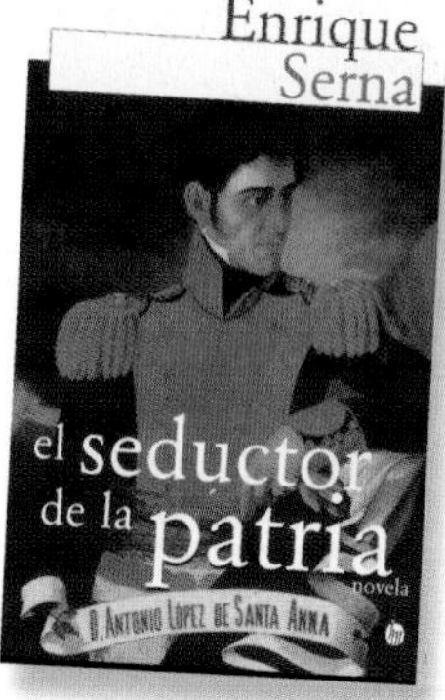

Novela de Enrique Serna

Familia de jornaleros seris de Sonora

Foto: Lourdes Almeida

national Language Center, de Inglaterra, y a la Asociación de Mujeres Universitarias.

SERIS ◆ Indios del grupo nómada más importante y numeroso de la época prehispánica en el noroeste del actual territorio mexicano y el suroeste de lo que hoy es Estados Unidos: ocupaba el territorio norte de Sonora, el norte de Baja California y gran parte del sur de Arizona. En la actualidad está convertido en un pueblo semisedentario, confinado en la isla Tiburón, que por decreto federal de 1975 tiene en posesión comunal, y en una pequeña franja desértica de la costa sonorense. La etnia seri pertenece a la familia lingüística jocameridional, tronco yumapacua, misma en la que se inscribían las etnias cocopas y cochimíes, ya extinguidas. Es, además, la única etnia de la región que no está emparentada con los pimas u ópatas-pimas. En 1938 se registró a 100 hablantes de seri, 450 en 1980 y 577 en 1987. De acuerdo con el Conteo Nacional de Población de 1995 había 482 hablantes de seri. Las familias nucleares o extensas son las unidades básicas de su sociedad. Hasta hace algunos años, los padres del novio solían hacer los arreglos para el matrimonio, entre los que estaban el pago de la novia, pues el padre de ella recibía diversos objetos y alimentos. Había ceremonias cuando las mujeres llegaban a la adolescencia, con una fiesta de iniciación, después de la cual eran consideradas adultas. En ocasión de la muerte, después del entierro tenía lugar un intercambio de objetos entre la familia del difunto y el especialista que había dirigido el ritual funerario. Con el sedentarismo y su incorporación a la economía de mercado, la mayor parte de estas costumbres se ha perdido, en tanto que ha adoptado patrones sociales que los identifican cada vez más con la población mestiza. La antigua religión seri era animista. Durante el siglo XVIII los misioneros católicos intentaron cristianizarlos, pero sus esfuerzos resultaron infructuosos. Más éxito han tenido algunos grupos protestantes, que han ganado adeptos entre ellos, si bien continúan realizando ceremonias asociadas con la fertilidad y para que los elementos naturales, principalmente el mar y el viento, les sean favorables. No tienen una organización sociopolítica tradicional, debido a sus antiguos patrones nómadas, pero el Consejo Supremo Seri y los encargados de la Cooperativa Pesquera poseen autoridad para resolver sus problemas. Antes de su sometimiento, los seris se calificaban como "los más bellos, los más fuertes, los más nobles, los más ágiles y los más valientes del mundo". En su concepto eran casi semidioses. Al igual que los tarahumaras, atrapaban las piezas de caza mayor después de haberlas cansado corriendo tras ellas. Se cree que el primer europeo que entró en contacto con los seris fue el fraile italiano Marcos de Niza, quien en 1539 exploró algunas regiones de Sonora. Un año después el explorador español Rodrigo Maldonado encontró en aquella región a un "indio gigante" (los seris eran de gran estatura). Desde entonces hubo numerosas expediciones en la nación seri, mismas que fueron rechazadas. Durante el virreinato, los seris, aún libres, efectuaron repetidos ataques contra las misiones y expediciones militares que invadían su territorio. Se calcula que en 1600 existían unos 5,000 seris. En 1677 la Compañía de Jesús se propuso someterlos al cristianismo, por lo que fundó Santa María del Pópulo y más tarde San Pedro de la Conquista o Pueblo de Seris, próximo a Hermosillo. No obstante, fueron pocos los que se acogieron a las costumbres cristianas. En 1749 el gobernador sonorense Diego Ortiz Parilla intentó nuevamente someterlos y envió una fuerza militar que, entre otras cosas, capturó a 80 familias indígenas y las deportó a Guatemala. Este hecho desencadenó una guerra prolongada, en la que los seris, los pimas y los apaches hicieron causa común contra los agresores. Las campañas militares para someterlos se iniciaron en el siglo XVI y se prolongaron hasta principios del XX, cuando la población seri, mermada, debió refugiarse en la zona que ahora habita. En 1930 iniciaron una vida relativamente sedentaria, pues debieron abandonar la caza, impracticable en la isla Tiburón, y se dedicaron a la pesca y la elaboración de artesanías, en especial las esculturas de palofierro, apreciadas internacionalmente, las que en 1987 les hicieron merecer el Premio Nacional de Artes y Tradiciones Populares. En 1974 lograron fincar tres poblados de importancia en la costa: Desemboque, Punta Chueca y Quino-Viga, gracias al programa Acción Indigenista. En 1987, el gobernador tradicional de la tribu, Enrique Romero Blanco, denunció que sus terrenos ejidales habían sido invadidos por los ganaderos sonorenses y que la empresa Televisa instaló un coto de caza privado en tierras de su comunidad, a cambio de un receptor de televisión y una antena parabólica.

SERNA, ENRIQUE ◆ n. en el DF (1959). Escritor. Licenciado en letras hispánicas por la UNAM. Ha colaborado en *Sábado*, suplemento del periódico *unomásuno* (1987-92), *La Jornada Semanal*, suplemento del periódico *La Jornada* y la revista *Letras Libres*. Coautor, con Carlos Olmos, del argumento de las telenovelas *Tal como somos*, *En carne propia* y *La sombra del otro*, producidas por Televisa. Fue coordinador de la colección de biografías de ídolos populares de la editorial Clío (1992-95). Autor de novela: *El ocaso de la primera dama* (1987, Premio Novela de Campeche 1986), *Uno soñaba que era rey* (1989), *El miedo a los animales* (1995) y *El seductor de la patria* (1999); cuento: *Amores de segunda mano* (1991); y ensayo: *Las caricaturas me hacen llorar* (1996).

SERNA, FRANCISCO ◆ n. en La Ciénega y m. en Hermosillo, Son. (1832-1895). Minero. Luchó contra la intervención francesa y el imperio. En 1865 participó en la toma de Hermosillo, donde fue dos veces prefecto y alcalde. En 1875 combatió al gobernador Pesqueira, al que acusó de fraude electoral. Fue vicegobernador (1877), gobernador sustituto (1877) y constitucional de Sonora (1878 y 1880).

SERNA, JACINTO DE LA ◆ n. y m. en la ciudad de México (¿1601?-1681). Estudió en la Real y Pontificia Universidad de México, de la que fue rector en tres ocasiones (1642,1642-43 y 1650-51). Cura de Jalatlaco y tres veces de la Catedral Metropolitana, Autor de un *Manual de ministros de indios, para el conocimiento de sus idolatrías y extirpación de ellas* (1892).

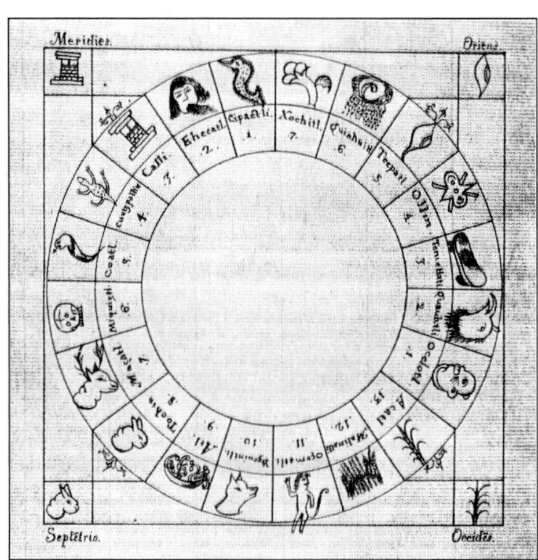

Una página del *Manual de ministros*, de Jacinto de la Serna

SERNA MARTÍNEZ, CLEMENTE ◆ n. en Monterrey y m. en el DF (1908-1998). Empresario. Trabajó en Oklahoma como peón ferrocarrilero y en Indiana como minero. Fue secretario de conflictos del Sindicato Ferrocarrilero. Inició sus actividades empresariales en el departamento de ventas de la emisora XEH de Monterrey (1930). Fue gerente de la XET (1933) y volvió a la XEH a petición de Emilio Azcárraga. Fue secretario del centro patronal de Tampico (1937), propietario de la XES (1937), impulsor de la Asociación Mexicana de Estaciones Radiodifusoras (1937), fundador de Radioprogramas de México (1941) donde lanzó la primera radionovela, *Anita de Montemar*, y el programa *La tremenda corte;* presidente de la Asociación Nacional de la Publicidad (1944), creador de la Cadena Azul (1948), director de la Confederación de Cámaras Nacionales de Comercio (1948-54), presidente del Club Ejecutivo de México (1954), presidente del Club Rotario de la ciudad de México, consejero de la Concamin, presidente del Comité México-Americano de Hombres de Negocios (1954), presidente de Ejecutivos de Ventas de México, fundador del Sistema Mexicano de la Radio, Vocero Mexicano, Arte Radiofónico de México, Canal 6 de Tijuana y otros medios más. En 1994 creó Medcom-Infored (con la adquisición del Grupo Red), manejadora del Canal 6 de Guadalajara, los noticieros de radio *Monitor*, el Grupo Editorial Expansión y la cadena estadounidense CBS-Noticias, entre otros.

SERRA, JUNÍPERO ◆ n. en España y m. en San Carlos de Monterrey, hoy Monterey, EUA (1713-1784). Franciscano. Tomó los hábitos en 1730. Llegó a la Nueva España en 1749, como misionero de las diócesis de México, Puebla, Oaxaca, Valladolid (hoy Morelia) y Guadalajara. En 1767 (luego de la expulsión de los jesuitas de la Nueva España) el virrey Carlos Francisco de Croix lo envió a la Alta California, donde fundó las misiones de San Fernando y San Diego (1769), San Carlos de Monterrey (1770), San Antonio de Padua y San Gabriel (1771), San Luis Obispo (1772), San Francisco de Asís y San Juan Capistrano (1776), Santa Clara (1777) y San Buenaventura (1782).

Junípero Serra

SERRA PUCHE, JAIME JOSÉ ◆ n. en el DF (1951). Licenciado en ciencias políticas por la UNAM (1973), maestro en economía por El Colegio de México (1975) y doctor en economía por la Universidad de Yale (1979). Profesor de la Universidad de Stanford (1982); profesor e investigador (1979-86), director interino (1981-82), director del Centro de Estudios Económicos (1983-86) y miembro del consejo editorial de la revista *Estudios Económicos* de El Colegio de México. Miembro del PRI desde 1978. A partir de 1972 trabajó en el sector público, en el que fue subsecretario de Ingresos de la Secretaría de Hacienda (1986-88); consejero de asuntos económicos del presidente electo (1988), secretario de Comercio y Fomento Industrial (1988-94) en el gabinete de Carlos Salinas de Gortari y secretario de Hacienda (del 1 al 29 de diciembre de 1994) del presidente Ernesto Zedillo. Ha sido presidente del Consejo de Administración de Banca Confía, consejero propietario del Infonavit, de los sistemas de Transporte Colectivo-Metro y de Transportes Eléctricos del DF, de ASA, Conafrut y de Caminos y Puentes Federales. Miembro del consejo editorial de *El Trimestre Económico* (1986). Autor de *Causas y efectos de la crisis en México* y *Políticas fiscales en México: un enfoque de equilibrio general* (1981). Premio Nacional de Economía Banamex (1979) y Premio Nacional de Ciencias Sociales de la Academia de la Investigación Científica (1986).

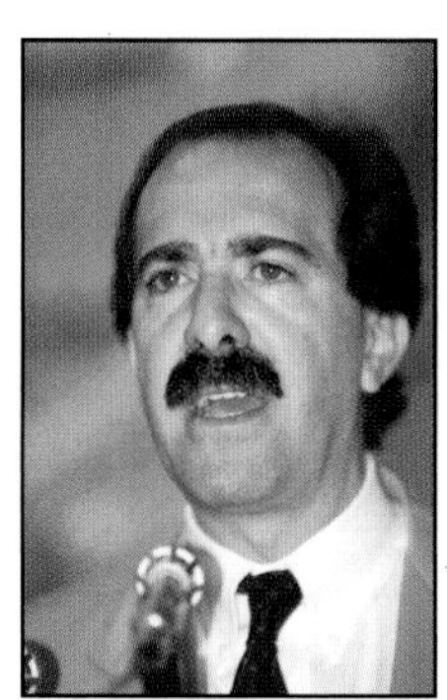
Jaime José Serra Puche

SERRA ROJAS, ANDRÉS ◆ n. en Pichucalco, Chis. (1904). Doctor en derecho. Profesor de la UNAM (1928-) y del IPN. Fue agente del Ministerio Público, diputado federal, senador, director general de Bienes Nacionales, jefe del Departamento Consultivo y Nacionalización de Bienes de la Procuraduría General de la República, representante de México ante la Conferencia de San Francisco, secretario del Trabajo (del 1 de diciembre de 1946 al 12 de enero de 1948) en el gabinete de Miguel Alemán y director del Banco Nacional Cinematográfico. Autor de *Derecho administrativo* (2 t.), *Ciencia política, Derecho económico* y una *Antología de la elocuencia mexicana* (1950). Maestro emérito y *doctor honoris causa* por la UNAM.

Andrés Serra Rojas

Foto: Eunice H. Chao

El arquitecto Francisco Serrano

Serradell, Narciso ◆ n. en Alvarado, Ver., y m. en la ciudad de México (1843-1910). Ingresó en el Seminario, presionado por su familia, pero escapó para estudiar música y medicina. Luchó contra la intervención francesa en las fuerzas de Ignacio Zaragoza. A la caída de Puebla (1863), fue aprehendido y deportado a Francia, país en el que concluyó la carrera de medicina. Volvió a México en 1865 y ejerció su profesión en Veracruz, donde organizó bandas de música y compuso danzas, polkas y mazurcas. En 1885 pasó a la ciudad de México para dedicarse a la docencia. En 1862 Serradell puso música a ciertos versos del poeta español Francisco Martínez de la Rosa, para crear la canción *La golondrina*, que él y otros prisioneros mexicanos cantaban en la prisión de Clermont-Ferrand. Con el nombre transformado en *Las golondrinas*, en México se interpreta desde entonces en ocasión de las despedidas.

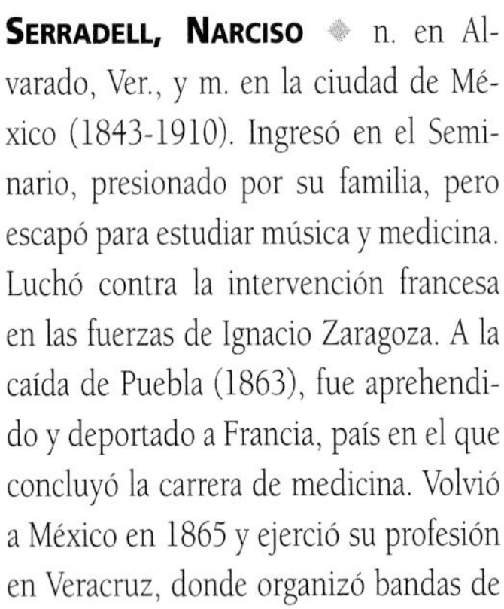

Foto: Archivo de Dirección Arquitectura INBA

Cine Encanto en el DF, edificio de Francisco Serrano

Serrano, Antonio ◆ n. en el DF (1948). Dramaturgo y director. Hizo estudios en la Real Academia Webber de Artes Dramáticas en Londres, Inglaterra, y en talleres con Eugenio Barba, Carlo Bosso y Philippe Gaullier. Además de una larga carrera como director de telenovelas, ha escrito y dirigido las obras teatrales *A destiempo, Doble cara* (1988), *Sexo, pudor y lágrimas* (1991) y *Café americano* (1995), y ha dirigido *Moliére* (1999) de Sabina Berman. Escribió y dirigió la adaptación cinematográfica de *Sexo, pudor y lágrimas*, estrenada en 1999.

Serrano, Francisco ◆ n. y m. en el DF (1900-1982). Arquitecto. En sus inicios trabajó dentro del *art decó* y el llamado estilo orgánico. Luego cultivó el estilo *barco* o *naval* en los 30 y 40 y más tarde el "modernista racional internacional" (funcionalista) y el "nacionalista". Entre 1930 y 1950 proyectó y edificó en la ciudad de México edificios de departamentos en la colonia Hipódromo Condesa y en Polanco, el Pasaje Polanco (en Julio Verne, Masaryk y Galileo); el edificio Sevilla, en Emilio Castelar y Galileo (1940); el edificio de Insurgentes y Quintana Roo (1940); el Basurto, en avenida México (1942) el edificio Jardín, de Sindicalismo y Martí; el Anáhuac, en Querétaro 109; y los casi gemelos de la glorieta de Chilpancingo, entre otros.

Serrano, Francisco ◆ n. en el DF (1949). Estudió ciencias políticas, filosofía y cine en la UNAM; guión cinematográfico en Nueva York y La Habana, y literatura francesa en París. Ha sido coordinador de una colección editorial de la SEP, director de Relaciones Internacionales del INBA (1983-85), subdirector editorial y director de *México en el Arte* (1986) y coordinador de asesores del CNCA (1991-). Ha colaborado en publicaciones literarias. Escribió los guiones cinematográficos *Sistema* (1971), *La otredad* (1972), *Tierra que arde* (1976, coautor) y *Relación de los hechos* (1977, coautor). Autor de cuento infantil: *Los vampiritos y el profesor* (1986) y *La loquita frente al mar* (1990); poesía: *Canciones egipcias* (1979), *Incubaciones* (1980), *Fin de mundo* (1980), *Poema del fino amor* (1981), *El cubo de los cambios* (1981), *Libro de hexaedros* (1982), *Alicuanta* (1984), *No es sino el azar* (1984), *Ángeles de llama y hielo* (1991), *Casas en el aire* (1991), *La rosa de Ariadna* (1992), *Tierra volando* (1992) y *Confianza en la materia* (1997); y antología: *La luciérnaga: poesía mexicana para niños* (1983), *La rosa de los vientos* (1992), *Los vampiritos y el profesor* (literatura infantil, 1986) y *24 poetas latinoamericanos*. Becario del Centro Mexicano de Escritores (1973-74) y del Museo de Arte Moderno de Nueva York (1977).

Serrano, Francisco R. ◆ n. en Quilá, Sin., y m. en Huitzilac, Mor. (1889-1927). Abuelo del anterior. Antirreeleccionista, en 1910 se unió a la insurrección maderista en las filas de Benjamín Hill. Fue secretario particular del gobernador Jósé María Maytorena (1912-13) y se incorporó a las fuerzas de Álvaro Obregón (1914), de quien fue jefe de Estado Mayor (1915). Combatió a los ejércitos de la Convención, en la que había participado con la representación de Miguel L. Cornejo. Alcanzó el grado de general de división. Diputado federal (1918), se unió al aguaprietismo en 1920. Subsecretario (1920-21) y secretario de Guerra y Marina (del 2 de diciembre de 1921 al 30 de noviembre de 1924) en el gabinete de Obregón y gobernador del DF (1926-27). Inició una campaña antirreeleccionista contra Obregón (1927). Luego del triunfo electoral de éste trató de iniciar un levantamiento armado, pero fue detenido y, sin jucio previo, fusilado junto con sus colaboradores en Huitzilac.

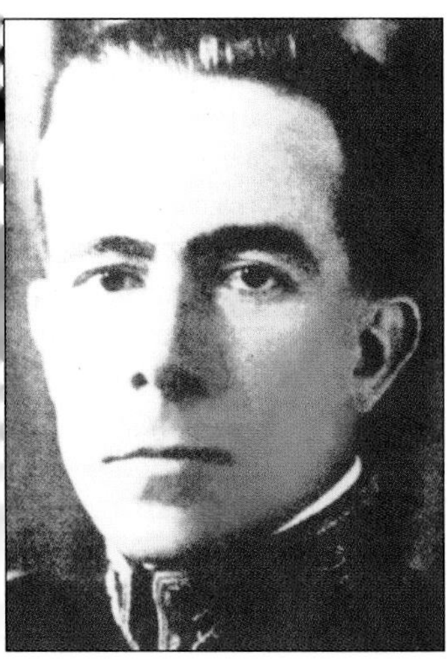
El general Francisco R. Serrano

SERRANO, GUSTAVO P. ◆ n. en Altar, Son., y m. en el DF (1887-1970). Licenciado en derecho. Fue diputado federal por Sonora (1920), secretario (1922) y presidente (1923) de la sección mexicana de la Comisión Internacional de Límites, secretario de Comunicaciones y Obras Públicas (del 21 de octubre de 1931 al 20 de enero de 1932) en el gabinete de Pascual Ortiz Rubio, director de la Comisión Nacional de Irrigación (1939), presidente de la Cámara Nacional de la Industria Extractiva (1940), secretario de Economía Nacional (del 1 de julio de 1944 al 30 de noviembre de 1946), durante el gobierno de Manuel Ávila Camacho, y miembro del Consejo Administrativo de la Comisión Federal de Electricidad (1951). Formó parte de la Comisión de Aguas México-Estados Unidos y fue embajador en Guatemala. Autor de *La minería y su influencia en el progreso y desarrollo de México*.

SERRANO, JOSÉ LUIS ◆ n. en Guadalajara Jal. (1947). Pintor. Estudió en La Esmeralda (1963-68). Fue profesor de pintura y dibujo en dicha institución. Ha expuesto individualmente 40 veces y ha participado en más de 100 muestras colectivas en México y el extranjero. En 1970 montó su primera exposición individual. En 1988 pasó a ser artista estable de las galerías Ana Quijano, México-Cancún. En 1989 exhibió en la galería Misrachi del DF. Alfonso de Neuvillate realizó un libro sobre su obra.

SERRANO CABRERA, MANUEL ◆ n. en Pachuca, Hgo. (1939). Pintor. Estudió en La Esmeralda, de 1955 a 1960. En 1961 participó en exposición de pintores del siglo XX en Bellas Artes. Desde 1962 se integró al Grupo Tlahmachcalli, con el cual expuso en los años siguientes en varias salas y galerías del país. Su obra se expuso en el Salón de la Plástica Mexicana, la OPIC y el Museo de Arte Moderno (1965). Fue restaurador del INAH (1963-64).

SERRANO CACHO, JUAN FRANCISCO ◆ n. en el DF (1937). Arquitecto. Hijo del también arquitecto Francisco Serrano. Estudió en la UIA (1960), donde fue profesor. Entre 1955 y 1960 colaboró con Augusto H. Álvarez y Juan Sordo Madaleno. Autor de un edificio en las calles de Nuevo León y Laredo (1960), la sede del Comité Olímpico Mexicano en Reforma 64 (1968) y otro en Insurgentes Sur 1552 (1977). Colaboró con Teodoro González y con Abraham Zabludovsky. Es coautor del Centro de Cómputo y Sala Bancaria de Nafinsa (1984-86), del parque Tomás Garrido Canabal de Villahermosa (1984-86) y del Centro Minero Nacional de Pachuca (1987-88). Trabajó en la firma de su padre, la empresa Serrano, Serrano y Nava Arquitectos entre 1960 y 1982. Diseñó la nueva UIA (1983-88, medalla de plata de la quinta Bienal de Arquitectura de Bulgaria en 1989).

SERRANO CASTRO, IRMA CONSUELO ◆ n. en Comitán, Chis. (1945). Cantante, actriz y política apodada *la Tigresa*. Estudió filosofía y letras y un posgrado en leyes en la UNAM. Trabajó en más de 25 películas, como *Santo contra los zombies* (1961), *El extra* (1962), *La conquista de El Dorado* (1965), *Los gavilanes negros* (1965), *Los amores de Juan Charrasqueado* (1967), *El caudillo* (1967), *La Martina (la mujer del sacristán)* (1971), *El monasterio de los buitres* (1972), *La Tigresa* (1972), *Noches de cabaret* (1977), *Las amantes del señor de la noche* (1983) y *Juana la cubana* (1992). Coautora de *A calzón amarrado* (1980). Senadora de la República por el PRD (1994-2000).

Irma Serrano

SERRANO DAZA, MIGUEL ◆ n. y m. en Puebla, Pue. (1842-1916). Licenciado en derecho por la Universidad de San Nicolás de Hidalgo. Fue secretario general de gobierno y secretario de Fomento en Puebla, durante los gobiernos liberales de Juan Crisóstomo Bonilla y Juan N. Méndez. Profesor y director del Colegio de Puebla (1884), profesor de la Escuela Normal de Puebla y diputado

FOTO: EUNICE H. CHAO

Juan Francisco Serrano Cacho

FOTO: FONDO EDITORIAL GRUPO AZABACHE

Parque Tomás Garrido Canabal de Villahermosa, obra de Teodoro González de León, Juan Francisco Serrano Cacho y Aurelio Nuño federal por ese estado. Junto con Ignacio Manuel Altamirano, Joaquín Miranda y Enrique Laubscher fundó la Escuela Nacional de Maestros, de la que fue el primer director (1887-1901). Participó en la comisión reorganizadora de la Escuela Nacional Preparatoria (1896) y en los congresos pedagógicos de 1889 y 1891. Desde 1912 dirigió la Escuela Normal de Puebla.

Serrano Limón, Jorge ◆ n. en el DF (1953). Estudió administración de empresas. Es corredor de bienes raíces. Imparte cursos de formación católica sobre noviazgo, sexo, familia y matrimonio. Desde 1987 es presidente del Comité Nacional Pro Vida (☛).

Serrano Migallón, Fernando ◆ n. en el DF (1945). Licenciado en derecho (1970) y en economía por la UNAM (1971) con estudios de posgrado en el Instituto Internacional de Administración Pública de París (1972) y la Academia de Derechos Internacionales de la Corte de La Haya (1972). Ha hecho estudios de doctorado en historia en la UNAM (1993), donde es profesor desde 1971. Catedrático de El Colegio de México (1982-). Ha sido gerente general comercial de Aeropuertos y Servicios Auxiliares (1976-79), director general de Análisis de la SAHOP (1979-82), coordinador de asesores del jefe del DDF (1986-88), director general de Asuntos Jurídicos de la Secofi (1989-93), abogado general de la UNAM (1993-95), director general del Derecho de Autor y del Instituto Nacional del Derecho de Autor (1995-). Ha colaborado en *Excélsior*, *Reforma* y otras publicaciones. Autor de *La descentralización regional. La región Languedoc Rousillón* (1972), *El particular frente a la administración* (1977), *El Grito de Independencia* (1981), *Isidro Fabela y la democracia mexicana* (1981), *La bandera de México* (1985), *Toma de posesión. El rito del poder* (1988), *El Sinaia* (1989), *Legislación electoral mexicana, génesis e integración* (1991), *La propiedad industrial en México* (1992), *Desarrollo electoral mexicano* (1995), *Nueva Ley Federal del Derecho de Autor* (1998) y *El asilo político en México* (1998), entre otras obras.

Serrano Rodríguez, Ambrosio ◆ n. en Atempan y m. en Puebla, Pue. (1818-1875). En 1863 se le designó primer obispo de Chilapa, Guerrero, y tomó posesión en 1866. Fue uno de los siete representantes mexicanos en el primer Concilio Vaticano (1869-70). Estuvo entre los firmantes de la carta pastoral de bienvenida a Maximiliano, en la que se calificaba la invasión francesa y el establecimiento del imperio como "bienes de la Providencia divina" y, por tanto, se exhortaba a los católicos a respetar y cumplir sus deberes "con la sociedad y el Gobierno" del austriaco, así como a dar "benevolencia y amor al ciudadano y al extranjero".

Serratos, Enrique ◆ n. en Guadalajara, Jal., y m. en el DF (1929-1960). Músico, hijo de los pianistas Ramón Serratos y Aurora Garibay. Estudió violín con Sandor Roth y José Simlovitz. Obtuvo una beca y perfeccionó sus conocimientos en el Instituto Curtis de Música, de Filadelfia, con Iván Golamin (1954). Se integró al Cuarteto de Cuerdas Curtis, dio clases en la Nueva Escuela de Música de Filadelfia y en la Escuela de Música de Wilmington. Regresó a México y fue profesor en el Conservatorio Nacional.

Serratos, Ramón ◆ n. en Compostela, Nay., y m. en el DF (1895-1973). Padre del anterior. Estudió piano en Guadalajara, con José Rolón. En 1915 el gobierno de Jalisco le expidió el título, sin precedente, de pianista. En 1919 fundó su propia academia musical. Se especializó con Josef Levine (1921-27), dirigió la Facultad de Música de la UNAM (1938-40) y fue profesor de investigación pianística de la misma (1940-60).

Serratos Amador, Alfredo ◆ n. y m. en el DF (1870-1955). Militó en el Partido Liberal al lado de los hermanos Flores Magón y Antonio Díaz Soto y Gama. En 1910 participó en la insurrección maderista como jefe de un regimiento de caballería. Fue uno de los más cercanos colaboradores de Emiliano Zapata y su representante en la Convención de Aguascalientes. Se encargó de concertar la reunión de Xochimilco entre el caudillo suriano y Francisco Villa (1914). Oficial mayor y titular de la Secretaría de Guerra y Marina (del 16 de enero al 27 de marzo de 1915) en el gobierno convencionista de Roque González Garza, cónsul de México en varias ciudades de Estados Unidos, jefe de la Policía Federal de Caminos y del Departamento de Caza y Pesca. Miembro de la Legión de Honor del Ejército Mexicano.

Servín Murrieta, Acela ◆ n. en Totutla, Ver. (1932). Maestra normalista por la Escuela Normal Veracruzana Enrique C. Rébsamen, donde fue profesora (1965-90). Pertenece al PRI desde 1952. Ha sido alfabetizadora en hospitales y profesora de primaria y secundaria (1952-65). Pertenece al SNTE (1961-) y al Sindicato Estatal de Trabajadores al Servicio de la Educación (fundadora; 1962-), en los cuales ha tenido cargos directivos. Integrante del Consejo Administrativo del Seguro Social de los Trabajadores de la Educación (1977-80) y del Consejo Directivo del Instituto de Pensiones de Veracruz (1980-). Diputada federal (1967-70) y senadora (1997-2000).

Sesma, Ramón ◆ n. en Puebla, Pue., y m. en las Filipinas (?-¿1819?). Se unió al movimiento de independencia en 1812, participó en el ataque a Tehuacán y se incorporó a las filas de Nicolás Bravo, con quien tomó San Agustín del Palmar. En 1813 preparó la entrada de José María Morelos a Oaxaca y en Chilpancingo dio su voto para que éste fuera nombrado generalísimo. En 1814 fue enviado a la Huasteca, donde rechazó a los realistas en Silacayoapan. En 1815 acompañó a Vicente Guerrero en su fallido ataque a Acatlán, plaza defendida por los realistas Antonio y Miguel Flon, primos de Sesma. En 1817 fue capturado y luego indultado. En 1818, acusado de conspirar nuevamente contra el gobierno colonial, fue deportado a las islas Filipinas.

Sesma, Raymundo ◆ n. en San Cristóbal de Las Casas (1954). Artista plástico. Estudió serigrafía en la Casa de la Cultura de Aguascalientes (1974), pintura en la Universidad de las Américas de Puebla (1976) y serigrafía y litografía en el Open Studio de Toronto (1977). Ha dado cursos en el Colegio Americano (1974-75), en la Casa de Cultura de Puebla (1974-80) y el Museo de Monterrey (1990), entre otras instituciones culturales. Becario de la Fundación Mary S. Jenkins (1975), del gobierno de Canadá (1977), del gobierno poblano (1978), de la SRE (1981) y de Fonapas (1982). Por su creación de libros de autor ha recibido reconocimiento internacional. Ha participado en cerca de 40 exposiciones colectivas y más de 90 individuales. Radica alternativamente en México e Italia.

Sesma y González, Antonio ◆ n. en Puebla, Pue. (?-?). Padre del anterior. En 1810 se unió a la lucha insurgente, pero fue aprehendido en 1811. Quedó libre en 1812 y se reunió con José María Morelos, en Izúcar. Tras la toma de Oaxaca fue designado intendente del ejército insurgente.

Sessé y Lacasta, Martín de ◆ n. y m. en España (?-1809). Se tituló como médico en la Universidad de Zaragoza (1772). Acompañó a las fuerzas españolas que atacaron Gibraltar. Pasó a América y, de 1779 a 1781, estuvo con los ejércitos que hicieron las campañas de Florida y Misisipi. Ejerció su profesión en Cuba y en 1785 se estableció en la ciudad de México, donde fue médico de la Inquisición y del Hospital del Amor de Dios. Recibió el nombramiento de comisionado del Jardín Botánico de Madrid, en 1785. En 1787 recibió la orden de encabezar una expedición científica, en la que participaron Mariano Mociño y el español Vicente Cervantes, con quienes recorrió gran parte del país y formó una importante colección de especies vegetales. Fue el primer director del Jardín Botánico de la capital virreinal (1788-1804). En este cargo tuvo un largo litigio con la Real y Pontificia Universidad (☛).

Sesto, Julio ◆ n. en España y m. en el DF (1879-1960). Su nombre completo era Julio Manuel Vicente y Sesto. Se estableció en México cuando era muy joven. Colaboró en *El Imparcial* y *El Mundo*, entre otras publicaciones. Fue profesor de la Universidad Nacional y publicó el poemario *Azulejos* (del que adquirió popularidad el poema *Las abandonadas*). Autor de *Biografías y anecdotario pintoresco de cien mexicanos célebres en el arte, muertos en la pobreza y el abandono, y estudio crítico de sus obras* (1929), *La tórtola del Ajusco, La casa de las bugambilias, La emperatriz morena* y *La bohemia de la muerte*.

Sequeyro, Adela *Perlita* ◆ n. y m. en Veracruz, Ver. (1901-1992). Su nombre completo fue Adela Sequeyro Haro. Inició su carrera como actriz teatral y fue una de las iniciadoras del cine mexicano. Actuó en las películas: *Atavismo* (1923), *No matarás* (1924), *Un drama en la aristocracia* (1924) y *El sendero gris* (1927), entre otras. Ya en el cine sonoro realizó unas actuaciones esporádicas antes de producir, escribir y protagonizar una cinta de ambiente taurino, *Más allá de la muerte* (1935), y dos años después fundó, junto con su marido, Mario Tenorio, la cooperativa Éxito, que produciría las dos películas que dirigió: *La mujer de nadie* (1937), que también editó, y *Diablillos de arrabal* (1938). Más tarde abandonó el cine para dedicarse a la crónica taurina.

Sevina, Lienzo de ◆ Documento del siglo XVI que, aparentemente, representa la expulsión de los frailes del pueblo o de la iglesia del poblado michoacano de Sevina. Está pintado en una tela de 125 por 47.5 centímetros y se encuentra en la Biblioteca Nacional de Antropología e Historia.

Sevilla, Ninón ◆ n. en Cuba (1926). Nombre profesional de la bailarina y actriz Emilia Pérez Castellanos. En su adolescencia integró el coro de un conjunto de variedades y se presentó en diversos foros de su isla natal. En México triunfó en las carpas de teatro de variedades y fue estrella del llamado *cine de rumberas*. Trabajó en *Carita de cielo* (1946), *Pecadora* (1947), *Revancha* (1948), *Perdida* (1949), *Aventurera* (1949), *Víctimas del pecado* (1950), *Sensualidad* (1950), *Mujeres sacrificadas* (1951), *Llévame en tus brazos* (1953), *Club de señoritas* (1955), *Yambaó* (1956), *Maratón de baile* (1957), *Mujeres de fuego* (1958). Ha actuado en las telenovelas *Rosa salvaje, Cuando llega el amor* y *Yo no creo en los hombres*. Obtuvo un Ariel por *Noches de carnaval* (1981). Sobre su vida y su trabajo, David Ramón escribió *Sensualidad* (1990).

FOTO: ARMANDO HERRERA

Ninón Sevilla

Sevilla, Raphael J. ◆ n. y m. en el DF (1905-1975). Cineasta. En Hollywood trabajó como asesor técnico de la Warner Brothers y se formó como director. A su regreso colaboró con Miguel Zacarías, Arcady Boitler y José Bohr. Dirigió 40 películas, entre ellas *Más fuerte que el deber* (1930, primera película con

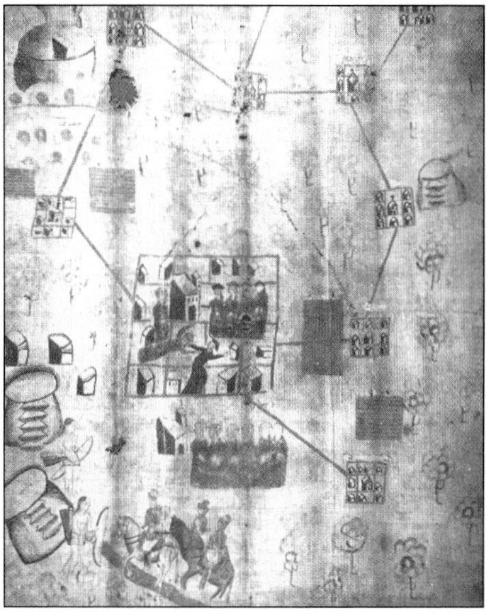

Lienzo de Sevina

FOTO: EXCÉLSIOR

Manuel Seyde

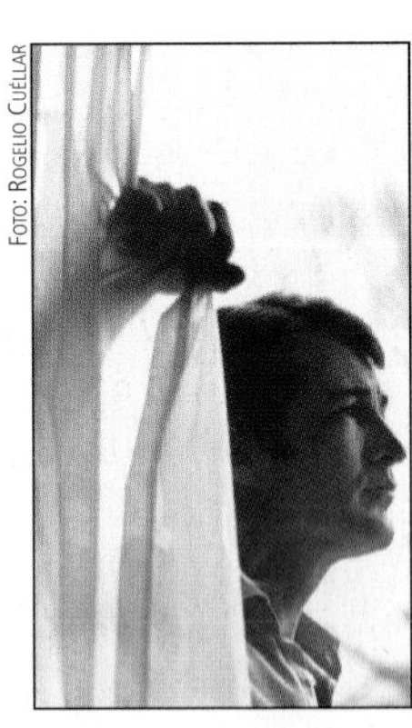
FOTO: ROGELIO CUÉLLAR

Jaime Augusto Shelley

sonido sincrónico hecha en México), *Almas encontradas* (1933), *Corazón bandolero* (1934), *María Elena* (1935), *Irma la mala* (1936), *Guadalupe la chicana* (1937), *La gran cruz* (1937), *Peruja* (1938), *El secreto de la monja* (1939), *El insurgente* (1940), *La torre de los suplicios* (1940), *Amor chicano* (1941), *La abuelita* (1942), *Maravilla del toreo* (1942), *Porfirio Díaz* (1944), *Asesinato en los estudios* (1944), *Como yo te quería* (1944), *La niña de mis ojos* (1946), *El amor abrió los ojos* (1946), *Una mujer con pasado* (1948) *El miedo llegó a Jalisco* (1949), *Canas al aire* (1949), *Quinto patio* (1950), *Tu vida entre mis manos* (1954) y *Paraíso escondido* (1958). En los años 50 se hizo coproductor de cine estadounidense.

SEYCHELLES, REPÚBLICA DE ◆ Estado insular africano, situado 1,600 kilómetros al este del continente, en el océano Índico. Tiene una superficie de 455 km², distribuida entre las 92 islas e islotes que conforman el país. Cuenta con 76,000 habitantes (1998), cuyo idioma oficial es el seselwa (francés criollo) aunque también hablan inglés y francés. Su capital es Victoria, que se halla en la isla de Mahé, la mayor del archipiélago (25,000 habitantes en 1993). *Historia:* en 1756 una expedición francesa tomó posesión de las islas y las bautizó con el apellido del ministro de Finanzas de Luis XV. En 1814, por los tratados de París, las islas pasaron a poder del imperio británico. En 1903 Seychelles se separó de la colonia de Mauricio y 45 años después accedió a la autonomía política, con un consejo legislativo de elección popular. En 1964 France-Albert René fundó el independentista Partido Popular Unido de Seychelles (PPUS), mientras James R. Mancham fundó el Partido Democrático de Seychelles (antiindependentista). En 1965 las islas de Aldabra, Farquhar y Desroches se incorporaron al Territorio Británico del Océano Índico. Luego de varias huelgas generales y movilizaciones promovidas por el PPUS, en 1974 esta organización obtuvo en las elecciones legislativas 47.6 por ciento de los votos. El gobierno inglés impuso en 1976 a Mancham como presidente, para otorgar al país la independencia, sin ceder el poder al PPUS. Ese mismo año Seychelles obtuvo la independencia como república de la Comunidad Británica. El presidente Mancham trató de posponer las elecciones de la nueva república, mientras estrechaba relaciones con Sudáfrica y vendía algunas de las islas del territorio (entre los compradores estuvo el actor Peter Sellers), por lo que un movimiento popular lo derrocó e impuso en el Ejecutivo a René, quien dos años después fue elegido presidente de la república y se declaró socialista y no alineado. En 1978 el PPUS se transformó en el Frente Progresista del Pueblo de Seychelles. De 1979 a 1982 fueron sofocados cinco intentos de golpe de Estado; el último, un cuartelazo organizado por militares sudafricanos. En 1983, Seychelles, Mauricio y Madagascar crearon la Comisión del Océano Índico para promover la cooperación regional. En 1984 René fue reelegido. México y Seychelles establecieron relaciones diplomáticas en junio de 1986.

SEYDE Y SEYDE, MANUEL ◆ n. en Paso del Macho, Ver., y m. en el DF (1914-1994). Periodista. Publicó una columna en *Excélsior*, llamada "Temas del día", del 28 de agosto de 1935 a marzo de 1983. Se distinguió por sus comentarios críticos e irónicos sobre diversas actividades deportivas. Impuso el mote de *ratones verdes* (1966) a los jugadores de la selección nacional de futbol y escribió que en Centroamérica se jugaba con *balón cuadrado*. Hizo una investigación sobre el origen del futbol en México. Sus artículos se compilaron en *La fiesta del alarido* (1970) y *Las copas del mundo* (1984). Autor de *Copa Mundial en 1986*. Premio Nacional de Periodismo.

SEYÉ ◆ Municipio de Yucatán situado en el occidente del estado, al sureste de Mérida y al sur de Motul. Superficie: 186.5 km². Habitantes: 8,170, de los cuales 1,977 forman la población económicamente activa. Hablan alguna lengua indígena 3,350 personas mayores de cinco años (maya 3,347). Indígenas monolingües: 91.

SHABOT, ESTHER ◆ n. en el DF (1947). Licenciada en sociología por la UNAM (1980), con maestría en sociología por la misma institución, especializada en estudios judaicos por la UIA. Profesora de diversas universidades desde 1981. Es analista de asuntos de Medio Oriente y con ese tema ha colaborado en *El Nacional* (1983-86), *Excélsior* (1986-) y *Radio Red*. Participó en el libro *Imágenes de un encuentro. La presencia judía en México en la primera mitad del siglo XX* (1992). Coordinó *Los propósitos de la mirada. Obra plástica de Eduardo Cohen* (1997). Coautora con Golde Cukier de *Panorama de Medio Oriente contemporáneo* (1986). Autora de *Los orígenes del sindicalismo ferrocarrilero* (1982).

SHABOT, EZRA ◆ n. en el DF (1956). Hermano de la anterior. Licenciado en ciencias políticas y administración pública por la UNAM, donde ha sido profesor desde 1979, jefe del Departamento de Ciencias Sociales (1984-85) y del Departamento de Planeación Académica de la ENEP-Acatlán (1989-92). Colaborador de los diarios *El Nacional* (1986-93) y *Reforma* (1994-) y analista político de los programas radiofónicos *Detrás de la Noticia*, *Decisión 97* y *Detrás del 2000*. Autor de *El pensamiento de la derecha* (1992), *La derecha mexicana 1960-80* (1985) y *Los refugiados judíos en México durante la segunda guerra mundial* (1993).

SHEDD, MARGARET ◆ n. en Persia y m. en EUA (1898-1986). Hija de misioneros protestantes estadounidenses. Colaboró en publicaciones como *New Yorker* y *Harpers Magazine*. En 1951, con apoyo financiero de la Fundación Rockefeller, creó el Centro Mexicano de Escritores, del cual fue directora honoraria hasta su muerte.

SHELLEY, JAIME AUGUSTO ◆ n. en el DF (1937). Escritor. Estudió letras en la UNAM y antropología en la Universidad Veracruzana (1961), instituciones donde ha sido profesor. Formó parte del Comité de Intelectuales que apoyó el movimiento estudiantil de 1968. En el INBA ha sido coordinador de Artes Plásticas (1962-63) y subdirector de teatro. Trabajó en la Casa del Lago (1963-64), fue inspector de la Dirección General de Cinematografía (1962-67), jefe de redacción de la sala de prensa de la Villa Olímpica (1968), corresponsal de la Agencia Mexicana de Noticias en Ottawa (1968-69), director de difusión de la Universidad Veracruzana (1974-75), jefe del Departamento de Publicaciones y Medios de Pemex (1979-81) y funcionario de Sicartsa. Codirector de la revista *Situaciones* (1959), director de *La Palabra y el Hombre* (1973-74), director de *Otro Cine* (1974-75), editor de la *Revista del Colegio de Licenciados en Administración de México* (1978-79) y cofundador de *La Jornada* (1984). Coescribió el guión de *El recurso del método* (1975). Perteneció al grupo La Espiga Amotinada (☛), con el que publicó los poemarios *La espiga amotinada* (1960) y *Ocupación de la palabra* (1965). Autor de *La gran escala* (1961), *Canción de las ciudades* (1963), *Hierofante* (1967), *Himno a la impaciencia* (1971), *Por definición* (1976), *Ávidos rebaños* (1981), *Victoria* (1984), *El abuso del poder* (poesía, 1987), *La gran revolución* (teatro, 1987), *Girasol de urgencias* (poesía, 1987), *Horas ciegas* (antología, 1987) y *Poesías* (1987). Becario del Centro Mexicano de Escritores (1961-62).

Sheridan, Beatriz ◆ n. en el DF (1934). Actriz. Estudió letras en la Universidad de Missouri y en el Mexico City College y arte dramático con Seki Sano. Se inició profesionalmente en 1959 y ha actuado en las obras dramáticas *La lección* (1959), *Penélope* (1960), *Fando y Lis* (1961), *Las troyanas* (1963), *Doce y una trece* (1965), *Diálogo entre el amor y un viejo* (1966), *La noche de los asesinos* (1967, que le valió un Heraldo como mejor actriz), *Un tranvía llamado deseo* (1968, Premio María Tereza Montoya a la mejor actriz), *¡Ah, los días felices!* (1977), *Las amargas lágrimas de Petra von Kant* (1980, con la que ganó dos premios a la mejor actuación), *Las tentaciones de María Egipcíaca* (1981), *De pétalos perennes* (1982) y *Jardín de invierno* (1986). Ha trabajado en las películas *Pedro Páramo* (1966), *Recuerdos del porvenir* (1969), *Jory* (1970), *La huelga de Cananea* (1978), *El jugador de ajedrez* (1980), *Confidencias* (1982, Ariel a la mejor actuación) y *Gaby Brimmer* (1986). Ha intervenido también en numerosos programas de televisión.

Sheridan, Guillermo ◆ n. en el DF (1950). Escritor. Ha ejercido la docencia en la Facultad de Filosofía y Letras y es investigador de poesía mexicana moderna en el Centro de Estudios Literarios de la UNAM. También fue profesor de El Colegio de México. Ha sido colaborador y miembro de la mesa de redacción de las revistas *Pauta*, *Biblioteca de México*, *Vuelta* y *Letras Libres*. Es director de la Fundación Octavio Paz, A.C. desde 1997. Escribió los guiones de varios documentales y de la película *Cabeza de Vaca* (1989), de Nicolás Echevarría, publicado en 1994. Autor de ensayo: *Los Contemporáneos ayer* (1985), *Índices de* Contemporáneos *1928-1931* (1988), *México en 1932: la polémica nacionalista* (1999) y *Los Hijos Pródigos: revistas y generaciones poéticas entre 1932 y 1946*; crónica: *Frontera norte* (1988) y *Cartas de Copilco y otras postales* (1994); biografía: *Un corazón adicto (la vida de Ramón López Velarde)* (1989, Premio Xavier Villaurrutia); y novela: *El dedo de oro* (1996). Ha realizado ediciones críticas de obras de Ramón López Velarde, José Juan Tablada, José Gorostiza, Carlos Pellicer e Ignacio Chávez.

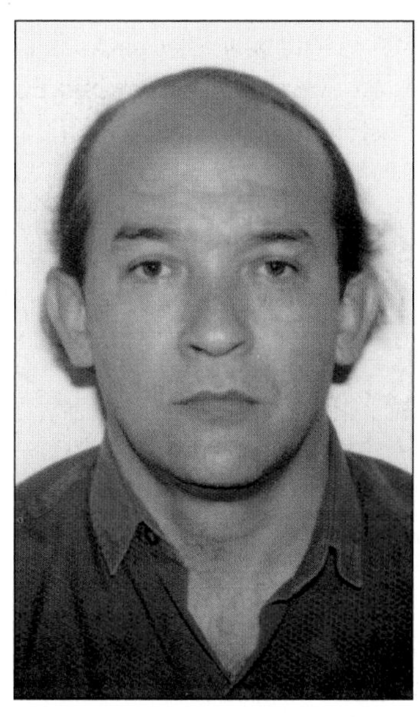

Guillermo Sheridan

Sherwell, Guillermo A. ◆ n. en Paraje Nuevo, Ver., y m. en EUA (1878-1926). Se tituló como profesor en la Normal Presbiteriana de Puebla. Dirigió la Primaria para Varones, de Jalapa, fue profesor en el Colegio Preparatorio, comisionado por el gobierno estatal para estudiar los sistemas de enseñanza secundaria en Estados Unidos; colaborador de Enrique Rébsamen, profesor de la Escuela Nacional de Maestros, director general de Enseñanza Primaria y jefe de la sección de Normales de la Secretaría de Instrucción Pública. Como jurista especializado en derecho internacional, asistió a diversos congresos con la representación nacional. Fue secretario de la Comisión Internacional Americana y catedrático de la Universidad de Georgetown. Autor de *El problema de la educación primaria de la América Latina*, del poemario *Capullos* (1906) y de biografías, en inglés, de Bolívar y de Sucre.

Foto: Colección Imcine

Stanislao Shilinsky y Manuel Palacios *Manolín* en *Las nenas del Siete*, película de Roberto Rodríguez

Shilinsky, Estanislao ◆ n. en Polonia y m. en el DF (1910-1985). Vivió en Japón, país del que salió después del terremoto de Tokio (1923). Actor cómico, hizo pareja con *Cantinflas* —que era su cuñado— y, desde 1930, con *Manolín*. Durante 30 años trabajaron en radio, cine, televisión y centros nocturnos en México, Estados Unidos y Sudamérica.

Foto: Rogelio Cuéllar

Javier Sicilia

Sicilia, Javier ◆ n. en el DF (1956). Poeta y ensayista. Estudió ciencias políticas y letras francesas en la UNAM. Ha sido coordinador de un taller literario en el Palacio de Minería, editor de la UNAM y la UAM, miembro de los comités de redacción de las revistas literarias *Cartapacios* y *Casa del Tiempo* y guionista. Ha colaborado en *Territorios*, *Sábado*, *Excélsior*, *Versus* y *La Gaceta del Fondo de Cultura Económica*. Coautor (con Tomás Calvillo) de *La revelación y los días* (ensayo, 1988). Autor del volumen de ensayos *Cariátide a destiempo y otros escombros* (1980) y de *Poesía y espíritu* (1999); de los poemarios *Permanencia en los puertos* (1982), *La presencia desierta* (1986) y *Trinidad* (1992), y las novelas *El bautista* (1991) y *El reflejo de lo oscuro* (1996).

Ma. Elena Sicilia Esquivel

Sicilia Esquivel, Ma. Elena ◆ n. en el DF (?). Licenciada en psicología con estudios de maestría en la UNAM y posgrado en psicoanálisis con especialización en adolescencia. Ha dirigido las revistas *Logros* (1977-84), *Individuo y Sociedad* (1982-1983), *Educación para la Salud* (1985-87) y *Agenda de la Mujer* (1987-1990). Fue directora de Fomento Cultural Somex y miembro del comité editorial de la revista *Somos-Somex*. Pertenece al Colegio de Sociólogos de México y a la Asociación de Egresados de Psicoterapia Psicoanalítica de la Adolescencia.

Sidar, Pablo L. ◆ n. en España y m. en el mar, cerca de Costa Rica (1895-1930). Piloto aviador graduado en la Escuela Militar de Aviación Mexicana (1922). Combatió contra los delahuertistas, los cristeros y los escobaristas (1923-29). Fue profesor de la Escuela Militar de Aviación y jefe del Primer Regimiento Aéreo, así como ayudante del secretario de Guerra y Marina, Plutarco Elías Calles (1929). En 1930 emprendió un vuelo sin escalas desde Cerro Loco, Oaxaca, hacia Buenos Aires, en compañía de Carlos Rovirosa. Frente a Puerto Limón, Costa Rica, una tormenta derribó su aparato y ambos pilotos murieron.

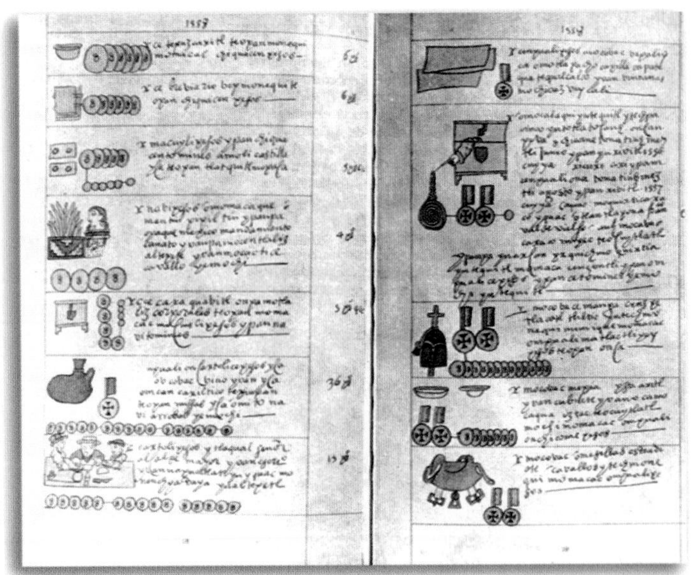

Códice Sierra

Sierra, Códice ◆ Documento conocido también como Códice de Santa Catarina Tejupan. El original está en la Academia de Bellas Artes de Puebla. Es fragmento de una nómina de las contribuciones y diezmos del pueblo mixteco de Santa Catarina Tejupan, en jeroglíficos popolocas traducidos al náhuatl con caracteres latinos. Abarca un periodo que va de 1550 a 1564.

Sierra, José Luis ◆ n. en Querétaro, Qro. (1949). Poeta. Licenciado en letras por la Universidad Autónoma de Querétaro, donde es docente. Ha realizado estudios especializados en España y ha sido profesor invitado en universidades de EUA. Colaborador de *Plural*, *La Palabra y el Hombre*, *Cuadernos Hispanoamericanos* y *Hora en Poesía*, entre otras. Autor de *Olga* (1979), *Paisaje con país y árboles nuevos* (1982), *Clamor desde lo hondo* (1986), *Ritual monográfico* (1993) y *Memoria ocupada* (1995).

Sierra, Susana ◆ n. en el DF (1942). Pintora y grabadora. Estudió en Europa (1960-62) y en San Carlos (1968-72). Becaria del CNCA (1989-90). Perteneció al grupo Nuevos Grabadores (1967-69). Desde 1977 ha expuesto individualmente en ciudades de México, Yugoslavia, Bulgaria, Alemania Federal, España, Francia y Suiza en más de 20 ocasiones. Ha colaborado en muestras colectivas en México, Estados Unidos, Alemania Federal, Ecuador, Cuba, Venezuela, Costa Rica, Canadá, España, Inglaterra, Puerto Rico y Francia. Becaria de la fundación Pollock-Krasner (1988) de Estados Unidos, por el Fonca en 1989 y por el SNCA en 1993. Premio de adquisición en los Salones Anuales de Pintura de 1980 y 1983. Fue seleccionada para participar en el Carnegie International de Pittsburg (1982).

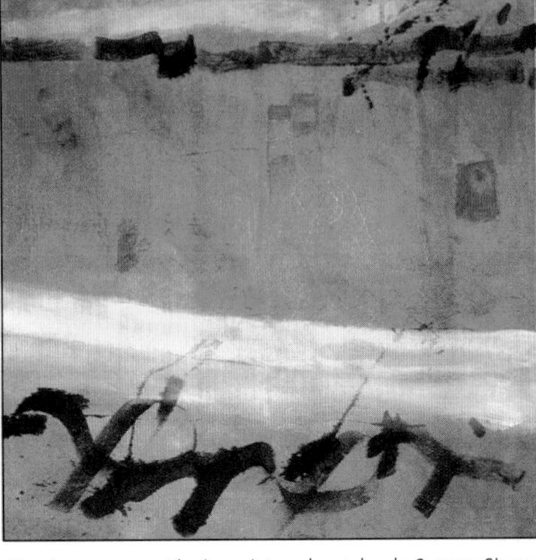

Parajes arenosos, técnica mixta sobre tela, de Susana Sierra

SIERRA LEONA, REPÚBLICA DE Estado de África situado en la costa del océano Atlántico. Limita al norte y noreste con Guinea y al sureste con Liberia. Tiene una superficie de 71,740 km² y 4,568,000 habitantes (1998). El idioma oficial es el inglés y también se hablan el krio (la lengua utilizada en las relaciones comerciales, y cuyo nombre es una corrupción de la palabra "créole"), el mende y el temne. Su capital es Freetown, uno de los puertos naturales más grandes del mundo, con 669,000 habitantes en 1990. *Historia*: En 1462 el navegante portugués Pedro da Cintra llegó a la región y la bautizó como Sierra Leona, pues desde la costa escuchó el eco de una tormenta reflejado por la cordillera, lo que le hizo pensar en el rugido de los leones. En la primera mitad del siglo XVI, bajo el dominio portugués, el comercio esclavista floreció en la costa del extremo occidental de África. La factoría de Cabo Verde concentraba la trata de los llamados ríos de Guinea, franja de litoral que comprendía de Senegal a Sierra Leona. En este último país, el principal negociante era Diego de Haro. A mediados del siglo XVII Inglaterra tuvo en Jamaica su primera base estable en el Caribe. Desde ahí introdujo en las posesiones españolas un variado contrabando que incluía seres humanos traídos involuntariamente de África. El tráfico se convirtió en legal por la firma de los tratados de Utrecht, mediante los cuales, entre otras cosas, Inglaterra se comprometió a introducir en los dominios de España 144,000 esclavos. El transporte se haría en embarcaciones de bandera británica y habría *factores*, esto es, representantes de las factorías inglesas, en Veracruz y Campeche. La empresa británica beneficiada con el negocio fue la Compañía del Mar del Sur, que a su vez contrató con la Compañía Real de África la entrega de 4,800 esclavos cada año, de los cuales provendrían 200 de Sierra Leona. Entre 1715 y 1736 entraron por Veracruz 2,449 "cabezas de ambos sexos" y, según Gonzalo Aguirre Beltrán, el número introducido por

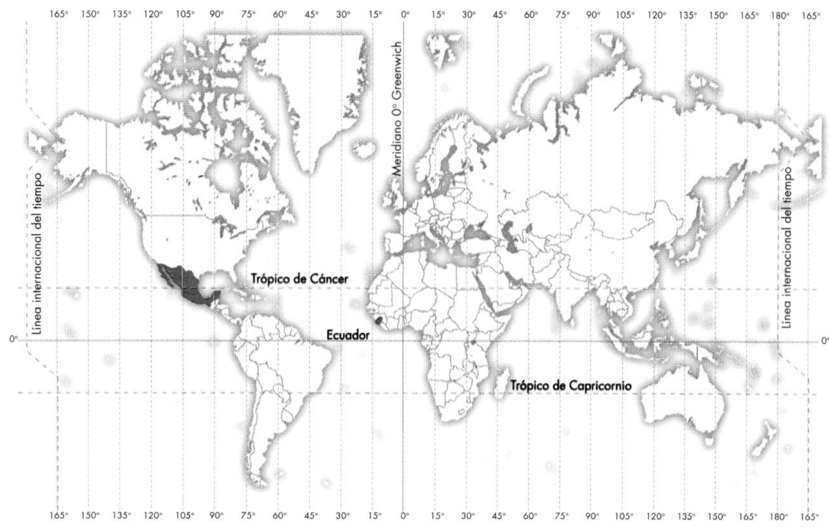

República de Sierra Leona

Campeche fue mayor, pero aparentemente destinados a trabajar en Belice. No es posible saber el número de esclavos procedentes de Sierra Leona que llegaron a la Nueva España. No obstante, se sabe que venían miembros de las tribus loko y mendé, conocidos aquí como xoxos y llamados también cumbá; y los vaí o krimvaí, mandingos llamados en México gallinas. Según el mismo estudioso fueron traídos esclavos de las tribus zapé y cumbá, ésta de origen mandingo, al igual que los bulom, buloes o banta; los limba y los loko; los yalunka, los kuranko y los kissí, los tres grupos conocidos aquí como gangá. Pese a lo anterior, agrega Aguirre Beltrán, los ríos de Sierra Leona "no dieron contingente apreciable a la trata de esclavos", pues la tarea de capturarlos "tropezaba a menudo con la hostilidad de las tribus costaneras, parte de las cuales recibieron el expresivo nombre de *malas gentes* por repeler con la fuerza la cautividad" y un grupo en especial, los kru, eran temidos por "su alta peligrosidad como inductores de motines en los navíos". En la segunda mitad del siglo XVIII había aumentado considerablemente la población negra de Gran Bretaña, entre otras razones por el flujo de libertos. La solución para el gobierno inglés la ofreció Granville Sharp, de la Sociedad Antiesclavista de Londres, quien compró en 1787 a los jefes tribales de Sierra Leona un territorio de 250 kilómetros cuadrados al que envió a un numeroso grupo de negros presuntamente "repatriados", quienes se integraron a una sociedad agrícola, al principio democráticamente organizada, pero que con el tiempo se convirtió en otro enclave colonialista inglés. Los supuestos "repatriados", que en realidad no tenían ninguna raíz en Sierra Leona, fueron llamados criollos y se convirtieron paulatinamente en intermediarios de los ingleses, cuya cultura decían poseer. En 1808 Sierra Leona se convirtió oficialmente en colonia británica, pese a la resistencia de los habitantes originales del país. En 1896 el territorio se transformó en protectorado. Dos años más tarde, uno de los dirigentes de la resistencia anticolonialista, Bai Buré, encabezó un levantamiento armado en casi todo el país, después de que el fisco británico intentó establecer un impuesto sobre cada choza. La contraofensiva de la Gran Bretaña aplastó la resistencia en un año. En 1951 se aprobó una Constitución que instauró un Consejo Legislativo. En 1953 Inglaterra designó a Milton Margai como ministro jefe del país. En 1957 la Cámara de Representantes sustituyó al Consejo Legislativo y Milton Margai, también por nombramiento de los británicos, se convirtió en primer ministro. En 1960 Syaka Pro Ben Stevens fundó el Con-

ARCHIVO XAVIER ESPARZA

Justo Sierra Méndez

greso de Todo el Pueblo (APC) y un año después Sierra Leona pasó a ser un Estado independiente, dentro de la Comunidad Británica. En 1964 murió Milton Margai y fue sucedido por su medio hermano, Albert Margai. Los gobiernos de ambos Margai crearon un clima de descontento entre la población de Sierra Leona, pues los dos primeros ministros otorgaron excesivas concesiones y prebendas a la élite de comerciantes sirio-libaneses, criollos y británicos; fomentaron la corrupción administrativa, el vicio organizado y el tráfico ilegal de diamantes, principal riqueza nacional. En 1967 el APC se convirtió en el primer partido político de oposición en África que ganó unas elecciones, al derrotar al Partido Popular de Sierra Leona (SLPP). El militar David Lansana declaró la ley marcial e impidió la toma de posesión del primer ministro electo, Stevens, quien se vio obligado a refugiarse en Conakry. Inmediatamente después, un grupo de oficiales del ejército depuso a Lansana y nombró al coronel A. Juxson-Smith líder del Consejo de Reforma Nacional. En 1968 un grupo de soldados (dirigido por Morlai Kamara) dio un golpe de Estado, conocido como el Golpe de los Sargentos, para dar posesión a Stevens como primer ministro. En 1971, con una nueva Constitución, Sierra Leona se proclamó república independiente (con Stevens como su primer presidente) y rompió los últimos lazos con la Comunidad Británica. En 1973, Sierra Leona y Liberia formaron la Unión del Río Mano. En 1976 Stevens fue reelegido. En ese año México estableció relaciones diplomáticas con Sierra Leona. En 1978 fue aprobada otra Constitución y se inició el primer periodo presidencial de siete años, nuevamente con Stevens como titular, quien en 1985 fue sucedido por Joseph Momoh y que, a su vez, fue derrocado por el primero de una serie de golpes militares que han afectado al país hasta la fecha.

SIERRA MÉNDEZ, JUSTO ◆ n. en Campeche, Camp., y m. en España (1848-1912). Hijo de Justo Sierra O'Reilly. Abogado. Estudió en el Colegio de San Ildefonso (1871). Fue profesor de la Escuela Nacional Preparatoria. Escribió en *El Renacimiento*, el *Monitor Republicano*, *El Domingo*, *La Tribuna*, *El Federalista*, *El Mundo*, *El Siglo XIX*, la *Revista Azul* y la *Revista Moderna*. Dirigió *La Libertad* hasta 1880. Fue diputado federal, suplente y propietario, por Sinaloa (1880-84), magistrado de la Suprema Corte de Justicia (1894), subsecretario de Instrucción Pública (1901) y secretario de Instrucción Pública y Bellas Artes (del 1 de diciembre de 1905 al 24 de marzo de 1911), en la etapa final del porfiriato. Promovió y logró la fundación de la Universidad Nacional de México (1910). En 1912 se le nombró ministro plenipotenciario de México en España. Publicó poemas en periódicos de la época. Sus *Cuentos románticos* aparecieron en *El Monitor*. Lo mismo puede decirse de sus crónicas de viaje, como las que forman *En tierra yankee*, que salieron en *El Mundo* (1897-98), y las que forman *En la Europa latina*, que primeramente se pudieron leer en *El Mundo Ilustrado* (1901-1903). Vio el estreno de su obra de teatro *Piedad* y su novela *El ángel del porvenir*, publicada por entregas en *El Renacimiento* (1869), fue editada como libro en 1873. El ensayo: *Evolución política del pueblo mexicano* se conoció primero como *México: su evolución social* (2 t., 1900-1902). *Juárez, su obra y su tiempo*, es probablemente su libro más leído.

SIERRA MÉNDEZ, SANTIAGO ◆ n. en Campeche, Camp., y m. en Tlalnepantla, Edo. de Méx. (1850-1880). Hijo de Justo Sierra O'Reilly y hermano del anterior. En 1863, en Veracruz, fundó el periódico literario *Violetas*, junto con Salvador Díaz Mirón y Rafael de Zayas Enríquez. Colaboró en los periódicos *Distrito Federal* (del que fue jefe de redacción), *La Vida en México*, *El Renacimiento*, *La Ilustración Espírita* (que dirigió), *El Federalista*, *El Bien Público* y *La Libertad*, entre otros. Fue oficial primero del Senado (1876) y secretario y encargado de negocios de la legación mexicana en Chile. Desde las páginas de *La Libertad* inició una polémica con el director del periódico *La Patria*, Ireneo Paz, misma que culminó en un duelo que le costó la vida. Autor del poema *Canto a México* y las novelas *Viajes por una oreja* (1869) y *Flor de fuego* (1870).

SIERRA MOJADA ◆ Municipio de Coahuila situado en el extremo occidental del estado, al norte de Torreón y al noroeste de Saltillo, en los límites con Chihuahua y Durango. Superficie: 6,996.2 km². Habitantes: 6,594, de los cuales 3,067 forman la población económicamente activa. Parte de su territorio lo ocupa la Zona del Silencio (☛).

SIERRA O'REILLY, JUSTO ◆ n. en Tixcacaltuyú y m. en Mérida, Yuc. (1814-1861). Se tituló como abogado en el Colegio de San Ildefonso (1838). Obtuvo el doctorado en ambos derechos en la Universidad Literaria de Yucatán. Fue juez de primera instancia (1839), comisionado por Yucatán para concertar con los estados del sur mexicano y con Texas una alianza contra el régimen centralista y, en 1843, derrotada la expedición del gobierno santanista contra Yucatán, como consejero del gobierno firmó el pacto por el que Yucatán se reincorporó a la República; fue vocal de la Asamblea Departamental y más adelante de la Asamblea Legislativa, que al inicio de 1846 dispuso que Yucatán reasumiese su soberanía. Al estallar la guerra entre México y Estados Unidos, Yucatán se declaró neutral. No obstante, tropas estadounidenses ocuparon la ciudad y la isla del Carmen. Sierra fue comisionado para negociar en Washington la desocupación del Carmen y solicitar ayuda para combatir la sublevación maya. Su misión diplomática fracasó y volvió a Yucatán en 1848, luego de haber comprometido la soberanía yucateca ante España e Inglaterra, al ofrecerle el dominio de la península a quien terminara con el levantamiento indígena. Fue diputado (1851 y 1857), agente de la Secretaría de Fomento de Yucatán (1852) y juez especial de Hacienda en Campeche, Fundó los periódicos *El Museo Yucateco* (1839), el *Registro Yucateco* (1845) y *El*

Justo Sierra O'Reilly

Fénix (1848) y *La Unión Liberal* (1855), que se convirtió en el periódico oficial del gobierno yucateco. En 1859-60 elaboró un código civil para el gobierno juarista. Autor de *La hija del judío* (novela publicada por entregas en su periódico *El Fénix*, 1849), *Lecciones de derecho marítimo internacional* (1854) y *Diario de nuestro viaje a los Estados Unidos de América y al Canadá* (4 t., 1850-51).

Sierra y Rosso, Ignacio ◆ n. en Jalapa, Ver., y m. en la ciudad de México (1811-1860). Secretario de Relaciones Interiores y Exteriores (del 28 de febrero al 21 de marzo de 1847 y del 21 al 26 de marzo de 1847) de Valentín Gómez Farías y de Antonio López de Santa Anna, y secretario de Hacienda (del 6 de agosto de 1853 al 26 de enero de 1854) de Santa Anna. Se le llamaba el "poeta cívico" del régimen santanista y su producción quedó dispersa.

Siete Leyes ◆ Conjunto de estatutos de rango constitucional del régimen centralista, cuyo nombre oficial es Leyes Constitucionales. La primera fue expedida el 15 de diciembre de 1835 y las restantes entraron en vigor el 30 de diciembre de 1836, publicadas por el presidente José Justo Corro. En su elaboración intervinieron, entre otros, Francisco Manuel Sánchez de Tagle, Miguel Valentín, Antonio Pacheco Leal y José María Cuevas, presumiblemente influidos por Lucas Alamán. El ordenamiento creó el Supremo Poder Conservador, especie de consejo de notables con facultades para anular leyes y actos de los otros poderes, disolver el Congreso, suspender a la Suprema Corte y destituir al presidente de la República. La vigencia de las Siete Leyes terminó al triunfo del alzamiento de las Bases de Tacubaya y la firma del convenio de Estanzuela con el presidente Bustamante, el 6 de octubre de 1841.

Siete Sabios ◆ Grupo formado en la Escuela Nacional de Jurisprudencia con el nombre de Sociedad de Conferencias y Conciertos. Lo integraron Manuel Gómez Morín, Vicente Lombardo Toledano, Teófilo Olea y Leyva, Alfonso Caso, Alberto Vázquez del Mercado, Antonio Castro Leal y Jesús Moreno Baca. Estos siete estudiantes formaban parte de un grupo más amplio, llamado Generación de 1915, en el que se incluían, entre otros, Miguel Palacios Macedo, Manuel Toussaint, Narciso Bassols y Daniel Cosío Villegas. El documento de fundación del grupo dice: "En la ciudad de México, a los cinco días del mes de septiembre de mil novecientos diez y seis y siendo las once de la mañana, se reunieron en la biblioteca de la Escuela Nacional de Jurisprudencia los señores Alfonso Caso, Antonio Castro, Manuel Gómez Morín, Vicente Lombardo Toledano, Jesús Moreno Baca, Teófilo Olea y Alberto Vázquez del Mercado y acordaron: I. Fundar una sociedad con el fin de propagar la cultura entre los estudiantes de la Universidad Nacional de México. II. La sociedad se llamará 'Sociedad de Conferencias y Conciertos'. III. Constituirse en socios fundadores reservándose el derecho de invitar a las personas que den conferencias". Existe un documento que indica que el 20 de marzo de 1918 Luis Enrique Erro, Miguel Palacios Macedo, Narciso Bassols y otros universitarios solicitaron formalmente su ingreso en la Sociedad. El nombre de los Siete Sabios, no sin sorna, le fue impuesto al grupo por el resto de los estudiantes de Jurisprudencia, quienes llamaban "monosabios" a los aspirantes a ingresar en la Sociedad.

Siglo xix, El ◆ Diario fundado el 8 de octubre de 1841 por Ignacio Cumplido. Se convirtió en abanderado de las luchas liberales y en decano del periodismo político mexicano. Por amenazas o censura, su publicación se vio interrumpida en 1842, 1843 y 1845-46, cuando Cumplido lo sustituyó con *El Memorial Histórico* y después con *El Republicano*. Reapareció el 1 de junio de 1848, cuando habían salido de la capital los invasores estadounidenses. El 12 de septiembre de 1856 el gobierno de Comonfort suspendió la aparición del diario y prohibió al editor la publicación de ése y cualquier otro periódico. El 1 de octubre volvió a salir. En enero de 1858, el gobierno golpista del Plan de Tacubaya prohibió la publicación del cotidiano, ausente del escenario de la prensa durante la guerra de los Tres Años. Reapareció en enero de 1861, cuando entró en la ciudad de México el gobierno liberal de Benito Juárez. El 31 de mayo de 1863, con los invasores franceses a las puertas de la capital, el presidente Juárez dejó el Distrito Federal y *El Siglo xix* suspendió otra vez su publicación hasta el triunfo de la República, en 1867. El órgano liberal se mostró todavía combativo, pero envejeció junto con su editor, quien murió el 30 de noviembre de 1887, a los 76 años de edad. El periódico, en plena decadencia, le sobrevivió hasta 1896. Fue dirigido por Francisco Zarco de 1855 a 1869, en lo que se considera su mejor época. Le sucedieron Manuel Payno, José María Vigil, Julio Zárate, Anselmo de la Portilla, Francisco Sosa y Antonio Torres Castro. La última época del periódico, dirigida por Luis Pombo y Francisco Bulnes, fue de corte oficialista.

Libro sobre *Los Siete Sabios de México*

El Siglo xix

EL SILGO DIEZ Y NUEVE.

N. 3.

AÑO I. MEXICO, DOMINGO 10 DE OCTUBRE DE 1841. Trim. I.

PARTE OFICIAL.

SIGNORET, LEÓN ◆ n. y m. en Francia (1857-1919). Comerciante llegado a México en 1878. En 1880, junto con su hermano Antonio, abrió la tienda de ropa Al Puerto de Veracruz, en la calle de la Monterilla de la ciudad de México. En 1882 se asoció con una camisería contigua, propiedad de M. Bourjac, quien en 1885 se retiró de la sociedad. En ese mismo año los hermanos Signoret se asociaron con Honorat, con lo que se creó Signoret, Honorat y Compañía, propietaria de la tienda que amplió sus rubros de venta a muebles, cristalería y otros giros. Signoret abrió sucursales del almacén en varias ciudades del país y de Latinoamérica y adquirió acciones de la empresa Mosler Bowen y Cook, que anexó a la tienda, ya convertida en almacén departamental. Regresó a Francia tras la muerte de su hermano.

SIGÜENZA Y GÓNGORA, CARLOS DE ◆ n. y m. en la ciudad de México (1645-1700). Sobrino del poeta español Luis de Góngora y Argote. En 1660 ingresó como novicio en la Compañía de Jesús, profesó sus votos simples en 1662 y, por sus escapatorias nocturnas del Colegio del Espíritu Santo, de Puebla, fue expulsado de la orden en 1668. Infructuosamente pidió su readmisión en 1669 y 1677. Aprendió matemáticas con su padre. Pasó a la Real y Pontificia Universidad de México, donde se supone que estudió derecho sin que haya obtenido grado; fue profesor de astrología y matemáticas (1672-92) y contador (1690-94). Desde 1690 aparecía como *Real Cosmógrapho*. Desde 1682 hasta su muerte fue capellán del Hospital del Amor de Dios (1682-1700). Se sabe que editó unos *Lunarios*, por lo menos en 1675 y 1681. En 1690 publicó *Los infortunios de Alonso Ramírez*, obra maestra del reportaje colonial, y en 1691 una obra similar a la que puso un título rigurosamente periodístico: *Mercurio volante con la noticia de la recuperación de las provincias del Nuevo México*. Del mismo año es la *Relación de lo sucedido a la Armada de Barlovento*. En 1692 rescató el archivo y la pinacoteca del edificio del Ayuntamiento, incendiado durante una insurrección popular. En el mismo año fue comisionado por el virrey para realizar una expedición a la bahía de Pensacola, en la que levantó varios mapas y realizó estudios diversos. En abril de 1693, en el mismo viaje, desembarcó en la bahía de Santa María de Galve, en la costa de Luisiana, donde elaboró un plano de la zona y declaró que a ese sitio habían llegado, en 1528, los náufragos de la expedición de Pánfilo de Narváez. Heredó su instrumental científico, su biblioteca, cartografía y numerosos textos inéditos al Colegio de San Pedro y San Pablo. Su legado fue destruido en 1847, cuando el ejército estadounidense ocupó la ciudad de México. Autor de *Primavera indiana. Poema sacro-histórico, idea de María Santísima de Guadalupe* (1668), *Glorias de Querétaro* (1668), *Teatro de virtudes políticas* (1680), *Manifiesto filosófico contra los cometas despojados del ingenio que tenían sobre los tímidos* (1681), *Triunfo parténico que en glorias de María Santísima inmaculadamente concebida* (poesía, 1683), *Paraíso occidental plantado y cultivado por la liberal benéfica mano de los muy católicos y poderosos Reyes de España* (1684), *Piedad heroica de don Hernando Cortés* (1689), *Trofeo de la justicia española en el castigo de la alevosía francesa* (1691), *Libra astronómica y filosófica* (1691) y *Oriental planeta evangélico* (1700; escrito cuando tenía 23 años).

Carlos de Sigüenza y Góngora

FOTO: MICHAEL CALDERWOOD

Danza típica de Silao, Guanajuato

SILACAYOAPAN ◆ Municipio de Oaxaca situado en el noroeste del estado, al suroeste de Huajuapan de León y al noroeste de Tlaxiaco. Superficie: 417.2 km². Habitantes: 8,293, de los cuales 1,992 forman la población económicamente activa. Hablan alguna lengua indígena 1,953 personas mayores de cinco años (mixteco 1,945), de las cuales 294 no saben español. En el cerro de Yucunondullo se encontraron tumbas y utensilios de cocina, vestigios de la cultura mixteca.

SILAO ◆ Municipio de Guanajuato situado al noroeste de Irapuato y al sureste de León. Superficie: 537.4 km². Habitantes: 131,527, de los cuales 29,672 forman la población económicamente activa. Hablan alguna lengua indígena 43 personas mayores de cinco años. Celebra su fundación el 25 de julio. La cabecera, del mismo nombre, es uno de los centros comerciales más importantes de la región del Bajío; en ella se conserva como atractivo turístico la casa en la que estuvo prisionero Francisco Javier Mina. En su jurisdicción están el cerro del Cubilete y el balneario de aguas termales de Comanjilla. El 12 de marzo de 1858, al inicio de la guerra de los Tres Años, el general liberal Manuel Doblado, fortificado en la ciudad de Silao, capituló ante las fuerzas conservadoras de Luis G. Osollo. Una de las batallas más importantes de ese conflicto se produjo en territorio de Silao, el 10 de agosto de 1860: el general liberal Jesús González Ortega, cuyos subalternos en esa ocasión fueron Ignacio Zaragoza e Ignacio Alatorre, derrotó a un ejército conservador más numeroso, comandado por Miramón y Mejía.

SILBERSTEIN TENENBAUM, JORGE ◆ n. en el DF (1959). Licenciado en matemáticas aplicadas por el ITAM (1978-82). Maestro en administración de empresas por el Instituto Tecnológico de Massachusetts (1985). Ha sido jefe del Departamento de Investigación de la Dirección General de Política Informática del INEGI (1980-82), asesor de Banamex (1984), asistente del tesorero de la Republic New York Corporation (1985-

86) y del Republic National Bank de Nueva York (1986), consultor interno de Safrabank (Estados Unidos, 1987-88); asesor del secretario (1989), director general de Ingeniería Financiera en la Unidad de Desincorporación de Entidades Paraestatales (1990-93) y subcoordinador general de la misma (1993-94), dentro de la SHCP; director general adjunto de Ingeniería Financiera y Proyectos Sectoriales de Banobras (1994) y coordinador general de la Unidad de Apoyo al Cambio Estructural (1995-99) y subsecretario de la SCT (1999-).

Silencio, Zona del ◆ Territorio sobre el cual la capa de la ionosfera es más delgada que en el resto del planeta y forma una especie de cono con la parte más angosta hacia la tierra. Está situado en la confluencia de los estados de Chihuahua, Coahuila y Durango, entre los paralelos 26 y 28. Comprende los municipios de Jiménez, Chihuahua; Francisco I. Madero y Sierra Mojada, Coahuila; y Mapimí y Tlahualilo, Durango. La descubrió el ingeniero químico Augusto Harry de la Peña en 1966. En ella no se captan las ondas hertzianas, lo que impide la comunicación por radio. Se producen también alteraciones magnéticas que no permiten a la brújula señalar al norte. Como las ondas provenientes del espacio exterior tienen paso franco, se observan peculiares fenómenos lumínicos y se ha registrado una radiación hasta 20 veces superior a la necesaria para tomar una radiografía torácica. Por la forma de embudo de la ionosfera, es un punto de atracción de objetos extraterrestres, como naves espaciales y aerolitos. Ahí se precipitó un cohete estadounidense Atenas que se esperaba descendiera en Nuevo México. El 8 de febrero de 1969 cayó el llamado meteorito de Allende, al que se calcula una antigüedad tres veces mayor que el sistema solar.

Zona del Silencio

Silerio Esparza, Maximiliano ◆ n. en el ejido Yerbabuena, Dgo. (1939). Licenciado en derecho por la Universidad Juárez de Durango. Pertenece al PRI desde 1958, en el que ha sido director estatal juvenil (1965), presidente del Comité Municipal en Durango (1966) y presidente del Comité Directivo Estatal en Durango (1969- 71), y presidente de la Comisión Coordinadora de Convenciones del CEN (1983). Secretario de Organización (1968-71) y secretario general de la Liga de Comunidades Agrarias y Sindicatos Campesinos de Durango (1975-78). Secretario general de la Confederación Nacional Campesina (1988-). Ha sido actuario notificador del juzgado segundo menor civil en Durango (1960-63), defensor de oficio, agente del Ministerio Público, asesor jurídico del Banjidal en Durango (1965-66), empleado del Programa Nacional Agrario del DAAC-CNC (1966-68), diputado local suplente, diputado local, presidente municipal de Durango, diputado federal (1976-79 y 1982-85) y senador (1988-91). Miembro de la Barra de Abogados de Durango. Secretario general de la CNC y gobernador de Durango (1992-1998).

Siliceo, Fernando ◆ n. en Guanajuato, Gto. (1864-?). Estudió en el Colegio Militar. En 1882 ingresó en la Escuela Naval de Campeche y se graduó como piloto de buques en 1887. En 1897 fue uno de los fundadores de la Escuela Naval Militar de Veracruz, en la que ejerció la docencia. En el Colegio Preparatorio de Veracruz fue profesor y subdirector. En 1919 fundó en el puerto de Veracruz, con apoyo de Venustiano Carranza y de Cándido Aguilar, la Escuela Náutica Mercante que en la actualidad lleva su nombre.

Maximiliano Silerio Esparza

Siliceo, Manuel ◆ n. en Silao, Gto., y m. en Orizaba, Ver. (?-1875). Abogado. Pasó de una posición política de liberal moderado a colaborador con los invasores franceses y el imperio. Secretario de Fomento (del 12 de diciembre de 1855 al 16 de septiembre 1857) en el gabinete de Ignacio Comonfort. Se adhirió al Plan de Tacubaya (1857). Miembro del Consejo de Gobierno (1864) y ministro de Instrucción Pública y Cultos (del 10 de abril al 16 de octubre 1865), en el gabinete de Maximiliano.

Siltepec ◆ Municipio de Chiapas situado en el sur del estado, al norte de Tapachula y al noreste de Acacoyagua. Superficie: 685.6 km^2. Habitantes: 30,777, de los cuales 7,764 forman la población económicamente activa. Hablan alguna lengua indígena 153 personas mayores de cinco años (mame 143).

Silva, Adriano ◆ n. en Querétaro, Qro. (1925). Egresado de la Escuela de Pintura y Escultura La Esmeralda (1959-61). Fue discípulo de José Chávez Morado. Es profesor en la Escuela Nacional de Maestros (1962-). Hay obras suyas en Morelia, Cancún y el Museo de Arte Moderno de México. En 1966 ganó el primer premio de escultura en el certamen de Nuevos Valores del Salón de la Plástica Mexicana y, tres años más tarde, el primer premio en el concurso de pintura de la Cámara de Comercio.

Silva, Agapito ◆ n. en Chilchota, Mich., y m. en la ciudad de México (1850-1896). Fue seminarista. Abandonó la escuela y en la capital del país militó en el Gran Círculo de Obreros de México. Se contó entre los promotores del Congreso Obrero de 1876, al que asistió como delegado de la Sociedad Unión y Concordia del Ramo de Meseros. Escribió el *El Socialista*, periódico del que fue coeditor. Cuando la prensa de derecha acusó al Congreso Obrero de radical, escribió en *El Siglo XIX*: "No es verdad que en el Congreso se encuentren delegados nihilistas o anarquistas. Nosotros somos socialistas, pero no petroleros o émulos de los comunalistas". Fue regidor del ayuntamiento de la ciudad de México, jefe de Hacienda en Sonora y director del *Diario de los Debates* del Congreso de la Unión. Al morir era diputado federal por Michoacán. Autor de los poemarios *Cantares, poesías mexicanas* (1873), *Páginas sueltas* (1875), *Poesías* (1875) y *Sueños y realidades* (1885); las novelas *Ernestina* (1885) y *Clemencia* (1891); y los dramas *Después de la falta* (1876, en colaboración con Alberto G. Bianchi), *El desenlace de un drama* (1880) y *Cazar al vuelo* (1886).

SILVA, ARNULFO ◆ n. en Oaxaca, Oax. (1874-?). Opositor del gobierno porfiriano desde 1907. En 1909 se afilió al antirreeleccionismo y en 1910 se incorporó a la insurrección maderista. Al producirse el golpe de Estado de Victoriano Huerta formó parte de las fuerzas constitucionalistas. En 1914 fue designado jefe de propaganda del Partido Nacional Democrático. Diputado al Congreso Constituyente de 1916-17. En 1920 se adhirió al Plan de Agua Prieta. Militó en el Partido Liberal Constitucionalista y fue contador mayor de Hacienda durante la presidencia de Álvaro Obregón.

Estela-la columna del sol, piedra de Xaltocan, obra de Federico Silva (1985)

SILVA, DAVID ◆ n. y m. en el DF (1917-1976). Abandonó la carrera de derecho para dedicarse a la actuación. Fue locutor de las estaciones XEB, XEW y XEQ e incursionó en el cine en 1939. Actuó en la primera fotonovela mexicana, *Póker de ases* (1942). Fue secretario de Organización y Propaganda de la Asociación Nacional de Actores (1964-67). Trabajó en Hollywood y se especializó en el Actor's Laboratory bajo la dirección de Miguel Chejov. Actuó en más de cien películas, dirigido entre otros por Rafael Corkidi, Alejandro Galindo y Juan López Moctezuma: *Brindis de amor* (en Hollywood), *El topo* y *La montaña sagrada* (de Jodorowsky), *La vida de Sam Houston* (filmada en Estados Unidos, hizo el papel de Antonio López de Santa Anna, de quien se declaraba admirador), *Hombre del aire, Café Concordia, Viviré otra vez, Cinco bikinis para el sordo, Esquina bajan, Ángeles del arrabal, Una familia de tantas, Espaldas mojadas, Hay lugar para dos, Rayito de luna, El amor es ciego, Ventarrón, Manos de seda, La isla de la Pasión* y *Humo en los ojos*. Obtuvo el Ariel a la mejor actuación (1946), por *Campeón sin corona*. Medalla Virginia Fábregas de la ANDA (1964) y mención honorífica del gobierno cubano por su trabajo en *Casta de roble*, filmada en Cuba (1957).

SILVA, FEDERICO ◆ n. en la ciudad de México (1923). Escultor. Se inició desde muy joven en las artes plásticas. Fue ayudante de David Alfaro Siqueiros en algunas obras públicas. Mostró por primera vez sus pinturas en el foyer del Palacio de Bellas Artes en una exposición colectiva en contra de la guerra y el fascismo. Su obra se centra en la cultura mexicana y ha encabezado propuestas vanguardistas. En 1967 presentó una exposición de pintura abstracta y después experimentó con arte cinético, lumínico, esculturas móviles con el uso de energía solar y eólica, láser, prismas, metales, etc. Profesor e investigador de la Coordinación de Humanidades de la UNAM. Autor de los libros *Federico Silva* (1977), *La escultura y otros menesteres* (1985) y *El viaje del nahual de Tonacacihuatl* (1989). Muestra de su arte se aprecia en los murales *La técnica al servicio de la paz*, en el IPN, *Historia de un espacio matemático*, realizado con rayo láser ubicado en la Facultad de Ingeniería de la UNAM; *La serpiente del Pedregal*, escultura de concreto y roca volcánica de 400 metros de longitud; *El vigilante*, monumento conmemorativo del Sistema de Satélites Morelos, el *Espacio Escultórico*, obra colectiva ubicada en la UNAM, que fue parteaguas de una nueva escultura en nuestro país, y la *Pintura Rupestre Huites*, de dimensiones colosales (5,000 metros cuadrados), elaborada sobre piedra granítica en el túnel de la presa Choix, en Sinaloa. Desde 1985 estableció su taller en Amaxac de Guerrero en Tlaxcala, transformando la ex fábrica de hilo La Estrella en un centro de creación de obras de arte, en donde se emplean los materiales de la región. En 1995 recibió el Premio Nacional de Ciencias y Artes, en el área de las Bellas Artes.

David Silva en *Esquina bajan*, película de Alejandro Galindo

SILVA, FIDEL ◆ n. en la hacienda de Apo, Tancítaro, Mich., y m. en el DF (1882-1950). Licenciado por la Escuela de Jurisprudencia de Morelia. Fue director de los periódicos *La Actualidad* (1906) y *El Heraldo* de Morelia, y *Verdad y Justicia* de Zamora. Redactor de *El Correo Michoacano* y *El Bien Social*. Autor de los opúsculos poéticos *Auras de juventud* (1905), *Quand l'amour meurt* (1924) y *Otoño sentimental* (1938).

SILVA Y ACEVES, MARIANO ◆ n. en La Piedad de Cabadas, Mich., y m. en el DF (1887-1937). Licenciado por la Eszcuela Nacional de Jurisprudencia (1905), de la que fue bibliotecario (1911-13). En 1910 se relacionó con el Ateneo de la Juventud. Fue profesor, director de la Escuela de Altos Estudios, secretario y rector de la Universidad Nacional de México (1921). En 1920 se le nombró secretario del Departamento Universitario y de Bellas Artes, en 1921 fundó la Escuela de Verano para Extranjeros y en 1933 el Instituto Mexicano de Lingüística y su *Revista Mexicana de Investigaciones Lingüísticas*. Fundó también las publicaciones *Conozca México, La Revista* y *Quincena Escolar*. Colaboró en *La Nave* (1916), *Pegaso* (1917), *Revista Nueva* (1919), *El Heraldo de México* (1921-23), *La Falange* (1923) y *El Nacional* (1942-46). Autor de *Arquilla de marfil* (1916), *Cara de Virgen* (1919), *Animula* (1920), *Campanitas de plata* (1925), *Calendario cívico mexicano* (1930), *Virgilio. Poeta mexicano. Estudio de formas del español en México* (1932), *Aventuras del tío Coyote* (1932) y *Muñecos de cuerda* (1936).

Silva y Álvarez Tostado, Atenógenes ♦ n. y m. en Guadalajara, Jal. (1848-1911). Sacerdote ordenado en 1871. Fue prebendado y canónigo lectoral de la catedral de Guadalajara. En 1892 fue preconizado y consagrado obispo de Colima y en 1900 se le trasladó a la arquidiócesis de Michoacán, que gobernó hasta su muerte.

Silva Cota, Guilebaldo ♦ n. en Ensenada, BC (1923). Licenciado en derecho por la UNAM (1951). Ha dado conferencias magistrales sobre derecho en la escuelas de derecho de BC. Pertenece al PRI desde 1946, donde ha sido presidente de la Comisión de Debates y Consejo Estatal, secretario de evaluación del Comité Directivo Estatal, miembro del Consejo Político Estatal, delegado nacional del CEN en Michoacán, Jalisco y Nayarit, presidente del CDE en BC y hoy es consejero político nacional. Diputado federal (1955-58), presidente municipal de Ensenada (1968) y senador (1994-2000). Ha sido presidente de la Comisión de Derechos Humanos de la Asociación Parlamentaria de BC y presidente del patronato de la Orquesta de BC.

Silva González, Miguel ♦ n. en Morelia, Mich., y m. en Cuba (1859-1916). Hijo de Miguel Silva Macías y nieto de José María Silva, ex gobernadores michoacanos. Cirujano (1883), se especializó en Europa como oftalmólogo. Fue profesor en la Escuela Nacional de Medicina y jefe de la sala de operaciones del Hospital General. Antirreeleccionista desde 1909. En 1910 era senador suplente y se unió a la insurrección maderista. Gobernador interino (1911) y constitucional de Michoacán (1912-13). Se negó a reconocer a Victoriano Huerta y, luego de un destierro de dos meses en Cuba, se unió a las fuerzas de Francisco Villa y se convirtió en su médico de cabecera durante la campaña del Bajío. Representó a la División del Norte en la firma del Pacto de Torreón, organizó hospitales de sangre en los campos de batalla y un sanatorio en Chihuahua. Tras la escisión revolucionaria y el triunfo de los carrancistas se exilió en Cuba, donde siguió ejerciendo la medicina hasta su muerte.

Silva Herrera, José ♦ n. en Cotija, Mich., y m. en la ciudad de México (1875-?). Abogado. Fue juez de primera instancia en Apatzingán, Jiquilpan y La Piedad, diputado federal (1911-13) y diputado al Congreso Constituyente de 1916-17, por Apatzingán.

Silva Herzog, Jesús ♦ n. en San Luis Potosí, SLP, y m. en el DF (1892-1985). Estudió economía en la Pain Up Town Business School de Nueva York (1914). Participó en la revolución en las fuerzas de Eulalio Gutiérrez, colaboró en los periódicos *El Demócrata* y *Redención* y fue su corresponsal en la Convención de Aguascalientes. Fundó la revista *Proteo* (mayo de 1917). En la ciudad de México, estudió en la Universidad Nacional (1920-22) y fue profesor de la Escuela Normal Primaria para Profesores (1919-24), de la Nacional de Maestros (1925-28), de la Escuela de Verano (1925-27) y de la Nacional de Agricultura (1924-38). Fundador del Instituto Mexicano de Investigaciones Económicas y de la *Revista Mexicana de Economía* (1928); coautor del primer proyecto de plan de estudios de la licenciatura de economía (1929) y profesor (1931-63) y director (1940-42) de la Escuela Nacional de Economía, donde fundó la revista *Investigación Económica*. Miembro de la Junta de Gobierno de la UNAM (1945-62), ministro en la Unión Soviética (1929-30), oficial mayor (1932-33) y subsecretario de la SEP (1933-34); miembro de la Junta de Gobierno del FCE (1935-62) y del Comité Editorial de la revista *Futuro* (1936-37). En 1937 coordinó la elaboración del informe sobre la industria petrolera que desembocó en el laudo de la Junta de Conciliación y en la sentencia de la Suprema Corte que llevaron a la expropiación petrolera. Presidente del Comité de Aforos y Subsidios al Comercio Exterior (1938-47), gerente general de la Distribuidora de Petróleos Mexicanos (1939-40), director fundador de *Cuadernos Americanos* (1942-85), subsecretario de Hacienda (1945-46) y presidente del Consejo Técnico de la Secretaría de Bienes Nacionales (1947-48). Autor, entre otras obras, de *Aspectos económicos de la Unión Soviética* (1930), *La reforma agraria en México y en algunos otros países* (1934), *El pensamiento socialista. Esquema histórico* (1937), *El pensamiento económico en México* (1947), *Tres siglos de pensamiento económico 1518-1817* (1950), *El agrarismo mexicano y la reforma agraria* (1959), *México y su petróleo. Una lección para América* (1959), *Breve historia de la revolución mexicana* (2 t., 1960), *Inquietud sin tregua. Ensayos y artículos escogidos, 1937-1965* (1965), *El pensamiento económico, social y político de México. 1810-1964* (1967), *Mensaje a un joven economista mexicano* (1967), *Una vida en la vida de México* (1972), *La larga marcha de un hombre de izquierda* (1972), *Mis últimas andanzas 1947-1970* (1973), *Una historia de la Universidad de México y sus problemas* (1974), *La economía política en México 1910-1974* (1975), *El pensamiento de Lázaro Cárdenas* (1975), Presidente de la Sociedad Mexicana de Geografía y Estadística (1944-46), miembro del Colegio Nacional de Economistas y de la Academia Mexicana (de la Lengua). Medalla Belisario Domínguez del Senado de la República (1984).

Silva Herzog Flores, Jesús ♦ n. en el DF (1935). Hijo del anterior. Licenciado en economía por la UNAM (1957)

Jesús Silva Herzog

FOTO: EIKÓN

Jesús Silva Herzog Flores

y maestro en economía por la Universidad de Yale (1962). Profesor de la UNAM (1963-70) y de El Colegio de México (1964-68). Pertenece al PRI. Ha sido analista del Departamento de Estudios Económicos (1956-64) y jefe de la Oficina Técnica del Banco de México (1964-70); director general de Crédito de la Secretaría de Hacienda (1970-72), director general del Infonavit (1972-76), gerente general del Banco de México (1977-78), director general de Crédito Público (1978-79), subsecretario (1979-82) y secretario de Hacienda (del 17 de marzo al 30 de noviembre de 1982 y del 1 de diciembre al 17 de junio de 1986) en los gabinetes de José López Portillo y Miguel de la Madrid; director general del Cemla (1988-91), embajador de México en España (1992-93); secretario de Turismo (1994); embajador en EUA (1995); precandidato y candidato del PRI al gobierno del DF (1999).

SILVA HERZOG MÁRQUEZ, JESÚS ◆ n. en el DF (1964). Licenciado en derecho por la UNAM y maestro en ciencias políticas por la Universidad de Columbia. Ha sido asesor de estudios legislativos del DDF (1988-93) y agregado de prensa en la embajada de México en Washington, EUA. Desde 1994 es profesor de tiempo completo del ITAM. Escribe en el diario *Reforma* (1993-). Autor de *Viejo régimen y transición democrática* (1999).

Fernando Silva Nieto

SILVA MACÍAS, MIGUEL ◆ n. en Ario de Rosales y m. en Morelia, Mich. (1821-1860). Hijo de José María Silva, ex gobernador michoacano. Médico cirujano (1847), realizó estudios de posgrado en Francia, Alemania, Inglaterra, Italia y Estados Unidos. En 1850, en Morelia, se le encomendó el control de una epidemia de cólera. Fue consejero de gobierno en Michoacán. Se adhirió a la revolución de Ayutla y llegó a la gubernatura interina de Michoacán (de enero de 1856 al 30 de junio de 1857), convocó a elecciones para diputados al Congreso Constituyente y promulgó la Constitución de 1857. Fue, asimismo, colaborador de los gobernadores liberales Melchor Ocampo y Epitacio Huerta.

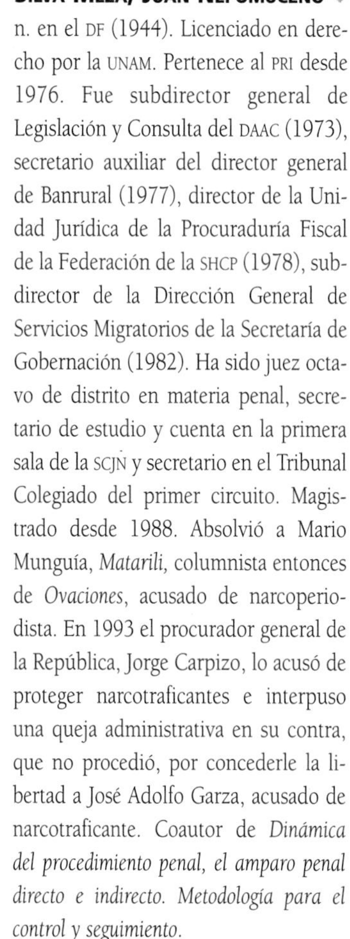

SILVA MEZA, JUAN NEPOMUCENO ◆ n. en el DF (1944). Licenciado en derecho por la UNAM. Pertenece al PRI desde 1976. Fue subdirector general de Legislación y Consulta del DAAC (1973), secretario auxiliar del director general de Banrural (1977), director de la Unidad Jurídica de la Procuraduría Fiscal de la Federación de la SHCP (1978), subdirector de la Dirección General de Servicios Migratorios de la Secretaría de Gobernación (1982). Ha sido juez octavo de distrito en materia penal, secretario de estudio y cuenta en la primera sala de la SCJN y secretario en el Tribunal Colegiado del primer circuito. Magistrado desde 1988. Absolvió a Mario Munguía, *Matarili*, columnista entonces de *Ovaciones*, acusado de narcoperiodista. En 1993 el procurador general de la República, Jorge Carpizo, lo acusó de proteger narcotraficantes e interpuso una queja administrativa en su contra, que no procedió, por concederle la libertad a José Adolfo Garza, acusado de narcotraficante. Coautor de *Dinámica del procedimiento penal, el amparo penal directo e indirecto. Metodología para el control y seguimiento*.

SILVA NAVA, CARLOS DE ◆ n. en el DF (1941). Licenciado en derecho por la Universidad Autónoma de Guadalajara (1964). Ha sido primer secretario del Tribunal Colegiado del Cuarto Circuito de Guadalajara (1966-68), secretario de Estudio y Cuenta de la Suprema Corte (1968-72), juez tercero de distrito en Nuevo Laredo (1972), juez segundo de distrito en materia administrativa en el DF (1972-77), magistrado del Tribunal Colegiado del Décimo Circuito (1977-78), magistrado del Segundo Tribunal Colegiado del Primer Circuito en materia administrativa del DF (1978-84) y ministro de la Suprema Corte de Justicia de la Nación (1984-).

SILVA NIETO, FERNANDO ◆ n. en San Luis Potosí, SLP (1950). Licenciado en derecho por la Universidad Autónoma de SLP (1973), posgraduado en planeación y política social (1970-77) y maestro en ciencia política por El Colegio de México (1977-79). Es investigador del INAP (1979-80). Ha sido asesor de la Dirección de Política Económica y Social y director de Asesoría a Estados de la SPP, secretario particular del titular de la Sedue, coordinador del Programa Solidaridad en el DF y asesor del secretario de Relaciones Exteriores (1993-94). En el gobierno potosino ha sido secretario particular del gobernador (1973), secretario de Planeación y Finanzas (1994), secretario de Educación (1995) y gobernador constitucional (1997-).

SILVA OCHOA, JORGE HUMBERTO ◆ n. en Colima, Col. (1937). Estudió en la Escuela Normal Gregorio Torres Quintero. Es licenciado en derecho por la Universidad de Colima. Miembro del PRI, en el que ha desempeñado diversas comisiones. Miembro fundador del Sindicato Único de Trabajadores de la Universidad de Colima. Profesor en la Escuela Normal Superior de Puebla (1971) y en la Universidad Autónoma de Guerrero (1972-73). Ha sido director técnico de la Escuela Primaria Federal Revolución, en Armería, Colima; director del Centro de Estudios Científicos y Tecnológicos 80, de Colima; secretario del Ayuntamiento de Cuauhtémoc, director de la Escuela Secundaria Técnica 1 de Colima, diputado local suplente (1964-67), corresponsal de *El Día* en Colima (1967-78), asesor del director general de Educación Pública en Guerrero (1972-73), jefe del Departamento de Servicios Sociales (1973-77), secretario general (1977-79), rector interino (1979-80) y rector de la Universidad de Colima (1980-84); director fundador del periódico *El Comentario* y diputado federal (1982-85). Ganó la presea de la Federación Nacional de Colegios y Asociaciones de Profesionistas.

SILVA VALDÉS, JESÚS ◆ n. en Morelia Mich., y m. en EUA (1914-1996). Compositor y guitarrista. En 1933 ingresó en el Conservatorio Nacional de Música a estudiar la Dirección y Composición con Carlos Chávez. Su primer maestro de guitarra fue Francisco Salinas, seguido por Manuel M. Ponce y, posteriormente, el español Andrés Segovia. También estudió en la Academia Chigiana de Siena, Italia, donde fue nombrado maestro de excelencia. Fue director de la Escuela Nacional de Música de Brooklym y de The North Carolina School of Performing Arts. Fue declarado Educador Sobresaliente de América, en Washington; se impuso su nombre a una beca que otorga la Virginia Commonwealth University, para estudiantes de guitarra; y logró que compositores como Manuel M. Ponce, Blas Galindo, Luis Sandi, entre otros, escribieran música para que fuera interpretada exclusivamente por él.

Silveti, Juan ◆ n. en Guanajuato, Gto., y m. en el DF (1893-1956). Se presentó como novillero en El Toreo de la Condesa, en 1915. Su arrojo en el ruedo le valió los motes de *Juan sin Miedo* y *El Tigre de Guanajuato*. En 1916 tomó la alternativa de manos de Luis Freg, misma que ese año refrendó en España, ante Rafael *el Gallo*. Se convirtió en personaje pintoresco en España por las anécdotas que se forjaron a su alrededor y por su vestuario: llevaba siempre traje de charro, pistola al cinto y un voluminoso mechón sobre la frente. Volvió a México en 1920 y continuó en la fiesta al lado de figuras como Gaona, Belmonte, Sánchez Mejías, Segura y Freg, entre otros. Durante su carrera sufrió numerosas cogidas, algunas de ellas de gravedad. Se retiró del toreo y vivió en Colombia, donde participó en las pugnas entre conservadores y liberales. En un movimiento armado alcanzó el grado de general.

Silveti Reynoso, Juan ◆ n. en el DF (1929). Torero. Hijo del anterior. Se inició como torero a los 16 años en la plaza de Aguascalientes. En 1949 se presentó exitosamente en la Plaza México. En 1950 tomó la alternativa de manos de Fermín Rivera y tuvo como testigo a Manolo Dos Santos. Ese mismo año viajó a España. En Madrid confirmó la alternativa con Antonio Bienvenida y otra vez Manolo Dos Santos como testigo. Esa tarde cortó oreja. Se retiró en 1968 en Tijuana.

Silla, de la ◆ Cerro de Nuevo León situado junto a la ciudad de Monterrey. La cima esta formada por dos eminencias que le dan una forma similar a la de una silla de montar.

Silla, de la ◆ Sierra de Durango. Es una de las estribaciones orientales de la sierra Madre Occidental. Es la prolongación meridional de la sierra de Coneto. Se halla al sur del valle de San Juan del Río, al norte de Malpaís de la Breña y al nor-noreste de la capital estatal.

Siller, Alfonso M. ◆ m. en el DF (1883-1966). Licenciado en derecho por la Escuela Nacional de Jurisprudencia (1903). Se unió al Ejército Constitucionalista en 1913 y fungió como secretario de gobierno de Coahuila en la gestión de Venustiano Carranza. Primer secretario (1915) y encargado de negocios (1916) y consejero en la legación mexicana en Washington (1916). Subsecretario encargado del despacho de Relaciones Exteriores (1916-17). Desempeñó diversos puestos en las representaciones mexicanas en Sudamérica, Francia e Italia.

Simeón, Rémi ◆ n. y m. en Francia (1827-1890). En 1839 vivió en México durante una breve temporada, en la que el americanista Joseph Auguste Aubin logró interesarlo por las culturas prehispánicas. Volvió a Francia, donde estudió derecho. En 1864 volvió a México apoyado por la Comisión Científica Francesa y con el auxilio del fraile Alonso de Molina inició la redacción de una gramática y un diccionario de náhuatl. En 1875 se encargó de la publicación de la *Gramática de la lengua náhuatl*, de Andrés de Olmos, tradujo los anales VI y VII de Chimalpáin (1889, lo que le valió un premio Loubat) y tradujo al francés la *Historia de las cosas de la Nueva España*, de Bernardino de Sahagún. Autor del *Dictionnaire de la langue nahuatl ou mexicaine* (1885), por el que obtuvo el premio Volney. Fue miembro de la Sociedad Americanista Francesa y, en 1884, presidente del Comité de Arqueología de la Sociedad de Etnografía de Francia.

Simojovel ◆ Municipio de Chiapas situado en el norte del estado, al noreste de Tuxtla Gutiérrez y al norte de San Cristóbal de Las Casas. Superficie: 476.9 km^2. Habitantes: 31,656, de los cuales 7,258 forman la población económicamente activa. Hablan alguna lengua indígena 17,126 personas mayores de cinco años (tzotzil 13,581 y tzeltal 3,545). Indígenas monolingües: 6,874. La cabecera es Simojovel de Allende.

Foto: Michael Calderwood

Cerro de la Silla, en Nuevo León

Simone, André ◆ n. y m. en Checoslovaquia (?-?). Periodista y escritor cuyo nombre real era Otto Katz. Radicado en Berlín desde 1922, era director del teatro de Piscator y de la editorial de la Ayuda Obrera Internacional. Al ascender Hitler al poder (1933) se refugió en Francia, donde colaboró en numerosas publicaciones y codirigió, con Alexander Abusch, la edición del *Libro pardo sobre el incendio del Reichstag y el terror de Hitler* (1933). Combatió por la República Española en las brigadas internacionales y en 1939 volvió como refugiado a Francia. Vino a México en 1940, donde logró que el gobierno avilacamachista concediera un número mayor de visados a los alemanes antifascistas. Redactor de la revista *Alemania Libre* (1941-42) y secretario del Movimiento Alemania Libre (1942). En mayo de 1942, al fundarse la editorial El Libro Libre, de los germanohablantes antinazis, propuso que se editaran textos en español para dar a conocer las posiciones del Movimiento Alemania Libre. Con el apoyo económico del gobierno mexicano dirigió entonces la edición del *Libro negro del terror nazi en Europa. Testimonios de escritores y artistas de 16 naciones* (1943). Regresó a Europa en 1946. Autor de *La batalla de Rusia* (México, 1943).

Foto: Boris de Swan

Transbordador La Paz-Mazatlán

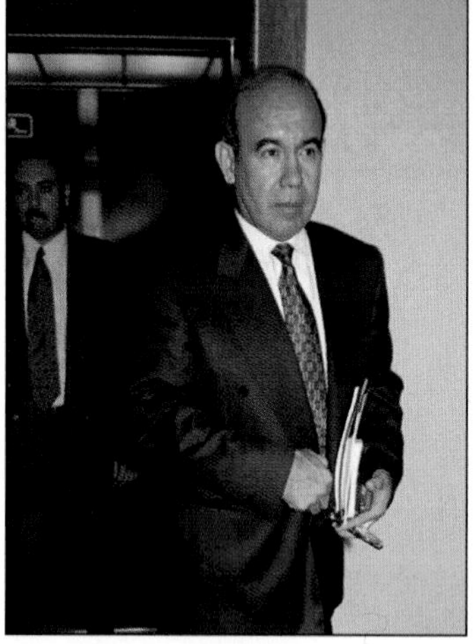

Juan S. Millán gobernador constitucional de Sinaloa

Sinaloa ◆ Estado de la República Mexicana situado en la costa del océano Pacífico. La parte norte de su litoral corresponde al golfo de California. Limita con Sonora, Chihuahua, Durango y Nayarit. Superficie: 58,328 km^2 (decimoséptimo lugar en extensión del país, equivalente al 2.98 por ciento del territorio nacional). La entidad está atravesada por las estribaciones de la sierra Madre Occidental, de la que se desprenden hacia la llanura costera las serranías de Sanabri, Cocapiro, Santa Rita, San Vicente, Tasajera, Ocoroni, Parras, Baragua, Capirato, el Potrero, Santiago y parte de la sierra de Durango. Las corrientes más importantes de Sinaloa son los ríos Fuerte, San Lorenzo, Piaxtla, Baluarte, Presidio, Sinaloa y Humaya. El estado se halla dividido en 18 municipios. Contaba en 1997 con 2,509,142 habitantes. Su producto interno bruto es de 2.24 del total nacional (1996). La población económicamente activa de Sinaloa en 1995 fue el 54.5 de las personas mayores de 12 años. La tasa de analfabetos mayores de 15 años fue de 8.68 por ciento de la población estatal mayor de 15 años. Hablan alguna lengua indígena 24,864 personas mayores de cinco años (mayo 9,603, mixteco 6,396, zapoteco 2,064 y náhuatl 1,129), de las cuales 2,429 no dominan el español. *Historia*: hace 12 o 14 mil años el territorio que se extiende desde Sinaloa hasta el norte de Arizona fue una zona de vegetación abundante, en la que vivían paquidermos y camélidos primitivos, lo que atrajo a los cazadores nómadas. Los primeros grupos sedentarios se establecieron hacia el año 250 a.n.e. en las inmediaciones del río Baluarte. A partir del año 900 el florecimiento cultural se desplazó hacia el norte del actual estado, a las regiones de Culiacán y Guasave. En esa época poblaban el actual territorio sinaloense diversas tribus de la familia lingüística yuto-azteca. Poco antes de la llegada de los españoles, el territorio del actual estado de Sinaloa estaba poblado por seis grupos sedentarios de agricultores y recolectores: cahítas, tahues, totorame, pacaxee, acaxee y xiximes. El 21 de diciembre de 1529, Nuño Beltrán de Guzmán inició una expedición de conquista al norte de la Nueva España; dos años después llegó al valle de Culiacán donde fundó la villa de San Miguel del Río San Lorenzo (29 de septiembre de 1531). Beltrán erigió el primer ayuntamiento de San Miguel y designó alcalde mayor a Diego de Proaño, quien trató de enriquecerse con el tráfico de esclavos. Los indios se rebelaron y Beltrán destituyó a Proaño. Presionados por la resistencia indígena, los españoles mudaron San Miguel del Río San Lorenzo a la confluencia de los ríos Humaya y Tamazula, y la llamaron San Miguel de Culiacán. Poco después, el caudillo indio Ayapin inició una sublevación y los españoles pidieron ayuda a Francisco Vázquez de Coronado, gober-

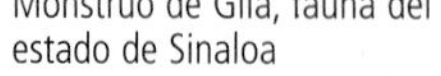

Monstruo de Gila, fauna del estado de Sinaloa

Paisaje aéreo de Cosalá, Sinaloa

Mayo con traje pascola de Sinaloa

FOTO: FONDO EDITORIAL GRUPO AZABACHE

nador de Nueva Galicia, quien sofocó la rebelión. En 1564, Francisco de Ibarra fundó San Juan Bautista de Carapoa, poblamiento pronto abandonado ante la resistencia indígena que liberó al territorio de invasores. En 1583, Pedro de Montoya consiguió autorización para reconquistar y fundó San Felipe y Santiago de Carapoa. Los indígenas ejecutaron a Montoya y a sus lugartenientes y el resto de los españoles huyó. El gobernador de Nueva Vizcaya envió un destacamento que obligó a los fugitivos a permanecer en San Felipe y después llegó él mismo para encabezar una campaña contra los indios, misma que acabó en fracaso. Sinaloa quedó de nuevo en poder de sus pobladores originales, aunque cinco españoles permanecieron en San Felipe y Santiago, en las riberas del Sinaloa, con la esperanza de encontrar oro. En 1591 los jesuitas Gonzalo de Tapia y Martín Pérez iniciaron la fundación de misiones en Sinaloa, lo que les permitió ganar prosélitos. En 1599, Diego Martínez de Hurdaide se hizo cargo del presidio militar y apoyó la tarea de evangelización por el noroeste. Entre 1595 y 1634 se crearon las misiones de Baca, Nío, Mocorito, Ahome, San Miguel Charay, San Jerónimo Tamazula, Mochicahui, Toro, Choix, Badiraguato, Atotonilco, Careatapa, San Juan, Bacubirito, Chicorato, San Ignacio, Guasave, Santa Polonia, Cabazán, Ajoya, Yecorato y San Agustín, que pronto devinieron centros autosuficientes, con alta producción de grano y ganado. Por cédula real de 1732 se creó la Gobernación de Sinaloa con la provincia de su nombre y las de Ostimuri y Sonora. Las de Culiacán y Chametla pertenecían a Nueva Galicia y Nueva Vizcaya, respectivamente. En 1776 se formaron las Provincias Internas de Occidente (Sonora y Sinaloa). Diez años después se creó la Intendencia de Arizpe, con las mismas provincias. Tras la expulsión (1767) de los jesuitas de la Nueva España las misiones resultaron abandonadas, en tanto que los indios fueron despojados de las tierras comunales y se convitieron en mineros o peones agrícolas. La guerra de Independencia contribuyó a un mayor aislamiento de Sinaloa, situación que favoreció el contrabando, gracias al cual surgieron grupos económicamente poderosos en El Rosario, Cosalá, Culiacán, Álamos y Pitic. En 1810 Miguel Hidalgo encargó a José María González Hermosillo levantar a Sonora y Sinaloa. Éste salió de

Foto: Fondo Editorial Grupo Azabache

Presa Sanalona, en Sinaloa

Timbre mexicano con el traje regional de Sinaloa

Pesca de camarón en Escuinapa, Sinaloa

Foto: Fondo Editorial Grupo Azabache

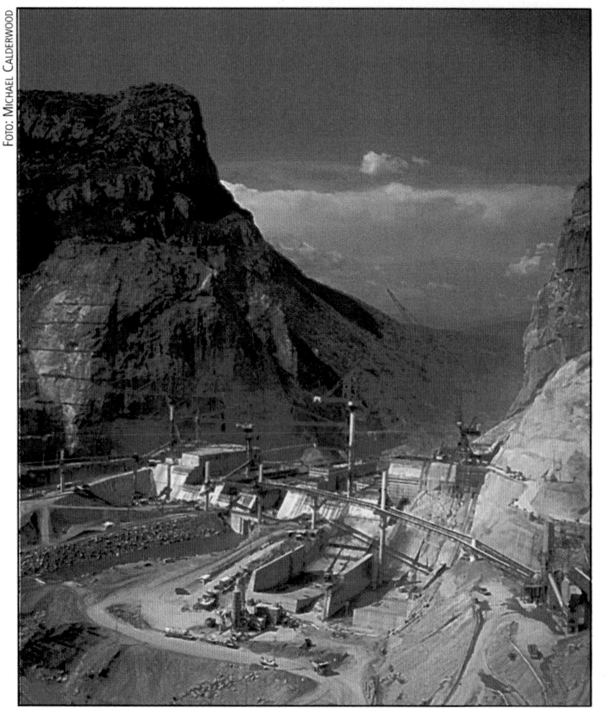

Presa Huites, en el estado de Sinaloa

Foto: Michael Calderwood

Jalisco y el 21 de diciembre tomó El Rosario, plaza defendida por el realista Pedro de Villaescusa, quien fue liberado y marchó al norte en busca del intendente Alejo García Conde. González Hermosillo fue derrotado por éste en San Ignacio, el 7 de febrero de 1811, con lo que prácticamente cesó la actividad de los insurrectos. En 1821, en El Rosario, el militar Fermín de Tarbé y el sacerdote Agustín José Chirlín se sublevaron en favor del Plan de Iguala. Sonora y Sinaloa, entonces, se convirtieron en parte del imperio iturbidista, con el nombre de provincia de Sonora. En 1823, los habitantes de El Rosario propusieron la creación del estado de Sonora, pero el Congreso General decidió dividir el territorio en Sinaloa, con capital en Culiacán, y Sonora, con sede en Ures. En enero de 1824, no obstante, el Congreso federal volvió a reunir a Sonora y Sinaloa en el Estado Libre de Occidente, cuya legislatura se asentaría en El Fuerte. Una insurrección indígena obligó al gobierno local a trasladarse a Cosalá, donde no hubo quórum para el Congreso Constituyente. El 14 de octubre de 1830 el Congreso de la Unión erigió los estados de Sinaloa y Sonora. A partir de

Foto: Museo de Arte de Sinaloa

Grupo de jóvenes a la sombra, pastel al óleo de Antonio López Sáenz, pintor originario de Mazatlán, Sinaloa

entonces, las oligarquías locales compitieron por el control económico y político de Sinaloa. Tales grupos eran las familias Iriarte y De la Vega, en Cosalá y Culiacán, respectivamente, y los comerciantes avecindados en Mazatlán. El Congreso Constituyente de Sinaloa se instaló en Culiacán el 13 de marzo de 1831. El estado se integró con los partidos de El Rosario, Concordia, Villa

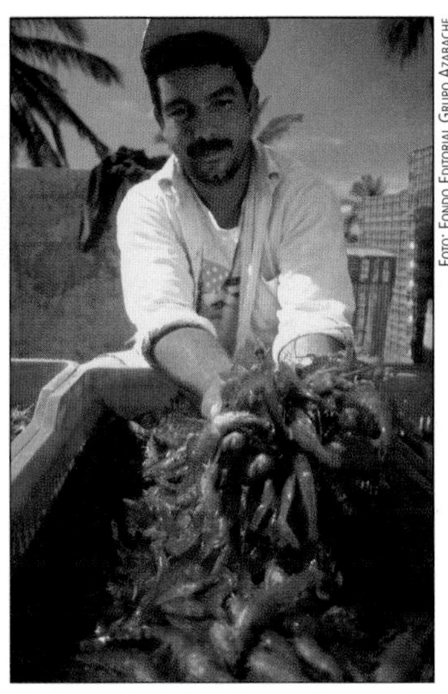

Foto: Fondo Editorial Grupo Azabache

Pesca de camarón en Escuinapa, Sinaloa

Unión, San Sebastián, Cosalá, Culiacán, Badiraguato, Mocorito, Sinaloa, El Fuerte y Choix. Su Constitución se expidió el 12 de diciembre de 1831. El primer gobernador fue Manuel María Álvarez de la Bandera, identificado con la familia Iriarte. La familia De la Vega, descontenta con esta designación, provocó en 1833 un motín que obligó al gobernador y a los legisladores a huir de Culiacán. Manuel María de la Vega y Rábago asumió el Ejecutivo local en 1835 e instauró un cacicazgo de veinte años, durante los cuales permitió a su familia enriquecerse mediante el contrabando, lo que afectaba los intereses de los comerciantes mazatlecos. En 1835, bajo el régimen centralista, Sinaloa se transformó en departamento. Tres años después, el gobernador Francisco Orrantia Antelo reivindicó la Constitución de 1824, lo que desató nuevamente la lucha civil. Durante las guerras intestinas Sinaloa contó con gobiernos paralelos, centralista y federalista, funcionando el primero en Culiacán y el segundo en Mazatlán. En 1847 los buques de guerra estadounidenses anclaron frente a Mazatlán y pidieron la rendición de la plaza, misma que fue evacuada de inmediato por la autoridad militar sin presentar batalla. El ejército invasor ocupó el puerto y permaneció en él, sin ser hostilizado, hasta el fin de la guerra. En 1852 accedió a la gubernatura Francisco de la Vega, ante lo cual, los comerciantes extranjeros de Mazatlán iniciaron una serie de manifestaciones y motines, molestos por las altas contribuciones que debían pagar. De la Vega trató de sofocar ese movimiento, pero el militar Pedro Valdés, pagado por el grupo mazatleco, aprehendió al gobernador, se autodesignó mandatario, proclamó la independencia de Mazatlán y saqueó Culiacán. Las pretensiones de Valdés fueron nulificadas por el gobierno central, pero tales hechos significaron el fin del cacicazgo delaveguista (1853) y el principio de la hegemonía de los comerciantes mazatlecos. Éstos mantuvieron el control del gobierno estatal mediante sucesivos gobiernos militares, situación que terminó con el triunfo de la revolución de Ayutla. Juan Álvarez designó gobernador a Pomposo Verdugo, aunque en 1858 los conservadores volvieron al poder gracias al golpe de Estado de Ignacio Comonfort. Plácido Vega, liberal, se sublevó en El Fuerte en 1859 y, apoyado por el gobernador sonorense Ignacio Pesqueira, avanzó hacia el sur. En La Noria, Mocorito, derrotó a los conservadores; éstos se retiraron a Mazatlán, plaza que fue sitiada por fuerzas conjuntas de Pesqueira y Vega. Al tenerse la noticia de que los sitiados recibirían refuerzos, Pesqueira se trasladó a Los Mimbres, cerca de Cosalá, donde presentó batalla y derrotó a los conservadores; más tarde, ya sin dificultad, tomó Mazatlán. Pesqueira regresó entonces a Sonora y nombró gobernador y jefe de armas a Vega. Éste combatió contra Manuel Lozada y aun acudió a Jalisco para auxiliar a Pedro Ogazón. Durante la guerra de los Tres Años, la armada inglesa envió a Sinaloa un contingente con el pretexto de proteger los intereses de los súbditos ingleses avecindados en Mazatlán y Culiacán, así como de un numeroso grupo de españoles, casi todos comerciantes, que tomaron las armas contra los liberales. En 1862, al iniciarse la intervención francesa, Vega creó la Brigada Sinaloa, que puso a las órdenes de Comonfort; poco después se le encomendó la tarea de comprar armas y municiones en Estados Unidos, para lo cual dejó en la gubernatura a Jesús García Morales. El 26 de marzo de 1864 la fragata *Cordelliere* bombardeó Mazatlán e intentó un desembarco que fue rechazado. Los republicanos Ramón Corona y Joaquín Sánchez depusieron a García Morales y lo sustituyeron con Antonio Rosales. El 13 de noviembre de 1864 los franceses lograron ocupar Mazatlán. Otro contingente imperialista tomó Altata el 21 de diciembre del mismo año y marchó sobre Culiacán, pero en

Foto: Gobierno del Estado de Sinaloa

Puente Negro en Culiacán, Sinaloa

Foto: Fondo Editorial Grupo Azabache

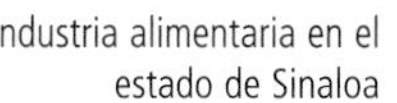

Industria alimentaria en el estado de Sinaloa

Foto: Gobierno del Estado de Sinaloa

Mujer rezando en el interior de la capilla de Jesús Malverde, en Culiacán, Sinaloa

San Pedro fue derrotada por Rosales. No obstante, los franceses entraron en Sinaloa desde Durango. Rosales tuvo algunas diferencias con Corona y fue sustituido en el gobierno por Domingo Rubí; más tarde murió en combate contra los imperialistas que avanzaban sobre Álamos. Los franceses, adueñados de Mazatlán, nombraron autoridades, asesinaron a reales o presuntos republicanos y recorrieron las zonas aledañas practicando la táctica de "tierra arrasada", hasta abandonar el puerto, el 13 de noviembre de 1866. Durante el periodo gubernamental de Eustaquio Buelna, la guarnición de Mazatlán se pronunció por el Plan de la Noria. Buelna fue a Sonora para pedir ayuda a Pesqueira, quien avanzó sobre las fuerzas de Manuel Márquez de León, gobernador nombrado por Donato Guerra, y lo venció en Culiacán. Luego de la derrota de los pronunciados de la Noria, Buelna volvió a Mazatlán, donde fue secuestrado por militares rebeldes, al parecer apoyados por el cónsul estadounidense, y liberado previo pago de un rescate. Sóstenes Rocha llegó a Sinaloa para restablecer el orden, el gobernador reasumió el poder y cambió la capital a Culiacán. En julio de 1876 Francisco Cañedo se pronunció por el Plan de Tuxtepec y depuso al gobernador Jesús María Gaxiola. Francisco Arce, comandante militar, aprovechó la confusión para asumir el gobierno, aunque el jefe de la guarnición de

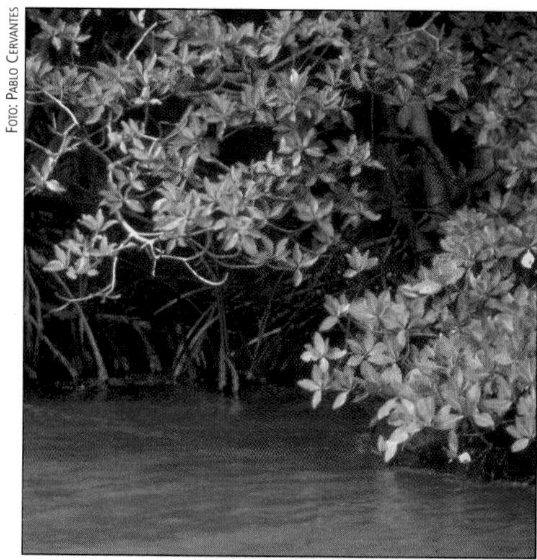
Foto: Pablo Cervantes

Manglar en Sinaloa

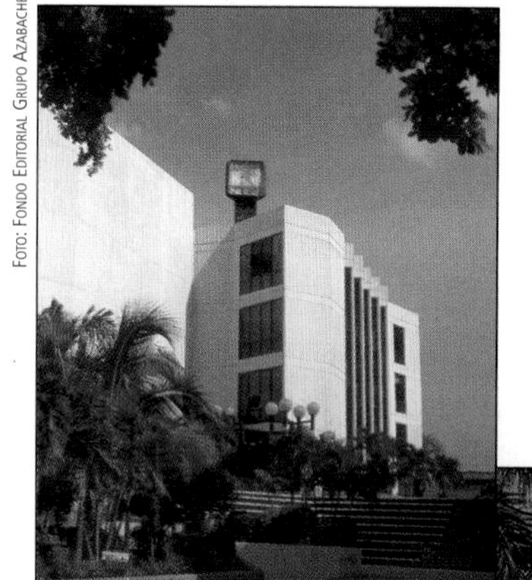
Foto: Fondo Editorial Grupo Azabache

Centro Cultural Genaro Estrada, en Culiacán, Sinaloa

Palacio municipal de Culiacán, Sinaloa

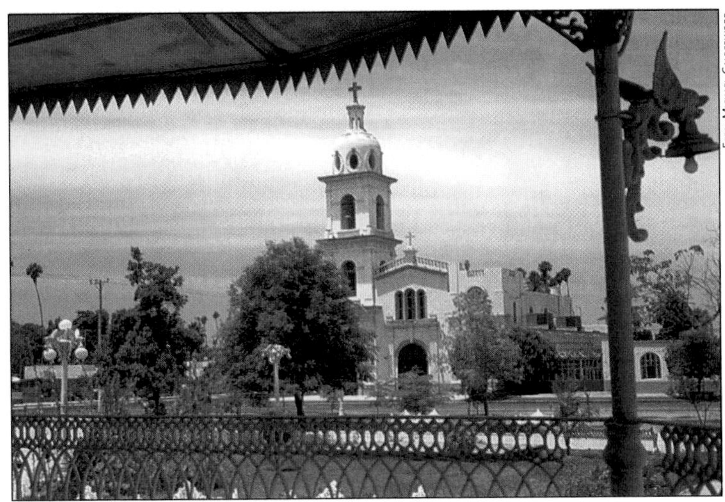

Foto: Michael Calderwood

Los Mochis, ciudad en el norte del estado de Sinaloa

Culiacán, Jesús Ramírez Terrón, lo enfrentó y derrotó en Cosalá y entregó el poder a Cañedo. Ramírez Terrón se sublevó en 1879, indignado por la matanza odenada por Porfirio Díaz y perpetrada por el gobernador veracruzano Mier y Terán. Ramírez Terrón fue derrotado y se refugió en Durango, donde fue asesinado. En junio de 1910 el antirreeleccionista Gabriel Leyva Solano se rebeló contra Porfirio Díaz; fue traicionado y asesinado tres días después de su levantamiento. El 20 de noviembre de ese año los maderistas iniciaron la revolución con un enfrentamiento contra las tropas federales en las afueras de Culiacán. Los seguidores del Plan de San Luis fueron, en Sinaloa, Juan M. Banderas, Ramón F. Iturbe, Herculano de la Rocha, Justo Tirado y Pomponio Acosta. Sitiaron y tomaron Culiacán (mayo de 1911) y Mazatlán (2 de junio de 1911). Aunque el gobernador Felipe Riveros reconoció a Huerta (5 de marzo de 1913), éste ordenó su aprehensión y nombró en su lugar a José Legorreta. Ramón F. Iturbe y Macario Gaxiola, quienes aún reconocían la autoridad de Riveros, iniciaron la revolución constitucionalista en Sinaloa con un ataque fallido sobre Topolobampo; en Estación San Blas, donde se replegaron, se les unieron Riveros y Manuel Mezta; gracias a éste, los constitucionalistas pudieron rechazar el contraataque de los federales. A su paso por Sinaloa (22 de enero de 1914), Venustiano Carranza intentó desconocer a Riveros, pero éste conservó el cargo gracias al apoyo de Juan Carrasco. Benjamín G. Hill tomó Los Mochis y Álvaro Obregón ocupó Culiacán el 14 de noviembre. Obregón sitió Mazatlán, encargó el asedio a Carrasco, Ángel Flores, Fructuoso Méndez, Elías Mascareño, Iturbe, Gaxiola y Mezta, y continuó su marcha al sur. Iturbe mantuvo el asedio y tomó Mazatlán el 9 de agosto de 1914. Luego de la escisión revolucionaria, Riveros y Gaxiola se declararon villistas, aunque el control del estado permaneció con los constitucionalistas. Iturbe tomó posesión de la gubernatura en 1917. La rebelión de Agua Prieta lo obligó a dimitir en 1920. No fue sino hasta el sexenio cardenista cuando se hicieron las primeras afectaciones a los latifundios sinaloenses, especialmente a los de la United Sugar Company, en cuyas tierras se desarrolló la Sociedad de Interés Colectivo Agrícola Ejidal de Emancipación Proletaria, que funcionó entre 1939 y 1953. En 1937, durante la administración de Alfredo Delgado, se inició la represión contra los campesinos, que continuó pese a la oposición del gobernador Rodolfo T. Loaiza, quien murió asesinado por las guardias blancas. Hacia 1940 se inició la construc-

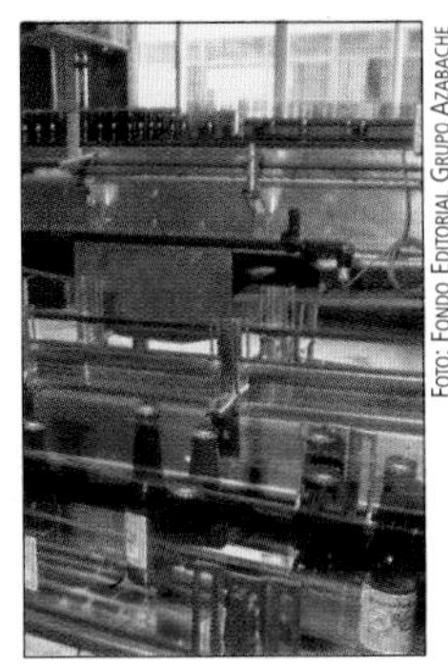

Foto: Fondo Editorial Grupo Azabache

Cervecería Pacífico, en el estado de Sinaloa

Foto: Museo de Arte de Sinaloa

Rincón Topolobampo, acuarela de Edgardo Coghlan, pintor sinaloense

Foto: Fondo Editorial Grupo Azabache

Capilla dedicada a Jesús Malverde, en Culiacán, Sinaloa

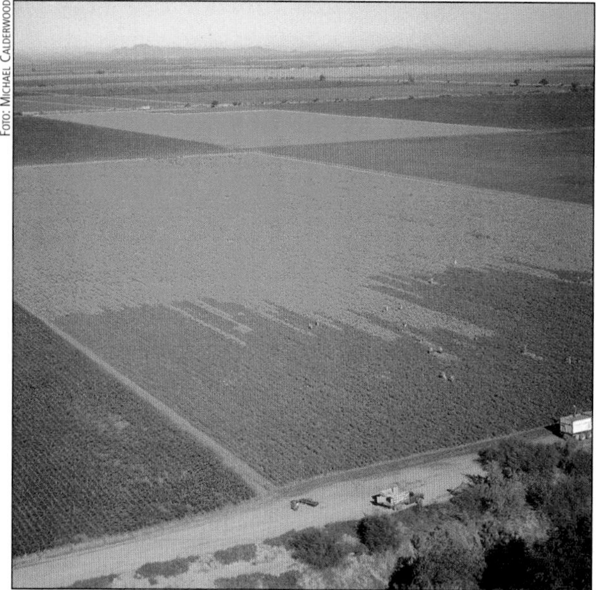
Foto: Michael Calderwood

Campo de zempazúchil en Los Mochis, Sinaloa

ción de los sistemas de riego, lo que benefició a los propietarios privados. Durante la segunda guerra mundial, se inició en la entidad el cultivo masivo y legal de amapola, para abastecer de opio y morfina al mercado de Estados Unidos, país que había entrado al conflicto y requería de materias primas para la elaboración de medicamentos. Terminada la conflagración, continuó en algunas zonas el cultivo de estupefacientes, ya de manera ilegal.

Poblado en la sierra de Tacuichamona, Sinaloa

Foto: Gobierno del estado de Sinaloa

POBLACIÓN DE 5 AÑOS Y MÁS HABLANTE DE LENGUA INDÍGENA, 1995

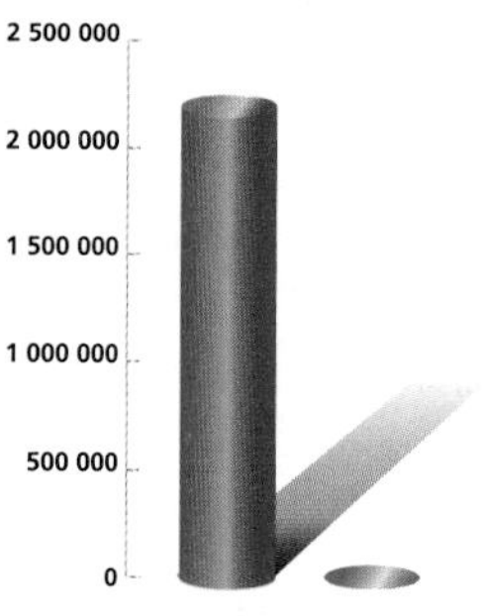

DISTRIBUCIÓN PORCENTUAL DE LA POBLACIÓN OCUPADA POR SECTOR DE ACTIVIDAD ECONÓMICA, 1995

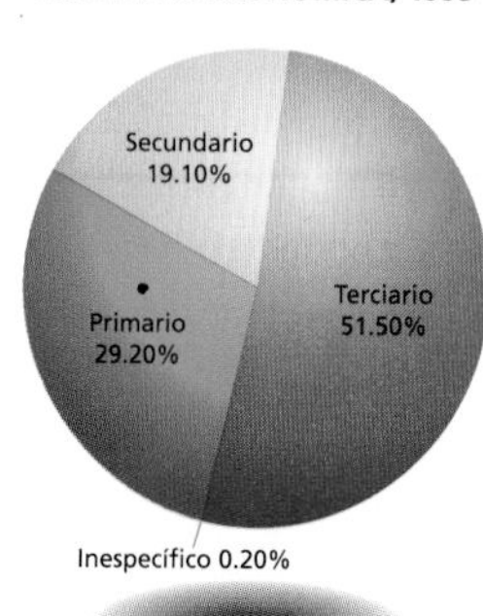

PROMEDIO DE ESCOLARIDAD DE LA POBLACIÓN DE 15 AÑOS Y MÁS, POR SEXO, 1995

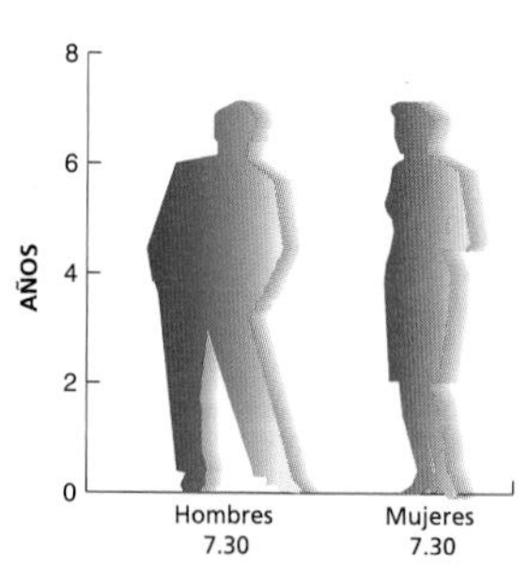

LONGITUD DE LA RED DE CARRETERAS POR SUPERFICIE DE RODAMIENTO, 1995

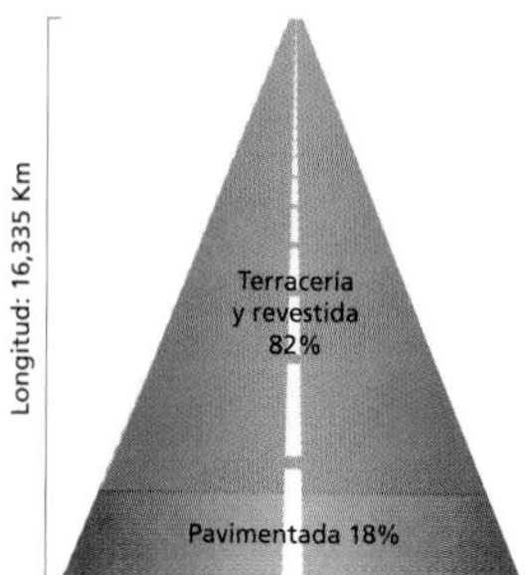

BIBLIOTECAS Y USUARIOS, 1993
Número de bibliotecas: 325

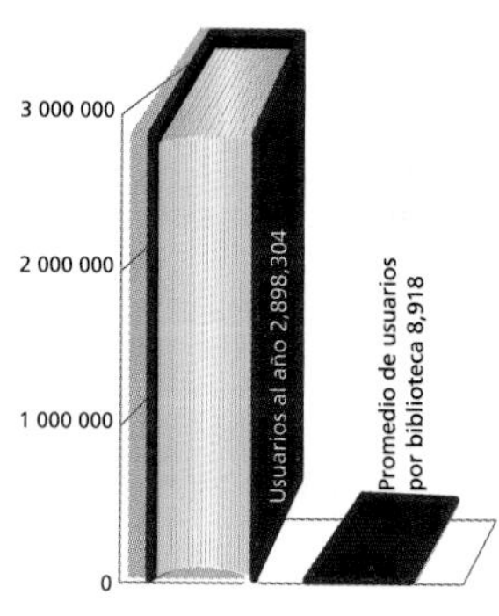

PRODUCTO INTERNO BRUTO (PIB) A PRECIOS CORRIENTES

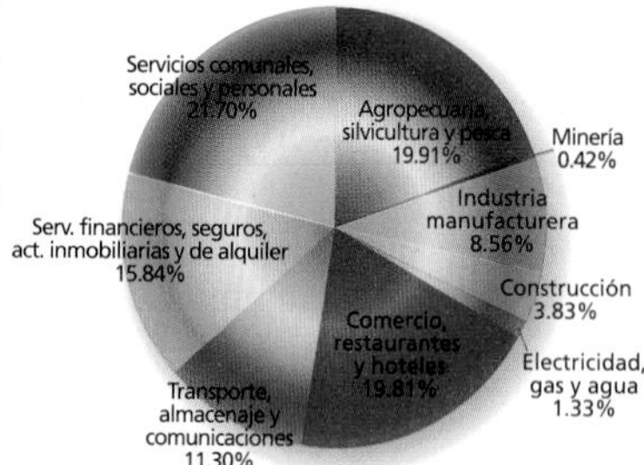

LÍNEAS TELEFÓNICAS EN SERVICIO Y APARATOS PÚBLICOS, 1994

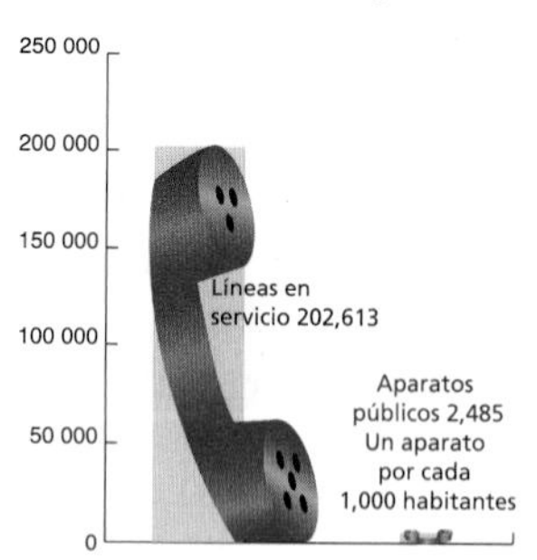

DISTRIBUCIÓN DE LA POBLACIÓN POR TAMAÑO DE LA LOCALIDAD, 1995

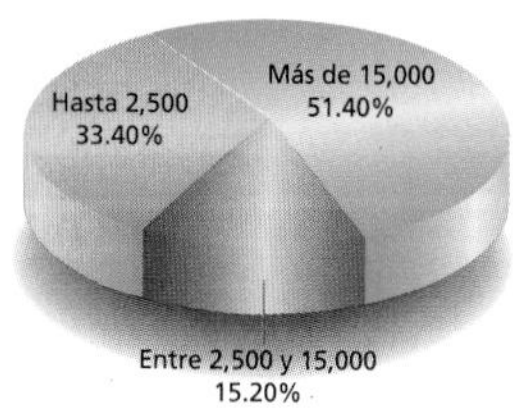

SINALOA ◆ Municipio de Sinaloa situado en el norte del estado, en los límites con Chihuahua. Superficie: 6,186.45 km². Habitantes: 90,283, de los cuales 23,354 forman la población económicamente activa. Hablan alguna lengua indígena 490 personas mayores de cinco años (mayo 259). Cuenta con importantes yacimientos minerales, como San José de Gracia, Gacubirito y Corini. La cabecera es Sinaloa de Leyva.

SINALOA ◆ Río de Durango y Sinaloa, también llamado Petatlán y Tamazula. Nace en la sierra Madre Occidental, en el centro del estado de Durango; le tributan los ríos San Simón, Tahona, San José de Gracia, Cabre y Ocorini. Entra en el estado de Sinaloa y surte la presa Sanalona, pasa al este de Culiacán y tras un recorrido de 400 km desemboca en el golfo de California, en la ensenada Pabellones. Su cuenca tiene una superficie de 13,500 km² y su escurrimiento medio anual es de 2,040 millones de metros cúbicos.

SINANCHÉ ◆ Municipio de Yucatán situado en el norte del estado, al norte de Motul y al noreste de Mérida, en el litoral del golfo de México. Superficie: 131.57 km². Habitantes: 3,027, de los cuales 921 forman la población económicamente activa. Hablan alguna lengua indígena 1,088 personas mayores de cinco años (maya 1,087). En su jurisdicción se halla la zona arqueológica de Uxmal, ciudad construida en el siglo VI de nuestra era por los mayas. Estuvo en auge entre los años 600 y 900. De acuerdo con el *Chilam Balam*, en el ciclo maya de Katún 2 Ahau (hacia 987-1007), Ah Zuytok Tutul Xiu, líder de un grupo tolteca, se estableció en ella mediante una invasión pacífica que logró fundir algunos elementos de su cultura con la original maya. En 1557 la familia de los xiúes presentó a las autoridades virreinales un mapa y una genealogía para reclamar sus derechos sobre Uxmal; en esa genealogía aparece como progenitor de la familia Hum Uitzil Chaac, por lo que, incorrectamente, se ha considerado a éste como fundador de la ciudad.

Foto: Fondo Editorial Grupo Azabache

Paisaje natural en Sinaloa, Sinaloa

La arquitectura pertenece al estilo Puuc o de la sierra, que se caracteriza por la forma paralelepípeda de los edificios, donde predomina la línea horizontal con abundantes adornos en las cornisas y numerosas representaciones de Chaac, dios de la lluvia. Los edificios que conforman Uxmal son: la pirámide del Adivino (la construcción más alta y conocida de la ciudad, erigida en diferentes épocas y en cuyo interior se encontró la figura conocida como "Reina de Uxmal", probable representación de Kukulkán), el Palacio del Gobernador, la Casa de las Tortugas, el juego de pelota, el Monumento de las Palomas, la Acrópolis, el Cuadrángulo de las Monjas y las construcciones conocidas como los edificios Norte, Oriente y Poniente, así como las casas del Enano y de la Vieja.

SINARQUISMO ◆ ☛ *Unión Nacional Sinarquista.*

Arquitectura virreinal en el municipio de Sinaloa, Sinaloa

Foto: Fondo Editorial Grupo Azabache

SINDICATO DE ACTORES INDEPENDIENTES ◆ Organismo formado en 1977 por un numeroso grupo de disidentes de la Asociación Nacional de Actores, cuando Jaime Fernández se reeligió en la secretaría general de la misma. Tuvo como antecedente la Coalición de Actores Independientes, formada en mayo de 1977 por un millar de profesionales de la escena, entre otros Carlos Ancira, Augusto Benedico, Claudio Brook, Luis Gimeno y Julio Castillo. En el mismo mes de su fundación, dicha coalición se transformó en Sindicato de Actores Independientes, que pidió registro laboral el 1 de junio sin que llegara a obtenerlo en toda su existencia. A mediados de 1978, un grupo de saístas, presionado por el cierre de fuentes de trabajo, volvió a la ANDA. El SAI fundó cooperativas que trataron de paliar el boicoteo a sus agre-miados. En octubre de 1981 abandonaron el sindicato Héctor Bonilla y Claudio Obregón, dos fundadores y prominentes activistas. El segundo declaró que el líder, Enrique Lizalde, anteponía "su moral personal a los intereses gremiales" y lo acusó de autoritario. El SAI se disolvió formalmente en 1985.

SINDICATO MEXICANO DE ELECTRICISTAS ◆ Fue fundado en 1914. En 1999 es titular del contrato con la empresa Luz y Fuerza. El SME fue una de las primeras y más importantes organizaciones obreras mexicanas y fungió, asimismo, como promotora de agrupaciones similares; así, participó en la creación de la Casa del Obrero Mundial, de la Confederación Nacional de Trabajadores Electricistas y de la Confederación de Trabajadores de México, de la que se retiró al poco tiempo. Constituyó la fuerza principal de la huelga general de 1916 (☛). Desde 1998 dirigencia y agremiados de este sindicato se han opuesto a las pretensiones de privatizar la industria eléctrica.

Maestra afiliada al Sindicato Nacional de Trabajadores de la Educación durante el movimiento magisterial de 1955-60

SINDICATO NACIONAL DE TRABAJADORES DE LA EDUCACIÓN ◆ Organización gremial fundada el 30 de diciembre de 1943. Entre sus antecedentes estuvo la Federación Nacional de Maestros, fundada el 4 de enero de 1927 por iniciativa de Vicente Lombardo Toledano, secretario de Educación de la CROM y primer secretario general de la Federación. Entre 1930 y 1943, además de las numerosas organizaciones sindicales regionales de profesores, se fundaron la Unión de Directores e Inspectores Federales de Educación, la Unión de Profesores de las Escuelas Técnicas, Industriales y Comerciales, la Confederación Mexicana de Maestros, la Liga de Trabajadores de la Enseñanza, el Frente Único Nacional de Trabajadores de la Enseñanza, el Sindicato Único de Trabajadores de la Enseñanza Superior Campesina, la Confederación Nacional de Trabajadores de la Enseñanza, la Unión Nacional de Encauzadores Técnicos de la Educación, la Federación Mexicana de Trabajadores de la Enseñanza, el Sindicato de Trabajadores de la Enseñanza de la República Mexicana (STERM), el Sindicato Único Nacional de Trabajadores de la Enseñanza (SUNTE), el Sindicato Mexicano de Maestros y Trabajadores de la Educación (SMMTE), el Sindicato Nacional Autónomo de Trabajadores de la Educación y el Frente Nacional Revolucionario de Maestros de México. Entre estas organizaciones las había dirigidas por fuerzas de izquierda y de derecha y varias contaron con los auspicios gubernamentales. Tal heterogeneidad fue causa de fricciones e incluso enfrentamientos violentos. Para acabar con la división entre las organizaciones magisteriales y facilitar su control, el presidente Manuel Ávila Camacho promovió la integración de un Comité Coaligado de Unificación Magisterial, con representantes del SUNTE, del SMMTE y del STERM. De ese comité surgió el Sindicato Nacional de Trabajadores de la

Logotipo del Sindicato Nacional de Trabajadores de la Educación

Educación (el 30 de diciembre de 1943), en el que confluyeron lombardistas, comunistas y gobiernistas. Su primer secretario general fue Ignacio Chávez Orozco, a quien sustituyó en 1945 el lombardista Gaudencio Peraza Esquiliano. En 1949 Jesús Robles Martínez llegó a la Secretaría General del SNTE y, pese a que su gestión sindical concluyó en 1952, estableció una suerte de *maximato* con algunos secretarios generales que sólo obedecían sus órdenes. A uno de ellos, Enrique W. Sánchez (1955-61), le correspondió enfrentar el movimiento magisterial de 1955-60 (☛). El 22 de septiembre de 1972, durante el sexenio de Luis Echeverría, un grupo encabezado por Carlos Jonguitud Barrios destituyó violentamente a Carlos Olmos Sánchez y se posesionó de la dirección del sindicato. El grupo se llamó Movimiento Reivindicador 22 de Septiembre y llevó a Eloy Benavides Salinas a la Secretaría General, con lo que concluyó el cacicazgo roblesmartinista. En 1974 se creó el grupo Vanguardia Revolucionaria, que institucionalizó el liderazgo vitalicio de Jonguitud, quien ejerció personalmente el cargo de secretario general o promovió para tal puesto a diversos seguidores. El 7 de marzo de 1979 se produjo en Chiapas una protesta de los profesores, motivada por el alto costo de la vida en el sureste mexicano. Las reivindicaciones salariales fueron asumidas en diversas entidades por los profesionales de la docencia, quienes exigieron democracia sindical. Los profesores disidentes constituyeron la Coordinadora Nacional de Trabajadores de la Educación, que dirigió grandes movilizaciones en 1979-80 y en 1983. En la primera mitad de 1989, medio millón de trabajadores de la enseñanza fueron a la huelga y el gobierno retiró del liderazgo sindical a Carlos Jonguitud y sus seguidores, con lo que se desintegró Vanguardia Revolucionaria. Se designó secretaria general del SNTE a Elba Esther Gordillo, quien fue ratificada mediante la elección en el congreso celebrado en Tepic. La nueva dirigente se deslindó del grupo de Jonguitud, impulsó una reforma en los procedimientos internos y detuvo el proyecto de disgregación del sindicato que se fraguaba en círculos gubernamentales. Hizo suyas numerosas demandas de los paristas, con quienes se pactó integrar proporcionalmente la dirección de las secciones, de acuerdo con el número de votos de cada corriente. Desde entonces el sindicato dejó de estar orgánicamente integrado al PRI y se respetó la militancia política de cada uno de sus integrantes. Sucedieron a Elba Esther Gordillo en la Secretaría General Humberto Dávila (1995-98) y Tomás Vázquez Vigil (1998-).

Sindicato Nacional de Trabajadores Minero-Metalúrgicos y Similares de la República Mexicana ◆ Fue constituido en Pachuca el 25 de abril de 1934 como sindicato nacional de industria. Agrupó algunas secciones de la Unión Mexicana de Mecánicos, de la Unión Minera Mexicana, varios sindicatos afiliados a la Confederación Revolucionaria de Obreros Mexicanos y muchos otros organismos gremiales independientes. Participó en la constitución de la Confederación de Trabajadores de México, de la que salió en el segundo Consejo Nacional (agosto de 1936). En enero de 1948 firmó un Pacto de Amistad y Solidaridad con los sindicatos de ferroviarios y petroleros. En mayo de 1950, con el voto de numerosos delegados que no contaban con apoyo de base, la VI Convención Nacional Ordinaria, impuso como secretario general a Filiberto Rubalcaba, quien ni siquiera pertenecía al sindicato. Diversas secciones y el Consejo General de Vigilancia del propio sindicato impugnaron tanto la convención como a los nuevos dirigentes. Los delegados democráticamente elegidos se reunieron aparte y nombraron secretario general a Antonio García Moreno, con lo que hubo dos direcciones, la primera reconocida por las autoridades y la de García Moreno por los trabajadores. Líderes impuestos, autoridades y empresas procedieron a despedir a los trabajadores que no se les sometían, lo que ocasionó brotes de resistencia en varias secciones. La mayor movilización se produjo en Nueva Rosita y Cloete (☛ *Huelga minera de 1950-51*), de donde los mineros y sus familias marcharon al Distrito Federal. Su combatividad contrastó con la tibieza de García Moreno. Los marchistas fueron reprimidos y el presunto líder oposicionista se extinguió políticamente. El órgano de gobierno del SNTMMSRM es su convención general, conformada por el Comité Ejecutivo General y por el Consejo General de Vigilancia y Justicia. Las secciones y fracciones pueden ejercer ciertas funciones de acuerdo con sus propios órganos de gobierno: comités ejecutivos locales, para las secciones; y comités ejecutivos de fracciones y comisionados de vigilancia, para las fracciones. Su secretario general desde 1960 es Napoleón Gómez Sada (☛).

Manifestación del Sindicato Nacional de Trabajadores Minero-Metalúrgicos y Similares de la República Mexicana en apoyo a Lázaro Cárdenas y contra el fascismo

Sindicato de Obreros Técnicos, Pintores y Escultores ◆ Organización formada entre los últimos días de noviembre y los primeros de diciembre de 1922. Llamado originalmente Unión Revolucionaria de Obreros Técnicos, Pintores y Escultores y Gremios Similares, fue impulsado por David Alfaro Siqueiros y Diego Rivera. For-

Foto: Héctor Herrera

Elba Esther Gordillo, secretaria general del SNTE de 1989 a 1995

Diego Rivera, fundador del Sindicato de Obreros Técnicos, Pintores y Escultores

maron parte de la agrupación, Ramón Alva de la Canal, Fermín Revueltas, Emilio García Cahero, Fernando Leal, Amado de la Cueva, Xavier Guerrero, Jean Charlot y Carlos Mérida, fundadores, y Máximo Pacheco, Roberto Reyes Pérez y José Clemente Orozco. Aunque su declaración de principios nunca se hizo pública y finalmente se perdió, de acuerdo con los testimonios de Rivera, Charlot, Orozco y Siqueiros, en la misma se establecían los siguientes puntos: "a) Una definición antiimperialista y revolucionaria. b) Adhesión a la III Internacional y a sus principios, abolición del capitalismo y dictadura del proletariado. c) Una concepción del trabajo artístico como producción artesanal, realizada por trabajadores del andamio y la brocha. d) Una concepción del trabajo artístico como un reflejo de la sociedad en que se vive y como una toma de posición frente a ésta. e) La proposición de un desarrollo del arte por un camino social, nacionalista y 'conectado íntimamente con las corrientes internacionales del arte moderno'. f) Establecimiento del sentido de la 'utilidad' de sus pinturas para las clases desposeídas. Vincularlas a la lucha de clases. 'Socialización del arte'. g) Prioridad al trabajo mural ante la pintura de caballete. 'Obras monumentales de dominio público'. h) Aprendizaje en el proceso de trabajo. i) Promoción del trabajo colectivo. 'Destrucción del egocentrismo reemplazándolo por el trabajo disciplinado de grupo'. j) Creación de la Cooperativa Francisco Tresguerras para buscar trabajo y administrar financieramente los resultados". El primer comité estuvo formado por Siqueiros como secretario general, Rivera y Guerrero como primero y segundo vocales, y Revueltas, Alva Guadarrama, Orozco, Mérida y Cueto. José Vasconcelos, secretario de Educación y contratador de los pintores, nunca aceptó de buen grado al sindicato. El órgano de la agrupación fue *El Machete* (☛), cuya primera dirección colectiva recayó en Rivera, Siqueiros y Guerrero. El periódico, como la mayoría de los miembros del sindicato, pasaron al Partido Comunista Mexicano (☛). Vasconcelos se fue de la SEP en julio de 1924 y el sindicato entró en crisis interna por divergencias en la estrategia a seguir. Rivera renunció al sindicato en julio y poco después todos los pintores fueron despedidos por el nuevo secretario de Educación, Bernardo Gastélum. (*Cfr.*: Paco Ignacio Taibo II. *Arcángeles. Cuatro historias no muy ortodoxas de revolucionarios*; México, 1988.)

SINDICATO DE TELEFONISTAS DE LA REPÚBLICA MEXICANA ◆ Sindicato nacional de industria constituido el 1 de agosto de 1950 con la fusión de las agrupaciones gremiales de las empresas Ericcson y Telefónica. El sindicato, formado por una sección matriz (en el Distrito Federal) y 86 foráneas, agrupa a 22,000 trabajadores y está afiliado al Congreso del Trabajo. Sus órganos son el Comité Ejecutivo Nacional y el Comité Ejecutivo de Vigilancia. En 1976 un movimiento democratizador interno llevó a Francisco Hernández Juárez a la Secretaría General del sindicato y depuso a Salustio Salgado, líder que había establecido una suerte de cacicazgo en la cúpula del organismo. Desde esa fecha, Hernández Juárez es el dirigente nacional de los trabajadores telefonistas. El STRM ha estallado numerosas huelgas en los últimos 10 años, pero en todos los casos el gobierno ha requisado las instalaciones de la empresa Teléfonos de México y la ha hecho funcionar. Este sindicato cuenta aproximadamente con 35,000 agremiados.

SINDICATO DE TRABAJADORES FERROCARRILEROS DE LA REPÚBLICA MEXICANA ◆ El proceso de unificación del gremio ferrocarrilero, que desde el siglo XIX contaba con numerosas agrupaciones regionales, culminó el 13 de enero de 1933 con la constitución del Sindicato de Trabajadores Ferrocarrileros de la República Mexicana, que no fue reconocido por el gobierno sino hasta un año y medio más tarde. En 1937 Lázaro Cárdenas nacionalizó la mayoría de las empresas del ramo. Al año siguiente entregó a los trabajadores la paraestatal Ferrocarriles Nacionales de México, en quiebra. El gobierno se opuso a que la administración obrera adecuara las tarifas a sus costos reales, con lo que fracasó este experimento autogestionario y la empresa volvió a manos del Estado. En

Marcha del Sindicato de Trabajadores Ferrocarrileros de la República Mexicana en contra de Luis N. Morones en 1933

Manifestación de la sección 4 del Sindicato de Trabajadores Ferrocarrileros de la República Mexicana contra Plutarco Elías Calles y a favor de Lázaro Cárdenas

1945 las fraternidades de trenistas y caldereros saboteron un tren de pasajeros y la dirección amenazó con expulsar a los miembros de ambas organizaciones. En 1947 el STFRM encabezó una manifestación obrera contra la carestía. En enero de 1948 firmó un Pacto de Solidaridad y Amistad con los sindicatos petroleros y minero-metalúrgicos. En febrero de 1948, Jesús Díaz de León, *el Charro*, informó que se había constituido una comisión con el gobierno, la Secretaría de Comunicaciones y la empresa. Meses después esta comisión recomendó suprimir 12,000 plazas y modificar el contrato colectivo de trabajo, lo que la empresa solicitó ante la Junta de Conciliación y Arbitraje. En julio se produjo una brusca devaluación del peso, de 4.85 a 8.65 por dólar, lo que motivó una movilización de los ferrocarrileros capitalinos, quien con otros gremios realizaron un mitin el 21 de agosto. Díaz de León, de acuerdo con el gobierno, se opuso a estas actividades y respondió acusando por vía judicial a Valentín Campa y Luis Gómez Z. de "abuso de confianza". El Comité de Vigilancia y cuatro miembros del Comité Ejecutivo, con apoyo de la base, intentaron destituir a Díaz de León, pero las autoridades intervinieron para ratificarlo y destituir a sus impugnadores, contra quienes se dictó orden de aprehensión. A esta intervención de las autoridades se le llamó "charrazo", por el mote del líder impuesto, lo que dio su nombre a hechos similares. Gómez Z. estuvo seis meses en la cárcel y Campa salió hasta 1953. Problemas salariales y de antidemocracia interna motivaron el movimiento ferrocarrilero de 1958-59 (☛), que fue reprimido y numerosos trabajadores resultaron encarcelados, algunos por varios años. Valentín Campa y el secretario general Demetrio Vallejo pasaron más de una década en prisión. El STFRM está afiliado al Congreso del Trabajo. En la dirigencia se sucedieron Praxedis Fraustro, que fue asesinado durante su gestión; Jorge Peralta Vargas y Víctor Flores.

SINDICATO DE TRABAJADORES PETROLEROS DE LA REPÚBLICA MEXICANA ◆ Fue constituido el 23 de agosto de 1935. En julio de 1936, durante su primera convención, acordó proponer la firma de un contrato colectivo de trabajo, lo que rechazaron las empresas extranjeras del ramo. El 31 de mayo de 1937 se inició una huelga que fue suspendida el 9 de julio, con la promesa de las autoridades de que se realizaría un estudio de la situación económica de las empresas, las que argüían insuficiencia financiera para satisfacer las demandas obreras. El estudio en cuestión reveló que las compañías podían conceder aumentos por 26 millones de pesos, pues sus utilidades en 1936 habían sido de 56 millones. Con esta base se emitió un laudo de la Junta Federal de Conciliación y Arbitraje, el que se negaron a acatar las empresas, que solicitaron amparo ante la Suprema Corte de Justicia. Ésta negó el recurso y las empresas demandantes se declararon en rebeldía. El sindicato hizo preparativos para reiniciar la huelga, pidió al gobierno que se dieran por terminados los contratos de trabajo y exigió la cancelación de las concesiones. El presidente Lázaro Cárdenas decidió decretar la expropiación de los bienes de 17 compañías extranjeras, el 18 de marzo de 1938. Las empresas retiraron a sus técnicos y las potencias dejaron de comprar crudo mexicano y se negaron a proporcionar los insumos, refacciones, maquinaria y equipo necesarios. Pese a todo, los trabajadores, dirigidos por su sindicato, hicieron operar la industria. En ese año se creó el organismo paraestatal Petróleos Mexicanos, con el que, desde entonces, el STPRM celebra contratos colectivos de trabajo cada dos años. En 1946 se realizaron paros escalonados en la industria contra los ajustes que pretendía la empresa y en favor de la nivelación salarial. Fidel Velázquez, secretario general de la Confederación de Trabajadores de México, a la que pertenecía el sindicato, desautorizó lo

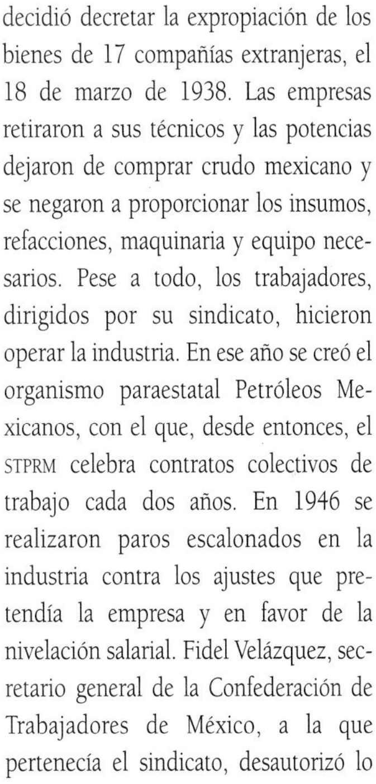

FOTO EIKÓN

Carlos Romero Deschamps

FOTO: FONDO EDITORIAL GUSTAVO CASASOLA

Los directivos del Sindicato de Trabajadores Petroleros de la República Mexicana recibidos por Lázaro Cárdenas en Palacio Nacional en 1937 que a su juicio eran "paros locos" y sugirió cesar a los líderes petroleros y militarizar la industria. Como respuesta, el 10 de julio de ese año, el STPRM desconoció al Comité Ejecutivo de la CTM y lo acusó de estar coludido con la empresa y el gobierno. Iniciado el sexenio del presidente Miguel Alemán, el 19 de diciembre de 1946 se realizó un paro total en la industria. El ejército ocupó los centros de trabajo y al día siguiente la empresa cesó a los líderes sindicales y a todos los trabajadores que se mostraran partidarios del paro. El 13 de enero de 1947 fue impuesto como secretario general el líder gobiernista Antonio Hernández Ábrego y el día 27 el sindicato volvió a la CTM. Como continuara la inconformidad de la base, en diciembre, durante la V Convención General Extraordinaria, se aplicó la cláusla de exclusión contra Hernández Ábrego y su comité, se denunció que los acuerdos entre la empresa y la depuesta dirección sindical atentaban contra los derechos obreros y se acordó separarse nuevamente de la CTM. El 10 de enero de 1948 el STPRM firmó un Pacto de Amistad y Solidaridad con los sindicatos ferroviario y minero-metalúrgico. En octubre de ese año, el Sindicato expresó su repudio al llamado "charrazo" en el Sindicato de Trabajadores Ferrocarrileros de la República Mexicana (☛). En mayo de 1949 el STPRM apareció entre los convocantes al Congreso Nacional de Unidad Obrera y Campesina del que surgió, en junio, la Unión General de Obreros y Campesinos de México. El 1 de diciembre, un grupo oficialista impidió iniciar la VI Convención General Ordinaria. El mismo grupo instaló una asamblea paralela que fue reconocida por las autoridades laborales. Al día siguiente, los delegados democráticamente elegidos intentaron realizar la Convención, pero la fuerza pública desalojó el salón donde sesionaban y la Secretaría del Trabajo reconoció como nuevo dirigente a Gustavo Roldán Vargas, *el Charro*, y de ese modo se consumó lo que se conoce como el "charrazo petrolero". El STPRM fue retirado de la UGOCM y volvió a la CTM. El órgano dirigente del sindicato es el Comité Ejecutivo General, conformado por los secretarios general, del interior, del exterior, de organización y estadística y tesorero. En enero de 1989, mediante una acción policiaco-militar, el "líder moral" del sindicato, Joaquín Hernández Galicia, *la Quina*, y el secretario general en turno, Salvador Barragán Camacho, fueron detenidos junto con otros dirigentes, a los que se acusó de homicidio, acopio de armas y otros delitos. El nuevo secretario general del sindicato fue Sebastián Guzmán Cabrera, quien fue sustituido por Carlos Romero Dechamps.

SINDICATO DE TRABAJADORES DE LA PRODUCCIÓN CINEMATOGRÁFICA DE LA REPÚBLICA MEXICANA ◆ ☛ *Cine Sonoro*.

SINDICATO ÚNICO DE TRABAJADORES ELECTRICISTAS DE LA REPÚBLICA MEXICANA ◆ Creado en 1972 con la unificación del Sindicato de Trabajadores Electricistas de la República Mexicana (STERM, organismo independiente que agrupaba a trabajadores de diversas empresas privadas, los que se habían incorporado a la Comisión Federal de Electricidad) con el Sindicato Nacional de Electricistas, Similares y Conexos de la República Mexicana (SNESCRM), creado al mismo tiempo que la CFE. La fusión de ambos sindicatos se dio luego de una disputa por la titularidad del contrato colectivo con esa empresa descentralizada del Estado. Se pactó entonces que representantes de ambas partes fusionantes compartirían cargos en la dirección del nuevo sindicato, del que Francisco Pérez Ríos fue elegido secretario general del Comité Ejecutivo Nacional, en tanto que Rafael Galván encabezó la Comisión Nacional de Vigilancia y Fiscalización. A la muerte de Pérez Ríos, en 1975, Leonardo Rodríguez Alcaine ocupó la secretaría general y se reinició el conflicto. Galván y sus seguidores, agrupados para entonces en la Tendencia Democrática, fueron hostilizados y expulsados del sindicato. El nuevo dirigente contó con el apoyo de las autoridades y de algunos galvanistas, quienes traicionaron a su antiguo líder y fueron recompensados con puestos públicos.

Leonardo Rodríguez Alcaine, líder del Sindicato Único de Trabajadores Electricistas de la República Mexicana

SINDICATO ÚNICO DE TRABAJADORES DE LA INDUSTRIA NUCLEAR ◆ Organización formada en 1979 por los trabajadores de las empresas Uranio Mexicano e Instituto Nacional de Investigaciones Nucleares. Sus antecedentes se remontan a la fundación, en 1964, del Sindicato Único de Trabajadores de la Comisión Nacional de la Energía Nuclear, formado aproximadamente por 254 trabajadores. Al crearse el Instituto Nacional de Energía Nuclear (1972) se constituyó el Sindicato Único de Trabajadores del Instituto Nacional de Energía Nuclear (SUTINEN), que en 1974 se incorporó al Sindicato Único de Trabajadores Electricistas de la República Mexicana como "secciones nucleares". En 1979, al dictarse una nueva ley nuclear que dividió al INEN en tres partes: Instituto Nacional de Investigaciones Nucleares (ININ), Uranio Mexicano y la Comisión Nacional de Seguridad y Salvaguardias (CNSS), se creó el SUTIN, aproximadamente con 1,500 trabajadores del ININ y de Uramex. Aunque no pudo agremiar a los trabajadores de la CNSS, sí logró que los trabajadores del ININ y Uramex que-daran unificados en el apartado A del artículo 123 constitucional. El 30 de mayo de 1983 el SUTIN estalló una huelga en demanda de aumento salarial de emergencia. Debido a que una de las dependencias del ININ, el Centro Nuclear de Salazar, no estalló la huelga, ésta fue declarada inexistente en relación con el Instituto, mientras el paro en Uramex era aceptado. Se procedió entonces a emplazar a huelga en solidaridad con los trabajadores de Uramex, lo que fue rechazado por la Junta Federal de Conciliación y Arbitraje. El 23 de junio de 1983 el sindicato se desistió de la huelga en Uramex, pues ya se había otorgado un aumento salarial. No obstante, la empresa declaró que era improcedente un desistimiento unilateral y que sólo negociaría con el sindicato la liquidación de los trabajadores. El 6 de agosto, la empresa aceptó el desistimiento de huelga, pero al día siguiente, domingo 7 de agosto, antes de que las instalaciones fueran entregadas por los huelguistas, Uramex declaró una suspensión de relaciones de trabajo con el SUTIN. Ninguna de las gestiones del sindicato ante las autoridades dio resultado. En 1985 el gobierno decidió cerrar la empresa Uramex y transformar al ININ en Instituto de Investigaciones Nucleares, de cuyo contrato colectivo el SUTIN también es titular.

SINDICATOS DE LA UNAM ◆ En 1929, al decretarse la autonomía de la Universidad Nacional de México, los trabajadores de la misma perdieron el estatuto de empleados federales, por lo que se inició un movimiento para integrar una agrupación sindical dentro de esa casa de estudios. En ese mismo año se formó el Sindicato Único de Empleados de la Universidad Nacional, que trató de afiliar a los profesores y buscó el apoyo de los estudiantes, el sector más organizado de la comunidad universitaria en aquellos años. Esta organización, dirigida por Diódoro Antúnez, se limitó a demandar aumentos salariales ante el Consejo Universitario. A finales de 1930 el sindicato fue reemplazado por la Unión de Empleados de la Universidad Nacional de México-Autónoma, dirigida por Manuel Vázquez Cadena y que logró la firma de un contrato colectivo vigente sólo durante un año. La Unión fue suplida el 7 de noviembre de 1932 por el Sindicato de Trabajadores de la Universidad Nacional de México-Autónoma, y el 18 de octubre de 1933 se fundó el Sindicato de Empleados y Obreros de la Universidad Autónoma de México (SEOUAM). A su secretario general, José Meixueiro Bonola, correspondió enfrentar la Ley Orgánica de 1933, que otorgaba plena autonomía a la Universidad, le retiraba el subsidio oficial, reorganizaba al personal y reducía los salarios. En 1935 Daniel Chávez fue elegido secretario general del SEOUAM. El 9 de octubre de 1945 se creó el Sindicato de Trabajadores de la UNAM, que se extinguió. En 1965 surgió el Sindicato de Empleados y Obreros de la UNAM (SEOUNAM), con Martín Hernández Granados como secretario general. Esta organización tampoco obtuvo registro formal, pero consiguió que el rector Ignacio Chávez se comprometiera a elaborar, junto con el sindicato, un estatuto para el personal administrativo, que fue aprobado en 1966, aunque prohibía la existencia de una agrupación que ostentara el nombre de "sindicato". Así, el 25 de abril de 1966 se constituyó la Asociación de Trabajadores Administrativos de la UNAM y se disolvió el SEOUAM. La ATAUAM tampoco obtuvo registro sindical, pero sí logró el reconocimiento de las autoridades universitarias. En 1970, la ATAUAM organizó el primer encuentro de trabajadores universitarios y volvió a solicitar el registro legal de la organización, que no se consiguió. Sin embargo, el 12 de noviembre de 1971 se creó el Sindicato de Trabajadores y Empleados de la UNAM (STEUNAM). Esta agrupación, dirigida por Evaristo Pérez Arreola, tampoco obtuvo el registro, por lo que inició una huelga (25 de octubre de 1972) que no se levantó sino hasta la firma de un convenio colectivo de trabajo, después de la renuncia del rector Pablo González Casanova, en febrero de 1973. El 13 de julio de 1974 se constituyó el Sindicato del Personal Académico de la UNAM. Como respuesta, círculos del gobierno de la República y de las propias autoridades universitarias promovieron el surgimiento de una Federación de Asociaciones de Personal Académico, la que poco después se transformaría en Asociación de Asociaciones de Personal Académico (AAPAUNAM). El 27 de marzo de 1977 el STEUNAM y el SPAUAM se fusionaron en el STUUAM: el 1 de abril se intentó negociar un contrato colectivo, que fue rechazado, y el 20 de junio de ese año el sindicato inició una huelga, declarada ilegal por la Junta Local de Conciliación y Arbitraje. El 7 de julio la policía entró en la Ciudad Universitaria y desalojó a los huelguistas. Pese a todo, el 10 de julio las autoridades universitarias reconocieron al STUUAM, que de ese año a 1989 estuvo dirigido por Evaristo Pérez Arreola, quien fue sustituido por Nicolás Olivos Cuéllar. En 1999 el dirigente era Agustín Rodríguez Fuentes.

SINGAPUR, REPÚBLICA DE ◆ Estado insular del sureste asiático situado en el extremo meridional de la península de Malaca. Está separado de la porción continental de la Federación de Malasia por el estrecho de Johore y de las islas indonesias cercanas a Sumatra por los estrechos de Malaca y Singapur. Tiene una superficie de 646 km^2 lo que incluye la isla principal y sus 54 islotes adyacentes. Su población en 1998 era de 3,476,000 habitantes. Su capital es la ciudad de Singapur (con 3,045,000 habitantes en 1996), que es también el puerto más importante del sureste asiático y principal centro mundial del comercio de caucho y estaño,

Timbre de Singapur

Ciudad de Singapur

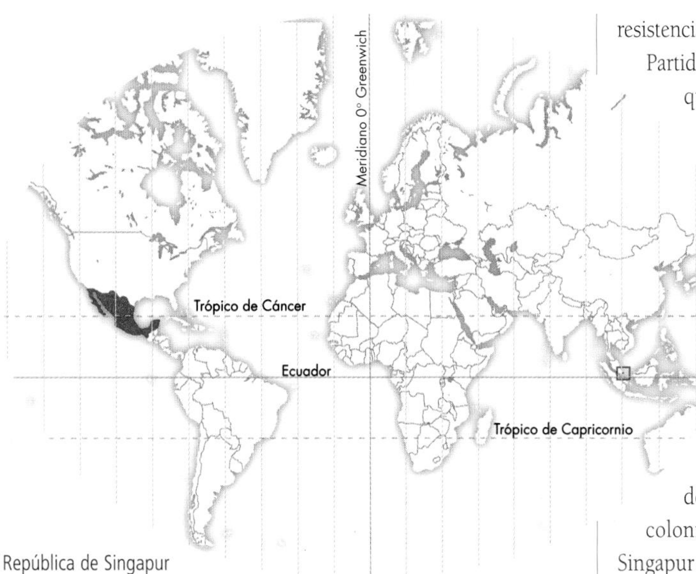

República de Singapur

Timbre de Singapur

Moneda de la República de Singapur

aunque en fecha reciente impulsaron las industrias textil, electrónica y petrolera. Los idiomas oficiales del país son malayo (considerado lengua nacional), mandarín, tamil e inglés (lengua "política" y comercial); además se hablan el punjabi, hindi, bengalí, tegelu, malayam y varios dialectos chinos. *Historia*: por su estratégica ubicación, a fines del siglo XII la isla, llamada entonces Temasek ("Pueblo del mar", en sánscrito), era ya un activo centro comercial dominado por Sumatra. En 1819, cuando el país ya tenía el nombre Singapur (de *Singa Pura*, o "Ciudad del león"), Thomas Stamford Raffles, agente de la Compañía Británica de las Indias Orientales, instaló en él la sede local de esa institución colonizadora. Cinco años después el gobierno inglés compró la isla al sultán malayo de Johore. En ese mismo año (1824), Stamford impuso en el trono singapurense al príncipe Hussein. A partir de entonces se propició la inmigración de chinos, quienes paulatinamente se convirtieron en población mayoritaria. En 1830 las autoridades británicas unieron a Singapur con Malaca y Penang para conformar los Establecimientos de los Estrechos, que en 1867 se convirtieron en colonia británica. En 1942, durante la segunda guerra mundial, el ejército japonés ocupó la isla; tres años después la resistencia singapurense, dirigida por el Partido Comunista de Malasia (PCM), que siempre consideró arbitraria la separación de Singapur y su país, derrotó a los invasores. Al término de la segunda guerra mundial el Reino Unido retomó el control de la colonia. En 1946 se restituyó el poder civil y Malaca y Penang se separaron de los Establecimientos dejando a Singapur como enclave colonial. La Unión Sindical de Singapur estalló una huelga general anticolonialista, y en 1948 el PCM inició una insurrección popular que fue reprimida. El gobierno colonialista efectuó en 1949 elecciones para nombrar a seis miembros de un Consejo Legislativo. El nuevo parlamento singapurense estuvo conformado sólo por ciudadanos de origen inglés. En 1954 se creó el Partido de Acción Popular (PAP, miembro de la Internacional Socialista), en el que militaban tanto personas de origen inglés como descendientes de inmigrantes chinos y de algunas de las minorías de la ciudad-Estado, con el objetivo de independizar a Singapur. En 1959, el PAP ganó en las elecciones parlamentarias y convirtió en primer ministro a Li Kuan Yu, fundador del partido. El jefe de gobierno del PAP planteó la independencia de Singapur en el marco de una federación con Malasia, país independizado en 1957. En 1963 se constituyó la Federación de Malasia, en la que se incluyeron Singapur, la península malaya, Sarawak y Sabah, aunque el control indirecto de la federación provenía aún de Londres. No obstante, las pugnas interraciales entre chinos y malayos hizo inviable la unión, por lo que Singapur se separó de la federación en 1965, se convirtió en república independiente adscrita a la Comunidad Británica, e ingresó en la ONU. El gobierno cifró la economía singapurense en el petróleo, por lo que la crisis mundial de los hidrocarburos en 1974 produjo dificultades financieras y un abatimiento del nivel de vida. A partir de entonces se reorientó la economía hacia la captación de capital extranjero. En la isla se instalaron numerosas plantas maquiladoras e importantes instituciones financieras abrieron oficinas para sus operaciones en el sureste asiático. En 1975 se establecieron relaciones diplomáticas con México. En el mismo año, la Internacional Socialista expulsó de sus filas al PAP, que había apoyado la represión contra las manifestaciones obreras y estudiantiles. En los años ochenta se implantó un severo régimen de control demográfico y se realizó una amplia campaña para difundir el confucianismo, especialmente la concepción determinista que considera inmodificable el destino humano. En 1990 Kuan Yu fue sustituido por Goh Chok Tong y en 1993 Ong Teng Cheong se convirtió en el primer presidente elegido por voto popular.

SINGUILUCAN ◆ Municipio de Hidalgo situado al suroeste de Tulancingo y próximo a Pachuca. Superficie: 334.1 km². Habitantes: 12,865, de los cuales 3,249 forman la población económicamente activa. Hablan alguna lengua indígena 17 personas mayores de cinco años (náhuatl 11).

SÍNTORA CONSTANTINO, FIDENCIO DE JESÚS ◆ ☛ *Niño Fidencio, el.*

SIONISMO ◆ ☛ *Israel, Estado de.*

SIQUEIROS, DAVID ALFARO ◆ ☛ *Alfaro Siqueiros, David.*

SIQUEIROS, JESÚS P. ◆ n. en Ures y m. en Hermosillo, Son. (1813-1890). Tipógrafo. Se inició en 1833 como meritorio de la imprenta del gobierno, de la que llegó a ser director. Tras la introducción de la imprenta en Arizpe, se convirtió en el editor de varios periódicos sonorenses.

SIRAHUÉN ◆ ☛ *Zirahuén.*

SIRIA, REPÚBLICA ÁRABE DE ◆ Estado del Medio Oriente situado en la costa del mar Mediterráneo. Limita al noroeste y norte con Turquía, al este con Irak, al sur con Jordania, y al suroeste con Israel y Líbano. Superficie: 185,180 km². Habitantes: 15,333,000

(1998). La capital es Damasco (1,549,932 habitantes en 1994) y otras ciudades importantes son Alepo (1,591,400 habitantes en 1994), Homs (644,204) y Latakia (306,535). El idioma oficial es el árabe y también se hablan kurdo y armenio. *Historia*: entre los siglos XXV y IV a.n.e. se sucedieron en territorio de la actual Siria los imperios canaanita, fenicio, hebreo, egipcio, arameo, asirio, babilonio y persa. El más notable fue el fenicio (siglos XII a VII a.n.e.) que creó la primera economía mercantil del mundo, inventó el alfabeto, construyó las primeras embarcaciones para la navegación de altura, amplió y sistematizó los conocimientos geográficos y efectuó la primera circunnavegación de África. En el 333 a.n.e., Alejandro de Macedonia conquistó Siria y 200 años más tarde el país fue provincia del imperio romano. En el 636 de nuestra era, los árabes derrotaron y expulsaron de la región a los bizantinos. En el 661 los omeyas establecieron la capital del imperio árabe en Damasco. En el 750 la dinastía abasí desplazó a la omeya del Califato y la capital del imperio árabe se trasladó a Bagdad. En el siglo X los handaníes fundaron una dinastía autóctona, aunque dominaban una provincia que había perdido peso político y que se desgastaba en rivalidades entre los emires locales. Esto explica que un reducido grupo de cruzados francos conquistase una franja de territorio sirio en la costa, lo que constituyó un enclave europeo durante 200 años. En el siglo XII, Saladino, al frente de tropas egipcias, inició la expulsión de los cruzados francos de Siria, quienes habían fortalecido la presencia de comunidades cristianas, como los maronitas. En 1516 Siria cayó en poder de los otomanos. En 1831 el líder egipcio Mehemet Alí conquistó Siria y, entre otras medidas, aplicó un severo régimen fiscal e impuso el servicio militar obligatorio, lo que originó un levantamiento conjunto de cristianos y musulmanes contra Egipto. La presencia de comunidades cristianas en Siria dio pretexto a la intervención de varios países europeos, cuyos contingentes rechazaron a Alí. A continuación, se encomendó la "protección de los cristianos sirios" a Francia, aunque el proceso culminó en 1840 con la restitución del dominio otomano y la aceptación, por parte de los sultanes turcos, de misiones y colegios cristianos. Las comunidades maronitas florecieron entonces en las regiones montañosas entre Damasco y Jerusalén y en 1858 cobró fuerza un movimiento antifeudal y autonomista. Los caciques musulmanes se consideraron amenazados e iniciaron una escalada represiva que desembocó en las grandes matanzas de junio de 1860. En julio de ese año la armada francesa desembarcó en Siria, supuestamente para proteger a los maronitas, y obligó al imperio turco a crear una provincia separada, el "Pequeño Líbano", territorio que disfrutaría de relativa autonomía bajo un gobernador cristiano designado por el sultán, con la aprobación de las potencias europeas. Así nació el actual Líbano. A fines del siglo XIX llegaron a México los primeros grupos importantes de siriolibaneses o "turcos", como se les llamaba por el pasaporte otomano. Durante la primera guerra mundial, Siria encabezó un movimiento panárabe de lucha anticolonialista y antifeudal, lo que afectaba a la aristocra-

Mezquita en Damasco, Siria

Timbre de la República de Siria

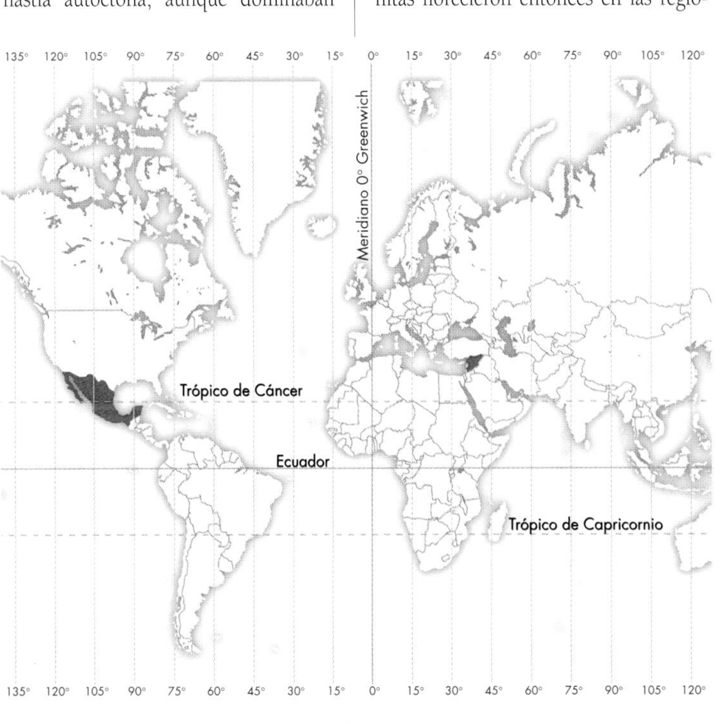

República Árabe de Siria

Noria de Damasco, en Siria

cia. El emir Faisal llevó a Damasco un ejército de beduinos que reprimió la insurrección. En 1918 una asamblea nacional proclamó a Faisal rey de Siria, Palestina y Líbano. No obstante, los tratados Sykes-Picot, firmados por Inglaterra y Francia, al término de la primera guerra mundial decretaban el "reparto" de Medio Oriente: Francia ocupó Siria y Líbano, mientras que la Corona británica se apoderó de Palestina, Jordania e Irak. Francia desplazó a Faisal en 1920 y dividió el país en cinco Estados: Gran Líbano (es decir, el Pequeño Líbano con algunas anexiones), Damasco, Alepo, Djabal Druza y Alawis (Latakia); los últimos cuatro Estados se reunificaron en 1924. De 1924 a 1932 Francia hizo creer a los árabes que preparaba la devolución del gobierno, aunque nunca se dieron pasos concretos en ese sentido. En 1932 un movimiento árabe que culminó en múltiples enfrentamientos callejeros obligó al gobierno francés a convocar a elecciones para nombrar un presidente y un parlamento; sin embargo, las elecciones fueron manipuladas y los cargos legislativos y el Poder Ejecutivo recayeron en personeros del gobierno francés, lo que generó nuevos disturbios. En esos años vino a México otra oleada migratoria de "siriolibaneses". En 1936, ante las movilizaciones árabes, Francia anunció la reunificación de Siria y Líbano, que no se efectuó. En ese año se reinició la movilización popular que culminó en 1939 con la renuncia del presidente sirio y con la suspensión de la Constitución con la que desde 1930 Francia gobernaba en Líbano y Siria. En 1941, durante la segunda guerra mundial, en los países árabes surgió una corriente de simpatía hacia la Alemania nazi, sentimiento estimulado por los agravios de otras potencias coloniales. Francia e Inglaterra, países beligerantes, procedieron a reforzar su presencia en la región mientras que alentaban la esperanza de un cambio en el régimen colonial. El comandante francés anunció la finalización del mandato de su país. En 1943 fueron elegidos presidentes Chikri al-Quwatli, en Siria, y Bechara al-Kuri, en Líbano; este último propuso entonces eliminar de la Constitución las cláusulas relativas al mandato, por lo que las fuerzas francesas lo hicieron prisionero con todo y gabinete. Violentas manifestaciones se generaron de inmediato en ambos Estados y el comandante de la "zona inglesa", para evitar la extensión de la inconformidad, intervino en favor de la liberación de Kuri. Desde entonces hasta el fin de la segunda guerra mundial, el gobierno francés transfirió paulatinamente la administración a las autoridades locales. Pese a lo anterior, en mayo de 1945 desembarcó en Beirut un contingente franco-senegalés, lo que volvió a encender la insurrección en Líbano y Siria: los franceses reprimieron el levantamiento árabe y bombardearon Damasco, hasta que se produjo un nuevo ultimátum inglés. En 1946 la ONU ordenó la retirada de las tropas francesas, que culminó al año siguiente. En 1947 Michel Aflaq, nacionalista cristiano, fundó el Partido Baas Árabe Socialista. En 1948 Siria y otros cinco países árabes atacaron al naciente Estado de Israel, que acabó por rechazarlos. En 1950 se establecieron las relaciones diplomáticas entre Siria y México. En 1956, tras la invasión anglofrancesa de Suez, Siria cerró el oleoducto al Mediterráneo y rompió relaciones con Francia y Gran Bretaña. En 1957 el Baas y el Partido Comunista ganaron las elecciones. En 1958 Siria y Egipto formaron la República Árabe Unida, con Gamal Abdel Nasser como presidente. En 1961 se disolvió la federación con Egipto, los conservadores ganaron los comicios, Nazim Kudsi llegó a la Presidencia de la República y Siria reingresó en la ONU. En 1962 un cuartelazo dio el poder a los militares durante 12 días, pasados los cuales Kudsi regresó al Ejecutivo. En 1963 una revolución popular llevó al partido Baas al gobierno y estableció el Consejo Nacional de Mando Revolucionario, encabezado por Silah al-Bitar. En 1964 una Constitución provisional estableció la República Popular Democrática de Siria, nacionalizó la banca y la industria y llevó a la jefatura del Estado a Amin el-Hafiz. En 1966 el ala radical del Baas, encabezada por Salah el-Jadid y Nureddin el-Atasi, de-rrocó a Hafiz. En 1967 estalló la guerra de los Seis Días entre varios países ára-bes e Israel, que ocupó las alturas del Golán y Quneitra, en el extremo suroccidental de Siria. Damasco rompió relaciones con Estados Unidos y el Reino Unido. En 1970 el ala moderada del Baas tomó el poder, conducida por Hafez el-Assad. En 1971 se promulgó una Constitución provisional, Assad ocupó la Presidencia y Siria, Egipto y Libia crearon la Federación de Repúblicas Árabes. En 1972 Assad unificó a la izquierda siria en el Frente Progresista de Unión Nacional. En 1973 se promulgó la Constitución que aún está vigente y Siria participó junto a otros países árabes en la guerra de Yom Kippur, en la que nuevamente fueron derrotados por Israel. Al año siguiente, un pacto de no agresión entre los gobiernos sirio e israelí devolvió a Siria parte de los territorios perdidos en la guerra de 1973. En 1975, mientras se agudizaban las diferencias con Irak por las aguas del Éufrates, se reanudaron las relaciones diplomáticas con Estados Unidos y con el Reino Unido. En 1976 Siria intervino en la guerra civil de Líbano en favor de una de las facciones beligerantes. En 1977, tras la visita a Israel del presidente egipcio Anuar el-Sadat, Damasco y El Cairo rompieron relaciones. En 1980 Siria se solidarizó

Timbre de la República de Siria

con Irán en la guerra que empezó entonces contra Irak y rompió relaciones con el gobierno de Bagdad. Pese a la retórica antiestadounidense de Hafez el-Assad, en 1991, durante la guerra del Golfo, Siria envió tropas al contingente antiraquí. En los años noventa se reanudaron las negociaciones con Israel.

SISAL ◆ Puerto yucateco situado en el municipio de Hunucmá (☛).

SISMOS ◆ El área central de la República Mexicana se localiza en una zona de actividad volcánica y cerca de la confluencia de algunas placas tectónicas, por lo que en diversas partes del país se producen con frecuencia movimientos telúricos. Las mitologías indígenas contaban en sus panteones con dioses de los temblores, como Tepeyollotli, para los nahuas; Pitaoxoo para los zapotecas y Cobracán para los mayas. De acuerdo con la mitología nahua, la era del cuarto sol, en la que vivían, terminaría mediante terremotos, por lo que cada vez que temblaba pensaban que el fin del mundo era inminente. Aun cuando los códices mencionan numerosos sacudimientos ocurridos en el siglo XIV, entre ellos uno probablemente ocurrido en 1354, provocado por una erupción del Popocatépetl, el primero que se puede fechar con certeza es el de 1475, durante el reinado de Moctezuma Ilhuicamina, cuando la mayoría de las casas de México-Tenochtitlan se derrumbaron y se abrieron enormes grietas. Entre los movimientos telúricos registrados como los más fuertes desde el siglo XIX se cuentan: el del 8 de marzo de 1800, llamado *temblor de San Juan de Dios*, del 25 de marzo de 1806, que provocó el derrumbe del templo de Zapotlán el Grande, Jalisco, cuando éste se encontraba lleno de feligreses; el ocurrido el 30 de mayo de 1818 que destruyó la ciudad de Colima y afectó severamente la de Guadalajara; varios en mayo de 1820, que destruyeron el templo del Campo Florido, de la ciudad de México; dos del 7 de abril de 1845 que destruyeron la capilla del Señor de Santa Teresa; el del 19 de junio de 1858, que causó numerosas muertes, así como daños en la mayor parte de las construcciones de la capital mexicana, cuyos habitantes pasaron varios días acampados en la Alameda Central. En 1911, la entrada de Francisco I. Madero en la ciudad de México estuvo rubricada también por un sismo que, aparentemente, no causó daños considerables. En 1928 un temblor destruyó la población de Pinotepa Nacional, Oaxaca. En 1957, otro sacudimiento afectó la ciudad de México, causó la muerte de más de 50 personas, derribó algunas construcciones y ocasionó la caída del Ángel de la Independencia. El 3 de febrero de 1973 otro movimiento telúrico afectó a la ciudad de México y causó graves daños en el sur de Jalisco y algunas zonas de Michoacán. Sin embargo, los terremotos del 19 y 20 de septiembre de 1985 han sido los más graves que ha resentido el país: a las 7:19 de la mañana del 19 de septiembre un sismo de 7.8 grados en la escala de Richter (algunas informaciones señalaron hasta 8.3 grados) y con más de 90 segundos de duración (según algunas fuentes duró 180 segundos), con epicentro localizado frente a las costas de Guerrero y Michoacán y cuyos efectos se sintieron en una zona de 800,000 km², afectó severamente a muchas poblaciones de Morelos, Michoacán, Jalisco, Colima, Guerrero y el Estado de México. Entre otros daños de consideración, hubo derrumbes en la ciudad de Colima; 3,000 personas quedaron sin vivienda en Zihuatanejo; más de 500 casas se derrumbaron en Ciudad Guzmán; la ciudad de Lázaro Cárdenas quedó casi completamente devastada, así como un área de aproximada 40 km² en la ciudad de México, principalmente en Tlatelolco, el primer cuadro de la ciudad y las colonias Juárez, Roma, Roma Sur, Guerrero, Lagunilla, Merced, Narvarte y Morelos. En la noche del 20 de septiembre, otro movimiento de tierra, de 6.5 grados en la escala de Richter, causó nuevos derrumbes en la capital del país. Aun cuando nunca se llegó a precisar cifras, se calcula que ambos

Rescatistas en la ciudad de México devastada por el sismo del 19 de septiembre de 1985

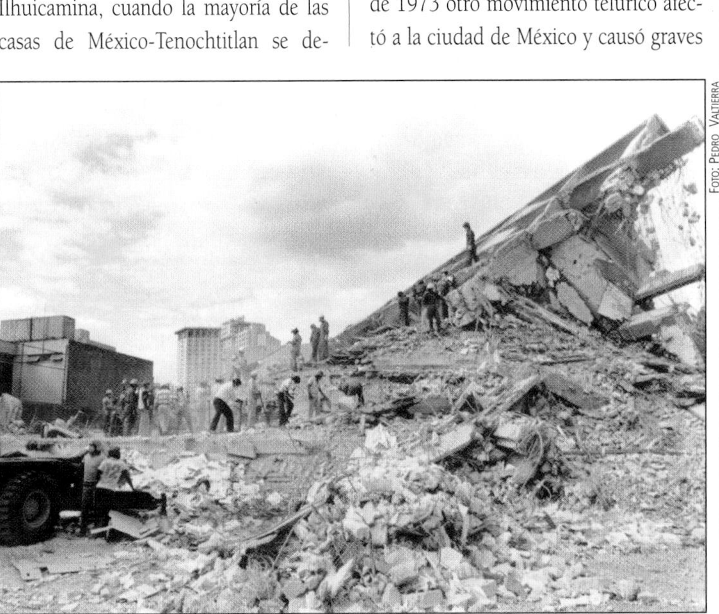

FOTO: PEDRO VALTIERRA

Destrucción causada por el sismo del 19 de septiembre de 1985 sismos provocaron entre 5,000 y 20,000 muertos, 50,000 heridos y 200,000 personas quedaron sin vivienda; se derrumbaron más de 550 edificios y unos 3,000 resultaron tan dañados que debieron ser evacuados; las comunicaciones telefónicas quedaron interrumpidas, resultaron dañadas las vías de transporte terrestre, las redes de agua potable y alcantarillado, así como el tendido de las líneas eléctricas. El monto de las pérdidas se calculó en unos dos billones de pesos (5,000 millones de dólares). Tal catástrofe generó un movimiento de solidaridad mundial hacia México: muchas naciones enviaron ayuda material y económica, mensajes de apoyo y grupos de socorristas que trabajaron durante varias semanas en el rescate de numerosas personas atrapadas entre los escombros de casas, hospitales, escuelas y centros de trabajo. El miércoles 25 de abril de 1989 un nuevo temblor, de siete grados en la escala de Richter, causó pánico en la ciudad de México. En años posteriores se registraron nuevos sismos, aunque ninguno con las consecuencias del de 1985; de todos modos, en la ciudad de México se han ensayado diversas medidas preventivas para disminuir los riesgos durante un sismo.

FOTO: EIKON

Ivar Sisniega

SISNIEGA, MARCEL ◆ n. en Cuautla, Mor. (1960). Ajedrecista, escritor y cineasta. Ha colaborado en el diario *unomásuno* y otras publicaciones. Está incluido en los libros colectivos *Versiones sobre un mismo campanario* y *Lluvia para una tarde de cuentos*. Autor del volumen de cuentos *Anda suelto un befo* (1986). Fue campeón nacional de ajedrez (1975) y obtuvo dos veces el cuarto lugar en los campeonatos mundiales juveniles de 1976 (Países Bajos) y 1977 (Cuba). Tiene título de maestro internacional de ajedrez, primera (1985) y segunda normas de gran maestro (1991) y primer gran maestro por la Federación Internacional de Ajedrez (1992). Primer lugar en el Certamen de Cuento del Ayuntamiento de Puerto Vallarta y la revista *La Brújula en el Bolsillo* (1983). Como cineasta realizó *Libre de culpas* (Ariel por fotografía y música 1998 y mejor cortometraje de ficción en el Cinemafest de Puerto Rico 1999).

SISNIEGA, IVAR ◆ n. en el DF (1958). Hermano del anterior. Licenciado en administración de empresas. Competidor de pentatlón moderno y triatlón. Primer lugar en el preolímpico de Atlanta (1984), primer lugar en el campeonato nacional de EUA (1981), ganador de todos los triatlones celebrados en México en 1986, y campeón panamericano en la competencia individual y por equipos (1990). Ha sido director de Deporte y cultura física del IMSS (1991-94), director de la unidad de becas de la Conade (1989-91), coordinador de Deporte en las campañas a la presidencia de Luis Donaldo Colosio y de Ernesto Zedillo. Ha laborado en el área deportiva de importantes empresas. Miembro permanente del Comité Olímpico Mexicano (1992-). Presidente de la Comisión Nacional del Deporte (1994-). Premio Nacional del Deporte (1990), medalla de plata en la Juegos Centroamericanos (1990). Fue considerado el mejor deportista mexicano internacional de 1978 a 1990.

SISTEMA ECONÓMICO LATINOAMERICANO ◆ Organismo regional de consulta, coordinación, cooperación y promoción económica y social conjunta, creado por iniciativa de Luis Echeverría Álvarez. El Convenio Constitutivo del Sistema Económico Latinoamericano (SELA) se firmó el 17 de octubre de 1975 en la ciudad de Panamá, luego de las reuniones ministeriales de julio y agosto de ese mismo año, en las que participaron representantes de Argentina, Barbados, Bolivia, Brasil, Colombia, Costa Rica, Cuba, Chile, República Dominicana, Ecuador, El Salvador, Granada, Guatemala, Guyana, Haití, Honduras, Jamaica, México, Nicaragua, Panamá, Paraguay, Perú, Trinidad y Tabago, Uruguay y Venezuela.

SISTEMA INTERAMERICANO ◆ ☛ *Organización de Estados Americanos*.

SISTEMA INTERNACIONAL DE PESAS Y MEDIDAS ◆ A fin de regular los sistemas de pesos y medidas que tradicionalmente se utilizaban en México, cuya arbitrariedad y flexibilidad provocaban confusiones o se prestaban a las acciones fraudulentas, el 15 de marzo de 1857 el país adoptó oficialmente el sistema métrico decimal o Sistema Internacional de Pesas y Medidas. Se impusieron diversas penas por el uso de medidas tradicionales como la vara, la legua, la brazada, el cordel, la arroba, el galón, el barril, el azumbre, el almud y aun otras más imprecisas, como el tiro de ballesta, la carga, el palmo o el codo, entre muchas otras. Según el nuevo patrón, implantado por primera vez en Francia el 4 de julio de 1837, las unidades básicas del nuevo sistema nacional de pesas y medidas fueron el metro, para las longitudes; el kilogramo, para la masa; el segundo, para el tiempo; el litro, para la capacidad y la peseta mexicana –pieza de plata de 10 gramos y 900 miligramos de ley– como unidad monetaria. A partir de estas unidades básicas, cualquier progresión de múltiplos y submúltiplos debía hacerse

FOTO: CARLOS HAHN

El litro, unidad básica del Sistema Internacional de Pesas y Medidas, fue adoptado en México en 1857

decimalmente. Sin embargo, aun a principios del siglo XX la mayor parte de las zonas rurales o semirrurales del país se mostraban reacias a aceptar este sistema y las mediciones se hacían en marcos, cordeles de 69 varas, aranzadas, caballerías, labores, haciendas o fanegas. El *Diario Oficial* del 14 de junio de 1928 publicó la Ley sobre Pesas y Medidas, la cual señala que el Sistema Nacional de Unidades de Medida tiene como fundamentales una de longitud, una de masa y una de tiempo y, en consecuencia, sus valores son independientes de la gravitación; dichas unidades son el metro, el kilogramo y el segundo de tiempo medio. Actualmente, el sistema métrico decimal se usa en todos los países del mundo con la única excepción de Estados Unidos y Reino Unido.

Sistema Volcánico Transversal ◆ Complejo orográfico también llamado Eje Volcánico Transversal, Faja Volcánica Mexicana y sierra Volcánica Transversal. Atraviesa el país de oeste-suroeste a este-noreste, a lo largo de unos 900 kilómetros. Para algunos geógrafos se extiende desde las costas de Nayarit hasta la sierra de los Tuxtlas, en el litoral veracruzano del golfo de México; en tanto que otros especialistas consideran que esta cordillera está limitada al oeste por la sierra Madre Occidental y al este por la sierra Madre Oriental. Consiste en grandes planicies escalonadas sobre las que se levantan numerosos volcanes. Pese a que el Sistema Volcánico Transversal es una zona de alto riesgo sísmico, a lo largo de él se han levantado algunas de las ciudades más importantes del país (México, Guadalajara, Pachuca, Morelia, Colima, Querétaro, Puebla y Toluca). El sistema cuenta, entre otros, con los volcanes Sangangüey, Popocatépetl, Iztaccíhuatl, Xitle, Citlaltépetl, Naucampatépetl, Xinantécatl, de Colima, Nevado de Colima, Tancítaro, Ceboruco, San Martín, Matlacuéyatl y, los más recientes, Paricutín y Jorullo, algunos de los cuales aún están activos.

Sisto Velasco, Eugenio ◆ n. en España (1924). En 1939 llegó exiliado a México, donde se naturalizó en 1947. Contador público (1955) y licenciado en administración por la UNAM (1963), donde ejerce la docencia desde 1955 y fue miembro del Consejo Técnico (1963-75) y jefe de la carrera de administración de la Facultad de Contaduría y Administración (1968-69). Ha sido profesor del Instituto Panamericano de Alta Dirección de Empresas (1970-) y de las universidades de Sonora y Coahuila (1962-65); director de Finanzas de Fundidora Monterrey (1972-77), socio fundador de la empresa Sisto, Agramonte y Asociados y director del Museo Franz Mayer (1978-). Miembro del Instituto Mexicano de Ejecutivos de Finanzas del Instituto Mexicano de Contadores Públicos, del Colegio de Licenciados en Administración y de la Asociación de Licenciados en Administración. Estudió pintura en la Escuela Nacional de Artes Plásticas. Ha presentado individualmente su obra desde 1954. Ha expuesto en el Ateneo Español de México, en el Instituto Cultural Hispano-Mexicano (1967), en las galerías de la ciudad de México (1970) y en el Museo de Arte Moderno de la Universidad Autónoma de Guerrero (1972).

Sitalá ◆ Municipio de Chiapas situado en el norte del estado, al noreste de Tuxtla Gutiérrez y de San Cristóbal de Las Casas. Superficie: 233.5 km². Habitantes: 5,940, de los cuales 1,670 forman la población económicamente activa. Hablan alguna lengua indígena 2,954 personas mayores de cinco años (tzeltal 2,911). Indígenas monolingües: 1,623.

Sitio de Xitlapehua ◆ Municipio de Oaxaca situado en el centro-sur del estado, al noreste y contiguo a Miahuatlán. Superficie: 66.34 km². Habitantes: 634, de los cuales 208 forman la población económicamente activa.

Siurob Ramírez, José ◆ n. en Querétaro, Qro., y m. en el DF (1886-1966). Antirreeleccionista desde 1909, en 1911 se unió a la insurrección maderista, en la que alcanzó el grado de general de división. Al término de la lucha armada se tituló en la Escuela Nacional de Medicina. Fue fundador y presidente del Partido Liberal Constitucionalista, que nombró candidato a la presidencia a Álvaro Obregón (1920). Gobernador de Guanajuato, de Querétaro y del territorio de Quintana Roo. Fue jefe del Departamento de Salubridad Pública (del 19 de junio de 1935 al 4 de enero de 1938 y del 5 de agosto de 1939 al 30 de noviembre de 1940) en el gabinete de Lázaro Cárdenas. Durante su gestión se construyeron los hospitales de Huipulco, Zoquiapan y Arcelia. También en el sexenio cardenista fue jefe del Departamento Central (del 4 de enero de 1938 al 5 de agosto de 1939). Varias veces diputado federal y comandante militar de diversas zonas del país, fue uno de los fundadores del

Foto: Juan Morín

El Popocatépetl y el Iztaccíhuatl forman parte del Sistema Volcánico Transversal

Semilla, óleo sobre tela de Waldemar Sjölander

Banco del Ejército y la Armada, inspector general del ejército, director de Sanidad Militar y director de Servicios Sociales de la Secretaría de la Defensa Nacional. Autor de *Tendencias modernas de la salubridad en la República Mexicana* (1936) y *La medicina social en México* (1940).

Sjölander, Waldemar ◆ n. en Suecia y m. en el DF (1908-1988). Estudió pintura y escultura en Suecia, Noruega y Dinamarca. Vino en 1946 y al año siguiente obtuvo la nacionalidad mexicana. En 1946 presentó su primera exposición individual. Profesor de la Academia de San Carlos y de La Esmeralda. A Sjölander se acercaron artistas deseosos de alejarse de la escuela mexicana de pintura, como Alberto Gironella, Pedro Coronel, Vlady, Vicente Rojo, Fernando García Ponce y Héctor Xavier. Expuso en México, Suecia, la Unión Soviética, Japón, Francia y Brasil. Hay obras suyas en los museos Nacional de Estocolmo, Moderno de Estocolmo, Gotemburgo, Tessin (Francia), Nacional de Bellas Artes (México), Nacional de Rodesia y de Arte Moderno de México. Premio Xipe-Totec de la primera Bienal de Escultura organizada por el INBA (1962) y primer premio en escultura del Salón de la Plástica Mexicana (1971). En 1998 el Museo Dolores Olmedo realizó una exposición retrospectiva de su obra, llamada Color, pasión y juego.

Alejandro Sobarzo Loaiza

Skirius, John ◆ n. en EUA (1938). Historiador egresado de la Universidad de Harvard. Su tesis profesional se convirtió en el libro *José Vasconcelos y la cruzada de 1929* (1976). En 1981 anunció que trabajaba en una biografía de Vasconcelos, de la que publicó adelantos en la revista *Vuelta*.

Slim, Julián ◆ n. en Líbano y m. en el DF (1887-1953). Llegó a Tampico a los 13 años y ahí estableció un puesto semifijo de ropa y mercería. En 1904 se trasladó a la ciudad de México para abrir la tienda La Estrella de Oriente en la plaza El Volador. En las calles de Correo Mayor y Corregidora adquirió una casa que fue sede de inmigrantes orientales, a quienes Slim apoyaba y otorgaba créditos para establecerse en México. En 1945 abrió la ferretería ADSA, que impulsó otros negocios que emprendió en México.

Slim Helú, Carlos ◆ n. en el DF (1940). Hijo del anterior. Ingeniero civil por la UNAM (1961), de la que fue profesor (1959-65). En 1975 abrió su propia correduría y en 1990 creó el Grupo Carso, que preside, firma controladora de empresas como la minera Nacobre, industrias y tiendas al menudeo que van desde la cigarrera Cigatam hasta Sears (40 tiendas), así como Sanborns (100 establecimientos). Otras propiedades suyas son Carso Global Telecom, que posee 24.8 por ciento de Teléfonos de México, y el Grupo Financiero Inbursa, casa de bolsa y aseguradora. Es el empresario más rico de México y uno de los más ricos del mundo: el valor de sus propiedades se estimaba en 1999 en 10,500 millones de dólares.

Foto: Dante Bucio

Carlos Slim Helú

Smith, Ken ◆ n. en EUA y m. en el DF (1918-1990). Locutor naturalizado mexicano. Fue cantante del grupo los *Teen Tops*. Se inició como locutor en 1935 en la estación XEBZ; más adelante trabajó en Estados Unidos y regresó a México en 1958 para montar los estudios de doblaje Ken Smith, que cerró en 1968. Locutor de televisión, fue el encargado de traducir las transmisiones de las misiones Apolo y fue miembro del equipo de *Stereo* Rey.

Sobarzo, Horacio ◆ n. en Magdalena y m. en Hermosillo, Son. (1896-1963). Licenciado en derecho por la Escuela Nacional de Jurisprudencia (1925). Fue juez de primera instancia en Nogales (1928), magistrado del Tribunal Supremo de Justicia (1929, 1933 y 1937), secretario de Gobierno (1946), gobernador sustituto e interino de Sonora (1948-49), en reemplazo de Abelardo L. Rodríguez. Autor de *Biografía de José Rafael Campoy* (1929), *Crónicas biográficas* (1949), *Crónica de la aventura de Raousset Boulbon en Sonora* (1954) e *Impugnación al laudo del Lic. Portes Gil sobre los límites entre Sonora y Chihuahua* (1956).

Sobarzo Loaiza, Alejandro ◆ n. en Hermosillo, Son. (1934). Hijo del anterior. Licenciado en derecho por la UNAM y doctor en la misma especialidad por la Universidad Central de Madrid (1961). Profesor de la UNAM (1965-68). Desde 1962 es miembro del PRI, en el que ha sido secretario particular del presidente del CEN (1972), presidente de la Comisión de Asuntos Internacionales (1975-76), director de Asuntos Internacionales (1977) y secretario de Asuntos Internacionales del CEN (1978-79 y 1987-). Ha sido notario público en Hermosillo (1964-65), asesor del director general de Pemex (1965-82), secretario de Estudio y Cuenta de la SCJN (1966), diputado federal (1973-76 y 1979-82), senador suplente (1976-82), director general de Gobierno de la Secretaría de Gobernación (1982-83), senador por Sonora (1982-88) y embajador en Venezuela (1988-91). Autor de *Régimen jurídico de alta mar* (1970), *México y su mar patrimonial; la zona económica exclusiva* (1976) y *Deber y conciencia. Nicolás Trist, el negociador norteamericano en la guerra del 47* (1991).

SOBERANES REYES, JOSÉ LUIS ◆ n. en Culiacán, Sin. (1950). Ingeniero civil por el ITESM, maestro en planeación urbana y desarrollo y maestro en ciencias de investigación y operaciones por la Universidad de Pennsylvania, EUA. Es profesor de posgrado de la Facultad de Ingeniería de la UNAM. Desde 1977 pertenece al PRI, donde formó parte de la Comisión de Estudios del DF y Zona Metropolitana del CEPES, fue tesorero general y secretario de Organización del CEN y representante de ese partido ante el IFE (1994). Vicepresidente de la Fundación Colosio. Ha sido asesor técnico de la Subsecretaría de Asentamientos Humanos y Obras Públicas, director de Programación y Presupuesto Regional de la SPP, coordinador de la Subsecretaría de Planeación del Desarrollo de la SPP, director general de Política Informática en el INEGI, director de Operaciones Urbanas de Diconsa y subsecretario de Desarrollo Urbano e Infraestructura de la Sedesol. Senador de la República (1994-2000). Pertenece a la Academia Mexicana de Informática y al Colegio de Ingenieros Civiles. Autor de *La reforma urbana*.

SOBERANISTAS ◆ ☛ *Oaxaca*.

SOBERÓN ACEVEDO, GUILLERMO ◆ n. en Iguala, Gro. (1925). Médico cirujano por la UNAM (1948) y doctor en química fisiológica por la Universidad de Wisconsin (1956). En la UNAM ha sido profesor desde 1958, investigador (1965-82) y director del Instituto de Investigaciones Biomédicas (1965-71), investigador del Centro de Investigaciones sobre la Fijación del Nitrógeno (Cuernavaca, 1981-82) y rector (1973-81). Fue investigador, jefe del Departamento de Bioquímica y director de la División de Investigación del Instituto Nacional de la Nutrición (1956-65); coordinador de los Servicios de Salud de la Presidencia (1981-82) y, en el gobierno del presidente Miguel de la Madrid, titular de la Secretaría de Salubridad y Asistencia, transformada durante su gestión en Secretaría de Salud (del 1 de diciembre de 1982 al 30 de noviembre de 1988). Editor de *Ensayos bioquímicos* (1970), coautor de *La universidad ahora, anotaciones, experiencias y reflexiones* (1983) y coordinador de *Hacia un sistema nacional de salud* (1983). Ha sido presidente de la Sociedad Mexicana de Bioquímica (1957), de la Academia de la Investigación Científica (1966-67), de la Academia Nacional de Medicina (1973-74), de la Unión de Universidades de América Latina (1976-79) y de la Asociación Internacional de Universidades (1980-) y presidente ejecutivo de la Fundación Mexicana para la Salud. Pertecene a corporaciones científicas de México y otros países. Es miembro de El Colegio Nacional (1981), *doctor honoris causa* por las universidades de Wisconsin (1976), Oviedo (1979), Tel-Aviv (1982) y Salamanca (1986). Premio Carnot de la Academia Nacional de Medicina (1965), de la Academia de la Investigación Científica (1965), Elías Sourasky (1968), Nacional de Ciencias (1980) y Abraham Horwitz (1991, de la Organización Panamericana de la Salud).

FOTO: DANTE BUCIO

Guillermo Soberón Acevedo

SOBERÓN Y PARRA, GALO ◆ n. en Chilpancingo, Gro., y m. cerca de Cuernavaca, Mor. (1896-1956). Se tituló en la Escuela Nacional de Medicina (1921), de la que fue profesor. Se especializó en la Universidad de París y en el Instituto de Enfermedades Tropicales de Hamburgo. Fue delegado de Salubridad en Iguala (1923), jefe de brigada, delegado federal, jefe de la Oficina de Sanidad Federal y director técnico de la Campaña para la Erradicación del Paludismo. Autor de *La reacción de Weil en el tabardillo o tifo exantemático* (tesis, 1921). Miembro de la Academia Nacional de Medicina. Murió en un accidente automovilístico.

SOCIAL, LA ◆ De acuerdo con un estudioso del movimiento obrero de la época, John M. Hart, esta organización se constituyó secretamente en 1868, con una docena de miembros que pertenecían al Club Socialista de Estudiantes. Según otro autor, José C. Valadés, la agrupación se fundó el 20 de marzo de 1871 para reunir "a todos aquellos elementos adictos a la causa socialista". En un *Manifiesto* (15 de abril de 1871) decía: "Queremos la abolición de todo sistema de gobierno y la libertad de los obreros manuales e intelectuales del universo", pues su programa no reconocía "nacionalidad ni origen ni distinción alguna". Entre sus fundadores estuvieron Plotino Rhodakanaty (☛), Ricardo B. Velatti (secretario de la organización en 1873), Benito Castro y Francisco Zalacosta. Según José C. Valadés, en La Social se manifestaba la tendencia "de los socialistas antipolíticos", contrarios a la participación electoral de los obreros. Después de un periodo de inactividad, fue reinstalada el 7 de mayo de 1876 en el templo de San Pedro y San Pablo, con la participación de miembros del ala radical del Congreso Obrero. El acto se celebró ante el retrato de Santiago Villanueva y un cuadro sobre las víctimas de la Comuna de París. Asistieron Jesusa Valadés, quien presidió la junta, Francisca y Soledad Sosa, Esther Fra-

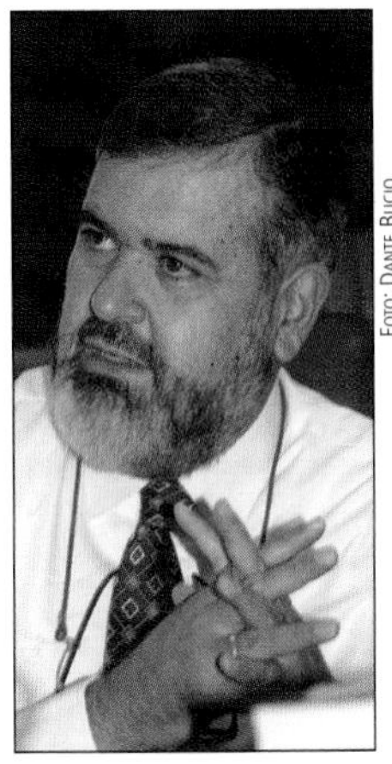
FOTO: DANTE BUCIO

José Luis Soberanes Reyes

goso y otras mujeres. Rhodakanaty pronunció el discurso de apertura, en el que dijo del socialismo: "Su fin inmediato es la transfiguración de la humanidad por medio de la ciencia, de la belleza y de la virtud. Su fin inmediato es la extinción de la pobreza y de la autoridad; la difusión y aumento de la riqueza pública entre todo el pueblo, la abolición de la prostitución y la conservación de nuestras facultades físicas y morales." De los militantes de La Social declaró: "Cosmopolitas de corazón, somos ciudadanos de todos los países; nuestra patria es el mundo entero y todos los hombres son nuestros hermanos; la tierra toda es el patrimonio común de los mortales y el género humano será feliz cuando no existan fronteras ni murallas." En esa reunión se acordó enviar una delegación al Congreso Obrero para denunciar ahí "las lacras políticas de los hombres que dirigen el Gran Círculo". La delegación estuvo integrada por Jesusa Valadés, Soledad Sosa, Santiago Enríquez e Ignacio Zavaleta, pero las mujeres enviadas como delegadas no fueron admitidas, "por reputarlas la ley como menores de edad y en tal virtud carecen de personalidad para ser representantes y además que nuestras leyes aun no conceden a la mujer los derechos del ciudadano". También, "por la conveniencia y decoro del sexo", fueron rechazadas en dos votaciones, por 49 a 29 votos la primera, y 37 a 27 la segunda. Como parte de sus trabajos, La Social realizó un ciclo de conferencias con te-mas como "¿Qué es el socialismo?", "Socialismo partidario y socialismo libre", "Federalismo y centralismo", "¿Qué es la Internacional?" y otros. En julio La Social se adhirió formalmente a la Asociación Internacional de Trabajadores (Federación del Jura) por conducto de la Federación Regional Española y llegó a ser considerada como la "sección mexicana" de esa organización, también conocida como Internacional anarquista (☛). El 15 de agosto de 1877, en medio de la agitación agrarista que vivía el centro del país, convocó a una asamblea de los trabajadores del campo, en la que se constituyó el Gran Comité Central Comunero, con Alberto Santa Fe como presidente, Félix Riquelme y Francisco Zalacosta como secretarios y el general Tiburcio Montiel como abogado de los pueblos en litigios agrarios. El 1 de enero de 1878 se inició una reunión que continuó el 8 y el 9. En ella se resolvió que "los afectos al socialismo verdadero se llamarán socialistas revolucionarios" para distinguirse de los que participan de las pugnas por el poder político. Se propuso enviar una delegación al siguiente congreso de la Internacional, ante el cual debería proponer la constitución de una Caja General de Socorros y Auxilios Internacionales "para los casos de huelga o revolución". Se acordó organizar a la clase por oficio y con carácter de resistencia, luchar por la jornada máxima de 50 horas semanales y el salario mínimo de un peso al día. Se declaró también: "Queremos la revolución socialista y la anarquía social. Se apoya el sistema de huelga, aislada o conjunta, pacífica o violenta, siempre que sea justa". Se acordó constituir "Ligas de Resistencia Campesina" y colonias agrícolas comunales para que el socialismo mostrara su viabilidad. "La tierra es de todos —se dijo— y se impone la expropiación de los usurpadores" (los terratenientes), por lo que "se declara: que el valor de la propiedad es nulo y se proclama la Ley Agraria". Ahí también se resolvió publicar un órgano que se llamaría *La Internacional* (☛). La circular con las resoluciones estaba firmada por Rhodakanaty, presidente; José Rico, vicepresidente; Félix Riquelme, primer secretario; José Muñúzuri, segundo secretario; Esther Sosa, tercera secretaria; E. Meza, cuarto secretario y Francisco Zalacosta, tesorero de La Social, "sección mexicana de la AIT". En septiembre de 1878 contaba con 62 secciones en la República, principalmente de campesinos que participaban en un activo movimiento de toma de tierras. Para ratificar su independencia de los manejos electorales que mantenían dividido al Gran Círculo, La Social organizó una manifestación el 14 de diciembre. Ese día, en la Plaza Colón se reunieron unas 5,000 personas que portaban mantas de la Internacional Anarquista. Entre los manifestantes se introdujeron varios disidentes del Gran Círculo que marcharon como todos hasta la Plaza de la Constitución, lo que dio pie para que los dirigentes porfiristas del Gran Círculo acusaran a La Social de estar comprometida con el candidato presidencial Trinidad García de la Cadena. En 1880 se convirtió en la principal fuerza del segundo Congreso Obrero, pero éste careció de fuerza y la Gran Confederación de Trabajadores Mexicanos que acordó crear no parece haber pasado del papel. Al año siguiente desapareció Zalacosta, uno de sus principales animadores, presumiblemente ejecutado en Querétaro. Rhodakanaty no pudo mantener cohesionada y en funcionamiento a la organización y decidió trasladarse a Chalco, donde fracasó en su intento de reabrir la Escuela de la Razón y del Socialismo (☛). Se dedicó entonces a la filosofía y La Social desapareció.

SOCIALISMO ◆ ☛ *Anarquismo* y *Comunismo*.

SOCIALISTA, EL ◆ Nombre del más importante periódico obrero del siglo XIX, fundado el 9 de julio de 1871. Fue su director Francisco del Paula González, y sus redactores Mariano García, Luis G. Miranda, Francisco J. Acosta, Manuel Chibrás, Manuel Escudero, José López, Carlos G. Rodríguez, Felipe Acosta, Enrique Trear, Fidencio Lara y Luis Sánchez. Posteriormente se incorporó Ángel Pola. Dio cabida a las diversas corrientes socialistas de su tiempo (utopistas, ácratas, marxistas, etcétera), informó sobre las actividades de la Internacional (☛), defendió la Comuna de París y, a la caída de ésta, demandó que se diera asilo en México a los comuneros, perseguidos entonces en casi toda Europa. El 1 de enero de 1872 se convirtió en "órgano oficial del Gran Círculo de Obreros de México". El 8 de septiembre de 1872, Juan de Mata Rivera asumió la dirección Francisco del

Paula González criticó al periódico y al Gran Círculo diciendo que "habían traicionado, con sus múltiples compromisos con los propietarios y con el gobierno, los ideales socialistas". El 1 de enero de 1876 cambió a un formato mayor y anunció que había adquirido una imprenta en San José de Gracia número 15, en la ciudad de México. Sus corresponsales eran: Tomás de Cuéllar, hijo, en Washington; Vicente García Torres, hijo, en París; Joaquín Gómez Vergara y Enrique Olavarría y Ferrari, en Madrid; Antonio Caulá en Barcelona; Luis Malanco en Roma; Ángel Núñez en Berlín y Roberto MacDowall en Colombia. Mantenía relaciones con el secretariado de la Internacional de Londres (marxista) y la secretaría de la Internacional del Jura (anarquista). En el número del 6 de febrero comunica que el *Boulletin de la Fedération Jurasienne* hace referencia al periódico mexicano. El 23 de marzo de 1876 se declaró "órgano oficial del Congreso Obrero" que estaba celebrándose en la capital. Como algunos delegados protestaron porque mutilaba sus intervenciones, respondió su director, Mata Rivera, que el órgano "ha albergado en sus columnas a todas las tendencias en defensa de la libertad de pensamiento. La prueba es que hemos dado lugar para que escriban algunos amigos comunalistas, españoles y rusos". Defendió el derecho a ejercer la censura porque algunos artículos "caen bajo la sanción de las leyes" y agregó que "*El Socialista* no está dispuesto a publicar desahogos personales ni cuestiones de tendencias". A la acusación de que el periódico unas veces apoyaba las huelgas y otras las combatía y de que en ocasiones sostenía la necesidad de una revolución social y después abogaba por sustituirla con filantropía y por la armonía entre el capital y el trabajo, respondió Mata Rivera: "Debemos de mantener la armonía entre el capital y el trabajo mientras pasan las revoluciones. Yo soy de los primeros socialistas mutualistas habidos en México y seguiré laborando por que se acaben los explotados y explotadores, opresores y oprimidos." Al convertirse Mata Rivera en activo partidario de Lerdo de Tejada, en *El Proteccionista* (20 de agosto de 1876) escribió Francisco Aduna, en referencia a *El Socialista*: "era en antaño el defensor del obrero, su guardián, su mentor, el que lo ilustraba, el que lo guiaba por el sendero glorioso del trabajo y la moral. Fundado por artesanos, por artesanos era leído con avidez, y por artesanos fomentado y enaltecido. ¿Y qué sucedió? La reelección lo encontró en su camino (o él a la reelección) y lo llevó con su editor ante el señor Lerdo, para que se quitara de esas pequeñeces de defender al obrero y defendiera a su gobierno. Ahí lo vemos ahora despreciado, vilipendiado y aborrecido por toda la clase obrera. No cabe, no puede caber en ningún taller, en ningún círculo obrero, un periódico que, habiendo sido uno de los nuestros, ha traicionado sus principios. ¿Qué importa que reciba dinero de la tesorería si la circulación y el crédito los ha perdido ante el pueblo." En abril de 1879 el periódico anunció que dejaba de ser órgano del Gran Círculo. Su director participó en la preparación del segundo Congreso Obrero. Sin embargo, a menos de una semana de iniciado éste, el periódico (8 de enero de 1880) anunció su adhesión a la candidatura presidencial de Trinidad García de la Cadena, lo que de hecho significó la ruptura con el Congreso, y el día 29 se pu-blicó un llamamiento de apoyo a su candidato, "el único hombre capaz de enfrentarse a la candidatura oficial del partido del general Porfirio Díaz". Sin embargo, celebradas las elecciones en las que resultó presidente Manuel González, el periódico apoyó la candidatura de Díaz a la gubernatura de Oaxaca. En 1881 publicó dos artículos de Nathan Ganz, quien por gestiones de Mata Rivera fue acreditado como representante de los obreros mexicanos ante el Congreso de la Internacional anarquista celebrado en ese año en Londres. En 1884 publicó el *Manifiesto del Partido Comunista*. En 1886 dejó de editarse.

Tomo I. MAZATLÁN, Estado de Sinaloa, Mayo 22 de 1892. Núm. 35.

EL SOCIALISTA.

PUBLICACION

Organo dedicado á las Sociedades Mutualistas de este Puerto.

Tiro Ordinario, 1,000 Ejemplares.

Editor propietario, A. H. Rodriguez.

CONDICIONES.

MESAS DIRECTIVAS

De las Sociedades Mutualistas de este puerto.

"Artesanos Unidos."

"Mutua de Zapateros."

"Antonio Rosales."

"EL SOCIALISTA."

Imprenta Comercial

—DE—

ANTONIO H. RODRIGUEZ

MAZATLÁN.

TALLER DE ENCUADERNACION.

LIBROS EN BLANCO.

TODO A PRECIOS MUY BARATOS.

IMPORTANTE.

J. J. Alexandre.

J. L. MARSHALL SUCESORES.

JOYEROS

MANUEL L. CHOZA,

Abogado y Escribano.

Calle Principal No. 26.

JOSE A. MEZA,

El Socialista del 22 de mayo de 1892

Socialista, El ◆ Órgano del Partido Socialista Obrero. Apareció como semanario en 1912, "dedicado a la defensa del proletariado" y bajo el lema "La emancipación de los trabajadores debe ser obra de los trabajadores mismos." En su primera época lo dirigió el ex magonista Juan Sarabia. El partido y su periódico desaparecieron durante la dictadura de Victoriano Huerta. El primero fue reconstituido a fines de 1916, como Partido Socialista Me-xicano, y en 1917 reapareció el semanario, que se transformó después en pu-blicación mensual y desapareció en 1918, aunque volvió a publicarse en enero de 1919. Reproducía artículos de *L'Humanité*, de *Vorwaerts*. Pese a su tendencia socialdemócrata, mostró simpatías por la revolución bolchevique.

Manuel M. Ponce, uno de los fundadores de la Sociedad de Autores y Compositores de México

SOCIEDAD AGRÍCOLA ORIENTAL ◆ Organización mutualista fundada en 1857. Desapareció poco después y en 1865 se creó una agrupación semejante que fue, según John M. Hart, durante largos periodos y hasta 1880, "el principal centro de actividad anarquista y de organización laboral urbana". La fundaron Santiago Villanueva y Hermenegildo Villavicencio, quienes agruparon a "escultores y pintores instruidos en la filosofía de Proudhon".

SOCIEDAD DE ARTESANOS Y JORNALEROS ◆ Organización obrera de Jalapa, fundada el 1 de junio de 1867. El 8 de julio de 1874 inició una huelga por la abolición del trabajo nocturno y la jornada máxima de 10 horas, haciéndose eco de los acuerdos de la Unión de Tejedores de las Fábricas Unidas del valle de México, del 24 de abril. La huelga persistió hasta el 6 de agosto, cuando lograron el acuerdo con la patronal de un máximo de 12 horas y, al cabo de un año, de 10 horas.

SOCIEDAD DE ARTESANOS SOMBREREROS ◆ Organización creada en 1854. El presidente era Ángel García Alonso y el reglamento fue redactado por José Delgado, Luciano Coronel y Manuel Barrera. El 13 de abril se dirigieron al secretario de Fomento, Joaquín Velázquez de León, para pedirle que aprobara el reglamento y autorizara la constitución de la Sociedad, a lo que el ministro respondió afirmativamente. El Congreso Obrero de 1876, por su antigüedad, le concedió el título de "Benemérita".

SOCIEDAD ARTÍSTICO-INDUSTRIAL ◆ Agrupación creada en la ciudad de México en 1846 por obreros ebanistas, con el fin "de perfeccionar a los trabajadores del ramo". El principal fundador fue Epifanio Romero. Desapareció en 1847 a consecuencia de la guerra contra los invasores estadounidenses. Su organización constituye uno de los principales antecedentes del sindicalismo mexicano. Fue reanimada hacia 1866 por Hermenegildo Villavicencio y Santiago Villanueva, quienes la convirtieron en centro de debates y conferencias socialistas. En 1868, sin embargo, Epifanio Romero, Juan Cano y otros líderes gobiernistas se incorporaron de nuevo a la Sociedad, al fusionar el Conservatorio Artístico-Industrial a la Sociedad, que quedó bajo su dirección. En 1870 un discurso de tono revolucionario de Francisco Zalacosta, en el que proponía una idea internacionalista de patria, motivó la escisión de Romero, Cano y otros. En 1873 se crearon filiales en Parral, Guadalajara y León. En ese año entró en conflicto con el Gran Círculo de Obreros de México, al que acusó de recibir subsidios del gobierno y de empresarios. Su órgano fue *El Obrero Internacional*. El 16 de noviembre de 1874 llamó a todas las organizaciones obreras para discutir sobre la necesidad de convocar a un congreso obrero socialista internacional que debería realizarse en México a fines de 1875. El llamamiento señalaba que "mientras todas las fuerzas de la Internacional se hagan radicar en Europa, la emancipación de los trabajadores no se llevará a la práctica, pues la América queda excluida en los trabajos positivos del socialismo". Decía también que "las persecuciones de las monarquías entorpecen el desarrollo que la Internacional puede tener en los países republicanos", donde se suponía que había mayores libertades. La iniciativa fracasó. Algunos de sus miembros promovieron la creación de cooperativas, como Ricardo B. Velatti, que imprimió este carácter a la Sociedad Progresista de Carpinteros (1872), que era mutualista. El mayor éxito de esta tendencia fue que la Colonia Obrera de Buenavista se constituyó en Asociación Cooperativa de Consumo de Obreros Colonos, con José Muñúzuri como presidente (1876).

SOCIEDAD DE AUTORES Y COMPOSITORES DE MÉXICO ◆ Organización creada como un instrumento de defensa de los derechos autorales y encargada del cobro de éstos a los usuarios de la música. Fue fundada el 7 de junio de 1945 por Alfonso Esparza Oteo, Mario Talavera, Ignacio Fernández Esperón *Tata Nacho*, Ernesto Cortázar, Manuel M. Ponce, Alberto Domínguez y otros creadores musicales. En 1958 se integró a la Confederación Internacional de Sociedades de Autores y Compositores, y fue aceptada como miembro en 1965. En 1971 inauguró la Casa del Compositor, en 1978 estrenó sus propios estudios de grabación, y un año después puso en funcionamiento cuatro salas cinematográficas, que en 1983 se convirtieron en sede de la Cineteca Nacional. Sus directores han sido Alfonso Esparza Oteo (1945-49), Ernesto Cortázar (1949-51 y 1953), Rodolfo Mendiolea (1953-63), Ignacio Fernández Esperón (1963-68), Consuelo Velázquez (1968-82) y Roberto Cantoral (1982-). Actualmente cuenta con más de 600 socios.

SOCIEDAD DE AUTORES MEXICANOS ◆ Organización fundada el 15 de enero de 1902, en el Teatro Abreu. Fue el primer organismo creado en México para la defensa de los intereses y la coordinación de labores de dramaturgos y literatos. Su primera mesa directiva tuvo a Juan de Dios Peza como presidente, a Hilarión Frías y Soto como vicepresidente, Alberto Michel como secretario, Carlos Valle y Garguen como protosecretario y a Enrique Olavarría y Ferrari como tesorero.

SOCIEDAD DANTE ALIGHIERI ◆ Fue fundada en Italia en 1880 por 150 personajes del mundo de las letras, la ciencia, la política y el derecho de ese país, con el objetivo de fortalecer los vínculos entre los mismos italianos, así como para promover su cultura y su lengua en todo el mundo. El nombre de la sociedad lo escogió el poeta Giosue Carduci, Premio Nobel de Literatura. Actualmente la sociedad tiene casi 500 comités en 58 países, con cinco millones de socios y 3,000 escuelas. En nuestro país fue fundada en 1901 con la participación de Geni Bonzano y María Appendini de Bigola, como una de las primeras instituciones culturales binacionales establecidas en México y uno de los primeros comités de dicha sociedad en el extranjero. Está presente en el Distrito Federal, Guadalajara, Monterrey, Puebla, Tampico, Aguascalientes, Tijuana, Orizaba, Cuernavaca, Veracruz, Querétaro y Acapulco.

Sociedad Filarmónica Mexicana ◆ Organismo fundado por Tomás León, Manuel Siliceo, José Ignacio Durán, Eduardo Liceaga y Aniceto Ortega el 14 de enero de 1866. Se convirtió en promotora de la creación musical en México. Su primera sede fue uno de los patios de la Escuela Nacional de Medicina, hasta que Benito Juárez, el 25 de octubre de 1867, le cedió el edificio de la antigua Universidad, en la calle de Cuba, donde posteriormente estuvo la Escuela Nacional de Música de la UNAM.

Sociedad General de Escritores de México ◆ Organismo fundado por José María Fernández Unsaín (☛) en 1976, sobre la base de la antigua Sociedad de Escritores Cinematográficos, de Radio y Televisión. Establecida como sociedad de autores de interés público, de acuerdo con la legislación vigente en ese tiempo, su propósito era defender los intereses de los escritores, asistirlos en el registro de su obra y en el cobro de sus derechos de autor y ofrecerles diversas prestaciones. Además de estas tareas, ha sido interlocutora en la discusión de numerosos proyectos legislativos sobre derechos de autor y temas afines y ha mantenido en el Distrito Federal, Bacalar, QR, y Álamos, Son., casas del escritor en las que ofrece estancia por diversos periodos a sus afiliados y a escritores destacados de México y otros países. En enero de 1987, la Sogem abrió su Escuela de Escritores a partir de un proyecto de Alejandro César Rendón (☛), quien fue su primer director (1987-98) y fue sucedido por José Antonio Alcaraz (1998-99) y Teodoro Villegas (1999). Fueron maestros fundadores, entre otros, Teodoro Villegas, José Antonio Alcaraz, Hugo Argüelles, Marcela del Río y José *Perro* Estrada. Posteriormente se han abierto otras escuelas en Guadalajara, Querétaro, Tijuana, San Cristóbal de Las Casas, Puebla y Metepec, Edo. de Méx. En 1995, después de la promulgación de una nueva Ley de Derechos de Autor, la sociedad pasó a ser de gestión colectiva de interés público. A la muerte de Fernández Unsaín en 1997, han ocupado la dirección Luis Reyes de la Maza (1997-99) y Víctor Hugo Rascón Banda (1999-).

Sociedad Mexicana de Escritores de Educación, Ciencia y Tecnología ◆ Fue creada en 1992 con el objetivo de promover la publicación de obras de divulgación e investigación científica y el acercamiento de éstas a la población, sobre todo infantil y juvenil. Actualmente cuenta con más de 60 miembros autores de libros de texto, educativos, técnicos o de corte científico, procedentes de instituciones de educación superior en México como el IPN, la UNAM y la Escuela Normal Superior. Su director es el maestro Arquímedes Caballero (☛).

Sociedad Mexicana de Geografía y Estadística ◆ Organismo creado por decreto presidencial de 28 de abril de 1851, con la fusión del Instituto Nacional de Geografía y Estadística y de la Comisión Estadística Militar. El Instituto había sido fundado el 18 de abril de 1833 por iniciativa de José Gómez de la Cortina, su primer presidente, con el apoyo del presidente (sustituto de Santa Anna) Valentín Gómez Farías. Entre los primeros socios de número y corresponsales del Instituto destacaron Manuel Gómez Pedraza y Andrés Quintana Roo. El 30 de septiembre de 1839, el secretario de Guerra, Almonte, creó la Comisión Estadística Militar (que presidió), para obtener y publicar datos para la estadística y la carta general de la República, así como un diccionario geográfico. El 28 de abril de 1851, a propuesta de Gómez de la Cortina, Santiago Blanco y Ramón Pacheco, se decretó la fusión del Instituto con la Comisión,

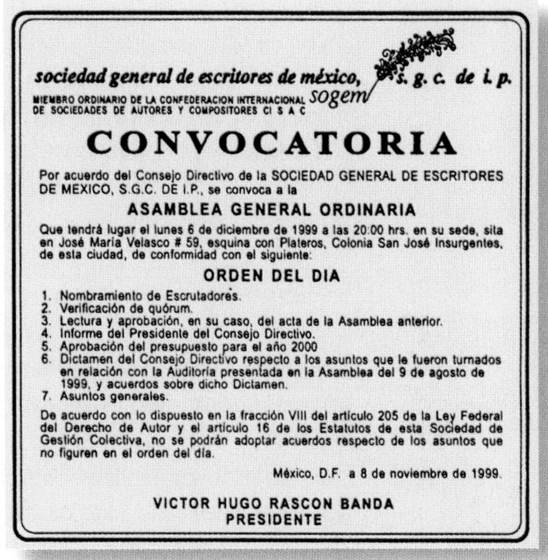

sociedad general de escritores de méxico, s. g. c. de i. p.
MIEMBRO ORDINARIO DE LA CONFEDERACION INTERNACIONAL DE SOCIEDADES DE AUTORES Y COMPOSITORES CI S A C
sogem

CONVOCATORIA

Por acuerdo del Consejo Directivo de la SOCIEDAD GENERAL DE ESCRITORES DE MEXICO, S.G.C. DE I.P., se convoca a la

ASAMBLEA GENERAL ORDINARIA

Que tendrá lugar el lunes 6 de diciembre de 1999 a las 20:00 hrs. en su sede, sita en José María Velasco # 59, esquina con Plateros, Colonia San José Insurgentes, de esta ciudad, de conformidad con el siguiente:

ORDEN DEL DIA

1. Nombramiento de Escrutadores.
2. Verificación de quórum.
3. Lectura y aprobación, en su caso, del acta de la Asamblea anterior.
4. Informe del Presidente del Consejo Directivo.
5. Aprobación del presupuesto para el año 2000
6. Dictamen del Consejo Directivo respecto a los asuntos que le fueron turnados en relación con la Auditoría presentada en la Asamblea del 9 de agosto de 1999, y acuerdos sobre dicho Dictamen.
7. Asuntos generales.

De acuerdo con lo dispuesto en la fracción VIII del artículo 205 de la Ley Federal del Derecho de Autor y el artículo 16 de los Estatutos de esta Sociedad de Gestión Colectiva, no se podrán adoptar acuerdos respecto de los asuntos que no figuren en el orden del día.

México, D.F. a 8 de noviembre de 1999.

VICTOR HUGO RASCON BANDA
PRESIDENTE

Convocatoria de la Sociedad General de Escritores de México para su asamblea general ordinaria de diciembre de 1999

de donde surgió la Sociedad Mexicana de Geografía y Estadística, a la que perteneció Benito Juárez. Sus labores se vieron interrumpidas durante la intervención francesa y el imperio de Maximiliano, pero las reanudó el 26 de marzo de 1868, con el concurso de Ignacio Manuel Altamirano, Eligio Ancona, Gabino Barreda, Antonio García Cubas, Alfonso Herrera, Manuel Payno, Ignacio Ramírez, Leopoldo Río de la Loza y Vicente Riva Palacio, entre otros. Es un organismo que trabaja las áreas de estadística, historia, geografía y otras disciplinas. Está afiliada a la Unión Geográfica Internacional y al Instituto Interamericano de Estadística. Desde el

Valentín Gómez Farías impulsó la creación de la Sociedad Mexicana de Geografía y Estadística

18 de marzo de 1839 ha editado un *Boletín*, una *Gaceta* mensual y numerosos libros y folletos.

Sociedad Mexicana de Historia Natural ◆ La primera organización que llevó este nombre fue fundada el 29 de agosto de 1868 por José Joaquín Arriaga, Antonio del Castillo, Francisco Cordero y Hoyos, Alfonso Herrera, Gumersindo Mendoza, Antonio Peñafiel, Manuel Río de la Loza, Jesús Sánchez, Manuel Urbina y Manuel Villada, a fin de reunir a los exponentes más destacados de la ciencia mexicana. Posteriormente se unieron a la Sociedad Gabino Barreda, Miguel Jiménez, Ignacio Alvarado, Agustín Andrade, Ignacio Manuel Altamirano y José María Velasco, entre otros. Esta sociedad se mantuvo en funciones durante 36 años, con apoyo gubernamental, y editó *La Naturaleza*, periódico científico dirigido por Manuel M. Villada. En 1912 esta primera sociedad desapareció, incapacitada para superar sus dificultades económicas. La segunda sociedad que llevó este nombre se fundó el 22 de enero de 1937, en una sesión efectuada en el Palacio de Bellas Artes. Sus fundadores fueron José R. Alcaraz, Ángel Roldán, Virgilio Camacho, Armando Vega y Enrique Beltrán. Su primer presidente fue Jesús Díaz Barriga. Edita desde 1939 la *Revista Mexicana de Historia Natural*. En su cincuentenario, el presidente era el maestro en ciencias Raúl Gio Argáez, tenía 374 socios numerarios, 14 corresponsales y cinco honorarios. De este organismo han surgido la Sociedad Botánica de Física (1949), la Sociedad Geológica Mexicana (1949), la Sociedad Mexicana de Ciencias Hidrobiológicas (1951), la Sociedad Mexicana de Entomología (1952) y la Sociedad Mexicana de Zoología (1977).

Sociedad Mutua del Ramo de Hilados y Tejidos del Valle de México ◆ Organización creada el 15 de mayo de 1865. Agrupaba a los obreros de dos fábricas de Tlalnepantla, La Colmena y San Ildefonso, que en junio de ese año protagonizaron la primera huelga concertada entre trabajadores de dos empresas, los que fueron baleados por la policía de Maximiliano. Muchos resultaron heridos y 50 fueron encarcelados.

Sociedad Mutua del Ramo de Sastrería ◆ Organización creada en julio de 1853. Epifanio Romero su presidente, fue encarcelado por el gobierno de Santa Anna y parece que durante su cautiverio desapareció la sociedad. (*Cfr.*: José C. Valadés. *El socialismo libertario*.)

Sociedad Mutualista de Escritores ◆ Organización creada para ofrecer un apoyo a los escritores, poetas, literatos y periodistas que tuvieran algún apremio económico. Se fundó en 1875 por iniciativa de Ignacio Manuel Altamirano, quien fue su presidente. El reglamento interno fue redactado por Ignacio Ramírez. Años después se extinguió.

Sociedad Mutualista Zarco de Artesanos ◆ Fundada en 1865 en Saltillo, Coahuila. En los años setenta del siglo XX todavía estaba en funciones.

Sociedad Nacionalista ◆ Partido político fundado en 1995 por el ex parmista Gustavo Riojas, quien lo preside. En 1996 presentó sus documentos ante el IFE para registrarse como partido político nacional, pero se rechazó su solicitud. En 1996 también fue rechazada como asociación política nacional, lo que consiguió hasta 1997. En junio de 1999 obtuvo sus registro como partido político al mostrar un padrón de 160,000 afiliados.

Logotipo del partido político Sociedad Nacionalista

Sociedad de Naciones ◆ Organismo de cooperación internacional creado el 28 de abril de 1919 por iniciativa del presidente estadounidense Thomas Woodrow Wilson e incorporado al Tratado de Paz de Versalles (29 de junio de 1919) que puso fin a la primera guerra mundial. México no figuró entre los 45 países fundadores debido a que Estados Unidos vetó su participación. Conocida también como Liga de las Naciones, tenía su sede en Londres y hacia 1930 contaba con 60 miembros. México fue admitido en septiembre de 1931. Entre sus objetivos estaba garantizar la observancia de los tratados internacionales y preservar la paz mundial, pero mostró su inoperancia cuando Francia e Inglaterra mostraron una temerosa pasividad ante la intervención de las potencias fascistas en España (1936-39), la invasión de Abisinia y Albania por la Italia de Mussolini, la anexión a la Alemania hitleriana de los Sudetes checoslovacos, parte de Dinamarca y Austria, o la ocupación de Finlandia y las repúblicas del Báltico por la Unión Soviética, hechos todos que México denunció en su momento ante la propia Sociedad de Naciones, sin que se resolviera actuar con la energía requerida, lo que propició el desencadenamiento de la segunda guerra mundial, que se inició oficialmente cuando Hitler y Stalin se repartieron Polonia. En los años de la conflagración la Liga dejó de funcionar para efectos prácticos. Fue disuelta oficialmente en 1946, después de la fundación de la ONU.

Sociedad Particular de Socorros Mutuos ◆ Organización obrera fundada el 5 de junio de 1853 en la ciudad de México. En sus bases constitutivas se condenaba "la esclavitud moderna que nos arrebata las ganancias de nuestro trabajo". La agrupación se declaró apolítica y se proponía abrir sucursales en otras ciudades, crear "un banco protector de las clases pobres", un asilo para mendigos y obreros inhabilitados y un "sistema de socorros a los socios enfermos y auxilios a las familias de los que fallezcan". Se inició con 33 socios y al mes eran 133. En julio del mismo año apoyó la creación de la Sociedad Mutua del Ramo de Sastrería. El 6 de julio de 1902, *La Convención Radical Obrera* se refería a esta sociedad "como la decana y fundadora del mutualismo mexicano", cuyos creadores "tuvieron que pasar por pruebas inconcebibles de persecución y de tortura que no los doblegaron; desde la disolución por la policía, hasta la prisión de algunos de sus honorables fundadores". Esta agrupación generó la formación de otras, "todas ellas cimentadas bajo un propio régimen, el legendario de las extinguidas cofradías, del cual no han podido independizarse, no obstante los esfuerzos de algunos de sus prohombres". Tuvo como antecedente al grupo llamado Hermanos del Petate, miembros de la Cofradía del Santísimo Sacramento, que auxiliaba a los deudos de miembros finados. Ésta existió hacia 1850. (*Cfr.*: José C. Valadés. *El socialismo libertario*.)

Sociedad de Tipógrafos Mexicanos ◆ Organización fundada en 1868, según José C. Valadés con el nombre de Asociación Socialista de Tipógrafos Mexicanos. Se reorganizó en 1871.

Socoltenango ◆ Municipio de Chiapas situado en el centro-sur del estado, al suroeste de Comitán y al sureste de Tuxtla Gutiérrez. Superficie: 775 km^2. Habitantes: 13,819, de los cuales 3,261 forman la población económicamente activa. Hablan alguna lengua indígena 879 personas mayores de cinco años (tzeltal 403 y tzotzil 370). En su jurisdicción se han encontrado restos de edificaciones prehispánicas.

Soconusco ◆ Municipio de Veracruz situado al suroeste de Coatzacoalcos y al oeste de Minatitlán. Superficie: 94.59 km^2. Habitantes: 11,661, de los cuales 2,475 forman la población económicamente activa. Hablan alguna lengua indígena 75 personas mayores de cinco años (náhuatl 53).

Soconusco ◆ Región de Chiapas situada en el sur del estado, en el litoral del océano Pacífico, al sureste de la sierra madre de Chiapas. Hacia el siglo VII la zona estaba poblada por los tapacholts, quienes fueron conquistados hacia 1486 por los mexicas, durante el señorío de Tizoc. Al concluir la conquista de México por los españoles, el Soconusco se convirtió en dependencia de la Audiencia de México. En 1542 pasó a formar parte de la Capitanía General de Guatemala. Al año siguiente quedó bajo la jurisdicción de la Audiencia de los Confines, que comprendía el sureste mexicano y Centroamérica. En 1565 volvió junto con Guatemala a la Audiencia de la Nueva España, hasta que en 1569, al reestablecerse la Audiencia de Guatemala quedó nuevamente bajo su autoridad. De acuerdo con la delimitación de 1794 y 1797, comprendía una franja entre la sierra y el mar de 58 leguas de largo en el actual estado de Chiapas, desde los límites con Oaxaca hasta la actual frontera con Guatemala. En algunos mapas de fines de la Colonia, el Soconusco comprende una extensión menor. Al consumarse la independencia, en 1821, junto con la provincias centroamericanas quedó dentro del Imperio Mexicano. El 14 de septiembre de 1824 se realizó un plebiscito, mediante el cual los partidos que formaban el estado de Chiapas se manifestaron por su incorporación a la República Mexicana, en tanto que el Soconusco votó por la unión con Centroamérica. Por vía diplomática, Guatemala reclamó como suyo el territorio, que por ser un partido del estado de Chiapas era considerado mexicano por las autoridades nacionales. En mayo, al mando de una fuerza militar guatemalteca, José Pierson ocupó el territorio en disputa, hizo jurar en Tapachula, capital del Soconusco, la Constitución de su país y se erigió en gobernador de la provincia. Chiapas consideró estos hechos como agresión y el 7 de julio de 1825 llegó un contingente mexicano a Tonalá, en tanto que se realizaban negociaciones entre ambos países. El 22 de agosto, la Cámara de Diputados de México resolvió poner el caso en manos del Ejecutivo, "para que obrando el presidente de la Federación conforme a sus atribuciones, hasta llegar al uso de las armas si así lo considera necesario, conserve la integridad de la República". El Senado no estuvo de acuerdo en que se optara por el uso de la fuerza y el Soconusco quedó en un estado de neutralidad al retirarse las fuerzas beligerantes. La primera Constitución local chiapaneca, del 19 de noviembre de 1825, decía que "El territorio del Estado es el mismo que antes componía la Intendencia y gobierno político del mismo, y consta de los partidos de la capital, Llanos, Tuxtlá,

Foto: Fondo Editorial Grupo Azabache

Socoltenango, Chiapas

Demetrio Sodi, el defensor de José de León Toral

Tonalá, Soconusco", etc. En 1831, el ex presidente guatemalteco Manuel José Arce reclutó en el Soconusco una fuerza expedicionaria con la que intentaba recuperar el poder en su país. Enterado el gobierno guatemalteco, envió un contingente militar que batió a Arce en Escuintla, el 24 de febrero de 1832, lo que motivó una protesta mexicana, sin que el asunto pasara a mayores. En agosto de 1842, el presidente Antonio López de Santa Anna envió un fuerte contigente militar, en tanto que daba a conocer una proclama en la que defendía el presunto derecho de México sobre el Soconusco. Bajo la ocupación militar, se realizaron juntas de autoridades y vecinos en Escuintla (día 10), Tapachula (día 15), Tuxtla (día 18) y luego en otras poblaciones, las que votaron por la anexión a México. Se enviaron estos resultados a la capital y, el 11 de septiembre del mismo año, el Congreso expidió un decreto mediante el cual declaraba al Soconusco unido al entonces departamento de Chiapas y, por lo mismo, a la República Mexicana. No se hizo esperar la protesta guatemalteca y se reinició un largo forcejeo diplomático. En 1878 se integró una comisión revisora de linderos con representantes de ambos países, cuyas delegaciones llegaron a un acuerdo después de cuatro años y el 27 de septiembre de 1882 se firmó un Tratado de Límites. Este documento tuvo carácter preliminar, pues la comisión siguió trabajando. En este periodo encabezó la representación mexicana Manuel E. Pastrana, en tanto que la delegación guatemalteca fue presidida por el estadounidense Miles Rock. El acuerdo final, que dejó la frontera como ahora existe, fue suscrito el 1 de abril de 1895. En diversos momentos se han presentado movimientos que reclaman la separación de Chiapas y la erección del estado del Soconusco. En 1983 se lanzó una proclama separatista desde el diario *Sur*, promovida por Augusto Villarreal Quezada y secundada por Alonso Rodríguez (quien incluso llamó a tomar las armas), Ángel Aguilar Díaz, el ex senador Ezzio del Pino Trujillo, así como comerciantes de café de Huixtlán. Se quejaban de la marginación en que el gobierno estatal tenía a esa región. El movimiento tuvo repercusiones en Tapachula, donde hubo marchas y otras formas de protesta en las elecciones de 1985, y se prolongó durante toda la década. En 1989, en la casa de José Cruz Toledo, ex rector de la Universidad Autónoma de Chiapas, se acordó "llegar hasta las últimas consecuencias para que el Sononusco se separe de Chiapas". El movimiento careció de apoyo popular y concluyó en 1990 con la firma de adhesión a la entidad chiapaneca de los 16 municipios que componen la región: Tapachula, Huixtlán, Mapastepec, Cacahoatán, Mazatlán, Metapa de Domínguez, Unión Juárez, Tuxtla Chico, Tuzantán, Acapetahua, Villa Comaltitlán, Acacoyahua, Escuintla, Huehuetán, Suchiate y Frontera Hidalgo.

Socorro ◆ Isla mexicana del océano Pacífico. Es la mayor del archipiélago de Revillagigedo, cuya jurisdicción corresponde al estado de Colima. Se halla 480 kilómetros al sur-suroeste del extremo sur de la península de Baja California y a la misma distancia al suroeste de las Islas Marías. Mide 16 kilómetros de noroeste a sureste y su anchura media es de 11 kilómetros. La isla es la cima del volcán Everman, que sobresale 1,051 metros de la superficie marina; en los extremos sureste y suroeste de la misma existen pequeñas bahías, propias para el calado de naves medianas. La armada mexicana cuenta con una base en esta isla.

Sochiapa ◆ Municipio de Veracruz situado al norte de Córdoba, al sur de Jalapa y contiguo a Huatusco. Superficie: 21.39 km^2. Habitantes: 2,792, de los cuales 666 forman la población económicamente activa. Hablan náhuatl cinco personas mayores de cinco años.

Sodi, Demetrio ◆ n. en Oaxaca, Oax., y m. en el DF (1866-1934). Se tituló como abogado en el Instituto de Ciencias y Artes de Oaxaca (1890). Fue profesor de la Escuela Libre de Derecho, de la Escuela Nacional Preparatoria y de la de Jurisprudencia. Ejerció diversos cargos judiciales en Colima, donde editó la revista *El Foro Colimense*, en Tehuantepec y en la ciudad de México, a la que llegó en 1895. Fue juez quinto de lo civil, magistrado del Tribunal Superior, así como ministro y presidente de la Suprema Corte (1908-10). Secretario de Justicia (del 25 de marzo al 25 de mayo de 1911) de Porfirio Díaz, cuyo discurso de despedida redactó. Francisco I. Madero le ofreció una cartera en su gabinete, la que declinó. En 1928 se encargó de la defensa del asesino de Álvaro Obregón, José de León Toral. Autor de *El jurado en México* (1909), *Mis sesenta días de mi-nistro*, *La justicia y la revolución*, *Nuestra ley penal* (1918) y *La nueva Ley Procesal Civil* (1933). Fue miembro de la Academia de Legislación y Jurisprudencia.

Sodi Miranda, Ariadna ◆ ☛ *Thalía*.

Sodi Morales, Demetrio ◆ n. y m. en el DF (1934-1982). Antropólogo e historiador. Fue profesor en las universidades Nacional Autónoma de México, Iberoamericana y de las Américas. Becario de la Fundación Guggenheim y secretario del Instituto Indigenista Interamericano. Autor de *La literatura de los mayas*, *Las máscaras de México*, *Mesoamérica*, *Los mayas, el tiempo capturado* y *The Maya World*.

SODI PALLARES, ERNESTO ♦ n. y m. en el DF (1919-1977). Ensayador y metalurgista por la UNAM (1939) y doctor en ciencias por la Universidad Neoboracensis de Nueva York (1946), especializado en criminalística. Fue profesor de química en colegios jesuitas y de los hermanos de las Escuelas Cristianas; profesor de criminalística, jefe de peritos, consejero y jefe de la Oficina Bibliográfica en Investigación Criminal de la Procuraduría General; inspector de Migración de la Secretaría de Gobernación; jefe de Servicios Federales adscrito a la secretaría privada de la Presidencia de la República y comentarista oficial de la provincia mexicana (1970). Colaboró en *La Prensa*. Autor de *Clasificación de tintas en la República Mexicana* (1947), *Clasificación de papeles en la República Mexicana* (1948), *Peritajes sobre la valuación de joyas* (1949), *Accidentes de tránsito* (1950), *Peritajes químicos en criminalística* (1951), *Clasificación de máquinas de escribir en la República Mexicana* (1952), *Cien lecciones sobre documentos falsificados* (1953), *Minerales mexicanos* (1954), *Impresión de valores* (1955), *Notas sobre ópalos mexicanos* (1956), *Notas sobre ágatas mexicanas* (1957), *El nopal en la historia de México* (1958), *Nuevo método para clasificar las cactáceas* (1959), *Fotografía con rayos X* (1960), *Fotografía en criminalística* (1962), *Envenenamientos* (1963), *Análisis de monedas mexicanas* (1964), *Fiestas, ferias y tianguis en la República Mexicana* (1965), *Espeleología turística* (1966), *Cocina vernácula mexicana* (1967), *Casonas antiguas de la ciudad de México* (1968), *Pinacoteca virreinal de San Diego* (1969), *La criminalística y su importancia en el campo del derecho* (1970), *Turismo mineralógico* (1971), *Turismo cinegético* (1972), *Turismo cultural* (1973), *Una vuelta al mundo tipo boumerang* (1974), *Turismo botánico* (1975), *Oaxaca turístico* (1975), *Aguascalientes turístico* (1975), *Investigación del delito* (1975) y *Excepta de máximas morales* (1975).

SODI ROMERO, FEDERICO ♦ n. en Oaxaca, Oax., y m. en el DF (1890-1969). Se tituló de abogado en el Instituto de Ciencias y Artes de Oaxaca (1913). Ejerció su profesión en la capital oaxaqueña y en la ciudad de México, donde alcanzó notoriedad como defensor en los jurados populares. Autor de las novelas *La ciudad tranquila*, *Feliciano cumple medio siglo* y *Clase media*, además de numerosas obras de teatro y la recopilación de sus mejores defensas: *El jurado resuelve. Casos reales ante el jurado popular* (1961).

SODI DE LA TIJERA, DEMETRIO JAVIER ♦ n. en el DF (1944). Licenciado en administración de empresas por la UIA (1966), posgraduado en la Universidad de Harvard (1973). Profesor de la UNAM (1973-74). De 1980 a 1990 perteneció al PRI, en el que formó parte del Consejo Nacional Consultivo del IEPES

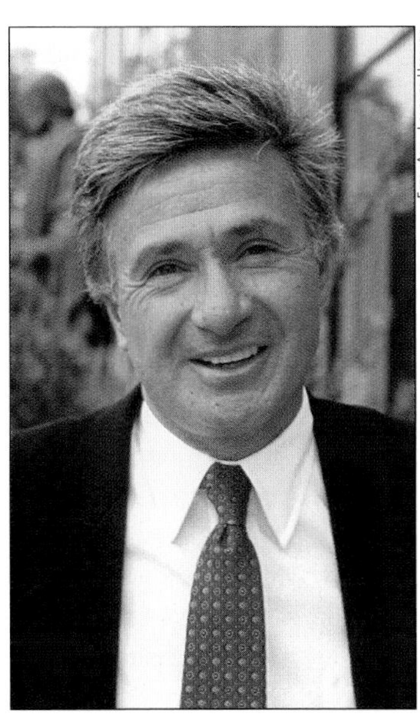

FOTO: ANA LOURDES HERRERA

Demetrio Sodi de la Tijera

(1983). Miembro del Consejo Directivo de la CNOP (1981). Ha sido subdirector de Tiendas Aurrerá (1963-73), director general de Suburbia (1973-74), director adjunto de Fertilizantes Fosfatados Mexicanos (1975-76), gerente de Operaciones Comerciales de Filiales Conasupo (1977), gerente general de Diconsa y representante de Conasupo ante la CTM, CCI, CNC y CNOP (1978-82); director general de la Comisión de Desarrollo Urbano del DDF (1982-83) y coordinador general de Abasto y Distribución del DDF (1983-). Miembro de la segunda Asamblea de Representantes del Distrito Federal (1991-94), diputado federal en dos ocasiones (1988-91, por el PRI y 1997-2000 por el PRD). Vicecoordinador del grupo parlamentario del PRD en la Cámara de Diputados durante la LVII Legislatura. Miembro del Consejo Nacional Directivo del Colegio Nacional de Licenciados en Administración (1979) y del Consejo Consultivo Nacional de la Sociedad Mexicana de Licenciados en Administración (1985). En 1999 se postuló como precandidato de su partido al gobierno del Distrito Federal

SOGEM ♦ ☛ *Sociedad General de Escritores de México*.

SOJO, FELIPE ♦ m. en la ciudad de México (?-1869). Escultor y pintor. Estudió en la Academia de San Carlos, donde fue alumno de Villar. Son obras suyas el altorrelieve *Descendimiento*, *Mercurio adormeciendo a Argos*, la escultura de *El Zarco* y un retrato de Maximiliano de Habsburgo que se conserva en el Museo de Historia de Chapultepec.

SOKOLOW, ANNA ♦ n. en EUA (1915). Bailarina y coreógrafa. Ha sido profesora en Canadá, Venezuela, Suecia, Suiza, Alemania, Holanda, Filipinas, Japón y en la Escuela Juilliard de Nueva York. Perteneció a la compañía de ballet de Martha Graham (1930-38). Desde 1934 formó diversos grupos dancísticos, entre ellos la Paloma Azul (1939), primer grupo mexicano de danza moderna, y la compañía Players Project (1988). Llegó a México en 1939, invitada por la SEP. Se interesó por el arte plástico mexicano e hizo amistad con Raúl Flores Canelo. Coreografías suyas, como *Opus 65* y *Rooms*, permanecen en los repertorios de diversas compañías de ballet en Tel Aviv y Londres y en el Ailey Dance Theater de Nueva York. Ha creado obras para el Paul Joffrey Ballet y el Netherlands Dance Theatre. Premio de la *Dance Magazine* (1962) por "integridad y audacia creativa" y Premio de las Artes Creativas de la Universidad de Brandeis (1974). El gobierno mexicano le impuso la Orden del Águila Azteca (1988).

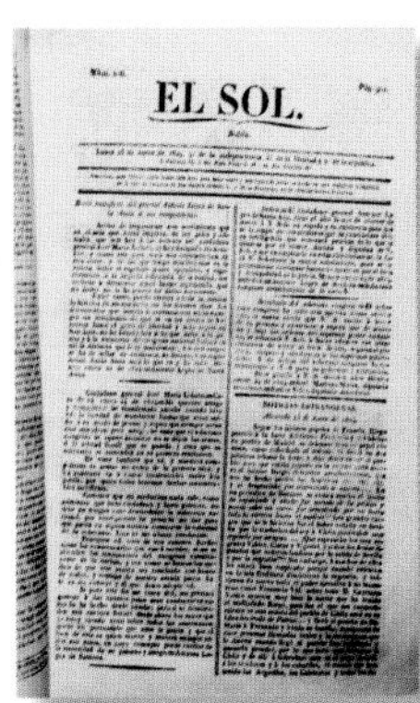

El Sol del lunes 26 de enero de 1824

Foto: Guillermo Aguilera

Rafael Solana

El Sol de México del 5 de noviembre de 1965

SOL, EL ◆ Órgano de la logia escocesa. Representó en sus inicios los intereses de la facción que pretendía guardar el trono del imperio mexicano a los Borbones. Tuvo como redactor a Manuel Codorniú y Ferreras durante su primera época, iniciada el 5 de diciembre de 1821. Iturbide ordenó cerrar el periódico en mayo de 1822. Reapareció el 15 de junio de 1823 como el principal vocero del centralismo. En esta segunda época mantuvo un tono marcadamente hispanista, aristocratizante y favorable a los sectores económicamente poderosos. Defendió los fueros eclesiástico y militar. Fue dirigido por Miguel de Santa María, quien firmaba con el pseudónimo de *Capitán Chinchilla*. Hacia 1828, según *El Correo de la Federación*, lo dirigió Carlos María Bustamante. Dejó de publicarse el 1 de diciembre de 1828, a raíz del llamado Motín de la Acordada (☛). Reapareció el 1 de julio de 1829. Realizó una permanente campaña contra el embajador de Estados Unidos, Joel R. Poinsett, hasta lograr que el presidente Guerrero pidiera a Washington su remoción. Al gobierno del mismo Guerrero lo atacó de manera sistemática y aprobó con entusiasmo el golpe de Estado de Anastasio Bustamante, quien le otorgó un generoso subsidio, a cambio de lo cual festejó la supresión de los órganos federalistas. El 1 de febrero de 1831 pidió que se aplicara a Guerrero la pena de muerte. Desde 1827 Luis Antepara era uno de sus redactores. Continuó en ese puesto hasta el 21 de junio de 1830, acompañado en la redacción por Antonio Pacheco. Polemizó con la prensa federalista, especialmente con *La Águila Mexicana*, el *Correo de la Federación* y *El Fénix de la Libertad* (☛). Desapareció a fines de diciembre de 1832, junto con el gobierno golpista de Bustamante.

SOL, EL ◆ Diario vespertino fundado en Monterrey por Rodolfo Junco de la Vega el 2 de abril de 1922. Con su infraestructura fue fundado *El Norte*.

SOL DE MÉXICO, EL ◆ Periódico del Distrito Federal. Apareció la edición vespertina el lunes 7 de junio de 1965, editado por la Cadena García Valseca que presidía José García Valseca (☛). Se anunció como director a Miguel Ordorica, muerto año y medio antes. La dirección efectiva recayó en Salvador Borrego. Fue el segundo periódico mexicano que se imprimió en sistema *offset* y color. El 25 de octubre se empezó a publicar la edición matutina, que dirigieron sucesivamente Mario Novoa, Fernando Alcalá Bates y J. de Jesús Taladrid. En 1974 la cadena fue intervenida por el gobierno y el Grupo Somex se convirtió en socio mayoritario. García Valseca continuó fungiendo como presidente y director general hasta que, a principios de 1975, el Estado vendió la Cadena García Valseca a un grupo empresarial encabezado por Mario Vázquez Raña, que transformó la razón social en Organización Editorial Mexicana.

SOLA DE SELLARÉS, MARÍA ◆ n. en Cataluña, España (1903). Maestra en pedagogía por la Escuela Normal de Tarragona y licenciada en literatura e historia por la Universidad de Valencia. Luego de la guerra civil se refugió en Guatemala y después en México. Fue profesora de la UNAM y de la Universidad de las Américas (1955-77). Colaboró en *Cuadernos Americanos*. Autora de *Educación integral* (1970).

SOLANA, MOISÉS ◆ n. en el DF y m. cerca de Valle de Bravo, Edo. de Méx. (1935-1969). Pelotari y piloto de automóviles de competencia. Hijo del también piloto José Antonio Solana. Empezó su carrera como jugador de jai-alai en 1950, en el Frontón Metropolitano, y la concluyó en 1968. Durante cuatro temporadas fue considerado el mejor delantero nacional en pelota vasca. Se inició en el automovilismo deportivo en 1954, en la quinta Carrera Panamericana, en la que obtuvo el sexto lugar de la categoría estándar. Participó en 269 competencias automovilísticas en México, Estados Unidos y varios países europeos. En Fórmula 1 fue integrante del equipo de Colin Chapman. Murió en un accidente durante la carrera Valle de Bravo-Bosencheve.

SOLANA, RAFAEL ◆ n. en San Andrés Tuxtla, Ver., y m. en el DF (1890-1965). Periodista. Fue uno de los fundadores del periódico *El Universal* (1916), donde se desempeñó como columnista, redactor, cronista taurino (durante 43 años, con el pseudónimo de *Verduguillo*) y subdirector. Dirigió el suplemento *El Universal Taurino*, que cambió su nombre a *El Taurino* y, luego a *Toros y Deportes*.

SOLANA, RAFAEL ◆ n. en Veracruz, Ver., y m. en el DF (1915-1992). Estudió actuación, derecho y filosofía en la UNAM (1930-37). Periodista desde 1929. Dirigió *Taller Poético* (1936-39) y fue cofundador de *Taller* (1938-39). Se desempeñó como secretario particular del titular de la SEP, Jaime Torres Bodet (1958-64), director de teatro foráneo y de publicidad del INBA, así como jefe de prensa del IMSS, rector del Centro de Estudios Universitarios de Periodismo y colaborador de *El Universal*, *El Hijo Pródigo*, *Tierra Nueva* (1942), *Siempre!*, *El Día* y *Excélsior*. Autor de poesía: *Ladera* (1934), *Los espejos falsarios* (1944), *Alas* (1958), *Pido la palabra* (1964), *Las estaciones* y *Sonetos* (1988); ensayo: *El crepúsculo de los dioses* (1943), *Veinte lecturas* (1964); cuento: *El envenenado* (1939), *El crimen de tres bandas* (1945), *Trata de muertos* (1947) y *El oficleido y otros cuentos* (1960); novela: *El sol de octubre* (1959), *La casa de la Santísima* (1960; se presentó una versión teatral en el mismo año) y *El palacio Maderna* (1960); teatro: *Las islas de oro* (1952), *Estrella que se apaga* (1954), *La ilustre cuna* (1954), *Debiera haber obispas* (1954), *Lázaro ha vuelto* (1955), *La edad media* o *El Plan de Iguala* (1955), *El círculo cuadrado* (1957), *A su imagen y semejanza* (1957), *Ni lo mande Dios* (1958), *Espada en mano* (1960), *Sólo quedaban las plumas* (1961), *Ensalada de Nochebuena* (1963), *El arca de Noé* (1965), *Vestida y alborotada* (1965), *El hombre de una sola mujer* (1970), *Pudo haber sucedido en Verona* (1984), *La pesca milagrosa* (1986), *Una vejez tranquila* (1987), *Pláticas de familia* (1988) y *Sangre de pollo*; y crónicas: *Noches de estreno* (1963), *Momijigari* (1964) y

Crónicas de Rafael Solana. Secretario del interior de la Unión Nacional de Autores, secretario general de la Federación de Uniones Teatrales, presidente de la Asociación de Críticos de Teatro de México y presidente de la Unión Mexicana de Cronistas de Teatro y Música. Premio Nacional de Ciencias y Artes (1986) y Premio Juan Ruiz de Alarcón (1991).

Solana Morales, Fernando ♦ n. en el DF (1931). Ingeniero civil (1952), licenciado en filosofía (1956) y en ciencias políticas y administración pública por la UNAM (1963), donde fue profesor (1962-76) y secretario general (1966-70). Miembro del PRI desde 1952. Ha sido miembro de la Comisión de Administración Pública del gobierno de México (1965-66), subdirector de Planeación y Finanzas de la Conasupo (1970-76), secretario de Comercio (del 1 de enero al 8 de diciembre de 1977) y de Educación Pública (1977- 1982) en el gabinete de López Portillo; director general del Banco Nacional de México (1982-88), secretario de Relaciones Exteriores (1988-1994) y nuevamente de Educación Pública (1994) en el gabinete de Carlos Salinas de Gortari; senador de la República (1994-2000). Primer presidente alterno del Parlamento Latinoamericano (1995-) y miembro de la mesa directiva de la Unión Interparlamentaria Mundial (1998-). Fue redactor (1952-56) y director (1957-66) de la revista *Mañana*, articulista de *Novedades* (1952-56), director de la revista *Transformación* (1963-64) y director de la agencia Informac (1965-66). Autor de *La planeación universitaria de México* (1970), *Historia de la educación pública en México* (1981) y *Tan lejos como llegue la educación* (1982). Miembro del Colegio de Licenciados en Ciencias Políticas y Administración Pública y de la Fundación Barros Sierra. Presidente de la Asociación Mexicana de Bancos (1987-88). Presidente de la Asociación de Educación y Desarrollo.

Solana Olivares, Fernando ♦ n. en el DF (1954). Estudió antropología en la ENAH. En la UAM fue coordinador de la serie *Molinos de Viento* y editor de la revista *Casa del Tiempo*. Fue colaborador de *unomásuno* y coeditor de *La Jornada Semanal* (1984-89) y de la sección cultural de *El Nacional*, en donde ha dirigido el suplemento *Dominical*. Fue subdirector de política del Canal 22 de televisión (1993-94), subdirector del Museo de Arte Moderno y director del Museo de Arte Contemporáneo de Oaxaca. Becario del Centro Mexicano de Escritores (1982-83). Autor de la novela *La rueca y el paraíso* (1995), la crónica *Oaxaca, crónicas sonámbulas* (1995) y el libro de relatos *El peso de la esperanza* (1996).

Solano, Rosalío ♦ n. en Bernal, Qro. (1916). Cinematografista. Ingresó al cine en 1932 como ayudante de electricista y fue ayudante de laboratorio de Guillermo Barqueriza, con quien se hizo fotógrafo. Hizo miles de tomas fijas de artistas y aspectos de filmaciones. Fue director de fotografía de 180 películas. En diversas cintas sus tomas sirvieron para ambientar o bien para destacar aspectos de la trama. Recibió el Ariel por *Talpa* (1985) y por *La pachanga* (1981). También fue reconocido por *Espaldas mojadas*, *La bandida*, *Tlayucan*, *La casa que arde de noche*, *Cuando ¡Viva Villa! es la muerte* y *La cárcel de Cananea*. Recibió la Diosa de Plata y el Premio Ónix. En 1993 se le rindió un homenaje.

Solares, Carlota *la Marquesa* ♦ n. y m. en el DF (1909-1980). Actriz de teatro y cine. Inició su carrera de actuación en la compañía teatral de Anita Blanch, de la que pasó a la de Virginia Fábregas, con la que realizó varias temporadas y algunas giras al extranjero. Pasó después a la estación radiofónica XEW y, finalmente, a la industria cinematográfica. Actuó en las cintas *Quinto patio*, *Curvas peligrosas* y *Salón de belleza*, entre otras. Medalla Virginia Fábregas de la ANDA (1962).

Solares, Ignacio ♦ n. en Ciudad Juárez, Chih. (1945). Escritor. Licenciado en letras hispánicas por la UNAM, donde ha sido profesor e investigador (1977-81), director de Teatro y Danza (1993-96) y director de Literatura (1996-). Ha sido jefe de redacción de *Plural* (1971-74), director de *Diorama de la Cultura* (1974-76), codirector de *La Semana de Bellas Artes* (1978-80). Director de la edición mexicana de *Quimera*, de *Hoy* (1988-91) y *La Cultura en México* (1991-). Autor de cuento: *El hombre habitado* (1975) y *Muérete y sabrás* (1995); novela: *Puerta del cielo* (1976), *Anónimo* (1979), *El árbol del deseo* (1980), *La fórmula de la inmortalidad* (1982), *Serafín* (1985), *Casas de encantamiento* (1987, Premio Magda Donato 1990), *Madero, el otro* (1989, finalista del Premio Rómulo Gallegos 1991), *La noche de Ángeles* (1991, Premio Internacional Novedades-Diana 1992), *El gran elector* (1993), *Nen, la inútil* (1994, Premio José Fuentes Mares 1996), *Columbus* (1996), *Los mártires y otras historias* (1997), *Lost in the City* (1998) y *El sitio* (1998, Premio Xavier Villaurrutia); teatro: *El problema es otro* (1969), *Delírium tremens* (1973, publicado como reportaje novelado en 1979), *El jefe máximo* (1990, Premio Julio Bracho 1992), *Desenlace* (1992), *El gran elector* (adaptación, 1993, obtuvo los premios Juan Ruiz de Alarcón, Sergio Magaña y Sor Juana Inés de la Cruz en 1994), *Infidencias* (1994), *Tríptico* (1994, Premio Mejor Autor 1995, otorgado por los críticos y periodistas teatrales), *La flor amenazada* (1995), *El fuego que no se apaga* (1995), *Los mochos* (1996) y *La vida empieza mañana* (1996); y la autobiografía: *Ignacio Solares. De cuerpo entero* (1990). Compilador del *Epistolario de Gustavo A. Madero*. También ha recibido los premios Tomás Valles (1988), Nacional de Periodismo (1994) y el José Fuentes Mares (1996). Becario del Centro Mexicano de Escritores (1974-75 y 1979-80), del Fonca (1992-93) y de la Fundación Guggenheim (1996-97). Miembro del SNCA desde 1993.

Solares Gutiérrez, Eduardo ♦ n. y m. en el DF (1888-1941). Pintor. Estudió en la Academia de San Carlos, donde fueron sus maestros Andrés Fabrés, Germán Gedovius y Julio Ruelas, entre otros. En Alemania obtuvo por

FOTO: DANTE BUCIO

Fernando Solana Morales

FOTO: ANA LOURDES HERRERA

Ignacio Solares

José Solé

concurso un lugar en la Academia Real de Pintura de Munich, donde fue alumno de Angelo Sang y Franz Stuk. En España estudió con Eduardo Chicharro (1911). Volvió a México en 1913. Practicó la pintura mural, el acuarelismo y fue profesor, decano y director de la Academia de San Carlos. Algunas de sus obras se exhiben en el Museo de la Acuarela de la Ciudad de México. Autor de murales en el castillo de Chapultepec (1931), en el Congreso del estado de Morelos (1932) y en la antigua Escuela de Agricultura de San Jacinto, así como de las acuarelas *Paisaje del valle de México, El Ajusco, La Iztaccíhuatl* y *Amanecer en el valle*. En el castillo de Chapultepec restauró las *Bacantes*, de Santiago Rebull.

Solé, José ◆ n. en el DF (1930). Estudió actuación en la Escuela de Arte Teatral del INBA y dirección escénica en París (1976). Se inició como actor en el Teatro Estudiantil Autónomo dirigido por Xavier Rojas (1946). Fue director de la Escuela de Arte Teatral (1965-68) y resultó cesado por su apoyo al movimiento estudiantil. Director del Departamento de Teatro (1977-87) y primer coordinador nacional de teatro (1991-95). Fundó la Compañía Nacio-

Foto: Armando Herrera

Los hermanos Soler: en la fila de abajo, de izquierda a derecha: Andrés, Fernando y Domingo

nal de Teatro y el Centro de Investigación Teatral Rodolfo Usigli (CITRU). Presidente del Centro Mexicano de Teatro (1983). Director teatral desde 1953, ha puesto en escena obras clásicas, de dramaturgos mexicanos y adaptaciones al español de teatro ligero, entre otras, *La mujer de mi vida*, de Verneuil (1953); *El tío Vania*, de Chéjov (1960); *Antígona*, de Anouilh (1960); *Juguetes olvidados*, de Hellman (1961); *Contigo pan y cebolla* (1961); *Los caballeros de la mesa redonda*, de Cocteau (1962); *Las troyanas*, de Eurípides (1963); *Peer Gynt*, de Ibsen (1964); *Los Argonautas*, de Magaña (1967); *Medusa*, de Carballido (1968); *Compañero*, de Leñero (1970); *Cenas y te acuestas*, de Popplewell (1972); *Asesinato de una conciencia*, de Basurto (1973); *Ahora no... cariño* (1973) y *Todos a la cama*, de Cooney y Chapman (1973); *Hipólito* (1974) y *Electra* (1976), de Eurípides, *La muralla china*, de Frisch (1980); *Moctezuma II*, de Magaña (1982), *La mujer del año* (1995), *Otelo*, de Shakespeare (1996), y *Juego de reinas*, entre otras. Ha hecho escenografía, actuado en cine, dirigido telenovelas como *Cenizas y diamantes* y montado obras para la Compañía Nacional de Ópera. Autor de *Correspondencia de movimiento* (1980) y *Creación colectiva, fórmula para el nuevo teatro* (Roma, 1981). Premio a la revelación juvenil (1953) y premio al mejor actor (1954). En 1999 se abrió un foro teatral con su nombre en la delegación regional sur del ISSSTE en el DF.

Soledad, de la ◆ Boca de Baja California Sur situada en el litoral del océano Pacífico, en el extremo meridional de la entrada a la bahía de Magdalena, en la punta norte de la isla del mismo nombre.

Soledad, Convenios de la ◆ ☛ *Preliminares de la Soledad*.

Soledad Atzompa ◆ Municipio de Veracruz situado al sur de Orizaba, en los límites con Puebla. Superficie: 65.8 km². Habitantes: 14,801, de los cuales 2,997 forman la población económicamente activa. Hablan alguna lengua indígena 12,404 personas mayores de cinco años (náhuatl 12,402). Indígenas monolingües: 5,082. En su cabecera se firmaron los preliminares del Tratado de la Soledad (☛).

Soledad Atzompa, Veracruz

Soledad Díez Gutiérrez ◆ ☛ *Soledad de Graciano Sánchez*, municipio de San Luis Potosí.

Soledad de Doblado ◆ Municipio de Veracruz situado al suroeste y próximo al puerto de Veracruz. Superficie: 370.96 km². Habitantes: 27,565, de los cuales 7,619 forman la población económicamente activa. Hablan alguna lengua indígena 19 personas mayores de cinco años (náhuatl 11).

Soledad Etla ◆ Municipio de Oaxaca situado en la zona central del estado, al noreste y próximo a la capital estatal. Superficie: 34.45 km². Habitantes: 3,352, de los cuales 917 forman la población económicamente activa. Hablan alguna lengua indígena 16 personas mayores de cinco años (mixteco 11).

Soledad de Graciano Sánchez ◆ Municipio de San Luis Potosí, contiguo a la capital de la entidad. Superficie: 221.4 km². Habitantes: 156,498, de los cuales 39,203 forman la población económicamente activa. Hablan alguna lengua indígena 421 personas mayores de cinco años (náhuatl 225 y huasteco 91). Se llamó Soledad Díez Gutiérrez.

Soler, Andrés ◆ n. en Saltillo, Coah., y m. en el DF (1898-1969). Nombre profesional del actor Andrés Díaz Pavía, hijo de los actores españoles Domingo Díaz García e Irene Pavía Ortiz. Se inició en la compañía teatral de su hermano Fernando, con quien recorrió varias ciudades de España y Latinoamérica (1930-32). Durante 1936 hizo presentaciones en Sudamérica al frente de su propia empresa. Ingresó en la actuación cinematográfica en ese mismo año, sin dejar la actividad teatral, y participó en más de 192 filmes. Fue director del Instituto Cinematográfico, Teatral y de Radio y Televisión de la Asociación Nacional de Actores (1950), ahora Academia Andrés Soler. Entre sus películas destacaron: *Chucho el Roto* (1934), *Celos* (1935), *Suprema ley* (1936), *Los tres mosqueteros* (1942), *Historia de un gran* *amor* (1942), *Lo que sólo un hombre puede sufrir* (1942), *Cinco fueron escogidos* (1942), *Doña Bárbara* (1943, Premio Ariel), *La mujer sin alma* (1943), *Los miserables* (1943), *La perla* (1945), *Negro es mi color* (1950), *Anacleto se divorcia* (1950), *Azahares para tu boda* (1950), *Los tres alegres compadres* (1951), *Si yo fuera diputado* (1951), *Con todo el corazón* (1951), *El bruto* (1952), *Tizoc* (1957), *Pueblo en armas* (1958), *¡Viva la soldadera!* (1958) y *Yo pecador* (1959). Compartió créditos con los mejores actores de cine de la época de oro e hizo mancuerna con *Tin Tán* en *El ceniciento*, *El vizconde de Montecristo* y *Lo que le pasó a Sansón*. La Federación Latinoamericana de Estudiantes Universitarios lo nombró "Hijo Predilecto de América" en 1958.

SOLER, DOMINGO ◆ n. en Chilpancingo y m. en Acapulco, Gro. (1902-1961). Hermano del anterior. En 1912 inició su carrera en la empresa de su padre, cuyo nombre artístico también fue Domingo Soler. En la década de los años treinta se incorporó al cine. Trabajó, entre otras, en la películas *La mujer del puerto* (1933), *El primo Basilio* (1934), *Tierra, amor y dolor* (1934), *Vámonos con Pancho Villa* (1935), *Bajo el cielo de México* (1937), *El señor alcalde* (1938), *Refugiados en Madrid* (1938), *Don Juan* (1939), *Los de abajo* (1939), *Perfidia* (1939), *Odio* (1939), *Con los dorados de Villa* (1939), *El Conde de Montecristo* (1941), *La gallina clueca* (1941), *Simón Bolívar* (1941), *El verdugo de Sevilla* (1942), *Historia de un gran amor* (1942), *La Virgen que forjó una patria* (1942), *El padre Morelos* (1942), *Las cinco noches de Adán* (1942), *El Rayo del sur* (1943), *La guerra de los pasteles* (1943), *Los miserables* (1943), *Sota, caballo y rey* (1943), *Imprudencia* (1944), *Más allá del amor* (1944), *El intruso* (1944), *Amor prohibido* (1944), *La barraca* (1945; Ariel al mejor actor), *Corazones de México* (1945), *Escuadrón 201* (1945), *El último amor de Goya* (1945), *Mujer* (1946), *Río Escondido* (1947), *El ladrón* (1947), *En cada puerto un amor* (1948), *Opio* (1949), *Comisario en turno* (1949), *Si me viera don Porfirio* (1950), *Nosotras las sirvientas* (1951), *Con todo el corazón* (1951), *El cardenal* (1951), *El rebozo de Soledad* (1952), *La sobrina del señor cura* (1954), *El crucifijo de piedra* (1954), *Tierra de hombres* (1956) y *Mi madre es culpable* (1959).

SOLER, FERNANDO ◆ n. en Saltillo, Coah., y m. en el DF (1903-1979). Actor y director de cine hermano de los anteriores. Realizó estudios de administración en Estados Unidos. Comenzó su carrera de actuación en Los Ángeles (1916) como integrante del Cuarteto Infantil Soler. En 1923, en Cuba, formó su propia compañía teatral, con la que recorrió varias ciudades de México, España y Sudamérica y en la que trabajaron sus hermanos Andrés, Domingo y Julián. Actuó en casi 500 películas, entre otras, *¿Cuándo te suicidas?* (1930), *Chucho el Roto* (1934), *Celos* (1935), *Abnegación* (1937), *Adiós, Nicanor* (1937), *La bestia negra* (1938), *La casa del ogro* (1938), *Refugiados en Madrid* (1938), *En tiempos de don Porfirio* (1939), *Papacito lindo* (1939), *Creo en Dios* (1940), *Al son de la marimba* (1940), *Cuando los hijos se van* (1941), *México de mis recuerdos* (1943), *La mujer sin alma* (1943), *El rey se divierte* (1944), *La mujer que engañamos* (1944), *Mis hijos* (1944), *La reina de la opereta* (1945), *Las cinco advertencias de Satanás* (1945), *Flor de durazno* (1945), *Los maderos de San Juan* (1946), *Que Dios me perdone* (1947), *Cuando los padres se quedan solos* (1948), *Una familia de tantas* (1948), *Rosenda* (1948), *Las tandas del Principal* (1949), *El gran calavera* (1949), *Ustedes los ricos* (1949), *La oveja negra* (1949), *Sensualidad* (1950), *Amor a la vida* (1950), *Azahares para tu boda* (1950), *Yo quiero ser tonta* (1950), *Mamá nos quita los novios* (1951), *La hija del engaño* (1951), *Prefiero a tu papá* (1952), *No te ofendas Beatriz* (1952), *Por ellas aunque mal paguen* (1952), *Maldita ciudad* (1954) y *El derecho de nacer* (1966). Fue director y actor en *Con su amable permiso* (1940), *El verdugo de Sevilla* (1942), *¡Qué hombre tan simpático!* (1942), *Tentación* (1943), *Como todas las madres* (1944), *Capullito de alhelí* (1944), *Mamá Inés* (1945), *El grito de la carne* (1950), *Los hijos artificiales* (1952), *Maridos a prueba* (1952) y *Educando a papá* (1954). Fue sólo director en *Me persigue una mujer* (1946), *La hija del penal* (1949), *Los enredos de una gallega* (1951) y *María del Mar* (1952). Presidió hasta 1950 la Academia Cinematográfica. En 1951 recibió un Ariel por su actuación en *No desearás la mujer de tu hijo*.

SOLER, JULIÁN ◆ n. en Jiménez, Chih., y m. en el DF (1910-1977). Actor y director de cine hermano de los anteriores. Inició su carrera de actor en Los Ángeles, a los dos años de edad, en la obra teatral *Sangre y democracia*, aunque su participación sistemática en los escenarios empezó en 1931, en España. Ingresó en la actuación cinematográfica en 1930 en la película *¿Cuándo te suicidas?*, filmada en Francia. Regresó a México a mediados de los treinta. Actuó en numerosas películas, entre otras, *Cruz Diablo* (1934), *El escándalo* (1934), *Chucho el Roto* (1934), *Una mujer en venta* (1934), *Clemencia* (1934), *La familia Dressel* (1935), *Noches de gloria* (1937), *Alma jarocha* (1937), *Estrellita* (1938), *Beso mortal* (1938), *Papacito lindo* (1939), *Odio* (1939), *Mi madrecita* (1940), *Simón Bolívar* (1941), *Mil estudiantes y una muchacha* (1941), *El que tenga un amor* (1942), *Tu mujer es la mía* (1942), *Caballería del imperio* (1942), *Miguel Strogoff* (1943), *Doña Bárbara* (1943), *Un beso en la noche* (1944), *Las dos huérfanas* (1944), *Sinfonía de una vida* (1945), *Los siete niños de Écija* (1946), *El secreto de Juan Palomo* (1946), *El canto de la sirena* (1946), *Que Dios me perdone* (1947), *Rostros olvidados* (1952) y *La maffia del crimen* (1957). Dirigió y actuó en *Tormenta en la cumbre* (1943) e *Imprudencia* (1944). Sólo dirigió en *Me ha besado un hombre* (1944), *Las cinco advertencias de Satanás* (1945), *Matrimonio sintético* (1947), *Tía Candela* (1948), *Una gallega en México* (1949), *Eterna agonía* (1949), *Azahares para tu boda* (1950), *Si usted no puede yo sí* (1950), *Una gringuita en México* (1951),

FOTO: ARMANDO HERRERA

Julián Soler

La duquesa del Tepetate (1951), *La miel se fue de la luna* (1951), *Los tres alegres compadres* (1951), *Un gallo en corral ajeno* (1951), *No te ofendas Beatriz* (1952), *La entrega* (1954), *La visita que no tocó el timbre* (1954), *El caso de la mujer asesinadita* (1954), *La mujer X* (1954), *Platillos voladores* (1955), *La tercera palabra* (1955), *Cuando México canta* (1956), *A media luz los tres* (1957), *El castillo del monstruo* (1957), *Aladino y la lámpara maravillosa* (1957), *Mi esposa me comprende* (1957), *Mis padres se divorcian* (1957), *Mi madre es culpable* (1959), *Las rosas del milagro* (1959) y *Calibre 44* (1959).

Foto: Armando Herrera

Javier Solís

Soler, Mercedes ◆ m. en el DF (1915-1971). Actriz. Hermana de los anteriores. Inició su carrera en las estaciones radiofónicas WEW y XEB y trabajó en las películas *Águilas de América* (1933), *Tierra, amor y dolor* (1934), *¡Así es mi tierra!* (1937) y *El pecado de ser pobre* (1950), entre otras.

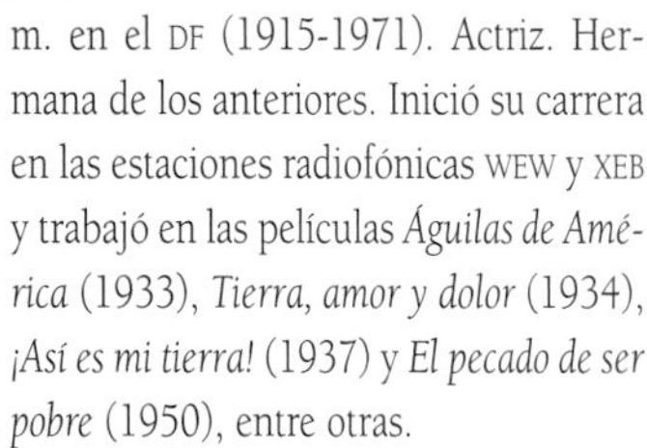

Soler Frost, Pablo ◆ n. en el DF (1965). Estudió en los colegios Alemán y Luis Vives. Colaborador de *Cartapacios, El Gallo Ilustrado, unomásuno, El Buscón, Comunidad Conacyt, La Jornada Semanal* y *Letras libres*. Autor de prosa: *De batallas* (1984); novela: *La mano derecha* y *Legión*; cuento: *El sitio de Querétaro* y *Lagartos terribles* (1995). Aparece en *Una ciudad mejor que ésta* (1998).

Soler Vinyes, Martí ◆ n. en Cataluña, España (1934). Vive en México desde 1939. Editor. Estudió arquitectura en la UNAM y tipografía en la UNESCO. Es profesor de la UIA (1979-). Trabajó para Siglo XXI Editores y fue director del departamento de ediciones de El Colegio de México (1996-1998). En 1997 fundó la editorial Libros del Umbral. Ha sido secretario de redacción de *Veu Catalana*. Colaborador de *Pont Blau, Cuadernos del Viento, Diálogos, Plural, La Gaceta del FCE, Sábado* y *El Gallo Ilustrado*. Autor de poesía: *Antología poética* (1959), *Tiempo de espera* (1962) y traducción y versiones de *Poesía negra norteamericana* (1977).

Solidaridad ◆ Municipio de Quintana Roo situado al norte de la entidad, en los límites con Yucatán al este y en litorales del mar Caribe al oeste; se creó con parte de Cozumel. Superficie: 4,331.7 km². Habitantes: 28,747, distribuidos en 174 localidades. Hablan alguna lengua indígena 9,832 personas mayores de cinco años (maya 9,651). Indígenas monolingües: 1,735.

Solís, Bernarda ◆ n. en el DF (1950). Licenciada en filosofía por la UNAM, donde ha sido profesora e investigadora, con estudios en Suiza e Inglaterra. Se especializó en psicoanálisis y psicoterapia. Ha sido gerenta de editorial Domés, editora y dictaminadora de Edamex. Fue editora de la revista *Ser Padres*. Ha colaborado en *Ovaciones, El Cuento, Excélsior, Cuestión* y *El Universal*. Bajo pseudónimo colabora en 64 diarios de la República. Ha sido jurado en concursos internacionales. Cuentos suyos han sido incluidos en los libros *El mismo camino* (1983) y *Sin permiso* (1984). Autora de *Con un bull para la cruda* (Premio Nacional de Cuento Efraín Huerta 1986), *Mi vida privada es del dominio público* (cuentos, 1988) y *Mariposa Nocturna* (novela, 1992).

Solís, Javier ◆ n. y m. en el DF (1931-1966). Nombre profesional del cantante Gabriel Siria Levario. Se desempeñó como mecánico, taxista, panadero, tablajero y boxeador. Ganó concursos de canto para aficionados en algunas carpas populares. Formó el Trío México, con Pablo Flores y Miguel García. Cantó ocasionalmente en la plaza Garibaldi hasta dedicarse de manera profesional a esta especialidad. Impulsado por el trío Los Panchos, en 1955 fue contratado para trabajar en algunos teatros y en las radiodifusoras XEQ y XEW. Hizo presentaciones en Estados Unidos y algunos países de Centro y Sudamérica, donde popularizó los "boleros rancheros". En los últimos años de su vida, sin que su nombre fuese revelado al público, actuó como payaso del circo Atayde. Entre sus interpretaciones más populares se cuentan *La mentira, Las rejas no matan, Bésame y olvídame, Esclavo y amo, Amigo organillero, Renunciación, En mi viejo San Juan, Julia, Me recordarás, Regalo de reyes, ¡Qué va!, Luz y sombra, Háblame, El malquerido, Cenizas, Payaso, Jamás, jamás* y *Entrega total*. Actuó en más de 30 películas: *Viaje al centro de la tierra, Diablos del cielo, Callejón sin salida, El gran pecador, Rateros último modelo, Los cuatro jinetes, Tres mosqueteros de Dios, Especialista en chamacas, Moliendo café, Los tres calaveras, Amor a ritmo de go go, Juan Pistolas, Los que no supieron amar* y *Campeón del barrio*. En 1963 ganó un Disco de Oro en Nueva York por haber vendido 100,000 copias de la canción *Llorarás*, marca que superó dos años después con *El loco* y *Sombras nada más*.

Solís, José Esteban ◆ n. y m. en Mérida, Yuc. (1825-1888). En 1852 inventó una desfibradora de hojas de henequén, llamada Máquina Solís, con la que ganó el premio de un concurso convocado por el gobierno yucateco y propició la expansión de la industria henequenera. En diciembre de 1865, por ese mismo invento, el imperio de Maximiliano le otorgó una medalla de oro.

Solís, *el Buky* Marco Antonio ◆ n. en Ario de Rosales, Mich. (1951). Compositor y cantante. Comenzó su carrera a los 12 años, en el dueto Los Hermanitos Solís, que formó con su hermano Joel. Posteriormente formó el grupo Los Bukis, con el que se presentó en bares de la ciudad de México y que en 1975 grabó *Falso amor*, su primer éxito de ventas, al que siguieron muchos más, en una veintena de discos de larga duración. En 1996 empezó a actuar como solista. Otras de sus canciones son *Tu cárcel, Cómo fui a enamorarme de ti, Y ahora te vas, Amor en silencio, Morenita* y *La venia bendita*, las que han sido interpretadas por numerosos cantantes. Ha recibido discos de oro y platino por sus ventas y se ha presentado en escenarios de México, Estados Unidos y América Latina. Actuó en las películas *La Coyota* (1987) y *Cómo fui a enamorarme* *de ti* (1991), supuestamente basada en la vida real de Los Bukis. Compuso parte de la música de *La muchacha* (1990).

SOLÍS ACERO, FELIPE ◆ n. en Tampico, Tams. (1956). Licenciado en derecho y en ciencias políticas. Miembro del PRI. Ha sido subdirector de Control y Apoyo del ISSSTE (1980), secretario particular del director de Recursos Humanos de la Secretaría de Salubridad y Asistencia (1981), jefe de proyectos especiales de la Coordinación General de Estudios Administrativos de la Presidencia (1981), asesor del secretario de Administración del gobierno mexiquense (1982), jefe de la Unidad de Control de Gestión del ISSSTE (1983), coordinador auxiliar de delegaciones estatales del ISSSTE (1983), miembro de la Comisión Federal Electoral (1991), director ejecutivo de Organización Electoral (1990-96) y secretario ejecutivo del IFE (1996-98).

SOLÍS BRUN, RENÉ ◆ n. en el DF (1936). Editor. Estudió en la UDLA y en la Universidad de Harvard, en la que obtuvo una maestría (1958). Fue profesor (1959-90), coordinador del área y presidente de la Academia de Mercadotecnia de la Facultad de Contaduría y Administración de la UNAM. Ha sido subtesorero de la empresa General Popo (1958-63), gerente de Organización y Planeación de Cifra (1963-70), director general del Grupo Editorial Expansión (1970-74) y de Promexa (más tarde Grupo Editorial Patria, 1974-95), director comercial de Citem (más tarde Casa Autrey, 1995-97) y director general del Grupo Editorial Planeta México (1997-).

SOLÍS CÁMARA Y JIMÉNEZ CANET, FERNANDO ◆ n. en el DF (1959). Economista por la Universidad Anáhuac, maestro en ciencias políticas y en economía por la Universidad de Harvard; maestro en economía por la Universidad de Boston. Miembro del PRI desde 1981, en donde fue secretario de Finanzas del MNJR (1982-83). Ha sido analista y subjefe de departamento de la dirección de Política Monetaria y Crediticia de la SHCP (1980-81), asesor de la Comisión de Hacienda de la Cámara de Diputados (1986-87), jefe de estudios económicos de la Coordinación General de Programación, Evaluación y Control del Infonavit (1986-88), director general de Recursos Materiales y Servicios Generales de la SPP (1988-92); coordinador para la descentralización educativa de la SEP (1992-94). Comisionado del Instituto Nacional de Migración (1994-98) y subsecretario de Población y Servicios Migratorios de la Secretaría de Gobernación (1998-99).

SOLÍS LUNA, ARTURO IGNACIO ◆ n. en Oaxaca (1951). Sociólogo por la UNAM. Se especializó en ecología y sociedad en el INE-Semarnap. En la Jica, de Japón, estudió política ecológica. Coordinador social del proyecto Sonntlan de México-Alemania para el uso de la energía solar (1978-81). Coordinador de la Editorial Bruguera Mexicana (1982). Jefe del proyecto de investigación social educativa en la Dirección General de Ciencia y Tecnología del Mar (1983-84). Director de Bachillerato Tecnológico (1993). Jefe del departamento de Gestión e Información Ambiental y subdirector de Desechos Industriales no Peligrosos del INE (1995-99). Secretario del subsecretario de coordinación delegacional y metropolitana del DF (1999-).

SOLÍS MANJARREZ, LEOPOLDO ◆ n. en la ciudad de México (1928). Licenciado en economía por la UNAM (1952) y maestro por la Universidad de Yale (1960). Profesor de El Colegio de México (1962-72) y otros centros de enseñanza. Investigador de El Colegio de México (1976). Desde 1960 pertenece al PRI. Ha sido jefe de Estudios Económicos del Banco de México (1964-70), director general de Programación Económica y Social de la Secretaría de la Presidencia (1971-75), subdirector general del Banco de México (1976-85), coordinador de asesores económicos del presidente de la República (1985-88), miembro de la junta de gobierno de Banco de México (1988-94) y director general del Instituto de Investigación Económica y Social Lucas Alamán (1989-). Autor de *La realidad económica mexicana: retrovisión y perspectivas* (1970), *Controversias sobre el crecimiento y la distribución* (1972), *La economía mexicana* (1973), *Planes de desarrollo económico y social en México* (1975), *La coyuntura actual de la economía mexicana* (1984), *Intento de la reforma económica en México* (1988), *La Perestroika: antecedentes, obstáculos y resultados preliminares* (1989), *Tendencias recientes y perspectivas probables del análisis económico* (1991), *Medio siglo en la vida económica de México. 1943-1993* (1994), *¿Crisis económico-financiera 1994-1995?* (1996) y *Evolución del sistema financiero mexicano hacia los umbrales del siglo XXI* (1997), entre otros. Miembro del Colegio Nacional de Economistas, El Colegio Nacional (1976-) y la Academia Mexicana (de la Lengua). Doctor *Honoris Causa* por la Universidad Autónoma de Nuevo León (1994), la Universidad Tecnológica de México (1995) y la Universidad Autónoma de Coahuila (1999). Miembro del Fondo Mexicano de Intercambio Académico.

Leopoldo Solís Manjarrez

SOLÍS MANJARREZ, MARCO AURELIO ◆ n. en Soyaló, Chis. (1925). Licenciado en economía por la UNAM (1952) y maestro en desarrollo económico por la Universidad Vanderbilt (1963). Ha sido jefe de la Oficina de Precios Oficiales de Importación (1959), subjefe del Departamento de Aranceles (1962), representante permanente de México ante la Alalc (1963), asesor económico de la Dirección de Estudios Hacendarios y Asuntos Internacionales (1966) y subdirector auxiliar de Integración y Aranceles de la Dirección de Estudios Hacendarios de la Secretaría de Hacienda (1967); director de Planeación y Estudios del IMCE (1970), director general de la Comisión Nacional del Cacao (1974-88) y director general de la Central de Abastos del DDF (1988-1991). Coordinador del Plan General de Asistencia Técnica en Comercio Exterior de la ONU y vicepresidente en los segundo y cuarto periodos extraordinarios de sesiones de la Alalc (1964-65). Dirigió la publicación de *Los aspectos fiscales de la Alalc* (1963).

Pertenece al Colegio de Economistas, al Consejo Internacional del Cacao (que presidió en 1979-81) y a la Liga de Economistas Revolucionarios del PRI.

Solís Quiroga, Héctor ♦ n. en la ciudad de México (1912). Licenciado (1936) y doctor (1961) en derecho por la UNAM. Ha sido profesor e investigador de la UNAM (1937-), director de la Escuela Normal de Especialización, juez y director general del Tribunal para Menores y presidente fundador del Consejo Tutelar del DF (1971-76); fundador del Albergue Tutelar Juvenil y del Instituto de Ciencias Penales de Michoacán (1968); director adjunto del Instituto Nacional de Ciencias Penales; creador de la carrera de maestro especialista en inadaptados e infractores; experto de la ONU en problemas de delincuencia juvenil en Latinoamérica y representante de México en reuniones internacionales sobre prevención del delito y tratamiento de delincuentes. Ha sido colaborador de *El Universal*, *Excélsior*, *El Nacional*, *El Sol de México*, *Criminalia* y *Eugenesia*. Autor de *Los menores inadaptados* (1936), *Visión sociológica de la Revolución Mexicana* (1959), *El ser y el deber ser de la Universidad de México* (1961), *Predelincuencia* (1961), *Código de menores*, *Introducción a la sociología criminal* (1962), *Educación correctiva* (1986), *Ley de asistencia al anciano* (1986) y *Justicia de menores*.

Libro de Carlos Solórzano

Solís Quiroga, Roberto ♦ n. y m. en el DF (1898-1967). Se tituló como médico en la Universidad Nacional (1922) y se especializó en neuropsiquiatría infantil y psicología de anormales. Profesor de la UNAM (1927-59) y de la Escuela Normal Superior (1928). En 1917 se incorporó al cuerpo médico de la Secretaría de Guerra y Marina y en 1921 fundó y fue jefe del Servicio de Anormales de las instituciones penales y correccionales del Distrito Federal. Director fundador del Tribunal para Menores (1926-47), del Instituto Médico Pedagógico del Parque Lira (1935-59) y de la Escuela Normal de Especialización (1959-64), instituciones cuya creación promovió. Colaborador de *Criminalia*, *Horizontes*, *Eugenesia* y *Boletín de Pediatría*. Corresponsal técnico de la ONU en México y miembro del Ateneo de Ciencias y Artes de México, de Tribuna Libre de México y de las sociedades Mexicana de Eugenesia, Pediátrica del Centro y Mexicana para Estudios Científicos de la Deficiencia Mental.

Sologaistoa, José C. ♦ n. en Guatemala y m. en el DF (1888-1966). Se tituló como abogado en la Universidad Nacional de Guatemala, de la que fue profesor, así como de la Universidad Nacional de Honduras. En Tegucigalpa fundó con Rafael Heliodoro Valle la revista *Actualidades* (1917), que dirigió. Viajó a Estados Unidos, donde fue director de *La Prensa*, de San Antonio, Texas, y publicó un *Directorio Mexicano* (1924). Llegó a México en 1945. Colaboró en periódicos de la cadena García Valseca y en *Excélsior, El Universal, Novedades, Jueves de Excélsior, Mañana, Hoy* y *Nosotros*. Durante 15 años fue editor de la revista *Caminos del Aire*, de la Compañía Mexicana de Aviación, y dirigió la revista de ficción *SOS, Policía* (1964-66).

Solórzano, Alfonso ♦ n. en Guatemala y m. en el DF (1911-1980). Estudió derecho y filosofía en Alemania y en México, país al que llegó en 1932 como refugiado político. En 1944 volvió a Guatemala, donde promovió la creación de la Confederación de Trabajadores de Guatemala, formuló el primer proyecto para el Código del Trabajo en ese país, fundó un partido político y el semanario marxista *Vanguardia*, desde el que promovió, entre otras, las tesis de Lázaro Cárdenas. Fue cónsul de Guatemala en La Habana y París. Volvió a su patria durante el gobierno de Jacobo Arbenz, participó en la elaboración de la Ley de Reforma Agraria y en la creación de la Confederación Nacional Campesina y dirigió el Partido de la Revolución Guatemalteca, el *Diario del Pueblo* y el Instituto Guatemalteco del Seguro Social. En 1954, tras el derrocamiento de Arbenz, volvió a exiliarse en México.

Solórzano, Carlos ♦ n. en Guatemala (1922). Llegó a México en 1939. Maestro (1944) y doctor en letras (1946) y arquitecto por la UNAM (1945). Estudió arte teatral en Francia (1949), becado por la fundación Rockefeller. Se ha desempeñado como director fundador del Teatro Universitario (1952-62), profesor de la UNAM (1962-), organizador y director del Teatro Nuevo de Latinoamérica (1968), coordinador ejecutivo del Teatro de la Nación del IMSS (1982) y presidente del Centro Mexicano del Instituto Internacional de Teatro de la UNESCO (1990-). Autor de *Del sentimiento de lo plástico en la obra de Unamuno* (1944), *Antología del teatro hispanoamericano contemporáneo* (1964), *Teatro guatemalteco contemporáneo* (1964) y *Testimonios teatrales de México* (1973), así como de las obras teatrales *Espejo de novelas* (1946), *Doña Beatriz, la sin ventura* (1954), *La mano de Dios* (1957), *Los fantoches* (1958), *Tres actos* (1959), *Los falsos demonios* (1963, convertida en novela en 1966), *Cruce de vías* (1969), *El zapato*; y la novela *Las celdas* (1971). Grabó un disco para la serie *Voz viva de México*. Profesor emérito de la UNAM (1985). Premio Universidad Nacional (1989) y Premio Miguel Ángel Asturias de Guatemala (1989).

Foto: Armando Herrera

Javier Solórzano

Solórzano, Javier ♦ n. en el DF (1954). Periodista. Su segundo apellido es Zínser. Estudió comunicación en la UIA y la UNAM. Profesor fundador de la carrera de comunicación de la UAM-Xochimilco. Se inició en la radio en el programa *Jóvenes de aquí y ahora*. Ha colaborado en *El Día*, *Ovaciones*, *unomásuno*, *El Universal* y *El Financiero*. Fue subdirector de Comunicación Internacional de la la Secretaría de Relaciones Exteriores, jefe de Análisis de Medios en la Presidencia de la República y en la Secretaría de Gobernación; y conductor y coordinador de contenidos de noticieros en el Canal 13 de Imevisión. Conduce el noticiero *Para empezar*, en Estereorey, y dirige y conduce el programa *En Blanco y Negro*, que se proyecta por Multivisión.

Solórzano, Jesús *Chucho* ♦ n. en

Morelia, Mich., y m. en el DF (1907-1987). Torero conocido como *el Rey del Temple*. Se inició en 1927 en la plaza de Acámbaro. En 1929 le fue concedida una primera alternativa que rehusó para actuar en España, donde en 1930 la tomó en Sevilla, y la confirmó al año siguiente en Madrid. Protagonizó célebres corridas en México y España. Se retiró en 1949. Fue el iniciador de una dinastía de toreros en México.

Solórzano, Julio ◆ n. en el DF (1945). Hijo de Alfonso Solórzano (☛) y Alaíde Foppa (☛). Maestro en historia por la Universidad Patricio Lumumba (1971). Pintor. Trabajó como reproductor de códices para el Museo Nacional de Antropología e Historia (1964) y fue ayudante de David Alfaro Siqueiros (1965-66). En 1971, en Suecia, figuró entre los cofundadores del Comité Internacional de Solidaridad con el Gobierno de la Unidad Popular de Chile. Investigador de la UNAM desde 1972. Ha ejercido el periodismo. Se dedica profesionalmente al canto desde 1964. Ha participado en numerosos conciertos individuales y colectivos y en 32 festivales internacionales. Director de la compañía disquera Nueva Cultura Latinoamericana. Ha participado en los discos *Nuestra es la voz, de todos la palabra* y *México-Chile Solidaridad*, grabó el disco de larga duración *Maderas latinoamericanas* (1974). Fundador y miembro de la dirección del Comité Mexicano de la Nueva Canción.

Soltepec ◆ Municipio de Puebla situado al este de la capital estatal y contiguo a Tepeaca. Superficie: 139.05 km^2. Habitantes: 10,906, de los cuales 2,736 forman la población económicamente activa. Hablan alguna lengua indígena cinco personas mayores de cinco años.

Solusuchiapa ◆ Municipio de Chiapas situado en el norte del estado, al noreste de Tuxtla Gutiérrez, en los límites con Tabasco. Superficie: 362.7 km^2. Habitantes: 6,926, de los cuales 1,595 forman la población económicamente activa. Hablan alguna lengua indígena 831 personas mayores de cinco años (tzotzil 561 y zoque 268).

Somalia ◆ Estado de África situado en el extremo oriental del continente, con costas hacia el golfo de Adén y el océano Índico. Su nombre oficial es República Democrática Somalí. Limita al suroeste con Kenia, al oeste con Etiopía y al noroeste con Djibouti. Ocupa la mayor parte del llamado Cuerno de África. Tiene una superficie de 637,657 km^2 y 9,237,000 habitantes (1998). Su capital es Mogadiscio, con 900,000 habitantes en 1990. Otras ciudades de importancia son Hargeisa (90,000 habitantes estimados para 1990), Kismaayo o Kismayu (90,000) y Berbera (70,000). Tiene dos idiomas oficiales, somalí y árabe, aunque también son comunes el suahili, italiano e inglés. *Historia*: Somalia era conocida por el antiguo Egipto como el País de Punt y los romanos la llamaron País de las Especias; ambos imperios mantenían relaciones comerciales con esa nación, en la que se desarrolló el grupo de los somalíes, que asimiló a los haussas y esclavizó a los bantúes. En los siglos VII y VIII de nuestra era, la región de la actual Somalia fue ocupada por inmigrantes yemenitas, quienes fundaron un sultanato; durante 300 años los musulmanes yemenitas construyeron un emporio comercial e intensificaron la islamización de los habitantes de la región. En el siglo XIII se consolidó el reino de Ifat, tributario de Etiopía, cuya capital, Zeila, entró en conflicto con los abisinios al tiempo que ampliaba su territorio y se convertía en el sultanato de Adal. A principios del siglo XV se agudizó la lucha entre este sultanato y Etiopía. Como adoptara la forma de un conflicto entre musulmanes y cristianos, los abisinios buscaron auxilio en Europa. La ayuda se demoró casi 100 años. En 1541 los marinos portugueses llegaron a la región y, con el apoyo de las tropas etíopes, arrasaron las ciudades de Zeila, Mogadiscio, Berbera y Brava. Durante 200 años, con la permanente amenaza de la flota portuguesa, aunque los lusitanos nunca ocuparon el territorio, el sultanato de Adal se fragmentó: las provincias norteñas quedaron sometidas al Egipto otomano, en tanto que las meridionales reconocieron la soberanía del sultán de Zanzíbar, quien en 1698 logró expulsar de la zona a los portugueses. La construcción del canal de Suez (1859-70) dio un nuevo valor estratégico a la región e hizo converger hacia ella a franceses, ingleses e italianos. El control de la nueva ruta comercial hacia la India era el eje de las negociaciones. En 1862 los franceses compraron el puerto de Obock, origen del actual Djibouti; los italianos se instalaron en Aseb, en 1869, y se extendieron luego por Eritrea, mientras que los ingleses, que ya ocupaban Adén, en la península Arábiga, se hicieron cargo en 1885 de los establecimientos egipcios en Zeila y Berbera. En 1899 el imán Mohamed ibn Abdullah Hassan se levantó en armas contra la invasión europea. De 1900 a 1904, Hassan derrotó a las fuerzas inglesas en varias ocasiones. En 1906, como compensación por su derrota frente a Etiopía, Italia obtuvo el litoral sur de Somalia. Por la presión de los nacionalistas somalíes comandados por Hassan, los ingleses se refugiaron en los puntos de la costa que podían defender y dejaron el interior en poder de los rebeldes. En 1920, Hassan fue derrotado con la utilización, por primera vez en África, de la aviación de guerra inglesa y el territorio quedó

República democrática de Somalia

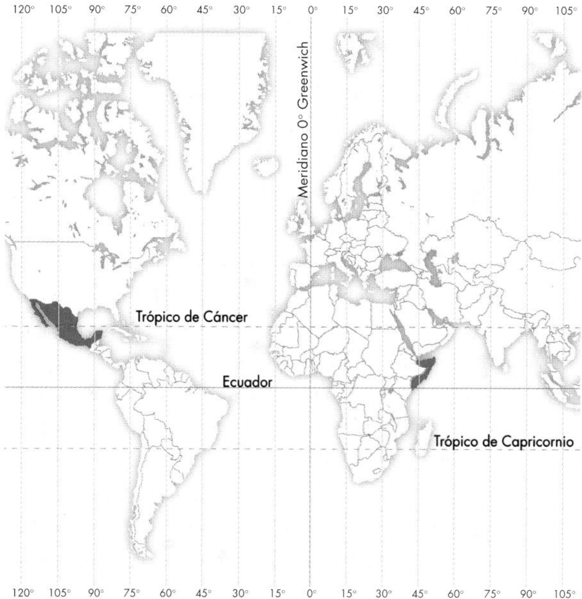

sometido al dominio británico. En 1941, durante la segunda guerra mundial, Inglaterra ocupó la parte italiana de Somalia y estableció un protectorado militar. En 1960 las regiones italiana y británica se unieron para formar la República de Somalia, tras el triunfo del movimiento nacionalista *Somalí Youth Club*. A la ceremonia de proclamación de la independencia de Somalia asistió Alejandro Carrillo Marcor, con la representación del gobierno mexicano. En 1963 el gobierno británico decidió incorporar el extremo sur somalí (Ogadén) al Estado keniano, por lo que Inglaterra y Somalia rompieron relaciones diplomáticas. En 1965 se produjeron graves incidentes fronterizos entre Somalia, Etiopía y Kenia en disputa por Ogadén, lo que provocó la intervencion de la Organización de la Unidad Africana. En 1969 fue asesinado el presidente Shermarke y el ejército tomó el poder. Se creó entonces el Consejo Supremo Revolucionario que proclamó la República Democrática Somalí. Un año después se manifestó por la implantación de un Estado socialista y nacionalizó la banca y las industrias. México y la República Democrática Somalí establecieron relaciones diplomáticas el 5 de agosto de 1975. En 1988, tras un fallido cuartelazo, el Movimiento Nacional Somalí (MNS) desató una nueva guerra civil, en marcha en 1999, aunque con la inclusión de diversas facciones en lucha, algunas apoyadas por Etiopía. El MNS, arrinconado en el norte del país, proclamó ahí la República de Somalilandia, que tiene un gobierno propio, no reconocido internacionalmente.

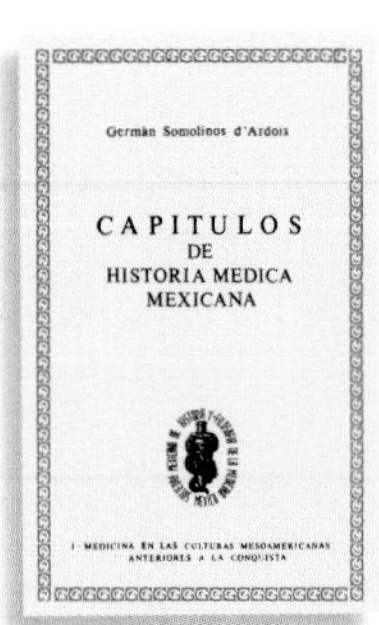

Llbro de Germán Somolinos

SOMBRERETE ◆ Municipio de Zacatecas situado en el noroeste del estado, contiguo a Fresnillo y al noroeste de la capital estatal, en los límites con Durango. Superficie: 4,105.33 km². Habitantes: 65,252, de los cuales 14,946 forman la población económicamente activa. Hablan alguna lengua indígena 17 personas mayores de cinco años. Su cabecera, del mismo nombre, es un importante centro minero que cuenta con una planta minerometalúrgica. Las primeras minas de Sombrerete fueron descubiertas en 1555 por Juan de Tolosa y Francisco de Ibarra. Martín Pérez y Juan Bautista de Llerena, fundaron la villa de San Juan Bautista de Llerenas, que más tarde cambió su nombre por el de Real de Minas de Sombrerete.

Dibujo de Jan Somolinos Palencia

SOMBRERETE, DE ◆ Sierra de Durango y Zacatecas, que forma parte de las estribaciones noroccidentales de la sierra de Zacatecas. Se extiende de sureste a noroeste, al noroeste de Fresnillo, al norte de la sierra de Chalchihuites y al sur de la de Santa María. Cuenta con importantes yacimientos minerales en explotación.

SOMOLINOS D'ARDOIS, GERMÁN ◆ n. en España y m. en el DF (1911-1973). Médico titulado en la Universidad Central de Madrid. Llegó exiliado a México en 1939 y obtuvo una beca del Instituto Nacional de Cardiología para hacer investigaciones sobre reumatismo cardiaco y sobre el factor Rh y su herencia (1944-46). Fue profesor del IPN y de la UNAM, así como colaborador de las publicaciones *Gaceta Médica de México* y *Anales de la Sociedad Mexicana de Historia de la Ciencia y la Tecnología*. Coautor de *Homenaje al profesor Ignacio Chávez por su XXV aniversario de vida profesional* (1945) y *Desarrollo de la anatomía patológica en México* (1964). Autor de *William Harvey, descubridor de la circulación sanguínea* (1952), *Historia de la medicina* (1952), *Historia y medicina. Figuras y hechos de la historiografía médica mexicana* (1957), *Lo mexicano en la medicina* (1961), *Desarrollo de la anatomía patológica en México* (1964), *25 años de medicina española en México* (1966), *El doctor Francisco Hernández y la primera expedición científica en América* (1971) y *El cirujano López de Hinojosa, su obra quirúrgica y la Compañía de Jesús* (1975). Miembro de la Academia Nacional de Medicina, institución que lo premió en 1962.

SOMOLINOS PALENCIA, JAN ◆ n. en Suecia (1938-1993). Hijo de exiliados españoles. Nieto de Ceferino Palencia (☛). Estudió dibujo en la Escuela de Arte de Boston (1953). Se tituló como médico cirujano en la UNAM (1961), de la que ha sido profesor, así como del IPN. Efectuó en 1961 su primera exposición individual, en la galería Diana de la ciudad de México. Como escritor ha colaborado en *El Gallo Ilustrado* (1971-73), *La Prensa Médica Mexicana* y *Arte-Noticias* (1971-74). Autor de *La belle époque en México* (1972), *El surrealismo y la pintura mexicana* (1974) y *Contribuciones mexicanas a la investigación médica* (1984). Presidente de la Academia Nacional de Medicina desde 1987 hasta su muerte.

SOMOZA ALONSO, MANUEL ◆ n. en el DF (1947). Licenciado en economía por la Universidad Anáhuac, de la que ha sido profesor, y maestro en administración de empresas por el ITESM. En Banamex fue ejecutivo del Departamento de Valores, gerente, subdirector de Inversiones Institucionales, subgerente y gerente del Fondo de Inversiones (1966-77) y director general de la Casa de Bolsa Banamex (1978-82). Ha sido director de Banca de Inversión Nafinsa (1983); director general de Operadora de Bolsa (1983); director adjunto financiero de Nafinsa (1984); director general de Fomento de Valores (1984-85) y presidente de la Bolsa Mexicana de Valores (1985-88), así como presidente de la Asociación Mexicana de Casas de Bolsa y director general de Inverlat (1985-). Colabora en programas del Canal 40 de televisión (1995-). Miembro del Instituto de Banca y Finanzas y del Instituto Mexicano de Ejecutivos de Finanzas.

SOMOZA SILVA, LÁZARO ◆ n. en España y m. en el DF (1895-1946). Periodista, llegó exiliado a México en 1939. Fue jefe de redactores del gobierno del Distrito Federal y colaborador de *El Nacional*. Autor de *El general Miaja. Biografía de un héroe* (1944) y *Lope de Vega. Historia de un hombre apasionado* (1944).

SONOÍTA ◆ Cabecera del municipio sonorense de General Plutarco Elías Calles (☛).

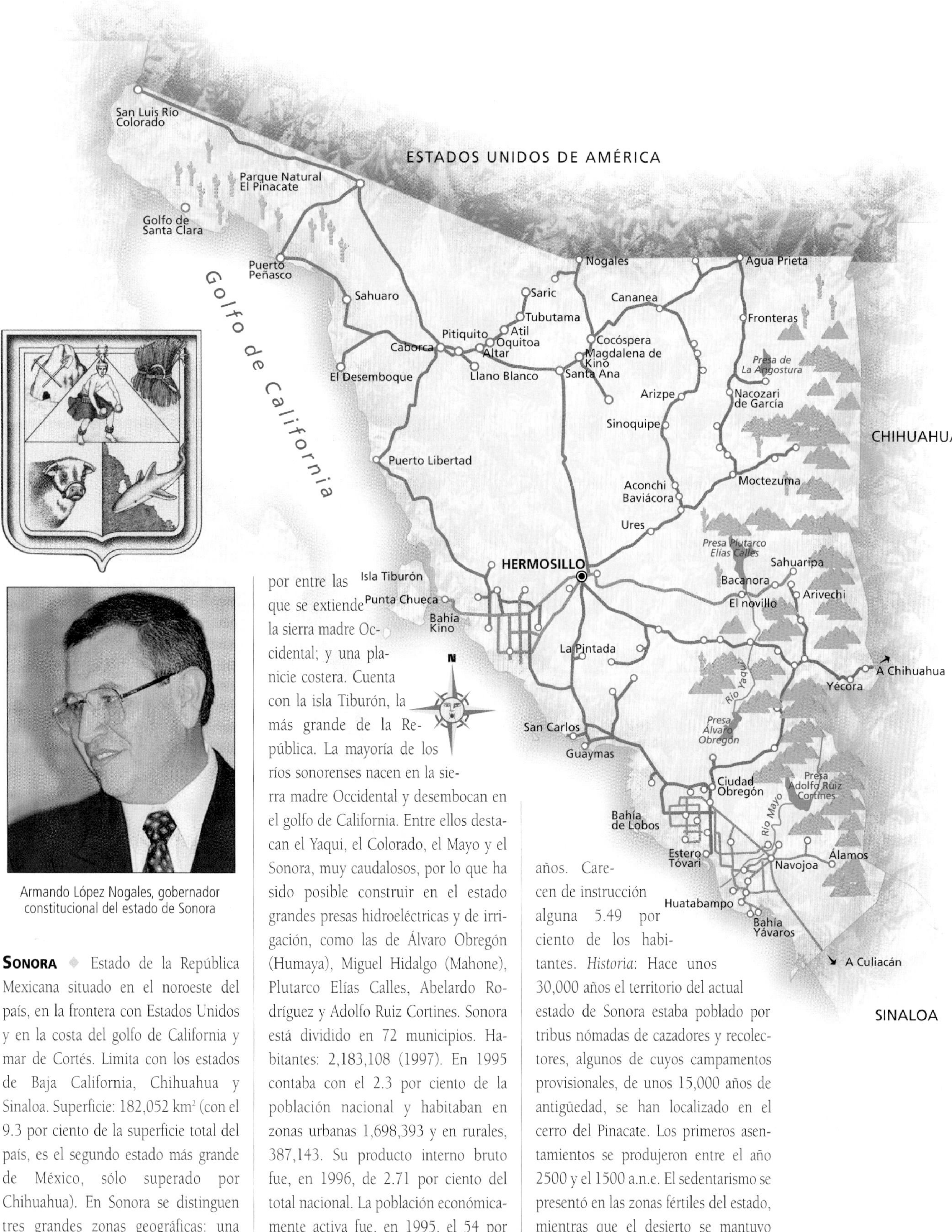

Armando López Nogales, gobernador constitucional del estado de Sonora

Sonora ◆ Estado de la República Mexicana situado en el noroeste del país, en la frontera con Estados Unidos y en la costa del golfo de California y mar de Cortés. Limita con los estados de Baja California, Chihuahua y Sinaloa. Superficie: 182,052 km^2 (con el 9.3 por ciento de la superficie total del país, es el segundo estado más grande de México, sólo superado por Chihuahua). En Sonora se distinguen tres grandes zonas geográficas: una franja oriental y una central (paralelas), por entre las que se extiende la sierra madre Occidental; y una planicie costera. Cuenta con la isla Tiburón, la más grande de la República. La mayoría de los ríos sonorenses nacen en la sierra madre Occidental y desembocan en el golfo de California. Entre ellos destacan el Yaqui, el Colorado, el Mayo y el Sonora, muy caudalosos, por lo que ha sido posible construir en el estado grandes presas hidroeléctricas y de irrigación, como las de Álvaro Obregón (Humaya), Miguel Hidalgo (Mahone), Plutarco Elías Calles, Abelardo Rodríguez y Adolfo Ruiz Cortines. Sonora está dividido en 72 municipios. Habitantes: 2,183,108 (1997). En 1995 contaba con el 2.3 por ciento de la población nacional y habitaban en zonas urbanas 1,698,393 y en rurales, 387,143. Su producto interno bruto fue, en 1996, de 2.71 por ciento del total nacional. La población económicamente activa fue, en 1995, el 54 por ciento de las personas mayores de 12 años. Carecen de instrucción alguna 5.49 por ciento de los habitantes. *Historia*: Hace unos 30,000 años el territorio del actual estado de Sonora estaba poblado por tribus nómadas de cazadores y recolectores, algunos de cuyos campamentos provisionales, de unos 15,000 años de antigüedad, se han localizado en el cerro del Pinacate. Los primeros asentamientos se produjeron entre el año 2500 y el 1500 a.n.e. El sedentarismo se presentó en las zonas fértiles del estado, mientras que el desierto se mantuvo habitado por nómadas. Las aldeas agrícolas sonorenses fueron influidas por las más complejas sociedades urbanas que se habían desarrollado en Hohokam (Arizona), Mogollón (Nuevo México) y Casas Grandes y Paquimé (Chihuahua), así como por las culturas mesoamericanas, que penetraron en territorio sonorense mediante el comercio. Hacia el 1340 de nuestra era aparentemente hubo una migración masiva de habitantes de Casas Grandes hacia la zona serrana de Sonora, quienes dieron origen a la tribu de los ópatas. A la llegada de los españoles el actual estado de Sonora estaba poblado por seris en la costa y por pápagos, pimas, ópatas, jovas, chínipas y cahítas (yaquis y mayos) en el interior. Los conquistadores incursionaron en Sonora a través de las rutas comerciales entre el Altiplano y el noroeste; de ese modo, los europeos distinguieron a los pueblos de acuerdo con los idiomas que hablaban, pertenecientes a las familias yuto-nahua (pimas, ópatas y cahitas) y hokana (especialmente los seris). En 1531, Nuño Beltrán de Guzmán fundó en Sinaloa el poblado de San Miguel de Culiacán, punto de partida de las expediciones que buscaron esclavos, minas y nuevas tierras hacia el norte. La primera de esas expediciones que entró en territorio sonorense fue la de Diego de Guzmán (1533), que llegó a las riberas del río Mayo; guiado por los mayos llegó al río Yaqui, de donde fue rechazado. Hacia 1536 pasaron por Sonora, procedentes del norte, Alvar Núñez Cabeza de Vaca y otros tres sobrevivientes de la expedición de Pánfilo de Narváez. En su libro *Naufragios*, Cabeza de Vaca dice que los indios de la región, posiblemente pimas bajos, llamados nebomes, lo acompañaron pacíficamente. Sus relatos, en los que menciona las ciudades de Cíbola y Quivira, inspiraron numerosas expediciones que pasaron por territorio sonorense. Las primeras fueron la del fraile Marcos de Niza (1539), enviado por el virrey Antonio de Mendoza, y la de Francisco Vázquez de Coronado (1540), a quien acompañaron Pedro Castañeda de Náxera y Juan Jaramillo, los que escribieron sendas *Relaciones*. También en 1539 y 1540, dos expediciones marinas, las de Francisco de Ulloa y Hernando de Alarcón, desembarcaron en la desembocadura del río Colorado. Aún con la esperanza de encontrar Cíbola o Quivira, Vázquez de Coronado fundó la villa de San Gerónimo de los Corazones como punto de aprovisionamiento. Los abusos cometidos por su lugarteniente

Foto: Fondo Editorial Grupo Azabache

Bahía de San Carlos y Cerro del Tela Kawi, en Sonora

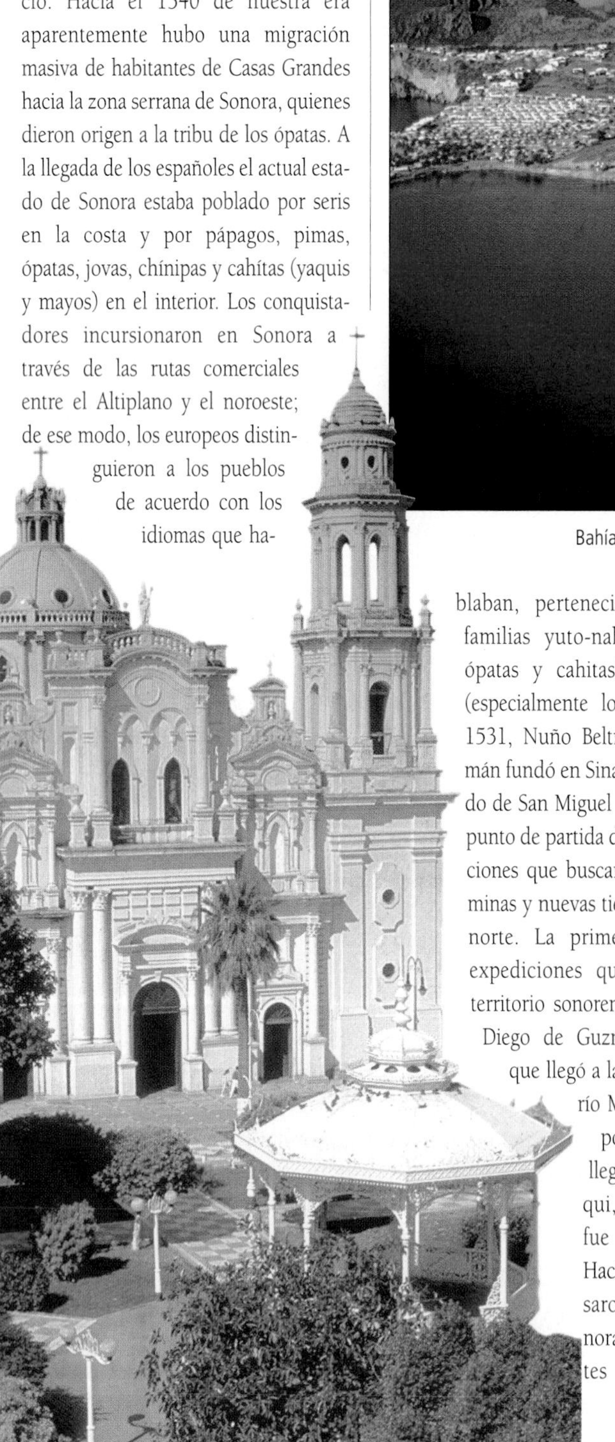

Foto: Fondo Editorial Grupo Azabache

Catedral de la Asunción en Hermosillo, Sonora

Diego de Alcaraz, comandante de la villa, provocaron una reacción violenta de los ópatas, quienes destruyeron el poblado. Mientras Vázquez de Coronado proseguía su viaje al norte, envió al oeste a Melchor Díaz, quien cruzó el desierto del Altar, atravesó el río Colorado y llegó al valle de Mexicali. La siguiente vía de entrada en Sonora fue la establecida en 1563 por Francisco de Ibarra, gobernador de la Nueva Vizcaya, quien cruzó la sierra Madre Occidental por el valle de Topia, fundó el fuerte de San Juan Bautista de Carapoa (1564) y colaboró con los yaquis en una guerra contra los mayos. Poco después, el fuerte de Carapoa fue atacado por los indios y la base española debió trasladarse a Sinaloa, donde se estableció el presidio de San Felipe y Santiago (1586). Diego Martínez de Hurdaide emprendió la conquista de las tribus sinaloa, tehueco, zuaque y ahome (1599). Desde 1531 hasta fines del siglo XVI, la población indígena disminuyó dramáticamente por los enfrentamientos violentos y las epidemias traídas por los europeos, así como por la sobreexplotación de la encomienda. En el siglo XVII se inició la entrada en Sonora de los misioneros jesuitas, quienes fundaron misiones en torno de las cuales se asentaron grupos indígenas que cultivaban la tierra y y proporcionaban mano de obra para las minas y soldados aborígenes cristianizados para oponerse a los indios insumisos. Hacia 1601 algunos mayos visitaron las misiones del río Zuaque e invitaron a los misioneros a que visitasen sus pueblos, lo que favoreció una penetración ideológica no violenta. Por su parte, Martínez de Hurdaide intentó infructuosamente realizar la conquista del valle del río Yaqui (1609). Derrotado, se replegó al río Zuaque donde fundó el fuerte de Montesclaros (1610), que sería su base de operaciones para una larga y siempre fallida campaña contra los indios. Después de un lustro de resistencia, éstos pidieron el cese de hostilidades y el establecimiento de misiones en su territorio. En esta situación, los jesuitas

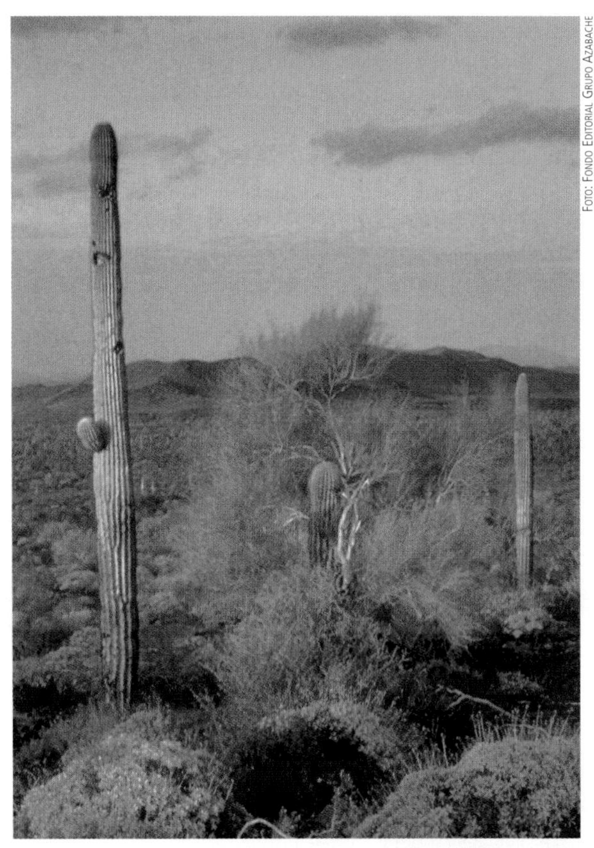

FOTO: FONDO EDITORIAL GRUPO AZABACHE

Parque Nacional El Pinacate, en Sonora

FOTO: MICHAEL CALDERWOOD

Campos de irrigación en Ciudad Obregón, Sonora

Sierra de Sonora

Halcón y correcaminos, fauna típica de Sonora

Andrés Pérez de Rivas y Tomás Basilio instalaron las primeras misiones del Yaqui (1617). Basándose, como los conquistadores militares, en las divisiones lingüísticas aborígenes, las misiones jesuitas se extendieron hacia el norte y crearon partidos o rectorados, cuyas cabeceras eran regidas por un misionero. En 1619 se fundó Cumuripa, primera misión jesuita en la Pimería, a la que siguieron Tecoripa (1625), Mátape, Batuco, Ures y Bavícora (1629). Para 1620`ascendía a 30,000l el número de mayos bautizados. En aproximadamente 100 años los jesuitas crearon seis rectorados en territorio de los actuales estados de Sonora y Sinaloa: San Felipe y Santiago, San Ignacio, San Francisco de Borja, Santos Mártires de Japón, San Francisco Javier y Dolores de Pimería Alta.

La obra misionera fue continuada a partir de 1687 por Gonzalo de Tapia, Martín Pérez y Francisco Eusebio Kino (☛), quien fue destacado a la Pimería Alta, donde estableció la misión de Dolores de Cosari. Paralelamente al avance de los jesuitas, los españoles de Nuevo México empezaron a entrar en Sonora desde el norte y descubrieron minas en Tuape y pastos aptos para la cría de ganado en los valles de San Pedro, Bavispe, Fronteras y el alto río Sonora. Pedro de Perea, "justicia mayor y capitán a guerra", estableció su cuartel cerca de Tuape (1641), dirigió campañas de exterminio contra los pimas, ópatas y sumas (1641-45), tomó esclavos para las haciendas y minas y llevó a cinco franciscanos de Nuevo México para que estableciesen misiones en el noreste de Sonora. Perea murió en 1645 y la provincia volvió a depender militarmente del presidio de Sinaloa y religiosamente de las misiones jesuitas. Entre las primeras grandes sublevaciones indígenas estuvieron la de los pueblos del río Grande en 1680, la de los pimas del Altar-Asunción (1695) y la protagonizada en 1696 por los ópatas del alto río Bavispe, en protesta por el trabajo forzado y el secuestro de niños, empleados como sirvientes de los españoles. Pese a todo, una vez sofocadas dichas sublevaciones, los europeos llevaron sus misiones cada vez más al norte, hasta Baja California, Nuevo México y Coahuila. En el siglo XVII se conformaron las provincias de San Juan Bautista de Sonora (1656) y San Ildefonso de Ostimuri (1676), que junto con la de Sinaloa dependieron del reino de Nueva Vizcaya. Durante el siglo XVIII los pápagos, pimas y seris que se habían mantenido independientes en el desierto fueron finalmente asimilados por las misiones. A las etnias locales se

Foto: Fondo Editorial Grupo Azabache

Complejos industriales en Sonora

sumaron, a partir del siglo XVII, numerosos grupos apaches expulsados de sus territorios. A partir de 1732 el gobierno de San Felipe y Santiago de Sinaloa incluyó la provincia de Culiacán y las alcaldías mayores de Rosario, Copala, Mayoola, Sinaloa, Ostimuri y Sonora. A principios del siglo XVII los mineros de Santa Bárabara y Parral entraron en Sonora en busca de nuevas vetas y mano de obra. El descubrimiento de los minerales de San Miguel (1666) y San Marcos (1668) propició el poblamiento español de Ostimuri. La *Gazeta de México* de octubre de 1737 decía: "Se ha tenido la noticia que en el mes de marzo antecedente, pervertido un Indio Guaíma como de edad de quarenta y cinco años, llamado *Augustín* Ascubul, difundió en los distritos de las dos Naciones Guaímas, y Pimas Bajos, la engañosa voz de haverse aparecido el *Dios Moctezuma*, y que por ministerio suyo, que era el Mayordomo *Arescibi, ó Propheta* de dicho *Moctezuma*, les ofrecía muchos dones, y citaba para ázia las vertientes del Mar del Sur, donde tenía su adoratorio, y que en él, y su Trono los recibiria bajo de su obediencia; añadiendo que á la Pimería alta, havian ido yá los *Tlatoles, ó Recados* sobre lo proprio, intimádoles al mismo tiempo, que á los que no le obedeciessen impondría rigorosissimos castigos". Así, Ascubul convocó a los ópatas y pimas, quienes iniciaron el culto de una imagen de Moctezuma. Juan Bautista de Anza, comandante del presidio de las Fronteras de la Pimería Alta, acudió al frente de la fuerza militar española, prendió a Ascubul y lo ejecutó el 1 de junio de ese mismo año. Los yaquis protagonizaron una gran rebelión en 1740. A mediados del siglo XVIII, el crecimiento económico de los asentamientos españoles fue una nueva amenaza para los indios, lo que generó nuevos conflictos que las misiones jesuitas, en crisis, no pudieron enfrentar; las rebeliones de yaquis, pimas y seris aumentaron considerablemente. En 1767 se decretó la expulsión de la Compañía de Jesús de todos los reinos de España y la mayor parte de las misiones en Sonora fueron secularizadas, pues sus nuevos administradores, los franciscanos, sólo daban importancia a la tutela religosa de los indios conversos. El ocaso de las misiones significó el fortalecimiento de los presidios. Hacia 1779 la Comandancia General de las Provincias Internas concentró el mando de todas las fuerzas militares del norte novohispano. A fines del siglo XVIII se abrieron nuevas rutas hacia la Alta California y Texas, con la finalidad de establecer una línea norteña de presidios y misiones que comunicaran el golfo de México con el océano Pacífico y cerraran el paso a la expansión de ingleses y franceses. Las expediciones encabezadas por Juan Bautista de

FOTO: PABLO CERVANTES

Paisaje característico del estado

Borregos cimarrones del Centro Ecológico de Hermosillo, Sonora

FOTO: FONDO EDITORIAL GRUPO AZABACHE

Máscara de pascola mayo, de Sonora

Mujer seri de Sonora

Anza entre 1774 y 1776 abrieron una ruta terrestre entre Sonora y Alta California. Al mismo Anza se debe la fundación de San Francisco, con soldados y colonos sonorenses y sinaloenses que partieron del presidio de San Miguel de Horcasitas. La expedición de Anza debía cruzar el desierto a través de la zona habitada por los yumas, uno de cuyos jefes había prometido su colaboración. No obstante, la fundación de la misión y colonia de San Pedro y San Pablo de Yuma provocó fricciones entre españoles e indios, lo que generó la sublevación india de 1781. Tanto el fracaso de Anza en su avance hacia el norte como el incremento de choques armados con los apaches, malogró la política expansionista en la frontera. La Instrucción de Gálvez (1786) ordenó la formación de rancherías para los apaches que aceptaran vivir en paz; se les ofrecieron tierras cerca de los presidios, así como raciones de alimentos y ropa. Con el establecimiento de la Ordenanza de Intendencias se creó la de Arizpe con las provincias y alcaldías que habían formado los gobiernos de Sonora y Sinaloa, cuyo intendente, militar, asumía las funciones del gobernador de la provincia. Pese a que la labor misional de jesuitas y franciscanos hizo innecesaria la presencia de párrocos en el noroeste de Nueva España, las provincias de Nueva Vizcaya, Sonora, Sinaloa y Nuevo México pertenecían al obispado de Durango (1620-1783). En 1783 se creó la diócesis

Trigo de los campos sonorenses

de Sonora, con jurisdicción sobre Sinaloa y las Californias. A principios del siglo XIX la minería sostuvo una población de españoles y castas que iba en ascenso y el comercio empezó a florecer. Pese a que Miguel Hidalgo envió a José María González Hermosillo y José Antonio López González a insurreccionar el noroeste del país, lo que sólo pudieron hacer entre diciembre de 1810 y febrero de 1811, auxiliados por José de Jesús y Nicolás Hidalgo y Costilla, la guerra de Independencia no encontró eco entre una población más preocupada por defenderse de las incursiones apaches. Alejo García Conde, intendente de Sonora y desde 1817 comandante general de las Provincias Internas de Occidente, envió tropas presidiales a combatir a los insurgentes, por lo que la frontera quedó desprotegida y las incursiones apaches se intensificaron. Este conflicto se resolvió en agosto de 1821, cuando García Conde se sumó al Plan de Iguala y la diputación provincial proclamó la independencia. Esa misma diputación, presidida por Bernardo del Espíritu Santo, obispo de Sonora, gobernó las provincias de Sonora y Sinaloa durante el imperio iturbidista (1822-23). A la caída de Iturbide, el Congreso de la Unión dividió la provincia en los estados de Sonora y de Sinaloa, con capital en Ures y Culiacán, respectivamente. La Constitución de 1824 fusionó de nuevo ambas entidades en el Estado Unido de Occidente, con capital en El Fuerte, cuya Constitución local fue promulgada en 1825. El primer gobernador constitucional del estado de Occidente fue Simón Elías González, quien en 1811 había formado parte del consejo de guerra que condenó a muerte a los primeros caudillos insurgentes. Indignados porque el comandante general José Figueroa pretendía utilizarlos como auxiliares en una campaña contra los apaches, los yaquis se sublevaron en 1825. Este enfrentamiento terminó al cabo de unos meses en una tregua negociada con el gobernador Elías González, quien aceptó conceder una amplia autonomía a los yaquis. Sin embargo, las autoridades no respetaron el acuerdo, por lo que Juan Ignacio Jusacamea (☛), conocido como Juan de la Cruz Banderas, encabezó una lucha de guerrillas (1826-33) e intentó unir a ya-

Sonorenses

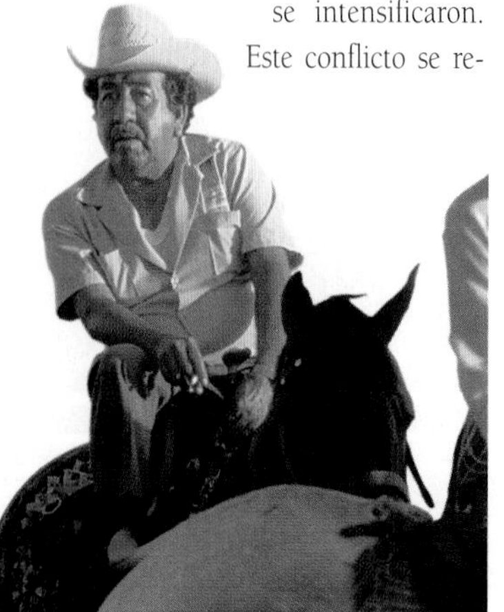

quis, ópatas, pimas y eudeves bajo instituciones propias. A la postre, Jusacamea fue ejecutado junto con Dolores Gutiérrez, su lugarteniene. Hacia 1826 los separatistas sonorenses fueron perseguidos por el gobernador José María Gaxiola y el comandante militar, Mariano Paredes y Arrillaga. Gaxiola fue derrocado en 1829, año en el que se inició en Álamos la publicación del periódico *Opinión Pública de Occidente*, primero en editarse en el estado. A los levantamientos indígenas el gobierno sonorense respondió con campañas de exterminio pero, simultáneamente, inició la política de nombrar entre los yaquis a capitanes y alcaldes dependientes de las autoridades estatales, con lo que logró romper la cohesión interna de la etnia. En enero de 1830 el ayuntamiento de Arizpe reconoció el Plan de Jalapa, proclamado por Anastasio Bustamante. El 14 de octubre de 1831 se dividió de nuevo la entidad en los estados de Sonora y Sinaloa, el primero de ellos con capital en Hermosillo y gobernado provisionalmente por Leonardo Escalante, quien poco después cedió el Ejecutivo local a Tomás Escalante. En 1832 la capital sonorense se estableció en Arizpe. El liberalismo propugnador del libre comercio y de la propiedad privada halló eco entre los sonorenses, aunque éstos no compartían el anticlericalismo, pues les convenía mantener las misiones en la frontera pima-apache. Después de la llegada de Antonio López de Santa Anna al poder (1834), Manuel María Gándara, terrateniente y comerciante con amplio poder en los valles de Ures y Horcasitas y en los mercados de Hermosillo y Guaymas, fue nombrado gobernador de Sonora y estableció un cacicazgo que se prolongó durante varios años. Al implantarse el centralismo, Sonora pasó a ser departamento (1835). En diciembre de 1837, por los problemas que se tenían con el gobierno del centro, que no prestaba ayuda a la entidad en su lucha contra los apaches y exigía de ella recursos que se necesitaban para su defensa, se pronunció en Arizpe José Urrea, militar que había hecho carrera en diversas campañas de exterminio contra seris y apaches y que tuvo una participación destacada en las guerras de Texas. El plan de Urrea restablecía el sistema federal y la Constitución de 1824. Gándara simuló adherirse al plan de Urrea y éste marchó a combatir a Sinaloa, donde fue derrotado por Paredes Arrillaga. Durante su ausencia, Gándara organizó una contrarrevolución so pretexto de combatir a los apaches y desató una lucha fratricida a la que se vieron arrastrados yaquis y mayos. El conflicto cesó al iniciarse la invasión estadounidense. Con Gándara al frente del gobierno, la capital estuvo en Ures desde 1839. En octubre de 1847 las fragatas *Congress* y *Portsmouth* fondearon en Guaymas y sus tripulantes ocuparon el puerto, mismo que desalojaron en abril de 1848, después de la firma del Tratado de Guadalupe-Hidalgo. A la derrota frente a los estadounidenses se sumó, en 1853, la venta de La Mesilla (☛). Entre tanto, los terratenientes y comerciantes sonorenses consolidaron su poder económico y aceleraron la secularización de las misiones. La revolución de Ayutla llevó al poder a la Coalición Liberal de Sonora, en la que militaban Ignacio Pesqueira, Jesús García Morales, Ángel y Joaquín Corella, Crispín S. de Palomares, José T. Otero y Próspero Salazar Bustamante, educados en el extranjero o en la capital del país y que representaban los intereses de los comerciantes locales o extranjeros. Esa coalición acabó con el gandarismo al llevar a Pesqueira a la gubernatura. Éste promulgó la Constitución local de 1861, acorde con la Norma Fundamental de 1857 y las Leyes de Reforma. El gobierno de Pesqueira promovió la construcción de caminos y vías férreas, así como la operación regular de embarcaciones para estrechar la comunicación con Estados Unidos; estimuló la industria y apoyó el expansionismo de los terranientes, para lo cual invadió los valles del Yaqui y del Mayo. Esta Coalición Liberal,

Sonora cuenta con una importante producción de vid

Mujeres del estado de Sonora

Foto: Michael Calderwood

Planta endustrial en Hermosillo, Sonora

en defensa de su proyecto modernizador nacionalista, se enfrentó a las invasiones extranjeras, tanto a las de los filibusteros William Walker (☛), Gastón Raousset de Boulbon (☛) y Henry Alexander Crabb (☛), como a la invasión francesa y el imperio de Maximiliano. Al iniciarse la guerra de los Tres Años, Pesqueira derrotó la sublevación local encabezada por Jesús Gándara y pasó a Sinaloa para colaborar con el liberal Plácido Vega, donde fue nombrado gobernador. En 1865, Guaymas, plaza defendida por José María Patoni, fue ocupada por el francés Castagny, cuyas fuerzas derrotaron también a Pesqueira en La Pasión. En julio del mismo año los imperialistas ocuparon la capital estatal y Pesqueira viajó a Estados Unidos en busca de apoyo, mientras la lucha de resistencia continuaba en Sonora encabezada por Jesús García Morales y el sinaloense Ángel Martínez. Gándara, conservador aliado con el imperio del Habsburgo, intentó recuperar el poder perdido, pero el triunfo republicano (tropas francesas desocuparon Guaymas el 6 de septiembre de 1866) fue su derrota definitiva. En octubre de 1871 la guarnición de Guaymas se adhirió al Plan de la Noria y ocupó Álamos; los rebeldes fueron derrotados al mes siguiente por Pesqueira, quien pasó a Sinaloa para someter en ese estado a los seguidores de Porfirio Díaz. La prolongada estadía de Pesqueira en el poder se vio amenazada, en 1872, al incorporarse a la Constitución local una cláusula que prohibía la reelección. No obstante, Pesqueira evitó que tal cláusula fuese publicada. En 1873 se reeligió, hubo una sublevación en su contra, pero la sofocó. En 1875 al ser impuesto José J. Pesqueira como gobernador, se rebeló Francisco Serna, ex candidato a la vicegubernatura. Para someter a los partidarios de Serna, Pesqueira pidió ayuda federal y Sonora se declaró en estado de sitio, situación agravada por un nuevo levantamiento yaqui. La crisis fue controlada cuando el gobierno central envió al militar Vicente Mariscal como gobernador. Al proclamar Porfirio Díaz el Plan de Tuxtepec, la familia Pesqueira se levantó en armas en favor de José María Iglesias. Las pugnas entre las distintas facciones sonorenses continuaron aun después de que Díaz asumiera la Presidencia de la República. En 1879, el gobernador Mariscal fue desconocido por Serna, que ocupó la capital estatal, fue reconocido por el gobierno central y trasladó la sede de los poderes a Hermosillo. El régimen porfirista se consolidó definitivamente en Sonora hacia 1880; éste llevó la modernización industrial a la agricultura y la minería, principalmente a base de capital extranjero, y la represión contra los trabajadores e indígenas a extremos que no alcanzaron los liberales juaristas. De 1883 a 1886 se ordenó una campaña represiva contra los vecinos de Pivita, quienes habían protestado por el despojo de sus tierras. En 1887 el último cabecilla apache, Gerónimo, fue expulsado de Sonora y el líder yaqui José María Leyva *Cajeme* (☛) fue derrotado y ejecutado. Luis Emeterio Torres, aliado de Díaz desde el pronunciamiento de La Noria, alternó la gubernatura del estado con la jefatura de la zona militar correspondiente. Este cacique fue sustituido en 1887 por Ramón Corral, otro viejo compañero de armas de Díaz. Corral, impulsor de la electrificación y los sistemas bancarios, a su vez fue sucedido por Rafael Izábal. En mayo de 1897 se firmaron los convenios de Estación Ortiz, entre Luis E. Torres, en calidad de comandante de la primera zona militar, y Juan Maldonado *Tetabiate* (☛). Dos años después la paz del yaqui volvió a romperse. En esa época, continuó la expansión industrial, así como la represión que Díaz había impuesto en todo el país. El ejemplo extremo de esa política se produjo en 1906, durante la huelga

Industria extractiva en el estado de Sonora

de los mineros de Cananea (☛). La guerra de guerrillas de los yaquis (☛) continuó hasta el siglo XX con la conducción de los líderes Ignacio Mori, Luis Bule, Luis Espinoza, Luis Matus y Sibalaume. A principios del siglo XX, como consecuencia de la crisis económica internacional, la situación de Sonora estaba afectada por la caída de los precios mineros y agrícolas del mercado mundial. En esos años, el magonismo tenía una amplia difusión entre los mineros de la entidad, quienes fueron la base del ejército que secundó el llamamiento maderista a la revolución (1910). La lucha armada se inició con pequeñas revueltas en Cananea y Sahuaripa, a las que vinieron a dar apoyo grupos armados procedentes de Chihuahua. Después de la toma de Ciudad Juárez y la renuncia de Díaz, José María Maytorena ocupó la gubernatura de Sonora (octubre de 1911). Al producirse la rebelión orozquista, Maytorena ordenó el reclutamiento de milicias irregulares para auxiliar a las tropas federales y de ese modo fundó una fuerza militar estatal apoyada financieramente por el gobierno central. En febrero de 1913, el gobierno sonorense fue el único en secundar al de Coahuila en la firma del Plan de Guadalupe, que desconocía a Victoriano Huerta. Maytorena, titubeante, se refugió en Arizona y el poder local fue asumido por Ignacio L. Pesqueira, quien formó el Cuerpo de Ejército del Noroeste, contingente militar disciplinado y eficaz, pese a que lo integraban en su mayoría mineros sin experiencia en la carrera de las armas. Este ejército contó también con el auxilio de los yaquis y mayos, a quienes se alistó con la promesa de que, al término del conflicto armado, se les restituirían sus tierras, lo que no se cumplió. En 1919, Venustiano Carranza decidió apoyar al sonorense Ignacio Bonillas para sucederlo en la Presidencia de la República, cuando era el también sonorense Álvaro Obregón el candidato con más prestigio entre los militares revolucionarios. Las diferencias de Benjamín Hill, Álvaro Obregón, Plutarco Elías Calles, Adolfo de la Huerta y otros caudillos del grupo de Sonora con Carranza se ahondaron y el 23 de abril de 1920 estos líderes locales lanzaron el Plan de Agua Prieta, que triunfó en unas cuantas semanas. La revuelta culminó con el asesinato de Carranza y la llegada a la Presidencia de la República de Adolfo de la Huerta, quien convocó a elecciones y en el mismo año dejó el cargo al líder Álvaro Obregón. En 1929 se proclamó el Plan de Hermosillo, apoyado por el gobernador Fausto Topete, que desconoció a Emilio Portes Gil y se manifestó partidario del militar José Gonzalo Escobar. En ese mismo año la rebelión escobarista fue aplastada. Precisamente a fines de los años veinte se abrieron al cultivo grandes extensiones de tierras en la costa y en las cuencas de los ríos Mayo y Yaqui. Paralelamente al crecimiento de la ganadería, la construcción de grandes presas en los años cuarenta propició un auge algodonero que terminó en la década siguiente con la abrupta caída de los precios internacionales del algodón, si bien la producción se orientó hacia otros cultivos de alta rentabilidad y el estado se mantuvo como una potencia ganadera. En los años setenta, en los valles del Yaqui y del Mayo, el presidente Luis Echeverría realizó una de las mayores expropiaciones de tierras que pasaron al régimen ejidal. En 1993 se designó candidato a la Presidencia de la República por el PRI a Luis Donaldo Colosio, nativo de Magdalena de Kino, quien fue asesinado en marzo de 1994.

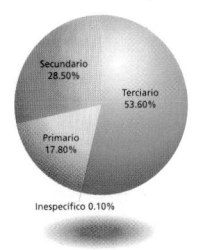

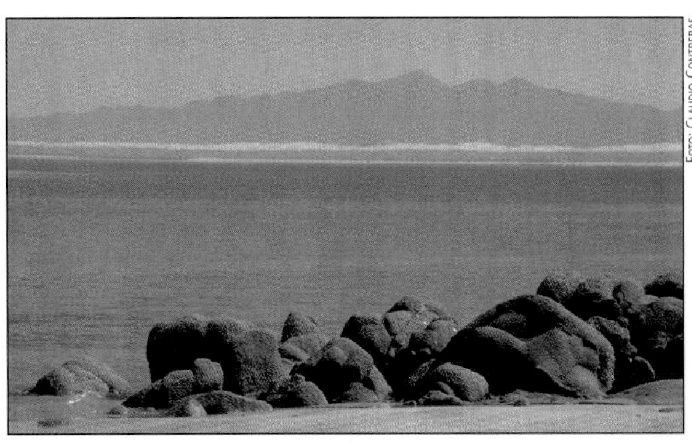

FOTO: CLAUDIO CONTRERAS

Playa del estado de Sonora

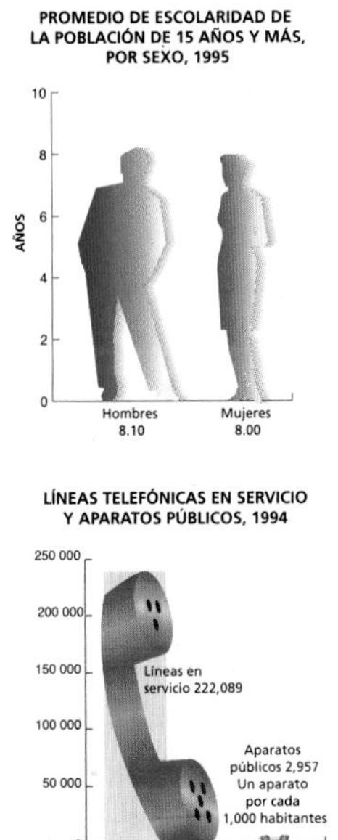

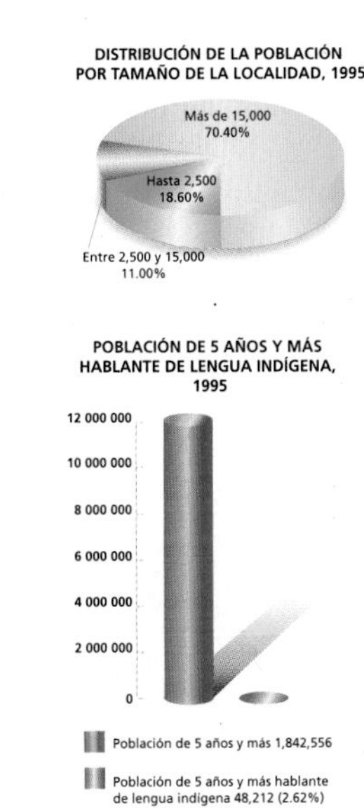

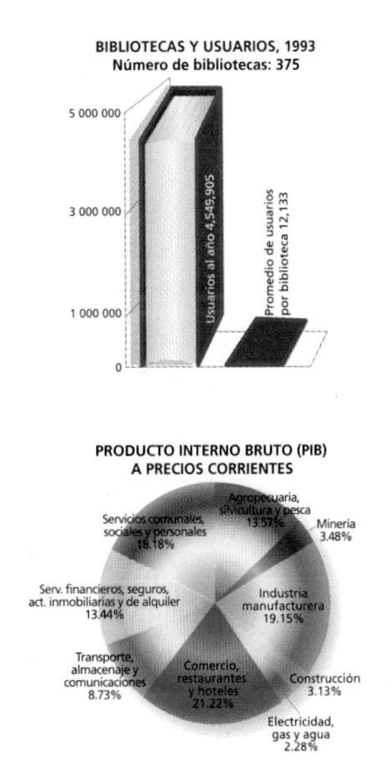

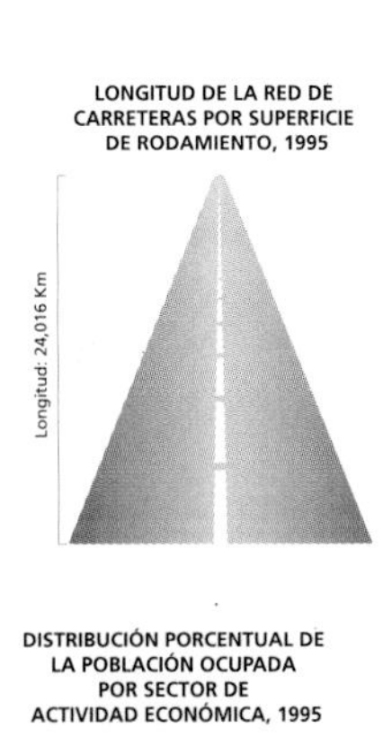

DISTRIBUCIÓN PORCENTUAL DE LA POBLACIÓN OCUPADA POR SECTOR DE ACTIVIDAD ECONÓMICA, 1995

Secundario 28.50%
Terciario 53.60%
Primario 17.80%
Inespecífico 0.10%

Alfonso Sordo Noriega

Centro Comercial Perisur, en el DF, obra de Javier y Juan Sordo Madaleno

SONORA ◆ Río de Sonora. Nace en el poblado de Arizpe, en la confluencia de los ríos Bacoachi y Bacanuchi, en la vertiente oeste de la sierra Madre Occidental. Corre de norte a sur, al oeste de la sierra de Batuc, tuerce al oeste, al sur de la sierra de Aconchi, recibe al río San Miguel de Horcasitas y ambos alimentan a la presa Abelardo Rodríguez, cercana a Hermosillo. El río Sonora atraviesa la zona desértica del estado y ahí se evapora o se pierde en la arena. En pocas ocasiones, cuando hay crecidas, desemboca en la bahía Kino, en el golfo de California.

SONOYTA ◆ Río de Sonora. Nace en el extremo noroccidental del estado, en la vertiente occidental de la sierra del mismo nombre, al este del cerro del Pinacate, cerca de la frontera con Estados Unidos. Corre de norte a sur en el oeste del desierto de Altar, donde la corriente es absorbida por la arena o se evapora. Sólo durante la época de lluvias desemboca en el golfo de California, al oeste de la bahía de San Jorge.

SONOYTA ◆ Sierra de Sonora. Se extiende de noroeste a sureste, paralelamente a la sierra Madre Occidental, desde la frontera con Estados Unidos. Su cumbre más alta es el cerro de Cubabi.

Palacio de Justicia del DF, obra de Javier Sordo Madaleno

SONTAG, HENRIETTE ◆ n. en Prusia y m. en la ciudad de México (1806-1854). Cantante egresada del Conservatorio de Praga. Formó parte en la compañía dirigida por Rossini y Mercadante, cantó en Viena y Berlín y tuvo un sonado éxito al interpretar la Rosina del *Barbero de Sevilla*, en París (1826). Estrenó la *Misa en re* y la *IX Sinfonía* de Beethoven. En 1848 inició una gira por varias ciudades europeas y estadounidenses. Contratada por René Masson llegó con su compañía a la ciudad de México, en 1854, para cantar en el Gran Teatro Nacional o de Santa-Anna. En abril de 1854, presentó la *Sonámbula*, de Bellini. En junio contrajo el cólera y murió. Fue sepultada en el Panteón de San Fernando y luego trasladados sus restos a Alemania, por gestiones de su esposo, el conde de Rossi.

SONTECOMAPAN ◆ Laguna de Veracruz situada en el litoral del golfo de México, al noreste de San Andrés Tuxtla y al norte de la laguna de Catemaco. Tiene una longitud de 7 km. Se comunica con el mar mediante la barra de Sontecomapan.

SOR FILOTEA ◆ ☛ *Fernández de Santa Cruz y Sahagún, Manuel.*

SOR JUANA INÉS DE LA CRUZ ◆ ☛ *Juana Inés de la Cruz.*

SORDO MADALENO, JAVIER ◆ n. en el DF (1956). Arquitecto. En sociedad con su padre, fundó y dirige la firma Sordo Madaleno y Asociados, la cual proyectó y construyó Plaza Universidad (1969), Plaza Monterrey (1970), Plaza Satélite (1971), Bosques de las Lomas (1975), Perisur (1982), el centro Soriana de Chihuahua (1985), la iglesia de la Beneficencia Española en el DF (1964), la Capilla Kingsville de Texas (1974), los cines Ermita (1964), París, El Dorado 70, Satélite y Bosques de las Lomas, el hotel Fiesta Americana de Guadalajara, el Marriot, Eureka de

FOTO: PABLO GONZÁLEZ DE ALBA

Puerto Vallarta, el Ritz Carlton y el Club de Industriales del DF, entre otras obras.

SORDO MADALENO, JUAN ◆ n. y m. en el DF (1916-1985). Padre del anterior. Arquitecto titulado en la UNAM (1939). Construyó numerosas unidades habitacionales, así como la Beneficencia Española, la ampliación Pablo Díez del Sanatorio Español, la iglesia de San Ignacio, la Central de Bomberos y el Palacio de Justicia de la ciudad de México. Fue miembro del Colegio Nacional de Arquitectos, de la Sociedad de Arquitectos Mexicanos, de la Academia Nacional de Arquitectos y del Instituto Americano de Arquitectos.

SORDO NORIEGA, ALONSO ◆ n. en España y m. en el DF (1900-1949). Vivió en México desde su infancia. En 1932 inició su carrera de locutor en la estación XEFA, de la que fue director. En 1934 pasó a la XEW, donde se convirtió en el primer cronista deportivo de la radiofonía mexicana. Coordinador de la campaña presidencial de Manuel Ávila Camacho y director de Información del gobierno federal. Precursor de las transmisiones a control remoto de los espectáculos deportivos, principalmente de las corridas de toros. Fue premiado en Estados Unidos como "primer cronista de América y mejor locutor de habla hispana".

SORIA, GABRIEL ◆ n. ¿en Morelia, Mich.?, y m. en el DF (1908-1971). Estudió periodismo en Estados Unidos, becado por el diario *Excélsior*. Trabajó en el periódico *Los Angeles Examiner* e inició sus contactos con la industria cinematográfica de Hollywood. Volvió a México en la década de los veinte y hacia 1930, con ayuda del fotógrafo Javier Sierra, puso sonido en algunos de los noticieros que hacía para la casa *Excélsior*, por lo que es, quizá, el iniciador del cine sonoro mexicano. Dirigió, entre otras, las películas *Chucho el Roto* (1934), *Martín Garatuza* (1935), *Los muertos hablan* (1935), *Mater nostra* (1936), *¡Ora Ponciano!* (1936), *La bestia negra* (1938), *Mala yerba* (1940), *La Virgen Morena* (1942), *Casa de mujeres* (1942) y *La dama de las camelias* (1943). En 1944 estuvo en España, donde realizó varios documentales para el franquismo.

SORIA TERRAZAS, JOAQUÍN ◆ n. en Chihuahua, Chih., y m. en el DF (1911-1990). Fue presidente del Sector Amateur de la Federación Mexicana de Futbol (1941-71), fundador, vicepresidente (1961-68) y presidente de la Confederación Norte, Centroamericana y del Caribe de Futbol (1968-90). Se le señaló como uno de los promotores del castigo impuesto a México por el llamado caso de "los cachirules", originado en la falsificación de documentos de algunos jugadores juveniles, lo que costó a México ser castigado con su exclusión de todas las competencias internacionales durante una parte de los ochenta y el campeonato mundial de 1990. Promovió la candidatura de México como sede de los mundiales de 1970 y 1986. Perteneció a la Comisión de Campeonatos Olímpicos.

La vuelta a Francia, óleo sobre tela de Juan Soriano

SORIANO, JUAN ◆ n. en Guadalajara, Jalisco (1920). Artista plástico autodidacto. Fue miembro de la Liga de Escritores y Artistas Revolucionarios (1936-38). En 1941 expuso su pintura individualmente en la Galería de la Universidad. De 1951 a 1955 trabajó y expuso en Italia. Vivió en Francia 25 años. Autor de la escultura en bronce *Toro echado*, que se colocó en el centro de una laguna del parque Tomás Garrido Canabal, en Villahermosa. Otra de sus obras se halla en el vestíbulo del Auditorio Nacional. En 1985 presentó una exposición retrospectiva en el Palacio de Bellas Artes. En 1987 recibió el Premio Nacional de Artes y el Premio Jalisco.

Xavier Sorondo Rubio

Foto: Ana Lourdes Herrera

Juan Soriano

SORONDO RUBIO, XAVIER ◆ n. y m. en el DF (1883-1957). Desde 1892 escribió poesía. Abandonó la carrera de derecho para dedicarse al periodismo. Con Rafael Alducin trabajó en la revista *El Automóvil en México* y en *El Imparcial*. Colaboró en *El Universal Ilustrado*, *Revista de Revistas* y *Excélsior*, diario del que fue subdirector durante 25 años y presidente del consejo de administración. En esa casa fundó *Jueves de Excélsior* y las dos ediciones de *Últimas Noticias*, en la primera de las cuales publicó la columna "El glosario de cada día". Se integró al servicio exterior mexicano y estuvo en Montevideo, Buenos Aires y La Paz. Autor de los poemarios *Estampas de torería* (1942), *Poemas mexicanos* (1947), *Viñetas* (1949), *Hacia la cumbre* (1954) y *El perpetuo rebelde*.

SORTÉ, MARÍA ◆ n. en el DF (1951). Actriz y cantante. Comenzó su carrera a fines de los setenta en programas cómicos de televisión; su primer papel destacado fue en la película *El barrendero* (1981), al lado de Mario Moreno *Cantinflas*. Posteriormente ha aparecido en telenovelas y ha grabado numerosos discos.

SORTO, MANUEL ◆ n. en El Salvador (1950). Cineasta y escritor. Ha trabajado con el realizador chileno Miguel Littín. Colaboró en *El Machete* y *unomásuno*. Autor de *Las cabezas infinitas* (1971, poesía en colaboración), *Frutos para Ana* (poesía, 1973) y la noveleta *Operación amor* (1980).

Francisco Sosa

SOSA, FRANCISCO ◆ n. en Campeche, Camp., y m. en el DF (1848-1925). Estudió filosofía y derecho en Mérida. En 1864 empezó a colaborar en *La Esperanza*, de la capital yucateca. Ahí mismo escribió para el *Álbum Meridano*. En 1868 pasó a la ciudad de México, donde fue prefecto de Coyoacán y colaboró en *El Renacimiento, El Federalista, El Siglo XIX, El Eco de Ambos Mundos, El Domingo, El Artista, La Libertad, La Juventud Literaria, El Nacional*, la *Revista Nacional de Letras y Ciencias* y la *Revista Universal*. Regresó a Mérida y fundó la *Revista de Mérida*, de oposición al gobierno lerdista, por lo que fue encarcelado en San Juan de Ulúa. Liberado al triunfo del Plan de Tuxtepec, en la capital del país se le encomendó la dirección del archivo de la Secretaría de Fomento. En 1873 fundó, con Vicente Riva Palacio, el periódico *El Radical*. Diputado federal, senador y director de la Biblioteca Nacional hasta 1912, cuando Francisco I. Madero lo destituyó. Autor de un *Manual de biografía yucateca* (1868), *Una venganza* (1874), *Doce leyendas* (1877), *El monumento de Colón* (1877), *El episcopado mexicano. Galería biográfica ilustrada* (1877), *Efemérides históricas y biográficas* (2 t., 1883), *Galería de contemporáneos* (1884), *Biografías de mexicanos distinguidos* (1884), *Anuario biográfico nacional* (1884), *Ecos de gloria* (poesía, 1885), *Apuntamientos para la historia del monumento a Cuauhtémoc* (1887), *Recuerdos* (poesía, 1888), *Bosquejo histórico de Coyoacán* (1890), *Notas biográficas de don Ponciano Arriaga* (1890), *Las estatuas de la Reforma* (1890), *Escritores y poetas sudamericanos* (1900), *Conquistadores antiguos y modernos* (1901) y *Breves notas tomadas en la escuela de la vida* (1910), entre otras obras. Fue miembro de la Academia Mexicana (de la Lengua) y de la Sociedad Mexicana de Geografía y Estadística.

SOSA, VÍCTOR ◆ n. en Montevideo (1956). Poeta y crítico de poesía. Ha colaborado en *Vuelta, Novedades, El Ángel, La Cultura en México* y otras publicaciones. Autor de *Sujeto omitido* (1983) y *Sunyata* (1992).

SOSA CENICEROS, PORFIRIO ◆ n. en Tezoatlán, Oaxaca, y m. en el DF (1879-1970). Licenciado en derecho por el Instituto de Ciencias y Artes de Oaxaca (1913). Afiliado al antirreeleccionismo, participó en la insurrección maderista. Por motivos políticos estuvo preso durante la dictadura de Victoriano Huerta. Diputado al Congreso Constituyente de 1916-17. Fue vicepresidente del Partido Constitucionalista de Oaxaca (1917) y agente del Ministerio Público en diversas ciudades del país (1917-23). En 1920 formó parte de la escolta de Venustiano Carranza en Tlaxcalantongo, lo que le valió la Medalla de la Lealtad, otorgada por la Asociación Venustiano Carranza. Dirigió el Instituto Juárez de Villahermosa, fue socio fundador de la Unión Nacional de Veteranos de la Revolución (1932) y abogado consultor del Departamento de Pensiones Civiles de Retiro (1934). Al morir era actuario del juzgado primero de distrito en el DF.

SOSA PAVÓN, MANUEL JACOBO ◆ n. en Chietla, Pue., y m. en el DF (1888-?). Descendiente de José María Morelos y Pavón. Ejerció diversos oficios y en 1901 se instaló en Cuautla como pagador de peones de la hacienda de Tenextepango. Ferrocarrilero desde 1910, en mayo de 1911 condujo el tren que llevó a Porfirio Díaz a Veracruz. Luego del cuartelazo huertista se alistó en el Ejército Libertador del Sur, donde se le dio el grado de mayor con mando sobre un cuerpo de dinamiteros. Operó en Oaxaca, Tlaxcala, Puebla y Morelos. En 1915 fue superintendente general de los ferrocarriles del gobierno convencionista. En 1916 fue expulsado de Oaxaca por los carrancistas y se refugió en El Salvador hasta 1917, cuando se acogió a la amnistía. Venustiano Carranza le encomendó la captura de Félix Díaz, que no llevó a cabo. En 1920 se reincorporó a su trabajo como ferrocarrilero, del que se jubiló en 1970. Miembro del comité directivo del Frente Zapatista.

SOSA TORRES, AURELIO ◆ n. y m. en Cárdenas, Tab. (?-1913). Militante del Partido Liberal Mexicano. En 1909 participó en el primer levantamiento armado antiporfirista de Tabasco, junto con Ignacio Gutiérrez. Retirado a la vida privada luego del triunfo maderista, en 1913 retomó las armas contra Huerta, con el grado de general brigadier. Murió en combate.

SOSA DE LA VEGA, MANUEL ◆ n. en San Luis Potosí, SLP (1916). Ingeniero mecánico electricista por el IPN (1930-34). Gerente general de Transportes Aéreos Mexicanos (Mérida, 1958), presidente del Departamento Especializado de Aviación de la Cámara Nacional de Transportes y Comunicaciones y del Comité de Tráfico de las Líneas Aéreas de México y Centroamérica (1959), consejero propietario de Datatrónic y miembro del comité ejecutivo de la Universidad de las Américas. En la Compañía Mexicana de Aviación ha sido trabajador de los departamentos de Tráfico, Express, Ventas y Aeropuertos, director comercial (1961), delegado ejecutivo (1964) y director general (1967-). Consejero propietario de Banca Confía, Multibanco Mercantil de México y Turborreactores, Aeropuertos y Terrenos, así como presidente del Consejo de Crédito Metropolitano de Banca Serfín. Miembro del Consejo de Administración de la Asociación Fundación de Seguridad Aérea, Club de Banqueros, Club de Industriales y miembro del comité ejecutivo (1973-78) y presidente (1975-76) de la

International Air Transport Association.

SOSAMONTES, RAMÓN ◆ n. en Chilpancingo, Gro., y m. en el DF (1911-1993). Pintor y grabador egresado de la ENAP. Fue profesor en Chapingo, la Escuela Normal Socialista de Hidalgo y en la Nacional de Maestros. Perteneció a la Liga de Escritores y Artistas Revolucionarios y al Taller de Gráfica Popular. Su obra comprende producción de caballete, murales y grabados de diversas técnicas.

SOSAMONTES HERRERAMORO, RAMÓN ◆ n. en Chilpancingo, Gro. (1951). Hijo del anterior. Licenciado en relaciones internacionales por la UNAM. Ingresó en 1968 a la Juventud Comunista de México, luego al Partido Comunista Mexicano, en el que perteneció a la Comisión Nacional Juvenil, al comité del DF hasta 1981 y al comité central. Participó en la campaña presidencial de Valentín Campa (1975-76) y la de Arnoldo Martínez Verdugo (1982). Cofundador del Partido Socialista Unificado de México (1981), del que fue miembro del comité central y dirigente en el DF (1981-87). Cofundador del Partido Mexicano Socialista (1987-89) y del PRD (1989-). Ha colaborado en *Oposición, Así Es, La Unidad, La Jornada* y *Crónica*. Miembro de la ARDF (1988-91), diputado federal (1994-97) y delegado del gobierno del Distrito Federal en Venustiano Carranza (1997-99) e Iztapalapa (1999-).

SOTEAPAN ◆ Municipio de Veracruz situado en el litoral del golfo de México, al noroeste de Coatzacoalcos y contiguo a Catemaco. Superficie: 528.07 km^2. Habitantes: 28,888, de los cuales 5,563 forman la población económicamente activa. Hablan alguna lengua indígena 18,948 personas mayores de cinco años (popoluca de Veracruz 17,939 y náhuatl 969). Indígenas monolingües: 1,470.

SOTELO, JULIO ◆ n. en la ciudad de México y m. en Irapuato, Gto. (1906-1970). Fue uno de los iniciadores de la crónica deportiva radiofónica en México. Trabajó en las estaciones XEX y XEB, para las cuales reseñó competencias de boxeo, futbol, beisbol y tenis.

SOTELO, PEDRO JOSÉ ◆ n. y m. en Dolores, Gto. (1790-?). Huérfano desde 1802, un año más tarde pasó al curato de Dolores, donde Miguel Hidalgo lo incorporó a uno de sus talleres de alfarería. En 1810 se unió al movimiento de independencia. Permaneció en Dolores custodiando a los españoles prisioneros y más tarde alcanzó al ejército insurgente en Guadalajara, donde se incorporó a las fuerzas de Mariano Hidalgo. Participó en las batallas del Monte de las Cruces y de San Jerónimo Aculco; enfermó y regresó a Dolores, donde permaneció oculto hasta 1821, cuando fue nombrado guardián de la casa de Hidalgo. Autor de *Memorias del último de los primeros soldados de la Independencia.* (1874), que dedicó al entonces presidente Sebastián Lerdo de Tejada.

SOTELO INCLÁN, JESÚS ◆ n. en la ciudad de México y m. cerca de San Felipe Torresmochas, Gto. (1913-1989). Estudió derecho en la UNAM. Profesor por la Escuela Nacional de Maestros. Historiador y dramaturgo. Fue uno de los fundadores de la radiodifusora XEW, donde condujo el programa *Los catedráticos*. Trabajó también en televisión. Fue fundador del Instituto Federal de Capacitación al Magisterio (1945), director del INBA y director de la Escuela Normal Ignacio Manuel Altamirano. Autor de estudios históricos: *Raíz y razón de Zapata* (1943) y teatro: *Malintzin, Medea americana* (1957).

SOTERAS MAURI, MARÍA ◆ n. en España y m. en el DF (1905-1976). Fue la primera mujer licenciada en derecho por la Universidad de Barcelona (1927). Doctora en derecho por la Universidad Central de Madrid, fue también la primera mujer admitida en el Ilustre Colegio de Abogados de Barcelona. Residió en París (1934-35) exiliada después de los sucesos políticos de 1934. Al inicio de la guerra civil se refugió en Bélgica y en 1939 pasó a México. Con su esposo, el abogado Antonio Vilalta y Vidal, fundó la Asociación Médico Farmacéutica. Trabajó en el Bufete Internacional fundado por Vilalta.

SOTO, ÁLVARO ◆ n. en el DF (1957). Periodista y fotógrafo. Se ha encargado de las secciones humorísticas en la revista *Contenido* desde 1976, entre ellas "Querida tía Alma.". También lo ha hecho en *Última Moda, Superdeportiva, Medio Tiempo* y *Reforma*. Premio Nacional de Periodismo del Club de Periodistas de México (1983, 1987, 1988 y 1990). Reside en Lisboa, Portugal, desde 1981.

Cecilia Soto

SOTO, CECILIA ◆ n. en Hermosillo, Son. (1950). Su nombre completo es Cecilia Guadalupe Soto González. Licenciada en Física por la UNAM. También estudió econometría, planeación energética y población y desarrollo. Participó en el movimiento estudiantil del 68 y en la marcha del 10 de junio de 1971, reprimida por el grupo paramilitar *Los Halcones*. Perteneció al Partido Laboral Mexicano (1975-1983). Fundó el Frente Campesino Pro-Plan Hidráulica del Noroeste (1980) y el Comité Pro-Defensa de los Derechos Humanos del Pescador. Ingresó al PARM en 1985. En 1988 participó en el Frente Democrático Nacional. Ha sido diputada local en Sonora (1980), diputada federal (1991-94) y candidata a la presidencia de la República por el Partido del Trabajo (1994). Ha colaborado en el periodico *Reforma* (1995-) y otras publicaciones.

SOTO, IGNACIO ◆ n. en Bavispe, Son., y m. en EUA (1890-1962). Ganadero e industrial. Luchó en la revolución constitucionalista y, como diputado local, apoyó el desconocimiento de Carranza, que dio pie al Plan de Agua Prieta. Fue gobernador de Sonora (1949-55). A su gobierno correspondió inaugurar la presa Álvaro Obregón.

SOTO, JESÚS ◆ n. en Monclova, Coah., y m. en Chihuahua, Chih. (?-1917). Luchó en la revolución maderista y más tarde se alistó en las fuerzas irregulares de los Carabineros de Coahuila, que combatieron la sublevación de Pascual Orozco. Constitucionalista en 1913, fue jefe de varias guarniciones. Murió en combate contra los villistas.

Foto: Colección Pecime

Fernando Soto *Mantequilla*

Soto, Roberto *el Panzón* ◆ n. en Zacatecas, Zac., y m. en la ciudad de México (1888-1960). Su segundo apellido era Astol. Inició su carrera teatral en 1913 como galán cómico en la compañía de Dora Vila y Ricardo Mutio y más tarde trabajó en zarzuelas. En 1920 formó una compañía propia. En 1925, con la compañía de Pepe Campillo, tuvo un gran éxito en el teatro Lírico por su trabajo en *Mexican Rataplán*, parodia de *Voilá le Ba-ta-clán*, espectáculo francés de *Madame* Rasimí. Presentó largas temporadas en los teatros Principal, Iris y Lírico.

Soto Allende, Rafael ◆ n. y m. en el DF (1905-1966). Pediatra. Estudió en la Escuela Nacional de Medicina de la Universidad Nacional (1929), de la que fue profesor. Trabajó en el Hospital Infantil de México, donde llegó a ser decano. Fue jefe del servicio de pediatría del Hospital Francés, miembro y tesorero de la Academia Nacional de Medicina, presidente de la Academia Mexicana de Pediatría y de la Asociación de Investigación Pediátrica y fundador de la Sociedad Mexicana de Pediatría.

Soto y Gama, Antonio Díaz ◆ ☛ *Díaz Soto y Gama, Antonio.*

Soto Guevara, Carlos ◆ n. en Puebla, Pue., y m. en el DF (1897-1957). Abogado. Se tituló en el Colegio de Puebla (1927). Profesor de idiomas en Estados Unidos (1919-21), diputado local en Puebla (1925), jefe de Estadística Económica de la Secretaría de Economía (1931), diputado federal, magistrado del Tribunal Supremo de Justicia del Distrito Federal, senador y magistrado del Tribunal Fiscal de la Federación (1942-57).

Soto Izquierdo, Enrique ◆ n. en Cusihuiriachic, Chih. (1935). Licenciado en derecho por la UNAM (1961). Desde 1958 pertenece al PRI, en el que fue director de *La República* (1968-70). Ha sido abogado de la Dirección General de Asuntos Jurídicos de la Secretaría de Gobernación (1960-66), director del Injuve (1970-76), diputado federal (1976-79 y 1982-85) y director del Instituto Mexicano de Cinematografía (1986-88). Tradujo al inglés la Constitución (1961). Fue responsable de la información económica internacional de las publicaciones del Bancomext (1962-65). Ha colaborado en *La Prensa*, *El Día*, *El Universal*, *El Nacional*, *Impacto* y la *Revista Técnica Financiera* (1963-82). Coautor de *Los derechos sociales del pueblo mexicano* (1978) y *Los derechos del pueblo mexicano* (1979). Autor de *El liberalismo y la Constitución de 57* (1957), *La Declaración de Derechos del Hombre y los propósitos de la* ONU (1958), *Misión a Oriente* (1964) y *Palabras por la juventud* (1976). Ganó el primer lugar del Concurso Internacional de Oratoria de *El Universal* (1957).

Soto *Mantequilla*, Fernando ◆ n. en Puebla, Pue., y m. en el DF (1911-1980). Hijo de Roberto *el Panzón* Soto. Se inició como actor cómico en la compañía teatral de su padre. Participó en numerosas películas, de entre las que destacan *Campeón sin corona* y *Pepe el Toro*.

Soto la Marina ◆ Municipio de Tamaulipas situado en el litoral del golfo de México, al este de Ciudad Victoria. Superficie: 5,499.3 km^2. Habitantes: 24,237, de los cuales 6,186 forman la población económicamente activa. Hablan alguna lengua indígena 195 personas mayores de cinco años (náhuatl 105). La desembocadura del río Soto la Marina, que se halla en su jurisdicción, fue el sitio en el que desembarcó la expedición de Francisco Javier Mina (1817), en el que resistió un sitio José Sardá, lugarteniente de Mina, y en el que desembarcó Agustín de Iturbide cuando pretendía volver a coronarse emperador de México.

Malecón de Soto la Marina, Tamaulipas

Foto: Fondo Editorial Grupo Azabache

Soto la Marina ◆ Río de Tamaulipas que nace en la presa Las Adjuntas, formado por la confluencia de los ríos Purificación y Corona, al este de la sierra Madre Oriental. Corre hacia el oriente, por la parte norte de la sierra de Tamaulipas, a través del cañón de Boca de la Iglesia; sale a la llanura costera, donde recibe al arroyo de Jiménez, tuerce al sur y nuevamente al este y le tributa el arroyo de las Palmas. Unos seis kilómetros antes de desembocar en el golfo de México, en la barra de Soto la Marina, se ensancha y forma dos ensenadas: la de las Garzas y la del Brito. Es navegable en sus últimos 50 kilómetros.

Soto Máynez, Óscar ♦ n. en Valle de Allende y m. en Chihuahua, Chih. (1904-1974). Abogado. Fue diputado federal (1949) y gobernador de Chihuahua (1950-55), puesto que debió dejar por presiones políticas, antes de cumplir su periodo sexenal. Durante su gobierno fundó la Universidad de Chihuahua (1954).

Soto Millán, Eduardo ♦ n. en el DF (1956). Compositor egresado de la Escuela Nacional de Música de la UNAM. Tomó cursos en el taller de Julio Estrada y con Ramón Barce, Rodolfo Halffter y Jean-Etienne Marie. Fundó y dirigió el grupo de Música Contemporánea de la Escuela Nacional de Música (1979-82) y el Ensamble Intermúsica (1984-86). Ha sido programador musical de Radio Educación, jefe del departamento de Música de Cámara de la UNAM, coordinador del Registro Nacional de Compositores del INBA, presidente fundador de la Sociedad Mexicana de Música Nueva (1989-1999) y creador del Centro de Apoyo para la Música de Concierto de la SACM (1993). Colaborador de los periódicos *unomásuno* y *La Jornada*. Compositor residente en la Arizona State University West (1995-96). Compilador del *Diccionario de compositores mexicanos de música de concierto. Siglo XX* (2 t., 1998 y 1999). El disco *Música del interior* reúne obras suyas (1994). Autor entre otras de *Improvisaciones I, II, III y IV* para uno a cuatro instrumentos de teclado (1979), *Dadalibitum* para tres o cuatro objetos sonoros (1982), *Metaphoras* (1982) y *Voces II* para orquesta sinfónica (1986), *Mexihco* para cinta magnétofónica (1982), *Corazón Sur* para cuarteto de percusión (1994), *Tloque-Nahuaque* para ensamble instrumental (1996) y *La Orestiada*. Mención honorífica en el Certamen Música Mexicana para Danza de la UNAM (1982) y en el Primer Concurso de Composición Felipe Villanueva (1986).

Soto Pastrana, Manuel Fernando ♦ n. en Tulancingo, en el actual estado de Hidalgo, y m. en la ciudad de México (1825-1896). Diputado al Congreso Constituyente de 1857. Como gobernador del Estado de México expidió la Ley de Desamortización (1861). Comandó fuerzas republicanas contra la intervención francesa y el imperio en la parte oriental del actual Hidalgo, en Puebla y San Luis Potosí. Fue magistrado de la Suprema Corte de Justicia. Desde 1857 promovió la erección del estado de Hidalgo, lograda en 1869, y cuya capital, en su honor, se llama Pachuca de Soto.

Soto Ponce, José ♦ n. en San Luis de la Paz, Gto., y m. en el DF (1902-1954). Periodista. Fue uno de los fundadores de la estación de radio XEFO-Radio Nacional, órgano de difusión del PNR. Fue agente de la Secretaría de Gobernación, profesor de la Escuela Industrial de Huérfanos de Santiago Tlatelolco y, desde 1938, colaborador del periódico *El Nacional*, del que también fue jefe de información.

Soto Ramos, Juan ♦ n. en Veracruz y m. en Alvarado, Ver. (1798-1859). Militar que inició su carrera a las órdenes de José Joaquín de Herrera. Fue ayudante de Antonio López de Santa Anna, participó en la campaña contra Isidro Barradas (1829), fue diputado local y gobernador de la fortaleza de San Juan de Ulúa (1838). Alcanzó el grado de general de brigada. Dos veces gobernador interino de Veracruz (1845 y 1846-49), durante su gestión suprimió el sistema bicamaral y reformó la Constitución local. En 1847 combatió la invasión estadounidense. Gobernador constitucional de Veracruz (1855-56), diputado federal y secretario de Guerra y Marina (del 26 de mayo de 1856 al 16 de septiembre de 1857) en el gabinete de Ignacio Comonfort.

Soto Reyes, Ernesto ♦ n. en Puruándiro, Mich., y m. en el DF (1899-1972). Estudió derecho en la Universidad Michoacana de San Nicolás de Hidalgo. Militó en el ejército constitucionalista y ascendió a teniente coronel de caballería. Participó en la fundación del Sindicato de Estudiantes Socialistas de la Casa del Obrero Mundial y del Partido Socialista Michoacano (1917). Miembro del CEN del PNR (1934) y del PRM, secretario del Comité Organizador del Frente Único Campesino, presidente del Comité Nacional de Orientación Política, promotor de la Federación de Partidos del Pueblo Mexicano (1951). Fue regidor del ayuntamiento de Zitácuaro (1921), presidente municipal de Morelia (1922), secretario particular del gobernador Lázaro Cárdenas (1928-30), cofundador de la Confederación Revolucionaria Michoacana del Trabajo, diputado federal (1930-32), oficial mayor de la campaña presidencial de Cárdenas, miembro y líder del Senado de la República (1934-37) y embajador en Paraguay (1941-44), Venezuela (1944-46), Uruguay (1946-49), la República Dominicana, Panamá, Haití y Turquía (1961-71). Autor de *La organización jurídica y contenido social del Estado Mexicano* (1942) y *Las democracias y el totalitarismo* (1942).

Soto Rodríguez, Humberto ♦ n. en Colima, Col. (1944). Ingeniero mecánico (1967) y doctor en ciencias administrativas (1981) por el IPN. Profesor de la Universidad Anáhuac (1974) y del Centro Nacional de Enseñanza Técnica Industrial (1974-77). Ha sido encargado de la programación y control de la producción de la Compañía Tornillos Spasser (1962-64), proyectista coordinador del Departamento de Diseño y Nuevos Proyectos de Hulera Euzkadi (1964-67), supervisor de proyectos del Instituto de Apoyo Técnico para el Financiamiento a la Industria (1967-77), director de Planeación y Control de Operaciones de Fertica, en Costa Rica (1977-79), así como gerente de Crédito (1979-80), subdirector de Crédito (1980-82), subdirector general (1982-88) y director general del Banco Mexicano de Comercio Exterior (1988-93). Autor de *La formulación y evaluación técnico económica de proyectos industriales* (1971).

SOTOMAYOR DE ZALDO, ARTURO ◆ n. en Veracruz, Ver. y m. en (1913-1995). Licenciado en derecho por la UNAM (1959). Fue policía preventivo y posteriormente profesor de historia en la Escuela Nacional Preparatoria (1938-91). Se dedicó al periodismo. Fue auxiliar, tipógrafo, redactor y secretario de redacción del periódico *Cooperación* (1934-35) y orador durante la campaña presidencial de Lázaro Cárdenas. Colaboró en *Hoy*, *Vea*, *Tiempo*, *Siempre!*, *El Hombre Libre*, *El Nacional*, *La Prensa*, *Novedades*, *unomásuno*, *Comunidad Conacyt*, *Revista de Revistas*, *Macrópolis*, *La Jornada*, *Excélsior* y *El Financiero*, así como del programa *En legítima defensa* de Radio Educación. Autor de poesía: *Vértigo azul* (1947), *El ángel de los goces* (1955) y *En esta tierra* (1956); y ensayo: *Nuestros niños héroes* (1947), *Sombras bajo la luna* (1948, incluye relatos), *Dos sepulcros en Bonampak* (1949), *Los bárbaros sobre la ciudad de México* (1960), *Historia de la economía internacional*, *La administración pública en México*, *Breve guía histórico-universal de la ciudad de México*, *Viajes al pasado de México* (1963), *México donde nací. Biografía de una ciudad* (1968), *Tehuantepec no es Panamá*, *Curso de historia de la ciudad de México*, *de la famosa México el asiento* (1969), *La metrópoli mexicana y su agonía* (1973), *Expansión de México*, *El antiguo y real Colegio de San Ildefonso*, *Crónicas extemporáneas* (1981), *Cortés según Cortés*, *La ciudad y sus personajes* (1988), *Aventuras de Víctor Dardo* (1991), *Ustedes la capital*, *La pérdida de Texas* y *El altruismo institucional: el Nacional Monte de Piedad*. Publicó, asimismo, antologías comentadas de Artemio del Valle Arizpe (*Don Artemio*, *México donde nací*) y de Manuel Rivera Cambas. Recibió la medalla Carlos M. Bustamante (1967) y el Premio Ciudad de México (1976).

SOTUTA ◆ Municipio de Yucatán situado al oeste de Chichén-Itzá y al sureste de Mérida. Superficie: 613.15 km². Habitantes: 7,739, de los cuales 2,039 forman la población económicamente activa. Hablan alguna lengua indígena 4,739 personas mayores de cinco años (maya 4,738). Indígenas monolingües: 278. Hasta antes de la guerra de castas la región de Sotuta, cacicazgo del maya Nachi-Cocom, era una de las más pobladas de la península. Actualmente el municipio es uno de los principales productores de henequén y de miel de abeja.

SOUST SCAFFO, ALCIRA ◆ n. en Uruguay (1924). Poeta. Becada por la CREFAL llegó a México en 1952 para estudiar pintura en Guanajuato. Trabajó en Radio UNAM como traductora y adaptadora de cuentos infantiles. Participó en el movimiento estudiantil de 1968 (☛). La entrada del ejército en la Ciudad Universitaria (18 de septiembre) la sorprendió en la Torre de Filosofía y se ocultó en uno de los baños, donde permaneció 11 días, luego de los cuales fue encontrada por Rubén Bonifaz Nuño. En 1975, ya con permiso de la Secretaría de Gobernación, empezó a trabajar en la Facultad de Filosofía y Letras, de donde la despidió en 1978 el director Abelardo Villegas. Entre 1984 y 1988 fue llevada varias veces a diversos hospitales psiquiátricos, donde indicaron que su experiencia de 1968 le había provocado "psicosis delirante crónica de características paranoides". De 1978 a 1988, aun sin trabajar ahí, pasaba la mayor parte del tiempo en la citada Facultad, donde colaboraba en las luchas laborales y estudiantiles y publicaba las hojas *Poesía en Armas*, con sus producciones. En 1988 regresó a Uruguay.

SOUSTELLE, JACQUES ◆ n. y m. en París, Francia (1912-1990). Doctor en letras por la Escuela Nacional Superior de Lyon. Etnólogo y político francés. En su país ocupó diversos cargos públicos. Fue jefe de los servicios secretos de Francia Libre durante la segunda guerra y ministro del general Charles de Gaulle. Gobernador de Argelia en 1955. Estuvo exiliado de 1962 a 1968 por tratar de asesinar a De Gaulle y pertenecer a una organización de extrema derecha. Se especializó en las culturas antiguas de México desde los años treinta, cuando llegó por primera vez a Veracruz. Su primera estancia prolongada en México fue entre 1932 y 1939. Autor de *México, tierra india* (1936), *La vida cotidiana de los aztecas en la víspera de la conquista* (1956), *El pensamiento cosmológico de los antiguos mexicanos* (1959), *El arte del México antiguo* (1966), *Los cuatro soles* (1967), *El universo de los aztecas* (1984), *Los olmecas* (1980) y *Los mayas* (1982). En su país fue miembro de la Academia Francesa desde 1983. En México recibió la Orden del Águila Azteca y el Premio Internacional Alfonso Reyes.

Jacques Soustelle

SOUTO ALABARCE, ARTURO ◆ n. en España (1930). Escritor, hijo del pintor Arturo Souto Feijóo. En 1938 salió de España con su familia. Vivió exiliado en Bélgica, Francia, Cuba y Estados Unidos (1938-42) antes de asentarse en México. Licenciado en letras españolas por la UNAM (1955). Profesor de la Universidad Femenina de México, de la Academia de la Danza Mexicana, de la UIA, del Centro Mexicano de Escritores, de la Universidad de Alabama (1968) y del Mexico City College-Universidad de las Américas (1960-72). En la UNAM se ha desempeñado como catedrático, asesor del Departamento de Graduados, jefe del Departamento de Lengua y Literatura Española, investigador del Centro de Estudios Literarios, jefe de publicidad de la Librería Universitaria (1957-68), coordinador del Departamento de Letras Hispánicas (1972-78), asesor de letras hispánicas en la División de Estudios de Posgrado (1978-81) y miembro de la Comisión Dictaminadora de Letras.

Colaborador de *Clavileño, Segrel, El Nacional, México en la Cultura, El Universal, Ideas de México, Revista de la Universidad y Comunidad Conacyt*. Coautor de *Romanticismo, realismo y naturalismo* (1976). Autor de *El romanticismo* (1955), *La plaga del crisantemo* (1960), *Grandes textos creativos de la literatura española* (1966), *La literatura mexicana en el siglo XX, La literatura española del siglo XX* (1973), *El lenguaje literario* (1973), *La literatura y las otras artes* (1972), *Literatura y sociedad* (1972) y *El ensayo* (1972).

Souto Feijóo, Arturo ◆ n. en España y m. en el DF (1902-1964). Padre del anterior. Pintor egresado de la Academia de San Fernando en Madrid (1925). En 1934 obtuvo el Premio Nacional y una beca para estudiar en Italia, Bélgica y Francia. Volvió a España en 1936. Durante la guerra civil fue miembro de la Alianza de Intelectuales Antifascistas. Presentó exposiciones en Francia, Bélgica, Cuba y Estados Unidos. Vivió en los últimos dos países antes de venir a México (1942), a donde llegó persuadido por Jaime Torres Bodet, a quien conoció en Bruselas.

Souza, Antonio ◆ n. y m. en el DF (1927-1989). Galerista. Con su recinto, Los Contemporáneos, a partir de los cincuenta fue el principal promotor de la corriente de ruptura (Manuel Felguérez, Francisco Toledo, José Luis Cuevas, Lilia Carrillo, Matías Goertiz, Günter Gherszo, Juan Soriano y Wolfgang Paalen). Luego fundó la Galería Antonio Souza, donde organizaba *happenings*. Expuso en México las obras de muchos artistas extranjeros, como Fernando Botero, a pesar de las tendencias nacionalistas de su época. En 1992 se le hizo un homenaje en La Casa del Lago y una exposición titulada *De la abstracción al happening* y se publicó *Galería Antonio Souza, vanguardia de una época*.

Souza Novelo, Narciso ◆ n. y m. en Mérida, Yuc. (1875-1952). Se tituló como médico por la Universidad de Columbia (1906), especializado en electricidad médica y rayos X (1907). Fue uno de los primeros en utilizar la fisioterapia en Yucatán y en hacer exploraciones con rayos X. Estudió las plantas medicinales, textiles y alimenticias yucatecas. Destacan sus estudios sobre las orquídeas. Autor de *Botánica* (1913), *Leyendas mayas, Zacates y gramíneas de Yucatán, Plantas alimenticias y de condimento que viven en Yucatán, Arboles maderables de Yucatán, Arboles frutales que viven en Yucatán, Curso de Botánica, Pochote* (1939), *Zicilte* (1939), *Farmacopea maya, Henequén. Ki* (1940), *Plantas melíferas y poliníferas que viven en Yucatán* (1940), *Sabila o zábila* (1940) y *Ciruelos americanos, con dibujos de los que se producen en Yucatán*.

Souza, Pilar ◆ n. y m en el DF (1923-1999). Actriz. En su infancia y juventud vivió en Colima. Estudió leyes en la ciudad de México. Trabajó en *Los signos del zodiaco* (1951), *Sueño de una noche de verano* (1948), *Antígona* (1949), *La danza macabra* (1949), *Rosalba y los llaveros* (1950), *El canto de los grillos* y muchas otras. En cine actuó en más de 15 películas, como *Pubertinaje* (1972), *Felicidad, Coronación, Dos crímenes* y *La madre* (1979), entre otras. Fue maestra y promotora de teatro por más de 25 años, sin abandonar sus papeles en televisión. Fue directora de la Escuela de Teatro del INBA (1980-83). En televisión comenzó como asistente de dirección de Salvador Novo. En ese medio grabó programas y telenovelas. Cuando falleció filmaba *Catalina y Sebastián*.

Soyaló ◆ Municipio de Chiapas situado al noreste del estado y próximo a Tuxtla Gutiérrez. Superficie: 178.9 km². Habitantes: 7,062, de los cuales 1,757 forman la población económicamente activa. Hablan alguna lengua indígena 1,851 personas mayores de cinco años (tzotzil 1,840).

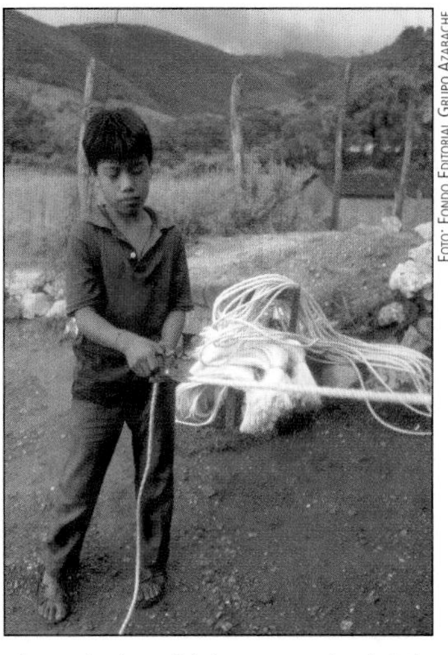

Foto: Fondo Editorial Grupo Azabache

Lugar donde se fabrican artesanías de ixtle en Soyaló, Chiapas

Soyaniquilpan de Juárez ◆ Municipio del Estado de México situado en el norte de la entidad, contiguo a Jilotepec, en los límites con Hidalgo. Superficie: 116.18 km². Habitantes: 8,370, de los cuales 2,369 forman la población económicamente activa. Hablan alguna lengua indígena ocho personas mayores de cinco años. La cabecera es San Francisco Soyaniquilpan.

Glifo de Soyaniquilpan de Juárez, Estado de México

Soyopa ◆ Municipio de Sonora situado al este de Hermosillo y al noreste de Guaymas. Superficie: 846.33 km². Habitantes: 1,931, de los cuales 628 forman

Castilla, óleo sobre tela de Arturo Souto

Herbert Spencer

Luis Spota

la población económicamente activa.

Spell, Jefferson Rea ◆ n. y m. en EUA (1886-1967). Doctor en filosofía por la Universidad de Pennsylvania (1931). Fue profesor de lenguas romances en la Universidad de Texas durante 40 años y profesor huésped de la UNAM (1944 y 46). En 1949 preparó y prologó una edición de *El periquillo sarniento*, de José Joaquín Fernández de Lizardi. Fue miembro de las asociaciones de Lenguas Modernas y la Americana de Profesores de Español. La Academia Mexicana (de la Lengua) le otorgó un diploma de honor por su trabajo en favor de las letras mexicanas.

Spencer, Herbert ◆ n. en Inglaterra y m. en EUA (1820-1903). Se tituló como ingeniero civil en 1837, pero se retiró de esa profesión (1845) para dedicarse a la filosofía y la sociología, de la que está considerado uno de los fundadores. Su obra ejerció una notoria influencia en varias generaciones de estudiosos mexicanos, especialmente en el área de la educación. Construyó un sistema filosófico, apoyado en las ideas evolucionistas de Charles Darwin y en sus propios estudios sobre las culturas precolombinas americanas. De su amplia producción, es de especial interés para México su *Descriptive Sociology of the Mexicans, Central Americans, Chibchas and Peruvians*, del que Daniel y Genaro García tradujeron y precisaron, echando mano de las fuentes citadas, las partes que forman los volúmenes *Los antiguos mexicanos* (1896) y *El antiguo Yucatán* (1898).

Spinoso Foglia, Roque ◆ n. en Venustiano Carranza y m. en el rancho El Relicario, Ver. (1930-1984). Miembro del PRI. Secretario general del Comité Ejecutivo Estatal del Sindicato de Empleados de la Industria Azucarera en Veracruz (1962-67), asesor del Sindicato de Despalilladores de Tabaco de la Región de Los Tuxtlas (1968-69), presidente del Comité Ejecutivo Estatal de la Federación Veracruzana de Productores de Caña de Azúcar (1971-76), secretario general del Consejo Directivo de la Alianza Nacional de Productores de Caña de Azúcar (1971-76), fundador y secretario general de la Unión Nacional de Productores de Caña de Azúcar (1977- 80), suplente del secretario general de la CNC ante el Fondo para Obras Sociales a Campesinos Cañeros de Escasos Recursos (1980-83) y presidente del Comité Ejecutivo de la Unión Nacional de Productores de Caña de Azúcar. Fue síndico suplente del ayuntamiento de Martínez de la Torre, Veracruz (1968-71), diputado local (1974-77), diputado federal suplente (1979-82) y diputado federal por Veracruz (1982-84). Murió asesinado.

Spitalier André, Emilio ◆ n. en Francia y m. en el DF (1892-1970). Empresario. Llegó a la ciudad de México en 1910 y se dedicó a los negocios comerciales, junto con su hermano Ernesto. Fue presidente de El Puerto de Veracruz, de la papelera San Rafael y de la Negociación Fabril de Soria.

Spitalier André, Ernesto ◆ n. en Francia y m. en el DF (1891-1971). Empresario. Hermano del anterior. Participó como combatiente en la primera guerra mundial. Estudió ingeniería industrial en Inglaterra y llegó a México para dedicarse a los negocios comerciales. Fue gerente de S. Robert y de El Puerto de Veracruz, presidente del consejo de administración de Negociación Fabril de Soria, vicepresidente del Banco Nacional de México y consejero de Industria Eléctrica de México, Celanese, Seguros América, La Carolina y Reforma y Lanera de México.

Spota, Luis ◆ n. y m. en el DF (1925-1985). Su nombre completo era Luis Mario Cayetano Spota Ruotti Castañares. Periodista y escritor. Autodidacto. Trabajó como fotógrafo de la revista *Hoy* (1939-43), de donde pasó, ya como reportero, a *Excélsior* (1943- 45), diario en el que, durante un mes y medio, ganó todos los días la primera plana con reportajes y entrevistas exclusivas. En 1945 se le designó director de la segunda edición de *Últimas Noticias*. Fue fundador de la Dirección de Educación Audiovisual de la SEP, director del suplemento *Heraldo Cultural* y de la revista *Espejo*. Colaboró en *Hoy, Mañana, El Heraldo de México, Esto, Así, Revista de América, Política* y *Novedades*. Condujo los programas de televisión *La hora 25* y *Fuera de serie*. Autor de los guiones y director de las películas *Nadie muere dos veces* (1952), *Amor en cuatro tiempos* (1954) y *Con el dedo en el gatillo* (1958). Autor de *José Mojica, hombre, artista y fraile* (1943) y *Biografía del licenciado Alemán* (1946); del volumen de cuentos *De la noche al día* (1945); de las obras de teatro *Ellos pueden esperar* (1949) y *Dos veces la lluvia* (1949); y de las novelas *El coronel fue echado al mar* (1947, ganadora del Concurso Nacional de Literatura), *Murieron a mitad del río* (1948), *Vagabunda* (1950), *La estrella vacía* (1950), *Más cornadas da el hambre* (1950, Premio Ciudad de México), *Las grandes aguas* (1954, llevada al cine), *Casi el paraíso* (1956), *Las horas violentas* (1958), *La sangre enemiga* (1959, llevada al cine), *El tiempo de la ira* (1960), *El aria de los sometidos* (1962), *La carcajada del gato* (1964), *La pequeña edad* (1964), *Los sueños del insomnio* (1966), *La plaza* (1972), *Las cajas* (1973), *El viaje* (1973), *Retrato hablado* (1975), *Palabras mayores* (1975), *Sobre la marcha* (1976), *El primer día* (1977), *El rostro del sueño* (1979), *Mitad oscura* (1982), *La víspera del trueno* (1982) y *Lo de antes* (1981); así como de los argumentos cinematográficos *Cadena perpetua* y *En la palma de tu mano* (1952, premiado con un Ariel). Dejó inconclusa la novela *Los que no volvieron*. Fue miembro de la Asociación Nacional de Box, presidente de la Comisión de Box y Lucha del DF y presidente fundador del Consejo Mundial de Boxeo. En 1988 se publicó el libro *La época de oro sin nostalgia (Luis Spota en el cine 1949-1959)*, de Elda Peralta.

Spratling, William ◆ n. en EUA y m. cerca de Iguala, Gro. (1900-1967). Arquitecto titulado en la Universidad de Auburn, Alabama. Fue profesor de la Universidad de Tulane (1921-29). Llegó a México en 1929 y fijó su residencia en Taxco, donde se dedicó a la elaboración de artesanías de plata y formó un taller de artesanos del ramo, que después se convirtió en una empresa productora de platería artística. Se dedicó también a la horticultura, la caricatura, la aviación y la arqueología. Promovió la plástica mexicana en Estados Unidos y, patrocinado por la institución Carnegie organizó una gran exposición de arte mexicano que se presentó durante tres años. Fue colaborador del *New York Herald Tribune*. Autor de *Little Mexico* (1926, reeditado en 1965 como *A Small Mexican World*), *Figures in a Mexican Renaissance* (1926, en colaboración con William Faulkner), *Old Plantation Houses in Louisiana* (1929), *The Frescoes of Diego Rivera* (1930), *File on Spratling: an Autobiography* (1932), y *More Human than Divine* (1960). Murió en un accidente automovilístico. Donó su colección de piezas arqueológicas a un museo de Taxco que ahora lleva el nombre de Guillermo Spratling. En 1944 la Warner Brothers produjo *The Man from New Orleans*, documental sobre los primeros años de Spratling en México. Fue miembro del Instituto Americano de Arquitectos.

Sri Lanka, República Socialista Democrática de ◆ Nación insular asiática situada en el océano Índico, al sureste de la India, de la que está separada por el estrecho de Palk. El nombre Sri Lanka, antes Ceilán, significa "La isla esplendorosa". Tiene una superficie de 65,610 km² y 18,455,000 habitantes (1998). Su capital administrativa es Colombo (615,000 habitantes en 1990) y la legislativa y judicial es Sri Jayewardenepura Kotte (109,000). Los idiomas oficiales son el cingalés y el tamil, aunque se utiliza también el inglés. *Historia*: poblada originalmente por los vedas, la isla de Ceilán fue invadida sucesivamente por migraciones cingalesas, indoeuropeas y tamiles. El *Mahavansa*, crónica de los reyes cingaleses escrita en el siglo V, narra la historia del país desde su colonización por el príncipe bengalí Vijaya hasta la muerte del rey Mahasena. En 1505 los portugueses llegaron a la isla, que se hallaba dividida en siete reinos, y la colonizaron; los lusitanos fueron desplazados en 1655 por los holandeses y éstos, a su vez, por los británicos en 1796, aunque los ingleses no pudieron derrotar la última resistencia cingalesa sino hasta 1815. El mango, fruto que se considera originario de este país, fue llevado a México en el siglo XVII por el Galeón de Filipinas. Un movimiento nacionalista que culminó en 1948 convirtió a Ceilán en un Estado de la Mancomunidad Británica de Naciones. Con Salomón W. R. D. Bandaranaike como primer ministro (1956-59), Ceilán inició una activa política exterior signada por el anticolonialismo y promovió la reunión Cumbre de Países Afroasiáticos, antecedente del Movimiento de Países no Alineados. A fines de los años cincuenta, un grupo separatista tamil protagonizó un levantamiento que culminó con el asesinato, en 1959, de Bandaranaike; un año después, la viuda del primer ministro, Sirimavo Bandaranaike, llegó al gobierno al frente del Partido de Liberación de Sri Lanka, y se convirtió en la primera jefa de Estado del mundo. En 1962, Bandaranaike nacionalizó las compañías petroleras y propiedades extranjeras y tuvo serias diferencias con Estados Unidos e Inglaterra, países afectados que no estuvieron de acuerdo con el monto de sus indemnizaciones. En 1965 Sirimavo Bandaranaike fue derrotada en los comicios por el Partido de Unión Nacional, dirigido por Dudley Senanayake. En 1970 una coalición del Partido Independentista con el Comunista y los trotskistas llevó a Bandaranaike de nuevo al poder. En 1972, ésta rompió con la Mancomunidad Británica, proclamó la República y promulgó la primera Constitución. En ese mismo año se establecieron las relaciones diplomáticas con México, país que Bandaranaike visitó el 17 de junio de 1975. El siguiente 24 de julio, el entonces presidente mexicano, Luis Echeverría, se entrevistó con ella en Colombo. Después de celebrarse en Colombo, en 1976, la Conferencia de Países no Alineados, Bandaranaike fue derrotada en los comicios por la oposición de derecha, que ha reavivado el conflicto con la etnia tamil, de la que una facción exige crear un Estado propio en la isla y se ha mantenido en guerra desde entonces.

WILLIAM SPRATLING

Taxco, 1930s

"MANY OF THE BEST-RUN SILVER SHOPS IN TAXCO HAVE BEEN SET UP BY SILVERSMITHS WHO HAVE BEEN ENCOURAGED BY DETACHED AMERICAN WOMEN."

BUYING THE HOUSE IN TAXCO HAD BEEN A SOlution for the writing of *Little Mexico;* being the first house I had ever owned, I rapidly fell in love with it. For the sixteen years I lived there, it never ceased to give me a deep and very personal satisfaction.

One of the first things I did was to make a map of the house as it was, locating and identifying every tree, bush and herb in the garden. The abruptness of the terrain in Taxco is probably what is mainly responsible for its charm. It is practically a vertical site—the variety of combinations, as rooms are adjusted to the separate levels, plus the fact that most of the domestic architecture is humble and

WILLIAM SPRATLING • 147

Texto de William Spratling sobre Taxco

Stack, Juan ◆ n. en el DF (1951). Su nombre es Juan Ernesto Martínez Stack. Estudió en el Centro Universitario de Teatro (1970). Licenciado en literatura dramática y teatro por la UNAM (1976). Como actor del teatro universitario (1969-84), representó a México en diversos festivales internacionales en Belgrado y Praga (1974), Berlín, Amsterdam y Zurich (1982), Boston, Washington y Nueva York (1984). En el Departamento de Teatro de la UNAM fue coordinador de publicaciones, coordinador técnico de teatros, coordinador de teatro estudiantil y jefe de personal del Centro Universitario de Teatro (1973-82). Ha sido locutor de Radio UNAM y de diversos programas de radio y televisión del sector público.

Jorge Stahl

Stahl, Jorge ◆ n. en Puebla, Pue., y m. en el DF (1886-1979). Fotógrafo de cine. En 1901 instaló un laboratorio de fotografía en Guadalajara. Tres años después viajó a Estados Unidos, donde adquirió su primera cámara de cine. Produjo *Ladrón de bicicletas* (1906). En 1921 hizo la fotografía de *El crimen de otro*. Produjo *Bolcheviquismo* (1922), *Aguiluchos mexicanos* (1924), *México, país de romance* (1925), *El secreto de la abuela* (1928), *Los hijos del destino* (1929), *La boda de Rosario* (1929) y *Tiburón* (1933) Se incorporó en 1942 a los estudios de Cinematográfica Lati-

Santa, película dirigida por Antonio Moreno y fotografiada por Jorge Stahl

noamericana (Clasa), de la que fue gerente hasta 1945, cuando fundó y pasó a dirigir los estudios San Ángel Inn. Procesó más de 500 películas y, como fotógrafo, destacó su trabajo en *Mi esposa y la otra* (1951).

STAMATIADES, KLEÓMENES ◆ n. y m. en el DF (1944-1991). Licenciado en pintura por la Academia de San Carlos (1971). Estudió producción teatral en la UNAM y en la Universidad Veracruzana. Fue profesor en preparatorias, en la UNAM y en la Universidad Veracruzana (1976-79). Pintor, escenógrafo y diseñador de vestuario. En 1971 se incorporó, como escenógrafo, al Taller Coreográfico de la UNAM. Como pintor expuso individualmente su obra 18 veces. Hizo más de 30 escenografías para teatro y danza, y numerosas escenografías y ambientaciones para cine, como las de *Simón Blanco*, *La mujer del prójimo*, *La ley del monte*, *Las mariposas disecadas*, *Los japoneses no esperan*, *El lugar sin límites*, *Los ojos de un niño* y *Noa Noa*, entre otras. Premio por la mejor escenografía y vestuario por *Las alegres comadres de Windsor* (1983) por la Unión de Críticos y Cronistas de Teatro. Premio a mejor vestuario en el festival del Chamizal por *Examen de maridos*.

Rodolfo Stavenhagen

STAMPA ORTIGOZA, MANUEL LUIS ◆ n. en Guadalajara, Jal., y m. en Cuernavaca, Mor. (1881-1930). Ingenierio civil y electricista por el Instituto Industrial del Norte de Francia (1906). Profesor en la Escuela Nacional de Artes y

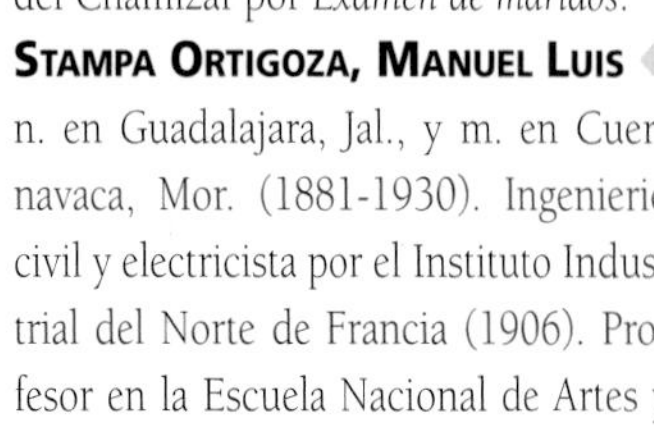

Oficios de la ciudad de México (1907-16). Trabajó en la Compañía de Luz y Fuerza (1908-19). Fue uno de los primeros mexicanos en operar aparatos radiorreceptores en el país. En 1915 fundó la Escuela Práctica de Ingenieros y Mecánicos Electricistas, que dirigió y cuyo primer plan de estudios formuló. Como ingeniero civil construyó el puente para ferrocarril de Surumuato, Querétaro, y las escolleras de Coatzacoalcos, Salina Cruz y Mazatlán. Edificó numerosas casas y fincas en Cuernavaca y el Distrito Federal, en las que introdujo el uso de materiales prefabricados. Autor de *Lecciones de electricidad industrial profesadas en la Escuela N. de Artes y Oficios para hombres, de México* (1908).

STAUFFER, TEDDY ◆ n. en Suiza y m. en Acapulco, Gro. (1907-1991). Músico. Llegó a México en los cuarenta, con su esposa, la actriz Heddy Lamarr. Se destacó su desempeño en el violín. Viajó a Acapulco y ahí creó los centros nocturnos La Perla y el Pavillón. Fue uno de los principales promotores del puerto turístico. Se hizo socio de varios hoteles.

STAVANS, ILÁN ◆ n. en el DF (1961). Escritor. Vive en Nueva York, donde es profesor de la Universidad de Columbia. Ha sido colaborador de *Excélsior*. Coautor, con Zuri Balkoff, de *Talía y el cielo o El libro de los ensueños* (novela corta, Venezuela 1979, reeditada en México en 1990). Autor de *Manual del (im)perfecto reseñista* (1989) y *Prontuario* (1992).

STAVENHAGEN, RODOLFO ◆ n. en Alemania (1932). Su segundo apellido es Gruenbaum. Naturalizado mexicano en 1949. Bachellor of arts por la Universidad de Chicago (1951), maestro en ciencias antropológicas por el INAH (1958) y doctor en sociología por la Universidad de París (1963). Ha sido investigador universitario; secretario general del Centro Latinoamericano de Ciencias Sociales, con sede en Brasil (1962-64), profesor (1972-), investigador y director del Centro de Estudios Sociológicos de El Colegio de México (1972-77), director general de Culturas Populares de la SEP (1977-79) y subdirector general de la UNESCO para ciencias sociales (1979-82) Coautor de *El ingenio del hombre* (1976). Autor de *Las clases sociales en las sociedades agrarias* (1969), *Agrarian Problems and Peasant Movements in Latin America* (1970), *Sociología del subdesarrollo* (1972), *Estructura agraria y desarrollo agrícola en México* (1974), *Capitalismo y campesinado en México* (compilación, 1975), *Testimonios* (1978), *Problemas étnicos y campesinos. Ensayos* (1980) y *Derecho indígena y derechos humanos en América Latina* (1988). Presidente de la Academia Mexicana de Derechos Humanos (1984-). Premio de Economía Banamex (1970), Premio de Ciencias Sociales Elías Sourasky (1973) y Premio de Universitario Sobresaliente de la UNAM (1982). Beca Guggenheim 1990-91. Premio Nacional de Ciencias y Artes (1997).

STÁVOLI, JOSÉ AGUSTÍN HILARIO ◆ n. en Italia y m. en Oaxaca, Oax. (1795-1853). Militar incorporado en 1810 al ejército napoleónico, con el que hizo las campañas de Rusia (1812) y de Alemania (1813-14) y con el que combatió en Waterloo (1815). Se ignora cuándo llegó a México, pero en 1821 formó parte del Ejército Trigarante. Se unió al Plan de Casa Mata (1823), contra Agustín de Iturbide, se unió a la sublevación de Lobato (1824) contra el Supremo Poder Ejecutivo y al fracasar ese movimiento, fue condenado a muerte por un tribunal militar. Le fue conmutada la pena por gestiones de su esposa, Leonarda Tolsá, hija de Manuel Tolsá. Se le desterró a Nueva Orleans y, acogido a la amnistía de 1825, volvió a México. Fue ayudante del comandante general del Estado Unido de Occidente, José Figueroa, y participó en las campañas contra apaches y seris. Se retiró con licencia a la ciudad de México (1826), pero volvió a filas en 1829 para combatir la invasión de Isidro Barradas, a las órdenes de Antonio López de Santa Anna. Durante el movimiento de Jalapa, encabezado por Anastasio Bustamante, permaneció fiel a Vicente Guerrero. Tras el asesinato de éste se retiró a la vida privada en Tampico, pero volvió a luchar en la sublevación contra Bustamante. Fue comandante militar de Matamoros (1833) y combatió a Mariano Arista (1834). Se retiró del ejército en 1840 y regresó a filas en 1846 para combatir la invasión estadounidense, en el curso de la cual obtuvo el grado de general. En 1851 se le asignaron funciones en Tehuantepec y en la ciudad de Oaxaca, donde murió en una epidemia de cólera.

Steck, Francis Borgia ◆ n. y m. en EUA (1884- 1962). Fraile franciscano. Doctor en historia por la Universidad Católica de Washington (1927). Se dedicó al estudio de la historia de la evangelización en México. Formó la Biblioteca Fraborese en el Colegio de Quincy, con unos 3,000 títulos sobre historia de la América española. Publicó una versión de la *Historia de las Indias*, de Motolinia. Coautor de *Historia de las misiones de California* (1921). Autor de *Colegio de Sta. Cruz de Tlatelolco* (1944) y *Marquette Legends* (1960).

Steele, Harry ◆ n. en Austria y m. en EUA (1890-1976). Empresario. Vivió en Estados Unidos desde su infancia. Durante su servicio militar fue destacado a Filipinas. Más tarde abrió una joyería en San Antonio, Texas, que pronto tuvo una sucursal en Monterrey, Nuevo León. En 1921 llegó a la ciudad de México, donde estableció la compañía H. Steele y fundó, entre otras, las fábricas Industrias Steele de México, Industria Relojera Mexicana, Oneida Mexicana y Tiempo, dedicadas a la elaboración de muebles de oficina, artículos de cocina, cubiertos y relojes.

Steele, Peter Wesley ◆ n. en EUA (1953). Periodista. Llegó a México en 1967 por un programa de intercambio académico. Licenciado en Relaciones Internacionales por la UNAM. Fue editor de las revistas *Contextos*, de la Secretaría de Programación y Presupuesto (1977-82) y *Ámbitos* (1982-84). Cofundador del diario *La Jornada*, donde dirigió la sección de información internacional (1984-85). En 1985 se trasladó a Italia, como funcionario de la agencia IPS. En septiembre de 1987, durante unas vacaciones, desapareció en Puerto Escondido, Oaxaca.

Stéfano Sahagún, Marco Antonio de ◆ n. en Chihuahua, Chih. (1951). Licenciado en derecho por la UNAM. Profesor de derecho en varias universidades. Comisionado del IEPES del PRI en las campañas presidenciales de 1988 y 1994. En la Secretaría de Comunicaciones y Transportes ha sido asesor del secretario (1976-78), director jurídico de la Comisión Nacional de Caminos y Puentes (1983-86), director de Organización (1986-88), director general de Modernización (1988-94) y director general de Puertos (1994-95). Director general de Asuntos Jurídicos de la SSA (1995-).

Steinsleger, José ◆ n. en Argentina (1947). Periodista y académico. Ha vivido en México de 1972 a 1978 y desde 1995. Con su nombre o con el pseudónimo de *Ricardo Parra* ha colaborado en *Personas*, *Los Universitarios*, *Excélsior*, *El Sol*, *Ovaciones*, *La Jornada* y otros medios. En Ecuador fue corresponsal de Alasei. Ha organizado talleres de periodismo y poesía en varias universidades. Fue representante del SUTERM en Sudamérica y miembro fundador de la Federación Latioamericana de Periodistas y de la Unión de Periodistas Democráticos de México. Organizó el primer Comité de Solidaridad con Nicaragua y fue secretario de prensa del Comité de Solidaridad con Argentina. Autor de *Imperialismo y sindicalismo en América Latina* (1976), *Bases militares en América Latina* (1980), *La batalla en Argentina* (1985) y *Panamá en el año del dragón* (1988).

Stephens, John Lloyd ◆ n. y m. en EUA (1805-1852). Licenciado en derecho por la Universidad de Columbia (1922). Se incorporó al servicio exterior y fue embajador de Estados Unidos en París, Roma y Londres. Realizó dos viajes de exploración a las zonas arqueológicas mayas (1839-40 y 1841-42), en compañía del dibujante inglés Frederick Catherwood. Autor de *Incidents of Travel in Central America, Chiapas and Yucatan* (2 t., 1841), *Incidents of Travel in Yucatan* (1843) y *Chichen* (1846).

Stephens García, Manuel ◆ n. en Bellavista, Nay. (1925). Estudió en la Escuela Normal Superior, donde se especializó en ciencias sociales. Ha sido dirigente de los estudiantes normalistas y de las Juventudes Obreras de Jalisco y Nayarit. Fue miembro de la Dirección Nacional del Partido Popular Socialista (1961-68), dirigente en el DF y secretario de Prensa de esa organización. Secretario general del Partido del Pueblo Mexicano (1976-82). Cofundador, miembro de la Comisión Política y jefe del departamento de Relaciones Políticas del Comité Central del PSUM (1982). Tres veces diputado federal (1961-64, 1970-73 y 1979-82) y editorialista de *Excélsior*. Dos veces candidato a gobernador de Nayarit (una por el PPS y otra por la Coalición de Izquierda). Fundador de la Organización para la Solidaridad de los Pueblos de Asia, África y América Latina (OSPAAAL) y miembro del Consejo Mundial de la Paz.

Stern, Claudio ◆ n. en el DF (1938). Su segundo apellido es Feitler. Licenciado en ciencias sociales y doctor en sociología por la Universidad de Washington. Ha sido profesor e investigador universitario, secretario ejecutivo del Programa de Investigaciones Sociales sobre Población en América Latina y director del Centro de Estudios Sociológicos de El Colegio de México. Coautor de *El ingenio del hombre* (1976), *Migración y desigualdad social en la ciudad de México* (1977), *Migraciones internas a la ciudad de México y su impacto sobre el mercado de trabajo* (1978) y *Hacia un modelo explicativo de las diferencias interregionales en los volúmenes de migración a la ciudad de México* (1979). Compilador de *La desigualdad social* (2 t., 1974). Autor de *Las regiones de México y sus niveles de desarrollo socioeconómico* (1973) y *Las migraciones rural-urbanas* (1974).

Stern, Miroslava ◆ n. en Checoslovaquia y m. en el DF (1926-1955). Actriz conocida como Miroslava. Salió

Marco Antonio Stéfano Sahagún

Libro escrito por John Lloyd Stephens

Foto: Colección Pascual Espinoza

Miroslava Stern

Margo Su

Claudio Suárez

Eduardo Suárez

de Checoslovaquia en 1938 y de ese año a 1945 estudió arte dramático en Estados Unidos y con Seki Sano, en México. Actuó en el teatro y el cine. Su primera película fue *Bodas trágicas* y la última *Ensayo de un crimen*, basada en la obra de Rodolfo Usigli. En 1954 formó parte de la delegación mexicana que asistió al Festival Cinematográfico de Venecia. Se suicidó. Sobre ella, en 1992 Guadalupe Loaeza escribió un libro que llevó al cine Alejandro Pelayo, ambos con el título *Miroslava*.

Stibi, George ◆ n. en Alemania (1901). Fue campesino, obrero y funcionario sindical antes de iniciarse en el periodismo. En 1930 era jefe de redacción del diario *Freiheit*, donde escribía contra el rearme de Alemania, por lo que pasó 28 meses en prisión, donde se dedicó a estudiar idiomas, arte y filosofía. Fue corresponsal en Moscú del diario comunista *Rote Fahne*. En 1935 dirigió las emisiones en alemán de Radio Moscú y a partir de julio de 1937, en Madrid, hizo lo mismo en *La Voz de España Republicana*. Al triunfo del franquismo pasó a Francia y de ahí vino a México. Aquí fue secretario del Movimiento Alemania Libre y se vinculó con los intelectuales de izquierda, a quienes invitó a colaborar en la revista *Alemania Libre*. Fue administrador del Taller de Gráfica Popular (1943-46) y organizador de sus exposiciones. En 1946 regresó a Alemania.

Stirner, Alfredo ◆ ☛ *Woog, Edgar*.

Stoopen, María ◆ n. en el DF (1940). Escritora. Su segundo apellido es Galán. Licenciada en lengua y literatura hispánicas y maestra en letras iberoamericanas por la UNAM y maestra en desarrollo humano por la Universidad Iberoamericana. Fue becaria del Taller de Ensayo Literario INBA-Fonapas (1979-80). Coordina talleres literarios. Ha colaborado en *Fem*, *Tierra Adentro*, *Casa Abierta al Tiempo*, *Páginas*, *Revista de la Universidad de México*, *La Semana de Bellas Artes*, *Reflejos*, *Texto Crítico*, *Comunidad* y *Educación* (de Puerto Rico). Coautora de *De la literatura. Homenaje a Sergio Fernández* (1983), *Todas mis amigas son poetas* (1983), *Nuestros mayores* (1984) y *Multiplicación de los Contemporáneos. Ensayos sobre la generación* (1989). Obtuvo en 1978 el Premio Nacional de Ensayo José Revueltas, del INBA y el gobierno de Durango, por su trabajo *La muerte de Artemio Cruz: una novela de denuncia y traición*, obra publicada en 1982.

Stoyanov, Rumen ◆ n. en Bulgaria (1941). Poeta. Doctor en filología y letras hispánicas por la Universidad de Sofía, de la que es catedrático. Fue profesor del Centro de Enseñanza de Lenguas Extranjeras de la UNAM (1983-88). Ha traducido al búlgaro *Cien años de soledad*, *Historia verdadera de la conquista de la Nueva España*, *El llano en llamas*, el *Popol Vuh* y poemas mexicas y mayas, que ha difundido en su país, principalmente en las revistas *LIK* y *Rodna Rech*. Durante su estancia en México colaboró en *Plural*, *Excélsior*, *El Nacional* y otras publicaciones. Autor de *El quinto sol* (1985, antología de poesía precolombina mexicana, en colaboración con Nikola Indzhov). Tradujo al español una selección de poesía búlgara, *Pegaso herido*, que se publicó con versiones de Eduardo Langagne (1983).

Su, Margo ◆ n. en el DF y m. en EUA (1930-1993). Nombre profesional de Margarita Su López. Fue corista de los teatros Follies, Colonial, Arbeu y Lírico y bailarina solista de la carpa Libertad y del Teatro Margo. Se presentó en los programas de televisión *Puerta al suspenso*, *la hora Nescafé* y *Cabaret Waikikí*. Actuó en las telenovelas *Extraños caminos del ayer* y *El pecado de Oyuki*. Trabajó en las películas *Madres solteras*, *Las Leandras*, *División narcóticos*, *El jurado resuelve*, *Club de señoritas* y *Juventud desenfrenada* y en las obras de teatro *Conejo blanco*, *El pájaro azul*, *Fuera ropa*, *Las hermanitas de Acámbaro*, *Frivolidades*, *Engordó la caballada*, *Atlántida*, *Sigue tu onda* y *Naná*. Empresaria del Teatro Blanquita (1968-81 y 1989-91) y productora de recitales o conciertos de figuras de los espectáculos. Dirigió los centros nocturnos King Kong y Margo. Produjo la película *Las noches del Blanquita* y la serie de televisión *Amor perdido*. Colaboró en las revistas *Diva* y *Viva* y en el diario *La Jornada*, del cual fue fundadora. Autora de las obras de teatro *Las hermanitas de Acámbaro* y *Frivolidades* y de los libros *Alta frivolidad* (1989) y *Posesión* (1991, novela), el libreto cinematográfico para *Las noches del Blanquita* y los guiones de los programas de televisión *Amor perdido*, *Las chambitas de Paquita* y *Par de pares*.

Suaqui Grande ◆ Municipio de Sonora situado al sureste de Hermosillo y contiguo a Guaymas y Cajeme. Superficie: 889.28 km^2. Habitantes: 1,313, de los cuales 350 forman la población económicamente activa.

Suárez, Claudio ◆ n. en el DF (1968). Futbolista. Su segundo apellido es Sánchez. Le dicen *El Emperador*. Se inició en la UNAM en 1989 como defensa central y de ahí pasó al Guadalajara. A la selección nacional ingresó en 1992 y ha jugado más de 130 encuentros, siendo el jugador mexicano con más partidos de selección y el número ocho en todo el mundo (con 120 contra otras selecciones); ha participado en los mundiales de EUA 1994 y Francia 1998, así como en tres copas América (1993, 1995 y 1997) y los juegos Olímpicos de 1996.

Suárez, Eduardo ◆ n. en Texcoco, Edo. de Méx., y m. en el DF (1894-1976). Licenciado por la Escuela Nacional de Jurisprudencia (1917) y doctor en derecho por la UNAM. Fue delegado a la Conferencia para la Codificación del Derecho Internacional, en La Haya (1930), agente ante la Comisión Mixta de Reclamaciones México-Gran Bretaña (1931-32), agente ante la Comisión Mixta de Reclamaciones México-Francia (1933), asistió a Londres a la Conferencia Monetaria Internacional (1933) y fue secretario de Hacienda y Crédito Público (del 18 de junio de 1935 al 30 de noviembre de 1940 y del 1 de diciembre de 1940 al 30 de noviembre de 1946) en los gabinetes de Lázaro Cárdenas y de Manuel Ávila Camacho; con ese cargo fue gestor de la nacionalización de las empresas Huasteca Petroleum (estadounidense) y

Compañía Mexicana de Petróleo El Águila (inglesa) y delegado ante la Conferencia Económica Mundial de Bretton Woods (Washington, 1944) de donde surgieron el Fondo Monetario Internacional y el Banco Mundial. Embajador en Inglaterra (1965-71), miembro del Patronato de la UNAM, cofundador del IMSS, promotor de la creación de Puertos Libres Mexicanos, presidente de la comisión redactora de la Ley Federal del Trabajo y vicepresidente del Banco Comercial Mexicano.

SUÁREZ, HÉCTOR ◆ n. en el DF (1938). Actor. Se inició en la televisión en el programa *Chucherías* y actuó después, entre otros, en *Cosa juzgada, La cosquilla, Sábado loco loco loco* y *¿Qué nos pasa?*, del que fue protagonista. Ha participado en numerosas telenovelas. Trabajó en las películas *Lanza tus penas al viento* (1966), *La mujer de seis litros* (1966), *Los años verdes* (1966), *No se mande, profesor* (1967), *Ambición sangrienta* (1967), *La sorpresa* (1969, que le valió una Diosa de Plata), *Doña Macabra* (1971), *De qué color es el viento* (1972), *Valentín Lazaña, el ratero de los pobres* (1978), *En la cuerda del hambre* (1979, con la que ganó otra Diosa de Plata), *Lagunilla, mi barrio* (1980), *Lagunilla 2* (1981) y *El mil usos* (1983). Se presenta en teatro y centros nocturnos.

SUÁREZ, JORGE ◆ n. en el DF (1944). Pianista. Fue alumno de Guillermo Salvador y estudió en el Instituto Curtis de Filadelfia, en el Conservatorio Tchaikovsky de Moscú, en el Instituto de Altos Estudios Musicales de Montreux, en la Universidad del Sur de California y en la Academia Ravel de Francia. Tuvo su primera presentación en público a los nueve años de edad y ha sido integrante del Trío México, con Manuel Suárez y Leopoldo Téllez, así como de orquestas y conjuntos de cámara. Investigador y director (1984-) de la Escuela Nacional de Música. Ha grabado ocho discos y ha participado en audiciones para la radio en Alemania, Corea, Cuba, China y Holanda. Primer premio en el Concurso Internacional de Música Mexiana (1981).

SUÁREZ, LUIS ◆ n. en España (1918). Periodista. Fue capitán de milicias en la guerra civil española. Vino a la caída de la República y se naturalizó mexicano en 1941. Fue reportero de *Tiempo* y *La Prensa*, jefe de información de *Mañana* y *Siempre!* y colaborador de numerosas publicaciones. Condujo el programa de televisión *Luis Suárez siempre en el 11* (1977-). Escribe en *Excélsior*. Autor de *España comienza en los Pirineos* (1944), *La paz de los Morales* (1945), *Boda en Juchitán* (1948), *Otro mundo* (1954), *México sobreviviente* (1961), *Confesiones de Diego Rivera* (1962), *México antiguo en el siglo XX* (1969), *La guerra en la paz: Vietnam, Camboya y Laos* (1969), *México. Días de una ciudad* (1969), *Cuernavaca ante el Vaticano* (1970), *México, imagen de la ciudad* (1974), *De Tenochtitlan a México* (1974), *La contaminación* (1974), *Los países no alineados* (1975), *Fin del chantaje atómico* (1975), *Lucio Cabañas, el guerrillero sin esperanza* (1976; Premio del Club Primera Plana en 1977), *Echeverría rompe el silencio* (1979), *Entre el fusil y la palabra* (1980), *Petróleo, ¿México invadido?* (1981), *Echeverría en el sexenio de López Portillo* (1984), y *Cárdenas, retrato inédito* (1987). Premio de la Organización Internacional de Periodistas (1978 y 1988), Premio de la Unión de Periodistas de la Unión Soviética (1986) y Premio de la Unión de Periodistas de Cuba (1988). Es miembro fundador de la Unión de Periodistas Democráticos de México, de la que fue secretario de Relaciones Internacionales. Vicepresidente de la Organización Internacional de Periodistas (1980-) y secretario general de la Federación Latinoamericana de Periodistas (1985-).

SUÁREZ, MANUEL ◆ n. en España y m. en el DF (1896-1987). Empresario. Llegó a México en 1910 y poco después se unió a la revolución, en las filas de la División del Norte. Creó varios centros especializados en hotelería, turismo y gastronomía, entre ellos el Casino de la Selva, en Cuernavaca, y destacó también como protector o patrocinador de algunos pintores mexicanos: otorgó becas con las que se beneficiaron, entre otros, José Reyes, Francisco Icaza, Mario Orozco Rivera y el *Dr. Atl*. Como presidente del Consejo Ejecutivo de Administración, Suárez inició el proyecto México 2000 (complejo hotelero, comercial, cultural y turístico) que se vio interrumpido por dificultades financieras. A ese conjunto corresponden el Hotel de México y el Polyforum Cultural Siqueiros.

FOTO: GUILLERMO AGUILERA

Héctor Suárez

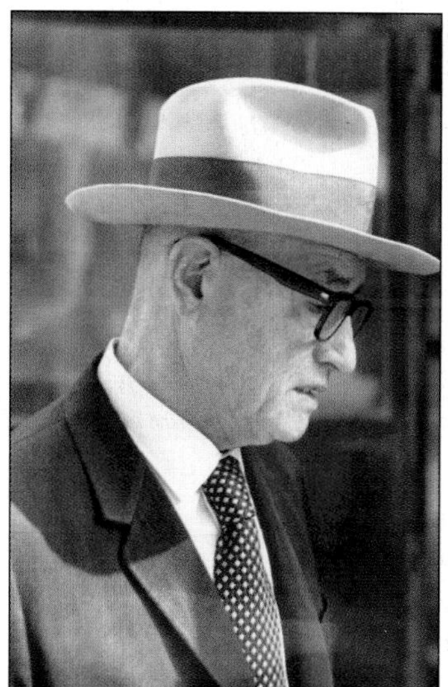

Manuel Suárez

SUÁREZ, MANUEL ◆ n. en el DF (1943). Violinista. Estudió en la Nueva Escuela de Música de Filadelfia, en el Instituto Curtis de Nueva York y en el Conservatorio Tchaikovsky de Moscú. Se inició profesionalmente en 1972, en el Carnegie Hall. Dirigió las escuelas de música de la Sociedad Orquestal de Thunder Bay y de la Universidad de Lakehead y dirigió la Orquesta Sinfónica Nacional (1973). Miembro fundador del Trío México, al lado de su hermano Jorge Suárez y Leopoldo Téllez (1975). Director de la Orquesta Sinfónica del Estado de México. Desde 1988 es profesor e investigador de la UNAM, del Conservatorio y de la Escuela Ollin Yoliztli. Ha sido dos veces jurado del concurso internacional de violín en Moscú (1982 y 1986).

SUÁREZ, VICENTE ◆ n. en Puebla, Pue., y m. en la ciudad de México (1833-1847). Su segundo apellido era

Vicente Suárez

Ferrer. Uno de los seis cadetes del Colegio Militar conocidos como los Niños Héroes. Fue el primero de ellos en morir ante la ofensiva de los invasores estadounidenses, cuando estaba en su puesto de centinela a la entrada del Castillo de Chapultepec, sede del Colegio.

Suárez Caamal, Ramón Iván ◆ n. en Calkiní, Camp. (1950). Escritor. Desde 1973 radica en Bacalar, Quintana Roo, donde ha sido director de Fomento Editorial y de la Casa Internacional del Escritor. Profesor de literatura y coordinador de talleres de poesía y cuento. Desde 1979 ha colaborado en numerosas publicaciones. Autor de *Poesía en acción* (1991; Premio Olga Arias 1991), *Pulir el jade* (1991, Premio Nacional de Poesía Jaime Sabines) y *Pejeluna* (1996), entre otros.

Suárez Cázares, Carlos ◆ n. en La Piedad, Mich. (1946). Sacerdote ordenado en 1972. Ha sido vicario cooperador de la parroquia de Pátzcuaro, presidente del Consejo Presbiterial, coordinador de la Comisión Arquidiocesana para la Promoción del Clero y director del Instituto Regional de Pastoral Don Vasco. Fue rector de los seminarios mayor y menor de Morelia hasta 1988, cuando se le designó obispo de Campeche.

Suárez Dávila, Francisco ◆ n. en el DF (1943). Licenciado en derecho por la UNAM (1961-65), maestro en economía por la Universidad de Cambridge (1965-67) con un posgrado en economía por la Universidad de París (1968-69). Profesor de la UNAM (1970-71) y del ITAM (1971). Integrante del Patronato de la UNAM (1991-). Miembro del PRI, en el que fue subsecretario de Asuntos Económicos Internacionales (1981-82). Ha sido economista de la Oficina Técnica (1970-71), director ejecutivo por México en el FMI (1974-76) y secretario de la Asamblea de Gobernadores de América Latina y Filipinas en el FMI y el Banco Mundial (1974- 76); gerente de Asuntos Económicos Internacionales (1977) y gerente general de Asuntos Internacionales del Banco de México (1978-80); director de Programación Financiera y Financiamiento Externo de Nafinsa (1980-82), subsecretario de Hacienda y Crédito Público (1982-88) y director general de Banca Somex (1988-91). Fue condecorado por el gobierno de Brasil. Miembro del Patronato de la UNAM (1991-). Representante de México ante la OCDE (1997-).

Lorenzo Suárez de Méndoza

Suárez Gamboa, Ricardo ◆ n. en Veracruz, Ver., y m. en Tampico, Tams. (1872-1915). Médico graduado en 1894. Se incorporó a la revolución maderista como miembro del Cuerpo Médico Militar y fue cirujano durante las campañas de Sonora, Guerrero y Oaxaca. Comisionado por el gobierno federal viajó a Europa para especializarse en técnicas quirúrgicas. Ingresó en la Academia Nacional de Medicina en 1899.

Suárez Inda, Alberto ◆ n. en Celaya, Gto. (1939). Se ordenó presbiterialmente en 1964 y su nombramiento episcopal como obispo de Tacámbaro ocurrió en 1985. Arzobispo de Morelia desde 1995.

Suárez Iriarte, Francisco ◆ m. en Toluca, Edo. de Méx. (?-1851). Abogado. Secretario de Hacienda (del 26 de enero al 18 de febrero de 1847) en el gabinete de Valentín Gómez Farías, y de Justicia (del 25 de marzo al 2 de abril de 1847) durante el gobierno de Antonio López de Santa Anna. Colaboró con los invasores estadounidenses a la caída del ayuntamiento encabezado por Manuel Reyes Veramendi; formó y presidió una asamblea municipal y, finalmente, ofreció un banquete a las fuerzas de ocupación en el que brindó por la anexión de México a Estados Unidos (1847). Tras la retirada de las tropas invasoras se inició un juicio en su contra por traición a la patria, pero aparentemente nunca se dictó el fallo.

Suárez de Mendoza, Lorenzo ◆ n. en España y m. en la ciudad de México (?-1583). Primo de Antonio de Mendoza, primer virrey de la Nueva España. Participó en la guerra de conquista de Túnez y fue patrono de la Universidad de Alcalá de Henares. Llegó a la ciudad de México en 1580 como quinto virrey de la Nueva España. Fue incapaz de controlar la corrupción generalizada entre los oidores, alcaldes y jueces de la audiencia y los corregimientos, por lo que solicitó un visitador a la Corona española. Felipe II envió con ese cargo a Pedro Moya de Contreras, quien sustituyó como virrey a Suárez, luego de su muerte. Autor de la novela *El pastor de Filida.*

Suárez Navarro, Juan ◆ n. en Guadalajara, Jal., y m. en la ciudad de México (1813-1867). Militar y político conservador. Fue partidario de Santa Anna y el encargado de traerlo de su destierro en 1853 para que ocupara por última vez la silla presidencial. En ese año alcanzó el generalato y más tarde fue oficial mayor de la Secretaría de Guerra. Luchó contra los revolucionarios de Ayutla y al triunfo liberal se exilió. Volvió a México en 1859, fue diputado por Yucatán y en 1860 combatió a los separatistas campechanos. Sirvió al imperio de Maximiliano y en 1865 se encargó de aplicar el decreto imperial de nacionalización de los bienes eclesiásticos.

Suárez Olvera, José ◆ n. en Querétaro, Qro., y m. en el DF (1922-1969). Pintor. Autor de la efigie de Benito Juárez que se halla en el Tribunal Superior de Justicia del Distrito Federal y de los cuadros que representan la vida de San Francisco de Asís, en el templo de San Francisco.

Suárez de Peralta, Juan ◆ n. en la ciudad de México y m. en España (¿1537?-¿1595?). Sobrino de Hernán Cortés. Encomendero. En 1579 marchó a España cuando Felipe II lo despojó de sus beneficios económicos, escandalizado por el "regocijo" con el que gastaba sus bienes al lado de su primo, Martín Cortés. Autor de un *Tratado de la caballería de la jineta y brida* (1580), primer libro escrito por un mexicano sobre temas profanos. Escribió también un *Tratado sobre alveitería* (inédito) y el *Tratado del descubrimiento de las Indias y su conquista* (1589) que no se publicó sino hasta 1878 como *Noticias históricas de la Nueva España*.

Suárez Pereda, José Rafael ◆ n. en Celaya, Gto. (?-1846). Algunos autores señalan que nació en Morelia, Michoacán. Abogado. Estudió en el Colegio de San Ildefonso. Doctor en derecho por la Real y Pontificia Universidad de México, de la que fue rector (1818-19 y 1819-20). También se desempeñó como rector del Colegio de Abogados, regidor y alcalde del ayuntamiento de Morelia, juez de distrito en la ciudad de México y en 1845 ministro de la Suprema Corte de Justicia de la Nación, de la que llegó a ser presidente.

Suárez de Peredo y Bezares, Francisco de Paula ◆ n. en Puebla, Pue., y m. en Italia (1823-1870). Abogado graduado en 1842 y sacerdote ordenado en 1848. Cura en Orizaba y en Puebla (1849-64), de donde fue expulsado por el gobernador Traconis. Primer obispo de Veracruz, ocupó ese cargo de 1864 hasta su muerte, ocurrida en Roma durante el Concilio Vaticano.

Suárez Rivera, Adolfo Antonio ◆ n. en San Cristóbal de Las Casas, Chis. (1927). Sacerdote ordenado en 1952. Ha sido profesor, director espiritual y prefecto de estudios del Seminario de San Cristóbal, secretario del oficio catequístico, capellán de Nuestra Señora de la Merced, confesor de religiosas y párroco de San Bartolomé de los Llanos, en la diócesis de San Cristóbal; miembro del equipo promotor de la Unión de Mutua Ayuda Episcopal, obispo de Tepic (1971-80) y de Tlalnepantla (1980-83) y arzobispo de Monterrey (1983-). En 1994 fue creado cardenal. En 1997 renunció, por motivos de salud, a la diócesis de Monterrey.

Suárez Torres, Ángel ◆ n. en Chiapa de Corzo y m. en Tuxtla Gutiérrez, Chis. (1929-1996). Licenciado en derecho por la UNAM (1947-51). Profesor de la Universidad Michoacana de San Nicolás de Hidalgo (1966) y de la Universidad de Coahuila (1970-71). Fue abogado postulante (1952-60), segundo secretario del Juzgado Segundo de Distrito en Materia Administrativa del DF (1960-62), secretario de Estudio y Cuenta de la Suprema Corte (1962-65), juez de distrito en Michoacán (1965-67), magistrado de circuito del Tribunal Colegiado de Saltillo (1967-79), presidente del Tribunal Superior de Justicia en Chiapas (1979-82), magistrado del Tribunal Colegiado del décimo circuito en Villahermosa (1983-84), magistrado del segundo tribunal Colegiado en Materia Administrativa del primer circuito del DF (1984), magistrado del Cuarto Tribunal Colegiado en Materia Administrativa del Primer Circuito del DF (1985-87) y ministro de la Suprema Corte (1987-96). Autor de un *Curso de actualización de amparo* (1975).

Suárez Torres, Gilberto ◆ n. en Oaxaca y m. en el DF (1912-1993). Abogado por la Facultad de Derecho de la UNAM (1932-37). Catedrático del Instituto de Ciencias y Artes de Oaxaca (1933-34), secretario (1933) y juez (1934) del juzgado segundo menor de la ciudad de Oaxaca, abogado consultor de la jefatura de policía (1935-46), abogado postulante, agente del Ministerio Público (1946-52) y subdirector de investigación de la PGJ del distrito y territorios federales. Jefe de la Dirección Federal de Seguridad (1952-58), subprocurador general de la República (1958-64) y procurador general de Justicia del Distrito y Territorios Federales (1964-70). Senador de la República (1970-76).

Suaste, Humberto ◆ n. en Champotón, Camp. (1954). Fotógrafo, tomó distintos cursos y asistió a seminarios en Estados Unidos y en la ciudad de México. Radica en Yucatán, donde promueve la actividad fotográfica. Ha expuesto sus obras en México y en Cuba. Participó en la edición de los libros *Capitalismo y vida rural en Yucatán* y *Ventanas de Latinoamérica*. Ha publicado fotografías en las revistas *Foto Zoom* y *Yucatán, Historia y Economía*. Autor del álbum *Tiempos del Mayab* (1988).

Suazo, Margarito ◆ n. y m. en la ciudad de México (1813-1847). Militar. Formaba parte del batallón Mina de la Guardia Nacional cuando ocurrió la invasión estadounidense. Participó, con el grado de capitán, en la batalla de Molino del Rey, el 8 de septiembre de 1847. Murió a consecuencia de las heridas recibidas en combate.

Subcomandante Marcos ◆ ☛ *Marcos.*

Subízar, Juan José ◆ n. en Durango, Dgo. (1804-1873). Abogado. Se tituló en 1827. Diputado local, presidente del Tribunal Superior de Justicia y varias veces gobernador interino de Durango (1848, 1850, 1850-51 y 1851, en sustitución de Marcelino Castañeda, y 1859, en reemplazo de Esteban Coronado). En 1859 fue llevado al Ejecutivo estatal por un motín que encabezó Tomás Borrego, pero se le desconoció casi de inmediato.

Sucilá ◆ Municipio de Yucatán situado en el noreste del estado y contiguo a Tizimín. Superficie: 256.76 km^2. Habitantes: 3,671, de los cuales 971 forman la población económicamente activa. Hablan maya 2,083 personas mayores de cinco años (monolingües: 48).

Suchiapa ◆ Municipio de Chiapas contiguo a Tuxtla Gutiérrez. Superficie: 355.2 km^2. Habitantes: 14,406, de los cuales 3,150 forman la población económicamente activa. Hablan alguna lengua indígena 19 personas mayores de cinco años (tzotzil 17).

Foto: Dante Bucio

Adolfo Suárez Rivera

Gilberto Suárez Torres

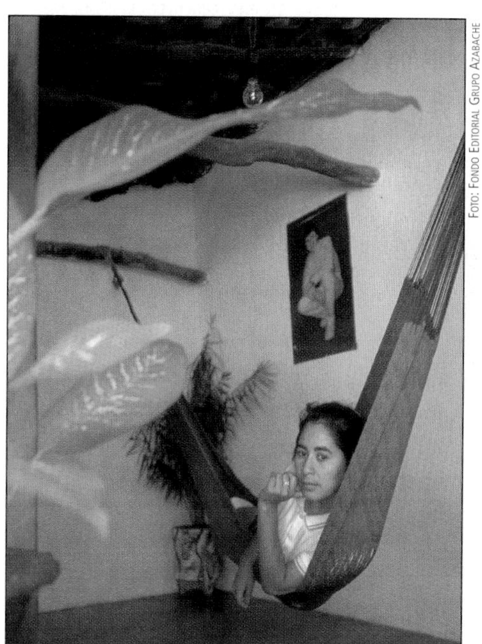
Foto: Fondo Editorial Grupo Azabache

Suchiapa, Chiapas

SUCHIATE ◆ Municipio de Chiapas situado en el extremo sur del estado, en los límites con Guatemala y en el litoral del océano Pacífico. Superficie: 303 km². Habitantes: 28,948, de los cuales 6,814 forman la población económicamente activa. Hablan alguna lengua indígena 36 personas mayores de cinco años (zapoteco 15). Su cabecera es Ciudad Hidalgo, antes Suchiate.

SUCHIATE ◆ Río de Chiapas. Nace cerca del volcán Tacaná, en la frontera México-Guatemala, y corre de norte a sur, marcando la línea divisoria entre ambos países, desde Unión Juárez hasta el océano Pacífico, en el que desemboca por la barra del mismo nombre. Recibe las aguas del río guatemalteco Cabús. En paso de Guarumo su curso se ve interrumpido por una presa irrigadora. Es sumamente caudaloso en verano y otoño.

SÚCHIL ◆ Municipio de Durango situado en el suroeste del estado, en los límites con Zacatecas. Superficie: 822.9 km². Habitantes: 7,512, de los cuales 1,631 forman la población económicamente activa. Hablan alguna lengua indígena 327 personas mayores de cinco años (tepehuano 325).

SUD ◆ Periódico editado por los insurgentes mexicanos. Se presume que José María Morelos encargó la elaboración de este órgano a José Manuel de Herrera, quien firmó con el pseudónimo de *Juan en el Desierto*. De acuerdo con la leyenda del cabezal de *Sud*, este era continuador de un desconocido *Despertador de Michoacán*. Sólo se conocen los números 51 y 53, el primero está datado en Oaxaca el 25 de enero de 1813 y el otro carece de fecha. Ambos aparecen como salidos de la Imprenta Nacional del Sur. En febrero del mismo año, sucedió a este periódico el *Correo Americano del Sur*, impreso también en Oaxaca, en el taller de José María Idíaquez.

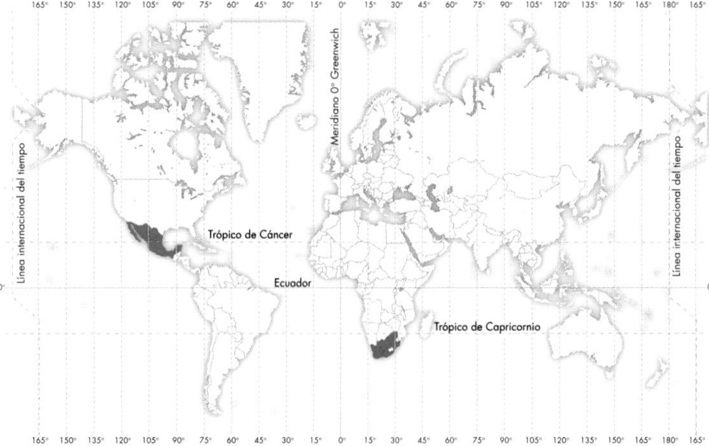

República de Sudáfrica

Timbre de la República de Sudáfrica

SUDÁFRICA, REPÚBLICA DE ◆ Nación ubicada en el extremo meridional del continente africano. Tiene costas en los océanos Atlántico e Índico y limita al norte con Namibia, Botswana y Zimbabwe. Superficie: 1,219,090 km². Habitantes: 39,357,000 en 1998. Su capital legislativa es Ciudad del Cabo (1,869,144 habitantes en 1991), la administrativa es Pretoria (1,080,187) y la judicial es Bloemfontein (300,150). Los idiomas oficiales son inglés y afrikaans, y también se hablan ndebele, swazi, xhosa, zulú, soto, tswana, tsonga y venda. Su moneda es el rand. *Historia*: en 1488 el navegante portugués Bartolomeu Dias llegó al cabo que llamó de Buena Esperanza, sitio donde hoy se levanta Ciudad del Cabo. A la llegada de los holandeses, en 1652, el actual territorio de Sudáfrica estaba ocupado por los bosquimanos (cazadores localizados en las zonas desérticas del oeste), los hotentotes (pastores de las costas meridional y oriental) y los bantúes (nómadas que ocupaban temporalmente zonas del norte y este). En 1652 los colonizadores holandeses fundaron la colonia Del Cabo. Durante el siglo XVIII las poblaciones nativas fueron desplazadas por sucesivas oleadas de guerreros zulúes, quienes acabaron por imponerse en la mayor parte del territorio sudafricano, desde donde atacaron, hasta principios del siglo XX, a los colonizadores blancos. En 1806 la colonia Del Cabo fue ocupada por los británicos. Ocho años después, como resultado de las guerras napoleónicas, Gran Bretaña obtuvo la posesión formal de la colonia. De 1835 a 1837 se produjo el "Gran Viaje", en el que los boers (descendientes de los colonizadores holandeses) emigraron hacia el norte para escapar del dominio británico y fundaron las naciones de Natal, Transvaal y Orange. En 1839 Natal se erigió en república y Transvaal lo siguió diez años después; en 1854 se declaró independiente el Estado Libre de Orange. Hacia 1866 se descubrieron enormes yacimientos de diamantes en Kimberley y en 1873 se encontró oro en Pilgrim's Rest. En 1877, Transvaal fue anexado por Gran Bretaña, pero se independizó en 1881. Debido al impulso anexionista británico se desató, en 1899, la llamada guerra de los Bóers, que concluyó en 1902 con el triunfo de los ingleses y su control sobre Transvaal y Orange. A principios del siglo XX era ya manifiesto el racismo exacerbado tanto de los bóers como de los nuevos detentadores del territorio; ningún sudafricano tenía acceso a los empleos calificados. En 1910 se constituyó la Unión de África del Sur, en los términos del *South Africa Act*, aprobada por la Cámara de los Comunes. En 1913 se promulgó el *Native Land Act*, que dio a los negros la propiedad de 8.9 millones de hectáreas, pero les prohibió poseer tierra en las áreas reservadas a los blancos. En la primera guerra mundial Sudáfrica participó al lado de los aliados y en 1915 ocupó el África Alemana del Sudoeste (Namibia). Igualmente, Sudáfrica se unió a los aliados en la segunda guerra mundial. En 1948 Sudáfrica aprobó la legislación separatista (*apartheid*) y, dos años más tarde, los decretos contra el terrorismo y contra el comunismo dieron al gobierno poderes casi ilimitados. En 1959, merced al Bantu Self-Government Act, se establecieron en Sudáfrica los bantustanes (hogares bantúes), que segregaban aún más a la población negra, relegándola a esa especie de campos de concentración. En 1961 Sudáfrica se constituyó en república y abandonó oficialmente la Comunidad Británica. Durante la década de los sesenta se creó el Congreso Nacional Africano (CNA) que organizó y dirigió la lucha de los sudafricanos negros que luchaban por sus derechos más elementales. En 1964 tuvo lugar el juicio de Rivonia, en el que ocho militantes del CNA, entre ellos Nelson Mandela, fueron condenados a cadena perpetua, acusados de subversión. En 1966 la ONU adoptó una resolución según la cual Sudáfrica perdía sus derechos de mandato sobre Namibia; tres años después el Consejo de Seguridad de la ONU condenó a Sudáfrica por desacatar dicha resolución. En 1976 se produjeron protestas antirracistas en Soweto, suburbio de la ciudad de Johannesburgo, que fueron reprimidas con saldo de varios cientos de muertos. Un año después, Steve Biko, líder de la resistencia negra, fue torturado hasta la muerte en una prisión; la ONU y Estados Unidos decretaron entonces un embargo a la venta de armas para Sudáfrica. En 1978 el ejército sudafricano entró en Angola para combatir a la guerrilla que pretendía la liberación de Namibia, y se involucró en la guerra civil de aquel país, al ocupar su porción sur y apoyar a los grupos paramilitares que combatían al gobierno de Luanda. Ese mismo año, Pieter Botha fue nombrado primer ministro, con lo que se inauguró en Sudáfrica la peor ola de represión contra negros y mestizos. En 1984 Botha fue elegido presidente y la resistencia antirracista aumentó, al grado que en 1986 el gobierno decretó el estado de emergencia en todo el país, mientras se ejecutaba selectivamente a las figuras (blancas o negras) más importantes del antirracismo. En 1987 aumentaron los disturbios y los 380,000 mineros del carbón y del oro se declararon en huelga, por lo que Botha decretó medidas dictatoriales de censura y aumentó la represión. En 1988 el arzobispo Desmond Tutu fue encarcelado; casi dos millones de trabajadores pararon en protesta por la eliminación del derecho de huelga mientras crecía la presión internacional para la liberación de Nelson Mandela. En 1989, alegando problemas de salud, Botha dejó en la presidencia a Frederik de Klerk, quien inició una serie de cambios en la tradicional política racista: acabó con la prohibición de los partidos políticos de izquierda, comenzó a excarcelar a militantes del CNA y eliminó la segregación en los transportes y sitios públicos de Johannesburgo. En 1990, Nelson Mandela quedó en libertad y comenzó una contraofensiva terrorista de organizaciones supremacistas blancas. Ese año Sudáfrica otorgó la independencia a Namibia. De Klerk anunció en 1991 que toda la población, sin importar su raza, podría votar. En 1994 Mandela ganó las elecciones presidenciales y tomó posesión ese mismo año. México estableció relaciones diplomáticas con Sudáfrica el 27 de octubre de 1993 y abrió su embajada en Pretoria en abril del año siguiente.

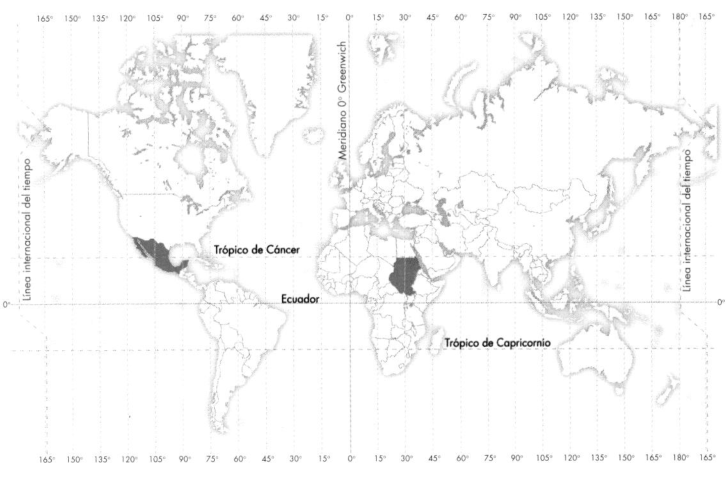

República del Sudán

SUDÁN, REPÚBLICA DEL ◆ Estado del noreste de África, situado en el litoral del mar Rojo. Limita al norte con Egipto, al este con Etiopía, al sureste con Kenia, al sur con Uganda y Zaire, al suroeste con la República Centroafricana, al oeste con Chad y al noroeste con Libia. Es el país más grande de África. La parte norte está ocupada por el extremo oriental del Sáhara y por el desierto de Libia. En el resto del territorio hay abundantes ríos que forman parte de la cuenca del Nilo. Superficie: 2,503,890 km². Habitantes: 28,292,000 (1998). Su capital ejecutiva es Jartum (924,505 habitantes en 1993) y la capital legislativa es Omdurmán (526,287). El idioma oficial es el árabe, pero en la región meridional del país es muy común el inglés y aún susbsisten unos 100 dialectos bantú, nilóticos y nilocamíticos. *Historia:* el actual territorio de Sudán era conocido por los egipcios como Khus y como Nubia por los griegos. En esta región no se consolidó un Estado hasta el siglo VIII a.n.e., cuando surgió el reino de Napata, que hacia el 730 a.n.e. conquistó al ya decadente imperio egipcio y los reyes de Napata fueron simultáneamente faraones, hasta el año 663 a.n.e., cuando Egipto fue conquistado por los asirios. Aun cuando éstos no incursionaron en Sudán, el reino Napata se disgregó y dio pie al surgimiento de los llamados Tres Reinos de las Cataratas: Nobatia, Dongola y Alodia, que mantendrían su autonomía durante unos 20 siglos y se convertirían en intermediarios de persas, griegos, romanos y árabes en su comercio de

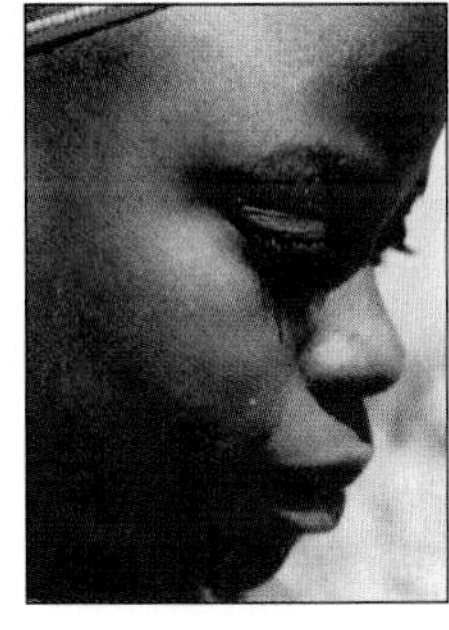
Joven sudanesa

esclavos, marfil o pieles provenientes del centro africano. Alrededor del siglo VI de nuestra era, debido a la influencia etíope, los Tres Reinos se convirtieron al cristianismo y en el siglo VII sufrieron una invasión árabe, lo que obligó al monarca de Dongola a pactar con los musulmanes la conversión de los Tres Reinos al islamismo, pero conservando la integridad territorial de su reino y de Alodia. En el siglo XIV los mamelucos egipcios destruyeron Dangola y hacia 1500 Alodia. Entre tanto, surgieron en el actual territorio sudanés tres reinos musulmanes: Sennar, Kordofan y Darfur. En 1820, el pachá egipcio Mahoma Alí inició la penetración en Sudán con el pretexto de exterminar a los mamelucos. Después de la derrota francesa del 5 de mayo de 1862, en Puebla, Napoleón III ordenó enviar a México 400 sudaneses del virreinato de Egipto, los que llegaron a Veracruz el 23 de febrero de 1863, destinados al servicio en tierras calientes. Para 1876, bajo un completo dominio egipcio, fue unificado el país. En 1881, el imán chiita Mahoma Ahmed, autoproclamado *mahdi* (redentor), inició una cruzada de "salvación del islamismo" y encontró inmediato apoyo entre la población, principalmente entre los árabes del norte. Las fuerzas británicas que habían ocupado Egipto en 1882 intervinieron en Sudán, pero no fueron capaces de dominar el país. En 1885 los mahdistas derrotaron a los ingleses, ocuparon Jartum y establecieron el primer gobierno nacional de Sudán, que se sostuvo hasta 1898, cuando se produjo la contraofensiva inglesa con apoyo de los franceses. Triunfantes los colonialistas, vino la disputa entre las dos potencias intervencionistas por la posesión de Sudán, lo que casi llevó a una guerra entre Francia e Inglaterra. Finalmente, el Reino Unido negoció la salida de los ejércitos franceses y a Sudán le impuso el estatus de "condominio" anglo-egipcio. Después de la primera guerra mundial, surgieron en África movimientos nacionalistas y antiimperialistas que poco a poco afianzaron sus posiciones. Para contrarrestar este fenómeno, la Corona británica procedió a dividir a los sudaneses con medidas como la prohibición de matrimonios interraciales, a fin de separar a la población negra del sur de los árabes del norte. Esa política rindió frutos. En 1950, los nacionalistas árabes sudaneses se organizaron; tres años más tarde, Sudán conquistó un estatuto de autogobierno y, en 1955, la elección de un parlamento, el que pronto proclamó la independencia. Sin embargo, la población negra del sur se vio desplazada de ese movimiento y, cinco meses antes de la proclamación de la independencia, se levantó en armas. La guerra civil duró 16 años y costó un millón de vidas. En 1969 el coronel Gaafar el-Nimeyri dio un golpe de Estado, proclamó la república democrática, otorgó autonomía administrativa al sur sudanés y le ofreció apoyo para la reconstrucción. En 1972, Nimeyri cambió su posición, rompió con los sectores que lo habían llevado al gobierno, se alió con las naciones conservadoras del área e ignoró los acuerdos tomados con la población negra. Los dirigentes del proscrito Partido Revolucionario Popular organizaron en Etiopía una fuerza guerrillera, la Anyanya, que ingresó al país y comenzó la lucha. En 1983 Nimeyri se reeligió y dos años después, en medio del mayor descrédito, fue derrocado por un grupo de militares dirigidos por el ministro de Defensa, Abdul Rahman Suwar al-Dahab, quien no consiguió la pacificación de los rebeldes del Ejército Popular de Liberación de Sudán, que controlaban casi todo el sur del país. México estableció relaciones diplomáticas con Sudán el 19 de octubre de 1982. En 1989 fue derrocado el primer ministro Sadik Mahdi, quien gobernaba desde 1986. Diez años después se realizaron elecciones y Omar al Bashir se convirtió en el hombre fuerte. Una intermitente guerra civil y las periódicas hambrunas caracterizan la vida del país, mientras el fundamentalismo islámico gana adeptos.

SUDZAL ◆ Municipio de Yucatán situado al este de Mérida y al sureste de Motul. Superficie: 436.87 km^2. Habitantes: 1,565, de los cuales 373 forman la población económicamente activa. Hablan maya 1,006 personas mayores de cinco años.

SUECIA, REINO DE ◆ Nación del norte europeo situada en la península de Escandinavia. Limita al oeste y norte con Noruega y al noroeste con Finlandia. El estrecho de Kattegat la separa de Dinamarca. Tiene costas en el golfo de Botnia y en el mar Báltico. Superficie: 449,964 km^2. Habitantes: 8,875,000 (1998). Su capital es Estocolmo (718,462 habitantes en 1997) y otras ciudades de importancia son Göteborg (454,016), Malmö (248,007) y Uppsala (184,507). El idioma oficial es el sueco y la enseñanza del inglés y una tercera lengua es obligatoria. Formalmente, la mayoría de la población está congregada en la Iglesia Luterana, pero de acuerdo con el Instituto Sueco "muy pocos demuestran interés en los servicios y actividades religiosas". En Suecia el rey es el jefe del Estado y el gobierno lo encabeza un primer ministro designado por el parlamento. Desde 1973 el rey de Suecia es Carlos XVI Gustavo. *Historia*: entre los años 7000 y 5000 a.n.e., Escandinavia era habitada por cazadores y recolectores que hacia el 3000 antes de nuestra era se asentaron alrededor de algunos de los 100,000 lagos del país y desarrollaron la agricultura. En el siglo IV de la era contemporánea, la tribu germánica *svear* (gente de mar), de la región del lago Mälaren, alcanzó cierta superioridad sobre las demás. La condición de buenos navegantes de los *svear* se manifestó principalmente en el llamado periodo vikingo, del año 800 al 1050, cuando hicieron viajes de exploración hacia América, establecieron colonias efímeras en Groenlandia y Vinlandia (nombre de una región que probablemente se localizaba en el oriente del actual Canadá), dominaban las rutas a Constantinopla y comerciaban con Asia y el resto de Europa. Se dice que Quetzalcóatl o Kukulkán era posiblemente un vikingo. Hacia el año 1000 se creó la Confederación Sverige, el reino de Svear, y los misioneros ingleses y alemanes iniciaron la cristianización del país que culminó en 1008, cuando el rey Skötkonung fue bautizado. Hacia el 1100 existía un embrionario Estado sueco, aunque sin un poder central efectivo. En el 1200 se inició un intercambio comercial cada vez más intenso entre los puertos alemanes de la Liga Hanseática y Escandinavia. En 1250 murió el rey Erik Eriksson y fue sustituido por su sobrino Valdemar, quien ocupó el sureste de Finlandia, unificó la legislación y estableció la capital nacional en Estocolmo. En 1275 llegó al trono Magnus Ladulas, quien introdujo las instituciones feudales. En 1397 la regente de Dinamarca, Margarita, logró la alianza de los cuatro reinos escandinavos (Suecia, Dinamarca, Noruega y Finlandia) en la Unión de Kalmar, para resistir la penetración económica y política de los alemanes. Hacia 1400 la supremacía danesa consagrada por la Unión de Kalmar suscitó en Suecia una rebelión dirigida por el caudillo campesino Engelbrekt. La segunda mitad del siglo XV se caracterizó por una agudización de las luchas por el poder entre las familias de la nobleza. Se constituyó la primera dieta con participación de los cuatro Estados: la nobleza, el clero, la burguesía y el campesinado. En 1523, dirigidos por el rey Gustavo Eriksson Vasa, los suecos se independizan de la Unión de Kalmar e iniciaron la reforma protestante. En 1611, el rey Gustavo II Adolfo inició el desarrollo sueco e involucró al país en la guerra de los Treinta Años, al lado de los protestantes, de la que salió victorioso. Después de la muerte de este rey, en 1632, los suecos continuaron su actividad militar en Europa. Axel Oxenstierna redactó la Constitución de 1634 y desempeñó el cargo de regente hasta la mayoría de edad de Cristina; ésta abdicó en 1654, se convirtió al catolicismo y se trasladó a Roma. Tras una serie de guerras con Dinamarca y Noruega, Suecia se anexó las provincias de Escania, Blekinge, Halland y Bohuslan (1658). Carlos XII luchó contra Dinamarca, Polonia y Rusia; después de los tratados de paz de 1719-21 se perdieron todas las provincias suecas al sur y al este del Báltico, excepto Pomerania y Finlandia. La reacción contra el absolutismo real culminó en la Constitución de 1719, que confirió atribuciones amplias al parlamento. De 1718 a 1772 la política estuvo dominada por el parlamento, en la llamada Era de Libertad, cuyo predominio se disputaban los partidos de los Sombreros (mercantilistas) y de los Gorros (liberales). En 1772, mediante un golpe de Estado, subió al trono Gustavo III, quien impuso su autoridad a la asamblea. Este rey fue asesinado luego de 20 años de monarquía despótica y Suecia se involucró en varias guerras internacionales, bajo el gobierno de Gustavo IV. En 1768 el marinero sueco Daniel Sidenstron o Sidcastron, conocido en la Nueva España como Daniel Siniestra, fue procesado en el virreinato acusado de herejía luterana; se le recluyó durante dos años en el convento de San Fernando; en 1774 fue nuevamente procesado por la Inquisición novohispana por herejía luterana y por bigamia y fue deportado a España. En 1805 Suecia se vio involucrada en las guerras napoleónicas. En 1809 el país perdió Finlandia en la guerra contra Rusia. Después de esta derrota, un movimiento popular obligó al rey a abdicar y se redactó una nueva Constitución, que equiparaba las atribuciones de la Corona y del Parlamento. Se dice que Felipe Lailson, quien tuvo una escuela de equitación en la ciudad de México durante el virreinato de Iturrigaray, era sueco. Este se unió a la insurgencia en 1812 y sirvió de enlace entre López Rayón y los Guadalupes. En 1814, el Tratado de Kiel unificó a Suecia y a Noruega, unión que terminó en 1905. En 1818, el mariscal francés Juan Bautista Bernadotte se convirtió en el rey Carlos XIV Juan, fundador de la dinastía que ocupa el trono. En 1826, representantes del gobierno sueco se entrevistaron con el presidente mexicano Guadalupe Victoria, para dar los primeros pasos hacia el establecimiento de relaciones diplomáticas, las que se formalizaron en 1885, cuando Suecia acreditó una representación diplomática ante el gobierno de Porfirio Díaz. En diciembre de 1865 el capitán sueco Erik

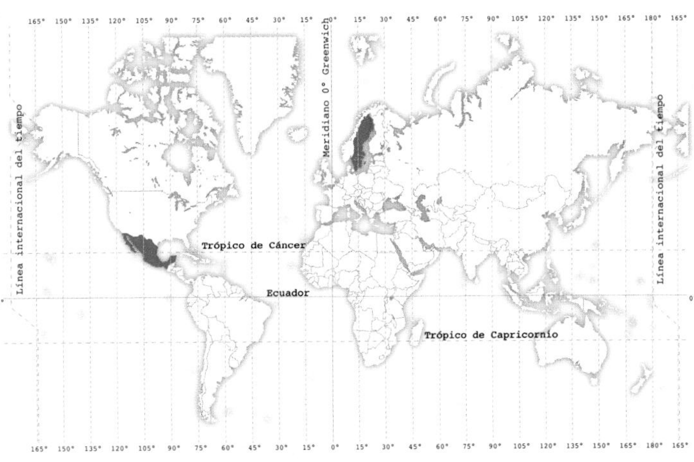

Reino de Suecia

Timbre del Reino de Suecia

Gustavo II Adolfo, rey de Suecia, inició el desarrollo de su país

Wulff manifestó a Matías Romero su decisión de combatir en las filas republicanas contra el imperio de Maximiliano y, por órdenes de Benito Juárez, en junio de 1866 fue incluido en el ejército de Mariano Escobedo. En 1865, en combate con los republicanos mexicanos, había muerto en Sonora el también sueco Emilio Langberg; éste había llegado a México en 1838, se unió a las fuerzas santanistas, en 1845 se pronunció con Paredes y Arrillaga en San Luis, participó en el cuartelazo de Mariano Salas en 1846, peleó contra los invasores estadounidenses en 1847, fue inspector de colonias militares en Chihuahua y formó parte del grupo comisionado para establecer la nueva línea divisoria de acuerdo con el Tratado de Guadalupe Hidalgo (1848), se unió a la revolución de Ayutla (1854) y en 1864 se adhirió al imperio de Maximiliano, quien lo hizo comandante general de Sinaloa. En 1866 la dieta sueca de los cuatro estados fue sustituida por un parlamento de dos cámaras. En 1954 se firmó un convenio de libre movimiento de población entre Suecia, Dinamarca, Finlandia, Noruega e Islandia. Una reforma constitucional en 1974 limitó las funciones del rey sueco a las meramente protocolarias. En 1975 el primer ministro Olof Palme visitó oficialmente México. El presidente mexicano José López Portillo viajó a Suecia y fue recibido en 1980 por el rey Carlos XVI Gustavo, quien dos años después correspondió a esa visita. En 1984 Palme volvió a visitar México para entrevistarse con el presidente Miguel de la Madrid. Palme y el presidente mexicano Miguel de la Madrid se reunieron en 1985, en la India, cuando se constituyó el Grupo de los Seis, en el que además de México, Suecia y la India participan Argentina, Grecia y Tanzania. El Reino de Suecia no se ha integrado a ningún pacto militar, permaneció neutral en las dos guerras mundiales del siglo XX y asiste como invitado a las reuniones del Movimiento de Países No Alineados.

SUFRAGIO EFECTIVO. NO REELECCIÓN ◆ Lema oficial del gobierno federal mexicano. En él sintetizó Francisco I. Madero, desde 1909, los objetivos de su lucha por la democracia. Empleó la frase en el Plan de Luis y en 1920 hicieron lo propio los firmantes del Plan de Agua Prieta.

Francisco I. Madero, creador de la frase "Sufragio efectivo. No reelección"

SUINAGA Y LUJÁN, PEDRO R. ◆ ¿n.? y m. en el DF (1905-1990). Estudió en Canadá (1921-25), donde también jugó futbol americano. Licenciado en derecho por la UNAM, en la que fue profesor. Jugador de futbol soccer, perteneció al equipo América (1925-28) y a la selección mexicana que asistió a los Juegos Olímpicos de Amsterdam (1928). En 1933 fundó el despacho de abogados Suinaga y Suinaga, donde laboró hasta 1965. Fue miembro y secretario del Consejo de Administración de *El Universal* (1955-65), embajador en Canadá (1965), vicepresidente de la Barra Mexicana-Colegio de Abogados. Miembro de la Asociación Mexicana de Golf y del Club Campestre de la Ciudad de México.

SUIZA ◆ País del centro de Europa que limita al norte con Alemania, al este con Liechtenstein y Austria, al sur con Italia, al suroeste y oeste con Francia. Su nombre oficial es Confederación Helvética. Superficie: 41,285 km². Habitantes: 7,116,000 (1997). La capital es Berna (127,469 habitantes en 1996) y otras ciudades de importancia son Zürich (343,869 habitantes), Basilea (174,007), Ginebra (173,559) y Lausana (115,878). Los tres idiomas oficiales de la Confederación son alemán, francés e italiano, aunque también es común el romanche o reto-románico. El gobierno suizo es ejercido por un Consejo Federal de siete miembros (elegidos cada cuatro años por la Asamblea Federal) que se alternan anualmente la presidencia del país. La Asamblea Federal, de dos cámaras, está integrada por el Consejo de los Estados (46 miembros) y el Consejo Nacional (200 miembros elegidos para un periodo de cuatro años). La economía suiza se basa en una intensa actividad turística y, sobre todo, en su calidad de sede de las principales organizaciones bancarias internacionales. *Historia*: alrededor del año 1000 a.n.e., el territorio de Suiza estaba habitado por el pueblo celta de los helvecios. Entre los siglos I antes de nuestra era y IV de nuestra era, los romanos dominaron el país y consolidaron una sociedad comercial. Por hallarse en una frontera natural entre el imperio romano y los "bárbaros" del norte, el territorio suizo sufrió invasiones de burgundios y alemanes que, al no poder internarse en territorio romano, se instalaron en el centro de los Alpes, lo que dio origen a la diversidad de culturas. En el año 800 el territorio pertenecía al imperio carolingio. En el 962 era parte del Sacro Imperio Romano Germánico. En los siglos XI y XII empezaron a conformarse los primeros estados feudales —el primero fue el de los Zahringen—. En el siglo XII se consolidaron los de los Kyburg y los Habsburgo, en tanto que los Zahringen desaparecieron. En 1273 Rodolfo de Habsburgo se coronó emperador de los cantones de Kyburg y Habsburgo; a su muerte se unieron a la incipiente confederación los de Schwyz, Uri y Unterwalden y, en 1291, los cinco cantones se unieron en un pacto perpetuo para mutua defensa. En 1308, tras el asesinato de Alberto de Austria, los cantones suizos lograron que Enrique VII de Luxemburgo confirmara sus derechos. En 1313 los suizos entraron en guerra contra el Sacro Imperio y resultaron vencedores dos años después. En 1352 el Sacro Imperio reconoció, mediante los tratados de Brandeburgo, la existencia de la Confederación. En 1474 una época de conflictos entre los cantones y el Imperio cesó con el tratado de paz perpetua. A partir de 1519 se produjeron enfrentamientos entre los cantones católicos y los protestantes, conflictos que terminaron con los Tratados de Westfalia (1648). En 1798, un grupo suizo, inspirado en la revolución francesa, proclamó la República Helvética, de tipo unitario. En 1803 fue dominada por Napoleón, quien le impuso un régimen federal. En 1815 el Congreso de Viena restauró la independencia de la Confederación, que a partir de entonces adoptó como Estado la más estricta neutralidad, al extremo de que no participa en bloques ni es miembro de la ONU, aunque sí pertenece a algunos organismos internacionales de cooperación. En 1817 vino a México en la expedición de Francisco Javier Mina, el mayor Maylefer, quien fue designado comandante de la caballería y destacó por su heroísmo. Murió por la Independencia Mexicana en el combate de la hacienda de Los Llanos. En 1827 Suiza abrió una oficina de negocios diplomáticos en México, a cargo de Karl Lavater. El 1 de enero de 1840, Antonio López de Santa Anna, a la sazón presidente, informó que estaban pendientes de aprobación los tratados celebrados con la Confederación Helvética. En 1847 se abrió el consulado suizo en la ciudad de México. En 1848 se promulgó en Suiza una Constitución federal que trató de poner fin a los conflictos religiosos surgidos entre los cantones. En 1855 el naturalista suizo Enrique Luis Federico Saussure (☛) participó en una expedición científica a México. En 1920 vino el suizo Edgar Woog (☛), futuro dirigente del Partido Comunista Suizo, quien bajo el pseudónimo de *Alfredo Stirner* participó en la fundación de la Federación de Jóvenes Comunistas en el mismo año. Don Jesús Silva Herzog escribió que el primer plan de estudios de la carrera de economía en la Universidad Nacional de México se debe a Fritz Bach, "suizo-alemán que había llegado a México en 1926 como representante" del Socorro Rojo Internacional y que al fundarse la Sección de Economía en la Facultad de Derecho fue nombrado profesor de economía industrial, "materia que conocía bien".

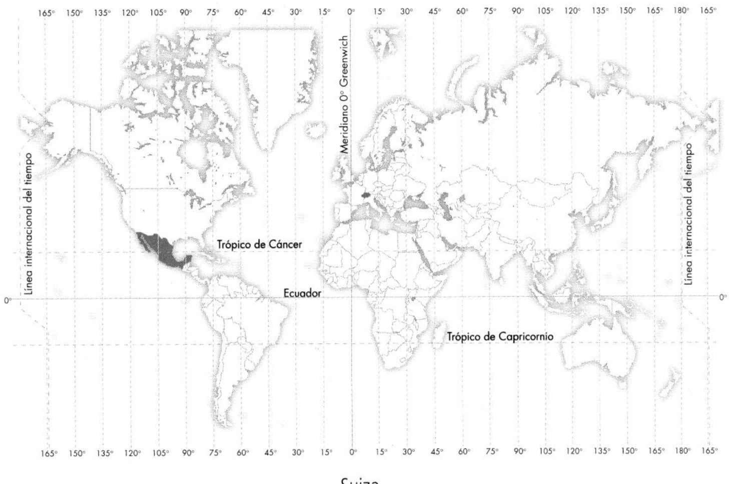

Suiza

Hacia 1940 llegó a México la fotógrafa y escritora suiza Gertrudis Duby (☛), quien se ha dedicado a promover la defensa y protección de la selva lacandona y de sus habitantes. Suiza se mantuvo neutral durante la primera guerra mundial y, aunque mantuvo esa neutralidad durante la segunda, las amenazas de agresión la obligaron a establecer relaciones comerciales con las potencias del eje y a ejercer domésticamente cierta represión sobre la prensa. En 1945 se establecieron las relaciones diplomáticas formales entre México y Suiza. A raíz de los terremotos de septiembre de 1985, Suiza fue uno de los países de mayor contribución per cápita para los damnificados.

Timbres de Suiza

Monedas y billetes Suizos

Paisaje suizo

Foto: Imagen Latina

José Sulaimán

Sulaimán Chagnon, José ◆ n. en Ciudad Victoria, Tams. (1931). Licenciado en administración de empresas por la Universidad de Michigan. Boxeador aficionado (1940-43) y auxiliar de la Comisión de Box de Ciudad Valles (1945). Beisbolista, en 1950 fue llamado a la selección nacional que participó en los Juegos Panamericanos de Buenos Aires, a los que su padre le impidió asistir; participó con el equipo de San Luis Potosí en los juegos nacionales de León (1949) y con el equipo de Tamaulipas en los juegos de Guaymas (1950). Campeón bateador y novato del año en 1951. Beisbolista profesional en la clase B, jugó en la Liga del Golfo y en la Petrolera. Con los equipos de Ciudad Valles y Ciudad Victoria jugó en la Liga de Otoño (1949-54). Estuvo un año en el equipo de Nueva Inglaterra, donde lanzó un juego sin hit ni carrera. Presidente fundador de la Asociación Estatal de Boxeo de Tamaulipas (1959), vicepresidente de la Federación Mexicana de Comisiones de Boxeo y fundador del Consejo Mundial de Boxeo (1963), vicepresidente (1969) y presidente de la Federación Norteamericana de Box (1967 y 1970), presidente del Comité de Clasificaciones (1970) y secretario general del CMB (1971). En 1975, en Túnez, fue electo presidente del CMB, cargo en el que fue ratificado en 1976 y reelecto en 1980. Presidente, asimismo, de la Comisión de Box y Lucha del DF (1989-91). Fundador del Consejo Mexicano del Deporte y Espectáculos Profesionales de México (1985-).

Foto: Ana Lourdes Herrera

Superbarrio

Sultepec ◆ Municipio del Estado de México situado en los límites con Guerrero, al suroeste de Toluca. Superficie: 507.2 km². Habitantes: 24,757, de los cuales 4,735 forman la población económicamente activa. Hablan alguna lengua indígena 67 personas mayores de cinco años (náhuatl 66). Su cabecera es Sultepec de Pedro Ascencio de Alquisiras. Durante la colonia y en el siglo XIX, cuando fue conocido como el Real de Sultepec, fue un importante centro minero. En 1812, las fuerzas insurgentes instalaron ahí la "Imprenta de la Nación", en la que con tinta de añil e improvisados tipos de madera, hechos a mano, editaron *El Ilustrador Nacional*, para difundir, decían, "la justicia, la necesidad y los nobles objetos de nuestra revolución".

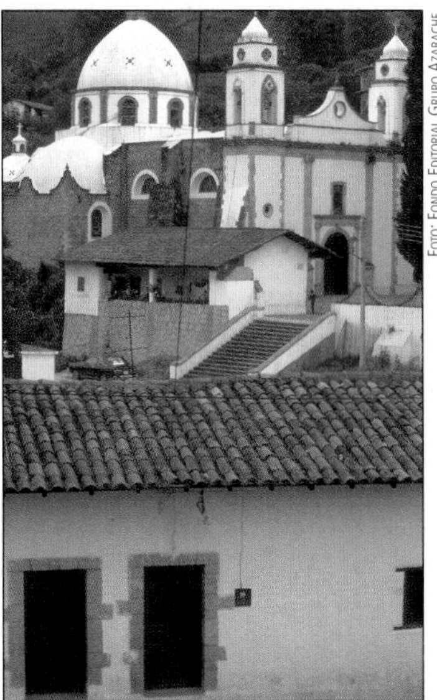
Foto: Fondo Editorial Grupo Azabache

Iglesia de la Veracruz en Sultepec, Estado de México

Sultepec, de ◆ Sierra del Estado de México que forma parte del Eje Volcánico; es la prolongación meridional de la sierra del Hospital. Se extiende de norte a sur desde el suroeste del Nevado de Toluca hasta los límites con Guerrero, donde se une a la sierra de Galeta. Paralelamente corre el río Chontalcuatlán. Tiene importantes yacimientos minerales.

Sumá ◆ Municipio de Yucatán situado al este y próximo a Motul. Superficie: 39.60 km². Habitantes: 1,901, de los cuales 508 forman la población económicamente activa. Hablan alguna lengua indígena 813 personas mayores de cinco años (maya 812).

Sumidero, del ◆ Cañón de Chiapas. Es una depresión en el Gran Río de Chiapa o Alto Grijalva. Tiene 15 kilómetros de longitud y se extiende de sureste a noroeste. Sus paredes, acantiladas, tienen alturas que van de los 150 a los 300 metros y son un muestrario de diversas capas geológicas. La fauna y la flora del extremo inferior son atípicas, por lo que la zona es objeto de estudio de botánicos y zoólogos. La presa de Chicoasén ocupa una parte de la hondonada.

Sunuapa ◆ Municipio de Chiapas situado al noroeste de Tuxtla Gutiérrez, cercano a Tabasco. Superficie: 178.9 km². Habitantes: 1,431, de los cuales 426 forman la población económicamente activa. Hablan alguna lengua indígena cinco personas mayores de cinco años.

Superbarrio ◆ n. en el DF (1985). Luchador social. Con un vistoso traje de luchador y oculto por una máscara, dice apellidarse Gómez. "Surgió de los terremotos" del 19 y 20 de septiembre de 1985 en la capital del país, donde se localiza su *Barriocueva*. Defiende los intereses de los habitantes más pobres de la ciudad de México. Ha derrotado en cuadriláteros públicos a *Catalino Creel* y al *Gusano de la Manzana*. El 6 de julio de 1988, en las elecciones presidenciales, recibió el voto de Cuauhtémoc Cárdenas. Pertenece a la dirección de la Asamblea de Barrios. Ha colaborado en el diario *La Jornada*, en el que sostuvo una polémica con Octavio Paz. A principios de 1989 fue muy comentada su forma de introducirse, protegido por su personalidad secreta, en la Asamblea de Representantes del Distrito Federal, donde ya se le había impedido el paso. En ese mismo año realizó un viaje a la ciudad de Los Ángeles, Estados Unidos, donde fue bien recibido por la comunidad mexicana y por la opinión pública, pero no por la policía, que lo detuvo debido a una ley del siglo XIX contra los individuos que cubren su rostro. El actor estadounidense Dustin Hoffman manifestó su deseo de llevar al personaje al cine.

Superior ◆ Laguna de Oaxaca también llamada Dicnahuanot, situada en el extremo sur del istmo de Tehuantepec, al este, sureste y sur de Juchitán de Zaragoza. Es una albufera de 30 kilómetros de largo que en su porción más ancha tiene 20 kilómetros. Al norte y al oeste está bordeada por tierra firme, por el sur está separada del mar Tileme por una barra y al este se halla limitada por una península que la separa de la laguna Inferior. En ella desemboca el río Juchitán.

SUPREMA JUNTA NACIONAL AMERICANA ◆ Creada por Ignacio López Rayón, comandante de las fuerzas insurgentes, en agosto de 1811, fue la primera instancia organizadora del movimiento de Independencia. Los propósitos organizativos fueron asentados en un acta firmada por el propio López Rayón, José María Liceaga y Joaquín López, quienes convocaron a una reunión en Zitácuaro a los jefes insurgentes que operaban en la zona de Michoacán para leerles el documento. A la también llamada Junta de Zitácuaro concurrieron Juan Albarrán, Ignacio Izaguirre, Benedicto López, Manuel Manso, Ignacio Martínez, Tomás Ortiz, Ignacio Ponce de León, Miguel Serrano, José Vargas y José Sixto Verduzco. Una vez leída el acta y aprobada por los presentes, estos se constituyeron en Suprema Junta Nacional Americana, nombraron presidente a López Rayón y vocales a José María Liceaga y a José Sixto Verduzco y expidieron un manifiesto que, en su parte medular, decía: "La falta de un jefe supremo en quien se depositasen las confianzas de la nación y a quien todos obedeciesen, nos iba a precipitar en la más completa anarquía, el desorden, la confusión, el despotismo y sus consecuencias eran los amargos frutos que comenzábamos a gustar después de once meses de trabajos y desvelos incesantes por el bien de la patria. Para ocurrir a tamaño mal y llenar las ideas adoptadas por nuestro gobierno y primeros representantes de la Nación, se ha considerado de absoluta necesidad erigir un tribunal a quien se reconozca por supremo y a quien todos obedezcan, que arregle el plan de operaciones en toda nuestra América y dicte las providencias oportunas al buen orden político y económico. En efecto, en junta de Generales celebrada el diez y nueve de este mes de ag., se acordó en su primera la instalación de una Suprema Junta Nacional Americana compuesta por ahora de tres individuos, quedando dos vacantes para que las ocupe, cuando se presente ocasión, igual número de sujetos beneméritos.

Ignacio López Rayón, creador de la Suprema Junta Nacional Americana

Se acordó también en el segundo que la elección recayese en las personas de los Exmos. SS. Lic. Ignacio López Rayón, Ministro de la Nación; Dr. José Sixto Verduzco y teniente general D. José María Liceaga. Y para que llegue noticia a todos y sus órdenes, decretos y disposiciones sean puntual y eficazmente obedecidos, se publica por bando, el que se fijará según estilo en los lugares acostumbrados para su observancia y debido cumplimiento, debiendo celebrarse con las demostraciones de júbilo un establecimiento que nos hace esperar muy en breve la libertad de nuestra patria, con la conminación de ser castigados los contraventores con proporción a su inobediencia. Dado en nuestro Palacio Nacional de la villa de Zitácuaro, a veintiún días del mes de ag. de mil ochocientos once". Esta Suprema Junta Nacional Americana o Junta de Zitácuaro adquirió una imprenta en la que se editó el *Ilustrador Americano* (☛). Enterado el gobierno virreinal de las funciones e importancia de la junta, ordenó a Félix María Calleja tomar la plaza de Zitácuaro, lo que ocurrió en enero de 1812. Los dirigentes de la junta huyeron de Zitácuaro y mantuvieron viva la organización hasta 1813, cuando las divergencias entre López Rayón, por un lado, y José Sixto Verduzco y José María Liceaga, por otro, la volvieron inoperante.

SUPREMA CORTE DE JUSTICIA DE LA NACIÓN ◆ ☛ *Poder Judicial.*

SUPREMO PODER CONSERVADOR ◆ El artículo cuarto de Las Bases Constitucionales de 1835 respetó la división de los poderes legislativo, ejecutivo y judicial, fijada en 1824, pero anunció el establecimiento de "un arbitrio suficiente para que ninguno de los tres pueda traspasar los límites de sus atribuciones". Este arbitrio fue dispuesto por la segunda de las Siete Leyes, aprobada en abril de 1836, que señalaba que "Habrá un supremo poder conservador que se depositará en cinco individuos, de los se renovará uno cada dos años". Las juntas departamentales debían proponer candidatos y enviar las listas de nombres a la Cámara de Diputados, la que debía, "a pluralidad absoluta de votos", integrar ternas para ocupar cada puesto vacante. Las ternas tenían que ser enviadas al Senado para que éste eligiera a uno de los candidatos, pudiendo ser reelegidos los que terminaran su periodo. Al tomar posesión de su cargo debían responder afirmativamente a la pregunta: "¿Juráis guardar y hacer guardar la Constitución de la República sosteniendo el equilibrio constitucional entre los poderes sociales, manteniendo o restableciendo el orden constitucional en los casos en que fuere turbado, valiéndose para ello del poder y medios que la Constitución pone en vuestras manos?" El sueldo anual de cada miembro sería de 6,000 pesos. Entre los requisitos para pertenecer a este cuerpo se hallaba ser mexicano por nacimiento, mayor de 40 años, en pleno goce de los derechos ciudadanos, tener un ingreso "físico o moral" de por lo menos 3,000 pesos anuales y haber sido presidente o vicepresidente de la República, senador, diputado, secretario del despacho o magistrado de la Suprema Corte de Justicia. Sus atribuciones eran: calificar, a petición de cualquiera de los otros poderes o un mínimo de 18 legisladores, la constitucionalidad de las leyes; declarar la nulidad de actos del Ejecutivo cuando fueran contrarios a la Constitución o a las leyes; hacer lo mismo ante actos de la Suprema Corte en caso de usurpación de facultades;

declarar, "por excitación del congreso general", "la incapacidad física o moral del presidente de la República cuando le sobrevenga"; suspender a la Suprema Corte cuando ésta desconociera a algunos de los otros poderes o tratara de trastornar el orden; suspender hasta por dos meses las sesiones del Congreso o, a solicitud del Ejecutivo, llamar a los suplentes "cuando convenga al bien público"; restablecer a uno o más de los poderes cuando hubieran "sido disueltos revolucionariamente"; declarar "cual es la voluntad de la nación, en cualquier caso extraodinario que sea conveniente conocerla"; declarar cuando estuviera el presidente de la República en el caso de "renovar todo el ministerio"; calificar la elección de senadores; y nombrar a los letrados que debían juzgar a los ministros de la Corte. Se consideraba "crimen de alta traición" la desobediencia de las disposiciones del Supremo Poder Conservador, que no era "responsable de sus operaciones " mas que ante Dios y la opinión pública. Sus miembros no podían ser juzgados ni reconvenidos por sus opiniones. Su sede estaba en el Palacio Nacional. En 1839 autorizó reformar la Constitución, antes del tiempo previsto para modificarla e invistió del carácter de constituyente al Congreso, donde en 1840 se propuso pasar el control de la constitucionalidad a la Suprema Corte y al año siguiente se planteó la desaparición del Supremo Poder Conservador, "cuerpo desconocido en las instituciones modernas" que desapareció al ser sustituidas las *Siete Leyes* por las *Bases Orgánicas* de 1843. En éstas se establecía la existencia de un Consejo de Gobierno integrado por 17 vocales, con carácter perpetuo, designados por el Presidente de la República. Este cuerpo, que se encargaría de dictaminar sobre la constitucionalidad de las leyes y sería asesor del ejecutivo, fue suprimido en 1847, al restablecerse la Constitución de 1824 con la adición del Acta de Reformas.

SUPREMO PODER EJECUTIVO ◆ ☛ *Poder Ejecutivo*.

SURÍA, TOMÁS DE ◆ n. en España y m. en la ciudad de México (1761-?). Grabador. Estudió en la Academia de San Fernando de Madrid, donde fue discípulo de Jerónimo Antonio Gil, quien lo trajo a México. Aquí continuó su aprendizaje en la Academia de San Carlos. Desde 1788 trabajó para la Casa de Moneda, donde ejecutó varias medallas. Grabó el túmulo levantado para las honras fúnebres de Carlos III (1789) y el monumento que se hizo a propósito de la proclamación de Carlos IV (1790). En 1791 participó en la expedición de Alejandro Malaspina a Nutka, hoy Canadá, viaje en el que realizó una serie de apuntes. Fue director de grabado en hueco en San Carlos (1798-) y en 1806 se le dio el nombramiento de "contador ordinario de pagos de tercera clase". Según Manuel Toussaint, murió después de 1834.

SURINAM, REPÚBLICA DE ◆ Antigua Guayana Holandesa. País sudamericano situado en el litoral del océano Atlántico. Limita al este con la Guayana Francesa, al sur con Brasil y al oeste con Guyana. Superficie: 163,820 km^2. Habitantes: 414,000 (1998). Su capital es Paramaribo (200,970 habitantes en 1993) y su idioma oficial es el holandés. *Historia*: en 1616 se establecieron en el territorio los primeros holandeses, patrocinados por la Compañía de las Indias Occidentales, e instauraron el tráfico de esclavos. En 1651, el inglés Willoughby estableció la primera población permanente e inició la penetración británica. En 1667, de acuerdo con el Tratado de Breda, Inglaterra cedió el territorio de Surinam a los Países Bajos. En 1848 adquirió independencia administrativa de las Antillas Neerlandesas y en 1954 obtuvo una relativa autonomía del Reino de los Países Bajos. El 25 de noviembre de 1975 logró su independencia y ese mismo día se establecieron las relaciones diplomáticas con México. En diciembre ingresó en la ONU.

SUROTATO, DE ◆ Sierra de Sinaloa. Es una de las estribaciones occidentales de la sierra Madre Occidental. Se extiende de noroeste a suroeste, paralelamente al río Petatlán, que la separa de las sierras Tarahumara y de Mohinora.

La obra de José Guadalupe Posada se considera en cierta forma precursora del surrealismo

SURREALISMO ◆ Movimiento artístico iniciado en 1924, en Francia, por André Breton (☛). Dentro de esa corriente, influida por la teoría psicoanalítica, cobraron importancia los elementos extraídos de los sueños, la fantasía, la conjunción de elementos incongruentes, la deformación de objetos y seres animados, la animación de cosas, el azar, las composiciones accidentales y "automáticas", ajenas a un plan, y otros factores no sujetos al racionalismo. Diversos críticos han encontrado que gran parte de la cerámica y otras artesanías mexicanas, lo mismo que la obra

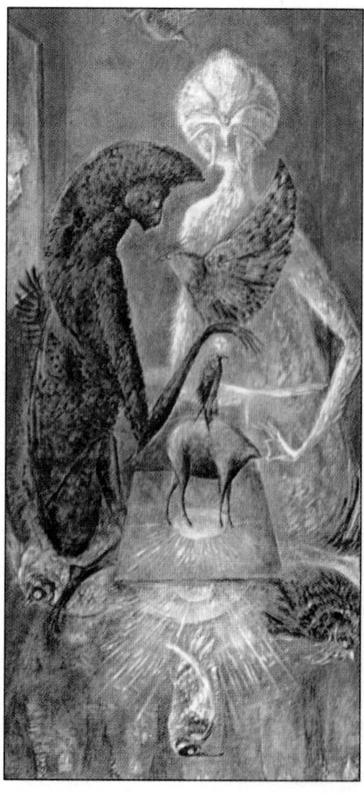

Reflection on the Oracle, óleo sobre tela de la pintora surrealista Leonora Carrington

Roulotte, óleo sobre masonite de la pintora surrealista Remedios Varo

de José Guadalupe Posada y otros creadores populares son ubicables en esta concepción. Breton vino a México en 1938 y firmó con Diego Rivera y León Trotsky el manifiesto *Por un arte revolucionario independiente*, que intentó conciliar surrealismo y marxismo. Otros artistas de esta filiación estética que vinieron en diferentes épocas, algunos para quedarse, fueron Antonin Artaud, Wolfang Paalen, Tomás Moro, Benjamín Peret, Paul Eluard, Alice Rahon, Remedios Varo, Luis Buñuel, Kati y José Horna, Leonora Carrington y algún otro. Según la crítica Raquel Tibol, "la práctica del surrealismo o las afinidades con él aparecieron en el arte mexicano antes del arribo de los militantes y fundadores del movimiento en Europa". El también crítico Jorge Alberto Manrique, observa que "la presencia de los surrealistas" significó "una novedad de apertura y de información, en un momento en que la cultura mexicana tendía a cerrarse excesivamente" y fue el germen de los cambios ocurridos en el arte local en los años cincuenta y sesenta. En 1940, en la Galería de Arte Mexicano, de Inés Amor, se realizó una Exposición Surrealista en la que se presentaron obras de Giorgio de Chirico, Dalí, Marcel Duchamp, Max Ernst, Alberto Giacometti, Kandinsky, Paul Klee, René Magritte, Joan Miró, Henry Moore, Francis Picabia, Picasso, y Man Ray. Junto a ellos figuró la producción de artistas locales como Rivera y Manuel Álvarez Bravo, catalogados en la sección internacional, Frida Kahlo, Antonio Ruiz, Manuel Rodríguez Lozano, Roberto Montenegro, Xavier Villaurrutia, Juan O'Gorman, Guillermo Meza, Carlos Mérida, Carlos Orozco Romero, Agustín Lazo y el trasterrado José Moreno Villa. Los trabajos que ahí se exhibieron, dice Ida Rodríguez Prampolini, "tienen muy poco que ver con esa escuela". En los años posteriores surgieron artistas influidos por esta corriente. En la literatura, se consideran surrealistas algunas obras de Octavio Paz, quien conoció a Breton y a algunos de sus colaboradores en sus "años crepusculares". Con todo, la misma Raquel Tibol señala que "no hay movimiento surrealista mexicano, pero sí hay arte mexicano surrealista".

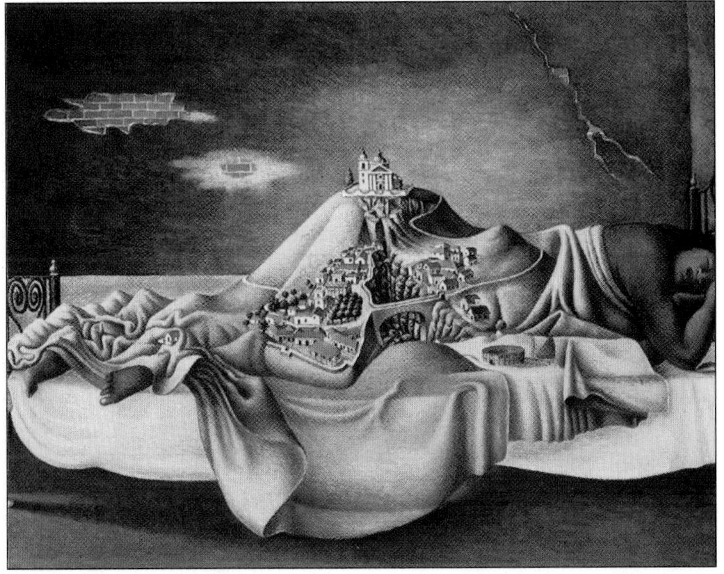

La Malinche, obra del pintor surrealista Antonio Ruiz

Autorretrato con monos, óleo sobre tela de la pintora surrealista Frida Kahlo

Sustaita Zavala, Alberto ◆ n. y m. en San Luis Potosí, SLP (1863-1909). Periodista y escritor. Inició colaboraciones en 1890 en *El Estandarte* de San Luis Potosí, con el pseudónimo de *P. K. Dor*, que usó en adelante tanto en su trabajo literario como en el periodístico. Colaboró en *El Correo de San Luis Potosí*. Autor de novela: *Las Bolado* (1906), *El crimen del pullman* (1907) y *Mutilado* (1909); cuento: *Siete pecados* (1894), *Mortales y veniales* (1907) y *Morralla* (1908); y teatro: *Nita* (1905) y *El padre Adrián*.

FOTO: ANA LOURDES HERRERA

Gerardo Suter

SUSTICACÁN ◆ Municipio de Zacatecas situado al suroeste de Fresnillo y al oeste-suroeste de la capital estatal. Superficie: 647.12 km². Habitantes: 1,453, de los cuales 273 forman la población económicamente activa.

SUSUPUATO ◆ Municipio de Michoacán situado en el oriente del estado, en los límites con el Estado de México, al sur de Zitácuaro y al sureste de Morelia. Superficie: 156.49 km². Habitantes: 8,173, de los cuales 1,911 forman la población económicamente activa. Hablan alguna lengua indígena 177 personas mayores de cinco años (mazahua 174). Su cabecera es Susupuato de Guerrero.

SUTER, GERARDO ◆ n. en Argentina (1957). Fotógrafo radicado en México desde 1970. Ha expuesto individualmente en el Instituto Goethe y en la Casa de la Cultura de Puebla (1979), en la Escuela de Diseño del INBA (1981), en la galería José Clemente Orozco (1982), en la galería Los Talleres (1983) y en la galería Fotografía Oltre, de Suiza (1984). Colectivamente ha expuesto en Estados Unidos, Inglaterra, Francia, México y Cuba. Ganó el primer premio del certamen de fotografía de la Casa del Lago (1979) y un premio de adquisición en la sección bienal de fotografía del Salón Nacional de Artes Plásticas (1982). Pertenece al Sistema Nacional de Creadores (1993-).

Juan de la Cabada en fotografía de Gerardo Suter

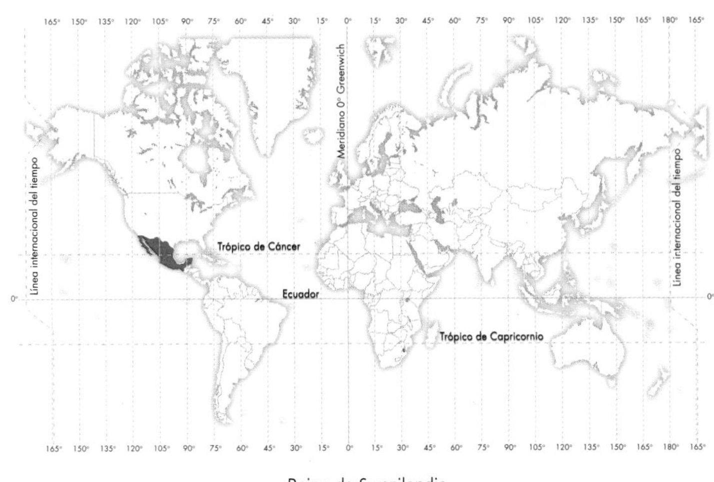

Reino de Swazilandia

SWADESH, MAURICIO ◆ n. en EUA (1909-1967). Doctor en lingüística por la Universidad de Yale. Durante tres años trabajó en México como alfabetizador en el Programa Tarasco, fue profesor en el Instituto de Historia de la UNAM y en la ENAH desde 1956. En la UNAM fundó la Sección de Investigaciones Lingüísticas del Centro de Cálculo Electrónico (1963) y el Seminario de Estudios de la Escritura Cultura Maya de la Coordinación de Humanidades (1967). Autor de *La lingüística como instrumento de la prehistoria* (1960), *Afinidades de las lenguas americanas* (1960), *Interrelaciones de las lenguas mayas* (1961), *Porhé y maya* (1966) y *El lenguaje y la vida humana* (1966).

SWANSEY, BRUCE ◆ n. en el DF (1955). Licenciado en ciencias y técnicas de la información por la UIA (1976), estudió letras en la UNAM (1976) y un posgrado en la Universidad de Navarra (1977). Maestro en comunicación por la UNAM (1979-81) y doctor en letras hispánicas por El Colegio de México. Profesor de la UAM-Xochimilco (1979-). Fue gerente ejecutivo editorial de la Subdirección de Publicaciones de Somex (1984-85). Ha sido director de la sección cultural de *Ser Joven*, revista del Crea (1980), miembro del consejo de redacción de la revista *Comunicación y Cultura* de la UAM (1980), comentarista y guionista de los canales 2 y 13 de televisión (1981), crítico de teatro de la revista *Proceso* desde 1981, guionista del Canal 7 de televisión (1984-85), director de la *Revista del Consumidor* (1985-86) y jefe de Información de la Dirección de Noticias del Canal 22 (1994). Ha sido colaborador de *Excélsior, Los Universitarios* (1975), *Escénica, Fem, Punto de Vida, Imágenes* (1978), *La Letra y la Imagen* (1980), *Territorios* (1980-83), *Diagonales, La Orquesta, México en la Cultura, uno**más**uno* y *La Jornada Semanal*, suplemento de *La Jornada*, en la que escribió la columna "La corte de los milagros". Autor de *La estructura de los mensajes en el best seller* (tesis de licenciatura) y *Prosas para el boudoir* (relatos, 1980). Ha recibido las becas Aktion Adveniat, de Pamplona (1977), INBA-Fonapas (1978-79), del Centro Mexicano de Escritores (1980-81) y del Taller Internacional de Escritores de la Universidad de Iowa (1982).

SWAZILANDIA, REINO DE ◆ Nación africana que limita al este con Mozambique, y al norte, sureste, sur y oeste con la República de Sudáfrica. Tiene una superficie de 17,364 km² y 952,000 habitantes (1998). Su capital administrativa y judicial es Mbabane (47,000 habitantes en 1990), la legislativa es Lobamba y la real es Lozitha. Sus idiomas oficiales, el sisiwati y el inglés. *Historia*: hacia 1750 el territorio de la actual Swazilandia fue poblado por la tribu swazi, de raza bantú. En 1840 los zulúes del actual territorio de Sudáfrica amenazaron al reino de Mswati, que solicitó ayuda a la Corona británica. En

1894 Swazilandia se convirtió en protectorado de Sudáfrica y en 1903, al término de la guerra Boer, el Reino Unido administró el protectorado. En 1967 Swazilandia se convirtió en una monarquía gobernada por el rey Sobhuza II y un año más tarde, como país independiente, llamado Ngwane, ingresó en la ONU. En 1973 Sobhuza derogó la Constitución y asumió el poder absoluto. Dos años después se establecieron las relaciones diplomáticas con México. En 1982 murió Sobhuza y fue sucedido por su viuda, Dzeliwe Shongwe quien, un año más tarde, fue depuesta y sustituida por otra viuda de Sobhuza, Ntombi Thwala.

Székely Sánchez, Alberto ◆ n. en el DF (1946). Licenciado en derecho por la UNAM (1968), maestro en derecho internacional (1969) y en derecho internacional y diplomacia (1970) por la Fletcher School of Law and Diplomacy de la Tufts University y doctor en derecho (1973-75) por la Universidad de Londres. Profesor de la UNAM (1970-) y El Colegio de México (1983-) e investigador del Instituto de Investigaciones Jurídicas de la UNAM (1970-82). Ha sido jefe interino del Departamento de Organismos Especializados de la Dirección General de Organismos Internacionales (1967-68), asesor del subsecretario de Relaciones Exteriores (1976-78), asesor del secretario de Relaciones Exteriores (1979-80), representante alterno de México ante la OEA (1980-81), asesor del secretario de Relaciones Exteriores (1981-82), representante permanente alterno de México ante la ONU en Suiza (1982-83), embajador del Servicio Exterior Mexicano (1986-), miembro por México de la Corte Permanente de Arbitraje Internacional de La Haya (1986-) y consultor jurídico de la SRE (1986-88). Autor de *Latin America and the Development of the Law of the Sea* (1976), *México y el derecho internacional del mar* (1978) e *Instrumentos fundamentales de derecho internacional público* (1981). Ha colaborado en *El Financiero*.

Szeryng, Henryk ◆ n. en Polonia y m. en la RFA (1918-1988). Músico. Inició su aprendizaje de piano con Aline Woznika, su madre. Hacia 1925, cuando ya era capaz de tocar el *Concierto para piano* de Félix Mendelssohn, inició sus estudios de violín. Estudió en Berlín con Carl Flesch (1925-28). En 1933, ya como violinista profesional, realizó una gira por Polonia, Rumania, Austria y Francia. Estudió composición en el Conservatorio de París con Nadia Boulanger y Gabriel Bovillon y se graduó en 1939. Durante la segunda guerra mundial se alistó como voluntario en el ejército del gobierno polaco en el exilio (en Inglaterra) y realizó numerosas actuaciones para los combatientes. Fue oficial de enlace e intérprete del primer ministro polaco, Ladislao Sikorsky, y en 1942 logró que México asilara a 4,000 compatriotas suyos. En 1945 fijó aquí su residencia y reorganizó la carrera de violinista de la UNAM. Obtuvo la nacionalidad mexicana en 1946. Fue profesor del Conservatorio Nacional, embajador cultural itinerante (1956-) y asesor especial en cuestiones musicales de la delegación de México en la UNESCO (1970-). Donó al INBA un violín Sancta Theresia, construido en 1683 por Andrea Guarneri. En 1953 ofreció un recital a petición del pianista Arthur Rubinstein. Presidente honorario de las Juventudes Musicales de México. En 1985 compuso e interpretó una obra para violín a beneficio de los damnificados por los terremotos de ese año. Actuó en el Festival Internacional Cervantino con la Orquesta Filarmónica del Bajío, dirigida por Sergio Cárdenas (1987). Hacia presentaciones con la Orquesta de la Radio del Sarre cuando murió. Difundió en el extranjero obras de Rodolfo Halffter y de compositores mexicanos como Carlos Chávez, Manuel M. Ponce, Higinio Ruvalcaba, Jiménez Mabarak, Sabre Marroquín, Silvestre Revueltas y Julián Carrillo.

Szmulewicz, Pablo ◆ n. en Argentina (1955). Pintor de nacionalidad mexicana. Inició sus estudios profesionales en Buenos Aires. Hizo cursos de posgrado en la Academia de San Carlos, de México, país al que llegó becado por la Secretaría de Relaciones Exteriores. Expone individualmente desde 1979. Ha presentado su obra en galerías de Argentina, Cuba y México. En Argentina obtuvo el Primer Premio de Pintura del Salón de Otoño de la Sociedad de Artistas Plásticos (1978), Medalla de Oro del Salón Anual de Santa Fe (1979) y el Primer Premio de Pintura del Primer Salón de San Isidro (1984).

Szymanski Ramírez, Arturo Antonio ◆ n. en Tampico, Tams. (1922). Estudió humanidades y lenguas clásicas en el Seminario de San Luis Potosí y en el Seminario Pontificio de Montezuma, Nuevo México. Sacerdote ordenado en 1947. Ha sido vicario cooperador de la Catedral, asistente de las Vanguardias de la Asociación Católica de la Juventud Mejicana, prefecto de disciplina, profesor, vicerrector y rector del Seminario de Tamaulipas, examinador prosinodal y oficial para las causas matrimoniales en esa diócesis; obispo titular de Cerosante y coadjutor del obispo de San Andrés Tuxtla (1960), obispo de esta diócesis (1965), obispo de Tampico (1968-87) y de San Luis Potosí (1987-89) y primer arzobispo de San Luis Potosí (1989-) y obispo emérito. Ha sido presidente de las comisiones nacionales de Liturgia (1979) y del Clero del Episcopado Mexicano (1985-88).

Díptico *Susurros épicos o galope de madera*, óleo sobre tela de Pablo Szmulewicz

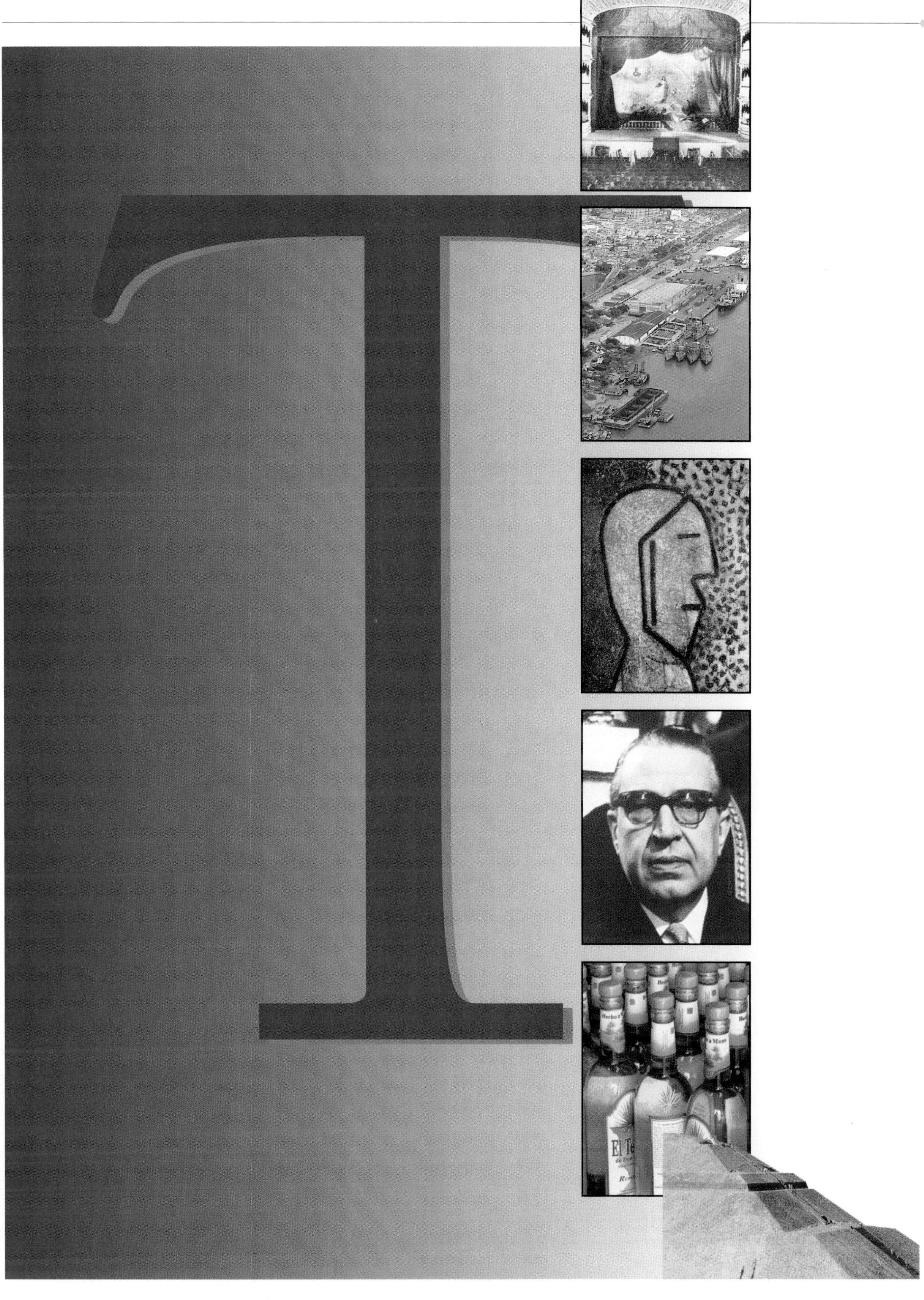

TABARES, MARIANO ◆ m. en Chilapa, Gro. (?- 1811). En 1810 era capitán del ejército realista que ocupaba Acapulco. A fines de ese año estableció contacto con las fuerzas de José María Morelos y les proporcionó información sobre las tropas oaxaqueñas que se acercaban para combatir a los insurgentes. Más tarde se incorporó al ejército de Morelos, quien en agosto de 1811 lo envió con David Faro a Estados Unidos en busca de dinero y reconocimiento diplomático para la insurgencia. Al pasar por La Piedad se encontró con las fuerzas de Ignacio López Rayón, quien lo ascendió a general brigadier, canceló su misión y lo envió a reunirse de nuevo con Morelos, pero éste desconoció lo actuado por Rayón. Poco después, Tabares, acusado de conspirar contra el caudillo, fue ejecutado.

TABASCO ◆ Municipio de Zacatecas situado en el sur del estado, al sur-suroeste de la capital estatal y al norte de Nochistlán, en los límites con Aguascalientes. Superficie: 403,8 km². Habitantes: 15,446, de los cuales 3,643 forman la población económicamente activa. Hablan alguna lengua indígena ocho personas mayores de cinco años.

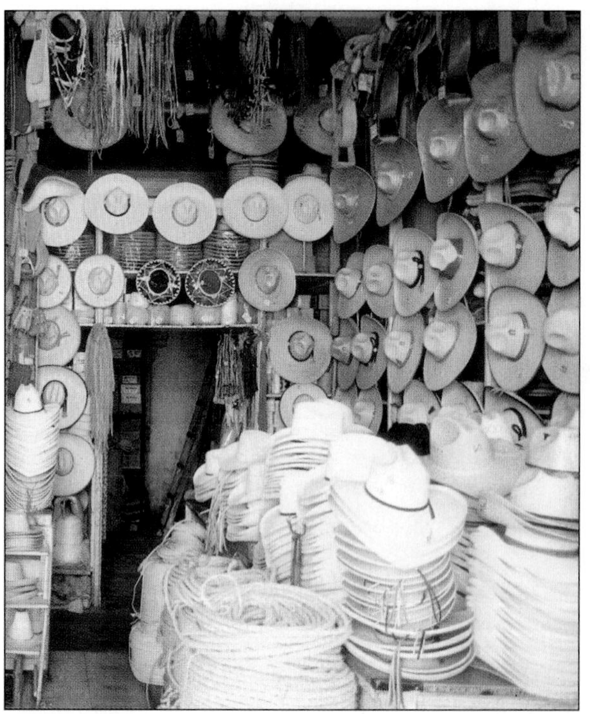

Tabasco, Zacatecas

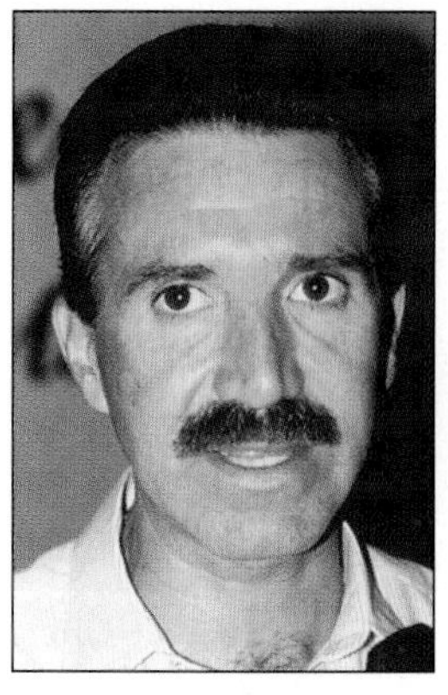

Roberto Madrazo Pintado, gobernador constitucional de Tabasco

TABASCO ◆ Estado de la República Mexicana situado en la costa meridional del golfo de México y en la frontera con Guatemala. Limita con Campeche, Chiapas y Veracruz. Superficie: 25,267 km². (equivalentes al 1.3 por ciento del territorio nacional), divididos en 17 municipios. La capital es Villahermosa. No existen accidentes orográficos de consideración, pero, en cambio, el sistema hidrológico es muy importante. Las principales corrientes, todas en la vertiente del golfo de México, son los ríos Tonalá, Grijalva, Usumacinta, Dos Bocas, San Pedro, San Pablo, Chilapa, El Hormiguero y el complejo Mezcalapa-Río Grande. El 60 por ciento del territorio tabasqueño está cubierto de agua. Habitantes: 1,817,703 en 1997. Hacia 1995 su población urbana la conformaban 911,254 personas y la rural, 837,515 (ambas totalizaban 1.9 por ciento del promedio nacional). Su índice de analfabetismo es de 9.64 por ciento entre los mayores de 15 años. Forman la población económicamente activa el 50.1 por ciento de los mayores de 12 años. Contribuye con 1.3 por ciento al producto interno bruto total nacional. Hablan alguna lengua indígena 51,364 personas mayores de cinco años (chontal de Tabasco 36,041, chol 9,459 y tzeltal 1,495), de las cuales 314 no dominan el español. *Historia*: hacia el año 1500 a.n.e., los olmecas (→) se

FOTO: FONDO EDITORIAL GRUPO AZABACHE

Guacamaya de Tabasco

instalaron en el actual territorio del estado, sobre todo en la ribera oriental del río Tonalá, en Cunduacán, Chiltepec, Tamulé y La Venta (☞), que vivieron sus mejores momentos en los últimos 500 años a.n.e. Durante el primer milenio de nuestra era, el extremo oriental fue ocupado por los mayas, quienes se asentaron en Macuspana y Comalcalco, y luego de la destrucción del imperio antiguo, primero los toltecas, hacia el siglo XIII, y más tarde los chontales (☞), hacia el XIV, se instalaron en la región. A partir de entonces, el comercio entre mayas y nahuas permitió el desarrollo de varias ciudades, como Cimatán, Teapa, Cunduacán y Xicalango. En los primeros años del siglo XVI, en la parte central del actual territorio del estado vivían unas 135,000 personas, chontales en su mayoría, sobre todo en los alrededores de Chocohtán. En 1518, los cinco barcos con los que Juan de Grijalva recorría el sur del golfo de México anclaron frente a la desembocadura de un río que, desde entonces, se llama Grijalva. Poco después, los españoles entraron en contacto con los chontales, de quienes recibieron varios obsequios de oro que despertaron la codicia de los europeos. Un año después, las fuerzas de Hernán Cortés llegaron a la desembocadura del Grijalva y lo siguieron río arriba. Se enfrascaron en combate con los chontales, y luego de dos días resultaron vencedores los españoles, quienes atribuyeran su victoria a la milagrosa aparición de Santiago Matamoros y celebraron la primera misa en territorio mesoamericano. Llamaron Villa de Santa María de la Victoria al pueblo costero de Potonchán y consiguieron que el *ta-*

FOTO: MICHAEL CALDERWOOD

Comalcalco, Tabasco

Timbre mexicano con el tema de Tabasco

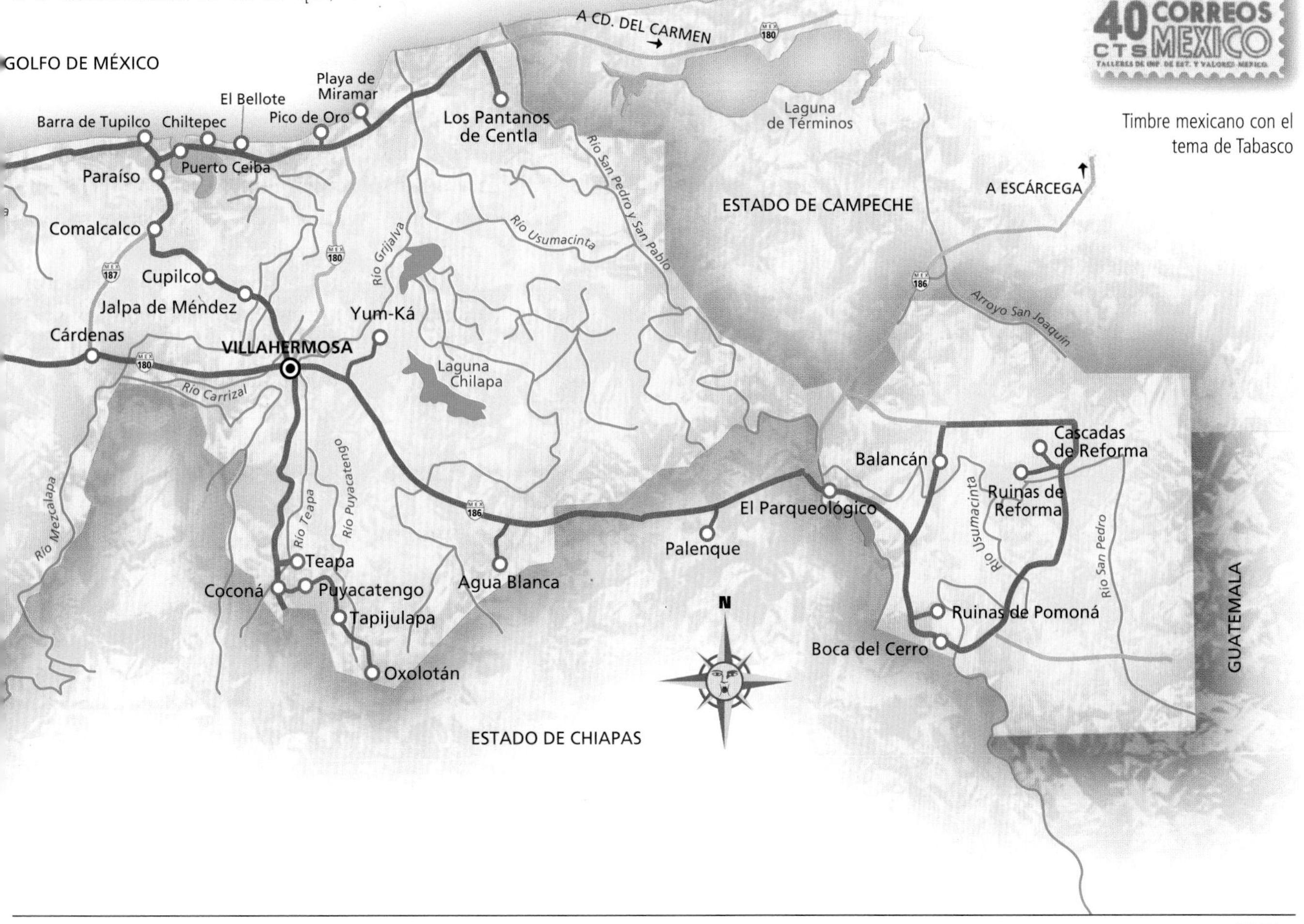

Foto: Fondo Editorial Grupo Azabache

Panorámica de Villahermosa, Tabasco

Foto: Fondo Editorial Grupo Azabache

Parque ecológico en Tabasco

bah-coh, el cacique de Chocohtán, les regalara una veintena de esclavas entre las que se encontraba una mujer de origen náhuatl, que se hacía llamar Malintzin y que más tarde sería conocida como doña Marina o *La Malinche*. En 1522, Gonzalo de Sandoval se instaló en la villa de Santa María de la Victoria y entregó indios a las encomiendas que creó en la costa. A principios de 1525, Juan de Vallecillo reinició la conquista del actual territorio tabasqueño, pero, al igual que Sandoval, fracasó en su intento por dominar el interior. En ese mismo año, una nueva expedición de Cortés, que se dirigía a Honduras, recorrió el sur de Tabasco. Según se dice, a orillas del río Usumascinta, el extremeño ahorcó a Cuauhtémoc, el último tlatoani mexica. En 1527, Baltazar Osorio Gallegos se hizo cargo del gobierno de Tabasco, y durante el año siguiente, realizó varias expediciones militares contra los cimatecos y los jaguayates. En 1528, apoyado en su nombramiento como adelantado de Tabasco, Francisco de Montejo destituyó a Osorio y se apoderó de la alcaldía de Tabasco. Al año siguiente, mientras combatía a los mayas yucatecos, los chontales de Xicalcingo y Cimatán se levantaron en armas contra la dominación europea, pero fueron derrotados por el hijo del alcalde, Francisco de Montejo y León, quien fundó, sobre las poblaciones arrasadas, las villa de Salamanca de Xicalcingo y Santiago Cimatlán. Nuevas sublevaciones impidieron a los conquistadores asentarse firmemente en territorio tabasqueño hasta 1535, cuando Montejo y León derrotó a los últimos alzados. Nueve años después, en 1543, la provincia de Tabasco se convirtió en dependencia de la Audiencia de Guatemala, pero en 1548, junto con Yucatán, el territorio tabasqueño volvió a depender de la ciudad de México. La Audiencia guatemalteca, sin embargo, retomó el control del sureste novohispano en 1550 y lo conservó durante una década, hasta que en enero de 1560 fue res-

Foto: Boris de Swan

Iglesia de la Virgen de la Asunción, Comalcalco

tablecida la autoridad de la Audiencia de México. En el plano religioso, desde 1538 Tabasco había dependido de la diócesis de Chiapas, y desde 1547 de la de Yucatán, aunque la presencia de los frailes mendicantes había sido muy esporádica, lo que provocó que la penetración del catolicismo romano fuera más bien superficial. Para fines del siglo XVI, la población indígena se había reducido hasta unas 8,500 personas, mientras que la europea no llegaba siquiera al centenar, por lo que se introdujeron esclavos africanos. Este tráfico humano, así como la abundancia de maderas preciosas en la zona y la excelente posición del puerto de la villa de Santa María de la Victoria, situado a medio camino entre Veracruz y Campeche, convirtió a la provincia en uno de los sitios de más actividad para los piratas ingleses, franceses y holandeses. En 1596, Francis Drake asaltó varias veces el puerto de Santa María de la Victoria, por lo que el ayuntamiento decidió trasladar la capital tierra adentro, hasta los llanos de la hacienda de San Juan Bautista. Pero mientras los complicados trámites burocráticos se realizaban, San ta María de la Victoria volvió a ser asaltada en 1614, 1615 y 1640, hasta que, en 1642, sin esperar las resoluciones de España, los habitantes del puerto se trasladaron a San Juan Bautista (☛ *Villahermosa*) y nueve años después, en 1650, consiguieron que las autoridades convirtieran al poblado de San Juan Bautista de Villa Hermosa en capital de la provincia de Tabasco. El traslado, por supuesto, no impidió las incursiones piratas, sobre todo las de los corsarios de la laguna de Términos, quienes, además de realizar ataques costeros, por lo menos en tres ocasiones, 1665, 1667 y 1677, remontaron el río Grijalva y saquearon San Juan Bautista. En el siglo XVII, los españoles comenzaron a practicar la ganadería. Hacia 1646, según registraron las autoridades eclesiásticas de Mérida, sólo vivían en Tabasco unos 2,797 indios. Aunque la peligrosidad de los corsarios decreció notablemente en el siglo XVIII, el gobierno colonial ordenó, en 1706, la construcción de un fuerte artillado en la desembocadura del río Grijalva, para impedir que los piratas entraran por el río y atacaran San Juan Bautista. En esa centuria se agudizaron los problemas de las comunidades indígenas del sur de Tabasco, a causa de la expansión de las haciendas ganaderas y cacaoteras, por lo que en 1712, cuando estalló un gran levantamiento de tzeltales (☛) al norte de San Cristóbal, muchos pueblos chontales se sumaron a la revuelta, pero a diferencia de la sublevación chiapaneca, la tabasqueña fue derrotada, en ese mismo año, por las fuerzas coloniales de Juan Francisco Medina Cachón. No obstante, en junio de 1727, los zoques de Teapa y Tecomajiaca eligieron un obispo y un rey propios, se levantaron en armas contra el gobierno virreinal y convocaron a los indios de Tlacotalpa, Jalapa, Tila y Oxolotlán, entre otros, para "acabar con los españoles". Aunque los sublevados establecieron contactos con otras comunidades indígenas del istmo de Tehuantepec, a fines de ese año, la insurrección fue derrotada. A mediados del siglo XVIII, el comercio de esclavos se reactivó a causa de un acuerdo entre España y Gran Bretaña, el que convirtió a los ingleses en los únicos

Foto: Michael Calderwood

Flor de macuilli de Tabasco

Foto: Fondo Editorial Grupo Azabache

Palacio Municipal Tabasco 2000

Foto: Fondo Editorial Grupo Azabache

Casa Museo Carlos Pellicer en Villahermosa, Tabasco

proveedores de africanos de las colonias americanas. Durante los últimos años del siglo se fundaron nuevos poblados en la parte central de la provincia, como San Carlos de Ocuatitlán (1766) y San Fernando de Ocuiltzapotlán (1768), e incluso en la costa del golfo, como Pueblo Nuevo de la Frontera (1780). Estos asentamientos, principalmente el último, se beneficiaron con la creación de las intendencias en 1787, pues Tabasco quedó incluido en la de Yucatán, y la cercanía con Campeche, Sisal y otros puertos de la península incrementaron sus posibilidades comerciales de la zona. No obstante, la baja densidad demográfica de la provincia constituía un problema. Hacia 1793, por ejemplo, la población tabasqueña estaba constituida por 151 europeos, 2,556 criollos, 11,184 mulatos y 19,438 indios. La guerra de Independencia prácticamente no provocó movimientos de tropas, salvo algunos del propio gobierno virreinal, que en 1811, ante las noticias de la insurrección en el centro de la Nueva España, decidió construir un cuartel especial en San Juan Bautista. En 1808 fue elegido el primer ayuntamiento de la capital provincial, cuyas autoridades, hasta entonces, eran designadas por el gobierno de Mérida. En los primeros meses de 1821, José María Jiménez Garrido organizó una conspiración independentista, la que fue descubierta por el gobernador Ángel del Toro. En agosto de ese año, mientras en el resto del virreinato se generalizaban los pronunciamientos iturbidistas, las fuerzas neoinsurgentes de Juan Nepomuceno Fernández Mantecón, enviado al sur de Veracruz por Antonio López de Santa Anna, cruzaron el río Tonalá, tomaron San Antonio de los Naranjos y Cunduacán, y en septiembre desalojaron a los españoles de San Juan Bautista y proclamaron la independencia. Dos años después, el diputado Manuel Crescencio Rejón, inició una campaña en el Congreso Constituyente para separar a Tabasco de la ex intendencia de Yucatán, pero interrumpió sus gestiones a causa del levantamiento santanista en Veracruz y el derrocamiento del emperador Agustín de Iturbide. A fines de 1823, Rejón consiguió que el Congreso aprobara la perseguida separación y, en el Acta Constitutiva de la Federación, publicada en enero de 1824, Tabasco, que entonces contaba con una población de 54,772 habitantes, figuró como uno de los estados miembros de la Unión. En mayo de ese año, Agustín Ruiz de la Peña fue electo gobernador provisional del estado, pero poco después, José Antonio Rincón, comandante militar del estado, se levantó

Foto: Michael Calderwood

Obrero petrolero de Tabasco

La petroquímica, actividad primordial en Tabasco

Foto: Michael Calderwood

Pozos petroleros de Tabasco

Foto: Michael Calderwood

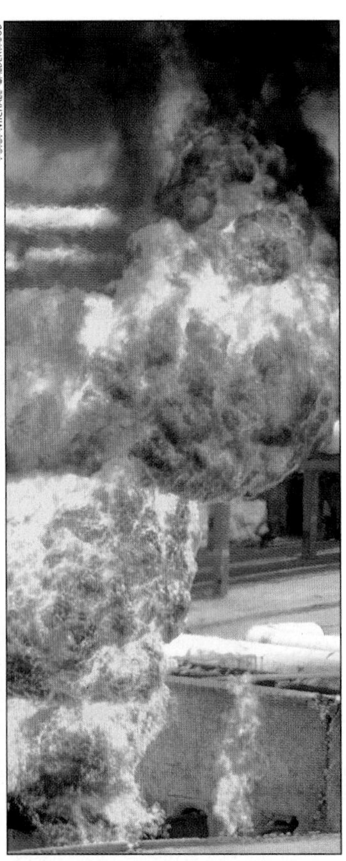

Exploración de pozos petroleros en Tabasco

en armas y obligó al gobierno de Ruiz de la Peña a refugiarse en Cunduacán. Otro pronunciamiento, el encabezado por José María Rivera, derrotó a Rincón en junio y el nuevo gobierno se negó a reconocer al comandante militar, nombrado en la ciudad de México, Francisco Hernández, por lo que, en agosto, Antonio Facio, al mando de una fuerza de 100 hombres, invadió Tabasco y sometió a las autoridades locales. En febrero del año siguiente, el Congreso local promulgó la primera Constitución tabasqueña, dividió la entidad en los departamentos de la Sierra, la Capital y la Chontalpa, avaló la elección de Ruiz de la Peña como primer gobernador constitucional y, en 1826, dispuso que el nombre de la capital del estado fuera San Juan Bautista de Tabasco; expidió el primer reglamento agrario que ratificó el estado de esclavitud en que vivían los campesinos, principalmente los indígenas. También, en 1826, se instaló una imprenta en el estado y comenzó a editarse el primer periódico local, *El Argos Tabasqueño*. En agosto del año siguiente, el vicegobernador, Marcelino Margalli, encabezó un levantamiento militar que derrocó al gobierno de Ruiz de la Peña. Margalli, de la logia escocesa, asumió la gubernatura y poco después, como parte de una actuación más afín a los yorkinos, promulgó una ley que prohibía a los españoles trabajar en Tabasco. En agosto de 1828, el vicegobernador Santiago Duque de Estrada, también escocés, logró desplazar a Margalli con el apoyo de la Legislatura local y se instaló en el Ejecutivo. En 1829, mediante una nueva sublevación militar, Ruiz de la Peña volvió al poder, pero en noviembre fue derrocado por el reunificado partido escocés, que a su vez fue derrotado en diciembre. En febrero de 1830, apoyados por el levantamiento del vicepresidente Anastasio Bustamante, en Jalapa, los centralistas de Sebastián López de Llergo y el propio Duque de Estrada invadieron el estado desde Campeche y tomaron San Juan Bautista. Durante los cuatro meses siguientes, varias facciones se disputaron el poder local hasta que, en agosto, el moderado José Rovirosa fue elegido gobernador. Los moderados, que también controlaban el Congreso, decidieron cambiar la Constitución del estado, al año siguiente promulgaron una nueva que poco tiempo se mantuvo en vigor, pues en junio de 1832, Mariano Martínez de Lejarza se adhirió a la insurrección federalista, acaudillada por Santa Anna. Con Manuel Buelta en el Ejecutivo, los liberales intentaron aplicar en Tabasco las medidas que el vicepresidente Valentín Gómez Farías promovía desde la ciudad de México, pero los conflictos entre el gobernador y Martínez de Lejarza, convertido en comandante militar al triunfo santanista, impidieron toda reforma y ambos acabaron por renunciar. Los centralistas, por su parte, aprovecharon las pugnas entre los liberales. En junio de 1835 consiguieron que la guarnición de San Juan Bautista se adhiriera a la maniobra golpista del presidente Santa Anna y eligieron gobernador a Eduardo Correa, quien, en noviembre, estableció el centralismo e inició una campaña contra los liberales. Cinco años después, los federalistas pudieron reorganizarse y en

Foto: Fondo Editorial Grupo Azabache

Bancos de Ostión en El Bellote, Tabasco

Copra de Tabasco

Foto: Michael Calderwood

Foto: Michael Calderwood

Plantación de papaya

febrero de 1840, Nicolás Maldonado, se levantó en armas en Tepetitlán, tomó Macuspana, Teapa y Huimanguillo, pero en julio fue derrotado cuando intentaba ocupar la capital del estado y se retiró a Campeche. Unos meses después, con la ayuda del cubano Francisco Sentamanat, Maldonado invadió Tabasco, derrotó a los centralistas en Teapa, Jalapa y Tlacotalpa, mientras Sentamanat los vencía en Cunduacán. En noviembre derrocó al gobierno. Los federalistas crearon una Junta Renovadora del Federalismo y nombraron gobernador a Ruiz de la Peña, quien se vió obligado a renunciar poco después por motivos de salud. Un nuevo Congreso Constituyente, reunido en febrero de 1841, decidió separar a Tabasco de la República, mientras subsistiera el gobierno centralista, pero el movimiento fue derrotado en mayo, en Comitán, por las fuerzas de Ignacio Barberena, y el gobierno federalista tuvo que huir a Yucatán, que por entonces también se había independizado. A fines de ese año, Simón Sarlat y Alonso Fernández formalizaron una coalición de Tabasco, Veracruz y Chiapas contra el gobierno de Bustamante y apoyaron el enésimo levantamiento de Santa Anna, quien, al llegar a la Presidencia, nombró gobernador y comandante militar al ex federalista Sentamanat. En julio de 1842, una flota texano-yucateca intentó tomar Frontera, pero fue rechazada por Sentamanat, que, como represalia, tomó Palizada y Campeche, que eran territorios de Yucatán y los incorporó a Tabasco. Al año siguiente, sin embargo, tropas centralistas de Yucatán, apoyadas por el gobierno de Santa Anna, invadieron Tabasco, tomaron San Juan Bautista y obligaron a renunciar a Sentamanat, quien en 1844 intentó derrocar al gobierno, pero fue apresado, fusilado y degollado. En enero de 1846, una parte de la guarnición tabasqueña se adhirió al levantamiento que Mariano Paredes y Arrillaga habían iniciado a fines de 1845 en San Luis Potosí, pero medio año después, descontenta con las pretensiones monárquicas de Paredes, la Asamblea Departamental de Tabasco se negó a sesionar y, en agosto, la guarnición de San Juan Bautista se levantó en favor del Plan de la Ciudadela de José Mariano Salas, y nombró comandante militar y gobernador del estado a Juan Bautista Traconis. Menos de medio año tenía de restablecido el

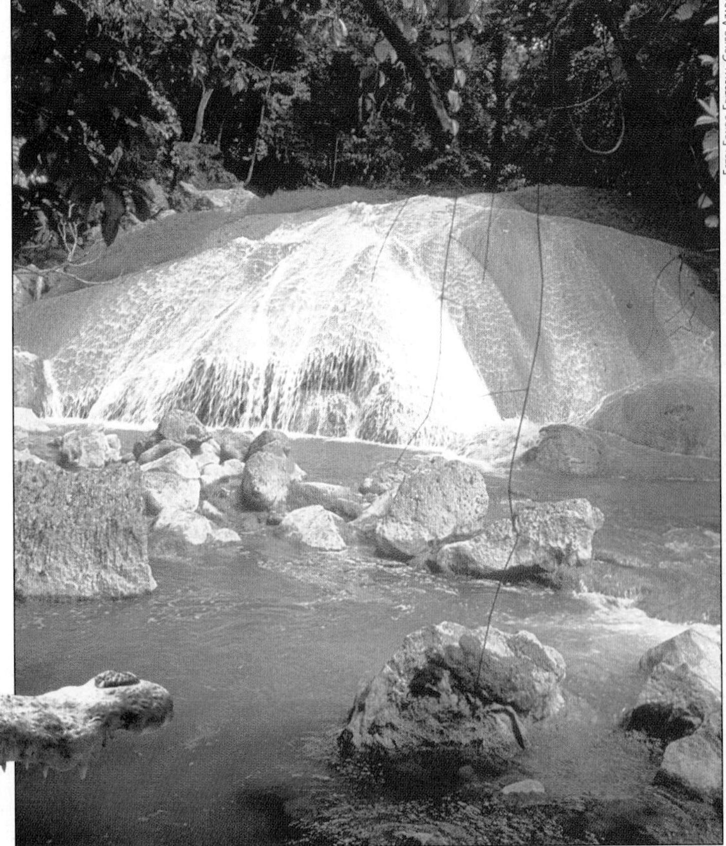

Foto: Fondo Editorial Grupo Azabache

Cascadas de Agua Blanca en Tabasco

Cocodrilo de Tabasco

Foto: Michael Calderwood

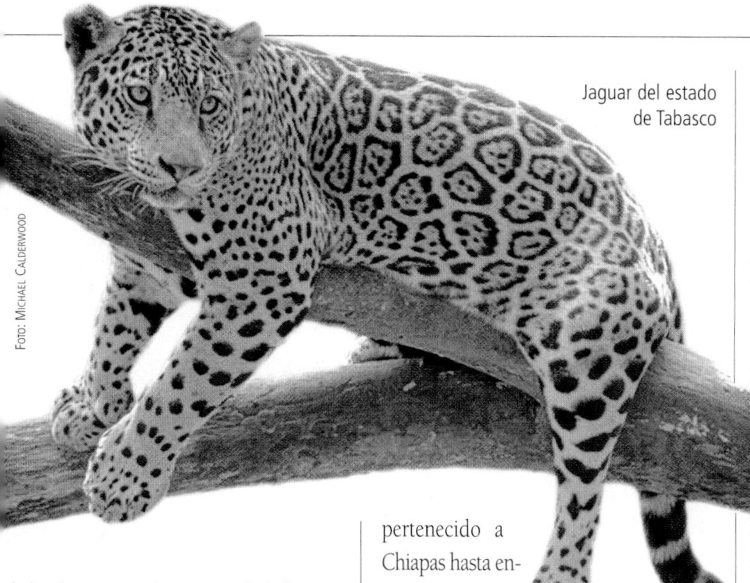

Jaguar del estado de Tabasco

Urna de Teapa en el Museo de Antropología de Tabasco

federalismo cuando, en octubre, fuerzas de la marina estadounidense al mando de Mathew C. Perry tomaron Frontera y remontaron el Grijalva hacia San Juan Bautista, pero el día 26 fueron derrotadas en los alrededores de la ciudad por la guardia nacional de Tabasco, al mando del gobernador Traconis, quien, sin embargo, fue destituido en enero de 1847, luego de un nuevo intento separatista. Unos días después, la guarnición de San Juan Bautista se sublevó para restituir a Traconis, pero fue derrotada por el ejército de Chiapas, comandado por el propio gobernador de ese estado. Seis meses después, en junio, los estadounidenses volvieron a atacar San Juan Bautista, derrotaron a las fuerzas de Domingo Echeagaray y tomaron la capital, pero sólo pudieron resistir en ella dos semanas debido a la insalubridad y las guerrillas de Miguel Bruno. El Congreso, por su parte, se trasladó a Tlacotalpa. Bruno conservó el mando militar del estado hasta noviembre de 1848, cuando fue destituido y fusilado por Manuel Peláez. En 1850 se promulgó una nueva constitución local. Por entonces, poco más de 63,000 personas vivían en el estado y de ellas, 4,000 se concentraban en la capital. A mediados de 1854, Victorio Dueñas se levantó en armas en Jalapa, adherido al Plan de Ayutla. Intentó, sin éxito, tomar San Juan Bautista pero fue hasta agosto del año siguiente cuando derrocó al gobierno conservador. En diciembre de 1856, la región de Huimanguillo, que había pertenecido a Chiapas hasta entonces, se incorporó a Tabasco.

Aunque en septiembre de 1857 se había promulgado una nueva constitución local, la mayor parte las fuerzas militares acantonadas en el estado se adhirieron al levantamiento conservador de Tacubaya. En diciembre y a principios de 1858 Francisco Colorado y Francisco Velázquez derrocaron al gobierno de Dueñas. Los liberales, por su parte, solicitaron ayuda al gobierno chiapaneco de Miguel Ángel Albino Corzo, y en octubre de ese año recuperaron el poder, que retuvieron hasta el fin de la guerra de los Tres Años. En marzo de 1863, las fuerzas invasoras francesas tomaron Frontera, en junio, los imperialistas de Eduardo González Arévalo ocuparon San Juan Bautista. Los republicanos se concentraron en Comalcalco, Tlacotalpa y Villa de Cárdenas, antes San Antonio de los Naranjos, y desde ahí, comandados por Gregorio Méndez, Lino Merino y Andrés Sánchez Magallanes, organizaron la resistencia republicana, hasta que, a fines de febrero de 1864, luego de dos meses de sitio, tomaron la capital. Los imperialistas se retiraron a Frontera, pero unos días más tarde fueron expulsados del estado por las tropas de Regino Hernández. Con Méndez al frente del gobierno, los republicanos resistieron va-

Puerto Ceiba, en Tabasco

Foto: Fondo Editorial Grupo Azabache

Jícaras labradas de Tabasco

Foto: Fondo Editorial Grupo Azabache

Ceiba, árbol sagrado de los mayas, en Tabasco

rios ataques franceses en Jonuta y Palizada. En junio de 1865, el gobierno de Tabasco se unió a la Coalición de Estados de Oriente, integrada por Veracruz, Chiapas y Oaxaca y, a principios de 1866, los republicanos conquistaron las últimas posiciones de los imperialistas en Tabasco: Frontera y Jonuta. Felipe de Jesús Serra fue elegido gobernador al triunfo de la República. Durante su mandato enfrentó los levantamientos de Rosario Bastar (1867), Narciso Sáenz (1868) y Ezequiel Jiménez (1868), hasta que en julio de 1871 fue derrocado por Dueñas. A principios de 1876, Ramón Ricoy y Faustino Sastré se levantaron en armas en Cárdenas y Teapa y se adhirieron al Plan de Tuxtepec. En mayo, luego del levantamiento de la guarnición de San Juan Bautista, las fuerzas porfiristas se instalaron en el poder. El gobierno lerdista, encabezado por Pedro Carrillo, se retiró a Frontera y en julio, con fuerzas mandadas por Pedro Sáenz de Barrada, reconquistó la capital. Sin embargo, el triunfo de la revuelta tuxtepecana en el resto del país obligó a Carrillo a rendirse. En 1880 se erigió la diócesis de Tabasco, que desde entonces tiene su sede en la capital. Tres años más tarde, la Legislatura tabasqueña promulgó la sexta constitución del estado. Entre 1895 y 1911, Abraham Bandala fue gobernador del estado en 19 ocasiones. En 1909 se creó la Sociedad Tabasqueña de Estudiantes, de carácter antirreeleccionista. En diciembre del año siguiente, al inicio de la insurrección maderista, Ignacio y Pedro Gutiérrez Torres se levantaron en armas contra el gobierno del presidente Díaz, pero fueron derrotados en abril de 1911. Sólo una pequeña fuerza al mando de Domingo C. Magaña continuó la lucha. Después del triunfo maderista hubo levantamientos en San Juan Bautista y Huimanguillo, uno magonista en Frontera, encabezado por Pedro Padilla. En febrero de 1913, luego del asesinato de Madero, el gobernador Manuel Mestre Ghigliazza reconoció al gobierno de Victoriano Huerta. Poco después se sublevaron Pedro C. Colorado, Fernando Aguirre Colorado y Aquileo Juárez. En diciembre, el Congreso aprobó una nueva constitución local, la que prácticamente no entró en

Foto: Michael Calderwood

Cascada de Tabasco

vigor, pues a principios de 1914, Alejandro Greene, Áureo Calles, Aurelio Sosa Torres y Ramón Sosa Torres se levantaron en armas en la región de la Chontalpa; tomaron Cunduacán, Huimanguillo, Cárdenas y Comalcalco antes de entrar, en septiembre, a San Juan Bautista. Un año más tarde, luego de varios meses de enfrentamientos entre las fuerzas locales, el gobierno de Venustiano Carranza nombró gobernador y comandante militar del estado a Francisco J. Múgica, quien prohibió la educación religiosa en el estado y, de acuerdo con su política laica, transformó San Juan Bautista en Villahermosa. En 1919, después de una campaña de hostigamiento contra los miembros del Partido Liberal Constitucionalista, la dirigencia del Partido Radical se apoderó del poder e impuso como gobernador a Greene, pero en marzo, los liberales organizaron un levantamiento militar en Frontera y tomaron el palacio de gobierno de Villahermosa, donde retuvieron unas horas al gobernador interino, Tomás Garrido Canabal, pero fueron derrotados en septiembre. En octubre del año siguiente, el gobierno de Greene fue desconocido por provocar una balacera en la sede del Congreso. En noviembre de 1922, Garrido Canabal fue elegido gobernador. Un año después, en diciembre de 1923, adheridos al delahuertismo, se levantaron en armas Francisco Lozano en Frontera y Greene en la Chotalpa. En enero de 1924 tomaron Villahermosa y derrocaron al gobierno de Garrido Canabal, quien, sin embargo, recuperó el poder en junio con el apoyo de fuerzas obregonistas. Poco después organizó ligas obreras de resistencia, inició el reparto agrario, creó el Partido Socialista Radical, dispuso que todos los ministros de los cultos religiosos fueran casados y creó unas brigadas de choque conocidas como *Camisas Rojas*. En 1928, el gobierno de Ausencio C. Cruz, dominado por el propio Garrido Canabal, prohibió las cantinas y el comercio de cualquier bebida alcohólica que no fuera cerveza. Después del asesinato del presidente Álvaro Obregón, destruyó la Catedral de Tabasco, intensificó la persecución religiosa y expulsó a los sacerdotes. Garrido Canabal volvió a ser elegido gobernador en 1930. Cuatro años después, el presidente Lázaro Cárdenas llamó al estado "el laboratorio de la revolución" y Garrido Canabal pasó a formar parte de su gabinete. Meses más tarde, al estallar el conflicto entre Cárdenas y Plutarco Elías Calles, Garrido Canabal permaneció leal a éste y salió del gabinete. En junio entró en Tabasco la "expedición punitiva" dirigida por Rodulfo Brito Foucher, supuestamente para participar en la campaña electoral del estado. Al mes siguiente, la fuerza de Brito fue atacada y resultaron muertos varios jóvenes, por lo que las organizaciones de derecha de todo el país hicieron grandes manifestaciones de protesta y el gobernador Manuel Lastra Ortiz, fue destituido. A partir de 1947 el periodo gubernamental es de seis años. En 1955, un alza en las tarifas del transporte motivo grandes manifestaciones de protesta, en una de las cuales fue herido el gobernador Manuel Bartlett Bautista, quien renunció el 22 de marzo. En 1974 se mencionó en la prensa internacional la existencia de grandes yacimientos de hidrocarburos en territorio tabasqueño. En la segunda mitad de los años setenta se intensificó la explotación petrolera, lo que produjo graves daños ecológicos, inflación, problemas sociales y, en los años ochenta, un crecimiento desmesurado de la población de Villahermosa.

DISTRIBUCIÓN PORCENTUAL DE LA POBLACIÓN OCUPADA POR SECTOR DE ACTIVIDAD ECONÓMICA, 1995

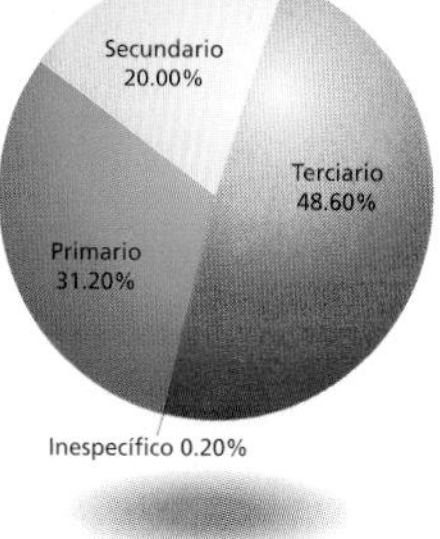

PRODUCTO INTERNO BRUTO (PIB) A PRECIOS CORRIENTES

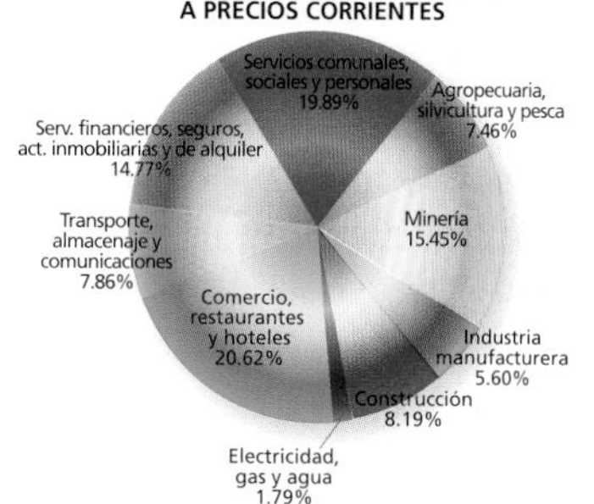

LONGITUD DE LA RED DE CARRETERAS POR SUPERFICIE DE RODAMIENTO, 1995

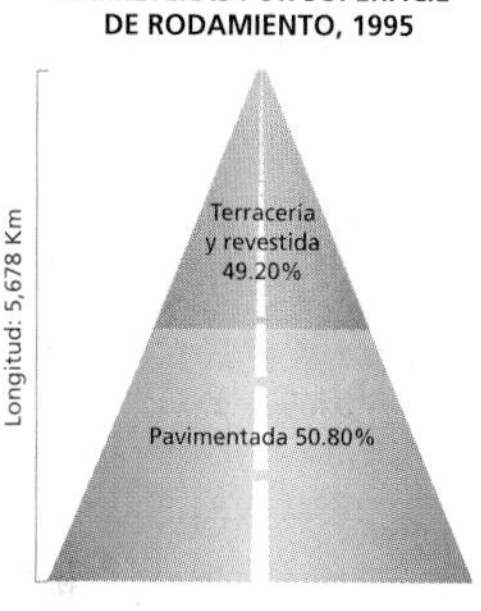

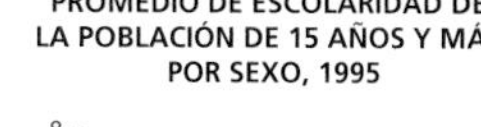

PROMEDIO DE ESCOLARIDAD DE LA POBLACIÓN DE 15 AÑOS Y MÁS, POR SEXO, 1995

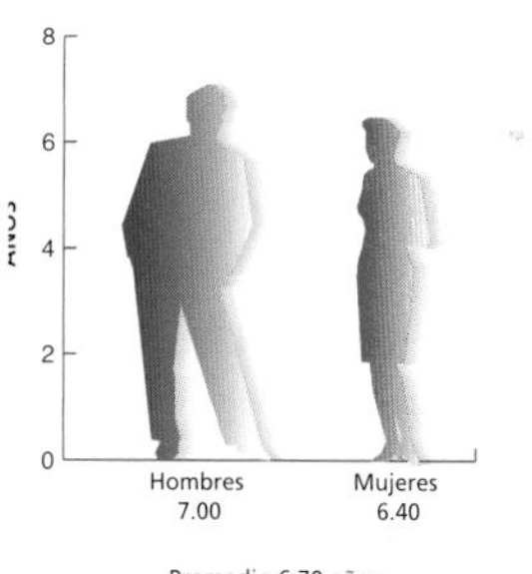
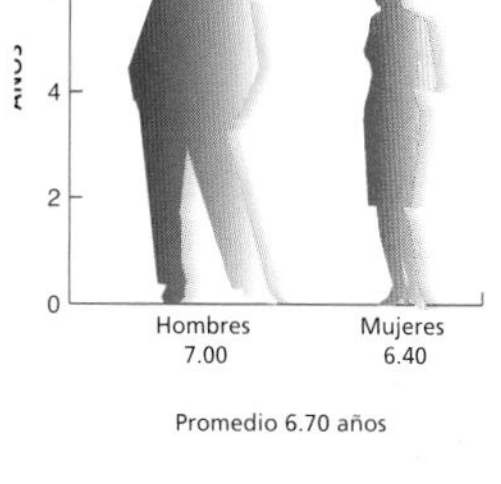

DISTRIBUCIÓN DE LA POBLACIÓN POR TAMAÑO DE LA LOCALIDAD, 1995

Más de 15,000 34.30%
Hasta 2,500 47.90%
Entre 2,500 y 15,000 17.80%

BIBLIOTECAS Y USUARIOS, 1993
Número de bibliotecas: 339

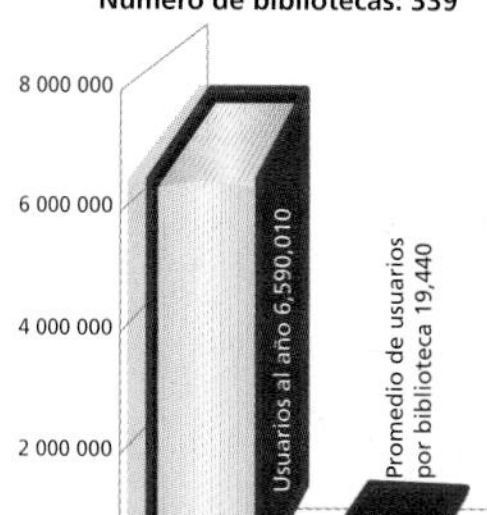

POBLACIÓN DE 5 AÑOS Y MÁS HABLANTE DE LENGUA INDÍGENA, 1995

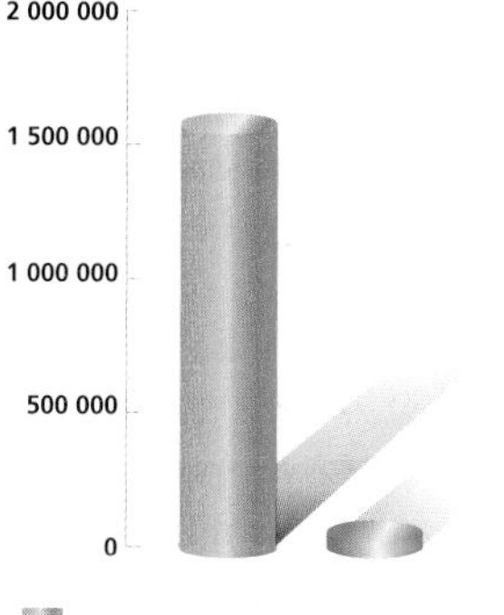

Población de 5 años y más 1,529,304

Población de 5 años y más hablante de lengua indígena 51,364 (3.36%)

Guaqueque de la fauna de Tabasco

FOTO: PABLO CERVANTES

José Juan Tablada

Diario de José Juan Tablada editado por Guillermo Sheridan

Tablada, José Juan ◆ n. en la ciudad de México y m. en EUA (1871-1945). Realizó estudios en el Colegio Militar y en una academia de pintura. Después de un viaje a Japón, hacia 1900, se convirtió en el primer mexicano en emplear la forma poética haikú. Escribió en *El Universal* (1890-), la *Revista Azul* (1894-96), la *Revista Moderna* (1898-1903) la *Revista Moderna de México* (1903-11), *El Mundo Ilustrado* y *Revista de Revistas*. Durante la dictadura de Victoriano Huerta fue jefe de redacción de *El Imparcial* (1913-14) y director del *Diario Oficial de la Federación* (1912-13). Al triunfo constitucionalista se exilió, pero en 1918 fue nombrado secretario de la embajada mexicana en Venezuela. En 1920 abrió una librería en Nueva York y escribió en las revistas estadounidenses *International Studio, Shadowland, The Arts* y *Survey Graphics*; y en las mexicanas *La Falange* (1922-23), *El Maestro* y *Número* (1934). Volvió a México en 1935. Aquí dirigió la revista *Mexican Art & Life* (1937-39). Vicecónsul en Nueva York (1945-). También colaboró en *Excélsior, El Universal* y *El Universal Ilustrado*. Autor de ensayo: *Cultura mexicana. Artes plásticas* (1920) e *Historia del arte en México* (1927); historia: *La defensa social. Historia de campaña de la División del Norte* (1913); memorias: *La feria de la vida* (1937); novela: *La resurrección de los ídolos* (1924); poesía: *Florilegio* (1899), *La epopeya nacional. Porfirio Díaz* (1909), *Al sol y bajo la luna* (1918), *Un día.* (1919), *Li-Po y otros poemas* (1920), *Retablo a la memoria de Ramón López Velarde* (1921), *El jarro de flores* (1922) y *La feria* (1928); relato: *Hirosigué, el pintor de la nieve y de la lluvia, de la noche y de la luna* (1914), *Los días y las noches de París* (1918) y *En el país del sol* (1919); teatro: *Madero-Chantecler. Tragicomedia zoológico-política de rigurosa actualidad* (1910, con el pseudónimo de *Girón de Pinabete Alcornoque y Astrágalo*); y textos humorísticos: *Del humorismo a la carcajada* (antología, 1944). Ingresó en 1928 a la Academia Mexicana (de la Lengua).

Tábora, Georgina ◆ n. en el DF (1959). Actriz. Estudió letras inglesas en la UNAM (1979-83). Ha actuado en *El deseo atrapado por la cola*, de Pablo Picasso, dirigida por Juan José Gurrola (1982), *Repaso de indulgencias*, de Óscar Liera, dirigida por Héctor Méndoza (1984), *El balcón*, de Jean Genet, dirigida por Georges Lavandant (1987), *Querida Lulú*, de varios autores, dirigida por Ludwik Margules (1987), *La rosa del tiempo*, de Juan José Gurrola (1987), *Nadie sabe nada*, de Vicente Leñero, dirigida por Luis de Tavira (1988), *De película*, de Julio Castillo (1989) y *Café americano* de y dirigida por Antonio Serrano (1995). Entre 1987 y 1989 formó parte del elenco del Centro de Experimentación Teatral del INBA. Trabajó en el Teatro-bar Guau (1985-87). Intervino en la película *Intimidad* (1989). Ha publicado poesía en revistas y suplementos literarios.

Tacámbaro ◆ Municipio de Michoacán situado al suroeste de Morelia y contiguo a Pátzcuaro. Superficie: 1,085.05 km². Habitantes: 53,113, de los cuales 12,871 forman la población económicamente activa. Hablan alguna lengua indígena 49 personas mayores de cinco años (náhuatl 12 y purépecha 10). Poco después de la conquista española, el territorio de Tacámbaro fue cedido en encomienda a Cristóbal de Oñate. Hacia 1538 se establecieron los frailes agustinos, quienes encabezaron la conquista espiritual en la región. El 11 de abril de 1865, una columna guerrillera republicana, comandada por Nicolás de Régules, derrotó a una fuerza formada por belgas e imperiales comandada por el coronel Tydgadt, y se apoderó de la población, pero tres meses más tarde, el 16 de julio, los imperialistas de Ramón Méndez contraatacaron y recuperaron Tacámbaro, que fue inútilmente defendida por el republicano José María Arteaga. La diócesis de Tacámbaro fue erigida el 26 de junio de 1913. Los principales atractivos turísticos son las cascadas de Santa Paula y de Caracho, la laguna de La Magdalena, el Cerro Hueco y el balneario de Chupío.

Tacámbaro ◆ Río de Michoacán que nace en el cerro de las Nieves o de San Andrés, de los manantiales conocidos como Ojos de Agua de los Puercos, al este-sureste de Uruapan; corre de noroeste a sureste, recibe los ríos Turicato o Caliente y Carácuaro; sobre su curso hay una pequeña presa irrigadora; desemboca en la frontera con Guerrero, en el río Balsas, al este de la presa El Infiernillo.

Tacaná ◆ Volcán de Chiapas situado

Tacacá, volcán de Chiapas

FOTO: FONDO EDITORIAL GRUPO AZABACHE

Tapijulapa, pueblo serrano en el municipio de Tacotalpa, Tabasco

en la frontera entre México y Guatemala, al sureste de la sierra del Soconusco y nor-noreste de Tapachula. Se eleva 4,057 metros sobre el nivel del mar y mide unos 2,000 metros. En la cima del volcán se construyó una marca fronteriza.

TACOTALPA ◆ Municipio de Tabasco situado en la porción centro-sur del estado, al sur-sureste de Villahermosa y al oeste de Tenosique, en los límites con Chiapas. Superficie: 794,77 km^2. Habitantes: 37,857, de los cuales 8,648 forman la población económicamente activa. Hablan alguna lengua indígena 6,632 personas mayores de cinco años (chol 6,425 y tzotzil 97). Entre los atractivos turísticos de Tacotalpa se halla el pueblo típico de Tapijulapa, que fue la cabecera municipal entre 1934 y 1937, en cuyas cercanías hay manantiales y pozas de aguas azufrosas de color azul. También, dentro de los límites del municipio, se encuentran las grutas de Poana y de Cuesta Chica, así como los manantiales de aguas sulfurosas en Villa Luz.

TACOTALPA ◆ Río de Tabasco, también llamado Oxolotán y Almendros. Nace en las cercanías de Tapijulapa, de la confluencia de los ríos Chacté y Plátano o San Pablo, provenientes de la vertiente septentrional de la Sierra Madre de Chiapas. Corre de sur a norte; en su primer tramo se llama Almendros. Recibe al río Concepción y se convierte en el Tacotalpa u Oxolotán, más abajo al Amatán y se une al Teapa, tributario del Grijalva, al sur-sureste de Villahermosa. Es navegable en los últimos 120 kilómetros de su recorrido, entre Oxolotán y la confluencia con el Teapa.

TACUBA ◆ Barrio de la ciudad de México que forma parte de la delegación Azcapotzalco del Distrito Federal. Fue el señorío de Tlacopan, que desde 1430 formó parte de la Triple Alianza con México-Tenochtitlan y Texcoco. Aunque sus dimensiones eran reducidas, logró imponer su hegemonía hasta la frontera con el reino purépecha y dominaba las poblaciones otomíes de Axocopan, Atotonilco, Cuautitlán, Cuahuacán, Jilotepec, Jacotitlán y Hueypochtla. Conquistada en 1521 por las fuerzas españolas de Pedro de Alvarado, quien se instaló en la población durante el sitio a la capital de los mexicas. Fue municipio hasta 1928. Se conservó como una población aparte hasta el siglo XX, cuando fue absorbido por la mancha urbana.

TACUBAYA ◆ Barrio de la ciudad de México situado en la delegación Miguel Hidalgo del Distrito Federal. En la era prehispánica era una población conocida como Atlacuihuayan o Atlacocuaya. Estuvo dominada, primero, por los tecpanecas y desde 1430 por los mexicas. Durante el virreinato, Tacubaya dependió del corregimiento de Coyohuacan (Coyoacán) del marquesado del Valle de Oaxaca. En 1841, en este pueblo se promulgaron las llamadas Bases de Tacubaya, que dieron fin al movimiento armado de Mariano Paredes y Arrillaga, y Antonio López de Santa Anna contra Anastasio Bustamante. En diciembre de 1857, los conservadores lanzaron el Plan de Tacubaya, mediante el cual desconocían la Constitución, lo que dio inicio a la guerra de los Tres Años. A mediados del siglo XIX, Tacubaya era una municipalidad que comprendía una gran zona desde Nonoalco hasta Narvarte, pasando por Santa Fe, San Lorenzo, el rancho de Nápoles, la hacienda de San Borja, la hacienda de Sola o Xola, La Piedad y la hacienda de la Condesa. Se decía que era "la capital de los pueblecillos cercanos a México". En 1928 desapareció como municipio y en

FOTO: BORIS DE SWAN

Aspecto del barrio de Tacubaya, en la ciudad de México

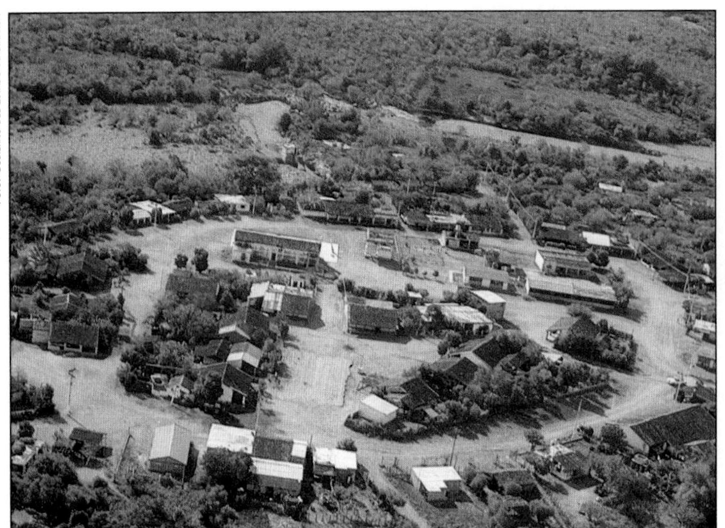
Foto: Gobierno del Estado de Sinaloa

Vista aérea de un poblado en la sierra de Tacuichamona, Sinaloa

Protasio Tagle

Paco Ignacio Taibo I

Foto: Rogelio Cuéllar

Paco Ignacio Taibo II

enero del año siguiente pasó a formar parte de la ciudad de México. En 1970 quedó dentro de la delegación Miguel Hidalgo del Distrito Federal.

Tacuichamona, de ♦ Sierra de Sinaloa que forma por el oeste una de las estribaciones de la sierra Madre Occidental. Se extiende de noroeste a sureste, paralela a la llanura costera, desde el río San Lorenzo, al sureste de Culiacán, hasta el río Piaxtla, al noroeste de la sierra Espinazo del Diablo.

Tagle, Protasio ♦ n. y m. en la ciudad de México (1839-1903). Su nombre completo era Protasio Pérez de Tagle. Abogado titulado en la Escuela Nacional de Jurisprudencia (1871), donde fue profesor. Se opuso a la intervención francesa y al imperio. Diputado federal al triunfo de la República (1867-75). En enero de 1871 participó en la creación de la Asociación Democrática Constitucionalista, que impulsó la candidatura presidencial de Porfirio Díaz, más tarde la insurrección de La Noria. Cinco años después redactó un borrador del que sería el Plan de Tuxtepec (☛) y desde la ciudad de México apoyó la nueva sublevación porfirista. A la caída del gobierno de Sebastián Lerdo de Tejada fue gobernador del Distrito Federal (del 21 al 28 de noviembre de 1876) y más tarde secretario de Gobernación (del 29 de noviembre al 6 de diciembre de 1876 y del 17 de febrero al 23 de mayo de 1877) y de Justicia (del 24 de mayo de 1877 al 15 de noviembre de 1879) en el gobierno de Porfirio Díaz. En 1879 se opuso a la candidatura presidencial de Manuel González, por lo que se retiró de la vida política.

Tahdziú ♦ Municipio de Yucatán situado en el sur del estado, al suroeste de Chichén Itzá y contiguo a Peto. Superficie: 53,65 km². Habitantes: 2,812, de los cuales 637 forman la población económicamente activa. Hablan alguna lengua indígena 2,285 personas mayores de cinco años (maya 2,275). Indígenas monolingües: 1,043.

Tahmek ♦ Municipio de Yucatán situado en el centro del estado, al sureste de Mérida y sur de Motul. Superficie: 139,24 km². Habitantes: 3,631, de los cuales 1,133 forman la población económicamente activa. Hablan alguna lengua indígena 2,629 personas mayores de cinco años (maya 2,626), de las cuales 111 son monolingües.

Taibo, Benito ♦ n. en el DF (1961). Escritor. Su apellido materno es Mahojo. Estudió historia en la UNAM. Colaborador de los diarios *El Universal* y *unomásuno*, de la revista *Siempre!* y del programa de televisión *Para gente grande*. Autor de *Siete primeros poemas*, *Vivos y suicidas* (1978) y *Recetas para el desastre* (1987).

Taibo I, Paco Ignacio ♦ n. en España (1924). Escritor. Llegó a México en 1958 y poco después se naturalizó mexicano. Ha sido director de noticieros de los canales de televisión 4, 5 y 8; director de Estrategia, Programación y Noticias del Canal 13 de televisión (1981) y editor, desde 1985, de la sección *El Universal en la Cultura* del diario *El Universal*. Coautor de *La regenta, cien años después*. Autor de gastronomía: *Breviario de la fabada*, *Breviario del mole poblano*, *Breviario del comer americano*, *Comiendo con Reyes* e *Historia de dos fogones* (2 t., 1993); historia: *Henry Langdon: el mejor de todos* (1966), *Los toros en el cine* (1969), *Enciclopedia del cine cómico* (3 t., 1978), *La música de Agustín Lara en el cine* (1983), *Los asombrosos itinerarios del cine*, *María Félix, cuarenta y siete años por el cine* (1985), *Indio Fernández: el cine por mis pistolas* (1986), *Cuevas: retratos y autorretratos* (1987), *Los toros en el cine mexicano* (1987), *Gloria y achaques del espectáculo en México* (tomo VIII de *Crónica general de México*; 1988), *De algún tiempo a esta parte* (2 t., 1990) y *La Doña* (1991); prosas varias: *Asturias imaginada*, *Risa loca* (1980), *Por el gusto de estar con ustedes* (1987), *Lecturas taurinas* (1987) y *El periodista* (1956); novela: *Juan M. N.* (1954), *Uno de los tres* (1970), *Pálidas banderas* (1975), *Fuga, hierro y fuego* (1979), *Para parar las aguas del olvido* (1980), *Todos los comienzos* (1983) y *Siempre Dolores* (1984); teatro: *La quinta parte de un arcángel* (1967), *Los cazadores* (1967), *El juglar y la cama* (1967) y *Morir del todo* (1973). En *El gato culto* (1994) reunió muchas de sus caricaturas para la sección de cultura de *El Universal*. En 1980 recibió un premio a la mejor obra de teatro estrenada en 1979.

Taibo II, Paco Ignacio ♦ n. en España (1949). Hijo del anterior. Llegó a México en 1958 y se naturalizó mexicano. Realizó estudios en la UNAM y en la ENAH, de las que fue profesor. Ha sido investigador de la UAM, director de la colección de historietas *México, historia de un pueblo*, de la *Crónica general de México* (1981-86) y del suplemento *La Cultura en México* de *Siempre!* (1987-

88). Director fundador del festival cultural La Semana Negra de Gijón. Coautor de *El caso Molinet* (1992) y *Frontera de espejos rotos* (1993). Autor, entre muchas otras obras, de cuento: *Doña Eustolia blandió el cuchillo cebollero* (1984) y *El regreso de la verdadera Araña y otras historias* (1988); historia: *La gran huelga del verano de 1920 en Monterrey* (1982), *Bolshevikis. Historia narrativa de los orígenes del comunismo en México (1919-1925)* (1986), *Arcángeles. Cuatro historias no muy ortodoxas de revolucionarios* (1988), *El año que estuvimos en ninguna parte* (1993), *Ernesto Guevara, también conocido como el Che* (1996) y *El general orejón ese* (1997); novela: *Días de combate* (1976) *Cosa fácil* (1976), *Héroes convocados* (1982), *La vida misma* (1987, Premio Hammett 1987), *Cuatro manos/Four Hands* (1990, Premio Hammett 1991), *La lejanía del tesoro* (1992, Premio Planeta-Joaquín Mortiz), *La bicicleta de Leonardo* (1993, Premio Hammett 1994) *Que todo es imposible* (1995); y testimonio: *68* (1991) e *Insurgencia mi amor* (1997). Ha recibido los premios Grijalbo de Novela (1982), Café Gijón (1985), Francisco Javier Clavijero del INAH (1986), de Cuento Ramón López Velarde (1990) y Bancarella (1998). Presidente de la Asociación Internacional de Escritores Policiacos (1989-).

TAILANDIA, REINO DE ◆ Nación del sureste asiático situada en la porción central de la península indochina. Limita al norte y noreste con Laos, al sureste con Camboya, al sur con Malasia y al este, noreste y norte con Myanmar. Tiene costas en el golfo de Siam y en el mar de Andaman. Superficie: 514,000 km^2. Habitantes: 60,300,000 (1998). La capital del reino es Bangkok, que en 1995 tenía 8,896,506 habitantes. Su idioma oficial es el tai o siamés, pero también se hablan laosiano, chino y malayo. La religión predominante es el budismo. *Historia*: los primeros habitantes del actual territorio de Tailandia fueron birmanos, mons e hindúes. Alrededor del último milenio a.n.e., los khmer se instalaron en el sureste del actual territorio de Tailandia. Hacia el siglo VI de la época contemporánea, los tais, pertenecientes a un grupo originario del centro del continente, se instalaron en la ribera occidental del río Mekong, establecieron el reino de Dvaravati y comenzaron a extenderse hacia el oeste. A principios del segundo milenio de nuestra era, sin embargo, los birmanos se adueñaron de la parte central del país. Poco después, los malayos se establecieron en Trambalinga. En 1238, los tai crearon el reino de Sukhotai, en el suroriente del territorio, pero poco después cayeron bajo la dominación del reino malayo de Angkor. Independizados de los malayos desde 1317, hacia 1350 fueron conquistados nuevamente por los birmanos, quienes establecieron el reino de Ayutthaya o Siam. En los primeros años del siglo XVI, los comerciantes portugueses y japoneses desplazaron de Siam a los traficantes musulmanes y, a mediados de esa centuria, los lusitanos establecieron una línea de comercio entre Siam, Filipinas y la Nueva España, por la que trajeron hasta el puerto de Acapulco grandes cantidades de especias y vinieron pequeños grupos de malayos y tais; éstos últimos fueron conocidos en México con el nombre de *syois*. A fines del siglo XVI, los tais encabezaron un gran levantamiento contra la dominación birmana y, en 1584, con Phra Naret al frente, se instaló la monarquía tai. Durante la siguiente centuria, el comercio exterior del reino fue controlado por portugueses, holandeses y británicos, hasta que a fines del siglo XVI, los franceses se adueñaron del comercio de especias y de Bangkok. Apoyados por los holandeses, los tai volvieron a levantarse en armas y destituyeron al rey colaboracionista. A mediados del siglo XVI los birmanos volvieron a conquistar Siam, pero en 1782, comandados por Phyra Tak, los tai reconquistaron el territorio tailandés, establecieron su capital en Bangkok y eligieron rey a Phyra Tak, quien tomó el nombre de Rama I y fundó la dinastía de los chakkri. A lo largo del siglo XIX, Francia, Holanda e Inglaterra se disputaron la colonización de Siam, pero finalmente prefirieron respetar la autonomía del reino a cambio de amplias prerrogativas comerciales e impositivas. En los últimos años del siglo XIX, las potencias coloniales comenzaron a despojar a Siam de sus colonias. Los franceses ocuparon los protectorados de Camboya (1897) y Laos (1907), y los ingleses,

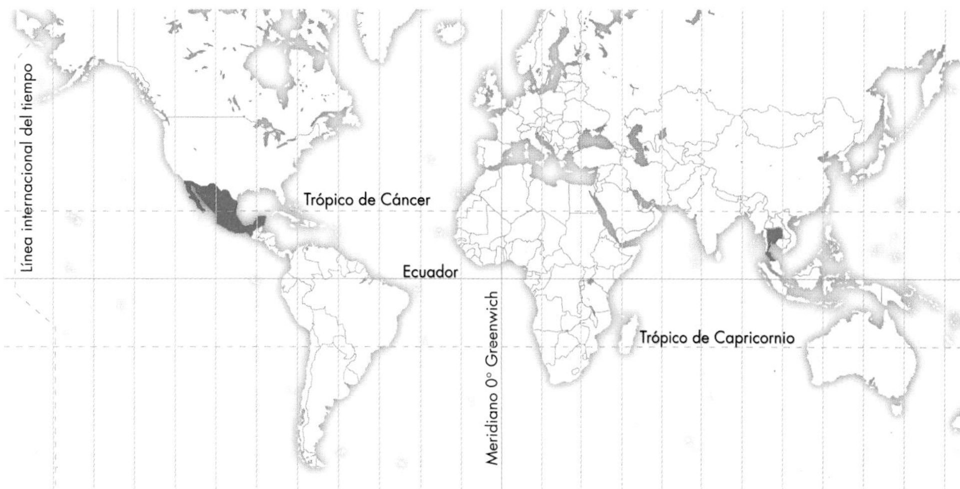

Monedas del Reino de Tailandia

Timbres del Reino de Tailandia

Transporte típico tailandés

los territorios de la península de Malaya (1907). En 1917, el gobierno de Siam le declaró la guerra a Alemania y un contingente de soldados siameses se trasladó a Francia, a combatir junto a los aliados. En 1919, el reino se integró a la Sociedad de Naciones. En 1932, un levantamiento armado obligó al rey a establecer una Asamblea Nacional y a promulgar una constitución. Tres años después, un nuevo movimiento popular hizo abdicar a Rama VII. Como el sucesor, Anada Mahidol, era menor de edad, los revolucionarios crearon una regencia, la que sin embargo no gobernó de manera efectiva. En 1938, un golpe de Estado instaló en el gobierno a Pibul Sonnggram. Al año siguiente, Siam se convirtió en Tailandia. En 1940, fuerzas tailandesas apoyadas por Japón obligaron a Francia a ceder varias zonas de Laos y Kampuchea, habitadas principalmente por tais, y en 1941, en correspondencia, el gobierno de Sonnggram permitió el tránsito del ejército nipón. En 1942, Tailandia declaró la guerra a los aliados y combatió con los japoneses hasta el fin de la segunda guerra mundial. En 1946, en circunstancias extrañas, murió Mahidol y fue sustituido por Bhumibol Adulyade, llamado Rama IX. Desde entonces, Tailandia se convirtió en uno de los aliados estadounidenses más confiables del sureste asiático. En 1954, por ejemplo, promovió la creación de la Organización del Tratado del Sureste Asiático (SEATO), que se instaló en Bangkok. Cuatro años después, los militares dieron un golpe de Estado y gobernaron el país hasta mediados de los años setenta. Hacia 1971, el ejército tailandés invadió varias zonas de Laos, Camboya y Vietnam, para apoyar a las fuerzas invasoras estadounidenses. En 1974 cayó el gobierno militar y Kukrit Pramoj fue elegido primer ministro. Al año siguiente, el 28 de agosto de 1975, México y el reino de Tailandia establecieron relaciones diplomáticas. En 1976 un nuevo golpe militar depuso a Pramoj. A partir de entonces, las guerrillas del Partido Comunista, activas desde los últimos años sesenta, intensificaron sus acciones, y a fines de los noventa aún subsistían. En 1977 ocurrieron varios enfrentamientos en la frontera de Tailandia con Camboya; en 1980, tropas vietnamitas atacaron a los camboyanos refugiados en Tailandia y tres años después, en 1983, el ejército tailandés sostuvo varios combates contra las fuerzas vietnamitas. En 1991 se produjo el golpe de Estado de Sunthorn Kongsompong y se promulgó una nueva constitución. En 1992, Chuan Leekpai fue nombrado jefe de gobierno y él mismo encabezó dos procesos electorales democráticos, en 1992 y 1995.

TAJIMAROA ◆ ☛ *Ciudad Hidalgo.*

TAJÍN, EL ◆ ☛ *Papantla.*

TAKAHASHI, KIYOSHI ◆ n. en Japón (1925). Escultor. Perteneció al ejército japonés durante la segunda guerra mundial. Estudió en la Academia de Arte de Tokio (1953) y formó parte del grupo Shinseisaku (1955-57). Llegó a México en 1960 y ese mismo año expuso por primera vez en el Palacio de Bellas Artes. Profesor de la Universidad Veracruzana (1961-¿1972?). En Jalapa fundó un taller de escultura. Sus obras se han presentado en EUA y Japón. Es autor de un busto de Francisco Javier Clavijero (1961), de cuatro relieves (1961), del *Pensador* (1961-62), que se encuentran en la Universidad Veracruzana, y de una escultura monumental en cemento (1968), situada en la Ruta de la Amistad del Anillo Periférico en la ciudad de México. Tiene obras en Japón y Francia. En 1957 recibió los premios Shinseisaka y Presidente de Osaka; en 1965, el Premio La Venta de la II Bienal de Escultura en México; en 1973, el Premio Teijiro Nakahara; en 1983, el Gran Premio de la Exposición de Escultura Moderna al Aire Libre, en Tokio. Fue ganador del Concurso de Escultura al Aire Libre de Nagano.

TALA ◆ Municipio de Jalisco situado en la porción central del estado, al oeste de Guadalajara y este de Ameca. Superficie: 389.24 km^2. Habitantes: 50,928,

Cabeza, escultura en madera de Kiyoshi Takahashi

de los cuales 12,362 forman la población económicamente activa. Hablan alguna lengua indígena 39 personas mayores de cinco años.

TALAMANTES, MELCHOR DE ◆ n. en Perú y m. en Veracruz, Ver. (1765-1809). Sacerdote. Su nombre completo era Melchor de Talamantes Salvador y Baeza. Ingresó a la orden de Nuestra Señora de la Merced en 1779. Doctor en teología por la Universidad de San Marcos de Lima, donde impartió cátedra. En 1786 inició los trámites para su secularización, pero a causa de la tardanza de El Vaticano se trasladó a Europa. Vivió en España (1798) y en Guayaquil, y en 1799 llegó a la Nueva España y se instaló en la ciudad de México, donde fue censor del *Diario de México* y autor, por órdenes del gobierno virreinal, de un estudio de límites entre Texas y Luisiana (1807). Tuvo una activa participación en el movimiento autonomista de Francisco Primo de Verdad y José de Iturrigaray en 1808. Autor de unos *Apuntes para el plan de independencia*, unas *Instrucciones al Ayuntamiento de México*, un texto llamado *Congreso nacional del reyno de Nueva España* y *Representación nacional de las colonias*. Fue aprehendido al producirse el golpe de Estado de los peninsulares acaudillados por Gabriel Yermo. Acusado de 120 delitos, fue condenado a muerte por la Inquisición, pero como la sentencia debía ser ejecutada en España, se le recluyó en el fuerte de San Juan de Ulúa en el puerto de Veracruz, donde murió al contraer la peste. Escribió también *Panegírico de Santa Teresa* (1802).

TALAMÁS CAMANDARI, MANUEL ◆ n. en Chihuahua, Chih. (1917). Estudió en los seminarios de Chihuahua y Durango y en la Universidad Gregoriana de Roma. Recibió las órdenes sacerdotales en 1943. Profesor y rector del Seminario de Chihuahua. Fue obispo de Ciudad Juárez (1957-). Es obispo emérito. Autor de *¿Cuál es su excusa?* y *Buen humor de un obispo, con gotitas de sabiduría*.

TALÁN RAMÍREZ, RAÚL ERIC ◆ n. en el DF (1942). Ingeniero de comunicaciones eléctricas y electrónicas maestro en ingeniería eléctrica por el IPN (1968), y maestro en investigación de operaciones por la Universidad de California (1973). Profesor del IPN (1965-78). Ha sido investigador de la Universidad de California (1973), director de la Unidad Profesional Interdisciplinaria en Ingeniería, Ciencias Sociales y Administración del IPN (1975-78), director general de Acreditación y Certificación (1979-81), secretario técnico del Programa Global de Mejoramiento Administrativo (1981-82), director general de Evaluación (1982-84) y director general de Educación Tecnológica Industrial de la Secretaría de Educación (1985). Director general del IPN (1985-88), subsecretario de Educación e Investigación Tecnológicas de la SEP (1988-94) y director general de Diconsa (1994-99). Pertenece al Colegio de Ingenieros Mecánicos y Electricistas y a la Asociación Mexicana de Ingenieros Industriales.

TALAVERA, JESÚS ◆ n. en La Barca, Jal. (1900). Museógrafo. En los años veinte colaboró con Roberto Montenegro, cuando éste era jefe del Departamento de Bellas Artes. Trabajó con Fernando Gamboa durante más de 37 años. Fue jefe de la Oficina Técnica (1951-56), director técnico del Museo Nacional de Bellas Artes (1956) y director técnico de museografía del Departamento de Bellas Artes de Jalisco (1971-). Recibió condecoraciones de los gobiernos de Francia y Suecia.

TALAVERA, JOSÉ ANTONIO ◆ n. en Pátzcuaro, Mich. (¿1777?-?). Sacerdote. Estudió en el Seminario de Valladolid, donde fue compañero de José María Morelos. Cura de Ajuchitlán y Pungarabato. En 1810 se levantó en armas contra el gobierno virreinal. En 1812 fue aprehendido y enviado a Oaxaca, donde permaneció preso hasta noviembre de ese mismo año, cuando fue liberado por las tropas de Morelos. Más tarde combatió a las órdenes de Nicolás Bravo; en diciembre de 1817 fue detenido por los realistas en los alrededores de Coyuca, enel actual estado de Guerrero.

TALAVERA, MARIO ◆ n. en Jalapa, Ver., y m. en el DF (1885-1960). Cantante y compositor. Hasta 1910 estudió canto en el Conservatorio Nacional de Música, donde fue alumno de José González Molina, José Vigil y Robles, Lamberto Castañares y Cenobio Paniagua, entre otros. Formó parte de la Impulsora de Ópera, con la cual interpretó la ópera *Bohemia* y trabajó como acompañante en varias salas cinematográficas. En 1920, con Carmen García Cornejo, Ángel R. Esquivel y Miguel Lerdo de Tejada, se presentó en varias ciudades de Estados Unidos. Hacia 1939, con Lerdo de Tejada , Alfonso Esparza Oteo y *Tata Nacho*, formó el grupo Los Cuatro Ases de la Canción, que se convirtió en el Trio Veneno a la muerte de Lerdo de Tejada (1941). Fue secretario del trabajo del Sindicato Mexicano de Autores, Compositores y Editores de Música, que por iniciativa suya se afilió a la Confederación Internacional de Sociedades de Autores y Compositores. Compuso, entre otras, *La china*, *Arrullo*, *Adiós*, *El nopal*, *Flor de mayo*, *El día que te vayas*, *Jesusita la vaquera*, *Luz de cirio*, *Muchachita mía*, *Así te quiero Cabellera*.

TALAVERA LÓPEZ, ABRAHAM ◆ n. en Tenango del Valle y m. en Naucalpan, Edo. de México (1949-1997). Licenciado en relaciones internacionales por El Colegio de México (1967-69). Profesor de la Universidad Autónoma del Estado de México (1969). En el PRI, partido al que perteneció desde 1967, fue director juvenil (1969-71) y director general del CEPES del Estado de México (1974), delegado general del CEN (1976), miembro de la Comisión de Asuntos Internacionales (1984) y secretario de Capacitación Política del CEN (1988-). Fue investigador del Instituto de Estudios Peruanos (1969) y de la Biblioteca del Congreso de Estados Unidos (1973); diputado federal (1973-76 y 1991-94), delegado del DDF (1977), director general de Investigaciones Políticas (1979), oficial mayor de la Secretaría de Gobernación (1980) y embajador en Guatemala (1985-88). Colaboró en *La Jornada*. Coautor de *México 1983*. *A la mitad* *del túnel* (1983) y autor de *Liberalismo y educación* (1973), *Desequilibrios regionales* (1976), *Entorno y propósitos de la educación en México* (1990) y *México electoral* (1991). Miembro de la Academia Nacional de Derecho Administrativo.

Talavera Ramírez, Carlos ◆ n. en la ciudad de México (1923). Sacerdote ordenado en 1948. Profesor del Seminario Conciliar de México y del Instituto Superior de Estudios Eclesiásticos de México. Ha sido presidente del Consejo Presbiterial de la arquidiócesis de México, asesor del Movimiento de Renovación en el Espíritu Santo, obispo auxiliar de México (1980-84), obispo de Coatzaocalcos (1984-95) y presidente del Departamento de Pastoral Social de la Conferencia Episcopal Latinoamericana (1995-).

Taller ◆ Revista mensual de "poesía y crítica" que apareció en la ciudad de México entre diciembre de 1938 y febrero de 1941, publicada por Editorial Cvltvra. Fue impulsada por el grupo de escritores que había editado la revista *Taller Poético* (☛), así como por algunos españoles asilados en México luego de la derrota de la República. Durante el primer año, Efraín Huerta, Octavio Paz, Alberto Quintero Álvarez y Rafael Solana figuraron como "responsables" de la publicación, pero desde octubre de 1938, Paz apareció como director, Juan Gil-Albert como secretario y Ramón Gaya, José Herrera Petere, Efraín Huerta, Alberto Quintero Álvarez, Antonio Sánchez Barbudo, Rafael Solana, Lorenzo Varela y Rafael Vela Albela como miembros de la redacción. Además de los anteriores, en sus páginas colaboraron Ermilo Abreu Gómez, Rafael Alberti, José Alvarado, Octavio G. Barreda, Neftalí Beltrán, José Bergamín, Juan de la Cabada, Luis Cardoza y Aragón, Antonio Castro Leal, Luis Cernuda, Jorge Cuesta, Enrique Díez Canedo, Francisco Giner de los Ríos, Enrique González Rojo, Andrés Henestrosa, María Izquierdo, Pablo Luis Lanssberg, León Felipe, Antonio Magaña Esquivel, José Moreno Villa, Pablo Neruda, Bernardo Ortiz de Montellano, Carlos Pellicer, Juan Rejano, José Revueltas, Alfonso Reyes, Adolfo Sánchez Vázquez, Salvador Toscano, Xavier Villaurrutia y María Zambrano.

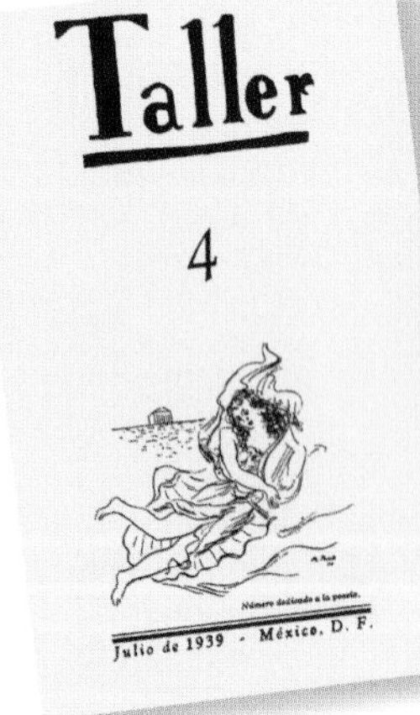

Taller

Bailarines del Taller Coreográfico de la UNAM en *Alabanzas*, coreografía de Gloria Contreras

Taller, El ◆ Periódico semanario, órgano de la Sociedad Progresista de Artesanos de Toluca, que apareció por primera vez el 20 de octubre de 1872 y, con algunas interrupciones, se publicó durante varios años.

Taller Coreográfico de la UNAM ◆ Grupo de danza fundado en septiembre de 1970 por Gloria Contreras, quien lo dirige desde entonces. En 1974 amplió sus funciones a la docencia, con la fundación del Seminario de Iniciación a la Danza. Hasta 1999 ha ofrecido 60 temporadas, en las que se han presentado más de 200 coreografías, la mayoría de la propia Contreras. Además, ha organizado concursos internacionales de fotografía, dibujo y poesía; exposiciones de dibujo, pintura, cartel, poesía y fotografía; audiovisuales, ballets videograbados en versiones distintas y programas de televisión. Del Seminario han egresado más de 10,000 bailarines y coreógrafos. El Taller ha editado 13 libros, entre ellos, *Taller Coreográfico de la* UNAM, *Espectro de la danza, Elogio de la danza, El espejo del cuerpo, Contrología* y *Bailando lo real maravilloso.* En 1970, el Taller recibió un premio "por mejorar el teatro y la danza en México", de la Unión Mexicana de Cronistas de Música; en 1972, el premio Ixtlilton del Festival Mundial del Folklore, celebrado en Guadalajara, y en 1981 el premio internacional de arte Copa de Plata del Ballet a la Excelencia Artística, otorgada por la revista estadounidense *Ópera popular*, además de una escultura, obra de Daniel Morales,

Foto: Nitzarindani Vega

Gloria Contreras en *Isolda*, coreografía de Gloria Contreras a cargo del Taller Coreográfico de la UNAM entregada a los miembros del taller por su público. Desde 1975, la agrupación pertenece al Consejo Internacional de la Danza. Su sede permanente es la sala Miguel Covarrubias, del Centro Cultural Universitario de la UNAM.

TALLER DE GRÁFICA POPULAR ◆ Centro de grabado surgido en el DF en abril de 1937. Lo formaron inicialmente Leopoldo Méndez, Pablo O'Higgings y Luis Arenal, luego de su salida de la Liga de Escritores y Artistas Revolucionarios (☛). Se adhirieron, casi inmediatamente, Ignacio Aguirre, Raúl Anguiano, Ángel Bracho, Jesús Escobedo, Isidoro Ocampo, Everardo Ramírez y Alfredo Zalce. Después se incorporaron cartel de la Confederación de Trabajadores de México, al que siguieron caricaturas sobre la expropiación petrolera y tres calendarios ilustrados para la Universidad Obrera de México. En el otoño de 1938 se ejecutó una serie de ocho carteles antifascistas que se pegaron en los muros por toda la ciudad. En favor de la causa republicana, por esos días apareció una serie de 12 litografías de Arenal, Anguiano, Guerrero y Méndez, que se conocieron como *La España de Franco*. Las paredes se llenaron nuevamente de grabados (32,000 ejemplares) para anunciar un ciclo de conferencias de la antifascista Liga de Cultura Alemana. Paralelamente, en el TGP se *Europa*. Entre 1943 y 1946, el Taller fue administrado por Jorge Stibi, a quien sucedió en este cargo Hannes Meyer, ex director de la Bauhaus. En 1944, el TGP fundó la editorial La Estampa Mexicana, que se dedicó, sobre todo, a editar calendarios, grabados y litografías. En marzo de 1945, el Taller dio a conocer su declaración de principios, en la que se definió como un "centro de trabajo colectivo para la producción funcional y el estudio de las diferentes ramas del grabado y la pintura", que realizaba un "esfuerzo constante para que su producción beneficie los intereses progresistas y democráticos del pueblo mexicano, principalmente en su lucha contra la

Argentina, la guerra sucia, obra de Jesús Álvarez Amaya ejecutada dentro de las actividades del Taller de Gráfica Popular

Grabado de Leopoldo Méndez para el Taller de Gráfica Popular

Jesús Álvarez Amaya, Alberto Beltrán, Celia Calderón, Fernando Castro Pacheco, José Chávez Morado, Francisco Dosamantes, Xavier Guerrero, Elena Huerta, Gonzalo de la Paz Pérez, Antonio Pujol y Fanny Rabel. Su primera sede estuvo en la calle de Belisario Domínguez 69, en la ciudad de México, donde se instaló una pequeña galería que desapareció en 1939. Inicialmente, las impresiones se realizaron en el taller de Jesús Arteaga, ubicado en la avenida Cuauhtémoc, hasta que los miembros del Taller comenzaron a utilizar una prensa mecánica que, se decía, había servido a los comuneros de París en 1871. Poco después se adquirió otra y ambas fueron operadas por José Sánchez. El primer trabajo del Taller fue un hacían mantas para manifestaciones, volantes, *calaveras*, corridos a la manera de Posada y dibujos. En 1939 el grupo editó el portafolios *En nombre de Cristo*, en defensa de los profesores rurales asesinados en el Bajío. Al inicio de la segunda guerra mundial se hizo una serie de 5,000 carteles pro soviéticos. En 1941, la sede del Taller se trasladó a la calle de Regina, de donde pasó más tarde a la calle de Quintana Roo y luego al número nueve de Nezahualcóyotl, donde permaneció hasta fines de los setenta. En 1942, el Taller diseñó varios carros alegóricos que participaron en algunas de las manifestaciones antifascistas de la ciudad de México. Al año siguiente, diez de los miembros del grupo editaron *El libro negro del terror nazi en* reacción fascista". Asimismo, consideraba "que la finalidad social de la obra plástica es inseparable de su buena calidad artística". Al término de la guerra, los grabadores dejaron de ceñirse exclusivamente a temas antifascistas y, en 1946, ilustraron una *Memoria* CAPFCE *1944-1946*. Al año siguiente, el Taller editó *85 estampas de la Revolución Mexicana* y en 1948, un portafolios de 10 grabados llamado *Asesinato de Jesús R. Menéndez en Cuba y lucha contra los provocadores de una nueva guerra*. Para 1949, unos 50 grabadores habían trabajado en el Taller, entre ellos Roberto Berdecio, Elizabeth Cattlet (incorporada en 1946), Antonio Franco, Óscar Frías, Arturo García Bustos, Guillermo Monroy, Francisco Mora, Agustín Villagra

Catelec y Mariana Yampolsky (desde 1944), y un número similar había colaborado eventualmente, como David Alfaro Siqueiros, Lena Bergner, Eleanor Coen, Coney Cohn, Jean Charlot, Jim Egleson, Gabriel Fernández Ledesma, Galo Galecio, Marshall Goodman, Jules Heller, Max Kahan, Carlos Mérida, Koloman Sokol, Ramón Sosamontes, Albe Steiner y Charles White. En ese mismo año, Hannes Meyer preparó la edición del álbum *El Taller de Gráfica Popular. Doce años de obra artística colectiva*. En 1960 apareció el albúm colectivo *450 años de lucha, homenaje al pueblo mexicano*. En el mismo año, por diferencias políticas, Méndez, Beltrán, Yampolski, Adolfo Mexiac, Íker Larrauri, Andrea Gómez y O'Higgins abandonaron la agrupación y poco después les siguieron Anguiano y Rabel. En 1965, Arenal organizó, en nombre del Taller, un homenaje público para celebrar el nombramiento de Adolfo López Mateos como presidente del Comité Organizador de los Juegos Olímpicos de México, por lo que, luego de protestar públicamente, Aguirre, Octavio Bajonero, Celia Calderón, Cattlet, José Luis Franco, Guerrero, María Luisa Martín, Norberto Martínez, Francisco Moral, Mercedes Quevedo y Alberto Rovira, se retiraron de la agrupación e intentaron, infructuosamente, constituirse en el Auténtico Taller de Gráfica Popular. En 1967 se celebró el trigésimo aniversario del Taller con una exposición en el Museo de Arte Moderno. En los años setenta, para solventar algunos problemas económicos, el Taller cedió al gobierno unas 3,000 obras de su archivo. En 1975, también con material del TGP, se creó el Museo de la Estampa Militante. En abril de 1986, la sede estaba en Serafín Olarte número 112, de donde pasó a Víctor Hugo y Filipinas, en la colonia Portales. En 1999 acabó el peregrinaje del Taller cuando el gobierno del Distrito Federal le entregó un inmueble en la colonia de los Doctores.

TALLER POÉTICO ◆ Revista de poesía y crítica editada en la ciudad de México. Apareció en mayo de 1936, noviembre de 1936, marzo de 1937 y junio de 1938. Fue dirigida por Rafael Solana y editada por Miguel N. Lira. En ella colaboraron, además de los citados, Enrique Asúnsolo, Octavio G. Barreda, Neftalí Beltrán, Luis Cardoza y Aragón, Jorge Cuesta, Genaro Estrada, Federico García Lorca, Mauricio Gómez Mayorga, Enrique González Rojo, Efrén Hernández, Efraín Huerta, Manuel Lerín, Clemente López Trujillo, Carlos Luquín, Vicente Magdaleno, José Moreno Villa, Elías Nandino, Octavio Novaro, Salvador Novo, Bernardo Ortiz de Montellano, Octavio Paz, Carlos Pellicer, Enrique Ramírez y Ramírez, Alberto Quintero Álvarez, Jaime Torres Bodet, Carmen Toscano, Rodolfo Usigli y Xavier Villaurrutia.

Frente al horizonte, óleo sobre tela de Eduardo Tamariz (1988)

TALPA DE ALLENDE ◆ Municipio de Jalisco situado en el occidente del estado, contiguo a Puerto Vallarta al oeste de Ameca. Superficie: 2,258.51 km². Habitantes: 14,276, de los cuales 3,183 forman la población económicamente activa. Hablan alguna lengua indígena 12 personas mayores de cinco años. En el municipio se encuentra el santuario (basílica menor) de Nuestra Señora de Talpa, donde desde 1644 es muy venerada la imagen, hecha en médula de caña de maíz. El 19 de septiembre es la fiesta de la Patrona del lugar, ante la que llegan grandes peregrinaciones. El municipio cuenta con recursos minerales.

TAMALÍN ◆ Municipio de Veracruz situado en la porción noroccidental del estado, al noroeste de Tuxpan y este-sureste de Tantoyuca. Superficie: 417.85 km². Habitantes: 11,670, de los cuales 3,017 forman la población económicamente activa. Hablan alguna lengua indígena 1,028 personas mayores de cinco años (náhuatl 1,000).

Tamariz, Eduardo ◆ n. en el DF (1945). Escultor. Estudió en la Escuela de Pintura y Escultura La Esmeralda (1963-67). Expuso por primera vez de forma individual en 1970, en la Galería de Arte Mexicano del DF. Sus obras se han presentado en Estados Unidos, Hungría, Jamaica, Puerto Rico y Yugoslavia. Es autor de unos medallones que se encuentran en el edificio de la Procuraduría General de la República (1988). En 1964 y 1965 ganó premios de La Esmeralda y, en 1969, el primer premio de un concurso de pintura convocado por el Instituto Nacional de la Juventud Mexicana.

Tamariz Galicia, Ernesto E. ◆ n. en Acatzingo, Pue. (1904). Escultor y pintor. Estudió en la Academia de Bellas Artes de Puebla (1918-23) y en la Academia de San Carlos (1923-25). Autor de una extensa obra en la que se cuentan bustos de Rafael Cabrera, en Puebla (1951); Ignacio Ramírez, en Toluca (1953); Carranza, Obregón y Calles, en La Paz (1958); varios aviadores, en el Aeropuerto del DF (1960); Arias Bernal, en Aguascalientes (1964); Luis Elizondo, en Monterrey (1967); Zaragoza, en el panteón de San Fernando, DF; León Felipe, en el DF (1969); e Hidalgo, en Taxco (1976), y otros; las estatuas de Madero, en Puebla (1928); Ignacio Vallarta y Mariano Otero, en la Suprema Corte de Justicia de la Nación, DF (1942); Allende, en San Miguel Allende (1944); José María Yáñez, en Guaymas (1954); Juárez, en la UABJO (1956); Alfonso Reyes, en la UANL (1960); Belisario Domínguez, en Nuevo Laredo (1965); Morelos, en Tenancingo (1968); Xicoténcatl, en Tlaxcala (1969); Mariano Escobedo, en el aeropuerto de Monterrey (1972); Isidro Fabela, en Toluca (1972); Antonio Caso, en la Plaza del Estudiante, DF (1973); Hidalgo, en León (1973); Cárdenas, en Huajuapan de León (1974); Martí, en Reforma e Hidalgo, DF (1975); Ignacio Chávez, en el Instituto de Cardiología (1980); Morelos y Matamoros, en Ecatepec (1980); Juan Pablo II, en la Basílica de Guadalupe (1980); Hidalgo, en Salvatierra (1981); Ávila Camacho, en Los Pinos (1981); Zapata, en Cuernavaca (1984); Morelos, en la carretera México-Cuernavaca (1986); e Ignacio de Loyola, en la Universidad Iberoamericana, DF (1987), entre otras. También hizo los monumentos a Vasco de Quiroga, en Irapuato (1943); a los Niños Héroes, en el DF (1951); a la Maternidad, en Toluca (1977); lo mismo que los relieves de la puerta de la Suprema Corte de Justicia de la Nación (1942); varias esculturas para la catedral de México (1957), y un Jesucristo, en la Catedral de Torreón (1963), así como otras piezas.

Tamariz y Sánchez, Eduardo ◆ n. en Puebla, Pue., y m. en el DF (1882-1957). Se tituló como abogado en la Escuela Nacional de Jurisprudencia (1905). Militante del Partido Católico Nacional. Fue diputado federal a la XXVI Legislatura (1911-13), secretario de Instrucción Pública (del 17 al 20 de septiembre de 1913) y de Agricultura y Colonización (del 19 de febrero al 26 de mayo de 1914) en el gobierno de Victoriano Huerta. Al triunfo del constitucionalismo (1914) salió del país y se instaló en Estados Unidos, donde vivió hasta 1920. En ese año regresó a México. Profesor de la Universidad Nacional y del Centro Rafael Dondé, y miembro del consejo de la Cruz Roja Mexicana.

La evangelización durante el siglo XVI, obra del escultor Ernesto Tamariz

Tamarón y Romeral, Pedro ◆ n. en España y m. en Baimoa, Sin. (?-1768). En 1749 viajó a Venezuela, donde fue capellán del obispo de Caracas y maestreescuela, chantre y vicario capitular de la diócesis caraqueña. Doctor en teología por la Universidad de Santa Rosa; en 1758 fue designado obispo de Durango. Llegó a la Nueva España al año siguiente y gobernó la diócesis hasta su muerte. Autor de *Triunfo glorioso y caro de Elías* (1732), *Triunfos de la gracia en la Santísima Imagen de María, que con el título del Socorro, se venera en la Nueva Valencia del obispado de Caracas* (1949), *Historia general de Caracas* y *La descripción del obispado de Durango, o diario de la visita de toda aquella diócesis*.

Tamasopo ◆ Municipio de San Luis Potosí situado al este de Río verde y contiguo a Ciudad Valles. Superficie: 1,296.7 km². Habitantes: 27,013, de los cuales 6,898 forman la población económicamente activa. Hablan alguna lengua indígena 1,909 personas mayores de cinco años (pame 1,824). En este municipio se hallan las lagunas de Tampasquín, Toro, Grande y Patos, y la cascada Puente de Dios, formada por el río Tamasopo.

Tamaulipas, de ◆ Sierra del sur de Tamaulipas situada al oeste de la llanura costera. Es una prolongación meridional de la Mesa de Solís. Se encuentra al sureste de la presa Las Adjuntas y al noreste de la sierra de Buenavista. Su parte central, la más elevada, es conocida también con el nombre de sierra Azul y ahí se encuentran los cerros de Mariquita, Tulipán y Venados.

Tomás Yarrington Ruvalcaba, gobernador de Tamaulipas

Tamaulipas ◆ Estado de la República Mexicana situado en en el extremo nororiental del país, en la frontera con Estados Unidos y en la costa del golfo de México. Limita con Veracruz, San Luis Potosí y Nuevo León. Superficie: 79,384 km^2 (que representan el 4.05 por ciento del territorio nacional), por lo que es el séptimo estado más extenso de México. Está dividido en 43 municipios. La capital del estado es Ciudad Victoria. Los principales ríos son el Bravo, que marca la frontera norte con EUA, el Conchos, el Purificación o Soto la Marina y el Tamesí, que sirve de límite con Veracruz. Habitantes: 2,628,839 (1997; el 2.8 por ciento del total nacional en 1995). En el conteo de 1995, la población urbana era de 2,103,324 personas y la rural, de 424,004. Son analfabetos 7.6 por ciento de los mayores de 15 años. Forman la población económicamente activa 53.2 por ciento de los mayores de 12 años. La entidad contribuye con 2.94 por ciento al producto interno bruto total nacional. Hablan alguna lengua indígena 10,061 personas mayores de cinco años (motocintleco 5,072 y huasteco 2,414), de las cuales 50 no saben español. *Historia:* los restos arqueológicos más antiguos, que forman lo que se conoce como Complejo Cueva del Diablo, permiten suponer que, por lo menos hace unos 8,000 años, el territorio del actual estado de Tamaulipas fue ocupado por grupos de cazadores y recolectores nómadas, que subistieron sobre todo al norte del río Soto la Marina. En el sur, hace 4,000 años aproximadamente, se inició el proceso de sedentarización. Esta zona fue ocupada por los olmecas y más tarde por los chichimecas, en la sierra de Tamaulipas, y los huastecos, en la actual Huasteca tamaulipeca, alrededor de la ciudad de Chila. Entre 1445 y 1466, las fuerzas mexicas de Moctezuma Ilhuicamina conquistaron la parte meridional de Tamaulipas y convirtieron a los pueblos huastecos y a los chichimecas en tributa-

Nauyaca arboricora, especie animal que se encuentra en el estado de Tamaulipas

Foto: Pablos Cervantes

Foto: Michael Calderwood

Tampico, Tamaulipas

Trajes típicos de la región tamaulipeca

rios de las ciudades del valle de Anáhuac, pero no pudieron someter a los apaches, comanches, pames, lipanes, tepemacas y cotomanes, que vivían al norte. Es probable que el primer europeo en recorrer la costa tamaulipeca, en el llamado Seno Mexicano, haya sido el florentino Américo Vespucio, quien, según relataba, viajó por la costa del golfo de México en 1497 y en 1502. 15 años más tarde, en 1517, los españoles, encabezados por Francisco Hernández de Córdoba, llegaron a la desembocadura del río Pánuco, pero fueron derrotados por los huastecos. Al año siguiente, las fuerzas de Francisco de Garay intentaron tomar Chila, pero también fueron vencidas por los indios. En 1519 fracasaron tres nuevos intentos europeos por apoderarse de la Huasteca, comandados por Juan de Grijalva, Alfonso Álvarez de Pineda y Diego de Camargo. En 1522, las fuerzas de Hernán Cortés se dirigieron a la Huasteca desde Pánuco, derrotaron a los indios y tomaron Chila. Poco después, Gonzalo de Sandoval y Sancho de Caniego intentaron avanzar más al norte, pero la falta de atractivos para los europeos, metales preciosos sobre todo, así como la hostilidad de los indios, impidió que los europeos se instalaran al norte del río de las Palmas. Tampoco tuvo éxito la expedición evangelizadora que Andrés de Olmos emprendió a mediados de ese mismo siglo. A principios de la centuria

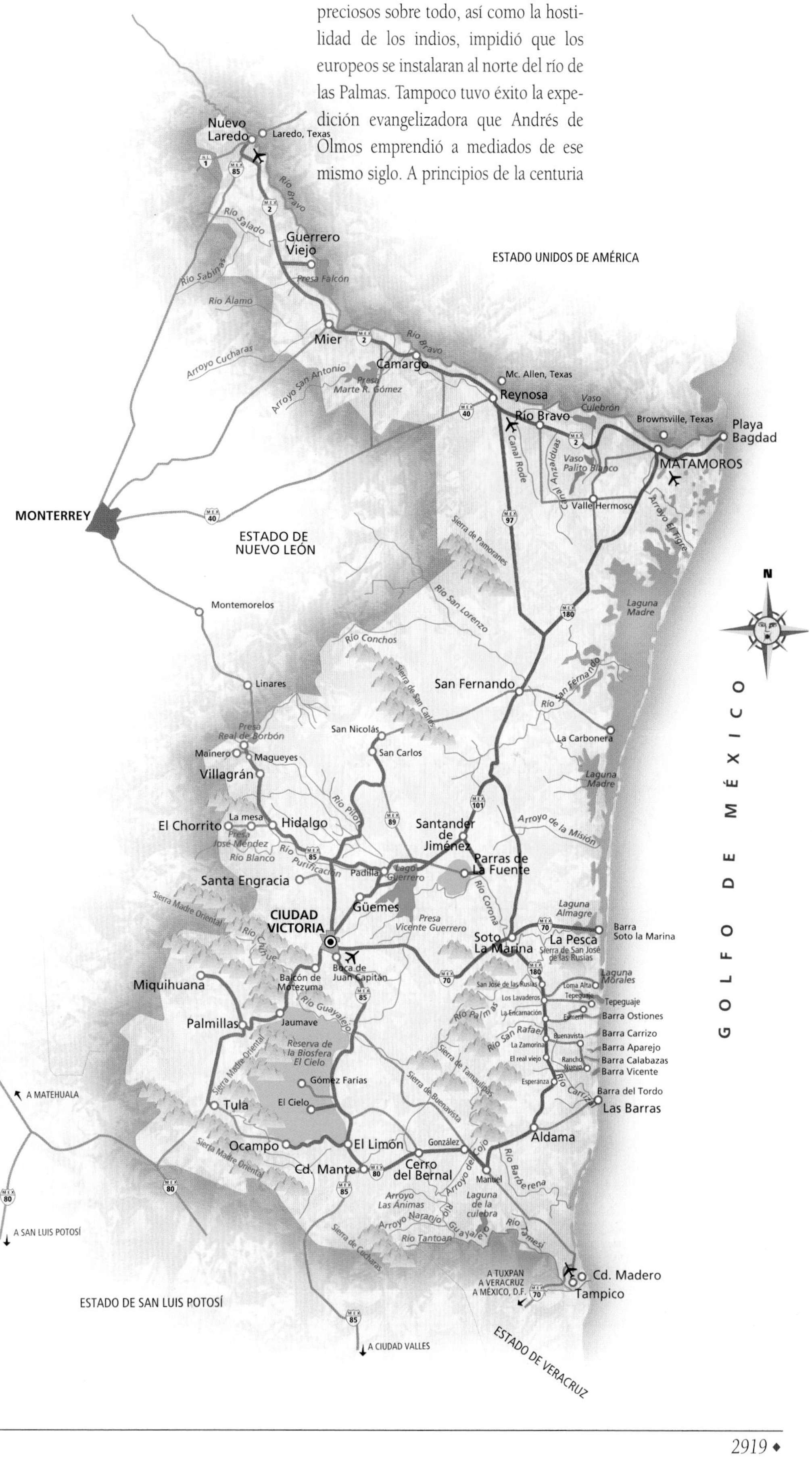

Foto: Michael Calderwood

Nuevo Laredo, Tamaulipas

siguiente, los franciscanos fundaron varias misiones en Tula, Jaumave y Palmillas, con lo que se introdujo la cría de ovejas en la región, cuya explotación se convirtió en la principal actividad económica durante los dos siglos siguientes. La ganadería, sin embargo, despojó a los indios de la poca tierra que les quedaba, por lo que a principios del siglo XVII, los huastecos se levantaron en armas y tomaron Palmillas y Jaumave, pero poco después fueron derrotados. Desde los años treinta del siglo XVIII, preocupados por la presencia de los franceses en la Luisiana y la lejanía de los asentamientos españoles de Texas, las autoridades españolas promovieron nuevas empresas de colonización al norte de la sierra de Tamaulipas. En mayo de 1748 crearon la Provincia de Nuevo Santander, que incluía el territorio situado al sur del río Nueces, que ahora se encuentra en Texas, al norte de la provincia de Tampico y al este de Nuevo Reino de León. El principal colonizador de la nueva provincia fue José de Escandón, quien, entre 1748 y 1770, fundó Aguayo, Güemes, Altamira, Padilla, Soto la Marina, Santander, Reynosa, Camargo y Laredo, entre otras. En 1776, la provincia de Nuevo Santander quedó bajo la jurisdicción de la Comandancia de las Provincias Internas; en 1785, con Texas, Coahuila y Nuevo León, formó parte de la Comandancia de Provincias Internas de Oriente. A fines de 1810, al iniciarse la guerra de Independencia, las autoridades españolas formaron milicias en Aguayo y Padilla, con

Cerro del Bernal, en Tamaulipas

Foto: Fondo Editorial Grupo Azabache

Foto: Pablo Cervantes

Águila elegante, fauna de Tamaulipas

FOTO: MICHAEL CALDERWOOD

Vista panorámica de Ciudad Victoria, Tamaulipas

la idea de combatir a los insurgentes, pero poco después, los milicianos desconocieron al gobierno español. Otros grupos insurgentes se formaron en Tula y Palma y, durante los seis meses siguientes, Juan Nepomoceno Jiménez, Luis de Herrera, José Ignacio Villaseñor, Bernardo Gómez de Lara, Mateo Acuña, José Julián Canales, Albino García y José María García *Cantareño*, entre otros, controlaron una buena parte del territorio de la provincia. A mediados de 1811, las fuerzas realistas de Joaquín de Arredondo tomaron Aguayo y desarticularon a la insurgencia; para 1815, las fuerzas insurgentes habían sido derrotadas. Dos años después, en abril de 1817, el contingente internacionalista de Francisco Javier Mina desembarcó en la barra de Soto la Marina, tomó la población y avanzó hacia Santander y más tarde hacia el Bajío. Una parte de esta fuerza permaneció acantonada en Soto la Marina, donde fue sitiada y derrotada en julio de ese año por las fuerzas de Arredondo. En mayo de 1821, Zenón Fernández, que formaba parte de la guarnición virreinal de Rioverde, se levantó en armas en favor del Plan de Iguala y, poco después, Antonio Fernandez de Córdoba se convirtió en insurgente en Aguayo. En julio, Fernández de Córdoba fue designado gobernador, pero fue sustituido por el también neoinsurgente Felipe de la Garza, quien en mayo de 1822 fue destituido por Agustín de Iturbide. Al año siguiente, a la caida del Imperio, De la Garza volvió a la gubernatura, estableció la capital en Padilla y apoyó el establecimiento de la República federal, por lo que en enero de 1824, en el Acta Constitutiva de la Federación, se estableció que uno de los estados de la Unión era el de "Nuevo Santander, que se llamará de los Tamaulipas". En julio de ese año, José Bernardo Gutiérrez de Lara fue elegido gobernador. Luego de unos días, el ex emperador Iturbide desembarcó en Soto la Marina e intentó sublevar el noreste de la República, pero fue aprehendido y fusilado. También en 1824, la capital del estado se instaló en Aguayo, que desde entonces se llama Ciudad Victoria, en honor del primer presidente de México. Cuatro años después, en agosto de 1829, las fuerzas invasoras españolas, comandadas por Isidro Barradas, que habían desembarcado cerca de Pueblo Viejo, Veracruz, en julio, cruzaron el río Pánuco y tomaron Tampico, de donde fueron desalojadas por Manuel Mier y Terán y Antonio López de Santa Anna. Al año siguiente, Francisco Vital Fernández se adhirió al Plan de Jalapa, se levantó en armas con-

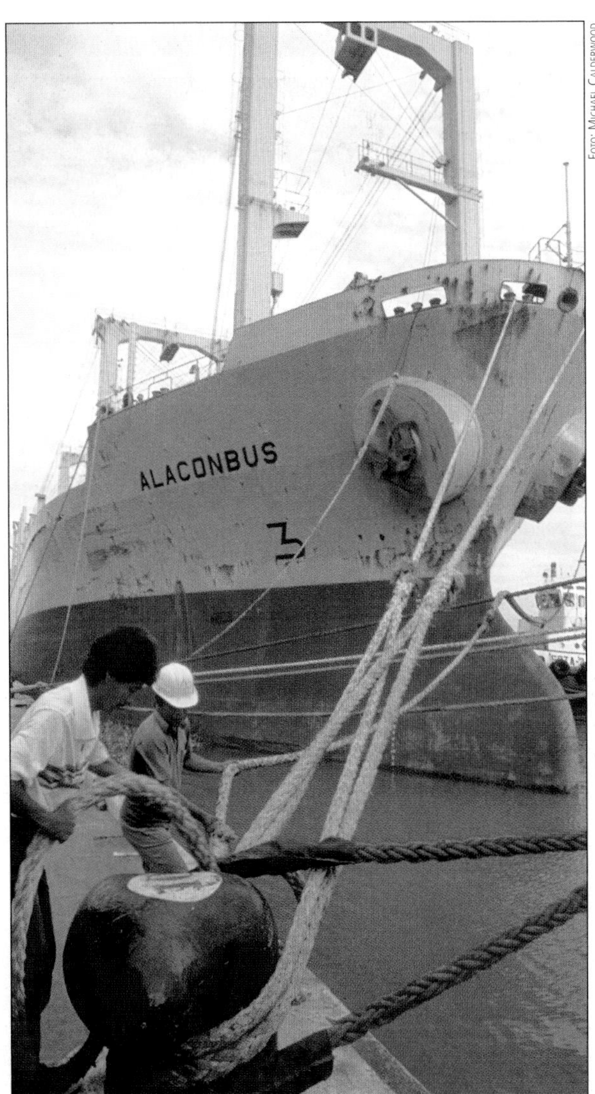

FOTO: MICHAEL CALDERWOOD

Puerto de Tampico, Tamaulipas

tra el gobierno del presidente Vicente Guerrero y derrocó al gobierno local, pero dos años después cambió de bando, apoyó a los liberales sublevados en 1832, tomó Matamoros y Ciudad Victoria y volvió a la gubernatura durante el gobierno intermintente de Valentín Gómez Farías. Durante el régimen centralista, el estado se convirtió en departamento. En 1836, las milicias tamaulipecas participaron en la campaña contra la secesión de Texas y, luego de la derrota de Santa Anna, el territorio tamaulipeco situado entre los ríos Bravo y Nueces permaneció en disputa entre Texas y México. Desde entonces, de hecho, el río Bravo fue el límite de las posesiones mexicanas del noreste. En 1838, un levantamiento de la guarnición militar de Tampico intentó derrocar al gobierno de Anastasio Bustamante, con el apoyo de José Antonio Mejía, pero el propio Bustamante se dirigió a Tampico y derrotó a los federalistas. En abril de 1846 se inició el avance de las fuerzas estadounidenses de Zachary Taylor sobre Tamaulipas. En mayo, los invasores tomaron Matamoros, en diciembre Ciudad Victoria y en febrero de 1847 Tampico. Al término de la guerra, el estado perdió la franja de tierra entre el Nueces y el Bravo, que se convirtió en territorio texano. En 1854, Juan José de la Garza se levantó en armas contra el gobierno de Santa Annna y se adhirió al Plan de Ayutla; tomó Matamoros, Tampico y más tarde colaboró con los liberales de Nuevo León. Aunque durante la guerra de los Tres Años no hubo levantamientos conservadores en el estado, luego del triunfo liberal aparecieron algunas guerrillas conservadoras en el sur, las que procedían principalmente de las Huastecas hidalguense y potosina. En julio de 1863, fuerzas de la marina francesa ocuparon Tampico y desde ahí organizaron una gran campaña hacia el norte, mientras los republicanos se concentraron en el extremo septentrional del estado, sobre todo en Nuevo Laredo y Matamoros. En 1864, el ejército imperialista de Tomás Mejía tomó Matamoros y en septiembre de ese año el gobernador Juan Nepomuceno Cortina se adhirió al imperio, con lo que los republicanos fueron prácticamente desalojados del estado. Desde los primeros meses de 1865, sin embargo, las fuerzas republicanas concentraron sus esfuer-

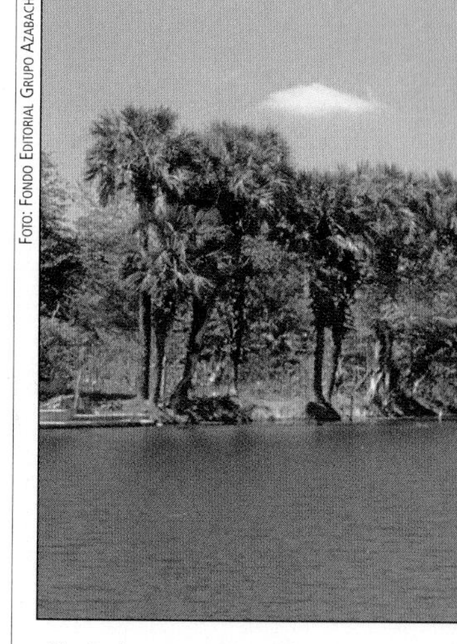

Foto: Fondo Editorial Grupo Azabache

Río Barberena, en Tamaulipas

Foto: Michael Calderwood

Refinería en Tampico, Tamaulipas

Foto: Elisa García

Rivera pesquera en Tamaulipas

zos en liberar Tamaulipas de los franceses, sobre todo de la contraguerrilla que Charles Dupin comandaba en la Huasteca, hasta que, a fines de 1866, el ejército del Noroeste, comandado por Mariano Escobedo, tomó Matamoros, y en junio de 1867, Tampico. A principios de 1876, Porfirio Díaz ocupó Matamoros y cerca de ahí proclamó el Plan de Palo Alto, que reformó al de Tuxtepec. Durante el porfiriato, Antonio Canales (1880-84), Alejandro Prieto (1888-96), Guadalupe Mainero (1896-1901), Pedro Argüelles (1901-08) y Juan B. Castelló (1908-11), gobernaron el estado. Hasta el asesinato del presidente Francisco I. Madero, en 1913, prácticamente no hubo acciones militares en el estado, pero en junio de ese año, cuatro meses después del golpe de Estado de Victoriano Huerta, una fuerza carrancista, al mando de Pablo González, tomó Matamoros, donde se constituyó en el Ejército del Noreste, mismo que ocupó Ciudad Victoria en noviembre y después Tampico en marzo de 1914. Tres meses después, Lucio Blanco, uno de los generales de González, desobedeció las órdenes de Venustiano Carranza de no repartir tierra y fraccionó la hacienda de los Borregos, situada en los alrededores de Matamoros. En el suroeste, varias comunidades campesinas se incorporaron al Ejército Libertador del Sur. Desde 1917, Francisco González Villarreal se encargó del gobierno de Tamaulipas, pero fue derrocado tres años después, por los partidarios del Plan de Agua Prieta, quienes designaron gobernador a Emilio Portes Gil.

Foto: Fondo Editorial Grupo Azabache

Quiosco de Ciudad Victoria, Tamaulipas

DISTRIBUCIÓN DE LA POBLACIÓN POR TAMAÑO DE LA LOCALIDAD, 1995

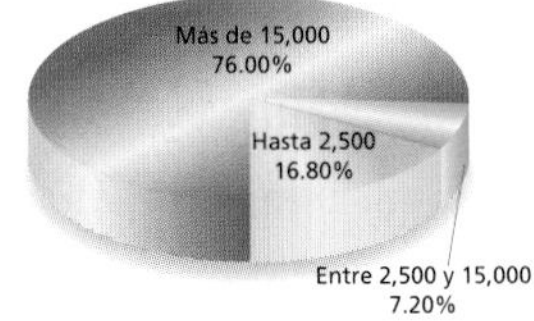

POBLACIÓN DE 5 AÑOS Y MÁS HABLANTE DE LENGUA INDÍGENA, 1995

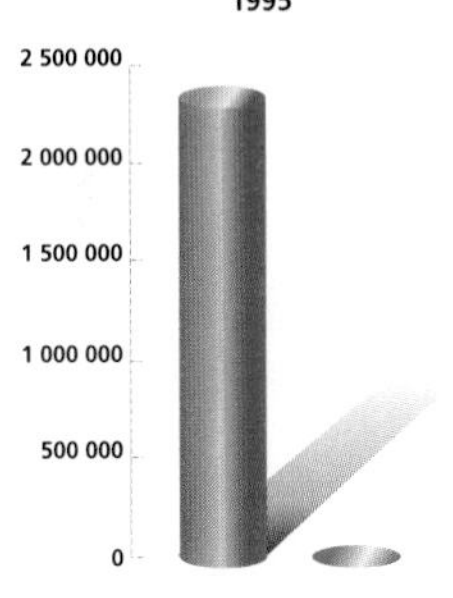

LÍNEAS TELEFÓNICAS EN SERVICIO Y APARATOS PÚBLICOS, 1994

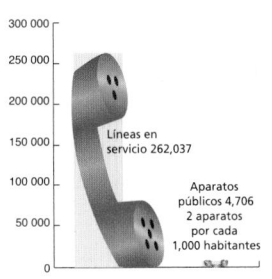

300 000
250 000
200 000
150 000
100 000
50 000
0
Líneas en servicio 262,037
Aparatos públicos 4,706
2 aparatos por cada 1,000 habitantes

LONGITUD DE LA RED DE CARRETERAS POR SUPERFICIE DE RODAMIENTO, 1995

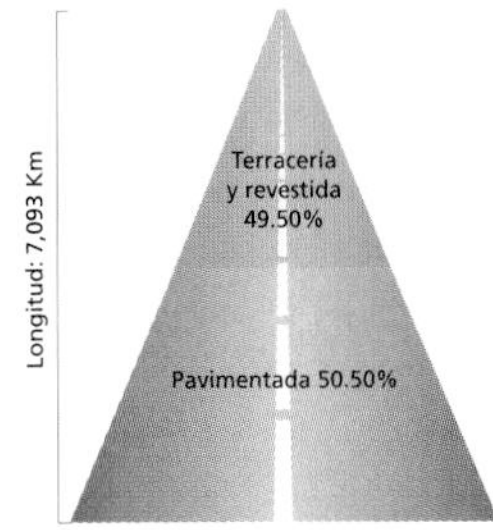

PRODUCTO INTERNO BRUTO (PIB) A PRECIOS CORRIENTES

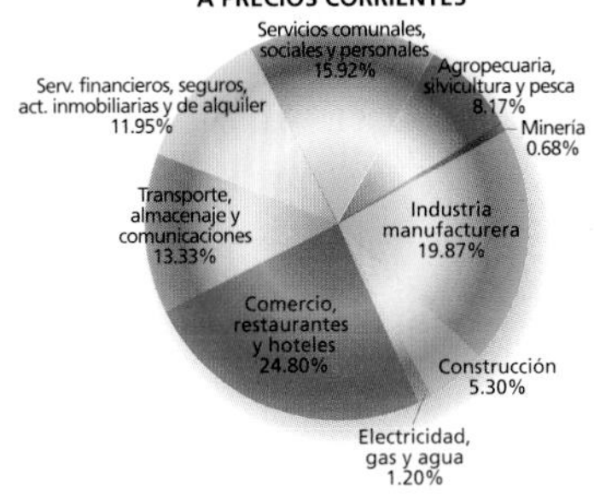

DISTRIBUCIÓN PORCENTUAL DE LA POBLACIÓN OCUPADA POR SECTOR DE ACTIVIDAD ECONÓMICA, 1995

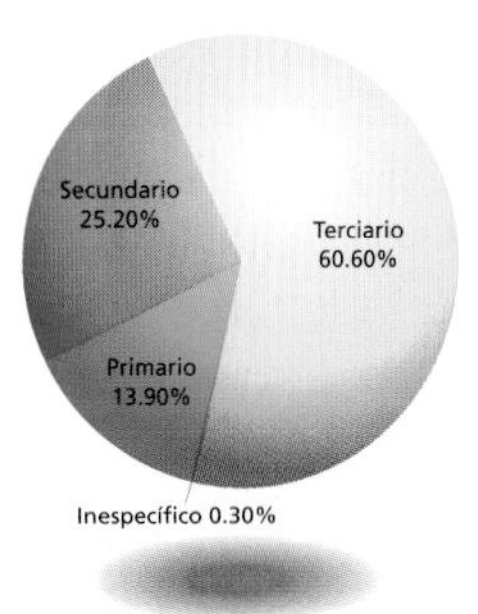

PROMEDIO DE ESCOLARIDAD DE LA POBLACIÓN DE 15 AÑOS Y MÁS, POR SEXO, 1995

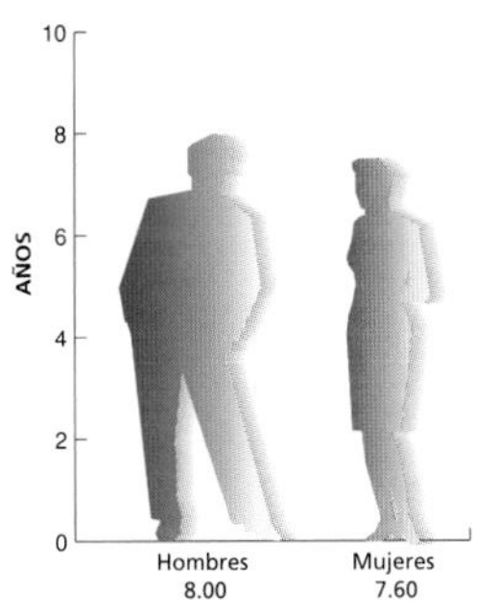

Jorge Tamayo

TAMAYO, ANDRÉS ◆ n. y m. en Valle de Santiago, Gto. (1787-1850). Insurgente. Se levantó en armas en 1810. Combatió en el Bajío hasta 1818, cuando se incorporó a las fuerzas de Vicente Guerrero, a quien en 1821 acompañó hasta Acatempan, donde éste se encontró con Agustín de Iturbide. Formó parte del Ejército Trigarante que desfiló por la ciudad de México en septiembre de ese año. Fue jefe político de Valle de Santiago.

TAMAYO, HUMBERTO G. ◆ ☛ *González Tamayo, Humberto.*

TAMAYO, JORGE ◆ n. en Oaxaca, Oax. (1937). Su apellido materno es López Portillo. Licenciado en economía por la UNAM (1955-59), posgraduado en planeación económica nacional en la Escuela Central de Planeación y Estadística de Varsovia (1962-63). Profesor (1961-63) y secretario general de la Escuela Nacional de Economía (1965-67) y secretario ejecutivo de la Comisión de Nuevos Métodos de Enseñanza (1968-70) de la UNAM. Presidente de la Junta de Gobierno del Colegio Madrid (1980-86). Fue brevemente detenido durante el movimiento estudiantil de 1968. En 1981 fue director del IEPES del PRI, partido al que pertenece desde 1970 y en el que ha sido miembro del Comité Estatal de Oaxaca (1997-) y del CEN (1997-). Ha sido contralor general de la CFE (1972-73), subdirector general de la Compañía de Luz y Fuerza del Centro (1973-76), subsecretario de Comercio Interior (1976-81), subdirector general de Empresas Filiales y Fideicomisos de Nacional Financiera (1981-82), director corporativo de Comercialización de Sidermex (1982-83), coordinador de comisarios y delegados de la Secretaría de la Contraloría General de la Federación (1983-88), director de la Constructora Nacional de Carros de Ferrocarril (1989-92), director general de Ferrocarriles Nacionales de México (1992-94) y oficial mayor de la SSA (1994-). Coautor de *Bases para la planeación económica de México* (1966) y *México, 75 años de revolución* (1988). Pertenece al Colegio Nacional de Economistas, del que fue presidente (1973-75).

TAMAYO, JORGE L. ◆ n. en Oaxaca, Oax. (1912-1978). Historiador y geógrafo. Ingeniero civil titulado en la UNAM (1936). Profesor de la Normal Superior (1943-52), la Universidad Obrera y la UNAM. Jefe de la oficina de Hidrología de la Comisión Nacional de Irrigación (1935-37), jefe del proyecto del Valle de Oaxaca (1937-38), ingeniero de la Secretaría de Recursos Hidráulicos (1939-43), contralor del Ferrocarril Mexicano (1946-49), contralor de los Ferrocarriles Nacionales de México (1947-49), fundador del Centro de Estudios de China Nueva (1949), consultor técnico de la ONU adscrito a la CEPAL (1950), gerente de ventas de Equipos Mexicanos, S. A. (1951-56), director de la empresa Constructores Oaxaqueños (1957-73), ingeniero consultor del gobierno de Chihuahua (1969-71), vocal ejecutivo de la Comisión del Papaloapan (1974-78) y director de Fábricas de Papel Tuxtepec (1974-78). Fundó el Centro de Investigación Científica que hoy lleva su nombre. Anotó y seleccionó los materiales de un *Epistolario de Benito Juárez* (1957), de un *Epistolario de Zaragoza* (1962) y de una *Antología de Juárez* (1972), así como de los 15 volúmenes de *Benito Juárez. Documentos, discursos y correspondencia* (1964). Coautor de *Catálogo de cartografía mexicana* (1941). Autor de *Saneamiento agrícola* (1942), *Datos para la hidrología de la República Mexicana* (1946), *Geografía general de México* (2 t., 1949), *Atlas general de la República Mexicana* (1949), *Geografía de Oaxaca* (1950), *Geografía de América* (1952), *El uso del agua y el uso del suelo en México* (1958), *Geografía de México y Centroamérica* (1959), *Geografía económica y política* (1962), *Estado de México. Panorama socioeconómico* (1963), *El problema fundamental de la agricultura en México* (1964), *Estudio de gran visión. Red de caminos de Chihuahua* (1968), *Juárez en Chihuahua* (1970), *Atlas de la salud de la República Mexicana* (1974) y *Atlas de agua de la República Mexicana* (1975). Presidió las sociedades mexicanas de Historia Natural (1974-75) y de Amistad con China Popular (1974-76). Premio de Economía Banamex (1962 y 1964).

Rufino Tamayo

TAMAYO, RUFINO ◆ n. en Oaxaca, Oax., y m. en el DF (1899-1991). Pintor. Estudió en la Academia de San Carlos (1915-21), de la que fue profesor (1928-30) y director (1932). En 1926 presentó su primera exposición individual y al año siguiente expuso en Nueva York. Fue jefe del Departamento de Bellas Artes de la SEP (1932). En 1934 se incorporó a la LEAR y en 1936 asistió al Congreso de Artistas de Nueva York, donde vivió hasta 1949 y fue profesor de la Escuela Dalton (1938-46) y de la Escuela de Arte del Museo de Brooklyn (1946-48). En 1948 se montó una retrospectiva de su trabajo en el Palacio de Bellas Artes; en 1950, en la Bienal de Venecia, se instaló una gran exposición de su obra. Fundó el Museo de Arte Prehispánico en la ciudad de Oaxaca (1974). Con su colección se creó el Museo de Arte Contemporáneo Rufino Tamayo, DF (1981). Entre 1981 y 1982

Naturaleza muerta con pie, óleo sobre tela de Rufino Tamayo (1928)

fue director de la Escuela de Bellas Artes de la UABJO. En 1985 donó la Casa-hogar Olga Tamayo, en Cuernavaca. Autor de los murales: *El canto y la música* (antiguo Conservatorio, 1933), *Revolución* (Museo Nacional de las Culturas, 1938), *La naturaleza y el artista* (Smith College de Northampton 1943), *Homenaje a la raza* (1951) y *Nacimiento de nuestra nacionalidad* (Palacio de Bellas Artes, 1952-53); *El hombre* (Museo de Bellas Artes de Dallas, 1953), *Naturaleza muerta*, en el Sanborn's de Lafragua (1954-55); *América* (Banco del Suroeste, en Houston, 1956); *Prometeo*, en la Universidad de Puerto Rico (1957); *Prometeo dando el fuego a los hombres* (UNESCO, París, 1959); *Israel de hoy e Israel de ayer* (barco israelí *Shalom*, 1963); *Dualidad* (Museo Nacional de Antropología, 1964); *El fuego creador* (Hemisferia de San Antonio, 1968); *Energía* (Camino Real, DF, 1969); *Eclipse total* (Monterrey, 1978). Ejecutó esculturas en Nueva York (1940), para el Centro Cultural Universitario de la UNAM (1981) y para el aeropuerto internacional de San Francisco (1983). Son suyos los vitrales *Homenaje al Sol* (Monterrey, 1980) y *El Universo* (1988). Su obra de caballete se encuentra en los principales museos de arte contemporáneo del mundo. Se han hecho ediciones de sus grabados por la Fundación Ford, Los Ángeles (1964); el Atelier Desjaubert, de París (1969); la editorial Polígrafa, de Barcelona, y la editorial Giorgio Alessandrina, de Roma. Recibió los premios de la segunda Bienal de São Paulo (1953), de la Fundación Guggenheim (1960), el Internacional de la Bienal de México (1960); el Nacional de Artes (1964); el Colouste Gulbekain del Instituto de Artes de París (1969); el Irico Reggino, de Ragio Calabria, Italia (1960); y el Albert Einstein del Technio Institute de Israel (1982). Recibió la Medalla Belisario Domínguez del Senado de la República (1988). Fue miembro de la Academia de Artes de Buenos Aires (1959), miembro honorario de la Academia Americana de Artes y Letras (1961), del Consejo de Crónica de la Ciudad de México (1987) y de El Colegio Nacional (1991). "Por estar en contra de los regímenes militares" rechazó la Orden del Quetzal del gobierno de Guatemala.

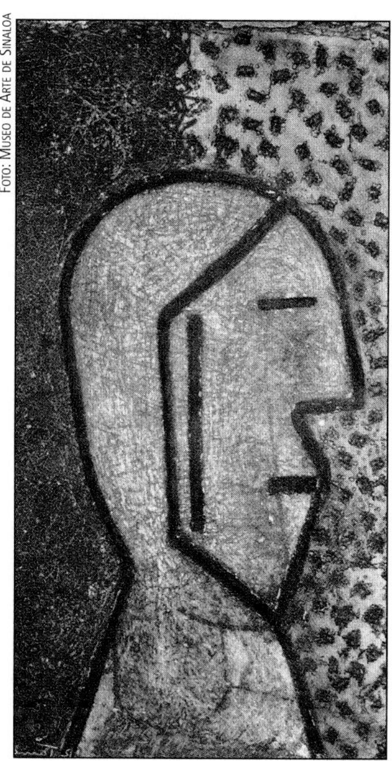

FOTO: MUSEO DE ARTE DE SINALOA

Perfil, mixografía de Rufino Tamayo

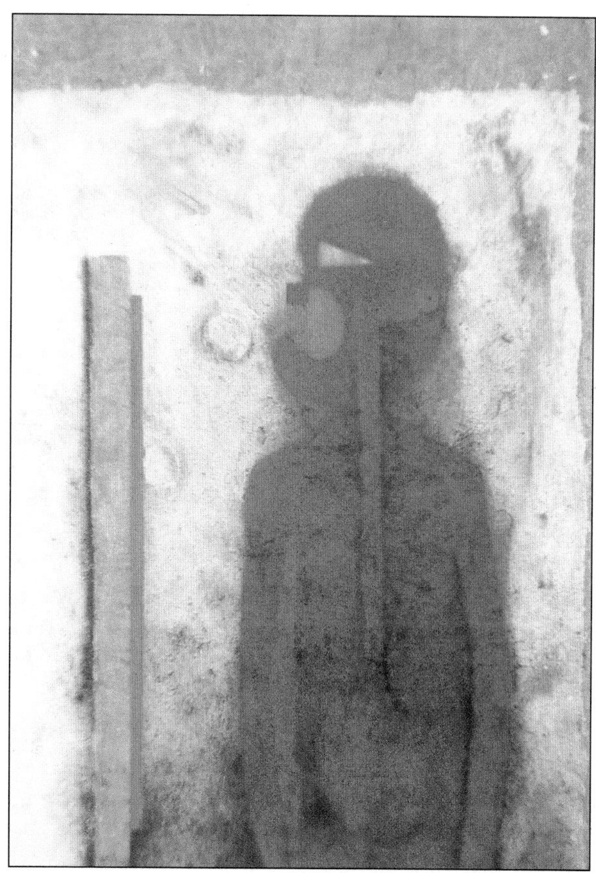

Hombre rojo, obra de Rufino Tamayo

Hombre radiante de alegría, óleo sobre tela de Rufino Tamayo

TAMAZULA ◆ Municipio de Durango situado en el extremo occidental del estado, al noroeste de la capital estatal y suroeste de Guanaveci, en los límites con Chihuahua y Sinaloa. Superficie: 5,188.10 km². Habitantes: 27,361, de los cuales 4,166 forman la población económicamente activa. Hablan alguna

Foto: Geney Beltrán

Poblado de Chapotán, en el municipio de Tamazula, Durango

Foto: Geney Beltrán

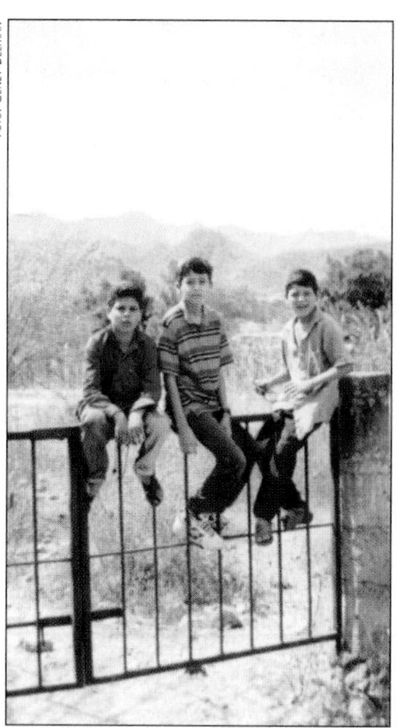

Niños de Tamazula, Durango

lengua indígena 27 personas (tarahumara 26). La cabecera municipal es Tamazula de Victoria.

Tamazula ◆ Río de Durango y Sinaloa. Lo forman las corrientes que bajan por las quebradas de Siánori y Topia, en la vertiente occidental de la sierra de Tepehuanes; corre hacia el oeste y se une al río Humaya, junto a la capital sinaloense, para formar el río Culiacán.

Foto: Gobierno del Estado de Sinaloa

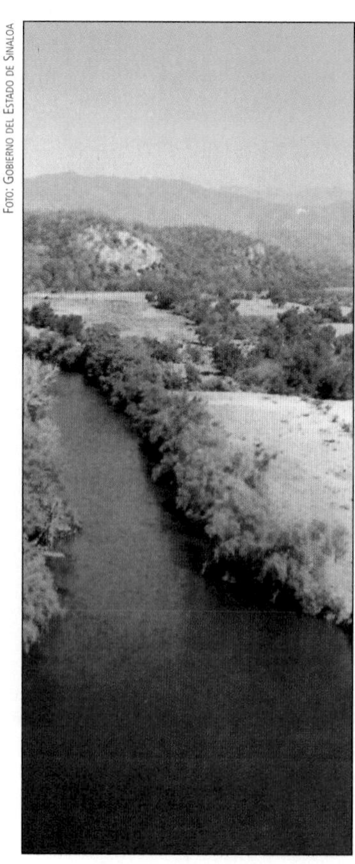

Río Tamazula, en Sinaloa

Tamazula de Gordiano ◆ Municipio de Jalisco situado en la porción suroriental del estado, al este de Ciudad Guzmán y suroeste de Atotonilco el Alto. Superficie: 1,303.13 km^2. Habitantes: 40,315, de los cuales 11,484 forman la población económicamente activa. Hablan alguna lengua indígena 118 personas mayores de cinco años (mixteco 57 y náhuatl 17). En el municipio hay un ingenio azucarero.

Tamazulapan ◆ Sierra de Oaxaca situada en la porción noroccidental del estado. Se extiende de norte a sur, al norte de la sierra de Tlaxiaco y este de la de Nochixtlán.

Tamazulapan del Espíritu Santo ◆ Municipio de Oaxaca situado al sureste de la capital del estado, en la región Sierra Norte. Superficie: 63.79 km^2. Habitantes: 5,391, de los cuales 1,715 forman la población económicamente activa. Hablan alguna lengua indígena 5,207 personas (mixe 5,204), de las cuales 2,066 no saben español.

Tamazulapan del Progreso ◆ ☛ *Villa de Tamazulapan del Progreso.*

Tamazunchale ◆ Municipio de San Luis Potosí situado en el extremo suroriental del estado, al sureste de Ciudad Valles, en los límites con Hidalgo y Veracruz. Superficie: 398.6 km^2. Habitantes: 83,458, de los cuales 26,534 forman la población económicamente activa. Hablan alguna lengua indígena 35,890 personas mayores de cinco años (náhuatl 35,773) y, de ellas, 2,791 son monolingües. Los primeros pobladores fueron huastecos, quienes fundaron el pueblo de Tam-uzum-tzalle, "Lugar de la Gobernación". En 1454, fuerzas mexicas invadieron la zona, pero fueron hostilizadas por los huastecos. En 1487 la población quedó firmemente en poder de los aztecas. A fines del 1522, los españoles ocuparon la población. Sin embargo, las disputas entre los propios europeos retrasaron la conquista efectiva de Tamazunchale durante una década, hasta que en 1539, una vez derrotado en el norte Francisco de Garay, los augustinos se instalaron en el pueblo. A mediados del siglo XVI, con la mayor parte del territorio ocupado por la encomienda de Juan de Cervantes, Tamazunchale dependía religiosamente de la arquidiócesis de México y jurídicamente del ayuntamiento de México. En 1787, con la instauración de las reformas borbónicas, la zona quedó bajo la jurisdicción de la intendencia de San Luis Potosí. Durante la guerra de Independencia operó una fuerza insurgente al mando de Francisco García, quien en 1811 y 1812 ocupó la actual cabecera, y desde 1813 se convirtió en guerrilla. En la guerra de los Tres Años, la ciudad permaneció en poder de los liberales. En 1862, los invasores franceses ocuparon la población. En 1873, el cura Mauricio Zavala abrió una escuela para indios, en la que se educaron varios de los 800 que a principios de 1879, al mando de Juan Santiago, tomaron y saquearon la ciudad, para forzar al gobierno a restituirles la tierra tomada por las haciendas. Poco después, un contingente al mando de Agustín Ugarte recuperó la ciudad, pero poco después se retiró. En agosto de ese año, las tropas de Bernardo Reyes recuperaron la población y obligaron a Santiago a huir hacia Hidalgo. Aunque el levantamiento campesino se prolongó hasta 1881, Tamazunchale permaneció en poder del gobierno. En 1901 se inauguró un gran reloj en la plaza principal.

Tamesí ◆ Río de Tamaulipas y Veracruz. Nace en la vertiente este de la sierra Madre Oriental, al sur de Ciudad Victoria, donde es llamado Guayalejo. Corre hacia el sureste y recibe al río Mante y los arroyos de las Ánimas, Naranjo y Tantoán. Al llegar a Veracruz se convierte en el Tamesí y su curso, hasta desembocar en el Pánuco, marca el límite entre ambos estados.

Tamez, Gerardo ◆ n. en EUA (1948). Compositor y guitarrista mexicano. Estudió en la Escuela Superior de Música y en el Conservatorio Nacional. Ha tomado cursos con Cristina Zárate, Abel Carlevaro y Leo Brouwer. En el Institute of Arts de California obtuvo el grado de licenciatura becado por Fonapas. Se ha presentado como intérprete en países de Norte y Sudamérica. Miembro fundador del grupo Los Folkloristas, con quienes grabó varios discos. Grabó el disco *Guitarra de América Latina* y forma parte del Terceto de Guitarras de la Ciudad de México. Sus composiciones han sido publicadas por las editoriales francesas Max Eschig y Salabert. En 1983, acompañado por la Sinfónica Nacional, estrenó su *Concierto San Ángel* para guitarra y orquesta. Ha escrito varias suites para guitarra sola, de las cuales destaca su pieza *Tierra mestiza*, de la cual también ha hecho versiones para dos, tres y cuatro guitarras y otra para orquesta sinfónica. Autor de la ópera-pop *Dos mundos* (1992).

Tamez, Jesús H. ◆ n. en Saltillo, Coah., y m. en el DF (1904-1989). Periodista. Su apellido paterno era Hernández. Estudió en la Universidad de Columbia (1923). En 1925 participó en la fundación de la Agencia Periodística Latinoamericana, en Nueva York. Regresó en 1928 a México, donde durante 25 años fue corresponsal y subgerente de la agencia United Press. Fue representante en la capital del país de *El Informador*, de Guadalajara; *El Mundo*, de Tampico; *El Dictamen*, de Veracruz; *El Siglo*, de Torreón; *Diario de Yucatán*, de Mérida; y *El Porvenir*, de Monterrey. Entrevistó a León Trotsky y a Manuel Ávila Camacho. Editor de varias historietas y de la revista *Cartel*. Colaboró en la revista *Siempre!*

Tamez Herrera, Manuel ◆ ☛ *Régulo*.

Tamiahua ◆ Albufera situada en el norte de Veracruz, frente a los municipios de Tampico Chico, Ozuluama, Chinampa de Gorostiza, Tamiahua y Tuxpan. Mide 110 kilómetros de largo por 25 de ancho y es navegable. En su interior se encuentran las islas Juana Ramírez, del Toro y del Ídolo, entre otras.

Tamiahua ◆ Municipio de Veracruz situado en la porción noroccidental del estado, al norte de Tuxpan y sureste de Tantoyuca, en la costa del golfo de México. Superficie: 985.4 km². Habitantes: 27,398, de los cuales 8,609 forman la población económicamente activa. Hablan alguna lengua indígena 359 personas mayores de cinco años (náhuatl 226 y huasteco 101). Importante productor de petróleo. Es uno de los mayores abastecedores de productos marinos del golfo. Parte del territorio municipal está ocupado por la laguna de Tamiahua.

Tampacán ◆ Municipio de San Luis Potosí situado en la porción suroriental del estado, al sur-sureste de Ciudad Valles y norte de Tamazunchale. Superficie: 260.8 km². Habitantes: 16,318, de los cuales 3,952 forman la población económicamente activa. Hablan alguna lengua indígena 6,925 personas mayores de cinco años (náhuatl 6,888). Indígenas monolingües: 576.

Tampamachoco ◆ Albufera situada en el extremo oriental del municipio veracruzano de Tuxpan, al sur de la de Tamiahua, con la que se comunica mediante un canal artificial. Está unida al río Tuxpan, junto a la barra del mismo nombre.

Tampamolón ◆ Municipio de San Luis Potosí situado en la porción suroriental del estado, al sur-sureste de Ciudad Valles y noreste de Tamazunchale, en los límites con Veracruz. Superficie: 100.9 km². Habitantes: 13,311, de los cuales 2,923 forman la población económicamente activa. Hablan alguna lengua indígena 7,629 personas mayores de cinco años (huasteco 4,456 y náhuatl 3,173), de las cuales 467 son monolingües. La cabecera es Tampamolón de Corona.

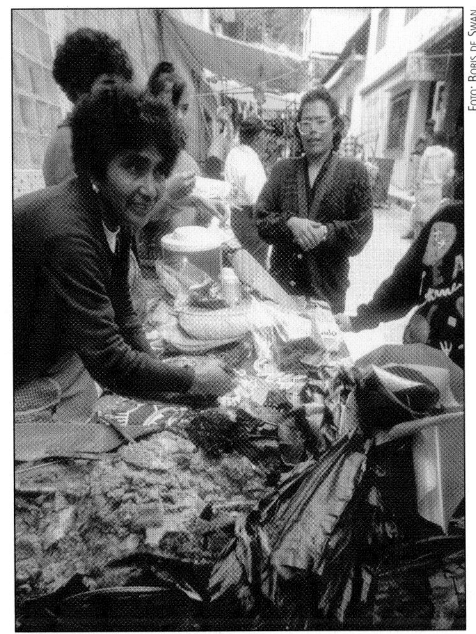
Foto: Boris de Swan

Zacahuil, platillo tradicional de Tamazunchale, San Luis Potosí

Tampaón ◆ Río de San Luis Potosí, también llamado Valles. Nace de la confluencia de los ríos Naranjos y de los Gatos o Mesillas, que bajan de la Sierra Madre Oriental. Corre de norte a sur, recibe al río Puerco y, al sur de Ciudad Valles, desemboca en el Tamuín.

Tampico ◆ Barra de Tamaulipas y Veracruz situada en la desembocadura del río Pánuco, a cuyos lados se construyó un par de escolleras paralelas de dos kilómetros de largo. La barra permite el acceso de los barcos de gran calado hasta la zona petrolera de Tampico.

Tampico ◆ Municipio de Tamaulipas situado en el extremo suroriental del estado, en los límites con Veracruz y contiguo a Ciudad Madero. Superficie: 68.1 km². Habitantes: 278,933, de los cuales 91,693 forman la población económicamente activa. Hablan alguna len-

Foto: Fondo Editorial Grupo Azabache

Tamiahua, Veracruz

gua indígena 1,925 personas mayores de cinco años (náhuatl 1,201 y huasteco 471). El territorio municipal fue habitado originalmente por los huastecos de Tam-piko (☛ *Pueblo Viejo*), que construyeron, en la actual cabecera municipal, una pequeña pirámide redonda que fue descubierta a principios de los años cuarenta. Los huastecos, sin embargo, desalojaron la ribera septentrional. Los españoles, por su parte, tampoco vivieron en el actual territorio del municipio, pero fundaron dos veces la villa de San Luis de Tampico; una en Pueblo Viejo (☛) y la otra en Tampico Alto (☛). En abril de 1823, Antonio López de Santa Anna, que unos meses antes se había levantado en armas contra el gobierno de Agustín de Iturbide, "autorizó" a los pobladores de Altamira a instalarse en la desembocadura del Pánuco, del lado tamaulipeco, donde fundaron un pueblo al que llamaron, en honor al veracruzano, Santa Anna de Tampico y más tarde Santa Anna de Tamaulipas. A mediados de 1929, una fuerza española al mando de Isidro Barradas desembarcó cerca de Tampico y en agosto tomó la población. Días después, mientras Barradas avanzaba hacia Altamira, las fuerzas mexicanas de Santa Anna intentaron tomar Tampico y durante dos semanas combatieron en sus alrededores, hasta que en septiembre, los españoles se rindieron. En 1832, Esteban Moctezuma se levantó en armas contra el gobierno de Anastasio Bustamante con la exigencia de crear un estado de las Huastecas, pero el movimiento fue derrotado. También derrotadas fueron las insurrecciones de 1838 y 1840, dirigidas ambas contra el propio Bustamante. La actual catedral comenzó a construirse en 1844. Durante la guerra de 1847, la marina estadounidense tomó Tampico sin combatir, gracias a las maniobras de Santa Anna, cuyo nombre fue quitado al municipio al triunfo de la revolución de Ayutla. Hasta 1862, la villa permaneció en poder de los liberales, pero en noviembre de ese año, los republicanos fueron desalojados por los invasores franceses. Tres meses después, las guerrillas de Asención Gómez y Juan José de la Garza recuperaron la plaza, pero una vez más, en agosto de 1863, los franceses y los imperialistas ocuparon el puerto. En agosto de 1865, luego de medio año de asedios y combates, los republicanos reconquistaron la plaza, que desde entonces permaneció en su poder. En los últimos años del siglo XIX, las exploraciones petroleras se incrementaron; a partir del establecimiento de la Waters Pierce Oil Company, en 1898, y la Huasteca Petroleum Company, en 1907, el puerto se convirtió en el principal exportador de crudo mexicano. En 1913, fuerzas del dictador Victoriano Huerta ocuparon el puerto, que a partir de diciembre fue asediado por los constitucionalistas. En abril de 1914, unos marinos estadounidenses del barco

Foto: Boris de Swan

Puerto de Tampico, Tamaulipas

Dolphin, que se encontraba frente a Tampico para "vigilar el asedio de los antihuertistas a la plaza", desembarcaron sin previo aviso y fueron aprehendidos y encarcelados por las autoridades portuarias. Pese a que fueron liberados de inmediato, el almirante Mayo, comandante de la flota extranjera, exigió que como desagravio las autoridades mexicanas rindiesen honores a la bandera de Estados Unidos, lo que fue rechazado por la Cancillería. Este incidente, preparado por el gobierno de Washington, dio origen a la ocupación, durante unos seis meses, del puerto de Veracruz. En mayo, por su parte, los constitucionalistas ocuparon Tampico. Después de la revolución y gracias al potencial petrolero de la llamada Faja de Oro, Tampico se convirtió en un importante centro de actividad económica, con una población flotante no cuantificada y donde circulaba el dólar como moneda corriente. La declinación se inició hacia 1921, cuando se encontró agua salada en los mantos de hidrocarburos y se incendiaron los pozos Meriwether 3 y Morrison 5, los más productivos, que luego se agotaron. En 1923, la diócesis de Tamaulipas cambió su sede de Ciudad Victoria a Tampico, nombre que tomó en 1958. La cabecera municipal es un importante centro comercial y pesquero que forma, con Ciudad Madero, una zona conurbada. En la jurisdicción se encuentran la Universidad Autónoma de Tamaulipas y varias refinerías de Petróleos Mexicanos. De ahí parte el oleoducto que surte a Monterrey. Sus instalaciones lo hacen el primer puerto industrial de México para embarcaciones de gran calado. Su aduana es la segunda más importante de la República.

Tampico Alto ◆ Municipio de Veracruz situado en el noroccidente del estado, al este de Pánuco y norte de Tuxpan. Tiene costas en el golfo de México. Superficie: 1,027.35 km². Habitantes: 13,604, de los cuales 4,272 forman la población económicamente activa. Hablan alguna lengua indígena 88 personas mayores de cinco años (náhuatl 40). El extremo norte de la laguna de Tamiahua queda dentro de la jurisdicción de este municipio, en el que, además, se ha desarrollado una mediana actividad petrolera. A principios del siglo XVIII, los habitantes de San Luis de Tampico (☛ *Pueblo Viejo*) se retiraron al sur y fundaron la población de Tampico Joya, situada en la actual jurisdicción municipal; en 1754 volvieron a fundar San Luis de Tampico, en el sitio que actualmente ocupa la cabecera municipal, Tampico Alto.

Tamuín ◆ Municipio de San Luis Potosí contiguo a Ciudad Valles y situado en los límites con Tamaulipas y Veracruz. Superficie: 2,427.5 km². Habitantes: 36,543, de los cuales 8,909 forman la población económicamente activa. Hablan alguna lengua indígena 3,355 personas mayores de cinco años (huasteco 2,225 y náhuatl 1,121). En la jurisdicción se encuentra la zona arqueológica de Tantoc, con dos grandes pirámides y un juego de pelota construidos en el estilo arquitectónico teotihuacano. En el siglo IX, los toltecas se instalaron a ocho kilometros de la actual cabecera y construyeron un templo que fue decorado con pinturas al fresco. Más tarde la zona fue ocupada por los huastecos, de cuya presencia se conservan 11 tumbas y varias esculturas, una de las cuales, el *adolescente huasteco*, se supone que es una representación de Quetzalcóatl. La cabecera municipal se llamó Guerrero y más tarde Villa Guerrero. En 1901, Edward L. Doheney inició la explotación del primer pozo petrolero, cuyo producto fue comercializado con éxito (☛ *Petróleo*). Cuenta con un balneario de aguas termales, Taninul, donde se construyó un complejo turístico.

Tamuín ◆ Río de San Luis Potosí. Nace al sur-sureste de Ciudad Valles, de la confluencia de los ríos Valles o Tampaón y Santa María, en la sierra Madre Oriental. Corre de oeste a este por la Huasteca potosina y se une al Pánuco al sur-suroeste de Ébano.

Tanabe *Ushio*, Atsuko ◆ n. en Japón (1935). Escritora. Vive en México desde 1956. Licenciada en estudios orientales y maestra en estudios latinoamericanos por la UNAM. Profesora de la Facultad de Filosofía y Letras de la UNAM. Ha sido jefa del departamento de Lenguas Asiáticas del Centro de Enseñanza de Lenguas Extranjeras de la UNAM. Colaboradora de *unomásuno*, *Diálogos*, *Revista de la Universidad*, *La Semana de Bellas Artes* y *Revista de Bellas Artes*. Ha publicado una *Antología de la poesía moderna de Japón* (1985), una *Antología del cuento japonés moderno y contemporáneo* (1985) y otra de *Cuento japonés del siglo XX* (1987). Tradujo y adaptó *El kojki*, obra mitológica japonesa (1981). Autora de *El japonismo de José Juan Tablada* (1981).

Tancanhuitz de Santos ◆ Municipio de San Luis Potosí situado en el suroriente del estado, al sur de Ciudad Valles y norte de Tamazunchale. Superficie: 187 km². Habitantes: 19,572, de los cuales 4,951 forman la población económicamente activa. Hablan alguna lengua indígena 11,887 personas mayores de cinco años (huasteco 6,514 y náhuatl 5,631). Indígenas monolingües: 795. La cabecera es General Pedro Antonio Santos y cerca de ella se encuentran los restos de una pirámide similar a la de Cuicuilco. El municipio, llamado antiguamente Ciudad Santos, cambió de nombre en 1981.

Tanciatot ◆ Río de Veracruz, también llamado Chicayán. Nace al oeste de Tuxpan, en la sierra de Tantima u Otontepec, en el oriente de la Huasteca; corre hacia el norte y tributa en el Pánuco, al sur de la laguna de Chairel.

Tancítaro ◆ Municipio de Michoacán situado al sur de Zamora y contiguo a Apatzingán. Superficie: 752.68 km². Habitantes: 23,412, de los cuales 4,900 forman la población económicamente activa. Hablan alguna lengua indígena 38 personas mayores de cinco años. La cabecera es Tancítaro de Medellín.

Tancítaro, Pico de ◆ Volcán apagado de Michoacán situado en la sierra de Apatzingán, cerca de Uruapan. Con 3,485 metros sobre el nivel del mar, es la mayor elevación del estado. Al norte de su base se encuentra el volcán Paricutín y lo rodean unos 250 pequeños conos volcánicos ya extinguidos.

Tancoco ◆ Municipio de Veracruz situado al noroeste de Tuxpan, sur-sureste de Pánuco y contiguo a Tamiahua. Superficie: 145.59 km². Habitantes: 7,019, de los cuales 1,743 forman la población económicamente activa. Hablan alguna lengua indígena 824 personas mayores de cinco años (huasteco 703 y náhuatl 113).

Tancochapan ◆ Río de Veracruz y Tabasco. Nace en la frontera entre ambos estados, al suroeste del lago de Rosario, de la confluencia de los ríos Playas o Xocuapan y Pedregal; corre de sureste a noroeste por la línea fronteriza y se une al Zanapa, al sur de La Venta, para formar el Tonalá. Es navegable para pequeñas embarcaciones.

Tanetze de Zaragoza ◆ Municipio de Oaxaca situado en el centro-norte del estado, al noreste de Oaxaca y sur de Valle Nacional. Superficie: 58.69 km². Habitantes: 1,821, de los cuales 690 forman la población económicamente activa. Hablan alguna lengua indígena 1,573 personas mayores de cinco años (zapoteco 1,570), de las cuales 165 no dominan el espanol.

Tangamandapio ◆ Municipio de Michoacán situado al este de Jiquilpan y oeste de Zamora. Superficie: 257.36 km². Habitantes: 22,151, de los cuales 5,177 forman la población económicamente activa. Hablan alguna lengua indígena 6,711 personas mayores de cinco años (purépecha 6,700), son monolingües 212.

Tangancícuaro ◆ Municipio de Michoacán situado al noroeste de Uruapan y contiguo a Zamora. Superficie: 408.67 km². Habitantes: 33,815, de los cuales 8,989 forman la población económicamente activa. Hablan alguna lengua indígena 902 personas mayores de cinco años (purépecha 892). La cabecera municipal se llama Tangancícuaro de Arista. El municipio cuenta con tres ojos de agua: Junguarán, Cupatchiro y Camécuaro, el último de los cuales es un centro turístico.

Tanhuato ◆ Municipio de Michoacán situado al norte de Zamora y este de La Piedad, en los límites con Jalisco. Superficie: 232.79 km². Habitantes: 14,514, de los cuales 3,575 forman la población económicamente activa. Hablan alguna lengua indígena 15 personas mayores de cinco años (purépecha 13). La cabecera municipal se llama Tanhuato de Guerrero.

Taniche ◆ Municipio de Oaxaca situado en el centro del estado, al noroeste de Miahuatlán y sur de Oaxaca. Superficie: 22.97 km². Habitantes: 990, de los cuales 239 forman la población económicamente activa.

Tanlajás ◆ Municipio de San Luis Potosí contiguo a Ciudad Valles. Superficie: 455.2 km². Habitantes: 16,634, de los cuales 3,935 forman la población económicamente activa. Hablan alguna lengua indígena 11,155 personas mayores de cinco años (huasteco 11,123). Indígenas monolingües: 788. En él se encuentran las lagunas Lagarto, Tabasquiche y el manatial de Ojo Caliente.

Tannenbaum, Frank ◆ n. en Austria y m. en EUA (1893-1969). Periodista, historiador y sociólogo. Vivió en México entre 1922 y 1945. Profesor de la Universidad de Columbia. Autor de *Wall Shadows: an Study in American Prisons* (1922), *The Mexican Agrarian Revolution* (1929), *Peace by Revolution: an Interpretation of Mexico* (1933), *Whiter Latin American? An Introduction to its Economic and Social Problems* (1934), *The Desting of the Negro in de Western Hemisphere* (1946), *Mexico, the Struggle for Peace and Bread* (1950), *A Philosophy of Labor* (1951) y *The Lay to Latin America* (1962). Luego de su muerte aparecieron *Toward and Appreciation of Latin America* (1972) y *The Future of Democracy in Latin America* (1974).

Tánori, Juan ◆ m. en Tuntunudé, Son. (¿1815?-1859). Caudillo de los ópatas y los pimas que encabezó varios levantamientos armados promovidos por los gandaristas sonorenses, a partir de 1842. En 1859 proclamó el Plan de Tepupa, mediante el cual se adhirió al Plan de Tacubaya y proclamó como gobernador de Sonora a Manuel María Gándara. Fue derrotado y fusilado.

Tánori, Refugio ◆ n. en Álamos y m. en Guaymas, Son. (1835-1866). Indio ópata, pariente de Juan Tánori, con quien se levantó en armas en 1842 y 1859. Se acogió a la amnistía luego del fusilamiento de Juan Tánori, pero a mediados de 1865 se sublevó en favor de Maximiliano de Habsburgo, quien le otorgó el grado de general y lo condecoró con la Cruz de la Orden de Guadalupe. Formó un ejército de ópatas, sitió Ures y liberó a los soldados argelinos que habían sido apresados en Sinaloa. Dos años después, al triunfo de la República, intentó huir del país por Guaymas, pero fue aprehendido frente a Santa Rosalía, regresado al puerto sonorense y fusilado.

Tanquián de Escobedo ◆ Municipio de San Luis Potosí situado al sureste de Ciudad Valles y noreste de Tamazunchale, en los límites con Veracruz. Superficie: 204.2 km². Habitantes: 13,162, de los cuales 3,028 forman la población económicamente activa. Hablan alguna lengua indígena 1,874 personas mayores de cinco años (huasteco 1,691 y náhuatl 179).

Tantima ◆ Municipio de Veracruz situado al noroeste de Tuxpan y sureste de Pánuco. Superficie: 267.32 km². Habitantes: 14,048, de los cuales 3,911 forman la población económicamente activa. Hablan alguna lengua indígena 921 personas mayores de cinco años (huasteco 883).

Tantima ◆ Sierra de Veracruz, también llamada Otontepec, situada en el noroccidente del estado, al oeste-noroeste de Tuxpan. Se extiende de norte a sur en la llanura costera.

Tantoyuca ◆ Municipio de Veracruz situado al noroeste de Tuxpan y sur de Pánuco, en los límites con Hidalgo. Superficie: 1,205.84 km². Habitantes: 89,492, de los cuales 23,463 forman la población económicamente activa. Hablan alguna lengua indígena 42,195 personas mayores de cinco años (huasteco 38,070 y náhuatl 4,080), de las cuales 2,786 no saben español. Los huastecos, primeros habitantes de la actual cabecera, fueron conocidos por la fabricación de cera, de donde derivó el nombre del poblado, "Lugar donde hay cera". Tantoyuca fue sometida por los ejércitos de la Triple Alianza a fines del siglo XV. En el siglo XVI, poco después de la conquista española, la población fue cabecera de la alcaldía mayor de Pánuco. Durante el levantamiento de los totonacas de Papantla en 1836, Tantoyuca fue ocupada por las fuerzas de Mariano Olarte y permaneció en su poder hasta 1837. En 1845, los huastecos se incorporaron al levantamiento de Santiago Esteves y Luciano Velázquez y tres años después, en febrero de 1848, Juan Nepomuceno Llorente llamó a combatir a los invasores estadounidenses y proclamó el Plan de Tantoyuca, que decía: "todas las propiedades territoriales serán comunes a todos los ciudadanos de la República". El levantamiento fue reprimido en 1849. Al año siguiente la población fue elevada a la categoría de villa. El 9 de agosto de 1856, "las clases oprimidas de obreros, indígenas y proletarios" proclamaron un segundo plan, redactado por Rafael Díaz, mucho más radical que el primero y claramente influido por el anarquismo europeo. Los sublevados consideraban que "no habiendo podido obtener otra base la propiedad en su principio más que la usurpación. es intolerable que unos hombres estén nadando en oro cuando otros no tienen un ochavo en el bolsillo" y "que cuando la vista de una mujer excita nuestros deseos amorosos, es absurdo que venga un marido a prevalerse de sus derechos y prohibirnos que nos acerquemos a la que amamos". Por ello, "Declaramos guerra a muerte a la propiedad privada para que quede por consiguiente la tierra de todos los hombres para que gocen de ella a su gusto" y así formar una sociedad en la que "el dinero será un mueble inútil" y en la que "todos participarán igualmente de los placeres como de los trabajos". El levantamiento fue derrotado. Sin embargo, luego de que se promulgó la Constitución liberal de 1857, el Congreso veracruzano erigió el Cantón de Tantoyuca. Un año después, en mayo de 1858, la villa fue tomada por fuerzas liberales al mando de Jesús Andrade. La localidad permaneció en poder de los republicanos hasta julio de 1864, cuando fue asaltada y ocupada por las fuerzas contraguerrilleras de Charles Dupin. Se le confirió la categoría de ciudad en 1901.

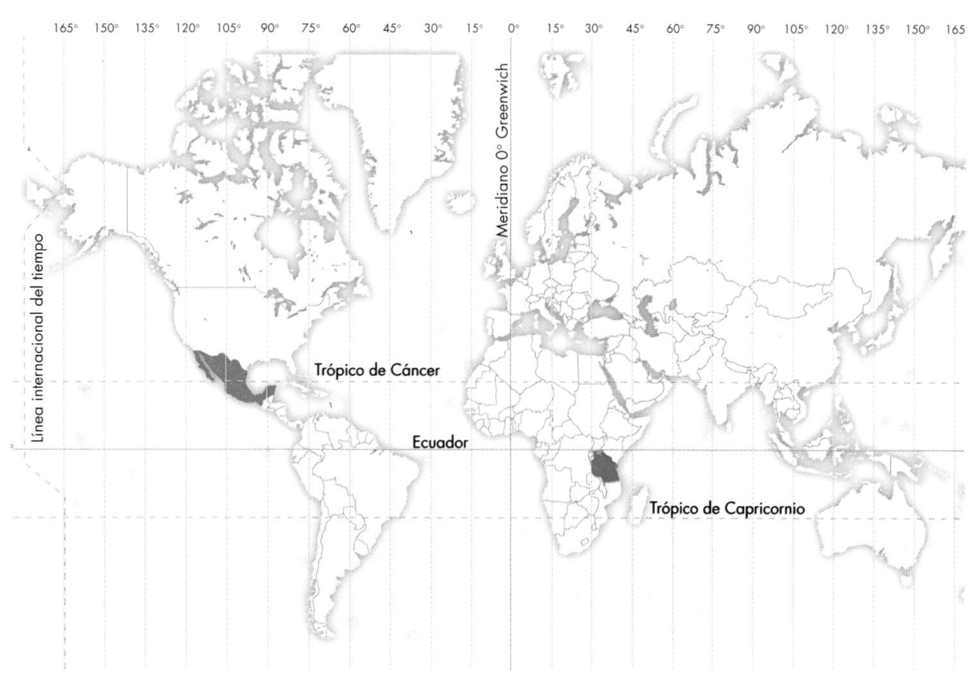

República Unida de Tanzania

TANZANIA, REPÚBLICA UNIDA DE Nación de África situada en el litoral del océano Índico. Está formada por el ex territorio de Tangañica y las islas de Zanzíbar, Pemba y Mafia. Limita al norte con Kenia y Uganda, al sur con Mozambique, Malawi y Zambia, al oeste con la República Democrática del Congo, y al noroeste con Ruanda y Burundi. Superficie: 945,087 km^2. Habitantes: 32,102,000 (1998). Su capital es Dar es Salaam, que en 1994 tenía 1,606,000 habitantes. Otras ciudades de importancia son Dodoma (capital designada, 1,461,000 habitantes), Mwanza (2,217,000) Tabora (1,223,000), Mbeya (1,742,000) y Tanga (1,546,000). Los idiomas oficiales son el suajili y el inglés, aunque también son comunes el árabe y lenguas locales. En territorio tanzanio se encuentran el Kilimanjaro, la cumbre más alta de África, que se eleva a 5,895 metros sobre el nivel del mar, y los lagos Victoria y Tangañica. *Historia:* los primeros hombres que utilizaron herramientas vivieron en el actual territorio de Tanzania. En 695, el príncipe Hazma de Omán se instaló en la isla de Zanzíbar y fundó un puerto que dio nombre a la región, que con muchas otras ciudades arabizadas de la costa oriental de África constituyó la cultura zandj. Desde Zanzíbar comerciaron con Persia, Siria, India y China. Vendían metales, marfil y esclavos; recibían libros, porcelanas y telas. A fines del siglo XV, la aparición de los portugueses en la costa oriental de África acabó con el desarrollo de los zandj. En 1498, Vasco de Gama desembarcó en Zanzíbar y cuatro años después, en 1502, conquistó el puerto. A partir de entonces, el comercio de esclavos, sobre todo bantúes provenientes del interior, se convirtió en el principal negocio de los ocupantes lusitanos. Muchos de esos esclavos fueron trasladados a la Nueva España durante la segunda mitad del siglo XVI y aquí fueron conocidos como *zíbaros* y *zamucos*. Durante los primeros 30 años del siglo XVIII, los árabes de Omán expulsaron a los portugueses y se adueñaron de la zona situada al norte del río Ruvuma, aunque de hecho sólo ejercieron un dominio efectivo en Zan-

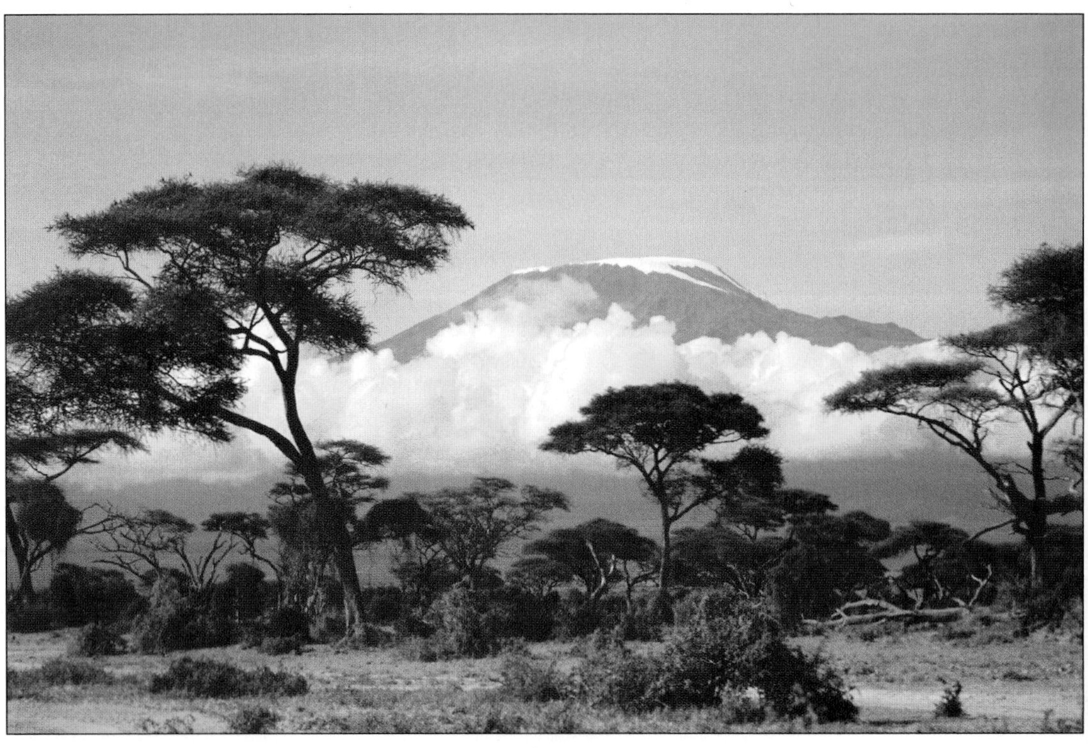

Paisaje de Tanzania

zíbar, Pemba y Mafia. La porción occidental de Tangañica permaneció habitada por tribus bantúes independientes, mientras que en la costa se formaron varios pequeños señoríos semiindependientes de Omán. En 1832, el sultanato de Omán estableció su capital en Zanzíbar y desde entonces los Estados de la costa de Tangañica fueron realmente absorbidos. El gobierno omaní restableció las rutas comerciales entre la costa y la región de los grandes lagos. Esas rutas fueron seguidas desde mediados del siglo XIX por varios exploradores anglosajones, entre ellos el célebre David Livingston, y más tarde por aventureros alemanes, en especial Karl Peters, quien, a mediados de los años ochenta, hizo que varios jefes tribales del interior firmaran unos acuerdos, los que fueron utlizados por el gobierno de Berlín para legitimar, ante las otras potencias coloniales europeas, el dominio del territorio situado al sur del lago Victoria, al este del Tangañica y al norte de las posesiones portuguesas de Mozambique. El sultanato de Zanzíbar, por su parte, se vio obligado a aceptar la ocupación alemana de Tangañica y unos años después, en 1890, el dominio británico de su propio territorio, que se convirtió en un protectorado de Londres, lo que al año siguiente movió a Alemania a hacer lo mismo y establecer su protectorado sobre Tangañica. 14 años después, en 1905, los musulmanes se levantaron en armas contra la dominación germana, pero, con la ayuda de la marina británica, los alemanes derrotaron, en 1907, a los insurrectos. Durante la primera guerra mundial, los ingleses y alemanes, que combatían en Europa, movilizaron varios contingentes de negros para conquistar, cada uno, la colonia del enemigo, pero como la guerra europea se decidió a favor de los anglosajones, en 1919 Inglaterra se adueñó de Tangañica, con el aval de la recién creada Sociedad de Naciones. 30 años después, al término de la segunda guerra mundial, la Organización de las Naciones Unidas revalidó la dominación británica (1946). En 1954 se creó la Unión Nacional Africana de Tangañica, dirigida por Julius K. Nyerere, y al año siguiente los ingleses establecieron un parlamento. En 1961, Tangañica consiguió que la Gran Bretaña lo reconociera como Estado independiente, pero dentro de la Comunidad Británica de Naciones. Un año después, el primer ministro, Nyerere, declaró la independencia del país, que adoptó el nombre de República de Tanzania. Dos años después, Inglaterra concedió la autonomía al sultanato de Zanzíbar, pero a principios de 1964 un levantamiento popular dirigido por el Partido Afro-Shirazi instauró la República. En abril de ese mismo año se estableció la República Unida de Tangañica y Zanzíbar, llamada República Unida de Tanzania desde octubre de ese año. Nyerere fue elegido presidente y en 1967 dio a conocer un documento llamado Declaración de Arusha, donde definió una forma particular de socialismo como meta nacional. Desde entonces, el gobierno de Nyerere siguió una linea de no alineamiento y apoyo los movimientos independentistas del sur de África. En febrero de 1973, Tanzania y México establecieron relaciones diplomáticas. A principios de los años setenta, el gobierno de Nyerere se opuso al golpe de Estado de Idi Amín Dada en Uganda, por lo que hubo varios enfrentamientos armados en las cercanías del lago Victoria e, incluso, una invasión ugandesa en 1978. En 1975, Nyerere visitó México. En 1984, con México, Argentina, Grecia, India y Suecia, Tanzania formó el Grupo de los Seis. En 1985, Alí Hassán Mwinyi fue elegido presidente de Tanzania, en lugar de Nyerere, quien murió poco después. En las elecciones de 1995, Benjamin Mkapa fue elegido presidente, Frederick Sumaye, primer ministro, y el Partido Revolucionario de Tanzania obtuvo la mayoría en la Asamblea Nacional.

TAPACHULA ◆ Municipio de Chiapas situado en la costa del océano Pacífico, en la región del Soconusco (☞) y en los límites con Guatemala. Superficie: 857 km^2. Habitantes: 244,855, de los cuales 66,195 forman la población económicamente activa. Hablan alguna lengua indígena 1,851 personas mayores de cinco años (mame 1,161 y zapoteco 432). En el siglo VIII de la época contemporánea, la región fue ocupada por los tapacholts, quienes a fines del siglo XV fueron conquistados por los mexicas. La población de Tapachula fue fundada en la última década del siglo XVI, luego de la ocupación europea del Soconusco. A mediados del siglo XVIII, poco más de 1,000 personas vivían en el pueblo. En 1794, luego de que un huracán destruyó el pueblo de Escuintla, la capital del partido de Soconusco pasó a Tapachula. En octubre de 1813, el gobierno de Chiapas elevó a Tapachula a la categoría de villa. En ese mismo año se creó el ayuntamiento local. En 1842, el Congreso de Chiapas elevó a Tapachula a la categoría de ciudad. De acuerdo con las sucesivas divisiones políticas del departamento o estado de Chiapas, Tapachula fue cabecera del distrito Suroeste (1844), del departamento de Soconusco (1846) y del distrito de Tapachula (1853). El 10 de mayo de 1887 el puerto de San Benito (hoy Puerto Madero), de este municipio, recibio la primera inmigración a México de japoneses, cuyos 35 integrantes buscaban establecer en Escuintla un emporio cafetalero. La misión fracasó y los inmigrantes se disgregaron por el territorio nacional. La diócesis católica de Tapachula fue creada en 1957. La cabecera es el más importante centro comercial del Soconusco. En ella se efectúa, durante los meses de enero y febrero, una exposición agrícola, ganadera, comercial y cultural. Del 22 al 29 de agosto se celebra una feria popular en honor del patrono: San Agustín.

TAPALAPA ◆ Municipio de Chiapas situado al norte de Tuxtla Gutiérrez y suroeste de Ixpangajoya. Superficie: 32.3 km^2. Habitantes: 3,286, de los cuales 792 forman la población económicamente activa. Hablan alguna lengua indígena 2,447 personas mayores de cinco años (zoque 2,432).

TAPALPA ◆ Municipio de Jalisco situado al noroeste de Ciudad Guzmán y noreste de Autlán. Superficie: 406.32 km^2. Habitantes: 14,099, de los cuales 3,206 forman la población económicamente activa. Hablan alguna lengua indígena 15 personas mayores de cinco años.

TAPALPA, DE ◆ Sierra de Jalisco que forma parte del Sistema Volcánico Transversal. Se extiende de sur a norte, al suroeste del lago de Chapala; es una prolongación septentrional del Nevado y del Volcán de Colima. Se une al noroeste con la sierra de Quilá.

TAPIA, ANDRÉS DE ◆ n. en España y m. en la ciudad de México (1485-?). Formó parte de la expedición de Hernán Cortés y participó en todas las acciones militares de la conquista. Como recompensa recibió las encomiendas de Cholula y Tizapán. Más tarde participó en las expediciones cortesianas a Baja California. Luego de una breve estancia en España, donde acompañó a Cortés, volvió a la Nueva España y fue alcalde de la ciudad de México. Escribió una *Relación* sobre la conquista, que empieza con el relato de la fundación de Veracruz y concluye con el combate entre las fuerzas de Cortés y las de Pánfilo de Narváez.

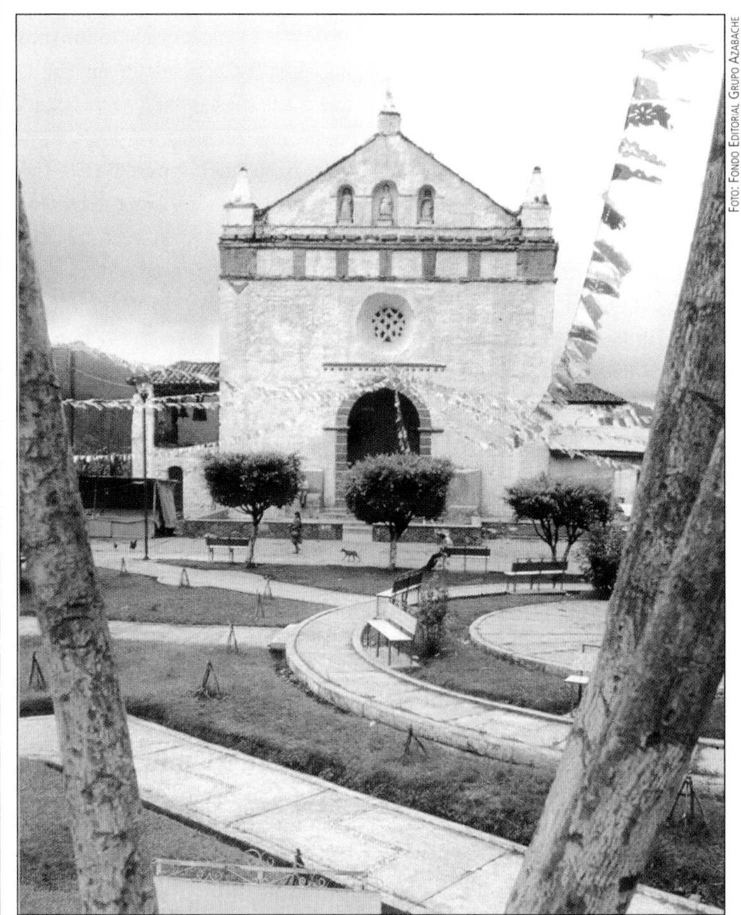

FOTO: FONDO EDITORIAL GRUPO AZABACHE

Iglesia de San Agustín en Tapalapa, Chiapas

TAPIA, GONZALO DE ◆ n. en España y m. en Toboropa, Sin. (1561-1595). Miembro de la Compañía de Jesús desde 1576. Llegó a la Nueva España en 1584 y se instaló en Guanajuato. Participó en las negociaciones que pusieron fin a la guerra chichimeca; en 1590 fundó San Luis de la Paz. Más tarde se incorporó a las misiones jesuitas del noroeste. Fue muerto por los indios.

TAPIA, JOSÉ DE ◆ n. en España y m. en el DF (1896-1989). Pedagogo. Su apellido materno era Bujalance. Profesor titulado en la Escuela Normal de Córdoba. Ejerció el magisterio en Peñarroya, Montemayor y Barcelona. Fue uno de los primeros en aplicar en España la educación activa de Célestin Freinet. Durante la guerra civil española dirigió un grupo escolar y perteneció a la Secretaría Regional Anarquista Catalana. En 1939, a la derrota de la República, se trasladó a Francia, donde fue recluido en varios campos de concentración. Se incorporó a la resistencia francesa durante la segunda guerra mundial y cayó en poder de los alemanes. Llegó a México en 1948 y trabajó para el Instituto Nacional Indigenista. Fue fundador y director de la escuela primaria Manuel Bartolomé de Cosio, en la ciudad de México. Colaborador de la *Enciclopedia UTEHA*.

TAPIA, MARIANO ◆ n. en Chiautla y m. en San José de Chiapa, en el actual estado de Puebla (?-1812). Insurgente. Era cura de Tlapa cuando, en noviembre de 1811, se incorporó a las fuerzas de José María Morelos. Participó en las tomas de Chiautla, Cuautla y Tehuacán. En 1812 se le encomendó auxiliar a Valerio Trujano, sitiado en Huajuapan, pero murió en el camino.

TAPIA, PRIMO ◆ n. en Naranja, hoy Naranja de Tapia, y m. en la hacienda de El Cortijo, cerca de Naranja, municipio de Zacapu, Mich. (1885-1926). Su apellido materno era De la Cruz. En 1900 ingresó al Seminario de Erongarícuaro. Tres años después fue expulsado y se contrató como jornalero en la hacienda de Cantabria. Fue a Estados Unidos en 1907 y ahí militó en la organización International Workers of the World y se relacionó con grupos magonistas. Fue organizador sindical en minas de Arizona y de michoacanos inmigrantes en zonas azucareras de Nebraska. En 1919 tuvo que huir de Estados Unidos, luego de que el sindicato de trabajadores azucareros fue derrotado en una huelga. Volvió a Naranja en 1920 y trabajó con los campesinos de la región de Zacapu. En octubre de 1921 ingresó en la Juventud Comunista de México y en noviembre fundó el Sindicato de Comunidades Agrarias. Más tarde organizó la delegación del Partido Comunista Mexicano en Michoacán y colaboró con la Casa del Obrero Mundial de Morelia, con la Federación de Sindicatos de Michoacán, con el Partido Socialista Michoacano y con el Partido Agrarista Michoacano. En diciembre de 1922 participó en la fundación de la Liga de Comunidades Agrarias de Michoacán, de la que fue su primer secretario general. Como dirigente de esta asociación realizó una intensa actividad política y sindical, lo que provocó la hostilidad de los terratenientes, que cuatro años después, cuando trabajaba en la creación de la Liga Nacional Campesina, lo secuestraron y fusilaron.

TAPIA, RAFAEL ◆ n. en Acatlán, Pue., y m. en la ciudad de México (1858-1913). Talabartero. Trabajó en Córdoba y Orizaba. Participó en la huelga de Río Blanco de 1907 e intervino en una conspiración antiporfirista con Heriberto Jara, Gabriel Gavira y Camerino Mendoza. Antirreeleccionista desde 1909, en ese año fundó el Club Ignacio de la Llave. Se levantó en armas en 1910. Combatió en Veracruz, Tlaxcala y Puebla y ascendió a general. Después del asesinato del presidente Francisco I. Madero fue detenido, encarcelado en la prisión militar de Santiago Tlatelolco y asesinado por la policía huertista.

TAPIA, RICARDO ◆ n. en el DF (1940). Médico y doctor en bioquímica. Ha sido investigador del Instituto de Fisiología Celular de la UNAM. Ha publicado más de un centenar de artículos científicos. Coautor de *Bioquímica* (1979) y *Neurobiología celular* (1991). Autor de *Las células de la mente* (1987).

TAPIA, SANTIAGO ◆ n. en Aguililla, Mich., y m. en Matamoros, Tams. (1820-1866). Militar. Luchó contra los invasores estadounidenses en 1847. Más tarde se dedicó al comercio, pero en 1854 se adhirió al Plan de Ayutla y combatió en las fuerzas de Epitacio Huerta. Formó parte del ejército liberal durante la guerra de los Tres Años. Gobernador de Puebla (1862) y gobernador y comandante militar de Michoacán (del 8 de febrero al 17 de julio de 1863). En 1864 fue detenido en Ixmiquilpan y recluido en Puebla. Fue liberado en 1866 y se encargó del gobierno de Tamaulipas (del 31 de agosto al 3 de noviembre de 1866). Murió de tifo durante el sitio de Matamoros.

TAPIA ACEVES, SANTIAGO ◆ n. en el DF (1941). Ingeniero en electrónica por el Instituto Modelo. Pertenece al PRI. Profesor en la Academia de Policía (1980). En la Dirección General de Policía y Tránsito del DDF fue jefe de área en las delegaciones Milpa Alta (1978-79) y Tláhuac (1979-83), comandante del Agrupamiento de Grúas (1983-88) y jefe del sector 16 en Azcapotzalco (1988). En la Secretaría General de Protección y Vialidad se ha desempeñado como jefe del sector 3 en Cuauhtémoc (1988), director general de Operaciones (1988-90) y titular de la dependencia (1990-92).

TAPIA BOLÍVAR, DANIEL ◆ n. en España y en el DF (1908-1985). Periodista y escritor. Colaboró en los periódi-

Daniel Tapia Bolívar

cos *La Libertad* y *La Voz* y de la revista *Crónica*. Durante la guerra civil española escribió para *La Vanguardia* y el *Servicio Español de Información*. A la derrota de la República pasó a México (1939). Fue miembro del Consejo Técnico de la Junta de Liberación Española (1944-45) y fundador del Ateneo Español de México. Fue colaborador de las revistas *Romance*, *Las Españas*, *Rueca*, *Ultramar* y *Litoral*. Traductor de Chesterton, Dumas, Bocaccio y Lawrence. Autor de *Ha llovido un dedito* (1935), *San Juan* (1935), *Teoría de Pepe-hillo* (1945) y *Breve historia del toreo* (1947). En 1932 recibió el Premio Zozaya para crónicas periodísticas.

Tapia Bolívar, Luis ◆ n. en España y m. en el DF (1905-1995). Licenciado en ciencias exactas por la Universidad Central de Madrid. Durante la guerra civil española dirigió el Centro de Capacitación del Sexto Cuerpo del Ejército y la Escuela Militar para Oficiales en Valencia y combatió en Madrid y Jarama. En 1939 fue hecho prisionero por las tropas franquistas y permaneció preso un año, hasta que escapó y se refugió en Portugal. Llegó a México en 1942. Trabajador de la compañía Proveedora Industrial, en 1942 ingresó como profesor en el Instituto Luis Vives, del que fue director técnico (1968-70) y director general (1969-83).

Tapia de Castellanos, Esther ◆ n. en Morelia, Mich., y m. en Guadalajara, Jal. (1842-1897). Poeta. Estudió en Morelia. Durante la guerra contra la intervención francesa trabajó como enfermera voluntaria en algunos hospitales republicanos en Guadalajara. Colaboró en los periódicos españoles *El Correo de Ultramar* y *La Ilustración Americana*. Autora de *Flores silvestres* (1871) y *Cánticos de los niños* (1881). Póstumamente aparecieron sus *Obras poéticas* (1905).

Esther Tapia de Castellanos

Tapia Colman, Simón ◆ n. en España y m. en el DF (1905-1993). Violinista y compositor. Estudió con Celso Díaz y Ramón Borobia en el Conservatorio de Zaragoza, con Vincent d'Indy en París (1925) y con Paul Hindemith (1935). Fue violín concertino del Teatro Apolo de Madrid (1924) y violinista principal del Cuarteto Colman. Republicano, al término de la guerra civil española estuvo preso en varios campos de concentración en Francia. Llegó a México en 1939. Fue primer violín de la Orquesta Sinfónica Nacional, fundador del coro del Colegio Ruiz de Alarcón (1940), director del programa radiofónico *Música de España*, transmitido por la XEW; director de la Orquesta del Ballet Español de Ana María (1943), director de la Asociación Musical Daniel, director del Coro de México, director del Coro del Conservatorio Nacional de Música (1971-72), fundador del coro de la CFE (1973) y coordinador musical del Colegio de Bachilleres (1975-77). Compuso *Una noche en Marruecos*, *Estampas de Iberia* (1939), *Sol de Aracena*, *Retratos*, *Leyenda gitana* (1956), *Seis caprichos*, *Trío prehispánico*, *Núcleos*, *Sísifo*, *Sonata para violín y piano*, *Gitanilla, gitanilla*, *Suite de danzas y retratos*, *Mi mozuca*, *N x 2*, *Secuencias nucleicas*, *Los días de la voz*, *Sandunguerías*, *Xtoloob*, *Humanidad*, *Rapsdodia aragonesa*, *Fantasía seri*, *Luz de noche*, *Cantar del yaqui* y *Canta Jalisco*. Autor de *Beethoven*, *Técnica abreviadísima del violín*, *Reflexiones musicales*, *La música en la historia y en las relaciones humanas*, *El arpa en la historia de la música y de la humanidad*, *El solfeo en nueve lecciones*, *El hombre. Idea y forma de su música* y *Música y músicos en México* (1991). En 1989 recibió un homenaje del Conservatorio Superior de Zaragoza, España.

Tapia Conyer, Roberto ◆ n. en Guanajuato, Gto. (1954). Médico cirujano por la UNAM y maestro en salud pública y ciencias por la Universidad de Harvard. Ha hecho estudios de administración de salud pública en la Universidad de California y de doctorado en ciencias en la UNAM, de cuya Facultad de Medicina es profesor. En la SSA, a la que ingresó en 1982, fue responsable del desarrollo del Sistema de Vigilancia Epidemiológica y subsecretario de Prevención y Control de Enfermedades. Presidente de la Sociedad Mexicana de Salud Pública (1997-98). Catedrático del Conacyt (1991-93) y asesor de la OMS. Ha colaborado en libros colectivos, revistas nacionales e internacionales, compendios y manuales. Coautor de *Vacunación en el adulto*. Autor de *Las adicciones en México: dimensión, impacto y perspectivas*. Pertenece al Sistema Nacional de Investigadores. Premio Jorge Rosenkranz 1998 en investigación epidemiológica, José Ruiloba en epidemiología, y Aída Weiss y Miguel Alemán en Salud. Miembro de la Academia Nacional de Medicina, de la Academia Mexicana de Ciencias, y del Community Epidemiology Work Group.

Roberto Tapia Conyer

Tapia Ruiz, Roderico ◆ n. en Sehuadehuachi, Son. (1956). Licenciado en derecho por la Universidad de Sonora. Afiliado al PAN desde 1985, ha sido secretario de Organización del Comité Estatal en Sonora. Diputado federal (1991-94). Recibió la medalla Encuentro de Parlamentarios Latinoamericanos y Europeos, otorgada por el Parlamento Francés en 1992.

Tapilula ◆ Municipio de Chiapas situado al norte de Tuxtla Gutiérrez y al suroeste de Palenque. Superficie: 126.7 km^2. Habitantes: 8,339, de los cuales 2,178 forman la población económicamente activa. Hablan alguna lengua indígena 753 personas mayores de cinco años (zoque 688).

Luis Tapia Bolívar

Tapiz y García, Pedro ◆ n. en España y m. en Durango, Dgo. (1673-1722). Fue visitador general de la diócesis de Tarragona. Llegó a la Nueva España en 1711. Obispo de Durango desde 1715 hasta su muerte.

Libro escrito por Alfonso Taracena

TAPONA, DE ◆ Llano de Durango situado al noreste de Durango y al suroeste de Torreón, al este de la sierra de Gamón y al norte de la sierra de Temazcal o del Pedregal.

TARACENA, ALFONSO ◆ n. en Cunduacán, Tab., y m. en el DF (1895-1995). Periodista, historiador y novelista. Fundador de los diarios capitalinos *El Universal* (1916), *Excélsior* (1917) y *Novedades*. Autor de *Bajo el fuego de Helios* (1928), *Los ángeles* (1930), *En el vértigo de la revolución* (1930), *Los abrazos* (1937), *Madero, víctima del imperialismo yanqui*, *La vida en México bajo Manuel Ávila Camacho*, *La vida en México bajo Miguel Alemán*, *La verdadera historia de la Revolución Mexicana. Decimotercera etapa. 1927-1928* (1963) e *Historia extraoficial de la Revolución Mexicana* (1987). Medalla Félix Fulgencio Palavicini (1994).

TARACENA, BERTA ◆ n. en el DF (1935). Maestra en historia de México por la UNAM, especializada en arte mexicano. Ha publicado artículos sobre el tema en catálogos y revistas del país. Fue presidenta de la Asociación Internacional de Críticos de Arte. Coautora de *Antonio Ramírez* (1989). Autora de *Manuel Rodríguez Lozano, Francisco Corzas, Diego Rivera. Pintura de Caballete y dibujo, El realismo fantástico de Antonio Suárez y Desiderio Hernández Xochitiotzin* y *Pintura de caballete y dibujo*, entre otras. Miembro de la Sociedad Defensora del Tesoro Artístico de México.

TARAHUMARA ◆ Sierra de Chihuahua, Sonora y Durango que forma parte de la cresta principal de la sierra Madre Occidental. Se extiende de noroeste a sureste, desde el sur del río Papigochic, en el oeste chihuahuense y el este sonorense, hasta el norte de Durango, donde se une a la sierra de Guanaceví. Comprende, de noroeste a sureste, la mesa del Venado, la sierra de Tutuaca, la de los Pandos y las cumbres del Gato. Los dos picos más altos son el cerro Jesús María, que se eleva 2,571 metros sobre el nivel del mar, y el Tabacotes de 2,359 metros. Su anchura máxima, en la parte central, es de unos 250 km. En esta cordillera se encuentran las barrancas del Cobre y de Tararecua, de casi 1,000 metros de profundidad.

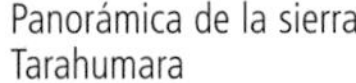
Panorámica de la sierra Tarahumara

Foto: Carlos Hahn

TARAHUMARA ◆ Vicariato de la Iglesia Católica Apostólica Romana establecido en la sierra Tarahumara en 1950. Abarca 35,923 km^2. La sede se halla en Sisoguichic.

TARAHUMARAS ◆ Indios del norte de México llamados realmente rarámuri, "los de los pies ligeros", que habitan en la zona montañosa del suroeste de Chihuahua, en la Alta Tarahumara. A la porción duranguense se le llama Baja Tarahumara o las Barrancas. En 1995, 62,555 personas mayores de cinco años hablaban tarahumara, de los cuales 13,774 eran monolingües. Los integrantes de esta etnia viven principalmente en Chihuahua (59,687), Sinaloa (845), Sonora (406) y Durango (490). La lengua tarahumara está clasificada al grupo nahua-cuitlateco, tronco yutonahua, familia pima-cora. Hacia el año 2000 a.n.e., los rarámuri comenzaron a practicar la agricultura, que desde entonces, junto con la caza y la pesca, se convirtió en su principal actividad económica. Hasta la llegada de los españoles vivieron en pequeños grupos en las llanuras del centro del actual estado de Chihuahua, pero desde el siglo XVI se replegaron a las montañas, a causa de la irrupción española en la meseta y el consiguiente establecimiento del trabajo forzado para los indios. A principios del siglo XVII, los europeos iniciaron la ocupación de la sierra Tarahumara. En 1600 los jesuitas se instalaron en la zona y en 1639 establecieron sus primeras misiones. En los últimos años del siglo XV se descubrieron importantes yacimientos minerales en la sierra Tarahumara y en 1631 se fundó el pueblo minero de San José del Parral, hoy Hidalgo del Parral. Reacios a la conquista material y espiritual, intentaron rechazar la dominación en 1646, cuando al mando de Tepox, Supichiochi, Ochárami y don Gregorio, cuatro pueblos se levantaron en armas y asaltaron e incendiaron la hacienda de Salto del Agua. Los españoles recurrieron a grandes contingentes de indios cristianizados y en 1648 derrotaron a los rebeldes y los concentraron en un pequeño número de poblaciones, con el fin de mantenerlos controlados. No obstante, dos años después Gabriel Teporame y Yagunaque volvieron a insurreccionar la zona. Tomaron Papigochic y Villa de Aguilar e incendiaron más de 10 conventos, pero en 1653 sus 2,000 hombres fueron derrotadas por los conquistadores y sus aliados indios. Teporame fue ahorcado en Papigochic. Entre 1684 y 1697, con el apoyo de tepehuanes, janos, sumas, conchos, tabaris y otros pueblos del desierto, los rarámuri, al mando de Corosia y Yepómera, intentaron rechazar la ocupación europea, pero, una vez más, a causa de la mayor efectividad de las armas españolas, fueron derrotados y tuvieron que retirarse hasta las cimas de

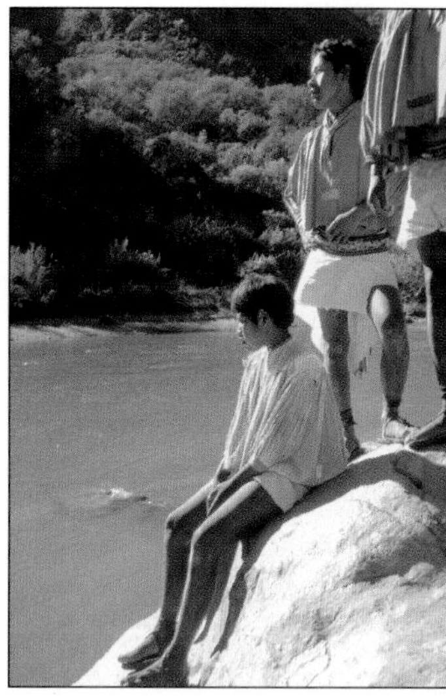
Indios Tarahumaras

la sierra, donde la inclemencia del entorno los mantuvo relativamente a salvo de la dominación política. No sucedió lo mismo en el plano religioso, pues la Compañía de Jesús estableció numerosas misiones en la sierra, donde, desde 1673, existió un importante contingente de frailes europeos no españoles. Tras la expulsión de los jesuitas en 1767, el control religioso quedó en manos de los franciscanos, quienes destruyeron la obra colectivizadora de la Compañía de Jesús. Cuando en 1900 volvió la Compañía de Jesús, hacía tiempo que habían cambiado sus ideas sobre las misiones. De hecho, a pesar de los jesuitas, o precisamente por ellos, hasta mediados del siglo XX la historia de los tarahumaras transcurrió al margen de la historia nacional, es decir, que en las comunidades serranas no tuvieron incidencia la revolución de independencia, las guerras de Reforma o la revolución de 1910-20, aunque, por supuesto, a partir de la segunda mitad del siglo XIX, los gobiernos liberales de Sonora y Chihuahua promulgaron varias leyes que afectaron las propiedades comunales de los indios. Desde los años cincuenta del siglo XX, los rarámuri han sido crecientemente incorporados a la vida económica norteña. Esto ha provocado el surgimiento del trabajo asalariado, la utilización de vestimenta de fabricación industrial e incluso la participación de jóvenes rarámuri en competencias de atletismo de larga duración. De todas formas, la mayoría de los hombres visten taparrabo de dos piezas, camisola, una banda blanca en la cabeza, faja tejida y sandalias de cuero; en invierno se protegen con cobijas de lana y cubren sus pies con pieles. Las mujeres, por su parte, visten blusa, falda amplia, faja, una banda roja en la cabeza y sandalias. La construcción de vivendas y el trabajo en el campo siguen realizándose colectivamente y cada familia que recibe ayuda de la comunidad ofrece a cambio una *tesgüinada*, es decir, comida y *tesgüino*, su aguardiente de maíz. La base de la organización social es la familia nuclear. Para efectuar el matrimonio, se acude al casamentero o *mayori*; la mayoría de los matrimonios son monógamos, aunque hay casos de poligamia. Las uniones matrimoniales no siempre son definitivas. Los entierros se llevan a cabo en las cuevas de las barrancas profundas, aunque la influencia católica ha introducido el uso de cementerios. Creen que los espíritus de las personas recientemente fallecidas rondan la tierra por un tiempo, ya que son incapaces de hallar el camino hacia el mundo de los muertos; por lo tanto, se efectúan tres fiestas funerarias para los hombres y cuatro para las mujeres, con las que se les ayuda a llegar a su destino final. Sus creencias religiosas animistas se han combinado con la adopción del catolicismo.

TARANDACUAO ◆ Municipio de Guanajuato situado en los límites con Michoacán y contiguo a Acámbaro. Superficie: 115.90 km². Habitantes: 11,949, de los cuales 2,915 forman la población económicamente activa. Hablan alguna lengua indígena 25 personas mayores de cinco años. En la presa Solís se practican deportes acuáticos.

Presa Solís en Tarandacuao, Guanajuato

TARÁNTULA, LA ◆ Periódico clandestino fundado en Guadalajara en 1857 y elaborado por un grupo de conservadores, entre quienes estaban Tomás Ruiseco, Remigio y Urbano Tovar, Ramón Barboza y Miguel España. Aparentemente, la publicación fue financiada por el sacerdote Rafael Homobono Tovar. Dejó de publicarse en octubre de 1858, cuando las fuerzas liberales de Santos Degollado ocuparon la capital jalisciense.

De la serie beso de obsidiana II, óleo sobre tabla de madera de Eloy Tarcisio (1995)

Foto: Fondo Editorial Grupo Azabache

TARASCOS ◆ ☛ *purépechas*.

TARCISIO, ELOY ◆ n. en el DF (1955). Pintor egresado de la Escuela Nacional de Artes Plásticas de la UNAM. A finales de los años setenta comenzó a interesarse por obras *modificables* que requirieran la *participación activa* de los espectadores y por el *happening*. Luego se inclinó por la instalación, disciplina en la que ha desarrollado una obra prolífica, basada en materiales como nopales y pétalos de flores, que pretenden una reflexión sobre el ser del mexicano. En 1991 promovió el festival anual Mes del Performance, y posteriormente fue fundador y director del centro cultural X-Teresa, Arte Alternativo, perteneciente al INBA. Obtuvo el Premio Nacional de Adquisición en la sección de dibujo del Salón Nacional de Arte del INBA (1983).

Tariácuri, "sacerdote del viento"

TAREA EDUCATIVA Y CULTURAL HACIA EL ORDEN Y LA SÍNTESIS ◆ Organización fascista creada en 1935 en la Universidad Autónoma de Guadalajara (☞). Sus miembros son conocidos como *tecos* por las siglas de la agrupación, aunque es posible que el grupo haya adoptado el nombre de Tarea Educativa para legitimar el apodo que recibían sus miembros. En los primeros años fue una organización secreta, infiltrada en la Federación de Estudiantes Universitarios. A fines de los años cuarenta y principios de los cincuenta, la organización tenía comisionado a Francisco Venegas como su representante en la ciudad de México. Participa en el Frente Estudiantil Mexicano Anticomunista y pertenece a la Federación Mexicana Anticomunista y a la Liga Mundial Anticomunista. De los *tecos*, Jean Meyer escribió que "las tácticas propiciadas por los jesuitas (infiltración, secreto y violencia) resultaron contraproducentes cuando no se pudo mantener el control. Así, los famosos 'tecos' de Guadalajara, destinados por algunos jesuitas a 'salvar la universidad de socialismo' resultaron rápidamente fascistas y antisemitas. Mientras tanto se habían apoderado de la UAG". El radicalismo de la organización la ha llevado a enfrentarse con grupos como la Asociación Católica de la Juventud Mejicana (☞), como en 1976, cuando dos militantes de esta última fueron asesinados en las cercanías del cerro del Cubilete. La intolerancia de los *tecos* llegó a tal punto, que incluso acusaron de "autodemoledor máximo y destructor diabólico de la Iglesia" al papa Juan XXIII. Entre sus dirigentes más destacados se contaban Carlos Cuesta Gallardo y los hermanos Leaño. En los años setenta aparecía como líder principal Antonio Leaño López, pero según Pablo Castellanos López, ex presidente de la ACJM, el verdadero dirigente era Raymundo Guerrero. El grupo editó la revista *Ariete*.

TARÉCUATO ◆ Río de Michoacán y Jalisco. Nace en la sierra de Tarécuato, en la porción noroccidental de Michoacán, al sureste de Sahuayo, de la confluencia de varios manantiales y arroyos menores; corre hacia el sur, vira al suroeste al entrar a la región suroriental de Jalisco y se une al río Quitupan para formar el Tepalcatepec.

TARETÁN ◆ Municipio de Michoacán situado al suroeste del lago de Pátzcuaro y al noreste de Apatzingán. Superficie: 351.78 km². Habitantes: 12,777, de los cuales 3,259 forman la población económicamente activa. Hablan alguna lengua indígena 27 personas mayores de cinco años (purépecha 22). La cabecera municipal es Taretán de Terán.

TARIÁCURI ◆ Personaje purépecha nacido en el siglo XIV y muerto en el siglo XV. Su nombre significa "Sacerdote del viento". Era hijo de Pauácame y de una mujer de la isla de Jarácuaro. Fue uno de los sacerdotes más importantes de los purépechas. Promovió una guerra religiosa, debido a la cual hizo crecer el imperio purépecha que a su muerte se dividió entre su hijo Hiquíngari y sus sobrinos Hiripan y Tangaxoan. Se sabe que fue enterrado en Pátzcuaro.

TARIÁCURI ◆ Trío de música popular formado en 1932 por los hermanos Norberto, Juan y Jerónimo Mendoza García, originarios de Huetamo, Michoacán. Tras la muerte de Jerónimo y la salida de Juan, Eligio Mendoza entró al conjunto y, sucesivamente, el trío fue completado con Roberto Gali, David Corpus, Chucho de la Rosa y Moisés Estevez. Pablo Flores sustituyó a Eligio tras su muerte. Aparecieron en las películas *Allá en el Rancho Grande*, *Ora Ponciano*, *El impostor*, *La paloma*, *Amapola del camino*, *Un viejo amor*, *Así es mi tierra* y *¡Ay Jalisco no te Rajes!*

TARIÁCURI, LA ◆ ☞ *Amalia Mendoza*.

TARÍMBARO ◆ Municipio de Michoacán situado al norte del de Morelia y al sur del lago de Cuitzeo. Superficie: 228.92 km². Habitantes: 36,637, de los cuales 8,347 forman la población económicamente activa. Hablan alguna lengua indígena 37 personas mayores de cinco años.

TARIMORO ◆ Municipio de Guanajuato situado en la porción suroriental del estado, al sur-sureste de Celaya y al este de Salvatierra. Superficie: 362.4 km². Habitantes: 37,291, de los cuales 7,605 forman la población económicamente activa. Hablan alguna lengua indígena 10 personas mayores de cinco años.

TARIO, FRANCISCO ◆ n en la ciudad de México y m. en España (1911-1977). Nombre profesional del escritor Francisco Peláez. Colaboró en la *Revista Mexicana de Literatura, Letras de México, Revista de la Universidad de Mexico* y *Vidas y Cuentos* entre otras. Vivió en España. Autor de *La noche* (1943), *Aquí abajo* (1943), *La puerta en el muro* (1946), *Equinoccio* (1946), *Yo de amores qué sabía* (1950), *Breve diario de un amor*

Trío Tariácuri

perdido (1951), *Acapulco en el sueño* (1951), *Tapioca inn: mansión para fantasmas* (1952), *La noche del féretro y otros cuentos de noche* (1958) y *Una violeta de más* (1968). En 1988 apareció *Entre tus dedos helados y otros cuentos*, recopilación realizada por Alejandro Toledo y prologada por Esther Seligson, y en 1994 su novela *Jardín secreto*.

Tárnava, Constantino de ◆ n. y m. en Monterrey, NL (1899-1974). Ingeniero eléctrico titulado en la estadounidense Universidad de Notre Dame. En 1919 instaló una estación experimental de radio en Monterrey y en 1921 inauguró la radiodifusora comercial CYO, la primera en México, de la que fue director, locutor y productor.

Tarrab, Irene ◆ n. en el DF (1954). Licenciada en física por la UNAM (1977), de la que fue profesora (1975-79). Doctora en astrofísica por la Universidad de París (1984), donde ejerció la docencia (1984-85). Ha investigado sobre poblaciones estelares y evolución de galaxias en el Instituto de Astrofísica de París (1980-86), el Instituto Max Planck, de Munich, Alemania (1986), y en el Observatorio de París (1986-). Regularmente traduce textos científicos del inglés al francés y de ambas lenguas al español. Ha publicado una docena de trabajos en *Astronomy and Astrophysics*. En 1977 obtuvo el Premio al Mejor Estudiante de México. Ha sido becaria del Conacyt (1980-82), del Colegio de Francia (1983) y del Centro de Estudios Atómicos de Francia (1984).

Tarrac Barrabía, Ángel ◆ n. en España y m. en Acapulco, Gro. (1898-1979). Escultor. Estudió en las escuelas de Bellas Artes de Barcelona y Madrid (1911-18). En París fue discípulo de Auguste Rodin y Aristide Maillol. Tras la derrota de la República Española estuvo en Francia y vino en 1942, año en que se naturalizó mexicano. Aquí realizó las siguientes obras: un busto de Maximino Ávila Camacho, en Teziutlán (1946); *Trofeo a los niños héroes*, cuyas copias se encuentran en cada una de las escuelas militares de América Latina (1947); *Águila monumental*, en el Club Rotario de Zitácuaro (1953); una estatua de Adolfo Ruiz Cortines, en Villahermosa (1957); *Nacimiento de México*, en la sede del PRI, en el DF (1963); una estatua de Abraham Lincoln, en Ciudad Juárez (1964); el busto de Lázaro Cárdenas del Sindicato de Trabajadores Petroleros de la República Mexicana en Reynosa, Agua Dulce y el DF (1971); un busto de Benito Juárez que se halla en Ciudad Satélite (1972); la estatua de José María Morelos del Museo Nacional de Historia (1972); la estatua de Jesús Clark Flores del Comité Olímpico Mexicano (1977); una estatua de Adolfo López Mateos, en Atizapán (1978); y *Otomí*, del parque Altamirano de Acapulco (1979). En 1923 ganó el primer premio del Concurso de Fuentes del Ayuntamiento de Barcelona y en 1936 la medalla de oro de la Exposición Nacional de España.

Tarragó, Leticia ◆ n. en Orizaba, Ver. (1940). Grabadora. Estudió en la Escuela de Pintura y Escultura La Esmeralda (1954-59), en el Taller Libre de Grabado del Instituto Nacional de Bellas Artes (1960-63) y en el Instituto de Bellas Artes de Varsovia (1963-64). Profesora de la Universidad Veracruzana y del Instituto Allende de San Miguel de Allende (1972-). Expuso por primera vez en 1959. Es fundadora del taller de Grabado de la Universidad Benito Juárez de Oaxaca (1972). En 1958 obtuvo el primer lugar en un concurso de carteles convocado por la aerolínea holandesa KLM; en 1961, el segundo lugar del Concurso Nacional de Artesanías; en 1963, el premio Nuevos Valores del Salón de la Plástica Mexicana; en 1967, el Premio Nacional de Grabado, y en 1977, la Orquídea de Plata de la Asociación de Universitarias de Orizaba.

Tarrazo, Francisco Antonio ◆ n. en Campeche y m. en la ciudad de México (?-1830). Fue gobernador del estado de Yucatán (del 23 de abril al 19 de julio de 1824) y senador de la República por la misma entidad a la segunda y tercera legislaturas (1827-28 y 1829-30).

Díptico, óleo sobre tela de Leticia Tarragó (1993)

Tarriba, Óscar ◆ n. en Culiacán, Sin., y m. en el DF (1908-1988). Bailarín y coreógrafo. En 1924, cuando vivía en Estados Unidos, comenzó a estudiar danza con Teodor Kosloff, Billy Richer y José Fernández. Formó parte de la Primera Compañía de Ballets Rusos de Monte Carlo. Se dedicó a la danza española desde 1928. En 1936 se presentó por primera vez en México. En los años cuarenta trabajó en la compañía de *Cantinflas*. En 1953 estableció su propia escuela. Algunas de sus alumnas fueron Pilar Rioja y Marta Forte. Se presentó en Cuba, Estados Unidos y varios países europeos.

Clásica, escultura en bronce de Ángel Tarrac Barrabía

TARTAKOWSKI, MALKE ◆ n. en el DF (1942). Escritora. Profesora de inglés titulada en el Instituto Madocs. Colaboradora de las revistas *Nosotros*, *Prensa Israelita*, *Wizo*, *Ecos de México* y *Na'amat*, así como del diario *Excélsior*, donde publica la columna "Tepis ti amo". Autora de *Una rosa, un pensamiento* (1976), *Sed por ser* (1977), *Tepis company* (1980), *Palabras en silencio* (1980), *Feria de conciencias* (1982), *L'ollita de frijoles* (1982), *En el vuelo* (1988), *Querencias* (1995) y *Alazar* (1997).

TASQUILLO ◆ Municipio de Hidalgo situado al norte de Tula y al noroeste de Pachuca. Superficie: 167 km². Habitantes: 16,392, de los cuales 3,498 forman la población económicamente activa. Hablan alguna lengua indígena 6,189 personas mayores de cinco años (otomí 6,171). En la cabecera municipal hay una parroquia construida en 1716.

TATA NACHO ◆ ☞ *Fernández Esperón, Ignacio.*

TATAHUICAPAN DE JUÁREZ ◆ Municipio veracruzano erigido el 20 de marzo de 1997. Cuenta con 12,181 habitantes, distribuidos en 23 localidades. Se ubica al este de Catemaco, en litorales del golfo de México.

TATALTEPEC DE VALDÉS ◆ Municipio de Oaxaca situado al este de Santiago Pinotepa Nacional y al noroeste de Puerto Escondido. Superficie: 369.99 km². Habitantes: 4,954, de los cuales 1,297 forman la población económicamente activa. Hablan alguna lengua indígena 2,438 personas mayores de cinco años (chatino 2,412).

FOTO: GUILLERMO AGUILERA

Tatiana

TATATILA ◆ Municipio de Veracruz situado al noroeste de Jalapa y al noreste de Perote. Superficie: 82.25 km². Habitantes: 3,961, de los cuales 1,273 forman la población económicamente activa. Hablan alguna lengua indígena 36 personas mayores de cinco años (náhuatl 30).

TATIANA ◆ n. en Monterrey, NL (1969). Nombre profesional de Tatiana Palacios Chapa. Cantante. Hizo estudios de música y gimnasia olímpica. Comenzó su carrera en la comedia musical *Kumán* (1984) y prosiguió grabando discos de baladas y música pop. En los años noventa optó por dedicarse a grabar canciones para niños y a conducir el programa *El mundo de Tatiana*. Ha participado en varias películas y grabado una decena de discos. Fue nombrada El Rostro de *El Heraldo de México* en 1984.

TAVERA ALFARO, XAVIER ◆ n. en Morelia, Mich. (1925). Realizó estudios de derecho en la Universidad Michoacana de San Nicolás de Hidalgo y de historia en El Colegio de México. Ha sido becario de la Coordinación de Humanidades de la UNAM (1954), investigador de El Colegio de México (1954-57) y del Instituto de Estudios Históricos de la Revolución Mexicana (1955), fundador y director de la Escuela de Verano (1957-59) y director de la Facultad de Filosofía y Letras de la UNAM (1958-59); director del Seminario de Historia Contemporánea de Veracruz e investigador de la Universidad Veracruzana (1959-61); director del Archivo Histórico del Congreso de Michoacán (1975-), cronista oficial de Morelia (1987) y director de la *Revista de la Universidad Michoacana de San Nicolás de Hidalgo* (1987-). Colaborador de *Historia Mexicana*, *Cuadernos Americanos*, *Filosofía y Letras*, *La Palabra y el Hombre*, *Revista de la Universidad de México*, *Universidad Michoacana*, *Humanitas*, *Boletín de la Sociedad Mexicana de Geografía y Estadística*, *Siempre!*, *Excélsior*, *El Nacional*, *El Día*, *Diario de Xalapa*, *El Espectador*, *Novedades* y *Gaceta de Literatura*. Es coautor de *Estudios históricos americanos, homenaje a Silvio Zavala* (1953) y *La Revolución Mexicana* (1960). Autor de *Tres votos y un debate del Congreso Constituyente 1856-1857* (1958), *El nacionalismo en la prensa mexicana del siglo XVIII* (1963), *Juan José Martínez de Lejarza, ilustrado mexicano* (1964), *Dos etapas de la Independencia de México* (1965), *Paseo por Morelia* (1967), *La jura de Carlos IV en Valladolid* (1969), *El nombre de Morelia* (1978), *Morelia* (1978), *José Juan Martínez de Lejarza, un estudio de luz y sombra* (1979), *Trinodonte* (1986), *Morelia en la época de la República restaurada* (1988) e *Historia mínima de Michoacán* (1988). Ha sido presidente de la Sociedad Michoacana de Historia.

TAVIRA, LUIS DE ◆ n. en el DF (1948). Director teatral y dramaturgo. Licenciado en literatura dramática por la UNAM (1973). Profesor fundador del Centro Universitario de Teatro y del Nucleo de Estudios Teatrales (1987) y profesor de la UIA y del INBA. Ha sido fundador del Taller Épico (1976), director del Centro Universitario de Teatro (1978-82), director de Actividades Teatrales de la UNAM (1982-84), director del Centro de Experimentación Teatral del INBA (1985), director interino de la Facultad de Teatro de la Universidad Veracruzana (1986) y director de La Casa del Teatro (1995-). Entre las obras que ha dirigido destacan *Apostasía* (1972), *Woyzeck* (1973), *The crew of Dyonisos* (1973), *Misa solemnis* (1974), *Esperando al zurdo* (1975), *La gran revolución* (1977), *La sombra del caudillo* (1980), *Lances de amor y fortuna* (1981), *El general madruga* (1982), *Novedad de la patria* (1983), *El martirio de Morelos* (1983), *Juana de Arco en la hoguera* (1984), *Grande y pequeño* (1985), *María Santísima* (1986), *Orestes Park* (1987), *Santísima* (1987), *Nadie sabe nada* (1988), *La pasión de Pentesilea* (1988), *Zozobra* (1989), *La conspiración de la cucaña* (1989), *Clotilde en su casa* (1990), *La noche de Hernán Cortés*

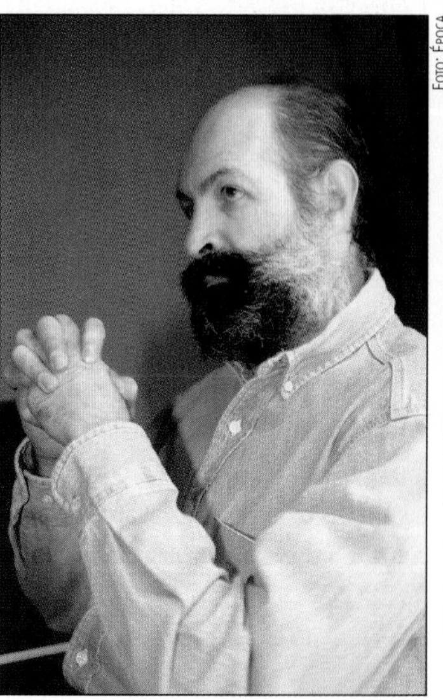
FOTO: ÉPOCA

Luis de Tavira

(1992), *Jubileo* (1993), *El rehén* (1993) y *Felipe Ángeles* (1999). Escribió en *La Jornada Semanal* (1989-95). Autor de los poemarios *Coloquio de la soledad* (1974), *Cantar de vísperas* (1975), *Crónica de viaje* (1976) y *Tarde perpetua* (1978), del ensayo *Un teatro para nuestros días* (1982), y de las obras de teatro *Novedad de la patria* (1983), *La pasión de Pentesilea* (1988) y *Ventajas de la epiqueya* (1996). Premio al mejor director escénico del Primer Festival de Teatro de las Américas, de Montreal (1986).

Tavira Urióstegui, Martín ♦ n. en Rincón Potrero, Gro. (1932). Licenciado en derecho por la Universidad Michoacana de San Nicolás de Hidalgo (1954-58), especializado en historia en la Escuela Normal Superior. Profesor (1954-79), regente del Colegio de San Nicolás (1973) y miembro de la junta de gobierno (1973-82) y secretario general de Federación de Profesores de la Universidad Michoacana de San Nicolás de Hidalgo. En el Partido Popular Socialista, al que pertenece desde 1952, ha sido miembro del comité estatal en Michoacán (1958-79) y miembro del comité central (1960-). Diputado federal en tres ocasiones (1979-82, 1985-88 y 1991-94).

Taxco, de ♦ Sierra de los estados de México y Guerrero situada en la vertiente meridional de Sistema Volcánico Transversal. Se extiende de noroeste a sureste, desde el sur del Estado de México hasta el norte de Guerrero, al noroeste de Iguala. Se prolonga hacia el sur con las sierras de Teloloapan y de Huitzuco, respectivamente. Su cumbre más elevada es el cerro Huisteco, que tiene 2,410 metros sobre el nivel del mar. Cuenta con importantes yacimientos minerales.

Taxco de Alarcón ♦ Municipio de Guerrero situado al norte de Chilpancingo, en los límites con Morelos. Superficie: 347 km². Habitantes: 95,144, de los cuales 23,155 forman la población económicamente activa. Hablan alguna lengua indígena 2,539 personas mayores de cinco años (náhuatl 2,407).

Ilustración de Santiago Ortega

Iglesia de Santa Prisca, en Taxco de Alarcón, Guerrero

El municipio y la cabecera se llaman Taxco de Alarcón por Juan Ruiz de Alarcón, a quien se supone nativo del lugar. La cabecera fue fundada por los españoles Miguel Díaz de Aux y Rodrigo de Castañeda, en 1528. Cuatro años más tarde, Juan Salcedo y Juan de Cabra descubrieron una vetas de oro y plata e iniciaron su explotación, especialmente en Taxco Viejo o Tlachco, Telelcingo, Cantarranas y Tenango, que fueron las primeras minas abiertas por los europeos en América. Poco después se estableció la provincia de Taxco, dentro de la cual quedaron incluidos los pueblos de Hueiztaca, Atzala, Acamixylahuaca, Tlamacazapán, Tenango, Nochtepec, Pilcayan, Teticpan, Coatlán, Acuitlapan y Teulistaca. Desde 1988 se celebra el festival cultural Jornadas Alarconianas, en la cabecera, que cuenta con numerosas construcciones coloniales, entre las que destaca Santa Prisca, templo barroco construido entre 1751 y 1759 por el minero José de la Borda. La orfebrería de plata, metal que abunda en la zona, se exporta a varios países. Entre sus lugares de interés destaca la parroquia de Santa Prisca, proyectada por el arquitecto Cayetano de Cigüenza y completada en 1758. Cada año se celebra en la ciudad la Feria Nacional de la Plata.

Tayikistán, República de ♦ Nación del centro de Asia. Limita al norte con Kirguistán, al este con China, al sur con Afganistán y al oeste y noroeste con Uzbekistán. Superficie: 143,000 km². Habitantes: 6,015,000 (1998). Su capital es Dushambé (524,000 habitantes en 1994). Otras ciudades importantes son Khujand (164,500 habitantes en 1989) y Kulob (79,300). El tayikistano es el idioma oficial, y también se hablan uzbeco y ruso. La moneda es el rublo tayikistano. *Historia*: la región de Tayikistán fue poblada originalmente por los tayikos, de origen persa. Estuvieron bajo dominio persa (siglos v a vii de

Panorámica de Taxco de Alarcón, Guerrero

Foto: Carlos Hahn

n.e.), árabe (siglos VIII a IX) y otomano (siglos X a XVIII). En 1750, cuando dependían del emirato de Bujara, vasallo de los otomanos, sufrieron la invasión afgana. A lo largo del siglo XIX la región fue paulatinamente dominada por Rusia. En 1923 pasó a formar parte de la Unión de Repúblicas Socialistas Soviéticas (☞), aunque la resistencia nacionalista se mantuvo bajo la forma de guerrilla durante los años veinte y treinta. En 1991 se independizó de la Unión Soviética y fue una de las repúblicas integrantes de la CEI. México estableció relaciones diplomáticas con Tayikistán en 1992.

TEABO ◆ Municipio de Yucatán situado en el sur del estado, al este de Tikul y al suroeste de Chichén Itzá. Superficie: 261.87 km^2. Habitantes: 4,848, de los cuales 978 forman la población económicamente activa. Hablan alguna lengua indígena 3,924 personas mayores de cinco años (maya), de los que 653 son monolingües.

TEACAPAN, DE ◆ Laguna de Sinaloa situada en el litoral de océano Pacífico, al sur de Escuinapa y al sureste de Mazatlán. Es el extremo septentrional de la albufera de Mezcaltitán, que se extiende desde el litoral de Nayarit. Se comunica al norte con la laguna del Lagartero y por el sur con la de Agua Brava. En ella desembocan los ríos Cañas y Acaponeta. Se comunica con el océano Pacífico por la boca de Teacapan.

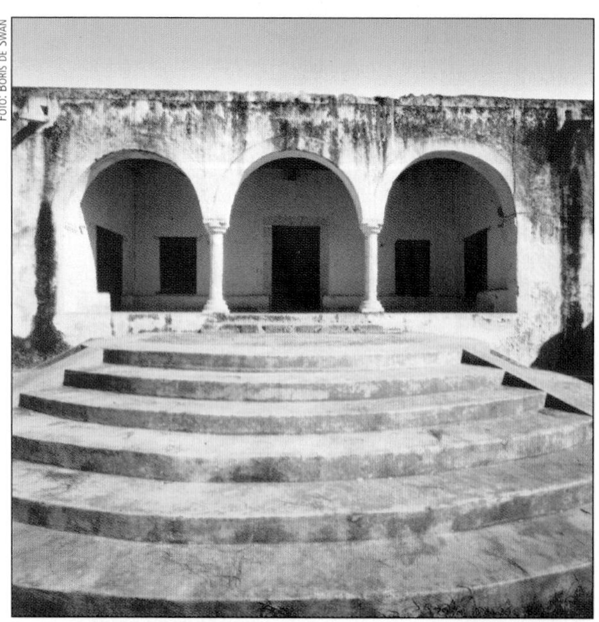

Foto: Boris de Swan

Portal de peregrinos en el convento de Teabo, Yucatán

Foto: Gobierno del Estado de Sinaloa

Palmeras al borde de la laguna de Teacapan, en Sinaloa

TEAPA ◆ Municipio de Tabasco situado al sur de Villahermosa y contiguo a Macuspana y Tacotalpa, en los límites con Chiapas. Superficie: 679.78 km^2. Habitantes: 42,657, de los cuales 10,686 forman la población económicamente activa. Hablan alguna lengua indígena 126 personas mayores de cinco años. En la jurisdicción se encuentran las grutas de Coconá, donde se presenta un espectáculo de luz y sonido; los balnearios de El Azufre y Puyacatengo, con aguas curativas; y los ríos Puyacatengo y Teapa, donde se practican deportes acuáticos.

TEAPA, DE ◆ Río de Chiapas y Tabasco, también llamado de la Sierra. Nace en la parte norte del estado de Chiapas, en la vertiente septentrional de la sierra de ese estado, al oeste de Simojovel de Allende. Corre de sur a norte, recibe al río Negro y entra al estado de Tabasco, cerca de Teapa. Más adelante recibe a los ríos Tacotalpa y Pichucalco y tributa en el Grijalva, al este de Villahermosa. Es navegable desde Teapa hasta la capital tabasqueña, en un tramo de 64 km.

TEATLAHUIANI ◆ Uno de los nombres del dios nahua de los borrachos, Tezcatzoncatl, llamado así, "El ahogador" en español, por la proclividad de los ebrios a ahogarse o, quizá, porque el dios los ahogaba de borrachos.

TEATRO ◆ Las representaciones dramáticas, generalmente unidas a manifestaciones dancísticas y musicales, formaban parte de las grandes culturas del México antiguo. El llamado teatro náhuatl, según los historiadores, tenía como características los diálogos entre personajes divinos y humanos; divertimientos cómicos y expresiones de la vida familiar y social, así como representaciones anecdóticas y semihistóricas. Entre los ejemplos que cita María del Carmen Millán se halla "la fiesta de Tlacaxipehualiztli o *desollamiento de los hombres* (que) era un grandioso espectáculo con un ceremonial que incluía bailes, simulacro de lucha, sacrificio, canto y música". Del teatro maya sólo se conoce una obra, el *Rabinal-Achí*. Los cronistas del siglo XVI consignaron las fiestas de la coronación de Moctezuma II o las anuales dedicadas a Tezcatlipoca: en la primera "hubo grandísimas fiestas, bailes, comedias y entremeses de día y noche"; con respecto a la segunda, consta que se asemejaba más a la concepción occidental del teatro, ya que tenía secuencias de una acción dramática, un personaje con características definidas, y accesorios como el maquillaje, vestuario y escenografía. Las representaciones de la mitología náhuatl fueron eliminadas por los conquistadores españoles, pero las piezas jocosas sobrevivieron a la conquista y se incorporaron como farsas ridículas al teatro que implantaron los sacerdotes católicos, en el que predominaron los autos sacramentales, misterios, alegorías, pastorelas y milagros del teatro castellano que se adaptaron a las condiciones americanas, de donde surgió una suerte de arte híbrido, altamente útil para la evangelización por su acento en lo didáctico. Pronto se hicieron representaciones en el interior de los templos, en los atrios y las plazas. Se sabe que en 1533 se escenificó una *Representación del fin del mundo* o *Auto del juicio final*, de fray Andrés de Olmos, que se cree es la misma obra que se puso poco después en náhuatl, en la capilla de San José de los Naturales. Se tiene noticia de que en Tlaxcala, para un público muy amplio, se representaron varias obras en 1538 y que al año siguiente se llevó a escena *La conquista de Jerusalem*, pieza atribuida a Motolinía. En la segunda mitad del siglo XVI, en la capital novohispana, en medio de la abundancia de drama litúrgico se abrió paso el teatro mundano, en especial la comedia juglaresca. De esa época datan los primeros locales adaptados expresamente para el teatro: los *corralones*, tablados al aire donde se controlaba el ingreso del público. En el Palacio Virreinal y en domicilios particulares solían ofrecerse funciones para solaz de los señores, sus familias e invitados. Se representaba a Lope de Rueda y otros autores peninsulares menos célebres. Algunos de ellos vinieron a México y aquí sus obras fueron llevadas a la escena, como fue el caso de Arias de Villalobos, Sancho Sánchez de Muñón, Luis de Belmonte Bermúdez, Juan de la Cueva, Fernán González de Eslava, que en el texto castellano mezcló largas parrafadas en latín y algunos nahuatlismos, y Gutierre de Cetina, más conocido por su *Madrigal* que por su producción dramática. De los criollos el más recordado es Juan Pérez Ramírez, autor del *Desposorio espiritual entre el pastor Pedro y la Iglesia mexicana*, obra de 1574. Alguna herejía debió advertir fray Juan de Zumárraga en las representaciones populares, pues introdujo la censura en 1574 y prohibió lo que consideraba "representaciones poco honestas". En el siglo XVII surge la primera figura universal de las letras novohispanas y el más alto exponente de la dramaturgia mexicana: el criollo Juan Ruiz de Alarcón, autor de 26 comedias, quien hace su carrera dramática en Madrid, donde compite con Lope de Vega, Tirso de Molina y Calderón de la Barca. Entre las obras más conocidas de Alarcón se cuentan *La cueva de Salamanca, Las paredes oyen, Mudarse por mejorarse, La verdad sospechosa, Los pechos privilegiados* y *El examen de maridos*. Funcionaba, a principios de ese siglo, una sala anexa al hospital Real de Naturales, institución administrada por la orden de San Hipólito, que de las funciones teatrales se allegaba fondos para su labor filantrópica. Dicha sala fue destruida en 1629 por una inundación. En 1621 había en la Nueva España tres compañías de actores, lo que evidencia cierto movimiento teatral. A esos conjuntos estables hay que agregar los grupos trashumantes y la permanente actividad teatral con fines religiosos. En la segunda mitad del siglo XVII es otra figura de alcance universal la que destella en las letras mexicanas: Sor Juana Inés de la Cruz, de extensa producción poética, quien dedica tiempo a escribir loas, entremeses, sainetes, autos sacramentales (*El divino Narciso*) y otras piezas para su representación, como las comedias *Los empeños de una casa* y *Amor es más laberinto*. Las representaciones se hacían en un "edificio permanente" que se empezó a construir en 1639 y que debió ser ocupado antes de su terminación. Este local, llamado el Coliseo Viejo, fue el primer teatro mexicano digno de ese nombre: era una construcción de madera, de dos pisos, con palcos bien puestos y un amplio escenario. Fueron sus primeros directores Mateo Jaramillo e Ignacio Márquez. Este local, al que se entraba por el hospital de Naturales, también era propiedad de la orden de San Hipólito, que en 1712 dejó de administrarlo por baja de la primera actriz y de su suplente. La respuesta la dieron las autoridades con unas ordenanzas que disponían alquilar el teatro a

Juan Ruiz de Alarcón, autor teatral de la primera mitad del siglo XVII

Sor Juana Inés de la Cruz, autora de las obras teatrales *Los empeños de una casa* y *Amor es más laberinto*

Representación teatral de guerreros tepanecas antes de la Conquista

Elenco de *Cosmopilitan Trouppe*, obra estrenada en el Teatro Nacional en junio de 1897

AVTOS
SACRAMENTALES,
ALEGORICOS, Y HISTORIALES.
DEDICADOS
AL PATRIARCA
SAN JVAN DE DIOS
COMPVESTOS
POR DON PEDRO CALDERON
de la Barca, Cavallero de la Orden de Santiago, Capellan de Honor de su Magestad, y de los Señores Reyes Nuevos de la Santa Iglesia de Toledo.
P.XXXXVI.
Pliegos
CON LICENCIA

Las obras teatrales de Pedro Calderón de la Barca tenían gran éxito en Nueva España

un particular, que era a la vez empresario y director. El teatro se incendió en 1722 y tres años después se puso en servicio un nuevo local, también de madera, situado en la esquina de las actuales calles de Motolinía y 16 de Septiembre. La gran figura de ese escenario fue Eusebio Vela, actor y dramaturgo tocado por la vena nacionalista, pues varias de sus obras refieren las grandezas de México. En diciembre de 1753 se inauguró en la actual calle de Bolívar el Coliseo Nuevo, construcción de cuatro pisos, hecha de mampostería, con 36 palcos. Este local se estrenó con *Mejor está que estaba*, de Calderón de la Barca, pese a que se habían solicitado obras a los dramaturgos José Eduardo de Herrera y Manuel Álvarez. En 1768, en su *Diario Literario*, José Antonio Alzate publicó un texto en que se pedía la reforma del teatro, necesaria para no privar "del Coliseo la porción más noble de la república" ni alejar de los escenarios a "aquellas personas que, o por su estado o por el dictamen de su conciencia, oyen con horror el solo nombre de comedia". Se decía que al introducir algunos cambios, al público que gustaba de las comedias se sumarían las "familias de honor, que desean vivir con crédito de su conducta" y que "doncellas abstraídas" que "viven temerosas de Dios y celosas de su reputación, se presentarían sin rubor en la comedia". El empresario o "asentista" "tendría más entradas", los autores, "asistidos de gente instruida, recibirán todos los aplausos a que son acreedores y darán a su profesión una estimación nada común, sacándola de la oscuridad que padece, y que ciertamente no merecen los actuales, por la regularidad de sus costumbres y la extensión de sus luces". De este modo, "el magistrado se complacería en ver ejecutado por vuestra merced sin turbulencias, lo que le ha costado muchos desvelos y no pudo conseguir aun a costa de repetidas providencias". La misma aprobación se obtendría de "los celosos de nuestras costumbres, los pastores, los padres espirituales". La reforma no debía consistir en una "destrucción general" ni en considerar crimen todo lo que no fuera "expresamente devoción". Quiero sólo, decía el autor del texto, "que los autores se ciñan a las leyes del arte, que proponiéndose para la tragedia un asunto elevado, hagan advertir la diferencia enorme que se encuentra entre ella y la comedia. Que tratándole con la majestad que merece el auditorio, nos inspiren sentimientos nobles, sentimientos compatibles con la moral cristiana. Que guarden inviolablemente el decoro a las personas que se representan, observando el carácter a cada una y conservándole sin declinación en todo el drama. Que persuadidos a la inverosimilitud de que un lacayo, un hombre de la más vil extracción, se familiarice con un príncipe y sea el archivo de sus secretos más serios, el consultor de los negocios más graves, le excluyan de la tragedia; pues siendo ésta perfecta, no habrá hombre de tan mal gusto que note la falta de los bufones". La carta, atribuible al propio Alzate, permite advertir que el teatro era poco respetuoso de las diferencias sociales y que estaba al margen de las preocupaciones morales de las "familias de honor". El virrey Bernardo de Gálvez escribió unas *Ordenanzas para el teatro de comedias de México* (1786). A fines del siglo XVIII era común que en los entreactos de las comedias se presentaran números musicales, o bien, que todo el programa lo integrara una *folla*, esto es, una mezcla de sainetes, zarzuelas, música y danzas. De acuerdo con el *Diario de México*, entre 1805 y 1812 se pusieron obras de medio centenar de autores, la mayoría españoles, entre los cuales se contaban Lope de Vega, Tirso de Molina, Calderón de la Barca, Francisco de Rojas Zorrilla, Tomás de Iriarte y Leandro Fernández de Moratín. También se representó una obra de Alarcón. En los intermedios se ofrecían tonadillas y, si la obra era larga, entre el

El Teatro Nacional, a mediados del siglo XIX

Interior del Teatro Nacional, hacia la mitad del siglo XIX

segundo y el tercer actos se ponía un sainete, generalmente anónimo. Del mismo periodo, el *Diario* da cuenta de 54 obras musicales. Los actores más populares eran Luciano Cortés y Agustina Montenegro. El primero fue el mejor pagado y entre 1812 y 1813 era tercer cantante. Eran reconocidos, aunque no tan bien pagados como los anteriores, Gertrudis Solís y el actor de carácter Francisco Carreño. En 1811 la empresa no renovó el contrato de María de la Luz Vallecillo, María Guadalupe Gallardo, Magdalena Lubert, Bartolomé Arias, José María Amador y los cantantes Dolores Munguía y Victorio Rocamora. El público armó un escándalo y el empresario salió a escena para dar una explicación, pese a lo cual el *Diario* no mejoró el juicio que le merecían los intérpretes, a los que tachaba de lánguidos, ignorantes y desmemoriados. Uno de sus redactores dijo: "Nadie puede negar que la compañía cómica que ha servido en la última temporada es la peor que jamás se ha visto". El citado periódico convocó en 1805 a un concurso de sainete, del que resultó ganador *El blanco por la fuerza*, de Antonio de Santa Ana, que se llevó a escena el 9 de junio de 1806. En el mismo año se celebró otro certamen que ganó *El miserable engañado y la niña de la media almendra*, de Francisco Escolano y Obregón, que se estrenó el 18 de junio de 1807 en el Coliseo. En segundo lugar quedó *El hidalgo en Medellín*, de Juan Policarpo de Veracruz. Estas obras, por así establecerlo la convocatoria, eran de tono moralizante. Una vez consumada la independencia, pugnas políticas y precariedad económica no impidieron la actividad teatral. En 1825 se construyó un edificio de madera, en las calles del Factor y Canoa (Donceles y Allende). Al año siguiente, el cubano José María Heredia retomó la crítica teatral y literaria abandonada por el *Diario de México*. Surgieron algunos dramaturgos que transitaron del neoclasicismo al romanticismo: Manuel Eduardo de Gorostiza (*Contigo pan y cebolla*), Fernando Calderón (*A ninguna de las tres*) e Ignacio Rodríguez Galván, quien introdujo temas de historia mexicana (*El privado del virrey*, *La capilla*). Asimismo, destaca el yucateco José Antonio Cisneros, considerado como el primer autor dramático en el mundo que suprimió monólogos y apartes, como en su obra *Mercedes*. En 1831 se fundó una Academia de Arte Dramático que tuvo efímera vida. El teatro de los Gallos era uno de los escenarios que ofrecían funciones regularmente en los años treinta. Casimiro del Collado y José María Lafragua fueron los redactores de *El Apuntador*, revista de crítica teatral editada por Vicente García Torres en 1841. Entre 1842 y 1844 se construyó el teatro de Santa Anna, en la calle de Vergara, que sobrevivió, ya como Nacional, hasta 1900, cuando se clausuró para ser derribado y dar paso a la avenida Cinco de Mayo. Por su parte, el Coliseo Nuevo, que se llamó teatro de México y Principal, fue remozado en 1845, cuando ya era propiedad de un particular. En 1863, el arquitecto Lorenzo de la Hidalga le dio nueva fachada y efectuó otros cambios de importancia. Otras reparaciones se le hicieron en 1895 y 1904; sería destruido por un incendio en 1931. El teatro propiamente dicho tenía que competir por los locales con músicos y compañías extranjeras de ópera. Uno de los pocos dramaturgos que vieron representadas sus obras en ese tiempo fue Pablo J. Villaseñor, quien vio estrenarse en el teatro Principal de Guadalajara sus dramas *El palacio de Medrano* y *Encarnación Rosas o el insurgente de Mescala*, en 1851, y *Heroica defensa de Guaymas por las armas mexicanas* y *Clementina*, en 1855. En la capital del país, en los años cin-

FOTO: ARCHIVO XAVIER ESPARZA

Interior del Teatro Juárez de Monterrey

FOTO: ARCHIVO XAVIER ESPARZA

José Peón Contreras, autor teatral mexicano de la segunda mitad del siglo XIX

Alfredo Chavero, dramaturgo que desarrolló temas prehispánicos en su obra

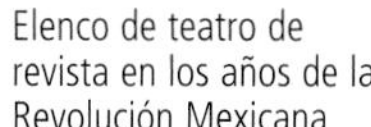

Elenco de teatro de revista en los años de la Revolución Mexicana

Foto: Archivo Casasola

cuenta, el modesto escenario de Factor y Canoa fue echado abajo y el empresario Francisco Arbeu hizo construir en su lugar el teatro de Iturbide, primero con iluminación de gas, que se abrió en febrero 1856 con varios bailes y el 25 de marzo se inició su primera temporada teatral con el drama en verso *¿Y para qué?*, de Pantaleón Tovar. Cierta insistencia nacionalista hizo que en el mismo año se pusieran en el Iturbide *Una deshonra sublime* y *La gloria del dolor*, del mismo Tovar, así como *Vasco Núñez de Balboa*, de Francisco González Bocanegra. A mediados de los años cincuenta se reponían las piezas más vistas de autores españoles y, de vez en cuando, en temporadas que rara vez pasaban de tres días, las obras de los mexicanos Gorostiza, Calderón y Rodríguez Galván. Más éxito obtuvo la compañía francesa de *vaudeville* de E. Lacroix y Auguste Crete, pese a que ofrecía un producto ajeno a la estética hispanista que se había impuesto en los escenarios mexicanos. En 1854 se presentaba en el Principal la compañía teatral del primer actor y director Manuel Fabre, en tanto que el modesto grupo del mexicano Pedro Viñolas actuaba en juguetes cómicos en el igualmente modesto teatro de Oriente. Ambas compañías fueron reunidas por el empresario Manuel Moreno en una temporada de poca fortuna en el teatro de Santa Anna.

Foto: Archivo Casasola

Teatro de revista a principios del siglo xx

Escenario pobre y dedicado casi exclusivamente a representaciones religiosas fue el teatro Nuevo México. De la misma época es el Teatro Provisional, situado en la calle del Puente de la Misericordia y delatado por su nombre como un foro sin mayores pretensiones. Por ese tiempo funcionaba también el Pabellón Mexicano y el teatro de los Gallos abría sólo los sábados. En 1855 llegó a México José Zorrilla, autor mediocre de la obra más exitosa en México: *Don Juan Tenorio*, que según informa Luis Reyes de la Maza ya había sido estrenada aquí en 1844. El mismo autor refiere que en el teatro del Relox se alternaban piezas breves, circo y bailables para solaz de una concurrencia popular. Lo circense se alternaba con juguetes cómicos en el teatro de La Esmeralda, de la calle de Corchero. Una de las escasas figuras del teatro español que vinieron a México fue Matilde Díez, quien, quizá por agradar al público local, el 15 de julio de 1855 presentó *La seducción*, del dramaturgo mexicano José Ignacio de Anievas. La ausencia de público hizo retirar la obra de inmediato y la Díez no volvió a ofrecer nada nacional, salvo la muy probada obra de Fernando Calderón, *A ninguna de las tres*, y, de José Tomás de Cuéllar, en 1856, *Deberes y sacrificios*. El teatro de Oriente ofreció *Equivocaciones de nombres y apellidos*, del escritor español Niceto de Zamacois, avecindado en México y en diciembre la obra mexicana de autor anónimo *Si el mundo es fiel amigo también es fiero enemigo, o el hijo pródigo*. Había, desde luego, buen número de autores nacionales, pero los escenarios les resultaban difícilmente accesibles, al extremo de que en 1857 no se montó una sola obra mexicana. Las obras de José Peón Contreras se empezaron a representar, en su natal Mérida, a principios de los años sesenta, pero sus mayores éxitos los obtuvo en la capital del país después de la intervención francesa, cuando se produjo en la dramaturgia, como en otros géneros literarios, una suerte de renacimiento. A los foros que ya existían se sumó en 1875 el Teatro Arbeu, situado en la calle República del Salvador, donde está desde 1968 la biblioteca Lerdo de Tejada de la Secretaría de Hacienda. Peón Contreras tuvo un gran éxito con *La hija del rey* (1876) y otras obras, que fueron bien recibidas por el público. Igual trayectoria recorrió el laguense José Rosas Moreno, cuyas obras se llevaron a la escena en ciudades de Guanajuato desde 1861; pero no sería hasta 1868 cuando su producción se viera representada en la ciudad de México. Su drama en verso *Sor Juana Inés de la Cruz* ha sido celebrado por varios estudiosos, los que destacan también su teatro infantil: *El año nuevo, Una lección de geografía* y *Amor filial*. Juan A. Mateos y Vicente Riva Palacio firmaron conjuntamente una amplia producción en la que dominan los temas históricos (*El abrazo de Acatempan, La catarata del Niágara*) y la sátira política (*El tirano doméstico, La ley del uno por ciento, La política casera*). Alfredo Chavero escribió óperas cómicas y una zarzuela. Sus obras propiamente teatrales intentaron rescatar personajes prehispánicos (*Xóchitl, Quetzalcóatl*) o se inscribieron en el registro federal de causantes de sollozos (*El valle de lágrimas, ¡Sin esperanza!*). Juan de Dios Peza, al igual que en su poesía, hizo importantes contribuciones a la cohesión doméstica (*La ciencia del hogar, En vísperas de la boda,*

Las dos muñecas) o extrajo de la historia algunos de sus temas. Manuel José Othón escribió dramas en prosa y en verso, anclado en un romanticismo que a fines de siglo se hallaba muy devaluado: *Después de la muerte, Lo que hay detrás de la dicha, A las puertas de la vida.* Las obras de Marcelino Dávalos, nacionalistas y bien construidas, son de la última década del porfirismo: *Guadalupe, ¡Viva el amo!* José Joaquín Gamboa se inicia al mismo tiempo que Dávalos, pero su producción fue, al igual que su vida, más prolongada: *La carne* o *Teresa, La muerte, El hogar, Via Crucis, Si la juventud supiera* y otras. En 1909 se incendió la Cámara de Diputados, instalada desde 1874 en lo que fuera el teatro Iturbide. En 1901 fue demolido el Teatro Nacional, pero de inmediato comenzó la construcción de un nuevo teatro, que eventualmente sería el Palacio de Bellas Artes. También se abrió el Renacimiento, convertido en 1905 en Teatro Virginia Fábregas, donde esta diva puso autores franceses y empezó a modificar el gusto españolizante que privaba hasta entonces. La zarzuela, conocida en su forma moderna desde mediados de los años cincuenta, vivió un prolongado auge que acabó por hacerle merecer el beneficio de la sátira. Así surgió la revista folklórica, que a la caída de Porfirio Díaz se teñiría de política y con esta característica se mantendría hasta 1940, cuando un grupo de pistoleros de la CROM asesinó de una golpiza al empresario del Teatro Lírico. Durante la revolución fue la revista el género más gustado y representado, pese a los riesgos que implicaba. En los años veinte, el propio presidente Álvaro Obregón sugería chistes, frecuentemente a su costa, a las compañías revisteriles. En el teatro de comedia y drama, como en otros campos, José Vasconcelos contribuyó a una interesante apertura hacia lo nuevo en 1921. En ese año trajo a la compañía de Camila Quiroga, cuyos integrantes se expresaban en perfecto argentino ante un público entre perplejo y regocijado. Esa fue una señal definitoria para el teatro mexicano, hasta entonces ajustado a los cánones españoles, al extremo de que obras de dramaturgos nacionales situaban la acción en la península y los actores debían pronunciar claramente la *s*, la *c* y la *z* a la manera de Castilla. Los argentinos demostraron que no se requería tal sumisión para hacer un teatro digno. Ricardo Parada León, del Grupo de los Siete Autores Dramáticos o Pirandellos, se empeñó exitosamente en que una obra suya se montara en el español de México. Surgió entonces un movimiento nacionalista que pasó en 1923 por una temporada de teatro municipal, lecturas dramatizadas y conferencias organizadas por la Unión de Autores Dramáticos en las que se dio a conocer a Ibsen y a Pirandello. Pero no fue hasta 1926, con María Tereza Montoya y Fernando Soler al frente, cuando en el Fábregas se presentó por primera vez en nuestra historia una temporada exclusiva de autores nacionales: Gamboa, Parada, Víctor Manuel Díez Barroso, Francisco Monterde, Amalia Castillo Ledón, Antonio Médiz Bolio, Julio Jiménez Rueda, Carlos Díaz Dufoo, Nemesio García Naranjo, María Luisa Ocampo y otros. El experimento prosiguió en los teatros Regis e Ideal hasta que tuvo que abandonarse por falta de apoyo del público, desconfiado de la producción local. Por su parte, Luis Quintanilla (el futuro estridentista Kinta-niya), Ermilo Abreu Gómez, Guillermo Castillo, el pintor Carlos González y el músico Francisco Domínguez crearon, inspirados en el *Chauve-Souris* de Nikita Balieff, el Teatro del Murciélago, que en su cortísima vida dio a conocer obras de José Gorostiza (*Ventana a la calle*), Manuel Horta (*Juana*) y Fernando Ramírez de Aguilar (*La tona*). En 1927, Antonieta Rivas Mercado conoció a Salvador Novo y Xavier Villaurrutia, con quienes fundaría a principios de 1928 el Teatro de Ulises, que sólo funcionó durante tres meses en la casa de Mesones 42, propiedad de la misma Antonieta, patrocinadora con María Luisa Cabrera de un experimento en que, según palabras de Novo, traducían y actuaban "las obras más desconocidas, nuevas y audaces de la época: O'Neill, Cocteau, Lenormand, Yeats", así como Claude Roger Marx, Shaw y Vildrac. Actuaron también Gilberto Owen, Isabela Corona y Clementina Otero de Barrios; Celestino Gorostiza dirigió e hicieron escenografías Agustín Lazo, Roberto Montenegro, Julio Castellanos y Manuel Rodríguez Lozano. El Teatro de Ulises desapareció en medio de un gran escándalo de los conservadores y ultranacionalistas de la escena, quienes no pudieron impedir que su labor fuera continuada por Los Escolares del Teatro, grupo creado por Isabela Corona y

Rodolfo Usigli, dramaturgo mexicano del siglo XX

FOTO: ARCHIVO XAVIER ESPARZA

Personajes de la zarzuela *La cuarta plana*, presentada en México en 1899

FOTO: ROGELIO CUÉLLAR

Salvador Novo

Cartel de una presentación de *Palillo* y *Tin Tan* en el Teatro Follies

Foto: Archivo Clementina Otero

Julio Bracho, director de teatro

Julio Bracho, que puso a Synge y Strindberg y luego *Proteo*, de Monterde. Después el mismo Gorostiza fundó el Teatro de Orientación, que en sólo tres años llevó a la escena a los clásicos griegos, autores del Siglo de Oro español, dramaturgos estadounidenses y mexicanos (Gorostiza y Villaurrutia), "pasando por Shakespeare, Molière y Goldoni. Desde la Rusia de Gogol y Chéjov hasta la Francia de Cocteau y Girardoux", según el mismo fundador. La escenografía estuvo a cargo de Lazo y Castellanos. Los actores fueron Clementina Otero, Carlos López Moctezuma, Josefina Escobedo, Stella Inda, Víctor Urruchúa y Ramón Vallarino, entre otros. Mauricio Magdaleno y Juan Bustillo Oro formaron el Teatro de Ahora para representar sus obras. Julio Bracho dirigió, con el Teatro de Masas, la obra *Lázaro rió*, de O'Neill, con Andrea Palma como protagonista. El mismo Bracho puso en escena a los clásicos griegos con el Teatro Universitario y Rodolfo Usigli organizó el Teatro de Media Noche, en el que participaron Rodolfo Landa, Ernesto Alonso, Víctor Velázquez, Carlos Riquelme y Víctor Junco. El Palacio de Bellas Artes se inauguró con tal nombre en 1934 con *La verdad sospechosa*, de Alarcón, interpretada por la compañía de María Tereza Montoya. Ésta y Fernando Soler, al regresar de España, incorporaron a su compañía a los actores y escenógrafos del movimiento renovador, aceptaron representar autores no tradicionales y estimularon a otros, como Alfredo Gómez de la Vega, a aventurarse por el mismo camino. Las hermanas Blanch, cuenta Gorostiza, seguían en el Teatro Ideal, "último reducto del 'astracán' español". Lejos de lo que ocurrió en otras áreas, el exilio republicano español traería pocas ideas nuevas a la escena mexicana. En 1936, enviada por el gobierno republicano, la compañía de Margarita Xirgu había tenido en México una temporada en la que sufrió la hostilidad de la colonia española, simpatizante del fascismo. Una novedad presentó esa compañía, y era que las "estrellas" podían desempeñar segundos papeles si así lo exigía la obra. El director era Cipriano Rivas Cheriff y en el cuadro de actores venía Pedro López Lagar. En ese mismo año, el empresario Félix Cervantes hizo construir el teatro que llevaba su nombre, y tenían gran popularidad los teatros Follies Bergere de la Plaza Garibaldi, Colonial de San Juan de Letrán y Apolo, de la Plaza de las Vizcaínas, en el que el empresario Jordiel Candela presentó a las primeras desnudistas en la historia del teatro frívolo en México. A la caída de la República, entre los transterrados llegaron Consuelo Guerrero de Luna, Ángel Garasa, Francisco Llopis, Amparo Morillo, Amparo Villegas, Rafael Banquells, Pepita Meliá, Benito Cibrián, José Cibrián, Augusto Benedico, Miguel Macía, las futuras actrices Ofelia Guilmáin, Pilar Sen, Aurora Molina, Sonia Furió, Alicia y Azucena Rodríguez; los directores Rafael López Miarnau y Luis de Llano; los escenógrafos Manuel Fontanals y Miguel Prieto; la pareja de Salvador Bartolozzi y Magda Donato, que entre otras cosas promovieron el teatro infantil. Max Aub fue el de mayor obra dramatúrgica, renglón en el que hubo variadas aportaciones de José María Camps, León Felipe, María Luisa Algarra y varios más, entre otros los críticos Sigfredo Gordon Carmona y Ceferino R. Avecilla. En 1941, la Compañía Mexicana de Comedia, más conocida como el grupo Proa, bajo la dirección de José de Jesús Aceves iniciaría una labor que a lo largo de dos décadas

Emilio Carballido, dramaturgo mexicano, autor de *Rosalba y los llaveros*

Foto: Archivo Clementina Otero

Carlos López Moctezuma y Clementina Otero en *Jaque a don Juan* de Claudio André Puget

Escenario del Teatro Lírico de la ciudad de México

llevaría el teatro a los sindicatos, con obras de Shaw, O'Neill y otros autores extranjeros, junto a dramaturgos mexicanos como Wilberto Cantón, Xavier Villaurrutia, Celestino Gorostiza, Luis G. Basurto, Magdalena Mondragón, José Attolini y otros, entre los que habría que incluir al transterrado Benjamín Jarnés, ya radicado aquí. Contó con Agustín Lazo, Julio Castellanos, María Izquierdo, José Julio Rodríguez y Jesús Bracho como escenógrafos. Entre los actores estuvieron Emma Fink, Stella Inda, María Douglas y los hermanos Rubén y Gustavo Rojo. En 1943 se constituyó el Teatro de México, sociedad integrada por Gorostiza, Julio Prieto, Miguel N. Lira, Conchita Sada, María Luisa Ocampo, Julio Castellanos y Villaurrutia. Tuvo como actores principales a Clementina Otero, Carlos López Moctezuma y Alberto Galán. Esta empresa desapareció en la misma década de los cuarenta, después de haber logrado temporadas de 10 y 12 semanas, impensables en aquel tiempo para el teatro nuevo. A los años cuarenta corresponden los grupos "experimentales" acaudillados respectivamente por Ignacio Retes (La Linterna Mágica), Xavier Rojas (Teatro Estudiantil Autónomo) y Hebert Darién y Lola Bravo (Teatro de Arte Moderno). La Linterna estrenó obras de Revueltas, Antonio Acevedo Escobedo, Xavier Rojas, Isabel Villaseñor y Rubén Bonifaz Nuño. Parte de la búsqueda o el encuentro del momento lo constituyen las obras en inglés presentadas por Fernando Wagner y el Teatro Panamericano, así como las escenificaciones en francés dirigidas por André Moreau con Les Comédiens de France. Dentro de esa heterogeneidad se sitúan los grupos Mexico City Players, de Earl Sennett, y el Aguileón, que dirigía William Linndom Clough en el Instituto Anglo Mexicano de Cultura, ambos para representaciones en inglés. El japonés Seki Sano tuvo un gran éxito de taquilla al montar *Un tranvía llamado deseo*, de Tennessee Williams. Salvador Novo, al frente del Departamento de Teatro del INBA, promovió a los entonces

Manolo Fábregas, hombre de teatro

muy jóvenes dramaturgos Sergio Magaña (*Los signos del Zodiaco*) y Emilio Carballido (*Rosalba y los llaveros*). Desde 1943 estaba en actividad el Instituto Cinematográfico de México, escuela de actores dirigida por Celestino Gorostiza, de donde salieron Miguel Córcega, Raúl Dantés, Lilia del Valle y Joaquín Cordero. En 1946 se fundó la Escuela de Arte Teatral del INBA, en cuyo proyecto participaron Clementina Otero, Ana Mérida y Fernando Torre Lapham. Su primer director fue Andrés Soler. Ignacio Retes dirigió de José Revueltas *Israel* (1948) y, con escenografía de Diego Rivera, puso en 1950 *El cuadrante de la Soledad*, pieza de escándalo, pues concitó la condena de los adoradores de Stalin, quienes vieron en esa obra un reprobable filo existencialista. Al mediar

Ignacio López Tarso, actor teatral

el siglo, se había ganado en definitiva la batalla con el habla hispanizante, debido a las rebeldías y a la tarea de la Escuela de Arte Dramático, fundada en 1946 y que pasó a formar parte del Instituto Nacional de Bellas Artes a la creación de éste, en 1947. Ejercían la crítica Francisco Monterde, Armando de Maria y Campos, Antonio Magaña Esquivel, Roberto Núñez y Domínguez y Rafael Solana, quien había estudiado actuación con Wagner y pronto vería la representación de su obra *Las islas de oro*, en el Teatro Colón. Miguel Guardia, que en ese tiempo estrenó *¡Ay, Dios mío!*,

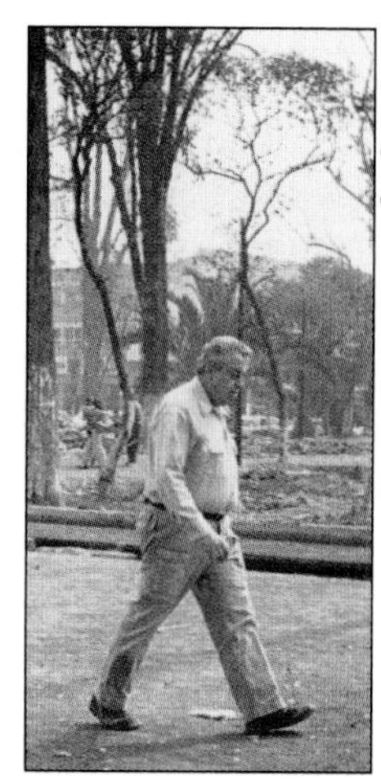

Jorge Ibargüengoitia, dramaturgo mexicano

Foto: Pablo González de Alba

El Teatro de la Ciudad, en el DF, hoy cerrado

Antología de teatro mexicano del siglo XX

Foto: Rogelio Cuéllar

Elena Garro, dramaturga mexicana del siglo XX

posteriormente se dedicaría a la crítica. Novo estrenó en 1951 *La culta dama*, exitosa obra que volvería una y otra vez a los foros. Otros dramaturgos surgidos en los primeros años cincuenta son Federico S. Inclán, Jorge Ibargüengoitia, Luisa Josefina Hernández, Carlos Prieto, Alfonso Anaya, Fernando Sánchez Mayans, Rafael Bernal, Roberto Blanco Moheno y Olga Harmony. Carlos Solórzano inició en ese tiempo una larga y provechosa carrera académica, después de presentar *Doña Beatriz la sin ventura* y *El hechicero*. Ruelas dirigió en Bellas Artes uno de los mayores fracasos en la historia del teatro mexicano: el *Cristóbal Colón*, de Fernando Benítez, quien para fortuna del periodismo ya no reincidió en la escena. En 1955, a 15 años de su primer estreno, Luis G. Basurto presenta en el Teatro Lírico *Cada quien su vida*, probablemente el mayor éxito de taquilla en la historia de la dramaturgia mexicana. El teatro de los Insurgentes, inaugurado a principios de estos años, quedaba todavía muy lejos de lo que era la ciudad vieja y tendría que esperar a la década siguiente para que Manolo Fábregas lo ambientara como sede de la comedia musical estilo Broadway. El exiliado español Álvaro Custodio fundó en 1953 el Teatro Clásico de México, que se mantendría en operación durante 20 años, a lo largo de los cuales transitó por repertorio español, transformó concepciones sobre escenografía, hizo crecer a Ignacio López Tarso y a Ofelia Guilmáin, se fue al frontón cerrado de la Ciudad Universitaria, donde puso varios espectáculos, trabajó en el Café Teatro Cancán y subió hasta el cerro de Teopanzolco, en la cima del cual escenificó *El regreso de Quetzalcóatl*. En los años cincuenta se inició la más trascendente labor de la UNAM en materia teatral. En esa década se formaron grupos estudiantiles en los planteles preparatorianos, donde en diferentes momentos despertarían vocaciones y dejarían sus enseñanzas Enrique Ruelas, Héctor Azar, Olga Harmony, Felipe de la Lama y otros maestros. En 1956 inició sus actividades, en el teatro del Caballito, el grupo Poesía en Voz Alta, que dramatizó composiciones líricas entre las que se incluyó *La hija de Rappacinni*, poema dramático de Octavio Paz, basado en un cuento de Nathaniel Hawthorne, que dirigió Héctor Mendoza, con escenografía de Leonora Carrington y música de Joaquín Gutiérrez Heras. El papel protagónico correspondió a Juan José Arreola, quien por su parte, dirigió un espectáculo con textos de Juan de la Encina, Diego Sánchez de Badajoz, Lope de Vega y García Lorca. Otros locales del teatro universitario, además del Caballito, antes Guimerá, fueron el Globo y el Arcos Caracol. En el Caballito se presentaron *Divinas palabras* y *Olímpica*, bajo la dirección de Juan Ibáñez, que asistieron al Festival de Nancy, Francia. Héctor Azar, autor de *Olímpica*, había obtenido en 1958 el Premio Xavier Villaurrutia por *La Appasionata*. En el teatro universitario, desde entonces, se han formado los más notables directores: Juan José Gurrola, Ludwik Margules, Julio y Germán Castillo, Luis de Tavira, Nancy Cárdenas y Jesusa Rodríguez. A fines de los años cincuenta empezó a figurar el dramaturgo Hugo Argüelles, que se ha dedicado tanto a su producción como a la formación de nuevos autores. Elena Garro publicó en la segunda mitad de esa década sus primeras obras, en la revista *La Palabra y el Hombre*, de la Universidad Veracruzana, institución que se ha distinguido desde entonces por su apoyo al teatro. Alexandro Jodorowsky, llegado en 1959 con el mimo Marcel Marceau, durante sus 15 años de residencia mexicana estuvo en el centro de varias polémicas, frecuentemente referidas a sus concepciones escénicas. Es el creador y aparentemente único cultivador del "teatro pánico". En 1961 vinieron dos compañías estadounidenses, The New York Repertory Theater y The Theater Guild American Repertory, y el público mexicano pudo ver en Bellas Artes, en inglés, tres obras de Tennessee Williams: *El zoológico de cristal, El dulce pájaro de la juventud* y *El último verano*. En los años sesenta ganaron sitio como críticos Fausto Castillo y Malkah Rabell. Surgieron, junto al veterano Julio Prieto, los escenógrafos Antonio López

Hugo Argüelles, autor teatral

Mancera, David Antón, Guillermo Barclay, Alejandro Luna, Félida Medina, Toni Sbert y Benjamín Villanueva, los dos últimos para abandonar muy pronto esta especialidad. Hubo nuevos directores: Adam Guevara, Miguel Sabido, José Estrada, Dimitrios Sarrás, Alejandro Bichir; y, por supuesto, actores, algunos con cierta experiencia, pero que vivieron su primer éxito en esta década: Bertha Moss, Meche Pascual, Beatriz Sheridan, Mónica Serna, José Carlos Ruiz, Alejandro Suárez, Enrique Rocha, Claudio Obregón, Héctor Bonilla, Julissa, Sergio Jiménez, Rosenda Monteros, Rosa Furman, Felio Eliel, Pina Pellicer, Héctor Ortega,

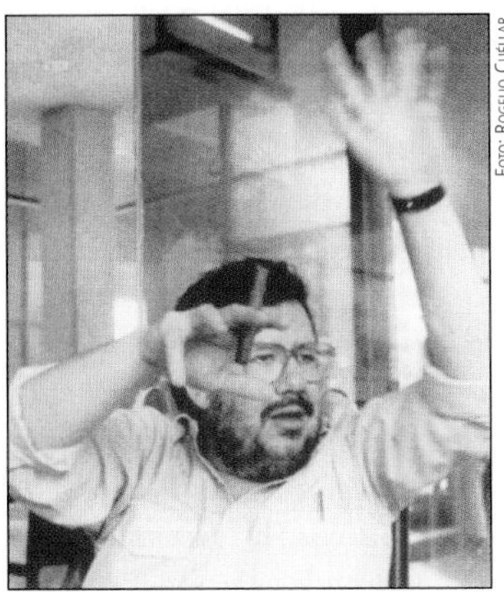

Foto: Rogelio Cuéllar

Hugo Hiriart, dramaturgo mexicano

Susana Alexander, Julián Pastor, Blanca Sánchez, Héctor Suárez y Alfonso Arau, quien después de una larga estancia en Cuba vino a poner *Locuras felices*, donde mostró sus variados talentos. Los nuevos dramaturgos fueron Eduardo Rodríguez Solís, Antonio González Caballero, Maruxa Vilalta, Vicente Leñero, Willebaldo López y Adela Fernández. Incursionan en la dramaturgia Abigael Bojórquez, José Estrada, Enrique Ballesté y Miguel Sabido, quien en 1963 fundó el Teatro de México, dedicado al rescate de obras tradicionales como las pastorelas. En años posteriores han ganado sitio los dramaturgos Juan Tovar, Hugo Hiriart, Tomás Urtusástegui, Carlos Olmos, Víctor Hugo Rascón Banda, Guillermo Schmidhuber, Óscar Villegas, Alejandro Aura, Sabina Berman, Jesús González Dávila, Óscar

Cartel que anuncia actividad teatral en la UAM-Ixtapalapa en 1989

Liera, Miguel Ángel Tenorio, José Ramón Enríquez, Germán Dehesa y Olivia de Montelongo. Entre los nuevos directores están los citados Hiriart y Oceransky, Salvador Garcini, José Caballero, José Luis Cruz y Morris Savariego, además de Jesusa Rodríguez, a quien mencionamos entre los egresados del teatro universitario. En 1977, con Juan José Bremer como director del INBA y José Solé al frente del Departamento de Teatro, se fundó con 34 integrantes la Compañía Nacional de Teatro, primer conjunto oficial de repertorio. En 1978 se fundó la compañía Serendipity, con un repertorio compuesto principalmente de obras infantiles. En 1982 se refundó la Unión de Cronistas de Teatro y Música (☞), que otorga premios anuales a las obras de teatro representadas en el DF. En las más recientes promociones de dramaturgos han destacado Luis Mario Moncada, Carmina Narro, Gerardo Luna, Gabriela Ynclán, Hugo Salcedo, David Olguín, Rocío Carrillo, Alejandra Montalvo, Elena Guiochins y Yasmina Reza. Entre los directores más jóvenes se cuentan Martín Acosta, Alejandro Ainslie e Israel Cortés.

Teayo ◆ ☞ *Castillo de Teayo*, municipio de Veracruz.

Tecajete ◆ Volcán de Hidalgo situado en la porción suroriental de la sierra de Pachuca, al este de la capital de la entidad y al noroeste de los llanos de Apan. Las erupciones de este volcán, y otros más pequeños que lo rodean, fueron las formadoras del suelo de lava y tobas de la región comprendida entre Tepa y Tulancingo.

Tecali de Herrera ◆ Municipio de Puebla situado al este-sureste de la capital de la entidad y contiguo a Tepeaca. Superficie: 184.97 km^2. Habitantes: 15,610, de los cuales 3,436 forman la población económicamente activa. Ha-

Foto: Rogelio Cuéllar

Vicente Leñero, dramaturgo mexicano de la segunda mitad del siglo XX

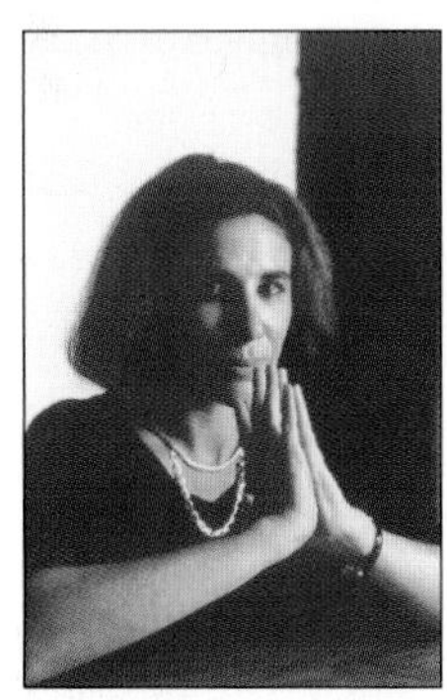

Sabina Berman dramaturga mexicana

Foto: Carlos Hahn

Teatro Juárez en Guanajuato, Guanajuato

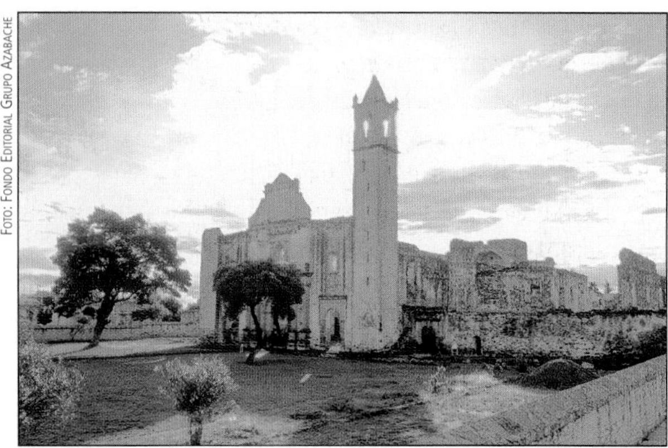
FOTO: FONDO EDITORIAL GRUPO AZABACHE

Ex convento de Santiago Apóstol en Tecali de Herrera, Puebla

blan alguna lengua indígena 85 personas mayores de cinco años (náhuatl 68). Hay en la jurisdicción canteras de mármol, en explotación. El 25 de agosto es la Feria de Muestras Artesanales de Onix. En la cabecera se halla una iglesia construida en 1569.

TECALITLÁN ◆ Municipio de Jalisco situado al sur-sureste de Ciudad Guzmán y al sur de Tamazula de Gordiano, en los límites con Michoacán. Superficie: 1,301.91 km². Habitantes: 17,564, de los cuales 4,533 forman la población económicamente activa. Hablan alguna lengua indígena 15 personas mayores de cinco años.

FOTO: FONDO EDITORIAL GRUPO AZABACHE

Iglesia en Tecamachalco, Puebla

TECÁMAC ◆ Municipio del Estado de México situado al oeste de San Juan Teotihuacán y al este de Cuautitlán, en los límites con Hidalgo. Superficie: 137.42 km². Habitantes: 148,432, de los cuales 36,156 forman la población económicamente activa. Hablan alguna lengua indígena 967 personas mayores de cinco años (náhuatl 430 y otomí 272). En la jurisdicción se encuentran las zonas arqueológicas de Iglesia Vieja y Ojo de Agua. La cabecera es Tecámac de Felipe Villanueva. Ahí se conserva la casa donde nació este compositor, así como las iglesias Agustiniana, de Santo Domingo y de Xolox, construidas en el siglo XVI, y el templo de Santa María Ozumbilla, edificado en el siglo XVII.

TECAMACHALCO ◆ Municipio de Puebla situado al este-sureste de la capital de la entidad y al nor-noroeste de Tehuacán. Superficie: 218.15 km². Habitantes: 52,764, de los cuales 10,285 forman la población económicamente activa. Hablan alguna lengua indígena 119 personas mayores de cinco años (náhuatl 56). En la jurisdicción hay importantes industrias de cordeles y de tejidos de ixtle. En la cabecera se celebra la fiesta de San Isidro, el 15 de mayo.

TECAMACHALCO, DE ◆ Sierra de Puebla que forma parte del Sistema Volcánico Transversal. Se extiende de noroeste a sureste, desde el sur de Tecamachalco hasta el extremo noroccidental de la sierra de Zongolica, al sur del valle de San Andrés Chalchicomula. Tiene yacimientos de yeso.

TECATE ◆ Municipio de Baja California situado al oeste de Mexicali y al este de Tijuana, en los límites con Estados Unidos. Superficie: 3,079.09 km². Habitantes: 62,629, de los cuales 17,527 forman la población económicamente activa. Hablan alguna lengua indígena 410 personas mayores de cinco años (purépecha 91, kumiai 68 y mixteco 66). El municipio cuenta con una importante industria cervecera.

TECHALUTA ◆ Municipio de Jalisco situado al sur de Acatlán y al norte de Ciudad Guzmán. Superficie: 87.86 km². Habitantes: 3,190, de los cuales 669 forman la población económicamente activa.

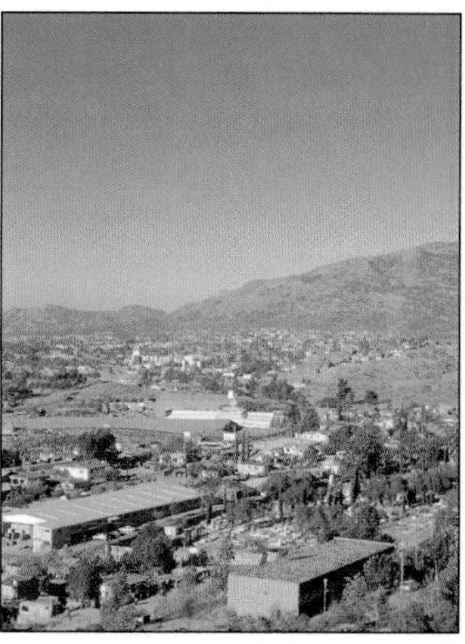

Tecate, Baja California

TECHIALOYAN, MANUSCRITOS DE ◆ Grupo de 21 pictografías novohispanas realizadas en papel de amate a fines del siglo XVII, llamadas así por la de San Antonio Techialoya y agrupadas por sus semejanzas en la realización: figuras humanas europeizadas y náhuatl escrito con caracteres latinos. Cada uno de los manuscritos ilustra y explica la historia y límites de un pueblo del centro de México, por lo que abundan las especificaciones geográficas e históricas de entre 1520 y 1540. Fueron realizados para proteger la integridad física y cultural de esos 21 pueblos. Según Federico Gómez de Orozco, los documentos fueron realizados en la Escuela de San José de los Naturales, dependencia del convento de San Francisco de la ciudad de México. Los 21 manuscritos, que fueron clasificados con letras, son los siguientes: A, de San Antonio de Techialoyan; B, o de la Biblioteca Nacional de París; C, de Quauhximalpan; D, de Metepec; E, de Zempoallan; F, Cuaderno de Ixtapalapa; G, o de Enciso; H, de Santa María Ocelotepec; J, de Santa Cecilia Acatitlán; K, de Santa María Calacohuayan, también llamado códice Sutro; L, de San Miguel Mimiahuapan; M, de San Bartolomé Tepanohuayan; N, de Santa María Tetelpan; P, de Tepozotlán; Q, o García Granados; R, de Chalco; S, de Azcapotzalco; T, de Tepozotlán; U, que es de un sitio cercano a Huehuetoca; V, de San Cristóbal Coyotepec; y X, de Coyoacán. Los códices se encuentran dispersos en la Biblioteca Nacional de Antropología e Historia, la Biblioteca del Estado de Guadalajara, la Biblioteca Newberry de Chicago, Biblioteca Carter Brown de Providence, el Instituto de Investigaciones de Mesoamérica de la Universidad de Tulane, la Biblioteca Nacional de París, el Museo Británico de Londres y la Biblioteca John Rylands de Manchester.

TECIUHTLAZQUE ◆ Hechiceros nahuas encargados, como su nombre lo indica, "El que espanta el granizo", de conjurar las tormentas de granizo y de enviar las nubes cargadas de hielo a los desiertos o a las tierras no cultivadas.

TECOANAPA ◆ Municipio de Guerrero situado al noreste de Acapulco y al sureste de Chilpancingo de los Bravo. Superficie: 776.9 km². Habitantes: 39,827, de los cuales 6,831 forman la población económicamente activa. Hablan alguna lengua indígena 150 personas mayores de cinco años (mixteco 91, náhuatl 29 y tlapaneco 28). En la jurisdicción se producen sombreros de palma, hamacas de ixtle y alfarería. Su nombre aparece también como Tecuanapa.

TECOH ◆ Municipio de Yucatán situado al sur-sureste de Mérida y al oeste de Chichén Itzá. Superficie: 452.2 km². Habitantes: 13,724, de los cuales 3,454 forman la población económicamente activa. Hablan alguna lengua indígena 8,381 personas mayores de cinco años (maya 8,379), de las cuales 309 son monolingües.

TECOLOTLÁN ◆ Municipio de Jalisco situado al sur de Ameca y al nor-noreste de Autlán. Superficie: 795.55 km². Habitantes: 15,878, de los cuales 4,190 forman la población económicamente activa. Hablan alguna lengua indígena ocho personas mayores de cinco años.

TECOLUTLA ◆ Municipio de Veracruz situado al norte de Jalapa y contiguo a Papantla y Martínez de la Torre, en la costa del golfo de México. Superficie: 471.31 km². Habitantes: 25,730, de los cuales 7,239 forman la población económicamente activa. Hablan alguna lengua indígena 1,114 personas mayores de cinco años (totonaco 953 y náhuatl 135). La cabecera, importante centro turístico, cuenta también con instalaciones portuarias para la navegación de cabotaje.

TECOLUTLA ◆ Río de Veracruz, también llamado Espinal. Nace en la porción noroccidental del estado, al sur de Poza Rica, de la confluencia de los ríos Necaxa, San Pedro, Axacal y Cempoala. Corre de suroeste a noreste; recibe a los ríos Laxaxalpan, Tecuantepec y Jaloapan y al arroyo de Chichicatzapa. Desemboca en la barra de Tecolutla, situada al sur de Tuxpan. El Tecolutla, cuyo curso es de unos 100 km, es navegable para embarcaciones de poco calado.

TECOMÁN ◆ Municipio de Colima situado en el extremo sur del estado, al suroeste de la capital de la entidad, en los límites con Michoacán y en la costa del océano Pacífico. Superficie: 807.63 km². Habitantes: 91,036, de los cuales 25,701 forman la población económicamente activa. Hablan alguna lengua indígena 565 personas mayores de cinco años (purépecha 306, náhuatl 184 y mixteco 31). Tecomán es el principal productor agrícola del estado; tiene industrias alimenticias y de extracción de aceites esenciales de cítricos, además de salinas. Cuenta con los balnearios Pascuales y Boca de Apiza.

FOTO: FONDO EDITORIAL GRUPO AZABACHE

En Tecomán se produce el 50% del limón mexicano

ILUSTRACIÓN DE SANTIAGO ORTEGA

Entrada principal de Tecoanapa, Guerrero

TECOMATLÁN ◆ Municipio de Puebla situado al sur de la capital de la entidad y al suroeste de Acatlán, en los límites con Oaxaca. Superficie: 181.15 km². Habitantes: 5,190, de los cuales 1,014 forman la población económicamente activa. Hablan alguna lengua indígena 26 personas mayores de cinco años.

TECOS ◆ ☛ *Tarea Educativa y Cultural hacia el Orden y la Síntesis*.

TECOZAUTLA ◆ Municipio de Hidalgo situado en el extremo occidental del estado, al oeste de Ixmiquilpan, en los límites con Querétaro. Superficie: 575.6 km². Habitantes: 28,529, de los cuales 7,099 forman la población económicamente activa. Hablan alguna lengua indígena 1,688 personas mayores de cinco años (otomí 1,678).

TECPAN ◆ Provincia creada el 8 de junio de 1813 por José María Morelos, "atendiendo al mérito del pueblo de Tecpan, que ha llevado el peso de la conquista de esta provincia", por lo que, agregaba Morelos, "he venido a erigirla por ciudad, dándole con esta fecha el nombre de Ntra. Señora de Guadalupe, cuya instalación se hará en la primera junta, y sólo se previene ahora para gobierno de los pueblos y lugares de esta provincia, que le reconocerán por cabecera de ella a dicha ciudad, especialmente en la peculiaridad de la guarda de los puertos". El mismo documento establecía como límite "el río de

Zacatula que llaman de las Balsas, por el poniente, y por el norte el mismo río arriba, comprendiendo los pueblos que están abordados al río, por el otro lado, distancia de cuatro leguas, entre los que se contará Cusamalá (Cutzamala) y de aquí siguiendo para el oriente a los pueblos de Totolzintla, Tlacozotitlán; para el sudeste, a la línea recta de la Palizada, portezuelo de mar que ha dado mucho quehacer en la presente conquista, quedando dentro Tixtla y Chilapa, y otros que hasta ahora hemos conquistado; todos los cuales reconocerán por centro de su provincia y capital a la expresada ciudad de Ntra. Sra. de Guadalupe, así en el gobierno político y económico, como en el democrático y aristocrático". El 22 de octubre de 1814, al ser sancionado el *Decreto Constitucional* o Constitución de Apatzingán, Tecpan aparecía como una de las 17 provincias en que se dividió a la América Mexicana.

Tecpan ◆ Río de Guerrero que nace en la vertiente meridional de la sierra Madre del Sur y recibe a los arroyos Tepalcatepec, Carrizal, Frío, Moreno y Chiquito. Al sur de Tecpan de Galeana se le une el arroyo Ajuquiaque. Desemboca en el océano Pacífico en la bahía de su mismo nombre, al noroeste de Acapulco.

Tecpan de Galeana ◆ Municipio de Guerrero situado en el occidente del estado, al noroeste de Acapulco y al suroeste de Chilpancingo, en la costa del océano Pacífico. Superficie: 2,537.8 km^2. Habitantes: 61,944, de los cuales 15,870 forman la población económicamente activa. Hablan alguna lengua indígena 140 personas mayores de cinco años (náhuatl 80). En la jurisdicción hay importantes recursos minerales.

Tecpatán ◆ Municipio de Chiapas situado al noroeste de Tuxtla Gutiérrez y al norte de la presa Nezahualcóyotl, en los límites con Veracruz y Oaxaca. Superficie: 770.1 km^2. Habitantes: 34,988, de los cuales 8,957 forman la población económicamente activa. Hablan alguna lengua indígena 6,495 personas mayores de cinco años (zoque 3,868 y tzotzil 2,499). En la jurisdicción se halla una zona arqueológica que no ha sido explorada y en la cabecera está el convento colonial de Santo Domingo.

Vista panorámica de Tecpan de Galeana, Guerrero

Tecuala ◆ Municipio de Nayarit situado al nor-noroeste de San Blas y al suroeste de Acaponeta, en los límites con Sinaloa y en la costa del océano Pacífico. Superficie: 1,137.3 km^2. Habitantes: 44,973, de los cuales 11,872 forman la población económicamente activa. Hablan alguna lengua indígena 70 personas mayores de cinco años (tepehuan 26).

Tecuanapa, de ◆ Barra de Guerrero situada en el extremo suroriental del estado, al este de la bahía Dulce, en la desembocadura del río Ometepec.

Tecuciztécatl ◆ Deidad nahua que ofreció inmolarse y así convertirse en el sol, cuando los dioses se reunieron en Teotihuacán para crear el mundo por quinta vez. Hizo penitencia durante cuatro noches y en la quinta se reunió con sus congéneres para sacrificarse. Cuatro veces intentó saltar a la fogata de la que nacería el sol, y sólo se arrojó luego de que lo hizo Nanaoatzin. Como se convirtió en una luna tan brillante como el sol, uno de los dioses le arrojó un conejo en la cara, que, según dice Bernardino de Sahagún, "oscurecióle la cara, ofuscóle el resplandor" y lo dejó "como ahora está".

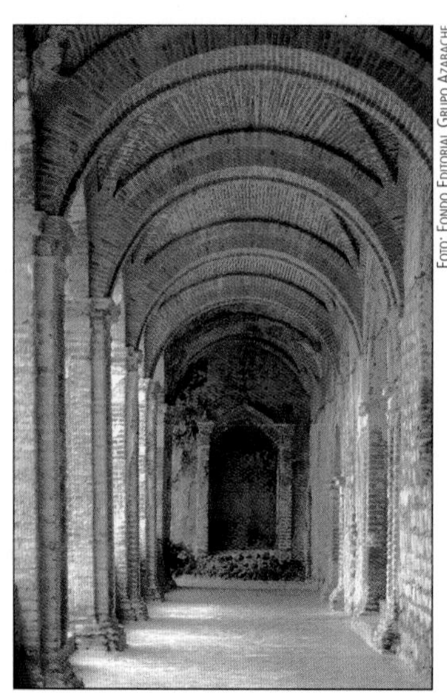
Foto: Fondo Editorial Grupo Azabache

Uno de los corredores del claustro de Santo Domingo en Tecpatán, Chiapas

Teódulo Rómulo ◆ ☛ *Rómulo, Teódulo.*

Tehuacán ◆ Municipio de Puebla situado en el suroriente del estado, al sureste de la capital estatal y al este-sureste de Izúcar de Matamoros. Superficie: 390.36 km^2. Habitantes: 190,468, de los cuales 47,563 forman la población económicamente activa. Hablan alguna lengua indígena 15,708 personas mayores de cinco años (náhuatl 10,605 y mazateco 3,389). Indígenas monolingües: 167. La cabecera es Tehuacán de Juan Crisóstomo Bonilla. En la jurisdicción abundan los manantiales de aguas sulfurosas con propiedades terapéuticas, en los que se han establecido balnearios como los de Garci-Crespo, El Riego, Peñafiel y Altepexi. Los mayores manantiales, San Lorenzo y Ahuelican, eran conocidos en el México prehispánico. Hay yacimientos de plata y plomo, canteras de pizarra, mármol y granito y una importante industria embotelladora. Importante plaza comercial, Tehuacán concentra la producción artesanal de los habitantes de la zona mixteca. Grupos nómadas habitaban el lugar hace aproximadamente 12,000 años. Hacia el año 5000 a.n.e. se inició la práctica de la agricultura. Hacia el 1200 a.n.e. se desarrolló la llamada Ciudad del Sol y poco después, en el año 1,000 aproximadamente, se construyeron las primeras pirámides. A partir del 200 de nuestra era el uso del riego, practicado incipientemente desde desde el 900 a.n.e., se generalizó y permitió el desarrollo de las comunidades de la región. A principios del siglo XVI, un señorío nahua, tributario de México-Tenochtitlan, dominaba una gran zona del valle de Tehuacán. En 1520, mientras el grueso de la expedición española se preparaba para sitiar la capital de los mexicas, tropas europeas conquistaron Tehuacán y trasladaron la población al sur. Diez años mas tarde, los franciscanos construyeron un convento, pero lo abandonaron hacia 1570, cuando los españoles se instalaron sobre los restos de la población indígena. Hasta 1534, el pueblo dependió de Segura de la Frontera y durante los 10 años siguientes quedó en la jurisdicción de Coxcatlán. En 1545 se creó el corregimiento de Tehuacán y poco después se estableció la provincia de Tehuacán, que hasta mediados del siglo XVII, se extendió por el norte de Oaxaca y el sur de Puebla. Durante los 40 años posteriores a la conquista, los principales encomenderos de la zona habían sido Alonso Castillo Maldonado, Juan Ruiz Alanís y Antonio Caicedo, pero para 1578 sus tierras se hallaban en poder de la Corona española. En los primeros años de la Colonia, Tehuacán se convirtió en centro comercial de alguna importancia, sobre todo por la producción de sal y por su situación geográfica, que la convertía en una de las escalas del camino entre Guatemala y México. El primer juez se estableció en la población en 1654. Seis años más tarde, un grupo de españoles ofreció mil pesos para la elevación del pueblo a Villa de Españoles, pero debido a que los nahuas y mazatecos del lugar ofrecieron 3,000, el 16 de marzo de 1660, Tehuacán fue bautizado como Ciudad de Indios de Nuestra Señora de la Concepción y Cueva. La denominación de "ciudad de indios" garantizaba a los pobladores originales los mismos derechos que otros grupos autóctonos privilegiados, como los tlaxcaltecas, aunque, de hecho, los indios continuaron marginados de la ciudad, concentrados en los pueblos de Guadalupe Tlacuempa, Santiago Tula y San Pedro Acoquiaco, que todavía a mediados del siglo XVIII tenían una población mayoritariamente indígena. Durante ese siglo, se construyeron algunos de los edificios más importantes de la ciudad: la iglesia parroquial (1724-28), el hospital de San Juan de Dios (1741) y el convento de Nuestra Señora del Carmen (1748-83). En 1742, cerca de 10,950 personas vivían en Tehuacán, casi todas dedicadas a las tareas agropecuarias. En la década de 1780, existían tres trapiches. A raíz de las reformas borbónicas de 1787, Tehuacán se convirtió en subdelegación de la intendencia de Puebla. En mayo de 1812, la ciudad fue tomada brevemente por insurgentes al mando del sacerdote José María Sánchez de la Vega. En agosto de ese año, la ocuparon las fuerzas de José María Morelos. Hasta noviembre de 1812, luego de la salida de Morelos hacia Oaxaca, funcionó como centro de operaciones de los insurgentes. Durante los dos años siguientes, la plaza estuvo ocupada por insurgentes y realistas, sin que ninguno consolidara su posición: Ignacio López Rayón la ocupó dos veces en 1814 y otro tanto hizo el realista Francisco Hevia. Más tarde, la ciudad estuvo en poder de Juan Nepomuceno Rosains y de José María Correa, quien fortificó el cerro Colorado, situado en las inmediaciones de la ciudad. A fines de 1815, Manuel Mier y Terán recibió al perseguido Congreso insurgente, pero poco después disolvió esta asamblea, detuvo a los diputados y formó una Comisión Ejecutiva de vida efímera. En enero de 1817, Mier y Terán fue derrotado y desalojado de la ciudad, y los realistas la ocuparon durante cuatro años, hasta que, en junio de 1821, Sánchez de la Vega volvió a levantarse en armas, ahora en favor del Plan de Iguala, y con el apoyo del neoinsurgente José Joaquín de Herrera se instaló en la

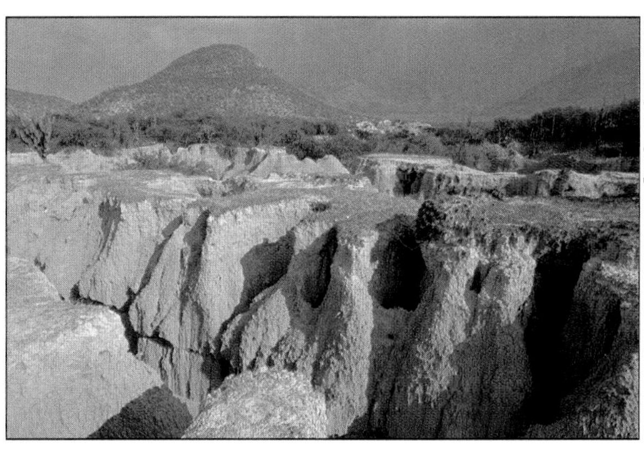

FOTO: CLAUDIO CONTRERAS KOOB

Valle de Tehuacán en Puebla

FOTO: CARLOS HAHN

Parroquia de Tehuacán, Puebla

localidad. A la caída del Imperio de Agustín de Iturbide, en 1823, en los alrededores se levantó en armas Vicente Gómez, quien al frente de un grupo llamado La Santa Liga, intentó, simultáneamente, la vuelta del emperador y la expulsión de los españoles del territorio nacional. Un año más tarde, también con la idea de reestablecer el imperio, se sublevó una parte de la guarnición tehuacanense, al mando de Antonio Reguera, pero fue derrotada rápidamente. En mayo de 1833 se produjo un nuevo levantamiento armado, ahora en contra del vicepresidente Valentín Gómez Farías, que fue dirigido por Lázaro Medrano y que también fue derrotado. En 1856, durante la insurrección de Antonio de Haro y Tamariz, la ciudad fue tomada por los conservadores y permaneció en su poder hasta el fin de la guerra de los Tres Años. En 1862, de acuerdo con lo estipulado en los Preliminares de la Soledad (☛), las tropas invasoras francesas ocuparon Tehuacán. En 1867, los republicanos de Luis Figueroa desalojaron a los imperialistas de la ciudad. En 1891 se estableció el ferrocarril entre Tehuacán y Oaxaca. Hacia 1900 se estableció el primer servicio de tranvías urbanos. Con el siglo se inició la explotación de los manantiales de agua mineral, desde entonces la principal actividad económica del municipio. Durante la revolución, la ciudad estuvo en poder de los maderistas (mayo de 1911) y los carrancistas (octubre de 1914), e intentó ser tomada por los zapatistas (noviembre de 1914). La diócesis de Tehuacán fue erigida en 1962 por el papa Juan XXIII. En 1967 se inauguró el Museo Arqueológico del Valle de Tehuacán.

TEHUACÁN, DE ◆ Valle de Puebla y Oaxaca situado en la porción suroriental del primer estado y en la noroccidental del segundo; se extiende de noroeste a sureste a lo largo de 120 km, paralelo al curso del río Salado, desde el sur de Tecamachalco hasta el norte de Tomellín. Lo limitan al norte y noreste la sierra de Tecamachalco; al este, la de Zongolica; al sur, el extremo noroccidental de la de Juárez; y al este el valle y la sierra de Zapotitlán.

TEHUANTEPEC ◆ ☛ *Santo Domingo Tehuantepec.*

TEHUANTEPEC, DE ◆ Golfo de Oaxaca y Chiapas situado en el litoral del océano Pacífico, al sur del istmo de Tehuantepec y en la porción suroriental de la República. Se considera que sus puntos extremos son, al oeste, Puerto Ángel, Oaxaca, y al este, la barra de Santiago, Chiapas. Mide aproximadamente 350 km de este a oeste, y 80 en su parte más ancha, de norte a sur. Dentro del golfo y en el litoral, se encuentran, de oeste a este, las bahías de Huatulco, el puerto de Salina Cruz, las lagunas Superior e Inferior y a la laguna costera Mar Muerto.

TEHUANTEPEC, DE ◆ Istmo situado en la porción suroriental de la República, que ocupa el sur de Veracruz, el este de Oaxaca y el oeste de Tabasco. Sus puntos extremos son la laguna de Ostión al noroeste, la barra de Tonalá al noreste, la bahía Ventosa al suroeste y el canal que comunica a la laguna costera Mar Muerto con el golfo de Tehuantepec, al sureste. La parte más estrecha del istmo mide 215 km y está definida por una recta imaginaria trazada de norte a sur, desde el puerto de Coatzacoalcos, extremo meridional del golfo de México, hasta el extremo septentrional del golfo de Tehuantepec, en un punto de la costa oaxaqueña localizado entre las lagunas Inferior y Oriental. Desde el siglo XVI se ha pensado abrir una vía o canal interoceánico por esa franja estrecha, tras un estudio del Consejo de Indias que determinó la factibilidad de la empresa. El rey Felipe II la prohibió por temor a que una potencia extranjera buscara apoderarse de la vía. Tras la apertura de un camino en el siglo XVIII, una expedición de Agustín Crammer y Miguel del Corral repitió el dictamen de que "podía abrirse un canal de comunicación entre los dos mares", pero el virreinato carecía de las atribuciones necesarias para ordenar la apertura y el asunto fue diferido hasta 1814, cuando se pensó en otorgar una concesión para abrir y operar el canal, pero la guerra de Independencia impidió todo progreso. En 1824, el gobierno de Guadalupe Victoria promovió la colonización de la zona para facilitar las obras, pero fracasó. En 1842, Antonio López de Santa Anna dio una concesión al español José Garay (conocida por ello como Concesión Garay) para la apertura del canal, ofreciéndole 50 años de percepción exclusiva de los derechos de tránsito y la propiedad de los terrenos a ambos lados del canal. Durante los 17 años siguientes, la Concesión Garay fue motivo de conflictos entre el gobierno mexicano y Garay y los inversionistas, británicos y norteamericanos que adquirieron derechos sobre la concesión y complicaron su situación legal, además de que con su participación propiciaban una eventual intervención militar del gobierno de los Estados Unidos con el pretexto de protegerlos. En 1848, tras la guerra con los Estados Unidos, se firmó el Tratado de Guadalupe-Hidalgo (☛), que en su versión original otorgaba también el libre tránsito perpetuo por el Istmo al ejército norteamericano. Esta cláusula fue finalmente eliminada. En 1850, el gobierno mexicano resolvió desconocer la concesión Garay, que ya había sido adquirida por el norteamericano P. A. Hargous. La amenaza de una nueva declaración de guerra llevó a la

Jóvenes de la ciudad oaxaqueña de Tehuantepec, en la región del istmo de Tehuantepec

FOTO: FONDO EDITORIAL GRUPO AZABACHE

firma, el 23 de junio, del Tratado de Tehuantepec, suscrito por el ministro mexicano Manuel Gómez Pedraza y el norteamericano Lechter, que comprometía a México a proteger a los concesionarios de la construcción del canal interoceánico y, en caso de que no pudiese, a aceptar la intervención de los Estados Unidos con el mismo propósito. Sin embargo, el tratado no fue ratificado por el Congreso mexicano. Al año siguiente, por orden del recién electo presidente Mariano Arista, una nueva comisión mexicana buscó invalidar definitivamente la Concesión Garay, lo que provocó nuevas amenazas y un decreto de Arista en el que se ofrecía libre paso "a todas las naciones del mundo" y neutralidad en caso de guerra. Este decreto fue derogado tras el derrocamiento de Arista, en 1852. El 21 de marzo del año siguiente, durante la fugaz presidencia del general Lombardini, se firmó un nuevo tratado, el de Neutralidad de Tehuantepec, más permisivo aún que el de Gómez Pedraza y suscrito por José María Tornel y Joaquín del Castillo en nombre de México y el embajador norteamericano, Conklin. El 20 de abril, sin embargo, Santa Anna regresó a la presidencia, desconoció el tratado y, poco después, consumó la venta de La Mesilla (☛) con su propio tratado; en él se ofrecía otra vez el libre tránsito para los Estados Unidos y la autorización de construir un ferrocarril interoceánico y "un camino de madera". Tras la revolución de Ayutla que derrocó a Santa Anna, las obras no progresaron, y en 1857, el gobierno de Juan Álvarez desconoció, una vez más, la Concesión Garay, ahora en poder de la compañía Sloo. El año siguiente, mientras las negociaciones seguían estancadas y Benito Juárez (☛) luchaba por imponer su presidencia contra la de Félix Zuloaga, Robert M. McLane fue nombrado embajador de Estados Unidos en México y enviado a resolver, de una vez por todas, la cuestión del istmo; de serle posible, debía además "obtener la cesión de Baja California", por la que estaba autorizado a pagar hasta 10 millones de dólares. Para lograr el reconocimiento de su gobierno por parte de los Estados Unidos, que lo condicionaba al respeto de los numerosos tratados sobre el istmo firmados previamente (y a uno más: el de Amistad y Comercio, suscrito por Lucas Alamán en 1832), Juárez aceptó la firma del Tratado McLane-Ocampo, en el que de nueva cuenta se ratificó el derecho de paso a perpetuidad y la autorización de una intervención militar en el istmo, y obtuvo el reconocimiento de los Estados Unidos en 1859. Sin embargo, el tratado no fue ratificado por el congreso norteamericano, que encontró inaceptables varias de sus cláusulas. La guerra civil norteamericana apartó la atención de ese país del istmo durante la década siguiente, y el gobierno mexicano, empobrecido por años de asonadas y guerras, optó por abandonar el proyecto. La cuestión no volvió a tratarse seriamente sino hasta 1936, cuando una fracción del congreso estadounidense recordó el Tratado de La Mesilla y propuso forzar el cumplimiento de su cláusulas sobre la zona del istmo, que se "compraría" y militarizaría. Al año siguiente, temeroso de la inminente guerra en Europa y de enemistarse con el gobierno de Lázaro Cárdenas, Franklin D. Roosevelt dio marcha atrás a esta iniciativa.

Tehuantepec ◆ Río de Oaxaca también llamado Grande. Nace en la porción central del estado, al sur de la sierra Villa Alta. Corre hacia el sur hasta llegar cerca de Laxichila, vira al suroeste y recibe las aguas del río Mijangos. Más adelante se desvía hacia el norte, luego al este y nuevamente al suroeste; al este de Juchitán su curso se ve interrumpido por la presa Benito Juárez, que también intercepta al Tequisistlán. Desemboca en el océano Pacífico, en la bahía Ventosa, al este de Salina Cruz, tras un recorrido de 335 km.

Tehuantepec, Territorio del Istmo de ◆ Entidad creada el 29 de mayo de 1853 por un decreto del presidente Antonio López de Santa, quien volvió a hacer efectiva una disposición promulgada por el Supremo Poder Ejecutivo el 14 de octubre de 1823, que estableció la erección de una "Provincia del Ystmo" con el territorio veracruzano de Acayucan y el oaxaqueño de Tehuantepec, pero que había desaparecido un año después, con el establecimiento de la Constitución de 1824. El proyecto santanista establecía que la nueva entidad comprendería "el área de su superficie desde la Barrilla en el Seno Méxicano, de donde se trazará un meridiano que encuentre al río Huillapan; de ahí seguirá el curso de este río sobre la orilla derecha hasta su origen, de donde se tirará una línea al paso de San Juan; desde este punto continuará el curso del río por la orilla derecha hasta su origen, de donde se llevará un meridiano a encontrar la costa del Océano Pacífico". La capital del territorio sería Minatitlán y el gobierno local quedaría a cargo de un comandante general y jefe superior político, que "deberá ser un general o jefe del Ejército o de la Marina". Cuatro años después, el 27 de mayo de 1857, el Congreso decidió restituir el territorio del istmo a Oaxaca, Veracruz y Tabasco. El 3 de marzo de 1865, durante el imperio de Maximiliano, fue erigido el departamento de Tehuantepec.

Tehuipango ◆ Municipio de Veracruz situado al suroeste de Córdoba y al noroeste de Tierra Blanca, en los límites con Puebla. Superficie: 111.04 km^2. Habitantes: 15,844, de los cuales 3,147 forman la población económicamente activa. Hablan alguna lengua indígena 12,879 personas mayores de cinco años (náhuatl 12,870) y de ellas 9,123 son monolingües.

Tehuitzingo ◆ Municipio de Puebla situado al sur de la capital de la entidad y al sureste y próximo a Izúcar de Matamoros. Superficie: 473.28 km^2. Habitantes: 12,044, de los cuales 2,228 forman la población económicamente activa. Hablan alguna lengua indígena 15 personas mayores de cinco años. En la jurisdicción existen yacimientos minerales.

Tehuixtla ◆ Balneario de Morelos situado en el municipio de Jojutla (☛). Se encuentra al sur de Cuernavaca, a orillas del río Amacuzac, cerca de la población de Tehuixtla, en los manantiales de aguas termales llamados de la Fundición.

TEICHMANN, REINHARD ♦ n. en la República Democrática de Alemania (1944). Escritor. Estudió letras hispánicas. Se dedica al análisis de la literatura mexicana contemporánea. Autor del libro de entrevistas *De la onda en adelante* (1987).

TEIXIDOR, FELIPE ♦ n. en España y m. en el DF (1895-1980). Bibliógrafo e historiador. Vivió en París, donde conoció a Diego Rivera. Llegó a México en 1919. Fue curtidor (1919-23), vendedor de libros viejos (1924), empadronador del municipio de Tacubaya (1925), traductor de francés e inglés del Colegio Militar, archivista de la Secretaría de Salubridad, empleado de la empresa Mexlibris, administrador de la revista *Contemporáneos* (1929-31), jefe de las secciones Administrativa y de Publicidad de la SRE (1929-35), jefe de personal de la Secretaría de Hacienda y Crédito Público (1935-37), jefe del Departamento Administrativo de la Secretaría de la Economía Nacional (1938-39) y secretario particular del director general de Petróleos Mexicanos (1940-46). Se naturalizó mexicano en 1928. Coordinó las cuatro primeras ediciones del *Diccionario Porrúa de historia, geografía y biografía de México* y la colección *Sepan cuantos...*, de la misma editorial (1959-80). Editor de *Noticia y reflexiones sobre la guerra que se tiene con los apaches en las provincias de Nueva España*, de Bernardo de Gálvez (1925), *Morelos. Documentos inéditos y poco conocidos* (3 t., 1927), *Cartas a Joaquín García Icazbalceta* (1937), *Adiciones a la imprenta en Puebla de los Ángeles de J.T. Mendina. Colección Gavito.* (1961) y *Memorias de Concepción Lombardo de Miramón* (1980). Autor de *Ex-libris y bibliotecas de México* (1931), *Anuario bibliográfico mexicano* (1931-34), *Bibliografía yucateca* (1937), *Viajeros mexicanos (siglos XIX y XX)* (1939) y *Catálogo de libros mexicanos o que tratan de América y de algunos otros impresos en España* (1949). En 1980 ingresó en la Academia Mexicana (de la Lengua).

Felipe Teixidor

Alfonso Teja Zabre

Adalberto Tejeda

TEJA ZABRE, ALFONSO ♦ n. en San Luis de la Paz, Gto., y m. en el DF (1888-1962). Historiador, abogado y escritor. Licenciado en derecho por la Escuela Nacional de Jurisprudencia (1911). Profesor e investigador de la UNAM. Fue agente del Ministerio Público, magistrado del Tribunal Superior de Justicia y del Tribunal Fiscal de la Federación, embajador en Cuba, República Dominicana y Honduras; presidente de la Comisión Revisora de las Leyes Penales, presidente del Tribunal Fiscal de la Federación y presidente del Consejo de Administración de la Productora e Importadora de Papel. Colaboró en *El Universal Gráfico*. Autor de semblanzas y ensayos históricos: *Vida de Morelos* (1917), *Historia y tragedia de Cuauhtémoc* (1929), *Biografía de México* (1931), *Ensayos de historia de México* (1935), *Historia de México. Una moderna interpretación* (1935), *Chapultepec. Guía histórica y descriptiva* (1938), *Panorama histórico de la revolución mexicana* (1939), *El adiós a Rubén Darío* (1941), *La estatua de Justo Sierra* (1942), *Exequias del orador Jesús Urueta* (1942) y *Memorias de López Velarde* (1949); *Guía de historia de México* (1944), *Breve historia de México* (1947), *Dinámica de la historia y frontera interamericana* (1947), *Teoría de la Revolución* (1947), *Historia de Cuauhtémoc* (1954) y *Leandro Valle. Un liberal romántico* (1956); novela: *Alas abiertas* (1920), *La esperanza* (1922), *Hatik* (1922) y *El nuevo Quetzalcóatl* (1927); y poesía: *Los héroes anónimos* (1910) y *Poemas y fantasías* (1914). Luego de su muerte aparecieron sus *Lecciones de California* (1962). Perteneció a la Academia Mexicana de la Historia (1960-62).

TEJADA Y DÍEZ DE VELASCO, FRANCISCO ♦ n. en España y m. en Guadalajara, Jal. (?-1760). Fraile franciscano. Su nombre completo era Francisco de San Buenaventura Martínez de Tejada y Díez de Velasco. Llegó a la Nueva España en 1746. Fue obispo de Mérida (1746-52) y obispo de Guadalajara (1752-60).

TEJEDA, ADALBERTO ♦ n. en Chicontepec, Ver., y m. en el DF (1883-1960). Su apellido materno era Olivares. Realizó estudios en la Escuela Nacional de Ingeniería. En 1913 era síndico del ayuntamiento de Chichontepec, pero se levantó en armas a causa del asesinato del presidente Francisco I. Madero. Jefe del Estado Mayor de la División de Oriente y jefe de operaciones en la Huasteca (1915-17), en 1916 resultó electo diputado al Congreso Constituyente, pero no asistió a las sesiones. Fue senador de la República (1917-20) y gobernador de Veracruz (1920-24). En 1922 se opuso a la represión de la huelga inquilinaria de Veracruz (☛) y en mayo del año siguiente promulgó una ley de vivienda a la que incorporó algunas demandas de los huelguistas. Durante el gobierno de Plutarco Elías Calles se encargó de las secretarías de Comunicaciones y Obras Públicas (del 1 de diciembre de 1924 al 25 de agosto de 1925) y de Gobernación (del 26 de agosto de 1925 al 18 de agosto de 1928), aunque continuó relacionado con los campesinos de Veracruz y apoyó la creación la Liga Nacional Campesina en 1926. En 1928 volvió a la gubernatura de Veracruz (1928-32). Al año siguiente se opuso a la creación del Partido Nacional Revolucionario, pero unos días después de la fundación del PNR, al comienzo de la rebelión escobarista, consiguió que la Liga Nacional Campesina cancelara su apoyo a la candidatura presidencial de Pedro V. Rodríguez Triana, del Bloque Obrero y Campesino, lo que le ganó la animadversión del Partido Comunista Mexicano. En Veracruz, sin embargo, impulsó la creación de cooperativas, fundó una institución financiera para obreros y campesinos llamada La Refaccionaria y realizó una gran campaña anticlerical, por lo que estuvo a punto de ser asesinado por un militante católico. Candidato independiente a la Presidencia de la República de 1934, en las elecciones obtuvo 15,765 votos y el mismo día de los comicios declaró haber votado por el líder comunista Hernán Laborde. Fue ministro plenipotenciario mexicano en Francia (1935-37), embajador de México en España durante la guerra civil (1937-39) y embajador en Perú (1942).

TEJERA HERNÁNDEZ, HUMBERTO ◆ n. en Venezuela y m. en el DF (1890-1971). Se tituló como abogado en la Universidad de los Andes, en la que ejerció la docencia. Profesor del Instituto Nacional de Panamá y de la Escuela Normal Superior. Llegó a México en 1920. Colaboró en *El Nacional* y en *México en la Cultura* de *Novedades*. Autor de *El árbol que canta* (1920), *La mujer de nieve* (1922), *Quetzalcóatl* (1924), *Biografía de don Miguel Hidalgo y Costilla* (1925), *Biografía de don Francisco A. de Icaza* (1926), *Cultores y forjadores de México* (1929), *Grecas mexicanas* (1930), *Cinco águilas blancas* (1932), *Acantilados* (1937), *Bolívar, guía democrática de América* (1944) y *Maestros indoiberos. Crónica de la escuela rural mexicana* (1963).

TEJUPILCO ◆ Municipio del Estado de México situado al sur de Valle de Bravo y al suroeste de Toluca, en los límites con Michoacán y Guerrero. Superficie: 926.95 km². Habitantes: 84,897, de los cuales 15,237 forman la población económicamente activa. Hablan alguna lengua indígena 151 personas mayores de cinco años. En el territorio municipal hay yacimientos minerales. Se han encontrados restos de asentamientos prehispánicos en Ocatitlán, Tejupilco, Ocotepec, el cerro de los Pericones, Ixtapan, Luvianos y el cerro de Nanchititla. En el siglo XVI, los misioneros españoles ordenaron la construcción de los templos católicos de Tejupilco, Ixtapan y Ocotepec. La cabecera municipal se llama Tejupilco de Hidalgo y ahí se encuentra la casa en la que vivió Cristóbal Hidalgo, el padre del iniciador de la independencia. El municipio fue erigido hacia 1850. El principal atractivo turístico son los manantiales de aguas termales que se encuentran en la hacienda de Ixtapan de la Panocha.

TEKAL DE VENEGAS ◆ Municipio de Yucatán situado al este-sureste de Motul y al sur de Temax. Superficie: 95.8 km². Habitantes: 2,318, de los cuales 552 forman la población económicamente activa. Hablan alguna lengua indígena 1,447 personas mayores de cinco años (maya 1,410), de las que 59 no saben español.

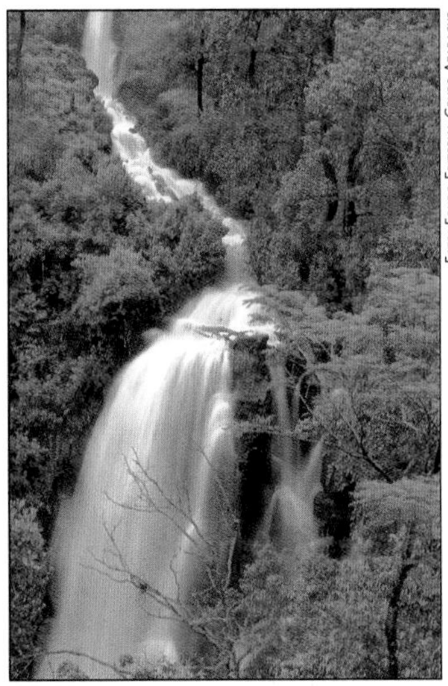

FOTO: FONDO EDITORIAL GRUPO AZABACHE

Manantiales de Luvianos en Tejupilco, Estado de México

TEKANTÓ ◆ Municipio de Yucatán situado al sureste de Motul y al suroeste de Temax. Superficie: 47.25 km². Habitantes: 3,971, de los cuales 1,078 forman la población económicamente activa. Hablan alguna lengua indígena 1,761 personas mayores de cinco años (maya 1,760).

TEKAX ◆ Municipio de Yucatán situado en el extremo sur del estado, al sureste de Tikul y al oeste de Peto, en los límites con Campeche y Quintana Roo. Superficie: 2,748.42 km². Habitantes: 32,668, de los cuales 7,939 forman la población económicamente activa. Hablan alguna lengua indígena 20,724 personas mayores de cinco años (maya 20,694), y 3,057 son monolingües. Su cabecera es Tecax de Álvaro Obregón.

TEKIT ◆ Municipio de Yucatán situado en el centro del estado, al sureste de Mérida y al oeste-suroeste de Chichén Itzá. Superficie: 219.71 km². Habitantes: 7,874, de los cuales 2,125 forman la población económicamente activa. Hablan alguna lengua indígena 4,900 personas mayores de cinco años (maya 3,895). Indígenas monolingües: 230.

TEKOM ◆ Municipio de Yucatán situado al suroeste de Valladolid y sureste de Chichén Itzá. Superficie: 201.83 km². Habitantes: 2,603, de los cuales 506 forman la población económicamente activa. Hablan alguna lengua indígena 2,174 personas mayores de cinco años (maya) y de ellas, son monolingües 763.

TELCHAC PUEBLO ◆ Municipio de Yucatán situado al norte de Motul y al oeste de Temax. Superficie: 81.75 km². Habitantes: 3,374, de los cuales 995 forman la población económicamente activa. Hablan maya 815 personas mayores de cinco años. A mediados del siglo XVI, después de la conquista de Yucatán, el actual territorio municipal formó parte de la encomienda de Francisco de Montejo.

Libro de Humberto Tejera

FOTO: BORIS DE SWAN

Pila Bautismal de la Iglesia de San Juan Bautista en Tekax, Yucatán

FOTO: CLAUDIO CONTRERAS KOOB

Tekax , Yucatán

Tele Guía

TELCHAC PUERTO ◆ Municipio de Yucatán situado al norte de Motul y al noroeste de Temax, en la costa del golfo de México. Superficie: 173.73 km². Habitantes: 1,413, de los cuales 323 forman la población económicamente activa. Hablan alguna lengua indígena 216 personas mayores de cinco años (maya 215).

TELE-GUÍA ◆ Revista semanal fundada en la ciudad de México por los hermanos Brígida, Carlos, Luis, Mariano y Rafael Amador. Apareció por primera vez el 7 de agosto de 1952. Publica la programación semanal de todos los canales de la televisión mexicana, así como reportajes sobre la industria televisiva nacional. El número 2,463, para la semana del 23 al 29 de octubre de 1999, informaba que Maüe Hernández Herrera era la directora editorial de la revista de Editorial Televisa que va en su año número 48. Está reputada como la primera revista en su género en el mundo y, según sus datos, su tiraje es de un millón de ejemplares.

Modelo de teléfono antiguo

FOTO: ARCHIVO XAVIER ESPARZA

TELÉFONO ◆ El 15 de marzo de 1878, dos años después de que el británico Alexander Graham Bell inventara un aparato de comunicación sonora a distancia, se realizó la primera comunicación telefónica en México, entre la capital de la República y el entonces pueblo de Tlalpan. Nueve días más tarde se repitió el experimento entre la Administración Central de Telégrafos y una de sus oficinas en Cuautitlán. En ese mismo año, Alfred Westrup trajo a México otro modelo de aparato y, en diciembre, firmó con el gobierno capitalino un contrato para instalar las líneas de comunicación entre las seis comisarías de policía con la oficina del inspector general y con la Secretaría de Gobernación. Entre 1879 y 1880 se instalaron los primeros teléfonos particulares y, un año más tarde, M. L. Greenwood obtuvo la concesión para instalar una red de servicio público en la ciudad de México. En 1882 se fundó la Compañía Telefónica Mexicana (CTM), que era subsidiaria de la Compañía Telefónica de Boston (que luego se transformó en la International Telehone and Telegraph Corp., la *ITT*), y a partir de entonces se establecieron varias compañías privadas, como la Mexican Bell Telephone y la Compañía Telefónica y Telegráfica del Norte, cada una de las cuales instaló sus propias líneas y aparatos. Seis años después, cuando se editó el primer directorio telefónico de la ciudad de México, 800 residencias porfirianas tenían teléfono. En el resto del país, mientras tanto, durante la última década del siglo XIX, se tendieron líneas telefónicas en Puebla, Veracruz, Mérida, Guadalajara, Jalapa, San Luis Potosí, Monterrey, Oaxaca, Progreso, Querétaro, Saltillo, Orizaba y Tampico, pero fue en 1987 cuando se inició el servicio público de larga distancia. En febrero de 1903, el británico John Sitzenstatter obtuvo una concesión para explotar durante 30 años el servicio telefónico en el Distrito Federal y sus alrededores y, en noviembre de ese año, la CTM consiguió otra concesión, también de 30 años para la ciudad de México, y se comprometió a establecer una red subterránea para evitar problemas entre las líneas telefónicas y las tranviarias. Sin embargo, Sitzenstatter no pudo enfrentar con éxito a la poderosa CTM, por lo que dos años después, en marzo de 1905, cedió sus derechos sobre la telefonía capitalina al consorcio sueco Telefonaktiebolaget L. M. Ericsson, que desde 1903 buscaba establecerse en México. Al recibir la concesión, y quizá para evitarles sufrimientos de pronunciación a los usuarios, la empresa escandinava creó una filial llamada Compañía de Teléfonos Ericsson (CTE), la que comenzó a funcionar en 1907 con 500 suscriptores. También a fines de la primera década del siglo XX, la CTM se convirtió en la Compañía Telefónica y Telegráfica

FOTO: ARCHIVO XAVIER ESPARZA

Teléfono automático de finales del siglo XIX

Mexicana (CTTM). En enero de 1915, el gobierno de Venustiano Carranza intervino la red y los bienes de la CTTM, que permanecieron controlados por el gobierno hasta 1925. En 1920, la CTE instaló las líneas de larga distancia entre la ciudad de México y Toluca, El Oro, Texcoco y Pachuca, pero la ventaja comercial le duró menos de una década, pues en en 1927, la CTTM inauguró el servicio de larga distancia hacia Estados Unidos y Canadá y en 1928 la comunicación con Europa. A principios de los años treinta se agravó el problema de la

La compañía telefónica Ericsson realiza en 1930 una exposición al público de sus servicios

duplicidad de las líneas, pues las dos empresas se habían extendido por casi todo el territorio nacional y resultaba demasiado caro para los usuarios contratar con las dos firmas. En 1936, el gobierno de Lázaro Cárdenas promulgó la primera Ley de Vías Generales de Comunicación, que dispuso la unificación de ambos sistemas, pero lo único que hicieron las trasnacionales fue crear un número especial para la comunicación de una red a otra. Diez años después, a fines de 1947, el gobierno de Miguel Alemán adquirió la mayoría de las acciones de la CTE y el 23 de diciembre creó Teléfonos de México; en 1950

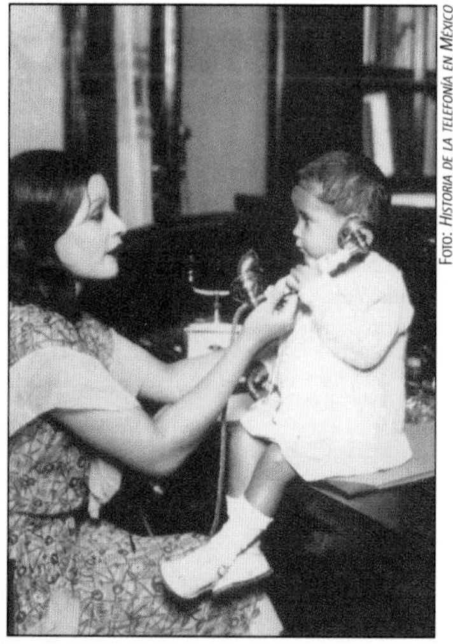

FOTO: *HISTORIA DE LA TELEFONÍA EN MÉXICO*

Uso del teléfono durante el periodo cardenista

compró la CTTM y la incorporó a Telmex y en 1952 concluyó la unificación de las redes. La empresa gubernamental, no obstante, permitió a las trasnacionales conservar el 37.5 por ciento de las acciones y se limitó a operar y a reparar las líneas, lo que permitió a la Ericsson, llamada Teleindustria Ericsson desde 1964, monopolizar de hecho la construcción de los aparatos telefónicos, las centrales y los cables. En 1980, por ejemplo, la Ericsson construyó 130,200 líneas locales y 42,000 de larga distancia, y 280,000 aparatos telefónicos. En 1953, Teléfonos de México puso como condición para dar servicio a nuevos usuarios, la adquisición por éstos de acciones y obligaciones de la compañía, lo que le pemitió manejar recursos en

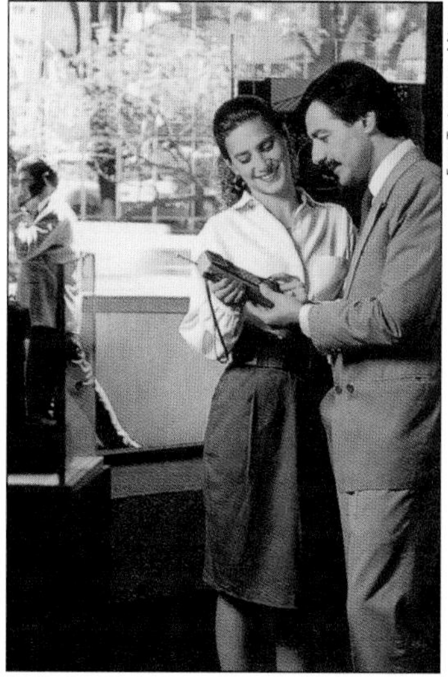

FOTO: TELÉFONOS DE MÉXICO

Para 1999 la telefonía celular cuenta en México con 6 millones y medio de usuarios

constante aumento. En 1958, un grupo de empresarios mexicanos encabezados por Carlos Trouyet adquirió las acciones que permanecían en poder de la CTTM y la CTE y a partir de 1960 las colocó la Bolsa Mexicana de Valores. El servicio de larga distancia automática nacional comenzó a funcionar en 1965, entre el Distrito Federal y Toluca. La comunicación directa con Canadá y Estados Unidos se estableció en 1969 y con el resto del mundo en 1978. En agosto de 1971 el gobierno de Luis Echeverría compró un nuevo lote de acciones, que convirtieron al Estado en el principal accionista de Teléfonos de México. En 1980, las líneas telefónicas operadas por Telmex abarcaban 27,092,641 km. En ese mismo año, Teléfonos de México era la duodécima empresa más importante del país. En los años ochenta se produjo un deterioro en el servicio, el que se agravó con los sismos de 1985. En la década siguiente el gobierno federal privatizó la empresa, que desde entonces se conoce como Telmex. En los años siguientes surgió la competencia en larga distancia con varias empresas. Desde fines de los ochenta se introdujo la telefonía celular y en 1999 se estimaba que en el país había 6 millones y medio de teléfonos celulares en operación.

TELÉGRAFO ◆ En mayo de 1849, el gobierno del presidente José Joaquín de Herrera otorgó una concesión al español Juan de la Granja, para que durante 10 años operara una red de telégrafos eléctricos, como los que Samuel Morse había inventado en 1832, a condición de que en los primeros dos años construyera una línea que debería enlazar la ciudad de México con el puerto de Veracruz. El 2 de noviembre de 1850 se hizo el primer ensayo de luz eléctrica en la Plaza de Armas y el miércoles 13 de ese mes se publicó en los diarios una *Proclama de progreso* firmada por Juan de la Granja y su socio William George Stewart, quienes anunciaban que habían "quedado removidos todos los obstáculos que se había opuesto hasta ahora a la comunicación de la electricidad entre el Palacio Nacional y el Colegio de Minería". En el desplegado se invitaba a cuantos quisieran para que "se satisfagan por sus propios ojos de lo maravilloso de esta invención", lo que podrían hacer asistiendo a Minería o a al Palacio, entre dos y cuatro de la tarde, para ver "en acción por algunos días las

FOTO: ARCHIVO XAVIER ESPARZA

Telegramas antiguos

FOTO: CARLOS HAHN

En la década de 1990 Teléfonos de México fue privatizada y a partir de entonces se conoce como Telmex.

máquinas telegráficas". Tres años después de esa primera comunicación sólo se había construido el tramo México-Nopalucan, que comenzó a funcionar en noviembre de 1851. Stewart y De la Granja abandonaron la empresa en diciembre, cuando tenían pendiente la comunicación con Veracruz, y la concesión quedó en manos de Hermenegildo de Viya y Cosío quien pudo, en apenas seis meses, terminar la línea, que fue inaugurada el 19 de mayo, en Jalapa. Dos años después, la red telegráfica medía 608 km y enlazaba la ciudad de México con León, Guadalajara, San Luis Potosí, Guanajuato, Veracruz y Orizaba. En mayo de 1859, el gobierno conservador prorrogó la concesión de De Viya, adicionada con las líneas que se construyeran o iniciaran en los siguientes 10 años. Al triunfo de la República, sin embargo, el gobierno del presidente Benito Juárez dispuso que la totalidad de las instalaciones telegráficas existentes pasaran a poder de la cuarta sección de la Secretaría de Fomento y se extendieran concesiones para el tendido de nuevas líneas a empresas particulares y a los gobiernos de los estados. Dos años después, en 1869, Juárez expidió el primer reglamento para la correspondencia telegráfica y decretó un sistema de subvenciones para los constructores de líneas. En 1878 fue creada la Dirección General de Telégrafos, dependiente de la Secretaría de Fomento. Al año siguiente, el gobierno de Porfirio Díaz contrató con la empresa estadounidense Mexican Telegraph el servicio de un cable submarino entre el puerto texano de Galveston y los puertos mexicanos de Tampico y Veracruz, que no fue incluido en la disposición de diciembre de 1889, por la que el gobierno dispuso que los telégrafos quedaban sujetos a la autoridad federal. En 1887, México y Guatemala celebraron un convenio para unir ambos países con este medio de comunicación. La Mexican Telegraph, por su parte, extendió sus cables submarinos a Coatzacoalcos y Campeche y tendió una línea terrestre de Coatzacoalcos a Salina Cruz. En 1891, la Dirección de Telégrafos Federales se incorporó a la Secretaría de Comunicaciones y Obras Públicas. Entre 1916 y 1917 se estableció la comunicación radiotelegráfica de México con Guatemala, El Salvador, Costa Rica y Honduras; en 1919 con Chile y en 1922 con La Habana, Cuba. En este último año se estableció también la comunicación telefónica simultánea con la telegráfica, por medio de aparatos telegrafónicos. En 1925 se convino con la Western Union Telegraph el intercambio de giros tentre México, Estados Unidos y Canadá. El 16 de junio de 1949 la Dirección General de Telecomunicaciones se hizo cargo del servicio telegráfico internacional. En la actualidad la transmisión de señales se hace a través de sistemas alámbricos e inalámbricos (cables coaxiales y sistemas de microondas) implantados por la Secretaría de Comunicaciones en combinación con Teléfonos de México. En 1960 el país quedó comunicado por télex con Canadá y Estados Unidos. En agosto de 1968 se inauguró en la ciudad de México la Torre Central de Comunicaciones, que aloja los servicios telegráfico internacional, de microondas, télex, canalización multiplex, así como los talleres y laboratorios. En octubre del mismo año se inauguró en México el servicio del sistema Intelsat, con una estación terrena en Tulancingo y estaciones repetidoras o relevadoras instaladas en satélites artificiales para la comunicación internacional por microondas. En 1989, el sistema Morse, que había sido la base de las telecomunicaciones en el país por más de un siglo, comenzó a ceder terreno a sistemas basados en enlaces satelitales, fibra óptica y microondas. En 1992, el sistema telegráfico mexicano dejó de operar definitivamente y se anunció que toda la red telegráfica nacional sería eventualmente desmantelada y quedaría sin uso. México forma parte de la Unión Internacional de Telecomunicaciones, antes Unión Telegráfica Internacional.

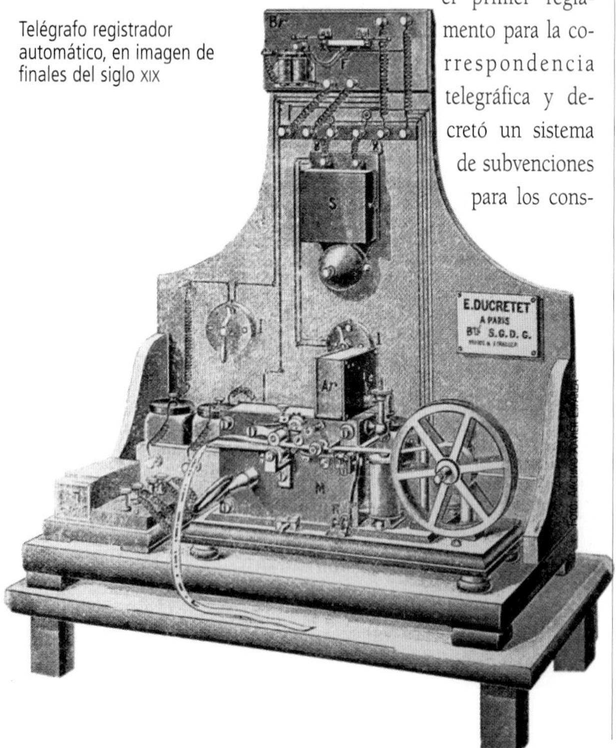

Telégrafo registrador automático, en imagen de finales del siglo XIX

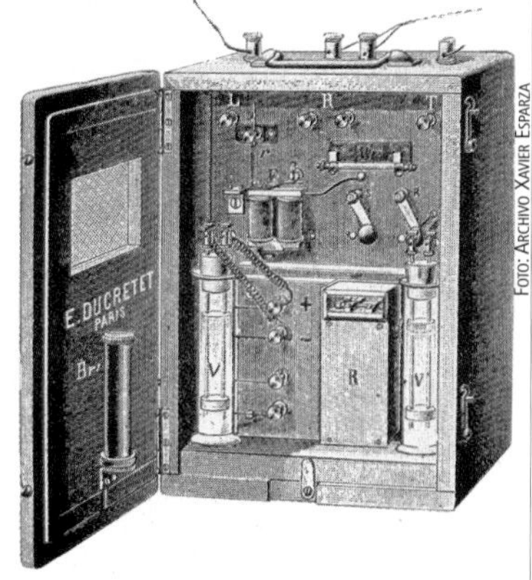

FOTO: ARCHIVO XAVIER ESPARZA

Teléfono receptor Ducretet

Guillermo González Camarena, pionero de la televisión en México

TELÉGRAFO DE GUADALAXARA, EL ◆ Periódico realista que apareció en la capital de Jalisco entre mayo de 1811 y febrero de 1812. Publicó 82 números. Fue dirigido por Francisco Severo Maldonado, quien poco antes había editado en *El Despertador Americano*, primer órgano insurgente.

TELEVISIÓN ◆ Los primeros experimentos fueron realizados en 1926 por el escocés John Logie Baird, quien tres años después efectuó las primeras transmisiones. No fue sino hasta principios de la década de los treinta cuando Vladimir K. Zworykin inventó el iconoscopio, principio electrónico de los actuales sistemas televisivos. Guillermo González Camarena efectuó los primeros ensayos de transmisión televisiva en México, hacia 1933, con un equipo construido por él mismo. En ese año, el Partido Nacional Revolucionario trajo al país un equipo de televisión en blanco y negro con el que hizo algunas demostraciones públicas. En Estados Unidos se considera que el inicio formal de las transmisiones fue en la Feria Mundial de Nueva York, en 1939. En el mismo año, en México, González Camarena inventó un sistema de televisión cromática, el que patentó aquí y en Estados Unidos. Siete años después inició una serie de transmisiones experimentales en blanco y negro, desde los laboratorios Gon-Cam, de su propiedad. Rómulo O'Farril fundó el primer canal de televisión comercial en nuestro país, XHTV-Canal 4, que inició sus emisiones de prueba el 27 de julio de 1950 desde el edificio de la Lotería Nacional. Ese canal transmitió, el 1 de septiembre del mismo año, el cuarto informe de gobierno del presidente Miguel Alemán. El 21 de marzo de 1951 se inauguró el Canal 2, dirigido por Emilio Azcárraga Vidaurreta, con González Camarena en la parte técnica. En 1952 funcionaban ya la XHLATV, de Matamoros, y el circuito cromático de la Universidad Nacional Autónoma de México. El 10 de mayo de 1952 se inauguró XHGC-Canal 5, propiedad de González Camarena. Tres años después, a sugerencia de Azcárraga, se unieron las tres estaciones (canales 2, 4 y 5) y formaron la empresa Telesistema Mexicano. Ese mismo año, debido a un convenio firmado entre Azcárraga, O'Farril y la International Standard Corporation, las señales de Telesistema Mexicano llegaron a los estados de Hidalgo, Puebla, Tlaxcala, México, parte de Veracruz y parte de Guerrero. En 1958 se inició la transmisión de telenovelas. La primera obra de ese género fue *Senda prohibida*, de Fernanda Villeli. El 2 de marzo de 1959 salió al aire XEIPN Canal 11, emisora cultural del Instituto Politécnico Nacional que era captado con dificultades en el Valle de México, sobre todo cerca del Casco de Santo Tomás, hasta que en 1969 se mejoró el equipo y se instaló una antena en el cerro del Chiquihuite. En 1963, la Secretaría de Comunicaciones y Transportes inició la construcción de la red nacional de telecomuni-

Transmisión por televisión de un lanzamiento espacial a principios de la década de los 60

Logotipo de la compañía de televisión Televisa

Logotipo de Televisión Azteca

Logotipo de Canal 22, señal de televisión estatal

Logotipo CNI canal 40

Logotipo de la empresa televisiva Multivisión

caciones, integrada básicamente por el servicio de microondas que conduce las señales telegráficas, telefónicas, radiofónicas y televisivas. El 1 de septiembre de 1968 inició sus transmisiones XHMTV Canal 8 (Televisión Independiente de México), propiedad de una empresa regiomontana, cuyos estudios y oficinas se instalaron en San Ángel; el contenido de la programación del nuevo canal siguió los mismos lineamientos de diversión que los canales de Telesistema Mexicano. El 12 de octubre de ese mismo año se inauguró XHDF Canal 13, propiedad de Francisco Aguirre. Esta emisora fue adquirida por el gobierno federal, a través de Somex, el 15 de marzo de 1972. El 8 de enero del año siguiente se fusionaron Telesistema Mexicano y Televisión Independiente de México para formar Televisa, cuyo cuerpo directivo quedó integrado por Rómulo O'Farril, Emilio Azcárraga Milmo y Miguel Alemán Velasco. El 10 de enero de 1979 se publicó el Reglamento del Servicio de Televisión por Cable. En 1984 se iniciaron las transmisiones del Canal 7, que formó parte del Instituto Mexicano de Televisión (Imevisión). La entrada en funcionamiento de este canal requirió convertir el 8 en 9. Para entonces ya existía el 22, que podía captarse por cable o mediante una sencilla adaptación de los receptores ordinarios. En 1989, la empresa Multivisión anunció que empezaría a operar ocho nuevos canales en el valle de México. En 1991, al anunciarse la venta de Imevisión, un grupo de intelectuales cercanos al gobierno promovió que en esa operación no se incluyera el Canal 22, lo que obtuvo el respaldo de cientos de firmantes para que el presidente Carlos Salinas accediera a la petición. En julio de 1993, un grupo de inversionistas encabezado por Ricardo Salinas Pliego adquirió por 643 millones de dólares estadounidenses las empresas Operadora de Teatros, Estudios América e Imevisión, que comprendía los canales 7 y 13 y sus repetidoras, las que en 1999 sumaban 250 distribuidas en el territorio nacional y 19 estaciones locales con instalaciones propias. El 2 de agosto de 1993 la antigua empresa Imevisión inició operaciones como Televisión Azteca. En 1997 esta firma adquirió estaciones de televisión en Chile, El Salvador y Guatemala, mientras que Televisa, su principal competidora, tenía fuertes intereses en Estados Unidos, en España y otros países. En 1998 se hicieron las primeras pruebas públicas de la televisión de alta definición, cuya entrada en el mercado se consideraba inminente. De acuerdo con la Comisión Federal de Telecomunicaciones, en 1999 había en México 16 millones de aparatos receptores de televisión, de los cuales 22 por ciento estaban conectados a los sistemas de paga, proporción que se esperaba aumentar a 70 por ciento de los usuarios en los primeros años del siglo XXI, cuando entre en operación la televisión interactiva, que permitirá aprovechar el mismo aparato para usar la Internet y sus servicios, por ejemplo telefonía; transacciones bancarias y financieras, correo y múltiples servicios, incluida la compra en la tienda de autoservicio o la comida a domicilio.

Logotipo de Canal 11, emisora televisiva del IPN

Téllez, Joaquín ◆ n. y m. en la ciudad de México (1861-1929). Militar. Se incorporó al ejército federal en 1881. Participó en la represión contra los yaquis y en 1997 asistió a las negociaciones entre el gobierno y el líder indio Tetabiate. Durante la rebelión maderista operó en Chihuahua y en 1912 sustituyó a Victoriano Huerta como jefe de las tropas encargadas de combatir a Pascual Orozco. Comandante militar de Guadalajara (enero de 1913), luego del asesinato del presidente Francisco I. Madero fue comandante militar en Monterrey (agosto de 1913), jefe de la división del Yaqui y gobernador de Sonora (de abril a julio de 1914). Al triunfo del constitucionalismo se exilió en El Salvador y volvió a México años más tarde.

Emilio Azcárraga Vidaurreta, fundador de Canal 2

Téllez, Manuel C. ◆ n. en Zacatecas, Zac., y m. en el DF (1885-1937). Diplomático. Realizó estudios en la Escuela Nacional Preparatoria. Ingresó al servicio exterior mexicano en 1918.

Manuel C. Téllez

Fue encargado de negocios en Japón (1918), primer secretario (del 7 de febrero al 20 de julio de 1920), encargado de negocios corrientes (del 20 de julio al 25 de noviembre de 1920), encargado de negocios (del 25 de noviembre de 1921 al 13 de diciembre de 1924) y embajador de México en Estados Unidos (del 1 de enero de 1925 al 16 de octubre de 1931); secretario de Gobernación (del 21 de octubre de 1931 al 20 de enero de 1932) en el gobierno de Pascual Ortiz Rubio, secretario de Relaciones Exteriores en los gabinetes de Ortiz Rubio (del 20 de enero al 2 de septiembre de 1932) y de Abelardo L. Rodríguez (del 5 de septiembre al 31 de diciembre de 1932); y embajador de México en Italia (1934).

Téllez, Othón ◆ n. en el DF (1957). Pintor. Estudió pintura y dibujo en La Esmeralda y filosofía en la UNAM (1974-79). Director del Centro de Educación Artística Diego Rivera del INBA, profesor en La Esmeralda y corresponsal cultural de la estación cubana Radio Progreso. Ha participado en 30 exposiciones colectivas y siete individuales. Su obra fue reconocida en el Quinto Encuentro Nacional de Arte Joven con una mención honorífica. Ha hecho escenografía, iluminación y vestuario para teatro, cine y danza. Coautor de *Conferencia de vampiros*.

Téllez Cruces, Agustín ◆ n. en Guanajuato, Gto. (1918). Licenciado en derecho por la UNAM (1938-42). Profesor del Instituto Politécnico de Hidalgo (1945) y profesor fundador de la Facultad de Leyes de la Universidad de Hidalgo (1945-46). Pertenece al PRI desde 1966. Ha sido secretario de juzgado en Hidalgo (1944) y Puebla (1945); jefe de la Oficina de Compilación de Leyes (1949) y secretario de Estudio y Cuenta de la Suprema Corte de Justicia de la Nación (1949); juez de distrito en Chiapas, Sonora y DF (1951-58), magistrado del Tribunal Colegiado del Segundo Distrito de Puebla (1960), magistrado del Primer Tribunal Colegiado del Primer Distrito del DF (1964), director general de Servicios Legales (1965-73) y director general jurídico y de gobierno del DDF (1974); ministro (1974-75) y presidente de la Suprema Corte de Justicia de la Nación (1977-81), presidente de la Suprema Corte de Justicia de Guanajuato (1981-82), senador de la República (1982-85), gobernador interino de Guanajuato (del 26 de junio al 25 de septiembre de 1985), y consultor legal de la Procuraduría General de la República (1988-92). Es miembro de las academias de Administradores Públicos, de Derecho Mercantil y de Derecho Turístico, de la Academia de Abogados de México y de la Real Academia de Legislación y Jurisprudencia Española.

Luis Téllez Kuenzler

Téllez Kuenzler, Luis ◆ n. en el DF (1958). Licenciado en economía por el ITAM y doctor por el Instituto Tecnológico de Massachusetts, instituciones donde ha sido profesor. Afiliado al PRI desde 1980. Ha sido asesor del presidente del INEGI (1984) y del subsecretario de Planeación y Control Presupuestal (1986), director del Sector Externo y Economía Internacional (1987), coordinador de asesores del secretario (1987-88) y director general de Planeación Hacendaria de la Secretaría de Hacienda (1989-90); subsecretario de planeación de la SARH (1990-94), coordinador de asesores del candidato a la Presidencia de la República por el PRI (1994), jefe de la Oficina de la Presidencia (1994-97) y secretario de Energía (1997-). Coautor de *El combate a la inflación* (1993), *Nueva legislación de bosques, tierras y aguas* (1993) y *La modernización del sector agropecuario y forestal* (1994).

Téllez Oropeza, Roberto ◆ n. en Zacatlán de las Manzanas, Pue. (1909). Músico. Estudió en el Conservatorio Nacional de Música (1929-38). Fue alumno de Silvestre Revueltas y José Rolón. Ha sido director de la Orquesta Sinfónica del Conservatorio (1935-36), director de la Orquesta Típica Miguel Lerdo de Tejada, director de las bandas de música de Bellas Artes (1943) y de la Secretaría de Educación (1957-66); y director del coro del DDF (1966). Su obra publicada o grabada comprende cinco óperas, cinco sinfonías, quince cuartetos, dos conciertos para piano, uno para violín, así como valses y música para cine.

Téllez Rincón, José María ◆ n. en Texcoco, Edo. de Méx. (1931). Fue obrero. Se afilió al PRI, del cual fue miembro fundador del IEPES (1954) y secretario de Capacitación Política en el XXV Comité Distrital (1972). Fue secretario general del SUTERM. Diputado federal (1979-82 y 1991-94). En 1991 renunció al PRI y se afilió al PFCRN.

Téllez Vargas, Armando ◆ n. y m. en el DF (1904-1927). Perteneció al Centro de Estudiantes de la Asociación Católica de la Juventud Mejicana. En 1923 fue encarcelado por haber escrito, con otros militantes católicos, una carta de protesta por la expulsión del delegado apostólico Ernesto Fillipi. Liberado poco después, en 1924 participó en la campaña presidencial de Ángel Flores. Militó en la Liga Nacional Defensora de la Libertad Religiosa y en 1927 tomó las armas contra el gobierno de Plutarco Elías Calles. Murió en combate en el Ajusco.

Téllez Vargas, Eduardo *el Güero* ◆ n. en Yautepec, Mor., y m. en el DF (1908-1991). Periodista. Comenzó su carrera como reportero de deportes en *Novedades*. En 1940 dio la exclusiva sobre el asesinato de León Trotsky. En 1944 pasó al diario *El Universal*, donde cubrió la fuente policiaca durante 37 años y destacó por su temeridad en la búsqueda de noticias. Autor de *Reportero de policía*.

TELLO, AURELIO ♦ n. en Perú (1951). Su nombre completo es Aurelio Efraín Tello Malpartida. Estudió pedagogía musical, composición, piano y dirección coral en Perú. Radica en México desde 1982, donde ha sido investigador y subdirector (1988-89) del Cenidim, y subdirector (1990-92) del INBA. Fundó en 1989 el ensamble de música barroca Capilla Virreinal de la Nueva España y ha rescatado la música virreinal de las catedrales de Oaxaca, DF y Puebla. Colaborador de *Pauta, Tono, Artes de México* y *México en el Arte.* Ha sido coordinador de *Archivo musical de la Catedral de Oaxaca* y *Catálogo de obras y archivo musical de la Catedral de Oaxaca. Antología* y autor del tercer tomo de *Tesoro de la música polifónica en México, 50 años de música en el Palacio de Bellas Artes, Salvador Contreras. Vida y obra.* Ha compuesto *Trifábula* (1982), *Danza-q* (1984), *Poema 9* (1987), *Jaray Arawi* (1988), *Constante* (1991) y *Las premoniciones de Añada* (1993), entre otras.

TELLO, MANUEL C. ♦ n. en Córdoba y m. en Orizaba, Ver. (1884-1963). Profesor normalista. Fue director de la Escuela Normal Veracruzana (1922, 1930-32 y 1941-45) y fundador de la Facultad de Pedagogía de la Universidad Veracruzana (1954). Autor de *Prácticas pedagógicas, Fundamentos generales de la pedagogía, Cursos de pedagogía, Principios de educación, Antropología pedagógica* y *El obrero.*

TELLO, RAFAEL J. ♦ n. y m. en el DF (1872-1974). Compositor. Estudió con Carlos J. Meneses (1884-88), Julio Ituarte (1889-98) y Ricardo Castro (1898-1904). Fue profesor (1902-14), subdirector (1914) y director del Conservatorio Nacional de Música (1914-1915 y 1938). Fundador (1917) y director del Conservatorio Libre (1917), profesor de la Escuela Nacional de Maestros, inspector de la SEP y profesor de la Escuela Universitaria de Música. Autor de las óperas *Juno* (1896), *Nicolás Bravo* (1910), *Due amori* (1916) y *El oidor* (1927); de una *Misa fúnebre* (1928), del poema sinfónico *Patria heroica* (1929) y de un *Tríptico mexicano* (1939), así como de *Mazurca* (1894), *Vals melodía* (1900), *Tarantela* (1900), *Madrigal para orquesta de cuerda* (1922), *Álbum de viaje* (1930), *Libera me Domine* (1931), *Brisas del ocaso* (1939), *Nieblas y albores* (1939) y *Pater Noster* (1945), entre otras.

TELLO ARRIAGA, GREGORIO ♦ n. en San Luis Potosí, SLP, y m. en el DF (1886-1976). Profesor normalista. Director de varias escuelas en Nayarit y Jalisco. Durante la revolución constitucionalista combatió en las fuerzas de Lucio Blanco. Fue diputado al Congreso Constituyente de 1916-17.

TELLO BARRAUD, MANUEL ♦ n. en Zacatecas, Zac., y m. en el DF (1898-1971). Se tituló como abogado en la Escuela Libre de Derecho. En 1924 ingresó al servicio exterior mexicano como vicecónsul en Brownsville, puesto que desempeñó también en Amberes y en Hamburgo. Fue cónsul en Berlín, Yokohama, Houston y Ginebra; secretario consejero de la embajada mexicana en Ginebra y delegado a las Conferencias Internacionales de Trabajo (1934-39), secretario y delegado suplente (1939) y delegado titular de México en la Sociedad de Naciones (1940-42); director del Servicio Diplomático y de Asuntos Políticos (1942-43), oficial mayor (1943) y subsecretario encargado del despacho Relaciones Exteriores (dos veces en 1944); secretario general de la Conferencia sobre Problemas Interamericanos de la Guerra y la Paz (1945), secretario de Relaciones Exteriores (1951-1952 y 1958-1964); embajador de México en EUA (1953-58) y senador de la República (1964-70). Autor de *Voces favorables a México en el Cuerpo Legislativo de Francia* (2 t., 1967).

Manuel Tello Barraud

TELLO MACÍAS, ALEJANDRO ♦ n. en el DF (1943). Hijo del anterior. Ingeniero civil (1962-67), especializado en planeación de obras en la UNAM (1967-68) y posgraduado en economía en la University of East Anglia, Gran Bretaña (1968-69). Ha sido subgerente de Comercio Exterior (1977-78) y subgerente encargado de Sistematización de Conasupo (1978); y jefe del Departamento de Planeación Financiera (1979), director de Estudios y Proyectos (1980) y director de Planeación y Fomento de Astilleros Unidos de la Secretaría de Energía (1981-92).

TELLO MACÍAS, CARLOS ♦ n. en Suiza (1938). Mexicano por nacimiento. Hermano del anterior. Licenciado en administración de empresas por la Georgetown University, EUA (1955-58), maestro en economía por la Universidad de Columbia (1958-59) y doctor por la Universidad de Cambridge (1961-63). Profesor de la UNAM (1960-87) y de El Colegio de México (1964-79), investigador del INAH (1978-) y del Wilson Center for US-Mexican Studies de la Universidad de California (1984-85). Ha sido subdirector general de Crédito (1971-74) y subsecretario de Ingresos de la Secretaría de Hacienda (1974-76); secretario de la Presidencia (1976) y de Programación y Presupuesto (1977); director general de Financiera Nacional Azucarera (1977-82), director general del Banco de México (1982), miembro de la Junta directiva de la UAM (1984-), embajador mexicano en Portugal (1987-88), presidente del Consejo Consultivo del Programa Nacional de Solidaridad

(1988-90) y embajador en Rusia (1990-92). Coautor de *La disputa por la nación* (1981), *México 83. A la mitad del túnel* (1983) y *El desafío mexicano* (1986). Compilador de *Las relaciones México-Estados Unidos* (1981) y *La desigualdad en México* (1984), Autor de *La tenencia de la tierra en México* (1968), *La política económica en México 1970-76* (1979), *La nacionalización de la banca en México* (1984) y *Cartas desde Mosaí* (1995). Miembro de la Academia Mexicana de Economía Política.

TELLO MACÍAS, MANUEL ◆ n. en el DF (1935). Licenciado en relaciones internacionales por la Georgetown University (1953-57) y maestro en relaciones internacionales por el Instituto de Altos Estudios Internacionales de Ginebra (1963-65). Profesor de varias universidades e institutos. Ingresó a la SRE en 1957, donde ha sido jefe del Departamento de Tratados Internacionales de la Dirección General de Servicio Diplomático (1957-59), representante alterno de México ante la OEA (1969-63), ante los organismos internacionales con sede en Suiza (1963-66) y ante la Conferencia del Comité del Desarme (1963-69); subdirector general (1967-70) y director general de Organismos Internacionales (1970-72); representante mexicano en el Consejo del Organismo para la Proscripción de las Armas Nucleares en América Latina (1970-73); embajador (1972), director en jefe para Asuntos de Organismos Internacionales (1972-74), director en jefe para Asuntos Políticos (1974-76), embajador de México en Gran Bretaña (1977- 79), subsecretario de Asuntos Multilaterales (1979-82), representante permanente de México ante los organismos internacionales con sede en Ginebra (1982-89), embajador de México en Francia (1989) y secretario (1994). Autor de *La política exterior de México* (1970-74), *Algunos de los problemas que tendrá que resolver la III Conferencia de las Naciones Unidas sobre el derecho del mar* (1974) y *Documentos de política internacional* (1975).

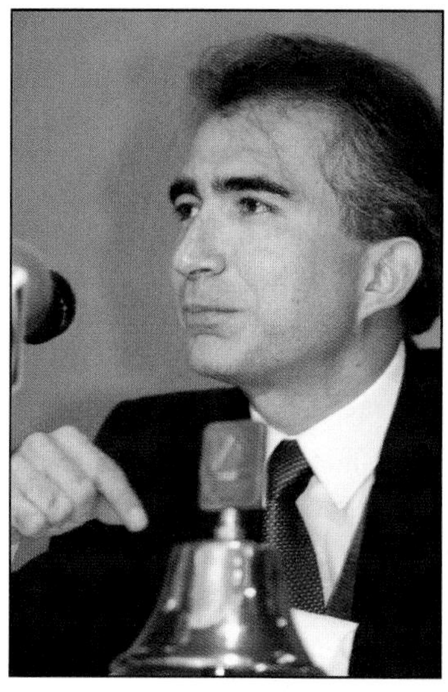

Jorge Tello Peón

TELLO PEÓN, JORGE ◆ n. en el DF (1956). Ingeniero civil titulado en la UAM con posgrado en hidráulica por la UNAM. Fue profesor de preparatoria y trabajó como ingeniero en empresas privadas. Ha sido subdirector de desarrollo tecnológico de la Dirección General de Investigaciones de Seguridad Nacional (1985-87), director de Servicios Técnicos del Centro de Investigación y Seguridad Nacional (1989-90), coordinador de asesores de la Coordinación para la Atención de los Delitos contra la Salud (1990-91) y del Centro de Planeación para el Control de Drogas (1991-93), director general del Centro de Investigación y Seguridad Nacional (1993-99) y subsecretario de Seguridad Pública de la Secretaría de Gobernación (1999-).

TELMO, EMMA ◆ n. en Cuba (1918). Actriz y locutora. Nombre profesional de Emmanuela Bruquetas Fernández. Desde su infancia formó parte de compañías teatrales. Llegó a México en 1930, donde actuó en el Teatro Ideal, al lado de sus padres. Ingresó en la XEW en 1935, y allí dio su voz a personajes de varias de las radionovelas más populares de ese tiempo, como *Elena Montalvo* (la primera hecha en México), *Anita de Montemar*, *Chucho el Roto* y *Una flor en el pantano*. Fue la primera locutora de *La hora nacional* y participó en la primera transmisión televisiva hecha en México (1942). Actuó en las películas *Los apuros de Narciso* (1939) y *La virgen que forjó una patria* (1942). Ha impartido clases de dicción y fraseo del español antiguo.

TELOLOAPAN ◆ Municipio de Guerrero situado en el norte de la entidad, al oeste de Iguala y al suroeste de Ixcateopan, en los límites con el Estado de México. Superficie: 1,116.1 km². Habitantes: 53,272, de los cuales 11,054 forman la población económicamente activa. Hablan alguna lengua indígena 1,401 personas mayores de cinco años (náhuatl 1,350). En la jurisdicción se encuentra Acatempan, lugar en el que, en 1821, unieron sus fuerzas Vicente Guerrero y Agustín de Iturbide, quienes constituyeron el Ejército de las Tres Garantías.

TELPOCHCALLI ◆ Escuela mexica a la que ingresaban los niños entre seis y nueve años. Ahí se les adiestraba para la guerra y se les ofrecían nociones elementales de religión. El nombre significa "Casa de los Jóvenes". Cada barrio o calpulli azteca tenía su propio telpochcalli y todos estaban consagrados a Tezcatlipoca. Quienes dirigían estos centros educativos recibían el nombre de telpochtlatos. Tanto los alumnos como los profesores tenían como uniforme un máxtlatl o taparrabo y una manta rala de fibras de maguey llamada clalcayatl. Los alumnos estaban obligados a conservar el celibato, so pena de severos castigos. La pereza se castigaba con la quema del cabello y la embriaguez con la muerte. Los estudiantes estaban obligados a trabajar en el mantenimiento de los templos y el cultivo común de la tierra para obtener su alimento. Los alumnos mayores que ya habían ido a la guerra, especialmente si habían ganado algún ascenso, podían llevar mujeres a sus habitaciones y ocasionalmente se les dejaba ir a dormir a sus casas. De aquellos centros salían cuando iban a casarse. Si deseaban retirarse antes, debían pagar un elevado precio al telpochtlato o esperar a que una orden sacerdotal los dejase libres.

Temamatla ◆ Municipio del Estado de México situado en la porción oriental de la entidad, al noreste de Amecameca y al sur de Chalco. Superficie: 48.72 km². Habitantes: 7,720, de los cuales 1,535 forman la población económicamente activa. Hablan alguna lengua indígena 35 personas mayores de cinco años (náhuatl 23 y mixteco 12). En la jurisdicción se halla la zona arqueológica del cerro de Tenayo. En la cabecera hay edificios coloniales, como la iglesia de Santiago Zula, construida en el siglo XVII, la iglesia de Reyes Acatlizhuayan, en el siglo XVIII, y la parroquia de Temamatla, construida en 1686.

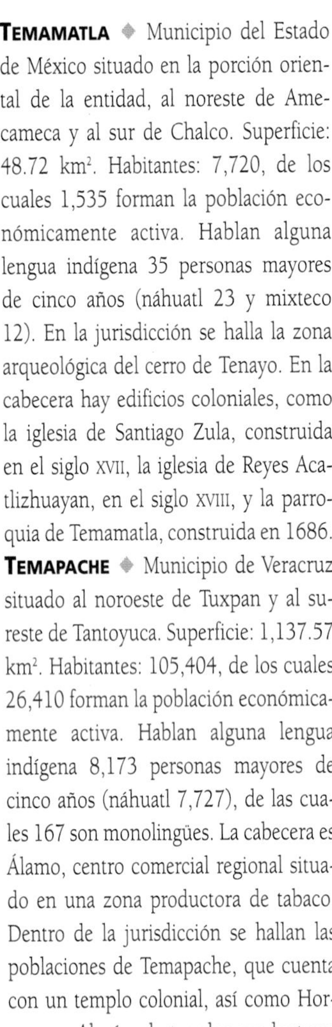

Francisco de Tembleque

Temapache ◆ Municipio de Veracruz situado al noroeste de Tuxpan y al sureste de Tantoyuca. Superficie: 1,137.57 km². Habitantes: 105,404, de los cuales 26,410 forman la población económicamente activa. Hablan alguna lengua indígena 8,173 personas mayores de cinco años (náhuatl 7,727), de las cuales 167 son monolingües. La cabecera es Álamo, centro comercial regional situado en una zona productora de tabaco. Dentro de la jurisdicción se hallan las poblaciones de Temapache, que cuenta con un templo colonial, así como Horcones y Alazán, destacados productores frutícolas, y el que fuera un importante campo petrolero de la Faja de Oro, Potrero del Llano, donde entre 1910 y 1937 se extrajeron más de 117 millones de barriles de crudo solamente del pozo Potrero del Llano 4.

Foto: Michael Calderwood

Temascaltepec, Estado de México

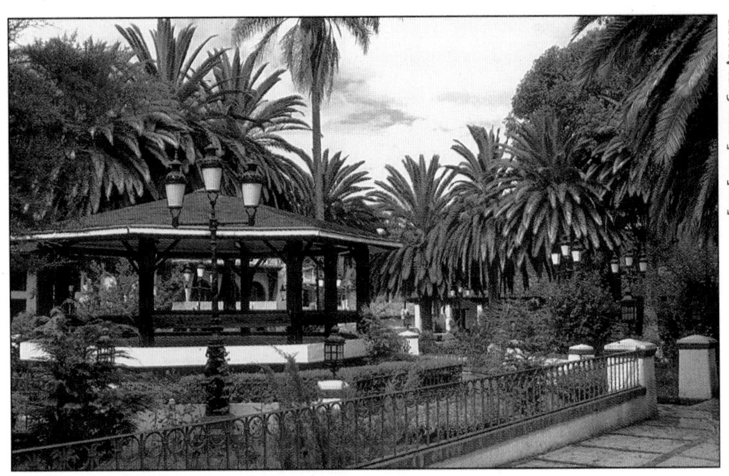

Foto: Fondo Editorial Grupo Azabache

Plaza de Armas de Temascaltepec, Estado de México

Temascalapa ◆ Municipio del Estado de México situado al norte de Texcoco y al este-noreste de Tepotzotlán, en los límites con Hidalgo. Superficie: 144.91 km². Habitantes: 24,440, de los cuales 5,098 forman la población económicamente activa. Hablan alguna lengua indígena 64 personas mayores de cinco años (mazahua 14 y otomí 11). En el municipio, que fue erigido en 1810, se encuentran las zonas arqueológicas de Teopancola y las Pastoras; la iglesia de San Juan Bautista, en Tercalco, y la parroquia de San Andrés de Ocotitlán.

Temascalcingo ◆ Municipio del Estado de México situado al noroeste de Atlacomulco y al oeste-suroeste de la laguna de Huapango, en los límites con Hidalgo y Michoacán. Superficie: 209.88 km². Habitantes: 59,140, de los cuales 11,279 forman la población económicamente activa. Hablan alguna lengua indígena 15,258 personas mayores de cinco años (mazahua 14,011 y otomí 1,247), de las cuales 209 son monolingües. En la jurisdicción se encuentran las ruinas de dos asentamientos prehispánicos, en Cerritos y Santa María Canchesda. La cabecera es Temascalcingo de José María Velasco y el ayuntamiento convirtió en museo la casa donde nació el pintor.

Temascaltepec ◆ Municipio del Estado de México situado al suroeste de Toluca y al sureste de Valle de Bravo. Superficie: 649.61 km². Habitantes: 26,643, de los cuales 6,770 forman la población económicamente activa. Hablan alguna lengua indígena 1,309 personas mayores de cinco años (metlatzinca 998 y náhuatl 311). En la jurisdicción se encuentran las zonas arqueológicas de Los Timbres, Pueblo Viejo, San Andrés de los Gama, San Lucas y San Pedro Tenayac. Entre 1560 y 1570, los conquistadores españoles fundaron el pueblo de Temascaltepec y construyeron un templo que todavía existe. Durante los primeros años de la Colonia hubo intensa actividad minera. El municipio fue erigido en 1824, poco después de que se segregara de Taxco el partido de Temascaltepec. En 1861, el Congreso mexiquense elevó a la categoría de villa al poblado. Desde entonces, la cabecera municipal se llama Temascaltepec de González. El principal atractivo turístico del municipio es un manantial de aguas termales situado en la localidad de Toxi.

Temascaltepec ◆ Río del Estado de México, Michoacán y Guerrero. Nace en la vertiente suroccidental del Nevado de Toluca, corre de este a oeste y recibe al río Ixtapantongo en los límites con Michoacán; vira al sureste, corre entre Michoacán y Guerrero y se une al Zitácuaro para tributar más adelante en el Cutzamala.

TEMASCALTEPEC, DE ◆ Sierra del Estado de México que forma parte del Sistema Volcánico Transversal. Está situada en la porción suroccidental de la entidad. Se extiende al oeste del Nevado de Toluca, al sur de Valle de Bravo y al norte del río de su mismo nombre. Tiene yacimientos minerales.

TEMAX ◆ Municipio de Yucatán situado al este de Motul y al noroeste de Valladolid. Superficie: 329.57 km². Habitantes: 6,672, de los cuales 1,636 forman la población económicamente activa. Hablan alguna lengua indígena 2,608 personas mayores de cinco años (maya 2,607). En la actual cabecera se asentó el señorío maya de Kin-chel.

TEMAZCAL, DEL ◆ Sierra de Durango, también llamada del Pedregal, situada al noreste de la sierra de Santa María. Es una de las estribaciones septentrionales de la sierra de Zacatecas. Se extiende hacia el sureste y separa al llano de Tapona de los de Estanzuela y la Purísima.

TEMBLEQUE, FRANCISCO DE ◆ n. en España y ¿m. en Puebla, Pue.? (?-¿1589?). Fraile franciscano. Llegó a la Nueva España hacia 1540 y aunque no tenía conocimientos de ingeniería o arquitectura, tres años después inició la construcción de un acueducto para unir el cerro de Tecajete con Otumba (45 km aproximadamente), que terminó 17 años después, en 1560.

TEMILOTZIN ◆ n. en Tlatelolco (?-1525). Poeta y guerrero mexica. Fue gobernador de Tzinacatlan. Participó en la defensa de México-Tenochtitlan en 1521 y en agosto de ese año fue capturado junto con Cuauhtémoc. Dos años después fue llevado en la expedición de Hernán Cortés a las Hibueras. Su obra poética fue recopilada y publicada en el volumen *Romances de los señores de Nueva España*.

TEMIXCO ◆ Municipio de Morelos situado al sur de Cuernavaca y al este de Cuautla. Superficie: 75.75 km². Habitantes: 87,967, de los cuales 19,416 forman la población económicamente activa. Hablan alguna lengua indígena 2,648 personas mayores de cinco años (náhuatl 2,475).

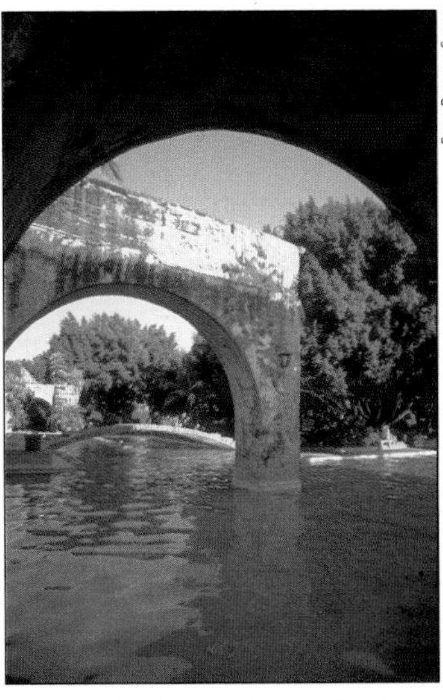
FOTO: BORIS DE SWAN

Antigua hacienda en Temixco, Morelos

TEMKIN, BENJAMÍN ◆ n. en Monterrey (1945). Emigró a Israel en 1961. Hizo estudios de relaciones internacionales en la Universidad de Jerusalén y un doctorado en la Universidad de Columbia. Fue el segundo judío de origen mexicano en ingresar al Parlamento israelí, tras triunfar en una elección como candidato del partido Meretz en 1992.

TEMOAC ◆ Municipio de Morelos situado al sureste y cerca de Cuautla, en los límites con Puebla. Superficie: 47.24 km². Habitantes: 11,896, de los cuales 2,365 forman la población económicamente activa. Hablan alguna lengua indígena 52 personas mayores de cinco años (náhuatl 47). El municipio fue erigido en marzo de 1977.

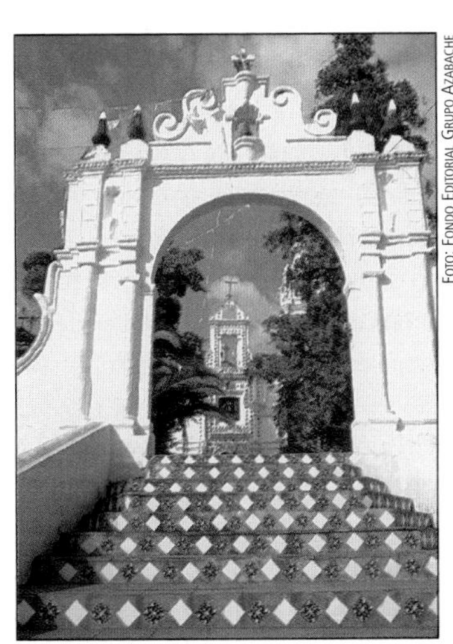
FOTO: FONDO EDITORIAL GRUPO AZABACHE

Templo del Señor de la Columna en Temoac, Morelos

TEMOAYA ◆ Municipio del Estado de México situado al norte de Toluca y al oeste de Naucalpan. Superficie: 111.18 km². Habitantes: 60,851, de los cuales 12,277 forman la población económicamente activa. Hablan alguna lengua indígena 19,772 personas mayores de cinco años (otomí 19,748), de las cuales 692 no saben el español. En la jurisdicción se hallan las zonas arqueológicas de Santiago Temoaya y Jiquipilco el Viejo. Durante la Colonia fueron construidas las iglesias de Santiago (siglo XVI), San Diego Alcalá y San José Pathé, así como la capilla de San Pedro. La cabecera ha adquirido renombre internacional por la manufactura de tapetes de lana o algodón, elaborados de acuerdo con la técnica autóctona de los otomíes. Cada uno de estos tapetes, en cuya confección los artesanos pueden demorar hasta 40 días, tiene estampados de colores firmes, con dibujos que representan las ideas y creencias de los indígenas de la región. A mediados de los setenta se erigió en su territorio el Centro Ceremonial Otomí, que preserva los valores culturales, la identidad y la cohesión de los otomíes, dentro de un parque ecológico.

FOTO: FONDO EDITORIAL GRUPO AZABACHE

Tapetes y tejedoras indígenas de Temoaya, Estado de México

TÉMORIS ◆ Cabecera del municipio chihuahuense de Guazapares (☛).

TEMÓSACHIC ◆ Municipio de Chihuahua situado al oeste de la capital de la entidad, en los límites con Sonora, y contiguo a Madera y Guerrero. Superficie: 5,361.91 km². Habitantes: 7,409, de los cuales 2,373 forman la población económicamente activa. Hablan alguna lengua indígena 296 personas (pima 252 y tarahumara 44). En 1676, los jesuitas Tomás de Guadalajara y José Tardá fundaron la población de San Francisco Javier de Temósachi, donde ahora se halla la cabecera municipal.

FOTO: FONDO EDITORIAL GRUPO AZABACHE

Hacienda en Temozón, Yucatán

TEMOZÓN ◆ Municipio de Yucatán situado al norte de Valladolid y al sur de Tizimín, en los límites con Quintana Roo. Superficie: 1,087.06 km^2. Habitantes: 11,659, de los cuales 2,638 forman la población económicamente activa. Hablan alguna lengua indígena 9,167 personas mayores de cinco años (maya 9,164) y de ellas, 1,960 son monolingües.

TEMPLETON, RINI ◆ n. en EUA y m. en el DF (1935-1986). Grabadora. Su nombre era Lucille Corinne Templeton. Escribió poesía, que publicó en diarios de Washington, y fue editora de un periódico en Nuevo México. Estudió escultura en Inglaterra (1956). Vivió en Cuba (1959-64), donde participó en la campaña de alfabetización y en la zafra, y donde fundó el Taller de Grabado de Catedral, en La Habana. Llegó a México en 1974. Estudió grabado en La Esmeralda. Participó en el Taller de Gráfica Popular. Estuvo ligada a movimientos populares, para lo que hizo ilustraciones, volantes, carteles y mantas. Al morir elaboraba material gráfico para los damnificados de Tlatelolco por el sismo de 1985. Póstumamente se montó una exposición de su obra, *Donde hay vida hay lucha*, y se editó *El arte de Rini Templeton. Donde hay vida hay lucha* (1989, edición en español e inglés).

FOTO: BORIS DE SWAN

Templo Mayor, en el DF

TEMPLO MAYOR ◆ Centro político y religioso de los mexicas, situado en el centro de la ciudad de México-Tenochtitlan, sobre la intersección de las calzadas Tepeyacac-Iztapalapa y Tlacopan. El recinto ocupaba un área rectangular de 3,900 m. (325 x 312 m), rodeado por la muralla Cohuatepantli, "bandera de víboras". Su principal construcción era el gran teocalli o templo mayor, del que actualmente puede observarse una parte de la base en la esquina de las actuales calles de Guatemala y Argentina. Era una pirámide de base rectangular, de 100 por 80 metros, que tenía cuatro o cinco cuerpos en talud, con pasillos entre uno y otro, escalinatas y un remate para los estandartes. En la cima, a 30 metros de altura, se encontraban dos templos, uno dedicado a Tláloc, el del norte, y el otro a Huitzilopochtli, el del sur. Ambos edificios tenían en su interior las estatuas de los dioses sobre pedestales. La localización del sitio preciso en el que se hallaba el Templo Mayor correspondió a Manuel Gamio, quien en 1913 inició una serie de excavaciones en el costado oriente de la Catedral Metropolitana y en el norte del Palacio Nacional. Ahí descubrió estructuras correspondientes a una de las etapas de erección del templo, en el ángulo suroeste, con lo que desmintió la creencia generalizada de que el más importante templo de los mexicas estaba exactamente debajo de la catedral, como lo afirmaban diversas crónicas. El 23 de febrero de 1978, un grupo de trabajadores de la Compañía de Luz y Fuerza que realizaban una labor rutinaria de mantenimiento, descubrieron la efigie de la diosa Coyolxauhqui. El hallazgo motivó un decreto presidencial por el que se autorizaba un trabajo mayor de exploración que quedó a cargo de Eduardo Matos Moctezuma, quien fue asesorado por Miguel León Portilla. Las exploraciones duraron cinco años. De acuerdo con los descubrimientos realizados por Matos y León-Portilla, el templo fue reedificado siete veces, ampliado 11 y su construcción se inició en el año 2 conejo (1390 en el calendario occidental); el estudio de los códices prehispánicos indica que el templo mayor era una representación del Cerro de la Serpiente (*Coatépetl*), donde, según la mitología náhuatl, nació Huitzilopochtli, hijo de Coatlicue. A los lados del templo mayor se descubrieron, asimismo, restos de santuarios menores, de un *tzompantli* (armazón en el que se conservaban, como trofeos de guerra, cráneos humanos) y un conjunto de habitaciones con frisos y pinturas murales, probablemente sitio de reunión de caballeros águila.

Un aspecto del Templo Mayor

TEMPOAL ◆ Municipio de Veracruz situado al noroeste de Tuxpan y al suroeste de Tampico, en los límites con San Luis Potosí. Superficie: 1,130.21

km². Habitantes: 35,600, de los cuales 9,357 forman la población económicamente activa. Hablan alguna lengua indígena 2,369 personas mayores de cinco años (huasteco 1,938).

TEMPOAL ◆ Río de Veracruz formado por la confluencia de las corrientes de Calabozo y del Hule, al norte de la población hidalguense de Huejutla. Corre de sur a norte, recibe al San Pedro y une su curso al Moctezuma, al oeste de El Higo, en los límites con San Luis Potosí.

TENA, FELIPE DE JESÚS ◆ n. en Panindícuaro, Mich., y m. en el DF (1873-1958). Se tituló en 1899 en la Escuela de Jurisprudencia de Michoacán, de la que fue profesor y director. También ejerció la docencia en la UNAM. En Michoacán fue gobernador interino (1911), secretario de Gobierno de Michoacán (1912-13), diputado a la Legislatura local y redactor del Código de Comercio (1926). Se desempeñó como jefe de los departamentos jurídicos de las secretarías de Salubridad y Asistencia y de Gobernación y ministro de la Suprema Corte de Justicia de la Nación (?-1954). Autor de *Derecho mercantil mexicano I* (1922) y *Derecho mercantil mexicano II* (1939).

TENA, LUCERO ◆ n. en el DF (1939). Bailarina. Nombre profesional de María de la Luz Tena Álvarez. Radica desde niña en España. Hizo estudios de danza clásica con Nina Scheskova, danza española con Emilia Díaz y baile flamenco con Carmen Amaya, con cuya compañía viajó a España. Regresó a México para su primera presentación en el Palacio de Bellas Artes en 1960. Ha hecho giras por todo el mundo. Es crotalista y para ella se han compuesto la *Suite para castañuelas y orquesta* de Joaquín Rodrigo (1975), la *Sonata Trianera* de Federico Moreno Torroba y *Tres anécdotas. Concierto para castañuelas y orquesta* de Leonardo Balada, entre otras.

TENA, MIGUEL ◆ n. en Cuitzeo y m. en Morelia, Mich. (¿1835?-1905). Médico. Fue profesor en los hospitales republicanos durante la invasión francesa y, como médico militar, participó en la batalla del 5 de mayo. Al triunfo de la República fue profesor del Colegio de San Nicolás de Hidalgo. Autor de un *Calendario Botánico de Michoacán* (1893).

TENA OROZCO, GERMÁN ◆ n. en Morelia, Mich. (1934). Ganadero. Miembro del Partido Acción Nacional. Ha sido presidente del Comité Directivo Regional del PAN en Michoacán, tesorero y secretario de la Unión Ganadera Regional de la misma entidad y diputado federal (1985-88).

TENA RAMÍREZ, FELIPE ◆ n. en Morelia, Mich., y m. en el DF (1905-1994). Licenciado en derecho por la UNAM (1929), donde ejerció la docencia y dirigió el Seminario de Derecho Constitucional y Administrativo. Fue ministro de la Suprema Corte de Justicia de la Nación. Autor de *Derecho constitucional mexicano* (1944) y *Leyes fundamentales de México* (1957). Premio Nacional de Jurisprudencia 1991.

TENABO ◆ Municipio de Campeche situado en el litoral del golfo de México y contiguo a la capital de la entidad. Superficie: 882 km². Habitantes: 7,630, de los cuales 1,792 forman la población económicamente activa. Hablan alguna lengua indígena 2,215 personas mayores de cinco años (maya 2,203).

TENACATITA ◆ Bahía de Jalisco situada en el litoral del océano Pacífico, en la porción suroriental del estado. Se encuentra al sur de la desembocadura del río Purificación, al suroeste de Autlán, y se abre hacia el suroeste, entre las puntas Hermanos y Cabeza de Navidad, al noroeste de la barra de Navidad.

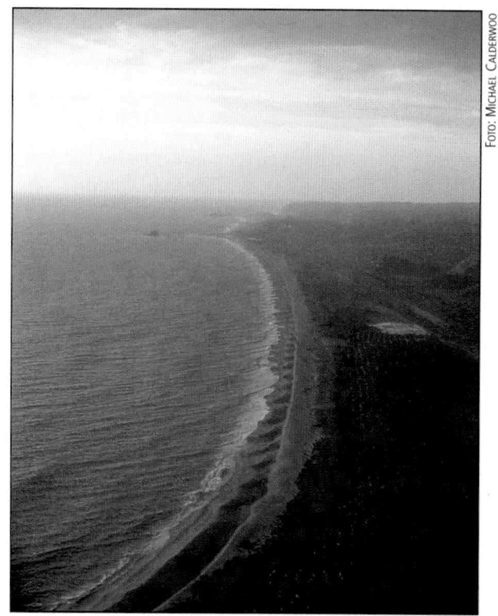
Foto: Michael Calderwoo

Bahía de Tenacatita, Jalisco

TENAMAXTLÁN ◆ Municipio de Jalisco situado al noreste de Autlán y al suroeste de Ameca. Superficie: 337.99 km². Habitantes: 7,195, de los cuales 1,671 forman la población económicamente activa.

TENAMPA ◆ Municipio de Veracruz situado al norte de Córdoba y al sur de Jalapa. Superficie: 69.92 km². Habitantes: 5,052, de los cuales 1,229 forman la población económicamente activa. Hablan alguna lengua indígena 27 personas mayores de cinco años (náhuatl 25).

TENAMPULCO ◆ Municipio de Puebla situado al oeste de Huauchinango y al norte de Teziutlán, en los límites con Veracruz. Superficie: 108.44 km². Ha-

Foto: Fondo Editorial Grupo Azabache

Tenabo, Campeche

bitantes: 7,002, de los cuales 2,037 forman la población económicamente activa. Hablan alguna lengua indígena 1,115 personas mayores de cinco años (náhuatl 604 y totonaco 510). La fiesta del santo patrono del municipio se celebra el 8 de septiembre, con jaripeos, música, danzas, procesiones y ofrendas.

TENANCINGO ◆ Municipio del Estado de México situado al sur-sureste de Toluca y al nor-noreste de Ixtapan de la Sal. Superficie: 127.42 km². Habitantes: 64,753, de los cuales 16,526 forman la población económicamente activa. Hablan alguna lengua indígena 123 personas mayores de cinco años (náhuatl 15 y mazahua 12). En la jurisdicción se realiza una intensa actividad artesanal que comprende el tejido de rebozos, la alfarería, la elaboración de licores de frutas y la manufactura de muebles de mimbre y de tule. Cuenta con canteras de mármol y ónix y depósitos de ópalo. En él se encuentran las zonas arqueológicas de Acatzingo, Tlapanalco, Coapastongo, La Muralla y Tenancingo. En ésta se han encontrado restos de un mamut, petroglifos y cerámica azteca. En Tenancingo está el monasterio carmelita del Santo Desierto, construido en el siglo XVIII, en el cual se halla el Cristo de las Siete Suertes, imagen de madera de tamaño natural. En la cabecera, Tenancingo de Degollado, se levanta la iglesia de Nuestra Señora de los Dolores o de Tenancingo, erigida donde antiguamente hubo una posada en la que se veneraba la imagen de la virgen María al pie de la cruz; a esta imagen se le atribuyeron milagros y se le erigió una ermita que en el siglo XIX se convirtió en parroquia, convertida después en la Basílica Clementina de Tenancingo.

Convento en Tenancingo, Estado de México

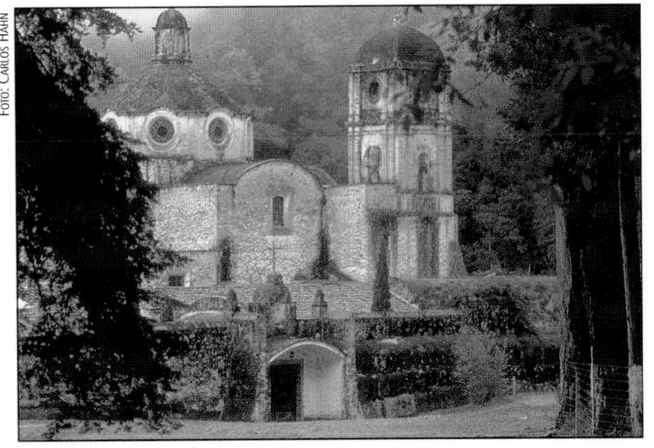
FOTO: CARLOS HAHN

FOTO: CARLOS HAHN

Panorámica de Tenancingo, Estado de México

TENANCINGO ◆ Municipio de Tlaxcala situado al sur de la capital de la entidad, en los límites con Puebla. Superficie: 17.1 km². Habitantes: 9,597, de los cuales 2,389 forman la población económicamente activa. Hablan alguna lengua indígena 509 personas mayores de cinco años (náhuatl 506).

TENANGO, DE ◆ Sierra del Estado de México que forma parte del Sistema Volcánico Transversal. Se extiende de oeste a este, desde el Nevado de Toluca hasta las estribaciones de las sierras del Ajusco y de las Cruces, al noroeste de Cuernavaca. Es el límite meridional del valle de Toluca.

TENANGO, DE ◆ Sierra de Guerrero que es una de las estribaciones septentrionales de la sierra Madre del Sur. Se extiende de este a oeste, al oriente del valle de Chilpancingo y al noroeste de la sierra de Malinaltepec.

TENANGO DEL AIRE ◆ Municipio del Estado de México situado al noroeste de Amecameca y al sur de Chalco. Superficie: 61.21 km². Habitantes: 7,282, de los cuales 1,784 forman la población económicamente activa. Hablan alguna lengua indígena 16 personas mayores de cinco años. En la cabecera municipal, Tenango de Tepopula, hay una parroquia que data de 1671. En la jurisdicción se encuentra la llamada pirámide de Tenango, descubierta en 1974.

TENANGO DE DORIA ◆ Municipio de Hidalgo situado al nor-noreste de Tulancingo y al noreste de Pachuca, en los límites con Puebla. Superficie: 210.7 km². Habitantes: 16,424, de los cuales 3,747 forman la población económicamente activa. Hablan alguna lengua indígena 4,356 personas mayores de cinco años (otomí 4,326), de las que son monolingües 507.

TENANGO DE RÍO BLANCO ◆ Cabecera del municipio veracruzano de Río Blanco (☛).

TENANGO DEL VALLE ◆ Municipio del Estado de México situado al sur de Toluca y al norte de Tenancingo. Superficie: 181.14 km². Habitantes: 54,789, de los cuales 12,471 forman la población económicamente activa. Hablan alguna lengua indígena 194 personas mayores de cinco años (otomí 30 y mazahua 15). La cabecera municipal, Tenango de Arista, recibió antes los nombres de Tenango y Tenango del Valle. Desde mediados del siglo VIII, grupos otomíes se instalaron en el cerro Tépetl, cerca de la cabecera municipal. En el siglo X fueron desplazados por otra etnia que, entre 900 y 1200, construyó en el cerro una pirámide con un estilo arquitectónico similar al de Teotihuacán. A principios del siglo XIII, el lugar fue conquistado por los matlaltzincas, quienes construyeron un pequeño templo en el cerro. En 1476, las tropas mexicas de Axayácatl tomaron la población y desde entonces se convirtió en tributaria de México-Tenochtitlan. En 1560 los españoles se adueñaron del lugar. Poco después construyeron la parroquia de Tenango, la capilla del monte Calvario y el templo de Atlatahuaca. Hacia 1670, las alcaldías mayores de Atlatlahuaca del Valle y Tenango del Valle se unieron para formar la provincia de Tenango del Valle, sufragánea de la del Valle de Matlacingo. En 1768 se convirtió en subdelegación o partido de la intendencia de México. En el cerro de Tenango, en junio de 1812, las tropas insurgentes de Ignacio López Rayón, que avanzaban sobre Toluca, fueron derrotadas por el ejército colonial mandado por Anastasio Bustamante. En la cabecera municipal se encuentra el Museo Arqueológico de Tenango.

Tenayuca ◆ Ciudad arqueológica situada en la delegación Gustavo A. Madero del Distrito Federal. Consta de una gran pirámide, que muestra huellas de ocho ampliaciones, con una base de 62 por 50 metros. Según los investigadores, cada ampliación corresponde a un ciclo de 52 años. La construcción original data, aproximadamente del año 960 de nuestra era. Tenayuca fue la capital de los acolhuas de Xólotl, Nopaltzin y Tlotzin, antes de que, en el siglo XIII, Quinatzin, el cuarto rey, trasladara la nueva capital a Texcoco.

Tenejapa ◆ Municipio de Chiapas contiguo a San Cristóbal de Las Casas. Superficie: 99.4 km². Habitantes: 27,614, de los cuales 8,043 forman la población económicamente activa. Hablan alguna lengua indígena 22,657 personas mayores de cinco años (tzeltal 22,602). Las principales fiestas son la de la Santa Cruz, el 3 de mayo; del apóstol Santiago, el 25 de julio, y de la Natividad de la Virgen, el 8 de septiembre.

Ténoch ◆ m. en México-Tenochtitlan (?-¿1363?). Segundo hijo de Iztacmixcóatl y uno de los caudillos de la peregrinación azteca de Aztlán a Tenochtitlan. Algunos autores sostienen que Ténoch es un mito; otros, como Cecilio A. Robelo, indican que se trató de un personaje real mitificado. Fue uno de los encargados de solicitar al señor de Colhuacan el permiso para establecerse en la zona lacustre del valle de México. Gobernó a los aztecas desde 1269 y en 1325 dirigió la construcción de Tenochtitlan, llamada así en su honor.

Tenochtitlan ◆ ☛ *México- Tenochtitlan.*

Tenochtitlan ◆ Municipio de Veracruz situado al noroeste del puerto jarocho y al nor-noroeste de Jalapa. Superficie: 82.25 km². Habitantes: 5,142, de los cuales 1,451 forman la población económicamente activa. Hablan alguna lengua indígena 12 personas mayores de cinco años.

Tenorio, Miguel Ángel ◆ n. en el DF (1954). Dramaturgo. Licenciado en ciencias de la comunicación por la UAM. Profesor de la UNAM. Tuvo la beca Salvador Novo (1975-77) y la del Fonca en dramaturgia (1989-90). Escribe guiones para televisión. Ha colaborado en *Punto de Partida, El Búho, El Heraldo de México* y otras publicaciones. Autor de cuento: *El burro baturro, Que sí, que no, que todo se acabó, Adán, Eva y la serpiente blanca* y *Ahí, te va una de piratas*; y teatro: *Colgar la vida, Un banana split, Naufragio, Las sirvientas y las tentaciones, El paletero tenía razón, Decisión, Mañana me caso, Cambio de valencia o el espíritu de lucha* (1975), *El día que Javier se puso águila* (1979), *En español se dice abismo* (1979), *Detrás de una margarita* (1983), *El cielo nuestro que se va a caer* (1984), *Dónde está la cajita* (1984), *Naufragio sobre una pareja de enamorados* (1985), *Y en el principio era sólo rock'n roll o de naufragios y otras miserias* (1987), *Nos vemos en el Ángel, ¿Quién paga?, La botana, Al romper el alba* (1989), *La casada imperfecta* (primer lugar del concurso dramaturgos de fin de Siglo de Socicultur, 1989), *Dormía soñándose bella, porque era de la clase media* (1990), *El hombre del sureste* (1990) y *La clave de Martinillo* (1993). Miembro de la Sogem. Desde 1994 pertenece al SNCA. En 1979 y 1984 obtuvo el premio de dramaturgia Celestino Gorostiza; en 1978 el Premio *Punto de Partida* y en 1987 el Cuauhtémoc de las Artes.

Tenorio Adame, Antonio ◆ n. en Tehuacán, Pue. (1936). Licenciado en economía por la UNAM. Profesor de la Universidad Autónoma de Sinaloa y de la UNAM (1971-75). Ha sido analista de la Gerencia de la Comisión del Río Balsas (1966-67), director de Planeación y Estadística de la Universidad Autónoma de Sinaloa (1967) y director de la Carta Nacional Agraria y del Centro de Estudios Históricos del Agrarismo en México de la Secretaría de la Reforma Agraria. Diputado federal en tres ocasiones (1976-79, 1985-88 y 1994-97). Perteneció al PRI, en el que fue delegado general del CEN en Chiapas (1979), representante ante el Movimiento Mexicano por la Paz (1979-81) y subsecretario de Capacitación Política del CEN. A fines de 1988 renunció a su militancia en el PRI para participar en el FDN y en la fundación y organización del PRD, partido al que pertenece desde 1989. Ha colaborado en la *Revista del México Agrario, La República* y otras publicaciones. Miembro fundador de la Unión de Periodistas Democráticos.

Tenorio Galindo, Tomás ◆ n. en Tierra Colorada, Gro. (1962). Periodista. Hizo estudios de pedagogía en la UNAM (1984). Se inició en la revista bibliográfica *Pie de Página* (1982-84). Ha sido secretario de redacción de *La Jornada, El Financiero* y *El Nacional*. Jefe de Noticieros de Radio UNAM (1995-97). Jefe de redacción de *Crónica* (1995-), periódico donde escribe sobre política nacional.

Foto: Eikon

Tomás Tenorio Galindo

Tenorio Muñoz Cota, Antonio ◆ n. en el DF (1966). Sociólogo egresado de la UNAM. Ha hecho estudios de letras modernas en la UIA, donde es profesor. Desde 1987 colabora en publicaciones culturales. Autor de ensayo: *Milan Kundera. La sabiduría de lo incierto* (1996); cuento: *No invoques mi amor en vano* (1997); y novela: *Más breve que una vida* (1999). Ha sido becario del Fonca (1995-96).

Tenosique ◆ Municipio de Tabasco situado en el extremo suroriental del estado, en los límites con Chiapas y Guatemala. Superficie: 2,098.10 km². Habitantes: 55,438, de los cuales 12,836 forman la población económicamente activa. Hablan alguna lengua indígena 2,480 personas mayores de cinco años (tzeltal 1,154, chol 1,007 y maya 86) y son monolingües 176. En la jurisdicción se encuentran las zonas arqueológicas de Boca del Cerro, Pomona y Penjalé. La cabecera municipal, Tenosique de Pino Suárez, es un importante centro comercial, maderero y ganadero de la región.

TENTACIÓN, DE LA ◆ Cumbres de Guerrero situadas en la región occidental del estado, que forman parte de la cresta principal de la sierra Madre del Sur. Se extienden de noroeste a sureste, al noreste de Petatlán. En su extremo suroriental se encuentra el cerro Grande, que se eleva 2,650 metros sobre el nivel del mar. De su vertiente meridional se desprenden los ríos San Jerónimo, Petatlán, Coyuquilla y San Luis de la Loma.

TENTZÓN ◆ Sierra de Puebla también llamada Tentzo. Se encuentra en el borde meridional del Sistema Volcánico Transversal, al sur de la presa de Valsequillo. Es la prolongación noroccidental de la sierra de Zapotitlán. Limita por el sur al valle de Puebla y por el oeste al de Tecamachalco. De su vertiente meridional surge el río Huehuetlán, tributario del Atoyac.

TEOAMOXTLI ◆ Libro sagrado de los toltecas compilado hacia el siglo VIII, que reunía textos de historia, moral, religión, arte, literatura, astronomía, filosofía, arquitectura y ciencia. Se sabe de él sólo por referencias.

TEOCALTICHE ◆ Municipio de Jalisco situado al oeste de Lagos de Moreno y al noreste de Guadalajara, en los límites con Zacatecas y Aguascalientes. Superficie: 895.60 km^2. Habitantes: 37,164, de los cuales 8,423 forman la población económicamente activa. Hablan alguna lengua indígena 17 personas mayores de cinco años.

TEOCELO ◆ Municipio de Veracruz situado al sur de Jalapa y al oeste-noroeste del puerto de Veracruz. Superficie: 54.29 km^2. Habitantes: 14,050, de los cuales 4,026 forman la población económicamente activa. Hablan alguna lengua indígena 24 personas mayores de cinco años. El municipio es conocido por su producción cafetalera. La cabecera fue elevada a la categoría de villa el 17 de mayo de 1881 y a la de ciudad, con el nombre de Teocelo de Díaz, el 11 de junio de 1899. Un año antes se había inaugurado en la jurisdicción la planta hidroeléctrica de Texolo.

TEOCOCUILCO DE MARCOS PÉREZ ◆ Municipio de Oaxaca situado al nor-noreste de la capital de la entidad, al sur-suroeste de Valle Nacional y al oeste de Ixtlán de Juárez. Superficie: 113.55 km^2. Habitantes: 1,729, de los cuales 242 forman la población económicamente activa. Hablan alguna lengua indígena 1,061 personas mayores de cinco años (zapoteco 852 y zapoteco de Ixtlán 207). El municipio se llamó San Pedro Teococuilco.

TEOCUITATLÁN DE CORONA ◆ Municipio de Jalisco situado al norte de Ciudad Guzmán y al sur de Guadalajara. Superficie: 409.88 km^2. Habitantes: 12,152, de los cuales 3,168 forman la población económicamente activa. Hablan alguna lengua indígena 13 personas mayores de cinco años.

TEOHUITZNÁHUAC ◆ Deidad nahua que por su nombre, "Dios rodeado de espinas", y por su origen, habría nacido de una virgen llamada Chalchihuitlicue, fue considerado como la versión nahua de Jesucristo por intelectuales novohispanos como Carlos de Sigüenza y Góngora, José Ignacio Borunda, Mariano Fernández de Echeverría y Veytia y Servando Teresa de Mier, entre otros, lo que les dio elementos para suponer que antes de la conquista española, el territorio mesoamericano había sido evangelizado por el apóstol Santiago o por Santo Tomás y que, por lo tanto, la cristianización de América, una de las principales justificaciones de la dominación española, había sido, en realidad, la conclusión de la obra de los apóstoles.

TEOIZTAC ◆ Deidad nahua que representaba y daba nombre a la tercera parte del cielo, identificado con el planeta Venus y el atardecer.

TEOLOCHOLCO ◆ Municipio de Tlaxcala situado al sureste de la capital de la entidad y al suroeste de Huamantla, en los límites con Puebla. Superficie: 58.4 km^2. Habitantes: 16,095, de los cuales 3,535 forman la población económicamente activa. Hablan alguna lengua indígena 1,212 personas mayores de cinco años (náhuatl 1,210).

TEOLOYUCAN ◆ Municipio del Estado de México contiguo a Tepotzotlán y Cuautitlán. Superficie: 34.98 km^2. Habitantes: 54,454, de los cuales 11,858 forman la población económicamente activa. Hablan alguna lengua indígena 203 personas mayores de cinco años (otomí 54 y náhuatl 35). El 13 de agosto de 1914, en las cercanías de la cabecera, representantes del gobierno de Francisco Carvajal y Venustiano Carranza firmaron los Tratados de Teoloyucan (☛), de acuerdo con los cuales se disolvió el viejo ejército federal. En la cabecera municipal hay una iglesia construida en el siglo XVII.

TEONNAPA ◆ Deidad nahua. Es una representación del dios del fuego, Xiuhtecutli, que era venerado por los comerciantes transhumantes, quienes, para reverenciarlo, se sangraban y esparcían varias gotas de sangre a los cuatro puntos cardinales.

TEOPANTLÁN ◆ Municipio de Puebla situado al sur y próximo a la capital de la entidad y al noreste de Izúcar de Matamoros. Superficie: 214.31 km^2. Habitantes: 5,203, de los cuales 1,331 forman la población económicamente activa. Hablan alguna lengua indígena 3,594 personas mayores de cinco años (náhuatl 3,594).

TEOPISCA ◆ Municipio de Chiapas situado al este-sureste de Tuxtla Gutiérrez y al sureste de San Cristóbal de Las Casas. Superficie: 173.9 km^2. Habitantes: 22,403, de los cuales 4,392 forman la población económicamente activa. Hablan alguna lengua indígena 6,966 personas mayores de cinco años (tzotzil 5,764 y tzeltal 1,177). En la jurisdicción hay una zona arqueológica y grutas que constituyen el principal atractivo turístico. Las principales fiestas son las de San Agustín, el 28 de agosto, y de San Sebastián, el 20 de enero. En la cabecera hay una parroquia colonial.

Retablo barroco del siglo XVIII de la Iglesia de San Agustín en Teopisca, Chiapas

TEOTENANTZIN ◆ Códice pictográfico elaborado sobre papel europeo del siglo XVIII, que se conserva en la Biblioteca Nacional de Antropología e Historia y que perteneció a Lorenzo Boturini. Representa a las diosas Chalchiuheucitl y Tonatzin, en una capilla sobre un cerro. En el reverso del documento, una leyenda señala: "Estas dos pinturas son unos diseños de la diosa que los indios nombran Teotenantzin, que quiere decir Madre de los Dioses, a quien en la gentilidad daban culto en el cerro de Tepeyácac, donde hoy lo tiene la virgen de Guadalupe".

TEOTEPEC ◆ Cerro de Guerrero situado en la cresta principal de la sierra Madre del Sur, al oeste de Chilpancingo. Con sus 3,700 metros sobre el nivel del mar, es la mayor elevación del estado. Tiene yacimientos de plata.

TEOTIHUACÁN ◆ Municipio del Estado de México situado en la porción nororiental de la entidad, al norte de Texcoco y al oeste de Cuautitlán. Superficie: 68.71 km^2. Habitantes: 39,183, de los cuales 8,692 forman la población económicamente activa. Hablan alguna lengua indígena 267 personas mayores de cinco años (mixteco 125 y otomí 52). Hacia el año 600 a.n.e., los primeros grupos nahuas se instalaron en el valle de Teotihuacán. 400 años después, cerca de 6,000 personas vivían en el valle y a partir del 200 a.n.e., luego del despoblamiento de Cuicuilco, el número aumentó hasta 10,000 habitantes. Paulatinamente los nahuas se concentraron en un solo pueblo, que alcanzó una superficie de más de 6 km^2, a orillas del lago de Texcoco que llegaba en ese tiempo hasta el poblado indígena. Teotihuacán se convirtió en uno de los principales centros económicos prehispánicos. Además de las primeras casas con cimientos de piedra, durante los últimos dos siglos anteriores de nuestra era se construyó la pirámide del Sol, se trazó la Micaotli o calzada de los muertos y se edificó la primera pirámide de la Luna. La del Sol se asienta sobre una base de 49,950 m^2. (222 x 225 m), mide 63 metros de altura y tiene cuatro cuerpos en talud y uno con tablero. La Micoatli era una avenida recta, orientada de nor-noreste a sur-suroeste, que terminaba en el actual río San Juan. La primera pirámide lunar, por su parte, limitaba por el norte la calzada de los muertos. El hecho de que en el diseño urbano sea más importante el templo de la luna, pues ahí desemboca la principal vía de la ciudad, se ha atribuido a la importancia que por entonces tenía entre los teotihuacanos el culto a la Madre Luna, suceso que refleja, quizá, la subsistencia del matriarcado como principal estructura familiar. Para los primeros años de nuestra era en Teotihuacán vivían unas 50,000 personas. Durante los tres y medio siglos posteriores, la ciudad creció hasta tener unos 100,000 habitantes, repartidos en 20 km^2. Se edificó, sobre el viejo templo, la pirámide de la Luna y se realizaron grandes edificios habitacionales, cuyas características permiten suponer que eran una suerte de multifamiliares mesoamericanos. La pirámide lunar se construyó sobre una base de 19,500 (150 x 130 m) y como su tamaño era mucho menor que la vieja pirámide del Sol, es posible suponer que por entonces se impuso definitivamente el culto solar en la ciudad. La otra construcción importante es la llamada Ciudadela, un recinto cuadrangular de 400 m^2 situado en el extremo meridional de la calzada de los muertos, más allá del río San Juan, donde se encuentra el templo de Ehécatl Quetzalcóatl. Estas dos construcciones fueron levantadas entre los siglos IV y VII. El Estado teotihuacano se consolidó y extendió su dominio económico, político y cultural hasta regiones como Kaminaljuyú, del altiplano guatemalteco, y algunas zonas situadas en el actual Belice.

Foto: Carlos Hahn

Calzada de los Muertos vista desde la Pirámide de la Luna en Teotihuacán, Estado de México

Foto: Claudio Contreras

Detalle de mural en Teotihuacán, Estado de México

Foto: Boris de Swan

Pirámide del Sol en Teotihuacán, Estado de México

Foto: Fondo Editorial Grupo Azabache

Ruinas de Teotihuacán, Estado de México

Entre los siglos IV y el VII, Teotihuacán alcanzó su mayor desarrollo. Si bien la superficie de la ciudad tenía unos 19 km², su población ha sido calculada en 200,000 personas. Entre los años 650 y 750, el Estado teotihuacano se desmoronó y la ciudad se despobló paulatinamente, hasta quedar abandonada. Desde el punto de vista cultural, de la etapa teotihuacana parecen derivar muchas de las instituciones adoptadas después por los diversos pueblos de la región central de México. Su arquitectura, escultura, cerámica, pintura mural, religión y organización política y social fueron modelo imitado por los diversos pueblos nahuas. El hecho de que acudieran a esta ciudad los señores de las provincias para ser coronados, ha hecho pensar que la palabra Teotihuacán significa "Lugar donde se hacen los señores", pero como, según la mitología, allí nació el quinto sol y fue creada nuevamente la luna, bien puede significar "Lugar donde se hacen los dioses" o "Lugar de los dioses". En los restos de los edificios de Teotihuacán hay también pinturas ejecutadas al fresco. A pesar del despoblamiento, en los alrededores de la ciudad subsistieron algunos asentamientos indígenas. En 1548, los franciscanos construyeron un convento en la recién fundada villa de San Juan Teotihuacán, contigua a las ruinas de la ciudad. Nueve años después, los constructores cedieron el inmueble a los agustinos, lo que provocó airadas protestas de la población indígena del lugar, por lo que en 1559 el convento volvió a ser administrado por la orden de Franciscanos Menores. El 8 de diciembre de 1987 la UNESCO declaró patrimonio cultural de la humanidad al conjunto arqueológico. En el municipio existen numerosos manantiales de aguas termales. La cabecera es Teotihuacán de Arista.

Iglesia de Teotitlán del Valle, Oaxaca

Foto: Fondo Editorial Grupo Azabache

Foto: Claudio Contreras

Fresco en las ruinas de Teotihuacán, Estado de México

TEOTITLÁN DE FLORES MAGÓN ◆ Municipio de Oaxaca situado en el norte del estado, al oeste y cerca de Huautla de Jiménez, en los límites con Puebla. Superficie: 95.69 km². Habitantes: 7,084, de los cuales 1,831 forman la población económicamente activa. Hablan alguna lengua indígena 1,506 personas mayores de cinco años (náhuatl 920 y mazateco 517). Hasta mediados del siglo XX, el municipio se llamó Teotitlán del Camino y se le impuso su actual nombre en honor de los hermanos Flores Magón, pues ahí nacieron Enrique y Jesús. En la jurisdicción se encuentran los manantiales de Tizatepec y la Villada, así como las ruinas arqueológicas de Cerrito Hidalgo. La cabecera es también cabecera del distrito judicial de Teotitlán.

TEOTITLÁN DEL VALLE ◆ Municipio de Oaxaca situado al este de la capital de la entidad, al noreste de Ocotlán y al sur de Ixtlán de Juárez. Superficie: 81.65 km². Habitantes: 5,330, de los cuales 1,283 forman la población económicamente activa. Hablan alguna lengua indígena 4,064 personas mayores de cinco años (zapoteco 4,059), y de ellas 307 no saben español. En el municipio se elaboran sarapes y tapices, tejidos en telares domésticos y teñidos a la manera antigua. En la jurisdicción hay una zona arqueológica. En la cabecera se encuentra una iglesia construida en el siglo XVII. La principal festividad se celebra el 6 de junio.

TEOTL ◆ Deidad de los pueblos nahuas que existía dualmente, creador y origen de todas las cosas. Su contraparte era llamada Omeyotl (☛).

TEOTLALCO ◆ Municipio de Puebla situado al suroeste de la capital de la entidad y al oeste-suroeste de Izúcar de Matamoros, en los límites con Morelos. Superficie: 167.11 km². Habitantes: 3,076, de los cuales 601 forman la población económicamente activa.

TEOTONGO ◆ Municipio de Oaxaca situado al este-sureste de Huajuapan de León y al noroeste de Teposcolula. Superficie: 39.55 km². Habitantes: 1,154, de los cuales 308 forman la población económicamente activa. Hablan alguna lengua indígena 37 personas mayores de cinco años.

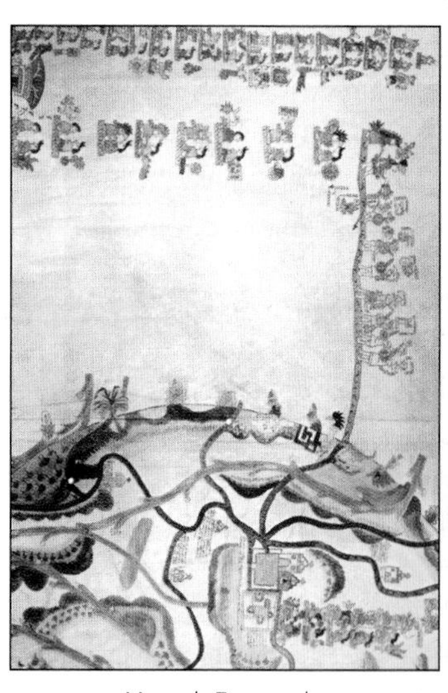

Mapa de Teozacoalco

TEOYAOMICQUI ◆ Deidad nahua. Una de las manifestaciones de la diosa Cihuacóatl, encargada de recoger las almas de los enemigos muertos en batalla, sobre todo los fallecidos en sacrificios o en las guerras floridas (☛). Con Huitzilopochtli, que tomaba el nombre de Teoyaotlatohua, formaba parte de la dualidad de los dioses guerreros.

TEOZACOALCO, MAPA DE ◆ Códice elaborado después de la conquista y que junto con una relación fue enviado al rey de España por el corregidor de Teozacoalco, Oaxaca. Contiene información geográfica e histórica de la zona mixteca y la genealogía de varios señores de Tilantongo y Teozacoalco (de 830 a 1580). El original que se encuentra en la biblioteca de la Universidad de Texas en Austin.

TEPACHE ◆ Municipio de Sonora situado al este de Ures y al sur de Moctezuma, cerca de Chihuahua. Superficie: 752.85 km^2. Habitantes: 1,611, de los cuales 856 forman la población económicamente activa. La actual cabecera fue fundada en 1670, con el nombre de Santa María de Depache. Más tarde se llamó Tepachi. Entre 1930 y 1932, el territorio quedó bajo la jurisdicción del ayuntamiento de Moctezuma. La fiesta más importante es la de Santa Teresa, que se celebra el 15 de octubre con bailes, juegos pirotécnicos, música, danzas y una feria popular.

TEPAKÁN ◆ Municipio de Yucatán situado al suroeste de Temax y al este-sureste de Motul. Superficie: 134.13 km^2. Habitantes: 2,193, de los cuales 663 forman la población económicamente activa. Hablan alguna lengua indígena 1,608 personas mayores de cinco años (maya 1,607).

TEPALCATEPEC ◆ Municipio de Michoacán situado al oeste de Apatzingán, al suroeste de Uruapan y contiguo a Coalcomán, en los límites con Jalisco. Superficie: 713.88 km^2. Habitantes: 24,678, de los cuales 6,677 forman la población económicamente activa. Hablan alguna lengua indígena 26 personas mayores de cinco años. La cabecera es Tepalcates.

TEPALCATEPEC ◆ Río de Michoacán y Jalisco, también llamado Grande. Nace en el suroriente del segundo estado, al sureste de Tamazula, de la confluencia de los ríos Quitupan y Tarécuato. Corre de norte a sur, recibe las aguas del San Diego y del San Jerónimo y entra en Michoacán, donde sus aguas son utilizadas para el Distrito de Riego de Tepalcatepec. La corriente, por su parte, tuerce al sureste al noroeste de Apatzingán, recibe al río del Marqués y desagua en la presa del Infiernillo, que también recibe al del Balsas.

TEPALCINGO ◆ Municipio de Morelos situado al sur-sureste de Cuautla, en los límites con Puebla. Superficie: 360.05 km^2. Habitantes: 23,329, de los cuales 4,911 forman la población económicamente activa. Hablan alguna lengua indígena 104 personas mayores de cinco años (náhuatl 71 y mixteco 19). En la jurisdicción se halla el balneario de Atotonilco y en la cabecera está el Santuario del Señor de las Tres Caídas.

TEPANECAS O TECPANECAS ◆ Indios nahuas que hacia el siglo XII de nuestra era, procedentes de Chicomoztoc, se instalaron en el valle de Anáhuac, que entonces estaba dominado por los chichimecas. El rey de éstos, Xólotl, al parecer casó a su hija Cuetlaxochitzin con el jefe de los recién llegados y les permitió asentarse en Azcapotzalco, donde, con el tiempo, formaron un señorío poderoso. Nueve reyes se sucedieron en el mando de los tepanecas hasta 1348, cuando Tezozómoc sucedió en el trono a su madre, Cihuaxóchitl; Tezozómoc llevó a los tepanecas a dominar el valle de Anáhuac, que disputaron exitosamente a los pueblos de Tlacopan, Xaltocan, Tenochtitlan, Texcoco, Colhuacan y Xochimilco. Bajo el reinado de Maxtlaton o Maxtla, hijo y sucesor de Tezozómoc, los tepanecas fueron derrotados en 1428 por los pueblos de Tlacopan, Tenochtitlan y Texcoco, confederados en la Triple Alianza.

TEPANCO DE LÓPEZ ◆ Municipio de Puebla situado al sureste de la capital de la entidad y al noroeste de Tehuacán. Superficie: 207.95 km^2. Habitantes: 14,714,

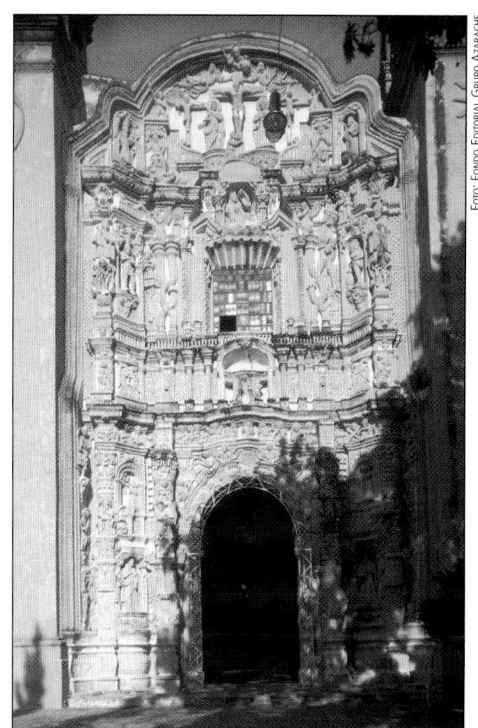

Foto: Fondo Editorial Grupo Azabache

Templo barroco en Tepalcingo, Morelos

de los cuales 3,191 forman la población económicamente activa. Hablan alguna lengua indígena 1,464 personas mayores de cinco años (popoloca 1,423).

TEPANGO DE RODRÍGUEZ ◆ Municipio de Puebla situado en la porción norte del estado, al nor-noreste de la capital de la entidad y al sureste de Huauchinango. Superficie: 20.42 km^2. Habitantes: 3,337, de los cuales 924 forman la población económicamente activa. Hablan alguna lengua indígena 2,641 personas mayores de cinco años (totonaco 2,627) y son monolingües 658.

TEPATITLÁN ◆ Sierra de Jalisco situada en el extremo oriental del estado, al noreste del lago de Chapala. Es el límite sur de la región de los Altos. Se extiende de oeste a este y enlaza con la sierra de Arandas.

TÉPATL, ASCENSIÓN ◆ n. en Pablo del Monte y m. en Tlaxcala, Tlax. (1883-1918). En 1909 se afilió al Partido Nacional Antirreeleccionista. Participó en la campaña electoral de Francisco I. Madero y en 1910 se levantó en armas. En 1913, perseguido por la policía huertista, se incorporó a las fuerzas carrancistas de Máximo Rojas; combatió en

Hidalgo, Puebla y Tlaxcala. Fue diputado al Congreso Constituyente de 1916-1917.

TEPATEPEC ◆ Cabecera del municipio hidalguense de Francisco I. Madero (☛).

TEPATITLÁN DE MORELOS ◆ Municipio de Jalisco situado al este de Guadalajara y al suroeste de San Juan de los Lagos. Superficie: 1,447.11 km². Habitantes: 109,300, de los cuales 26,626 forman la población económicamente activa. Hablan alguna lengua indígena 51 personas mayores de cinco años. La cabecera es el centro agrícola, ganadero, comercial e industrial más importante de la región de los Altos.

TEPATLAXCO ◆ Municipio de Veracruz situado al sur-sureste de Jalapa y al oeste del puerto de Veracruz. Superficie: 99.53 km². Habitantes: 6,841, de los cuales 2,070 forman la población económicamente activa. Hablan alguna lengua indígena 25 personas mayores de cinco años (náhuatl 23).

TEPATLAXCO DE HIDALGO ◆ Municipio de Puebla situado al noreste y próximo a la capital de la entidad, en los límites con Tlaxcala. Superficie: 51.03 km². Habitantes: 14,275, de los cuales 3,032 forman la población económicamente activa. Hablan alguna lengua indígena 3,302 personas mayores de cinco años (náhuatl 3,291).

TEPEACA ◆ Municipio de Puebla situado al este de Puebla y al noroeste de Tecamachalco. Superficie: 179.88 km². Habitantes: 56,665, de los cuales 11,839 forman la población económicamente activa. Hablan alguna lengua indígena 159 personas mayores de cinco años (náhuatl 99). Desde el siglo XI, el actual territorio del municipio estuvo habitado por grupos chichimecas, que a fines del siglo XII fueron conquistados por los toltecas, quienes fundaron el señorío de Tepeyacac hacia 1182. Dos siglos más tarde, en 1398, fuerzas de Tlatelolco conquistaron el señorío y lo sometieron al dominio del valle de México. Poco después los tlatelolcas fueron derrotados y expulsados y el señorío tolteca recuperó la independencia. Entre 1400 y 1442, durante el reinado de Cuetzpalin, Tepeyacac vivió una época de florecimiento económico y cultural, que terminó bruscamente luego de que, en 1459, se apoderó de la región el señorío de Cuauhtinchán. A causa de la derrota, muchos habitantes de Tepecayac emigraron hacia el valle de Toluca. Los que quedaron, reorganizaron el señorío en 1464, pero dos años más tarde fueron conquistados por los mexicas al mando de Axayácatl, los que desde 1491 debieron combatir contra Tlaxcala y Cholula. Fue a principios del siglo XVI cuando el senorío quedó firmemente bajo el dominio tenochca. En 1520, fuerzas de Hernán Cortés derrotaron a la guarnición azteca y fundaron la villa Segura de la Frontera, la segunda población establecida por los europeos. Ahí instalaron lo que se conoce como Rollo de Tepeaca, una columna de piedra coronada con una cruz, que se encontraba en la plaza principal de la villa y que servía como picota y horca. En 1532, el gobierno de Felipe II otorgó un escudo de armas a la población, que poco después recuperó su nombre original y a fines del siglo XVI se convirtió en Tepeaca. Dos años antes, en 1530, los franciscanos habían iniciado la construcción de un convento-fortaleza en Tepeaca, que fue concluido en 1580. En 1555, el gobierno virreinal creó la provincia de Tepeaca, que incluía Chalchicomula, Huatlatlauco, Nopaluca, Santiago Tecali, Tecamachalco y Tepeji. En 1559 la población se elevó a la categoría de ciudad. A principios del siglo XVII, en Tepeaca existían cuatro obrajes textileros y el desarrollo económico de los otros pueblos de la provincia obligó a las autoridades a fundar nuevas alcaldías mayores en el territorio de Tepeaca. Así, en 1605, Santiago Tecali se separó de la provincia y en 1665 se fundaron las alcaldías de Tepeji y Huatlatlauco. Sin embargo, la provincia continuó como importante centro mercantil y manufacturero, por su cercanía con Puebla y por la tradición del mercado prehispánico. En 1706, Tepeaca quedó bajo la jurisdicción del marquesado de Atlixco y en 1710, el primer marqués, José Sarmiento de Valladares, adquirió el derecho de nombrar a las autoridades locales. En 1787, sin embargo, a raíz de las reformas borbónicas, la provincia de Tepeaca se incorporó a la intendencia de Puebla. Muchas de la casas del siglo XVIII, construidas con muros cubiertos de ladrillos y fachadas de azulejos, han logrado sobrevivir. Durante la guerra de Independencia, la ciudad fue tomada por las fuerzas realistas de Ciriaco del Llano y desde entonces permaneció bajo su poder. El 24 de abril de 1821, los realistas de Francisco Hevia derrotaron, aunque con grandes pérdidas en sus filas, a los insurgentes de Nicolás Bravo y del ex realista José María de Herrera, pero poco después, en ese mismo año, el propio Herrera tomó la ciudad. Entre las festividades más importantes de la cabecera destacan la Feria del Mole, del 28 al 30 de septiembre, y la feria regional, agrícola, artesanal, industrial y comercial el 4 de octubre. En la jurisdicción existen varias canteras de mármol.

TEPEACA, DE ◆ Sierra de Puebla situada en la vertiente meridional del Eje Volcánico y en la región central del estado. Se extiende de este a oeste, como límite suroriental del valle de Puebla, paralelamente a la sierra de Tentzo, de la que está separada por el río Atoyac. Su límite occidental se halla al sureste de la capital poblana y contiguo al extremo oriental de la presa de Valsequillo. Cuenta con yacimientos de yeso y canteras de mármol.

Convento-fortaleza del siglo XVI, Tepeaca, Puebla

FOTO: FONDO EDITORIAL GRUPO AZABACHE

ILUSTRACIÓN DE SANTIAGO ORTEGA

Ayuntamiento de Tepecoacuilco de Trujano, Guerrero

TEPEAPULCO ◆ Municipio de Hidalgo situado al sureste de Pachuca y al noroeste de Apan, en los límites con el Estado de México. Superficie: 239 km². Habitantes: 48,241, de los cuales 13,041 forman la población económicamente activa. Hablan alguna lengua indígena 167 personas mayores de cinco años (náhuatl 102). Fue sede de un señorío acolhua dependiente de Texcoco. En 1528 los franciscanos iniciaron la construcción de una iglesia y un convento, en donde Bernardino de Sahagún realizó una parte de sus investigaciones sobre el México antiguo. Hacia 1545, las autoridades españolas construyeron un acueducto y su caja de agua. La ciudad fue feudo de Hernán Cortés hasta 1566. En 1952, alrededor del poblado de Irolo, se construyó el complejo industrial llamado Ciudad Sahagún, donde se instalaron la Siderúrgica Nacional, Diesel Nacional y Constructora Nacional de Carros de Ferrocarril.

TEPECOACUILCO ◆ Río de Guerrero que nace en la vertiente meridional de la sierra de Huitzuco, al este-sureste de Iguala. Corre hacia el noroeste y luego al sur. Recibe al río Atopula, en cuya confluencia se construía, a mediados de la década de 1980, la presa de Huitzuco. Más al sur su curso se ve interrumpido por la presa Tepecoacuilco, que riega unas 5,000 hectáreas en las inmediaciones de Iguala; el río Tepecoacuilco desemboca en el Balsas.

TEPECOACUILCO DE TRUJANO ◆ Municipio de Guerrero situado al sur de Iguala y al norte de Chilpancingo. Superficie: 984 km². Habitantes: 33,102, de los cuales 7,752 forman la población económicamente activa. Hablan alguna lengua indígena 8,057 personas mayores de cinco años (náhuatl 8,011) y de ellas, 1,493 son monolingües. En la jurisdicción hay importantes recursos minerales.

TEPECHITLÁN ◆ Municipio de Zacatecas situado al sur-suroeste de Zacatecas y al noroeste de Nochistlán, en los límites con Jalisco. Superficie: 517.70 km². Habitantes: 9,193 de los cuales 2,068 forman la población económicamente activa. Hablan alguna lengua indígena 16 personas mayores de cinco años.

TEPECHPAN, TIRA DE ◆ Códice acolhua posterior a la conquista española. Está elaborado sobre papel a la manera tradicional de los nahuas y narra la historia del valle de Anáhuac desde la llegada de los mexicas a Chapultepec hasta los primeros años de la Colonia. Tiene 6 metros de largo por 21 centímetros de ancho.

TEPEHUACÁN DE GUERRERO ◆ Municipio de Hidalgo situado al oeste de Huejutla de los Reyes y al nor-noroeste de Molango, en los límites con San Luis Potosí. Superficie: 426.6 km². Habitantes: 25,221, de los cuales 5,675 forman la población económicamente activa. Hablan alguna lengua indígena 9,247 personas mayores de cinco años (náhuatl 9,247). Indígenas monolingües: 1,692.

TEPEHUANES ◆ Nombre con que se conoce a los odamí, indios que vivieron en la provincia de Nueva Vizcaya durante la Colonia, y en los estados de Chihuahua, Durango, Nayarit y Sinaloa, a partir de la independencia de la Nueva España. Fueron llamados *saelo* (campamochas) por los tarahumaras y tepehuanes por los españoles, probablemente a partir de un nombre náhuatl que incluía la palabra *tépetl* (montaña). Su lengua pertenece al grupo nahuacuitlateco, tronco yutonahua, familia pima-cora. Se ha clasificado a los sobrevivientes en tres ramas: tepehuanes del norte (☛), que habitan en el sur de Chihuahua; tepehuanes del sur (☛), en Durango; y tepecanos, que viven en Durango. En todo el país, en 1995, hablaban tepehuan o tepecano 22,651 personas mayores de cinco años, concentradas casi exclusivamente en Durango (16,874, de las que 1,823 no saben español) y Chihuahua (3,986, de las cuales 407 son monolingües), aunque algunos vivían en Nayarit (1,241, y 32 no hablan español) y Sinaloa (131). Antes de la conquista española, los odamí ocuparon las zonas templadas de la sierra Madre Occidental, en la región que sería Nueva Vizcaya durante el virreinato, principalmente en lo que hoy son los municipios de Tepehuanes y Santiago Papasquiaro, Durango, y la región suroeste de Chihuahua; es posible que se hubiesen extendido hasta las inmediaciones de la región lagunera, en el actual estado de Coahuila. Por su cercana filiación lingüística y debido a que las fuentes españolas del siglo XVI no establecen diferencias, es probable que en épocas antiguas los tepehuanes del norte y del sur formaran un solo grupo o que sólo estuviesen divididos por ligeras variantes dialectales, aunque con un patrimonio cultural común. Según algunas fuentes, la separación entre ambos grupos se produjo hacia 1530. Los odamí se consideraban a sí mismo superiores a los rarámuri (tarahumaras), acaxees y otros pueblos vecinos, con los que frecuentemente estaban en guerra.

Como el resto de los pueblos indígenas del noroccidente, los odamí fueron conquistados por los españoles hacia 1530, aunque, de hecho, los europeos sólo dominaron unas pocas ciudades. Ya en 1539, varios pueblos nayaritas, posiblemente coras (☛) y tepehuanes, habían intentado levantarse en armas contra los españoles. Es probable, también, que algunos pueblos de odamí se hayan sumado a las rebeliones del Mixtón (1541) y de la sierra de Topia (1601-04). La Compañía de Jesús, a partir de 1600, se encargó de la conquista espiritual. A principios de 1616, dice José Arlegui en la versión de Luis González Obregón, un "indio de los contornos de Nuevo México, 'demonio en traje de bárbaro', salió de aquellos lugares, y dirigiéndose a la ciudad de Durango, hacía, en todos los pueblos y rancherías de los indios tepehanes a donde llegaba, un oración tan bien razonada en su idioma, y tan eficaz para conmover los ánimos sosegados de los indios, que acabándola de oír, al punto se enardecían en cólera contra los españoles, detestando la ley que profesaban y el modo de vivir en que los tenían". Impulsados por ese indio, que se decía Hijo de Dios, los chamanes auguraron la llegada de un "hombre muy poderoso" que los libraría de los españoles y establecería un reino en el que los indios vivirían felices. El 16 de noviembre de 1616, prácticamente todos los pueblos odamí se levantaron en armas, asaltaron Santiago Papasquiaro, Santa Catalina y El Zape, ejecutaron a los españoles y establecieron su centro de operaciones en Tenexapa, donde rindieron culto a un ídolo del que los chamanes decían recibir instrucciones para promover la sublevación y destruir a los blancos y a los sacerdotes del dios de los blancos. Después de atacar el Real de Topia, los odamí lograron la colaboración de los xiximes, acaxées y tarahumaras. Al año siguiente, 25,000 indios marcharon sobre Durango, pero fueron derrotados por el gobernador de Nueva Vizcaya, Gaspar de Alboar. Poco después, éste organizó una columna de 600 españoles, quienes en 1617 asesinaron a cerca de 15,000 indios. Aunque con una fuerza ya muy menguada, los odamí volvieron a levantarse en armas en 1635 y tras una nueva derrota se sumaron a las insurrecciones tarahumaras de 1639, 1684 y 1690, entre otras. Durante el medio siglo en que florecieron las misiones jesuitas (1708-67), los tepehuanes vivieron concentrados en pequeños pueblos, con lo cual perdieron una gran parte de sus costumbres, pero todavía intentaron resitirse a la dominación occidental. Hacia 1808, las autoridades españolas descubrieron una conspiración encabezada por el gobernador de la región, José Domingo de la Cruz Valdés, pero ni así pudieron evitar que dos años después, los tepehuanes se levantaran en armas adheridos a la insurrección independentista de Miguel Hidalgo. Medio siglo más tarde se integraron a los ejércitos coras de Manuel Lozada (☛).

TEPEHUANES ◆ Municipio de Durango situado al noroeste de Santiago Papasquiaro y al sur de Guanaceví, en los límites con Chihuahua. Superficie: 6,401.5 km^2. Habitantes: 13,588, de los cuales 3,545 forman la población económicamente activa. Hablan alguna lengua indígena 49 personas (tarahumara 41). La cabecera municipal es Santa Catarina de Tepehuanes.

TEPEHUANES ◆ Río de Durango también llamado Santa Catarina Tepehuanes. Nace en los altos de Tarahumar, en el eje principal de la sierra Madre Occidental, en la región noroeste del estado; corre hacia el sureste, entre las sierras de la Candela y de Tepehuanes y al noroeste de la sierra de la Magdalena se une al río Santiago Papasquiaro, para formar el de Ramos.

TEPEHUANES, DE ◆ Cordillera de Durango situada en la cresta principal de la sierra Madre Occidental, en el oeste del estado, al noroeste de la capital de la entidad. Limita al norte y al oeste con los Altos de Topia, al noreste con el río Tepehuanes y al este con el Santiago Papasquiaro. Su altitud media supera los 2,000 metros sobre el nivel del mar. Cuenta con yacimientos minerales.

TEPEHUANES DEL NORTE ◆ Indios que viven en el suroeste del estado de Chihuahua. Según el Conteo Nacional de Población de 1995, había en esta región 3,986 hablantes de tepehuan, idioma del grupo nahua-cuitlateco, tronco yutonahua, familia pima-cora. Los miembros de la etnia conservan algo de su vestimenta tradicional: blusa suelta de manga larga, enaguas de colores llamativos y pañoleta en la cabeza, para las mujeres; y camisa y pantalón comerciales, huaraches de cuero con suela de llanta, faja y paliacate al cuello, para los hombres. Hay, sin embargo, tepehuanes septentrionales que aún usan calzón y camisa de algodón blanco, y cotense, una especie de pañoleta atada con nudos en la cadera. La agricultura para consumo familiar y la cría de animales son las actividades preponderantes de los tepehuanes del norte, aunque también practican la cacería para complementar su alimentación. La unidad básica de producción es la familia nuclear, aunque las labores pesadas, la construcción de una casa o la cosecha, por ejemplo, las realizan varias familias. La unidad social básica también es la familia nuclear, aunque ocasionalmente se dan casos de familias extensas. Los ritos matrimoniales se inician cuando el novio se "roba" a la novia, que generalmente está de acuerdo, y la lleva a vivir a su casa familiar, hasta que los parientes de la mujer "perdonan" el hecho y los aceptan como pareja, sin que medien ceremonias civiles ni religiosas. La mujer da a luz arrodillada, detenida de las axilas por su marido. La placenta y el cordón umbilical son quemados, antes de que los coma algún perro, lo que traería mala suerte. Apenas nacido, el niño es bañado y se le da de mamar y en caso de que nazcan gemelos se le da muerte al que abandona la matriz en segundo lugar. Los tepehuanes del norte creen que el alma de los recién fallecidos permanece cerca de su casa alrededor de un mes y que no se aleja en forma definitiva sino hasta que se realiza una fiesta de despedida, en la cual se coloca ropa, comida y un licor de maíz llamado *tesgüino* para que el muerto los use en su viaje al más allá. Después se hacen otras dos fiestas, una a los cuatro meses y la otra al año del fallecimiento. Los tepehuanes del norte practican un catolicismo fuertemente influido por sus ritos ancestrales: veneran a una deidad creadora a la que llaman Diusuroga o Nuestro Padre Dios, que es el creador del mundo; al Dios Venado, dueño de los animales; al espíritu del viento y a dos seres sobrenaturales relacionados con la muerte: el dios o espíritu de la montaña, que toma la forma de un guajolote para anunciar la muerte de las personas, y Ugai, ser espiritual que produce una luz en el cielo cuando fallece uno de los miembros del grupo. A todos ellos se les hacen ofrendas para agradarlos y recibir sus favores, así como para que haya lluvia y buenas cosechas. La curación por medio de la hechicería es realizada por los chamanes, llamados bajadioses porque se comunican con las deidades, aunque su papel es sobre todo de diagnóstico. La enfermedad se supone causada por una persona en particular y cuando el paciente fallece el bajadiós lleva al "criminal" ante el capitán del pueblo para que éste ordene que se le azote en público. De las fiestas católicas que celebran, destacan la de los Santos Reyes, en la que se ejecuta la danza de Los Matachines, se sacrifican algunos toros y se bebe *tesgüino*; la de Semana Santa, con procesiones y la representación de la Pasión de Jesucristo, impregnada de elementos locales; y la de San Francisco, en la que además de venerar al santo se hacen rituales para agradecerle las cosechas. La organización político-religiosa es paralela a la que existe en la comunidad mestiza, con facultades para juzgar los crímenes en que se ven implicados los tepehuanes. La tribu entera está regida por la autoridad del capitán general, electo por sus gobernadores. Por lo demás, los tepehuanes del norte se rigen por el sistema municipal del país.

TEPEHUANES DEL SUR ◆ Indios que viven principalmente en el extremo meridional de Durango, en la sierra de Mezquital, aunque existen pequeños grupos en el oeste del municipio de Pueblo Nuevo, Durango, y cerca de Huajicori, en Nayarit. Los sobrevivientes tepecanos, por su parte, están agrupados en la localidad de Azqueltán, Durango. Los hablantes de tepehuan, en 1995, eran 16,874 en Durango (de los cuales 1,823 no saben español) y 1,241 en Nayarit (32 no hablan español). Su idioma está clasificado en el grupo nahua-cuitlateco, tronco yutonahua, familia pima-cora, y aunque su clasificación es la misma que la del tepehuan del norte, ambas son variantes ininteligibles entre sí. La indumentaria que utilizan hombres y mujeres consta por lo regular de prendas de fabricación comercial, aunque algunos hombres usan todavía camisa y calzón de manta y pañuelo rojo en el cuello; hay mujeres que llevan vestidos de colores con falda amplia y pañoleta amarrada en la cabeza. Las actividades económicas primordiales de los tepehuanes del sur son la agricultura y la ganadería, pero hay quienes se dedican al comercio en pequeñas tiendas y otros emigran para emplearse temporalmente como asalariados. La unidad de su sociedad es la familia extensa; el matrimonio es arreglado por los padres del joven en visitas que hacen a la familia de la mujer para solicitar su consentimiento; cuando el matrimonio se realiza, el joven permanece un tiempo con sus suegros para ayudar en las labores agrícolas. El ritual asociado con la muerte de uno de los miembros del grupo tiene una duración de cinco días, durante los cuales el chamán se encarga de realizar el ceremonial para que el alma se dirija a su destino final y evitar, en consecuencia, que regrese a importunar a los vivos y no es sino hasta el quinto día cuando se crema el cadáver. Cuando se cumplen dos años del fallecimiento se hace otra ceremonia similar en la que el chamán vuelve a indicar al alma el camino hacia el más allá, con objeto de que no vuelva a la tierra. Los tepehuanes del sur practican la religión católica, combinada con elementos de sus creencias antiguas: veneran a deidades como el Dios Padre, que se asocia con el sol; a Jesús Nazareno, al que relacionan con la luna; a la estrella de la mañana; a la Virgen María, que tiene varios ayudantes entre los que está la Virgen de Guadalupe; y a su

Foto: Lourdes Almeida

Familia de campesinos tepehuanes del sur, originarios de Nayarit

Foto: Lourdes Almeida

Familia de campesinos tepehuanes del sur, nativos de Durango héroe cultural, llamado Ixcaitiung ("el que gobierna"), héroe legendario parecido al nahua Quetzalcóatl. Los chamanes son los encargados de dirigir la vida religiosa de la comunidad; su entrenamiento dura cinco años. Cuando una persona enferma, los chamanes realizan una ceremonia que dura cinco días, durante los cuales entonan largas oraciones, dan masaje al enfermo o le soplan humo de tabaco mientras el paciente hace una confesión ritual, para lograr el alivio completo. Otras de las ceremonias más importantes son los "mitotes", ritos colectivos de cinco días acompañados de ayunos y rezos, realizados, uno en la primavera, para pedir que la tierra fructifique, otro en otoño, para celebrar los primeros frutos; un tercero al finalizar la cosecha y el último en invierno, para que los seres sobrenaturales protejan a las personas del frío. Del santoral católico celebran la Pasión de Jesucristo, la Virgen de Guadalupe, la Navidad y al santo patrono de cada pueblo. En esas fechas hay danzas de matachines y manifestaciones festivas propias de esta comunidad. Los grupos de apellido común parecen ser el remanente de clanes parilineales no localizados; un muestreo hecho en el registro de bodas de la iglesia del Mezquital reveló que no hay uniones entre individuos del mismo apellido, aun cuando los contrayentes sean de diferentes pueblos. El líder de cada apellido, un anciano y frecuentemente chamán, es llamado jefe de patio y dirige los mitotes de su grupo. La organización tradicional política sigue teniendo importancia: cada año se elige a los gobernadores primero, segundo y tercero; alguaciles, un fiscal y un topil, que se encargan de los asuntos de la comunidad, solucionan problemas locales y organizan las festividades religiosas; los pueblos tepehuanes del sur también pertenecen a sus respectivas cabeceras municipales y se encuentran sujetos a los lineamientos que las rigen.

TEPEHUAS ◆ Indios que viven en las huastecas hidalguense y veracruzana y en la sierra Norte de Puebla. En 1995, hablaban tepehua 8,942 personas mayores de cinco años, distribuidas en Hidalgo (1,974), Veracruz (5,937) y Puebla (243). La lengua tepehua está clasificada en el grupo maya-totonaco, tronco totonaco, familia totonaca. Aun cuando el tepehua y el totonaco formaron un solo idioma en épocas remotas, empezaron a separarse hacia el siglo VI a.n.e. Dominados por los acolhuas desde el siglo XIV, los tepehuas fueron conquistados por los mexicas a fines del siglo XV o principios del XVI y más tarde, a partir de la década de 1520, por los españoles. Luego de la conquista europea, la población tepehua descendió sensiblemente, al punto que en 1596, las autoridades españolas dispusieron su concentración en el pueblo de Pataloyan, para frenar la inmigración al centro del virreinato. La palabra tepehua deriva del náhuatl *tepehuaque*, que significa "dueños de los cerros". Muchos tepehuas siguen utilizando el traje tradicional, que consiste en camisa blanca o de color y calzón blanco ancho, que se anuda en los tobillos, en tanto que las mujeres llevan blusa y falda blancas, ceñidor y *quechquémitl*. Su actividad económica básica es la agricultura, complementada por una ganadería de autoconsumo, aunque algunos tepehuas emigran temporalmente para contratarse como asalariados y otros producen artesanías. Las mujeres confeccionan las prendas de vestir y algunas elaboran objetos de barro y tejen cestos. La unidad social es la familia nuclear. Para hacer la petición matrimonial, los padres del novio visitan a la familia de la novia. Cuando llegan a un acuerdo, se fija la fecha de la entrega de la muchacha y ese día los padres de ella la llevan a la casa del joven, donde se ofrece una comida, mientras éste construye una casa; algunas parejas legalizan su matrimonio más adelante y muy pocas realizan la boda religiosa. Cuando alguien muere, su cuerpo es bañado y vestido con sus mejores ropas, lo velan durante toda la noche, rezan, prenden copal y sirven comida y bebida a los acompañantes. En algunos lugares se acostumbra poner algo de comida para el muerto y en el ataúd, a veces, su ropa; a los siete días del entierro hay una ceremonia en la que ofrecen comida al alma, para despedirla y para que no vuelva a la tierra a molestar a los vivos; las almas de quienes mueren trágicamente permanecen junto a los seres malignos y no llegan al cielo. Practican la religión católica combinada con elementos de sus creencias antiguas, que le dan un matiz mágico: Wilcháan, el sol, por ejemplo, es una deidad que rige la vida de los seres humanos, en tanto que Malkuyú, la luna, es un ente masculino asociado con lo maligno; la Virgen o *Hachiuxtinin* y San José cuidan a su vez al sol; las estrellas o *staku* son guardianes que vigilan mientras el sol está ausente y disparan sus flechas contra los aerolitos, para evitar que éstos lleguen a la tierra y se conviertan en tigres devoradores de humanos; otros seres sobrenaturales son los dueños de la naturaleza, como el dueño del agua, Xalapának Xkán, a quien cuidan Sireo y Sirena, sus padres; Lapanak, el viento, es un hombre alto y barbón, que corre por encima de los árboles; el dueño de la tierra, Xalapának Lakat'un, tiene como peones a los muertos; el señor de la muerte se llama Sautazoma (Moctezuma); el dueño del monte, Xachan'achín, lleva guajes con jugo de caña, que ofrece a quien encuentra en sus dominios; el espíritu maligno, Tlakakikuru (del náhuatl *tlacatecólotl*, "hombre tecolote"), invoca a los espíritus de los muertos y se hace acompañar por los malos aires, el remolino y los seres de la oscuridad, que deambulan por los caminos; el lugar de los muertos es Lak'nin; los medios para el control de lo sobrenatural los tienen los curanderos o adivinos (hapapaná); los brujos (jaxkayanan), en cambio, son malignos. La enfermedad es concebida como producto de la brujería, la "pérdida del alma" o el castigo divino. Los hapapaná, mediante sueños, conocen la causa y el tratamiento para cada enfermedad. Cada año se elige un fiscal para los asuntos de la iglesia; se nombran también mayordomos y sus ayudantes, quienes organizan las fiestas de los santos. Celebran varias fechas del santoral católico, como la del santo patrón, el carnaval, el día de muertos y la fiesta de San Miguel Arcángel, cuando se agradecen las buenas cosechas. Su organización política está supeditada al sistema municipal del país.

Tepeji del Río de Ocampo ◆ Municipio de Hidalgo antes llamado Tepeji del Río. Está situado al sur y próximo a Tula, en los límites con el Estado de México. Superficie: 393.2 km². Habitantes: 61,950, de los cuales 14,803 forman la población económicamente activa. Hablan alguna lengua indígena 2,968 personas mayores de cinco años (otomí 2,884). Los primeros habitantes del actual territorio municipal se instalaron ahí hacia el año 500 a.n.e. Entre los siglos X y XVI de nuestra era, los mexicas y otros grupos desconocidos se instalaron en El Tesoro, 2 km al noroeste de la cabecera, de cuya presencia sobrevivieron cuatro monumentos en torno a una plaza cuadrangular y una pirámide que fueron descubiertos en 1952. La evangelización católica se inició en 1558; 28 años más tarde, los franciscanos concluyeron la construcción de un convento, en Utlaxpan, en el que lograron reunir y adoctrinar a los otomíes y a los nahuas.

Tepelmeme de Morelos ◆ Municipio de Oaxaca situado al este-noreste de Huajuapan de León y al suroeste de Huautla de Jiménez, en los límites con Puebla. Superficie: 495 km². Habitantes: 1,645, de los cuales 246 forman la población económicamente activa. En la cabecera municipal hay una iglesia del siglo XVIII. La principal fiesta del municipio se celebra el 4 de agosto.

Tepemaxalco ◆ Municipio de Puebla situado al suroeste de Atlixco y al noroeste de Izúcar de Matamoros. Superficie: 30.62 km². Habitantes: 1,170, de los cuales 299 forman la población económicamente activa. Hablan alguna lengua indígena ocho personas mayores de cinco años. El 19 de abril se celebra la fiesta del santo patrono, con juegos pirotécnicos, danzas, procesiones y feria popular.

Tepeojuma ◆ Municipio de Puebla situado al suroeste de la capital de la entidad y al norte y próximo a Izúcar de Matamoros. Superficie: 121.19 km². Habitantes: 8,378, de los cuales 2,030 forman la población económicamente activa. Hablan alguna lengua indígena 1,201 personas mayores de cinco años (náhuatl 1,159).

Tepepa, Gabriel ◆ n. en Tlaquiltenango y m. en Jojutla, Mor. (1841-1911). Algunos autores dicen que nació en 1847. Su apellido materno era Herrera. Incorporado al contingente republicano de Francisco Leyva, participó en la batalla de Puebla del 5 de mayo de 1862. Combatió en Morelos la intervención francesa y el imperio. Al triunfo de la República se dedicó a la agricultura. En 1876 se adhirió al Plan de Tuxtepec. Luego del triunfo de Porfirio Díaz volvió a dedicarse a la agricultura y fue capataz de la hacienda de Temilpa. Antirreeleccionista desde 1909 y partidario del Plan de San Luis Potosí, el 7 de febrero de 1911 se levantó en armas en Tlaquiltenango. En Metepec se reunió con Emiliano Zapata y Pablo Torres Burgos. A mediados de marzo de 1911 regresó a Morelos y tomó Tlaquiltenango y Jojutla, donde, contra las órdenes de Torres Burgos, permitió que sus tropas incendiaran varias casas de españoles, lo que provocó la renuncia de aquél a la jefatura de los revolucionarios. En abril, ya a las órdenes de Zapata, combatió en los límites de Morelos, Puebla y Guerrero y a principios de mayo participó en las tomas de San Juan Chinameca, Amayuca, Jonacatepec y Cuautla. Todavía en mayo volvió a Tlaquiltenango y poco después fue asesinado por soldados a las órdenes de Ambrosio Figueroa.

Tepetitla de Lardizábal ◆ Municipio de Tlaxcala situado en el suroccidente del estado, al oeste de Cacaxtla y al suroeste de Tlaxcala, en los límites con Puebla. Superficie: 35.2 km². Habitantes: 12,771, de los cuales 3,114 forman la población económicamente activa. Hablan alguna lengua indígena 52 personas mayores de cinco años (náhuatl 47). La cabecera municipal es Tepetitla.

Tepetitlán ◆ Municipio de Hidalgo situado al norte de Tula y al sur de Alfajayucan. Superficie: 179.9 km². Habitantes: 6,635, de los cuales 1,723 forman la población económicamente activa. Hablan alguna lengua indígena 111 personas mayores de cinco años (otomí 105).

Tepetitlán ◆ Río de Tabasco que nace de la confluencia del Macuspana con el Tulijá, en la región centro-sur del estado, al este-sureste de la población de Macuspana. Corre hacia el noreste, norte y noroeste trazando un curso semicircular en torno a la población de Benito Juárez; al nor-noreste de ésta se bifurca en los ríos Chilapa y Chilapilla. Su curso es navegable durante todo el año.

Tepetlán ◆ Municipio de Veracruz situado al noreste de Jalapa y al noroeste del puerto de Veracruz. Superficie: 83.9 km². Habitantes: 8,155, de los cuales 2,298 forman la población económicamente activa. Hablan alguna lengua indígena nueve personas mayores de cinco años.

Tepetlaoxtoc ◆ Municipio del Estado de México situado al noreste de Texcoco y al sur-sureste de Teotihuacán, en los límites con Tlaxcala. Superficie: 234.86 km². Habitantes: 19,380, de los cuales 4,433 forman la población económicamente activa. Hablan alguna lengua indígena 114 personas mayores de cinco años (náhuatl 54 y otomí 11). En la jurisdicción hay dos zonas arqueoló-

Convento dominico de Tepetlaoxtoc, Estado de México

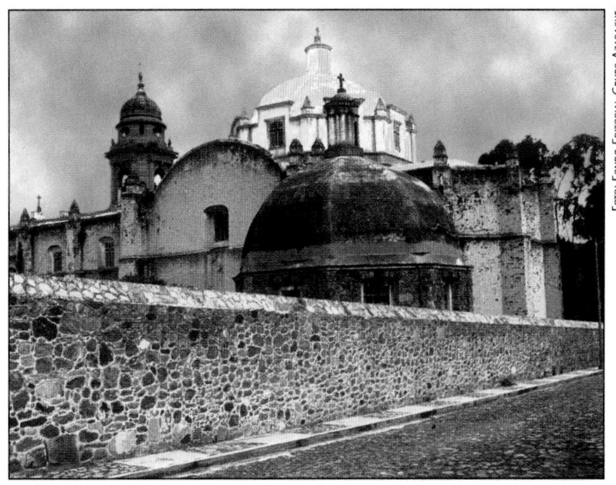

Foto: Fondo Editorial Grupo Azabache

gicas, Tepetlaoxtoc y Techachal y se halla el convento dominico de Tlaxcontla, construido por Domingo de Betanzos a partir de 1529 y reconstruido en 1549. En la cabecera, Tepetlaoxtoc de Hidalgo, se encuentra la iglesia de Santa María Magdalena, construida en el siglo XVII.

TEPETLIXPA ◆ Municipio del Estado de México situado al suroeste de Amecameca y al sur de Chalco, en los límites con Morelos. Superficie: 103.69 km². Habitantes: 15,181, de los cuales 3,183 forman la población económicamente activa. Hablan alguna lengua indígena 49 personas mayores de cinco años (náhuatl 20 y mixteco 18). En el poblado de San Miguel Nepantla se encuentra una de las casas que pertenecieron a Sor Juana Inés de la Cruz.

TEPETONGO ◆ Municipio de Zacatecas situado en el sur del estado, al suroeste de Zacatecas y al sureste de Valparaíso, en los límites con Jalisco. Superficie: 714.42 km². Habitantes: 9,116, de los cuales 1,953 forman la población económicamente activa.

TEPETZINTLA ◆ Municipio de Puebla situado al sureste de Huauchinango, al nor-noreste de la capital del estado y contiguo a Zacatlán. Superficie: 127.57 km². Habitantes: 9,182, de los cuales 1,709 forman la población económicamente activa. Hablan alguna lengua indígena 7,547 personas mayores de cinco años (náhuatl 6,693 y totonaco 853) y de ellas son monolingües 2,846. El Jueves de Corpus se celebra una feria en la que se ejecutan las danzas de Negritos, Huehues, Toreros y Aztecas.

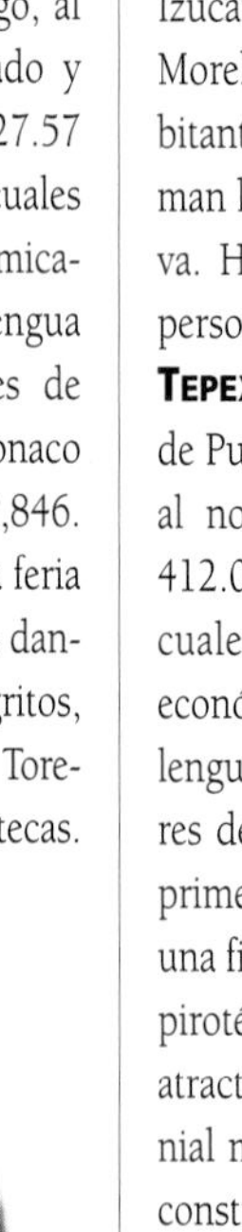

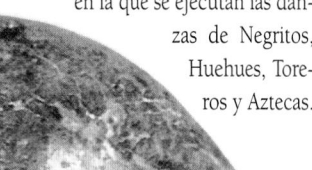

Cráneo del Hombre de Tepexpan

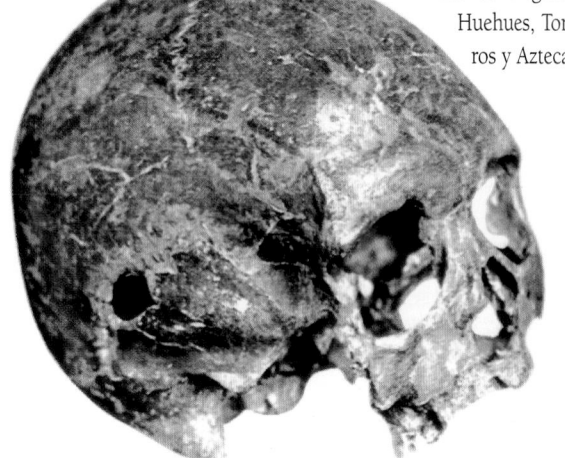

Fósil encontrado en Tepexi de Rodríguez, Puebla

TEPETZINTLA ◆ Municipio de Veracruz situado al oeste-noroeste de Tuxpan y al sureste de Tantoyuca. Superficie: 245.56 km². Habitantes: 13,278, de los cuales 3,347 forman la población económicamente activa. Hablan alguna lengua indígena 2,225 personas mayores de cinco años (náhuatl 2,219).

TEPEXCO ◆ Municipio de Puebla situado al suroeste de Puebla y al oeste de Izúcar de Matamoros, en los límites con Morelos. Superficie: 121.19 km². Habitantes: 5,394, de los cuales 1,105 forman la población económicamente activa. Hablan alguna lengua indígena 10 personas mayores de cinco años.

TEPEXI DE RODRÍGUEZ ◆ Municipio de Puebla situado al sureste de Puebla y al nor-noreste de Acatlán. Superficie: 412.05 km². Habitantes: 16,812, de los cuales 2,636 forman la población económicamente activa. Hablan alguna lengua indígena 1,241 personas mayores de cinco años (popoloca 1,075). El primer viernes de Cuaresma se celebra una fiesta tradicional con danzas, juegos pirotécnicos y una feria. El principal atractivo turístico es el centro ceremonial mixteco de Tepeji el Viejo, que fue construido entre los siglos X a XVI de nuestra era. En 1987, los investigadores René Hernández Rivera y Shelton P. Apelgate, ambos del Instituto de Geología de la UNAM, descubrieron en la cantera de Tlayua, a 50 km de la cabecera, los restos fósiles de un dinosaurio que vivió hace 190 y 135 millones de años y de un cocodrilo que vivió hace unos 100 millones de años. Estos descubrimientos modificaron el concepto que se tenía sobre la formación geológica de América, pues fósiles semejantes sólo habían sido hallados en las regiones septentrionales del continente.

TEPEXPAN, HOMBRE DE ◆ Restos de huesos humanos descubiertos a principios de 1947 en el pueblo de Tepexpan, perteneciente al municipio de Acolman, Estado de México, por una expedición de arqueólogos mexicanos y estadounidenses dirigida por Helmut de Terra, Hans Iundberg y Javier Romero, que fue patrocinada por la Viking Fundation, el Instituto Nacional de Antropología e Historia y el Instituto de Geología de la UNAM. Al principio se pensó que los restos, un cráneo, una mandíbula inferior, unas rótulas, unas clavículas y unos trozos de costillas, habían pertenecido a un hombre de entre 55 y 65 años y de 1.70 metros de altura, que había muerto hace unos 12,000 años a.n.e. en un pantano situado a la orilla del lago que se extendía hasta esa zona, pero unos años después, Santiago Genovés examinó los huesos y estableció que, en realidad, habían pertenecido a una mujer de 30 años de edad aproximadamente, que medía 1.60 metros de altura.

TEPEYAHUALCO ◆ Municipio de Puebla situado al noreste de Puebla y al sur de Teziutlán, en los límites con Veracruz. Superficie: 426.08 km². Habitantes: 14,803, de los cuales 3,645 forman la población económicamente activa. Hablan alguna lengua indígena 27 personas mayores de cinco años. En el municipio hay respiraderos azufrosos, llamados humeros.

TEPEYAHUALCO DE CUAUHTÉMOC ◆ Municipio de Puebla situado al sureste de Puebla y al noroeste de Tehuacán. Superficie: 19.15 km². Habitantes: 2,710, de los cuales 588 forman la población económicamente activa. Hablan alguna lengua indígena 21 personas mayores de cinco años (náhuatl 20).

TEPEYANCO ◆ Municipio de Tlaxcala contiguo a la capital del estado. Superficie: 22.2 km². Habitantes: 8,672, de los cuales 4,244 forman la población económicamente activa. Hablan alguna lengua indígena 48 personas mayores de cinco años (náhuatl 43).

TEPEYOLOTLI ◆ Deidad nahua de los cerros, cuyo nombre significa "corazón del monte". Los nahuas creían que los montes estaban llenos de agua, pues veían que de ellos brotaban los ríos y manantiales, y que podían romperse y anegar la tierra, por lo que les colocaban imágenes de Tláloc para representar el corazón acuático del monte. Era, además, el Octavo Señor de la Noche y se le consideraba el eco o voz de la noche. Se le asignaba como animal simbólico el tigre. En los códices se le representaba con el glifo de una cueva, como boca de la tierra.

TEPEZALÁ ◆ Municipio de Aguascalientes situado al nor-noreste de la capital de la entidad y al este de Rincón de Romos, en los límites con Zacatecas. Superficie: 209 km². Habitantes: 16,175, de los cuales 3,381 forman la población económicamente activa.

TEPIC ◆ Municipio de Nayarit contiguo a San Blas y Santiago Ixcuintla. Superficie: 1,983.8 km². Habitantes: 292,780, de los cuales 75,213 forman la población económicamente activa. Hablan alguna lengua indígena 4,375 personas mayores de cinco años (huichol 3,276, cora 527 y purépecha 121). La cabecera municipal es también la capital del estado. El territorio fue habitado originalmente por los coras, quienes se establecieron en un pueblo al que llamaron Tepique, "Lugar entre cerros". En 1531, las fuerzas españolas de Nuño Beltrán de Guzmán ocuparon el pueblo cora y sobre él fundaron la villa del Espíritu Santo, que fue la primera que los europeos establecieron en territorio nayarita. Al año siguiente, poco después de que se creara el Reino de la Nueva Galicia, Beltrán de Guzmán rebautizó la población con el nombre de Santiago de Galicia de Compostela y la convirtió en capital. Cien españoles fueron los primeros habitantes. A mediados de 1540, Cristóbal de Oñate trasladó la capital al sur, adonde ahora se encuentra Santiago de Compostela y la población cora recobró su nombre original, que poco después se contrajo hasta convertirse en Tepic. Hasta el último tercio del siglo XVIII, aunque era sede de una alcaldía mayor y su gobierno eclesiástico había sido elevado a la categoría de parroquia en 1761, Tepic fue un pequeño poblado dependiente de Santiago de Compostela, pero debido a que el camino entre el puerto de San Blas y Guadalajara pasaba por ahí, la villa triplicó la población y se estableció una de los ferias regionales más importantes de Nueva Galicia, por lo que en 1786 pudo absorber el territorio de Acaponeta y, en 1811, convertirse en ciudad. Como durante la revolución de independencia las fuerzas insurgentes bloquearon el camino entre México y Acapulco, el tráfico marítimo se hacía por San Blas, con lo que Tepic incrementó su prosperidad. En agosto de 1859, la ciudad fue tomada por las fuerzas liberales de Esteban Coronado, quien tuvo que entregar la plaza luego de dos meses de asedio por parte de los conservadores y los ejércitos coras de Manuel Lozada. Un año después, las guerrillas liberales de Antonio Rojas derrotaron a las fuerzas de Gerónimo Calatayud, y recuperaron la ciudad. En junio de 1862, desconocidos los Convenios de Pochotitlán, las fuerzas campesinas de Lozada tomaron la ciudad. Entre 1884 y 1917, Tepic fue capital del territorio federal de Nayarit (☛). La diócesis de Tepic fue erigida por el papa León XIII el 23 de junio de 1891. Los principales atractivos turísticos de la ciudad son una catedral de estilo neogótico construida en el siglo XIX, el templo de la Santa Cruz, edificado en 1741 en donde desde mediados del siglo XVI había existido una cruz de zacate formada naturalmente; el ex convento anexo al templo de la Santa Cruz, del cual partieron Junípero Serra y Eusebio Kino a la expedición misionera de las Californias; el Museo Regional de Antropología y la Casa Museo de Amado Nervo.

TEPIC, DE ◆ Sierra de Nayarit. Se extiende de noroeste a sureste, dentro de la sierra Madre Occidental. Limita por el este al valle de Tepic y en su

FOTO: FONDO EDITORIAL GRUPO AZABACHE

Ex convento de San Francisco de Tepeyanco, Tlaxcala

FOTO: FONDO EDITORIAL GRUPO AZABACHE

Detalle labrado de la fachada del convento de Tepeyanco, Tlaxcala

FOTO: MICHAEL CALDERWOOD

Tepic, Nayarit

extremo sur se encuentra el volcán de Sangangüey.

TEPIC, DE ◆ Valle de Nayarit que se encuentra unido con el de Santa María del Oro. Se extiende hacia el sureste desde la base occidental de la sierra de Tepic. Limita al este con el volcán Sangangüey, al sur con la sierra del Carretón y al oeste con la de San Juan.

TEPITOTON ◆ Dioses domésticos de la mitología nahua, de los cuales, los reyes debían tener seis, los nobles cuatro y los plebeyos dos. Además, se encontraban en los campos y en los montes.

TEPOCA, DE ◆ Bahía de Sonora situada en el litoral del golfo de California. Se localiza al sur del cabo Tepoca, al suroeste de Caborca y al noreste de la isla Ángel de la Guarda; se abre hacia el sur y el oeste y es fondeadero para embarcaciones de poco calado. En la parte norte de la bahía se halla el puerto de Lobos.

TEPOCA ◆ Cabo de Sonora situado en la región noroccidental del estado, al suroeste de Caborca, en el litoral del golfo de California. Limita por el noroeste a la bahía del mismo nombre.

TEPORAME *TEPEROCA*, GABRIEL ◆ ¿n. cerca del peñón de Nonolat?, y m. en Papigóchic, en el actual estado de Sonora (?-1653). Caudillo tarahumara que en 1650 encabezó la segunda gran sublevación de los tarahumaras (☛) del siglo XVII. Tomó Papigóchic y Villa de Aguilar y reunió un ejército de más de 2,000 hombres. Tres años después, en 1653, fue capturado por los españoles y ahorcado y descuartizado por los indios sumisos aliados de los europeos. Murió, dijeron sus contemporáneos, "vomitando injurias contra los españoles y contra la cobardía de los suyos, que lo habían entregado".

TEPOSCOLULA ◆ ☛ *San Pedro y San Pablo Teposcolula.*

TEPOTZOTLÁN ◆ Municipio del Estado de México situado al norte de Naucalpan y al suroeste de la laguna de Zumpango, en los límites con Hidalgo. Superficie: 208.88 km^2. Habitantes: 54,419, de los cuales 11,967 forman la población económicamente activa. Hablan alguna lengua indígena 170 personas mayores de cinco años (otomí 61 y náhuatl 46). La actual cabecera fue habitada originalmente por los otomíes. Entre los siglos XVII y XVIII, los jesuitas construyeron un Colegio, que actualmente es sede del Museo Nacional de Virreinato, y su iglesia adjunta, donde ejecutaron los retablos que fueron considerados los mejores de la Nueva España. En la jurisdicción se encuentra la capilla del poblado de Tepojoco, la iglesia de San José de Huilango, una escultura barroca de Cristo tallada en un árbol y el acueducto de Xalpa, construido en el siglo XVIII. Entre los lugares de recreo están los Arcos del Sitio y la presa de la Concepción.

Retablo barroco en Tepotzotlán

FOTO: BORIS DE SWAN

Convento de Tepoztlán, Morelos

TEPOZTLÁN ◆ Municipio de Morelos situado en los límites con el Distrito Federal y contiguo a Cuernavaca y Huitzilac. Superficie: 279 km^2. Habitantes: 26,503 de los cuales 8,064 forman la población económicamente activa. Hablan alguna lengua indígena 1,864 personas mayores de cinco años (náhuatl 1,672). El nombre significa "Lugar de metal". Las exploraciones arqueológicas han descubierto cerámica y otros objetos de una etapa contemporánea a la de Zacatenco (aproximadamente del siglo I antes de nuestra era) y del periodo conocido como Azteca IV. Hay una iglesia colonial en la cabecera, que está al pie de un cerro, el Tepozteco, en cuya cima hay un templo dedicado a Tepoztécatl, variante de Quetzalcóatl, y una placa con el glifo de Ahuízotl y la fecha 10-conejo (1502 del calendario gregoriano). En la jurisdicción hay yacimientos minerales. La celebración del carnaval atrae a gran número de visitantes.

TEPOZTLÁN, DE ◆ Sierra de Morelos situada al sur de la sierra del Ajusco. Se extiende de oeste a este, aproximadamente 15 km al sur del Distrito Federal y 20 al norte de Cuernavaca. En su porción suroccidental se encuentra el cerro Tepozteco.

TEQUECHMECANIANI ◆ Uno de los nombres del dios nahua de la embriaguez, Tezcatonatl, llamado así, "El Ahorcador", por los supuestos efectos asfixiantes de la borrachera.

TEQUEPA, DE ◆ Bahía de Guerrero situada en la región occidental del estado, al oeste-noroeste de Atoyac y al sureste de Zihuatanejo. Se halla en la desembocadura del río Coyuquilla, al sureste de la punta Japutica y al noroeste del morro de Papanoa, en el litoral del océano Pacífico.

TEQUESQUITENGO, DE ◆ Lago de Morelos situado en la parte meridional del valle de Cuernavaca, 48 km al sur de la capital del estado. Es un depósito lacustre de forma elipsoidal con un eje mayor de 3.7 km y uno menor de 2.7; su profundidad media es de 60 metros.

En los años cuarenta del siglo XIX, los propietarios de la hacienda de Vista Hermosa inundaron deliberadamente el pueblo vecino de Tequesquitengo, con el fin de despojar a la comunidad de la tierra adyacente y dedicarla a la producción azucarera. En las riberas de este lago existe un balneario que es visitado por turistas nacionales y extranjeros; ahí se pueden practicar deportes acuáticos. Hay numerosas casas de campo de habitantes de la ciudad de México.

Foto: Michael Calderwood

Panorámica de Tequila, Jalisco

TEQUILA ◆ Bebida alcohólica resultado de la fermentación y destilación del aguamiel de la piña de la planta *agave tequilana*, en sus variedades *azul* y *xiguin*, abundante sobre todo en el municipio de Tequila, aunque también existe en algunas partes de Nayarit, los Altos de Jalisco y Michoacán. Antes de la conquista española, los tiquilos, habitantes de Tequila, reservaban su uso a los ancianos y los sacerdotes, pero también lo empleaban, frotado, para aliviar los dolores provocados por la artritis. Durante los 100 años posteriores a la invasión europea, los conquistadores trataron de impedir su fabricación y consumo, pero fracasaron. Hacia 1640 retiraron las prohibiciones y establecieron un estanco o monopolio para el "vino mezcal de Tequila". Unos años después, sin embargo, los españoles desaparecieron el estanco y volvieron a prohibir la producción de tequila; sin embargo, en 1673 se vieron obligados a autorizar nuevamente la producción tequilera y a reestablecer el estanco. El ingreso derivado de los impuestos fue destinado por la Audiencia de Guadalajara a la construcción de las obras hidráulicas en la capital neogallega. El desarrollo de la industria licorera en Nueva Galicia comenzó a amenazar la riqueza de los productores y comerciantes del centro de la Nueva España, quienes a principios de la década de 1780 iniciaron una nueva campaña contra la producción de tequila y en 1785 consiguieron que, una vez más, la Corona española la prohibiera. Diez años después, en 1795, de nuevo obligadas por la realidad, las autoridades virreinales autorizaron la producción y venta del tequila. En ese año, José María Guadalupe Cuervo recibió una concesión real para la elaboración y comercialización de tequila. Surgió así la firma Cuervo, que desde entonces es una de las empresas tequileras más importantes del país. La otra gran destilería, la Sauza, fue fundada a principios del siglo XIX por José María Castañeda y adquirida en 1873 por Cenobio Sauza, quien en ese mismo año comenzó a exportar el producto. De entre los aguardientes que se elaboran en México, el tequila se ha convertido en el más conocido en todo el mundo. En 1986 se exportaron casi 50 millones de litros del licor y la venta doméstica fue de sólo 15 millones de litros anuales. En 1996, la exportación de la bebida representó 240 millones de dólares para el país. En 1998 se produjeron 111,772,943 litros, de los cuales se exportaron 81,451,180.

TEQUILA ◆ Municipio de Jalisco situado al noroeste de Guadalajara y al este-noreste de Puerto Vallarta, en los límites con Zacatecas y Nayarit. Superficie: 1,364.14 km². Habitantes: 33,155, de los cuales 7,028 forman la población económicamente activa. Hablan alguna lengua indígena 16 personas mayores de cinco años. Su cultivo principal es el agave tequilero y su industria básica es la destilación del tequila, cuya denominación de origen posee. La cabecera municipal fue elevada a la categoría de villa el 16 de octubre de 1656 y fue bautizada con el nombre de Villa de Torre Argas de Ulloa y Chávez, en honor del gobernador de la Nueva Galicia.

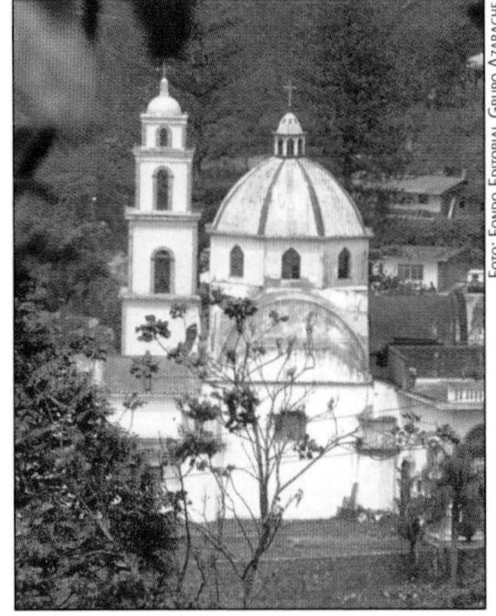

Foto: Fondo Editorial Grupo Azabache

Iglesia de San Pedro, en Tequila, Veracruz

TEQUILA ◆ Municipio de Veracruz situado al sur de Orizaba y al suroeste de Córdoba. Superficie: 74.85 km². Habitantes: 10,676, de los cuales 2,688 forman la población económicamente activa. Hablan alguna lengua indígena 8,416 personas mayores de cinco años (náhuatl 8,397) y de ellas 3,040 son monolingües.

Foto: Michael Calderwood

Agave, planta de donde se extrae el tequila

Volcán Tequila, en Jalisco

TEQUILA ◆ Volcán de Jalisco que forma parte del Sistema Volcánico Transversal. Está situado al oeste-noroeste de Guadalajara y al sur de Tequila. Se eleva 3,000 metros sobre el nivel del mar.

TEQUISISTLÁN ◆ Río de Oaxaca formado por la confluencia del Chapahuana con el Carrizal, en la vertiente oriental de la sierra de Miahuatlán. Corre de suroeste a noreste y, al sur de la sierra de Mixes, desemboca en el río Tehuantepec, del que es el afluente más importante.

TEQUISQUIAPAN ◆ Municipio de Querétaro situado al este-sureste de la capital de la entidad y al norte de San Juan del Río, en los límites con Hidalgo. Superficie: 343.6 km². Habitantes: 45,779, de los cuales 11,552 forman la población económicamente activa. Hablan alguna lengua indígena 59 personas mayores de cinco años. En la jurisdicción hay manantiales de aguas sulfurosas que lo han convertido en importante centro turístico. El municipio también es reconocido por sus artesanías de mimbre y la cría de ganado bravo.

TEQUISQUIAPAN, DE ◆ Valle de Querétaro situado en la altiplanicie mexicana, en las estribaciones septentrionales de la sierra Gorda, al nor-noreste de San Juan del Río. Lo limita al noroeste la sierra del Pinal de Zamorano y, al norte, el valle de Cadereyta. El suelo del valle de Tequisquiapan es rico en ópalos y topacios y en el sur hay numerosos manantiales de aguas termales.

TEQUITLALATO DE ZAPOTITLÁN ◆ Códice también conocido como de Tributos de Santiago Zapotitlán, población del actual estado de Puebla. De carácter tributario, es una tira de piel, de 25.6 por 85 centímetros, dividida horizontalmente por líneas rojas en seis bandas; representa 101 casas, cada una con pequeños círculos a los lados y, sobre ellos, una leyenda en mixteco en la que se asienta el nombre cristiano de cada habitante, su estado civil y los nombres, en náhuatl, de otros miembros de su familia. En el reverso la tira dice: "Pintura de Pedro Rodrigo de Santiago, Tequitlalato de Zapotitlán, presentada en nueve de agosto de mil quinientos sesenta y un años". El documento original se encuentra en la Biblioteca Nacional de Antropología e Historia.

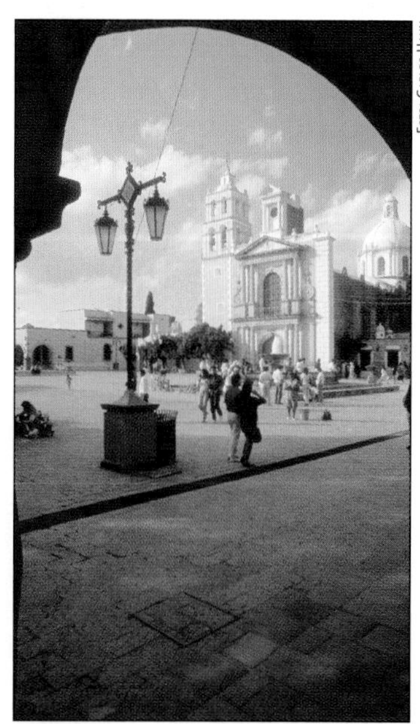

Plaza y parroquia de Tequisquiapan, Querétaro

TEQUIXQUIAC ◆ Municipio del Estado de México situado al nor-noreste de Tepotzotlán y al noroeste de Teotihuacán, en los límites con Hidalgo. Superficie: 127.42 km². Habitantes: 24,766, de los cuales 5,579 forman la población económicamente activa. Hablan alguna lengua indígena 59 personas mayores de cinco años (otomí 18 y náhuatl 9). En la localidad de Tlapanaloya hay una zona arqueológica y los principales lugares de recreo son El Salto, El Charrito, Palo Grande y el manantial El Bije. En la cabecera hay una parroquia construida en el siglo XVI y un museo regional de antropología e historia.

TEQUIXTEPEC, LIENZO DE ◆ Códice mixteco posterior a la conquista elaborado con técnica indígena. Procede de San Miguel Tequixtepec, Oaxaca, en la Mixteca Alta. Se divide en dos partes: el lienzo 1, de algodón, mide 3.05 por 2.48 metros. Tiene dibujados 25 cuadros con glifos toponímicos de la región, 24 de los cuales fueron traducidos al español en el siglo XVI. Está pintado en negro, anaranjado, rojo y verde; su contenido es topográfico y genealógico y está fechado con el signo mixteco para el año 6-técpatl (aproximadamente 1576). El lienzo 2, también de algodón, mide 2.85 metros por 70 centímetros. Presenta a 51 personajes, aunque sólo se anotan tres nombres indígenas. Está pintado en verde, negro, rosa y anaranjado. Ambos lienzos se encontraban en la presidencia municipal de San Miguel Tequixtepec y fueron descubiertos y estudiados en 1970 por Luz Irma de la Fuente y Salvador Cruz. Ahora forman parte del archivo del Instituto Nacional de Antropología e Historia.

TERÁN, ANA ◆ n. en Hermosillo, Son. (1949). Escritora. Estudió filosofía. Ha publicado crónicas y ensayos en *Casa del Tiempo*, *La Orquesta*, *Revista Mexicana de Cultura*, *La Plaza*, *Blancomóvil* y otras publicaciones. Autora de cuento:

Tiempo mutuo (1989), y biografía: *Más vale morir ahogado que de sed* (1995).

TERÁN, MIREYA ◆ n. en el DF (1941). Licenciada en lengua y literatura españolas por la UNAM. Fue profesora de preparatoria y colaboradora de suplementos culturales. Ingresó en el Servicio Exterior Mexicano en 1970, en el que fue intérpete oficial de la Presidencia de la República (1970-85), consejera de Asuntos Políticos de la embajada en España, ministro de asuntos culturales en el consulado en Nueva York, ciudad en la que fundó el Instituto Cultural Mexicano de Nueva York, que presidió hasta 1996; jefa de la cancillería de la embajada en Italia y directora adjunta de Protocolo de la SRE.

TERÁN LIRA, MANUEL ◆ n. en Torreón, Coah. (1939). Escritor. Médico cirujano titulado en el IPN. Ha sido editor de la *Revista Revolución*. Colaborador de las revista *Jueves de Excélsior* y de los periódicos *El Siglo de Torreón*, *El Porvenir* de Monterrey, *El Sol de Durango*, *La Opinión* y *Noticias* de Torreón. Autor de las novelas *Francisco Villa y la toma de Torreón* (1970), *Desde Macondo* (1973), *Lotería* (1975), *Cómo la ves* (1976), *El niño Fidencio* (1980), *Página roja* (1981), *Los indios laguneros* (1984), *La muerte del mexicano* (1984) y *El cholo Ladislao* (1985), así como de una *Historia de Torreón* (1978).

TERÁN PEREDO, JESÚS ◆ n. en Aguascalientes, Ags., y m. en Francia (1821-1866). Se tituló como abogado en el Seminario de Zacatecas (1845). Fue jefe político del partido de Aguascalientes (1849), gobernador interino de Aguascalientes (1849-50), fundador (1849) y director del Instituto Científico y Literario de esa entidad (1850), diputado a la Legislatura de Zacatecas (1850) y diputado federal (1853). Gobernador interino de Aguascalientes al triunfo de la revolución de Ayutla (1855-57) y gobernador constitucional (mayo de 1857). Fue secretario de Gobernación (del 18 de junio al 16 de septiembre de 1857) en el gabinete de Ignacio Comonfort. Durante la guerra de los Tres Años militó en las fuerzas de Vicente Rosas Landa en Veracruz y Oaxaca. Secretario de Justicia (del 8 de diciembre de 1861 al 23 de noviembre de 1863) y encargado del despacho de Gobernación (del 6 al 12 de abril de 1862) en el gobierno de Benito Juárez. En 1864 fue nombrado ministro plenipotenciario de México en España e Inglaterra. Durante su gestión intentó disuadir a Maximiliano de Habsburgo de sus propósitos imperialistas en México y aunque fracasó, pudo conseguir la declaración británica de neutralidad.

TERÁN DE LOS RÍOS, TOMÁS ◆ ¿n. en España? y m. en Puebla, Pue. (¿1670?-1724). Militar. Fue gobernador y capitán general de Nueva Galicia (1716-24). Durante su gestión encabezó a las fuerzas españolas que en 1722 derrotaron la última gran sublevación de los coras (☛) en el siglo XVIII.

TERÁN TERÁN, HÉCTOR ◆ n. en Moctezuma, Son., y m. en Mexicali, BC (1931-1998). Licenciado en administración de empresas por el Tecnológico de Monterrey. En el PAN, organización a la que perteneció desde 1952, fue secretario de Propaganda del Sector Juvenil, editor del periódico *El Debate*, presidente del partido en Baja California, delegado del Comité Ejecutivo Nacional en Sonora, consejero nacional regional, miembro del Comité Ejecutivo Nacional y candidato a la gubernatura de Baja California en 1977. Diputado a la Legislatura de Sonora (1980-83), diputado federal (1985-88), senador de la República (1994-95), secretario general de Gobierno (1989-94) y gobernador de Baja California (1995-98).

TERÁN ZOZAYA, HORACIO ◆ n. en Ciudad Victoria, Tams., y m. en EUA (1905-1970). Abogado. Fue agente del Ministerio Público y juez de lo civil en Tamaulipas, y en la ciudad de México, jefe del Departamento Jurídico de la regencia capitalina, oficial mayor de la Secretaría de Gobernación, gobernador de Tamaulipas (1951-57) y delegado del Consejo Nacional de Turismo en Texas.

TERAS, DE ◆ Sierra de Sonora situada en la región nororiental del estado, al este de la presa de La Angostura y al sureste de Agua Prieta. Forma parte de la sierra Madre Occidental. Se extiende de noroeste a sureste, y enlaza al este con la sierra de Huachinera. En ella se explotan yacimientos de cobre y plata.

TERCER IMPERIO ◆ Semanario político de oposición que apareció en 1896 en la ciudad de México. Fue dirigido por Inocencio Arreola. Algunos de sus colaboradores fueron Ramón Prida, Juan Sarabia y los hermanos Flores Magón.

TERCERA INTERNACIONAL ◆ ☛ *Internacional Comunista*.

TERCERO, JUAN D. ◆ n. en Ciudad Victoria, Tams., y m. en el DF (1895-1987). Músico. Su nombre completo era Juan Diego Tercero Farías. Compositor egresado del Conservatorio Nacional de Música, donde estudió con Gustavo E. Campa, y profesor de armonía y contrapunto titulado en la Escuela Normal de Música de París, donde estudió con Nadia Boulanger. Fue miembro del coro de Henry Expert, director del coro parisiense Au Temps de Ronsard, Francia (1933-35), director de la Escuela Nacional de Música de la UNAM (1946-54) y director de la Sociedad Coral Universitaria (1952-69). Autor de los ensayos *Pláticas sobre música* (1963). En 1969 editó 10 de sus composiciones corales. Compuso, entre otras, las siguientes obras: *Sinfonía del IV Centenario*, *O quam suavis*, *Ave regina coelorum*, *Veni sponsa Christi*, *Asumpta est María*, *Puella mea*, *El afilador*, *El vino de Lesbos*, *No me mueve, mi Dios*, *El gran teatro del mundo*, *Sonatina para violín y piano* y *Tres trozos para piano*. Además, utilizó poesía de Manuel M. Flores, para *Oda a la patria*; de Carlos Pellicer, para *Himno universitario*; de Manuel Gutiérrez Nájera, para *Non omnis moriar*; de Sor Juana Inés de la Cruz, para *Detente sombra de mi bien esquivo*; de Enrique González Martínez, para *Milagro de la tarde*; de Gutierre de Cetina, para *Ojos claros, serenos*; de Francisco Monterde, para *Tres haikais*; y de Francisco Díaz de León, para *Señor, deja mis ojos*. Miembro del Seminario de Cultura Mexicana desde 1963. Vicepresidente de la Confederación Nacional de Coros de América (1965) y presidente de la Federación

FOTO: CARLOS HAHN

Héctor Terán Terán

Nacional de Coros de México (1965). Maestro emérito por la UNAM (1967). Medalla Pedro José Méndez (1968) y presea Manuel M. Ponce (1986).

Foto: Michael Calderwood

Laguna de Términos, en Campeche

Términos, de ◆ Laguna de Campeche situada en la parte suroccidental de la península de Yucatán. Mide 70 por 40 km. Es una albufera separada del golfo de México por la isla del Carmen; se comunica con aquél por las barras Principal y de Puerto Real. En la laguna desembocan los ríos Palizada, Chumpán y Candelaria, y las lagunas de Pom, Atasta, del Corte, San Carlos, del Este, de Balchacah y de Palau.

Terrazas, Alberto ◆ n. en Chihuahua, Chih., y m. en EUA (1869-1925). Hijo de Luis Terrazas Fuentes. Empresario y político porfirista. Fue gerente del Banco Minero Chihuahuense, constructor del rastro de la ciudad de México y gobernador de Chihuahua (de diciembre de 1910 a enero de 1911). En 1913 combatió a las fuerzas de la División del Norte que intentaron tomar Chihuahua y en 1914 participó en la batalla de Ojinaga. Se exilió en El Paso a la caída del gobierno de Victoriano Huerta (1914). Volvió a México en 1920, pero tres años más tarde regresó a EUA.

Manuel Terrazas

Terrazas, Manuel ◆ n. en el DF (1923). Su apellido materno es Guerrero. Estudió en la Escuela Nacional de Maestros y en la Escuela Nacional de Jurisprudencia de la UNAM. Fue profesor de educación primaria (1945-49). En 1939 ingresó al PCM, en el que se desempeñó como miembro de la Comisión Juvenil del DF (1939-40), director del órgano *La Voz de México* (1952-60), secretario general del Comité del DF (1955) y miembro del Comité Central, del presídium, de la Comisión Política y secretario de Organización, de Acción Sindical y de Finanzas (1945-73). Fue miembro del Comité Nacional y secretario de Prensa, Propaganda y Acción Social de la CJM (1945 y 1951-52); miembro del Comité Nacional de la CCI (1961-66) y miembro de la Comisión Ejecutiva Nacional del MLN (1961-64). En 1973 formó un organismo al que llamó Asamblea Permanente del PCM y en noviembre de ese año, acusado de "actividad abiertamente escisionista", fue expulsado. En diciembre formó la Unidad de Izquierda Comunista, que dirigió hasta 1987, cuando se fusionó en el Partido Mexicano Socialista, de cuya dirección formó parte. Fue diputado federal en coalición con el PST (1979-82) y con el Partido Socialista Unificado de México (1985-88). En 1989 rehusó incorporarse al PRD y formó la Corriente de Izquierda Socialista. En el mismo año se afilió al PFCRN y fue nuevamente diputado (1991-94). Miembro del Movimiento Mexicano por la Paz y del Consejo Mundial de la Paz.

Terrazas, Silvestre ◆ n. y m. en Chihuahua, Chih. (1873-1944). Periodista. Estudió en el Instituto Científico y Literario de Chihuahua. Fue oficial mayor de la diócesis de Chihuahua (1894) y director de la *Revista católica* (1896-1901), de la *Lira Chihuahuense* (1896-1901) y de *La Idea*. En 1899 fundó el periódico *El Correo de Chihuahua*, que dirigió hasta 1913, y en 1906 llevó el primer linotipo a Chihuahua. Por oponerse al gobernador Enrique C. Creel y al presidente Porfirio Díaz fue encarcelado varias veces. Liberado poco después, se exilió en Estados Unidos. Volvió a México a la caída de Díaz y reabrió *El Correo*, pero en 1912 fue detenido por soldados orozquistas que habían cerra-

Tomo I, Año I. Chihuahua, Miércoles 1º de Enero de 1902. Núm 1

EL CORREO DE CHIHUAHUA.

Diario Independiente, de información

1902.

A la Ciencia, á las Artes al Ejército Comercio é Industria, que hacen la prosperidad de Chihuahua; A los hogares que la engalanan á nuestros subscriptores, lectores anunciantes amigos y compañeros, saludamos al principiar el año, deseándoles prosperidad y dicha.

La Redacción

Directorio.

INDICADOR.

PROGRAMA.

Temas

El Correo de Chihuahua, periódico dirigido por Silvestre Terrazas

do una vez más el diario. Liberado luego del asesinato del presidente Francisco I. Madero, se unió a la División del Norte. Fue secretario general de Gobierno (1913-15) y gobernador interino de Chihuahua (del 13 al 20 de mayo de 1914 y del 4 de octubre al 13 de noviembre de 1914). Al ser derrotado el villismo por los carrancistas se retiró a El Paso y ahí publicó el periódico *La Patria* (1919-31). Volvió al país y reeditó *El Correo de Chihuahua*. Fue diputado local y federal. Autor de *Curiosidades históricas, Mártires de la Tarahumara* y *El verdadero Pancho Villa*. Presidió la Sociedad de Estudios Históricos de Chihuahua.

Terrazas Allen, Patricia ◆ n. en Delicias, Chih. (1943). Ingeniera agrónoma graduada en la Universidad Autónoma de Chihuahua. Ha pertenecido a los consejos de administración de diversas empresas agrícolas. Afiliada al PAN desde 1966, ha sido coordinadora de campañas, secretaria de Organización en su ciudad y miembro del Consejo Estatal. Regidora en el Ayuntamiento de Delicias (1976-79) y diputada federal (1991-94). Premio a la Mujer Profesional, otorgado por la Facultad de Ciencias de la Universidad Autónoma de Chapingo (1987).

Terrazas Fuentes, Luis ◆ n. y m. en Chihuahua, Chih. (1829-1923). Ganadero y militar. Hizo estudios en el

Luis Terrazas Fuentes

Seminario de Chihuahua. Fue fiscal de la Tesorería (1851), regidor (1854-55) y síndico del ayuntamiento de Chihuahua. Militó en las filas liberales durante la guerra de los Tres Años. Fue jefe político del distrito de Iturbide (1859), presidente de la junta de guerra contra los apaches y comanches (1860) y gobernador interino (1860-61), constitucional (1861-64) y nuevamente interino de Chihuahua (1865-67). Durante la intervención francesa formó una Junta Patriótica Central en Chihuahua, organizó el Batallón Primero del estado, rechazó el cargo de prefecto imperial que le ofreció Maximiliano y comandó las fuerzas republicanas que expulsaron de Chihuahua a los franceses (1866). Reelegido gobernador constitucional al triunfo de la República (1869-73), en 1871 combatió la sublevación de la Noria y en 1872, luego de ser derrotado por los porfiristas, trasladó su gobierno a Ciudad Guerrero, pero volvió a Chihuahua a la muerte del presidente Benito Juárez. Durante el gobierno de Sebastián Lerdo de Tejada fundó los periódicos *El Radical* y *El Rasca-Rabias*. En 1876 se opuso a los rebeldes del Plan de Tuxtepec. Al triunfo de éstos se retiró a la vida privada, pero en 1879 participó en la insurrección que derrocó al gobernador Ángel Trías. Reconciliado con Díaz, durante el porfiriato se hizo de un latifundio de más de 2.5 millones de hectáreas, fue nuevamente gobernador de Chihuahua (1880-84 y 1903-1904), diputado federal y senador de la República (1886-90). Se exilió en Estados Unidos en 1913 y volvió a México en 1920.

TERRAZAS GARCÍA, ISAAC ◆ n. en el DF (1973). Futbolista. Ha jugado como defensa central del equipo América. Seleccionado nacional, participó en el Campeonato Mundial de 1998 y en la Copa América de Paraguay en 1999.

TERRAZAS QUEZADA, JOAQUÍN ◆ n. en Labor de Dolores y m. en Chihuahua, Chih. (1829-1901). Militar. Desde 1850 dirigió numerosas campañas de represión contra los apaches, lo que le valió el mote de *El azote de los indios*; herido en la batalla de Ojo de la Laguna se retiró del ejército. En 1857, sin embargo, desconoció al gobierno de Félix María Zuloaga, se levantó en armas y se unió a las fuerzas liberales. Durante la intervención francesa fue comandante militar de Chihuahua, pero en 1864 se incorporó a la guardia del presidente Benito Juárez y en 1865 lo escoltó hasta Paso del Norte. Al año siguiente participó en la ofensiva republicana que recuperó Chihuahua y Durango. Se opuso a los planes de la Noria (1871-72) y Tuxtepec (1875-76), pero luego se sometió a Porfirio Díaz y fue inspector de colonias militares y jefe de la segunda zona militar. Es autor de un volumen de *Memorias* (1905).

TERRAZAS VALDÉS, ANA CECILIA ◆ n. en el DF (1969). Periodista y escritora. Licenciada en comunicación por la UIA. Ha hecho estudios de posgrado en literatura y periodismo. Ha sido coordinadora de prensa del Centro de Investigación y Análisis del Campo (1991-93), editora y reportera de la agencia APRO (1992-97) y reportera de cultura (1992-99) de *Proceso*. Ha colaborado en *Equis*, *Fractal*, *Viceversa* y *Letras Libres*, *Reforma* y en diversos programas de radio y televisión. Coautora de *La prensa en la calle* (1994). Fue becaria de intercambios México-Estados Unidos y Canadá (1995).

TERRENATE ◆ Municipio de Tlaxcala situado al norte de Huamantla y al noreste de Apizaco, en los límites con Puebla. Superficie: 297.30 km^2. Habitantes: 10,505, de los cuales 3,530 forman la población económicamente activa. Hablan alguna lengua indígena 15 personas mayores de cinco años (náhuatl 13).

TERRÉS, JOSÉ ◆ n. y m. en el DF (1864-1924). Se tituló en la Escuela Nacional de Medicina (1885), en la que ejerció la docencia (1888-1921). Fue inspector de las escuelas municipales de la ciudad de México, jefe de la sección de terapéutica clínica del Instituto de Medicina, director de la Escuela Nacional Preparatoria, director del Instituto Médico Nacional, director de la *Revista Médica* y secretario de la Escuela Nacional de Medicina. Colaboró en los *Anales del Instituto Médico Nacional* y en la *Gaceta Médica de México*. Autor de *Manual de propedéutica clínica*, *La etiología del tabardillo*, *El paludismo en México* y *Manual de patología interna*. Fue tres veces presidente de la Academia Nacional de Medicina (1900, 1907 y 1912), institución a la que ingresó en 1895.

Ana Cecilia Terrazas

José Terrés

TERRÍQUEZ SÁMANO, ERNESTO MAXIMINO ◆ n. en Colima, Col. (1938). Licenciado en comercio y administración por el Colegio Luis Silva de Guadalajara. Ha sido tesorero del ayuntamiento de Colima, secretario general de la Federación de Organizaciones Populares de Colima y fundador de *Panorama Cultural*, suplemento del periódico *Panorama*. Colaborador de *Ecos* *de la Costa* y *Diario de Colima*. Autor de *La Iglesia en la historia de México* (1963), *Margarita Maza de Juárez, una vida ejemplar* (1971), *Con ejemplos como Juárez no podemos fracasar* (1972), *Colima en la ruta de Juárez* (1972), *Una visión de Revueltas. Ideología y mito en El luto humano* (1976) y *Monografía del estado de Colima* (1982).

Terroba Wolff, Guillermo Felipe ◆ n. en el DF (1950). Licenciado en derecho por la UNAM (1972), especializado en programación-presupuestación en el Centro de Capacitación para el Desarrollo de la SPP (1976). Pertenece al PRI desde 1969. Ha sido jefe de la Oficina del Registro Nacional de Extranjeros (1971-73), subjefe del Departamento de Servicios Generales (1973-77) y secretario del titular (1977) en la Secretaría de Gobernación, subdirector de Análisis Social para la Evaluación de la SPP (1977-79), asesor del subsecretario de Regulación y Abasto (1979) y subgerente coordinador del Programa PIDER-Conasupo de la Secretaría de Comercio (1979); director de Infraestructura y Servicios de Apoyo de la Secretaría de la Contraloría General de la Federación (1983-88) y director general de la Corporación Mexicana de Impresión del DDF (1988-94).

Terrones Benítez, Alberto ◆ n. en Villa del Nombre de Dios, Dgo. (1887-1981). Se tituló como abogado en el Instituto Juárez de Durango (1910). Fue diputado al Congreso Constituyente de 1916-17, presidente del Tribunal Superior de Justicia de Durango, diputado federal suplente (1918-24), diputado federal (1924-26) y miembro del Bloque Antirreeleccionista que se oponía al regreso de Álvaro Obregón a la Presidencia; fundador del Sindicato de Campesinos Agraristas de Durango y gobernador interino del mismo estado (1929-30). Trabajó como gerente de minas y colaboró en las publicaciones estadounidenses *Engineering and Mining Journal* y *Mining Journal*, y en el diario capitalino *Excélsior* (1937-46). En 1988 fue publicado su *Anecdotario político de Durango*.

Tesechoacán ◆ Río de Oaxaca y Veracruz, también llamado Playa Vicente. Nace de la confluencia de los ríos Manso y Ayutla o Cajones, en el oriente de Oaxaca, al norte de la sierra de Villa Alta; entra al estado de Veracruz, corre de suroeste a noreste y en la llanura costera del golfo tuerce al noroeste y se une al Papaloapan, al sur de Tlacotalpan. Es navegable en la mayor parte de su curso.

Tesechoacán ◆ ☛ *José Azueta.*

Testigos de Jehová ◆ Grupo religioso fundado en 1878 en Pittsburgh por Charles Taze Russell, quien se dedicó a la reinterpretación de los textos bíblicos de acuerdo con los trabajos de William Miller, quien afirmaba que el mundo se acabaría en 1844. Russell murió en 1916 y fue sustituido en la dirección de los testigos de Jehová por Joseph Rutherford. El grupo ha tenido varios nombres: Sociedad de Publicaciones de la Torre del Vigía, Asociación Internacional de Estudiantes de la Biblia, Reino Teocrático, Aurora Milenial, Russellismo, Sociedad Bíblica de Publicaciones de la Torre del Vigía y Púlpito del Pueblo; su nombre actual fue adoptado en 1931. Este grupo rechaza la Trinidad cristiana y la preñez divina de María y afirman que Jesucristo tuvo varios hermanos y hermanas. Carece de templos para celebrar sus oficios y sus lugares de reunión son llamados *Salones del Reino*; se opone al servicio militar, a rendir honores a los símbolos patrios y a recibir vacunas, trasplantes de órganos o transfusiones de sangre. Considera que todos los miembros de la organización son "ministros de la palabra" y tienen la obligación de hacer proselitismo religioso. En México edita las revistas *La Atalaya* (por lo que a veces sus miembros son llamados *atalayos*), versión en español de *The Watchtower and Herald of Christ's Presence*, y *¡Despertad!*, versión castellana de *Awake!* Además, poseen su propia editorial. En agosto de 1999, se calculaba que en México había 525,230 testigos de Jehová, lo que quintuplicaba las cifras de 10 años atrás.

Tetabiate ◆ m. cerca de Mazocoba, Son. (1867-1901). Jefe de los indios cahítas pobladores del valle del Yaqui. Su nombre castellano era Juan Maldonado y fue lugarteniente y sucesor de José María Leyva *Cajeme*. Al morir éste, Tetabiate asumió el mando de la rebelión del valle del Yaqui hasta mayo de 1897, cuando firmó la paz con el gobierno federal y fue designado capitán general de la zona. En 1899, sin embargo, ante la violación de los tratados firmados en Estación Ortiz, volvió a dirigir una sublevación indígena; dos años después fue muerto en combate y sucedido por Luis Bule.

Tetecala ◆ Municipio de Morelos situado al suroeste de Cuernavaca y al este de Zacatepec. Superficie: 89.16 km^2. Habitantes: 6,843, de los cuales 1,792 forman la población económicamente

Calles rústicas de Tetecala, Morelos

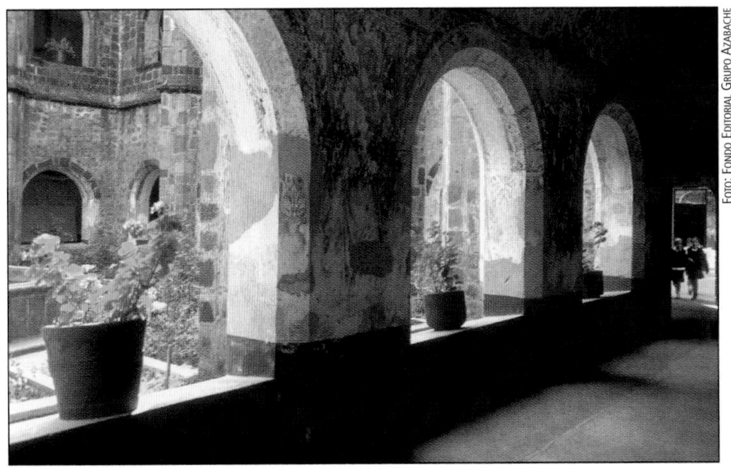

Claustro del convento dominico de San Juan Bautista en Tetela del Volcán, Morelos

activa. Hablan alguna lengua indígena 48 personas mayores de cinco años (náhuatl 44). El municipio cuenta con yacimientos minerales.

TETELA DE OCAMPO ◆ Municipio de Puebla situado en la porción norte del estado, al nor-noreste de la capital de la entidad y al este de Zacatlán. Superficie: 304.89 km². Habitantes: 24,106, de los cuales 6,287 forman la población económicamente activa. Hablan alguna lengua indígena 5,591 personas mayores de cinco años (náhuatl 5,565). El municipio celebra, el 15 de agosto, la fiesta de la Asunción.

TETELA DEL VOLCÁN ◆ Municipio de Morelos situado al noreste de Cuautla, en los límites con el Estado de México y Puebla. Superficie: 111.6 km². Habitantes: 15,673, de los cuales 3,476 forman la población económicamente activa. Hablan alguna lengua indígena 2,629 personas mayores de cinco años (náhuatl 2,612).

TETELES DE ÁVILA CASTILLO ◆ Municipio de Puebla situado al sureste de Huauchinango, al este de Zacatlán y contiguo a Teziutlán. Superficie: 8.93 km². Habitantes: 4,531, de los cuales 996 forman la población económicamente activa. Hablan alguna lengua indígena 797 personas mayores de cinco años (náhuatl 783). El 7 de octubre, en la cabecera se realiza un festival de danzas autóctonas.

TETEOINNAN ◆ Deidad mexica, posiblemente de origen humano, cuyo nombre significa "Madre de los dioses". De acuerdo con la *Historia* de Francisco Javier Clavijero, fue hija de un cacique de Colhuacan. En la época de la fundación de México-Tenochtitlan los sacerdotes aztecas pidieron al caudillo de Colhuacan una de sus hijas, "para consagrarla como madre de su dios protector", Huitzilopochtli. El cacique accedió sin saber que su hija sería sacrificada ante el altar del dios y que su cadáver sería desollado para que la piel sirviese de vestimenta, durante la ceremonia, a un joven mexica. De este modo, la joven fue convertida en diosa y madre honoraria no sólo de Huitzilopochtli, sino de todos los dioses aztecas y reverenciada desde entonces como Teteoinnan. Por ser madre de los dioses y éstos, a su vez, padres de la raza humana, Teteoinnan era llamada también Toci, "nuestra abuela". Desempeñaba múltiples funciones en el panteón azteca: era, por ejemplo, la creadora de los movimientos telúricos, por lo que se le adoraba con el nombre de Tlaliyolo, "corazón de la tierra"; patrocinaba también a los médicos y adivinos bajo la faceta de Yoaltícitl, "médica de la noche", y como una de las terapias más utilizadas entre los antiguos mexicanos era la del baño de vapor, el temazcal, era conocida también como Temazcalteci, "abuela de los baños". Otro de sus nombres era Cihuatéotl, diosa femenina. Entre los tlaxcaltecas, Teteoinnan era la patrona de las lavanderas. Uno de los templos más importantes de la diosa se hallaba en el cerro del Tepeyac, donde actualmente se levanta la basílica de Guadalupe.

TETEPANGO ◆ Municipio de Hidalgo situado al este de Tula y al oeste de Pachuca. Superficie: 56.5 km². Habitantes: 8,805, de los cuales 1,860 forman la población económicamente activa. Hablan alguna lengua indígena 36 personas mayores de cinco años (náhuatl 23).

TETIPAC ◆ Municipio de Guerrero situado al norte de Taxco y al noreste de Ixcateopan, en los límites con el Estado de México. Superficie: 269.3 km². Habitantes: 12,649, de los cuales 2,655 forman la población económicamente activa. Hablan alguna lengua indígena 15 personas mayores de cinco años. En la jurisdicción hay yacimientos minerales, varias cascadas y un manantial de aguas termales en Huaxtelica. En la cabecera se producen artificios pirotécnicos.

Entrada a la ciudad de Tetipac, Guerrero

Tetiz ♦ Municipio de Yucatán situado al oeste de Mérida y al este de Sisal. Superficie: 180.11 km². Habitantes: 4,013, de los cuales 926 forman la población económicamente activa. Hablan alguna lengua indígena 2,195 personas mayores de cinco años (maya 2,193).

Tetla de la Solidaridad ♦ Municipio de Tlaxcala situado al noreste de la capital de la entidad. Superficie: 153.8 km². Habitantes: 19,722, de los cuales 4,051 forman la población económicamente activa. Hablan alguna lengua indígena 44 personas mayores de cinco años (náhuatl 27).

Tetlama ♦ Río de Morelos, también llamado Jojutla. Nace de la confluencia de varios arroyos en las laderas meridionales de la sierra de Ocuilan, al sureste de las ruinas de Xochicalco. Corre de noroeste a sureste. Recibe a los ríos Xochitepec y Yautepec, al sur de Jojutla de Juárez y al sureste del lago de Tequesquitengo, y desemboca en el río Grande de Amacuzac. Es utilizado para irrigar los cañaverales de la zona, así como las plantaciones de arroz.

Tetlatlahuca ♦ Municipio de Tlaxcala situado al suroeste de la capital de la entidad y al este de Cacaxtla. Superficie: 44.6 km². Habitantes: 10,230, de los cuales 4,281 forman la población económicamente activa. Hablan alguna lengua indígena 10 personas mayores de cinco años.

Tetzahuitl ♦ Uno de los nombres del dios mexica Huitzilopochtli. Significa "espanto" y le fue aplicado luego de que asesinó a sus 400 hermanos. Los mexicas también lo llamaron Tetzauteotl, esto es, "dios espantoso".

Tetzauhcíhuatl ♦ Deidad nahua que habitaba en el segundo cielo y que, cuando terminara el mundo, bajaría a la tierra para comerse a los hombres. Su función y el hecho de que fuera un esqueleto, daba origen a su nombre, que significa "mujer espantosa".

Teuchitlán ♦ Municipio de Jalisco situado al oeste de Guadalajara y al norte de Cocula. Superficie: 285.53 km². Habitantes: 8,133, de los cuales 2,081 forman la población económicamente activa. Hablan alguna lengua indígena nueve personas mayores de cinco años.

Teuffer San Ciprián, Salvador ♦ n. y m. en el DF (1905-1972). Estudió en la Escuela Superior de Ingeniería Mecánica y Eléctrica del IPN. Líder campesino. Fue oficial mayor (1934-40) y secretario general del Departamento de Asuntos Agrarios y Colonización (1940-46), embajador de México en Bolivia, ingeniero contratista de la Secretaría de Agricultura y Recursos Hidráulicos y jefe de pensionados de Aeropuertos y Servicios Auxiliares.

Teúl de González Ortega ♦ Municipio de Zacatecas situado al oeste de Nochistlán y al sur-suroeste de la capital de la entidad, en los límites con Jalisco. Superficie: 1,261.81 km². Habitantes: 9,327, de los cuales 1,824 forman la población económicamente activa. Desde el siglo IX, en el actual territorio municipal se instaló uno de los más importantes puntos de intercambio de los pueblos del occidente mesoamericano e incluso del actual suroeste de Estados Unidos. De las construccciones prehispánicas, subsiste un templo, que es el principal atractivo de la zona arqueológica de El Teúl, pero también se han encontrado diversas tumbas, figuras de cerámica, herramientas de cobre, pipas de piedra, malacates, molcajetes y ornamentos de concha y caracol.

Teutli Otero, Guillermo ♦ n. en el DF (1946). Licenciado en derecho por la UNAM, tomó cursos en problemas económicos y sociales del desarrollo en la Escuela de Administración Pública, España (1970) y en economía y finanzas en el Instituto Internacional de Administración Pública, Francia (1971); doctor en economía del desarrollo por la Universidad de París (1973), llevó un curso de economía industrial y evaluación de proyectos en el Instituto de Estudios del Desarrollo Económico y Social, Francia (1973-74). Desde 1963 pertenece al PRI, en cuyo CEN ha sido coordinador de Divulgación Ideológica (1980-81) y coordinador de la Comisión de la Frontera Norte (1982). Subsecretario de Divulgación Ideológica del CEN de la FOP (1984). Se ha desempeñado como profesor en la UNAM (1975-), secretario auxiliar en la Secretaría Privada de la Presidencia de la República (1975), subdirector sectorial de la Industria Electrónica Fronteriza y Maquiladora de la Secretaría de Patrimonio y Fomento Industrial (1977-82), comisario A en entidades paraestatales del Sector Turismo (1983), director general de Análisis y Evaluación (1983-85), comisario A del Sector Comercio (1985-86) de la Secogef, contralor general de Conasupo (1988-91) y asesor general y director financiero (1991) del Infonavit. Coautor de *El comercio exterior de México* (1982) y de *Asian Productivity Organization* (1983).

Teutli Talavera, Honorato ♦ n. en Cholula, Pue., y m. en el DF (1893-1959). Antirreeleccionista. Fue uno de los fundadores, junto con los hermanos Serdán, del Club Luz y Progreso. En 1913 se levantó en armas contra el gobierno de Victoriano Huerta, alcanzó el grado de general de división y fue designado jefe de operaciones en Puebla y presidente del Consejo de Guerra en México. Fue presidente municipal de Cholula y de Huejotzingo e inspector general de policía en Puebla.

Texas ♦ Nombre que recibió desde fines del siglo XVII el territorio situado en el extremo nororiental de la Nueva España, al norte del río Nueces, al norte y este del río Bravo, al sur del río Rojo y al oeste del río Sabinas, que formó parte del Imperio Mexicano (1821-23) y de los Estados Unidos Mexicanos (1824-36) y que, con la franja situada entre el Nueces y el Bravo, fue ocupado militarmente por Estados Unidos en la guerra de 1846-47, nación al que pertenece desde 1848, según lo establecen los Tratados de Guadalupe-Hidalgo. Hasta el siglo XVI, la región estuvo habitada por comanches, apaches, asinais, carancahuases, coxates y dancoeses, indios nómadas dedicados principalmente a la caza, la pesca y la recolección. En 1519,

cana por su idioma y su religión; que, como lo decían en el documento de noviembre, el establecimiento del centralismo destruía el acuerdo que los unía a México; y que la consolidación del gobierno centralista era muestra de que "los mexicanos no están hechos para la libertad". Ese mismo día, David Gouverneur Burnet y Lorenzo de Zavala fueron elegidos, respectivamente, presidente y vicepresidente de la República. Burnet (1788-1870), que había combatido en las fuerzas de Francisco de Miranda en Venezuela (1806), llegó a Texas a principios de la década de los treinta y, como la mayoría de sus paisanos, se opuso a los intentos conciliadores de Austin y promovió, desde 1835, la separación texana. Que Austin no hubiera sido elegido presidente se explica porque, a causa de la guerra, su política moderada había sido desplazada. El 3 de marzo, la convención creó un comité encargado de dirigir la guerra, que fue integrado por Houston y Zavala, entre otros. Cuatro días más tarde, Santa Anna tomó el pequeño fuerte de El Álamo y pasó a degüello a sus defensores, lo que acabó de exacerbar el odio que promovían los separatistas más activos. Durante marzo y abril, mientras una fuerza naval al mando de Francisco de Paula López intentó bloquear las costas texanas, el ejército de José Urrea avanzó hasta las márgenes del río Colorado: tomó Matagorda, New Washington, Brazoria y San Felipe, donde, a principios de abril, se instaló Santa Anna. A fines de abril, un contingente del ejército de Estados Unidos comandado por Edmund Gaines cruzó el río Sabinas y tomó Nacogdoches, supuestamente para evitar que la guerra afectara los intereses de su país, pero en realidad para impulsar la avalancha de mercenarios que se incorporaban a las tropas texanas. Días después, al mando de 100 hombres, Santa Anna cruzó el Brazos y fracasó en su intento por capturar al gobierno de Burnet en Harrisburg, por lo que, durante los cinco días siguientes, con 500 soldados de refuerzo, se dedicó a perseguir a 800 milicianos dirigidos por Houston, que se retiraba hacia el río Trinidad. En ese movimiento, el 21 de abril las tropas santanistas fueron sorprendidas y derrotadas por los texanos y, al día siguiente, una patrulla de milicianos capturó a Santa Anna, quien de inmediato ordenó la paralización de toda la campaña. Poco después, el presidente mexicano fue conducido al puerto de Velasco, donde, el 14 de mayo, firmó un acuerdo con el presidente Burnet en el que se establecía que "El general Antonio López de Santa Anna, se conviene en no tomar las armas ni influir en que se tomen contra el pueblo de Texas durante la actual contienda de independencia", acordó el retiro de las tropas mexicanas al sur del río Bravo y la devolución de "toda propiedad particular incluyéndose ganado, caballos, esclavos negros, o gente contratada de cualesquiera denominación (.) aprehendida por una parte del ejército mexicano o que se hubiere refugiado en dicho ejército desde el principio de la última invasión". Además, Santa Anna y Burnet firmaron un acuerdo secreto donde se establecía que el veracruzano "preparará las cosas en el gabinete de México para que sea admitida la comisión que se mande por el gobierno de Texas, a fin de que por toda negociación sea todo transado, y reconocida la independencia que ha declarado la Convención", y que en un futuro próximo, Texas y Mexico celebrarían un tratado de límites, "no debiendo extenderse el territorio de este último más allá del Río Bravo del Norte". Filisola inició la retirada hacia el sur, pero días más tarde fue desconocido por Urrea, que se empeñaba en continuar la guerra. En mayo, el gobierno de José Justo Corro declaró que Santa Anna estaba incapacitado para celebrar tratados con Texas mientras estuviera preso y apoyó a Urrea, quien a mediados de junio sustituyó a Filisola y reunió a las fuerzas mexicanas en Matamoros, con la idea de preparar la recuperación del territorio perdido. Al mes siguiente, el gobierno de Estados Unidos extendió su reconocimiento formal a la República de Texas, decisión que ratificó a principios de 1837. Poco después, Francia, Gran Bretaña y Bélgica reconocieron a la nueva República. Los texanos, por su parte, celebraron en octubre sus primeras elecciones y Houston se convirtió en el primer presidente constitucional. En diciembre de 1836, al promulgarse la Constitución centralista, el estado de Coahuila y Tejas se convirtió en los departamentos de Coahuila y Tejas, quizá con la vana intención de convencer a los texanos de reincorporarse a la República, pero esta última denominación nunca tuvo vigencia efectiva. De todas formas, y según los acuerdos entre Burnet y Santa Anna, el límite entre Coahuila y Texas se estableció en el río Bravo y, sin que México lo reconociera, el territorio del departamento de Tamaulipas quedó reducido al sur del Bravo. Durante 1837, los enfrentamientos entre México y Texas se desarrollaron principalmente en el golfo de México, pero no alcanzaron la intensidad de los años anteriores. En 1838 fue elegido presidente Mirabeu Bonaparte Lamar, quien inició una campaña de exterminio contra los indios del norte y en 1839 trasladó la capital texana a Austin. En septiembre de 1838, una columna de milicianos texanos al mando de Ruben Ross se incorporó a las fuerzas federalistas de Antonio Zapata, Antonio Canales y José María González, que en enero de 1839, con el apoyo de otra fuerza texana, ésta al mando de William S. Fisher, se constituyeron en la República de Río Grande, con la idea de formar un gobierno independiente al sur de Texas y al noreste de México. De hecho, durante la primera mitad de la década de 1840, el territorio situado entre los ríos Bravo y Nueces no tuvo un gobierno estable y reconocido. En mayo de 1839, Lamar intentó obtener el reconocimiento de México, pero su enviado, Bardnard E. Bee, fue detenido en el puerto de Veracruz y enviado a Cuba. Al año siguiente, el gobierno texano apoyó el levantamiento federalista de Yucatán y, en noviembre, el ataque

En marzo de 1836, Santa Anna atacó el cuartel texano de El Álamo

Acta de Independencia de Texas

Glifo de Texcalyacac, Estado de México

de Juan Pablo Anaya contra Tabasco. Un año después, en septiembre de 1841, Lamar firmó un tratado de amistad con el gobierno yucateco de Santiago Méndez y poco después alquiló tres barcos de la marina texana a la República de Yucatán. En julio de 1842, una flota de las dos Estados independientes intentó tomar el puerto tabasqueño de Frontera, pero fue rechazada. A fines de ese año, el nuevo gobierno de Houston (1841-44) rechazó los tratos oficiales con Yucatán y durante los años siguientes, aunque la colaboración entre Texas y Yucatán continuó, ésta se desarrolló de manera extraoficial. Todavía en 1842 continuaban los enfrentamientos entre tropas mexicanas y texanas, pero éstos eran muy esporádicos. En septiembre de ese año las cosas parecieron cambiar, cuando un contingente tamaulipeco al mando de Adrián Woll ocupó San Antonio. Sin embargo, la ofensiva de Woll careció de apoyo del resto de las fuerzas mexicanas instaladas sobre el río Bravo y el general francés tuvo que retirarse. Houston, mientras tanto, impulsó la anexión de Texas a Estados Unidos, lo que logró el 12 de abril de 1844. Durante los tres meses siguientes, el Congreso mexicano se ocupó en discutir una ley impositiva para reiniciar la guerra contra Texas antes que el tratado de anexión entrara en vigor. Sólo en agosto comenzaron los preparativos para la guerra, pero la insurrección de Mariano Paredes y Arrillaga, en noviembre de 1844, que fue calificada por el presidente Santa Anna como maniobra de los texanos, pospuso por medio año las acciones. A fines del mismo 1844, Alison Jones fue elegido presidente de Texas. El 28 de febrero de 1845, el Congreso estadounidense aprobó la anexión de Texas y unos días más tarde, el embajador mexicano en Washington, Juan Nepomuceno Almonte, rompió las relaciones diplomáticas entre los dos países. Los estadounidenses y los texanos, sin embargo, plantearon la posibilidad de llegar a un arreglo diplomático que evitara la inminente guerra. El Congreso mexicano aprobó a principios de mayo iniciar negociaciones con los texanos y durante junio, una comisión secreta redactó un proyecto de acuerdo que establecía que México consentía "en reconocer la independencia de Texas", a cambio del compromiso de la nueva República de no agregarse a ningún Estado. El gobierno de José Joaquín de Herrera parecía estar dispuesto a aceptar el acuerdo, pero a mediados de junio, el cónsul mexicano en Nueva Orleans, Francisco de Paula Arrangóiz, informó que los estadounidenses se preparaban a tomar Galveston, por lo que el Congreso mexicano advirtió que "desde el momento en que el gobierno supiere que el Departamento de Texas se ha agregado a la Unión Americana, o que tropas de ella lo han invadido, declarará hallarse la nación en guerra con los Estados Unidos del Norte América". Naturalmente, las negociaciones entre Texas y México habían sido una maniobra de los texanos y los estadounidenses para ganar tiempo y, el 4 de julio de 1845, una nueva convención texana reunida en Washington-on-the-Brazos ratificó la decisión del Congreso estadounidense y se agregó a Estados Unidos. Una semana después, las fuerzas enviadas por Washington, al mando de Zachary Taylor, cruzaron el río Sabinas hacia el oeste y a principios de agosto alcanzaron la ribera del río Nueces. Durante los seis meses siguientes no hubo movimientos de tropas hacia Texas, debido a un nuevo intento de negociación impulsado por el gobierno estadounidense, pero también y sobre todo, al nuevo pronunciamiento de Paredes y Arrillaga en diciembre de ese año. A principios de 1846, el ejército estadounidense inició su avance hacia el río Bravo y en marzo se instaló frente a Matamoros. Entonces comenzó la guerra contra Estados Unidos.

Feria Internacional del Caballo en Texcoco, Estado de México

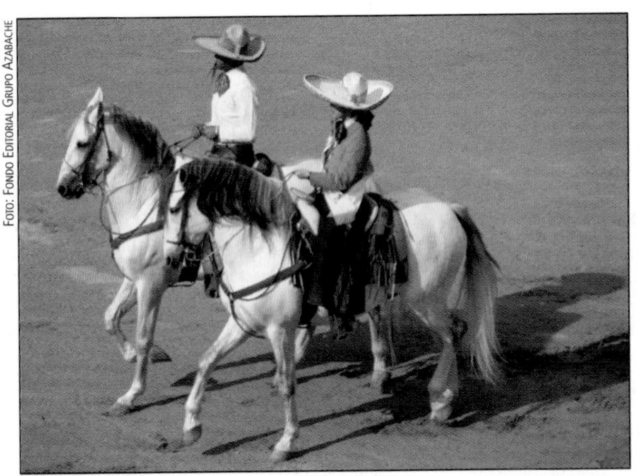

FOTO: FONDO EDITORIAL GRUPO AZABACHE

TEXCALYACAC ◆ Municipio del Estado de México situado al noreste de Tenancingo y al sureste de Toluca. Superficie: 13.75 km². Habitantes: 3,744, de los cuales 750 forman la población económicamente activa. Hablan alguna lengua indígena 25 personas mayores de cinco años (náhuatl 18 y otomí 7). En la jurisdicción se encuentra la zona de recreo del cerro de la Gloria. En la cabecera hay una iglesia construida en el siglo XVII.

TEXCATEPEC ◆ Municipio de Veracruz situado al oeste de Tuxpan y al suroeste de Tantoyuca, en los límites con Hidalgo. Superficie: 153.81 km². Habitantes: 8,243, de los cuales 2,106 forman la población económicamente activa. Hablan alguna lengua indígena 5,250 personas mayores de cinco años (otomí 5,208), y de ellas, 1,295 son monolingües.

TEXCATITLÁN ◆ Municipio del Estado de México situado al suroeste de Toluca y al sureste de Valle de Bravo. Superficie: 218.62 km². Habitantes: 13,970, de los cuales 2,687 forman la población económicamente activa. Hablan alguna lengua indígena 87 personas mayores de cinco años. En la jurisdicción hay varias zonas arqueológicas y atractivos turísticos como la laguna del Aserradero de Venta Morales, el cerro del Molcajete y el Ojo de Agua. En la cabecera se encuentra un templo del siglo XVIII.

TEXCOCO ◆ Municipio del Estado de México situado al noreste de Chalco y al sureste de Cuautitlán, en los límites con Puebla. Superficie: 503.53 km². Habitantes: 173,106, de los cuales 40,752 forman la población económicamente activa. Hablan alguna lengua indígena 2,362 personas mayores de cinco años (náhuatl 2,294 y totonaco 68). Los primeros habitantes del actual territorio municipal fueron otomíes, quienes fundaron la población de Catenichco. Ocupada más tarde por los teotihuacanos, que se establecieron en Coatlinchán, Tláloc, Huexotla, Texcotzingo y el Contador, y más tarde por los toltecas, en el siglo XI de nuestra era la población fue sometida por Xólotl al señorío acolhua de Tenayuca y dos siglos más tarde, a principios del siglo XIII, se convirtió en capital del señorío de Acolhuacan, aunque el primer rey que vivió permanentemente en ella, Quinantzin, lo hizo desde 1324. Los dominios de Texcoco llegaban al norte hasta Tepeapulco y al sur hasta Mixquic. Poco antes, hacia 1298, se iniciaron las guerras entre Texcoco y Azcapotzalco por el dominio del norte del lago. Durante los enfrentamientos, los tecpanecas ocuparon varias veces la zona de Huehuetoca, mientras que, por su parte, los acolhuas tomaron brevemente Azcapotzalco, a principios del siglo XIV. Cien años después, en 1418, las fuerzas de Tezozómoc, señor de Azcapotzalco, tomaron Texococo y derrocaron y asesinaron a Ixtlilxóchitl, el monarca acolhua, pero el hijo de éste, Nezahuacóyotl, formó una alianza con Tlacopan y México-Tenochtitlan, cuyas tropas derrotaron y expulsaron a los tecpanecas de Texcoco en 1430. Una vez instalado en el trono, Nezahualcóyotl (1430-72) reconstruyó la ciudad, la adornó con unos grandes jardines que se conocen con su nombre y la convirtió en el principal centro cultural del valle de Anáhuac. Durante el gobierno de su hijo Nezahualpilli (1472-1516), el señorío texcocano participó en las numerosas guerras de conquista organizadas por los mexicas y amplió sus dominios hasta la Huasteca, al norte, y los valles de Chalco y Cuernavaca, al sur. A principios del siglo XVI, la población texcocana era de 100,000 personas, aproximadamente. En diciembre de 1519, luego de la captura de Moctezuma Xocoyotztin, una pequeña fuerza de españoles incursionó en Texcoco y aprendió a Cacamatzin, rey de los acolhuas, y lo condujo a México-Tenochtiltan. Días más tarde, Pedro de Alvarado saqueó el palacio de Nezahualcóyotl. Al año siguiente, a fines de diciembre de 1520, las fuerzas españolas de Hernán Cortés, auxiliadas por un contingente de acolhuas disidentes comandados por un nuevo Ixtlilxóchitl, derrotaron a las fuerzas texcocanas en Matlatzingo y tomaron y saquearon la ciudad. El gobierno acolhua, por su parte, se retiró a la capital de los mexicas. Una vez instalado en Texcoco, y con la colaboración de los acolhuas, Cortés organizó desde ahí el sitio contra México-Tenochtitlan (☛ *Conquista*). En 1523, los tres primeros franciscanos que llegaron a la Nueva España, los flamencos Johan Dekers (Juan de Tecto), Johan van der Auwera (Juan de Aora) y Pedro de Gante, se instalaron en Texcoco y en ese mismo año De Gante fundó la primera escuela americana organizada de acuerdo con la tradición europea. Luego de la conquista, los españoles impusieron en Texcoco un gobierno de indios, que conservó muchas de las características prehispánicas, al que se le añadió un corregidor español. En 1552 fue creada la provincia de Tezcuco, que ocupaba una región entre los actuales estados de México y Tlaxcala, desde el extremo oriental del lago de Texcoco hasta los llanos de Apan. En 1570, los acolhuas sobrevivientes a la conquista española sumaban 77,000. A principios del siglo XVII, los españoles autorizaron al gobierno indígena de Texcoco la instalación de obrajes textiles y en 1604 existían ocho en la ciudad. Hacia 1620, a causa de la dominación de españoles y aristócratas colaboracionistas, un gran número de acolhuas comenzó emigrar, casi a escapar, a la ciudad de México. Unos años después, entre 1629 y 1631, una epidemia de *cocoliztli* diezmó a la población. La corriente migratoria fue detenida por el gobierno virreinal en 1640, mediante la persecución de los texcocanos en los barrios de indios de la ciudad de México, pero hacia 1644 la migración y la epidemia habían hecho descender la población de Texcoco a unos 8,000 habitantes. En 1786, la provincia de Tezcuco se convirtió en subdelegación de la intendencia de México. Entre febrero y julio de 1827, la cabecera municipal fue también capital del Estado de México. En diciembre de 1827, una parte de la guarnición local, al mando de José Nuño de Rivera, se levantó en armas en favor del plan que Manuel Montaño había proclamado en Otumba unos días antes. Las fuerzas de Rivera se dirigieron a Tulancingo (☛), donde se incorporaron a los contingentes conservadores de Nicolás Bravo. En la segunda mitad del siglo XIX se inició la desecación del lago de Texcoco. También a fines del siglo, durante el gobierno de Porfirio Díaz, se fundó la Escuela Nacional de Agricultura, que desde entonces se encuentra en el pueblo de Chapingo, contiguo a la hacienda del mismo nombre. La capilla de Chapingo fue decorada por Diego Rivera. El 23 de agosto de 1911, Andrés Molina Enríquez se levantó en armas contra el gobierno de Francisco León de la Barra y proclamó el Plan de Texcoco, en el que exhortaba a desconocer a De la Barra y proponía la creación de un gobierno provisional revolucionario,

Cazador de patos de Texcoco en la época precortesiana

encabezado por Emiliano Zapata, Francisco Vázquez Gómez, Manuel Bonilla y Pascual Orozco. El obispado de Texcoco fue creado por el papa Juan XXIII en abril de 1960. A principios de los años setenta se iniciaron los trabajos para regenerar el lago y se procedió a la construcción de varios embalses, como el lago Churubusco, el lago Recreativo y el lago Nabor Carrillo (☛). En la cabecera, llamada Texcoco de Mora en honor de José María Luis Mora, están la catedral y un convento franciscano, ambos construidos en el siglo XVI, así como un Museo Arqueológico dedicado a la cultura acolhua.

TEXHUACÁN ◆ Municipio de Veracruz situado al sur de Córdoba y al sureste de Orizaba. Superficie: 32.9 km^2. Habitantes: 4,077, de los cuales 1,028 forman la población económicamente activa. Hablan alguna lengua indígena 2,751 personas mayores de cinco años (náhuatl 2,750). Indígenas monolingües: 172.

TEXISTEPEC ◆ Municipio de Veracruz situado al sureste de Minatitlán y de Coatzacoalcos. Superficie: 615.26 km^2. Habitantes: 20,026, de los cuales 4,595 forman la población económicamente activa. Hablan alguna lengua indígena 611 personas mayores de cinco años (popoluca de Veracruz 566). En 1987, en la localidad de San Lorenzo Tenochtitla se descubrieron nueve esculturas olmecas.

TEYA ◆ Municipio de Yucatán situado al noreste de Motul y al noroeste de Temax. Superficie: 65.15 km^2. Habitantes: 2,075, de los cuales 479 forman la población económicamente activa. Hablan alguna lengua indígena 1,286 personas mayores de cinco años (maya).

Tezcatlipoca en el códice Borgia

TEYRA ◆ Pico de Zacatecas situado en el extremo sur de la sierra de los Novillos o de Teyra, al norte de los llanos de la Gruñidora y al noroeste de Fresnillo. Se eleva 2,866 metros sobre el nivel del mar. Cuenta con yacimientos minerales.

TEZCATLIPOCA ◆ Deidad nahua. Se le reconocía incluso superior a Huitzilopochtli y a Quetzalcóatl. Durante mucho tiempo se pensó que el nombre de este dios significaba "Espejo negro que humea", ya que el jeroglifo de la deidad está formado por un espejo redondo de obsidiana del que brota humo. Sin embargo, algunos autores sostienen que este jeroglifo es ideográfico y que, en realidad, su nombre significa "el ofrendado en sacrificio" o "el sacrificado". De acuerdo con el códice Zumárraga, los dioses originales, Tonacatecutli y Tonacacíhuatl, que habitaban el decimotercer cielo, tuvieron cuatro hijos: Tlatlauhqui Tezcatlipoca, que nació rojo; Yayauhqui Tezcatlipoca, que nació negro; Quetzalcóatl y Omitéotl, también llamado Inaquizcóatl o Huitzilopochtli, del que nació sólo el esqueleto. El primer Tezcatlipoca, Tlatlauhqui, fue adorado principalmente por los nahuas de Tlaxcala y Huejotzingo, por lo que prácticamente fue eliminado del panteón mexica. El segundo, Yayauhqui, al que Bernardino de Sahagún llamó el Júpiter mexicano, fue venerado principalmente por los pueblos del valle de México y se creía que "estaba en todo lugar, sabía todos los pensamientos y conocía todos los corazones". Según la mitología náhuatl, Tonacatecutli y Tonacacíhuatl encomendaron a sus cuatro hijos la creación del mundo, aunque sólo Yayauhqui Tezcatlipoca y Quetzalcóatl fueron autores de la creación; después de eso, ambas divinidades iniciaron una lucha en la que, alternativamente, cada uno de ellos vencía y era vencido, como representación de la pugna entre el día y la noche. Finalmente, Yayauhqui Tezcatlipoca derrotó a Quetzalcóatl y lo expulsó de Tula. Yayauhqui Tezcatlipoca tenía diversos nombres, según la función que desempeñase en determinado momento: era llamado Necocyautl, sembrador de discordias en ambas partes; Moyocoyatzin, el que hace cuanto quiere o el aire; Teyocoyani, el creador; Techimaltini, el protector; Xiuhtecuhtli, señor del fuego; Mictlantecuhtli, señor de la muerte; Yaotl, el enemigo, que era patrono de los guerreros, en una simbiosis con Huitzilopochtli; Telpochtli, Mancebo, puesto que, al representar también el vigor, no podía envejecer; y Yoalehécatl, viento de la noche, patrono de los salteadores y de los hechiceros, para quien se habían mandado poner bancas de piedra en todas las esquinas de las ciudades de la Triple Alianza; Titlacahua, "Cuyos Esclavos Somos", la única deidad ante la que se arrodillaban los mexicas; y, según Francisco Javier Clavijero, "el dios de la providencia, el alma del mundo, el creador del cielo y de la tierra y el señor de todas las cosas". Tras la conquista y la consiguiente imposición del catolicismo, los indígenas sometidos identificaban a Tezcatlipoca en la figura de Jesucristo, pues éste también había sido sacrificado.

TEZCATZONCATL ◆ Deidad nahua de la embriaguez y de los borrachos. Era esposo de Mayahuel y hermano de Colhuacatzincatl, Izqutecatl, Pantecatl, Papaztac, Tepoztecatl, Tlatecayohua, Tlihua, Toltecatl, Tototecatl y Yiauhtecatl.

TEZIUTLÁN ◆ Municipio de Puebla situado en la porción nororiental del estado, al noreste de la capital de la entidad. Superficie: 84.20 km^2. Habitantes: 71,228, de los cuales 20,239 forman la población económicamente activa. Hablan alguna lengua indígena 4,503 personas mayores de cinco años (náhuatl 4,361). Hasta mediados de 1640, cuando se convirtió en provincia del reino de México, Teziutlán fue un corregimiento sufragáneo de la provincia de Xalapa. Un siglo después, en

1787, con la implantación de las reformas borbónicas, la villa fue incorporada a la intendencia de Puebla. En la jurisdicción hay yacimientos minerales. En el pueblo de Mexcalcuautla se encuentra el mineral La Aurora. La cabecera destaca por sus curtidurías, la elaboración de vinos y licores y la fabricación de puros. Las fiestas más importantes son las del Jueves de Corpus y la Feria Nacional de Teziutlán, del 29 de julio al 6 de agosto.

TEZOATLÁN DE SEGURA Y LUNA ◆ Municipio de Oaxaca situado al sur-suroeste y cerca de Huajuapan de León y al noroeste de Chilapa de Díaz. Superficie: 334.27 km². Habitantes: 12,008, de los cuales 3,489 forman la población económicamente activa. Hablan alguna lengua indígena 5,220 personas mayores de cinco años (mixteco 5,218). En la jurisdicción hay yacimientos minerales. En la localidad de San Juan Diquiyú hay restos arqueológicos de un conjunto de construcciones semejantes a las de Monte Albán.

TEZONAPA ◆ Municipio de Veracruz situado al noroeste de la presa Miguel Alemán, al sur-sureste de Córdoba y al oeste de Tierra Blanca, en los límites con Puebla y Oaxaca. Superficie: 351 km². Habitantes: 49,805, de los cuales 14,005 forman la población económicamente activa. Hablan alguna lengua indígena 8,822 personas mayores de cinco años (náhuatl 7,711 y mazateco 929), de las cuales 147 son monolingües. En el municipio, creado en 1960 con territorio de Zongolica, hay dos ingenios azucareros, uno en Tezonapa y otro en Motzorongo. En 1900 llegaron al puerto de Veracruz 1,500 braceros italianos, enganchados para trabajos en "la finca azucarera y cafetera de Motzorongo", propiedad del general porfirista Carlos Pacheco (☛ *Italia*).

TEZONTEPEC ◆ Cabecera del municipio hidalguense de Pacula (☛).

TEZONTEPEC DE ALDAMA ◆ Municipio de Hidalgo situado al norte de Tula y al sur de Alfajayucan. Superficie: 120.8 km². Habitantes: 35,722, de los cuales 7,704 forman la población económicamente activa. Hablan alguna lengua indígena 219 personas mayores de cinco años (otomí 197).

TEZONTLALPAN ◆ Sierra de Hidalgo y México. Es la prolongación suroccidental de la de Pachuca. Se extiende de este a oeste, desde el oriente de Tula hasta el suroeste de la capital hidalguense. Por el suroeste está ligada a los cerros de Xalpa mediante un lomerío que, actualmente, está perforado por los túneles de Tequixquiac, que dan salida a las aguas negras de la cuenca de México.

TEZOYUCA ◆ Municipio del Estado de México situado al noroeste de Texcoco y al suroeste de Teotihuacán. Superficie: 17.49 km². Habitantes: 16,338, de los cuales 3,388 forman la población económicamente activa. Hablan alguna lengua indígena 70 personas mayores de cinco años (otomí 30 y náhuatl 29). En la jurisdicción se halla la zona arqueológica de Cuanalán, que no ha sido explorada.

TEZOZÓMOC ◆ m. en Azcapotzalco (1427). Fue rey de Azcapotzalco de 1348 a 1427. En 1413 conquistó Texcoco, ordenó el asesinato del rey Ixtlilxóchitl y desterró al heredero legítimo del trono, Nezahualcóyotl. Más tarde se impuso sobre los señoríos de Xaltocan y Culhuacan. Casó a una de sus hijas, Ayauhcíhuatl, con el señor mexica Huitzilíhuitl, con lo que consiguió dominar casi todo el valle de México.

THALÍA ◆ n. en el DF (1971). Nombre profesional de la cantante y actriz Ariadna Sodi Miranda. Hija de Ernesto Sodi Pallares. Egresada del Centro de Capacitación Artística de Televisa, comenzó su carrera en obras de teatro patrocinadas por la televisora. Fue integrante del grupo vocal Timbiriche y a fines de los años ochenta comenzó una carrera como solista. Ha grabado los discos *Thalía*, *Mundo de cristal*, *Love*, *En éxtasis* y *Amor a la mexicana*. Ha tenido papeles estelares en numerosas telenovelas, entre ellas la trilogía *María Mercedes*, *Marimar* y *María la del Barrio*, de gran éxito en Centro, Sudamérica y Asia. Condujo programas de televisión en España.

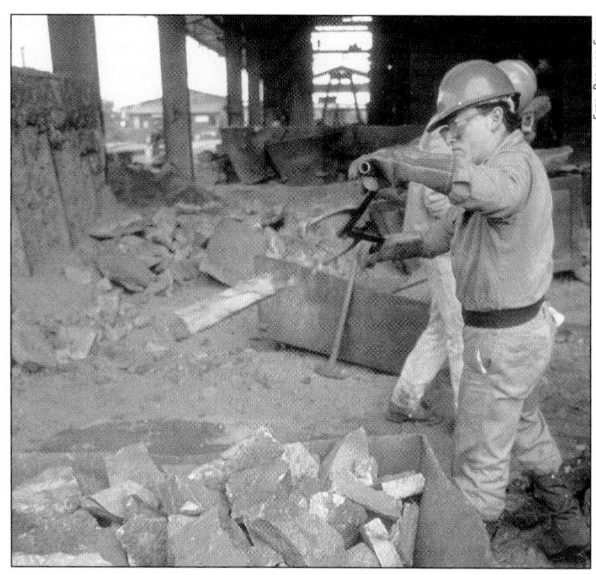

FOTO: BORIS DE SWAN

Actividad minera en Teziutlán, Puebla

THIERRY, DAVID ◆ m. en el DF (?-1988). Contador Público. En 1919 ingresó en la Asociación Católica de la Juventud Mejicana y formó parte de la Liga Defensora de la Libertad Religiosa (1926-30). Estudió en la Escuela Superior de Comercio y Administración, en la que durante 15 años fue profesor de cálculo financiero, auditoría y contabilidad de costos. En la UNAM ejerció la docencia a lo largo de 20 años, fue tesorero con los rectores Martínez Ocaranza y Chico Goerne, perteneció al Consejo Universitario y se desempeño como auditor externo y miembro del Patronato Pro Construcción de la Ciudad Universitaria. Trabajó como auditor general en la Dirección de Pensiones, Pemex y el Banco de México. Cofundador del Instituto Mexicano de Contadores Públicos y del Instituto de Administración Pública. Al morir era el decano de los contadores públicos.

Tezozómoc

THOMAS, HUGH ◆ n. en Inglaterra (1931). Historiador. Autor de *La guerra civil española* (1961), *La Conquista de México* (1996) y *Yo Moctezuma* (1998).

THOMPSON, CHARLES ALEXANDER ◆ n. y ¿m.? en Inglaterra (?-?). Diplomático enviado por el gobierno británico a México, luego de la consumación de la independencia. Tradujo al inglés el *Diccionario Geográfico-Histórico de las Indias Occidentales o América*, del ecuatoriano Antonio Alcedo. Autor de *Na-*

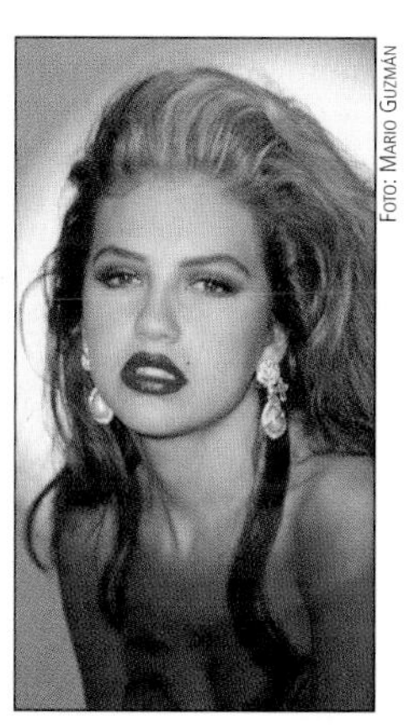

FOTO: MARIO GUZMÁN

Thalía

rración de una visita oficial a Guatemala, viniendo de México* (1829); publicó las descripciones del cañón del Zopilote y del fuerte de San Diego, con numerosas anotaciones estratégicas y alguna información sobre la complicidad de las autoridades españolas con los piratas.

THOMPSON, EDWARD HERBERT ◆ n. y m. en EUA (1860-1935). Arqueólogo titulado en el Instituto Tecnológico Worcester (1879). Mientras era cónsul estadounidense en Yucatán (1885-1909), se dedicó a la investigación de las ruinas mayas, auspiciado por el Museo Peabody. Exploró sobre todo en los alrededores de Chichén Itzá; ahí descubrió la Venus Maya, el Mausoleo del Gran Sacerdote, el Templo de las Columnas Pintadas y la Antigua Chichén, y saqueó una gran cantidad de ofrendas del Cenote Sagrado. En 1926 fue acusado de robo arqueológico, pero el juicio se suspendió por su muerte. Colaboró en *Proceedings of the American Association for Advacement of Science, Memories of Peabody Museum* y *National Geographic Society Magazine*. Autor de *People of the Serpent. Life and Adventure Among the Mayas* (1932). Luego de su muerte apareció *The High Priest's Grave. Chichén Itzá, Yucatán, México* (1938).

Glifo de Tianguistenco, Estado de México.

THOMPSON, JOHN ERIC SIDNEY ◆ n. y m. en Inglaterra (1898-1975). Mayista. Antropólogo titulado en la Universidad de Cambridge y doctor por las universidades de Michigan (1958) y Pennsylvania (1962). Vivió e investigó en Yucatán, patrocinado por la Carnegie Institution de Washington. Fue profesor de la Universidad de Winchester y miembro del Seminario de Cultura Maya de la UNAM y de la Sociedad Mexicana de Estudios Antropológicos. Tradujo al inglés los *Viajes al nuevo mundo* de Thomas Gage. Colaborador de la *Enciclopedia yucatanense*. Autor de *The Meaning of the Mayan Monthly* (1925), *Correlation in the Mayan and European Calendars* (1927), *The Causeways of the Coba District, Eastern Yucatan* (1928), *The Children of the Sun and the Central America* (1929), *The Solar Year of the Mayas at Quirigua, Guatemala* (1932), *A Maya Calendar from the Alta Verapaz, Guatemala* (1932), *Maya Chronology: the Fifteen Ton Glyph* (1934), *Maya Chronology: the Correlation Question* (1935), *The Dates on Altar U Copan* (1935), *La civilización de los mayas* (1936), *The Dates of the Temple of the Cross, Palenque* (1936), *A New Method of Deciphering Yucatecan Dates with a Special Reference to Chichen Itza* (1937), *Lunar Inscription in the Usumacinta Valley* (1937), *Apuntes sobre la estela número 5 de Balajbal, Quintana Roo* (1940), *Mexico Before Cortes* (1941), *Observations on Glyph G of the Lunar series* (1942), *The Fish as a Maya Symbol for Counting and Further Discusion af Directional Glyphs* (1944), *Maya Hieroglyphic Writing* (1950), *The Rise and Fall of Maya Civilization* (1954), *A Catalog of Maya Hieroglyphics* (1962) e *Historia y religión de los mayas* (1975).

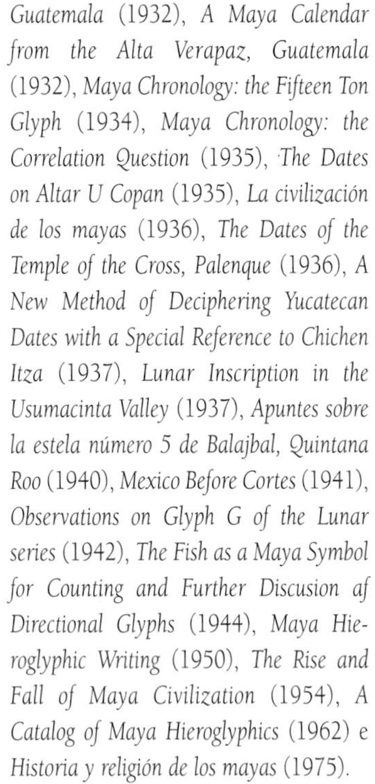

TIACAPAN ◆ Deidad nahua de los placeres carnales, la primogénita de las cuatro que existían. Con sus hermanas, acertó al punto cardinal por el que apareció el sol, cuando se creó el mundo por quinta ocasión.

TIANGUISMANALCO ◆ Municipio de Puebla situado al oeste de la capital estatal y al norte de Atlixco. Superficie: 114.81 km². Habitantes: 9,122, de los cuales 2,169 forman la población económicamente activa. Hablan alguna lengua indígena 1,520 personas mayores de cinco años (náhuatl 1,518).

TIANGUISTENCO ◆ Municipio del Estado de México situado al sureste de Toluca y al nor-noreste de Tenancingo, en los límites con Distrito Federal. Superficie: 114.93 km². Habitantes: 51,149, de los cuales 11,768 forman la población económicamente activa. Hablan alguna lengua indígena 694 personas mayores de cinco años (otomí 404 y náhuatl 273). La cabecera municipal, Tianguistenco de Galeana, se llamó Santiago Tianguistenco. En la jurisdicción se halla el pueblo de Guadalupe Yancuitlalpan, conocido como Gualupita, donde cada martes se celebra el mercado más importante de la región, célebre por los sarapes y gabanes trabajados en telares primitivos y los quezquémetl hechos a mano. En la misma localidad hay dos templos construidos en el siglo XVII: uno dedicado a la virgen de Guadalupe y otro llamado La Capillita.

TIANGUISTENGO ◆ Municipio de Hidalgo situado al sureste de Tepehuacán y al suroeste de Huejutla de Reyes, en los límites con Veracruz. Superficie: 282.7 km². Habitantes: 14,091, de los cuales 3,491 forman la población económicamente activa. Hablan alguna lengua indígena 4,349 personas mayores de cinco años (náhuatl 4,341). Indígenas monolingües: 350. En la jurisdicción se encuentran la gruta Tezcatetl y la cascada Hueyatlapa. Se han encontrado esculturas zoomorfas con cabezas de forma humana. Hacia 1530 los frailes augustinos iniciaron la conquista espiritual de la región y en 1540 construyeron un templo en la actual cabecera municipal. Durante la guerra de Independencia, el cura del lugar, Juan de Bustamante, reunió un ejército de aproximadamente 6,000 hombres, con quienes hizo la campaña insurgente en esta zona. El municipio fue erigido en 1850.

TIBOL, RAQUEL ◆ n. en Argentina (1923). Se naturalizó mexicana en 1961. Crítica de arte. Estudió en la Universidad de Buenos Aires. En 1953 vino a México como secretaria de Diego Rivera. Ha sido museógrafa y jurado de arte en México y otros países. Secretaria de redacción de *Política* (1962-67), conductora de *La plástica y la crítica* del Canal 11 (1971-81), crítica de arte de *Proceso* (1976-), conductora de *Museos en el aire* en Radio Universidad y de *Aproximaciones* del Canal 11. Ha colaborado en la mayoría de las publicaciones importantes de México. Autora del volumen de cuentos: *Comenzar es la esperanza* (1950); y de los libros de ensayo: *Veinte años del Taller de Gráfica Popular* (1957), *Arturo Estrada y sus caminos en el arte mexicano* (1961), *Siqueiros, introductor de realidades* (1961), *Época moderna y contemporánea* (tercer tomo de la *Historia general del*

Raquel Tibol

arte mexicano, 1964), *David Alfaro Siqueiros* (1965), *David Alfaro Siqueiros* (1969), *Pedro Cervantes* (1974), *Orozco, Rivera, Siqueiros, Tamayo* (1974), *Siqueiros, vida y obra* (1974), *Fernando González Gortázar: espacio-urbe-comunidad* (1977), *Frida Kahlo* (1980), *José Chávez Morado: imágenes de identidad mexicana* (1980), *Hermenegildo Bustos: pintor de pueblo* (1981), *Pasos en la danza mexicana* (1982), *Frida Kahlo, una vida abierta* (1983), *Luis Nishizawa: realismo, expresionismo, abstracción* (1984), *José Clemente Orozco* (1984), *Orozco, artista gráfico* (1984), *Feliciano Peña: de la honradez y el arraigo profesional* (1985), *Guía de los murales de Diego Rivera en Chapingo* (1986), *Epílogo a las memorias de Angelina Beloff* (1986), *Diego Rivera ilustrador* (1986), *Gráficas y neográficas en México* (1987), *Palabras de Siqueiros* (selección, prólogo y notas, 1996), *Los murales de Siqueiros* (coordinación, introducción y textos, 1998), *Antología de Frida Kahlo* (selección y proemio, 1999) y de varios prólogos. Antologó *Julio Antonio Mella en El Machete* (1968), *Documentación sobre el arte mexicano* (1974), *Textos de David Alfaro Siqueiros* (1974), *Frida Kahlo: crónica, testimonios y aproximaciones* (1977) y *Diego Rivera: arte y política* (1979). Premio Fernando Benítez de la Feria Internacional del Libro de Guadalajara (1998).

TIBÓN, CARLETTO ◆ n. en Italia y m. en Cuernavaca, Mor. (1903-1981). Escritor y coreógrafo. Hermano de Gutierre Tibón. Durante años dirigió compañías de danza en Italia y México. También dirigió óperas en el Palacio de Bellas Artes y colaboró en la redacción de los tres primeros tomos de la *Enciclopedia de México*. Autor de un *Calendario de fiestas mexicanas* (1968) y de las novelas *Los pitipititos* (1973) y *Los tatarabuelos* (1975).

TIBÓN, GUTIERRE ◆ n. en Italia y m. en Cuernavaca, Mor. (1905-1999). Filólogo, antropólogo e historiador. Estudió en Suiza, donde inventó la máquina de escribir *Hermes Baby* (1932). Vino en 1949 y fue profesor de la UNAM. En 1962 empezó a elaborar la *Enciclopedia de México*, cuyos tres primeros tomos, los únicos que dirigió, aparecieron en 1966, 1967 y 1968. En 1969 vendió los derechos de la obra. Colaborador de *Excélsior*. Autor de *América. Setenta siglos de la historia de un hombre* (1945), *Aventuras de Gog y Magog* (1946), *Origen, vida y milagros de su apellido* (1946), *Divertimientos lingüísticos* (1947), *México 1950. Un país en futuro* (1950), *Vuelo con 800 pegasos* (1950), *Prehistoria del alfabeto* (1956), *Diccionario etimológico de los nombres propios de personas* (1956), *Kijmon* (1959), *Venatana al mundo invisible* (1960), *Olinalá* (1960), *Onomástica hispanoamericana* (1961), *Pinotepa Nacional. Mixtecos, negros y triquis* (1961), *Aztlán Aztatlán* (1962), *Mujeres y diosas en México* (1967), *México en Europa y en África* (1970), *El mundo secreto de los dientes* (1972), *Historia del nombre y de la fundación de México* (1975), *Aventuras en cinco continentes* (1977), *El ombligo como centro erótico* (1981), *El ombligo como centro cósmico. Una contribución a la historia de las religiones* (1981), *La tríade prenatal* (1981), *El jade en México: el mundo esotérico del chalchihuite* (1983), *La ciudad de los hongos alucinantes* (1983), *Aventuras en México 1937-1983* (1983), *Los ritos mágicos y trágicos de la pubertad femenina* (1984) y *Diccionario etimológico comparado de los apellidos españoles, hispanoamericanos y filipinos* (1988). Premio Internacional Alfonso Reyes 1987. Presea Ciudad de México y Orden al Mérito de la República Italiana, con el grado de Gran Oficial (1991).

Foto: Rogelio Cuéllar

Gutierre Tibón

TIBÓN, JUAN MANUEL ◆ n. en Italia y m. en Cuernavaca, Mor. (1900-1979). Agrónomo. Hermano del anterior. Llegó a México en 1956. Fue colaborador de la *Enciclopedia de México*. Coautor, con Gutierre Tibón, de *Introducción al budismo* (1957) y autor de *Historia del peso mexicano* (1961).

TIBURÓN, DEL ◆ Isla de Sonora situada en el golfo California, al noroeste de la bahía Kino y al este-sureste de la isla Ángel de la Guarda. Está separada del litoral sonorense por un canal de 4 km de ancho, llamado estrecho del Infiernillo, muy peligroso para la navegación, y por la bahía de Agua Dulce. Es la isla más grande de México. Mide 52 km de norte a sur y tiene una anchura media de 30 km. La recorren dos sierras para-

Reserva de la biosfera en Isla del Tiburón, Sonora

Foto: Fondo Editorial Grupo Azabache

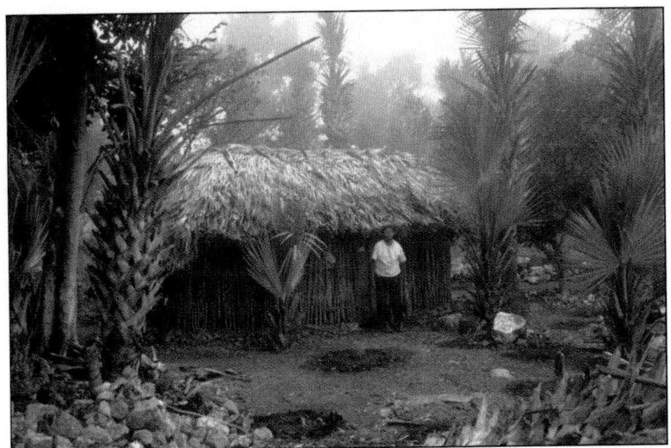
Plantío de palmas en Ticul, Yucatán

lelas, de norte a sur: la Kunkaak, al oriente, y la Menor, al occidente. Abundan los venados y las caguamas. Pertenece a los seris.

TICUL ◆ Municipio de Yucatán situado al sur-sureste de Mérida y al noroeste de Tekax. Superficie: 355.12 km². Habitantes: 31,028, de los cuales 7,756 forman la población económicamente activa. Hablan alguna lengua indígena 15,831 personas mayores de cinco años (maya 15,820). Cerca de la cabecera se hallan las grutas de Loltún. Indígenas monolingües: 575.

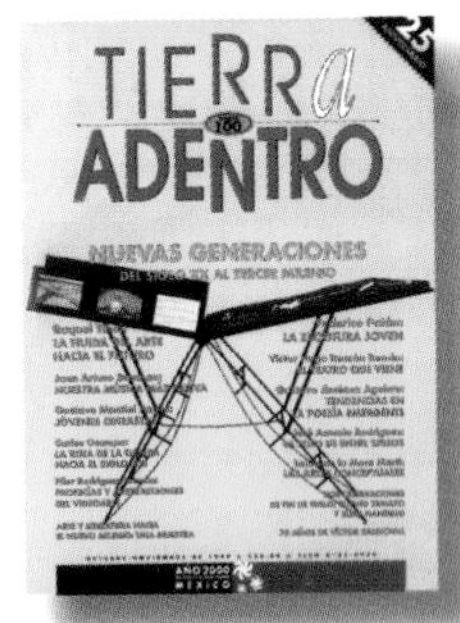

Tierra Adentro

TIERRA ADENTRO ◆ Publicación bimestral editada en su segunda época por la Dirección de Descentralización del CNCA. Su primer número, editado por Carmen Masip, Víctor Sandoval, José María Landín y José Manuel Pintado, apareció en 1974, y su existencia se interrumpió tras 46 números. En 1990 apareció el número 47, dedicado a la difusión de la obra de escritores y artistas plásticos jóvenes, agrupados en cada número alrededor de un tema común. En octubre de 1999 apareció su número 100, "dedicado a la creación, el análisis y la reflexión en torno de las nuevas generaciones artísticas", dirigido por Jorge von Ziegler, con Juan Domingo Argüelles como subdirector, Ignacio Ortiz Monasterio como asesor editorial y Carlos Miranda en la jefatura de redacción.

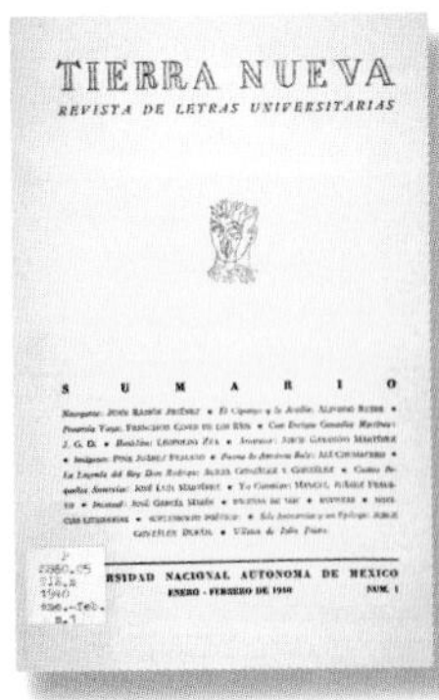

Tierra Nueva

TIERRA BLANCA ◆ Municipio de Guanajuato situado al este-noreste de San Miguel de Allende y al sureste de San Luis de la Paz, en los límites con Querétaro. Superficie: 332.80 km². Habitantes: 13,614, de los cuales 2,695 forman la población económicamente activa. Hablan alguna lengua indígena 39 personas mayores de cinco años (otomí 19).

TIERRA BLANCA ◆ Municipio de Veracruz situado al sur del puerto de Veracruz y al oeste de Alvarado, en los límites con Oaxaca. Superficie: 1,363.76 km². Habitantes: 90,123, de los cuales 23,834 forman la población económicamente activa. Hablan alguna lengua indígena 2,240 personas mayores de cinco años (chinanteco 1,830, mazateco 133 y náhuatl 102), de las que son monolingües 109.

TIERRA COLORADA ◆ Poblado guerrerense fundado en 1848, en la confluencia de diversas rutas comerciales. Fue convertido en ejido en 1925 y en 1952 en cabecera del municipio de Juan R. Escudero (☛), llamado así en honor del fundador del Partido Obrero de Acapulco.

TIERRA NUEVA ◆ Revista literaria bimestral editada en la ciudad de México por la UNAM. Apareció entre enero de 1940 y diciembre de 1942, bajo la responsabilidad de Alí Chumacero, Jorge González Durán, José Luis Martínez y Leopoldo Zea. El nombre de la revista fue propuesto por Alfonso Reyes. Además de los anteriores, en ella colaboraron Ermilo Abreu Gómez, Manuel Alcalá, Raúl Anguiano, Neftalí Beltrán, Juan de la Cabada, Manuel Cabrera, Manuel Calvillo, Alfredo Cardona Peña, Bernardo Casanueva Mazo, Manuel Gonzalo Casa, Antonio Caso, Víctor Ceja Reyes, Juan Cruz, Jorge Cuesta, José Chávez Morado, Enrique Díez-Canedo, Arturo Echeverría Loria, José Fuentes Mares, José Gaos, José Garabito Martínez, José García Marín, Francisco Giner de los Ríos, Antonio Gómez Robledo, Enrique González Martínez, Enrique González Rojo, Alfonso Gutiérrez Hermosillo, Andrés Henestrosa, María Luisa Hidalgo, Efraín Huerta, José E. Iturriaga, Juan Ramón Jiménez, Pina Juárez Frausto, León Felipe, María del Carmen Millán, José Moreno Villa, Pablo Neruda, Isidoro Ocampo, Octavio Paz, Emilio Prados, Julio Prieto, Alberto Quintero Álvarez, José Revueltas, María Ramona Rey, Rafael del Río R., Rafael Solana, Juan Soriano, Juan Manuel Terán, Julio Torri, Xavier Villaurrutia y Joaquín Xirau.

TIERRANUEVA ◆ Municipio de San Luis Potosí situado al suroeste de Río Verde y contiguo a Santa María del Río, en los límites con Guanajuato. Superficie: 615.1 km². Habitantes: 9,669, de los cuales 1,827 forman la población económicamente activa. Hablan alguna lengua indígena seis personas mayores de cinco años (náhuatl cinco).

TIGRE, DEL ◆ Sierra de Jalisco que forma parte del Sistema Volcánico Transversal, situada al noreste de Ciudad Guzmán y al sur del lago de Chapala. Se extiende de oeste a sureste. La porción septentrional desciende hacia la sierra de Tizapán; se prolonga al occidente hasta el lago de Sayula y al suroriente continúa en la sierra de las Bufas.

TIGRE DE ÁLICA ◆ ☛ *Lozada, Manuel.*

TIGRE DE TACUBAYA ◆ ☛ *Márquez, Leonardo.*

TIHUATLÁN ◆ Municipio de Veracruz situado al norte de Poza Rica y al suroeste de Tuxpan, en los límites con Puebla. Superficie: 828.29 km². Habitantes: 81,660, de los cuales 20,357 forman la población económicamente activa. Hablan alguna lengua indígena 2,901 personas mayores de cinco años (totonaco 1,739, náhuatl 732 y otomí 361).

TIJERINA, JUAN B. ◆ n. en Matamoros y m. en Ciudad Victoria, Tams. (1857-1912). Profesor normalista. Ejerció la docencia antes de dedicarse al periodismo. Fue diputado local durante el porfiriato y desde el Congreso atacó a la dictadura de Díaz, por lo que debió abandonar el país. En San Antonio, Texas, fundó el periódico *La libertad*. Al volver a México fue encarcelado durante un tiempo. Más tarde fundó la Escuela Normal de Ciudad Victoria. Autor de poesía que firmó con el pseudónimo de *Harmodio*. Póstumamente apareció el volumen *Poesías escogidas* (1921).

Tijerina Almaguer, Luis ♦ n. en Linares, NL (1897-1978). Fue profesor de educación primaria y secundaria, regidor y presidente municipal suplente de Monterrey, diputado a la Legislatura de Nuevo León, director de la Escuela Nacional de Maestros, oficial mayor de la Secretaría de Educación y director federal de Educación en Nuevo León y Jalisco. Autor de *Canto al escudo de Nuevo León, Alma charra* y *Vetas del pensamiento*. En 1960 recibió la medalla Ignacio Manuel Altamirano.

Tijuana ♦ Municipio de Baja California situado en el extremo noroccidental del estado, al oeste de Tecate y al norte de Ensenada, en el litoral del océano Pacífico y en los límites con Estados Unidos. Superficie: 1,392.45 km². Habitantes: 991,592, de los cuales 267,878 forman la población económicamente activa. Hablan alguna lengua indígena 6,383 personas mayores de cinco años (mixteco 2,741, purépecha 913 y zapoteco 468), de las que 146 no dominan el español. En 1829, Santiago Argüello obtuvo una concesión de tierra sobre el río Tecate y cerca de la costa del océano Pacífico, en un lugar conocido como rancho de la Tía Juana, situado al sur de San Diego. Después de la guerra contra Estados Unidos y de la firma del Tratado de Guadalupe-Hidalgo (1848), que estableció la linea fronteriza justo al norte del asentamiento de la Tía Juana, éste quedó bajo la jurisdicción del municipio de Frontera. A principios de la década de 1860, el lugar estaba habitado, principalmente, por las familias Argüelles y Bandini. En 1864, el cabildo de Frontera nombró al primer juez residente en Tía Juana y en 1878 se instaló el primer puesto aduanal en el lugar. Hacia 1891, el poblado comenzó a ser conocido como Tijuana, luego de que, a causa del desbordamiento del río Tecate, la población se retiró hasta su asentamiento actual. (Otras versiones derivan el nombre de las palabras *ticuán*, "lugar de tortugas", o *teguana*, "sin alimentos".) En 1900, Tijuana, con menos de 300 habitantes, fue convertida en subprefectura municipal. Diez años depués la población aumentó a 700 personas. El 9 de mayo de 1911, derrotadas las tropas gubernamentales de José María Larroque, Tijuana fue ocupada por una fuerza de estadounidenses comandada por Carl Rhys Pryce, aparentemente en apoyo de la insurrección del Partido Liberal Mexicano en Baja California (☛). Días después se hicieron evidentes los propósitos separatistas de Pryce, quien recibía apoyo de los grandes diarios de California, en tanto que los anarquistas eran hostilizados por el ejército estadounidense. El 3 de junio, un día después de la proclamación de independencia de la República de Baja California, los milicianos anarquistas rompieron con Pryce, fusilaron a algunos mercenarios y expulsaron al resto de la ciudad. A fines de junio, fuerzas federales al mando de Celso Vega recuperaron la ciudad. En 1917 fue erigido el municipio de Tijuana y en 1925 se le agregó a la cabecera municipal el apellido de Ignacio Zaragoza, pero cuatro años después, ante el rechazo por el nuevo nombre, el gobierno del estado le restituyó la denominación original. A partir de 1919, al implantarse en Estados Unidos la abstinencia alcohólica obligatoria, el paso de turistas de ese país hacia Tijuana se incrementó considerablemente. Surgieron cantinas, casinos, prostíbulos, agencias de divorcios y otros servicios. En 1921, los habitantes de la ciudad eran poco más de un millar. En 1940, la población estaba formada por más de 16,000 personas. A fines de los años treinta se construyó la presa Rodríguez, que desde entonces es la principal fuente de abastecimiento de agua de la ciudad. Durante la segunda guerra mundial aumentó el número de cantinas y prostíbulos, al incrementarse la afluencia de soldados estadounidenses acantonados en California. La cercanía con el mercado norteamericano convirtió a la ciudad en punto de paso, y frecuentemente de destino, para trabajadores migratorios, muchos de ellos indocumentados. La diócesis fue creada en 1963. Durante los años setenta se comenzó a desarrollarse la industria maquiladora, que a fines del siglo es la actividad que absorbe más fuerza de trabajo.

CECUT en Tijuana, Baja California

Tila ♦ Municipio de Chiapas situado al noreste de San Cristóbal de Las Casas y al suroeste de Palenque, en los límites con Tabasco. Superficie: 390 km². Habitantes: 48,708, de los cuales 12,297 forman la población económicamente activa. Hablan alguna lengua indígena 37,935 personas mayores de cinco años (chol 33,306 y tzeltal 4,573). En la cabecera municipal se encuentra el Santuario del Señor de Tila, iglesia construida durante el virreinato.

Tilapa ♦ Municipio de Puebla situado al sur-suroeste de Atlixco y contiguo a Izúcar de Matamoros. Superficie: 102.05 km². Habitantes: 7,872, de los cuales 1,699 forman la población económicamente activa. Hablan alguna lengua indígena 38 personas mayores de cinco años.

Tileme, Mar ♦ Nombre con el que se conoce el extremo occidental de la laguna Inferior en Oaxaca. Es un brazo que se extiende de este a oeste, separado de la laguna Superior por una barra arenosa llamada cabo Santa Teresa, y del golfo de Tehuantepec por la barra donde se encuentra la población de San Mateo del Mar.

Tilghmann, Hugo ♦ n. en Guadalajara, Jal., y m. en el DF (1909-1949). Caricaturista. Hizo estudios de medicina en la ciudad de México. Se inició como cartonista en la revista *Policromías* y más tarde colaboró en los diarios *El*

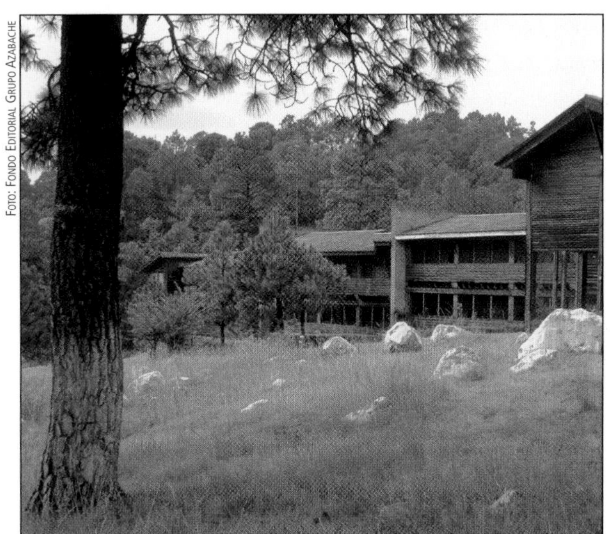

FOTO: FONDO EDITORIAL GRUPO AZABACHE

Construcciones de madera en el Parque Nacional El Ocotal, en Timilpan, Estado de México

Universal y en *El Universal Ilustrado*. Autor de las tiras cómicas "Dos mexicanos en la guerra", "Mamerto y sus conocencias" y "Nagulás y Laburio". Fue gerente de la empresa Producciones Hugo Tilghmann.

TILÍN ◆ n. en el DF (¿1928?). Locutor. Nombre profesional de Salvador Gómez Castellanos. Comenzó su carrera en la emisora XEQ (1945), de la que pasó a la XEW. Con el mote "El fotógrafo de la voz", se hizo famoso como imitador y conductor de diversos programas cómicos, entre los que se recuerda *El Risámetro*. También actuó en teatro, televisión y cabaret.

TIMILPAN ◆ Municipio del Estado de México situado al norte de Toluca y al noroeste de Tepotzotlán. Superficie: 187.39 km². Habitantes: 13,871, de los cuales 2,856 forman la población económicamente activa. Hablan alguna lengua indígena 840 personas mayores de cinco años (otomí 826 y mazahua 14).

TIMÓN ◆ Revista semanal fundada por José Vasconcelos, cuyo primer número apareció el 22 de febrero de 1940. Acusada de recibir financiamiento de la embajada alemana era, de acuerdo con Héctor Orestes Aguilar, "una revista de sociales (que incluía) los con frecuencia sanguinolentos partes de guerra; cultural pero con un acento periodístico de actualidad; antialiada y progermana; frívola pero con un contenido propagandístico complicadamente ideologizado y en ocasiones francamente militarista". Opuesta a los Estados Unidos, poco a poco tendió a la promoción de la ideología nacionalsocialista. Fue prohibida tras la aparición de su número 16, el 15 de junio de 1940.

TIMUCUY ◆ Municipio de Yucatán contiguo a Mérida y Acanceh. Superficie: 65.15 km². Habitantes: 5,407, de los cuales 1,409 forman la población económicamente activa. Hablan alguna lengua indígena 4,600 personas mayores de cinco años (maya 4,588), de los cuales 333 no dominan el español.

TINGAMBATO ◆ Municipio de Michoacán situado al noreste de Uruapan y contiguo a Pátzcuaro. Superficie: 254.77 km². Habitantes: 11,079, de los cuales 2,245 forman la población económicamente activa. Hablan alguna lengua indígena 1,000 personas mayores de cinco años (purépecha 998). La región de Tingambato fue evangelizada por los agustinos en el siglo XVI, quienes a mediados del siglo XVII construyeron un templo dedicado al apóstol Santiago en la actual cabecera. La iglesia se incendió en 1844 y poco después fue reconstruida.

TINGÜINDÍN ◆ Municipio de Michoacán situado al sureste de Zamora y al noroeste de Uruapan. Superficie: 271.59 km². Habitantes: 12,355, de los cuales 3,215 forman la población económicamente activa. Hablan alguna lengua indígena 412 personas mayores de cinco años (purépecha 390).

TINOCO RUBÍ, VÍCTOR MANUEL ◆ n. en Zitácuaro, Mich. (1946). Licenciado en derecho por la UNAM (1967), de la que ha sido profesor (1964-66), así como de la Universidad La Salle (1973-78) y la UIA (1980-83). Militante del PRI desde 1976. Ha sido secretario del interior de la sección 26 del Sindicato de Trabajadores del DDF (1968-70) y miembro de la Asociación Sindicalista de Michoacán; diputado local en Michoacán y presidente de la Gran Comisión del Congreso del estado (1989-91), senador de la República (1991-95) y gobernador constitucional de Michoacán elegido para el periodo (1995-2001). Pertenece al Colegio de Abogados de México.

Víctor Manuel Tinoco Rubí

TIN TAN ◆ ☛ *Valdés, Germán*.

TINUM ◆ Municipio de Yucatán situado al oeste de Valladolid. Superficie: 393.44 km². Habitantes: 8,679, de los cuales 2,194 forman la población económicamente activa. Hablan alguna lengua indígena 6,098 personas mayores de cinco años (maya 6,087), y de ellas, 525 son monolingües. En la jurisdicción, al suroeste de la cabecera, se encuentra Chichén Itzá (☛).

TIQUET, JOSÉ ◆ n. en Las Flores, municipio de Paraíso, Tab. (1924). Poeta. Profesor titulado en la Escuela Normal Rural La Granja de Villahermosa. Realizó estudios de derecho en la UNAM, pero los interrumpió para dedicarse al periodismo. Ha trabajado en los diarios *El Universal Gráfico* (1949) y *El Universal* (1950-59), en la revista *Impacto* (1956-59), en el INBA (1959-72), en la Secretaría de Turismo (1972-75) y en el PRI de Tabasco (1975-). En 1958 fundó la revista *Veamos*. Colaborador de *Revista Mexicana de Cultura* de *El Nacional*, de *Poesía de América* y de los diarios *Excélsior* y *Novedades*. Coautor de *Quinteto de cámara* (1986). Autor de *Nuestra voz* (1951), *Sangre de lejanía* (1953), *Los remeros del alba* (1961), *Sólo un hombre* (1964), *Marzo del labriego* (1965), *A la altura del sueño* (1986) y *Por estas hojas anda un árbol* (1990).

TIQUICHEO DE NICOLÁS ROMERO ◆ Municipio de Michoacán situado al sureste de Morelia y al suroeste de Zitácuaro, en los límites con los estados de México y Guerrero. Superficie:

Ilustración de Javier Guadarrama

Ayuntamiento municipal de Tixtla de Guerrero, Guerrero

2,909.85 km^2. Habitantes: 16,355, de los cuales 2,850 forman la población económicamente activa. Hablan alguna lengua indígena 27 personas mayores de cinco años.

Tirado Benedí, Domingo ◆ n. en España y m. en el DF (1898-1971). Pedagogo. Trabajó en el Ministerio de Instrucción Pública de España y en 1939, tras la derrota de la República, se refugió en México. Se naturalizó mexicano en 1941. Fue asesor de Octavio Véjar Vázquez, cuando éste era secretario de Educación Pública (1941-43); organizador y profesor del Servicio de Información Pedagógica y supervisor de Enseñanza Técnica Superior de la Secretaría de Educación. Profesor de la UNAM y de la Escuela Normal Superior. Traductor de la UNESCO. Tradujo *De las cosas del campo*, de Marco Terencio Varrón. Autor de *La ciencia de la educación* (2 t., 1939), *Cooperativas talleres, huertos y granjas escolares* (1940), *Bases para una ciencia de la educación en México* (1944), *Problemas de organización escolar* (1945), *Orientaciones pedagógicas*, *Matemáticas y pedagogía*, *Métodos de educación y de enseñanza en México* y *El tesoro del maestro*.

Tirado Fuentes, René ◆ n. en Zacapoaxtla, Pue., y m. en el DF (1908-1990). Periodista. Hizo estudios en la UAP. Comenzó su carrera en *Jueves de Excélsior* y *Revista de Revistas*. Colaboró en *Hoy*, *El Universal Ilustrado*, *El Nacional* y *La Prensa* y fue socio de *Excélsior*; diario en el que colaboró durante 31 años. Diputado federal en la década de los setenta. Autor de poesía: *Tu paso por la tierra* y *Umbral*; y crónica: *Reencuentro con Azorín* y *Treinta días en la casa del vecino*.

Tirado Pedraza, José de Jesús ◆ n. en Santa Ana Maya, Mich., y m. en Monterrey, NL (1908-1993). Sacerdote ordenado en 1931. Estudió en el Seminario Conciliar de Morelia. Fue vicerrector y rector del Seminario de Morelia, canónigo y deán de la catedral moreliana, obispo auxiliar de la diócesis de Morelia (1963-65), obispo de Ciudad Victoria (1965-73), auxiliar de la arquidiócesis de Monterrey (1973-76) y arzobispo de Monterrey (1976-83).

Tixcacalcupul ◆ Municipio de Yucatán situado al sur-suroeste de Valladolid y al sureste de Chichén Itzá, en los límites con Quintana Roo. Superficie: 719.98 km^2. Habitantes: 5,121, de los cuales 1,093 forman la población económicamente activa. Hablan maya 4,316 personas mayores de cinco años, y de ellas, 1,109 son monolingües. En la jurisdicción se halla la población de Tepich, que fue tomada por las fuerzas mayas de Cecilio Chi el 30 de julio de 1847, acción que marcó el inicio de la guerra de castas (☛ *Yucatán*).

Tixkokob ◆ Municipio de Yucatán situado al este de Mérida y al suroeste de Motul. Superficie: 159.67 km^2. Habitantes: 14,746, de los cuales 4,129 forman la población económicamente activa. Hablan alguna lengua indígena 3,597 personas mayores de cinco años (maya 3,589). Es el principal productor de henequén de la península de Yucatán. También produce miel de abeja. En la cabecera hay talleres de talabartería y tejido de hamacas. Está unida a Izamal por una calzada construida en tiempos prehispánicos, en territorio municipal están las ruinas de la ciudad maya de Aké, la cual floreció de los años 250 al 900 de nuestra era. En ella se encuentra una plataforma a la que se llega por una escalera de 45 metros de ancho. En la parte superior están 36 columnas que sostenían el techo de esta edificación.

Tixméuac ◆ Municipio de Yucatán situado al sureste de Ticul y al suroeste de Chichén Itzá. Superficie: 251.65 km^2. Habitantes: 3,786, de los cuales 1,037 forman la población económicamente activa. Hablan alguna lengua indígena 3,132 personas mayores de cinco años (maya 3,131).

Tixpéual ◆ Municipio de Yucatán situado al este y próximo a Mérida. Superficie: 68.98 km^2. Habitantes: 4,663, de los cuales 1,385 forman la población económicamente activa. Hablan alguna lengua indígena 1,795 personas mayores de cinco años (maya 1,789).

Tixtla de Guerrero ◆ Municipio de Guerrero contiguo a Chilpancingo. Superficie: 290 km^2. Habitantes: 33,657, de los cuales 6,904 forman la población económicamente activa. Hablan alguna lengua indígena 5,964 personas mayores de cinco años (náhuatl 5,876). En

René Tirado Fuentes

Venta de armadillo en Tixkokob, Yucatán

Mujer de Tixkokob, Yucatán

la actual cabecera, en 1782, nació Vicente Guerrero. El 26 de mayo de 1811, las fuerzas insurgentes de José María Morelos tomaron la población y dejaron un destacamento al mando de Hermenegildo Galeana. El 15 de agosto de ese año los realistas pusieron sitio a la plaza, pero al día siguiente Morelos dejó Chilpancingo y derrotó a las fuerzas coloniales. Entre 1849 y 1871 fue capital de Guerrero. En la jurisdicción se producen artesanías de cuero, mezcal y juegos pirotécnicos.

Tizapán el Alto ◆ Municipio de Jalisco situado en la ribera sur del lago de Chapala, al sureste de Guadalajara y al noreste de Ciudad Guzmán, en los límites con Michoacán. Superficie: 273.32 km². Habitantes: 19,963, de los cuales 4,984 forman la población económicamente activa. Hablan alguna lengua indígena 16 personas mayores de cinco años (purépecha 12).

Tizayuca ◆ Municipio de Hidalgo situado al suroeste de Pachuca y al oeste de Tepeapulco, en los límites con el Estado de México. Superficie: 92.5 km². Habitantes: 39,357, de los cuales 9,103 forman la población económicamente activa. Hablan alguna lengua indígena 458 personas mayores de cinco años (náhuatl 315 y otomí 55). En la cabecera se encuentra una parroquia construida en 1569.

Tizimín ◆ Municipio de Yucatán situado en el extremo nororiental del estado, al nor-noreste de Valladolid, en el litoral del golfo de México y en los límites con Quintana Roo. Superficie: 4,132.37 km². Habitantes: 61,447, de los cuales 15,332 forman la población económicamente activa. Hablan alguna lengua indígena 29,141 personas mayores de cinco años (maya 29,110). Indígenas monolingües: 1,963. En 1838, Santiago Imán se levantó en armas en la actual cabecera contra el gobierno centralista de Antonio López de Santa Anna, en lo que fue el inicio de la rebelión que terminó con la independencia temporal de Yucatán (☛).

Ilustración de Antonio Esparza

Palacio municipal de Tlacoachistlahuaca, Guerrero

Tizoc ◆ ¿n. y m. en México-Tenochtitlan? (1436-1486). Séptimo emperador de los mexicas, cuyo nombre significa "el sangrador" o "el agujereado con esmeraldas". Era hijo primogénito de Moctezuma Ilhuicamina y hermano de Ahuízotl y de Axayácatl. Fue elegido tlatoani en 1481, luego de la muerte de su padre. Aunque emprendió 14 campañas militares, no pudo ampliar los dominios de la Triple Alianza. En cambio, desarrolló el primer sistema de correos del imperio y terminó la reconstrucción del Templo Mayor. Murió envenenado, aparentemente por una conjura de Techoylala y Maztla, señores de Tlachco e Iztapalapa, respectivamente.

Tizoc

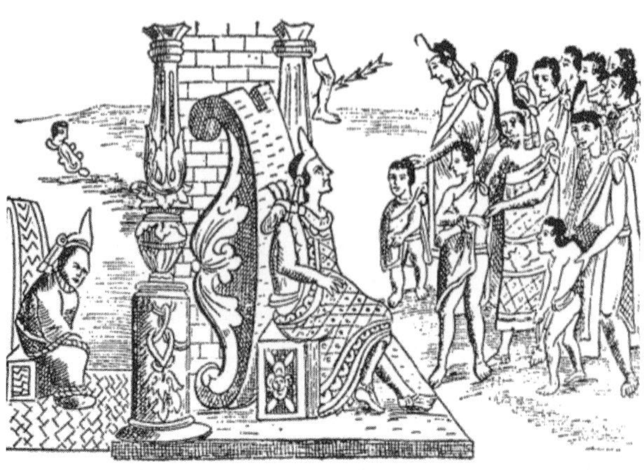

Tlacahuepan ◆ Deidad nahua venerada principalmente en Texcoco. Era uno de los hermanos menores de Huitzilopochtli y en México-Tenochitlan recibía un trato similar al dios de la guerra. En la mitología, Tlacahuepan ayudó a Tezcatlipoca en su enfrentamiento con Quetzalcóatl.

Tlacateotl ◆ m. en Tlatelolco (?-1428). Rey de Tlatelolco, cuyo nombre significa "dios humano". Era hijo de Cuacuahpitzahuac. Ascendió al trono en 1418. Durante su mandato normó la actividad de los pochtecas, comerciantes guerreros. Realizó incursiones fuera del valle de México e intentó liberar a su señorío de la dominación de Azcapotzalco, pero murió, ahorcado o apedreado, por órdenes del cacique de esta ciudad.

Tlacoachistlahuaca ◆ Municipio de Guerrero situado al sur-sureste de Tlapa y contiguo a Ometepec, en los límites con Oaxaca. Superficie: 450.6 km². Habitantes: 12,477, de los cuales 2,901 forman la población económicamente activa. Hablan alguna lengua indígena 7,050 personas mayores de cinco años (mixteco 4,269 y amuzgo 2,571), de las cuales, 3,539 son monolingües.

Tlacoapa ◆ Municipio de Guerrero situado al sureste de Chilpancingo y al noreste de Ayutla de los Libres. Superficie: 326.3 km². Habitantes: 7,645, de los cuales 1,906 forman la población económicamente activa. Hablan alguna lengua indígena 5,633 personas ma-

Vista panorámica de Tlacoapa, Guerrero

yores de cinco años (tlapaneco 5,593). Indígenas monolingües: 2,279.

Tlacoatzintepec, Lienzo de ◆ Códice chinanteco realizado a fines del siglo XVI o principios del siglo XVII para explicar ante las autoridades españolas los conflictos territoriales del pueblo de San Andrés Teolilalpa con otros pueblos del norte de Oaxaca. Es un pliego de tela de 116 por 149 centímetros. El original se encuentra en el templo católico de San José Tlacoatzintepec, de ahí su nombre, y existe una copia en la Biblioteca Nacional de Antropología e Historia, en la ciudad de México.

Tlacochahuaya de Morelos ◆ ☛ *San Jerónimo Tlacochahuaya*, municipio de Oaxaca.

Tlacojalpan ◆ Municipio de Veracruz situado al sureste de Tierra Blanca y al suroeste de Cosamaloapan, en los límites con Oaxaca. Superficie: 91.3 km^2. Habitantes: 4,594, de los cuales 1,361 forman la población económicamente activa. Hablan alguna lengua indígena 17 personas mayores de cinco años.

Tlacolula, de ◆ Valle de Oaxaca situado al este de la capital del estado y al norte de Miahuatlán. Se extiende de este a oeste, al sur de la sierra de Ixtlán y al norte del valle de Ocotlán, del que lo separan varios cerros volcánicos. En este valle se encuentran las zonas arqueológicas de Mitla y Tlacolula.

Tlacolula de Matamoros ◆ Municipio de Oaxaca situado al sureste de la capital estatal, al sur de Teotitlán del Valle, al noreste de Ocotlán y contiguo a San Pablo Villa de Mitla. Superficie: 244.96 km^2. Habitantes: 12,733, de los cuales 3,427 forman la población económicamente activa. Hablan alguna lengua indígena 3,091 personas mayores de cinco años (zapoteco 2,820). En la jurisdicción se encuentran los restos de la ciudad zapoteca de Yagul, que floreció hacia el siglo XIV de nuestra era, situada en las faldas de un cerro rematado por rocas escarpadas, en lo que constituye la fortaleza; en la parte baja se localizan los palacios, el de los Seis Patios entre ellos (palacio del gobernante), el juego de pelota, tumbas y pinturas rupestres; numerosas piezas cerámicas y ornamentales se han encontrado en Yagul y son conservadas en el Museo de Oaxaca. La cabecera es el más importante centro regional de acopio y distribución de madera. Ahí se celebra, alrededor del 10 de octubre, una gran feria regional en la que se muestra el mezcal de producción local.

Tlacolulan ◆ Municipio de Veracruz situado al noroeste de Jalapa y al este de Perote. Superficie: 137.36 km^2. Habitantes: 8,307, de los cuales 2,019 forman la población económicamente activa. Hablan alguna lengua indígena 15 personas mayores de cinco años.

Tlacotalpan ◆ Municipio de Veracruz situado al sureste de Alvarado y al oeste-noroeste de San Andrés Tuxtla. Superficie: 646.51 km^2. Habitantes: 15,183, de los cuales 5,265 forman la población económicamente activa. Hablan alguna lengua indígena siete personas mayores de cinco años. Hasta el siglo XII de nuestra era, el actual territorio municipal estuvo habitado por los totonacas, pero entre el siglo XIII y el XV, la región fue ocupada por los toltecas. Hacia 1475, luego de tomar Cempoala y Cotaxtla, los ejércitos mexicas de Axayácatl sometieron el original asentamiento indígena, al que pusieron su nombre, que significa "en el medio de la

Tlacolula de Matamoros, Oaxaca

Foto: Michael Calderwood

Tlacotalpan, Veracruz

tierra". Poco después de la conquista española, el poblado fue dado en encomienda a uno de los soldados de Hernán Cortés, Alonso Romero, cuya familia gobernó el lugar hasta mediados del siglo XVI. En 1541 se estableció el corregimiento, que poco después se transformó en alcaldía mayor. A principios del siglo XVII, el gobierno virreinal intentó que Tlacotalpan quedara bajo la jurisdicción de Cosamaloapan, pero la oposición de los indios, cuyas principales actividades económicas eran el comercio, la pesca y la navegación, impidió la realización del proyecto. Los límites del municipio fueron definidos a fines del siglo XVIII. En 1824 y 1827, en este lugar funcionó una de las primeras escuelas de la marina mexicana. A mediados del siglo XIX se construyó el palacio municipal. Hacia 1860 la población tlacotalpeña era de unos 3,000 habitantes. En 1862 la ciudad fue ocupada por los franceses, pero tres años más tarde la guerrilla republicana, al mando de Manuel Gómez, desalojó a los invasores. También en 1865, el gobierno republicano de Veracruz dio a Tlacotalpan el rango de ciudad. Desde ahí, Porfirio Díaz organizó el levantamiento contra el gobierno de Sebastián Lerdo de Tejada, iniciado a fines de 1875 en Tuxtepec. En 1889, el ayuntamiento fraccionó las dos haciendas más importantes de la jurisdicción: El Zapotal, que era de Dolores Tosta, la esposa de Antonio López de Santa Anna y la de los hermanos Cházaro, que había pertenecido hasta mediados del siglo a la Cofradía de la Virgen de la Candelaria. A partir de entonces la producción de azúcar se convirtió en uno de los giros económicos más importantes del lugar. La otra actividad relevante era el transporte fluvial, que decayó a principios del siglo XX con el establecimiento del ferrocarril del istmo. En 1896 la ciudad se convirtió en Tlacotalpan de Porfirio Díaz, pero acortó nuevamente su nombre después de la revolución. En 1998 fue nombrada por la UNESCO patrimonio cultural de la humanidad.

Tlacotepec ◆ Cabecera del municipio guerrerense de general Heliodoro Castillo (☛).

Tlacotepec ◆ Cerro de Guerrero situado en la cresta principal de la sierra Madre del Sur, al norte de Coyuca de Benítez. Se eleva 3,495 metros sobre el nivel del mar.

Tlacotepec de Benito Juárez ◆ Municipio de Puebla situado al sur-sureste de Tecamachalco y al noroeste de Tehuacán. Superficie: 340.61 km². Habitantes: 36,606, de los cuales 7,245 forman la población económicamente activa. Hablan alguna lengua indígena 9,539 personas mayores de cinco años (popoloca 7,634 y náhuatl 1,873). El 4 de julio se realiza una feria popular en honor del Señor del Calvario.

Tlacotepec de Mejía ◆ Municipio de Veracruz situado al norte de Córdoba y al oeste-suroeste del puerto de Veracruz. Superficie: 90.48 km². Habitantes: 2,906, de los cuales 966 forman la población económicamente activa.

Tlacotepec Plumas ◆ Municipio de Oaxaca situado al este-noreste de Huajuapan de León y al norte de Teposcolula. Superficie: 37 km². Habitantes: 572, de los cuales 99 forman la población económicamente activa.

Tlacotontli ◆ Deidad nahua que, con Zacatontli, dominaba los caminos. Al principio de cada viaje, la tribu pochteca realizaba grandes ofrendas en su honor. Lo representaban con una mariposa.

Tlacuilotepec ◆ Municipio de Puebla situado en la porción septentrional del estado, al norte de Huauchinango y contiguo a Xicotepec. Superficie: 153.08 km². Habitantes: 16,183, de los cuales 4,502 forman la población económicamente activa. Hablan alguna lengua indígena 2,946 personas mayores de cinco años (totonaco 2,613, otomí 222 y náhuatl 105).

Tlachichilco ◆ Municipio de Veracruz situado al oeste-suroeste de Tuxpan y al suroeste de Chichontepec, en los límites con Hidalgo. Superficie: 291.18 km². Habitantes: 10,602, de los cuales 2,485 forman la población económicamente activa. Hablan alguna lengua indígena 5,189 personas mayores de cinco años (tepehua 2,295, otomí 1,645 y náhuatl 1,247). Indígenas monolingües: 289.

Tlachichuca ◆ Municipio de Puebla situado al noreste de Tecamachalco y al noroeste del Pico de Orizaba, en los límites con Veracruz. Superficie: 459.25 km². Habitantes: 26,366, de los cuales 6,271 forman la población económicamente activa. Hablan alguna lengua indígena 15 personas mayores de cinco años.

Tláhuac ◆ Delegación situada en el sureste del Distrito Federal. Limita con Iztapalapa, Xochimilco, Milpa Alta y el Estado de México. Superficie: 93 km². Habitantes: 255,891 (1995), de los cuales 44,937 forman la población económicamente activa, dedicada principalmente a las tareas agropecuarias, la construcción, la minería y la producción manufacturera. Hablan alguna lengua indígena 2,430 personas mayores de cinco años (náhuatl 592, otomí 459, mixteco 426 y zapoteco 364). El pueblo de Tláhuac, contracción de Cuitláhuac, que significa "en el lugar de quien cuida el agua", fue fundado en una isla situada en el centro del lago de

Xochimilco por un grupo nahua de cultura tolteca que antes, a fines del siglo XII o principios del XIII, se había instalado en Chalco, en la ribera oriental del lago. Otra parte de ese grupo fue expulsado del valle de México y fundó Cuernavaca (☛ *Morelos*). Hacia 1262, Cohuatomatzin fue elegido primer rey de Cuitláhuac. Hacia 1299, el señor de Cuitláhuac se alió con el de Azcapotzalco y durante los dos siglos siguientes el poblado permaneció sometido a los tecpanecas, hasta que en 1430, luego de la destrucción de Azcapotzalco, los ejércitos combinados de Texcoco y México-Tenochtitlan, comandados por Nezahualcóyotl e Izcóatl, ocuparon Cuitláhuac, así como el resto de los dominios tecpanecas del sureste del valle de México. Los mexicas construyeron una calzada a lo ancho del lago de Xochimilco, que tuvo como centro la isla de Cuitláhuac, que a principios del siglo XVI tenía más de 2,000 habitantes. Después de la conquista el poblado comenzó a ser conocido como Tláhuac. La evangelización fue realizada por los frailes de la Órden de Predicadores, los que a mediados del siglo XVI edificaron el templo y convento de San Pedro. Luego de las reformas borbónicas de fines del siglo XVIII, Tláhuac se convirtió en parte del corregimiento de Chalco y de la intendencia de México. Con el establecimiento de la República, en 1824, Tláhuac quedó incluido en el Estado de México, dentro del municipio de Chalco. La calzada de Tláhuac funcionó, precariamente, hasta fines del siglo XIX, cuando el lago de Chalco fue desecado. En 1890, la población de Tláhuac fue calculada en 5,000 personas. En 1898, al establecer nuevos límites para la capital el gobierno de Porfirio Díaz, Tláhuac quedó dentro del Distrito Federal. Al año siguiente se estableció el primer ayuntamiento tlahuica, que desapareció en 1903, durante otra reorganización del territorio capitalino. Durante la revolución de 1910-17, casi todos los alzados de Tláhuac se incorporaron al Ejército Libertador del Sur. En 1918, el gobierno de Venustiano Carranza convirtió en ejido la tierra de la Compañía Agrícola de Xico y Anexas, que durante el porfiriato había acaparado la mayor parte de la tierra cultivable del municipio. El ayuntamiento de Tláhuac fue restablecido en 1924, luego de dos años de lucha vecinal, pero en agosto de 1928, el gobierno de Plutarco Elías Calles decretó la desaparición de las municipalidades del DF. Al año siguiente, Tláhuac fue convertido en una de las 13 delegaciones del nuevo Departamento Central del Distrito Federal. En 1950 vivían en el territorio de la delegación 9,511 personas. Diez años más tarde, la población había aumentado a 29,880 habitantes, de los cuales tres cuartas partes vivían en el campo. Forman parte de la delegación las localidades de Mixquic (☛), San Juan Ixtayopan, Santa Catarina Yecahuizol y Tetelco.

TLAHUALILO, DE ◆ Sierra de Coahuila y Durango situada en la porción norte de la altiplanicie mexicana. Se extiende de norte a sur en el límite de ambos estados, al norte de Torreón y al noroeste del vaso de la antigua laguna de Mayrán.

TLAHUALILO ◆ Municipio de Durango situado en el extremo nororiental de la entidad, al norte de Gómez Palacio y al noreste de Mapimí, en los límites con Coahuila y Chihuahua. Superficie: 3,709.80 km². Habitantes: 22,924, de los cuales 6,254 forman la población económicamente activa. Hablan alguna lengua indígena 27 personas mayores de cinco años. La cabecera es Tlahualilo de Zaragoza. En 1887, el secretario de Fomento del gobierno de Porfirio Díaz, Carlos Pacheco, otorgó una concesión de aguas a la Compañía Agrícola Industrial y Colonizadora del Tlahualillo, fundada por José de Teresa y Miranda para explotar la cuenca del río Nazas. Tres años más tarde, la empresa quebró y pasó a manos de los acreedores ingleses de Teresa y Miranda. Éstos cometieron algunas irregularidades que afectaban a los vecinos de la zona, por lo que el nuevo ministro de Fomento, Olegario Molina, expidió en 1907 una ley de aguas que afectó a la compañía, al grado de que poco tiempo después la abandonaron. Una porción del territorio municipal se encuentra en la Zona del Silencio (☛ *Silencio, zona del*).

TLAHUAPAN ◆ Municipio de Puebla situado al noroeste de la capital estatal y al nor-noroeste de Atlixco, en los límites con el Estado de México y Tlaxcala. Superficie: 298.51 km². Habitantes: 29,642, de los cuales 6,093 forman la población económicamente activa. Hablan alguna lengua indígena 38 personas mayores de cinco años. La fiesta principal es la de Santa Rita, que se celebra el 22 de mayo con carreras de caballos, fuegos artificiales y danzas.

TLAHUELILPAN ◆ Municipio de Hidalgo situado al oeste de Pachuca y al norte de Tepeji del Río. Superficie: 31.25 km². Habitantes: 13,400, de los cuales 3,120 forman la población económicamente activa. Hablan alguna lengua indígena 84 personas mayores de cinco años (otomí 58).

TLAHUILTEPA ◆ Municipio de Hidalgo situado al noreste de Zimapán y al oeste-noroeste de Molango. Superficie: 467.7 km². Habitantes: 11,245, de los cuales 2,966 forman la población económicamente activa. Hablan alguna lengua indígena 36 personas mayores de cinco años (náhuatl 19).

TLAHUIZCALPAN ◆ Deidad nahua del amanecer y del crepúsculo que era la representación del planeta Venus. Se supo que Quetzalcóatl adoptó esta forma después de muerto.

TLAJOMULCO ◆ Municipio de Jalisco situado al sur de Guadalajara y al este de Acatlán. Superficie: 636.93 km². Habitantes: 100,797, de los cuales 20,238 forman la población económicamente activa. Hablan alguna lengua indígena 136 personas mayores de cinco años (purépecha 39 y náhuatl 27). La cabecera municipal es Tlajomulco de Zúñiga. En la jurisdicción hay fábricas de teja y ladrillo y se producen cerámica, metates y molcajetes.

TLALCHAPA ◆ Municipio de Guerrero situado al oeste-suroeste de Ixcateopan y al noreste de Zihuatanejo, en los lí-

Ilustración de Javier Guadarrama

Ayuntamiento municipal de Tlalchapa, Guerrero

mites con el Estado de México. Superficie: 414.3 km². Habitantes: 13,832, de los cuales 2,417 forman la población económicamente activa. Hablan alguna lengua indígena 25 personas mayores de cinco años. Hay minas de plata en explotación.

Tlalixcoyan ♦ Municipio de Veracruz situado al suroeste de Alvarado y al sureste del puerto jarocho, en el litoral del golfo de México. Superficie: 974.71 km². Habitantes: 36,697, de los cuales 9,899 forman la población económicamente activa. Hablan alguna lengua indígena 165 personas mayores de cinco años (chinanteco 132). En 1991 ocurrió una matanza de siete policías judiciales a manos de presuntos narcotraficantes, a quienes perseguían en avioneta, aunque finalmente se vinculó en la emboscada a militares que fueron sometidos a juicio y sentenciados.

Tlalixtac de Cabrera ♦ Municipio de Oaxaca contiguo a la capital del estado. Superficie: 61.24 km². Habitantes: 6,042, de los cuales 1,224 forman la población económicamente activa. Hablan alguna lengua indígena 1,034 personas mayores de cinco años (zapoteco 993).

Tlalixtaquilla de Maldonado ♦ Municipio de Guerrero situado al sureste de Olinalá y al norte de Ometepec, en los límites con Oaxaca. Superficie: 331.50 km². Habitantes: 6,681, de los cuales 1,541 forman la población económicamente activa. Hablan alguna lengua indígena 1,078 personas mayores de cinco años (mixteco 1,074). En el municipio se encuentra el cerro Campo de Guerrero, donde durante algún tiempo se estableció el cuartel general de las fuerzas insurgentes de Vicente Guerrero.

Tlaliyolo ♦ Nombre que recibía la deidad nahua Teteoinnan, la madre de los dioses, cuando se le consideraba la causante de los temblores de tierra. Su nombre significa "corazón de la tierra".

Tlalmanalco ♦ Municipio del Estado de México situado en el oriente de la entidad, al norte de Amecameca y al sureste de Chalco, en los límites con Puebla. Superficie: 162.40 km². Habitantes: 38,396, de los cuales 9,544 forman la población económicamente activa. Hablan alguna lengua indígena 75 personas mayores de cinco años. En la jurisdicción está una parte del parque nacional de Zoquiapan. En la cabecera, Tlalmanalco de Velázquez, está el acueducto de Los Arcos y un convento franciscano construido entre 1585 y 1591, el que cuenta con una capilla abierta construida en 1560, decorada con relieves de personas, plantas y animales entrelazados y una escultura conocida como Cristo rumbo al Calvario.

Tlalmanalco ♦ Río del Estado de México, también llamado de la Compañía. Nace en la ladera occidental del volcán Iztaccíhuatl, al noreste de Amecameca, en el oriente de la entidad; corre de sureste a noroeste y entra al vaso del antiguo lago de Chalco, donde un canal lo conduce, entre la sierra de Santa Catarina y el cerro del Pino, al lago de Texcoco. Sus aguas son utilizadas por las fábricas papeleras de San Rafael y Miraflores.

Tlalnelhuayocan ♦ Municipio de Veracruz contiguo a Jalapa. Superficie: 29.61 km². Habitantes: 9,750, de los cuales 2,014 forman la población económicamente activa. Hablan alguna lengua indígena 15 personas mayores de cinco años (náhuatl ocho).

Ilustración de José de Santiago

Palacio municipal de Tlalixtaquilla de Maldonado, Guerrero

TLALNEPANTLA ◆ Municipio de Morelos situado en los límites con el Distrito Federal y el Estado de México y contiguo a Tepoztlán. Superficie: 131.25 km². Habitantes: 4,948, de los cuales 1,077 forman la población económicamente activa. Hablan alguna lengua indígena 59 personas mayores de cinco años.

TLALNEPANTLA DE BAZ ◆ Municipio del Estado de México situado al noreste de Naucalpan y al sur de Tepotzotlán, en los límites con el Distrito Federal. Superficie: 82.45 km². Habitantes: 713,143, de los cuales 237,649 forman la población económicamente activa. Hablan alguna lengua indígena 6,280 personas mayores de cinco años (náhuatl 2,090 y otomí 1,626). Hasta el siglo XVI, el actual territorio municipal estuvo habitado, sucesivamente, por otomíes y toltecas, quienes se instalaron en lo que hoy es Santa Cecilia Acatitlán. Hacia el siglo XIII, la región fue ocupada por los acolhuas de Tenayuca. La cabecera, Tlalnepantla de Comonfort, fue fundada a mediados del siglo XVI por misioneros franciscanos, entre dos pueblos, uno de otomíes y otro de nahuas, y por eso fue llamado Tlalnepantla, que significa "tierra de en medio". La conquista espiritual fue realizada por los franciscanos, quienes construyeron un convento hacia 1554 y una iglesia, ahora catedral, que fue terminada en 1557. De la colonia sobreviven algunas construcciones como el templo y el puente de Tenayuca, el acueducto de Guadalupe y la ex hacienda de Santa Mónica. El territorio de Tlalnepantla formó parte de la intendencia de México y, desde 1824, del Estado de México, hasta que en 1843 el gobierno de Antonio López de Santa Anna creó el Distrito de México, denominación centralista del Distrito Federal, donde quedó comprendida la localidad de Tlalnepantla que, al reimplantarse el federalismo, en 1846, se reincorporó al Estado de México. Once años después, en el último gobierno de Santa Anna, se restableció el Distrito de México y Tlalnepantla volvió a ser incluido en él y se creó, el 16 de febrero, la Prefectura de Tlalnepantla, también llamada del Norte, que incluía territorio del actual municipio de Tlalnepantla y de San Cristóbal Ecatepec, Guadalupe Hidalgo, Monte Bajo y Monte Alto. Dos años después se instaló el primer ayuntamiento tlalnepantlense y en 1857 el municipio quedó definitivamente integrado al Estado de México. Durante la intervención francesa actuó en territorio municipal la guerrilla republicana de Catarino Fragoso, que en febrero de 1867 estuvo a punto de aprehender a Maximiliano de Habsburgo, quien se retiraba de la ciudad de México hacia Querétaro. El 2 de septiembre de 1874, la cabecera municipal fue elevada a rango de villa y se le agregó el apellido del ex presidente Ignacio Comonfort. El 13 de septiembre de 1948 adquirió el rango de ciudad. La diócesis de Tlalnepantla fue erigida en enero de 1964 por el papa Paulo VI. A partir de los años cuarenta del siglo XX, con el crecimiento desmesurado de la ciudad de México (☛ *Valle de México, Área Metropolitana del*), Tlalnepantla se ha convertido en uno de los mayores centros industriales de México. En noviembre de 1984, en el pueblo de San Juan Ixhuatepec, situado en los límites con el Distrito Federal, 11 explosiones de los depósitos de gas butano instalados en la población destruyeron 15 manzanas, mataron a más de 1,000 personas (el gobierno reconoció sólo 500), dejó heridas a 2,000 y damnificadas a 20,000, aproximadamente. Una explosión menor ocurrió en 1996.

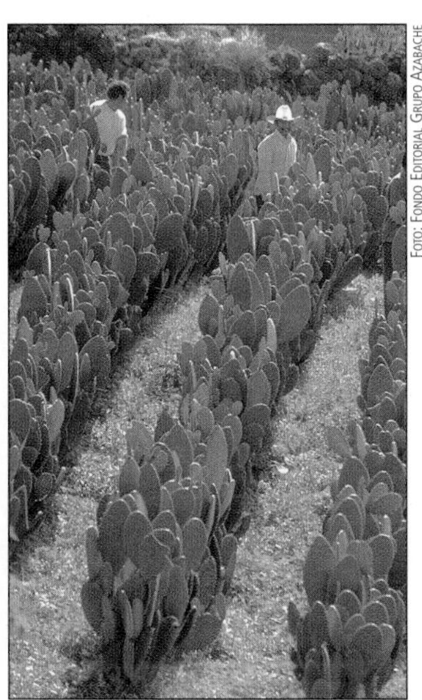
FOTO: FONDO EDITORIAL GRUPO AZABACHE

Cultivo del nopal en Tlalnepantla, Morelos

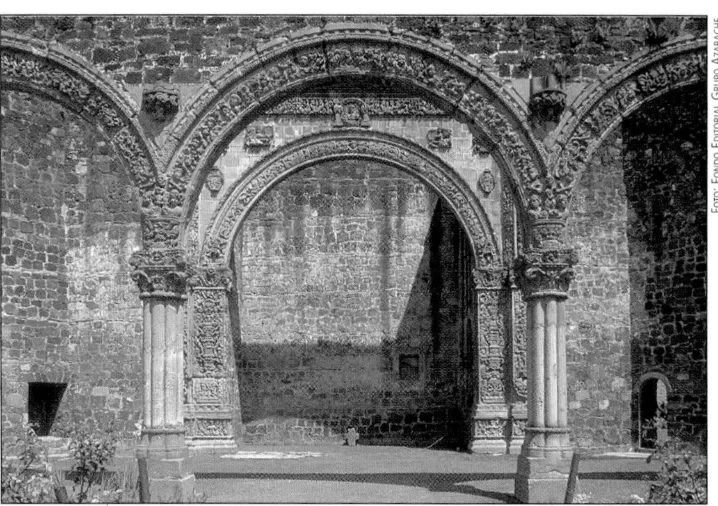
FOTO: FONDO EDITORIAL GRUPO AZABACHE

Capilla abierta en Tlalmanalco, Estado de México

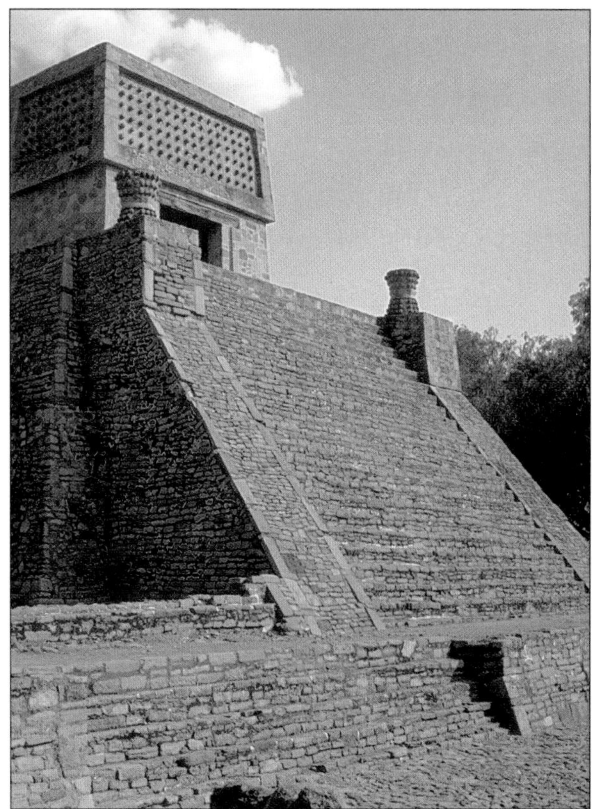

Zona arqueológica de Tenayuca en Tlalnepantla de Baz, Estado de México

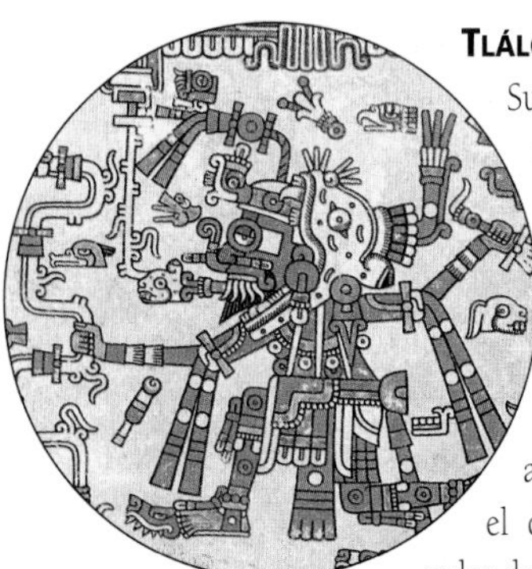

Tláloc en el Códice Laúd

TLÁLOC ◆ Dios nahua de la lluvia. Su nombre deriva de *tlalli*, tierra, y *octli*, licor: "El vino de la tierra", es decir, lluvia. Era, pues, el dios de las aguas del cielo, a diferencia de Chalchiuhicueye, diosa de las aguas de la tierra. Se le atribuía la dádiva de la vida y el dominio de las almas separadas de los cuerpos. Los autores que se han dedicado al estudio de la mitología náhuatl difieren al referirse al origen de esta deidad: algunos señalan que los hermanos Tlatlauhqui Tezcatlipoca, Yayauhqui Tezcatlipoca, Quetzalcóatl y Omitéotl, hijos de la pareja original divina de Ometecutli y Omecíhuatl, fueron encargados de crear el mundo, así como a los dioses subalternos; entre sus obras, dieron al agua una organización particular y, para regirla, formaron a Tlaloccantecutli y a su esposa Chalchiuhicueye. Algunos otros afirman que Tláloc era la divinidad más antigua del panteón náhuatl. Los nahuas llamaban Tlalocan al lugar donde suponían que se formaba la lluvia y Tlaloccantecutli, "Señor del lugar del vino de la tierra", al numen que residía allí. Esta deidad, con distintos nombres pero con las mismas características, era adorada por las diversas etnias que habitaban el actual territorio mexicano: en zapoteco se llamaba Cocijo ("Rayo") y con igual significado, en totonaco se nombraba Tajín; en mixteco era Tzahui y los purépechas lo llamaron Chupi-Tirípeme ("Agua preciosa azul"). Su imagen aparece ya en la cultura olmeca, con máscara de tigre-serpiente. De acuerdo con la mitología náhuatl, Tláloc tenía cuatro ayudantes, los tlaloques, uno en cada punto cardinal, que simbolizaban a las nubes. Ellos portaban una vasija con agua y empuñaban un bastón. Al luchar entre sí rompían sus cántaros con los bastones y producían el trueno, el relámpago y la lluvia. Se le rendía culto en el templo mayor de México-Tenochtitlan, junto a Huitzilopochtli.

TLALPAN ◆ Delegación situada en el sur del Distrito Federal. Limita con las delegaciones de Magdalena Contreras, Álvaro Obregón, Coyoacán, Xochimilco y Milpa Alta y con los estados de México y Morelos. Superficie: 312 km². Habitantes: 552,516 (1995), de los cuales 133,260 forman la población económicamente activa, dedicada principalmente a la producción manufacturera, la construcción, la minería y las tareas agropecuarias. Hablan alguna lengua indígena 7,200 personas mayores de cinco años (náhuatl 2,088, mixteco 1,149, otomí 817, zapoteco 758 y totonaco 457). Los primeros habitantes del actual territorio fueron varios grupos seminómadas de filiación otomí, que unos 600 o 700 a.n.e. comenzaron a practicar la agricultura en el Ajusco, Topilejo y más tarde en Cuicuilco (☛), donde construyeron una ciudad de más de 400 hectáreas de extensión y que en su mejor momento fue habitada por unas 20,000 personas. Poco antes del inicio de la época clásica prehispánica, esa ciudad fue destruida por la erupción del Xitle, uno de los volcanes de la sierra del Ajusco. Los sobrevivientes se dispersaron y probablemente algunos de ellos emigraron hacia Teotihuacán. Durante el siglo XIII, los xochimilcas se instalaron en Topilejo y, poco después, un grupo de tepanecas de Coyoacán refundó Ajusco, más tarde llamado San Miguel Ajusco, y creó la localidad de Tlalpan, nombre que significa "en la tierra". Poco después de la conquista de México-Tenochtitlan, los españoles se instalaron en la región y bautizaron el pueblo de Tlalpan con el nombre de San Agustín de las Cuevas, que se incorporó al marquesado del valle de Oaxaca. En 1637, los frailes dominicos construyeron su convento, iglesia y hospicio en San Agustín. A partir del siglo XVII, la región de Tlalpan comenzó a ser utilizada como lugar de recreo por los habitantes de la ciudad de México. Con el establecimiento de las intendencias, en 1787 el corregimiento de San Agustín de las Cuevas se incorporó a la de México. Ese mismo año se construyó la Calzada de Tlalpan, que hasta mediados del siglo XX fue el corredor vial más importante de la creciente ciudad de México. Al establecerse la República federal, en 1824, quedó dentro de la jurisdicción del Estado de México. Tres años después, el 14 de junio de 1827, el gobernador Lorenzo de Zavala convirtió en sede de los poderes mexiquenses a San Agustín. Meses después, en septiembre, la población fue elevada a la categoría de ciudad y recuperó su nombre nahua. Tlalpan fue capital del estado hasta el 14 de agosto de 1830, cuando los poderes se trasladaron a Toluca. En 1854, el gobierno centralista de Antonio López de Santa Anna inventó un Distrito de México, sede del gobierno nacional, y Tlalpan fue incluido en él. Al año siguiente,

Foto: Carlos Hahn

Tláloc, en el Museo Nacional de Antropología e Historia de la ciudad de México

El Ajusco, en Tlalpan, Distrito Federal

los liberales que habían derrocado a Santa Anna intentaron devolver al Estado de México el partido de Tlalpan, pero los vecinos del lugar solicitaron que éste fuese parte del Distrito Federal. En 1861, el gobierno de Benito Juárez creó el partido de Tlalpan, formado por todo el sur del DF. En 1896, la población tlalpense era de 7,000 habitantes, por lo que dos años después, el gobierno de Porfirio Díaz estableció el primer ayuntamiento local. A fines del siglo XIX se edificaron las fábricas de papel de Loreto y Peña Pobre. En 1903 se instaló, al sur de la cabecera, la Escuela Militar de Aspirantes. Poco antes del inicio de la insurrección maderista, más de 13,000 personas vivían en el municipio. En febrero de 1913, los cadetes de la Escuela Militar de Aspirantes se sumaron al movimiento de la Ciudadela y participaron en el golpe de Estado que acabó con el gobierno de Francisco I. Madero. Hasta 1920, en la zona operaron numerosas guerrillas del Ejército Libertador del Sur. En 1929 desapareció el municipio y el territorio de Tlalpan se convirtió en una de las delegaciones del Distrito Federal. Algunos de los atractivos turísticos de la delegación son los Bosques de Tlalpan, las zonas arqueológicas de Cuicuilco, Tenantongo y del cerro Zacatépetl, una parroquia del siglo XVI, la casa de Antonio López de Santa Anna, la Casa Chata, la Casa de Moneda, la prisión de José María Morelos y el ex Palacio Municipal. En Tlalpan existen algunos conventos, numerosos sanatorios siquiátricos y otros centros hospitalarios.

TLALPUJAHUA ◆ Municipio de Michoacán situado al noreste de Zitácuaro, en los límites con el Estado de México. Superficie: 231.49 km². Habitantes: 18,411, de los cuales 5,264 forman la población económicamente activa. Hablan alguna lengua indígena 43 personas mayores de cinco años. En la jurisdicción, que se encuentra en una importante región minera, hay yacimientos de oro, plata, cobre y plomo que eran aprovechados, si bien mínimamente, antes de la conquista española. En el siglo XVIII fueron explotados por José de la Borda, quizá el minero más célebre del México colonial. El municipio fue erigido el 10 de diciembre de 1831. Una porción de su territorio está ocupada por el Parque Nacional Hermanos Rayón. Otras actividades importantes son las artesanías de vidrio soplado, el arte plumario y la peletería. En la cabecera se encuentra la parroquia que data del siglo XVIII, el Museo de Mineralogía e Historia y el monumento a Ignacio López Rayón. El 19 de marzo se realiza una feria en honor de San José, patrono municipal; el 16 de julio se festeja a la Virgen del Carmen con una verbena popular, tianguis y danzas, y el 2 de noviembre hay una feria agrícola, comercial y artesanal.

TLALPUJAHUA, DE ◆ Sierra de Michoacán y del Estado de México que forma parte del Sistema Volcánico Transversal. Se encuentra al norte de la sierra de Angangueo, en el límite de ambos estados. Tiene importantes yacimientos de oro y otros minerales que se explotan en El Oro y Tlalpujahua. Su pico más alto es el cerro de Tarimangacho, que se eleva 3,104 metros sobre el nivel del mar.

TLALTECUTLI ◆ Deidad nahua de la tierra, cuyo nombre significa "el señor tierra". Era uno de los cuatro elementos formadores del mundo (agua, aire, fuego y tierra) y también el dios vengador del adulterio. Se presentaba como una dualidad femenino-masculina.

TLALTENANGO ◆ Municipio de Puebla situado al noroeste de la capital estatal y al este de Huejotzingo, en los límites con Tlaxcala. Superficie: 37 km². Habitantes: 5,078, de los cuales 906 forman la población económicamente activa. Hablan alguna lengua indígena 20 personas mayores de cinco años (náhuatl 15).

TLALTENANGO DE SÁNCHEZ ROMÁN ◆ Municipio de Zacatecas situado al suroeste de la capital estatal y al noroeste de Nochistlán, en los límites con Jalisco. Superficie: 859.37 km². Habitantes: 23,670, de los cuales 6,070 forman la población económicamente activa. Hablan alguna lengua indígena 58 personas mayores de cinco años (huichol 21). En la jurisdicción se encuentra la presa Miguel Alemán Excamé, que recibe aguas del río Tlaltenango.

TLALTETELA ◆ Municipio de Veracruz situado al sur de Jalapa y al norte de Huatusco. Superficie: 266.5 km². Habitantes: 11,904, de los cuales 2,996 forman la población económicamente activa. Hablan alguna lengua indígena 30 personas mayores de cinco años (náhuatl 26). La cabecera se llama Axocuapan.

TLALTIZAPÁN ◆ Municipio de Morelos situado al suroeste de Cuautla y al su-

FOTO: FONDO EDITORIAL GRUPO AZABACHE

Mausoleo zapatista en Tlaltizapán, Morelos

reste de Cuernavaca. Superficie: 301.14 km². Habitantes: 43,401, de los cuales 10,460 forman la población económicamente activa. Hablan alguna lengua indígena 579 personas mayores de cinco años (tlapaneco 300 y náhuatl 188). Entre 1915 y 1916, en la actual cabecera se instaló el cuartel general del Ejército Libertador del Sur (☛ *Morelos*). Seis kilómetros al norte se encuentra el balneario Las Estacas.

TLALTIZAPÁN, DE ◆ Sierra de Morelos que forma parte del Sistema Volcánico Transversal. Está situada al sur del valle de Yautepec y al oeste del de Cuautla. Se extiende de norte a sur, paralela y al este de la sierra de Yautepec o Tetillas, al norte del río Chinameca. Sus cimas más altas son los cerros de Tlaltizapán, Temilpa o Chiquihuite y el de Peaña.

TLALTONATIUH ◆ Nombre del cuarto mundo en la mitología nahua. Está representado en el Códice Vaticano. Se le atribuye una duración de 5,206 años.

TLALXICTENTICA ◆ Morada de la deidad nahua del fuego, Mictlantecutli, que se encontraba en el centro de la tierra, donde se concentraba el fuego.

TLANALAPA ◆ Municipio de Hidalgo situado al sureste de Pachuca y contiguo a Tepeapulco, en los límites con el Estado de México. Superficie: 156.7 km². Habitantes: 9,648, de los cuales 2,380 forman la población económicamente activa. Hablan alguna lengua indígena 21 personas mayores de cinco años. El actual territorio minucipal fue evangelizado en el siglo XVI por los franciscanos.

TLANCHINOL ◆ Municipio de Hidalgo situado al este de Tepehuacán y al suroeste de Huejutla de Reyes, en los límites con San Luis Potosí. Superficie: 380.3 km². Habitantes: 31,193, de los cuales 6,827 forman la población económicamente activa. Hablan alguna lengua indígena 14,388 personas mayores de cinco años (náhuatl 14,378). Indígenas monolingües: 2,954. El actual territorio municipal fue evangelizado en el siglo XVI por los frailes agustinos; en la cabecera se encuentra un templo construido en 1735.

TLANEPANTLA ◆ Municipio de Puebla situado al sureste de la capital estatal, al sur de Tepeaca y al norte de Tepexi de Rodríguez. Superficie: 14.04 km². Habitantes: 3,638, de los cuales 698 forman la población económicamente activa. Hablan alguna lengua indígena 86 personas mayores de cinco años (náhuatl 84).

TLAOLA ◆ Municipio de Puebla situado al sur de Xicotepec, al norte de Zacatlán y contiguo a Huauchinango. Superficie: 108.44 km². Habitantes: 15,822, de los cuales 4,346 forman la población económicamente activa. Hablan alguna lengua indígena 9,938 personas mayores de cinco años (náhuatl 9,926) de las cuales 469 son monolingües.

TLAPA DE COMONFORT ◆ Municipio de Guerrero situado al este de Chilapa y al sureste de Olinalá, cerca de Oaxaca. Superficie: 1,054 km². Habitantes: 50,040, de los cuales 9,198 forman la población económicamente activa. Hablan alguna lengua indígena 24,642 personas mayores de cinco años (náhuatl 13,790, mixteco 8,126 y tlapaneco

ILUSTRACIÓN: ANTONIO ESPARZA

Tlapa de Comonfort, Guerrero

2,704). La cabecera, el centro comercial más importante de la región, fue ocupada por las tropas insurgentes de José María Morelos en noviembre de 1811. En 1992, el papa Juan Pablo II erigió la diócesis de Tlapa.

TLAPA, LIENZO DE ◆ Códice del siglo XVI, realizado en una tira de tela de 2.85 metros de largo por 0.76 de ancho, que narra la historia política de los pueblos de Tlapa, Acatepec, Totoltepec, Tlachinolli, Chicuey, Acpetzintli y Yohualamax. En el reverso, además de casi un centenar de jeroglifos geográficos, se cuenta que el documento fue utilizado como título de propiedad de los tlapanecos de Azoyú, para defenderse de los conquistadores españoles. El original se encuentra en la Biblioteca Nacional de Antropología e Historia.

TLAPACOYA ◆ Municipio de Puebla situado al este de Huauchinango y al nor-noreste de Zacatlán. Superficie: 80.38 km². Habitantes: 5,914, de los cuales 1,555 forman la población económicamente activa. Hablan alguna lengua indígena 2,830 personas mayores de cinco años (náhuatl 2,816). Indígenas monolingües: 128. Los primeros habitantes del actual territorio municipal fueron grupos de cazadores y recolectores, que se instalaron hace más de 20,000 años. La agricultura se comenzó a practicar 4,000 años a.n.e., y entre los años 1200 y 700, los habitantes de la región recibieron influencia olmeca. Hacia los años 700 se construyó el centro ceremonial de Tlapacoya, que existió hasta 100 a.n.e. De sus edificios ha sobrevivido una pequeña pirámide, en cuya parte posterior se edificaron tres tumbas con grandes huesos. La fiesta más importante, la del Santo Entierro, se celebra el segundo viernes de Cuaresma con música, danza, procesiones, bailes y juegos pirotécnicos.

TLAPACOYAN ◆ Municipio de Veracruz situado al norte de Jalapa y al sur de Papantla, en los límites con Puebla. Superficie: 142.3 km². Habitantes: 48,941, de los cuales 13,092 forman la población económicamente activa. Hablan alguna lengua indígena 696 personas mayores de cinco años (náhuatl 636).

TLAPANALÁ ◆ Municipio de Puebla situado al nor-noroeste de Izúcar de Matamoros y al sur-suroeste de Atlixco. Superficie: 80.38 km². Habitantes: 7,950, de los cuales 1,706 forman la población económicamente activa. Hablan alguna lengua indígena 33 personas mayores de cinco años (náhuatl 31).

TLAPANECO ◆ Río de Guerrero también llamado Huamuxtitlán. Nace en la porción oriental del estado, de la confluencia de los ríos Alcozauca y Coycoyán; corre de sur a norte, recibe al arroyo Zapotitlán y tuerce al noroeste; una parte de su cauce corre en el límite con Puebla, antes de unirse al río Mezcala.

TLAPANECOS ◆ Nombre con el que se conoce, desde mediados del siglo XVI, a los yoppimes, indios de origen nahua cohuxca tlapaneco y yoppime tlapaneco, que vivían en la la porción oriental del actual estado de Guerrero. A fines del primer milenio de la época contemporánea, una migración de nahuas teotihuacanos ocupó la zona de Chilpancingo, Tlapa, Olinalá y Chilapa y se mezcló con los yoppime. Hacia 1480, las tropas mexicas de Tízoc iniciaron la conquista de los señoríos yoppimes del norte, los más vinculados a las culturas del valle de México, y en 1486, luego de una sangrienta contienda, los guerreros aztecas de Ahuízotl conquistaron Tlapa. En ese mismo año, para celebrar el triunfo, los sacerdotes mexicas sacrificaron a 24 mil guerreros yoppimes en el Templo Mayor de México-Tenochtitlan. Los yoppimes meridionales, por su parte, se agruparon alrededor del señorío de Yoppitzingo y durante 40 años resistieron el avance de las fuerzas de la Triple Alianza. El territorio de Yoppitzingo llegó a extenderse por el centro del actual estado de Guerrero; estaba limitado por el río Nexpa o Ayutla al oriente, por el océano Pacífico al sur, por el río Papagayo al poniente y por el río Omitlán al norte. Entre 1521 y 1522, tropas españolas al mando de Pedro de Alvarado y Gonzalo de Sandoval realizaron numerosas incursiones en la Costa Chica y sometieron a los indios. En marzo de 1531, sin embargo, los yoppimes de Cuauhtepec se levantaron en armas contra los conquistadores y sus aliados, los indios de Puzutla y Cuscotitlán; tomaron Cuscotitlán y convocaron a un levantamiento generalizado en la Costa Chica contra los invasores, que fue apoyado en Acapulco, Citla, Citlala, Xaltiango y Acamaluta. Unos meses después, Hernán Cortés envió una fuerza de españoles e indios al mando de Vasco Porcallo, que en ese mismo año diezmó a los indios. Poco después, los yoppimes sobrevivientes se concentraron en los alrededores de Tlapa y desde entonces fueron conocidos como tlapanecos. Los frailes agustinos se encargaron de la conquista espiritual. En el siglo XVIII, los tlapanecos fueron hostilizados por la familia Moctezuma, que se apropió de una gran cantidad de la tierra comunal de los indios. En noviembre de 1811, cuando las fuerzas de José María Morelos ocuparon Tlapa, un gran número de tlapanecos se sumó a la revolución de independencia. Treinta años más tarde, a principios de 1842, los indios de Quechultenango y Chilapa se levantaron en armas para oponerse a la voracidad de las haciendas y luego de enfrentar con éxito a las tropas gubernamentales durante medio año, llegaron con Juan Álvarez a un acuerdo que incluía una amnistía generalizada para los insurrectos y la promesa de restitución de la tierra. El gobierno de Nicolás Bravo entorpeció la reforma agraria y en abril de 1843, los tlapanecos de Ixcateopan, Acatepec, Tlalquesolapa, Copantoyac, Tlapa y Chilapa volvieron a sublevarse; dos de los principales dirigentes eran Domingo Santiago y Miguel Casarrubias. El alzamiento se generalizó en el centro y noreste de Guerrero y llegó hasta el occidente de Oaxaca. El movimiento indígena volvió a ser reprimido a fines de ese año. Aunque derrotados, todavía en 1844, 1849 y 1857, los tlapanecos volvieron a insurreccionarse para forzar la restitución de sus tierras. Desde fines de la década de 1850, sin embargo, los sucesivos gobiernos liberales consiguieron despojar a los indios e impedir, al mismo tiempo, los levantamientos armados. En 1995, 74,448 personas mayores de cinco años hablaban tlapaneco, de las cuales 23,012 eran monolingües y 53,130 vivían en Guerrero. El idioma tlapaneco ha sido clasificado en el grupo joca-meridional, tronco tlapaneco, familia tlapaneca. A pesar de la continua agresión a la que han sido sometidos desde el siglo XVI, los tlapanecos conservan su vestimenta tradicional: los hombres usan el calzón de manta anudado en los tobillos, camisa de manta, faja, sombrero de palma y huaraches; las mujeres visten falda larga, blusa de manta con bordados, una especie de mantilla o un rebozo y huaraches. La agricultura es su actividad económica básica, aunque también elaboran artesanías de palma. La base de su sociedad es la familia nuclear, constituida por los padres y los hijos solteros. El matrimonio se realiza, de preferencia, entre habitantes del mismo pueblo. Cuando un joven desea casarse contrata a un casamentero que visita a la familia de la novia, junto con el padre del novio, llevando diversos regalos; se fija la fecha de la ceremonia, después de la cual hay un baile. La pareja de recién casados vive un tiempo con los padres de la mujer, pues el hombre debe trabajar para sus suegros como "pago por la novia". El matrimonio no se considera definitivo sino hasta que nace el primer hijo; entonces se efectúa la fiesta de la "quema de la leña", cuando en una fogata se creman las ofrendas para sus dioses. Al morir un miembro del grupo, su cuerpo es lavado y amortajado con tela blanca. Más tarde se le envuelve y se le sepulta en un petate o se le deposita en un ataúd; si la familia tiene recursos económicos, se hace un velorio. Según sus creencias, el alma recorre todos los caminos por los que pasó en vida; luego, toma la forma de una mariposa que es devorada cuatro veces por el diablo, quien más tarde la defeca. Si el demonio la atrapa con facilidad, el alma trabajará eternamente en las milpas de poca fertilidad; pero si le es difícil hacerlo, su trabajo será en tierras fértiles. Practican la religión católica mezclada con sus creencias ancestrales; así, veneran a dos deidades principales, Akunba y Akunmbatso, relacionadas con el agua y la fertilidad.

TLAPEHUALA ◆ Municipio de Guerrero situado al este de Coyuca de Catalán y al norte de Atoyac, cerca del Estado de México y de Michoacán. Superficie: 266.70 km². Habitantes: 20,851, de los cuales 3,118 forman la población económicamente activa. Hablan alguna lengua indígena 27 personas mayores de cinco años. Se elaboran artesanías de palma y alfarería.

Ilustración de Javier Guaderrama

Vista panorámica de Tlapehuala, Guerrero

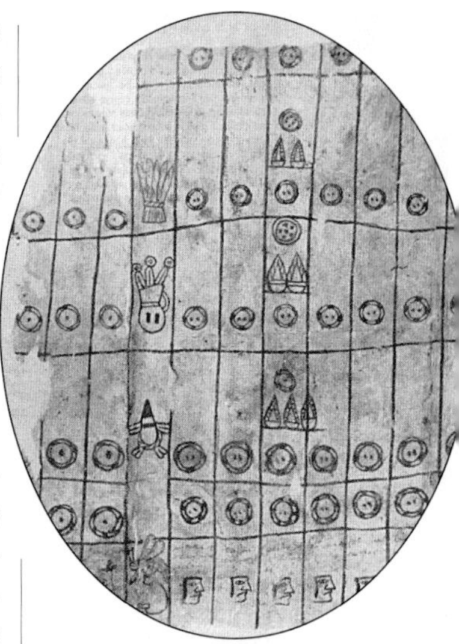

Códice Tlaquiltenango

TLAQUEPAQUE ◆ Municipio de Jalisco contiguo a Guadalajara. Superficie: 270.88 km². Habitantes: 449,238, de los cuales 103,809 forman la población económicamente activa. Hablan alguna lengua indígena 1,828 personas mayores de cinco años (otomí 564, purépecha 415, náhuatl 145 y mixteco 117). El municipio es reconocido por sus artesanías de barro, vidrio soplado y textiles. La cabecera, antiguamente llamada San Pedro Tlaquepaque, es un importante centro turístico.

TLAQUILPAN ◆ Municipio de Veracruz situado al sur-suroeste de Orizaba y al oeste de Zongolica, en los límites con Puebla. Superficie: 58.4 km². Habitantes: 5,444, de los cuales 1,066 forman la población económicamente activa. Hablan alguna lengua indígena 4,541 personas mayores de cinco años (náhuatl 4,539). Indígenas monolingües: 657.

TLAQUILTENANGO ◆ Códice nahua del siglo XVI elaborado en papel amate, seis de cuyas partes se encuentran en la Biblioteca Nacional de Antropología e Historia y el resto, más de 100 fragmentos, en el Museo Americano de Historia Natural de Nueva York. Es una relación de tributos pagados en monedas, con fechas de los pagos. Fue descubierto por Mauricio de la Arena en la iglesia

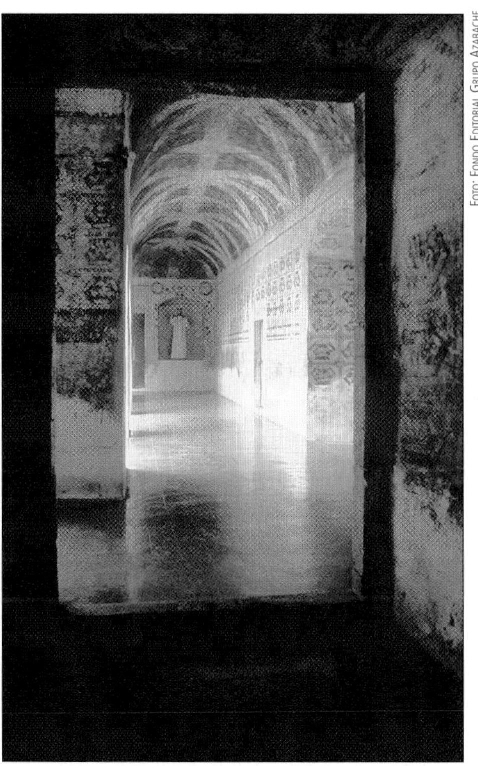
Foto: Fondo Editorial Grupo Azabache

Claustro del convento de Santo Domingo en Tlaquiltenango, Morelos

parroquial de Tlaquiltenango y cedido al Museo Nacional de Antropología en 1909. Los fragmentos del códice estaban pegados en las paredes, como pinturas murales.

Tlaquiltenango ◆ Municipio de Morelos situado en el extremo sur del estado, al sur-suroeste de Cuautla y al sur-sureste de Cuernavaca, en los límites con Puebla y Guerrero. Superficie: 467.6 km^2. Habitantes: 29,843, de los cuales 7,761 forman la población económicamente activa. Hablan alguna lengua indígena 579 personas mayores de cinco años (náhuatl 138). El territorio fue evangelizado por los franciscanos de Cuernavaca, quienes dejaron esa labor a los dominicos, los que ordenaron la construcción de la iglesia y su casa conventual al arquitecto Francisco Becerra. Estos edificios fueron decorados con murales por los indígenas de la zona.

Tlaquitenango ◆ ☛ *Yautepec*.

Tlatelolco ◆ Códice nahua que registra, sin referencias cronológicas precisas, algunos de los acontecimientos más notables de la historia de los tlatelolcas en la segunda mitad del siglo XVI, como su participación como aliados de los españoles en la guerra contra los caxcanes, zacatecas y otros grupos en el cerro del Mixtón, en la Nueva Galicia (1540-42), y la muerte del virrey Juan de Velasco (1564). Probablemente fue elaborado hacia 1565. Es un papel de amate, de 365 por 40 centímetros, montado en tela, que se conserva en la Biblioteca Nacional de Antropología e Historia. Se le ha llamado también Manuscrito o Pintura de Xochipilla.

Tlatelolco ◆ Zona de la ciudad de México fundada sobre un islote del lago de Texcoco situado al noroeste de México-Tenochtitlan (☛). Aunque es muy probable que hubiera sido habitado desde el siglo X de nuestra época, el asentamiento definitivo ocurrió en 1337, cuando un grupo de mexicas descontentos por la distribución de las chinampas de la recién fundada capital de los aztecas, se exilió y fundó un pequeño señorío independiente, que recibió el nombre de Tlatelolco, "lugar del promontorio de tierra". Para protegerse de sus paisanos, los tlatelolcas aceptaron la dominación de Azcapotzalco, que, sin embargo, desde 1360 permitió la elección independiente de los señores locales. Durante los 100 años siguientes, gobernados sucesivamente por Cuacuauhpitzáhuac (1380-1418), Tlacatéotl (1418-28) y Cuauhtlatoa (1428-60), los tlatelolcas extendieron sus dominios hasta Tepeyacac y Tecamachalco, hasta que en 1473 el señor Moquihuix (1460-73) fue derrotado y muerto por las fuerzas mexicas de Axayácatl. Tlatelolco se convirtió en una especie de ciudad satélite de México-Tenochtitlan, aunque conservó una relativa independencia interna. Su integración a los dominios de la Triple Alianza permitió a los comerciantes tlatelolcas convertir su mercado en el más importante de Mesoamérica. En 1520, a la muerte de Cuitláhuac, el gobierno mexica quedó en manos del señor de Tlatelolco, Cuauhtémoc, quien dirigió la resistencia azteca contra los españoles (☛ *Conquista*). En junio de 1521, luego de ser desalojadas del Templo Mayor, las fuerzas mexicas se retiraron a Tlatelolco y ahí combatieron hasta principios de agosto, cuando Cuauhtémoc

Códice Tlatelolco

Colegio de Santiago Tlatelolco

fue capturado. Los españoles establecieron en Tlatelolco uno de los primeros pueblos de indios, al cual bautizaron como Santiago Tlatelolco, e impusieron a Cuauhtémoc como gobernante (1521-23). En 1524, los franciscanos fundaron su primer convento, a un lado del antiguo local del mercado. En 1536, a instancias de Juan de Zumárraga y Luis de Velasco, los mismos franciscanos crearon el Imperial Colegio de Indios de la Santa Cruz de Santiago Tlatelolco, para educar a los jóvenes aristócratas mexicas. Ahí, de sus discípulos, hablantes de náhuatl, español y latín, Bernardino de Sahagún recogió una buena parte de la información con la que redactó su *Historia general de las cosas de la Nueva España*. La institución fue gobernada por los franciscanos hasta 1546, cuando comenzó a ser regida por los propios estudiantes. Cuatro años después, sin embargo, el edificio se hallaba destruido y el Colegio dejó de funcionar. A mediados del siglo XVI, la ciudad de México absorbió a Tlatelolco, que se convirtió desde entonces en un barrio de indios de la capital de la Nueva España. En los primeros años del siglo XVII, la mayoría de las actividades que antes controlaba el mercado de Tlatelolco fueron asumidas por el mercado de San Juan, más cercano al centro de la ciudad de México. A causa de la conquista española, la población indígena disminuyó drásticamente. En 1623, por ejemplo, sólo 12,000 tlatelolcas vivían en la ciudad; diez años más tarde, en 1634, la población se había reducido a la mitad; y en 1646 eran menos de 5,000. A mediados del siglo XIX, luego de las reformas impulsadas por los liberales, las construcciones que franciscanos conservaban en Tlatelolco pasaron a manos del gobierno, que convirtió el convento en oficinas y en prisión militar, donde estuvieron presos muchos de los opositores de los gobiernos de Benito Juárez, Sebastián Lerdo de Tejada, Porfirio Díaz y Francisco I. Madero, entre ellos Miguel Negrete, Juan Nepomuceno Cortina, Gildardo Magaña, Francisco Villa, Bernardo Reyes y Félix Díaz. Durante el gobierno de Díaz se construyó, al oriente del templo y en la acera norte del jardín, la principal aduana pulquera de la ciudad de México y en la acera oeste se construyó una ampliación de la cárcel militar. El ex Colegio, situado en el lado este del jardín, sufrió varias modificaciones, la última en los años treinta, cuando se le impuso una fachada del llamado estilo colonial mexicano. El edificio alojó la secundaria 16. Desde fines del siglo XIX se cubrió de vías y otras instalaciones ferrocarrileras la superficie que ahora ocupa la Unidad Habitacional Nonoalco-Tlatelolco, en torno a la cual surgieron barrios y campamentos más o menos permanentes de trabajadores ferrocarrileros y sus familias. En los años cincuenta, al oriente del jardín estaba el viejo barrio de Santiago, habitado por obreros, artesanos, pequeños comerciantes y músicos populares. El edificio de la aduana pulquera estaba ocupado por el Registro Federal de Automóviles, la secundaria 16 funcionaba en lo que había sido el Colegio y, al sur del templo seguía la Prisión Militar de Tlatelolco. Durante el movimiento ferrocarrilero de 1958-59 (☛), en el jardín y sus alrededores se produjeron grandes encuentros entre los obreros ferroviarios y la fuerza pública. A principios de los años sesen-

Estudiantes en Tlatelolco el 2 de octubre de 1968

ta fueron derribadas la ex Aduana y la cárcel para construir la unidad habitacional proyectada por los arquitectos Mario Pani y Luis Ramos Cunningham. Al jardín se le puso una extraña rotonda en el centro y en su perímetro una balaustrada que se copió de la que existe en el jardín de San Marcos, en Aguascalientes. Las vecindades de la acera sur se demolieron, la secundaria desapareció para abrir la ampliación del Paseo de la Reforma y del ex Colegio sólo quedó parte de los muros, ahora en medio de un espejo de agua, pues la fachada se trasladó piedra por piedra al lado oeste. Al ser habitado el conjunto urbano de Nonoalco-Tlatelolco, alcanzó una población de más de 70,000 personas. El 2 de octubre de 1968, en la plaza de las Tres Culturas, situada sobre el sitio donde estuvo el mercado indígena, la fuerza pública disparó sobre la multitud inerme que realizaba un mitin. Según las autoridades, los muertos no llegaron a 30. De acuerdo con la prensa internacional, las víctimas de la agresión fueron cientos, en su mayoría jóvenes que participaban en el movimiento estudiantil de 1968 (☛). Tlatelolco fue una de las zonas más dañadas por el terremoto de septiembre de 1985, y a partir de entonces las organizaciones vecinales han desplegado una permanente actividad.

TLATILCO ◆ Zona arqueológica del Estado de México. El nombre significa "en los entierros". Fue descubierta en 1936, pero su exploración se inició hasta 1942. Se le ha calculado una antigüedad que va de 1,400 a 1,700 años a.n.e. En su perímetro se encontraron más de 250 entierros. De acuerdo con los restos óseos, se cree que los dos grupos étnicos que habitaron originalmente Tlatilco eran descendientes de los olmecas. Las figuras de barro encontradas en la zona sugieren que esta cultura reverenciaba la belleza femenina, acaso como una forma de exaltar la fertilidad (las representaciones de mujeres superan a las de hombres en proporción de 100 a uno). Se piensa que esta comunidad vivió largos periodos de paz, durante los que alcanzaron, a pesar de la sencillez de su sociedad, cierto grado de sofisticación, manifestado en sus peinados y adornos corporales.

Plano en papel de maguey del siglo XVI que representa un barrio en el oriente de Tlatelolco

TLATLAUHQUICENTÉOTL ◆ Deidad nahua, dependiente de Centéotl, la diosa del maíz, que protegía el maíz rojo.

TLATLAUQUITEPEC ◆ Municipio de Puebla situado al oeste de Teziutlán y al sureste de Zacapoaxtla. Superficie: 246.22 km². Habitantes: 45,036, de los cuales 10,703 forman la población económicamente activa. Hablan alguna lengua indígena 9,375 personas mayores de cinco años (náhuatl 9,322). En la jurisdicción, rica en recursos minerales, se encuentra la presa Mazatepec, en la que pueden practicarse deportes acuáticos. En la cabecera se realiza, del 13 al 20 de septiembre, una feria regional agrícola, ganadera, artesanal, industrial y comercial.

TLATLAYA ◆ Municipio del Estado de México situado al sur de Valle de Bravo y al oeste-suroeste de Ixtapan de la Sal, en los límites con Guerrero. Superficie: 693.34 km². Habitantes: 33,170, de los cuales 3,995 forman la población económicamente activa. Hablan alguna lengua indígena 57 personas mayores de cinco años. En la jurisdicción, que cuenta con yacimientos minerales, se encuentran las zonas arqueológicas de Cerro del Tecolote, Copaltepec, Las Parotas, Rincón Grande, Santa Ana, San Francisco y Zicatecoyan, así como la presa Vicente Guerrero, en la que se pueden practicar deportes acuáticos. En la cabecera hay una parroquia construida en el siglo XVII.

Archivo Xavier Esparza

Figurilla de Tlatilco, Estado de México

TLAXCALA ◆ Estado de la República Mexicana que limita al norte con Hidalgo, al norte, este, sur y suroeste con Puebla y al oeste con el Estado de México. Superficie: 4,060.93 km^2 (0.21 por ciento de la superficie nacional). Es el estado más pequeño del país. Está dividido en 60 municipios. La capital es Tlaxcala de Xicoténcatl. Otras ciudades importantes son Apizaco, Huamantla, Santa Ana Chiautempan y Tlaxco. Habitantes: 911,696 (1997). En 1995 contaba con el uno por ciento de la población nacional. Ese año la población urbana era de 706,526 personas y la rural de 177,398. Forman la población económicamente activa 56.5 por ciento de los mayores de doce años. Contribuye con 0.5 al producto interno bruto nacional. Su índice de analfabetismo es de 8.86 por ciento de los mayores de 15 años. Hablan alguna lengua indígena 26,886 personas (náhuatl 24,728), de las cuales 248 no dominan el español. Los primeros asentamientos humanos en el actual estado de Tlaxcala ocurrieron probablemente 15,000 o 10,000 años a.n.e., cuando arribaron a la zona los primeros recolectores y cazadores nómadas; éstos fueron desplazados mucho después por los quinametin, que posiblemente fueran de origen teotihuacano y otomí. A su vez, los quinametin fueron desalojados por los olmeca-xicalancas, "gente del lugar de las canoas" en español, de marcada influencia maya. Por ejemplo, dos de las esculturas tlaxcaltecas de esa época, el chac-mool llamado de Tlaxcala, que ahora se encuentra en el Museo Nacional de Antropología, y el monolito encontrado en Tizatlán, llamado dios jaguar de Molinahtla, son de influencia olmeca-tolteca-maya. Los olmeca-xicalancas, también llamados olmeca-zacatecas u olmecas tardíos, establecieron su capital en Cacaxtla, en cuyas ruinas se han descubierto pinturas monumentales, y edificaron otras poblaciones como Mixco, Xochitecatl (Xochitécatitla), Tenanyecac, Xiloxochitla y Xocoyucan. Hacia el siglo X, los olmeca-xicalancas fueron expulsados de la región tlaxcalteca por los tolteca-chichimecas y por los chichimeca-poyauhtecas. Los primeros eran una de las ramas toltecas, de nariz aguileña y cuerpo y labios delgados, que habían vivido en la Huasteca hasta los siglos V y VI, más tarde en Tula y hacia el siglo IX se establecieron en el Valle de Anáhuac, Morelos, Tlaxcala y Cholula. Por su parte, los chichimeca-poyauhtecas, llamados también teochichimecas o tlaxcaltecas, formaban una de las siete tribus nahuatlacas de Chicomoztoc. Habían llegado en 1206 a Puhuaxtlan o Poyauhtlan, a la orilla del lago de Texcoco, pero a causa del hostigamiento al que fueron sometidos por acolhuas, tecpanecas, texcocanos y especialmente por la gente de Coatlichan, prefirieron emigrar hacia el actual territorio de Tlaxcala, después de derrotar en 1330 a los de Coatlichan. Instalados en la región tlaxcalteca después de asesinar a su jefe principal, Colopechtli, los tlaxcaltecas ocuparon la totalidad del territorio que actualmente forma el estado e incluso se instalaron en Tulancingo, Huauchinango, Orizaba, Zacatlán Xilotepec y Xicochimalco. Guiados por el caudillo Culhuatecuhtlicuanex, los tlaxcaltecas fundaron Tepectícpac en 1348, el primer señorío de lo que más tarde

Alfonso Sánchez Anaya, gobernador de Tlaxcala

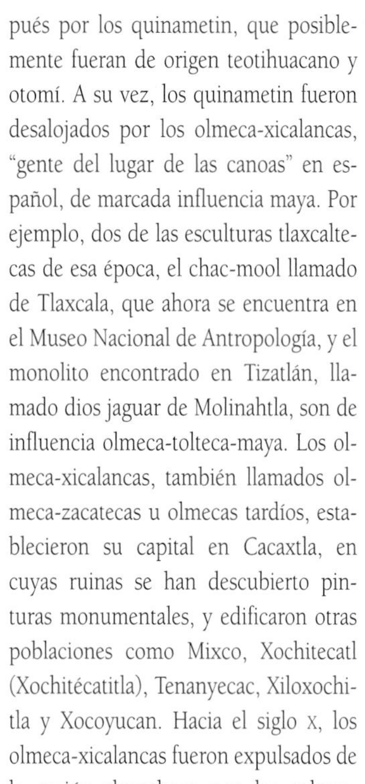

FOTO: FONDO EDITORIAL GRUPO AZABACHE

Palacio de Gobierno de Tlaxcala

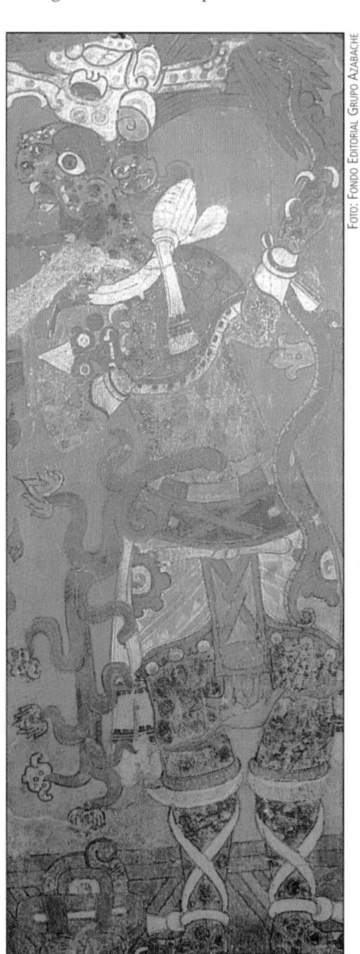

FOTO: FONDO EDITORIAL GRUPO AZABACHE

Mural de Cacaxtla, en Tlaxcala

Camaxtli originario de Tlaxcala

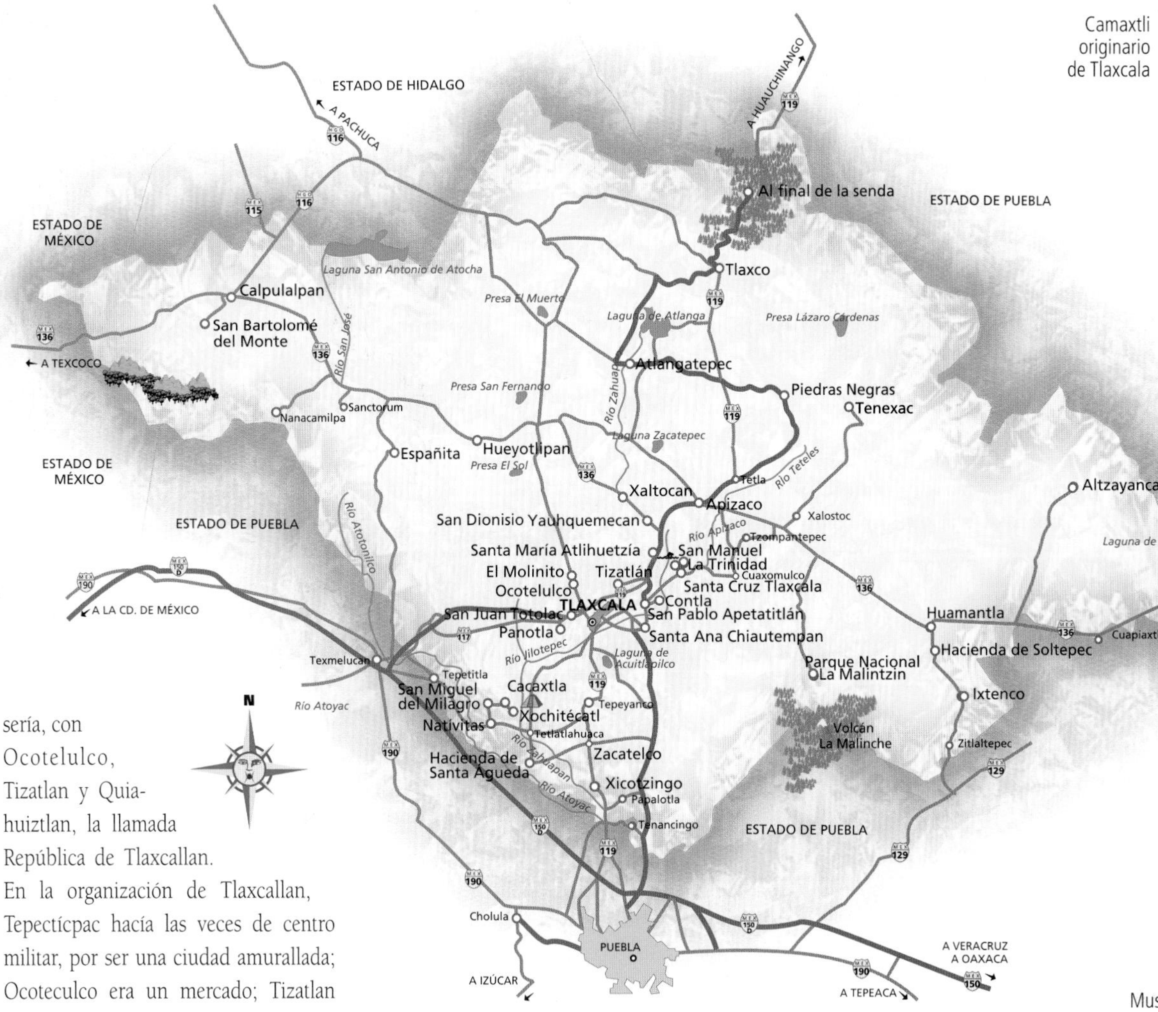

Mapa de Tlaxcala

sería, con Ocotelulco, Tizatlan y Quiahuiztlan, la llamada República de Tlaxcallan.

En la organización de Tlaxcallan, Tepectícpac hacía las veces de centro militar, por ser una ciudad amurallada; Ocoteculco era un mercado; Tizatlan fungía como centro administrativo y Quiahuiztlan era el centro de producción artesanal. Entre 1418 y 1430, los tlaxcaltecas rescataron, educaron y ayudaron a Nezahualcóyotl, hijo del asesinado rey acolhua Ixtlilxóchitl y uno de los más cercanos aliados de México-Tenochtitlan, en su lucha por la reconquista de Texcoco, pero a partir de la creación de la Triple Alianza en 1430, se iniciaron los enfrentamientos entre la zona de Puebla-Tlaxcala y el valle de Anáhuac. El florecimiento y expansión de los tlaxcaltecas generó de inmediato serias fricciones con los mexicas de Tenochtitlan, quienes apoyados por los nahuas de Huexotzinco, Cholollan, Itzocan y Tecamachalco, iniciaron una serie de campañas militares, en las que nunca tuvieron éxito y que más tarde derivaron en las guerras floridas. La continua agresión de los pueblos del valle de Anáhuac obligó a los tlaxcaltecas a observar una estricta disciplina y a poner en práctica un sistema de gobierno democrático, en el que los caciques de cada señorío actuaban siempre de común acuerdo y supeditados a las necesidades de supervivencia de su nación; esta administración asombró a los conquistadores españoles, quienes popularizaron la denominación de República de Tlaxcala y llamaron "senadores" a los señores tlaxcaltecas. A principios del siglo XVI, el directorio tlaxcalteca estaba integrado por Tlehuexolotzin, Maxixcatzin, Xicoténcatl y Citlalpopocatzin. En septiembre de 1519, informado de la enemistad que había entre mexicas y tlaxcaltecas, Hernán Cortés propuso a éstos

FOTO: FONDO EDITORIAL GRUPO AZABACHE

Detalle de uno de los escudos de la Capilla Real de los Indios en Tlaxcala

Museo Nacional del Títere Rosete Aranda en Tlaxcala

FOTO: FONDO EDITORIAL GRUPO AZABACHE

Foto: Michael Calderwood

Tlaxcala, Tlaxcala

Foto: Michael Calderwood

Ocotlán y la Malinche, en Tlaxcala

Foto: Fondo Editorial Grupo Azabache

Máscara tallada, de uso tradicional en el carnaval de Tlaxcala

que le permitieran el paso por sus tierras y se aliaran con él para derrotar al imperio azteca, pero los cuatro senadores y Xicoténcatl Axayacatzin, llamado *El Joven*, decidieron guerrear contra los españoles. Comandados por Xicoténcatl Axayacatzin, los tlaxcaltecas tuvieron dos enfrentamientos desafortunados con las fuerzas de Cortés, por lo que los senadores de Tlaxcala aceptaron aliarse con los invasores. Xicoténcatl Axayacatzin se negó a aceptar la rendición y poco antes de la conquista de Tenochtitlan se separó de la fuerza española y comenzó a organizar un grupo para combatir a los europeos, pero poco después fue aprehendido por una partida de soldados españoles y colgado, acusado de traición. Con ayuda de los tlaxcaltecas, la Corona española conquistó México-Tenochtitlan y el resto de la Nueva España, incluidos Nuevo México, Arizona, Texas y Florida; los actuales países centroamericanos, Ecuador, Perú y Filipinas. Los tlaxcaltecas fueron también repobladores de Cuba y la actual República Dominicana. En muchos de estos lugares, a fines del siglo XX, todavía era posible identificar a descendientes de los tlaxcaltecas transterrados, debido a sus apellidos nahuas, pues gracias a su colaboración con los invasores españoles, éstos les permitieron conservar sus nombres originales. Poco después de la conquista, entre 1520 y 1522, los españoles establecieron el primer ayuntamiento tlaxcalteca, integrado por un cabildo de aristócratas indios presididos por un español. Además, y como una forma de corresponder a la colaboración durante la conquista, los españoles prometieron un trato especial para los tlaxcaltecas, que incluía la condonación de impuestos. En 1525, el obispado de Yucatán se trasladó a Tlaxcala, pero sólo funcionó ahí 18 años, pues en 1543 pasó a Puebla de los Án-

Foto: Fondo Editorial Grupo Azabache

Troje de construcción tradicional en el estado de Tlaxcala

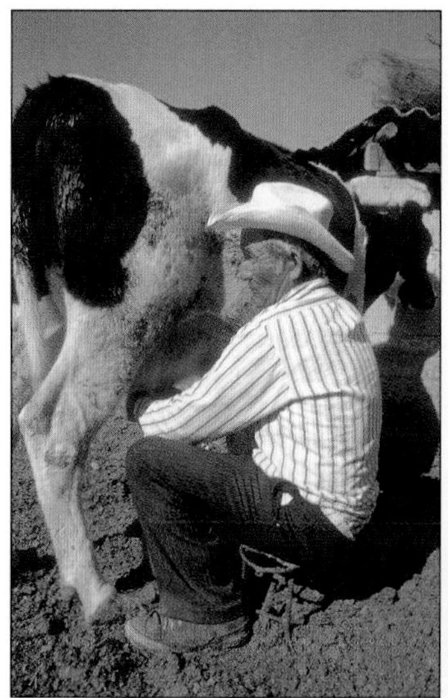

Actividad ganadera en el estado de Tlaxcala

geles. De todas formas, los obispos tlaxcaltecas habían vivido en Puebla desde 1539, debido a la lentitud con que se construía la catedral, pero sobre todo por el conflicto permanente entre las órdenes mendicantes, los franciscanos en particular, que poseían el control eclesiástico de los indios, y las autoridades seculares, en especial los obispos. En 1535, el gobierno español concedió el título de ciudad a Tlaxcala. En la primera división política de la Nueva España se respetaron los límites prehispánicos entre los pueblos, por lo que el territorio de la República de Tlaxcala fue conocido como provincia de Tlaxcala, integrante del Reino de México, pero debido al crecimiento de la provincia de Puebla, el territorio tlaxcalteca se redujo. Aunque en los primeros años posteriores a la conquista los españoles mantuvieron su promesa de no cobrar impuestos a los señoríos tlaxcaltecas, desde la segunda mitad del siglo XVI se les empezó a exigir una cierta cantidad de maíz al año. En 1583, los cuatro señores principales de la República de Tlaxcala, Zacarías de Santiago, Antonio de Guevara, Pedro de Torres y Diego de Téllez, viajaron a España con el propósito de refrendar ante Felipe II las disposiciones coloniales, pero fracasaron en su intento por conservar un estatuto especial respecto del resto de los indios americanos. A principios del siglo XVII, sin embargo, Tlaxcala se había convertido en la segunda zona manufacturera más importante de la Nueva España. Sólo en la capital, por ejemplo, existían 11 obrajes textiles. En esos años, la población de la capital era de 12,000 personas aproximadamente. Durante la primera mitad del siglo XVII, el conflicto entre las órdenes mendicantes y la jerarquía diocesana se agudizó, sobre todo con la llegada al obispado poblano de Juan de Palafox y Mendoza (☛), en junio de 1640, quien intentó despojar a los frailes del gobierno de las parroquias de indios, hasta que en la madrugada del 29 de diciembre de 1640, una fuerza de sacerdotes y laicos del obispado poblano invadió Tlaxcala y obligó a los franciscanos, dominicos y agustinos a ceder las parroquias. En el episodio, conocido como la "toma de Tlaxcala", los religiosos mendicantes perdieron más de 36 parroquias. Unos años después, la población de la ciudad de Tlaxcala se había reducido a menos de 4,000 habitantes. El 14 de junio de 1692, poco después de la sublevación de los indios de la ciudad de México

Foto: Fondo Editorial Grupo Azabache

Museo Regional de Tlaxcala

Arquitectura tradicional en Tlaxcala

Foto: Fondo Editorial Grupo Azabache

Foto: Pablo Cervantes

Momoto, pájaro del estado de Tlaxcala

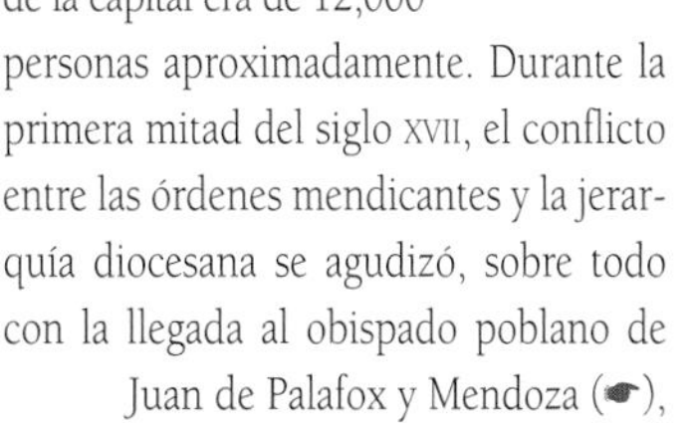

Foto: Pablo Cervantes

Foto: Michael Calderwood

Mariposa de alas transparentes de Tlaxcala y gusano de maguey de Tlaxcala

Timbre mexicano con la imagen del Santuario de Ocotlán, Tlaxcala

Foto: Fondo Editorial Grupo Azabache

Jardín Botánico de Tizatlán, Tlaxcala

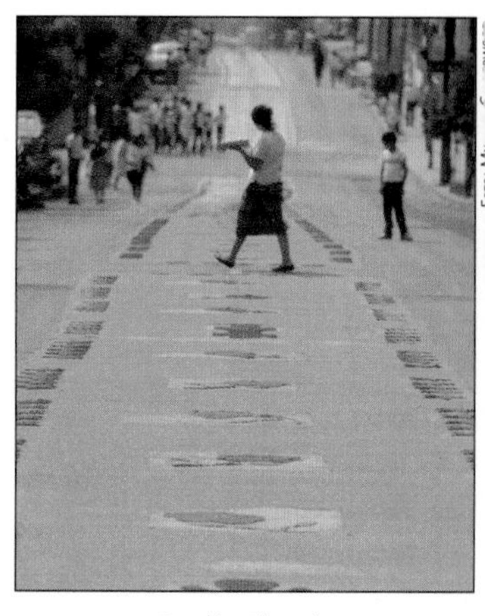
Ocotlán, Tlaxcala

que acabó con el Palacio Virreinal, los tlaxcaltecas de tres pueblos protestaron por el aumento del precio de la carga de maíz, que había aumentado a cinco pesos. Los indios exigieron la disminución del precio, pero como su petición no fue oída, irrupieron en los almacenes para tomar el grano y después se dirigieron a la casa del alcalde mayor de Tlaxcala, Fernando de Bustamante, la apedrearon e intentaron quemarla, pero fueron rechazados por la guarnición española, que, además, pidió ayuda a la ciudad de México. El 26 de julio, las tropas enviadas por el virrey se retiraron, tras haber asesinado a unos 100 tlaxcaltecas, 60 de ellos degollados personalmente por Bustamante. Aunque en los años siguientes hubo por lo menos tres malas cosechas, las de 1697, 1717 y 1786, los tlaxcaltecas no volvieron a insurreccionarse. En octubre de 1787, menos de un año después del establecimiento de las reformas borbónicas, el gobierno de Tlaxcala obtuvo una dispensa real, mediante la cual conservó casi todos los privilegios que había recibido por su colaboración en la conquista, pero durante los tres años siguientes, las autoridades virreinales intentaron cobrar los mismos tipos de impuestos a las comunidades tlaxcaltecas. Desde 1789, el ayuntamiento de Tlaxcala inició un movimiento contra la incorporación de la provincia a la intendencia de Puebla y el 2 de mayo de 1793, una cédula real dispuso la creación de un corregimiento especial, cuyo gobierno dependería únicamente del virrey. Iniciada la guerra de independencia, el ayuntamiento tlaxcalteca reafirmó su lealtad al gobierno virreinal, pero el acto tuvo poca influencia, pues desde mediados de 1811, una fuerza insurgente al mando de Mariano Aldama comenzó a operar en los actuales límites de Hidalgo y Tlaxcala, en los llanos de Apan. En septiembre, las fuerzas de Aldama derrotaron a los realistas de Ciriaco del Llano en Calpulalpan, pero unas semanas después Aldama fue traicionado y asesinado. La dirección de la insurgencia tlaxcalteca quedó en manos de Juan Francisco Osorno, cuyas tropas operaron en el norte de la provincia, así como en la sierra norte de Puebla y el centro del actual estado de Hidalgo. Hacia 1813, las tropas de Nicolás Bravo incursionaron en la parte meridional de Tlaxcala, pero poco después se retiraron y la región se mantuvo en poder de las fuerzas virreinales. En el Decreto Constitucional que las fuerzas insurgentes de José María Morelos promulgaron en 1814, Tlaxcala figuró como una de las 17 provincias mexicanas; es decir, por primera vez se colocó al territorio tlaxcalteca en plan de igualdad con el resto de las antiguas intendencias virreinales. En 1821, poco después de la proclamación del Plan de Iguala, las fuerzas de Nicolás Bravo tomaron la capital tlaxcalteca sin combatir. A la caída del Imperio Mexicano de Agustín de Iturbide, una parte de la diputación tlaxcal-

Danzante con máscara tradicional de Tlaxcala

Foto: Fondo Editorial Grupo Azabache

Paseo de los Portales en Tlaxcala

Mujer indígena de Tlaxcala

Altar de la Catedral de Tlaxcala

Cristo de pasta de caña, símbolo que contribuyó a la evangelización en Tlaxcala

Tlaxcala. En 1846, al reimplantarse el federalismo, Tlaxcala conservó su condición de territorio. En 1847, un mes después de tomar la ciudad de México, las tropas invasoras estadounidenses que perseguían al presidente Antonio López de Santa Anna penetraron en Tlaxcala por el sureste, pero el 9 de octubre fueron derrotadas en Huamantla por los mexicanos comandados por Eulalio Villaseñor. En abril de 1851, el gobierno del presidente Mariano Arista aprobó el primer Estatuto Orgánico del Territorio de Tlaxcala. En febrero de 1857, al promulgarse la Constitución liberal, Tlaxcala se convirtió en estado libre y soberano. En diciembre de ese mismo año, el primer gobernador tlaxcalteca, Guillermo Valle, apoyó el golpe de Estado del presidente Ignacio Comonfort y disolvió el Congreso local. Tres semanas después, el 6 de enero de 1858, las tropas liberales de Miguel Negrete tomaron la capital del estado y reestablecieron la Constitución de 1857. El 9 de enero, Negrete se reunió en Tlaxco con las fuerzas poblanas de Miguel C. Alatriste y, con el Congreso disuelto por Valle, designó

Foto: Fondo Editorial Grupo Azabache

La Virgen de Ocotlán, óleo anónimo del siglo XVII, expuesta en el Museo Regional de Tlaxcala

teca inició las gestiones para convertir a Tlaxcala en estado y consiguieron que en el Acta Constitutiva de la Federación, promulgada en enero de 1824, Tlaxcala apareciera como uno de los estados integrantes de la República. Durante el resto del año, sin embargo, con el apoyo de la diputación y el gobierno poblanos, los ayuntamientos de Huamantla, Apetatitlán, Ixtlacuixtla y Yauhquemehcan realizaron una campaña para incorporarse a Puebla. El enfrentamiento entre los "independentistas" y los "unionistas" llegó a tal extremo, que en la Constitución, promulgada en octubre de 1824, se estableció que el carácter de la antigua gobernación de Tlaxcala sería definido posteriormente. Un mes después, el 24 de noviembre, el Congreso federal promulgó una ley que establecía la creación del territorio de Tlaxcala, hecho que dejó inconformes a ambos grupos. En 1835, el nuevo gobierno centralista desapareció el territorio de Tlaxcala e incorporó la región al departamento de México. Ocho años después, de acuerdo con las Bases Orgánicas, se reestableció el territorio de

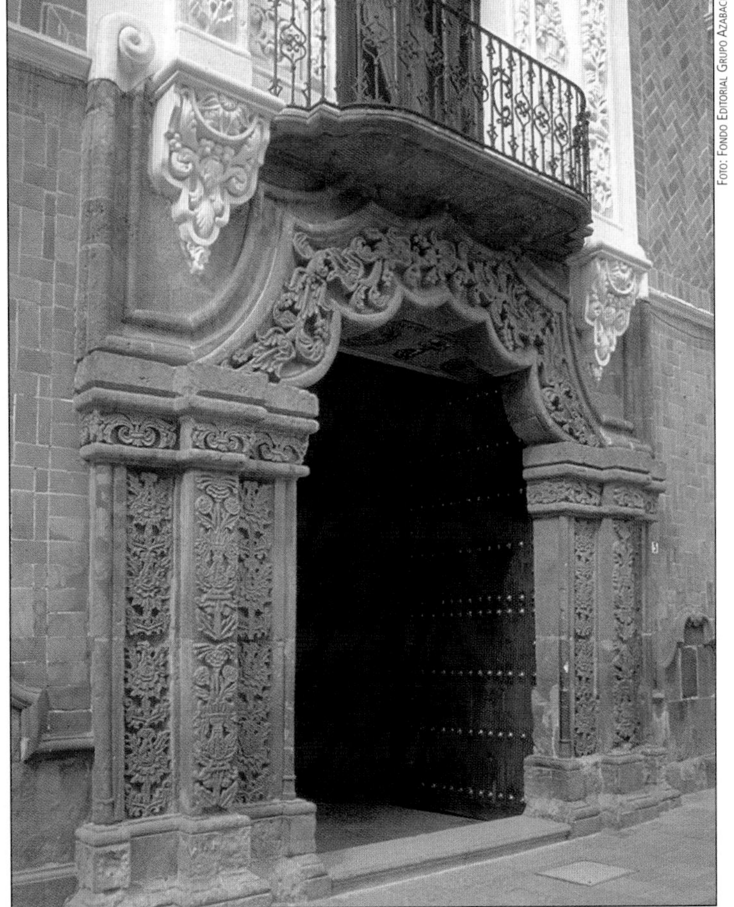
Foto: Fondo Editorial Grupo Azabache

Portón del Palacio de Gobierno de Tlaxcala

Foto: Fondo Editorial Grupo Azabache

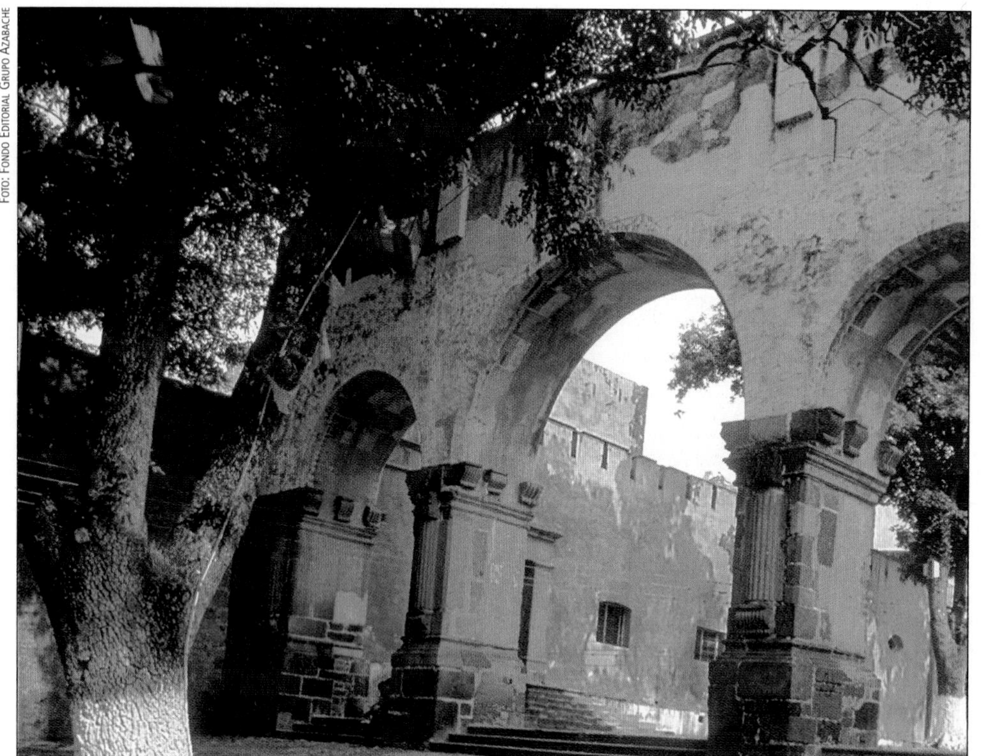

Arcos platerescos de la catedral de Tlaxcala

gobernador a José Manuel Saldaña. El gobierno conservador de Félix María Zuloaga, por su parte, suprimió el estado en mayo. Poco después, los conservadores tomaron Tlaxco, Huamantla, Tlaxcala, Apetitlán y Chiautempan. Los liberales de Antonio Carbajal ocuparon brevemente la capital del estado en septiembre; tomaron Apetatitlán, en abril de 1859, Chiautempan en agosto de ese mismo año y Calpulalpan en agosto de 1860, pero a pesar de las victorias constitucionalistas, los conservadores permanecieron en la capital del estado hasta el fin de la guerra de los Tres Años. Durante 1861, las guerrillas conservadoras de Marcelino Cobos, Leonardo Márquez, Miguel Negrete y Félix María Zuloaga, cuyo centro de operaciones era Puebla, realizaron numerosas incursiones en Tlaxcala. En marzo de 1862, el gobierno de Benito Juárez impuso el estado de sitio en la entidad. A la caída de Puebla en manos de los franceses, a fines de junio de 1863, el gobierno de Tlaxcala abandonó la capital del estado y se refugió en la sierra norte de Puebla. Poco después, los invasores ocuparon las principales poblaciones del estado. En marzo de 1865, Maximiliano de Habsburgo decretó la erección del Departamento Imperial de Tlaxcala, que comprendía más o menos los límites del estado. A mediados de ese año comenzó a operar la guerrilla republicana de Antonio Rodríguez y en noviembre las tropas de Rafael Cuéllar derrotaron a una fuerza de 600 austriacos. En enero de 1867, los republicanos tomaron Tlaxcala. Tres meses después, en abril, las fuerzas de Porfirio Díaz, que acababan de tomar Puebla, derrotaron en San Diego Notario a los imperialistas comandados por Márquez. En diciembre de 1871, poco después de la proclamación del Plan de La Noria, las fuerzas insurrectas de Díaz atravesaron el estado de suroeste a noreste, camino de la sierra norte de Puebla. Cuatro años después, en noviembre de 1876, durante la también porfirista sublevación de Tuxtepec, los rebeldes penetraron a Tlaxcala desde Puebla y en las lomas de Teocac se enfrentaron al ejército lerdista de Ignacio R. Alatorre, al que derrotaron gracias a la llegada sorpresiva de las fuerzas de Juan N. Méndez. A partir de la caída del gobierno de Sebastían Lerdo de Tejada, dos grupos porfiristas, encabezados por Miguel Lira y Ortega y J. Mariano Grajales respectivamente, se enfrentaron por el control político del estado hasta que, en 1885, el gobierno de Díaz impuso en la gubernatura a Próspero Cahuantzi, quien gobernó Tlaxcala hasta 1911. Durante su gobierno se desarrolló la industria textilera en el corredor que une la capital del estado con la ciudad de Puebla y entre 1877 y 1906, la cantidad de fábricas pasó de 21 a 40. Por otro lado, entre 1899 y 1901, el gobierno de Díaz convirtió una parte de Tlaxcala en campo de concentración

Fuente de cantera en la Plaza de la Constitución de Tlaxcala

Bosque de pinos en el estado de Tlaxcala

para los yaquis de Sonora. En 1905, dos movimientos de protesta, uno en Xacoltan y otro en Tenancingo, fueron reprimidos violentamente por Cahuantzi. En mayo de 1910, los pueblos de Zacatelco, Amaxac de Guerrero, Contla y Tepehitec se levantaron en armas contra el gobierno de Díaz, pero fueron derrotados un mes más tarde. En septiembre, durante las celebraciones del centenario de la independencia, las manifestaciones antigubernamentales de Panzacola, Zacatelco y Xicochtzinco fueron reprimidas. A fines de 1910, volvieron a levantarse en armas algunos de los sublevados de mayo y al mando de Juan Cuamatzi, uno de los líderes del anterior movimiento, operaron en los alrededores del cerro de la Malinche hasta febrero de 1911, cuando fueron derrotados por las tropas federales de Aureliano Blanquet, que asesinaron a Cuamatzi. En mayo de ese año las fuerzas maderistas de Isidro Ortiz y Carmen Vélez tomaron Tlaxcala y obligaron a renunciar al gobernador Cahuantzi. Éste, sin embargo, consiguió imponer en el gobierno local a Agustín Sánchez, quien promovió una imposible coexistencia entre las tropas rebeldes y las del gobierno, que fue aceptada por los maderistas en junio, luego de un breve enfrentamiento entre las fuerzas de Vélez y la guarnición de Apizaco, donde se habían concentrado los federales. En 1913, tras el asesinato del presidente Francisco I. Madero, Máximo Rojas, Pedro M. Morales, Felipe Villegas y Domingo Arenas se levantaron en armas. Caída la dictadura de Victoriano Huerta, el Ejército Libertador del Sur tomó la capital del estado y desalojó al gobierno carrancista de Pedro M. Morales. Los constitucionalistas, sin embargo, recuperaron la ciudad e intentaron realizar una tímida reforma agraria a la que se opusieron las fuerzas campesinas de Arenas que, incorporadas al zapatismo, intentaron derrocar al gobierno. Para 1917, sin embargo, los grupos campesinos habían sido prácticamente derrotados.

FOTO: FONDO EDITORIAL GRUPO AZABACHE

Platillos de la gastronomía de Tlaxcala

BIBLIOTECAS Y USUARIOS, 1993
Número de bibliotecas: 135
1 000 000
800 000
600 000
400 000
200 000
0
Usuarios al año 984,212
Promedio de usuarios por biblioteca 7,291

POBLACIÓN DE 5 AÑOS Y MÁS HABLANTE DE LENGUA INDÍGENA, 1995

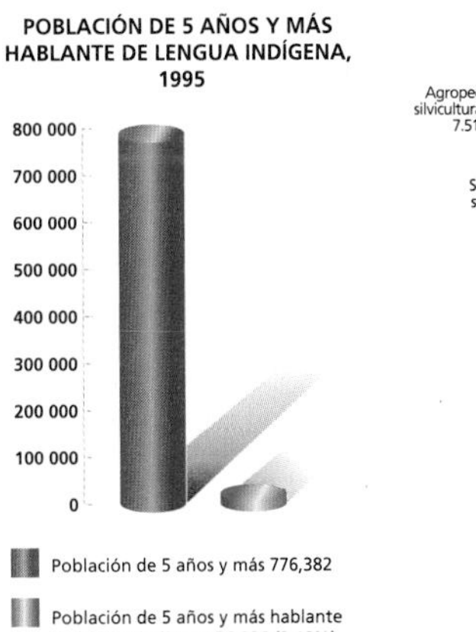

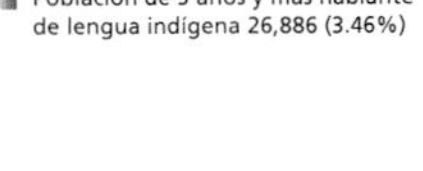

PRODUCTO INTERNO BRUTO (PIB) A PRECIOS CORRIENTES

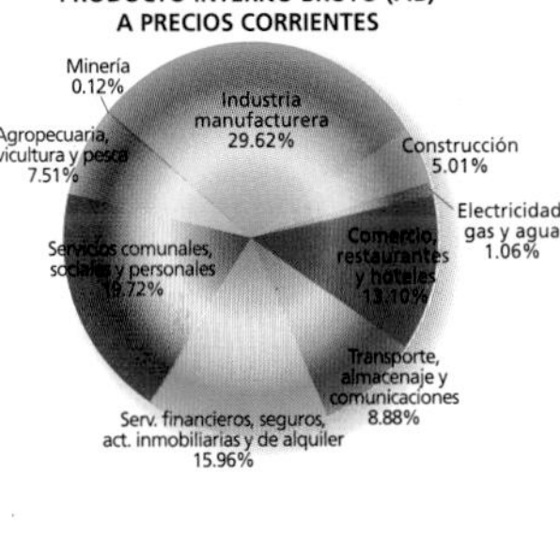

LÍNEAS TELEFÓNICAS EN SERVICIO Y APARATOS PÚBLICOS, 1994

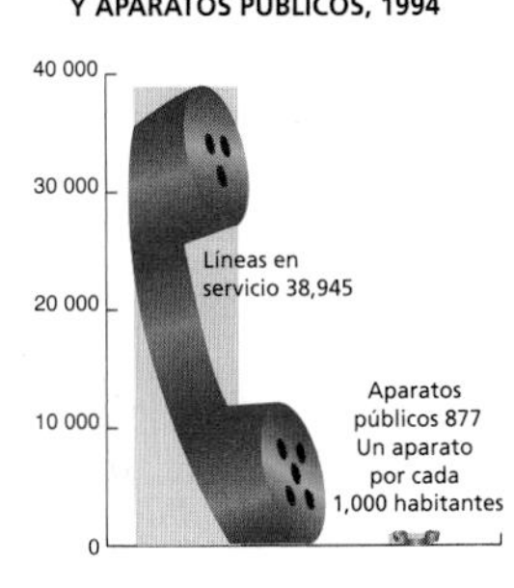

LONGITUD DE LA RED DE CARRETERAS POR SUPERFICIE DE RODAMIENTO, 1995

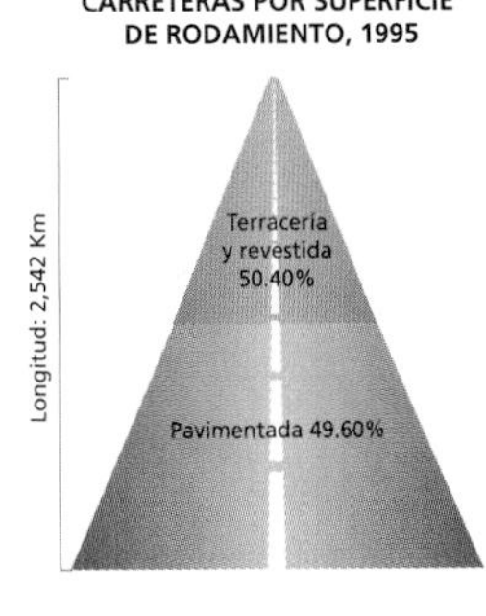

PROMEDIO DE ESCOLARIDAD DE LA POBLACIÓN DE 15 AÑOS Y MÁS, POR SEXO, 1995

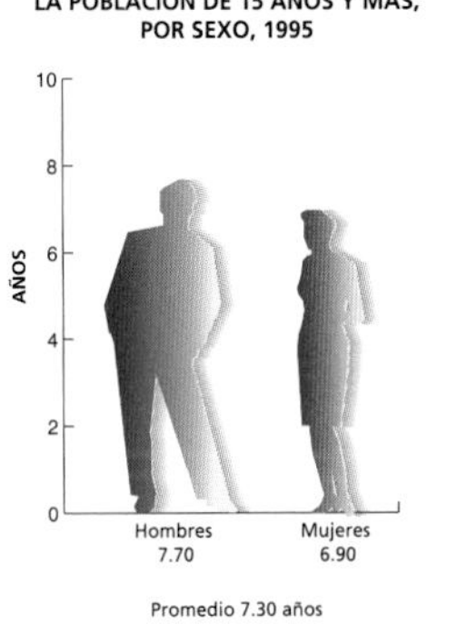

DISTRIBUCIÓN PORCENTUAL DE LA POBLACIÓN OCUPADA POR SECTOR DE ACTIVIDAD ECONÓMICA, 1995

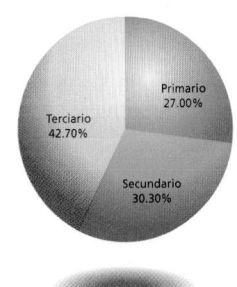

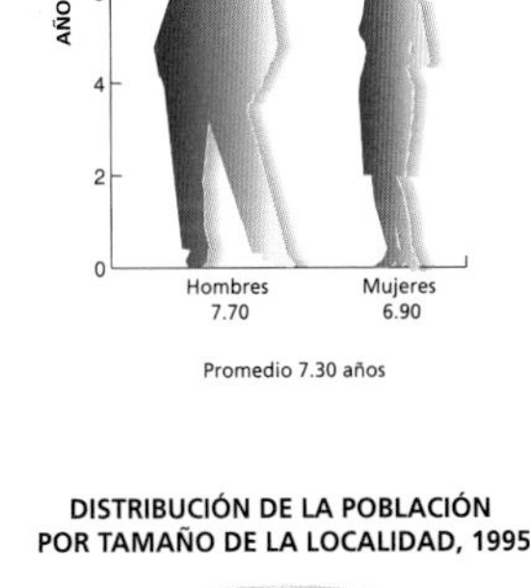

DISTRIBUCIÓN DE LA POBLACIÓN POR TAMAÑO DE LA LOCALIDAD, 1995

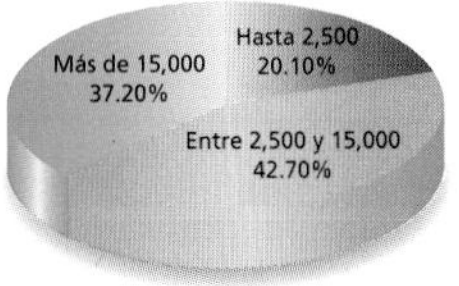

Foto: Fondo Editorial Grupo Azabache

Palcos del Teatro Xicoténcatl en la ciudad de Tlaxcala, Tlaxcala

Tlaxcala ◆ Municipio de Tlaxcala situado en la porción centro-sur de la entidad, al suroeste de Apizaco y al oeste de Huamantla. Superficie: 44.6 km². Habitantes: 63,423, de los cuales 16,104 forman la población económicamente activa. Hablan alguna lengua indígena 792 personas mayores de cinco años (náhuatl 378 y totonaco 256). En el territorio del municipio se encuentra la zona arqueológica de Tizatlán. La cabecera, llamada Tlaxcala de Xicoténcatl desde 1932, es también capital del estado, desde la erección de éste en 1857, y sede de la diócesis católica de Tlaxcala desde 1959, año de refundación del obispado. Hacia 1519, los españoles hicieron construir algunas casas en la actual cabecera. A fines de 1520, los conquistadores establecieron el primer ayuntamiento de la ciudad y, en 1535, la Corona española elevó la población a la categoría de ciudad. El edificio que actualmente ocupa el Poder Ejecutivo local fue construido en la segunda mitad del siglo XVI, y es sede del poder tlaxcalteca desde mediados del siglo XVIII. El municipio destaca por la importancia de su producción textil; cuenta con numerosas fábricas de hilados y tejidos de lana, algodón y fibras sintéticas.

Tlaxcala, Lienzo de ◆ Documento elaborado en 1550 por órdenes del virrey Luis de Velasco, que, con la técnica y la forma indígena pero desde el punto de vista de los españoles, narra la participación de los tlaxcaltecas en la conquista y evangelización española de Mesoamérica. De los tres originales de la obra, uno fue enviado a España, otro a la ciudad de México y el tercero a los archivos del ayuntamiento de Tlaxcala, de donde fue sustraido por órdenes de Maximiliano de Habsburgo. Aunque los tres han desaparecido, existe una copia, elaborada en 1773, que se encuentra en la Biblioteca Nacional de Antropología. El documento está compuesto por cuatro lienzos de tela de algodón, de 105 por 203 centímetros cada uno.

Tlaxcalantongo ◆ Población del municipio poblano de Xicotepec (☛), donde, en la madrugada del 21 de mayo de 1920, fue asesinado el presidente Venustiano Carranza.

Tlaxco ◆ Municipio de Puebla situado en la porción septentrional de la entidad, al norte de Pahuatlán, en los límites con Hidalgo. Superficie: 90.57 km². Habitantes: 5,743, de los cuales 1,697 forman la población económicamente activa. Hablan alguna lengua indígena 276 personas mayores de cinco años (otomí 287).

Tlaxco ◆ Municipio de Tlaxcala situado en el extremo septentrional de la entidad, al norte de Apizaco, en los límites con Hidalgo y Puebla. Superficie: 497.3 km². Habitantes: 30,776, de los cuales 7,040 forman la población económicamente activa. Hablan alguna lengua indígena 52 personas mayores de cinco años (náhuatl 32). En la jurisdicción hay ganaderías de reses bravas. La cabecera se llama Tlaxco de Morelos.

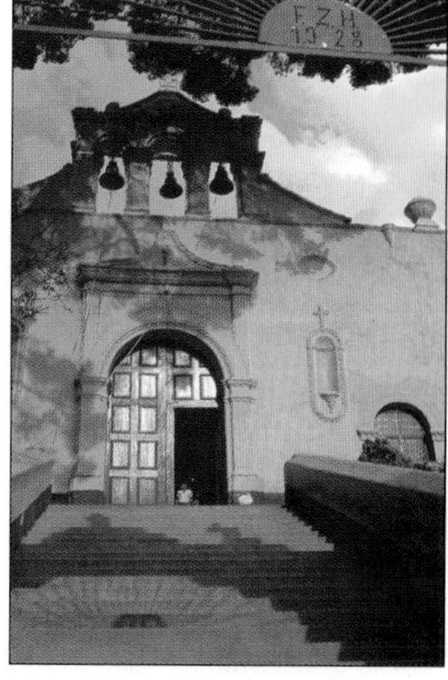

Parroquia de Tlaxco, Tlaxcala

Tlaxcoapan ◆ Municipio de Hidalgo situado al oeste de Pachuca y al noreste de Tepeji del Río. Superficie: 79.25 km². Habitantes: 21,159, de los cuales 4,819 forman la población económicamente activa. Hablan alguna lengua indígena 62 personas mayores de cinco años (otomí 44). En la jurisdicción está la localidad de Tlahuelilpa de Ocampo, que cuenta con una iglesia con claustro y capilla abierta que están considerados entre los más bellos del periodo colonial.

Tlaxiaco ◆ ☛ *Heroica Ciudad de Tlaxiaco* y *Santa María Asunción Tlaxiaco.*

Tlaxiaco, de ◆ Sierra de Oaxaca situada en el noroccidente del estado, en la Mixteca Alta. Se extiende de noroeste a sureste, al suroeste de la sierra

Lienzo de Tlaxcala

de Tamazulapan, al sur del río Huajuapan, al este del Mixtepec o Santo Domingo y al noreste de Nochixtlán. Posee yacimientos minerales.

TLAYACAPAN ◆ Municipio de Morelos situado al nor-noroeste de Cuautla y al este de Tepoztlán. Superficie: 84.17 km². Habitantes: 11,864, de los cuales 2,679 forman la población económicamente activa. Hablan alguna lengua indígena 605 personas mayores de cinco años (mixteco 276 y náhuatl 266). En la cabecera se encuentran un convento y una iglesia construidos por los frailes agustinos en el siglo XVI.

TLAYACAPAN, BANDA MUNICIPAL DE ◆ Conjunto de música de viento que interpreta obras del repertorio tradicional para acompañar festividades religiosas, populares y ritos fúnebres. Formada hacia 1870 con el nombre de Los Alarcones por Vidal Santa María (?-1916) y Juan Chilopa junto con un grupo de amigos y parientes. Tras un periodo inactivo a causa del levantamiento armado de 1910, recomenzaron en 1916 bajo la dirección del coronel zapatista Cristino Santa María (hijo de Vidal), recorriendo casi todo el estado de Morelos "para alegrar los días de aquellos que esperaban morir en la revolución". En la actualidad la conforman 37 miembros de distintas edades, cuya ocupación principal son las labores del campo. Emplean trompetas, cornetas, flautas, ocarinas, pitos y caracoles, entre otros instrumentos. Obtuvo el Premio Nacional de Ciencias y Artes en la categoría de Artes y Tradiciones Populares (1998).

FOTO: FONDO EDITORIAL GRUPO AZABACHE

Capilla de San Martín en Tlayacapan, Morelos

TLAZAZALCA ◆ Municipio de Michoacán situado al sur de La Piedad, al este y próximo a Zamora. Superficie: 297.45 km². Habitantes: 9,294, de los cuales 2,958 forman la población económicamente activa. Hablan alguna lengua indígena 32 personas mayores de cinco años. En la época virreinal la región noroccidental del actual estado de Michoacán fue erigida en provincia de Tlazazalca. Más tarde fue corregimiento de Michoacán y luego de Zamora. En el siglo XVIII se transformó en provincia, con capital en Aramutaro, la antigua población purépecha de Ayaramutaro, convertida después en Nuestra Señora de la Piedad, actual La Piedad de Cabadas. En 1787 la provincia de Tlazazalca se convirtió en subdelegación de la intendencia de Valladolid.

TLAZOLCUAINI ◆ Una de las tres advocaciones de Tlazoltéotl, la diosa nahua de la lubricidad, llamada así, "la que come cosas sucias", porque confesaba a los lujuriosos y les perdonaba sus faltas.

TLAZOLTÉOTL ◆ Deidad nahua de la basura y de la lujuria, cuyo culto probablemente se originó en la Huasteca y más tarde se extendió hasta las culturas mixteca y zapoteca. Según algunos autores, en un principio esta divinidad era la diosa madre, la parte femenina de la deidad

Tlazoltéotl

original; cuando su culto se propagó por la Mesa Central, la diosa adoptó el patrocinio de las relaciones sexuales, ligadas con la fecundidad de la tierra; por este motivo Bernardino de Sahagún la calificó de "Venus mexicana". Su templo principal se hallaba en Chalma.

TLETONATIUH ◆ Nombre del tercer mundo de la cosmogonía nahua, que, como su nombre lo indica, "sol de fuego", terminó con una lluvia de lumbre, lo que algunos autores suponen que fue en realidad una serie de temblores. Según el Códice Vaticano, la tercera edad de la tierra duró 4,804 años.

TLILAPAN ◆ Municipio de Veracruz situado en la porción central del estado, al sur de Orizaba y al nor-noroeste de Zongolica. Superficie: 23.85 km². Habitantes: 3,172, de los cuales 875 forman la población económicamente activa. Hablan alguna lengua indígena 1,363 personas mayores de cinco años (náhuatl 1,358). Indígenas monolingües: 55.

TLILPOTONQUI ◆ Planta de la herbolaria mexica, cuyo nombre fue advocación de Quetzalcóatl como patrono de los calmécac, tal vez por la pintura negra con que se cubrían los sacerdotes-maestros de dicha institución.

TLOQUE NAHUAQUE ◆ Deidad nahua principal. Representaba el origen del mundo y para varios de los cronistas del siglo XVI, Bernardino de Sahagún entre ellos, era la versión mesoamericana del dios de los cristianos. Existía dualmente: en Ometecutli y en Omecíhuatl.

TLOTZIN, MAPA ◆ Códice acolhua elaborado, junto con el Mapa Quinatzin, posiblemente entre 1541 y 1545 por los alumnos de la Escuela de Texcoco. Con técnica indígena narra la historia de los acolhuas desde su sedentarización (en el siglo XIII) hasta el reinado de Nezahualpilli (a fines del siglo XV). Incluye su migración al valle de Anáhuac y la fundación de Texcoco (☛). Es una tira de piel de 31.5 por 127.5 centímetros y se encuentra en la Biblioteca Nacional de París, en la colección Aubin-Goupil. El original perteneció sucesivamente a Fernando de Alva Ixtlilxóchitl, Lorenzo Boturini y Joseph Marius Alexis Aubin.

TLOTZIN-PÓCHOTL ◆ Rey de los acolhuas de Tenayuca. Hijo de Xólolt, el fundador del reino de Acolhuacan. Sucedió en el trono a su hermano Nopaltzin en 1263 y gobernó hasta 1298. De su gestión destaca el empeño que puso para que su pueblo abandonara definitivamente el nomadismo a que los obligaba su actividad básica de cazadores, para lo cual introdujo los métodos agrícolas utilizados por los toltecas. Es probable que durante su reinado se fundara Texcoco.

TOBÓN, MAURO ◆ m. en Orizaba, Ver. (?-1928). Obrero textil. Fundador del PCM (1919), organizó sindicatos en Puebla y Tlaxcala. En 1920, su despido de una fábrica de Metepec provocó que los obreros se amotinaran, tomaran por asalto las oficinas de la empresa y apuñalaran al administrador y al cajero cuando éstos intentaron disparar contra los trabajadores. Pasó algo similar en 1928, cuando fue despedido de la fábrica Cocolapan de Orizaba. Fue asesinado por pistoleros de la CROM.

FOTO: FONDO EDITORIAL GRUPO AZABACHE

Calle de un antiguo señorío indígena en Tochimilco, Puebla

TOCATLÁN ◆ Municipio de Tlaxcala situado al sureste de Apizaco y al noroeste de Huamantla. Superficie: 5.9 km^2. Habitantes: 4,213, de los cuales 892 forman la población económicamente activa. Hablan alguna lengua indígena 16 personas mayores de cinco años.

TOCI ◆ Deidad nahua cuyo nombre significa "Nuestra abuela". Era la Teteoinnan (☛) o la "Madre de los dioses" y se le conocía también como Tonantzin, "Nuestra madrecita". Desempeñaba distintas funciones y advocaciones: así, era Tlalli Iyollo, "corazón de la tierra", la que provocaba los sismos; Yoaltízitl, "la médica de la noche", patrona de curanderos, suertistas y adivinadores; Temascalteci, "abuela de los baños de vapor", por ser los temascales un método terapéutico usual entre las parturientas nahuas; y Omecíhuatl o Cihuatéotl, parte femenina de la pareja original, patrona de las lavanderas y a quien los tlaxcaltecas rendían un culto especial. Bajo este último nombre tenía un templo, Cihuateocalli, en las afueras de Tenochtitlan, donde ahora se encuentra la Basílica de Guadalupe. La Pehuame, "parturienta" en español, de los purépechas era una divinidad idéntica a Toci, tenía diferentes advocaciones: Cuerauáperi, deidad de la vida y de la muerte, y Xarátanga, madre de los dioses. Tanto entre los nahuas como entre los purépechas, Toci-Cuerauáperi era también diosa de la luna, de la tierra y de la comida. Luego de la conquista europea, los sacerdotes españoles trataron de sustituir el culto a Toci con el de Santa Ana, abuela de Jesucristo.

TOCUMBO ◆ Municipio de Michoacán situado al suroeste de Zamora y al noroeste de Uruapan, en los límites con Jalisco. Superficie: 293.57 km^2. Habitantes: 12,237, de los cuales 3,189 forman la población económicamente activa. Hablan alguna lengua indígena 24 personas mayores de cinco años.

TOCHIMILCO ◆ Municipio de Puebla situado al oeste de Atlixco y en la ladera suroriental del Popocatépetl, en los límites con Morelos. Superficie: 233.45 km^2. Habitantes: 15,795, de los cuales 3,210 forman la población económicamente activa. Hablan alguna lengua indígena 2,049 personas mayores de cinco años (náhuatl 2,044). La principal fiesta está dedicada a la Santa Cruz y se celebra el 3 de mayo.

TOCHTEPEC ◆ Municipio de Puebla situado al oeste de Tecamachalco y al sureste de Tepeaca. Superficie: 44.66 km^2. Habitantes: 16,060, de los cuales 3,237 forman la población económicamente activa. Hablan alguna lengua indígena 29 personas mayores de cinco años (náhuatl 23).

TODD PÉREZ, LUIS EUGENIO ◆ n. en Monterrey, NL (1935). Médico cirujano titulado en la UANL (1958). Hizo su residencia en los hospitales de Enfermedades de la Nutrición (1961), Infantil de México (1961) y de la Universidad de Georgetown, EUA (1964), y en la Escuela de Medicina de la Universidad de Washington (1963). En la UANL fue profesor (1959-), director de la Unidad Metabólica del Hospital Universitario (1965-), director de Graduados de la Facultad de Medicina (1967), director de la Facultad de Enfermería (1968), director del Instituto de Investigaciones Científicas (1969-70 y 1973) y rector (1973-79). Miembro del PRI. Ha sido jefe de los Servicios Coordinados de Salud Pública del gobierno de Nuevo León (1979-82), diputado federal (1982-85), subsecretario de Educación Superior e Investigación Científica de la SEP (1988-92), representante de México ante la UNESCO (1992-97) y candidato a gobernador por el estado de Nuevo León (1997). Colaborador de los periódicos *El Porvenir* y *El Norte* de Monterrey. Autor de *Testimonios universitarios* (1974), *Metas y aspiraciones de la universidad* (1974), *Revolución educativa* (1975), *Reflexiones sobre el pensamiento social de un mexicano universal: Alfonso Reyes* (1977), *Papel del universitario en el momento político actual* (1978), *La universidad es unidad en la pluralidad* (1978) y *Pedro Garfías, rebeldía creativa* (1979). Miembro de la Academia de Ciencias de Nueva York, de la Junta Directiva del Conacyt (1975) y del Instituto Mexicano de Investigaciones Nefrológicas.

Todos Santos ◆ Bahía de Baja California situada en el litoral del océano Pacífico, en el noroccidente del estado. Se abre entre las puntas San Miguel, al norte, y Banda, al sur. En su litoral se encuentra Ensenada.

Todos Santos, de ◆ Islas de Baja California situadas en el océano Pacífico, frente a la bahía de su mismo nombre. Son dos promontorios rocallosos, de 2,000 por 800 metros uno, y 800 por 400 el otro. Durante la primavera y el verano sirven de criadero a diversas especies de aves marinas.

Togo ◆ Nación situada en el oeste de África, en la costa del golfo de Guinea. Su nombre oficial es República Togolesa. Limita al norte con Burkina Faso, al este con Benin y al oeste con Ghana. Superficie: 56,785 km^2. Habitantes: 4,397,000 (1998). Su capital es Lomé (366,476 habitantes en 1990). El idioma oficial es el francés, aunque también son usuales unas 40 lenguas locales. Los grupos étnicos predominantes son los ewé, kabye y mina. *Historia*: hacia el siglo xii, el territorio fue poblado por tribus de la familia ewé-fon, procedentes del valle del Níger, una de las cuales constituyó, en el actual suroeste de Togo, cerca de Lomé, el reino Coto, que fue destruido por los portugueses hacia 1471. Unos años después los lusitanos construyeron algunos fuertes en la costa, desde donde perseguían y secuestraban a los ewés, con el fin de convertirlos en esclavos. A la Nueva España los negreros trajeron grupos de *cotos*, los habitantes de Coto, así como de *anas*, *popós* y *tarís*, negros que vivían cerca de la actual frontera entre Benin y Togo. A partir de entonces, la costa del golfo de Guinea fue conocida como "Costa de los Esclavos", por la gran cantidad que procedían de ahí. La mayor parte de los ewés esclavos fueron conducidos a Brasil. A principios del siglo xvii, los holandeses sustituyeron a los lusitanos en el comercio humano. En 1874 los alemanes se instalaron en territorio togolés. A principios de los años ochenta del siglo xix, el alemán Gustav Nachtigal realizó una gran exploración por el actual territorio de Togo y la porción oriental de Ghana y consiguió firmar varios cientos de tratados con los señoríos locales, los que fueron utilizados por el gobierno imperial de Alemania para legitimar, frente a los reclamos ingleses y franceses, la colonización alemana en el golfo de Benin. Las potencias europeas llegaron a un acuerdo en la Conferencia de Berlín, en 1884, y se creó el protectorado alemán de Togo. A fines del siglo las autoridades alemanas permitieron la inmigración de un gran número de negros brasileños liberados en su país. Durante la primera guerra mundial, los ejércitos coloniales de Francia e Inglaterra, que dominaban Benin y Ghana, respectivamente, invadieron Togo y desalojaron a los alemanes. En 1919, con el aval de la Sociedad de Naciones, los británicos se apoderaron de la porción occidental del país, mientras que los franceses se instalaron en la oriental. En 1956, el gobierno británico incorporó administrativamente la porción occidental a su colonia de Ghana, entonces llamada Costa de Oro. En ese mismo año los franceses dejaron de llamar colonia a su fracción de Togo y crearon el Territorio Francés de Ultramar de Togo, dotado de autonomía interna. Para entonces, los descendientes de los esclavos brasileños dominaban buena parte de la vida económica de la colonia, aunque estaban divididos en dos "familias": los Olympio y los Souza. En 1958, Sylvanus Olympio, uno de los jerarcas, ganó las elecciones presidenciales e inició negociaciones con la metrópoli para conseguir la independencia, que fue reconocida por Francia en 1960. En ese mismo año se creó la República Togolesa y Olympio fue elegido presi-

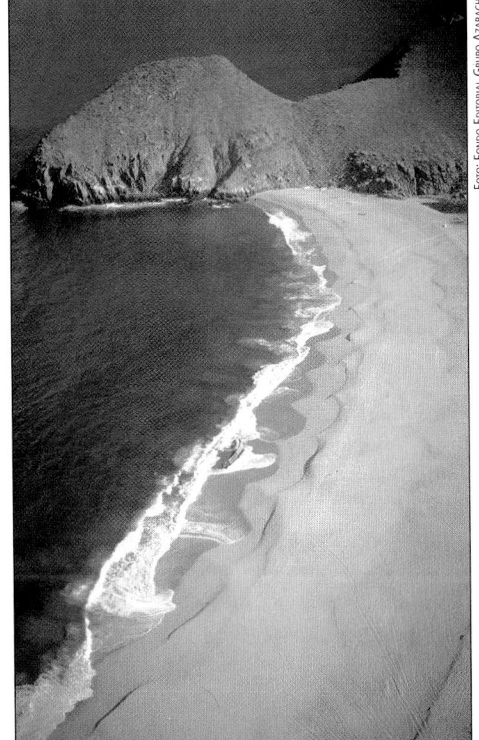

Bahía de Todos Santos, en Baja California

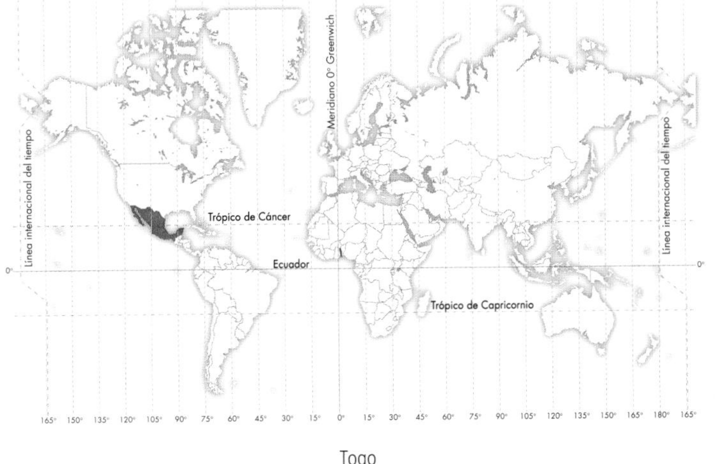

Togo

dente. Como intentara nacionalizar los yacimientos de fosfatos, principal fuente de divisas en manos de empresas francesas, tres años después fue asesinado. En 1967, el sucesor de Olympio, Nicolás Grunitzky, fue derrocado por un golpe militar encabezado por Etienne Eyadema. Dos años después, impulsado por Eyadema, se fundó el partido Agrupación del Pueblo Togolés. En 1972, el gobierno de Eyadema nacionalizó 35 por ciento de las acciones de las empresas mineras francesas; tres años después elevó la participación togolesa a 51 por ciento y en 1975 nacionalizó totalmente la minería del país. En ese mismo año se establecieron relaciones diplomáticas con México. También en 1975, un grupo de naciones africanas, asiáticas y americanas firmaron con la Comunidad Económica Europea un acuerdo de comercio, conocido como la Convención de Lomé, que fue ratificado cinco años después. También en 1980 Eyadema proclamó la tercera república togolesa. En 1982 se produjeron varios enfrentamientos armados en la frontera de Togo y Ghana. Ambas naciones reestablecieron relaciones diplomáticas en 1995 y en ese año Europa reanudó la ayuda humanitaria al país, suspendida por la guerra y los atropellos a los derechos humanos. El jefe de gobierno es Étienne Gnassingbé Eyadema (1986-) y el primer ministro, Klutse Kwassi Klutse (1996-).

TOJOLABALES ◆ Indios que viven en el sureste de Chiapas, cerca de la frontera con Guatemala. En 1995 hablaban tojolabal 37,181 personas mayores de cinco años, la mayoría vivían en Chiapas y 6,810 eran monolingües. Su idioma está clasificado en el grupo maya-totonaco, tronco mayense, subfamilia yax. No tiene variantes dialectales de consideración. La ropa tradicional de esta etnia ha empezado a desaparacer, aunque hay algunos hombres que usan pantalón de manta bordada y camisa de mangas anchas, bordada en el cuello y los puños; las mujeres llevan una falda llamada *juna*, adornada con encajes, blusa bordada, pañoleta de popelina y unos huaraches conocidos como *xanab*. La base de su economía es la agricultura, pero algunos tojolabales deben emigrar para contratarse como peones agrícolas. Se dedican también a la crianza de animales de corral y practican la caza. Su organización social se basa en la familia nuclear y aún se concede importancia a la familia extensa. La forma tradicional de petición de mano ha sido sustituida paulatinamente por el rapto, con el consenso de la novia. Aunque son católicos, conservan algunas de sus creencias tradicionales: adoran al sol, como deidad creadora y protectora, y a la luna, entes asociados con el fuego y el agua, respectivamente, y que viven en el cielo, junto al dios de los cristianos. Suponen que las enfermedades son causadas por los brujos, que son conocidos como *pukuj*. Para contrarrestarlos cuentan con unos curanderos llamados *pita chik'*. En cada pueblo la asamblea comunal es la máxima autoridad, pues tiene injerencia y poder de decisión en todos sus problemas; no obstante, siempre se halla supeditada a las autoridades municipales. Se cree que los tojolabales, también llamados chañabales, los choles y los lacandones, fueron los fundadores del imperio maya clásico; incluso el *Popol Vuh* los menciona y los sitúa en el territorio que actualmente ocupan.

TOLA, LUIS ◆ n. y m. en la ciudad de México (1802-1881). Militar. Estudió en el Colegio de Minería. Se incorporó al ejército en 1823. Miembro del Cuerpo de Ingenieros desde 1829. En 1832 se opuso al levantamiento liberal de Antonio López de Santa Anna. Dos años después participó en la campaña que trató de impedir la independencia de Texas. Comandante del ejército del norte luego de la derrota santanista (1838-42), durante su gestión organizó varias expediciones contra Texas y se encargó de fortificar Matamoros durante la guerra de los Pasteles (1838). Fue subdirector del Colegio Militar (1843-44), jefe de la Sección de Ingenieros (1844-47), encargado de la fortificación del puerto de Veracruz (1846) y del sur de la ciudad de México (1847); director interino de Ingenieros Militares (1847-49), comandante de ingenieros de la ciudad de México (1850-53), oficial mayor de la Secretaría de Guerra y Marina (1853-55) y director del Colegio Militar (1856-57). Despedido en febrero de 1857 por oponerse a la Constitución liberal, en diciembre de ese año se levantó en armas contra el gobierno de Ignacio Comonfort y en enero de 1858, el gobierno de Félix Zuloaga lo repuso en el cargo. Renunció en junio de 1859. Durante el gobierno de Maximiliano de Habsburgo fue director del Colegio de Minería (1866). Encarcelado al triunfo de la República (1867-69), pudo, sin embargo, ser profesor del Colegio Militar (1877-81).

TOLA DE HABICH, FERNANDO ◆ n. en Perú (1941). Escritor. Realizó estudios en las universidades de San Marcos de Lima, Central de Madrid e Hispanoamericana de Santa María de la Rábida, en España. Ha editado *Sátiros y amores*, de Ricardo Gómez Robledo (1984); *Las Rulfo y otros chismes de barrio*, de Ángel de Campo (1985); *Narraciones, confidencias y otros textos*, de Alberto Michel (1985); *El amor por los niños*, de Manuel Gutiérrez Nájera (1986); *Obras poéticas*, de Fernando Calderón (1986); y *Algunas consideraciones sobre la literatura mexicana*, de José María Vigil (1986). Autor del volumen de entrevistas *Los españoles y el boom*; de los ensayos *Museo literario*, *Homenaje a I. M. Altamirano*, *La crítica literaria mexicana en el siglo XIX* y *Poesía de Manuel Carpio*; y de los poemarios *Lulú la meona* y *Canción de amor*.

TOLCAYUCA ◆ Municipio de Hidalgo situado al oeste de Zempoala y al suroeste de Pachuca, en los límites con el Estado de México. Superficie: 120.8 km². Habitantes: 9,997, de los cuales 2,256 forman la población económicamente activa. Hablan alguna lengua indígena 37 personas mayores de cinco años (náhuatl 19).

TOLEDO, ALEJANDRO ◆ n. en el DF (1963). Licenciado en ciencias políticas y administración pública por la UNAM, donde imparte talleres literarios, así como en la UAM y el INBA. Editor de los libros de *Punto de Partida* (1984-89), coordinador de Publicaciones de la Dirección de Literatura de la UNAM y miembro del consejo de redacción del *Periódico de Poesía*. Ha sido coordinador de la serie *Cuadernos del Nigromante*, editor de *Macrópolis*, colaborador de *Este País*, *Brecha*, *El Ángel* y *Diario de Monterrey* y reportero especial de *El Universal*. Es autor de narrativa: *Tres cuentos del mar* (1993) y *Atardecer con lluvia* (1996); de ensayo: *Dujardín y el monólogo interior* (1994); entrevista: *Cuento mexicano/cuento hispanoamericano: conversaciones de Luis Leal y Seymour Menton* (1987) y *Los márgenes de la palabra* (1995, Premio de Periodismo Cultural, INBA, 1992); reportaje *Chávez-De la Hoya: viaje mágico y misterioso* (1996); y antología: *Entre tus dedos helados y otros cuentos* (1988, selección de la obra de Francisco Tario), *El imperio entre las voces. Fernando del Paso ante la crítica* (1997), *Cuentos dispersos* (1999, selección de cuentos de Fernando del Paso). Ha obtenido las becas Salvador Novo (1983-1984), del Centro Mexicano de Escritores (1991-92) y del Fonca (1992-93). Premio de Periodismo Deportivo Ciudad de México (1995).

TOLEDO, ALEJO ◆ n. en Álamos y m. en Navojoa, Son. (¿1830?-1880). Militar. Alistado en la Guardia Nacional, luchó en las filas liberales en la guerra de los Tres Años y más tarde combatió la intervención francesa y el imperio. Al triunfo de la República participó en varias campañas contra yaquis y mayos (1867). Fue presidente municipal de Navojoa (1969) y en 1871 se opuso a los sublevados del Plan de la Noria; en 1875 combatió a las fuerzas del gobernador Ignacio Pesqueira; y en 1876 en favor de Francisco Serna. En 1876 reconoció al gobernador Vicente Mariscal.

TOLEDO, FRANCISCO ◆ n. en Juchitán, Oax. (1940). Pintor y grabador. Estudió en el Instituto de Ciencias y Artes de Oaxaca, en el Taller Libre de Grabado de la Escuela de Diseño y Artesanías de la ciudad de México (1959) y con Stanley William Hayter en París (1963). Expuso por primera vez en 1959, en el Centro Artístico de Fort Worth, Dallas. Hay obras suyas en los museos de Arte Moderno de México, París, Nueva York y Filadelfia, en la Biblioteca Pública de Nueva York, en la Galería Tate de Londres y en la Kunstnaneshus de Oslo. Diseñador de tapices, los que realiza junto con los artesanos de Teotitlán del Valle, y ceramista. Autor del mural *La cangrejera* en el Club de Industriales del DF (1995). Donó una importante colección de obras artísticas a la Casa de la Cultura de Juchitán y otra al Museo de Oaxaca. Patrocinó la revista literaria *Guchachi' Reza* (iguana rajada), que difundió la cultura zapoteca. Fundador de Ediciones Toledo. Su contribución ha sido decisiva para organizaciones políticas como la Coalición Obrero Campesina Estudiantil del Istmo y para diversas empresas culturales, entre otras la fundación del diario *La Jornada*, la creación del Museo de Arte Contemporáneo de Oaxaca, el Instituto de Artes Gráficas de Oaxaca y el museo fotográfico al que puso el nombre de Manuel Álvarez Bravo. Autor de las carpetas de grabados *Toledo Chilam Balam* (1974), *Toledo Sahagún* (1974), *Toledo Guchachi* (1976) y *Nuevo catecismo para indios remisos* (1981), e ilustrador de ediciones del *Chilam Balam* (1976) y el *Manual de zoología fantástica* de Jorge Luis Borges (1983), así como de *Una historia antigua de la mierda* de Alfredo López Austin (1988) y *Álbum de zoología* de José Emilio Pacheco

El camino, obra en técnica mixta de Francisco Toledo

Francisco Toledo

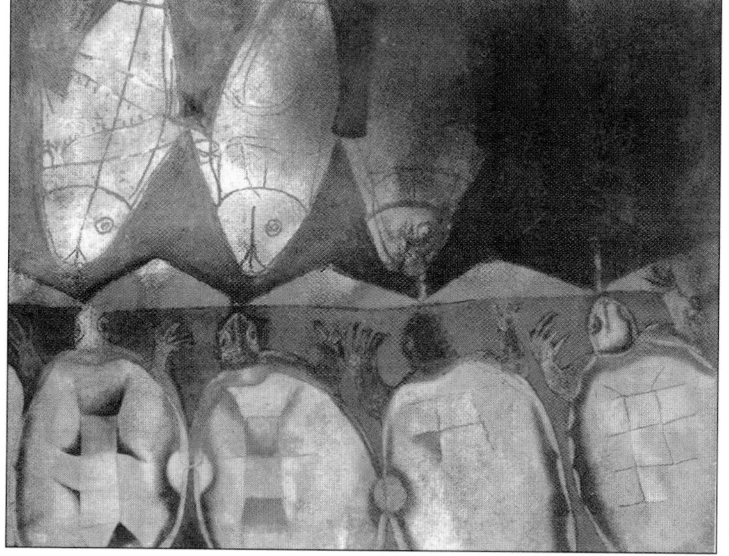

Peces y tortugas, óleo sobre tela de Francisco Toledo

FOTO: JESÚS SÁNCHEZ URIBE

Benda, escultura en plata de Francisco Toledo

Conejo y pescado, tinta y acuarela sobre papel de Francisco Toledo

Antonio Sebastián de Toledo Molina y Salazar

(1998). Creador emérito del SNCA (1993-) y Premio Nacional de Ciencias y Artes (1998).

Toledo, Jesús ◆ n. en Álamos, Son., y m. en la ciudad de México (1839-1892). Militar. En 1854 combatió a los mercenarios de Gastón de Raousset de Boulbon. Cuatro años después, durante la guerra de los Tres Años, se incorporó a las fuerzas liberales de Jesús García Morales, las que ocuparon Sinaloa en 1858. En 1863 se integró al Ejército de Oriente, comandado por Porfirio Díaz. Participó en la defensa de Oaxaca, en la toma de Zamora y en el sitio de Querétaro. En 1869 se levantó en armas contra el gobierno del presidente Benito Juárez, pero fue derrotado y apresado. Tres años después, en 1871, se adhirió al Plan de la Noria y volvió a insurreccionarse. De nuevo derrotado, participó en el levantamiento porfirista de 1875-76. Al morir tenía el grado de general de brigada.

Toledo, Luis ◆ n. en Ixcatepec, Oax. (1924). Pintor. Estudió en la Escuela de Pintura y Escultura La Esmeralda. Expuso por primera vez en 1960. Obras suyas se han presentado en Bélgica, Estados Unidos y Francia. En 1966, 1968 y 1976, recibió el Premio de la Crítica del Salón Mexicano de la Acuarela. En 1968 obtuvo el Premio de Adquisición del Instituto Nacional de Bellas Artes.

Toledo, Víctor ◆ n. en Córdoba, Ver. (1957). Estudió letras hispánicas en la UNAM. Ha sido jefe de la Oficina de Literatura de la Delegación Álvaro Obregón y consejero de redacción de la revista *Graffiti*. Trabajó en el programa Charlas y Lecturas de Poesía del ISSSTE. Colaborador de *Plural, Tierra Adentro, El Ojo Hormiguero, El Día de los Jóvenes, La Nigua, Guchachi' Reza* y *El Día*. Autor de poesía: *Poemas de Didxaza* (1985), y de ensayo: *El águila en las venas, Neruda en México, México en Neruda* (1994). Becario del Centro Mexicano de Escritores (1983) y del Instituto Nacional de Bellas Artes (1984). Premio Poesía Joven de México (1983).

Toledo, Víctor M. ◆ n. en el DF (?). Dedicado a la docencia de temas ecológicos. Fundador y editor de la revista *Etnoecológica*. Ha colaborado en la *Encyclopaedia of Biodiversity*. Catedrático de la Universidad de Barcelona (1977). Coordinó la redacción del *Plan Pátzcuaro 2000* (1994). Coautor de *La producción rural en México: alternativas ecológicas* (1989). Autor de *Ecología y autosuficiencia alimentaria* (1985) y *La diversidad biológica de México* (1988). Obtuvo los premios Nacional Serfín del Medio Ambiente (1985) y Nacional al Mérito Ecológico (1999). Es investigador del Instituto de Ecología de la UNAM, campus Morelia, y miembro del SNI. Ha sido becario de la Fundación John Simon Guggenheim (1992-93).

Toledo Corro, Antonio ◆ n. en Escuinapa, Sin. (1919). Político y empresario. Pertenece al PRI, en el que ha sido secretario general en Sinaloa (1951), diputado a la Legislatura de esa entidad (1951-53), presidente de la Cámara de Comercio de Sinaloa (1957), presidente municipal de Mazatlán (1960-63), encargado de mecanización de zonas ejidales de Campeche (1970), diputado federal (1976-77), gerente general de Servicios Ejidales S.A. (1977), secretario de la Reforma Agraria (del 9 de junio de 1978 al 28 de abril de 1980) y gobernador de Sinaloa (1 de enero de 1981 al 31 de diciembre de 1987).

Toledo Molina y Salazar, Antonio Sebastián de ◆ n. y m. en España (¿1625?-1715). Tenía el título de marqués de Mancera. Fue mayordomo de la reina Isabel de Borbón (1668), embajador español en Venecia y virrey de la Nueva España (1664-73). Llegó a la ciudad de México en octubre de 1664. Al año siguiente, a causa del aumento de la actividad pirata en la Florida, reorganizó la Armada de Barlovento. En 1666 ordenó que una buena parte del presupuesto virreinal se dedicara a la decoración interna de la Catedral de la ciudad de México. Cuatro años después, mientras equipaba una nueva expedición a California, suspendió las obras de desagüe del valle de México y las de construcción del convento de Guanajuato para impulsar las de fortificación de San Juan de Ulúa.

Tolentino Hernández, Arturo ◆ n. en Sierra Mojada, Coah., y m. en Ciudad Juárez, Chih. (1888-1954). Compositor. Contador titulado en el Colegio Palmore de Chihuahua (1908). Fue cofundador (1941), profesor y director de la Academia de Artes y Literatura de Chihuahua y fundador y director de la Biblioteca Municipal de Chihuahua (1941-54). Compuso *Sonrisas de primavera, Ojos de juventud, Tricolor, Hora del encanto, Dora, En alas del ensueño, Ven para siempre, Maravilla, Tus ojos, Flor María, La dama blanca, Alma parralense, Uranus, Almas gemelas* y *Ven para siempre*.

Tolimán ◆ Municipio de Jalisco situado al oeste-suroeste de Ciudad Guzmán y al sureste de Autlán de Navarro, en los límites con Colima. Superficie: 460, km^2. Habitantes: 9,370, de los cuales 1,818 forman la población económicamente activa. Hablan alguna lengua indígena ocho personas mayores de cinco años.

Tolimán ◆ Municipio de Querétaro situado al noreste de la capital estatal y al norte de Tequisquiapan, en los límites con Guanajuato. Superficie: 724.7 km^2. Habitantes: 20,019, de los cuales 3,837 forman la población económicamente activa. Hablan alguna lengua indígena 4,884 personas mayores de cinco años (otomí 4,867). En diciembre de 1855, José López Uraga se levantó en armas contra el gobierno de

Ignacio Comonfort. Durante los dos meses siguientes, López Uraga utilizó el municipio como centro de operaciones, hasta que en febrero de 1856 las fuerzas liberales de Luis Ghilardi tomaron la cabecera.

Tolotzin ◆ Dios principal de los matlatzincas. Su nombre significa "el que tiene la cabeza inclinada". Parece que el dios Coltzin, "el venerado encorvado" que adoraban los colhuas y que dio nombre a Colhuacan, es Tolotzin. También se le llamaba Tolo, Toloqui o Tolocatzin. El cerro en que se hallaba su templo, construido posiblemente por los toltecas, dio nombre a Toluca. Algunos autores sostienen que Tolotzin y Coltzin eran variantes de Huehuéteotl, el dios viejo del fuego en el panteón mexica.

Tolsá, Manuel ◆ n. en España y m. en la ciudad de México (1757-1816). Arquitecto y escultor. Estudió escultura con José Puchol en la Academia de San Carlos de Valencia y arquitectura con Ribelles, Gascó y Gilabert en la Academia de San Fernando de Madrid. Llegó a la Nueva España en 1791 para encargarse de la dirección de la Academia de las Tres Nobles Artes de San Carlos. Terminó la construcción de la Catedral Metropolitana (1791-1813). Proyectó una plaza de toros (1793), supervisó las obras de drenaje y de abastecimiento de agua potable para la ciudad de México, concluyó la construcción de la Catedral de Aguascalientes, edificó una fuente en el

Manuel Tolsá

inicio del camino real a Toluca (1794), hizo el busto en bronce para la tumba de Hernán Cortés (1795), reforestó la Alameda Central de la ciudad de México, levantó un obelisco y una pirámide en el camino real a Toluca (1795), ejecutó la estatua ecuestre de Carlos IV, más conocida como *El Caballito* (1796-1803), construyó el Palacio de Minería (1707-1813), elaboró los planos del Hospicio Cabañas de Guadalajara y el primer proyecto de un cementerio civil en la ciudad de México (1808). Edificó numerosas casas particulares, como las del marqués del Apartado, situada en la esquina de las actuales calles de Donceles y Argentina; la de Buenavista, en Puente de Alvarado; y la que perteneció a la marquesa de Selva Nevada. Desde su llegada a la Nueva España abrió una casa de baños e instaló una fábrica de coches.

El Palacio de Minería, en la ciudad de México, obra de Manuel Tolsá, en grabado de Pedro Gualdi de 1853

Foto: Fausto Ramírez

El Caballito, en la ciudad de México, obra de Manuel Tolsá

Toltecas ◆ Indios de filiación nahua, creadores de una cultura y de un imperio que florecieron entre los siglos IX a XI de nuestra era. Tuvieron hegemonía sobre casi toda Mesoamérica. Su capital fue Tullan, 70 kilómetros al norte de la ciudad de México, donde aún existen vestigios de sus creaciones arquitectónicas, escultóricas y de cerámica. Aparentemente los toltecas fueron uno de los grupos emigrados de Teotihuacan, luego del ocaso de dicho imperio, guiados por Mixcóatl, "serpiente de nubes". Este grupo se fundió con otro de chichimecas provenientes del norte y crearon la cultura tolteca-chichimeca. Mixcóatl se casó con Chimalma, "la que porta escudo", quien murió al dar a luz a Ce Ácatl Topiltzin; por tal razón, Chimalma fue consagrada como una de las deidades del poniente, las Ciuteteo, mujeres diosas muertas del primer parto. Cuando Topiltzin nació en Tepoztlán, Mixcóatl ya había muerto, por lo que el niño fue educado por sus abuelos maternos. Al llegar Topiltzin a la edad adulta, un grupo de tolteca-chichimecas lo buscó para entregarle el trono de su padre: Topiltzin accedió, se dirigió al cerro de la Estrella, dominio de Culhuacán, y ahí estableció su gobierno, que más tarde, en el siglo X, se trasladó a Tulancingo (☛) y luego a Tula (☛), donde fueron conquistados los grupos nonoalcas de Veracruz que se habían establecido en la región unos años antes. La influencia cultural tolteca fue tan grande, que la palabra *toltécatl* llegó a convertirse, entre los pueblos nahuas, en sinónimo de artista. Los tolteca-chichimecas y nonoalcas fueron grandes astrónomos y elaboraron calendarios muy precisos. Conocían las propiedades curativas de las plantas, por lo que hicieron de la herbolaria una ciencia. Algunos de sus médicos más célebres fueron Oxomoco, Cipactonal, Tlaltecuin y Xochicahua. Además, los toltecas descubrieron y explotaron minas de cobre, plata, plomo, oro y estaño e iniciaron en Tula la edad de los metales. Crearon el servicio de correos y se cree que las estatuas conocidas como *chac mool*, originales de los toltecas, representan al corredor que espera los mensajes que ha de transportar. Algunas fuentes históricas dicen que 10 reyes gobernaron Tullan de 856 a 1168, año en que la ciudad fue destruida y abandonaba a consecuencia del conflicto entre los dirigentes político-militares, generalmente toltecas, y los líderes comerciantes, casi todos nonoalcas, pero sobre todo por las invasiones de chichimecas y otomíes venidos del norte.

FOTO: IRMGARD GROTH KIMBAL

Olla de la cultura tolteca con la efigie de Tláloc

TOLUCA ◆ Municipio del Estado de México situado al este de Valle de Bravo y al oeste del Distrito Federal. Se encuentra a 2,680 metros sobre el nivel del mar. Superficie: 377.28 km^2. Habitantes: 564,476, de los cuales 149,953 forman la población económicamente activa. Hablan alguna lengua indígena 21,071 personas mayores de cinco años (otomí 20,368 y mazahua 703). La cabecera, Toluca de Lerdo, es también capital del Estado de México. En el siglo VII de la época contemporánea, los matlatzincas (☛) se asentaron en el actual valle de Toluca y fundaron las poblaciones de Toloche, Tecaxic y Calixtlahuaca. Hacia 1120, fundaron Nepintatuhui, Tolocan para los nahuas, que se convirtió en una de las principales de los dominios matlatzincas. En 1474, las fuerzas mexicas de Axayácatl tomaron Nepitatuhui y convirtieron a los pueblos del valle de Toluca en tributarios de la Triple Alianza. A principios de 1521, un grupo de conquistadores españoles comandado por Gonzalo de Sandoval penetró al valle de Toluca por el este y derrotó a los matlatzincas en Nepitatuhui; se apoderó de la ciudad y de esa forma impidió que los matlatzincas colaboraran con los mexicas en la defensa de México-Tenochtitlan. Con el establecimiento de la dominación española, Toluca fue incorporada a los extensos dominios de Hernán Cortés y recibió el nombre de Ciudad de San José. En la década de 1550, los frailes franciscanos se instalaron en el viejo poblado matlatzinca. A principios del siglo XVII, por su parte, los carmelitas construyeron la iglesia del Carmen del Tercer Orden, que tiene una capilla abierta. A fines de octubre de 1810, las fuerzas insurgentes de Miguel Hidalgo ocuparon Toluca durante algunos días, pero luego del triunfo del ejército colonial en Aculco (noviembre), la ciudad quedó en poder de los españoles. En los alrededores, sin embargo, comenzaron a operar las guerrillas de Tomás Ortiz y Benedicto López. A raíz de la promulgación de la Carta de Cádiz, en diciembre de 1812 se creó el municipio de Toluca, instalado efectivamente en

Vista del Nevado de Toluca

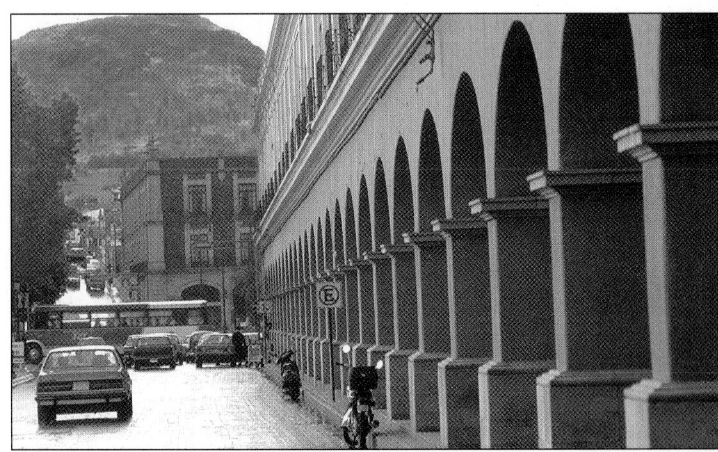
Portales de Toluca, Estado de México

mayo del año siguiente. Fue suprimido entre 1814 y 1820. En 1830, el gobernador del Estado de México, el yorkino Lorenzo de Zavala, trasladó la capital del estado de Tlalpan a Toluca. Poco después aparecieron los primeros diarios de la ciudad: *El Conservador* (1831), *El Fanal* (1831-32), *Miscelánea* (1831-32) y *Minerva* (1834), los dos últimos fundados por José María Heredia. Los portales que se encuentran en el centro de la ciudad fueron construidos entre 1832 y 1836, a instancias de José María González Arratia. En 1836, al establecerse el centralismo, Toluca dejó de ser municipio y capital del estado. Volvió a serlo hasta 1846, luego que se reestableció la Constitución de 1824. En noviembre de 1861, unos meses después de la muerte de Miguel Lerdo de Tejada, la Legislatura mexiquense añadió el apellido del liberal veracruzano al nombre de la cabecera municipal. Como muchas de las construcciones religiosas, el enorme convento de franciscanos fue fraccionado al triunfo definitivo de los liberales y en esos terrenos se edificaron el Palacio Municipal, el Palacio de Gobierno del estado y una iglesia católica. A fines del siglo XIX, se establecieron algunas fábricas. Entre 1912 y 1915, la zona oriental del municipio, la más cercana al Nevado de Toluca, permaneció en poder del Ejército Libertador del Sur. En julio de 1915, acosado por las tropas carrancistas, el gobierno convencionista de Francisco Lagos Cházaro se instaló en Toluca, donde se extinguió en octubre ante la persecución de los carrancistas. La diócesis de Toluca fue creada en 1950.

Toluca, Nevado de ◆ Volcán del Estado de México, también llamado Xinantécatl, que forma parte del Sistema Volcánico Transversal, situado 22 kilómetros al sureste de Toluca de Lerdo. Por el este se une a la sierra de Tenango; por el noroeste a los montes de la Gavia; por el oeste a la sierra de Temascaltepec y por el suroeste a la del Hospital. En el cráter del volcán, ya extinguido, hay dos lagunas, la del Sol y la de la Luna, y varias eminencias, entre ellas el pico del Fraile, cuya cima se halla a 4,558 metros sobre el nivel del mar.

Tomás Pons, Francisco ◆ n. en Cataluña, España (1931). Matemático. Fue traído a México en 1939, a la derrota de la República Española. Estudió la licenciatura en la UNAM, la maestría en la Universidad de Princeton (1955) y el doctorado en el Centro de Investigación y Estudios Avanzados del IPN (1961). Profesor de la UNAM (1956-), de la Escuela Militar de Ingenieros de México (1956-61), de la Universidad de París (1962-63), del CIFA (1962-67) y de la Universidad Autónoma de Barcelona (1973-74). Desde 1968 es investigador del Instituto de Matemáticas de la UNAM. En 1961 definió la que se conoce como integral de Bruhat-Tomás. Colaborador del *Boletín de la Sociedad Matemática Mexicana* y de los *Anales del Instituto de Matemáticas de la UNAM*. Coautor de *Álgebra superior* (1974) y *Teoría de los números algebraicos* (1975). Autor de *Los números racionales* (1972) y *Los números reales* (1973).

Tomás Rosich, Juan ◆ n. en Cataluña, España, y m. en el DF (1894-1968). Crítico teatral y cinematográfico. Llegó a México en 1939, poco después de la derrota de la República Española. Aquí colaboró en las publicaciones *Esto*, *Cinema Reporter*, *Mañana* y *Claridades*. Fue miembro de la Agrupación de Críticos de Teatro de México.

Tomatlán ◆ Municipio de Jalisco situado al sur de Puerto Vallarta y al oeste de Ciudad Guzmán, en la costa del océano Pacífico. Superficie: 2,657.5 km². Habitantes: 33,872, de los cuales 8,177 forman la población económicamente activa. Hablan alguna lengua indígena 35 personas mayores de cinco años.

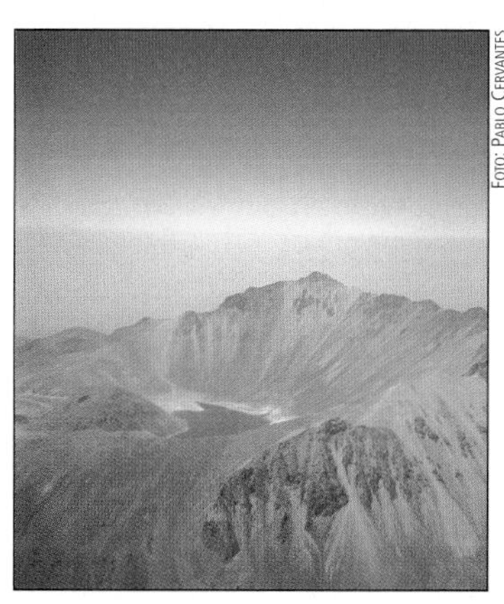

Foto: Pablo Cervantes

Cráter del Nevado de Toluca

Foto: Michael Calderwood

Nevado de Toluca

Tomatlán ◆ Municipio de Veracruz situado al nor-noroeste de Córdoba y al noreste de Orizaba. Superficie: 31.26 km². Habitantes: 5,880, de los cuales 1,696 forman la población económicamente activa. Hablan alguna lengua indígena 24 personas mayores de cinco años (náhuatl 19).

Tomatlán ◆ Río de Jalisco situado en la porción occidental del estado. Nace en la ladera suroccidental de la sierra del Desmoronado, de la confluencia de los ríos Desmoronado y Coyol, al suroeste de Talpa de Allende. Corre de norte a sur, entra a la llanura costera y tuerce al suroeste. Desemboca en el océano Pacífico, al sureste de Cabo Corrientes, tras un recorrido de 90 kilómetros.

Tomellín, de ◆ Cañón de Oaxaca situado en la porción central del estado, en cuyo fondo corre el río Tomellín. Es recorrido en su totalidad por el ferrocarril que va a la ciudad de Oaxaca.

Tomellín ◆ Río de Oaxaca que nace de la confluencia del Parián y del Huaucilla, al noroeste de la capital estatal. Corre de sur a norte y atraviesa el escudo Mixteco por el cañón de Tomellín. Desemboca en el río Grande de Quiotepec, al oeste de la sierra de Juárez.

TOMMASI, ENRIQUE ALFONSO ◆ n. en Mérida, Yuc. (1927). Médico cirujano y partero graduado en la Escuela Médico Militar (1949), de la que ha sido profesor. Ha impartido clases en la UNAM, la Universidad de Costa Rica y la Escuela de Enfermería del ISSSTE. Ha trabajado en hospitales militares y civiles. En el ISSSTE ha sido director general del Centro Hospitalario 20 de noviembre (1972-77) y titular de la Coordinación de Planificación Familiar (1977-79). Fue director de Planeación de la Coordinación Nacional de Planificación Familiar de la SSA (1980-83) y director del Hospital Mocel de la ciudad de México (1993-97). Coautor de *Los desafíos del desarrollo social* (1989). Autor de *Hacia una nueva forma de vivir* (1998). Miembro del Colegio de Médicos Militares Francisco Montes de Oca (1950), la Asociación Mexicana de Ginecología y Obstetricia (1957), la Asociación Mexicana para Estudios de la Esterilidad (1961), la Federación Internacional de Ginecología y Obstetricia, el Consejo Mexicano de Ginecología y Obstetricia (1972), la Asociación Médica del Hospital Mocel y el Colegio Americano de Ginecología y Obstetricia.

TOMMASI LÓPEZ, LEOPOLDO ◆ n. y m. en Mérida, Yuc. (1898-1976). Escultor, arquitecto y escritor. Aprendió escultura en el taller de su padre, un inmigrante italiano, y en 1916 ganó una beca del gobierno estatal para estudiar arquitectura y escultura en la Real Academia de San Fernando, en Madrid.

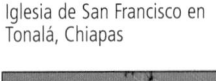

Iglesia de San Francisco en Tonalá, Chiapas

FOTO: FONDO EDITORIAL GRUPO AZABACHE

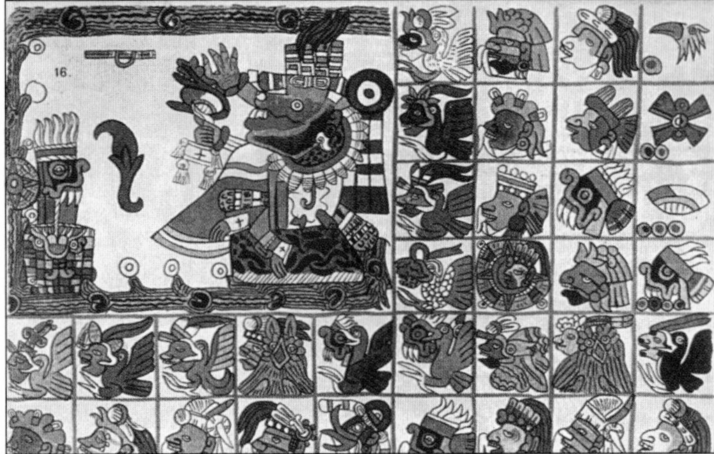

Tonalámatl del códice Aubin

Volvió a México en 1921. Siete años después, en 1928, con Manuel Amábilis construyó el pabellón de México de la Feria de Sevilla. En 1946, con otros meridanos residentes en la ciudad de México, fundó la Asociación Zamná, que entre 1946 y 1953 editó 18 libros de autores yucatecos. Más tarde fue director de Bellas Artes de Yucatán (1970-75). Proyectó numerosos edificios en las ciudades de México, León, Morelia, Veracruz y Mérida. En 1926, realizó un monumento a Felipe Carrillo Puerto, que se encuentra en el Paseo Montejo de Mérida. Autor de *El feísmo en la pintura contemporánea* (1936), *La ciudad de ayer, hoy y mañana* (1951), *Fuego junto al ejido*, *La otra costilla de Adán* y *Mis otras manos*. En 1972 recibió la Medalla Yucatán.

TOMÓCHIC ◆ Población del municipio chihuahuense de Guerrero (☛), donde, en 1891, el ejército porfirista ejecutó una de sus grandes matanzas.

TONACATECUTLI Y TONACACÍHUATL ◆ ☛ *Ometecutli y Omecíhuatl.*

TONALÁ ◆ Municipio de Chiapas situado al suroeste de Tuxtla Gutiérrez y al noroeste de Tapachula, en el litoral del océano Pacífico. Superficie: 1,766.2 km². Habitantes: 73,673, de los cuales 18,346 forman la población económicamente activa. Hablan alguna lengua indígena 327 personas mayores de cinco años (zapoteco 210). El municipio cuenta, como sitios de atractivo turístico, con los esteros de Cabeza de Toro, Boca del Cielo y Paredón, y con las playas de Puerto Arista. En la cabecera hay un museo arqueológico. Las fiestas más importantes son las de San Francisco, del 1 al 4 de octubre. Del 20 al 31 de diciembre se realiza una feria comercial y ganadera.

TONALÁ ◆ Municipio de Jalisco contiguo a Guadalajara. Superficie: 119.58 km². Habitantes: 271,857, de los cuales 49,468 forman la población económicamente activa. Hablan alguna lengua indígena 456 personas mayores de cinco años (náhuatl 116, purépecha 100 y mixteco 92). En la jurisdicción se hallan los manantiales de San Elías, La Alberca, La Escondida de Galán y El Ocote, así como las fuentes de aguas termales de Zalatitlán, San Gaspar y Atotonilquillo. En la cabecera hay una importante producción de alfarería.

TONALÁ ◆ Río de Veracruz y Tabasco situado en la parte noreste del istmo de Tehuantepec. Nace de la confluencia de los ríos Tancochapa y Zanapa, al norte de Las Choapas; corre 30 kilómetros de sur a norte sobre el límite entre Tabasco y Veracruz y desemboca en el golfo de México, en la barra de Tonalá, al noroeste de la zona arqueológica de La Venta.

TONALÁMATL ◆ Especie de almanaque de fechas destacadas. El nombre significa "papel de los días". Consignaba un lapso de 260 días, dividido en 20 partes de 13 días cada una, llamadas trecenas. Los mexicas llamaban a este cómputo cemilhuitlapohualiztli, "cuenta de fiestas o de días rituales". Algunos autores, como Manuel Orozco y Berra, señalan que los zapotecas fueron los creadores del tonalámatl, al cual llamaban pije o piyé. Otros, sin embargo, entre ellos Alfredo Chavero, le atribuyeron la invención de este calendario ritual a los toltecas. Los códices Borgia, Borbónico y Aubin, entre otros, incluyen algunos tonalámatl.

TONAMECA ◆ Río de Oaxaca que nace en la vertiente meridional de la sierra de Miahuatlán. Corre de norte a sur y desemboca en el océano Pacífico, al oeste de Puerto Ángel, en donde forma la barra de Tonameca. Sus tres últimos kilómetros son navegables.

TONATICO ◆ Municipio del Estado de México situado al sur-suroeste de Tenancingo y al sur de Toluca, en los límites con Guerrero. Superficie: 48.72 km^2. Habitantes: 9,966, de los cuales 2,358 forman la población económicamente activa. Hablan alguna lengua indígena 18 personas mayores de cinco años. En la jurisdicción se hallan las zonas arqueológicas del cerro de la Estrella, Pueblo Viejo y Tonatico. Tiene diversos sitios de interés turístico, como las grutas de la Estrella, la cascada de Tzumparilla y el balneario municipal, con aguas termales. Se han hallado restos fósiles de fauna prehistórica. En la cabecera están el santuario diocesano de la Virgen de Tonatico, iglesia construida en el siglo XVII, y un templo católico que fue edificado en el siglo XVIII.

TONATIUH ◆ Nombre del Sol entre los antiguos nahuas, cuyo nombre significa "el que va dando luz". En el panteón mexica, Tonatiuh o Teotl, era considerado el creador de todas las cosas y causa de ellas. Su culto se extendió por casi toda Mesoamérica.

TONAYA ◆ Municipio de Jalisco situado al este de Autlán de Navarro y al noroeste de Ciudad Guzmán. Superficie: 463.67 km^2. Habitantes: 6,749, de los cuales 1,640 forman la población económicamente activa.

TONAYÁN ◆ Municipio de Veracruz situado al norte de Jalapa y al sureste de Teziutlán. Superficie: 74.03 km^2. Habitantes: 4,563, de los cuales 999 forman la población económicamente activa. Hablan alguna lengua indígena 16 personas mayores de cinco años.

FOTO: ARMANDO HERRERA

Tongolele

TONGOLELE ◆ n. en EUA (1931). Bailarina. Nombre profesional de Yolanda Ivonne Móntez Farrington. A los 15 años decidió dedicarse profesionalmente a la danza, por lo que abandonó el hogar familiar e ingresó al Ballet Internacional de San Francisco. Se inició en 1946, en el Joe Di Maggio Club y luego en el cabaret tahitiano El Huracán. En Los Ángeles, Miguel Valdés la contrató para bailar rumba. Después de actuar en el Hotel Tropics de Tijuana, en 1947 se presentó en el Distrito Federal en la Arena Coliseo y en el Teatro Tívoli, donde causó verdadero furor. Organizaciones de padres de familia, mujeres devotas y ministros eclesiásticos, en nombre de la decencia, trataron inútilmente de impedir sus presentaciones. Ella misma eligió su nombre, mitad africano y mitad tahitiano. Fue amiga de Elías Nandino, quien la introdujo en los círculos intelectuales mexicanos. Se inició en el cine en *Nocturno de amor* (1947), a la que siguieron *Han matado a Tongolele* (1948), *El rey del barrio* (1949), *Amor de locura* (1952), *El misterio del carro express* (1952), *Mátenme porque me muero* (1956), *Música de hoy y de siempre* (1956), *Las mujeres pantera* (1966), *El crepúsculo de un dios* (1968), *Las noches del Blanquita* (1981), *La mujer de otro, Chucho el remendado, La mujer viviente, Las fabulosas del reventón I y II* y *Superespectáculos del mundo*, entre otras. Actuó en el extranjero en las cintas *Cherchez la Femme* (en Alemania), *Rey del terror* (España), *Biombo chino* (Italia), *El detective* (Argentina) y *Snake People* (EUA, última película de Boris Karloff). También ha trabajado en televisión.

TONILA ◆ Municipio de Jalisco situado al sur de Ciudad Guzmán y al sureste de Autlán, en los límites con Colima. Superficie: 293.89 km^2. Habitantes: 7,386, de los cuales 2,098 forman

FOTO: CARLOS HAHN

Parroquia de Tonatico, Estado de México

Toña la Negra

la población económicamente activa. El 24 de diciembre de 1859, durante la guerra de los Tres Años, en territorio del municipio se produjo una batalla en la que los conservadores Miguel Miramón, José María Moreno y Miguel Quintanilla derrotaron a los liberales Juan N. Rocha, Leandro Valle, Manuel García Pueblita y Antonio Rojas.

TONTO ◆ Río de Veracruz y Oaxaca. Nace con el nombre de Altotoco en la vertiente oriental de la sierra de Zongolica, al sur de Orizaba. Corre hacia el sureste, paralelamente a la sierra, desde la que es alimentado con numerosos afluentes, el Petlapa y el Tilpan, entre ellos; con el nombre de río Tonto entra a Oaxaca y surte la presa Miguel Alemán, de la que sale hacia el este, recibe al arroyo de Enmedio y al río Amapa. Parte de su curso marca el límite entre ambos estados y, finalmente, se une al río Santo Domingo, al noreste de Tuxtepec, para formar el Papaloapan.

Fausto Topete

TOÑA LA NEGRA ◆ n. en Veracruz, Ver., y m. en el DF (1912-1982). Cantante. Su nombre era María Antonia del Carmen Peregrino. En 1922 ganó un concurso para aficionados de una estación radiofónica de Veracruz. Llegó a la ciudad de México en 1929. Comenzó a cantar en el Centro de Dependientes y en el Teatro Variedades. Inició su carrera profesional hacia 1933, en el Teatro Iris y en el Teatro Politeama. Más tarde se presentó en la estación radiofónica XEW. Grabó más de 30 discos. Apareció, entre otras, en las películas *Payasadas de la vida* (1934), *María Eugenia* (1942) y *La mulata de Córdoba* (1945). Interpretó sobre todo canciones de Agustín Lara, de las cuales algunas de las más conocidas son *Veracruz, Mujer, Pecadora, Noche de ronda* y *Revancha*.

TOOR, FRANCES ◆ n. y m. en EUA (1890-1956). Periodista. Estudió periodismo y literatura en la Universidad de California. Llegó a México en los años veinte y se dedicó a estudiar algunas de las costumbres y tradiciones mexicanas. Entre 1925 y 1933 editó mensualmente la revista bilingüe *Mexican Folkways*, en la que colaboraron, entre otros, Diego Rivera, José Clemente Orozco y David Alfaro Siqueiros. Autora de *Español fácil para sus visitas a México y Cuba* (1926), *Nueva Guía de México* (1930), *A Treasury of Mexican Folkways* (1947) y *Three Worlds of Peru* (1949). El gobierno mexicano la condecoró con la Orden del Águila Azteca.

TOPELSON, SARA ◆ n. en el DF (1947). Arquitecta. Es egresada de la UNAM, en la que ha sido profesora. También ha ejercido la docencia en la UAM, la Universidad Anáhuac y la Academia Internacional de Arquitectura de Sofía, Bulgaria. Autora de numerosos proyectos entre los que se cuentan edificios de interés social y la Casa de Cultura de Huayamilpas. Ha sido secretaria de Relaciones Internacionales de la Federación de Colegios de Arquitectos de la República Mexicana y consejera de varias sociedades y federaciones de arquitectos. Pertenece a la Academia Nacional de Arquitectura y la Academia Mexicana de Arquitectura. Ha sido vicepresidenta y presidenta de la Unión Internacional de Arquitectos (1996-99). Premio a la Excelencia Académica de la Universidad Anáhuac. Ganó el Concurso Nacional de Modernización de Espacios Educativos (1990). Mujer del Año por el Patronato Nacional de la Mujer del Año (1996).

TOPETE, BONIFACIO ◆ n. en Guadalajara, Jal., y m. en la ciudad de México (¿1835?-1896). Militar. Formó parte de las fuerzas liberales durante la guerra de los Tres Años. Combatió la intervención francesa. Defendió Puebla en 1863 y luego de la derrota de las fuerzas de Jesús González Ortega fue apresado y conducido a Francia, de donde escapó poco después y regresó a México. Al triunfo de la República fue gobernador y comandante militar del territorio de Baja California. Ascendido a general de brigada en 1894, murió cuando acababa de ser nombrado oficial mayor de la Secretaría de Guerra.

TOPETE, FAUSTO ◆ n. en Álamos, Son., y m. en Mexicali, BC (1890-1954). Era empleado de una tienda cuando, en 1913, se incorporó a las fuerzas de Benjamín Hill, a cuyo estado mayor perteneció (1915). Realizó la campaña de pacificación en el río Mayo, en 1916, y más tarde fue comandante militar de Álamos. En 1920 se adhirió al Plan de Agua Prieta y en 1923 combatió la rebelión delahuertista. Elegido gobernador constitucional de Sonora para el periodo 1927-31, en 1929 se separó del cargo y se levantó en armas contra el gobierno de Emilio Portes Gil. Fue derrotado en Naco y en Mariaca (abril de 1929) y bombardeado en Hermosillo (abril de 1929). Se exilió en Estados Unidos.

TOPETE DEL VALLE, ALEJANDRO ◆ n. y m. en Aguascalientes, Ags. (1908-1999). Historiador y cronista. Maestro normalista. Impartió clases de historia y antropología en la Universidad Autónoma de Aguascalientes y el Colegio Militar. Miembro del PRI , fue diputado local. Fue historiador y cronista vitalicio de la ciudad de Aguascalientes y fundó la Casa de Cultura de la ciudad, posteriormente convertida en el Instituto Cultural Aguascalientes. Miembro del

Seminario de Cultura Mexicana y las academias Nacional de Historia y Geografía y Mexicana (de la Lengua). Recibió la Medalla de Plata del Reconocimiento Francés, Las Palmas de la Academia Nacional de Historia y Geografía y de la Academia de Historia y Geografía de Aguascalientes y la Medalla Ignacio Manuel Altamirano.

Topia ◆ Municipio de Durango situado al noroeste de Santiago Papasquiaro y al suroeste de Guanaveci. Superficie: 1,617 km². Habitantes: 8,808, de los cuales 2,123 forman la población económicamente activa. Hablan alguna lengua indígena 15 personas mayores de cinco años. El actual territorio municipal fue habitado originalmente por los acaxees, que fueron conquistados por los españoles en la segunda mitad del siglo XVI. Al descubrirse yacimientos minerales en la región, la minería se convirtió en la principal actividad económica, sustentada en la explotación de los acaxeés, quienes en 1591 se levantaron en armas acaudillados por un grupo de hechiceros que los impulsaron a acabar con la religión católica que había sido introducida por los conquistadores. Los indios tomaron los reales de Topia y San Andrés y destruyeron medio centenar de templos católicos, pero a fines de ese año fueron derrotados por un contingente enviado por el gobierno de Nueva Vizcaya. Diez años más tarde, sin embargo, los acaxees volvieron a insurreccionarse y durante tres años resistieron las ofensivas de las fuerzas virreinales y los intentos negociadores del obispo de Guadalajara, Alonso de la Mota y Escobar, pero en 1604 fueron derrotados y diezmados por los españoles. De fines de 1930 a principios de 1931, el municipio de Topia estuvo incorporado al de Canelas.

Topilejo ◆ Pueblo de la delegación de Tlalpan, Distrito Federal, situado al sur de la ciudad de México, en las estribaciones de la sierra del Ajusco. Fue fundado 600 o 700 años a.n.e., por grupos de filiación otomí que comenzaron a practicar la agricultura en el sur del valle de Anáhuac. Hacia el siglo XIII, la población fue ocupada por los xochimilcas y más tarde por los mexicas. A partir de la conquista española, el pueblo quedó bajo la jurisdicción de Tlalpan (☛). A fines de 1929, en los alrededores de Topilejo ocurrió el asesinato de por los menos un centenar de militantes vasconcelistas, jóvenes obreros, estudiantes y veteranos de la revolución en su mayoría, que habían sido apresados luego de las elecciones de 1929. En 1968, en Topilejo, una brigada de jóvenes universitarios que participaban en el movimiento estudiantil de 1968 (☛) creó una comuna socialista que desapareció después de la matanza del 2 de octubre, en Tlatelolco.

Topiltzin ◆ Deidad nahua de las siembras de temporal, también llamado Piltzintli, "dios niño". Se le consideraba primogénito de la primera pareja humana.

Topiltzin ◆ n. en Tepoztlán, en el actual estado de Morelos (?-?). Su nombre completo era Ce Acatl Topiltzin y fue el último rey tolteca. Acerca de la vida de este personaje existen versiones diferentes y aun contradictorias. Después de su muerte fue divinizado e identificado con el dios Quetzalcóatl. Era hijo del rey tolteca Mixcóatl y de Chimalma. Huérfano de padre desde antes de nacer y de madre desde su alumbramiento, fue educado por sus abuelos maternos en la región que ahora es el valle de Morelos. Cuando creció, un grupo de toltecas fue a ofrecerle el trono de su padre; Topiltzin aceptó y se dirigió al cerro de la Estrella, donde fundó una ciudad capital de los toltecas. Aproximadamente en el año 856 fundó la ciudad de Tullan (Tula) que se convirtió en su nueva capital. Otras versiones señalan que Topiltzin gobernó a los toltecas entre 1111 y 1116 y que era hijo del rey Tecpancaltzin. La leyenda que más tarde se tejió en torno a este personaje señala que enseñó a su pueblo todos los adelantos científicos (agricultura, astronomía, arquitectura, medicina) y predicó la moderación, la prohibición de los sacrificios humanos y la penitencia. Como los toltecas de Tullan convivían con los chichimecas, adoradores del dios guerrero Tezcatlipoca, el pacifismo de Topiltzin, sacerdote de Quetzalcóatl, no fue bien visto y este rey fue expulsado de la ciudad. La mitología dice que Topiltzin se embriagó y, avergonzado, huyó hacia el oriente, se metió al mar en una balsa hecha de serpientes y aseguró que algún día regresaría a recuperar sus posesiones. Otro mito señala que Topiltzin, luego de su expulsión de Tullan, se inmoló en una gran pira, de la que surgió convertido en Venus, estrella de la mañana o estrella del atardecer, astro que para los nahuas era Quetzalcóatl.

Topolobampo ◆ Puerto del municipio sinaloense de Ahome (☛).

Toral, Francisco de ◆ n. en España y m. en la ciudad de México (1501-1571). Fraile franciscano. Llegó a la Nueva España en 1542. Fundador del convento de Tecamachalco. Fue provincial de su orden (1557-59) y obispo de Yucatán (1562-1571). En Mérida tuvo conflictos con Diego de Landa y sus compañeros franciscanos. Autor de un *Arte y vocabulario de la lengua popoloca o totonaca*.

Toral, José de León ◆ ☛ *León Toral, José de*.

Toral, María Teresa ◆ n. en España (1912). Grabadora. Estudió en la Escuela de Artes y Oficios de Madrid (1936). Llegó a México en 1959. Formó parte del Taller de Grabado de la

A la víbora de la mar, obra de María Teresa Toral

Foto: Ana Lourdes Herrera

Regina Torné

José María Tornel y Mendívil

Alfonso Toro

Libro de Alfonso Toro publicado en 1949

Ciudadela (1959-63) y fue discípula de Isam Ishukawa y Yukio Fukazawa (1963). Expuso por primera vez en 1963. Sus obras se han presentado en Checosolovaquia, Chile, España, Estados Unidos, Holanda e Israel. En 1972 recibió una mención honorífica del Salón de la Plástica Mexicana.

Toraya Baqueiro, José Manuel ◆ n. en Mérida, Yuc. (1948). Licenciado en derecho por la UNAM. Hizo estudios de posgrado en el IPADE. Afiliado al PRI desde 1967, ha sido asesor de campañas electorales en su estado y del CEN de ese partido, así como secretario general del Comité Directivo Estatal y miembro del Consejo Político Estatal. Ha tenido cargos en el Ayuntamiento de Mérida y ha sido director de la Comisión Ordenadora del Uso del Suelo en Yucatán, director general de la Comisión de Regularización de la Tenencia de la Tierra, director del Registro Agrario Nacional, regidor secretario del municipio de Mérida y senador de la República (1994-2000). Ha sido consejero de la Cámara Nacional del Autotransporte.

Torcacita, La ◆ n. en Tequila, Jal., y m. en el DF (1924-1988). Nombre profesional de la cantante Matilde Sánchez Elías. Después de ganar un concurso radiofónico de aficionados, formó con su hermana Fausta el dueto Las Tapatías. Como solista grabó más de 50 discos. Entre las canciones que le dieron popularidad se cuentan *Aires del Mayab, Dos arbolitos* y *Virgencita de Talpa*. Actuó en el cine al lado de Pedro Armendáriz en *Juan Charrasqueado*, de Pedro Infante en *Cuidado con el amor* y de Fernando Casanova en *El hombre del alazán*.

Toriz Cobián, Alfonso ◆ n. en Juchiltán, Jal. (1913). Sacerdote ordenado en 1939. Estudió en el Seminario Conciliar de Guadalajara y en la Universidad Gregoriana de Roma. Profesor del Seminario Conciliar de Guadalajara. Fue asesor de la Asociación Católica de la Juventud Mejicana y de la Juventud Católica Femenina Mexicana en Guadalajara. Ha sido coadjutor del obispo de Chilapa (1954-56), obispo de Chilapa (1956-58) y obispo de Querétaro (1958-).

Torné, Regina ◆ n. en Villahermosa, Tab. (1944). Actriz. Su verdadero nombre es Rosa Vierben del Pilar Marina Incháustegui Anaya. Comenzó su carrera cinematográfica en los años sesenta y ha actuado en cerca de 40 películas, entre las que destacan *Nosotros los jóvenes* (1965), *Despedida de soltera* (1965), *Adiós cuñado* (1966), *El as de oros* (1967), *Los hijos de Satanás* (1971), *Viento salvaje* (1972), *Tiempo y destiempo* (1975) y *Como agua para chocolate* (1990, Ariel a la mejor actuación femenina en 1992). Como cantante y animadora ha trabajado en televisión, y también ha participado en obras de teatro.

Tornel y Mendívil, José María ◆ n. en Orizaba, Ver., y m. en la ciudad de México (1789-1853). Militar. Realizó estudios en el Seminario de Tehuacán. Se incorporó a las tropas insurgentes de Epitacio Sánchez en 1813 y más tarde sirvió en Michoacán, a las órdenes de Ramón López Rayón. En marzo de 1814 fue detenido por los realistas y condenado a muerte, pero se salvó gracias a la intervención de Ignacio Arévalo. Estuvo preso en México, Puebla y Orizaba, donde volvió a colaborar con la insurgencia, y en 1821 se adhirió al Plan de Iguala. Fue secretario particular de Antonio López de Santa Anna (1821) y del presidente Guadalupe Victoria (1824-29), gobernador y comandante militar del Distrito Federal (1828-29) enviado del presidente Victoria para parlamentar con los rebeldes de la Acordada (1828), diputado federal (1827-28 y 1829-30), enviado extraordinario y ministro plenipotenciario de México en Estados Unidos (1829-31), oficial mayor de la Secretaría de Guerra (1832), secretario de Guerra y Marina (1833) en el gobierno de Santa Anna y nuevamente gobernador del Distrito Federal (1833-34). A partir de entonces, fue secretario de Guerra y Marina en los gabinetes de Santa Anna (1834-35, 1839, 1841-42, 1843, 1844, 1853), Miguel Barragán (1835-36), José Justo Corro (1836), Anastasio Bustamante (1838-39), Nicolás Bravo (1839, 1846), Valentín Canalizo (1843-44) y Mariano Paredes y Arrillaga (1846). Estuvo encargado del despacho de la Secretaría de Relaciones Exteriores en el primer gobierno de Bustamante (1839) y fue director del Colegio de Minería (1843-53). Fue uno de los primeros traductores mexicanos de Lord Byron. Autor de *La muerte de Cicerón, Tejas y los Estados Unidos de América en sus relaciones con la República Mexicana* (1837) y *Breve reseña histórica de los acontecimientos más notables de la Nación Mexicana* (1852).

Toro, Alfonso ◆ n. en Zacatecas, Zac., y m. en el DF (1873-1952). Se tituló de abogado en el Instituto de Ciencias de Zacatecas (1898). Profesor de la Universidad Nacional. Fue agente del Ministerio Público en Zacatecas y en la ciudad de México, magistrado del Tribunal Superior de Justicia del DF, presidente de la comisión encargada de reformar los códigos Penal y de Procedimientos Penales de Aguascalientes, diputado federal (1918-20) y jefe del Departamento de Etnografía de la Dirección de Antropología y Arqueología de la SEP. Fundador y director de la *Revista Zacatecana* y de los periódicos *El Tribuno* y *El Estado*, de Zacatecas. Colaboró en los diarios *Excélsior* y *El Nacional* y en *Zig-Zag, Revista de Revistas* y *Don Quijote*. Autor del prólogo y las notas de los *Breves apuntes de la pintura en México*, de Agustín F. Villa. Compilador de *Los judíos en la Nueva España* (1932) y autor de *El origen del hombre en América y su vida en los tiempos prehistóricos, Importancia del estudio de la historia, Métodos de investigación histórica, Breves apuntes sobre iconografía de algunos héroes de la independencia, Biografía de Agustín Rivera y Sanromán, El gran cardenal Francisco Jiménez de Cisneros y la cultura española, La Iglesia y el Estado en México, La familia Carvajal, Estudio histórico sobre los judíos en la Nueva España (1944), La Inquisición en la Nueva España en el siglo XVI, Un crimen de Hernán Cortés* (1922), *Dos constituyentes del año de 1824: biografías de D.*

Miguel Ramos Arizpe y D. Lorenzo Zavala (1925) *Compendio de historia de México* (1926), *Historia de la Suprema Corte de Justicia de la Nación* (1934).

Toro, Carlos ◆ n. en Zacatecas, Zac., y m. en el DF (1875-1914). Escritor y periodista. Hermano del anterior. Escribió en *El Universal, El Imparcial, El País* y *El Tiempo*. Estuvo en prisión por sus colaboraciones de tono antiporfirista en *Tilín-Tilín* y *Diógenes*. Autor de *La cárcel de Belén, La fórmula Díaz-Corral y el porvenir de la República* (1913), *La caída de Madero por la revolución felicista* (1913), *Vencedores y vencidos* (1916) y *Pedruscos recogidos en la sombra* (1938).

Toro, Francisco de Paula ◆ n. en Nueva Granada, hoy Colombia, y m. en Tlacotalpan, Ver. (1799-1840). Militar. Era cuñado de Antonio López de Santa Anna. En 1834 era comandante militar de Yucatán y se levantó en armas contra el gobierno del vicepresidente Valentín Gómez Farías. Fue gobernador de Yucatán en dos ocasiones (1834-35 y 1835-37).

Toro, Guillermo del ◆ n. en Guadalajara, Jal. (1964). Cineasta. Realizó estudios de efectos especiales y maquillaje con Dick Smith y de guión con Jaime Humberto Hermosillo, con quien colaboró en 1985 en la producción de *Doña Herlinda y su hijo* y filmó el cortometraje *Doña Lupe*. También fundó Necropia, empresa de maquillaje y efectos especiales cuyo trabajo ha destacado en *Cabeza de Vaca* (1990), *Mi querido Tom Mix* (1991) y *Cronos* (1991), primera película de Del Toro (Ariel en ópera prima, guión, argumento, dirección y mejor película en 1993 y Gran Premio y Premio al Mejor Actor del Festival de Oporto 1994). En Hollywood dirigió *Mimic* (1997).

Toros ◆ La primera corrida de toros que se celebró en la Nueva España, cuando la lidia se realizaba a caballo y el toro era muerto con una lanza, fue el 24 de junio de 1526. Las reses que se emplearon descendían del ganado traído a Veracruz después de la destrucción de México-Tenochtitlan. La corrida fue organizada por los miembros del ayuntamiento de la ciudad de México para celebrar el regreso de la expedición de Hernán Cortés a las Hibueras. En julio de 1528, el cabildo metropolitano dispuso que cada año, con motivo de las fiestas de San Hipólito, San Juan y Santiago, "se corran toros (.) so pena de diez pesos de oro", y en agosto de 1529, la Audiencia de la Nueva España, entonces presidida por Nuño Beltrán de Guzmán, ratificó la decisión. La primera ganadería de reses bravas que hubo en México fue fundada por Juan Gutiérrez Altamirano, el futuro conde de Santiago de Calimaya, quien estableció la Hacienda de Atenco en el valle de Toluca e importó varios sementales navarros. Poco después se establecieron otras ganaderías como la de Peredo y la de los Salcedos. La crianza de reses bravas se extendió por algunas regiones del virreinato, particularmente en Tlaxcala y, desde principios del siglo XVII, en las regiones septentrionales. Como en España, los aristócratas de la colonia conservaron una gran afición por la fiesta y así, por ejemplo, el virrey Luis de Velasco toreaba todos los sábados en Chapultepec, lo que contribuyó a difundir el gusto por la fiesta entre la población. Hasta fines del siglo XVII la fiesta estuvó limitada a los caballeros, pero en los pueblos se acostumbraba organizar pequeñas corridas durante las celebraciones religiosas. Como los españoles realizaban corridas casi con cualquier motivo, desde la llegada de un virrey hasta las victorias del ejército español en Europa, el gusto por mirar los enfrentamientos entre toros y notables aumentó de manera considerable. En los primeros años de la Colonia, las corridas se celebraban en ruedos improvisados que se construían en la plazuela del Marqués y en las plazas de los marqueses de Santa Fe de Guardiola y de los Palos, así como en las faldas del cerro de Chapultepec. De todos los cosos, cuya existencia duraba sólo un par de meses, el más importante fue el de la Plaza del Volador, donde se realizaban las corridas oficiales, a las que asistían con toda pompa las corporaciones civiles y religiosas. En el verano de 1611, el virrey García Guerra organizó varias corridas en los patios del palacio virreinal. En el siglo XVII, los toreros de a caballo comenzaron a adornar sus trajes con remaches de plata y todo tipo de hilos brillantes, con lo que prefiguraron el traje de luces y la indumentaria charra. Hacia 1690, el torero más célebre en la ciudad de México era Francisco Goñi de Peralta, quien, como la inmensa mayoría de los practicantes, provenía de las familias más distinguidas de la aristocracia novohispana. Sin embargo, los nuevos reyes borbones, franceses de nacimiento y afrancesados por convicción, que se instalaron en el gobierno de España al inicio del siglo XVIII, no sentían aprecio por la fiesta y la marginaron de sus actividades sociales, por lo que el gusto por las corridas decreció considerablemente en las colonias. El fenómeno fue aprovechado por los aficionados pobres que carecían de caballos y que intervenían en la fiesta desde 1680, aunque de manera subalterna, quienes comenzaron a figurar en las corridas de manera cada vez más destacada hasta que, en 1722, durante las fiestas de recepción al virrey Juan de Acuña, el marqués de Casafuerte, una cuadrilla de "toreadores" de a pie figuró como atractivo principal en la Plaza del Volador. Este hecho permitió el estallido de *chulos*, que era como se conocía a los andantes, al grado de que durante el resto de la dominación europea y durante el siglo XIX, en todas las ferias o con cualquier pretexto, en la mayoría de los pueblos del virreinato se celebraron corridas de toros. Durante la segunda mitad del siglo XVIII, los inmigrantes españoles se convirtieron en los toreros más célebres y el más renombrado de todos fue Tomás Venegas, apodado *el Gachupín Toreador*, quien introdujo en México algunas de las normas del toreo español. Otros matadores de la época fueron Pedro Montero, Juan Sebastián *el Jerezano*, Alonso Gómez *el Zamorano* y Miguel García, natural de Querétaro, que quizá fue la primera figura ameri-

Carlos Toro

Foto: Colección Gustavo García

Guillermo del Toro

Actividad taurina durante el último siglo de la Colonia

cana. Hasta entonces, salvo las ceremonias de la lidia propiamente dicha adoptadas de España, la actividad taurina carecía de cualquier reglamentación, pero en 1770, el ayuntamiento de la ciudad de México publicó un bando en el que dispuso que, salvo los toreros, "ninguna persona, de cualquier edad o condición" podría permanecer en la arena mientras se celebraran las corridas, ni tampoco nadie "será osado de picar los toros (.) con espada, garrocha, púas o jaretas, ni entrar a la plaza a vender dulces, pasteles, bebidas ni alguna otra cosa", so pena "de un año de destierro a los nobles, cien azotes a los de color quebrado, y de dos meses de cárcel para los españoles". A mediados de los años ochenta, el virrey Bernardo de Gálvez intentó reanimar el toreo como actividad cortesana, pero la influencia borbónica entre los aristócratas novohispanos había menguado o desaparecido su interés por la fiesta. Los pocos jóvenes que se sumaron al entusiasmo taurófilo de Gálvez optaron por cubrirse los rostros con máscaras, para evitar el bochorno público. Por otra parte, desde los primeros años de esa década, la Real y Pontificia Universidad de México inició una campaña para que se retirara el coso de la Plaza del Volador, pues impedía casi totalmente la entrada a la casa de estudios, sobre todo en tiempos de lluvias, y la aglomeración de comerciantes en el angosto callejón que quedaba entre el coso y la Universidad producía un bullicia que alteraba el orden académico. Desde luego, la afición de las autoridades universitarias estaba fuera de duda, pues aun en las épocas de mayor apremio económico, los miembros del claustro universitario ocupaban localidades preferentes, que resultaban muy caras. En 1788, el gobierno de la ciudad mandó edificar una plaza permanente, construida con madera, que se llamó Real Plaza de Toros de San Pablo, por estar en la Plaza de San Pablo, situada cerca del actual Hospital Juárez, y maniobró para que las plazas temporales se instalaran en las afueras de la ciudad, sobre todo en el recién abierto Paseo de Bucareli. Los borbones, no por consideración a los toros, sino porque la juzgaban una actividad primitiva, mantuvieron su hostilidad contra la tauromaquia y, en 1805, el rey español Carlos IV prohibió la realización de corridas en sus dominios, medida que, por supuesto, se acató pero no se cumplió. Uno de los infractores fue Ignacio Allende, entonces capitán del Regimiento Provincial de Dragones de la Reina, que a mediados de 1810 participó en una corrida realizada para celebrar la consagración del Santuario de Guadalupe en San Luis Potosí, a la cual asistieron, como espectadores, el militar Félix María Calleja, comandante de las tropas españolas de la Nueva España, y el sacerdote Miguel Hidalgo y Costilla, que era dueño de tres haciendas en las que criaba ganado bravo. De acuerdo

ARCHIVO XAVIER ESPARZA

Anuncio de corrida de toros realizada para obras de caridad a finales del siglo XIX

con algunos historiadores, al terminar la corrida, Hidalgo y Allende intentaron convencer a Calleja de que se sumara a la conspiración independentista de Querétaro, pero, por lo que sucedió después, es evidente que sus coincidencias se limitaban a la pasión por la fiesta. A fines de ese año, por lo menos dos toreros se incorporaron a las fuerzas insurgentes, comandadas por el ganadero Hidalgo: en octubre, Agustín Marroquín, un español que había formado parte del séquito del virrey José de Iturrigaray y que se encontraba detenido en Guadalajara, fue liberado por el ejército de José Antonio *el Amo* Torres y participó en la batalla del Puente de Calderón; fue detenido y fusilado en Acatita de Baján en 1811. También a fines de 1810, Juan José Luna, un matador novohispano que

Corrida de toros a principios del siglo XIX

NUEVA EMPRESA
"EL TOREO," S. A.

Foto: Archivo General de la Nación

Grupo de empresarios que construyeron la Plaza El Toreo a principios del siglo XX

había actuado en la ciudad de México, se sumó a las fuerzas de Hidalgo y más tarde a las de Luis Mier y Terán, para quien capturó, a mediados de 1815, a Juan Nepomuceno Rossains. En julio de 1815, el virrey Calleja, que necesitaba dinero para enfrentar a los insurgentes, reconstruyó la Plaza de San Pablo, la convirtió en dependencia del gobierno y comisionó su administración a Ramón Gutiérrez del Mazo, quien controló el coso hasta fines de la década de 1810. Dos años después de la consumación de la independencia, el gobernador del Distrito Federal, Luis Quintanar, publicó el primer reglamento taurino completo, que, como su similar de Aguascalientes de 1839, dispuso subastar la exclusividad de los ganaderos. El reglamento sólo se aplicó en las plazas temporales, pues en ese mismo año se incendió la Plaza de San Pablo. En los primeros años del México independiente, el toreo se volvió muy impopular, debido sobre todo a que los sentimientos antiespañoles se exacerbaron, lo que en 1832 llevó a las autoridades de Guadalajara a prohibir las corridas. La procedencia peninsular de la fiesta, sin embargo, no fue la única razón que convocó a los opositores del toreo, sino también su inutilidad económica, argumento que fue utilizado por el cubano José María de Heredia, entre otros, quien escribió que era preferible utilizar a las reses bravas como bestias de trabajo en la agricultura. Diez años duró el declive del toreo hasta que, en abril de 1835, se reconstruyó la Plaza de San Pablo para recibir al español Bernardo Gaviño Rueda (1812-1886), que ya era célebre en Cuba y que se convertiría en la principal figura taurina del segundo tercio del siglo. Además de ser el primero que utilizó en México un traje de luces cordobés y el primer torero formado a la española, Gaviño incorporó parte de la técnica local y su estilo influyó en varios toreros mexicanos, como Mariano Rodríguez *la Monja* y Pablo Mendoza. Sin embargo, sólo unos pocos matadores se adaptaron al ritual importado, pues era menos vistoso y circense que el improvisado aquí, y la mayor parte de los toreros siguió colocando banderillas con cohetes que estallaban al momento de fijarse en el lomo del toro o permitiendo que subalternos a caballo derribaran al animal por la cola. Quizá por el estruendo de las banderillas, por el ajetreo de los caballos o por las lluvias, para 1848 la Plaza de San Pablo se hallaba en pésimo estado, casi toda la madera estaba podrida y el gobierno decidió cerrarla. Dos años después, el coso volvió a funcionar, pero ya muy deteriorado, por lo que el presidente José Joaquín de Herrera decidió abrir una nueva plaza permanente, construida en el extremo norte del Paseo de Bucareli, en el sitio donde actualmente se encuentra el antiguo edificio de la Lotería Nacional. La inauguración fue en noviembre de 1851. La Plaza de San Pablo, por su parte, funcionó hasta 1864. Durante la primera mitad del siglo, los principales empresarios taurinos fueron José María López de Nava y los hermanos Luis y Sóstenes de Ávila, que fueron particularmente activos en la Feria de San Marcos en Aguascalientes. Con el ascenso de los liberales al poder, a mediados de los años cincuenta, la tauromaquia perdió el apoyo oficial del que hasta entonces había gozado, porque los liberales, de los cuales sólo Ponciano Arriaga, Santos

Archivo Xavier Esparza

Toreros en imagen publicada en *El Mundo Ilustrado* en 1897

Foto: Archivo General de la Nación

Plaza de toros el Toreo de la Condesa, en la ciudad de México

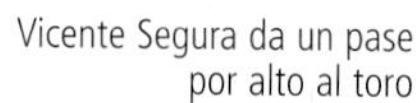

Vicente Segura da un pase por alto al toro

Foto: Archivo General de la Nación

Foto: Archivo General de la Nación

Cuadrilla de toreros se prepara para dar el paseíllo en corrida de toros de 1939

Degollado y Miguel Negrete eran taurófilos conocidos, vieron en el toreo una reminiscencia del pasado colonial e iniciaron una larga campaña contra la fiesta brava, que sin embargo amainó en ciertos momentos, como en 1862, cuando incluso el presidente Benito Juárez organizó algunas corridas destinadas a recabar fondos para resistir la intervención extranjera. En noviembre de 1867, meses después del triunfo de la República, el propio Juárez ordenó la publicación de un decreto por el que quedaron prohibidas las corridas de toros en el Distrito y Territorios Federales. En los tres años siguientes, casi todas las legislaturas estatales siguieron el ejemplo del gobierno federal y a principios de los años setenta el toreo estaba prohibido en casi todo el país. A partir del triunfo del Plan de Tuxtepec, el gobierno porfirista adoptó una política tolerante y permitió el resurgimiento de la fiesta, aunque en el estado de Oaxaca continuó vigente la prohibición que databa del juarismo. En 1887, finalmente, el gobierno capitalino permitió la celebración de corridas y la gente volvió a la Plaza de San Rafael, fundada un año antes, y más tarde se concentró en las de Colón, Paseo y Coliseo, levantadas en 1887. La plaza de la Hacienda de los Morales fue construida en 1888. El reestablecimiento de la fiesta permitió a los toreros mexicanos alcanzar gran popularidad, pero ninguno fue tan conocido como *el Charro* Ponciano Díaz, un antiguo discípulo de Gaviño, quien luego de una década como profesional pudo sufragar los gastos que transformaron el coso de Bucareli en la primera plaza de mampostería de México (1888). Además, la fama del *Charro* Díaz estaba tan extendida, que en 1889 fue contratado para actuar en España. Como era el primer matador mexicano que se presentaba en la península, actuó vestido de charro y con un gran bigote. Por entonces, las principales ganaderías eran El Berenjenal, El Desierto, Chamuco, La Cieneguilla, El Capulín, Torreón y El Venadero. En los últimos años de gobierno de Porfirio Díaz, comenzaron a actuar dos de los toreros más importantes nacidos en México. Uno, el principal, fue Rodolfo Gaona, *el Califa de León* o *el Indio Grande*, que recibió la alternativa en 1905 y que, entre otras cosas, inventó el pase de capa que se llama *gaonera*. El otro fue Vicente Segura, profesional desde 1907 pero que interrumpió brevemente su carrera en 1910, para incorporarse a la rebelión maderista. Quizá influido por los liberales, de los que casi era contemporáneo, el presidente Venustiano Carranza prohibió las corridas de toros en la ciudad de México entre 1916 y 1920, pero los sonorenses que lo desplazaron del gobierno reestablecieron la fiesta en la capital, que durante esa década se concentró en el Toreo de la Condesa. También durante los años veinte, la actividad taurina comenzó a ser seguida de manera sistemática por la prensa. En 1923, el diario *El Universal Taurino* instituyó el premio *La Oreja de Oro*. Tres años después, en 1926, Armando de Maria y Campos fundó la revista *El Eco Taurino*, que, debido al impulso de Abraham Bitar y Alfonso de Icaza Green, su principal cronista, en 1928 se transformó en *El Redondel* (1928-87), periódico en el que se hicieron famosas las crónicas del propio Icaza Green, "Puyas y Pinchazos", que eran firmados por *Ojo*. En los años veinte comenzaron a torear Pepe Ortiz *el Orfebre Tapatío* (1925), Fermín Espinosa *Armillita* (1926) y Silverio Pérez, *el Faraón de Texcoco* (1928), quienes, con Luis Castro *el Soldado* (1933) y Lorenzo Garza (1935), célebres además por sus *mano a mano* en España, dominaron la tauromaquia nacional en los años treinta y los primeros cuarenta. Pese a la presencia de esas figuras, a fines de los años treinta todavía sobrevivían espec-

Ases mexicanos del toreo: Fermín Espinosa Armillita, Alberto Balderas, Jesús Solórzano, Lorenzo Garza, Luis Castro *el Soldado* y Silverio Pérez

Foto: Boris de Swan

Trajes de torero

La fiesta de los toros, tradicional en México

táculos exóticos como el que se presentó en el Estadio Nacional en ocubre de 1939, que consistió en enfrentar un toro contra un oso. El exilio republicano español no aportó figuras importantes al toreo mexicano, pero en cambio contribuyó con Pepe Alameda, cronista radiofónico desde 1941, quien durante 40 años reseñó corridas en México y España. Durante el gobierno de Manuel Ávila Camacho se dispuso que una parte de las ganancias de las plazas se destinaran a la asistencia pública. Durantre los años cuarenta se profesionalizaron Carlos Arruza (1940), Luis Procuna (1943), Manuel Capetillo (1948) y Joselito Huerta. En febrero de 1946, mientras tanto, se celebró la primera corrida en la Plaza de Toros México, en el DF, en la que participaron Luis Castro *el Soldado*, Manuel Rodríguez *Manolete* y Luis Procuna. El coso, situado en el sur de la ciudad de México, tiene 45,000 localidades y se dice que es el mayor del mundo. En los sesenta se iniciaron Manolo Martínez (1965), Eloy Cavazos (1966) y *Curro* Rivera (1968), y en los setenta Mariano Ramos (1972), Manolo Arruza (1973), Miguel Espinosa *Armillita Chico* (1977) y Jorge Gutiérrez (1978). En 1987 había 232 plazas fijas.

El pase de pecho, lance taurino

TORQUEMADA, JUAN DE ◆ n. en España y m. en la ciudad de México (¿1557?-1624). Llegó a la Nueva España hacia 1560. Ingresó a la Orden de Franciscanos Menores en 1579 y posiblemente estudió con Bernardino de Sahagún. Guardián del convento de Santiago de Tlatelolco (1600-09) y director del Colegio de la Santa Cruz de Santiago de Tlatelolco, entre 1603 y 1610 dirigió la construcción del templo católico de Santiago, contiguo al convento. En 1607, luego de una de la más grandes inundaciones de la ciudad de México (☛), participó en la recostrucción de las calzadas de los Misterios, de San Cristóbal y de Chapultepec, así como de las represas de Zumpango y Citlaltépetl. Fue cronista de la orden de San Francisco (1609), guardián de los conventos de Zacatlán y Tlaxcala (1612) y gobernador de la provincia franciscana del Santo Evangelio (1614-17). En 1615 publicó, en Sevilla, *Los veintiún Libros Rituales i Monarchía Indiana, con el origen y guerras de las Indias Occidentales, de sus poblaciones, descubrimientos, conquistas, comercio y otras cosas maravillosas de la misma tierra*, obra redactada con información recogida en los conventos franciscanos y los relatos de algunos indios sobrevivientes a la conquista. Además, fue autor de una *Vida de Fray Sebastián de Aparicio* (1600) y de varias obras de teatro en náhuatl. Póstumamente apareció un tomo con sus *Opúsculos* (1622).

Juan de Torquemada

Miguel Espinosa *Armillita Chico*, torero mexicano

TORRE, GERARDO DE LA ◆ n. en Oaxaca, Oax. (1938). Escritor. Estudió teatro con Carlos Ancira y Rodolfo Valencia. Formó parte del taller literario de

Foto: Rogelio Cuéllar

Gerardo de la Torre

Juan José Arreola. Trabajó 18 años como obrero en la refinería de Azcapotzalco. Militó en el PCM. Ha sido guionista de *Plaza Sésamo* (1972-81), *Tony Tijuana*, *Hora marcada* y otros programas. Investigador del Centro de Estudios Históricos del Movimiento Obrero, director de la Casa del Lago de la UNAM (1985), profesor de la Sogem (1990-) y coordinador del taller de guiones del Centro de Capacitación Cinematográfica. Ha colaborado en periódicos y revistas. Sus textos han sido incluidos en las antologías *Narrativa joven de México* (1969), *Onda y escritura en México* (1971) y *Dos siglos de cuento mexicano* (1979). Coautor de *De los tres ninguno* (1975, cuentos), *El hombre equivocado* (1988, novela) y *Ruiz Massieu: el mejor enemigo* (1995, reportaje). Autor de *El otro diluvio* (1968), *El vengador* (1973), *Viejos lobos de Marx* (1981), *Relatos de la vida obrera* (1988), *La lluvia en Corinto* (1993), *Tobalá y otros mezcales oaxaqueños* (1998), *Ensayo general* (1970), *La línea dura* (1971), *Muertes de aurora* (1980), *Hijos del águila* (1989), *Los muchachos locos de aquel verano* (1994, Premio de Novela José Rubén Romero 1992) y *Morderán el polvo* (1999); y la autobiografía *Gerardo de la Torre. De cuerpo entero* (1990). Premio del Festival Cinematográfico de La Habana por su guión *Los niños de Morelia* (1997). Becario del Centro Mexicano de Escritores (1967-68). Pertenece al Sistema Nacional de Creadores (1994-).

Torre, Juan de la ◆ n. en España (?-?). Llegó a la Nueva España en 1525, procedente de Santo Domingo, donde había desempeñado diversos cargos en el gobierno de Diego Colón. Fue regidor (1525 y 1528) y alcalde ordinario de la ciudad de México (1526, 1527 y 1532).

Torre, Juan de la ◆ n. en Tacámbaro, Mich., y m. en el DF (1852-1920). Su apellido materno era Hurtado. Abogado titulado en el Colegio de San Nicolás de Hidalgo (1875). Fue director de la Biblioteca del Colegio Nicolaíta, director de la Biblioteca Pública de Morelia (1874), juez de letras en Zinapécuaro (1875-81), oficial mayor de gobierno de Michoacán (1881-85) y diputado federal (1875 y 1885-1910). En su Biblioteca Jurídica Mexicana publicó, anotados y comentados, *Constitución federal de 1857*, *Código de renta del timbre*, *Legislación de patentes de marcas*, *Código mexicano de minería* y el *Texto vigente de la Constitución mexicana*. Autor de *Historia y descripción del Ferrocarril Nacional Mexicano*, *Historia y descripción del Ferrocarril Central Mexicano*, *Guía para el estudio del derecho constitucional mexicano*, *Crónica de la inauguración de la calzada construida en el lago de Cuittzeo*, *Lecciones de moral*, *Bosquejo histórico-estadístico de la ciudad de Morelia* (1883), *Compendio de geografía de México*, *Geografía universal*, *El amigo de los niños mexicanos* y *El amigo de las niñas mexicanas*.

Torre, Luis de la ◆ n. en España (?-?). Hermano de Juan de la Torre. Fue regidor (1526), alcalde ordinario (1528, 1538 y 1544) y alcalde de mesta de la ciudad de México (1545).

Torre, Nicolás de ◆ n. en la ciudad de México y m. en Cuba (?-1653). Doctor en filosofía por la Real y Pontificia Universidad de México, de la que fue rector en dos ocasiones (1628-29 y 1639-40). Canónigo y deán de la catedral metropolitana y obispo de Honduras y de Cuba (1644-53). Autor de un capítulo del libro *Viaje de tierra y mar que hizo el Excmo. marqués de Villena* (1640).

Torre Abedrop, Rafael de la ◆ n. en Concepción del Oro, Zac. y m. en el DF (1932-1993). Licenciado en economía por la UNAM (1959). Hizo estudios de administración pública en París (1963). Fue secretario del ayuntamiento de Naucalpan (1964-65), director de licencias sanitarias de la SSA (1965-69), administrador de rentas en Naucalpan y Tlalnepantla (1969-71), presidente municipal de Naucalpan (1971-72), director general del Programa de Regeneración de la Zona Oriente del Estado de México (1974-75) y delegado del DDF en Miguel Hidalgo (1977-82). Fue director general de la empresa Arrendadora de Carros de Ferrocarril.

Torre Bermúdez, José María ◆ n. en España y m. en el DF (1922-1981). Fotógrafo cinematográfico. Llegó a México en 1948. Realizó estudios de medicina en la UNAM y de antropología en la ENAH (1944- 47). Profesor del CUEC de la UNAM. Se inició en la fotografía como ayudante del Noticiero Clasa y más tarde fue camarógrafo de la Compañía Cinematrográfica Teleproducciones (1951-53). Fue secretario de la Asociación Nacional de Productores de Cortometrajes (1967-74). Hizo foto fija para agencias publicitarias (1953-60) y en 1967 instaló su propia empresa, Servicios Fotográficos Torre, que dirigió hasta su muerte. Además de varios documentales para la CFE, realizó el cortometraje *El mes más cruel* y dirigió la fotografía de la película *El balcón vacío* (1961) y del cortometraje *Remedios Varo* (1966), ambos realizados por Jomi García Ascot.

Torre Blanco, José ◆ n. en España (1895-?). Médico titulado en la Universidad Central de Madrid (1918). Fue jefe del servicio de ginecobstetricia de la Maternidad Provincial de Madrid (1919), inspector médico general del Seguro de Maternidad del Instituto Nacional de Previsión (1932-37), profesor de la Universidad Central de Madrid (1934-36) y secretario de la sección médica de la editorial Calpe. Durante la guerra civil española trabajó en el Cuerpo de Sanidad de Carabineros. Luego de la derrota de la República Española (1939) se exilió y en 1940 se naturalizó mexicano. Profesor del IPN, del Hospital Juárez, del Hospital Militar y del Hospital General. Ha sido jefe del servicio de ginecobstetricia del Sanatorio de los Trabajadores de la Educación (1951) y jefe de la División de Ginecobstetricia del Hospital 20 de Noviembre del Instituto de Seguridad y Servicios Sociales para los Trabajadores del Estado (1959). Autor de *Obstetricia para comadronas* (1922), *La mujer, el amor y la vida* (1940) y *Uno de tantos* (1976). Miembro fundador de la Sociedad Mexicana de Ginecología y Obstetricia.

Torre Díaz, Álvaro ◆ n. en Mérida, Yuc. (1889-1944). Médico graduado en Mérida y posgraduado en París. Fue oficial mayor y secretario general de gobierno del estado de Yucatán, embajador en Brasil, agregado comercial de México en Washington, encargado provisional de la embajada mexicana en Estados Unidos (del 6 de junio al 3 de julio de 1920) y gobernador constitucional de Yucatán (1926-30).

Torre Grajales, Abelardo de la ◆ n. en Chiapa de Corzo, Chis., y m. en el DF (1913-1976). Fue secretario general del sindicato de la Secretaría de Hacienda y Crédito Público, diputado federal, secretario general de la Federación de Sindicatos de Trabajadores al Servicio del Estado, senador de la República (1958-64), oficial mayor y subsecretario de la Secretaría de Patrimonio Nacional (1964), secretario de organización del CEN del PRI (1960-64) y jefe de los Servicios Generales del Instituto Mexicano del Seguro Social. Perteneció a la Sociedad Mexicana de Geografía y Estadística.

Torre Lapham, Fernando ◆ n. en el DF (1918). Maestro, director y actor de teatro. Estudió en la Escuela de Iniciación Artística de Peralvillo. Fundador, junto con Francisco Monterde, Ana Mérida y Clementina Otero, de la Escuela de Arte Teatral del INBA (1946), donde ha sido profesor y director en dos ocasiones. Fundador del teatro universitario en Morelos y en la UV. Inició su carrera como actor con las obras *Los Alzados* de Luis Octavio Madero y *Volpone o el zorro* de Ben Jonson. Ha dirigido obras de Luisa Josefina Hernández, Federico Inclán y Rafael Bernal, entre otros, y dirigió la Compañía Nacional de Teatro de 1956 a 1958. Ha sido maestro de actores por más de 55 años, en especialidades y materias como esgrima, expresión verbal, análisis de textos dramáticos y actuación, e impartido clases en el CUT, la UV, el Centro de Capacitación Artística de Televisa, el Centro Cultural Virginia Fábregas y el Foro Teatro Contemporáneo. También ha participado en las películas *Donde el círculo termina* (1955), *En cualquier parte del mundo* (1993), *Sin remitente* (1994) y *Santitos* (1999). Fue becario del Centro Mexicano de Escritores (1955-56).

Torre Lloreda, Manuel de la ◆ n. y m. en Pátzcuaro, Mich. (1786-1836). Sacerdote ordenado en 1801. Estudió en el Seminario de Valladolid y en la Real y Pontificia Universidad de México. Profesor del Seminaro de Valladolid y párroco de Santa Clara del Cobre. En 1808 fue acusado de simpatizar con el movimiento independentista de la ciudad de México y encarcelado brevemente en el convento del Carmen de Valladolid. Fue párroco de Santa Clara del Cobre (1812-20) y de Pátzcuaro (1820-36) y diputado al primer Congreso Constituyente de Michoacán (1824). Colaboró en los periódicos *El Michoacano Libre* y *El Astro Moreliano*. Tradujo obras de los latinos Tibulo, Catulo, Propercio y Metastasio y *Las Vigilias* de Torcuato Tasso (1827).

Torre y Rabasa, Mario de la ◆ n. en el DF (1921). Editor. Hizo estudios de posgrado en la Universidad de Pittsburgh. Ha sido vicepresidente de Cartón y Papel de México. Se ha dedicado a la edición de libros de arte de gran formato, entre los que destacan *Los calendarios mexicanos* (1973), *El México de Guadalupe Victoria* (1974), *Artes Gráficas Panamericanas* (1980, premio de la Feria Industrial del Libro de Leipzig, 1982), *Chapultepec* (1988), *Las castas mexicanas* (1989) y *Testimonios de viaje. 1823-1873* (1989). Fue premiado en la Feria del Libro de Frankfurt en 1992.

Torre Repetto, Carlos ◆ n. y m. en Mérida, Yuc. (1904-1978). Ajedrecista. En 1915 se estableció con su familia en Nueva Orleans, donde fue discípulo de E. Z. Adams. En 1922 ganó el campeonato local y al año siguiente el del estado de Louisiana. En 1924 ganó el campeonato de Nueva York y el Western Championship y derrotó a David Janowsky en una partida de exhibición. En 1925, en un torneo en Baden Baden, quedó tablas con Alekhine; compitió en el torneo internacional de Marienbad, donde quedó en tercer lugar, y en el internacional de Moscú, en el que derrotó a Emmanuel Lasker con una jugada de su invención, llamada *la lanzadera*, y poco después empató con José Raúl Capablanca para quedar en quinto lugar. Siguió participando en torneos el año siguiente, pero una crisis nerviosa, aunada a una frágil salud, insomnio y mala alimentación, lo retiró de las competencias definitivamente. Autor de *El desarrollo de la habilidad del ajedrecista*. Fue nombrado Gran Maestro Internacional por la Federación Internacional de Ajedrez en 1979.

Carlos Torre Repetto

Torre Ruiz, Luis de la ◆ n. en Mezquitic, Jal. (1932). Caricaturista y dibujante. Se inició en el diario de Guadalajara *El Informador*. En la capital del país fue ilustrador de *El Cuento, Contenido, La Capital* y *Caballero*. Cartonista de la revista *Hoy* (1965-75). Ingresó en 1976 en la casa *Excélsior*, donde ha sido ilustrador de la sección "Ideas" y del suplemento *El Búho*, cartonista editorial de *Últimas Noticias* y *Revista de Revistas*. Una muestra de 200 de sus cartones se ha exhibido en diversas ciudades del país. Participó en el II Salón Internacional de la Caricatura (Bruselas, 1988). Ha presentado exposiciones individuales en el DF, Cuernavaca, Guadalajara y Acapulco. Es suyo *El Quijote lector*, mural en cerámica que se halla en el Museo Franz Mayer. Premio Nacional de Periodismo 1987.

Torre y Ulivarri, Alfonso de la ◆ n. en Aguascalientes, Ags., y m. en Agua Fría, Son. (1908-1935). Ingresó en la Asociación Católica de la Juventud Mejicana en 1918. Fue presidente de las delegaciones de la ACJM en Tampico (1920) y Magdalena (1920). Vivió en Estados Unidos a mediados de los años veinte y volvió a México en 1929. En ese mismo año fundó en Sonora un grupo de católicos llamado Agustín de Iturbide y en 1935 se levantó en armas contra el gobierno de Lázaro Cárdenas. Murió en combate.

Torre Villar, Ernesto de la ◆ n. en Tlatlauqui, Pue. (1917). Historiador. Licenciado en derecho y maestro y doc-

Ernesto de la Torre Villar

tor en historia. Estudió en la UNAM, El Colegio de México, la ENAH y la Universidad de París. Profesor de la UNAM y de otras instituciones de enseñanza superior. Fue subdirector del Archivo General de la Nación (1945-48). Ha sido director del Archivo Histórico de la Secretaría de Hacienda (1951-54), director del Instituto de Investigaciones Bibliográficas de la UNAM (1965-78) e investigador del Instituto de Investigaciones Históricas de la misma universidad. Colabora en *Excélsior* y otras publicaciones. Autor de *El nacimiento entre los pueblos prehispánicos* (1944), *El triunfo de la república liberal* (1960), *La Constitución de Apatzingán y los creadores del Estado mexicano* (1965), *El triunfo de la República y el fin del Imperio* (2 t., 1967-70), *Lecturas históricas mexicanas* (5 t., 1965-71), *Fray Pedro de Gante, maestro y civilizador de América* (1973), *Códice Mendocino* (1978), *La biografía en las letras históricas mexicanas* (1980), *Mexicanos ilustres* (1980), *La expansión hispanoamericana en Asia. Siglos XVI y XVII* (1980), *Los grabados de la "Historia antigua de México" de Francisco Javier Clavijero* (1980), *La doctrina cristiana en lengua castellana de fray Pedro de Gante* (1981), *Testimonios guadalupanos* (1982), *La independencia mexicana* (1982) y *Breve historia del libro en México* (1987), entre otros. Secretario de la comisión de historia del Instituto Panamericano de Geografía e Historia y presidente del Comité Internacional de Ciencias Históricas (1985-). Miembro de la Academia Mexicana (de la Lengua), de la Sociedad Mexicana de Geografía y Estadística, el Seminario de Cultura Mexicana, la Sociedad de Historia Moderna y Contemporánea de Francia, la Academia Mexicana de la Historia y el Sistema Nacional de Investigadores. Ha recibido los premios Elías Sourasky (1965), Nacional de Artes y Ciencias en la rama de Historia (1987), Universidad Nacional (1987) y Puebla (1995).

TORREA, JUAN MANUEL ♦ n. en Ciudad Victoria, Tams., y m. en el DF (1874-1960). Estudió en el Colegio Militar. Profesor de la Escuela de Maestros Constructores y del Colegio Militar. Se incorporó al Ejército Mexicano en 1895. Fue jefe de los archivos de la Secretaría de Relaciones Exteriores. Perteneció a las fuerzas de Venustiano Carranza, donde alcanzó el grado de general. Autor de *Las virtudes del guerrero mexicano, Apuntes de geografía e historia militares, La asonada militar de 1913, La Polonia guerrera, Diccionario geográfico, histórico, biográfico y estadístico de la República Mexicana, Las banderas históricas, La vida de una institución gloriosa, El reclutamiento del ejército, Entre el pasado y entre los muertos, El Colegio Militar, La lealtad en el Ejército Mexicano* y *La decena trágica.* Fue secretario y presidente de la Asociación del Colegio Militar y presidente de la Sociedad Mexicana de Geografía y Estadística, del Ateneo Nacional de Ciencias y Artes y de la Asociación Mexicana de Historia y Geografía.

TORREBLANCA, JUAN NEPOMUCENO ♦ n. y m. en el DF (1878-1960). Músico y compositor. En 1920 fundó la Orquesta Típica de México, más tarde conocida como Orquesta Típica Presidencial Torreblanca.

TORREBLANCA, MARCELO ♦ n. y m. en el DF (1907-1986). Estudió la carrera de educación física. Profesor de la Academia de la Danza Mexicana del Instituto Nacional de Bellas Artes. Formó parte del Teatro Sintético y de las Misiones Culturales de la Secretaría de Educación (1931-35). Fue director de la Compañía de Danza Tradicional de la Academia de la Danza Mexicana, colaborador del Fondo Nacional para el Desarrollo de la Danza Mexicana y asesor de la Escuela Nacional de Danza Folclórica del INBA. Autor de la coreografía de la ópera *Tata Vasco* y de la obra *Cuauhtémoc.*

TORREBLANCA CONTRERAS, FERNANDO ♦ n. y m. en el DF (1895-1980). Empleado de los Ferrocarriles Nacionales de México desde 1910. Hacia 1915 era secretario particular de Alberto J. Pani, director de los Ferrocarriles Constitucionalistas de México. En 1916 se incorporó al Ejército del Noroeste y trabajó en la Secretaría de Guerra y Marina. Fue secretario particular de Álvaro Obregón (1917-24), de Plutarco Elías Calles (1924-28) y Emilio Portes Gil (1929-30); visitador de Consulados (1930-32) y subsecretario de Relaciones Exteriores en el gobierno de Pascual Ortiz Rubio (1932-33). Acompañó al ex presidente Elías Calles en su destierro en Estados Unidos y más tarde fue presidente de la Junta de Asistencia Privada para el Distrito y Territorios Federales (1947-77) y vicepresidente de la Asociación Cívica General Álvaro Obregón.

TORREBLANCA GALINDO, ZEFERINO ♦ n. en Guadalajara, Jal. (1955). Desde su infancia se trasladó a Acapulco. Contador Público por el ITESM, especializado en finanzas en Londres. Empresario, propietario de Operadora Togal. Ha dirigido la Canaco local. Fundador (1987) y director (1990) de la Coparmex de Acapulco, diputado federal (1994-97) y presidente municipal de Acapulco por el PRD (1999-2002).

TORREBLANCA REYES, MAGÍN C. ♦ n. en Huajuapan de León, Oax. (1929). Sacerdote ordenado en 1953. Asistente de la Acción Católica de Puebla. Ha sido cura de San Martín Texmelucan y, en Texcoco, auxiliar del obispo (1973-77), administrador apostólico (1977-78) y obispo (1978-).

TORREBLANCA Y TAPIA, LUCIO ♦ n. en Huajuapan de León, Oax., y m. en Durango, Dgo. (1894-1961). Sacerdote ordenado en 1922. Estudió en el Seminario de Huajuapan de León y en la Universidad Gregoriana de Roma. Fue profesor, vicerrector y rector del Seminario de Huajuapan, obispo de Chiapas (1944-59) y obispo de Durango (1959-61).

TORREJÓN, ÁNGELES ♦ n. en el DF (1963). Fotógrafa. Licenciada en ciencias de la comunicación por la UAM. Fue editora del periódico *Tiempo de niños* de la SEP. Ha sido fotógrafa de *La Jornada* (1990) y reportera gráfica (1987-89) y coordinadora (1991-) de la agencia Imagen Latina. Su trabajo ha aparecido

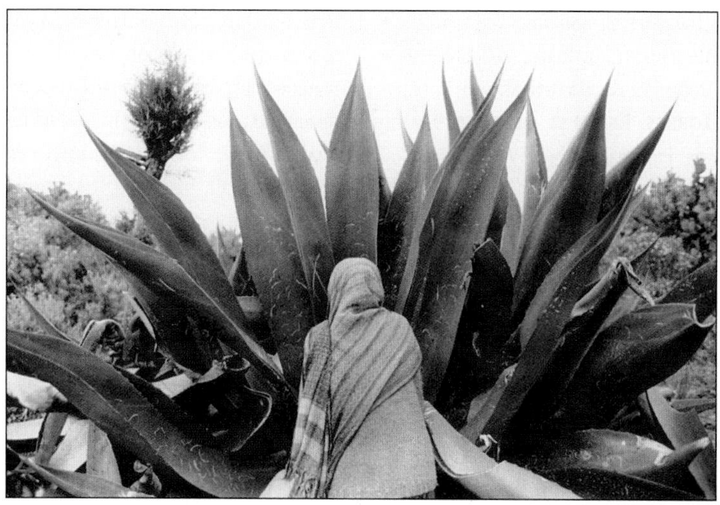

Buenavista, Otumba, Estado de México, fotografía de Ángeles Torrejón

en *Proceso*, *La Jornada*, *El Economista*, *México Indígena*, *Voz y Voto*, *Por Esto*, *Voices of Mexico* y *Luna Córnea*, entre otras publicaciones, y ha sido incluido en los libros *La fotografía de prensa en México. 40 reporteros gráficos* (1992), Primera bienal de fotoperiodismo (1994) y *La mirada inquieta. Nuevo fotoperiodismo mexicano 1976-1996* (1996). Ha participado en exposiciones individuales y colectivas en México y otros países. Premio "Mujeres vistas por mujeres" (1990), en Venezuela. Mención honorífica en el Premio de Periodismo Cultural Fernando Benítez (1997) y la segunda Bienal de Fotoperiodismo (1997). Primer lugar en el Concurso de Fotografía Antropológica del INAH (1997). Becaria del Fonca (1993-94).

Torrente, Mariano ◆ n. en España y m. en Cuba (1792-1856). Historiador. En 1809 salió de España, a causa de la invasion francesa. Se trasladó a la Gran Bretaña y ahí conoció a Agustín de Iturbide, quien le proporcionó numerosos materiales sobre la historia de México. En 1843 se estableció en La Habana. Autor de una *Historia general de la revolución hispanoamericana* (1829) y de un *Mapa de la provincia de Venezuela, Reino de Santa Fe y Nueva España* (1831). Luego de su muerte apareció su *Historia de la independencia de México* (1918).

Torreón ◆ Municipio de Coahuila situado al suroeste de Cuatrociénegas y al oeste de Saltillo, en los límites con Durango. Superficie: 1,947.70 km². Habitantes: 508,076, de los cuales 151,796 forman la población económicamente activa. Hablan alguna lengua indígena 437 personas mayores de cinco años (náhuatl 168). Entre los siglos IX y XV de la época contemporánea, el actual territorio municipal fue habitado por un grupo de matarajes, indios nómadas del grupo irritila, de cuya presencia subsisten, en la sierra de Noas, situada en la porción meridional del municipio, textiles, calzado, cordelería vegetal y de pelo, cestas, arcos, puntas de flecha, piezas de pedernal y varios petroglifos que no han podido ser descifrados. Durante la segunda mitad del siglo XVI los franciscanos intentaron la evangelización del territorio. Desde 1730, la actual jurisdicción del municipio fue parte del marquesado de San Miguel de Aguayo. En 1812, los terrenos de la margen suroriental del río Nazas se incorporaron al recién creado municipio de Matamoros de la Laguna. En 1825, el sexto marqués de San Miguel de Aguayo vendió esas tierras a las compañías británicas Baring Brothers & Company y Staples & Company. Los ingleses, sin embargo, se vieron obligados a ceder a sus acreedores los terrenos, que en 1840 los vendieron a la familia Sánchez Navarro, propietaria de grandes latifundios en Coahuila y Durango. Ocho años después, en 1848, las antiguas propiedades del marqués de San Miguel de Aguayo fueron adquiridas por el español Leonardo Zuloaga, quien en 1850 mandó construir una torre cerca del río Nazas, con el triple propósito de permitir la construcción de un dique que impidiera las inundaciones, de vigilar las crecidas y proteger a los vecinos de las incursiones chichimecas. Poco después, El Carrizal, rancho de Zuloaga, comenzó a ser conocido como El Torreón. A principios de los años ochenta, poco después de la muerte de Zuloaga, el rancho de El Torreón comenzó a ser administrado, en nombre de la viuda, por el alemán Andrés Eppen von Aschenborn, quien en 1883 autorizó el paso del ferrocarril México-Ciudad Juárez. La nueva vía aumentó el valor de la tierra y el número de habitantes. En 1888, para permitir la construcción del entronque entre el ferrocarril Durango-Monterrey y el México-Ciudad Juárez, Eppen fraccionó el rancho, sobre un diseño realizado por Federico Wulff. En ese mismo año, los presbiterianos comenzaron a actuar en la zona y poco después, siempre promovidos por la presencia de los estadounidensese empleados en el ferrocarril, proliferaron diversos grupos protestantes: en 1894 llegaron los bautistas y en 1902 los metodistas. El 25 de febrero de 1893 el pueblo se erigió en Villa del Torreón, aunque permaneció dentro de la jurisdicción de Matamoros de La Laguna. Hasta 1893 se construyó el primer templo católico en la localidad. En 1902 se tendió la vía

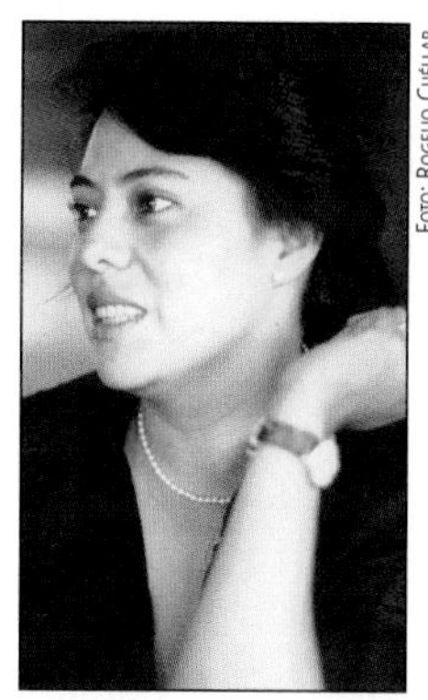

Foto: Rogelio Cuéllar

Ángeles Torrejón

Plaza de Armas de Torreón, Coahuila

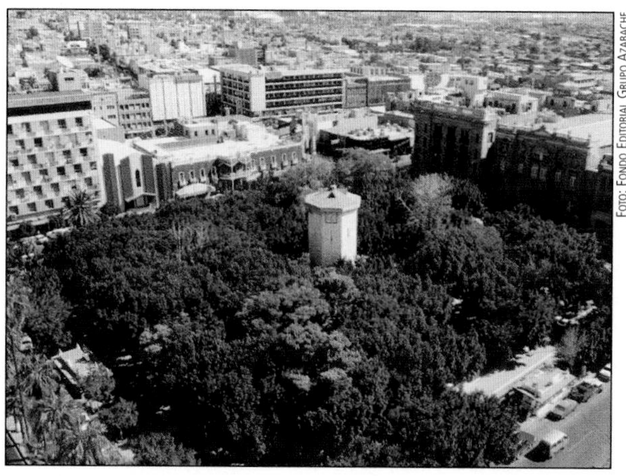

Foto: Fondo Editorial Grupo Azabache

del ferrocarril Torreón-Saltillo, con lo que aumentó la importancia estratégica y comercial de la villa, e incluso se estableció un Banco Chino. El 15 de septiembre de 1907, la Legislatura coahuilense otorgó a Torreón el rango de ciudad. En mayo de 1911, fuerzas maderistas al mando de Sixto Ugalde, Orestes Pereyra y Agustín Castro derrotaron a los federales de Emiliano Lojero. El primero de octubre de 1913, luego de dos días de combates, la División del Norte ocupó la ciudad, con lo que desarticuló la ofensiva huertista contra el norte del país, pero se retiró poco después. A fines de marzo de 1914, los villistas contraatacaron y luego de 14 días de combates, el 2 de abril desalojaron a los federales. El 4 de julio, Francisco Villa y unos representantes de Venustiano Carranza firmaron un documento conocido como Pacto de Torreón, mediante el cual, la División del Norte reconoció la autoridad presidencial de Carranza, a condición de que éste no tratara de intervenir en la conducción militar de la división, que quedaría a cargo de Villa. Los firmantes reformaron el Plan de Guadalupe cuando establecieron que al triunfo del levantamiento constitucionalista, el presidente interino debería convocar de inmediato a elecciones presidenciales, en las cuales no podrían participar los jefes militares vencedores; y dispusieron la desaparición del Ejército Federal, que sería sustituido con las divisiones del Norte y del Noroeste. En diciembre de 1916, las menguadas fuerzas villistas ocuparon por última vez Torreón, aunque sólo pudieron retenerla pocos días, a causa del hostigamiento carrancista. A partir del gigantesco reparto agrario realizado en La Laguna (☛) por el presidente Lázaro Cárdenas en 1936, la producción agropecuaria permitió que la ciudad se convirtiera en un importante centro bancario y comercial. En 1957 se erigió la diócesis de Torreón.

Efrén *el Alacrán* Torres

Torres, Adolfo ◆ n. en Monterrey, NL (1950). Actor, director y dramaturgo. Profesor de la Universidad Autónoma de Nuevo León. Coautor de *Amor se dice a veces* y *Tres historias y un concierto*; y autor de *El ególatra*, *Amor eterno* y *¡Todas queremos ser reinas!*

Torres, Efrén *el Alacrán* ◆ n. en Las Palmas, Mich. (1943). Boxeador. Inició su carrera profesional en 1957, en Guadalajara, y en su primera pelea, contra Félix Padilla, venció por nocaut. En febrero de 1969, en el Distrito Federal, derrotó al tailandés Chartai Chionoi y se coronó campeón mosca del Consejo Mundial de Boxeo. Un año después, en marzo de 1970, perdió el campeonato frente al propio Chionoi.

Torres, Felizardo ◆ n. en El Fuerte, Sin., y m. en Álamos, Son. (1848-1906). Estudió en el Liceo de Sonora. Fue regidor del ayuntamiento de Álamos (1875), director de la Casa de Moneda de Sonora (1877-78), tesorero del comité organizador del Instituto Científico y Literario, diputado a la Legislatura local, socio de la minera La Sonorense, concesionario para instalar el alumbrado en Hermosillo y gobernador interino de Sonora (19 de diciembre de 1882 al 31 de agosto de 1883).

Torres, José Antonio ◆ n. en Cocupano, Mich., y m. en la Hacienda La Tlachiquera, cerca de Silao, Gto. (¿1770?-1818). Estudió en el Seminario de Valladolid. Era vicario de Cuitzeo del Porvenir en 1810, cuando se incorporó a las tropas insurgentes de Albino García, con quien participó en la toma de Valladolid de junio de 1811. Ascendido a mariscal en 1814, en diciembre de ese año fue derrotado por las tropas de Agustín de Iturbide en la Hacienda de Cuerámano, pero en marzo de 1815, ya recuperado, tomó Irapuato y La Piedad y poco después mandó construir el fuerte de los Remedios, en los alrededores de Pénjamo, que convirtió en su cuartel general. En marzo de 1816 fue nombrado vocal de la Junta Subalterna Gubernativa (☛) y poco después del traslado de la asamblea a Jaujilla, ésta lo designó teniente general de las tropas insurgentes, grado que conservó hasta 1817, cuando el mando se le otorgó a Francisco Javier Mina. Resentido por el desplazamiento, mantuvo una tensa relación con Mina y, según se dice, intentó sabotear la expedición internacionalista. En noviembre, muerto Mina, reasumió el cargo de comandante. En enero de 1818 capituló ante los realistas que sitiaban el fuerte de los Remedios y aunque consiguió escapar de los españoles, en abril fue destituido como jefe de los insurgentes por la Junta Subalterna instalada en Puruándiro, por lo que desconoció a este órgano y designó como gobernante a Ignacio Ayala. Durante el resto del año, perseguido por las tropas virreinales de Anastasio Bustamante y desconocido por los propios insurgentes, mantuvo una pequeña fuerza que, sin embargo, era la única independentista que sobrevivía en Guanajuato. Murió asesinado por el capellán Juan Manuel Zamora, aparentemente por una deuda de juego.

Torres, José Antonio *el Amo* ◆ n. en San Pedro Piedra Gorda, hoy Manuel Doblado, Gto., y m. en Guadalajara, Jal. (¿1755?-1812). Era mayordomo de una hacienda cercana a Irapuato cuando, en septiembre de 1810, se incorporó a las fuerzas de Miguel Hidalgo, quien lo comisionó para insurreccionar el sur de Nueva Galicia. En octubre de ese año tomó Sayula y en noviembre derrotó a los realistas en Zocoalco y ocupó Guadalajara. Durante la batalla del Puente de Calderón (enero de 1811) dirigió la retaguardia insurgente y tras el triunfo de las fuerzas coloniales marchó al norte. En abril, con Ignacio López Rayón, tomó Zacatecas y, más tarde, solo, La Piedad y Tacámbaro. En mayo de 1811 participó en el ataque contra Valladolid y desde entonces operó en los alrededores de Pátzcuaro y Uruapan. Aunque miembro formal de la Junta de Zitácuaro, nunca asistió a las reuniones y en su lugar envió a Remigio Zarza. Capturado por los realistas en abril de 1812 en Palo Alto, cerca de Tupátaro, y conducido a Guadalajara, en mayo de ese año fue juzgado, condenado a muerte, ahorcado y descuartizado.

TORRES, JUAN ◆ n. en Celaya, Gto. (¿1946?). Músico. Hizo estudios informales de piano y órgano. Se hizo famoso en la década de los setenta por sus grabaciones de baladas y música ligera en versiones instrumentales, en los discos de la serie *Juan Torres y su órgano melódico*.

TORRES, JUAN MANUEL ◆ n. en Minatitlán, Ver., y m. en el DF (1938-1980). Director de cine y escritor. Llegó al Distrito Federal en 1955. Dos años después, en la revista *Futuro*, publicó sus primeros cuentos. Más tarde colaboró en *Cuadernos del Viento* y *Revista de la Universidad*. Entre 1962 y 1968 estudió cine en Lodz, Polonia. A su regreso a México estudió en la Escuela Teatral del INBA. Perteneció al PCM y colaboró en *Nuevo Cine, Snob, Revista de Bellas Artes* y *Revista Mexicana de Literatura*. Hizo traducciones del polaco. Dirigió un episodio de la película *Yo, tú, nosotros* (1970) y los largometrajes *Diamantes, oro y amor* (1971), *La otra virginidad* (1974, Ariel a la mejor película en 1975), *La vida cambia* (1975), *El mar* (1976) y *La mujer perfecta* (1977). Fue incluido en la antología *Onda y escritura en México*, de Margo Glantz (1971). Autor del ensayo *Las divas* (1962), de los volúmenes de cuento *El mar* (1967) y *El viaje* (1969) y de la novela *Didascalias* (1970).

TORRES, JUAN MANUEL DE ◆ n. en Comitán de las Flores, Chis., y m. en Cunduacán, Tab. (?-1870). Fue gobernador interino de Tabasco, del 15 de octubre al 15 de noviembre de 1850.

TORRES, LORENZO ◆ n. en Mochicahui, Sin., y m. en EUA (1836-1912). Militar. Combatió a la intervención francesa y participó en la toma de Álamos (1866). En 1871 se adhirió al Plan de la Noria y en 1876 se levantó en armas contra el gobernador de Sonora, Ignacio Pesqueira; proclamó el Plan de Álamos, pero fue derrotado en Sinaloa. Diputado a la Legislatura de Sinaloa y subinspector de colonias militares en Sonora (1880), durante 20 años combatió a los apaches y a los yaquis de Cajeme y en 1892 participó en la represión de Tomóchic. Elegido gobernador constitucional de Sonora para el periodo 1887-91, en 1888 pidió una licencia y fue nombrado jefe de las tropas del Yaqui. Además, fue comandante militar de Sonora y senador de la República (1898-1910), aunque no ocupó su escaño.

TORRES, LUIS EMETERIO ◆ n. en el mineral de Guadalupe y Calvo, Chih., y m. en EUA (1844-1935). Militar. Combatió la intervención francesa y el imperio. En 1866 participó en la toma de Álamos. Expulsado del ejército en 1868 por haber intentado derrocar al gobierno sinaloense de Domingo Rubí, en 1871 se adhirió al Plan de la Noria; operó en el norte de Sinaloa y el sur de Sonora. Amnistiado a la muerte del presidente Benito Juárez, fue diputado federal (1873-75) y en 1875 se levantó en armas en favor del Plan de Tuxtepec. Cuatro años más tarde, en 1879, encabezó una asonada contra el gobierno de Ignacio Pesqueira y lo derrocó. Fue gobernador de Sonora (1879-81, 1883-87, 1899-1900, 1903 y 1907-11), jefe político y comandante militar de Baja California (1888-94), comandante de la zona militar de Mérida (1893-99) y senador de la República por Morelos aunque nunca ocupó el escaño (1904-08). Al triunfo de la insurrección maderista se exilió en Estados Unidos.

TORRES, MACARIO ◆ n. en Quiroga, Mich., y m. en Valle de Santiago, Gto. (1854-1885). Se tituló de abogado en el Colegio de San Nicolás de Hidalgo, de Morelia, donde ejerció la docencia. Fue profesor del Colegio de Guanajuato, secretario del Juzgado de Letras de Zitácuaro (1878) y del de Tacámbaro, así como funcionario del gobierno de Guanajuato. En 1920 apareció su poemario *Versos*, con prólogo de Pascual Ortiz Rubio.

TORRES, MARCELO ◆ n. en Yahualica, Hgo., y m. en Orizaba, Ver. (1876-1948). Médico titulado en la ciudad de México. Trabajó en el Hospital de la Luz y más tarde en Zongolica. Maderista desde 1910 y carrancista desde 1913. Fue diputado al Congreso Constituyente de 1916-17.

TORRES, MARIANO DE JESÚS ◆ n. y m. en Morelia, Mich. (1838-1922). Escritor. Estudió en el Colegio de San Nicolás. Durante la guerra de los Tres Años colaboró en los periódicos liberales *El Partido Puro, La Sombra de Morelos, La Causa del Pueblo* y *La Idea*. En 1862, en Guadalajara, obtuvo el título de abogado. Fue juez de letras de Ario (1862), La Piedad (1863) y Pátzcuaro (1864). Al triunfo de la República editó el periódico *El Cinco de Mayo*. En 1877 ganó un premio de pintura, con una serie de óleos sobre Valladolid. Fue diputado federal suplente y diputado a la Legislatura michoacana (1882-84), director del *Diario Oficial* del gobierno de Michoacán (1879-85) y director de los periódicos *La Lira Michoacana, La Mujer Mexicana, La Diadema de Gloria* y *El Centinela*. Partidario desde 1902 del antirreeleccionismo, en 1914 fue síndico del ayuntamiento de Morelia. En su imprenta editó *El álbum michoacano, La rosa de Michoacán, Parnaso michoacano, Parnaso español y mexicano* y *El odeón michoacano*. Autor de *El nuevo autor de comedias, La primavera en invierno, La mujer marido, Diccionario de legislación y jurisprudencia michoacana, Diccionario histórico, biográfico, geográfico, estadístico, zoológico, botánico y mineralógico de Michoacán, Historia civil y eclesiástica de Michoacán, El héroe de Dolores o la independencia de México, La aurora de la libertad, Laurel por laurel, Las obras de misericordia, Andrés, el cazador, La fuerza*

Escena de *La mujer perfecta*, filme dirigido por Juan Manuel Torres

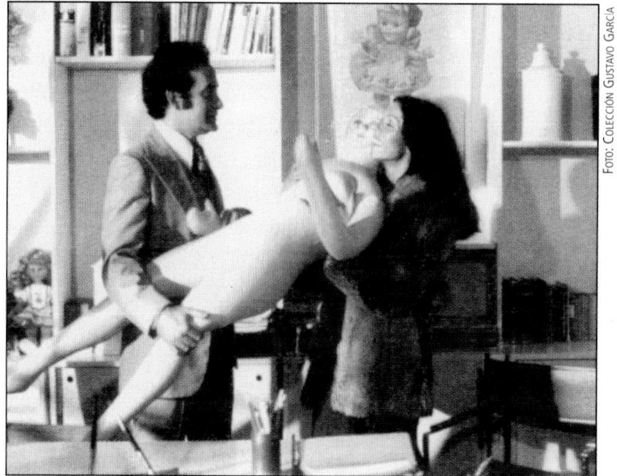

FOTO: COLECCIÓN GUSTAVO GARCÍA

ARCHIVO XAVIER ESPARZA

Casa de Ignacio Torres Adalid en la avenida Juárez de la ciudad de México

del destino, *Los amores de un ángel*, *Un dineral o castillos en el aire* y *La última noche de máscaras*.

TORRES, MORELOS ◆ n. en Zitácuaro, Mich. (1967). Licenciado en historia, con estudios de antropología, en la UNAM. Tomó clases de actuación con Leonid Stein. Fue jefe de redacción de la revista *Escénica*, editor de *La Cabra* y redactor de *La Cultura en México*. Colaborador de diversas publicaciones. Autor de guión cinematográfico: *El futuro ya está aquí* (1987); poesía: *Tierra abierta* (1989); y teatro: *Abecedario* (1987), *Vocabulario* (1987) y *Cuatrocientos puntos* (1990). Ha recibido los premios Punto de Partida (1987), Universitario de Cuento (1988 y 1989) y Carmen Báez (1994). Becario del Centro Mexicano de Escritores (1994-95) y el Fonca (1999-2000).

TORRES, RAIMUNDO *BATTLING* ◆ n. en San Luis Potosí, SLP, y m. en Reynosa, Tams. (1941-1972). Boxeador. Inició su carrera pugilística en 1957. Fue campeón mundial de peso welter entre 1961 y 1964. Perdió el campeonato ante Jorge Rosales. Murió asesinado.

TORRES, TEODORO ◆ n. en Villa de Guadalupe, SLP, y m. en el DF (1891-1944). Periodista y escritor. Llegó a la ciudad de México en 1914 y en ese año se inició en el periodismo. A la caída del gobierno de Victoriano Huerta se exilió en San Antonio, Texas, donde colaboró en *La Prensa*. Volvió a México en 1921. Colaborador de *Excélsior*. Cofundador de la Escuela de Periodismo ahora llamada Carlos Septién García. Fue director de *Revista de Revistas*, *Saber* y *México al Día*. Autor de las novelas *La patria perdida* (1935) y *Golondrina* (1944) y de los textos periodísticos *Pancho Villa: una vida de romance y tragedia* (1924), *Como perros y gatos* (1925), *Orígenes de las costumbres* (1934), *Periodismo* (1937) y *El humorismo y la sátira en México* (1943). En 1941 ingresó en la Academia Mexicana (de la Lengua).

TORRES, VICENTE FRANCISCO ◆ n. en el DF (1953). Escritor. Ha sido profesor universitario y colaborador del suplemento *Sábado* de *unomásuno*. Autor de ensayo: *José Revueltas el de ayer*, *La novela bolero latinoamericana*, *La otra literatura mexicana*, *El cuento policial mexicano* (1982), *Visión global de la obra literaria de José Revueltas* (1985) y *Narradores mexicanos de fin de siglo* (1989, Premio Nacional de Periodismo Cultural 1988), reeditado como *Esta narrativa mexicana* (1991).

TORRES ADALID, IGNACIO ◆ n. en la ciudad de México y m. en Cuba (1836-1914). Empresario. Fue propietario de la Hacienda de San Antonio Ometusco, que era la mayor mayor productora de pulque a fines del siglo XIX. Se exilió en La Habana en 1914, luego de la caída del gobierno de Victoriano Huerta. Una parte de su fortuna la destinó a obras de beneficencia.

TORRES BODET, JAIME ◆ n. y m. en el DF (1902-1974). Escritor. Estudió en la Escuela Nacional de Jurisprudencia y en la Facultad de Altos Estudios de la Universidad Nacional. Fue profesor de la Universidad Nacional y secretario de la Escuela Nacional Preparatoria, secretario del rector José Vasconcelos (1921), codirector de la revista *Falange* (1922-23), jefe del Departamento de Bibliotecas de la Secretaría de Educación (1922-24), secretario de Bernardo J. Gastélum cuando éste era jefe del Departamento de Salubridad (1925-29) y codirector de la revista *Contemporáneos* (1928-31). Entre 1929 y 1943 desempeñó cargos diplomáticos. Fue secretario de Educación Pública (1943-46) en el gobierno de Manuel Ávila Camacho, director de la revista *México y la Cultura* (1946), secretario de Relaciones Exteriores en el gabinete de Miguel Alemán (1946-48), representante mexicano en la reunión constitutiva de la OEA (1948), director general de la UNESCO (1948-52), embajador de México en Francia (1952-58) y nuevamente titular de la SEP en el gobierno de Adolfo López Mateos (1958-64), cuando se inició la publicación de los libros de texto gratuitos. Autor de cuento: *Sombras* (1937); ensayo: *Contemporáneos* (1928), *El escritor en su libertad* (1953), *Tres inventores de la realidad* (1955) y *Patria y cultura* (1964), entre otros; novela: *Margarita de niebla* (1927), *La educación sentimental* (1929), *Proserpina rescatada* (1931), *Estrella de día* (1933) y *Primero de enero* (1934); poesía: *Fervor* (1918), *Canciones* (1922), *El corazón delirante* (1922), *Nuevas canciones* (1923), *Los días* (1923), *La casa* (1923), *Biombo* (1925), *Poesías* (antología, 1926), *Destierro* (1930), *Cripta* (1937), *Sonetos* (1949), *Selección de poemas* (antología, 1950), *Fronteras* (1954), *Sin tregua* (1957), *Trébol de cuatro hojas* (1958) y *Obra poética* (compilación, 1967), entre otros; relato: *Nacimiento de Venus y otros relatos* (1955); y siete volúmenes de memorias (1955-74). Perteneció a El Colegio Nacional, el Instituto de Francia y a las academias Mexicana (de la Lengua) y del Mundo Latino. Premio Nacional de Letras 1966.

FOTO REFORMA

Jaime Torres Bodet

TORRES BURGOS, PABLO ◆ n. en Villa de Ayala y m. cerca de Rancho Viejo, Mor. (?-1911). Profesor normalista titulado en Cuautla. Entre 1900 y 1906 trabajó en Villa de Ayala, de donde pasó a Anenecuilco. Ahí se dedicó al comercio y conoció a Emiliano Zapata. Más tarde volvió a Ayala y en 1909, con Refugio Yáñez y Luciano Cabrera, fundó el Club Liberal Melchor Ocampo, para apoyar la candidatura de Patricio Leyva a la gubernatura de Morelos. Por esta actividad política estuvo preso entre enero y marzo de 1910. A fines de ese año, enviado por un grupo de campesinos entre los que se encontraban Zapata, Gabriel Tepepa, Rafael Merino y Catarino Perdomo, viajó a San Antonio, Texas, donde se entrevistó con Francisco I. Madero, quien lo nombró jefe del ejército revolucionario en Morelos. El 10 de marzo de 1911, con Zapata y Merino, se levantó en armas en la Villa de Ayala. A fines del mes renunció a la comandancia de las tropas revolucionarias por su oposición al saqueo de Jojutla. Fue asesinado.

TORRES CAMPOS, EDUARDO CONSTANTINO ◆ n. en Aguascalientes, Ags. (1957). Ingeniero agrónomo zootecnista por el Instituto Autónomo Agropecuario 20. Afiliado al PAN desde 1979, en el que ha sido sido presidente del Comité Directivo Municipal en Pabellón de Arteaga, regidor de ese municipio y diputado federal (1991-94).

TORRES CASTAÑEDA, JOSÉ SOLEDAD ◆ n. en Río Grande, Zac., y m. cerca de Durango, Dgo. (1918-1967). Sacerdote ordenado en 1943. Fue obispo de Ciudad Obregón (1959-67), diócesis que gobernó hasta su asesinato.

TORRES CASTILLO, JORGE ◆ n. en Gómez Palacio, Dgo. (1947). Licenciado en derecho por la UNAM. Afiliado al PRI, fue secretario de Información y Propaganda y secretario general del Comité Directivo Estatal de ese partido en Durango, diputado local y asesor de la CNC, entre otros cargos. Pasó al PRD en 1989 y ha sido, desde entonces, coordinador del Comité Promotor Estatal y presidente del Comité Directivo Estatal de ese partido, así como diputado federal (1991-94). Fue director del Centro de Seguridad Social del IMSS en Gómez Palacio.

TORRES CHAVARRÍA, CELIA ◆ n. en Iztapaluca, Edo. de Méx. y m. en el DF (1936-1994). Licenciada en derecho por la Universidad Iberoamericana (1983), especializada en pedagogía (1978). Militante del PPS (1957-88), del Movimiento de Liberación Nacional (1959) y del PRD (1989-), del que fue fundadora y a cuyo CEN perteneció. Secretaria de Organización y Propaganda del Frente Único de Inquilinos (1962), dirigente de la Coalición de Comerciantes (1963), representante del Grupo de Mujeres Indígenas (1970), presidenta del Movimiento Revolucionario de Indigenistas (1970), presidenta del Movimiento Revolucionario de Integración Nacional (1986), representante popular de la Asociación de Taxistas y Tianguistas (1989) y fundadora y dirigente de la Confederación Nacional de Comerciantes Cardenistas (1989). Fue directora del Centro Cultural Mazahua (1973), directora del Centro Cultural Indigenista de la SEP (1973-83) y profesora en la Escuela para Trabajadores y en la Escuela para Indígenas (1980). Diputada federal por el PPS (1976-79) y por el FDN (1988-91).

TORRES GALLARDO, GILBERTO ◆ n. en Oaxaca, Oax., y m. en el DF (1886-1947). Periodista. Llegó a la ciudad de México a principios del siglo XX. Colaboró en los periódicos *El Diario* y *El Imparcial*. Simpatizante de la Convención Revolucionaria, en 1915 acompañó a Toluca a sus representantes, para quienes editó un periódico. Más tarde fue colaborador y jefe de edición de *El Demócrata* de Villahermosa, colaborador de *La Prensa* desde 1928 y director de *El Demócrata* de San Luis Potosí. Utilizó el seudónimo de *Gil-Tor*. Autor de novela: *Las tragedias de la carne, ¡Lujuria bendita!* y *La nostalgia del burdel*; y memorias: *Yo: historia de un hombre sin historia*.

TORRES GAYTÁN, RICARDO ◆ n. en Coalcomán, Mich. (1911). Licenciado en economía por la UNAM (1944), de la que fue profesor (1943-77), director del Instituto de Investigaciones Económicas (1950-52), director de la Escuela Nacional de Economía (1953-61) y miembro de la Junta de Gobierno (1962-75). Ha sido fundador del INAP (1966), delegado en foros internacionales, economista de la SHCP (1942-44), oficial mayor de la Secretaría de la Economía Nacional (1953-58), director del Banco Nacional de Crédito Ejidal (1958-60) y director de la Industria Nacional de Química Farmacéutica (1960-64), entre otros cargos. Colaborador de *Revista de Economía, Investigación económica, Cuadernos americanos* y *Problemas del desarrollo*, entre otras publicaciones. Autor de *Aspectos monetarios del comercio internacional* (1969), *Teoría del comercio internacional* (1972), *Un siglo de devaluaciones del peso mexicano* (1980), y *Memoria conmemorativa de la Facultad de Economía* (1981) y *La política comercial* (tomo dos). Miembro del Colegio Nacional de Economistas (1980), Premio Universidad Nacional (1988), miembro de número de la Academia Mexicana de Economía Política (1989) y Premio Nacional de Economía (1990).

Ricardo Torres Gaytán

TORRES HARO, JOSÉ FÉLIX ◆ n. en Tepic, Nay. (1935). Estudió en Tepic en la Escuela Normal Urbana (1960-64) y en el Instituto de Ciencias y Artes (1964-66). Fue secretario de Acción Popular (1969-75) y presidente del Comité Directivo Estatal del PRI de Nayarit (1975-78), partido al que pertenece desde 1953. Ha sido secretario general de la Confederación Nacional de Organizaciones Populares en Nayarit (1969-75), diputado a la Legislatura de Nayarit (1972-75), presidente municipal de Tepic (1978-81), coordinador de las federaciones de transportes de la CNOP (1980-87), secretario general de gobierno de Nayarit (1981-85), presidente de la Comisión Electoral del estado (1981-85), diputado federal (1985-88) y secretario de Transporte del CEN de la CNOP.

TORRES Y HERNÁNDEZ, AGUSTÍN DE JESÚS ◆ n. en Alfajayucan, Hgo., y m.

en el DF (1818-1889). Sacerdote ordenado en 1843. Perteneció a la Congregación de los Padres Paúles desde 1847. Fue director del Colegio Clerical de Morelia, rector de los seminarios de León, Pátzcuaro y Zacatecas (1869), obispo de Tabasco (1882-85) y obispo de Tulancingo (1885-89).

Juan José Torres Landa

Torres Hurtado, Felipe ◆ n. en Ario de Rosales, Mich. (1901). Sacerdote ordenado en 1924. Estudió en el Seminario de Morelia. En 1917 ingresó en la orden de los Misioneros del Espíritu Santo. Ha sido vicario apostólico de Baja California (1939-49) y obispo de Saltillo (1949-75).

Torres Landa García, Juan Ignacio ◆ n. en León, Gto. (1959). Contador público titulado en la Universidad Autónoma de Querétaro (1980-82). Miembro del PRI desde 1976. Ha sido presidente municipal de San José Iturbide (1983-85), delegado del Fonhapo (1986-88), diputado al Congreso local de Guanajuato (1988-91) y diputado federal (1991-94).

Carlos Torres Manzo

Torres Landa, Juan José ◆ n. en Cuerámaro, y m. en San José de Iturbide, Gto. (1911-1980). Padre del anterior. Licenciado en derecho por la UNAM (1935). Fue director de la Escuela Preparatoria de Guanajuato (1943-44), diputado federal (1949-52), gobernador de Guanajuato (1961-67), delegado del PRI en Baja California (1969-70), embajador de México en Brasil (1970-74) y asesor de la Secretaría de Gobernación.

Ricardo Torres Nava

Torres Manzo, Carlos ◆ n. en Ticomán, Mich. (1923). Licenciado en economía por la UNAM (1947-52), realizó estudios de posgrado en la London School of Economics and Political Science (1955-57) y se diplomó en planeación económica en Tokio (1962). Fue presidente de la Federación Estudiantil Universitaria (1950), gerente de la Asociación de Comerciantes del Banco del Pequeño Comercio (1950-51), supervisor (1952-54) y economista de la Secretaría de Economía (1958), economista del Banco de Crédito Rural (1959-61), fundador de la revista *El Economista Mexicano* (1961), supervisor y jefe del Departamento de Política Comercial de la Secretaría de Industria y Comercio (1961-64), gerente de Administración y de Ventas de la Conasupo (1965-70), secretario de Industria y Comercio (1970-74), gobernador de Michoacán (1974-80), director del IEPES del PRI (1980-81 y 1986-87), subsecretario de Promoción de Turismo (1989), director de Azúcar S.A., hasta 1991, y coordinador general de la Comisión Nacional de Alimentos (1991-). Autor de la novela *El ameritado profesor Urzúa* (1986). En 1961 recibió un premio del Banco Nacional de México por su tesis de licenciatura. Fue presidente del Colegio Nacional de Economistas.

Torres Mesías, Luis ◆ n. y m. en Mérida, Yuc. (1916-1996). Profesor normalista. Miembro del PRI, en el que fue presidente del Comité Directivo Estatal en Yucatán (1956-58). Fue secretario general de Gobierno de Yucatán (1958), alcalde de Mérida (1959-60), diputado federal (1961-64) y gobernador del estado elegido para el periodo 1964-1970.

Torres Montes, Luis ◆ n. en Querétaro, Qro. (1934). Ingeniero químico industrial por el IPN. Estudió conservación de materiales arqueológicos en la Universidad de Nueva York. Profesor de la ENAH, la UNAM, del INBA y el Centro Latinoamericano de Estudios para la Conservación y Restauración de Bienes Culturales México-UNESCO. Ha introducido en México numerosas técnicas de conservación y restauración de bienes culturales. Ha sido jefe del grupo de restauración del Museo Nacional del Virreinato (1963-64), jefe de laboratorio de diversos departamentos de conservación y restauración en el INAH y el INBA (1966-77). Ha participado en proyectos de restauración y conservación, como los de los murales de Bonampak, la piedra de Copán, el parque arqueológico Tikal (Guatemala), el Museo Nacional de Arte, el Templo Mayor, el monumento de la independencia y el acueducto de Guadalupe. Presidente fundador del grupo mexicano del Instituto Internacional de Conservación (1972-74), jefe (1981-83) y asesor de Restauración (1985) del Museo Franz Mayer y secretario ejecutivo del Comité Nacional Permanente de Conservación de Documentos, Libros, Manuscritos y Artes Gráficas (1988-). Coautor de *Conservación de madera húmeda. Estudio comparativo de dos métodos* (1970). Autor de *Antropología y técnica* (1982) y *Antropología y técnica no. 2* (1987). Becario de la Fundación Rockefeller (1962-63), el ICCROM (Gobierno de Italia y Amigos de Spoleto, 1964) y la Dirección Nacional de Museos de la Secretaría de Cultura de Argentina (1986).

Torres Nava, Ricardo ◆ n. en el DF (1955). Alpinista. Estudió farmacología. En mayo de 1989, en una expedición internacional, fue el primer mexicano en alcanzar la cima del Everest, la montaña más elevada del mundo. Autor de *La conquista del Everest* (1990).

Torres Ordóñez, Luis ◆ n. en Los Llanos de San Juan Bautista, Chih., y m. en el DF (1912-1972). Profesor normalista y licenciado en economía por la UNAM. Fue funcionario de la Universidad Obrera, fundador del Partido Popular (1948), secretario de Organización del Movimiento Mexicano por la Paz, fundador y presidente de la Sociedad Mexicana de Amistad con China Popular, y director de Promoción Económica y jefe de la Comisión Técnica Consultiva del Instituto Nacional Indigenista.

Torres Portillo, Adolfo ◆ n. y m. en el DF (1920-1996). Guionista. Fue escritor radiofónico. En 1950 pasó al cine. De su primera película, *La hija de la otra*, siguieron cerca de 130, entre ellas *Cuando levanta la niebla* (1952), *Vainilla, bronce y morir* (1956), *Alazán y enamorado* (1963), *El cuerpazo del delito* (1968), *El Arracadas* (1977), *Lagunilla mi barrio* (1980), *El rey de la vecindad* (1985) y *Que Dios se lo pague* (1989). Dirigió *Los tres reyes magos* (1974), una de las pocas películas de animación que se han hecho en México, e hizo papeles pequeños en películas como *El principio* (1972). Socio fundador de la sección de autores y adaptadores del Sindicato de Trabajadores de la Industria Cinematográfica y de la Sogem, de la que fue vicepresidente y presidente honorario. Lleva su nombre la escuela de la Sogem en Querétaro, que fundó y dirigió.

Torres Quintero, Gregorio ◆ n. en Colima, Col., y m. en el DF (1866-1934). Profesor normalista titulado en la ciudad de México (1891). En Colima fue director de la Escuela Porfirio Díaz (1892), jefe de las secciones de Educación y de Beneficencia de la Secretaría de Gobierno e inspector general de los establecimientos de enseñanza del estado. Creó el método onomatopéyico para la alfabetización. Autor de *Cuentos colimotes* y *Descripciones, cuentos y sucedidos* (1931).

Torres Romero, Alfredo ◆ n. en Puruándiro, Mich. (1922). Sacerdote ordenado en 1945. Estudió en los seminarios de Morelia y de Montezuma. Ha sido secretario de Miguel Darío Miranda, asesor de la Acción Católica de Morelia (1966-67), director espiritual del Seminario Conciliar de Morelia (1967-68), obispo auxiliar de México (1968-74), obispo coadjutor (1974-75) y administrador apostólico de la diócesis de Aguascalientes (1975-80), secretario general de la Conferencia del Episcopado Mexicano (1976-79) y obispo de Toluca (1980-).

Torres y Rueda, Marcos de ◆ n. en España y m. en la ciudad de México (1588-1649). Sacerdote. Estudió en la Universidad de Alcalá de Henares. Profesor de la Universidad de Osma y del Colegio de Santa Cruz de Valladolid. Fue canónigo de la catedral de Burgos y rector del Colegio de San Nicolás de Burgos. Nombrado obispo de Yucatán en 1655, llegó a la Nueva España en 1646. Consagrado en Puebla por el obispo Juan de Palafox y Mendoza (☛), se instaló en Mérida en noviembre. En agosto de 1647, con el apoyo de Palafox, fue nombrado gobernador de la Nueva España y presidente interino de la Real Audiencia de México, en sustitución del virrey García Sarmiento de Sotomayor (☛). Llegó a la ciudad de México en diciembre, pero fue obligado a vivir en Tacuba hasta mayo de 1648, a causa de la lentitud con que Sarmiento preparaba su viaje a Perú. El 13 de mayo, finalmente, tomó posesión del gobierno de la Nueva España, con el título de obispo-gobernador, y de inmediato desató una campaña contra los enemigos de Palafox: los jesuitas, la Inquisición y casi todos los colaboradores de Sarmiento, a quienes destituyó de sus cargos o desplazó de toda posición de poder. En diciembre, intentó imponer la elección del cabildo de la ciudad de México, con lo que se ganó la animadversión de los criollos de la capital, partidarios de Palafox, quienes lo acusaban de haberse embolsado más de medio millón de pesos durante los 11 meses de su gobierno. Enemistado con el obispo de Puebla, para los primeros meses de 1649 ya había perdido todo apoyo y su situación era insostenible. En abril enfermó gravemente y no pudo asistir a dos de los acontecimientos más importantes de la vida colonial del siglo XVII: el asesinato de medio centenar de judaizantes y herejes realizado por la Inquisición el día 11, y la consagración de la Catedral de Puebla, realizada el 18.

Torres Sánchez, Rafael ◆ n. en Culiacán, Sin. (1953). Escritor. Licenciado en economía por la UNAM y maestro en historia por la Universidad de Guadalajara. Profesor de la Universidad de Guadalajara. Fue becario del INBA-Fonapas (1980-81). Ha colaborado en *La Cultura en México*, suplemento de la revista *Siempre!*, así como en *La Semana de Bellas Artes*, *Incluso* y *Tierra Adentro*. Autor de ensayo: *Las disquisiciones del Che Guarufa* (1986); y poesía: *Entre la ? y el !* (1976), *Cuatro fechas y un son para niños* (1983), *Fragmentario* (1985) y *Juego de espejos* (1990). En 1978 ganó el segundo lugar del Premio Nacional de Poesía Joven Francisco González de León; en 1986 el Premio de Poesía Carlos Pellicer y en el mismo año el Premio Internacional de Ensayo Malcom Lowry.

Torres Torija, Antonio ◆ ¿n. y m. en la ciudad de México? (1840-1922). Arquitecto. Se tituló en la Escuela de Bellas Artes (1861), donde fue profesor (1863-1916). Jefe de la Dirección de Obras Públicas de la ciudad de México (1877-1903). En 1885, sobre unos bocetos de Lorenzo de la Hidalga, elaboró los planos del Palacio de Lecumberri (☛). Autor de *Introducción al estudio de la construcción práctica*, *Tratado de geometría elemental para obreros*, *Curso de estabilidad de construcciones* y *Desarrollo de cálculos del curso de construcción*.

Torres Torija, José ◆ n. y m. en el DF (1885-1952). Médico cirujano graduado en la Escuela Nacional de Medicina (1908). Profesor de las escuelas nacionales de Medicina y Jurisprudencia. Entre 1904 y 1948 trabajó en los hospitales Juárez, General y de Jesús. Fue secretario de la Sociedad de Cirugía y director general del Hospital Juárez (1921), secretario general de la UNAM, oficial mayor del Departamento de Salubridad Pública y presidente de la Academia Nacional de Medicina (1929), a la que pertenecía desde 1925. Formó parte de la Junta de Gobierno de la UNAM hasta 1952. Autor de *Anales de clínica del Hospital Juárez* (1931). Perteneció a la Academia Nacional de Ciencias, a la Academia Nacional de Ciencias Penales y a la Academia Mexicana de Cirugía, de la que fue secretario perpetuo.

Torres Tuñón, Luis Antonio ◆ n. en Panamá y m. en la ciudad de México (?-1756). Doctor en jurisprudencia por las universidades de México y de Sevilla. Fue rector de la Real y Pontificia Universidad de México (1753-54) y prebendado y arcediano de la Catedral Metropolitana, en la que fundó la biblioteca pública.

Torres Villaseñor, Manuel ◆ n. en el DF (1943). Doctor en ciencias por la UNAM. Investigador especialista en metales del Instituto de Materiales de la UNAM, durante ocho años estudió nuevas aleaciones del zinc hasta lograr una: el *zinalco*, mezcla de aluminio, cobre y zinc, dos veces más resistente que

Gregorio Torres Quintero

Marcos de Torres y Rueda

el aluminio, 30 por ciento más barato y más apto para trabajar a muy bajas temperaturas. En 1986 recibió el Premio Manuel Noriega de la Organización de Estados Americanos; en 1987, el Premio de Investigación de la UNAM y el Premio Anual de la Canacintra.

Julio Torri

Torri, Julio ◆ n. en Saltillo, Coah., y m. en el DF (1889-1970). Escritor. Su apellido materno era Maynes. Licenciado en derecho por la Escuela Nacional de Jurisprudencia (1913) y doctor en letras por la UNAM (1933). Perteneció al Ateneo de la Juventud y en agosto de 1921, con Vicente Lombardo Toledano, Xavier Guerrero y José Clemente Orozco, fundó el Grupo Solidario del Movimiento Obrero. Fue codirector, con Agustín Loera, de la Editorial Cvltvra (1916-23); fundador (1920) y jefe del Departamento de Bibliotecas (1920-21) y jefe del Departamento Editorial de la Universidad; director de la colección "Clásicos" de la SEP, miembro del Comité Organizador del Tercer Congreso Internacional de Escritores (1939) y profesor de la Escuela Nacional Preparatoria y de la Facultad de Filosofía y Letras hasta 1964. Tradujo, entre otras obras, *Discurso sobre las pasiones del amor*, de Blas Pascal (1918), y *Las noches florentinas*, de Henrich Heine (1918). Autor de *Ensayos y poemas* (1917), *Romances Viejos* (1918), *De fusilamientos* (1940), *Sentencias y lugares comunes* (1945), *La literatura española* (1952), *Antología* (1959) y *Prosas dispersas* (1964). En 1987, apareció *El ladrón de ataúdes*, volumen de su prosa de ficción recopilada por Serge I. Zaitzeff. Perteneció a la Academia Mexicana (de la Lengua) desde 1952. En 1953 fue nombrado profesor emérito de la UNAM.

Columba Domínguez, Miguel Torruco y José Elías Moreno en *El río y la muerte*, pelícla de Luis Buñuel

Torroella, Alfredo ◆ n. en Cuba (1845-1879). Periodista y dramaturgo. Vivió algunos años en México, donde ejerció el periodismo y estrenó sus obras teatrales *El milagro*, *El istmo de Suez* y *El mulato*.

Torroella, Enrique ◆ n. en Cuba y m. en el DF (1853-1928). Hermano del anterior. Llegó a México alrededor de 1867 y estudió en el Colegio Militar. Fue agregado de la legación mexicana en Guatemala, subdirector del Colegio Militar (1896-1909), jefe del del estado mayor en la Secretaría de Guerra y Marina, jefe del estado mayor del presidente Francisco León de la Barra y nuevamente jefe del Estado Mayor de la Secretaría de Guerra y Marina (1911-13). Se retiró del ejército al producirse el golpe de Estado de Victoriano Huerta.

Torruco Castellanos, Miguel ◆ n. en Palenque, Chis., y m. Orizaba, Ver. (1917-1956). Fue piloto de la Compañía Mexicana de Aviación, pero a raíz de su matrimonio con María Elena Marqués se dedicó a la actuación. Estudió con Seki Sano. Trabajó, entre otras, en las películas *Negro es mi color* (1950), *La mujer desnuda* (1951), *La estatua de carne* (1951), *Acapulco* (1951), *El misterio del carro express* (1952), *Acuérdate de vivir* (1952), *El plagio de un millonario* (1952), *Casa de muñecas* (1953), *La intrusa* (1953), *Cuando me vaya* (1953), *La sospechosa* (1954), *La desconocida* (1954) y *El río y la muerte* (1954).

Tort, César ◆ n. en Puebla, Pue. (1928). Músico y maestro. Su apellido materno es Oropeza. Fue alumno de Ramón Serrato, Pedro Michaca y Aaron Copland. Estudió en el Real Conservatorio de Madrid (1949-52). Ha sido profesor de la SEP y de la UNAM, donde también es investigador (1975-). Director para México, Centroamérica y el Caribe de la Sociedad Internacional de Educación Musical de la UNESCO (1988). Fundador del Instituto Artene, Centro de Pedagogía Infantil Musical (1976). Creador de un método de pedagogía musical que desde 1967 se aplica en la Escuela Nacional de Música y a partir de 1969 en el Conservatorio Nacional de Música. Ha compilado la música de numerosas canciones infantiles como *Chocolate molinillo*, *Los veinte ratones* y *Señora Santa Ana*. Autor de la ópera *Hilitos de oro* (1985), el poema sinfónico *Estirpes*, la obra para orquesta de cámara *La comedia*, la cantata *La espada*, *La voz del huéhuetl* (ejercicios) y otras obras de cámara, para piano, para coro y sinfónicas. Su serie de discos de larga duración *La música y el niño* (1971, 1978, 1985) apareció con el sello de la UNAM. Ha diseñado instrumentos musicales para su uso en escuelas. Autor de *Micro-pauta* (1971), *Educación musical en el jardín de niños* (1971), *Educación musical en el primer año de primaria* (1975), *Educación musical en el segundo grado* (1976), *Educación musical en las primarias* (1982), *El coro y la orquesta escolares* (1988), *El ritmo musical y el niño* (1995) y *Posadas y villancicos* (1997). Cédula Real de la Fundación de la Ciudad de Puebla, otorgada durante un homenaje por el gobierno de ese estado (1995).

Tortolero, Francisco ◆ n. en Mazatlán, Sin., y m. en San Luis Potosí, SLP (1901-1957). Tenor, discípulo de Ángel Esquivel y José Pierson en el Conservatorio Nacional de Música. Fue primer solista de la Orquesta Típica de Lerdo de Tejada, miembro de la Compañía de Ópera de Bracalli y, durante 18 años, de la Metropolitan Opera House de Nueva York.

Tortugas ◆ Isla de Baja California Sur situada en el golfo de California frente al puerto de Santa Rosalía, al noreste de la isla San Marcos. En su territorio existe un volcán extinguido.

Toscana, David ◆ n. en Monterrey, NL (1961). Escritor. Ingeniero industrial por el ITESM. Fue profesor de enseñanza secundaria. Ha colaborado en las revistas *Coloquio* y *Cultura Norte*. Fue becario del Centro de Escritores de Nuevo León. Autor de novela: *Estación Tula* (1991), *Las bicicletas* (1992) y *Santa María del Circo* (1998). Becario del Centro de Escritores de Nuevo León (1990-91) y del Fonca.

Toscano, Carmen ♦ n. en la ciudad de México y m. en Aguascalientes, Ags. (1910-1988). Escritora. Realizó estudios en la Escuela Normal Superior y en la Facultad de Filosofía y Letras de la Universidad Nacional. En 1941, con María del Carmen Millán, fundó la revista *Rueca* (1941-52). Fue colaboradora de *Taller Poético*, *América* y *Revista de la Universidad de México*, y guionista de televisión. Con el material fílmico reunido por su padre, Salvador Toscano, escribió y produjo las películas *Memorias de un mexicano* (1950) y *Ronda Revolucionaria* (1980). Autora de biografía: *Rosario la de Acuña, mito romántico* (1948); poesía: *Trazo incompleto* (1934) e *Inalcanzable y mío* (1936); y teatro: *El huésped*, *El amor de la tía Cristina*, *Cierto día* (1950), *Leyendas del México colonial* (1955), *La llorona* (1959) y *Las senadoras suelen guisar* (1964). En 1949 obtuvo un premio en el concurso cultural de la Cooperativa Talleres Gráficos de la Nación.

Toscano, Salvador ♦ n. en Ciudad Guzmán, Jal., y m. en el DF (1872-1947). Cineasta. Ingeniero civil titulado en la Escuela Nacional de Ingenieros (1897). A mediados de 1896, en la calle de Jesús, en la ciudad de México, instaló una pequeña sala de exhibición cinematográfica, donde se presentaron varios de los cortometrajes traídos en ese mismo año por Gabriel Vayre, representante de los hermanos Lumiére en México (☛ *Cine, Inicios del*). Al año siguiente, en la calle de Plateros, instaló la sala *Cinematógrafo Lumiére* y viajó por Celaya, Chihuahua, Guadalajara, Puebla, San Luis Potosí, Tehuacán y Zacatecas, donde presentó por primera vez el cine. En 1899 exhibió cortometrajes que adquirió en Europa de Thomas Alva Edison y Georges Méliès. También compró una cámara y un pequeño laboratorio de revelado que le permitieron realizar, en 1899, los primeros cortos de ficción mexicanos: *Don Juan Tenorio* y *Luisa Obregón y su esposo en Canarios de café*. A partir de entonces combinó el oficio de camarógrafo transhumante con el de exhibidor. En los primeros años del siglo XX fundó en la ciudad de México el salón La Metrópoli, uno de los primeros cines estables, y recorrió gran parte del país y algunas regiones del sur de Estados Unidos. En 1905 fotografió la llegada a Veracruz, y su traslado a la ciudad de México, del cadáver de Manuel Aspíroz, embajador de México en Estados Unidos. En 1906 realizó un documental, quizá el primero con argumento, sobre la *Visita del presidente Porfirio Díaz a Yucatán*, y en 1907 filmó varias "vistas" sobre una gran inundación de Guanajuato. La mayor parte de su obra son escenas de la revolución de 1910-17, que fueron editadas por su hija, Carmen Toscano, en los largometrajes *Memorias de un mexicano* (1950) y *Ronda revolucionaria* (1980). En los años veinte instaló otra sala de proyección cinematográfica, conocida como Salón Rojo, en la ciudad de México.

Toscano, Salvador ♦ n. en Atlixco, Pue., y m. en el volcán Popocatépetl, en el Edo. de Méx. (1912-1949). Historiador y arqueólogo. Hijo del anterior. Licenciado en derecho por la UNAM (1937). Profesor en las escuelas Normal Superior y Nacional de Artes Plásticas. Fue investigador y fundador del Instituto de Investigaciones Estéticas de la UNAM (1936), secretario del Instituto de Antropología y director de la colección *Fuentes para la historia de México* (1947-48). Murió en un accidente de aviación. Colaboró en *Barandal*, *Armas y letras* y *Revista de la Universidad de México*. Autor de *El Dr. Mora* (1936), *Derecho y organización social de los aztecas* (1937), *Arte precolombino de México y de la América Central* (1944), *México antiguo* (1946), *Federico Cantú. Obra realizada de 1922 a 1948* (1948) y *Cuauhtémoc* (1953).

Totatiche ♦ Municipio de Jalisco situado al norte de Guadalajara y al noroeste de Teocaltiche, en los límites con Zacatecas. Superficie: 542.98 km². Habitantes: 6,125, de los cuales 1,365 forman la población económicamente activa. Hablan alguna lengua indígena 10 personas mayores de cinco años.

Totolac ♦ Municipio de Tlaxcala contiguo a la capital del estado. Superficie: 28.4 km². Habitantes: 14,962, de los cuales 4,597 forman la población económicamente activa. Hablan alguna lengua indígena 142 personas mayores de cinco años (náhuatl 64 y totonaco 62).

Totolapa ♦ Municipio de Chiapas situado al sur de San Cristóbal de Las Casas y al noroeste de Comitán. Superficie: 186.3 km². Habitantes: 4,671, de los cuales 1,114 forman la población económicamente activa. Hablan alguna lengua indígena 184 personas (tzotzil 159). Entre el 13 y el 15 de agosto se celebra la fiesta de la Asunción de la Virgen.

Salvador Toscano

Totolapan ♦ Municipio de Morelos situado al este de Tepoztlán y al nornoreste de Cuautla, en los límites con el Estado de México. Superficie: 70.14 km². Habitantes: 8,201, de los cuales 1,506 forman la población económicamente activa. Hablan alguna lengua indígena 239 personas mayores de cinco años (náhuatl 63 y mixteco 34).

Totoltepec de Guerrero ♦ Municipio de Puebla situado al noreste de Acatlán y al oeste-suroeste de Tehuacán, en los límites con Oaxaca. Superficie: 164.56 km². Habitantes: 1,066, de los cuales 249 forman la población económicamente activa. Hablan alguna lengua indígena 71 personas mayores de cinco años (mixteco 70).

Totonacos ♦ Indios que viven en las estribaciones orientales de la sierra Norte de Puebla y en la región centro norte de Veracruz. En 1995, hablaban totonaco 214,192 personas mayores de cinco años (3.91 por ciento de los hablantes de lenguas indígenas). En Puebla vivían 86,392 (de los cuales 18,655 no sabían español) y en Veracruz 115,455 (14,448 monolingües). En el

Distrito Federal vivían 3,187 y en el Estado de México 5,433. El idioma totonaco está clasificado en el grupo maya-totonaco, tronco totonaco, familia totonaca. Los restos arqueológicos totonacas más antiguos tienen 4,000 años de antigüedad. Fueron encontrados en el municipio veracruzano de Actopan, aunque es posible que estos primeros habitantes constituyeran un grupo totonaca primitivo, que se estableció en el centro del actual estado de Veracruz. Hacia el siglo I de nuestra época algunos, grupos indígenas venidos de Chicomoztoc, que se retiraban hacia el este debido a la hostilidad de los chichimecas, se establecieron en la sierra Norte de Puebla y en la llanura costera de Veracruz, al sur de la Huasteca veracruzana. Los inmigrantes se mezclaron con los originales habitantes de la región, se instalaron en El Tajín y en Yohualichán y más tarde en Cempoala, Papantla y Nautla. Los pequeños señoríos totonacas se agruparon en la confederación de Totonacapan y se extendieron hasta la desembocadura del río Papaloapan, el norte de Oaxaca y el este de Puebla. A partir del siglo XIII, el centro político se trasladó hacia el sureste y los jefes de la confederación se establecieron en Cempoala. Entre 1450 y 1470, las fuerzas nahuas de la Triple Alianza sometieron el centro veracruzano y convirtieron a los pueblos totonacas en tributarios del Anáhuac. Los nahuas se instalaron firmemente en la región y desalojaron del Papaloapan a los totonacas, que se concentraron al norte del actual puerto de Veracruz y en la sierra Norte de Puebla. A principios del siglo XVI, los totonacas eran más de 750,000. En mayo de 1519, las tropas españolas de Hernán Cortés entraron pacíficamente en Cempoala, donde, con ofertas y amenazas, despertaron el deseo independentista de los totonacas y consiguieron su colaboración para enfrentarse a los aztecas. Al mismo tiempo, los españoles destruyeron las imágenes religiosas autóctonas y las sustituyeron por las suyas. En septiembre de ese año, mientras los conquistadores avanzaban hacia México-Tenochtitlan, los totonacas de Nautla se levantaron en armas contra la guarnición mexica, a la que poco después derrotaron. En mayo de 1520, impulsados por Cuitláhuac, los guerreros aztecas organizaron una fuerza para enfrentar a los españoles, pero fueron derrotados por un ejército de totonacas dirigido por los europeos. Un año más tarde, en abril de 1521, los señores de la confederación totonaca viajaron a Texcoco, donde se sometieron a Cortés. En 1523, los frailes franciscanos iniciaron la evangelización en la zona y en 1533 los agustinos se establecieron en las cercanías de Papantla. Aunque consiguieron bautizar a casi todos los indios, no pudieron impedir la sobrevivencia de muchas de las creencias prehispánicas, como la de la creación, que consistía en suponer que el mundo había sido formado en cinco ocasiones. Además, los totonacas mezclaron su propia tradición religiosa con la impuesta por los españoles y, por ejemplo, atribuyeron al cristiano San Juan los poderes de sus antiguos dioses de la lluvia y los rayos; consideraron a Venus y a la Luna como deidades maléficas, emparentadas con el Demonio judeocristiano; conservaron la fe en el sol y en la tierra, que estaban relacionados con el cultivo del maíz y llamaron Jerusalem al extremo oriental del mundo, donde se dirigían las almas de los danzantes, los músicos, las comadronas, las mujeres muertas en el parto y quienes morían por la mordedura de las serpientes. Durante los primeros años de la Colonia conservaron algunas prerrogativas ganadas por su alianza con los conquistadores, pero desde los últimos años del siglo XVI, la aristocracia totonaca desapareció y los indios fueron agrupados en reducciones y congregaciones. En el curso del siglo XVII fueron empujados tierra adentro, al ocupar europeos y mestizos las tierras. Hasta 1787, cuando debido a las reformas borbónicas, los totonacas se repartieron en las intendencias de Puebla y Veracruz, la zona en que vivían había formado parte de la provincia de Papantla, dependiente del reino de México. Durante el virreinato, los totonacas fueron despojados de una gran cantidad de sus bienes territoriales y para principios del siglo XIX, los hacendados, ganaderos y azucareros principalmente, poseían casi toda la tierra laborable. En 1813, los indios de las cercanías de Papantla se levantaron en armas y al mando de Serafín Olarte controlaron la región hasta 1819, cuando fueron derrotados por los realistas. Dos años después se adhirieron al Plan de Iguala. Sin embargo, la independencia iturbidista no resolvió el problema de la tierra y, más aún, lo complicó, pues los hacendados de la región totonaca se vieron libres de la legislación colonial que protegía a los indios y a mediados de los años treinta del siglo XIX, el conflicto entre campesinos y hacendados volvió a estallar. Desde 1833, los terratenientes de la región de Papantla

Claustro del convento de San Guillermo en Totolapan, Morelos

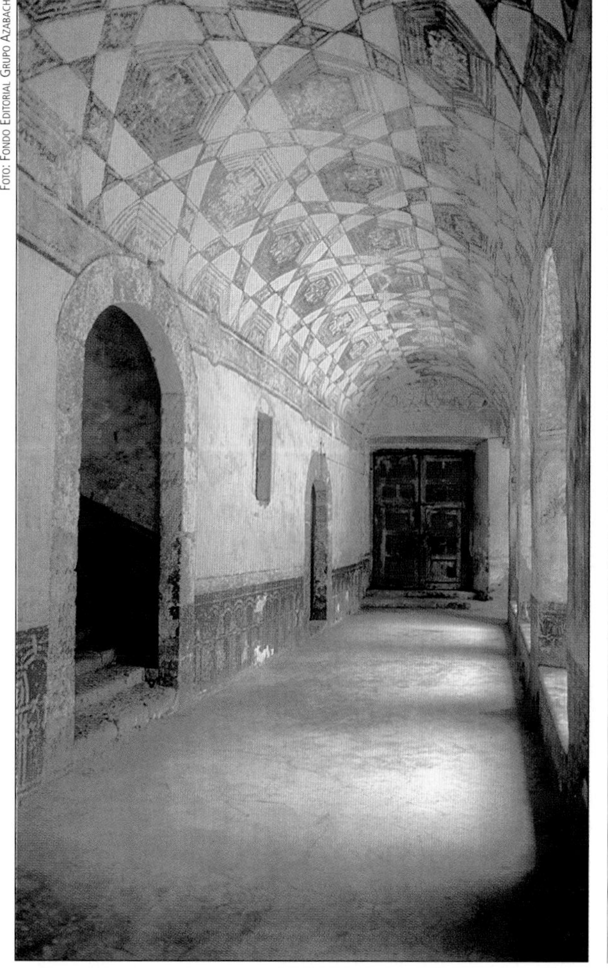

FOTO: FONDO EDITORIAL GRUPO AZABACHE

Familia de campesinos totonacas de Papantla, Veracruz

habían ocupado gran parte de la tierra comunal de los alrededores de Papantla. A principios de 1836, el obispado de Puebla prohibió a los indios de Papantla celebrar la Semana Santa de acuerdo con sus costumbres, lo que provocó una insurrección que fue apoyada por Mariano Olarte, el *hombre fuerte* de la región y pariente del guerrillero insurgente. En noviembre de 1836, los totonacas tomaron Papantla y entraron en negociaciones con el gobierno centralista de José Justo Corro, pero un mes después las fuerzas gubernamentales asaltaron la plaza y desalojaron a las fuerzas de Olarte. En los últimos días de diciembre, Olarte proclamó el federalista Plan de Papantla y la insurrección se extendió a Chichontepec y Tuxpan, que entonces pertenecían a Puebla; Tantoyuca y Misanta, en Veracruz; Huauchinango, Zacatlán y Zacapoaxtla, en Puebla; y Tulancingo, Huejutla y Zacualtipán, en el actual estado de Hidalgo. En febrero de 1837, el gobierno envió a Papantla al ex presidente Guadalupe Victoria, quien consiguió la revocación del edicto diocesano sobre las celebraciones indígenas y convenció a varios de los dirigentes totonacas de abandonar la lucha. Solucionada la demanda inmediata, muchos campesinos depusieron las armas y se redujo el ejército de Olarte, que llegó a contar con 5,000 efectivos, hecho que fue aprovechado por las fuerzas del gobierno, las cuales asolaron la región en la primera mitad de 1837 sin que los guerrilleros de Olarte, apenas 200 en ese momento, pudieran defender los pueblos. A fines de ese año, terminada la época de siembras, los totonacas volvieron a insurreccionarse, pero en mayo de 1838 Olarte fue asesinado y el movimiento se extinguió. Diez años después, los totonacas del norte se incorporaron al levantamiento de los huastecos de Tantoyuca (☛). En julio de 1853, los totonacas de Misanta se levantaron en armas contra una disposición del gobierno que establecía la realización de sorteos entre los jóvenes campesinos para señalar a quienes debían incorporarse al ejército. Poco después, grupos de Papantla y Tlapacoyan se incorporaron al movimiento, que se extingió un mes más tarde, ante el arribo de fuerzas gubernamentales desde Puebla. A partir de la llegada de los liberales al poder, a mediados del siglo, la capacidad insurreccional de los totonacas se redujo considerablemente, aunque todavía en 1891, 1896 y 1906, grupos armados de campesinos se levantaron en armas en la región de Papantla. Durante el porfiriato, las estructuras de poder de los totonacas resultaron definitivamente suprimidas y los indios fueron incorporados al sistema de municipalidades. Desde los primeros años del siglo XX los jóvenes totonacas se han incorporado al mercado de trabajo de la ciudades y han comenzado a usar ropa de fabricación comercial, pero los viejos todavía conservan su vestimenta tradicional: los hombres camisa y calzón de manta, sombrero y huaraches y las mujeres falda blanca, faja, blusa con bordados de colores y quechquémitl de lana con bordados y una pañoleta. La principal actividad económica todavía es la agricultura, aunque cada familia posee, además, aves de corral y cerdos para el consumo doméstico. En la llanura costera de Veracruz también se come pescado. También se dedican a la elaboración y venta de artesanías como cerámica, tejidos de fibras naturales, máscaras de madera y, en la región de Papantla, figuras de vainilla. Cuando una persona muere, su cadáver es aseado y vestido con ropa nueva, se coloca en el ataúd junto con una botella de agua, tortillas y unas cuantas monedas, efectos que servirán para que el alma del muerto pueda efectuar su viaje al inframundo. El cadáver es velado durante una noche y, después, enterrado. De acuerdo con su tradición, el alma de los muertos tarda algunos días en emprender su viaje, por lo que los familiares suelen servir la comida en el lugar del ausente.

Indígena totonaca de Puebla

Libro de Manuel Toussaint

Manuel Toussaint

FOTO: ROGELIO BAEZA
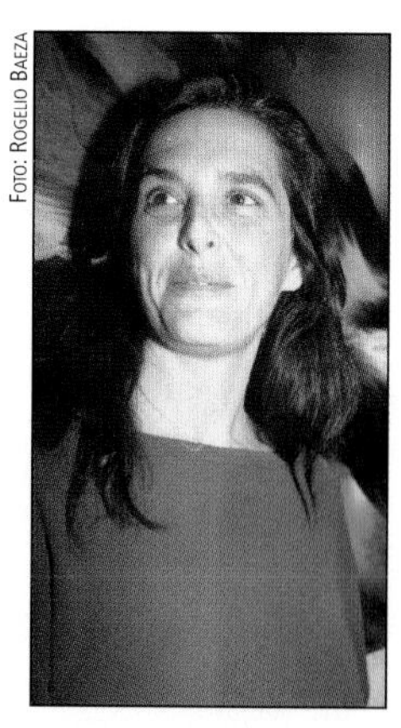
Cecilia Toussaint

Totontepec Villa de Morelos ◆ Municipio de Oaxaca situado al noreste de Oaxaca y al sur-sureste de Tuxtepec. Superficie: 318.95 km². Habitantes: 5,438, de los cuales 1,439 forman la población económicamente activa. Hablan alguna lengua indígena 4,441 personas mayores de cinco años (mixe 4,347 y zapoteco 85), de las cuales 740 son monolingües.

Tototlán ◆ Municipio de Jalisco contiguo a Zapotlanejo y Atotonilco el Alto. Superficie: 292.85 km². Habitantes: 19,819, de los cuales 5,103 forman la población económicamente activa. Hablan alguna lengua indígena ocho personas mayores de cinco años.

Totutla ◆ Municipio de Veracruz situado al noreste de Orizaba, al suroeste de Jalapa y al oeste-noroeste del puerto de Veracruz. Superficie: 80.61 km². Habitantes: 14,022, de los cuales 3,099 forman la población económicamente activa. Hablan alguna lengua indígena 14 personas mayores de cinco años (náhuatl 11).

Toussaint, Cecilia ◆ n. en el DF (1955). Cantante. Comenzó en los grupos La Nopalera y Rehilete. Después de interpretar composiciones de la nueva trova y boleros optó por el rock con el grupo Abril y, posteriormente, Arpía, formado por ella. En su repertorio destacan sus versiones de canciones de Jaime López (☛), como *Me siento bien, pero me siento mal*, *La primera calle de la Soledad*, *Ámame en un hotel*, *Sácalo*, *Caite cadáver*, *La almohada eléctrica* y otras. Ha grabado los discos *Arpía* (1985), *En esta ciudad* (1987), *Tírame al corazón* (1990), *Noche de día. En vivo* (1992), *Sirena de trapo* (1993) y *Detrás del silencio* (1998). También ha hecho coros en grabaciones del grupo Caifanes, actuado en teatro y telenovelas y participado en películas como *Frida, naturaleza viva* (1983), *¿Cómo ves?* (1985), *La leyenda de una máscara* (1989) y *Dama de noche* (1993).

Toussaint, Florence ◆ n. en el DF (1950). Su segundo apellido es Alcaraz. Periodista. Licenciada en periodismo y comunicación colectiva, maestra en ciencias de la comunicación y doctora en sociología por la UNAM, donde es profesora (1977-) e investigadora. Ha sido coordinadora del Centro de Estudios de la Comunicación (1992-94). Colabora en *Proceso* (1980-) y *El Universal* (1997-), en Radio Universidad y en diversas publicaciones. Pertenece al consejo editorial de la *Revista Mexicana de Comunicación*. Editora y coautora de *¿Televisión pública en México?* (1992) y *Democracia y medios de comunicación: un binomio inexplorado* (1995). Autora de *Escenario de la prensa en el porfiriato* (1989), *Prensa y nueva tecnología* (1989), *Recuento de medios fronterizos* (1990) y *Televisión sin fronteras* (1998). Fue presidenta de la Asociación Mexicana de Investigadores de la Comunicación (1989-91). Pertenece a la Fundación Manuel Buendía y a la Asociación Internacional de Investigación en Comunicación Social. Medalla Alfonso Caso al mérito universitario (1998).

Toussaint, Manuel ◆ n. en Puebla, Pue., y m. en la ciudad de México (1858-1927). Médico titulado en Puebla (1884). Ingresó al cuerpo médico militar. Con una beca estudió en Alemania y fue interno del Hospital de la Charité en París. Regresó a México en 1890 y se inició como docente en la Universidad Nacional. Fue director de los hospitales General y Francés, jefe del Servicio de Fisiología Experimental en el Instituto Médico Nacional, profesor en la Facultad de Medicina, fundador del Museo e Instituto de Anatomía Patológica, que además dirigió, y miembro (1894-1927) y presidente de la Academia Nacional de Medicina (1905 y 1910). En 1901 aplicó por primera vez en México la cirugía gástrica y la raquianestesia. Colaborador de la *Gaceta Médica de México*, del *Boletín del Instituto de Anatomía Patológica* y de la *Revista de Anatomía Patológica y Clínicas Médica y Quirúrgica*.

Toussaint, Manuel ◆ n. en la ciudad de México y m. en EUA (1890-1955). Historiador del arte. Su segundo apellido era Ritter. Hijo del anterior. Estudió en la Universidad Nacional. En 1919, con Agustín Loera y Enrique González Martínez, fundó la editorial México Moderno. Profesor de las escuelas nacionales Preparatoria y de Antropología, de la Universidad y de El Colegio de México. Fue secretario particular de José Vasconcelos (☛) en el Departamento Universitario y la SEP; director de San Carlos (1928-29), fundador del Laboratorio de Arte de la UNAM (1934), director fundador del Instituto de Investigaciones Estéticas de la UNAM (1938-55) y director del Departamento de Monumentos Coloniales del INAH (1945-55). Preparó la edición de numerosas antologías. Autor de *Saturnino Herrán y su obra* (1920), *Viajes alucinados. Rincones de España* (1921), *Taxco. Su historia, sus monumentos, características actuales y posibilidades turísticas* (1931), *D. José de la Borda restituido a España* (1933), *Litografía de México en el siglo XIX* (1934), *La pintura en México durante el siglo XVI* (1936), *Paseos coloniales* (1939), *Compendio bibliográfico del "Triunfo parténico" de don Carlos de Sigüenza y Góngora* (1941), *Pátzcuaro* (1942), *Arte mudéjar en América* (1946), *Arte colonial en México* (1948), *Acolman* (1948), *La conquista del Pánuco* (1948), *Catedral de México y Sagrario Metropolitano. Su historia, su tesoro, su arte* (1948), *La catedral y las iglesias de Puebla* (1954), *Las aventuras de Pipiolo en el bosque de Chapultepec* (1954) y *Pintura colonial en México* (1965). Fue miembro de El Colegio Nacional, la Academia Mexicana de la Historia y la Academia Mexicana (de la Lengua). En 1953 recibió el doctorado *honoris causa* de la UNAM.

Toussaint, Marianne ◆ n. en Torreón, Coah. (1958). Poeta. Hija de Enriqueta Ochoa. Realizó estudios de literatura hispanoamericana en la UNAM. Profesora del IPN (1984). Ha sido auxiliar administrativo de la Escuela de Periodismo Carlos Septién García (1978), analista de prensa de la Comisión Nacional de Cacao (1979) y comentarista del programa *Proyección 2000* (1987). Ha impartido talleres literarios. Pertenece al consejo editorial de *Viceversa*. Colaboradora de *El Correo del Libro*, de las revistas *El Caracol Marino, Alejandría, Revista de la Universidad* y *Tierra Adentro*, de los periódicos *La Opinión*, de Torreón, *Excélsior* y *La Jornada*. Coautora de *Caligrafía de Adriana* (1987). Autora de *Esta cuchilla móvil* (1982), *Murallas* (1996) y *El paisaje era la casa* (1996). Becaria del Fonca (1990-91) y del Centro Mexicano de Escritores (1991-92).

Toussaint Ribot, Mauricio ◆ n. el DF (1953). Licenciado en Ciencias Políticas y Administración Pública por la UNAM, especializado en administración pública. Entre otros cargos en la administración pública, ha sido secretario del Fideicomiso del Gobierno Federal Minerales no Metálicos Mexicanos (1975-79), ministro del Servicio Exterior Mexicano (1980), secretario del secretario de Relaciones Exteriores (1979-82), contralor interno de la SRE (1983-89), director general de Operación Minero-Metalúrgica (1990-93) y de Política Energética (1993 y 1995-96) de la SEMIP, subdirector de aeropuertos de ASA (1996-99) y director de modernización y cambio estructural de la CFE (1999-).

Tovalín, Alberto ◆ n. en el DF (1961). Su segundo apellido es Ahumada. Fotógrafo. Licenciado en lingüística por la ENAH. Ha colaborado en publicaciones mexicanas y extranjeras y participado en exposiciones individuales y colectivas en México, España, Estados Unidos, Turquía, Israel y Arabia Saudita. Editor de la *Agenda Cultural*, con obra de fotógrafos mexicanos contemporáneos (1994-) y del libro *Joaquín Santamaría. Sol de Plata/Silver Sun* (1998). Coeditor de *Young Mexican Photographers* (Japón, 1998). Organizó el encuentro binacional Crónicas Fotográficas I, México-Estados Unidos (1995) y ha encabezado, a partir de entonces, programas de promoción de la fotografía mexicana. Premio de adquisición Sotero Constantino (1993). Ha sido becario (1993-94) y beneficiario del Programa de Apoyo a Proyectos Culturales del Fonca (1996-97) y miembro de los consejos consultivos de los Fondos para la Cultura y las Artes de Campeche y Veracruz.

Tovar, Juan ◆ n. en Puebla, Pue. (1941). Escritor. Realizó estudios de ingeniería química en la UAP y de literatura dramática en la UNAM. Profesor del IPN, del INBA (1967-74), del Centro Universitario de Teatro, del Centro de Experimentación Teatral y del Centro de Capacitación Cinematográfica. Fue jefe de redacción de *Diorama de la Cultura* y ha colaborado en las principales publicaciones literarias. Coautor de los guiones cinematográficos *Pueblo fantasma* (1966) y *Reed: México insurgente* (1970); de las obras teatrales *De paso* (1984) y *Manga de Clavo* (1985) y la antología *Asedio a Alfonso Reyes* (1989). Autor de cuento: *Hombre en la oscuridad* (1965), *Los misterios del reino* (1966, Premio de Cuento de la revista *La Palabra y el Hombre*), *La plaza y otros cuentos* (1968, Premio INJUVE 1966), *De oídas* (1973), *El lugar del corazón* (1974), *Criatura de un día* (1980) y *Memoria de apariencias* (1989); novela: *El mar bajo la tierra* (1967), *La muchacha en el balcón o la presencia del coronel retirado* (1970, Premio de Novela en el I Concurso de la Juventud, SEP), *La madrugada* (1979) y *Lo que tengas de mí* (1995); teatro: *Coloquio de la rueda en su centro* (1970), *La madrugada* (1979), *Las adoraciones* (1981), *El destierro* (1982), *Cura de locura* (1982), *Muera Villa* (1985), *Luz del norte* (1989) y *Fort Bliss (agonía de Victoriano Huerta)* (1993); y adaptaciones como *Manuscrito encontrado en Zaragoza* (de Jean Potocki, 1984), *El monje* (de Mathew H. Lewis, 1986) y *Mi querida Lulú* (de Frank Wedekind, 1987). Recibió el Premio Alfonso X de Traducción Literaria del INBA (1984) y compartió un Ariel por el guión de *Crónica de familia* (1987). Becario del Centro Mexicano de Escritores (1964-65 y 1974-75) y del Fonca (1991-92). Miembro del Sistema Nacional de Creadores (1993-).

Tovar, Juan de ◆ n. y m. en la ciudad de México (1541-1626). Sacerdote. En 1572 se unió a la Compañía de Jesús. Fue profesor de los conventos de San Gregorio y Tepozotlán. Por mandato del virrey Martín Enríquez de Almanza, recopiló documentos sobre el mundo prehispánico y escribió una *Historia antigua de México*, la que se perdió durante su traslado a España. De otra versión, más corta, de la misma obra, se conserva sólo la segunda parte, que fue publicada, en 1860, con el título de *Historia de los indios mexicanos*.

Tovar, Lupita ◆ n. en Matías Romero, Oax. (1911). Actriz. Se inició en Hollywood, donde trabajó en *Drácula* (1931, actuación que en 1999 le valió ser designada Reina del Terror del festival Halloween Horror Nights) y en el *Tenorio de Harlem*, *Border Law* y *Al este de Bordeo*. En México estelarizó la primera versión sonora de *Santa* (1931). Participó en papeles estelares en *Mariguana* (1936), *El rosario de Amozoc* (1938), *María* (1938), *Miguel Strogoff* (1943) y *Resurrección* (1943). Se retiró en los años cuarenta.

Tovar, Mauro de ◆ n. en España y m. en Ciudad Real, hoy San Cristóbal de Las Casas, Chis. (?-1666). Monje benedictino. Fue obispo de Caracas (1639-52) y obispo de Chiapas (1652-66).

Tovar, Pantaleón ◆ n. y m. en la ciudad de México (1828-1886). Escritor. Luchó contra la invasión estadounidense de 1847. Elegido diputado al término de la guerra de los Tres Años, en septiembre de 1861 pidió con otros legisladores la renuncia de Juárez. Al año siguiente se incorporó a las fuerzas de Ignacio Zaragoza en Acatzingo y ahí editó el boletín *La Idea del Ejército*. Durante el imperio de Maximiliano fue perseguido y se exilió en Nueva Orleans, La Habana y Nueva York. En 1865 apoyó la prórroga del mandato presidencial de Juárez y al año siguiente volvió a México y se unió a las fuerzas de Porfirio Díaz. En 1867 participó en la batalla de Puebla y en el sitio de la ciudad de México. Al triunfo de la

Foto: Rogelio Cuéllar

Marianne Toussaint

Lupita Tovar

Libro de Juan Tovar

República fue administrador de rentas municipales, redactor de *El Siglo XIX* y diputado federal (1869-71). Colaboró en *El Guardia Nacional*, *El Cabrión*, *Las Cosquillas*, *El Constitucional* y *El Federalista*. Autor de las obras de teatro *Misterios del corazón* (1848), *Justicia del cielo* (1849), *La Catedral de México* (1850), *La toma de Oaxaca por Morelos*, *La conjuración de México* (1852), *Una deshonra sublime* (1854), *¿Y para qué?* (1856), *Risa de llanto* (1856), *La gloria del dolor* (1857), *Don Quijote de la Mancha* y *El rostro y el corazón*; de la novelas *Ironías de la vida* (1851) y *La hora de dios* (1865); de la recopilación de textos periodísticos *Horas de ostracismo* (1865) y de una *Historia del cuarto Congreso constitucional* (1872-74). Póstumamente aparecieron sus *Poesías* (1886).

Foto: Héctor López

Rigo Tovar

Tovar, Rigo ◆ n. en Matamoros, Tams. (1950). Cantante. Fue repartidor, tapizador, cantinero, lijador, soldador y troquelador. En 1972, cuando trabajaba en Houston, fundó el grupo de música afroantillana *Costa Azul*, que desde entonces dirige. Comenzó a componer en 1973. Algunas de sus canciones son *La sirenita*, *Mi Matamoros querido*, *En esta Navidad*, *Quítate la máscara*, *Dos tardes de mi vida*, *Triste Navidad*, *Me quiero casar*, *En las estepas del Asia central*, *Mi testamento*, *Mi amiga, mi esposa y mi amante*, *Cómo será la mujer* y *Lamento de amor*. Ha protagonizado el documental *Rigo, una confesión total*, de Víctor Vío (1978) y dos películas de ficción, ambas dirigidas por Felipe Cazals: *Rigo es amor* (1980) y *El gran triunfo* (1980).

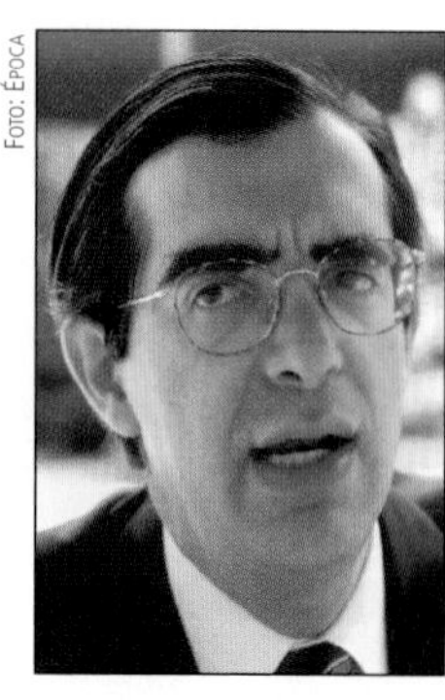
Foto: Época

Guillermo Tovar y de Teresa

Tovar, Urbano ◆ n. en Mascota, Jal. (?-1887). Abogado y político conservador. Fue gobernador de Jalisco (1858), procurador general de la Nación, magistrado del Supremo Tribunal de Justicia y secretario de Hacienda (del 5 de noviembre de 1859 al 13 de agosto de 1860) en el gobierno de Miguel Miramón. Perteneció al Colegio Nacional de Abogados.

Tovar Luna, Raúl ◆ n. en Querétaro, Qro. (1913). Fotógrafo, pintor, grabador y escultor. Estudió en la Escuela Nacional de Artes Plásticas. Expuso por primera vez en 1965. En 1976 ganó un premio del Salón de la Plástica Mexicana.

Tovar Montañez, Jorge ◆ n. en el DF (1939). Maestro normalista por la Escuela Normal Superior, con especialidad en matemáticas. Afiliado al PPS desde 1965, ha desempeñado diversos cargos en los comités estatales de ese partido en Chihuahua y Nuevo León; también ha sido diputado federal suplente (1979-82) y diputado federal (1991-94). Ha sido profesor de primaria, secundaria, preparatoria y normal en escuelas del gobierno de Chihuahua, el Instituto Tecnológico de Chihuahua y el Colegio de Bachilleres (1965-89).

Tovar y de Teresa, Guillermo ◆ n. en el DF (1956). Historiador. Realizó estudios en la UAM. Fue asesor del presidente Gustavo Díaz Ordaz (1968-70), de Pedro Ramírez Vázquez cuando éste ocupó la SAHOP (1977-82) y de Juan José Bremer cuando fue subsecretario de Cultura de la SEP (1983). Cronista de la ciudad de México (1986-87), renunció al cargo para convertirse en miembro fundador del Consejo de la Crónica de la Ciudad de México (1987-). Colaborador de las revistas *Artes de México*, *Archivo Español de Arte*, *Space Design*, *Cuadernos de Arte Virreinal*, *Historia Mexicana* y *Vuelta*, de cuyo consejo editorial fue miembro. Coautor de *El retablo de los reyes de la Catedral de México. Historia y restauración* (1985). Autor de *Pintura y escultura del renacimiento en México* (1978), *México barroco* (1980), *El renacimiento en México. Artistas y retablos* (1982), *La ciudad de México y la utopía en el siglo XVI* (1987), *Bibliografía novohispana de arte* (2 t., 1988-90), *Un rescate de la fantasía. El arte de los Lagarto, iluminadores novohispanos de los siglos XVI y XVII* (1988), *Gerónimo de Balbás en la Catedral de México* (1990), *Los escultores mestizos del barroco novohispano* (1991), *Pintura y escultura en Nueva España (1557-1640)* (1992), *El arte de la herrería en México* (1994) y *Repertorio de artistas mexicanos* (3 t., 1995-97), entre otros. Medalla al mérito ciudadano de la ARDF (1993). Fue becario de la Fundación Guggenheim (1985).

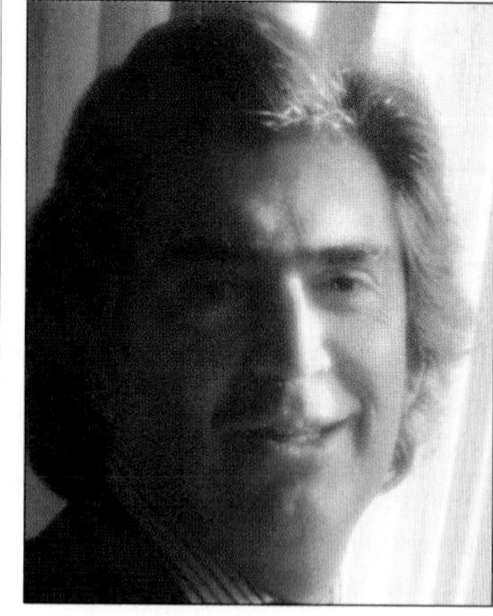

Rafael Tovar y de Teresa

Tovar y de Teresa, Rafael ◆ n. en el DF (1954). Licenciado en derecho por la UAM. Diplomado en inglés profesional por la Universidad de Cambridge; maestro en historia de las relaciones internacionales del siglo XX, y doctorado en historia de América Latina por la Universidad de París, Francia. Pertenece al PRI, donde fue subcoordinador del sector cultural del IEPES y miembro de la Comisión Consultiva de Política Exterior (1982). Ha sido jefe de relaciones culturales de la SHCP (1974-76), asesor del director general del INBA (1976-78), director de Asuntos Culturales (1979-82) y ministro de la Embajada de México en Francia (1983-88); asesor del secretario de Relaciones Exteriores (1987-88), coordinador nacional de Proyectos Especiales e Intercambios Culturales (1988-91), director general del Instituto Nacional de Bellas Artes (1991-92) y presidente del Consejo Nacional para la Cultura y las Artes (1992-) y del Fondo Nacional para la Cultura y las Artes (1992-). Pertenece a la Asociación del Servicio Exterior Mexicano y a la Federación de Alianzas Francesas.

Tovilla Cristiani, Eduardo Homero ◆ n. en Comitán, Chis. (1940). Licenciado en economía (1962) y doctor en administración pública por la

UNAM (1969), de la que fue profesor (1964-66) y subdirector de Administración (1966-70). Ha sido gerente de Administración de Aeroméxico (1970-73), gerente de Filiales Industriales y de Servicios de Conasupo (1973-76), oficial mayor de la CNOP(1975-76), diputado federal (1976-79 y 1982-85), gerente de Administración y Relaciones Públicas de Fertimex (1976-82), representante del gobierno de Chiapas en el Distrito Federal (1985) y subdelegado del DDF en Cuauhtémoc (1985-85). Pertenece al Colegio Nacional de Economistas y a la Liga de Economistas Revolucionarios del PRI.

Townsend, William Cameron ◆ n. y m. en EUA (1896-1982). Lingüista titulado en el Occidental College de Los Ángeles (1919). En 1917 se trasladó a Guatemala. Se dedicó a aprender lenguas americanas, a las cuales tradujo la *Biblia*. Llegó a México en 1936 y, apoyado por el presidente Lázaro Cárdenas, se dedicó a evangelizar indios en su propia lengua, así como a estudiar sus idiomas. En junio de 1936 fundó el Instituto Lingüístico de Verano, del que fue director hasta 1982, y en 1977 el Museo México-Cárdenas, en el estado de Carolina del Norte. Autor de los folletos *La verdad del petróleo mexicano* (1938), *Spanish Primer Sycofonemic Methods* (1936), *El Instituto Lingüístico de Verano* (1944) y *Mayan Studies I* (1961); y de los libros *Lázaro Cárdenas: demócrata mexicano* (1954), *The Found a Common Language: Community through Bilingual Education* (1972) y *La Unión Soviética como la vimos, de Armenia a Rusia* (1975). En 1958 fue condecorado por el gobierno mexicano con la Orden del Águila Azteca.

Toxqui Fernández de Lara, Alfredo ◆ n. en Cholula, Pue. (1913). Médico cirujano titulado en la Escuela de Medicina de la Universidad de Puebla (1940), de la que fue profesor (1948-51). Ha sido médico del Hospital General de Puebla, jefe de la Cruz Verde del estado, coordinador de los servicios de cirugía del Hospital Regional de IMSS, regidor suplente del ayuntamiento de Puebla (1948-51), diputado federal (1955-58), subdirector (1966-67) y oficial mayor de la Secretaría de Gobernación del gobierno de Puebla (1967); presidente interino del Comité Directivo Estatal del PRI en la misma entidad (1970), senador de la República (1970-75) y gobernador de Puebla (1975-81).

Toxtle Tlamani, Rodolfo ◆ n. en Coronango, Pue. (1948). Médico cirujano por la UAP, con especialidades en el Hospital Universitario de Puebla y el Hospital Infantil de México. Perteneció al PCM, del que fue secretario de Organización (1975-78) y al PFCRN, por el que fue diputado federal (1991-94). Ha ejercido su profesión y es profesor universitario. Miembro de la Sociedad Nacional de Profesores de Pediatría. Fue presidente de la Academia de Pediatría de la UAP.

Trabulse, Elías ◆ n. en el DF (1942). Historiador. Su apellido materno es Atala. Químico titulado en la UNAM y doctor en historia por El Colegio de México (1973). Profesor de la UNAM, de la Universidad Iberoamericana y del Instituto Tecnológico Autónomo de Monterrey. Es investigador del Centro de Estudios Históricos de El Colegio de México y codirector de historia cultural y científica de la humanidad de la UNESCO. Compilador de los cuatro volúmenes de la *Historia de la ciencia en México* (1983-87). Autor de *Ciencia y religión en el siglo XVII* (1974), *Las revoluciones de independencia en México y Estados Unidos. Un estudio comparativo* (1976), *Fluctuaciones económicas en Oaxaca durante el siglo XVIII* (1977), *El círculo roto. Estudios históricos sobre la ciencia en México* (1982), *La ciencia y la técnica en el México colonial* (1982), *Cartografía mexicana* (1983), *Le Développement Scientifique* (1984), *La ciencia perdida. Fray Diego Rodríguez, un sabio del siglo XVII* (1985), *Francisco Xavier Gamboa. Un político criollo en la ilustración mexicana 1717-1794* (1985), *Francisco Xavier de Gamboa and his Comentaries on the Minning Ordinances* (1987), *Francisco Javier Clavigero. Historiador ilustrado 1731-1787* (1987), *La ciencia en el siglo XIX* (1987) y del prefacio y la bibliografía de *Los manuscritos perdidos de Sigüenza y Góngora* (1988). Pertenece a la Academia Mexicana de la Historia desde 1980. En 1965, por sus trabajos sobre cinética química, recibió el premio internacional de la American Society for Testing and Materials; en 1984 obtuvo el Premio Juan Pablos y en 1986 el Premio Sor Juana Inés de la Cruz.

Libro de Elías Trabulse

Traconis, Daniel ◆ n. en Mérida, Yuc. (1836-?). Estudió en el Colegio de San Ildefonso y el Colegio Militar. En 1855 combatió el levantamiento conservador de Tolimán y en 1857 el de Puebla. Se incorporó a las fuerzas liberales de Miguel Cástulo Alatriste en diciembre de 1857. En 1858 participó en un frustrado asalto liberal contra la ciudad de México y fue hecho prisionero, encarcelado en la prisión de Santiago Tlatelolco y condenado a muerte. Escapó poco después y se unió a las fuerzas de Pedro Ampudia. A principios de los años sesenta volvió a Yucatán y combatió a los mayas de Chan Santa Cruz. Fue comandante de celadores de Sisal y del batallón fijo de Yucatán. En 1864 reconoció al imperio. Nombrado comandante de la ofensiva imperial contra los mayas en junio de 1865, realizó varias incursiones victoriosas en la selva yucateca, pero en septiembre de 1866 fue sitiado en la población de Tihosuco. En noviembre, luego de 50 días de asedio, derrotó a los mayas. A principios de 1867 reprimió un alzamiento en la isla del Carmen y atacó a las fuerzas de Pablo García que sitiaban Campeche, pero en marzo tuvo que volver rápidamente a Mérida, a causa de la ofensiva republicana de Manuel Cepeda Peraza. Al frente de la guarnición de Mérida, fue sitiado durante 51 días por los republicanos, hasta que el 15 de junio se rindió y entregó la plaza. En diciembre de ese año se levantó en armas contra el presidente Benito Juárez y en febrero de 1868 ocupó brevemente el puerto de Sisal. Fue derrotado y amnistiado y se reincorporó al ejército. En 1871 dirigió una gran ofensiva contra los mayas y en julio de 1872 derrotó una insurrección conservadora en Valladolid. Durante el porfiriato fue gobernador de Yucatán (1890-94) y jefe de colonias militares.

Juan Bautista Traconis

Traconis, Juan Bautista ◆ n. en Mérida, Yuc., y m. en la ciudad de México (1809-1870). Militar. Su apellido materno era Rodríguez. Era comandante militar del departamento de Tabasco cuando, en agosto de 1846, se adhirió al Plan de la Ciudadela (☛), se levantó en armas contra del gobierno del presidente Mariano Paredes y Arrillaga y el 12 de agosto derrocó a José Víctor Jiménez Falcón y asumió la gubernatura. En octubre de ese año derrotó en las afueras de San Juan Bautista a las fuerzas invasoras estadounidenses de Mathew C. Perry y como el presidente Mariano Salas se negaba a proporcionarle ayuda, intentó independizar el estado, lo que se evitó porque en diciembre el gobierno de Valentín Gómez Farías le envió material de guerra. El 5 de enero de 1847 fue derrocado por fuerzas del gobierno de Chiapas. No obstante, se incorporó al Ejército Mexicano y participó en la batalla de Churubusco, el 20 de agosto de ese año. En 1855 se adhirió al Plan de Ayutla y durante el gobierno de Ignacio Comonfort fue gobernador de Puebla (1856-57). Durante la guerra de los Tres Años combatió a los conservadores en Veracruz y Oaxaca. Fue comandante militar y gobernador interino de Tamaulipas (del 15 de septiembre al 23 de octubre de 1862). Desde 1863 aceptó colaborar con los invasores franceses, por lo que al triunfo de la República fue degradado y encarcelado. Autor de una *Acusación al Soberano Congreso de la Unión contra los cc. presidente de la República Benito Juárez y Miguel Blanco, su ministro de la Guerra, por haber violado la Constitución, varias leyes y la ordenanza del Ejército* (1863).

Armando Trasviña Taylor

Trait d'Union, Le ◆ Periódico de la ciudad de México editado en francés por René Masson. El subtítulo era *Journal Francais Universel*. Se inició su publicación en 1849 y fue bisemanario hasta el 2 de junio de 1856, en que empezó a publicarse diariamente, excepto domingos. Defendió los intereses empresariales desde un punto de vista liberal. Durante el debate en torno a la Constitución de 1857 abogó por la libertad de cultos. Criticó la Ley Lafragua del 29 de diciembre de 1855, que limitaba severamente la libertad de expresión. Apoyó con entusiasmo la Ley de Desamortización del 8 de junio de 1856, que afectaba los bienes de las corporaciones civiles y eclesiásticas. El 23 de enero de 1858, bajo el gobierno conservador, el periódico fue suspendido. Masson volvió a publicarlo bajo el nombre de *Le Courrier Français*, que también fue censurado y el editor lo transformó en *Les Deux Mondes*, que corrió la misma suerte. Masson se trasladó a Veracruz, donde se hallaba el gobierno liberal, y volvió a publicar *Le Trait d'Union*. A principios de 1861, al instalarse el presidente Benito Juárez en la ciudad de México, continuó la publicación del periódico en la capital. En agosto de 1864, bajo la ocupación francesa, este órgano fue clausurado y Masson enviado al exilio. El periódico volvió a aparecer al triunfo de la República. En 1896 mudó su nombre a *Courrier du Mexique et de l'Europe*.

Le Trait d'Union

Le Trait d'Union

Trapero, Cándido ◆ n. Villamoras, Sin. (1932). Jugador de futbol americano. Estudió en el IPN. En 1948 ingresó como *fullback* en el equipo *Iguanas* del internado del Politécnico. Fue conocido como *El Expreso de Santo Tomás*. Entre 1950 y 1955 jugó con los *Burros Blancos* del IPN, en la Liga Mayor de Futbol Americano y, con Eduardo Tapia y Ramiro *Tigre* Medina, formó un grupo llamado *Los Tres Mosqueteros*. En dos ocasiones perteneció a la Selección Nacional. En 1952 recibió el título de Jugador del Año.

Trasviña Taylor, Armando ◆ n. en La Paz, BCS (1933). Estudió en la Escuela Normal Urbana de Baja California Sur (1952) y en la Escuela Normal Superior de México (1960). En el PRI, partido al que pertenece desde 1946, se ha desempeñado como director juvenil (1952-84) y oficial mayor del Comité Directivo del Territorio de Baja California Sur (1952), presidente del Comité Directivo Estatal de Baja California Sur (1972-74) y delegado del CEN en Durango (1982) y Campeche (1985). Ha sido juez del Tribunal para Menores de La Paz (1965-72), director de Acción Social del gobierno del territorio de Baja California Sur (1966-72), diputado y presidente del Congreso Constituyente de Baja California Sur (1974-75), secretario general de Gobierno de la entidad (1975-79), diputado federal (1979-82), delegado de la CNOP en Durango (1980) y senador de la República (1982-88). Autor de *A. envíos poéticos* (1966), *El estado de Baja California* (1969), *La literatura en Baja California Sur*, *Loreto, madre y cuna de las Californias* y *Europa, la marina y la pesca*. Pertenece a la Comisión de las Californias, a la Asociación de Escritores de la Península de Baja California y a la Academia de Historia Sudcaliforniana.

Tratado de Guadalupe-Hidalgo ◆ Nombre con el que se conoce, por el pueblo del Distrito Federal donde se firmó, el *Tratado de Paz, Amistad y Límites* con el que formalmente terminó la guerra entre México y Estados Unidos (☛). Fue signado el 2 de febrero de 1848 por Bernardo Couto, Miguel Aristáin y Luis G. Cuevas, en nombre del gobierno mexicano, y Nicholas P. Trist, en representación del estadounidense. Las negociaciones se habían iniciado el 21 de agosto de 1847, un día después de las derrotas mexicanas en las batallas de Padierna y Churubusco, cuando a propuesta del cónsul británico en la ciudad de México, el comandante de las fuerzas invasoras, el general Winfield Scott, había enviado un mensaje al presidente Antonio López de Santa Anna, en el que consideraba que "Demasiada sangre se ha vertido ya en esta desnaturalizada tierra, entre las dos grandes repúblicas de este continente" y que era "tiempo de que las diferencias entre ellas sean amigable y honrosamente arregladas". Santa Anna aceptó y, el 23 de agosto, dos representantes del gobierno, Ignacio de Mora y Villamil y Benito Quijano se encontraron en Tacubaya con Persifor J. Smith y J. A. Quitman, los dos enviados de Scott, y redactaron un convenio de armisticio "con el objeto de dar lugar al gobierno mexicano para tomar en consideración las proposiciones que tiene que hacerle el comisionado por parte del Excmo. Sr. Presidente de los Estados Unidos". Dicho armisticio entró en vigor un día después, luego del intercambio de ratificaciones. El 27 de agosto, José Joaquín de Herrera, Bernardo Couto, Ignacio de Mora y Villamil y Miguel Aristáin se encontraron en Azcapotzalco con Nicholas P. Trist, el comisionado estadounidense, quien había sido nombrado agente confidencial de Estados Unidos en abril. Días después, Trist comunicó a los representantes mexicanos las propuestas del gobierno de Washington, que consistían en la cesión de Texas, incluida la franja de tierra situada entre los ríos Nueces y Bravo, que era reclamada por los texanos desde el fin de su guerra de independencia; la cesión de las dos Californias y Nuevo México y algunas zonas septentrionales de Tamaulipas, Coahuila, Chihuahua y Sonora, así como la autorización de libre tránsito de tropas estadounidenses por el istmo de Tehuantepec. A cambio, Estados Unidos se comprometía a pagar todas las reclamaciones de ciudadanos estadounidenses contra México, renunciaba al cobro de indemnizaciones de guerra y aceptaba pagar una cantidad por el territorio cedido. El gobierno de Santa Anna respondió que sólo en el caso de Texas se podía hablar de cesión, que si los estadounidenses querían más territorio lo compraran y que el tránsito por Tehuantepec no era objeto de negociación. El 6 de septiembre, a nombre de la comisión, Couto presentó una nota en la que recordaba que la guerra se había iniciado por la posesión de Texas y que sólo en ese caso el gobierno estadounidense podía alegar derechos, no así con los territorios del noroeste y que ni Nuevo México ni las Californias eran objeto de las negociaciones. Trist contestó que los Estados Unidos "no se presentan como compradores que pretenden obligar a la venta de territorio, sino a título de conquista". Ese mismo día se suspendieron las conferencias y el 7 de septiembre se reiniciaron los combates. El 20 de octubre, luego de la ocupación de la ciudad de México y la huida de Santa Anna, Trist envió una una nota a Luis de la Rosa, secretario de Relaciones del gobierno de Manuel de la Peña y Peña que se encontraba en Querétaro, en la que proponía reanudar las negociaciones. De la Rosa contestó siete días más tarde, el 27 de octubre, y en su comunicación aseguraba que "el gobierno de México está animado de los mismos ardientes deseos (.) de que cese una guerra cuyas calamidades pesan actualmente sobre esta República" y volvió a llamar a los miembros de la comisión, pero como Herrera y Mora y Villamil tenían cargos en el gobierno, De la Rosa nombró en su lugar a Luis G. Cuevas y a Manuel Rincón, pero éste se negó a participar. El 22 de noviembre, De la Rosa informó a Trist que la comisión estaría formada por Couto, Aristáin y Cuevas. El gobierno estadounidense, sin embargo, estaba molesto por la incapacidad de Trist para imponer los términos propuestos por Washington, sobre todo la parte referida a la anexión de la franja de tierra entre el Nueces y el Bravo, y el 24 lo desconoció como negociador, pero el 6 de diciembre, una vez que había obtenido el apoyo de Scott y del gobierno mexicano, Trist informó a Washington que las negociaciones se habían reiniciado y que por lo tanto su desconocimiento no tenía sentido. Además argumentó que si las negociaciones se suspendían nuevamente y el ejército de Estados Unidos permanecía más tiempo en México, provocaría el incremento de la resistencia mexicana; "Déjese que el espíritu de la desesperación llegue a despertarse —escribió— y entonces las cosas presentarán un aspecto muy diverso del que han presentado hasta aquí". La nueva ronda de negociaciones se inició el 2 de enero de 1848 en la ciudad de México. Durante enero, mientras crecía la oposición interna a las negociaciones e incluso se había producido un levantamiento militar en San Luis Potosí, los comisionados mexicanos consiguieron excluir del tratado las cláusulas sobre el tránsito por el istmo de Tehuantepec, que los estadounidenses se comprometieran a respetar las vidas, propiedades y creeencias religosas de los mexicanos de Nuevo México y la Alta California, que la península de Baja California permaneciera en México y que el territorio de Chihuahua se conservara intacto. En cambio, no pudieron evitar que la frontera nororiental se estableciera en el río Bravo y aceptaron 15 millones de pesos de indemnización, en vez de los 30 millones de pesos que el gobierno de Querétaro necesitaba para derrotar a la oposición, porque, según escribía De la Rosa el 26 de enero, "sin recursos tan cuantiosos (.) para hacer frente a las dificultades que van a suscitarse con la terminación de los tratados, el gobierno está seguro de su disolución en muy pocos días". El 29 de enero, los comisionados terminaron de redactar el proyecto de tratado y lo firmaron tres días más tarde. La línea divisoria, que "será religiosamente respetada por cada una de las dos Repúblicas", se estableció del "río Grande, llamado por otro nombre río Bravo del Norte", hasta la población de El Paso; de ahí la frontera subía hacia el norte "por el lindero occidental de Nuevo México hasta donde este lindero esté cortado por el primer brazo del río Gila (y si no está cortado por ningún brazo del río Gila, entonces hasta el punto del mismo lindero occidental más cercano a tal brazo, y de allí, en una línea recta al mismo brazo continuará después por la mitad de este brazo); y del río hasta su confluencia con el río Colorado"; donde se iniciaba una línea recta hacia el oeste que atravesaba California y terminaba en el océano Pacífico. El corte separaba de México la franja septentrional de Tamaulipas, precisamente la tierra entre el Nueces y el Bravo; la

Nicholas P. Trist, representante de los Estados Unidos en la negociación del Tratado de Guadalupe-Hidalgo

Portada del cartapacio del Tratado de Guadalupe-Hidalgo

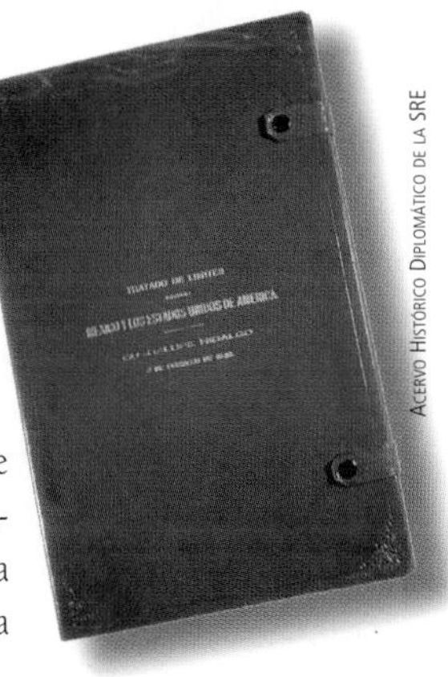

ACERVO HISTÓRICO DIPLOMÁTICO DE LA SRE

totalidad de los territorios de Texas, Nuevo México y de la Alta California y la porción de Sonora situada al norte del río Gila. En total, Estados Unidos se apropiaba de 2,500,000 km², aproximadamente. Los mexicanos que vivieran en el territorio cedido, decía el documento, "podrán permanecer en donde ahora habitan, o trasladarse en cualquier tiempo a la República Méxicana; conservando en los indicados territorios los bienes que poseen". En caso de quedarse, "podrán conservar el título y derechos de ciudadanos mexicanos", pero si un año después no habían manifestado su determinación, "se considerará que han elegido ser ciudadanos de los Estados Unidos". Respecto a los comanches, apaches y otros grúpos nómadas que habitaban la zona recién ocupada, Estados Unidos aseguraba que "contendrá" sus incursiones en territorio mexicano "por medio de la fuerza, siempre que sea necesario". Washington se comprometía a pagar 15 millones de pesos al gobierno de Querétaro, tres de ellos al momento del intercambio de las ratificaciones y el resto en pagos anuales de tres millones cada uno; asimismo, pagaría todas las reclamaciones de estadounidenses contra México. La parte final del documento establecía que con la firma del tratado terminaría el bloqueo de los puertos mexicanos y se haría entrega de las aduanas; un mes más tarde, las fuerzas que ocupaban la ciudad de México se retirarían, y dos meses después la totalidad de los efectivos estadounidenses abandonarían territorio mexicano. El 17 de febrero se iniciaron las negociaciones para el armisticio, que fue redactado por los mexicanos Mora y Villamil y Benito Quijano, y los estadounidenses Worth y Smith, y firmado a principios de marzo. El proceso de ratificaciones, por su parte, se inició a finales de febrero en Estados Unidos y principos de mayo en México. En el Congreso de Washington sólo el diputado Crittenden se opuso, por considerarlo desventajoso para México, pero el 10 de marzo, el Senado lo aprobó. En Querétaro, mientras tanto, la discusión de inició el 10 de mayo, y a pesar de que la Cámara de Diputados estaba dominada por los moderados, fue necesaria la intervención de los ministros De la Rosa y Anaya para que el día 13, por 51 votos contra 35, el tratado fuera aprobado. El dictamen pasó al Senado el 21, y el 24 de mayo fue aprobado por 33 votos en favor. Sólo votaron en contra de la cesión de territorio los senadores Robredo, Mariano Otero, Ramón Morales y Bernardo Flores. El 30 de mayo, finalmente, se intercambiaron las ratificaciones. En 1853, tropas estadounidenses ocuparon La Mesilla (☛) y Santa Anna optó por vender los casi 110 mil kilómetros cuadrados que comprendía, además de que liberaba a Washington del compromiso de evitar las incursiones de indios. De esta manera, Estados Unidos se apoderó de un territorio que comprende la totalidad de los actuales estados de California, Nevada, Utah, Arizona, Nuevo México y Texas y, parcialmente, Wyoming, Colorado, Kansas y Oklahoma.

Cartapacios del Tratado de Guadalupe-Hidalgo

Acervo Histórico Diplomático de la SRE

Tratado McLane-Ocampo ◆ Nombre con el que se conoce, por los apellidos de los negociadores, el *Tratado de Tránsito y Comercio entre los Estados Unidos Mexicanos y los Estados Unidos de América*, firmado en el puerto de Veracruz el 14 de diciembre de 1859, por el "ciudadano Melchor Ocampo, secretario de Estado y del Despacho de Relaciones Exteriores" del gobierno constitucional de Benito Juárez, y por el "ciudadano Robert M. McLane, enviado extraordinario y Ministro plenipotenciaro de Estados Unidos de América cerca del Gobierno Mexicano". A mediados de abril de 1859, McLane había iniciado conversaciones con Ocampo y Miguel Lerdo de Tejada, secretario de Fomento, Colonización, Industria y Comercio del gobierno liberal, con la idea de formalizar un acuerdo que permitiera el tránsito de ciudadanos y mercancías estadounidenses por el istmo de Tehuantepec. Para los liberales, entonces derrotados en todo el centro del país, el acuerdo les permitiría obtener recursos económicos y pertechos militares para enfrentar con éxito al ejército conservador. Por eso, desde finales de abril, Ocampo insinuó que el gobierno de Juárez estaba dispuesto a ceder Baja California a Estados Unidos y a permitir el libre tránsito de estadounidenses por Tehuantepec y a través de otras vías en el norte. El mismo Ocampo propuso el establecimiento de una alianza militar entre ambos Estados y la celebración de dos tratados, uno sobre la cesión de Baja California y otro sobre los derechos de paso por el istmo. Los estadounidenses, por su parte, rechazaron las propuestas de Ocampo, pero, impulsados por la aparente disposición del gobierno de Juárez, continuaron con las conversa-

Miguel Lerdo de Tejada, con quien se iniciaron conversaciones para el Tratado McLane-Ocampo

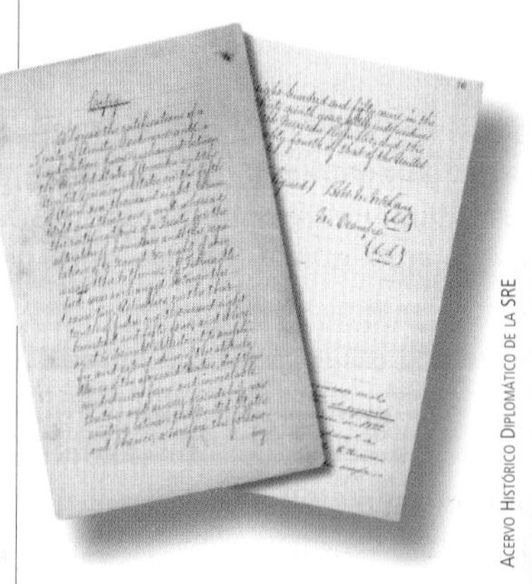

Acervo Histórico Diplomático de la SRE

Manuscrito del Tratado McLane-Ocampo

James Buchanan, presidente estadounidense al momento de la firma del Tratado McLane-Ocampo

ciones y, el 20 de junio, McLane presentó un proyecto que incluía, además de la autorización a perpetuidad del tránsito estadounidense por Tehuantepec, la creación de otros dos corredores: uno entre Camargo y Mazatlán y otro entre Nogales y Guaymas; la cesión de Baja California a Estados Unidos y la autorización para que, "usando de su arbitrio", el gobierno de Washington pudiera "emplear sus fuerzas" con el fin de proteger a quienes utilizaran los tres corredores. El 10 de julio, Ocampo presentó una contrapropuesta en la que rechazaba la cesión de la península, pero aceptaba la creación de los tres corredores, en el entendido de que la seguridad de los pasos era responsabilidad del gobierno mexicano y que las fuerzas extranjeras sólo podrían ocuparlos militarmente "previo permiso del gobierno mexicano". Además, el proyecto de Ocampo prohibía la construcción de instalaciones militares extranjeras en territorio nacional. Durante el resto de julio, los representantes de la Casa Blanca insistieron en la cesión de Baja California, y el presidente James Buchanan se manifestó contrario a la celebración de un tratado que no incluyera la entrega de la península, mientras que los mexicanos reafirmaron la necesidad de establecer una alianza militar entre los dos países. A mediados de agosto, Ocampo fue sustituido por Juan Antonio de la Fuente, quien mantuvo las posiciones del gobierno de Juárez. En diciembre, Washington aceptó, en términos generales, la propuesta de Ocampo, y con el michoacano de nuevo al frente de la Cancillería se firmó el tratado. El documento se consideró como un acuerdo para "ampliar y extender algunas de las especificaciones" del tratado, que en diciembre de 1853 habían firmado los gobiernos de Antonio López de Santa Anna y Franklin Pierce para concluir la venta de La Mesilla (☛). Por el Tratado MacLane-Ocampo, el gobierno mexicano cedía "a los Estados Unidos en perpetuidad (.) el derecho de vía por el istmo de Tehuantepec, de un océano hasta otro por cualquier clase de camino que exista hoy o existiera en adelante". México, para promover el tránsito interocéanico, asumía el compromiso de establecer "dos puertos, el uno al este y el otro al oeste" del istmo, en los que sólo se cobrarían los gastos "del acarreo y almacenaje". Además, el gobierno nacional renunciaba a cobrar cualquier "gravamen o derecho de portazgo" a las mercancías del país del norte que transitaran por Tehuantepec, salvo los que también se aplicaran a las "personas y propiedades mexicanas", y aceptaba el libre paso del correo estadounidense. La seguridad del corredor quedaba a cargo del Ejército Mexicano, pero en caso de que éste no la garantizara, "el Gobierno de los Estados Unidos podrá, con el consentimiento o a pedimento del Gobierno de México", emplear sus propias fuerzas militares para garantizar el libre tránsito de mercancías y personas. McLane consiguió la inclusión de un párrafo que permitiría al ejército estadounidense intervenir en cualquier momento, pues en él se especificaba que en "el caso excepcional (.) de un peligro imprevisto o inminente para las vidas o propiedades de los ciudadanos de Estados Unidos, las fuerzas de dicha República tendrán facultad de obrar (.) sin que dicho consentimiento previo haya sido obtenido". Más adelante, el tratado establecía la creación de los corredores Nogales-Hermosillo-Guaymas y Camargo-Monterrey-Durango-Mazatlán, en los cuales se garantizaban "a perpetuidad" los derechos de tránsito para el país vecino. Se estipulaba también que por el paso Nogales-Hermosillo-Guaymas, así como por Tehuantepec, podrían desplazarse libremente "tropas, pertrechos y municiones de guerra" del ejército estadounidense, que pagarían la mitad de los gastos de transporte de materiales y personas civiles; que las creencias religiosas de los extranjeros serían respetadas; que, de una lista de 41 productos, el Congreso de EUA escogería aquellos que podrían circular libremente entre ambos países y que México conservaba el derecho de celebrar acuerdos de libre comercio con cualquier nación, sólo que sin ofrecer más privilegios que los otorgados a Estados Unidos. Finalmente, "en consideración de las anteriores estipulaciones, y en compensación de las rentas a las cuales renuncia México (.), el Gobierno de los Estados Unidos conviene en pagar al Gobierno de México la suma de cuatro millones de pesos, de los cuales, dos millones se pagarán luego de que se verifique el canje de ratificaciones". El resto del pago, sin embargo, sería retenido por Washington para el "pago de las reclamaciones de los ciudadanos de los Estados Unidos contra el Gobierno de la República de México". Ese mismo día, Ocampo y McLane firmaron una *Con-*

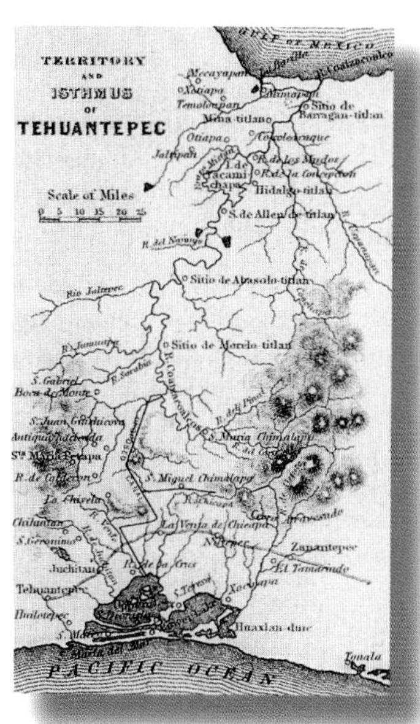

Litografía del istmo de Tehuantepec, punto central del Tratado McLane-Ocampo (1854)

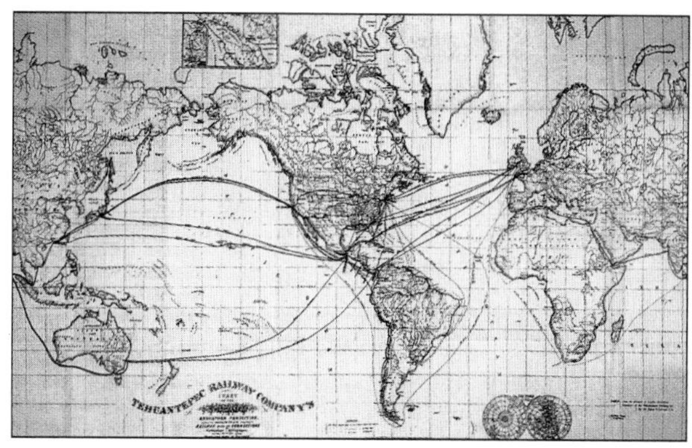

Mapa con las rutas de todo el mundo a través del istmo de Tehuantepec, ambición de los Estados Unidos a partir del Tratado McLane-Ocampo *vención entre la República Mexicana y los Estados Unidos* que era, de hecho, la alianza que desde junio había propuesto el secretario de Relaciones de México. Este segundo documento establecía que si "el resguardo y seguridad de los ciudadanos de cualquiera de las dos Repúblicas fueren arriesgados dentro del territorio de la otra, y que el Gobierno legítimo y reconocido de ella no pueda, por cualquier motivo (.) prevenir tal resguardo y seguridad, será obligación de aquel Gobierno solicitar el socorro del otro para mantener (.) el orden y seguridad en el territorio de aquella República". La ratificación de tratado debía realizarse en los seis meses siguientes. Durante los primeros meses de 1860 se libró una batalla diplomática entre Gregorio Barandarián, representante del gobierno conservador de Miramón, y José María Mata, embajador de México en Washington, quienes trataron de convencer a los senadores estadounidenses de rechazar o ratificar el tratado, que concitó la oposición de los empresarios que pretendían abrir un canal en Panamá o Nicaragua, opuestos naturalmente a la creación de un paso en Tehuantepec; de los miembros del Partido Repúblicano, reacios a permitir el fortalecimiento económico de los esclavistas estados sureños, que serían los más beneficiados con la proyectada vía; y, por último, de los partidarios del proteccionismo estadounidense, quienes consideraban peligrosa la posibilidad de que México celebrara acuerdos semejantes con gobiernos europeos. En mayo, el Senado estadounidense, que en dos ocasiones había rechazado el documento, solicitó al gobierno de Juárez la ampliación del plazo para la ratificación. El gobierno mexicano accedió, pero el 5 de octubre, vencida esta prórroga, Juárez rechazó una nueva posposición, e *ipso facto* se canceló el tratado. Aunque todavía en diciembre el presidente Buchanan abogó por la aprobación del Congreso, éste no volvió a discutirlo. Para entonces, el ejército liberal había pasado a la ofensiva.

Protesta del gobierno mexicano en contra del Tratado Mon-Almonte el 30 de enero de 1860

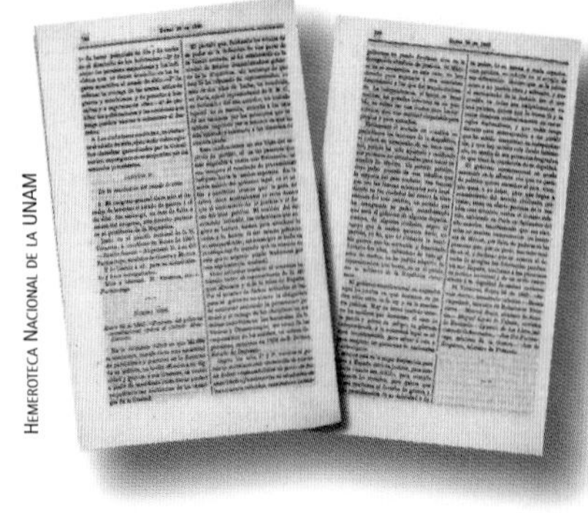
HEMEROTECA NACIONAL DE LA UNAM

TRATADO MON-ALMONTE ◆ Convenio firmado en París el 26 de septiembre de 1859 por Juan Nepomuceno Almonte, ministro plenipotenciario del gobierno conservador de Félix María Zuloaga, y Alejandro Mon, representante de la reina Isabel II de España, con lo que se restablecieron las relaciones diplomáticas entre ambos países, rotas por el gobierno peninsular a finales de 1856, luego del asesinato de varios ciudadanos españoles en las haciendas mexiquenses de San Vicente y Chiconcuac y el mineral duranguense de San Dimas. Mediante el documento, el gobierno conservador aseguraba que "continuará activamente la persecución y castigo de los cómplices" de las personas condenadas y ejecutadas por los asesinatos en el Estado de México, mientras que, respecto de los crímenes de Durango, se comprometía a activar "todos los procedimientos" para que, una vez desalojados los liberales del estado, los culpables "tengan el debido castigo". Aunque el gobierno conservador "está convencido de que no ha habido responsabilidad de las autoridades" en los asesinatos, consentía en "indemnizar a los súbditos españoles" afectados, para "que se corten de una vez las diferencias que se han suscitado entre la República y España". Finalmente, el gobierno de España aceptaba que "las referidas indemnizaciones no pueden servir de base ni antecedente para otros casos de igual naturaleza", por lo que "los daños y perjucios cuyas reclamaciones se hallaban pendientes al interrumpirse las relaciones (.) serán objeto de arreglos ulteriores". En enero de 1860 se celebró el intercambio de las ratificaciones, pero la derrota de los conservadores en la guerra de los Tres Años, dejó sin efecto el acuerdo que los liberales se negaron a reconocer.

TRATADO DE TLATELOLCO ◆ Convenio internacional firmado el 14 de febrero de 1967 en la sede de la Secretaría de Relaciones Exteriores, situada en el barrio de Tlatelolco de la ciudad de México, que prohíbe a los Estados firmantes la utilización de la energía nuclear con fines militares. Cuatro años antes, el 21 de marzo de 1963, el presidente mexicano, Adolfo López Mateos, envió una iniciativa a los jefes de Estado de Bolivia, Brasil, Chile y Ecuador, en la que proponía la firma de un acuerdo que proscribiera el uso, compra, fabricación o almacenamiento de armas nucleares en el continente americano, desde México hasta el extremo sur de América, aunque permitía la utilización de la energía nuclear con fines pacíficos. Un mes después, el 29 de abril, los mandatarios convocados por López Mateos aceptaron la iniciativa e invitaron al resto de los presidentes latinoamericanos. El texto del tratado fue redactado por una comisión especial de la Organización de las Naciones Unidas. Para vigilar el cumplimiento de lo acordado, en 1969 se creó el Organismo para la Proscripción de las Armas Nucleares en la América Latina (OPANAL).

TRATADOS DE BUCARELI ◆ Nombre que se ha dado a las actas de las Conferencias de Bucareli, que dieron como resultado la firma de una Convención Especial de Reclamaciones y otra Convención General de Reclamaciones. El 13 de agosto de 1923 fueron firmados ambos documentos en el número 85 de la calle de Bucareli, de donde tomaron su nombre. Fueron la culminación de las conversaciones sostenidas desde 1921 entre representantes de los gobiernos de México y Estados Unidos, cuyas relaciones se habían interrumpido desde el 7 de mayo de 1920. Por el gobierno de Washington firmaron Charles Beecher Warren y John Burton Payne, en tanto que la parte mexicana estuvo representada por Fernando González Roa y Ramón Ross. La Convención Especial de Reclamaciones tenía por objeto canalizar las exigencias de ciudadanos estadounidenses por presuntos daños causados a sus bienes

Edificio en el cual se discutieron los Tratados de Bucareli

durante la revolución. La Convención General de Reclamaciones establecía que los ciudadanos de ambos países harían las demandas pertinentes por daños sufridos de 1868 a 1910. Las discusiones en torno a estos documentos tratados fueron ásperas en los congresos de ambas naciones, e incluso se dijo que el asesinato del senador mexicano Field Jurado se debió a su oposición a la firma de los mismos. La ratificación del Convenio General fue firmada en Washington el 8 de septiembre de 1923, por Charles Evan Hughes, Charles Beecher Warren y John Burton Payne, por el lado de Estados Unidos, y por Manuel C. Téllez, en representación del gobierno mexicano. El Convenio Especial fue ratificado dos días después en la ciudad de México y firmado por George F. Summerlin y Alberto J. Pani. Según Aarón Sáenz, quien era secretario de Relaciones Exteriores cuando se inició la negociación, "las actas de las conferencias no alcanzaron el grado de una obligación contractual, de un deber constitucional que cumplir, ni de una obligación de derecho internacional que se pudiera exigir. Fue un *modus vivendi* que se obtuvo por virtud de la buena fe entre los dos gobiernos, sin formalidad legal, pero con los efectos de haber solucionado el estancamiento en las relaciones internacionales. La solución consistió en reanudar las relaciones diplomáticas entre México y los Estados Unidos, incondicionalmente, pacíficamente".

Tratados de Córdoba ◆ Documento que marca el fin de la dominación española sobre México. Su nombre completo es *Tratados celebrados en la Villa de Córdoba el 24 del presente mes, entre los señores don Juan de O'Donojú, Teniente General de los ejércitos de España, y don Agustín de Iturbide, Primer Jefe del Ejército Imperial Mexicano de las Tres Garantías*. Fue firmado el 24 de agosto de 1821, cuando sólo Acapulco, Chihuahua, Durango, Veracruz y la ciudad de México permanecían en poder de las fuerzas coloniales. La decisión de firmar los acuerdos provino, paradójicamente, de O'Donojú, capitán general y jefe político superior de la Nueva España, quien seis días después de haber desembarcado en Veracruz y luego de haber redactado dos proclamas en que manifestaba su determinación de ocupar el virreinato, el 5 de agosto le escribió una carta a Iturbide en la que explicaba que su misión no consistía en prolongar "la dependencia colonial" sino, al contrario, "poner a los numerosos pueblos en estado de conseguir, con más seguridad y sin sacrificios horribles, lo que la propagación de las luces les hizo desear", es decir, la independencia. Para lograr la emancipación de manera pacífica, O'Donojú aceptaba una propuesta que Iturbide le había hecho en marzo al entonces virrey Juan Ruiz de Apodaca, que consistía en que una Regencia integrada por el virrey y los principales conspiradores de la Profesa (☛) se encargara de cumplir el Plan de Iguala (☛). Finalmente, O'Donojú proponía encontrarse con Iturbide para "poder conciliar (.) las medidas necesarias para evitar toda desgracia (.) en tanto que el rey y las Cortes aprueban el tratado que celebremos y por que V. tanto ha anhelado". Tres semanas después se realizó la entrevista. El acuerdo, hecho para desatar "sin romper los vínculos que unieron a los dos continentes", establecía que "Esta América se reconocerá por nación soberana e independiente". El nuevo Estado, llamado Imperio Mexicano (☛), tendría carácter "monárquico constitucional moderado" y sería gobernado por Fernando VII o, "por su renuncia o no admisión", por los infantes Carlos, Francisco de Paula o Carlos Luis, a quienes se les ofrecería sucesivamente el trono. Si ninguno de los borbones españoles aceptaba, las Cortes mexicanas designarían un emperador. Mientras dos enviados viajaban a España y transmitían las ofertas, se formaría una "Junta Provisional Gubernativa", compuesta por "los primeros hombres del reino por sus virtudes, por sus destinos, por sus fortunas, representación y concepto", uno de los cuales sería el propio O'Donojú. La Junta elegiría un presidente y a tres personas, "de su seno o fuera de él", que se encargarían del Poder Ejecutivo mientras se determinaba quién sería el emperador. Además, la Junta tendría la obligación de convocar a las Cortes constituyentes mexicanas y hasta antes de la instalación de éstas, ejercería el Poder Legislativo. Por último, el acuerdo establecía que toda persona "queda en libertad natural para trasladarse con su fortuna a donde le convenga", salvo los "empleados públicos o militares, que notoriamente son desafectos a la independencia mexicana", quienes "necesariamente saldrán de este imperio, dentro de los términos que la regencia prescriba". O'Donojú fue comisionado para convencer a la guarnición virreinal de la ciudad de México de que desalojara la plaza. En abril de 1822, las Cortes españolas

Madero y su gabinete durante la negociación de los Tratados de Ciudad Juárez

declararon nulo el tratado y desconocieron la independencia del imperio mexicano, con lo que el camino para la coronación de Iturbide quedó abierto.

Tratados de Ciudad Juárez ◆ Nombre del acuerdo de paz firmado el 21 de mayo de 1911 en la población fronteriza de Ciudad Juárez, por "don Francisco S. Carbajal, representante del Gobierno del señor General don Porfirio Díaz; don Francisco Vázquez Gómez, don Francisco Madero y Lic. don José María Pino Suárez como representantes los tres últimos de la revolución", que puso fin a la insurrección iniciada en noviembre de 1910. Desde los primeros días de abril de 1911, a causa del avance maderista sobre Ciudad Juárez, cuya posible ocupación facilitaría a los rebeldes adquirir armas en El Paso, las autoridades porfiristas habían anunciado su disposición a negociar un acuerdo de paz. El día 20, dos representantes gubernamentales, Toribio Esquivel Obregón y Oscar Braniff, llegaron a Ciudad Juárez para entrevistarse con Madero, que encabezaba el ejército rebelde instalado cerca de la población. Madero, por su parte, parecía poco dispuesto a emprender una acción armada contra la ciudad, y el 23 de abril acordó una tregua con Juan N. Navarro, comandante de las fuerzas federales de Ciudad Juárez, para permitir las negociaciones. En la última semana de abril, Braniff y Esquivel propusieron que, a cambio del licenciamiento de las fuerzas revolucionarias y fin de las hostilidades, el gobierno de Díaz aceptaría algunos triunfos de los candidatos maderistas a diversas gubernaturas y legalizaría el Partido Nacional Antirreeleccionista. Aunque la propuesta gubernamental no consideraba la principal demanda del Plan de San Luis Potosí (☛), la renuncia del presidente Díaz, Madero pareció aceptar la propuesta. El gobierno de Díaz envió a Ciudad Juárez a Francisco S. Carbajal para establecer los detalles del acuerdo. Durante su viaje, sin embargo, Vázquez Gómez y otros de los más cercanos colaboradores de Madero, convencieron al coahuilense de exigir la renuncia del presidente antes que acordar cualquier otras cosa, lo que hizo el 4 de mayo. Las negociaciones se estancaron y parecía que los revolucionarios reemprenderían el ataque contra la población fronteriza, pero a causa de que la guarnición estadounidense de El Paso advirtió que si alguna bala cruzaba la fronterza, los soldados de Estados Unidos entrarían a México a castigar a quienes dispararan, Madero prefirió retirarse hacia Chihuahua, a pesar de la oposición del ejército rebelde. El 7 de mayo se reanudaron las negociaciones en Ciudad Juárez, Al día siguiente, sin embargo, las fuerzas de Pascual Orozco y Francisco Villa atacaron Ciudad Juárez a pesar de la oposición de Madero, y la ocuparon el día 10. Las conversaciones de paz se reiniciaron nuevamente, y el 21 se firmó el acuerdo. El documento establecía que "Desde hoy cesarán en todo el territorio de la República las hostilidades que han existido entre las fuerzas del Gobierno y de la Revolución", debido a que "el señor General Porfirio Díaz ha manifestado su resolución de renunciar a la presidencia de la República antes de que termine el mes en curso" y a que "se tienen noticias fidedignas de que el señor Ramón Corral renunciará igualmente a la Vicepresidencia". Los firmantes acordaron que "por ministerio de la ley, el señor licenciado don Francisco L. de la Barra (.) se encargará interinamente del Poder Ejecutivo de la Nación y convocará a elecciones generales dentro de los términos de la Constitución". El gobierno de León de la Barra, además, se encargaría de licenciar a las tropas revolucionarias "a medida que en cada Estado se vayan dando los pasaos necesarios para restablecer y garantizar la paz y el orden públicos", si bien Chihuahua, Coahuila y Sonora quedaron en manos de los maderistas. Fuera del documento se convino en que los antirreeleccionistas ocuparían las carteras ministeriales del nuevo gobierno.

Tratados de la Soledad ◆ ☛ *Preliminares de la Soledad.*

Tratados de Teoloyucan ◆ Nombre con el que se conocen las *Condiciones en que se verificará la evacuación de la plaza de México por el Ejército Federal y la disolución del mismo*, documento firmado en la localidad de Teoloyucan, Estado de México, el 13 de agosto de 1914 por Álvaro Obregón, Lucio

Firma de los Tratados de Teoloyucan

Blanco, Othón P. Blanco y Gustavo A. Salas, con lo que concluyó la revolución constitucionalista. Las negociaciones entre Lauro Villar y Alfredo Robles Domínguez, representantes del gobierno del presidente Francisco Carbajal y del ejército de Venustiano Carranza, respectivamente, habían empezado desde mediados de julio, poco después de la huida hacia España del dictador Victoriano Huerta, pero sólo a principios de agosto, ante el avance hacia la ciudad de México de las fuerzas de Álvaro Obregón y Pablo González, el gobierno de Carbajal decidió negociar sin condiciones. El 9 de agosto, Robles Domínguez se entrevistó con José Refugio Velasco, secretario de Guerra y Marina del gabinete de Carbajal, y luego de una larga plática en la que adujo como razones para la rendición incondicional la invasión estadounidense de Veracruz y Tampico y la urgencia de evitar nuevos combates, lo convenció de que el ejército federal se retirara de la ciudad de México sin combatir. El 11 de agosto, acompañado por los ministros plenipotenciarios de Brasil, Gran Bretaña y Guatemala, el encargado de negocios de Estados Unidos y el secretario de la legación francesa, gobernador huertista del Distrito Federal, Eduardo Iturbe, se trasladó al campamento de Obregón en Teoloyucan para establecer la forma de la rendición del ejército federal y su disolución. Dos días después, en un punto del "camino nacional de Cuautitlán a Teoloyucan, la delegación del gobierno, integrada por Salas y Blanco, se encontró con Obregón y Lucio Blanco, los representantes de las fuerzas constitucionalistas, y los cuatro, en la salpicadera de un automóvil, firmaron las *Condiciones*. El breve documento establecía que las fuerzas federales "dejarán la plaza de México, distribuyéndose en las poblaciones a lo largo del ferrocarril de México a Puebla" y ahí esperarían a los enviados del gobierno a los que entregarían sus armas. El resto de las guarniciones federales sobrevivientes, las de Manzanillo, Córdoba y Jalapa, así como las jefaturas militares de Chiapas, Tabasco, Campeche y Yucatán, se disolverían en esos lugares. Los barcos de la Armada Nacional, por su parte, debían concentrarse en Manzanillo y Puerto México, hoy Coatzacoalcos. Respecto de los oficiales y jefes del ejército federal, éstos quedaban "a disposición del Primer Jefe de los Constitucionalistas", mientras que para los soldados, se ofrecía proporcionales "los medios para volver a sus hogares". Finalmente, los carrancistas dispusieron que las tropas federales establecidas en San Ángel, Tlalpan y Xochimilco, que habían combatido contra las fuerzas del Ejército Libertador del Sur, se retirarían sólo cuando sus posiciones fueran ocupadas por los constitucionalistas.

TRAVEN, B. ◆ n. ¿en Alemania? y m. en el DF (¿1882?-1969). Pseudónimo del escritor Ret Marut (Mauricio Rathenau, según algunas fuentes), quien, según su viuda, no estaba seguro de cuál era su lugar de nacimiento. Fue activista político, actor y periodista. Editó en Munich el periódico *Ziegelbrenner* (1916-18) y tras la caída del imperio alemán perteneció a la Comisión de Propaganda de la República Socialista de Baviera (1918-19); detenido a la caída del gobierno revolucionario, escapó de ser fusilado y huyó de Alemania a Gran Bretaña, de donde fue deportado en 1923. Pasó a México; en Tampico adoptó el nombre de *T. Torsvan* y trabajó en una compañía petrolera. Estudió arqueología en la Universidad Nacional y en los años treinta vivió en Yucatán. En 1951 obtuvo la nacionalidad mexicana. Por entones ya había adoptado la identidad de *B. Traven*, aunque más tarde apareció como *All Croves*, supuesto traductor de las obras de Traven, que también fueron traducidas por Esperanza López Mateos. Otras versiones lo hicieron aparecer como *Hal Croves*, sueco o alemán, o *Croves Torvan Traven* o *Traven Torsvan*, estadounidense nacido en 1890 y avecindado en México. Usó el nombre de *Ret Marut* para numerosas colaboraciones periodísticas. Escribió en alemán y en inglés. Autor de un *Estudio antropológico de Chiapas*; de cuento: *Canasta de cuentos mexicanos* (1946) y *Cuentos de B. Traven* (1963); y de novela: *La rosa blanca* (1933), *Puente en la selva* (1936), *La rebelión de los colgados* (1938), *La carreta* (1950), *El tesoro de la sierra Madre* (1951), *Gobierno* (1951), *El barco de la muerte* (1951) y *Aslan Norval* (1968). A partir de ellos se han realizado, entre otras, las películas *El tesoro de Sierra Madre* (1947) de John Huston, *La rebelión de los colgados* (1954) de Emilio Fernández y Alfredo Crevenna, *Canasta de cuentos mexicanos* (1955) de Julio Bracho, *Macario* (1959) de Roberto Gavaldón. En 1987, Juan Luis Buñuel realizó la serie televisiva *La rebelión de los colgados*.

B. Traven

TREINTA-TREINTA ◆ ☛ *Grupo de Artistas Independientes ¡30-30!*

TREJO, BLANCA LYDIA ◆ n. en Comitán, Chis., y m. en el DF (1906-1970). Escritora. Estudió en la Casa Central de Guatemala y en la Universidad Nacional de México. Fue canciller del consulado mexicano en Barcelona durante la guerra civil española (1936-39). Colaboradora de la *Revista de Occidente*. Realizó la antología *Cantos a la madre* (1936). Autora de *El ratón Panchito roe-libros* (1935), *La marimba* (1935), *Cantos a la madre* (1936), *El héroe de Nacozari* (1936), *Paradojas-contrastes* (1937), *Convenciones y convencionistas. Problemas del proletariado* (1938), *Lo que vi en España* (1940), *Lo que sucedió al nopal* (1941), *Un país en el fango* (1942), *El padrastro* (1944), *El congreso de los pollitos* (1945), *La literatura infantil en México, desde los aztecas hasta nuestros días* (1950), *Maravillas de un colmenar* (1954), *El quetzal* (1955), *Copo de algodón* (1955), *Cuentos o leyendas indígenas para los niños* (1959), *La espiga sabelotodo* y *La escopeta de Filemón*. En 1935 fue premiada por la Secretaría de Educación Pública, en 1954 recibió una mención honorífica del gobierno de Chiapas.

TREJO, ERNESTO ◆ n. en Fresnillo, Zac. (1950). Poeta. Licenciado en economía titulado en California y licenciado en literatura por la Universidad de

Iowa. Ha sido editor del *Boletín de Análisis Bibliográfico* y de la Editorial Latitudes. Autor de *El día entre las hojas* (1984).

Trejo, Francisco Eulogio ◆ n. en Guadalajara, Jal., y m. en Colima, Col. (1830-1880). Abogado. Estudió en Guadalajara. En 1863 se instaló en Colima, para huir de las tropas francesas que habían tomado la capital jalisciense, pero dos años después fue aprehendido por los invasores. Fue juez. Escribió para los periódicos *La Independencia, La Aurora del Progreso, La Unidad Nacional* (1870-71), *El Defensor de la Paz* (1871) y *El Noticiero* (1872). En 1876 apoyó el levantamiento porfirista de Tuxtepec. Autor de *La sombra de Guzmán* (1872), *La filosofía del matrimonio* y *La riqueza de los pobres*.

Trejo, Paulina ◆ n. en la ciudad de México (1925). Grabadora y pintora. Estudió en la Escuela Nacional de Artes Plásticas (1947) y en la Escuela de Artes del Libro, donde obtuvo diploma de maestra grabadora. Expuso por primera vez en 1944. Recibió el Premio Ignacio Cumplido para las Artes Gráficas.

Cárcel, grabado de Paulina Trejo

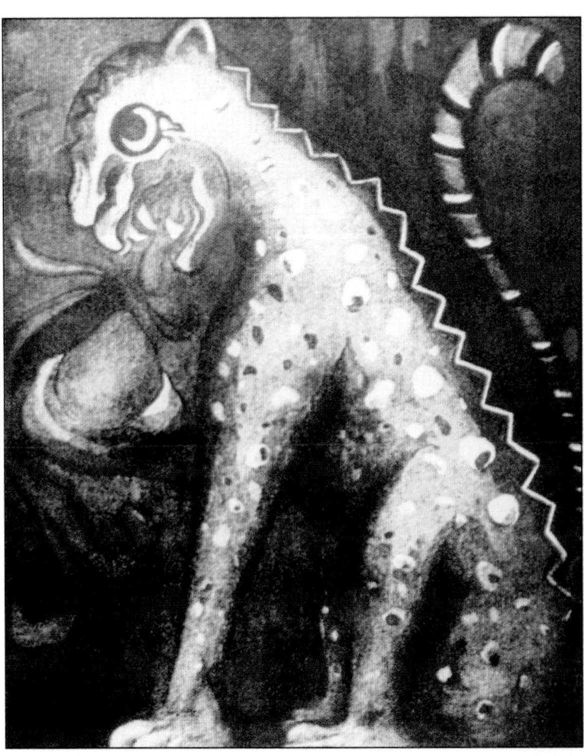

Trejo, Pedro de ◆ n. en España (¿1534?-?). Poeta. Llegó a la Nueva España hacia 1556. Vivió en Michoacán, Zacatecas, Nueva Galicia y Colima. A mediados de 1569 fue acusado de blasfemo. El proceso pasó del párroco de Colima a la Audiencia Episcopal de Michoacán, que en marzo del año siguiente lo condenó al pago de 400 pesos de oro, pero Trejo apeló y el juicio fue remitido al Tribunal del Santo Oficio de México. En 1572 fue condenado a cuatro años de galeras y a que "perpetuamente no haga coplas". Autor de un *Cancionero general de obras del poeta Pedro de Trejo plasenciano Dirigidas al muy alto y muy poderoso y esclarecido Señor y monarcha Don phelipe Segundo deste nombre Majestad Real por divina permisión para defensa De su chatolica Yglesia, Rei despaña*, escrito hacia 1570.

Trejo Delarbre, Raúl ◆ n. en el DF (1953). Periodista. Licenciado en periodismo (1975), maestro en estudios latinoamericanos (1996) y doctor en sociología (1999) por la UNAM, donde ha sido profesor (1973-) e investigador (1985-). Militó en el MAP (1981) y el PSUM (1981-84). Cofundador del Sindicato del Personal Académico de la UNAM (1974) y el STUNAM (1977). Ha sido jefe de redacción de *Unión* (1977-78), *Solidaridad* (1978-82) y *Así Es* (1982); codirector de *Punto* (1984-86), comentarista del noticiero *Enlace* del Canal 11 (1987-88), y director de *Política*, suplemento de *El Nacional* (1989-92, 1994) y de *etcétera* (1993-). Ha colaborado en las principales publicaciones de la ciudad de México. Coautor de *La democracia acaba donde empieza el rating* (1988) y *Los sindicatos mexicanos ante el Tratado de Libre Comercio* (1993), entre otros. Coordinador de *México. El reclamo democrático* (1988), *Así cayó la Quina* (1989) y, entre otros, *Chiapas. La guerra de las ideas* (1994). Autor de *La prensa marginal* (1975), *De Adolfo Ruiz Cortines a Adolfo López Mateos*, tomo XII de la *La clase obrera en la historia de México* (1981); *Este puño sí se ve* (1987), *Las agencias de información en México* (1989), *Crónica del sindicalismo en México (1976-1988)* (1990), *Los mil días de Carlos Salinas* (1991), *Ver pero también leer* (1992), *La sociedad ausente* (1992), *Chiapas, la comunicación enmascarada* (1994), *La nueva alfombra mágica* (1996) y *Volver a los medios* (1997). Premio Nacional de Periodismo (1994) y de la Fundación Social para las Comunicaciones (España, 1996). Medalla al Mérito Universitario (1999). Cofundador de la Unión de Periodistas Democráticos y de la Asociación Mexicana de Investigadores de la Comunicación, que presidió (1985-87). Miembro del Instituto de Estudios para la Transición Democrática (1989-), la Fundación UNAM (1993-), la Internet Society (1996-) y el SNI (1996-).

Trejo Fuentes, Fausto ◆ n. en Pachuca, Hgo. (1925). Médico cirujano por la UNAM (1952), donde hizo cursos de posgrado y fue profesor (1956-89). Director de Orientación Vocacional del Politécnico (1964-68). Director de Preparatorias Populares (1973-80). Miembro de la Juventud Comunista (1947-50) y del PCM (1950-81), miembro del Comité Nacional del Frente Electoral del Pueblo (1964). Durante el movimiento estudiantil de 1968 (☛) destacó como uno de los líderes de la Coalición de Maestros, por lo que fue preso político (1968-71) y exiliado en Uruguay y Chile (1971). En 1981 fue secuestrado por la policía y torturado bajo la acusación de estar ligado a grupos armados. Miembro del PRD desde 1980. Candidato a diputado local por el VII Distrito de Hidalgo (1999). Ha colaborado en *Por Qué?* y otras publicaciones.

Trejo Fuentes, Ignacio ◆ n. en Pachuca, Hgo. (1955). Licenciado en periodismo por la UNAM y maestro en literatura hispanoamericana por la Universidad Estatal de Nuevo México. Profesor de la UNAM y de la Universidad Iberoamericana. Jefe de redacción de *La Semana de Bellas Artes*, promotor cultural y coordinador en la Dirección de Literatura del INBA. Ha sido coordinador del taller de crítica literaria de *Punto de Partida* y del taller literario de DIFOCUR en Culiacán, Sinaloa. Es dictaminador y asesor literario de Editorial Grijalbo. Colaborador de *El Gallo Ilustrado*,

Sábado, El Semanario Cultural de Novedades, Punto, El Universal, Excélsior, Pie de Página, Revista de la Universidad de México, Vaso Comunicante, Revista Mexicana de Ciencia Política, Diálogos, Revista de Bellas Artes, Revista de Revistas, Tierra Adentro, Quimera, El Segundo Piso y *Primera Plana*. Coautor de los ensayos *Revueltas en la mira* (1984) y *José Emilio Pacheco* (1987); y del relato *Amor de la calle* (1990). Autor de la antología: *Inés Arredondo para jóvenes* (1990); los ensayos: *Segunda voz. Apuntes sobre novela mexicana* (1987), *De acá de este lado. Una aproximación a la novela chicana* (1987, Premio Comitán de Domínguez en 1988), *Faros y sirenas. Aspectos de crítica literaria* (1988) y "Sergio Galindo: tres tristes tópicos" (1992, en *Sergio Galindo narrador*, Premio de Ensayo Literario, Instituto Veracruzano de Cultura); de narrativa: *Crónicas romanas* (1990), *Aztecas en Kafkania* (1991), *Amiga a la que amo* (1994), *Loquitas pintadas* (1995). Becario INBA-Fonapas (1983) y del Centro Mexicano de Escritores (1983-84).

TREJO GONZÁLEZ, MARIO ◆ ☛ *Martré, Gonzalo.*

TREJO Y LERDO DE TEJADA, CARLOS ◆ n. y m. en el DF (1879-1941). Abogado. Fue diputado federal (1911-13), ministro plenipotenciario de México en Argentina, Chile y Cuba en los años veinte; subsecretario encargado del despacho de Educación Pública (del 8 de octubre al 9 de diciembre de 1930) en el gobierno de Pascual Ortiz Rubio y gobernador del territorio de Baja California Norte (del 27 de diciembre de 1930 al 7 de noviembre de 1931). Coautor, con Manuel Urquidi, de *Estudio y proyecto de organización de la Beneficencia Pública* (1920). Autor de *Nuestra verdadera situación política y el Partido Democrático* (1910), *Derecho administrativo mexicano. Su formación y desarrollo de 1810 a 1910* (1911), *La revolución y el nacionalismo. Todo para todos* (1916), *Evolución educacional de México* (1922), *¿Por qué no tenemos nacionalismo? Las funciones del Estado y la formación de nuestra nacionalidad* (1926), *Norte contra sur. Obregón-Calles-Ortiz Rubio. Ensayo de sociología política mexicana* (1931), *La educación socialista* (1935) y *Sin rumbo y sin alma. Maquinismo suicida* (1937).

TREJO RESÉNDIZ, WONFILIO ◆ n. en Maquihuana, Tams., y m. en el DF (1927-1987). Maestro en filosofía por la UNAM, de la que fue secretario de la coordinación de Humanidades y coordinador del Colegio de Filosofía de la Facultad de Filosofía y Letras. Corealizador de la antología *Temas de Filosofía* (1976) y de una *Antología de ética* (1976). Coautor de *La filosofía y la ciencia de nuestros días* (1976). Autor de *Introducción a Dilthey* (1962), *El problema de la filosofía americana* (1965), *El fundacionismo normativo de Ernesto Sosa, Antología de ética* (1976), *Ensayos epistemológicos* (1976), *Fenomenalismo y realismo* (1983) y *Filosofía de la historia de la filosofía*.

TREJO SIRVENT, SOCORRO ◆ n. en Tuxtla Gutiérrez, Chis. (1954). Escritora. Hizo estudios de periodismo en la UNAM y la Universidad del Claustro de Sor Juana. Ha coordinado talleres de literatura infantil y otros proyectos de promoción cultural. Ha colaborado en revistas literarias y publicado en antologías. Autora de *Soles de agua* (1995, poesía).

TREJO VILLAFUERTE, ARTURO ◆ n. en Ixmiqulpan, Hgo. (1953). Escritor. Estudió en la UNAM, en la Escuela Nacional de Locutores y en El Colegio de México. Profesor de la UNAM, de la Universidad Femenina de México y de la Universidad Autónoma Metropolitana, plantel Azcapotzalco. Fue becario INBA-Fonapas (1981-82). Ha sido redactor de los noticieros de Radio Educación y Radio Universidad, coordinador editorial de *La Semana de Bellas Artes*, fundador y miembro del consejo editorial de la revista *Sitios*, coordinador de actividades de la Dirección de Literatura del INBA, fundador del Taller de Poesía Sintética, fundador y miembro del consejo editorial de la revista *As de Corazones Rotos-Letra* y jefe de redacción de *Su Otro Yo* y *Ser Joven*. Colaborador de la *Gaceta* de la UNAM, *Nexos, Proceso, Revista de la Universidad, Punto de Partida, Pie de Página, El Machete, Casa del Tiempo, Revista Mexicana de Literatura, Era de Michoacán, Sábado* (suplemento de *unomásuno*) y *El Gallo Ilustrado* (suplemento de *El Día*). Coautor de *Doce modos* (1976) y *Andan por ahí* (1987). Autor de poesía: *Mester de hotelería* (1979), *A quien pueda interesar* (1982), *Como el viento que pasa* (1985), *Malas compañías* (1988); ensayo: *Palabras de la fe* (1989); y novela: *Lámpara sin luz* (1999).

TRELLES, IGNACIO *NACHO* ◆ n. en Guadalajara, Jal. (1919). Futbolista y entrenador. Su apellido materno es Campos. Estudió dos años de la carrera de ingeniería mecánica en la Escuela Superior de Ingeniería Mecánica y Eléctrica. En 1934 se inició como futbolista profesional en el equipo Necaxa (1934-43). Actuó también para el Monterrey, el América (1943-46), los *Vikingos* de Chicago (1947-48) y el Atlante (1948). Se retiró como jugador en 1948 y en ese año inició su carrera de director técnico. Ha sido entrenador del Zacatepec (1948-52 y 1954-61), el Cuautla (1952-53), el Marte (1953-54), el América (1961-65), el Puebla (1972-77), el Cruz Azul (1977-83), el Atlante (1983-86) y el Universidad de Guadalajara (1986-). Director técnico de la selección nacional (1958-66 y 1976) y a la que ha llevado a los campeonatos mundiales de Suecia (1958) e Inglaterra (1966) y a los juegos olímpicos de Tokio (1964) y México (1968). Fue comentarista de la televisión estatal en los campeonatos mundiales de futbol de Argentina (1978), España (1982) y México (1986). En 1954-55 y 1957-58, hizo campeón de liga al Zacatepec; en 1953-54, al Marte, al que llevó, además, al título de campeón de campeones; en 1966-67 y 1967-68, al Toluca; y en 1978-79 y 1979-80, al Cruz Azul, de cuyas fuerzas básicas ha sido asesor.

FOTO: ÉPOCA

Ignacio *Nacho* Trelles

TRENS LANZ, MANUEL BARTOLOMÉ ◆ n. en Frontera, Tab., y m. en el DF (1893-1963). Médico e historiador. Doctor por la Escuela de Medicina de

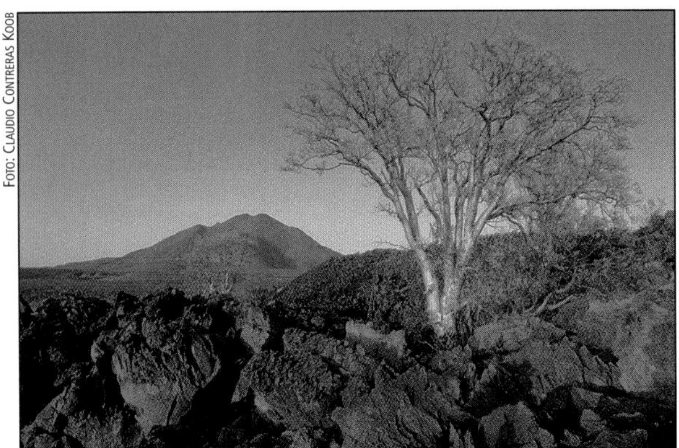
Foto: Claudio Contreras Koob

Volcán Tres Vírgenes, BCS

Yucatán (1920). Fue director del Hospital Domingo Chanona, de Tuxtla Gutiérrez (1929-40), jefe del Servicio del Consejo Superior de Salubridad de Mérida, jefe de investigaciones históricas del gobierno de Veracruz y director del Archivo General de la Nación (1953-59). Colaboró en el diario *El Nacional*. Autor de *Los indios lacandones. Su vida y su historia* (1929), *Apuntes para la historia estadística de México* (1930), *Historia de Chiapas desde los tiempos prehispánicos hasta la caída del imperio de Maximiliano* (1942), *Historia de Veracruz* (1947-50), *Historia de la H. ciudad de Veracruz y de su ayuntamiento* (1952), *Arte curativo de las enfermedades. Farmacia y hechicería. La brujería y el paludismo* (1954), *Síntesis histórica de la nación mexicana* (1954), *El imperio en Chiapas* (1957), *Bosquejos históricos de San Cristóbal de Las Casas* (1957) y *México de antaño* (1957).

Francisco Eduardo de Tresguerras

Tres Palos, de ◆ Albufera de Guerrero también llamada Papagayo, situada en el litorial del océano Pacífico, al sureste y muy cercana a Acapulco, cuyo aeropuesto se localiza en el cordón litoral que bordea, por el sur, a la laguna. Mide 15 km de largo y unos seis de ancho. Se extiende de noroeste a sureste. En su extremo noroeste desemboca el río Sabana y al sureste pasa el río Papagayo, antes de tributar en el mar. Se comunica con el Pacífico mediante un canal situado en su extremo suroriental; cerca de este canal se localizan las playas Encantada y Barra Vieja.

Tres Valles ◆ Municipio de Veracruz erigido el 28 de noviembre de 1988 y situado al sur de la capital del estado, en los límites con Oaxaca. Superficie: 378.60 km^2. Habitantes: 46,175, de los cuales 11,998 forman la población económicamente activa. Hablan alguna lengua indígena 3,298 personas mayores de cinco años (chinanteco 2,256 y mazateco 809), de ellas, son monolingües 117.

Tres Vírgenes ◆ Volcán de Baja California Sur situado en la sierra de Santa Lucía, al noroeste de Santa Rosalía. Se eleva 1,995 metros sobre el nivel del mar. Hizo erupción en 1746 y 1857.

Tres Zapotes ◆ Zona arqueológica situada en el municipio veracruzano Santiago Tuxtla (☛).

Tresguerras, Francisco Eduardo de ◆ n. y m. en Celaya, Gto. (1759-1833). Pintor, arquitecto y grabador. Realizó estudios irregulares en la Academia de San Carlos de la ciudad de México. Simpatizante de la revolución de Independencia, en 1811 fue aprehendido, juzgado y encarcelado. En 1820, sin embargo, fue diputado provincial de Guanajuato. Edificó la Fuente de Neptuno, en Querétaro (1797); un obelisco y una fuente dedicados al rey Carlos IV, en Celaya (1797); el Palacio del conde de Casa Rul, en Guanajuato; un puente sobre el río de la Laja, cerca de Celaya (1803-09); el teatro Alarcón, en la ciudad de México (1827); y el obelisco conmemorativo de la independencia, en San Luis Potosí. Entre 1802 y 1807 dirigió la reconstrucción de la iglesia del Carmen de Celaya y diseñó el altar mayor. En el Museo Nacional de Historia de Chapultepec se encuentran dos de sus cuadros, un *Retrato de María Guadalupe Ramírez* (1787) y un *Autorretrato* (1794). Además, ejecutó numerosos frescos en diversos conventos de

Foto: Fondo Editorial Grupo Azabache

La Fuente de Neptuno, obra de Francisco Eduardo de Tresguerras, en Querétaro

Celaya, Querétaro y San Luis Potosí. Autor de *Ocios literarios* y *Tres zamoranos ilustres*.

TRESPALACIOS, JOSÉ FÉLIX ◆ n. en Chihuahua, Chih. (1781-1838). Militar. En 1812 era militar realista y rechazó un ataque insurgente contra Monterrey. En 1814, sin embargo, organizó con Pablo Caballero y Gaspar Ochoa una conspiración independentista en Chihuahua; en noviembre de ese año, infructuosamente, intentó apoderarse del cuartel de la ciudad, pero fue derrotado, juzgado y condenado a 10 años de prisión en Ceuta y desterrado a perpetuidad en el norte de la Nueva España. En San Luis Potosí fue indultado pero se le exigió ir a España, orden que no cumplió, pues luego de enfermar en La Habana, huyó a Estados Unidos. Regresó a la consumación de la independencia y se encargó del gobierno de Coahuila y Texas. En 1823 se levantó en armas en favor del derrocado emperador Agustín de Iturbide, pero fue derrotado. Más tarde ocupó una senaduría (1831-34) y fue secretario de gobierno y comandante general de Chihuahua.

TRESIERRAS Y CANO, ALONSO ◆ n. en España y m. en Arizpe, Son. (1762-1818). Abogado. Se instaló en Sonora en 1790. Fue comandante militar y jefe político de Sonora en dos ocasiones (1793-96 y 1813-14).

TREVI, CRISTINA ◆ n. y m. en el DF (1929-1956). Soprano. Su nombre completo era Cristina Benítez Treviño. Estudió con Fanny Anitúa. Se dedicó a la interpretación de óperas y operetas. Fue integrante de la Ópera Nacional y alternó con María Callas, Rossi Lemeni y Del Mónaco. Participó en algunos programas de televisión.

TREVI, GLORIA ◆ n. en Monterrey, NL (1971). Nombre profesional de Gloria de los Ángeles Treviño Ruiz. Cantante. Comenzó en el grupo Boquitas Pintadas y continuó como solista. Grabó los discos *¿Qué hago aquí?*, *Pelo suelto*, *Tu ángel de la guarda*, *Me siento tan sola* y *Más turbada que nunca*. Ha participado en las películas *Pelo suelto* (1991), *Zapatos viejos* (1993) y *Una papa sin catsup* (1995); ha conducido programas de televisión. En los noventa apareció en calendarios. Colaboró en la revista *Generación*. Desapareció en 1998; acusada junto con su productor, Sergio Andrade, de corrupción de menores.

TREVIÑO, ANA CECILIA ◆ n. en Morelia, Mich. (1931). Periodista. Es conocida por el pseudónimo *Bambi*. Su apellido materno es Del Villar. Licenciada en periodismo por la Universidad Femenina de México (1949), realizó estudios especiales en la Facultad de Filosofía y Letras de la UIA. En 1948 se incorporó al diario *Excélsior* y desde 1973 dirige la "Sección B", a la que dio un marcado acento cultural. Autora de ensayo: *El ojo de Polifemo (Visión de la obra de Agustín Bartra)* (1957, Premio Andreu Xandri a la mejor obra de un periodista sobre literatura catalana), *Arte de leer la tierra: geomancia* (1974) y *Basura de oro* (1990, sobre el asesinato del líder de los pepenadores); y del reportaje *París a dos mil años* (1951, Premio de Periodismo de París, con motivo del Bimilenario de dicha ciudad). Premio Nacional de Periodismo (1980). Becaria del Centro Mexicano de Escritores (1964-65).

TREVIÑO, CELIA ◆ n. en Monterrey, NL. (1912). Violinista. Estudió en el Conservatorio Nacional de Música. En 1928 estudió en Italia, becada por el gobierno del presidente Lázaro Cárdenas. Autora del poemario *Rimas sinfónicas* (1949) y de los libros de memorias *Mi vida atormentada* (1965) y *Su majestad el violín* (1978). En 1927 ganó el segundo lugar del concurso anual de Conservatorio Cart Hein; en 1932, la Unión Filarmónica de Polonia la bautizó como "la novia de los músicos de América". Años más tarde, el gobierno mexicano le obsequió un Amati de 1670.

TREVIÑO, FRANCISCO L. ◆ n. en Villa Guerrero y m. en Torreón, Coah. (1887-1937). Se incorporó a la revolución constitucionalista en 1913. Dos años después se unió a las tropas de Jacinto B. Treviño y combatió a la División del Norte. Fue administrador de la aduana de Piedras Negras, tesorero del estado, gobernador interino de Chihuahua (de febrero a mayo de 1916) y diputado federal (1918-20). En 1920 apoyó la precadidatura presidencial de Pablo González y se sumó a la revuelta de Agua Prieta. Más tarde fue designado jefe del Estado Mayor de la Jefatura de Operaciones Militares en Torreón, cargo que desempeñó hasta su muerte.

TREVIÑO, GERÓNIMO ◆ n. en la hacienda La Escondida, cerca de Cadereyta, NL, y m. en EUA (1836-1914). Militar. En 1858, al inicio de la guerra de los Tres Años, se incorporó a las fuerzas liberales de San Luis Potosí y combatió en Zacatecas, San Luis Potosí, Jalisco y Guanajuato. Comandante en 1860 y coronel en 1863, participó en el sitio de Puebla y formó parte de la columna republicana comandada por Tomás O'Horan, que en abril de 1863 rompió el sitio y se unió al ejército del Centro. Combatió en la batalla de San Lorenzo (mayo de 1863) y luego se retiró a Oaxaca, donde en noviembre se incorporó a las fuerzas de Porfirio Díaz. Un año después atravesó el país, de Oaxaca a Nuevo León, y desde entonces, al mando de la Legión del Norte, combatió a las órdenes de Mariano Escobedo y Francisco Naranjo. Participó en las batallas de Santa Gertrudis y San Jacinto y en el sitio de Querétaro. Al triunfo de la República fue comandante del Ejército de Oriente, comandante militar del Distrito Federal (del 22 de julio al 4 de diciembre de 1867) y gobernador constitucional de Nuevo León (1867-71). Participó en los levantamientos porfiristas de 1871-72 y 1875-76. Triunfante la insurrección tuxtepecana, fue ascendido a general de división y ocupó brevemente el gobierno de Nuevo León (1877). Fue jefe de las Segunda Zona Militar, secretario de Guerra y Marina (del 1 de diciembre de 1880 al 31 de diciembre de 1881) en el gobierno de Manuel González, comandante de la División del Norte, enviado del gobierno a Europa para estudiar técnicas militares (1883), presidente del

FOTO:ÉPOCA

Gloria Trevi

FOTO:ÉPOCA

Ana Cecilia Treviño

Retrato y firma de Géronimo Treviño

Francisco Amado Treviño Abatte

Ferrocarril Monterrey-Golfo y jefe de la Tercera Zona Militar (1909-12). Se retiró del ejército en 1912. Al año siguiente, poco después del asesinato del presidente Francisco I. Madero, fue apresado por órdenes de Victoriano Huerta y expulsado a Nueva Orleans, pero volvió en abril para encargarse de la presidencia del Supremo Tribunal Militar, puesto que no ocupó, pues se encargó interinamente del gobierno de Nuevo León (1913). En 1914, al triunfo del movimiento constitucionalista, se exilió en El Paso.

Treviño, Jacinto B. ◆ n. en Ciudad Guerrero, Coah., y m. en el DF (1883-1971). Militar. Su nombre completo era Jacinto Blas Treviño González. Estudió en el Colegio Militar (1900-08). En noviembre de 1911 formó parte del Estado Mayor del presidente Francisco I. Madero. Al año siguiente combatió la rebelión orozquista; a principios de 1913 organizó milicias rurales en Coahuila. Se levantó en armas contra Victoriano Huerta y firmó el Plan de Guadalupe (☛). Participó en los combates de Monclova y Torreón y en 1914 tomó Pachuca. Al triunfo de los constitucionalistas fue jefe del Estado Mayor de Venustiano Carranza y se encargó del despacho de la Secretaría de Guerra y Marina (del 8 al 26 de septiembre de 1914). Participó en la campaña carrancista contra la División del Norte en San Luis Potosí y en abril de 1915, al mando de la Brigada Hidalgo, derrotó a los villistas de Tomás Urbina en El Ébano, Tamaulipas, y a fines de 1915 tomó Chihuahua, lo que le valió su ascenso a general de división. Comandante militar de Chihuahua (1916-17). En 1920 se adhirió al Plan de Agua Prieta. Durante el interinato de Adolfo de la Huerta fue secretario de Industria, Comercio y Trabajo (del 1 de junio al 30 de noviembre de 1920). En la presidencia de Álvaro Obregón presidió la comisión revisora de hojas de servicio de la Secretaría de Guerra (1921). En 1929 se sumó a la rebelión escobarista y, derrotado, se exilió en Estados Unidos. Volvió a México en 1941. Fue consejero del Banco Nacional del Ejército y la Armada (1947) y senador de la República (1952-58). En 1951, con José Gonzalo Escobar, Raúl Madero y Samuel M. Santos, fundó la Asociación Política y Social Revolucionaria de Hombres de la Revolución, que en 1954, con el apoyo de Ruiz Cortines, se transformó en Partido Auténtico de la Revolución Mexicana (☛), del que fue presidente (1954-65). Fue vocal gerente (1957-66) y director de Puertos Libres Mexicanos (1964-70). Autor de *Nunca un desleal*.

Treviño, Radamés ◆ n. en Monterrey, NL, y m. en Calpulalpan, Tlax. (1942-1970). Ciclista. Obtuvo medalla de oro en los Juegos Centroamericanos de Panamá. Participó en competencias en la RFA, Checoslovaquia y Holanda. Impuso una marca mundial de la hora.

Treviño, Ramón ◆ n. y m. en Monterrey, NL (1841-1891). Abogado. Combatió la intervención francesa y el imperio de Maximiliano de Habsburgo. Fue gobernador de Nuevo León (1873-74) y se retiró de la política al triunfo de la rebelión tuxtepecana.

Treviño Abatte, Francisco Amado ◆ n. en Mexicali, BC (1953). Licenciado en derecho por la Universidad Iberoamericana (1976). Pertenece al PRI desde 1972. Ha sido secretario del Interior del sector popular del Movimiento Nacional de la Juventud Revolucionaria (1975-77), asesor jurídico del Fondo de Garantía y Fomento de la Industria Mediana y Pequeña (1978-80), subdelegado jurídico y de gobierno del Departamento del Distrito Federal en Tláhuac (1980-82) y delegado del DDF en Magdalena Contreras (1982-88).

Treviño Cantú, Javier ◆ n. en Monterrey, Nuevo León (1960). Hizo estudios de derecho en la Universidad de Monterrey. Licenciado en relaciones internacionales por El Colegio de México, donde coordinó la licenciatura en administración. Maestro en políticas públicas por la Universidad de Harvard (1987). Miembro del PRI. Fue director de planeación del Centro Arturo Rosenblueth de la SEP, asesor del director de Comunicación Social de la Presidencia de la República, consejero y ministro de información en la embajada mexicana en Estados Unidos (1989-93), asesor del secretario de Desarrollo Social (1993), consejero de Luis Donaldo Colosio durante su candidatura presidencial (1993-94) y asesor para asuntos internacionales del candidato Ernesto Zedillo (1994). Subsecretario de Cooperación Internacional de la SRE (1994-98) y oficial mayor de la SHCP (1998-). Ha sido copresidente y asesor de la Comisión México-Estados Unidos para el Intercambio Educativo y Cultural, que otorga las becas Fullbright-García Robles. Miembro de número de la Academia Mexicana de Derecho Internacional.

Treviño Castro, Alejandro *Alex* ◆ n. en Monterrey, NL (1957). Beisbolista. Jugó en las ligas mayores con los *Gigantes* de San Francisco los *Dodgers* de Los Ángeles.

Treviño Martínez, Jorge ◆ n. en Monterrey, NL (1935). Licenciado en derecho por la UNAM y doctor en derecho administrativo por la Universidad de París (1963). Profesor de la Universidad Autónoma de Nuevo León, de la Universidad de Monterrey y del Instituto Tecnológico y de Estudios Superiores de Monterrey. Ha sido secretario del Tribunal Fiscal de la Federación (1957-59), asesor fiscal del gobierno de Nuevo León (1968-70), subtesorero general del gobierno neoleonés (1970-73), administrador fiscal regional del noroeste (1973-82), diputado federal (1982-85) y gobernador de Nuevo León (1985-1991). Autor de *Jurisprudencia y tesis del Tribunal Fiscal de la Federación 1917-1959* (1960). Es miembro de la Academia de Derecho Fiscal de Nuevo León y del Colegio de Abogados de Nuevo León.

Treviño Olivares, Amado ◆ n. en Tampico, Tams. (1925). Periodista. Licenciado en derecho por la Universidad de San Luis Potosí (1945). Es miembro del PRI (1952-). Perteneció a la Organización Sindical de los Trabajadores de las Artes Gráficas de Mexicali. Ha sido jefe de redacción de los diarios *El Sol de León* (1948), *El Occidental* de Guadalajara (1949) y ABC de Mexicali; director de los cotidianos *Nuevo Mundo* y *La Extra* (1960) de Mexicali; director de la revista *Presente,* de Mexicali, subdirector de prensa de la SSA (1961), director de Información y Relaciones Públicas (1962) y director de Turismo del gobierno de Tamaulipas (1968); director de Prensa y Relaciones Públicas de la Cámara de Diputados (1969-70), director de Relaciones Públicas e Información del DDF (1971), jefe del Departamento de Prensa y Difusión del IMSS (1977-82), secretario auxiliar del jefe del DDF (1982-83), director general de Información y Difusión de la Secretaría del Trabajo (1983-) y coordinador de Relaciones Públicas del DDF (1995-97).

TREVIÑO ZAPATA, NORBERTO ◆ n. en Matamoros, Tams., y m. en ¿el DF? (1911-1973). Se tituló como médico cirujano en la UNAM, donde fue profesor. Miembro del PRI. Diputado federal y presidente de la Gran Comisión (1952-55), gobernador de Tamaulipas (1957-63), director general del Instituto Nacional de Protección a la Infancia (1970-72) y embajador en Italia (1972-76). Escribió libros con el pseudónimo de *Norberto Trenzo*. Fundó la Facultad de Medicina Veterinaria y Zootecnia de Ciudad Victoria.

TRIANA GUZMÁN, MARTÍN ◆ n. en Zacatecas, Zac., y m. en el DF (?-1934). Militar. Se levantó en armas contra el gobierno de Porfirio Díaz en noviembre de 1910. Combatió principalmente en Durango. En 1913 se incorporó a la División del Norte y participó en las dos tomas de Torreón (1913 y 1914). Fue gobernador interino de Aguascalientes en dos ocasiones (del 23 al 24 de septiembre de 1914 y 10 de agosto de 1915 al 16 de enero de 1916); durante la guerra de facciones combatió a los convencionistas; tomó parte en la batalla de Celaya (1915). En 1916 alcanzó el grado de general de brigada.

TRÍAS ÁLVAREZ, ÁNGEL ◆ n. en Chihuahua y m. en Labor de Trías, hoy Quintas Carolinas, Chih. (1809-1867). En Europa estudió comercio y administración. Entre 1834 y 1838, al mando de una pequeña fuerza de civiles y en su calidad de presidente de la Junta de Policía de Chihuahua, emprendió cuatro campañas contra los apaches. Fue regidor (1836) y alcalde de Chihuahua (1838), prefecto político (1838), miembro de un grupo militar llamado Defensores de la Patria, organizado para combatir a los franceses (1838-39), magistrado suplente del Supremo Tribunal de Justicia de Chihuahua (1840-41), juez de hacienda (1840-41) y diputado federal a la Legislatura que en 1842 disolvió Nicolás Bravo. Designado vocal de la Junta Nacional Legislativa de 1843, se negó a participar en las sesiones. En agosto de 1845, apoyado por un levantamiento liberal, se apoderó del gobierno de Chihuahua, pero fue destituido en enero de 1846, al triunfo de la insurrección de Mariano Paredes y Arrillaga. En agosto de ese año, luego de la reinstauración del federalismo, volvió a la gubernatura chihuahuense, en diciembre fue elegido gobernador constitucional. Derrotado por las tropas estadounidenses en Sacramento, en febrero de 1847, en marzo dejó el gobierno local y viajó a la ciudad de México, donde se incorporó al Estado Mayor del presidente Antonio López de Santa Anna. Participó en la batalla de Cerro Gordo. En septiembre volvió a Chihuahua y reasumió la gubernatura. En febrero de 1848 intentó detener un nuevo avance estadounidense en Chihuahua, pero en marzo fue derrotado y hecho prisionero por Sterling Price. Liberado en julio, instaló su gobierno en Parral y más tarde en Chihuahua. En marzo de 1849 volvió a ser elegido gobernador constitucional y se retiró en noviembre de 1850, pero volvió al poder dos años después (de diciembre de 1852 a abril de 1853), luego de adherirse al Plan del Hospicio, que llevó a Santa Anna por última vez a la Presidencia. En 1854 se opuso a la venta de La Mesilla y fue destituido. Al triunfo de la revolución de Ayutla fue otra vez gobernador de Chihuahua (de noviembre a diciembre de 1855) y comandante del Ejército de Operaciones. En diciembre de 1857, cuando era segundo jefe de la guarnición de la ciudad de México, se opuso al golpe de Estado del presidente Ignacio Comonfort y se levantó en armas. Se enfrentó a los conservadores en la ciudad de México, pero fue obligado a retirarse a Veracruz. Combatió en el oriente hasta mediados de 1858, cuando abandonó a las tropas constitucionalistas, se retiró a Chihuahua y consiguió una concesión para construir un ferrocarril entre Chihuahua y Guaymas. En 1860 se reincorporó a la lucha y combatió en Chihuahua y Sonora, donde fue comandante militar de Hermosillo. Al término de la guerra de los Tres Años fue gobernador del Distrito Federal (del 23 al 30 de abril de 1862), organizador de la Guardia Nacional de la ciudad de México, comandante de la segunda división del Ejército del Centro en la batalla de San Lorenzo (1863) y gobernador y comandante militar de Chihuahua (del 11 de julio de 1864 a 14 de julio de 1865).

TRÍAS OCHOA, ÁNGEL ◆ n. en Chihuahua, Chih., y m. en la ciudad de México (1839-1912). Hijo del anterior. Ingeniero y ensayador titulado en el Colegio de Minería de la ciudad de México. En 1858, cuando todavía era estudiante, fue detenido por el gobierno conservador de Félix María Zuloaga. En 1862 se incorporó a las fuerzas republicanas de José María Patoni. Formó parte del ejército de Jesús González Ortega que, entre marzo y mayo de 1863, fue sitiado en Puebla por los franceses y al triunfo de los invasores hecho prisionero y encarcelado. Como casi toda la oficialidad republicana, escapó mientras era conducido a Francia y se reincorporó a las fuerzas mexicanas. Combatió en Nuevo León, Sonora y Sinaloa. En 1865, cuando era diputado local en Chihuahua, apoyó las pretensiones presidenciales de González Ortega y fue expulsado del ejército. Once años más

Foto: Época

Viola Trigo

Foto: Guillermo Aguilera

Guadalupe Trigo

Miguel Trillo al lado de Francisco Villa

tarde, en enero de 1876, adherido al Plan de Tuxtepec, se levantó en armas y tomó Chihuahua, pero en septiembre fue rechazado por las fuerzas lerdistas de Luis Terrazas. En agosto de 1877, poco después del triunfo porfirista, fue elegido gobernador de Chihuahua para el periodo 1877-1881. En 1878 intentó retirarse del gobierno a causa de la oposición terracista, pero el Congreso local no aceptó su dimisión. Al año siguiente fue derrocado por Terrazas. Ascendido a general brigadier en 1880, fue jefe de armas en Durango y Guerrero y constructor del telégrafo Chihuahua-Sonora.

Tributos de Mizquiahuala ◆ Códice nahua realizado en la segunda mitad del siglo xvi. Es una tira de papel de amate en la que los indios de la hoy hidalguense población de Mizquiahuala registraron el tributo que entregaron, a fines de los años sesenta y principios de los setenta, al corregidor Manuel de Olvera. Fue propiedad de Lorenzo Boturini hasta principios del siglo xix, cuando lo adquirió Joel R. Poinsett, quien, años más tarde, lo donó a la Sociedad Filosófica Americana de Filadelfia, que en 1942 lo cedió al acervo de la Biblioteca Benjamin Franklin de la ciudad de México.

Trigo, Guadalupe ◆ n. en Mérida, Yuc., y m. en el DF (1941-1982). Nombre profesional del músico y compositor José Alfonso Ontiveros Carrillo. Licenciado en derecho por la Universidad Autónoma de Yucatán (1967). En Mérida formó parte de varias agrupaciones de música regional, entre ellas el grupo "Los Monjes". Llegó a la ciudad de México en 1969 y comenzó a usar el nombre de Guadalupe Trigo. Murió en un accidente automovilístico. Coautor, con Eduardo Salas, de la canción *Mi ciudad*; y autor de más de 120 canciones, entre ellas *Romance a sor Juana, El pescador, Oiga usted don Emiliano, La yunta y el arado, Te lo juro corazón, Mi poeta de cristal, El nuevo cancionero, Canto a mi tierra, Gitana, Hoy no salgo a la cantina, Caribeña, Marissa, Compañera, Me quedé solo, La milpa de Valerio, Canción con sombrero, Oiga corazón, Homenaje a Gabriela Mistral* y *Homenaje a León Felipe*. Perteneció a la Sociedad de Autores y Compositores de Música.

Trigo, Viola ◆ n. en Monclova, Coah. (?). Nombre profesional de la cantante Violeta Tapia Flores. Esposa del anterior, a quien acompañó durante muchos años. Ha participado en congresos y encuentros culturales y feministas, entre los que destaca la Cumbre Internacional de la Mujer 1995, celebrada en China. En 1997 fue candidata a la jefatura de gobierno del DF por el Partido del Trabajo.

Trigos, Juan Jacobo ◆ n. en el DF (1941). Escritor y crítico musical. Estudió en el Conservatorio Nacional de Música y en la Academia Andrés Soler de la Asociación Nacional de Actores. Ha trabajado en agencias publicitarias e hizo música para películas. Colaborador de la revista *Mester*, del periódico *Excélsior* y de la *Revista Mexicana de Cultura*, suplemento de *El Nacional*. Autor de cuento: *La guillotinita* (1978) y *El sótano* (1978); teatro: *Contra-sujeto* (1978), *El moco* (1979), *A falta de dios, nuestro señor Presidente* (1992), *De padres ausentes hijos imaginarios* (1992), *Déjame que te mate para ver si te extraño* (1992) y *Yo digo que soy yo, pero quién sabe* (1992); y novela: *La culpa* (1979), *La zarpa* (1980), *La leyenda de don Juan Manuel* (1981), *El tapado* (1981), *La llorona* (1984), *El callejón de las ratas* (1986), *Rincón de las calaveras* (1987), *Confesión de una muerta* (1987), *Amor del bueno* (1989) y *El perro bailarín* (1992).

Trigueros, Ignacio ◆ n. en Veracruz, Ver., y m. en la ciudad de México (1805-1879). Fue alcalde del puerto de Veracruz, secretario de Hacienda en los gobiernos de Antonio López de Santa Anna (del 21 de noviembre de 1841 al 26 de octubre de 1842; del 4 de marzo al 4 de octubre de 1843, y del 4 de junio al 12 de septiembre de 1844), Nicolás Bravo (del 26 de octubre de 1842 al 4 de marzo de 1843); Valentín Canalizo (del 4 de octubre de 1843 al 4 de junio de 1844 y del 21 de septiembre al 28 de octubre de 1844) y José Joaquín de Herrera (del 12 al 21 de septiembre de 1844), senador de la República (1845-47) y gobernador del Distrito Federal (del 24 de marzo al 3 de junio de 1847). En 1867 fundó la Escuela de Sordomudos y en 1870 la Escuela para Ciegos.

Trigueros Saravia, Eduardo ◆ n. en Pasaje, Dgo., y m. en el DF (1907-1955). Licenciado en derecho por la Escuela Libre de Derecho (1928), de la que fue profesor (1928-54). También ejerció la docencia en la UNAM (1942-55). Fue jefe del Departamento Jurídico, consultor, subdirector y secretario del Consejo de Administración del Banco Nacional de México y rector de la Escuela Libre de Derecho (1950-54). Autor de *Flexibilidad de la interpretación de las constituciones rígidas* (1928), *La devolución de los depósitos bancarios constituidos en oro* (1934), *La evolución doctrinal del derecho internacional privado* (1939), *La apertura de créditos en bancos* (1939), *La nacionalidad mexicana* (1940) y *Trayectoria del derecho mundial* (1953). Perteneció a la Barra Mexicana-Colegio de Abogados, a la Academia Mexicana de Jurisprudencia y Legislación y al Instituto de Derecho Comparado.

Trillo, Miguel ◆ n. en Chihuahua y m. en Parral, Chih. (1883-1923). En 1913 se incorporó a la revolución constitucionalista. Desde 1914 militó en la División del Norte. Fue secretario particular de Francisco Villa y alcanzó el grado de coronel. Murió en el mismo atentado en el que Villa fue asesinado.

TRINCHERAS ◆ Municipio de Sonora situado al norte de Hermosillo y el sur-suroeste de Nogales. Superficie: 3,764.26 km². Habitantes: 1,900, de los cuales 626 forman la población económicamente activa. Hablan alguna lengua indígena cinco personas mayores de cinco años. En varias cuevas situadas en la jurisdicción se han encontrado pinturas rupestres.

TRINIDAD, DE LA ◆ Río de Oaxaca y Veracruz. Nace en la región del Zempoaltépetl, de la confluencia de los ríos del Chisme y Puxmetacán. Corre de suroeste a noreste, entra en Veracruz y en la llanura costera del golfo de México se une al río de La Lana para formar el San Juan Evangelista.

TRINIDAD, DE LA ◆ Sierra situada en el sureste de Baja California Sur. Se extiende de norte a sur, al norte-noreste de San José del Cabo. Alcanza alturas superiores a los mil metros sobre el nivel del mar. Está separada de la sierra de San Lázaro por el río San José.

TRINIDAD, DE LA ◆ Valle situado en el norte de Baja California, al sureste de Ensenada. Se extiende de este a oeste entre el extremo sur de la sierra de Juárez y el norte de la de San Pedro Mártir.

TRINIDAD FERREIRA, ÁNGEL ◆ n. en el DF (1932). Periodista. Estudió en la Escuela de la Cadena García Valseca (1950). Fue reportero de la oficina de Prensa de la Secretaría de Educación (1949-51), de *Últimas Noticias* (1951-) y de *Excélsior* (1963-76), donde firmaba la columna diaria "Frentes Políticos" y la dominical "Documental Política"; jefe de la sección política de *El Heraldo de México* (1976-77), reportero de la fuente de Presidencia del Canal 13 (1977-82), director de *El Sol de México* (1983), director de Noticiarios de Imevisión (1986-92) y director de *La Afición* (1995-99). Ha entrevistado a decenas de jefes de Estado y de gobierno. Autor de un libro sobre la visita del papa Paulo VI a Colombia (1968) y de otro sobre la campaña electoral de Miguel de la Madrid (1982). Desde 1986 es miembro del consejo consultivo del Instituto de Estudios Políticos, Económicos y Sociales del PRI.

TRINIDAD GARCÍA DE LA CADENA ◆ Municipio del estado de Zacatecas situado en el suroeste de la entidad, en los límites con Jalisco. Superficie: 212.27 km². Habitantes: 3,710, de los cuales 857 forman la población económicamente activa.

TRINIDAD SÁNCHEZ SANTOS ◆ ☛ *Zitlaltepec de Trinidad Sánchez Santos.*

TRINIDAD Y TOBAGO, REPÚBLICA DE ◆ Estado insular americano situado a 24 kilómetros del delta del río Orinoco, en el mar Caribe, frente a la costa de Venezuela. Está formado por las islas de Trinidad, Tabago, Pequeño Tabago, Monos, Chacachacare, Gasparee y Huevos. Superficie: 5,128 km². Habitantes: 1,283,000 (1998). Su capital es Puerto España (52,451 habitantes en 1992). Otras ciudades de importancia son San Fernando (30,092 habitantes en 1990) y Arima (29,695). El país es miembro de la Comunidad Británica y el idioma oficial es el inglés. *Historia:* los primeros habitantes del actual territorio de Trinidad y Tabago fueron caribes, dedicados principalmente a la caza y la recolección. En julio de 1498, durante la tercera expedición de Cristóbal Colón por el Caribe, fuerzas españolas desembarcaron en Trinidad, que fue llamada Trinidad de Barlovento y se convirtió en dominio de España. Poco después se introdujo el cultivo de la caña de azúcar. En 1532, Madrid estableció una gobernación en la isla, que a principios del siglo XVII se hallaba prácticamente despoblada, pues la sobreexplotación y violencia de los conquistadores acabaron con los indios caribes, por lo que se inició la importación de esclavos africanos. En 1632 desembarcaron en Tabago los holandeses, pero no pudieron constituir un asentamiento permanente. Piratas y fuerzas militares de las potencias europeas se alternaron en su afán de controlar las islas, pero fue hacia 1781 cuando los franceses establecieron una colonia en Tabago, hasta donde llegaron las convulsiones de la revolución, que alentaron los levantamientos de esclavos y obligaron a los colonos blancos a trasladarse a Trinidad. Diez años más tarde, Tabago fue ocupada por fuerzas británicas que hallaron la isla prácticamente deshabitada. Ahi nacieron en 1790, Juan José Codallos (☛) y Felipe Codallos (☛), quienes formaron parte del ejército colonial de la Nueva España; en 1821 se incorporaron al Ejército Trigarante y luego participaron activamente en la política mexicana de la primera mitad del siglo XIX. Juan José fue yorkino, quien en 1830 se levantó en armas contra el gobierno golpista de Anastasio Bustamante, proclamó un plan federalista y murió fusilado en 1831. Felipe, por su parte, fue enviado en 1822 a Guatemala con la orden de garantizar la incorporación de los países centroamericanos al imperio de Agustín de Iturbide, más tarde fue gobernador de Puebla y combatiente contra la invasión estadounidense de 1847. En 1797, los ingleses ocuparon Trinidad en 1802, por medio del tratado de Amiens, España renunció a su posesión. En Tabago, mientras tanto, franceses y británicos se disputaron el control de la isla, hasta que, vencidos los primeros en Europa, los ingleses se adueñaron de la isla. A partir de la abolición de la esclavitud en las colonias inglesas del Caribe (1838), el gobierno metropolitano impulsó la contratación de inmigrantes de India, quienes se ocuparon principalmente de la producción azucarera, mientras que los ex esclavos se concentraron en las ciudades. En 1899, Trinidad y Tabago fueron unificadas administrativamente. En los años veinte de este siglo comenzaron a manifestarse algunos grupos independentistas. En 1950, las dos islas fueron integradas, aunque con autonomía interna, a la Federación de las Antillas Británicas, que se disolvió 11 años después, en 1961, con el retiro de Jamaica. El 31 de agosto de 1962, la nación se independizó, aunque conservó la forma monárquica y se integró a la Comunidad Británica de Naciones. En ese año

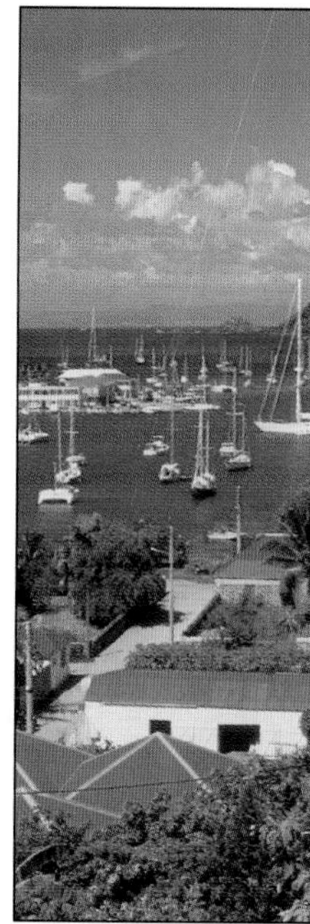

Paisaje tropical en República de Trinidad y Tobago

Ángel Trinidad Ferreira

ingresó en la Organización de las Naciones Unidas. El primer jefe de gobierno fue Eric Eustace Williams, quien gobernó hasta su muerte, en 1981. Las relaciones diplomáticas entre México y Trinidad y Tabago se establecieron en 1966. Hacia 1973, en los alrededores de Trinidad y Tabago se descubrieron grandes yacimientos petrolíferos, cuya explotación fue acaparada por la firma anglo-holandesa Royal Dutch Shell y la estadounidense Texaco. En agosto de 1975, el presidente mexicano Luis Echeverría se entrevistó con el primer ministro Williams y el gobernador Ellis Clarke, en Puerto España. En 1976, el gobernante Movimiento Nacional del Pueblo impulsó la promulgación de una nueva constitución, la cual se firmó el 1 de agosto, convirtió al país en República, rompió los vínculos con Gran Bretaña. En 1985, el gobierno de Chambers compró las propiedades de la Texaco y nacionalizó, de hecho, la industria petrolera. Su jefe de gobierno es Basdeo Panday (1987-) y su jefe de Estado, Noor Mojammed Hassanali (1995-).

FOTO: ÉPOCA

Trino

Las aventuras de Pipo, por *Trino*

TRINIDAD VISTA HERMOSA, LA ◆ Municipio de Oaxaca situado al este-sureste de Huajuapan de León y al nor-noroeste de Teposcolula. Superficie: 31.9 km². Habitantes: 293, de los cuales 96 forman la población económicamente activa.

TRINIDAD ZAACHILA ◆ Municipio de Oaxaca situado al sur-suroeste de la capital estatal, al noreste de Huixtepec y el noroeste de Ocotlán. Superficie: 34.45 km². Habitantes: 2,833, de los cuales 727 forman la población económicamente activa. Hablan alguna lengua indígena 11 personas mayores de cinco años.

TRINITARIA, LA ◆ Municipio de Chiapas situado al sureste de Comitán y al norte de Tapachula, en los límites con Guatemala. Superficie: 1,840.7 km². Habitantes: 58,827, de los cuales 16,041 forman la población económicamente activa. Hablan alguna lengua indígena 5,556 personas mayores de cinco años (kanjobal 3,157, chuj 1,559 y tzeltal 275). En la jurisdicción se encuentran la zonas arqueológicas de Juncana, El Rosario, San Caralampio y La Cañada, el balneario de aguas sulfurosas de La Trinitaria, las cuevas de San Francisco y, en el extremo nororiental, las lagunas de Montebello. Es uno de los municipios que recibió al mayor número de refugiados guatemaltecos durante la guerra civil que sacudió a ese pais en la década de los ochenta.

TRINO ◆ n. en Guadalajara, Jal. (1961). Nombre profesional del caricaturista José Trinidad Camacho Orozco. Licenciado en ciencias de la comunicación por el ITESO. Colaboró en la revista *Galimatías*, de Guadalajara, y participó en *Monobloc. Todos Venimos del Mono*, sección del periódico *El Occidental*. Posteriormente colaboró en *unomásuno*, *El Financiero* y *La Jornada* (en las tiras *La Croqueta*, *Humor Perro*, *La Mamá del Abulón*, *La chora interminable*, *Gárgaras de Humor Flemático*). Cofundador de *El Chamuco*. Autor de las tiras cómicas *Historias del Rey Chiquito*, *Historias paralelas*, *Fábulas de policías y ladrones* y *Crónicas marcianas*. También ha hecho caricatura, animación y video para cine y televisión y ha colaborado en programas de radio. Coautor, con el caricaturista *Jis* (☛), de *El Santos contra la Tetona Mendoza I* y *II*, *El Santos contra Godzilla*, *El Santos y el Peyote en la Atlántida* (1999) y *La chora interminable*. Autor de *Fábulas de policías y ladrones I* y *II*, *Historias paralelas* e *Historias del Rey Chiquito*.

TRIQUIS ◆ Indios que habitan en el oeste de Oaxaca, principalmente en cinco pueblos de la sierra de Chicahuaxtla: San Juan Copala, San José Chicahuaxtla, San Andrés Chicahuaxtla, Santo Domingo Chicahuaxtla y San Martín Itunyoso. En 1995, hablaban triqui 18,715 personas mayores de cinco años. Vivían en Oaxaca 14,058, de los cuales 4,600 son monolingües. La lengua triqui está clasificada en el grupo otomangue, tronco savizaa, familia mixteca, que tiene tres variantes dialectales (Copala, Chicahuaxtla e Itunyoso), que dificultan la comunicación. Los individuos de esta etnia conservan su vestimenta tradicional: calzón de manta, camisa con bordados en puños y cuello, faja, sombrero y huaraches, para los hombres; enredo negro si son casadas o azul marino si son solteras, faja y huipil, para las mujeres. La agricultura es la actividad económica básica de este grupo, aunque en algunos casos rentan sus terrenos como pastizales o cuidan el ganado de los mestizos; cada familia triqui posee dos o tres cabezas de ganado mayor, aves de corral, cabras, ovejas y burros; además, los hombres emigran temporalmente para trabajar como asalariados y algunas mujeres han empezado a hacer lo mismo, sobre todo a las ciudades de Oaxaca o México. La base social es la familia nuclear, aunque hay algunas familias extensas. La edad casadera para las mujeres oscila entre los 12 y los 15 años de edad, en tanto que para los varones es entre los 18 y los 21 años. Para concertar un matrimonio, el padre del novio hace tres visitas a los padres de la novia, hasta que se acuerda el monto de la dote. Cuando un triqui muere, su cuerpo es velado una noche y luego es enterrado junto con un itacate que, de acuerdo con sus creencias, le dará fuerza para llegar al mundo de los muertos. Según su mitología, la vida empezó con una pareja original y sus descendientes se dispersaron hasta que los triquis, dirigidos por una mujer, se establecieron en San Andrés. El sol y la luna fueron seres que vivían en una calabaza y que, tras algunas peripecias, montaron en un gato y un conejo y llegaron hasta lo alto del cielo, desde donde empezaron a iluminar al mundo. Asimismo, veneran y hacen ofrendas a la lluvia, al rayo, a la tierra, al viento, al fuego y a las estrellas. Cada pueblo trique tiene una autoridad principal que arbitra cuando se presentan dificultades en la comunidad. Los triquis viven en las montañas desde el siglo XIII, cuando fueron atacados por grupos guerreros de la región de Tlaxiaco. A principios del siglo XV fueron dominados por los aztecas y convertidos en tributarios de México-Tenochtitlan, aunque los dominadores no pudieron defender a los triquis de la agresión de los mixtecos. Después de la conquista, los triquis se mantuvieron en zonas apartadas, donde los misioneros españoles no podían llegar con facilidad. Sin embargo, paulatinamente fueron cooptados para la religión cristiana, sobre todo debido al trabajo del misionero Gonzalo Lucero. En 1843, a causa de los tributos que los españoles todavía cobraban y del despojo de sus tierras comunales, los pueblos triquis se levantaron en armas, pero en ese año el movimiento fue reprimido por las fuerzas gubernamentales de Manuel Ruiz, que tomaron Copala y Juxtlahuaca. Dos años después los indios volvieron a insurreccionarse y tomaron Putla, Tlaxiaco, Juxtlahuaca y Copala y recibieron apoyo del guerrerense Juan Álvarez, quien nombró comandante del levantamiento triqui a Feliciano Martín y dispuso que dejaran de pagar los diezmos y los impuestos, por lo que el movimiento se extendió a toda la Mixteca e incluso hubo un intento de tomar Huajuapan. En 1845 la sublevación fue derrotada por tropas oaxaqueñas, pero algunos grupos guerrilleros sobrevivieron hasta 1848. En 1956, los triquis se aliaron con los mestizos y ejecutaron a tres militares de bajo rango, por lo que las fuerzas federales bombardearon varios pueblos y un destacamento se acuarteló en Copala, donde permanecía aún en la década de los ochenta.

TRISTÁN Y ESMENOTA, ESTEBAN LORENZO DE ◆ n. en España y m. en San Juan de los Lagos, Jal. (1723-1794). Sacerdote. Doctor en cánones por la Universidad de Granada. Fue chantre de la Catedral de Guadix, obispo de Nicaragua (1775-83) y obispo de Durango (1783-94). Murió envenenado.

TRITSCHLER Y CÓRDOVA, GUILLERMO ◆ n. en San Andrés Chalchicomula, Pue., y m. en Monterrey, NL (1878-1952). Sacerdote ordenado en 1903. Doctor en filosofía, teología y derecho canónico por la Universidad Gregoriana de Roma. Profesor del Seminario Conciliar de México. Fue canónigo penitenciario de la Catedral Metropolitana, obispo de San Luis Potosí (1931-41) y arzobispo de Monterrey (1941-52). Nombrado miembro de la Academia Mexicana de la Historia, aunque no aceptó la designación.

TRITSCHLER Y CÓRDOVA, MARTÍN ◆ n. en San Andrés Chalchicomula, Pue., y m. en Mérida, Yuc. (1868-1942). Sacerdote ordenado en 1891. Estudió en el Seminario Palafoxiano. Doctor en filosofía, teología y derecho canónico por la Universidad Gregoriana. Fue director espiritual del Seminario Palafoxiano, secretrario particular del arzobispo de Puebla (1896-1900), obispo (1900-06) y arzobispo (1906-42) de Yucatán. En dos ocasiones se vio obligado a abandonar la arquidiócesis por la persecución religiosa (1914-19 y 1926-29). Fue editor de un *Boletín Eclesiástico del Obispado*.

TRONCOSO, FRANCISCO DE PAULA ◆ n. en Veracruz, Ver., y m. en la ciudad de México (1839-1919). Estudió en el Colegio Militar, donde más tarde fue profesor. Combatió la intervención francesa y el imperio de Maximiliano de Habsburgo, sobre todo en la región de Tlacotalpan. Ascendió a general de brigada en 1868. Fue diputado federal. Autor de *Las guerras con las tribus yaqui y mayo del estado de Sonora* (1905) y *Diario de las operaciones militares del sitio de Puebla en 1863* (1909).

FOTO: LOURDES ALMEIDA

Familia de campesinos triquis de San Andrés Chicahuaxtla, Oaxaca

TRONCOSO, JUAN NEPOMUCENO ◆ n. en Veracruz y m. en Tlacotepec, Ver. (1779-1830). Abogado y sacerdote. Estudió en la Real y Pontificia Universidad de México (1795) y en el Seminario Palafoxiano de Puebla (1804). Dedicado al periodismo, entre el 30 de noviembre de 1820 y el 17 de diciembre de 1821 publicó el semanario *La Abeja Poblana*, en donde, el 2 de marzo de 1821, apareció por primera vez el Plan de Iguala, por lo cual fue confinado al curato de Molcajac y más tarde procesado por un tribunal militar. A la consumación de la independencia fundó, con José María Troncoso, la editorial Troncoso Hnos. Autor de los folletos *A los americanos amantes de la justicia, Pascuas de un militar, Mi carta al pueblo, Cartas al Pensador Mexicano* y *Avisos al pueblo*.

TRONCOSO Y SOTOMAYOR, BALTASAR ◆ (1725-1791). Pintor y grabador mexicano. Autor de imágenes de San Luis Gonzaga, Santa María Magdalena, la Virgen de Guadalupe, el Cristo de la Piedad, San Ignacio de Loyola y San Francisco Javier; también pintó los retratos de Pedro de San José Betancourt (1751) y de Juan Antonio de Oviedo (1760), entre otros.

TROTSKISMO ◆ El primer grupo trotskista que hubo en México se aglutinó, a finales de 1930, en torno de Manuel Rodríguez, un profesor interesado en el marxismo desde principios de los años veinte, y que luego de participar en las campañas organizadas por los comunistas en favor de Augusto César Sandino, se había incorporado al Partido Comunista Mexicano. Ahí conoció a Rusell Blackwell, un estadounidense miembro del Partido Comunista Norteamericano que usaba el seudónimo de Rosalío Negrete. Éste llegó a México a finales de los años veinte y trabajó en la reorganización de la Juventud Comunista, hasta que fue excluido del PCM por su afinidad con los trotskistas estadounidenses y volvió a su país. A finales de 1930, Rodríguez también fue expulsado del PCM por simpatizar con la Oposición de Izquierda Internacional, la organización de los trotskistas europeos y estadounidenses, y poco después proclamó abiertamente su adhesión a León Trotsky (☛) y fundó la Oposición Comunista de Izquierda, organización a la que poco después se incorporaron Eduardo Calero, Guillermo Solís, Bernardo Claraval y Alberto Martínez, entre otros expulsados del PCM. La Organización Comunista de Izquierda (OCI) publicó el boletín *Izquierda* y sus escasos militantes se dedicaron fundamentalmente a la propaganda en círculos obreros y a la discusión interna, pues estaba por definirse el rumbo político e ideológico del incipiente trotskismo mexicano. La OCI participó en varios de los movimientos obreros de 1933 y 1934. En marzo de ese último año, el Partido Comunista expulsó a otro grupo de simpatizantes trotskistas, encabezado por los profesores Luciano Galicia, Benjamín Álvarez y Octavio Fernández, que se fusionó con la OCI y creó la Liga Comunista Internacionalista, cuyo órgano de prensa fue la revista *Nueva Internacional*. Este grupo tuvo particular incidencia en algunos núcleos de obreros textiles y de artes gráficas. Debido a la represión gubernamental, a los enfrentamientos políticos con el Partido Comunista y con la dirección lombardista de los sindicatos, pero también a las divergencias de carácter táctico de sus propios miembros, en los primeros meses de 1935 la Liga entró en un periodo de reflujo, el que intentó ser superado a finales de ese año con la publicación de la revista *Octubre*, de Fernández y Rodríguez, pero el fortalecimiento de la organización sólo se logró a principios de 1936, con la incorporación de Diego Rivera, quien se había separado del PCM. Poco después se empezó a publicar el periódico *Cuarta Internacional* y se incrementó notablemente la actividad de la Liga en sindicatos de panaderos y albañiles, lo que le permitió organizar un frente llamado Comité de Acción y Unificación Obrero Campesino Independiente, el que organizó un mitin en el teatro Imperial de la capital del país el 18 de octubre. Al día siguiente se realizó otro del PCM en el que se acusó a los trotskistas de organizar una "conspiración contrarrevolucionaria". A finales de 1936, la Liga inició gestiones para que México diera asilo a Trotsky. El 12 de diciembre, en un acto público, el Partido Comunista y la Confederación de Trabajadores de México, dirigida por Vicente Lombardo Toledano, expresaron su rechazo a esa pretensión. Con el mismo fin, en enero de 1937 se realizó otro mitin del PCM y la CTM que fue disuelto por la policía. El día 9 de ese mes llegó el viejo bolchevique a Tampico, después de que Francisco J. Múgica y Diego Rivera gestionaran exitosamente ante Lázaro Cárdenas la petición de asilo. A mediados de ese año, se presentaron diferencias entre los miembros del buró político de la Liga, lo que en la práctica significó su desaparición, por lo que entre 1937 y 1939 prácticamente no existió un grupo trotskista en México. De un lado quedaron Galicia y Félix Ibarra, y por el otro Fernández, Rivera y José Ferrel, quienes durante esos dos años se dedicaron a editar *Clave*, revista teórica y política aparecida durante la estancia de Trotsky en México y cuya finalidad fue presentar, en español, las posiciones del trotskismo, que eran continuamente tergiversadas. A finales de enero de 1939 fueron expulsados del PCM otros 12 militantes acusados de "trotskistas". En marzo, el Partido Comunista afirmó que en el Centro Pro Múgica "se han colado los provocadores trotskistas". En los primeros meses de 1939, los dos grupos, separados en 1937, volvieron a reunirse y la Liga se reorganizó y publicó un nuevo periódico, *El Bolchevique*. Los trotskistas respondieron al Partido Comunista que "con el pretexto de la unidad a toda costa" querían entregar la revolución "a las derechas". En septiembre, la Liga cambió su nombre al de Partido Obrero Internacionalista (POI) y comenzó a editar el periódico *Lucha Obrera*, que apareció entre 1939 y 1947. En 1939, Diego Rivera, distanciado de Trotsky, fundó el Partido Revolucionario Obrero y Campesino, que al año siguiente

Grabado de Baltasar Troncoso y Sotomayor ejecutado en 1743 sobre una obra de José de Ibarra

apoyó la candidatura presidencial de Juan Andrew Almazán. Desde finales de 1944, luego de la derrota del movimiento sindical encabezado por el Frente Nacional Proletario, las diferencias volvieron a surgir entre Galicia y Fernández, por lo que en 1945 éste se separó del POI y formó el Grupo Socialista Obrero. Dos años después, el POI y GSO se disolvieron y sus miembros se limitaron a la actividad sindical, especialmente entre electricistas, telefonistas, maestros y ferrocarrileros. Durante ocho años, ninguna organización reivindicó las posturas del trostkismo hasta que, en 1957, un grupo de militantes, salidos de la Juventud Comunista del PCM y de la Juventud Popular del PP, se unieron con algunos veteranos trostkistas y comenzaron a editar el periódico *Linterna*, en torno al cual formaron la Juventud Socialista Mexicana. El grupo entró en contacto con la Cuarta Internacional y dos años después, en enero de 1959, un núcleo de sus militantes entre los que se encontraban Felipe Galván, Francisco Moranga y Vidal Solís se constituyó en Partido Obrero Revolucionario (☛), que se sumó a la corriente internacional posadista. Otros miembros de la JSM, por su parte, dirigidos por Francisco Navarrete y Manuel Aguilar Mora, formaron la Liga Estudiantil Marxista a fines de ese año, que se transformó en Liga Obrera Marxista en los últimos meses de 1960. En el Partido Obrero Revolucionario, identificado como POR-(t), además de los fundadores, militaron Eunice Campirán, David Aguilar Mora, Fernando López Limón y Alfonso Lizárraga, entre otros. Su periódico fue *Voz Obrera*. En sus primeros años, el POR(t) se concentró sobre todo en realizar trabajo propagandístico entre grupos estudiantiles, pero desde mediados de los años sesenta, sus miembros sufrieron una fuerte represión y varios de ellos fueron encarcelados, la organización desapareció en la década siguiente. La LOM, por su parte, también concentró su actividad entre los estudiantes, particularmente los de la UNAM. En 1964, sin embargo, se escindió, a causa de las diferencias surgidas en torno a la afiliación internacional. El núcleo, dirigido por Navarrete y Rafael Torres, se vinculó a la corriente internacionalista que dirigía Pierre Lambert y editó un *Boletín Obrero*. El otro grupo, que era encabezado por Aguilar Mora y Carlos Sevilla, apoyó al secretariado de la Cuarta Internacional y publicó el periódico *El Obrero Militante*. A fines de 1967, sin embargo, el grupo decidió disolverse. La situación en que se encontraban todas estas vertientes del trotskismo imposibilitó que los trotskistas participaran organizadamente en el inicio del movimiento estudiantil de 1968. Días después de la manifestación silenciosa del 13 de septiembre, Aguilar Mora y Sevilla constituyeron, con José Revueltas, Roberto Escudero y Luis González de Alba, el Movimiento Comunista Internacionalista, con carácter de frente amplio en cuanto sus concepciones ideológicas. La represión generalizada contra el movimiento estudiantil de 1968 acabó con los pocos cuadros de MCI, y algunos de ellos como Aguilar Mora, Alfonso Peralta, Alfredo López, Ricardo Hernández, Antonio Sánchez y Salvador Hernández, fundaron el Grupo Comunista Internacionalista, que desde febrero de 1969 editó la revista *La Internacional*. Su actividad, como la del resto de los grupos trotskistas, se limitó a la UNAM y al IPN. A partir del resurgimiento del movimiento estudiantil en 1971, en el que el CGI tuvo una activa participación, el grupo se fortaleció y entró en contacto con organizaciones no trotskistas con la idea de formar un partido. A fines de ese año se alió con el Partido Mexicano del Proletariado y los grupos Teoría y Práctica y Pregrupo e inició la publicación de la revista *Perspectiva*. Poco después la coalición se extinguió. En agosto de 1972, el CGI comenzó a editar *Bandera Roja*, pero al mes siguiente se escindió y fundó la Juventud Marxista Revolucionaria, convertida desde diciembre de 1973 en Liga Socialista. El resto del CGI, sin embargo, impulsó la reunificación, pero en abril de 1975, un tercer grupo, que se oponía al reingreso de los miembros de la Liga Socialista, se separó del CGI y se concentró en la redacción del periódico *Rojo*. La Liga tampoco pudo conservar la unidad y poco antes de las elecciones de 1976 se dividió en la Tendencia Militante y en la Fracción Bolchevique Leninista. Todos los grupos, sin embargo, apoyaron a Valentín Campa, el candidato del PCM en las elecciones de 1976, y a partir de entonces, aunque cada uno conservaba distintos puntos de vista e incluso el grado de colaboración con los comunistas había variado notablemente, la tendencia hacia la unificación se aceleró. En abril de 1976, el CGI y los redactores de *Rojo* se unieron para formar la Liga Comunista Internacionalista. En noviembre, la LCI se fusionó con la Tendencia Militante y crearon el Partido Revolucionario de los Trabajadores (☛). La Fracción Bolchevique Leninista se unió a la Fracción Trotskista Leninista de la LOM y, en 1977, la nueva organización se sumó al PRT. En agosto de 1979 Ricardo Hernández encabezó a un grupo de militantes que salieron del PRT y se incorporaron al PCM. En noviembre, la Tendencia Bolchevique se separó del partido por diferencias en torno al proceso revolucionario de Nicaragua, a sus salida, adoptó el nombre de Partido Obrero Socialista, cuya principal fuerza se encontraba en el municipio mexiquense de Naucalpan. En 1982, un grupo de militantes del POS que habían pertenecido a la Liga Socialista, se separó de ese grupo y volvió al PRT. En 1987, un numeroso grupo de militantes del PRT se separó del partido y participó en la creación del Movimiento al Socialismo, que en 1989 se incorporó al Partido de la Revolución Democrática. Con la caída de los gobiernos de la URSS y Europa Oriental, el trotskismo entró en crisis en todos los países donde actuaba. En México, el PRT, la principal fuerza organizada que pudo construir esta corriente, se extinguió en los noventa. (*Cfr.*: *Breve historia del trotskismo en México* (mimeo) de José Chávez Jaimes. PRT, 1984).

León Trotsky

Carlos Trouyet

TROTSKY, LEÓN ◆ n. en Ucrania y m. en el DF (1879-1940). Nombre adoptado en el clandestinaje por Lev Davidovich Bronstein. Estudió en la Universidad de Odesa. En 1896 se incorporó a la Liga Obrera de Nocolaiev y en 1897 fundó la Unión Obrera de la Rusia del Sur. En 1899 fue detenido por la policia zarista, encarcelado en Moscú y desterrado a Siberia en 1900. Dos años después escapó y se refugió en Finlandia y Gran Bretaña. Ahí conoció a a Plejanov, se incorporó al grupo dirigente del Partido Social Demócrata Ruso y editó, con Lenin, el periódico *Iskra*. En 1903 rompió con Lenin. A principios de 1905 regresó clandestinamente a Rusia. En Petrogrado fundó el primer consejo de obreros de la ciudad y fue el principal dirigente de la fracasada revolución de ese año, a fines del cual volvió a ser detenido y deportado a Siberia, de donde escapó en 1907. Se instaló en Francia y más tarde en Viena y ahí fundó, en 1908, el periódico *Pravda*. Expulsado de Francia en 1914 por su oposición a la guerra, viajó a España y a Estados Unidos, donde editó *Novy Mir*. Enterado del estallido de la revolución de febrero de 1917, se embarcó hacia Rusia, a donde llegó en marzo, después de la abdicación del zar. Presidió el soviet de Petrogrado y en agosto ingresó con su grupo en el Partido Bolchevique, del que formó parte del buró político. En noviembre (octubre en el viejo calendario), dirigió la insurrección que instauró el poder soviético. Como comisario del Pueblo para Asuntos Extranjeros, a principios de 1918 firmó los tratados de paz de Brest-Litovsk y poco después fue nombrado Comisario del Pueblo para la Guerra. Organizó y dirigió el Ejército Rojo, que derrotó a las fuerzas contrarrevolucionarias rusas y rechazó la invasión de 22 países. A partir de la muerte de Lenin, fue objeto de una enconada campaña de José Stalin, quien lo privó de sus cargos públicos en 1925, lo expulsó del Partido Comunista (bolchevique) en 1927 y dos años después lo desterró de la Unión Soviética. Se exilió en Turquía (1929-31), Francia (1933-35) y Noruega (1935-36) y en enero de 1937 llegó a México, donde le concedió asilo el gobierno de Lázaro Cárdenas por gestiones, entre otros, de Francisco J. Múgica y Diego Rivera. Fue recibido por Frida Kahlo al desembarcar en Tampico. Poco después se instaló en Coyoacán, en la casa de Rivera. En abril, con un grupo de partidarios alemanes y estadounidenses, sobre todo, organizó una réplica al juicio al que había sido sometido en Moscú en 1925. El jurado, conocido como el Comité Dewey, lo exculpó de las acusaciones del PCUS. Para responder al Partido Comunista Mexicano y a Vicente Lombardo Toledano, quienes lo señalaban como "aliado de Hitler" y agente del imperialismo. En noviembre de 1937 publicó una "Carta al proletariado mexicano", en la que hacía su defensa. Durante 1937 y 1939 vivió en Coyoacán y algunas semanas en Taxco y San Miguel Regla, pero en abril de 1939, a causa de su rompimiento con Rivera, se trasladó a otra casa, también en Coyoacán, ahora convertida en museo. En mayo de 1940, un grupo de comunistas, entre los que se encontraba David Alfaro Siqueiros, intentó tomar la casa por asalto, pero los atacantes fueron rechazados por la pequeña guarnición que la custodiaba. Cinco meses después, en agosto, el agente estalinista Ramón Mercader del Río (☛), quien había ganado su confianza, consiguió introducirse en su casa y le partió el cráneo con un piolet. Horas después murió. Es autor de *Nuestras tareas políticas* (1904), *Balance y perspectivas* (1906), *La guerra y la Internacional* (1914), *Nuestra revolución* (1918), *Defensa del terrorismo* (1920), *Lenin* (1924), *Las lecciones de octubre de 1917* (1925), *Literatura y revolución* (1925), *La revolución desfigurada* (1929), *Mi vida* (1930), *Historia de la revolución rusa* (3 t., 1932), *El desaparecido testamento de Lenin* (1935), *La revolución traicionada* (1937) y *La escuela de falsificación de Stalin* (1937). Luego de su muerte aparecieron *Stalin* (1946), *La revolución permanente* (1947) y diversas antologías de su obra.

TROUYET, CARLOS ◆ n. y m. en el DF (1903-1971). Empresario. Su apellido materno era González. Fue mensajero del Banco Francés de México, calígrafo, corredor de valores y socio de la casa de cambio J. Lacaud; presidente de la Bolsa de Valores de México (1933-36 y 1939-44), fundador de la empresa bursátil Casa Trouyet (1944), cofundador y codueño, con Eloy S. Vallina, del Complejo Industrial Chihuahua (1952); codueño de las filiales mexicanas de las empresas telefónicas Ericsson e International Telephone and Telegraph (1958); socio y presidente del Banco Comercial Mexicano y presidente de la junta de gobierno de la Universidad Iberoamericana (1966-69). Fue también el principal accionista de las empresas Equipos Mecánicos, Crédito Minero y Mercantil, Cervecería Moctezuma, Central de Malta, Seguros la Comercial, Techo Eterno Eureka, Asbestos de Monterrey, Compañía Industrial de Orizaba, Banco Comercial Mexicano, Bosques de las Lomas; de los hoteles Las Brisas, de Acapulco, y El Tapatío, de Guadalajara. En 1969 se estableció el Premio Nacional de Literatura Carlos Trouyet.

TRUCHAS ◆ Río de Guerrero, también llamado Yolotla. Nace en la vertiente septentrional de la sierra Madre del Sur, al noreste de Atoyac de Álvarez; corre de sur a norte, recibe al río Yextla y desemboca en el Balsas, junto a Tetela del Río.

TRUCHUELO, JOSÉ MARÍA ◆ n. en Querétaro, Qro., y m. en el DF (1880-1953). Licenciado en derecho por el Colegio Civil de Querétaro. Fue juez de lo civil, abogado consultor del gobierno de Querétaro (1911), secretario general de Gobierno en la misma entidad (1914-15), director del Colegio Civil del estado (1915), síndico del Ayuntamiento de Querétaro (1915), secretario de Instrucción Pública del gobierno local y diputado al Congreso Constituyente de 1916-17, donde redactó la mayor parte de los artículos referidos a la estructura del Poder Judicial. Candidato derrotado al gobierno de Querétaro en 1919, al año siguiente se adhirió al Plan de Agua Prieta. Gobernador constitucional de Querétaro (del 28 de noviembre de 1920 al 30 de septiembre de 1923). Su gobierno expidió la primera ley reglamentaria del artículo 123 constitucional. Más tarde fue presidente del Tribunal Supremo de Justicia del Distrito Federal y ministro de la Suprema Corte de Justicia de la Nación.

Trueba Olivares, Eugenio ♦ n. en Silao, Gto. (1921). Escritor. Licenciado en derecho por la Universidad de Guanajuato. Ha sido profesor, director de la Facultad de Derecho y rector de la Universidad de Guanajuato. Director de las revistas *Umbral* y *Garabato*. Coautor, con Manuel de Ezcurdia y Alfonso Prado, de *Tres cuentos* (1947). Autor de cuento: *Cuentos* (1951), *Antesala* (1956) y *La pupila del gato* (1957); ensayo: *Marx, Platón, San Agustín. Ensayo sobre utopías* (1983) y *Vitoria, su pensamiento* (1987); novela: *La turba imagen* (1962); y teatro: *Los intereses colectivos* (1959), *El integérrimo Madrazo* (1959), *Mortis arbitrium* (1981), *Edicto de gracia* (1981) y *El río revuelto* (1982), y de *Una mala mirada* (1979).

Trueba Urbina, Alberto ♦ n. en Campeche, Camp., y m. en el DF (1903-1984). Licenciado en derecho por la Universidad Nacional de Sureste (1927) y doctor en derecho por la UNAM (1950), en la que ejerció la docencia. Fue juez menor de lo civil en Mérida, agente del Ministerio Público Federal (1935-36), presidente de la Junta Central de Conciliación y Arbitraje del Distrito Federal (1937-39), diputado federal (1940-43 y 1949-51), senador de la República (1952-55) y gobernador de Campeche (1955-56). Autor de *Nueva jurisprudencia sobre suspensión del acto reclamado en el amparo* (1935), *Diccionario de derecho obrero* (1935), *La ley federal del trabajo reformada* (1941), *La ley de amparo reformada* (1941), *Nuevo derecho administrativo del trabajo* (1973) y *Nuevo derecho internacional social* (1979).

Trujano, Valerio ♦ n. en Tepecoacuilco, en el actual estado de Guerrero, y m. en Tepeaca, Pue. (1767-1812). Se dice que a fines del siglo XVIII fue arriero y que desde entonces era amigo de José María Morelos y de Vicente Guerrero. Se levantó en armas a principios de 1811 y poco después tomó Chilacayoapa, sublevó varios pueblos de la Mixteca y en marzo, en Cuicatlán, derrotó a las tropas virreinales de Manuel Guendulàin y tomó Huajuapan. A principios de abril de 1812 fue sitiado en Huajuapan por un millar de soldados coloniales, entre ellos un regimiento de frailes; el asedió concluyó en julio, 111 días después, con la llegada de las fuerzas de Morelos. Durante el resto del año operó, desde Tehuacán, en el sur de Puebla, norte de Oaxaca y noreste de Guerrero. Murió en una emboscada.

Trujillo, Gilberto ♦ n. en Guadalajara, Jal., y m. en el DF (1878-1946). Licenciado en derecho. Fue subsecretario de Hacienda, encargado del despacho en el gabinete de Victoriano Huerta (del 10 al 14 de julio de 1914) y secretario de Hacienda (del 14 de julio al 13 de agosto de 1914) en el gobierno de Francisco S. Carbajal.

Trujillo, Julio ♦ n. en el DF (1969). Escritor. Licenciado en lengua y literatura hispánicas por la UNAM. Ha sido redactor de la revista *Universidad de México* (1992-93) y del suplemento *Lectura* (1993) y miembro del consejo directivo de la *Revista Mexicana de Cultura* de *El Nacional* (1996). Secretario de redacción de *Letras Libres* (1998-). Autor de poesía: *Una sangre* (1998, Premio Nacional de Poesía Elías Nandino 1994). Segundo lugar en el concurso de poesía UNAM-*El Nacional* (1991). Primer lugar en el concurso de poesía de la revista *Punto de partida* (1992). Becario del INBA (1993-94) y del Fonca (1994-95).

Trujillo, Víctor ♦ n. en el DF (1962). Actor y locutor. Comenzó su carrera en la radio. En el teatro universitario conoció a Ausencio Cruz, con el que hizo crítica política durante varios años. En 1987 condujeron el programa *En tienda y trastienda*, en Canal 13, al que siguió *La caravana* (1988), en el

Foto: Archivo Xavier Esparza

Valerio Trujano, en el sitio de Huajuapan

que Trujillo presentó a *Brozo, el payaso tenebroso* y a otros personajes que hizo populares. En 1992 montó con Cruz la sátira política *El dedo del Señor*. Ya disuelto el dúo, Trujillo continuó con *Brozo* en televisión, radio y prensa, así como con *la Beba Galván*. En 1999 empezó a conducir el programa *Las once y sereno* en el Canal 40 de televisión.

Trujillo Bolio, Iván ♦ n. en Villahermosa, Tab. (1954). Cineasta graduado en el CUEC y biólogo por la UNAM. Ha hecho documentales sobre la fauna y flora de México. Entre sus películas destacan *Tortuga Laúd* (1984, Di-ploma de Honor en el XXXIV Festival de la Asociación Internacional de Cine Científico) y *Monarca, adivinanzas para siempre* (1987, Ariel al mejor cortometraje documental). En 1985 condujo la serie televisiva *Vida en peligro*, en 1995 dirigió el programa *Xochimilco, la lucha por la supervivencia* (premio Primer Filme Científico de Iberoamérica de la Semana de Cine Científico de Ronsa, España). Ha sido profesor de la UNAM, jefe de la Sección de Cine Científico de la Filmoteca de la UNAM (1980-85), jefe del Departamento de Información y Relaciones Públicas (1985-87), subdirector de Cinematografía (1987-89), director general de Actividades Cinematográficas y de la Filmoteca de la UNAM (1989-), así como vicepresidente (1993-99) y presidente de la Federación Interna-cional de Archivos Fílmicos (1999-). Produjo la serie *18 lustros de la vida en México en este siglo (1900-1989)*,

Francisco Trujillo Gurría

Foto: Armando Herrera

Emilio Tuero

ganadora de cuatro Arieles. Ha sido miembro de la Comisión de Premiación de la Academia Mexicana de Artes y Ciencias Cinematográficas y jurado en festivales de cine.

TRUJILLO Y GUERRERO, FELIPE IGNACIO ◆ n. en España y m. en Valladolid, hoy Morelia, Mich. (1652-1721). Sacerdote. Estudió en la Universidad de Salamanca. Fue fiscal del Tribunal del Santo Oficio en Barcelona, inquisidor mayor de Palermo, juez del Tribunal Real, abad de Santa María de Herrana y obispo de Michoacán (1711-21).

TRUJILLO GURRÍA, FRANCISCO ◆ n. en San Juan Bautista, hoy Villahermosa, Tab., y m. en el DF (1898-1946). Se trasladó a la ciudad de México a estudiar, pero en 1913 se incorporó a la revolución constitucionalista. En Tabasco fue secretario general de Gobierno (del 1 de enero de 1931 al 31 de diciembre de 1934) encargado del Poder Ejecutivo local (del 1 al 22 de febrero de 1931, del 17 al 26 de junio de 1931 y del 13 al 15 de agosto de 1931) en ausencia del gobernador Tomás Garrido Canabal, y gobernador constitucional (del 1 de enero de 1939 al 31 de diciembre de 1942). Secretario del Trabajo y Previsión Social (del 1 de marzo de 1943 al 30 de noviembre de 1946) con el presidente Manuel Ávila Camacho.

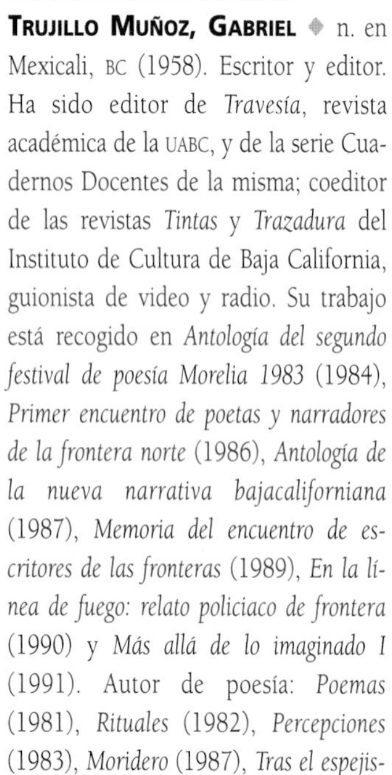

TRUJILLO MUÑOZ, GABRIEL ◆ n. en Mexicali, BC (1958). Escritor y editor. Ha sido editor de *Travesía*, revista académica de la UABC, y de la serie Cuadernos Docentes de la misma; coeditor de las revistas *Tintas* y *Trazadura* del Instituto de Cultura de Baja California, guionista de video y radio. Su trabajo está recogido en *Antología del segundo festival de poesía Morelia 1983* (1984), *Primer encuentro de poetas y narradores de la frontera norte* (1986), *Antología de la nueva narrativa bajacaliforniana* (1987), *Memoria del encuentro de escritores de las fronteras* (1989), *En la línea de fuego: relato policiaco de frontera* (1990) y *Más allá de lo imaginado I* (1991). Autor de poesía: *Poemas* (1981), *Rituales* (1982), *Percepciones* (1983), *Moridero* (1987), *Tras el espejismo* (1989), *Mandrágora* (1989), *Atisbos* (1991), *A plena luz* (1992) y *Permanent Work. Poems 1981-1992* (antología, Estados Unidos, 1993); ensayo: *Tres ensayos sobre el ensayo bajacaliforniano* (1988), *Rubén G. Benavides* (1988), *Alabanzas y vituperios* (1990), *La ciencia ficción. Literatura y conocimiento* (1991) y *Señas y reseñas* (1992); narrativa: *Mexicali. Crónicas de infancia* (1990), *Laberinto (as time goes by)* (1995, Premio Estatal de Novela 1994) y la trilogía *Orescu* (en prensa). Premio Mauricio Richter 1986 en artes. Premio Estatal de Literatura en ensayo (1990) y periodismo cultural (1992).

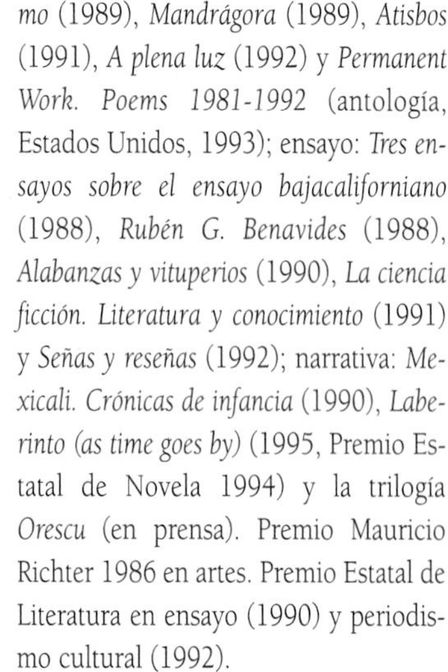

TUBUTAMA ◆ Municipio de Sonora situado al suroeste de Nogales y al este de Caborca. Superficie: 1,351.6 km^2. Habitantes: 1,893, de los cuales 523 forman la población económicamente activa. Entre 1930 y 1934, el municipio desapareció y fue absorbido por el de Altar. En la cabecera hay una misión de estilo plateresco, construida hacia 1791 por los franciscanos.

TUDELA ◆ Códice mexica realizado hacia 1553, conocido generalmente por el apellido de su descubridor, José Tudela de la Orden, quien lo estudió por primera vez en 1940, aunque a veces se identifica por el sitio donde se conserva y donde lo encontró Tudela, el Museo de América de Madrid. El documento, realizado con la técnica nahua, pero sobre papel europeo, es una descripción de costumbres y formas de organización de los aztecas e incluye representaciones de dioses y señores.

TUERO, EMILIO ◆ n. en España y m. en el DF (1912-1971). Actor y cantante. Su apellido materno era Cubillas. Llegó a México en 1923. Estudió música con José Eduardo Pierson y fue empleado de una panadería. Se inició como actor en 1931, en el Teatro Politeama. Más tarde fue cantante de las estaciones de radio XEFO y XEW, así como de varios centros nocturnos. Pedro de Lille lo llamó *El Barítono de Argel*. Actuó en las películas *Tras la reja* (1936), *La india bonita* (1938), *Juan Soldado* (1938), *El rosario*

Iglesia de San Pedro y San Pablo en Tubutama, Sonora

de Amozoc (1938), *En tiempos de don Porfirio* (1939), *Cuando la tierra tembló* (1940), *Al son de la marimba* (1940), *Dos mexicanos en Sevilla* (1941), *Mil estudiantes y una muchacha* (1941), *Noche de recién casados* (1941), *Cuando los hijos se van* (1941), *El ángel negro* (1942), *Yo bailé con don Porfirio* (1942), *El baisano Jalil* (1942), *El que tenga un amor* (1942), *Internado para señoritas* (1943), *No matarás* (1943), *La dama de las camelias* (1943), *Resurrección* (1943), *El

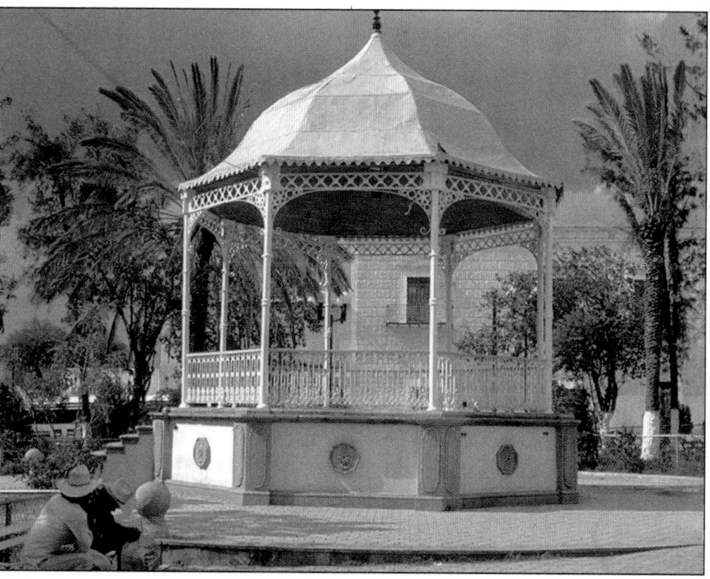
FOTO: FONDO EDITORIAL GRUPO AZABACHE

Quiosco porfiriano en Tula, Tamaulipas

camino de los gatos* (1943), *El recuerdo de aquella noche* (1944), *Club Verde*, *El recuerdo de un vals* (1944), *Las casadas engañan de cuatro a seis* (1945), *Ave de paso* (1945), *Tú eres la luz* (1945), *Vértigo* (1945), *Yo fui una usurpadora* (1945), *Otoño y primavera* (1947), *La sentencia* (1949), *Canas al aire* (1949), *El miedo llegó a Jalisco* (1949), *La dama del alba* (1949), *Quinto patio* (1950), *El dinero no es la vida* (1951), *Historia de un amor* (1955) y *Viva el amor* (1956). Produjo algunas de estas cintas. También fue conductor del programa de televisión *Cita musical*.

TUIRÁN, RODOLFO ◆ n. en Nicaragua (1955). Licenciado en economía por la UASLP, maestro en demografía por El Colegio de México y doctor en sociología por la Universidad de Texas en Austin. Profesor de El Colegio de México y la Facultad Latinoamericana de Ciencias Sociales. Ha sido miembro del Estudio Binacional sobre la Migración México-Estados Unidos (1995-), miembro del grupo de expertos sobre Producción Alimentaria y Crecimiento convocado por la FAO (1996), delegado ante la Comisión de Población y Desarrollo de la ONU (1997-98), presidente del Comité Especial de Población y Desarrollo de la CEPAL (1997-98), presidente de la Comisión de Población y Desarrollo de la ONU (1997-98) y secretario general del Consejo Nacional de Población (1997-). Ha sido becario del Population Council y la Hewlett Foundation (1986-90) y miembro de los consejos editoriales de las revistas *Papeles de Población* y *Universidad Autónoma del Estado de México*. Miembro del Sistema Nacional de Investigadores (1991-). Fue presidente de la Sociedad Mexicana de Demografía.

TULA ◆ Municipio de Tamaulipas situado al suroeste de Ciudad Victoria y oeste de Ciudad Mante, en los límites con San Luis Potosí. Superficie: 2,660.62 km². Habitantes: 28,639, de los cuales 7,496 forman la población económicamente activa. Hablan alguna lengua indígena 14 personas mayores de cinco años. En la cabecera se realiza un tianguis semanal en el que se venden artesanías en cera.

TULA ◆ Río de Hidalgo formado por los de Tepeji, Cuautitlán y del Salto o Desagüe. Nace en la región occidental del estado, al noroeste de la sierra de Tezontlalpan y al oeste de Pachuca. Corre de sur a norte y tuerce al noroeste al llegar a la sierra de Pachuca. Se une al río San Juan, en los límites con el estado de Querétaro, para formar el Moctezuma.

TULA DE ALLENDE ◆ Municipio de Hidalgo situado al oeste de Pachuca y al norte de Tepeji del Río, en los límites con el Estado de México. Superficie: 305.8 km². Habitantes: 82,333, de los cuales 19,905 forman la población económicamente activa. Hablan alguna lengua indígena 258 personas mayores de cinco años (otomí 114). A mediados del siglo II de la época contemporánea, algunos grupos de huastecos se instalaron en el actual territorio municipal y fundaron la ciudad de Chingú. Más tarde fueron sustituidos por los otomíes y desde el siglo VIII por los nonoalcas. Hacia el año 900 de nuestra era, los toltecas (☛), que vivían en el valle de Tulancingo, se trasladaron al oeste y se instalaron en un bosque de tules, donde fundaron un poblado llamado Tullan, "lugar de tules". Poco después, los nonoalcas fueron incorporados a la sociedad tolteca y aportaron mucho del refinamiento y la organización con la que sería conocida la ciudad, que rá-

FOTO: MICHAEL CALDERWOOD

Río de Tula, Hidalgo

Rodolfo Tuirán

pidamente se convirtió en un importante centro urbano, al grado que, con los años, los pueblos nahuas del valle de Anáhuac hicieron de Tullan el nombre genérico de las ciudades. Las construcciones más importantes eran el Coatepantli o Muro de Culebras, el Tzompantli o Muro de las Calaveras, dos juegos de pelota, el templo de Tlahuizcalpantecuhtli, "Señor de la Casa del Alba"; una pirámide de 1,424 m² de base y 10 metros de altura, y el templo de las Mil Columnas, como se conoce una construcción de la que sólo ha sobrevivido una serie de pequeños pilares. Durante más de dos siglos, la ciudad fue el principal centro comercial, minero y manufacturero de la altiplanicie mexicana, pero a mediados del siglo XII comenzaron a manifestarse conflictos entre los líderes político-militares, casi todos toltecas, y los grandes comerciantes, nonoalcas en su mayoría, hasta que en 1168, luego de varios enfrentamientos armados entre nonoalcas y toltecas, fuerzas chichimecas y otomíes destruyeron e incendiaron la ciudad. Desde entonces, la región fue ocupada por los otomíes, pero a mediados del siglo XIII, éstos fueron conquistados por los futuros acolhuas de Texcoco. Desde el siglo XIV, la región fue tributaria de la Triple Alianza del valle de Anáhuac. El territorio fue conquistado por los españoles en los años treinta del siglo XVI. En 1539, los franciscanos se instalaron en Tula, pero sólo 20 años después, en 1550, construyeron una iglesia y un convento, realizados probablemente por Antonio de San Juan. En Tula, en septiembre de 1811, se levantó en armas Julián Villagrán (☛), uno de los principales insurgentes hidalguenses. Entre 1852 y 1854, primero en favor de Antonio López de Santa Anna y después en su contra, pero en realidad siempre para evitar el cobro de impuestos excesivos, los otomíes de los alrededores de Tula se mantuvieron sublevados, y sólo se rindieron al triunfo de la revolución de Ayutla. A partir de entonces se enfrentaron a los repetidos intentos liberales de acabar con la propiedad comunal de la tierra. La cabecera es sede de la diócesis de Tula desde su erección, en 1961. En 1976 entró en funcionamiento la refinería Miguel Hidalgo.

TULANCINGO DE BRAVO ◆ Municipio de Hidalgo situado al este de Pachuca y norte de Apan, cerca de Puebla. Superficie: 290.4 km². Habitantes: 110,140, de los cuales 27,865 forman la población económicamente activa. Hablan alguna lengua indígena 4,583 personas mayores de cinco años (otomí 3,698 y náhuatl 771). Es probable que los primeros habitantes del actual territorio municipal se hayan instalado en el valle de Tulancingo hacia el año 5000 a.n.e. 6,000 años después, hacia el 977 de nuestra era, los toltecas (☛), que comandados por Topiltzin habían abandonado Culhuacán poco tiempo antes, se establecieron en el va-lle, en la margen derecha del río Tulan-cingo. Cuatro años después aproximadamente, los toltecas se retiraron hacia el oeste y poco después fundaron Tula (☛). Hasta el siglo XII, sin embargo, la zona estuvo habitada por toltecas, pero luego de la destrucción de Tula, Tulancingo cayó en poder de los otomíes y más tarde, en el siglo XIII, de los acolhuas, que dominaron la región hasta el siglo XVI. Poco después de la conquista de las ciudades del valle de Anáhuac, los españoles se instalaron en Tulancingo y dos de ellos, Francisco de Terrazas y Francisco de Ávila, se repartieron el territorio en encomiendas. Hacia 1527, los franciscanos iniciaron la evangelización y un año después comenzaron a construir un convento. Desde los años cuarenta del mismo siglo, la población fue tomada como lugar de descanso de los europeos, por lo que fue conocida como Retiro de los Conquistadores. En 1657, los franciscanos construyeron el templo de San Francisco, la actual catedral, que en 1764 pasó a depender del obispado de México y fue reconstruida por José Damián Ortiz en 1788. En abril de 1821, la guarnición española abandonó la ciudad, ante el avance del ejército trigarante, comandado por Guadalupe Victoria

FOTO: TELÉFONOS DE MÉXICO

Antena de telecomunicaciones en Tulancingo, Hidalgo

y Nicolás Bravo, que en ese mes entraron en la ciudad y publicaron el primer periódico de la localidad, *El Mosquito de Tulancingo*. A principios de enero de 1828, Bravo, que entonces era vicepresidente de la República, volvió a la ciudad, para levantarse en armas en contra de su ex compañero, el presidente Victoria. Una semana antes, el masón escocés Manuel Montaño había proclamado un plan en Otumba, cuyas principales demandas eran la disolución de las sociedades masónicas y la expulsión del embajador estadounidense Joel R. Poinsett, aunque, en realidad, pretendía imponer a los escoceses en el gobierno y acabar con la República Federal. Días después, Bravo salió de la ciudad de México, redactó un manifiesto en el que acusaba a los yorkinos de promover la anarquía en México y en Tulancingo se reunió con Montaño y 600 soldados, con la idea de esperar más sublevaciones en otras partes del país. Éstas, sin embargo, no se produjeron. El 6 de enero, las fuerzas de Vicente Guerrero llegaron a las afueras de Tulancingo, revisaron la zona y se establecieron en la hacienda de San Francisco. Al día siguiente, vencido un plazo de ocho horas que Guerrero había dado a Bravo para que se rindiera, atacó la ciudad y derrotó a los escoceses. Desde 1863, año de la erección de la diócesis, la cabecera es también sede del obispado de Tulancingo.

TULANE ◆ Códice realizado hacia 1550 con técnica prehispánica, que narra la historia de los mixtecos entre 1438 y 1512. Al reverso tiene notas en mixteco escritas con caracteres latinos. El documento, que también se conoce como Códice Muro, perteneció originalmente a Samuel Daza, quien lo legó a Félix Muro; éste lo cedió a una estadounidense, quien, a su vez, lo donó a la Universidad de Tulane en 1932 .

TULCINGO ◆ Municipio de Puebla situado al suroeste de Acatlán y sur de Izúcar de Matamoros, en los límites con Guerrero y Oaxaca. Superficie: 223.25 km^2. Habitantes: 8.707, de los cuales 1,349 forman la población económicamente activa. Hablan alguna lengua indígena 22 personas mayores de cinco años. La cabecera es Tulcingo del Valle.

TULE, EL ◆ Municipio de Chihuahua situado al oeste de Hidalgo del Parral y este de Batopilas. Superficie: 409.42 km^2. Habitantes: 2,566, de los cuales 421 forman la población económicamente activa. Hablan tarahumara 68 personas. Fue dependencia de Huejotitlán hasta 1859, cuando se erigió el municipio, que durante mucho tiempo se llamó San Antonio del Tule. La cabecera es El Tule.

TULIJÁ ◆ Río de Chiapas y Tabasco. Nace en el norte de Tabasco, al noreste de Yajalón, de la confluencia de los ríos Encanto y Bascán; corre de sureste a noroeste, recibe al Chacamax y, en territorio tabasqueño, al sureste de Villahermosa, se une al Macuspana para formar el Tepetitlán.

TULPETLAC ◆ Población del municipio mexiquense de Ecatepec (☛), que forma parte del área metropolitana del valle de México.

TULTEPEC ◆ Municipio del Estado de México situado al sureste de Tepotzotlán y al noroeste de Texcoco. Superficie: 22.49 km^2. Habitantes: 75,996, de los cuales 13,436 forman la población económicamente activa. Hablan alguna lengua indígena 266 personas mayores de cinco años (náhuatl 98 y otomí 92). Dentro de la jurisdicción se encuentra la zona arqueológica de Xahuento, que no ha sido explorada. En la cabecera hay un acueducto construido en el siglo XVIII y un templo católico, el santuario de Nuestra Señora de Loreto, edificado en el siglo XVI.

TULTITLÁN ◆ Municipio del Estado de México situado al noreste de Naucalpan y sureste de Tepotzotlán, en los límites con el Distrito Federal. Superficie: 55.99 km^2. Habitantes: 361,434, de los cuales 74,371 forman la población económicamente activa. Hablan alguna lengua indígena 1,446 personas mayores de cinco años (náhuatl 370 y otomí 347). Antiguamente se llamó San Antonio Tultitlán. En la jurisdicción se hallan la zona arqueológica de Tultitlán y el lago de Guadalupe, donde se practican deportes acuáticos. La cabecera, Tultitlán de Mariano Escobedo, fue uno de los pueblos del señorío de Cuauhtitlán. Después de la conquista perteneció a la encomienda de Juan Jaramillo, esposo de la Malinche; en 1569 se erigió en esta población un convento franciscano, construido por Bernardino de la Fuente. También en el siglo XVI se levantaron las iglesias de San Antonio de Padua y Santa María Cuautepec.

TULUM ◆ Nombre con el que se conocen las ruinas de la ciudad maya de Zana, situada en el municipio quintanarroense de Cozumel, en la costa del mar Caribe. Construido hacia el siglo XII, el emplazamiento maya fue una fortaleza destinada a proteger el comercio marítimo. Es un rectángulo de 170 por 400 metros, limitado por tres lados por una muralla de 6 metros de ancho y entre 3 y 6 de alto, mientras que el cuarto se encuentra sobre la costa. Dentro de los muros se encuentran El Castillo y los templos de los Frescos, del Dios Descendente y de la Serie Inicial.

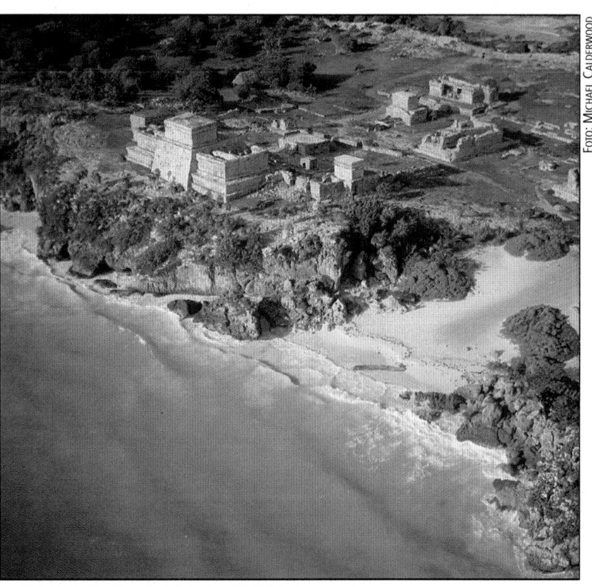

FOTO: MICHAEL CALDERWOOD

Ruinas de Tulum, Quintana Roo

TUMBALÁ ◆ Municipio de Chiapas situado al suroeste de Palenque y al noreste de San Cristóbal de Las Casas. Superficie: 705.5 km^2. Habitantes: 25,011, de los cuales 5,560 forman la población económicamente activa. Hablan alguna lengua indígena 17,970 personas (chol 17,225). En la jurisdicción se encuentra la Cascada de Agua Azul. El 2 de febrero es la fiesta de la Candelaria, la más importante de la cabecera.

TUMBISCATÍO DE RUIZ ♦ Municipio de Michoacán situado al sur de Apatzingán y al noroeste de Arteaga. Superficie: 1,626 km². Habitantes: 10,128, de los cuales 1,646 forman la población económicamente activa. Hablan alguna lengua indígena nueve personas mayores de cinco años.

TUNAL, DEL ♦ Río de Durango que nace de la confluencia de varios arroyos, en la vertiente norte de la sierra de Durango. Corre de sur a norte, recibe al río Chico, entra al valle de Durango y tuerce al este. Más adelante recibe las aguas del arroyo Vaca y de los ríos de la Sauceda y Santiago Bayacora; cruza la región suroccidental de Malpaís de la Breña y se une al río Poanas para formar el Mezquital.

TUNAS, DE LAS ♦ Sierra de Chihuahua que es una de las estribaciones del este de la sierra Madre Occidental. Se extiende de norte a sur, desde el extremo meridional de los médanos de Samalayuca hasta la vertiente noroccidental de la sierra de Choreachic, al noroeste de la ciudad de Chihuahua; la sierra se extiende paralelamente al curso del río Santa Clara y al este de la sierra del Arco, en el oeste del estado.

TÚNEZ, REPÚBLICA DE ♦ Nación de África situada en el norte del continente, en la costa del mar Mediterráneo. Limita al sureste con Libia y al oeste con Argelia. Superficie: 164,150 km². Habitantes: 9,335,000 (1998). La capital es Túnez (674,100 habitantes en 1994). El idioma oficial es el árabe y también se hablan francés y bereber. *Historia*: en el año 814 a.n.e., los fenicios fundaron la ciudad de Cartago, en el actual territorio tunecino, que se convirtió en un importante centro político y económico, rival de Roma. Entre el 149 y el 146 a.n.e., en la última guerra Púnica, el romano Publio Cornelio Emiliano Escipión, *El Africano II*, conquistó Cartago, la bautizó África y se apoderó de los

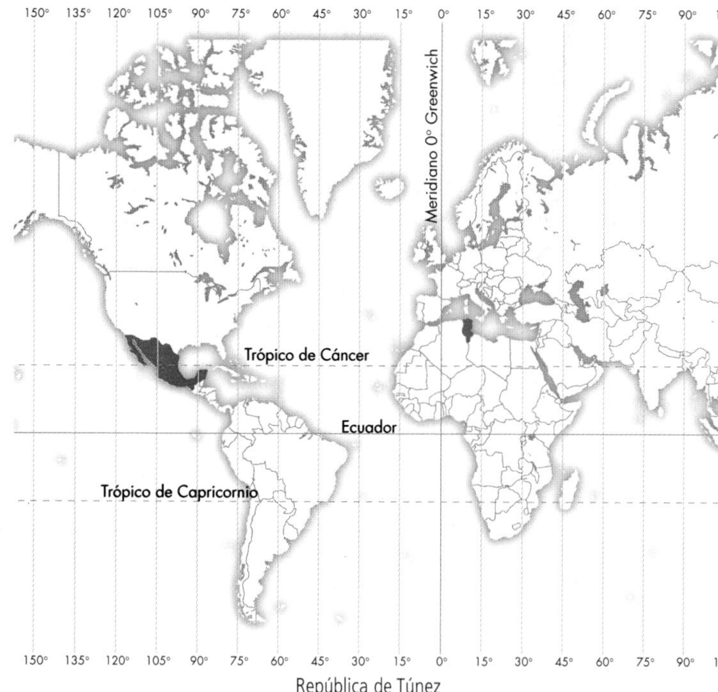

República de Túnez

dominios cartagineses del continente que, a partir de entonces, sería llamado como la ciudad. En el siglo III de nuestra era, África-Cartago fue un baluarte de los cristianos. En 439 la ciudad fue conquistada por los vándalos, grupo germánico que, capitaneado por Genserico, expulsó a los romanos del norte africano. En 533 y 534, las fuerzas bizantinas de Belisario desalojaron a los vándalos y se apoderaron de la región costera, pero en 647 fueron desalojados por los árabes, quienes fundaron Kairuán en 670 y establecieron el reino de Ifriquiya Islámica, nación cuya superficie corresponde aproximadamente a la de la actual República de Túnez. En el 698, los árabes tomaron Cartago y fundaron la ciudad de Túnez. Entre 1148 y 1160 el país fue ocupado por los normandos. En el siglo XIII, tras la conquista de los almohades, Túnez se constituyó en reino independiente, bajo la soberanía de los hafsidas. En 1574, los otomanos convirtieron a Túnez en provincia de su imperio. Tres siglos más tarde, en 1881, fuerzas francesas invadieron y conquistaron el país y dos años después, luego de un frustrado levantamiento independentista, Francia estableció un protectorado sobre la región. En 1920 se creó el Partido Destour; en 1934, Habib, Bourguiba fundó el Partido Neo-Destour, con carácter nacionalista, e inició la lucha por la independencia, que fue reconocida por Francia en 1956. La monarquía fue conservada y Bourguiba, electo primer ministro, promulgó una constitución y consiguió que Túnez fuera aceptado en la ONU. El 25 de julio de 1957 el Parlamento suprimió la monarquía y estableció la República, con Bourguiba como presidente. En 1963, Túnez se incorporó a la Organización de Unidad Africana. Al año siguiente, el Partido Neo-Destour se convirtió en el Partido Socialista Desturiano y se establecieron relaciones diplomáticas entre Túnez y México. En 1975, Bourguiba se autonombró presidente vitalicio. Tres años después, la Unión General de Trabajadores Tunecinos organizó una huelga nacional contra él, pero el movimiento fue reprimido por el ejército. En 1979, la Liga Árabe estableció su sede en la ciudad de Túnez. En 1995, Túnez firmó con la Unión Europea un tratado de asociación, según el cual en 12 años el país pasaría a formar parte de la Unión Económica Europea. Su presidente es Zine al-Abidine (1994-).

TUNKÁS ◆ Municipio de Yucatán situado al noroeste de Chichén Itzá y sureste de Motul. Superficie: 514.79 km². Habitantes: 3,694, de los cuales 934 forman la población económicamente activa. Hablan alguna lengua indígena 1,986 personas mayores de cinco años (maya). Indígenas monolingües: 76.

TUN TUN ◆ n. en Tampico, Tams., y m. en el DF (1932-1993). Actor. Nombre profesional de José René Ruiz. De baja estatura y grandes aptitudes para la comedia y el baile; debutó en la película *El rey del barrio* (1949) al lado de Germán Valdés *Tin Tan* (☛), con quien alternó en numerosas ocasiones. Participó en *La marca del zorrillo* (1950), *Los olvidados* (1950), *El revoltoso* (1951), *¡Mátenme porque me muero!* (1951), *El bello durmiente* (1952), *Miradas que matan* (1953), *El violetero* (1960), *El monasterio de los buitres* (1972), *A paso de cojo* (1978), *El día de los albañiles* (1983), *Bajo el volcán* (1983) y *La guerrera vengadora* (1987), entre otras. También actuó en obras de teatro, programas de televisión y espectáculos para centro nocturno.

Foto: Colección Imcine

René Ruiz *Tun Tun*, en *El violetero*

TURATI ÁLVAREZ, EDUARDO ◆ n. en la ciudad de México (1944). Médico cirujano oftalmólogo graduado en la UNAM (1967). Profesor de la Escuela Nacional Preparatoria (1964-70) y de la Escuela Nacional de Estudios Profesionales Iztacala de la UNAM (1978-81), de la Universidad La Salle (1979-80) y de la Universidad Autónoma de Chihuahua (1981-85). Militante del Partido Acción Nacional. Ha sido presidente de la Unión Nacional de Padres de Familia (1978-82) y diputado federal (1985-88).

TURBIO ◆ Río de Guanajuato que nace en la vertiente suroccidental de la sierra de Comanjá, al suroeste de León. Corre de norte a sur y tuerce al este, sureste y sur para rodear la sierra de Pénjamo; recibe los ríos de Gómez y de Pénjamo y desemboca en el Lerma al sureste del valle de la Piedad, en los límites con el estado de Michoacán.

TURICATO ◆ Municipio de Michoacán situado al sur de Morelia y sureste de Apatzingán. Superficie: 1,175.32 km². Habitantes: 36,112, de los cuales 5,879 forman la población económicamente activa. Hablan alguna lengua indígena 332 personas mayores de cinco años (náhuatl 224, otomí 37 y totonaco 24). En enero de 1814, en los llanos de Puruarán, las fuerzas realistas de Ciriaco de Llano derrotaron a la columna insurgente de Mariano Matamoros, a quien aprehendieron.

TURKMENISTÁN, REPÚBLICA DE ◆ Nación asiática que limita al norte con Kazajistán, al este con Uzbekistán, al sur con Afganistán y al suroeste con Irán. Tiene costas en el mar Caspio. Superficie: 488,100 km². Habitantes: 4,309,000 (1998). Su capital es Ashjabad (548,500 habitantes en 1996). Otras ciudades importantes son Chardzhou (166,400 habitantes en 1991) y Dashhowuz (117,000). El turcomano es el idioma oficial, y también se hablan uzbeco y ruso. La moneda es el manat. *Historia*: los primeros turcomanos llegaron a la región hacia el siglo X, pero hasta comienzos del siglo XX no se había dado un Estado nacional, ya que las diversas regiones del actual Turkmenistán estuvieron dominadas por diferentes tribus. En 1717, la primera expedición colonizadora rusa, la del príncipe Aleksandr Biekóvitc-Tcherkáskki, fue repelida por la tribu teke. En 1869, un regimiento ruso fundó, en la costa del Caspio, el puerto de Krasnovodsk, y fomentó la lucha de las tribus yomud y goklan contra los tekes. A partir de entonces comenzó una paulatina expansión rusa en Turkmenistán, que culminó en 1881 con la batalla de Geok-Tepe, en la que Mikhail Skobeliov derrotó definitivamente a los tekes. Se creó entonces la provincia Transcaspiana del imperio ruso, misma que en 1899 fue convertida en gobernación general. En 1916 comenzó una rebelión contra la dominación rusa y se desencadenó una guerra civil, en la que intervino Gran Bretaña con apoyo a los independentistas contra el avance bolchevique. En 1919, el Ejército Rojo dominó la región y expulsó a los británicos. En 1924 se creó la República Soviética de Turkmenistán que se integró a la Unión de Repúblicas Socialistas Soviéticas (☛). En 1991 se independizó de la URSS y pasó a formar parte de la CEI. México estableció relaciones diplomáticas con Turkmenistán en 1992.

República de Turkmenistán

TURNER, ETHEL DUFFY ◆ n. en EUA y m. en Cuernavaca, Mor. (1885-1969). Periodista. Esposa de John Kenneth Turner. Militó en el Partido Liberal Me-xicano. Dirigió la página en inglés del periodico magonista *Regeneración*. Autora de *Ricardo Flores Magón y el Partido Liberal Mexicano* (1960). El gobierno mexicano le asignó una pensión.

TURNER, JOHN KENNETH ◆ n. y m. en EUA (1878-1948). Periodista. Estudió en la Universidad de California en Berkeley. A principios del siglo XX ingresó en la redacción del *Republican* de Fresno. En 1906 se trasladó a San Francisco y más tarde a Portland, su lugar de ori-

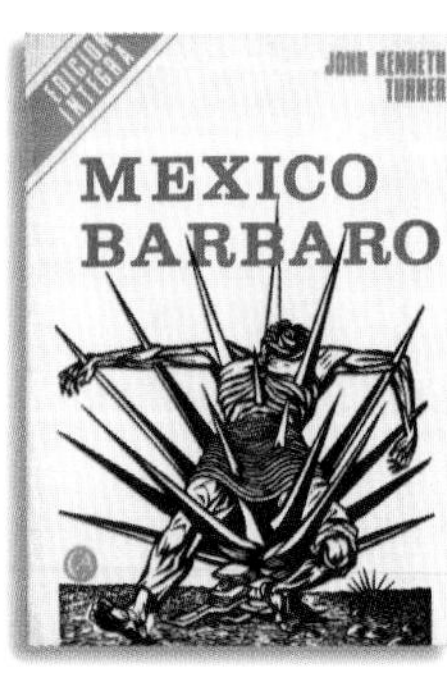

México Bárbaro, de John Kenneth Turner

gen, donde dirigió la sección deportiva del *Journal*. Mas tarde se trasladó a Los Ángeles y cuando trabajaba para el *Record* conoció a Librado Rivera, Ricardo Flores Magón y Antonio I. Villarreal, que entonces estaban presos; poco después se incorporó al Partido Liberal Mexicano. Vino a México por primera vez en 1908, como corresponsal del *American Magazine* de Nueva York y, acompañado por Lázaro Gutiérrez de Lara, recorrió Valle Nacional, el valle del Yaqui y Yucatán. Volvió un año después, enviado por el *Record*, y colaboró en la sección deportiva del *Mexican Herald*, al mismo tiempo que escribía para *Regeneración*. En 1911 entrevistó al presidente Francisco I. Madero y dos años después, durante la Decena Trágica (febrero de 1913), denunció la injerencia del embajador estadounidense Henry Lane Wilson, por lo que debió salir del país a la muerte de Madero. Regresó a México en 1914 y escribió sobre la invasión estadounidense de Veracruz. En 1920 entrevistó a Genovevo de la O, Gildardo Magaña, Otilio Montaño y otros miembros del desaparecido Ejército Libertador del Sur. También colaboró en *Scripps* y *McRae* y en el periódico *The Nation*. Algunos de sus reportajes sobre México fueron recopilados en *México bárbaro* (1910). Autor de *Shall it be Again?* (1914) y *Hands off Mexico* (1920).

TURNER, JORGE ◆ n. en Panamá (1922). Su nombre completo es Jorge Enrique Turner Morales. Licenciado en derecho (1956) y maestro (1982) y doctor (1984) en estudios latinoamericanos por la UNAM, de la que ha sido profesor e investigador. En Panamá fue dirigente estudiantil, organizador sindical (actividades que le valieron cárcel y destierro), fundador de la Escuela de Periodismo de la Universidad de Panamá, director del diario *El País*, columnista del periódico *El Día*, asesor laboral y en leyes de la Presidencia, diputado nacional y embajador en México, cargo que dejó en 1989 por no reconocer al gobierno impuesto por los invasores estadounidenses. En México ha sido coordinador de la sección internacional de *El Nacional* y columnista de *El Universal*, colaborador de *Siempre!*, *La Jornada* y otras publicaciones. Autor de ensayo: *El deporte en la historia y en el derecho penal*, *Panamá: espejismo y realidad*, *Nuestra lucha actual contra el imperialismo* y *Perspectivas del movimiento obrero*; y de narrativa: *Viento de agua* (1977). Presidente del Sindicato de Periodistas de Panamá (1959-60), miembro del secretariado de la Federación Latinoamericana de Periodistas. Medalla Gabino Barreda de la UNAM (1982) y Premio Nacional de Periodismo en Panamá (1988).

TUROK WALLACE, MARTA ◆ n. en el DF (1952). Antropóloga titulada en 1974. Estudió en las universidades Tufts, Harvard, Cambridge y Massachusetts. Realizó estudios de maestría en antropología social en la UNAM (1977). Ha sido profesora de la ENAH, la UIA y la Universidad Autónoma de Chiapas (1979). Fue becaria del Harvard Chiapas Proyect (1972-73), la UNAM (1975-77) y el INI (1977-78). Ha sido coordinadora de la Galería Universitaria Aristos (1975-77), jefa del Departamento de Investigaciones Antropológicas del INI en Chiapas (1978-80), jefa de la zona de Chiapas del Área de Organización para la Comercialización (1980-82) coordinadora estatal en Chiapas de la Subgerencia de la Región Sureste (1981-82) y coordinadora Corporativa de Capacitación de la subgerencia Corporativa de Operaciones Rurales en el Programa Conasupo-Coplamar (1982); coordinadora del Programa de Protección y Estímulo a los Valores Tradicionales en las Artesanías y Culturas Populares (1983-85) y, en la Dirección General de Culturas Populares de la Secretaría de Educación, jefa del Departamento de Capacitación (1983-84), subdirectora de Vinculación (1984-85) subdirectora técnica (1985-86) y directora general (1986-88). Ha sido presidenta de la Asociación Mexicana de Arte Popular, A.C. Ha colaborado en *La Jornada*. Coautora de *Antropología e historia de los mixe-zoques y mayas: Homenaje a Frans Blom* (1983) y *Bordando sobre la escritura y la cocina* (1984). Autora de *El proceso de producción de textiles de lana de Chamula* (1979) y *Cómo acercarse a la artesanía* (1988).

TURÓN, CARLOS EDUARDO ◆ n. en Morelia y m. en Uruapan, Mich. (1935-1992). Escritor. Ingeniero químico titulado en la UNAM. Director fundador de la revista *Confluencias*. Fue colaborador de las revistas *Vuelta*, *Siempre!* y *La Vida Literaria*, y de los diarios *Excélsior*, *El Heraldo de México* y *El Sol de México*. Tradujo la novela *Mi madre* (1980) de Georges Bataille. Autor de ensayo: *Frente a Delfos* (1970), *La iconoclastia de José Revueltas* (1974), *Algunas claves de Gerard de Nerval* (1976) y *José Revueltas, el hijo del hombre* (1984); novela: *Sobre esta piedra* (1981); y poesía: *En los lindes del día* (1965), *Tríptico de verano* (1970), *Exaltación de la extranjera* (1974), *Compasión de Eleusis* (1977), *Crucifixiones* (1978), *La libertad tiene otro nombre* (1979, premio Xavier Villaurrutia), *La clepsidra* (1985) y *Quehaceres del amante* (1989).

TURQUÍA, REPÚBLICA DE ◆ Nación euroasiática que limita con Grecia y Bulgaria al noroeste, con Georgia al noreste, con Armenia e Irán al este, y con Irak y Siria al sur. Tiene costas en los mares Negro, al norte, y Mediterráneo, al sur y suroeste. Superficie: 779,452 km^2. Habitantes: 64,479,000 (1998). La capital es Ankara o Angora (con 2,837,937 habitantes en 1995). Otras ciudades de importancia son: Estambul (antigua Constantinopla, con 7,774,169 habitantes) e Izmir o Esmirna (2,017,669). La moneda es la lira turca. El idioma oficial es el turco y se hablan también kurdo, árabe, griego, armenio y ladino o judezhmo. *Historia*: 2,000 a.n.e. años antes de nuestra era los hititas establecieron su imperio en el Asia Menor. Después, la región fue sede, sucesivamente, de los imperios de Persia, Grecia y Roma. En el año 330 de la época contemporánea, Constantino fundó la ciudad de Constantinopla, que fue capital del Imperio Romano de

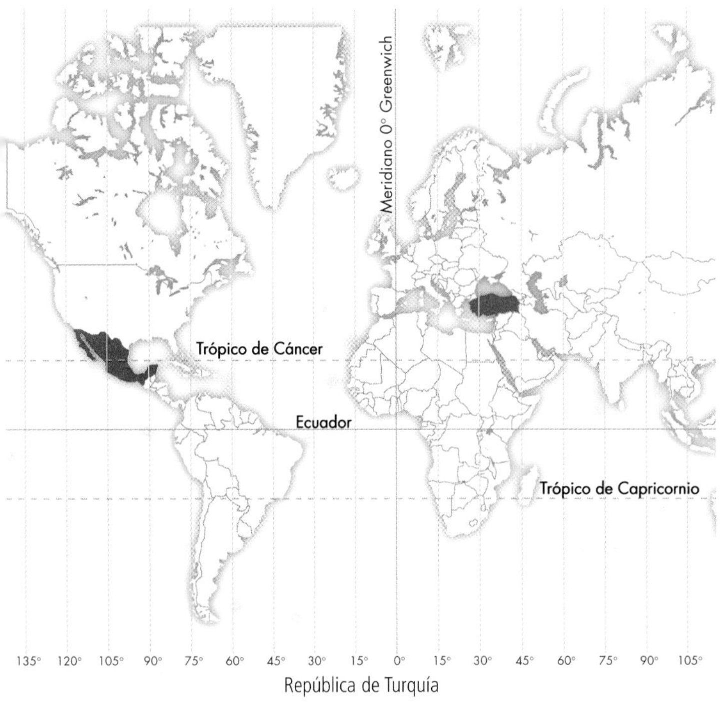

República de Turquía

Oriente, primero, y más tarde del Imperio Bizantino. En el siglo XI los turcos, hostigados por los mongoles, emigraron del Turkestán y se instalaron en Asia Menor. En 1071 los seléucidas derrotaron a los bizantinos y fundaron un sultanato en la península de Anatolia. En el siglo XIV, los seléucidas fueron derrotados y Osmán fundó la dinastía otomana, del imperio turco-otomano. En 1389 los otomanos conquistaron Serbia y Bulgaria, y entre 1403 y 1451, durante los imperios de Mahomet I y Murad II, el imperio otomano se consolidó. En 1453, las fuerzas otomanas de Mahomet II tomaron Constantinopla, destruyeron el Imperio Bizantino y bautizaron Estambul a la ciudad. Entre 1520 y 1566, el imperio turco alcanzó su auge, durante el sultanato de Solimán I, *el Magnífico*, quien dominó Rumania, Hungría, Yugoslavia, Siria, Irak, Israel, parte de la península Arábiga y una zona del norte de África, que iba desde Egipto hasta Argelia. En 1653, los otomanos fueron derrotados cerca de Viena y el poderío del imperio comenzó a decaer. En 1864, el diplomático mexicano Pablo Martínez del Río, enviado por Maximiliano de Habsburgo, pretendió infructuosamente comprar a Turquía los Santos Lugares. En 1878, al término de la guerra contra Rusia, Turquía perdió algunas posesiones en los Balcanes. En 1908, el sultán Abdul Hamid II promulgó una Constitución y estableció el primer parlamento. Al año siguiente, un levantamiento colocó en el trono a Mohamed V. En 1912, Bulgaria, Grecia y Serbia, derrotaron a los ejércitos turcos y el imperio perdió sus posesiones en Macedonia y el oeste de Tracia. Durante la primera guerra mundial, Turquía combatió contra Francia, Inglaterra y Rusia, pero en 1918 fue derrotada, lo que desencadenó un movimiento popular dirigido por Mustafá Kemal (Atatürk), que acabó con la

Troya se encontraba en la actual Turquía

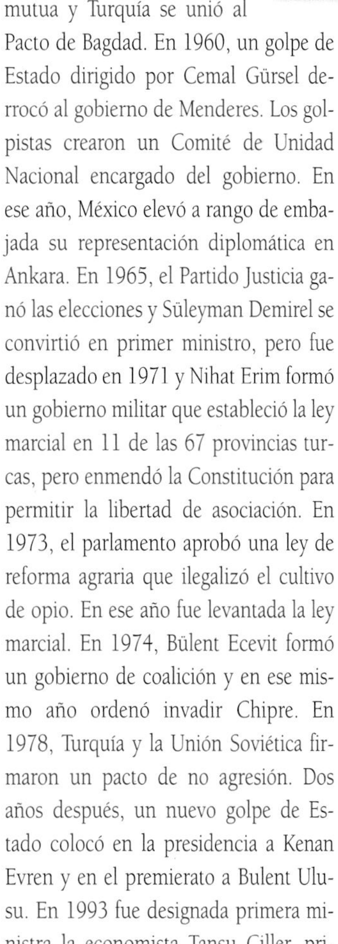

monarquía. Al fin del conflicto bélico, el Tratado de Sevres condenaba a Turquía a la desintegración, hecho que se evitó en 1923, cuando Atatürk expulsó a las fuerzas griegas de ocupación y proclamó la república secular. En 1927, los gobiernos de México y Turquía suscribieron un Tratado de Amistad y cinco años después se establecieron las relaciones diplomáticas. En 1950, Adnan Menderes asumió la jefatura del gobierno como primer ministro y dos años después, el país se adhirió a la Organización del Tratado del Atlántico Norte, hecho que permitió al gobierno de Estados Unidos instalar numerosas bases militares en el norte, cerca de la frontera con la Unión Soviética. En 1955 estallaron varios motines antigriegos en Estambul, a raíz del conflicto en Chipre (☛). En ese mismo año Turquía e Irak firmaron un acuerdo de defensa mutua y Turquía se unió al Pacto de Bagdad. En 1960, un golpe de Estado dirigido por Cemal Gürsel derrocó al gobierno de Menderes. Los golpistas crearon un Comité de Unidad Nacional encargado del gobierno. En ese año, México elevó a rango de embajada su representación diplomática en Ankara. En 1965, el Partido Justicia ganó las elecciones y Süleyman Demirel se convirtió en primer ministro, pero fue desplazado en 1971 y Nihat Erim formó un gobierno militar que estableció la ley marcial en 11 de las 67 provincias turcas, pero enmendó la Constitución para permitir la libertad de asociación. En 1973, el parlamento aprobó una ley de reforma agraria que ilegalizó el cultivo de opio. En ese año fue levantada la ley marcial. En 1974, Bülent Ecevit formó un gobierno de coalición y en ese mismo año ordenó invadir Chipre. En 1978, Turquía y la Unión Soviética firmaron un pacto de no agresión. Dos años después, un nuevo golpe de Estado colocó en la presidencia a Kenan Evren y en el premierato a Bulent Ulusu. En 1993 fue designada primera ministra la economista Tansu Ciller, pri-

Timbre de Turquía

mera mujer que accede a ese puesto en Turquía. En 1996, una corte turca condenó a 20 meses de cárcel a Yaser Kemal, el escritor turco más renombrado, por criticar las restricciones oficiales a la libertad de expresión. Ese mismo año y el siguiente se recrudecieron los combates con los separatistas kurdos, quienes estaban levantados en armas desde 1985. Se calcula que desde entonces han muerto más de 22,000 personas por ese conflicto étnico. En 1999, Abdula Ocaram, el líder de los separatistas kurdos, fue capturado en Italia, y Turquía solicitó su extradición para ser juzgado y aplicarle la pena de muerte. Desde 1993, Suleyman Demirel es presidente de Turquía, y Mesut Yilmaz, primer ministro desde 1998.

Foto: Rogelio Cuéllar

Isabel Turrent

Eduardo Turrent Rozas

TURRENT, ISABEL ◆ n. en el DF (1947). Licenciada en historia del arte por la UIA (1969) y en relaciones internacionales por El Colegio de México (1975), donde estudió la maestría en ciencia política (1977). Maestra en política por la Universidad de Oxford (1983). Ha impartido clases en la UIA, el ITAM, el Centro de Arte Mexicano, la Universidad de las Américas y El Colegio de México, en cuyo Centro de Estudios Internacionales fue investigadora (1980-91). Ha colaborado en *Vuelta*, *Época*, *Foro Internacional*, *Mujeres de Contenido* y *Letras Libres*; ha sido editorialista de los diarios *Reforma* y *El Norte* y comentarista de noticias internacionales en el noticiero radial *Monitor*. Ha sido miembro de la Comisión Consultiva de Ingreso al Servicio Exterior Mexicano (1982-85). Autora de *La Unión Soviética en América Latina. El caso de la Unidad Popular Chilena (1970-1973)* (1984), *El deshielo del este* (1991) y *Las voces del cambio* (1992).

TURRENT, JAIME ◆ n. en San Andrés Tuxtla, Ver. (1946). Escritor. Su apellido materno es Fernández. Estudió derecho en la Universidad Veracruzana y letras en la UNAM. Ha sido jefe del Departamento Editorial de la Universidad Autónoma Metropolitana (1987). Colaborador de *La Palabra y el Hombre*, *Revista de la Universidad*, *Diario de Xalapa*, *La Cultura en México*, suplemento de la revista *Siempre!* y *El Gallo Ilustrado*, suplemento del cotidiano *El Día*. Autor de las novelas *Los encantados* (1982) y *La eterna noche del desconsuelo* (1987).

TURRENT, LOURDES ◆ n. en el DF (1950). Hizo estudios de sociología en la UNAM y de música en el Conservatorio Nacional de Música y en la Escuela Vida y Movimiento, donde cursó la licenciatura en fagot. Ha sido colaboradora de Radio UNAM, del Departamento de Música y de la Orquesta Filarmónica de la misma institución y subdirectora del Centro de Arte Mexicano. Autora de *La conquista musical de México* (1995).

TURRENT, MIGUEL ÁNGEL ◆ n. en San Andrés Tuxtla, Ver. (1938). Nombre profesional del actor, dramaturgo y poeta Ángel Rodríguez Turrent. Inició su carrera como actor en 1955. Tres años después se trasladó a la ciudad de México. Estudió en el Instituto Cinematográfico y Teatral y en Instituto de Arte Dramático Andrés Soler. Ha trabajado en medio centenar de espectáculos. Autor del *collage* escénico *Cantares y poemas* (1977); de los volúmenes de cuento: *Quimeras* (1983) y *¡Hola, humanos!* (1987); de poesía: *Florilegio poético* (1977), *Reflexiones* (1980), *Erótica y romántica* (1982), *Sentires* (1985) y *Algo erótico* (1986); y teatro: *El autorretrato* (1978), *El tridente*, *Un día de locuras*, *Como en el principio*, *La gloria de Dios* (1985), *Claveles blancos*, *El empleado* (1987), *Shila o el día que se acabó* y *Los días tristes*.

TURRENT ROZAS, EDUARDO ◆ n. en Galería, municipio de Catemaco, Ver., y m. en el DF (1892-1974). Escritor. Perteneció al grupo Noviembre. Autor de *Añoranzas* (1948), *Ayer* (1951), *Veracruz de mis recuerdos* (1953), *Estampas de mi tierra* (1954), *Remolino* (1958), *Magdalena* (1960), *Los Tuxtlas* (1963), *Mente en vuelo* (1965) y *Catemaco, retablos y recuerdos* (1967).

TURRENT ROZAS, LORENZO ◆ n. en Catemaco, Ver., y m. en el DF (1903-1941). Escritor. Licenciado en derecho por la Universidad Veracruzana (1926). Fue funcionario judicial, director de la revista jalapeña *Noviembre*, fundador y director de la editorial Integrales. Perteneció a la Liga de Escritores y Artistas Revolucionarios (1935-38). Miembro de Comité de Redacción y colaborador de la revista *Ruta* (1938-39), magistrado del Tribunal Superior de Justicia de Veracruz y director de una escuela para hijos de trabajadores (1939-41). En 1932 publicó la antología *Hacia una literatura proletaria*. Autor de *Camino* (1934), *22 de diciembre. Diario de un estudiante* (1937) y *Jack* (1940). En 1973, preparada por Miguel Bustos Cerecero, apareció una edición con la *Obra completa de Lorenzo Turrent Rozas*.

TUXCACUESCO ◆ Municipio de Jalisco situado al este-sureste de Autlán y al oeste de Ciudad Guzmán. Superficie: 257.46 km². Habitantes: 4,027, de los cuales 924 forman la población económicamente activa. En la jurisdicción se produce una bebida alcohólica llamada tuxca, destilada del maguey mezcalero. Juan Rulfo (☛) le dio celebridad mundial al municipio al incluirlo en su narrativa.

TUXCACUESCO ◆ Río de Jalisco que nace de la confluencia de varios arroyos en la vertiente suroriental de la sierra de Quilá, al suroeste de Cocula. Corre de norte a sur entre las sierras de Tapalpa y de Cacoma. Recibe al río Tapalpa y al oeste-suroeste de Ciudad Guzmán, cerca de los límites con Colima, se une al Ayuquila o San Pedro para formar el Armería.

TUXCUECA ◆ Municipio de Jalisco situado en la ribera suroccidental de la laguna de Chapala, al sur de Guadalajara y al sureste de Acatlán. Superficie: 298.94 km². Habitantes: 5,509, de los cuales 1,276 forman la población económicamente activa.

TUXPAN ◆ Municipio de Jalisco situado en los límites con Colima y contiguo a Ciudad Guzmán. Superficie: 541.75 km². Habitantes: 33,652, de los cuales 8,472 forman la población económicamente activa. Hablan alguna lengua indígena 109 personas mayores de cinco años (náhuatl 100). El 23 de marzo de

1915, luego de dos días de combates, una parte de la División del Norte al mando de Roberto Fierro y Calixto Contreras fue derrotada por las fuerzas carrancistas de Manuel M. Diéguez y Francisco Murguía.

TUXPAN ◆ Municipio de Michoacán situado al noroeste de Zitácuaro y al sureste de Ciudad Hidalgo. Superficie: 206.92 km². Habitantes: 23,511, de los cuales 5,051 forman la población económicamente activa. Hablan alguna lengua indígena 38 personas mayores de cinco años. En la jurisdicción se elaboran quesos, mosaicos y herrería artística. Cuenta con una zona arqueológica y yacimientos de plata. El 25 de julio, en la cabecera, se celebra la fiesta del santo patrono en la que se ejecutan las danzas de los Espadachines y de las Plumas. El 30 de septiembre se conmemora el nacimiento de José María Morelos. Hacia 1560 fue creada la provincia de Tuspa (Tuxpan), que tenía jurisdicción sobre Mazamitla, Tamazula, Zapotlán, Zapotiltic, Tonila y Pihuamo. En 1630, el alcalde mayor trasladó su residencia de Tuspa a Zapotlán y la provincia se llamó entonces de Zapotlán el Grande. En 1787 se convirtió en subdelegación de la intendencia de Guadalajara.

TUXPAN ◆ Municipio de Nayarit situado al norte de San Blas y al sur de Acaponeta. Superficie: 474.3 km². Habitantes: 31,867, de los cuales 10,450 forman la población económicamente activa. Hablan alguna lengua indígena 56 personas mayores de cinco años (cora 21).

TUXPAN ◆ Municipio de Veracruz situado al norte de Poza Rica y al sureste de Tantoyuca, en el litoral del golfo de México. Superficie: 1,061.89 km². Habitantes: 127,622, de los cuales 35,629 forman la población económicamente activa. Hablan alguna lengua indígena 2,233 personas mayores de cinco años (náhuatl 1,017 y totonaco 792). La cabecera es Tuxpan de Rodríguez Cano. Los huastecos, primeros habitantes de la región, se instalaron en el pueblo de Tam-buc, "siete lugares", situado al sureste de la actual cabecera, casi en la desembocadura del río Tuxpan, que más tarde fue ocupada por los totonacos. A finales del primer milenio de la época contemporánea, bajo la influencia de los toltecas, la población comenzó a ser conocida con el nombre náhuatl de Tochpan, "lugar de conejos". En los últimos años del siglo XV, las fuerzas mexicas de Ahuízotl conquistaron Tochpan y convirtieron a la región en tributaria de Tenochtitlan. En 1522, poco después de la conquista de Pánuco, las fuerzas de Hernán Cortés ocuparon la desembocadura del Tuxpan y se establecieron junto al sitio del asentamiento totonaco. A mediados del siglo XVI, el pueblo de Tuxpan fue incorporado a la alcaldía mayor de Huauchinango y al obispado de Puebla. Durante el siglo XVII, el puerto fue atacado en varias ocasiones por piratas ingleses y franceses y por lo menos en 1678 los corsarios británicos saquearon la población. Además de las incursiones, el pueblo se veía frecuentemente afectado, sobre todo en verano, por las crecidas del río Tuxpan, por lo que en la segunda mitad del siglo XVIII, las autoridades españolas decidieron trasladar la población al noroeste, cerca de la ribera occidental de la laguna de Tampamachoco, donde se encuentra desde entonces. En 1787, al instaurarse la división política por intendencias, los pueblos de Tuxpan y Chichontepec quedaron dentro de la jurisdicción de Puebla. A pesar de su excelente posición geográfica, a medio camino, entre Tampico y Veracruz, a principios del siglo XIX, el puerto de Tuxpan era poco utilizado. Durante la revolución de independencia casi no hubo acciones militares en el actual territorio municipal, pero sí y muchas en los alrededores, sobre todo en Papantla, que fueron combatidas por las tropas coloniales acantonadas en el puerto. Poco después de consumada la independencia, la población de Tuxpan era de casi 3,000 habitantes. En agosto de 1829, las fuerzas de Antonio López de Santa Anna que marchaban hacia Tampico para combatir a la expedición de reconquista de Isidro Barradas, acamparon brevemente en Tuxpan y fueron auxiliadas por sus habitantes, por lo que en 1830 el Congreso de Puebla elevó la población a la categoría de villa. En 1845, luego de varios meses de infructuosas solicitudes y de la detención del líder del movimiento, Luciano Velázquez, los totonacas de Tuxpan, Tantoyuca, Papantla, Ozulama, Amatlán, Pánuco y Tampico se levantaron en armas para conseguir la restitución de sus tierras comunales y durante más de dos años combatieron a las fuerzas del gobierno (☛ *Papantla* y *Tantoyuca*). En abril de 1847, los invasores estadounidenses ocuparon el puerto. En diciembre de 1853, el gobierno de Santa Anna decretó la separación de Tuxpan de Puebla y su integración a Veracruz. Tres años después, durante el Congreso Constituyente, el diputado Isidoro Olvera propuso crear el Territorio de Iturbide, que estaría formado por los distritos de Tuxpan, Tampico, Tancanhuitz y

FOTO: FONDO EDITORIAL GRUPO AZABACHE

Tuxpan, Veracruz

Huejutla, pero la moción fue rechazada. También en 1856 se terminó la construcción, iniciada en 1842, de la principal iglesia de Tuxpan, que en siglo XX sería convertida en catedral. Hacia 1863, las fuerzas invasoras francesas ocuparon la población, pero tres años más tarde fueron desalojadas por los guerrilleros republicanos de Desiderio Pavón, José María Carbajal y Esteban Mascareñas. En 1881, la Legistatura de Veracruz convirtió a Tuxpan en ciudad. Aunque los campos chapopoteros del territorio municipal se conocían por lo menos desde el siglo XVI, sólo hasta los últimos años del siglo XIX se realizaron los primeros intentos de explotación comercial. En 1880, por ejemplo, un grupo de empresarios británicos estableció una refinería en la ciudad, pero la carencia de tecnología y la falta de mercados inmediatos la hicieron quebrar en 1890. Diez años después, sin embargo, el estadounidense Edward L. Doheney descubrió los yacimientos de la hacienda de Trujillo y la explotación petrolera se generalizó (☛ *Petróleo*). A principios de 1914, las fuerzas carrancistas de Cándido Aguilar derrotaron en las cercanías de la cabecera municipal a un contingente federal. Poco después, en mayo de ese mismo año, la población fue convertida provisionalmente en capital de Veracruz, mientras Venustiano Carranza, el primer jefe del ejército constitucionalista, se hallaba ahí. En agosto, todavía en Tuxpan, el gobierno de Carranza publicó una de las primeras leyes sobre la industria petrolera en México. El 9 de junio de 1955, la Legislatura veracruzana añadió al nombre de la cabecera los apellidos de Enrique Rodríguez Cano. En octubre de 1956, del puerto de Tuxpan partieron, a bordo del yate *Granma*, 82 revolucionarios, algunos de los cuales (como Fidel Castro, Raúl Castro y Ernesto *Che* Guevara) encabezarían la revolución cubana. En 1962 se erigió la diócesis de Tuxpan. A finales de los años ochenta se estaba construyendo, en la laguna de Tampamachoco, una gran planta termoeléctrica. El municipio tiene una próspera industria pesquera (ostión, cazón, robalo y camarón) alimentada, básicamente, por la laguna de Tampamachoco, pero la agricultura y la extracción de petróleo ocupan a la mayor parte de los trabajadores. Tuxpan es puerto de altura y cabotaje y tiene una aduana marítima. Está comunicado con Tampico por un canal que cruza las lagunas de Tampamachoco y Tamiahua.

TUXPAN ◆ Río de Michoacán también llamado Tajimaroa. Nace de la confluencia de varios arroyos en la vertiente sur de la cordillera de las Mil Cumbres, en el eje Volcánico, al sureste de Ciudad Hidalgo. Corre de norte a sur y se une al río Zitácuaro para formar el Tuzantla.

TUXPAN ◆ Río de Veracruz formado en la vertiente este de la sierra Madre Oriental por la confluencia de los ríos Vinazco y Pantepec, al noroeste de Poza Rica. Corre de oeste a este por la llanura costera del golfo de México, recibe a los arroyos Hondo, de Mequetela y de Cañas y al río Buenavista, así como las aguas de la laguna de Tampamachoco. Desemboca en el golfo de México y forma la barra de Tuxpan, 12 km antes de la cual se localiza el puerto de Tuxpan de Rodríguez Cano. El río Tuxpan es navegable en sus últimos 67 km.

TUXTEPEC, DE ◆ Sierra de Oaxaca situada en el extremo norte del estado, inmediatamente al este de la presa Miguel Alemán, al norte del río Santo Domingo y al sur del Tonto, en los límites con el estado de Veracruz. Sus principales crestas son los cerros de Soyaltepec, Paso de Vigas, Playa Obispo y Piedra Corral.

TUXTEPEC ◆ ☛ *San Juan Bautista Tuxtepec.*

TUXTEPEC, PLAN DE ◆ ☛ *Plan de Tuxtepec.*

TUXTILLA ◆ Municipio de Veracruz situado al suroeste de Cosamaloapan y al sureste de Tierra Blanca, en los límites con Oaxaca. Superficie: 168.62 km^2. Habitantes: 2,128, de los cuales 641 forman la población económicamente activa. Hablan alguna lengua indígena 11 personas mayores de cinco años.

TUXTLA ◆ Municipio de Chiapas situado al oeste de San Cristóbal de Las Casas. Superficie: 412.4 km^2. Habitantes: 386,135, de los cuales 96,112 forman la población económicamente activa. Hablan alguna lengua indígena 5,952 personas mayores de cinco años (tzotzil 2,223, tzeltal 1,930, zapoteco 524 y zoque 509). La cabecera, Tuxtla Gutiérrez, es capital del estado. En la parte central del municipio se encuentran el cañón del Sumidero, formado por el río Grijalva, y las grutas de Montecristo y Palmacristi. Hacia el siglo V a.n.e., los zoques se instalaron en el actual territorio municipal. Doscientos años des-

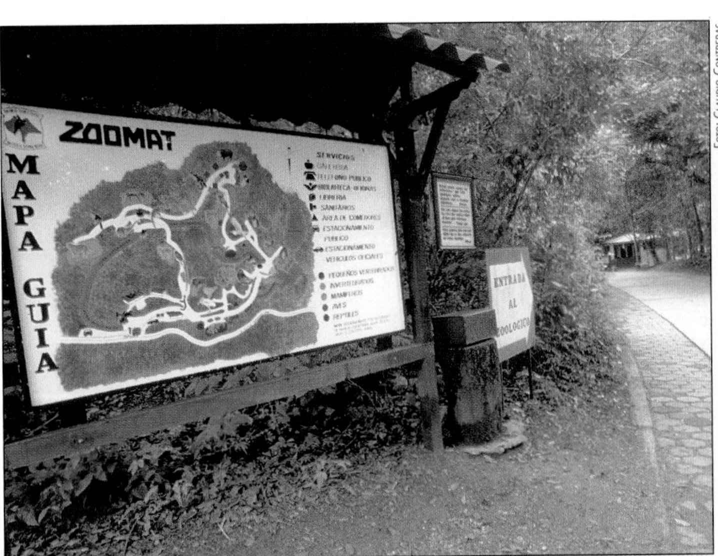

FOTO: CLAUDIO CONTRERAS

Tuxtla Gutiérrez, cabecera municipal de Tuxtla, Chiapas

pués, aproximadamente, fundaron el poblado de Cayotocmó, "casa de conejos". En los últimos años del siglo XV, los mexicas ocuparon el poblado y lo rebautizaron con el nombre de Tochtla, "donde abundan los conejos". Aunque las incursiones españolas en la región se sucedieron desde 1522, no fue sino hasta 1527 cuando una fuerza europea al mando de Diego de Mazariegos que se dirigía al cañon del Sumidero a combatir a los chiapa acampó en Tochtla. Sin embargo, los conquistadores se retiraron poco después. En 1546, los frailes dominicos Alonso de Villalba y Tomás de las Casillas comenzaron a evangelizar la región y a finales del siglo se instalaron definitivamente en el pueblo y bautizaron la localidad con el nombre de San Marcos Tuxtla. Durante el siglo XVII, a causa de la presencia de los conquistadores en la región, los zoques fueron despojados de su tierra y segregados, hasta que, en 1693, los indios se sublevaron y ejecutaron al alcalde mayor de San Cristóbal y a su representante en San Marcos. En 1768, la Audiencia de Guatemala creó la alcaldía de San Marcos Tuxtla, que abarcaba la porción occidental de Chiapas. Diez años después, la población tuxtleca era de casi 3,000 habitantes. En 1790, la población de San Marcos fue integrada, como cabecera de partido, a la Intendencia de Chiapas, dependiente de la Capitanía General de Guatemala. En 1813, las Cortes españolas elevaron a la categoría de villa al poblado. Ocho años después, en septiembre de 1821, el ayuntamiento de Tuxtla se pronunció por la independencia de España. Un año más tarde, los jefes militares de la villa se manifestaron en favor del imperio de Agustín de Iturbide y en octubre de 1823, unos meses después de su caída, se adhirieron al Plan de Chiapa Libre que había sido proclamado en Comitán. En noviembre, sin embargo, las fuerzas mexicanas derrotaron a la guarnición de Tuxtla e incorporaron el partido a México. En 1829, la Legislatura chiapaneca convirtió a Tuxtla en ciudad. En 1833, a causa de un levantamiento centralista en San Cristóbal, la capital del estado, el gobernador y el Congreso se trasladaron a Tuxtla. Dos años después, las tropas federalistas de Joaquín Miguel Gutiérrez fueron derrotadas y Tuxtla quedó en manos de los centralistas. Al establecerse el gobierno centralista, Tuxtla perdió su condición de cabecera de partido. En 1838, al mando de una fuerza liberal, Gutiérrez intentó tomar la ciudad, pero murió durante el asalto. Diez años después, en mayo de 1848, el Congreso local, entonces dominado por los liberales, decidió suprimir el nombre de San Marcos y la localidad se convirtió en Tuxtla Gutiérrez. Tradicionalmente bastión de los liberales, en enero de 1858, al inicio de la guerra de los Tres Años, el gobierno estatal se trasladó nuevamente a Tuxtla y ahí permaneció hasta febrero del año siguiente, cuando regresó a San Cristóbal. Cuatro años después, las fuerzas imperialistas obligaron al gobierno a refugiarse una vez más en Tuxtla, donde permaneció hasta el triunfo de la República. En 1892 la sede de los poderes pasó definitivamente a Tuxtla Gutiérrez. En 1964 se creó la diócesis de Tuxtla Gutiérrez. En la cabecera se encuentran los museos de Antropología e Historia y de Historia Natural, el Instituto de Ciencias y Artes, el Jardín Botánico de Tuxtla y el zoológico Miguel Álvarez del Toro. Las principales fiestas de la ciudad son la de San Marcos Evangelista (del 20 al 25 de abril), Santo Domingo de Guzmán (del 1 al 5 de agosto), San Roque (del 16 al 25 de agosto), la Purísima Concepción (del 8 al 12 de diciembre) y los días de Todos los Santos y de Muertos (del 1 y 2 de noviembre).

TUXTLA CHICO ◆ Municipio de Chiapas situado en los límites con Guatemala y contiguo a Tapachula. Superficie: 64.6 km^2. Habitantes: 32,395, de los cuales 7,502 forman la población económicamente activa. Hablan alguna lengua indígena 69 personas mayores de cinco años (mame 27). El municipio es el más importante productor de café de la República Mexicana. En su jurisdicción se hallan las ruinas de Rosario Izapa, centro ceremonial de la cultura olmeca-maya, donde están el Árbol de la Vida, la Piedra de Sacrificios, un calendario y un monolito antropomorfo llamado el Guerrero. Las principales fiestas son el 2 de febrero, día de la Candelaria; del 11 al 14 de marzo, cuando se realiza una feria comercial; y los días 28 y 29 de abril, celebración de San Pedro.

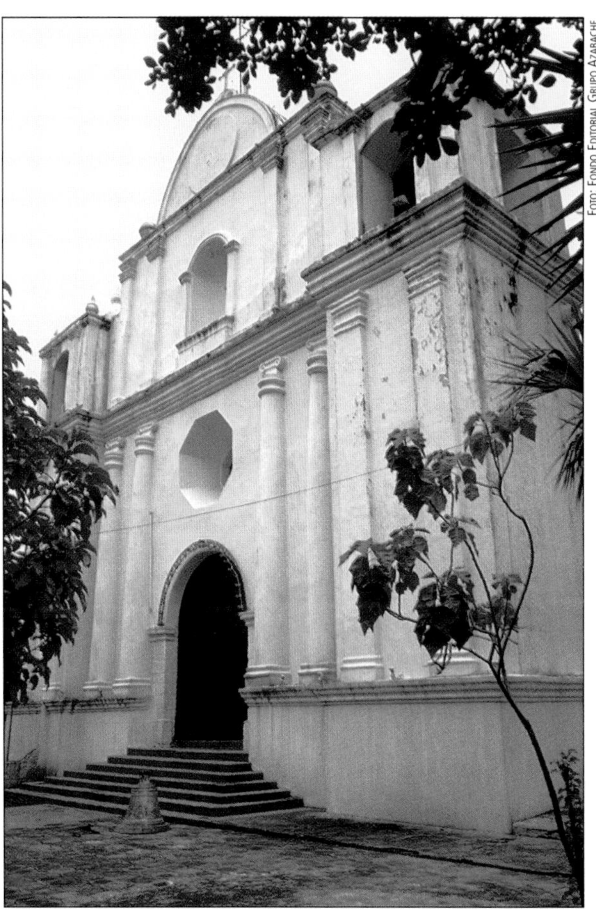
FOTO: FONDO EDITORIAL GRUPO AZABACHE

Iglesia de la Candelaria en Tuxtla Chico, Chiapas

TUXTLA GUTIÉRREZ ◆ Cabecera del municipio chiapaneco de Tuxtla (☛) y capital de Chiapas.

TUZAMAPÁN DE GALEANA ◆ Municipio de Puebla situado al noroeste de Teziutlán y al este de Huauchinango, en los límites con Veracruz. Superficie: 45.92 km^2. Habitantes: 5,679, de los cuales 1,538 forman la población económicamente activa. Hablan alguna lengua indígena 2,882 personas mayores de cinco años (náhuatl 1,466 y totonaco 1,414). Indígenas monolingües: 112.

TUZANTÁN ◆ Municipio de Chiapas situado al noroeste de Tapachula y al sureste de Acacoyagua. Superficie: 268.3 km². Habitantes: 22,833, de los cuales 5,905 forman la población económicamente activa. Hablan alguna lengua indígena 197 personas mayores de cinco años (mame 62, tzotzil 52).

TUZANTLA ◆ Municipio de Michoacán situado al suroeste de Zitácuaro y al sureste de Morelia, en los límites con el Estado de México. Superficie: 827.69 km². Habitantes: 17,828, de los cuales 3,251 forman la población económicamente activa. Hablan alguna lengua indígena 36 personas mayores de cinco años.

TZAPOTLATENAN ◆ Deidad nahua de la medicina. De acuerdo con la tradición, inventó un remedio llamado oxitl u ojote del rey. Durante su celebración anual se realizaban sacrificios humanos en su honor.

TZARÁRACUA ◆ Cascada de Michoacán situada en Uruapan, al sur de la cabecera municipal. Se forma en la salida del río Cupatitzio a la superficie, después de recorrer un tramo subterráneo. La caída mide unos 40 metros.

TZELTALES ◆ Indios también llamados zendales, cuyo nombre significa "los que vienen de lado". Habitan en el centro y norte de Chiapas, en una zona comprendida entre los ríos Grijalva y Usumacinta. En 1995, hablaban tzeltal 283,260 personas mayores de cinco años. Vivían en Chiapas 279,015, de los cuales 97,072 no saben español. El idioma tzeltal está clasificado en el grupo maya-totonaco, tronco mayanse, familia mayanse, subfamilia yax. Hacia el siglo X a.n.e., quizá provenientes de Centroamérica, los tzeltales se instalaron en las montañas occidentales de Guatemala. En el siglo V de nuestra era se retiraron hacia el norte, se asentaron en la meseta Central de Chiapas y en el siglo VI se establecieron en Yaxbité. Desde entonces se dedicaron principalmente a la agricultura y adoptaron la costumbre de que la siembra sólo es realizada por varones que hayan previamente ayunado y practicado la abstinencia. Más tarde se incorporaron al antiguo imperio maya, en el que permanecieron hasta su disolución, en el siglo X. Unos 200 años después, el poder político de los tzeltales se fragmentó en varios pequeños señoríos, lo que propició la separación cultural entre los tzotziles, concentrados alrededor de Zinacantán, los choles, que vivían en Tumbalá, y los tzeltales propiamente dichos, que permanecieron en la región de Ocosingo. A finales del siglo XV, los tzeltales sostuvieron varios enfrentamientos con las fuerzas mexicas y lograron conservar su independencia. A principios de la década de 1530 el territorio tzeltal fue conquistado por los españoles, pero sólo 10 años después, hacia 1540, al establecerse las congregaciones de indios, los tzeltates fueron realmente sometidos. En 1545, el obispo Bartolomé de las Casas inició la conquista espiritual en la región; los tzeltales, no obstante, consiguieron integrar los ritos cristianos a los suyos. De su antigua vida religiosa conservaron el culto a los nahuales, los espíritus domésticos gemelos de las personas, que una vez al año viajaban hasta un sitio llamado Atimaltik, donde por medio del Libro de las Vidas, en el que estaban registrados los nombres y destinos de todos los tzeltales, conocían la identidad de quienes morirían durante el año que comenzaba. Se consideraba a los nahuales como causantes de las enfermedades, que eran curadas por los *dzunbiles*, curanderos y pulsadores, por medio de ofrendas, rezos, limpias, yerbas medicinales y baños de vapor. Los tzeltales creen que las personas poseen dos almas, una de las cuales, al morir, es devorada por los nahuales. Han preservado el culto a Chulmetik, la diosa de la tierra; a Uch, el ser protector del crecimiento de las milpas y encargado de curar las enfermedades; a la montaña Ikal Ajau, situada cerca de Oxchuc, lugar que consideraban sagrado y viviente; y a los lagos, poblados de vírgenes que velaban por el bienestar de las comunidades. Cuando iniciaron el culto a los santos patronos con que los evangelizadores bautizaron sus pueblos, los convirtieron, como a sus antiguos dioses, en deidades parlantes y los vistieron como ellos mismos se vestían desde la conquista, es decir, con falda larga de manta, blusa o huipil decorados con bordados de colores, faja de lana y a veces una pañoleta de lana en el caso de las santas y calzón corto y camisa de manta, faja de lana o algodón, huaraches y un sombrero de palma decorado con listones para los santos. De los conquistadores también adoptaron la veneración a la cruz, a la Virgen María, que se mezcló con el culto a la diosa de la luna y de la fecundidad, Ixchel; y a Jesucristo, a quien convirtieron en Dios Tatik Jesucristo, deidad que era auxiliada por 13 ayudantes, los fiadores del cielo. Lejos de contribuir a la sumisión, la mezcla de las religiones sirvió a los tzeltales como arma de lucha contra los españoles. En 1584, por ejemplo, un grupo llamado Los Doce Apóstoles encabezó una insurrección armada de corte milenarista, que enlazaba elementos de la tradición religiosa judeocristiana, de la tzeltal y de la tzotzil. Desde fines del siglo XVI, pero sobre todo durante el XVII, los conquistadores se dedicaron a destruir las formas de organización política de los tzeltales. Sin embargo, los indios pudieron conservar, no sin esfuerzos, la costumbre de dividir a cada pueblo en dos calpules que eran dirigidos por un *katinab* o "jefe supremo", a quien asistía un *okil kabil* o secretario, mientras que el gobierno de la comunidad entera estaba en poder de dos *cornales* o gobernadores y cuatro *xtules*, o

FOTO: CLAUDIO CONTRERAS

Tzeltales de Ocosingo, Chiapas

regidores. No sucedió lo mismo respecto con la libertad y la propiedad, pues los conquistadores pudieron reducir significativamente la extensión de la tierra comunal y esclavizaron a un gran número de indios, muchos de los cuales fueron utilizados por los comerciantes y hacendados españoles, para transportar productos entre San Cristóbal y Veracruz. A esto se sumó la introducción de la caña de azúcar en la región y la consiguiente elaboración de chicha, una bebida alcohólica hecha de jugo de caña fermentada. Durante el siglo XVII, la explotación y las epidemias diezmaron a los tzeltales, quienes, a pesar de todo, pudieron organizar un gran levantamiento contra la dominación española a principios del siglo XVIII. En abril de 1711, a una tzeltal de Cahancú llamada María de la Candelaria se le apareció la "Virgen Santísima María de la Cruz" en los alrederores del pueblo y le ordenó la construcción de una ermita en ese lugar. Unas semanas después, los *cornales* de Cahancú inciaron la construcción del templo, pero en junio, la aparición de la Virgen fue puesta en duda por el sacerdote Simón de Lara, quien fue expulsado del pueblo, y desconocida por el obispo de Chiapas, Juan Bautista Álvarez de Toledo. La jerarquía eclesiástica prohibió el culto a la Virgen en el sitio en que se había aparecido y, en julio, María de la Candelaria comenzó a redactar unos llamamientos a los pueblos cercanos, en los que convocaba a los tzeltales, en nombre de la Virgen, a reunirse en Cahancú porque ya no había "ni Rey, ni Presidente, ni Obispo". En agosto, durante una fiesta en honor a la Virgen, los representantes de 32 pueblos tzeltales y tzotziles redactaron una proclama en la que llamaban a todos los indios a unirse al culto a la Virgen, a que mataran a los españoles, los mestizos y los negros, para que los indios vivieran tranquilos, sin pagar tributos. El gobierno religioso quedó en manos de María de la Candelaria y del chamán mestizo Sebastián Gómez de la Gloria, mientras que las fuerzas campesinas fueron comandadas por Juan García. Poco después, los tzeltales tomaron Chiilum, donde asesinaron a todos los españoles. La rebelión se extendió hacia Ocosingo y Cuira y más tarde, con la unión de los tzotziles de San Juan Chamula al movimiento, hasta Simojovel. Más de 15,000 tzeltales y tzotziles estaban sublevados. Por entonces se organizó una "república de indios" profundamente religiosa y militarizada, similar a la que los mayas de Chan Santa Cruz establecieron en el siglo XIX en Yucatán: crearon una Audiencia en Gueitiapan, bautizaron a Cahancú "Ciudad Real de Nueva España" y convirtieron en esclavos a los españoles prisioneros. En noviembre, las fuerzas españolas al mando de Toribio Cosío tomaron Cahancú, luego de incendiar varios pueblos, pero la rebelión sobrevivió y todavía a principios de 1713, 4,000 tzeltales intentaron tomar San Cristóbal de Las Casas. En marzo de ese año, los conquistadores capturaron y asesinaron a Juan García y la sublevación fue derrotada, aunque algunos pueblos continuaron alzados hasta 1716, cuando falleció María de la Candelaria. El otro dirigente tzeltal, Gómez de la Gloria, no fue detenido y es posible que en 1727 hubiera participado, con otros de los líderes sobrevivientes del movimiento de Cahancú, en una conspiración de tzeltales y zoques que reivindicaban el culto a la Virgen de Cahancú. En junio 1727, los indios de Ocosingo y Bachajón se levantaron en armas, pero fueron derrotados. Desde el siglo XIX, después de las reformas liberales de mediados de la centuria, muchos tzeltales comenzaron a abandonar temporalmente la región para contratarse como peones agrícolas en las fincas cafetaleras del Soconusco. En el siglo XX se iniciaron en la elaboración de cerámica y textiles para venderlos como artesanías, pues la destrucción de la propiedad comunal había minado de manera definitiva sus formas de organización. En 1936, el gobierno de Chiapas estableció que en los municipios en que la mayoría de la población fuera tzeltal, el presidente municipal debía pertenecer a la etnia, aunque los mestizos que generalmente asesoraban a los ediles se convirtieron, de hecho, en los verdaderos alcaldes. Medio siglo después, el Instituto Nacional Indigenista estableció en San Cristóbal un centro para ayudar a los indios a resolver problemas sanitarios, educativos y eventualmente económicos. A finales del siglo XX, sin embargo, los tzeltales había podido conservar, además de una buena parte de su religión y el vestido, los ritos que acompañan al nacimiento, el matrimonio y la muerte. Antes del bautizo católico, los tzeltales celebran la ceremonia de la "siembra el alma del niño", es decir, el entierro de la placenta del recién nacido. El matrimonio, por su parte, es arreglado por los padres del novio, que visitan y llevan obsequios a los de la novia. Después de la boda, el nuevo esposo permanece un año en la casa de los suegros para colaborar en las faenas agrícolas. Si el matrimonio es satisfactorio para la pareja, el esposo hace una fiesta llamada *mukel-ja*, en la que ofrece aguardiente a los suegros y con la que se considera oficialmente consumada la unión. Finalmente, cuando muere un tzeltal, su cuerpo es bañado y vestido con ropas nuevas; el cadáver es velado durante dos días y dos noches, con dos cirios, mientras a los asistentes se les ofrece chicha y se les anima con música. El cuerpo se entierra con la cabeza hacia el oeste, junto con sus objetos personales, una aguja y un carrete de hilo y, en el caso de los hombres, con comida y aguardiente.

TZICATLACOYAN ◆ Municipio de Puebla situado al sureste de la capital del estado y al oeste de Tecamachalco. Superficie: 174.77 km^2. Habitantes: 5,943, de los cuales 1,450 forman la población económicamente activa. Hablan alguna lengua indígena 15 personas mayores de cinco años (náhuatl).

TZIMOL ◆ Municipio de Chiapas al norte de la presa de La Angostura y contiguo a Comitán. Superficie: 32.3 km^2. Habitantes: 10,887, de los cuales 2,862 forman la población activa. Hablan alguna lengua indígena 61 personas mayores de cinco años (tzotzil 36).

TZINTZUNTZAN ◆ Municipio de Michoacán situado en la ribera del lago de Pátzcuaro y contiguo a Quiroga. Superficie: 156.49 km². Habitantes: 12,408, de los cuales 3,149 forman la población económicamente activa. Hablan alguna lengua indígena 2,311 personas mayores de cinco años (purépecha 2,308). En la jurisdicción se encuentra la zona arqueológica de Ihuatzio, también llamada de las Yácatas, a la orilla del lago. Las ruinas constan de dos plataformas principales: en la primera hay tres yácatas y dos en la segunda, construidas de lajas; alrededor de estas construcciones se han encontrado entierros acompañados de piezas de cerámica y objetos de metal, obsidiana y jade; en el espacio entre los dos grupos de edificios se encontró un chac mool desnudo, característico de esta región de Michoacán. En el Museo Nacional de Antropología, en la ciudad de México, hay otros dos chac mool de esta zona y un altar en forma de coyote. La cabecera municipal fue sede del imperio purépecha. En la cabecera están el convento franciscano de Santa Ana, la capilla abierta del Hospital, que fue construida en 1619, y la iglesia de la Soledad. De 1533 a 1539, Vasco de Quiroga encabezó el primer obispado de Michoacán, con sede en esta ciudad.

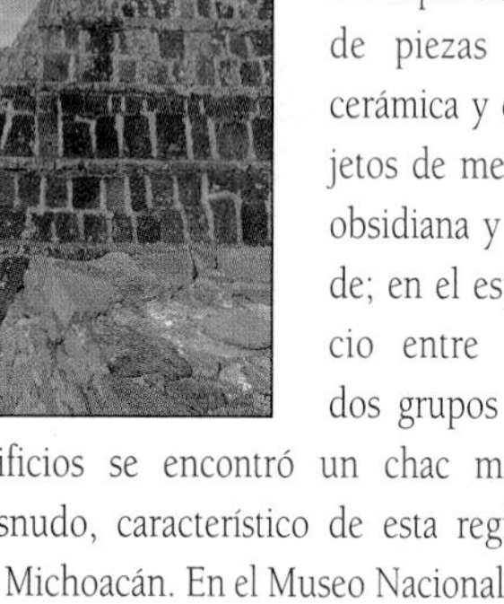

FOTO: CLAUDIO CONTRERAS

Zona arqueológica de Ihuatzio en Tzintzuntzan, Michoacán

TZITZIO ◆ Municipio de Michoacán contiguo a Morelia. Superficie: 906.58 km². Habitantes: 11,498, de los cuales 2,346 forman la población económicamente activa. Hablan alguna lengua indígena 11 personas mayores de cinco años.

TZOMPANTEPEC ◆ Municipio de Tlaxcala situado al noreste de la capital estatal y al sureste de Apizaco. Superficie: 48.2 km². Habitantes: 7,551, de los cuales 2,525 forman la población económicamente activa. Hablan alguna lengua indígena 21 personas mayores de cinco años (náhuatl 12).

TZONTEHUITZ ◆ Volcán extinguido de Chiapas situado en la meseta central del estado, al norte de San Cristóbal de Las Casas. Se eleva 2,858 metros sobre el nivel del mar.

TZONTEMOC ◆ Deidad nahua que era uno de los cuatro soportes del universo. Su nombre significa "Cabeza que cae". Se le identificaba con el sol poniente, pero sólo de día, pues en la noche era Mictlantecuhtli, el dios del infierno que acudía a dar luz a los muertos. En los códices se le representaba como un águila o una guacamaya que baja a beber de una urna la sangre de los sacrificados.

TZOTZILES ◆ Indios que viven en el centro y noroeste de Chiapas, en la zona de los Altos, y los límites con Tabasco. Los tzotziles pueblan una región que colinda al este con la habitada por los tzeltales, con quienes están emparentados cultural y lingüísticamente. Los principales pueblos tzotziles son Zinacantán, Simojovel, Mitonic, Pentalhó y San Juan Chamula. En 1995, hablaban tzotzil 263,611 personas mayores de cinco años, de las cuales 96,602 son monolingües. El idioma tzotzil está clasificado en el grupo mayatotonaco, tronco mayense, familia mayense, subfamilia yax; la lengua tzotzil tiene pequeñas variantes dialectales que no impiden la comunicación entre individuos de diferentes pueblos. Aun cuando la ropa tradicional tiene ligeras diferencias de una a otra comunidad, en general consta, para las mujeres, de una blusa o huipil blanco, con bordados de colores, falda larga de color oscuro, faja, pañoleta de manta y un chal cuadrado, de lana o algodón; los hombres, por su parte, visten calzón y camisa de manta, faja de algodón o lana, huaraches, sombrero de palma adornado con listones y un poncho de lana, llamado chamarro. Su actividad económica básica es la agricultura, tanto para autoconsumo como para comercialización, y la mayoría de las familias posee ganado menor, de carga y aves de corral. Un gran número de hombres emigra temporalmente para contratarse en las fincas cafetaleras del Soconusco. En su organización social coexisten las familias nucleares con las extensas. Para la concertación del matrimonio, los padres del novio o un mediador piden a la novia mediante sucesivas visitas a los padres de la joven en las que se llevan obsequios que, las primeras veces, deben ser rechazados, pues el aceptarlos implica acceder al matrimonio; al llegarse a un acuerdo, se fija la fecha de la boda, que se formaliza cuando el novio y sus padres son aceptados en casa de la novia; una vez sellado el matrimonio, deben llevarse regalos y dinero en efectivo, como pago por la desposada. Cuando un tzotzil muere, su cadáver es colocado sobre un petate, con la cabeza hacia el oeste; una persona anciana, del mismo sexo que el muerto, lo lava y viste con sus mejores ropas; una vez que el cadáver es sacado de la casa, el piso de la misma se riega con agua salada, se quema chile y se orienta al alma del fallecido para que se dirija al cementerio; el cuerpo es enterrado al atardecer, con la cabeza hacia el oeste y acompañado de comida, dinero y diversos objetos que le servirán en su tránsito al purgatorio, primero, y al cielo, después, donde el alma vivirá tantos días como vivió su dueño, tiempo durante el cual rejuvenecerá hasta renacer en un niño del sexo opuesto. El compadrazgo es una institución que establece lazos muy sólidos y sólo se formaliza en ocasión de los ritos cristianos como bautizos, confirmaciones o matrimonios. Aunque católicos, los tzotziles

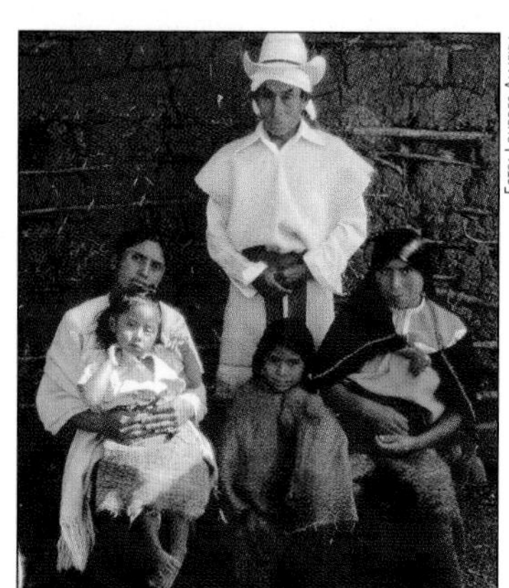

FOTO: LOURDES ALMEIDA

Familia de campesinos tzotziles de San Juan Chamula, Chiapas conservan aún numerosos elementos de su antigua religión: para ellos, el mundo es un cubo rodeado por agua y sostenido por cuatro u ocho pilares (montañas, hombres o reptiles), cuyos movimientos provocan los sismos. Jesucristo se identifica con el sol y la virgen María con la luna y con la fertilidad; San Salvador es también el dios creador. La tierra es una deidad femenina y el dios de la lluvia reina sobre el trueno, los montes y los animales del bosque, envía el agua y, por ende, propicia las buenas cosechas; los santos que veneran son considerados parientes de Cristo y de la Virgen, pero de menor jerarquía. La cruz es guardiana de los hombres, así como un símbolo sagrado que se identifica con un árbol y con la entrada al mundo inferior. Hay cruces en pozos, cuevas, caminos, en la entrada de los pueblos y sobre las casas. Creen en la existencia de seres malignos que habitan en el inframundo, a los que se da el nombre genérico de *pukuh*, entre los que se cuenta el fantasma de una mujer que vive en los bosques, un diablo de pelo largo, un diablo de dos caras y un caníbal al que llaman *h'ik'al*. Tienen una concepción animista de la naturaleza. Creen que el alma humana consta de 12 o 13 partes, una de las cuales es la del animal compañero (vayihel, wayjel o chulel). Los tzotziles se ciñen a la organización muncipal, aunque mantienen a sus autoridades religiosas. Hasta el siglo XII de nuestra era, los tzotziles formaron parte de los tzeltales, pero a la desaparición del imperio antiguo maya y el consiguiente establecimiento de los pequeños señoríos tzeltales, comenzaron a diferenciarse. En el siglo XV, las fuerzas mexicas de Tiltototl conquistaron Zinacantán, que por entonces era uno de los principales asentamientos tzotziles. En 1524, las fuerzas españolas de Luis Marín conquistaron el territorio y sometieron a los tzotziles. A mediados del siglo XVI, los dominicos y los mercedarios evangelizaron la región. Durante el siglo XVII, debido a los constantes despojos, la extensión de las tierras comunales se redujo considerablemente, lo que hizo crecer el descontento. A principios del siglo XVIII, a los tzotziles de Zinacantán y Chamula se les apareció la Virgen María en varias ocasiones y los instruyó para organizar un culto sin sacerdotes blancos. Las autoridades coloniales negaron tales apariciones e intentaron suprimir el culto, pero lo único que provocaron fue irritar a los tzotziles. En 1710, la jerarquía de San Cristóbal de Las Casas ordenó destruir una de las parroquias de la Virgen en Zinacantán y, en 1711, la ermita de Santa Marta, población cercana a Chamula, fue demolida. Por eso, cuando a mediados de 1712 se levantaron en armas los tzeltales (☛) de Cahancú, casi todos los pueblos tzotztiles se sumaron a la insurrección y juntos pelearon hasta 1713, cuando las fuerzas coloniales capturaron y asesinaron a Juan García, el comandante militar de los indios. No obstante, entre los indios subsistió la tendencia a reinventar la religiosidad católica para enfrentar a los hacendados y comerciantes de San Cristóbal. Cuando en diciembre de 1867 una niña de San Juan Chamula llamada Agustina Gómez Checheb miró caer del cielo tres piedras, que fueron consideradas parlantes y por lo tanto divinas por Pedro Díaz Cuscat, uno de los ayudantes del párroco de Chamula, los tzotziles las convirtieron en objetos de culto. Poco después, en febrero de 1868, Gómez Checheb a "dio a luz" a tres pequeños dioses de barro, que, según informaba Díaz Cuscat a los pueblos vecinos, habían nacido para reconfortar a los indios y para apoyarlos en contra de los hacendados. A partir de entonces, los indios dejaron de bajar a San Cristóbal para comerciar y establecieron un sistema de autoconsumo que tenía como centro el pueblo de Tzajalhmel, el mismo donde se celebraban los oficios religiosos. En abril de ese año, Díaz Cuscat y Gómez Checheb, que dirigían el culto y transmitían la voz de los dioses, comunicaron que la voluntad divina era sustraer a los tzotziles de las fiestas de Semana Santa de San Cristóbal, porque los indios requerían de un Jesucristo propio, y el Viernes Santo de ese año crucificaron a un hermano de Gómez Checheb. Las autoridades de San Cristóbal utilizaron el hecho como pretexto y en diciembre capturaron a los principales líderes del culto nuevo. Aún así no pudieron impedir la continuación de los ritos de Tzajalhemel ni tampoco el aumento de las inquietudes políticas de los tzotziles, pues en mayo de 1869, Ignacio Fernández Galindo, un mestizo de la ciudad de México, se incorporó a la iglesia tzotzil, narró cómo los mayas, coras y yaquis habían podido liberarse de los conquistadores e impulsó a los indios a luchar por la liberación de Gómez Checheb y Díaz Cuscat, así como por la restitución de las tierras comunales. Fernández Galindo organizó un gobierno religioso y militarizado y, en junio, los tzotziles se levantaron en armas. Días después, las fuerzas indígenas se presentaron en San Cristóbal y consiguieron la liberación de Díaz Cuscat y Gómez Chechen a cambio de dejar a Fernández Galindo en la ciudad, con la promesa de que sería liberado unos días después. Pero las autoridades encarcelaron, a Fernández Galindo y en julio lo fusilaron. Los tzotziles intentaron tomar San Cristóbal en dos ocasiones, pero fueron derrotados, mientras que las fuerzas gubermanentales tomaron Tzajalhemel. Durante la segunda mitad del año, el gobierno combinó la negociación con el exterminio y en octubre de 1870, Díaz Cuscat se rindió. Desde entonces, quizá para recordar la insurrección, la Semana Santa es la principal fiesta de los tzotziles.

Tzucacab ◆ Municipio de Yucatán situado en la porción meridional del estado, al sureste de Tekax y al suroeste de Peto, en los límites con Quintana Roo. Superficie: 692.99 km^2. Habitantes: 12,170, de los cuales 2,920 forman la población económicamente activa. Hablan alguna lengua indígena 7,125 personas mayores de cinco años (maya 7,118), de las cuales 793 son monolingües. Ubicado en una zona cañera, en el municipio se encuentran los ingenios de Catmís, Kakalná y Thul.

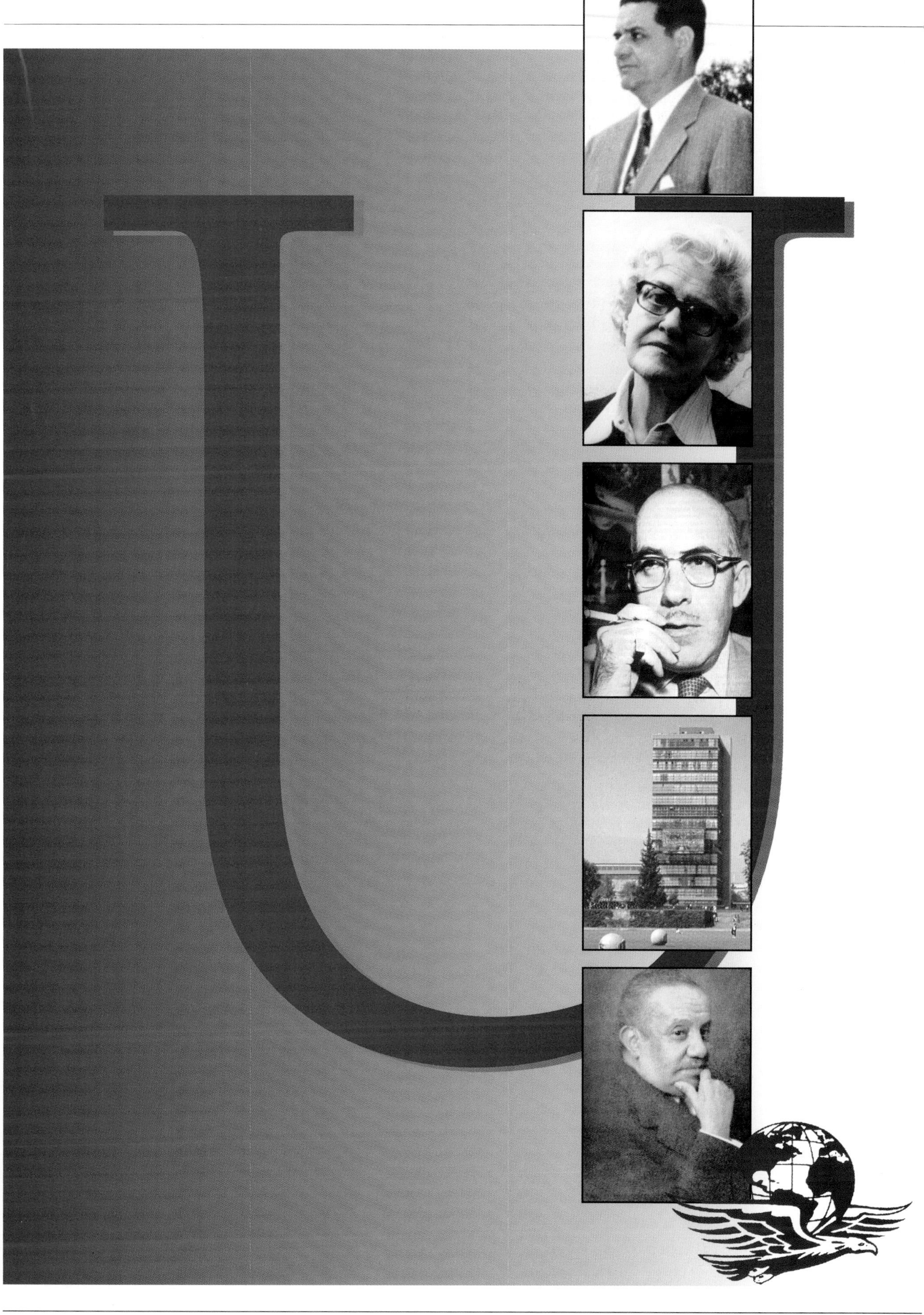

UAYMA ◆ Municipio de Yucatán situado al este de Chichén Itzá y al oeste de Valladolid. Superficie: 196.72 km². Habitantes: 2,804, de los cuales 723 forman la población económicamente activa. Hablan alguna lengua indígena 2,012 personas (maya), de las cuales 484 son monolingües.

UBACH, JOSÉ ALBERTO ◆ n. en Tijuana, BC (1958). Compositor y guitarrista egresado del Conservatorio Nacional de Música, donde estudió con Guillermo Flores Méndez y Guillermo Noriega. Tomó cursos con Robert Guthrie, Andrés Segovia, John W. Duarte y Christopher Parkening. Estudió dirección orquestal con Donald Barra en la Universidad Estatal de San Diego. Llegó al descubrimiento, como musicólogo, de una sonata para guitarra terza de Beethoven. Terminó el *Cuarteto para guitarra* (1991) que Manuel M. Ponce dejara inconcluso. Grabó por vez primera la música de Manuel Y. Ferrer e inventó la *guitarrina* que interpreta repertorio para mandolina y algunos tipos de laúd. Es autor de un *Preámbulo* (1991) para dicho *Cuarteto* de Ponce, de unas *Diferencias sobre la* Sarabande *de Poulenc* (1983), de un *Tríptico* (1991), *Dos tonadas mexicanas* (1993), *Recordatus* (1995), *Vals del minuto y double* (1996), *Siete meditaciones sobre el amor de Dios* (1996), *De allá* (1993) para coro infantil y otras obras.

UBILLA, ANDRÉS DE ◆ n. en España y m. en Chiapas (¿1540?-1603). Vivió desde su infancia en la Nueva España. En 1559 ingresó en la Orden de Predicadores. Doctor por la Real y Pontificia Universidad de México, fue superior de los conventos de Oaxaca, México y Puebla y provincial de los dominicos (1582-?). Desde 1586 se opuso al virrey Álvaro Manrique de Zúñiga, el marqués de Villamanrique, quien intentó quitar parroquias de indios a los dominicos. En 1589 viajó a España para convencer a Felipe II y al Consejo de los perjuicios que la política del virrey en favor del clero secular acarreaba a la colonia. Fue obispo de Chiapas dos años después de la caída del virrey (1592-1601). En 1603 fue nombrado obispo de Michoacán, pero murió antes de tomar posesión.

UCAREO, DE ◆ Sierra de Michoacán y Guanajuato que forma parte del Sistema Volcánico Transversal. Se extiende del noreste michoacano al sureste guanajuatense, al sureste del lago de Cuitzeo, al sur de Acámbaro y al noreste de Morelia y de la sierra de Mil Cumbres. Presenta aún diversas manifestaciones de actividad volcánica: el cerro de las Humaredas emite gases sulfurosos y el surtidor llamado de El Chillador arroja agua a 94 grados centígrados. En ella se encuentran la laguna llamada del Azufre y los manantiales termales de La Tacita. Su pico más elevado es el cerro de San Andrés, que alcanza los 3,340 metros sobre el nivel del mar.

UCRANIA, REPÚBLICA DE ◆ Estado europeo que limita con Belarús al norte, con Rusia al noreste y este, con Rumania y Moldavia al sureste, con Hungría y Eslovaquia al oeste y con Polonia al noroeste. Tiene costas en los mares Negro y de Azov, en el sur. Superficie: 603,700 km². Habitantes: 50,861,000 (1998). Su capital es Kiev (2,630,000 habitantes en 1996). Otras ciudades importantes son Kharkov (1,555,000) y Dnepropetrovsk (1,147,000). El ucraniano es el idioma oficial y también se hablan ruso y tártaro-crimeo. La moneda es el grivna. *Historia*: En el primer milenio de nuestra era, el territorio ucraniano fue habitado por pueblos a quienes los eslavos llamaban "rus" (extranjeros), que formaron el Kievski Rus, embrión de Estado nacional cristianizado por el príncipe Vladimir, quien extendió sus territorios hasta formar dos principados: Volodimir y Gálitch. En 1199 el príncipe Roman Volinski unificó ambos principados. Entre 1237 y 1241 la región padeció numerosas invasiones tártaras que debilitaron a la dinastía Volinski hasta hacerla desaparecer en 1323. Un año después la región quedó en manos del príncipe polaco Boleslaw de Mazowice para que, en 1340, Casimiro *el Grande*, de Polonia, absorbiera completamente a Ucrania. En 1836 se aceleró la colonización polaca de Ucrania, lo que obligó a numerosos campesinos insumisos a huir a las regiones semidesérticas al este del río Dniéper, desde donde organizaron la resistencia; tales rebeldes fueron llamados "cosacos zaporojes" (es decir, fugitivos al otro lado de las montañas). Estos cosacos, convertidos en avezados guerreros, fueron contratados durante el siglo XVI por las noblezas rusa y polaca para defender sus fronteras de los ataques tártaros. En 1569 el reino unificado de Polonia y Lituania intentó cristianizar por la fuerza a los ucranianos y trató, también, de imponerles la esclavitud. A finales del siglo XVI, la Corona polaca reconoció y registró a los cosacos que habia contratado,

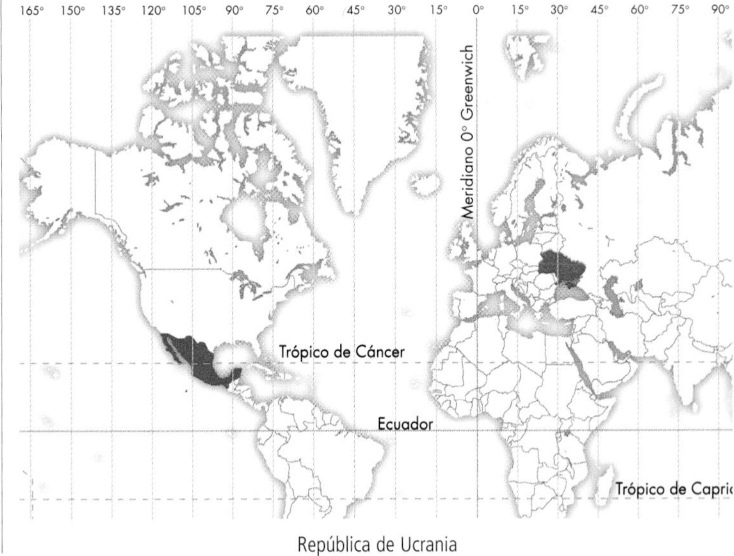

República de Ucrania

permitiéndoles ejercer cargos públicos, mientras persiguió y atacó a los que se mantuvieron en rebeldía. De 1635 a 1638 se produjo una gran rebelión cosaca contra el intento de construir una fortaleza polaca en su territorio. Al finalizar la rebelión, el gobierno polaco expulsó a los cosacos de su parlamento; algunos se refugirón con sus coterráneos y en 1647 eligieron al ex parlamentario Bogdan Khmelnitski como jefe supremo. Khmelnitski encabezó en 1648 una contraofensiva que invadió numerosas ciudades de Polonia, donde los terratenientes así como los judíos y los sacerdotes católicos fueron asesinados. Derrotado, el rey de Polonia se vio obligado, en 1649, a aceptar el regreso de los rebeldes al parlamento, y el aumento del número de cosacos registrados y con derechos. Durante los siguientes tres años se produjeron nuevas rebeliones de cosacos, hasta que en 1652 éstos pidieron al monarca ruso, Alekséi Mijáilovich Romanov, protección contra los polacos; comienza así la primera guerra Ruso-polaca (1653-56), al término de la cual, con la victoria de las fuerzas del Romanov, Ucrania se convirtió en protectorado de Moscú. En 1657, a la muerte de Khmelnitski, su sucesor, Iván Vykhóvski, rechazó la protección rusa y pidió que Ucrania quedara unida al reino de Polonia-Lituania. Se desató la segunda guerra Ruso-polaca (1658-67), después de la cual Ucrania quedó dividida entre los dos países. Un año después, inconformes, los cosacos pidieron ayuda al sultán otomano Mohamed IV, a quien ofrecieron el país como protectorado. En 1672 los otomanos atacaron y ocuparon la porción polaca de Ucrania, en la que permanecieron hasta 1684, cuando Jan III Sobieski la recuperó. En 1708, el nuevo líder cosaco, Iván Mazeppa, se alió con Carlos II de Suecia y ambos se rebelaron contra Pedro *el Grande*, pero fueron derrotados un año después y los cosacos perdieron incluso el derecho de nombrar a sus líderes. En 1775 los rusos eliminaron los últimos focos de resistencia cosaca. En 1793 Ucrania quedó completamente bajo el dominio ruso. A mediados del siglo XIX se comenzaron a organizar grupos de nacionalistas ucranianos que pretendian sacudirse la tutela rusa, lo que desató medidas de represión y censura de parte de Moscú, que fueron en aumento hasta llegar, en 1905, a prohibirse el uso del idioma ucraniano y, en 1914, a declarar rusos a todos los habitantes de Ucrania. En 1917, al producirse la revolución rusa, Ucrania se declaró independiente, Moscú envió tropas y en 1918 estableció un gobierno soviético en Kiev al tiempo que Ucrania era invadida por alemanes y austriacos, quienes nombraron otro gobierno en la parte del territorio que dominaban. En 1919 el avance del Ejército Rojo fue total y Ucrania quedó integrada al poder bolchevique y en 1922 se convirtió en una de las repúblicas constituyentes de la Unión Soviética (☛). En 1991 el parlamento acordó crear un ejército nacional propio y el electorado votó por la independencia de la entonces Unión Soviética. México estableció relaciones diplomáticas con Ucrania en 1992.

Ucú ◆ Municipio de Yucatán situado al noroeste de Mérida y al suroeste de Progreso. Superficie: 192.89 km². Habitantes: 2,789, de los cuales 771 forman la población económicamente activa. Hablan maya 980 personas mayores de cinco años.

Ugalde Pérez, José ◆ n. en Querétaro, Qro., y m. en el DF (1883-1959). Profesor normalista especializado en física y química. Creador de un método para precipitar lluvias, que utilizó exitosamente en Querétaro, La Laguna y Tlaxcala.

Uganda, República de ◆ Nación de África situada en el centro-oeste del continente. Limita al norte con Sudán, al este con Kenia, al sur con Tanzania y Ruanda y al oeste con la República Democrática del Congo. Con Tanzania comparte el lago Victoria y con la República Democrática del Congo el Alberto. Superficie: 241,040 km². Habitantes: 20,554,000 (1998). Su capital es Kampala (773,463 habitantes en 1991).

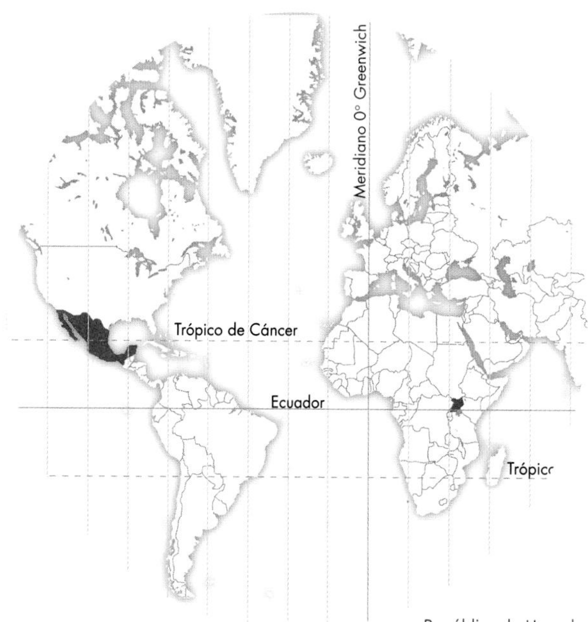

República de Uganda

El idioma oficial es el inglés y se utilizan numerosas lenguas locales. *Historia*: aun cuando los pobladores originales del actual territorio de Uganda fueron los bantúes, labradores y herreros llegados aproximadamente en el siglo I de nuestra era, las primeras huellas de una civilización urbana datan del siglo X y son las del reino de Bigo. Hacia el siglo XIII llegó a la región el pueblo bacwezi, de origen nilótico, conquistó a los bantúes y fundó el reino de Bunyoro, aunque al paso del tiempo los bantúes y los bacwezi se fusionaron cultural y racialmente. Entre los siglos XVII y XVIII se consolidó el reino de Bunyoro y surgieron los de Buganda, Busoga y Ankole; los cuatro estaban vinculados con el tráfico de esclavos pero tenían diferencias interregionales que llevaron a una polarización entre los reinos de Buganda (apoyado por los shirazis de Zanzíbar) y de Bunyoro (que contaba con el auxilio de los traficantes sudaneses). A principios del siglo XIX los shirazis fundaron el reino de Toro y retiraron su apoyo a Bunyoro, con lo que Buganda consiguió la hegemonía del actual territorio ugandés. En 1830 los mercaderes árabes entraron en contacto con Buganda e introdujeron la religión islámica. En 1862 llegaron los exploradores británicos que buscaban las fuentes del Nilo; el primero en arribar al lago Victoria fue

John Speke. En 1875 otro explorador, Henry Morton Stanley, visitó al rey Mutesa de Buganda y observó la aceptación que había tenido el islam. Debido a las advertencias que Stanley hizo en Europa, en 1877 empezaron a llegar misioneros católicos y protestantes. En 1888 la Compañía Imperial Británica de África del Este (IBEA) se estableció en la zona, pero respetó la división entre las regiones católica, protestante e islámica. En 1893 los ingleses convirtieron en protectorado a Buganda. En 1962 Uganda accedió a la independencia dentro de la Comunidad Británica. Un año después el país se declaró república y Edward Mutesa, llamado Mutesa II, fue elegido presidente. En 1966, el primer ministro Milton Obote dio un golpe de Estado incruento, impuso una nueva Constitución y se autonombró presidente. Mutesa, por su parte, se refugió en Inglaterra. El 25 de enero de 1971, Idi Amín dio un cuartelazo contra Obote. Al año siguiente, Amín ordenó una matanza de militares de las tribus langi y acholi; el ejército quedó constituido por miembros de la tribu de Amín y por mercenarios nubios. Amín rompió relaciones con Israel y expulsó del país a todos los asiáticos; los seguidores de Obote organizaron una invasión desde Tanzania, pero fueron derrotados. En 1973 todos los negocios extranjeros fueron expropiados sin pago de indemnización. Tres años después Inglaterra rompió relaciones con Uganda. En 1978 tropas ugandesas invadieron parte de Tanzania, pero el contraataque tanzano de 1979 llegó hasta Kampala; Amín huyó y en su lugar se estableció un Consejo Ejecutivo Nacional presidido por Yusuf Lule, sustituido poco después por Godfrey Binaisa. En 1980 Obote fue electo presidente de la república y un año más tarde surgieron las primeras manifestaciones de descontento popular contra Obote y estalló la violencia en Kampala. En 1983, unos 200,000 ugandeses se refugiaron en Sudán, Ruanda y Zaire. El 27 de julio de 1984 un consejo militar dirigido por Bazilio Olara Okello y Tito Okello depuso a Obote. Un año después se celebraron elecciones y Tito Okello fue electo presidente, con Abraham Waligo como primer ministro. Este gobierno fue derrocado en 1986 por el Movimiento de Resistencia Nacional, encabezado por Iueri Kaguta Museveni, quien asumió la presidencia.

UGARTE, GERZAYN ◆ n. en Terrenate, Tlax., y m. en el DF (1881-1955). Profesor rural. Inició su carrera política como secretario particular del gobernador tlaxcalteca Próspero Cahuantzi, pero más tarde apoyó el antirreeleccionismo y militó en el Partido Democrático. Cuando fue diputado federal por Tlaxcala (1911-13) perteneció al grupo renovador de la Cámara, por lo que el dictador Victoriano Huerta lo hizo arrestar. Liberado al triunfo de los constitucionalistas, dirigió el periódico *El Liberal* (1914) y fue secretario particular y miembro del Estado Mayor de Venustiano Carranza (1915). Diputado por el Distrito Federal al Congreso Constituyente de 1916-17, representante de México, con Luis Cabrera y Ernesto Hidalgo, al Congreso de Buenos Aires, que intentó lograr la paz mundial (1918), y ministro de México en Colombia, Ecuador y Venezuela. En mayo de 1920 acompañaba a Carranza cuando éste fue asesinado. Luego fue senador por Tlaxcala y se opuso a la firma de los Tratados de Bucareli. Participó en la rebelión escobarista (1929). Fue ministro plenipotenciario de México en Francia, subjefe de Inspección del Departamento de Tránsito (1934-40) y nuevamente senador de la República (1940-46). Autor de *¿Por qué volví a Tlaxcalantongo?*

UGARTE, JOSÉ DE ◆ n. y m. en la ciudad de México (1803-1877). Militar. A mediados de 1835, cuando era coronel, participó en la insurrección que derrocó al gobierno federalista de Michoacán. Más tarde formó parte de la Asamblea Departamental michoacana, el remedo centralista del Congreso Local, y en marzo de 1844, como era el más antiguo miembro de ese órgano, fue nombrado gobernador del estado (del 6 de marzo de 1844 al 5 de septiembre de 1846). Ascendido a general de división por Antonio López de Santa Anna, combatió a los estadounidenses en la guerra de 1847 y en 1852 se sumó al levantamiento del Plan de Jalisco. Fue gobernador y comandante militar de Michoacán durante el último gobierno de Santa Anna (del 2 de febrero de 1853 al 1 de junio de 1854) y combatió a los liberales durante la revolución de Ayutla (1854-55). Durante la intervención francesa y el imperio fue prefecto de Michoacán y director de policía de la ciudad de México.

UGARTE, JUAN DE ◆ n. en Honduras y m. en San Pablo, BC (1662-1730). Vivía en la Nueva España cuando, en 1679, ingresó en la Compañía de Jesús. Fue profesor del Colegio Máximo de San Pedro y San Pablo. En 1696 participó en la misión jesuita a Baja California, en la que también fueron Francisco Kino y Juan María Salvatierra. Al año siguiente estableció el Fondo Piadoso de las Californias. Hacia 1700 se le encomendó el cuidado de la misión de San Javier, en California. Luego de explorar la costa occidental de la península de Baja California en busca de un fondeadero para el galeón de Manila, en 1708 fundó las misiones de San José de Comondú y en 1714 la de San Miguel de Comondú. Superior de la California (1717), fundó las misiones de La Paz (1720) y de Guadalupe Huasinapí. Escribió una *Relación* de su viaje por el litoral californiano.

UGARTE, MAURICIO ◆ n. en San Antonio de Béjar, Texas (1803-¿1853?). Militar. Como cadete, en 1821 secundó el Plan de Iguala y desde ese año fijó su residencia en Chihuahua. En 1823 se unió al Plan de Casa Mata para derrocar al emperador Agustín de Iturbide; en ese año le correspondió transportar a la ciudad de México las urnas en las que se depositaron los restos de Miguel Hidalgo, Ignacio Allende, Ignacio Aldama y Mariano Jiménez. Combatió la invasión frustrada de Isidro Barradas en Tampico (1829), realizó varias campañas contra los apaches y en tres ocasiones fue jefe político y militar de Paso del Norte. En 1846, se levantó en armas y se autonombró gobernador de Chihuahua. Al año siguiente colaboró en la organización de la resistencia contra los invasores estadounidenses y combatió en Sacramento y en Villa de Rosales. Fue subinspector de colonias militares (1850) y contador mayor de Hacienda (1852).

Ugarte y Pagés, Eduardo ◆ n. en España y m. en el DF (1906-1955). Escritor. Licenciado en derecho por la Universidad Central de Madrid y en filosofía por la Universidad de Salamanca. Fue guionista de la Metro Goldwyn Mayer y director de diálogos en Hollywood (1930). De nuevo en España, perteneció a la compañía Filmófono y colaboró con Federico García Lorca en el teatro Universitario. Trabajó en la Institución Pedagógica de Extensión Universitaria en los Medios Rurales y en la Escuela Dramática para Estudiantes de Teatro. Durante la guerra civil española fue agregado a la embajada en Francia y representante en el Congreso Internacional de Teatro. Exiliado en México en 1939, fue director del Departamento Literario de Clasa Films Mundiales (1943), coguionista de *La monja Alférez* de Emilio Gómez Muriel (1944) y realizador de *Bésame mucho* (1944) y *Cautiva del pasado* (1952), entre otras. También trabajó en Cuba. Autor de *Rutas del teatro* (1953). En 1928 ganó un primer premio por la obra teatral *De la noche a la mañana*, publicada en Nueva York y estrenada en España, Portugal e Inglaterra.

Ugarte y Sarabia, Agustín de ◆ n. en España y m. en Perú (?- 1650). Fue obispo de Chiapas (1628-30), de Guatemala (1630-41), de Arequipa (1641) y de Quito.

Ugarte Vizcaíno, Salvador ◆ n. en Guadalajara, Jal., y m. en el DF (1880-1962). Hizo estudios de ingeniería. Se dedicó a la industria eléctrica y estableció una casa de cambios. En 1926 incorporó su negocio al Banco Nacional de México y fue designado gerente de la casa matriz de esa institución. En 1932 fundó el Banco de Comercio y fue su director general hasta 1958, cuando se convirtió en presidente del consejo y consejero delegado del mismo. En 1949 promovió una colecta nacional destinada a financiar un monumento a Juan de Zumárraga, que se halla en Durango, España. Conformó una biblioteca de crónicas mexicanas del siglo XVI y textos sobre lenguas indígenas que donó al Instituto Tecnológico de Monterrey. Autor de *El vocabulario manual de las lenguas castellana y mexicana, compuesto por D. Pedro de Arenas* (1936), *Notas de bibliografía mexicana* (1943), *Catálogo de obras escritas en lenguas indígenas de México o que tratan de ellas* (1954) y dos volúmenes de *Poesías* (1959). Fue miembro de la Academia de Historia y Geografía de México.

Uhse, Bodo ◆ n. en Alemania (1904). Hijo de un oficial alemán muerto en la primera guerra mundial. En su juventud se afilió al partido nazi, pero pronto se desengañó y militó en organizaciones antifascistas. Cuando Hitler llegó al poder se refugió en Francia. En 1936, en España, se unió a las brigadas internacionales en defensa de la República. Enfermo, en 1938 volvió a Francia, donde trabajó para la recién fundada organización de ayuda a los ex combatientes alemanes y austriacos del ejército republicano español. Invitado por Joseph W. Angell, hijo de un ex rector de Yale, se instaló en Nueva York, donde continuó su trabajo de apoyo a los brigadistas alemanes. Del 2 al 4 de junio de 1939 participó con Ludwig Renn (☛) en el congreso de la League of American Writers; ambos trataron infructuosamente de crear en Estados Unidos un centro para el exilio antifascista alemán. En diciembre de ese año las autoridades estadounidenses lo urgieron para que abandonara el país antes del 3 de febrero de 1940. En marzo obtuvo visa mexicana y, una vez en la ciudad de México, se alojó en una casa alquilada por los alemanes antifascistas en Tacuba y se incorporó a los trabajos de la Liga pro Cultura Alemana, que le encomendó la obtención de visas mexicanas y coordinar la ayuda económica para los antifascistas alemanes amenazados en Francia. Simultáneamente desarrolló su labor literaria y dio algunos cursos y conferencias en el IPN, aunque sobrevivía gracias al apoyo solidario de la Liga pro Cultura Alemana, la League of American Writers y el Joint Antifascist Refugee Committee, de Nueva York. En octubre de 1941 fue cofundador (con Anna Seghers, Egon Erwin Kisch y Rudolf Feistmann) del Club Enrique Heine, de intelectuales antifascistas germanoparlantes, de cuya presidencia fue miembro (1941-46). Cofundador del Movimiento Alemania Libre (1942) y redactor de su órgano, *Alemania Libre*, así como codirector de la editorial El Libro Libre (1942-46). Coautor de *El libro negro. Antología del terror y la resistencia* (1943). Autor de *Nosotros, los hijos*, *Ataque contra Wyst* y *Teniente Bertram* (1944). Volvió a su país en 1948.

Uhthoff, Enrique ◆ n. y m. en el DF (1887-1950). Periodista y escritor. Después de la decena trágica se refugió en Cuba y España. Regresó a México hacia 1939. Autor de las piezas de teatro *Pancho macho* (estrenada en Madrid, 1930), *Rayo en la encina* (Madrid, 1937), *La niña Lupe* (opereta estrenada en el Teatro Esperanza Iris, 1946), *Amar, eso es todo* (1949), *Mi compañero el gallo* y *Nopal*.

Uirauanecha ◆ Deidades purépechas asignadas al sur o a la parte izquierda del mundo, también llamados dioses de la tierra caliente, cuyo nombre significa "Conejos echados". Aún se les rinde culto en la región del Bajío, principalmente durante las festividades del primero de noviembre. Sus correspondientes nahuas eran los centzontotochtin.

Ulacia, Manuel ◆ n. en el DF (1954). Escritor. Arquitecto titulado en la UNAM, maestro y doctor en letras hispánicas por la Universidad de Yale. Ha sido profesor de ambas instituciones. Codirector y editor fundador de *El Zaguán*. Ha colaborado en *Vuelta*, *Revista de la Universidad de México*, *Revista Mexicana de Cultura*, *Cambio 16* y *Diálogos*, así

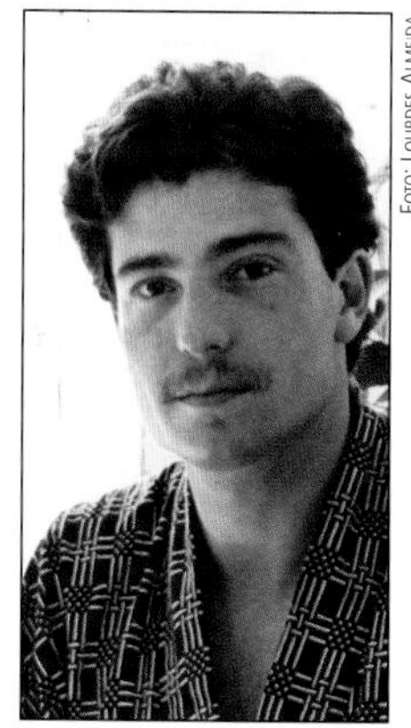
Foto: Lourdes Almeida

Manuel Ulacia

como en los diarios: *El Día*, *Excélsior*, *El Nacional* y *unomásuno*. Coautor, con Eduardo Milán, de *Obra poética de Haroldo de Campos* (1987); con Víctor Manuel Mendiola y José María Espinasa de *La sirena en el espejo* (1990); y con Mendiola y Nedda G. de Anhalt de *La fiesta innombrable: trece poetas cubanos* (1992). Autor de ensayo *Luis Cernuda: escritura, cuerpo y deseo* (1986); y de poesía: *La materia como ofrenda* (1980), *El río y la piedra* (1989) y *Origami para un día de lluvia* (1990). Becario del Centro Mexicano de Escritores (1977-78).

ULISES ◆ Revista literaria bimestral fundada en abril de 1927 por Salvador Novo y Xavier Villaurrutia. Aparecieron seis números, el último en febrero de 1928. En su nómina de colaboradores figuraron, entre otros, José Gorostiza, Gilberto Owen, Julio Castellanos, Manuel Rodríguez Lozano y los propios fundadores. A partir de esta publicación se gestó el Teatro de Ulises y fue el antecedente de la revista *Contemporáneos*.

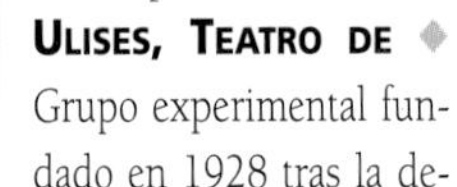

ULISES Revista de Curiosidad y Crítica
EDITORES, SALVADOR NOVO Y XAVIER VILLAURRUTIA
NUM. 1 MAYO 1927 – MEXICO TOMO I

SUMARIO

MAX JACOB: Poesías.
MAXIMO BONTEMPELLI: Sobre una locomotora.
SALVADOR NOVO: Espejo.
GILBERTO OWEN: Desvelo.
SAMUEL RAMOS: Antonio Caso.

NOTAS:
JORGE CUESTA: La pintura de Agustín Lazo.
XAVIER VILLAURRUTIA: Oaxaca, de Manuel Toussaint.
GILBERTO OWEN: Pájaro Pinto, de Antonio Espina.
JORGE CUESTA: Reflejos, de Xavier Villaurrutia.
EL CURIOSO IMPERTINENTE:
Jacob, Bontempelli, Murand, Dos Passos, Díaz Mirón, etc.
REPRODUCCIONES de Agustín Lazo.

REDACCION Y ADMINISTRACION
BRASIL 42-10 – MEXICO, D. F.

CONDICIONES – Un Cuaderno .... $ 0.50
Subscripción a 6 números 2.50
" a 12 " 5.00
(moneda mexicana)

Número uno de la revista *Ulises*

ULISES, TEATRO DE ◆ Grupo experimental fundado en 1928 tras la desaparición de la revista literaria *Ulises*, por Xavier Villaurrutia, Salvador Novo y Gilberto Owen, entre otros, auspiciados por Antonieta Rivas Mercado, quien cedió para la primera temporada del grupo teatral un salón de su casa en el número 42 de la calle de Mesones, en la ciudad de México. De acuerdo con sus integrantes, el de Ulises pretendía ser "el pequeño teatro experimental adonde se representen obras nuevas por nuevos actores no profesionales". La segunda y última temporada del grupo experimental (1929) tuvo lugar en el local del Teatro Virginia Fábregas. El Teatro de Ulises tradujo y representó obras de Paul Claudel, Roger Marx, Charles Vildrac, Eugene O'Neill y Lord Dunsany, entre otros; los actores, directores y escenógrafos fueron los mismos integrantes del grupo: Villaurrutia, Novo, Owen, Roberto Montenegro, Manuel Rodríguez Lozano, Julio Castellanos, Isabela Corona, Agustín Lazo y Clementina Otero.

Salvador Novo, integrante del grupo Teatro de Ulises

Foto: Fondo Editorial Grupo Azabache

Fortaleza de San Juan de Ulúa, Veracruz

ULLOA, BERTA ◆ n. en la ciudad de México (1927). Su nombre completo es Berta Guadalupe Ulloa Ortiz. Maestra en historia de México por la UNAM (1963). Ha sido directora del Centro de Documentación del Museo Nacional de Historia (1951-57) y profesora-investigadora (1957-), directora de la Biblioteca (1966), coordinadora académica (1981-82) y directora (1983-88) del Centro de Estudios Históricos de El Colegio de México. Coautora de *Así fue la revolución mexicana* (1985). Autora de *La revolución mexicana a través del archivo de la Secretaría de Relaciones Exteriores* (1963), *Revolución mexicana. 1910-1920* (1963 y 1985), *La revolución intervenida. Relaciones diplomáticas entre México y Estados Unidos. 1910-1914* (1971 y 1997), *La lucha armada. 1911-1920* (1976), *La revolución escindida* (1979), *La encrucijada de 1915* (1979), *La Constitución de 1917* (1983), del tomo IV de *De la República restaurada a la revolución. 1862-1921* (1980), de *Veracruz, capital de la nación. 1914-1915* (1986), *La revolución más allá del Bravo. Guía de documentos relativos a México en archivos de EUA 1900-48* (1991), *La lucha revolucionaria, 1910-1917* (1991) y *Una semblanza de don Daniel Cosío Villegas* (en prensa). Medalla Constituyentes 1917 de la Asociación de Hijos de Diputados Constituyentes (1997).

Ejemplar de la revista *Ultramar*

ULLOA CARREÓN, GUILLERMO ◆ n. en Zacatecas (1957). Licenciado en derecho. Realizó sus estudios profesionales en la Universidad Autónoma de Zacatecas. Posteriormente realizó un posgrado sobre economía laboral y formación política en Washington DC. Pertenece al PRI desde 1972, en el que ha participado como secretario general de la Juventud Popular; secretario general del Movimiento Nacional de la Juventud Revolucionaria; secretario suplente de Acción Obrera; secretario de Organización y presidente del CDE del PRI en Zacatecas. Dentro de la administración pública, se ha desempeñado como auxiliar de la Secretaría Particular de Gobierno del Estado; subdelegado de la Comisión Coordinadora del Servicio Social de Instituciones de Educación Superior, y coordinador del Programa de Vivienda de Infonavit en el estado. Ha sido diputado federal suplente; diputado local al Congreso del Estado de Zacatecas y senador de la República (1994-2000).

Ulloa y Chávez, Antonio de ◆ n. en España y m. ¿en Guadalajara, Jal.? (¿1600?-1661). Doctor en cánones por la Universidad de Salamanca. Fue rector de la Real y Pontificia Universidad de México de noviembre de 1654 a mayo de 1655, cuando fue designado miembro de la Audiencia de México y gobernador de Nueva Galicia (1655-1661).

Ultramar ◆ Revista literaria fundada por los exiliados españoles Juan Rejano y Miguel Prieto, director y director artístico, respectivamente, y en la que Daniel Tapia figuró como secretario de redacción. La publicación sólo apareció una vez, en junio de 1947.

Ulúa, San Juan de ◆ Islote de Veracruz, unido a tierra firme mediante un rompeolas construido en 1902. Se encuentra frente al puerto de Veracruz y en él fue erigida en el virreinato una fortaleza. Durante muchos años fue el punto de desembarque de las naves provenientes de España, función de la que fue desplazada al construirse el muelle de Veracruz, y hasta principios del siglo XX fue también una prisión en la que fueron encarcelados muchos de los precursores y protagonistas de la independencia y de la revolución. Fray Servando Teresa de Mier, Lorenzo de Zavala, Benito Juárez, Francisco Zarco, Manuel M. Diéguez y Esteban Baca Calderón son algunos de los que, por sus ideas políticas, estuvieron recluidos en las "tinajas" de Ulúa, celdas llamadas así por su reducido tamaño y por estar siempre inundadas. Ulúa fue el último reducto de España en territorio mexicano. La fortaleza estuvo dominada sucesivamente por los comandantes españoles José Dávila, Francisco Lemour y José Coppinger, quienes durante cuatro años mantuvieron un bombardeo constante pero inofensivo sobre el puerto de Veracruz. En 1825, el presidente Guadalupe Victoria ordenó la toma de San Juan de Ulúa, lo que se logró el 18 de noviembre de ese año con una flotilla adquirida a Inglaterra y comandada por Pedro Sáinz de Baranda. En 1838, al ocurrir la guerra de los Pasteles, la fortaleza fue brevemente ocupada por la armada francesa. Más tarde fue utilizada como sede de los poderes federales por los presidentes Benito Juárez y Venustiano Carranza, cuando debieron abandonar la ciudad de México. Una vez concluida la revolución, la fortaleza fue remozada y convertida en museo y monumento histórico.

Umán ◆ Municipio de Yucatán situado en el occidente del estado, al suroeste de Mérida y al noroeste de Ticul. Superficie: 434.30 km². Habitantes: 45,892, de los cuales 12,006 forman la población económicamente activa. Hablan alguna lengua indígena 12,209 personas mayores de cinco años (maya 12,201), de las cuales son monolingües 258. En su jurisdicción hay numerosas desfibradoras y limpiadoras de henequén.

Umbert Santos, Luis ◆ n. en Cataluña, España, y m. ¿en el DF? (1883-?). Periodista y editor. Fue interventor del Consejo de Sanidad de Guerra. Vino a México a la caída de la República española (1939). Fue auditor, colaborador de *El Monitor Masónico* y *Mundo Masónico* de La Habana y director de la Editorial Humanidad. Autor de *Fichero piadoso* (1945) y *Cincuenta lecciones de cultura masónica* (1945).

Unda Manterola, Adolfo ◆ n. en la ciudad de México (1907). Ortodoncista. Pionero del frontenis. A los ocho años de edad comenzó a jugar con pelotas de tenis, a las que les quitaba el forro para que rebotaran mejor en la pared. En 1930, ya instituido el frontenis, ganó los primeros Juegos de la Revolución, como pareja de Paco Buj. Coautor del primer reglamento de frontenis. Miembro del Club Rotario desde 1938.

UNESCO ◆ ☛ *Organización de las Naciones Unidas para la Educación, la Ciencia y la Cultura.*

Unidad de Izquierda Comunista ◆ Organización política fundada en septiembre de 1973 por un grupo de expulsados del Partido Comunista Mexicano (☛), dirigido por Manuel Terrazas. Antes se llamó Asamblea Permanente del Partido Comunista Mexicano. Obtuvo su registro en la Secretaría de Gobernación el 28 de noviembre de 1978, ya con el nombre de Unidad de Izquierda Comunista. En 1979 se alió con el Partido Socialista de los Trabajadores y en 1987 se fusionó con otras organizaciones para formar el Partido Mexicano Socialista.

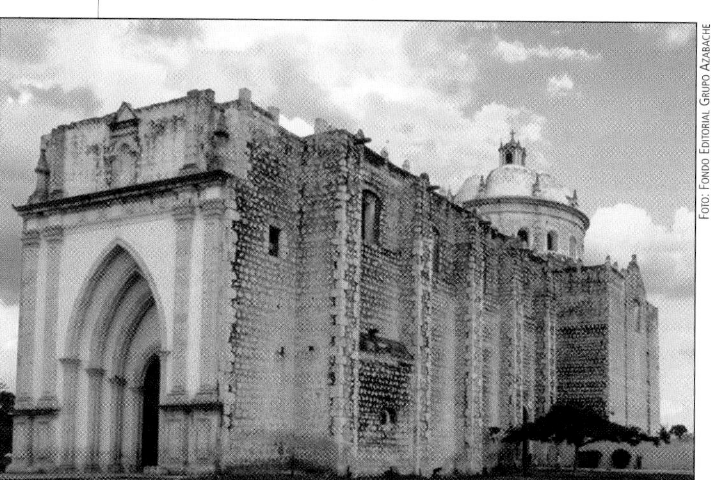

Foto: Fondo Editorial Grupo Azabache

Iglesia de San Francisco de Asís de Umán, Yucatán

Unión, La ◆ Cabecera municipal del municipio guerrerense Unión de Isidoro Montes de Oca (☛).

Unión Continental ◆ Confederación creada por los gobiernos de Perú, Chile y Ecuador en 1861, en Santiago de Chile. México se incorporó a ella el 11 de junio de 1862, gracias a la acción del embajador peruano ante el gobierno de Benito Juárez, Manuel Nicolás Corpancho. De acuerdo con el tratado firmado por México, las cuatro naciones se comprometían a prestarse ayuda militar mutua y las expediciones agresoras serían "reputadas y tratadas como expediciones piratas". Los ciudadanos mexicanos, peruanos, chilenos y ecuatorianos recibirían "tratamiento de nacionales" en cualquiera de las otras naciones; los barcos de estos países gozarían "de las mismas exenciones, franquicias y concesiones que las naves nacionales"; la correspondencia emitida en los cuatro países "circulará libremente (.) y no se cobrará por ella ningún derecho o impuesto", las sentencias emitidas por los tribunales de una nación "surtirán en los territorios de cualquiera de las otras los mismos efectos que los otorgados en su propio territorio" y los representantes diplomáticos de cada país "prestarán a los ciudadanos o naturales de las otras (.) la misma protección que a sus nacionales". Además, las partes se comprometían a "unir sus esfuerzos para la difusión de la enseñanza primaria y de los conocimientos útiles" y a impulsar la adopción de "un sistema uniforme en monedas (.) y un sistema uniforme de pesas y medidas". Para la consolidación y vigilancia del tratado, los países contratantes se comprometían a crear un "Congreso de Plenipotenciarios" que "en ningún caso y por ningún motivo puede tomar como materia de sus deliberaciones los disturbios intestinos, movimientos o agitaciones interiores de los diversos Estados de la Unión".

Unión de Colonias Populares del Valle de México ◆ Su primer antecedente se remonta a 1968, cuando el movimiento estudiantil estableció nexos con las colonias populares de la ciudad de México, que, junto con algunos sindicatos independientes, integraron en 1973 el Frente Popular Independiente (FPI) en el que participaban, entre otras, las colonias San Agustín de Ecatepec, Santo Domingo de los Reyes, Cerro del Judío, Padierna y el Movimiento Restaurador de Colonos de Nezahualcóyotl. Este frente, por cierto, sin éxito pero adelantándose a lo que estaba por venir, postuló candidatos populares independientes para las elecciones de 1976. Año con año la UCP ha ido dejando constancia de sus análisis, principios, trayectoria y actitud responsable de lucha social.

Unión de Cronistas de Teatro y Música ◆ Organización creada el 8 de enero de 1938 con el nombre de Asociación de Cronistas de Espectáculos Teatrales y Musicales. Entre sus fundadores estuvieron Francisco Monterde, Víctor Reyes, Gerónimo Baqueiro Foster, Armando de Maria y Campos, José Barros Sierra, Salomón Kahan, Manuel Horta, Alfonso de Icaza, Xavier Villaurrutia, Ramón García, José Morales Esteves y José F. Elizondo.

Unión General de Obreros y Campesinos de México ◆ Organización fundada con la participación del Sindicato de Trabajadores Petroleros de la República Mexicana, el Sindicato de Trabajadores Minero-metalúrgicos y Similares de la República Mexicana y la Alianza de Obreros y Campesinos de México, reunidos en el Congreso Nacional de Unidad Obrera y Campesina, que se celebró del 20 al 22 de junio de 1949 en la ciudad de México. En sus inicios contó con 300,000 miembros.

Unión Hidalgo ◆ Municipio de Oaxaca situado en el oriente del estado, al este-noreste de Juchitán de Zaragoza y al norte de la laguna Superior. Superficie: 132.69 km^2. Habitantes: 12,910, de los cuales 2,991 forman la población económicamente activa. Hablan alguna lengua indígena 8,363 personas (zapoteco 8,355), de las cuales 386 son monolingües.

Unión de Iglesias Independientes ◆ ☛ *Pentecostales*.

Unión de Isidoro Montes de Oca ◆ Municipio de Guerrero situado en el extremo occidental de la entidad, al noroeste de Zihuatanejo, en el litoral del océano Pacífico y en los límites con Michoacán, estado del que lo separa el río Balsas. Superficie: 1,142 km^2. Habitantes: 27,515, de los cuales 6,309 forman la población económicamente activa. Hablan alguna lengua indígena 56 personas mayores de cinco años. Su cabecera municipal es La Unión.

Unión Juárez ◆ Municipio de Chiapas situado en el sur del estado, al noreste y próximo a Tapachula, en la frontera con Guatemala. Superficie: 72 km^2. Habitantes: 12,835, de los cuales 3,403 forman la población económicamente

Ilustración de Santiago Ortega

Plaza cívica de La Unión, cabecera municipal de Unión de Isidoro Montes de Oca, Guerrero activa. Hablan alguna lengua indígena 231 personas mayores de cinco años (mame 229). En la jurisdicción se encuentra el volcán Tacaná (☛) y la poza de Muxbal.

UNIÓN LIBERAL ◆ Organismo político creado con la anuencia de Porfirio Díaz, para sustentar su reelección de 1892. Sin ocultar que se identificaban con las tesis de la burguesía europea de fines del siglo XIX, los dirigentes de esta formación se apegaron al positivismo para darle fundamentos "científicos" al gobierno de Díaz. La organización, que fue comúnmente llamada Partido Científico (☛), se convirtió en la fuerza política más importante de esos años. Luego del fraudulento triunfo porfirista de 1892, el poder de la Unión Liberal aumentó y sus miembros, "los científicos", controlaron rápidamente casi la totalidad de las finanzas y de la enseñanza, así como importantes inversiones en la agricultura y en la industria.

UNIÓN MINERA MEXICANA ◆ Organización gremial fundada en julio de 1911 por trabajadores mineros de la zona carbonífera de Coahuila. Combatió la rebelión orozquista en 1912, para lo cual formó el Batallón Mariano Escobedo, disuelto por Victoriano Huerta. En 1915 apoyó la candidatura de Gustavo Espinosa Mireles a la gubernatura de Coahuila. Participó en el Congreso Obrero de Saltillo, en el que se fundó la CROM, de la cual fue, en sus inicios, la organización afiliada más numerosa.

UNIÓN MUTUA DE TEJEDORES DEL DISTRITO DE TLALPAN ◆ Organización obrera creada el 27 de enero de 1868 con trabajadores de La Fama Montañesa, La Abeja y otras fábricas. El 8 de julio de 1868 los obreros de La Fama iniciaron una huelga y el día 9 los secundaron los trabajadores de otras empresas. Los huelguistas pedían mejor material, respeto a los trabajadores, jornada máxima de 12 horas para las obreras y pago para el trabajo infantil por cuenta del patrón. Benito Juárez intervino en favor de los obreros y los patrones aceptaron entonces sus demandas. En 1873, la Unión había quedado reducida a los trabajadores de La Fama Montañesa y decidió convocar a una asamblea, el 5 de febrero, a todos los obreros textiles del valle de México, quienes acordaron constituir la Unión de Resistencia de Tejedores del Valle de México (☛), coordinada por un consejo con delegados de fábrica que elegirían una mesa directiva con un presidente, un secretario y un tesorero.

UNIÓN NACIONAL SINARQUISTA ◆ Organización política fundada en León, Gto., el 23 de mayo de 1937. Sus antecedentes más importantes fueron las agrupaciones católicas Base (☛) y Legión (☛), así como la Sociedad de Empleados y Obreros Nuevo México, de León, y el Círculo de Estudios Vasco de Quiroga, grupo estudiantil de Morelia. Entre los 137 fundadores figuraron José Ángel Urquiza, a quien se considera su principal promotor, José Trueba Olivares, su primer jefe nacional; Manuel Zermeño, subjefe, y Antonio Trueba Olivares. Salvador Abascal ingresó en junio. El nazi Helmut Oscar Schreiter fue, según ciertas fuentes, uno de los fundadores de la UNS, en tanto que para otras era una suerte de asesor de los dirigentes en la primera etapa. Hugh G. Campbell, en *La derecha radical en México*, afirma que había un liderazgo secreto de la unión que era simultáneamente el alto mando de Base, que a su vez estaba controlado por jerarquía católica. Algunos autores, convencidos del carácter germanófilo de la organización, afirman que el nombre de ésta fue adoptado para que la sigla fuera UNS, palabra que en aleman significa "nosotros". La unión mantenía relaciones con la Falange Española y se inspiró en la estructura militarizada del Partido Nacional Socialista de Alemania. Otras semejanzas con las organizaciones fascistas europeas eran su anticomunismo, la obediencia incondicional a los jefes, el saludo con el brazo extendido, el uso de uniformes militares y el brazalete con la insignia sinarquista. En 1944 Abascal escribió que la UNS pugnaba por la instauración de un "orden social cristiano" en el que "es necesario que Cristo gobierne en las leyes, en los palacios de gobierno, en los hogares, en las escuelas, en los medios de difusión de ideas: libros, periódicos, cine, radio; en el vestir, en la calle, en los comercios, en las fábricas y en el campo". A juicio del mismo autor, "El catolicismo es el padre y la esencia de México; pero en relación a los hombres, el primer padre de la patria es Hernán Cortés". México, para Abascal, ha estado "evidentemente dirigido por la masonería, que es el instrumento oculto en manos fundamentalmente de los judíos norteamericanos". Juárez representa a "los indígenas astutos, traicioneros y sirvientes de las logias y de los intereses norteamericanos". Otro autor de la misma filiación afirma que "el comunismo

FOTO: HEMEROTECA NACIONAL

Salvador Abascal, líder de la Unión Nacional Sinarquista

FOTO: HEMEROTECA NACIONAL

Propaganda de la Unión Nacional Sinarquista en 1943

soviético y el capitalismo norteamericano son manifestaciones de la misma revolución, cuyo cuerpo se localiza en el judaísmo fanático, y cuyos frutos surgieron de la Revolución Francesa, de la Revolución Mexicana y de la Revolución Rusa". En 1941, ante las acusaciones de germanofilia, el entonces jefe nacional, Manuel Torres Bueno, declaró: "Alemania basa sus pretensiones en una superioridad y predominio racial, en la unidad y pureza de la raza aria; este principio, aparte de ser científicamente falso, es antinatural y completamente inaplicable al pueblo de México. México es una nación mestiza". Abascal, por su parte, afirmó: "Hitler es un enemigo de Dios; su teoría es bárbara, anticristiana y fundamentalmente falsa". Los miembros de la unión se aglutinaban en grupos de 30 hombres; tres de estos grupos y su personal formaban una centuria y tres de éstas una compañía. Un *Folleto para jefes* establecía: "No debe haber discusiones en las asambleas; todas las decisiones las debe tomar el jefe. La regla general y absoluta es que ningún asunto debe ser sujeto a votación en la asamblea". En el primer año de su existencia logró reclutar a 5,000 miembros. En junio de 1938 inició la publicación de su órgano, *Sinarquismo*. En mayo de 1938 ya eran 10,000 militantes y un año después llegaban a 30,000. En 1938 Manuel Zermeño asumió la jefatura nacional y Abascal quedó como subjefe. Como el primero fuera herido en Tepic, Abascal tomó el mando efectivo de la organización en enero de 1939 y asumió formalmente la jefatura en agosto de 1940. Hizo aumentar el número de miembros ("soldados", como solían decir los jefes) a 250,000 en julio de 1940 y, al retirarse del cargo en diciembre de 1941, la UNS contaba con más de medio millón de militantes. En abril de 1938 fue asesinado José Antonio Urquiza, a quien desde entonces se llamó *El Ausente*. Los sinarquistas muertos por la represión gubernamental fueron 17 en 1939, 38 en 1940 y 32 en 1941. Al dejar Abascal la jefatura de la unión, a fines de 1941, encabezó un proyecto de colonización en Baja California, en tanto que José Trueba Olivares hizo lo mismo en Sonora. En la dirección de la UNS quedó Manuel Torres Bueno, quien inició un viraje hacia posiciones moderadas, lo que pudo advertirse cuando manifestó su apoyo al presidente Manuel Ávila Camacho, tanto en política exterior como en la "trascendental labor de incrementar nuestra producción nacional". En materia internacional, la tradicional yancofobia sinarquista se abandonó en marzo de 1942, cuando se anunció el interés de la UNS por cooperar con Estados Unidos en un programa para elevar el nivel de vida en Latinoamérica y contrarrestar la propaganda comunista. Cuando México declaró la guerra a los países del eje, no sin reticencias, la unión llamó a sus miembros a combatir a quienes trabajaban en favor de las potencias totalitarias y contra las democracias. A mediados de 1943 fue destituido de la dirección de *El Sinarquista* Alfonso Trueba, miembro del ala radical, y por ésta y otras razones Abascal anunció internamente que se separaba de la organización y el 31 de marzo de 1944 se vio obligado a entregar la jefatura de la colonia María Auxiliadora que había fundado en Baja California. En mayo, después de que se hizo pública su baja de la UNS, declaró a un periódico que el sinarquismo de entonces era un fraude y reanudó sus ataques a Estados Unidos, que eran "la verdadera amenaza", aun peor que el comunismo y la Unión Soviética. Detrás de Abascal salieron Rubén Mendoza y Alfonso Trueba Olivares, miembros de la dirección nacional, y José Trueba Olivares, el hombre más popular de la UNS después de Abascal. El 22 de julio de 1944 se acusó en *El Sinarquista* al presidente Ávila Camacho de permitir que avanzaran los intentos de sovietizar a la nación y se llamó al ejército para defender a la patria del comunismo. En las semanas siguientes el gobierno desató una de las mayores oleadas represivas contra la UNS, que la llevaron a replegarse al mayor clandestinaje, pues se prohibió la circulación de *El Sinarquista* y en ocho estados de la República se impidió toda reunión de sus afiliados. En octubre del mismo año, el alto mando decidió aceptar la renuncia a la jefatura que Torres Bueno había presentado meses antes. Sin embargo, Torres Bueno se negó a entregar el cargo. Como respuesta, la dirección secreta nombró jefe nacional a Carlos Athié Carrasco, conocido sólo en el círculo dirigente. Entre 1945 y 1946 hubo dos grupos que se ostentaban como Unión Nacional Sinarquista, el de

Manifestación de la Unión Nacional Sinarquista en el Hemiciclo a Juárez, en la ciudad de México

Torres Bueno, que pretendía ingresar a la política electoral, y el de Athié, cuya actividad estaba centrada en labores sociales, como la formación de cooperativas de consumo y la alfabetización. El primero siguió editando *El Sinarquista*, pese a la prohibición gubernamental, y la facción de Athié editó un *Boletín de Información*. Al levantarse la prohibición gubernamental, en junio de 1945, se editaron sendos *Sinarquistas*. El nombre del periódico motivó un litigio jurídico que llegó a la Suprema Corte, la que falló en favor de la facción de Athié, por lo que el grupo de Torres Bueno tuvo que sacar un nuevo órgano, al que llamó *Orden*, igual que la revista que había publicado la UNS entre 1942 y 1944. Signo del acercamiento a las esferas oficiales fue el encabezado con que saludó el nuevo periódico al presidente entrante: "Alemán incorpora a su gobierno las ideas sociales y políticas del sinarquismo". Por su parte, los abascalistas, quienes antes predicaban que "ningún asunto debe ser sujeto a votación de la asamblea", desconocieron a los dos presuntos dirigentes y convocaron a una reunión nacional para elegir los líderes capaces de cohesionar a la unión. Este intento fracasó por la renuencia de Abascal a participar en estas actividades. En mayo de 1945, Torres Bueno anunció que cedía la jefatura nacional a Gildardo González Sánchez, uno de sus seguidores más cercanos. En 1946 se reformaron los estatutos y el nombramiento de jefe nacional dejó de ser atribución del antecesor, para convertirse en facultad de la junta directiva. En febrero de ese año se anunció, contraviniendo la tradición, que el sinarquismo crearía un partido político. Éste se fundó el 23 de marzo del mismo año y adoptó el nombre de Partido Fuerza Popular. El 13 de mayo se le concedió el registro electoral y presentó seis candidatos a senadores y 38 a diputados, varios de ellos miembros del PAN, con lo que se inició un periodo de colaboración entre el sinarquismo y Acción Nacional. Fuerza Popular sólo triunfó en un distrito, pero poco después este diputado desertó de la Unión Nacional Sinarquista y se mostró sumiso ante el PRI. En abril de 1947 Luis Martínez Narezo sucedió en la jefatura nacional a González Sánchez, quien paulatinamente retomó las posiciones radicales de los fundadores, se distanció del gobierno y volvió al antiyanquismo tradicional. Otro éxito de Martínez Narezo fue lograr el retorno de Zermeño a la UNS y la reconciliación con Abascal, pese a que éste se negó a volver al activismo. En la novena Junta de Jefes, celebrada en Córdoba en diciembre, fueron oradores algunos connotados hispanistas y yancófobos como el citado Abascal, Jesús Guisa y Acevedo, José Vasconcelos y Alfonso Junco. El 19 de diciembre de 1948, los sinarquistas realizaron un mitin en el Hemiciclo a Juárez, en el que acusaron al Benemérito de "robar iglesias" e inflamados por los oradores, varios de los presentes llegaron a la parte superior del monumento, donde cubrieron con una capucha la cabeza del Juárez de mármol. Este hecho desató una campaña de desplegados periodísticos, declaraciones de los sectores gobiernistas y de izquierda, así como diversos actos "de desagravio" por el sacrilegio cívico. Como consecuencia, el 28 de enero de 1949, la Secretaría de Gobernación canceló el registro electoral de Fuerza Popular. De este modo, el sinarquismo, que entonces contaba con unos 100,000 miembros, perdió su "brazo político". El 10 de octubre de 1954, la UNS realizó un mitin en el que se llamó a los héroes nacionales "caterva de bellacos", lo que motivó una nueva avalancha de protestas. La unión, decaída durante el resto de los años cincuenta, cobró cierta notoriedad después del triunfo de la revolución cubana, cuando se realizó una larga e intensa campaña bajo el lema "Cristianismo sí, comunismo no". Después de otro periodo de postración, el sinarquismo inició en 1971 los trabajos de organización de otro "brazo político", el Partido Demócrata Mexicano (☛). Fueron sus principales promotores Ignacio González Gollaz, Baltazar Ignacio Valadés, Juan Aguilera Azpeitia y Leonardo Durán Juárez, quienes culminaron sus esfuerzos en 1975, al constituir formalmente el partido, que obtuvo registro electoral en 1978 y lo perdió en 1988, al no alcanzar el 1.5 por ciento de la votación total. De 1986 a 1990, el dirigente nacional de la Unión Nacional Sinarquista fue Víctor Atilano Gómez, quien sucedió a Baltazar Ignacio Valadés Montoya. En abril de 1990 se nombró jefe nacional de la UNS a José Valadés Montoya. El PDM recuperó el registro y en 1994 tuvo como candidato a la Presidencia al ex panista y ex miembro del Partido de Foro Doctrinario y Democrático, Pablo Emilio Madero. En 1996, Clemente Gutiérrez Pérez fue elegido jefe nacional de la unión. En la elección de jefe de gobierno del DF de 1997, el candidato fue Baltazar Ignacio Valadés Montoya, quien quedó en último sitio y el PDM fue disuelto el 29 de marzo de 1998. Sus militantes constituyeron en 1998 el Partido Alianza Social (☛), actual heredero de la tradición sinarquista. En el primer Consejo Nacional del PAS están Pablo Emilio Madero, Adalberto Rosas, Ignacio González Gollaz, Roberto Claderón, Víctor Atilano Gómez, Baltazar Ignacio Valadés Montoya y José Antonio Calderón Cardoso. Jesús Ruiz Munilla aparecía como director en 1999.

Unión de los Obreros, La ◆ Periódico "escrito por varios obreros mexicanos y dedicado exclusivamente a defender los derechos de su clase y a procurar la protección al trabajo". Lo dirigió Vicente S. Reyes, antiguo lerdista que se incorporó al porfirismo. Según *El Hijo del Trabajo* recibía del gobierno un subsidio de 50 pesos quincenales. Aparecieron 12 números entre el 29 de julio y el 21 de octubre de 1877.

Unión de Repúblicas Socialistas Soviéticas ◆ Nación comunista euroasiática surgida tras el colapso del último imperio zarista de Rusia (☛). Su periodo histórico comprende formalmente de 1922 (aunque la Revolución de Octubre ocurrió en 1917) hasta 1991. Limitó al sur con Corea del Norte, China, Mongolia y Afganistán; al

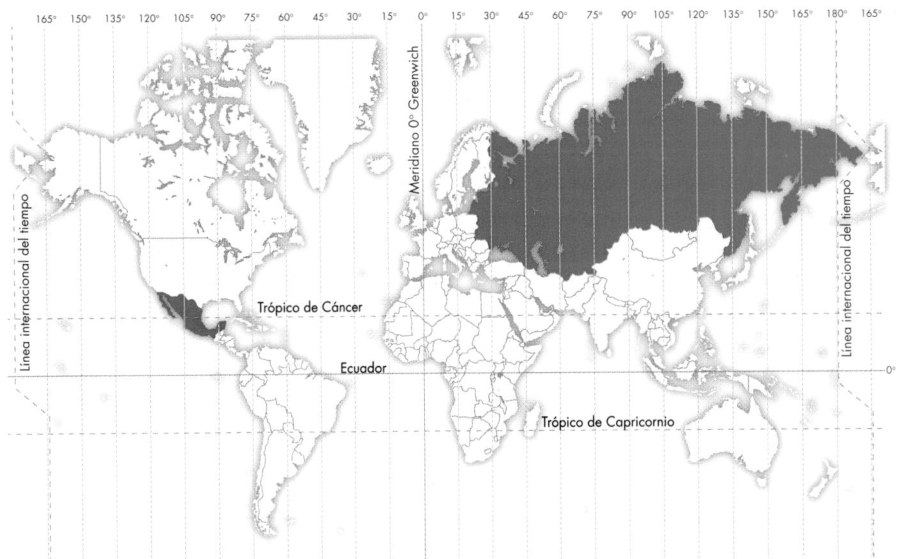

Unión de Repúblicas Socialistas Soviéticas

suroeste con Irán, y Turquía; al oeste con Rumania, Hungría, Checoslovaquia y Polonia; y al noroeste con Finlandia y Noruega. Tenía costas, al norte, en el océano Glacial Ártico; al noreste, en el estrecho de Bering; al este, en el océano Pacífico; al sur, en el mar Caspio; al suroeste, en el mar Negro, y al noroeste, en el mar Báltico. Su superficie era de 22,402,200 km² y ocupaba aproximadamente la sexta parte del área no marítima del planeta. En 1987 tenía 281,000,000 habitantes. Su capital fue Moscú, con 8,546,000 habitantes en 1984. Otras ciudades de importancia eran Leningrado (4,832,000 habitantes, cuyo nombre anterior y actual es San Petersburgo), Kiev (2,411,000), Tashkent (1,985,000) y Bakú (1,661,000). Aunque el ruso se utilizó como lengua franca, no hubo idioma oficial en la Unión Soviética porque fue una confederación de 15 repúblicas soviéticas, 20 repúblicas autónomas, ocho regiones autónomas, 10 comarcas nacionales y 129 territorios y regiones en los que se hablan unas 130 lenguas con cinco alfabetos diferentes. Su moneda era el rublo. *Historia:* en febrero de 1904 estalló la guerra entre Rusia y Japón, en la cual fue destruida la mayor parte de la flota del zar en el océano Pacífico. Luego de la derrota, la inquietud se generalizó por toda Rusia y resurgieron los grupos oposicionistas que habían sido destruidos por el zarismo. Desde enero de 1905 se produjeron continuas sublevaciones, luego de una manifestación de obreros de San Petersburgo reprimida por el ejército. En la capital se creó un consejo de obreros llamado soviet, que se apoderó del control de la ciudad y obligó al zar Nicolás II a establecer un parlamento (duma) y a aceptar algunas reformas. En 1914 Rusia entró en la primera guerra mundial y la prolongación del conflicto ocasionó graves problemas económicos, malas cosechas y hambre, lo que aunado al reclutamiento masivo, generó un sentimiento antibélico en la población. El descontento creció y volvieron a constituirse soviets. Incapaz de ejercer la autoridad, el zar abdicó en marzo de 1917. En Petrogrado (San Petersburgo desde 1914), la asamblea creó una inestable República, cuyos dirigentes se negaron a terminar la guerra. En noviembre, una nueva insurrección derrocó al gobierno de Alexander Kerensky y dio el poder a los soviets, presididos por León Trotsky (☛). En los consejos la mayoría estaba formada por delegados bolcheviques, quienes eligieron un gobierno encabezado por Vladimir Ilich *Lenin*, quien prometió paz a los soldados, tierra a los campesinos y pan a los obreros. Al año siguiente, el nuevo gobierno firmó el tratado de Brest-Litovsk, que puso fin a la guerra con Alemania y Turquía. El gobierno organizó apresuradamente el Ejército Rojo, con Trotsky como comandante en jefe, para contrarrestar las fuerzas contrarrevolucionarias. Siguieron varios años de guerra civil y de intervención militar de más de 20 países, entre otros Alemania, Estados Unidos, Francia, Inglaterra, Hungría, Japón y Turquía. En 1921, para remediar el hambre y el desmantelamiento de la industria, el Consejo de Comisarios del Pueblo, presidido por Lenin desde su creación en 1918, impulsó la *nueva política económi-*

Soldados de la Revolución Rusa de 1917

Plaza Roja de Moscú, en la antigua URSS, hoy Rusia

Stanislav Petskovsky, primer embajador de la URSS en México

ca, que autorizó a los campesinos a cultivar parcelas propias y estableció una moderada libertad de comercio. Al año siguiente, un representante personal de Lenin asistió a la toma de posesión, como gobernador de Yucatán, de Felipe Carrillo Puerto (☛), líder del Partido Socialista del Sureste. El Partido Comunista Mexicano conmemoró por primera vez en 1921 el triunfo de la Revolución de Octubre, con un mitin celebrado en el Teatro Hidalgo al que asistieron 400 personas y en el que hablaron Genaro Gómez, del Sindicato de Obreros Panaderos del DF, y José C. Valadés. En 1922 el Estado ruso se transformó en la Unión de Repúblicas Socialistas Soviéticas. El 7 de noviembre de 1922, en el Tívoli del Elíseo, el PCM conmemoró por segunda vez el triunfo de la Revolución de Octubre con un mitin en el que hablaron Genaro Gómez, Rosendo Gómez Lorenzo y una obrera de la fábrica El Buen Tono; José Vasconcelos, secretario de Educación, proporcionó una orquesta para amenizar el acto. En los primeros años de la década, muchos rusos que huían de la guerra se instalaron en México y un gran número de ellos fue extorsionado por el barón Vladimir Wendhausen von Rozenberg, el ex cónsul de Rusia en Yucatán y Campeche, quien se había encargado provisionalmente del consulado en la ciudad de México en 1914 y que colaboraba con el Ejército Blanco de Manchuria. Al año siguiente, el gobierno soviético, que comenzaba a recuperarse de la guerra civil y la invasión extranjera, volvió a insistir en que el gobierno de México reabriera su consulado en Moscú, pues salvo los viajes exploratorios de José María Sánchez y Lázaro Basch, realizados en 1922, y algunos acercamientos de los representantes soviéticos en Nueva York a Ramón P. Negri, desde 1919 no había contactos oficiosos entre ambas naciones. En septiembre de 1923 se iniciaron las negociaciones entre el representante soviético en Washington, B. E. Skvirsky, y el encargado de Negocios de México en Estados Unidos, Manuel C. Téllez. Las conversaciones continuaron en Berlín en octubre de ese año, entre Manuel Álvarez del Castillo y Nikolái Nikoláievich Kretinsky, y más tarde entre Pascual Ortiz Rubio y Etienne Brodovski, hasta que en agosto de 1924 el gobierno mexicano nombró embajador a Basilio Vadillo. El poder soviético, por su parte, le encargó la misión a Stanislav Petskovsky (1880-1943), que fue recibido en la ciudad de México el 7 de noviembre de ese año con un acto organizado por el PCM en la Escuela Nacional Preparatoria, en el que participó el senador Luis G. Monzón (☛). México fue el primer país de América que estableció relaciones con la URSS. Durante los dos años siguientes, Petskosvky colaboró con diversas organizaciones obreras opuestas a la CROM, por lo que se ganó la enemistad de esa central y quizá la del gobierno de Plutarco Elías Calles. Lenin, mientras tanto, había muerto en enero de 1924 y desde fines de ese año se inició una lucha por el poder entre Trotsky y José Stalin, en la que venció este último. En noviembre de 1925, durante una corta visita a México, el poeta Vladimir Mayakovsky se relacionó con Diego Rivera, Luis G. Monzón, Úrsulo Galván, Xavier Guerrero, el grupo de los estridentistas (☛) y con Luis Puig Casauranc, secretario de Educación de Calles. En noviembre de 1926, Petskosvki fue relevado por Alejandra Kollontai (☛). Tres años des-

Entrega de la Orden del Águila Azteca a Alejandra Kollontai en 1946

Alexandr Makar (tercero de izquierda a derecha), embajador de la URSS en México, en una reunión de la Sociedad de Estadística, en México, en 1929

El poeta soviético Vladimir Maiakovsky con Francisco Moreno durante su visita a México en 1925

pués, Stalin se apoderó del control del gobierno y expulsó a Trotsky de la URSS. A fines de los años veinte, Yucatán y la Unión Soviética firmaron acuerdos comerciales que sin embargo no se concretaron. En ese tiempo, las ideas educativas de Anatoli Lunacharski, el ministro soviético de Cultura, influyeron notablemente entre los profesores de la península. A mediados de julio de 1929, cuando la campaña represiva del gobierno de Emilio Portes Gil contra los comunistas se encontraba en su apogeo, el Comité Ejecutivo de la Internacional Comunista (☛) hizo publicar en el diario *Pravda* de Moscú un "Manifiesto a los obreros y campesinos de México y del mundo" en el que condenaba la represión contra los comunistas y llamaba a los obreros y campesinos de todos los países a levantar su voz de protesta "contra el fascismo mexicano". Durante los meses siguientes, en varias de las misiones diplomáticas de México hubo concentraciones para exigir el cese de los asesinatos de comunistas y varias de ellas fueron atacadas a pedradas, como ocurrió, en enero de 1930, en la embajada en Buenos Aires, donde, además, los manifestantes arrojaron, según el embajador Alfonso Reyes, "papeles que dicen '¡Abajo el gobierno fascista mexicano. Asesino y masacrador de comunistas!'" El gobierno mexicano, a fines de enero, retiró a su embajador en Moscú y rompió relaciones diplomáticas con la Unión Soviética. Tres meses después, la policía mexicana asaltó la sede diplomática soviética, secuestró a su personal durante varias semanas y, luego de confiscar parte de su equipaje, expulsó al embajador Alexandr Makar. En diciembre, sin embargo, llegó a la ciudad de México el cineasta letón Sergei Eisenstein (☛), quien, con Grigori Alexandrov y Eduard Tissé, durante dos años filmó por todo el país el material para *¡Que viva México!*, cinta inconclusa que Alexandrov reconstruyó en los años setenta. En mayo de 1934, el gobierno de Abelardo L. Rodríguez manifestó su interés por reanudar las relaciones diplomáticas. Los soviéticos condicionaron la aceptación a que México apoyara el ingreso de la URSS a la Sociedad de Naciones y en septiembre, el gobierno mexicano presentó la moción para el ingreso de la Unión Soviética. Sin embargo, las negociaciones no continuaron. Desde el inicio de la década, Stalin había iniciado la colectivización de la tierra, pero como los campesinos se opusieron, las fuerzas del ejército y de la policía política realizaron grandes matanzas para imponer la decisión del dirigente. Durante la guerra civil española, soviéticos y mexicanos combatieron en favor de la República. En 1937 el gobierno de Lázaro Cárdenas concedió asilo político a Trotsky, cuya presencia fue criticada por los comunistas y algunos de ellos, como David Alfaro Siqueiros, incluso intentaron asesinarlo. El crimen fue ejecutado en 1940 por un agente de la policía política soviética llamado Ramón Mercader de Río. El asesinato de Trotsky fue la culminación de una serie de juicios y asesinatos que Stalin había iniciado desde 1917 y que destruyó al grupo dirigente de los bolcheviques en 1935 y diezmó los mandos del ejército. Los asesinados más importantes fueron Nikolai Ivanovich Bujarin, Lev Borissovich Rosenfeld alias *Kamenev* y Grigori Yevseievich Apfelbaum alias *Zinoviev*, pero la represión se extendió por toda la estructura del gobierno y del Partido Comunista. Cientos de miles de personas fueron asesinadas o recluidas en campos de concentración, de las cuales no todas eran soviéticas, pues la intolerancia estalinista afectó a los comunistas del resto del mundo, como al mexicano Evelio Badillo y a *Julio Gómez*, cuyo verdadero nombre era Julio Isakovich Rosovsky, nacido en Rusia pero traído desde la infancia a México. Ambos fueron detenidos en 1935 y estuvieron confinados en Siberia durante 20 años. Otros personajes de la vida mexicana, si bien nacidos en Italia, como Vittorio Vidali y Tina Modotti, pudieron salvarse. En 1939, la URSS firmó un pacto de no agresión con Alemania y a fines de ese año invadió Letonia, Estonia, Lituania, parte de Polonia y Finlandia, hecho que México condenó ante la Sociedad de Naciones. Dos años después, en junio de 1941, los alemanes violaron el pacto e invadieron la Unión Soviética. Carente de mandos, pues 30,000 oficiales habían sido asesinados durante las purgas y varios miles más, entre ellos Georgi Konstantinovich Zhúkov, estaban presos, el ejército soviético no pudo contener la ofensiva nazi y a fines de ese año,

La URSS tiene su origen en la Revolución de 1917

los alemanes estaban frente a Moscú y Leningrado. Desde 1942, sin embargo, Stalin reincorporó a los purgados y en febrero de 1943, luego de cinco meses de lucha, los soviéticos derrotaron a los nazis en Stalingrado e iniciaron una gran ofensiva dirigida por Zhúkov que culminó en abril de 1945, con la ocupación de Berlín. Unos días después, 50,000 personas se reunieron en la ciudad de México para celebrar la victoria. En los años previos, en México se desplegó una amplia solidaridad con la URSS. En esa campaña en favor del pueblo soviético destacaron el Taller de Gráfica Popular, el PCM, la Confederación de Trabajadores de México y, desde 1944, el Instituto de Amistad e Intercambio Cultural México-URSS (☛), constituido por un grupo de intelectuales. El gobierno de Manuel Ávila Camacho, por su parte, envió algunos mensajes de aliento a las autoridades soviéticas y en noviembre de 1942, luego de la entrada de México en la segunda guerra mundial, acordó el reestablecimiento de las relaciones diplomáticas. En abril del año siguiente, las representaciones fueron elevadas al rango de embajadas y en junio llegó a México el primer embajador, Konstantin Oumansky (☛), quien murió en la capital de la República en 1945. Al término de la guerra, la URSS, además de los territorios ocupados desde 1939, se anexó partes de Checoslovaquia, Rumania y Mongolia, así como la mitad de la isla de Sajalín y el archipiélago de las Kuriles, perdidos en

Foto: Lucio Blanco

Oleg Darvsenkov, último embajador de la URSS en México

1904. Desde la segunda guerra estableció su modelo político y económico sobre Polonia, Hungría, Checoslovaquia, Albania, Bulgaria y Rumania y el sector soviético del territorio germano que se convertiría en República Democrática de Alemania. Con estos países, en 1949, constituyó el Consejo de Ayuda Mutua Económica. En ese año la disputa ideológica con los comunistas yugoslavos se convirtió en un distanciamiento entre los gobiernos de Moscú y Belgrado. En 1953 murió el dictador José Stalin. En 1954 la península de Crimea fue incorporada al territorio soviético. Un año después, Moscú reconoció la soberanía de la República Democrática de Alemania, Nikolái Bulganin fue nombrado primer ministro y la Unión Soviética, Alemania Oriental; Polonia, Rumania, Bulgaria, Hungría, Albania y Checoslovaquia firmaron el

Moscú, capital de la URSS

Tratado de Amistad, Colaboración y Ayuda Mutua, que fue conocido como Pacto de Varsovia. En 1956, durante el vigésimo congreso del Partido Comunista de la Unión Soviética, Nikita Jruschov criticó la política estalinista y trató de iniciar un proceso modernizador, pero en noviembre de ese año, fuerzas del ejército soviético invadieron Hungría (☛) y fue aplastado a sangre y fuego el movimiento renovador iniciado unos meses antes, lo que fue aprobado por los marxistas mexicanos. En 1957 la URSS puso en órbita los primeros dos satélites artificiales de la Tierra. Un año después, Jruschov fue nombrado primer ministro. En febrero de 1959, varios diputados del PRI acusaron a la embajada soviética de dirigir el movimiento que los trabajadores de los Ferrocarriles Nacionales de México habían iniciado en febrero de 1958. Durante los tres meses siguientes se desarrolló una intensa campaña antisoviética y, en abril, el gobierno de Adolfo López Mateos expulsó a Nicolái M. Remisov y a Nicolái V. Aksenov, agregado militar y segundo secretario, respectivamente, de la representación soviética en México. A fines de ese año, sin embargo, Anastas Mikoyan, vicepresidente del Consejo de Ministros de la URSS, visitó Poza Rica, Monterrey, Monclova y la ciudad de México, donde inauguró una gran exposición de productos soviéticos que fue visitada por más de un millón de personas. En 1960, Leonid Brezhnev

Sergei Eisenstein, cineasta soviético, durante la filmación de la película *¡Que viva México!* en 1932

Anastas Mikoyan (izquierda), vicepresidente del Consejo de Ministros de la URSS, visita al entonces presidente de México, Adolfo López Mateos (centro)

De derecha a izquierda: el pintor David Alfaro Siqueiros, el embajador de la URSS en México, N. Bazárov, su esposa y el escritor soviético Boris Polevói, llegado a México para entregar al artista mexicano el Premio Internacional Lenin

Mijail Gorbachov, último presidente de la URSS

fue nombrado presidente del Soviet Supremo, el máximo órgano gubernamental de la URSS, pero Jruschev conservó la secretaría general del Partido Comunista. Al año siguiente, la Unión Soviética envió al espacio a Yuri Gagarin y detonó su primera bomba de hidrógeno. Dos años después, los soviéticos instalaron cohetes nucleares en Cuba, pero tuvieron que retirarlos poco después, a causa de la amenaza estadounidense de iniciar una guerra nuclear. En ese año se produjeron varios cambios en la dirigencia soviética: Brezhnev fue sustituido por Mikoyan como presidente del Soviet Supremo, Jruschev fue retirado de sus cargos, Brezhnev ocupó el primer secretariado del PCUS y Mikoyan fue sustituido por Nikolái Podgorny en la presidencia del Soviet Supremo. En 1963, Gagarin y Valentina Tereshkova, la primera mujer cosmonauta, visitaron México. En agosto de 1968, fuerzas combinadas del Pacto de Varsovia invadieron Checoslovaquia para reprimir el movimiento democrático conocido como la Primavera de Praga, hecho que fue condenado por el Partido Comunista Mexicano, que hasta entonces había celebrado todas las decisiones soviéticas en materia internacional. Un año más tarde se agudizó la tensión entre los gobiernos chino y soviético e incluso se produjeron algunos enfrentamientos armados en ciertos puntos de su frontera. En marzo de 1971, luego de que en varios periódicos de la ciudad de México se había publicado que los miembros del grupo guerrillero Movimiento de Acción Revolucionaria habían sido entrenados en la Unión Soviética, el gobierno de Luis Echeverría expulsó al encargado de negocios y a otros tres diplomáticos soviéticos. Dos años después, el mismo Echeverría realizó un viaje oficial a la Unión Soviética y lo mismo hizo su sucesor, José López Portillo, en 1978. En 1979, los gobiernos de la URSS y de Estados Unidos firmaron el segundo Tratado de Limitación de Armas Nucleares, que se conoce por su sigla en inglés: SALT II. En diciembre de ese año, tropas soviéticas invadieron Afganistán para apoyar a un acosado gobierno afín a Moscú, lo que provocó la protesta oficial de México en los foros internacionales. Internamente, el conjunto de la izquierda aprobó la intervención militar, con la sola excepción del Partido Comunista Mexicano. En 1982 murió Brezhnev y lo sucedió Yuri Andropov, quien impulsó un proceso de renovación que se interrumpió con su muerte, en 1984. Konstantin Chernenko, su sustituto, se encargó del gobierno hasta marzo de 1985. Desde entonces, bajo la direccción de Mijaíl Gorbachov, se inició una profunda renovación de la vida sovietica, conocida como *perestroika*, que a la postre marcaría el fin de la Unión Soviética. En mayo de 1986 se produjo uno de los peores accidentes en la historia de la energía nuclear, en la localidad ucraniana de Chernobyl, donde un reactor fuera de control liberó grandes cantidades de gases radioactivos, los que contaminaron gran parte de Europa. En 1987, los gobiernos de Estados Unidos y la Unión Soviética acordaron retirar sus misiles de alcance intermedio del continente europeo. En ese año, la *perestroika* dio pie a una muy amplia remoción de funcionarios corruptos y la subsecuente llegada de cuadros jóvenes y reformistas a los puestos de poder así como a una corriente de reivindicaciones de las minorías étnicas. En 1988, al tiempo que se inició la retirada de las fuerzas soviéticas de Afganistán, se presentaron movimientos independentistas en las repúblicas bálticas y el Soviet Supremo aprobó la creación del Congreso de los Diputados del Pueblo. El año siguiente trajo más demandas de independencia, de Moldavia, Georgia y Uzbekistán. En 1990 el Congreso terminó con el monopolio del Partido Comunista, aunque refrendó el cargo de presidente a Gorbachov. Estonia, Letonia y Lituania se declararon independientes y Moscú ordenó el bloqueo económico de esas naciones bálti-

Recibimiento del presidente mexicano Luis Echeverría en la URSS el 12 de abril de 1973

cas. Simultáneamente, la Federación Rusa, encabezada por el presidente Boris Yeltsin, declaró su soberanía en tanto que el Congreso decidió la transición del país a una "economía de mercado planificada". En 1991 tropas soviéticas ocuparon las repúblicas bálticas y en algunos lugares, como en la capital lituana, se produjeron numerosas muertes de civiles. Ucrania, mientras tanto, se unió al clamor por la disolución de la Unión Soviética y la independencia de las repúblicas que la formaban. Boris Yeltsin, presidente de Rusia, exigió la renuncia de Gorbachov, aún presidente de la URSS. Georgia se declaró independiente. En agosto de ese año, un grupo de cuadros dirigentes de la vieja guardia y militares de alto rango, calificados como de la línea dura y apoyados por fuerzas de la seguridad del Estado, detuvieron a Gorbachov y a su familia en un intento de cuartelazo. El repudio popular y una inusitadamente audaz defensa de Yeltsin hicieron desistir a los golpistas. El fallido golpe precipitó las declaraciones de independencia de muchas repúblicas, ante lo cual Gorbachov ofreció su renuncia y el Soviet Supremo suspendió las actividades del Partido Comunista. El Congreso transfirió el poder central de la unión a las repúblicas, lo que les abrió paso a la independencia. En diciembre de 1991 quedó oficialmente disuelta la Unión Soviética y se constituyó la Comunidad de Estados Independientes, con la Federación de Rusia a la cabeza.

UNIÓN DE RESISTENCIA DE TEJEDORES DEL VALLE DE MÉXICO ◆ Organización creada el 5 de febrero de 1873 con representantes de los obreros textiles de La Fama Montañesa, Río Hondo, El Águila, San Fernando, La Magdalena, San Ildefonso, La Colmena y otras fábricas del ramo. En julio y agosto de ese año respaldó la huelga en La Fama Montañesa por la jornada de 13 horas, movimiento que resultó victorioso, y otra huelga en la fábrica de Tepeji del Río, en agosto, en la que la patronal también accedió a las demandas obreras, aunque finalmente despidió a 50 de los trabajadores más combativos, los que fueron colocados en otras empresas por sus compañeros de la unión. Por esos días se produjeron huelgas en Río Hondo y San Ildefonso, contra la rebaja del pago a destajo y el aumento de la jornada laboral. Ambos movimientos triunfaron, aunque después, con el acuerdo del gobierno lerdista, los patrones rebajaron nuevamente los salarios.

UNIÓN DE SAN ANTONIO ◆ Municipio de Jalisco situado en el noreste del estado y contiguo a Lagos de Moreno, en los límites con Guanajuato. Superficie: 639.36 km². Habitantes: 15,172, de los cuales 3,625 forman la población económicamente activa. Hablan alguna lengua indígena 20 personas mayores de cinco años.

UNIÓN DE TEJEDORES DE LAS FÁBRICAS UNIDAS DEL VALLE DE MÉXICO ◆ Organización obrera creada en abril de 1874, en una reunión celebrada en el ex templo de San Pedro y San Pablo, con asistencia de 58 representantes de 14 sociedades convocados por los trabajadores de La Colmena. En la asamblea de fundación se acordó luchar por la abolición del trabajo nocturno y una jornada máxima de 10 horas. Como el Gran Círculo de Obreros retrasara el inicio del movimiento, otra asamblea resolvió ir a la huelga el 1 de febrero de 1875. Los líderes del Gran Círculo juzgaron "demasiado atrevido y prematuro este paso, instigado por malos elementos adictos a doctrinas extremistas". En agosto de 1874 la Sociedad de Artesanos y Jornaleros de Jalapa había realizado una huelga de un mes, mediante la cual lograron de inmediato rebajar la jornada a 12 horas y obtuvieron de la patronal el acuerdo de reducirla a 10 horas al cabo de un año. En enero, el presidente Lerdo de Tejada recibió a una comisión con las demandas de la unión y ordenó al gobernador del DF que interviniera para obtener un acuerdo obrero-patronal. Antes de que las gestiones oficiales llegaran a su fin, los obreros de La Fama Montañesa y San Fernando realizaron una huelga, del 9 al 15 de enero. Los dirigentes del Gran Círculo los expulsaron con el pretexto de que rompían la disciplina y acordó que toda huelga debía contar con su aprobación. Esta falta de solidaridad ocasionó la extinción de este agrupamiento.

UNIÓN DE TULA ◆ Municipio de Jalisco situado al sur-suroeste de Ameca y contiguo a Autlán. Superficie: 323.34 km². Habitantes: 14,594, de los cuales 3,487 forman la población económicamente activa. Hablan alguna lengua indígena 29 personas mayores de cinco años. En su jurisdicción se levanta la presa de Tacotán, en el río Ayuquilla, que brinda irrigación a los cultivos frutícolas. Destaca por su producción de maguey mezcalero.

UNIÓN DE VARIEDADES ◆ Organización de resistencia fundada en 1930 por Juan Lavat, Rodolfo Bugarini, Claudio Estrada, Armando Soto la Marina *Chicote* y otros actores de carpa. En 1934 se fusionó con la Unión Mexicana de Actores en la naciente ANDA (☛).

UNIÓN DE VECINOS Y DAMNIFICADOS 19 DE SEPTIEMBRE ◆ Organización fundada en la colonia Roma de la ciudad de México el 4 de octubre de 1985, 15 días después del terremoto del 19 de septiembre. Su objetivo específico era pugnar por una solución al grave problema de vivienda que se padece en la capital del país, y en general fortalecer la organización de la sociedad civil para la transformación democrática de México. Además, su Comisión Cultural se propuso contribuir al desarrollo integral de los ciudadanos y ganar espacios para la expresión artística independiente. Tras 14 años de actividad ininterrumpida, la Unión de Vecinos y Damnificados 19 de septiembre se ha convertido en una de las principales organizaciones vecinales en la lucha por la vivienda. Su Comisión Cultural, además de organizar festivales artísticos, actos culturales y talleres de iniciación artística, apoya las actividades de la Escuela Popular de Arte y la Galería Frida Kahlo.

EL UNIVERSAL,
PERIÓDICO INDEPENDIENTE.

El Universal, 18 de noviembre de 1848

EL UNIVERSAL,
PERIÓDICO INDEPENDIENTE.

El Universal, 7 de julio 1849

EL UNIVERSAL
Limitan apoyo a estados
Aumentará GDF agua y predial

El Universal del 17 de noviembre de 1999

El Universal anuncia en 1916 "La rotativa más grande de la República"

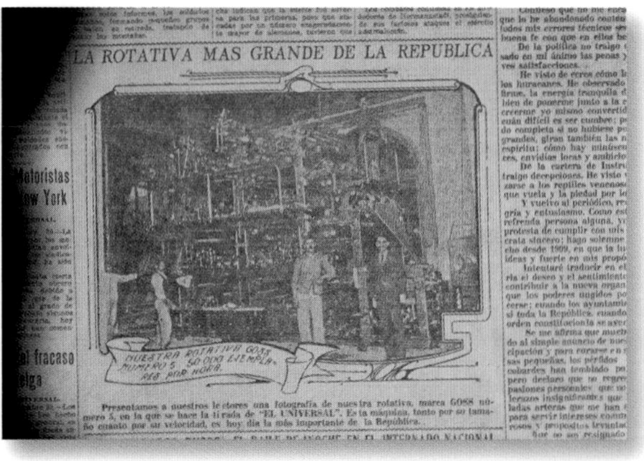
LA ROTATIVA MAS GRANDE DE LA REPUBLICA

NUESTRA ROTATIVA GOSS NUMERO 5 50,000 EJEMPLARES POR HORA

Presentamos a nuestros lectores una fotografía de nuestra rotativa, marca GOSS número 5, en la que se hace la tirada de "EL UNIVERSAL". Es la máquina, tanto por su tamaño como por su velocidad, es hoy día la más importante de la República.

UNIVERSAL, EL ◆ Diario conservador fundado en 1848 por Rafael de Rafael, con el apoyo económico y la orientación política de Lucas Alamán. Este periódico fue el principal foro de los opositores al liberalismo, cuya tribuna fue el diario *El Siglo XIX*; entre ambas publicaciones llegaron a producirse serios enfrentamientos. *El Universal* fue cerrado el 11 de agosto de 1855, dos días después de la salida del país de Antonio López de Santa Anna.

UNIVERSAL, EL ◆ Diario fundado el 1 de julio de 1888 por Rafael Reyes Spíndola y editado en la ciudad de México por la compañía de O. R. Spíndola, que más tarde vendió el periódico a Ramón Prida; éste, a su vez, lo cedió a Luis del Toro. En diciembre de 1901 se clausuró el diario, pues su director fue encarcelado por algunas críticas al gobierno. Este periódico alcanzó renombre por ser el primero en dar preferencia a las noticias en primera plana.

UNIVERSAL, EL ◆ Diario fundado el 1 de octubre de 1916 por Félix F. Palavicini. Es el periódico más antiguo del Distrito Federal. Contó en su origen con los equipos de impresión más modernos de la época y reflejaba una marcada influencia del estilo periodístico estadounidense. Apoyó las posiciones vanguardistas del Congreso Constituyente de 1916-17 y en sus prensas se imprimió la Constitución. Durante el gobierno de Venustiano Carranza, al que criticaba con severidad, fue clausurado (del 29 de marzo al 17 de abril de 1917) y su director, Palavicini, detenido. En sus primeros lustros de vida contó en su nómina de colaboradores con Amado Nervo, Luis Cabrera, José Vasconcelos, Antonio Caso, Francisco Zamora y Vicente Lombardo Toledano, entre otros. En 1922 se inició el tiraje de su edición vespertina, primera en su género en Latinoamérica: *El Universal Gráfico*. De 1923 a 1940, Miguel Lanz Duret asumió la dirección; posteriormente han dirigido el periódico Miguel Lanz Duret Sierra (1940-1959), la familia Lanz Duret Valdez (1959-1969) y Juan Francisco Ealy Ortiz (1969-).

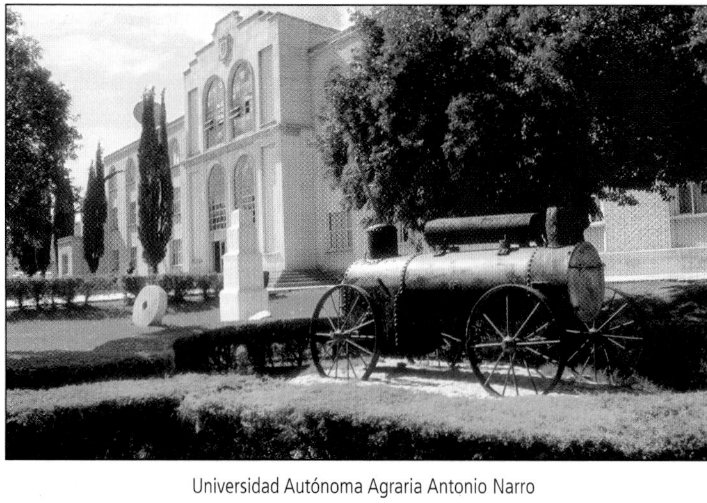
Universidad Autónoma Agraria Antonio Narro

UNIVERSIDAD DE LAS AMÉRICAS ◆ Institución fundada en 1940 por Henry L. Cain, primer presidente de la misma (1940-53), y Paul V. Murray, con el nombre de Mexico City College, sucursal de la Fundación de Escuelas Americanas, primero, y afiliada después a la Asociación de Colegios de Texas, dedicada a la educación de los jóvenes estadounidenses residentes en México. Su primer local se hallaba en la colonia Roma de la ciudad de México. En 1954 adquirió terrenos en el kilómetro 16 de la carretera México-Toluca y erigió ahí nuevas instalaciones. Tres años después inauguró un Centro de Estudios Regionales en Oaxaca, especializado en antropología y arqueología, que más tarde se convirtió en el Instituto de Estudios Oaxaqueños. En 1962 el Mexico City College se convirtió en Universidad de las Américas y, bajo la dirección de Ray Lindley, empezó a aceptar estudiantes de todo el mundo. En 1968 el gobierno federal le cedió unos terrenos cerca de Cholula, Puebla, donde la universidad construyó, con dinero proveniente de varias fundaciones culturales estadounidenses, unas instalaciones más modernas, las que fueron inauguradas en 1970. En 1998 tenía 1,254 alumnos de licenciatura en su plantel Ciudad de México y 5,753 en el de Puebla.

UNIVERSIDAD ANÁHUAC ◆ Institución que tuvo su origen en el Centro de Investigación y Estudios Superiores fundado en 1964 por los Legionarios de Cristo y el fundador de la congregación, el padre Marcial Maciel. La institución comenzó sus actividades en aquel año, en una casa ubicada en Lomas Virreyes y con 48 alumnos en dos carreras: administración de empresas y economía. Bajo la rectoría del padre Faustino Pardo, L.C., en los años siguientes el centro abrió las carreras de psicología y ciencias humanas (1965) y de arquitectura y derecho (1966). Al mismo tiempo, se emprendió la construcción de las nuevas instalaciones en Lomas Anáhuac; el 4 de junio de 1968 se inauguró la nueva sede, la cual tenía 4,703 alumnos de licenciatura en 1998. Desde 1980 está incorporada a la UNAM. La universidad cuenta con más de 20 licenciaturas y ha dado origen a tres universidades filiales: Universidad Anáhuac del Sur (1,826 alumnos de licenciatura en 1998), en el DF; Universidad del Mayab (891 alumnos de licenciatura en 1998), en Mérida, Yuc., y Universidad Anáhuac en Jalapa (331 alumnos de licenciatura en 1998).

UNIVERSIDAD AUTÓNOMA AGRARIA ANTONIO NARRO ♦ Con sede en Saltillo, Coahuila, esta universidad tiene como antecedente la Escuela Regional de Agricultura Antonio Narro (financiada por Antonio Narro Rodríguez), inaugurada el 4 de marzo de 1923. En 1938 la escuela fue administrada por el estado de Coahuila y cambió su nombre a Escuela Superior de Agricultura Antonio Narro. En 1957 fue adscrita a la administración de la Universidad de Coahuila y en 1975 adquirió la autonomía y su nombre actual. Su Ley Orgánica fue publicada el 3 de mayo de 1975 en el periódico oficial coahuilense y sus fuentes de financiamiento son el gobierno de Coahuila y el gobierno federal. En 1998 tenía 3,173 alumnos de licenciatura.

UNIVERSIDAD AUTÓNOMA DE AGUASCALIENTES ♦ Tiene como antecedentes la Escuela de Agricultura, fundada por Jesús Portugal en 1867 y transformada, en 1871, en Instituto Científico y Literario, que tuvo diversas denominaciones hasta que se convirtió en Instituto Autónomo de Ciencias y Tecnología de Aguascalientes, que fue la base de la actual universidad, creada el 19 de junio de 1973 como organismo público descentralizado, cuya Ley Orgánica fue promulgada en febrero del año siguiente. Esta casa de estudios cuenta con cuatro centros de licenciatura (con 8,060 alumnos en 1998), tres de carreras técnicas y uno de bachillerato. Edita las revistas *Voz Universitaria* y *Correo Universitario*.

UNIVERSIDAD AUTÓNOMA DE BAJA CALIFORNIA ♦ Institución de servicio público, con sede en Mexicali y unidades descentralizadas en Tecate, Tijuana y el valle de Mexicali, fundada en 1957. Su Ley Orgánica se publicó en el periódico oficial del estado el 28 de febrero de aquel año. Cuenta con nueve facultades, seis escuelas, siete institutos y tres departamentos. En 1998 tenía 21,031 alumnos de licenciatura.

UNIVERSIDAD AUTÓNOMA DE BAJA CALIFORNIA SUR ♦ Organismo público descentralizado cuya Ley Orgánica fue publicada el 31 de diciembre de 1975. Este centro de estudios cuenta con subsidio de los gobiernos estatal y federal. Tiene su sede en La Paz y en 1998 su matrícula de licenciatura era de 2,524 alumnos.

UNIVERSIDAD AUTÓNOMA DE CIUDAD JUÁREZ ♦ En 1973 el presidente Luis Echeverría decretó que todas las instituciones de educación superior ubicadas en Ciudad Juárez, Chihuahua, se fusionasen en la Universidad Autónoma de Ciudad Juárez, cuya Ley Orgánica fue expedida en octubre de ese año. En 1998 esta institución contaba con casi 500 profesores y 7,801 alumnos de licenciatura. Edita *Tribuna Universitaria*, *Educación* e *Imágenes* y tiene una estación de radio.

Universidad Autónoma de Baja California

Foto: Fondo Editorial Grupo Azabache

Edificio de la Universidad Autónoma de Baja California Sur en La Paz

UNIVERSIDAD AUTÓNOMA DE COAHUILA ♦ Fue creada por decreto del gobierno estatal el 2 de octubre de 1957. Con sede en Saltillo, tiene unidades descentralizadas en Torreón y Monclova. En total cuenta con 28 centros de enseñanza, entre facultades y escuelas superiores y de bachillerato, además de haber incorporado numerosos institutos estatales. Obtuvo su autonomía en abril de 1973. En 1998 su matrícula era de 19,891 alumnos en licenciatura.

UNIVERSIDAD AUTÓNOMA DE COLIMA ♦ Fundada en 1867 como Universidad Popular de Colima, fue reorganizada en 1962, cuando adoptó su nombre actual. Su sede se localiza en la capital estatal. Cuenta con seis escuelas de educación superior (con 8,711 alumnos de licenciatura en 1998), dos de nivel medio, tres de bachillerato y una de artes y ha incorporado diversas escuelas de nivel medio-superior del estado.

UNIVERSIDAD AUTÓNOMA DE CHAPINGO ♦ Institución pública de educación superior creada por decreto presidencial el 30 de diciembre de 1974. Se basó en la estructura académica de la Escuela Nacional de Agricultura, establecimiento fundado el 22 de febrero de 1854, por decreto de Antonio López de Santa Anna expedido 19 de agosto de 1853. Su primer director fue José Guadalupe Arreola. Funcionó

FOTO: FONDO EDITORIAL GRUPO AZABACHE

Universidad Autónoma de Chapingo

en el ex convento de San Jacinto, en la ciudad de México, hasta el 20 de noviembre de 1923, cuando se estableció en la ex Hacienda de Chapingo, en el municipio de Texcoco. Los antecedentes de la ENA son los cursos de agricultura establecidos en el Colegio de San Gregorio en los años treinta del siglo XIX, que se llevaban a cabo en San Jacinto, establecimiento dominico como lo fue San Gregorio. En agosto de 1853 se creó un Colegio Nacional de Agricultura que recogió la experiencia de las décadas previas para planear estudios elementales, secundarios y superiores relacionados con las ciencias de la tierra. Al momento de constituirse, la ENA formaba administradores agrícolas y mayordomos de fincas rústicas. En enero de 1856, el gobierno de Ignacio Comonfort reorganizó los planes de estudios de la escuela, para formar agricultores teórico-prácticos y profesores de agricultura, así como mariscales y mayordomos. Entre 1883 y 1893 se expidieron títulos de ingeniero agrónomo y médico veterinario, y a partir de ese año se constituyeron como carreras separadas. Así, en 1907 la escuela impartía tres carreras: agrónomo, ingeniero agrónomo y médico veterinario, que se ampliaron a cuatro en 1909, cuando se creó un plantel forestal en Santa Fe, DF. Desde 1908 se llamó Escuela Nacional de Agricultura y Veterinaria. Durante el porfiriato, algunos de los científicos más importantes del momento, como Manuel María Villada, Gumersindo Mendoza, Alfonso Herrera y Mariano Bárcena, fueron profesores de la institución. Su presupuesto, controlado por la Secretaría de Fomento desde 1881, era semejante al de las otras grandes escuelas superiores, como la Preparatoria y la de Medicina, aunque el número de sus egresados era mucho menor. La ENA permaneció cerrada entre 1914 y 1919, periodo durante el que muchos de sus alumnos se incorporaron a la revolución, mientras que otros formaban parte del Ateneo Ceres (1917-19), especie de escuela "extramuros" donde continuaron sus estudios. Al trasladarse a Chapingo, la escuela adoptó el lema "Enseñar la explotación de la tierra, no la del hombre". Un año después la escuela preparaba ingenieros agrónomos que podían especializarse en agricultura general, industrias agrícolas y en irrigación y servicios, así como técnicos forestales. En 1941 se fijó como requisito para ingresar a la escuela la terminación de los estudios de secundaria, se estableció una "preparatoria agrícola", que subsiste hasta nuestros días, y la duración de los cursos superiores se fijó en cuatro años. Entre 1943 y 1971 la ENA fue una escuela militarizada, aunque desde 1969 se relajaron algunas de sus normas más extremas. En 1959 se fundó el Colegio de Posgraduados de la Escuela Nacional de Agricultura para otorgar grados de maestría y doctorado. La preparatoria agrícola, cuya existencia aseguraba el ingreso de jóvenes campesinos, fue suprimida entre 1963 y 1966, pero cuando se reabrió se establecieron dos formas de ingreso: una para los alumnos con secundaria concluida y otra para quienes hubieran terminado la preparatoria. Aunque se constituyó como universidad en 1973, su estatuto no fue expedido sino hasta 1978. En 1975 se creó el Centro Regional Universitario del Sureste, en Tabasco, el primero de los planteles desentralizados de la UACh, al que siguieron los del Oriente, en Veracruz (1980); del Sur, en Oaxaca (1980); del Noroeste, en Sonora (1981); de la Península de Yucatán, en Yucatán (1981); del Centro Occidente, en Michoacán (1981); del Occidente, en Jalisco (1986), y del Centro Norte, en Zacatecas (1987), así como la Unidad Regional Universitaria de Zonas Áridas, en Durango (1982). En la actualidad la UACh imparte 20 licenciaturas y la preparatoria agrícola y cuenta con centros de investigación, campos de experimentación propios, invernaderos y laboratorios. Hacia 1998 contaba con aproximadamente 400 profesores y 3,432 alumnos. Publica la revista *Agrociencia*.

UNIVERSIDAD AUTÓNOMA DE CHIAPAS ◆ Con el antecedente de la Universidad Literaria Nacional y Pontificia de las Chiapas (☛), fundada en 1826, se creó este organismo descentralizado cuya Ley Orgánica fue promulgada el 28 de septiembre de 1974, aunque no la ejerció sino hasta el 17 de abril de 1975. En 1998 contaba con 11,701 alumnos de licenciatura distribuidos en los centros de estudio de Tuxtla Gutiérrez, su sede, Tapachula y San Cristóbal de Las Casas. Edita las revistas *Criterio Universitario* y *Vida Universitaria*.

UNIVERSIDAD AUTÓNOMA DEL ESTADO DE HIDALGO ◆ Institución con sede en Pachuca, cuyo antecedente fue el Instituto Científico y Literario de Hidalgo; su Ley Orgánica, que le confiere autonomía, fue promulgada el 25 de febrero de 1961. Cuenta con planteles de educación superior en Pachuca, Tula y Ciudad Sahagún y con escuelas preparatorias en Pachuca, Tulancingo y Tula, con una población escolar de 6,223 alumnos (1998).

UNIVERSIDAD AUTÓNOMA DEL ESTADO DE MÉXICO ◆ Nombre que adoptó, el 21 de marzo de 1956, el Instituto Científico y Literario de Toluca. Al momento de constituirse como universidad, el instituto contaba con escuelas Preparatoria, de Medicina, Jurisprudencia, Comercio, Enfermería y Pedagogía Superior. Su primer rector fue Juan Josafat Pichardo. La ciudad universitaria y la sede Colón, ambas en Toluca, se inauguraron en 1964, y en la década

Foto: Fondo Editorial Grupo Azabache

Universidad Autónoma del Estado de Morelos

siguiente se puso en funcionamiento la sede Cerillos, también en la capital del estado. La ley orgánica que ampara su existencia fue reformada en 1976 y en 1992. A partir de 1984, con la inauguración del plantel de Atlacomulco, se inició el establecimiento de sedes regionales de la universidad: actualmente existen unidades en Amecameca, Atizapán de Zaragoza, Ecatepec de Morelos, Temascaltepec, Texcoco, Valle de Chalco y Zumpango. En 1999, la UAEM impartía un bachillerato, 47 licenciaturas, dos carreras técnicas, 37 especializaciones, 36 maestrías y nueve doctorados, con alrededor de 2,000 profesores y una matrícula total de 57,000 estudiantes, 21,000 de ellos en licenciatura. Contaba también con 12 centros de investigación y un sistema de educación a distancia. En 1996 se reformó el Estatuto Universitario.

Universidad Autónoma del Estado de Morelos ◆ Con sede en Cuernavaca, fue fundada en 1939; su actual Ley Orgánica y la autonomía datan de 1978. Cuenta con varios planteles de educación profesional, 19 escuelas preparatorias, un Centro de Preparación para Profesores y una División de Estudios Superiores. En 1998 tenía más de 600 profesores y 9,268 alumnos. Publica mensualmente la *Gaceta Universitaria*.

Universidad Autónoma del Estado de Querétaro ◆ Institución ubicada en el Centro Universitario de la ciudad de Querétaro. Su origen se halla en el Colegio Civil del Estado de Querétaro, fundado en 1869 y clausurado en 1950. En 1951 se fundó la universidad, que obtuvo la autonomía en 1958. Este organismo cuenta con diversas escuelas profesionales, preparatorias e institutos de idiomas y de bellas artes y cuenta con 6,403 alumnos de licenciatura. Publica *Universidad*, *Diálogo Universitario* y *Nuestra Verdad*.

Universidad Autónoma de Guadalajara ◆ Institución creada en 1935 con sede en Guadalajara, Jalisco, con el nombre de Universidad Autónoma de Occidente, fue la primera universidad privada de México. Hacia 1998 contaba con 7,435 alumnos, 20 por ciento de ellos extranjeros, 14 escuelas y facultades y tres institutos.

Universidad Autónoma de Guerrero ◆ El 16 de septiembre de 1869 el gobernador de Guerrero, Francisco O. Arce, fundó en la ciudad de Tixtla el Instituto Literario para la Enseñanza Secundaria, cuyo primer director fue Francisco Granados Maldonado. En 1870 se trasladó a Chilpancingo y en 1885 se convirtió en escuela preparatoria y profesional, sólo con la carrera de derecho. El 26 de octubre de 1901 se transformó en Escuela Normal para Profesoras y a fines de ese año se convirtió nuevamente en institución mixta, como escuela normal y preparatoria. En 1942 se especializó en la impartición de carreras técnicas con el nombre de Colegio del Estado de Guerrero y 18 años después adquirió el rango de universidad, cuya autonomía obtuvo en 1963. En 1980 contaba con una facultad, ocho escuelas profesionales (una incorporada), dos subprofesionales y 10 preparatorias (cuatro incorporadas). Su matrícula era en 1998 de 25,907 alumnos en licenciatura.

Universidad Autónoma Metropolitana ◆ Con sede en la ciudad de México, esta universidad fue creada tras una propuesta de la Asociación Nacional de Universidades e Institutos de Enseñanza Superior. Inició sus actividades preliminares el 10 de enero de 1974, con Pedro Ramírez Vázquez como su primer rector. Tiene tres planteles: Azcapotzalco, Iztapalapa y Xochimilco, con 40,975 alumnos de licenciatura en 1998.

Universidad Autónoma de Nayarit ◆ Tiene como antecedente el Instituto de Ciencias y Letras fundado en Tepic en 1930. La Universidad Autónoma se constituyó el 19 de agosto de 1969. Es una institución con personalidad jurídica propia, cuyo objetivo de acuerdo con su ley Orgánica, es impartir la educación media superior y superior, formar profesionistas investigadores y profesionales universitarios, con investigaciones científicas acerca de la realidad estatal, regional, nacional e internacional. En 1998 contaba con 7,510 alumnos.

Universidad Autónoma de Nuevo León ◆ Ubicada en la Ciudad Universitaria de Monterrey, data de 1932 y obtuvo la autonomía el 26 de noviembre de 1969; su Ley Orgánica fue publicada en 1971. Tiene como antecedente el Colegio Civil del estado. Cuenta con diversos programas de educación superior, bachillerato y posgrado en varios planteles distribuidos en el estado. Publica *Universidad*, *Armas y Letras* e *Interfolia Biblioteca Universitaria Alfonso Reyes*. Contaba en 1998 con 54,469 alumnos de licenciatura.

Universidad Autónoma de Occidente ◆ ☛ *Universidad Autónoma de Guadalajara*.

Timbre conmemorativo del 70 aniversario de la fundación de la Universidad (hoy Autónoma) de Sinaloa

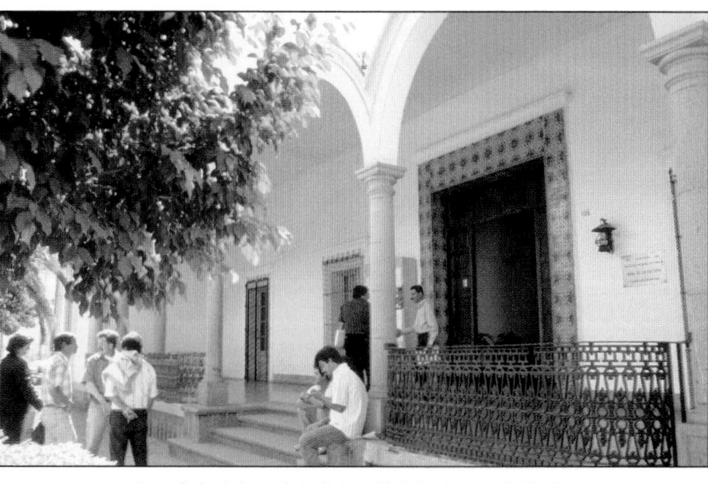

Casa de la Cultura de la Universidad Autónoma de Sinaloa

Universidad Autónoma de Puebla ◆ Institución cuyos antecedentes se remontan al 15 de abril de 1587, cuando se fundó en la ciudad de Puebla el Colegio del Espíritu Santo, de los jesuitas. Esta institución aceptó estudiantes seglares en 1594, como consta en sus actas: "El curso de Artes se ha proseguido hasta ahora con fervor y se llevará al fin, graduándose en la Universidad de México los estudiantes seglares que se han aprovechado bien del cuidado de los nuestros". En 1790 se estableció "Que en el Colegio del Espíritu Santo se reúnan los de San Jerónimo y San Ignacio bajo el título o advocación de Colegio Carolino", que en 1805 se transformó en Real Colegio Carolino del Espíritu Santo. En 1820, al producirse el retorno de los jesuitas, el Real Colegio Carolino fue transformado en Real Colegio del Espíritu Santo de San Jerónimo y San Ignacio de la Compañía de Jesús. La institución fue reorganizada y rebautizada en 1822 como Imperial Colegio del Espíritu Santo, en 1824 como Muy Ilustres Colegios del Espíritu Santo, de San Jerónimo y San Ignacio; en 1825, Colegio del Estado; en 1834, Colegio de San Jerónimo y San Ignacio del Estado Libre y Soberano de Puebla; en 1846, Colegio Departamental; en 1860, Colegio Nacional del Espíritu Santo; en 1864, Colegio Imperial del Espíritu Santo; en 1867, Colegio del Estado y, en 1937, Universidad de Puebla, la que en 1956 se convirtió en autónoma y adquirió la denominación de Benemérita. Contaba en 1998 con 28,184 alumnos de licenciatura. Publica la revista *Universidad*.

Universidad Autónoma de San Luis Potosí ◆ Creada el 10 de enero de 1923 por decreto del Congreso local a iniciativa del gobernador Rafael Nieto. Tuvo como antecedente el Instituto Científico y Literario fundado en 1859. De acuerdo con el decreto fundacional, la constituyeron la Escuela Preparatoria, las facultades de Medicina, Jurisprudencia e Ingeniería; las escuelas Comercial y de Estudios Químicos, el Hospital Civil Dr. Miguel Otero, la Biblioteca Pública del estado, el Observatorio Meteorológico y el ramo de enseñanza normal de la Dirección de Educación del gobierno potosino. Fue la primera universidad autónoma del país, calidad que le fue confirmada el 23 de febrero de 1934. En 1980 impartía 12 carreras y contaba con el Instituto de Investigación de Zonas Desérticas y con dos planteles de bachillerato. En 1998 tenía 17,063 alumnos de licenciatura.

Universidad Autónoma de Sinaloa ◆ En 1873, el gobernador Eustaquio Buelna creó el Liceo Rosales, ubicado en el puerto de Mazatlán. Este instituto fue trasladado a Culiacán en 1874, cambió su nombre a Universidad de Occidente en 1918 y a Universidad Socialista del Noroeste en 1937. Se convirtió en Universidad de Sinaloa en 1941 y obtuvo la autonomía el 7 de diciembre de 1965. Su Ley Orgánica data de abril de 1972. En 1980 contaba con ocho facultades, una Escuela de Estudios Profesionales, un Taller de Artes Plásticas, una Escuela de Meteorología, varias preparatorias y centros de estudios de idiomas y música. En 1998 tenía 33,999 estudiantes distribuidos en Mazatlán, Guamúchil, Guasave, Culiacán y Los Mochis.

Universidad Autónoma de Tamaulipas ◆ Inaugurada en 1950, obtuvo la autonomía en 1967 y su Estatuto Orgánico fue aprobado el 5 de noviembre de 1972. Con sede en Ciudad Victoria, cuenta también con planteles en El Mante, Tampico, Reynosa y Nuevo Laredo. En 1998 tenía 26,228 alumnos. Publica mensualmente el *Boletín de Investigaciones*.

Universidad Autónoma de Tlaxcala ◆ Fue establecida en 1986, durante el gobierno de Emilio Sánchez

Interior del edificio central de la Universidad Autónoma de Puebla

FOTO: CARLOS HAHN

Foto: Fondo Editorial Grupo Azabache

Teatro Héroes de la Universidad (hoy Autónoma) de Chihuahua

Piedras. Su antecedente es el Instituto de Estudios Superiores del Estado (IESE), que tenía escuelas de Enfermería y Obstetricia, Derecho, Normal Superior, superior de Comercio y Odontología. La universidad comenzó sus actividades ofreciendo estas carreras. En 1998 su población escolar era de 6,609 alumnos.

UNIVERSIDAD AUTÓNOMA DE ZACATECAS FRANCISCO GARCÍA SALINAS ◆ Su origen se localiza en la Casa de Estudios de Jerez, fundada en 1832 y trasladada en 1837 a la capital zacatecana, ya como Instituto Literario de García. En 1880 se transformó en el Instituto de Ciencias de Zacatecas que en 1959 adquirió la autonomía y, finalmente, el 6 de septiembre de 1968 se transformó en universidad autónoma. Imparte 14 carreras y enseñanza media superior en sus planteles, distribuidos en los muncipios de Guadalupe, E. Estrada y Fresnillo, además de su sede en la capital estatal. En 1998 tenía 9,031 alumnos en licenciatura.

UNIVERSIDAD DE COLIMA ◆ Fue establecida en 1960. Su propósito era "la búsqueda de una identidad académica propia, a propósito de impartir toda enseñanza posterior a la educación primaria: la enseñanza preparatoria y la profesional, en sus niveles medio y superior; fomentar la investigación científica y social, principalmente en relación con los problemas estatales y nacionales, y extender con mayor amplitud los beneficios de la cultura superior". Declara entre sus objetivos el apoyo de "la docencia, la investigación, la difusión de la cultura y la crítica sociopolítica". En 1998 tenía 8,711 alumnos de licenciatura.

UNIVERSIDAD DE CHIHUAHUA ◆ Fundada el 8 de diciembre de 1954 por decreto del Congreso local, abrió aulas y locales improvisados en enero de 1955 e inició la construcción de su sede en el perímetro de la ciudad deportiva de la capital chihuahuense. Sus primeros planteles fueron inaugurados entre 1955 y 1956 y en 1968 obtuvo la autonomía. En 1998 su población escolar era de 11,814 alumnos. Publica *Lecturas Jurídicas* y el *Boletín Bibliográfico*.

UNIVERSIDAD FEMENINA DE MÉXICO ◆ Fundada en 1943 a iniciativa de Adela Formoso de Obregón Santacilia, quien fue su primera directora. Impartía las carreras de periodismo, diplomacia, decoración y química y tenía una normal de educadoras. En 1996 desapareció y sus instalaciones conforman el *campus* Chapultepec de la Universidad del Valle de México.

UNIVERSIDAD DE GUADALAJARA ◆ Se inauguró en 1792 con el nombre de Real y Literaria Universidad de Guadalajara. Sus antecedentes datan de 1774, cuando los sacerdotes de San Felipe Neri de Guadalajara pidieron a la Real y Pontificia Universidad de México que se creara una "casa de estudios públicos a fin de que la juventud de aquel dilatado reino tenga mayor proporción de decicarse a ellos, a causa de no haber en aquella ciudad otra más que la del Real Colegio Seminario de San José". La Real y Pontificia Universidad creyó inconveniente la creación de una universidad en Guadalajara, pues, según el catedrático de aquélla, Francisco Gómez: "Los pocos estudiantes que en el día hay en esta Universidad, y que de los hijos de fuera de esta ciudad es de donde se habilita esta Universidad y Colegio de estudiantes, y que así desmembrada la ciudad de Guadalajara, con los que necesariamente habían de concurrir a su Universidad, era casi el total exterminio de ésta" (la de México). Las peticiones, tanto del clero como de la administración civil, continuaron y fueron finalmente recompensadas: en 1791 Carlos IV dispuso la fundación de la Real Universidad de

Estudiantes en el recinto de la Universidad Autónoma de Tamaulipas

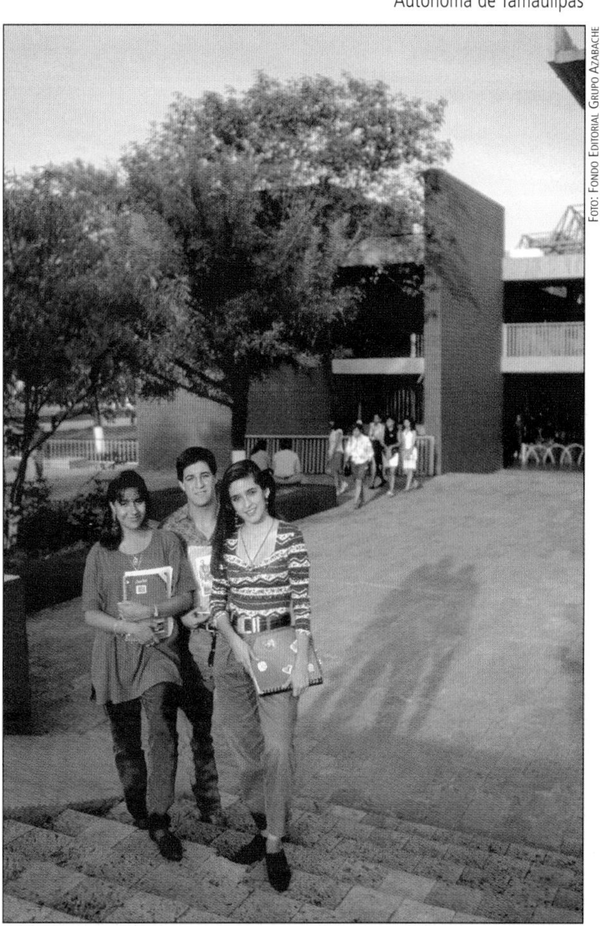

Foto: Fondo Editorial Grupo Azabache

Foto: Carlos Hahn

Edificio de la Universidad de Guadalajara

Guadalajara, que se instaló 12 de abril de 1792, según su primer rector, José María Gómez y Villaseñor, quien el 3 de noviembre envió un comunicado al rector de la Real y Pontificia Universidad de México, donde se leyó ante el claustro el 12 de abril de 1793. La carta decía: "Muy Ilustre Señor. En execución de las Reales Cédulas en que nuestro Augusto Soverano animado del zelo por la felicidad de estos sus Reynos, manda que en esta Ciudad se erija Universidad. Se abrió ésta finalmente el 3 del corriente cuyos respetos tenemos el honor de rendir a Vuestra Señoría los que logramos el de haber sido los primeros en formarla con la sumisión que exige la gloria a que ella aspira proponiéndose a Vuestra Señoría por modelo, y la de que siempre se lisonjearán sus Fundadores contándose por miembros de ese muy Noble y Sabio Cuerpo". Fue clausurada en 1827 por el gobernador Prisciliano Sánchez, quien fundó el Instituto de Ciencias. Restaurada por el conservador José Antonio Romero (1834), en 1836 fue sujeta a una nueva legislación por Antonio Escobedo (centralista) y el 2 de diciembre de 1860 Pedro Ogazón la suprimió. La restauró el gobernador José Guadalupe Zuno en 1925 y su administración fue absorbida por el gobierno de Jalisco. En 1934 la cerró Sebastián Allende. Al año siguiente, el también gobernador Everardo Topete la tomó como base para crear el Instituto Socialista de Altos Estudios que en 1937 adoptó su nombre actual. En 1980 contaba con 12 facultades, ocho institutos de investigación, ocho escuelas de estudios profesionales y de ella dependían 12 preparatorias, cuatro vocacionales y una escuela regional. En 1998 tenía 52,148 alumnos de licenciatura. Publica trimestralmente la *Revista de la Universidad de Guadalajara*.

Universidad de Guanajuato ♦ Institución cuyo antecedente fue el Colegio Jesuita de la Purísima Concepción, fundado en 1732. Se transformó después en Colegio del Estado y en 1945 en universidad. En 1998 tenía un número aproximado de 1,150 profesores y 6,692 estudiantes. Publica la revista mensual *Colmena Universitaria*.

Universidad Iberoamericana ♦ Centro privado de enseñanza. Fue fundado en 1943, con sede en la ciudad de México y con el nombre de Centro Cultural Universitario. En 1973, la Secretaría de Educación Pública le otorgó el reconocimiento de validez oficial a sus estudios y, más tarde, en 1976, amplió este reconocimiento a cualquier parte de la República Mexicana, lo que le permitió abrir planteles en León (1978; con 1,684 alumnos en 1998), Tijuana (Noreste, 1982; con 842 alumnos en 1998), Torreón (Laguna, 1982; con 2,081 alumnos en 1998) y Puebla (Golfo-Centro, 1983; con 3,750 alumnos en 1998). El decreto presidencial del 27 de abril de 1981 le otorgó la validez oficial a sus programas de bachillerato y de educación superior. La institución está conformada por 17 departamentos, dedicados a cultivar las humanidades, el arte, las ciencias básicas sociales y de salud, las disciplinas económico-administrativas, el derecho y la ingeniería. En 1979 un sismo derribó el plantel que la institución tenía en la colonia Campestre Churubusco, por lo que la comunidad universitaria promovió una campaña de reconstrucción. Sus nuevas instalaciones se hallan en Santa Fe, en el occidente del Distrito Federal, en la cual ofrece 33 licenciaturas, 20 maestrías, seis doctorados y dos programas de especialización, además de más de 100 cursos y diploma-

Foto: Fondo Editorial Grupo Azabache

Universidad de Guanajuato

dos. En 1998 tenía 10,088 alumnos en licenciatura. Tiene un catálogo editorial con más de 800 títulos y publica las revistas *Didac, Historia y Gráfica, Jurídica, Poesía y Poética, Prometeo, Psicología Iberoamericana, Sociología y Política, Revista de Filosofía, Revista Iberoamericana de Derecho a la Información* y *Umbral XXI*.

Universidad Juárez Autónoma de Tabasco ◆ Fundada en la ciudad de Villahermosa en 1958. Contaba en 1980 con ocho facultades o escuelas de enseñanza profesional y en 1998 contaba con 18,851 alumnos.

Universidad Juárez del Estado de Durango ◆ Inició sus tareas en agosto de 1957 en la ciudad de Durango y obtuvo la autonomía el 30 de abril de 1962. En 1980 contaba con siete facultades o escuelas profesionales, dos institutos de investigación. En 1998 tenía 7,561 estudiantes.

Universidad La Salle de México ◆ Institución privada incorporada a la UNAM. Fue fundada en 1962 en la ciudad de México. En 1980 otorgaba títulos de licenciatura y de maestría. En 1998 contaba con 7,145 alumnos en su plantel del DF. Edita una *Gaceta, Indicador Diez Días, Boletín de Biblioteca* y el *Boletín de Preparatoria*. Su antecedente se localiza en los colegios fundados por los santos lasallistas en 1905; en los años treinta, éstos fundaron las preparatorias de los colegios Francés de La Salle y Cristóbal Colón. El primer rector de la universidad fue Manuel J. Álvarez Campos. Para 1995 contaba con seis planteles foráneos ubicados en Guadalajara (213 alumnos en 1998), Morelia (191 alumnos en 1998), Cuernavaca (622 alumnos en 1998), Cancún (651 alumnos en 1998), Ciudad Obregón (414 alumnos en 1998) y Pachuca (356 alumnos en 1998).

Universidad Literaria Nacional y Pontificia de las Chiapas ◆ Fundada en 1826, impartió cursos de latín, filosofía, derecho canónico, derecho civil, medicina y, desde 1862, francés, matemáticas, cronología e historia. En 1872, en decadencia, se transformó en el Instituto Literario y Científico del Estado de Chiapas.

Universidad Michoacana de San Nicolás de Hidalgo ◆ Creada en 1917 a partir del Colegio Primitivo y Nacional de San Nicolás (que en 1782 obtuvo de la Real y Pontificia Universidad de México el permiso para establecer las cátedras de cánones y leyes), fundado en Pátzcuaro y trasladado después a Morelia. En 1962, al iniciarse el periodo del gobernador Agustín Arriaga Rivera, en la Universidad Nicolaíta se había iniciado una reforma que pretendía elevar el nivel académico y dar a ese centro de enseñanza una orientación más apegada a los intereses de obreros y campesinos. Como respuesta, los sinarquistas, el PAN, la Cámara de Comercio y otros sectores de la derecha local apoyaron, incluso mediante la violencia, a un grupo minoritario de profesores empeñado en defender sus posiciones dentro de la casa de estudios. Con la intención de poner fin al proceso de cambios y a los conflictos suscitados por éste, el gobernador envió al Congreso local un proyecto de Ley Orgánica de la Universidad, el que una vez aprobado motivó que estudiantes y profesores realizaran una multitudinaria marcha de protesta por las calles de Morelia, donde fueron reprimidos por la fuerza pública con saldo de un muerto y varios heridos. Poco después resultaron encarcelados cuatro maestros y dos estudiantes partidarios de la reforma. En octubre hubo un alza en las tarifas del transporte urbano en Morelia, lo que ocasionó una extensa protesta popular encabezada por los estudiantes. El 2 de octubre la policía mató a un estudiante y, como respuesta, el día 3 se inició una huelga de los universitarios, quienes calificaron al gobierno de Arriaga de "torpe y agresor" y de emplear a grupos de golpeadores contra los huelguistas. Las demandas eran tres: castigo a los asesinos, eliminación de los latifundios existentes en el estado y desaparición de poderes locales. El Consejo Universitario, encabezado por Jaime Labastida, y el rector Nicanor Gómez apoyaron las exigencias estudiantiles y, por su parte, campesinos de la entidad formaron un Comité Estatal de Lucha para respaldar a los universitarios. Para poner fin al movimiento, que se extendía a diversos núcleos sociales, el día 8 de octubre de 1966 el ejército entró en la universidad. Quince personas, entre líderes estudiantiles y campesinos, fueron encarceladas. El Congreso local aprobó con celeridad una nueva Ley Orgánica que daba al gobierno mayor control sobre ese centro de enseñanza, se clausuró la Escuela de Altos Estudios, se desligó a las secundarias de la universidad y fueron cerradas las casas del estudiante. En 1998 esta universidad contaba con 23,381 alumnos de licenciatura.

Universidad Iberoamericana

Foto: Carlos Hahn

Escudo original de la Universidad Nacional de México, antecedente de la unam

Universidad Nacional Autónoma de México ◆ Institución creada como Universidad Nacional de México, a iniciativa de Justo Sierra y Ezequiel A. Chávez y por decreto presidencial del 26 de mayo de 1910, como una dependencia de la Secretaría de Instrucción Pública y Bellas Artes. Pese a que de hecho y formalmente esta institución no deriva de la Real y Pontificia Universidad de México (☛), suele considerarse a ésta como su antecedente. Inició sus labores el 22 de septiembre del mismo año de 1910, "despojada de toda reliquia escolástica, de toda filosofía de rutina". Los cuatro primeros artículos de su Ley Constitutiva establecían: "Se instituye, con el nombre de Universidad Nacional de México un cuerpo docente cuyo objeto primordial será realizar en sus elementos superiores la obra de la educación nacional. La Universidad quedará constituida por la reunión de las Escuelas Nacionales Preparatorias, de Jurisprudencia, de Medicina, de Ingenieros, de Bellas Artes (en lo concerniente a la enseñanza de la arquitectura) y de Altos Estudios. El ministro de Instrucción Pública y Bellas Artes será el Jefe de la Universidad; el gobierno de ésta quedará, además, a cargo de un rector y un consejo universitario. El rector de la Universidad será nombrado por el Presidente de la República; durará en su cargo tres años; pero podrá renovarse su nombramiento para uno o varios trienios". Durante la dictadura de Victoriano Huerta fue separada la Escuela Nacional Preparatoria de la universidad. En diciembre de 1914, un grupo de profesores universitarios firmó un proyecto de autonomía formulado por Ezequiel A. Chávez, documento que se presentó al gobierno convencionista sin que haya prosperado por la propia inestabilidad política de este órgano. Carranza, por su parte, en el decreto de reorganizacion de las secretarías y departamentos de Estado del 5 de febrero de 1917, suprimió la Secretaría de Instrucción Pública y creó el Departamento Universitario y de Bellas Artes, que ocupó José Natividad Macías en mayo de ese año. Según el decreto, quedaban bajo jurisdicción de dicho departamento "todas las escuelas que dependan actualmente de la Universidad Nacional y todos los demás establecimientos docentes o de investigación científica que se crearen en lo sucesivo. Escuelas de Bellas Artes, Música y Declamación, de Artes Gráficas, de Archiveros y Bibliotecarios. Propiedad literaria, dramática y artística. Bibliotecas, museos y antigüedades nacionales. Fomento de Artes y Ciencias. Exposiciones de obras de arte. Congresos científicos y artísticos. Extensión universitaria". Según el artículo 15 del decreto "El Departamento Universitario y de Bellas Artes se denominará 'Universidad Nacional' y estará bajo el rector de esta institución". El departamento era, de hecho y derecho, la universidad misma. El 10 de julio de 1917, el Senado modificó la parte del decreto referente al Departamento Universitario para incluirlo entre las dependencias de la Secretaría de Educación. El debate continuó y, mientras tanto, subsistió el departamento con las facultades que le había conferido Carranza. Bajo la presidencia de Álvaro Obregón, la universidad se convirtió en dependencia de la Secretaría de Educación Pública al crearse esta cartera, el 28 de septiembre de 1921. El 31 de diciembre de ese año, el secretario de Educación, José Vasconcelos, giró un oficio al rector Antonio Caso, en el que le informaba que formaban parte de la universidad "las siguientes instituciones: Facultad de Altos Estudios, Facultad de Jurisprudencia, Facultad de Medicina, Facultad Odontológica, Escuela de Medicina Homeopática, Facultad de Ingenieros, Escuela Nacional Preparatoria, y que está a su cargo también la Extensión Universitaria". Otro oficio, del 17 de enero, comunicaba que la Facultad de Ciencias e Industrias Químicas no dependería de la Dirección de Educación Técnica y que a partir del día primero anterior debería "ser considerada con la categoría de facultad dependiente de esa Universidad". El 27 de agosto de 1923, la Federación de Estudiantes de México solicitó a la Cámara de Diputados que se concediera autonomía a la Universidad Nacional en lo referente a su estructura técnica y el manejo de sus recursos, dominio directo sobre los inmuebles donde se hallaban los centros de enseñanza y facultad para profesores y estudiantes de proponer al presidente una terna para la elección de rector. Después de casi dos décadas de existencia de esta casa de estudios, el 6 de mayo estalló la huelga universitaria de 1929 (☛) que desembocó, el 10 de julio de ese año, en la expedición de la Ley Orgánica de la Universidad Nacional de México que concedía la autonomía a esta casa de estudios. Bajo el rectorado de Roberto Medellín y promovido y dirigido por Vicente Lombardo Toledano, en septiembre de 1933 se celebró el Congreso de Universitarios Mexicanos, que resolvió normar la enseñanza superior por el método del materialismo dialéctico, de acuerdo con el concepto de educación socialista que impulsaba el partido oficial. Los acuerdos de este Congreso resultaron inaceptables para un amplio sector de profesores y estudiantes, quienes juzgaron que se atentaba contra la libertad de cátedra. Se inició entonces un conflicto en el que abundaron los choques violentos. La huelga universitaria de 1933 (☛) culminó con la expedición de la Ley Orgánica del 21 de octubre de ese año, que ampliaba la autonomía de esa casa de estudios, pues eliminaba el derecho de veto del pre-

Escudo de la UNAM

sidente de la República, cancelaba el subsidio anual y le otorgaba 10,000,000 de pesos por única vez, pero le quitaba el carácter de "nacional". De hecho, convertía a la Universidad Autónoma de México en una institución privada. De acuerdo con la nueva norma jurídica, fue elegido rector Manuel Gómez Morín, futuro fundador del PAN, a quien otra huelga, ocurrida en 1934, lo obligó a renunciar. En esta época, la Universidad se componía de la Escuela Nacional Preparatoria, la Escuela de Verano, los Cursos de Invierno, los Cursos Especiales, las unidades de investigación y cuatro facultades que, a su vez, agrupaban escuelas. La Facultad de Filosofía y Bellas Artes comprendía las escuelas de Filosofía y Letras, de Arquitectura, de Artes Plásticas y Superior de Música; la Facultad de Derecho y Ciencias Sociales estaba formada por las escuelas de Derecho, Economía y Comercio y Administración; la Facultad de Ciencias Médicas y Biológicas englobaba el Departamento de Ciencias Biológicas, las escuelas de Medicina Veterinaria, Odontología y de Medicina, ésta a su ves dividida en dos secciones: Medicina propiamente dicha y Enfermería y Obstetricia; y, por último, la Facultad de Ciencias Físicas y Matemáticas, donde estaban el Departamento de Ciencias Físicas y Matemáticas y las escuelas de Ingenieros y de Ciencias Químicas. En 1935, el rector Fernando Ocaranza, quien creó el ciclo de iniciación universitaria, correspondiente a la educación secundaria, obtuvo un subsidio extraordinario de dos millones de pesos, lo que alivió momentáneamente la precaria situación económica de la Universidad, pero abrió la puerta a las presiones oficiales para introducir la educación socialista. El rector informó que había recibido una carta del presidente Lázaro Cárdenas con esa intención, lo que llevó a varios profesores a presentar su renuncia el 16 de septiembre de 1935. El texto del documento, redactado por Ezequiel A. Chávez, decía: "la carta dirigida por el señor Presidente a usted, acerca de la condición que en lo venidero habrá de tener la Universidad, deja completamente claro que el Gobierno de la Unión ha resuelto hacer desaparecer la libertad de cátedra y por lo mismo la autonomía universitaria". Al grupo de profesores renunciantes, en el que estaban Alfonso Caso, Pablo Martínez del Río, Artemio de Valle-Arizpe, Federico Gamboa, Federico Mariscal, se unió el rector Ocaranza, quien dejó su cargo el 17 de septiembre. Le sucedió Luis Chico Goerne, quien hizo aprobar en 1936 un nuevo Estatuto que creó el Departamento de Acción Social, para difusión externa, y dejó en cuatro el número de institutos de investigación: Geología, Astronomía e Investigaciones Físico-Matemáticas; el de Biología; el de Investigaciones Sociales y el de Investigaciones Estéticas. En 1937 se fundó Radio Universidad, con Alejandro Gómez Arias al frente, y en 1938 el Instituto de Física. En marzo de 1938, la relación con el gobierno, tradicionalmente conflictiva, se transformó momentáneamente por efecto de la expropiación petrolera, pues los universitarios realizaron una manifestación de apoyo a la medida y un mitin en el que Gómez Arias habló en nombre de la institución. Con Gustavo Baz a la rectoría, desde mediados de 1938, se aprobó un nuevo Estatuto y mejoraron sustancialmente las relaciones entre las autoridades universitarias y el gobierno, que entregaron regularmente un subsidio a la institución. Quienes desempeñaban cargos en la universidad ocparon simultáneamente puestos públicos o empezaron a pasar de unos a otros. El propio Baz renunció a la rectoría para incorporarse al gabinete del presidente Manuel Ávila Camacho. El rector Rodulfo Brito Foucher se propuso introducir diversas reformas apoyado en un grupo de pistoleros conocido como la *Bristapo*, nombre que quería evidenciar su filiación nazi. El pistolerismo cobró varias víctimas y el asesinato del joven José García Castillo, del que los estudiantes acusaron al rector, lo que desembocó en la huelga universitaria de 1944 (☛). Brito renunció ante el Consejo Universitario, que nombró rector a Samuel Ramírez Moreno, quien no aceptó, y luego a José Aguilar Álvarez. Por otra parte, el movimiento antibritista había creado un directorio en el que figuraban maestros prominentes, quienes, a su vez, designaron rector a Pedro Argüelles y, como éste declinara, a Manuel Gual Vidal. Los bandos buscaron el apoyo, y el subsidio, del presidente Ávila Camacho, quien impuso como fórmula conciliatoria la integración de una Junta de Avenimiento formada por los ex rectores, salvo Brito y los más recientes, quienes eligieron rector a Alfonso Caso. El gobierno encargó al Consejo Universitario la elaboración de un proyecto de Ley Orgánica que el 30 de diciembre de 1944 fue aprobado por el Congreso y surgió así la Universidad Nacional Autónoma de México. Esta ley, vigente desde entonces, no logró evitar nuevos conflictos. En 1948 el rector Salvador Zubirán elevó en 10 por ciento las colegiaturas, lo que produjo una nueva huelga que llevó a presentar su renun-

Timbre conmemorativo del LXXV aniversario de la apertura de la Universidad Nacional de México

Biblioteca Central de la Universidad Nacional Autónoma de México

Foto: Jorge Contreras Chacel

cia. Después de un interinato de Alfonso Ochoa Ravizé, la Junta de Gobierno nombró rector a Luis G. Garrido, pero un sector de los estudiantes eligió a Antonio Díaz Soto y Gama, a quien dieron "posesión" en el edificio de Justo Sierra 16. Sin reconocimiento de los órganos universitarios y, en consecuencia, sin presupuesto, Soto y Gama desistió y Garrido pudo asumir el cargo. Durante su gestión se crearon el Departamento de Psicopedagogía y la Escuela Nacional de Ciencias Políticas y Sociales; se conmemoró el supuesto cuarto centenario de la universidad, considerando que la Nacional era la misma que la Real y Pontificia, y en 1950 se inició la construcción de la Ciudad Universitaria, que aún inconclusa se inauguró ("dedicó", se dijo entonces) el 20 de noviembre de 1952. El 10 de febrero de 1953 renunció Garrido y le sucedió Nabor Carrillo Flores, quien al tomar posesión del cargo dijo que la universidad, "pese a sus penurias, pese a sus angustias físicas y pese a sus problemas de todo orden es una milagrosa cantera de hombres extraordinarios". Durante el rectorado de Carrillo Flores se escrituraron en favor de la UNAM los terrenos de la Ciudad Universitaria, se fomentó la difusión cultural, aumentó el interés por los espectáculos deportivos, sobre todo el futbol americano, la porra adquirió una fuerza sin precedente y estalló una huelga en 1958 contra el alza en las tarifas del transporte urbano. Después de dos periodos completos, Carrillo fue sucedido por Ignacio Chávez, quien amplió el ciclo de bachillerato de dos a tres años, estableció los exámenes de admisión, tanto para el primer ingreso como para el paso de uno a otro ciclo, pese a que la misma universidad hubiera dado calificaciones aprobatorias; hizo construir planteles preparatorianos fuera del centro de la ciudad y, para elevar el nivel académico y hacer más rigurosa la disciplina adoptó diversas medidas que fueron impuestas frecuentemente contra la opinión de la comunidad. La disidencia fue reprimida por la fuerza y en 1966, en la Facultad de Derecho, estalló una huelga que se extendió a otros planteles universitarios. Con representantes de todas las escuelas se constituyó el Consejo Estudiantil Universitario (CEU), que demandó, entre otros puntos, la desaparición del cuerpo de vigilancia, el pase autómatico a licenciatura para los egresados de la Escuela Nacional Preparatoria y la realización de una reforma universitaria de carácter democrático. En abril, un grupo de estudiantes de Derecho y Economía se posesionó de la Rectoría y obligó a renunciar a Ignacio Chávez. Le sucedió Javier Barros Sierra (☛), quien inició el proceso de reforma que habían exigido los huelguistas. Durante el movimiento estudiantil de 1968 (☛), la casa de estudios fue ocupada por el ejército y el rector fue objeto de una campaña infamante promovida por políticos del partido gubernamental. Barros Sierra optó por dejar la UNAM, pero la Junta de Gobierno esa vez coincidió con el punto de vista de la mayoría universitaria al rechazar su renuncia. El movimiento fue sometido a una creciente represión que culminó con el asesinato de manifestantes inermes el 2 de octubre, en Tlatelolco. La matanza fue ejecutada por órdenes del presidente Gustavo Díaz Ordaz. Después de Barros Sierra fue rector Pablo González Casanova, quien creó el Colegio de Ciencias y Humanidades e inició el proceso de desconcentración de la UNAM que continuarían otros rectores a lo largo de los años setenta. A principios de esa década dio principio el proceso para sindicalizar a los trabajadores universitarios. El 12 de octubre de 1971 se constituyó el Sindicato de Trabajadores y Empleados de la UNAM, que en octubre del año siguiente estalló una huelga en demanda de contratación colectiva. El rector Pablo González Casanova renunció y en su lugar entró Guillermo Soberón, quien firmó no un contrato, pues el STEUNAM no contaba con personalidad jurídica ante las autoridades laborales, sino un convenio que modificó el Estatuto del Personal Administrativo. En junio de 1974 se fundó el Sindicato de Personal Académico y, para contrarrestarlo, simpatizantes de las

Represión contra el movimiento estudiantil de 1968, en el cual participaron alumnos de la comunidad de la Universidad Nacional Autónoma de México

Manifestación de estudiantes de la UNAM en contra del alza de tarifas del transporte urbano

FOTO: HÉCTOR GARCÍA

autoridades universitarias y políticos afines al gobierno constituyeron la Asociación de Asociaciones (*sic*) de Personal Académico de la UNAM. El 27 de marzo de 1977, STEUNAM y SPAUNAM se fusionaron y crearon el STUNAM que en junio fue a la huelga en demanda de contrato colectivo, lo que fue rechazado por la Rectoría. Las autoridades laborales declararon la huelga "ilegal" y el 7 de julio 14,000 policías tomaron las instalaciones universitarias y fueron detenidos brevemente algunos líderes sindicales. Pese a lo anterior, el 10 de julio la Rectoría accedió a negociar con el sindicato un nuevo convenio de trabajo. Al reformarse la legislación laboral y aceptarse el registro de los sindicatos universitarios, la Rectoría firmó sendos contratos colectivos con el STUNAM y la AAPAUNAM. En 1985, el rector Jorge Carpizo presentó al Consejo Universitario un extenso documento conocido como *Fortaleza y debilidad de la UNAM*. En él presentaba una relación de los problemas universitarios y concluía que todo se iba a resolver cuando los investigadores investiguen, los profesores enseñen y los estudiantes estudien, lo que excluía de toda responsabilidad al sector administrativo. El Consejo Universitario aprobó sin discusión un paquete de medidas propuestas por el rector, las que despertaron el rechazo mayoritario de la comunidad. Todo mundo estuvo de acuerdo con el rector en que la casa de estudios atravesaba por una crisis, pero no se aceptó su conclusión de que los culpables eran investigadores, profesores y alumnos, contra quienes se dirigían los acuerdos del Consejo Universitario, los que en 1986 tuvieron como consecuencia una nueva huelga que demandaba la derogación de lo resuelto por las autoridades, la democratización de la UNAM, mayor presupuesto, el control del gasto y de la burocracia y la celebración de un congreso para discutir libremente las mejores vías hacia la elevación del nivel académico. Se creó, como 20 años antes, un Consejo Estudiantil Universitario (CEU) que exigió diálogo público con las autoridades, el que se transmitió por Radio UNAM. Pese a una costosísima campaña de prensa para desprestigiar al movimiento estudiantil, éste logró que se aceptara la celebración del congreso, que tuvo lugar del 14 de mayo al 5 de junio y cuyas resoluciones fueron adoptadas por el Consejo Universitario el 18 de octubre. En 1990 la UNAM contaba con 271,358 alumnos, 28,389 miembros profesores y empleados académicos y 25,664 empleados administrativos; impartía 70 carreras y 284 cursos de posgrado en 12 facultades y nueve escuelas nacionales; ofrecía educación media superior en nueve escuelas preparatorias y cinco colegios de ciencias y humanidades. En 1991, la UNAM adquirió una supercomputadora Cray que, además de facilitar numerosos proyectos de investigación, permitía administrar una gran cantidad de servicios, especialmente los de conexión a internet. En 1992 la Biblioteca Nacional fue ampliada y sus Fondos de Origen y Reservado fueron trasladados a Ciudad Universitaria desde el antiguo templo de San Agustín. En 1993 se abrió el Museo de las Ciencias Universum en el Centro Cultural Universitario. En 1995 se lanzó al espacio, sin éxito, el primer satélite de la UNAM, el UNAMSAT-I, diseñado y construido enteramente por universitarios. En 1996, se informó de la aplicación del Examen General de Calidad Profesional, lo que sujeta a la Universidad Autónoma a supervisión externa. Igualmente, el Centro Nacional para la Evaluación de la Educación Superior (Ceneval) estableció un examen único de ingreso al bachillerato en la zona metropolitana del DF, el que al ofrecer varias opciones a los aspirantes quitó a la UNAM la presión de una de-

Foto: Jorge Contreras Chacel

Edificio de Rectoría de la Universidad Nacional Autónoma de México

Foto: Pablo González de Alba

Estadio Olímpico de Ciudad Universitaria, en la UNAM

Foto: Jorge Contreras Chacel

Sala Nezahuacóyotl de la Universidad Nacional Autónoma de México

manda excesiva, pero nuevamente quedó en manos de un órgano externo la decisión de cuáles y cuántos aspirantes podían ingresar a la Universidad Nacional. En el mismo año tuvo lugar el lanzamiento exitoso del satélite UNAMSAT-B, dedicado a la investigación científica, y en ese año se abrieron también los institutos de Matemáticas y Astronomía y la Unidad del Centro de Ecología en Morelia, Michoacán. En 1997, en su sesión del 9 de junio, el Consejo Universitario aprobó modificaciones a los principios y criterios para regular el ingreso y la permanencia de estudiantes en la universidad. Igualmente, el 1 de julio aprobó modificaciones a los reglamentos generales de Inscripciones y Exámenes de la UNAM. En 1999, en una sesión realizada fuera de las sedes de la propia universidad, el Consejo Universitario aprobó sin discusión un aumento de las cuotas de inscripción y colegiatura. Los estudiantes declararon que las cuotas eran anticonstitucionales y demandaron, entre otros puntos, la dimisión del rector Barnés, -quien renunció, en noviembre de ese año-, la derogación del reglamento, la cancelación del convenio con el Ceneval y la celebración de un congreso para discutir los problemas de la UNAM El 20 de mayo se inició la huelga estudiantil más prolongada en la historia de la universidad mexicana.

Escudo de la Universidad Pontificia de México

Universidad Obrera de México ◆ Institución fundada el 8 de febrero de 1936 por Vicente Lombardo Toledano, tres años después de su salida de la UNAM. Con sede en la calle de San Ildefonso número 72, de la ciudad de México, ofrece cursos de alfabetización, secundaria abierta y educación superior. Sus directores han sido Vicente Lombardo Toledano (1936-68) y Adriana Lombardo Otero (1968-). En su plantilla de profesores se han contado, entre otros, Alexander Abush, Carlos Zapata Vela, Andre Simone, Enrique Yáñez, Laszlo Radvanyi, Rudolf Neumann, Carmen Otero Gama, Leo Lambert, Leo Katz, Paul Westheim, Anna Seghers, Hannes Meyer, Egon Erwin Kisch, Lázaro Peña, Juan Marinello, Aníbal Ponce, Enrique Délano, Alonso Aguilar, Agustín Yáñez, Mario Rivera, Carlota Guzmán, Leopoldo Ancona, Bodo Uhse, Enrique Arreguín, Ángel Bassols y Clementina Batalla de Bassols.

Universidad Panamericana ◆ Institución educativa privada fundada en 1978. Mantenida por el Opus Dei (☛), su antecedente inmediato fue el Instituto Panamericano de Humanidades, fundado en 1968 y elevado al rango de universidad 10 años más tarde. En 1981, la universidad abrió un plantel en Guadalajara, que en 1998 contaba con 2,286 alumnos. Más tarde abrió, en Aguascalientes, la Universidad Bonaterra, cuya población era de 727 alumnos en 1998. En Tamaulipas abrió otro plantel, con 618 alumnos en 1998. Actualmente, la universidad ofrece las carreras de administración y mercadotecnia, administración y finanzas, administración y negocios internacionales, administración y relaciones internacionales, contaduría pública, pedagogía, derecho, ingeniería civil, ingeniería electromecánica e ingeniería civil administrativa. En 1998 tenía 3,389 alumnos.

Universidad Pontificia de Mérida ◆ Fue fundada en 1824 y extinguida en 1861. Impartió las cátedras de gramática, filosofía, teología, moral, derecho canónico, derecho civil, medicina y cirugía, matemáticas, química, física y literatura. En 1864 su infraestructura fue aprovechada para fundar la Academia de Literatura y Ciencias Eclesiásticas.

Universidad Pontificia de México ◆ Después del cierre definitivo de la Real y Pontificia Universidad de México (☛), la jerarquía eclesiástica logró crear una institución heredera de aquélla, la Nueva Pontificia Universidad Mexicana (☛), erigida por bula del papa León XIII del 14 de diciembre de 1895. Sin embargo, los conflictos entre la Iglesia y el Estado obligaron a cerrarla nuevamente en 1932. La reapertura de una universidad pontificia fue pedida al Vaticano por el arzobispo Luis María Martínez (1949), por el arzobispo Miguel Darío Miranda (1958) y por la Conferencia de Institutos Religiosos de México (1960). Finalmente, el papa Juan Pablo II aprobó la creación de la Universidad Pontificia de México el 29 de junio de 1982. Como gran canciller de la institución figura Sergio Obeso Rivera y como vice gran canciller, Ernesto Corripio Ahumada. Es su rector Jorge Medina Orozco. Edita *Efemérides Mexicana, Ágora* y el *Boletín Informativo*. En 1986 esta universidad fundó un Instituto de Investigación Histórica.

Universidad Popular Mexicana ◆ Fue fundada en la ciudad de México el 3 de diciembre de 1912 por los miembros del Ateneo de México (antes Ateneo de la Juventud), con el fin de impartir educación superior a los trabajadores. Su primer rector fue Alberto J. Pani, a quien en 1914 sustituyó Alfonso Pruneda; éste fue rector hasta la clausura de la institución (1922). De carácter privado, fue cerrada cuando las donaciones de particulares fueron insuficientes. Tuvo dos secretarios de la Junta de Gobierno: Martín Luis Guzmán (1912-17) y Vicente Lombardo Toledano (1917-22). De 1915 a 1916 publicó un *Boletín*. Entre los colaboradores más destacados de la institución se contaron Antonio Caso, Alfonso Reyes, Pedro Henríquez Ureña, Jesús Acevedo, Manuel Gómez Morín, Guillermo Zárraga, Alfonso Caso, Salvador Ordóñez, Everardo Landa y José Terrés.

Universidad Regiomontana ◆ Institución particular fundada en 1957, con sede en la capital de Nuevo León.

En 1980 contaba con 509 profesores y 7,200 alumnos de bachillerato, licenciatura, maestría y doctorado. En 1998 tenía 2,694 alumnos de licenciatura. Publicaba la revista *Urbi*.

UNIVERSIDAD DE TIRIPETÍO ◆ Se le considera la primera universidad de América. Fue fundada por fray Alonso de la Veracruz, su primer rector (1540-51), por cédula real de Carlos V.

UNIVERSIDAD DE TLAXCALA ◆ Fue creada el 20 de noviembre de 1976 por decreto del gobierno estatal; imparte 12 carreras profesionales, carreras de nivel medio terminal y cursos de idiomas.

UNIVERSIDAD VERACRUZANA ◆ Institución fundada en 1944, con sede en Xalapa. Tiene planteles también en Orizaba, Córdoba, Coatzacoalcos y Minatitlán. Además de los estudios superiores que imparte, en diversas áreas, incide en la vida científica y cultural del estado de Veracruz mediante numerosos institutos de investigación, publicaciones, museos, un observatorio, compañías de teatro y la Orquesta Sinfónica de Xalapa. Fue creada por decreto del gobernador Jorge Cerdán. Tuvo su antecedente en el Instituto Literario de Veracruz, creado por el gobernador Francisco Hernández y Hernández hacia 1870. Es autónoma desde 1996, y funciona de manera descentralizada. Edita *La Palabra y el Hombre, Extensión* y otras publicaciones.

UNIVERSIDAD DE YUCATÁN ◆ Creada el 27 de febrero de 1922 como Universidad Nacional del Sureste, por un convenio suscrito entre el secretario de Educación Pública, José Vasconcelos, y el gobernador Felipe Carrillo Puerto. En 1938 el gobernador Humberto Canto Echeverría promulgó un nuevo estatuto, la convirtió en Universidad de Yucatán (aunque de 1951 a 1958 volvió a ser Universidad Nacional del Sureste) y le otorgó la autonomía. En 1980 contaba con dos facultades, siete escuelas profesionales y una de enseñanza media superior. En 1998 su población de licenciatura era de 7,430 alumnos. Publica la *Revista de la Universidad de Yucatán*.

UNO, PRIMITIVO ◆ n. en General Terán, Chih., y m. en Salamanca, Gto. (1881-1966). Militante del Partido Liberal Mexicano. A fines del porfiriato se afilió al antirreeleccionismo. En 1913 se incorporó a la División del Norte, de la que fue proveedor general y en la que alcanzó el grado de coronel por méritos en combate. Al término de la lucha armada ocupó puestos públicos en Chihuahua. En 1926 fundó el Frente Nacional Villista. Se le otorgó un reconocimiento de la Legión de Honor Mexicana como veterano de la revolución.

UNOMÁSUNO ◆ Diario publicado en la ciudad de México. El primer número apareció el 14 de noviembre de 1977. En el directorio aparecía Manuel Becerra Acosta como director general y Carlos Payán como subdirector; José Solís García, subdirector técnico; Marco Aurelio Carballo, coordinador de información; Jorge Hernández Campos y Manuel Moreno Sánchez, coordinadores editoriales, y Sonia Labadié como gerente. Su diseño gráfico fue obra de Pablo Rulfo. En 1989 la dirección del diario fue asumida por Luis Gutiérrez Rodríguez y en 1998 por Rafael Cardona. Edita los suplementos *Sábado*, fundado por Fernando Benítez y dirigido desde 1986 por Huberto Batis; y *Página Uno*, que dirige Luis Gutiérrez Esparza.

MIÉRCOLES 17 DE NOVIEMBRE DE 1999

unomásuno

Enérgico y contundente mensaje del presidente en la IX Cumbre Iberoamericana

EZ: sólo hay libertad con democracia plena

Insuficientes recursos para demandas sociales: Gurría

Zedillo exalta la libertad para disentir; Fidel se esfuma como negra oveja

Ofrece FLO lucha total contra la delincuencia

Más allá de la tolerancia

Periódico unomásuno del 17 de noviembre de 1999

UNZUETA, GERARDO ◆ n. en Tampico, Tams. (1925). Periodista. Hizo estudios de leyes y artes plásticas en la UNAM. Militante del PCM (1946-81), del PSUM (1981-88), del PMS (1988-89) y del PRD (1989-). Ha sido director de *La Voz de México* y *Oposición*, órganos del PCM, así como de *La Unidad* (PMS) y *6 de Julio* (PRD). Editó las revistas *Socialismo* y *Memoria*. Colaboró en las revistas *Política* y *Siempre!* Es colaborador de la página editorial de *El Universal* desde 1985. En el PCM y el PSUM fue miembro del Comité Central y de la Comisión Política de ambos partidos. Es miembro del Consejo Nacional del PRD desde

FOTO: BORIS DE SWAN

Universidad Veracruzana

Universidad (hoy Autónoma) de Yucatán

FOTO: FONDO EDITORIAL GRUPO AZABACHE

Gerardo Unzueta

1992. Fue presidente del Servicio Electoral del mismo partido de 1996 a 1998. Como consecuencia de su participación como secretario general del Partido Comunista en el DF y de su apoyo al movimiento estudiantil, sufrió prisión política de 1968 a 1971. Ha sido diputado federal por el Partido Comunista y la Coalición de Izquierda (1979-82) y por el PSUM (1985-88). Autor de *Lombardo Toledano y el marxismo-leninismo, La concepción materialista de la historia, Nuevo programa para la nueva revolución, Ocho puntos de vista sobre la teoría marxista del Estado* y *Comunistas y sindicatos*. Ha sido miembro del Sindicato de Redactores de la Prensa, de la Asociación Mexicana de Periodistas y de la Unión de Periodistas Democráticos. Actualmente se desempeña como asesor del gobierno del DF para asuntos legislativos.

URANGA, EMILIO ◆ n. y m. en el DF (1921-1988). Realizó estudios de medicina y la maestría en filosofía en la UNAM, se doctoró en Alemania. Llevó cursos de especialización en las universidades Albertina de Friburgo, de Tübingen, de Colonia, de Oxford y en la Sorbona. Investigador en el Instituto de Investigaciones Sociales en la UNAM, en donde también fue profesor de las facultades de medicina y de filosofía. Dio clases en la Escuela Normal Superior y en diversas universidades del país y del extranjero, como la de San Marcos de Lima, Perú y la de La Habana, Cuba. En 1949 trabajó en el Departamento de Prensa de la UNESCO. Miembro de la Academia Peruana de Filosofía (1951), de la Academia Mexicana de Filosofía y de la Sociedad Cubana de Filosofía en 1953. Fue secretario de la Sociedad Mexicana de Filosofía en 1957. Colaboró en *Cuadernos Americanos, Revista de la Facultad de Filosofía y Letras, Historia de México, Epígrafes, Novedades, El Nacional* y *El Universal*. Autor de los ensayos: *Análisis del ser del mexicano* (1952), *Apología y vejamen de la fenomenología* (1957), *Introducción a la lectura de Jorge Lukács* (1957), *Astucias literarias* (1971), *Mi camino hacia Marx* (1973), *Andanzas de mocedad* (1976), *¿De quién es la filosofía?* (1977) y *El tablero de enfrente* (1979). Recibió la Medalla Antonio Caso en 1949 y fue becario del Centro Mexicano de Escritores en dos ocasiones (1957-58 y 1958-59).

URANGA Y SÁENZ, FRANCISCO ◆ n. en Santa Cruz de Rosales, Chih., y m. en el DF (1863-1930). Sacerdote ordenado en 1886. Fue párroco de varias iglesias en Chihuahua y contribuyó a formar la Sociedad Mutualista de Artesanos de Ciudad Lerdo. Obispo de Sinaloa (1903-17), se exilió en Estados Unidos y volvió a México en 1919 como obispo de Tloe y auxiliar del arzobispo de Guadalajara. Obispo de Cuernavaca (1922-30), de 1926 a 1929, durante la guerra cristera, volvió a refugiarse en Estados Unidos.

URBALEJO, FRANCISCO ◆ n. en el Mineral de Bayoreca y m. en La Esperanza, Son. (1880-1950). Militar. En 1900 participó, como soldado raso, en una de las campañas federales contra los yaquis. En 1910 combatió a las fuerzas maderistas y dos años después defendió al gobierno de Francisco I. Madero contra el levantamiento orozquista. Se unió a la revolución constitucionalista y durante unos días de 1914 se alineó con la Convención de Aguscalientes. Seguidor del Plan de Agua Prieta, combatió nuevamente contra los yaquis y en 1929 se sumó a la rebelión escobarista.

URBÁN, VÍCTOR ◆ n. en Tultepec, Edo. de Méx. (1934). Organista egresado del Conservatorio Nacional, en el que estudió con Jesús Estrada (1951-60) y del que más tarde fue profesor y director (1974-77). Se especializó en el Instituto Pontificio de Música Sacra, en la Academia Chigiana de Siena con Fernando Germani, en el Instituto Pontificio de Música Sacra en el Vaticano con Ferruccio Vignarelli, y en Alemania con Helmuth Rilling. También estudió canto gregoriano con Raffaele Baratta, dirección coral con Domenico Bartolucci e historia de la música con Higinio Avilés. Ha sido profesor de la Escuela Nacional de Música y de la Escuela de Bellas Artes de Toluca, de la que fue director (1977-78). Asistente del organista titular en el Auditorio Nacional y organista titular en la iglesia de San Ignacio de Loyola, como concertista ha grabado programas para Radio Universidad y para la Radio de Frankfurt. Cofundador del Festival de Órgano de Morelia y de la Escuela Superior de Música Sacra de Toluca. Realiza giras anuales por Italia, donde ha sido jurado de concursos internacionales; en 1987, la RAI proyectó en televisión un concierto suyo en la ciudad de Perugia y su grabación de música navideña fue difundida el 24 de diciembre por Radio Vaticano. También ha hecho giras por Estados Unidos, Rusia, Francia, España y Alemania e investigaciones sobre el *Retablo medieval* para órgano y orquesta de Miguel Bernal Jiménez (☛). Primer premio en composición y segundo premio como solista, en un concurso del gobierno del Estado de México (1957). Ha obtenido también la Presea Estado de México.

URBIETA, JESÚS ◆ n. en Juchitán, Oax., y m. en el DF (1959-1997). Pintor. Terminó la carrera de ingeniero civil y trabajó como topógrafo. Estudió en el Taller de Gráfica de la Casa de Cultura del Istmo, en Juchitán (1980-83) donde llevó estudios de cerámica (1989-90), en la Escuela de Artes Plásticas, Pintura

Sin título, obra sobre papel amate de Jesús Urbieta (1996)

y Grabado del INBA en Oaxaca (1983-84) y en la Escuela Nacional de Pintura, Escultura y Grabado La Esmeralda en el DF (1984-85). Montó veinte exposiciones individuales en Oaxaca, Guanajuato, DF, el Estado de México y San Antonio, EUA. Obras suyas se encuentran en los museos de Arte Contemporáneo de Monterrey, de Arte Moderno de México, el Würt de Künzelsau, Alemania y en la Fundación Cultural Artensión. Ejerció la herrería, fue editor y cantante de sones y boleros. Creó la Fundación Guiée Xhúuba dedicada a promover la cultura juchiteca. Autor de *Siempre en llamas* (poesía, 1989) y de *Zeferino y su hermana Mariana Pombo* (novela corta, 1995). Primer Premio de Adquisición en el IX Encuentro Nacional de Arte Joven de Aguascalientes 1989. Gran Paleta de Oro del XXVI Festival Internacional de Pintura del Castillo-Museo Grimaldi en Francia, 1994.

URBINA, LUIS G. ◆ n. en la ciudad de México y m. en España (1864-1934). Su nombre completo era Luis Gonzaga Urbina Sánchez. Poeta y periodista. Se inició como redactor en *El Siglo XIX*. Fue secretario particular de Justo Sierra, cuando éste se desempeñó como secretario de Instrucción Pública y Bellas Artes; profesor de la Escuela Nacional Preparatoria y director de la Biblioteca Nacional (1913). Con Manuel Gutiérrez Nájera fue uno de los editores de la *Revista Azul*. Radicó en La Habana (1915) y en Madrid (1916), donde fue corresponsal de *El Heraldo de Cuba* y primer secretario de la legación mexicana (1918-20). Regresó a México y al triunfo del Plan de Agua Prieta volvió a España, como encargado de la Comisión de Investigación Histórica. Cronista y crítico de teatro de *El Mundo Ilustrado, El Universal* y *El Imparcial*. Autor de los poemarios *Versos* (1890), *Ingenuas* (1902), *Puestas de sol* (1910), *Lámparas en agonía* (1914), *El glosario de la vida vulgar* (1916), *El corazón juglar* (1920), *Los últimos pájaros* (1924), *El cancionero de la noche serena* (1941), *Retratos líricos* (1946) y *Poesías completas* (2 t., 1946); los ensayos *Antología del Centenario* (2 t., 1910, en colaboración con Pedro Henríquez Ureña y Nicolás Rangel) y *La vida literaria de México* (1917); y los volúmenes de narrativa *Cuentos vividos y crónicas soñadas* (1915), *Bajo el sol y frente al mar* (1916), *Estampas de viaje* (1919), *Psiquis enferma* (1922), *Hombres y libros* (1923) y *Luces de España* (1923).

URBINA, SALVADOR ◆ n. y m. en el DF (1885-1963). Abogado. Profesor de la UNAM. Fue jefe del Departamento Consultivo, oficial mayor y subsecretario de Hacienda; procurador general de la Nación, delegado a la Conferencia Internacional Panamericana, celebrada en 1928 en Cuba; presidente de la Suprema Corte, senador (1952-58) y director de la Lotería Nacional. Autor de *El Estado en sus dos aspectos: como entidad soberana y como persona de derecho civil* (1906), *La doble personalidad del Estado* (1930) y *Breve comentario al estudio de George Jaffin* (1942).

URBINA, TOMÁS ◆ n. y m. en Congregación de Nieves, Dgo. (1877-1915). Al dar comienzo la revolución de 1910 se incorporó a las fuerzas de su compadre Francisco Villa, con quien hizo las campañas de Durango y el sur de Chihuahua. En 1911, al triunfo del maderismo, se le reconoció el grado de coronel. En 1912 combatió a Pascual Orozco en las filas de la División Federal del Norte, comandada por Victoriano Huerta. Tras el asesinato de Madero volvió a levantarse en armas y, al frente de tropas irregulares, tomó la ciudad de Durango el 18 de junio de 1913, donde nombró gobernador a Pastor Rouaix. Avanzó después sobre Gómez Palacio y Lerdo, pero fracasó en su ataque a Torreón. Esperó la llegada de Francisco Villa y los ejércitos de ambos conformaron la División del Norte constitucionalista, que asaltó con éxito aquella ciudad en 1914. Se mantuvo fiel a la Convención de Aguascalientes y Villa le encomendó la gubernatura provisional de San Luis Potosí; tomó la capital de dicho estado, la ciudad de León y más tarde avanzó sobre Tampico, pero fue derrotado en El Ébano por Jacinto B. Treviño. Cuando Francisco Villa se retiró del Bajío, Urbina desertó y regresó a su pueblo natal, donde lo aprehendió y ejecutó Roberto Fierro, por órdenes del propio Villa.

URCELAY, NICOLÁS ◆ n. en Mérida, Yuc., y m. en Tampico, Tams. (¿1900?-1959). Cantante. Inició su carrera en la estación radiofónica XEW, empresa en la que trabajó hasta su muerte; cantó también en teatro, cine y televisión. Su interpretación más célebre fue la canción *Júrame*.

Nicolás Urcelay

URDANETA, ANDRÉS DE ◆ n. en España y m. en la ciudad de México (1508-1568). Marino, en 1525 participó con Juan Sebastián Elcano en la expedición de Jofre de Loaysa a las islas Molucas (en Indonesia). En 1538 se alistó en la expedición que Pedro de Alvarado pretendía llevar a Oriente. Salió con él de Guatemala y al llegar a su primera escala, el puerto de Navidad, en la Nueva España, recibieron órdenes del virrey Antonio de Mendoza para auxiliar a Cristóbal de Oñate en su guerra contra los caxcanes de la Nueva Galicia. En 1542, terminada la campaña, Mendoza lo nombró corregidor de la provincia de Ávalos. En 1553 profesó como agustino y seis años después Felipe II lo incluyó en la expedición de Miguel López de Legaspi a las islas que más tarde serían llamadas Filipinas, hacia donde partió en 1564. Fue el encargado de encontrar la ruta de regreso de Manila a Nueva España, lo que consiguió en 1565 para dejar abierto el camino a la llamada Nao de China. Autor de una *Relación del viaje del comendador Loaysa y cartas al rey Felipe II con descripciones de los puertos de Acapulco y Navidad*.

Retrato y firma de Luis G. Urbina

URDANIVIA, MARIANO D. ◆ ☛ *Díez de Urdanivia, Mariano.*

URDAPILLETA TRUEBA, LAURA ◆ n. en Guadalajara, Jal. (1933). Bailarina. Estudió con Sergio Unger y Nelsy Dambré. Cofundadora del Ballet Nelsy Dambré, del que fue primera bailarina, así como del Ballet Concierto de México, del Ballet Clásico de México y de la Compañía Nacional de Danza. Ha sido

Andrés de Urdaneta

bailarina huésped de los ballets de San Salvador, Houston, Guatemala y el Ballet Theater de Nueva York. El coreógrafo yugoslavo Boris Tonin creó para ella la obra *Pas de deux*. Fue la primera mexicana en bailar la obra de *Giselle*. Radicada en Ciudad Juárez, estableció una escuela de danza.

Urdimalas, Pedro de ◆ n. en 1911 en Guadalajara, Jal., y m. en el DF (1911-1995). Su verdadero nombre era Jesús Camacho Villaseñor. Guionista, actor, compositor y uno de los pioneros de radio y televisión mexicanas. Fue guionista de las películas *Nosotros los pobres* y *Ustedes los ricos*, *A toda máquina*, *Los tres García*, *Los tres Huastecos* y *La oveja negra*. Compositor de *Amorcito corazón*, *Mi cariñito*, *Perdón no pido*, *Pobre del pobre*, *Dicen que soy mujeriego*, entre otras 600 registradas en la Sociedad de Autores y Compositores de México, que lo nombró *El Poeta Insigne de México*. Fue coguionista de *Los Olvidados* (1950).

Urdiñola, Francisco de ◆ n. en España y m. en Santa Elena, Zac. (1552-1618). Llegó a la Nueva Galicia hacia 1572 y se alistó en las fuerzas de Alonso López de Lois, a quien sucedió en el mando. Alcanzó renombre al combatir a los indios de la región en Saltillo, Matehuala y Mazapil. Retirado a la vida privada se dedicó a la minería, la agricultura y la ganadería. Acusado de uxoricidio fue encarcelado hasta 1599, cuando se le absolvió. Gobernó Nueva Vizcaya (1603-13) y fue el iniciador de la vitivinicultura en la Nueva España.

Urecho ◆ ☛ *Nuevo Urecho*.

Ures ◆ Municipio de Sonora situado al nor-noreste de Guaymas y contiguo a Hermosillo. Superficie: 2,618.56 km². Habitantes: 10,206, de los cuales 3,074 forman la población económicamente activa. Hablan alguna lengua indígena 18 personas mayores de cinco años. En su jurisdicción se localizan las construcciones coloniales de la misión de San Miguel (1642) y la iglesia de San Miguel Arcángel (1655). La cabecera, del mismo nombre y fundada en 1644 por el jesuita Francisco Paris, obtuvo la categoría de ciudad en 1838 y ha sido dos veces capital de Sonora (1838-42 y 1847-79).

Urgell, Francisco de P. ◆ n. en España (¿1840?-?). Escritor que pasó casi toda su vida en México. Fundó, con Manuel Olaguíbel, Agustín F. Cuenca, Pedro Castera y Juan de Dios Peza, el Círculo Literario Gustavo A. Bécquer y editó el periódico mensual *Páginas Literarias*. Autor de *Amor*, *Apuntes sobre la mitología azteca* e *Historia de los grandes hombres de Anáhuac* (1878, con las biografías de Huemantzin, Xólotl, Huitziton, Acamapatzin, Nezahualcóyotl, Moctezuma I, Moctezuma II, Nezahualpilli, Tlahuilcole, Maxicatzingo, Xicoténcatl *el Viejo*, Xicoténcatl *el Joven*, Cuauhtémoc, Fernando P. Ixtlilxóchitl, Antonio de Tovar Cano Moctezuma y Fernando de Alva Ixtlilxóchitl).

Uriangato ◆ Municipio de Guanajuato situado en el sur del estado, contiguo a Yuriria y en los límites con Michoacán. Superficie: 147.90 km². Habitantes: 49,391, de los cuales 12,930 forman la población económicamente activa. Hablan alguna lengua indígena 45 personas mayores de cinco años.

Uriarte Castañeda, María Teresa ◆ n. en el DF (1947). Licenciada, maestra y doctora en historia por la UNAM, donde es investigadora y directora del Instituto de Investigaciones Estéticas (1998-). Fue directora de Investigaciones y Fomento a la Cultura Regional, responsable del Programa Cultural de Gobierno y presidenta del Patronato de Promotores Voluntarios del Gobierno de Sinaloa (1987-1992). Presidenta del Consejo de Reincorporación Social (1998-99). Autora de *Pintura rupestre de Baja California* (1981), *El juego de pelota en Mesoamérica. Raíces y supervivencias* (1992) y *Tepantitla en Teotihuacán* (1996).

Uriarte y Pérez, Jesús María ◆ n. en Batopilas, Chih., y m. en Culiacán, Sin. (1825-1887). Sacerdote ordenado en 1850. Fue cura de Quila, profesor y rector (1853-70) del Seminario Conciliar de Sonora, gobernador de la mitra, vicario capitular y obispo de Hermosillo (1870). En 1883 logró que la sede apostólica dividiera su territorio en dos jurisdicciones: Sonora y Sinaloa.

Urías Álvarez, Patricia ◆ n. en el DF (1950). Licenciada en ciencias y técnicas de la información por la UIA, con posgrado en historia por la UNAM. Participó en el seminario de Edmundo O'Gorman (1986-96). Reportera de Notimex (1969-73), jefa de Difusión y Publicaciones por el ITAM (1973-76), asistente de investigación en el IIA de la UNAM (1977-80), profesora de la UNAM (1979-83), directora de información y análisis en la Unidad de la Crónica Presidencial (1982-90), editora de la revista *Memoria de papel*, del Consejo Nacional para la Cultura y las Artes (1990-95); y, en el Canal 11 de televisión, directora de *Café Express* (1995-96) y *Hoy en la Cultura* (1996), así como productora de *Águila o Sol* (1998-). Coautora de *Así fue la Revolución Mexicana* (1985).

Uribe, Álvaro ◆ n. en el DF (1953). Escritor y editor. Residió en París, en dos ocasiones, donde fue coeditor de la revista bilingüe *Altaforte* (1978-84) y consejero cultural de la embajada mexicana (1989-93). Desde 1994 ha coordinado las colecciones editoriales Memorias mexicanas, Práctica mortal y Sello bermejo del SNCA. Autor de *Topos* (relatos breves, 1980), *El cuento de nunca acabar* (cuento 1981) *La audiencia de los pájaros* (relato, 1986), *La linterna de los muertos* (1986), *La lotería de San Jorge* (nevela, 1995), *Recordatorio de Federico Gamboa* (biografía literaria, 1999 y *La otra mitad* (ensayos, 1999). Desde 1999 pertenece al SNCA.

Uribe, Lucio ◆ n. y m. en Colima, Col. (¿1840-1894?). Albañil en su juventud, llegó a ser un renombrado constructor, aun sin haber realizado estdios profesionales. En Colima construyó el teatro Hidalgo, el Palacio de Gobierno, la catedral y un puente sobre el río Naranjo. Fue tres veces diputado local.

Uribe, Marcelo ◆ n. en el DF (1953). Poeta y editor. Licenciado en letras españolas por la UNAM y maestro por la Universidad de Maryland, de la que fue investigador. Desde 1992 es gerente de Editorial Era. Ha sido secretario de redacción de *La Gaceta del Fondo de Cultura Económica* (1976-81) y colaborador de *Mesa Llena* y *Sábado*. Autor de *Las delgadas paredes del sueño* (1987, Premio de Poesía Carlos Pellicer).

URIBE, REBECA ◆ n. en Guadalajara, Jal., y m. en la ciudad de México (1914-1949). Autora de los poemarios *Esfinge* (1933), *Versos* (1937), *Llovizna* (1940) y *Poesía* (1949).

URIBE, VIRGILIO ◆ n. ¿en la ciudad de México? y m. en Veracruz, Ver. (1896-1914). Cadete de la Escuela Naval Militar de Veracruz, en la que había ingresado en 1912. Dos años más tarde, al ocurrir la invasión estadounidense, Uribe fue uno de los organizadores de la resistencia y murió en la defensa de su escuela. Póstumamente se le ascendió a subteniente.

URIBE ORTEGA, HERNÁN ◆ n. en Chile (1924). Periodista y escritor. Profesor de la Universidad de Chile (1971), donde trabajó en los diarios *El Siglo*, *Las Noticias Gráficas* y *Las Noticias de Última Hora*, del Partido Socialista, del que era director en septiembre de 1973. Director del semanario *Vistazo* (1968-71) y corresponsal en Chile de Radio Habana y de las agencias noticiosas Sinjua y ADN (1960-72). Se asiló en México en 1974. Ha sido profesor de la UNAM (1975-), articulista de *El Sol de México*, *unomásuno* y *Excélsior*; corresponsal de la revista chilena *Análisis*, colaborador de *Noticiero Latinoamericano* (de Ginebra), *Argumentos* (de Madrid), *El Periodista Demócrata* (de Praga) y de la agencia Prensa Latina. Ha publicado ensayos en la *Revista Mexicana de Ciencias Políticas* y en los *Cuadernos del Centro de Estudios de la Comunicación* de la UNAM. Coautor de *Professional Codes in Journalism* (Praga, 1979) e *Imperialismo y medios masivos de comunicación* (1979). Autor de *Fulgor y muerte de Pablo Neruda* (1983), *Ética periodística en América Latina* (1984), *La guerra secreta de las noticias* (1987) y *Operación Tía Victoria* (1987), así como de los ensayos *América Latina: impacto de las nuevas tecnologías en la profesión periodística*, por encargo de la UNESCO, y *Guía para el estudio de los géneros periodísticos interpretativos* para la Facultad de Ciencias Políticas y Sociales de la UNAM. Secretario general del Colegio de Periodistas de Chile (1964-66), vicepresidente de la Organización Internacional de Periodistas (1966-71) y Cofundador (1975) y vicesecretario general de la Federación Latinoamericana de Periodistas (1985-88). Volvió a Chile en 1988.

URIBE ORTIZ, SUSANA ◆ n. y m. en el DF (1912-1975). Licenciada en derecho y en historia por la UNAM y maestra en historia por El Colegio de México. Estudió bibliotecología en la Biblioteca del Congreso de Washington y en la Biblioteca Pública de Nueva York (1949). Trabajó en la Comisión de Historia del Instituto Panamericano de Geografía e Historia y fue encargada de la formulación de los índices y la bibliografía de la *Revista de Historia de América*. En El Colegio de México, donde inició la edición de *Bibliografía Histórica Mexicana*, se desempeñó como profesora investigadora (1942-45), bibliotecaria (1945-56), bibliotecaria directora (1964-65), bibliotecaria catalogadora (1966-67), jefa de sección (1967-69) y profesora investigadora A (1969-71). Dirigió la biblioteca B del INAH (1949-57) y fue profesora de la UNAM. Representante de América Latina ante el Consejo Internacional de Ciencias Históricas con sede en París y representante de México al Congreso Internacional de Ciencias Históricas celebrado en San Francisco. Colaboró en *Fuentes para la historia contemporánea de México, 1910-1940*. Autora de *Juárez. Ensayo bibliográfico* (1972) y *Manuel Orozco y Berra en la historiografía mexicana* (1970).

URIBE RUIZ, JESÚS ◆ n. en Uruapan, Mich., y m. en el DF (1919-1997). Ingeniero agrónomo por la Escuela Nacional de Agricultura y doctor en ciencias por la Universidad de París, diplomado en extensión agrícola por el Departamento de Agricultura de Estados Unidos. Presidente de los consejos técnicos de la CNOP y la CNC. Profesor de Chapingo, la UNAM, el IPN y la Universidad La Salle y jefe de los departamentos de Preparatoria y Fitotecnia de Chapingo. Fue representante de la SAG en la Comisión de la Cuenca de Tepalcatepec (1934-40), director de agricultura del Instituto Nacional Indigenista, investigador de la Comisión Nacional de Energía Nuclear para la Aplicación del Átomo a la Agricultura, investigador de la Dirección de Planeación de la Secretaría de la Presidencia, investigador de zonas áridas del Instituto de Investigaciones Agrícolas, cofundador del Banrural, director de asuntos internacionales de la Secretaría de Agricultura y Ganadería, asesor científico de la Presidencia de la República y asesor de la dirección general del Conacyt. Autor de *La agonía del bosque*, *Lágrimas del monte*, *Cuentos del campo mexicano*, *Problemas y soluciones en el desarrollo agrícola de México*, *La crisis agrícola en la reforma agraria de México*, *Agricultura sin tecnocracia* y *Desplome agrícola en México. Causas y soluciones*. Presidente de la Academia Mexicana de Ciencias Agrícolas. Premio Nacional de Economía (1964).

URIBE ZÚÑIGA, PATRICIA ◆ n. en el DF (1956). Médica especializada en pediatría e infectología, egresada de la UNAM y el Instituto Nacional de Pediatría. Ha sido profesora en la UNAM (1977-86) y en la Universidad La Salle. En 1987 se incorporó al Conasida, en el que ha ocupado puestos directivos y del que asumió la Presidencia en 1999. Fue asesora del Programa Mundial de Sida (1992-95). Es miembro del Sistema de Investigadores de la Secretaría de Salud. Ha publicado más de 30 artículos en revistas nacionales e internacionales y presentado más de 50 trabajos en conferencias internacionales. Es autora del libro para adolescentes *¿Qué onda con el Sida?* y de la *Guía para la atención domiciliaria* de OPS/OMS para Latinoamérica. Ha sido coautora de libros sobre sexualidad, salud reproductiva y enfermedades de transmisión sexual.

Píndaro Urióstegui Miranda

Víctor L. Urquidi

URIÓSTEGUI MIRANDA, PÍNDARO ◆ n. en Iguala, Gro., y m. en EUA (1937-1998). Licenciado en derecho por la UNAM (1958). Profesor de la Escuela Nacional Preparatoria y de la ENEP-Acatlán (1980-82). Miembro del PRI, en el que fue secretario de Organización y oficial mayor en el DF (1975-76) y delegado general del CEN en varias entidades. Miembro del Consejo Técnico de la CNC (1968-70). Agente del Ministerio Público (1959-63), director general de Injuve (1964-70), delegado del DDF en Gustavo A. Madero (1970-73), dos veces diputado federal por Guerrero (1973-76 y 1985-88), gerente general administrativo de la Comisión Federal de Electricidad (1976-80) y coordinador de Programas Regionales de Empleo de la Secretaría de Programación y Presupuesto en Chihuahua, Coahuila y Nuevo León (1982-84). Autor de *La revolución, voz joven de México* (1960), *Imagen de una democracia* (1963), *En torno a nuestra historia* (1966), *Testimonios del proceso revolucionario de México* (1970), *Juventud y educación: dos reflexiones permanentes* (1968), *Aquí no ha pasado nada* (novela, 1977) y *Guardar las formas* (1990).

Río Urique, Chihuahua

FOTO: CARLOS HAHN

URIQUE ◆ Municipio de Chihuahua situado en el suroeste del estado, contiguo a Batopilas, en los límites con Sinaloa. Superficie: 3,968.06 km^2. Habitantes: 19,271, de los cuales 3,094 forman la población económicamente activa. Hablan alguna lengua indígena 5,690 personas (tarahumara). En su territorio se localizan las barrancas del Cobre y Tararecua, cruzadas por el ferrocarril Chihuahua-Pacífico.

URIQUE ◆ Río de Chihuahua. Nace de la confluencia de varios arroyos en la región suroccidental del estado, en la cresta principal de la sierra Tarahumara. Corre de sureste a noroeste, tuerce al suroeste y cruza la sierra por la barranca del Cobre; cerca de los límites con Sinaloa se une al río Verde o San Miguel, para formar el río Fuerte.

URQUIDI, JOSÉ DE ◆ n. en la Villa de San Bartolomé, hoy Villa de Allende, Chih., y m. en la ciudad de México (1771-1826). Militar. Fue aprehendido por piratas ingleses cuando viajaba a Cuba en la fragata *Pomona*, encarcelado en Panzacola, Estados Unidos, y finalmente canjeado. Prestó servicios en Cuba hasta 1816, cuando volvió a la Nueva España como escolta del virrey Juan Ruiz de Apodaca. En 1821 se retiró del ejército y fue diputado al primer Congreso mexicano, disuelto por Agustín de Iturbide. Fue primer vocal (1823) y dos veces jefe político (1824) de la provincia de Chihuahua, diputado al primer Congreso local y dos veces gobernador provisional del estado de Chihuahua (1825 y 1825-26, fue el primer gobernador de la entidad). Le correspondió promulgar la Constitución local de 1825. Elegido senador en 1826, murió antes de ocupar el escaño.

URQUIDI, JUAN FRANCISCO ◆ n. en la ciudad de México (1881-?). Ingeniero. Trabajó en las obras de provisión de aguas potables de la ciudad de México (1906-12). Antirreeleccionista, al triunfo del maderismo fue ingeniero de los edificios públicos dependientes del DDF. Fue secretario de la agencia confidencial del movimiento constitucionalista en Washington y le correspondió informar a Venustiano Carranza la decisión estadounidense de evacuar Veracruz (septiembre de 1914). Fue secretario de varias legaciones mexicanas (1915-21) y enviado extraordinario y ministro plenipotenciario en Colombia, Uruguay y El Salvador.

URQUIDI, JUAN NEPOMUCENO DE ◆ n. en la ciudad de México y m. en la hacienda de la Concepción, Chih. (1813-1880). Licenciado en derecho (1837), pasó a Chihuahua donde se dedicó a la política y a administrar la hacienda de la Concepción, que había heredado. Fue secretario de gobierno (1840-42 y 1845-46), varias veces diputado local, magistrado y dos veces presidente del Supremo Tribunal de Justicia. Gobernador interino de Chihuahua (1850-52), insaculado por el Congreso tras la renuncia de Trías (1855-56) y ratificado por el presidente Juan Álvarez. Durante la intervención francesa permaneció en prisión varios meses y después alojó en su casa al presidente Benito Juárez, cuando éste se dirigía a Paso del Norte.

URQUIDI, VÍCTOR L. ◆ n. en la ciudad de México (1919). Licenciado por la Escuela de Economía de Londres (1940). Ha sido economista de los bancos de México (1940-47) y Mundial (1947-49), de la Secretaría de Hacienda (1949-51) y de la Comisión Económica para América Latina (1951-52), de cuya Oficina Regional en México fue director (1952-58); asesor en política de desarrollo económico de la Secretaría de Hacienda y del Banco de México (1958-64). Cofundador, con Daniel Cosío Villegas, de El Colegio de México, en el que ha sido director del Centro de Estudios Económicos y Demográficos (1965-66), presidente (1966-85) y profesor e investigador (1985-). Cofundador de la Universidad Autónoma Metropolitana. Coautor de *El desarrollo económico de México y su capacidad para absorber capital del exterior* (1953). Autor de *Trayectoria del mercado común latinoamericano* (1960), *Viabilidad eco-*

nómica de América Latina (1962) y *Educación superior, ciencia y tecnología en el desarrollo de México: un estudio preliminar* (1964, en colaboración con Adrián Lajous). Miembro de El Colegio Nacional y de los comités ejecutivos del Club de Roma y de la Asociación Económica Internacional, así como del Comité de la ONU sobre Aplicación de la Ciencia y la Tecnología al Desarrollo. Premio Nacional de Ciencias Sociales (1977), Premio Interamérica (1988) y primer Premio Iberoamericano de Economía Raúl Prebisch (1990) otorgado por España.

URQUIZA, CONCHA ◆ n. en Morelia, Mich., y m. cerca de Ensenada, BC (1910-1945). Escritora. Publicó su primer poema a los 13 años de edad en *Revista de Revistas*. Trabajó en el departamento de publicidad de la Metro Goldwyn Meyer, en Nueva York (1928-33). Fue militante del Partido Comunista Mexicano y en 1938 ingresó en la Congregación de las Hijas del Espíritu Santo, en Morelia; sin embargo, renunció a la vida religiosa y viajó a San Luis Potosí, donde fue profesora de historia y literatura (1939-43). Colaboró en *Rueca, Aula, Labor, Ábside, México al Día, Juventud, Saber* y *Logos*. Autora de *Obras* (1946), *Poemas de Concha Urquiza* (1955), *El párroco ideal según yo lo había soñado* (1955), *Poesías y prosas* (1971) y *Antología* (1979). Murió ahogada.

URQUIZO, FRANCISCO L. ◆ n. en San Pedro de las Colonias, Coah., y m. en el DF (1891-1969). Militar y escritor. A fines de 1910 se incorporó a la revolución en las fuerzas de Emilio Madero. En 1911 perteneció a la guardia personal del presidente Francisco I. Madero. Fue prisionero de Victoriano Huerta tras el cuartelazo de 1913 y más tarde liberado. Viajó al norte para unirse al ejército constitucionalista y perteneció al Estado Mayor de Venustiano Carranza; combatió en las fuerzas de Pablo González y en 1916 fue nombrado comandante de la plaza de México. En ese mismo año fue jefe del Departamento de Estado Mayor de la Secretaría de Guerra y Marina. En 1917 se integró a la comisión encargada de reorganizar el Ejército Nacional. Secretario de Guerra y Marina (del 22 de febrero al 21 de mayo de 1920) en el gabinete de Venustiano Carranza, a quien acompañó en su viaje a Veracruz. Tras el asesinato del presidente en Tlaxcalantongo, fue aprehendido y recluido en la prisión militar de Santiago Tlatelolco. En ese mismo año fue liberado y degradado, por lo que se exilió en Europa. En 1925, a su regreso a México, ocupó puestos menores en oficinas federales y de inspección fiscal. En 1934 fue readmitido en el ejército y siete años más tarde alcanzó el grado de general de división. Fue subsecretario de Guerra y Marina durante la segunda guerra mundial y secretario de la Defensa Nacional (del primero de septiembre de 1945 al 30 de noviembre de 1946) en el gabinete de Manuel Ávila Camacho. Jefe del Departamento de Industria Militar (1952-58) y presidente del Consejo Consultivo de la Secretaría de la Defensa Nacional (1960-69). Fue colaborador de *El Universal Ilustrado, Marte, Mañana, Tópicos, El Legionario, El Nacional* y *El Universal*. Escribió el prólogo de *Ocho mil kilómetros en campaña*, de Álvaro Obregón. Autor de *La caballería constitucionalista, su organización e instrucción* (1914), *Organización del ejército constitucionalista* (1916), *Colonias militares* (1916), *Almanaque militar* (1919), *Proyecto para la formación del Estado Mayor del ejército* (1919), *Manual del oficial constitucionalista. Infantería* (1920), *Europa Central en 1922* (crónicas, 1922), *Lo incognoscible* (novela, 1922), *Cosas de la Argentina* (crónicas, 1923), *De la vida militar mexicana* (relatos, 1930), *México-Tlaxcalantongo: mayo de 1920* (crónica, 1932), *El primer crimen* (teatro, 1933), *Mi tío Juan* (novela, 1934), *Recuerdo que.* (crónicas, 1934), *Don Venustiano Carranza, el hombre, el político, el caudillo* (1935), *H.D.T.U.P. (Hay de todo un poco)* (relatos, 1935), *Charlas de sobremesa* (1937), *Tropa vieja* (novela, 1943), *Morelos, genio militar de la independencia* (biografía, 1945), *Cuentos y leyendas* (1945), *Al viento* (teatro, 1953), *¡Viva Madero!* (1954), *Tres de diana* (1955), *Páginas de la revolución* (1956), *Un pedazo de historia de la revolución: vida del general Federico Montes* (1959), *Siete años con Carranza* (1959), *Madrid de los años veinte* (crónicas, 1961), *Breviario humorístico* (1963), *El desván* (1964), *Símbolos y números* (1965), *Aquellos veintes* (1965) y *La ciudadela quedó atrás* (1965). Medalla Belisario Domínguez (1967).

URRAZA SARACHO, ÁNGEL ◆ n. en España y m. en el DF (1891-1946). Llegó a México en 1910 y fijó su residencia en la región lagunera, donde fue empleado de la familia algodonera de los Arocena; con éstos y con Fernando Rodríguez, José Larrea y Enrique Buj, fundó la Compañía Agrícola de Lequeitio. En 1928 se trasladó a la ciudad de México y estableció la empresa hulera Euzkadi, dedicada en un principio, a la producción de zapatos tenis y ampliada después a la elaboración de diversos productos de hule vulcanizado. Esta empresa se asoció después con la B. F. Goodrich, de Estados Unidos, para formar la firma Goodrich-Euzkadi. Fue fundador de otras empresas y miembro de los consejos de administración de Canada Dry, Seguros la Provincial, Banco de Londres y México, Seguros Monterrey, Maderera del Trópico, Lomas de Chapultepec y Crédito Afianzador. Fue presidente de la Sociedad Española de Beneficencia de México.

URREA, BERNARDO DE ◆ n. en Culiacán, Sin., y m. en Altar, Son. (¿1710?-1777). Militar. En 1752 se le dio el mando de la Compañía Presidial de Sinaloa y se le encomendó trasladarla al extremo norte de Sonora, donde fundó el presidio militar y poblado de Altar (1755). A lo largo de su carrera militar comandó más de 100 campañas contra los seris y pimas. Fue tres veces gobernador interino de las Provincias Internas de Occidente (1760-61, 1762-63 y 1773).

URREA, JOSÉ ◆ n. en el presidio de Tucson, ahora en EUA, y m. en Durango, Dgo. (1797-1849). Militar. Combatió a

Concha Urquiza

ARCHIVO XAVIER ESPARZA

Francisco L. Urquizo

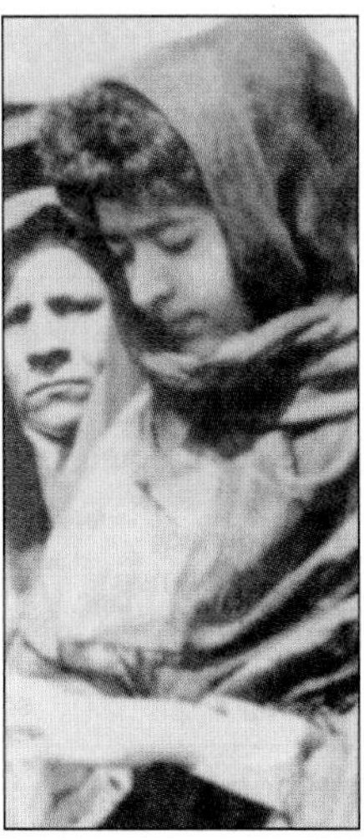

Teresa Urrea

Foto: Rogelio Cuéllar

Alicia Urreta

los insurgentes en el sur de Sinaloa, Jalisco y Michoacán. En 1821 secundó el Plan de Iguala. En 1829, a las órdenes de Antonio López de Santa Anna, rechazó la expedición de Isidro Barradas. Anastasio Bustamante lo nombró comandante militar de Durango. En 1834 asumió el mando del Regimiento Permanente de Cuautla y un año después, ya con el grado de general, fue gobernador y comandante militar de Durango. En ese cargo combatió a los comanches. En 1836 participó en la expedición de Texas y acompañó a Santa Anna hasta la derrota en San Jacinto. Comandante de Sonora y Sinaloa (1837), se rebeló contra el gobernador Manuel María Gándara, asumió el gobierno e instauró el federalismo. En 1838, derrotado en Mazatlán por Mariano Paredes y Arrillaga, entregó el poder al vicegobernador Escalante y se refugió en Durango. Fue encarcelado (1839), por apoyar a los franceses durante la guerra de los Pasteles, escapó de prisión (1840) y asaltó, con un grupo de partidarios, el Palacio Nacional, donde el 15 de julio de 1840 mantuvieron como rehén al presidente Anastasio Bustamante. Después de esta acción escapó hacia Durango y se sublevó dos veces más en 1841. Al asumir Santa Anna la Presidencia se reincorporó al ejército. Gobernó Sonora (1842-44) y realizó una campaña con fines de exterminio contra los los seris. Fue comandante militar de Tamaulipas (1846) y en esa plaza combatió a los invasores estadounidenses. Autor de un *Diario de las operaciones militares de la división que al mando del general José Urrea, hizo la Campaña de Tejas* (1838).

Urrea, Mariano de ◆ n. en Altar, Son., y m. ¿en Ecuador? (1765-1852). Militar. En 1804 comandaba la Compañía de Indios Auxiliares de Bacoachi que combatió a los apaches y otras etnias insumisas. Desde 1810 luchó contra los insurgentes en Nayarit, Jalisco, Zacatecas y Michoacán. En 1821 secundó el Plan de Iguala. Se le encomendó, junto con Pedro Celestino Negrete, el asedio de Durango y, al tomar la plaza, asumió el gobierno de la Nueva Vizcaya (1821-22). En 1822 fue comandante militar de las Provincias Internas de Occidente y un año después apoyó el Plan de Casa Mata y entró en la ciudad de México con las tropas republicanas. El Congreso lo designó jefe político y militar de las provincias de Sonora y Sinaloa, proclamó la creación del Estado Libre de Sonora y lo gobernó de hecho; el Congreso le pidió que entregase el mando, a lo que se negó. En 1824 organizó una campaña contra los ópatas y convocó a elecciones de diputados para un Congreso local constituyente del estado de Occidente. Entregó el mando político, trató de retener el militar y fue derrotado y aprehendido en 1825, acusado de querer convertirse en "rey de Sonora". En 1826, desde la ciudad de México, se afilió al Plan de Montaño, asonada de la logia escocesa contra el presidente Guadalupe Victoria. A la derrota de ese movimiento fue desterrado a Ecuador.

Urrea, Miguel ◆ n. en Culiacán, Sin. (1801-1876). Minero. En 1838 secundó a los federalistas de José Urrea. Vicegobernador liberal de Sonora (1857-60), en 1858 rehusó hacerse cargo del Ejecutivo local. Durante la intervención francesa financió a un grupo guerrillero republicano y en 1866 participó en la liberación de Álamos.

Urrea, Teresa ◆ n. en Ocorini, Sin., y m. en EUA (1872-1906). Fue conocida como *Santa Teresita de Cabora* o la *Santa de Cabora* por el nombre de la hacienda en la que vivía. Desde los 12 años de edad sufría ataques de epilepsia y la imaginación popular le atribuyó facultades curativas que supuestamente ejercía por hipnosis y sugestión. Lauro Aguirre se convirtió en su administrador. Desde 1890, los periódicos *El Monitor Republicano*, de México, y *El Tiempo*, de Nuevo México, dedicaban numerosas notas a sus pretendidas curaciones milagrosas. En 1891 los rebeldes de Tomochic derrotaron a una partida federal cuando se dirigían a conocer a la Santa de Cabora y le atribuyeron ese triunfo, lo que aumentó su popularidad. En 1892 los indios del río Mayo se sublevaron con la consigna de "¡Viva la Santa de Cabora!" Aunque no estaba involucrada en la sublevación, el gobierno federal la deportó a Estados Unidos, donde se convirtió en "patrona" de los indios de aquel lado de la frontera. Según algunos autores, fue la impulsora de la rebelión de Temosáchic, reprimida en 1896. En 1895 empezó a editarse en Nogales, Arizona, un periódico en el que se le hacía aparecer como redactora de textos antiporfiristas. La escritora Brianda Domecq publicó, con base en su biografía, la novela *La insólita historia de la Santa de Cabora* (1990).

Urreta, Alicia ◆ n. en Veracruz, Ver., y m. en el DF (1930-1986). Pianista egresada del Conservatorio Nacional. Fue alumna de Brendel, Flavigny, Iglesias y De la Rocha y se especializó en composición de música electrónica y electroacústica en la Schola Cantorum de París. Fue profesora de acústica en el IPN (1957), pianista titular de la Orquesta Sinfónica Nacional (1957), coordinadora general de la Compañía Nacional de Ópera del INBA, coordinadora de música de la Casa del Lago, directora de actividades musicales de la UNAM y fundadora de la Camerata de México. Impulsó la celebración del Festival Hispano Mexicano de Música Contemporánea. Fue también solista de las orquestas Filarmónica de la UNAM y Sinfónica de la Universidad de Harvard. Autora de las partituras para las películas *Narda o el verano*, *5000 años de deporte* y *La muerte viva*; la música para las puestas en escena de *La gatomaquia*, de Lope de Vega; *El gesticulador*, de Rodolfo Usigli; *La mujer del abanico*, de Yukio Mishima; *Sotoba komachi* (teatro noh del siglo XIV); *Patio de Monipodio* (con la que obtuvo un premio en 1974); *Los novios de la Torre Eiffel*, de J. Cocteau; *Leoncio y Lena*, de Büchner; *Higiene de los placeres y de los dolores*, de Héctor Azar; *Mata Hari y Landrú*, de Álvaro Custodio; *Platero y yo*, de Juan Ramón Jiménez, y *El diálogo del amor con un viejo*, de Rodrigo de Cota; así como de diversas composiciones corales, electrónicas, electroacústicas y sinfónicas: *De la pluma al ángel, Hugo de la letra nocturna, Arcana, Salsópera* (con textos de Salvador Novo), *El espejo encantado, Salmodias para piano, Estudios para guitarra, Romance de Doña Balada* (ópera, 1972), *Natura Mortis o la verdadera historia de Caperucita Roja* (1972), *Rallenti* (1969), *Estudio sonoro para una escultura, Homenaje a Castro* y *Teogonía mexica*. Primer lugar en el Concurso Juan Sebastián Bach (1951), primer premio en el Concurso de Música para Cine Experimental con la partitura de la cinta *El ídolo de los orígenes* (1967) y Premio de la Unión de Cronistas de Teatro y Música de Orense (1970).

URRUCHÚA DURAND, FEDERICO ◆ n. en el DF (1940). Licenciado en derecho por la UNAM (1963), posgraduado en economía internacional en El Colegio de México. Ha sido secretario auxiliar del segundo subsecretario (1966-71), secretario particular del subsecretario (1975-77) y subdirector encargado de la Dirección de Conferencias y Organismos Autónomos de la Secretaría de Relaciones Exteriores (1970-80). Adscrito al servicio diplomático, ha sido consejero de la embajada en Italia (1975-76), encargado de la apertura de la embajada en Albania (1976), embajador del Servicio Exterior Mexicano (1980), comisionado en las embajadas en Canadá, España y Panamá; así como embajador en Jamaica y en El Salvador (1985-89) y en Belice (1989-91). Director general de África y de Medio Oriente de la SRE (1999).

URRUSTI, LUCINDA ◆ n. en el Marruecos Español (1930). Pintora y museógrafa, exiliada con su familia en México desde 1939. Estudió en el taller de Ricardo Martínez y en La Esmeralda (1953). Ha sido museógrafa del INBA y reside actualmente en Nueva York. Primer premio del Salón de Otoño del INBA (1953), primer premio de Jóvenes Valores del Salón de la Plástica Mexicana (1957) y primer premio del segundo Salón de la Plástica Femenina (1962). Recibió una mención de honor en la segunda Bienal Interamericana de México. En 1993 ingresó en el SNCA.

URRUSTI SANZ, JUAN ◆ n. en España (1927). Se asiló en México en 1939. Obtuvo el título de médico cirujano en la UNAM (1951), de la que ha sido profesor (1956-) y fundador de la especialidad de perinatología. Realizó estudios de posgrado en el IMSS (1952) y en el Hospital Dolores Sanz de Lavie (1953). En el IMSS fue médico interno, pediatra, jefe del servicio de pediatria del Hospital de Gineco-obstetricia del Centro Médico Nacional, jefe de Educación Médica Continua de la Jefatura de Servicios de Enseñanza e Investigación, titular de la Subjefatura y técnico normativo de la Jefatura de Nuevos Programas. Ha colaborado en los *Archivos de Investigación Médica*. Coeditor de *Avances recientes en pediatría perinatal*. Coautor de *Los factores de riesgo perinatal en la población adscrita al Instituto Mexicano del Seguro Social, investigación epidemiológica (1974-1976)* (1977), *La toxemia del embarazo* (1964), *Nuevos conceptos sobre viejos aspectos de la desnutrición* (1973) y *Diagnóstico y manejo de algunos problemas del recién nacido* (1968). Miembro de la Academia Nacional de Medicina, de la Academia Mexicana de Pediatría, de la Academia de Investigación Pediátrica, de la Asociación de Estudios Perinatales y de la Sociedad Mexicana de Pediatría.

URRUTIA, AURELIANO ◆ n. en la ciudad de México y m. en EUA (1872-?). Egresado de la Escuela Nacional de Medicina, desde 1896 fue médico militar. Conoció en el ejército a Victoriano Huerta, a quien un día salvó la vida y del que fue compadre. Reincorporado a la vida civil, tuvo un sanatorio en Coyoacán y fue profesor y director (1911-13) de la Escuela Nacional de Medicina. Tras la Decena Trágica, Huerta lo hizo secretario de Gobernación (del 13 de junio al 14 de septiembre de 1913), con la oposición de Jorge Vera Estañol, quien debió renunciar. Se le menciona como uno de los autores intelectuales del asesinato de Serapio Rendón. Fue director del Hospital General (1913-14). A la caída de Huerta se refugió en Estados Unidos. En los años veinte el gobierno mexicano lo juzgó en ausencia, pero más tarde Emilio Portes Gil le ofreció garantías para su regreso a México, aunque no aceptó la oferta. Tampoco se acogió a la amnistía general decretada por Lázaro Cárdenas.

Aureliano Urrutia

URRUTIA, ELENA ◆ n. en el DF (1932). Nombre profesional de María Elena Lazo de Mendizábal. Licenciada en psicología por la UIA y licenciada en letras francesas por la Universidad Libre de Bruselas. En la empresa Teleproducciones (1951-54), participó en la elaboración de las películas *Raíces* (1953, Benito Alazraki), en la que además fue adaptadora, y *Torero* (1956, Carlos Velo). Trabajó en la Casa del Lago (1972-75). Ha sido colaboradora (1967-86) y directora del programa *Foro de la mujer* en Radio Universidad (1982-86), directora del Museo Universitario del Chopo (1975-77), subdirectora de Difusión Cultural de la SRE (1981-83) y coordinadora del Programa Interdisciplinario de Estudios de la Mujer de El Colegio de México (1983-). Fundadora (1976) y codirectora de *Fem* (1986-87); fundadora y colaboradora de *unomásuno* (1977-83) y *La Jornada* (1984-). Realizó las antologías *Imagen y realidad de la mujer* (1975) y *El cuento en el Museo del Chopo* (1978). Coautora de *Evocación de mujeres ilustres* (1980), *Bordando sobre la escritura y la cocina* (1984), *Nuestros mayores* (1984), *Las mujeres frente a la crisis de America Latina y el Caribe* (1985), *Diego Rivera hoy* (1986), *Antología tributaria* (1986), *Fem. 10 años de periodismo feminista* (1988) y *Mujer y literatura mexicana y chicana: culturas en contacto* (1988). Pertenece al Pen Club y a la Asociación de Escritores de México.

Elena Urrutia

URRUTIA, ÓSCAR ◆ n. en el DF (1928). Su apellido materno es Tazzer. Arquitecto titulado en la UNAM, donde es profesor desde 1955. Ha sido subdirector de Capacitación Técnica de la Secretaría de Comunicaciones (1953), comisario general del gobierno ante la Exposición

Óscar Urrutia

Internacional de Bruselas (1956), director fundador de la revista *Calli* (1959), comisario general del gobierno de México ante las exposiciones Trienal de Milán (1960) y Siglo XXI de Seattle (1962), coordinador general de los Juegos Olímpicos de México (1968), director del primer Festival Internacional Cervantino (1972), director de Artes Plásticas del INBA (1977), director del Museo de Arte Moderno de la Ciudad de México (1984) y arquitecto consultor de Empresas Copal (1988). Es autor del proyecto artístico del Centro Médico Siglo XXI (1987). Coautor de los libros *Francisco Artigas* y *La magia de la forma*. Autor de *Ese cuerpo que era yo* (1993). Pertenece a la Sociedad de Arquitectos de México, al Colegio de Arquitectos y a la Academia de Arquitectos. Ha sido condecorado por los gobiernos de Bélgica, Finlandia y Senegal.

URRUTIA Y ARANA, JUAN ♦ n. en España y m. en la ciudad de México (1670-1743). Heredó el marquesado del Villar del Águila, en Querétaro, donde fijó su residencia y donde construyó el acueducto y varias fuentes públicas. Fueron esculpidas tres estatuas suyas de las cuales una fue robada y otra decapitada en 1867 por una granada.

URSÚA DE ESCOBAR, AURORA ♦ n. en Guadalajara, Jal., y m. en el DF (1896-1967). Secretaria particular de Francisco I. Madero. Fue la última persona con la que el presidente habló antes de su asesinato y quien brindó refugio al padre del mismo. Se unió a la revolución constitucionalista y fue agente de enlance entre Francisco Villa (quien le otorgó el grado de coronela), Emiliano Zapata y Lucio Blanco. Proveyó de armamento a los rebeldes Andrés y Rómulo Figueroa. Tras la escisión revolucionaria permaneció al lado de Felipe Ángeles, como su secretaria. Más adelante participó en la campaña presidencial de Manuel Ávila Camacho y trabajó con los dirigentes priistas Carlos A. Madrazo, Javier Rojo Gómez y Lauro Ortega. Fundadora y profesora de la escuela Sara P. de Madero y una de las fundadoras de la Unión de Veteranos de la Revolución, de cuyo comité era secretaria de Acción Femenil al morir.

ÚRSULO GALVÁN ♦ Municipio de Veracruz situado en el litoral del golfo de México, al noroeste del puerto de Veracruz. Superficie: 149.70 km^2. Habitantes: 28,158, de los cuales 8,436 forman la población económicamente activa. Hablan alguna lengua indígena 65 personas mayores de cinco años (náhuatl 17 y totonaco 11). En su territorio se localizaba Cempoala, capital del imperio totonaca, donde Hernán Cortés se entrevistó con el "cacique gordo", uno de sus primeros aliados mexicanos. El conquistador se enfrentó en el mismo lugar a las fuerzas de Pánfilo de Nárváez. Cempoala es actualmente una zona arqueológica donde se conservan los restos de los templos Mayor, de las Chimeneas y de las Caritas. A un lado del poblado totonaco de Cempoala se erigió el asentamiento español de Cempoala que actualmente es el más importante centro comercial e industrial de la zona. En 1764, tropas inglesas ocuparon el presidio de San Miguel de Panzacola, en la Florida, por lo que la guarnición española debió abandonar el sitio; el gobernador del presidio, Diego Ortiz Parrilla, encomendó a Pedro Amoscotogui y Bermudo la conducción de los colonos hacia la costa de Veracruz; Amoscotogui custodió a los vecinos españoles y a un grupo de indios yamases y apalachinos hasta territorio del actual municipio de Úrsulo Galván, donde fue fundado el pueblo de San Carlos, a orillas del río Chachalacas.

URTUSÁSTEGUI, TOMÁS ♦ n. en el DF (1933). Dramaturgo y cronista de teatro. Médico cirujano por la UNAM especializado en pediatría. Participó en los talleres de Hugo Argüelles y Vicente Leñero. Dirige un taller de teatro en una clínica del IMSS. Ha colaborado en la *Revista Mexicana de Cultura, El Nacional, El Día* y *unomásuno*. Autor de las obras de teatro *Cinco monólogos* (1984), *Ponte en mi lugar* (1984), *Cuando veas la cola de tu vecino arrancar* (1984), *Profanación* (1985, Premio Salvador Novo en 1984), *El poder de los hombres* (1984), *Coyote sol, venado luna* (1985, Premio Wilberto Cantón en 1987), *¿Huele a gas?* (1985, Premio Salvador Novo en 1981), *Ruega por nosotros* (1985), *Sabes, voy a tener un hijo* (1985), *Y retiemble en sus centros la tierra* (1985, Premio de Teatro Histórico del INBA y los estados de Campeche, Sonora, Yucatán, Querétaro y Tlaxcala), *Tiempo de heroísmo* (1986), *Más allá* (1986), *Vida, estamos en paz* (1986, Premio Wilberto Cantón), *Agua clara* (1987), *Yo te quiero, tú me quieres, eso está muy bien* (1987), *Sólo para hombres* (1987), *Hoy estreno* (1987), *Hombre y mujer* (1987), *Yo sólo sé que te vas. Yo sólo sé que me quedo* (1987, Premio Plural), *Libertad de expresión* (1988, Premio de Teatro Histórico del INBA), *Apenas son las cuatro* (1989), *Sangre de mi sangre* (1992), *Carretera del norte* (1992), *Danzón dedicado a.* (1993); y de las piezas de teatro para niños *La canción del sapito Cro-cro* (1984), *El manzano prodigioso* (1984), *El niño que podía leer el mañana* (1984), *Al fin niños* (1984), *Baldomero verdadero* (1985), *Árbol del tiempo* (1985), *La nueva arca de Noé* (1985), *El lápiz rojo* (1987), *Cupo limitado* (1988, Premio de Teatro Infantil del INBA y el gobierno de Coahuila) y *El fabricante de nubes* (1988, Premio de Teatro para Niños del INBA). *Drácula gay* (1990), *La duda* (1991) y *Radioranzas 42* (1994). Escribió *Manual de dramaturgia*.

URUÁCHI ♦ Municipio de Chihuahua situado en el occidente del estado, al oeste-suroeste de la capital estatal, en los límites con Sonora. Superficie: 3,058.31 km^2. Habitantes: 8,587, de los cuales 1,168 forman la población económicamente activa. Hablan alguna lengua indígena 1,131 personas mayores de cinco años (tarahumara 1,131).

URUAPAN ♦ Municipio de Michoacán situado al noreste de Apatzingán y al oeste-suroeste de Morelia. Superficie: 830.28 km^2. Habitantes: 250,794, de los cuales 63,926 forman la población económicamente activa. Hablan alguna lengua indígena 10,830 personas mayores de cinco años (purépecha 10,805). Indígenas monolingües: 1,944. Es el más importante centro comercial, agrícola y ganadero de la región llamada Tierra Caliente. En su territorio se localizan la cascada de la Tzaráracua (☛), el salto de Camela y el parque nacional La Quinta. En la cabecera, Uruapan del Progreso, entre las principales artesanías están las lacas hechas a mano. Este asentamiento fue sede de uno de los cacicazgos en que estuvo dividido el imperio purépecha. En 1522, a la llegada del conquistador Cristóbal de Olid, el rey purépecha Tangaxoan II debió refugiarse temporalmente en Uruapan. Hacia 1530 llegaron a la población los evangelizadores franciscanos, quienes pusieron al lugar San Francisco Uruapan. En 1815 fue sede del poder insurgente, encabezado por José María Morelos. En este poblado se produjo en mayo de 1854, durante la revolución de Ayutla, un combate en el cual los liberales Epitacio Huerta y García Pueblita derrotaron al santanista José Manuel Escudero. En 1858, Epitacio Huerta, gobernador michoacano, elevó el asentamiento a rango de ciudad y le llamó Uruapan del Progreso. Durante la intervención francesa fue provisionalmente la capital republicana de Michoacán; el 17 de junio de 1865 la plaza fue atacada por los republicanos Arteaga, Riva Palacio y Régules, quienes derrotaron al conservador Francisco de P. Lemus, quien fue fusilado.

URUCHURTU, ALFREDO P. ◆ n. en Hermosillo, Son., y m. en el DF (1884-1939). Pedagogo egresado de la Escuela Normal de Maestros. El gobierno de Sonora lo becó para estudiar en Alemania y Suiza. Fue subdirector y director de la Escuela Nacional de Maestros, director de la Normal de San Luis Potosí, director de Educación Primaria en Baja California Norte, inspector general de escuelas primarias, jefe del Departamento de Enseñanza Normal y Primaria y oficial mayor de la SEP.

URUCHURTU, ERNESTO P. ◆ n. en Hermosillo, Son., y m. en el DF (1907-1997). Su nombre completo era Ernesto Peralta Uruchurtu. Licenciado en derecho por la UNAM (1931). Fue agente del Ministerio Público, juez y magistrado del Supremo Tribunal de Justicia de Sonora, director jurídico del Banjidal y de la Secretaría de Agricultura y Ganadería, director general de Población de la Secretaría de Gobernación, secretario general del PRI durante la campaña presidencial de Miguel Alemán, subsecretario y dos veces secretario de Gobernación (del 12 de febrero al 30 de junio de 1948 y del 14 de octubre de 1951 al 30 de noviembre de 1952) en el gabinete de Miguel Alemán y tres veces jefe del Departamento del Distrito Federal (del 1 de diciembre de 1952 al 30 de noviembre de 1958, del 1 de diciembre de 1958 al 30 de noviembre de 1964 y del 1 de diciembre de 1964 al 14 de septiembre de 1966), en los gabinetes de Adolfo Ruiz Cortines, Adolfo López Mateos y Gustavo Díaz Ordaz. Durante su larga gestión, prolongó el Viaducto Miguel Alemán, tapó o entubó los canales y ríos de la ciudad; convirtió la calzada de Tlalpan en vía rápida, hizo edificar construcciones modernas para sustituir los viejos mercados y alojar los puestos callejeros de La Merced, La Lagunilla y numerosas colonias; ordenó una permanente tarea de desazolve del drenaje que acabó con las inundaciones; remozó el Zócalo y le dio nueva y mejor vialidad al retirar los tranvías, pero destruyó o mutiló valiosos monumentos al ampliar la avenida Pino Suárez; prohibió la creación de nuevos fraccionamientos en el Distrito Federal y se negó a proporcionar servicios municipales a los que se habitaron sin su consentimiento; llenó de gladiolas jardines y camellones; y, por último, acabó con la vida nocturna de la capital al ordenar el cierre de centros de diversión a la una de la mañana. Después de un violento desalojo de colonos en Santa Úrsula, diputados de varios partidos, sobre todo Enrique Ramírez y Ramírez, del PRI, y Juan Landerreche Obregón, del PAN, exigieron su destitución, por lo que renunció. Lo llamaban el *Regente de Hierro* y fue el único que gobernó la capital del país durante 14 años.

URUCHURTU, MANUEL R. ◆ n. en Hermosillo, Son., y m. en el mar (1874-1912). Se tituló como abogado en la Escuela Nacional de Jurisprudencia (1899), después de haber sido profesor normalista. Se desempeñó como magistrado fiscal del Supremo Tribunal de Justicia de Sonora (1901-1903), diputado federal y representante de México en el juicio arbitral sobre el Chamizal. Autor de *Apuntes biográficos del señor D. Ramón Corral (1854 a 1900)* (1910). Murió en el naufragio del trasatlántico *Titanic*.

URUCHURTU PERALTA, GUSTAVO A. ◆ n. en Hermosillo, Son., y m. en el DF (1899-1987). Hermano de Ernesto P. Uruchurtu. Luchó en la revolución constitucionalista a las órdenes de Álvaro Obregón. Médico cirujano especializado en cardiología, fue diputado federal por Sonora, funcionario de la Secretaría de Salubridad y Asistencia, senador por Sonora y presidente del Patronato del Nacional Monte de Piedad.

URUETA, CORDELIA ◆ n. y m. en la ciudad de México (1908-1995). Pintora. Hija del diplomático Jesús Urueta. Inició sus estudios en la escuela al aire libre de Alfredo Ramos Martínez. Su primera exposición de dibujos se realizó a instancias de Gerardo Murillo. Fue profesora en varias escuelas de la SEP, funcionaria del Servicio Exterior Mexicano y promotora de arte del INBA

Ernesto P. Uruchurtu

Uruapan, Michoacán

FOTO: MICHAEL CALDERWOOD

Foto: Rogelio Cuéllar

Cordelia Urueta

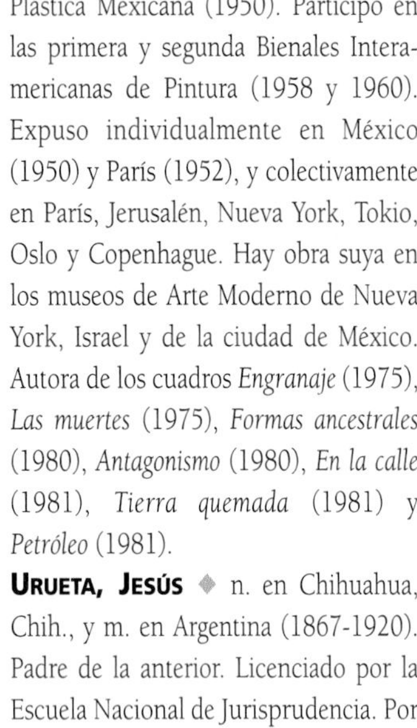

(1955-). Cofundadora del Salón de la Plástica Mexicana (1950). Participó en las primera y segunda Bienales Interamericanas de Pintura (1958 y 1960). Expuso individualmente en México (1950) y París (1952), y colectivamente en París, Jerusalén, Nueva York, Tokio, Oslo y Copenhague. Hay obra suya en los museos de Arte Moderno de Nueva York, Israel y de la ciudad de México. Autora de los cuadros *Engranaje* (1975), *Las muertes* (1975), *Formas ancestrales* (1980), *Antagonismo* (1980), *En la calle* (1981), *Tierra quemada* (1981) y *Petróleo* (1981).

Urueta, Jesús ♦ n. en Chihuahua, Chih., y m. en Argentina (1867-1920). Padre de la anterior. Licenciado por la Escuela Nacional de Jurisprudencia. Por sus dotes oratorias lo llamaron *El Príncipe de la Palabra*. Colaboró en la *Revista Moderna* y *El Siglo XIX*. Fue bibliotecario y profesor de la Escuela Nacional de Jurisprudencia, dos veces diputado federal y profesor de la Escuela Nacional Preparatoria. Crítico del dictador Victoriano Huerta, éste lo mandó encarcelar. Secretario de Relaciones Exteriores (del 12 de diciembre de 1914 al 18 de junio de 1915) de Venustiano Carranza. Fue fundador del Partido Democrático y en 1919 se le designó ministro plenipotenciario en Argentina y encargado de negocios ante el gobierno uruguayo, puestos que desempeñó hasta su muerte. Autor de *Fresca* (1893), *Alma poesía. Conferencias sobre literatura griega* (1904), *Pasquinadas y desenfados políticos* (1911), *Conferencias y discursos literarios* (1919) y *Obras completas* (1930).

Foto: Archivo Casasola

Jesús Urueta, crítico de Huerta

Puerto desconocido, óleo sobre tela de Cordelia Urueta (1964)

Urueta, Jesús *Chano* ♦ n. en el mineral de Cusihuiriáchic, Chih., y m. en el DF (1895-1979). Hijo del anterior. Participó en algunas acciones durante la revolución y más tarde emigró a Estados Unidos. Se inició como cineasta en Hollywood, con el largometraje *El destino* (1930) y el cortometraje *Gitanos* (1930). Volvió a México y en 1933 realizó su primera película, *Profanación*, a la que siguieron *Enemigos* (1933), *El escándalo* (1934), *Una mujer en venta* (1934), *Clemencia* (1934), *Canción del alma* (1937), *Jalisco nunca pierde* (1937), *Mi candidato* (1937), *María* (1938), *Hombres del mar* (1938), *Los de abajo* (1939), *El signo de la muerte* (1939), *La noche de los mayas* (1939), *¡Que viene mi marido!* (1939), *La liga de las canciones* (1941), *El conde de Montecristo* (1941), *El misterioso señor Marquina* (1942), *Ave sin nido* (1943), *El camino de los gatos* (1943), *No matarás* (1943), *El corsario negro* (1944), *El recuerdo de aquella noche* (1944), *Mujer* (1946), *La feria de Jalisco* (1947), *De pecado a pecado* (1947), *La carne manda* (1947), *Ahí viene Vidal Tenorio* (1948), *La norteña de mis amores* (1948), *Dos almas en el mundo* (1948), *Si Adelita se fuera con otro* (1948), *En los Altos de Jalisco* (1948), *La santa del barrio* (1948), *Se la llevó el Remington* (1948), *La gota de sangre* (1949), *El gran campeón* (1949), *No me quieras tanto* (1949), *Ventarrón* (1949), *Rayito de luna* (1949), *El desalmado* (1950), *Resortes* (1950), *Al son del mambo* (1950), *Serenata de Acapulco* (1950), *Peregrina* (1950), *La estatua de carne* (1951), *Manos de seda* (1951), *Del can-can al mambo* (1951), *La bestia magnífica* (1952), *El monstruo resucitado* (1953), *El vendedor de muñecas* (1954), *La desconocida* (1954), *La bruja* (1954), *La ilegítima* (1955), *La fuerza del deseo* (1955), *El túnel seis* (1955), *El seductor* (1955), *El ratón* (1956), *El jinete sin cabeza* (1956), *La cabeza de Pancho Villa* (1957), *La marca de Satanás* (1957), *Los tigres del ring* (1957), *Cuando se quiere se quiere* (1958), *Del suelo no paso* (1958), *No soy monedita de oro* (1958), *Luciano Romero* (1959), *Guantes de oro* (1959), *El demonio azul* (1964), *Alma Grande, el yaqui justiciero* (1965) y *El as de oros* (1967), *Tu camino y el mío* (1971) y *Los leones del ring* (1972), entre otras. Además, codirigió *Los hermanos Diablo* (1959) y *La mujer del carnicero* (1968).

Urueta, Margarita ♦ n. en el DF (1918). Estudió teatro en Alemania, París y Nueva York. Ha sido poeta, dramaturga, ensayista, novelista y directora teatral. Construyó un teatro y lo dedicó a la memoria de su padre, Jesús Urueta, donde se iniciaron Héctor Suárez, el teatrista Alejandro Jodorowsky y muchos más. De sus principales obras sobresalen: *Almas de perfil, San Lunes, Espía sin ser, Mediocre, Conversación sencilla, Biografía de Jesús Urueta, Confesiones de Sor Juana, Hasta mañana, Compadre y Malinche*. La primera telenovela de la televisión mexicana fue escrita por ella en 1952 y se llamó *La familia Bellavista*. Otras telenovelas fueron: *Aprender a vivir* e *Historia de México*. Es autora de la comedia *Tianguis*, que ganó el Premio Mundial de Teatro en Nueva York y en México. En 1992 publicó el libro *Teatro de Margarita Urueta*, y en 1998 presentó su biografía titulada *El juicio de mi tiempo*.

Uruguay, República Oriental del ♦ Nación de Sudamérica situada en el litoral del océano Atlántico. Limita con Brasil y Argentina. Superficie: 176.215 km^2. Habitantes: 3,289,000 (1998). Su capital es Montevideo (1,378,707 habitantes en 1996). El idioma oficial es el español. *Historia*: El territorio del actual Uruguay estuvo poblado originalmente por los charrúas, chanás, yaros y guenoas, subramas de la etnia guaraní, todos los cuales fueron exterminados completamente entre los siglos XVI y XIX. En 1515 el español Juan Díaz de Solís descubrió el Río de la Plata, desembarcó al año siguiente y fue ejecutado por los charrúas. Entre 1527 y 1528, Sebastián Cabot navegó por el Río de la Plata, llamado así por él, se internó en el continente, exploró los ríos Paraná y Paraguay y construyó un fuerte en la desembocadura del río San Salvador. En

1603 el gobernador de Paraguay, Hernando Arias de Saavedra, intentó penetrar en la Banda Oriental (nombre del territorio al este del río Uruguay), pero fue repelido por los charrúas. En 1617 se creó la Gobernación del Río de la Plata, a la que se adjudicaron los territorios del acual Uruguay; siete años después se inició la evangelización jesuita, lo que marcó el inicio de la colonización definitiva de la Banda Oriental. En 1680 los portugueses de la colonia de Brasil, dirigidos por Manuel Lobo, fundaron en territorio oriental, frente a Buenos Aires, la Nova Colonia do Sacramento, que se convertiría en punto de conflicto entre las coronas española y portuguesa. En 1726, Mauricio de Zabala fundó la ciudad de San Felipe y Santiago de Montevideo. Cincuenta años más tarde, la Banda Oriental se incorporó al virreinato del Río de la Plata. En 1777, Portugal reconoció la jurisdicción de España sobre el territorio, de acuerdo con el Tratado de San Ildefonso. A partir de 1778, Montevideo empezó a convertirse en rival comercial de Buenos Aires. En 1801 los portugueses invadieron los territorios de las misiones orientales, lo que fijó el límite de la Banda Oriental en el río Ibicuí; cinco años más tarde Montevideo fue invadida por los ingleses, cuyo dominio sobre Uruguay concluyó en 1807. Al ocurrir la invasión napoleónica a España, en 1808, y ante la ausencia de un rey hispano, se formó en Montevideo una Junta de Gobierno que declaró la soberanía del pueblo. En 1811, José Artigas encabezó el primer movimiento independentista y venció a los realistas en Las Piedras; tres años después terminó la dominación española en el Río de la Plata, con la capitulación de Montevideo. En 1815 fue dictada en Uruguay, por Artigas, la primera reforma agraria de Latinoamérica. Por ser Uruguay un territorio de pastizales propio para la ganadería, rama que ya se había impulsado en el país, y por su importancia estratégica fue un sitio codiciado por los países vecinos: en 1816 se inició una invasión brasileña que, en 1820, obligó a Artigas a refugiarse en Paraguay y que en 1821 convirtió la Banda Oriental en la provincia brasileña Cisplatina. La liberación uruguaya se inició en abril de 1825, cuando Juan Antonio Lavalleja, con 33 orientales refugiados en Buenos Aires, invadió el país; el 25 de agosto, Lavalleja proclamó la independencia de Montevideo y declaró su unión con las Provincias Unidas del Río de la Plata. El 20 de febrero de 1827 "los 33", que ya eran un ejército regular de 2,000 hombres, pertrechados por Argentina, vencieron a los brasileños en Ituzaingó. Finalmente, el 27 de agosto de 1828 se firmó un Tratado de Paz, por el que Brasil y Argentina renunciaron a sus pretensiones sobre la Banda Oriental y dos años más tarde, el 18 de julio de 1830, se promulgó la Constitución de la República Oriental del Uruguay. A partir de entonces se conformaron dos partidos políticos conocidos como Colorado (fundado y dirigido por el general Rivera) y Blanco o Nacional (de Manuel Oribe), cuya rivalidad condujo a numerosas guerras civiles durante el siglo XIX y parte del XX. La más importante de estas luchas intestinas fue la guerra Grande, que se produjo entre 1839 y 1852. En el curso de ésta, Oribe recibió apoyo del dictador argentino Juan Manuel de Rosas, y mantuvo a Montevideo sitiada de 1843 a 1851. En 1863, luego de la defensa que el general mexicano Ignacio Zaragoza hizo de la ciudad de Puebla, el gobierno uruguayo decidió otorgarle una medalla a este militar; sin embargo, cuando la confección de la presea estaba casi concluida ocurrió la muerte de Zaragoza, por lo que la misma medalla le fue conferida a Benito Juárez, quien la recibió un año después. De 1863 a 1865 se produjo una nueva guerra civil, luego de un fallido intento de fusión entre los partidos Blanco y Colorado. Entre 1865 y 1879, Uruguay se unió a Brasil y Argentina en la Triple Alianza, en guerra contra Paraguay. Hacia finales del siglo XIX, durante la presidencia de Lorenzo Latorre, Uruguay se consolidó como una nación exportadora que no acumulaba capital, pues éste fluía invariablemente hacia Inglaterra. En 1897 se produjo una primera fórmula de coparticipación entre los partidos Blanco y Colorado, durante la presidencia de Juan Lindolfo Cuesta. En 1903 llegó al Ejecutivo el colorado José Batlle y Ordóñez, quien consolidó el progreso económico uruguayo, fincado en la ganadería. Un año más tarde se produjo la última lucha entre Blancos y Colorados, que ganaron los segundos y se inició un largo periodo de paz que hizo llamar a Uruguay "la Suiza de América". En 1951 se promulgó una nueva Constitución que suprimió el cargo de presidente y estableció un Consejo Nacional de Gobierno compuesto por nueve miembros. El 30 de noviembre de 1958, el Partido Blanco ganó las elecciones, tras 93 años de gobierno colorado, y en 1966 el Ejecutivo volvió a ser ejercido por un presidente de la República. La riqueza de Uruguay estaba en manos de oligarcas y especuladores, lo que generó altos niveles de inflación y la depauperación de los trabajadores orientales; en 1968, como consecuencia, se generaron las primeras grandes huelgas nacionales y el 13 de junio de ese año, el gobierno de Jorge Pacheco Areco declaró la ley marcial; el 22 de septiembre se clausuraron las universidades y escuelas de segunda enseñanza de Montevideo y simultáneamente empezó a operar el Movimiento de Liberación Nacional-Tupamaros, grupo guerrillero que luchaba por

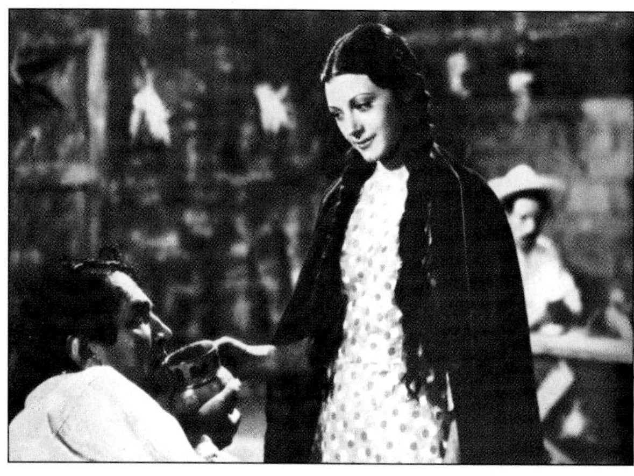

Esther Fernández y Miguel Ángel Ferriz en Los de abajo, filme dirigido por Jesús Chano Urueta

Jesús *Chano* Urueta

Timbre de la República Oriental del Uruguay

Timbres de la República Oriental del Uruguay

República Oriental del Uruguay

reivindicaciones populares. En 1971 se formó el Frente Amplio, que agrupó al conjunto de la izquierda y lanzó la candidatura presidencial de Líber Seregni. Dos años después, el 27 de junio de 1973, Juan María Bordaberry dio un golpe de Estado, declaró ilegal al Frente Amplio, encarceló a Seregni y declaró una guerra interna contra los Tupamaros. En 1976 el ejército destituyó a Bordaberry. Se inició entonces la mayor emigración en la historia de los uruguayos. Muchos se asilaron en México, donde pemanecieron hasta 1984, cuando se restableció la democracia en su país. Entre estos refugiados se contaron numerosos profesores universitarios y periodistas como Carlos Quijano, director de *Marcha*; así como grandes artistas, como los integrantes de la Camerata Punta del Este, la compañía de teatro El Galpón y el músico Alfredo Zitarrosa. El 30 de noviembre de 1980 un referéndum repudió el intento militar de legalizar su gobierno mediante una nueva constitución; a partir de entonces la represión se agudizó, aumentó el número de prisioneros políticos y salieron del país unos 300,000 uruguayos (en 1981 se calculaba en 2,000 el número de uruguayos exiliados en México). Ante su impopularidad y las presiones políticas internas y externas, el gobierno militar se vio obligado a devolver el poder a los civiles. En 1984 fue liberado Seregni y llegó a la presidencia el civil Julio María Sanguinetti. En 1985 se reinstaló el Poder Legislativo en Uruguay y se decretó una amnistía para los sobrevivientes del Movimiento de Liberación Nacional-Tupamaros. El 90 por ciento de los uruguayos refugiados en México regresó a Uruguay. Del 5 al 7 de mayo de 1986 el presidente Sanguinetti realizó una visita oficial a México y vino de nuevo en noviembre de 1987 para asistir a la reunión del Grupo de los Ocho, al que México también pertenece. Desde 1995 se publica en la ciudad de México *El Entrevero*, periódico dirigido a la comunidad uruguaya en México.

Urzúa y Arizmendi, Martín de ◆ n. en España y m. en las Filipinas (1653-1715). Alcalde ordinario de la ciudad de México (1679) y gobernador interino de Yucatán (1695 y 1699). Fue excomulgado por el obispo Pedro de los Rios y Lamadrid, acusado de unos homicidios ocurridos en la iglesia de Valladolid, por lo que debió marchar a España para ser enjuiciado. Una vez absuelto (1706) regresó a ocuparse por tercera ocasión del gobierno yucateco y en 1708 se le designó gobernador y capitán general de las Filipinas, así como presidente de la Real Audiencia de Manila.

Usigli, Rodolfo ◆ n. y m. en el DF (1905-1979). Dramaturgo. Realizó estudios en el Conservatorio Nacional y en la Escuela de Arte Dramático de la Universidad de Yale. En 1924 empezó a escribir crónicas teatrales en la revista *El Sábado*. Fue profesor (1933-47) y director de Cursos de Teatro de la UNAM (1937), así como profesor de la Academia Cinematográfica (1942); director de Prensa de la Presidencia de la República (1936), director del Teatro Radiofónico de la SEP (1938) y del Departamento de Teatro de la Dirección de Bellas Artes (1938-39) y director del Teatro Popular Mexicano (1972-75). Ingresó en el cuerpo diplomático y se desempeñó como agregado cultural en Francia y embajador en Líbano (1956-62) y en Noruega (1962-71). Fue delegado de México a los festivales cimatográficos de Bélgica, Checoslovaquia, Venecia (1950) y Cannes (1949 y 1950). Autor de las obras teatrales: *Quatre chemins* (1929), *El apóstol* (1930), *Falso drama* (1932), *Noche de estío* (1933), *La última puerta* (1934-35), *Estado de secreto* (1935), *El niño y la niebla* (1936), *Alcestes* (1936), *Medio tono* (1937), *Mientras amemos* (1937), *El gesticulador* (1937), *Otra primavera* (1938), *La mujer no hace milagros* (1939), *Aguas estancadas* (1939), *Vacaciones* (1940), *Sueño de un día* (1940), *La familia cena en casa* (1942), *Corona de sombra* (1943), *Dios, batidillo y la mujer* (1943), *Vacaciones II* (1945), *La función de despedida* (1949), *Los fugitivos* (1950), *Jano es una muchacha* (1952), *Un día de éstos* (1953), *La exposición* (1959), *La corona de fuego* (1960), *La diadema* (1960), *Corona de luz* (1964), *Un navío cargado de* (1966), *Las madres* (1966), *El encuentro* (1966), *El testamento y el viudo* (1966), *El gran circo del mundo* (1969), *Carta de amor* (1972), *El caso Flores* (1972), *Buenos días señor presidente* (1972) y *Teatro completo* (3 t., 1963-79); el poemario *Conversación desesperada* (1938); las novelas *Ensayo de un crimen* (1944) y *Obliteración* (1971) y los ensayos *México en el teatro* (1932), *Caminos del teatro en México* (1933), *Itinerario del autor dramático* (1940), *Antonio Ruiz et L'art dangereux de la peinture* (1960) y *Anatomía del teatro* (1966). Premio América (1970) y Premio Nacional de Letras (1972).

Rodolfo Usigli

Usumacinta ◆ Río de Chiapas y Tabasco. Nace de la confluencia de los ríos Salinas o Chixoy (guatemalteco) y el de la Pasión (mexicano), en el extremo oriental de Chiapas, en la frontera con Guatemala, al este de la selva Lacandona. Corre de sureste a noroeste como línea divisoria entre Chiapas y Guatemala; recibe al río Chancalá, entra por el extremo sureste de Tabasco y toma el rumbo norte para torcer al oeste, cerca de Balancán de Domínguez. Parte de su curso sirve de límite entre Chiapas y Tabasco. Tuerce al norte y de su curso se desprende el río San Antonio; llega al límite entre Tabasco y Campeche, vira al noroeste y da nacimiento al río Palizada, que atraviesa

Campeche y desagua en la laguna de Términos; sigue su trayectoria al oeste, vuelve a recibir las aguas del San Antonio, tuerce al noroeste y genera al río San Pedro y San Pablo, que desemboca en el golfo de México; sigue su curso hacia el noroeste, recibe al arroyo Chichicaste, forma el río de las Islas, cuyas aguas retoma el Grijalva inmediatamente antes de unir su curso al del Usumacinta, en el punto llamado Tres Bocas, 16 kilómetros al sur de Frontera, donde ambos forman una sola corriente que desemboca en el golfo de México. El Usumacinta tiene un curso aproximado de 800 Km, de los cuales 300 son navegables. Su cuenca, de 64,000 km², es la tercera de la vertiente del golfo. Su escurrimiento medio anual es de 56,000 de metros cúbicos, aproximadamente.

Utah ◆ Actual estado de Estados Unidos que fue territorio de la Nueva España. Antes de la llegada de los conquistadores españoles, el valle de Utah estuvo poblado por los indios mimbreros y otras etnias. En 1776 llegaron los franciscanos Silvestre Vélez de Escalante y Francisco Atanasio Domínguez, quienes trataban de abrir una ruta entre Santa Fe y las misiones recién establecidas en Monterrey, Alta California. Pese a las recomendaciones y descripciones favorables del lugar que hicieron los franciscanos, el virreinato, primero, y el gobierno mexicano, después de 1821, no dispusieron la colonización de Utah por falta de recursos económicos. La zona, ignorada por los mexicanos, fue lugar de tránsito de cazadores y comerciantes canadienses y estadounidenses. En 1847 los mormones, dirigidos por Brigham Young, ocuparon Utah, territorio que México perdió en 1848, por los tratados de Guadalupe-Hidalgo.

Uxmal ◆ Ciudad arqueológica maya localizada en el municipio de Sinanché, Yucatán (☛).

Uxpanapa ◆ Municipio veracruzano erigido el 30 de enero de 1997. Cuenta con 38,035 habitantes, distribuidos en 83 localidades. Se ubica al este de Cosamaloapan, de cuyos terrenos orientales fue creado, y al sur de Alvarado, cerca de los límites con Oaxaca.

Uzbekistán, República de ◆ Estado asiático que limita al noroeste, norte y este con Kazajstán, al sureste con Kirguistán y Tayikistán, al sur con Afganistán y al oeste con Turkmenistán. Aproximadamente la mitad del mar de Aral se halla en su territorio. Superficie: 447,400 km². Habitantes: 23,574,000 (1998). Su capital es Tashkent (2,107,000 habitantes en 1994). Otras ciudades importantes son Samarcanda (362,000 habitantes en 1995) y Namangán (362,000). El uzbeko es el idioma oficial y también se hablan ruso, tártaro, kasajo y tayikistano. La moneda es el sum. *Historia*: hay huellas de presencia humana en el actual territorio de Uzbekistán que se remontarían a 70,000 años a.n.e. En el primer milenio antes de nuestra era se crearon ahí los primitivos Estados nacionales de Bactriana, Khuarezm y Sogdiana, que fueron sometidos por los persas (en el siglo VI a.n.e.), Alejandro de Macedonia (siglo IV a.n.e.), los árabes (siglo VIII) y los mongoles (siglo XIII). En el siglo XIV Shibaka, nieto de Gengis Kan, recibió el territorio como herencia, lo llamó Kiptchak y fundó la dinastía sheibanida. A finales de ese siglo el Kan Ozbeg convirtió la región al islamismo y, por su nombre, comenzó a llamarse "uzbekos" a los habitantes del kanato. Durante sucesivas dinastías de orígenes mongol y persa Uzbekistán conoció periodos de relativo auge, en gran medida gracias a encontrarse en el paso de las rutas comerciales más importantes de la época. Al comenzar el siglo XIX, Uzbekistán estaba dividida en los condados de Bujara, Kiva y Kokand, que no tenían fronteras bien definidas y que luchaban constantemente entre sí, excepto cuando se trataba de frenar invasiones externas, como ocurrió con las expediciones rusas de 1817 y 1839. Entre 1855 y 1876 se produjo una lenta penetración rusa, que paso a paso se apoderó de los tres condados de Uzbekistán. En 1924, luego de un lustro de resistencia, Uzbekistán quedó incluida en la Unión Soviética (☛). En 1990 declaró su independencia de la URSS, que Moscú reconoció hasta 1991. México estableció relaciones diplomáticas con Uzbekistán en 1992.

Uzeta Murcio, Sergio ◆ n. en el DF (1961). Licenciado en Comunicación por la UIA (1984). Fue reportero y redactor del periódico *La Afición* (1982-1984), analista e investigador de la Secretaría de Salud (1984). En la Presidencia de la República ha sido analista e investigador (1984-87), jefe de información (1984-88) y director de información (1988-91). En el Canal 11 se ha desempeñado como asesor de la Dirección General (1991), director de noticiarios y programas informativos (1991-) y conductor de *Enlace*. Ha sido miembro del Comité Ejecutivo de la Sociedad de Alumnos de Comunicación y representante universitario y consejero técnico de la UIA (1983-84). Ha participado en diversos seminarios sobre periodismo. Obtuvo el premio de Periodismo José Pagés Llergo 1998 y por la Asociación Nacional de Locutores el Micrófono de Oro (1999).

Uzpanapa ◆ Río de Veracruz. Su nombre se escribe indistintamente Uzpanapa, Uspanapa o Uxpanapa. Nace en la vertiente septentrional de la sierra Atravesada, corre de sur a norte y recibe al río Nanchital, donde empieza a ser navegable para embarcaciones de poco calado; tuerce al noroeste, al sureste de Minatitlán, y se une al río Coatzacoalcos, al sur del puerto del mismo nombre.

Obras dramáticas de la autoría de Rodolfo Usigli

República de Uzbekistán

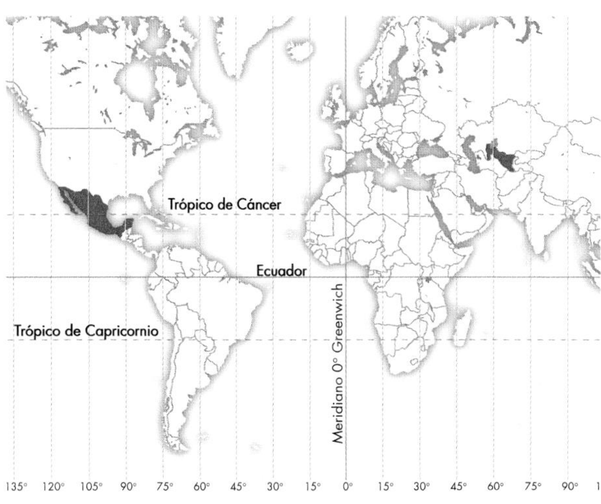

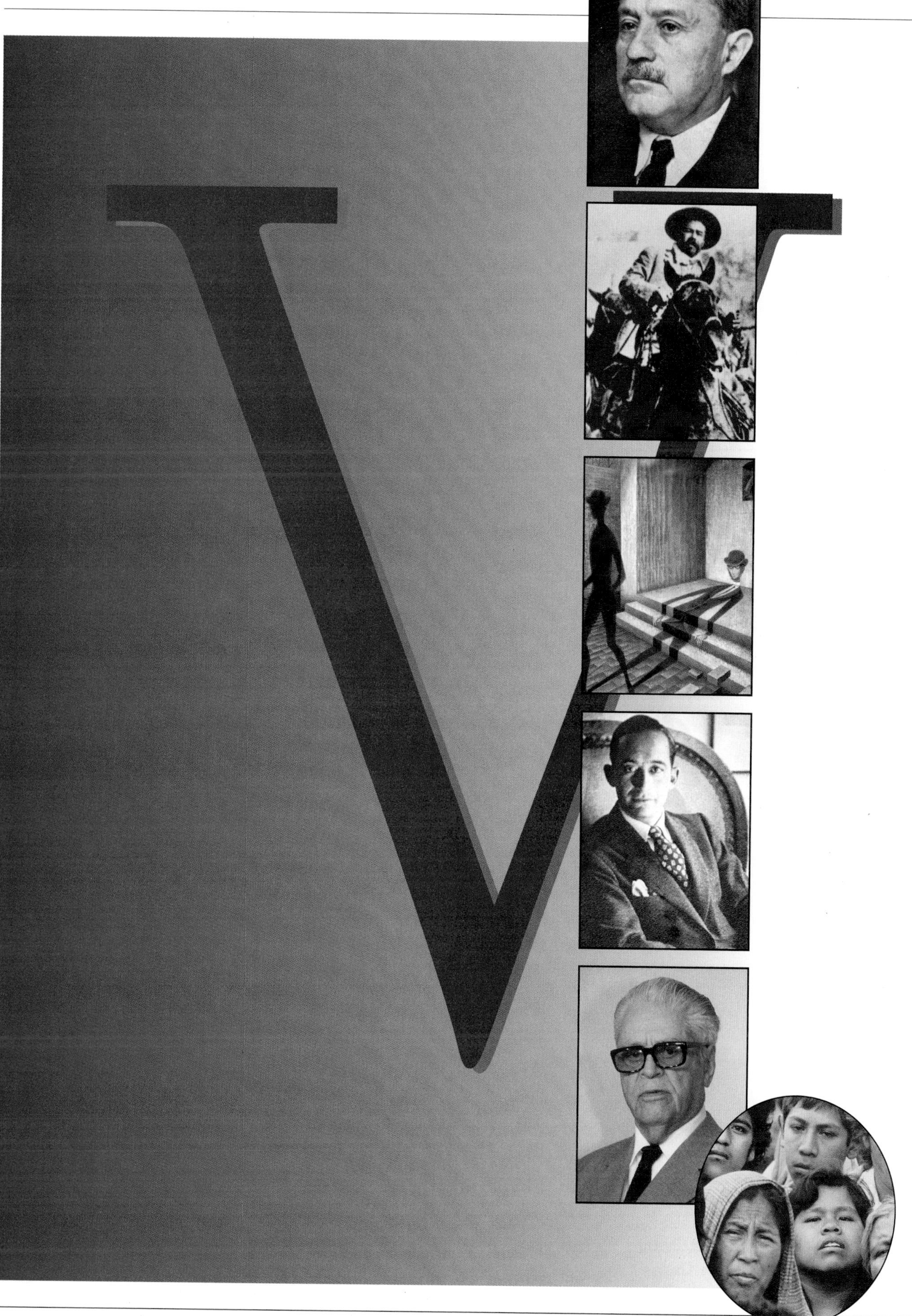

VADILLO ◆ n. y m. en el DF (1929-1983). Caricaturista. Su nombre completo era Leonardo Vadillo Paulsen. Estudió dibujo y pintura en La Esmeralda. Fue cartonista de *Paquín*, *Don Timorato*, *Diógenes*, *Zócalo*, *Ovaciones*, *Diario de la Tarde*, *Excélsior*, *Sucesos*, *El Día*, *Siempre!* y *El Sol de México*. Presentó exposiciones de su obra pictórica. Premio del Club de Periodistas (1974).

VADILLO, BASILIO ◆ n. en Zapotitlán, Jal., y m. en Uruguay (1885-1935). Padre del anterior. Estudió en el seminario de Colima. Profesor normalista graduado en 1913. Fue director de una escuela primaria y secretario de redacción de la revista *Vida y Luz*, así como colaborador de *Colliman* (1907). Ingresó en 1908 en la Escuela Nacional de Maestros, a la que representó en el primer Congreso Nacional de Estudiantes (1910). En 1913 organizó a un grupo de condiscípulos, con los que se dirigió a Mazatlán para unirse al ejército constitucionalista. De nuevo en Colima fue director general de Educación (1915-17), restableció las escuelas Preparatoria y Normal del estado y dirigió el periódico local *El Baluarte*. Diputado federal (1918-20), en 1919 fundó *El Monitor Republicano*, para apoyar la candidatura presidencial de Obregón. Gobernador constitucional de Jalisco (del 1 de marzo de 1921 al 14 de marzo de 1922), durante su gestión inició el reparto agrario, enfrentó la primera huelga ferrocarrilera del estado y combatió a la "banda del pañuelo negro", dirigida por Pedro Zamora. Un grupo político encabezado por José Zuno y apoyado por Obregón provocó un motín en Guadalajara, luego del cual Vadillo fue destituido. Ministro mexicano en Noruega, la URSS y Suecia, en 1929 fue miembro fundador del Partido Nacional Revolucionario, primer director de su órgano de prensa, *El Nacional Revolucionario*, y segundo presidente del Comité Ejecutivo (1930). Al morir era embajador en Uruguay (1931). Dejó inédito el libro *El campanario*.

Fray Diego Valadés

VADILLO, EVELIO ◆ n. en Ciudad del Carmen, Camp., y m. en el DF (?-1958).

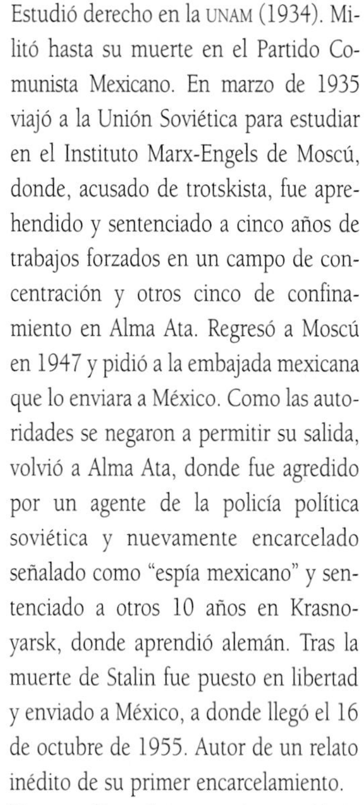

Estudió derecho en la UNAM (1934). Militó hasta su muerte en el Partido Comunista Mexicano. En marzo de 1935 viajó a la Unión Soviética para estudiar en el Instituto Marx-Engels de Moscú, donde, acusado de trotskista, fue aprehendido y sentenciado a cinco años de trabajos forzados en un campo de concentración y otros cinco de confinamiento en Alma Ata. Regresó a Moscú en 1947 y pidió a la embajada mexicana que lo enviara a México. Como las autoridades se negaron a permitir su salida, volvió a Alma Ata, donde fue agredido por un agente de la policía política soviética y nuevamente encarcelado señalado como "espía mexicano" y sentenciado a otros 10 años en Krasnoyarsk, donde aprendió alemán. Tras la muerte de Stalin fue puesto en libertad y enviado a México, a donde llegó el 16 de octubre de 1955. Autor de un relato inédito de su primer encarcelamiento.

VADO Y RUZ, IGNACIO ◆ n. en Mérida, Yuc., y m. en Veracruz, Ver. (1837-1898). Médico graduado en 1862. Ejerció su profesión en la ciudad de México y en Tabasco, estado del que fue gobernador interino (del 31 de julio de 1871 al 1 de enero de 1872).

VAILLANT, GEORGE CLAPP ◆ n. y m. en EUA (1901-1945). Arqueólogo egresado de la Universidad de Harvard (1922). Fue profesor de las universidades de Yale y Columbia. Dirigió el museo de la Universidad de Pensylvania, efectuó en Mesoamérica tres grandes exploraciones (1919, 1926 y 1928-36), realizó excavaciones en Zacatenco, Ticomán y El Arbolillo y, de acuerdo con sus descubrimientos, elaboró una nueva clasificación de los periodos u horizontes prehispánicos. Autor de *Aztecs of Mexico* (1941), traducido al español como *La civilización azteca* (1944).

VAL BLANCO, ENRIQUE DEL ◆ n. en el DF (1946). Licenciado en economía por la UNAM (1976), tomó cursos de administración de empresas en Ginebra (1972 y 1975) y de organización de ventas en Bogotá (1973). En la UNAM fue consejero técnico y profesor (1976). Trabajó para empresas privadas (1965-76). Ha sido asesor técnico de la Compañía de Luz y Fuerza (1976), secretario técnico del subsecretario de Comercio Interior (1977-78), secretario del Comité de Comercialización del Inmecafé (1977-78), secretario del Comité de Cooperación Hispano-Mexicano en materia de Comercio Interior (1977-78), secretario del Consejo de Cafés y Cafeterías de México (1977-78), director general de Normas sobre Adquisiciones y Almacenes de la Secretaría de Comercio (1978-82), consejero de las empresas Compañía Mexicana de Tubos, Hilos Cadena, Torres Mexicanas y Duralmex (1978-82), director de Responsabilidades y Situación Patrimonial (1982-87), subsecretario de la Contraloría General de la Federación (1987-91), director del Fonatur (1991) y coordinador del Programa Nacional de Empresas de Solidaridad (1992-94) y subsecretario de la Sedesol (1994-98). Ha colaborado en *Controversia*, *unomásuno*, *El Gallo Ilustrado*, *Punto*, *Nueva Universidad*, *Revista de Administración Pública* y *Praxis*. Vicepresidente del Colegio Nacional de Economistas (1979-81). En 1977 fue condecorado por el gobierno español.

VAL BLANCO, JOSÉ MANUEL DEL ◆ n. en el DF (1949). Licenciado en economía por la UNAM (1969) y etnólogo graduado en la ENAH (1980). Ha sido director del Museo Nacional de las Culturas del INAH (1985-89), de Investigación y Promoción Cultural del Instituto Nacional Indigenista de la SEP (1989-92), de Promoción Cultural (1992) y de Culturas Populares del Consejo Nacional para la Cultura y las Artes (1993-94) y del Instituto Indigenista Interamericano (1995).

VALADÉS, DIEGO ◆ n. en Tlaxcala, Tlax., y m. ¿en Italia? (1533-¿1582?). Tomó el hábito franciscano en 1550. Se dedicó a la evangelización, principalmente de los chichimecas. Discípulo y secretario de fray Pedro de Gante, en 1571 fue enviado al capítulo general franciscano, reunido en Francia. Fue procurador de la Orden de Franciscanos Menores desde 1575, cuando fijó su residencia en Roma. Autor de un catecismo y un libro sobre ascética, ambos escritos en náhuatl y ya perdidos, y de *Rhetorica christiana* (1579), escrito en latín e ilustrado con grabados de él mismo, que fue el primer libro de un mexicano editado en Europa, reeditado dos veces y traducido al alemán.

VALADÉS, DIEGO ◆ n. en Mazatlán, Sin. (1945). Hijo de José C. Valadés. Licenciado en derecho por la UNAM (1969), donde ha sido investigador del Instituto de Investigaciones Jurídicas, director general de Difusión Cultural (1973-76), abogado general (1977-80), presidente de la Comisión Técnica de Estudios y Proyectos Legislativos (1977-79), coordinador de Humanidades (1981) y presidente de la Comisión Editorial (1981). Pertenece al PRI desde 1965. Ha sido coordinador jurídico de Servicios de Salud de la Presidencia (1981-82), director de Asuntos Jurídicos de la Secretaría de Gobernación (1982-84), subsecretario de Regulación Sanitaria de la SSA (1984-85), secretario de Gobierno en Sinaloa (1986), diputado federal (1986-88), embajador en Guatemala (1988), coordinador general Jurídico (1988-91) y secretario A de Gobierno del DDF (1991), secretario general de Coordinación Metropolitana (1991-92), procurador del DF (1992-94) y procurador general de la República (1994). Coordinador, con Mario Ruiz Massieu, de la recopilación *La transformación del Estado mexicano* (1989). Autor de *La dictadura constitucional en América Latina* (1974), *La UNAM, formación, estructura y funciones* (1974) y *Las leyes orgánicas de la UNAM* (1980). Pertenece al Colegio de Abogados de México. Cruz al Mérito a la Investigación Jurídica (1978) otorgado por el Instituto Mexicano de Cultura.

VALADÉS, EDMUNDO ◆ n. en Guaymas, Son., y m. en el DF (1915-1994). Escritor y periodista. En 1936 se inició en el periodismo en la revista *Hoy*. Fundó en 1939 la revista *El Cuento*, de la que sólo pudo publicar cinco números debido a la escasez de papel provocada por la segunda guerra mundial;

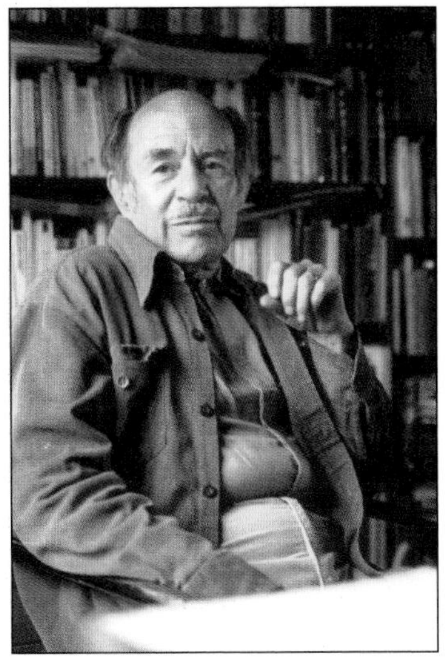

Edmundo Valadés

en 1964 inició de nuevo la publicación de la revista que desde entonces dirigió. Miembro de la Unión de Estudiantes Progresistas Obreros y Campesinos, donde organizó escuelas nocturnas para trabajadores y dirigió una de ellas. Fue secretario de redacción y director editorial de *Novedades*, subjefe de la Oficina de Prensa de la Presidencia (1958-64), profesor del Centro Mexicano de Escritores (1965-66), director de la sección cultural de *Excélsior*, director de la revista *Cultura Norte* y colaborador de *El Día*, *El Nacional*, *América*, *Cuadernos Americanos* y *unomásuno*. Autor, entre otras obras, de los volúmenes de cuento *La muerte tiene permiso* (1955), *Antípoda* (1961), *Las dualidades funestas* (1966) y *Sólo los sueños y los deseos son inmortales, palomita* (1980) y de las antologías *El libro de la imaginación* (1970) *Los grandes cuentos del siglo XX* (1979), *Los cuentos de El Cuento* (1981), *23 cuentos de la Revolución Mexicana* (1985), *Con los tiernos infantes terribles* (1988), *La picardía amorosa* (1988) e *Ingenios del humorismo* (1988). Fue presidente de Pecime, de la Asociación Mexicana de Periodistas de Radio y Televisión y de la Asociación de Escritores de México. Medalla Nezahualcóyotl de la Sociedad General de Escritores de México (1978) y Premio Nacional de Periodismo (1981).

VALADÉS, JOSÉ C. ◆ n. en Mazatlán, Sin., y m. en el DF (1901-1976). Historiador. Figuró entre los fundadores del grupo Jóvenes Igualitarios (1920) y dirigió su periódico, *Juventud Mundial*. Cofundador de la Federación de Jóvenes Comunistas (1920), secretario general de la Confederación General de Trabajadores (1921) y secretario del Buró Latinoamericano de la Tercera Internacional (1922). Fue uno de los dirigentes de la huelga inquilinaria del Distrito Federal (☛). Se separó del Partido Comunista en 1925. Secretario particular de Ezequiel Padilla en la SRE (1940-42), director de *El Correo de Occidente*, de Mazatlán (1942-45) y del semanario *Ya* (1946), profesor de la UNAM (1941-59), secretario general de la Federación de Partidos del Pueblo Mexicano (1946), embajador en Líbano, Siria e Irak (1951-53), Colombia (1953-56), Uruguay (1956-57), Portugal (1963-66) y en Marruecos (1966). Autor, entre otras obras, de *Orígenes del movimiento obrero en México* (1927), *Las memorias de don Adolfo de la Huerta* (1930), *Santa Anna y la guerra de Texas* (1936), *El porfirismo. Historia de un régimen* (3 t., 1941-48), *Breve historia de la guerra con los Estados Unidos* (1947), *Imaginación y realidad de Francisco I. Madero* (2 t., 1960), *Historia general de la Revolución Mexicana* (10 t., 1963-65), *Mis confesiones* (1966), *Introducción a la obra de Daniel Thomas Egerton. Historia del pueblo de México* (3 t., 1967), *Brevísima historia de México* (1975), *El porfirismo y la revolución* (1975, sexto tomo de *México a través de los siglos*) y *Maximiliano y Carlota. Historia del Segundo Imperio* (1976).

VALADEZ, SOCORRO ◆ n. el DF (1955). Fue secretaria ejecutiva del subdirector (1980-81) y del director de *unomásuno* (1982-83). Es socia fundadora de la empresa Desarrollo de Medios, editora del diario *La Jornada* (1984), en el que ha sido secretaria ejecutiva del director general (1984-96) y responsable de la sección *El Correo Ilustrado* (1992-).

VALBUENA SÁNCHEZ, GILBERTO ◆ n. en Chietla, Pue. (1929). Sacerdote ordenado en 1955. Ha sido misionero diocesano, director de la Escuela Apostólica,

Diego Valadés

José C. Valadés

FOTO: RICARDO SALAZAR

Carlos Valdés

Manuel *Loco* Valdés

vicerrector del Seminario Menor Palafoxiano, miembro del grupo promotor del Movimiento por un Mundo Mejor y párroco de Izúcar de Matamoros, obispo auxiliar de Tacámbaro (1973), vicario apostólico de La Paz (1976-88) y obispo de Colima (1988-).

VALDELAMAR, EMA ELENA ◆ n. en el DF (1926). Compositora de música popular. Se inició en 1945 cantando en la radiodifusora XEW, y en 1946 compuso el bolero *Mil besos*. Sus canciones fueron interpretadas por Los Panchos, Lola Flores y Sara Montiel, entre otros, y entre las más conocidas están *Mírame bien, Volver a besarte, Sin mañana ni ayer, Amor sin pasado* y *Devuélveme el corazón*.

VALDÉS, AGUSTÍN A. ◆ n. en Cuba y m. en el DF (1860-1924). Militar. Durante la guerra cubana de independencia se exilió en México. Aquí se naturalizó e ingresó en el ejército. En 1913 fue gobernador interino de Tabasco y un año más tarde Huerta lo ascendió a general de división. Al término de la revolución fue jefe de circulación del periódico *El Universal*.

VALDÉS, ANTONIO JOSÉ ◆ n. en Cuba y m. en la ciudad de México (1780-¿1830?). Pedagogo, en 1803 fundó una escuela en La Habana y fue premiado por la Sociedad Patriótica de esa ciudad. Establecido en la ciudad de México desde 1808, fundó una escuela en 1809. Al iniciarse la guerra de Independencia volvió a Cuba, donde en 1812 estableció una imprenta y fundó el diario *La Cena*, que se publicó hasta 1814 y en el que se difundían los pormenores de las luchas independentistas americanas. Fundó en Buenos Aires el periódico *El Censor* (1815). De nuevo en México fue secretario de la provincia de Nueva Galicia (1821-22) e impresor de cámara del emperador (1822-23). Cofundador de la logia yorquina (1825). Publicó *La Águila Mexicana* (☛) y sucedió a Zavala en la dirección de este periódico, de mayo de 1825 a agosto de 1826. Desde México se asoció a la Junta Promotora de la Libertad Cubana. De diciembre de 1828 a abril de 1829 fue comisario general de México en el gobierno de Guadalupe Victoria. Coautor de una *Memoria estadística del estado de Occidente* (1928). Autor de *Principios generales de la lengua castellana* (1806) y una *Historia de la isla de Cuba* (1828).

VALDÉS, CARLOS ◆ n. en Guadalajara, Jal., y m. en el DF (1928-1991). Escritor. Estudió en El Colegio de México. Cofundador de *Cuadernos del viento* (1961). Fue colaborador de *Ariel, México en la Cultura, La Cultura en México, Nueva Revista de Filología Hispánica, Ideas de México* y *Revista de la Universidad de México*. Tradujo *Al borde de la guerra*, de Norman Cousins (1966). Autor de *Ausencias* (cuento, 1955), *Dos ficciones* (cuento, 1958), *Dos y los muertos* (cuento, 1960), *El nombre es lo de menos* (cuento, 1961), *Crónicas del vicio y la virtud* (1963), *Los antepasados* (novela, 1963), *José Luis Cuevas* (1966), *La voz de la tierra* (novela, 1972) y *La catedral abandonada* (1992).

VALDÉS, MANUEL *LOCO* ◆ n. en Ciudad Juárez, Chih. (1931). Cómico. Su nombre completo es Manuel Gómez Valdés Castillo. Hermano de Germán Valdés *Tin Tan*. Su actividad más destacada la ha realizado en televisión, con programas como *Variedades de media tarde, El show del Loco Valdés, Ensalada de locos* o *Variedades de medianoche*. Ha actuado en las películas *Cada quien su música* (1958), *Caperucita roja* (1959), *El tigre negro* (1961), *Tintansón Crusoe* (1964), *Las mujeres pantera* (1966) y *Detectives y ladrones* (1966), entre otras. Durante 35 años ha puesto en escena una farsa tradicional que glosa el *Don Juan Tenorio*.

VALDÉS, RAMÓN ◆ n. y m. en el DF (1923-1988). Cómico. Su nombre completo era Ramón Gómez Valdés Castillo. Hermano del anterior. Actuó en las películas *Calabacitas tiernas* (1948), *El rey del barrio* (1949), *Yo soy charro de levita* (1949), *La marca del zorrillo* (1950), *Simbad el mareado* (1950), *Novia a la medida, Tres mosqueteros y medio* (1956), *El traga sables* (1964), *Tintansón Crusoe* (1964), *El capitán Mantarraya, El chanfle* y *Chanoc*. En televisión ha trabajado en las series *Chespirito, El Chapulín Colorado* y *El Chavo del Ocho*, donde hizo el personaje de *Don Ramón*.

VALDÉS, ULISES ◆ n. en Morelia, Mich., y m. en el DF (1874-1938). Médico (1898) y administrador (1907) del Hospital Morelos, profesor (1908) y director (1914) de la Escuela Nacional de Medicina, visitador general de la Beneficencia Pública, director del Hospital Juárez y secretario general de Salubridad Pública. Presidente de la Academia Nacional de Medicina (1913) y miembro fundador de la Academia de Cirugía.

VALDÉS AGUILAR, RAÚL ◆ n. en el DF (1933). Licenciado en Relaciones Internacionales por la UNAM (1959), donde ejerció la docencia (1972-75). Miembro del Servicio Exterior en el que ha estado adscrito a las embajadas en la RFA, El Salvador, India, Cuba e Italia (1960-71). En la Secretaría de Relaciones Exteriores ha sido subdirector general, director general, secretario particular del titular (1971-76) y director en jefe para Asuntos Bilaterales (1979-83). Embajador en la República Federal de Alemania (1977-79), Venezuela (1978-79), Israel (1983-88) y la República Democrática de Alemania (1988-90), director general para América Latina y el Caribe (1990) y embajador en Colombia (1990-94). Presidente de la Asociación del Servicio Exterior Mexicano (1981-83).

VALDÉS GARCÍA, SANTOS JOSÉ ◆ n. en Coahuila y m. en el DF (1905-1990). Profesor. Ejerció la docencia en escuelas primarias, fue director de la Normal Rural de San Marcos, Zacatecas, y de la de Saucillo, Chihuahua. Contribuyó a la organización del magisterio, en la tarea de impulsar y perfilar la educación en el campo: primaria rural, misiones culturales y escuelas normales rurales, convertidas durante el gobierno de Lázaro Cárdenas en Escuelas Regionales Campesinas. Colaboró en *El Mundo de Tampico, El Heraldo de San Luis Potosí, El Siglo* y *La Opinión*, de Torreón; *El Día*, del DF y, entre otras, en las revistas *Política* y *Siempre!* Autor de *Motivos sociales de la educación, La religión y la escuela socialista, Democracia y disciplina escolar, Meditaciones sobre el artículo tercero constitucional, La reforma educativa, Participación de los maestros mexicanos en la*

Revolución de 1910, El movimiento sindical magisterial mexicano, Civismo y madera, La batalla por la cultura, Matamoros, ciudad lagunera y *Dos hombres del pueblo.*

VALDÉS GONZÁLEZ, LUZ MARÍA ◆ n. en el DF (1940). Licenciada en antropología social por la UIA (1963), maestra en demografía por El Colegio de México (1966) y maestra en antropología social por el University College, de Inglaterra (1970). Militante del PRI desde 1971. Ha sido investigadora de la Oficina de Recursos Humanos del Banco de México (1969), asesora del subsecretario de Gobernación (1973), profesora de la UNAM (1973-77 y 1985-88), secretaria técnica del Programa Nacional Indicativo de Investigación Demográfica del Conacyt (1974-79), profesora en la UAM (1976-79), asesora del secretario general de Planeación de la Política de Población para Grupos Indígenas de la Secretaría de Gobernación (1980-83), jefa del Proyecto sobre Minorías Étnicas del Centro de Estudios Económicos y Sociales del Tercer Mundo (1980-83), miembro del Sistema Nacional de Investigadores (1986) y secretaria general del Consejo Nacional de Población (1988-90). Autora de *Diagnóstico sobre la investigación y necesidades de fortalecimiento de la infraestructura científica en demografía* (1977), *Memorias étnicas: una aproximación teórica* (1984), *Migración indígena en los censos de 1980* (1986), *Dinámica de población de hablantes de lenguas indígenas* (1987) y de *El perfil demográfico de los hablantes de lenguas indígenas* (1987). Pertenece al Colegio de Etnología y a la Sociedad Mexicana de Demografía.

VALDÉS MEDELLÍN, GONZALO ◆ n. en el DF (1963). Periodista y dramaturgo. Profesor del Núcleo de Estudios Teatrales. Colaborador de *unomásuno, El Nacional* y otras publicaciones. Ha escrito y montado los espectáculos *Encuentros de amor y poesía* (1983), *Transa poética: in memoriam Efraín Huerta* (1984), *Todos los Novos el Novo* (1986), *Ni a tontas ni a locas o La buena gente* (1985, en colaboración con José Antonio Alcaraz) y *A tu intocable persona* (1994). Ha dirigido *Las criadas* y *La carcajada* de Jean Genet (1987), *Los vampiros jóvenes*, de Muñoz (1989), *La última noche con Laura*, de Inclán (1991), *Los protagonistas de la literatura mexicana del siglo XX*, de Carballo (1990), *La construcción*, de Martínez (1993) e *Invitación a la muerte*, de Villaurrutia (1995). Autor de *Corazones apasionados en manos del buzón sentimental* (1985). Becario del INBA y del Fonca (1989-90). En 1995 obtuvo el Premio de la Casa de América Latina por su cuento "En la casa de las semejanzas".

VALDÉS Y MUNGUÍA, MANUEL ANTONIO ◆ n. y m. en la ciudad de México (1742-1814). Impresor del Colegio de San Ildefonso, de la Compañía de Jesús (1764-67), trabajó en el taller de Felipe de Zúñiga y Ontiveros (1767-1807); pasó a Guadalajara (1807) para trabajar en la imprenta de su hijo, Mariano Valdés Téllez Girón, y en 1808 regresó a la ciudad de México, donde fundó su propia imprenta, en la que redactó y publicó las *Gazetas de México*. Fue también propietario de una empresa de coches de alquiler (1793).

VALDÉS RODRÍGUEZ, MAURICIO ◆ n. en Texcoco, Edo. de Méx. (1948). Licenciado en ciencias políticas por la UNAM (1970), donde es profesor, y maestro por la Universidad de Londres (1983). En 1967 ingresó al PRI, en el que fue secretario general de la FOP mexiquense, delegado del CEN en Tlaxcala (1987-88) y secretario de Divulgación Ideológica (1981-82) y presidente del Comité Estatal (1990-91). Renunció a ese partido en 1998 y se sumó al PRD. Ha sido presidente municipal de Texcoco (1973-75), diputado federal (1979-82 y 1988-91), senador de la República (1991-93) y embajador de México en Dinamarca (1994).

VALDÉS OSORIO, GARCÍA DE ◆ n. en España y m. en Mérida, Yuc. (?-1652). En 1650 fue designado gobernador y capitán general de Yucatán. Durante su gestión se produjeron una epidemia de fiebre amarilla (1650), una hambruna provocada por los especuladores del maíz (1651) y numerosas incursiones piratas. Aparentemente murió asesinado por alguno de sus enemigos políticos. Su vida dio origen a la novela *El conde de Peñalva*, de Eligio Ancona.

VALDÉS PEZA, ARMANDO ◆ m. en el DF (1917-1970). Pintor, periodista y diseñador. Nieto del poeta Juan de Dios Peza. Estudió pintura en Estados Unidos y en Europa. Fue diseñador de vestuario y escenógrafo en los estudios de la Metro Goldwyn Mayer. Regresó a México en 1940. Fue profesor en la Academia de San Carlos, diseñador de modas (actividad en la que alcanzó mayor notoriedad) y cronista de sociales de *El Heraldo de México* y *Novedades*.

VALDÉS *TIN TAN*, GERMÁN ◆ n. en Progreso, Yuc., y m. en el DF (1915-1973). Cómico cuyo nombre era Germán Gómez Valdés Castillo. Hermano de Ramón y Manuel Valdés. Vivía en Ciudad Juárez, Chihuahua, cuando inició en 1943 su carrera como locutor y animador en una estación local de radio. Realizó una gira por Estados Unidos donde hizo popular el tipo cómico del "pachuco" y en la que conoció a su "carnal Marcelo" (Marcelo Chávez), quien sería su pareja artística más de 20 años. Actuó por primera vez en la ciudad de México en 1945, en el Teatro Iris, donde alternó con *Cantinflas* y Agustín Lara. Adquirió renombre debido a las más de 200 películas que filmó, entre ellas: *El hijo desobediente* (1945), *El niño perdido* (1947), *Calabacitas tiernas* (1948), *El rey del barrio* (1949), *No me defiendas compadre* (1949), *La marca del zorrillo* (1950), *¡Ay amor, cómo me has puesto!* (1950), *Simbad el mareado* (1950), *El ceniciento* (1951), *Chucho el remendado* (1951), *El bello durmiente* (1952), *El vizconde de Montecristo* (1954), *Lo que le pasó a Sansón* (1955), *Escuela de verano* (1958), *La casa del vampiro* (1959), *El violetero* (1959), *¡¡¡Mátenme porque me muero!!!* (1951), *El campeón ciclista* (1956), *El gato sin botas* (1956), *Teatro del crimen* (1956), *Las mil y una noches* (1957), *Viaje a la luna* (1957), *La odalisca numero 13* (1957), *El fantasma de la opereta* (1960) y *El tesoro del rey Salomón* (1962). Produjo y protagonizó las películas *Tintasón Crusoe* (1964) y *El capitán Mantarraya* (1970).

Germán Valdés *Tin Tan*

Foto: EDOMEX

Octaviano Valdés Valdés

Fernando Valdez

Rubén Valdez

Valdés Valdés, Octaviano ♦ n. en Cacalomacán, Edo. de Méx., y m. en el DF (1902-1991). Sacerdote ordenado en 1927. Estudió en el Colegio Pío Latinoamericano. Fue profesor del Seminario Conciliar de México, protonotario apostólico *ad instar* y vicario general del arzobispado de México, así como capellán del convento del Dulce Nombre de María y San Bernardo, deán de la catedral de México, canónigo desde 1950 y coordinador de la Mitra ante la Comisión Diocesana de Orden y Decoro. Especialista en arte sagrado. Promovió una tertulia dominical conocida como el Círculo Mate, en la que participaban intelectuales de diversas ideologías y religiones. Antologó: *Poesía neoclásica* (1946), *El humanismo mexicano* (de Gabriel Méndez Plancarte, 1970) y *Crítica de críticas. Alfonso Méndez Plancarte defiende a Sor Juana* (1984). Autor de poesía: *El pozo de Jacob* (1929) y *Bajo el ala del ángel* (1952); novela: *La cabellera de Berenice* (1968); ensayo: *El prisma de Horacio* (1937), *El barroco, espíritu y forma del arte de México* (1956) y *Amado, Manuel José y otros exámenes* (1975), y biografía: *El padre Tembleque* (1945) y *Ángel María Garibay* (1985). Miembro de la Academia Mexicana (de la Lengua), de El Colegio de México, de El Colegio Nacional, del Instituto Mexicano de Cultura y miembro honorario del Instituto de Investigación Venustiano Carranza. Medalla Sor Juana Inés de la Cruz (1958) y medalla de plata de la Sociedad Cultural Sor Juana, por *Críticas de críticas*.

Valdeschak, Martín ♦ n. en el DF (1966). Violinista egresado del Conservatorio Nacional, donde fue alumno de Carlos Esteva, Vladimir Vulfmann, Ivo Valenti, Fernando Raudales, Hermilo Novelo y Rasma Lielmane. Estudió en Houston con Fredell Lack y Sergio Ortiz y en la Academia Juilliard de Nueva York (en la que obtuvo el título de *bachelor of music* en 1989), con Margaret Pardee. Fue discípulo en Suiza de Igor Ozim. Ha sido solista de la mayoría de orquestas sinfónicas de México y ha actuado en varias ciudades de Europa y Norteamérica. Seleccionado como concertino de la Orquesta Internacional de Jóvenes (1987 y 88), participante en el Festival de Schleswig Holstein, donde fue dirigido por Leonard Bernstein, Christoff Eschenbach y Sergiu Celibidache. Solista de la Orquesta Sinfónica Nacional. Premio Nacional de la Juventud y mención de excelencia Jesús Reyes Heroles del Crea (1986).

Valdespino Castillo, Roberto ♦ n. en Pachuca, Hgo. (1932). Licenciado en derecho por la UNAM (1957). Tomó un curso en el Instituto Internacional de Administración Pública de Francia (1972). Miembro del PRI, del que ha sido representante ante la comisión electoral en Hidalgo (1964), director del CEPES (1970) y presidente del Comité Directivo Estatal (1984). Ha sido agente del Ministerio Público en Apan (1959) y en Ciudad Sahagún (1960), presidente municipal de Tulancingo (1961-63), subprocurador general de Justicia de Hidalgo (1970), diputado local (1970-72), procurador general de Justicia de Hidalgo (1972), director de Servicios Descentralizados de la SEP (1978), director jurídico (1981) y secretario general de Gobierno de Hidalgo (1983-84). Diputado federal (1985-88). Autor de *El estado de Hidalgo* (1980). Presidente del Club 20-30 (1960), presidente del Club de Leones (1965) y presidente de la Junta de Mejoramiento Moral, Cívico y Material de Tulancingo.

Valdespino y Díaz, Ignacio ♦ n. en Chalchihuites, Zac., y m. en EUA (1861-1928). Estudió en el Seminario de Durango. Sacerdote ordenado en 1885, fue cura de Santiago Papasquiaro, miembro del cabildo de la catedral de Durango, obispo de Hermosillo (1902-13) y de Aguascalientes (1913-28). Durante la guerra cristera estuvo exiliado. Autor de la novela *Lupe* (1924), de la autobiografía *El calvario de un obispo* y de un poemario.

Valdez, Fernando ♦ n. en el DF (1948). Periodista y editor. Estudió en la Escuela de Periodismo Carlos Septién García (1968), mercadotecnia y publicidad (1968), producción y dirección de televisión (1970) en la Escuela Columbia. Participó en el movimiento estudiantil de 1968. Fundador del periódico *Eclipse* (1967) y editor de la revista *Quimera* (1988). Director de la editorial Seix-Barral de México (1969-82), dueño de la editorial Leega (1981), de la que conserva el 50 por ciento de las acciones, y dueño, presidente y director de la editorial Plaza y Valdez (1986-).

Valdez, Jorge ♦ n. en Torreón, Coah. (1955). Poeta. Sus obras se han publicado en los periódicos: *La Jornada, México en el Arte, Tierra Adentro, Sábado, Casa del Tiempo, Periódico de Poesía, La Nación, Casa de las Américas, Cuadernos Hispanoamericanos* y *Sibila*. Aparece en *Anuaro de poesía* (1990), *Poemas eróticos hispanoamericanos* (Argentina, 1990), *Innovación y permanencia en la literatura coahuilense, 1987-1991* (1993) y *Ruido de sueños, Noise of Dreams, Panorama de la nueva poesía mexicana, la generación 1940-1960* (1994). Autor de *Libros Voz Temporal* (1985), *Aguas Territoriales* (1989), *Cuerpo cierto* (1995) y la plaquette *Materia en vilo* (1995), y de las antologías *La poesía argentina hoy* y *Poetas españoles de dos generaciones*. Premio Internacional de Poesía Plural (1985). Premio Nacional de Poesía Aguascalientes (1998).

Valdez, Manuel M. ♦ n. en Córdoba, Ver., y m. en el DF (1897-1965). Egresado de la Escuela de Odontología de la ciudad de México, en 1913 se unió al ejército constitucionalista, en el que fundó el servicio dental. Fue trabajador del Hospital Central Militar. Alcanzó el generalato.

Valdez Abascal, José Rubén ♦ n. en el DF (1951). Licenciado en derecho por la UNAM (1975). Profesor de la Universidad Panamericana. Miembro del PRI. Ha sido subjefe del Departamento de Asesoría Jurídica de Impuestos al Ingreso y subjefe del Departamento de Simplificación Tributaria de la Dirección General de Legislación Tributaria de la SHCP (1976), jefe del Departamento de Legislación y Normatividad (1977-79), subdirector (1979-80) y director de Legislación y Asuntos Jurídicos Paraestatales (1981-82) y director general de Asuntos Jurídicos de la SPP (1982-88), director general de Asuntos Jurídicos de la Presidencia (1988-94) y procurador general de Justicia del Distrito Federal (1994-95). Miembro de la Barra Mexicana-Colegio de Abogados, fue vicepresidente de la Agrupación Nacional de Abogados al Servicio del Estado de la CNOP (1982-86).

VALDIOSERA BERMAN, RAMÓN ◆ n. ¿en Tuxpan, Ver.? (1918). En 1932 se ganaba la vida vendiendo sus dibujos en los mercados y en ese mismo año se hizo novillero, junto con Carlos y Manolo Arruza. Se retiró meses después. Fue dibujante y redactor de *Eco Taurino* y de *México Gráfico* (1937). En 1936 creó una empresa de historietas que fracasó. En 1939 era director artístico de Publicaciones Herrerías e historietista de *El ladrón de Bagdad*, que aparecía en *Chamaco Chico*, revista que llegó a tener un tiraje de 600,000 ejemplares. Creó la historieta *Pepín* para la cadena García Valseca. Hacia 1942 hizo la primera fotonovela mexicana, *Póker de Ases* (con David Silva, Víctor Manuel Mendoza, Rafael Baledón y Ricardo Montalbán). Radicado en Estados Unidos, se dedicó al diseño de modas, telas y joyería inspiradas en motivos prehispánicos; expuso sus diseños en los museos de arte moderno de Nueva York y Tokio, así como en varias ciudades europeas. Realizó los primeros programas de modas en el Canal 4. Colaborador de *Excélsior*. Autor de *Mil preguntas y mil respuestas sobre sexo y lesbianismo en México* y *La vida íntima de la Malinche*. En 1988 retomó su actividad como diseñador de modas. Tiene un taller artesanal en Puebla y otro en Ixtlahuaca. Ganó un Ariel por la cinta *Una reina para Latinoamérica* y por la primera película hablada en totonaco.

VALDIVIA, BENJAMÍN ◆ n. en Aguascalientes, Ags. (1960). Licenciado en filosofía por la Universidad de Guanajuato y maestro en la materia por la UNAM, con cursos en estética, investigación social y poética. Ha sido profesor, investigador y editor en la Univer-

Ramón Valdiosera Berman

sidad de Guanajuato, coordinador de talleres literarios y editor de Silencio Editorial (1989-). Coautor de *Granuja*, *Alabarda* y *Folios*. Autor de poemarios: *Desde la mano en alto* (1983), *El juego del tiempo* (1985), *Asuntos de la lluvia* (1986), *Demasiado tarde* (1987), *Otro espejo de la noche* (1988), *Combates de lo efímero* (1990); novela: *El pelícano verde* (Premio Internacional de Novela Nuevo León, 1988); ensayo: *El friso de nuestros dioses de Saturnino Herrán* (1987), *La Convención de Aguascalientes de 1914* (coautor, 1989), *El camino del fuego* (1991), *El eco de la imagen. Vanguardia y tradición en Gabriel Fernández Ledezma* (1992), *Indagación de lo poético* (1993), *Imágenes y vida de Irapuato* (1993) y teatro: *El nahual de Paramillo* (1986). Becario Salvador Novo (1980), del Fonca (1991-92) y del Conaculta (1994-95). Miembro del Sistema Nacional de Investigadores (1990-94). Ha ganado los premios Nacional de Poesía Punto de Partida, de Crítica del Arte del INBA (1987), Internacional de Ensayo Ludwig von Mises (1987), Internacional de Poesía Le Courrier de l'Orenoque (1991) y Nacional de la Juventud (1986).

VALDIVIA, JOSÉ ANTONIO ◆ n. en Baja California Sur (1938). General brigadier diplomado de Estado Mayor. Licenciado en administración militar por la Escuela Superior de Guerra (1966) y maestro en administración y seguridad nacional por el Colegio de Defensa Nacional (1986), ha realizado estudios de relaciones internacionales e historia de México en la SRE. Militante del PRI desde 1964, donde fue coordinador regional en Quintana Roo y Sonora, asesor del presidente del CEN y miembro del CPN. Ha sido agregado militar y aéreo en la embajada de México en EUA y delegado del Ejército Mexicano ante la Junta Interamericana de Defensa y de la Comisión México-EUA. Dos veces senador (1988-91 y 1994-2000) y diputado federal (1991-94). Autor de *Compendio de estrategia general*, *Grandes personajes de la historia* y *Origen, evolución y futuro del blindaje*. Medallas al Mérito Técnico Militar y de la Legión de Honor Mexicana.

VALDIVIA, JUAN ◆ n. ¿en Guadalajara, Jal.? y m. en Cerro del Grillo, Zac. (¿1777?-1811). Insurgente. Se alistó en las fuerzas de José Antonio Torres, con quien hizo la campaña de Zacatecas. Durante la batalla del Cerro del Grillo, el 14 de abril de 1811, los independentistas contaban sólo con un pequeño cañón que no podían utilizar, pues le faltaba la cureña; Valdivia, de gran corpulencia, se ofreció a actuar como soporte de la pieza de artillería; el único disparo que pudo hacerse de esa forma decidió la batalla en favor de los rebeldes, pero costó la vida a Juan Valdivia, quien desde entonces fue conocido como *Juan cureña* o *El hombre cureña*. Este episodio fue narrado en un romance por Guillermo Prieto. Algunos autores indican, sin embargo, que Valdivia no murió en esa batalla, sino que quedó paralítico porque el disparo le rompió la espina dorsal.

VALDIVIA AGUILERA, ANDRÉS ◆ n. en Aguascalientes, Ags. (1930). Profesor por el Instituto Federal de Capacitación del Magisterio de Durango (1950), especializado en física, química y pedagogía en la Escuela Normal Superior (1954-60). Desde 1948 es miembro del PRI, del que fue presidente del Comité Directivo Estatal de Aguascalientes (1974-81). Secretario de Organización de la Liga de Comunidades Agrarias y Sindicatos Campesinos de Aguascalientes (1967-70). En el SNTE se ha desempeñado como secretario general de Delegaciones (1950-56), secretario de Organización de la sección I (1956-59),

José Antonio Valdivia

Andrés Valdivia Aguilera

Ignacio Valdivielso

Angélica Vale

secretario de Educación Sindical del Comité Ejecutivo Nacional (1971-73), representante ante la Federación Mundial de Educadores de Rumania (1973) y secretario de Fomento Cultural del Comité Ejecutivo Nacional (1967-70). Ha sido diputado local (1967-70) y senador por Aguascalientes (1982-88).

Valdivielso, Ignacio ◆ n. en la ciudad de México y m. en Francia (1805-1861). Se integró al cuerpo diplomático como agregado a la primera misión mexicana en Roma, de la que fue secretario (1830). Fue agregado a la misión en Londres (1832) y en París, cónsul en las Ciudades Hanseáticas y en Prusia, secretario de Miguel Santa María, quien tenía la misión de reanudar las relaciones diplomáticas entre México y España; plenipotenciario y encargado de negocios ante España (a la muerte de Santa María), ministro plenipotenciario y enviado extraordinario ante el mismo gobierno (1842) y secretario de legación en Madrid (1844-46). Donó una renta con la que en 1875 se fundó en México el Instituto Oftalmológico Valdivielso.

Valdovinos, Mucio ◆ n. y m. en Morelia, antes Valladolid, Mich. (1808-1864). Tomó el hábito agustino en 1824 y se ordenó sacerdote en 1831. Fue profesor de teología, secretario de la Provincia, prior del convento de Querétaro, administrador de la hacienda de San Nicolás y procurador general. En 1845 volvió a la vida secular. Dos veces diputado federal por Guanajuato y consejero de Estado de Antonio López de Santa Anna. En 1855 volvió a Morelia y se dedicó a la docencia. Colaboró en *El Zurriago Literario*, *La Verdad*, *La Cruz*, *El Mosaico* y *El Universal*. Autor de "Noticias relativas a la matanza de los españoles presos en Valladolid" y "Noticias sobre los sucesos que precedieron a la entrada del brigadier Cruz a Valladolid", apéndices 1 y 6 del segundo tomo de la *Historia de Méjico* de Lucas Alamán, documentos que fueron impugnados en 1850 por José Ignacio y José Mariano Ansorena, lo que dio pie a una polémica. Escribió también *Manual de la virtud* (1851), *El libro indispensable de los niños* (1852), *Elaboración del azúcar en Michoacán* (1854), *Cartilla de las madres de familia* (1855), *Cartilla de los casados* (1855), *Penitenciaría y reforma de cárceles* (1855), *Carta al partido conservador* (1856), *La cuestión del día o sea la tiranía del clero* (1856), así como de *Consejos a una esposa* y *El evangelio de los mansos y humildes de corazón*.

Vale, Angélica ◆ n. en el DF (1976). Cantante y actriz. Hija de Angélica María y Raúl Vale. Apareció por primera vez en la telenovela *El milagro de vivir*, a los dos meses de edad. En teatro ha actuado en *Papacito piernas largas* (1978), *Zoila sonrisas* (1980-81), *El club de la amistad* (1982-84), *El mago de Oz* (1985-86), *Imaginación* (1987), *La estrella* (1988), *Vaselina* (1988), *Mamá ama el rock* (1990), *Los tenis rojos* (1991) y *Blanca Nieves* (1999) y en la telenovela *Muñeca rota* (1978).

Vale, Tere ◆ n. en el DF (1950). Comunicadora. Licenciada en psicología por la Universidad Anáhuac especializada en neuropsicología por la UNAM y maestra en antropología social por la UIA. Fue responsable del programa de la SEP para el rescate de niños de la calle. Ha sido conductora del noticiero del Canal 13 de televisión (1980-83), directora de noticieros de Radio 1440, del grupo Radio Centro. Ha colaborado en *Siempre!*, *El Sol de México* y otras publicaciones. Presidenta y directora del consejo de administración de Radiosistema Mexicano (XEN), codirectora de grupo Multimedia, directora general de Publicidad Estelar, conductora del noticiero *Hora Siete* de la estación Ondas del Lago. Fue moderadora del debate de los partidos políticos sobre reforma electoral (1997). Forma parte de los consejos directivos de la Asociación de Radiodifusores del Valle de México y de la Cámara de la Industria de la Radio y la Televisión. Recibió de la Presidencia de la República el reconocimiento 19 de Septiembre por su trabajo en las escuelas dañadas por los sismos de 1985.

Valencia, Gabriel ◆ n. y m. en la ciudad de México (1799-1848). Militar realista. Combatió a los insurgentes. En 1921 se adhirió al Plan de Iguala. Estuvo destacado en San Juan de Ulúa hasta la salida de los españoles. Participó en la guerra de Texas (1836) y fue uno de los defensores de Anastasio Bustamante (1840), contra quien, sin embargo, se pronunció en 1841. Primer presidente de la Junta Nacional Legislativa designada por Nicolás Bravo en 1842, cuerpo que elaboró las Bases Orgánicas de 1843.

Valencia, Rubén ◆ n. y m. en el DF (1949-1990). Pintor. Estudió en la ENAP (1972). A principios de los setenta, junto con otros artistas, formó el Grupo Cero y, a finales de la misma década, formó el No-Grupo, junto con Alfredo Núñez, Maris Bustamante y Melquiades Herrera, que presentaron varios *performances* como *Montaje de momentos plásticos* (en el Museo de Arte Moderno) y *Caliente Caliente* (Facultad de Artes Plásticas en Jalapa, UNAM y la ENAP). Durante los ochenta presentó el espectáculo *El usurpador de sombras* y, más tarde, la controvertida obra *El Pornochou*.

Valencia, Sixto ◆ n. en Tezontepec, Hgo. (1943). Dibujante de historietas. Se inició profesionalmente a finales de los cincuenta en *La Prensa*, con *El Halcón*. En 1960 creo *Memín Pinguín*. Hizo la serie de *Episodios Mexicanos*, publicada por la SEP.

Memín Pinguín, historieta creada por Yolanda Vargas Dulché y Sixto Valencia

Valencia, Tita ◆ n. en el DF (1938). Escritora. Estudió piano en el Conservatorio Nacional y en la Escuela Normal de Música de París. Ha sido coordinadora de los programas de extensión cultural de la UNAM-SRE en la Universidad de Texas en San Antonio (1977-84), subdirectora del Museo de Arte Moderno (1985-86) y redactora de notas para los discos editados por la SEP. Participó en un taller literario de Juan José Arreola. Ha colaborado en *Cuadernos del Unicornio, Revista de la Universidad de México, Mester, Plural, México en la Cultura, La Palabra y el Hombre* y *Zarza*. Autora de *Minotauromaquia* (prosa poemática 1976, premio Xavier Villaurrutia en 1977), *Testimonio carcelario* (1976, antología de Ricardo Flores Magón) y *El trovar clus de las jacarandas* (poesía, 1995).

Valencia, Vicente ◆ n. en Zacatecas, Zac., y m. en Chihuahua, Chih. (¿1776?-1811). Ingeniero en metalurgia (1801) por el Colegio de Minería de la ciudad de México, donde fue condiscípulo de Mariano Jiménez. Se unió en 1811 a las fuerzas de Miguel Hidalgo e Ignacio Allende y fue director de ingenieros del ejército insurgente. Se le aprehendió junto con los caudillos de la independencia en Acatita de Baján, fue conducido a Chihuahua, juzgado y fusilado. Un mineral descubierto por Andrés del Río lleva el nombre de valencia o valencita, como homenaje al insurgente, quien descubrió un proceso de beneficio para metales "dóciles", mismo que no tuvo tiempo de divulgar o poner en práctica.

Valencia Benavides, Andrés Leopoldo ◆ n. en el DF (1949). Licenciado en derecho por la UNAM (1973). Miembro del PRI. Profesor de la UNAM (1972 y 1975-76) y de la UAM-Azcapotzalco (1975, 1979 y 1983), coordinador del Programa de Especialización para Formación de Profesores de la UAM-Azcapotzalco (1975, 1979 y 1983) e investigador de la Universidad Pedagógica Nacional (1980-82). Ha sido representante suplente adscrito a la misión permanente de México ante la OEA (1973-75), subdirector general adjunto de Asuntos Jurídicos de la SRE (1975-77), secretario particular del subsecretario de Cultura y Recreación (1977-78), subdirector administrativo del Registro Nacional de Electores (1979-80), subdirector de la Unidad de Coordinación del Sector Agrario de la SRA (1981), director general de Organismos Internacionales de la SRE (1983-88), secretario técnico del CNCA (1989-92) y subprocurador de Asuntos Jurídicos de la SRA (1992-94).

Valencia Ortiz, Tito ◆ n. en Achotal, Ver. (1932). Licenciado en administración militar por la Escuela Superior de Guerra, Universidad del Ejército y Fuerza Aérea (1963) y maestro en seguridad nacional en el Colegio de Defensa Nacional (1982). Ha sido agregado militar y aéreo en la embajada de México en Brasil (1982-84), director del Colegio de Defensa Nacional (1984), comandante de Guarnición en Tamaulipas. (1984-85), director de la Escuela Militar de Clases en Puebla (1986-87), comandante de la zona militar de Mérida (1987-88), director general de Caballería (1989-90), director general de la Armada Blindada (1990), comandante de la octava zona militar de Tampico (1990-91), comandante de la cuarta zona militar de Hermosillo (1991-92), subinspector y contralor general del Ejército y Fuerza Aérea Mexicanos (1992-94) y coordinador general del Centro de Planeación contra el Combate a las Drogas (1994-).

Valenti, Rubén ◆ n. en Comitán, Chis., y m. en Guatemala (1879-1915). Perteneció a la Sociedad de Conferencias, que más tarde se convertiría en Ateneo de la Juventud. Subsecretario de Instrucción Pública y Bellas Artes durante el gobierno de Victoriano Huerta y secretario del ramo (del 14 de julio al 13 de agosto de 1914) en el gabinete de Francisco S. Carvajal. Autor de *Poemas amatorios* (1908) y de la colección de novelas cortas "Rojo y negro" (1913).

Valentín Gómez Farías ◆ Cabecera del municipio chihuahuense de Gómez Farías (☛).

Valentín y Tamayo, Miguel ◆ n. en Tlaxiaco, Oax., y m. en la ciudad de México (1779-1843). Sacerdote ordenado en 1805 y doctor en cánones por la Real y Pontificia Universidad de México. Cura de Córdoba, Huamantla y Amozoc. Fue diputado por Oaxaca a las Cortes de Cádiz (1820), diputado suplente por Tlaxcala al Congreso Constituyente (1821), miembro de la Regencia del Imperio (1822), consejero por Puebla y nuevamente diputado por Oaxaca al Congreso Constituyente (1824), miembro de la Junta de Instrucción Pública (1827), diputado federal por Oaxaca (1830), uno de los redactores de las Siete Leyes (1836) y cura del Sagrario Metropolitano (1839-43). Presidió el Ateneo Mexicano y fue miembro de los institutos de literatura y beneficencia.

Valentina, La ◆ Una de las más famosas canciones de la época revolucionaria. Fue popularizada en todo el país a partir de 1914, pero se conocía en Sinaloa desde 1909 y supuestamente había sido compuesta por algún soldado de las fuerzas de Gabriel Leyva, uno de los precursores de la revolución, según consta en el libro *Los destripados* (1909, de Heriberto Frías). Aun cuando la canción no estaba inspirada en ella, Valentina Gatica (☛), soldadera en las fuerzas de Álvaro Obregón, la hizo suya e incluso inspiró algunos cambios en la letra de la misma. Según Ricardo Perete, Valentina Gatica "parecía hecha a la medida de la canción o viceversa". De acuerdo con el periodista Javier Cruz Aguirre, la inspiradora de la canción era la coronela Valentina Vázquez Ramírez, quien en 1986 aún vivía en Ensenada y contaba con 113 años de edad.

Valenzuela, Fernando ◆ n. en Etchohuaquila, Son. (1960). Beisbolista. Como aficionado se dio a conocer con la selección de Navojoa. Se inició en el beisbol profesional como lanzador en la Liga del Noroeste (1977) de donde pasó al Puebla (1978) y al Guanajuato (1978) de la Liga Central. Jugó después en el Club Leones de Yucatán (1979). En 1980 pasó a Estados Unidos como integrante de los equipos Lodi (1979) y

Fernando Valenzuela

Misioneros de San Antonio (1979-80). Desde 1981 fue lanzador titular de *los Dodgers* de Los Ángeles, equipo del que fue despedido en 1991; pasó entonces al *Serafines* y, a mediados de los noventa, regresó al beisbol mexicano. En 1981 destacó por el lanzamiento de la "bola de tirabuzón". Ganó los trofeos Cy Young (1981), Novato del Año (1981, primer lanzador en ganarlo), Bat de Plata (1983) y Guante de Oro (1986). Asimismo, fue el lanzador abridor en el juego de las estrellas de las Ligas Mayores de 1981; empató la marca en grandes ligas de ocho blanqueadas por un novato (1981); lanzó 285 entradas en una temporada (1982); ponchó a 15 bateadores en un partido (1984); empató la marca de cinco ponches consecutivos en un juego de estrellas (1986) y lanzó un juego sin hit ni carrera (1990). Ha asistido a dos series mundiales.

Gilberto Valenzuela Ezquerro

VALENZUELA, JESÚS E. ◆ n. en Guanaceví, Dgo., y m. en la ciudad de México (1856-1911). Se tituló de abogado en la Escuela Nacional de Jurisprudencia. Fue diputado federal (1880-1904) y responsable de las publicaciones de la Secretaría de Instrucción Pública y Bellas Artes. Fue cofundador y codirector, con Amado Nervo, de la *Revista Moderna* (1898-1911), en torno a la cual se formó un grupo de poetas a quienes él mismo patrocinaba. Autor de los poemarios *Almas y cármenes* (1904), *Lira libre* (1906) y *Manojo de rimas* (1907). En 1907 fue electo miembro del Ateneo de Santiago de Chile, de la *Juris Positivi Poenales Scholae* y del Centro de Ciencias y Letras de la misma ciudad. Recibió la distinción *I Nostri Contemporani*, de Roma.

VALENZUELA, JOSÉ CAMILO ◆ n. en Guasave, Sin. (1946). Estudió economía en la Universidad Autónoma de Sinaloa (1972), donde fue presidente de la Federación de Estudiantes (1971-72). Miembro de la dirección nacional de la Corriente Socialista (1976-83), secretario general del Partido Patriótico Revolucionario (1983-87), cofundador del PMS (1987-89) y del PRD (1989-). Dos veces diputado federal (1985-88 y 1991-94).

VALENZUELA, RAFAEL ◆ n. en Chicontepec, Ver., y m. en el DF (1877-1927). Pedagogo por la Escuela Normal Veracruzana (1895). Fue profesor en varias escuelas de Tuxpan y Ozuluama, director de Escuelas Primarias y director general de Educación, en Veracruz, y profesor en la Escuela Normal Superior. Autor de *Método Rébsamen*, *Biología general*, *Aritmética pedagógica*, *Guía de los maestros*, *Geografía de Veracruz* y *Geografía del estado de Hidalgo*.

VALENZUELA, TERESA ◆ n. en Irapuato, Gto. (1951). Licenciada en teatro por la Escuela de Arte Teatral del INBA, estudió arquitectura, teatro y danza en la Universidad de Guanajuato, y composición dramática con Emilio Carballido. Se inició como actriz en el primer Festival Cervantino. Ha sido profesora de la Escuela de Arte Teatral y directora del Centro de Teatro Infantil del INBA. Colaboradora de *Tramoya* (de la Universidad Veracruzana) y *Repertorio* (de la Universidad Autónoma de Querétaro). Coautora de *Detrás de una margarita* (1984) y de *Jardín con animales* (1985). Autora de las obras de teatro *Chispas, rayos y centellas* (pastorela, 1985), *Estela y la geografía política* (1985), *Mundo nocturno* (1985), *Dijeron que a todas* (1986), *Ganadores* (1986), *Entre todos se puede* (1987, mención honorífica en el segundo Concurso Celestino Gorostiza), *Alegría la lotería* (1987, premio en el tercer Concurso Celestino Gorostiza) y *Dulce niño de aguamiel* (1993). Ha dirigido la puesta en escena de algunas de sus obras, la mayoría infantiles. Premio a la mejor actriz en el quinto Festival de Teatro del Chamizal.

VALENZUELA EZQUERRO, GILBERTO ◆ n. en el DF (1922). Se tituló de ingeniero civil en la UNAM (1947). Ha sido jefe de Pavimentos, subdirector de Planeación y Programa, subdirector de Construcción y Conservación (1953-58) y director general de Obras Públicas del DDF (1958-64); secretario de Obras Públicas en el gabinete de Gustavo Díaz Ordaz (1964-70), vocal ejecutivo de la Comisión Técnica del Metro (1977), presidente y director general de la empresa Parque Reforma (1980-84) y director general del Proyecto Nuevo Club de Industriales (1985-88). Miembro desde 1948 y presidente (1979-80) del Colegio de Ingenieros Civiles; miembro de la Sociedad Mexicana de Ingenieros, de la Unión Mexicana de Asociaciones de Ingenieros y de la Academia Mexicana de Ingeniería. Fue presidente de la Sociedad de ex Alumnos de la Facultad de Ingeniería (1964-70).

VALENZUELA GALINDO, GILBERTO ◆ n. en Sahuaripa, Son., y m. en el DF (1891-1978). Fundó la Unión Estudiantil Antirreeleccionista (1910), con algunos de sus condiscípulos de la Escuela de Jurisprudencia, en la que se graduó en 1914. Se unió en Veracruz a las fuerzas de Carranza (1914). Fue juez instructor militar y agente del Ministerio Público en Veracruz, comisionado para reorganizar el Supremo Tribunal de Justicia de Sonora, del que fue presidente (1915-16); diputado y presidente del Congreso local (1916), gobernador provisional de Sonora (de diciembre de 1916 a enero de 1917), por licencia de Adolfo de la Huerta, y nuevamente diputado local (1919). Algunos historiadores lo consideran uno de los autores intelectuales del Plan de Agua Prieta. Secretario de Gobernación (del 1 de junio al 4 de agosto de 1920) en el gabinete de De la Huerta, subsecretario del ramo, encargado del despacho, en el gobierno de Obregón, y nuevamente titular de Gobernación (del 8 de enero al 25 de agosto de 1925) con Plutarco Elías Calles. En 1925 rompió con los aguaprietistas y fue enviado como embajador a Bélgica y ministro a Inglaterra. Volvió a México en 1928. Un año después se unió a la rebelión escobarista y, derrotado, debió exiliarse. Regresó a México en 1934 y fue candidato presidencial de oposición. Secretario de la Suprema Corte de Justicia de la Nación, profesor universitario y presidente ejecutivo del Supremo Consejo Nacional de la Asociación Nacional de Abogados.

Valenzuela Yera, Policarpo ◆ n. en San Antonio de los Naranjos, hoy Cárdenas, y m. en San Juan Bautista, hoy Villahermosa, Tab. (1831-1914). Se incorporó a las fuerzas de Porfirio Díaz, en las que alcanzó el grado de coronel en la lucha contra la intervención francesa y el imperio. Fue gobernador interino de Tabasco en 1886 y 1887. Renunció presionado por Díaz, pero reconciliado con el régimen porfirista, fue elegido gobernador constitucional para el periodo 1911-1914, pero abandonó el Ejecutivo local al triunfo de la revolución maderista.

Valera Aparicio, Fernando ◆ n. en España (1889-?). Fue director de *El Pueblo*, funcionario del Instituto Geográfico y Estadístico (1925), diputado a Cortes (1931 y 1936), director general de Agricultura y de Industria y subsecretario de Agricultura y Obras Públicas (1932-37). A la caída de la República española se asiló en México (1942). Fue profesor de la Academia Hispano-Mexicana, traductor del griego clásico en la Facultad de Filosofía y Letras, director literario de las editoriales Tyris y Surya y jefe del gobierno republicano en el exilio. Autor de *Liberalismo* (1942), *Introducción a la filosofía* (1942), *Reencarnación, Karma, mística cristiana* (1942), *El sendero inmóvil* (1943), *Diálogos de las Españas* (1943), *Cuentos y leyendas de Juan Valera* (1944, en colaboración), *La guía de los descarriados de Salomón Ben Maimún* (1945), *Evolución de España* (1967), *Reivindicación de un pueblo calumniado* (1968) y *Mitos de la burguesía* (1976).

Valeriano ◆ Códice realizado en papel, que tiene el carácter de título de propiedad: se mencionan en él 22 personas (indios y españoles), porciones de terreno y la fecha de 1574. Tiene jeroglíficos y caracteres latinos. Se halla desde 1940 en la Biblioteca Nacional de Antropología e Historia.

Valerio, Robert ◆ n. en Inglaterra y m. en Oaxaca (1959-1998). Cuentista, poeta y crítico de artes plásticas. Estudió letras en la Universidad de Liverpool (1977-81). Vino en los años ochenta y se naturalizó mexicano. Colaboró con el Instituto de Artes Gráficas de Oaxaca como escritor y traductor independiente (1992-93), fue responsable de la videoteca y del área de relaciones del Museo de Arte Contemporáneo (1994) y, desde 1996, fue coordinador de difusión del mismo recinto. Colaboró en diversas revistas mexicanas y británicas como *El Alcaraván, Tierra Adentro, Curare* y *Guchachi'reza; Envoi, Orbis* y *Poetry and Audience*. Es autor de los poemarios *Fifty-fifty* (1996), *Cuando amanezca otra vez* (1997) y del ensayo *Atardecer en la maquiladora de utopías* (1998).

Valerio Trujano ◆ Municipio de Oaxaca situado en el norte del estado, al sur-suroeste de Huajuapan de León y al noroeste de la capital estatal. Superficie: 53.58 km². Habitantes: 1,631, de los cuales 389 forman la población económicamente activa. Hablan alguna lengua indígena 249 personas (mixteco 219). Se llamó Hacienda de Guendulain.

Valero, Francisco ◆ n. en el DF (1941). Escritor. Su segundo apellido es Becerra. Contador público por el IPN. Ha sido coordinador de exposiciones y museografía de la Casa del Lago (1976-77), secretario general de la Asociación de Escritores de México, promotor de actividades culturales, prologuista y editor. Colaborador de la sección cultural de *Ovaciones*, de *El Gallo Ilustrado*, la *Revista Mexicana de Cultura, Amatlacuilo* y *Presencia Educativa*. Autor de ensayo: *Diálogos con el arte* (1980), *Ellos son las palabras* (1984) y *La profecía de los malditos* (1987); y de poesía: *Soy el ave que vuela hacia encontrar su sombra* (1984), *Reverberación de silencios* (1985), *Elegía oceaniana* (1986), *Génesis de un remordimiento* (1987) y *Reverberación de silencios* (1989).

Valero, Manuel Antonio ◆ n. en la ciudad de México y m. en Colombia (1790-1863). Militar. Estudió en España, donde combatió la invasión napoleónica. Coronel del ejército trigarante, hacia 1824 fue a Venezuela y sirvió a las órdenes de Simón Bolívar, en cuyas filas alcanzó el generalato. Fue ministro de Guerra y Marina de Venezuela (1830 y 1857) y en 1861 se alistó en el ejército colombiano.

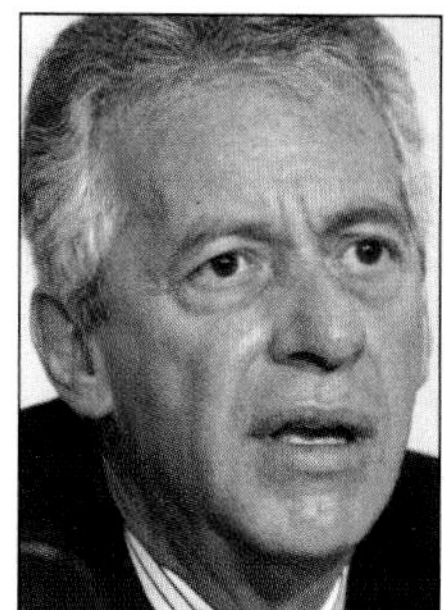
Ricardo Valero

Valero, Ricardo ◆ n. en el DF (1942). Sus apellidos son Valero Recio Becerra. Licenciado en relaciones internacionales por la UNAM (1963) y maestro por El Colegio de México (1968), instituciones donde ha sido profesor. Perteneció al PRI, en el que fue director de la Comisión Nacional Editorial (1975-76), director de la revista *Línea* (1976), secretario de la Comisión Consultiva (1976), subsecretario (1981-82) y secretario de Asuntos Internacionales (1982) y miembro de la Comisión Nacional de Ideología (1983). En 1988 dejó el PRI y al año siguiente fue uno de los fundadores del PRD. Trabajó en la Secretaría de la Presidencia. Ha sido director general de Documentación y Asuntos Internacionales de la Secretaría del Trabajo (1972-76), coordinador de Publicaciones y Bibliotecas de la SEP (1977-78), gerente general de los Talleres Gráficos de la Nación (1978-82), asesor del secretario de Gobernación (1979-81) y, en la SRE, asesor del director en jefe para Asuntos Multilaterales (1968-70), asesor del secretario (1979-80), miembro de la Comisión Consultiva de Política Exterior (1979-80) y subsecretario de Cooperación Internacional (1985-88). Diputado federal plurinominal por el PRD (1991-94) y senador (1997-2000).

Roberto Vallarino

VALERO, SERGIO ◆ n. en el DF (1969). Poeta. Licenciado en letras hispánicas por la UNAM. Autor de los poemarios *Designio de los pies cansados* y *Cuaderno de Alejandra* (Premio Nacional de Poesía Joven Elías Nandino 1997). Obtuvo mención honorífica en la rama de poesía en el concurso de la revista *Punto de Partida* (1993).

VALEZZI ZAFRA, HÉCTOR ◆ n. en el DF (1957). Licenciado en derecho por la UIA. Ingresó a la SRE como analista (1980) y ha sido secretario técnico en las oficinas de la secretaría particular del titular del ramo (1983-84), comisionado en la embajada de México en Brasil (1984-88) y en la embajada en EUA estuvo en el área de Asuntos Políticos (1989-90). Fue jefe de cancillería en la embajada de México en la India (1990-92) y en 1991 ascendió a la categoría de consejero. Ese mismo año alcanzó el grado de ministro. Director adjunto de la Dirección General de Protocolo (1992-95), jefe de cancillería en la Representación Permanente de México ante la Unión Europea (1995-98) y director del Servicio Exterior y de Personal (1998-).

Foto: Claudio Contreras

Valladolid, Yucatán

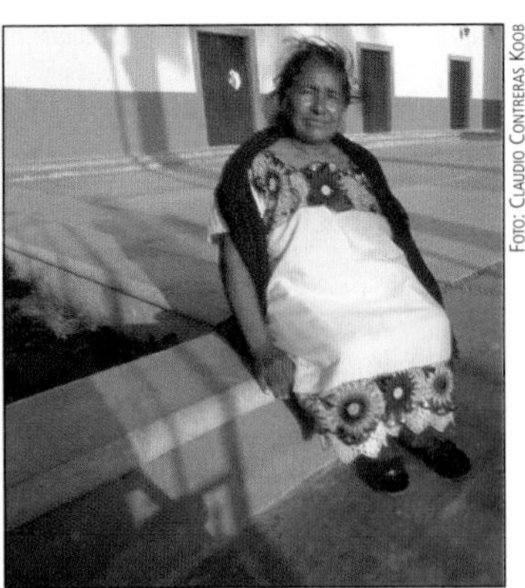
Foto: Claudio Contreras Koob

Mujer maya de Valladolid, Yucatán

VALLADOLID ◆ Municipio de Yucatán situado en los límites con Quintana Roo, al este de Chichén Itzá y al sur de Tizimín. Superficie: 867.77 km^2. Habitantes: 52,496, de los cuales 12,124 forman la población económicamente activa. Hablan alguna lengua indígena 23,707 personas (maya 23,636 y mixe 171), de las cuales 3,640 son monolingües. La cabecera fue fundada por Francisco de Montejo, sobrino del conquistador de Yucatán, en mayo de 1543, en el lugar llamado Chouac. En 1545 fue trasladada al poblado de Zací. En la ciudad se halla el convento de San Bernardino, construido a la orilla del cenote de Sisal, ahora de Valladolid, desde donde se realizó la evangelización franciscana. Pedro Sáinz de Baranda (☛) y Juan L. MacGregor fundaron en 1833 la fábrica de hilados y tejidos La Aurora Yucateca, primera en México con maquinaria de vapor. En esta ciudad se promulgó, el 10 de mayo de 1910, el Plan de Valladolid, mediante el cual los militares Maximiliano R. Bonilla, José Crisanto Chi, Juan Mata Pool, José Candelario May, Teodoro Núñez, José Antonio Balam, Juan Bautista Pec, Mónico Tus y Lázaro Báez denunciaban la situación de miseria e injusticia que imperaba en la península, desconocían al gobernador Enrique Muñoz Aréstegui, nombraban una junta gubernativa y restablecían el territorio de Quintana Roo. El 4 de junio del mismo año, los firmantes del Plan de Valladolid se levantaron en armas, en lo que algunos historiadores consideran el auténtico movimiento precursor de la Revolución Mexicana, aunque fueron sometidos poco después por el ejército federal.

VALLADOLID ◆ ☛ *Morelia*.

VALLADOLID, BERNARDINO DE ◆ n. en España y m. en Mérida, Yuc. (1616-1652). Fraile franciscano. Llegó a la Nueva España en 1634 como secretario de la provincia franciscana de San José. Tradujo al maya gran parte de la *Materia médica*, del griego Dioscórides Pedanius, que ilustró con un catálogo de plantas yucatecas. Autor de *Conclusiones teológicas* (1641, representación dramática en maya y latín).

VALLADOLID, CONSPIRACIÓN DE ◆ ☛ *Michoacán*.

VALLARÍ, MANUEL *PIBE* ◆ n. en el DF (1923). Deportista, arquitecto y periodista. Fue uno de los mejores jugadores de la Liga Mayor de Futbol Americano en México. En 1939 ingresó en el Instituto Técnico Industrial del IPN, donde se inició como jugador y en los años cuarenta formó parte del "cuarteto de los burros galopantes". Como corredor logró un promedio de 7.91 yardas por jugada. Con el equipo del IPN obtuvo dos campeonatos (1943 y 1949) y encabezó el seleccionado nacional que venció al equipo estadounidense de Randolph Field (1947). Fue el primer mexicano en ingresar al Salón de la Fama de la Fundación Internacional del Deporte de Los Ángeles (1981). Durante varios años escribió la columna "Punto Extra" en *El Universal*.

VALLARINO, ROBERTO ◆ n. en el DF (1955). Ha sido fundador y reportero de *unomásuno*, fundador y codirector de la revista *Cuadernos de Literatura*, agregado cultural de la embajada de México en Yugoslavia (1981), coordinador de la Colección Letras Nuevas de la SEP y de talleres de periodismo cultural del ISSSTE, organizador de los encuentros de Poetas Jóvenes de la Frontera Norte (1984-86) y asesor del Programa Cultural de las Fronteras. Fue corresponsal de guerra en Irán, investigador en la Universidad de Utah y asesor del Museo Amparo en Puebla. Coautor de *Cinco poetas jóvenes* (1977).

Autor de poesía: *Cantar de la memoria* (1977), *Elogio de la lluvia* (1979), *Invención del otoño* (1980), *Crónicas cotidianas* (1982), *Exilio interior* (1983) y *La conciencia de la duda* (1993); novela: *Las aventuras de Euforión* (1996); ensayo: *Textos paralelos* (1980), *Taller, Taller poético y tierra nueva por sus protagonistas* (1989), *La historia del Banco de Londres y México* (1990), *El Caballito de Sebastián* (1995), *Catorce perfiles* (1997) y *Las noches desandadas* (1998); antología: *Salvador Novo, sus mejores obras* (1979), *Los grandes poemas del siglo XX* (1979) y *Antología del primer Encuentro de Poesía Joven en la Frontera Norte de 1984* (1986); y narrativa: *El rostro y otros cuentos* (1986). Premio Diana Moreno Toscano (1975). Becario del Centro Mexicano de Escritores (1975-76 y 1978-79) y de la Fundación Fullbright (1988-90).

Vallarta, Ignacio Luis ◆ n. en Guadalajara, Jal., y m. en la ciudad de México (1830-1893). Licenciado en derecho por la Universidad de Guadalajara (1854). Fue secretario particular del gobernador de Jalisco Santos Degollado (1855), profesor, colaborador del periódico liberal *Revolución*, diputado al Congreso Constituyente de 1856-57 y magistrado del Tribunal Superior de Justicia de Jalisco (1857). Durante la guerra de los Tres Años fue secretario particular del gobernador jalisciense Pedro Ogazón, colaborador del *Boletín del Ejército Federal* y coronel del Batallón Hidalgo (1861). Durante el segundo periodo de gobierno de Ogazón fue varias veces insaculado para ocupar la gubernatura interina. Fue elegido diputado federal (1862), pero no ocupó la curul pues, en su opinión, no había tenido un número suficiente de votos. Nombrado gobernador de Jalisco (1863), no ocupó el cargo porque José María Arteaga se negó a entregar su puesto. Desde Zacatecas, en 1866, acompañó a Benito Juárez, de quien fue secretario de Gobernación (del 15 de enero al 14 de septiembre de 1868). Gobernador constitucional de Jalisco (1871-75), secretario de Relaciones Exteriores (del 28 de noviembre al 6 de diciembre de 1876, del 6 de diciembre de 1876 al 17 de febrero de 1877 y del 17 de febrero de 1877 al 18 de junio de 1878) en los gabinetes de Porfirio Díaz y Juan N. Méndez. Presidente de la Suprema Corte de Justicia de la Nación (1878-82). Autor de *Votos de Vallarta sobre el juicio de amparo y comentarios a la Constitución* (5 t., 1894-95).

Vallarta Ceceña, José Álvaro ◆ n. en Santiago Ixcuintla, Nay. (1939). Estudió en la Escuela Superior de Guerra; maestro en administración de seguridad y defensa por el Colegio de Defensa Nacional, hizo posgrados en inteligencia estratégica, operaciones psicológicas y de altos estudios militares en Fort Bragg, Fort Huachuca y el Army War College de EUA. Pertenece al PRI, en el que ha sido coordinador administrativo y de vuelos de la campaña presidencial de 1976 y secretario de Comités Estatales de la CNOP en 1999. En el servicio exterior ha sido ayudante del agregado militar y aéreo adjunto a la embajada de México en EUA y agregado militar en la de la RFA. Autor de *Origen y principio* y colaborador de *El Universal* y *Reforma*. En 1998 fue precandidato al gobierno de Nayarit. Senador de la República para el periodo 1994-2000.

Vallarta Robles, José Antonio ◆ n. en Santiago Ixcuintla, Nay. (1930). Licenciado en derecho por la Universidad Autónoma de Guadalajara (1953). Ha sido representante legal de la Comisión Nacional del Maíz y de Pronase (1953), secretario de acuerdos, dictaminador, auxiliar del presidente de la Junta Especial y secretario de Conflictos Colectivos de la Junta Federal de Conciliación y Arbitraje (1959-85), apoderado legal de la Compañía Mexicana de Aviación (1960-66), asesor jurídico de la Dirección General de Servicios Jurídicos de la SIC (1962), jefe del Departamento Jurídico de la Comisión Mixta Nacional de Servicios Médicos para Trabajadores de la Caña (1966), editorialista y director jurídico de *La Prensa* (1970), secretario de Estudio y Cuenta del Tribunal Colegiado en Materia de Trabajo de la Suprema Corte (1970), apoderado general de Líneas Aéreas Costarricenses (1978), director de Prensa de la PGJDF (1982), subdirector jurídico de la Comisión Nacional de la Industria Azucarera (1984), asesor del oficial mayor de la SPP (1985) y presidente de la Junta Local de Conciliación y Arbitraje (1985-88).

Valle, Cristina del ◆ n. en el DF (1963). Pintora. Estudió arquitectura en la Universidad Iberoamericana (1985), pintura y diseño en el Bennington College de Estados Unidos (1985-87), donde fue alumna de Pat Adams y Sidney Tillim, y en la ENAP (1987). Trabajó en el Centro Internacional de Arte, de Florencia (1987). Desde 1987 ha participado en exposiciones colectivas en México y el extranjero y en 1991 presentó su primera exposición individual.

Valle *el Buhó*, Eduardo ◆ n. en el DF (1947). Estudió economía en la UNAM (1974), donde fue profesor (1974-77). Participó en el movimiento estudiantil de 1968, por lo que fue preso político (1968-71). Cofundador del PMT (1975-87), del PMS (1987) y del PRD (1989). Ha sido asesor del subsecretario de Hacienda (1974), diputado federal (1985-88) y funcionario de la Procuraduría General de la República (1990-93). Desde 1994 vive en EUA. Autor de *Allende: cronología de la Unidad Popular* (1974) y *Escritos sobre el movimiento del 68* (1983). Fue secretario general de la UPD (1989-90).

Valle, J. Felipe ◆ n. en Colima, Col., y m. ¿en Acapulco, Gro.? (¿1890?-1928). Pedagogo. En 1909 era profesor en Mazatlán, donde había fundado un colegio particular, cuando fue aprehendido y encarcelado por sus ideas antirreeleccionistas. Durante la revolución maderista regresó a Colima y fue nombrado oficial mayor del Congreso local. Gobernador de Colima (1917-19), durante su gestión fundó la Cámara de Comercio, construyó un observatorio meteorológico e instaló el servicio telefónico rural. Le correspondió en 1919 jurar la Constitución local. Fue administrador de la aduana de Acapulco (1919) y profesor.

Ignacio L. Vallarta

José Cecilio Valle

Leandro Valle

Rafael Heliodoro Valle

Valle, Jesús del ◆ n. y m. en Saltillo, Coah. (1853-1938). Abogado egresado del Ateneo Fuente. Fue síndico del ayuntamiento de Saltillo (1877), juez de lo civil y de lo penal en Viesca y Saltillo, fiscal y magistrado del Tribunal Supremo de Justicia y gobernador interino y constitucional de Coahuila (1909-11).

Valle, José Cecilio del ◆ n. en Honduras y m. en Guatemala (1780-1834). Doctor en derecho civil y canónico. Estudió en la Universidad de San Carlos, en Guatemala, de la que fue profesor de economía (1812-20). Fue diputado de la Comisión Gubernativa, censor de la *Gaceta de Guatemala* (1805) y diputado de la Junta Central de España e Indias, por León de Nicaragua (1809). Como miembro de la diputación provincial fue redactor del Acta de Independencia de Centroamérica, promulgada el 15 de septiembre de 1821, y representó a Honduras en la Junta Provisional Consultiva. Cuando Agustín de Iturbide invitó a Guatemala a unirse al Imperio Mexicano, Valle se opuso, pero acató la decisión aprobatoria de la asamblea. Diputado al primer Congreso General de México (1822), fue miembro de la Comisión de Constitución; por sus críticas a Iturbide estuvo preso en el convento de Santo Domingo, aunque fue liberado para ocupar el Ministerio de Relaciones Interiores y Exteriores (del 23 de febrero al 19 de marzo de 1823) en el gabinete imperial. En abril de 1823 reasumió su curul al reinstalarse el Congreso. En 1824 fue diputado a la Asamblea Nacional de Guatemala y firmó la primera Constitución federal de ese país.

Valle, Leandro ◆ n. en la ciudad de México y m. en el monte de las Cruces, Edo. de Méx. (1833-1861). Liberal. Estudió en el Colegio Militar donde fue condiscípulo de Miguel Miramón. En 1847 combatió la rebelión de los polkos y la invasión estadounidense, a las órdenes de Juan Álvarez. En 1852 redactó el periódico *El Chapulín*. En 1854, cuando su padre fue encarcelado, se unió a la revolución de Ayutla, al triunfo de la cual fue agregado de la legación mexicana en París. Regresó a México en 1857 para participar en la guerra de los Tres Años, durante la cual estuvo a las órdenes, sucesivamente, de Parrodi, Santos Degollado, Ignacio Zaragoza y Jesús González Ortega, a quien acompañó en su campaña victoriosa por el Bajío. En 1859, con el grado de general de brigada, tuvo a su cargo la campaña del sur de Jalisco, estado al que representó en el Congreso Federal en 1860. En 1861 se le hizo general de brigada, comandante general del Distrito Federal y diputado federal por Jalisco. Salió a batir una partida de conservadores, pero fue aprehendido y fusilado por órdenes de Leonardo Márquez.

Valle, Mario del ◆ n. en Jalapa, Ver. (1954). Poeta y editor. Estudió letras españolas en la UNAM. Fundador y director de la editorial Papeles Privados, en la que ha publicado numerosos títulos de poetas mexicanos y extranjeros. Fue director de la revista *El Rehilete*. Autor de los poemarios *Línea rota* (1973), *Del río a la memoria* (1980), *Trazos de la serpiente* (1992) y *Luz de plomo* (1996).

Foto: Barry

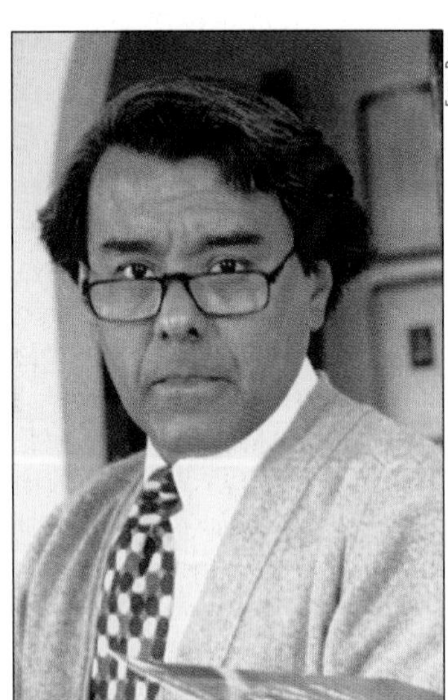

Mario del Valle

Valle, Rafael Heliodoro ◆ n. en Honduras y m. en el DF (1891-1959). Profesor egresado de la Escuela Nacional de Maestros (1911). Maestro en historia (1946) y doctor en ciencias históricas (1948) por la UNAM. Profesor de la Escuela Nacional de Maestros, de la Nacional Preparatoria (1921-28) y de la UNAM (1936-49). Cónsul de Honduras en Mobile, EUA (1915) y en Belice (1916), jefe de publicaciones del Museo Nacional de México (1921-22), director de las revistas *El Libro y el Pueblo* (1921-24) y *Bibliografía Mexicana*; jefe de la Sección de Bibliografía de la SEP (1926-28) y embajador de Honduras ante EUA y la OEA (1949-55). Establecido en México escribió en diversas publicaciones de Latinoamérica las columnas "Cosmópolis", "Gazapos" y "Columna de humo", con los pseudónimos de *Próspero Mirador*, *Guillermo Galindo*, *Miguel A. Osorio*, *Ángel Sol* y *Luis G. Mila*. Autor, entre otras obras, de los poemarios: *El rosal ermitaño* (1911), *Unísono amor* (1940), *Contigo* (1943) y *La sandalia de fuego* (1952); los relatos *Imaginación de México* (1945) y *Flor de Mesoamérica* (1955); las antologías: *Poetas de América* (1922), *Cartas hispanoamericanas* (1945), *Un diplomático mexicano en París* (1948) y *Oro de Honduras* (2 t., 1948-54); y las obras de historia: *La anexión de Centro América a México* (6 t., 1924-29), *Visión del Perú* (1943), *Bolívar en México* (1946) y *Héroes de 1847* (1947). Premio Marie Moors Cabot de periodismo (1940). El gobierno mexicano lo condecoró póstumamente con el Águila Azteca.

Valle, Ramón ◆ n. en Guanajuato, Gto., y m. en la ciudad de México (1841-1901). Estudió en los seminarios de León (1857) y de Pátzcuaro (1860) y en el Colegio del Estado de Guanajuato. Durante la intervención francesa obtuvo el grado de coronel en las filas republicanas. Fue diputado local, juez del Registro Civil y secretario del Ayuntamiento de Guanajuato (1876). Se ordenó sacerdote en 1879 y se desempeñó como promotor fiscal de la Curia en León (1880-95), capellán en la ciudad de México, consultor en el Concilio Provincial de Oaxaca y delegado al noveno Congreso de Americanistas (1895). Colaborador del semanario *El Gorro Frigio*. Autor de las obras teatrales: *Por un gato* (1866), *El no de las niñas*, *Un asesinato*, *El segundo amor* (1870), *La vida íntima* (1870) y *Cidalia* (1888); de la *Colección de las obras poéticas del C. Ramón Valle* (1869) y de los poemarios: *Algunas poesías* (1887), *Obras poéticas* (1869) y *Virgen del valle* (1875). Fue presidente perpetuo de la Arcadia Mexicana.

VALLE, RÓMULO DEL ◆ n. en Cuautla, en el actual estado de Morelos, y m. en la ciudad de México (1792-1866). Militar, padre de Leandro Valle. Participó en la guerra de Independencia (1811-21) y combatió en 1847 a los invasores estadounidenses. Fue comandante general de Guerrero (1853) y de Puebla. Perseguido por Antonio López de Santa Anna, se unió a la revolución de Ayutla; combatió a las órdenes de Santos Degollado en la guerra de los Tres Años y éste lo nombró jefe militar de Colima (1859). Murió cuando luchaba contra la intervención francesa y el imperio.

VALLE ALQUICIRA, EUTIQUIO DEL ◆ n. en la ciudad de México (1921). Inició la carrera de maestro normalista. Profesor por la Escuela Nacional de Educación Física. Ha sido jugador profesional de beisbol, softbol y volibol, fundador del Club Venados (1949) y entrenador de los atletas mexicanos que compitieron en los Juegos Centroamericanos de Caracas (1959), los Panamericanos de Chicago (1959, los Olímpicos de Roma (1960) y Tokio (1964). Presidente de la Asociación de Atletismo del DF (1952-59), de la Federación Mexicana de Atletismo (1959-61 y 1972), de la Confederación Centroamericana y del Caribe de Atletismo.

VALLE-ARIZPE, ARTEMIO DE ◆ n. en Saltillo, Coah., y m. en el DF (1884-1961). Licenciado en derecho (1910). Fue diputado federal por Chiapas (1910-12). Ingresó en el servicio exterior (1919) y fue segundo secretario de las legaciones en Madrid y Bruselas. Se estableció en España (1922-28), donde se incorporó a la Comisión de Investigaciones y Estudios Históricos Francisco del Paso y Troncoso. Volvió a México en 1928 y colaboró en el periódico *El Universal* con la columna "Del Tiempo Pasado". Fue secretario de la Facultad de Filosofía y Letras (1934-42) y cronista de la ciudad de México (1942-61). Autor de ensayos, cuentos, textos sobre historia, antologías y novelas entre los que destacan: *Ejemplo* (1919), *Vidas milagrosas* (1921), *Amores y picardías* (1932), *Historias de vivos y muertos* (1936), *Por la vieja calzada de Tlacopan* (1937), *Historia de la ciudad de México, según relatos de sus cronistas* (1939), *Cuentos del México antiguo* (1939), *El canillitas* (1941), *Leyendas mexicanas* (1943), *Amor que cayó en castigo* (1945), *Calle vieja y calle nueva* (1949), *Espejo del tiempo* (1951), *Fray Servando* (1951), *Cosas de sombras* (1951), *Lejanías entre brumas* (1951), *Piedras viejas bajo el sol* (1952), *Papeles amarillentos* (1954), *Engañar con la verdad* (1955), *De otra edad que es esta edad* (1957), *Santiago* (1959), *Historias, tradiciones y leyendas de las calles de México* (1959) y *La casa de los Ávila* (1960). Miembro de la Academia Mexicana (de la Lengua), de la Academia Colombiana de la Historia y de la Academia de Historia de Ecuador.

Artemio de Valle-Arizpe

VALLE DE BRAVO ◆ Municipio del Estado de México situado en el occidente de la entidad, al suroeste de Toluca y al noroeste de Tenancingo. Superficie: 453.48 km^2. Habitantes: 47,502, de los cuales 10,736 forman la población económicamente activa. Hablan alguna lengua indígena 254 personas mayores de cinco años (mazahua 222 y otomí 15). Llamado San Francisco del Valle de Temascaltepetl entre 1830 y 1878, cuenta con las presas irrigadoras La Peña y Avándaro (esta última captura las aguas de los ríos del Molino y Amanalco), en las que se pueden practicar deportes acuáticos; y las zonas arqueológicas de Valdelisa y Valle de Bravo. En la barranca del Diablo hay seis grupos de pinturas ejecutadas directamente sobre la roca; uno de esos grupos es la única muestra pictórica existente de la cultura tolteca. Tiene construcciones de la época virreinal: la

Ramón Valle

FOTO: BORIS DE SWAM

Valle de Bravo, Estado de México

capilla del convento franciscano del siglo XVI, el acueducto de Pipioltepec y el Cristo Negro de Santa María Ahuacatlán. En la jurisdicción se hallan los manantiales de aguas termales de El Salto y Tilostoc, así como el de Tenería, a cuyas aguas se atribuyen propiedades terapéuticas. En el Estado de México es uno de los más importantes productores de aguacate y madera de pino y encino. En septiembre de 1971 se celebró, en la localidad de Avándaro, el festival Rock y Ruedas, que congregó a unos 150,000 jóvenes. Su cabecera, del mismo nombre y situada en la ribera de la presa de Avándaro, cuenta con un museo regional.

VALLE DE CHALCO SOLIDARIDAD ◆ Municipio del Estado de México situado en el oriente de la entidad, en los límites con el Distrito Federal. Superficie: 44.57 km². Habitantes: 287,073, distribuidos en cinco localidades. Hablan alguna lengua indígena 9,389 personas mayores de cinco años (mixteco 3,008, náhuatl 2,473, otomí 780 y zapoteco 718). El municipio fue erigido en noviembre de 1994, en su mayor parte con territorio de Chalco, aunque también con áreas de Chicoloapan, Ixtapaluca y La Paz. La cabecera es Xico.

Ramón del Valle-Inclán

VALLE GONZÁLEZ, ARMANDO ◆ n. en Aguascalientes, Ags. (1936). Médico cirujano por la Escuela Médico Militar (1959), maestro en gastroenterología por la UNAM y el Hospital de Enfermedades de la Nutrición (1965), posgraduado en cirugía general en los hospitales Central Militar, Juárez, Tacubaya, Rubén Leñero y 20 de Noviembre. Profesor del Hospital 20 de Noviembre (1974), de la Universidad Anáhuac (1977-82) y de la UAM (1986), asesor de área de la UAM (1984-86), subdirector médico (1979-81) y director del Hospital 20 de Noviembre (1981-84), así como subdirector general médico del ISSSTE (1984-). Autor de *Manual de microcirugía* (1983), *Manual de medicina general* (1986), *Cuide a sus hijos* (1986) y *Educación para la salud del magisterio* (1987). Miembro fundador de la Asociación Mexicana de Cirugía Experimental (1978).

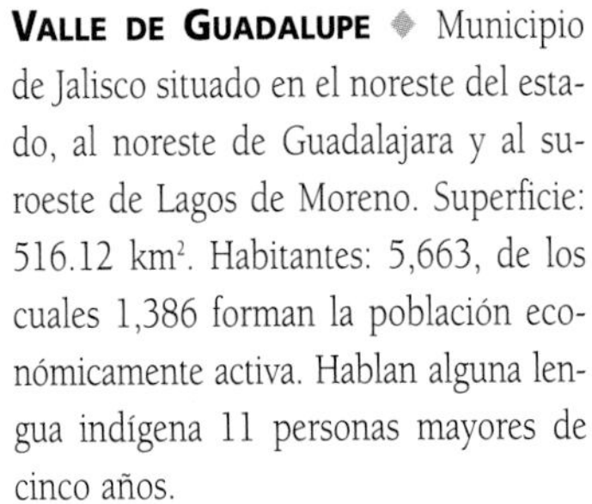

VALLE DE GUADALUPE ◆ Municipio de Jalisco situado en el noreste del estado, al noreste de Guadalajara y al suroeste de Lagos de Moreno. Superficie: 516.12 km². Habitantes: 5,663, de los cuales 1,386 forman la población económicamente activa. Hablan alguna lengua indígena 11 personas mayores de cinco años.

VALLE HERMOSO ◆ Municipio de Tamaulipas situado en el norte del estado, contiguo a Matamoros, en la frontera con Estados Unidos. Superficie: 1,770.25 km². Habitantes: 55,286, de los cuales 14,698 forman la población económicamente activa. Hablan alguna lengua indígena 45 personas mayores de cinco años (náhuatl 22). En su jurisdicción se localiza la laguna Palito Blanco. A fines de los años treinta, muchos de los trabajadores temporales mexicanos que fueron expulsados de Estados Unidos se asentaron en las cercanías de las ciudades tamaulipecas de Matamoros y Reynosa. Uno de los centros poblacionales así formado fue la Colonia 18 de Marzo, que después se convertiría en Valle Hermoso, cabecera del municipio.

VALLE-INCLÁN, RAMÓN DEL ◆ n. y m. en España (1866-1936). Escritor perteneciente a la Generación del 98. Colaborador del diario madrileño *El Globo*, viajó por primera vez a México, según él, por ser éste el "único país que se escribe con X" (1892-93). Colaboró en el periódico *El Correo Español*, fue redactor especializado en temas españoles de *El Universal* de Rafael Reyes Spíndola y estuvo a punto de trabarse en duelo con Victoriano Agüeros, director de *El Tiempo*. Volvió a México en 1921 como invitado de honor a las fiestas del centenario de la consumación de la independencia. Durante su segunda estancia en México criticó a los "gachupines", españoles acaudalados, de quienes dijo que "encarnan el espíritu más reaccionario" y los calificó de "extracto de la barbarie ibérica" y "enemigos de la justicia e ignorantes de las cualidades del indio mexicano, a cuya raza pertenecieron Juárez, Altamirano y el mismo general Díaz". A la pregunta de "¿qué le hubiera gustado ser?", respondió: "general mexicano". En 1922 viajó a Estados Unidos, donde se convirtió en defensor de México, de sus indios, de la reforma agraria y de la educación popular. Al regresar a España declaró: "La tierra es de quien la labra." Autor de novela, drama, poesía y *esperpento*, forma narrativa dialogada, de su propia invención: *Femeninas* (1894), *Sonata de otoño* (1902), *Comedias bárbaras* (1907-23), *Tirano Banderas* (1926, inspirada parcialmente en la figura de Porfirio Díaz), *La corte de los milagros* (1927), *Viva mi dueño* (1928) y *Baza de espadas* (1958).

VALLE DE JUÁREZ ◆ Municipio de Jalisco situado en el sureste del estado, al este de Ciudad Guzmán, en los límites con Michoacán. Superficie: 79.32 km². Habitantes: 5,646, de los cuales 1,391 forman la población económicamente activa. Hablan alguna lengua indígena 16 personas mayores de cinco años.

VALLE DE MÉXICO ◆ Estado de la República erigido por decreto del gobernador militar del Distrito Federal Álvaro Obregón, el 23 de febrero de 1916. Dejó de existir al entrar en vigor la división política establecida por la Constitución de 1917.

VALLE DE MÉXICO, ÁREA METROPOLITANA DEL ◆ Para la Comisión de Coordinación Metropolitana de los gobiernos del Estado de México y el Distrito Federal, comprende las 16 delegaciones políticas de la capital de la República y los municipios mexiquenses de Coacalco, Chalco, Ecatepec, Huixquilucan, Juchitepec, Naucalpan, Nezahualcóyotl, Ocoyoacac, La Paz, Tenango del Aire, Tlalnepantla, Tultitlán, Valle de Chalco Solidaridad y Xalatlaco, con una población total de 14,194,360 habitantes. De acuerdo con otras apreciaciones, también forman parte de la zona conurbada Atizapán de Zaragoza, Cuautitlán de Romero Rubio, Cuautitlán Izcalli, Chicoloapan, Chimalhuacán, Ixtapaluca, Nicolás Romero y Teoloyucan, con lo que sumarían 16,59,397 habitantes, de acuerdo con los datos censales de 1995.

VALLE NACIONAL ◆ ☛ *San Juan Bautista Valle Nacional.*

VALLE NACIONAL ◆ Río de Oaxaca que nace de la confluencia de varios arroyos en la vertiente suroriental de la sierra de Juárez, en el norte del estado; corre de suroeste a noreste, recibe al río Soyalapan o San Cristóbal, tuerce al norte y entra en la llanura costera del golfo, donde se une al río Santo Domingo para formar el Papaloapan, en la vertiente suroriental de la sierra de Tuxtepec, al suroeste de San Juan Bautista Tuxtepec.

VALLE DE SANTIAGO ◆ Municipio de Guanajuato situado en el sur del estado, contiguo a Salamanca y en los límites con Michoacán. Superficie: 835.70 km². Habitantes: 131,460, de los cuales 29,906 forman la población económicamente activa. Hablan alguna lengua indígena 166 personas mayores de cinco años. Fue originalmente un asentamiento otomí llamado Camémbaro. En mayo de 1607 los conquistadores españoles fundaron el poblado de Valle de Santiago. El 26 de junio de 1811 se produjo en este sitio la acción de Valle de Santiago, en la que el realista Miguel del Campo derrotó al guerrillero insurgente Albino García. La fiesta del Señor Santiago, patrono de la localidad, es el 26 de julio.

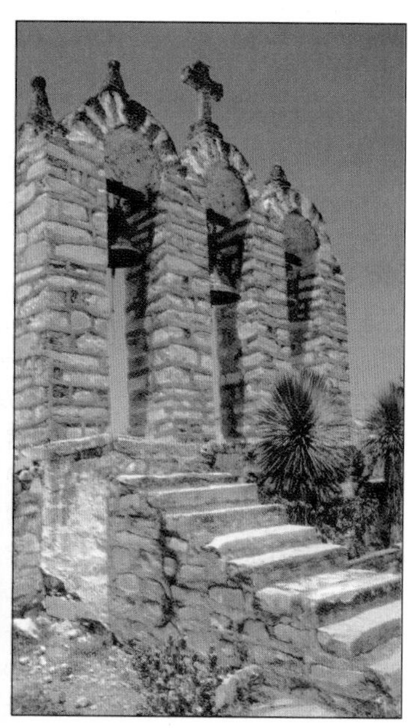

Iglesia de San Carlos Borromeo en Vallecillo, Nuevo León

FOTO: FONDO EDITORIAL GRUPO AZABACHE

Paraje en Valle de Santiago, Guanajuato

VALLE DE ZARAGOZA ◆ Municipio de Chihuahua situado en el sur del estado, al sur-sureste de la capital estatal y contiguo a Hidalgo del Parral. Superficie: 4,168.18 km². Habitantes: 6,123, de los cuales 1,700 forman la población económicamente activa. Hablan alguna lengua indígena 40 personas mayores de cinco años (tarahumara 39).

VALLECILLO ◆ Municipio de Nuevo León situado en el norte del estado, contiguo a Sabinas Hidalgo, en los límites con Tamaulipas. Superficie: 1,859.90 km². Habitantes: 2,188, de los cuales 743 forman la población económicamente activa.

VALLEJO, DE ◆ Sierra del suroeste de Nayarit. Forma parte de la sierra Madre Occidental. Se extiende de suroeste a noreste, al sur-suroeste de Tepic; está limitada al noreste por la sierra de Zapotlán, al sureste y sur por el río Ameca, que marca el límite entre Nayarit y Jalisco, y al noroeste por la bahía de Banderas, en el océano Pacífico; su extremo suroeste llega a la costa para formar la punta Mita, al sur de las islas Marías. Su cumbre más elevada alcanza 1,535 metros sobre el nivel del mar.

VALLEJO, DEMETRIO ◆ n. en Espinal, Oax., y m. en el DF (1910-1985). Su segundo apellido era Martínez. Fue arriero, campesino y telegrafista. Militante del PCM, del que fue expulsado en los años cuarenta. Formó parte de Acción Socialista Unificada y fue cofundador del Partido Obrero Campesino Mexicano (1950-1963). Fundador de la Federación de Trabajadores del Istmo (1936). Ingresó en 1934 a la empresa Ferrocarriles Nacionales de México, en la que fue presidente de la Gran Comisión pro Aumento de Salarios (1958) y en la que organizó los paros de los días 26, 27, 28 y 29 de junio de 1958. El 13 de agosto de ese año fue elegido secretario general del Sindicato de Trabajadores Ferrocarrileros de la República Mexicana (por 56,000 votos contra nueve) y dirigió la huelga que se inició el 25 de febrero de 1959 (☛ *Movimiento ferrocarrilero*). Detenido el 28 de marzo de 1959, fue acusado de sabotaje y disolución social y fue preso político hasta 1970. En 1970 fue uno de los fundadores del Comité Nacional de Organización y Auscultación, antecedente del Partido Mexicano de los Trabajadores, del que fue cofundador y uno de los dirigentes (1974).

Demetrio Vallejo

Fue expulsado del PMT en 1983 e ingresó en el Partido Socialista Unificado de México (1983), por el cual fue diputado federal (1985). Autor de *Yo acuso, Mis experiencias y decepciones en el palacio negro de Lecumberri, La monstruosidad de una sentencia* y *Las luchas ferrocarrileras que conmovieron a México.*

Vallejo, Fernando ◆ n. en Colombia (1942). Escritor, cineasta y biólogo. Estudió letras en universidades de Colombia, y dirección de cine en el Centro Spiremental di Cinematografía de Roma. Radica en México desde 1971, donde ha escrito sus libros y filmado sus películas. Ha dirigido las cintas de largometraje *Crónica roja, En la tormenta* y *Barrio de campeones*, y escrito los libros *Logoi: una gramática del lenguaje literario, Barbara Jacob el mensajero, La Virgen de los sicarios* (1998), *La tautología darwinista y otros ensayos de biología* y *El río del tiempo.*

Valles, Adolfo ◆ n. en Chihuahua, Chih., y m. en el DF (1873-1937). Abogado. Fue agente del Ministerio Público, juez de lo penal, magistrado del Tribunal Superior de Justicia del Distrito Federal y, en el régimen de Francisco I. Madero, procurador general de la República. Profesor de derecho en la Escuela Nacional de Jurisprudencia (1920-35) y de esgrima en la Nacional Preparatoria. Durante varios años fue campeón nacional de sable. Autor de *Código Penal para el Distrito Federal anotado* (1907).

Vallina García, Eloy S. ◆ n. en España y m. en Chihuahua, Chih. (1903-1960). Empresario. Radicó en Chihuahua desde su infancia. Fue gerente del Banco Mercantil de Chihuahua, cofundador (1933) y director del Comercial Mexicano y fundador de las empresas Financiera y Fiduciaria de Chihuahua, Descuento Agrícola, Celulosa de Chihuahua, Plywood Ponderosa, Cementos de Chihuahua, Bosques de Chihuahua y Viscosa de Chihuahua, así como del Instituto de Chihuahua. En 1959 fue uno de los promotores de la mexicanización de la empresa Ericsson, que se convertiría en Teléfonos de México. Compró las acciones de la empresa Ferrocarril Noroeste de México, junto con Carlos Trouyet, José de la Mora y Sam Rosso. Se desempeñó, asimismo, como consejero de Aeronaves de México, Tubos de Acero de México, Fierro Comercial, Aceros de Chihuahua e Industrias de Madera.

Fotografía de Pedro Valtierra

Valner Onjas, Gregorio ◆ n. en Toluca, Edo. de Méx. (1929). Médico por la UNAM (1953), especializado en psiquiatría y psicoanálisis en la Universidad de Chicago. Ha sido profesor universitario (1967-69), médico de diversos hospitales, director general del Instituto de Acción Urbana e Integración Social y del Instituto de Desarrollo de Recursos Humanos del Estado de México, subsecretario de Asentamientos Humanos y Obras Públicas (1977-82) y presidente de la Comisión de Asentamientos Humanos de la ONU (1980-81). Autor de *Urbanística: las ciencias del desarrollo humano.* Vicepresidente de la Asociación Mundial de Vivienda Rural (1979-80).

Valparaíso ◆ Municipio de Zacatecas situado en el occidente del estado, en los límites con Durango y Jalisco, al oeste de la capital estatal. Superficie: 5,663.59 km². Habitantes: 36,393, de los cuales 8,514 forman la población económicamente activa. Hablan alguna lengua indígena 760 personas mayores de cinco años (tepehuan 55).

Valparaíso, de ◆ Sierra del occidente de Zacatecas. Está situada al oeste-suroeste de Fresnillo. Se extiende de noroeste a sureste; está limitada al norte por la sierra de Chalchihuites y al este y suroeste por el río Valparaíso.

Gregorio Valner Onjas

Valsequillo ◆ Presa de Puebla, también llamada Manuel Ávila Camacho, situada al sur de la capital del estado y al este de Atlixco, en el curso del río Atoyac. Su cortina fue construida en el sitio llamado Balcón del Diablo, entre el oeste de la sierra de Tepeaca y el norte de la de Tentzo. Tiene una capacidad de 403 millones de metros cúbicos y se utiliza para el regadío de los valles de Tecamachalco, Tehuacán y Atoyatempan.

VALTIERRA, PEDRO ◆ n. en Fresnillo, Zac. (1955). Fotógrafo de la oficina de prensa de la Presidencia (1975), del periódico *El Sol de México* (1977-78) y del *unomásuno* (1978-84). Fundador del Grupo 5 (1980) y cofundador de Fotógrafos Unidos (1981). Cofundador y director de la agencia *Imagenlatina* (1983-84), cofundador (1984) y jefe del departamento de fotografía (1984-86 y 1995-) de *La Jornada*. En 1986 reorganizó *Imagenlatina*, de la que se retiró para fundar la agencia *Cuartoscuro*, de la que es director (1987-). Dirigió la revista *Mira* (1990-91). Autor o coautor gráfico de varios libros y folletos, entre los que destacan: *La batalla por Nicaragua* (1980), *El magisterio en lucha* (1981), *Guatemala: las líneas de su mano* (1982), *Nicaragua: la mujer en la revolución* (1982), *Obreros somos* (1983), *Los refugiados en México* (1983), *Testimonios Conamup* (1983), *Ciudad quebrada* (1985) y *Nicaragua, una noche afuera* (1992). Ha recibido, entre otros, los premios y distinciones de la primera Bienal de Fotografía de México (1980), dos veces Fotógrafo del Año en la rama de fotoperiodismo de la revista *Fotozoom* (1980 y 1995), Premio Nacional de Periodismo (1983), premio de adquisición en la tercera Bienal de Fotografía del INBA (1984), Fotógrafo de la Década en el campo del periodismo de la revista *Fotozoom* (1985), medalla Testimonio Roque Dalton, de El Salvador (1986), Premio José Pagés Llergo (1998), Premio Rey de España (1998) y Premio Fotoprensa México (1998).

VALTIERRA, VICENTE M. ◆ n. y m. en León, Gto. (1880-1929). Graduado en la Escuela Nacional de Ingeniería. Militó en el Partido Constitucional Progresista y, al triunfo de la revolución maderista, fue alcalde suplente de la ciudad de México y miembro de la administración de la ciudad de León. Diputado por Guanajuato al Congreso Constituyente de 1916-17.

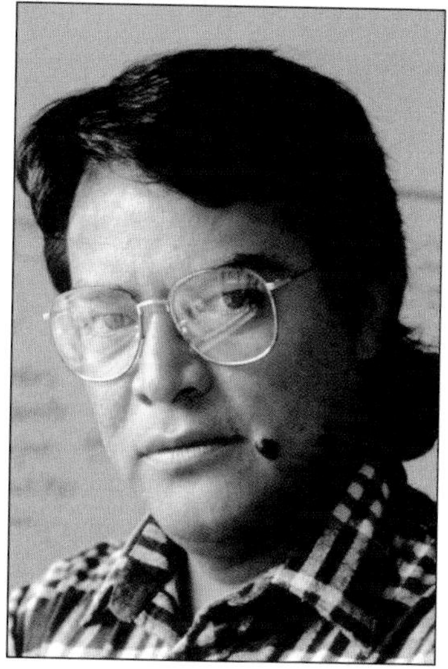

Pedro Valtierra

VALTÓN, EMILIO ◆ n. en Salvatierra, Gto., y m. en EUA (1880-1963). Doctor en filosofía por la Universidad de París. Ordenado sacerdote, fue cura de Actopan y otras parroquias. Colaborador del diario *Excélsior*. Coautor de *IV centenario de la Asociación de Libreros de México* (1940) y *Homenaje a don Francisco Gamoneda. Miscelánea de estudios de erudición, historia, literatura y arte* (1946). Autor de *Impresos mexicanos del siglo XVI. Estudio bibliográfico con una introducción sobre los orígenes de la imprenta en América* (1935) y *El primer libro de alfabetización en América. Cartilla para enseñar a leer impresa por Pedro Ocharte en México, 1569. Estudio crítico, bibliográfico e histórico* (1947).

VALVERDE TÉLLEZ, EMETERIO ◆ n. en Villa del Carbón, Edo. de Méx., y m. en León, Gto. (1864-1948). Sacerdote. Doctor en filosofía por el Seminario Conciliar de México (1887), del que fue profesor (1882-90). Obispo de León (1909-48), vivió exiliado a causa de la revolución constitucionalista (1914-16) y de la guerra cristera (1926-29). Promovió la construcción del Cristo monumental en el cerro del Cubilete. Reunió una biblioteca de 20,000 volúmenes que se conserva como Fondo Valverde Téllez en la Biblioteca Alfonso Reyes de la Universidad Autónoma de Nuevo León. Autor de *Apuntaciones históricas sobre la filosofía en México* (1896), *Crítica filosófica* (1898), *Bibliografía filosófica mexicana* (2 t., 1913-14), *Poema de amor divino* (1922), *Cartas pastorales y edictos* (1923) y *Biobibliografía eclesiástica mexicana* (3 t., 1949).

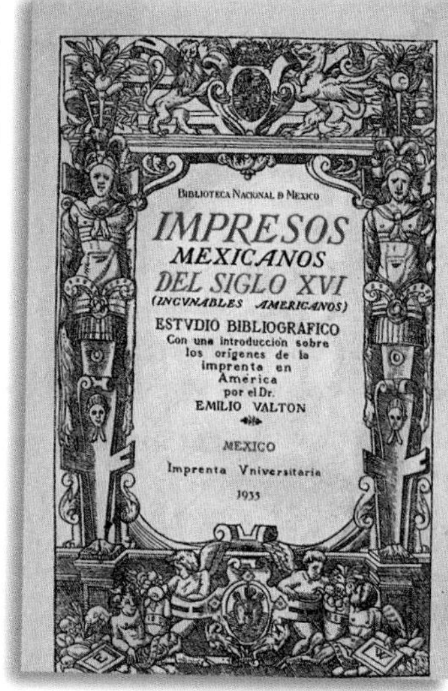

Biblioteca Nacional de Mexico

IMPRESOS MEXICANOS DEL SIGLO XVI

(INCVNABLES AMERICANOS)

ESTVDIO BIBLIOGRAFICO

Con una introducción sobre los orígenes de la imprenta en América

por el Dr. EMILIO VALTON

MEXICO

Imprenta Vniversitaria

1935

Libro de Emilio Valtón

VANEGAS ◆ Municipio de San Luis Potosí situado en el extremo norte del estado, al nor-noroeste de Matehuala, en los límites con Nuevo León y Zacatecas. Superficie: 2,667.2 km^2. Habitantes: 8,179, de los cuales 1,992 forman la población económicamente activa. Hablan alguna lengua indígena nueve personas mayores de cinco años.

Emeterio Valverde Téllez

VANEGAS ARROYO, ANTONIO ◆ n. en Puebla, Pue., y m. en la ciudad de México (¿1852?-1917). Editor. Residió desde 1867 en la capital del país y trabajó en el taller de encuadernación de su padre. En 1874 instaló su propia imprenta, en la que publicó hojas y folletos con oraciones, letanías, juegos, loterías, corridos, cuentos, canciones y calaveras, así como una serie de obras dramáticas que formaron su *Galería de Teatro Infantil. Colección de comedias para representarse por niños o títeres*, ilustradas por el grabador José Guadalupe Posada (☛), con quien Vanegas formó un equipo de trabajo desde 1890. En su imprenta, en la que más tarde trabajó también su hijo, Blas Vanegas, publicó asimismo los periódicos *La Casera*, *El Volador*, *Don Chepito*, *La Gaceta Callejera*, *El Jicote*, *El Teatro*, *El Centavo Perdido* y *El Boletín*, con la colaboración de los poetas Constancio S. Suárez y Manuel Romero y el *Secretario de los amantes*, recopilación de cartas de amor.

VANMELLE, FREDERICK ◆ n. en Bélgica y m. en el DF (1936-1985). Estudió teatro y artes plásticas en Francia, donde fue alumno de Etienne Decroux, y en Bélgica. Fue profesor de artes plásticas en Bruselas (1960-70). En 1963 montó su primer espectáculo con números de pantomima. Llegó a México en 1978; puso la obra *Las hermosas locuras*, realizó una gira por el país y trabajó en un programa especial del DDF (1974), fundó (1974) y dirigió (1974-85) la Compañía de Teatro Frederick, presentó el espectáculo *Luzzinaciones* en Mexicali y en la ciudad de México (1980), participó en el undécimo Festival Internacional Cervantino con *Historia de un caballo*, basada en un cuento de León Tolstoi (1980), montó *Hermosas locuras* (1982) y actuó en *El Fantástico mundo del teatro sin palabras*, espectáculo de la SEP (1982 y 1984). Impartió seminarios y talleres de teatro y mímica. Como pintor expuso en Bélgica, España y México. En 1985 montó los espectáculos *En trapos atrapados* y *El gran espectáculo del Teatro Frederick para niños*. Murió en el terremoto del 19 de septiembre de 1985.

VARELA RUIZ, GUSTAVO ◆ n. en el DF (1942). Licenciado en economía por la UNAM (1970), de la que fue profesor (1971-73). Pertenece al PRI, donde fue subdirector regional del IEPES (1981-82). Ha sido jefe de asesoría de ventas en el Banjidal (1961-65), subjefe de Estudios Económicos, de Juntas Estatales de Electrificación (1965-66) y jefe de proyectos especiales de la CFE (1971-73), contralor general de la Compañía de Luz y Fuerza (1973-76), director de delegaciones federales de la Secofi (1976-81), director fiduciario de Fidein (1981-84), director general del Fondo de Fomento Industrial (1984-89), gerente proveedor y de almacenes de Pemex (1990-98) y oficial mayor de la Semarnap (1998-). Presidente de la Asociación de Economistas de la Industria Eléctrica, vicepresidente y presidente del Comité Ejecutivo del Colegio Nacional de Economistas (1976-76 y 1985-86) y presidente de la Asociación de Economistas de América Latina (1985-86). Medalla al Mérito Civil del Reino de España (1980).

VARGAS, CARLOS ◆ n. en La Reforma, Hgo. (1924). Escritor y periodista. Licenciado en derecho por la UNAM (1957), donde ejerce la docencia desde 1963. Ha colaborado en los periódicos *Excélsior* (1944-55), *El Sol de Hidalgo*, que dirigió en 1950, y *El Universal* (1950-72). Autor de *El hombre sin muros* (1945), *Filosofía del derecho* (1956), *Las palabras de los hombres* (1958), *Cárcel espiritual* (1961), *Filosofía de la felicidad social* (1964) y *Poema del hombre sin muros* (1974).

VARGAS, ELVIRA ◆ n. en Tlalpujahua, Mich., y m. en el DF (1906-1967). Periodista. Cursaba la preparatoria cuando participó en la huelga de 1929, que dio la autonomía a la Universidad Nacional. Fue activista de la campaña presidencial de José Vasconcelos y se inició en el periodismo en 1930 en la publicación vasconcelista *El Momento*. Fue redactora (1931) y jefa de redacción de *El Nacional* (1938), colaboradora de *El Universal*, columnista de la cadena García Valseca (1946-52), colaboradora del *Novedades* (1953) y cofundadora del *Diario de la Tarde* (1959), periódico del que fue jefa de redacción y, ocasionalmente, directora. Colaboró en las revistas *Hoy*, *Mañana* y *Siempre!* Autora de *Por las rutas del sureste*.

VARGAS, FÉLIX ◆ n. en Los Mezquites, Jal. (1943). Escritor. Contador público y auditor por la Universidad de Guadalajara. Estudió pintura y escultura en el Jardín del Arte de la capital jalisciense y letras en la Universidad de Guadalajara. Ha sido profesor de literatura y folclor mexicano, coordinador del Departamento de Enseñanza Preparatoria y coordinador de Eventos Especiales de la Universidad de Guadalajara, así como coordinador de teatro del Instituto Cultural Cabañas. Ha colaborado en *Comunidad Latinoamericana de Escritores*, *Summa* e *Intento*, publicación que dirige. Autor de los volúmenes de cuento *La muerte del rostro azul* (1975), *El milagro atropellado* (1977), *Chinto Luna* (1980), *La casa de los caballos muertos* (1980) y *Castigo de castidad* (1986); y de las obras teatrales *Las dos soledades* (1979) y *Jesús, María y José* (1980).

Fulgencio Vargas

VARGAS, FULGENCIO ◆ n. en Jaral del Progreso y m. en Guanajuato, Gto. (1875-1962). Historiador. Fue profesor en la Universidad de Guanajuato, diputado y presidente del Congreso local (1914). Autor de *Flores del Centenario*

(1910), *La insurrección de 1810 en el estado de Guanajuato* (1910), *Yuririapúndaro* (1923), *Fray Bartolomé de las Casas. Su vida y su obra* (1924), *Anecdotario de provincia* (1925), *Apaseo 1523-1933. Datos históricos* (1933), *El estado de Guanajuato* (1933), *Camécuaro* (1935), *Apuntes de literatura* (1936), *Estudio biográfico sobre don Manuel Doblado* (1938), *Historia elemental de Guanajuato* (1938), *Proceso histórico de la metrópoli guanajuatense* (1948) y *Granaditas y su proceso histórico* (1951). Perteneció a la Sociedad Mexicana de Geografía y Estadística y a las academias Mexicana de la Historia y Nacional de Ciencias Antonio Alzate.

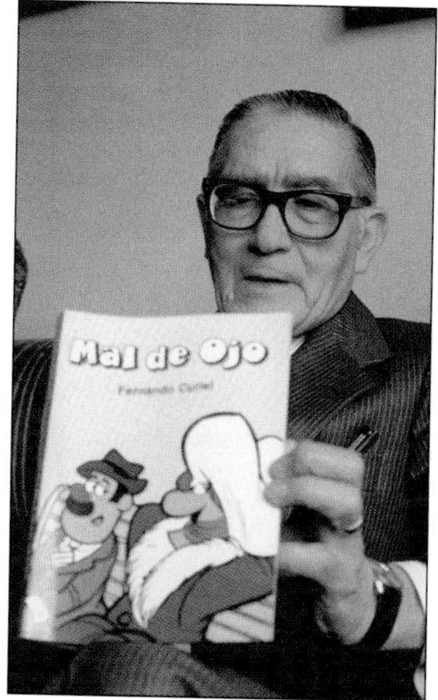

Gabriel Vargas

Vargas, Gabriel ◆ n. en Tulancingo, Hgo. (1918). En 1927 ganó un concurso de dibujo internacional infantil en Osaka y en 1930 fue becado por el gobierno mexicano para estudiar en París. No quiso ir a Francia pero se le pensionó para que estudiara en la ciudad de México, después de que Alfonso Pruneda viera sus dibujos "El día del tráfico" y "Construcción de la catedral de México". Creador de las historietas *La vida de Cristo, Sherlock Holmes, Los chiflados, Los del doce, Don Jilemón Metralla y Bomba, El caballero rojo, Poncho López, Los Superlocos* y *La familia Burrón*. Esta historieta ha sido objeto de estudios sociológicos, históricos y literarios. Dueño de la editorial G y G. Fue jefe del departamento de dibujo de *Excélsior* y cartonista de *El Universal Gráfico* (1955-). Premio y diploma por 25 años de trabajo en *El Universal Gráfico* otorgado por la Asociación Nacional de Periodistas (1980), premio del Club de Periodistas (1981), Premio Nacional de Periodismo (1983), condecoración como Gran Humanista Mexicano (1984) por el Club Internacional de Mujeres, nombramiento simbólico de Cronista del Tercer Mundo e Hijo Predilecto del Estado de Hidalgo (1985).

Pedro Vargas

Vargas, Pedro ◆ n. en San Miguel de Allende, Gto., y m. en el DF (1908-1989). Cantante conocido también como *el Samurai de la Canción* y *el Tenor Continental*. En la parroquia de su pueblo natal aprendió solfeo, órgano y piano (1918), viajó después a la ciudad de México donde estudió canto con José Pierson. Se inició profesionalmente en 1928 en la ópera *Cavallería Rusticana* en el Teatro Esperanza Iris. Tras una gira por Estados Unidos y Canadá con la Orquesta Típica Lerdo de Tejada, fue contratado por la radiodifusora XEW (1930), desde la cual empezó a cobrar renombre como intérprete, sobre todo de las composiciones de Agustín Lara. En 1942 cantó en la Casa Blanca, invitado por Franklin D. Roosevelt y actuó para Getulio Vargas, ex presidente brasileño y compadre suyo, y para Augusto Pinochet, así como para Lázaro Cárdenas, Manuel Ávila Camacho, Adolfo Ruiz Cortines, Adolfo López Mateos, Gustavo Díaz Ordaz, Luis Echeverría, José López Portillo y Miguel de la Madrid. Grabó su primer disco en 1928, en Chicago. Compuso *Tú me haces falta, Porteñita mía* y *Me fui*. Orden de Caballero de la Cruz del Sur, Mister Amigo y Ciudadano Honorario de Texas (1975) y presea Isabel la Católica del gobierno español (1988). Perteneció a la Orden de Malta.

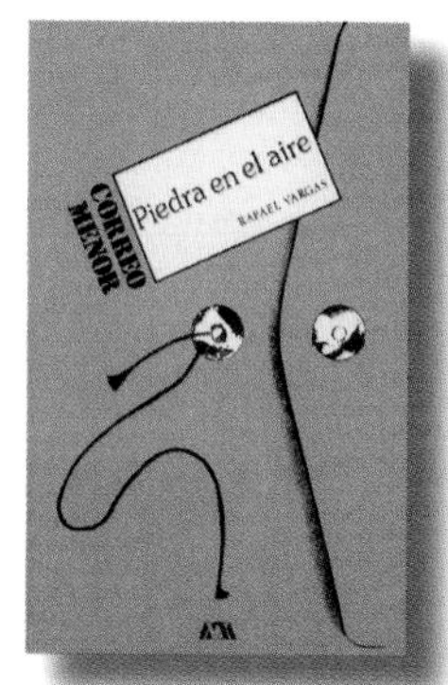

Poesías de Rafael Vargas

Vargas, Rafael ◆ n. en el DF (1954). Estudió ciencias de la comunicación en la UNAM. Trabajó para el Departamento de Publicidad del FCE, donde formó parte del equipo editor de la *Gaceta del* FCE. Agregado cultural de la embajada mexicana en Perú (1987). Colaborador de la *Revista de la Universidad de México, Melodía, El Rehilete, Territorios* (jefe de redacción), *Sitios, Proceso, La Semana de Bellas Artes, La Cultura en México, Sábado* y *Nexos*. Coautor de *Doce modos* (1976). Autor de *Conversaciones* (1979), *Piedra en el aire* (1984), *El habitante de la niebla* (1987), *Pacífico* (1988) y *Escritura la flor* (1995). Becario del Programa Inter-

Ramón Vargas

Simón Vargas Aguilar

nacional de Escritores de Iowa (1980) y del CNCA desde 1998.

VARGAS, RAMÓN ◆ n. en el DF (1960). Tenor. Estudió con Antonio López en el Instituto de Música y Arte. Fue miembro del coro infantil de la Basílica de Guadalupe (1968-72). En 1982 ganó el concurso Carlo Morelli y en 1983 debutó en Bellas Artes en el papel de Fenton de la ópera *Falstaff*, de Verdi, dirigida por Eduardo Mata. En 1986 tuvo su primer papel protagónico en *The Rake's Progress*, de Stravinski. En 1987 se fue a Europa y en ese año ganó el concurso Enrico Caruso. En 1991 triunfó en el papel de Amenofi de la nueva producción del Moisés de Rossini, en el Teatro Communale de Bolonga. Desde 1992 se ha presentado con éxito en escenarios como La Scala de Milán, El MET de Nueva York, el Covent Garden de Londres, el San Carlo de Nápoles, el Colón de Buenos Aires, la Arena de Verona y las óperas de Viena, París, Munich, Chicago y San Francisco. La prensa de Europa se refiere a él como *Rey de la Ópera para el 2000*. Ha recibido los premios Lauri Volpi (Italia, 1993), Gino Tani para Artes y Espectáculo (1995) y la medalla de la Sociedad de Autores y Compositores Mexicanos (1997).

VARGAS, SILVESTRE ◆ n. en Tecalitlán y m. en Guadalajara, Jal. (1901-1985). Hijo del mariachi Gaspar Vargas. Se inició como violinista en 1914 y en 1921 se incorporó al Mariachi Vargas de Tecalitlán, de su padre, grupo que dirigió a partir de 1932 y con que obtuvo popularidad internacional. Fue el primero en incorporar trompetas al mariachi (1940). Su conjunto ha acompañado a Lucha Reyes, Pedro Infante, Jorge Negrete, Amalia Mendoza, José Alfredo Jiménez, Miguel Aceves Mejía, Pedro Vargas, María Victoria, Javier Solís, Juan Gabriel, Estela Núñez, y Lola Beltrán. Se retiró en 1976. Hizo arreglos de sones jaliscienses, como *Las alazanas*, *El carretero*, *El son de la negra* y *Camino real de Colima*. Autor de *Los arrieros*, *El pasajero*, *Lupita*, *El cuatro*, *La madrugada*, *El gusto*, *El palmero*, *Las abajeñas*, *El perico loro*, *El meracumbé*, *El tecalitleco* y *El lunar que te vi*. Grabó 23 discos. Se presentó cientos de veces en radio, televisión, teatro y cine. Hizo popular el grito: "¡No te rajes, Jalisco!" Miembro de la Sociedad de Autores y Compositores de Música.

VARGAS AGUIAR, MARIO ◆ n. en La Paz, BCS (1948). Licenciado en derecho por las universidades de Sonora y Guanajuato y maestro en derecho constitucional y administrativo por la UNAM. Es miembro del PRI desde 1966, del que ha sido dirigente Juvenil del Sector Popular, secretario del Comité Directivo Estatal de Baja California Sur, delegado en La Paz, Los Cabos, Comondú y Mulegé, coordinador de acción electoral del CEN en Sinaloa y delegado general del CEN en Puebla. Presidente municipal de Mulegé (1978-80), diputado federal (1991-94) y senador de la República para el periodo 1994-2000. Coautor de *Constitución Política de Baja California Sur* y autor de una *Monografía del municipio de Mulegé* (1989).

VARGAS AGUILAR, SIMÓN ◆ n. en Torreón, Coah. (1957). Licenciado en derecho por la Universidad Autónoma de Coahuila. Fue secretario del ayuntamiento de Torreón y, en la PGR, jefe de la Unidad Coordinadora de Supervisión de la Campaña Permanente contra el Narcotráfico, director de Orientación Legal y Quejas, director de Participación Social y encargado del despacho de la Contraloría Interna y Visitaduría General. Dirigió el Instituto de Capacitación de Ferronales, el Centro de Análisis del Instituto de Estudios Educativos y Sindicales de América, así como Normatividad en la Dirección General de Investigación y Seguridad Privada de la Segob. En el Tribunal Superior Agrario fue secretario de Estudio y Cuenta y en la Procuraduría Federal Preventiva coordinó la Unidad de Desarrollo y Control Interno. Administrador central de Regulación del Despacho Aduanero de la Secretaría de Hacienda (1999-).

VARGAS APEZACHEA, RAFAEL ◆ n. en Tehuacán, Pue., y m. en el DF (1884-1946). Ingeniero por la Escuela Nacional de Agricultura. En 1913 actuó como agente para la unificación de las fuerzas revolucionarias dispersas en Veracruz, Puebla y Oaxaca. En diciembre de 1913 se incorporó en Tamaulipas a la Brigada Caballero. Comandante del cañonero *Guerrero* (1914), en 1915 participó en las tomas de San Blas y Guaymas y llegó a ser jefe de la escuadrilla del Pacífico. En 1916, enviado por Carranza, viajó a Japón para comprar maquinaria destinada a la elaboración de cartuchos y a su regreso fue fundador y director de la fábrica de municiones del Ejército Constitucionalista. Fue jefe del Departamento de Ingenieros y del Departamento de Infantería, comandante de Marina en el golfo y jefe del Estado Mayor. General de brigada en 1920. Fue subdirector de los Establecimientos Fabriles Militares y en 1929 instaló el equipo para fabricar fusiles Máuser. Autor de *Submarinos y sumergibles* (1917).

VARGAS COMSILLE, HUGO CÉSAR ◆ n. en Ciudad Madero, Tams. (1956). Realizó estudios de derecho y ciencias sociales en la Universidad Autónoma de Tamaulipas (1975). Cursó la carrera de comunicación en la UNAM (1980). Ha sido subjefe de Publicidad y Promoción de Siglo XXI Editores (1976-80), editor de la revista *Controversia* (1978-82), reportero y redactor de *El Machete*, editor y colaborador de *Cuadernos de*

Yolanda Vargas Dulché

Marcha (1981-84), corrector de *unomásuno* (1982), guionista de Radio y Televisión Mexiquense (1983-84), director de Publicaciones de la UAP (1985-87), jefe de redacción de *Gambito,* revista mexicana de ajedrez (1985-87), gerente de producción de Pangea Editores (1988-89), colaborador de *El Nacional* (1990-93), director de Publicaciones del Instituto de Investigaciones Doctor José María Luis Mora (1989-), colaborador de *Este país* (1994-) y redactor de *El Bagre* (1995-).

Vargas Dulché, Yolanda ◆ n. y m. en el DF (1925-1999). Directora, editora y autora de historietas (*Lágrimas, Risas y Amor*, entre ellas) y autora de teatro: *Celos, La solterona, Madres puras* y *Ocho en París*. Fundadora de la Editorial Vid. Recibió el Ariel al mejor argumento original por *Cinco rostros de mujer* (1948). Autora de *Cristal. Una parte de mi vida* (memorias, 1965). La I Convención de Cómics y Ciencia Ficción del DF le otorgó un reconocimiento en 1997.

Vargas Gómez, Joaquín ◆ n. en la ciudad de México (1925). Estudió en el Colegio Militar (1944). Empresario. Fundó una fábrica de herramientas y en los cincuenta entró en el negocio de importación de tubería. En 1965 obtuvo la concesión de una gasolinería en la que instaló un avión de desecho, que se convirtió en el primer local de la cadena de restaurantes Wings. En 1968 se hizo cargo de la presidencia y dirección general de Televisión Independiente de México, Canal 8, donde impulsó los programas *Domingos Espectaculares* y *El Chavo del 8*. Instaló la primera radiodifusora de frecuencia modulada en México. Fundó en 1976 la empresa productora Tele Rey. En 1989 era dueño de 26 estaciones de radio (entre las que se hallan las primeras del país en usar tecnología láser), numerosos restaurantes de lujo, 35 cafeterías Wings, y en ese año fundó la empresa JV Corporación, a la que pertenecen la televisora Multivisión y la radiodifusora Multi-Radio.

Vargas y Gutiérrez, Francisco Melitón ◆ n. en Ahualulco de Mercado, Jal., y m. en Puebla, Pue. (1822-1896). Sacerdote ordenado en 1850, se graduó en teología en el Seminario de Guadalajara, del que fue profesor y rector. Cura de Zapopan, Acatlán, Colotlán y Aguascalientes, fue prebendado de la catedral de Guadalajara, canónigo lectoral, primer obispo de Colima (1884-88) y obispo de Puebla (1888-96).

Lágrimas, risas y amor, historieta de Yolanda Vargas Dulché

Vargas Lugo, Bartolomé ◆ n. en Tulancingo, Hgo., y m. en el DF (1890-1972). Ingeniero egresado de la Escuela Nacional de Agricultura. Se unió en 1914 al Ejército Libertador del Sur. Al término de la revolución fue, sucesivamente, dirigente de la Comisión Nacional Agraria (antecedente de la Secretaría de la Reforma Agraria), gobernador de Hidalgo (1929-33), director del Banco Nacional de Crédito Agrícola y asesor del Departamento de Asuntos Agrarios y Colonización.

Joaquín Vargas Gómez

Vargas Machado, Leonardo ◆ n. en Izúcar de Matamoros, Pue. (1930). Profesor por la Escuela Nacional de Maestros (1954) y doctor en pedagogía por la Normal Superior de México (1982). Ha ejercido la docencia en escuelas federales (1947-49 y 1955-57), en la Nacional de Maestros (1964-67), la Normal Ignacio Manuel Altamirano (1964-77) y la Normal Superior (1967-70). En la SEP ha sido jefe de la Oficina de Becas de Secundarias Particulares Incorporadas (1967), jefe de la Oficina de Control Escolar de Secundarias Particulares Incorporadas (1968-69), asesor de la Dirección General de Segunda Enseñanza (1969-70) y de la Dirección General de Coordinación Educativa (1971-74); coordinador general del Programa de Secundaria Abierta (1974-76), subdirector de Sistemas Abiertos (1976-78), director del Sistema de Telesecundaria (1978), jefe del Departamento de Educación Secundaria para Adultos (1979-81), director general de la Unidad de Telesecundaria (1981-85) y director general de Telesecundaria (1985-88). Autor de *La secundaria abierta* (1974), *Guías de estudio de telesecundaria* (1980), *Opciones educativas para campesinos egresados de telesecundaria* (1982) y *Jornadas de alfabetización en telesecundaria para 1982* (1982). Miembro de la Academia Mexicana de la Educación.

+ Franco Melitón. Obpo. de Puebla.

Retrato y firma de Francisco Vargas y Gutiérrez

Remedios Varo

El ermitaño, óleo y nacar sobre masonite de Remedios Varo

Tránsito en espiral, obra de Remedios Varo

Vargas Machuca, Santos ◆ n. y ¿m.? en la ciudad de México (1775-¿1830?). Insurgente. Fue gobernador de la parcialidad de Santiago Tlatelolco. Durante la guerra de Independencia pidió autorización al virrey Francisco Xavier Venegas para instruir en el manejo de las armas a los indígenas de su jurisdicción y defender a la colonia, pero acusado de preparar un grupo insurgente debió huir de la capital de la Nueva España para unirse a las fuerzas rebeldes. Una vez consumada la independencia fue regidor de la ciudad de México.

Vargas y Rivera, Juan Manuel ◆ n. en Perú y m. en San Bartolomé, Chis. (?-1774). Fraile mercedario. Fue primer definidor, calificador de la Suprema y General Inquisición y teólogo consultor de su orden. Comendador en Panamá y obispo de Chiapas (1770-74). Fue designado obispo de Yucatán, pero murió antes de asumir ese cargo.

Vargas Saldaña, Mario ◆ n. en Boca del Río, Ver., y m. en el DF (1935-1995). Licenciado en derecho. Perteneció al PRI, donde fue secretario general de los Comités Directivos Estatales en Sinaloa y Veracruz y secretario general del comité directivo en el DF. Fue secretario de Profesionales y Técnicos de la CNOP. Se desempeñó como director general de Investigaciones Políticas y Sociales de la Secretaría de Gobernación. Tres veces diputado federal por el DF (1973-76, 1982-85 y 1988-91).

Vargas Zapata Luján Ponce de León, Diego de ◆ n. en España y m. en Nuevo México (¿1650?-1704). Llegó a la Nueva España en 1672 como correo real. Alcalde mayor de Teutila y de Tlalpujahua, gobernador y capitán general de Nuevo México (1691), reconquistó ese territorio, cuyos habitantes originales se habían rebelado desde 1680 y que volverían a hacerlo en 1692. En 1693 emprendió la segunda expedición de reconquista y la primera de exterminio contra los apaches; pasó tres años en prisión, acusado por el cabildo de Santa Fe, pero fue restituido y designado varias veces gobernador de Nuevo México. Dirigió numerosas campañas contra los indios de la región, en una de las cuales murió. Recibió el título de marqués de la Nava de Braziñas.

Vargaslugo Rangel, Elisa ◆ n. en Pachuca, Hgo. (¿1942?). Maestra (1964) y doctora (1972) en filosofía por la UNAM, de la que ha sido profesora e investigadora en el Instituto de Investigaciones Estéticas. Colaboradora de los *Anales del Instituto de Investigaciones Estéticas*, *Archivo Español del Arte* y otras publicaciones. Coautora de *El Colegio de San Ignacio de las Vizcaínas* (1987), *Bosquejos de México* (1987), *La construcción en el arte* (1987), *La colección pictórica del Banco Nacional de México* (1992), *Santa Prisca restaurada* (1990), *Hechizo de Oaxaca* (1991) y *Regionalización en el arte* (1992). Autora de *Portadas religiosas en México* (1969), *La iglesia de Santa Prisca de Taxco* (1972), *El claustro franciscano de Tlatelolco* (1975), *Juan Correa. Su vida y obra* (4 t., 1985-95) y *México Barroco* (1992), entre otros. Premio Universidad Nacional 1994. Miembro del Seminario de Cultura Mexicana (1983-) y del SNI. Miembro correspondiente de la Academia de Bellas Artes de Santa Isabel de Hungría, Sevilla e investigadora emérita de la UNAM desde 1995.

Varo, Remedios ◆ n. en España y m. en el DF (1913-1963). Pintora egresada de la Academia de San Fernando, de Madrid. En 1935 expuso en Barcelona con el grupo Logicófobo. Casada con el poeta Benjamín Péret, durante la guerra civil española viajó a París, donde conoció a los representantes del movimiento surrealista, al que se afilió. Llegó a México en 1942, cuando Francia fue ocupada por los nazis. En 1947, Péret volvió a Francia, pero su esposa decidió quedarse en México. En 1964 el INBA realizó una muestra retrospectiva de su obra completa y en 1966 el cineasta Jomi García Ascot realizó un documental sobre su trabajo. Entre sus cuadros se cuentan *Recuerdo de la Walkiria* (1938, con el que concurrió a la Exposición Surrealista de París), *Armonía* (1956), *Tailleur pour dames* (1957), *Vagabundo* (1958) y *Mimetismo* (1960).

Vasconcelos, Eduardo ◆ n. en Oaxaca, Oax. (¿1895?-1953). Licenciado en derecho por la Escuela Nacional de Jurisprudencia. Fue diputado federal y presidente de la gran comisión de la Cámara de Diputados, procurador de Justicia de Guerrero, secretario de gobierno del Estado de México, rector del Instituto Científico y Literario de Toluca, secretario de Gobernación (del 5 de septiembre de 1932 al 9 de mayo de 1934) y de Educación Pública (del 9 de mayo al 30 de noviembre de 1934) en el gobierno de Abelardo L. Rodríguez, ministro de México en Italia (1934-40), ministro de la Suprema Corte de Justicia de la Nación (1940-46) y gobernador interino de Oaxaca (1947-50), en

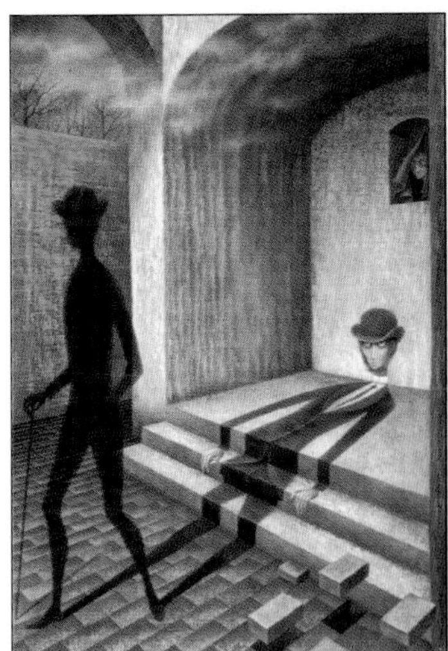

Fenómeno, obra de Remedios Varo

sustitución de Edmundo Sánchez Cano.

VASCONCELOS, JOSÉ ◆ n. en Oaxaca, Oax., y m. en el DF (1882-1959). Abogado. Presidió en 1909 el Ateneo de la Juventud, del que fue fundador. Participó en el movimiento maderista como uno de los secretarios del Centro Antirreeleccionista de México y fue codirector de *El Antirreeleccionista*. Agente de Madero en Washington y fundador del Partido Constitucionalista Progresista. Después del cuartelazo de Huerta, Carranza lo designó agente confidencial en Inglaterra y Francia. Director de la Escuela Nacional Preparatoria (1914), criticó a Carranza y éste ordenó su arresto, por lo que huyó a EUA. Asistió a la Convención de Aguascalientes y fue secretario de Instrucción Pública (del 6 de noviembre de 1914 al 16 de enero de 1915) en el gabinete de Eulalio Gutiérrez. En 1920 ofreció su apoyo al Plan de Agua Prieta y Adolfo de la Huerta lo designó jefe del Departamento Universitario y de Bellas Artes (del 9 de junio de 1920 al 2 de octubre de 1921). Impuso a la Universidad Nacional el actual escudo y el lema "Por mi raza hablará el espíritu". Obregón lo designó primer titular de la SEP (del 2 de octubre de 1921 al 2 de julio de 1924). Después de la firma de los Tratados de Bucareli condenó el asesinato del senador Field Jurado y renunció a su puesto. Nuevamente exiliado tras una campaña fallida por el gobierno de Oaxaca, en París y Madrid publicó la primera época de la revista *La Antorcha* (1924-25). Regresó a México en 1928 y un año después fue candidato a la Presidencia por el Partido Nacional Antirreeleccionista. Tras su derrota proclamó el Plan de Guaymas, mediante el cual llamó sin éxito a un levantamiento armado. Encarcelado después de promulgar su plan, fue liberado poco después, se exilió y en París volvió a publicar *La Antorcha*. Autor de ensayos, historia y filosofía: *Estudios indostánicos* (1920), *La raza cósmica* (1925), *Tratado de metafísica* (1929), *Breve historia de México* (1937) y *En el ocaso de mi vida* (1957); teatro: *Prometeo vencedor* (1916) y *Los robachicos* (1946); cuentos y relatos: *La sonata mágica* (1933), *La cita* (1945), *El viento de Bagdad* (1945) y *La flama* (1959); y memorias noveladas: *Ulises criollo* (1935), *La tormenta* (1936), *El desastre* (1938) y *El proconsulado* (1939), entre otras obras. Fue miembro de la Academia Mexicana (de la Lengua) y fundador de El Colegio Nacional.

VASCONCELOS ALDANA, RUBÉN ◆ n. en Oaxaca, Oax. (1910). Médico titulado en la UNAM (1934). Subdirector de la Escuela Superior de Medicina Rural (1945-47), director de la Vocacional de Ciencias Biológicas (1947), subdirector del Hospital General de México (1951-53), jefe del Departamento Médico de la Dirección de Asistencia en el DF (1953-54), secretario general auxiliar de la UNAM (1954-60), director de Servicios Médicos y Sociales (1961-62) y jefe del Servicio del Trabajo de la SOP (1953-65), director de la Clínica de la Conducta (1965), de Ación Social Educativa (1965-70), así como coordinador del Servicio Nacional de Orientación Vocacional de la SEP (1968-70). Autor de *Cartas médicas* (1969), *Evolución de la medicina* (1970) y *Gerontorama de un médico* (1976). Presidente del Colegio de Médicos Eduardo Liceaga (1950-52) y director fundador de su órgano, *Panorama Médico de México*. Miembro de la Academia Nacional de Medicina y presidente de la Sociedad Mexicana de Historia y Filosofía de la Medicina (1974-75).

VASCONCELOS CRUZ, HÉCTOR ◆ n. en el DF (1945). Licenciado en ciencias políticas por la Universidad de Harvard (1968) y doctor en historia política por la de Cambridge (1972). Miembro del PRI, fue asesor de la Dirección General del IEPES (1975-76). Profesor e investigador de la UNAM (1973-76), director general de Difusión Fiscal de la Secretaría de Hacienda (1976-78), director general del Festival Internacional Cervantino (1977-82), coordinador general de Asuntos Especiales Internacionales de la SRE (1979-81), secretario ejecutivo del Fondo Nacional para la Cultura y las Artes (1989-95) y secretario general del Consejo de la Crónica de la Ciudad de México (1989-). Premio Rey de España (1985) por el mejor trabajo sobre el quinto centenario de la llegada de los españoles a América, con los programas *Historiadores novohispanos*, *Inquisición en la Nueva España*, *Evangelización en la Nueva España* y *Educación en la Nueva España*.

VÁSQUEZ COLMENARES, PEDRO ◆ n. en Tuxtepec, Oax. (1934). Hijo de Genaro Vicente Vásquez Quiroz. Licenciado en derecho por la UNAM (1958). Desde 1963 es miembro del PRI, en el que ha ocupado diversos puestos directivos. Miembro del Consejo Técnico Consultivo de la CNC (1968-70). En la UNAM fue profesor y subdirector general de Servicios Escolares. Ha sido agente del Ministerio Público (1959-64), empleado de la Tesorería de la Federación y de la Secretaría del Trabajo y Previsión Social (1960-63), oficial mayor de la Secretaría de la Presidencia (1971-73), director general de Aeropuertos y Servicios Auxiliares (1973-75), subsecretario de Nuevos Centros de Población Ejidal de la Secretaría de la Reforma Agraria (1976), director general de Aeroméxico (1976-80), gobernador de Oaxaca (1980-85), director general de Investigación y Seguridad Nacional de la Secretaría de Gobernación (1985-88) y embajador en Guatemala (1989-95). Es miembro de la Sociedad Mexicana de Geografía y

José Vasconcelos

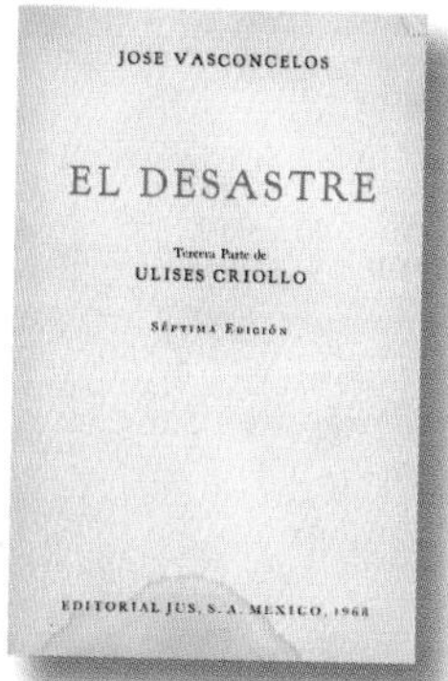

Libro de José Vasconcelos

Héctor Vasconcelos

Estadística, de la Asociación Nacional de Abogados, de la Academia Mexicana de Derecho Internacional y de la Academia Iberoamericana de Derecho Aeronáutico y del Espacio.

Vásquez Quiroz, Genaro Vicente ◆ n. en Oaxaca, Oax., y m. en el DF (1892-1967). Licenciado en derecho por la Escuela Nacional de Jurisprudencia. Fue diputado federal (1918), senador de la República, gobernador interino (1925-28) y constitucional de Oaxaca (1928-32), director de Derechos Agrarios del Departamento de Asuntos Agrarios y Colonización, miembro de la comisión que redactó el Plan Sexenal (1933), secretario general del DDF, jefe del Departamento de Trabajo (del 18 de junio de 1935 al 20 de junio de 1937) y procurador general de la República con Lázaro Cárdenas, así como ministro de la Suprema Corte de Justicia. Fue promotor del primer Congreso Indigenista Panamericano y fundador del Departamento de Asuntos Indígenas. Se le atribuye la frase "Al indio hay que darle la razón, aunque no la tenga". Autor de *Biografía de Juárez*, *Historia de Oaxaca*, *El camino de la reconstrucción*, *Doctrinas y realidades en la legislación para indios*, *Sociología del estado de Oaxaca* y *Biografía de Morelos*. Miembro del Consejo Vitalicio de la Sociedad Mexicana de Geografía y Estadística y de la Academia Mexicana de Derecho Internacional.

Interior de la catedral de San Pedro en el Vaticano

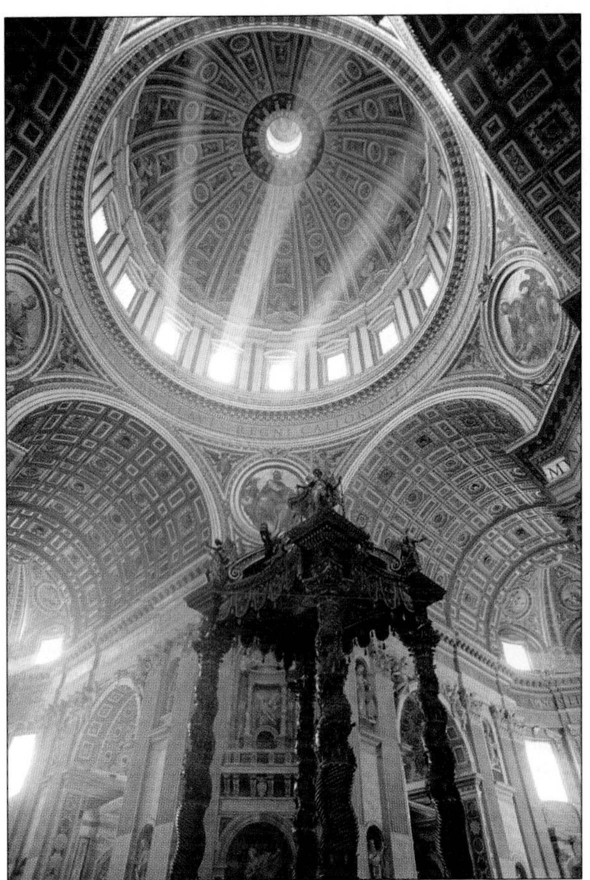

Vásquez Ramírez, Arnulfo ◆ n. en Patambán, Mich. (1938). Filósofo por el Seminario de Zamora (1957). Agricultor y ganadero. Pertenece al PAN desde 1964, donde ha sido presidente del Comité Municipal de Zamora (1984-87). Presidente municipal de Zamora, diputado federal (1991-94) y secretario de la Comisión de Agricultura y Recursos Hidráulicos.

Vaticano, El ◆ Ciudad-Estado de Europa. La totalidad de su territorio se halla dentro de la capital italiana, con excepción de la residencia papal de verano, situada en Castelgandolfo, municipio situado 25 km al sureste de Roma. Su nombre oficial es Estado de la Ciudad del Vaticano o Santa Sede, por ser el centro espiritual de la Iglesia Católica Apostólica Romana (☛). Superficie: 0.44 km^2. Habitantes: 1,000 en 1995. La moneda es la lira italiana y los idiomas oficiales son el latín y el italiano. El jefe de Estado y de gobierno es el papa en funciones, quien igualmente reúne en su persona los poderes Legislativo y Judicial. *Historia*: El Vaticano tiene su origen en los Estados Pontificios, territorios que quedaron en poder de la Iglesia al desmembrarse el Imperio Romano. En México, durante el periodo colonial, las relaciones entre la Iglesia y el Estado fueron normadas por el Regio Patronato Indiano, constituido por tres bulas expedidas por los papas Alejandro VI y Julio II, mediante las cuales se reconocían como derechos de la Corona española enviar misioneros que evangelizaran a los indios, construir iglesias, hospitales y monasterios; elaborar ternas de candidatos a arzobispos, obispos, abades, canónigos y otros ministros, que luego debían ser presentadas al El Vaticano, que finalmente elegiría a quienes debían asumir las diversas dignidades; recolectar los diezmos, que fueron una contribución obligatoria hasta 1833, y entregarlos a la Iglesia. Otros privilegios del trono de Madrid fueron la posibilidad de revisar las sentencias eclesiásticas y modificarlas, si así lo deseaba el poder civil, y la exigencia del pase regio, facultad de la Corona para permitir o impedir la circulación de documentos pontificios. A fines del siglo XVIII, como consecuencia de la revolución francesa, se creó la República romana, que privó al papado de casi todos sus poderes. Napoleón, en 1807, incorporó los dominios del Pontificado a Francia, pero a la caída de Bonaparte se restableció el poder de los papas, que en los años siguientes se opusieron a la unificación de Italia, temerosos de quedar bajo dominio del poder civil. Al consumarse la independencia de México, se supuso que las atribuciones que concedía al trono español el Regio Patronato Indiano pasarían al nuevo gobierno o que, por lo menos, no habría dificultad para establecer un concordato entre el imperio mexicano y El Vaticano. En marzo de 1822 se reunieron los obispos mexicanos y resolvieron que había cesado "el uso del Patronato que en sus iglesias se concedió por la Silla Apostólica a los Reyes de España" y que era "necesario esperar igual concesión de la Santa Sede" en beneficio del gobierno imperial. Con el fin de definir las relaciones entre la Iglesia y el nuevo Estado, en 1823 el Congreso Constituyente envió a José María Marchena como representante ante el papa León XIII, a quien debía informar que la religión única de los mexicanos era la católica. El pontífice, sin embargo, se negó a reconocer la independencia de México, donde la jerarquía optó por mantener una prudente espera. Otro representante mexicano ante el trono papal fue José María Michelena. En 1825 el gobierno envió a Roma al clérigo Francisco Vázquez, quien debía gestionar el establecimiento de una relación regular con El Vaticano, donde se presentó hasta 1830. Mientras el país se iba quedando sin obispos, Vázquez, quien había renunciado a su misión durante la presidencia de Vicente Guerrero, recibió del gobierno de Anastasio Bustamante el nombramiento de enviado extraordinario y ministro plenipotenciario. El papa Gregorio XVI no lo recibió como diplomático, pues no reconocía la independencia mexicana y, por lo tanto, rechazó toda posibilidad de establecer un concordato. En cambio, el pontífice accedió a preconizar *motu proprio* (esto es, sin que tal acto implicara el reconocimiento del gobierno mexicano) a los obispos de Chiapas, Linares, Guadalajara, Michoacán y Puebla. Para esta diócesis designó al mismo Vázquez, quien fue consagrado en Roma y él mismo, a su regreso, se encargó de consagrar a los otros obispos nombrados. Para que de acuerdo con la legislación mexicana procedieran esos nombramientos, se hizo necesario expedir la ley del 16 de mayo de 1831, que autorizaba a la Iglesia para hacer tales designaciones. En diciembre de 1833 el Congreso aprobó una ley que autorizaba al presidente y a los gobernadores de los estados a "ejercer las atribuciones que las leyes coloniales concedían a los virreyes, presidentes de audiencias o gobernadores" y establecía sanciones para los dignatarios que se negaran a acatarla. Lo anterior era una manera de reivindicar los derechos del Patronato en favor de la nación. Todas estas medidas ocasionaron que Ignacio Tejeda, quien era embajador de Nueva Granada ante El Vaticano y desde 1831 encargado de negocios de México ante la sede papal, renunciara a su gestión en noviembre de 1833, por lo cual se designó a Lorenzo de Zavala encargado de la legación mexicana en Roma, aunque nunca visitó esta ciudad. Santa Anna ocupó nuevamente la Presidencia y desechó las leyes reformistas, nombró ministro de Justicia al obispo de Michoacán, anuló la orden de expulsión contra el obispo de Puebla, aceptó la bula papal que designaba obispo de Yucatán a José María Guerra, nombramiento que el Congreso había rechazado, y ordenó reabrir la Universidad y otras instituciones que volvieron a manos de la Iglesia. Entre mayo y agosto de 1835 el colombiano Tejeda se encargó nuevamente de los asuntos mexicanos en la sede papal, hasta que a Manuel Díez de Bonilla se le designó (septiembre de 1835) enviado extraordinario y ministro plenipotenciario, carácter con el que lo recibió el pontífice el 9 de diciembre de 1836 y de esta manera quedó reconocida la independencia de México. Sin embargo, Díez de Bonilla, quien había gestionado exitosamente el reconocimiento del gobierno de México por El Vaticano, fracasó en su intento de negociar el restablecimiento del patronato y en 1839 fue sustituido por José María Montoya, quien fue representante diplomático ante la sede pontificia hasta 1848, año en que la segunda República romana quitó nuevamente el poder al papa, hasta que al año siguiente se lo restituyeron Francia y Austria. Ignacio Valdivieso fue ministro plenipotenciario en Roma (1848-49) y José María Montoya volvió a ocuparse de los asuntos de México en El Vaticano en 1850, como encargado de negocios. En 1851 llegó de Roma el primer delegado apostólico, Luis Clementi, quien permaneció en México hasta 1861, cuando junto con el obispo de Puebla, Pelagio Antonio de Labastida y Dávalos, fue expulsado por el gobierno de Juárez. Durante el último periodo de Santa Anna en el poder (1853-55) fungió como embajador ante El Vaticano Manuel Larráinzar. En abril de 1857, el gobierno liberal designó a Ezequiel Montes enviado extraordinario y ministro plenipotenciario en Roma, a donde llegó en junio. La Iglesia se negó a obedecer la Constitución de 1857 y a fines de ese año, al grito de "Religión y fueros", inició junto a los conservadores la guerra de los Tres Años. En ese lapso, los liberales promulgaron las Leyes de Reforma, que consumaron la separación entre la Iglesia y el Estado, establecieron la libertad de cultos, suprimieron el

El Vaticano es el centro espiritual de la Iglesia Católica Apostólica Romana

poder económico del clero y reglamentaron su injerencia en la educación. El Vaticano reconoció a los gobiernos conservadores, que acreditaron como representante diplomático a Pelagio Antonio de Labastida y Dávalos (1859-60), al que Ezequiel Montes se negó a entregarle los archivos de la legación. Al producirse la invasión francesa (1862-67), la Iglesia católica recobró en México algunas posiciones. El 8 de julio de 1862, después de dos siglos y medio de gestiones ante El Vaticano, Pío IX canonizó a Felipe de Jesús. Con Maximiliano, la Iglesia y El Vaticano tuvieron una estrecha colaboración hasta que se promulgó la llamada ley de tolerancia de cultos, que ocasionó el regreso a Roma del segundo delegado papal, Pedro Francisco Meglia, quien duró apenas medio año en su cargo (diciembre de 1864 a junio de 1865). El resultado de estas diferencias fue una ruptura entre el imperio y El Vaticano, por lo que Ignacio Aguilar y Marocho, embajador imperial ante el trono pontificio (1864-65), cesó en su función. En 1865, Maximiliano envió a Roma una Comisión de Plenipotenciarios integrada por el obispo Francisco de la Concepción Ramírez, Joaquín Degollado y Joaquín Velázquez de León, quienes presentaron una fórmula de avenimiento que fue rechazada por El Vaticano. También en busca de un arreglo se presentó Agustín Fischer ante Pío IX, pero fracasó en su gestión oficiosa. En 1870, con el triunfo de las fuerzas del Piamonte quedó unificada Italia con Roma como capital. El papa se negó a aceptar

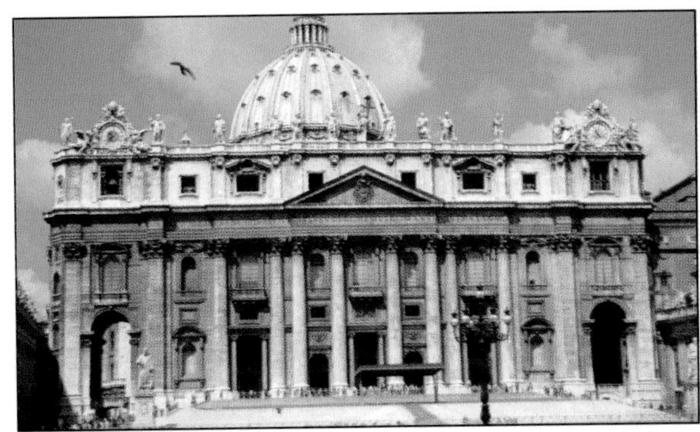
En enero de 1929 el Vaticano se convirtió en Estado

la hegemonía de los triunfadores, que le quitaban todo poder temporal y reducían los dominios del pontífice a El Vaticano, Letrán y la villa de Castelgandolfo. Durante el porfiriato, habiéndose mantenido vigentes las Leyes de Reforma, las relaciones entre la Iglesia y el Estado tendieron a normalizarse. La jerarquía se mostraba respetuosa de las autoridades civiles y éstas no impidieron los actos de culto externo. En esas condiciones vino a México un visitador apostólico, Nicolás Averardi, quien permaneció en el país de mayo de 1896 a diciembre de 1899. En marzo 1902, con la intención de tramitar el establecimiento de una delegación apostólica, vino el camarlengo privado del papa León XIII, Ricardo Sanz de Samper, quien en los dos meses que estuvo aquí desplegó una gran actividad, gestionó infructuosamente el restablecimiento de relaciones diplomáticas entre México y El Vaticano, pero logró que el gobierno mexicano permitiera la reapertura de la delegación pontificia que año y medio después, el 5 de enero de 1904, ocuparía Domingo Serafini, ya como delegado papal. Le sucedieron José Ridolfi (1905-11) y Tomás Pío Boggiani (1912-14). Entre 1915 y 1921, el delegado apostólico en Washington fue encargado de negocios para México. El 22 de julio de 1921 hubo nuevamente delegado apostólico, al llegar a la capital mexicana Ernesto Filippi, quien fue expulsado del país en enero de 1923. Durante su gestión, en septiembre de 1921, los delegados de la Asociación Católica de la Juventud Mejicana tuvieron una recepción de héroes en el Congreso Internacional de Juventudes Católicas, celebrado en Roma, donde el papa Benedicto XV los recibió en audiencia privada y ofició para ellos una misa especial. A su regreso promovieron exitosamente la erección del Monumento a Cristo Rey en el cerro del Cubilete, debido a una colecta popular que permitió al delegado apostólico poner la primera piedra el 11 de enero de 1923, en un acto multitudinario en el que los asistentes recibieron indulgencia plenaria del papa. Filippi fue formalmente sustituido el 1 de abril de 1925, cuando llegó a la ciudad de México Serafín Cimino, quien mes y medio después tuvo que abandonar el país por enfermedad, sin que las autoridades le permitieran regresar. Desatadas nuevamente las hostilidades entre la Iglesia y el Estado mexicano, en mayo de 1925 se fundó la Liga Nacional Defensora de la Libertad Religiosa. Giorgio Giuseppe Caruana fue el siguiente delegado, del 5 de marzo de 1926 al 12 de mayo del mismo año, cuando fue expulsado por las autoridades mexicanas. El 2 de julio Calles promulgó las reformas al Código Penal y la Ley de Cultos, que restringían las actividades eclesiásticas y establecían severas penas por incumplimiento. Este hecho generalizó el enfrentamiento entre la Iglesia y el Estado (☛ *Cristeros*), que fue desde actos de rebeldía civil hasta la lucha armada. En enero de 1929, el papa Pío XI firmó con el gobierno italiano los Acuerdos de Letrán, con lo que El Vaticano se convirtió en Estado. Como sucesor de Caruana, el papa nombró en junio a un mexicano, Leopoldo Ruiz y Flores, arzobispo de Morelia que se convirtió en delegado apostólico el 10 de octubre de 1929 y fue desterrado el 4 de octubre de 1932. Ruiz y Flores volvió en junio y fue recibido por el presidente Emilio Portes Gil. La primera entrevista con el jefe del Poder Ejecutivo se realizó el día 12 y el 22, después de otra reunión con la máxima autoridad civil, el delegado apostólico anunció que el conflicto había sido solucionado. Ruiz y Flores, aunque exiliado nuevamente (1932-37), continuó como representante papal hasta su muerte (1941). Le sucedió como encargado de negocios el arzobispo de México, Luis María Martínez (1942-49), quien entregó la delegación a Guillermo Piani, enviado de El Vaticano (1949-56), a quien sucedió Luigi Raimondi (1957-67). Otros delegados pontificios han sido el cardenal Guido dei Mestri (1967-70), Carlo Martini (1970-73), Mario Pío Gaspari (1973-77) y Sotero Sanz Villalba, que permaneció en el cargo unos cuantos días, del 26 de noviembre de 1977 a enero de 1978. El 7 de febrero de 1978 llegó a México el último delegado apostólico, Girolamo Prigione, a quien durante casi dos décadas le tocaría estar en el centro de un cambio radical en las relaciones entre la Iglesia y el Estado y entre México y El Vaticano. En 1979 visitó el país el papa Juan Pablo II. Después de un proceso electoral severamente impugnado, Carlos Salinas de Gortari asumió el poder en 1988. Urgido de apoyos y legitimación, a su toma de posesión invitó a un grupo de dignatarios eclesiásticos y al delegado apostólico Girolamo Prigione. Empezó así un proceso que culminó en 1992, al promulgarse las reformas constitucionales

El Papa Juan Pablo II

y la ley reglamentaria que reconocieron personalidad jurídica a las agrupaciones religiosas y derechos limitados a los ministros de culto. Un año antes, el papa Juan Pablo II hizo una segunda visita a México. El lunes 22 de septiembre de 1992 se anunció el establecimiento de relaciones diplomáticas entre ambos Estados, "a nivel de embajada por parte de México y de nunciatura apostólica por parte de la Santa Sede". Embajador de México fue designado Enrique Olivares Santana y El Vaticano informó que Girolamo Prigione, hasta entonces delegado apostólico, sería a partir del 12 de octubre el nuncio. El gobierno mexicano aceptó dar título de "nuncio" al embajador vaticano, pero rechazó la pretensión de otorgarle el decanato del cuerpo diplomático. Pese a ser representante de un Estado extranjero, en nombre de todos los católicos mexicanos a él le correspondió, el 25 de noviembre de 1992, presentar a la Secretaría de Gobernación la solicitud de registro de la Iglesia Católica Apostólica Romana. En 1996, Prigione fue sustituido en la nunciatura por Justo Mullor. En 1993 el papa estuvo en Mérida y en 1999 efectuó su cuarta visita al país.

VATICANUS ◆ Códice llamado también *Códice Vaticano B*, *Códice Vaticano 3773 B* o *Códice Vaticano Ritual*. Desde 1570 pertenece al acervo de la Biblioteca Apostólica Vaticana. De origen probablemente nahua prehispánico, procede de la región cholulteca o de la Mixtequilla (Puebla-Tlaxcala). Está elaborado sobre 96 planas de piel de venado. Es de carácter calendárico, astronómico y mitológico.

VÁZQUEZ, AGUSTÍN ◆ n. en Villa Corona y m. en Jiménez, Chih. (1836-1912). Militar. En 1865, el presidente Benito Juárez lo nombró jefe político del distrito de Hidalgo, Chihuahua, y comandante militar de la línea sur del estado. Ocupó Parral (1865), de donde fue desalojado por una ofensiva francesa. En marzo de 1866 recuperó la plaza. Al triunfo de la República dejó el ejército y más tarde fue diputado a la Legislatura chihuahuense.

VÁZQUEZ, ANA MARÍA ◆ n. en el DF (1961). Dramaturga. Estudió letras en la UNAM y en la escuela de escritores de la Sogem. Su primera obra fue *Piel de cemento* (1991), a la que siguieron *Pan de muerto* (1992, con la cual obtuvo el Premio Nacional del INBA 1991) y *La dama de las camelias* (1992).

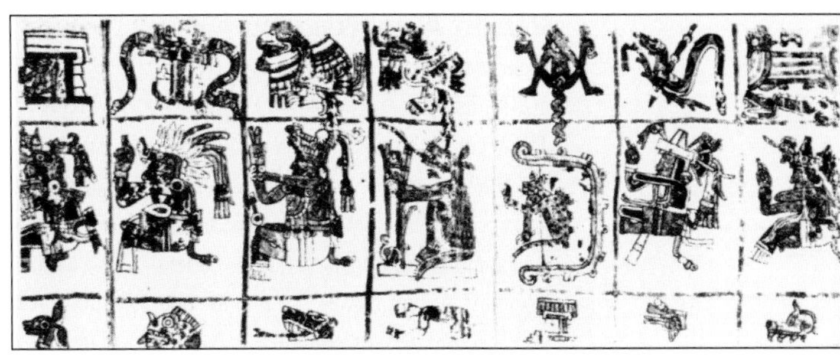

Códice Vaticano B, de la región poblano-Tlaxcalteca, en piel plegada

VÁZQUEZ, ALONSO ◆ n. en España y m. en la ciudad de México (¿1565?-1608). Pintor. Llegó a la Nueva España en 1603 en el séquito del virrey Juan de Mendoza y Luna. Autor de los cuadros del altar mayor de la Universidad y de un *Martirio de Santa Margarita* que se encuentra en la capilla del Palacio de los Virreyes.

VÁZQUEZ, CECILIA ◆ n. en el DF (1967). Pintora. Licenciada en artes visuales por la UNAM (1993) con estudios de maestría en bellas artes en la Universidad de Massachusets. Fue gerenta de la Galería Azul (1990-93). Asistió al primer Encuentro de Arte Contemporáneo en la Casa Dusmet de Chinchón, España, de la Fundación Arte y Artistas Contemporáneos (1997). Ha participado en una veintena de muestras colectivas y ha presentado cinco exposiciones individuales en la ciudad de México. Está incluida en una exposición itinerante para recorrer Estados Unidos como parte de las fiestas del milenio. Beca para Jóvenes Creadores del Fonca (1992-93 y 1997-98) y Beca Fulbright (1999-2001).

VÁZQUEZ, JORGE ADALBERTO ◆ n. en Alaquines, SLP, y m. en el DF (1886-1959). Escritor. Estudió derecho. Fue profesor de literatura en el Instituto Científico y Literario de San Luis Potosí y en la Universidad Autónoma de San Luis (1916-59). En 1918 se trasladó a la ciudad de México y fue subjefe de los departamentos de Bellas Artes y de Bibliotecas de la SEP (1925-32) y secretario particular de Miguel Álvarez Acosta, director del INBA (1954-58). Autor de poesía: *Rincón del olvido* (1912), *Senda huraña* (1917), *El espíritu intacto* (1923), *La sombra invisible* (1944), *Parva. Poemas no coleccionados* (1945), *La sed inexhausta* (1947), *Arriba brillaba el sol* (1948) y *Voz en el viento* (1950); y ensayo: *Por campos ubérrimos* (1940) y *Perfil y herencia de la poesía mexicana* (1955). Miembro fundador de la Academia Potosina de Artes y Ciencias.

VÁZQUEZ, JOSÉ MARÍA ◆ n. en la ciudad de México (?-?). Pintor que trabajó a fines del siglo XVIII y principios del XIX. En la Academia de San Carlos fue discípulo de Rafael Ximeno y Gerónimo Antonio Gil. En 1801 fue designado teniente de director de Pintura y dirigió interinamente (1825) la Academia de San Carlos (1825). Autor de *Sacrificio de Isaac* (1796), *El niño Juan Crisóstomo Martínez* (1800), *Retrato de María Luisa Gonzaga Fonserrada y Labarrieta* (1806), *Retrato de María Antonia Dávalos y Aguilar* (1814), *Calvario* (1817), *Virgen de Guadalupe*, *San Ignacio y Jesús con los niños* (para la iglesia de Loreto), *San Antonio* (para el Sagrario Metropolitano) y *La santa cena* (para la catedral).

VÁZQUEZ, SERAFÍN ◆ n. en San Martín Xaltocan, Tlax. (1922). Sacerdote ordenado en 1948. Estudió en el Seminario Palafoxiano de Puebla. Ha sido vicario cooperador de las parroquias de Atlixco y Analco, superior del equipo de misioneros diocesanos, presidente de las misiones internas y de indígenas, párroco de Santa Teresita de Puebla, canónigo del cabildo de Nuestra Señora de Ocotlán, obispo de Huejutla (1968-78) y obispo de Ciudad Guzmán (1978-).

Francisco Vázquez de Coronado

Francisco Vázquez Gómez

VÁZQUEZ ÁVILA, FERNANDO ◆ n. en Rioverde, SLP, y m. en el DF (1891-1977). Estudió en el Colegio Militar. En 1912 combatió la rebelión orozquista en Nuevo León y al año siguiente se incorporó a las fuerzas de Venustiano Carranza. Comandó la artillería contra los villistas en la batalla del Ébano. Fue subdirector de Armamento y Municiones (1948) y director de Ingenieros del Ejército Mexicano (1953); cofundador del Partido Auténtico de la Revolución Mexicana (1954), general de división (1963) y diputado federal (1967-70). Presidió la Asociación del Colegio Militar (1931).

VÁZQUEZ CANO, JOSÉ FRANCISCO ◆ n. en Guadalajara, Jal., y m. en el DF (1895-1961). Compositor, pianista y chelista graduado en el Conservatorio Nacional de Música. Fue alumno de Rafael J. Tello, Ignacio y César del Castillo, Horacio Ávila y Julián Carrillo. Estudió composición con el profesor Bortelein, de la Escuela Internacional de París. Profesor de la Facultad de Música de la UNAM. Fue fundador y director de la Escuela Libre de Música, fundador y director de la Escuela de Música y Declamación (1920-61), fundador de la Compañía Mexicana de Ópera (1926), cofundador de la Facultad de Música de la UNAM (1929) y codirector, con José Rocabruna, de la la Orquesta Sinfónica de la UNAM (1936). Autor de una *Suite para instrumentos de arco* (1927).

VÁZQUEZ CANO, LUIS IGNACIO ◆ n. en Chihuahua, Chih. (1949). Licenciado en administración de empresas por la Universidad Iberoamericana (1973) y maestro en administración pública por la Universidad Internacional de Florida (1981). Profesor de la Universidad Iberoamericana (1973-85), del Instituto de Fomento Cooperativo de la Secretaría de Comercio (1976) y del INAP (1979-86). Ha sido jefe del Departamento de Sistemas de la Dirección General de Registro Agrario Nacional de la SRA (1973-76), subdirector de Programación y Presupuesto de la Secretaría de Hacienda (1976-79), director de Sistemas de Administración de Personal (1979-82), coordinador de Organización del Gobierno Federal (1983), director general de Modernización Administrativa (1984-85) y director general de Servicio Civil de la Secretaría de Programación (1985-88), así como subsecretario B (1988-90) y subsecretario A de la Secretaría de la Contraloría General de la Federación (1990-94).

VÁZQUEZ CISNEROS, PEDRO ◆ n. en Tapalpa y m. en Guadalajara, Jal. (1895-1969). Periodista. Licenciado en derecho graduado en 1916. Durante la cristiada fundó el periódico *La Época*, en Guadalajara, pero poco después se exilió en Estados Unidos. Fue director-gerente fundador de *El Occidental* (1944-48) y colaborador de *Excélsior* y de la cadena García Valseca con la columna "Observatorio", que firmaba con sus iniciales. Autor de *Balas perdidas*.

VÁZQUEZ DE CORONADO, FRANCISCO ◆ n. en España y m. en la ciudad de México (1510-1554). Sobrino del virrey Antonio de Mendoza. Llegó a la Nueva España en 1535. Hacia 1538 fue nombrado miembro vitalicio y regidor del cabildo de la ciudad de México y gobernador de Nueva Galicia. En 1540, al mando de una fuerza de españoles, salió de Compostela hacia el norte con la idea de encontrar las Siete Ciudades de Cíbola y Quivira que Marcos de Niza creyó ver un año antes. Recorrió la costa del actual estado de Sonora y en río yaqui fundó la Villa de los Corazones, que fue la primera población del noroeste del virreinato. Más tarde recorrió el noroeste de Chihuahua, el sureste de Nuevo México, el oeste de Texas, el noroeste de Oklahoma y el sur de Kansas, sin encontrar las ciudades de oro. Volvió a Nueva Galicia en 1542 y reasumió la gubernatura. Poco después reprimió una sublevación de indios en Ostotipac. Fue procurador mayor y regidor de la ciudad de México (1545-54).

VÁZQUEZ DE ESPINOSA, ANTONIO ◆ n. y m. en España (?-1630). Fraile carmelita. Recorrió Perú y la Nueva España como misionero catequista y regresó a España en 1622, como censor de la Inquisición. Autor de *Confesionario general, luz y guía del cielo y método para poder confesar, Descripción de las Indias Occidentales, Viaje y navegación del año de 1622 que hizo la flota de Nueva España y Honduras* (1623), *Sumario de indulgencias* (1623) y *Circunstancias para los tratos y contratos de las Indias del Perú y Nueva España* (1624).

VÁZQUEZ GÓMEZ, EMILIO ◆ n. en Tula, Tams., y m. en el DF (1858-1926). Licenciado en derecho por la Escuela Nacional de Jurisprudencia (1885). Fue síndico del ayuntamiento de Saltillo (1880). En 1888 y 1892 publicó sendos folletos contra las reelecciones de Porfirio Díaz. Presidente del Centro Antirreeleccionista (mayo de 1909), fundó filiales del mismo en toda la República. Fue uno de los organizadores de la convención de abril de 1910 de los partidos nacionales Democrático y Antirreeleccionsta y precandidato a la Presidencia de la República. Fue brevemente encarcelado y más tarde se exilió en Estados Unidos. Al triunfo del movimiento maderista se opuso al licenciamiento de las fuerzas revolucionarias. Secretario de Gobernación (del 26 de mayo al 2 de agosto de 1911) del presidente interino Francisco León de la Barra, renunció por considerar a ese gobierno como prolongación del de Porfirio Díaz. En la convención del Partido Constitucional Progresista fue desplazado del maderismo, acusado de apoyar las demandas de Emiliano Zapata. En 1912 se levantó en armas con Pascual Orozco y, tras la derrota de éste, se exilió. Se le atribuye la frase: "Revolución que transa, revolución que se pierde."

VÁZQUEZ GÓMEZ, FRANCISCO ◆ n. en Tula, Tams., y m. en el DF (1860-1933). Hermano del anterior. Graduado en la Escuela Nacional de Medicina, de la que fue profesor. Estudió en Europa y después se estableció en la ciudad de México, donde fue médico personal de Porfirio Díaz. Antirreeleccionista, fue candidato a la vicepresidencia de la República, designado por la convención de los partidos nacionales Antirreeleccionista y Democrático (1910). Tras las elecciones de ese año se exilió en EUA junto con el resto de los maderistas, aunque se opuso a la lucha armada. Secretario de Relaciones Exteriores (del 10 de marzo al 21 de mayo de 1911) en el gobierno provisional de Madero. Se opuso al licenciamiento de las tropas revolucionarias. Secretario de Instrucción Pública (del 26 de mayo al 27 de octubre de 1911) en el gabinete de León de la Barra, se alejó del maderismo luego de que la convención del Partido Constitucional Progresista impulsara la fórmula Madero-Pino Suárez. En 1912 tuvo un acercamiento político con Zapata. Se opuso a Huerta aunque no se unió a la revolución constitucionalista, pues tenía marcadas diferencias con Villa y Carranza, por lo que se exilió en Estados Unidos. En 1918 Zapata le propuso la jefatura nacional de la rebelión propuesta por las reformas al Plan de Ayala, con la esperanza de que todos los anticarrancistas se unieran bajo su mando. Vázquez Gómez declinó la oferta y no regresó a México sino hasta 1929. Autor de *Memorias políticas (1909-1913)* (1933).

VÁZQUEZ HERRERA, LORENZO ◆ n. en Tlaquiltenango y m. en Buenavista de Cuéllar, Mor. (1879-1917). Jornalero de la hacienda de Tenextepango, fue alistado por leva en el ejército federal y conoció a Emiliano Zapata. En febrero de 1911 se unió al levantamiento de Gabriel Tepepa y en marzo pasó a las filas de Pablo Torres Burgos y de Zapata, con quienes participó en las tomas de Tlaquiltenango y Jojutla y en el sitio y toma de Cuautla. Fue uno de los firmantes del Plan de Ayala. Combatió al huertismo y tomó parte en los sitios y ocupaciones de Santa Rosa Treinta y Zacatepec, de cuyo ingenio fue administrador. En agosto de 1914 fue sustituto del gobernador provisional de Morelos, Genovevo de la O; estuvo en el cargo hasta 1916, cuando Cuernavaca fue tomada por los carrancistas. Su derrota le granjeó la desconfianza de Zapata; fue acusado de traición y murió ahorcado.

VÁZQUEZ HUMASQUÉ, ADOLFO ◆ n. en España y m. en el DF (1887-1975). Egresado de la Escuela Especial de Ingenieros Agrónomos. Ocupó diversos puestos en el gobierno republicano español, entre ellos los de inspector del Banco Hipotecario, director del Instituto de Reforma Agraria (1931 y 1936) y subsecretario de Agricultura. Llegó exiliado a México en 1939 y se dedicó al cultivo de viñedos y olivares en Baja California y Michoacán. Fue coautor del proyecto de ley del seguro agrícola y ganadero.

VÁZQUEZ JUÁREZ, DIEGO ◆ n. en San Francisco Caxonos, Oax. (1933). Profesor egresado de la Escuela Nacional de Maestros (1955). Trabaja para el Instituto Nacional Indigenista, en el que es coordinador estatal de Oaxaca. Ha participado en acciones de desarrollo comunitario de 16 etnias oaxaqueñas, así como con coras y huicholes de Nayarit y Jalisco y con tepehuanes y nahuas de Durango. Colaboró en la reubicación de los chinantecos desplazados por la construcción de la presa Cerro del Oro. En 1987 recibió la presea Manel Gamio al Mérito Indigenista del INI.

VÁZQUEZ LIRA, ALEJO ◆ n. en Tulantepec, Hgo. (1928). Caricaturista. Estudió dibujo publicitario en la Academia de San Carlos. Ha sido cartonista político de *Excélsior*, *Sucesos*, *Diario de México*, *El Heraldo de México*, *unomásuno* y *Página Uno*. Ha sido ilustrador de algunas columnas y libros de Raúl Prieto, como *Madre Academia*.

VÁZQUEZ LOMBERA, JUAN ◆ n. en Progreso de Obregón, Hgo. (1940). Ingeniero egresado del IPN (1962), donde fue profesor. Catedrático fundador de la ENEP-Cuautitlán. Se inició en la industria automotriz después de recibir capacitación en Columbus, Indiana, para después desarrollarse en el campo de la industria textil y la aplicación del diseño mecánico en el campo alimentario. Ha diseñado, fabricado e instalado más de 70 plantas completas para diferentes procesos de tratamiento y envase de alimentos, además de 4,000 máquinas de proceso con tecnología y diseño propios. Su proceso hidrotérmico para envasar mango le valió un reconocimiento del Departamento de Agricultura de Estados Unidos. A los 19 años obtuvo el Primer Lugar en el concurso Ford Motor Company de Artes Manuales 1959, con modelos a escala de maquinaria agrícola. Bird's Eye de México le brindó un reconocimiento por sus 25 años de servicio en la fabricación de maquinaria y la Asociación Mexicana de Ingenieros Mecánicos y Electricistas le otorgó el Testimonio a la Excelencia Profesional y Mención Honorífica. Premio Nacional de Ciencias y Artes (1994).

VÁZQUEZ LÓPEZ, ELOÍ ◆ n. en Oaxaca, Oax. (1955). Arquitecto egresado de la Universidad Autónoma Benito Juárez de Oaxaca (1978) y maestro en planificación y desarrollo regional por el Instituto Tecnológico de Oaxaca (1986). Director de la Preparatoria 2 (1977-80). Militante del PSUM, dirigió el Comité Estatal de Oaxaca (1982-87) y fue miembro del Comité Central (1983-87). En el PMS fue secretario general del Comité Estatal y miembro del Consejo Nacional (1987-89). Pertenece al PRD desde 1989, donde ha sido miembro del Consejo Nacional (1989-94). Diputado federal (1991-94).

VÁZQUEZ DEL MERCADO, ALEJANDRO ◆ n. en Sombrerete, Zac., y m. en el DF (1841-1923). Comerciante radicado en Aguascalientes, durante la intervención francesa brindó protección a los republicanos perseguidos y, finalmente, se alistó en la lucha contra Maximiliano. Al triunfo de la República fue diputado a la Legislatura de Aguascalientes (1867), jefe político de Rincón de Romos, diputado federal, jefe político del estado (1882-83) y gobernador interino (1903-07) y constitucional de Aguascalientes (1887-95 1907-11). Renunció poco antes del triunfo de la insurrección maderista.

Retrato y firma de Alejandro Vázquez del Mercado

VÁZQUEZ DEL MERCADO, DIEGO ◆ n. en España y m. en Filipinas (?-1616). Fue canónigo de la catedral de Guatemala y deán de las de Manila y de Valladolid. En 1603 fue nombrado primer

María Elena Vázquez Nava

Natalio Vázquez Pallares

Héctor Vázquez Paredes

obispo secular de Yucatán y en 1608 fue promovido al arzobispado de Manila.

Vázquez del Mercado, Ginés ◆ n. en España y m. en Juchipila, Zac. (?-1552). Sobrino y yerno del conquistador Bernardino Vázquez de Tapia. En Nueva Galicia se dedicó a la minería. La audiencia de Guadalajara le encomendó reprimir a los indios de Tolotlán y, en 1552, la exploración de las llanuras de Guadiana, en las que, se decía, había montañas de plata; encontró, en cambio, una montaña de hierro que desde entonces lleva el nombre de cerro del Mercado, al pie del cual se fundaría la ciudad de Durango. Murió a consecuencia de las heridas sufridas durante un ataque indio en Saín.

Vázquez Nava, María Elena ◆ n. en el DF (1954). Licenciada en economía por la UNAM (1977). Tomó un curso de análisis económico y programación financiera en el Fondo Monetario Internacional (1979). En el PRI ha sido integrante del consejo consultivo del IEPES (1986) y secretaria de finanzas del CEN (1987-88). Profesora del INAP. En la Secretaría de Hacienda ha sido analista de la Dirección General de Crédito Público (1976), subjefa (1977-78) y jefa del Departamento de Análisis del Financiaminto del Gobierno Federal (1978-79), subdirectora auxiliar de la Dirección de Crédito Público (1979-81) y encargada de la coordinación de estudios especiales (1981-82). En la Secretaría de Programación y Presupuesto se ha desempeñado como técnica de la Dirección General de Política Presupuestal (1982) y directora general de Normatividad de Obras Públicas, Adquisiciones y Bienes Muebles (1982-84). Secretaria de la Contraloría General de la Federación (1988-94) en el gabinete de Carlos Salinas. Asesora de la Presidencia (1994-).

Vázquez Ortiz, Gonzalo ◆ n. en Cuautla y m. en Cuernavaca, Mor. (?-1945). Obrero. A principios de 1911 se incorporó a las fuerzas de Pablo Torres Burgos y en mayo de ese año participó en el sitio y toma de Cuautla. Fue el encargado de llevar el Plan de Ayala a los periodistas de la ciudad de México y a Pascual Orozco. En 1912 sirvió de enlace entre Zapata y los hermanos Vázquez Gómez. General brigadier (1913), luego del triunfo del Plan de Agua Prieta se incorporó al nuevo ejército federal.

Vázquez Pallares, Natalio ◆ n. en Coalcomán, Mich., y m. en el DF (1913-1981). Licenciado en derecho por la Universidad Michoacana de San Nicolás de Hidalgo (1938). En 1935, cuando estudiaba en la Universidad de Guadalajara, participó en la fundación de la Federación de Estudiantes Socialistas de Occidente. Más tarde fundó la Confederación de Jóvenes Mexicanos y en julio de 1938 era secretario general interino de la Juventud Socialista Unificada de México. En 1939 presidió la Federación de Estudiantes Antiimperialistas de América y encabezó un movimiento estudiantil que dio una nueva ley orgánica a la Universidad Michoacana, donde se desempeñó como rector (1939). Fue procurador de Justicia de Michoacán, secretario particular del gobernador y diputado federal (1949-52), senador (1958-64), secretario auxiliar de la CNC (1961-64), embajador en Yugoslavia (1966-68), director general del Banco Nacional de Crédito Agrícola (1969-70), coordinador del Cuerpo Consultivo Agrario, director del Centro de Estudios Históricos del Agrarismo en México, asesor jurídico de la Cámara Coordinadora para el Desarrollo Agropecuario del DDF y director del Instituto de Capacitación Agraria de la SRA. Colaboró en el periódico *Excélsior*. Presidió el Movimiento Mexicano por la Paz y perteneció al Comité Ejecutivo del Consejo Mundial de la Paz. Autor de *Hacia una reforma universitaria* (1939), *Un nuevo régimen de propiedad y un pueblo* (1945) y *En defensa de la revolución* (1989).

Vázquez Paredes, Héctor ◆ n. en San Cosme Xaloztoc, Tlax. (1936). Licenciado en derecho por la UNAM (1959). Profesor de la Universidad de Tlaxcala (1965-71). Desde 1967 es miembro del PRI, en el que ha desempeñado, entre otros cargos, la presidencia del comité directivo de Tlaxcala (1970-75). Fue secretario general de la Federación de Organizaciones Populares de Tlaxcala (1969-70). Director de Planeación y Promoción Industrial del gobierno de Tlaxcala (1975-80), secretario general de Gobierno de la misma entidad (1981-82), representante ante el Consejo Consultivo Estatal del IMSS (1981-82) y senador (1982-88). Autor de *Tlaxcala y su problema agrario* (1961) y *El nuevo municipio mexicano* (1986).

Vázquez Ramírez, Esther Martina ◆ n. en Pluma Hidalgo, Oax. (1964). Licenciada en historia por la ENAH y maestra por el Instituto José María Luis Mora. Ha sido investigadora en el Programa de Artesanías y Culturas Populares (1984-85) y en el Departamento de Estudios de Proyectos de la Dirección General de Culturas Populares (1986-89), así como profesora en el Colegio Clásico de México (1990-99). Autora de *Organización y resistencia popular en la ciudad de México durante la crisis de 1929-1932* (1998). Becaria del Instituto Estudios Históricos de la Revolución Mexicana (1996-97). Premio Nacional de Administración Pública 1988 y mención honorífica en la categoría de investigación en el concurso Salvador Azuela (1997) del INEHRM.

Vázquez Raña, Mario ◆ n. en España (1933). Llegó a México en 1949. Empresario y comerciante. Codueño de las mueblerías Hermanos Vázquez. En 1976 adquirió la Organización Editorial Mexicana que publica decenas de diarios, entre otros: *El Sol de México*, el deportivo *Esto*, *El Occidental* de Guadalajara y *La Prensa* del DF, en los que figura como director general. Es concesionario de varias estaciones de radio y canales de televisión. Presidente del Comité Olímpico Mexicano desde 1974, de la Organización Deportiva Panamericana desde 1975 y de la Organización de Comités Olímpicos Nacionales desde 1979, organismo al que están afiliados 169 países. Miembro del Comité Olímpico Internacional

(1991-). En 1988, el libro *Los más ricos del mundo*, de la revista francesa *L'Expansion*, colocó a Vázquez Raña como el quinto hombre más rico de México.

VÁZQUEZ ROJAS, GENARO ◆ n. en San Luis Acatlán, Gro., y m. cerca de Morelia, Mich. (1931-1972). Estudió en la Escuela Normal Rural de Ayotzinapa (1950). Fue profesor en Guerrero. Militó en el Movimiento Revolucionario del Magisterio y en el Movimiento de Liberación Nacional. En 1959 participó en la fundación de la Asociación Cívica Guerrerense, organización que logró derrocar al gobernador Raúl Caballero Aburto (1961) y que se transformó, más tarde, en la Asociación Cívica Nacional Revolucionaria. Detenido en noviembre de 1966 por la policía guerrerense en la ciudad de México, fue conducido a Chilpancingo y encarcelado. El 22 de abril de 1968 fue liberado por un grupo armado que comandaba Roque Salgado, se unió a la guerrilla y fue responsable del secuestro de Jaime Castrejón Díez, rector de la Universidad Autónoma de Guerrero. Murió, según información oficial, a consecuencia de un accidente automovilístico ocurrido en el kilómetro 226 de la carretera México-Morelia. Según algunos investigadores y periodistas fue emboscado y asesinado por un grupo paramilitar.

VÁZQUEZ Y SÁNCHEZ VIZCAÍNO, FRANCISCO PABLO ◆ n. en Atlixco y m. en Cholula, Pue. (1769-1847). Doctor en teología por la Real y Pontificia Universidad de México (1795). Fue cura de San Jerónimo Coatepec, de San Martín Texmelucan y del sagrario de Puebla. El 25 de abril de 1825 el gobierno de la República lo nombró enviado extraordinario y ministro plenipotenciario ante El Vaticano, cuando la Iglesia católica aún no reconocía la independencia mexicana. Su viaje a Roma se demoró tres años por cuestiones de protocolo, pero una vez en la Ciudad del Vaticano logró para el país el reconocimiento apostólico (1831) y fue nombrado obispo de Puebla (1831-1847). Tradujo unas *Cartas de unos judíos alemanes y polacos a Mr. Voltaire* y la *Historia antigua de México*, de Francisco Javier Clavijero.

VÁZQUEZ SANTA ANA, HIGINIO ◆ n. en Atemajac de Brizuela, Jal., y m. en Nicaragua (1888-1962). Pedagogo y periodista. Fue director de educación en Michoacán, inspector en Durango, consultor pedagógico del Colegio Militar, profesor de la Escuela de Verano de la UNAM y del Instituto Técnico Industrial, delegado de educación en Querétaro y Tlaxcala, secretario del Congreso Nacional Pedagógico y oficial mayor de la SEP. Colaboró en varios periódicos de México, Mazatlán y Guadalajara; dirigió la revista *Sursum*, órgano de la Asociación Nacional de Maestros, y el periódico masón *Acción*. En 1939 ingresó en el Seminario de Montezuma, en Estados Unidos, donde se ordenó sacerdote en 1943. Autor de *Hombres ilustres nacionales*, *Arte dramático infantil*, *Hombres ilustres de América*, *Hombres ilustres de Jalisco*, *Hombres ilustres michoacanos*, *Morelos*, *Cantares mexicanos*, *El Congreso Pedagógico de México*, *Historia de la canción mexicana*, *Danzas mexicanas*, *Tepotztlán* y *Juan Diego y fray Martín de Valencia*.

VÁZQUEZ SILOS, JOSÉ MACLOVIO ◆ n. en San Luis Potosí, SLP, y m. en Autlán, Jal. (1918-1990). Sacerdote ordenado en 1943. Ha sido profesor del Seminario Conciliar de San Luis Potosí, subasistente diocesano de la Unión de Católicos Mexicanos y del Movimiento Estudiantil y Profesional, asistente de la Asociación Nacional de Trabajadores Guadalupanos, vicario cooperador de la parroquia del Sagrario, párroco de Charcas, canónigo de la catedral, capellán del templo de San José, secretario canciller de la curia, vicario general y obispo de Autlán (1969-90).

VÁZQUEZ TAMEZ, ILDEFONSO V. ◆ n. en Piedras Negras, Coah., y m. en Icamole, NL (1890-1915). Militar. En 1911 se unió a las fuerzas de Pablo González. En 1912 combatió a los orozquistas y al Ejército Libertador del Sur. En febrero de 1913 escoltó al presidente Francisco I. Madero del castillo de Chapultepec al Palacio Nacional y luego del golpe de Estado de Victoriano Huerta viajó a Coahuila y se unió a las fuerzas carrancistas de Antonio I. Villarreal. Fue jefe de la primera División del Noreste y en mayo de 1915 asumió la comandancia militar y la gubernatura provisional de Nuevo León. Murió en combate contra la División del Norte.

VÁZQUEZ DE TAPIA, BERNARDINO ◆ n. en España y m. en la ciudad de México (¿1493?-1559). Llegó a América en 1513. Cuatro años después se alistó en la expedición de Juan de Grijalva que exploró las costas del golfo de México y en 1519 se unió a la expedición de Hernán Cortés. Mensajero de Cortés en México-Tenochtitlan, participó en la matanza del Templo Mayor, en el sitio y derrota de la capital de los mexicas. En 1522 realizó un proyecto para la construcción de la ciudad española, que fue utilizada por Alonso García Bravo. Participó en la conquista del Pánuco. Fue factor de la real Hacienda, alcalde y regidor de la Villa Rica de la Vera Cruz, alcalde y regidor de la ciudad de Mexico (1524) y regidor perpetuo (1528), procurador mayor (1538), alcalde (1541), así como alférez real y regidor decano (1552). Autor de una *Relación de la conquista*.

VÁZQUEZ TORRES, IGNACIO ◆ n. en Sauz de Méndez, Gto. (1939). Licenciado en derecho por la UNAM. Miembro del PRI, en el CEN de ese partido ha sido secretario de Organización (1982) y presidente de la Comisión de Información y Evaluación; en la CNC fue secretario de Acción Juvenil (1962), secretario auxiliar del Comité Nacional (1964) y secretario de la Comisión Política (1968); asesor general en Guanajuato (1965) y secretario general (1966) de la Liga de Comunidades Agrarias. Ha sido tres veces diputado federal por Guanajuato (1967-70, 1973-76 y 1979-82), asesor jurídico del Programa de Descentralización de las Explotaciones Lecheras del DF en el Banrural (1971-73), senador suplente por Guanajuato (1976-82); director general de Investigaciones Políticas

Mario Vázquez Raña

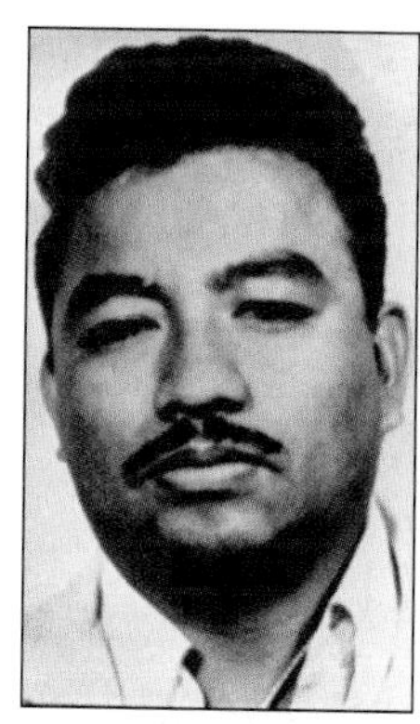

Genaro Vázquez Rojas

Tomás Vázquez Vigil

Josefina Vázquez Vera

Gonzalo Vega

(1976-78), oficial mayor (1978-79) y asesor del titular de la Secretaría de Gobernación (1982-83); director general de delegaciones (1983) y coordinador general para la Descentralización Educativa de la SEP (1982-86); y, en el DDF, delegado en Cuauhtémoc (1988-90) y coordinador general de Abasto y Distribución (1992). Senador para el periodo 1997-2000.

VÁZQUEZ VELA, GONZALO ♦ n. en Jalapa, Ver., y m. en el DF (¿1897?-1963). Licenciado en derecho por la Escuela Nacional de Jurisprudencia. En Veracruz fue secretario de Gobierno durante la gestión de Adalberto Tejeda, gobernador constitucional del estado (1932-34). Oficial mayor encargado del despacho de la Secretaría de Gobernación, en el gabinete de Plutarco Elías Calles, y secretario de Educación Pública del presidente Lázaro Cárdenas (del 17 de junio de 1935 al 30 de noviembre de 1940). Durante su gestión fue inaugurado el IPN y fundó la Oficina Editora Popular, el INAH, las secundarias para hijos de trabajadores, el Instituto Nacional de Psicopedagogía, escuelas para hijos del ejército y el Instituto de Preparación del Profesorado de Escuelas Secundarias, antecedente de la Escuela Normal Superior. Consejero de la Presidencia de la República, de la Compañía Mexicana de Luz y Fuerza y del Banco Nacional Hipotecario, así como gerente de la Aseguradora Mexicana.

VÁZQUEZ VERA, JOSEFINA ZORAIDA ♦ n. en el DF (1932). Maestra y doctora en historia por la UNAM y doctora en historia de América por la Universidad Central de Madrid, con cursos en la Universidad de Harvard. Ha sido directora del Centro de Estudios Históricos de El Colegio de México, miembro del comité editorial de la colección Sepsetentas y miembro de los consejos editoriales de *Historia Mexicana* y *Newsletter for the History of Education*. Coautora de *Historia de la educación en México* (1976), *Historia general de México* (1976), *Historia de México* (1978), *Historia moderna y contemporánea de México* (1980) y *Mexico and United States*. Autora de *Historia de la historiografía*, *Nacionalismo y educación en México*, *Tropiezos para establecer un Estado: Historia de México 1921-1948* (1976), *Mexicanos y norteamericanos ante la guerra del 47* y *La intervención norteamericana 1846-1848* (1997). Premio Nacional de Ciencias y Artes (1999).

VÁZQUEZ VIGIL, TOMÁS ♦ n. en Guadalajara, Jal. (1944). Profesor egresado de la Normal Rural de Jalisco y de la Normal Superior de Nayarit en la especialidad de matemáticas. Licenciado en derecho por la Universidad de Guadalajara (1985). Ha sido regidor del ayuntamiento de Guadalajara, jefe de control de gestión y subdirector general de Educación Básica en Jalisco. Delegado político del Departamento del Distrito Federal en Coyoacán (1994-96). Miembro de los consejos editoriales de *Nuevos Horizontes* y de *15 de Mayo*. Secretario general del Comité Ejecutivo Nacional del Sindicato Nacional de Trabajadores de la Educación elegido para el periodo 1998-2001.

VEERKAMP, FEDERICO ♦ n. en Alemania y m. en el DF (1881-1975). Empresario radicado en México desde 1906. En 1908 fundó, junto con su hermano Alberto, la Casa Veerkamp, dedicada a la venta de instrumentos musicales. Fundó también las empresas Cuerdas Musicales, de la que fue director, y Selva Negra Mexicana. Cofundador de la fábrica El Ánfora.

VEGA, ALBERTO DE LA ♦ n. en Coxcatlán, Pue., y m. en el DF (1923-1969). Escultor egresado de Escuela de Pintura y Escultura La Esmeralda, donde fue alumno de Francisco Zúñiga, Juan Cruz, Luis Ortiz Monasterio y Esteban Francis. Profesor (1954) y consejero técnico (1958) de La Esmeralda. En 1960 fue uno de los redactores de los estatutos de la Bienal Interamericana. Ha realizado trabajos públicos en Morelos y Michoacán y hay obra suya en el Museo de Arte de Boston. Autor de *Monumento a Miguel Hidalgo* (1954), *Vendedora de tortillas* (1955), *La espina* (1956), *Maternidad* (1958), *Mujer reclinada* (1959) y *La negra y la paloma* (1962). Miembro del Salón de la Plástica Mexicana (1956). Fue jurado de la Bienal Interamericana. Premio de adquisición del Salón de la Plástica Mexicana (1955, 1956, 1958 y 1959), premio Tolsá en la primera Exposición Nacional de Escultura (1960) y mención honorífica en la primera Bienal Nacional de Escultura (1962).

VEGA, GABRIELA DE LA ♦ n. en el DF (1946). Licenciada en letras modernas por la UNAM (1972), maestra en pedagogía y literatura por la Sorbona (1975) y doctora en ciencias sociales por la Escuela Práctica de Altos Estudios de París. Profesora en la UNAM (1972-74) y directora del Centro de Estudios Universitarios Londres (1980-1992). Es socia fundadora y directora de Jomar Arte y Literatura (1985-92) y socia de la Casa de la Acuarela (1984-92). Premio Nacional de Cuento en 1985.

VEGA, GONZALO ♦ n. en el DF (1946). Actor de cine, teatro y televisión. Estudió literatura dramática y teatro en la UNAM, así como en el INBA. Se inició profesionalmente en 1967. Ha actuado en las películas *Pubertinaje* (1971), *Por qué nací mujer* (1968), *Los recuerdos del porvenir* (1968), *La agonía de ser madre*, *Las pirañas aman en cuaresma* (1969), *Más allá de la violencia*, *Las Poquianchis* (1976), *Crónica de un amor*, *Aquellos años* (1972), *Ante el cadáver de un líder* (1973), *Los renglones torcidos de Dios*, *Lo que importa es vivir* (1986), *Antonieta*, *Knock-out*, *La seducción* y *El lugar sin límites* (1977); en las obras de teatro *La ronda de la hechizada* (1969), *El show de terror de Rocky*, *Hipólito*, *La ópera de tres centavos*, *Bodas de sangre*, *El beso de la mujer araña*, *Don Juan Tenorio* y *La señora presidenta*, así como en varias telenovelas, entre ellas: *En carne propia* y *La vida en el espejo* (1999). Ha ganado dos Arieles, dos Diosas de Plata y el premio Goya, de España.

VEGA, ISELA ♦ n. en Hermosillo, Son. (1940). Inició su carrera como modelo

Isela Vega

y cantante en la década de los sesenta, para después tomar clases de actuación. Se inició en cine en la cinta *La rabia por dentro* (*The Rage*, 1962). Su primer papel importante fue en *Las pecadoras* (1967). En los setenta llegó a ser considerada el símbolo sexual del cine mexicano. En su filmografía destacan *Las pirañas aman en cuaresma* (1969), *Las golfas* (1969), *Las reglas del juego* (1970), *Fin de fiesta* (1971), *El monasterio de los buitres* (1972), *La celestina* (1973), *La india* (1974), *El llanto de la tortuga* (1974), *Las apariencias engañan* (1977), *La viuda negra* (1977, Ariel a la mejor actuación en 1984), *Las cariñosas* (1978), *Naná* (1979), *Las 7 Cucas* (1981) y *El amor es un juego extraño* (1984). Produjo y dirigió las cintas *Una gallina muy ponedora* (1981), *Los amantes del señor de la noche* (1983) y *Dos chichimecas en Hollywood* (1989), las tres con guiones suyos. Incursionó en el teatro con algunas obras como *Zaratustra* (1970) y *Sexicienta* (1983). Radica en Los Ángeles, donde trabaja como periodista, y regresa ocasionalmente a México para actuar en teatro.

Vega, *Lolita* de la ◆ n. en Ciudad Juárez, Chih. (1960). Estudió psicología en la Universidad de las Américas y comunicación en la Anáhuac. Ha sido conductora de *La hora de los aficionados* (1972, Mexicali), *Palco de Prensa* (1972-75, Baja California), *La hora de los locutores* (1974-77, en Televisa) y *Panorama Cultural* (1981-83, en el Instituto Mexicano de la Radio). Iniciadora del Canal 7, desde 1998 conduce el programa *Hablemos Claro*, en TV Azteca. Ha colaborado en *Impacto*, *México Hoy* y *Cuarto Poder*. Directora y conductora de *Frente a Frente* de Radio Fórmula (1998-). Ha recibido la Presea Ejecutiva (1992, 93, 94 y 95), Presea AB (1993), premios del Certamen Nacional de Periodismo (1992, 93, 94 y 95), la Estrella de Plata (1994) y el Premio Beca Shalom.

Vega, Netzahualcóyotl de la ◆ n. en Coyuca de Catalán, Gro. (1931). Maestro normalista por la Escuela Nacional de Maestros (1948) y licenciado en derecho por la UNAM (1956). Desde 1949 pertenece al PRI, donde ha sido representante ante la comisión electoral de Guerrero (1979), presidente del consejo consultivo del CEPES (1987) y representante ante el Consejo General del IFE. Secretario general del Sindicato de Trabajadores de la Industria de Radio y Televisión y miembro del CEN de la CTM. Diputado federal (1982-85 y 94-97), senador (1988-94) y diputado a la Asamblea Legislativa del DF para el periodo 1997-2000.

Vega, Patricia ◆ n. en Tijuana, BC (1957). Periodista, poeta y fotógrafa. Licenciada en comunicación social por la Universidad Anáhuac. Reportera de cultura de *La Jornada* desde 1984, donde cubrió seis años la fuente de cine. Fundadora de la revista cultural *Entremés* y conductora del programa *Arena en Radio* UNAM. Su serie de poemas Parodias de Guerra se incluyó en el volumen colectivo *Por la piel* (1986), publicado por la UNAM, y en las antologías poéticas *Parvada* (Universidad Autónoma de Baja California Norte) y *Vidas mareas* (Universidad Autónoma de Zacatecas). Tercer lugar del premio de periodismo cultural El Gallo Pitagórico (1980) y Premio de Periodismo Cultural del INBA (1989) con el trabajo *El caso Rushdie: testimonios sobre la intolerancia* (editado en 1991). Autora de *A gritos y sombrerazos* (1996). Mención honorífica del Club de Periodistas de México por la exclusiva mundial de los textos inéditos de Juan Rulfo (1997).

Vega, Plácido ◆ n. en El Fuerte, Sin., y m. en Acapulco, Gro. (1830-1878). Militar. Durante la guerra de los Tres Años combatió a los conservadores en Sinaloa. Ascendido a general en 1860, al año siguiente fue elegido gobernador de Sinaloa. Durante el verano de 1862 combatió a los ejércitos coras de Manuel Lozada, pero desde fines de ese año, se negó a colaborar con las fuerzas jaliscienses de Ramón Corona, eludió las solicitudes de tropas para combatir a los franceses en el centro del país y se dedicó a los negocios. En febrero de 1863, sin embargo, organizó una fuerza con la que desembarcó en Acapulco y participó en algunos combates anteriores al sitio de Puebla. Luego volvió a Sinaloa, reinició las hostilidades con Corona y a fines de ese año se embarcó para San Francisco, con el propósito de comprar armas. Sin embargo, demoró tres años y medio en concretar la compra y cuando volvió a Sinaloa, el triunfo de la República era inminente. Acusado de traición y encarcelado en Durango, se fugó al poco tiempo y se exilió en Estados Unidos.

Vega, Santiago R. de la ◆ n. en Monterrey, NL, y m. en el DF (1885-1950). Periodista y militante del Partido Liberal. Se inició como caricaturista del periódico de oposición *Mefistófeles*, lo que le valió ser encarcelado en 1902. Quedó libre dos años después y se instaló en San Antonio Texas, donde fundó *La Humanidad*. Volvió a México en 1909 y participó en la fundación de la Casa del Obrero Mundial. En 1911 fue, junto con Francisco Castrejón, Francisco J. Múgica, Juana B. Gutiérrez de Mendoza y Camilo Arriaga, uno de los conspiradores del llamado Complot de Tacubaya, que pretendía capturar a Porfirio Díaz. Fue más tarde secretario particular de José E. Santos y de Antonio I. Villarreal y colaborador (redactor o caricaturista) de las publicaciones *Multicolor, La Risa, El Padre Padilla, Arlequín, Claridades* y *El Universal*; asimismo, editó hojas sueltas de contenido político en las que utilizó el pseudónimo de *Kiff*.

Nezahualcóyotl de la Vega

Santiago R. de la Vega

VEGA AMADOR, RENATO ◆ n. en el DF y m. en Culiacán, Sin. (1911-1993). Ingresó al Colegio Militar en 1928 y recibió el grado de subteniente en 1931. Fundador del Partido Nacional Revolucionario. Con el grado de general fue comandante de zona militar en Tlaxcala y Michoacán. Formó las guardias de Sinaloa (1951) y fue subdirector del penal de Lecumberri (1954), coordinador de las campañas electorales del PRI en San Luis Potosí (1959), director de Tránsito del DDF (1967) y jefe de la policía capitalina (1969). Presidió la Asociación General Leandro Valle y fue coordinador de la Unidad Revolucionaria del PRI (1989-93).

VEGA DE ALATORRE ◆ Municipio de Veracruz situado en el litoral del golfo de México, al noreste de Jalapa y al sureste de Papantla. Superficie: 310.92 km^2. Habitantes: 19,412, de los cuales 5,598 forman la población económicamente activa. Hablan alguna lengua indígena 46 personas mayores de cinco años.

Jorge de la Vega Domínguez

VEGA CAMARGO, JAVIER ◆ n. en el DF (1959). Licenciado en administración por la Universidad Anáhuac, de la que fue profesor (1980-81); maestro en administración pública y candidato a doctor por la London School of Economics and Political Science. Pertenece al PRI desde 1982, donde ha sido delegado municipal en el Estado de México (1983) y coordinador de asesores del gobernador mexiquense (1985-86). Director de Asuntos Internacionales de la Secretaría de Energía (1989-94), secretario de Desarrollo Social del Departamento del Distrito Federal 1994-97) y subsecretario de Promoción Turística de la Secretaría de Turismo (1997-).

VEGA DOMÍNGUEZ, JORGE DE LA ◆ n. en Comitán, Chis. (1931). Licenciado en economía por la UNAM (1955). Profesor del Instituto Tecnológico Regional de Ciudad Madero (1956-59), así como profesor (1959-65) y director de la Escuela Superior de Economía del IPN (1963-65). En el PRI ha sido asesor del presidente del partido (1962-65), director del IEPES (1969-70) y presidente del CEN (1986-88). Gerente del Banco del Pequeño Comercio en Tampico (1956-59), jefe del Departamento de Gasto Público de la Secretaría de la Presidencia (1960), subdirector de Dina Nacional (1960-63), subdirector del Banco del Pequeño Comercio (1963-64), diputado federal (1964-67), gerente de Ventas (1965-69) y director general de Conasupo (1970-76), gobernador de Chiapas (1976-77), secretario de Comercio (1977-82) en el gobierno de Miguel de la Madrid y de Agricultura y Recursos Hidráulicos (1988-89), en el de Carlos Salinas de Gortari Embajador de México en Canadá (1991-). Autor de *La expropiación petrolera* (1958). Fue presidente del Colegio Nacional de Economistas (1960-62).

VEGA ESCAMILLA, RAMÓN R. DE LA ◆ n. en Zapotlán el Grande, hoy Ciudad Guzmán, Jal., y m. en Colima, Col. (1811-1896). Radicado en Colima y asociado en 1830 con Ramón Fajardo, editó los primeros periódicos locales: *El Observador de las Leyes, El Popular* y *La Unión*. Fue secretario del ayuntamiento de Colima (1839), fundador de la fábrica de hilados y tejidos de San Cayetano, de la que fue subdirector y gerente (1842), presidente del Tribunal Mercantil (1844-46), diputado federal por Morelia (1845-46), vocal de la diputación territorial (1847), jefe político de Colima (1848-49 y 1849-50), diputado suplente al Congreso Constituyente de 1856-57, diputado federal (1861), gobernador interino de Colima designado por Manuel Doblado (1862) y gobernador constitucional de Colima (1862-64). Abandonó el estado en 1864, cuando los invasores franceses se apoderaron de la entidad, pero volvió al año siguiente. Fue presidente de la Junta de Mejoras Materiales. Ramón Corona lo nombró gobernador y comandante militar de Colima (1867) y luego fue nuevamente elegido. Regidor en varias ocasiones e inspector general de educación (1880-92). Coautor, con Longinos Banda y Antonio Ferrer, de un *Ensayo estadístico del territorio de Colima* (1846).

VEGA-GIL RUEDA, ARMANDO ◆ n. en el DF (1955). Músico y poeta. Antropólogo titulado en la ENAH, de la que ha sido profesor. Periodista, ha colaborado en el diario *unomásuno,* en *La Onda*, de *Novedades*, y en *Milenio;* jefe redacción de *Melodía, Diez Años Después* y coordinador de *rock* de *Las Horas Extras*. Violinista del grupo folclórico Canek y bajista del grupo de *rock* Botellita de Jerez, con el que grabó los discos *Botellita de Jerez* (1983), *La venganza del hijo del guacarrock* (1985), *Naco es chido* (1987), *Niña de mis ojos* (1989) y *La despedida* (1998). Asesor del Instituto de Cultura de la Ciudad de México (1997-). Ha publicado poesía en la revista *Gilgamesh* y es autor del poemario *Entre sueños te veas* (1988) y de *La semiótica de la semita o ¡Ay, qué ricos tus cocoles!* (prosas varias, 1990).

VEGA SÁNCHEZ, RAFAEL ◆ n. en Huichapan, Hgo., y m. ¿? (1888-1946). Estudió en el Instituto Científico y Literario de Hidalgo, del que fue profesor. Desde 1905 perteneció al grupo Bohemia Hidalguense y en enero de 1910 organizó el Club Antirreeleccionista Benito Juárez. Participó en la revolución. Fue diputado al Congreso Constituyente de 1916-17, editor del periódico *El Constituyente*, vocero de la fracción radical de los diputados a la asamblea de Querétaro; inspector de la Secretaría de Hacienda y jefe de la oficina de Hacienda de San Juan del Río. Autor de los poemarios *El tesoro del espíritu, En la cumbre suprema* (1928), *Vidas exactas* y de una *Antología de poetas hidalguenses* (1944).

VEJACIONES, DE LAS ◆ Códice también llamado Lienzo de Aztactepec y Citlaltepec o Códice protesta contra las vejaciones de los primeros encomenderos. Se encuentra en la Casa del Alfeñique, en Puebla. Procede de Tlapa, Guerrero. Elaborado en el siglo XVI, sobre tela, muestra los dos cerros de su nombre y una batalla fechada en 1572.

VÉJAR VÁZQUEZ, OCTAVIO ◆ n. en Jalapa, Ver., y m. en el DF (1900-1974). Licenciado en derecho por la Escuela Nacional de Jurisprudencia (1924). En

1925 se incorporó al ejército, donde fue jefe del Cuerpo de Defensores de Oficio Militares, procurador general de Justicia Militar y profesor en el Colegio Militar. Fue procurador de Justicia del Distrito y Territorios Federales (1940-41), asesor jurídico y titular de la Secretaría de Educación Pública (del 12 de septiembre de 1941 al 20 de diciembre de 1943), en el gabinete de Manuel Ávila Camacho. Fundador del Partido Nacional Demócrata Independiente (1944). Autor de *Hacia una escuela de unidad nacional* y *Autonomía del derecho militar*. En 1938 el presidente Cárdenas le otorgó la condecoración al mérito militar, por su participación en la elaboración del Código de Justicia Militar.

VELA, ARQUELES ◆ n. en Tapachula, Chis., y m. en el DF (1899-1977). Profesor normalista, realizó cursos de posgrado en las universidades de Madrid, París, Berlín y Roma (1925-32). Fue profesor de la Escuela Nacional de Maestros (1935) y de la UNAM, director de la Secundaria 1 y de la Escuela Secundaria Experimental (1939-58), así como profesor y director de la Normal Superior. Redactor de *El Demócrata* (1920), secretario de redacción de *El Universal Ilustrado* (1921) y director del suplemento dominical de *El Nacional* (1933). Fue una de las principales figuras del estridentismo. Autor de los poemarios *El sendero gris y otros poemas inútiles 1919-1920* (1921) y *Cantata a las muchachas fuertes y alegres de México* (1940); de los cuentos, relatos y novelas *La señorita Etcétera* (1922), *El café de nadie* (1926), *El viaje redondo* (1929), *Cuentos del día y de la noche* (1945), *El picaflor* (1961) y *Luzbel* (1966); y de los ensayos *Historia materialista del arte* (1936), *Evolución histórica de la literatura universal* (1941), *Literatura universal* (1951) y *Fundamentos de la literatura mexicana* (1953), entre otras obras. Miembro de la Sociedad Internacional de Críticos de Arte. Maestro en letras *ex oficio* por la Escuela Normal Superior (1939). En 1949 el gobierno francés lo condecoró con las Palmas Académicas.

VELA, EULALIO ◆ n. en Veracruz, Ver., y m. en Chihuahua, Chih. (1838-1890). Militar. Luchó en las filas liberales en la guerra de los Tres Años y en las republicanas durante la intervención francesa. Secundó en 1876 el Plan de Tuxtepec y al triunfo de éste ascendió a general. Fue gobernador de Veracruz durante unos días de diciembre de 1879 y más tarde comandante militar de Veracruz, Matamoros (donde reprimió una rebelión indígena) y de Chihuahua.

VELA, SERGIO ◆ n. en el DF (1964). Egresado de la Escuela Libre de Derecho (1988), de la que es profesor. Estudió piano con Héctor Rojas, canto con María Julius, composición musical con Humberto Hernández Medrano y dirección orquestal con Roswitha Heintze en la Escuela Superior de Música de Viena, y con Murray Sidlin en la Escuela de Música de Aspen. Director general del Festival Internacional Cervantino (1992-). Ha sido director escénico de las óperas *Fausto* (1990), *La clemencia de Tito* (1993), *El holandés volador* (1994), *Tristán e Isolda* (1996), *Idomeneo, rey de Creta* (1998) y *Los visitantes* (1999), con la Compañía Nacional de Ópera del INBA que también dirigió (1992). Director de escena e iluminación en *Salomé* en la Ópera de Virginia (1994) y en *Turandot* en el Festival Puccini de Torre del Lago (1996). Conduce las transmisiones operísticas del Canal 22 (1994-) y un programa de debate cultural en el Canal 40 (1999-). Orden del Mérito de la República Italiana (1997) y Orden de las Artes y las Letras del gobierno francés (1998).

VELA QUINTERO, ENRIQUE ◆ n. en la ciudad de México y m. en Villa Ocampo, Dgo. (1908-1990). Bailarín y coreógrafo. Estudió en la Escuela Superior de Música y danza con las profesoras Amelia Costa y Armen Ohanian (1921-23). Como bailarín se inició profesionalmente en 1923, fue miembro de la Compañía Americana de Ballet (Boston, 1923-26), fundador y director del Cuadro Infantil de Ballet (1928-31) y profesor en la Escuela Nacional de Danza (1931-33 y 1938-87). Creador de coreografías para *La sílfide*, *El lago de los cisnes* y *El amor brujo*.

VELARDE, MARIO ◆ n. y m. en el DF (1940-1997). Futbolista. Se inició con el Necaxa en 1962 y fue convocado a la selección nacional en 1970. Jugó después en la UNAM, equipo del que fue director técnico y al que llevó a una final (1984-85). Dirigió al Cruz Azul (al que en 1989 llevó a la final) y al Toluca (1991-92). Asumió durante algunos meses la dirección técnica de la selección mexicana tras el Campeonato Mundial de 1986, en el que fue integrante del cuerpo técnico.

VELARDE GOROSTIETA, VÍCTOR M. ◆ n. y m en el DF (1904-1997). Periodista, lingüista y traductor. Ingresó a *Excélsior* en 1920 como traductor de cables y durante 11 años fue auxiliar de ese departamento, así como primer jefe de redacción de *Últimas Noticias* (1936), periódico del cual fue subdirector y director. Fue reconocido por su peculiar estilo de redactar encabezados. Publicó la cabeza más famosa en *La Extra* de *Últimas Noticias*, el 5 de marzo de 1953, la que con un lacónico "¡Ya!" anunció el fallecimiento de Stalin. Fue premiado en México, Europa y Latinoamérica. Ejerció el periodismo durante 72 años, 70 de ellos en *Excélsior*.

VELARDE PÉREZ, ADELA ◆ n. en Ciudad Juárez, Chih., y m. ¿en el DF? (?-1971). Enfermera, presunta inspiradora de la canción *La Adelita*. Se fugó de su casa y el 7 de febrero de 1913 se unió a las tropas carrancistas del coronel Alfredo Breceda, donde fungió como enfermera después de los combates de Camargo, Torreón, Parral y Santa Rosalía. Trabajó durante 32 años en un puesto burocrático de la Secretaría de Industria y Comercio. Contaba con una carta del arzobispo de la ciudad de México, Luis María Martínez, que decía: "Para la auténtica Adelita, con mi bendición" y poseía un decreto presidencial de 1963 en el que se le concedía una pensión por sus servicios prestados a la Revolución Mexicana y una nota de

Octavio Véjar Vázquez

Pirámide del sol, obra de José María Velasco

José María Velasco

algún periódico que decía que el Senado la había reconocido como la auténtica Adelita.

Velasco, Francisco Lorenzo de ◆ n. en Guadalajara, Jal., y m. en Playa Vicente, Ver. (1784-1816). Doctor en cánones por la Universidad de Alcalá de Henares (1807). Volvió a Nueva España en 1812 y obtuvo una prebenda en la Colegiata de Guadalupe, la que abandonó para unirse a las fuerzas insurgentes. Dirigió a partir del número 21 *El Ilustrador Americano*. Pasó a Michoacán como secretario de José Sixto Verduzco. Fue derrotado por Linares en las lomas del Calvario. En agosto de 1813 intervino en las negociaciones previas a la capitulación del fuerte de San Diego. Promulgada el Acta de Independencia (6 de noviembre de 1813) se le nombró mariscal de campo. Entró en conflicto con otros insurgentes y en 1814 se acogió al indulto. Fue recluido en Puebla y la autoridad eclesiástica lo condenó a destierro en Puerto Rico, pero camino a Veracruz se fugó. Se unió en Tehuacán a las fuerzas de Juan Nepomuceno Rossains; y, por instrucciones de éste, incendió la población de San Andrés Chalchicomula (enero de 1815); trató de huir cuando Rossains fue destituido (20 de agosto), cayó en manos de Guadalupe Victoria y éste lo devolvió a Tehuacán (18 de diciembre) en calidad de prisionero. Reapareció al lado de Manuel Mier y Terán luchando contra el español José Barradas, a quien derrotaron cerca de Tepeji de la Seda (27 de diciembre). Murió en combate contra los realistas.

Hacienda de Chimalpa, obra de José María Velasco

Velasco, Horacio G. ◆ n. en España y m. en el DF (1926-1988). Periodista y escritor. En 1946 ganó un concurso de cuento. En 1949 llegó a México y se incorporó a las Librerías de Cristal. Incursionó en el periodismo televisivo. Fue director de *60 Minutos* y creador de *6 en Punto*. Crítico de cine en varias publicaciones y jurado de la Asociación de Periodistas Cinematográficos. Autor de *La primavera de los urogallos* (novela, 1989).

Velasco, José Francisco ◆ n. ¿en Hermosillo, Son.? (1790-?). Era secretario de la Comandancia General de las Provincias Internas de Occidente en 1821, cuando se unió al Plan de Iguala. En ese mismo año fue el primer presidente municipal de Hermosillo y le correspondió jurar el acta de independencia en Sonora. Diputado al primer Congreso General (1822) y fue miembro de la Junta Nacional Instituyente creada por Iturbide; diputado a los congresos constituyentes de Occidente (1824) y de Sonora (1831), secretario general de Gobierno (1828-29), administrador de la aduana de Guaymas, juez de primera instancia en Hermosillo (1845) y secretario de gobierno de Sonora (1846). Autor de *Noticias estadísticas del estado de Sonora* (1850).

Velasco, José María ◆ n. en Temascalcingo, Edo. de Méx., y m. en la ciudad de México (1840-1912). Pintor. Realizó la carrera de agrimensor en el Instituto Científico y Literario de Toluca. Ingresó en 1858 en la Academia de San Carlos, donde fue alumno de Santiago Rebull, Pelegrín Clavé y Eugenio Landesio. Incursionó más tarde en la botánica, la zoología y la anatomía. Hizo estudios sobre el ajolote. Profesor de perspectiva y paisaje en San Carlos (1868), dibujante (1880-82) y fotógrafo del Museo Nacional (1882-84) e inspector de dibujo y escultura de la Escuela Nacional de Bellas Artes (1910-12). Es el más afamado paisajista mexicano. Se especializó en panorámicas del valle de México, apreciadas desde diversos ángulos. El Museo de Arte Moderno del INBA, donde existe una sala que lleva su nombre, cuenta con una amplia colección de su obra, en la que se cuentan, entre muchas otras, *Río de San Ángel* (1861), *Puente rústico de San Ángel* (1862), *Un paseo en los alrededores de México* (1866), *Cerro de Guadalupe en Guerrero* (1873), *Peñascos del cerro de Atzacoalco* (1874), *Barranca de Tepotzotlán* (1874), *Valle de México* (1875), *México* (1877, considerada su obra maestra), *Baño de Netzahualcóyotl* (1878), *Catedral de Oaxaca* (1887), *Lumen in coelo* (1892), *Hacienda de Chimalpa* (1893), *Rocas del Tepeyac* (1894) y *El Citlaltépetl* (1897). En los cincuenta, algunas de sus obras más conocidas se hallaban en colecciones particulares. Hizo una serie de lienzos para el Instituto de Geología. Dejó un *Autorretrato* ejecutado en 1894. Fue miembro de la Sociedad Mexicana de Historia Natural, a la que ingresó en 1868 con el trabajo *La flora en el valle de México*. En 1874 y 1876 ganó sendas medallas de oro en las exposiciones nacionales de Bellas Artes, en 1876 llevó algunos cuadros a la exposición del centenario de Filadelfia, donde recibió una medalla. Primer premio de la Academia Nacional de México (1878). En 1893 obtuvo una medalla de oro en Madrid y expuso en la Feria Mundial de Chicago, donde también fue premiado. Presidió en 1889 la delegación mexicana a la Exposición Universal de París y ahí recibió otra medalla y el gobierno francés le impuso la Legión de Honor. Diploma y medalla en la Exposición de Bellas Artes de Puebla

(1900). El gobierno austriaco lo condecoró en 1902 con la Cruz de Francisco José.

VELASCO, JOSÉ REFUGIO ◆ n. en Aguascalientes, Ags., y m. en el DF (1851-1919). Egresado del Colegio Militar, luchó contra la intervención francesa y el imperio. En 1867 intervino en la batalla de San Jacinto y en el sitio de Querétaro, a las órdenes de Mariano Escobedo. Participó en diversas campañas de represión contra los indios de Chihuahua, San Luis Potosí, Michoacán y Sonora (1872-1906). Sirvió al dictador Victoriano Huerta. En 1913, año en el que ascendió a general de división, recuperó la plaza de Torreón, defendida por los villistas Calixto Contreras y los hermanos Arrieta. En abril de 1914, Francisco Villa lo derrotó en esa misma plaza. Gobernador y comandante militar de los estados de México, San Luis Potosí y Coahuila, durante el régimen huertista. Secretario de Guerra y Marina en el gabinete transitorio de Francisco Carbajal (del 14 de julio al 13 de agosto de 1914), procedió a disolver el ejército federal, de acuerdo con los tratados de Teoloyucan (☛), después de lo cual se exilió en Estados Unidos.

VELASCO, LUIS DE ◆ n. en España y m. en la ciudad de México (1511-1564). Participó con el rey Carlos I (Carlos V de Alemania) en las guerras de Francia (1525), fue veedor y capitán general de las guardias de España y virrey de Navarra (1547-49). Llegó en 1550 a la Nueva España como segundo virrey, cargo que ejerció hasta su muerte. En 1551 abolió la esclavitud de los indios, un año más tarde se produjo la primera inundación de la ciudad de México, en 1553 inauguró la Real y Pontificia Universidad y promovió, en 1554, la fundación de las poblaciones de Durango y Nombre de Dios.

VELASCO, LUIS DE ◆ n. y m. en España (1539-1617). Hijo del anterior. Llegó a la Nueva España en 1550, con su padre. En 1585 se le designó regidor de la ciudad de México, pero sus diferencias con el virrey Álvaro Manrique de Zúñiga lo obligaron a viajar a España, donde Felipe II lo nombró embajador en Florencia. Regresó a la Nueva España en 1589 con el nombramiento de virrey, cargo que asumió en 1590. En 1591 pactó la paz con los chichimecas y envió varias partidas de colonos tlaxcaltecas a mezclarse con aquéllos para imbuirles hábitos sedentarios; eximió de pago a los indios que tuvieran litigios administrativos, pero duplicó sus tributos para financiar las campañas bélicas de la metrópoli; en 1593 ordenó la construcción del Paseo de la Alameda y en 1594 encomendó a Juan de Oñate la conquista de Nuevo México. En 1595 fue designado virrey de Perú, cargo que ejerció hasta 1603, cuando regresó a la Nueva España, de la que volvió a ser nombrado virrey en 1607. Tras la inundación de ese año encomendó a Enrico Martínez y al jesuita Juan Sánchez la construcción del canal de Huehuetoca (☛). Durante su segundo virreinato se produjo en Veracruz la rebelión de esclavos encabezados por Yanga. Volvió a España en 1610 y desde el año siguiente hasta su muerte fue presidente del Consejo de Indias.

VELASCO, MARÍA ELENA, *LA INDIA MARÍA* ◆ n. en Puebla (¿1935?). Actriz y directora de cine. Su carrera empezó en el teatro universitario, en el que actuó en *El séptimo sello*, de Bergman (1970), *Dos viejos pánicos*, de Piñera, dirigida por Gonzalo Celorio (1972) e *Inmaculada*, de Héctor Azar (1972). Con el personaje de *la India María* se inició en la televisión, con apariciones frecuentes en Siempre en Domingo. Se ha presentado en teatro y otros escenarios. La primera película en que actuó fue *Tonta, tonta, pero no tanto* (1971). La primera película que dirigió fue *Desempleo* (1978), a la que siguieron *El coyote emplumado* (1982), *Ni Chana ni Juana* (1984), *Ni de aquí ni de allá* (1987), *Se equivocó la cigüeña* (1992) y *Las delicias del poder* (1998), todas protagonizadas por ella misma.

VELASCO, MIGUEL ÁNGEL ◆ n. en Jalapa, Ver., y m. en el DF (1903-1999). Panadero. Cofundador (1921) de la Unión Gremial de Obreros Panaderos de Jalapa, de la Federación de Obreros Panaderos de Veracruz (1924) y de la Federación de Sindicatos de Obreros y Campesinos de Córdoba (1925). Militante del Partido Comunista, formó parte de su comité central (1928-34). En 1932 fue detenido y enviado como preso político a las islas Marías. Representó a la Confederación Sindical Unitaria en la constitución del Comité Nacional de Defensa Proletaria (1935) y fue cofundador de la CTM, en la que formó parte del primer comité nacional (1936). En 1942 fue director de *La Voz de México*, órgano del PCM, del que fue expulsado en 1943. Formó el Círculo Socialista Morelos, Acción Socialista Unificada (1948-50) y el Partido Obrero y Campesino Mexicano (1950), que se disolvió en 1963 cuando sus miembros ingresaron al Partido Popular Socialista (1963), de donde salió en 1971 para fundar el Movimiento de Acción y Unidad Socialista, una de las organizaciones que en 1982 constituyeron el PSUM, donde fue integrante del comité central. Cofundador del PMS (1987-89) y del PRD (1989). Subdirector del Centro de Estudios del Movimiento Obrero y Socialista (1982-99). Autor de *La administración obrera en las empresas* (1939), *La Unión Soviética frente a la guerra interimperialista* (1939), *El Partido Comunista durante el gobierno de Cárdenas* (1975), y *Vicente Lombardo Toledano y el movimiento obrero* (1975).

VELASCO, RAÚL ◆ n. en Celaya, Gto. (1933). Llegó al DF en 1953. Fue reportero de *Novedades*, fundador y jefe de la sección de espectáculos de *El Heraldo de México*, conductor de un programa en *Radio Variedades*, locutor de Televisión Independiente de México, conductor de los programas *Confrontación 68*, *Medianoche*, *Domingos espectaculares* y *Siempre en domingo* (1969-98). Ha colaborado en *Novelas del Radio*, *Cine Universal*, *Cine Novelas*, *Cine Álbum*. Creó los programas televisivos *Estrellas de los 80*, *Video Éxitos*, *Noche de Valores*, *El Sabor de la Noche* y *Galardón a los Grandes*. Autor de

Retrato y firma de Luis de Velasco padre

Retrato y firma de Luis de Velasco hijo

María Elena Velasco, *la India María*

Raúl Velasco

Manuel M. Velasco Suárez

los libros *Mi rostro oculto* (1989) y *Vibraciones cósmicas* (1998).

Velasco, Verónica ◆ n. el DF (1962). Estudió periodismo y teatro en la UNAM. Ha sido conductora y actriz del programa *El nuevo a capa y espada* (1985) y de la serie *Los amorosos de Jaime Sabines* (1986); jefa del Departamento de Acuerdos Bilaterales del Festival Internacional Cervantino (1986-87), asesora técnica de la Dirección de Fomento Cultural del Crea (1987), conductora de los programas *espectáculo de la ciudad* (1987), *La guía de cada día*, *Telecartelera cinematográfica* y *Mundo ganadero* (1988-89), *Partidos políticos* (1988), del Centro de Producción de Programas Informativos y Especiales de la Presidencia (Cepropie), de *Fin de Siglo* (1988-90) y del noticiero *Imevisión Informa* (1989-92). Corresponsal de Univisión (1991-94), conductora y directora general de los programas *Expediente 13/22: 30* (1993-96), *Se vale soñar, A corazón abierto* (1998), *Se busca justicia, Chiquitos pero picosos* y *Ciberkids*, y directora general de Argos Noticias (1999).

Velasco Cevallos, Rómulo ◆ n. en Oaxaca, Oax., y m. en el DF (1884-1948). Fue redactor de los periódicos *El Imparcial, El Universal, El País, El Globo* y *Excélsior*; subdirector de *El Maestro Rural* y de la revista *Asistencia*; jefe de prensa de la Secretaría de la Asistencia Pública e investigador del Archivo General de la Nación. Autor de *La infamia yanqui* (1914), *Aquiles Serdán* (1920), *¿Se apoderará Estados Unidos de América de Baja California?* (1920), *El Hospital Juárez, antes Hospital de San Pablo* (1934), *Las loterías. Historia* (1934), *El niño mexicano ante la caridad y el Estado* (1935), *Asistencia pública: un año bajo la administración del presidente Cárdenas* (1939), *Fichas bibliográficas sobre asistencia social en México* (1943), *La alfabetización en la Nueva España* (1944), *La cirugía mexicana en el siglo XVIII* (1944), *La administración de fray Antonio María de Bucareli y Ursúa* (1946), *Visita y reforma de los hospitales de San Juan de Dios de Nueva España en los años de 1772-1774* (1946) y de la novela *El hombrecillo inútil*.

Velasco Fernández, Rafael ◆ n. en Pánuco, Ver. (1927). Médico cirujano (1951), posgraduado en psiquiatría en la UNAM (1966), de la que ha sido profesor. Secretario general de la Universidad Veracruzana (1963-65), director de la Clínica de la Conducta de la SEP (1965-71), director general de Salud Mental de la Secretaría de Salubridad y Asistencia (1971 y 1973- 77), rector de la Universidad Veracruzana (1971-73), secretario general de la ANUIES (1977-85), subsecretario de Educación Superior e Investigación Científica de la SEP (1985-88), secretario de Salud y Asistencia del estado de Veracruz (1989-94) y director de Salud Mental de la SSA (1995-). Autor de *El niño hiperquinético. Los síndromes de disfunción cerebral* (1978), *Salud mental, enfermedad mental y alcoholismo* (1980) y *Esa enfermedad llamada alcoholismo* (1981). Pertenece, entre otras agrupaciones, a la Asociación Internacional de Presidentes de Universidades, Panel de Expertos en Salud Mental de la OMS, Seminario de Cultura Mexicana, Consejo Mexicano de Psiquiatría, International Council on Alcohol and Addictions, Organización Universitaria Interamericana, Asociación Médica Franco-Mexicana, Asociación Psiquiátrica Mexicana, Asociación Mexicana de Psiquiatría Infantil, Asociación Mundial de Psiquiatría y a la Asociación Psiquiátrica de América Latina. *Doctor honoris causa* por las universidades Veracruzana (1980) y de Quebec (1986). Premio de Cooperación de la Organización Interuniversitaria Interamericana (1985).

Velasco Gil, Carlos Manuel ◆ ☛ *Gill, Mario.*

Velasco Gómez, Raúl ◆ n. en el DF (1941). Ingeniero químico egresado de la UNAM, especializado en administración pública en el IPN (1971-72). Militante del PAN. Profesor en el Colegio Fray Junípero Serra y en la Universidad Autónoma de Querétaro (1977-78). Ha sido diputado local en Baja California (1986-89) y diputado federal (1991-94).

Velasco Sotomayor, Gabriel ◆ n. en el DF (1949). Matemático y ajedrecista. Hizo estudios de maestría y doctorado en las universidades de Kiev, Ucrania y Maine, EUA. En 1977 quedó empatado en primer lugar en un torneo de primera categoría de ajedrez en Kiev, y en 1991 fue subcampeón del estado de Guanajuato. Varias de sus colaboraciones fueron publicadas en *British Chess Magazine* (1977-78). Tuvo a su cargo la página de ajedrez de la revista *Tiempo* (1984-85). Autor de *Geometría plana* (1979) y *Tratado de geometría* (1981).

Velasco Suárez, Manuel M. ◆ n. en San Cristóbal de Las Casas, Chis. (1914). Médico cirujano por la UNAM (1939). Realizó estudios de posgrado en neurología y neurocirugía en las universidades de Harvard y Washington (1941-43). Ha sido profesor de la UNAM (1944-), neurocirujano (1947-58) y jefe del servicio de neurocirugía del Hospital Juárez (1948-63), jefe del Departamento de Neurología y Asistencia Psiquiátrica (1951-58) y director general de neurología y Salud Mental y Rehabilitación de la SSA (1958-64); fundador (1964) y director general del Instituto Nacional de Neurología y Neurocirugía (1964-70), gobernador de Chiapas (1970-76), fundador de la Universidad Autónoma de Chiapas, director general del Hospital Juárez (1987-89) y secretario del Consejo de Salubridad General de la Presidencia (1989-94). Autor de *Correlaciones fronto-temporales* (1952), *Hipopatía del dolor* (1955), *Tumores ventriculares* (1957), *La salud mental en México* (1962) y *Neurobiología* (1979). Miembro de la Liga Mexicana contra la Epilepsia, de la Liga Mexicana contra el Alcoholismo, de la Academia Mexicana de Cirugía y de la Academia Nacional de Medicina; presidente del capítulo mexicano y miembro del comité ejecutivo de la organización Médicos Contra la Guerra Nuclear, que recibió el Nobel de la Paz (1985). Medalla de Honor de la Federación Mundial de Sociedades de Cirugía Neurológica, medalla de oro Spiegel-Wycis de Neurocirugía Funcional Estereotáctica (1986), diploma de la Academia Mexicana de Cirugía (1987) y Premio Chiapas de Ciencias (1987).

Velasco Zimbrón, Alejandro ◆ n. y m. en el DF (1907-1959). Médico cirujano titulado en la UNAM (1930). Fue profesor en las escuelas de Odontología y de Medicina, fundador del Banco de Huesos del Hospital Infantil (introdujo al país la técnica del enclavijamiento e investigó la aplicación ortopédica del acrílico), de la Clínica Primavera, de la Asociación Civil Tepeyac, del Hospital para Niños Incurables y de los sanatorios de Santa María de Guadalupe y de Nuestra Señora de la Consolación. Fue funcionario de la Beneficencia Privada y de los hospitales de los Ferrocarriles Nacionales y Germán Díaz Lombardo. Miembro de las academias Nacional de Medicina y Francesa de Cirugía Ortopédica. El gobierno francés lo nombró caballero de la Legión de Honor.

Velatti, Ricardo Benvenuto ◆ n. ¿en Italia? (1850-?). Hijo de obreros. Autodidacto. Carpintero de oficio. En 1867-68 se unió al grupo socialista de Santiago Villanueva y H. Villavicencio, que en febrero de 1869 sería el Círculo Proletario. En marzo de 1871 fue cofundador de La Social (☛) y secretario de ésta en 1873. Cofundador y activista del Gran Círculo de Obreros de México, en 1875 fue elegido tercer secretario de la mesa directiva de éste, en la que representó al ala izquierda. En 1876 escribió en *La Huelga*, periódico aparecido en Jalapa para oponerse a los compromisos de los líderes del Gran Círculo con Lerdo de Tejada. Fue delegado de la Sociedad Artístico-Industrial al Congreso Obrero de 1876 y una de las principales figuras del ala radical. Llegó a presidir algunas sesiones. En los años setenta impulsó la creación de cooperativas. Colaboró en *El Obrero Internacional* (1874).

Velázquez, Consuelo ◆ n. Ciudad Guzmán, Jal. (1924). En 1939 se tituló como profesora de piano en la Escuela Normal de Música. Concertista graduada en el Conservatorio. En los cuarenta adquirió renombre como compositora en la XEW y dejó la música sinfónica cuando compuso la canción *Bésame mucho*, que le ganó reconocimiento mundial y ha sido interpretada en más de 20 idiomas, por cantantes como Elvis Presley, Frank Sinatra, Elton John, Charles Aznavour y los Beatles. Autora, entre muchas otras, de *Pedacito, Cachito mío, Déjame quererte, Para ti, para ti, Amar y vivir, Yo no fui, Al nacer este día, Dondequiera, Enamorada, Corazón, Enamorado perdido, No insistas más, Amar, No volveré, Te espero, Sólo amor, Pasional, Te lo dije, Anoche, Tú, mi amor, Tu respuesta, Amor sobre ruedas, Vivir y amar, Volverás a mí, Aunque tengas razón, Que seas feliz* (de la que se grabaron 21 versiones en tres meses, en 1956) y *Verdad amarga*. Fue diputada federal por el PRI (1979-82). El Consejo Panamericano de sociedades autorales latinoamericanas le otorgó el título de *La Compositora de América*. Presidenta (1970-82) y presidenta vitalicia (1982-) de la Sociedad de Autores y Compositores de México y vicepresidenta de la Confederación Internacional de Sociedades de Autores y Compositores. Premio José Clemente Orozco (1975) y Premio Jalisco (1990). La Sociedad de Autores y Compositores le otorgó la Credencial de Oro (1996) y, en la Feria de Octubre de Guadalajara, recibió El Ave de Plata (1997).

Velázquez, Fidel ◆ n. en San Pedro Azcapotzaltongo, hoy Villa Nicolás Romero, Edo. de Méx., y m. en el DF (1900-1997). Trabajó en el campo durante su infancia. Pasó a la ciudad de México hacia 1914, donde fue aprendiz de carpintero (1915). En 1920 era trabajador de la Compañía Lechera del Rosario, donde intentó en vano formar un sindicato (1922), por lo que fue despedido. En 1924 fue obrero de una planta pasteurizadora, donde conoció a los hermanos Justino y Alfonso Sánchez Madariaga, con quienes fundó la Unión Sindical de Trabajadores de la Industria Lechera, de la que fue secretario general, afiliada a la CROM. En 1929 fundó la Federación Sindical de Trabajadores del DF y participó en la fundación del PNR. En junio de 1933 la Unión se escindió de la CROM y concertó un pacto de unidad con otras organizaciones obreras independientes y, junto con Vicente Lombardo Toledano, convocó al congreso constituyente de la Confederación General de Obreros y Campesinos de México (CGOCM). En los primeros días de febrero de 1936, durante su segundo

Foto: Armando Herrera

Consuelo Velázquez

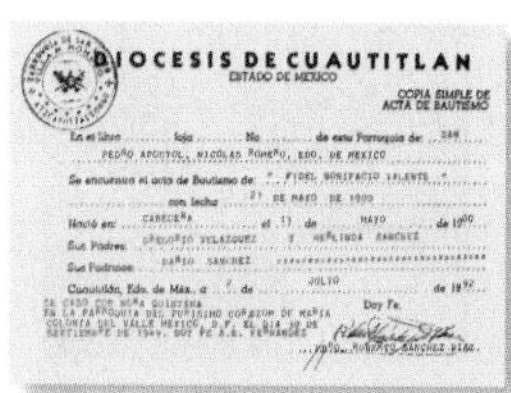

DIOCESIS DE CUAUTITLAN
ESTADO DE MEXICO
COPIA SIMPLE DE ACTA DE BAUTISMO
PEDRO APOSTOL, NICOLAS ROMERO, EDO. DE MEXICO
Se encuentra el acta de Bautismo de: FIDEL BONIFACIO VALENTE
con fecha 21 DE MAYO DE 1900
Nació en: CABECERA el 17 de MAYO de 1900
Sus Padres: GREGORIO VELAZQUEZ Y HERLINDA SANCHEZ
Sus Padrinos: MARIO SANCHEZ
Cuautitlán, Edo. de Méx., a ... de JULIO de 19..
Doy Fe.

Retrato y acta de nacimiento de Fidel Velázquez

congreso, la CGOCM se disolvió y, del 21 al 24 de febrero de ese año dio pie a la creación de la Confederación de Trabajadores de México, de la que el fue primer secretario de organización y propaganda. En 1941 fue elegido secretario general de la CTM, cargo en el que se mantuvo hasta su muerte, con excepción del periodo 1947-50 en que ocupó el puesto Fernando Amilpa. Fue diputado federal y tres veces senador (1946-52, 1958-64 y 1970-76). Recibió la medalla Belisario Domínguez en 1979.

Tere Velázquez

Velázquez, Gerardo ◆ n. en Cárdenas, SLP (1949). Dramaturgo. Ingeniero químico por el IPN y pasante en letras inglesas por la UNAM. Asistió al taller de composición dramática de Emilio Carballido. Ha colaborado en *Revista de la Universidad de México, Punto de Partida, El Cuento, Tramoya* y en los suplementos culturales de *Excélsior, El Día* y *El Heraldo de México*. Coautor de *Aleluyas para dos desempleos y un tema de amor* (1969). Autor de las obras de teatro *Chana volante o la jaula de los canarios* (1973, premio del IPN), *El cuarto más tranquilo* (1975, Premio Punto de Partida), *En la tupida oscuridad* (1976, premio Museo del Chopo), *Toño Basura. Retrato cubista* (1977, premio de la Universidad de Panamá), *Sobre las lunas* (1979), *Vía libre* (1980, premio Punto de Partida) y *Aunque vengas en figura distinta, Victoriano Huerta* (1984, premio INBA-Casa de la Cultura de Mexicali). Otras obras suyas son *Hasta hacernos polvo juntos, El telar rojo (Huelga de Río Blanco)* y *El último viaje*.

Velázquez, Leonardo ◆ n. en Oaxaca, Oax. (1935). Compositor. Aprendió composición en el Conservatorio Nacional de Música y en el Conservatorio de Los Ángeles. Ha sido maestro de música. Fue jefe de discoteca y productor de programas en Radio UNAM, así como presidente de la Liga de Compositores de Música de Concierto de México (1973-75). Fundó y dirigió la Orquesta de Cámara de la SEP y fue jefe del Departamento de Música y director de Actividades Musicales de la UNAM. Ha desempeñado el cargo de vocal del Comité de Vigilancia de la SACM, presidente de Música de Concierto en México y miembro de la Academia de Artes. Desde 1994 pertenece al Sistema Nacional de Creadores de Arte.

Velázquez, Miguel Ángel ◆ n. en el DF (1950). Periodista. Ha sido reportero de la revista *Tiempo* y *El Universal*. Fundador de los periódicos *unomásuno* y *La Jornada;* jefe de información de Canal 11; jefe de la corresponsalía de California, subdirector de información y director de Operaciones Nacionales de Notimex; director de servicios informativos y jefe de la sección "La Capital" de *La Jornada*. Ha colaborado en *El Nacional* y en el noticiero radiofónico *Para Empezar*. Comentarista de la BBC de Londres.

Velázquez, Tere ◆ n. y m. en el DF (1942-1998). Nombre profesional de la actriz María de los Ángeles Teresa Villar Dondé. Estudió en la Academia Andrés Soler. Se inició en la obra teatral *Quinceañera impaciente*. Filmó más de 180 películas, 29 de las cuales fueron rodadas en Italia, España y Sudamérica. Algunos de sus filmes más importantes fueron: *Sube y Baja, Soy millonario, Mi madre querida, Piernas de oro, Suicídate mi amor, La bala perdida, Fray don Juan, Dos criados malcriados, Suerte te dé Dios, En carne propia* y *Monte escondido*.

Velázquez Cárdenas de León, Joaquín de ◆ n. y m. en la ciudad de México (1732-1786). En la Real y Pontificia Universidad fue profesor titular de astrología y matemáticas desde 1765, cuando era bachiller en medicina y astrología. En 1768 el virrey lo envió a Sultepec a reconocer el beneficio de metales. En 1773 tenía nombramiento de abogado de la Real Audiencia y ese año renunció a la cátedra universitaria. En 1780 todavía sirvió a la Universidad como examinador. Dedicado a las ciencias exactas, fundó una Academia de Matemáticas. En 1774 viajó a España como representante de los propietarios de minas y dos años después logró organizar el gremio, por lo que, en 1777, el virrey Antonio María de Bucareli formalizó la creación del Real Tribunal General de Minería, especie de cámara patronal del ramo que presidió Velázquez de León, quien impulsó desde ahí la fundación del Colegio de Minería, del que fue director. Trianguló el valle de México y fue el primer americano en hacer un corte estratigráfico e interpretarlo correctamente. Coautor de las *Reales ordenanzas para la dirección, régimen y gobierno del importante cuerpo de la minería de la Nueva España y de su Real Tribunal General* (puestas en vigor en 1783).

Velazquez Duarte, Diego ◆ n. en Chapalilla, Nay. (1932). Licenciado en filosofía por el Montezuma College de la Universidad Católica de Washington (1957) y licenciado en derecho por Escuela Superior de Derecho de la Universidad Autónoma de Nayarit (1987). Pertenece al PAN desde 1989, donde fue secretario de Acción Electoral de Tepic (1991). Fue asesor jurídico de la SARH en Nayarit (1986-87). Diputado federal (1991-94).

Velázquez H., Pedro ◆ n. en Valle de Bravo, Edo. de Méx., y m. en el DF (1913-1968). Sacerdote ordenado en 1937. Era doctor en teología por la Universidad Gregoriana y sociólogo egresado del Centro de Economía y Humanismo, de París. Regresó a México en 1939 y dos años más tarde ingresó en el Secretariado Social Mexicano, del que fue vocero y director hasta su muerte. Profesor en los seminarios Mayor, Menor y de Misiones Extranjeras y secretario de Acción Social del Consejo Episcopal Latinoamericano, en el que editó las series de folletos "Desarrollo integral" y "Cuadernos para hoy" y dirigió la revista *Contacto*. Fundador de la Unión Mexicana de Escuelas de Trabajo Social, de la Confederación Mexicana de Cajas Populares, del Movimiento de Cooperativas Agropecuarias y Artesanales y del Instituto de Desarrollo de la Comunidad. Amigo de Vicente Lombardo Toledano (☛), se le considera precursor del diálogo entre cristianos y marxistas. Autor de *Miseria de México. Tierra desconocida, métodos de educación popular, Reformas de estructura* *de la empresa, Dimensión social de la caridad, La pastoral social, La verdadera redención del proletariado, Misión social del empresario, Ruta social del católico* y *El pensamiento social de Juan XXIII*.

VELÁZQUEZ DE LEÓN, JOAQUÍN ◆ n. y m. en la ciudad de México (1803-1882). Estudió en el Colegio de Minería. En 1821 se adhirió al Plan de Iguala y alcanzó el grado de coronel de ingenieros en el ejército trigarante. Fue comisionado especial en Washington e integrante de la junta mixta de reclamaciones (junio de 1840), encargado de negocios *ad ínterim* en Washington (1842), fundador y director de la Escuela Práctica de Minas y Metalurgia y secretario de Fomento en uno de los gabinetes de Antonio López de Santa-Anna (del 26 de abril de 1853 al 9 de agosto de 1855). Fue uno de los encargados de ofrecer a Maximiliano el trono del Segundo Imperio y en 1865 éste lo envió a Roma como presidente de una comisión diplomática. Perteneció a la Sociedad Universal para el Desarrollo de las Ciencias (creada en Londres en 1851 y de la que fue presidente honorario), a la Sociedad de Geología de Francia y al Instituto de África.

VELÁZQUEZ RIVERA, LUIS ◆ n. en Paso de Ovejas, Ver. (1947). Licenciado en periodismo por la Universidad Veracruzana, de la que es profesor. Ha sido colaborador de *El Dictamen* y jefe de redacción de *La Tarde*, ambos del puerto de Veracruz. Autor de *Un infierno llamado Veracruz* (1984), *Bamba violenta* (1985) y *El café, ese desconocido genocidio*. Recibió el Premio del Club de Periodistas de México (1982).

VELÁZQUEZ RODRÍGUEZ, PRIMO FELICIANO ◆ n. en Santa María del Río y m. en San Luis Potosí, SLP (1860-1953). Estudió en el Seminario de San Luis Potosí (1880), del que fue profesor. Se dedicó al periodismo y al estudio de la historia. Fundó en 1883 el periódico *La Voz de San Luis* y en 1885 *El Estandarte*, que se publicaría hasta 1890. Tradujo del náhuatl el *Códice Chimalpopoca o Anales de Cuauhtitlán* y *El gran acontecimiento. Historia de la aparición de ntra. sra. de Guadalupe publicada en México por Luis Lazo de la Vega en 1649*. Autor de *Colección de documentos para la historia de San Luis Potosí* (4 t., 1897-99), *La aparición de Santa María de Guadalupe* (1931), *San Francisco de Asís* (1940) e *Historia de San Luis Potosí* (4 t., 1946-48). Fue miembro de la Sociedad Mexicana de Geografía y Estadística, de la Academia de Ciencias Antonio Alzate, Academia Mexicana de Santa María de Guadalupe, Academia Mexicana (de la Lengua) y de la Academia Mexicana de la Historia (1919-53).

VÉLEZ, ÁNGEL MARÍA ◆ n. en la ciudad de México y m. en Veracruz, Ver. (1805-1886). Militar. Unido al ejército trigarante combatió en agosto de 1821 en Azcapotzalco. Fue empleado de la Administración de Correos de Veracruz (1824-28) y oficial de la Comisaría General del mismo puerto. En 1838 combatió a los franceses en la guerra de los Pasteles y en 1847 a los invasores estadounidenses. Volvió a trabajar en la Administración de Correos de Veracruz y en 1860 fue titular de la dependencia. En 1864, durante la intervención francesa, fue gobernador republicano y comandante miltar de Veracruz. En 1868 volvió a ser administrador de Correos en el puerto jarocho, cargo que desempeñó casi hasta su muerte.

VÉLEZ, FRANCISCO A. ◆ n. en Jalapa, Ver., y m. en el DF (?-1919). Estudió en el Colegio Militar. En 1847, durante la invasión estadounidense, tomó parte en la defensa del puerto de Veracruz. Alcanzó el grado de general de brigada durante la guerra de los Tres Años, en el bando conservador. Gobernador y comandante militar de Guanajuato (1859) y de San Luis Potosí (1860). El 22 de diciembre de 1860 participó en la batalla de Calpulalpan, en la que fueron definitivamente derrotados los conservadores. Amnistiado en 1861 se retiró del ejército, pero retomó las armas en 1866 contra la intervención francesa. En enero de 1867 unió sus fuerzas a las de Vicente Riva Palacio y, en el sitio de Querétaro, tomó el convento de la Cruz. Fue gobernador del Distrito Federal (del 6 de septiembre de 1869 al 27 de enero de 1871), diputado federal y comandante militar del DF.

VÉLEZ, GONZALO ◆ n. en el DF (1964). Estudió letras hispánicas en la UNAM. Autor del poemario *La hoja verde del jueves*, del guión de *El pesadillante* (1997) y de la novela *Perforaciones* (1998). Becario de novela del Fonca (1996-97) y Premio Joaquín Mortiz (1998).

VÉLEZ, LUPE ◆ n. en San Luis Potosí, SLP, y m. en EUA (1910-1944). Nombre profesional de la actriz Guadalupe Villalobos Vélez y conocida en México como *la Chinampina Mexicana* y *la Niña Lupi*. Se inició en el teatro de revista en 1924 con las obras *Ya apareció la cadena, Una hora de matrimonio, No lo tapes* y *Humo de opio*. Pasó a Hollywood, donde actuó en su primera película, *El gaucho*, al lado de Douglas Fairbanks, y donde realizó casi toda su carrera cinematográfica. Trabajó en revistas musicales en Nueva York y Londres y actuó con la pareja cómica de Stanley Laurel y Oliver Hardy. Fue esposa de los actores estadounidenses Gary Cooper y Johnny Weismüller. Actuó en las películas *Naná* y *La Sandunga* (1937), filmadas en México; *La canción del lobo* (1929, con Gary Cooper), *Lady of the Pavements* (de D. W. Griffith), *El ala rota, The Squaw Man* (1931), *Oriente es occidente, El puerto del infierno, Resurrección* y *La pelirroja de Manhattan*. Participó en la serie del personaje *Mexican Spitfire*, realizada en Los Ángeles, donde se suicidó.

Foto: Hemeroteca Nacional

Joaquín Velázquez de León

LA APARICIÓN

SANTA MARÍA DE GUADALUPE

PRIMO FELICIANO VELÁZQUEZ

MÉXICO, D. F.
1931

Obra de Primo Feliciano Velázquez Rodríguez

Francisco Vélez

Foto: Archivo General de la Nación/Fondo Teixidor

Lupe Vélez

Pedro Vélez

VÉLEZ, PEDRO ◆ n. en Zacatecas, Zac., y m. en la ciudad de México (1787-1848). Abogado. Como presidente de la Suprema Corte de Justicia accedió a la Presidencia de la República el 23 de diciembre de 1829, luego de que el Plan de Jalapa obligara a la renuncia del presidente interino José María Bocanegra; el mismo día, de acuerdo con la Constitución, quedó integrada una junta de gobierno con Vélez, Lucas Alamán y Luis Quintanar, que estuvo en funciones hasta el 31 de diciembre del mismo año, cuando entregó el Ejecutivo a Anastasio Bustamante.

VÉLEZ ALATRISTE, JORGE ◆ n. en Puebla, Pue., y m. cerca del DF (1911-1970). Actor. Se inició como locutor de la estación de radio XEW y pasó después a trabajar en el cine. Su primera película fue *Doña Malvada*. En 1945 se retiró de la industria cinematográfica y fijó su residencia en Estados Unidos, tras casarse con Margarita Riccardi, viuda de Maximino Ávila Camacho. Murió en un accidente automovilístico. Actuó en las películas *La familia Dressel* (debido a la cual adquirió fama), *Jalisco nunca pierde* (1937), *Ojos tapatíos, La tierra del mariachi, Amor chinaco* y *Virgen de medianoche*.

VÉLEZ ESCALANTE, MANUEL ◆ n. y m. en Hermosillo, Son. (¿1825?-1881). Profesor en Guaymas y fiscal del Supremo Tribunal de Justicia de Sonora. En 1865 reconoció al imperio de Maximiliano. Éste lo designó prefecto imperial del departamento de Sonora (febrero de 1866). Acompañó al austriaco en el sitio de Querétaro, en 1867, donde fue aprehendido por los republicanos.

Retrato y firma de Francisco Javier Venegas de Saavedra

VELO, CARLOS ◆ n. en España y m. en el DF (1909-1988). Cineasta. Licenciado en entomología (1932) y doctor en ciencias biológicas (1934) y en entomología por la Universidad Central de Madrid, de la que fue profesor (1933-35), así como del Instituto Nacional de Segunda Enseñanza (1934-36), en España, y de la Escuela Nacional de Ciencias Biológicas (1942-43) y del Centro Universitario de Estudios Cinematográficos, en México. Llegó a México en 1939. Fue director cinematográfico de Ultea Films y del *Noticiero Mexicano* (1941-51), trabajó para Clasa Films Mundiales (1941-66) y fundó el Padroado da Cultura Galega (1947). Se asoció con Manuel Barbachano Ponce (1953) en Teleproducciones, donde fue director, consejero técnico y jefe de montaje de los noticieros *Telerrevista, Cine Selecciones, Cámara* y *Cine Verdad*. Director del Centro de Producción del Cortometraje (1971), fundador del Centro de Producción Audiovisual de la SEP (1976), fundador y director del Centro de Capacitación Cinematográfica (1975-77) y director de Cine y Televisión de la Dirección General de Comunicación Social de la Presidencia (1984-88). En 1981 fue encarcelado por órdenes de Margarita López Portillo. Dirigió, entre otras, las películas documentales *Pintura mural mexicana* (1953, premio del Festival de Edimburgo) y *La tierra del chicle*, así como los largometrajes *Torero* (1956, mención honorífica y premio Flaherty de Nueva York) y *Pedro Páramo* (1966, que lo hizo acreedor a un Ariel). Autor del libro *Sonora* (1982).

VENADO ◆ Municipio de San Luis Potosí situado en el occidente del estado, al nor-noroeste de la capital estatal y al sur-suroeste de Matehuala. Superficie: 1,360.6 km². Habitantes: 14,794, de los cuales 3,549 forman la población económicamente activa. Hablan alguna lengua indígena 17 personas mayores de cinco años. En la jurisdicción se producen alfarería y dulces de leche. Cuenta con fábricas de hilados y tejidos.

VENEGAS, SOCORRO ◆ n. en San Luis Potosí, SLP (1972). Escritora. Ha conducido programas culturales de radio y coordina el taller de cuento del Centro Morelense de las Artes. Textos suyos aparecen en las antologías *Cuentistas de Tierra Adentro III* (1997), *Apocalipsis* (1998), *Antología de letras y dramaturgia. Jóvenes creadores* (1998) y *Bestiario contemporáneo* (1999). Autora del volumen de cuento *La risa de las azucenas* (1998). Ha sido becaria del Fondo para la Cultura y las Artes del Estado de Morelos (1996-97) y del Fonca (1997-98).

VENEGAS DE SAAVEDRA, FRANCISCO JAVIER ◆ n. y m. en España (1760-1838). Militar. En España combatió en 1808 la invasión napoleónica. En 1810 fue gobernador de Cádiz y en ese mismo año fue designado virrey de la Nueva España. Durante su gestión al frente del gobierno virreinal frustró la conspiración de Valladolid, convirtió la sede de la Real y Pontificia Universidad de México en cuartel, creó tribunales especiales de policía, fundó una junta militar en cada capital provincial y organizó

Escudo de armas de Francisco Javier Venegas de Saavedra

al ejército para oponerse a la lucha de Miguel Hidalgo, primero, y a la de José María Morelos, después. Asimismo, le correspondió promulgar la Constitución española de Cádiz (1812) y la Ley de Imprenta, las que días después suspendió, al declarar el virreinato el estado de sitio. Fue destituido en 1812 y sustituido en 1813 por Félix María Calleja. Regresó a España y en 1818 fue capitán general de Galicia.

VENEZUELA ◆ República de Sudamérica con costas en el mar Caribe y el océano Atlántico. Limita con Guyana, Brasil y Colombia. Superficie: 912,050 km². Habitantes: 23,242,000 (1998). Su capital es Caracas (con 1,964,846 habitantes en 1992) y otras ciudades de importancia son: Maracaibo (1,363,873 habitantes en 1990), Valencia (1,031,941), Maracay (799,884), Barquisimeto (745,444), Barcelona (429,072), San Cristóbal (336,100) y Maturín (257,683). El idioma oficial es el español y su moneda el bolívar. Cuenta con los yacimientos de hidrocarburos más ricos de América del Sur y es el tercer productor de petróleo del mundo. *Historia:* el territorio estuvo originalmente habitado por los indios arauacos, caribes y guajiros (nómadas de los llanos y las mesetas del sur), y los timotes y cuicas (agricultores andinos). El 5 de agosto de 1498, en su tercer viaje, Cristóbal Colón pisó por primera vez tierra continental americana en la costa sur de la península de Paria, en Venezuela, y el 15 de agosto desembarcó en la isla Margarita. En 1499 una expedición dirigida por Alonso de Ojeda, en la que participaban también Américo Vespucio y Juan de la Cosa, bordeó las costas venezolanas y llegó al lago Maracaibo. En 1500 se fundó el primer asentamiento español en la isla de Cubagua, mientras Vicente Yáñez Pinzón llegaba al río Orinoco, el mayor de Venezuela. Dos años después, el fraile Bartolomé de las Casas fundó la primera misión en tierra firme, cerca de la actual ciudad de Cumaná, la que sería destruida casi de inmediato por los indios cumanagotos. En ese mismo año una sublevación indígena fue reprimida por Jácome Castellón, quien erigió una fortaleza en Cumaná. En 1525 fue erigida la gobernación de Margarita y el 26 de julio de 1527, Juan de Ampués fundó Santa Ana de Coro, que sería la primera capital venezolana. El 27 de marzo de 1528 quedó establecida la capitanía general de Venezuela. Debido a una cesión de Carlos V, empresarios alemanes, principalmente la firma bancaria Welser, iniciaron la exploración sistemática del territorio. En 1529 el alemán Ambrosio Alfinger se convirtió en el primer gobernador de Venezuela y estableció su capital en Santa Ana de Coro (24 de febrero). El sucesor de Alfinger, Felipe de Hutten, fue asesinado en 1546 por órdenes del explorador español Juan de Carvajal, con lo que terminó la injerencia germana en la zona. En 1548, Juan de Villegas fue designado gobernador. Una sublevación indígena, dirigida por el cacique Guaicaipuro, fue reprimida en 1568 y su líder ejecutado. En 1570 el sucesor de Guaicaipuro, Paramaconi, fue derrotado y se vio forzado a pactar la paz con los conquistadores españoles. En 1573 se produjo una nueva sublevación, esta vez de indios mariches, encabezados por Tamanaco; ésta fue reprimida y su líder, también ejecutado. En 1578, Caracas se convirtió en capital de Venezuela y en 1591 fue constituida la gobernación de Trinidad-Guayana. Durante el siglo XVII, la política genocida de los conquistadores obligó a importar mano de obra esclava. En 1777, Carlos III erigió la Gran Capitanía General de Venezuela, que tuvo una relación estrecha con Nueva España, lo que influyó en la cultura de ambos países. Desde 1699 la nobleza criolla (los mantuanos), propietaria de esclavos y grandes plantaciones cacaoteras, mantuvo una sorda lucha económica con los gobernantes peninsulares. Para acabar con esa situación, Felipe V fundó en 1730 la Real Compañía Guipuzcoana, que controló la producción del cacao, restó poder a los mantuanos y prohibió el comercio con México. El monopolio comercial de esta compañía provocó en 1730 la primera rebelión mestiza en el país, dirigida por Andrés López, llamado *Andresote*. En 1749 se produjo otro alzamiento similar, encabezado por Francisco de León. Ambos movimientos fueron reprimidos. En 1784 los mantuanos optaron por introducir el cultivo del café. El primer movimiento independentista fue la conjuración de Manuel Gual y José María España, descubierta el 13 de julio de 1797. En marzo de 1799, Simón Bolívar viajó a México. Llegó a Veracruz y se hospedó en la casa de José Donato de Austria, padre de José de Austria, quien sería secretario particular del libertador y autor del libro *Historia militar de Venezuela*. A Bolívar, que entonces tenía 16 años de edad, se le atribuyen un romance con *la Güera* Rodríguez y una discusión con el virrey Miguel José de Azanza sobre el derecho de los pueblos iberoamericanos de alcanzar su libertad. La primera carta que se conoce de Bolívar está fechada en Ve-

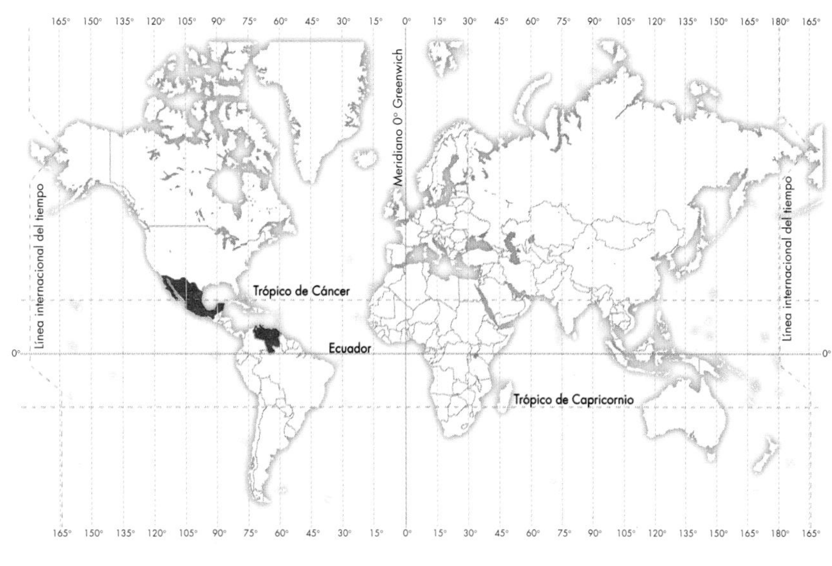

Venezuela

Timbres de Venezuela

racruz el 20 de marzo de 1799. Por su parte, Francisco de Miranda, llamado *el Precursor*, quien desde 1776 buscaba en Europa apoyo para independizar a Venezuela, intentó en abril de 1806 invadir al país desde Ocumare. Fue derrotado y se refugió en Trinidad, donde los ingleses financiaron una nueva intentona de Miranda. Un cabildo abierto en Caracas en abril de 1810 destituyó al capitán general de Venezuela, Vicente Emparán, y constituyó una junta de gobierno. Ésta desconoció a las Cortes de Cádiz y convocó a un congreso nacional que proclamó la independencia el 5 de julio de 1811. Venezuela designó generalísimo a Miranda y se inició entonces la guerra para expulsar a los españoles; Miranda fue capturado y remitido a Cádiz, donde murió en 1816. En 1812 la metrópoli envió al militar Domingo Monteverde, quien derrotó a los insurgentes. Entre diciembre de 1812 y enero de 1813, Bolívar dirigió una campaña libertadora desde el Bajo Magdalena, Colombia. Entró en Venezuela en mayo de 1813 y el 7 de agosto hizo una entrada triunfal en

Simón Bolívar, héroe venezolano, viajó a México en marzo de 1799

Caracas, donde se le dio el título de Libertador y se le nombró capitán general de los ejércitos insurgentes. Otro militar enviado por España, José Tomás Boves, puso en práctica tácticas guerrilleras y logró que pelearan en sus tropas los esclavos negros. Pudo derrotar a Bolívar, quien debió refugiarse en las Antillas a fines de 1814. En una carta fechada en Jamaica en 1815, Bolívar sugería que la estrategia indicada entonces para liberar a Iberoamérica del yugo español debía empezar por una expedición a México. En enero de

Simón Bolívar en la batalla de Ingaüi

1815 Fernando VII, reinstalado en el trono de España, envió a Venezuela un ejército dirigido por Pablo Murillo, para combatir tanto a los pocos insurgentes que se mantenían en lucha, como a los esclavos negros de José Antonio Páez, quienes armados por Boves habían decidido hacer su propia lucha. Así, los llaneros se convirtieron en aliados naturales de los rebeldes. Desde Haití y apoyado por el presidente de ese país, Petión, Bolívar regresó a Venezuela y reagrupó a los numerosos líderes rebeldes que actuaban por separado (Páez, Piar, Arismendi, Urdaneta y Bermúdez), logró apoderarse de Bogotá, llevó a los ejércitos venezolanos hasta el Alto Perú (actual Bolivia, en su honor) y se creó la Gran Colombia (Venezuela, Colombia, Ecuador y Panamá). En 1817 y 1818, Bolívar, con ayuda de Páez, liberó nuevamente la mayor parte de Venezuela, cuya capital estableció provisionalmente en Angostura (hoy Ciudad Bolívar); cruzó la cordillera de los Andes y el 7 de agosto de 1819 batió a los realistas en la batalla del puente de Boyacá. En diciembre de ese año el Congreso de Angostura proclamó la Constitución de la Gran Colombia, que comprendía el antiguo virreinato de la Nueva Granada, la capitanía general de Venezuela y la presidencia de Quito. El primer ministro plenipotenciario de la Gran Colombia ante el imperio de Agustín de Iturbide fue el mexicano Miguel Santa María (☛). El 24 de junio de 1821 los rebeldes ganaron la batalla de Carabobo, tras la que se consolidó la libertad venezolana. En 1824, España intentó recuperar sus ex colonias americanas con el apoyo de la flota rusa, por lo que México y Venezuela firmaron un tratado mutuo de defensa. Manuel Antonio Valero (☛), militar mexicano educado en España, sirvió a las órdenes de Bolívar, alcanzó el grado de general y fue ministro de Guerra y Marina (1830 y 1857). En 1830 la unidad iberoamericana ansiada por Bolívar se malogró por obra de los intereses regionalistas:

Flores en Ecuador, Santander en Colombia y Páez en Venezuela decidieron crear gobiernos nacionales separados. El 17 de diciembre de 1830 murió Simón Bolívar. El Congreso de Valencia declaró la separación de Venezuela y nombró jefe militar y político a Páez, quien se erigió en dictador. Después de tres constituciones (1830, 1857 y 1859), la de 1864 estableció una república federal llamada Estados Unidos de Venezuela. El presidente José Gregorio Monagas abolió la esclavitud el 25 de marzo de 1854. Entre 1859 y 1863 se produjo la llamada guerra federal, al término de la cual Páez y los conservadores fueron derrotados. En 1863, Páez se entrevistó con el diplomático mexicano Matías Romero y se ofreció como voluntario para combatir la intervención francesa, en favor de Benito Juárez. Hasta 1870 se sucedieron gobiernos provisionales, guerras internas y derrocamientos. En abril de 1870 el liberal Antonio Guzmán Blanco entró victorioso en Caracas y gobernó hasta 1888, pacificó al país, confiscó los bienes del clero, estableció la educación obligatoria y saneó las finanzas, aunque mantuvo un régimen de propiedad favorable de la pequeña minoría de 4 por ciento que poseía todas las tierras. De 1888 a 1889 se alternaron varios gobiernos dictatoriales, hasta que el caudillo andino Cipriano Castro invadió Venezuela con 60 hombres, suscitó la traición contra el presidente Andrade y se apoderó de Caracas para instaurar una dictadura que duró hasta el 19 de diciembre de 1908. El gobierno de Castro debió enfrentar en 1902 el bloqueo y bombardeo de Puerto Cabello por una flota conjunta de Italia, Inglaterra y Alemania, naciones que con las armas trataban de obligar al pago de la deuda venezolana. Un año después de la intervención armada, el 13 de diciembre de 1903, el conflicto terminó con la firma del Protocolo de Washington. En 1903 terminó otro litigio financiero, éste con México, que databa de 1826, cuando el entonces encargado mexicano de negocios en Londres, Vicente Rocafuerte, prestó al gobierno de la Gran Colombia 63,000 libras esterlinas. Al dividirse el país en tres naciones, Colombia, Ecuador y Venezuela asumieron la deuda. No obstante, en 1856, y aún sin haber cobrado el débito, el gobierno mexicano cedió los derechos a la casa Martínez del Río, misma que debió apelar a una comisión mixta de reclamaciones para que Venezuela finiquitara el adeudo. En 1903, por laudo arbitral, Venezuela tuvo que pagar 102,075 libras (el monto de su parte de la deuda, más intereses). El 19 de diciembre de 1908, Castro fue derrocado por Juan Vicente Gómez, su lugarteniente, quien instauró su propia dictadura hasta el 17 de diciembre de 1935, cuando murió, después de pacificar al país mediante el terror y la represión. Varios contingentes de venezolanos opuestos a Castro y a Gómez participaron en la Revolución Mexicana, en el ejército constitucionalista. En 1918 las compañías extranjeras iniciaron la explotación del petróleo venezolano. Álvaro Obregón, desde la Presidencia de México, permitió a un grupo de venezolanos opuestos a la dictadura de Gómez organizar, desde el territorio nacional, una expedición armada. Estos venezolanos exiliados en México eran: Luis y Luis Alfredo López Méndez, Humberto Tejera, Guillermo Egea Mier, Carlos León, Pedro Elías Aristigueta, Diego Córdoba, Ramón Ayala, Salvador de la Plaza, Víctor Volcán, Carlos y Manuel María Aponte, Gustavo Machado, Horacio Blanco Fombona, los generales Ortega Martínez y Emilio Arévalo Cedeño, Bartolomé Ferrer y Alberto Ravell. Aún en México, los exiliados venezolanos Salvador de la Plaza y Gustavo Machado fundaron el Partido Revolucionario Venezolano. De 1927 a 1935 se suspendieron las relaciones diplomáticas entre México y Venezuela. En 1931 se organizó en México otra expedición fallida de venezolanos que deseaban derrocar a Gómez; en esta expedición, organizada por Carlos León, viajaron unos 200 internacionalistas mexicanos; el desembarco de esta invasión en las costas del estado Falcón, motivó aquel siniestro telegrama de León Jurado a su jefe Juan Vicente Gómez: "Mañana comerán carne mexicana los zamuros corianos". Sucedieron a éste los presidentes Eleazar López Contreras (1935-1941) e Isaías Medina Angarita (1941-1945). En su viraje reaccionario de 1937, López Contreras disolvió los partidos populares, suprimió la prensa de oposición y expulsó a 37 revolucionarios que fueron asilados en México por Lázaro Cárdenas: entre ellos estaban varios personajes de la futura política venezolana, como Jóvito Villalba, Gustavo Machado, Inocente Palacios, Carlos Augusto León y José Tomás Jiménez Arráiz, así como Salvador de la Plaza, Miguel Acosta Saignes o Inocente Palacios, quienes estudiaron la realidad mexicana; Carlos Irazábal que editó, con prólogo de Luis Chávez Orozco, la primera edición de *Hacia la democracia*; Carlos Augusto León, autor del poemario aparecido en México *Los pasos vivientes*; y Miguel Otero Silva, quien en la ciudad de México vio aparecer su primer libro de poemas, *Agua y cauce*, y su primera novela: *Fiebre*. El 18 de octubre de 1945 una junta cívico-militar derrocó a Medina y llevó al poder a Rómulo Batancourt, quien también había vivido exiliado en México. Betancourt legalizó los partidos políticos, promulgó una nueva Constitución y convocó a elecciones. En 1946 fue electo presidente el novelista Rómulo Gallegos (☛), otro veterano del exilio mexicano. Gallegos fue depuesto el 24 de noviembre de 1948 por un triunvirato militar integrado por Carlos Delgado Chalbaud, secretario de la Defensa, Marcos Pérez Jiménez y Felipe Llovera Páez. Gallegos se refugió nuevamente en México, donde continuó su obra litearia. De este modo, a fines de los años cuarenta se produjo otra y más grande oleada migratoria hacia México. Por primera vez, al lado de intelectuales de prestigio, aparecieron obreros y campesinos, dirigentes sindicales, mujeres que habían

Rómulo Gallegos, novelista y presidente de Venezuela

sido víctimas de torturas, gente sin filiación ideológica que la dictadura había perseguido infundadamente, jefes de partidos políticos diferenciados por sus doctrinas pero hermanados en la acción coincidente de enfrentarse a los usurpadores. Los núcleos de desterrados venezolanos publicaron en México sus órganos de expresión política, *Venezuela Democrática* y *Noticias de Venezuela*, y colaboraron en la revista *Humanismo* del cubano Raúl Roa. El presidente mexicano Lázaro Cárdenas escribió a Rómulo Gallegos en esa oportunidad: "Fiel a sus tradiciones, el México de la Revolución lo acogió a usted con beneplácito. Como escritor y como estadista tiene usted títulos suficientes para honrar al país que le brinda su albergue. Durante los últimos años, nuestra bandera ha amparado en el extranjero a perseguidos de todas las ideas políticas y en nuestro territorio han encontrado protección mujeres y hombres de todos los credos. Es fácil explicar esta conducta: los mexicanos de nuestro tiempo hemos pagado un altísimo tributo en vidas humanas para alcanzar el triunfo del movimiento iniciado en 1910". En 1950, Delgado Chalbaud, presidente de la junta militar, fue asesinado y lo sustituyó Pérez Jiménez. Éste convocó a unas elecciones en las que ganó Jóvito Villalba, pronto derrocado por el mismo Pérez Jiménez, a quien correspondió el inicio del auge petrolero venezolano, durante el cual subieron los ingresos fiscales, se emprendieron grandes obras y se auspició la inmigración de 500,000 europeos; simultáneamente, sin embargo, se desatendieron la educación, la salud y la vivienda y se proscribieron casi todos los partidos políticos. En 1953 los Estados Unidos de Venezuela se transformaron en República de Venezuela. En 1957, Pérez Jiménez pretendió prolongar su mandato concediendo el voto a los extranjeros, pero el 23 de enero de 1958 una acción conjunta de militares prodemocráticos y dirigentes políticos derrocó al dictador, que se refugió en Estados Unidos; una junta provisional (Wolfgang Larrazábal y Edgar Sanabria) convocó a eleciones y en diciembre de 1958 fue elegido presidente Rómulo Betancourt. Éste procesó y extraditó a Pérez Jiménez. En 1960, Venezuela encabezó la formación de la Organización de Países Exportadores de Petróleo. En ese año, el presidente mexicano Adolfo López Mateos realizó una visita oficial a Venezuela. En 1963, Betancourt visitó oficialmente México, luego de sobrevivir a un atentado. En 1973, Venezuela se unió al Pacto Andino. En 1975 el presidente venezolano Carlos Andrés Pérez, otro de los asilados por Cárdenas, realizó una visita oficial a México y en el mismo año Luis Echeverría se entrevistó con él en Caracas. En 1976, Venezuela nacionalizó el petróleo. En 1977, José López Portillo visitó oficialmente Venezuela. El mandatario Luis Herrera Campins viajó a México en 1981 y 1983. El presidente Jaime Lusinchi vino a México en 1984, cuando se renovó el Pacto de San José. Miguel de la Madrid visitó oficialmente a Lusinchi en Caracas en 1984 y éste viajó a México en 1985, 1986 y 1987, esta última vez para asistir a la reunión del Grupo de los Ocho en Acapulco. En 1989, con Carlos Andrés Pérez nuevamente en la presidencia, a raíz de una serie de aumentos en los precios de los bienes y servicios básicos se desataron violentos motines en Caracas, con saldo de varios cientos de muertos, heridos y detenidos y con el saqueo de comercios. El incidente fue llamado "el caracazo". En 1992 se produjeron dos intentos de golpe de Estado dirigidos por el coronel Hugo Chávez. Los intentos fallaron y Chávez fue encarcelado mientras crecía el repudio popular al gobierno de Pérez, cuya política de austeridad golpeó fuertemente la economía familiar. En 1993 un juez exigió que se juzgara a Pérez por corrupción y el Congreso autorizó la destitución del presidente, que fue procesado y hallado culpable. Purgó una condena de 30 meses teniendo su casa como cárcel. En 1995 el coronel golpista Hugo Chávez, ya en libertad, encabezó una organización política legal (Movimiento Bolivariano) que lo llevó a la presidencia en 1999. En el poder, Chávez convocó a un Congreso Constituyente.

Venta, de la ◆ Río de Chiapas también llamado Pueblo Viejo. Nace en la porción suroccidental del estado, al norte del extremo noroccidental de la sierra Madre de Chiapas, por la confluencia de los ríos Jiquipilas o Zoyatenco y Cintalapa, al este de Cintalapa de Figueroa; corre hacia el norte, tuerce al noroeste y recibe a los ríos La Ciénega y Encajonado antes de desembocar en la presa Netzahualcóyotl, al suroeste de Raudales de Malpaso.

Venta, La ◆ Zona arqueológica de Tabasco (☛ *Huimanguillo*).

Ventanas, de las ◆ Sierra de Durango. Forma parte de la cresta principal de la sierra Madre Ocidental, en el extremo suroeste del estado. Se extiende de noreste a suroeste, al suroeste de la ciudad de Victoria de Durango; colinda al este con la sierra de Durango, al suroeste con el estado de Sinaloa y al noroeste con el río Presidio y con la sierra Espinazo del Diablo.

Ventosa, de la ◆ Bahía de Oaxaca situada en el golfo de Tehuantepec, en la desembocadura del río del mismo nombre, al este de Salina Cruz y al sursuroeste de Juchitán de Zaragoza. Colinda al oeste con el cerro del Morro o de la Ventosa y al este con la punta del Morro. Mide 1,590 metros de largo por 450 de ancho y permite la entrada de barcos de poco calado.

Ventura López, Pablo ◆ n. en Temascal, Oax. (1953). Profesor por la Escuela Normal Superior de Oaxaca. Miembro del PAN. Fundador y dirigente estatal de la Organización de Indígenas Oaxaqueños y asesor de la Alianza Nacional de Profesionales Indígenas Bilingües. Ha sido profesor y director de primaria, asesor de cursos de capacitación de promotores culturales bilingües, asesor de cursos de formación de supervisores escolares bilingües, jefe de la Oficina de Extensión Educativa de la Dirección General de Educación Indígena, responsable del Plan Oaxaca, supervisor

Delegación Venustiano Carranza en el Distrito Federal

escolar en la zona 169 de Jalapa de Díaz, Oaxaca, y diputado federal plurinominal (1985-88). Coautor de *El Estado mexicano y los grupos étnicos*.

VENUSTIANO CARRANZA ◆ Delegación política del Distrito Federal. Limita con el Estado de México y las delegaciones Gustavo A. Madero, Iztacalco y Cuauhtémoc. Superficie: 35.55 km^2 (por su extensión ocupa el decimosegundo lugar entre las delegaciones políticas y equivale al 2.47 por ciento de la superficie total del Distrito Federal). Habitantes: 485,623 (1995), de los cuales 76,697 forman la población económicamente activa, dedicada principalmente a la explotación de minas y canteras, la producción manufacturera, la construcción y las tareas agropecuarias. Hablan alguna lengua indígena 4,794 personas mayores de cinco años (náhuatl 1,094, zapoteco 825, otomí 744, mixteco 453 y mazahua 416). Fue creada por la Ley Orgánica del Distrito Federal, del 29 de diciembre de 1970. En su perímetro se localiza el cerro del Peñón de los Baños, formación volcánica que cuenta con una fuente de aguas termales. De acuerdo con la mitología náhuatl, en este peñón, que durante mucho tiempo fue una isla dentro del lago de México, el dios Huitzilopochtli sacrificó a su sobrino Cópil, cuyo corazón arrojó al fondo lacustre. Mientras las tribus aztecas peregrinaban de Chapultepec a Tizapán, el corazón de Cópil floreció hasta convertirse en el nopal sobre el que se posó el águila que, al devorar a una serpiente, dio a los peregrinos la señal que esperaban para fundar su ciudad. Por su céntrica ubicación, el Peñón fue punto de referencia para los navegantes del lago. Cuando los conquistadores españoles emprendieron la campaña final contra Tenochtitlán, edificaron en la actual jurisdicción la que probablemente sea la primera construcción española en la capital: las Atarazanas, fortaleza desde la cual se planeó y ejecutó el asalto final contra la capital mexica, y que fue después vivienda provisional de los conquistadores. Con este poblamiento en lo que más tarde sería el barrio de San Lázaro, se inició la urbanización de lo que es ahora la delegación Venustiano Carranza; el proceso de poblamiento y la urbanización acelerada no se produjeron plenamente, sino hasta la primera mitad del siglo XX, cuando la desecación total del lago así lo permitió. Sin embargo, durante la época colonial y a lo largo del siglo XIX, la garita de San Antonio Abad marcaba el extremo oriental de la ciudad, después del cual sólo se hallaban los llanos de San Lázaro y el Peñón de los Baños. En 1884 se descubrieron en este cerro los restos del llamado "Hombre del Peñón". Dentro de esta delegación se localizan el Aeropuerto Internacional Benito Juárez (inaugurado en 1954), el Palacio Legislativo, los mercados de Jamaica, Sonora y La Merced; el pueblo de la Magdalena Mixhuca (donde nació la hija de Moctezuma Xocoyotzin, quien en 1528 pidió a Hernán Cortés que llamara así al asentamiento, pues deseaba ponerlo bajo la protección religiosa de María Magdalena) y el Archivo General de la Nación, antigua penitenciaría del Distrito Federal, conocida como Palacio de Lecumberri, inaugurada en 1900 y a un costado de la cual fueron asesinados Francisco I. Madero y José María Pino Suárez el 22 de febrero de 1913.

VENUSTIANO CARRANZA ◆ Municipio de Chiapas situado en el centro del estado, al oeste de Comitán y al sureste de Tuxtla Gutiérrez. Superficie: 1,396.10 km^2. Habitantes: 51,756, de los cuales 12,629 forman la población económicamente activa. Hablan alguna lengua indígena 7,144 personas (tzotzil 4,226 y tzeltal 2,918). Indígenas monolingües: 730. En su jurisdicción se localizan la presa de La Angostura (la mayor del país), la laguna de Santa Ana y los baños del Carmen, como principales atractivos turísticos. La cabecera, hoy del mismo nombre, se llamó San Bartolomé.

VENUSTIANO CARRANZA ◆ ☛ *San Gabriel*.

VENUSTIANO CARRANZA ◆ Municipio de Michoacán situado en el noroeste del estado, al noroeste de Zamora, en los límites con Jalisco. Superficie: 237.97 km^2. Habitantes: 22,945, de los cuales 4,951 forman la población económicamente activa. Hablan alguna lengua indígena 32 personas mayores de cinco años. Su cabecera, del mismo nombre, se llamó antes San Pedro Caro.

VENUSTIANO CARRANZA ◆ Municipio de Puebla situado en el norte del estado, al noreste de Huauchinango, en los límites con Veracruz. Superficie: 308.71 km^2. Habitantes: 25,066, de los cuales

5,661 forman la población económicamente activa. Hablan alguna lengua indígena 1,118 personas mayores de cinco años (náhuatl 569 y totonaco 531).

Vera, Agustín ◆ n. en Acámbaro, Gto., y m. en San Luis Potosí, SLP (1889-1946). Escritor. Licenciado en derecho (1914) por el Instituto Científico y Literario de San Luis Potosí. Fue juez y magistrado del Supremo Tribunal de Justicia de San Luis, profesor en la Universidad Potosina y de la Escuela Nacional Preparatoria. Colaboró en *Vida Nacional*, *La Razón* y *Bohemia*. Autor de *La cena de Margot*, *La culpa de todos*, *El nahual*, *La mujer caída*, *¡Huelga!*, *Una pasión*, *Extraña aventura*, *El retrato de Chopin*, *Último amor*, *La novia de cera*, *Triste ilusión* (teatro, 1911), *Como en los cuentos* (teatro, 1916), *En la profunda sombra* (novela, 1916), *La vida rota* (teatro, 1920), *El humo de la gloria* (teatro, 1930), *La revancha* (novela, 1930) y *Tradiciones potosinas* (2 t., 1941).

Vera, Luis Roberto ◆ n. en Chile (1947). Poeta. Licenciado y maestro en letras clásicas por la Universidad de Chile, maestro en estudios de Asia por El Colegio de México y maestro en literatura española por la Universidad de Nuevo México. Asistió al taller literario de Hernán Lavín Cerda. Ha sido profesor e investigador de la UNAM. Fue miembro del grupo literario El Zaguán. Ha colaborado en *Punto*, *Cero en Literatura*, *El Zaguán*, *La Letra y la Imagen*, *Versus*, *Cuadernos de Literatura*, *Vuelta* y *Sábado*. Autor de los poemarios *La piedra en el pozo* (1978), *Bajo la ola* (1979), *Pintura en tiempo presente* (1982), *Guardabajo* (1982), *Permanencia voluntaria* (1983) y *Tesserae* (1989). Becario INBA-Fonapas de poesía (1978-79).

Vera, Santiago de ◆ n. en España y m. en Guadalajara, Jal. (?-1606). Doctor en cánones por la Real y Pontificia Universidad de México (1579), a la que en 1580, como alcalde de Corte de la Audiencia, dio posesión del solar de Alonso Dávila, entregado por la Corona "para que en él se edificasen unas escuelas". Rector de esta casa de estudios (1582-83), ordenó al obrero mayor de la ciudad hacer la traza de "diez tiendas" que debían constituir "un edificio leve" y se obtuvo "licencia para sacar tres mil vigas de los montes de Chalco". Fue oidor de la Audiencia de Guadalajara, presidente de la Audiencia de Filipinas (1584-93) y gobernador de la Nueva Galicia (1593-1606).

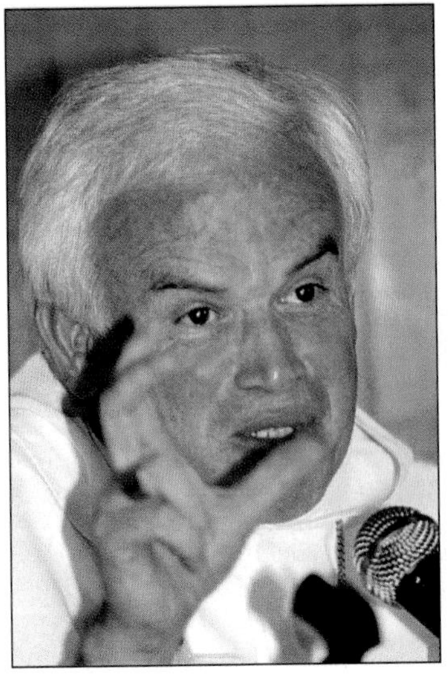
Raúl Vera López

Vera Estañol, Jorge ◆ n. y m. en el DF (1873-1958). Licenciado en derecho por la Escuela Nacional de Jurisprudencia, de la que director. En 1912 fue cesado y con un grupo de profesores y estudiantes fundó la Escuela Libre de Derecho. Ocupó la Secretaría de Instrucción Pública (del 19 de febrero al 13 de junio de 1913) de Victoriano Huerta. Vivió exiliado en Europa (1914-16) y en Estados Unidos (1916-31). Coautor de *México y su evolución social* (1920) y *Ensayo sobre la reconstrucción de México* (1920). Autor de *Partido Evolucionista* (1911), *Al margen de la Constitución de 1917* (1920), *Carranza and his Bolshevik Regime* (1920) e *Historia de la revolución mexicana. Orígenes y resultados*.

Vera López, Raúl ◆ n. en Acámbaro, Gto. (1945). Estudió ingeniería química en la UNAM y en 1968 ingresó a la Provincia de la Orden de Predicadores de México (dominicos). Fue ordenado sacerdote en Roma por el papa Paulo VI (1975). En México ha trabajado en la Parroquia Universitaria de los dominicos y ha sido maestro de novicios y socio provincial. Obispo de la diócesis de Ciudad Altamirano (1988-95), designado por Juan Pablo II. Ha sido miembro de la comisión que coordina las relaciones entre la CEM y la Conferencia de Superiores y Superioras Mayores Religiosos, y de la Comisión Episcopal para Indígenas del Episcopado Méxicano. En 1992 representó al Episcopado Mexicano en la cuarta Conferencia General del Episcopado Latinoamericano. Obispo coadjutor (1995-1999) de la diócesis de San Cristóbal de Las Casas y sustituto (1999-) del obispo Samuel Ruiz.

Vera y Talonia, Fortino Hipólito ◆ n. en Tequixquiac, Edo. de Méx., y m. en Cuernavaca, Mor. (1834-1898). Sacerdote. Estudió en el Seminario Conciliar y se ordenó en 1857. Fue vicario, cura, prebendado y canónigo en diversas plazas y primer obispo de Cuernavaca (1894-96). Cuando era párroco de Amecameca fundó el Colegio Católico, instituto que editó, entre otras obras, la *Biblioteca hispano-americana septentrional*, de Beristáin y Souza (1883), *Colección de documentos eclesiásticos de México* (3 t., 1887), *Tesoro guadalupano* (2 t., 1889) e *Informaciones sobre la milagrosa aparición de la Sma. V. de Guadalupe en 1666 y 1723* (1889). Autor de *Escritores eclesiásticos de México* (1880) y *Catecismo geográfico, histórico y estadístico de la Iglesia Mexicana* (1881).

Archivo Xavier Esparza

Fortino Hipólito Vera y Talonia

VERACRUZ ◆ Estado de la República Mexicana situado en la costa del golfo de México. Su nombre oficial es Veracruz-Llave. Limita con Tabasco, Chiapas, Oaxaca, Puebla, Hidalgo, San Luis Potosí y Tamaulipas. Superficie: 72,420.07 km^2. Su línea costera tiene una extensión de 684 km. En el estado se ubica la montaña más alta del país, el Pico de Orizaba o Citlaltépetl, con más de 5,700 metros. Cuenta con 35 por ciento de los ríos mexicanos, entre los que destacan el Pánuco, el Coatzacoalcos, el Tuxpan y el Papaloapan. Habitantes: 7,176,735 (1999, es la tercera entidad más poblada del país, con 7.4 por ciento del total nacional). Su población urbana es de 4,281.094 personas y la rural de 2,895,641. Son analfabetas 13.22 por ciento de los mayores de 15 años. La población económicamente activa la conforman el 53.9 por ciento de los mayores de 12 años. El producto interno bruto de Veracruz en 1996 represetó el 4.7 por ciento del nacional. Actualmente tiene 210 municipios y cuenta con la ciudad portuaria más importante del país: Veracruz. Hablan alguna lengua indígena 590,829 personas mayores de cinco años (náhuatl 314,121, totonaco 115,455, huasteco 47,620, popoluca 34,261, zapoteco 20,121, chinanteco 17,394 y otomí 15,688), de las cuales 69,807 no saben español. *Historia*: se han encontrado rastros de presencia humana en el actual territorio del estado con una antigüedad de 12,000 años. Las tres culturas autóctonas de Veracruz fueron la huasteca, en el norte; la totonaca, que se desarrolló en el centro; y la olmeca tardía, que ocupó el sur del actual territorio del estado. La cultura totonaca primitiva se extinguió hacia el año 900 de nuestra era. A ésta siguió el predominio del militarismo tolteca y la influencia de los nonoalcas y pipiles. A partir de 1450 los pueblos veracruzanos fueron sometidos por los ejércitos de la Triple Alianza, que los convirtieron en tributarios. La opresión mexica propició la adhesión de los totonacas a Hernán Cortes, que al marchar hacia el altiplano aumentó considerablemente sus fuerzas. La primera expedición española que llegó a costas de Veracruz fue organizada en Cuba por el gobernador Diego Velázquez en 1518 y comandada por Juan de Grijalva. En su tripulación

Miguel Alemán Velasco, gobernador constitucional del estado de Veracruz

Castillo de Teayo, en Veracruz

FOTO: MICHAEL CALDERWOOD

Presa Miguel de la Madrid, en Veracruz

venían, también, Pedro de Alvarado, Francisco de Montejo y Bernal Díaz del Castillo. Esta expedición llegó a Cozumel, bordeó la península de Yucatán y tocó la barra de Tonalá, desde donde los españoles pudieron avistar el Citlaltépetl. Pedro de Alvarado, capitán de una de las naves, entró por el río Papaloapan hasta el poblado que llamó Río Banderas, actual Boca del Río. El 24 de junio (día de San Juan) de 1518, Juan de Grijalva desembarcó en un islote que llamó San Juan de Ulúa, pues oyó a los indígenas pronunciar la palabra Aculúacan, con la que designaban a la nación Acolhua, de Texcoco. Alvarado regresó a Cuba para mostrar a Velázquez los objetos de oro que habían trocado con los indígenas, mientras Grijalva siguió su exploración hasta avistar las sierras de Misantla y Tuxpan; llegó, asimismo, a Pánuco, donde fue atacado por los hustecos. Velázquez encomendó una nueva expedición, esta vez a Hernán Cortés, quien siguió la ruta de Grijalva y llegó el 22 de abril de 1519 frente a San Juan de Ulúa. En el sitio de desembarco fundó la Villa Rica de la Vera Cruz. Cortés permaneció en ese sitio durante 20 días y luego mudó el asentamiento de la Vera Cruz a 80 km al norte; pactó su primera alianza con el cacique totonaca de Cempoala, Chicomácatl, e inició la campaña que lo llevaría a derrotar al imperio mexica. En 1522, Cortés partió a Pánuco a batir a los huastecos y el 26 de diciembre fundó la villa de Santisteban del Puerto. La rebelión huasteca siguió hasta que Gonzalo Sandoval la reprimió al frente de un ejército indio. Después de la conquista, la población indígena de Veracruz fue diezmada por las guerras, la

FOTO: FONDO EDITORIAL GRUPO AZABACHE

Antiguo oratorio de San Felipe Neri en Orizaba, Veracruz

FOTO: FONDO EDITORIAL GRUPO AZABACHE

Manufactura de puros en Santiago Tuxtla, Veracruz

FOTO: FONDO EDITORIAL GRUPO AZABACHE

Zozocolco, Veracruz

Huasteco

peste, la viruela y los trabajos forzados, en tanto que los españoles buscaban asentarse preferentemente en el altipano y fundaban en Veracruz diversos ingenios. Para el trabajo cañero se importaron, legal e ilegalmente, esclavos procedentes de África. Durante el virreinato se constituyó la provincia de Veracruz, formada por las alcaldías mayores Córdoba, Cozamaloapa (Cozamaloapan), Guachinango (Huauchinango), Cuayacocotla (Huayacocotla), Orizaba, Pánuco, Papantla, San Juan de los Llanos, Tuxtla, Veracruz la Nueva, Veracruz la Vieja, Villa Alta y Xalapa de la Feria, además de una parte de la provincia de Guazacualco (Coatzacoalcos). A mediados del siglo XVI se construyó la fortaleza de San Juan de Ulúa, para proteger el puerto de Veracruz, convertido en la puerta de entrada de la Nueva España. En 1601, en una nueva mudanza, la ciudad de Veracruz se trasladó al sitio que ocupa actualmente. Los piratas atacaron numerosas veces el puerto. John Hawkins tomó la fortaleza de San Juan de Ulúa en 1568 y más tarde Veracruz resentiría las incursiones de los más activos corsarios del golfo de México, entre ellos Lorencillo, quien saqueó el puerto y la ciudad en 1683. Por otra parte, el desmedido tráfico de esclavos dio a Veracruz una amplio porcentaje de población de origen africano. La sobreexplotación y el mal trato que recibían los esclavos causó una rebelión de 500 negros cimarrones encabezada por Yanga, en 1609, quien logró crear un asentamiento en el que los negros eran libres y poseían sus propias tierras de labranza; las autoridades de la Nueva España enviaron a Pedro González de Herrera, quien logró derrotar a Yanga el 23 de febrero de 1609, pero no pudo hacer otra cosa que aislar a los sublevados, quienes fundaron el pueblo de San Lorenzo de los Negros, actual Villa de Yanga. El 4 de diciembre de 1786, la Ordenanza de Intendencias creó el 4 de diciembre la de Veracruz, que reunía los corregimientos o las alcaldías mayores de Veracruz la Nueva (corregimiento con jurisdicción sobre Tlaliscoya, Tlacotalpa y Alvarado), Veracruz la Vieja (con jurisdicción sobre Misantla, Cempoala, Zongolica, Perote y Guazacoalco), Xalapa, Córdoba, Orizaba, Cosamaloapan, Tuxtla, Acayucan, Papantla y Pánuco. La capital quedó establecida en Veracruz la Nueva. En 1811, una vez iniciada la guerra de independencia, en Veracruz se integró la llamada Junta Independiente Americana, formada por Mariano Rincón, Tamariz, Cardeña, los hermanos Ortiz, Fiayo y Teresa Medina de la Sota Riva. El 13 de marzo de 1812 fue descubierta en Veracruz una conspiración insurgente encabezada por José Evaristo Molina, de 17 años de edad, y Cayetano Pérez, quienes fueron aprehendidos y fusilados el 29 de julio. En ese año, las campañas insurgentes de José María Morelos y Nicolás Bravo se extendieron hasta abarcar el territorio veracruzano. A Bravo, jefe de operaciones en la zona, se unieron los sacerdotes Mariano Rincón, Manuel de las Fuentes, Alarcón, Juan Moctezuma Cortés, José María Sánchez de la Vega e Ignacio Luna, quienes mantuvieron la actividad independentista en Veracruz, recurriendo muchas veces a la guerra de guerrillas. Guadalupe Victoria se convirtió en el

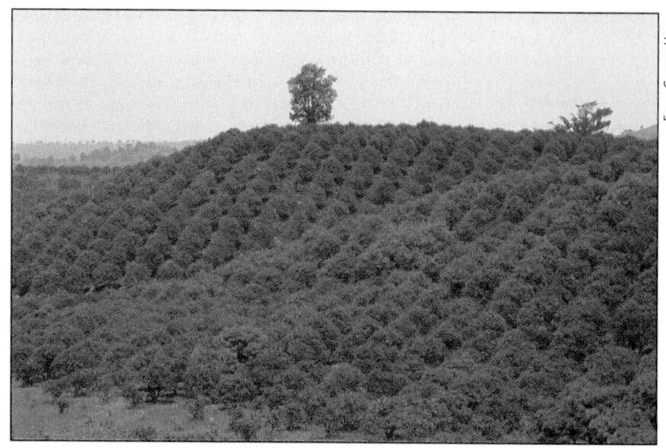

FOTO: CARLOS HAHN

Plantío de cítricos en Veracruz

FOTO: FONDO EDITORIAL GRUPO AZABACHE

Vista aérea del Tajín, Veracruz

FOTO: FONDO EDITORIAL GRUPO AZABACHE

Café La Parroquia, en Veracruz

Foto: Michael Calderwood

Pajaritos, Veracruz

Foto: Fondo Editorial Grupo Azabache

Detalles del casco urbano de Tlacotalpan, Veracruz

Orquídeas, flores regionales de Veracruz

Foto: Michael Calderwood

principal líder insurgente en Veracruz en 1814, luego de serias disputas internas entre los caudillos Ignacio López Rayón y Juan N. Rossains. Victoria mantuvo la lucha guerrillera en Veracruz, sin grandes acciones militares, pero como un obstáculo permanente al comercio entre Veracruz y la ciudad de México. Desde la promulgación del Plan de Iguala hasta la firma de los tratados de Córdoba (23 y 24 de agosto de 1821), el comandante insurgente de Veracruz fue Antonio López de Santa Anna. Una vez consumada la independencia, éste se autodesignó comandante general de la Procuraduría de Veracruz, cargo del que fue relevado por el entonces emperador Agustín de Iturbide, lo que motivó, el 2 de diciembre de ese año, el inicio de la lucha por la instauración de la República, sustentada poco más tarde por el Plan de Casa Mata. La Constitución de 1824 erigió el estado de Veracruz, con la misma jurisdicción que tenía la intendencia, pero con capital en Jalapa. La primera Constitución política de Veracruz se promulgó el 3 de junio de 1825. La fortaleza de San Juan de Ulúa, último reducto español en México, capituló el 18 de noviembre de 1825. El 27 de julio de 1829 desembarcó en Cabo Rojo el militar Isidro Barradas, quien tenía la intención de reconquistar el país para la Corona española, pero fue derrotado por Santa Anna. En 1830 la capital estatal pasó de Jalapa a Veracruz, ciudad que se vio acosada por la armada francesa entre 1838 y 1839, en la llamada guerra de los Pasteles. En noviembre de 1845 se inició uno más de los levantamientos populares que eran frecuentes en el estado. Éste fue dirigido por el ex militar Luciano Vázquez, quien convirtió la sublevación en una lucha agraria en la que participaron tanto indígenas huastecos como ex esclavos negros y mulatos. En 1846, al iniciarse la invasión de Estados Unidos, la marina de este país, comandada por Winfield Scott, ancló el 18 de mayo en las afueras del puerto de Veracruz, cuyo bloqueo comenzó el 20 de mayo. Las hostilidades empezaron el 23 de marzo de 1847 con un bombardeo sobre la ciudad y el desembarco de tropas, las que se encontraron con la resistencia de la población. El ejército y la armada de Estados Unidos desalojaron Veracruz y el resto del país a partir del 30 de julio de 1848. El 25 de agosto de 1852 asumió el gobierno estatal el liberal Ignacio de la Llave, quien restauró el federalismo. El 27 de septiembre de ese año se produjo un intento fallido de convertir a la región llamada Huasteca en el estado de Iturbide. Durante la guerra de los Tres Años, Benito Juárez se vio obligado a trasladar la sede de los poderes federales al puerto de Veracruz, el 4 de mayo de 1857. En 1861, con la llegada de la flota de la Triple Alianza, se inició la guerra de intervención francesa, que formaría el efímero imperio de Maximiliano de Habsburgo, quien llegó

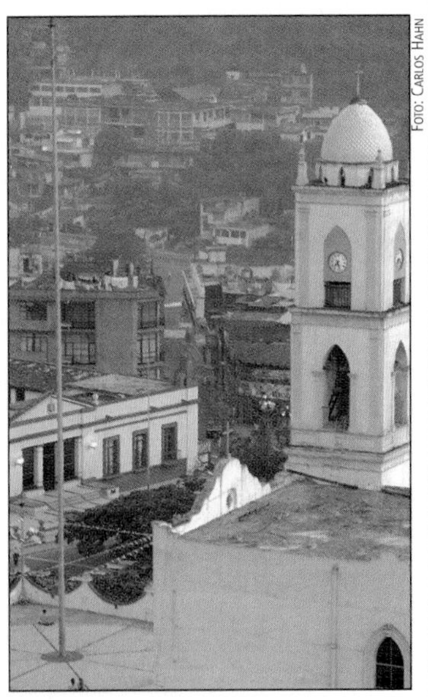
Foto: Carlos Hahn

Vista panorámica de Papantla, Veracruz

Jóvenes músicos de Veracruz

Foto: Michael Calderwood

Río Filobobos, Veracruz

Foto: Fondo Editorial Grupo Azabache

Palacio municipal de Córdoba, Veracruz

a México por Veracruz, el 28 de mayo de 1863. El 10 de julio de 1863 el gobierno del estado expidió un decreto ordenando que la entidad se designara, en lo sucesivo, Veracruz-Llave, en honor de Ignacio de la Llave. En junio de 1906, un grupo de militantes magonistas entre los que se hallaba Miguel Alemán, padre del futuro presidente de la República, lanzaron la Proclama de los Tuxtlas y protagonizaron un levantamiento que fue sofocado. A fines del mismo año, en Río Blanco (☛), se inició un movimiento de huelga que en enero fue salvajemente reprimido por las autoridades porfiristas. Tanto la insurrección maderista como la constitucionalista tuvieron seguidores en el estado de Veracruz. El 21 de abril de 1914, tras el cuartelazo de Victoriano Huerta, la flota estadounidense, comandada por Fletcher, bloqueó la entrada del puerto de Veracruz, con el pretexto de impedir que el vapor *Ypiranga* llevara suministros al dictador Victoriano Huerta. El 23 de noviembre del mismo año, aprovechando un incidente provocado por ellos mismos, la infantería de marina estadounidense desembarcó en Veracruz y se encontró con la resistencia de los cadetes de la Escuela Naval y la población civil, que fue vencida por la superioridad de efectivos y armamento de los invasores. Huerta aprovechó la ocupación para llamar a filas a numerosos trabajadores, quienes, engañados, fueron obligados a combatir no a los agresores estadounidenses, sino a las tropas constitucionalistas. Tanto la ocupación como el bloqueo de Veracruz cesaron pocos días después por las negociaciones del gobierno de Venustiano Carranza, quien estableció su gobierno en Veracruz, el 3 de diciembre de 1914.

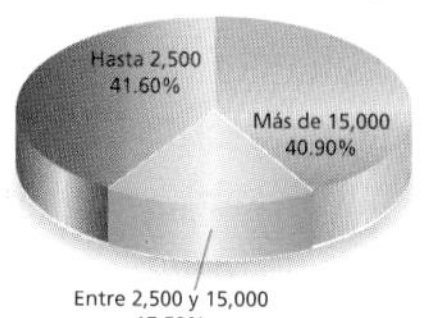

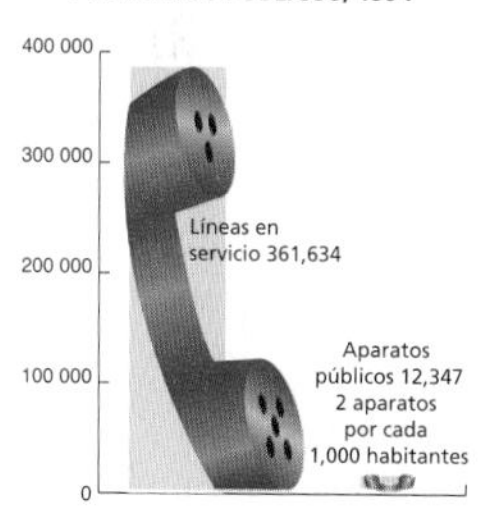

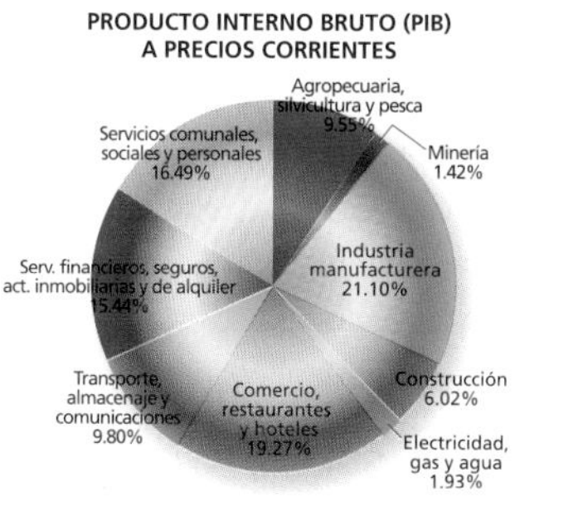

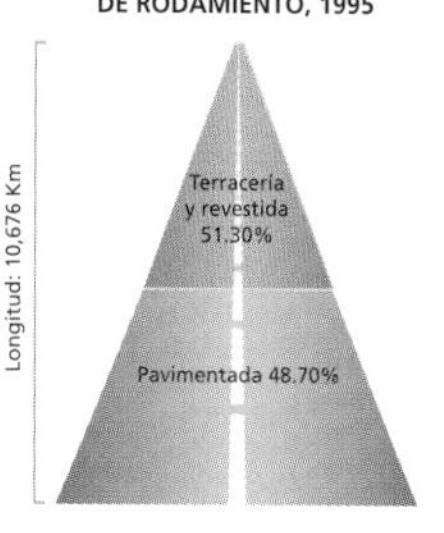

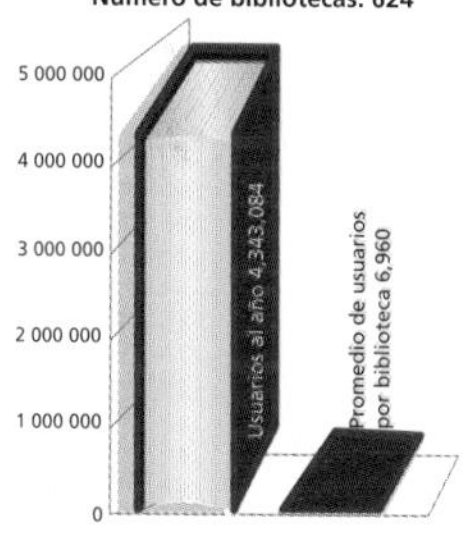

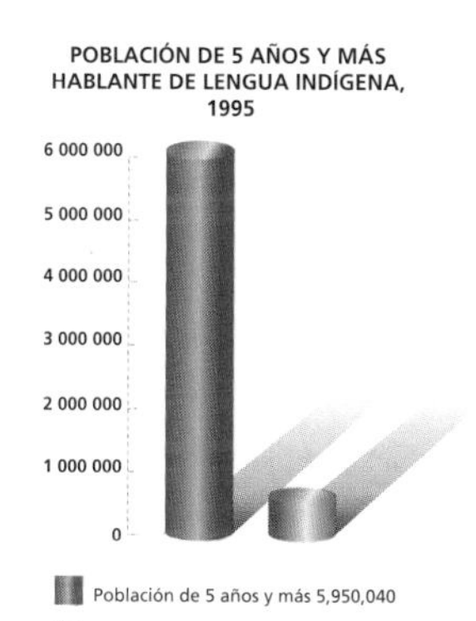

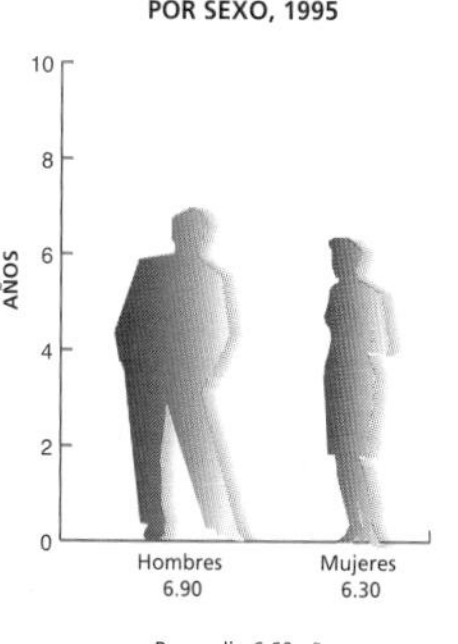

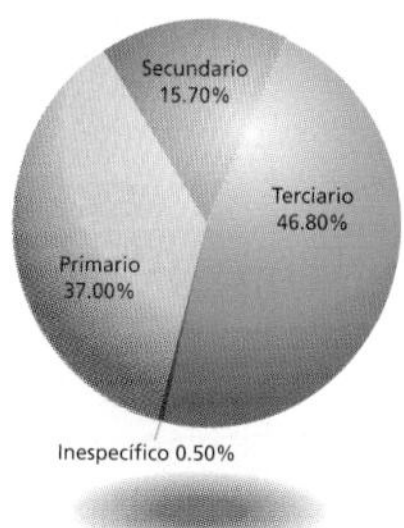

Veracruz, Veracruz

Alonso de la Veracruz

Veracruz ◆ Municipio de Veracruz situado en el litoral del golfo de México, al noreste del puerto de Veracruz. Superficie: 241 km². Habitantes: 425,140, de los cuales 111,084 forman la población económicamente activa. Hablan alguna lengua indígena 2,276 personas mayores de cinco años (zapoteco 615 y náhuatl 609). En la cabecera, del mismo nombre, se halla el principal puerto del país, construido entre las puntas Gorda y Mocambo. El islote y fortaleza de San Juan de Ulúa quedó unido a tierra por el rompeolas norte, cuando se construyó el puerto actual, que sustituyó al puerto natural utilizado desde la llegada de los conquistadores españoles. Alrededor se han levantado astilleros, plantas siderúrgicas y empacadoras. En esta ciudad están la Escuela Naval y el Instituto Veracruzano. En las playas de Chalchimecan, frente a Ulúa, Hernán Cortés constituyó el 22 de abril de 1519 el ayuntamiento de la Villa Rica de la Vera Cruz, el más antiguo de México. Durante el siglo xvi, la ciudad fue cabecera de alcaldía mayor; en el siglo xvii figuraron, de modo independiente, las alcaldías mayores de la Antigua y la Nueva Veracruz; la primera comprendía todo el viejo territorio ocupado por pueblos indígenas, y la segunda, el puerto donde desembarcaban las flotas procedentes de España.

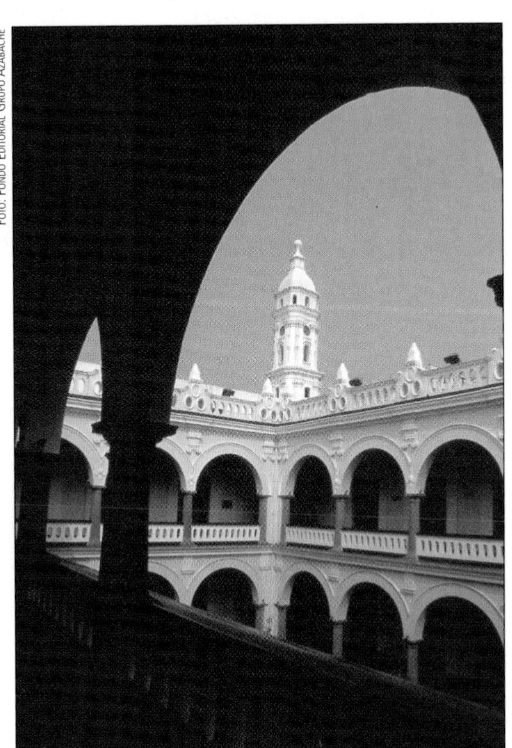

Palacio del Ayuntamiento en Veracruz, Veracruz

Veracruz, Alonso de la ◆ n. en España y m. en la ciudad de México (¿1507?-1584). Su nombre era Alonso Gutiérrez. Estudió en Alcalá y Salamanca. Viajó a la Nueva España como sacerdote. Al llegar en 1536 a Veracruz ingresó en la orden de San Agustín y tomó el nombre de Alonso de la Veracruz. En esa orden llegó a ser maestro de novicios (1537-40) y lector de filosofía y teología en el Gimnasio Mayor de Tiripitío (1540-45). Él y Jacobo Daciano fueron los primeros en administrar la comunión a los purépechas. Gobernador de la diócesis de Michoacán (1542) en ausencia de Vasco de Quiroga, vicario provincial de su orden (1543), prior y lector en Tacámbaro (1545), lector en Atotonilco el Grande (1546-48) y provincial (1548-51 y 1557). En 1553, al inaugurarse la Real Universidad de México ocupó, a partir del "viernes postrero de junio", la cátedra de *Biblia*. Era bachiller por la Universidad de Salamanca y la Universidad mexicana lo incorporó el 12 de julio como maestro en artes y lo reconoció como maestro en teología. Trató de eximir del pago del diezmo a los indígenas michoacanos, por lo que en 1561 fue llamado a España por su orden, para ser sometido a proceso. Absuelto, volvió a la Nueva España en 1573 como vicario general. Fue nuevamente provincial (1575-78). Autor de *Recognitio Summularum* (1554), *Dialectica Resolutio* (1556), *Physica Speculatio* (1557), *Speculum conjugiorum* (1557) y *Constitutiones Collegii Divi Pauli* (1624).

Verdad y Ramos, Francisco Primo de ◆ n. en Ciénega del Rincón, Ags., y m. en la ciudad de México (1760-1808). Estudió en el Colegio de San Ildefonso. Fue abogado de la Real Audiencia y miembro del Colegio de Abogados. Era síndico del ayuntamiento de la ciudad de México en 1808, cuando ocurrió la invasión napoleónica a España; junto con el regidor Juan Francisco Azcárate propuso al virrey José de Iturrigaray que reuniera a todos los ayuntamientos de la Nueva España para formar un gobierno independiente provisional, en tanto estuviese presa la familia real española. Argumentó que, a falta de un rey, la soberanía volvía automáticamente al pueblo. Su proyecto contó con la adhesión de los criollos. El 15 de septiembre de 1808 los españoles, viendo amenazados sus privilegios, aprehendieron y destituyeron al virrey Iturrigaray y encarcelaron o desterraron a todos los munícipes comprometidos con el proyecto de Verdad, quien fue encerrado en el arzobispado, donde amaneció muerto el 4 de octubre de ese año, probablemente asesinado.

VERDE ◆ Río de Durango y Chihuahua, también llamado San Miguel. Nace en el estado de Durango, en la vertiente occidental de la sierra Tarahumara, al oeste de Santa María del Oro; corre de sureste a noroeste, entra en el estado de Chihuahua y recibe las aguas de los ríos Chinatú o Turuachic, de los Loera o Guadalupe y Calvo, Tenariva y Batopilas; cerca del límite con Sinaloa, al sur del la sierra Cumbres del Gato, se une al río Urique para formar El Fuerte.

VERDE ◆ Río de Jalisco. Nace en el noreste del estado, al oeste de Lagos de Moreno, en la región de los Altos, de la confluencia de los ríos Aguascalientes y Encarnación; corre de noreste a suroeste y recibe las aguas de los ríos San Juan de los Lagos, Jalostotitlán, San Miguel, Teocaltiche y Apulco; se une al Grande de Santiago, 8 km al noreste de Guadalajara.

VERDE ◆ Río de Oaxaca. Nace al noreste de Pinotepa Nacional, de la confluencia de los ríos Atoyac y Yolotepec o Ciruelo; corre de noreste a suroeste y desemboca en el océano Pacífico, al oeste del lago Chacagua.

VERDUCHI, ENZIA MARÍA ◆ n. en Italia (1967). Desde los cinco años vivió en Campeche, donde estudió periodismo y asistió al taller de cuento de Rafael Ramírez Heredia. Trabajó en la Dirección de Publicaciones de la UNAM y fue directora del Instituto Campechano de Cultura. Ha colaborado en publicaciones estatales y en *Casa del Tiempo, Tierra Adentro, Excélsior, El Sol de México* y *unomásuno*. Autora de *Lecturas de Campeche* (1990, libro de texto) y *Cartas de usurpación* (1992, poemario). Premio Nacional de Cuento Efraín Huerta 1992, por "La breve complicidad del recuerdo". Becaria del Centro Mexicano de Escritores (1992-93).

VERDUGO, AGUSTÍN ◆ n. en Culiacán, Sin., y m. en la ciudad de México (1858-1906). Abogado. Ejerció su profesión en Guadalajara. Fue profesor de la Escuela Nacional de Jurisprudencia y director de las revistas *Ciencia Jurídica* y *El Derecho*, órgano de la Academia Mexicana de Jurisprudencia y Legislación. Tradujo *Derecho internacional privado*, de Pasquale Fiore, y *Manual de derecho comercial*, de Ch. Lyon Caen y L. Renault. Recopiló la *Colección legislativa de la República Mexicana. desde el año 1899 hasta 17 de octubre de 1902*. Autor de *Principios de derecho civil mexicano* (5 t., 1885-87) y *Discursos, alegatos y estudios jurídicos* (2 t., 1894).

VERDUGO-FUENTES, WALDEMAR ◆ n. en Chile (1955). Licenciado en letras españolas por la Universidad Católica de Santiago de Chile. Reside en México desde 1980. Ha sido profesor del Tecnológico de Monterrey y de la Universidad Autónoma de Baja California Norte. Jefe de redacción de la edición mexicana de la revista *Vogue* (1980-85). Ha colaborado en *Clarín* de Buenos Aires, *Mercurio* de Chile, *Panameño, Prensa Libre* de Guatemala, *La Opinión* de Estados Unidos, *New Orleans International, unomásuno, Cosas del Mundo* de Estados Unidos, *El Sol de Lima* y *Universal* de Venezuela. Autor de *Guardián del umbral* (cuentos, Buenos Aires, 1976), *El barquero de las almas* (cuentos, Buenos Aires, 1978), *Recopilaciones taoístas* (ensayo, 1983), *En voz de Borges* (1986), *El sendero mágico* (novela, 1987), *Ocho mujeres del siglo XX* (entrevistas, 1987, premio de periodismo cultural) y *La isla de los inmortales* (1987).

VERDUZCO, JOSÉ SIXTO ◆ n. en Zamora, Mich., y m. en la ciudad de México (¿1770?-¿1830?). Sacerdote. Su apellido aparece también como Verdusco y Berduzco. Estudió en el Seminario Conciliar y en el Colegio de San Nicolás Obispo, de Valladolid, el que fue profesor y rector. Era cura de Tuzantla (1811) cuando los principales caudillos de la independencia fueron aprehendidos en Acatita de Baján; Ignacio López Rayón escapó a esa celada y se refugió con Verduzco. Éste, más tarde, fue uno de los miembros de la Junta de Zitácuaro, organización que lo nombró gobernador y jefe militar de Michoacán, donde mantuvo una campaña desastrosa contra el realista Pedro Celestino Negrete; incluso trató infructuosamente de tomar la plaza de Valladolid, acción en la que perdió a la mayoría de sus hombres. Representó a Michoacán en el Congreso de Chilpancingo, asamblea que presidió, y fue uno de los firmantes de la Constitución de Apatzingán. De 1814 a 1817 volvió al curato de Tuzantla, alejado de la lucha insurgente, pero en ese año retomó las armas. La Junta de Jaujilla lo nombró comandante militar de las provincias de México y del Sur. En diciembre de 1817 fue capturado por los realistas Cueva y Salazar, en Purechucho, y remitido a Cuernavaca. Nicolás Bravo trató de rescatarlo, pero fue aprehendido en el intento. Verduzco estuvo encarcelado en la ciudad de México, en la Inquisición primero y en el convento de San Fernando, después. En 1820, debido al indulto general decretado por las Cortes Españolas, fue liberado. Residió en Zamora. En 1821 se negó a unirse al Plan de Iguala. Una vez proclamada la independencia, fue cura de Valle de San Francisco, San Luis Potosí, senador por ese estado en dos legislaturas (1825-26 y 1827-28) y diputado por un distrito potosino y otro michoacano (1829-30).

VERDUZCO, MARTA ◆ n. en el ¿DF? (¿1942?). Actriz. Egresada de la Escuela de Arte Teatral del INBA. Becaria por el gobierno de Francia en la Escuela del Este en Estrasburgo y en el Centro de Búsquedas Teatrales, y por el gobierno polaco en el Teatro Laboratorio de Jerzy Grotowsky. Ha trabajado en las películas *Crónica de familia* (1985) y *Trazos en blanco* (1985). En teatro ha actuado en *Historia de un anillo* (1962), *La parodia* (1962), *Teseo* (1962), *Los poseídos* (1963), *Las bizarrías de Belisa* (1969), *Nostalgia de la muerte* (1972), *Santísima* (1980), *El árbol* (1983), *El examen de maridos* (1986), *Intimidad* (1988), *La danza de la muerte* (1989), *Viaje de un largo día hacia la noche* (1992), *Salomé* (1994) y *Los signos del Zodiaco* (1997), entre otras. Ha incursionado en el cine, la televisión y el cabaret. Becaria del

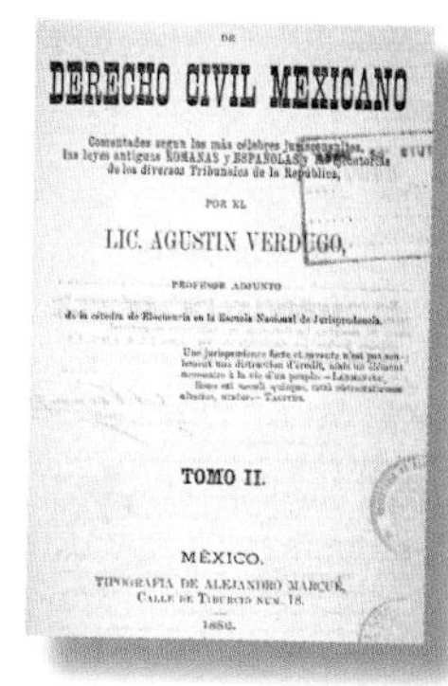

DE
DERECHO CIVIL MEXICANO
POR EL
LIC. AGUSTIN VERDUGO,
PROFESOR ADJUNTO
de la cátedra de Elocuencia en la Escuela Nacional de Jurisprudencia.
TOMO II.
MÉXICO.
TIPOGRAFIA DE ALEJANDRO MARCUÉ,
CALLE DE TIBURCIO NUM. 18.

Obra de Agustín Verdugo

José Sixto Verdugo

Foto: Lourdes Almeida

Martha Verduzco

Fonca (1993-95). Premio a la mejor actriz por *La noche de los asesinos* (1967) y *Kafka* (1973) de la Unión de Críticos y Cronistas de Teatro.

Francisco de Paula Verea y González

VEREA Y GONZÁLEZ, FRANCISCO DE PAULA ◆ n. en Guadalajara, Jal., y m. en Cuyuaco, Pue. (1813-1884). Doctor en cánones y en derecho civil por la Universidad de Guadalajara y por el Seminario Conciliar de esa ciudad, donde ejerció la docencia. Fue prosecretario, secretario de la mitra y canónigo doctoral de la catedral. En 1853 fue electo obispo de Linares, Nuevo León, y se le trasladó a Puebla en 1879.

VERGARA, PROGRESO ◆ n. en España y m. en Tepic, Nay. (1900-1951). Periodista. Combatió en defensa de la República Española. Fue militante del Partido Socialista y secretario particular de Indalecio Prieto. Exiliado en México en 1939, colaboró en *Excélsior*. Murió en un accidente durante una gira de trabajo del presidente Miguel Alemán.

José María Vértiz y Delgado

VERSEN, JORGE E. VON ◆ n. y m. en Saltillo, Coah. (1882-1944). Dirigente minero. Combatió al porfirismo desde la prensa y se unió a la revolución constitucionalista, en las fuerzas de Jesús Carranza. Venustiano Carranza lo envió varias veces a Estados Unidos para resolver conflictos diplomáticos. Cofundador (1915), con Ernesto Meade Fierro, del periódico *La Raza*, editado en San Antonio, Texas. Fue diputado suplente (1911-13) y diputado al Congreso Constituyente de 1916-17, donde formó parte del ala radical.

VÉRTIZ Y DELGADO, JOSÉ MARÍA ◆ n. y m. en la ciudad de México (1812-1876). Médico titulado en la Escuela de Cirugía (1835) y en el Establecimiento de Ciencias Médicas (1836), de la que fue profesor. Se especializó en oftalmología en Francia. Fue médico y director del Hospital de Jesús, médico del Hospital San Andrés, director del consultorio oftalmológico inaugurado por Fagoaga, donde se convirtió en especialista en la extirpación de cataratas; profesor y director de la Escuela de Medicina y cofundador de una corporación precursora de la Academia de Medicina. Inventor del tratamiento de los abscesos hepáticos mediante la canalización continua con ductos metálicos.

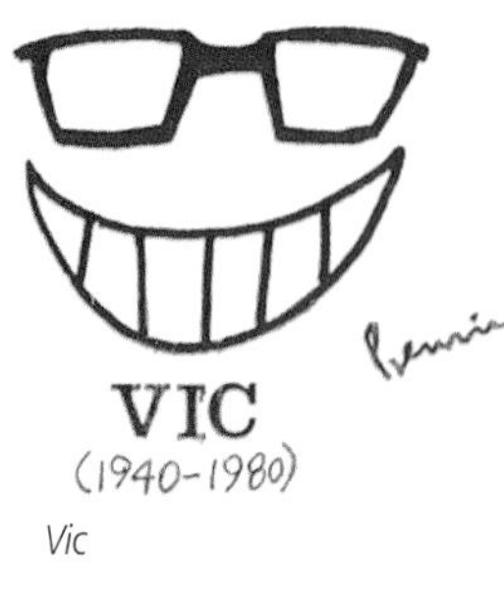

Vic

VÉRTIZ Y HONTAÑÓN, JUAN JOSÉ DE ◆ n. en España y m. en Real del Parral, en el actual estado de Durango (1682-1738). En 1707 fue designado gobernador y capitán general de Yucatán, aunque su llegada a Campeche ocurrió en 1715. En 1719 renunció al cargo. Fue alcalde mayor de los partidos de Teozacualco y Teococuilco y gobernador y capitán general de Nueva Vizcaya (1731-38).

VÉRTIZ Y SALCEDO, JUAN JOSÉ ◆ n. en Mérida, Yuc., y m. en España (1719-1798). Hijo del anterior. Llegó a España hacia 1737 e ingresó en el ejército. Se le envió a varias ciudades europeas a estudiar táctica militar y en 1770 se le designó gobernador de Buenos Aires. En 1778 recibió el nombramiento de virrey de Buenos Aires. Gobernó hasta 1784, cuando regresó a España, donde fue uno de los principales accionistas del Banco de San Carlos.

VETAGRANDE ◆ Municipio de Zacatecas situado en el centro del estado, contiguo a la capital estatal, en los límites con San Luis Potosí. Superficie: 212.26 km². Habitantes: 6,969, de los cuales 1,485 forman la población económicamente activa. Durante la época colonial y parte de la independiente, este municipio fue un emporio minero casi tan importante como el de Zacatecas; en él aún existen instalaciones, campamentos y minas abandonados, así como unas cuantas vetas en explotación.

VEYRE, GABRIEL ◆ n. en Francia y m. en Marruecos (1871-1936). Iniciador de la cinematografía en México. Estudió farmacéutica en la Universidad de Lyon. Ingresó a la Sociedad Lumiere y, a mediados de 1896 viajó a Bélgica, en la primera de sus misiones para presentar al diario *Le Figaro* filmes sobre la coronación del zar. En 1897 vino a México, donde, en compañía del concesionario Claude Ferdinand Bon Bernard, presentó el cinematógrafo a Porfirio Díaz, así como a la prensa y al público. Tras dos meses de éxito de las primeras exhibiciones fílmicas, en las que presentó material francés y breves tomas de la Ciudad de México, fue a Guadalajara antes de abandonar el país.

VIAL, OCTAVIO ◆ n. y m. en el DF (¿1920?-1989). Futbolista. Fue jugador aficionado en los equipos España y Lusitania y profesional en el América (1936-48) y el Atlante (1948-50). Fue campeón goleador con el equipo América en la temporada 1940-41. Entrenador del Universidad, al que llevó a la primera división en 1961, del Atlante y de la selección mexicana que asistió al campeonato mundial de 1950. Retirado en 1963, se dedicó al comercio.

VIC ◆ n. y m. en el DF (1940-1980). Nombre profesional del caricaturista Víctor Monjaraz. Realizó estudios de derecho. Se inició como caricaturista en algunas publicaciones estudiantiles. Fue cartonista de *El Nacional* y del noticiero *24 Horas*. Premio en el Certamen Nacional del Club de Periodistas (1980).

VICARIO, LEONA ◆ n. y m. en la ciudad de México (1789-1842). Insurgente cuyo nombre completo era María de la Soledad Leona Camila Vicario Fernández de San Salvador. En el despacho de su tutor, el abogado Agustín Pomposo Fernández de San Salvador, conoció al entonces pasante de derecho Andrés Quintana Roo, quien la involucró en la lucha por la independencia. Aquél, descubierto como conspirador, huyó en 1812 de la Ciudad de México y se unió en Tlalpujahua a las fuerzas de Ignacio López Rayón. Ella le enviaba dinero e información acerca de los movimientos políticos y militares que se observaban en la capital del virreinato y trató de convencer a algunos armeros vizcaínos de que se unieran a la revolución de independencia, por lo que fue delatada, aprehendida y recluida en su casa, bajo la vigilancia de su tutor. Escapó y fueron confiscados sus bienes. Trató de alcanzar a Quintana Roo, pero fue recapturada y recluida en el convento de Belén de las Mochas, de donde escapó el 6 de abril de 1813, ayudada por Antonio Vázquez Aldama y Luis

Leona Vicario

Rodríguez Alconedo. Viajó hacia territorio insurgente llevando bajo su amplia falda un retal de imprenta, pues los rebeldes editaban en forma rudimentaria su periódico *El Ilustrador Nacional*, con tipos de madera y tinta de añil. En la zona liberada contrajo matrimonio con Quintana Roo. La pareja siguió al Congreso de Chilpancingo hasta la captura de Morelos y más tarde huyó. En 1818 fueron delatados por dos ex insurgentes indultados, se les capturó y se vieron obligados a acogerse al indulto. Fueron confinados a la ciudad de Toluca, donde permanecieron hasta 1820. A la consumación de la independencia, y en virtud de que había perdido su capital en favor de la causa, el Congreso de 1822 le otorgó en recompensa la hacienda de Ocotepec, en los llanos de Apam, y tres casas en la ciudad de México.

Vicencio, Celso ♦ n. en San Francisco Zonacatlán y m. en Toluca, Edo. de Méx. (1839-1908). Abogado. Fue magistrado del Tribunal Superior de Justicia del Estado de México, secretario general de Gobierno durante la gestión de Alberto García, director del periódico *El Presente*, senador, director del Conservatorio Nacional de Música y del Instituto Científico y Literario de Toluca y, en 1889, delegado al Congreso Nacional de Instrucción Pública.

Vicencio Tovar, Abel Carlos ♦ n. y m. en el DF (1925-1994). Licenciado en derecho por la UNAM. Miembro del PAN, donde ocupó cargos tanto en el comité regional del DF como en el Comité Ejecutivo Nacional. Fue representante de su partido ante la Comisión Federal Electoral, Ha sido profesor universitario, diputado federal (1964-67, 1973-76, 1979-82 y 1988-91) y presidente nacional del PAN (1978-1984). Fue colaborador del diario *Excélsior*. Autor de *El desarrollo económico de México* (1962), *Principios de sociología y panorama sociológico de México* (1973), *Semejanzas en el sistema mercantilista y las relaciones económicas contemporáneas* (1975) e *Implicaciones socioeconómicas del crecimiento urbano en México y América Latina* (1975).

Vicencio Tovar, Astolfo ♦ n. en el DF (1927). Hermano del anterior. Contador público por la Escuela Bancaria y Comercial (1952). Miembro del PAN, donde ha sido propagandista juvenil (1949-52), integrante de la Comisión Política del DF (1954-61), jefe del sexto distrito (1958-60), secretario general (1960-62), secretario de asuntos electorales, fundador del Instituto de Estudios Sociales y Políticos, jefe regional en el Estado de México, miembro del CEN, consejero nacional y miembro de la Comisión de Promociones Económicas. Ha sido tres veces diputado federal (1967-70, 1982-85 y 1988-91).

Vicens, Josefina ♦ n. en Villahermosa, Tab., y m. en el DF (1911-1988). Su segundo apellido era Maldonado. Escritora. Fue secretaria particular del jefe del Departamento Agrario, secretaria de Acción Femenil de la CNC, dirigente del sector femenil agrario del PMR, oficial mayor de la Sección de Técnicos del Sindicato de Cinematografistas y miembro del Consejo Consultivo de Premiación de la Academia de Ciencias y Artes Cinematográficas. Con el pseudónimo de *Diógenes García* colaboró en diversas publicaciones y, con el de *Pepe Faroles*, en la revista *Sol y Sombra* y en el periódico *Torerías*. Autora de los guiones cinematográficos de *Los perros de Dios* (1972, Ariel al mejor argumento), *Los problemas de mamá, Los novios de mis hijas, Renuncia por motivos de salud* (1977, Ariel al mejor argumento), *Las señoritas Vivanco* y *El proceso de las señoritas Vivanco*. Autora de las novelas *El libro vacío* (1958, premio Xavier Villaurrutia) y *Los años falsos* (1982, premio Juchimán de la Universidad Juárez Autónoma de Tabasco). Vicepresidenta de la Sociedad General de Escritores de México, miembro de la Sección de Autores Cinematográficos del Sindicato de Trabajadores de la Producción Cinematográfica y presidenta de la Academia de Ciencias y Artes Cinematográficas (1970-76).

Celso Vicencio

Vicens de la Llave, Juan ♦ n. en España y m. en China (1895-1958). Fue delegado de propaganda del gobierno de la República Española en Francia. Llegó exiliado a México en 1940. Trabajó en las Bibliotecas Populares del DDF (1940-44) y en la Biblioteca, Hemeroteca y Archivo de Documentación Económica de la Secretaría de la Economía Nacional. Director del periódico mensual *Aragón* (1943-55). Autor de *Cómo se organiza una biblioteca* (1942) y *Manual del catálogo diccionario* (1942).

Foto: Eloy Valtierra

Abel Carlos Vicencio Tovar

Vicente Guerrero ♦ Cabera del municipio chihuahuense de Guerrero (☛).

Vicente Guerrero ♦ Municipio de Durango situado en el sureste del estado, al sureste de la capital estatal, en los límites con Zacatecas. Superficie: 432.30 km². Habitantes: 20,126, de los cuales 4,766 forman la población económicamente activa. Hablan alguna lengua indígena 131 personas mayores de cinco años (tepehuan 123).

Josefina Vicens

Vicente Guerrero ♦ Municipio de Puebla situado en el sureste del estado, al noreste de Tehuacán, en los límites con Veracruz. Superficie: 234.73 km². Habitantes: 20,345, de los cuales 4,226 forman la población económicamente activa. Hablan alguna lengua indígena 3,969 personas (náhuatl 3,968) y de ellas, son monolingües 740. Su cabecera municipal es Santa María del Monte.

Victoria ♦ Municipio de Guanajuato situado en el noreste del estado, al estenoreste de Dolores Hidalgo y al noreste de San Miguel de Allende, en los límites con San Luis Potosí. Superficie: 939.20 km². Habitantes: 17,746, de los cuales 3,864 forman la población económicamente activa. Hablan alguna lengua indígena 24 personas mayores de cinco años.

VICTORIA ◆ Municipio de Tamaulipas situado al noroeste de Tampico y al oeste de Soto la Marina, en los límites con Nuevo León. Superficie: 1,634.08 km². Habitantes: 243,960, de los cuales 67,098 forman la población económicamente activa. Hablan alguna lengua indígena 253 personas mayores de cinco años (náhuatl 112 y huasteco 51). En la jurisdicción se halla el zoológico de Tamatán. La cabecera, Ciudad Victoria, es también la capital del estado. En ella se encuentran la sede de la Universidad Autónoma de Tamaulipas y cuenta con edificios coloniales, como la catedral y la iglesia de los Siete Señores. La ciudad fue fundada el 6 de octubre de 1750 por José de Escandón, con el nombre de Villa de Santa María de Aguayo; el 21 de abril de 1825 la capital tamaulipeca se trasladó de la ciudad de Padilla a la de Aguayo, que entonces recibió el nombre de Ciudad Victoria. La diócesis fue erigida por Paulo VI el 21 de diciembre de 1964.

VICTORIA, DELFINO ◆ n. en Córdoba y m. en Jalapa, Ver. (¿1874?-?). Graduado en la Escuela Nacional de Medicina, ejerció en Córdoba y en 1913 se unió a la revolución constitucionalista en las fuerzas de Cándido Aguilar. Fue gobernador interino de Veracruz (1919). Al triunfo del aguaprietismo se retiró a la vida privada.

VICTORIA, FRANCISCO ◆ n. en Tamazula, Dgo., y m. en Puebla, Pue. (?-1830). Insurgente, hermano del primer presidente de la República. Su nombre era Francisco Fernández pero, como su hermano, adoptó el apellido Victoria. Combatió por la independencia en las fuerzas de Vicente Guerrero, con quien operó en el sur. Formó parte del ejército trigarante. En 1829 combatió en Tampico la invasión del español Isidro Barradas. Acompañó en su retiro a Guerrero, cuando éste fue depuesto, y más tarde se unió al pronunciamiento de Juan Álvarez contra Anastasio Bustamante. Fue capturado y encarcelado en Morelia, escapó y se refugió en Puebla, donde organizó una nueva conspiración contra Bustamante. La conjura se descubrió y fue fusilado.

VICTORIA, GUADALUPE ◆ n. en Tamazula, Dgo., y m. en Perote, Ver. (1786-1842). Insurgente cuyo nombre original era José Miguel Ramón Adaucto Fernández y Félix. Estudió en el Seminario de Durango. En 1811 se unió a la lucha independentista y adoptó el nombre de Guadalupe Victoria. Combatió en las filas de José María Morelos y se distinguió en el asalto a Oaxaca, el 25 de noviembre de 1812. Dos años después el Congreso de Chilpancingo lo ascendió a general. Acompañó a Morelos a Veracruz y se quedó a operar en esta provincia después de la retirada del caudillo. Al estallar la pugna entre Rossains y Rayón, los líderes locales desconocieron al primero y le dieron su cargo a Victoria, quien obtuvo triunfos en Tolomé y Puente del Rey. En 1815 sufrió su primera gran derrota y en febrero de 1817 ocupó brevemente Nautla y fue derrotado en Palmillas. A partir de entonces su zona de operaciones se redujo a una angosta franja entre la costa al norte del puerto de Veracruz y las montañas cercanas a Huatusco, donde resistió acosos y persecuciones sin aceptar el indulto. Reapareció en 1821, una vez proclamado el Plan de Iguala, con la publicación de un relato de sus vicisitudes de los últimos cuatro años, al final del cual exhortaba a la concordia de los distintos caudillos independentistas para pacificar el país. Salió al encuentro de Agustín de Iturbide, ante quien se presentó en San Juan del Río, aunque éste no le concedió ningún crédito político o militar. Propuso modificar el Plan de Iguala para llamar al gobierno de México a un ex combatiente insurgente y no a un extranjero. Después de la coronación de Iturbide, manifestó sus ideas republicanas y fue encarcelado. Escapó y dio su apoyo al Plan de Casa Mata. A la caída del imperio se formó un triunvirato ejecutivo (en funciones entre el 31 de marzo de 1823 y el 10 de octubre de 1824) integrado por Pedro Celestino Negrete, Nicolás Bravo y el propio Victoria; sin embargo, éste no ocupó su puesto sino hasta julio de 1823, pues, nuevamente al mando de las fuerzas veracruzanas, debió enfrentar el bombardeo que sobre el puerto de Veracruz iniciaron los españoles atrincherados en la fortaleza de San Juan de Ulúa. En esa oportunidad negoció un armisticio para evacuar del puerto a los extranjeros. Fue diputado por Durango al Congreso Constituyente de 1824, mismo que el 2 de octubre de ese año lo nombró primer presidente de la República, cargo que asumió el 10 de octubre siguiente. Durante su gestión, centralizó la hacienda pública, agobiada por el gasto del ejército y las insuficiencias de todo orden; interesado en la educación popular, facilitó las tareas de la Sociedad Lancasteriana; estableció relaciones diplomáticas con la Gran Bretaña, Estados Unidos, América Central y la Gran Colombia, a invitación de la cual envió un representante al Congreso Anfictiónico de Panamá (1826); y ordenó constituir la marina de guerra que liberó San Juan de Ulúa, último reducto español en el país (1825). En lo político, intentó aplicar una política para atraerse

Retrato y firma de Guadalupe Victoria

a los diferentes bandos, para lo cual integró su primer gabinete con miembros prominentes de las distintas facciones. No obstante, los conflictos soterrados durante el imperio de Iturbide salieron a la superficie. En el plano legal afrontó la contradicción entre la intolerancia religiosa y la libertad de expresión y prensa, que respetó escrupulosamente. Intentó mantener cierta distancia de las logias masónicas, la escocesa y la yorkina, pero ambas trataron por todos los medios de influir en su gobierno. Unos procuraban obtener ventajas para las inversiones inglesas, otros para las estadounidenses. Los primeros pugnaban por conservar el orden jerárquico heredado de la Colonia; los otros porque se impusiera un régimen de oportunidades para todos. Los hispanistas promovieron la rebelión de Joaquín Arenas, que fue sofocada y despertó una oleada de indignación contra los españoles acaudalados que la habían patrocinado, por lo que tuvo que firmar el decreto de expulsión de los peninsulares el 20 de diciembre de 1827. El mismo sector apoyó la intentona de golpista de Manuel Montaño, quien fue derrotado en Otumba. En 1828, Manuel Gómez Pedraza convirtió la derrota electoral de su partido en una victoria de las presiones, el uso indebido del poder, las amenazas y el soborno, con lo cual consiguió, a principios de septiembre, que las legislaturas locales lo eligieran presidente. El partido yorkino respondió con el pronunciamiento de Perote y la insurrección popular conocida como el Motín de la Acordada, que obligó a Gómez Pedraza a renunciar al Ministerio de Guerra y a sus aspiraciones presidenciales, tras de lo cual el Congreso designó presidente a Vicente Guerrero, a quien Victoria entregó el poder el 1 de abril de 1829 y se retiró a la hacienda El Jobo, en Veracruz. Ocasionalmente fue llamado por el gobierno para algunas misiones conciliatorias. Murió en el hospital del Castillo de Perote, donde era tratado de sus ataques de epilepsia. El 25 de agosto de 1843 el Congreso lo declaró Benemérito de la Patria.

Gabinete del presidente Guadalupe Victoria

10 de octubre de 1824 al 1 de abril de 1829

Secretaría de Relaciones Interiores y Exteriores:	
Juan Guzmán	10 de enero de 1824 al 11 de enero de 1825
Lucas Alamán	12 de enero al 26 de septiembre de 1825
Manuel Gómez Pedraza	27 de septiembre al 2 de noviembre de 1825
Sebastián Camacho	3 de noviembre de 1825 al 5 de julio de 1826
Juan José Espinosa de los Monteros	6 de julio de 1826 al 7 de marzo de 1828
Juan de Dios Cañedo	8 de marzo de l828 al 25 de enero de 1829
José María de Bocanegra	26 de enero al 1 de abril de 1829
Secretaría de Hacienda:	
José Ignacio Esteva	10 de octubre de 1824 al 26 de septiembre de 1825
Pablo de la Llave	27 de septiembre al 27 de noviembre de 1825
José Ignacio Esteva	28 de noviembre de 1825 al 4 de marzo de 1827
Tomás Salgado	5 de marzo al 1 de noviembre de 1827
Francisco García	2 de noviembre de 1827 al 15 de febrero de 1828
José Ignacio Pavón	16 de febrero al 7 de marzo de 1828
José Ignacio Esteva	8 de marzo de 1828 al 12 de enero de 1829
Bernardo González Angulo	13 de enero al 1 de abril de 1829
Secretaría de Guerra y Marina:	
Manuel de Mier y Terán	10 de octubre al 18 de diciembre de 1824
José Castro	19 de diciembre de 1824 al 7 de enero de 1825
Manuel Gómez Pedraza	8 de enero al 7 de junio de 1825
José Ignacio Esteva	8 de junio al 14 de julio de 1825
Manuel Gómez Pedraza	15 de julio de 1825 al 9 de febrero de 1827
Manuel Rincón	10 de febrero al 3 de marzo de 1827
Manuel Gómez Pedraza	4 de marzo de 1827 al 3 de diciembre de 1828
José Castro	4 al 7 de diciembre de 1828
Vicente Guerrero	8 al 25 de diciembre de 1828
Francisco Moctezuma	26 de diciembre de 1828 al 1 de abril de 1829
Secretaría de Justicia:	
Pablo de la llave	10 de octubre de 1824 al 29 de noviembre de 1825
Miguel Ramos Arizpe	30 de noviembre de 1825 al 7 de marzo de 1828
Juan José Espinosa de los Monteros	8 de marzo de 1828 al 31 de marzo de 1829

Victoria Aguilar, Héctor ◆ n. en Conkal y m. en Mérida, Yuc. (1886-1926). Mecánico. En 1911 fundó la Unión Obrera de Ferrocarrileros y encabezó la primera huelga de ferrocarrileros en Yucatán. Fue miembro del ayuntamiento de Mérida (1915) y diputado al Congreso Constituyente de 1916-17, donde formó parte del ala radical. Diputado local (1918-22) y consejero de los Ferrocarriles Unidos de Yucatán.

Vidal, Carlos A. ◆ n. en Pichucalco, Chis., y m. en Huitzilac, Mor. (1885-1927). Militar. Se unió en 1913 a la revolución constitucionalista en Chiapas, en las filas de Pedro C. Colorado. Ascendió en julio de 1915 a general de brigada. Fue gobernador y comandante militar de Quintana Roo (1916-17) y de Tabasco (1918-19). En 1920 se adhirió al Plan de Agua Prieta. Partidario de Francisco R. Serrano en la campaña presidencial de 1927, con él y otros colaboradores fue asesinado en Huitzilac el 3 de octubre de ese año.

Vidal, Pilar ◆ n. en el DF (1941). Cursó la carrera de pianista en la Escuela Nacional de Música. Becada por el Conservatorio Nacional y por el Consejo Nacional de Música para especializarse en dirección orquestal. Ha sido subdirectora de la banda de la delegación Cuauhtémoc y directora huésped de las bandas de la Secretaría de

Marina y de la delegación Azcapotzalco. En 1978 fundó la Orquesta Sinfónica de la delegación Magdalena Contreras, la Camerata Tlatiizalli y la Orquesta de la Cámara de la delegación Benito Juárez. Desde 1986 es directora huésped de la Orquesta del Arcady Festival Simphony. En 1990 recibió un reconocimiento de la UNAM y en 1991 el premio Sol de Oro, del Círculo Nacional de Periodistas de Espectáculos.

Vidal Guijo, Jaime ♦ n. en Francia (1940). Hijo de españoles republicanos, llegó a México en 1947. Fundador y director del restaurante El Tirol (1964-69), desde 1970 se dedica al diseño de joyas. Premio Nacional de Diseño (1974).

Vidal Sánchez, J. Amílcar ♦ n. en Pichucalco, Chis., y m. en el DF (1890-1978). Ingeniero por el Instituto Politécnico Rensealaer de Troy, Estados Unidos. Fue diputado por Chiapas al Congreso Constituyente de 1916-17, jefe del cuarto distrito de Puertos, Faros y Marina Mercante de la Secretaría de Comunicaciones y Obras Públicas (1917-26), jefe de la Comisión Receptora de Materiales de Guerra (1924-33), jefe del Departamento de Maquinaria y Obras Públicas (1932-35) y jefe de la Comisión Agraria en Tabasco.

Vidal y Ubeda, Gabriel ♦ n. en España (1910). Ingeniero industrial y teniente de artillería por la Academia de Artillería de Madrid (1931). Trabajó en el Consorcio de Industrias Militares y en el Parque del Ejército 1. Durante la guerra civil fue comandante de varias unidades de artillería y ayudante del ministro de Defensa. En 1939 se exilió en Francia, de donde pasó a México en 1942. Aquí fundó una fábrica de cartón, fue superintendente de la fábrica Cementos Hidalgo, fundador y gerente de Cementos Anáhuac, fundador de Cementos Maya, director de Cementos California (1956-63), ayudante técnico de la Dirección General del Conjunto Industrial Ciudad Sahagún, director técnico de Forjamex, así como asesor y codirector de Concarril.

Vidales, Amadeo S. ♦ n. en Tecpan, Gro., y m. en el DF (1883-1932). Su familia inició en Acapulco una empresa constructora de barcos, asesorada por Juan R. Escudero, que pronto tuvo sucursales en varios puertos del país. Ingresó en el Partido Obrero de Acapulco, fundado por Escudero, y en 1923 tomó las armas contra la rebelión delahuertista. En esa campaña obtuvo el grado de general brigadier. Fundó la cooperativa agrícola Unión de Ambas Costas (1925). En 1926 proclamó el Plan del Veladero, en el que proponía la expulsión de los españoles del territorio nacional y la confiscación de sus bienes. Fundó, en el municipio de Atoyac, la población agrícola Juan R. Escudero (1930). Murió asesinado.

Vidales, Aura María ♦ n. en el DF (1958). Poeta y periodista. Licenciada en periodismo por la escuela Carlos Septién. Miembro del taller de poesía del Museo Universitario del Chopo. Fue fundadora del periódico *Cuestión* (1979), donde se desempeñó como reportera y jefa de sociales. Ha sido reportera y coordinadora de varios medios impresos, así como de televisión. A partir de 1999, jefa del Departamento de Distribución de Publicaciones de la Secretaría del Trabajo y Previsión Social. Coautora de *Caligrafía de Ariadna* (1987). Autora de los poemarios *Ensueño* (1979), *Estalactitas* (1984), *Ventanas vacías* (1990), *Cantos para el guerrero* (1995) y *Arcoiris* (1997). Fue primera mención honorífica del premio de poesía femenina Dolores Castro, Oaxaca (1998).

Vidali, Vittorio ♦ n. y m. en Italia (1900-1983). En 1917 ingresó en el Círculo Juvenil Socialista de Trieste, del Partido Socialista, y colaboró en su órgano, *Il Lavoratore*. Cofundador de la Federación Juvenil Comunista de Italia (1921), país del que salió en 1923, después de sufrir varios atentados de las bandas del gobierno fascista. Vivió en Nueva York, donde bajo el pseudónimo de Enea Sormenti hizo trabajo político para la Federación Italiana del Partido de los Trabajadores de Estados Unidos (Comunista). Fue expulsado en 1927 y viajó a la Unión Soviética, de donde vino a México como representante del Socorro Rojo Internacional para Centroamérica. En México se unió a la Liga Antimperialista de las Américas, tomó parte en el apoyo a la lucha de Sandino en Nicaragua e intervino en las actividades del Partido Comunista Mexicano, del que fue delegado al sexto congreso de la Internacional Comunista (1928) y al de la Internacional Juvenil Comunista (1928), ambos en Moscú, a donde viajó con un pasaporte a nombre del panadero Carlos Contreras, miembro del PCM. En 1928 trabajó en Jalisco con David Alfaro Siqueiros en la organización de mineros. En 1930 fue deportado junto Tina Modotti (☛) y otros comunistas de diferentes nacionalidades. Volvió a la Moscú, se afilió al Partido Comunista de la Unión Soviética y recorrió varios países europeos como militante del Socorro Rojo Internacional. En 1934 tuvo que salir de la Unión Soviética, antes de ser eliminado junto con la Modotti por una purga estalinista. El Socorro Rojo Internacional lo envió a España con ayuda para los mineros encarcelados en Asturias. Desempeñó misiones en diversos países europeos y en 1936 volvió a España, donde al estallar la guerra civil organizó el Quinto Regimiento, base del ejército republicano, en el que cobró celebridad como el Comandante Carlos (Contreras), comisario comunista y organizador de la resistencia en Madrid. Al triunfo del franquismo, herido y enfermo, se refugió en Francia, de donde fue nuevamente a Estados Unidos y de ahí a México, donde fue cofundador de la Asociación Anfascista Giuseppe Garibaldi, hizo trabajo sindical entre los tranviarios y fue expulsado del PCM. Vivió con Tina Modotti y al quedar viudo formó otra familia. Colaboró en el diario *El Popular* y tuvo una estrecha relación con la intelectualidad de izquierda. Señalado, sin serlo, como participante en el ataque encabezado por Siqueiros a la casa de Trotsky, fue secuestrado varias semanas por la policía secreta. Regresó a Italia en 1947 y se incorporó al Partido Comunista de

Venecia Julia (de Trieste), donde se opuso a la anexión a Yugoslavia. Fundador y secretario general del Partido Comunista del Territorio Libre de Trieste (1948) y delegado del mismo al XX congreso del PCUS (1956). En 1957, al fusionarse la organización triestina en el Partido Comunista Italiano, formó parte del comité central y fue diputado (1958) y senador (1963). A partir de los años cincuenta se opuso al monopolio ideológico marxista de Moscú y abogó por un socialismo democrático. Ha sido acusado de múltiples crímenes políticos sin que se le haya probado uno solo. Tratan con mayor o menor amplitud sobre México o algunos mexicanos sus libros *Il Quinto Reggimento* (1973), *Tina Modotti* (1973), *Diario del XX Congreso* (1974), *De México a Murmansk* (1975), *La Caduta della Repubblica* (1979), *Retrato de mujer. Una vida con Tina Modotti* (1982; ed. mexicana de 1984) y *Comandante Carlos* (1983; ed. mexicana de 1986).

VIDARGAS, FRANCISCO ♦ n. en el DF (1963). Escritor y autor de investigaciones especializadas en México y España. Colaborador de *El País* y director de Textos Dispersos Ediciones. Coautor de *México y Cusco, ciudades hermanas 1987-1988* (1998) y *San Agustín de Acolman* (1990). Autor de *Frontera de lo irremediable. El patrimonio cultural en circunstancia* (1994), *Un pintor manierista. Baltazar de Echave Ibia* (1995) y *Tres visiones norteamericanas sobre el Arte Novohispano* (1995). Es miembro del Consejo Internacional de Monumentos y Sitios (ICOMOS) y de la Sociedad Defensora del Tesoro Artístico de México. Becario del Centro Mexicano de Escritores (1991-92), del Fonca (1993-94) y del Fideicomiso para la Cultura México/EUA (1995).

VIDAURRI, SANTIAGO ♦ n. en Lampazos, NL, y m. en la ciudad de México (1808-1867). Fue oficial mayor y secretario general del gobierno de Nuevo León (1835). En 1854 se adhirió al Plan de Ayutla y un año después emitió su Plan Restaurador de la Libertad. Mantuvo contactos con la Junta Revolucionaria de Brownsville (formada por Benito Juárez, Melchor Ocampo y otros liberales), que le encargó insurreccionar los estados del norte. Tomó la plaza de Monterrey y ahí se declaró gobernador y comandante militar; ocupó Matamoros y Saltillo y decretó la anexión de Coahuila a Nuevo León. Durante el Congreso Constituyente se le consideró tan poderoso e influyente como Ignacio Comonfort, a quien dio asilo tras su golpe de Estado. Dejó la gubernatura de Nuevo León en 1858 por haber desconocido al secretario de Guerra, Santos Degollado. Combatió a los conservadores en la guerra de los Tres Años; fue derrotado en Ahualulco por Miguel Miramón. En 1860 ocupó de nuevo el gobierno de Nuevo León y fue reelegido en 1863. Estuvo a punto de aprehender a Juárez en Monterrey. En 1865 reconoció al imperio de Maximiliano, quien lo designó consejero imperial y ministro de Hacienda. Al triunfo de la República, Porfirio Díaz lo capturó en la ciudad de México. Fue juzgado por traidor y fusilado.

VIENA, CÓDICE ♦ Documento prehispánico mixteco conservado en la Biblioteca Nacional de Viena. Se conoce también como Códice Vindobonensis Mexicanus I, Códice Elementine o Codex Indiae Meridianalis. Realizado probablemente en 1357, consta de 52 hojas en piel de venado; al igual que los códices Bodley y Nuttall, trata temas mitológicos, con algunas interpolaciones de carácter histórico. Se inicia con la creación del hombre, sigue con la historia de Quetzalcóatl y el origen del pueblo mixteco y refiere la cronología de las tres primeras dinastías de los caciques de Tilantongo (1270-1357). Hernán Cortés lo envió, junto con el Códice Nuttall, como regalo al emperador Carlos V, quien lo obsequió al rey Manuel de Portugal y éste al cardenal Julio de Médicis, quien lo legó al papa Clemente VII; el documento siguió cambiando de manos hasta que Leopoldo I de Austria lo donó a la Biblioteca Imperial, ahora Nacional.

VIERA, JUAN DE ♦ n. en Puebla, Pue., y m. en la ciudad de México (¿1720?-?). Sacerdote, fue mayordomo administrador de las rentas de los colegios de San Ildefonso y de San Pedro y San Pablo. Cronista de la ciudad de México. Autor de *Breve compendiosa narración de la ciudad de México, corte y cabeza de toda la América Septentrional. Tenostictlan. Año de 1777.*

Santiago Vidaurri

VIESCA ♦ Municipio de Coahuila situado en el suroeste del estado, próximo a Torreón, en los límites con Durango y Zacatecas. Superficie: 4,203.50 km^2. Habitantes: 19,510, de los cuales 5,217 forman la población económicamente activa. Hablan alguna lengua indígena 19 personas mayores de cinco años. En la jurisdicción se explota el salitre del lecho de la laguna de Viesca o Parras, ya desecada.

VIESCA, ANDRÉS S. ♦ n. en Parras y m. en Torreón, Coah. (1827-1908). Militar liberal. Se unió a la revolución de Ayutla (1854). Tras el fallido autogolpe de Estado de Ignacio Comonfort se unió a las tropas de Santiago Vidaurri (☛) y peleó en San Luis Potosí, en el bando liberal, durante la guerra de los Tres Años. Republicano, alcanzó el generalato (1865) en su lucha contra la intervención francesa y el imperio. Hizo la campaña en Coahuila, fue derrotado dos veces en Parras y triunfó en Santa Isabel. Gobernador de Coahuila (1867 y 1886) y senador de la República (1875-76 y 1888-1900).

Dunas de Bilbao en Viesca, Coahuila

FOTO: FONDO EDITORIAL GRUPO AZABACHE

Agustín Viesca y Montes

Viesca y Montes, Agustín ◆ n. y m. en Parras, Coah. (1779-1845). Abogado. Fue gobernador de Coahuila y secretario de Relaciones Interiores y Exteriores (del 3 de noviembre al 18 de diciembre y del 18 al 23 de diciembre de 1829), en los gabinetes de Vicente Guerrero y José María Bocanegra.

Vietnam, República Socialista de ◆ Estado de Asia situado en el oriente de la península Indochina. Tiene costas en el golfo de Tonkín, el mar Meridional de China y el golfo de Tailandia. Limita al norte con China, al oeste con Laos y al suroeste con Camboya. Superficie: 331,041 km². Habitantes: 77,562,000 (1998). Su capital es Hanoi (2,154,900 habitantes en 1996); otras ciudades de importancia son Ciudad Ho-Chi-Minh (antes Saigón, con 3,600,000 habitantes), Haiphong (449,747), Da Nang (382,674) y Long Xuyen (132,681). Su moneda es el nuevo dong y el idioma oficial es el vietnamita o anamita, aunque también se hablan chino, francés, inglés y laosiano. *Historia*: originalmente, el territorio vietnamita estuvo poblado por tribus indonesias y malayas, que fueron confinadas a las montañas por los grupos de invasores mongoles, con los que, finalmente, se produjo una fusión racial. Annam, el reino así creado en el valle del río Songkoi (Rojo), atrajo la atención de China, mientras en el delta del río Mekong (en el sur) se formaba el Estado de Champa, con influencia de la India. El imperio de la dinastía china de Han invadió y dominó el norte del actual Vietnam, desde el año 112 a.n.e. hasta el 938 de la era contemporánea, cuando el pueblo en armas logró su liberación. En el año 946, el líder Ngo Quyen impidió un nuevo intento de invasión china en la batalla de Bach Dang y fundó la dinastía Ngo. En 968 Dinh Bo Linh creó el Estado de Dai Co Viet, sometido nuevamente al vasallaje de China. Entre los años 1009 y 1225 (periodo de la dinastía vietnamita Ly), Vietnam adoptó el budismo e inició una política expansionista. Entre 1225 y 1400, la dinastía Tran libró una guerra constante contra el Estado de Champa y, por el norte, derrotó a los mongoles de Gengis Khan, primero, y de Kublai Khan, después. Entre 1406 y 1428 volvió a instalarse el dominio chino (esta vez, el de la dinastía Ming), que terminó con la victoria de los guerrilleros de Le Loi, fundador de la dinastía Le. Durante el siglo XVII el territorio estuvo dividido en dos Estados: al norte, Tonkín, y al sur, Cochinchina. Ese mismo siglo fue repelida una invasión china de la dinastía Ching. En 1695, el antiguo reino de Champa se fundió con el Estado de Dai Viet (Vietnam). En 1776, un movimiento popular derrocó a la dinastía Le y el país empezó a resentir las incursiones de los khmer. En 1802, Nguyen Anh venció a la dinastía de los Tay Son, fundó la Nguyen y creó el reino de Vietnam, con capital en Hue. Las persecuciones contra los católicos produjeron la intervención franco-española en la península Indochina; en 1858, Francia realizó una campaña tras la cual, en 1884, estableció un protectorado en Indochina (Vietnam, Laos y Camboya; a su vez, el territorio vietnamita quedó dividido en tres partes: Tonkín, Annam y Cochinchina, al norte, centro y sur, respectivamente). En la tercera década del siglo XX surgieron las primeras organizaciones nacionalistas. En 1930, Nguyen Ai Quoc adoptó el nombre de Ho-Chi-Minh y agrupó a las numerosas organizaciones marxistas en el Partido Comunista de Indochina (PCI), que inició la lucha contra la ocupación francesa. Al inicio de la segunda guerra mundial, Japón ocupó la península y el PCI organizó la resistencia. Al final del conflicto, el Vietminh (Liga para la Independencia de Vietnam, fundada en 1941 por Ho-Chi-Minh), ocupó militarmente Hanoi, proclamó la República Democrática de Vietnam (1945), y el emperador Bao-Dai se trasladó al sur. En 1946, con el bombardeo de Haiphong, Francia inició una nueva guerra contra Vietnam, Laos y Camboya. En 1951 dejó de existir el protectorado de la Indochina Francesa, aunque el ejército mantuvo su ofensiva. El Partido Comunista de Indochina se dividió en tres secciones, para Camboya, Laos y Vietnam (esta última se llamó Partido de los Trabajadores de Vietnam). En mayo de 1954, tras la victoria vietnamita de Dien Bien Phu y mediante los arreglos de Ginebra, el Vietminh obligó a Francia a retirarse al sur del paralelo 17. Se convocó entonces a unas elecciones de reunificación, a celebrarse en 1956, que nunca se llevaron a cabo, pues los franceses cedieron el papel de ocupantes a los estadounidenses, quienes iniciaron una matanza sistemática de comunistas en Vietnam del Sur, donde reinaba el emperador Bao Dai, quien fue derrocado por un golpe de Estado por Ngo Dinh Diem. En 1955, bajo la tutela de Estados Unidos, se proclamó en Saigón la República de Viet Nam, Diem se

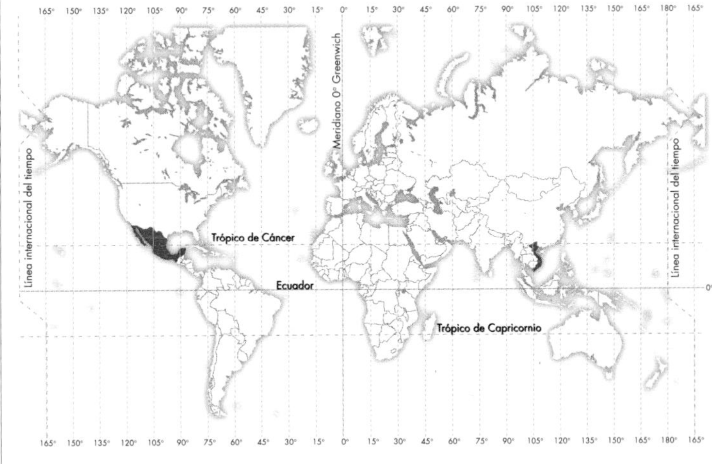

República Socialista de Vietnam

autodesignó presidente y actuó en forma dictatorial. La resistencia contra la ocupación estadounidense en el sur fue dirigida por el Frente de Liberación Nacional, apoyado por la República Democrática de Vietnam. En 1963 el gobierno mexicano estableció relaciones diplomáticas con el gobierno de Vietnam del Sur. Al año siguiente cayó el dictador Ngo Dinh Diem y siguió una serie de golpes de Estado en el sur hasta que Nguyen Van Thieu se hizo cargo del gobierno en 1965. En ese año, en la ciudad de México, el gobierno de Gustavo Díaz Ordaz reprimió brutalmente una manifestación estudiantil de solidaridad con Vietnam. Estados Unidos inició una agresión militar en gran escala contra Vietnam en 1964. El general Curtis Lemay, jefe de operaciones del ejército invasor, declaró entonces que su objetivo era "hacer retroceder a Vietnam a la edad de piedra", para lo que se aplicó la guerra química y bacteriológica, se ensayaron toda clase de armas y se descargaron sobre el territorio vietnamita más bombas que todas las usadas durante la segunda guerra mundial. Estados Unidos llegó a tener 580,000 soldados en el país. La agresión costó dos millones de vidas y concluyó formalmente en enero de 1973, después de grandes movilizaciones pacifistas en todo el mundo, especialmente en Estados Unidos. El acuerdo para poner fin a la invasión lo firmaron el gobierno del norte y el Frente de Liberación (Vietcong), de un lado, y Estados Unidos y el gobierno militar del sur, por la otra parte. En octubre de 1974 hicieron una visita oficial a México Phan, Duy Tuan, miembro de la Comisión de Relaciones Exteriores de la República Democrática de Vietnam, y Nguyen Khac Thin, corresponsal de la agencia de noticias de Vietnam; fueron recibidos por Luis Echeverría y Horacio Flores de la Peña, titular de la Secretaría del Patrimonio Nacional. En la primavera de 1975 se inició la ofensiva final contra el gobierno militar de Vietnam del sur y el 30 de abril cayó Saigón. Se estableció un gobierno del Frente de Liberación Nacional y se cambió el nombre de la capital sureña a ciudad Ho-Chi-Minh, en honor del líder comunista muerto en 1969. A la salida de las tropas estadounidenses, en Saigón, una de cada cuatro personas padecía alguna enfermedad venérea y en todo Vietnam del Sur había 3 millones de desempleados, 4 millones de analfabetos, un millón de viudas, 800,000 huérfanos y un millón de tuberculosos. Del 16 al 21 de noviembre de 1975 se realizaron en Ciudad Ho-Chi-Minh las conferencias de unificación, que dieron origen a la República Socialista de Vietnam, con la que México estableció relaciones diplomáticas en ese mismo año. El 26 de abril de 1976 quedó formalmente constituido el gobierno único de Vietnam, país que al año siguiente fue admitido en la Organización de las Naciones Unidas. En 1978 el régimen de Kampuchea, dirigido por Pol Pot y con apoyo del gobierno chino, entró en conflicto con Vietnam y se rompieron las hostilidades entre ambos países. Vietnam invadió el país vecino en apoyo del Frente de Salvación Nacional de Camboya, derrocó a Pol Pot y, como represalia, el ejército chino penetró en Vietnam con 650,000 hombres. Los invasores chinos salieron del país pocos días después, en una costosa retirada, y luego de haber causado cuantiosos daños. Tanto la unificación de Vietnam como los conflictos subsecuentes generaron una corriente migratoria de sudvietnamitas, algunos de origen chino y otros ex colaboradores de Estados Unidos, los que se embarcaban en lanchones y se perdían a la deriva en el mar Meridional de China. Se calcula en más de medio millón el número de estas *boat people* que murieron de hambre, sed, insolación o a manos de los piratas. En los noventa, Vietnam realizó cambios constitucionales: aceptó la economía de mercado y restringió el poder del Partido Comunista. Además, reestableció relaciones diplomáticas con Estados Unidos (en 1994 Washington levantó el embargo comercial y en 1996 designó embajador) y se incorporó a la Asociación de Naciones del Sudeste Asiático (1995).

VIGAS DE RAMÍREZ, LAS ◆ Municipio de Veracruz situado al oeste de Jalapa y contiguo a Perote. Superficie: 108.57 km². Habitantes: 13,535, de los cuales 3,057 forman la población económicamente activa. Hablan alguna lengua indígena 32 personas mayores de cinco años. La cabecera es Profesor Rafael Ramírez.

VIGIL, JOSÉ MARÍA ◆ n. en Guadalajara, Jal., y m. en la ciudad de México (1829-1909). Escritor y periodista. Abandonó la carrera de derecho para dedicarse a la literatura, como miembro del grupo La Falange de Estudio, cuyo órgano de divulgación era *El Ensayo Literario*, donde inició su carrera periodística. Fue profesor del Liceo de Jalisco (1855), oficial mayor del Congreso de la Unión (1861), donde fundó la biblioteca con el acervo de los conventos suprimidos; director del periódico oficial *El País*, colaborador de *El Siglo XIX*, *El Porvenir*, *El Monitor Republicano*, *El Álbum* y *El Nuevo Mundo* y editor de la *Revista Filosófica*. Durante la intervención francesa se refugió en Estados Unidos, desde donde apoyó la causa juarista con su trabajo periodístico. Al triunfo de la República volvió a México, editó en Guadalajara el *Boletín de Noticias*, publicó en la ciudad de México *La Prensa* (1866) y fue elegido diputado a cinco legislaturas, aunque sólo ocupó la curul en dos de ellas. Fue profesor en las escuelas Nacional Preparatoria y Normal para Señoritas y magistrado de la Suprema Corte de Justicia (1875) y director de la Biblioteca Nacional (1880-1909), cuyo catálogo publicó en ocho tomos. Hizo traducciones, editó *Historia de las Indias*, de Bartolomé de las Casas, *Crónica mexicana*, de Fernando Alvarado Tezozómoc, y *Memorias para la historia de México independiente*, de José María Bocanegra. Autor de los poemarios: *La aurora poética de Jalisco* (1851) y *Realidades y quimeras* (1857); de las obras teatrales: *Dolores o una pasión* (1851), *La hija del carpintero* (1854), *Flores de Anáhuac* y *Composiciones dramáticas* (1867) y *Un demócrata al uso*

José María Vigil

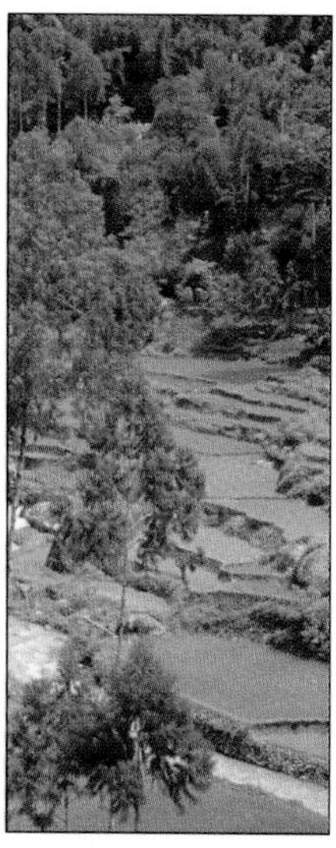
Paisaje natural en la República Socialista de Vietnam

(1872); de textos sobre literatura: *Isabel Prieto de Landázuri* (1883), *Poetisas mexicanas. Siglos XVI, XVII, XVIII y XIX* (1893), *Antología de poetas mexicanos* (1894). *Reseña histórica de la literatura mexicana* (1894) y *Lope de Vega* (1904); y de los textos de historia: *Ensayo histórico del Ejército de Occidente* (1874) e *Historia de la reforma, la intervención y el imperio* (1889, quinto tomo de *México a través de los siglos*). Ingresó en 1881 a la Academia Mexicana (de la Lengua), de la que fue bibliotecario (1883-1909) y director (1894-1909).

VIGUERAS LÁZARO, FILIBERTO ◆ n. en Tlalchapa, Gro. (1918). Profesor rural (1934). Tomó un curso de derecho laboral en la Universidad Obrera. Miembro del PRI, en el que ha sido secretario de Acción Obrera, secretario de Organización y secretario general del Comité Directivo Estatal de Morelos; presidente del Comité (1969), secretario general en Acapulco y secretario de Acción Obrera en Guerrero. Miembro fundador de la CTM (1936). Secretario de prensa y propaganda (1945) y secretario general de la Federación de Trabajadores de Morelos (1945-55). Secretario de Actas y Acuerdos, de Organización y Promoción Sindical y de Trabajo y Conflictos de la Federación Morelense; secretario general de la sección 72 de azucareros en el Ingenio Zacatepec y secretario de la Federación de Trabajadores de Guerrero (1983). En 1942 encabezó una huelga en Zacatepec, por lo que en 1944 fue secuestrado junto con otros líderes. En 1944 organizó un sindicato minero en Taxco y ganó varios sindicatos de la CROM para la CTM. Ha sido profesor rural en Tlaquiltenango (1934-37), presidente municipal de Acapulco, juez menor municipal en Acapulco, regidor de Obras Públicas del ayuntamiento de Acapulco, dos veces diputado local, diputado federal (1979-82) y senador por Guerrero (1982-88).

Maruxa Vilalta

VILA CUENCA, JOSÉ ◆ n. en España y m. en el DF (1898-1981). Militante del Partido Socialista Obrero Español (1917-), luchó en la guerra civil y alcanzó el grado de teniente coronel en el ejército republicano. Exiliado en Francia (1939) y en México (1942), trabajó en la iniciativa privada y fue colaborador de *El Socialista* y de la revista *Francia*. Desempeñó algunos puestos en la Benéfica Hispana.

VILA MAUNER, JOSÉ ANTONIO ◆ n. en Cataluña, España (1925). Vino en 1942 y obtuvo la nacionalidad mexicana en 1947. Se tituló como médico por la UNAM (1952), se especializó en administración de hospitales en la Escuela de Posgraduados de la Secretaría de Salubridad y Asistencia y en la UNAM (1963), de la que ha sido profesor (1960-63 y 1965-72), así como de la Asociación Mexicana de Hospitales (1965-) y de los cursos para directivos del IMSS (1974-). Fue residente en administración de hospitales de la Universidad de Chicago, médico residente (1958-60), médico adjunto (1960-65) y subdirector administrativo del Instituto Nacional de Cardiología (1965-74); jefe del departamento de Programas Médico-arquitectónicos de la Subdirección General Médica y asesor médico de la Jefatura de Planeación, Supervisión y Evaluación Médica del IMSS (1974-76). Jefe del Servicio de Cardiología (1958-63) y médico consultor en cardiología de la Benéfica Hispana (1981-), así como asesor médico de la dirección científica del Grupo Roussel (1974-). Colaborador de *Principia Cardiológica* y de los *Archivos del Instituto de Cardiología de México*. Autor de *Waiting Time in the Out Patient Department* (Chicago, 1964). Miembro de la Sociedad Mexicana de Historia y Filosofía de la Medicina y del Colegio Mexicano de Cardiología, secretario tesorero (1976-81) y presidente de la Federación Mexicana de Hospitales (1982-).

VILALTA, MARUXA ◆ n. en Cataluña, España (1932). Nombre profesional de la escritora María Vilalta Soteras, hija de Antonio Vilalta y Vidal. Fue traída a México luego de la derrota de la República Española. Estudió letras en la UNAM y en la Universidad de Cambridge. Colaboradora de *Excélsior* (1956-) y conductora de diversos programas de televisión, entre ellos *Mujeres que trabajan* y *El libro de hoy*. Ha dirigido obras de teatro de su propia autoría y de Ustinov, Chéjov, Anovilli, Wallach y Husson. Autora de las novelas *El castigo* (1957), *Los desorientados* (1958) y *Dos colores para el paisaje* (1961); de los relatos *El otro día, la muerte* (1974); y de las obras de teatro *Los desorientados* (1960), *A manera de sinopsis, Un país feliz, La última letra, Soliloquio del tiempo, Un día loco, El 9, Cuestión de narices, Esta noche juntos, amándonos tanto* (1970, Premio Juan Ruiz de Alarcón de la Asociación de Críticos de Teatro a la mejor obra del año), *Nada como el piso 16* (1976), *Historia de él* (1978), *Una mujer, dos hombres y un balazo* (1981), *Pequeña historia de horror (y de amor desenfrenado)* (1984), *Una voz en el desierto* (1991) y *Francisco de Asís* (1992).

VILALTA Y VIDAL, ADRIÁN ◆ n. en Cataluña, España, y m. en el DF (1906-1968). Periodista. Licenciado en derecho por la Universidad de Barcelona, fue redactor del periódico republicano *El Diluvio* y funcionario del gobierno de la Generalitat, en Cataluña. Exiliado en México en 1938, trabajó como reportero de la fuente de economía en el diario *Excélsior*.

VILALTA Y VIDAL, ANTONIO ◆ n. en Cataluña, España, y m. en el DF (1905-1981). Hermano del anterior. Licenciado en derecho por la Universidad de Barcelona (1926). Fundador del Partido Esquerra Republicana de Catalunya, regidor y vicealcalde de Barcelona (1931 y 1934); fundador e integrante del Consejo Ejecutivo del Partit Nacionalista Republicá d'Esquerra y jefe de su fracción parlamentaria. Vino a México en 1939, a la caída de la República española, y obtuvo la nacionalidad mexicana en 1940. Fue editor de la revista *Noticiero de Seguros, Previsión y Ahorro*, fundador de la Asociación Médico Farmacéutica y abogado de la Secretaría de Hacienda (1958-81). Autor de *La premeditación como circunstancia atenuante* (1949) y *La individualización de la ley civil* (1982). Perteneció al Ilustre Colegio de Abogados de Barcelona.

Vilalta y Vidal, Emiliano ◆ n. en Cataluña, España, y m. en el DF (1908-1971). Periodista, hermano de los anteriores. Estudió la carrera de derecho. Se inició como editorialista del diario republicano *El Diluvio*, fue juez de distrito en Barcelona y Guadix, Granada, y oficial del cuerpo jurídico militar. Vino a México en 1938 y obtuvo la nacionalidad mexicana. Fundó y dirigió la revista *La Propiedad* y fue corresponsal de la agencia France Press.

Vilar, Manuel ◆ n. en España y m. en la ciudad de México (1812-1860). Escultor. Tras estudiar en Barcelona y Roma fue contratado en 1846, junto con Pelegrín Clavé, como profesor de la Academia de San Carlos, de México, cuyo sistema de enseñanza reorganizó. De sus obras se conservan las estatuas de Cristóbal Colón (1852), del caudillo tlaxcalteca Tlahuicole (1852) y los bustos de Moctezuma y Malintzin.

Vilchis, Fernando ◆ n. en Veracruz, Ver. (1932). Pintor egresado de la ENAP (1954) y del Centro Superior de Artes Aplicadas del INBA (1960), especializado en técnicas litográficas, cartel y grabado en el Instituto de Bellas Artes de Varsovia. En 1963 fundó el Taller de Grabado de la Universidad Veracruzana. Puso en funcionamiento, con Leticia Tarragó, el Taller de Grabado de la Universidad Autónoma Benito Juárez, de Oaxaca y fue director de la Unidad Interdisciplinaria de Investigaciones Estéticas y Creación Artística de la Universidad Veracruzana. Ha expuesto individual o colectivamente desde 1962 en Israel, México y en las bienales de Puerto Rico (1971 y 1979), Italia (1974) y Yugoslavia (1981). Primer premio en el Salón de la Estampa y el Dibujo del INBA (1975).

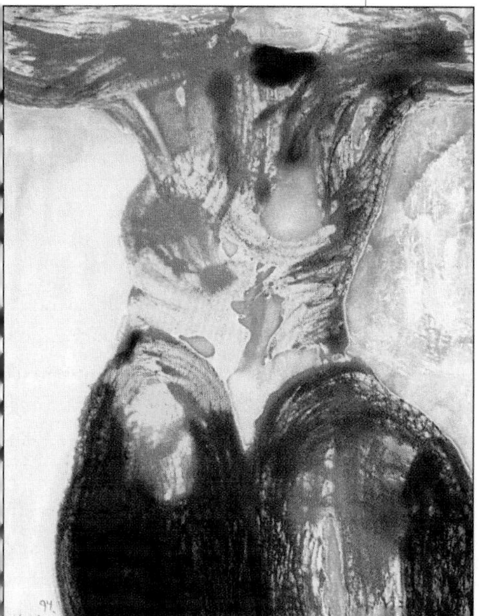

Serie "Torsos", arenas y óleo sobre tela de Fernando Vilchis

Vilchis Gil de Arévalo , Rafael ◆ n. en Toluca, Edo. de Méx. (1936). Periodista. Se inició como auxiliar en el periodismo en 1957. Ha sido redactor, subdirector y director de *El Sol de Toluca*. Presidente de la Asociación de Periodistas del Valle de Toluca (1984-85). Presea de Periodismo e Información José María Cos por artículo de fondo (1985).

Viljoen, Benjamín ◆ n. en Transvaal, hoy Sudáfrica, y m. en EUA (1868-1916). Militar. Luchó contra el ejército británico en la segunda guerra anglo-bóer (1899-1902) y fue segundo jefe del ejército de los colonos holandeses, a las órdenes de Luis Rotha. En enero de 1903 llegó a México con un grupo de sus compatriotas (derrotados en la guerra), para establecer una colonia agrícola en el municipio de Julimes, Chihuahua. En febrero de 1911 se unió a la revolución. Participó en algunas acciones al lado de Francisco I. Madero, a quien acompañó en la toma de Ciudad Juárez. Una vez en el poder, Madero lo comisionó para reprimir a los yaquis. Obtuvo la nacionalidad mexicana y se mantuvo al margen de las actividades políticas. Residió sus últimos años en Arizona.

Villa, Francisco ◆ n. en Río Grande, Dgo., y m. en Hidalgo del Parral, Chih. (1878-1923). Revolucionario cuyo nombre era Doroteo Arango Quiñones. Huérfano desde la adolescencia, fue leñador, agricultor y vendedor ambulante. En 1894, él y sus hermanos llegaron a trabajar como medieros en la hacienda de la familia López Negrete, donde uno de los propietarios, Agustín López Negrete, trató de raptar a Martina Arango, hermana de Doroteo; éste impidió el rapto e hirió a su patrón, por lo que tuvo que esconderse. Perseguido por los guardias de la hacienda, se refugió en la sierra, donde entró en contacto con la banda de Ignacio Parra, a la que se unió ya con el pseudónimo de *Pancho Villa*, que adoptó por su abuelo Jesús Villa. Vivió varios años como abigeo y estuvo brevemente preso en Durango. Se alejó de la banda de Parra cuando uno de sus integrantes asesinó a un anciano. Se trasladó a Chihuahua, donde fue minero, obrero, albañil y comerciante, actividad en la que conoció al entonces gobernador Abraham González. Perseguido aún por la policía, se refugió de nuevo en la sierra y se dedicó al bandolerismo. Abraham González lo hizo participar en la insurrección maderista. Tres días antes del inicio anunciado de la revolución, el 17 de noviembre de 1910, comenzó las hostilidades con el ataque a la hacienda de Chavarría. Al frente de un pequeño contingente se presentó en la hacienda de Bustillo ante Francisco I. Madero, quien le dio el grado de coronel. Él y Pascual Orozco condujeron la lucha en el estado de Chihuahua, misma que concluyó con la toma de Ciudad Juárez, en mayo de 1911, tras la cual se produ-

Manuel Vilar

Rafael Vilchis Gil de Arévalo

Francisco Villa

FOTO: ARCHIVO CASASOLA

Francisco Villa, el Centauro del Norte

jo la renuncia de Porfirio Díaz. Al término de la insurrección, dejó sus tropas al mando de Raúl Madero y se retiró a Chihuahua, donde se dedicó a criar ganado y estableció una carnicería. En 1912 retomó las armas para combatir la rebelión orozquista, en la que se negó a participar. Madero envió a Victoriano Huerta como comandante de la División del Norte y Villa se puso a sus órdenes en Torreón. Destacó en los combates de Tlahualilo, Conejos y Rellano y fue ascendido a general brigadier por Huerta, quien luego lo acusó de insubordinación y ordenó su fusilamiento, lo que se evitó por la intervención de Madero. La pena fue conmutada por la de reclusión y se le trasladó a la prisión militar de Santiago Tlatelolco, donde conoció al zapatista Gildardo Magaña, quien lo enseñó a leer. Escapó de la cárcel a fines de 1912 y se refugió en Estados Unidos. En marzo de 1913, tras los asesinatos de Madero, José María Pino Suárez y Abraham González, entró a México por Chihuahua, con apenas nueve seguidores. Recibió ayuda del gobernador sonorense, José María Maytorena, y formó un numeroso ejército, que puso a las órdenes de Venustiano Carranza. En septiembre de 1913 quedó constituida, en Ciudad Jiménez, la División del Norte, con la que creció su prestigio y fue llamado *el Centauro del Norte*. Tomó Torreón (en septiembre), Chihuahua (noviembre), Ciudad Juárez (el 15 de noviembre), Tierra Blanca (24 de noviembre, cuando aniquiló una división federal completa) y nuevamente Chihuahua, el 8 de diciembre. Los brigadieres de la División del Norte, Maclovio Herrera, José E. Rodríguez y Manuel Chao, lo nombraron gobernador provisional de Chihuahua, cargo que dejó a su subalterno Manuel Chao el 8 de enero de 1914, aunque siguió gobernando la entidad, de facto, hasta finales de 1915. Durante su gestión al frente del Ejecutivo local instaló el primer telégrafo inalámbrico del norte del país, expulsó de la entidad a los comerciantes españoles acusados de colaborar con Huerta, abarató los artículos de consumo básico, abrió el Instituto Científico y Literario, condonó las contribuciones atrasadas y emitió moneda. El inglés William Benton se acercó a él, con el pretexto de denunciar abusos de algunos soldados villistas, y trató de asesinarlo, por lo que fue muerto de inmediato, lo que originó una reclamación del gobierno británico. Villa dejó el gobierno de Chihuahua y siguió su campaña militar con el combate de Gómez Palacio (en marzo de 1914, ya con Felipe Ángeles, Raúl Madero y José Isabel Robles integrados a la División del Norte), la segunda toma de Torreón (22 de marzo a 2 de abril de 1914) y las ocupaciones de San Pedro de las Colonias (5 a 9 de abril de 1914) y de Paredón (20 de mayo de 1914, con una carga de 6,000 *dorados*, como llamaban a los combatientes de élite y a la escolta personal de Villa, por el color de sus camisas. Su autosuficiencia resultó incompatible con la jefatura unificada que pretendía Carranza, con quien se inició un largo conflicto. Villa se negó a atacar Saltillo, como ordenaba Carranza, y en cambio tomó Zacatecas, (el 23 de junio de 1914), acción que fue definitiva en el curso de la guerra, pues precipitó la caída de Huerta. La pugna entre Villa y Carranza se agudizó durante la Convención de Aguascalientes. Ambos fueron desttituidos de sus cargos por esa asamblea, pero Carranza se negó a acatar el acuerdo entró en rebeldía y se inició la lucha de facciones. Eulalio Gutiérrez, elegido presidente por la Convención, designó a Villa jefe de operaciones militares. Con la firma del Pacto de Xochimilco, el 4 de diciembre de 1914, se estableció una alianza entre la División del Norte y el Ejército Libertador del Sur, dirigido por Emiliano Zapata, quien logró que el caudillo norteño se adhiriese al Plan de Ayala. Las fuerzas convencionistas ocuparon la ciudad de México el 6 de diciembre de 1914, y los dirigentes se retrataron juntos, con Villa en el sillón presidencial. Ambos contingentes aban-

Tropas fieles a *Francisco Villa*

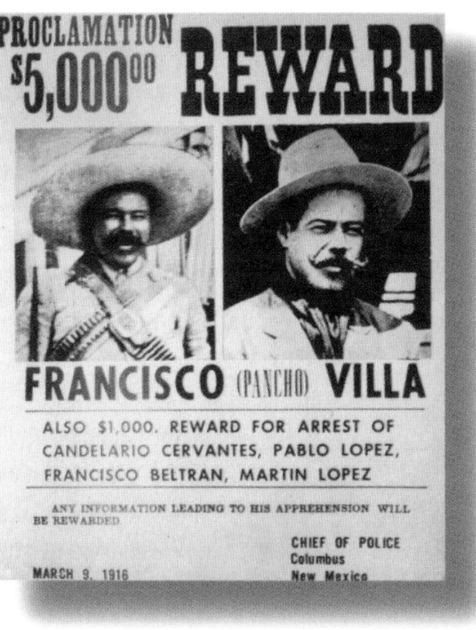

El jefe de la policía de Columbus, Nuevo México, ofrece cinco mil dólares por información que conduzca a la captura de *Francisco Villa*

donaron la capital y se inició su declive. Villa fue derrotado por Obregón, sucesivamente, en Celaya, León y Trinidad y obligado a replegarse hacia el norte del país, donde combatió a lo largo de 1915 y 1916. Al frente de 10,000 hombres, fracasó en su intento de apoderarse de Agua Prieta, donde fue derrotado por Plutarco Elías Calles, quien fue autorizado a transitar con sus tropas por territorio estadounidense. Después de esa batalla, la División del Norte se disolvió y Villa se convirtió en un guerrillero que sólo operaba en Chihuahua. Estados Unidos impidió el paso de pertrechos para los villistas y congeló sus cuentas en el Columbus State Bank, por lo que se produjo el ataque a la población de Columbus, Nuevo México, el 9 de marzo de 1916. Este hecho dio pretexto al gobierno estadounidense para intervenir nuevamente en México. Washington envió la llamada Expedición Punitiva, comandada por John J. Pershing, héroe de la primera guerra mundial, y a quien acompañaba George Patton. La expedición permaneció en el país, sin autorización del gobierno carrancista, del 15 de marzo al 21 de junio de 1916, sin lograr atrapar a Villa. Este se mantuvo casi inactivo desde entonces y, finalmente, se amnistió mediante la firma de los Convenios de Sabinas. De acuerdo con éstos, le fue reconocido el grado de general de división, se le entregó la hacienda de Canutillo y se le permitió mantener una guardia de 50 *dorados*, pagados por el gobierno. En su hacienda organizó el trabajo comunal, convirtió la iglesia en troje, compró maquinaria agrícola, sembró, plantó y almacenó trigo, maíz y frijol; construyó una escuela para los hijos de los campesinos, así como casas para sus empleados, trazó calles; introdujo los servicios de correo y telégrafo, instaló talleres de carpintería, carnicerías y zapaterías; fudó un banco de crédito agrícola e impulsó la industria ganadera. A fines de 1922 expresó al periodista Regino Hernández Llergo, sus simpatías por el precandidato a la Presidencia, Adolfo de la Huerta, quien estaba en competencia por el cargo con Plutarco Elías Calles. El 20 de junio de 1923, Villa y tres acompañantes fueron asesinados en una emboscada, en Hidalgo del Parral, por Jesús Salas Barraza. Reconocido como héroe popular en leyendas y corridos populares, fue hasta 1967 que se puso su nombre en el recinto de la Cámara de Diputados, después de un largo debate.

VILLA, HIPÓLITO ◆ n. en Río Grande, Dgo. (¿1881?-1925). Revolucionario llamado Hipólito Arango, hermano del anterior. Acompañó a su hermano en la lucha revolucionaria desde 1910. Hizo las campañas de Chihuahua, Durango y Coahuila; participó en la formación de la División del Norte, actuó en las tomas de Torreón, en el combate de Gómez Palacio y en la toma de Zacatecas. Convencionista en 1914, se amnistió en 1920, durante el gobierno de Adolfo de la Huerta. Participó en la rebelión delahuertista.

VILLA, JOSÉ SANTOS ◆ n. ¿en Guanajuato, Gto.? y m. en Chihuahua, Chih. (¿1750?-1811). Insurgente, pariente de Miguel Hidalgo. Era director de la orquesta del curato de Dolores, Guanajuato, y auxiliaba a Hidalgo en su labor educativa con los indígenas de la región. En septiembre de 1810 participó en el inicio de la guerra de Independencia y durante la campaña alcanzó el grado de coronel. Fue aprehendido, junto con los caudillos insurgentes, en Acatita de Baján, conducido a Chihuahua y fusilado.

Lucha Villa

VILLA, LUCHA ◆ n. en Ciudad Camargo, Chih. (1936). Nombre profesional de la cantante Luz Elena Ruiz Bejarano. Se inició en 1959 en la ciudad de México en teatro, cabaret y televisión. Ha grabado decenas de discos. Entre sus mayores éxitos como intérprete están las canciones *¿Sabes de qué tengo ganas?*, *A medias de la noche*, *Amanecí en tus brazos*, *Qué bonito amor*, *Si nos dejan*, *Te solté la rienda* y *Vámonos*. En teatro tuvo una larga temporada con *El quelite* (llevada a cine) y ha participado en otras obras. Ha trabajado en televisión y radio. Participó en más de 100 películas, como *El Gallo de Oro* (1964), *El quelite* (1969), *Lagunilla mi barrio* (1970), *Mecánica nacional* (1971), *El lugar sin límites* (1977), *Encuentro inesperado* (1991), *Lolo* (1991). Ha obtenido dos Diosas de Platas y dos Arieles. Medalla Virginia Fábregas de la ANDA (1987).

VILLA AHUMADA ◆ Antes Villa González. Cabecera del municipio chihuahuense de Ahumada (☛).

VILLA ALDAMA ◆ Municipio de Veracruz situado al noroeste de Jalapa. Superficie: 78.96 km². Habitantes: 7,337, de los cuales 1,711 forman la población económicamente activa. Hablan alguna lengua indígena nueve personas mayores de cinco años.

VILLA ALTA ◆ Sierra de Oaxaca situada en el centro del estado, al este y noreste de la capital estatal; forma parte de la sierra Madre Oriental. Se extiende de sur a norte, al noroeste de la sierra de Mixes, al oeste del nacimiento del río del Chisme, y al este y paralela al río Villa Alta o Cajonos.

VILLA DE ÁLVAREZ ◆ Municipio de Colima situado en el norte del estado y contiguo a la capital estatal. Superficie: 428.39 km². Habitantes: 66,300, de los cuales 12,279 forman la población económicamente activa. Hablan alguna lengua indígena 24 personas mayores de cinco años.

VILLA DE ALLENDE ◆ Municipio del Estado de México situado al norte de Valle de Bravo y al oeste-noroeste de Toluca, en los límites con Michoacán. Superficie: 202.38 km². Habitantes: 37,105, de los cuales 6,670 forman la población económicamente activa. Hablan alguna lengua indígena 969 personas (mazahua 958). En la jurisdicción se hallan la zona arqueológica de San Cayetano, el parque nacional de Bosencheve con el vivero San Cayetano. La cabecera es San José Villa de Allende.

VILLA DE ARISTA ◆ Municipio de San Luis Potosí contiguo a la capital estatal. Superficie: 498.97 km². Habitantes: 13,487, de los cuales 2,635 forman la población económicamente activa.

Portales de Villa Flores, Chiapas

FOTO: FONDO EDITORIAL GRUPO AZABACHE

VILLA DE ARRIAGA ◆ Municipio de San Luis Potosí situado en los límites con Zacatecas, Jalisco y Guanajuato y contiguo a la capital del estado. Superficie: 1,156.4 km². Habitantes: 13,933, de los cuales 3,300 forman la población económicamente activa. Hablan alguna lengua indígena 25 personas mayores de cinco años.

VILLA AZUETA ◆ Cabecera del municipio veracruzano de José Azueta (☛).

VILLA DEL CARBÓN ◆ Municipio del Estado de México situado en los límites con Hidalgo y contiguo a Tepotzotlán. Superficie: 93.69 km². Habitantes: 30,726, de los cuales 6,663 forman la población económicamente activa. Hablan alguna lengua indígena 414 personas mayores de cinco años (otomí 147). En su jurisdicción se localizan las zonas arqueológicas de Atexcapa, las Moras y San Jerónimo, así como el llano de San Lucas, el cerro de la Bufa y el río de San Rafael. En la cabecera, del mismo nombre, se halla el templo de la Virgen de la Peña de Francia, construido en el siglo XVIII.

VILLA COMALTITLÁN ◆ Municipio costero de Chiapas situado en la porción sur del estado, al noroeste de Tapachula. Superficie: 606.10 km². Habitantes: 25,535, de los cuales 5,994 forman la población económicamente activa. Hablan alguna lengua indígena 142 personas mayores de cinco años (tzeltal 67 y tzotzil 40). Se llamó Pueblo Nuevo Comaltitlán.

VILLA CORONA ◆ Municipio de Jalisco contiguo a Acatlán. Superficie: 179.37 km². Habitantes: 16,055, de los cuales 3,951 forman la población económicamente activa. Hablan alguna lengua indígena 15 personas mayores de cinco años.

VILLA CORZO ◆ Municipio de Chiapas situado en el occidente del estado, al sur de Tuxtla Gutiérrez y contiguo a Tonalá. Superficie: 4,026.70 km². Habitantes: 63,351, de los cuales 13,924 forman la población económicamente activa. Hablan alguna lengua indígena 416 personas mayores de cinco años (tzotzil 328 y tzeltal 55).

VILLA DE COS ◆ Municipio de Zacatecas situado al noreste y próximo a la capital estatal, en los límites con San Luis Potosí. Superficie: 5,824.08 km². Habitantes: 32,502, de los cuales 6,742 forman la población económicamente activa. Hablan alguna lengua indígena 22 personas mayores de cinco años (chontal de Oaxaca 11 y mixteco 11).

VILLA CUAUHTÉMOC ◆ Cabecera del municipio mexiquense de Otzolotepec (☛).

VILLA CUAUHTÉMOC ◆ Cabecera del municipio veracruzano de Pueblo Viejo, (☛).

VILLA DE CHILAPA DE DÍAZ ◆ Municipio de Oaxaca situado al noroeste de la capital del estado, al sureste de Huajuapan de León y cercano a Puebla. Superficie: 234.75 km². Habitantes: 1,865, de los cuales 343 forman la población económicamente activa. Hablan alguna lengua indígena 132 personas (mixteco 129). Su cabecera municipal es Santa María Chilapa de Díaz.

VILLA DÍAZ ORDAZ ◆ Municipio de Oaxaca situado en el centro del estado, al este de la capital de la entidad. Superficie: 209.23 km². Habitantes: 5,791, de los cuales 1,746 forman la población económicamente activa. Hablan alguna lengua indígena 4,818 personas (zapoteco 4,816). El nombre, antes Santo Domingo del Valle, se le impuso en honor del general José María Díaz Ordaz.

VILLA DE ETLA ◆ Municipio de Oaxaca situado en el centro del estado, al nor-noroeste de la capital de la entidad. Superficie: 17.86 km². Habitantes: 6,319, de los cuales 1,602 forman la población económicamente activa. Hablan alguna lengua indígena 411 personas (zapoteco 221 y mixteco 190). En la cabecera, del mismo nombre, hay un convento dominico construido a fines del siglo XVI, y un acueducto colonial; el bosque cercano es, además, un parque recreativo. En su jurisdicción existen zonas arqueológicas poco exploradas. La principal festividad se efectúa el 16 de junio. El nombre anterior del municipio era San Pedro y San Pablo Etla.

VILLA FLORES ◆ Municipio de Chiapas situado al norte de Tonalá y al suroeste de Tuxtla Gutiérrez, cerca del océano Pacífico. Superficie: 1,232.10 km². Habitantes: 79,925, de los cuales 20,059 forman la población económicamente activa. Hablan alguna lengua indígena 396 personas mayores de cinco años (tzotzil 264 y zoque 67). La cabecera, del mismo nombre, es el principal centro de comunicaciones y de distribución comercial de la vertiente occidental de la sierra Madre de Chiapas. La principal fiesta es la del Señor de Esquipulas, que se celebra la segunda y tercera semanas de enero.

VILLA GARCÍA ◆ Municipio de Zacatecas situado en el oriente del estado, al sur-sureste de Villa González Ortega, en los límites con Aguascalientes. Superficie: 683.36 km². Habitantes: 13,467, de los cuales 3,609 forman la población económicamente activa.

VILLA GENERAL ESCOBEDO ◆ Cabecera del municipio General Escobedo (☛), de Nuevo León.

VILLA GONZÁLEZ ORTEGA ◆ Municipio de Zacatecas situado en el oriente del estado, al este-sureste de la capital estatal, en los límites con San Luis Potosí. Superficie: 253.67 km². Habitantes: 11,613, de los cuales 2,657 forman la población económicamente activa.

VILLA DE GUADALUPE ◆ Municipio de San Luis Potosí situado al noreste de la capital estatal, contiguo a Matehuala, en los límites con Nuevo León y Tamaulipas. Superficie: 1,486.1 km². Habitantes: 10,907, de los cuales 2,902 forman la población económicamente activa. Hablan alguna lengua indígena 21 personas mayores de cinco años.

VILLA DE GUADALUPE HIDALGO ◆ ☛ *Guadalupe, Villa de* y *Gustavo A. Madero.*

VILLA GUERRERO ◆ Municipio del Estado de México situado al sur y próximo a Toluca. Superficie: 239.86 km². Habitantes: 43,283, de los cuales 11,220 forman la población económicamente activa. Hablan alguna lengua indígena 54 personas mayores de cinco años. Fue fundado el 20 de abril de 1867. En la jurisdicción se hallan el salto de la Neblina y el balneario del Salitre. En la cabecera, del mismo nombre y anteriormente llamada Tecualoya, están las iglesias de San Gaspar y de San Mateo, construidas en el siglo XVIII.

VILLA GUERRERO ◆ Municipio de Jalisco situado en el norte del estado, al nor-noroeste de Guadalajara, en los límites con Zacatecas. Superficie: 1,092. km². Habitantes: 5,766, de los cuales 1,287 forman la población económicamente activa. Hablan alguna lengua indígena 79 personas (huichol 74).

VILLA GUSTAVO A. MADERO ◆ ☛ *Gustavo A. Madero.*

VILLA HIDALGO ◆ Municipio de Jalisco situado en el noreste del estado, contiguo a Teocaltiche, en los límites con Aguascalientes. Superficie: 496.60 km². Habitantes: 13,715, de los cuales 3,108 forman la población económicamente activa. Hablan alguna lengua indígena 12 personas mayores de cinco años.

VILLA HIDALGO ◆ Municipio de Oaxaca situado al noreste de la capital del estado y contiguo a San Melchor Betaza, Totontepec Villa de Morelos, San Mateo Cajonos y San Francisco Cajonos. Superficie: 35.72 km². Habitantes: 2,287, de los cuales 522 forman la población económicamente activa. Hablan alguna lengua indígena 1,890 personas (zapoteco 1,776 y mixe 333), de las cuales 302 son monolingües. Se llamó Hidalgo Yalalag.

VILLA DE HIDALGO ◆ Municipio de San Luis Potosí situado en el occidente del estado, al sur y contiguo a la capital estatal, en los límites con Guanajuato. Superficie: 1,658.93 km². Habitantes: 15,724, de los cuales 3,438 forman la población económicamente activa. Hablan alguna lengua indígena 59 personas mayores de cinco años.

VILLA HIDALGO ◆ Municipio de Sonora situado en el noreste del estado, contiguo a Nacozari de García. Superficie: 951.17 km². Habitantes: 1,955, de los cuales 639 forman la población económicamente activa. Hablan alguna lengua indígena seis personas mayores de cinco años. El municipio, antes llamado Oputo, formó parte del de Pilares de Nacozari, actual Nacozari de García, del 26 de diciembre de 1930 al 13 de mayo de 1931. En la cabecera, del mismo nombre y antiguo asentamiento de los ópatas, se celebra una feria popular, del 8 al 12 de octubre.

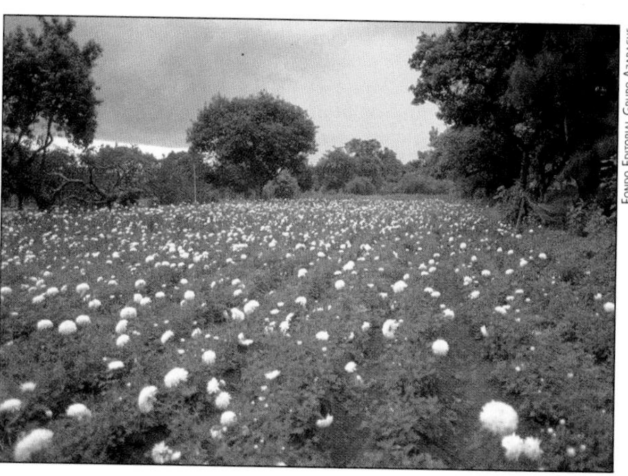

Floricultura en Villa Guerrero, Estado de México

VILLA HIDALGO ◆ Municipio de Zacatecas situado en el oriente del estado, al sureste de la capital estatal, en los límites con San Luis Potosí. Superficie: 522,87 km². Habitantes: 16,490, de los cuales 2,782 forman la población económicamente activa.

VILLA ISSA, MANUEL RAFAEL ◆ n. en Mexicali, BC (1943). Ingeniero agrónomo por la Escuela Nacional de Agricultura de Chapingo (1967), maestro en ciencias por el Colegio de Posgraduados de Chapingo (1970), del que ha sido profesor (1971-), investigador, funcionario y director (1985-86); y doctor en economía por la Universidad de Purdue, EUA (1973).

Villa Guerrero, Jalisco

Primo Villa Michel

Desde 1974 pertenece al PRI. Ha sido delegado regional de la SPP en Puebla (1978-82), diputado federal (1982-85), subsecretario de Desarrollo y Fomento Agropecuario y Forestal de la SARH (1986-88) y director general del Instituto Nacional de Investigaciones Agropecuarias y Forestales (1988-89). Autor de *El mercado de trabajo y la adopción de tecnología nueva de producción agrícola: el caso del Plan Puebla* (1974). Premio Anual de Economía Banamex (1976).

VILLA JIMÉNEZ ◆ Cabecera del municipio michoacano de Jiménez (☛).

VILLA JUÁREZ ◆ Municipio de San Luis Potosí situado al noreste de la capital estatal y al sur de Matehuala. Superficie: 661.9 km². Habitantes: 11,867, de los cuales 2,586 forman la población económicamente activa. En la jurisdicción se localiza Guaxcamá, una de las plantas azufreras más grandes del país. La cabecera, del mismo nombre, se llamó anteriormente Carbonera.

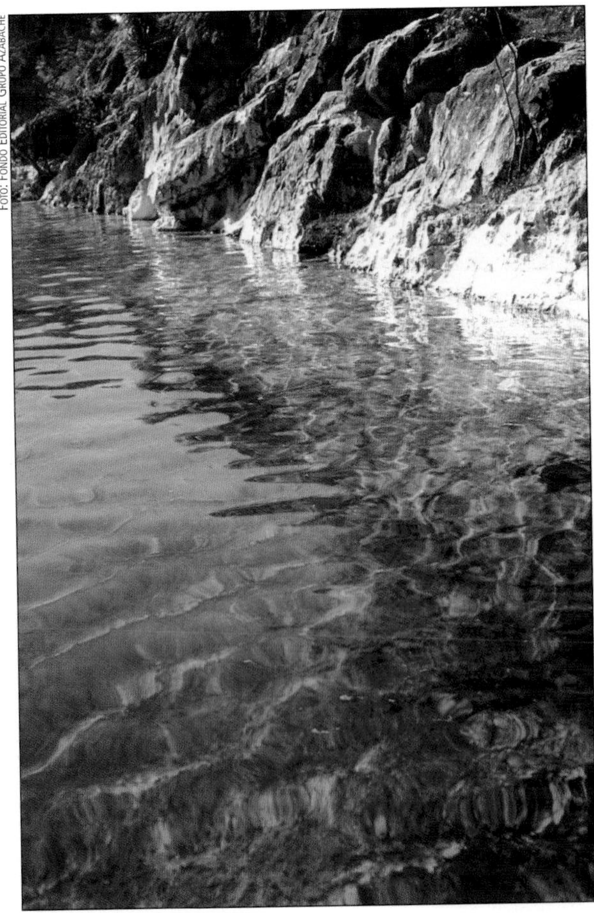
Aguas sulfurosas en Villa de Tamazulapan del Progreso, Oaxaca

Foto: Fondo Editorial Grupo Azabache

VILLA LÓPEZ ◆ Cabecera del municipio chihuahuense de López (☛).

VILLA MADERO ◆ ☛ *Madero.*

VILLA MAINERO ◆ Cabecera del municipio tamaulipeco de Mainero (☛).

VILLA MARIANO MATAMOROS ◆ Cabecera del municipio tlaxcalteca de Ixtacuixtla (☛). Antes se llamó San Felipe Ixtacuixtla.

VILLA MATAMOROS ◆ Cabecera del municipio chihuahuense de Matamoros (☛).

VILLA MICHEL, PRIMO ◆ n. en San Gabriel, hoy Venustiano Carranza, Jal., y m. en el DF (1893-1970). Abogado. Inició su carrera como defensor de oficio y llegó a ser magistrado en el estado de Sonora. Miembro de la Comisión Técnica y de Legislación de la Secretaría de Gobernación (1922), oficial mayor de la Secretaría de Industria y Comercio (1923), secretario general de Gobierno del Distrito Federal (1925), cargo en el que promovió la creación del Tribunal para Menores (1926). Fue gobernador del Distrito Federal (encargado del despacho de junio de 1927 a noviembre de 1928 y titular durante diciembre de 1928), secretario de Industria, Comercio y Trabajo (del 5 de septiembre de 1932 al 30 de noviembre de 1934) en el gabinete de Abelardo L. Rodríguez; embajador en Alemania, Uruguay, Holanda, Japón, Guatemala, Canadá, Inglaterra (1938) y Bélgica; oficial mayor (1940-45) y secretario de Gobernación (del 18 de junio de 1945 al 30 de noviembre de 1946), en sustitución de Miguel Alemán en el gobierno de Manuel Ávila Camacho. Presidente del Comité Coordinador de Importaciones y de la Comisión Mexicano-Norteamericana de Cooperación Económica, consejero diplomático de la delegación mexicana a la Conferencia de Cancilleres de Río de Janeiro, delegado a la Conferencia de San Francisco y director del Instituto Nacional de la Vivienda.

VILLA MORELOS ◆ Cabecera del municipio de Morelos en el estado de Michoacán (☛).

VILLA OBREGÓN ◆ Nombre anterior del municipio Cañadas de Obregón (☛), municipio de Jalisco.

VILLA DE LA PAZ ◆ Municipio de San Luis Potosí situado en el noroeste del estado y contiguo a Matehuala. Superficie: 228.8 km². Habitantes: 5,060, de los cuales 1,397 forman la población económicamente activa. Hablan alguna lengua indígena 11 personas mayores de cinco años. Cuenta con variados recursos minerales. Su cabecera es La Paz.

VILLA PESQUEIRA ◆ Municipio de Sonora situado al este-noreste de Hermosillo y al sureste de Ures. Superficie: 1,834.13 km². Habitantes: 1,701, de los cuales 540 forman la población económicamente activa. Hablan alguna lengua indígena cuatro personas mayores de cinco años.

VILLA DEL PUEBLITO ◆ Cabecera del municipio queretano de Corregidora (☛).

VILLA PURIFICACIÓN ◆ Municipio de Jalisco situado en la porción sudoccidental del estado, al oeste de Autlán. Superficie: 1,937.61 km². Habitantes: 12,014, de los cuales 3,187 forman la población económicamente activa. Hablan alguna lengua indígena 24 personas mayores de cinco años.

VILLA DE RAMOS ◆ Municipio de San Luis Potosí situado en el noroeste del estado y contiguo a Matehuala. Superficie: 2,145.5 km². Habitantes: 32,484, de los cuales 5,419 forman la población económicamente activa. Hablan alguna lengua indígena 28 personas mayores de cinco años. En la jurisdicción se localizan numerosas lagunas de agua salada, como el Barril, el Salitral, la Difunta y el Naranjo. Cuenta con yacimientos minerales. La cabecera es Ramos.

VILLA DE REYES ◆ Municipio de San Luis Potosí situado al sur y próximo a la capital estatal, en los límites con Guanajuato. Superficie: 1,122 km². Habitantes: 38,926, de los cuales 8,012 forman la población económicamente activa. Hablan alguna lengua indígena 52 personas mayores de cinco años. En la jurisdicción se localizan las lagunas del Refugio y San Vicente y una parte del parque nacional El Gogorrón.

VILLA SOLA DE VEGA ♦ Municipio de Oaxaca situado en el centro-sur del estado, al suroeste de la capital de la entidad. Superficie: 680.01 km². Habitantes: 12,414, de los cuales 2,022 forman la población económicamente activa. Hablan alguna lengua indígena 436 personas (zapoteco 427).

VILLA TALEA DE CASTRO ♦ Municipio de Oaxaca situado en el centro-norte del estado, al noreste de la capital de la entidad y al sur de Tuxtepec. Superficie: 54.86 km². Habitantes: 2,685, de los cuales 842 forman la población económicamente activa. Hablan alguna lengua indígena 1,733 personas (zapoteco 1,969). Tiene yacimientos minerales sin explotar y se han hallado tumbas prehispánicas.

VILLA DE TAMAZULAPAN DEL PROGRESO ♦ Municipio de Oaxaca situado al sureste de Huajuapan de León y al nor-noreste de Chilapa de Díaz. Superficie: 102.06 km². Habitantes: 6,202, de los cuales 1,272 forman la población económicamente activa. Hablan alguna lengua indígena 90 personas mayores de cinco años (zapoteco 38 y mixteco 32). El municipio tiene numerosos balnearios de aguas termales. En 1947, cerca de uno de estos balnearios se encontraron restos humanos y piezas de cerámica de la cultura mixteca primitiva. En la cabecera municipal se halla un templo construido en el siglo XVIII.

VILLA TEJUPAM DE LA UNIÓN ♦ Municipio de Oaxaca situado en el noroeste del estado, al sureste de Huajuapan de León. Superficie: 71.45 km². Habitantes: 2,201, de los cuales 494 forman la población económicamente activa. Hablan alguna lengua indígena 83 personas (mixteco 82).

VILLA DE TEZONTEPEC ♦ Municipio de Hidalgo situado en el sur del estado, al sur-suroeste de Pachuca y contiguo a Zempoala, en los límites con el Estado de México. Superficie: 133.6 km². Habitantes: 8,817, de los cuales 2,109 forman la población económicamente activa. Hablan alguna lengua indígena 25 personas mayores de cinco años. En la cabecera, del mismo nombre, existe un convento agustino edificado entre 1554 y 1571.

VILLA TREVIÑO, SAÚL ♦ n. en el DF (1933). Médico cirujano por la UNAM (1956), doctor en bioquímica por la Universidad de Tulane (1964) y posdoctorado en bioquímica por la Universidad de Pittsburgh (1964). Instructor en el Departamento de Patología en la UNAM y en las universidades de Tulane y Pittsburgh (1964), investigador en el Medical Research Council Laboratory de Inglaterra (1964-66), profesor investigador en el Departamento de Biología Celular del Cinvestav (1966-83) y miembro del grupo internacional de expertos en carcinogénesis química (1977). Ha sido jefe del Departamento de Biología Celular del Cinvestav (1969-80), miembro del Comité de Selección de Becas del Área Biológica del Conacyt (1974-77), coordinador de la sección de trabajo para el desarrollo de un programa de biología general para la enseñanza media superior de la SEP (1978) y secretario ejecutivo del Consejo del Sistema Nacional de Educación Tecnológica de la SEP (1983-88). Autor de *Patología clínica del daño celular* (1969), *Biosíntesis de proteínas* (1970), *Los ácidos nucleicos, moléculas de la herencia* (1979) y *Las bases químicas de la información celular* (1979). Miembro de la Academia Nacional de la Investigación Científica, del Consejo Editorial de la revista *Toxicology* (1980), vocal del Fondo Ricardo Zevada (1984) y secretario de la Sociedad Mexicana de Bioquímica.

VILLA DE TUTUTEPEC DE MELCHOR OCAMPO ♦ Municipio de Oaxaca situado en el litoral del océano Pacífico, al sureste de Santiago Pinotepa Nacional. Superficie: 1,249.03 km². Habitantes: 40,501, de los cuales 9,149 forman la población económicamente activa. Hablan alguna lengua indígena 1,922 personas (chatino 1,119, mixteco 815). El parque nacional y la laguna de Chacahua, refugio de diversas especies animales, se hallan 25 km al sur de la cabecera. En la jurisdicción hay vestigios de la cultura mixteca. La pista del aeropuerto, en Río Grande, está cubierta con pedacería de cerámica prehispánica muy cerca de la cabecera, en San Pedro Tututepec, fue desenterrado un monolito de dos metros de alto: es una obra escultórica prehispánica en mediorrelieve, con la representación de un jaguar a punto de devorar a una mujer. La principal festividad del municipio es el 2 de febrero, día de la Candelaria.

VILLA UNIÓN ♦ Cabecera del municipio duranguense de Poanas (☛).

VILLA UNIÓN ♦ Municipio de Coahuila situado en el noreste del estado, al este-noreste de Múzquiz. Superficie: 1,540.30 km². Habitantes: 6,228, de los cuales 1,890 forman la población económicamente activa.

VILLA UNIÓN ♦ Población del municipio de Mazatlán, Sinaloa, al este de la cabecera municipal y 15 km al norte de la laguna El Caimanero.

VILLA VICENTE GUERRERO ♦ Cabecera del municipio tlaxcalteca de San Pablo del Monte (☛).

VILLA VICTORIA ♦ Municipio del Estado de México situado al noreste de Valle de Bravo y al noroeste de Toluca. Superficie: 504.70 km². Habitantes: 63,978, de los cuales 14,735 forman la población económicamente activa. Hablan alguna lengua indígena 4,853 personas (mazahua 4,827). Indígenas monolingües: 94. En la jurisdicción se localiza la presa de Villa Victoria, en la que se pueden practicar deportes acuáticos.

VILLA DE ZAACHILA ♦ Municipio de Oaxaca situado al sur de la capital estatal y al norte de Zimatlán. Superficie: 54.86 km². Habitantes: 15,512, de los cuales 3,013 forman la población económicamente activa. Hablan alguna lengua indígena 432 personas (zapoteco 416). En el valle de Ocotlán se localiza la zona arqueológica de Zaachila, donde se hallan las ruinas de la ciudad del mismo nombre. Capital zapoteca en el periodo Monte Albán IV (1000-1521); en ella hay un túmulo funerario en el que se encontraron los restos de 25 personas, al parecer un personaje principal

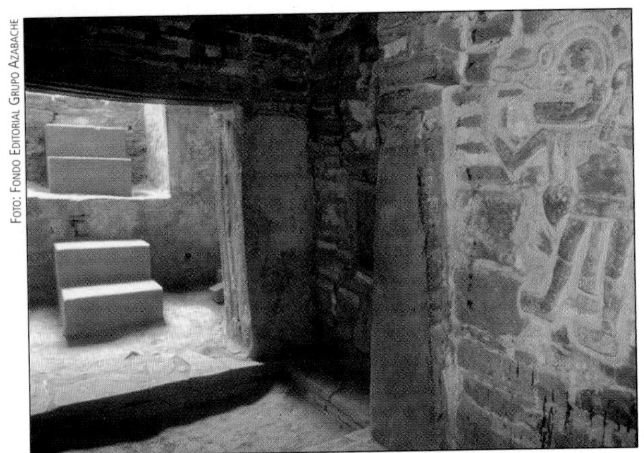

Cámara funeraria en Villa de Zaachila, Oaxaca

y miembros de su séquito, así como pectorales de oro, vasijas, anillos, mosaicos de turquesa y un vaso de mármol. En la cabecera hay una iglesia construida en el siglo XVII. El nombre de Zaachila corresponde, asimismo, a tres reyes de la nación zapoteca, consignados en su historia desde el año 1386. Zaachila I dirigió las guerras zapotecas contra los huaves, mixes y chontales y fue el constructor del fuerte y de la ciudad de Zaachila-Yoo (que los mexicas llamaban Teotzapotlan). A Zaachila III, quien vivió y gobernó durante el siglo XV, correspondió establecer una alianza con los mexicas para combatir a los mixtecos.

José Vicente Villada

Villada, José Vicente ◆ n. en la ciudad de México y m. en Toluca, Edo. de Méx. (1843-1904). Militar republicano. Abandonó un pequeño comercio en Pachuca para alistarse, en 1857, en las filas conservadoras de Miguel Miramón, durante la guerra de los Tres Años. Al ocurrir la intervención francesa se unió a las fuerzas republicanas. Participó en 1863 en la defensa de Puebla, fue aprehendido pero escapó cuando era conducido a Veracruz. Se reincorporó a filas en San Luis Potosí y realizó la campaña en Michoacán, a las órdenes de Régules: participó en diciembre de 1863 en la acción de Morelia; en febrero de 1865, en la batalla de Villa de Reyes, al frente de un ejército que derrotó y dio muerte al coronel zuavo Banderbak; el 26 de marzo de 1865, en la toma de Puruándiro, donde se apropió de una imprenta con la que editó el *Boletín del Ejército en Campaña*; y en abril, en la batalla de Tacámbaro. En octubre de 1865 fue aprehendido en Santa Ana Amatlán y conducido a Uruapan, donde se le juzgó y condenó a muerte, aunque finalmente fue canjeado. Al triunfo de la República fue dos veces diputado federal. En 1885 fundó y dirigió el diario *El Partido Liberal*, dirigió después *La Revista Universal* y *Los Derechos del Hombre*. Gobernó el Estado de México (1889-1904).

Manuel Villafuerte Mijangos

Villafuerte Mijangos, Manuel ◆ n. en Tuxtla Gutiérrez, Chis. (1921). Licenciado en derecho por la UNAM (1949). Fundador de la Federación Regional de Trabajadores de la CTM en San Cristóbal de Las Casas (1945), fundador de la Asociación de Profesores y Trabajadores Administrativos de la Escuela Nacional Preparatoria 5 (1958), fundador del Sindicato de Profesores de la UNAM (1965), asesor jurídico de los sindicatos de Trabajadores Terraceros y Conexos de la República Mexicana, Industria Eléctrica de México, Telefonistas de la República Mexicana, Industria del Gas, Radio Aeronáutica Mexicana y Sobrecargos de Aviación de México (1952-82). Ha sido juez municipal de San Cristóbal de Las Casas (1944-45), regidor segundo del ayuntamiento de la misma ciudad (1947), abogado postulante (1952-75), procurador federal de la Defensa del Trabajo (1975-76), diputado federal (1976-79) y senador por Chiapas (1982-88).

Villafranca, Juan de ◆ n. en el DF (1954). Licenciado en derecho por la UIA. Ha Participado en el Comité de Representación de la Comisión Nacional de Inversiones Extranjeras (1983-1991) ha ocupado cargos en la Secofi (1983-1988). En el Banco Nacional Cinematográfico trabajó en el Departamento Fiduciario y ha sido secretario particular del director general de esa institución. Director general de Asuntos Jurídicos de la SRE y secretario particular del titular (1991-1993); secretario técnico de la Comisión Mexicana de Cooperación con Centroamérica, presidente de la Asamblea General de la Organización Mundial de la Propiedad Intelectual, con sede en Ginebra (OMPI), embajador de México en Singapur (1993-98) y oficial mayor de la SRE (1999-).

Villagarcía, Rocío. ◆ n. en Guadalajara Jal. (?). Estudió pedagogía y se inició en la televisión tapatía como comentarista del programa *Arte y Cultura*. En 1972 se trasladó al DF como reportera de televisión con Jacobo Zabludovsky. Es escultora y ha expuesto en la ciudad de México. Coautora de *Carlota, el mundo cladestino del aborto* (1977).

Villagómez, Adrián ◆ n. en Tuxpan, Ver., y m. en Cancún, QR, (1922-1998). Estudioso del Arte Nacional. Fue director del Centro Nacional de Conservación de Obras Artísticas del INBA (1964-71). Se desempeñó como maestro de historia en la ENAP, y director de Artes Plásticas del INBA (1988-98). Medalla al Mérito Universitario (1991).

Villagómez, J. Trinidad ◆ n. en Valle de Santiago, Gto., y m. en Uruapan, Mich. (1838-1865). Militar republicano. Dejó los estudios en el Colegio de San Nicolás para incorporarse a las filas de Vicente Riva Palacio, al ocurrir la intervención francesa. En octubre de 1865, ya con el grado de coronel, fue aprehendido en Santa Ana Amatlán, junto con numerosos luchadores republicanos, conducido a Uruapan y fusilado.

Villagordoa Lozano, José Manuel ◆ n. en el DF (1930). Licenciado en derecho por la UNAM (1952). Miembro del PRI desde 1965. Ha sido subgerente fiduciario de Financiera México (1953-65), consejero del Banco Azteca (1953-65) y del Banco del Ahorro para la Propiedad (1963-65); asesor jurídico de la Subdirección Técnica (1965-71), jefe del Departamento de Convenios de la Jefatura de Servicios Técnicos (1971-77) y subtesorero del IMSS (1977); subtesorero de Ingresos de la Secretaría de Hacienda (1977-78), director general de Asuntos

Semana, óleo sobre tela de Armando Villagrán

Jurídicos de la SPP (1978-82); director general Jurídico y de Gobierno (1982-84), coordinador general jurídico del DDF (1984-86) y ministro de la Suprema Corte de Justicia (1986-94). Autor de *Doctrina general del fideicomiso* (1976) y *El fideicomiso en México* (1977). Presidente de la Asociación de Abogados al Servicio del Estado.

Villagrá, Agustín ◆ n. en Cuautitlán, Edo. de Méx., y m. en Chihuahua, Chih. (1819-1866). Militar. Ingresó en el ejército en 1828 y en 1839 fue dado de baja por participar en un pronunciamiento contra el presidente Anastasio Bustamante, aunque en 1841 fue readmitido en filas. Combatió la rebelión separatista en Yucatán y Tabasco y participó en la toma de San Juan Bautista. Luchó contra la invasión estadounidense (1847). Fue jefe del Estado Mayor de Ángel Trías Álvarez y presidente de la Junta de Defensa Nacional. Partidario de Antonio López de Santa Anna, luchó contra los revolucionarios de Ayutla. Al triunfo liberal sirvió al presidente Ignacio Comonfort, a quien se mantuvo fiel al proclamarse el Plan de Tacubaya. Peleó en el bando liberal durante la guerra de los Tres Años. Al iniciarse la intervención francesa era comandante del Cuerpo Municipal de la ciudad de México. Estuvo a las órdenes de Leandro Valle en la derrota de Las Cruces y sirvió a las órdenes de Jesús González Ortega, con quien participó, en 1863, en el sitio de Puebla, luego del cual fue capturado y enviado a Francia como prisionero. En 1864 fue liberado en Tours, después de negarse a firmar su adhesión al imperio de Maximiliano. Regresó a México por Estados Unidos y se reincorporó al ejército republicano en Chihuahua (febrero de 1865), batió al coronel Pyot en Hidalgo del Parral y luego pasó a las fuerzas de José María Patoni. De septiembre a noviembre de 1865, ya con el grado de general de brigada, ocupó la gubernatura de Chihuahua.

Villagrá, Gaspar de ◆ n. en Puebla, Pue. (1555-?). Participó en la conquista de Nuevo México (1595). En 1596, Juan de Oñate lo nombró procurador general del ejército y capitán en territorio de Nuevo México (1596-1607). Autor de *Historia de Nuevo México* (1610) y de *El capitán Gaspar de Villagrá para justificarse de las muertes, justicias y castigos que el adelantado don Juan de Oñate dizen que hizo en la Nuevo México* (1612).

Villagrán ◆ Municipio de Guanajuato contiguo a Salamanca y Celaya. Superficie: 98.60 km². Habitantes: 42,653, de los cuales 9,899 forman la población económicamente activa. Hablan alguna lengua indígena 120 personas mayores de cinco años (otomí 95). La cabecera, del mismo nombre, se llamó El Huaje hasta 1910, cuando se elevó a la categoría de villa con el nombre de Encarnación Ortiz, misma que en 1930, fecha de erección del municipio, se transformó en Villagrán, en honor del insurgente Julián Villagrán.

Villagrán ◆ Municipio de Tamaulipas situado en el occidente del estado, al nor-noroeste de Ciudad Victoria, en los límites con Nuevo León. Superficie: 1,435.06 km². Habitantes: 7,578, de los cuales 2,330 forman la población económicamente activa. Hablan alguna lengua indígena ocho personas mayores de cinco años.

Villagrán, Armando ◆ n. y m. en el DF (1938-1991). Pintor egresado de la Escuela Nacional de Pintura, Escultura y Grabado La Esmeralda, del INBA. Presentó 45 exposiciones individuales y más de 60 colectivas en diversas ciudades de la República y el extranjero. Premios Ciudad de México y Quintana Roo y mención honorífica en el Concurso Nacional de Pintura de la Canaco (1969), mención honorífica en el Concurso Nacional El Acero (1971) y pre-

Presa Real de Borbón en Villagrán, Tamaulipas

Foto: Fondo Editorial Grupo Azabache

José Villagrán García

mio del Concurso Nacional de Carteles (1972) del Programa Nacional Fronterizo.

VILLAGRÁN, CARLOTA ◆ n. en el DF (1950). Actriz y locutora. Hermana del anterior. Estudió en la Escuela Nacional de Maestros y en la Escuela de Arte Teatral del INBA. Ha trabajado en las películas *Los motivos de Luz* (1985, Felipe Cazals) y *Redondo* (1986, Raúl Busteros). Ha sido también locutora, reportera, guionista y productora de Radio Universidad y Radio Educación. Coautora de las obras *Y sin embargo se mueven* y *Lección de anatomía*.

VILLAGRÁN, FRANCISCO *EL CHITO* ◆ n. y m. en Huichapan, en el actual estado de Hidalgo (?-1813). Insurgente. Era hijo de Julián Villagrán. En noviembre de 1810, perseguido por homicidio, decidió unirse a la lucha por la independencia. Tomó San Juan del Río, plaza de la que poco después fue desalojado por las fuerzas realistas. Más tarde se apoderó de Huichapan, donde se fortificó y mantuvo una campaña de hostigamiento a los convoyes del ejército realista que provenían de Veracruz. Se convirtió en máxima autoridad de la zona, sin reconocer al resto de los jefes insurgentes, y se destacó por su despotismo y afán de lucro. A mediados de 1811, la Junta de Zitácuaro lo nombró mariscal de campo, pero declinó el grado para no reconocer la autoridad de aquélla. A principios de 1812 atacó sin éxito Tulancingo, pero derrotó al realista Llorente en Atotonilco. En septiembre, Ignacio López Rayón intentó apoderarse de Ixmiquilpan, acción en la que fracasó porque Villagrán retiró sus fuerzas antes del asalto final. Rayón intentó reprenderlo, pero fue atacado por aquél y debió refugiarse en Tlalpujahua. El 3 de mayo de 1813, el realista Pedro Monsalve atacó Huichapan, dispersó a los insurgentes, capturó a Villagrán y lo fusiló el 14 de mayo.

Iglesia de la Concepción en Villahermosa, Tabasco

FOTO: MICHAEL CALDERWOOD

VILLAGRÁN, JULIÁN ◆ n. en Huichapan, en el actual estado de Hidalgo (1760-1813). Padre del anterior. Arriero, se unió a principios del siglo XIX al ejército virreinal, como capitán del regimiento de Tula. Fue uno de los conspiradores insurgentes de Querétaro. Tras el inicio de la lucha armada, en septiembre de 1810, el virreinato abrió una causa formal contra los conspiradores, dirigida por el oidor Collado; Villagrán, unido a la lucha armada, capturó a Collado y consiguió que la causa fuese disuelta y que se diera libertad a los conspiradores aún presos. Junto con su hijo, Francisco Villagrán, tomó la plaza de San Juan del Río, de la que poco después fueron desalojados; intentó apoderarse de Querétaro, pero fue repelido por Félix María Calleja. Tras asesinar a Miguel Sánchez, codirigente de la insurrección en la Huasteca, Villagrán se erigió en líder del movimiento guerrillero en aquella región, donde, según Calleja, se hacía llamar "Julián I, emperador de la Huaxteca". Operó en Ixmiquilpan y Zimapán, población que convirtió en su cuartel general y actuó como cacique del Mezquital sin obedecer a los jefes insurgentes. Se negó a reconocer la autoridad de la Junta de Zitácuaro, aunque en ocasiones actuaba de acuerdo con aquélla. En mayo de 1812 intentó infructuosamente apoderarse de Tulancingo. En acciones conjuntas con su hijo mantuvo una campaña de hostigamiento a los convoyes realistas que, provenientes de Veracruz, debían transitar por su zona de dominio. En mayo de 1813 su hijo fue capturado por el realista Pedro Monsalve, quien ofreció perdonarlo y liberarlo si Julián Villagrán accedía al indulto. Cuando éste se negó, aquél fue fusilado. Días después, denunciado por su lugarteniente Felipe Maya, fue capturado en San Juan Amaxac y fusilado.

VILLAGRÁN GARCÍA, JOSÉ ◆ n. y m. en el DF (1901-1982). Arquitecto titulado en la Universidad Nacional de México (1923). Fue profesor (1924-77), director de la Escuela Nacional de Arquitectura (1933-35) y miembro de la Junta de Gobierno de la UNAM (1953-70). Trabajó para el Departamento de Salud Pública (1924-35), el Consejo de Arquitectura de la Ciudad de México (1934-37), el Comité Nacional de Lucha contra la Tuberculosis (1939-47) y para el Comité Administrador del Programa Federal de Construcción de Escuelas (1949-81), del que fue vocal ejecutivo. Construyó los mercados San Cosme y San Lucas (1953-54). Fue consultor para Iberoamérica de la Organización Mundial de la Salud en materia de hospitales (1951). Entre sus obras están el Hospital de Huipulco (1929), el Instituto Nacional de Cardiología (1937), el Hospital Infantil (1941), la Maternidad Mundet (1943), el Centro Universitario México (1944), la Escuela Nacional de Arquitectura (1951), el cine Las Américas (1952) y el Centro Inmobiliario América (1952), el Instituto Cumbres (1953), el Seminario Nacional de Misiones en Tlalpan (1953), el cine Reforma (1957), la Unidad de Congresos del Centro Médico Nacional (1958), el hotel María Isabel (1962) y los planteles 4, 6 y 7 de la Escuela Nacional Preparatoria (1963). Miembro de la Sociedad de Arquitectos

El tiempo y sus lugares, técnica mixta sobre tela de José Villalobos

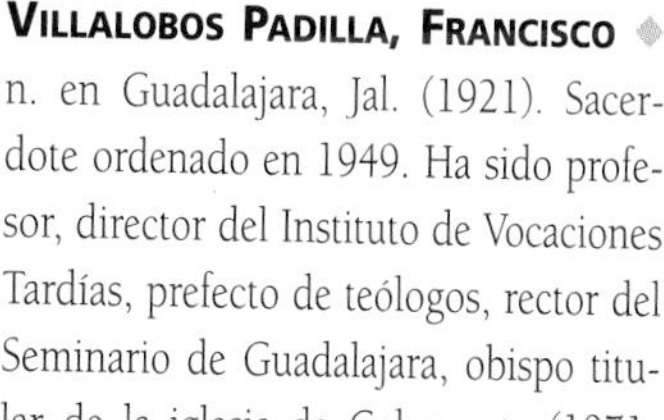

Mexicanos y de El Colegio Nacional. Premio Nacional de Artes en la rama de arquitectura (1968). En 1987 se le rindió un homenaje nacional.

VILLAHERMOSA ◆ Cabecera del municipio de Centro (☛) y capital del estado de Tabasco. En 1557, a causa de los constantes ataques piratas, los habitantes de Santa María de la Victoria, primera población española fundada en territorio tabasqueño, remontaron el río Grijalva hasta el paraje llamado Tres Lomas, donde el 24 de junio de ese año fundaron la población de San Juan Bautista de Tabasco. El alcalde mayor de Yucatán, Cozumel y Tabasco, Diego de Quijada, trazó los solares y expidió títulos, aunque llamó Villa de Carmona al asentamiento. El nombre de Villahermosa y el derecho de usar escudo le fueron concedidos en 1598 por Felipe II. El 24 de junio de 1641, la ciudad adoptó el nombre de San Juan de Villahermosa y se convirtió en la capital de la provincia de Tabasco. El 5 de febrero de 1825 se promulgó la Constitución de Tabasco y el 4 de noviembre siguiente se decretó que su capital sería Villahermosa, con el nombre de San Juan Bautista de Tabasco. El 3 de febrero de 1916, el gobernador Francisco J. Múgica restituyó a la capital del estado su antiguo nombre.

VILLALDAMA ◆ Municipio de Nuevo León situado en el norte del estado, al norte de Monterrey y contiguo a Sabinas Hidalgo. Superficie: 870.50 km^2. Habitantes: 4,354, de los cuales 1,243 forman la población económicamente activa. El 15 de abril se conmemora la fundación de la cabecera municipal, Ciudad de Villaldama.

VILLALOBOS, ANTONIO I. ◆ n. en la ciudad de México (1884-1964). Abogado. Fue diputado federal, oficial mayor de la Secretaría de Gobernación, presidente de la Junta de Conciliación y Arbitraje, procurador de Justicia Militar, senador de la República, presidente del Partido de la Revolución Mexicana (del 2 de diciembre de 1940 al 17 de enero de 1946) y embajador en Brasil (1946).

VILLALOBOS, JOAQUÍN ◆ n. y m. en la ciudad de México (1830-1879). Liberal. Hizo trabajo periodístico en contra de los conservadores, la intervención francesa y el imperio de Maximiliano. Colaboró en *El Siglo XIX*, *El Correo de México* y *El Globo*. Fue empleado de la Tesorería del DF. Autor de las obras de teatro *Walker*, *Apuros de un sastre en un jueves santo*, *El brillo del mundo* (1854), *¡La Patria!* (1868), *Safo* (1872) y *El amor de los amores* (1877).

VILLALOBOS, JOSÉ ◆ n. en Ixtepec, Oax. (1950). Pintor. Arquitecto por la UNAM, en cuya Escuela de Arquitectura ha sido profesor de diseño. También ha sido profesor de la Universidad de Puebla y la Universidad de las Américas. En 1981 presentó su primera exposición individual. Ha expuesto en México y los Estados Unidos y obtenido dos veces (1995 y 1996) el premio MARCO del Museo de Arte Contemporáneo de Monterrey. Becario del Arts International (Instituto Cultural Mexicano de la Ciudad de Nueva York), produjo una carpeta de grabados: *El Mar Baldío* (1994).

VILLALOBOS PADILLA, FRANCISCO ◆ n. en Guadalajara, Jal. (1921). Sacerdote ordenado en 1949. Ha sido profesor, director del Instituto de Vocaciones Tardías, prefecto de teólogos, rector del Seminario de Guadalajara, obispo titular de la iglesia de Columnata (1971-

Antonio Villalobos

Templo inconcluso de San Pedro en Villaldama, Nuevo León

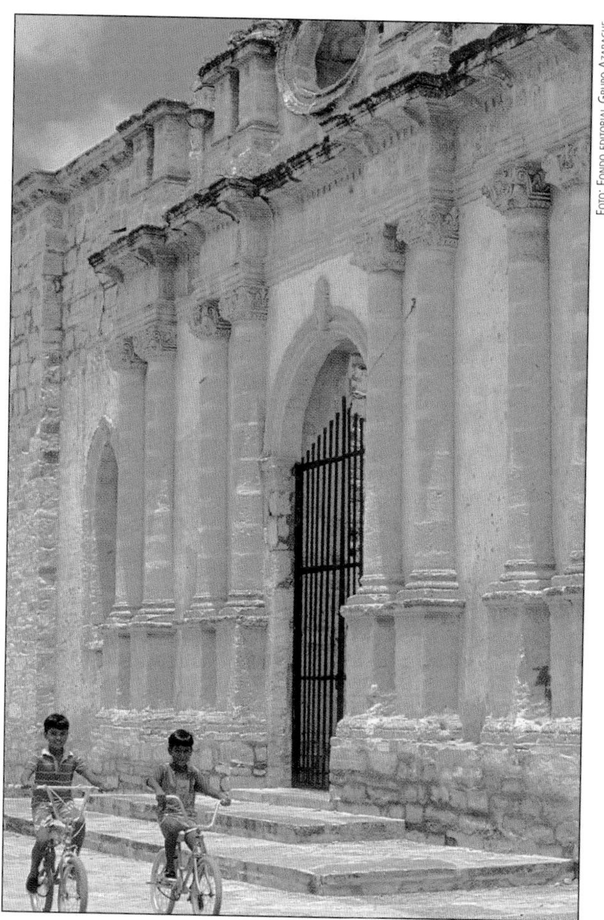

Foto: Fondo Editorial Grupo Azabache

72), auxiliar del obispo de Saltillo (1972-75) y obispo de Saltillo (1975-).

VILLALONGÍN NAVARRO, MANUEL ◆ n. en Valladolid, hoy Morelia, y m. en Puruándiro, Mich. (1777-1814). Hacendado. En 1810 se unió a las fuerzas insurgentes de Miguel Hidalgo y en noviembre de ese año participó en la ocupación de Guadalajara. Fue ascendido a mariscal de campo y combatió en la batalla del Puente de Calderón. Luego del triunfo de los realistas formó una guerrilla que operó en Michoacán. En 1811 realizó una incursión a la capital michoacana, para liberar a su esposa. Participó en varias acciones al lado de José María Morelos, Albino Trujillo, Mariano Matamoros y Manuel Muñiz. Murió en combate en Puruándiro, frente a las tropas realistas de Felipe Castañón.

VILLALPANDO, CÉSAR ◆ n. en el DF (1957). Abogado por la Escuela Libre de Derecho y maestro en historia de México por la UNAM. Trabajó para el Fondo Nacional de Estudios y Proyectos, Fideicomiso de Fomento Económico del Gobierno Federal (1980-88). Editor responsable de la revista *Fonep* (1980-88) e investigador en el Instituto de Investigaciones Jurídicas de la Escuela Libre de Derecho (1989-). Ha publicado *El Panteón de San Fernando* (1981), *Introducción al Derecho Militar Mexicano* (1991) y *Crónica de Viejos Amores* (1992), además de varios ensayos y artículos periodísticos. Fue comisionado por el presidente Salinas para realizar la búsqueda de los restos mortales de José María Morelos y Pavón (1990-91). Huésped distinguido de la ciudad de Querétaro (1986), Premio al Mérito Académico otorgado por la Escuela libre de Derecho (1997) y primer lugar en el Concurso Literario Nacional sobre los Símbolos Patrios (1990).

La anunciación, óleo sobre tela de Cristóbal de Villalpando

La iglesia triunfante, óleo sobre tela de Cristóbal de Villalpando

VILLALPANDO, CRISTÓBAL DE ◆ n. y m. en la ciudad de México (1650-1714). Pintor. Su primera obra, un retablo en Huaquechula, Puebla, fue realizada en 1675. Autor de *La transfiguración* (1683), cuatro murales en la sacristía de la Catedral Metropolitana (1685-88), *La sagrada familia* y la cúpula del altar de los Reyes, en la Catedral de Puebla (1688); *La gloria de San Miguel*, en la sacristía de la Catedral Metropolitana (1688); *Vista de la plaza mayor de México* (1695), 11 cuadros de *La vida de la Virgen*, en Zacatecas (1706); 22 lienzos con *La vida de San Ignacio*, en Tepotzotlán (1710); dos murales llamados *La iglesia militante y triunfante*, en las catedrales de México y Guadalajara; 15 escenas de *La vida de San Francisco*, en la Universidad de San Carlos de Antigua, Guatemala; *San Ignacio* y *San Francisco Javier*, en el Colegio del Estado de Puebla; *San Miguel*, en la parroquia de Cholula; *La sagrada familia con Santa Ana y San Joaquín*, en Guadalupe, Zacatecas; *Santa Teresa con San José y la Virgen* y *Ecce homo*, en la Profesa; siete cuadros en el ex convento del Carmen, en San Ángel; la *Virgen de Aranzazú* y *Crucifixión*, en el Museo de las Vizcaínas y la *Virgen del apocalipsis*, en el Museo Bello, de Puebla.

VILLALPANDO, FERNANDO ◆ n. y m. en Zacatecas, Zac. (1844-1902). Músico. En 1855 era miembro de la banda del segundo batallón de Zacatecas y ahí estudió con Juan Nepomuceno Rosales. Fue director de la banda municipal de Zacatecas, violín concertino de la orquesta de la Compañía Mexicana de ópera Italiana (1867), acompañante de Ángela Peralta, director de la Orquesta del Instituto de Ciencias (1873), cofundador, con Jesús Alejandri, de la Academia de Música Zacatecana (1874), fundador de las escuelas dominicales de Propaganda Musical Zacatecana (1879), organizador de la Banda del estado de Aguascalientes (1887), director de la Academia de Música de Aguascalientes (1887-91) y nuevamente director de la Banda Municipal de Zacatecas. En 1901 fundó el taller litográfico La Lira Zacatecana, destinado a editar piezas musicales. Es probable que su primera obra sea una marcha fúnebre para el sepelio de González Ortega, que fue estrenada en 1881 y que luego fue interpretada en los funerales de Ulysses Grant, Víctor Hugo, Sadi Carnot y Sebastián Lerdo de Tejada. Autor de la marcha *Batallón González Ortega* (1895), *Misa solemne, Salutación americana* (1892) y de chotises, danzas, boleros, canciones, misas (algunas de las cuales han sido interpretadas en El Vaticano) y coros: *Lazos de amor, Luz y sombra, Fiesta tapatía, Patria, La mariposa, El trabajo, Mi dulce hogar, La lectura, Un beso a mi madre, El niño jugando, Mi nacimiento, El recreo, Las vacaciones* y *La tarde de febrero*.

Villalpando Nava, José Manuel ◆ n. en Aguascalientes, Ags. (1926). Estudió en la Escuela Nacional de Maestros (1947). Se tituló como técnico en educación por la Escuela Normal Superior (1951). Maestro en filosofía (1959) y doctor en pedagogía por la UNAM (1962), donde es profesor de carrera. Ha ejercido la docencia en la Escuela Nacional de Maestros, la Escuela Nacional de Educadoras, la Escuela Normal Superior y la UNAM. Inspector de Enseñanza Normal Superior y asesor jurídico en la SEP. Autor de *Manual de psicotécnica pedagógica, Los fundamentos de la orientación profesional, Didáctica de la psicología, Sociología de la educación, Didáctica general, Filosofía de la educación, Pedagogía comparada, Didáctica de la pedagogía, Manual de lógica, Manual de ética, Manual de estética, Didáctica de la filosofía, Manual de historia de la educación, Manual de investigación pedagógica, Manual de capacitación pedagógica para oficiales de la Armada y fundamentos del mando militar*.

Villalpando Núñez, Sara ◆ n. en Jiquilpan, Mich. (1939). Estudió comercio. Miembro del PRI. Ha sido secretaria del Interior del Sindicato de Empleados de Boticas, Droguerías, Laboratorios y Similares de la Federación de Trabajadores del DF (1976-), secretaria de Trabajo de la Federación Obrera de Organizaciones Femeniles de la República Mexicana (1980-) y presidenta de la Comisión de Prensa y Propaganda de la Federación de Trabajadores del DF (1977-82). Dos veces diputada federal por el DF (1982-85 y 1988-91).

Villalvazo y Rodríguez, Germán Ascensión ◆ n. en Atenguillo, Jal., y m. en San Cristóbal de Las Casas, Chis. (1829-1879). Sacerdote ordenado en 1852 y doctor en cánones graduado en 1853. Fue prebendado y penitenciario, así como teólogo consultor en el Concilio Vaticano y obispo de Chiapas (1869-79).

Villamar ◆ Municipio de Michoacán situado en el noroeste del estado, al oeste de Zamora y al norte de Tancítaro. Superficie: 332.37 km². Habitantes: 22,066, de los cuales 4,222 forman la población económicamente activa. Hablan alguna lengua indígena 32 personas mayores de cinco años. Tanto el municipio como la cabecera, antes Guarachita, recibieron su actual nombre en honor del abogado liberal Eligio Villamar.

Villamar, Eligio ◆ n. en Guarachita, hoy Villamar, y m. en Cointzio, Mich. (1825-1852). Abogado. En 1847 se alistó en el Batallón Bravo para combatir la invasión estadounidense y, a las órdenes de Pedro María Anaya, participó en la batalla de Churubusco, en agosto de ese año. Ejerció después la abogacía y escribió algunos poemas, la mayor parte de los cuales quedaron inéditos.

Villamil Rodríguez, Jenaro ◆ n. en Mérida, Yuc. (1969). Licenciado en periodismo por la UNAM (1993). Ha sido coodinador del suplemento *Informe Especial* de *El Financiero* (1990-94), coordinador editorial de *El Financiero del Sureste* (1994-96), colaborador de *Proceso* (1996-97), *El Universal* (1998-99), *Equis, Bucareli Ocho* y *Expansión*, entre otros. Coordinador de la Unidad de Información, Comunicación y Análisis de la Secretaría de Gobierno del Distrito Federal (1998-99). Coautor de *Sucesión pactada* (1993, elaborado por la Unidad de Análisis Prospectivo de *El Financiero*). Autor de *Ruptura en la cúpula* (1996) y *Los desafíos de la transición* (1998).

Villanueva ◆ Municipio de Zacatecas situado en los límites con Jalisco y Aguascalientes y contiguo a la capital del estado. Superficie: 2,567.77 km². Habitantes: 32,014, de los cuales 7,807 forman la población económicamente activa. Hablan alguna lengua indígena nueve personas mayores de cinco años. En su jurisdicción se localiza la ciudad arqueológica amurallada de La Quemada (Tuitlan, Teutlan o Teul, en náhuatl), construida tal vez por los teotihuacanos en la frontera septentrional de su Estado, para contener los avances de los nómadas norteños. Se cree que en su peregrinación hacia el centro del país, los nahuas pasaron por ésta y la poblaron durante algún tiempo. A la llegada de los conquistadores españoles la ciudad amurallada estaba aún habitada. Poco después fue incendiada por los nahuas que acompañaban a los conquistadores, de donde tomó su actual nombre. La ciudad consta de una gran pirámide edificada sobre un cerro, patios ceremoniales con pequeñas pirámides centrales y restos de otros edificios.

Villanueva, Alfonso ◆ n. en Zamora, Mich. (?). Artista Plástico. Se

Sorpresa femenina, grabado de Alfonso Villanueva

Felipe Villanueva

René Villanueva

Los Folkloristas, grupo musical fundado por René Villanueva

inició en el Taller Escuela de Gráfica y Pintura del INBA, de Uruapan. Se ha especializado en el grabado a color. Autor de los grabados *Pareja en reposo*, *Personaje* (1980), *Interior con sol* (1984), *Cacharros* (1984) y *Sorpresa femenina* (1984). Premio Nacional de Grabado (1969) otorgado por la Casa del Lago.

Villanueva, Ernesto ◆ n. en el DF (1966). Licenciado en derecho por la UAM (1989) y doctor en derecho de la información por la Complutense de Madrid y la Universidad de Alcalá (1998). Candidato a doctor en comunicación pública en la Universidad de Navarra (1999). Ha sido profesor-investigador asociado de teoría general en derecho en la UAM (1995) y consultor jurídico externo de la Comisión de Comunicación Social de la Cámara de Diputados (1996-). Dictaminador para las becas de posgrado en comunicación y derecho otorgadas por el Instituto de Cooperación Iberoamericana-Embajada de España en México (1998-) y consultor internacional de la UNESCO en materia de derecho de la información. Es miembro de los consejos editoriales de *Revista Mexicana de Comunicación*, *Espacios de Comunicación* y *Le Monde Diplomatique*. Es director de la revista *Iberoamericana de Derecho de la Información* y articulista de *Proceso* (1999-). Ha escrito más de 300 artículos de divulgación científica. Autor de *Autonomía electoral en Iberoamérica. Una visión de derecho comparado* (1994), *El sistema jurídico de los medios de comunicación en México* (1995) y *Régimen jurídico comparado de la ayuda del Estado a la prensa* (1996), entre otros. Representante de América Latina y España ante la Bellagio Alliance Oxford University Network on Media Law.

Villanueva, Felipe ◆ n. en Tecámac, Edo. de Méx., y m. en la ciudad de México (1862-1893). Músico y compositor. A los seis años de edad tocaba el violín en el coro de la iglesia de su pueblo, a los 10 compuso su primera pieza, *Cantata patriótica (retrato del benemérito cura Hidalgo)*; y a los 11 la mazurca *El último adiós*. Estudió en el Conservatorio Nacional de Música, donde fue alumno de Alfredo Bablot y Antonio Valle. En 1887, inconforme con los métodos y el nivel de enseñanza del Conservatorio, abandonó esa escuela y fundó, con Ricardo Castro, Gustavo E. Campa y Juan Hernández Acevedo, el Instituto Musical, donde fue profesor. Con Campa, Castro, Hernández Acevedo, Carlos J. Meneses e Ignacio Quezadas formó el Grupo de los Seis, que difundió las obras de los autores románticos extranjeros. Fue, asimismo, primer violín en varias orquestas. Autor de numerosas mazurcas, valses, minuetos, motetes, danzas, habaneras, piezas de salón, misas y las óperas *Un día de asueto* y *Keofar*.

Villanueva, René ◆ n. en Oaxaca, Oax. (1933). Músico y pintor. Ingeniero químico titulado en la UNAM (1955). Estudió pintura en La Esmeralda y en la Academia de San Carlos (1958), donde fue alumno de Raúl Anguiano, Benito Messeguer, Santos Balmori y Fernando Castro Pacheco; y estética e historia del arte en la UNAM (1968). Militó en el PCM (1973-81), el PSUM (1981-87) y el PMS (1987-89). Expuso por primera vez en 1962. En 1966 fundó el grupo Los Folkloristas (☛). Ha sido productor de los programas *Letra y música en América Latina* para Radio Universidad (1969-79 y 1989-92), Radio Educación (1979-83) y XEQ (1995-96). Ha presentado exposiciones individuales y colectivas y producido infinidad de discos y casetes de música indígena mexicana. Fue cofundador de la Peña de los Folkloristas (1970) y de la compañía Discos Pueblo (1973), organizador del primer Festival de Música Folklórica y Nueva Canción (1973), coordinador de la barra musical de los talleres infantiles del programa *Pampa pipiltzin* del Canal 13 (1976), organizador del foro central del segundo Festival de Oposición (1979), director de la serie de discos del INAH (1985-1988). Cofundador de *Zurda* (1985) y colaborador de *Espejo* (1995), *El Financiero* (1991-97) e *Insumisa* (1998). Propuso crear la Fonoteca Nacional (1996 y 1997). Ha sido asesor del FZLN. En 1999 formó la Fundación Cultural Fonotecaria de México. Autor de *Cantares de la memoria* (1994), *El coro de la selva* (1997, para el libro colectivo *Memorial de Chiapas*), *Música popular de Michoacán* (1998), *El tiempo y la palabra* (1998).

Villanueva, Ricardo ◆ n. en Los Mochis, Sin. (1950). Licenciado en administración de empresas en la UAP. Pertenece al PRI desde 1983. Ha sido tercer secretario de la embajada en Egipto (1975), segundo secretario en la embajada en la URSS (1981), subdirector general en Europa Occidental (1983), director de Protocolo (1983), consejero de la delegación de México ante la UNESCO (1988), director general del Servicio Exterior y de Personal de la SRE (1989-90), embajador de México en Finlandia (1990-91) y embajador en Arabia Saudita (1991-).

Villanueva, Santiago ◆ n. y m. en la ciudad de México (1838-1872). De niño trabajó como ebanista. En 1861 tomó cursos de dibujo en San Carlos y de anatomía en la Escuela de Medicina. Se inició en la escultura y fue "un joven bohemio y poco ordenado" hasta que conoció a Plotino Rhodakanaty, de quien se convirtió en discípulo. En 1865, con Francisco Zalacosta y Hermenegildo Villavicencio, fundó el Club Socialista de Estudiantes. Promovió la fundación de la Sociedad Mutua del

Ramo de Sastrería en 1864 y con Zalacosta impulsó la creación de la Sociedad Mutua del Ramo de Hilados y Tejidos del Valle de México con obreros de las fábricas San Ildefonso y La Colmena, de Tlalnepantla, el 15 de mayo de 1865, que el 10 de junio estallaron la primera huelga y fueron reprimidos por la autoridad imperial. Con Villavicencio reanimó la Sociedad Artístico-Industrial hacia 1867, en la que participaban otros pintores, escultores y militantes obreros. Impulsó la creación de la Unión Mutua de Tejedores del Distrito de Tlalpan, con obreros de la Fama Montañesa y otras fábricas, como La Abeja, de Tizapán (1868). Éstas se fueron a la huelga en julio y Villanueva estuvo en la comisión que se entrevistó con Juárez, quien intervino para que los patrones aceptaran las demandas obreras. En 1869, después de la derrota y fusilamiento del líder agrarista Julio Chávez López, organizó un ciclo de conferencias en la Sociedad Artístico-Industrial en San Pedro y San Pablo. En enero de 1871 firmó un llamamiento que, en septiembre, se concretó en el Gran Círculo de Obreros de México, que lo eligió presidente en su asamblea constitutiva. Defendió la independencia de las organizaciones obreras, se opuso a la participación electoral de los trabajadores y rechazó todo subsidio gubernamental. A su muerte, el Gran Círculo aceptó un subvención de 200 pesos mensuales del presidente Lerdo de Tejada.

Villanueva Arreola, Aquilino ◆ n. en Torreón, Coah., y m. en el DF (1889-1988). Cirujano titulado en la Escuela Nacional de Medicina (1918), especializado en urología. Fue director general del Departamento de Salubridad (1929), creador de la Asociación Nacional de Protección a la Infancia, director general del Hospital General (1940-45). Presidente de la Academia Nacional de Medicina (1955) y de la Academia Mexicana de Cirugía. Profesor emérito de la UNAM.

Villanueva y Gómez de Eguiarreta, José Epigmenio ◆ n. en Taxco, Gro., y m. en la ciudad de México (1792-1840). Sacerdote. Doctor en cánones, bachiller en derecho civil, bachiller en filosofía por la Real y Pontificia Universidad y profesor de derecho civil en la misma. Fue cura en varias plazas, prebendado y canónigo de la Catedral Metropolitana, diputado federal (1831-32) y senador por el Estado de México. Fue promovido al episcopado en 1839, pero murió antes de ser consagrado.

Villanueva Madrid, Mario Ernesto ◆ n. en Chetumal, QR (1948). Ingeniero agrónomo por la Universidad de Chihuahua y maestro en ciencias agrícolas por el Colegio de Posgraduados de Chapingo. Miembro del PRI desde 1968, donde presidió el Comité Directivo Estatal de Quintana Roo (1984-85). Coordinador del Consejo Consultivo de la Liga de Comunidades Agrarias (1984-86), secretario de Finanzas (1980-83) y de Acción Agrícola (1986-89) del CEN de la CNC. Senador (1991-93) y gobernador de Quintana Roo (1993-99). Acusado de narcotráfico y asociación delictuosa al final de su gestión, huyó.

Villanueva Páramo, Luis ◆ n. en la ciudad de México (1913). Boxeador. Sastre de oficio. Inició su carrera pugilística en 1927 con un combate en Nuevo Laredo, en esa ocasión con el sobrenombre de *Kid Chino*, que cambió a *Kid Azteca*. En 1932 peleó por primera vez en la ciudad de México, en la división welter, contra Battling Shaw, al que derrotó por puntos. En ese año ganó el campeonato nacional welter al derrotar a David Velasco y mantuvo su categoría de campeón hasta 1948. Defendió su título más de 50 veces, hasta que renunció a él. Se retiró en 1954, luego de 300 combates profesionales. Filmó las películas *El gran campeón* (1949, de Chano Urueta), *Kid Tabaco* (1954, de Zacarías Gómez Urquiza), *Guantes de oro* (1959, de Chano Urueta). y *En busca de un campeón*. Se dedica a dar clases particulares de pugilismo. En 1988 ingresó en el Salón de la Fama.

Villanueva y Salinas, José ◆ n. en San Jerónimo, hoy Ciudad Cuauhtémoc, Col., y m. en Santiago Apóstol, Tultepec, Edo. de Méx. (1937-1985). Escultor. Ingresó al Colegio de los Carmelitas en Quéretaro 1938, donde hizo estudios de bachiller, pero se le impidió continuar la carrera sacerdotal por sus ideas "contrarias a la enseñanza religiosa". Estudió escultura en la Academia de San Carlos y (1953), recibiendo clases de Fidias Elizondo, Luis Sahagún y Benjamín Coria, entre otros. Fue depositario honorario del ex templo de Santiago Apóstol en Teyahualco (1955-85). Restaurador de las esculturas religiosas de los templos católicos de la ciudad de Orizaba (1947) y de gran parte de las parroquias de las diósesis de Texcoco y Cuautitlán (1963-85). Creador de esculturas, óleos y acuarelas de carácter religioso para templos de la mayor parte de los estados del país, así como para Estados Unidos y Centroamérica. Escultor oficial de los templos de Cancún (1983). Murió asesinado.

Villanueva Sansores, Alberto Eduardo ◆ n. en Chetumal, QR (1936). Arquitecto titulado en la UNAM y en la Universidad Autónoma de Puebla. Pertenece al PRI, en el que ha sido director del CEPES (1972-75) y presidente del Comité Directivo Estatal de Quintana Roo (1980). En el gobierno de Quintana Roo ha sido jefe del Departamento de Arquitectura (1958-70), director del Catastro (1968-72), tesorero de la Junta Local de Caminos y presidente de la Junta Territorial de Agua (1969-72); miembro de la Comisión Tripartita (1974), oficial mayor del gobierno estatal (1975-80), representante del sector gubernamental ante el consejo estatal del Infonavit (1975-80) y senador de la República (1982-88). Trabajó en el despachó del arquitecto José Villagrán García (1961-65). Fue arquitecto de la Dirección de Obras Públicas y Comisión Técnica de Planeación del gobierno de Puebla (1965-68) y director del Inco (1972-75).

Aquilino Villanueva Arreola

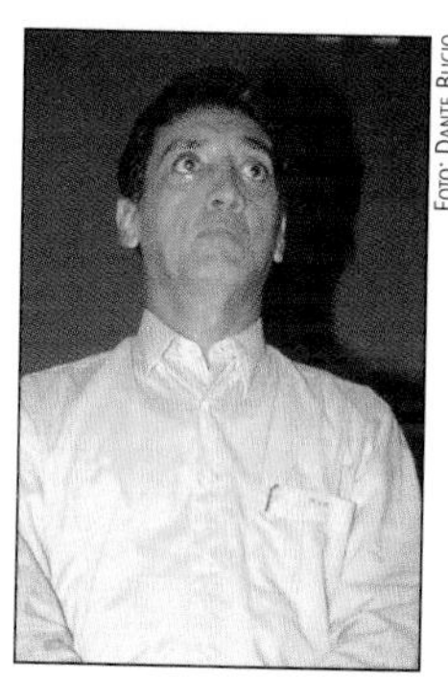

Foto: Dante Bucio

Mario Villanueva

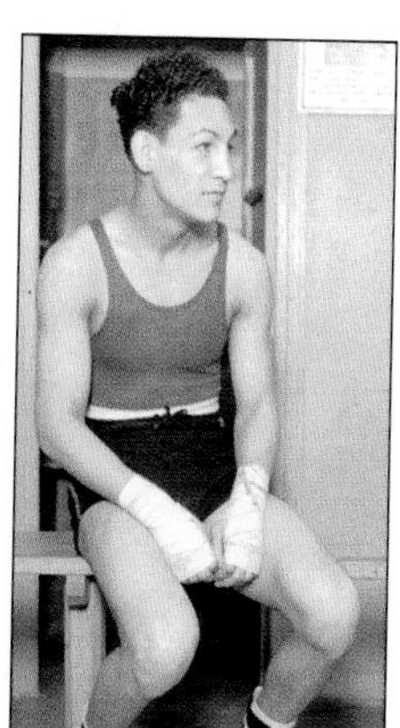

Luis Villanueva Páramo, *Kid Azteca*

Alfredo Eduardo Villanueva Sansores

VILLAR, LAURO ◆ n. en Matamoros, Tams., y m. en la ciudad de México (1849-1923). También se cree que nació en Soto la Marina, Tamaulipas. Ingresó en el ejército en 1865, en el Estado Mayor de Juan N. Cortina, y en Matamoros combatió contra la intervención francesa y el imperio de Maximiliano de Habsburgo. Permaneció en el ejército federal durante los gobiernos de Benito Juárez, Sebastián Lerdo de Tejada, Porfirio Díaz, Francisco León de la Barra y Francisco I. Madero. Al inicio de la decena trágica estaba encargado de la defensa del Palacio Nacional. Al ocurrir el ataque de Bernardo Reyes fue herido y sustituido por Victoriano Huerta.

VILLAR, SAMUEL DEL ◆ n. en el DF (1945). Licenciado en derecho por la UNAM (1968), maestro en leyes y doctor en jurisprudencia por la Universidad de Harvard. Estudió economía y política en las universidades de Londres y París (1964). Ha sido profesor de El Colegio de México y de la UNAM. Estuvo afiliado al PRI (1972-1988), en el cual fue tesorero del CEN (1972-75). Organizador del PRD en SLP y fundador del mismo (1989), consejero nacional por SLP (1989-), integrante del CEN de ese partido (1989-1992 y 1995-1996), representante ante el IFE (1994-1995) y asesor jurídico del presidente nacional perredista (1996-99). Ha sido consultor externo del presidente de la República (1977-78), director ejecutivo del Fideicomiso *Excélsior* (1972-76), asesor de asuntos especiales del presidente de la República (1983-85) y procurador general de Justicia del DF (1997-). Editor de *Pensamiento Europeo* y *Pensamiento Iberoamericano* en *Excélsior* (1965-69) y articulista de ese diario (1965-1976); fundador (1976) y tesorero del Consejo de Administración de *Proceso* y director general de *Razones* (1980-82). Autor de *El sistema mexicano de regulación de la inversión extranjera: elementos y deficiencias generales* (1975), *Depresión en la industria azucarera mexicana* (1976), *El manejo y la recuperación de la economía mexicana* (1979), *Estado y petróleo en México: experiencias y perspectiva* (1979), *La justicia y la guerra de las drogas entre Estados Unidos y México* (1993), "La guerra de las drogas de EUA y los derechos humanos en México", y "La guerra de las drogas de EUA y la corrupción en México" en *Justicia y narcóticos entre México y Estados Unidos* (1993), *La legitimidad partidocrática, el control electoral 1988-1994* (1996).

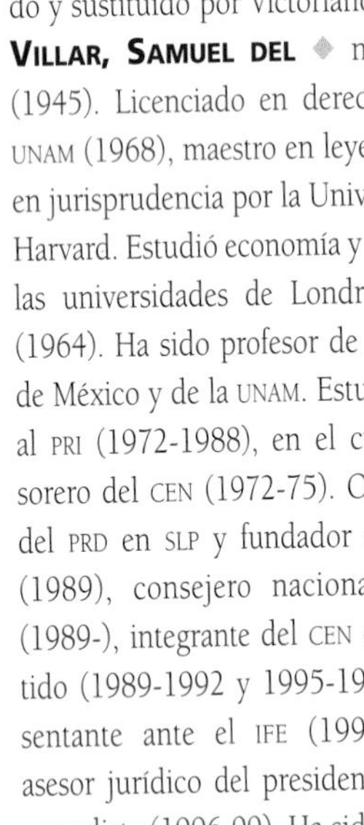

Foto: Archivo Casasola

Antonio I. Villarreal

Foto: Eikón

Samuel del Villar

VILLARREAL, ANTONIO I. ◆ n. en Lampazos, NL, y m. en el DF (1879-1944). Su apellido materno era González. Profesor titulado en la Escuela Normal de Monterrey (1899). Fue secretario del Círculo Liberal Ponciano Arriaga de San Luis Potosí (1896-98). En 1900 dirigía la primaria de Villa Aldama, Nuevo León, cuando editó el periódico oposicionista *El Liberal* y fue encarcelado. En 1901 participó en el Congreso de Clubes Liberales, celebrado en San Luis Potosí, por lo que volvió a ser encarcelado. Una vez en libertad se reunió con los hermanos Flores Magón en Estados Unidos y colaboró en el diario *Regeneración*. Secretario del Comité Organizador del Partido Liberal Mexicano, en San Luis Misuri (1906), y firmante de su programa. Perseguido por la policía estadounidense a petición del gobierno porfirista, fue detenido y encarcelado en Los Ángeles y en Florence, Nuevo México. En 1908 encabezó un fallido levantamiento armado desde Las Vacas, Coahuila. Rompió con los Flores Magón y se unió al antirreeleccionismo en 1909 y un año después participó en la insurrección maderista. Combatió en la batalla de Santa Rosalía y fue ascendido a coronel en la toma de Ciudad Juárez. A la caída de Porfirio Díaz formó parte del Partido Constitucional Progresista y, en 1911, el presidente Francisco I. Madero lo nombró cónsul general en España. Volvió a México en 1913 y se unió a la revolución constitucionalista en el ejército del noreste; participó en las acciones de Monterrey, Matamoros, Linares, Ciudad Victoria y Tampico. En 1914 reabrió la Casa del Obrero Mundial, que había sido clausurada un año antes por Victoriano Huerta, y en ese mismo año se encargó del gobierno de Nuevo León. Fue presidente de la Soberana Convención Revolucionaria (1914) e intentó resolver las diferencias entre Venustiano Carranza y las fuerzas de Villa y Zapata. A fines de ese año viajó a Córdoba para entrevistarse con Carranza, quien lo convenció de sumarse a sus fuerzas y lo envió otra vez a Nuevo León como gobernador del estado. Sin embargo, renunció poco después y se exilió en Estados Unidos. Volvió a México en 1920, luego de la rebelión de Agua Prieta. Fue secretario de Agricultura y Fomento (del 1 de junio al 30 de noviembre de 1920 y del 1 de diciembre de 1920 al 26 de noviembre de 1921) en los gobiernos de Adolfo de la Huerta y Álvaro Obregón. Candidato derrotado al Senado (1922), en 1923 se sumó la rebelión delahuertista y participó en la toma de Puebla. En 1927 apoyó la campaña política de Francisco Serrano. Dos años después fue candidato presidencial y en ese mismo año se unió a la rebelión escobarista. Derrotado, se exilió de nuevo en Estados Unidos, pero volvió a México en 1934 y fue candidato presidencial de la Confederación Revolucionaria de Partidos Independientes. Colaboró en el diario *Excélsior*. En 1940 reingresó en el ejército y fue miembro de la Asociación de Veteranos de la Revolución.

VILLARREAL, FELÍCITOS ◆ n. en Monterrey, NL, y m. en el DF (1875-1917). En 1913 dejó su profesión de ingeniero para unirse a la revolución. Fue subsecretario de Hacienda, encargado del despacho (del 20 de agosto al 18 de septiembre de 1914) en el gabinete de Venustiano Carranza. Distanciado del líder constitucionalista, fue secretario de Hacienda (del 4 de diciembre de 1914 al 16 de enero de 1915) en el gabinete del presidente convencionista Eulalio Gutiérrez.

Villarreal, José Javier ◆ n. en Tijuana, BC (1959). Licenciado en letras españolas por la Universidad Autónoma de Nuevo León, de la que es profesor. Coordinador de talleres de creación literaria y de lectura en el ISSSTE. Coeditor, con Minerva Margarita Villarreal, de la hoja de poesía *Hogaza.* Colaborador de *Casa del Tiempo*, *Síntesis*, *El Buscón*, *Plural*, *Siempre!*, *La Gaceta del Fondo de Cultura*, *El Norte* y *Punto*. Poemas suyos se han incluido en *Segundo Festival de Morelia* (1984), *20 años de poesía en Monterrey* (1985) y *Parvada* (1986). Coautor, con Víctor Manuel Cárdenas y Gabriel Trujillo, de *Voces y canciones* (1983). Preparó la *Antología mínima de la poesía de Alfonso Reyes* (1982) y una *Recopilación de la obra en verso de Fray Servando Teresa de Mier* (1985). Autor de los volúmenes de poesía: *En torno a monumentos* (1983), *Poemas bajacalifornianos* (1984), *Mar del norte* (1988), con el que obtuvo el Premio Nacional de Poesía Aguascalientes 1987) y *Portuaria* (1994). Mención en el Premio *Plural* (1984) y Premio de Poesía Alfonso Reyes 1989.

Villarreal, Julián ◆ n. en Saltillo, Coah., y m. en el DF (1869-1934). Meteorólogo titulado en la Escuela Civil de Monterrey y cirujano (1893) por la Escuela Nacional de Medicina; se especializó en oftalmología en hospitales de Estados Unidos, Francia, Gran Bretaña, Alemania y Austria. Profesor (1895) y director de la Escuela Nacional de Medicina (1911). Trabajó como meteorólogo del observatorio del Colegio Civil de Monterrey, jefe de trabajos anatómicos de la Escuela Nacional de Medicina (1894) y cirujano del Hospital Morelos (1897), donde introdujo la radioterapia y la entonces poco conocida técnica de la asepsia quirúrgica. Fue director del Hospital de la Cruz Roja Mexicana. Colaborador de la *Gaceta Médica.* Miembro (1899) y presidente de la Academia Nacional de Medicina (1910) y fundador de la Academia de Cirugía.

Villarreal, Minerva Margarita ◆ n. en Montemorelos, NL (1957). Licenciada en sociología por la Universidad Autónoma de Nuevo León (1981), donde también estudió teatro. Tomó cursos de posgrado en Israel y en El Colegio de México. Profesora de la UANL y directora de un taller de investigación social sobre la mujer. Ha sido coordinadora de talleres del ISSSTE y codirectora de la hoja literaria *Hogaza* de Monterrey (1987). Coautora de *Montemorelos: cuestiones regionales* (1980) y del volumen de cuentos *Juegos cotidianos* (1983). Autora de los poemarios: *Hilos de viaje* (1982), *Entretejedura* (1988), *Palabras como playas* (1990), *Dama infiel al sueño* (1991), *Pérdida* (1992), *Desde la vieja casa* y *Adamar* (1998). Ha recibido los premios Plural (1986), de Poesía Alfonso Reyes (1990) y el de las Artes, otorgado por la UANL (1991).

Villarreal, Viviano L. ◆ n. en la Villa de San Nicolás Hidalgo, NL (1838-1918). Abogado. Suegro de Gustavo A. Madero. Al ocurrir la intervención francesa tomó las armas en la Legión del Norte, comandada por Gerónimo Treviño, y participó en las acciones de Charco Escondido, la Bufa y San Bernabé. Fue diputado federal dos veces (1867 y 1872-76), senador de la República (1877), secretario general de Gobierno (1868-72) y gobernador de Nuevo León (1878-81). En este cargo, la hacienda local tuvo superávit luego de 40 años de cuentas deficitarias. Reelegido en 1911, renunció en 1913 como protesta por el asesinato de Francisco I. Madero.

Villarreal Arrambide, René Patricio ◆ n. en Monterrey, NL (1947). Licenciado en economía por la Universidad Autónoma de Nuevo León (1969), maestro en economía por El Colegio de México (1971) y doctor en economía por la Universidad de Yale (1975). En el PRI, partido al que pertenece desde 1971, fue secretario técnico de la Comisión de Desarrollo Industrial del plan de gobierno de Miguel de la Madrid (1982) y secretario de la Comisión Política, Económica y Social del IEPES, donde tomó un curso de especialización en planificación agrícola e industrial (1969). Profesor de la Universidad Anáhuac (1971-72), del ITAM (1975), de El Colegio de México (1978-79) y de la UNAM. Ha sido jefe de Programación y Proyectos de Nafinsa (1971-72), director general y secretario técnico de la Comisión Coordinadora de Política Industrial del Sector Público (1975-77), director de Finanzas Internacionales (1977-79) y subdirector general de Planeación Hacendaria de la Secretaría de Hacienda (1979- 82); subsecretario de Planeación Industrial y Comercial de la Secretaría de Comercio (1983-85), coordinador general del Centro de Promoción y Evaluación de Proyectos de la Secretaría de Energía (1985-88) y director general de Productora e Importadora de Papel (1988-98). Autor de *El desequilibrio externo en la industrialización de México, 1929-1975. Un enfoque estructuralista* (1976), *Economía internacional* (compilador, 2 t., 1979), *La contrarrevolución monetarista* (1986) y *Hacia una nueva economía de mercado* (1998). Miembro del Colegio Nacional de Economistas. Premio Nacional de Economía Banamex (1975).

Villarreal Dávila, Rosendo Alfredo ◆ n. en Saltillo, Coah. (1942). Milita en el PAN desde 1990, donde ha sido consejero nacional y estatal, así como presidente del Comité Directivo Estatal (1999-2002). Presidente municipal de Saltillo (1991-1993); candidato a gobernador (1994); senador de la República (1994-2000); cofundador y directivo de Fundación México 2000.

Villarreal Guerra, Américo ◆ n. en Ciudad Victoria, Tams. (1931). Ingeniero civil por la UNAM (1953).

Américo Villarreal Guerra

Desde 1956 pertenece al PRI, en el que fue miembro de las Juventudes Liberales de Tamaulipas (1946-48) y de las Juventudes Liberales de México (1949-53). Ha sido jefe de Obras de Pequeña Irrigación en Tamaulipas (1956-60); subdirector de Pequeña Irrigación (1960-67), encargado del despacho de la Subsecretaría de Construcción (1976), subsecretario de Infraestructura de la Subsecretaría de Construcción (1976) y subsecretario de Infraestructura Hidráulica de la Secretaría de Agricultura (1978-80); senador de la República (1982-87) y gobernador constitucional de Tamaulipas (1987-93). Miembro de la Asociación de Ingenieros y Arquitectos de México, de la Asociación Nacional de Hidráulica, de la Sociedad Mexicana de Ingeniería Económica y de Costos y del Colegio de Ingenieros y Arquitectos. Presidente de la Sociedad Mexicana de Ingenieros (1983- 86).

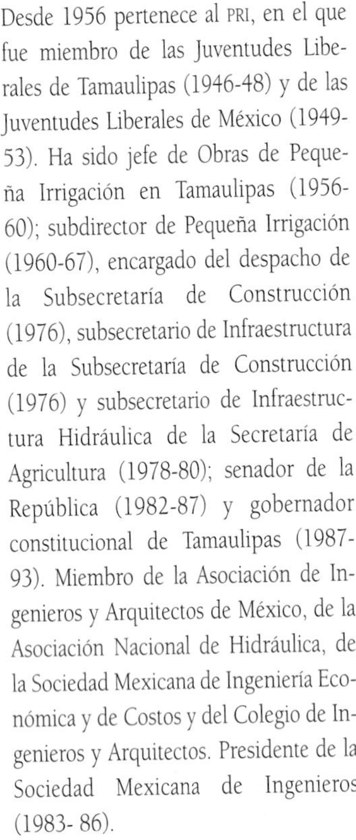

Autorretrato de José María Villasana

Villasana, José María ◆ n. en Veracruz, Ver., y m. en la ciudad de México (1848-1904). Periodista y caricaturista. Radicado en la ciudad de México fue fundador de una de las principales columnas del periódico *El Ahuizote*. En 1891 fundó el periódico *El Mundo Ilustrado*, donde redactó sus célebres "Cuadros de costumbres". Colaboró en *México Gráfico* y *La Orquesta*. Fue diputado federal y profesor de dibujo en la Escuela Nacional Preparatoria.

Archivo Xavier Esparza

Obra de José María Villasana reproducida en *El Mundo Ilustrado*

Archivo Xavier Esparza

Obra de José María Villasana reproducida en *El Mundo Ilustrado*

Villasana, Marcos ◆ n. en Acapulco, Gro. (1960). Boxeador. Obtuvo la corona en los Guantes de Oro de Acapulco en peso gallo. Después de cinco derrotas buscando el campeonato mundial, de la división pluma, en 1990 obtuvo el triunfo. Se retiró del boxeo en 1991 un año despues.

Villasana, Vicente ◆ n. en Querétaro, Qro., y m. en Ciudad Victoria, Tams. (1886-1947). Periodista. En 1918 fundó el diario *El Mundo*, en Tampico, y en 1941 *El Heraldo de San Luis Potosí*. Murió asesinado por el jefe de la policía de Tamaulipas, lo que aceleró la destitución del gobernador Hugo Pedro González.

Villasana López, Juan Guillermo ◆ n. en Pachuca, Hgo., y m. en el DF (1891-1959). En 1909 participó en la organización de la Sociedad Impulsora de Aviación, de la que fue primer presidente. En 1910 voló sobre la capital hidalguense en el aeroplano *Pachuca*, que él construyó y diseñó. En un segundo vuelo en 1910 alcanzó 700 metros de altura. Ingeniero en aeronáutica por la Universidad de Buffalo. En 1912 fabricó cinco aeroplanos tipo Doperdussin para la Secretaría de Guerra. En 1912 dio a conocer la hélice Anáhuac, creada por él, cuya patente donó a la nación. Fundador y primer jefe del Departamento de Aeronáutica Civil (1928) e instructor de aviación.

Villaseca Quintero, Juan Bautista ◆ n. y m. en el DF (1932-1969). Médico. Fue presidente del Instituto de Intercambio Cultural México-Checoslovaquia. Autor de los poemarios *Azoteas del insomnio*, *Litoral de ti*, *Siete pétalos en el preludio de la primavera*, *En el sur de la tormenta*, *Diurnos*, *El viento de las cadenas*, *Diario para María Azahar*, *La luz herida*, *La soledad rescatada*, *Canciones para una sorda*, *De la tierra a la rosa* y

Variaciones de invierno; y de la novela *Pánfilo Godínez.*

VILLASEÑOR, EDUARDO ◆ n. en Angamacutiro, Mich., y m. en el DF (1896-1978). Estudió ingeniería en la Universidad de Londres, así como leyes y filosofía. Profesor de la Escuela Nacional de Agricultura (1921-25) y de la Universidad Nacional (1927-32). Fue secretario general de la UNAM, director del Departamento de Sociedades Cooperativas del Banco Nacional Agrícola (1926-28), agregado comercial de México en Londres (1929-31), director del Departamento Consular de la SRE (1931-32), miembro de la Comisión Nacional Bancaria (1932-33), secretario y organizador del Consejo Nacional de Economía (1932-34), cónsul general en Nueva York (1935), director del Banco Nacional de Crédito Agrícola (1936-37), subsecretario de Hacienda (1938-40), director general del Banco de México (1940-46) y del Banco del Atlántico (1949-65). Autor de *Éxtasis* (poemas, 1934), *En la orilla de la revolución* (1937), *Las zonas nuevas y el indio* (1938), *El fracaso de los economistas* (1940), *Interamerican Trade and Financial Problems* (1941), *De la curiosidad y otros papeles* (1945), *Los recuerdos y los días* (1960), *Nuestra industria textil del algodón, El Banco Interamericano* y *Problemas de crédito en un país productor.*

VILLASEÑOR, ISABEL ◆ n. en Guadalajara, Jal., y m. en el DF (1914-1953). Pintora, poeta y actriz. Esposa del también pintor Gabriel Fernández Ledesma. Ingresó en el Centro Popular de Pintura de San Antonio Abad (1928) y en 1930 presentó su primera exposición individual, en la Biblioteca Nacional. Colaboró con Alfredo Zalce en la ejecución de un mural en la escuela primaria de Ayotla. Recorrió en 1931 el estado de Hidalgo como profesora misionera y en ese mismo año Serguei Eisenstein le ofreció el papel principal de una parte de su película inconclusa *¡Que viva México!* Ganó la flor natural de un concurso de poesía convocado por *El Universal Gráfico.*

VILLASEÑOR, JORGE ◆ n. en Guadalajara, Jal. (1884-1944). Ingeniero titulado en Guadalajara. Se dedicó a la construcción de obras de infraestructura en Jalisco. Cofundador del Partido Liberal Jalisciense. Luchó en la revolución constitucionalista. Fue diputado por Jalisco al Congreso Constituyente (1916-17) y diputado federal (1918-20).

VILLASEÑOR, JOSÉ MARÍA ◆ n. y m. en Morelia, Mich. (1880-1961). Sacerdote egresado del Seminario de Morelia, del que también fue profesor. Canónigo de la capital michoacana, en 1914 fundó en esa ciudad la Escuela Superior de Música Sagrada, que dirigió hasta su muerte, ocurrida cuando era deán de la catedral moreliana.

VILLASEÑOR, PEDRO ◆ n. ¿en Jalisco? y m. en Morelia, Mich. (?-¿1849?). Insurgente, se unió a las fuerzas de Miguel Hidalgo en noviembre de 1810, cuando éste entró en Guadalajara, y lo acompañó en la batalla del puente de Calderón. Siguió en las filas de Ignacio Allende, en su retirada hacia Saltillo, y más adelante pasó con Ignacio López Rayón a Zacatecas. Con mando de tropas derrotó al realista Bringas en Ojo Caliente en abril de 1811. Herido de bala poco después, en la batalla del Maguey, se ocultó en la sierra de Colotlán para ser atendido. Año y medio después, una vez recuperado, se unió en el sur a José María Morelos, quien le encomendó la administración de la provincia de Tecpan, en sustitución de Leonardo Bravo. Fue diputado al Congreso de Chilpancingo (1815) en sustitución de Andrés Quintana Roo, pero marchó a Michoacán cuando el Congreso se retiró a Tehuacán. En marzo de 1816 reconoció la autoridad de la Junta de Uruapan y negoció con la Junta de Tehuacán la unificación del mando insurgente, por lo que se integró a la Junta de Jaujilla. En 1817 fue enviado por la Junta a recibir la expedición internacionalista de Francisco Javier Mina. El 26 de septiembre de 1817 fue copado en Jaujilla, plaza que abandonó para refugiarse en la ranchería de Zárate. En marzo de 1818 formó una nueva junta en Las Balsas, que pronto fue desmantelada. Tras este descalabro se refugió en la sierra, sin acogerse al indulto, e incluso se negó a secundar el Plan de Iguala. Una vez consumada la independencia participó en la política local y llegó a formar parte del Consejo de Estado de Michoacán.

VILLASEÑOR, VÍCTOR MANUEL ◆ n. y m. en el DF (1903-1981). Estudió derecho en las universidades del Sur de California (1924), de Michigan (1926) y Nacional de México (1928). Campeón universitario de atletismo en la carrera de 400 metros planos, asistió en 1928 a los Juegos Olímpicos de Amsterdam. Trabajó en el bufete jurídico de Luis Cabrera (1927-28) y fue abogado de la Comisión General de Reclamaciones entre México y Estados Unidos (1929-33), delegado a la séptima Conferencia Panamericana, celebrada en Montevideo (1933), consejero jurídico de la embajada mexicana en Estados Unidos (1934), jefe del Departamento de Biblioteca y Archivos Económicos de la Secretaría de Hacienda (1935), miembro del Consejo Nacional de Educación Superior y de la Investigación Científica (1936-38), miembro fundador de la Confederación de Trabajadores de México y su representante ante los congresos de la Federación Sindical Internacional (1938-39); director de la Escuela Superior Obrera Karl Marx y de la revista *Futuro* (1936-40), presidente de la Sociedad de Amigos de la Unión Soviética (1936-41), jefe del departamento del Plan Sexenal de la Secretaría de Gobernación (1938-40), miembro de la Liga de Acción Política (1941-47) y redactor de su órgano *Combate* (1941); fundador y secretario general del Instituto de Amistad e Intercambio Cultural México-URSS (1944-50), fundador (1948) y vicepresidente del Partido Popular (1948-49), director de la Constructora Nacional de Carros de Ferrocarril (1952-70), director de Diesel Nacional y de Siderúrgica Nacional (1959-70) y gerente general de los Ferrocarriles Nacionales de México (1970-73). Coautor, con Vicente Lombardo Toledano, de *Viaje al mundo del porvenir* (1936). Autor de *La nacionalidad de las sociedades y la protección diplomática de los intereses extranjeros en México* (1930), *Problemas del mundo contemporáneo* (1937), *Al otro lado de la "cortina de hierro"* (1946) y *Memorias de un hombre de izquierda* (2 t., 1976).

VILLASEÑOR AMAYA, PEDRO ◆ n. en Candela, Coah., y m. en el DF (1880-1959). Apoyó la insurrección maderista de 1910. En 1912, con Alfonso Madero, creó el Cuerpo de Carabineros de Nuevo León para combatir al orozquismo en Durango y Coahuila. También en 1912 pasó a Veracruz para luchar contra Félix Díaz. Constitucionalista desde 1913, militó en las fuerzas de Jesús Carranza y de Antonio I. Villarreal en Nuevo León, Tamaulipas y San Luis Potosí. En 1914 se incorporó al Cuerpo de Ejército del Noreste y participó en el sitio y toma de Monterrey. Fiel al carrancismo, fue ascendido a brigadier y operó en Puebla, a las órdenes de Francisco Coss. Al frente de la brigada Poncho Vázquez participó con Álvaro Obregón en la toma de Puebla (1915). Fue jefe de la guarnición de Tehuacán y comandante militar de Puebla (octubre de 1915). En 1916 se le destacó a Oaxaca para combatir a los rebeldes Higinio Aguilar y Juan Andrew Almazán. Al término del conflicto armado fue jefe de operaciones militares en Piedras Negras y en Torreón, presidente del Supremo Tribunal Militar (1938). General de división en 1939.

VILLASEÑOR ARANO, IGNACIO ◆ n. en Tres Valles, Ver. (1942). Licenciado en relaciones internacionales por la UNAM (1966) y licenciado especial en relaciones internacionales por la Universidad Católica de Lovaina (1969). En la Secretaría de Relaciones Exteriores ha sido profesor del Instituto Matías Romero, jefe del Departamento de África, Asia y Oceanía (1970), jefe del Departamento de Europa (1971), jefe del Departamento de América (1972), subdirector general adjunto del Servicio Diplomático (1973-75), subdirector general del Servicio Diplomático (1976-77), consejero de la embajada en Gran Bretaña (1977-79), director general de Organismos Regionales (1979-82), ministro y encargado de negocios en Estados Unidos (1982-83), director en jefe para Asuntos Bilaterales (1983-89), embajador en Ecuador (1989-91) y embajador en Uruguay (1991-).

VILLASEÑOR DÍAZ, ALDEGUNDO ◆ n. en El Parnaso, distrito de Ayutla, Jal., y m. en Toluca, Edo. de Méx. (1888-1918). Era comerciante cuando se unió a la revolución constitucionalista en las filas de Manuel M. Diéguez. Diputado al Congreso Constituyente de 1916-17, donde participó en el ala radical. Instalado en Toluca se dedicó al periodismo y criticó duramente a las autoridades locales, por lo que fue aprehendido y condenado a muerte. Se dice que él mismo dirigió al pelotón que lo fusiló.

VILLASEÑOR LOMELÍ, JOSÉ ◆ n. en Pénjamo, Gto., y m. en el DF (1876-1945). Obrero antiporfirista. Militó en el Partido Nacional Antirreeleccionista y luchó en la revolución constitucionalista. Fue diputado por Guanajuato al Congreso Constituyente de 1916-17.

VILLASEÑOR M., SALOMÓN ◆ n. en Tzutzio, Michoacán (1964). Licenciado en actuación por el INBA. Ha realizado lecturas de poesía en diferentes foros y en encuentros de poesía. Ha publicado en algunos suplementos y revistas literarias nacionales y extranjeras. Profesor de teatro en Preparatorias de la UNAM. Ha publicado: *El mar donde vivo ahogado* (1993), *Azul en llamas* (1996) y *Guardián de los jardines* (1997). Ganador del V Concurso Internacional de Poseía La Porte des Poetes (París, 1997) con el poema "Agua Luna".

VILLASEÑOR NORMAN, ADOLFO ◆ n. en Zacatecas, Zac., y m. en el DF (1888-1971). Ingeniero titulado en la Escuela Nacional de Ingenieros de la ciudad de México. Fue diputado por Zacatecas al Congreso Constituyente de 1916-17, diputado local en Zacatecas (1917), gobernador interino de Zacatecas (del 1 al 11 de septiembre de 1928) y miembro de la Comisión Geográfica de ese estado.

VILLASEÑOR PEÑA, EDUARDO ◆ n. en La Piedad, Mich., y m. en Guanajuato (1945-1994). Estudió administración de empresas, desarrollo agroindustrial, tecnología de alimentos y comercio internacional en México y en el extranjero. Perteneció al PRI. Desempeñó varios cargos en depedencias porcícolas (1987-1989). Presidente municipal de la Piedad (1990-91), diputado federal (1991-1992) y durante 21 días gobernador de Michoacán (1992). Director general del Fideicomiso de Fomento Minero (1993-94). Presea al Mérito Ganadero de la Confederación Nacional Ganadera (1993).

VILLASEÑOR SANABRIA, MARGARITA ◆ n. en el DF (1934). Licenciada en letras francesas por el IFAL, maestra en letras españolas por la Universidad de Guanajuato, doctora en letras españolas por la UNAM y doctora en literaturas comparadas por la Universidad de París. Ha sido jefa de Difusión Cultural de la delegación Cuauhtémoc (1974), traductora en Nafinsa (1971-75), investigadora en ciencias de la comunicación de la Subdirección Administrativa del IMSS (1971-76) y en la Dirección de Estudios de la Comunicación de Televisa (1972-75) y asesora de la vicepresidencia de Investigaciones y de Estudios de la Comunicación de Televisa (1978-85). Colaboradora de *La Rana Sabia*, *Excélsior*, *El Nacional*, *El Sol de México*, *Letras Nuevas* y *Estaciones*. Autora de poesía: *Poemas* (1956), *Tierra hermana* (1958), *Poemas cardinales* (1962), *La ciudad de cristal* (1965), *El rito cotidiano* (1981, Premio Xavier Villaurrutia) y *De muerte natural* (1984); de ensayo: *El tiempo y el espacio en la obra de Ramón del Valle Inclán* (1962, tesis de maestría); las adaptaciones de *La Celestina* (1969, en colaboración con Miguel Sabido, Premio Festival de Manizales en 1970), *La ilustre fregona*, *Bodas de sangre*, *Casa de muñecas* y *Diego el mulato*; el guión de cine: *La Celestina* (1973, en colaboración); las obras de teatro: *La gesta de Juárez* (1972, premio del DDF), *Apocalipsis 1910* (1973), *El árbol de la vida* (1973), *Los sueños de*

Quevedo (1974), *Entremeses de la Nueva España* (1974) y *Camino negro*, así como de la telenovela *El extraño retorno de Diana Salazar* (1988). Premio a la Mejor Adaptación de la Asociación de Escritores por *Comala y otros murmullos* (1986).

Villaseñor y Sánchez, José Antonio ◆ n. en la ciudad de México (?-?). Historiador, cartógrafo y matemático. Fue colegial de San Ildefonso, oficial mayor de la Contaduría General de Reales Tributos, contador general de la de Azogues (1741) y cosmógrafo del reino de la Nueva España. Autor de un *Informe a la Audiencia Gobernadora de la Nueva España, sobre rebaja del precio del azogue, que solicitan los mineros* (1742), *Observación del cometa que apareció en el hemisferio de México en los Meses de febrero y marzo de 1742* (1746), *Theatro americano, Descripción general de los reinos y provincias de la N. España y sus jurisdicciones* (2 t., 1746-48), *Pantómetra matemática combinatoria de las leyes de la plata* (1733), *Tabla o logaritmos del azogue y plata de toda ley* (1741), *Romance lírico en elogio de Fernando VI, Rey de España* (1749), *Matemático cómputo de los astros* (1756), así como *Calendarios y pronósticos lunarios*, un *Mapa geográfico de la Provincia de la Compañía de Jesús* e *Yconismo hidrotérreo, o mapa geográphico de la América Septentrional*.

Villaseñor Villanueva, Carlos ◆ n. y m. en Guadalajara, Jal. (1875-1955). Médico cirujano (1907) y farmacéutico (1908) por la Facultad de Medicina de Guadalajara, de la que fue profesor. También ejerció la docencia en la Escuela de Ciencias Químicas y en la Escuela Normal. Fue diputado suplente por Jalisco al Congreso Constituyente de 1916-17, médico de Sanidad (1916-24), miembro honorario de la Ciudad Química de Guadalajara, profesor honorario vitalicio de la Facultad de Medicina y director vitalicio de la Escuela de Ciencias Químicas de Guadalajara. Miembro de honor del Congreso de Farmacia.

Villaseñor y Villaseñor, Alejandro ◆ n. y m. en la ciudad de México (1864-1912). Abogado, historiador y periodista. Licenciado en derecho por la Escuela Nacional de Jurisprudencia (1887). Se dedicó al estudio de la historia y al periodismo. Colaboró en el diario *El Tiempo* y fue fundador y colaborador de las publicaciones *La Tribuna* (1885) y *La Lira* (1886). Autor de *Los condes de Santiago* (1901), *Reclamaciones a México por los Fondos de Californias* (1902), *Gobernantes de México y formas de gobierno* (tercera edición en 1910) y *Biografías de los héroes y caudillos de la Independencia* (2 t., 1910).

Villatoro Escobedo, Gustavo ◆ n. en Comitán, Chis. (1895-1950). Profesor normalista. Se unió en 1914 al Cuerpo de Ejército del Noroeste y participó, entre otras, en las batallas de Celaya y Trinidad. Profesor de literatura de las escuelas superiores Florencio M. del Castillo y José M. Chávez, y de la Nacional Preparatoria. Fue oficial del Estado Mayor de Álvaro Obregón (1915), secretario del director general de Bellas Artes (1915), jefe de la sección de Arte Teatral del Departamento de Bellas Artes (1916), subjefe del Departamento de Bibliotecas de la SEP (1922) y jefe del Departamento de Leyes Nacionales y Extranjeras de la Cámara de Diputados (1922). Desempeñó misiones diplomáticas en Italia, Holanda, España (1925), Argentina (1927) y Uruguay, donde fue encargado de negocios (1929) y fundó la Asociación de Escritores de Teatro. Dirigió la Academia de Arte Dramático y Cinematografía de la ciudad de México. Tradujo obras de dramaturgos italianos, entre otras: *Seis personajes en busca de autor*, de Luigi Pirandello.

Villaurrutia, Antonio de ◆ n. en España y m. en la ciudad de México (?-1793). Fue ministro honorario del Consejo de Indias y oidor decano de las audiencias de Santo Domingo y de México. Llegó a Guadalajara en 1787 como intendente gobernador y presidente de Nueva Galicia, cargos que ocupó hasta 1791.

Villaurrutia, Jacobo de ◆ n. en Santo Domingo y m. en la ciudad de México (1757-1833). Viajó muy joven a la Nueva España, donde hizo la carrera eclesiástica en el Seminario de la ciudad de México. Fue a España, se graduó como abogado y en 1785 figuró entre los fundadores de la Academia de Literatos Españoles y como colaborador de la publicación *El Correo de Madrid* o *Correo de los Ciegos*. Fue oidor de Guatemala (1792-1804). De nuevo en la Nueva España fundó, con Carlos María de Bustamante, el *Diario de México* (1805), primer cotidiano de Hispanoamérica. En 1808 participó en el movimiento autonomista de Primo Verdad, por lo que fue desterrado a Europa. Regresó a México en 1821 y se desempeñó como presidente de la Suprema Corte de Justicia. Autor de *La escuela de la felicidad* (con el pseudónimo de *Diego Rulavit y Laur*), *Pensamientos escogidos de las máximas filosóficas de Marco Aurelio y de Federico II de Prusia* (1786) y *Sistema de instrucción pública* (1807, recopilación de artículos periodísticos).

Villaurrutia, Xavier ◆ n. y m. en el DF (1903-1950). Poeta y dramaturgo. Abandonó los estudios de derecho para

Plano de la ciudad de México realizado por José Antonio Villaseñor y Sánchez en 1750

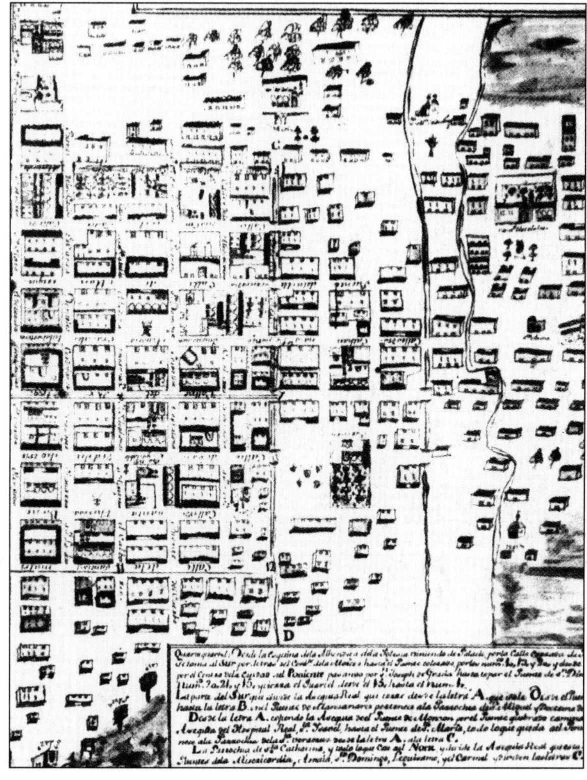

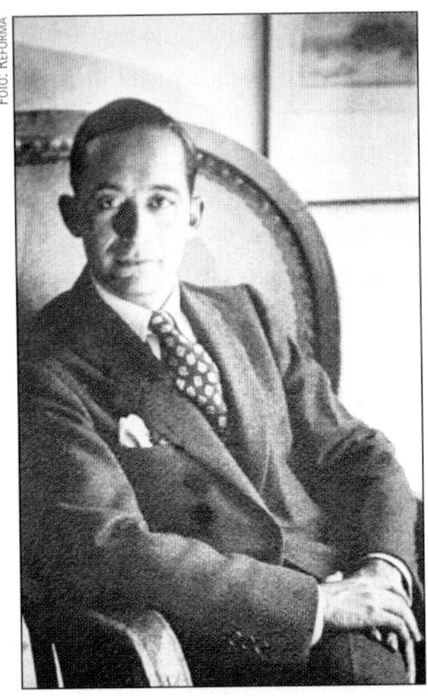

FOTO: REFORMA

Xavier Villaurrutia

dedicarse a la literatura. Dirigió con Salvador Novo la revista *Ulises* (1927-28). Fue cofundador del grupo teatral Ulises (1928), colaborador de la revista *Contemporáneos* (1928-31), estudiante de teatro de la Universidad de Yale (1936) becado por la Fundación Rockefeller; profesor de la UNAM y jefe de la sección de teatro del Departamento de Bellas Artes. Guionista, con Fernando de Fuentes, de *Vámonos con Pancho Villa* (1934); con Rafael F. Muñoz, de *Cinco fueron escogidos* (1942); y con Mauricio Magdaleno, de *La mujer de todos* (1946). Autor de los guiones de *El espectro de la novia* (1943), *La mujer sin cabeza* (1943), *Distinto amanecer* (1943), *La mujer legítima* (1945), *El monje blanco* (1945), *La casa de la zorra* (1945), *La mulata de Córdoba* (1945), *Bailando en las nubes* (1945), *Don Simón de Lira* (1946), *Bel Ami (El buen mozo o Historia de un canalla)* (1946), *San Felipe de Jesús (el divino conquistador)* (1949) y *La dama del alba* (1949). Colaborador de *Letras de México* (1937-47), *Examen* y *El Hijo Pródigo* (1943-46). Autor de los poemarios: *Reflejos* (1926), *Dos nocturnos* (1931), *Nocturnos* (1931), *Nocturno de los ángeles* (1936), *Nocturno mar* (1937), *Nostalgia de la muerte* (1938), *Décima muerte y otros poemas no coleccionados* (1941) y *Canto a la primavera y otros poemas* (1948, por el que recibió el primer premio del concurso de las Fiestas de Primavera, organizado por el DDF); de los relatos: *Mauricio Leal, retrato* (1924), *Dama de corazones* (1928, con ilustraciones del autor) y *El éxodo* (1928); de los ensayos: *La poesía de los jóvenes de México* (1924), *El retrato* (1947) y *Textos y pretextos* (1949); y de las obras teatrales: *Parece mentira* (1933), *¿En qué piensas?* (1934), *Ha llegado el momento* (1934), *Sea Ud. breve* (1934), *El ausente* (1937), *Invitación a la muerte* (1940), *La hiedra* (1941), *La mujer legítima* (1942), *Autos profanos* (1943, antología), *El solterón* (1945), *El yerro candente* (1945), *El pobre Barba Azul* (1946), *La mulata de Córdoba* (1948), *Juego peligroso* (1949) y *La tragedia de las equivocaciones* (1950). En 1953 se editó su obra completa.

Portada de Xavier Villaurrutia

VILLAVICENCIO, HERMENEGILDO ♦ n. y m. en la ciudad de México (1842-1869). Estudió medicina. Discípulo de Plotino Rhodakanaty. Cofundador del Club Socialista de Estudiantes, con Francisco Zalacosta y Santiago Villanueva (1863), y de La Social (☛). En octubre de 1864 participó en la creación de la Sociedad Particular de Socorros Mutuos y en noviembre vigorizó la Sociedad Mutua del Ramo de Sastrería. Participó en la huelga de la fábrica La Colmena de Tlalnepantla en junio de 1865, que fue reprimida por el gobierno de Maximiliano de Habsburgo. Reorganizó la Sociedad Agrícola Oriental. Con Villanueva reanimó la Sociedad Artístico-Industrial hacia 1867. Promovió la creación de la Unión Mutua de Tejedores del Distrito de Tlalpan, con obreros de la Fama Montañesa y otras fábricas, como la Abeja, de Tizapán (1868).

VILLAVICENCIO, PABLO DE ♦ n. en el Real del Rosario, Sin., y m. en Toluca, Edo. de Méx. (1792-1832). Escritor conocido como *el Payo del Rosario*. Llegó a la ciudad de México en 1822 y publicó numerosos folletos acerca de temas políticos. Militó en la logia yorkina. Fue encarcelado por sus opiniones en 1824 y en 1830. Por la misma razón se le recluyó dos meses en el fuerte de San Diego, en Acapulco (1825-26) y *el Pensador Mexicano* recogió a su familia. Participó en la insurrección popular conocida como Motín de la Acordada. Fue asesinado por las fuerzas golpistas del general Mariano Ortiz de la Peña. Publicó más de un centenar de obras, algunas de ellas en fascículos periódicos como sus *Nuevas zorras de Sansón*. o las *Funciones de Maroma en casa de doña Prudencia de Mendiola*, del que aparecieron 13 entregas. Entre sus folletos políticos destacan: *Defensa del Pensador, o sea reflexión sobre su causa y estado* (1822), *La libertad de imprenta no se ataca impunemente.* (1823), *Serviles metan las manos que ya se desplomó el templo* (1823), *De coyote a perro inglés voy al coyote ocho a tres* (1825), *Plan de desgachupinar si vienen los de la Liga* (1826), *Si el presidente sigue como va, como subió bajará* (1826), *Si vienen los godos nos cuelgan a todos* (1826), *Tronó en el Senado el cohete y salió un domingo siete* (1826), *El gobierno de la Unión sopla la revolución* (1828), *El perdón de Bravo no es moco de pavo* (1828), *Proclama del servil obispo de Puebla* (1928), *Culebrina fulminante para el señor Bustamante* (1831), *Ya los gatos se mudaron al Palacio Nacional* (1831) y *O se van los gachupines o nos cortan el pescuezo* (1831), entre otros.

VILLEGAS, ABELARDO ♦ n. en el DF (1934). Su apellido materno es Maldonado. Maestro (1958) y doctor en filosofía (1971) por la UNAM, en la que ha sido profesor (1954-), secretario de la Facultad de Filosofía y Letras (1966-69), jefe del Departamento de Humanidades de la Dirección General de Difusión Cultural (1970-73), director de Radio Universidad (1977), director de la Facultad de Filosofía y Letras (1978-81), secretario ejecutivo de la Coordinación General de Estudios de Posgrado (1985-87) y secretario general académico (1987-). Fue jefe de Cursos, Conferencias y Congresos de la Secretaría de Relaciones Exteriores (1960-64). Coautor de una *Antología del pensamiento social y político de América Latina* (1964) y *La formación del mundo moderno* (1977). Autor de *La filosofía de lo mexicano* (1960), *Panorama de la filosofía latinoamericana actual* (1963), *La filosofía en la historia política de México* (1966), *Positivismo y porfirismo. Antología* (1972), *Reformismo y revolución en el pensamiento latinoamericano* (1972), *Cultura y política en América Latina* (1978), *Autognosis. El pensamiento mexicano en el siglo XX* (1985), *Violencia y racionalidad* (1985) y *Democracia y dictadura, el destino de una idea bolivariana* (1987).

VILLEGAS, AMPARO ◆ n. en España y m. en el DF (1890-1969). Actriz. Inició su carrera en el teatro de la Princesa, en Madrid, en la compañía de María Tubau. Trabajó, también en España, con María Guerrero y Fernando Díaz de Mendoza. Aquí se incorporó al grupo Teatro Español de México, dirigido por Alvaro Custodio. Participó en numerosas puestas, donde destacaron sus interpretaciones de Belisa en el drama *La discreta enamorada*, de Lope de Vega; Violante en *Reinar después de morir*, de Vélez de Guevara; y la Muerte en *Bodas de sangre*, de García Lorca. Su última aparición, un mes antes de morir, fue en *La medusa*, de Emilio Carballido.

VILLEGAS, GASTÓN ◆ n. en Tampico, Tams., (1943). Licenciado en derecho por la UNAM, con especialización en áreas corporativas, derecho corporativo y derecho fiscal. Participó en la firma Abogados Noriega y Escobedo (1981-86), socio de Abogados Villegas, Cassis y Asociados (1986-94), miembro de la Barra Mexicana de Abogados y de la Asociación Nacional de Empresas (1994). Subprocurador Jurídico y de Derechos Humanos de la PGJDF (1997-).

VILLEGAS, ÓSCAR ◆ n. en Ciudad del Maíz, SLP (1943). Ceramista y director teatral. Estudió artes plásticas y composición dramática en la UNAM y dirección escénica en la Escuela de Arte Teatral del INBA. Colaborador de la revista *Tramoya*. Autor del poemario *Este viaje* (1966) y de las obras de teatro *La paz de la buena gente* (1967), *El renacimiento* (1967), *Marlon Brando es otro* (1969), *Santa Catarina* (1969), *El señor y la señora* (1969), *La pira* (1970), *Atlántida* (1976), *Mucho gusto en conocerlo* (1984), *El reino animal* y *Lo verde de las hojas* (1990). Premio SEP 1969, Protea 1976 y Juan Ruiz de Alarcón 1981. Becario del Fonca 1994-96.

VILLEGAS, PALOMA ◆ n. en el DF (1951). Estudió Letras en la UNAM. Formó parte del Consejo de Redacción del sumplemento *La Cultura en México* y de la revista literaria *La Mesa Llena*. Autora de *Mapas* (poesía, 1981) y *La luz oblicua* (novela, 1995).

VILLEGAS, SIDARTA ◆ n. en el DF (1964). Tomó cursos de literatura dramática, teatro, lengua y literatura hispánicas en la UNAM, en donde ha trabajado como redactor de discursos y conferencias en la Dirección General de Servicios de Cómputo Académico. Formó parte de la Delegación Mexicana en el Barco para los Jóvenes del Mundo y visitó diferentes países. Colaborador de *unomásuno*. Obtuvo el Premio Nacional de la Juventud 1987 por *Quemazón y otros siniestros*. Becario del Centro Mexicano de Escritores (1990-91).

VILLEGAS CHÁVEZ, MARGARITA ◆ n. en Chihuahua, Chih., y m. en el DF (1929-1978). Actriz. Inició su carrera en 1950, como animadora de programas de televisión. Actuó también en teatro y en las películas *El derecho de la vida* (1958), *El sordo* (1958), *Sube y baja* (1958), *El analfabeto* (1960), *Los falsos héroes* (1961), *Para morir iguales*, *Maratón de baile* y *Mecánica nacional* (1971).

VILLEGAS GUEVARA, EDUARDO ◆ n. en Palmillas, Tams. (1962). Escritor. Estudió literatura dramática y teatro en la UNAM. Ha colaborado en *El Sol de México*, *Vínculos*, *La Jornada* y la *Revista de la UAEM*, de cuyo Consejo de Redacción es miembro. Autor de testimonio: *Las orillas del asfalto* (1987, Premio Nacional de Testimonio); cuento: *El blues del chavo banda* (1991, Premio Nacional de Cuento Gilberto Owen), *La noche de la desnudez* (1996, mención honorífica en el Premio Nacional de Cuento de San Luis Potosí, 1993) y *Cuentos de magos para niños* (1999); novela: *El misterio del tanque* (1989); y teatro: *El despertar de los siete magníficos* (1991), *Preparativos de viaje* (1991), *El complot asesino* (1991) y *La noche de los dulces* (1991). Ha obtenido los premios de cuento Juan B. Tijerina del Programa Nacional de las Fronteras (1988), de Novela Corta Carlos González Salas (1988) y los de dramaturgia Óscar Liera y de la revista *Punto de Partida*. Ha sido becario del Fonca (1997-98).

VILLEGAS M., VÍCTOR MANUEL ◆ n. en Toluca, Edo, de Méx. (1913). Doctor en arquitectura titulado en Madrid (1936). Por iniciativa suya, en 1944 se fundó la Escuela Municipal de Ingeniería del Instituto Científico y Literario del Estado de México. En la Universidad de Guanajuato fundó la Escuela de Arquitectura y la maestría en restauración de monumentos, En la UNAM ha sido profesor e investigador del Instituto de Investigaciones Estéticas. Restaurador del Teatro Juárez, de la iglesia de la Valenciana y Cata, la casa natal de Diego Rivera en Guanajuato, el panteón de Belén en Guadalajara, el santuario de Guadalupe en Aguascalientes y la sacristía del convento de la Asunción en Toluca. Coautor, con Antonio Bonet Correa, de *El barroco en España y en México* (1967). Autor de *Hierros coloniales en Toluca* (1936), *Hierros coloniales en Zacatecas* (1955), *El gran signo formal del barroco* (1956), *Tresguerras, arquitecto de su tiempo* (1964), *Arte popular de Guanajuato* (1964), *El panteón romántico de Guadalajara* (1969), *La arquitectura de Refugio Reyes* (1973), *Guadalupe. Santuario de Aguascalientes* (1973), *Valenciana. La basílica de Guanajuato* (1974), *La iglesia del mineral de Cata* (1974), *La iglesia de la Compañía de Jesús y la Universidad de Guanajuato* (1975), *Un pleito tristemente célebre en la ciudad de México en el siglo XX* (1977) y *La sacristía del convento de la Asunción de Toluca* (1977).

FOTO: FONDO HISTÓRICO ALFONSO SÁNCHEZ GARCÍA

Víctor Manuel Villegas M.

VILLEGAS VILLALOBOS, ANTONIO ◆ n. en el DF (1947). Ingeniero químico (1965) y licenciado en derecho por la UNAM (1970), con posgrado en relaciones internacionales por la Universidad Sophia de Japón (1974). Ha sido abogado del despacho de Ricardo Franco Guzmán (1969-72), vicecónsul y consejero en Japón (1972-80), adscrito a la embajada de México en Francia (1980-83), director general para África, Asia y Oceanía (1983-86) y director general para América Latina y el Caribe de la SRE (1986-91); embajador en El Salvador (1999-) Recibió la Orden Imperial del Sol Naciente.

VILLELA, JUAN DE ◆ n. y ¿m.? en España (¿1560?-?). Fue oidor de la Audiencia de Lima. Llegó a la Nueva España en los primeros años del siglo XVII como visitador general. Fue presidente de la Audiencia (1607) y gobernador de Nueva Galicia (1608-09). Durante su gestión eximió a los indios del pago de tributos por un periodo de diez años. En 1610 volvió a España. Dejó inédito el manuscrito *Informe sobre los arbitrios propuestos por Agustín de Reyna al virrey D. Luis de Velasco sobre la moneda y plata de Indias*.

VILLELA, VÍCTOR ◆ n. en Ciudad Altamirano, Gro. (1937). Estudió periodismo en la escuela Carlos Septién García. Trabajó en compañías constructoras, de seguros y en Intendencia Naval como marinero oficinista. Fue empleado administrativo en la UNAM, secretario de redacción del suplemento *Sábado* (1988-91 y 1994-95), subdirector del Centro de Documentación en la Secretaría de Gobernación (1992-93), redactor del periodico *El Día* (1995) y secretario de redacción de la revista *Memoranda*. Ha colaborado en diversas publicaciones. Autor de *Palabras para convencer* (1974, cuentos), los poemarios *Las líneas precisas* (1964) y *Paisaje desde una hora* (1972); y la traducción *Zumárraga y la Inquisición mexicana* (1988). Becario del Centro Mexicano de Escritores (1979-71).

VILLELA GÓMEZ, JOSÉ ◆ n. y m. en el DF (1915-1992). Ingeniero civil por la UNAM (1939). Becario del Museo Nacional de la Aviación y el Espacio de la Institución Smithsoniana (Washington, 1986-87). En Washington, en el Instituto Smithsoniano, dirigió durante un año las investigaciones acerca de la historia de la Fuerza Aérea Mexicana y la participación del Escuadrón 201 en la campaña de Filipinas durante la segunda guerra mundial. Fue instructor de teoría aeronáutica en el Centro Internacional de Adiestramiento de Aviación Civil, la Escuela Aeronáutica Panamericana, escuela Mexicana del Aire y a la Aeroescuela. En la Dirección General de Aeronáutica Civil trabajó en el Departamento de Aeródromos y Aeropuertos Civiles, en el Departamento de Inspección Aeronáutica y en la Oficina de Relaciones Públicas del Aeropuerto Internacional de la Ciudad de México. Durante 11 años fue gerente del Club Aéreo de México. Fue asesor técnico de la Gerencia de Comunicación Social de Aeropuertos y Servicios Auxiliares y de la Asociación Mexicana de Redactores de Aviación. Colaboró en la *Revista Aérea Latinoamericana, Aviación México* y *Hélice*. Autor de *Historia gráfica de la aviación mexicana* (vol. I, 1960), *Pioneros de la aviación mexicana* (1964), *Historia gráfica de la aviación mexicana* (vol. II, 1971) y *Aircraft of the Mexican Air Force* (1987). Secretario de la vicepresidencia para América Latina de la Federación Aeronáutica Internacional (1956).

Fernanda Villeli

VILLELI, FERNANDA ◆ n. en el DF (1914). Nombre profesional de la guionista de telenovelas Ofelia Villenave Garza. Estudió inglés y escritura dramática en Estados Unidos. Fue secretaria del director del Banco de México y asistente ejecutiva del representante del Fondo Monetario Internacional, Harry White, antes de dedicarse a escribir. Realizó libretos para radionovelas. Autora del libreto de la primera telenovela mexicana, *Senda prohibida* (1958), a la que siguieron *San Martín de Porres, Los extraños caminos del amor, La mesera, No quiero lágrimas, El ídolo de barro, Al filo de la muerte, La sonrisa del diablo, El maleficio, Lo blanco y lo negro* y *La traición*, entre las 60 de su autoría. Pertenece a la Sociedad General de Escritores de México.

VILLERÍAS, JUAN ◆ m. en Real de Catorce, SLP (¿1775?-1811). Insurgente. Pertenecía a la orden de San Juan de Dios. En 1810 se levantó en armas en San Luis Potosí, pero, hostigado por Rafael Iriarte, se retiró a Guanajuato, donde se entrevistó con Ignacio Allende, quien lo destacó en las tropas de Mariano Jiménez. Participó en la acción de Aguanueva y realizó la campaña en Nuevo León. Tras la captura de los líderes de la revolución, se incorporó a las fuerzas de Ignacio López Rayón; participó en la batalla de Piñones y luego se se distanció de este caudillo. Fue a Nuevo Santander y sufrió sucesivas derrotas a manos del realista Joaquín de Arredondo. Volvió a San Luis Potosí, donde fue batido y muerto en combate por el ex insurgente José María Semper.

VILLORO, JUAN ◆ n. en el DF (1956). Escritor. Estudió sociología en la UAM. Ha sido conductor del programa *El lado oscuro de la luna* en Radio Educación (1977-81), jefe de Actividades Culturales de la UAM-Iztapalapa (1980-81), agregado cultural de la embajada mexicana en la República Democrática de Alemania (1981-84), jefe de redacción de *Pauta* y director de *la Jornada Semanal* (1995-1998). Colaborador de

FOTO: ANA LOURDES HERRERA

Juan Villoro

La Gaceta del Fondo, Revista de la Universidad, Crisis, La Palabra y el Hombre, Nexos, Vuelta, Proceso, Siempre!, La Orquesta, Diorama de la Cultura, El Gallo Ilustrado, Sábado, unomásuno, La Jornada, Cambio y *Humboldt*. Becario del INBA en narrativa (1976-77). Traductor de Gregor von Rezzori, Arthur Schnitzler, Truman Capote, Georg Christoph, Hugo von Hofmannsthal y Graham Greene. Coautor de *El rock en silencio* (1980). Autor de los cuentos: *El mariscal de campo* (1978), *La noche navegable* (1980), *Albercas* (1985), *Tiempo transcurrido* (1985), *La alcoba dormida* (1992) y *La casa pierde* (1999); crónica: *Palmeras de la brisa rápida. Un viaje a Yucatán* (1989); novela: *El disparo de argón* (1994) y *Materia dispuesta* (1997); y libros para niños: *Las golosinas secretas* (1985), *El profesor Zíper y la fabulosa guitarra eléctrica* (1991, ganador del premio del International Board on Books for the Young al mejor libro para niños publicado en México), y *Autopista sanguijuela* (1998).

VILLORO, LUIS ♦ n. en Cataluña, España (1922). Su segundo apellido es Toranzo. Naturalizado mexicano. Médico cirujano (1944) y maestro y doctor en filosofía por la UNAM (1950), con estudios de posgrado en la Universidad de París y en la Ludwigsuniversitat de Munich (1952). En la UNAM fue profesor (1950-74), investigador (1971-74), secretario de la Rectoría (1961-62), coordinador del Colegio de Filosofía (1967-69), jefe de la División de Estudios Superiores de la Facultad de Filosofía y Letras (1970-72) y miembro de la Junta de Gobierno (1972-82). En la UAM ha sido profesor (1974-82), director de la División de Ciencias Sociales y Humanidades del plantel Iztapalapa (1974-78) y miembro de la Junta Directiva (1979-83). Embajador de México ante la UNESCO (1983-). Codirector de la revista *El Espectador*, director de la *Revista de la Universidad de México* y fudador y coeditor de *Crítica*. Autor de *El proceso ideológico de la revolución de independencia* (1953), *Los grandes momentos del indigenismo en México* (1959), *La crítica del positivismo básico a la metafísica* (1961), *Páginas filosóficas* (1962), *La idea y el ente en la filosofía de Descartes* (1963), *Estudios sobre Husserl* (1974), *Signos políticos* (1974), *Creer, saber, conocer* (1982), *El concepto de ideología* (1985) y *El poder y el valor, fundamentos de una ética política* (1998). Fue presidente de la Asociación Filosófica de México (1980-81). Pertenece a El Colegio Nacional. Premio Nacional de Ciencias y Artes (1986). Premio Universidad Nacional 1989.

Luis Villoro

VINAZCO ♦ Río de Veracruz. Nace en la sierra Madre Oriental, en las montañas de Huayacocotla de la sierra Madre Oriental, en el noroeste de la entidad. Corre de suroeste a noreste y recibe las aguas de los ríos Zacualpan, Texcatepec, Tlachichilco y Chiflón; en la llanura costera se une al Pantepec para formar el Tuxpan, al suroeste de la ciudad homónima.

VINORAMA ♦ Isla de Sinaloa, también llamada Güinorama, Guinoraba o Winorama. Se localiza en el golfo de California, muy próxima a la costa y frente a la bahía de Navachiste, al suroeste de Guasave y al sureste de Topolobampo. Forma un cordón con las islas Macapule, San Ignacio y San Juan. Mide 2,500 por 1,200 metros.

VINÓS SANTOS, RICARDO ♦ n. en España y m. en el DF (1888-1957). Doctor en ciencias por la Universidad Central de Madrid, posgraduado en las universidades de París, Roma y Berlín. Fue director-fundador de la Escuela de Orientación Profesional de Madrid, vocal del Consejo Nacional de Cultura, presidente de la Junta Central de Formación Profesional y vicepresidente de la Junta de Reorganización de la Enseñanza Secundaria y Profesional. Exiliado en México desde 1939, fundó y dirigió (1940-57) la Academia Hispano-Mexicana y colaboró en *España Peregrina*.

Ricardo Vinós Santos

VIÑAS LUNA, JOSÉ MOISÉS ♦ n. en el DF (1951). Estudió en la Facultad de Filosofía y Letras de la UNAM. Ha trabajado en la Cineteca de la UNAM (1981-85). Es jefe de información del Centro de Documentación e Investigación Fotográfica (1985-). Ha sido colaborador del *unomásuno* (1980-82), *Esto* (1983-84), *Revista Cine* (1983-) y *El Universal* (1985-). Autor de *Historia del cine mexicano* (1987).

VIOLANTE, CARLOS ♦ n. en Zinapécuaro, Mich., y m. cerca de Nueva Ciudad Guerrero, Tams. (1903-1953). Periodista. Inició su carrera como auxiliar en el diario *Excélsior*, que tiempo después lo envió a Nueva York a trabajar con Rodrigo de Llano. Regresó a México en 1923 e ingresó en la planta de redactores de *El Universal*, donde destacó como cronista parlamentario. Murió en un accidente de aviación.

VIQUEIRA, CARMEN ♦ n. en España (1923). Exiliada en México en 1939.

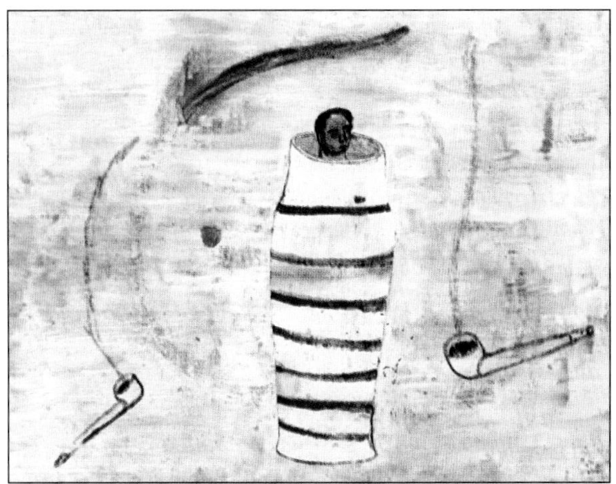

Sin título, encáustica sobre papel de Boris Viskin

Maestra en psicología por la UNAM (1951) y doctora en antropología por la Universidad Iberoamericana. Ha sido psicóloga del Internado Santa Isabel en Washington, profesora y jefa del Departamento de Antropología de la UIA (1977-) y colaboradora de la *Revista Española de Antropología*. Coautora de *Magia, brujería y homicidio*. Autora de *Hospitales para locos e "inocentes" en Hispanoamérica. Antecedentes españoles* y *Percepción y cultura* (1976).

VIQUEIRA LANDA, JACINTO ♦ n. en España (1921). Ingeniero mecánico electricista titulado en la UNAM (1951) y posgraduado en Francia (1961) y en Estados Unidos (1964). Ha sido ingeniero del Departamento de Estudios Especiales (1946-51) e ingeniero del Departamento de Construcción de la Compañía Mexicana de Luz y Fuerza Motriz (1952-63), superintendente A (1964-66) y jefe del Departamento de Ingeniería Mecánica y Eléctrica de la Facultad de Ingeniería de la UNAM, jefe de Ingeniería Eléctrica de la Compañía de Luz y Fuerza del Centro (1968-71), gerente general de Planeación y Programa de la Comisión Federal de Electricidad (1974-76), jefe del Departamento de Energía de la UAM-Azcapotzalco (1977-79) y coordinador de la carrera de ingeniero mecánico electricista de la UNAM (1979-). Colaborador de *Revista AMIME, Ingeniería, Revista Mexicana de Electricidad* y *Revista Técnica IEM*. Autor de *Análisis de las opciones energéticas de México* (1977).

Vitola

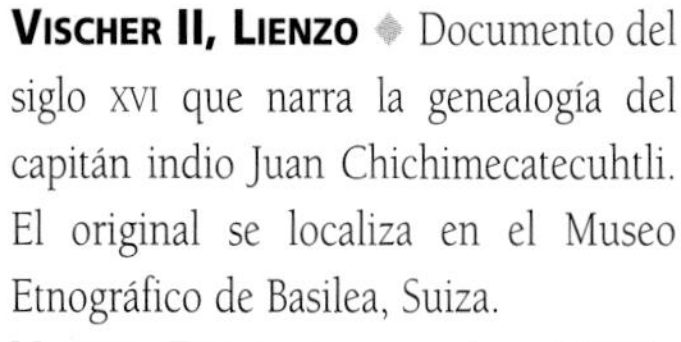

VISCHER II, LIENZO ♦ Documento del siglo XVI que narra la genealogía del capitán indio Juan Chichimecatecuhtli. El original se localiza en el Museo Etnográfico de Basilea, Suiza.

VISKIN, BORIS ♦ n. en el DF (1960). Pintor. Ha expuesto individualmente desde 1983 en la ciudad de México, Morelia, Guadalajara, Veracruz y Florencia; colectivamente en México, Monclova, Morelia, Aguascalientes, La Habana, Nueva York y Seattle. Premio Arte Joven del INBA en Aguascalientes (1988), Premio Salón de Pintura del INBA (1988) y mención honorífica en la Sección Bienal de Dibujo del INBA (1988).

VISTA HERMOSA ♦ Municipio de Michoacán situado en el noroeste del estado, al noroeste de Zamora y al suroeste de La Piedad, en los límites con Jalisco. Superficie: 200.46 km^2. Habitantes: 18,651, de los cuales 4,048 forman la población económicamente activa. Hablan alguna lengua indígena 20 personas mayores de cinco años.

VITAL FERNÁNDEZ, FRANCISCO ♦ n. en Ciudad Victoria y m. en Los Ébanos, Tams. (1802-1850). Militar. En 1829, durante la expedición de reconquista del español Isidro Barradas, defendió la barra de Tampico y mantuvo a salvo el puerto homónimo. Llegó al generalato en 1832. Fue gobernador de Tamaulipas (de diciembre de 1829 a enero de 1830; de agosto de 1831 a marzo de 1832; agosto de 1832 a marzo de 1833; de septiembre de 1833 a julio de 1834; de septiembre de 1834 a marzo de 1835; de abril a septiembre de 1835; septiembre de 1841 a junio de 1843; de noviembre de 1846 a septiembre de 1848). En 1847, ante el avance de los invasores estadounidenses, se vio obligado a desplazar su gobierno de Ciudad Victoria a Tula.

VITOLA ♦ n. en Canadá (1927). Su nombre es Fanny Kauffman Winner. Vivió en Cuba, donde se inició como cantante. Más tarde hizo carrera como comediante y vino a México. Se presentó en 1943 en el teatro Arbeu de la capital. En 1946 comenzó su trayectoria en el cine mexicano, en la cinta *Se acabaron las mujeres*. Al lado de *Tin Tan*, *Cantinflas*, *Schilinsky*, *Palillo*, Medel y de algunos otros cómicos, actuó en numerosas comedias de los años cuarenta, cincuenta y sesenta, entre las que destacan *El rey del barrio* (1949), *¡Ay amor, cómo me has puesto!* (1950), *Mi papá tuvo la culpa* (1952), *De ranchero a empresario* (1953), *El vizconde de Montecristo* (1954), *Club de señoritas* (1955), *La cigüeña distraída* (1964) y *Autopsia de un fantasma* (1966). Actuó también en teatro y televisión.

VIVAR Y BALDERRAMA, JUAN ♦ n. en la ciudad de México y m. en Chihuahua, Chih. (1800-1858). Médico y periodista. En 1830 la Secretaría de Guerra y Marina lo nombró director del Hospital Militar de Arizpe, Sonora, y fue también diputado local por esa circunscripción. Se trasladó en 1834 a Chihuahua, donde ejerció su profesión. En 1835 se inició como redactor de *El Noticioso de Chihuahua*, periódico oficial del gobierno de José Joaquín Calvo. Fue director del Hospital Militar de Chihuahua y del periódico *La Palanca* (1837), miembro del Consejo Superior de Salubridad de Chihuahua (1849), diputado local (1851 y 1853), miembro del triunvirato que ejerció el Ejecutivo chihuahuense (1853), magistrado del Supremo Tribunal de Justicia, jefe político y administrador de Tabacos en el Valle de Allende.

VIVERO Y VELASCO, RODRIGO DE ♦ n. en la ciudad de México y m. en Orizaba, Ver. (1564-1636). Sobrino del virrey Luis de Velasco, hijo. Fue corregidor de Cholula y gobernador de la Nueva Vizcaya hasta 1603, cuando entregó el poder a Francisco de Urdiñola. Durante su gobierno organizó varias expediciones para reprimir a los apaches y a los comanches. En 1608, Velasco lo designó gobernador interino de las Filipinas, cargo que desempeñó hasta 1609, cuando se embarcó de regreso a la Nueva España. Una tormenta hizo naufragar su nave y lo arrojó a las costas japonesas, donde fue recibido por el shogún, Ieyasu Tokugawa, como enviado oficial de España, lo que significó el primer vínculo diplomático de Japón con el exterior. En 1610, Tokugawa le facilitó el regreso a la Nueva España en compañía de 23 enviados, encabezados por Tanaka Shosuke o Jocuquendono, según algunos autores, lo que dio pie a Luis de Velasco para formalizar los lazos con el shogunato nipón. En 1620 se le nombró presidente de la Audiencia de Panamá.

Viveros Barradas, Francisca ♦ ☛ *Paquita la del Barrio.*

Vizarrón y Eguiarreta, Juan Antonio de ♦ n. en España y m. en la ciudad de México (¿1685?-1747). Sacerdote, fue designado arzobispo de México en 1730, cargo que asumió en 1731 y que desempeñó hasta su muerte. Asimismo, de 1734 a 1740 fue virrey de la Nueva España. Como arzobispo, en 1737 proclamó a la Virgen de Guadalupe como patrona de México y en 1746 la hizo patrona de la Nueva España. Durante su gestión virreinal confiscó los bienes del duque de Monteleone, descendiente de Hernán Cortés, por haberse involucrado en la guerra contra Felipe V; aumentó el número de presidios en el norte, temeroso por la vecindad de los colonos franceses; reprimió levantamientos indígenas en California y Guatemala y edificó la Casa de Moneda. En 1736 enfrentó la epidemia llamada del gran matlazáhuatl, que diezmó a la población indígena de la ciudad de México. Promovió la migración hacia los minerales de Arizona y ordenó la represión del levantamiento místico indígena de Agustín Ascuchul, en Sonora.

Vizcaíno, Rogelio ♦ n. en el DF (1949). Periodista e historiador. Su nombre completo es Felipe Rogelio Vizcaíno Álvarez. Estudió ciencias políticas en la UNAM. Profesor de la Escuela Nacional de Antropología e Historia (1975-83), donde fundó los talleres de historia del movimiento obrero. Ha sido investigador de la Dirección de Investigaciones Históricas del INAH (1983-85), director de *Unidad Proletaria* (1982-83) de la Coordinadora Minera del SNTMMRM, cofundador de *Información Obrera* (1983) y director de la revista *Encuentro de la Juventud* del Crea (1984-88). Colaborador de *Página Uno, Excélsior* y *Punto.* Coautor de *Cárdenas y la izquierda mexicana* (1972), *Historia y crónicas de la clase obrera en México* (1982), *El socialismo en un solo puerto* (1983) y *Memoria roja* (1983).

Vizcaíno, Sebastián ♦ Marino y explorador activo a fines del siglo XVI y principios del XVII. Realizó numerosos viajes entre la Nueva España y las Filipinas. En 1596 el virrey Gaspar de Zúñiga y Acevedo, por órdenes de Felipe III, le encomendó una expedición a California, en la que fundó el puerto de La Paz; desalentado por la aridez del terreno y la hostilidad de los indios regresó a la ciudad de México en 1597. Dos años después, Felipe III le encomendó otra expedición a California, destinada a localizar el llamado estrecho de Anián. Zarpó en 1602, recorrió la costa occidental de California desde el Cabo Blanco de San Sebastián hasta la actual ciudad de San Diego y fundó Monterrey, hoy Monterey. En 1603, al agotársele las provisiones, regresó a la metrópoli. El nuevo virrey, Juan de Mendoza y Luna, lo nombró alcalde mayor de Tehuantepec; sin embargo, Vizcaíno viajó a España para proponer a Felipe III la conquista de California, aun costeada por él, a lo que el soberano español se negó. Navegó por el Pacífico en busca de relaciones comerciales con Japón. Tras el accidente de Rodrigo de Vivero (☛), Vizcaíno fue nombrado primer embajador español y novohispano en Japón, país al que entró en 1611; el shogún aceptó establecer relaciones diplomáticas con España, pero se negó a admitir a los evangelizadores católicos. Realizó varios viajes de exploración por las costas japonesas. Regresó a la Nueva España en 1612. Escribió relaciones de todos sus viajes.

Vizcaíno Murray, Francisco ♦ n. en Guaymas, Son. (1935). Licenciado en comercio y administración pública por la UNAM y doctor por el IPN. Ha sido auditor general de la Secretaría de la Reforma Agraria, secretario y subdirector general del IMSS, subsecretario de la Secretaría de Salubridad y Asistencia y director del Instituto Nacional de Energía Nuclear y de Uramex. Autor de *Presencia de Uramex en el desarrollo de México, Aportación al estudio de las nuevas energías* y *La contaminación en México.*

Vizcaya Canales, Francisco ♦ n. en Monterrey, NL (1929). Licenciado en derecho por la Universidad de Nuevo León (1954), posgraduado en la UNAM (1965). Tomó cursos de banca central y política monetaria en el CEMLA (1966) y de alta dirección de empresa en el IPADE (1976). Ha sido subjefe y jefe del Departamento de Bancos y Moneda (1964-73), subdirector auxiliar de Crédito (1973-74), subdirector y director de Bancos, Seguros y Valores de la Secretaría de Hacienda (1978-82) y director general del Banco del Atlántico (1982-90). En 1989 fue elegido presidente de la Asociación Mexicana de Bancos.

Vlady ♦ n. en la URSS (1920). Nombre profesional del pintor Vladimir Kibalchich Rosakob. Hijo del escritor bolchevique Víctor Serge. Salió de la Unión Soviética en 1936. Expuso individualmente, por primera vez, en Bruselas, en 1937. Vino en 1942 y obtuvo la nacionalidad mexicana en 1949. Fue becado por el gobierno de Francia (1966) y por la Fundación Guggenheim (1968) para estudiar en Europa, donde trabajó en los talleres de Arístides Maillol, Víctor Brauner, Óscar Domín-

Juan Antonio Vizarrón y Eguiarreta

Francisco Vizcaíno Murray

Desierto que lleva el nombre del explorador Sebastián Vizcaíno

Foto: Fondo Editorial Grupo Azabache

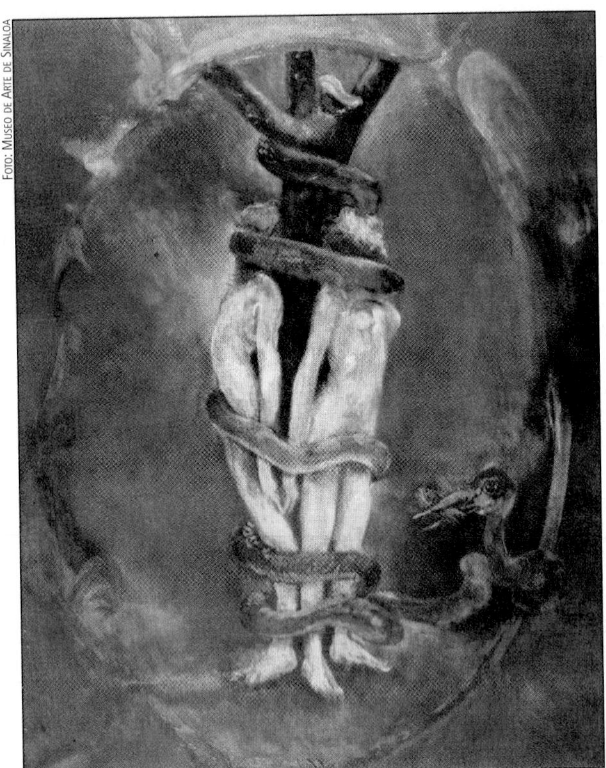

Adán y Eva en el Paraíso, obra de Vlady

Vlady

Verónica Volkow

guez, Wilfredo Lam, André Masson y Max Ernst. Hay obras suyas en el Museo de Arte Moderno, en el restaurante Carmel y en la Casa Koenin, de Cuernavaca. Ejecutó murales en el hotel Casino Hornos de Acapulco y en un edificio particular de la colonia Polanco. Decoró la biblioteca Miguel Lerdo de Tejada de la Secretaría de Hacienda, una de las mayores obras muralísticas de México. Ludwik Margules realizó la película *Cuaderno veneciano* (1978), sobre la obra homónima de Vlady. Ha colaborado con textos e ilustraciones en *La Jornada* y los suplementos *Sábado*, de *unomásuno*, y *El Búho*, de *Excélsior*. Autor de *Abrir los ojos para soñar* (prosas varias, 1998). Premio Anual de Dibujo (1971) y de Grabado (1972) del Salón de la Plástica Mexicana.

Vlady, Andrew ◆ n. en EUA (1943). Litógrafo. En Los Ángeles trabajó para Claus Oldenberg, Robert Rauschenberg, Roy Lichtenstein y Frank Stella en el taller Gemini GEL. Adquirió después el taller Ediciones Gráficas Kyron, de Nueva York. En 1972 fundó en México un taller de impresión, Ediciones Gráficas Kyron, en el que han trabajado Francisco Toledo, Rufino Tamayo, Leonora Carrington, Francisco Corzas, Francisco Zúñiga, Raúl Anguiano y José Luis Cuevas, entre otros artistas.

Volkow, Verónica ◆ n. en el DF (1955). Escritora. Licenciada en letras hispanoamericanas por la UNAM y maestra en literatura comparada por la Universidad de Columbia. Ha escrito catálogos para Arnold Belkin, Francisco Toledo, Christine Couture y Nicholas Sperakis. Colaboradora de *Cuadernos de Literatura, Versus, Vuelta, Revista de la Universidad de México, Revista Mexicana de Cultura, El Día, Sábado, Diálogos* y *El Zaguán*. Coautora de la *Antología de Michael Hamburger* (1990). Autora de *Antología de Elizabeth Bishop* (1987) y de *John Asbery. Antología en un espejo convexo*; poesía: *La Sibila de Cumas* (1974), *Litoral de tinta* (1979), *El inicio* (1983), *Los caminos* (1989), *La noche del pez* (1996) y *Arcanos* (1996); ensayo: *Graciela Iturbide, los disfraces* (1984) y *La mordedura de la risa. Ensayos sobre el pintor Francisco Toledo*; y del volumen de crónicas *Diario de Sudáfrica* (1988). Cofundadora del Comité Mexicano contra el *Apartheid* (1988). Obtuvo las becas Salvador Novo (1978-79), del Centro Mexicano de Escritores (1991-92) y del Fonca (1993-94). Pertenece al Sistema Nacional de Creadores de Arte (1996-).

Volpi, Jorge ◆ n. en el DF (1968). Su segundo apellido es Escalante. Licenciado en derecho, maestro en letras por la UNAM y doctor en filología hispánica por la Universidad de Salamanca. Fue coordinador de la Escuela Vida y Movimiento y jefe de redacción del suplemento *Instancia*, de *El Nacional*. Ha colaborado en *Punto, El Búho, Pauta, Letras Libres, Viceversa* y *Equis*. Coautor de *Tres bosquejos del mal* (1994). Autor de narrativa: *Pieza en forma de sonata* (1990); ensayo: *La imaginación y el poder* (1998); y las novelas: *A pesar del oscuro silencio* (1992), *Días de ira* (1994), *La paz de los sepulcros* (1995), *El temperamento melancólico* (1996), *Sanar tu piel amarga* (1997) y *En busca de Klingsor* (1999, Premio Biblioteca Breve otorgado por la editorial Seix Barral). Obtuvo las becas Salvador Novo (1988-89), del Centro Mexicano de Escritores (1991-92) y del Fonca para jóvenes creadores (1993-94). Premio *Plural* Latinoamericano de Ensayo por *El magisterio de Jorge Cuesta* (1991).

Vos, Jan de ◆ n. en Bélgica (1936). Historiador. Estableció su residencia en Chipas en 1973. Desde 1974 investiga la historia chiapaneca. Autor de *Viajes al desierto de la soledad. Cuando la selva lacandona aún era selva* (1988), *No queremos ser cristianos, Las rebeliones indígenas, La batalla del Sumidero, La guerra de las vírgenes, Bajaron tres piedras del cielo, San Cristóbal, ciudad colonial, Oro verde. La conquista de la selva lacandona por los madereros tabasqueños (1822-1949)* (1989), *La paz de Dios y del rey. La conquista de la selva lacandona (1525-1821)* (1989), *Fray Lorenzo de la nada*. Recibió el Premio Chiapas 1986 y el Premio Francisco Javier Clavijero 1987. Pertenece al Sistema Nacional de Investigadores (1988-). Mención honorífica como finalista en el Primer Concurso Nacional de Investigación Regional, por el trabajo inédito *Los enredos de Romensal* 1990.

Voz de México, La ◆ Diario publicado en la ciudad de México entre 1870 y 1909. De corte católico, fue contrincante de los diarios *El Siglo XIX* y *El Monitor Republicano* en la palestra política. Su fundador y primer director fue Rafael Gómez, a quien sucedieron Ignacio Aguilar y Marocho y Trinidad Sánchez Santos; en 1875 se transformó en vocero de la Sociedad Católica, aunque casi de inmediato fue reemplazado por *El Mensajero Católico*.

Voz de México, La ◆ Órgano del Partido Comunista Mexicano. Sustituyó a *El Machete*. El primer número apareció el 16 de septiembre de 1938. Fue diario en sus inicios y durante un breve periodo de los años cincuenta. Sus talleres fueron asaltados en varias ocasiones por la policía, entre otras, en 1954, el 26 de julio de 1968 y el mismo día de 1969. En 1958 el Comité Central retiró del cuerpo de redacción a Manuel Terrazas,

Gerardo Unzueta y José Montejano, lo que dio inicio a una larga lucha interna que terminó con la derrota de la dirección encabezada por Dionisio Encina. En febrero de 1968 fue detenido el director del periódico, Hugo Ponce de León. En abril de 1970 el PCM empezó a publicar *Oposición* y *La Voz de México* se convirtió en un irregular órgano interno hasta su extinción a mediados de los años setenta.

VUELTA ◆ Revista mensual de literatura, política y otros temas. Dirigida desde su fundación por Octavio Paz, el primer número apareció en diciembre de 1976, publicado por Amigos del Arte, A.C. En su directorio aparecían Alejandro Rossi, como director suplente; José de la Colina, Salvador Elizondo, Juan García Ponce, el mismo Rossi, Kazuya Sakai, Tomás Segovia y Gabriel Zaid como miembros del Consejo de Redacción, todos ellos colaboradores. De la Colina era el secretario de redacción, Abel Quezada Rueda el director artístico y Celia García Terrés la gerenta. Publicó textos de Borges, Adolfo Bioy Casares, Ramón Xirau, José Emilio Pacheco, Hugo Margáin, Enrique Krauze, Javier Sologuren, Juan Acha, Alberto Ruy-Sánchez, Milan Kundera, Guillermo Sheridan, Susan Sontag, Luis Villoro, Tomás Segovia, Esther Seligson, Rafael Segovia, Italo Calvino, Gastón García Cantú y Ulalume González de León. Su primer editorial, obra de Paz, decía: "*Vuelta*, como su nombre lo dice, no es un comienzo sino un retorno. En octubre de 1971 apareció una revista, *Plural*; navegó contra viento y marea durante cerca de cinco años; al llegar al número 58, desapareció; hoy reaparece, con otro nombre. ¿Es la misma? Sí y no. El consejo de redacción, los colaboradores y los propósitos son los mismos. (.) *Vuelta* quiere decir regreso al punto de partida y, asimismo, mudanza, cambio. ¿Dos sentidos contradictorios? Más bien complementarios: dos aspectos de la misma realidad, como la noche y el día. (.) En 1971 el director de *Excélsior*, Julio Scherer, nos propuso la publicación de una revista literaria, en el sentido amplio de la palabra literatura: invención verbal y reflexión sobre esa invención, creación de otros mundos y crítica de este mundo. Aceptamos con una condición: libertad. Scherer cumplió como los buenos y jamás nos pidió suprimir una línea o agregar una coma. Actitud ejemplar, sobre todo si se recuerda que más de una vez los puntos de vista de *Plural* no coincidieron con los de *Excélsior*. Es sabido lo que ocurrió después: un conflicto en la cooperativa que edita *Excélsior* provocó la salida del grupo que dirigía el periódico. Nosotros, todos los que hacíamos la revista, sin vacilar un instante, decidimos irnos también." En agosto de 1989 la revista era publicada por Editorial Vuelta, S.A. de C.V., empresa de la que Paz era presidente, Enrique Krauze secretario, José Carral Escalante tesorero y Gabriel Zaid, Ulalume González de León, José de la Colina, Julieta Campos, Alejandro Rossi y Salvador Elizondo vocales. Figuraban en el directorio, después de Paz, Enrique Krauze como subdirector y Aurelio Asiáin como secretario de redacción. En el Consejo de Colaboración aparecían algunos de los mencionados y Natalio R. Botana, Guillermo Cabrera Infante, Juan Gustavo Cobo Borda, Pablo Antonio Cuadra, Haroldo de Campos, Jorge Edwards, Jaime Gil de Biedma, Pere Gimferrer, Alberto Girri, Juan Goytisolo, Roberto Juarroz, Juan Liscano, Eduardo Lizalde, Enrique Molina, Álvaro Mutis, Silvina Ocampo, Olga Orozco, José Miguel Oviedo, Gonzalo Rojas, Severo Sarduy, Fernando Savater, Guillermo Sucre, José Miguel Ullán y Mario Vargas Llosa. La Mesa de Redacción estaba integrada por Fabienne Bradu, Jorge Brash, Adolfo Castañón, Christopher Domínguez, José María Espinasa, Julio Hubard, Eduardo Milán y Guillermo Sheridan. El editor responsable era el mismo Krauze, quien más tarde fue sustituido en el cargo por Asiáin. En 1993 *Vuelta* recibió el Premio Príncipe de Asturias de Comunicación y Humanidades. En septiembre de 1998, poco después de la muerte de Octavio Paz, apareció el número 261 y último de la revista.

VUELTAS, DE LAS ◆ Río de Oaxaca que nace en la vertiente occidental de la sierra de Ixtlán, al nor-noroeste de la capital estatal; corre hacia el nor-noroeste y al suroeste de la sierra de Juárez se une al río Grande de Ixtlán para formar el Grande de Quiotepec, en la cuenca del Alto Papaloapan.

VUSKOVIC, PEDRO ◆ n. en Chile y m. en el DF (1924-1993). Investigador y catedrático en la UNAM, así como del Centro de Investigación y Docencia Económica (CIDE). Ex ministro de Economía del gobierno de Salvador Allende y consultor internacional de la CEPAL. Desde 1974, tras el golpe militar al gobierno de Allende, se exilió en la ciudad de México. Fue vicepresidente ejecutivo de la Corporación de Fomento de Chile, director del Instituto de Economía de la universidad de su país, funcionario internacional de la CEPAL, director del área de América Latina en el CIDE y colaborador del Centro de Investigaciones Interdisciplinarias de la UNAM. Publicó investigaciones en antologías y libros especializados. Autor de *Pobreza y desigualdad en América Latina* (1994, libro póstumo). Fundador de la Casa de Chile en México.

FOTO: EIKÓN

Jorge Volpi

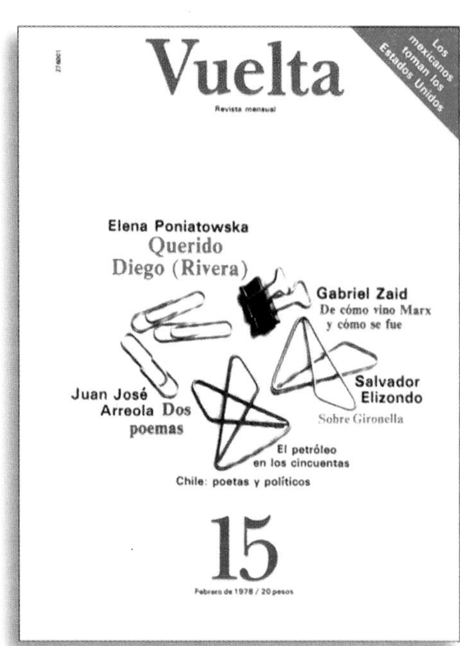

Revista *Vuelta*

Fernando Wagner

WAGNER, FERNANDO ◆ n. en la ciudad de México y m. cerca de Cuernavaca, Mor. (1905-1973). Actor y director de teatro. Estudió en Alemania, con Max Reinhardt. Volvió a México en 1930. Profesor de la escuela de teatro del INBA. Fue director de teatro experimental de la UNAM, fundador del Pan American Theatre, director de teleteatros y telenovelas desde 1951 y director de escena de las óperas *La flauta mágica, Fausto, Mefistófeles* y *La traviata*. Murió en un accidente automovilístico. De sus montajes teatrales destacan *Cada quien su vida*, de Luis G. Basurto; *Anna Christi*, de Eugene O'Neill; *Judith*, de Cristian Friedrich Hebbel; y *Los de abajo*, de Mariano Azuela. Actuó, entre otras, en las películas: *La familia Dressel* (1935), *La perla* (1945), *El señor fotógrafo* (1952), *Los tres Villalobos* (1954) y *Flor de canela* (1957). Coautor, con Emilio Carballido y Luisa Baurer, de la obra de teatro *Las lámparas del cielo y de la tierra*. Autor del libro *Técnica teatral*.

WAITE, CHARLES B. ◆ n. en EUA (1861-?). Fotógrafo. Trabajó en Los Ángeles en una compañía fotográfica y abrió su propio estudio en 1983. Colaboró en la revista *Land of Sunshine* y publicó un libro con imágenes citadinas. Emigró a México en 1896 y reunió un acervo de imágenes paisajísticas sobre el país, destinadas a guías turísticas, trabajando lo mismo para Porfirio Díaz que para científicos, arqueólogos y compañías ferroviarias. Colaboró en diversos periódicos mexicanos a finales del siglo XIX y principios del XX. Retrató los diversos estratos de la sociedad mexicana de la época. Logró hacer una considerable fortuna y adquirió numerosas propiedades. Al inicio de la Revolución Mexicana los indígenas de Magdalena Etla quemaron su rancho y decapitaron a su hermano en 1911, por lo que su familia regresó a EUA. Sus últimas fotos datan de 1913, año en el que se pierde su rastro. En el Archivo General de la Nación se conservan 3,500 de sus fotos.

WALDECK, JUAN FEDERICO MAXIMILIANO ◆ n. y m. en Checoslovaquia (1766-1875). Pintor, dibujante y grabador. Era ciudadano francés. Estudió pintura clásica en París. Fue soldado y viajó por Chile y Guatemala, donde dibujó algunas ruinas prehispánicas. Llegó a México en 1825, como ingeniero de las minas de Tlalpujahua y un año después se instaló en la ciudad de México, donde se asoció para presentar espectáculos "fantasmagóricos" y donde fue profesor de dibujo y pintura. En 1827 ejecutó las litografías de la Colección de antigüedades mexicanas que existen en el Museo Nacional e hizo la invitación a las fiestas de aniversario de la independencia. Entre 1834 y 1836, con patrocinio gubernamental, estuvo en Yucatán dedicado al "examen y la reproducción rigurosa de las ruinas de la América Central". Estuvo en Uxmal y Palenque. Como enviara informes y objetos arqueológicos a Inglaterra, el gobierno le retiró su apoyo y le confiscó dibujos y manuscritos. No obstante, publicó en París *Voyage Pintoresque et Archéologique dans la Province d'Yucatan (Amérique Central) Pendant les Années 1834 et 1836* (1838). Ilustró el libro *Monuments Anciens du Mexique. Palenque et Autres Ruines*, de Charles E. Brasseur (1866).

Yucateca, litografía de Juan Federico Maximiliano Waldeck

WALDEEN ◆ n. en EUA y m. en Cuernavaca, Mor. (1913-1993). Nombre profesional de la bailarina y coreógrafa Waldeen von Falkestein. Estudió ballet clásico en la Escuela de Ballet Ruso Kosloff de Los Ángeles, danza moderna en la escuela centroeuropea con Benjamin Zemach, y tomó cursos con Harold Kreutzberg. Se presentó en Canadá, Japón y Estados Unidos con el grupo de Michio Ito, con el que llegó a México en 1934, donde fue invitada por el gobierno para crear una escuela de danza moderna. En 1940 dirigió el Ballet de Bellas Artes y estrenó el ballet *La Coronela* con música de Revueltas, con el que inició, junto con la recién llegada Ana Sokolow, el movimiento mexicano de danza moderna. Con el Ballet de Waldeen se presentó en el Palacio de Bellas Artes (1942-45) y ese último año creó su primer ballet masivo, *Siembra,* con más de 5,000 integrantes, para apoyar una campaña de alfabetización. Trabajó en el Coreographers Workshop de Nueva York (1946-48). Con el Ballet Moderno realizó giras por milpas, ingenios y astilleros. Se naturalizó mexicana en 1958. Fundó y dirigió la Escuela de Danza Moderna en Cuba (1962-66). De nuevo en México, abrió el Centro de Danza y Artes Escénicas (1966). Autora de las coreografías *Helena la traicionera, Sinfonía concertante, Tiempo entre dos tiempos* (1969), *El espacio y el tiempo* (1970) y *Coro de primavera*, entre otras, así como un poema coreográfico sobre Carmen Serdán (1989). Autora de la antología *La danza. Imagen de creación continua* (1982). En 1988 recibió el Premio José Limón, del INBA y el gobierno de Sinaloa.

WALKER, WILLIAM ♦ n. en EUA y m. en Honduras (1824-1860). Filibustero. Estudió derecho y medicina en Europa. Vivió en San Francisco, donde colaboró en el *San Francisco Herald* con artículos antimexicanos. En 1853 organizó un grupo de mercenarios con el que desembarcó en el sur de la península de Baja California. Tomó La Paz y se proclamó presidente de una supuesta República de Sonora y Sinaloa, que incluía el territorio bajacaliforniano. En los primeros días de noviembre fue desalojado por fuerzas mexicanas y se embarcó a Ensenada, que ocupó con ayuda de otro grupo de mercenarios comandado por Gary Frazer. A principios de 1854 emprendió la marcha a Sonora, pero el viaje por el desierto le llevó más de tres meses y sólo en abril pudo cruzar el delta del río Colorado. Fue hostilizado por milicianos sonorenses, hasta que a principios de mayo, protegido por una columna del ejército estadounidense, regresó a su país. A principios de 1855 se alió con los liberales de Nicaragua, que entonces estaban en guerra contra los conservadores, y en junio desembarcó en El Realejo. En julio tomó Granada, la capital conservadora y durante los días siguientes realizó varias matanzas que diezmaron a la población local, derrocó al gobierno liberal de Patricio Rivas y se autonombró presidente de Nicaragua. Reestableció la esclavitud y convirtió el inglés en idioma oficial. En 1857 fue derrocado por los ejércitos de Honduras, Costa Rica y Nicaragua y salvado por fuerzas de la marina estadounidense. Cuatro años después integró una nueva fuerza e invadió Honduras, pero fue derrotado y fusilado.

WALKER LÓPEZ, ALBERTO ♦ n. en el DF (1947). Arquitecto egresado de la UNAM (1965). Miembro del PRI, en el que fue miembro del Consejo Político Nacional (1997-99). Ha sido coordinador técnico de la Comisión Constructora y de Ingeniería Sanitaria de la SSA (1968-71), director del Centro de Estudios de Desarrollo Regional y Urbano de la Secretaría de la Presidencia (1976), coordinador general del Programa Coplamar-SAHOP (1979-83), director general de Promoción y Fomento Portuario de la SCT (1983-88) y del Centro para el Desarrollo de la Infraestructura en Salud de la SSA (1989-90), coordinador del programa Por una Escuela Digna, de la Sedesol (1990-93), vocal ejecutivo del Centro Nacional de Desarrollo Municipal (1994-95), subdirector de Evaluación Técnica del Infonavit (1995-98) y coordinador del Fondo Nacional de Apoyo a Empresas Sociales, de la Sedesol (1998-99).

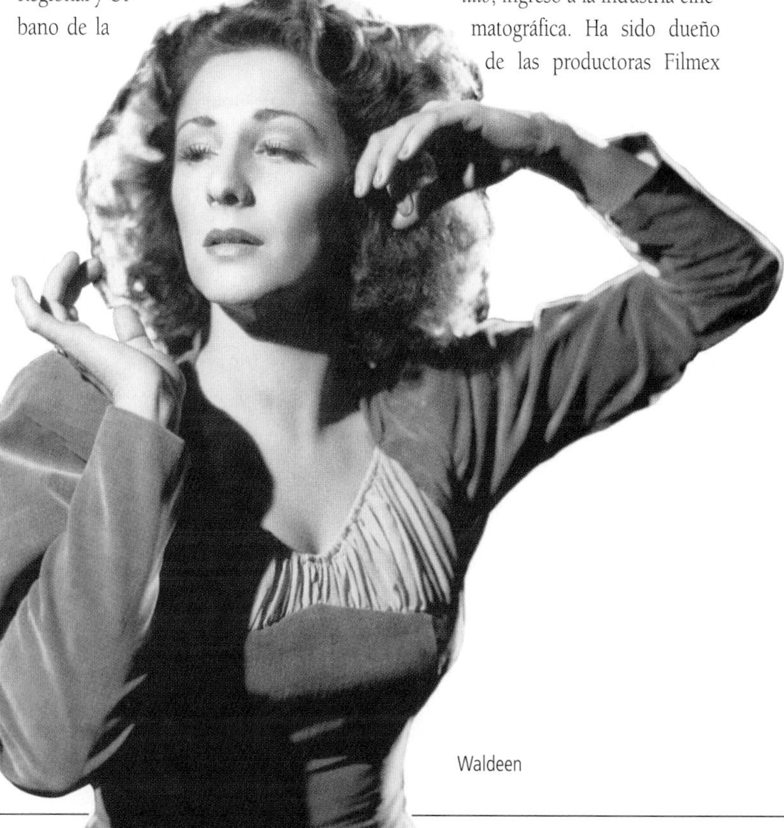

Waldeen

WALLERSTEIN, EUGENIA ♦ ☛ *Meyer Wallerstein, Eugenia.*

WALLERSTEIN, GREGORIO ♦ n. en la ciudad de México (1913). Productor cinematográfico. Contador público titulado en la Universidad Nacional de México y alumno fundador de la Escuela Nacional de Economía de la UNAM. Participó en el movimiento estudiantil de 1929, que consiguió la autonomía universitaria. Fue auditor del Hotel Reforma. En 1941, con la película, *Lo que el viento trajo* (1941), de José Benavides *jr.*, protagonizada por Jesús Martínez, *Palillo*, ingresó a la industria cinematográfica. Ha sido dueño de las productoras Filmex

William Walker

FOTO: ÉPOCA

Gregorio Wallerstein

(1941-64) y Cima Films (1964-), para las cuales trabajaron, entre otros, Antonio Aguilar, Julio Alemán, Arturo de Córdova, María Félix, Vicente Fernández, Pedro Infante, Libertad Lamarque, Jorge Negrete, Joaquín Pardavé, Silvia Pinal y Jorge Rivero. Fue vicepresidente de Películas Nacionales.

Wallerstein, Marcela ◆ n. en el DF (1971). Actriz. Nieta del anterior. Pasó su juventud en Venezuela. Hizo estudios de actuación en EUA. Vive en España, donde ha participado en las obras *Solo o en compañía de otros, La viuda del capitán Estrada* y *El amor sí tiene cura*, en la película *Le compro a su chica* y en el capítulo "Como por arte de magia" de la serie televisiva *Crónicas urbanas*.

Walls Armijo, Armando ◆ n. en el DF (1931). Químico titulado en la UNAM (1952). Doctor en ciencias, especializado en química, por la Universidad de Harvard (1957), donde estudió becado por la Fundación Rockefeller (1954-55). Ha sido profesor, secretario (1966-70), investigador y jefe de departamento del Instituto de Química de la UNAM (1970-79). En 1968 obtuvo el Premio de Ciencias de la Academia de la Investigación Científica y, en 1979, el Premio Nacional de Química Andrés Manuel del Río, de la Sociedad Química de México.

Walsh, Edmundo A. ◆ n. y m. en EUA (1885-1956). Sacerdote ordenado en 1916. Perteneció a la Compañía de Jesús. En la Universidad de Georgetown fue profesor, fundador y director de la Escuela del Servicio Exterior y vicepresidente (1924-56). Representante de la Iglesia Católica en la Unión Soviética (1922-23), en 1929 participó, como enviado del Papa, en las negociaciones entre el gobierno mexicano y la jerarquía eclesiástica que pusieron fin al levantamiento de los cristeros.

Ward, Henry George ◆ n. y ¿m.? en Inglaterra (?-?). Llegó a México en 1823, como miembro de una comisión británica encargada de estudiar las condiciones económicas y políticas del país, con el fin de decidir el otorgamiento de un eventual empréstito del gobierno inglés. Dos años después, en mayo de 1825, fue nombrado encargado de negocios de la Gran Bretaña en México, cargo en el que se mantuvo hasta 1827. Durante su gestión diplomática cultivó buenas relaciones con el presidente Guadalupe Victoria y con el secretario de Relaciones Exteriores, Lucas Alamán, y se dedicó a contrarrestar la política del embajador de Estados Unidos, Joel R. Poinsett, por lo que impulsó las logias masónicas escocesas. Al igual que Poinsett, sin embargo, se opuso a que el obispo de Puebla, Antonio Pérez Martínez, se integrara al gabinete. Más tarde logró que Manuel de Mier y Terán dirigiera la Comisión de Límites entre México y Estados Unidos, con el afán de frenar el expansionismo de ese país; después de estudiar las potencialidades mineras de México, logró la firma de un Tratado de Comercio entre ambas naciones. A su regreso a Inglaterra publicó *México en 1827* (1828).

Obra de Henry George Ward

Warman, Arturo ◆ n. en el DF (1937). Antropólogo. Licenciado en etnología por la ENAH (1968). Militó en el Movimiento de Acción Popular y en el Partido Socialista Unificado de México. Director del Instituto Nacional Indigenista (1989-94); secretario de Agricultura y Ganadería (1994-95) y de la Reforma Agraria (1995-99) en el gabinete de Ernesto Zedillo. Coautor de *Los productores de maíz en México: restricciones y alternativas* y *El desafío Mexicano* (1982), y autor de *La danza de moros y cristianos (Un estudio de aculturación)* e *Historia de un bastardo. Maíz y capitalismo* (1988). Premio al Mérito Fray Matías de Córdova 1991 del gobierno de Chiapas.

Foto: Época

Arturo Warman

Warman, Nathán ◆ n. en el DF (1930). Hermano del anterior. Arquitecto egresado de la UNAM (1950) y licenciado en economía por la misma universidad (1955); realizó estudios de posgrado en las universidades británicas de Manchester (1961) y Glasgow (1963) y fue profesor de esta última (1963-71). Ha sido economista (1955-57), subjefe del Departamento de Aranceles (1957-59) y jefe del Departamento de Estudios Especiales de la Dirección de Estudios Hacendarios de la Secretaría de Hacienda (1959-60), coordinador de investigaciones de la oficina mexicana de la Comisión Económica para América Latina (1971-74), subdirector de Crédito de Financiera Nacional Azucarera (1974-75) y subsecretario de Fomento Industrial de la Secretaría del Patrimonio (1976-82).

Wasserstrom, Dunia ◆ n. en Rusia y m. en el DF (1919-1991). Escritora. Vivió gran parte de su vida en Francia, donde estudió lenguas vivas en la Universidad de La Sorbona de París. Debido a su actividad política fue deportada. Pasó tres años en el campo de concentración de Aushwitz, donde fue ocupada como traductora y del que logró escapar. En 1964 testificó en el proceso de Aushwitz en Frankfurt. Desde 1959 y hasta su muerte radicó en México. Fundó el Museo del Holocausto en el Centro Comunitario Nidje de Jerusalén, Israel, y la Unión de Sobrevivientes de Campos de Concentración y Partisanos de la Segunda Guerra Mundial. Narró sus experiencias en el campo de concentración en el libro *Nunca jamás* (1975), que en el momento de su muerte llevaba 15 ediciones. Fue condecorada con la Cruz de Francia.

Watty Urquidi, Ricardo ♦ n. en EUA (1938). Sacerdote ordenado en 1968. Es miembro de la Congregación de los Misioneros del Espíritu Santo. Estudió en el Seminario Superior de Estudios Eclesiásticos de Tlalpan. Ha sido profesor en el Seminario Menor de Alajuela (Costa Rica), formador en el Seminario Menor de Quetzaltenango (Guatemala), párroco de San Marcos Mexicaltzingo (1971-75), vicesuperior de la Provincia de México de los Misioneros del Espíritu Santo (1974-80), obispo auxiliar de México (1980-89), vicario espiscopal de la arquidiócesis de México (1980-89) y primer obispo de Nuevo Laredo (1989-).

Weckmann Muñoz, Luis ♦ n. en Lerdo, Dgo. (1923). Licenciado y maestro en historia (1944), doctor en letras (1949) y licenciado en derecho por la UNAM (1950). Hizo estudios de posgrado en la Universidad de California en Berkeley (1946-48). Es doctor en derecho internacional por la Universidad de París (1951-52). Ha sido encargado de negocios y secretario de las embajadas mexicanas de Checoslovaquia y Francia (1952), delegado alterno de México ante la Asamblea General de la ONU (1952-53), director general de Asuntos Internacionales de la SEP, secretario general ejecutivo del Consejo Nacional de México para la UNESCO, presidente del Comité de Acción Cultural de la OEA, consejero de la embajada mexicana en París (1965-67), embajador en Israel (1967-69), Austria (1969-73), la RFA (1973-74), Irán (1976-79), Italia (1981-86) y Bélgica (1986-); representante mexicano ante el Organismo Internacional de Energía Atómica (1969-73), subsecretario general y enviado especial de la ONU a Irán e Irak (1974) y Chipre (1974-75), representante de México ante la ONU (1979-80) y representante de México ante la Comunidad Europea (1986-). Autor, entre otras obras, de *La sociedad feudal. Esencia y supervivencias* (1944), *El pensamiento político medieval y una nueva base para el derecho internacional* (1950), *Panorama de la cultura medieval* (1960) y *Las relaciones franco-mexicanas 1823-1885* (3 t., 1956-72).

Weinberg Marchevsky, Liliana Irene ♦ n. en Argentina (1956). Vino en 1980 y adquirió la ciudadanía mexicana. Es profesora e investigadora del Centro de Estudios Latinoamericanos de la UNAM. Fue editora de *Cuadernos Americanos* (1985-96). Premio de Ensayo Latinoamericano Lya Kostakowsky 1996 por *Entre el paraíso y el infierno.*

Weingarsthofer, Federico ♦ n. en el DF (1946). Cineasta. Realizó estudios de física y matemáticas en el IPN y de ingeniería en la UNAM. Tomó cursos de fotografía y publicidad en el Columbia College Panamericano. Es egresado del Centro Universitario de Estudios Cinematográficos. En 1968 participó como uno de los fotógrafos del documental *El grito*. Fue fotógrafo de las películas *Derrota* (1973) y *La víspera* (1982). Dirigió los largometrajes *Quizá siempre sí me muera* (1970), *Caminando pasos, caminando* (1975) y *Bajo el mismo sol y sobre la misma tierra* (1979) y los mediometrajes *Cuando la niebla levante* (1980) y *Semilla del cuarto sol* (1982).

Weintlaner, Roberto Julio ♦ n. en Austria y m. en el DF (1883-1968). Etnólogo. Se tituló como ingeniero metalúrgico en 1908 y al año siguiente emigró a Estados Unidos, donde comenzó a interesarse en la etnología. Llegó a México en 1922. Trabajó en el Museo Nacional de Arqueología y realizó varios estudios entre los mazahuas, los mazatecos, los mixes y los pames. Fundador de la Sociedad Alemana Mexicanista y del Consejo de Lenguas Indígenas y colaborador del Instituto Lingüístico de Verano. Perteneció a la Sociedad Antropológica Americana. Colaboró en las revistas *México Antiguo*, *Anales del Museo Nacional de Antropología e Historia y Etnografía*. Autor de *Un calendario de los zapotecas del sur* (1956).

Weisz Carrington, Pablo ♦ n. en el DF (1947). Pintor y escultor. Hijo de Leonora Carrington. Expone desde 1971 en México y Estados Unidos. Es autor de la serie de 98 piezas *Los siete pecados capitales* y de 30 esculturas en bronce de pequeño formato a las que pertenecen *La cantante calva* y *El hombre hueco*. Ejecutó también las *Cartas del Tarot*.

Foto: Christa Cowrie

Liliana Weinberg

Foto: Javier Hinojosa

La soberbia, obra de Pablo Weisz Carrington

Welter, Ariadne ♦ n. y m. en el DF (1930-1998). Actriz. Su segundo apellido era Borhauer. Comenzó su carrera en 1954. Entre otras, participó en las películas *Sombra verde* y *La rebelión de los colgados*. En el teatro lo hizo en

FOTO: COLECCIÓN PECIME

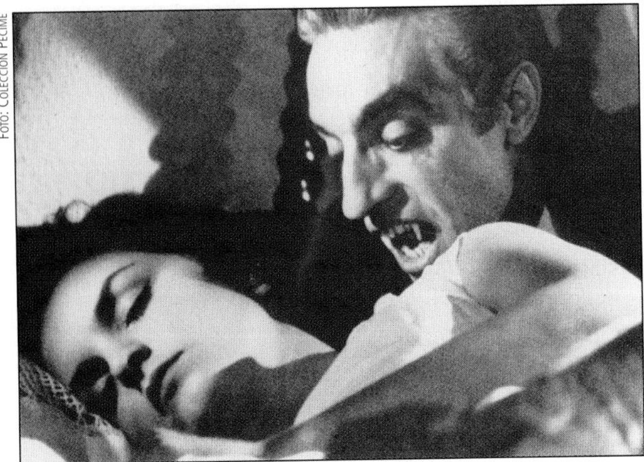

Ariadne Welter y Germán Robles en *El vampiro*

Equus, Una ciudad para vivir, La criada malcriada y *No me manden flores*. Asimismo, actuó en las telenovelas *María la del barrio, Mi querida Isabel* y *Sin ti*. Premio Menorah como mejor actriz por *El boxeador* (1959) y Premio El Heraldo como mejor actriz por *Tiempo de Lobos* (1982).

WERNER WAINFELD, MARTÍN ◆ n. en el DF (1963). Licenciado en economía por el ITAM (1986) y doctor en economía con especialización en finanzas internacionales por la Universidad de Yale. Profesor del ITAM (1991-94). Ha sido asesor del subsecretario de Hacienda (1985-87) y del secretario de Programación y Presupuesto (1991), coordinador de asesores del subsecretario (1992), director de Deuda Pública (1992-94) y director general de Banca de Desarrollo de la Secretaría de Hacienda (1994); subsecretario de Comunicaciones y Desarrollo de la SCT (1994-95); director general de Crédito Público (1995-96) y subsecretario de la SHCP (1997-). Autor de *La medición del déficit operacional del sector público* (1987), *Indización e inflación* (1990), *Dealing with a High Public Debt: The Mexican Experience* (1991), *La solvencia del sector público: el caso de México* (1993) y *La banca de desarrollo. 1988-1994. Balance y perspectivas* (1994). Segundo lugar del Premio Nacional de Economía 1992 de Banamex.

WESTHEIM, PAUL ◆ n. en Alemania y m. en el DF (1885-1963). Historiador. Durante 17 años dirigió en Berlín la revista *Das Kunstblatt*, donde impulsó la corriente expresionista alemana, hasta que en 1933, perseguido por los nazis, se exilió en París. Al año siguiente fue privado de su nacionalidad por el gobierno hitleriano. En 1940 se alistó en el ejército francés para combatir la invasión alemana, pero huyó luego de la rendición de Petain. Llegó a México en 1941. Colaborador de la *Enciclopedia judaica castellana* (1947-51). Escribió en *México en la Cultura*, suplemento de *Novedades*. Autor de *El pensamiento artístico moderno* (1945), *Arte antiguo de México* (1950), *La calavera* (1953), *El grabado en madera* (1954), *La escultura del México antiguo* (1956), *Ideas fundamentales del arte prehispánico en México* (1957) y *La cerámica del México antiguo. Fenómeno artístico* (1962). Luego de su muerte aparecieron *Obras maestras del México antiguo* y *Escultura y cerámica del México antiguo* (1980). Fue miembro del Pen Club Internacional.

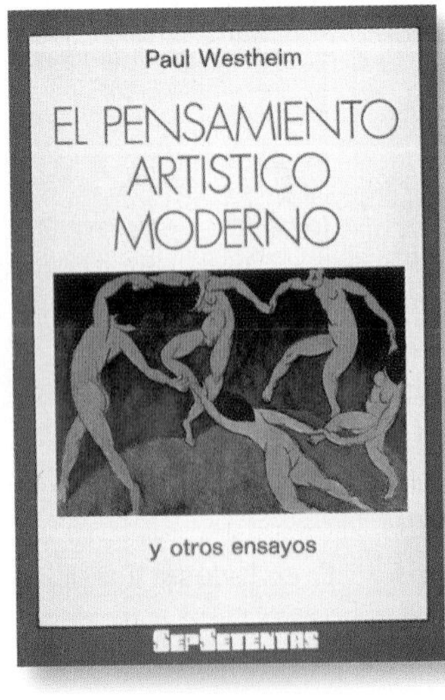

Obras de Paul Westheim

WESTON, EDWARD ◆ n. y m. en EUA (1886-1958). Fotógrafo. Se inició hacia 1902. Trabajó para la Marshall Field Company de Chicago, para los ferrocarriles de California y fue fotógrafo comercial. En 1911 abrió su propio estudio en Glendale, California, y poco después, con sus innovaciones, el uso de la luz natural sobre todo, revolucionó el arte fotográfico estadounidense. Expuso en San Francisco en 1915 y en Nueva York en 1922. Llegó a Manzanillo en julio de 1923, acompañado por Tina Modotti, entonces su mujer, modelo y asistente. Se instaló en Tacubaya y después vivió en la calle de Lucerna, en la colonia Juárez. Entró en contacto con Diego Rivera, David Alfaro Siqueiros, Jean Charlot y José Clemente Orozco, entre otros. Influyó en Manuel Álvarez Bravo y en el desarrollo de la fotografía mexicana. Trabajó en San Cristóbal Ecatepec, Teotihuacán, Tepotzotlán, Guadalajara y la ciudad de México. Volvió a Estados Unidos en 1926 y se estableció en San Francisco. En 1931, con Ansel Admas y Willard Van Dyke, fundó el Grupo F.64. Durante la segunda guerra mundial formó parte de la fuerza aérea de Estados Unidos. En 1946 se presentó una retrospectiva de su obra en el Museo de Arte Moderno de Nueva York y en 1950 expuso en París y Londres. Varias de las fotos que tomó en México están entre las más importantes de su producción. En 1937 se convirtió en el primer fotógrafo becado por la Fundación Guggenheim.

WHALEY, ARTURO ◆ n. en Teloloapan, Gro. (1948). Ingeniero en comunicaciones y electrónica titulado en el IPN (1969) y físico egresado de la UNAM (1971-73), de la que fue profesor. Militó en el Movimiento de Acción Popular (1981) y en el Partido Socialista Unificado de México (1981-87), a cuyo comité central perteneció. Ha sido investigador del Programa de Reactores de la Comisión Nacional de Energía Nuclear, en el Instituto Nacional de Energía Nuclear y en el Instituto Nacional de Investigaciones Nucleares (1970-85); secretario general del Sindicato Unico de Trabajadores de la Industria Nuclear (1972-85) y diputado federal (1985-88). Desde 1997 es miembro del CEN del Partido Democracia Social.

WILLIAMS, CAMILO JUAN ◆ n. en Inglaterra y m. en el DF (?-1922). Llegó a México en 1899, donde fundó, el 7 de enero, el Colegio Williams, en la calle

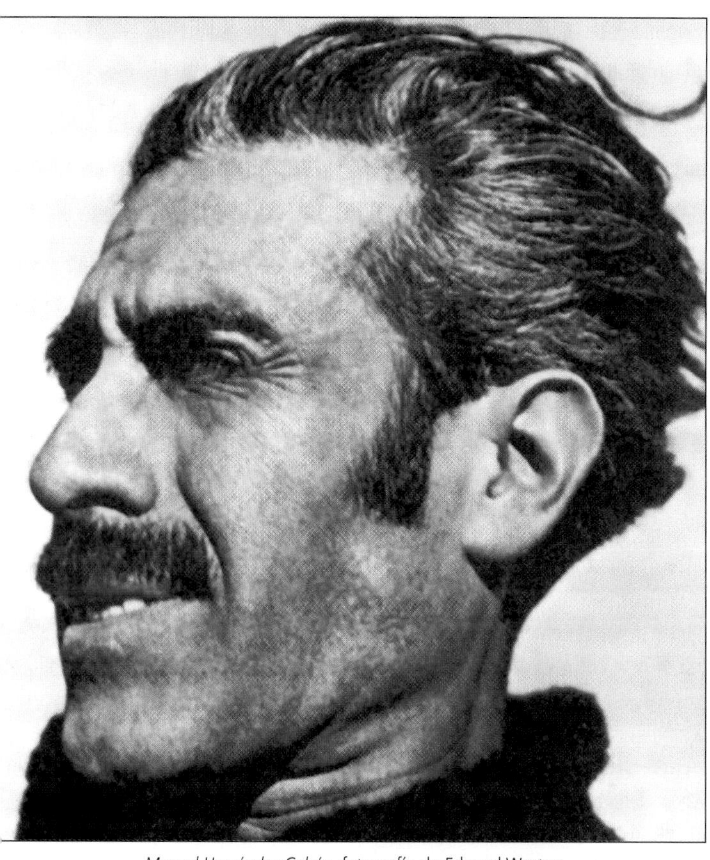

Manuel Hernández Galván, fotografía de Edward Weston

de la Mariscala de la ciudad de México, con un grupo de profesores ingleses que impartían la enseñanza en ese idioma y que incorporaban la enseñanza artística y deportiva en el internado y el cultivo de hortalizas para la alimentación propia.

Williams Rani, Ana ◆ n. y m. en el DF (1902-1992). Hija del anterior. Estudió pedagogía en Los Ángeles, EUA (1910-22). Desde 1928 fue directora del Colegio Williams de Niñas y Señoritas.

Wilmot Mason, Juan Jorge ◆ n. en Monterrey, NL (1928). Ceramista. Realizó estudios de cerámica en la Academia de San Carlos y en el Instituto Franco-Italiano de París (1953) y de diseño en la Escuela de Oficios en Basilea, Suiza (1953-57). Realizó sus trabajos iniciales durante un recorrido por la selva lacandona (1949). Diseñador gráfico de Empaques de Cartón Titán (1952). En Europa fue aprendiz en el taller de Richard Bampi, fue a Alemania para estudiar diseño gráfico y, en Gustavberg, Suecia, trabajó con el ceramista Limberg Koge Londgren. Fue profesor de la UIA (1957). En 1958 fundó su taller y una escuela de cerámica en Tonalá, Jalisco. Ha expuesto individual o colectivamente desde 1972 en México, Francia y Canadá. Medalla de Oro en tres concursos de diseño del Instituto Mexicano de Comercio Exterior, en la Segunda Bienal de Ceramique D'Art de Vallauris y en la Feria Internacional de Artesanías de Munich. Galardón Presidencial del IV Premio Nacional de la Cerámica de Tlaquepaque 1982 en Jalisco. Premio Nacional de Ciencias y Artes 1995, en la categoría de Artes y Tradiciones Populares.

Wilson, Henry Lane ◆ n. y m. en EUA (1857-1932). Diplomático. Estudió derecho. Ingresó al servicio exterior estadounidense en 1897. Ministro de Estados Unidos en Chile (1897-1904) y en Bélgica (1905-09). En 1910 fue nombrado embajador de Estados Unidos en México, a donde llegó en el mismo año. A mediados de 1912, a causa de un impuesto de tres centavos que el gobierno intentó imponer a cada barril de petróleo exportado, dijo que México debía "librarse a la mayor brevedad" del presidente Francisco I. Madero y envió varias comunicaciones a su gobierno en las que presentaba al país al borde de la anarquía. El tono tan notoriamente hostil de los mensajes hizo que incluso el presidente William H. Taft dudara de su veracidad. Desde los primeros días de febrero de 1913, participó en las conspiraciones que desencadenaron la Decena Trágica y el derrocamiento de Madero. En la sede de la representación estadounidense, el 18 de febrero, reunió a Victoriano Huerta y a Félix Díaz, quienes firmaron el Pacto de la Embajada (☛), en el que se establecían los términos del golpe de Estado que implicó el asesinato de Madero y Pino Suárez y llevó al poder a Victoriano Huerta, cuyo reconocimiento gestionó infructuosamente ante Washington. En julio fue destituido por el nuevo presidente estadounidense, Woodrow Wilson. Autor de *Diplomatic Episodes in Mexico, Belgium and Chile* (1927).

Wimer, Javier ◆ n. en el DF (1933). Doctor en derecho por la Universidad de París (1958). En el PRI fue miembro de las comisiones de Relaciones Internacionales (1981) y de la Nacional de Ideología (1983), así como del Consejo Consultivo del IEPES (1986-87). Fundador y codirector de la revista *Medio Siglo* (1952-54), director de la revista *El Libro y el Pueblo* (1959-63), asesor de la Presidencia (1959-64, 1970-76 y 1984-88), agregado cultural de las embajadas en Costa Rica, Argentina y Uruguay (1966-70), director general de Consejo Nacional de Cultura y Recreación de los Trabajadores (1974-76), coordinador general de Educación Audiovisual de la SEP (1976-78), director de la revista *Nueva Política* (1977-81), director general del Centro Latinoamericano de Estudios Políticos (1977-81), director de Espiral Editores (1978-81), director general de Archivo, Biblioteca y Publicaciones de la SRE (1979-81), embajador especial en Francia, Polonia y la URSS (1980-81), embajador en Yugoslavia y Albania (1981-82), subsecretario de

Adrián Woll

Gobernación (1982-84), director general de la Comisión Nacional de los Libros de Texto Gratuito (1984-92), delegado ante el Comité de Derechos Económicos, Sociales y Culturales de la ONU (1987-96), consejero del Comité Editorial de Derecho del FCE (1989-92), miembro del Consejo Editorial (1991-94) y asesor de la presidencia del Conaculta (1992-94). Autor de *Juicio crítico de la revolución mexicana* (1955) y *Sor Juana Inés de la Cruz* (1973). Becario (1959-60) e integrante del Consejo Consultivo del Centro Mexicano de Escritores (1996-).

Wionczek, Miguel S. ◆ n. en Polonia y m. en el DF (1919-1988). Economista titulado en la Universidad de Varsovia. Llegó a México después de la segunda guerra mundial. Profesor de El Colegio de México. Fue director de información económica del Centro de Estudios Monetarios Latinoamericanos (1958-70), codirector del *Journal of Common Market Studies* de Oxford, miembro de la delegación mexicana que participó en la redacción de la Carta de los Derechos y Deberes Económicos de los Estados (1973-74), director adjunto del Conacyt (1974-76), asesor de la ONU, miembro de la Comisión Puswash, director de la colección Entre la Guerra y la Paz del Fondo de Cultura Económica y coordinador del Programa de Energéticos de El Colegio de México. Colaboró en el diario *Excélsior*. Autor de *El nacionalismo mexicano y la inversión extranjera* (1968), *Economic Coperation in Latin America, Africa and Asia* (1969) y *El primer y el tercer mundo: confrontaciones* (1974).

Witt Greene, Andrés de ◆ n. en Villahermosa, Tab. (1921). Médico cirujano titulado en la UNAM (1946) especializado en pediatría en la Universidad de Nueva York (1949) y maestro en salud pública por la Johns Hopkins University de Washington (1959). Profesor de la UNAM, de la Escuela de Administración del Hospital para Graduados de la SSA y de la Escuela de Enfermería del ISSSTE. Ha sido jefe del Departamento de Protección Materno-Infantil (1946) y director de la Policlínica Infantil Antonio Márquez de la Cruz Blanca Neutral (1953-55), subjefe del Departamento de Asistencia Materno-Infantil de la SSA (1953-54), jefe del Departamento de Asistencia Materno-Infantil (1955-58), jefe de la División de Pediatría (1961-70), subdirector médico (1964-65) y director del Hospital 20 de Noviembre del ISSSTE (1971-72); subdirector general médico del ISSSTE (1972-76 y 1982-84), jefe del Departamento de Servicios Médicos de la CFE (1976-80), director general de Higiene Escolar (1980-82) y director general de Regulación de los Servicios de Salud de la SSA (1984-88). Autor de *La salud pública en México, su problemática y alternativas de solución* (1982).

José Woldenberg

Woldenberg, José ◆ n. en Monterrey, NL (1952). Licenciado en sociología (1975) y maestro en estudios latinoamericanos por la UNAM (1987), de la que ha sido profesor y en la que realizó estudios de doctorado en ciencia política. Ha sido miembro fundador (1974) y funcionario del Sindicato de Personal Académico de la UNAM (1976-77) y del Sindicato de Trabajadores de la UNAM (1977-78). Cofundador y miembro del Consejo Nacional del MAP (1981); cofundador e integrante del comité central del PSUM (1981-87), miembro fundador (1987), integrante del Consejo Nacional (1987) y del Comité Ejecutivo del PMS (1988) y miembro del PRD (1989-91). Presidió el Instituto de Estudios para la Transición Democrática (1989-94). Consejero ciudadano (1994-96) y consejero presidente del Consejo General del Instituto Federal Electoral (1996-). Ha sido colaborador de *La Cultura en México, unomásuno* (1979-83), *La Jornada* (1984-96), *Etcétera*, *Nexos* y otras publicaciones. Coautor de *La desigualdad en México* (1984), *La sucesión presidencial en 1988* (1987) y *La reforma electoral de 1996. Una descripción general* (1997), entre otras obras. Autor de *Antecedentes del sindicalismo* (1983), *Revuelta y Congreso en la UNAM*, *Historia documental del SPAUNAM* (1989), *Las ausencias presentes* (novela, 1992), *Violencia y política* (1995), *Francisco Zarco* (antología, 1996) y *Memoria de la izquierda* (1998). Es miembro del Sistema Nacional de Investigadores.

Wolf, Gregorio ◆ n. en EUA y m. en la hacienda de Guanímaro, Gto. (?-1818). Insurgente. Formó parte de la expedición internacionalista de Francisco Javier Mina, que desembarcó en la costa tamaulipeca en 1817. Murió en combate y fue decapitado. Por órdenes de Anastasio Bustamante, su cabeza se expuso en Irapuato.

Wolfe, Bertram D. ◆ n. en EUA (1896-?). Periodista y escritor. Militó en el Partido Comunista de Estados Unidos. Llegó a México a principios de los años veinte, como profesor de la Escuela Nacional Preparatoria, y en 1922 se incorporó al Partido Comunista Mexicano. Fue secretario de prensa del comité central y en 1924 delegado al IV Congreso de la Internacional Comunista (☛). Colaboró en *El Machete* y dirigió *El Libertador*, órgano de la Liga Antiimperialista de las Américas. Desde finales de 1924 colaboró con la Confederación Ferrocarrilera y a mediados de 1925 fue elegido consejero del comité de huelga, por lo que en junio de ese año, luego de reprimido el movimiento obrero, fue expulsado del país. En julio de 1928, sin embargo, formó parte de la delegación mexicana que asistió al VI Congreso de la Komintern. Convertido al trotskismo, en los años cuarenta se unió a la Cuarta Internacional. Volvió a México en los sesenta. Realizó estudios de literatura latinoamericana en la Universidad de Columbia. Colaboró en *The Nation, Liberator, The Communist* y *The Daily Workwer*. Autor de *La fabulosa vida de Diego Rivera* (1939), *A Life in Two Centuries, Strange Communists I Have Known* y *Three Who Made a Revolution*.

WOLL, ADRIÁN ◆ n. y m. en Francia (1795-1875). Militar. Llegó a México en 1817, en la expedición internacionalista de Francisco Javier Mina y perteneció a su estado mayor. A la derrota de este caudillo se estableció en Tampico. Cuatro años después, en 1821, se adhirió al Plan de Iguala. En ese año se naturalizó mexicano. En 1832 se levantó en armas en contra del gobierno de Anastasio Bustamante y en noviembre tomó Colima. Tres años después fue ascendido a general de división y en 1836 formó parte del ejército con el que Santa Anna intentó impedir la independencia de Texas. Fue apresado por los texanos poco después de la batalla de San Jacinto. Más tarde fue comandante militar de Tamaulipas y en septiembre de 1842 combatió nuevamente en Texas y tomó San Antonio, pero se vio obligado a retirarse. Luchó contra los estadounidenses durante la guerra de 1847 y luego se trasladó a Francia. Volvió en 1853, llamado por Santa Anna, y fue gobernador y comandante militar de Tamaulipas (del 2 de mayo de 1853 al 28 de enero de 1855). Al triunfo de la revolución de Ayutla regresó a Francia, donde vivió hasta 1858, cuando se incorporó al ejército conservador de Jalisco, durante la guerra de los Tres Años. Volvió a exiliarse luego de la victoria liberal. En 1862 llegó por tercera vez a México, pero un año después viajó de nuevo a Europa, como miembro de la comisiión de conservadores que en octubre de 1863 ofreció a Maximiliano de Habsburgo el trono de México. Combatió contra los republicanos hasta 1867, cuando regresó definitivamente a su país.

WOLPERT BARRAZA, ENRIQUE ◆ n. en Culiacán, Sin. (1939). Médico cirujano por la UNAM (1962) con especialidad en medicina interna (1966) y gastroenterología (1967) por el Instituto Nacional de Nutrición y esta última también por la Mayo Graduate School of Medicine de la Universidad de Minnesotta, EUA (1969). Profesor de la UNAM. Pertenece al PRI desde 1983. Ha sido médico jefe del servicio clínico, jefe del departamento de gastroenterología y de la Clínica del Hígado (1971-88) del Instituto Nacional de la Nutrición y subsecretario de Servicios de Salud de la SSA (1988-94). Autor de *Temas selectos de hepatología* (1982) y *Enfermedades del hígado y de las vías biliares* (1982). Presidente de la Asociación Mexicana de Gastroenterología (1984). Premio Nacional de Cirugía de la Academia Nacional de Medicina (1973) y Premio Alejandro Celis de la Academia Nacional de Medicina (1976).

WOMACK, JOHN ◆ n. en EUA (1937). Historiador. Doctor en historia por la Universidad de Harvard (1965), de la que es profesor (1968-). Ha colaborado en *La Cultura en México, Sábado, La Jornada Semanal* y otras publicaciones. En 1977 tradujo *La cristiada*, de Jean Meyer. Es autor de *Emiliano Zapata y la revolución en Morelos* (1965) y *Emiliano Zapata y la Revolución Mexicana* (1969).

WONG, ÓSCAR ◆ n. en Tonalá, Chis. (1948). Poeta. Estudió letras hispánicas en la UNAM. Fue subsecretario de Cultura y Recreación del gobierno de Chiapas (1982-84), redactor y reportero de *Excélsior* y *El Nacional*, coordinador de ediciones especiales de *Siempre!* y articulista de *La Jornada*. Colaborador de revistas y suplementos culturales. En 1983 realizó la antología *Nueva poesía de Chiapas* (1986). Autor de ensayo: *Eso que llamamos poesía* (1974), *La salvación y la ira. Nueva poesía mexicana* (1986), *La pugna sagrada. Comunicación y poesía* (1997); relato: *La edad de las mariposas* (1990); y poesía: *Si te das al viento* (1978), *Fragmentaciones* (1979), *En un lugar del mundo* (1981), *He brotado raíces* (1982), *Yo soy el mar* (1986), *Enardecida luz* (1992), *Vocación de espuma* (1993), *A pesar de los escombros* (1994), *Ritual de ausencias* (1995) y *Espejo a la deriva* (1996), entre otras obras. Becario del INBA-Fonapas (1978-79) y del Centro Mexicano de Escritores (1985-86). Ha recibido los premios Puerto Vallarta y Sahuayo (1986), Ramón López Velarde de Poesía (1988), Rosario Castellanos de Cuento (1989), de los Juegos Florales de Cunduacán, Tabasco (1997), y de los Juegos Florales Anita Pompa de Trujillo, Sonora (1998).

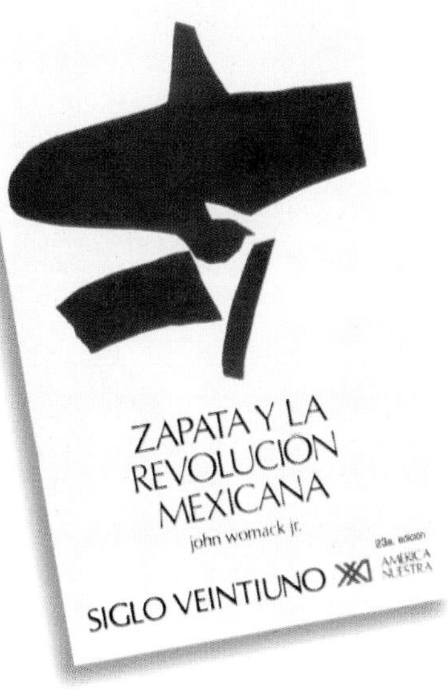

Libro escrito por Jonh Womack

Benjamín Wong Castañeda

WONG CASTAÑEDA, BENJAMÍN ◆ n. en Concepción del Oro, Zac. (1934). Periodista. Inició su carrera profesional a mediados de los años cincuenta en *El Sol de San Luis*. Más tarde participó en la fundación de *El Sol del Norte*, de Saltillo, y *El Sol de México*, de la capital de la República, del que fue reportero durante 20 años. Ha sido director general de Organización Editorial Mexicana (1977), director fundador del semanario *Punto* (1982-87 y 1988-), subdirector general del diario *El Universal* (1986) y consejero encargado de los asuntos políticos y de prensa de la embajada mexicana en China (1987-88).

WONG URREA, ROBERTO ◆ n. en Sinaloa (1950). Ingeniero civil por la UNAM (1969-74). Pertenece al PRI desde

Jaime Wooldrich

Paloma Wooldrich

1970, en el que ha sido delegado estatal en Michoacán, Nuevo León, Morelos y Veracruz (1973-75) y coordinador de Estudios de Perspectiva Internacional del IEPES (1989). Ha sido asesor de la SARH (1973), coordinador del Programa Nacional de Capacitación Técnica Económica de la Secretaría de la Presidencia (1974-76), jefe de asesores en el ISSSTE (1977-78), jefe de la Unidad de Coordinación Sectorial (1979-81), coordinador del Programa Internacional de Apoyo a Centroamérica de la SRE (1987-88) y, en la Secretaría de Gobernación, asesor del secretario (1989-90), director del Registro Nacional de Electores (1990), del IFE (1991) y del Registro Nacional de Población e Identificación Personal (1991-94).

Woog, Edgar ◆ n. en Suiza (1898-?). Estudió en Basilea y Hamburgo. Militó en la Juventud Socialdemócrata Suiza y en el Partido Socialdemócrata Alemán (1917). Vino con su familia a México, donde su padre estableció una joyería. Aquí usó el pseudónimo de Alfred Stirner. Se incorporó al Partido Comunista Mexicano y en agosto de 1920, con Rafael Carrillo, Rosendo Gómez Lorenzo y José C. Valadés, fundó la Federación de Jóvenes Comunistas. Dos años después, en noviembre de 1922, formó parte de la delegación mexicana al cuarto Congreso de la Internacional Comunista. Miembro del Comité Ejecutivo de la Internacional (1922-24) y de su comisión Internacional de Control (1924-27). Detenido en España en 1931 fue deportado a México, de donde partió a la Unión Soviética. Fue secretario general del Partido Suizo del Trabajo (comunista).

Wooldrich, Jaime ◆ n. en Oaxaca, Oax., y m. en Naucalpan, Méx. (1918-1986). Médico cirujano titulado en la UNAM (1940-46), especializado en urología en el Hospital General de México (1947-48). Becado, hizo estudios en el Instituto Nacional de Cancerología (1949-50). Profesor de la UNAM y del Centro México Nacional. Fue médico de la Secretaría de Agricultura y Fomento (1947-48); médico (1947-86), jefe de servicio, consultor técnico y jefe de la Unidad de Urología del Hospital General (1965-86); y jefe de la Unidad de Urología del Instituto Nacional de Cancerología (1950-58). Tradujo el capítulo sobre las enfermedades renales de *Medicina interna*, de T.R. Harrison (1964). Autor de *Urología* (1960) y *Breve introducción a la nefrología* (1960). En 1968 ingresó en la Academia Nacional de Medicina, de la que fue tesorero (1971-72), secretario general (1975), vicepresidente (1977) y presidente (1978). Perteneció a la Sociedad Mexicana de Urología (1949), a la Sociedad Médica del Hospital General (1952), a la Asociación Costarricense de Urología (1961), al Colegio de Médicos Cirujanos de la República de Costa Rica (1961), a la Sociedad Ecuatoriana de Urología (1962), a la Societé Internationale D'Urologie (1964) y al Consejo Mexicano de Urología (1970). Miembro fundador de la Sociedad Médica del Instituto Nacional de Cancerología (1961), de la Sociedad Mexicana de Estudios Oncológicos (1961) y de la Sociedad Mexicana de Urología (1962).

Woolrich, Paloma ◆ n. en el DF (1953). Actriz. Estudió actuación en la Escuela de Arte Dramático del INBA, con Sergio Bustamante, con el grupo Roy Hart, con Julio Castillo en el Núcleo de Estudios Teatrales y de danza contemporánea en el Carnegie Hall de Nueva York. Perteneció al grupo Sombras Blancas de Julio Castillo. Ha participado en las obras *Tres cuentos de autores latinoamericanos* (1968), *La última flor* (1970), *La excepción y la regla* de Brecht (1970), *Yo* de Maiakovsky (1970), *El espejo encantado* de Salvador Novo (1973), *Tierra* de Oceransky, *Antropos* de Cummings (1975), *Frankenstein* (1977), *Gipsy* (1977), *El contrario Luzbel* (1982), *Sueño de una noche de verano* (1984), *Yourcenar o cada quien su Marguerite* (1989), *De algún tiempo a esta parte* (1996) y otras puestas en escena con Jesusa Rodríguez en El Hábito (1991-93). Participó en las películas *Los años duros* (1970), *Entre violetas* (1974), *Alucarda* (1974), *México, México ra ra ra* (1975). También participó en series de televisión. Becaria del Fonca (1994-95).

Woolrich Bejarano, Manuel Alberto ◆ n. en Huixtla, Chis. (1913). Historiador. Ha sido responsable de las bibliotecas del Banco Nacional de Comercio Exterior, la Sociedad Mexicana de Geografía y Estadística, el Instituto de Biología de la UNAM, el Museo de la Ciudad de México y el Centro de Estudios de Historia de México-Condumex. Autor de *Efemérides históricas y biográficas chiapanecas* (1930), *La obra santiaguista en Chiapas* (1945) *El istmo de Tehuantepec* (1945), *Biobibliografía del doctor Nicolás León* (1946) y *Bibliografía sobre Belice* (1958).

Wörner Baz, Marysole ◆ n. en el DF (1936). Pintora y escultora. Estudió en París, becada por el Instituto Francés para América Latina (1957). Expuso por primera vez en 1955, en la Galería Baz-Fisher de San Miguel de Allende. Hay obras suyas en los museos de Arte Moderno de México y Tel Aviv, en el de Arte de Birmingham y en el Centro de Arte de Texas. Ha expuesto en Canadá, Colombia, Estados Unidos, Francia y Venezuela.

Wright, Burnis Wild Bill ◆ n. en EUA (1925-?). Beisbolista. Bateador ambidiestro, era jardinero central. Se inició en las ligas negras estadunidenses, pero como en aquel país las ligas mayores estaban cerradas a los negros, vino a México. Jugó en los *Diablos Rojos* del México y con los Gallos de Santa Rosa de la Liga Mexicana desde 1940, circuito en el que bateó arriba de .300 en nueve temporadas consecutivas y fue campeón de bateo en 1942 y 1943. Su promedio global fue de .355 y dio 966 hits. Ingresó al Salón de la Fama de Monterrey en 1981.

Wright, Chalky ◆ n. en Durango, Dgo., y m. en EUA (¿?-1957). Se inició en el boxeo en 1927. Fue campeón mundial de peso pluma en 1941, título que perdió al año siguiente ante Willie Pep. Su marca profesional fue de 148 triunfos, 39 derrotas y 16 empates.

Wright de Kleinhans, Laureana ◆ n. en Taxco, Gro., y m. en la ciudad de México (1846-1896). Periodista y escritora. En 1865 publicó algunos poemas en el periódico liberal *El Estudio*.

Laureana Wright de Kleinhans

León Felipe en su estudio, acrílico sobre masonite de Marysole Wörner Baz

Fue socia honoraria de la Sociedad Netzahualcóyotl (1869) y del Liceo Altamirano de Oaxaca (1885). Perteneció a la Sociedad Científica, Artística y Literaria El Porvenir (1872) y al Liceo Hidalgo (1873). Hacia 1884 comenzó a publicar en *El Diario del Hogar*, pero sus ataques a la política represiva del presidente Manuel González estuvieron a punto de costarle la expulsión de México, pues fue acusada de extranjera. Dirigió *Violetas del Anáhuac* (1887-89), publicación en la que defendió el sufragio femenino y la igualdad de derechos de ambos sexos. Colaboró en *El Federalista*. Autora de *La emancipación de la mujer por medio del estudio* (1891) y *Educación errónea de la mujer y medios prácticos para corregirla* (1892). Luego de su muerte aparecieron sus *Mujeres notables mexicanas* (1910).

Wybo Alfaro, Luis ◆ n. en el DF (1935). Diplomático. Ingeniero civil titulado en la UNAM (1955) y licenciado en relaciones internacionales por la UNAM (1958). Profesor de la UNAM y del Instituto Matías Romero de Estudios Diplomáticos. Ingresó al servicio exterior mexicano en 1959. Ha sido canciller en el consulado mexicano en Montreal (1959-63), vicecónsul (1963-66) y cónsul en Londres (1966-71); subdirector general del Servicio Consular (1971-76), cónsul general en Hamburgo (1976-77), director general de Protocolo (1977-78), director general de Asuntos Consulares (1978-80), director general de Protección (1980-81), embajador en Rumania (1981-86), en Kenia concurrente en Tanzania y Zimbabwe (1986-89), director general de Fronteras de la SRE (1989-94) y embajador en China (1997-). Autor de *Terminología consular* (1980).

Ilustración de Javier Guadarrama

Xalpatláhuac, Guerrero

Xalapa ◆ ☛ *Jalapa*.

Xalatlaco ◆ ☛ *Jalatlaco*.

Xalisco ◆ Municipio de Nayarit contiguo a Tepic, cercano a Jalisco. Superficie: 290.6 km². Habitantes: 34,595, de los cuales 7,671 forman la población económicamente activa. Hablan alguna lengua indígena 162 personas mayores de cinco años (náhuatl 54 y tlapaneco 40). Se llamó Jalisco.

Xaloztoc ◆ Municipio de Tlaxcala situado en la porción centro-oriental del estado y contiguo a Apizaco. Superficie: 58.10 km². Habitantes: 15,490, de los cuales 3,351 forman la población económicamente activa. Hablan alguna lengua indígena 50 personas mayores de cinco años (náhuatl 25). La cabecera se llama Xaloztoc, pero antes fue conocida como San Cosme Xaloztox. A mediados del siglo XX le fue segregada una porción de territorio en el que se creó el municipio de Santa María Tocatlán.

Xalpatláhuac ◆ Municipio de Guerrero situado en el oriente del estado, al este de Chilpancingo y al noroeste de Ometepec. Superficie: 393.60 km². Habitantes: 3,353, de los cuales 1,301 forman la población económicamente activa. Hablan alguna lengua indígena 8,189 personas (mixteco 4,771 y náhuatl 3,418). Indígenas monolingües: 2,217.

Xaltocan ◆ Municipio de Tlaxcala situado al norte de la capital estatal y al oeste de Apizaco. Superficie: 84.90 km². Habitantes: 6,911, de los cuales 1,898 forman la población económicamente activa. Hablan alguna lengua indígena 16 personas mayores de cinco años. En la jurisdicción se cultivan plantas medicinales y resinosas. A mediados del siglo XX se le quitó una parte del territorio para crear el municipio de Domingo Arenas.

Xaman Ek ◆ Deidad maya de los viajeros, en especial de los comerciantes, que se asociaba con Chac, el dios de la lluvia. Se le representaba en los códices con una gran nariz y unas marcas negras en su tocado; su glifo, una cabeza excesivamente estilizada, semeja la representación de un mono.

Xaltocan, Tlaxcala

Xaratanga ◆ Deidad purépecha, diosa madre y patrona de las siembras y de los comestibles, probablemente contraparte femenina del dios Curicaueri, cuyo nombre significa "La que se deja ver en lo alto" o "La que se deja ver en todas partes". Su animal simbólico era, tal vez, la serpiente y se le consagraban el maíz y la plata, así como a Curicaueri se le ofrendaba el oro. Su culto se centraba en Jarácuaro, ciudad en la que tenía cinco templos, uno por cada una de las direcciones del universo.

Xayacatlán de Bravo ◆ Municipio de Puebla situado en el sur del estado y contiguo a Acatlán. Superficie: 70.16 km². Habitantes: 1,419, de los cuales 144 forman la población económicamente activa. Hablan alguna lengua indígena 819 personas (mixteco 818).

Xel-Ha ◆ Zona arqueológica del municipio de Cozumel, situada al norte

Foto: Fondo Editorial Grupo Azabache

Xel-Ha, Quintana Roo

de Tulum. La principal construcción es una pirámide monumental llamada Castillo del Meco, que consta de cinco cuerpos escalonados.

XICO ◆ Municipio de Veracruz situado en la porción occidental del estado, al suroeste de Jalapa y al sureste del Cofre de Perote. Superficie: 176.85 km². Habitantes: 27,258, de los cuales 7,301 forman la población económicamente activa. Hablan alguna lengua indígena 78 personas mayores de cinco años (náhuatl 55). La cabecera se llamaba San Francisco Xicochimalco Viejo, que quiere decir "Pueblo de ardaga". También se le conoce como Xico Viejo y cerca de ahí se encuentra el sitio arqueológico del mismo nombre, sobre la meseta del cerro de Yoticpac, que cuenta con un montículo circular rodeado de pequeñas elevaciones. En la zona se localiza el Citlaltépetl o Pico de Orizaba y el Naucampatépetl o Cerro de las Cuatro Esquinas.

XICOHTÉNCATL ◆ Municipio de Tlaxcala situado al sur de la capital del estado y al suroeste de Huamantla, en los límites con Puebla. Superficie: 27 km². Habitantes: 19,901, de los cuales 4,550 forman la población económicamente activa. Hablan alguna lengua indígena 352 personas (náhuatl 329 y totonaco 23). En 1943 le fue quitada una porción de territorio en la que se erigió el municipio de José María Morelos. La cabecera es Papalotla de Xicohténcatl.

XICOHTZINCO ◆ Municipio de Tlaxcala situado al sur de la capital estatal y al noroeste de Vicente Guerrero, en los límites con Puebla. Superficie: 16.2 km². Habitantes: 9,485, de los cuales 2,251 forman la población económicamente activa. Hablan alguna lengua indígena 31 personas mayores de cinco años (náhuatl 21). Fue erigido en 1941 en territorio que perteneció a Zacatelco, su cabecera municipal es Xicohtzingo.

XICOTÉNCATL ◆ Municipio de Tamaulipas situado al sur-sureste de Ciudad Victoria y al noroeste de Tampico. Superficie: 1,267.46 km². Habitantes: 23, 023, de los cuales 6,270 forman la población económicamente activa. Hablan alguna lengua indígena 34 personas mayores de cinco años (náhuatl 14). En la jurisdicción se halla uno de los ingenios azucareros más grandes del país, construido entre 1946 y 1948, así como una fábrica de celulosa que procesa bagazo de caña.

Foto: Fondo Editorial Grupo Azabache

Hacienda de Santa Águeda en Xicohtzinco, Tlaxcala

XICOTÉNCATL ◆ n. y m. en Tlaxcala, Tlax. (?-¿1522?). Es llamado *el Viejo*, para distinguirlo de su hijo, Xicoténcatl Axayacatzin. Su nombre, en español, sería "Habitante de Xicotenco". A principios del siglo XVI era uno de los cuatro gobernantes del señorío de Tlaxcala. En 1519 se opuso a que la nación tlaxcalteca se aliara con Hernán Cortés, pero acató la voluntad de la mayoría luego de la derrota de las fuerzas tlaxcaltecas que comandaba su hijo y renunció a su jerarquía. Fue uno de los primeros indios bautizados. De acuerdo con algunos autores, tuvo alrededor de 90 esposas.

XICOTÉNCATL, FELIPE SANTIAGO ◆ n. en Tlaxcala, Tlax., y m. en la ciudad de México (1805-1847). Militar. Formó parte de las fuerzas santanistas que en 1832 derrocaron al gobierno golpista de Anastasio Bustamante. En 1839 participó en la expedición que el gobierno centralista organizó para reprimir el levantamiento independentista de Santiago Ímaz en Yucatán. En septiembre de 1847, durante la guerra contra Estados Unidos, fue nombrado comandante del Batallón de San Blas. Murió en combate durante el asalto estadounidense al castillo de Chapultepec.

Felipe Santiago Xicoténcatl

Foto: Boris de Swam

Xico, Veracruz

Xicoténcatl Axayacatzin, *el Joven*

XICOTÉNCATL AXAYACATZIN ◆ n. en Tlaxcala, Tlax., y m. en Texcoco, Edo. de Méx. (¿1484?-1521). Es llamado *el Joven*, para distinguirlo de su padre, Xicoténcatl. Fue regidor del señorío tlaxcalteca de Titzatlan. En 1519, los de Tlaxcala lo responsabilizaron de las fuerzas armadas locales para defenderse del avance español. En septiembre enfrentó a los europeos en dos ocasiones y en ambas fue derrotado. Formalizada la alianza entre Tlaxcala y España se unió a las fuerzas de Cortés y participó en los primeros ataques a Tenochtitlán, pero en mayo de 1521, meses antes de la caída de la capital mexica, retiró a sus tropas del valle de Anáhuac y se dirigió a Tlaxcala, con la idea de organizar la resistencia contra los europeos. Cortés lo acusó de "prófugo en frente de guerra" y ordenó su aprehensión y ejecución, que fue realizada por Alonso de Ojeda unos meses más tarde. Escribió poesía y algunos de sus textos fueron compilados en *Cantares mexicanos*.

XICOTEPEC ◆ Municipio de Puebla situado en la porción norte del estado, al norte de Zacatlán y al noreste de Huauchinango, en los límites con Veracruz. Superficie: 283.20 km². Habitantes: 64,815, de los cuales 16,409 forman la población económicamente activa. Hablan alguna lengua indígena 3,918 personas mayores de cinco años (náhuatl 2,885 y totonaco 605). En la cabecera, Xicotepec de Juárez, se celebra del 21 al 30 de marzo la feria del café, con una exposición agrícola, ganadera, artesanal, industrial y comercial; del 8 al 13 de abril se realiza la feria de primavera y una exposición regional, y el 24 de noviembre es la fiesta de San Juan. En la jurisdicción se encuentra Tlaxcalantongo, donde fue asesinado Venustiano Carranza en la noche del 20 al 21 de mayo de 1920.

Muerte de Xicoténcatl Axayacatzin, *el Joven*

XICOTLÁN ◆ Municipio de Puebla situado al sur-suroeste de Izúcar de Matamoros y al oeste de Acatlán. Superficie: 145.44 km². Habitantes: 1,147, de los cuales 224 forman la población económicamente activa. Sus habitantes elaboran artesanías de palma.

XICHÚ ◆ Municipio de Guanajuato situado al noreste de San Miguel de Allende y al este de San Luis de la Paz, en los límites con San Luis Potosí. Superficie: 855.40 km². Habitantes: 11,182, de los cuales 2,550 forman la población económicamente activa. Los primeros habitantes del territorio fueron otomíes y chichimecas. El nombre del municipio es nahua y significa "hermana de mi abuela". La cabecera fue fundada en 1580 por Alejo de Guzmán. La principal fiesta está dedicada a San Francisco de Asís y se celebra el 4 de octubre.

XICHÚ ◆ Río de San Luis Potosí y Querétaro. Nace en la vertiente noroccidental de la sierra Gorda, al este de San Luis de la Paz; corre de noroeste a sureste, entra al estado de Querétaro y al oeste de Peñamiller se une al río Tolimán para formar el Extoraz.

XILITLA ◆ Municipio de San Luis Potosí situado al sur de Ciudad Valles y al noroeste de Tamazunchale, en los límites con Hidalgo y Querétaro. Superficie: 403.5 km². Habitantes: 46,757, de los cuales 12,214 forman la población económicamente activa. Hablan alguna lengua indígena 16,656 personas (náhuatl 15,788 y huasteco 868). Indígenas monolingües: 955. En la porción de selva huasteca de este municipio, el escocés Edward James (☛) plasmó sus fantasías escultóricas y arquitectónicas: levantó construcciones de concreto que no cumplen función alguna y que se consideran ejemplos del arte surrealista.

XILITLA, DE ◆ Sierra de San Luis Potosí y Querétaro. Es una de las estribaciones frontales de la sierra Madre Oriental; se extiende de norte a sur, de la porción nororiental de Querétaro a la suroriental de San Luis Potosí, al noreste de la sierra de Jalpan y al norte de la de Zimapán.

XIMÉNEZ, FRANCISCO ◆ n. en España y ¿m. en la ciudad de México? (1560-?). Llegó a la Nueva España hacia 1605. Fue médico en el Hospital de Huaxtepec. Fraile dominico desde 1612. Autor de *Quatro libros de la naturaleza y virtudes de las plantas y animales que están recevidos en el uso de medicina en la Nueva España* (1915), que en realidad es una traducción anotada, corregida y aumentada de un libro del italiano Nando Antonio Recchi, que resumía las investigaciones sobre herbolaria de Francisco Hernández.

XIMÉNEZ, FRANCISCO ◆ n. en España y m. en Guatemala (1666-1723). Fraile dominico. Llegó a Guatemala hacia 1688. Fue párroco de San Pedro de las Huertas, Xcenacó, Chimaltenango, Rabinal y Santo Tomás Chichicastenango. Aprendió quiché, tzoltzil y cakchikel. En una ocasión, los quichés de Santo Tomás le mostraron el *Popol Vuh*, que copió y más tarde tradujo al español. El original de esta primera traducción, que fue publicado en 1857, en Austria, se encuentra en la Biblioteca Newberry de Chicago. Es autor de una *Historia de la provincia de San Vicente de Chiapa y Guatemala de la Orden de Predicadores*, que fue publicado en 1929, así como de *Historias del origen de los indios de esta provincia de Guatemala* y *Tesoro de las lenguas cakchikel, quiché y subtuxil en que las dichas lenguas se traducen en la nuestra española*.

Ximénez González, Héctor ◆ n. en Tlalmanalco, Edo. de Méx. (1938). Licenciado en derecho por la UNAM (1959). Fue profesor de la Escuela Normal de Chalco (1965). Es miembro del PRI desde 1962 en el que ha sido delegado regional (1982-83), secretario de organización (1984-86) y presidente (1988-89 y 1994) del CDE del Estado de México; subdelegado en Michoacán (1989), delegado en Puebla (1990), coordinador del Movimiento Popular Territorial (1992) y secretario de Acción Electoral (1993) del CEN. Ha sido secretario del ayuntamiento de Tlalnepantla (1966), presidente municipal de Chalco (1970-72), subdirector de Egresos del gobierno del Estado de México (1975-76), procurador General de Justicia en el Estado de México (1987-88), director general de Asuntos Jurídicos (1994) y delegado estatal en el Estado de México de la Sedesol (1995), diputado federal en dos ocasiones (1976-79 y 1985-88), secretario general de Gobierno en el Estado de México (1995-97) y senador de la república (1997-2000).

Xinantécatl ◆ ☛ *Nevado de Toluca.*

Xirau, Ramón ◆ n. en España (1924). Escritor y filósofo. Llegó a México en 1939, y obtuvo la nacionalidad mexicana en 1955. Maestro en filosofía por la UNAM (1946) de la que es investigador emérito. Fundador de la revista *Presencia* (1948), subdirector del Centro Mexicano de Escritores (1952-64), director del Departamento de Filosofía de la Universidad de las Américas (1953-70) y fundador (1964) y director de la revista *Diálogos* (1964-85). Autor de poesía: *10 poemes* (1951), *Graons* (1979), *Ocells* (1986) e *Indrets del temps* (1999); crítica literaria: *Tres poetas de la soledad: Gorostiza, Villaurrutia y Paz* (1955), *Genio y figura de sor Juana Inés de la Cruz* (1967), *Octavio Paz, el sentido de la palabra* (1970) y *Ars brevis. Epígrafe y comentarios* (1985); y ensayo filosófico: *Método y metafísica en la filosofía de Descartes* (1946), *Introducción a la historia de la filosofía* (1964), *Idea y querella de la Nueva España* (1974), *Entre ídolos y dioses. Tres ensayos sobre Hegel* (1978), *Ortega y Gasset: razón histórica y razón vital* (1983) y *Sentido de la presencia* (1998), entre otras obras. Becario de las fundaciones Rockefeller (1951-52 y 1955-56 y 1963-64) y Guggenheim (1969 y 1972). *Doctor honoris causa* por las universidades de las Américas (1970) y de Barcelona (1984), ha recibido las Palmas Académicas de Francia (1976), la medalla de la Orden de Isabel *la Católica* (1979) y, entre otros, los premios UNAM (1988) y Nacional de Ciencias y Artes (1995). Miembro del Sistema Nacional de Investigadores, de El Colegio Nacional y de la Academia Mexicana (de la Lengua).

Foto: Rogelio Cuéllar

Ramón Xirau

Xirau Icaza, Joaquín ◆ n. y m. en el DF (1950-1976). Estudió economía. Fue colaborador de *Diálogos*, *Plural*, *Línea*, *Diorama de la Cultura* y la *Revista de Bellas Artes*. Coautor, con Miguel Díaz, de *Nuestra dependencia fronteriza* (1976). Autor de *Poemas* (1976, con prólogo de Octavio Paz). Realizó la película *El cuervo*, basada en el relato homónimo de Poe.

Xirau y Palau, Joaquín ◆ n. en España y m. en el DF (1895-1946). Filósofo. Doctor en filosofía y letras y en derecho. Estudió en Barcelona, Madrid, París, Bruselas, Ginebra, Lovaina y Cambridge. Ejerció la docencia en el Instituto de Lugo y en las universidades de Salamanca, Zaragoza y Barcelona. Profesor invitado en las universidades de Oxford, París, Londres, La Habana y Cambridge. Fundó y dirigió el seminario de Filosofía y Pedagogía de la Universidad de Barcelona. Llegó a México en 1939, a la caída de la República Española. Aquí fue profesor de la UNAM y del Instituto Francés de América Latina y fundador de la Casa de España. Murió en un accidente automovilístico. Autor de *Las condiciones de la verdad eterna en Leibniz* (1921), *Rousseau y las ideas políticas modernas* (1923), *Descartes y el idealismo subjetivista moderno* (1927), *El sentido de la verdad* (1927), *La filosofía de Husserl* (1940), *Amor y mundo* (1940), *Dimensión del tiempo* (1941), *Lo fugaz y lo eterno* (1942), *En torno a Spinoza* (1944), *El pensamiento vivo de Juan Luis Vives* (1944), *Vida, pensamiento y obras de Bergson* (1944), *Ramón Llull, filosofía y mística* (1945) y *Manuel B. Cosío y la educación en España* (1945).

Xitle ◆ Volcán extinguido del Distrito Federal situado en la delegación Tlalpan, al noroeste del pueblo del Ajusco y al suroeste del ex pueblo de Tlalpan. Forma parte de la sierra del Ajusco. Hizo erupción por última vez hacia el año 400 a.n.e. y la lava arrojada formó el pedregal de San Ángel y acabó con el asentamiento de Cuiculco.

Xiuhtecutli ◆ Deidad nahua del fuego producido por los hombres cuyo nombre significa "Señor de la yerba y del año".

Xiutetelco ◆ Municipio de Puebla situado en la porción nororiental del estado, contiguo a Teziutlán, en los límites con Veracruz. Superficie: 93.12 km^2. Habitantes: 27,728, de los cuales 6,371 forman la población económicamente activa. Hablan alguna lengua indígena 142 personas (totonaco 137). El municipio tiene industrias madereras y minería, así como buenos cultivos de vainilla; existen en su territorio numerosos vestigios arqueológicos. En la cabecera municipal, San Juan Xiutetelco, se encuentra una pirámide truncada.

Xiximíes ◆ Indios nómadas de filiación yuto-azteca que vivían en territorio de los actuales estados de Durango y Sinaloa, en la sierra de Topia, sobre todo entre los ríos Piaxtla y San Lorenzo.

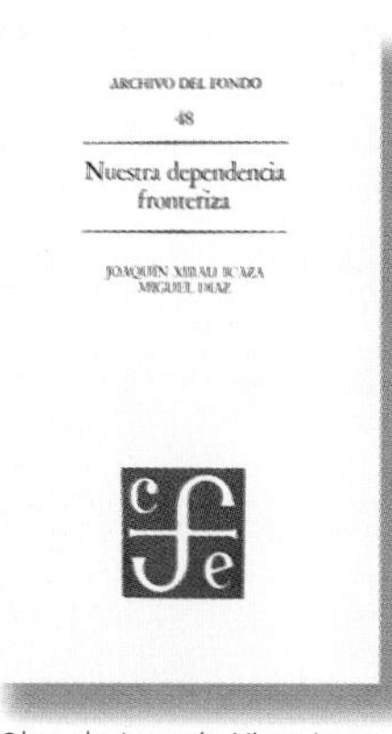

Obra de Joaquín Xirau Icaza

Fueron exterminados por los españoles en el siglo XVII. Se dedicaron principalmente a la caza y a la recolección. Vivían desnudos, con el cuerpo pintado de ocre, amarillo o negro, pero algunos usaban tilma de algodón o de pita de maguey para cubrirse el torso, o pieles de venado para las piernas. Todos, sin embargo, usaban collares de caracoles y narigueras rudimentarias. Combatían con arcos y lanzas y sostuvieron largas guerras contra sus vecinos, en especial con los acaxeés, y practicaron la antropofagia. Como todos los pueblos de esa región, los xiximíes se opusieron a la conquista y desde finales del siglo XVI combatieron a los europeos, quienes durante muchos años no pudieron asentarse en la zona. En 1604, una fuerza española comandada por el gobernador de Nueva Vizcaya, Francisco de Urdiñola, se internó en la sierra y, luego de algunos combates, forzó a los indios a congregarse alrededor de la misión jesuita de San Andrés, en los pueblos de Llexupa, San Gregorio, Coapa, Tecaya, Chalala, San Pedro y Las Vegas, con lo que quedaron destruidas casi todas sus formas de organización. Siete años después, en 1611, los xiximíes se levantaron en armas contra la dominación y expulsaron a los jesuitas, pero en ese mismo año, las fuerzas de Urdiñola derrotaron a los sublevados e hicieron una gran matanza entre los sobrevivientes. Los 6,000 restantes fueron de nuevo confinados a sus pueblos y unos años después desaparecieron como etnia.

XOCCHEL ◆ Municipio de Yucatán situado al este-sureste de Mérida y al sureste de Motul. Superficie: 53.65 km^2. Habitantes: 2,922, de los cuales 674 forman la población económicamente activa. Hablan alguna lengua indígena 1,900 personas mayores de cinco años (maya 1,899).

XOCHCUA ◆ Deidad nahua cuyo nombre significa "Come flores". Era, con Nanahuatl, responsable de la destrucción de la flora.

XOCHIAPULCO ◆ Municipio de Puebla situado al oeste de Teziutlán y al este de Zacatlán. Superficie: 110.99 km^2. Habitantes: 4,275, de los cuales 966 forman la población económicamente activa. Hablan alguna lengua indígena 1,702 personas (náhuatl 1,697).

XOCHIATIPÁN ◆ Municipio de Hidalgo situado al sureste de Huejutla de Reyes y al noreste de Tianguistengo, en los límites con Veracruz. Superficie: 149 km^2. Habitantes: 15,894, de los cuales 3,681 forman la población económicamente activa. Hablan alguna lengua indígena 11,759 personas (náhuatl 11,756). Indígenas monolingües: 3,692. La región fue un asentamiento prehispánico del señorío de Metztitlán. Hay numerosas zonas arqueológicas.

XOCHICALCO ◆ Ciudad nahua situada en un cerro del actual municipio morelense de Cuernavaca, encima de los cerros Xochicalco, La Bodega y La Malinche y a 114 kilómetros al sur-suroeste de la ciudad de México, cuyo nombre significa "Lugar de la casa de las flores". Hacia el año 300 a.n.e., los primeros habitantes de la región construyeron varias terrazas escalonadas en las laderas del monte, cuyos taludes fueron revestidos con piedra, y en su cumbre aplanaron una meseta de unos 70,000 m^2. Ahí construyeron la pirámide de las Serpientes Emplumadas —que mencionan en sus escritos Fray Bernardino de Sahagún (1591), José Antonio Alzate (1791) y Guillermo Dupaix (1805), descripciones sobre las cuales fue reconstruida en 1909 por Leopoldo Batres—, el juego de pelota, el templo de las Estelas, la necrópolis, el edificio de los Bajorrelieves y el Observatorio, una cueva natural. De acuerdo con las inscripciones descifradas en la pirámide de las Serpientes Emplumadas, es posible que hacia el año 650 de nuestra era se reunieron en esta ciudad los más destacados astrónomos nahuas, mayas y zapotecas, entre otros, para realizar un ajuste calendárico. Para Román Piña Chan es el Temoanchan, sitio donde los antiguos mexicanos ubicaban el origen de los dioses y los hombres. La ciudad fue abandonada hacia el año 900, aproximadamente, parece que hay evidencias de que hubo una revuelta y la ciudad fue incendiada. En 1996 se inauguró un Museo de Sitio que exhibe piezas y ofrece información sobre sus antiguos pobladores.

XOCHICOATLÁN ◆ Municipio de Hidalgo situado al este de Molango y al noroeste de Tianguistengo. Superficie: 159.30 km^2. Habitantes: 7,846, de los cuales 2,156 forman la población económicamente activa. Hablan alguna lengua indígena 125 personas mayores de cinco años (náhuatl 122). En la cabecera municipal se encuentra un templo católico construido en 1536, que fue secularizado en 1750 y casi destruido por un incendio en 1849.

XOCHIHUEHUETLÁN ◆ Municipio de Guerrero situado en el extremo nororiental del estado, al noreste de Chilpancingo y al norte de Tlapa, en los límites con Puebla y Oaxaca. Superficie: 191.6 km^2.

ILUSTRACIÓN DE ANTONIO ESPARZA

Xochihuehuetlán, Guerrero

Habitantes: 7,183, de los cuales 683 forman la población económicamente activa. Hablan alguna lengua indígena 51 personas (náhuatl 47).

Xochiltepec ◆ Municipio de Puebla situado al este-noreste de Izúcar de Matamoros y al sur-sureste de Atlixco. Superficie: 75.26 km². Habitantes: 3,145, de los cuales 710 forman la población económicamente activa. Hablan alguna lengua indígena 97 personas (náhuatl 87).

Foto: Archivo Xavier Esparza

El lago de Xochimilco en 1898

Xochimilco ◆ Delegación del Distrito Federal. Limita con Iztapalapa, Tláhuac, Milpa Alta y Tlalpan. Superficie: 122 km². Habitantes: 332,314 (1995), de los cuales 76,697 forman la población económicamente activa, dedicada principalmente a la producción manufacturera, las tareas agropecuarias, la construcción y la minería. Hablan alguna lengua indígena 5,362 personas mayores de cinco años (náhuatl 1,888, otomí 1,136, mixteco 561, zapoteco 385, mazateco 375 y mazahua 318). En la jurisdicción se hallan los pueblos de San Andrés Ahuacoyan, San Francisco Tlalnepantla, San Gregorio Atlapulco, San Lorenzo Atemoaya, San Lucas Xochimanca, San Luis Tlaxialtemanco, San Mateo Xalpa, Santa Cecilia Tepetlapa, Santa Cruz Acalpixcan, Santa Cruz Xochitepec, Santa María Nativitas Zacapan, Santa María Tepepan, Santiago Tepalcatlapan y Santiago Tulyehualco. Los primeros habitantes se instalaron en Acalpixpan, donde se han descubierto restos arqueológicos. Hacia el año 919 de nuestra era, luego de explorar durante 20 años las costas de los lagos del valle de Anáhuac, un grupo nahua de Chicomoztoc, dirigido por Huetzalin o Quetzali, se instaló en un isla situada en el más meridional de los lagos y fundó un pueblo "en el sembradío de flores" o en "el lugar de la sementera florida", Xochimilco. Sus habitantes fueron los primeros en construir chinampas (☛) para ampliar las zonas de cultivo. Poco después, los xochimilcas ocuparon Culhuacán, Chinameca, Mixquic, Tepozotlán, Tláhuac, Tlayacapan y Xumiltepec, entre otros pueblos, y más tarde dominaron todo el sur del actual Distrito Federal. A principios del siglo XIV, durante el reinado de Acatonale o Tecuhtonalli, los xochimilcas iniciaron una larga guerra contra culhuacanos y los mexicas y en 1378, las fuerzas mexicas de Acamapichtli, que trabajaban para Azcapotzalco, conquistaron Xochimilco. La región permaneció en poder de los tecpanecas hasta 1428, cuando los acolhuas de Nezahualcóyotl y los mexicas de Izcóatl derrotaron a Tezozómoc y destruyeron Azcapotzalco. La dirigencia xochimilca, encabezada por Tecopaintzin, se negó a someterse la recién creada Triple Alianza, por lo que en 1429 las fuerzas acolhuas de Tlacaelel invadieron el señorío y tomaron Xochimilco. Poco después, por órdenes de Itzcóatl, los vencedores destruyeron todos los documentos históricos de la ciudad. A partir de entonces, Xochimilco se convirtió en tributario de México-Tenochtitlan y sus pobladores fueron utilizados por los mexicas como obreros, para la construcción de la calzada de Iztapalapa, el templo Mayor y el acueducto de Coyoacán, y como soldados en las campañas de Tehuantepec, Meztitlan y Oztoman, entre otras. El territorio del señorío, por su parte, fue convertido en una especie de huerto de la ciudad azteca. A mediados del siglo XVI, poco después de la

Palacio municipal de Xochimilco durante la Revolución Mexicana

Foto: Michael Calderwood

Chinampa de Xochimilco

Foto: Michael Calderwood

Vista de Xochimilco, en el Distrito Federal

conquista española, Xochimilco fue encomienda de Pedro de Alvarado, quien mantuvo la producción de las chinampas para abastecer a la ciudad de México. En 1541, a la muerte de Alvarado, Xochimilco se convirtió en corregimiento. En 1552, el xochimilca Juan Badiano tradujo al latín el primer escrito sobre medicina que se elaboró en América: el *Libellus de medicinalibus indorum herbis*, del también xochimilca Martín de la Cruz, quien lo escribió en náhuatl. El pueblo de Xochimilco adquirió en 1559 el rango de ciudad y a finales del siglo XVI se creó la provincia de Xochimilco. La conquista espiritual fue realizada por los frailes franciscanos, quienes construyeron el convento de San Bernardino de Sena (1535-1604) y el convento y templo de la Visitación en el cerro de Tepepan (1599). En 1786, al crearse las intendencias, Xochimilco fue declarado subdelegación de la intendencia de México. En 1891, Alonso Íñigo Noriega estableció un servicio de vapores que transitaba por los canales entre Xochimilco e Iztacalco. Entre 1911 y 1917, Xochimilco fue escenario de numerosas acciones de guerra entre el Ejército Libertador del Sur y las tropas federales o constitucionalistas. En diciembre de 1914, Francisco Villa y Emiliano Zapata se reunieron en esta ciudad y firmaron el Pacto de Xochimilco (☛), poco antes de avanzar sobre la ciudad de México. En 1968, varios canales del norte de la delegación fueron empleados para la construcción de la pista olímpica de Cuemanco, que fue utilizada en los Juegos Olímpicos de México. Unos metros al norte, en 1975, se instaló el plantel Xochimilco de la Universidad Autónoma Metropolitana. Desde 1980, en la sede de la delegación se encuentra el Museo Arqueológico de Xochimilco, junto a las ruinas de un asentamiento nahua. En 1987, la zona de las chinampas fue declarada Patrimonio Cultural de la Humanidad por la UNESCO.

XOXHIMOCHPOCHTLI ◆ Deidad nahua encargada, con Meichpochtli, de la protección de las mujeres ebrias.

XOCHIPILLI ◆ Deidad nahua de la juventud, la poesía, la fecundidad masculina y la jardinería, cuyo nombre significa "Brote florido" o "Hijo florido". Se le consideraba una representación juvenil de Tonatiuh, el sol nahua, y a veces se le identificaba con Macuilxóchitl, deidad de la danza.

XOCHIQUETZAL ◆ Deidad nahua de la alegría, las flores y el amor, cuyo nombre es un apócope de Xochiquetzalli, "Flor preciosa". Se le identificaba con Tonacacíhuatl, parte femenina de la pareja original y madre de los dioses, que habitaba en un cielo llamado Tamoanchan. Esposa de Tláloc, fue raptada por Tezcatlipoca y aquél la busca eternamente. Era patrona de los hortelanos, de las bordadoras y, en Tlaxcala, de las prostitutas.

XOCHISTLAHUACA ◆ Municipio de Guerrero situado al sur-sureste de Tlapa y contiguo a Ometepec, en los límites con Oaxaca. Superficie: 321.10 km². Habitantes: 18,513, de los cuales 4,111 forman la población económicamente activa. Hablan alguna lengua indígena 12,690 personas (amuzgo 11,832 y mixteco 858).

XOCHITEPEC ◆ Municipio de Morelos situado al sur de Cuernavaca y al norte de Zacatepec. Superficie: 99.13 km². Habitantes: 40,657, de los cuales 8,483 forman la población económicamente activa. Hablan alguna lengua indígena 411 personas mayores de cinco años (náhuatl 292).

Foto: Michael Calderwood

Xochipilli

Ilustración de Santiago Ortega

Palacio municipal Xochistlahuaca, Guerrero

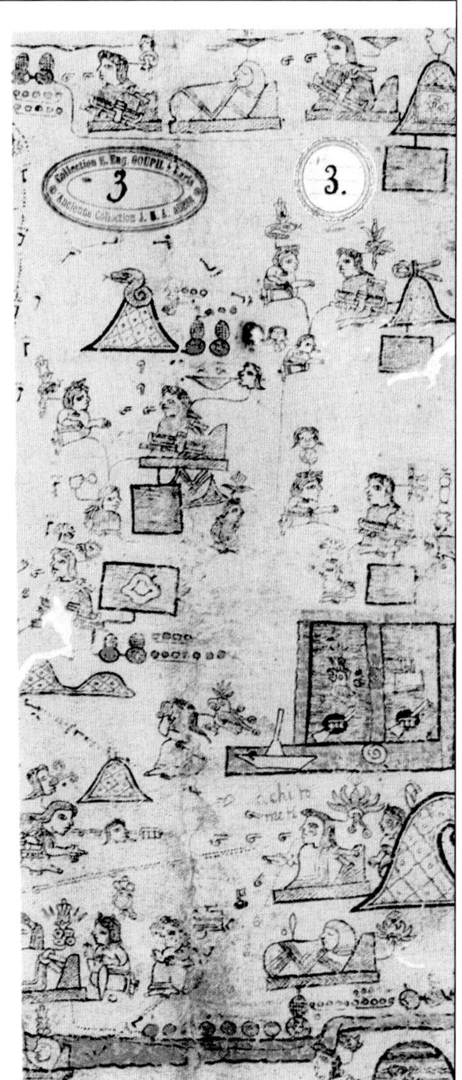

Códice Xólotl

Xóchitl ◆ ☛ *Pulque.*

Xochitlán de Vicente Suárez ◆ Municipio de Puebla situado al noroeste de Teziutlán y al sureste de Huauchinango. Superficie: 45.92 km^2. Habitantes: 11,588, de los cuales 2,764 forman la población económicamente activa. La cabecera es Xochitlán de Romero Rubio.

Xochitlán Todos Santos ◆ Municipio de Puebla situado al noroeste de Tehuacán y al sureste de la capital del estado. Superficie: 141.61 km^2. Habitantes: 4,569, de los cuales 1,051 forman la población económicamente activa. Hablan alguna lengua indígena 12 personas mayores de cinco años. La cabecera es Xochitlán.

Xólotl ◆ Deidad nahua de los monstruos y de las cosas extraordinarias, cuyo nombre significa "Mozo". De acuerdo con la mitología, fue uno de los 1,600 semidioses que nacieron al romperse el pedernal que dio a luz a la diosa Omecíhuatl; era uno de los destinados a morir en Teotihuacán para que renaciera el sol, pero fue el único que escapó.

Xólotl ◆ Códice acolhua conocido también como "Historia de la nación chichimeca", que narra la vida de los texcocanos desde la migración a Culhuacán, en el siglo x, hasta el reinado de Nezahualcóyotl, en el siglo xv. El documento, elaborado hacia 1542, está formado por diez hojas de amate y ocho de papel europeo y se encuentra en la sección Manuscritos Mexicanos de la Biblioteca Nacional de París. Perteneció a Lorenzo Boturini y después a J. M. Aubin.

Xonacatlán ◆ Municipio del Estado de México situado al oeste de Naucalpan y al noreste de Toluca. Superficie: 179.89 km^2. Habitantes: 36,141, de los cuales 7,370 forman la población económicamente activa. Hablan alguna lengua indígena 1,393 personas (otomí 1,384). En la cabecera hay un templo construido en el siglo xvii. Éste y los ojos de agua de Mimiapan y de Xolotepec son los principales atractivos turísticos.

Xólotl

Xonachi Quecuya ◆ Diosa zapoteca de la muerte. Era esposa de Coqui Bezelao o "Señor demonio". Se le adoraba principalmente en Mitla, necrópolis destinada a los altos aristócratas y sacerdotes.

Xoxippa ◆ Nombre de una de las tres principales deidades de los otomíes.

Xoxocotla ◆ Municipio de Veracruz situado al suroeste de Córdoba y al oeste-noroeste de Zongolica, en los límites con Puebla. Superficie: 63.34 km^2. Habitantes: 4,212, de los cuales 831 forman la población económicamente activa. Hablan alguna lengua indígena 931 personas mayores de cinco años (náhuatl 931).

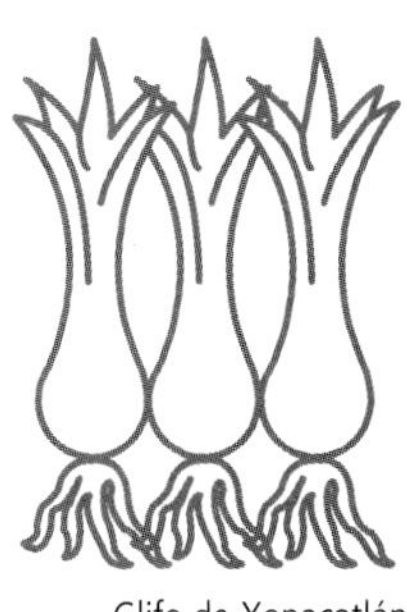

Glifo de Xonacatlán

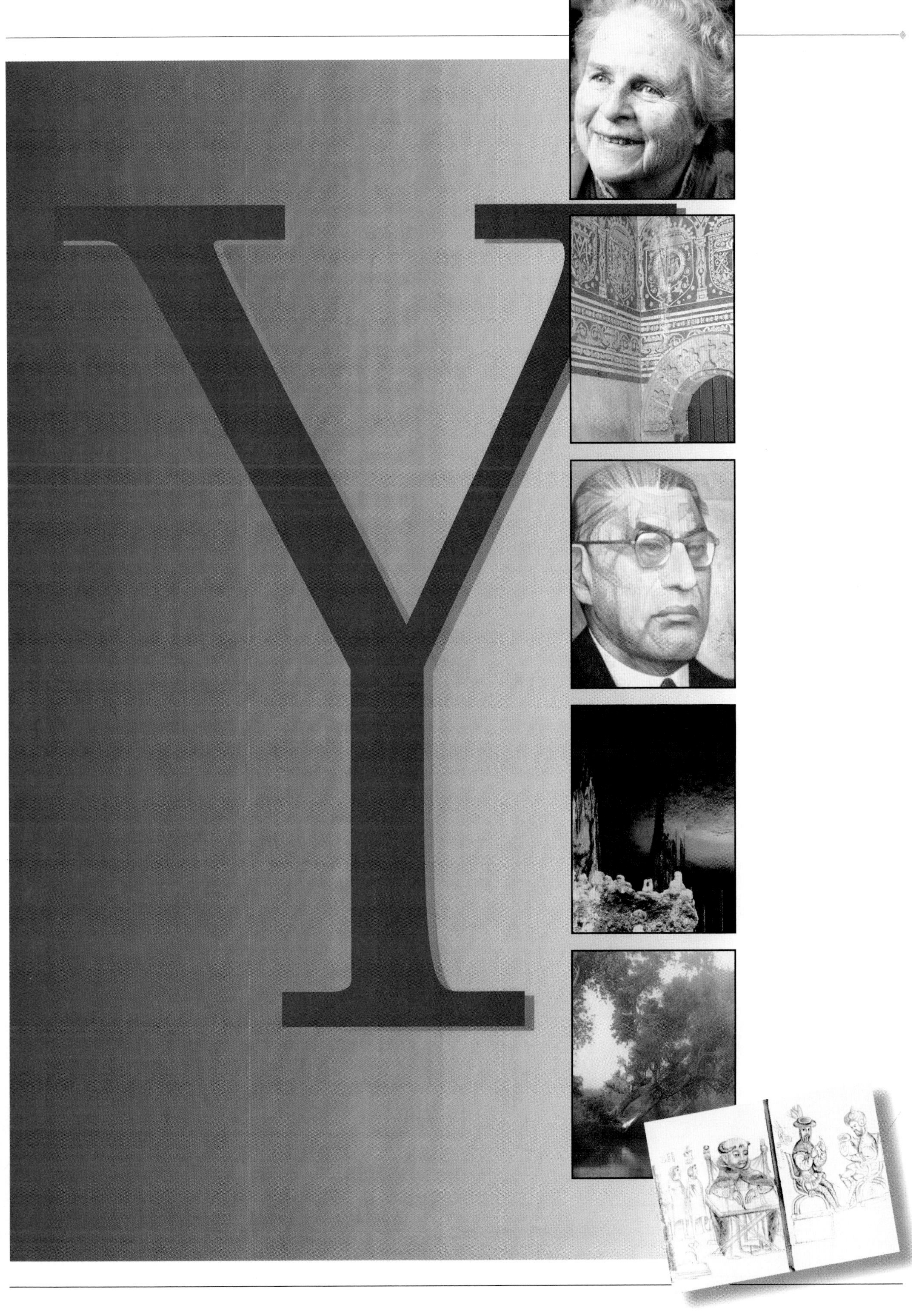
Y

YACAMÁN, JOSÉ MIGUEL ◆ ☛ José Yacamán, Miguel.

YACATECUHTLI ◆ Deidad nahua de los comerciantes, cuyo nombre significa "El que sirve de guía". Tenía cinco hermanos, Cochimetl, Chichonquiavitl, Nacxitl, Xomocuil y Yacapitzahua, y una hermana, Chalmecacioatl. Era considerado una de las facetas de Quetzalcóatl. Antes de iniciar cada viaje, los pochtecas sacrificaban un esclavo en su honor, para que los ayudara durante la travesía.

Mariana Yampolsky

YAGUL ◆ ☛ *Tlacolula de Matamoros.*

YAHUALICA ◆ Municipio de Hidalgo situado al sur de Huejutla de Reyes y al noreste de Molango, en los límites con Veracruz. Superficie: 164.50 km². Habitantes: 19,889, de los cuales 4,545 forman la población económicamente actva. Hablan alguna lengua indígena 13,556 personas mayores de cinco años (náhuatl 13,555). En el territorio municipal existen numerosas zonas arqueológicas.

YAHUALICA DE GONZÁLEZ GALLO ◆ Municipio de Jalisco situado en la porción nororiental del estado, al noreste de Guadalajara y al suroeste de Teocaltiche, en los límites con Zacatecas. Superficie: 478.30 km². Habitantes: 23,539, de los cuales 5,143 forman la población económicamente activa. Hablan alguna lengua indígena 33 personas mayores de cinco años. A la antigua Yahualica se le agregó el nombre del que fuera gobernador del estado, Jesús González Gallo.

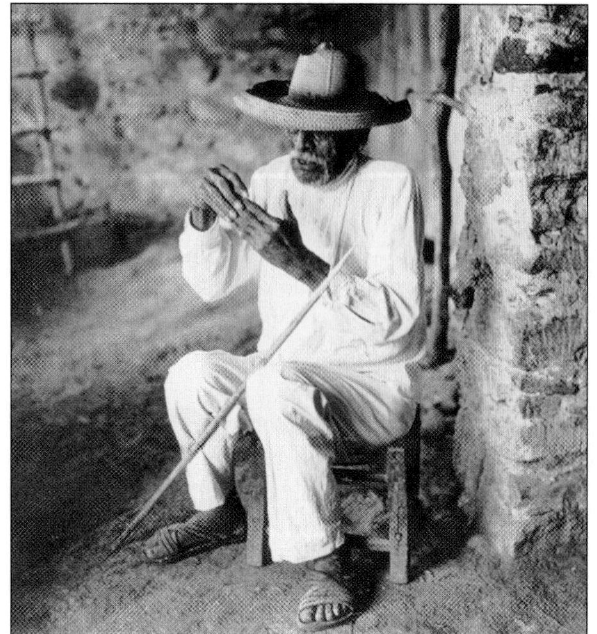

Fotografía de Mariana Yampolsky

YAJALÓN ◆ Municipio de Chiapas situado al noreste de San Cristóbal de Las Casas y al suroeste de Palenque. Superficie: 109.30 km². Habitantes: 24,216, de los cuales 5,519 forman la población económicamente activa. Hablan alguna lengua indígena 12,909 personas mayores de cinco años (tzeltal 11,012 y chol 1,897). Indígenas monolingües: 5,065.

YALAHAU ◆ Estero de Quintana Roo situado en la porción noreste de la península de Yucatán, entre la isla de Holbox y tierra firme, al norte de Chiquilá. Por la boca de Conil se comunica con el golfo de México, al este, y con el canal de Yucatán, al noroeste. En sus aguas hay abundante pesca.

YALALAG ◆ ☛ *Hidalgo Yalalag.*

YAMPOLSKY, MARIANA ◆ n. en EUA (1925). Fotógrafa y grabadora. Licenciada en artes y humanidades por la Universidad de Chicago (1945). Llegó a México en 1945 y adquirió la nacionalidad en 1954. Ese año se incorporó al Taller de Gráfica Popular, al que perteneció hasta 1958. Estudió en las escuelas de Pintura y Escultura La Esmeralda (1948) y de Artes del Libro (1949). En 1950 colaboró con Carmen Toscano en la edición de la película *Memorias de un mexicano* (1950). Ha sido fundadora y profesora del Centro de Enseñanza de Lenguas Extranjeras del IPN (1966), coeditora del Fondo Editorial de la Plástica Mexicana, colaboradora del Centro de Investigaciones de las Artesanías y coordinadora e ilustradora del área de ciencias naturales de la Comisión Nacional de los Libros de Texto Gratuitos (1972-76). Comenzó a tomar fotografías en 1954 y para 1998 había acumulado 60,000 negativos; en 1999 se inauguró la retrospectiva *Mariana Yampolsky. Imagen. Memoria.* Editora de la colección Colibrí de la SEP (1978) y de los libros *La imagen de Zapata* (1979), *Niños* (1980), *Imaginación y realidad* (1980), *El ciclo mágico de los días* (1980), *Diego Rivera y los frescos de la Secretaría de Educación Pública* (1980), *Francisco Toledo* (1981) y *Juguetes mexicanos* (1981). Con su obra fotográfica se han integrado los volúmenes *La casa que canta*, *La casa en la tierra* (1981) *La raíz y el camino* (1985), *Tlacotalpan* (1987), *Estancias del olvido* (1987) y *The Edge of Time* (1998).

YANGA ◆ n. en África y m. ¿en San Lorenzo de los Negros, Ver.? (?-?). Esclavo de la nación Bron. Fue traído de África como esclavo en 1579 y afirmaba que, de no haber sido capturado, hubiera sido rey en su tierra. A su llegada escapó y con un grupo de esclavos se asentó en las faldas del Pico de Orizaba, donde mantuvo 30 años un pequeño Estado independiente del virreinato, en el que acogió a otros prófugos. El Estado independiente de Yanga creció y adquirió poder, por lo que en 1609 el virrey Luis de Velasco II envió una expedición de 550 hombres, comandada por Pedro González de Herrera. Los cimarrones capturaron a un español con quien mandaron una arrogante carta a Herrera, retándolo a combatir. Éste atacó el poblado en que se asentaban los ex esclavos, pero ya había sido abandonado y sólo pudo destruir las chozas que halló. Al no poder capturar a los insurrectos, se pactó su rendición ante el virrey, a condición de que se les concediera establecerse en un lugar cercano a su palenque para fundar un pueblo exclusivo de negros, que todos los esclavos huidos antes de 1608 quedasen libres, tener a Yanga como gobernador y conceder la sucesión a sus descendientes. A cambio, se comprometieron a pagar tributo a la Corona, entregar a cualquier fugitivo de haciendas aledañas y auxiliar en caso de ataques externos. En 1630 se asentaron en un paraje cercano a Palmillas en las faldas del monte Totutla. En 1654 solicitaron el traslado del pueblo y en 1655 se asentaron en San Lorenzo de los Negros, actualmente Yanga.

YANGA ◆ Municipio de Veracruz situado 12 km al sureste de Córdoba y al noreste de Zongolica, entre los cerros de San Miguel al sur y Atoyac al norte.

Superficie: 102.82 km^2. Habitantes: 16,959, de los cuales 4,632 forman la población económicamente activa. Hablan alguna lengua indígena 65 personas mayores de cinco años (náhuatl 34). Su capital es la ciudad de Yanga, antiguamente conocida como San Lorenzo de los Negros, fundada el 4 de enero de 1655 como resultado de la lucha armada de los negros esclavos por obtener su libertad. Actualmente, en los días previos a la festividad de San Lorenzo (10 de agosto) se organiza un carnaval en recuerdo del negro Yanga.

Yanhuitlán ◆ Códice mixteco elaborado entre 1541 y 1550 que narra la historia de los mixtecos desde mediados del siglo XIV, cuando fueron conquistados por los mexicas, hasta mediados del siglo XVI, cuando los españoles sometieron la región. Se supone elaborado por un español, porque si bien el registro del tributo se hace como en los códices prehispánicos, el trazo corresponde a las técnicas europeas y la ropa de los personajes blancos es morisca. El documento está formado por más de 16 hojas de papel europeo, de 31 por 22.5 centímetros. La Academia de Bellas Artes de Puebla conserva 12 hojas y varios fragmentos de este documento, en tanto que el Archivo General de la Nación guarda otras cuatro hojas del mismo.

Yanhuitlán ◆ Provincia de la Nueva España creada en 1553 con el territorio de la Mixteca Alta, el que dominicos habían evangelizado desde 1529. Tenía jurisdicción sobre Cuestlaguaca, Chicaguastepec, Iztactepec, Guautla, Tequecistepec, Tonaltepec y Xatepetongo. En 1688 la provincia de Yanhuitlán fue abolida y su territorio repartido entre las de Teposcolula y Nochistlán. En el pueblo de Yanhuitlán fue construida una iglesia sobre los cimientos de un edificio prehispánico del que se rescató un pectoral de oro y turquesas, conservado en el Museo Nacional de Antropología e Historia. En el mismo pueblo fue construido, entre 1550 y 1575, un convento dominico, financiado por el encomendero Francisco de las Casas, primo de Hernán Cortés. ☛ *Santo Domingo Yanhuitlán.*

Agustín Yáñez

Yáñez, Agustín ◆ n. en Guadalajara, Jal., y m. en el DF (1904-1980). Licenciado en derecho por la Escuela de Jurisprudencia de Guadalajara (1929) y maestro en filosofía por la UNAM (1951). Profesor de la preparatoria de la Universidad de Guadalajara (1931-32), de la Escuela Nacional Preparatoria (1932-53) y de la UNAM (1942-1953 y 1959-1962). Entre otros cargos desempeñó los de director del periódico católico tapatío *La Época* (1925-26) y de la revista *Bandera de Provincias*, director de Educación Primaria de Nayarit, rector del Instituto Científico y Literario de Tepic, director de radio de la SEP (1932-34), coordinador de Humanidades de la UNAM (1945), gobernador de Jalisco (1953-59), subsecretario de la Presidencia (1962-64), secretario de Educación Pública (del 1 de diciembre de 1964 al 30 de noviembre de 1970) en el gobierno de Díaz Ordaz y presidente de la Comisión Nacional de los Libros de Texto Gratuitos (1977-80). Autor de ensayo: *El contenido social de la literatura iberoamericana* (1943), *Fichas mexicanas* (1945), *Yahualica* (1946), *Proyección universal de México* (1963), *Conciencia de la revolución* (1964) y *Dante, concepción integral del hombre y de la historia* (1965); narrativa: *Baralipton* (1931), *Espejismo de Juchitán* (1940), *Flor de juegos antiguos* (1942), *Melibea, Isolda y Alda en tierras cálidas* (1946) y *Tres cuentos* (1964); y novela: *Archipiélago de mujeres* (1943), *Al filo del agua* (1947), *La creación* (1959), *La tierra pródiga* (1960), *Las tierras flacas* (1962) y *Las vueltas del tiempo* (1973), entre otras obras. En 1949 ingresó al Seminario de Cultura Mexicana, del que fue presidente (1949-51); y en 1952 a El Colegio Nacional y a la Academia Mexicana (de la Lengua), que también presidió (1973-80). Premio Nacional de Ciencias y Artes (1973).

Yáñez, José María ◆ n. y m. en la ciudad de México (1804-1880). Militar. Se unió al ejército trigarante en 1821. Dos años después se adhirió al Plan de Casa Mata que derrocó a Iturbide. Combatió la expedición española de Isidro Barradas y participó en la sublevación liberal de 1832-33, que llevó a Santa Anna por primera vez a la Presidencia. En 1838 participó en la guerra de los Pasteles. En 1846 intervino en la sublevación federalista de José Mariano Salas, que derrocó al gobierno de Paredes y Arrillaga, por lo que en 1847 la legislatura jalisciense lo declaró benemérito del estado. En septiembre desalojó a las fuerzas estadounidenses del puerto de San Blas y al principio de 1848 luchó contra los invasores en Sinaloa y Zacatecas. En 1852 se adhirió al Plan de Jalisco, que reimpuso a Santa Anna en la Presidencia. Fue gobernador de Jalisco (del 12 de noviembre de 1852 al 9 de junio de 1853) y gobernador y comandante militar de Sinaloa y Sonora (1854). Secretario de Guerra y Marina de Comonfort (del 6 al 29 de abril de 1856), en 1857 fue nombrado gobernador de Sinaloa, pero el Congreso le impidió tomar posesión. Se levantó en armas en diciembre de ese año, derrocó al gobierno liberal, se encargó del gobierno sinaloense (del 4 de enero al 24 de

José María Yañez

Códice Yanhuitlán

Mariano Yáñez

Foto: Rogelio Cuéllar

Ricardo Yáñez

abril de 1858) y militó en las filas conservadoras durante la guerra de los Tres Años. En 1862 se alistó para combatir la intervención francesa, pero más tarde reconoció al imperio y gobernó el departamento de Guanajuato (del 13 de diciembre de 1863 al 22 de septiembre de 1864). Al triunfo de la República fue juzgado y condenado a prisión. Quedó en libertad en 1872.

Yáñez, Juan ◆ n. en Puebla, Pue., y m. en la ciudad de México (¿1791?-1836). Bandolero. En 1821 fue comandante militar de Acatlán y, más adelante, mayor de plaza en Puebla. Fue asistente militar del presidente Antonio López de Santa Anna desde 1834 y, al mismo tiempo, jefe de una banda de salteadores que operó durante varios años en las ciudades de México y Veracruz y a lo largo del camino que las une, principalmente en los alrededores de Río Frío. El 8 de noviembre de 1835, tres de sus compañeros, a los que proporcionó armas y transportes, asesinaron a Carlos Mairet, el cónsul suizo en México, por lo que fue aprehendido en ese mismo año y, con algunos de los miembros de su banda, juzgado y condenado a muerte. Murió meses después, luego de un intento de suicidio. Su vida inspiró el personaje *Relumbrón*, de la novela *Los bandidos de Río Frío*, de Manuel Payno.

Yáñez, Mariano ◆ n. y m. en la ciudad de México (¿1795?-1881). Abogado. Fue secretario de Relaciones Exteriores (del 16 de enero al 28 de abril de 1851 y del 23 de octubre al 10 de diciembre de 1852), y de Hacienda (del 29 de abril al 24 de mayo de 1851), en el gabinete de Mariano Arista.

Yáñez, Puri ◆ n. en España (1936). Pintora. Fue traída a México en 1939, a la caída de la República española. Estudió decoración en la Universidad Femenina de México (1952-55) y artes plásticas en la UIA (1956-58). Ha expuesto sus obras en Beirut (1962), las galerías Excélsior (1965 y 1968), Chapultepec (1967), Plástica de México (1968), José María Velasco (1970) y Arvil (1972), así como en los museos de Antropología (1971) y de Arte Moderno del Distrito Federal (1972).

Yáñez, Ricardo ◆ n. en Guadalajara, Jal. (1948). Poeta y periodista. Estudió en la Universidad Autónoma de Guadalajara y en la UNAM. Ha sido editor de *El Ciervo Herido* (1976-78), coordinador de los talleres de poesía del INBA, redactor de Radio Universidad, reportero, corrector y redactor del periódico *unomásuno* (1977-84) y secretario de redacción del diario *La Jornada* (1984-86) y de la revista *Mira* (1991-94). Es fundador de los talleres de poesía del gobierno de Jalisco, del Centro para el Estudio del Floklore en México y del Ágora de Jalapa. Mantiene, desde 1986, talleres de creación artística en el DF, Puebla, Monterrey, Guadalajara, Saltillo, Pachuca, Celaya y Tepic. Autor de *Divertimiento* (1972), *Escritura sumaria* (1977), *Ni lo que digo* (1985), *Dejar de ser* (1994), *Antes del habla* (1995) y *Prosaísmos* (crónicas periodísticas, 1995). En 1971 ganó el premio de poesía de la revista *Punto de Partida*.

Yáñez de la Fuente, Enrique ◆ n. y m. en el DF (1908-1990). Estudió arquitectura en la Academia de San Carlos (1927-31). Profesor del IPN (1934-42), de la UNAM (1937-38) y de la UAM (1986-88). Perteneció a la Unión de Arquitectos Socialistas (1938-40). Fue vocal técnico del Comité de Construcción de Escuelas (1944-46), primer director de Arquitectura del INBA (1946-52), subdirector de Inmuebles y Construcciones y jefe de Proyectos y Construcciones del IMSS (1964-70), consejero del Instituto Nacional de la Vivienda (1964-70), director técnico del Fideicomiso Puerto Vallarta (1972-73) y jefe del Departamento Técnico del Fideicomiso Lago de Tequesquitengo y Agua Hedionda. De las obras que proyectó y dirigió destacan los hospitales General de Veracruz (1944-50), La Raza (1945-52) y el Centro Médico Nacional (1954-61), todos del IMSS; y los hospitales General de Ciudad Juárez (1964) y Adolfo López Mateos del DF (1968-70), así como la Clínica de Diagnóstico Automatizado (1973-1974), éstos del ISSSTE. Construyó la sede del Sindicato Mexicano de Electricistas (1936-40), la Normal Superior (1944-46) y el Instituto Mexicano del Petróleo (1966). Autor de *Hospitales de seguridad social* (1973), *Arquitectura, teoría, contexto, diseño* (1983) y *Del funcionalismo al posracionalismo. Ensayo sobre la arquitectura contemporánea* (1990). Académico emérito de la Academia Nacional de Arquitectura y Gran Premio de la Academia (1990). Miembro de número de la Academia de Artes. En 1988 fue nombrado *doctor honoris causa* por la UAM.

Yáñez Hernández, Magdaleno ◆ n. en Coroneo, Gto. (1950). Licenciado en derecho por la Universidad Autónoma de Querétaro (1980), licenciado en ciencias sociales por la Escuela Normal Superior (1982) y maestro en derecho social por la Universidad Autónoma del Estado de México (1983). Militó en el Partido Demócrata Mexicano y en 1986 fue designado presidente del mismo en Querétaro y secretario de Acción Obrera de su Comité Ejecutivo Nacional. Ha sido secretario general del sindicato de Polynova (1977), secretario de Organización de la Federación de Trabajadores de Querétaro y diputado federal (1985-88).

Yáñez Pinzón, Vicente ◆ n. en España (?¿-1515). Marino. Fue capitán de la carabela *La Niña* durante el primer viaje de Cristóbal Colón a América (1492). En 1500 atravesó por su cuenta el Atlántico y llegó a la desembocadura del Amazonas. En 1506, durante su segunda expedición, arribó al Río de la Plata. Dos años después, en junio de 1508, realizó su tercer viaje de exploración, con la misión de descubrir un paso entre el Mar del Sur y el océano Atlántico. Navegó por las costas de Honduras, costeó la Península de Yucatán, recorrió parte del golfo de México y probablemente desembarcó en las costas del actual estado de Tamaulipas. Fue el primer capitán español en avistar tierras mexicanas; su derrotero está indicado en el mapa editado en 1511 por Pedro Mártir de Anglería. Después de ese viaje no se volvieron a tener noticias de él.

YÁÑEZ VARGAS, LEONARDO ◆ n. en Esqueda, Son. (1937). Licenciado en administración de empresas por el Instituto Tecnológico de Nogales y contador público por la Escuela Bancaria y Comercial. Como miembro del PAN, en el que militó de 1978 a 1997, fue consejero estatal y presidente del CDE en Sonora, y consejero nacional. Fue secretario del ayuntamiento de Agua Prieta, Sonora. Senador para el periodo 1994-2000.

YAONÁHUAC ◆ Municipio de Puebla situado en la porción norte del estado, al nor-noroeste de Teziutlán y al sureste de Cuetzalan. Superficie: 54.85 km². Habitantes: 6,392, de los cuales 1,381 forman la población económicamente activa. Hablan alguna lengua indígena 3,339 personas mayores de cinco años (náhuatl 3,336).

YAQUI ◆ Río de Sonora, de más de 800 kilómetros de curso. Nace en la porción oriental del estado, en la sierra de Molinares, con el nombre de Papigóchic o Aros; corre hacia el noroeste y recibe las aguas del Bavispe; tuerce al sur y, al norte de Sahuaripa, vira al oeste; atraviesa la sierra Madre Occidental; en la presa Plutarco Elías Calles, en la vertiente suroriental de la sierra de Batuc, une su curso al del río Moctezuma, recibe el nombre de Yaqui, tuerce hacia el sur y corre paralelo a la cresta principal de la sierra Madre Occidental, por su vertiente oeste; al entrar en la llanura costera tuerce hacia el suroeste y su curso se ve interrumpido por la presa Álvaro Obregón; corre después hacia el sur, paralelo a la sierra de Baroyeca y al norte de Ciudad Obregón dirige su curso al oeste para desembocar en el golfo de California, al oeste de Pótam y al sur de la bahía de Guaymas. En la llanura costera, sus aguas son aprovechadas para el riego. Su cuenca comprende unos 66,000 km².

YAQUIS ◆ Indios que viven en la porción sur del estado de Sonora, principalmente en Vícam, Pótam, Ráhum, Tórim, Cócorit, Huírivis, Pitahaya o Belén y Bácum, localidades situadas en las márgenes del bajo río Yaqui, aunque también hay colonias de esta etnia en las reservaciones estadounidenses de Guadalupe, Pascua y Scattel y en las ciudades mexicanas de Magdalena, Caborca, Nogales, Hermosillo, Obregón, Tijuana y Mexicali. Además, existen grupos en Veracruz, Jalisco y Yucatán, descendientes de los prisioneros deportados durante la guerra del Yaqui. Su lengua está clasificada en el grupo nahua-cuitlateco, tronco yutonahua, familia pima-cora. En 1945 fueron catalogados, junto con los mayos, como los únicos sobrevivientes de la subfamilia cahíta, de la familia taracahíta, de aquel tronco lingüístico. En 1995, 13,061 personas mayores de cinco años hablaban yaqui. Las autoridades yaquis, sin embargo, aseguran que el número total de individuos de su etnia, dispersos en México y en el sur de Estados Unidos, asciende a 40,000; éstos suelen reunirse en el valle del Yaqui, en ocasión de las festividades religiosas. Su principal actividad económica es la agricultura: cultivan frutas, cereales, hortalizas y legumbres tanto para la venta como para el consumo doméstico. Muchos se han convertido en peones agrícolas o aparceros. Para complementar su dieta, practican la caza y la pesca; trabajan en cooperativas y cada pueblo cuenta con una central de maquinaria agrícola. La base social yaqui es la familia nuclear, que se forma cuando las personas son aún muy jóvenes. La máxima autoridad de cada familia es el padre, aunque la opinión de los ancianos, hombres o mujeres, tiene gran peso. Cuando una persona agoniza, se le asignan padrinos y madrinas; al ocurrir la muerte, éstos deben sufragar los gastos del velorio y del entierro. Poco después del deceso, los padrinos hacen estallar un cohete que, según sus creencias, avisa que el alma del muerto se dirige al cielo. En el velorio suele haber danzas y música. Durante el entierro, los familiares del muerto permanecen de espaldas a la sepultura y, una vez concluida la inhumación, los asistentes a la ceremonia fúnebre regresan rápidamente a sus casas para evitar un encuentro con el alma de la persona fallecida. Un año después del deceso tiene lugar una ceremonia de dos o tres días de duración, en la que hay danzas, rezos, cantos, comida y bebida. El compadrazgo o parentesco ritual es relevante en la vida de los yaquis, ya que consolida las relaciones sociales; por ende, hay padrinos para bautizos, matrimonios y defunciones. Practican la religión católica matizada por sus antiguas creencias. La máxima autoridad religiosa es el conjunto de maestros, presidido por el *yoohue*, quien cuida el templo del poblado y presta servicio, auxiliado principalmente por el sacristán mayor. En la Semana Santa el control lo asumen dos hermandades cuyos miembros están dedicados a dar servicio a Jesús y al Niño-Cristo: los llamados *chapayecas* o "fariseos", y los danzantes (matachines, pascolas, coyotes y venados). Poseen sus propias autoridades tradicionales; en cada pueblo o *comunila*, como también se le llama, hay un gobernador llamado *cobanahua*, un mayor del pueblo o pueblo *yoohue*, un capitán, un comandante, un gran consejero llamado *temastimole*, que puede criticar lo dicho o hecho por el *cobanahua*, así como la gran consejera llamada *kiyohteiyohue*. Todos los cargos se ejercen vitaliciamente, con excepción del de gobernador, que dura un año. Las autoridades de cada pueblo se reúnen normalmente los domingos para discutir los problemas de cada localidad. Cuando surge un conflicto mayor, capaz de afectar a toda la etnia, realizan una *comunila* ge-

Río Yaqui, Sonora

Foto: Michael Calderwood

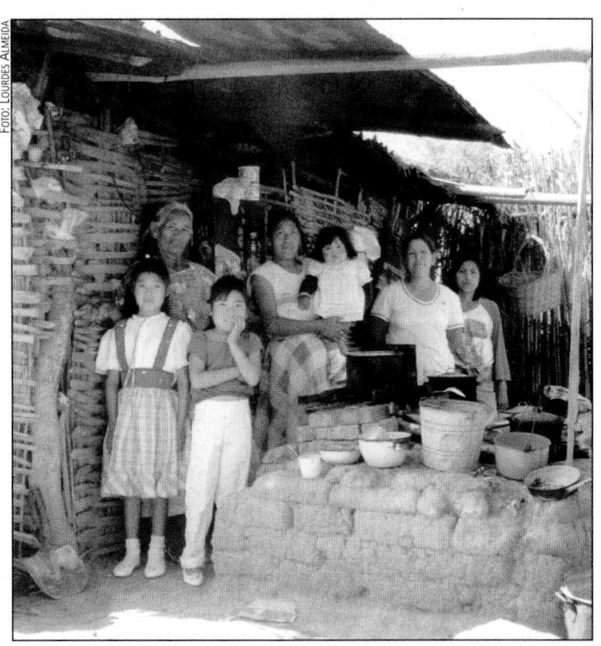
FOTO: LOURDES ALMEIDA

Familia de jornaleros yaquis de Vicam, Sonora

neral, en la que se reúnen las autoridades de los ocho pueblos. A principios del siglo XVI, en las riberas del río Yaqui vivían unos 60,000 yaquis y mayos, que entonces sólo tenían leves diferencias de lenguaje. En octubre de 1533, una fuerza española al mando de Diego de Guzmán, quien venía de Nueva Galicia, cruzó hacia el norte el río Yaqui, pero fue derrotado por los yaquis y se retiró. En 1564, sin embargo, Francisco de Ibarra logró establecer contacto con la etnia y la hizo combatir contra los mayos. En 1608, una fuerza de 40 jinetes españoles y 2,500 indios comandada por Diego Martínez de Hurdaide, que perseguía a los caciques zuaques Lautaro y Babilomo, cruzó el Yaqui y se internó en la región, pero de nuevo los españoles fueron derrotados. Al año siguiente Hurdaide volvió con 50 españoles y 4,000 indios cristianos, atacó a los yaquis y de nuevo fue derrotado, pero en 1615, el comandante español hizo transportar una parte de su ejército por mar hasta la bahía de Guaymas y, sorprendidos por el ataque marítimo, los yaquis decidieron negociar y aceptaron el establecimiento de misiones jesuitas en la zona, la primera de las cuales se estableció en mayo de 1617. La misión quedó al mando de Andrés Pérez de Rivas, quien, tres años después, consiguió bautizar a 4,900 niños y a 3,000 adultos, y decidió concentrar a los indios en los pueblos de Cócorit, Bácum, Tórim, Vícam, Pótam, Ráhum, Belén y Guíviris. En 1734 se reunieron en una sola las provincias norteñas de Rosario, Culiacán, Sinaloa, Ostimuri y Sonora y se designó a Manuel Bernal de Huidobro como su primer gobernador. La política española de aplicar impuestos a los comestibles y repartir las tierras comunales provocó la oposición de los indios, por lo que en 1740, dirigidos por Juan Calixto, los yaquis, los pimas y los mayos se levantaron en armas, exigieron la salida de los *yoris* (los blancos), el retiro del ejército del valle del Yaqui y respeto a la propiedad comunal. El gobernador Huidobro encabezó la campaña contra los indios y fue derrotado. El gobierno virreinal envió una expedición de refuerzo al mando de Agustín de Vildósola, que derrotó a los sublevados en Tecoripa, el cerro del Tambor y Otancahui y firmó un acuerdo con los pueblos yaquis y mayos para respetar sus formas de organización. En 1743, sin embargo, Vildósola, que entonces era gobernador de Sonora, sospechó que se preparaba una insurrección y mandó detener y ejecutar a los caciques yaquis y mayos Juan Calixto, Juan Ignacio Muni y Esteban. Desde entonces, el gobierno sonorense adoptó la costumbre de nombrar comandante militar del valle del Yaqui a un indio de la región, porque creyó que los yaquis respetarían a sus autoridades si éstas pertenecían a la etnia. La fórmula funcionó durante el resto del siglo XVIII y los primeros años del siglo XIX, pero en 1825, varios pueblos desconocieron a los caciques y, encabezados por Juan Ignacio Juscamea, llamado Banderas, se levantaron en armas. Los indios crearon una Confederación India de Sonora para exterminar a los *yoris* y consiguieron aliarse con los mayos y los ópatas. Durante casi una década, debido a la utilización de las armas de fuego, los yaquis se manejaron con independencia y pudieron reorganizar sus comunidades, pero en enero de 1833 Banderas fue derrotado y fusilado junto con Virgen y Dolores Gutiérrez, los dirigentes ópatas. En 1842, las comunidades yaquis se incorporaron al levantamiento centralista de Manuel María Gándara y tomaron Hermosillo y Guaymas, pero más tarde fueron derrotados. En 1860, aprovechando un nuevo levantamiento de los militares que debían combatirlos, los yaquis se adhirieron al Plan de la Magdalena y se levantaron en armas. Una vez más, sin embargo, volvieron a ser derrotados. En 1865, José María Tranquilino Almada logró que un gran número de yaquis y mayos se unieran al ejército de intervención que trataba de imponer el imperio de Maximiliano. Durante ese año y el siguiente, batallones indígenas hicieron la guerra a las tropas republicanas de Antonio Rosales y de Ángel Martínez. En 1866, las fuerzas de Refugio Tanori y Emilio Langberg tomaron Ures y, en junio, las de Almada ocuparon Álamos. Aunque fueron desalojadas por los republicanos poco después, los yaquis se mantuvieron activos en el sur de Sonora, norte de Sinaloa y oeste de Chihuahua hasta el triunfo de la República. Eran, de hecho, la principal fuerza imperialista de la región. Nuevas sublevaciones yaquis fueron combatidas por el liberal Próspero Salazar en 1867, 1868 y 1873. En esas campañas, las fuerzas de Salazar recurrieron a la mayor brutalidad. En febrero de 1868, por ejemplo, las fuerzas de Jesús García Morales entraron en negociaciones con varias comunidades yaquis, pero en vez de respetar los acuerdos de paz, los concentraron en las ruinas de una iglesia, esperaron a que los indios trataran de huir y asesinaron a más de un centenar de ellos. En 1874 el gobierno sonorense nombró alcalde mayor de la zona a José María Leyva Cajeme (☛), un yaqui con gran autoridad entre su pueblo, que había servido al ejército republicano en su combate contra los yaquis imperialistas y, al año siguiente, a causa de una nueva agresión del gobierno sonorense de Ignacio Pesqueira, Cajeme se levantó en armas y se inició la guerra del Yaqui. Durante 10 años, Cajeme gobernó una nación prácticamente independiente, pero en 1885 un comando militar se adentró en territorio indio y asesinó a la familia de Cajeme. Hasta entonces, los yaquis se habían limitado a rechazar las ofensivas del ejército mexicano, pero a partir de la agresión, comenzaron a realizar incursiones contra el resto del territorio sonorense. El gobierno organizó una gran campaña militar y, en 1887, asesinó a Cajeme, pero de inmediato fue sustituido por Juan Maldonado Tetabiate, quien quedó al frente de un ejército y una nación debilitados, por lo que recurrió a la guerra de guerrillas. En 1897, Tetabiate pactó la paz con el gobierno federal, pero dos años después, el ejército violó el acuerdo y renació la insurrección. Cuatro años combatieron de nuevo los yaquis, pero en 1901, a la muerte de Tetabiate, la sublevación se disolvió. En febrero de 1902 se produjo un nuevo alzamiento, dirigido esta vez por Luis Bule. El gobierno respondió con deportaciones masivas de indios prisioneros a Yucatán, Jalisco, Tlaxcala y Veracruz y, en 1909, Bule se rindió. Fueron reclutados mediante el sistema de leva por el ejército porfirista, que los utilizó contra la rebelión maderista. Durante la presidencia de Madero fueron lanzados contra los alzados orozquistas y, a partir de 1913, la gran mayoría formó parte de los batallones de voluntarios creados por Álvaro Obregón, a quien ayudaron decisivamente en la lucha contra el huertismo. Al margen de estos indígenas asimilados al ejército, había otro grupo rebelde, conocido como los "broncos", cuyos comandantes eran Luis Espinosa, Ignacio Mori y Luis Matus, que mantuvo el hostigamiento contra todas las fuerzas, revolucionarias o no, que entraban a su territorio. En 1917, el gobernador sonorense Adolfo de la Huerta pactó una nueva paz con los yaquis. En ese mismo año, el pacto fue violado y se generalizó otra rebelión que el mismo De la Huerta canceló con otro tratado, en 1919. Insurrecciones similares habrían de sucederse durante los años veinte, sobre todo entre 1926 y 1927, cuando el gobierno del presidente Plutarco Elías Calles decidió bombardear las riberas del río y concentrar a un gran número de indios en las cercanías de Perote, hasta que el 27 de octubre de 1937, el presidente Lázaro Cárdenas dictó el "Acuerdo para resolver el problema agrario de la región del Yaqui", mediante el cual se concedieron a la tribu 500,000 hectáreas, 20,000 de ellas de riego. En 1958 el gobierno sonorense efectuó un plebiscito entre los yaquis para ofrecerles una organización municipal; éstos prefirieron conservar su organización tradicional, aunque aceptaron la coordinación con las autoridades constitucionales para resolver cuestiones de riego, sanidad, educación y crédito.

Foto: Imagen Latina

Tomás Yarrington Ruvalcaba

Yarrington Ruvalcaba, Tomás ◆ n. en Matamoros, Tams. (1957). Licenciado en economía por el Instituto Tecnológico y de Estudios Superiores de Monterrey (1979) y maestro en administración pública por la Universidad del Sur de California (1987). Integrante del PRI, fue miembro de su Consejo Político Nacional (1995-96). Diputado federal (1991), presidente municipal de Matamoros (1993-95), secretario de Hacienda de Tamaulipas (1997-98) y gobernador de ese estado elegido para el periodo 1998-2004.

Yarza, Remigio ◆ n. en Zitácuaro, Mich. (¿1775?-1819). Abogado. A finales de 1810 se unió a las fuerzas insurgentes de Ignacio López Rayón. Un año después fue nombrado representante de José Antonio Torres ante la Suprema Junta Gubernativa de América que se reunió en Zitácuaro. Fue secretario de José María Cos (1812) y del Congreso insurgente (1814-15). Firmó, como secretario del Congreso, la Constitución de Apatzingán de octubre de 1814. Se separó del Congreso al año siguiente y a principios de 1816, con José María Vargas, reorganizó la Junta Nacional Gubernativa en Uruapan e impulsó su traslado a Jaujilla. En 1817 organizó una fuerza militar que operó en Michoacán y Guanajuato. Se negó a colaborar con Francisco Javier Mina y con el propio Torres, quien ordenó su captura y lo hizo fusilar.

Yarza Gutiérrez, Alberto ◆ n. en la ciudad de México y m. en Tacubaya, DF (1857-1923). Estudió en el Colegio Militar. En 1913 apoyó el golpe de Estado de Victoriano Huerta, por lo que ascendió a general de división en 1914. Fue gobernador de Tlaxcala (en abril de 1913), de Michoacán (mayo y junio de 1913), y de Tabasco (del 30 de agosto de 1913 al 1 de septiembre de 1914).

Yatini, Lienzo de ◆ Códice zapoteco realizado en el siglo XVIII. Es un pliego de tela pintada de 160 por 117 centímetros. El original se encuentra en la Biblioteca Nacional de Antropología.

Yauhquemehcan ◆ Municipio de Tlaxcala situado al noreste de la capital estatal y al suroeste de Apizaco. Superficie: 29.20 km^2. Habitantes: 16,844, de los cuales 3,321 forman la población económicamente activa. Ha-

Iglesia de San Dionisio en Yauhquemehcan, Tlaxcala

Foto: Fondo Editorial Grupo Azabache

Convento de Santiago el Mayor en Yautepec, Morelos

blan alguna lengua indígena 51 personas mayores de cinco años (náhuatl 29). En la jurisdicción se cultivan plantas medicinales.

YAUTEPEC ◆ Municipio de Morelos situado al este de Cuernavaca y al oeste de Cuautla. Superficie: 140.90 km². Habitantes: 79,108, de los cuales 17,574 forman la población económicamente activa. Hablan alguna lengua indígena 236 personas mayores de cinco años (náhuatl 122, mixteco 36). En la jurisdicción se encuentra la población de Oaxtepec, que antes de la conquista europea fue uno de los sitios de recreo de la aristocracia mexica, donde los dominicos construyeron un convento a mediados del siglo XVI y en 1569 los Hermanos de la Caridad establecieron el hospital de la Santa Cruz, uno de los nosocomios novohispanos más importantes hasta el siglo XVIII, cuando desapareció. En 1966 se abrió al público el Centro Vacacional de Oaxtepec, del IMSS. Cerca de la cabecera, Yautepec de Zaragoza, está el ingenio azucarero de Oacalco.

Flecha, relieve en piedra volcánica de Jorge Yázpik

Yaxcabá, Yucatán

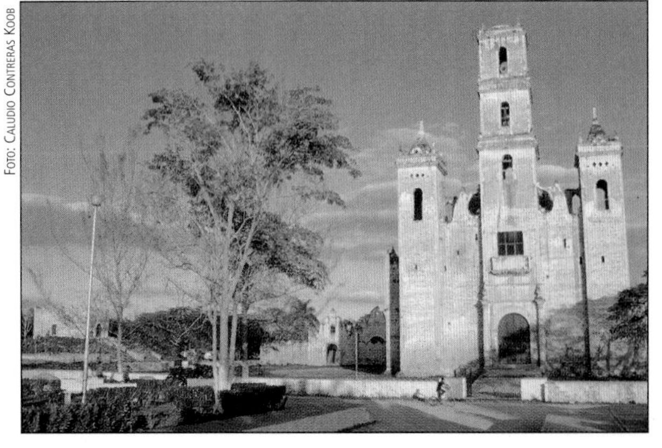

Foto: Claudio Contreras Koob

YAUTEPEC ◆ Río de Morelos también llamado Tlaquiltenango. Nace de los manantiales de Oaxtepec, en la porción norte del estado, en la vertiente meridional de la sierra de Tepoztlán. Corre de norte a sur, entre las sierras de Yautepec y de Tlaltizapán; al este de Tlaltizapán, la corriente tuerce hacia el suroeste, recibe a los ríos Agua Dulce y Tetlama o Jojutla y desemboca en el Amacuzac, al sureste del lago de Tequesquitengo, en los límites con el estado de Guerrero.

YÁVAROS ◆ ☛ *Huatabampo*.

YAXCABÁ ◆ Municipio de Yucatán situado al suroeste de Chichén Itzá y al este de Ticul. Superficie: 1,079.40 km². Habitantes: 11,855, de los cuales 3,492 forman la población económicamente activa. Hablan alguna lengua indígena 8,834 personas mayores de cinco años (maya 8,833). Indígenas monolingües: 1,252.

YAXCHILÁN ◆ ☛ *Ocosingo*.

YAXE ◆ Municipio de Oaxaca situado al sur-sureste de la capital estatal y al nor-noreste de Miahuatlán. Superficie: 65.07 km². Habitantes: 2,003, de los cuales 487 forman la población económicamente activa.

YAXKUKUL ◆ Municipio de Yucatán situado al noreste de Mérida y al suroeste de Motul. Superficie: 43.43 km². Habitantes: 2,245, de los cuales 628 forman la población económicamente activa. Hablan alguna lengua indígena 645 personas mayores de cinco años (maya 645).

YAYAUHQUICINTÉOTL ◆ Deidad nahua cuyo nombre significa "El dios del maíz prieto". Era la encargada de la protección de las mazorcas rojas, pintas y moradas.

YAZBEK, CHARLOTTE ◆ n. en Puebla, Pue., y m. en el DF (?-1989). Escultora y pintora. Estudió con Uxio Souto, Hermilo Castañeda, Pedro Medina Guzmán y Mathías Goeritz (1952-62). Expuso por primera vez en 1963, en la Galería Fulton de Nueva York, y al año siguiente presentó varias de sus obras en el Pabellón Mexicano de la Feria Mundial de Nueva York. Ha sido asesora de artesanías del gobierno del Estado de México (1970-76). En su casa de campo, en Avándaro, tenía montada una exposición permanente. Hay obra suya en el Museo de Arte Moderno. Autora de los óleos *Pareja* y *Autorretrato* (1981), de las esculturas *La familia*, que se encuentra en la Unidad Adolfo López Mateos de la ciudad de México (1963); *El vendedor de esperanzas*, *Los novios* y *Adagio*, que están en el circuito interior de la ciudad de México (1971); 18 piezas del Parque Escultórico de Cuautitlán Izcalli (1971); y una estatua de Carlos Hank González, que está en Tequesquitengo (1982). En 1962, 1964 y 1977 el cineasta Rafael Corkidi realizó cortometrajes sobre su obra.

YÁZPIK, JORGE ◆ n. en el DF (1955). Escultor. Estudió en la Escuela de Artes Plásticas de la UNAM (1977). Ha expuesto su obra desde 1982 en museos y galerías del país como la Juan Martín, de Arte Mexicano y del ITAM y en Uruguay, Perú, Colombia, Francia y EUA. En 1997 montó *Jorge Yázpik. Escultura* en los museos de Arte Moderno y Rufino Tamayo de la ciudad de México. Becario del Fonca (1991). Desde 1993 pertenece al SNCA. Tercer premio en escultura del XV Concurso Nacional de Artes Plásticas en 1980.

YECAPIXTLA ◆ Municipio de Morelos situado al este de Cuautla y al oeste de Tetela del Volcán, en los límites con el estado de México. Superficie: 180.50 km². Habitantes: 33,578, de los cuales 7,020 forman la población económicamente activa. Hablan alguna lengua indígena 229 personas mayores de cinco años (mixteco 125 y náhuatl 43). En 1534, los agustinos Jorge de Ávila y Andrés de San Esteban se instalaron en la actual cabecera, que era un antiguo pueblo nahua, la llamaron San Juan de Yecapixtla e iniciaron la construcción de un convento y un templo que fue terminado hacia 1540.

YÉCORA ◆ Municipio de Sonora situado al noreste de Guaymas y al sureste de Hermosillo, en los límites con Chihuahua. Superficie: 3,312.05 km². Habitantes: 6,114, de los cuales 1,327 forman la población económicamente activa. Hablan alguna lengua indígena 251 personas mayores de cinco años (pima 250). Entre el 26 de diciembre de 1930 y el 8 de abril de 1935 fue suprimido como municipio y su territorio pasó a formar parte del de Sahuaripa.

YECUATLA ◆ Municipio de Veracruz situado al noreste de Jalapa y al sur de Misantla. Superficie: 135.72 km². Habitantes: 12,764, de los cuales 3,624 forman la población económicamente activa. Hablan alguna lengua indígena 305 personas mayores de cinco años (totonaco 293).

YEHUALTEPEC ◆ Municipio de Puebla situado en al sureste de la capital del estado y contiguo a Tecamachalco. Superficie: 170.95 km². Habitantes: 17,448, de los cuales 3,414 forman la población económicamente activa. Hablan alguna lengua indígena 108 personas mayores de cinco años (náhuatl 103).

YEHYA, NAIEF ◆ n. en el DF (1963). Periodista. Ingeniero industrial titulado en la UNAM (1992). Comenzó a escribir ensayos y reseñas críticas sobre cine y música en el suplemento *Sábado*, del periódico *unomásuno* (1990-97). Mantiene la columna "La Jornada Virtual" en *La Jornada Semanal* (1995-). Colabora en *Crónica* (1996-) y en *El Financiero* (1998-). Textos suyos han aparecido en las revistas *Viceversa*, *Origina*, *Etcétera*, *Generación*, *Gallito Comics*, *La PUSmoderna*, *Poliéster*, *Somos*, *X*, *LA Weekly*, *Complot Internacional* y otras. Radicado en Nueva York, es corresponsal en esta ciudad de la revista *Letras Libres*. Está incluido en las antologías *El fin de la nostalgia. Nueva crónica de la ciudad de México* (1992), *Por amor al sax* (1992), *Dispersión multitudinaria* (1997) y *Líneas aéreas* (España, 1999). Autor de novela: *Obras sanitarias* (1992), *Camino a casa* (1994) y *La verdad de la vida en Marte* (1995); cuento: *Bajo la luz del cinescopio* 1994); y ensayo: *Caos y rabia en la cultura de la máquina* (1993) y *Los sueños electrónicos de las ovejas cibernéticas* (1994).

YEMEN, REPÚBLICA DEL ◆ Nación de Asia situada en el sur de la península Arábiga, en los litorales de los mares Rojo y Arábigo. El estrecho de Bab el-Mandeb la separa de Etiopía. Limita al norte con Arabia Saudita y al noreste con Omán. Superficie: 527,970 km², que incluyen las islas Socotora, Los Hermanos, Perim y Kamarán. Habitantes: 16,887,000 (1998). La capital es Sana'a (972,000 habitantes en 1995) y otras ciudades de importancia son Adén (562,000), Taizz (290,107) y Hodeida (246,068). El idioma oficial es el árabe y la moneda el riyal yemenita. *Historia*: entre los siglos VII a.n.e. y VI de la era actual, se desarrolló una cultura basada en el comercio, que llevó al surgimiento de ciudades como Ma'in, Marib, Timna o Nagram, ubicadas en las rutas de las caravanas que transportaban especias de Dhufar, ahora situado en Omán, y Punt, que actualmente pertenece a Somalia, y que luego seguían camino hasta los mercados mediterráneos o de Mesopotamia. Esas ciudades se unificaron en reinos, primero el de Mina y luego el de Saba, cuya vinculación con el litoral africano dio origen al imperio de Axum. Saba mantuvo sus lazos con África durante varios siglos y resultado de ello fue la propagación del cristianismo entre los yemenitas, a partir del siglo IV, por obra de predicadores etiopes. Cuando la secta hebrea himyarita ejerció su hegemonía sobre el sur árabe, poco después del ocaso de Saba, y estableció la judía como religión oficial, se desencadenaron conflictos con los cristianos, que desembocaron en ocupaciones extranjeras: Etiopía conquistó la región en el año 525, pero fue desplazada por los persas en el 570. Desde el siglo VII, a partir de la unificación árabe impulsada por Mahoma, Yemen fue dominado por los califatos de Damasco y Bagdad y más tarde por el imanato autóctono de Yahya al-Hadi ila'l-Haqq. En 1517 los otomanos ocuparon la franja costera yemenita. En el interior, mientras tanto, un imán siguió gobernando. En 1618, los ingleses instalaron en el puerto de Moka una agencia de la Compañía de las Indias para comerciar con café. La presencia británica se amplió en el siglo XIX: como consecuencia de la conquista del país por el egipcio Mehmet Alí, los británicos ocuparon el extremo suroccidental de la península, mientras los turcos trataban de consolidar su dominio en el interior, lo que consiguieron en 1872; para lograrlo, tuvieron que mantener en su cargo al imán yemenita, que incluso reafirmó su posición al hacer hereditario su cargo, antes electivo. En 1869, con la apertura del canal de Suez y la consolidación del dominio otomano sobre el norte de Yemen, Adén cobró gran importancia para la estrategia global británica. Entre 1870 y 1934 los ingleses extendieron su hegemonía, mediante tratados de amistad o establecimiento de protectorados sobre las tribus locales, hasta consolidar un país que llegaba, por el oeste, a la frontera con Omán. De 1911 a 1913 el imán Yahya ad-Din condujo una rebelión nacionalista, después de la cual el imperio turco reconoció la autoridad plena de los imanes sobre el territorio, a cambio de la aceptación por éstos de una formal

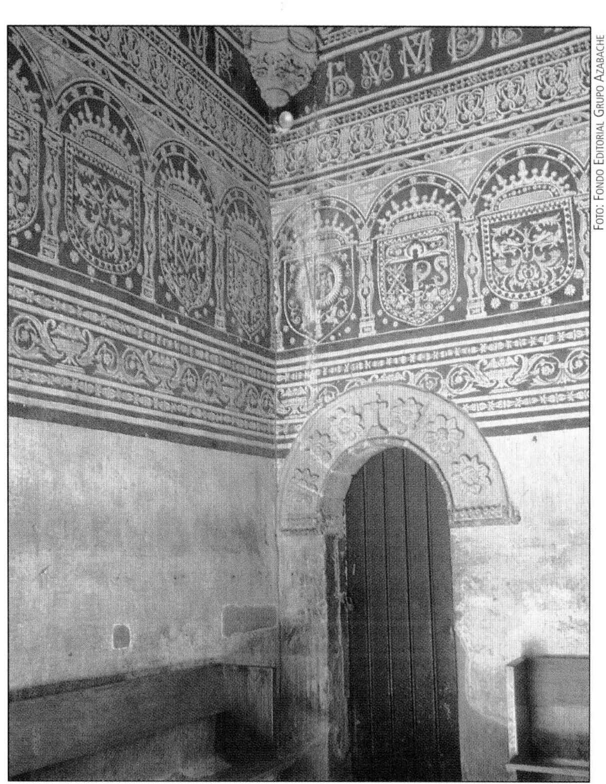

FOTO: FONDO EDITORIAL GRUPO AZABACHE

Convento de San Juan Bautista en Yecapixtla, Morelos

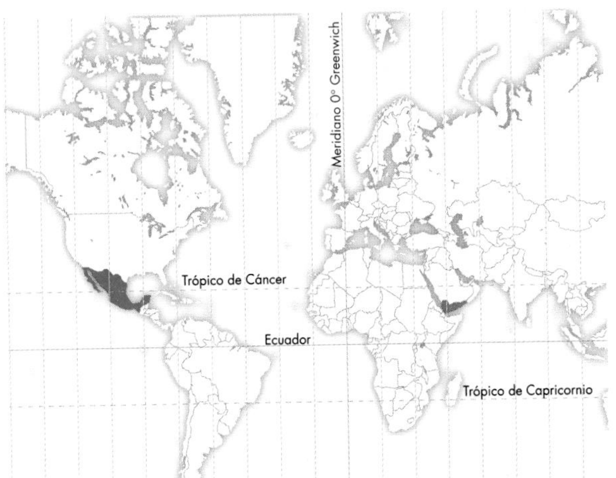

República del Yemen

soberanía otomana. Luego de la primera guerra mundial, Yahya ad-Din se proclamó soberano independiente de Yemen, lo que llevó a conflictos con el emir saudita de Najd y con los ingleses instalados en Adén, que en 1937 se convirtió en colonia. Los sauditas lanzaron una ofensiva militar contra el imán Yahya ibn Mohammed, que en el tratado de paz de 1934 tuvo que aceptar la pérdida de algunos territorios al norte del país, pero mantuvo su independencia, de acuerdo con el Tratado de Taif. Los ingleses no se involucraron en la guerra, pero alentaron los conflictos internos de Yemen y apoyaron a los grupos contrarios al imán, que murió asesinado en 1948. Al término de la segunda guerra mundial, la explosión del nacionalismo árabe condujo a la formación de diversos grupos en Adén, que en 1955 formaron el Frente Nacional Unido, promotor de manifestaciones callejeras y huelgas entre 1956 y 1960. Los ingleses trataron de dividir el movimiento mediante algunas concesiones y con la instauración de un parlamento, pero no pudieron evitar que el Frente de Liberación Nacional, brazo armado del Frente Nacional Unido, iniciara la revolución en el interior. En Yemen del Norte, Ahmad, sucesor de Yahya ibn Mohammed, se sumó en 1958 a la República Árabe Unida, formada por Egipto y Siria, pero la abandonó en 1961. En Adén, en 1959, se constituyó la Federación de los Emiratos Árabes del Sur y en 1963 la Federación de Arabia Meridional. Ahmad, en tanto, murió en 1962 y fue sucedido por su hijo Muhammad al-Badr, quien en septiembre de 1962 fue depuesto por el militar Abdullah al-Sallal, que estaba apoyado por Egipto. Sallal proclamó la República Árabe de Yemen en tanto que Badr, con apoyo saudita e inglés, inició una guerra civil contra el gobierno republicano. En 1963 el ejército egipcio intervino en favor de la República y, al año siguiente, tropas sauditas invadieron Yemen para apoyar a Badr. En 1964, con una nueva Constitución, Sallal llegó a la Presidencia. En 1965, el ex imán presentó su propia Constitución y se recrudecieron las hostilidades. En 1965 las tropas sauditas se retiraron de Yemen y las egipcias hicieron lo mismo entre 1967 y 1968. Por otra parte, el FLN ocupó en 1967 el puerto de Adén, proclamó la independencia e inició una revolución socialista. Ésta fue hostilizada desde luego por Inglaterra y Arabia Saudita, primero, y por Estados Unidos después, por lo que el gobierno de Yemen del Sur, o República Popular de Yemen, se vio obligado a preparar militarmente a su pueblo. En el norte, un cuartelazo llevó a la presidencia al moderado Abdul Rahman al-Iryani, mientras el ex imán Badr era depuesto por su propio hijo, Muhammad ibn Hussein, en 1968. En octubre de 1972, Iryani firmó un tratado con el gobierno de Yemen del Sur, que preveía una futura reunificación de ambos Estados. México estableció relaciones diplomáticas con Yemen del Sur en agosto de 1975. El acuerdo de futura unificación disgustó al monarca saudita Faisal, quien alentó en junio de 1974 un cuartelazo dirigido por Ibrahim al-Hamadi. Sin embargo, Hamadi se enfrentó al dirigente saudita, que intentaba controlar el gobierno yemenita, por lo que en 1977 fue asesinado. El gobierno quedó a cargo de una junta cívico militar, comandada por Ahmed al-Gashmi, quien continuó la política nacionalista y antisaudita de Hamadi y, como su antecesor, murió asesinado en 1978. En Yemen del Sur, mientras tanto, el trabajo político se encaminó a la formación de un partido que defendiera la revolución, pero la infiltración de las potencias occidentales dio frutos: en julio de 1978 el entonces presidente Alí Robaye intentó dar un golpe para desviar el proceso e impedir la creación del partido. El cuartelazo fue derrotado y el Frente Nacional integró un triunvirato ejecutivo. En Yemen del Norte, el militar Alí Abdullah Saleh, designado presidente en 1978, no pudo evitar que las disensiones internas estallaran en enero de 1979 en conflictos armados. En el sur, a comienzos de 1979 Abdel Fattah Ismail, secretario general del recientemente creado Partido Socialista Yemenita, fue nombrado jefe de Estado. En 1980, Alí Nasser sustituyó en la presidencia a Ismail. Arabia Saudita intensificó su campaña de hostigamiento sobre Yemen del Sur, con la reclamación de algunas partes de su territorio, aquellas en las que la empresa petrolera estatal argelina había descubierto yacimientos de hidrocarburos. Cuando el Frente Nacional Democrático, que agrupaba a todas las fuerzas progresistas del norte, estaba a punto de tomar el poder, por instigación saudita el conflicto derivó en una guerra contra Yemen del Sur. La mediación de Siria, Irak y Jordania logró un alto al fuego y un acuerdo por el cual se retomaron las negociaciones tendientes a la reunificación, suspendidas desde 1972. Después de la pacificación, la capital del nuevo Estado norteño fue establecida en la ciudad de Sana'a; se impuso el islamismo como religión oficial y se elaboró una Constitución que respetaba y procuraba integrar las características e ideologías divergentes de los dos regímenes. Después de ser discutida por los respectivos parlamentos, la futura Constitución sería también sometida a referéndum de los pueblos yemenitas. El gobierno, asimismo, firmó en enero de 1980 un acuerdo con el FND para permitir su inserción en la vida política. Hubo, sin embargo, un enfrentamiento más entre la república y el Frente, que terminó en abril de 1982, cuando fue suscrito el quinto acuerdo de cese el fuego entre Saleh y el líder del FND, el sultán Omar. En 1990 se produjo la unificación de la República Árabe de Yemen y la República Democrática Popular de Yemen para crear la República del Yemen. Sin embargo, en 1994 se produjo una breve guerra civil entre el norte y el sur, ganada por el primer bando. A finales de 1995 tropas de Eritrea desembarcaron en la isla Hanish, que reclaman como suya, y se produjo una breve guerra con Yemen. La mediación de Egipto acabó con las hostilidades y los gobiernos beligerantes acetaron llevar su diferendo ante los tribunales internacionales.

Yerbanís, del ◆ Sierra de Durango situada en la porción oriental del estado. Se extiende de noroeste a sureste, a lo largo de 20 km, al noreste de Peñón Blanco y al oeste-suroeste de Cuencamé; está limitada al este por el río Cuencamé; al sur por la sierra de Santa María; al suroeste y oeste por el río del Peñón, que la separa del valle de San Juan del Río; y al norte por el río Nazas. En su extremo noroccidental se encuentra el Cerro Blanco, una de las eminencias más importantes del estado de Durango.

Yermo, Gabriel de ◆ n. en España y m. en la ciudad de México (1757-1813). Comerciante avecindado en la Nueva España. Se casó con la heredera de las haciendas de Temixco y San Gabriel, en el valle de Cuernavaca. Levantó un emporio que controlaba el abasto de carne de la ciudad de México y que surtía de reses de lidia las principales plazas novohispanas, por lo que entró en conflicto con el virrey José de Iturrigaray, quien impuso elevados impuestos a sus productos. Como el resto de los grandes comerciantes capitalinos, se opuso al intento autonomista del Ayuntamiento de la ciudad de México y en la noche del 15 de septiembre de 1808 dirigió el golpe de Estado que destituyó al virrey.

Yermo y Parres, José María de ◆ n. en la Hacienda de Jalmolonga, Edo. de Méx., y m. en Puebla, Pue. (1851-1904). Su madre falleció 50 días después de su nacimiento, tras lo cual fue llevado por su padre a la ciudad de México. Ingresó a la congregación de la Misión Paules en 1867 y emitió sus votos religiosos en 1869. Fue enviado a París en 1871 para completar su formación. Dos años después regresó al país. Fue ordenado sacerdote en León, en 1879. En 1885 fundó con cuatro monjas la congregación de las Siervas del Sagrado Corazón de Jesús y de los Pobres en el Calvario de León. En 1888 instaló en Puebla el Asilo de Caridad de Santa Inés donde al año siguiente incardinó la congregación y trasladó su gobierno general. En 1893 fundó también en Puebla la Casa de la Misericordia Cristiana para la regeneración de la mujer y educación de la infancia y la juventud donde ayudaba a prostitutas y daba atención a huérfanos. Sus fundaciones de beneficencia se sucedieron por la república, se fundaron escuelas e internados indígenas en la Tarahumara. Sus restos fueron depositados en la Casa Central de la congregación, en Puebla. La congregación tiene 64 casas de ayuda, 50 en el país y 14 en EUA, Guatemala, Honduras, Nicaragua, Colombia y África. Fue beatificado en 1990 por el Papa Juan Pablo II.

Yesca, La ◆ Municipio de Nayarit situado al este de Tepic y al norte de Ixtlán del Río, en los límites con Jalisco. Superficie: 2,218.50 km². Habitantes: 14,349, de los cuales 2,432 forman la población económicamente activa. Hablan alguna lengua indígena 1,762 personas mayores de cinco años (huichol 1,757).

Yesca, de la ◆ Sierra de Nayarit y Jalisco. Es el extremo suroriental de la de Buenavista o Pinabete. Se extiende de suroeste a noreste, desde el norte del río Grande de Santiago, en Nayarit, hasta la vertiente suroccidental de la sierra de Bolaños, de la que está separada por el río del mismo nombre, en Jalisco.

YMCA ◆ Siglas de la Young Men's Christian Association, institución protestante fundada en Londres en 1844 y extendida a Estados Unidos en 1851. En México se conoce como la *Guay* por la pronunciación inglesa de la "y". En enero de 1891 se abrió el primer establecimiento de la asociación en la ciudad de México, en un pequeño local en la calle de San Juan de Letrán, con el propósito expreso de brindar a los jóvenes estadounidenses y británicos residentes en este país un ambiente cultural y religioso similar al de sus países. Inició sus actividades sólo con una sala de lectura, pero rápidamente se le agregaron un gimnasio, boliche, baños y salones de juegos. El primer secretario general de la YMCA en México fue el estadounidense George M. Taylor, sustituido por su compatriota I. E. Manger, quien fue reemplazado a su vez por E. P. Gastón. A principios del presente siglo la asociación construyó su edificio sede en la calle de Balderas, en el que está el diario *Novedades*. A mediados del siglo se trasladó a unas instalaciones modernizadas en la avenida Ejército Nacional y pronto abrió más sucursales en la capital y en provincia, como el centro social de Camomihla, varias clínicas, casas en Torreón y Chihuahua; instalaciones deportivas en la avenida Río Churubusco y el club deportivo Mallorca. Asimismo, existe una asociación similar femenina, la Young Women's Christian Association.

Gabriel de Yermo

José María de Yermo

Yoaltícitl ◆ Deidad nahua, una de las advocaciones de Teteoinnan, cuyo nombre significa "La médica de la noche". Era la patrona de los médicos, adivinos y "suertistas", así como de los niños recién nacidos.

Yobaín ◆ Municipio de Yucatán situado al noreste de Motul y al noroeste de Temax, en el litoral del golfo de México. Superficie: 81.75 km². Habitantes: 1,983, de los cuales 543 forman la población económicamente activa. Hablan alguna lengua indígena 722 personas mayores de cinco años (maya 721).

Yocippa ◆ Deidad otomí de la fecundidad, cuyo nombre significa "Venerable coyote". Al inicio de la primavera, los otomíes celebraban la *yocippatotoco* o persecución del viejo coyote, que duraba tres días, durante los cuales comían

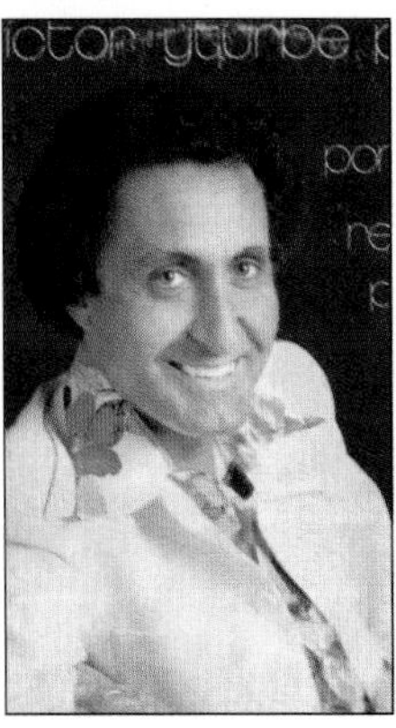

Víctor Yturbe *el Pirulí*

abundantemente, se emborrachaban y organizaban grandes orgías. El culto de este dios fue imitado por los pueblos nahuas, quienes convirtieron a Yocippa en Huehuecóyotl y a su fiesta en el tepílhuitl.

Yocupicio, Román ◆ n. en Masiaca y m. en Navojoa, Son. (1890-1950). Militar. En 1913 se levantó en armas en contra el gobierno de Victoriano Huerta y dos años después combatió a las fuerzas de la Convención. Desde finales de 1915, con Fausto Topete, dirigió una campaña contra los mayos. En 1920 se sumó a la insurrección de Agua Prieta. Fue presidente municipal de Navojoa (1921-23) y en 1929 se unió a la rebelión escobarista y al ser derrotado se exilió en Estados Unidos. Volvió a México durante el gobierno del presidente Lázaro Cárdenas y fue gobernador de Sonora (del 4 de enero de 1937 al 31 de agosto de 1939).

Yodocono de Porfirio Díaz ◆ ☛ *Magdalena Yodocono de Porfirio Díaz.*

Yogana ◆ Municipio de Oaxaca situado al noroeste de Miahuatlán y al sur-suroeste de Ejutla. Superficie: 91.86 km². Habitantes: 1,807, de los cuales 369 forman la población económicamente activa.

Yolotepec ◆ Río de Oaxaca, también llamado Ciruelo o Colorado. Nace en la porción occidental del estado, al noroeste de la capital de la entidad, de la confluencia del río Sordo y varias corrientes menores, provenientes de las sierras de Nochixtlán y de Tlaxiaco. Corre hacia el sur-suroeste; en la vertiente suroriental de la sierra de Yocuyacua recibe las aguas del río Putla o de las Cucharas. Luego tuerce hacia el sureste y, al noreste de Santiago Pinotepa Nacional, en la vertiente septentrional de la sierra de Miahuatlán, se une al río Atoyac para formar el Verde.

Yolotepec, Lienzo ◆ Códice mixteco, también llamado Lienzo de Amoltepec, pintado sobre una tela rectangular de algodón a mediados del siglo XVI. Describe los pueblos de Yolotepec y Santiago Amoltepec, situados en la Mixteca Alta. El original se encuentra en la Museo Americano de Historia Natural de Nueva York.

Yon Sosa, Marco Antonio ◆ n. en Guatemala y m. cerca de Ocosingo, Chis. (1929-1970). Estudió en la Escuela Politécnica del Ejército de Guatemala (1947-50) y asistió a los cursos del centro estadounidense de adiestramiento de Fort Gulik, en Panamá. El 13 de noviembre de 1960 se levantó en armas, con Luis Augusto Turcios Lima y Alejandro de León, contra el gobierno dictatorial de Miguel Ydígoras Fuentes. Fue vencido por sus ex compañeros del ejército guatemalteco e integró el Movimiento Revolucionario 13 de Noviembre (MR-13), organización guerrillera de la que formaron parte los mexicanos David Aguilar Mora, Eunice Campirán, Manuel Suárez y Adolfo Gilly. Durante casi una década dirigió el MR-13 y participó directamente en muchas de sus acciones, hasta que en mayo de 1970, perseguido por el ejército guatemalteco, cruzó el río Usumacinta cerca de la desembocadura del Lacantún y fue sorprendido por una patrulla militar mexicana que le dio muerte.

Ypiranga ◆ Vapor de la línea transatlántica Hamburguesa Americana en el que salió de México, a finales de mayo de 1911, el ex presidente Porfirio Díaz para trasladarse a Europa. En 1914, el presidente Victoriano Huerta compró a comerciantes de Estados Unidos un cargamento de armas que, por cuestiones diplomáticas, debió viajar primero a Rusia y luego a Alemania, desde donde las transportó a México este mismo buque. La intercepción de este cargamento dio pie a la invasión estadounidense del puerto de Veracruz, en 1914. No obstante, el *Ypiranga* logró hacer el desembarco en Puerto México. En ese año, al triunfo de la revolución constitucionalista, Huerta salió del país a bordo de la misma nave.

Ysusi Farfán, Guillermo ◆ n. en el DF (1946). Estudió en la Escuela Nacional de Arquitectura de la UNAM (1969). Ha sido proyectista, arquitecto y asesor técnico de la Dirección de Obras Públicas de Quintana Roo (1970), encargado de proyectos y construcción (1966-69) y coordinador de la gerencia general de Constructora Art-Vito Alessi (1971-72). Fue presidente de la Asociación de Vecinos de la colonia de Lomas Quebradas, Magdalena Contreras (1986-94), presidente de la Asociación Pro-defensa Civil y Ecológica del Surponiente del DF (1995-97), representante del Colegio de Arquitectos en la Magdalena Contreras. Delegado en Magdalena Contreras (1997-).

Ytuarte, Agustín ◆ n. en el DF y m. en Puerto Vallarta, Jal. (¿1936?-1986). Escenógrafo de cine. Trabajó en películas mexicanas y estadounidenses, entre ellas *Bajo fuego, Rambo II, Rescatemos a Harry* y *Cazador.* Era uno de los escenógrafos más solicitados a nivel mundial. Pereció en un accidente aéreo. Pertenecía al Sindicato de Técnicos y Manuales de la Producción Cinematográfica.

Yturbe *el Pirulí*, Víctor ◆ n. en el DF y m. en Naucalpan, Edo. de Méx. (1936-1987). Cantante. Realizó estudios de arquitectura. Fue fotógrafo en Acapulco, donde también trabajó en una alberca como el payaso *Pirulí*. Se trasladó a Puerto Vallarta y ahí se inició como cantante. Más tarde fue locutor de Radio Mil y Televisa. En 1971 obtuvo su primer éxito con la melodía *Felicidad*, de Armando Manzanero. Se presentó en teatro, centros nocturnos y televisión. Algunas de sus interpretaciones más populares fueron *Mi segundo amor*, *Miénteme* y *Verónica*. En 1973 recibió un premio Xóchitl. Murió asesinado.

Yucatán ◆ Canal de Quintana Roo situado al noreste de la península de Yucatán, entre el extremo oriental de México y el suroccidental de Cuba. Limita al noroeste con el extremo suroccidental del canal de la Florida y al sureste con el golfo de Honduras; comunica al mar Caribe con el golfo de México, al que lleva una parte de la corriente caliente del Atlántico septentrional. Entre los cabos San Antonio, de Cuba, y Catoche, de Quintana Roo, el canal tiene una anchura de 230 km, aproximadamente.

FOTO: MICHAEL CALDERWOOD

Mérida, capital del estado de Yucatán

Victor Cervera Pacheco, gobernador de Yucatán

YUCATÁN ◆ Estado de la República Mexicana situado en la península del mismo nombre, en el litoral del golfo de México. Limita con Quintana Roo y Campeche. Superficie: 38,402 km² (equivalente al 1.95 por ciento de la superficie total del país). Habitantes: 1,617,120 (1997). En 1995 su población representaba 1.7 por ciento de la total de México, y vivían en zonas urbanas 1,250,589 personas y en rurales 306,033. Su índice de analfabetismo es de 11.94 por ciento de los mayores de 15 años. Forman la población económicamente activa 58.5 por ciento de las personas mayores de 12 años. El producto interno bruto de Yucatán en 1996 fue de 1.3 por ciento del PIB nacional. Hablan alguna lengua indígena 545,902 personas mayores de cinco años (maya 544,021), de las cuales 46,918 no dominan el español. La entidad, con 106 municipios, se localiza en la región denominada plataforma de Yucatán, planicie rocosa formada por la sedimentación del agua marina durante el mesozoico y el cenozoico, por lo que carece de formaciones montañosas y sólo cuenta con pequeños lomeríos; entre éstos destacan la Sierrita

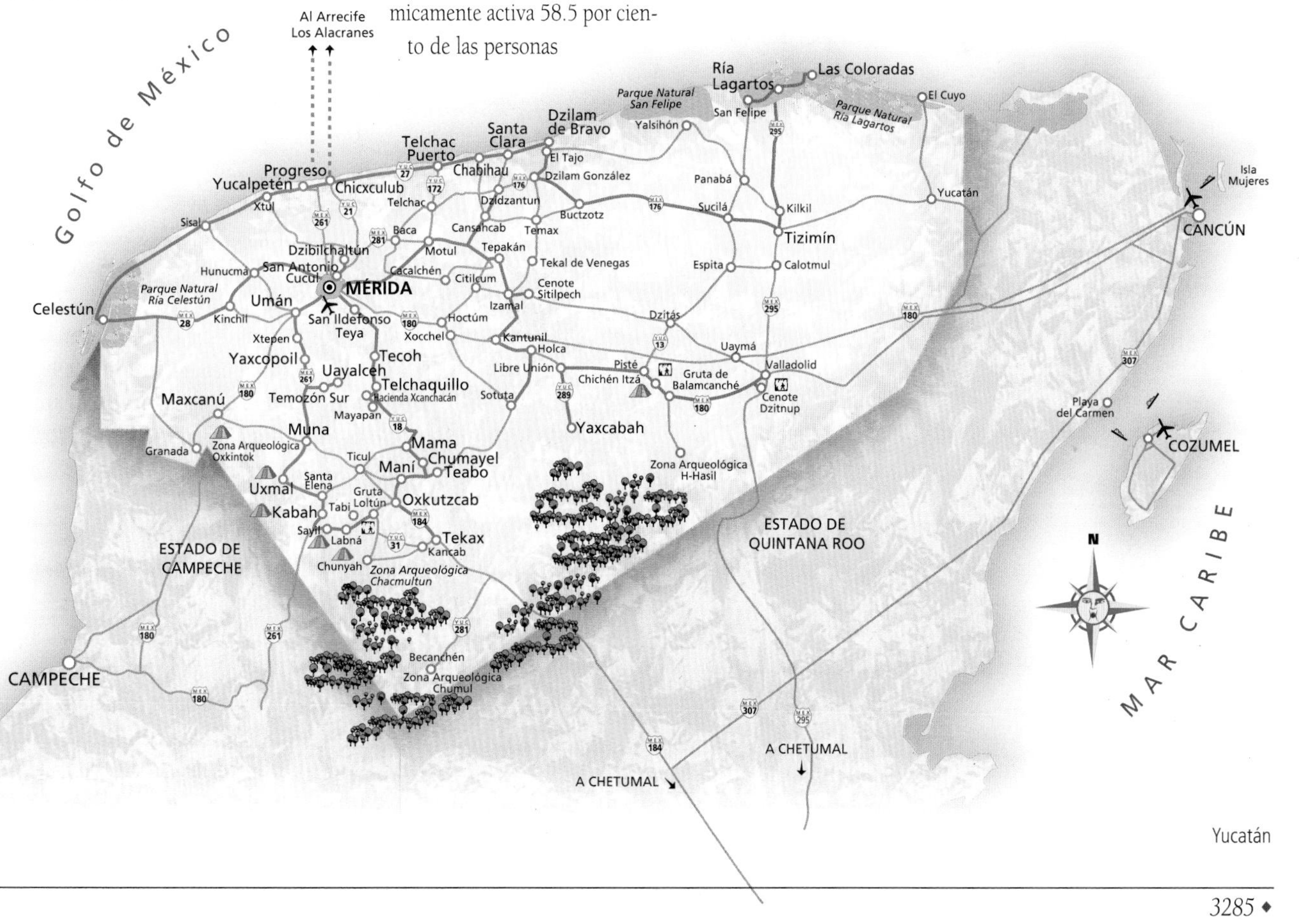

Yucatán

Foto: Michael Calderwood

Dzitnup en Yucatán

Foto: Michael Calderwood

Celestún, Yucatán

(cuya altitud promedio es de 100 metros) y la sierra de Ticul (con eminencias de 300 metros en promedio). La excesiva permeabilidad del suelo calizo del estado impide la formación de corrientes superficiales. Existen en cambio mantos freáticos que en algunos sitios se comunican a la superficie mediante pozos naturales, llamados cenotes, de los que se obtiene el abasto de agua para la población. La capital del estado de Yucatán es Mérida; otras ciudades de importancia son: Motul, Progreso, Ticul, Tizimín, Uxmal y Valladolid. El papa León X dispuso en enero de 1519 erigir la diócesis de Yucatán, en la creencia de que ya existía un templo en Santa María de los Remedios de Cozumel, nombre que recibió en Europa la península, considerada entonces como isla. La orden del pontífice no pudo acatarse por no haber todavía en territorio peninsular los elementos indispensables para establecer el gobierno de la Iglesia y el obispado se instaló en Tlaxcala en 1527. Fue hasta el 16 de diciembre de 1561 cuando se erigió la diócesis definitiva, elevada a arquidiócesis el 11 de noviembre de 1906. *Historia*: El territorio del actual estado de Yucatán fue poblado aproximadamente hacia el año 300 de nuestra era por avanzadas de la cultura maya clásica, que fundaron numerosas ciudades-estado, abandonadas hacia el año 900. En el año 987 llegaron a Yucatán los toltecas, dirigidos por Kukulkán (nombre maya de Quetzalcóatl), acompañados por los itzáes (grupos mayenses asimilados a la cultura nahua) y los tutul-xiúes. Los toltecas se fusionaron racialmente con los mayas clásicos, pero lograron imponer su cultura, religión y organización política y social. Unos 40 años antes de la migración tolteca, había sido fundada la ciudad-estado de Mayapán, gobernada por la dinastía Cocom, misma que más tarde estableció la llamada Liga de Mayapán, con sus similares de Uxmal (capital de los tutul-xiúes) y Chichén Itzá (de los itzáes). La Liga de Mayapán fue efímera, pues en el año 1194 se inició una guerra entre Mayapán y Chichén Itzá, que terminó con el triunfo de los Cocom hacia el año 1200 y con la subsecuente destrucción de las civilizaciones de los tutul-xiúes e itzáes; las fuentes indígenas señalan que la tiranía

Cenote Dzitnup Yuc, también llamado cenote X'keken

Foto: Claudio Contreras Koob

Cenote sagrado en Chichén Itzá, Yucatán

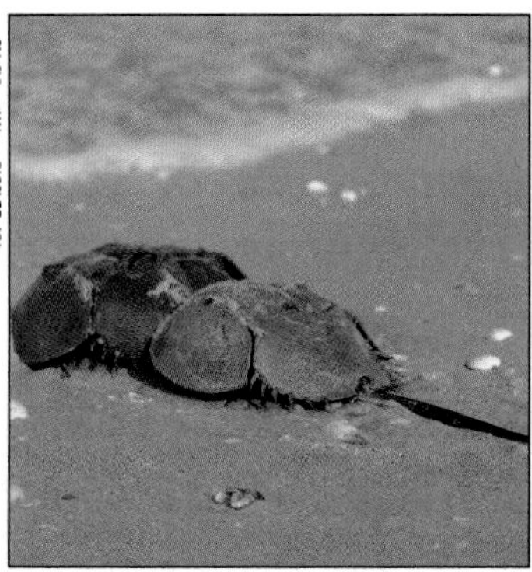

Cacerolita de mar

Cocom se prolongó dos siglos y medio. El predominio maya postclásico decayó, como su antecesor, hacia el año 1250, cuando las ciudades fueron abandonadas y sólo permanecieron algunas pequeñas aldeas de sus alrededores, que mantenían constantes guerras entre sí. Los primeros españoles que llegaron a Yucatán fueron los náufragos de la expedición de Pedro de Valdivia, que salió en 1511 del Darién (Panamá) rumbo a Santo Domingo y que zozobró frente a la costa oriental de la península; atacados por los indígenas, sólo dos náufragos se salvaron: Jerónimo de Aguilar, rescatado años después por Hernán Cortés, y Gonzalo Guerrero, quien se integró a la civilización maya, se casó con la hija del cacique de Chetumal y tuvo la primera descendencia mestiza en la historia de México. El 26 de junio de 1513, Juan Ponce de León avistó la costa norte de Yucatán, en su viaje hacia Florida; tres años más tarde volvió a costear la península, aunque no desembarcó en ninguno de sus puntos. En marzo de 1517, Francisco Hernández de Córdoba tocó tierra en Cozumel y el Cabo Catoche, llegó a Campeche y en Champotón sus hombres fueron rechazados por los indios. Regresó a Cuba e informó del descubrimiento de Yucatán, considerado entonces como isla. Juan de Grijalva llegó a Cozumel el 3 de mayo de 1518, entró a la bahía de la Ascensión, en el actual Quintana Roo, rodeó la costa, arribó a Campeche y Champotón, donde también peleó con los indígenas, y entró poco después al río que llevaría su nombre. En 1517, España supo de la existencia de Yucatán, territorio al que se le dio el nombre de isla de Santa María de los Remedios. En noviembre de 1518, Carlos V firmó las capitulaciones para su conquista en favor de Diego Velázquez, gobernador de Cuba. Éste organizó una expedición que confió a Hernán Cortés, quien salió de la isla el 18 de febrero de 1519, llegó a Cozumel, pasó por Isla Mujeres, rescató a Jerónimo de Aguilar y siguió su viaje hacia el centro del país. No se interesó por Yucatán y la península quedó al margen de los intereses hispanos. El 8 de diciembre de 1526, Carlos V firmó nuevas capitulaciones para la conquista de las islas de Yucatán y Cozumel, esta vez en favor de Francisco de Montejo, quien dio inicio a su expedición en 1527; intentó avanzar desde la costa oriental, pero fue rechazado por los indios; tres años después, acompañado por su hijo, Francisco de Montejo y León, reinició la conquista, esta vez desde el occidente; durante cinco años ambos Montejo lucharon contra los indígenas, a los que no pudieron derrotar. En un tercer intento de conquista, Montejo y León ocupó Champotón en 1537 y avanzó hacia el

Catalinetas de Yucatán

Foto: Michael Calderwood

Progreso, Yucatán

Foto: Fondo Editorial Grupo Azabache

Puerto de Chicxculub, Yucatán

norte hasta fundar Campeche en 1540 y Mérida en 1542. La conquista de la costa oriental, hasta Bacalar, la llevó a cabo Gaspar Pacheco, célebre por su crueldad, y la conquista espiritual estuvo a cargo de los franciscanos, quienes llegaron a edificar hasta 30 conventos, los de Valladolid, Izamal, Maní, Ticul y Chumayel, entre otros. A finales de 1565, Yucatán, dominado en un principio por los Montejo, fue convertido en una gubernatura cuyo primer titular fue Luis Céspedes de Oviedo. Hacia el final de la dominación española se implantó

Foto: Caludio Contreras Koob

Xlapak, Yucatán

el sistema de intendencias: una de ellas fue la de Mérida, cuya jurisdicción abarcaba toda la península, con sus islas, y la alcaldía mayor de Tabasco. El levantamiento indígena más importante en Yucatán, antes de la guerra de Castas, fue el de Jacinto Canek: este caudillo, cuyo nombre real era Jacinto Uc de los Santos, inició una rebelión el 20 de noviembre de 1761 contra los blancos y mestizos. Canek, nombrado rey de los mayas, dijo que el triunfo de su rebelión estaba escrito en el *Chilam Balam*; sus primeras acciones militares fueron exitosas, por lo que el gobierno yucateco envió un gran destacamento militar que derrotó a los rebeldes, tras de lo cual fueron quemados 500 indios. Canek huyó a Huntulchac, donde fue nuevamente derrotado, se refugió en Sibac y ahí fue finalmente aprehendido; se le juzgó y condenó a muerte y su ejecución tuvo lugar en la plaza mayor de Mérida, el 14 de diciembre del mismo año. Yucatán se mantuvo al margen de la revolución de independencia; no obstante, esa época quedó marcada por la lucha entre los sanjuanistas (llamados así por tener su centro de reunión en la sacristía de la ermita de San Juan, en Mérida), sacerdotes y seglares encabezados por Vicente María Velázquez, y los rutineros o serviles (partidarios del absolutismo monárquico). A partir de la convocatoria a las cortes españolas, publicada en 1810, las reuniones de los sanjuanistas tomaron un matiz político, acentuado cuando la Constitución de Cádiz se proclamó en Yucatán, en octubre de 1812. En julio de 1814 se abolió la Constitución de 1812 y se anunció en Mérida el restablecimiento del régimen absolutista de Fernando VII. Los sanjuanistas fueron encarcelados. Una vez restablecida la Constitución y liberados los sanjuanistas, éstos, unidos con antiguos rutineros vueltos liberales, organizaron la Confederación Patriótica, mezcla de credos políticos, religiosos y sociales cuya cohesión no duró

Mascarón de Chaac, dios maya de la lluvia

Foto: Caludio Contreras Koob

Foto: Caludio Contreras Koob

Ruinas de Labná

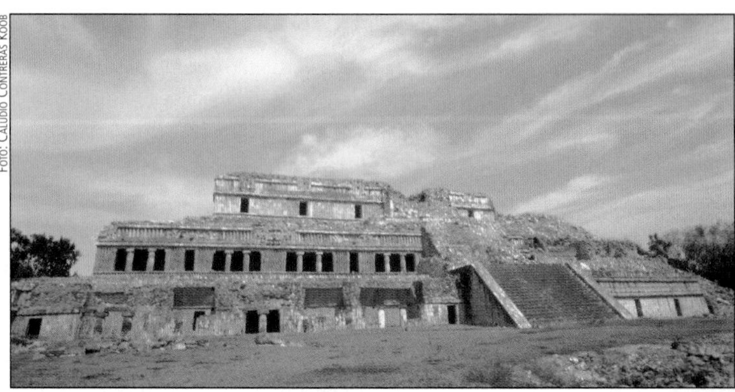

Foto: Caludio Contreras Koob

Ruta Puuc, Sayil

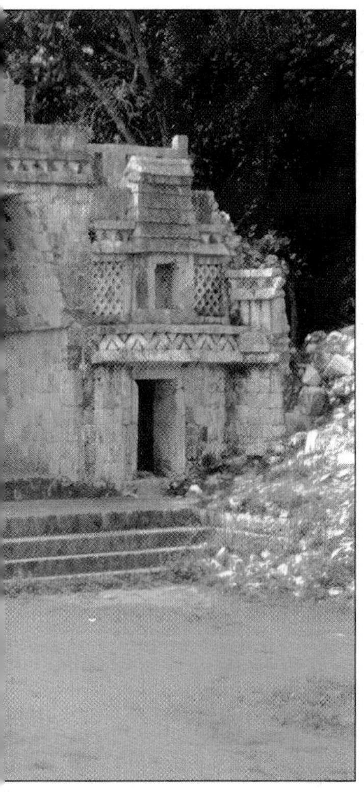

mucho, pues a finales de 1820 ya estaban divididos en dos bandos antagónicos: uno, encabezado por Zavala, en el que empezaba a germinar la idea de la independencia de Yucatán; y otro presidido por el gobernador Mariano Carrillo y Albornoz. A mediados de 1821 se conocieron en Yucatán la proclamación del Plan de Iguala y la celebración de los Tratados de Córdoba. El 15 de septiembre de ese año, cuando las fuerzas iturbidistas estaban en Tabasco y Campeche mostraba simpatías por ese movimiento, el gobernador Juan María Echeverri declaró la independencia de la provincia y su deseo de formar parte de la nación mexicana. En agosto de 1823 se instaló en Mérida el Congreso Constituyente del estado, que manifestó su preferencia por el sistema federal. El 21 de noviembre de 1824 se juró la Constitución mexicana y el 23 de abril de 1825 se proclamó la de Yucatán. A partir de entonces se sucedieron en el poder liberales y rutineros, federalistas y centralistas, de acuerdo con las corrientes políticas imperantes en el centro del país. En octubre de 1835, al implantarse en la República el sistema unitario, Yucatán se convirtió en departamento, se impusieron gobernantes desde el centro, aumentaron los aranceles al comercio de exportación, vital para un territorio aislado, y se exigió el envío de un contingente militar para la campaña de Texas. El descontento fue en aumento y en mayo de 1839 estalló una insurrección en Tizimín, encabezada por Santiago Imán, que fue secundada por otros grupos. En febrero de 1840 culminó el levantamiento al pronunciarse Anastasio Torrens, en Mérida, quien restableció el régimen federal. El Congreso local, a su vez, declaró rotas las relaciones con México. El 1 de octubre de 1841 se presentó ante la legislatura un proyecto para decretar la independencia de Yucatán; los diputados aprobaron la iniciativa, pero los senadores y el gobernador Santiago Méndez la bloquearon. Ya constituida en esa época la República de Texas, Yucatán firmó con ella un tratado de amistad y comercio. En 1841, el presidente Antonio López de Santa Anna envió a Mérida a Andrés Quintana Roo para arreglar las diferencias con Yucatán, lo que logró el 28 de diciembre de ese año, al firmar con el gobierno local un tratado de reincorporación a México. Santa Anna, sin embargo, desconoció los términos del pacto y pretendió que Yucatán aceptara sin reservas las Bases de Tacubaya, con lo que se reiniciaron las hostilidades. El 7 de mayo de 1842 se excluyó del Congreso federal a los legisladores yucatecos y se declaró a Yucatán enemigo de la nación. En octubre de 1842 marchó una expedición militar del centro contra Yucatán, comandada por Vicente Miñón, primero, y por Matías de la Peña Barragán, después. Éste, derrotado en la ciudad de Campeche, intentó sin éxito avanzar

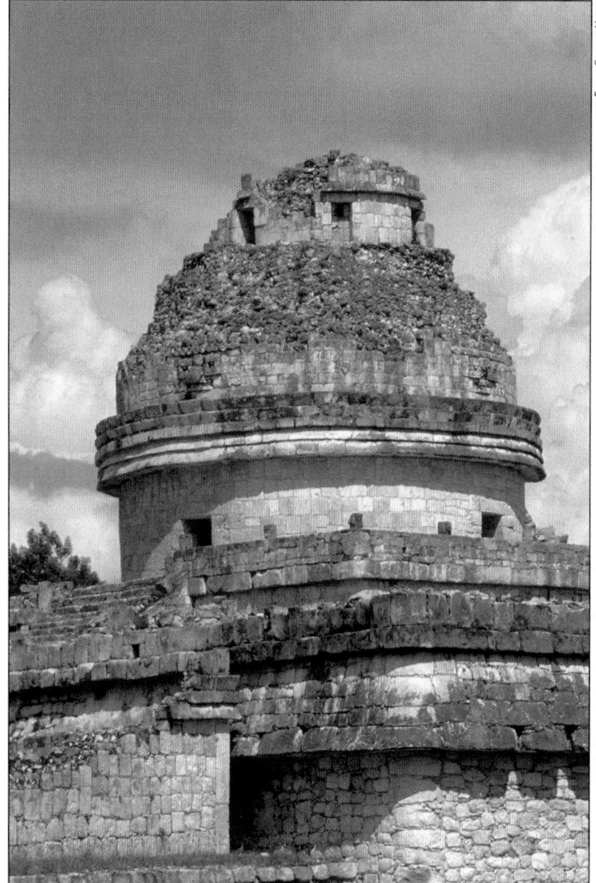

Foto: Carlos Hahn

Observatorio situado en Chichén Itzá·, Yucatán

Chacmultun, Yucatán

Foto: Caludio Contreras Koob

Casa maya en Noc Ac, Yucatán

sobre Mérida por la costa norte y capituló en Tixpéual el 15 de mayo de 1843, derrotado por Sebastián López de Llergo. El conflicto terminó el 11 de enero de 1844, al ser aprobados en el estado los convenios celebrados en la capital del país, el 14 de diciembre anterior, por los cuales Yucatán aceptó las Bases Orgánicas y quedó incorporado a México como departamento. Poco después, el gobierno central revocó varias de las concesiones otorgadas en los convenios de diciembre de 1843, de modo que el 1 de enero de 1846, Yucatán desconoció por segunda vez al régimen unitario. Al restablecerse en agosto de 1846 la Constitución de 1824, el gobernador yucateco Miguel Barbachano y el Congreso decidieron reconocer al nuevo gobierno federal, pero los campechanos, inconformes, se levantaron en armas el 8 de diciembre y pusieron en vigor la Constitución yucateca de 1841. La reincorporación a México quedó aplazada. Estados Unidos, ya en guerra con México, ocupó la isla del Carmen y amenazó con bloquear los puertos de la península, pero los campechanos manifestaron su neutralidad al gobierno estadounidense y consiguieron que éste permitiera el tráfico marítimo por Sisal y Campeche. En 1847 se inició la llamada guerra de Castas de Yucatán, último intento de los mayas por recobrar su independencia. El conflicto se prolongaría durante más de medio siglo. El 18 de julio de 1847, las autoridades yucatecas descubrieron una gran concentración de mayas armados en la hacienda Culumpich, propiedad de Jacinto Pat, cacique de Tihosuco; éste había planeado una sublevación que debería comenzar el 15 de agosto de ese año, con el degüello simultáneo de todos los blancos y mestizos de Yucatán, y para la cual contaba con el apoyo de los caciques de Tepich y de Chichimila, Cecilio Chi y Manuel Antonio Ay; luego de la eliminación de sus enemigos, los mayas proclamarían su independencia y coronarían a Chi como su rey. Descubierta aquel día la conspiración, Ay fue capturado y fusilado el 26 de julio; Chi y Pat huyeron y las tropas federales, en represalia, aniquilaron a la población maya de Tepich, el 29 de julio. La respuesta indígena vino al día siguiente, con la aniquilación de los blancos y mestizos de la misma localidad. La primera etapa de esta guerra, de avance de los mayas, se prolongó hasta julio de 1848. En más de 250 pueblos fueron exterminados los blancos, mestizos y los pocos mulatos que sobrevivían en Yucatán. Por su parte, las fuerzas gubernamentales practicaban el genocidio con los indígenas, en las localidades por las que pasaban en su constante retirada. Los sublevados dominaban Peto, Valladolid, Izamal, Bacalar y la región de los chenes, en tanto que el gobierno yucateco controlaba sólo la capital, su camino real a Campeche y algunas poblaciones de la costa norte. La situación del gobierno Yucateco de Méndez fue tan desesperada, que envió en marzo de 1848 comunicaciones a los gobiernos de Gran Bretaña, España y Estados Unidos, en las que ofrecía enajenar la soberanía de Yucatán a cambio de la represión de los indígenas. Estas negociaciones no fructificaron, pues al mes siguiente dejó el gobierno nuevamente a Barbachano. El

Foto: Caludio Contreras Koob

Manglar cerca de Progreso, en Yucatán

Foto: Caludio Contreras Koob

Henequén, planta ligada a la historia de Yucatán

Foto: Caludio Contreras Koob

Hacienda de Yaxcopoc, Yucatán

19 de abril de 1848 representantes de éste y de Pat firmaron el Convenio de Tzucacab, de acuerdo con el cual se eximía a los indígenas de impuestos, se les condonaban las deudas y se les entregaban sus tierras de labor. El convenio también establecía que Barbachano sería gobernador perpetuo de Yucatán, en tanto que Pat sería cacique vitalicio de todos los mayas, medida que no agradó a Chi; simultáneamente a la firma del convenio, Barbachano comisionó a Pedro Regil Estrada y a Joaquín García Rejón para solicitar auxilios bélicos del exterior; se autorizó a estos enviados a plantear la agregación de Yucatán a la corona española, a condición de que España dominara a los mayas. Estas negociaciones no fructificaron y los enviados viajaron a la ciudad de México para hacer el mismo ofrecimiento al presidente José Joaquín de Herrera. Éste aceptó. El 17 de agosto siguiente, en respuesta al apoyo mexicano, Barbachano declaró que Yucatán se reincorporaba a la federación. El 19 de abril de 1848, el nuevo líder de la sublevación, Venancio Pec, ocupó la plaza de Bacalar y pudo comprar legalmente armamento a los británicos, que antes lo proporcionaban de contrabando. El superintendente de Belice reconoció a los mayas como fuerza beligerante para forzar al gobierno mexicano a firmar un tratado de límites con la colonia inglesa, lo que ésta no consiguió, sino hasta 1893. La segunda etapa de la guerra se inició en julio de 1848: en virtud de que los mayas se dispersaron para atender sus cultivos, Barbachano pudo tomar la iniciativa militar, confiada a Sebastián López de Llergo. Las tropas yucatecas avanzaron hasta Dzitás por el oriente, a Yaxcabá por el centro y Tecax por el sur. Sucesivamente reconquistaron otras plazas: Peto, Valladolid y Tihosuco, hasta que entraron en la región de los chenes. En noviembre de 1848 Barbachano dispuso vender como esclavos a los mayas capturados, quienes fueron enviados a los hacendados cubanos. Este comercio fue terminado por decreto del presidente Benito Juárez el 6 de mayo de 1861. En mayo de 1849, Chi fue asesinado por Anastasio Flores, su lugarteniente. Pat, a su vez, fue eliminado por Venancio Pec el 9 de septiembre de ese año. Éste y Florentino Chan asumieron el mando de la rebelión, rechazaron las negociaciones con las autoridades civiles y eclesiásticas y se declararon súbditos de la reina Victoria de Inglaterra. El 5 de febrero de 1850, Manuel Micheltorena sustituyó en el mando militar a López de Llergo y se inició la tercera etapa de la guerra, durante la cual ambos bandos se afianzaron en sus posiciones. Después de haber perdido la plaza de Bacalar, los mayas fundaron una nueva capital en la selva, el poblado de Chan Santa Cruz (Pequeña Santa Cruz), donde se adoraba a una "cruz parlante". En marzo de 1851, Micheltorena asaltó esta plaza, pero no pudo acabar con la rebelión,

Foto: Caludio Contreras Koob

Estación de ferrocarril, Yucatán

Foto: Caludio Contreras Koob

Municipio de Kopoma, Yucatán

Mujeres de Yucatán

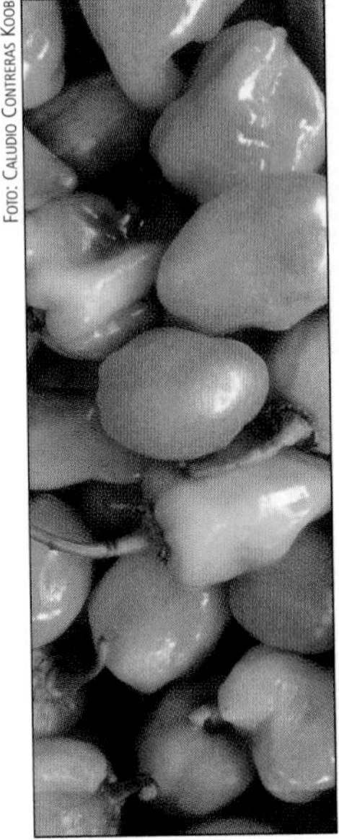

Chile habanero de Yucatán

Boda mestiza en Yucatán

por lo que en 1852 entregó el mando a Rómulo Díaz de la Vega; éste organizó una batida general contra los indígenas, en tanto que se producía una crisis en el gobierno local, tras la cual se sucedieron en la gubernatura el propio Díaz de la Vega, Pedro Ampudia, Santiago Méndez y Pantaleón Barreda, todo lo cual relegó la guerra de Castas a segundo plano. La Constitución Federal de 1857 elevó a Yucatán a la categoría de estado; ese mismo año se produjo la sublevación de Campeche, territorio que al año siguiente se segregó de Yucatán y se convirtió en entidad federativa. Los mayas aprovecharon esta coyuntura para retomar Tekax, Valladolid y Bacalar. Sin embargo, el 2 de enero de 1860 el gobernador Agustín Acereto envió una nueva expedición a Chan Santa Cruz, plaza que fue ocupada el día 12. Poco después, las tropas yucatecas fueron casi aniquiladas por la guerrilla maya: de los 2,850 efectivos de la expedición sólo sobrevivieron 600. El creciente auge de las haciendas henequeneras y la contratación de indígenas para que laboraran en ellas, en condiciones menos crueles que las tradicionales, mermaron el número de efectivos sublevados. En 1862, al ocurrir la intervención francesa, los puertos de Sisal y de Campeche fueron bloqueados por el enemigo y el comercio local se vio afectado. Un año después, Felipe Navarrete se levantó contra el gobierno estatal, asumió la gubernatura, reconoció a la regencia y luego al gobierno de Maximiliano. El régimen de Navarrete, que duró tres años, creó el comisariato imperial de Yucatán, al que Maximiliano otorgó amplia libertad y casi autonomía. La última acción importante de la guerra de Castas fue el sitio que los rebeldes pusieron a Tihosuco, en 1865, durante 50 días. El 1 de febrero de 1898 llegó a la gubernatura estatal Francisco Cantón Rosado, quien reanudó la campaña contra los mayas, quienes sólo efectuaban eventuales incursiones contra los poblados. La rendición definitiva de los indígenas la consiguió Ignacio A. Bravo, quien en 1899 arribó como jefe de la zona militar de Yucatán. Éste emprendió un avance paulatino y sistemático, a fin de consolidar todas y cada una de las posiciones ganadas, hasta ocupar definitivamente Chan Santa Cruz el 5 de mayo de 1901; simultáneamente, José María de la Vega atacó desde el mar y ocupó Payo Obispo y Bacalar, con lo que la parte oriental de la península quedó bajo control directo del gobierno federal, que en 1902 erigió territorio de Quintana Roo, con lo que nuevamente se redujo la extensión de Yucatán. En los primeros años del presente siglo, y como colofón a la guerra de Castas, hubo levantamientos indígenas, todos ellos aplastados antes de que pudieran adquirir fuerza: Yok'Not en 1901; Xocén en 1904; Mérida en 1909; Dzelkop y Valladolid en 1910 y Peto, Temax, Sotuta y Yaxcabá en 1911. El 6 de junio de 1910 el Congreso nombró gobernador interino a José María Pino Suárez; el 8 de agosto dejó el poder a Jesús L. González, que había sido secretario de Francisco I. Madero, y empezó a trabajar por su propia candidatura al gobierno, para cerrar el periodo que terminaría el 31 de enero de 1914. Madero concurrió como observador a las elecciones. Aunque Moreno Cantón gozaba de mayores simpatías, resultó elegido Pino Suárez, quien tomó posesión de la gubernatura, por segunda vez, el 8 de octubre de 1911. Designado candidato a la vicepresidencia de la República, dejó en el Ejecutivo local como interino a su cuñado, Nicolás Cámara Vales, quien a su vez ganó en los siguientes comicios y se convirtió en gobernador constitucional el 30 de diciembre. Algunos sectores juzgaron que estos movimientos eran producto de la imposición y surgieron nuevas rebeliones en Opichén, Conkal, Maxcanú y Temax, las cuales fueron sofocadas. Asesinados Madero y Pino Suárez, Victoriano Huerta nombró sucesivamente gobernadores de Yucatán a Arcadio Escobedo, Eugenio Rascón y Prisciliano Cortés. Entre 1913 y 1915, Quintana Roo volvió a formar parte de Yucatán. Derrotada la usurpación, Venustiano Carranza designó gobernador de Yucatán a Eleuterio Ávila, quien tomó posesión en septiembre de 1914. El batallón Cepeda Peraza, de la fuerza de seguridad pública local, que Carranza había solicitado para combatir a Villa y a Zapata, se sublevó en Mérida y se retiró al oriente del estado. A causa de este hecho, Ávila fue llamado a Veracruz, donde radicaba el gobierno carrancista, y se hizo cargo del gobierno Toribio V. de los Santos, cuyos consejeros y colaboradores pronto suscitaron la animosidad pública. Por esos días se dispuso que los oficiales del ejército federal, disuelto por los Tratados de Teoloyucan, se concentraran en Veracruz. Los afectados, con Ortiz Argumedo a la cabeza, aprovecharon el descontento que existía y se levantaron en armas; cundió el movimiento y De los Santos huyó de Mérida, llevándose los caudales de la hacienda pública. Ortiz Argumedo ocupó Mérida el 12 de febrero de 1915 y se hizo cargo del gobierno. Carranza, a su vez, anunció el nombramiento de Salvador Alvarado como gobernador de Yucatán y éste envió un largo mensaje intimando la entrega incondicional de la plaza. El ex oficial porfirista presentó estos hechos al pueblo como una violación de la soberanía del estado y se preparó para la defensa. Alvarado desembarcó en Campeche, al mando de un poderoso contingente. De

Mérida salieron a encontrarlo el Batallón de Voluntarios y otros efectivos; ambas fuerzas se enfrentaron en Blanca Flor, Pocboc y Halachó; los argumedistas fueron derrotados y el 19 de marzo de 1915 entró el ejército de Alvarado en Mérida. El nuevo gobernador expidió el decreto de liberación de los jornaleros del campo y dictó leyes para la emancipación de los sirvientes domésticos; reglamentó la Ley Agraria promulgada por Carranza el 6 de enero de 1915; promovió la creación del Partido Socialista Obrero; y propició la celebración del primer Congreso Feminista celebrado en la República. En las elecciones de 1917 resultó electo gobernador el líder ferrocarrilero Carlos Castro Morales, quien tomó posesión el primero de febrero de 1918. En marzo siguiente se reunió en Motul el primer Congreso Obrero Socialista de Yucatán, convocado por Felipe Carrillo Puerto, presidente del Partido Socialista Obrero. Esta organización cambió ahí su denominación por la de Partido Socialista del Sureste. En 1920, con el triunfo del Plan de Agua Prieta, se levantaron en armas las fuerzas militares de Mérida y nombraron gobernador a Tomás Garrido Canabal. Éste renunció a los pocos días y lo sustituyó Enrique Recio, a su vez desconocido por el Senado. El 26 de julio asumió el Ejecutivo Antonio Ancona Albertos, quien fue sucedido por Hircano Ayuso O'Horibe, y más tarde por Manuel Berzunza. La campaña electoral de 1921 constituyó una sangrienta lucha entre los socialistas y las fuerzas tradicionalistas. Electo Felipe Carrillo Puerto, tomó posesión el 1 de febrero de 1922. La rebelión delahuertista encabezada en Yucatán por Juan Ricárdez Broca obligó a Carrillo a salir de Mérida con unos cuantos colaboradores; se dirigieron a la costa oriental a fin de embarcarse rumbo a La Habana, pero cayeron en una emboscada; presos, se les llevó a Mérida y después de un simulacro de consejo de guerra, Felipe Carrillo Puerto, sus hermanos Wilfrido, Edesio y Benjamín, Manuel Berzunza, presidente municipal de Mérida, y otros ocho acompañantes fueron asesinados el 3 de enero de 1924. El 17 de abril llegó a Yucatán el general Eugenio Martínez e hizo huir a los delahuertistas. En 1931, el presidente Pascual Ortiz Rubio suprimió el territorio federal de Quintana Roo y repartió su superficie entre los estados de Yucatán y Campeche. En 1934, el presidente Abelardo L. Rodríguez restituyó a Yucatán las islas de Cozumel, Mujeres y Holbox, hasta entonces bajo administración federal. De 1931 a 1934 se suspendió totalmente la desfibración del henequén en las haciendas. Por decreto del 11 de enero de 1935 fue erigido nuevamente el territorio de Quintana Roo, perdido en definitiva por Yucatán. En 1935 se inició el reparto de las haciendas henequeneras entre los campesinos y se autorizó la ocupación de los equipos de desfibración por los ejidatarios. Las fuerzas conservadoras reaccionaron contra las medidas agrarias y en julio de 1936 ocurrió un sangriento motín que arrojó del poder al gobernador interino. Un año después, Lázaro Cárdenas visitó la península y el 8 de agosto de 1937 dictó un acuerdo, complementado por el del 18 del mismo mes, que disponía la entrega de ejidos a los pueblos; la reducción de la propiedad territorial de las fincas henequeneras a 150 hectáreas como máximo y la expropiación de los equipos de desfibración y de las vías férreas. Sin embargo, las instalaciones industriales y de los medios de transporte volvieron a manos de los latifundistas por un fallo de la Suprema Corte. Se refundieron entonces todas las parcelas individuales en el gran ejido henequenero, controlado por el gobierno local a través de un nuevo organismo: Henequeneros de Yucatán. En febrero de 1955, Adolfo Ruiz Cortines acordó la disolución del gran ejido y la liquidación de Henequeneros de Yucatán, con lo que la situación de ese cultivo empeoró: el 90 por ciento de la superficie sembrada en Yucatán (17 por ciento del territorio estatal) está dedicada al cultivo de esta planta que ocupa a 55,000 familias, cuando sólo con 30,000 se cultivaría la misma área. (☛ *Campeche*, *Mayas* y *Quintana Roo*).

PROMEDIO DE ESCOLARIDAD DE LA POBLACIÓN DE 15 AÑOS Y MÁS, POR SEXO, 1995

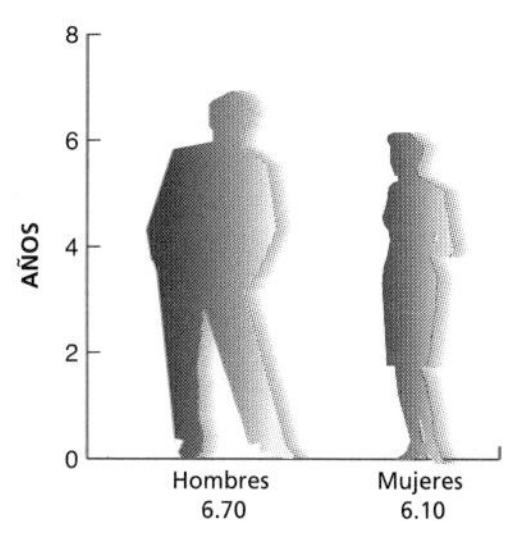

POBLACIÓN DE 5 AÑOS Y MÁS HABLANTE DE LENGUA INDÍGENA, 1995

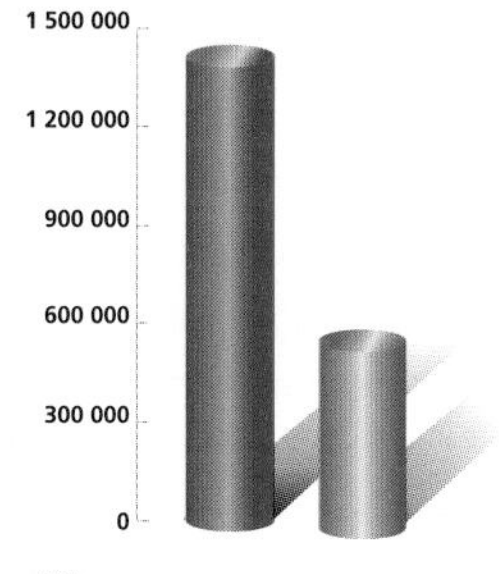

BIBLIOTECAS Y USUARIOS, 1993
Número de bibliotecas: 230

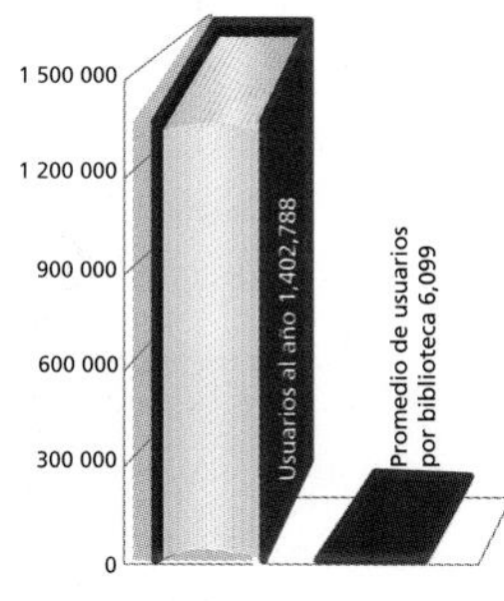

DISTRIBUCIÓN DE LA POBLACIÓN POR TAMAÑO DE LA LOCALIDAD, 1995

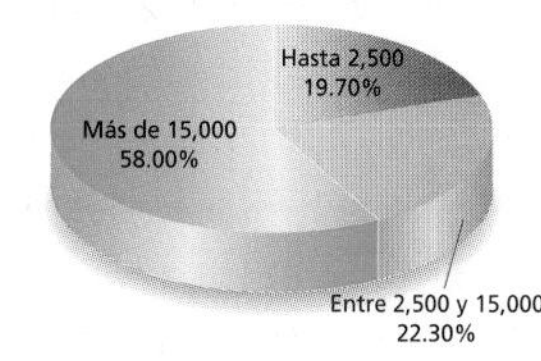

LONGITUD DE LA RED DE CARRETERAS POR SUPERFICIE DE RODAMIENTO, 1995

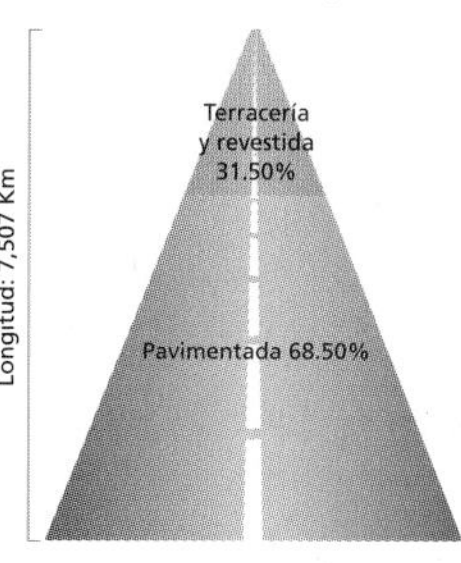

LÍNEAS TELEFÓNICAS EN SERVICIO Y APARATOS PÚBLICOS, 1994

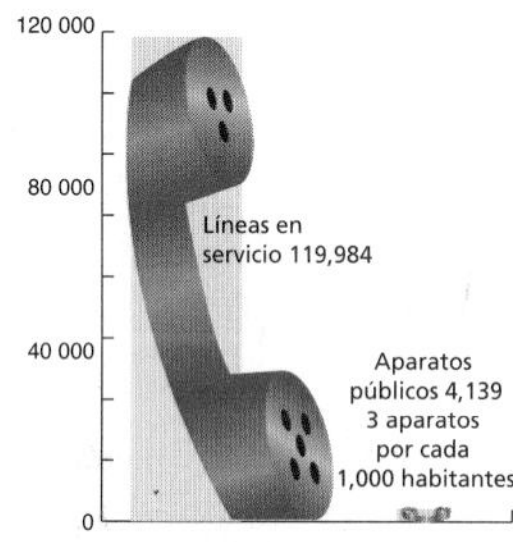

DISTRIBUCIÓN PORCENTUAL DE LA POBLACIÓN OCUPADA POR SECTOR DE ACTIVIDAD ECONÓMICA, 1995

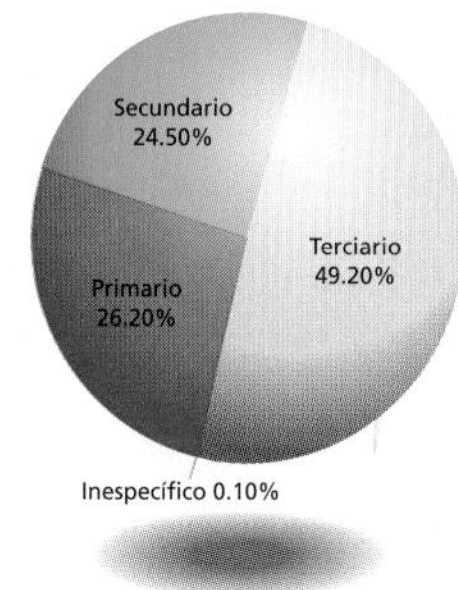

PRODUCTO INTERNO BRUTO (PIB) A PRECIOS CORRIENTES

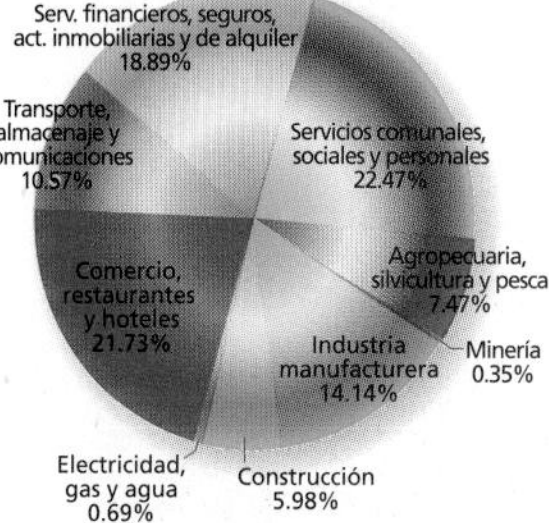

Ciudad de Hoctún en la península de Yucatán

Timbre de Yugoslavia

Cocodrilo de río, fauna de la península de Yucatán

YUCATÁN ◆ Península situada en el extremo oriente de la República Mexicana. Comprende parte de Belice y Guatemala y los estados de Yucatán, Campeche y Quintana Roo. Tiene unos 200 km^2 de superficie de los cuales tres cuartas partes están en territorio mexicano.

YUGOSLAVIA, REPÚBLICA FEDERATIVA DE ◆ Nación de Europa situada en el litoral del mar Adriático. Limita al norte con Hungría, al noreste con Rumania, al este con Bulgaria, al sur con Macedonia y Albania, y al oeste con Bosnia y Herzegovina. Superficie: 102,173 km^2. Habitantes: 10,632,000 (estimación para 1997). La capital es Belgrado (1,168,454 habitantes en 1994) y otras ciudades de importancia son Novi Sad (179,391), Pristina (155,499), Nis (175,391) y Podgorica (117,875). La moneda es el nuevo dinar yugoslavo y el idioma oficial es el serbiocroata, aunque también se hablan húngaro y albanés. Constituyen al Estado federal las repúblicas de Serbia y Montenegro y las provincias autónomas de Kosovo y Voivodina. *Historia*: Los pobladores originales del actual territorio yugoslavo fueron serbios, croatas y eslovenos. Bajo la influencia de Bizancio, los serbios adoptaron la religión ortodoxa, en tanto que los croatas se convirtieron al catolicismo y el resto de los grupos étnicos abrazaron el islam. Hacia el siglo XII, Serbia, sometida al imperio bizantino, conquistó su independencia y se erigió en nación líder de los pueblos eslavos del sur. No obstante, en 1389 el imperio otomano conquistó Serbia y la hegemonía turca en la región se mantuvo durante 500 años. A principios del siglo XVII el médico dálmata Peter Romson se instaló en Veracruz y fundó un pequeño hospital en el puerto. El otro yugoslavo que vivió en la Nueva España durante la colonia fue el barón Ratkej, que pertenecía a la Compañía de Jesús, quien se estableció en la sierra Tarahumara hacia 1680 y se dedicó a evangelizar a los rarámuri. En 1878 Yugoslavia se independizó de Turquía. En 1908, Austria-Hungría se anexó el territorio de Bosnia-Herzegovina. Cuatro años después, Serbia y Montenegro se unieron a Grecia y a Bulgaria en su lucha contra Turquía, país al que finalmente arrebataron las regiones de Kosovo y Macedonia. Desde los primeros años del siglo, Stevo Seljan, de Zagreb, había vivido en México y en 1913 recibió un diploma de la Sociedad Méxicana de Geografía y Estadística. En 1914, Austria hizo responsable a Serbia del asesinato, en Sarajevo, del archiduque Francisco Fernando, hecho que desencadenó la primera guerra mundial. Mediante el Pacto de Corfú (20 de julio de 1917), el Comité Sureslavo y Serbia acordaron la unión de eslovenos, croatas y serbios en un solo reino. Un año después, Bosnia-Herzegovina y Montenegro se adhirieron al Pacto de Corfú y quedó constituido (diciembre de 1918) el Estado Sureslavo, cuyas fronteras serían fijadas en 1919 por la Conferencia de Paz y los posteriores Tratados de Rapallo. El país fue gobernado por la dinastía serbia de los Karajorgevich. En 1921 una nueva Constitución, centralista, desató un movimiento croata contra la hegemonía serbia. En el mismo año, Alejandro I dio

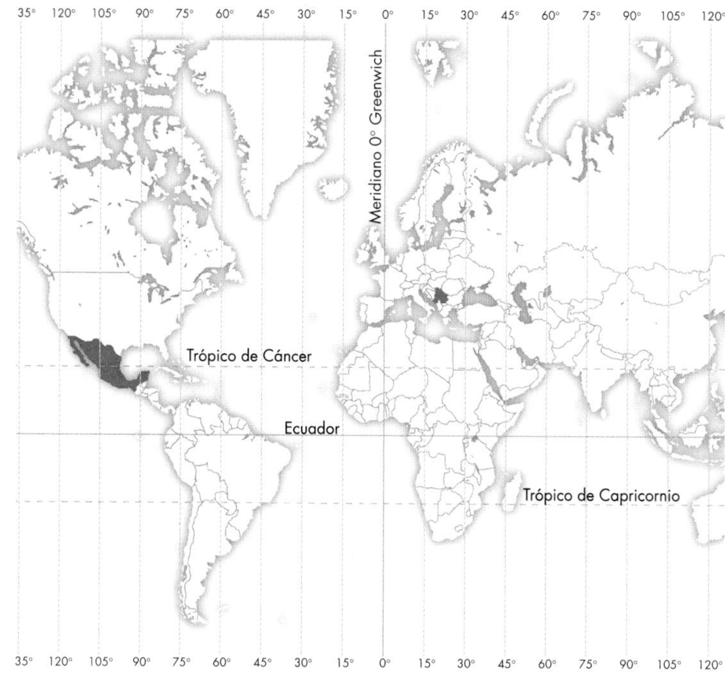

República Federativa de Yugoslavia

un golpe de Estado, instauró una dictadura que unificó al país, ya con el nombre de Yugoslavia (que significa "Nación de los Eslavos del Sur" o Sureslavia), y lo dividió en banatos, juridicciones administrativas que no respetaban las nacionalidades, lo que intensificó el movimiento nacionalista croata. En 1934, Alejandro I fue asesinado en Francia y sucedido en el trono por Pedro II, menor de edad que quedó sujeto a la regencia del príncipe Pablo. De hecho, el poder fue detentado por el primer ministro, Milan Stojadinovic, quien inscribió al país en la órbita de la Alemania nazi. Hacia 1938 el movimiento nacionalista croata adquirió una clara tendencia separatista, dirigido por Matchek, quien en 1939 obtuvo la autonomía para Croacia y fue designado vicepresidente. En 1941, durante la segunda guerra mundial, que costó al país 1,700,000 vidas, Stojadinovic autorizó el libre tránsito de tropas nazis a través de territorio yugoslavo, lo que dio origen a una rebelión popular en Belgrado. A este levantamiento siguió un cuartelazo dirigido por el militar Cimovitchi, auspiciado por los aliados, quien reemplazó al príncipe regente Pablo por Pedro II, entonces un adolescente. Hitler envió a sus divisiones a invadir el occidente de Yugoslavia, en tanto que los búlgaros ocuparon la porción oriental. El 17 de abril de 1941, el ejército imperial yugoslavo se rindió y los invasores dividieron al país e impusieron gobernantes títeres, en tanto que la familia real se exilió en Londres. Se produjo entonces una gran insurrección popular que, al ser aplastada por los nazis, se atomizó en numerosos movimientos armados, entre los que destacaban los de los chetniks, realistas dirigidos por Draza Mihajlovic, y los partisanos, guerrilleros comunistas comandados por Josip Broz Tito (de origen croata). En tanto que Mihajlovic negociaba con los nazis, Tito creó un poderoso frente interno en el que movilizó a toda la población y la comprometió, simultáneamente, en una revolución socialista. En 1942 se creó el Consejo Antifascista de Yugoslavia, que fue sustituido un año más tarde por el Comité Yugoslavo de Liberación Nacional, de hecho, un auténtico gobierno nacional, cuya legitimidad fue reconocida incluso por los aliados y por el exiliado Pedro II. En 1944 Belgrado fue liberada por la acción conjunta del ejército soviético y los partisanos; la liberación total del país ocurrió en 1945, cuando los guerrilleros comunistas y el ejército rojo ocuparon Trieste y Zagreb. De inmediato fue abolida la monarquía y se elaboró una nueva Constitución. Tras unas elecciones ganadas por el Partido Comunista se proclamó, el 29 de noviembre de 1945, la República Federal Popular de Yugoslavia, con la que México estableció relaciones en 1946. En 1948, la Unión Soviética intentó subordinar al gobierno yugoslavo, mismo que se rebeló y Stalin sometió al país a un bloqueo económico. Tito, jefe del Estado desde su fundación, eliminó del Partido Comunista y del aparato estatal a los elementos prosoviéticos, proclamó una política neutralista y solicitó apoyo económico a las potencias occidentales.

Visita oficial de Miguel de la Madrid a Yugoslavia

Jesús Yurén

Tímbre de Yugoslavia

A partir de 1950, con la propiedad económica en manos del Estado, se fomentó la creación de cooperativas agrícolas y se implantó la autogestión obrera en la industria, con un amplio margen de autonomía para las empresas. Dos años más tarde, el Partido Comunista se transformó en la Liga de los Comunistas. En 1956 se produjo un movimiento político interno, tendiente a combatir la hegemonía absoluta de Tito. La oposición se aglutinó en torno al vicepresidente Milan Djilas, quien a la postre debió pasar diez años en prisión. Del 1 al 6 de septiembre de 1961 se celebró en Belgrado la primera conferencia de jefes de Estado del Movimiento de Países No Alineados, del que Tito fue una de las principales figuras. Éste realizó, en 1963, una visita oficial a México. En ese mismo año, el presidente Adolfo López Mateos visitó Belgrado. También en 1963, la República Popular Federal de Yugoslavia se convirtió en República Federativa Socialista de Yugoslavia. En 1971 y 1972 renacieron los movimientos nacionalistas de Croacia y Montenegro, primero; y de Serbia, Macedonia y Bosnia-Herzegovina, después, que provocaron una crisis interna. De la Liga de los Comunistas y del aparato estatal fueron expulsados varios dirigentes croatas y serbios, en tanto que la represión generó resistencia y actos de terrorismo. Tito fue designado presidente vitalicio en 1974. En ese mismo año, el presidente Luis Echeverría visitó Yugoslavia en dos ocasiones. Tito volvió a México en 1976 y murió el 4 de mayo de 1980. Se efectuó entonces la transición hacia una presidencia colegiada. En marzo y abril de 1981 se produjeron disturbios en la región de Kosovo, donde se concentra la población de origen albanés, teóricamente autónoma y con derecho a la secesión, pero en la práctica impedida de optar por la autodeterminación. A estos disturbios se sumaron en 1985 otros problemas surgidos en algunas repúblicas, expresados en el crecimiento de grupos militantes de musulmanes y católicos. En 1984, el presidente Miguel de la Madrid visitó Yugoslavia y, dos años después, el presidente Lazar Mojsov estuvo en México. En 1989, al tiempo que la población kosovar efectuaba manifestaciones contra la medida que le restaba autonomía a la provincia de Kosovo, la república de Eslovenia proclamó su independencia de la federación yugoslava. En 1990, la Liga de los Comunistas renunció al monopolio del poder político y el parlamento de Kosovo declaró a su nación independiente de Serbia, aunque aún federada a Yugoslavia, lo que provocó una intervención del ejército serbio, que ocupó la capital kosovar y encarceló a los legisladores locales que promovieron la secesión. Ese mismo año, Bosnia y Herzegovina se declaró independiente de Yugoslavia, federación a cuya presidencia llegó entonces el serbio Slobodan Milosevic. En 1991 se desató la crisis política: cuando correspondía al croata Stipe Mesic la presidencia de la federación (cargo que debía rotarse entre los representantes de las seis repúblicas coligadas), los serbios le impidieron asumir el cargo; Croacia, entonces, decidió separarse de Yugoslavia y, en rápida sucesión, el resto de las repúblicas confirmaron o anunciaron su intención de independizarse de la federación; asimismo, el ejército serbio invadió Croacia y Bosnia y Herzegovina, lo que provocó una intervención de las fuerzas de paz de la ONU, de poca efectividad. En 1992, tras la desintegración de la República Socialista Federativa de Yugoslavia y la conformación de la República Federal de Yugoslavia (integrada sólo por las repúblicas de Serbia y Montenegro), México siguió respetando el marco legal establecido con aquélla en las relaciones diplomáticas. Las atrocidades cometidas por los serbios en las guerras contra croatas y bosnios provocó un rechazo internacional casi unánime: Yugoslavia fue expulsada de la ONU, la OMS y del FMI, en tanto que la Cruz Roja pidió que se eliminaran los campos de concentración de prisioneros de guerra, que rápidamente se hicieron famosos por las crueldades ahí cometidas. Un año después, Yugoslavia comenzó a padecer todo tipo de bloqueos y sanciones internacionales, luego de que Belgrado rechazó el plan de paz propuesto por la ONU. En 1996 se firmaron acuerdos de paz entre Yugoslavia y los países a los que atacó, y Belgrado reconoció la independencia de Macedonia, Bosnia y Herzegovina, Croacia y Eslovenia. A finales de 1998 y durante 1999, el conflicto en Kosovo resurgió: las pretensiones autonomistas de los kosovares de origen albanés fueron duramente reprimidas por el ejército yugoslavo. Tras saberse de numerosas matanzas de albano-kosovares, fuerzas de la ONU intervinieron y obligaron al repliegue de los serbios; cuando las víctimas albanesas tuvieron el apoyo internacional, comenzaron a realizar, a su vez, matanzas de serbios. Un grupo de artistas pertenecientes al Comité México por Yugoslavia ofrecieron un concierto en 1999 para la reconstrucción de la Escuela de Música de Belgrado.

YUKALPETÉN ◆ ☛ *Progreso.*

YUM KAAX ◆ Deidad maya de la agricultura que era representada como una deidad joven. En su glifo se mostraba con una mazorca de maíz, como tocado, y esparciendo granos sobre la tierra. Su correspondiente nahua era Cinteotl.

YURÉCUARO ◆ Municipio de Michoacán situado al norte de Zamora y al oeste de La Piedad, en los límites de Jalisco. Superficie: 195.28 km². Habitantes: 26,487, de los cuales 5,832 forman la población económicamente activa. Hablan alguna lengua indígena 25 personas mayores de cinco años.

YURÉN, JESÚS ◆ n. y m. en el DF (1901-1973). Líder obrero. Fue secretario general del Sindicato de Panaderos del Distrito Federal (1927), del de trabajadores de limpia de la ciudad de México y del de choferes. Participó en la Confederación de Trabajadores del Distrito Federal (1936) y con Fidel Veláz-

Foto: Fondo Editorial Grupo Azabache

Laguna de Yuriria, en Guanajuato

quez, Fernando Amilpa, Alfonso Sánchez Madariaga y Blas Chumacero formó el grupo conocido como "los cinco lobitos". Fue dos veces diputado federal (1937-40 y 1943-46) y en dos ocasiones senador de la República (1952-58 y 1964-70).

Yuri ◆ n. en Veracruz, Ver. (1964). Nombre profesional de la cantante y actriz Yuriria Valenzuela Canseco. Inició su trayectoria como cantante del grupo La Manzana Eléctrica en 1975. Ha tenido éxito comercial con canciones como *Hombres al borde de un ataque de celos*, *Pequeño panda de Chapultepec*, *Qué te pasa*, *Aire*, y otras. Participó en las películas *Milagro en el circo* (1978), *Tohui, el pequeño panda de Chapultepec* (1982), *Canta Chamo (Siempre te amaré)* (1983), *Siempre en Domingo* (1983) y *¡Soy libre!* (1991). Ganó el Festival OTI con la canción *Tiempos mejores*. Recibió la Gaviota de Plata en el Festival de Viña del Mar, en Chile.

Foto: Época

Yuri

Yuriria ◆ Laguna de Guanajuato, también llamada Yuririapúndaro. Cubre parcialmente el territorio de los municipios de Yuriria y de Valle de Santiago. Limita al suroeste con el cerro Culiacán, al oeste con el valle de Salvatierra, al este con la mesa de San Agustín, al sureste con el cerro Blanco y al sur con el valle de Santiago. Ocupa una cuenca cerrada, a 1,733 metros sobre el nivel del mar. Mide 17 km de largo y su anchura máxima es de siete. En 1548, el agustino Diego de Chávez construyó un canal que comunica la laguna con el río Lerma. Es el mayor depósito natural de agua del estado, cuenta con varias islas y en sus aguas hay abundante pesca de bagre.

Yuriria ◆ Municipio de Guanajuato situado en el sur del estado, al sureste de Salamanca y al oeste de Salvatierra, en los límites con Michoacán. Superficie: 778.80 km^2. Habitantes: 75,248, de los cuales 15,902 forman la población económicamente activa. Hablan alguna lengua indígena 116 personas mayores de cinco años. Los otomíes, primeros habitantes del actual territorio municipal, fueron desalojados por los purépechas, quienes llamaron a la región Yuririhapúndaro, "Lugar del lago de sangre", pues en la laguna de Yuriria los otomíes arrojaban los cadáveres de sus enemigos muertos en combate, mismos que con su sangre teñían de rojo el agua. En la cabecera se encuentra un monasterio agustino construido por Diego Chávez entre 1540 y 1550, cuya portada, de estilo plateresco, es una copia modificada de la de Acolman. Las festividades de Navidad y Año Nuevo se festejan en Yuriria con desfiles de carros alegóricos, exhibición de nacimientos, pastorelas y serenatas.

Yustiaza Ulloa Serrano, Miguel ◆ n. en El Espinal, Oax. (1970). Actor. Formó parte del grupo El Taller de la Comunidad (1992-98) con el que participó en las obras *La vida según Tadeco*, *Una noche de diciembre en la Alameda*, *En un lugar de La Mancha*, *La trilogía del hombre*, *Liando* y *Los colores del tiempo*. Subdirector de Esférica Ludens, compañía con la que ha montado *Letanía*, *Tríptico telefónico* y *Hamlet sin Dinamarca*. Asesor artístico del Centro de Arte y Ballet. Autor de la obra *Hotelito*. Prosecretario y bibliotecario del Ateneo Español. Vocal de cultura de la Asociación Cultural Espinaleña. Miembro del Grupo Cultural Minotauro.

Yutanduchi de Guerrero ◆ Municipio de Oaxaca situado al oeste de la capital del estado, al sureste de Tlaxiaco y al sur de Asunción Nochixtlán. Superficie: 223.27 km^2. Habitantes: 1,313, de los cuales 595 forman la población económicamente activa. Hablan alguna lengua indígena 984 personas mayores de cinco años (mixteco 980).

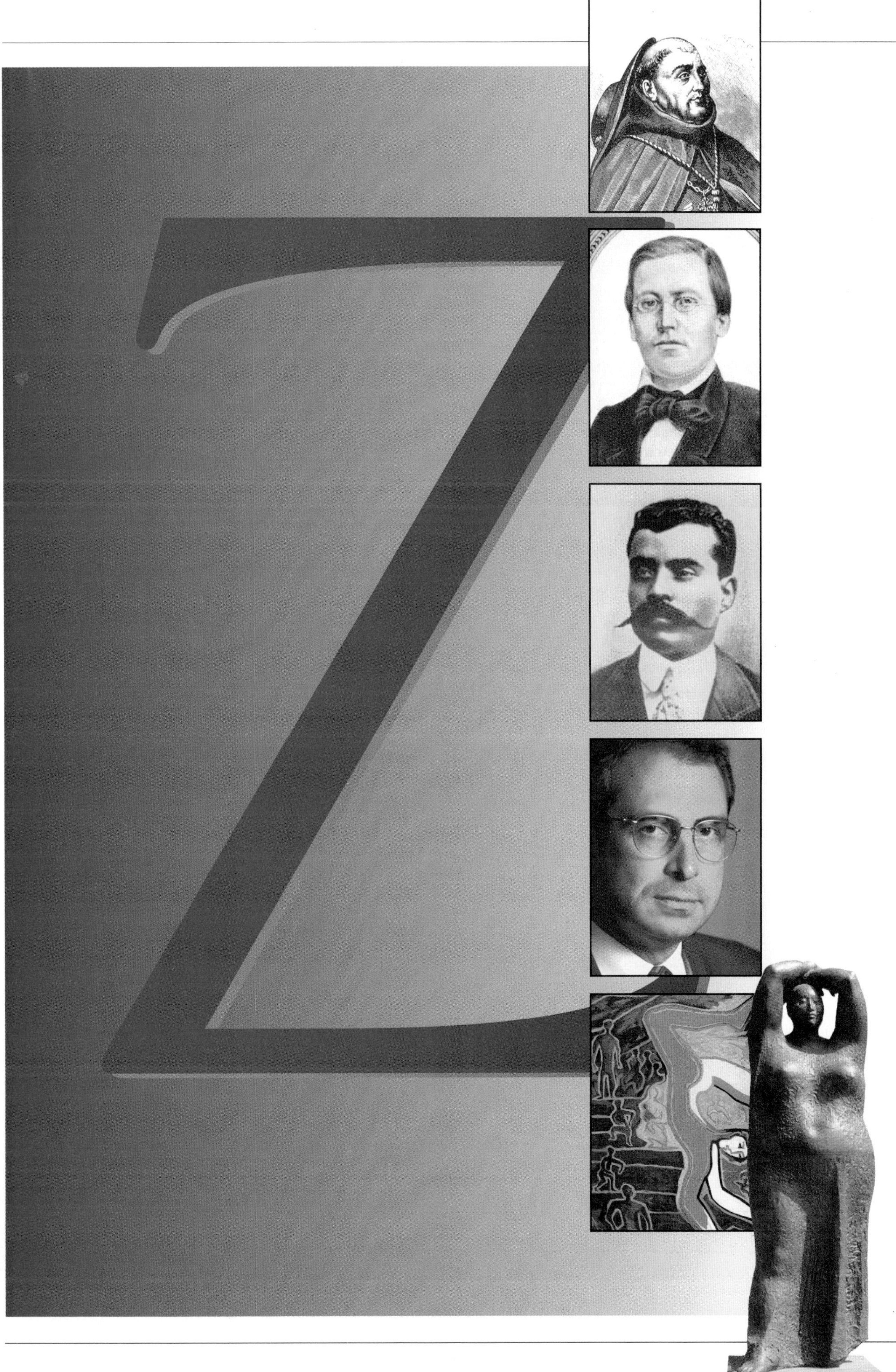

ZAACHILA ◆ ☛ *Villa de Zaachila* y *Trinidad de Zaachila.*

ZABALETA, SUSANA ◆ n. en Monclova, Coah. (1964). Estudió canto en la Escuela Superior de Música de Monterrey, en Roma (1984) y, con Enrique Patrón, María Julius e Irma González, en la Escuela Vida y Movimiento, donde formó parte de la orquesta de cámara. Grabó en España el disco *¿O fue un sueño?* (1992) y en México *Desde el baño* (1997). Ha participado en obras de teatro, en la telenovela *La sombra del otro* y en las películas *Sobrenatural*, *Pocahontas* (doblando la voz protagónica) y *Sexo, pudor y lágrimas*. Premio Revelación Musical 1992 por *El Heraldo de México*.

Susana Zabaleta

ZABLUDOVSKY, ABRAHAM ◆ n. en Polonia (1924). Arquitecto. Fue traído a México en 1927. Cursó la carrera en la Academia de San Carlos y se tituló en 1949. Fue profesor de la UNAM (1965-67). Trabajó en el taller de Mario Pani. Fue asesor del Fondo de Operaciones y Descuento Bancario para la Vivienda (1966-70), director general de Inurba (1973-75), asesor de la Comisión de Desarrollo Urbano del DF (1978- 81) y asesor técnico del Infonavit. Realizó los estudios urbanísticos de Molango, Naucalpan y Chalma y de las zonas del Ajusco, la Marquesa y Chiconcuac. Ha proyectado los conjuntos habitacionales Lomas de Plateros (1967-71), Torres de Mixcoac (1969-71) y Vallejo-Patera (1970-73); el Teatro de la Ciudad de Tuxtla Gutiérrez (1979), el Multibanco Mercantil de México (1984) y la transformación de la Biblioteca de México de la Ciudadela en Centro Bibliotecario México (1988). Asociado con su colega Teodoro González de León hizo el edificio de la delegación Cuauhtémoc del DDF (1972), la embajada mexicana en Brasilia (1974), la sede del Infonavit (1975), El Colegio de México (1975), la Universidad Pedagógica Nacional (1979), el Museo Tamayo (1981), el Auditorio del Estado de Guanajuato (1989) y el remozamiento del Auditorio Nacional (1991), entre otras obras. Expuso fotomurales de su obra en el Chicago Athenaeum de EUA (1994). Coautor, con Teodoro González de León, de *Arquitectura contemporánea mexicana* (1969) y *Ocho conjuntos de habitación* (1976). En 1978 se publicó *Mexican Architecture: the Work of Abraham Zabludovsly and Teodoro González de Leon*, de Paul Heyer. Socio académico emérito del Colegio de Arquitectos, Premio Nacional de Ciencias y Artes 1982, Premio Latinoamericano de la Bienal de Buenos Aires, Argentina (1989), Medalla de Oro de la

Foto: Rogelio Cuéllar

Abraham Zabludovsky

Foto: Carlos Hahn

Auditorio Nacional, en la ciudad de México, obra remodelada por Abraham Zabludovsky y Teodoro González de León

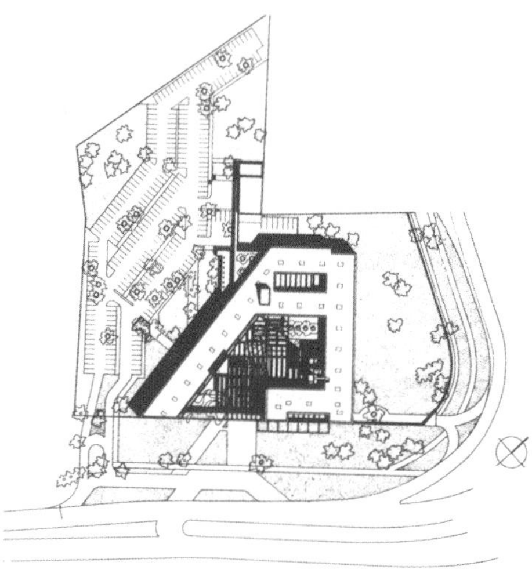

Plano del Colegio de México, obra arquitectónica de Abraham Zabludovsky y Teodoro González de León

Bienal de Arquitectura de Sofía, Bulgaria (1991), Premio de la Ciudad de México (1991), Premio de la Bienal de Recife, Brasil, y de la Bienal de México (1994).

Zabludovsky, Abraham ◆ n. en el DF (1956). Periodista. Su apellido materno es Nerubay. Licenciado en ciencias políticas por la Universidad Trinity de San Antonio, Texas (1979). Dentro de la empresa Televisa ha sido reportero de la fuente presidencial (1980-82), productor ejecutivo del programa *Contrapunto* del Canal 9 (1982-90), productor y guionista de los programas anuales de noticias *Resumen del año* (1985-), la serie *Fundadores* (1986) y los programas *El siglo de las maravillas* (1999), de la serie *Milenio Televisa*; director y conductor de *24 Horas de la tarde* (1986-98) y *El noticiero con Abraham Zabludovsky* (1998-), director del programa *Mundo de dinero* (1985-87) y de su versión radial, transmitida por la XEW, y director general del programa *Conexión financiera*. Fue fundador y presidente de la revista *Época* (1991) y ha sido conductor y director del programa de radio *De la A a la Z*. Premio Nacional de Periodismo 1997.

Abraham Zabludovsky

Zabludovsky, Gina ◆ n. en el DF (1954). Su segundo apellido es Kuper. Licenciada, maestra y doctora en sociología por la UNAM (1990), donde es profesora e investigadora. Imparte cursos en diversos centros de enseñanza superior. Ha colaborado en *Excélsior*, *El Nacional*, *unomásuno*, *Revista Mexicana de Ciencias Políticas y Sociales*, *Sociológica*, *International Sociology* y otras publicaciones. Coautora y coordinadora de *La sociedad a través de los clásicos* (1988) y de *El sexenio de Miguel Alemán: gobierno, obreros y empresarios* (1985). Autora de *México: Estado y empresarios* (1980), *La dominación patrimonial en la obra de Max Weber* (1989), *Patrimonialismo y modernización. Poder y dominación en la sociología del Oriente de Max Weber* (1994) y *Sociología y política. El debate clásico y contemporáneo*. Distinción UNAM Jóvenes Académicos en el área de investigación en ciencias sociales (1990). Becaria del Programa de Estudios de la Mujer del Colegio de México (1991-92).

Zabludovsky, Jacobo ◆ n. en el DF (1928). Periodista. Licenciado en derecho por la UNAM, de la que ha sido profesor. Comenzó como locutor en la XEX en 1945. Fue auxiliar de redacción de los noticieros de la cadena Radio Continental (1946), subjefe de Servicios Informativos de la radiodifusora XEX (1947), productor y director del *Noticiero General Motors* del Canal 4 (1950), director del noticiero cinematográfico *El Mundo en Marcha*, conductor de los programas informativos *Primera Plana*, *Siglo XX*, *La verdad en el espacio*, *Telemundo*, *Diario Nescafé* y *Hoy sábado*; coordinador de Radio y Televisión (1958-64) y consejero de Difusión y Relaciones Públicas de la Secretaría de la Presidencia (1964-70); director de información y director general de los noticieros de Televisa y director general y conductor de los programas *24 Horas* (1970-86 y 1987-1998) y *Somos*, así como de *Contrapunto*, *Ecoentrevista*, *Ecomentario*, *Domingo a domingo*, *Hoy domingo* y *De nuevo* (1999-); también ha sido subdirector general de Televisa (1986), director de la agencia de noticias de televisión Econoticias y vicepresidente de Univisa (1986). Presidente y director general de *Ovaciones* y *Summa*. Colaborador de las revistas *Foto Guión*, *Claridades*, *Revista de Revistas*, *Cine Mundial*, *El Redondel* y *Siempre*, y del diario *Novedades*. Autor de *La conquista del espacio*, *La libertad y la responsabilidad en la radio y la televisión mexicanas*, *Charlas con pintores*, *Siqueiros me dijo*, *En el aire* y *Cinco días de agosto*. *Doctor honoris causa* por la Universidad de Jesusalén. Premio Nacional de Periodismo, Premio Internacional de Periodismo Rey de España (1983 y 1986), Monje de Oro del gobierno de Nicaragua y Premio de la Asociación de Cronistas de Espectáculos de Nueva York, por *24 Horas* (1986).

Foto: Héctor Herrera

Jacobo Zabludovsky

Foto: Dante Buccio

Gina Zabludovsky

Zacapoaxtla, Puebla

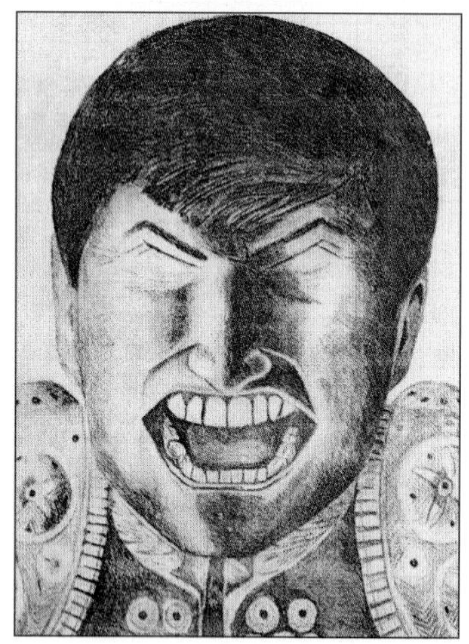
Autorretrato de Moisés Zabludovsky

Zabludovsky, Moisés ◆ n. en el DF (1959). Pintor y grabador. Realizó estudios de diseño en la Parsons School of Design de Nueva York, EUA (1982) y en la UAM (1979). Asistió al taller de Silvia González (1972) y al Arcai de París (1978). Coautor de la carpeta litográfica *Tablas y tercios* (1990). Ha expuesto individual y colectivamente desde 1977. Su obra se ha presentado en el Museo Carrillo Gil (1981), la galería Miró (1978), la galería Lourdes Chumacero (1987 y 1991), el Museo de la Ciudad de México (1991) y en Nueva York (1988) y Ohio, EUA (1991). Mención honorífica en la primera Bienal Iberoamericana de Pintura de la Ciudad de México, en 1979.

Zabludovsky Kuper, Jaime ◆ n. en el DF (1956). Licenciado en economía por la Universidad Anáhuac y el ITAM, instituciones en las que fue profesor. Maestro y doctor en economía por la Universidad de Yale. Afiliado al PRI desde 1989. Ha sido ayudante de investigación en Conasupo (1974-76), asesor de Compañía Operadora de Teatros, S.A. (1977), asistente de investigación en la Dirección de Investigación Económica (1977-85), economista en el Banco de México (1985-88), miembro del Comité de Asesores Económicos de la Presidencia de la República (1985-88); director general de Política de Comercio Exterior (1988-90), asesor del subsecretario de Comerico Exterior (1990), coordinador de la Oficina de Negociación del TLC (1990-94), y subsecretario de Negociaciones Comerciales Internacionales en la Secofi (1994-98) y embajador de México ante la Unión Europea (1998-). Coautor de *Trade and Industry Policy for Structural Adjustment in Mexico* (1990).

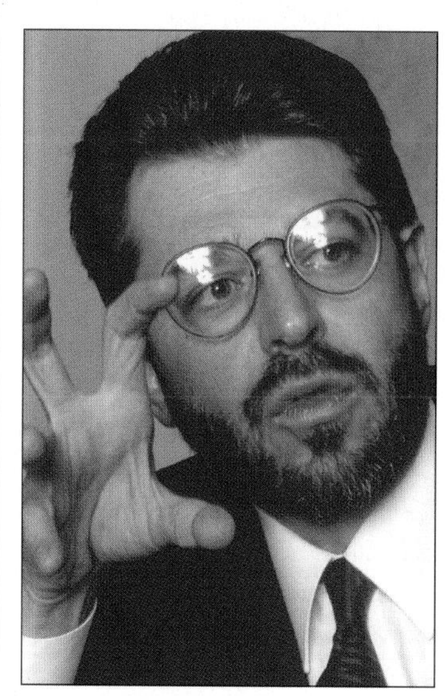
Jaime Zabludovsky Kuper

Zabre, Solón ◆ n. en Ciudad Camargo, Chih., y m. en Saltillo, Coah. (1904-1981). Su apellido materno era Morel. Dirigente obrero y campesino. Fue rector de la Universidad Autónoma de Sinaloa. Perteneció al jalapeño Grupo Noviembre y salió de Veracruz cuando el gobierno del estado expulsó a sus integrantes. Se trasladó a la ciudad de México y colaboró en la revista *Ruta* (1938-39). Militó en la Liga de Escritores y Artistas Revolucionarios. Fue director de un internado para hijos de trabajadores y profesor de la Escuela Nacional de Economía de la UNAM, de la que llegó a ser decano. Fundó la librería e imprenta Don Quijote y editó la revista *Letras de Ayer y de Hoy*. Autor de los poemarios *Alba en el pozo* (1946), *Retablo de la ausencia* (1946), *Nocturnos* (1947), *Áspero nombre de mi tierra* (1960) y *Siete nocturnos sin ella* (1961); y de los ensayos *Paul Verlaine* (1949) y *El pronunciado Gabriel Leyva* (1963).

Zacapala ◆ Municipio de Puebla situado al sur de la capital del estado y al oeste de Tehuacán. Superficie: 392.92 km^2. Habitantes: 4,269, de los cuales 964 forman la población económicamente activa. Hablan alguna lengua indígena 24 personas mayores de cinco años (náhuatl 20).

Zacapoaxtla ◆ Municipio de Puebla situado en el norte del estado, al oeste de Teziutlán y al este de Zacatlán. Superficie: 188.81 km^2. Habitantes: 45,546, de los cuales 10,348 forman la población económicamente activa. Hablan alguna lengua indígena 15,027 personas mayores de cinco años (náhuatl 18,774 y totonaco 204). En la jurisdicción se localiza la zona arqueológica de Youalichan. En la cabecera, del mismo nombre, se celebra el primer domingo de mayo el *Mitoticuicalli*, festival de danzas autóctonas.

Zacapoaxtla, de ◆ Sierra de Puebla y Veracruz. Forma parte de la sierra Madre Oriental. Se extiende de noroeste a

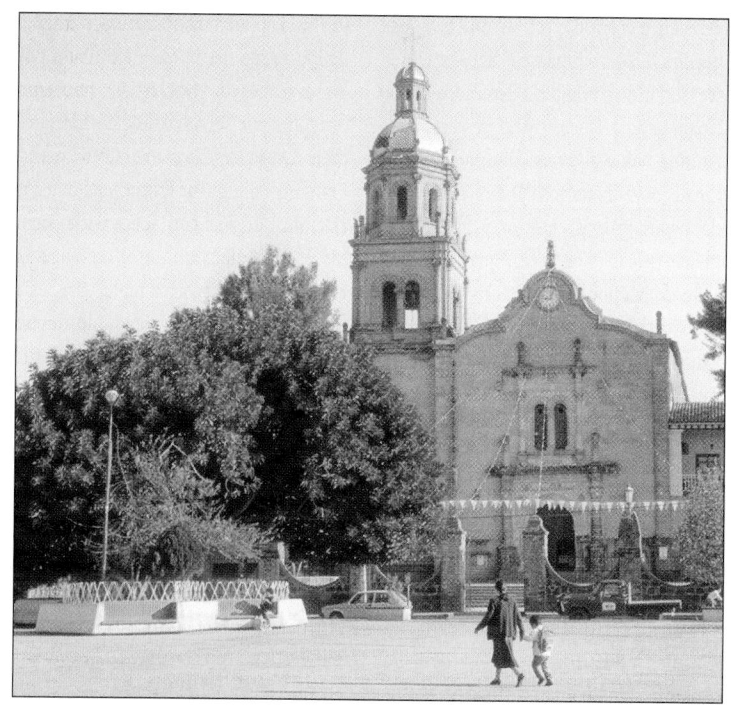
FOTO: CARLOS HAHN

Parroquia de Zacapu, Michoacán

sureste, entre el extremo surooriental de la sierra de Huauchinango y la vertiente noroccidental del Cofre de Perote.

ZACAPU, DE ◆ Laguna de Michoacán, también llamada de Zipimeo. Se localiza en el occidente del municipio de Zacapu, 60 kilómetros al nor-noroeste de Pátzcuaro. Aun cuando es de tamaño reducido, en sus aguas abunda la pesca y sus derrames alimentan al río Lerma.

ZACAPU ◆ Municipio de Michoacán situado en el norte del estado, al oeste-noroeste de Quiroga y al sureste de Zamora. Superficie: 322.02 km². Habitantes: 69,019, de los cuales 16,135 forman la población económicamente activa. Hablan alguna lengua indígena 1,082 personas mayores de cinco años (purépecha 1,069). Tiene gran potencial agrícola por el aprovechamiento de las tierras ganadas a la ciénega de Zacapu, que fue desecada por la familia española Noriega a fines del siglo XIX. En la jurisdicción se explotan los bosques y hay aserraderos que alimentan la industria de la celulosa. La cabecera, Zacapu de Mier, fue el mayor centro industrial de Michoacán, hasta que el puerto de Lázaro Cárdenas la desplazó. En las afueras está la fábrica Celanese Mexicana. Existen evidencias arqueológicas de que en Zacapu existía, hace unos 2,000 años, un Estado agrario. La *Relación de Michoacán* señala que hacia el siglo XIII llegaron los purépechas al Bajío y que tiempo después el señorío de Naranxan obligó a Ziranzirancámaro, señor de Zacapu, a expulsar de sus dominios a los chichimecas. En el siglo siguiente gobernaba Quenomen, viuda de Carómaco, quien fue sometida por los señores de Pátzcuaro, Ihuatzio y Tzintzuntzan. Tras la conquista, Zacapu formó parte de la encomienda de Hernando de Jerez. La evangelización la inició, en 1548, el franciscano Jacobo Daciano, quien fundó el convento de Santa Ana, del que aún queda el templo.

ZACARÍAS, MIGUEL ◆ n. en el DF (1908). Cineasta. Hijo de emigrados libaneses. Se formó en colegios maristas y estudió en Estados Unidos. Inició su carrera fílmica en 1932 con *Sobre las olas*, e hizo melodramas, comedias, musicales y películas cómicas. Dirigió *El peñón de las ánimas,* primera película de María Félix. Dirigió, entre otras películas, *Soledad, El cilindrero, La loca, Flor de durazno, El dolor de los hijos, Juana Gallo, El enamorado, Payasadas de la vida, Papá se desenreda, Carta de amor, Tierra baja, Cuidado con el amor* y *Necesito dinero.* Autor del poemario *Voces de amor* (1990). En 1993 recibió el Ariel de Oro. Fue presidente de la Asociación de Productores Cinematográficos, de la Asociación Nacional Cinematográfica y director de la Academia Nacional Cinematográfica. Representó al país en los festivales de Cannes, Francia y del Río de la Plata en Argentina.

Consuelo Guerrero de Luna y Libertad Lamarque en *Soledad*, película de Miguel Zacarías

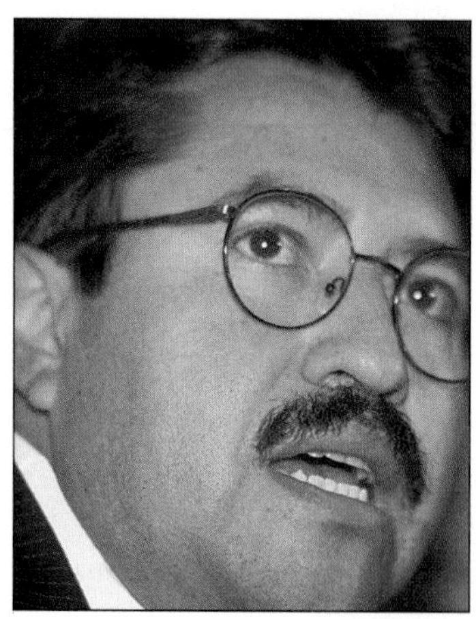

Ricardo Monreal, gobernador del estado de Zacatecas

ZACATECAS ◆ Estado de la República Mexicana que limita con Coahuila, Nuevo León, San Luis Potosí, Jalisco, Aguascalientes y Durango. Superficie: 73,252 km^2 (3.74 por ciento del territorio nacional). Tiene 56 municipios. El principal sistema montañoso es la sierra de Zacatecas, que corre de noroeste a sureste en la parte media del estado. Habitantes: 1,332,683 (1997). En 1995 tenía 1.5 por ciento de la población del país y habitaban en zonas urbanas 670,579 personas y en rurales 665,917. Es la segunda entidad con mayor emigración: 37.7 por ciento de su población de origen radica en otra entidad. Su índice de analfabetismo es de 11.43 por ciento de los mayores de 15 años. Forman la población económicamente activa 51 por ciento de los mayores de 12 años. En 1996 participaba con 0.8 por ciento del producto interno bruto nacional. En 1995 hablaban alguna lengua indígena 1,262 personas mayores de cinco años (tepehuan 289, náhuatl 173 y huichol 148), de las cuales 61 no sabían español. *Historia*: el territorio del actual estado estuvo poblado originalmente por los zacatecos, que vivían en el centro y en el norte, y los guachichiles, ocupantes del extremo sureste, indios nómadas dedicados principalmente a la caza y la recolección, aunque había algunas comunidades de zacatecos sedentarios. Todos vivían en pequeñas grupos aislados y frecuentemente peleaban entre sí. Hacia el tercer siglo de la época contemporánea se inició la penetración cultural mesoamericana, que trajo consigo la agricultura, la que no llegó a convertirse en la actividad económica principal. Hacia el siglo VIII, los nahuas construyeron algunas ciudades fortificadas como La Quemada, Chalchihuites y La Florida, en la zona que posteriormente fue ocupada por los caxcanes. A principios de 1530, dos de los capitanes de Nuño Beltrán de Guzmán (☛), los vascos Cristóbal de Oñate y Peralmíndez Chirinos, organizaron dos fuerzas militares de mexicas, tlaxcaltecas y purépechas con las que se adentraron en territorio zacateco y caxcán. Chirinos marchó directamente al norte y llegó hasta el sitio donde levantó después la ciudad de Zacatecas, pero no encontró nada que lo impulsara a seguir y volvió a Compostela; desde entonces se consideró que toda la región situada al norte de Michoacán formaba parte del reino de Nueva Galicia. Oñate, por su parte, viajó hacia el noreste por territorio de los caxcanes, llegó hasta Nochistlán y muy cerca del asentamiento indígena fundó la villa del Espíritu Santo de Guadalajara (1532), población que fue atacada por los caxcanes hasta que los españoles la abandonaron. Durante la segunda mitad de los años treinta, los conquistadores intentaron someter a los caxcanes, hasta que en 1540, los indios se levantaron en armas y comenzaron a hostilizar las expediciones españolas. En abril de 1541 el encomendero vasco Miguel de Ibarra fue derrotado y ejecutado por los caxcanes de Nochistlán, que eran dirigidos por Tenamaxtle, llamado también *Diego el Zacateco*. Otro vasco, Francisco de Aguilar Ibarra, inició negociaciones de paz con Tenamaxtle, pero los indios atacaron otro contingente español y lo obligaron a replegarse hasta la nueva Guadalajara. En junio de ese año, Pedro de Alvarado lanzó desde Guadalajara dos ataques contra los caxcanes en los que fue derrotado y que, en julio, le causaron la muerte. Los caxcanes, por su parte, tomaron Guadalajara a finales de septiembre, pero tuvieron que retirarse y, en octubre, el virrey Antonio de Mendoza organizó una fuerza de tlaxcaltecas y purépechas con la que avanzó hasta encontrarse con el ejército de Oñate, que combatía sin éxito en los actuales límites entre Zacatecas, Jalisco y Aguascalientes, y se dirigió a Nochistlán, donde, en noviembre, luego de cuatro días de combates, 50,000 mexicas, tlaxcaltecas y purépechas derrotaron a 12,000 caxcanes y zacatecos comandados por Tenamaxtle, con lo que terminó la que se conoce como guerra del Mixtón. Los españoles asesinaron a los

Calle de Jerez, Zacatecas

8,000 indios sobrevivientes y detuvieron a Tenamaxtle, quien pudo huir y refugiarse en el Mixtón de Juchipila, donde organizó nuevos grupos de indios, que durante los ocho años siguientes realizaron algunas incursiones en el territorio ocupado por los españoles, que fueron rechazadas por Oñate y por Juan Fernández de Hijar, que también era vasco. La mayor parte de los caxcanes meridionales fue incorporada a los dominios españoles y eso permitió que se realizaran algunas expediciones en territorio de los zacatecos. En septiembre de 1546, varios exploradores comandados por el vasco Juan de Tolosa, quienes habían seguido la ruta de Chirinos, llegaron a un cerro con forma de vejiga de cerdo, al que desde entonces se conoce como cerro de La Bufa. Los zacatecos del lugar les regalaron algunas pepitas de plata y los europeos se enteraron de la existencia de uno de los yacimientos argentíferos más grandes del mundo. En enero de 1848, Tolosa, el vasco Diego de Ibarra y el español Baltazar Temiño de Bañuelos, fundaron la ciudad de Zacatecas y prosiguieron sus exploraciones hacia el noroeste, hasta que, en 1555, descubrieron las minas de Sombrerete. Poco después se estableció una alcaldía mayor en Zacatecas y se creó la provincia de los Zacatecas, integrante del Reino de Nueva Galicia. A pesar de que entre la

Foto: Carlos Hahn

Arquitectura zacatecana

Foto: Carlos Hahn

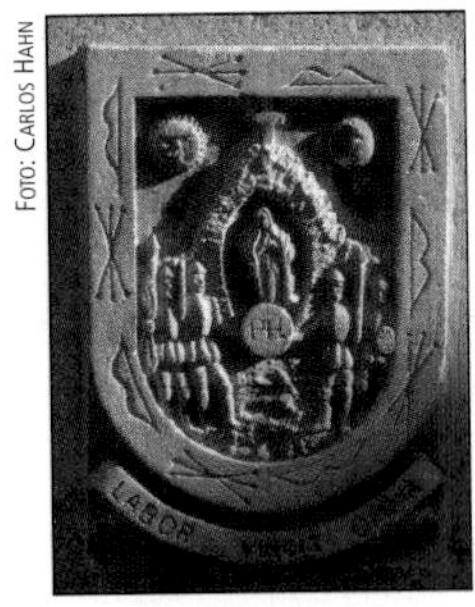

Escudo del estado de Zacatecas

nueva población y la frontera septentrional de la Nueva España se extendía un gran territorio habitado por zacatecos, guachichiles y guamares que se negaban a aceptar la dominación europea, dos años después de la fundación de Zacatecas en los alrededores de la ciudad había más de 35 explotaciones mineras. Los principales propietarios eran Tolosa, Ibarra, Temiño y Oñate. A partir de 1550, los zacatecos que vivían entre Zacatecas, Guadalajara y Querétaro asaltaron con frecuencia las caravanas que transportaban la plata a la ciudad de México. A partir de los años setenta, diestros ya en el uso de caballos, se dedicaron a asaltar las poblaciones fronterizas, con lo que dificultaron el comercio y la subsistencia de Zacatecas y de los nuevos centros mineros, fundados en los años sesenta al noroeste de la ciudad por el vasco Francisco de Ibarra, e incluso en 1561, grandes contingentes de zacatecos y guachichiles armados se instalaron en los alrededores de Zacatecas. Al principio, los españoles reaccionaron con violencia y asesinaron a todos los zacatecos que capturaron en las expediciones de Hernán Pérez de Bocanegra, pero lo único que consiguieron fue que los zacatecos establecieran una alianza con los guachichiles de San Luis Potosí y Coahuila y comenzaran a violar y secuestrar mujeres, empalar frailes, saquear iglesias católicas, incendiar ranchos, descerebrar niños y sacarles el corazón o cortarles los testículos o la cabellera a los soldados. Para 1561, unos 200 españoles y más de 2,000 indios mesoamericanos habían muerto en los "caminos de la plata". Las mercancías destruidas o robadas equivalían a 400,000 pesos de oro aproximadamente y el valor de los ranchos y estancias asaltadas era de unos 600,000 pesos de oro. Por entonces, en el camino que unía Zacatecas con Guadalajara, comenzaron a actuar varios grupos guerrilleros de esclavos africanos que habían huido de las minas, pese a lo cual, en 1570, cuando los españoles sumaban apenas 300 personas, más de 500 esclavos vivían en la provincia. En los años setenta, los españoles crearon varias congregaciones para los zacatecos derrotados y algunos pueblos amurallados como Jerez. En los ochenta establecieron presidios en Palmillas, sobre el camino de México; Cuicillo, sobre el de Aguascalientes; y Fresnillo, que protegía el camino hacia las minas de Sombrerete. A estas medidas se agregaron el trabajo misional de los frailes mendicantes, que fundaron misiones a lo largo de la frontera; la utilización masiva de tlaxcaltecas, purépechas, otomíes, mexicas y caxcanes como soldados y colonos, así como la firma de tratados con los zacatecos, a quienes se les prometieron exenciones impositivas y condonación de los servicios personales, todo lo cual permitió derrotar a los indios a pesar de una gran ofensiva desatada por los zacatecos en la segunda mitad de la década de 1580. En 1585, Zacatecas fue elevada al rango de ciudad por Felipe II, y en 1588 se le otorgó su escudo de armas. Para los primeros años del siglo XVII, los españoles estaban firmemente instalados el sur, el centro y el oeste de los actuales límites del estado. A principios del siglo XVII, la población zacatecana estaba formada por unos 1,500 españoles, 5,000 indios, más de 800 esclavos africanos y alrededor de 12 italianos y portugueses. En esos años, Zacatecas era la tercera ciudad más importante del virreinato. Durante el primer tercio del siglo, el rendimiento de las minas zacatecanas continuó en ascenso, pero desde 1635, debido a que el mercurio necesario para la amalgamación de la plata era importado de Europa y a causa de que las minas comenzaron a inundarse, la minería de la región dejó de crecer y, en 1636, cuando el gobierno virreinal re-

Valle de los Órganos, en Zacatecas

Foto: Michael Calderwood

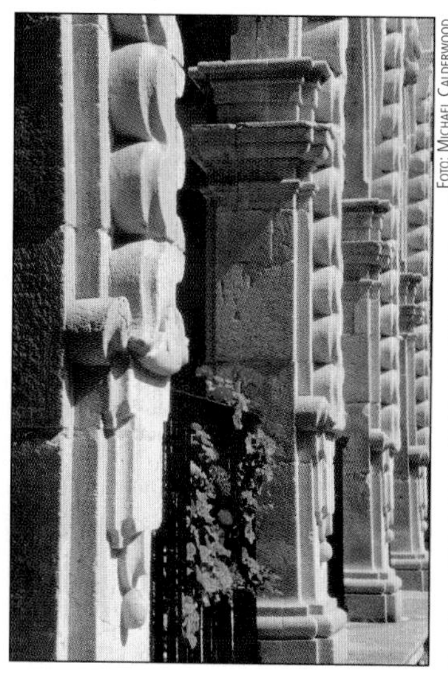

Cantera de Zacatecas

colectó dinero para mantener la armada de Barlovento, los propietarios de Zacatecas sólo pudieron aportar 10,000 pesos. Durante los treinta años siguientes, prácticamente se interrumpió toda actividad minera y gran parte de la región se despobló. En 1646, por ejemplo, sólo permanecían en la zona unos 500 españoles. El renacimiento de la minería zacatecana se inició en los años setenta del siglo XVII, pero fue a principios de la centuria siguiente cuando las minas volvieron a producir cantidades considerables. En 1727, en los alrededores de Zacatecas se establecieron el conde de Santiago de la Laguna y el conde de San Mateo de Valparaíso; por su parte, Francisco de Valdivieso, más tarde conde de San Mateo del Álamo, se estableció en Mazapil en 1734 y en Sombrerete en 1738. La reactivación de la minería atrajo nuevo mineros y comerciantes y a partir de 1770, sobre todo debido a José de la Borda, se iniciaron 40 años de bonanza para los propietarios de las minas, lo que de alguna manera benefició al resto de la población. En 1772, el vasco Francisco Cayetano Fagoaga, el marqués del Apartado, refundó el campo minero de Sombrerete, que en los años noventa vivió sus mejores momentos, siempre controlado por la familia Fagoaga. En Zacatecas, mientras tanto, las mayores minas fueron explotadas por Borda y más tarde por el vasco Manuel de Rétegui. Debido al rápido crecimiento económico de la región, en diciembre de 1786, cuando se publicaron las leyes que establecieron la división política en intendencias, los distritos mineros de Fresnillo, Sombrerete, Mazapil y Zacatecas, así como Nochistlán, Tlaltenango, Valparaíso y Aguascalientes quedaron dentro de la intendencia de Zacatecas. Poco después se creó la Hacienda de Zacatecas, donde se concentró la plata extraída en las minas, que hasta entonces tenía que ser trasladada a la ciudad de México para su valuación y traslado a España. Durante los últimos años del siglo XVIII y los primeros del siglo XIX, la minería zacatecana fue una de las más importantes de la Colonia, pero la actividad decayó al inicio de la revolución de independencia, pues muchos propietarios y casi todas las autoridades huyeron hacia el centro del país y los mineros desertaron y se incorporaron a los insurgentes. En octubre de 1810 se inició un levantamiento en Fresnillo; en el sur, Daniel Camarena se levantó en armas y tomó Nochistlán, mientras Rafael Iriarte atacaba Aguascalientes. Ignacio Cervantes, conde de Santiago, el comandante de las fuerzas españolas, envió a José María Cos a espiar los movimientos de Iriarte, pero el sacerdote se pasó a los insurgentes y en noviembre, las fuerzas de Iriarte tomaron la capital. En enero de 1811, el derrotado ejército de Miguel Hidalgo que huía de Guadalajara pasó por Zacatecas y, en febrero, las fuerzas realistas de José Manuel Ochoa tomaron la ciudad. Un mes más tarde, sin embargo, las tropas de Ignacio López Rayón derrotaron a las coloniales de Ochoa en Piñones y las de Pedro Villaseñor a las de Francisco Bringas en Ojocaliente, por lo que, en abril, los insurgentes ocuparon la capital de la intendencia, desde donde López Rayón intentó convencer a José María Calleja, el comandante de los colonialistas, para que se pasara a la insurgencia, a lo que se negó el militar realista y marchó sobre Zacatecas. Unos días más tarde, Miguel Emparan derrotó a López Rayón en el rancho del Maguey y, en mayo, luego de vencer a Víctor Rosales, Calleja tomó la ciudad. En el sur de la intendencia, mientras tanto, operaban las guerrillas de José María Calvillo, quien incluso había montado una fábrica de cañones en Nochistlán. En septiembre de 1812, una fuerza insurgente dirigida por Rosales atacó Zacatecas, pero fue derrotada. Al año siguiente, en Noria de Ángeles, se levantó en armas Guadalupe Díaz y en 1817 la fuerza internacionalista de Francisco Javier Mina se internó por el este de la intendencia; derrotó a los españoles en Peotillos y la Hedionda y en junio tomó Pinos. Poco a poco, sin embargo, el ejército colonial recuperó el

Antigua Plaza de Toros de San Pedro y, al fondo, el Acueducto de El Cubo, en Zacatecas

Huerto de nogales en Zacatecas

FOTO: FONDO EDITORIAL GRUPO AZABACHE

Ex hacienda de Bernárdez, en el estado de Zacatecas

control militar de la intendencia y, para 1820, la rebelión había prácticamente desaparecido. Al año siguiente, en junio de 1821, el ayuntamiento de Nochistlán se adhirió al Plan de Iguala y proclamó la independencia del imperio mexicano; durante los días siguientes, todas las autoridades locales se convirtieron repentinamente en independentistas. En abril de 1823, después de la abdicación de Agustín de Iturbide, Juan Peredo se levantó en armas en Aguascalientes, derrotó en Zacatecas a los simpatizantes del emperador, se apoderó de la comandancia militar y en octubre de ese año, poco después de la instalación del Congreso Constituyente local, fue elegido gobernador. En enero, mediante el Acta Constitutiva de la Federación, se creó el estado de los Zacatecas. La primera Constitución del estado se aprobó en enero de 1825. Desde entonces, tanto la Legislatura local como los puestos asignados al estado en el Congreso general fueron dominados por los liberales, entre ellos Valentín Gómez Farías y Francisco García Salinas, quien, además, se encargó interinamente de la gubernatura desde agosto de 1829, apoyado por los alzados contrarios a la elección presidencial de Manuel Gómez Pedraza, quienes habían tomado Fresnillo a finales de 1828 y Sombrerete en enero de 1829. A finales de 1829, la Legislatura local aprobó una ley que disponía la confiscación de los bienes de la Iglesia para la creación de un "banco agrario", ley que fue declarada anticonstitucional por el Congreso federal en marzo del año siguiente. El gobernador García Salinas se opuso al levantamiento que derrocó al gobierno de Vicente Guerrero. Desde principios de 1830, vista la tendencia centralizadora de los escoceses, García Salinas fortaleció la Guardia Nacional, un cuerpo de voluntarios creado por el Congreso en 1823, el que rápidamente y a pesar de la oposición del gobierno golpista de Anastasio Bustamante, se convirtió en una fuerza bien armada y entrenada, la que en 1832 estaba nominalmente constituida por casi 8,000 soldados de caballería y unos 8,500 de infantería, aunque sólo 4,000 estaban armados de manera permanente. Durante los años del gobierno de Bustamante, Zacatecas se convirtió en el principal bastión de los liberales y, desde 1831, Gómez Farías y García Salinas impulsaron a varios gobernadores y legisladores contra los sublevados de Jalapa. Por eso, en enero de 1832, al iniciarse el levantamiento de Antonio López de Santa Anna contra Bustamante, el gobierno de Rodríguez exigió al presidente la destitución de todos los ministros y, a finales de ese año, impulsó el regreso de Gómez Pedraza a la Presidencia, pero se opuso a los Acuerdos de Zavaleta, porque éstos pretendían disolver las legislaturas locales. Durante la gestión intermitente de Gómez Farías, García Salinas pudo realizar algunas de las reformas liberales por las que luchaba desde finales de la década anterior y, por eso, cuando en mayo de 1834 Santa Anna desplazó al vicepresidente, clausuró el Congreso y alentó los pronunciamientos procentralistas, el gobierno de Zacatecas formó una alianza con Jalisco, Michoacán y San Luis Potosí, la que se disolvió unos meses más tarde. Finalmente, en febrero de 1835, el Congreso santanista ordenó la reducción de las guardias nacionales de los estados, disposición a la que naturalmente se opuso el gobierno zacatecano, que decidió reasumir su soberanía y no reconocer al gobierno central. A principios de abril, Santa Anna se puso al frente de un ejército de 5,000 hombres con el que atacó Aguascalientes a finales de ese mes y fomentó insurrecciones contra el gobierno de García Salinas en Nieves y Fresnillo. En mayo, las fuerzas santanistas asaltaron la capital del estado, derrotaron a la Guardia Nacional y arrasaron la ciudad. También en mayo, como represalia, el Congreso federal decretó la erección del estado de Aguascalientes, con lo que Zacatecas perdió su zona agrícola más importante. En diciembre del año siguiente, cuando se estableció formalmente la República Unitaria, Zacatecas se convirtió en departamento. Al triunfo de la revolución de Ayutla, Victoriano Zamora se encargó del gobierno local y en junio de 1857, promulgada la Constitución liberal, fue elegido gobernador y, desde enero de 1858, apoyó al gobierno de Benito Juárez. A principios de abril, el ejército conservador de Miguel Miramón tomó la capital del estado y obligó a las fuerzas de Zamora a retirarse al norte del estado, pero unos días más tarde, los liberales de Juan Zuazua

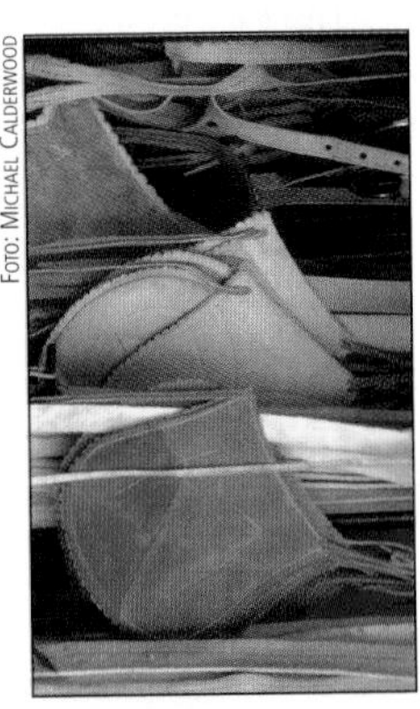
FOTO: MICHAEL CALDERWOOD

Artículos de piel de Zacatecas

FOTO: FONDO EDITORIAL GRUPO AZABACHE

Habitantes de Zacatecas

tomaron Zacatecas y fusilaron a los jefes reaccionarios que defendían la ciudad. En octubre de ese año, los conservadores de Leonardo Márquez ocuparon brevemente la capital del estado y luego se dirigieron hacia el sur, para unirse a Miramón. El gobierno liberal quedó a cargo de Jesús González Ortega, quien en junio de 1859 promulgó una ley que condenaba a muerte a los sacerdotes que hicieran campaña contra la Constitución y, naturalmente, casi todos los sacerdotes huyeron del estado y se refugiaron en Jalisco. En octubre, González Ortega fue desalojado de la capital por las fuerzas de Adrian Woll y se retiró a Sombrerete, donde volvió a ser derrotado por los conservadores, que, de esta manera, se apoderaron de la mayor parte del estado. Los liberales volvieron al ataque y en junio de 1860, luego de una victoria de González Ortega al sur de Aguascalientes, los constitucionalistas avanzaron hacia el norte y tomaron la capital del estado. Al año siguiente, González Ortega fue nombrado comandante militar de Zacatecas, San Luis Potosí y Aguascalientes, con facultades para disponer de las rentas y organizar un cuerpo de ejército. En febrero de 1864, los franceses entraron en Zacatecas y convirtieron al estado en el Departamento Imperial de Zacatecas. Un año después, en junio de 1864, Ignacio Mateo Mena fue consagrado primer obispo de Zacatecas. En el norte del estado, mientras tanto, combatían las fuerzas guerrilleras de González Ortega, pero en septiembre de 1864 fueron derrotadas por los franceses en la hacienda de Estanzuela, con lo que todo el estado quedó bajo el dominio de los invasores y así permaneció hasta noviembre de 1866, cuando, una vez retirados los franceses, las fuerzas del gobernador Miguel Auza entraron en la capital. En enero de 1867, el presidente Juárez se instaló en Sombrerete, Fresnillo y Zacatecas, de donde tuvo que huir apresuradamente el día 27 ante el sorpresivo ataque del ejército de Miramón. Juárez se retiró a Jerez y a Fresnillo, mientras Miramón, acosado por el ejército de Mariano Escobedo, se retiraba hacia el sur. En los primeros días de febrero, los republicanos sorprendieron a las fuerzas de Miramón en Cuisillo y las derrotaron estrepitosamente en San Jacinto, con lo que el ejército de los imperiales quedó destruido. En diciembre de 1869, el gobernador Trinidad García de la Cadena se adhirió a un levantamiento antijuarista iniciado en San Luis Potosí y proclamó, junto con la Legislatura local, un *Plan restaurador del orden constitucional de la República*. En enero, las fuerzas del gobierno al mando de Antonio Neri ocuparon la capital del estado, por lo que García de la Cadena se retiró hacia Jalisco, pero volvió en marzo, y fue derrotado por las fuerzas de Donato Guerra en Santa Cruz y ocupó brevemente Zacatecas antes de ser finalmente vencido. Al año siguiente, García de la Cadena se sumó al levantamiento porfirista de la Noria y en 1875 al de Tuxtepec. En 1877 ocupó la guberantura de Zacatecas. Tres años después, con apoyo de organizaciones obreras, el gobernador fue candidato presidencial y, derrotado en las elecciones, se levantó en armas. Durante el porfiriato gobernaron el estado Jesús Arréchiga (1880-96), Genaro García (1900-04), Eduardo G. Pankhurst (1904-08) y Francisco de Paula Zárate, contra quien se sublevó Luis Moya en febrero de 1911 y tomó Nieves, Tlaltenango, Teúl y Nochistlán. En abril, Moya intentó ocupar la capital, fue rechazado en Fresnillo, pero derrotó a los federales en Sombrerete. Días después, Gertrudis Sánchez tomó Mazapil y en mayo renunció el gobernador Zárate. En abril de 1913, Pánfilo Natera se levantó contra el régimen de Victoriano Huerta y tomó Zacatecas en junio, pero fue desalojado por las fuerzas de José Delgado. Dos veces más, en octubre de ese año y a principios junio de 1914, Natera atacó la capital del estado, pero en ambas ocasiones fue derrotado. La impericia de Natera fue aprovechada por las fuerzas de la División del Norte comandada por Francisco Villa, que el día 23, pese a las órdenes de Venustiano Carranza, quien insistía en que Natera realizara el asalto, se lanzaron contra la ciudad y derrotaron a los federales. Para finales de 1916, los carrancistas se habían instalado firmemente en el poder, aunque sobrevivieron guerrillas villistas hasta 1917. En agosto de 1926, Pedro Quintanar se levantó en armas en Valparaíso contra la ley reglamentaria del artículo 130 constitucional, que el presidente Plutarco Elías Calles había promulgado unos meses antes y, desde entonces, por todo el sur y centro del estado se generalizaron los levantamientos cristeros hasta que, en abril de 1929, 660 federales fueron derrotados en el Tesorero por una fuerza de 530 cristeros. Dos meses después, el gobierno de Emilio Portes Gil llegó a un acuerdo o *modus vivendi* con la jerarquía de la Iglesia católica que puso fin al conflicto.

POBLACIÓN DE 5 AÑOS Y MÁS HABLANTE DE LENGUA INDÍGENA, 1995

1 200 000
1 000 000
800 000
600 000
400 000
200 000
0

Población de 5 años y más 1,173,681
Población de 5 años y más hablante de lengua indígena 1,262 (0.11%)

PROMEDIO DE ESCOLARIDAD DE LA POBLACIÓN DE 15 AÑOS Y MÁS, POR SEXO, 1995

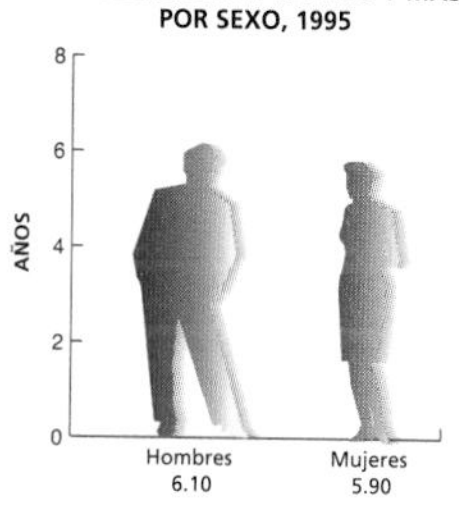

PRODUCTO INTERNO BRUTO (PIB) A PRECIOS CORRIENTES

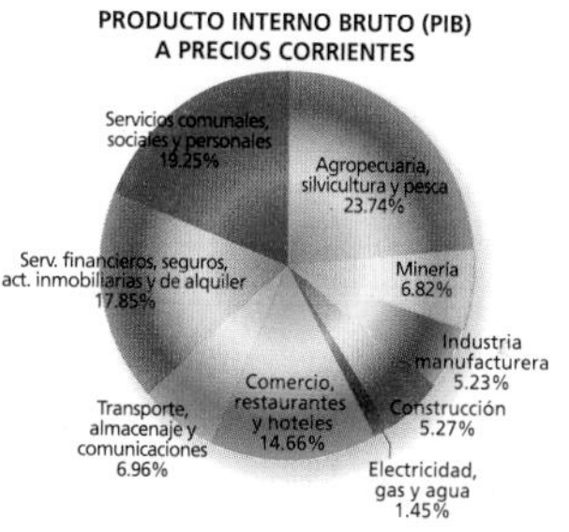

LONGITUD DE LA RED DE CARRETERAS POR SUPERFICIE DE RODAMIENTO, 1995

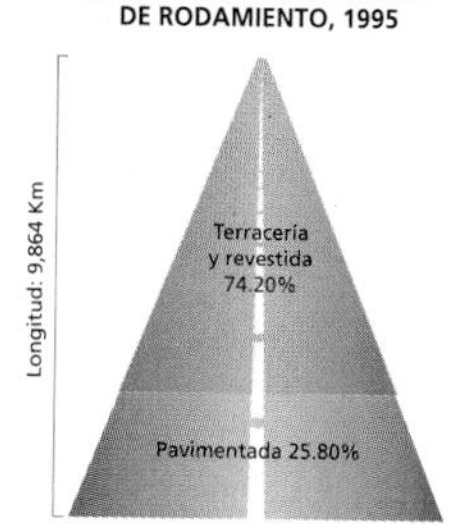

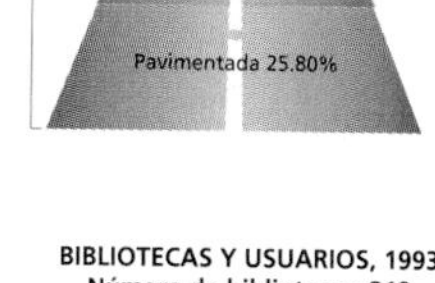

DISTRIBUCIÓN PORCENTUAL DE LA POBLACIÓN OCUPADA POR SECTOR DE ACTIVIDAD ECONÓMICA, 1995

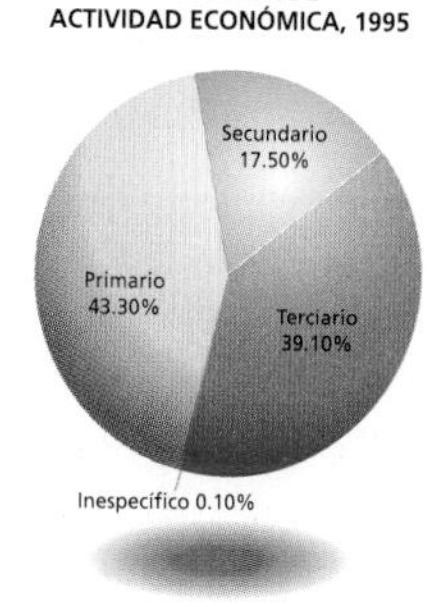

BIBLIOTECAS Y USUARIOS, 1993
Número de bibliotecas: 318

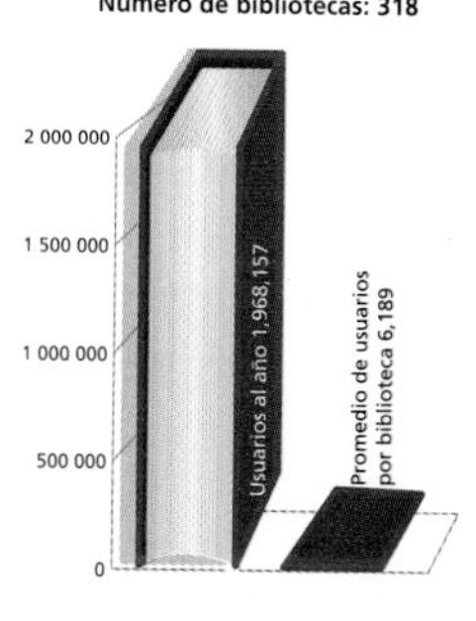

DISTRIBUCIÓN DE LA POBLACIÓN POR TAMAÑO DE LA LOCALIDAD, 1995

LÍNEAS TELEFÓNICAS EN SERVICIO Y APARATOS PÚBLICOS, 1994

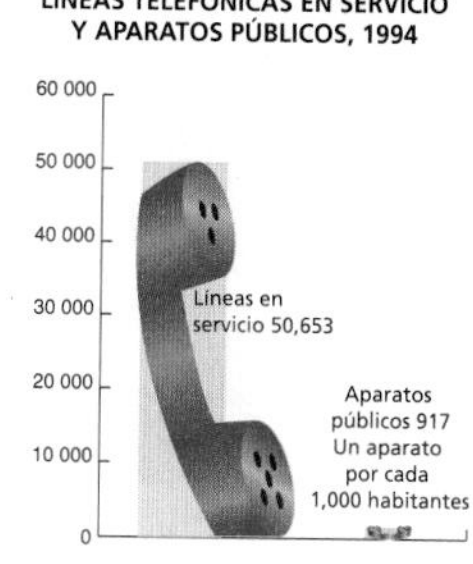

Zacatecas ◆ Municipio de Zacatecas situado al sureste de Fresnillo y al este de Jerez. Superficie: 719.60 km². Habitantes: 118,742, de los cuales 33,841 forman la población económicamente activa. Hablan alguna lengua indígena 103 personas mayores de cinco años (náhuatl 29). Cuenta con prósperas ganadería e industria de lácteos. Su principal riqueza es la minería: se explotan numerosos yacimientos de oro, estaño, plata, plomo, cinc, hierro y sulfuros. En la cabecera, del mismo nombre y también capital del estado, existe una planta minerometalúrgica; es, además, sede de la Universidad Autónoma de Zacatecas y cuenta con el Museo de Arte Virreinal, localizado en el ex convento de Guadalupe (monasterio fundado en el primer tercio del siglo XVIII por Antonio Margil de Jesús). En el cerro de La Bufa, junto a la ciudad, hay un observatorio meteorológico. El nombre significa "Lugar donde abunda el zacate". A la llegada de los conquistadores españoles la región estaba habitada por los zacatecos; el territorio atrajo a muchos aventureros, pues se descubrió de inmediato su riqueza mineral. Uno de ellos, Juan de Tolosa, *Barbalonga*, en 1546 supo que había plata en un lugar a 15 jornadas de Tlaltenango. El 8 de septiembre, al término de un segundo viaje, llegó hasta una cañada en cuya parte superior sobresalía un promontorio rocoso al que puso el nombre de Bufa ("vejiga de cerdo", en vasco). En la falda del cerro vivían unos 500 indios zacatecos. Con Diego y Miguel de Ibarra, Baltazar Termiño de Bañuelos y algunos otros fundó el 20 de enero de 1548 la población que fue conocida como Real de Minas de Nuestra Señora de los Remedios. En 1580 se nombró al primer corregidor, pues ya para entonces Zacatecas era alcaldía mayor dependiente de Nueva Galicia. En 1585, Felipe II le dio título de Muy Noble y Leal Ciudad de Nuestra Señora de los Zacatecas y en 1588 le otorgó escudo de armas. Hacia 1800 la población de Zacatecas era de 20,000 personas. A la fecha no sobrevive en Zacatecas ninguna de las construcciones del siglo XVI. Su edificación más antigua es el convento gótico de San Francisco, del siglo XVII, y el resto de las joyas arquitectónicas de la ciudad datan del XVIII, como la Compañía de Santo Domingo (construida en 1746), el convento de San Agustín, la capilla barroca del cerro de La Bufa y la catedral (edificada entre 1731 y 1748). En esta ciudad ocurrió uno de los más brillantes ataques de *Pancho Villa* contra las fuerzas huertistas: el 23 de junio de 1914, desobedeciendo las disposiciones de Venustiano Carranza, Villa atacó y tomó la plaza, con lo que causó un daño irreparable al viejo ejército federal, que poco después se rindió en Teoloyucan.

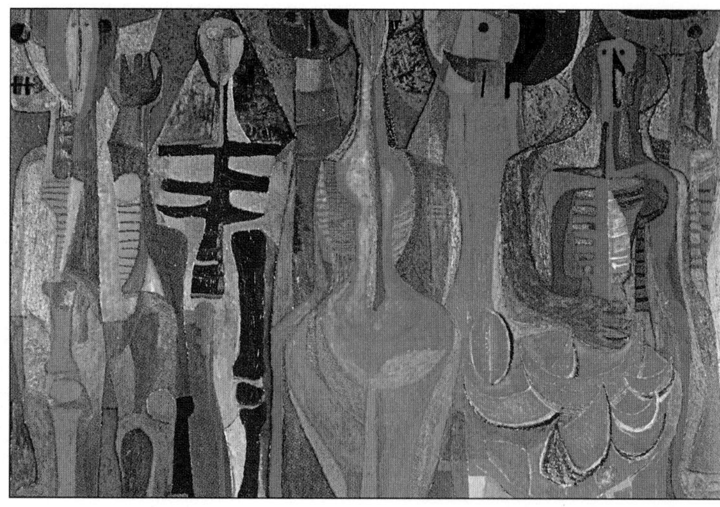

Los personajes del callejón azul, óleo sobre tela del pintor zacatecano Pedro Coronel

Foto: Carlos Hahn

Zacatecas, capital del estado de Zacatecas

Zacatecas, de ◆ Sierra de Zacatecas situada en el occidente del estado. Se extiende de noroeste a sureste, al oeste de la ciudad de Zacatecas. La limitan al noroeste, la sierra de Santa María; al oeste, las de Chalchihuites y Valparaíso; al sur, la de los Montes de García y, al sureste, la de Jerez de Colotlán, las cuales forman el conjunto conocido como sierras de Zacatecas.

Zacatelco ◆ Municipio de Tlaxcala situado en el sur del estado, al sur de la capital estatal, en los límites con Puebla. Superficie: 30.30 km². Habitantes: 30,574, de los cuales 9,540 forman la población económicamente activa. Hablan alguna lengua indígena 252 personas mayores de cinco años (náhuatl 186). En 1941 perdió parte de su territorio para la creación del municipio de Xicohtzingo.

Detalle de la fachada de la parroquia de Zacatelco, Tlaxcala

ZACATEPEC ◆ Municipio de Morelos situado al sur de Cuernavaca y al suroeste de Cuautla. Superficie: 26.81 km². Habitantes: 32,719, de los cuales 9,394 forman la población económicamente activa. Hablan alguna lengua indígena 109 personas mayores de cinco años (náhuatl 54 y zapoteco 21). En la cabecera, Zacatepec de Hidalgo, se localiza el ingenio Emiliano Zapata, uno de los más importantes del país.

ZACATEPEC ◆ Ganadería fundada por Daniel Muñoz y su esposa, María Cristina González, en 1924. Se estableció en la hacienda de Santiago Zotoluca (☛ *Zotoluca*), en el municipio de Tlaxco, Tlax. Los colores de su divisa son plomo y rojo.

ZACATEPEC, LIENZO DE ◆ Documento también llamado Códice Martínez Gracida o Códice mixteco. Procedente del poblado de Zacatepec, Oaxaca, el original se conserva en la Biblioteca Nacional de Antropología e Historia y existen copias en Zacatepec y en el Museo Etnográfico de Berlín. Pintado sobre tela, el documento contiene nombres de lugares de la región de Yamiltepec, figuras genealógicas y una iglesia cristiana.

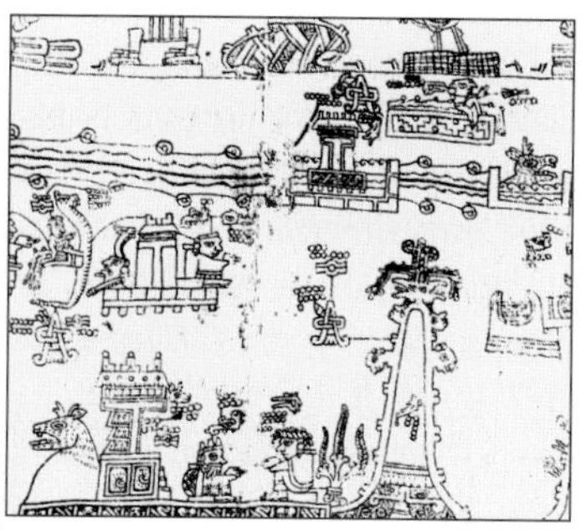

Lienzo de Zacatepec

ZACATLÁN ◆ Municipio de Puebla situado en el norte del estado, contiguo a Huauchinango, en los límites con Hidalgo. Superficie: 512.82 km². Habitantes: 62,778, de los cuales 15,135 forman la población económicamente activa. Hablan alguna lengua indígena 7,976 personas mayores de cinco años (náhuatl 6,876 y totonaco 1,007). Destaca por la producción de manzanas, lo que ha determinado la celebración de una feria anual, del 13 al 21 de agosto. En la cabecera, del mismo nombre, aunque conocida como Zacatlán de las Manzanas, se celebra el 15 de mayo la fiesta de San Pedro Labrador, para bendecir el cultivo de maíz. Cuenta con industria productora de sidra. En la ciudad se halla una basílica del siglo XVI. En la vertiente septentrional de la sierra Madre Oriental, en el estado de Puebla, se creó en 1556 la provincia de Hueytlalpa con jurisdicción sobre un territorio que se extendía hasta el litoral del golfo de México; hacia 1600 se le segregó la parte nororiental para crear la provincia de Papantla, y Hueytlalpa se convirtió en 1620 en la provincia de Zacatlán, que en 1787 fue convertida en subdelegación de la intendencia de Puebla. Cerca de la cabecera se localiza el valle de las Piedras Encimadas, formación basáltica natural. Desde principios de siglo se localiza en Zacatlán una fábrica de relojes monumentales que surte a iglesias, parques y edificios públicos de todo el país. Hacia 1955 se montó en la misma población una fábrica de pistolas, que dejó de funcionar en 1970, cuando el Estado adquirió el monopolio de la producción de armas.

FOTO: CARLOS HAHN

Zacatlán, Puebla

ZACAZONAPAN ◆ Municipio del Estado de México situado en el suroeste de la entidad, contiguo a Valle de Bravo. Superficie: 92.45 km². Habitantes: 3,161, de los cuales 640 forman la población económicamente activa. En la jurisdicción se localizan las zonas arqueológicas de Potrerillos y Pueblo Viejo, sin explorar, así como la hacienda de Santa María, edificada en el siglo XVIII.

ZACOALCO DE TORRES ◆ Municipio de Jalisco situado al oeste del lago de Chapala, al sureste de Guadalajara y contiguo a Acatlán. Superficie: 488.06 km². Habitantes: 25,836, de los cuales 6,200 forman la población económicamente activa. Hablan alguna lengua indígena 28 personas mayores de cinco años (purépecha 16). En la jurisdicción se localiza la laguna de San Marcos. En este sitio se produjo en noviembre de 1810 la batalla de Zacoalco, en la que el insurgente José Antonio Torres venció a una división de 500 realistas bisoños comandados por Tomás Ignacio Villaseñor. Como homenaje a ese insurgente, el Congreso local decidió en 1829 dar al municipio su actual nombre.

ZACUALPAN ◆ Municipio del Estado de México situado en el sur de la entidad, al sur-suroeste de Toluca, en los límites con Guerrero. Superficie: 198.63 km². Habitantes: 14,115, de los cuales 2,551 forman la población económicamente activa. Hablan alguna lengua indígena 23 personas mayores de cinco años. Cuenta con yacimientos de plata, cobre, cinc, hierro y plomo que se explotan desde 1529. En la jurisdicción se hallan las zonas arqueológicas del cerro de la Tentación, Ocostitlán, Coloxtitlán, Mamatla, Tepextitlán y la Trinidad. En la cabecera, del mismo nombre, hay una iglesia franciscana del siglo XVI.

Gabriel Zaid

La economía presidencial

V
Vuelta

Libro de Gabriel Zaid

Zacualpan ◆ Municipio de Morelos situado en el noreste del estado, al este de Cuautla, en los límites con Puebla. Superficie: 58.75 km². Habitantes: 7,569, de los cuales 1,649 forman la población económicamente activa. Hablan alguna lengua indígena 13 personas mayores de cinco años (náhuatl 13). La cabecera es Zacualpan de Amilpas.

Zacualpan ◆ Municipio de Veracruz situado al oeste de Poza Rica, en los límites con Hidalgo. Superficie: 219.62 km². Habitantes: 6,955, de los cuales 2,131 forman la población económicamente activa. Hablan alguna lengua indígena 151 personas mayores de cinco años (otomí 127).

Zacualpan ◆ Sierra de los estados de México y Guerrero, que forma parte del Eje Volcánico. Se extiende de noroeste a sureste, desde el extremo suroriental de la sierra de Sultepec, en el Estado de México, hasta la vertiente sur de la sierra de Taxco, en Guerrero. Sus principales elevaciones son los cerros Coronas, Tres Cruces, Mamatla, Espinazo del Diablo, Picacho y Canal.

Zacualtipán, de ◆ Sierra de Hidalgo situada en el centro-oriente del estado. Forma parte de la sierra Madre Oriental. Se extiende de noroeste a sureste, al este del lago de Metztitlán y del río Amajac, y al norte del río Tulancingo. Cuenta con yacimientos minerales.

Zacualtipán de Ángeles ◆ Municipio de Hidalgo situado al norte de Atotonilco el Grande, en los límites con Veracruz. Superficie: 241.60 km². Habitantes: 22,785, de los cuales 6,084 forman la población económicamente activa. Hablan alguna lengua indígena 705 personas mayores de cinco años (náhuatl 697). Los agustinos iniciaron las tareas de evangelización desde 1578.

Zahuapan, de ◆ Río de Tlaxcala. Nace en la porción central del estado, al noroeste de Apizaco; corre hacia el sur, a través del extremo oriental del valle de Tlaxcala; al este de la capital estatal y al norte de Chiautempan tuerce al suroeste, avanza hasta San Vicente Xiloxochitla donde tuerce al sur, y al este de Zacatelco vuelve a cambiar su rumbo hacia el sureste. Al sur de Xicohtzingo entra en el estado de Puebla, donde se convierte en el río Atoyac.

Zaid, Gabriel ◆ n. en Monterrey, NL (1934). Poeta, traductor y ensayista. Su segundo apellido es Giacoman. Ingeniero mecánico administrador por el ITESM (1955). Ha colaborado en *Revista de Bellas Artes, Cuadernos del Viento, La Vida Literaria, Plural, Diálogos, El Gallo Ilustrado, México en la Cultura, Revista de la Universidad de México* y *Vuelta*. Tradujo *Canciones* de Vidyapati (1978). Autor de poesía: *Fábula de Narciso y Ariadna* (1958), *Seguimiento* (1964), *Campo nudista* (1969), *Práctica mortal* (1973), *Cuestionario* (1976) y *Sonetos y canciones* (1992); de ensayo: *La poesía, fundamento de la ciudad* (1963), *La máquina de cantar* (1967), *Los demasiados libros* (1972), *Leer poesía* (1972), *Cómo leer en bicicleta* (1975), *El progreso improductivo* (1979), *La poesía en la práctica* (1986), *Un amor imposible de López Velarde* (1986), *Adivinos o libreros* (1986), *La economía presidencial* (1987), *De los libros al poder* (1988) y *Muerte y resurrección de la cultura católica* (1991); y de antologías: *Ómnibus de poesía mexicana* (1970), y *Asamblea de poetas jóvenes de México* (1980). Miembro de El Colegio Nacional (1984-) y de la Academia Mexicana (de la Lengua). Ha recibido los premios Xavier Villaurrutia 1972 y Magda Donato 1986.

Zaire ◆ ☛ *Congo, República Democrática del.*

Zaitzeff, Serge I. ◆ n. en Francia (1940). Maestro y doctor en letras hispánicas por la Universidad de Indiana. Ha sido profesor de diversas instituciones de enseñanza superior en Estados Unidos. Colaborador de las publicaciones mexicanas *Nexos, La Palabra y el Hombre* y *Sábado*. Realizó la compilación y notas de *De casa a casa: correspondencia entre Manuel Toussaint y Alfonso Reyes* (1990). Autor de *Crónicas escogidas de Rafael López* (1970), *Rafael López, poeta y prosista* (1972), *La Venus de la Alameda. Antología de Rafael López* (1973), *Fuerza y dolor. Antología poética de Roberto Argüelles Bringas* (1975), *Julio Torri y la crítica* (1981), *Obras de Ricardo Gómez Robelo y Carlos Díaz Dufoo jr.* (1981), *La obra literaria de Rubén M. Campos* (1983), *Ad Altare Dei y todos los poemas de Francisco González Guerrero* (1983) y *El arte de Julio Torri*. Se encargó del prólogo, recopilación y bibliografía de *Lira ruda*, obra completa de Roberto Argüelles Bringas (1986).

Záizar, David ◆ n. en Tamazula de Gordiano, Jal., y m. en el DF (1930-1982). Cantante, actor y compositor, era hijo de un mariachero. Llegó a la ciudad de México en 1949 y formó el grupo musical Cantores del Bosque. Trabajó en radio, cine, televisión y teatro. Con Juan formó el dueto Hermanos Záizar (1958), que grabó más de 50 discos de larga duración. Participó, entre otras, en las películas *Cruz de olvido, Cielo rojo, La malagueña salerosa, India mía* y *San Juan de Ulúa*.

Záizar, Juan ◆ n. en Tamazula de Gordiano, Jal., y m. en el DF (1933-1991). Músico, hermano del anterior. Estudió solfeo, armonía, violín y piano en San Luis Potosí. Llegó a la ciudad de México en 1949 y formó el grupo Cantores del Bosque. En 1958 formó el dueto Hermanos Záizar con su hermano David y se dedicó a la composición. Fue también actor de cine y teatro. Compuso las canciones *Apártate de mí* (1951), *Entre cadenas, No soy culpable, Una paloma herida, Cielo rojo, Cruz de olvido, La basurita, Vuelve gaviota, Canto al obrero* (1971), *¿Qué le debo a la vida?, Partes iguales, El corrido del chicano, Cárcel perpetua, ¡Qué padre es la vida!, No tiene la culpa el indio* y *Suenen guitarrones*. Como solista grabó ocho discos de larga duración. Recibió la medalla Virginia Fábregas por 25 años de actividad profesional.

Zalacosta, Francisco ◆ n. en Durango, Dgo., y m. en Querétaro, Qro. (1844-1881). Hijo de un oficial del ejército liberal, quien lo condujo a la ciudad de México, donde quedó huérfano y fue recogido por una familia acomodada que le dio estudios. Estaba por ingresar a la carrera de medicina cuando conoció a Plotino Rhodakanaty, de quien se convirtió en discípulo. Fundó con Santiago Villanueva (☛) y Hermenegildo Villavicencio (☛), en enero de 1865, el Club Socialista de Estudiantes en la ciudad de México. Con Villanueva promovió la creación de la Sociedad Mutua del Ramo de Hilados y Tejidos del Valle de México, con obreros de las fábricas de San Ildefonso y La Colmena de Tlalnepantla, el 15 de marzo de 1865, los que estallaron la huelga el 10 de junio y fueron reprimidos por las autoridades imperiales. Fundó y dirigió el periódico *La Internacional* (1878). Estuvo un tiempo con Rhodakanaty en Chalco y volvió a la escuela, que tuvo que dejar ante los apremios económicos en que cayó su familia adoptiva, para dedicarse a la ebanistería y luego a la sombrerería. Ocasionalmente suplía a Rhodakanaty en la escuela de Chalco, con lo cual entró en contacto con los campesinos de la región. En 1868-69 estuvo en Ixmiquilpan, Hidalgo, donde impulsó la lucha agrarista de los peones de las haciendas. Perseguido por los terratenientes volvió a la ciudad de México en febrero de 1869. A mediados de ese año trató de unirse en Huamantla al grupo de insurrectos de Julio Chávez López (☛), pero las autoridades intentaron aprehenderlo y huyó hacia Puebla disfrazado de campesino, pasó a la ciudad de México y, a principios de agosto, cuando quiso ir hacia la zona rebelde, fue detenido en la Villa de Guadalupe. Recuperó la libertad, por gestiones de Villanueva, a principios de septiembre, después del fusilamiento de Chávez López. En 1871 fue cofundador de La Social y en septiembre de ese año, cuando se creó el Gran Círculo de Obreros, participó en él activamente. En 1872 fue secretario de la Sección Mexicana de la Internacional Anarquista (☛). Residió algún tiempo fuera de la capital y volvió al celebrarse el Congreso General Obrero (marzo-abril de 1876) y reunió a los delegados opuestos a los líderes del Gran Círculo, de acuerdo con Rhodakanaty, Francisco de Paula González y otros militantes radicales, quienes el 19 de abril acordaron separarse del Congreso Obrero y fundar un periódico, *El Hijo del Trabajo*, que apareció el día 21. En la reapertura de La Social, el 7 de mayo de 1876, declaró: "Que venga la revolución social es lo que queremos. El fracaso del Congreso Obrero no es el fracaso del socialismo, como lo asegura la prensa clerical. Es el fracaso de los leguleyos políticos, de los centralistas que se creen los llamados a dirigirnos eternamente, de los que quieren ponernos a subasta pública entre los capitanes: Lerdo de Tejada y Porfirio Díaz." Consumado el triunfo de la rebelión de Tuxtepec, clausurados los locales de las asociaciones proletarias y con la prensa bajo censura, Zalacosta, en junio de 1877, salió de la capital a organizar grupos campesinos a los que llamó comunidades, cuyo fin sería proclamar y aplicar la "ley agraria", que definía como "el acto de expropiar a los terratenientes y hacendados de las posesiones que mantienen por el desgraciado privilegio concedido por las leyes antinaturales". Operó en los estados de México, Tlaxcala, Puebla e Hidalgo. En éste reunió a los campesinos de la hacienda de San Javier, quienes detuvieron al administrador y a los empleados y eligieron democráticamente una nueva administración. En 1881, después de participar en insurrecciones de Hidalgo y Guanajuato, fue detenido en Querétaro junto con otros trabajadores, acusado de "atentar contra las personas y los bienes". Fue juzgado sumariamente y ejecutado en la misma ciudad.

ZALCE, ALFREDO ◆ n. en Pátzcuaro, Mich. (1908). Pintor, escultor y grabador. Estudió en la Escuela Nacional de Bellas Artes (1927), donde fue alumno de Diego Rivera; en la Escuela de Talla Directa (1930) y en el taller de litografía de Emilio Amero (1931). Profesor de La Esmeralda y de la Academia de San Carlos (1944). Director de la Escuela Popular de Bellas Artes (1950). Fundó la Escuela de Pintura de Taxco (1930), creó el Taller de Artes Plásticas de Uruapan (1949) y la Escuela de Pintura y Artesanías de Morelia (1950). Cofundador de la LEAR (1933-37) y del Taller de Gráfica Popular (1937-47). Expone individualmente desde 1931. Hay obras suyas en los museos Metropolitano y de Arte Moderno, de Nueva York; de Estocolmo, nacionales de Varsovia y Sofía, de La Jolla, de Arte Contemporáneo en Morelia y de Arte Moderno, en México. Autor de una cuantiosa obra de caballete; del volumen de litografías *Estampas de Yucatán* (1945); de escultura: *Pájaro* (1960), *Columna de la muerte* (1962), *El abrazo* (1968); y de los murales de la escuela rural de Ayotla (1930, con Isabel Villaseñor), *Lavanderas* (1932, primaria Rafael Delgadillo), *Mujeres trabajando* (1932, Escuela Industrial para Mujeres), *Las luchas sociales del estado de*

La ventana, óleo sobre masonite de Alfredo Zalce

Foto: Reforma

Alfredo Zalce

Foto: Museo de Arte de Sinaloa

El contorsionista, obra de Alfredo Zalce

Niceto de Zamacois

Puebla (1938, con Ángel Bracho y Rosendo Soto, en la Escuela Normal de Puebla), *Éxodo de la población de la región del Paricutín* (1950, con Ignacio Aguirre y Pablo O'Higgins), *Los defensores de la integridad nacional* (1951, Museo Michoacano), *Fray Alonso de la Vera Cruz* (1952, Museo Michoacano), *Lo social en el desarrollo de los deportes* (1958, mosaico de vidrio en el parque deportivo de Nuevo Laredo), *La solidaridad* (1959, altorrelieve en el Centro Médico Nacional), *La conversión de los indios al credo cristiano* (1962, Cámara de Diputados de Michoacán) y varios paños en el Museo Nacional de Antropología 1964), entre otros. Premio de adquisición del Salón Anual de Pintura del Salón de la Plástica Mexicana (1961), presea Generalísimo Morelos del Ayuntamiento de Morelia (1969) y premio del Salón de la Plástica Mexicana (1978).

ZALDÍVAR, SERGIO ◆ n. en el DF (1934). Su segundo apellido es Guerra. Arquitecto por la UNAM (1957), posgraduado en restauración por la Universidad de Roma (1961). Profesor de la Universidad Autónoma de Guadalajara (1959-60) y de la UNAM (1960 y 1972-74). Afiliado al PRI desde 1969. Ha sido subdirector de Construcción del CAPFCE (1967-71), jefe de Monumentos Coloniales y director de Monumentos Históricos del INAH (1971-76); jefe de la oficina de Ordenación Urbana y Restauración de Monumentos (1977-80) y director de Sitios Patrimoniales y Monumentos del DDF (1981-85), director técnico del Consejo del Centro Histórico (1984-91), director de Sitios y Monumentos del Patrimonio Cultural de la Sedue (1991-92) y de la Sedesol (1992-94). Ha dirigido las obras de restauración del Palacio Nacional, la Casa de los Condes de Heras y Soto, el antiguo Colegio de San Ildefonso, partes del acueducto de Guadalupe, el ex convento de San Juan Bautista de Coyoacán, el Palacio de Minería y la Catedral Metropolitana, en el DF; monumentos coloniales en Coixtlahuaca, Teposcolula y Yanhuitlán, Oaxaca; Tzintzuntzan, Tupátaro y Cuitzeo, Michoacán; Tepeyanco, Atlihuetzía y San Francisco, Tlaxcala; Cuauhtinchan y Huejotzingo, Puebla, y otros. Por iniciativa suya se trasladó la estatua de Carlos IV a su actual emplazamiento. Diseñó el monumento a Hidalgo en Madrid y el de Zapata en Los Ángeles. Autor de *Arquitectura del valle de Atemajac* (1959), *Arquitectura barroca de Jalisco* (1960), *Barroco popular en Jalisco* (1962), *Actividades en monumentos dañados por el sismo de 1973* (1975), *Arquitectura colonial en Guadalajara* (1976), *Memoria de restauración del Palacio Nacional* (1976), *Libro monumental Palacio Nacional* (1976, en colaboración), *El atrio de San Bernardino, Xochimilco* y *Traslado de "el Caballito"* (1984). Secretario del Comité Nacional Mexicano del Icomos (1982).

Roberto Zamarripa

ZAMACOIS, NICETO DE ◆ n. en España y m. en la ciudad de México (1820-1885). Periodista y escritor. En México dirigió el periódico conservador *La Espada de Don Simplicio* (1855-56). En 1858 regresó a España, donde colaboró, entre otros, en los periódicos *Irurac-bat* y *El Museo Universal*. Regresó a México durante la intervención francesa y fue jefe de redacción de los periódicos imperiales *El Cronista* y *La Sociedad Mercantil*. Al triunfo de la República volvió a España, pero regresó otra vez a México, donde declinó la naturalización, pese a que se le había ofrecido hacérsele diputado federal por Oaxaca. Tradujo *La destrucción de Pompeya*, de Bulwer-Lytton. Coautor de *Los mexicanos pintados por sí mismos* (1855) y *México y sus alrededores* (1855). Autor de teatro: *El sitio de Monterrey* (1846), *Los misterios de México* (1851), *El testamento de El Gallo Pitagórico* (1855), *La herencia de un barbero* (zarzuela, 1859), *El jarabe* (1860), *Las dos suegras* (1860), *El corregidor* (zarzuela, 1861) y *El músico y el poeta* (zarzuela, 1861); poesía: *Los ecos de mi lira* (1849) y *Los misterios de México* (1851); novela: *El mendigo de San Ángel* (1864-65) y *El capitán Rossi* (1864); relato: *Un ángel desterrado del cielo* (1885); y una *Historia de México* (18 t., 1876-82).

ZAMACONA, MANUEL MARÍA DE ◆ n. en Puebla, Pue., y m. en la ciudad de México (1826-1904). Periodista. Estudió derecho en el Seminario Palafoxiano de Puebla. Fue director del periódico *El Siglo XIX* y secretario de Relaciones Exteriores (del 13 de julio al 22 de noviembre de 1861) en el gabinete de Benito Juárez; renunció a su cargo luego de que el Congreso de la Unión rechazó el convenio que había firmado con el representante inglés, Charles Wyke, mediante el cual se reconocía una elevada deuda ante Gran Bretaña (21 de noviembre de 1861). Diputado federal (1867); encabezó en el Congreso y desde la prensa una campaña contra la reelección de Juárez, quien, no obstante, lo nombró miembro de la Comisión de Reclamaciones entre México y Estados Unidos (1872).

ZAMARRIPA, ÁNGEL ◆ n. en Morelia, Mich., y m. en el DF (1912- 1990). Su segundo apellido era Landi y firmaba sus trabajos como *Fa-Cha*. Caricaturista. Pintor, dibujante y grabador egresado de la Academia de San Carlos y de la Escuela de Artes del Libro, donde tuvo como profesor a Andrés C. Audiffred. Fue profesor de la Escuela Nacional de Artes Gráficas y expuso su obra pictórica en varias ciudades de México y del extranjero. Desde 1930 colaboró en las publicaciones *El Universal Ilustrado*, *Ja-já*, *Don Timorato*, *Magazine de Policía*, *Revista de Revistas*, *Jueves de Excélsior*, *Vea*, *Todo*, *Excélsior* y *Esto*. Miembro fundador de la Sociedad Mexicana de Grabadores, que presidió. Miembro del Club de Caricaturistas de México y de la Sociedad Mexicana de Acuarelistas.

ZAMARRIPA, FERNANDO ◆ n. en Soledad de los Ranchos, SLP (¿1775?-?). Sacerdote insurgente. Fue cura de varias parroquias en San Luis Potosí y en Guanajuato, donde conoció a Miguel Hidalgo. Estuvo ligado a la conspiración de Querétaro y tras el inicio de la guerra de independencia participó en el pronunciamiento de San Luis Potosí (10 de noviembre de 1810). Con el grado de coronel dirigió la lucha en Durango y Zacatecas. El 9 de abril de 1812 fue aprehendido y condenado al destierro.

ZAMARRIPA, ROBERTO ◆ n. en el DF (1960). Periodista. Estudió comunicación en la UAM-X (1982). Fue miembro del Partido Comunista Mexicano (1977-81) y responsable de la Comisión Nacional Juvenil (1980-81). Miembro fundador del PSUM, en el que fue dirigente nacional juvenil (1981-1986). Ha sido redactor de internacionales (1984-88) y reportero de *La Jornada* (1989-93); reportero de *Proceso* (1993); editor del suplemento *Enfoque* (1994-96) y coordinador de Información del diario *Reforma* (1996-). Trabajos suyos están incluidos en la antología *El fin de la nostalgia: nueva crónica de la ciudad de México* (1992). Es autor de *Sonora 91. Historia de políticos y policías* (1992).

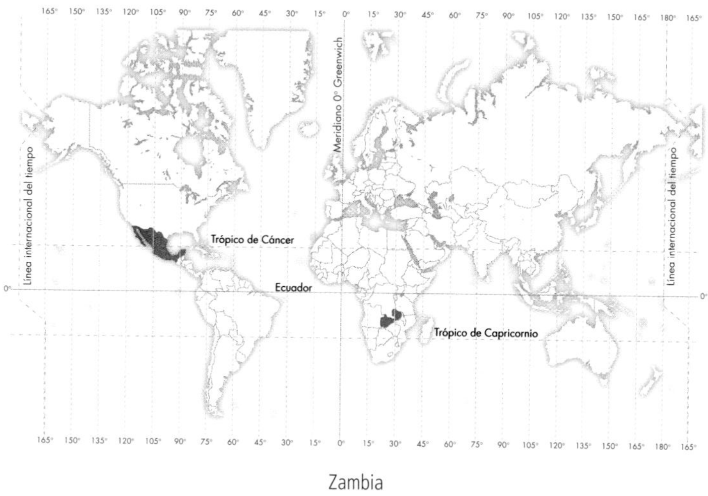

Zambia

ZAMBIA ◆ República del sur de África que limita al norte con la República Democrática del Congo y con Tanzania, al este con Malawi y Mozambique, al sur con Zimbabwe, Botswana y Namibia y al oeste con Angola. Superficie: 752,614 km². Habitantes: 8,781,000 (1998). Su capital es Lusaka (con 982,362 habitantes en 1990). Su moneda es el kwacha y los idiomas oficiales son el inglés y las lenguas bantúes nyanja, bemba, lozi, luvale y tonga. *Historia*: entre los siglos I y VII de nuestra era se estableció en territorio de la actual Zambia una población de agricultores y herreros perteneciente a la primera migración bantú, que fue la base del Estado Luanda, localizado en la confluencia de los ríos Kafue y Zambezi. La nación Luanda comenzó a sufrir un proceso de desgaste a finales del siglo XVIII debido a la penetración de traficantes de esclavos, mozambiqueños y árabes, que desviaban hacia el este parte de los cargamentos humanos que los balunda destinaban a los puertos del Atlántico. Con la decadencia de la trata de negros, en el siglo XIX la autoridad de los mwata yambo (reyes luandas) se debilitó y permitió que, a partir de la creciente independencia de los kazembe (gobernadores locales), surgiese una serie de pequeños reinos dispersos. Los portugueses atravesaron varias veces el país entre 1798 y 1811, en busca de una ruta que conectara sus colonias de Mozambique y Angola; sin embargo, la belicosidad de los zulúes los obligó a abandonar esos proyectos. Aun algunos pueblos, como los soto, expulsados de sus tierras al sur de la actual Zambia, llegaron a establecer un reino en el suroeste del país, hacia 1835. En 1851 arribó a la región el británico David Livingstone, quien fue hacia las cataratas Victoria, en el río Zambezi y fue el primer europeo en verlas (1855). Después llegaron algunos comerciantes y exploradores al servicio de Cecil Rhodes, comerciante inglés, dueño de numerosas empresas en Sudáfrica, quien deseaba expandir sus dominios hacia el norte. En 1889, Rhodes obtuvo de la Corona británica los derechos para que su compañía, la British South-Africa, monopolizara el comercio y la minería en esa área, considerada desde entonces esfera de influencia inglesa. Un año más tarde, Rhodes firmó un tratado con el rey soto Lewanika y se estableció así el protectorado de Rhodesia del Norte. En 1924, Inglaterra asumió el control colonial directo de la región. En 1931 se descubrieron en el país nuevos y más ricos yacimientos de cobre, que colocaron a Rhodesia del Norte en el tercer lugar de la producción mundial de ese metal. Seis años más tarde eran ya 40 mil los africanos que trabajaban en las minas y vivían en condiciones miserables; esto dio pie a la formación de algunos sindicatos, que a la larga se transformaron en los primeros movimientos nacionalistas, como el Congreso Nacional Africano de Rhodesia del Norte (NRANC). En 1952 el entonces profesor de primaria Kenneth Kaunda se transformó en secretario general del NRANC, presidido entonces por Harry Nkumbula. En 1953, preparando su dominación neocolonial futura, los británicos organizaron una federación entre Rhodesia del Norte (Zambia), Rhodesia del Sur (Zimbabwe) y Nyassalandia (Malawi), gobernada por Roy Welensky, colono blanco, desde Salisbury. Se buscaba con ello una división del trabajo que encomendaba a Zambia la producción minera y a Zimbabwe la agrícola. El NRANC encabezó entonces la lucha contra la discriminación racial y por la independencia, pero cuando Nkumbula se mostró titubeante frente a un proyecto constitucional destinado a institucionalizar el predominio de la minoría blanca, Kaunda optó por separarse y fundar el Congreso Nacional Africano de Zambia (ANCZ), además de declarar un boicoteo a las elecciones. El ANCZ fue proscrito y Kaunda encarcelado en 1959; sin embargo, sus seguidores crearon el Partido Unido de la Independencia Nacional (UNIP), que Kaunda presidió luego de ser liberado (1960). También el UNIP fue ilegalizado pocos meses después, cuando los ingleses comprobaron el arraigo popular de las propuestas independentistas. Como resultado de la represión y marginación de la mayoría, en 1961 estalló la violencia en Rhodesia del Norte. Al año

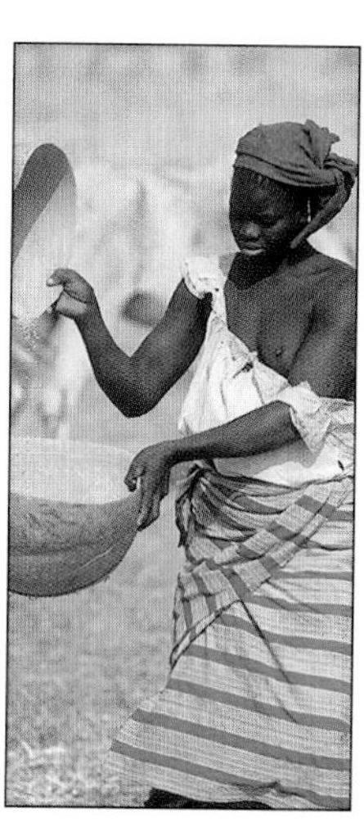
Mujer de Zambia

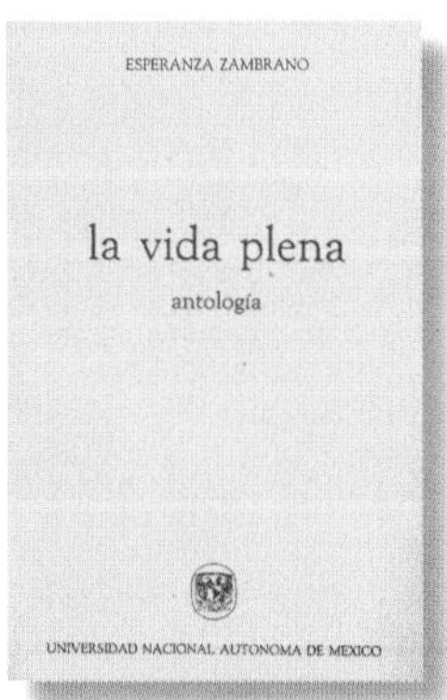

Antología poética de Esperanza Zambrano

Guillermo Zambrano

siguiente el gobierno británico se vio obligado a anunciar una "revisión constitucional" que satisficiera algunas demandas de la UNIP y convocó a elecciones, en las que triunfó el partido de Kaunda sobre la organización de Welensky, de modo que la federación se disolvió el 31 de diciembre de 1963. En octubre de 1964 el UNIP proclamó la independencia de la nación, llamada desde entonces República de Zambia. La presidencia fue ocupada por Kaunda; éste orientó su política exterior hacia una estrecha colaboración con los países africanos opuestos al régimen racista de Ian Smith en Rhodesia. Kaunda, reelegido presidente en 1968, decretó el control estatal sobre las compañías extranjeras concesionarias de la explotación del cobre; en 1969 nacionalizó la banca y en 1970 las compañías aseguradoras. Simultáneamente, tendió a personalizar el poder y a eliminar toda oposición, lo que originó una escisión en el UNIP, encabezada por S. Kapwepwe. Éste fue encarcelado en marzo de 1972 y Kaunda reforzó sus posiciones en el gobierno y en el partido. En 1973, Kaunda volvió a ser reelegido y dos años después estableció relaciones diplomáticas con México. Zambia integró, junto con Angola, Botswana, Mozambique y Tanzania, el grupo de países de la Línea del Frente en el Combate Contra el Racismo. Por su apoyo a la lucha del Frente Patriótico de Zimbabwe, Zambia fue agredida en varias ocasiones por el régimen de Ian Smith, que en 1979 destruyó sus principales vías de comunicación y la obligó a transportar su comercio exterior por los ferrocarriles rhodesianos. La independencia de Rhodesia (Zimbabwe) en 1980 llegó a tiempo para Zambia, que comenzaba a sentir los efectos de la presión económica y militar de los racistas. Por otra parte, con el pretexto de perseguir a miembros de la Organización Popular del Suroeste Africano (SWAPO), fuerzas del ejército sudafricano realizaron reiteradas incursiones en Zambia, donde atacaban campamentos de refugiados namibios. En 1991 el opositor Frederick Chiluba sucedió en la presidencia a Kaunda.

Zambrano, Antonio Basilio ♦ n. en Valladolid, hoy Morelia, Mich. (?-?). Insurgente. Estudiante de leyes en la ciudad de México, fue aprehendido por conspirar contra el gobierno virreinal y encarcelado en Perote, en San Juan de Ulúa y finalmente en España. Regresó a México en 1811, se vinculó con la lucha por la independencia y se reunió con Ignacio López Rayón, quien lo nombró en 1812 secretario de la Junta Nacional Americana; en septiembre de ese año estuvo en Tehuacán, donde se unió a las fuerzas de José María Morelos, con las que en noviembre tomó Oaxaca.

Zambrano, Esperanza ♦ n. en Dolores Hidalgo, Gto., y m. en el DF (1901-1992). Poeta. Estudió en el Conservatorio Nacional y la Escuela de Altos Estudios. Trabajadora de la SEP, asesora de la Unión Panamericana (antecedente de la OEA), asesora técnica y directora de Publicaciones de la Comisión Interamericana de Mujeres de la OEA. Autora de *De la inquietud joyante* (1927), *Los ritmos secretos* (1931), *Canciones del amor perfecto* (1939), *Retablos del viejo Guanajuato* (1943), *Los romances* (1945), *Oración por la Francia cautiva*, *Fuga de estío* (1952), *Sonetos del amor ensimismado* (1954), *Obras completas* (1988, con prólogo de Emmanuel Carballo) y *La vida plena* (antología preparada por José Emilio Pacheco). Miembro de la Legión de Honor Mexicana. Fundadora (1934) y presidenta (1953-54) del Ateneo Mexicano de Mujeres. Por su contribución literaria a la liberación de Francia, el gobierno de ese país le otorgó las Palmas Académicas en 1945 y la Medalla del Reconocimiento al año siguiente, preseas que recibió en 1987. Condecoración Juan Pablo Duarte de la República Dominicana (1945) y Medalla al Mérito, del gobierno de Guanajuato (1963).

Zambrano, Francisco ♦ n. en Monterrey, NL, y m. en Guadalajara, Jal. (1888-1973). Jesuita. Fue ordenado sacerdote en España (1923). Establecido en México desde 1925, se dedicó al estudio de la historia de su orden en el país. Autor de *Diccionario biobibliográfico de la Compañía de Jesús en México* (12 t., 1961-73).

Zambrano, Guillermo ♦ n. en Monterrey, NL (1946). Periodista y escritor. Estudió periodismo en la Universidad Iberoamericana (1969), sociología en la Universidad de París (1971) y literatura en El Colegio de México (1973). Ha sido reportero de policía de *El Sol de México*, director de noticieros de Canal 8 (1974), corresponsal en Centro y Sudamérica de *El Universal* (1974), redactor de información internacional de *El Día* (1975) y de *unomásuno* (1977-80), corresponsal en París de *unomásuno* (1981), escritor, corrector, editor y traductor independiente (1982-); redactor suplente de la agencia AFP (1984), reportero de la agencia UPI (1988) y reportero de *unomásuno* (1988-). Coautor de *El día menos pensado* (cuentos, 1969). Autor de las novelas *Larva* (1973) y *Los crímenes de la calle del Seminario* (1987), así como del guión cinematográfico *Los hombres de arena* (1984).

Zambrano, José Antonio ♦ n. en Tepeji del Río, Hgo. (1953). Escritor. Participó en el taller de cuento de Orlando Ortiz en el INBA (1981). Ha sido director y editor del periódico *Espartaco* y subdirector de *La Voz de Hidalgo*. Adaptó para niños cuentos de Kafka, Borges, Cortázar, así como de *Las mil y una noches* para el programa *El rincón de los niños*, en Radio Universidad. Ha colaborado en *El Sol de Hidalgo, La Región* (de Tula), *Tepexi*, *Actualidades*, *El Gallo Ilustrado*, *Mi Periodiquito*, *Pie de Página*, *Di*, *Tropos*, *La Crítica de la Crítica*, *La Semana de Bellas Artes*, *Tierra Adentro*, *Enciclopedia Infantil Colibrí*, *Revista de Revistas*, *El Heraldo Cultural* y en los suplementos culturales de *El Universal*, *El Nacional* y *Excélsior*. Editó la *Monografía de Villa del Carbón* (1987, de Gilberto Hernández Monroy). Coautor de *Rounds de sombra* (1981) y *Costal de versos y cuentos* (1985). Autor de *Un tesoro para dos monitos* (1982, Premio Nacional de Cuento Infantil Juan de la Cabada 1980), *El ratón compositor. El mosquito escritor. Don hablantín* (1982, edición bilingüe japonés-español), *El libro de las mil puertas* (1982, finalista del Premio Lazarillo, de España) y *La zona arqueológica de Tula* (1985).

ZAMBRANO, MARÍA ◆ n. y m. en España (1907-1991). Escritora y filósofa. Fue discípula de Ortega y Gasset. Simpatizó con el bando republicano durante la guerra civil española. Vino en 1939 a México, donde fue profesora de la Universidad Michoacana de San Nicolás de Hidalgo. Regresó a Europa en 1964 y a España en 1984. Autora de *Pensamiento y poesía en la vida española* (1939), *Filosofía y poesía* (1939), *Isla de Puerto Rico: nostalgia y esperanza de un mundo mejor* (1940), *Pensamiento vivo de Séneca* (1944), *La agonía de Europa*, *La tumba de Antígona*, *La España de Galdós*, *De la aurora*, *El sueño creador*, *Poesía e historia* y *El hombre y lo divino*. *Doctora honoris causa* por la Universidad de Málaga (1987), donde en 1990 se estableció la fundación que lleva su nombre. Premio Cervantes (1989).

ZAMBRANO, NICÉFORO ◆ n. y m. en Monterrey, NL (1862-1940). En 1909 se afilió al Partido Antirreeleccionista y fue presidente municipal de Monterrey durante el periodo presidencial de Francisco I. Madero. En 1913, tras el cuartelazo de Victoriano Huerta, se alistó en el ejército constitucionalista. Fue diputado al Congreso Constituyente de 1916-17, gobernador de Nuevo León (1917-19), tesorero general de la Nación y cónsul de México en San Francisco. Se retiró a la vida privada luego del asesinato de Venustiano Carranza.

ZAMORA ◆ Municipio de Michoacán situado al sur-suroeste de La Piedad y al norte de Tancítaro, cercano a Jalisco y Guanajuato. Superficie: 438,42 km². Habitantes: 160,079, de los cuales 42,920 forman la población económicamente activa. Hablan alguna lengua indígena 770 personas mayores de cinco años (purépecha 759). La cabecera, Zamora de Hidalgo, es un importante centro comercial, agrícola y ganadero en el que se producen rebozos, chalinas, joyería, alfarería y calzado. 14 kilómetros al este de la misma ciudad se localizan los manantiales y el lago Camécuaro. Cuando el virrey Antonio de Mendoza marchó a Jalisco, en 1540, fundó el Fuerte de Zamora, donde intentó establecer una villa, para la cual nunca hubo pobladores. El mismo gobernante intentó de nuevo la fundación de ese asentamiento, como punto de contención de los chichimecas. La fundación definitiva de la villa ocurrió el 18 de enero de 1574, año en el que en la porción noroccidental del estado fue erigida la provincia de Zamora (antes corregimiento de Xacona), que tenía jurisdicción sobre tierras de Coxumatlán, Sahuayo, Pajacuarán, Ario, Caro, Ixtlán, Tangamandapio, Tangancícuaro y Xaripo. En 1787 se transformó en subdelegación de la intendencia de Valladolid. El 21 de noviembre de 1810, Miguel Hidalgo y su ejército insurgente pasaron por la villa de Zamora, a la que confirieron la categoría de ciudad; esta fue designada, en 1825, capital del departamento michoacano del Poniente. El 4 de febrero de 1867 se produjo la toma de Zamora, en la que los militares republicanos Nicolás Régules, Villada, Martiniano León y Méndez Olivares, en un segundo intento, desalojaron de la plaza a los imperialistas comandados por Juan Berna. La diócesis de Zamora fue erigida el 26 de enero de 1862 por bula de Pío IX y ejecutada el 8 de mayo de 1864.

ZAMORA, FRANCISCO ◆ n. en Nicaragua y m. en el DF (1890-1985). Su segundo apellido era Padilla. Periodista. En 1905 editó en Masaya el periódico *El Eco*. Llegó a México en 1908, estudió en la Escuela Nacional de Jurisprudencia y en 1910 inició su carrera periodística como colaborador de *El Constitucional*, último periódico revolucionario clausurado por el régimen de Porfirio Díaz. Al triunfo de la revolución maderista fue colaborador (con el pseudónimo de *Jerónimo Colgnard*) de *El Noticioso*, *El Diario Oficial*, *El Diario del Hogar* y *Nueva Era*. Fue fundador de *El Gladiador* y *Excélsior* y colaborador de *El Radical* y *ABC*. Naturalizado mexicano en 1925, fue profesor de la UNAM (1932-67). Trabajó en *El Universal* (1918-48), donde escribió la columna "Apuntes del natural", con el pseudónimo de *Zeta*, y fue secretario de redacción, cronista, editorialista y articulista. Desde las páginas de ese diario inició en 1935 una polémica con Antonio Caso, la que continuó Vicente Lombardo Toledano y dio por resultado el libro *Idealismo y marxismo*. Colaboró en *El Universal Ilustrado*, *El Universal Taurino*, *Futuro*, *Esto*, *Tiempo*, *El Mundo* y *Novedades*. Autor de *El salario mínimo* (1932), *La clase media. Apuntes de teoría económica* (1941), *Elementos de teoría económica* (1943), *Introducción a la micro y macrodinámica económica* (1958), *La sociedad económica moderna. Capitalismo, planeación y desarrollo* (1966) y *Mensaje a un joven periodista mexicano* (1969). Su *Tratado de teoría económica*, editado inicialmente en 1953, es todavía libro de texto en varias escuelas de la especialidad. Autor de la declaración de principios y del reglamento del Sindicato Nacional de Redactores, organismo que presidió en dos ocasiones. Fue miembro del Instituto Mexicano de Investigaciones Económicas (1928), secretario general de la Federación de Uniones y Sindicatos de Artes Gráficas, fundador del Congreso General de Trabajadores y de la Universidad Obrera (1939) y miembro del Colegio Nacional de Economistas. En 1937 formó parte de la comisión internacional presidida por John Dewey, que analizó el caso Trotsky. Profesor emérito de la UNAM (1963).

ZAMORA, GUILLERMO ◆ n. en el DF (1945). Periodista. Su segundo apellido es Villa. Fue reportero de *Oposición*, órgano del PCM (1976-77), y corresponsal de guerra en El Salvador y Nicaragua (1979-85) para Radio Educación, *El Día*, Notimex, Canal 11, Canal 13, el Servicio Latinoamericano de Noticias (EUA), Radio Canadá Internacional, Radio Cadena Nacional (Colombia) y *El Mundo* (Colombia). Productor y conductor de *Sin cortapisas*, de Radio UNAM (1985-88); corresponsal de National Public Radio (1985-87), del Servicio Latinoamericano de Noticias (1985-87), de Radio Bilingüe (EUA, 1985-91), la BBC de Londres (1989-93) y la Comunidad Europea (1991-92). Reportero de *Proceso* (1986-89), *Mira* (1991-93),

FOTO: CARLOS HAHN

Zamora, Michoacán

Apro (1992-93) y *De par en par* (1994). Jefe de prensa del Comité Central del PRD para las elecciones de consejeros ciudadanos del DF (1995) y asesor de las comisiones legislativas encargadas de la investigación del caso Conasupo (1995-96 y 1998). Coautor de *Democracia y medios de comunicación* (1995). Autor de *La caída de la hoz y el martillo* (1994) y *Caso Conasupo: la leche radiactiva* (1997, Premio Internacional Rodolfo Walsh de Literatura de No Ficción 1998).

Zamora, Senorina Mercedes ♦ n. y m. en Colima, Col. (1866-1925). Fue becada por el gobierno de Colima para estudiar en la Academia de San Carlos de la ciudad de México, donde fue discípula de José María Velasco. Paisajista, pintó parajes de Colima, ríos, arboledas y sus volcanes; estos últimos le hicieron ganar una medalla de oro en la Exposición Internacional de París de 1899. Participó en la Exposición Mundial de Chicago y en las exposiciones nacionales de Bellas Artes. De regreso a Colima, impartió clases en la Escuela Normal de Señoritas y en la Escuela Normal de Maestros.

Zamora Alcántara, Mario ♦ n. en Honduras (1920). Escultor. Fue alumno del español José Bauxanli, en Honduras, y de Jenaro Amador Lira, en Nicaragua. Estudió en la Academia de Bellas Artes de Roma con los profesores Atilio Selva y Calori y Giovanni Ardini. Llegó en 1944 a México y estudió en la Academia de San Carlos con Fidias Elizondo. Fue agregado cultural de la embajada hondureña en Italia (1950-53). Ha expuesto, individual o colectivamente, en varias ciudades de México y Estados Unidos. Autor de los monumentos a los Niños Héroes (1950, en Ciudad Victoria), a José María Aguilera (1952), a Vicente Suárez (1956), a Francisco Morazán (1956, en Nueva Orleans), a Amado Nervo (1963), a Nezahualcóyotl (1963) y a Francisco Morazán (1967, en Santiago de Chile); y de los bustos de Bach y de Beethoven (1950, en el Conservatorio de Guatemala), de Pedro Nufio y Francisco Morazán (1954, en Honduras) y de Lempira (1960, en Quito). Primer premio Rubén Darío, de Nicaragua (1942).

Zamora Bátiz, Julio ♦ n. en Guadalajara, Jal. (1937). Licenciado por la UNAM (1960), maestro por la Universidad de Massachusetts y doctor en economía por la Universidad de Texas (1963). Ha sido director general de Crédito de la Secretaría de Hacienda (1970-71), embajador en Uruguay (1971-74), Perú (1974-76) y ante la Asociación Latinoamericana de Libre Comercio; observador de México en el Grupo Andino (1974-76), diputado federal (1976-79) y embajador en Nicaragua. Autor de *La corrupción en Estados Unidos* (1988).

Zamora Camacho, Esteban ♦ n. en Angostura, Sin. (1935). Periodista. Militante del PAN desde 1958, ha sido presidente de la organización juvenil y el comité regional, así como miembro del consejo nacional de ese partido. Jefe de información de *El Sol de San Luis*, de *Tribuna de San Luis* y de *El Mundo*, de Tamaulipas; colaborador de *Noroeste*, de Culiacán y dos veces diputado federal plurinominal (1982-85 y para el periodo 199-94).

Zamora Flores, Jesús ♦ n. en el DF (1931). Periodista por la escuela Carlos Septién García (1959-62). Militante del Partido Demócrata Mexicano, en el que ha sido secretario nacional de prensa (1986) y director del periódico *El Demócrata* (1987). Diputado federal plurinominal (1985-88).

Zamora Millán, Fernando ♦ n. en el DF (1922). Licenciado en economía y en derecho por la UNAM, donde ha ejercido la docencia. Ha sido director general de Estudios Económicos de la Secretaría de Economía (1949-58), director de los programas de gobierno de Sonora (1955), el Estado de México (1956), Guerrero (1957), Yucatán (1958) y Michoacán (1958); subgerente técnico y de filiales de la Conasupo (1960-61), director general del Plan de Gasto Público de la Secretaría de la Presidencia (1962-64), director general del Instituto Nacional de la Vivienda (1965-69), presidente de la junta directiva de la Sociedad Mexicana de Geografía y Estadística (1969), director técnico del *Estudio de economía urbana para el DDF* (1976), presidente de Construcciones Metálicas (1977), presidente de la Asociación de Industriales de Veracruz (1977-79), asesor del Banco Interamericano de Desarrollo en Nicaragua (1979) y consejero del secretario de Industria y Comercio (1981). Autor de *El Banco Interamericano* (1944), *Industrialización y planeación de México* (1950), *La industria minera mexicana* (1955), *La planeación económica de México. Teoría y práctica* (1962), *La habitación popular* (1966), *La demanda efectiva de vivienda* (1967), *Un deber de la revolución: la habitación rural* (1969), *Economía mixta* (1975), *Mitos, utopías y límites de crecimiento* (1975), *Economistas en predicamentos* (1975), *México, hora de decisión* (1979), *Año cero, cuatro aspectos económicos* (1981) y *México, ¿ahora hacia dónde?* (1987).

Zamora Orozco, Valentín ♦ n. y m. en el DF (¿1912?-1968). Escritor. Fue profesor en varias escuelas del Distrito Federal y, durante once años, director de Enseñanza Primaria de la SEP. Director general de Educación en Hidalgo, inspector general y profesor en la Escuela Nacional de Maestros, fundador de la escuela Emiliano Zapata, periodista y sindicalista. Autor de *Verde y azul, Campo y azul, Campo de flores, Mis juguetes y yo, Sobre las nubes de América, Cielo, tierra y mar* y *Metodología de la enseñanza de la escritura*.

Zamora y Penagos, Mateo de ♦ n. en Colombia y m. en Valladolid, Yuc. (?-1744). Franciscano. Doctor en teología por la Universidad de Santa Fe de Bogotá. Fue custodio, maestro provincial, procurador ante las cortes de Madrid y Roma, calificador de la Inquisición y obispo de Yucatán (1743- 44).

Zamudio V., Justo A. ♦ n. en Alvarado, Ver. (1914). Licenciado en derecho por la UNAM (1942) y maestro en lengua y literatura españolas por la Escuela Normal Superior (1946). En la SEP ha prestado sus servicios como jefe de la Sección de Escuelas Secundarias para Trabajadores (1938-40), jefe de Legislación Escolar (1941) y jefe del De-

Cañas de la ceremonia, obra de Rodolfo Zanabria

partamento de Escuelas Secundarias Particulares (1942-50 y 1953-58) de la Dirección General de Segunda Enseñanza; subdirector general (1959-60) y director general de Segunda Enseñanza (1961-70), jefe de la Sección de Supervisión Escolar de la Dirección General de Enseñanza Media (1971-76), presidente de la Comisión Permanente de Libros de Texto del Consejo Nacional Técnico de la Educación (1977-) y director general de Educación Secundaria (1977-).

Zanabria, Rodolfo ◆ n. en Metepec, Edo de Méx. (1930). Pintor. Estudió litografía, cerámica y grabado con los profesores Francisco Dosamantes, Juan Soriano, Yukio Fukasawa e Ysamo Ishukawa (1964). Estuvo becado en el Atélier 77, de París, con Hitier (1969), y en La Esmeralda. Paleografió escritos medievales de la Biblioteca Nacional de París. Autor del volumen de cuentos *Eme o el triunfo de los apaches* (1989). Primer premio del Salón de Otoño 1969 por su obra *La geisha*. Beca Guggenheim (1970-71).

Zanolli, Uberto ◆ n. en Italia y m. en el DF (1917-1994). Músico. Estudió violín, viola y composición en los conservatorios de Verona, Bolzano y Milán, donde fue discípulo de Pietro Mascagni y Enrico Bossi. Se doctoró en historia del arte e ingeniería. Vino en 1953 contratado por la ópera nacional y se naturalizó mexicano. Fue profesor del Conservatorio Nacional y de la UNAM, en la que enseñó italiano. Fue nombrado director permanente de la orquesta de la Academia de la Ópera del INBA y del Coro y la Orquesta del Teatro de Bellas Artes. En 1966 creó el Coro de la Viga, que se convertiría en el Coro de la Escuela Nacional Preparatoria. Fundó y dirigió la Orquesta de Cámara de la Escuela Nacional Preparatoria (1972-94). Se le deben cerca de 700 obras, entre composiciones propias y arreglos e instrumentaciones para el rescate y divulgación de compositores mexicanos y de la vida y la obra de Giacomo Facco, músico del véneto del siglo XVIII. Autor de *Organología musical* (t., 1990) y de *Giacomo Facco, Maestro de reyes* (edición facsimilar de 1998). Grabó, entre otros, los discos *Cantata Clori* de Facco, *Sonata de Navidad*, *Concierto de Epifanía 1990*, *El arte de la fuga*, *La France Éternelle*, *México romántico*, *Homenaje al maestro preparatoriano* y *Concierto de Navidad 1993*. Compuso música sinfónica, de cámara, vocal y cinematográfico, entre ellas *Tres Danzas Antiguas*, *Retablo Romántico*, *Elegía a un Hombre*, *Cabalgata*, *France Eternelle*, *Cántico a Fray Sol*, *Imagen*, *Leyenda*, *Tarantella* y *Siete miniaturas del Mayab*. Caballero de la Orden del Mérito de la República Italiana (1962). Músico del año de la Unión de Cronistas de Música y Teatro de México (1963). Medalla de Oro al Mérito Académico de la UNAM (1975). Águila de Tlatelolco de la SRE (1978). Lira de Oro del Sindicato de Trabajadores de la Música (1986).

Zapata, Emiliano ◆ n. en San Miguel Anenecuilco y m. en Chinameca, Mor. (1879-1919). En 1906 participó en Cuautla en una junta en la que se planteó la necesidad de defender la tierra de los campesinos morelenses de la voracidad de los hacendados porfiristas. Como represalia, en 1908 se le forzó a incorporarse al noveno regimiento de Cuernavaca. Ingresó como soldado raso, pero pronto fue ascendido a caballerango de Pablo Escandón, jefe del Estado Mayor de Porfirio Díaz, y más tarde ocupó el mismo cargo a las órdenes de Ignacio de la Torre en la ciudad de México. Este último autorizó su baja. El 12 de septiembre de 1909 se le eligió presidente de la Junta de Defensa de las Tierras de Anenecuilco. En ese año apoyó la candidatura de Patricio Leyva para la gubernatura del estado, en oposición a Pablo Escandón. Cuando éste fue declarado triunfador, Anenecuilco sufrió un despojo de tierras, las que en mayo de 1910 recuperó Zapata

Foto: Fondo Editorial Grupo Azabache

Emiliano Zapata en retrato de Alfredo Zalce

Emiliano Zapata con el Plan de Ayala en la mano

para su comunidad. En noviembre de ese año acudió a Villa de Ayala a una reunión convocada para conocer y discutir el Plan de San Luis, de Francisco I. Madero, después de lo cual envió a Estados Unidos a Pablo Torres Burgos para negociar con aquél la participación de los campesinos morelenses en el levantamiento. Como resultado, 72 hombres tomaron las armas el 10 de marzo de 1911, comandados por Torres Burgos. El grupo armado inició una marcha desde Villa de Ayala hacia el sur, perseguido por el federal Aureliano Blanquet. En el camino, el grupo se transformó en un ejército que tomó Jonacatepec, Chinameca, Tlayacac, Tlaquiltenango y Jojutla. Después de esta última acción, Torres Burgos dejó a Zapata la jefatura de la revolución maderista en Morelos y poco después fue asesinado, junto con sus hijos, por una partida de soldados porfiristas. Zapata continuó su avance y tomó Yautepec, Cuautla y Cuernavaca. Al triunfo de la revolución maderista se negó a deponer las armas mientras no se hiciera efectivo el reparto de tierras. Francisco León de la Barra, presidente interino, declaró a Zapata "bandido y rebelde" y encomendó a Victoriano Huerta y Aureliano Blanquet que lo combatieran.

FOTO: ARCHIVO CASASOLA

Emiliano Zapata

Madero, no obstante, se entrevistó con él en Yautepec, en agosto de 1911, y trató de convencerlo de que depusiera las armas y licenciara a sus tropas. No llegaron a ningún acuerdo, pues Madero se negó a aceptar el reparto agrario, única condición de los campesinos morelenses. La campaña de Blanquet y Huerta contra los zapatistas no se detuvo, por lo que el caudillo se replegó hasta los límites de Morelos con Guerrero, desde donde reorganizó a sus tropas, llamadas ya Ejército Libertador del Sur. Hubo otra conversación entre Madero y Zapata, en la que el primero se comprometía a que, al llegar a la Presidencia, nombraría como autoridades de Morelos sólo a los revolucionarios, lo que no cumplió y continuó con la campaña contra los zapatistas, que se habían disuelto en guerrillas. El 25 de noviembre de 1911 lanzó el Plan de Ayala (☛), en el que se exigía la redención de los indígenas y el reparto de latifundios, se desconocía a Madero y se nombraba a Pascual Orozco dirigente de la revolución armada. En septiembre, Madero encomendó la campaña militar de Morelos a Felipe Ángeles, quien intentó entrevistarse con Zapata para llegar a un acuerdo pacífico. Aun cuando las tropas zapatistas eran relativamente débiles y desorganizadas, en 1912 sobresalieron las tomas de Yautepec, Tepalcingo, Cuautla y Cuernavaca. En febrero de 1913, Victoriano Huerta usurpó el poder y envió a Morelos al padre de Pascual Orozco con la intención de que Zapata depusiera las armas. Éste, que entonces dominaba el Estado de Morelos y partes de Puebla, Guerrero, Tlaxcala y del Estado de México, hizo fusilar al enviado del dictador. El 30 de mayo reformó el Plan de Ayala, declaró a Huerta indigno de ocupar la Presidencia, desconoció el Plan de Guadalupe y retiró a Orozco la jefatura de la lucha armada. En los primeros meses de 1914, el Ejército Libertador del Sur tomó Jonacatepec, Chilpancingo y Cuernavaca. En junio llegó a Cuajimalpa, Xochimilco y Milpa Alta, desde donde hostilizaba la ciudad de México, en la que no entró, pues ésta fue ocupada por los carrancistas. En septiembre de 1914, Carranza envió a Juan Sarabia, Antonio I. Villarreal y a Luis Cabrera a conferenciar con Zapata; éste exigió la renuncia de Carranza al Poder Ejecutivo y el reconocimiento del Plan de Ayala, lo que no fue aceptado por los emisarios carrancistas. El estado quedó, así, bajo control del Ejército Libertador del Sur. Desde su cuartel general en Cuernavaca, Zapata inició el reparto agrario. Fue invitado a la Convención de Aguascalientes y envió una delegación integrada por Antonio Díaz Soto y Gama, Leobardo Galván, Paulino Martínez, Manuel J. Santibáñez y Manuel Uriarte, quienes permanecieron como observadores hasta el desconocimiento de Carranza. Zapata entonces reconoció como presidente a Eulalio Gutiérrez y se

FOTO: ARCHIVO XAVIER ESPARZA

Tropas fieles al general Emiliano Zapata

De izquierda a derecha, sentados: Benjamín Argumedo, Emiliano Zapata y Manuel Palafox; atrás: Ignacio Ocampo Amescua, George Carothers y Amador Salazar

alió a Francisco Villa. El 26 de noviembre de 1914 la División del Norte y el Ejército Libertador del Sur ocuparon la ciudad de México y el 4 de diciembre se efectuó en Xochimilco la entrevista de los dirigentes de ambas fuerzas. Villa se comprometió a surtir de armas a las tropas zapatistas al tiempo que aceptaba el Plan de Ayala. Zapata partió después hacia Amecameca y tomó Puebla el 17 de diciembre de 1914, aunque en enero Álvaro Obregón lo desalojó de esa plaza. Durante 1915 los zapatistas se afanaron en imponer un orden para el desenvolvimiento de la vida social, bajo la autoridad civil de los tradicionales consejos de ancianos: se estimuló el trabajo en el campo y en las fábricas, los hombres trabajaron con fusil al lado y se procedió a revisar los problemas de límites entre los pueblos. En 1916, Carranza ordenó a Pablo González lanzar una nueva ofensiva, en la que con apoyo de la aviación bastaron 72 horas para apoderarse de las principales poblaciones. Los zapatistas, más que ofrecer resistencia a un ataque en forma, se habían replegado al campo y desde ahí, con el clima como aliado, hostilizarían a los carrancistas hasta que éstos se retiraron, en diciembre. Los campesinos reconquistaron Jonacatepec (7 de enero de 1917), Yautepec (8 de enero), Cuautla (10 de enero), Micatlán, Tetecala y Cuernavaca, donde Zapata, en marzo, expidió una Ley Administrativa General para el Estado. Promulgada la Constitución y con Carranza como presidente, éste ordenó una nueva embestida contra los campesinos morelenses. Pablo González, sabiendo que se enfrentaba a un enemigo que estaba en todas partes y en ninguna, desistió de buscar batallas frontales y recurrió al soborno, la extorsión y otros métodos para acabar con el caudillo suriano. Los métodos de este general dieron resultado y el 10 de abril Zapata murió en Chinameca, en una emboscada que le tendió Jesús Guajardo, agente carrancista que había ganado su confianza. Algunos núcleos zapatistas mantuvieron la guerra de guerrillas hasta que en 1920 se adhirieron al Plan de Agua Prieta y, tras la muerte de Carranza, se incorporaron al ejército federal. En declaración fechada el 1 de octubre de 1916, Zapata afirmó que Carranza había desencadenado su campaña antirreligiosa sólo para ocultar la falta de contenido revolucionario de su programa político y social: "Se ha vuelto loco en una serie de accesos de epilepsia anticlerical, sin comprender que estos ataques al culto religioso y a la conciencia popular son contraproducentes y perjudiciales, pues a nadie persuaden, a nadie convencen, y sí exacerban las pasiones, crean mártires, hacen despertar más vivas las supersticiones que se quieren dominar y dan fuerza al enemigo que se pretende combatir". Para él, los objetivos de la revolución eran destruir los latifundios, liberar a los trabajadores de la esclavitud feudal y "proteger a los obreros urbanos de la avidez de los capitalistas". En 1918, Zapata escribió al general Amezcua: "Es preciso no olvidar que en virtud del respeto a la solidaridad del proletariado, la emancipación del obrero no puede lograrse si no se realiza a la vez la liberación del campesino. De no ser así, la burguesía podría poner estas dos fuerzas la una frente a la otra y aprovecharse, *v. gr.*, de la ignorancia de los campesinos para combatir y refrenar a los justos impulsos de los trabajadores citadinos; del mismo modo que, si el caso se ofrece, podría utilizar a los obreros poco conscientes y lanzarlos contra sus hermanos del campo. Así lo hicieron en México, Francisco Madero, en un principio, y Venustiano Carranza últimamente, si bien los obreros han salido ya de su error y comprenden ahora perfectamente que fueron víctimas de la perfidia carrancista".

Zapata, Eufemio ◆ n. en Villa de Ayala y m. en Cuautla, Mor. (1873-1917). Revolucionario, hermano del anterior. Era comerciante en Veracruz cuando estalló la insurrección maderista. Regresó al estado de Morelos, donde se puso a las órdenes de Pablo Torres Burgos, primero, y de Emiliano Zapata, después. En agosto de 1911 su hermano lo envió a parlamentar con Francisco I. Madero. Fracasados los intentos de avenimiento, se proclamó el Plan de Ayala, del que Eufemio fue uno de los firmantes, ya con el grado de general. Durante 1912 operó militarmente en el sur y el oeste del estado de Puebla y el 30 de abril de 1912 efectuó, en Ixcamilpa, el primer reparto agrario del país. Durante 1913 y 1914 mantuvo su campaña en Puebla. En agosto de 1914 se estableció en Cuautla, donde fue el encargado de nombrar a las comisiones de agricultores que debería hacer los repartos de tierra y dictaminar sobre conflictos de límites entre las comunidades. El 4 de diciembre presenció, en Xochimilco, la entrevista de su hermano con Francisco Villa. A mediados de 1915 se le encomendó la dirección del ingenio de Cuahuixtla. Fue asesinado en una riña.

Eufemio Zapata

Luis Zapata

ZAPATA, LUIS ◆ n. en Chilpancingo, Gro. (1951). Escritor. Estudió letras francesas en la UNAM. Ha sido codirector de *El Nuevo Mal del Siglo*, colaborador de *Punto de Partida* y del periódico *Alianza Francesa*. Publicó por entregas en el suplemento *Sábado* su novela *Ese amor que hasta ayer nos quemara* (1987-88), incluida en el libro homónimo de 1989. Autor de novela: *Hasta en las mejores familias* (1975, Premio Quetzalcóatl), *El vampiro de la colonia Roma* (1979, Premio Juan Grijalbo), *De pétalos perennes* (1981, llevada al cine como *Confidencias*), *A tontas y a locas*, *En jirones* (1985), *Melodrama* (1983, llevada al teatro como *La fuerza del amor* en 1989), *La hermana secreta de Angélica María* (1989) y *¿Por qué mejor no nos vamos?* (1992); cuento: *De amor es mi negra pena* (1983); teatro: *La fuerza del amor* (1989), *La generosidad de los extraños* 1990) y *Sábado* (1990), y la autobiografía *Luis Zapata, de cuerpo entero* (1990). Primer premio del concurso de cuento en francés del IFAL y la Alianza Francesa con *Deuxieme pont* (1977).

ZAPATA, MARIO ◆ n. en España y m. en el DF (1920-1980). Su nombre era Antonio Pérez García. A los 16 años se incorporó al ejército republicano y combatió durante la guerra civil española. En 1939 ingresó en el Partido Comunista de España, del que fue organizador y dirigente durante el franquismo. Estuvo preso en la cárcel de Burgos entre 1940 y 1953. Clandestinamente salió en muchas ocasiones de España. Fue asesor del gobierno cubano de Fidel Castro. Vino 13 veces a México, la última y definitiva en 1962. Crítico tenaz del socialismo autoritario, dejó el PCE en 1968, pero continuó ligado a proyectos políticos de carácter democrático. Aquí trabajó para el Fondo de Cultura Económica, condujo programas de televisión y escribió para *El Día*, *El Machete*, *Nexos* y *Dí*, entre otras publicaciones. Autor de *¿Qué está pasando en la educación básica?* (1976; reeditado en 1983 como *Reforma educativa ¿para qué?*) y *Burgos, cárcel de la dictadura franquista* (1983). Al morir trabajaba en una monografía de México.

ZAPATA, NICOLÁS ◆ n. en Mineral de Catorce, SLP, y m. en Chihuahua, Chih. (1770-1811). Insurgente. Fue alcalde de Mineral de Catorce y en 1806 era mayordomo de alhóndiga de la ciudad de San Luis Potosí. Fue uno de los conspiradores de esa ciudad descubiertos por Félix María Calleja. Se le encarceló y desde su prisión trabajó en favor de la lucha insurgente; fue liberado poco después y se incorporó a la rebelión el 10 de noviembre de 1810, por lo que fue nuevamente encarcelado. Lo puso en libertad Mariano Jiménez, con quien hizo la campaña en las Provincias Internas de Oriente. Ascendió a mariscal de campo. En marzo de 1811 fue capturado en Acatita de Baján con los líderes independentistas. Lo realistas lo trasladaron a Chihuahua, donde fue fusilado.

ZAPATA, ROSAURA ◆ n. en La Paz, BCS, y m. en el DF (1876-1963). Su segundo apellido era Cano. Se tituló como profesora en la Escuela Nacional de Maestros (1899). Estudió también psicología y pedagogía en la Universidad Nacional. En Estados Unidos tomó cursos sobre educación preescolar (1902). Continuó su especialización en Europa. A su regreso al país promovió el establecimiento de jardines de niños (1904) y presidió los jurados para nombrar a las primeras educadoras. Fue directora de varias escuelas, profesora en la Nacional de Maestros e inspectora general de Jardines de Niños de la SEP (1928). Autora de *Cuentos y conversaciones para jardines de niños y escuelas primarias*, *Rimas para jardines de niños*, *Cantos y juegos*, *Técnica de la educación preescolar* y *Educación preescolar*. En 1954 recibió la medalla Belisario Domínguez, otorgada por el Senado de la República, y más tarde la medalla Ignacio Manuel Altamirano, por sus 50 años de actividad profesional pedagógica.

ZAPATA BUTTNER, ENRIQUE ◆ n. en la ciudad de México (1921). Piloto aviador militar (Escuela Militar de Aviación, 1944), naval (Armada de Estados Unidos, 1944) y de combate (Fuerza Aérea de Estados Unidos, 1945). Miembro del PRI, fue secretario de su Comisión Nacional de Estudios sobre Aviación Civil (1964). Ha sido instructor en la Escuela Militar de Aviación y en unidades de la Fuerza Aérea Mexicana (1945-46), comandante supervisor de adiestramiento y ayudante técnico de la Compañía Mexicana de Aviación (1947-75); asesor técnico de transportes aéreos en diversas dependencias oficiales (1955-65), presidente de la Comisión de Estudios y Proyectos Técnicos Aeronáuticos y de la Comisión Coordinadora de Tránsito Aéreo Civil, Militar y Naval y miembro de la Comisión Nacional de Aeropuertos de la SCT (1959-67); asesor técnico de la ASPA (1964-78), miembro del Consejo de Administración de Radio Aeronáutica Mexicana (1967-76), delegado mexicano ante la Confederación Interamericana de Transporte Aéreo y ante las conferencias de la Organización de Aviación Civil Internacional (1968), miembro del Consejo de Administración de la Nacional Abastecedora de Combustible de Aviación (1973-77), supervisor general de desarrollo tecnológico de Aeropuertos y Servicios Auxiliares (1983-86); director general de Transporte Aéreo Federal (1986-88) y director general de Aeronáutica Civil (1988-).

ZAPATA GARCÍA, JORGE DOROTEO ◆ n. en Chihuahua, Chih. (1949). Licenciado en derecho por la Universidad Autónoma de Chihuahua. Director del Departamento de Asistencia Jurídica del Comité Directivo estatal del PRI en Chihuahua (1980-82). Asesor jurídico, secretario de Organización, secretario general adjunto y secretario general de la Federación de Trabajadores del Estado de Chihuahua y secretario general del Sindicato de la Industria Maquiladora. Ha sido secretario del Ayuntamiento de Delicias, secretario general de Aguas y Saneamiento, secretario particular del gobernador de Chihuahua, oficial mayor de la Procuraduría General de la República, delegado ante la ONU, primer subprocurador general de la República y diputado federal por Chihuahua (1985-88).

ZAPATA FRAYRE, GILBERTO ◆ n. en Guadalupe, Zac. (1953). Ingeniero minero metalúrgico y civil por la UAZ. Afiliado al PAN desde 1982, ha desempeñado varios cargos en su estado, entre los que destacan la presidencia del Comité Directivo Estatal. Ha sido diputado local (1986-89) y federal (1991-94). Ha trabajado en la industria de la construcción y ha sido responsable de la Oficina de Catastro e Inmuebles Federales de la SAHOP (1981-82), de la Oficina de Catastro de Inmuebles Federales de la Sedue (1982-85) y perito minero de la SEMIP, entre otros cargos. Es consejero de la delegación zacatecana de Canacintra.

Zapata Loredo, Fausto ◆ n. en San Luis Potosí, SLP (1940). Licenciado en derecho por la Universidad Autónoma de San Luis Potosí (1958-61), estudió ciencias de la información en el World Press Institute (1964). Profesor de la UNAM (1967-68). En el PRI ha sido miembro del consejo nacional (1967) y subsecretario de prensa y propaganda del CEN (1969), así como coordinador de prensa de la campaña de Luis Echeverría (1970). Secretario de Prensa y Propaganda de la Confederación Nacional Campesina (1965). Ha sido jefe de información de *La Prensa* (1962-65), diputado federal suplente (1967-70), subsecretario de Información de la Secretaría de la Presidencia de la República (1970-76), senador por San Luis Potosí (1976-82), embajador en Italia y Malta (1977), asesor del presidente de la República (1981), embajador para Asuntos Especiales (1982), columnista de *Excélsior* (1986-87), embajador en la República Popular China (1987-88), delegado del DDF en Coyoacán (1988-91), cónsul general en Los Ángeles y embajador para asuntos especiales de la SRE (1996) y. gobernador de San Luis Potosí durante 14 días (1991). Autor de *Kennedy* (1964), *Desarrollo en libertad: la política del cambio en México* (1972), *Información y opinión* (1972) y *México: notas sobre el sistema político y la inversión extranjera* (1975).

Zapata y Sandoval, Juan de ◆ n. en la ciudad de México y m. en Guatemala (¿1547?-1630). Agustino, fue profesor en el Colegio de San Pablo. Viajó a España, donde fue lector de la sagrada escritura y regente de estudios del Colegio de San Gabriel de Valladolid. En 1613 se convirtió en el séptimo obispo de Chiapas y en 1621 fue trasladado al obispado de Guatemala. Autor de *De justitia distributiva et acceptione personarum ei opposita* (1609), *Commentaria in primam partem divi thomae aquinatis* (1611) y *Disputatio celebris ac singularis circa fidei professionem et juramentum fidelitatis ab episcopis praestandum* (1623).

Zapata Vela, Carlos ◆ n. en San Juan de la Punta, Ver., y m. en el DF (1906-1997). Fue expulsado de la secundaria por editar el periódico *La Chispa* de "ideas subversivas". Encabezó un Partido Comunista Estudiantil en la Escuela Nacional Preparatoria, donde editó *La Avalancha*, hizo estudios en la Escuela Nacional de Agricultura y se tituló como abogado por la UNAM (1931), en la que participó en el movimiento autonomista (1929). Se afilió en 1938 al PRM, donde fue secretario de Heriberto Jara (☛), con el que trabajó hasta la muerte de éste en 1968. Fue diputado federal (1930, 1940 y 1961-64), asesor de la Secretaría de Marina (1940-46), subdirector del Banco Nacional de Crédito Agrícola (1946-52), jefe de la Oficina de Colonias del DF (1951), embajador de México en la URSS (1967-71) y presidente del Instituto de Intercambio y Amistad Mexicano-Soviético (1971-89). Autor de *Conversaciones con Heriberto Jara* (1992) y de *Cartas de África* (1995).

Zape ◆ Río del noroeste de Durango. Nace en la vertiente norte de un contrafuerte que une las sierras de Guanaceví y de la Candela. Corre de sur a norte, paralelo a la sierra de Canoas, recibe a los arroyos Biogamé, Guanaceví y San Esteban; al noroeste de Santa María del Oro tuerce al este y se encajona en la región del Salto. Cerca de la población de Sestín recibe al río Matalotes y se transforma en el Del Oro o Sestín.

Zapfe, Guillermo ◆ n. y m. en el DF (1933-1992). Nombre profesional de Wilhelm Karl Guillermo Zapfe Mateos. Pintor egresado de La Esmeralda (1960) y de la Escuela del Museo de Louvre (1960). Ha sido profesor de la Escuela de Restauración y Museografía del INAH (1972). Expuso individualmente por primera vez en 1958 y dos años después recibió el primer premio en el concurso de pintura del Instituto Latinoamericano de Cinematografía Educativa. En 1963 se le designó jefe de Pintura del Museo Nacional de Antropología, donde realizó varios cuadros para las salas Maya y de Los orígenes. En 1964 fue escenógrafo del Museo de las Culturas y en 1968 coordinó el Taller de Artes Plásticas de la Universidad de Nuevo León. Primer premio de Nuevos Valores del Salón de la Plástica Mexicana (1959) y primer premio de adquisición en la Bienal Rufino Tamayo (1985).

Carlos Zapata Vela

Zapopan ◆ Municipio de Jalisco contiguo a Guadalajara. Superficie: 893.15 km². Habitantes: 925,113, de los cuales 227,513 forman la población económicamente activa. Hablan alguna lengua indígena 3,744 personas mayores de cinco años (náhuatl 1,183, purépecha 891, zapoteco 236, mazahua 215, huasteco 178, huichol 119, mixteco 119, totonaca 118, otomí 102 y mixe 56). Forma parte del área metropolitana de Guadalajara. Es un importante centro industrial. En su jurisdicción se localiza la zona arqueológica del Ixtépete, sitio ceremonial de los teotihuacanos con cinco capas superpuestas de otras tantas épocas. La cabecera se fundó como asentamiento de españoles por Francisco de Bobadilla en 1541. En esta ciudad se halla el santuario de la Virgen de Zapopan, gemelo del de San Juan de los Lagos. La imagen que se venera en esta iglesia fue llevada por el franciscano Antonio de Segovia, quien se dice que durante la rebelión del Mixtón de Juchipila la enarboló frente a los caxcanes y éstos se retiraron. En noviembre de 1730 el obispo de Guadalajara, Gómez de Cervantes, dedicó el santuario. Desde 1735, anualmente se lleva la imagen a todos los templos de la capital tapatía, donde permanece varias semanas y es regresada el 12 de octubre al frente de una gran peregrinación. Den-

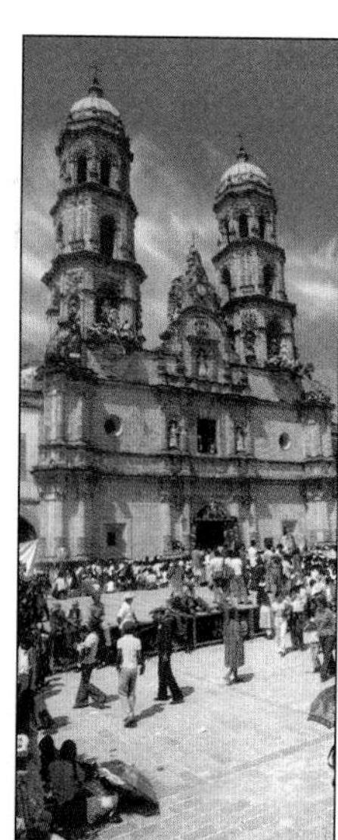

Zapopan, Jalisco

tro del municipio tuvo lugar, el 28 de enero de 1873, la acción de la Mojonera, en la que Ramón Corona derrotó a Manuel Lozada (☛), quien defendía el Plan Libertador de los Pueblos de la Sierra de Álica.

ZAPOTAL, EL ◆ ☛ *San Lucas*, municipio de Chiapas.

ZAPOTECOS ◆ Indios que habitan principalmente los municipios oaxaqueños de El Centro, Etla, Zimatlán, Ejutla, Tlacolula, Ixtlán, Villa Alta, Choapan, Ocotlán, Miahuatlán, Yautepec, Tehuantepec, Juchitán, Pochutla y Juquila, así como, en menor proporción, Tlaxiaco y algunas zonas de los estados de Guerrero, Veracruz y Chiapas. De acuerdo con los datos del censo de 1995, en México hay 415,247 personas mayores de cinco años hablantes de zapoteco, idioma del grupo otomangue, tronco savizaa, familia zapoteca; existen unas 15 variantes dialectales del mismo, por lo que la comunicación entre individuos de comunidades diferentes se realiza en español. Algunos investigadores sugieren la existencia de seis dialectos (serrano, nexitzo, villalteco, valle, tehuano y miahuateco), otros sugieren nueve, que a lo largo de 1,500 años se han diferenciado tanto, que ya podrían considerarse idiomas distintos. La zona zapoteca se divide en las regiones de la sierra de Ixtlán, al norte del estado; la zona de Pochutla y Miahuatlán, al sur; así como la zona del istmo y la región de los valles centrales, alrededor de la capital estatal. Los zapotecas están en contacto con los mixtecos en las montañas, con los chatinos en el sureste y con los chuchones, chinantecos, mexicanos y popolucas en el norte. Dentro de su área hay localidades mixes, zoques, huaves y chontales. Aun cuando la vestimenta tradicional zapoteca ha sido paulatinamente desplazada por la ropa comercial, en algunas localidades las mujeres aún usan huipil, rebozo, huaraches, falda de enredo, faja y algún tipo de tocado, especialmente el *tlacoyal* (turbante trenzado de lana). El atuendo masculino tradicional consta de calzón plegado, camisa de color y sombrero de paja o palma. En la mayor parte de las comunidades zapotecas la actividad económica básica es la agricultura; algunas colocan sus cultivos en el marcado nacional, pero la mayoría produce para el autoconsumo. En las zonas urbanizadas, como Juchitán y Tehuantepec, el comercio es la actividad económica primordial. La pesca, caza y recolección son actividades menores, destinadas a la complementación alimenticia. En toda la zona zapoteca los hombres emigran temporalmente para emplearse como asalariados; asimismo, producen artesanías de lana, barro, cuero, palma e ixtle. La mayoría de los grupos son endogámicos, aunque hay excepciones; los matrimonios entre parientes son objetados. La monogamia es la regla, aunque se conocen casos de poligamia en la región de los valles centrales. La residencia es patrilocal hasta que nace el primer hijo; algunos autores señalan que el novio pasa un año viviendo y trabajando en la casa de la novia, antes de independizarse. La unidad básica es la familia nuclear, aunque generalmente no se recuerdan las genealogías antiguas. Cuando una mujer se casa no adopta el apellido del marido, pero sí los hijos. En algunas comunidades la concertación del matrimonio la llevan a efecto los padres o los padrinos del novio, o un intermediario designado por ellos. En otras localidades es frecuente el rapto de la novia (acción simbólica), que poco después se legaliza mediante una ceremonia; en ambos casos, la boda se formaliza con una fiesta. Los rituales con motivo de la muerte varían de un pueblo a otro. Aun cuando los zapotecas son católicos, conservan elementos de sus creencias antiguas. Aunque éstas varían, de una comunidad a otra, hay algunas ceremonias similares: se hacen rituales con diversas ofrendas en cerros y cuevas destinados al dios del rayo, para propiciar buenas lluvias y buenas cosechas; creen en la existencia de seres como la Matlacihua (demonio femenino que causa el infortunio de los hombres), los *cheneques* o *chaneques* y otros duendes que pueden provocar enfermedades. Creen, asimismo, que cada persona, desde su nacimiento, queda ligada con un animal compañero

Foto: Lourdes Almeida

Familia de campesinos zapotecos de Juchitán, Oaxaca

Pareja de zapotecos de finales del siglo XIX

Mujeres zapotecas

Foto: Fondo Editorial Grupo Azabache

o *tona*, cuyo destino comparte. Su organización política y religiosa es jerárquica, está graduada por edades y es mantenida en función de los servicios públicos; un hombre casado pasa por ciertos cargos hasta llegar a ser principal o anciano. Funcionan las juntas del pueblo, los tequios y los sistemas locales de contribución. Los ciudadanos con algún grado escolar superior al común ocupan puestos medios sin tener que ascender desde topiles o policías, y pueden llegar a ser alcaldes. La zona zapoteca se rige por las disposiciones municipales. Cuando las autoridades cambian, después de haber cumplido su periodo reglamentario, se realiza la ceremonia del cambio de varas; aún hay comunidades en las que los principales siguen siendo consultados con respecto a problemas que atañen a todo el grupo. En sus orígenes, la etnia zapoteca, desprendida del núcleo paleo-olmeca que emigró de la región del Pánuco hacia el este, entró en el actual estado de Oaxaca por el Soconusco. En la zona del istmo encontró y venció a los huaves y en el área del Cempoaltépetl a los mixes, que opusieron la más dura resistencia. La tribu invasora se abrió paso, llegó a Xa Quixe ("Al pie de la montaña", hoy Teotitlán del Valle), avanzó al valle de Oaxaca y ocupó el cerro del Tigre (*Denibée* en zapoteco, *Yucuñana* en mixteco o Monte Albán), donde alcanzó su periodo clásico entre los siglos V y IX; en esa época ocurrió la migración mixteca y se formaron nuevas fronteras entre el Zapotecan y el Mixtecapan. Los zapotecas entraron en guerra con sus vecinos, su hegemonía empezó a ceder y entre los años 1000 y 1200 Monte Albán se despobló. Entonces alcanzaron preponderancia los caudillos militares y se fundó Zaachila, su nueva capital. Paulatinamente se produjo una fusión mixteco-zapoteca que dio origen a un nuevo Estado con sede en Mitla. A mediados del siglo XV los mexicas invadieron la zona: Coyolicaltzi, sobrina de Ahuízotl, se casó con Cosijoesa, señor de los zapotecas, y de este modo se formó una alianza frente a los mixtecos. Los españoles sometieron a ambos pueblos indígenas.

ZAPOTILTIC ♦ Municipio de Jalisco situado en el sureste del estado, contiguo a Ciudad Guzmán. Superficie: 497.82 km². Habitantes: 28,961, de los cuales 7,098 forman la población económicamente activa. Hablan alguna lengua indígena 29 personas mayores de cinco años.

ZAPOTITLÁN ♦ Municipio de Puebla situado en el sureste del estado, contiguo a Tehuacán, en los límites con Oaxaca. Superficie: 484.77 km². Habitantes: 8,132, de los cuales 2,145 forman la población económicamente activa. Hablan alguna lengua indígena 709 personas mayores de cinco años (mixteco 571 y chocho 48). En unas cuevas del poblado de Santana Teloxtoc, de su jurisdicción, en 1986 se encontraron altares, bodegas y numerosos objetos manufacturados (máscaras y escudos de madera con incrustaciones y jícaras policromas, elaborados entre los siglos XII y XV) de la cultura mixteco-popoluca, en lo que se consideró el más importante hallazgo arqueológico de la década. Su cabecera es Zapotitlán Salinas.

ZAPOTITLÁN, DE ♦ Sierra de Puebla situada en el sur del estado. Se extiende de noroeste a sureste, al oeste y suroeste de Tehuacán y al sur de la sierra de Tecamachalco; está limitada al noreste por el río Salado y al sureste por el valle de Zapotitlán.

ZAPOTITLÁN LAGUNAS ♦ Municipio de Oaxaca situado en el occidente del estado, al suroeste de Mariscala de Juárez, en los límites con Guerrero. Superficie: 112.27 km². Habitantes: 2,915, de los cuales 431 forman la población económicamente activa. Hablan alguna lengua indígena 10 personas mayores de cinco años.

ZAPOTITLÁN DE MÉNDEZ ♦ Municipio de Puebla situado en el norte del estado, al sureste de Huauchinango y al noroeste de Teziutlán. Superficie: 35.72 km². Habitantes: 4,857, de los cuales 1,374 forman la población económicamente activa. Hablan alguna lengua indígena 3,179 personas mayores de cinco años (totonaco 3,040), de las cuales 604 son monolingües.

ZAPOTITLÁN PALMAS ♦ Municipio de Oaxaca situado en el noroeste del estado, próximo a Huajuapan de León, en los límites con Puebla. Superficie: 59.96 km². Habitantes: 1,551, de los cuales 161 forman la población económicamente activa. Hablan alguna lengua indígena 269 personas mayores de cinco años (mixteco 383).

ZAPOTITLÁN DEL RÍO ♦ Municipio de Oaxaca situado en el centro del estado, al suroeste de la capital estatal. Superficie: 492.47 km². Habitantes: 2,688, de los cuales 580 forman la población económicamente activa. Hablan alguna lengua indígena 10 personas mayores de cinco años.

ZAPOTITLÁN TABLAS ♦ Municipio de Guerrero situado en el sureste del estado, al este de Chilpancingo y al noroeste de Ometepec. Superficie: 820.90 km². Habitantes: 11,222, de los cuales 4,523

FOTO: CLAUDIO CONTRERAS KOOB

Vegetación de Zapotitlán, Puebla

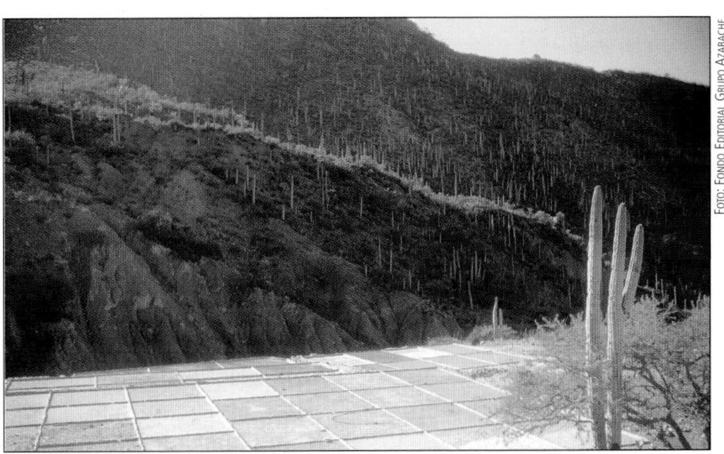
FOTO: FONDO EDITORIAL GRUPO AZABACHE

Zapotitlán Salinas, cabecera de Zapotitlán, Puebla

Ilustración de Santiago Ortega

Entrada principal de Zapotitlán Tablas, Guerrero

forman la población económicamente activa. Hablan alguna lengua indígena 11,222 personas mayores de cinco años (tlapaneco 11,222) y de ellas, son monolingües 5,921.

Zapotitlán de Vadillo ◆ Municipio de Jalisco situado en el sur del estado, al suroeste de Ciudad Guzmán, en los límites con Colima. Superficie: 480.74 km². Habitantes: 6,516, de los cuales 1,189 forman la población económicamente activa. Su cabecera es Zapotitlán de Vadillo, mismo nombre que tenía antes el municipio.

Daniel Zaragoza

Zapotlán, de ◆ Laguna de Jalisco situada en el sur del estado, al suroeste del lago de Chapala, al sureste de Sayula y al noreste del Nevado de Colima. A 1,495 metros sobre el nivel del mar, ocupa la parte más baja de una cuenca cerrada, en el Eje Volcánico, en cuyo margen sur se localiza Ciudad Guzmán.

Zepotlán el Grande ◆ Municipio jalisciense cuya cabecera es Ciudad Guzmán (☛).

Zapotlán de Juárez ◆ Municipio de Hidalgo situado en el sur del estado, contiguo a Pachuca, en los límites con el Estado de México. Superficie: 131.10 km². Habitantes: 13,597, de los cuales 3,412 forman la población económicamente activa. Hablan alguna lengua indígena 27 personas mayores de cinco años (náhuatl 16 y otomí 11). Fue erigido el 5 de septiembre de 1935 con territorio segregado al municipio de Tolcayuca.

Zapotlán del Rey ◆ Municipio de Jalisco situado en el oriente del estado, al sureste de Guadalajara y al suroeste de Atotonilco el Alto, cerca de Michoacán. Superficie: 320.90 km². Habitantes: 15,016, de los cuales 3,499 forman la población económicamente activa. Hablan alguna lengua indígena 46 personas mayores de cinco años.

Zapotlanejo ◆ Municipio de Jalisco contiguo a Guadalajara. Superficie: 643.02 km². Habitantes: 51,961, de los cuales 11,354 forman la población económicamente activa. Hablan alguna lengua indígena 61 personas mayores de cinco años (huichol 22). El 1 de noviembre de 1860 se produjo una batalla en la que el general republicano Ignacio Zaragoza derrotó al conservador Leonardo Márquez, cuando éste se dirigía a Guadalajara a tratar de romper el sitio impuesto por Jesús González Ortega.

Zaragoza ◆ Municipio de Coahuila situado en el norte del estado, cerca de la frontera con Estados Unidos y contiguo a Piedras Negras. Superficie: 8,183.50 km². Habitantes: 12,403, de los cuales 3,609 forman la población económicamente activa.

Zaragoza ◆ ☛ *Santa Inés de Zaragoza*, municipio de Oaxaca.

Zaragoza ◆ Municipio de Puebla situado en el norte del estado, al sureste de Huauchinango y al noroeste de Teziutlán. Superficie: 51.03 km². Habitantes: 8,976, de los cuales 2,797 forman la población económicamente activa. Hablan alguna lengua indígena 563 personas mayores de cinco años (mixteco 535).

Zaragoza ◆ Municipio de San Luis Potosí contiguo a la capital del estado. Superficie: 703.7 km². Habitantes: 21,235, de los cuales 4,333 forman la población económicamente activa. Hablan alguna lengua indígena 19 personas mayores de cinco años.

Zaragoza ◆ Municipio de Veracruz situado al oeste de Minatitlán y al este de Acayucan. Superficie: 41.13 km². Habitantes: 7,998, de los cuales 1,504 forman la población económicamente activa. Hablan alguna lengua indígena 3,766 personas mayores de cinco años (náhuatl 3,757).

Zaragoza ◆ ☛ *Atizapán de Zaragoza*.

Zaragoza, Antonio ◆ n. en Guadalajara, Jal., y m. en Tepic, Nay. (1855-1910). Periodista. Abogado por el Instituto de Ciencias de Guadalajara (1878). Colaboró desde su juventud en diversas publicaciones. Fue director del *Diario Oficial* de Jalisco y secretario de gobierno del territorio de Tepic (1890), donde publicó y dirigió el periódico *Lucifer*. Autor de los poemarios *Armonías* (1882), *Recuerdos* (1882) y *Versos* (1890).

Zaragoza, Daniel ◆ n. en el DF (1957). Boxeador profesional desde 1980, tras participar en los Juegos Olímpicos de Moscú. Campeón nacional (1985) y cuatro veces mundial, dos en peso gallo (1985 y 1988-90) y campeón norteamericano y mundial (del CMB) de peso supergallo (1991 y 1995-97). A los 40 años, fue el campeón mundial más longevo del boxeo. Se retiró en 1997 con una marca de 55 triunfos, ocho derrotas y tres empates.

Zaragoza, Ignacio ◆ n. en Bahía del Espíritu Santo, Texas, y m. en Puebla, Pue. (1829-1862). Militar. Realizó estudios en el Seminario de Monterrey, pero los interrumpió cuando quiso incorporarse a filas durante la guerra contra Estados Unidos y más tarde los abandonó en definitiva, para dedicarse al comercio. En 1853 se alistó en la Guardia Nacional de Nuevo León y al año siguiente se levantó en armas contra el gobierno de Antonio López de Santa Anna. En junio de 1855 participó en la batalla de Saltillo. A finales de 1856 tomó parte en la defensa de Monterrey contra los conservadores. En diciembre de 1857 se encontraba en la ciudad de México y luego de la maniobra golpista del presidente Ignacio Comonfort formó un grupo de rifleros y marchó a Nuevo León, donde se unió a las fuerzas de Santiago Vidaurri. Comandante de los liberales de Jalisco desde mayo de 1860, en julio de ese año, con Pedro Ogazón, derrotó a Leonardo Márquez cuando se retiraba de Sinaloa. En agosto colaboró con Jesús González Ortega durante la batalla de Silao y en septiembre lo sustituyó en la jefatura del ejército liberal y tomó

Guadalajara. En noviembre volvió a derrotar a Márquez en Zapotlanejo y al mes siguiente se reunió con González Ortega y participó en la batalla de Calpulalpan. Fue secretario de Guerra y Marina (del 13 de abril al 22 de diciembre de 186l) en el gabinete de Benito Juárez, pero a finales de 1861 se trasladó a Veracruz como comandante del Ejército de Oriente. Dirigió la defensa mexicana en Acultzingo y el 5 de mayo de 1862 derrotó al ejército francés que intentaba tomar Puebla. Murió de tifoidea seis meses después, mientras intentaba reorganizar las fuerzas mexicanas.

Zaragoza, Miguel ◆ n. en Veracruz, Ver. (1806-¿1850?). Militar. Padre del anterior. Destacado en Texas, participó en 1832 en la defensa de Nacogdoches y en el combate de Angelina contra los separatistas. En 1834 se le envió a Michoacán y en septiembre de 1836 volvió a Texas, en las filas del ejército del norte. En 1840 peleó a las órdenes de Mariano Arista y en 1842 a las de Anastasio Parrodi. En 1844 fue jefe de Detall en Monterrey y más tarde en Zacatecas. Combatió a los invasores estadounidenses en 1847.

Zárate, Carlos *el Cañas* ◆ n. en el DF (?). Boxeador. Fue campeón mundial de peso gallo del CMB, que lo nombró boxeador del año, luego de mantener 10 defensas invicto. Su marca profesional fue de 34 victorias. En 1992 comenzó a entrenar a boxeadores jóvenes en el gimnasio Lupita, donde él lo hizo bajo la guía de Arturo *Cuyo* Hernández.

Zárate, Julio ◆ n. en Jalapa, Ver., y m. en la ciudad de México (1844-1917). Periodista e historiador. Estudió abogacía en el Colegio Carolino de Puebla. Combatió al imperio de Maximiliano con sus artículos en *El Eco del País*, periódico editado en Atlixco. Fue diputado federal por Puebla, Veracruz y el Distrito Federal (1862), colaborador de Sebastián Lerdo de Tejada, secretario de gobierno en Veracruz durante el periodo de Juan de la Luz Enríquez, secretario de Relaciones Exteriores (del 12 de diciembre de 1879 al 22 de septiembre de 1880) en el gabinete de Porfirio Díaz, ministro de la Suprema Corte de Justicia (1902) y senador por Campeche (1912). Autor de *Los estados de la federación mexicana*, una *Monografía del estado de Veracruz*, un *Compendio de historia de México, Elementos de historia general* y *La guerra de independencia*, tercer tomo de *México a través de los siglos*.

Zárate, Luis ◆ n. en Santa Catarina Cuanana, Oaxaca (1951). Estudió en la Escuela Nacional Superior de Artes Decorativas y en el "Atelier 17" de París, donde vivió por 13 años. Ha realizado exposiciones individuales y colectivas en España, Alemania, Francia, Italia, Estados Unidos y México.

Zárate Flores, Alfonso ◆ n. en el DF (1946). Académico, analista político y consultor privado. Licenciado en derecho por la UNAM (1968). Siguió un curso de investigación en la Universidad de Londres (1979-80), por la que es maestro en sociología política (1981). Profesor de la UNAM. La UIA y otras instituciones. Ha sido asesor de la SHCP (1977-78), director de información de la Coordinación General del Sistema Nacional de Evaluación de la Presidencia de la República (1981-82), fundador de la revista *Evaluación* (1982), asesor del secretario de Relaciones Exteriores (1986-88), director general de análisis de la Unidad de Información y Análisis de la Oficina de Coordinación de la Presidencia de la República (1989-90), fundador y director general del Grupo Consultor Interdisciplinario (1991-), analista del noticiero *Punto por punto* (1995) y del noticiero *Monitor* (1996-). Ha colaborado en *Expansión* y *Milenio*. Coautor de *México: estabilidad y luchas por la democracia 1900-1982* (1988) y *Fin de siglo, fin de ciclo* (1997). Autor de *Los usos del poder* (1995). Miembro de la Asociación de Estudios Latinoamericanos (1994-95). Fue miembro de la comisión coordinadora del Grupo San Ángel (1995). Fundador y dirigente de Causa Ciudadana (1996-).

Zárate Herrera, José Luis ◆ n. en Puebla, Pue. (1966). Escritor. Hizo estudios de ingeniería y medicina. Fue fundador del Círculo Puebla de Ciencia

Ignacio Zaragoza

Ficción y de la revista *Prolepsis*, que también dirigió. Textos suyos aparecen en las antologías *Más allá de lo imaginado II* (1991), *Frontera de espejos rotos* (1993), *Silicio en la memoria* (1997) y *Rock. Cuentos compactos* (1998). Publicó por entregas la novela *Fe de erratas* (1997-98) en el diario *La Jornada de Oriente*. Autor de cuento: *Permanencia voluntaria* (1990, Premio JOMAR de narrativa) e *Hyperia* (1999); y novela: *Xanto. Novelucha libre* (1994) y *La ruta del hielo y la sal* (1998, Premio Internacional MECyF de Novela Fantástica). Ha obtenido los premios Puebla (1985) y Kalpa (1990) de cuento de ciencia ficción y los premios internacionales Más Allá y Axxón Primordial. Ha sido becario del Fondo para la Cultura y las Artes del Estado de Puebla (1998-99).

Julio Zárate

Zarca, de la ◆ Meseta del norte de Durango y sur de Chihuahua. Se extiende de noroeste a sureste y se halla limitada al norte por el río Conchos, al noreste por la sierra de los Remedios, al este por la de Atotonilco (que la separa del bolsón de Mapimí), al sureste por el río de la Cadena, al sur y suroeste por la sierra Cuchillas de la Zarca, al oeste por la de Guajolotes y al noroeste por la de Santa Bárbara. Mide unos 120 km de largo por 80 de ancho, con una altitud media de 1,800 metros sobre el nivel del mar.

Alfonso Zárate Flores

Zarco, Francisco ◆ n. en Durango, Dgo., y m. en la ciudad de México (1829-1869). Periodista. Su nombre completo era Joaquín Francisco Zarco

Mateos. De manera autodidáctica estudió idiomas, historia, derecho y otras ciencias sociales. En 1844 (a los 15 años de edad) entró a trabajar como meritorio en el Ministerio de Relaciones Exteriores. Cuando el gobierno mexicano debió marchar a Querétaro (octubre de 1847), tras la invasión estadounidense, Luis de la Rosa, ministro universal, lo nombró oficial mayor de las cuatro secretarías que componían el gabinete de Manuel de la Peña y Peña. El presidente Pedro María Anaya lo designó oficial mayor interino de la Secretaría de Relaciones Exteriores (noviembre de 1847 a junio de 1848). Periodista desde 1842, en 1849 colaboró en *El Álbum Mexicano* y en 1850 redactó y publicó *El Demócrata*, del que aparecieron 103 números, hasta que fue encarcelado por sus críticas a Mariano Arista. En 1851 presidió el Liceo Hidalgo, publicó *La Ilustración Mexicana*, redactó *El Presente Amistoso Dedicado a las Señoritas Mexicanas*, colaboró en *La semana de las señoritas* y fue elegido diputado suplente por Yucatán. El 1 de enero de 1852 empezó a escribir en *El Siglo XIX* bajo el pseudónimo de *Fortún*. Entre mayo y junio fue uno de los redactores del periódico *Las Cosquillas* y Arista, ya presidente, pretendió enjuiciarlo pese a su fuero de diputado, lo que obligó a Zarco a ocultarse hasta diciembre, cuando el Congreso emitió un segundo dictamen absolutorio. El 30 de abril de 1853 se convirtió en editor responsable de *El Siglo XIX*, cargo que ocuparía hasta su muerte. Durante la dictadura del último periodo santanista se le impusieron varias multas, fue obligado a no publicar editoriales y para preservar la vida del periódico lo limitó a la mera reproducción de partes del gobierno y noticias generales. A la caída de su Alteza Serenísima insertó en el diario el Plan de Ayutla, cuando la guarnición capitalina todavía no decidía apoyar la revolución encabezada por Juan Álvarez. Se opuso a que se tomaran represalias contra los órganos conservadores y defendió su derecho a la libre expresión. En 1856 fue elegido diputado por Durango al

Francisco Zarco

Congreso Constituyente, donde ocupa 150 veces la tribuna y es, simultáneamente el cronista más puntual de esta asamblea, en la que defendió su derecho a elaborar una nueva Norma Fundamental y no simplemente a reformar alguna de las anteriores, logró que se garantizara la gratuidad en la impartición de justicia, que se entendiera la libertad de imprenta como "la más preciosa de las garantías del ciudadano" y evitó, siempre que pudo, que se pusieran taxativas a los derechos individuales. Abogó por la tolerancia en materia de cultos, se opuso a la supresión del Senado, pugnó por el federalismo y, por el voto unánime de sus colegas, redactó y leyó el Manifiesto a la Nación que precedió a la nueva Constitución. Después del golpe de Estado de Comonfort, Zarco decidió no tratar asuntos políticos para proteger a su periódico, pero ante la hostilidad de los conservadores, el 29 de enero dejó de ser editor responsable y, perseguido por los golpistas, decidió ocultarse y publicar el *Boletín Clandestino*. Como respuesta a los asesinatos ordenados por Leonardo Márquez el 11 de abril, Zarco publicó, también desde su escondite, el folleto *Las matanzas de Tacubaya*. En esa rigurosa clandestinidad, sirvió en la capital en diversas misiones al gobierno de Benito Juárez, hasta que el 13 de mayo de 1860 fue aprehendido y torturado. Durante siete meses de encarcelamiento estuvo reducido a una pequeña celda donde contrajo la tuberculosis. Con las fuerzas liberales en la capital, salió de prisión el 25 de diciembre de 1860. De inmediato editó un *Boletín de Noticias* que dejó a Pantaleón Tovar al volver a la dirección de *El Siglo XIX*. Se opuso al intento de Juárez de dictar una amnistía en favor de los golpistas. Se opuso también al destierro dictado contra varios obispos y exigió que se les sometiera a juicio para aplicar el principio de igualdad ante la ley. El 12 de enero de 1861 fue nombrado secretario de Relaciones Exteriores del gabinete juarista, puesto que asumió el día 21 y después se encargó del despacho de Gobernación. Instituyó como día de fiesta el 5 de febrero, día de la Constitución; expidió la Ley de Secularización de Hospitales y Establecimientos de Beneficencia y la disposición que impedía al Estado intervenir en la administración de sacramentos; levantó el estado de sitio y expidió una nueva ley de imprenta. El 9 de mayo de 1861 dejó el gabinete. Fue elegido diputado a la segunda Legislatura, pero no pudo ocupar su curul. Nuevamente diputado en 1863, salió de la ciudad de México con el gobierno juarista y fundó en San Luis Potosí, el 15 de junio de 1863, *La Independencia Mexicana*, en el que llamó a emplear todos los medios para "generalizar la guerra contra el invasor"; en Saltillo, a partir del 16 de marzo de 1864, publicó *La Acción*. Enfermo, se trasladó a Estados Unidos con su familia. En Nueva York, mientras trabajaba como traductor en imprentas y editoriales, continuó su defensa de la causa mexicana en el *Herald* y en sus colaboraciones para el *Mercurio*, de Valparaíso, Chile; la *Reforma Pacífica*, de Montevideo; *El Comercio* y *El Nacional*, de Lima; *La Nación Argentina*, *La Tribuna* y *El Pueblo* de Buenos Aires; *El Porvenir*, de Caracas; y los periódicos mexicanos *El Noticioso* y *El Criterio*, de Veracruz, *Idea Liberal*, de Puebla, y *El Ferro-Carril*, de Orizaba. En noviembre de 1867 volvió a la ciudad de México, fue nuevamente diputado y reasumió la dirección de *El Siglo XIX*, de la que su enfermedad lo retiró el 1 de septiembre de 1869. Todavía presidió el Congreso en noviembre. Murió el 22 de diciembre y ese mismo día la Cámara de Diputados acordó que se inscribiera su nombre en el salón de sesiones. Colaboró en *Hombres ilustres mexicanos*, obra aparecida en 1873-74. Autor de *Historia del Congreso Extraordinario Constituyente de 1856-1857* (2 t., 1857) y *Comentarios del Tratado de Miramar y dificultades prácticas para la transformación monárquica de México* (1864). Con sus artículos se han integrado varias antologías.

ZARFATE, GASPAR ◆ n. ¿en la ciudad de México? y m. ¿en las Filipinas? (1571-1620). Ingresó en 1587 en la orden de los dominicos. Fue lector de artes en Puebla y más tarde se le envió a las Filipinas, donde gobernó el convento principal de la ciudad de Manila y fue definidor y vicario provincial. Autor de *Primer arte y gramática de la lengua de la Nueva Segovia*.

ZÁRRAGA, ÁNGEL ◆ n. en Durango, Dgo., y m. en el DF (1886-1946). Su segundo apellido era Argüelles. Pintor. Estudió en la Academia de San Carlos, que en 1904 lo becó para continuar su preparación en Europa. En ese año ingresó en la Academia Real de Bruselas y en 1910 en la de Bellas Artes de París.

La dádiva, obra de Ángel Zárraga

Expuso en el Salón de Otoño, al lado de Picasso, Bracque y otros iniciadores del cubismo (1910). Durante la primera guerra mundial realizó los murales de las iglesias de Meudon y Saint Ferdinand des Ternes, en París. Al término del conflicto, fue profesor de los soldados estadounidenses estacionados en Europa y dio clases en la Chaumiére. Decoró la capilla del castillo de Vert Coeur, cerca de Versalles (1922), la capilla de Nuestra Señora de Salette, en Suresnes (1924), la iglesia de los Mínimos, en Réthel (1926), los salones de la legación mexicana en París (1927) y la iglesia de Fedhala, en Marruecos; el fresco de *El Redentor*, en Guébriant, y el de la Casa del Café en la Plaza de la ópera, de París (1932). Regresó a México en 1942. Autor de las pinturas de la cúpula del Mal Paso, en Mégreve, y las de San Fernando de las Ternas y la iglesia de la Ciudad Universitaria de París; los retratos de Renoir, Bonard, Hervieu, Eugenio D'Ors y Lucien Romier; los murales en el edificio Guardiola de la ciudad de México (sede del Club de Banqueros), *La voluntad de construir*, en la Biblioteca México; la decoración de la Catedral de Monterrey y de obras de caballete. Escribió una *Oda a la virgen de Guadalupe* (1915), *Tres poemas* (1934) y una *Oda a Francia* (1938) que publicó en París.

Las futbolistas, óleo sobre tela de Ángel Zárraga

ZARUR MÉNEZ, AMÍN ◆ n. en Arcelia, Gro. (1936). Licenciado en biología por la UNAM (1957) y doctor en biología marina por la UNAM y la Universidad de Hamburgo. Miembro del PRI. Ha sido ayudante de investigador en el Instituto de Biología de la UNAM (1956-57), profesor e investigador fundador del Instituto Técnico Pesquero de Veracruz (1957-59); profesor investigador (1961-66), director de la Escuela de Ciencias (1963-66) y secretario general interino de la Universidad Autónoma de Guerrero (1966); y profesor de la UNAM (1967-70). En el sector público se ha desempeñado como investigador de la Dirección General de la Fauna de la Secretaría de Agricultura y Ganadería (1960-61), presidente del Comité Organizador del primer Congreso Nacional Oceanográfico (1963), director general del Instituto Nacional de la Pesca de la SIC (1968-71), delegado de Pesca en San Diego (1971-75), delegado y director de Pesca en Guerrero (1976-78), director general de Acuicultura del Departamento de Pesca (1978-80), presidente municipal de Acapulco (1981-83), director general de Acuicultura de la Secretaría de Pesca (1984-85) y diputado federal por Guerrero (1985-88). Presidente del Colegio de Biólogos de México (1979).

Ángel Zárraga

Glorificación de la Virgen bajo el misterio de la Trinidad, obra de Ángel Zárraga

ZARZA BERNAL, ANSELMO ♦ n. en Atlixco, Pue. (1916). Sacerdote ordenado en 1939. Estudió en el Seminario Palafoxiano y en la Pontificia Universidad Gregoriana de Roma. Ha sido secretario de los arzobispos de Puebla: Ignacio y Octaviano Márquez y Toriz, secretario canciller de la curia, promotor de justicia, canónigo prebendado de la catedral; capellán de varias comunidades, así como obispo de Linares (1962-66) y de León (1966-92). Es obispo emérito.

ZARZOSA, JESÚS CHUCHO ♦ n. en San Luis Potosí, SLP (1919). Pianista y director de orquesta. Fue alumno de Juan León Mariscal. Ha hecho arreglos sinfónicos de piezas populares mexicanas. Autor de las bandas sonoras para las películas *México lindo y querido, La muerte de un gallero, El gallo de oro, El aviso inoportuno* y *Los pequeños privilegios*, así como *Bosquejos* (pieza para cuarteto de cuerdas). Fue miembro del Comité Ejecutivo de la sección de compositores del Sindicato de Trabajadores de la Producción Cinematográfica. Ganó un Ariel por la música de la película *El otro* (1985).

Lorenzo de Zavala

ZAUTLA ♦ Municipio de Puebla situado en el norte del estado, al suroeste de Teziutlán y al sureste de Zacatlán. Superficie: 274.27 km^2. Habitantes: 19,048, de los cuales 3,373 forman la población económicamente activa. Hablan alguna lengua indígena 8,137 personas mayores de cinco años (náhuatl 8,132). Indígenas monolingües: 704.

ZAVALA, FRANCISCO JOSÉ ♦ n. en Tepic y m. en Guadalajara, Jal. (1840-1915). Se tituló como licenciado en derecho en la Universidad de Guadalajara (1861). Colaboró en *La Prensa, La Verdad, La Civilización, El Pabellón Mexicano* y otras publicaciones tapatías (1865). Fue diputado federal por Jalisco (1880); asesor de la cuarta división militar (1881) y magistrado del Tribunal Superior de Jalisco (1884). Desde 1873 fue profesor de la Escuela Católica de Jurisprudencia en la que ocupó la dirección. Colaboró en *La Linterna de Diógenes, El Regional* y otras publicaciones católicas. Autor de *Elementos de derecho internacional privado* (1886), *Libertad religiosa y libertad de enseñanza* (1905), *El socialismo y la Iglesia* (1907) y *El positivismo* (1909).

ZAVALA, JESÚS ♦ n. en San Luis Potosí, SLP, y m. en el DF (1892-1956). Escritor. Se tituló como abogado en el Instituto Científico y Literario de San Luis Potosí (1917). Establecido en la ciudad de México desde 1920, fue profesor de las escuelas nacionales Preparatoria y de Jurisprudencia y de la Libre de Derecho. Colaborador de *Juventud, Revista de Revistas, El Nacional, Estilo, El Heraldo de San Luis Potosí* y *El Universal*. Compilador de *Cuatro siglos de literatura mexicana* (1946). Autor de los poemarios *Flores del alba* (1911), *Vendimia juvenil* (1917), *De la hermandad* (1918, en colaboración con Luciano Joublanc Rivas y Manuel Ramírez Arriaga) y *Jardines de provincia* (1919); y de los ensayos *Antología de Manuel José Othón* (1945), *Manuel José Othón, su vida y su obra* (1945), *Cuatro siglos de literatura mexicana* (1946), *Epistolario de Manuel José Othón* (1946) y *Manuel José Othón, el hombre y el poeta* (1952). Miembro fundador de la Academia Potosina de Ciencias y Artes.

ZAVALA, LAURO ♦ n. en el DF (1954). Licenciado en ciencias de la comunicación en la UAM, maestro por la UNAM y doctor en literatura prehispánica por El Colegio de México. Traductor y corrector en Siglo XXI Editores (1970-1974) y en El Colegio de México (1975-1978). Profesor de enseñanza superior. Autor de *La edición de libros universitarios* (colectivo, 1989), *Material inflamable. Reseñas y crítica cinematográfica* (1989), *Multiplicación de los Contemporáneos. Ensayos sobre la generación* (colectivo, 1989), *Paquete: cuento. La ficción en México* (colectivo (1990), *Ámbito tres. Reflexiones sobre nuestro espacio cultural* (colectivo, 1991), *Interpretaciones a la obra de Carlos Fuentes* (colectivo, 1991), *Seminario La Posmodernidad* (colectivo, 1991), *Generación de conocimientos y formación de comunicadores* (colectivo (1992), *Diálogos y fronteras. El pensamiento de Mijalil Bajitin en el mundo contemporáneo* (1993) y *Posibilidades y límites de la comunicación museografía* (1993); antologó *Humor e ironía en el cuento mexicano* (1979-1991, (1992, 2 t.), *La palabra en juego. Antología del cuento mexicano contemporáneo, 1986-1992* (1993), *Teorías de los cuentistas* (1993), *Towards the Museum of the Future. Some New European Perspectives* (1993).

ZAVALA, LORENZO DE ♦ n. en Mérida, Yuc., y m. en Texas (1788-1836). Hizo sus primeros estudios en el Seminario Tridentino de Mérida. Pasó a la escuela de Pablo Moreno (1802-1807), donde fue condiscípulo de Andrés Quintana Roo. Perteneció al grupo de los sanjuanistas, simpatizante de la independencia novohispana que abrió un colegio del que fue profesor. Escribió en *El Misceláneo* (1813-14), fundó e imprimió en el taller de Francisco Bates los periódicos *El Aristarco Universal* (1813), *El Redactor Meridano*, órgano del ayuntamiento de Mérida (1813), y *El Filósofo Meridano*, donde polemizó con los *rutineros*, que representaban al pensamiento conservador. En 1814 fue elegido diputado a las Cortes que disolvió Fernando VII, aprehendido con Bates y José Matías Quintana y enviado a la fortaleza de San Juan de Ulúa, donde en forma autodidacta aprendió inglés y mêdicina. Quedó en libertad en 1817 y ejerció la medicina en Mérida. En 1820, al restablecerse la Constitución de Cádiz, fundó *El Hispano Americano Constitucional*, reorganizó la Sociedad de San Juan y fue nuevamente elegido diputado a Cortes. Víctima del golpe de mano de Mariano Carrillo, jefe de armas de Mérida, se exilió en La Habana, donde publicó el folleto *Pruebas de la estensión del despotismo o idea del estado actual de la capital de Yucatán*. Pasó Madrid en enero de 1821 y ocupó su curul. Ahí conoció el Plan de Iguala y se trasladó a París, a Londres y a Nueva York. Llegó a México a principios de 1822. Fue diputado por Yucatán al primer Congreso Constituyente y miembro de la Junta Nacional Instituyente creada por Iturbide en ese año, la que aprobó el *Reglamento político de Imperio* redactado por él. A la caída del imperio colaboró en *El Sol* (1823), donde inició su lucha en favor del federalismo; *El Correo de la Federación* (1826-30), del que fue director (1829-30); *El Fénix de la Libertad* (1932-33) y *La Águila Mexicana*, donde publicó una serie de textos que reunió en el folleto *Colección de artículos selectos sobre política* (1828). Hizo traducciones y fue diputado al Congreso Constituyente (1823-24), que presidía al aprobarse la Constitución. En 1825 fue cofundador de la logia yorkina, en la que figuró en forma prominente. En octubre del mismo año fue elegido senador por Yucatán (1825-26). Gobernador del Estado de México (1827-29 y 1832-33). Fue el director intelectual del llamado motín de la Acordada (☛), que llevó a la presidencia a Vicente Guerrero, de quien fue secretario de Hacienda (del 18 de abril al 2 de noviembre de 1829). Dejó su cargo para ir a Yucatán a negociar con los centralistas, pero éstos le impidieron desembarcar en la península. Al producirse el golpe de Estado de Anastasio Bustamante, fue acusado por este dictador de promover por correo la insurrección de Zacatecas, a lo que respondió: "jamás hago revoluciones por cartas". El 2 de junio, hostilizado por el gobierno, debió abandonar el país y se dirigió a Nueva Orleans. Recorrió Estados Unidos y pasó a Europa. Volvió a finales de 1832, reasumió la gubernatura del Estado de México, fue diputado federal por Yucatán en 1833 y a finales de ese año regresó a Francia como ministro plenipotenciario. En agosto de 1834 renunció a su cargo diplomático y entregó la legación el 26 de marzo de 1835. Se estableció en Texas, donde tenía una concesión de tierras, obtenida hacia 1829, que era la segunda en extensión. Opuesto al régimen centralista, participó en el movimiento texano por el restablecimiento de la Constitución federal de 1824. En noviembre de 1835 asistió, como diputado por Harrisbourg, a la convención de Austin donde los texanos ratificaron su demanda de respeto a la Carta Magna de 1824. En marzo de 1836 firmó en Nueva Washington el acta de independencia y el el 1 de mayo, en Brazoria, participó en la reunión que proclamó la erección de la República de Texas, de la que fue el primer vicepresidente hasta el 22 de octubre, cuando renunció y, enfermo, se retiró a Zavala's Point, cerca de San Jacinto, donde murió el 16 de noviembre. Autor de *Ensayo histórico de las revoluciones de Mégico, desde 1808 hasta 1830* (2 t., 1831-32), *Viaje a los Estados Unidos del Norte de América* (1834) y *Viaje a Holanda, Suiza y Alemania* (inédito).

ZAVALA, MAURICIO ◆ n. en San Luis Potosí, SLP, y m. ¿en Mérida, Yuc.? (¿1832?-¿1914?). Sacerdote. Fue párroco de Ciudad del Maíz, fundó en ese sitio una escuela técnica militarizada, sostenida y dirigida por él; adherido a las corrientes anarquistas, en auge a finales del siglo XIX, ideó un proyecto de reforma agraria para el reparto de los latifundios potosinos y, para impulsar su proyecto, llegó a encabezar una rebelión, hacia 1885. Al fracasar su levantamiento armado fue aprehendido y condenado a muerte. Se le conmutó la pena por destierro a Yucatán. Fue cura de Progreso, secretario del Capítulo (1900), racionero, párroco del sagrario y canónigo. Autor de *Juárez y la reforma* (1896), *Polémica. Colección de artículos sueltos* (1896), *Gramática maya* (1896), *Miscelánea teológica y canóniga* (1897) y *Vocabulario español-maya* (1898, en colaboración con A. Medina).

ZAVALA, SILVIO ◆ n. en Mérida, Yuc. (1909). Estudió en las universidades del Sureste y Nacional de México y se doctoró en derecho en la Universidad Central de Madrid (1931). En El Colegio de México fundó y dirigió el Centro de Estudios Históricos (1940-56) y presidió la institución (1963-66). Ha sido secretario del Museo Nacional (1937-38), fundador y director de la *Revista de Historia de América* (1938-65), director de la Biblioteca Histórica Mexicana de Obras Inéditas, director del Museo Nacional de Historia (1946-54), presidente de la Comisión de Historia del Instituto Panamericano de Geografía e Historia (1947-65); delegado permanente (1956-63) y miembro del Consejo Ejecutivo de la UNESCO (1960-66); presidente del Consejo Internacional de Filosofía y Ciencias Humanas (París, 1965-71) y embajador en Francia (1966-75). Coautor de *Historia de América* (1940-41). *Fuentes para la historia del trabajo en Nueva España* (5 t., 1939-41) e *Historia universal. Antigüedad y edad media* (1953). Autor de *Los intereses particulares en la conquista de la Nueva España* (1933), *Las instituciones jurídicas en la conquista de América* (1935), *La encomienda indiana* (1935), *La utopía de Tomás Moro en la Nueva España y otros estudios* (1937), *Francisco del Paso y Troncoso. Su misión en Europa, 1892-1916* (1938), *De encomiendas y propiedad territorial en algunas regiones de la América Española* (1940), *Ideario de Vasco de Quiroga* (1941), *The Spanish Colonization of America* (1943), *New View Points of the Spanish Colonization of America* (1943), *El norte de México y el sur de los Estados Unidos; servidumbre natural y libertad cristiana según los tratadistas españoles de los siglos XVI y XVII* (1944), *Ensayos sobre la colonización española en América* (1944), *Contribución a la historia de las instituciones coloniales en Guatemala* (1947), *Síntesis de la historia del pueblo mexicano* (1947), *La filosofía política en la conquista de América* (1947), *Ordenanzas del trabajo. Siglos XVI y XVII* (1947), *Estudios indianos* (1948), *América en el espíritu francés del siglo XVIII* (1949), *Historia universal moderna y contemporánea* (1949), *Hispanoamérica septentrional y media. Periodo colonial. México* (1953), *Aproximación a la historia de México* (1953), *Programa de historia de América en la época colonial* (1961), *El nuevo mundo en los intercambios mundiales postcolombinos* (1961), *La defensa de los derechos del hombre en América Latina. Siglos XVI-XVIII* (1963), *Recuerdo de Vasco de Quiroga* (1966), *Geschichte des Mexikanischen Volkes, Bine Synthese* (1966), *Apercus sur l'histoire du Mexique* (1967), *Los esclavos indios en la Nueva España* (1968), *El mundo americano en la época*

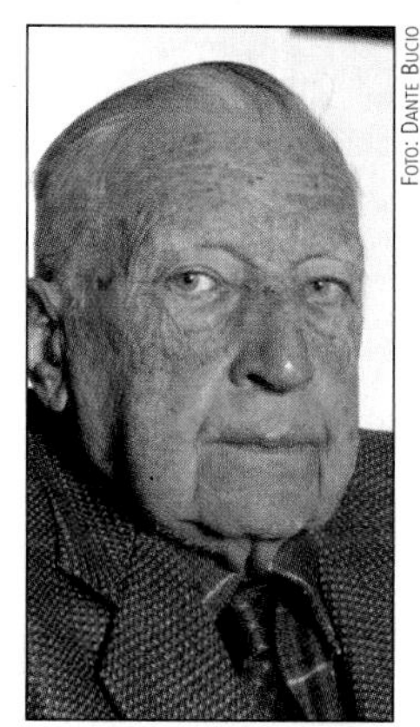

Silvio Zavala

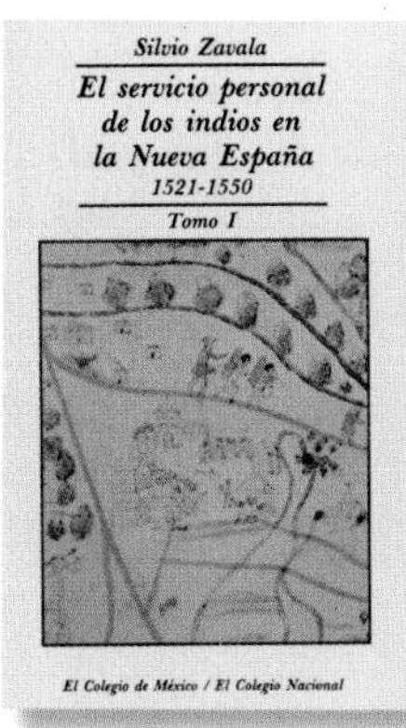

Obra de Silvio Zavala

Dionisio Zavala Armendáriz

Leszek Zawadka

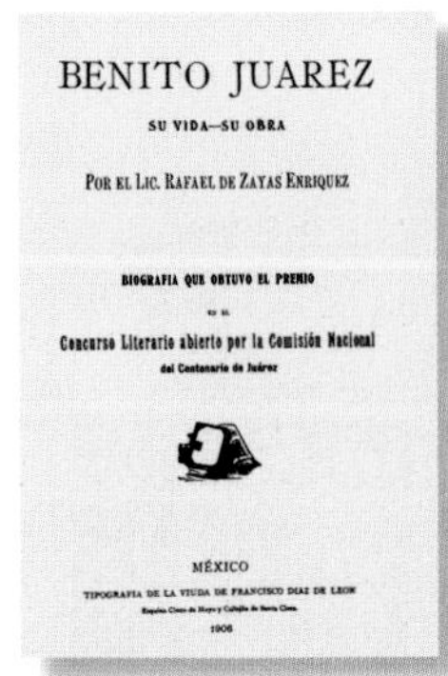

BENITO JUAREZ

SU VIDA—SU OBRA

POR EL LIC. RAFAEL DE ZAYAS ENRIQUEZ

MÉXICO

1906

Obra de Zayas Enríquez

colonial (2 t., 1968), *Apuntes de historia nacional, 1808-1974* (1975), *Orígenes de la colonización en el Río de la Plata* (1978), *El servicio personal de los indios en el Perú* (1979), *Fuentes para la historia del trabajo en la Nueva España* (8 t., 1980), *Fray Alonso de la Veracruz. Primer maestro de derecho agrario en la incipiente Universidad de México 1553-1555* (1981), *El servicio personal de los indios en la Nueva España, 1576-1599* (1987), *Apuntes de historia nacional 1808-1974* (1990) y *Temas del virreinato* (1990). Miembro de El Colegio Nacional, del Consejo de la Crónica de la Ciudad de México y de la Academia Mexicana de la Historia. Profesor emérito de El Colegio de México, Premio Nacional de Letras (1969), Presea Vasco de Quiroga (1986), Premio Rafael Heliodoro Valle (1988), medalla Eligio Ancona del gobierno de Yucatán y Premio Príncipe de Asturias de Ciencias Sociales 1993. Medalla al Mérito Ciudadano de la ARDF (1991).

ZAVALA ARMENDÁRIZ, DIONISIO ◆ n. en Real de Catorce, SLP, y m. en Aguascalientes, Ags. (1882-1973). Minero (1900-1902). Pasó a Monterrey donde fue aseador de caballos y cochero. Fundó la Liga Socialista de Cocheros de Sitio, la Sociedad de Carretoneros Mariano Escobedo y la Sociedad Mutualista de Cocheros Particulares. Afiliado al Partido Liberal de Nuevo León (1909). En 1913 se unió a la revolución constitucionalista. Diputado por Matehuala al Congreso Constituyente de 1916-17, participó en la redacción de los artículos 27 y 123. Dos veces diputado federal (1917-18 y 1920-22), inspector federal del trabajo y presidente de las juntas regionales de Conciliación en Pachuca, Guanajuato, Mexicali, Toluca, Veracruz, El Oro, Zacatecas, San Luis Potosí, Cananea, Mazatlán y Aguascalientes (1918-48).

ZAVALA ECHAVARRÍA, ROBERTO ◆ n. en Eldorado, Sin. (1943). Licenciado en derecho por la Universidad Autónoma de Sinaloa, de la que ha sido profesor (1971-1973). Ejerció la docencia en la Escuela Libre de Derecho de Sinaloa (1973-1994). Secretario del Ayuntamiento de Guasave (1975-1977), director de Asuntos Jurídicos del Gobierno de Sinaloa, director general del Instituto de Readaptación Social de Sinaloa. Ha sido subsecretario del gobierno de Sinaloa, diputado local (1989-1992), subdirector jurídico de la empresa descentralizada Caminos y Puentes Federales de Ingresos y Servicios Conexos, director general jurídico de la Secretaría de Agricultura, Ganadería y Desarrollo Rural del Gobierno Federal, subsecretario de Seguridad Pública de la Secretaría de Gobernación y jefe de la Unidad de Estudios Legislativos de la Secretaría de Gobernación (1999-).

ZAVALA PEÑA, HUMBERTO ANDRÉS ◆ n. en Acapetahua, Chis. (1943). Licenciado en derecho por la UNAM (1965). Tomó cursos de contratación colectiva en Estados Unidos (1977) y sobre políticas de empleo en Ginebra (1980). En el PRI fue secretario general del Comité Directivo Estatal de Chiapas (1983-85). Fundador y secretario de Acción Política de la Federación de Organizaciones Obreras Juveniles de Chiapas. Asesor jurídico de la Federación de Trabajadores de Chiapas y secretario de la Comisión de Honor y Justicia del Instituto de Educación Obrera de la CTM. Ha sido juez de primera instancia en Motozintla (1969), en Tapachula (1972-74) y en Pichucalco (1974-76); asesor de la Comisión Coordinadora de Acuerdos del Ejecutivo en Chiapas (1976), diputado local en Chiapas (1979-82), magistrado en la sala civil del Tribunal Superior de Justicia de Chiapas (1982-83) y diputado federal (1985-88).

ZAVALETA, CONVENIOS DE ◆ Fueron firmados el 23 de diciembre de 1832 en la hacienda de Zavaleta por los militares Antonio Gaona, Mariano Arista y Lino Alcorta, representantes de Anastasio Bustamante, y Juan Pablo Anaya, Gabriel Valencia e Ignacio Basadre, en nombre de Manuel Gómez Pedraza. Los convenios establecían el fin del gobierno golpista de Bustamante y entregaban el Ejecutivo a Gómez Pedraza.

ZAWADKA, LESZEK ◆ n. en Polonia (1954). Músico. Graduado en la Academia Federico Chopin, de Varsovia. Llegó a México en 1977. Se ha presentado en diversos escenarios y ha sido profesor del Conservatorio Nacional. En 1990 fundó el Coro de Niños de Chalco para una presentación ante el papa Juan Pablo II. El grupo ha continuado bajo su dirección, ha hecho giras internacionales y tiene dos discos. Zawadka recibió la Orden del Águila Azteca en 1996.

ZAYAS, MARIUS DE ◆ n. en Veracruz (1880-1961). Caricaturista y poeta. Su familia, desterrada por Porfirio Díaz, se exilió en Nueva York, ciudad en la que montó una exposición de sus caricaturas en la Iglesia de La Asunción (1909), promovió distintas vanguardias artísticas entre 1913 y 1920, fundó dos galerías y participó en la primera exposición de arte moderno en América (1913). Fue autor de los primeros poemas visuales. Autor de *La evolución del arte moderno* (1928, publicado en 1998). En 1997 se publicó la correspondencia que mantuvo con Alfred Barr, director del MOMA de Nueva York, con el título *How, When and Who Modern Art came to New York: Marius de Zayas*.

ZAYAS ENRÍQUEZ, RAFAEL DE ◆ n. en Veracruz, Ver., y m. en EUA (1848-1932). Abogado, periodista y escritor. Estudió filosofía y derecho romano en Alemania. Obtuvo el título de licenciado en jurisprudencia en Veracruz (1872). Colaboró en *El Eco del Comercio*, cofundó de la revista *Las Violetas* (1869) y reabrió *El Progreso*, periódico fundado por su padre. Opositor al gobierno, tuvo que refugiarse en Perú, donde fue redactor de *El Heraldo* y *Grand Journal du Perú*. Nuevamente en Veracruz fundó *El Ferrocarril*, que clausuró el comandante militar (1876). Fundó el periódico *El Pueblo*, que 10 días después también fue cerrado. Fue diputado (1877) y juez de distrito (1878), cargo al que renunció para reabrir *El Ferrocarril*. Dirigió el órgano socialista *La Comuna*, donde planteó la supresión del ejército e hizo una defensa de los comuneros de París de 1871 y definió al comunismo como el régimen "donde cada hombre tiene derecho a los dones de la naturaleza y de la sociedad, en proporción a sus necesidades, y cada individuo tiene el deber de concurrir al bienestar de sus semejantes en proporción a sus facultades". Fue también defensor de oficio de la comandancia militar y cónsul general en San Francisco. Participó, con Francisco I. Madero y Alberto Leduc, en el Congreso Nacional Espírita de 1906. Colaboró en *El 5 de Mayo de 1862*, la *Revista Azul* y *El Mundo Ilustrado*. Autor de las obras de teatro *Paula* (1870), *El expósito* (1874), *El esclavo* (1879) y *El conde de Villamediana* (1906); de las novelas *Remordimiento* (1881), *Oceánida* (1887) y *El teniente de los gavilanes* (1902); de los ensayos *Cartas sobre el comunismo* (1875), *El alcoholismo: sus causas, sus consecuencias, disposiciones penales, modo de combatirlo* (1884), *Los Estados Unidos Mexicanos, sus progresos en veinte años de paz, 1877-1897. Estudio histórico y estadístico fundado en los datos oficiales más recientes* (1897), *Avicultura práctica: apuntes sobre el origen de las aves de corral* (1897), *Les Etats-Unis Mexicains, leur ressources naturelles, leur situation actuelle* (1899), *Benito Juárez. Su vida. Su obra* (1906, primer premio del concurso del centenario del nacimiento de Benito Juárez), *Porfirio Díaz, la evolución de su vida* (1908), *El estado de Yucatán* (1908), *El caso México y la política del presidente Wilson* (1914), *La verdad sobre el 25 de junio. Apuntes para la historia* (1919) e *Historia de la reforma de México* (1926); y de los poemarios: *Tropicales* (1883), *Anacreonte* (1891), *Poemas sudras* (1903) y *Épicas* (1929). Usó los pseudónimos de *Anacreonte, Guarrete, Jamapa, Leporello, Liporello, Razay*, entre otros.

Zazueta Aguilar, Jesús Humberto ◆ n. en Costa Rica, Sinaloa (1956). Maestro normalista especializado en ciencias sociales por la Normal Superior de La Laguna, Durango. Afiliado al PRD desde 1989, ha sido miembro del Comité Ejecutivo Nacional de ese partido y diputado federal (1991-94).

Leopoldo Zea

Zea, Leopoldo ◆ n. en el DF (1912). Maestro (1943) y doctor en filosofía por la UNAM (1944), donde ha sido profesor (1942-), investigador (1954-65), secretario (1948-53), director de la Facultad de Filosofía y Letras (1966-70), director de Difusión Cultural (1970-73) y director del Centro Coordinador y Difusor de Estudios Latinoamericanos (1982-88). Director del IEPES del PRI (1959). Coeditor de *Tierra Nueva* (1940). Secretario de la Comisión Permanente del Consejo Consultivo de la UNESCO (1953-54), jefe de los departamentos de Cooperación Intelectual y de Estudios Universitarios de la SEP (1953-55), director general de Relaciones Culturales de la SRE (1960-66), director del Consejo Nacional de Difusión Cultural y presidente de la Conferencia Latinoamericana de Difusión Cultural y Extensión Universitaria (1972), coordinador de la Federación Internacional y de la Sociedad Latinoamericana de Estudios Sobre América Latina y el Caribe (1982), director de *Cuadernos Americanos* (1986-) y coordinador general de la Comisión Nacional Conmemorativa del quinto Centenario del Encuentro de Dos Mundos (1988-). Director de las revistas *Deslinde* y *Universidad de México*. Ha sido colaborador regular de *El Nacional, Novedades, Excélsior* y *El Día*. Autor de *El positivismo en México* (1943), *Apogeo y decadencia del positivismo en México* (1944), *En torno a una filosofía americana* (1947), *Dos etapas del pensamiento en Hispanoamérica* (1949), *Conciencia y posibilidad del mexicano* (1952), *América como conciencia* (1953), *La filosofía en México* (1955), *El pensamiento latinoamericano* (1965), *Filosofía de lo americano* (1983), *Ideas y presagios del descubrimiento de América* (antología, 1991) y otras obras. *Doctor honoris causa* por las universidades de París, Estatal de Moscú (1984), de Montevideo (1985), la UNAM y de La Habana (1997). Premio Nacional de Historia, Ciencias Sociales y Filosofía (1980) y Premio UNAM (1988).

Zea Arreguín, Agustín ◆ n. y m. en la ciudad de México (1886-1968). Se tituló como contador en la Escuela Superior de Comercio y Administración (1908). Profesor y director (1931-33) de la Facultad de Contaduría y Administración y profesor (1918-61) y director (1921-29) de la ESCA. Fue empleado del Banco Central, contador general de la pagaduría de Hacienda y auditor de los Ferrocarriles Nacionales de México, de bancos descentralizados y del gobierno federal. Autor de *Prácticas comerciales y administrativas*. Miembro fundador del Colegio de Contadores Públicos de México y del Instituto Mexicano de Contadores Públicos.

Zebadúa, Emilio ◆ n. en el DF (1961). Su segundo apellido es González. Licenciado en derecho por la UNAM (1984) y en economía por el ITAM (1984), maestro (1986) y doctor (1991) en ciencia política por la Universidad de Harvard. Investigador y profesor del Centro de Estudios Históricos de El Colegio de México (1992-96). Trabajó en la Oficina de Coordinación de la Presidencia de la República con Joseph-Marie Cordoba. Consejero ciudadano del Consejo General del IFE (1996-). Ha colaborado en *La Jornada* y *Expansión*. Fue coordinador de *El Financiero Internacional*. Autor de *El gran debate: Estados Unidos en el mundo contemporáneo* (1994), *Banqueros y revolucionarios: la soberanía financiera de México, 1914-1929* (1999) y *La política económica de México en el Congreso de la Unión (1970-1982)* (1999, con Leonardo Lomelí). Becario Full-

Emilio Zebadúa

bright-Citicorp (1984-86) y del ITAM (1979-83). Miembro del Sistema Nacional de Investigadores.

ZEDILLO PONCE DE LEÓN, ERNESTO ◆ n. en el DF (1951). Licenciado en economía por el IPN (1972) y maestro y doctor en economía por la Universidad de Yale (1978). Tomó cursos de evaluación de proyectos de inversión en capital humano en la Universidad de Bradford, Inglaterra (1973) y de economía en la Universidad de Colorado (1974). Profesor del IPN (1973-74 y 1978-80) y de El Colegio de México (1981-83). Afiliado al PRI desde 1971, colaboró en diversas comisiones del IEPES, fue coordinador de la campaña del candidato a la Presidencia de la República Luis Donaldo Colosio (1993-94) y candidato él mismo a la Presidencia de la República (1994). Ha sido investigador económico de la Dirección General de Programación Económica y Social de la Secretaría de la Presidencia (1971-74); economista (1978-82) y subgerente de Investigación Económica y Financiera (1982), director del Fideicomiso para la Cobertura de Riesgos Cambiarios, del Banco de México (1982-88), secretario de Programación y Presupuesto (1988-92), secretario de Educación Pública (1992-94) y presidente de la República elegido para el periodo 1994-2000. Pertenece al Colegio Nacional de Economistas. Fue presidente del Centro Latinoamericano de Administración para el Desarrollo.

ZEGBE SANEN, ALFONSO ◆ n. en Huauchinango, Pue. (1938). Licenciado en derecho por la UNAM (1961). Miembro del PRI. Secretario ejecutivo de la Copal (1980-86). En la CNOP fue secretario de Acción Política Juvenil (1961-62). En la Secretaría del Trabajo fue jefe de mesa de trabajo de la Oficina de

GABINETE DEL PRESIDENTE ERNESTO ZEDILLO PONCE DE LEÓN
1 de diciembre de 1994, en ejercicio

GOBERNACIÓN:	
ESTEBAN MOCTEZUMA BARRAGÁN	**1 de diciembre de 1994 a 28 junio de 1995**
EMILIO CHUAYFFET CHEMOR	**28 de junio de 1995 a enero de 1998**
FRANCISCO LABASTIDA OCHOA	**enero de 1998 a mayo de 1999**
DIÓDORO CARRASCO ALTAMIRANO	**mayo de 1999-**
RELACIONES EXTERIORES:	
JOSÉ ÁNGEL GURRÍA TREVIÑO	**1 de diciembre de 1994 a enero de 1998**
ROSARIO GREEN MACÍAS	**enero de 1998-**
DEFENSA NACIONAL:	
ENRIQUE CERVANTES AGUIRRE	**1 de diciembre de 1994-**
MARINA:	
JOSÉ RAMÓN LORENZO FRANCO	**1 de diciembre de 1994-**
HACIENDA Y CRÉDITO PÚBLICO:	
JAIME SERRA PUCHE	**1 al 29 de diciembre de 1994**
GUILLERMO ORTIZ MARTÍNEZ	**29 de diciembre de 1994 al 1 de enero de 1998**
JOSÉ ÁNGEL GURRÍA	**1 de enero de 1998-**
CONTRALORÍA Y DESARROLLO ADMINISTRATIVO:	
NORMA SAMANIEGO BREACH	**1 de diciembre de 1994 a diciembre de 1995**
ARSENIO FARELL CUBILLAS	**diciembre de 1995-**
ENERGÍA:	
JOSÉ IGNACIO PICHARDO PAGAZA	**1 de diciembre de 1994 a diciembre de 1995**
JESÚS REYES HEROLES	**diciembre de 1995 a octubre de 1997**
LUIS TÉLLEZ KUENZLER	**octubre de 1997-**
COMERCIO Y FOMENTO INDUSTRIAL:	
HERMINIO BLANCO MENDOZA	**1 de diciembre de 1994-**
AGRICULTURA Y GANADERÍA:	
ARTURO WARMAN GRYJ	**1 de diciembre de 1994 a enero de 1995**
FRANCISCO LABASTIDA OCHOA	**enero de 1995 a enero de 1998**
ROMÁRICO ARROYO MARROQUÍN	**enero de 1998-**
COMUNICACIONES Y TRANSPORTES:	
GUILLERMO ORTIZ MARTÍNEZ	**1 al 29 de diciembre de 1994**
CARLOS RUIZ SACRISTÁN	**29 de diciembre de 1994-**
DESARROLLO SOCIAL:	
CARLOS ROJAS GUTIÉRREZ	**diciembre de 1994 a mayo de 1998**
ESTEBAN MOCTEZUMA	**mayo de 1998 a agosto de 1999**
CARLOS JARQUE URIBE	**agosto de 1999-**
EDUCACIÓN PÚBLICA:	
FAUSTO ALZATI ARAIZA	**1 de diciembre de 1994 a enero de 1995**
MIGUEL LIMÓN ROJAS	**enero de 1995-**
SALUD:	
JUAN RAMÓN DE LA FUENTE	**1 de diciembre de 1994 al 17 de noviembre de 1999**
TRABAJO Y PREVISIÓN SOCIAL:	
SANTIAGO OÑATE LABORDE	**1 de diciembre de 1994 a agosto de 1995**
JAVIER BONILLA GARCÍA	**agosto de 1995 a mayo de 1998**
JOSÉ ANTONIO GONZÁLEZ FERNÁNDEZ	**mayo de 1998 a abril de 1999**
MARIANO PALACIOS ALCOCER	**abril de 1999-**
REFORMA AGRARIA:	
MIGUEL LIMÓN ROJAS	**1 de diciembre de 1994 a enero de 1995**
ARTURO WARMAN GRYJ	**enero de 1995 a abril de 1999**
EDUARDO ROBLEDO RINCÓN	**abril de 1999-**
TURISMO:	
SILVIA HERNÁNDEZ ENRÍQUEZ	**1 de diciembre de 1994 a diciembre de 1997**
ÓSCAR ESPINOSA VILLARREAL	**diciembre de 1997-**
MEDIO AMBIENTE, RECURSOS NATURALES Y PESCA:	
JULIA CARABIAS	**1 de diciembre de 1994-**
PROCURADURÍA GENERAL DE LA REPÚBLICA:	
ANTONIO LOZANO GRACIA	**1 de diciembre de 1994 a noviembre de 1996**
JORGE MADRAZO CUÉLLAR	**diciembre de 1996-**
DEPARTAMENTO DEL DISTRITO FEDERAL:	
ÓSCAR ESPINOSA VILLARREAL	**1 de diciembre de 1994 a noviembre de 1997**

Sanciones (1963), ayudante del titular (1963-64), comisionado para la integración de las comisiones regionales de los salarios mínimos (1963-64), secretario particular del oficial mayor (1965-70), jefe del Departamento de Investigaciones Industriales (1970) y del Departamento de Registro de Asociaciones (1977-78), subdirector de Registro de Asociaciones (1977-78) y asesor del subsecretario (1979). Secretario particular del director de Inversiones Públicas de la Secretaría de la Presidencia (1964-65), jefe del Departamento de Servicios Administrativos de la CFE (1971-74), coordinador de Prensa, Difusión y Relaciones Públicas del Indeco (1974-76), diputado federal (1979-82) y senador (1982-88). Miembro de la Academia Mexicana de Derecho del Trabajo y de la Academia Mexicana de Finanzas Públicas.

Zeevaert Wiechers, Leonardo ◆ n. en Veracruz, Ver. (1914). Ingeniero civil por la UNAM (1939). Hizo una especialidad en ingeniería estructural y obtuvo el grado de maestro en ingeniería civil en el Instituto Tecnológico de Massachusetts (1940). Fue investigador visitante de ingeniería estructural en la Universidad de Illinios, por la que obtuvo el grado de doctor en filosofía de la ingeniería civil. Diseñó y supervisó la cimentación de la Torre Latinoamericana, entre otros numerosos proyectos de ingeniería. También es autor de un método de construcción de edificios colgantes, que no necesitan columnas en el frente y permiten más flexibilidad arquitectónica en su diseño, e inventor del péndulo de torsión libre, aparato empleado para mediciones de ingeniería sísmica. Premio Universidad Nacional 1989.

Zehe, Alfred ◆ n. en Alemania (1939). Doctor en física y ciencias naturales. Profesor de la Universidad Carlos Marx de Leipzig. Ha publicado 190 trabajos de investigación, dirigido 11 tesis de doctorado y registrado 13 patentes. En 1976 llegó a México gracias a un programa de intercambio entre las universidades Autónoma de Puebla y Técnica de Dresden. Fue investigador titular del Instituto de Ciencias de la UAP (1976-80) y profesor visitante de la UAP y de la UAS (1980-83). En la UAP colaboró en el Departamento de Semiconductores y en la UAS contribuyó al establecimiento del Instituto de Investigaciones Metalúrgicas. En 1983 fue arrestado por el FBI en Boston, acusado de ser espía de la República Democrática de Alemania. De acuerdo con el periodista Miguel Ángel Granados Chapa, su captura obedeció, probablemente, a que en la UAS impulsó un proceso para separar el cobre del molibdeno, elemento de usos industriales y estratégicos de gran importancia. México vende al país del norte cobre en bruto que contiene 23 por ciento de molibdeno, más valioso que el resto del metal. Premio Nacional de Ciencia y Tecnología de la RDA (1973). *Doctor honoris causa* por la UAP (1980).

Zelaya Alger, Alfonso ◆ n. en Torreón, Coah., y m. Chihuahua, Chih. (1936-1994). Su nombre era Alfonso Guillén Zelaya Alger. En su infancia vivió en Ciudad Juárez. Militante de la Juventud Socialista del Partido Popular, en 1955 abandonó sus estudios en la vocacional del IPN para unirse al Movimiento 26 de Julio, dirigido por Fidel Castro. Aún en México, fue detenido y torturado en junio de 1956. En noviembre se embarcó en el *Granma* e inició, con Fidel Castro, la revolución cubana. Fue aprehendido en el combate de Alegría de Pío y deportado a México. Al triunfo de la revolución se estableció en La Habana, donde se le conocía como el *Comandante Zelaya*. Fue miembro del comité central del Partido Comunista Cubano y comandante de las fuerzas armadas de ese país, así como vicepresidente del Instituto Cubano de Amistad con los Pueblos. Al morir era presidente de la Asociación de Educadores Latinoamericanos y del Caribe.

Zelaya Alger, Héctor Alejandro ◆ n. en el DF y m. en Nicaragua (1937-1960). Hermano del anterior. Incorporado al Frente de Liberación Sandinista, fue muerto en combate contra las fuerzas somocistas en El Dorado, Las Segovias.

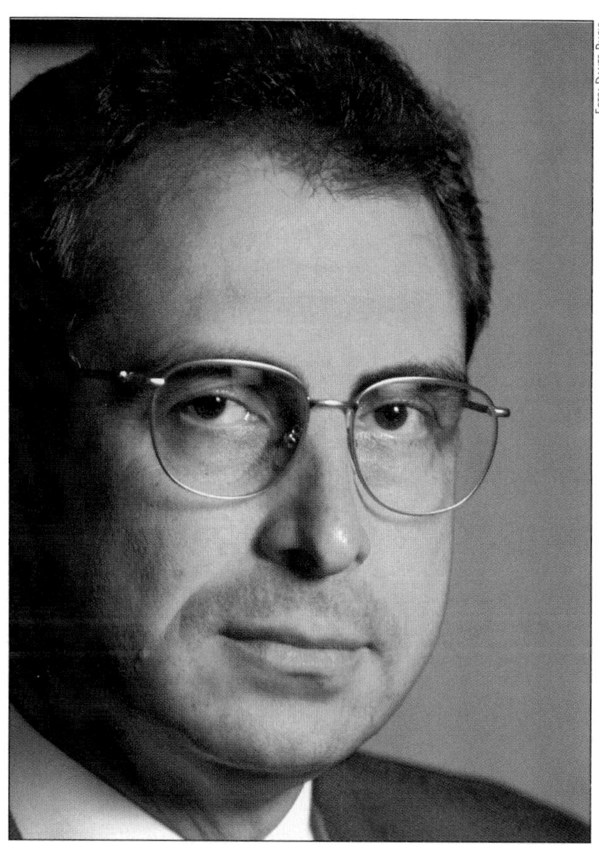
Foto: Dante Bucio

Ernesto Zedillo Ponce de León

Zelis, Rafael de ◆ n. en Veracruz, Ver., y m. en Italia (1747-1798). Ingresó en 1765 a la Compañía de Jesús y debió salir de la Nueva España en 1767. Radicó en Bolonia, donde fue secularizado antes de la extinción de la Compañía. Autor de *Viajes en su destierro* y *Catálogo de los sugetos de la Compañía de Jesús que formaban la Provincia de México el día del arresto, 25 de junio de 1767* (1871).

Zempoala, de ◆ Lagunas de los Estados de México y Morelos, localizadas en la vertiente sur de la sierra del Ajusco, al noroeste de Cuernavaca. Se formaron en varios cráteres volcánicos, a 2,900 metros sobre el nivel del mar. Son, de este a oeste: Zempoala, Compila, Tonatihua, Seca, Ocoyotongo, Quila y Hueyapan. Esta última abastece de agua potable a las poblaciones de Huitzilac y Coajomulco.

Zempoala ◆ Municipio de Hidalgo situado en el sur del Estado, al sur de Pachuca, en los límites con el Estado de México. Superficie: 305.80 km^2. Habi-

Lagunas de Zempoala

tantes: 23,148, de los cuales 5,915 forman la población económicamente activa. Hablan alguna lengua indígena 61 personas mayores de cinco años (náhuatl 30). Fue evangelizado por los franciscanos, quienes en 1585 terminaron la construcción de su convento, secularizado a mediados del siglo XVIII. Miembros de la misma orden construyeron también un acueducto, en el siglo XVI, obra dirigida por Francisco Tembleque.

ZEMPOALA, CONGREGACIÓN DE ◆ ☛ *Úrsulo Galván*, municipio de Veracruz.

ZENDEJAS, FRANCISCO ◆ n. y m. en el DF (1917-1985). Escritor. Su segundo apellido era Gómez. Estudió economía en la UNAM y en las universidades de Washington y Columbia. Fue profesor de idiomas en secundarias nocturnas de la SEP, secretario particular del secretario del Trabajo (1943), jefe del Departamento de Publicidad y Espectáculos del INBA (1943), editor del primer número de la revista *Artes de México*, representante de México en Londres en el primer Congreso de Salud Mental (1947), conductor de programas sobre libros en las estaciones XEQ, XEW (1947), XELA (1960-72) y Radio Universidad (1972-84). Dirigió las galerías *Excélsior*. Fundó el Premio Hispanoamericano Xavier Villaurrutia (1955), del que fue vocal ejecutivo, y en 1972 la Sociedad Alfonsina Internacional y el Premio Internacional Alfonso Reyes. Colaboró en *Letras de México, El Hijo Pródigo, Cuadernos Americanos, Las Moradas* (Perú) y *Cuadernos* (Francia), *Revista Mexicana de Cultura* de *El Nacional* (1937-40), *Novedades, Hoy* y *Excélsior* (1955-85, con la columna "Multilibros"). Fue editor de las revistas literarias *Prometeus* (1949) y *El Pan Duro* (1969). Autor de *Novelas cortas y cuentos dialogados* (1966), *Hacia décima flor* (poesía, 1966), *La pasión de Pasternak* (ensayo, 1968) y las obras de teatro *Cuando el príncipe muere, ¡Jerónimo!* y *La hoz o el martillo*.

Herencia, óleo sobre tabla de Nahum B. Zenil

ZENDEJAS GÓMEZ, ADELINA ◆ n. y m. en el DF (1909-1993). Licenciada en letras y maestra en ciencias de la educación y en historia por la UNAM. Fue profesora en diversas escuelas secundarias y preparatorias, colaboradora de *El Universal Gráfico* (1925), *El Nacional, El Universal, Excélsior, El Popular, El Día* (donde publicó la columna "Ellas y la vida"), *Tiempo, Revista de Revistas, Ferronales, Magisterio* y *La Maestra*; directora del boletín *Servicios Sociales* de la Secretaría de Hacienda, miembro de la Comisión Redactora de los Programas de Civismo e Historia de México para secundaria; directora de la Escuela Taller para Obreras y Empleadas de Extensión Universitaria, delegada a la primera Conferencia Mundial de Trabajadoras (1956) en Budapest; presidenta del Instituto de Amistad e Intercambio Cultural México-URSS (1964-74), coordinadora de Organizaciones e Instituciones Progresistas durante el Año Internacional de la Mujer (1975), comentarista del noticiero *Enlace* del Canal 11 (1981-82) y redactora de la columna "Binomio", en *Excélsior* (1983-93). Autora de *Habitación: delincuencia infantil y juvenil, la crisis de la educación en México, La mujer en la intervención francesa, Las luchas de la mujer mexicana (de 1776 a 1975)* y *Frida Kahlo en la preparatoria*. Fundadora y dirigente del Frente Único pro Derechos de la Mujer. Medalla de Veteranas de la Unión de Sociedades de Amistad e Intercambio Cultural con los pueblos de la URSS (1975), medalla de Caballero de la Amistad del Soviet Supremo (1982) y Premio Nacional de Periodismo (1988).

ZENDEJAS DE LA PEÑA, MIGUEL JERÓNIMO ◆ ¿n.? y m. en Puebla, Pue. (1724-1815). Pintor, discípulo de Pablo Talavera y Joaquín Magún y protegido del obispo Antonio Joaquín Pérez. Autor de los murales de la iglesia de San Marcos, en Puebla (destruida en 1863 por las tropas invasoras francesas), los cuatro lienzos murales del Santuario de la Virgen de los Dolores de Acatzingo (*Calle de la Amargura, Los apóstoles dando el pésame a la virgen, El descendimiento y la piedad* y *La crucifixión* 1775-78), *La oración del huerto* (1815, en el Sagrario de Puebla), *San Juan Nepomuceno, Episodios de la vida de San Felipe Neri*, en el templo de la Concordia; numerosas pinturas en la catedral y en las iglesias de San José, El Carmen, el Sagrario, San Juan de Dios y Santa Rosa. En el Museo Nacional de Historia se conserva, de él, la decoración de una botica, fechada en 1797.

ZENIL, NAHUM BERNABÉ ◆ n. en Chicontepec, Ver. (1947). Artista plastico profesor titulado en la Escuela Nacional de Maestros (1964) y pintor egresado de La Esmeralda (1972). Ha expuesto su obra desde 1971 en México, Estados Unidos, Cuba, Francia, Brasil, Ecuador, Venezuela, Inglaterra, Canadá y Suecia. Ha montado 17 exposiciones individuales desde 1974, entre las que destacan *Del circo y sus alrededores* en la Galería de Arte Mexicano (1994) y *El gran circo del mundo* en el MAM (1999). Cofundador del Grupo 72, con Ramón Martínez Villar, Miguel Ángel Ramírez, Eduardo Serrano Pérez, María Antonieta Tovar y Víctor Manuel Vázquez. Desde 1997 pertenece al Sistema Nacional de Creadores. Mención honorífica del Concurso Nuevos Valores del Salón de la Plástica Mexicana en 1976. Segundo lugar en el concurso La Plástica en la Seguridad Social del ISSSTE de 1976. Premio de adquisición, Sección de pintura, del Salón Nacional de Artes Plásticas del INBA (1980 y 1982). Mención honorífica en el concurso Imágenes Guadalupanas del Centro Cultural Arte Contemporáneo de 1987.

ZENKER HACKETT, ALEJANDRO ◆ n. en el DF (1955). Traductor. Estudió en la Fachoberschule für Sozialpadagogik, de Colonia (1977), y en el Programa para la Formación de Traductores, de El Colegio de México (1980). Ha sido traductor independiente (1978-), asesor editorial del IEPES del PRI, (1981); asesor editorial, coordinador de actividades socioculturales y editor del *Boletín* del Centro de Lenguas Extranjeras de la UNAM (1982); director general de las revistas *El Traductor* y *Reflexiones*, de la Asociación de Traductores Profesionales (1982); director de Difusión Cultural y asesor académico de la Dirección General del Instituto Superior de Intérpretes y Traductores (1982-83), director general y editor de *Gaceta, panorama de la traducción e interpretación en México*, del Instituto Superior de Intérpretes y Traductores (1982-86) y director general del Instituto Superior de Intérpretes y Traductores (1983-86). En 1999 dirigía la editorial Minimalia. Ha colaborado en la *Revista de Bellas Artes*. Presidente fundador de la Asociación de Traductores Profesionales (1980-86) y secretario general y cofundador de la Sociedad Iberoamericana de Estudios Sobre la Traducción (1982-86). Miembro de la Federación Internacional de Traductores, donde ha sido integrante de varios comités y corresponsal de la revista *Babel* (1984-1987).

ZENTENO BUJÁIDAR, FRANCISCO ◆ n. en Puebla, Pue. (1933). Pintor egresado en 1954 de la Real Academia de Bellas Artes de San Fernando, en Madrid. En Guadalajara, España, participó en la decoración mural del templo de Alarilla, bajo la dirección de Carlos P. de Lara, y colaboró con ilustraciones para el *Correo Literario*. Regresó a México en 1954. Realizó un mural en el Centro Cultural de Puebla (1955) y un fresco en el templo de Cristo Rey, de Uruapan (1958). En 1970 fundó el Comité Nacional Mexicano de la Asociación Internacional de Artes Plásticas de la UNESCO. Por su iniciativa se creó el Museo de Arte Mexicano de Plovdiv, Bulgaria (1981). Fue colaborador de la revista *Visión* (1971- 81).

ZENTLA ◆ Municipio de Veracruz situado al noreste de Córdoba y contiguo a Huatusco, cerca de Puebla. Superficie: 241 km^2. Habitantes: 11,562, de los cuales 3,386 forman la población económicamente activa. La cabecera, del mismo nombre, fue fundada entre 1882 y 1884 por inmigrantes italianos que la llamaron Colonia Manuel González.

ZEPEDA, CRISTINA ◆ n. en Querétaro, Qro. (1949). Pintora, actriz y dramaturga. Ha actuado en unas 40 obras, dirigido alrededor de 15 y diseñado escenografía y vestuario para 20. Autora de las obras de teatro *Lunarcito, el elefante* (1980), *El mantelito mágico* (1984), *Mariana mañana* (1985) y *La visita de Unic* (1986).

ZEPEDA, DANIEL A. ◆ n. en San Cristóbal de Las Casas y m. en Tuxtla Gutiérrez, Chis. (1856-1941). Abogado (1881). Ocupó diversos puestos judiciales en Chiapas. Fue juez de distrito en Salina Cruz, Veracruz y Zacatecas, diputado al Congreso Constituyente de 1916-17, magistrado (1931-37) y defensor de oficio del Tribunal Superior de Justicia de Chiapas (1938). Autor de *El caballo de la molendera, cuento tradicional de Chiapas* (1910) y *Cuentos regionales del estado de Chiapas* (1926).

ZEPEDA, ERACLIO ◆ n. en Tuxtla Gutiérrez, Chis. (1937). Escritor. Cursó el bachillerato en la Universidad Militar Latinoamericana. Estudió antropología social en la Universidad Veracruzana (1962), donde fue profesor (1958-60). También ejerció la docencia en instituciones de Cuba, China, la URSS y EUA. Participó en un movimiento contra el gobernador de Chiapas, Efraín Aranda Osorio (1955-56), quien aplicó el delito de disolución social por primera vez en el estado. Militó en el Partido Obrero Campesino (1958-59) y en PCM (1960-81), del que fue miembro del Comité Central y de la Comisión Política, corresponsal en Moscú del órgano *La Voz de México*. Al ocurrir el ataque estadounidense a Playa Girón (1961), fue oficial de milicias en Cuba. Cofundador y miembro del Comité Central del PSUM (1981-87). Cofundador del PMS (1987-89), por el que fue precandidato a la Presidencia y candidato a senador por Chiapas. Cofundador del PRD (1989-94). En la Conasupo (1967) fundó el Teatro de Orientación Campesina, produjo la radionovela *San Martín de la Piedra* y fundó el periódico mural *El Correo Campesino*. Cofundador de la Dirección de Cultura del gobierno del estado de Chiapas (1977), director nacional de Promoción Cultural y asesor del director general del Fonapas (1978-79), asesor del subsecretario de Cultura y miembro del consejo editorial de la SEP (1982-84) y diputado federal (1985-88). En 1994 fue miembro de la Comisión Especial Autónoma para el conflicto en Chiapas, de la presidencia de la Convención Nacional Democrática y de la Conai. Fue secretario general de gobierno en Chiapas (1994-97). Es miembro fundador y directivo del Partido de la Democracia Social. Ha participado como actor en las películas *Reed, México insurgente* y *Campanas rojas*, *El norte*, *Figuras de la pasión*, y *Mañana de cobre*. Ha sido comentarista de Canal 13 y Radio Educación. Grabó un disco para la colección *Voz Viva de México*, de la UNAM. Formó parte del grupo La Espiga Amotinada (☛). Coautor de los poemarios *La espiga amotinada* (1960) y *Ocupación de la palabra* (1965); y de *Tres cuentos* (1960). Autor de los volúmenes de cuento *Benzulul* (1959), *Trejito* (1967), *Asalto nocturno* (1974, Premio Nacional de Cuento), *El caguamo* (1980), *Andando el tiempo* (1982, Premio Xavier Villaurrutia) y *Ratón que vuelve* (infantil, 1991); de la obra de teatro *El tiempo de agua* (1960) y de los poemarios *Compañía de combate* (1961), *Asela* (1962), *Elegía a Rubén Jaramillo* (1963) y *Relación de travesía* (1985). Premio Chiapas (1983).

FOTO: REFORMA

Eraclio Zepeda

ZEPEDA, MASHA ◆ n. en Moscú, Rusia (1964). Hija del anterior. Pintora.

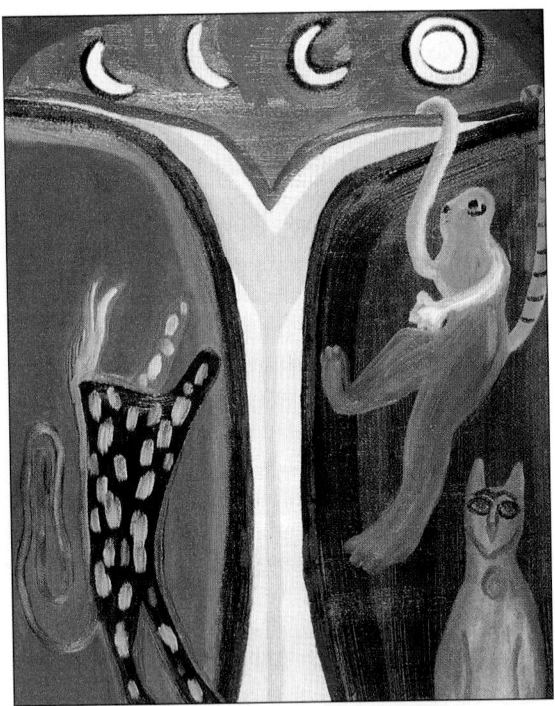

Tres personajes con eclipse de luna, óleo sobre tela de Masha Zepeda

Estudió en la ENAP de la UNAM. Reportera del programa *Pampa Pipiltzin* (1974-76) y productora de *A capa y espada* (1981-82) de Canal 13. Dirigió la biblioteca infantil del Parque España de la SEP en la ciudad de México. Curadora del Museo Carrillo Gil (1986-88) y directora del Instituto de Artes Gráficas de Oaxaca (1988-90). Fundadora del programa *Aprendiendo a través del Arte* para México. Coordinadora de los talleres de artes plásticas para niños de escasos recursos del programa *La calle es de todos* del Instituto de Cultura de la Ciudad de México. Ha participado en más de 70 muestras colectivas y 10 exposiciones individuales desde 1985. Como ilustradora ha colaborado en varias revistas y en el libro *Tiempo de adivinar*. Autora de *Artistas plásticos de Chiapas* (1999). Su obra forma parte del acervo del Instituto de Artes Gráficas de Oaxaca, del Museo Nacional de la Estampa, Pinacoteca 2000, Banco Internacional, revista *Época* y TV Azteca. Becaria del Fonca (1991-92 y 1994-95).

La boda, obra dirigida por Raúl Zermeño

Zepeda Méndez, Juventino Borrao ◆ n. y m. en Monterrey, NL (1919-1996). Ciclista. Fue el máximo ganador de la competencia Clásica de la Constitución, donde sus *fugas* se hicieron famosas. También ganó la Vuelta García Valseca. Haciendo equipo con Joaquín Martínez, Julio Zepeda, Simón Sánchez y Alfonso *Pelón* Salinas ganó el título del mejor equipo en la última vuelta del Centro de la República. Tras su retiro vendía bicicletas.

Zepeda Bermúdez, Pedro Pablo ◆ n. en San Cristóbal de Las Casas, Chis. (1952). Contador Privado por la Escuela Técnica Industrial Comercial y Vocacional 28 y economista por la Universidad Anáhuac. Ha sido asesor de la SPP (1975-1976), subdirector del Sector Agropecuario (1976-1978), director general del Patronato Nacional de Promotores Voluntarios (1978-1979), diputado federal (1979-1982), asesor del Secretario del Trabajo y Previsión Social (1982), y colaborador del secretariado de gabinetes de la Presidencia (1983). Ha ocupado cargos en Banca Cremi (1983-1989), en el Banco Internacional (1989-1992) y en las nueve empresas de Servicios Portuarios de Puertos Mexicanos (1992-1996). Coordinador general de Puertos y Marina Mercante (1996-).

Zepeda Patterson, Jorge ◆ n. en Mazatlán, Sin. (1952). Periodista. Licenciado en economía por la Universidad de Guadalajara y maestro en sociología por la Facultad Latinoamericana de Ciencias Sociales del DF. Ha hecho estudios de doctorado en ciencias políticas en la Universidad de París. Fundador y director del periódico *Siglo XXI* (1989), ganador de los premios de Periodismo Iberoamericano Rey de España, José Martí de Cuba y Nacional de Periodismo, entre otros. En 1997 fundó y dirigió el diario *Público*. Columnista político, colaborador de *Expansión* y de *Detrás de la noticia*, coordinador de proyectos editoriales de la Asociación de Editores de los Estados y presidente de la Sociedad de Periodistas. También ha sido investigador de tiempo completo en la Universidad Nicolaíta (1982-85) y El Colegio de Michoacán (1985-89). Autor de *Economía y poder en Michoacán* y *Las sociedades rurales hoy*. Premio María Moors Cabot, por sus contribuciones al desarrollo del periodismo en México, otorgado por la Universidad de Columbia (1999).

Zerecero, Anastasio ◆ n. y m. en la ciudad de México (1799-1875). Se tituló de abogado en 1821. En ese año se adhirió al Plan de Iguala y entró en la ciudad de México con el ejército trigarante. Fue diputado al Congreso General (1822) y estuvo en la cárcel al disolver Iturbide la asamblea. A la caída del imperio participó como federalista y yorkino. Partidario de Vicente Guerrero fue, junto con Lorenzo de Zavala, uno de los promotores de la rebelión de la Acordada. En 1847 se alistó en la Guardia Nacional para combatir la invasión estadounidense. Se adhirió al Plan de Ayutla en 1854, peleó al lado de los liberales en la guerra de los Tres Años y combatió la intervención francesa y el imperio de Maximiliano. Al triunfo de la República fue juez de lo civil en México, decano del Colegio de Abogados y magistrado del Tribunal Supremo de Justicia del Distrito Federal. Autor de *Observaciones del ciudadano Anastasio Zerecero a la Constitución* (1857), *Benito Juárez* (1866) y *Memorias para la historia de las revoluciones en México* (1869).

Zermeño, Raúl ◆ n. en el DF (1940). Director teatral. Su segundo apellido es Saucedo. Realizó estudios en la Escuela de Arte Teatral del INBA y es maestro en realización cinematográfica por la Escuela Superior de Cine, Teatro y Televisión de Polonia (1974). Profesor fundador y director (1976-84) de la Facultad de Teatro de la Universidad Veracruzana, director fundador de la

Compañía Titular de Teatro (1975-77). Profesor de la Escuela de Arte Teatral (1975-77), del CUEC (1971-72) y director del CUT (1989-) de la UNAM. Dirige la revista *Repertorio* (1987-) de la Universidad Autónoma de Querétaro. Como actor, participó en *Arpa de pasto*, *La comedia de las equivocaciones*, *Los cuervos están de luto* y *La excepción y la regla*, entre otras. Ha dirigido *Collage* (1964), *Antes del desayuno*, *Tartufo* (1965), *Las brujas de Salem* (1976), *La boda* (1980), *El orden de los factores* (1983), *Los cabellos de Absalón* (1983), *Martha la piadosa* (1986), *Historia de un anillo* (1987) y *El anzuelo de Fenisa* (1991), entre otras. Dirigió las películas *Mea culpa* (premio en el Festival de Oberhausen, 1960), *Media vuelta* (premio a la mejor ficción en Varsovia, 1970). Premio Nacional de Teatro en Kalisz por *La ópera de los tres centavos* (1974, en Polonia) y premio al segundo mejor espectáculo televisivo por *Los albañiles*. Premio de la Unión de Cronistas y Críticos de Teatro al mejor espectáculo de provincia y el de la Asociación Mexicana de Cronistas de Teatro como director revelación por *La boda* (1980). Premio a la Mejor Dirección Profesional (1983) y seis premios por *Marta la piadosa* (1986), del Festival del Siglo de Oro en Chamizal.

Zermeño Araico, Manuel ◆ n. y m. en el DF (1901-1986). Egresado de la Escuela Naval Militar. Combatió contra los delahuertistas en Tabasco y Campeche (1923), fue comandante interino y pagador en Guaymas (1927), comandante del buque *Acapulco* (1928), perito balista en Veracruz (1933), ayudante de Lázaro Cárdenas (1935), agregado naval en Washington (1939) y director de la Escuela Naval Militar (1944). Recibió despacho de vicealmirante en 1950. Fue enviado extraordinario y ministro plenipotenciario en Noruega (1951) y secretario de Marina (del 1 de diciembre de 1958 al 30 de noviembre de 1964) en el gabinete de Adolfo López Mateos. Militó después en el PARM.

Zermeño Infante, Jorge ◆ n. en el DF (1949). Licenciado en derecho por la UIA. Afiliado al PAN desde 1968, donde ha sido secretario de Organización del Comité Regional del Estado de México (1973-74), secretario del Comité Municipal de Torreón, Coah. (1977-80), consejero estatal en Coahuila (1979-91), presidente del Comité Directivo Municipal de Torreón, Coah. (1982-84 y 1988-91), presidente del Comité Directivo Estatal de Coahuila (1984-85), consejero nacional (1984-) y diputado federal (1991-94).

Zertuche Muñoz, Fernando ◆ n. en el DF (1936). Licenciado en derecho por la UNAM (1959). Tomó cursos de historia en El Colegio de México. Profesor de la Universidad Femenina de México (1957-58) y de la UNAM (1962-64 y 1969-70), así como investigador en El Colegio de México (1959-60). Miembro del PRI, en el que fue director del Fondo para la Historia de las Ideas Revolucionarias en México (1976-78). Abogado y jefe del Departamento de Relaciones de Trabajo de Teléfonos de México (1961-66), prosecretario general del Consejo Técnico del IMSS (1966-70), oficial mayor (1970-74) y presidente de la Junta Federal de Conciliación y Arbitraje (1974-76); secretario general del IMSS (1976-82), subsecretario de Trabajo y Previsión Social (1982-85), director general del Instituto Nacional de Educación para Adultos (1985-89), secretario del Consejo de la Crónica de la Ciudad de México (1989-91), subdirector general de Promoción Nacional y Conservación del Patrimonio del INBA (1991-) y secretario ejecutivo del IFE (1998-). Editor de *El territorio mexicano* (2 t., 1982) y coordinador de *Muerte del presidente Juárez* (1971). Coautor de *Fuentes de la historia contemporánea de México* (1965-67). Autor de *La primera presidencia de Benito Juárez* (1971-72), *Si el tiempo te consulta. Palabras sobre Benito Juárez* (1981), *Historia y justicia social* (1987) y *Francisco J. Mújica* (1987), así como del prólogo y selección de *Luis Cabrera: una visión de México* (1988).

Zetina, Carlos B. ◆ n. en San Andrés Chalchicomula, Pue., y m. en el DF (1864-1927). Fundador de la fábrica de zapatos Excélsior. Fue diputado federal (1911-13), presidente del Ayuntamiento de la ciudad de México (1918), senador por Puebla y, en 1923, candidato presidencial. Fue, asimismo, fundador del pueblo Guadalupe Victoria, en el municipio de Chalchicomula.

Zevada, Ricardo J. ◆ n. y m. en el DF (1904-1979). Minero en su juventud. Se tituló como tenedor de libros y tomó cursos en la Facultad de Altos Estudios. Licenciado por la Escuela Nacional de Jurisprudencia (1925), de la que fue profesor (1927-34). Fue jefe de abogados del Comité Liquidador de los Antiguos Bancos de Emisión (1930), jefe del Departamento Legal del Banco Nacional Hipotecario Urbano y de Obras Públicas (1933), director general de Crédito de la Secretaría de Hacienda (1934), consejero de la embajada mexicana en Inglaterra (1936), miembro de las Juntas Directivas Londinenses del Ferrocarril Mexicano, del Interoceánico y de la Terminal de Veracruz; jefe del Departamento de Crédito del Banco Ejidal (1937), vocal ejecutivo del Comité Regulador del Mercado de las Subsistencias (1938-40), fundador y director del Banco del Ahorro Nacional (1942-58 y 1965) y director general del Banco Nacional de Comercio Exterior (1958-65). Redactor del periódico *Combate* (1941), órgano de la Liga de Acción Política (1941-47). Autor de *Pensamiento político de Ponciano Arriaga*, *La lucha por la libertad en el Congreso Constituyente de 1857* y *Calles, el presidente*. Tesorero del Patronato del Centro de Estudios Avanzados y de la Investigación Científica del IPN, patrono del Instituto Nacional de Astrofísica, Óptica y Electrónica, así como consejero o director de las empresas Sky-Line, Alkamex, Rigar, Síntesis Orgánicas, Derivados Maleicos, Industrias Derivadas del Etileno, Inmuebles Tlalpan, Casas América, Inmuebles de la Ciudad de México, Azucarera del Río Guayalejo, Azucarera de Los Mochis, Mexicana de Seguros La Equitativa e Impulsora Minera de Angangueo. Fundador del Fondo para la Donación Bibliotecaria

FOTO: REFORMA

Fernando Zertuche Muñoz

Narciso Bassols (1975) y del Fondo de Estudios e Investigaciones que lleva su nombre (1979).

ZIEROLD, PABLO ◆ n. en Alemania y m. en el DF (1864-1938). Llegó a México en 1888. Fue trabajador de la casa Levien, donde llegó a ser jefe de taller. Por sus ideas políticas fue echado de esa empresa y se dedicó a la afinación de pianos. En hojas sueltas difundía traducciones de los socialistas europeos y mantenía correspondencia con Bebel, Liebknecht y Rosa Luxemburgo. Realizó trabajo sindical con los obreros de la cervecería de Toluca. Cofundador del Partido Socialista Obrero (20 de agosto de 1911), junto con Adolfo Santibáñez, José R. Rojo, Fredesvino E. Alonso, Enrique Erding, Jesús M. González, Juan Humblot, Emilio V. Rojo, Luis A. Rojo, Alberto Galván, Enrique Quintanar y Zenaido Cárdenas. En los años treinta fundó, con otros alemanes, la Liga pro Cultura Alemana, de carácter antifascista. Escribió para *El Socialista*, órgano del Partido Socialista Obrero, y para *El Machete*. Tradujo *El ABC del socialismo*, de H.P. Meyer, y *¿Por qué los trabajadores deben ser socialistas?*, de H.G. Wilshire. Autor de *Plática entre el Popocatépetl y el Ixtaccíhuatl*. Su archivo fue legado al Partido Comunista Mexicano, de donde desapareció luego de un allanamiento policiaco. De él dijo Gastón García Cantú que "en una labor ejemplar y sostenida había logrado, a través del Partido Socialista Obrero y del periódico *El Socialista*, establecer un puente entre las tradiciones de finales del siglo XIX y las luchas sociales previas a la Constitución de 1917".

ZIHUATANEJO ◆ Bahía de Guerrero situada en el litoral del océano Pacífico. Está limitada al sur por la punta Descanso. Frente a la entrada se localiza el islote Roca Negra o Solitaria. En el fondo de la bahía está el puerto del mismo nombre.

ZIHUATANEJO ◆ Cabecera del municipio de José Azueta, Guerrero (☛). Con la población e isla de Ixtapa forma uno de los más importantes complejos turísticos del país.

ZIHUATEUTLA ◆ Municipio de Puebla situado en el norte del estado, al noreste de Huauchinango, en los límites con Veracruz. Superficie: 177.33 km². Habitantes: 10,983, de los cuales 3,034 forman la población económicamente activa. Hablan alguna lengua indígena 3,700 personas mayores de cinco años (totonaco 2,062 y náhuatl 1,538).

Vista panorámica de Zihuatanejo, Guerrero

FOTO: MICHAEL CALDERWOOD

ZIMAPÁN ◆ Municipio de Hidalgo situado al noroeste de Ixmiquilpan, en los límites con Querétaro. Superficie: 860.90 km². Habitantes: 38,412, de los cuales 7,374 forman la población económicamente activa. Hablan alguna lengua indígena 4,383 personas mayores de cinco años (otomí 4,267 y náhuatl 116). Indígenas monolingües: 54 personas. Sus yacimientos de plomo, plata, cinc y cobre fueron explotados desde el siglo XVI hasta 1840. La región fue evangelizada por los franciscanos, primero, y por agustinos, después, y pasó al clero secular en 1729. Una iglesia construida en el siglo XVI por los agustinos fue destruida en el siglo XVII.

ZIMAPÁN, DE ◆ Sierra de Hidalgo situada en el noroeste del estado, al sur del río Moctezuma, al oeste del Amajac, al noroeste de la sierra de Pachuca y al norte del río Tula. Es una de las estribaciones de la sierra Madre Oriental. Su parte oriental está formada, a su vez, por las sierras de la Bonanza, la Pechuga y Cardonal.

ZIMATLÁN ◆ Río de Oaxaca que nace en la vertiente sur de la sierra de Miahuatlán; corre de norte a sur hasta desembocar en el océano Pacífico, en la barra de su nombre, al este-noreste de Puerto Ángel. Tiene una longitud de 50 kilómetros.

ZIMATLÁN DE ÁLVAREZ ◆ Municipio de Oaxaca situado al norte de Ejutla y al sur de la capital del estado. Superficie: 255.16 km². Habitantes: 16,311, de los cuales 3,974 forman la población económicamente activa. Hablan alguna lengua indígena 570 personas mayores de cinco años (zapoteco 520 y mixteco 20). Activo centro comercial, produce mezcal, maderas, cerámica y tejidos. Como principal atractivo turístico cuenta con las grutas de granito en San Pedro Totomachapan, que constan de varias galerías con estalactitas y estalagmitas. Una de ellas que, según la imaginación popular semejaba un demonio, fue destruida para evitar prácticas supersticiosas.

ZIMBABWE, REPÚBLICA DE ◆ Nación del sur de África. Limita al norte con

Zambia, al este con Mozambique, al sur con Sudáfrica, y al suroeste y oeste con Botswana. Superficie: 390,580 km². Habitantes: 11,377,000 (1998). La capital es Harare, antes Salisbury (con 1,184,169 habitantes en 1992). La moneda es el dólar de Zimbabwe. Su idioma oficial es el inglés y se emplean comúnmente lenguas bantúes. *Historia*: los habitantes originales del territorio del actual Zimbabwe fueron los bosquimanos. Entre los siglos I y V de nuestra era ocurrió la inmigración de la etnia bantú, poseedora ya de ciertas técnicas agrícolas, mineras y metalúrgicas, quienes establecieron numerosos asentamientos en la cuenca del río Zambeze, se fusionaron con los bosquimanos y dieron origen al Estado Karanga. Los nuevos pobladores de la región descubrieron yacimientos de oro, cobre y estaño, con lo que desarrollaron la orfebrería. Hacia el siglo VIII, cuando los árabes fundaron el puerto de Sofala (en el actual Mozambique), el Estado karanga tuvo una salida directa para su producción metalúrgica. El monomotapa (rey de los karanga) sometió a los musulmanes, como ya había hecho con otros pueblos menores del área, y logró la hegemonía sobre una región que comprendía partes de Malawi (el entonces reino de Kitwara), Mozambique y la mayor parte del ahora Zimbabwe. En el siglo X, el Estado Karanga inició la construcción de las grandes ciudades amuralladas de Khami, Naletali, Dhlo-Dhlo, Mapungubwe y Gran Zimbabwe, cuyas ruinas descubrieron los portugueses hacia el siglo XVI. A mediados del siglo XV, al agotarse las minas de sal de la región, los karangas se desplazaron al norte. En esa época los rotsi, pueblo del sur perteneciente al mismo grupo shona que los karanga, desplazaron a éstos hacia el norte y hacia la costa y ocuparon el territorio. Cuando los portugueses llegaron a la región, a principios del siglo XVI, y destruyeron los puertos de Sofala y de la isla de Mozambique, el antiguo Estado karanga era un pequeño reino que necesitó la protección europea para sobrevivir. En la ciudadela y el palacio de Gran Zimbabwe habitaban entonces los rotsi, cuyo changamira (rey) había extendido su dominio sobre la región minera, aunque sin llegar a controlar un área tan vasta como los antiguos karanga. Entre 1834 y 1838, los zulúes, procedentes del Natal, asolaron la región. Los rotsi fueron expulsados hacia el oeste, y la ciudad monumental de Gran Zimbabwe decayó completamente. En la primera mitad del siglo XIX el territorio estaba dividido entre los pueblos shonas, que ocupaban la región noreste, y el reino zulú de Matabele, que ocupaba el suroeste. En 1888, el gobierno inglés declaró zona de influencia británica a la región comprendida entre Bechuanalandia y el río Zambeze; simultáneamente, Charles Rudd, agente del empresario inglés Cecil Rhodes, obtuvo del jefe matabela Lobenguela las concesiones mineras de su territorio. En 1889, un real privilegio concedió el gobierno de la zona a la British South Africa Company, propiedad de Rhodes, que inició la ocupación en 1890, facilitando tierras a los colonizadores europeos, quienes fundaron Salisbury, su capital. Gran parte de la población negra fue privada de sus tierras y confinada en reservas o condenada a la servidumbre. Las rebeliones matabeles de 1893 y 1896 fueron aplastadas por el ejército británico. En 1895, el territorio adoptó el nombre de Rhodesia, por el apellido del dueño del territorio. En ese mismo año, la compañía asesinó al rey Lobenguela, y Rhodes asumió plenamente el gobierno de lo que entonces se llamó Rhodesia del Sur. En 1923, sin embargo, expiró el privilegio de la BSA y Gran Bretaña administró directamente la colonia de Rhodesia del Sur, en cuyo seno se forjó un régimen racista, similar al de Sudáfrica. En 1953, el Reino Unido estructuró la Federación de África Central, entre Rhodesia del Norte (actual Zambia), Rhodesia del Sur y Nyasalandia (actual Malawi). En las elecciones de 1962 se repartieron la victoria dos organizaciones derechistas: el Frente Rhodesiano, dirigido por Ian Smith, y el Partido Federal Unido, de E. Whitehead. En 1963 quedó disuelta la federación. Comenzaba en esa época el proceso descolonizador en África: Rhodesia del Norte y Nyasalandia rechazaron los intentos de los colonos blancos de perpetuar su dominación y se independizaron en 1964. En Rhodesia del Sur, el Congreso Nacional Africano intensificó su movilización independentista. Las elecciones de 1965 fueron ganadas por el Frente Rhodesiano y, simultáneamente, se crearon dos movimientos negros nacionalistas: la Unión Popular Africana de Zimbabwe (ZAPU) y la Unión Nacional Africana de Zimbabwe (ZANU), fundadas en 1962 y 1963, respectivamente. En 1964, los

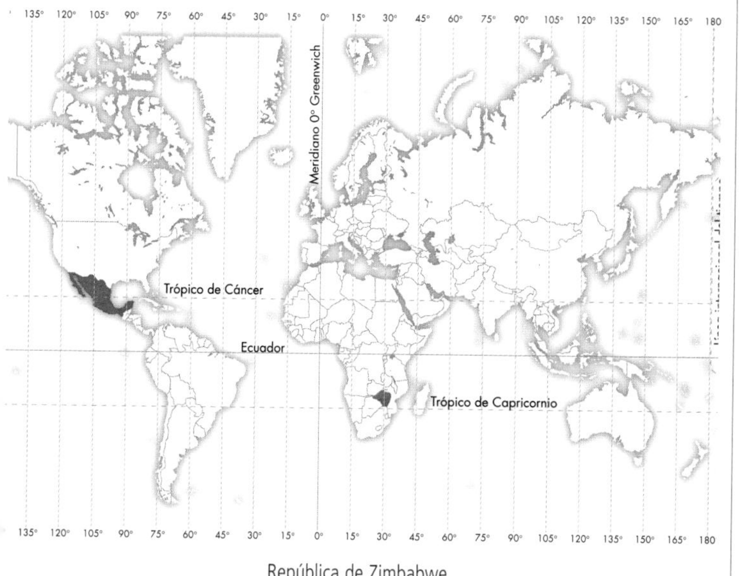

República de Zimbabwe

Monedas de Zimbabwe

Mujer de Zimbabwe

laboristas ganaron las elecciones en Inglaterra, por lo que las relaciones de ese país con el gobierno del Frente Rhodesiano se volvieron tirantes. El 11 de noviembre de 1965, Ian Smith proclamó unilateralmente la independencia de Rhodesia del Sur, con el nombre de Rhodesia, se aprobó una nueva constitución en febrero de 1966 y, en diciembre de ese año, abandonó la Comunidad Británica de Naciones. Londres desconoció tales medidas y el régimen rhodesiano fue castigado con un boicoteo comercial impuesto por la ONU, acuerdo que fue desconocido por Sudáfrica y Portugal y burlado por las potencias occidentales. Los independentistas rhodesianos de la ZANU y la ZAPU optaron entonces por la lucha armada, por lo que Smith ordenó el encarcelamiento de los máximos dirigentes de ambas organizaciones (Robert Mugabe y Joshua Nkomo), aunque no pudo evitar el inicio de la gran insurrección de agosto de 1967, misma que sólo pudo reprimir con auxilio de las tropas sudafricanas y portuguesas. En 1969, Smith organizó un referéndum amañado que aprobó la forma republicana de gobierno, hecha efectiva a partir de marzo de 1970; en las elecciones de abril de ese año, Clifford Dupont fue electo presidente y Smith llegó al cargo de primer ministro. Éste intensificó su lucha contra las guerrillas de la ZANU y la ZAPU, cuya actividad se consolidaba y extendía. El régimen de Salisbury intentó internacionalizar el conflicto al bombardear, en repetidas ocasiones, a Zambia y Mozambique, países a los que acusaba de apoyar la lucha guerrillera. Los agredidos no respondieron y, junto con Angola, Botswana y Tanzania constituyeron el Grupo de la Línea del Frente en la Lucha Contra el Racismo. La ZAPU y la ZANU, por su parte, se fusionaron en el Frente Patriótico que intensificó la lucha armada y política llevándola hasta Salisbury. Este hecho opacó el papel de los líderes negros que limitaban la lucha a los marcos impuestos por la legalidad de los blancos: Abel Muzorewa (obispo y dirigente del Consejo Nacional Africano) y N. Sithole, del ala moderada de la ZANU. En noviembre de 1977, luego de un bobardeo masivo de la aviación rhodesiana sobre Mozambique, Smith propuso a Muzorewa y Sithole una transferencia del poder a la mayoría negra; éstos aceptaron negociar con el régimen de Salisbury, pero Mugabe y Nkomo rechazaron la proposición. En 1979, después de unas elecciones en las que los votantes fueron llevados a las urnas a punta de fusil, Muzorewa asumió el cargo de primer ministro y cambió el nombre del país por el de Zimbabwe-Rhodesia. En el nuevo gobierno, la minoría blanca conservó el control absoluto del país. El Frente Patriótico denunció al nuevo gobierno como una continuación del de Smith e intensificó las acciones armadas. Tras una "conferencia constitucional", convocada por Gran Bretaña a finales de 1979, en 1980 Zimbabwe-Rhodesia obtuvo la independencia como República de Zimbabwe. En ese año, en las primeras elecciones libres del país, la ZANU obtuvo el triunfo; se integró un gobierno de coalición (del Frente Patriótico) con Robert Mugabe como primer ministro, Joshua Nkomo en el Ministerio del Interior y Canaan Banana en la Presidencia. A partir de entonces se inició la rivalidad entre las organizaciones ZANU y ZAPU, hasta que Mugabe debió separar a Nkomo de su puesto y designarlo ministro sin cartera. En 1982, la crisis estalló cuando los adeptos de Nkomo crearon, coordinados por el agente sudafricano Malcolm Gallaway, un movimiento llamado Superzapu, que inició una campaña terrorista destinada a crear pánico entre la población blanca, para desacreditar al gobierno de Mugabe. En ese año, Salisbury, la capital, mudó su nombre a Harare. En marzo de 1983, Nkomo huyó a Botswana, después de ser detenido en el aeropuerto de Harare, cuando pretendía viajar al exterior con una cantidad de dólares superior a la permitida por la ley. El líder de la ZAPU fue más tarde a Londres, desde donde pretendía intensificar su campaña contra Mugabe, pero su influencia sobre Zimbabwe prácticamente desapareció. El establecimiento de relaciones diplomáticas con México se produjo el 25 de marzo de 1985.

ZIMBRÓN, ÁNGEL ♦ n. en Ixtlahuaca, Edo. de Méx., y m. en el DF (1854-1934). Abogado. Fue secretario general de gobierno (1897) y dos veces gobernador del Distrito Federal (del 19 de septiembre al 3 de noviembre y en diciembre de 1900) y magistrado del Tribunal Superior de Justicia (1906-11). Dueño del antiguo rancho de San Lucas, en Azcapotzalco, fundó en ese sitio la colonia El Imparcial.

ZINACANTÁN ♦ Municipio de Chiapas contiguo a San Cristóbal de Las Casas. Superficie: 171.40 km². Habitantes: 24,631, de los cuales 5,799 forman la población económicamente activa. Hablan alguna lengua indígena 19,118 personas mayores de cinco años (tzotzil 17,992). Indígenas monolingües: 8,124.

ZINACANTEPEC ♦ Municipio del Estado de México contiguo a Toluca. Superficie: 306.07 km². Habitantes: 105,566, de los cuales 22,263 forman la población económicamente activa. Hablan alguna lengua indígena 949 personas mayores de cinco años (otomí 738 y mazahua 98). En la jurisdicción se hallan las zonas arqueológicas del Nevado de Toluca y de Santa María del Monte, así como el Parque Nacional de Toluca. Su cabecera, San Miguel de Zinacantepec, cuenta con un convento franciscano construido entre 1569 y

Zinacantán, Chiapas

FOTO: FONDO EDITORIAL GRUPO AZABACHE

1585, probablemente por encargo del fraile Martín de Aguirre. Esta cabecera se erigió sobre el poblado prehispánico de Tzincantlán ("Lugar de murciélagos"), situado cerca de los centros culturales de Calixtlahuaca y Tecaxic.

ZINACATEPEC ◆ Municipio de Puebla situado en el sureste del estado, al sureste de Tehuacán, cerca de los límites con Oaxaca. Superficie: 86.76 km^2. Habitantes: 11,976, de los cuales 3,153 forman la población económicamente activa. Hablan alguna lengua indígena 7,467 personas mayores de cinco años (náhuatl 7,271). En la cabecera, San Sebastián Zinacatepec, hay un convento

Vista panorámica de Zirándaro, Guerrero

del siglo XVI. En una de sus capillas se encuentra una pila bautismal que es una obra de arte del periodo colonial.

ZINÁPARO ◆ Municipio de Michoacán situado en el noroeste del estado y contiguo a La Piedad, cerca de Guanajuato y Jalisco. Superficie: 50.45 km^2. Habitantes: 4,631, de los cuales 1,099 forman la población económicamente activa. Hablan alguna lengua indígena ocho personas mayores de cinco años.

ZINAPÉCUARO ◆ Municipio de Michoacán situado en el noreste de Morelia, en los límites con Guanajuato. Superficie: 519.89 km^2. Habitantes: 48,902, de los cuales 11,324 forman la población económicamente activa. Hablan alguna lengua indígena 99 personas mayores de cinco años.

ZINAPÉCUARO ◆ Río de Michoacán. Nace en el rancho de Yerbabuena, en el noreste del estado; corre de sureste a noroeste y recibe numerosos tributarios: los arroyos de los manantiales Ojo de Jesús, Colmena, Rosal, Ojo de Sauz, Tzimeo, Peñitas y Chapitiro. Tras un recorrido de 35 km desemboca en la laguna de Cuitzeo.

ZINCÚNEGUI, MIGUEL ◆ n. en Pátzcuaro y m. en Morelia, Mich. (1799-1872). Militar. En 1821 se adhirió al Plan de Iguala. Fue diputado local y federal. General en 1856, fue consejero de gobierno y gobernador interino de Michoacán (1858).

ZINCÚNEGUI TERCERO, LEOPOLDO ◆ n. en Zinapécuaro, Mich., y m. en el DF (1885-1972). Licenciado en derecho por la Universidad Michoacana de San Nicolás de Hidalgo. Vivió en Toluca, donde fundó *El Heraldo, El Noticioso* y *Alma Bohemia*. Combatió en las filas constitucionalistas desde 1914, bajo las órdenes de Francisco Murguía, primero, y de Gertrudis M. Sánchez, después. Militante del Partido Liberal Constitucionalista, fue cinco veces diputado federal entre 1917 y 1930, juez del Registro Civil en la ciudad de México, visitador de la Secretaría de Hacienda y subjefe del Departamento Técnico, Industrial y Comercial de la SEP. Colaboró en *El Nacional*. Autor de *Capullos*, *Los ojos de Aladino* (1934), *Anecdotario prohibido de la revolución* (1936), *Bajo el cielo de Tzintzuntzan* (1940), *Zinapécuaro* (1941), *Alguna vez fui poeta* (1957), *Sótanos* (novela, 1959), *Don dinero* y *Toluca de mis recuerdos*.

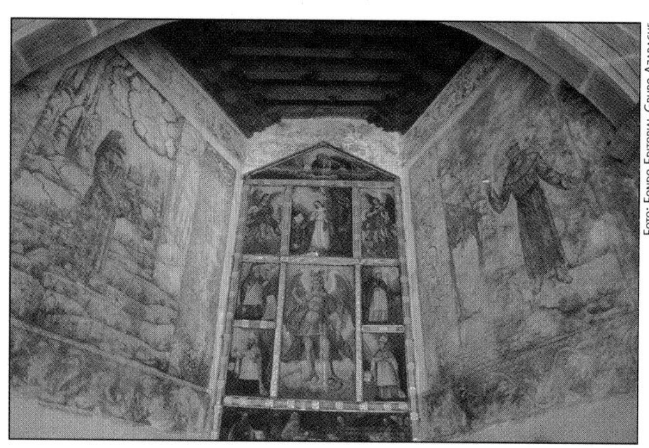

FOTO: FONDO EDITORIAL GRUPO AZABACHE

Museo de Arte Virreinal de Zinacantepec, Estado de México

ZIRACUARETIRO ◆ Municipio de Michoacán situado al suroeste de Morelia y al noreste de Apatzingán. Superficie: 143.56 km^2. Habitantes: 11,479, de los cuales 2,987 forman la población económicamente activa. Hablan alguna lengua indígena 78 personas mayores de cinco años (purépecha 73).

ZIRAHUÉN ◆ Lago de Michoacán situado al sur-suroeste del lago de Pátzcuaro y al este de la ciudad de Uruapan. Se localiza en una cuenca cerrada del eje volcánico.

ZIRÁNDARO ◆ Municipio de Guerrero situado al nor-noreste de Zihuatanejo, en los límites con Michoacán. Superficie: 2,475.60 km^2. Habitantes: 22,382, de los cuales 3,755 forman la población económicamente activa. Cuenta con abundantes reservas minerales. En su jurisdicción se localizan las eminencias

FOTO: CLAUDIO CONTRERAS KOOB

Lago de Zirahuén, Michoacán

Plaza principal de Zitácuaro, a finales del siglo XIX

del Pico de Armenta y el cerro de Barrabás, donde tenía su base de operaciones la guerrilla de Vicente Guerrero.

ZITÁCUARO ◆ Municipio de Michoacán situado al este-sureste de Morelia, en los límites con el Estado de México. Superficie: 508.25 km^2. Habitantes: 130,593, de los cuales 28,303 forman la población económicamente activa. Hablan alguna lengua indígena 3,077 personas mayores de cinco años (mazahua 2,722 y otomí 355). Indígenas monolingües: 85. En la jurisdicción se localizan los balnearios de aguas termales de San José Purúa y de Agua Blanca. Se han encontrado numerosos vestigios arqueológicos: entre el pueblo de San Felipe de los Alzati y el viejo mineral de Angangueo están las ruinas de una ciudad fortificada, con pirámides, templos y juego de pelota. Zitácuaro fue habitada originalmente por pirindas, otomíes y mazahuas y fue ocupada por los purépechas hacia 1330. Tras la conquista española, los franciscanos mudaron de sitio el asentamiento hasta el lugar que ahora ocupa y lo llamaron San Juan Zitácuaro; edificaron la parroquia que aún existe y en la primera mitad del siglo XVIII fundaron un convento. Durante la colonia, la entonces villa de Zitácuaro era centro de peregrinación por la veneración de los fieles hacia la Virgen María y la imagen de Nuestra Señora de los Remedios, traída por Hernán Cortés a la Nueva España y cedida por los franciscanos a esta ciudad a finales del siglo XVI, y para la cual se construyó un santuario en el siglo XVII. A principios de 1811 el insurgente Benedicto López tomó la ciudad de Zitácuaro; el gobierno virreinal comisionó a Juan Bautista de la Torre para limpiar el camino entre México y Michoacán, por lo que este realista atacó dos veces la plaza, el 20 de febrero y el 22 de mayo; en ambas ocasiones fue rechazado por López y en el combate de mayo perdió la vida. Zitácuaro era un sitio de gran importancia estratégica por lo que, después de los ataques fallidos de De la Torre, Ignacio López Rayón decidió fortificarla, en previsión de inminentes presiones realistas. El 22 de junio Emparán inició las hostilidades, pero sus fuerzas fueron completamente aniquiladas por los insurgentes. A finales de 1811, López Rayón, José María Liceaga y Joaquín López se reunieron en un inmueble, que poco después sería llamado Palacio Nacional de Zitácuaro, y levantaron un acta en la que se declaraba la necesidad de establecer un organismo rector de la lucha por la independencia. El documento convocaba a los principales caudillos revolucionarios que operaban en Michoacán, Guanajuato y Jalisco (Remigio Yarza, Ignacio Martínez, Tomás Ortiz, Benedicto López, José María Vargas, Mariano Tercero, Juan Albarrán, Ignacio Ponce de León, Manuel Manso, Miguel Serrano, José Ignacio Izaguirre y José Sixto Verduzco), mismos que se reunieron el 18 de agosto de 1811 y el día 21 dieron origen a la llamada Junta de Zitácuaro o Suprema Junta Nacional Americana, cuyo primer presidente fue el propio López Rayón; este organismo, que se proclamaba fiel al rey español Fernando VII, adquirió una imprenta y publicó *El Ilustrador Americano*. A finales de 1811 la Junta se debilitó por pugnas internas, lo que propició que el realista Félix María Calleja ocupara la plaza el 2 de enero de 1812, día en el que ordenó fusilar a todos los prisioneros, autorizó el saqueo indiscriminado y por último prendió fuego a la ciudad; asimismo, despojó de sus derechos a los pueblos indígenas de la comarca. La junta entonces inició su retirada hacia Tuzantla y posteriormente se disolvió ante la creación del Congreso de Chilpancingo. Al ocurrir la revolución de Ayutla, la mayoría de los habitantes de Zitácuaro se manifestaron en favor del liberal Juan Álvarez, por lo que las tropas santanistas pusieron sitio a la población, la ocuparon y la incendiaron el 1 de abril de 1855. Durante la intervención francesa, mientras el resto del estado de Michoacán estaba en poder de los imperialistas, Zitácuaro se mantuvo como plaza republicana. A mediados de 1864 llegó Vicente Riva Palacio y la fortificó. El 1 de julio, el imperialista Leonardo Márquez atacó el lugar y desalojó a Riva Palacio, pero tres días después éste recuperó la ciudad. Un año después, el 15 de abril de 1865, las tropas belgas y el realista mexicano Ramón Méndez, que habían sido derrotados días antes en Tacámbaro, tomaron desquite mediante el expediente de prender fuego a la ciudad. Por estas acciones, la cabecera de este municipio recibe la denominación de Heroica Zitácuaro. El área aledaña a Zitácuaro fue escenario de las correrías de los Hermanos de la Hoja, capitaneados por el coronel Astucia, inmortalizado por el novelista Luis G. Inclán.

Palacio municipal de Zitácuaro, Michoacán

FOTO: CARLOS HAHN

ZITÁCUARO ◆ Río de Michoacán. Nace en la vertiente sur de la sierra de Angangueo, al norte de la ciudad de Zitácuaro; corre de norte a sur y se une al río Tuxpan para formar el Tuzantla.

ZITARROSA, ALFREDO ◆ n. y m. en Uruguay (1936-1989). Fue locutor desde 1954 y escribió poesía, por lo que ganó un premio del Ayuntamiento de Montevideo, todo antes de iniciarse como compositor y cantante. Militó en el anarquismo, en el Partido Comunista Uruguayo y en el Frente Amplio. Hostilizado por la dictadura se exilió en España (1974) de donde pasó a México en 1979, aunque ya en 1977 había actuado en este país, durante las Jornadas de la Cultura Uruguaya en el exilio. Aquí se presentó inicialmente con el grupo Sanampay, cuyas cantantes eran Guadalupe Pineda y Hebe Rosell, grabó discos, hizo presentaciones y dirigió el programa *En privado*, en Radio Educación. Colaboró en *Excélsior* con la columna "El oficio de cantor". Volvió a Uruguay en 1984. Autor de las canciones *Adagio a mi país* ("himno uruguayo en el exilio", según Miguel Ángel Granados Chapa), *Crece en el pie, Beethoven, Mi tierra en invierno, Mariposa negra, Tanta vida en cuatro versos, Milonga de ojos dorados, Candombe del olvido, El violín de Becho, Los puñales, Vidalita, Pa'l que se va, Canto de nadie, Milonga en do, Si te vas, Baila la mara, María serena mía, Melodía larga, Negra chao, Hoy vive aquí, Stéfanie, Doña Soledad* y *Guitarra negra*. Su último disco es *Sobre pájaros y almas* (1988). Autor del libro de cuentos *Por si recuerdo* (1987).

El Zócalo de la ciudad de México a mediados del siglo XIX en grabado de Casimiro Castro

ZITLALA ◆ Municipio de Guerrero situado al noreste de Chilpancingo y contiguo a Chilapa. Superficie: 308.20 km². Habitantes: 17,786, de los cuales 3,335 forman la población económicamente activa. Hablan alguna lengua indígena 7,922 personas mayores de cinco años (náhuatl 7,922), de las cuales 2,233 son monolingües. Cuenta con numerosas lagunas pequeñas, entre ellas las de Xinxinapa, Zolenatla, Zoquiapa, Xoxocotitlán y Laguna Seca, y con los cerros Zacatzonapa, Cuatzón y Campanario. En la cabecera se produce un mezcal muy apreciado regionalmente.

ZITLALTEPEC DE TRINIDAD SÁNCHEZ SANTOS ◆ Municipio de Tlaxcala situado en la porción suroriental de la entidad, al sur de Huamantla y al este del volcán la Malinche, en los límites con Puebla. Superficie: 101.40 km². Habitantes: 8,095, de los cuales 1,943 forman la población económicamente activa. Su cabecera municipal es Zitlaltepec.

ILUSTRACIÓN DE JAVIER GUADARRAMA

Parroquia de San Nicolás de Tolentino, en Zitlala, Guerrero

ZÓCALO ◆ Nombre con el que se conoce la Plaza de la Constitución o Plaza Mayor de la ciudad de México, explanada cuadrada de 240 metros por lado. Está limitado al norte por la catedral y el Sagrario Metropolitanos, al noreste por la zona arqueológica del Templo Mayor, al este por el Palacio Nacional, al sureste por la sede de la Suprema Corte de Justicia, al sur por los dos edificios del Departamento del Distrito Federal, al oeste por el portal de Mercaderes y al noroeste por el Nacional Monte de Piedad. El actual Zócalo se localiza aproximadamente en el mismo espacio que ocupó la plaza mayor de México-Tenochtitlan, que medía 325 metros de este a oeste y 312 de norte a sur y estaba flanqueada por el Gran Teocalli o Templo Mayor, los templos de Tezcatlipoca, Quetzalcóatl, Tonatiuh, Yopico y Temacalatl; el Juego de Pelota, el Coateocalli, el Telpochcalli, la Casa de las Águilas, el Templo de Mujeres y la Casa de los Servidores; en su costado este se localizaba la Casa Nueva o de Moctezuma II y al oeste se hallaba la Casa Vieja o de Axayácatl. En 1521 los conquistadores españoles hicieron la traza de la que sería la nueva ciudad y diseñaron un cuadrado que medía 367 metros de norte a sur, 246 en un lado y 236 en el otro, pero construyeron una iglesia en la parte norte, con lo que la plaza quedó reducida a su porción meridional. De los diez solares que bordeaban la plaza, Hernán Cortés se apropió de los que correspondían a las casas de Axayácatl y de Moctezuma II y en 1529, en la parte occidental, que

El Zócalo de la ciudad de México es 1999.

FOTO: CARLOS HAHN

Celebración del 15 de septiembre en el Zócalo de la ciudad de México

no pertenecía a Cortés, se construyó el Portal de Mercaderes. El extremo sur estaba bordeado por un canal. En 1533, Gonzalo Ruiz fue autorizado a instalar pequeñas tiendas de ropa frente al Portal de Mercaderes, cuyas ganancias se aplicarían a los servicios municipales. La Casa de Moctezuma fue heredada por Martín Cortés, quien en 1562 la vendió al gobierno, que la convirtió en la residencia de los virreyes (☛ *Palacio Nacional*). La Casa de Axayácatl, por su parte, se convirtió en el Palacio de los Marqueses del Valle de Oaxaca. En el extremo sur se levantó el Portal de las Flores y la Casa del Cabildo de la ciudad (☛ *Palacio del Ayuntamiento*). Durante la inundación de 1629 se destruyó el empedrado de la explanada, así como los establecimientos situados en el sur. En junio de 1692, durante el levantamiento popular contra las autoridades, además del Palacio Virreinal fueron destruidos los locales de los comerciantes que se encontraban sobre la explanada y sobre sus restos, en 1703, se erigió el mercado del Parián (☛). Con la construcción del Sagrario Metropolitano (1749-68) quedó cerrada la parte norte de la plaza. En 1790, durante las obras de nivelación del piso de la plaza, iniciadas dos años antes, durante las cuales se desecó el canal del sur, Antonio León y Gama descubrió el calendario azteca y el Cuauhxicalli de Tizoc. En enero de 1782 se inauguró el Mercado del Volador, situado donde ahora se levanta la Suprema Corte de Justicia. En diciembre de 1796 se colocó un basamento en el centro de la plaza donde en 1803 se instaló la estatua ecuestre de Carlos IV (*El Caballito*) realizada por Manuel Tolsá. En mayo de 1812, en honor de la Carta de Cádiz, la explanada tomó oficialmente el nombre de Plaza de la Constitución. La estatua fue cubierta durante el gobierno de Agustín de Iturbide y retirada a finales de 1824, por órdenes del presidente Guadalupe Victoria. En 1840 se plantaron fresnos enfrente del atrio de la Catedral. A finales de 1843, sobre una parte de lo que había sido el Parián, destruido desde el levantamiento popular conocido como motín de la Acordada (☛), Lorenzo de la Hidalga inició la construcción de un monumento a la independencia que le había encomendado el presidente Antonio López de Santa Anna, pero debido a la caída del gobierno santanista, De la Hidalga tuvo que interrumpir las obras en 1844, cuando sólo había construido el basamento o zócalo de la columna. La gente comenzó a utilizar el pedestal como punto de reunión y a identificarlo con toda la plaza, que se convirtió en el Zócalo. En 1866, la línea de cadenas que limitaban el atrio de la catedral desde finales del siglo XVIII fue extendida alrededor de toda la plaza, y por eso el Paseo de las Cadenas se convirtió en Paseo del Zócalo. A partir de 1875, con la instalación de una terminal de tranvías, la plaza se fue cubriendo de vías metálicas. Tres años después, sobre el zócalo de De la Hidalga se construyó un kiosco. En 1879, al este de la catedral se edificó un Mercado de Flores, a un lado del cual, en 1881, se colocó una estatua de Enrico Martínez. En 1891 la plaza fue asfaltada y en 1894 se le instaló el alumbrado eléctrico. Cuatro años después se construyó el inmueble del Centro Mercantil en el límite suroeste de la plaza. En 1914, los árboles fueron retirados del Zócalo y en el espacio libre se construyó un jardín que fue adornado con cuatro esculturas de Agustín Querol. En años posteriores ese jardín desapareció y la calle del Seminario fue ampliada, en tanto que el monumento a Enrico Martínez era trasladado al extremo opuesto, frente a la desembocadura de la actual calle 5 de Mayo. El Mercado de las Flores fue eliminado y en 1924 se colocó, en el costado oriental de la Catedral, la estatua de Bartolomé de las Casas y se construyeron unos baños públicos en el subsuelo. En 1934 el jardín fue remozado. Al año siguiente, el callejón que desembocaba por el sur en el Zócalo fue ampliado y convertido en la avenida 20 de Noviembre, en tanto que el antiguo Portal de las Flores era demolido y se iniciaba en ese lugar la construcción de la sede del Departamento del Distrito Federal. En 1940 se construyó el edificio de la Suprema Corte de Justicia donde había estado el Mercado del Volador. Entre 1953 y 1958 se efectuaron diversas tareas de remozamiento en el Zócalo: se retiraron prados, vías y construcciones, se cubrió de concreto y en el centro se colocó un astabandera; las banquetas de la catedral fueron ampliadas, quedó prohibido el estacionamiento de automóviles y fueron retirados los puestos del Portal de Mercaderes. En 1970 se colocó, a un costado del edificio del DDF y frente a la Suprema Corte de Justicia, un monumento conmemorativo de la fundación de México-Tenochtitlan; se pusieron fuentes en las aceras laterales de la catedral, se volvió a levantar el monumento a Bartolomé de las Casas en el costado oriental de la misma y en su costado occidental se instaló la estatua de Pedro de Gante. A inicios de 1999 el gobierno capitalino realizó un concurso para remozar el Zócalo.

Zohn, Alejandro ◆ n. en Viena, Austria (1930). A temprana edad se naturalizó mexicano. Arquitecto e ingeniero civil por la Universidad de Guadalajara (1955), en la que ha sido profesor de composición y edificación (1959-63). Ha realizado y supervisado la construcción de proyectos arquitectónicos como el Mercado Libertad (1958-59, remozado en 1981-82), la Unidad Deportiva Presidente Adolfo López Mateos (1962), la unidad habitacional Miravalle IV (1975) y el hotel Hermanos Reyes de Guadalajara (1976-80); el mercado Río Cuale de Puerto Vallarta (1978), así como el mejoramiento vial y visual del centro de Tlaquepaque (1977-79), y la Unidad Habitacional Ciudad Oriente en Ecatepec (1982-83). Miembro del Colegio de Arquitectos de Jalisco. Miembro académico emérito de la Sociedad de Arquitectos Mexicanos. Insignia José Clemente Orozco del gobierno de Jalisco (1957). Premio Jalisco 1964. Premio Cementos Guadalajara por diseño estructural (1972) y por la mejor obra en concreto (1974). Gran Premio de la Academia Internacional de Arquitectura de la VI Bienal Mundial de Arquitectura de Sofía (1991).

Zohn Muldoon, Ricardo ◆ n. en Guadalajara, Jal. (1962). Licenciado en música por la Universidad de California, con maestría y doctorado en composición por la Universidad de Pennsylvania. Ha tomado cursos en la Academia Chigiana de Siena, Italia, con Franco Donatoni y con Georges Crumb. Coordinó el festival Callejón del Ruido en Guanajuato. Maestro de composición en el College-Conservatory of Music de la Universidad de Cincinnati. Autor de música para piano: *Quasimodo* (1984) y *Migajas* (1986); oboe: *Cantiga del merolico* (1990); guitarra: *Dimes y diretes* (1985); quinteto: *Danza búlgara* (1995); conjuntos instrumentales: *Tango* (1993) y *El rizar de la tarde* (1994); orquesta de cámara: *Happy Ernst* (1985) y otros. Compositor residente de la Camargo Foundation de Francia (1992). Becario del festival de Música de Tanglewood (1993), de la fundación Guggenheim (1965) y del Taller Interamericano de Composición de la Universidad de Indiana (1996). Medalla Mozart del INBA (1994).

Zollman, Ronald ◆ n. en Bélgica (1950). Inició sus estudios musicales a los cuatro años de edad. Asistió al Conservatorio Real de Amberes y en París tomó cursos con Nadia Boulanger e Igor Markevitch. Se graduó en el Conservatorio Real de Bruselas y recibió el Diploma al Mérito Académico en la Academia Chigiana de Siena, Italia (1971). Creó la Filarmónica Juvenil de Bélgica. Ha dirigido orquestas en Bélgica, Inglaterra, Francia, Alemania, Italia, Holanda, Suiza, Suecia, España, Rusia y Australia. Ha sido director de la Ópera Nacional de Bélgica, Inglaterra y Escocia. Fue nombrado director musical de la Orquesta Nacional de Bélgica (1989-1994), y desde 1994, de la Orquesta Filarmónica de la UNAM. Resultó premiado en el Concurso Internacional de Jóvenes de Florencia (1972).

Ronald Zollman

Zongolica ◆ Municipio de Veracruz situado al sur-sureste de Orizaba y al sur de Córdoba. Superficie: 347.33 km². Habitantes: 35,615, de los cuales 9,077 forman la población económicamente activa. Hablan alguna lengua indígena 24,002 personas mayores de cinco años (náhuatl 23,634), de las que son monolingües 4,428. Durante la guerra de Independencia Rafael Argüelles y los sacerdotes Mariano de las Fuentes y Juan Moctezuma Cortés formaron en Zongolica un contingente con el que en mayo de 1812 ocuparon la ciudad de Orizaba, de donde extrajeron un gran cargamento de tabaco, lo vendieron y con el producto así obtenido instalaron un taller de acuñación de monedas que llevaban en el anverso un arco y una flecha, con la inscripción "Viva Fernando VII y América". En el reverso tenían una hoja de palma y una espada cruzadas.

Zongolica, de ◆ Sierra de Puebla, Veracruz y Oaxaca. Se extiende de noroeste a sureste. Su extremo noroccidental se localiza en el estado de Puebla, al sureste de la sierra de Tecamachalco; su vertiente oriental, que desciende hacia la llanura costera del golfo de México, se encuentra en el estado de Veracruz, al suroeste de Orizaba; limita por el este al valle poblano de Tehuacán y entra en el estado de Oaxaca hasta un punto al norte del río Santo Domingo.

Zongozotla ◆ Municipio de Puebla situado en el norte del estado, al noreste de Zacatlán y al sureste de Huauchinango. Superficie: 19.15 km². Habitantes: 3,804, de los cuales 1,160 for-

Vista de Zongolica, Veracruz

Foto: Fondo Editorial Grupo Azabache

man la población económicamente activa. Hablan alguna lengua indígena 2,827 personas mayores de cinco años (totonaco 2,763). Indígenas monolingües: 750. Destaca por su producción de ajonjolí, café, caña de azúcar, tabaco y vainilla y por la elaboración de aguardientes, vinos y licores, así como de artesanías de lana, palma e ixtle.

ZONTECOMATLÁN ◆ Municipio de Veracruz situado al oeste de Tuxpan, en los límites con Hidalgo. Superficie: 216.33 km². Habitantes: 11,632, de los cuales 2,599 forman la población económicamente activa. Hablan alguna lengua indígena 7,068 personas mayores de cinco años (náhuatl 5,616, otomí 1,049 y tepehua 421) y de ellas, 1,664 son monolingües.

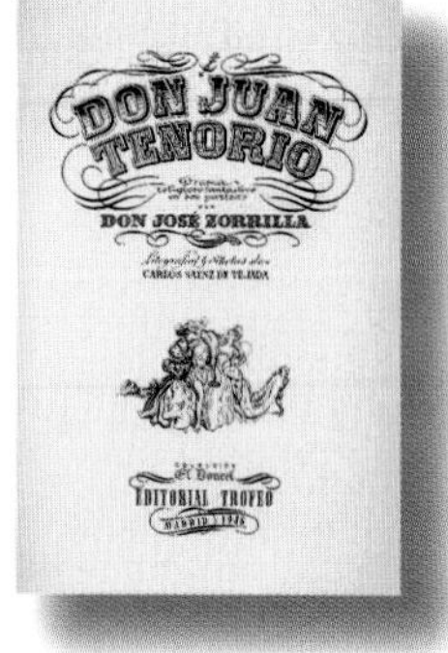

Portada de *Don juan* Tenorio de José Zorrilla

ZOQUES ◆ Indios que habitan varios municipios en las planicies de Tuxtla Gutiérrez y Pichucalco, Chiapas; en los municipios de San Miguel y San Martín Chimalpa y Niltepec, en Oaxaca, así como en las cercanías de los pueblos de Teapa, Topopilapa y Ayopa, Tabasco. En 1995 había en el país 44,398 personas mayores de cinco años hablantes de zoque, idioma del grupo maya-totonaco, tronco mixeano, familia mixeana, subfamilia zoque, con cinco variantes dialectales que dificultan la comunicación entre individuos de distintas regiones. A raíz de la erupción del volcán Chichonal, los zoques sufrieron graves cambios en su organización; muchos de ellos debieron ser reubicados en campamentos provisionales, con tierras impropias para el cultivo, lo que aceleró el proceso de migración en busca de trabajo asalariado. Una vez pasada la crisis, los zoques han regresado paulatinamente a sus asentamientos tradicionales. Su actividad económica básica es la agricultura, generalmente para el autoconsumo, la cría de cerdos y aves de corral y la elaboración de artesanías textiles, de palma, bejuco o mimbre y algo de cerámica. De acuerdo con sus distintas filiaciones religiosas, los zoques se subdividen en tres grandes grupos: los costumbreros, los católicos y los adventistas. Los primeros siguen el patrón religioso tradicional; los católicos pertenecen al culto apostólico romano y son dirigidos por el sacerdote, en tanto que los adventistas o sabáticos poseen sus propios templos, son dirigidos por el pastor y procuran evitar el contacto cultural con el resto de la etnia. Entre los costumbreros prevalece la familia extensa y entre los otros dos grupos se combinan ésta y la nuclear. Los costumbreros y católicos practican la endogamia, aunque se dan casos de matrimonios mixtos entre ambos grupos; en el caso de los primeros, la petición de la novia se efectúa por conducto de un intermediario que visita y hace obsequios a los padres de la joven, para después fijar la fecha de la ceremonia y celebrar la fiesta; los católicos acuden a su sacerdote para que negocie los términos de la boda, cuya ceremonia se celebra en la iglesia y con una fiesta. Por su parte, los adventistas practican con rigor la endogamia; la petición de la novia la hacen los padres del pretendiente o él mismo y se efectúan las bodas por lo civil y en su templo, sin que haya fiesta. También la muerte reviste distintas connotaciones: los costumbreros creen que el alma se dirige al mundo de los muertos, ubicado hacia el oeste; los católicos, que se dirige al cielo, al infierno o al purgatorio, tal como lo estipula su iglesia; y los adventistas suponen que el alma de un muerto que profesó su religión llega directamente, por ese solo hecho, al reino de Dios. Entre los costumbreros el compadrazgo es una institución importante que se establece preferentemente entre individuos del mismo grupo y lleva implícitas relaciones de respeto; los católicos establecen el compadrazgo con los mestizos, pues suponen que eso les da un mejor estatus social; los adventistas eligen como padrinos de sus hijos a personas de su misma religión y su misma familia. Los costumbreros conservan ritos y mitos prehispánicos: creen en seres sobrenaturales que son dueños de las cuevas, ríos, bosques, montes, de la lluvia y del viento; estos seres pueden causar daño a los hombres y, para evitar las calamidades, los costumbreros efectúan ceremonias propiciatorias, conducidas por los ancianos. Creen que las enfermedades son provocadas también por factores sobrenaturales o por brujería; para contrarrestar esos males, los brujos y curanderos hacen ceremonias con ofrendas y dan tratamiento a base de limpias, rezos y yerbas medicinales. Durante el primer año de vida de un niño costumbrero, sus padres acuden al especialista para conocer la identidad de su *tona* (llamada *a'nson*) o animal compañero, con el que compartirá su destino. Los católicos veneran a distintos santos, van a misa y tienen asociaciones que organizan fiestas de los santos patrones; aun cuando saben que las enfermedades tienen causas naturales y acuden a los centros de salud, en ocasiones sienten la necesidad de tratarse con los curanderos. Los adventistas, en cambio, siguen los lineamientos de su religión, nunca participan en las festividades tradicionales y, en caso de enfermedad, acuden a los centros médicos de su iglesia en la zona. En algunos sitios aún está vigente el sistema de cargos tradicionales, que cuenta con fiscales, sacristanes y auxiliares para el cuidado de la iglesia y la organización de las fiestas. Los ancianos que han desempeñado varios de estos cargos alcanzan una posición preponderante y designan a quie-

Familia de campesinos zoques de Copoya, Chiapas

FOTO: LOURDES ALMEIDA

nes desempeñarán cada año los cargos. Celebran las fiestas para los santos patronos y algunas otras como el Carnaval, la Semana Santa, Pascua de Resurrección y Navidad. El sistema de cargos políticos por escalafón ha caído en desuso y las comunidades zoques se ciñen a los lineamientos municipales, cuyos puestos de dirección recaen en los mestizos.

Zoquiapan ◆ Municipio de Puebla situado en el norte del estado, al noroeste de Teziutlán y al noreste de Zacatlán. Superficie: 22.96 km². Habitantes: 2,951, de los cuales 667 forman la población económicamente activa. Hablan alguna lengua indígena 2,052 personas mayores de cinco años (náhuatl 2,036). Indígenas monolingües: 395.

Zoquitlán ◆ Municipio de Puebla situado en el sureste del estado, al este de Tehuacán y al sureste de Tecamachalco. Superficie: 311.27 km². Habitantes: 18,042, de los cuales 4,226 forman la población económicamente activa. Hablan alguna lengua indígena 13,710 personas mayores de cinco años (náhuatl 13, 512). Indígenas monolingües: 4,930.

Zorrilla, Begoña ◆ n. en Tampico, Tams. (1956). Pintora. Licenciada y maestra en artes visuales por la ENAP. Ha participado en exposiciones individuales y colectivas en México, España y Estados Unidos. Participó en el VI Encuentro Nacional de Arte Joven (1986).

Zorrilla, José ◆ n. y m. en España (1817-1893). Dramaturgo y poeta. Pasó en 1855 a México, donde colaboró con poesías para algunas publicaciones. Residió hasta 1859 en Cuba y volvió a México. En 1864 Maximiliano y Carlota lo designaron poeta de cámara, instaló un teatro dentro del Palacio Nacional y en 1865 presentó ahí su *Don Juan Tenorio*, conocido en México desde 1844. Autor, además, de *Drama del alma* (1868) y *Cartas al duque de Rivas*.

Zorrilla Arena L., Santiago ◆ n. en el DF (1937). Profesor por la Escuela Nacional de Maestros y licenciado en sociología por la UNAM, realizó estudios de posgrado sobre desarrollo e integración económica en la Antigua Universidad de Alcalá de Henares. Profesor de la Facultad de Contaduría y Administración de la UNAM (1970-) y miembro del Centro de Investigación de la misma. Coautor, con José Silvestre Méndez, de *Cien preguntas y respuestas de la economía mexicana* (1983) y *México por entidades federativas* (1985), así como de *Dinámica social* (2 t.) e *Introducción socioeconómica al panorama de México*. Autor de *Cómo aprender economía*, *Aspectos socioeconómicos de la problemática en México*, *Introducción a la metodología de la investigación* y *Diccionario de economía*.

Zorrilla Martínez, Pedro ◆ n. en Monterrey, NL (1933). Licenciado en derecho por la UNAM (1965) y doctor en derecho y ciencias políticas y económicas por la Universidad de París y la London School of Economics (1958). Profesor de la UNAM (1959-), de la Universidad Iberoamericana (1966-67), del ICAP, de las universidades de Nuevo León y de Tamaulipas, del CEMLA, profesor visitante de la Universidad de Texas y de la Universidad de París y del Instituto de Administración Pública, de Francia. Ha sido secretario de la Presidencia del Tribunal Superior de Justicia del Distrito y Territorios Federales (1955), secretario auxiliar de la Junta de Gobierno de los Organismos y Empresas del Estado de la Secretaría del Patrimonio Nacional (1959), abogado general del Programa Nacional Fronterizo (1961), abogado consultor de la Canacintra (1964), subdirector jurídico de la Secretaría de la Presidencia (1965), secretario general de Gobierno en Tamaulipas (1968), director general de Población de la Secretaría de Gobernación (1970), oficial mayor del DDF (1971), procurador de Justicia del Distrito y Territorios Federales (1972), gobernador de Nuevo León (1973-79), asesor de la Secretaría de Programación y Presupuesto (1980-82), director general de Concarril (1982-85) y coordinador de asesoría del gobierno de Nuevo León en el DF (1989-). Miembro del Colegio de Abogados y miembro fundador del INAP y de la Sociedad Mexicana de Planificación.

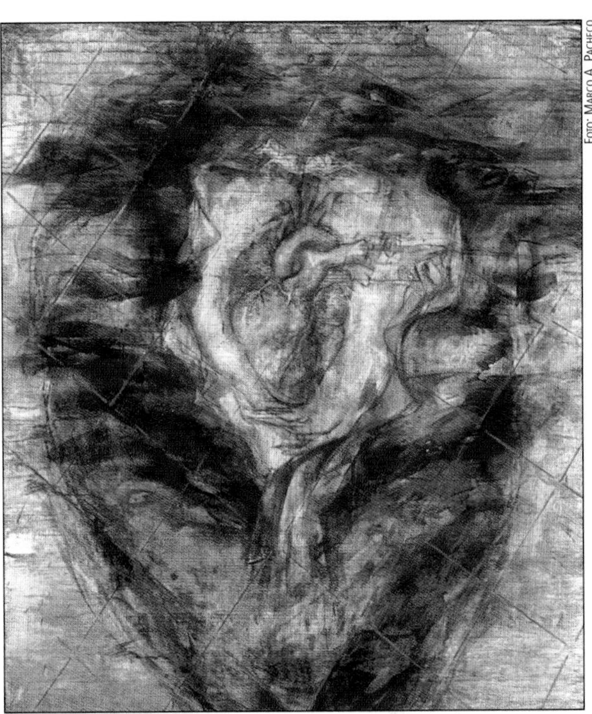

El ciervo, obra de Begoña Zorrilla, 1989

Zorrilla Pérez, José Antonio ◆ n. en Zimapán, Hgo. (1942). Miembro del PRI, en el que fue subdirector juvenil del Comité Ejecutivo Nacional (1965-68), subsecretario de Organización (1976-79) y delegado general en Morelos (1977-79), así como presidente del Comité Directivo Estatal en Hidalgo (1979). En la CNC se desempeñó como secretario de Acción Juvenil, miembro de la comisión política (1969-71), secretario de Organización (1977), delegado en Morelos (1977) y secretario coordinador de uniones (1977). Ha sido asesor de la Oficialía Mayor del gobierno de Hidalgo (1965-68), secretario particular del subsecretario de Gobernación (1970-76), diputado federal (1976-79), secretario general de Gobierno en Hidalgo (1979-82) y titular de la Dirección Federal de Seguridad (1982-85); candidato a diputado federal por su partido en 1985, renunció y salió del país el 27 de mayo de ese año. En 1989 fue aprehendido y se le acusó de mantener nexos con narcotraficantes, de proporcionar a delincuentes credenciales de la dirección a su cargo, de ser el autor intelectual del homicidio de

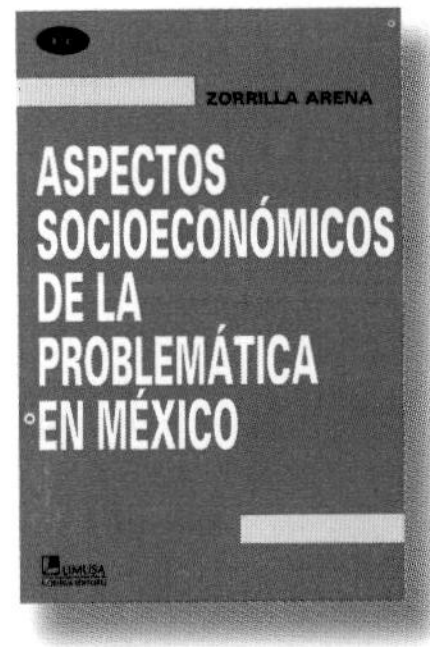

Obra de Santiago Zorrilla Arena

Pedro Zorrilla Martínez

Manuel Buendía (☛) y de otros delitos por los que en 1993 fue declarado culpable y sentenciado a 35 años de prisión.

ZOTOLUCA ◆ Ganadería fundada por José María González Pavón, dueño también de las ganaderías de Piedras Negras y la Laguna. Su nombre proviene de la hacienda de Santiago Zotoluca, en el municipio de Tlaxco, Tlax., en la que se estableció en 1888. Comenzó su crianza "con vacas de Tepeyahualco y sementales" importados de España. Su divisa tiene los colores rojo y azul. Se hizo popular desde su primera corrida, en El Toreo de la ciudad de México, en 1913, en la que alternaron Rodolfo Gaona y Luis Freg.

Fortunato Zuazua

ZOVEK ◆ n. en Torreón, Coah., y m. en Cuautitlán, Edo. de Méx. (1940-1972). Nombre profesional de Francisco Xavier Chapa del Bosque. Profesor de artes marciales. Desde principios de los años setenta, como *Profesor Zovek*, realizaba acrobacias y actos de escapismo. Participó en varios programas de televisión y actuaba en distintos foros. Fue protagonista de la película *El ídolo maldito*. El 10 de marzo de 1972 murió mientras realizaba uno de sus actos acrobáticos, contratado por el Circo Hermanos Suárez: debía viajar colgado de un helicóptero, pero el aparato maniobró con brusquedad para evitar una colisión y *Zovek* cayó desde una altura de 200 metros.

ZOZAYA BERMÚDEZ, JOSÉ MANUEL ◆ n. en Salvatierra, Gto., y m. en la ciudad de México (1775-1853). Diputado examinador y rector del Colegio de Letras de la Audiencia de México. Durante la primera regencia mexicana y el gobierno de Agustín de Iturbide se desempeñó como ministro plenipotenciario ante el gobierno de Estados Unidos. En 1823 regresó con maquinaria y trabajadores para instalar la primera fábrica de papel del México independiente, que se localizaba en Tizapán. La segunda edición de la Constitución de 1824 se imprimió en papel fabricado por Zozaya. Diputado federal por Guanajuato. Miembro del Colegio de Abogados.

ZOZOCOLCO DE HIDALGO ◆ Municipio de Veracruz situado al suroeste de Papantla, en los límites con Puebla. Superficie: 106.11 km². Habitantes: 11,346, de los cuales 3,021 forman la población económicamente activa. Hablan alguna lengua indígena 8,401 personas mayores de cinco años (totonaco 8,275 y náhuatl 126) y de ellas, son monolingües 2,262.

ZUAZO, ALONSO DE ◆ n. en España y m. en Santo Domingo (1466-¿1539?). Abogado al servicio de la Corona de España. Fue enviado a Santo Domingo como justicia mayor en 1517. Pasó en 1520 a Cuba para tomar residencia al gobernador Diego Velázquez. Participó en 1523 en la expedición de Francisco de Garay a Pánuco para servir de intermediario entre éste y Hernán Cortés, pero el navío en que viajaba encalló. En una embarcación improvisada llegó hasta Veracruz, desde donde Cortés lo hizo llevar a México. Al iniciar su expedición a las Hibueras, el conquistador extremeño lo dejó al frente del gobierno de la Nueva España, como alcalde mayor y asesor del contador y del tesorero sin embargo, las intrigas palaciegas del contador, el tesorero, el veedor y el factor hicieron que fuese llevado preso y encadenado a Cuba. Liberado más adelante, residió en Santo Domingo, donde fue oidor.

ZUAZUA, FORTUNATO ◆ n. en Lampazos de Naranjo, NL, y m. en EUA (1890-1938). Militar. Se incorporó en 1910 a la insurrección maderista. En 1912 combatió al orozquismo y en 1913 se unió al constitucionalismo, a las órdenes de Pablo González. Participó con Lucio Blanco en la toma de Matamoros y en el reparto agrario de la hacienda de los Borregos. En 1915 combatió a la División del Norte en el Bajío, en las fuerzas de Francisco Murguía, y

FOTO: FONDO EDITORIAL GRUPO AZABACHE

Pueblo totonaca en Zozocolco de Hidalgo, Veracruz

después en Chihuahua y Coahuila, a las órdenes de Jacinto B. Treviño. En ese año obtuvo el grado de general de brigada y más tarde se desempeñó como jefe de operaciones en varias plazas del país. Combatió en 1918 a los zapatistas y era el comandante de la ciudad de México en mayo de 1920, cuando el gobierno de Venustiano Carranza huyó de la capital, por lo que entregó la plaza a Treviño. En 1920 fue administrador del timbre en Tacubaya, combatió la rebelión escobarista (1929) y fue inspector del ejército (1932-34). Candidato al gobierno de Nuevo León, ganó las elecciones en 1935, pero éstas fueron anuladas. En 1936 contendió por el Ejecutivo local nuevamente y volvió a ganar, aunque el triunfo se le concedió a Anacleto Guerrero Guajardo, candidato del Partido Nacional Revolucionario.

Zuazua, Juan ◆ n. en Lampazos de Naranjo, NL, y m. cerca de Saltillo, Coah. (1821-1860). En 1841 participó en varias campañas de represión contra los indios de Nuevo León. Durante la guerra contra Estados Unidos combatió en las batallas de Palo Alto, Resaca de la Palma, Tampico, Matamoros y La Angostura. En 1854 se unió a la revolución de Ayutla y militó a las órdenes de Santiago Vidaurri en Nuevo León, Coahuila y Tamaulipas; peleó en el lado liberal durante la guerra de los Tres Años. Cuando Vidaurri rompió con Benito Juárez, Zuazua siguió al jefe norteño al exilio en Estados Unidos. Regresó a México en 1860 y fue asesinado por José Silvestre Aramberri.

Zubarán Capmany, Juan ◆ n. en Campeche, Camp., y m. en el DF (1872-1932). Estudió abogacía en el Instituto del Estado. Fue diputado federal (1911-13) y polemizó en el Congreso con Querido Moheno, con quien estuvo a punto de batirse. Al ocurrir el cuartelazo de Victoriano Huerta marchó a Mérida, donde fue detenido y trasladado a una cárcel de la ciudad de México. Escapó de prisión y se refugió en Cuba, donde vivió hasta 1915. Regresó a México y en 1916 ingresó en el Partido Liberal Constitucionalista. Diputado al Congreso Constituyente de 1916-17, nunca asistió a las sesiones. Nuevamente diputado federal en 1917-18 y 1920-21, en este último año presidió la Cámara.

Zubarán Capmany, Rafael ◆ n. en Campeche, Camp., y m. en el DF (1875-1948). Abogado, hermano del anterior. Participó en 1910 en la insurrección maderista. En 1913 se incorporó al constitucionalismo. Fue secretario de Gobernación (del 26 de noviembre de 1914 al 24 de junio de 1915) en el gabinete de Venustiano Carranza; agente confidencial de éste en Washington y presidente municipal de la ciudad de México. Dirigió el Partido Liberal Constitucionalista, fue senador, desempeñó algunos puestos diplomáticos en Europa y fue secretario de Industria, Comercio y Trabajo (del 1 de diciembre de 1920 al 26 de diciembre de 1921) de Álvaro Obregón. En 1923 apoyó la rebelión delahuertista, tras la cual debió exiliarse en Estados Unidos. Regresó a México en 1937 y fue colaborador de *El Universal* (1937- 48).

Zubieta, Francisco ◆ n. y m. en el DF (1870-1932). Caricaturista y dibujante. En 1889 abandonó sus estudios en el Colegio Militar para aprender dibujo con los profesores Santiago Rebull, Jesús Corral y Miguel Hernández. Fue profesor de dibujo en el Instituto Zea, en la Escuela Nacional Preparatoria (de la que fue prefecto de 1904 a 1911) y secretario del Museo Nacional de Arqueología, Historia y Etnografía (1913). Tuvo también diversos cargos públicos. Como caricaturista colaboró en *El Cómico, El Alacrán* y *Tilín-tilín*.

Zubirán, Salvador ◆ n. en Cusihuiriachic, Chih., y m. en el DF (1898-1998). Su segundo apellido era Anchondo. Se tituló en la Escuela Nacional de Medicina de la Universidad Nacional de México (1923), en la que fue profesor (1925-66), rector (1946-48) y miembro de la Junta de Gobierno (1958-62). Hizo estudios de posgrado en el hospital Peter Bent Brigham de la Universidad de Harvard (1925). Jefe del Servicio de Alimentos del Departamento de Salubridad Pública (1931-34), miembro de la Comisión de Estudios de la Presidencia de la República (1935-37), jefe fundador del Departamento Autónomo de Asistencia Infantil (1937), encargado del despacho (1939) y subsecretario de Asistencia Pública (1940-43), director fundador del Hospital de las Enfermedades de la Nutrición, director del Instituto Nacional de la Nutrición (1944-80), miembro del Consejo de Salubridad General (1964-80) y vocal ejecutivo del Programa Nacional de Alimentación del Conacyt (1970-82). Coautor de un *Estudio sobre la reorganización física y funcional de la Escuela de Medicina de la* UNAM (1948). Autor de *Ideario, realizaciones y proyectos* (1948). Presidente de la Academia Nacional de Medicina (1946) y fundador de la Sociedad Mexicana de Nutrición y Endocrinología. Profesor emérito de la UNAM (1967), *doctor honoris causa* de las universidades de Yucatán (1948), Nacional Autónoma de México (1979), Autónoma del Estado de México (1981), Autónoma de Puebla (1984) y Autónoma de Chihuahua (1990), Premio Nacional de Ciencias 1968, director emérito del Instituto Nacional de la Nutrición Salvador Zubirán (1980), Medalla Belisario Domínguez (1986) y Medalla Eduardo Liceaga (1989).

Zubiría y Campa, Luis ◆ n. en Durango, Dgo., y m. en Torreón, Coah. (1878-1936). Licenciado en derecho. Destacó como historiador y pintor. Diputado federal por Durango (1911-13), se afilió al Bloque Renovador. Al ser disuelto el Congreso por Victoriano Huerta fue encarcelado. Se unió al ejército zapatista. Fue secretario de Hacienda (del 14 de junio al 29 de julio de 1915) en el gabinete del presidente convencionista Francisco Lagos Cházaro. Al desaparecer el gobierno de la convención se exilió en Estados Unidos. Tiempo después regresó al país y se dedicó a la minería.

Zubiría y Escalante, José Antonio Laureano ◆ n. en Arizpe, Son., y

Juan Zuazua

Rafael Zubarán Capmany

Salvador Zubirán

Obra de *Zukor*

m. en la hacienda de Cacaria, Dgo. (1795-1862). Sacerdote ordenado en 1817. Fue cura de Nazas, Sombrerete y del Sagrario; diputado provincial (1820), misionero en Zacatecas, Chihuahua y Nuevo México y sinodal en Durango. En 1831 el papa Gregorio XVI lo nombró obispo de Durango. Dos años después protestó contra las reformas de Valentín Gómez Farías, por lo que debió dejar el país. A la caída de éste regresó a México. En 1844 concluyó y consagró la Catedral de Durango y durante su gestión le fueron segregadas a su obispado las diócesis de Zacatecas y Nuevo México. En 1856 manifestó su repudio a la ley de desamortización de los bienes eclesiásticos y en 1857 se opuso a la Constitución, por lo que fue confinado al asentamiento de Nieves, Zacatecas. Tras el pronunciamiento de Tacubaya (diciembre de 1857) volvió a Durango y en el transcurso de la guerra de los Tres Años permaneció oculto en una cueva de la hacienda de Cacaria, en la que murió y en la que sus restos permanecieron dos años. Fue el único obispo mexicano al que no desterró el gobierno liberal.

Zubiría y Sánchez de Manzanera, Santiago de ◆ n. y m. en Durango, Dgo. (1834-1909). Sacerdote consagrado en 1858. Fue cura de Sombrerete, canónigo de la catedral (1891), vicario capitular (1894) y arzobispo de Durango (1895-1909). Convocó y presidió el primer concilio provincial de Durango (1896).

Zuckerman Duarte, Conrado ◆ n. en Mérida, Yuc. (1900-1979). Graduado en la Escuela Nacional de Medicina (1924), se especializó en ginecología y cancerología en España, Francia y Estados Unidos. Fue director de la Clínica de Cirugía y Radioterapia y del Instituto Nacional de Cardiología, jefe de la Campaña Anticancerosa en México, director de la *Revista Mexicana de Cirugía, Ginecología y Cáncer*, presidente de la Sociedad Mexicana de Cancerología y profesor en la Escuela de Graduados de la UNAM. Autor de *Los cánceres* (1928), *Colecistectomía* (1932), *Patología quirúrgica* (1935), *Viaje de un cirujano* (1938), *Estado actual de la cirugía en los tumores cerebrales* (1939), *Estudios cancerológicos* (1943), *La vida de los médicos en México* (1945), *Temas del presente* (1974) y *Emerge mi inquietud* (1992). Fue miembro de la Academia Mexicana de Cirugía, Academia de Cirugía de Madrid, Sociedad Mexicana de Cancerología, Sociedad Mexicana de Biología, Sociedad Mexicana de Eugenesia, Sociedad Cubana de Cancerología, Sociedad Francesa de Ginecología y de la Asociación Mexicana de Ginecología y Obstetricia.

Zuk, Eva María ◆ n. en Polonia (1946). Pianista. Fue llevada por su familia a Venezuela, donde inició sus estudios musicales a los cuatro años de edad. Desde los seis años ofrece recitales y a los 10 fue solista de la Orquesta Sinfónica de Venezuela. Profesora ejecutante del piano por el Ministerio de Educación de Venezuela (1959), licenciada en música y maestra en ciencias por la Juilliard School of Music de Nueva York (1966). Discípula de Gerty Haas, Eduardo Steuermann, Rosina Lhevinne, Zbigniew Drewiecki y Leon Barzin. Vino en 1971 y se naturalizó mexicana en 1994. Se ha presentado como solista de más de 50 orquestas de Europa y América y prácticamente todas las mexicanas. Ha grabado discos con música de Chopin, De Falla, Haydn y, con investigaciones suyas, una antología del género de la polonesa, otras de Felipe Villanueva y Ricardo Castro, así como *La fuente armoniosa* (obras para piano de compositores mexicanos contemporáneos). Fue premiada en los concursos de piano Queen Elizabeth de Bélgica y Chopin de Varsovia. Ha recibido la Orden Andrés Bello y la Medalla del Bicentenario de Simón Bolívar del gobierno venezolano, el Escudo de Armas de San Juan de Puerto Rico y la Medalla del Centenario de Carol Szimanowsky del gobierno polaco.

Zukor ◆ n. en Puebla, Pue. (1938). Nombre profesional del pintor Enrique Zúñiga Cordero. Estudió en la Academia de San Carlos y en La Esmeralda del INBA, en Querétaro con Jesús Guerrero Galván y en León, Guanajuato, con Segoviano. Expone individualmente desde 1970 en el país y desde 1955 colectivamente en Checoslovaquia (1984), la URSS (1987) y México. Obras suyas pertenecen al acervo del Museo Nacional de Arte de Praga y del Instituto Smithsoniano de Washington, EUA. Miembro fundador del Jardín del Arte, pertenece a las asociaciones Mexicana de Artistas Plásticos e Internacional de Artistas Plásticos y a la Asamblea Permanente de Artistas Plásticos de México.

Zuloaga, Félix María ◆ n. en Álamos, Son., y m. en la ciudad de México (1813-1898). Militar conservador. Abandonó los estudios en el seminario para alistarse en la Milicia Cívica de Chihuahua (1834), en cuyas filas participó en las campañas de represión contra comanches y apaches. En 1838 ingresó en el ejército. Defendió al gobierno de Anastasio Bustamante (1840) y en 1841 al de Antonio López de Santa Anna; combatió en Yucatán a los separatistas y en 1846 dirigió las obras de fortificación de Monterrey, ante la inminente guerra contra Estados Unidos. Combatió a los invasores en la ciudad de México (1847). Fue regidor y alcalde constitucional de la ciudad de Chihuahua. Reincorporado al ejército, en diciembre de 1853 se le nombró presidente del Consejo de Guerra de la Plaza de México. Combatió la revolución de Ayutla, alcanzó el grado de general de brigada y fue apresado por los liberales, aunque más tarde Ignacio Comonfort lo liberó e incorporó a sus fuerzas. En la junta de representantes de los estados, reunida en Cuernavaca en 1855, representó a Chihuahua. Participó en las dos campañas de Puebla contra los conservadores. Se le dio el mando de una de las brigadas de la ciudad de México y con una de ellas inició la asonada del Plan de Tacubaya, el 17 de diciembre de 1857. El 22 de enero de 1858 los pronunciados lo designaron presidente interino y asumió el Ejecutivo al día siguiente, en tanto que Benito Juárez, al amparo de la Constitución, hacía lo mismo, con lo que inició la guerra de los Tres Años, en la que cada bando tuvo su presidente. De inmediato expidió un decreto mediante el cual derogaba todas las leyes y disposiciones liberales que afectaban los fueros militares y eclesiásticos y desconocía la Constitución de 1857. Se le involucró en el asesinato de Melchor Ocampo. Del 20 de diciembre de 1858 al 24 de enero de 1859 su interinato se vio interrumpido por la defección de Miguel María de Echegaray; sin embargo, Miguel Miramón lo repuso al frente del Ejecutivo. Zuloaga se separó del cargo el 2 de febrero de 1859 y nombró sustituto a Miramón. En mayo de 1860 desconoció a Miramón y se autodesignó presidente, por lo que éste lo apresó y lo hizo acompañarlo en sus campañas, para que viera "cómo se gana la Presidencia de la República". Al triunfo liberal fue declarado fuera de la ley y se exilió en Cuba, donde vivió hasta después de la muerte de Benito Juárez. Regresó a México y se dedicó a atender un negocio en la capital del país.

Zuloaga, Luis ◆ n. en Álamos, Son., y m. en Chihuahua, Chih. (1802-1864). Hermano del anterior. Residió desde 1816 en la ciudad de Chihuahua. Atendió la Caja de la Tesorería Real y, después de la consumación de la independencia, fue oficial mayor y secretario general de Gobierno del estado (1825). Magistrado del Supremo Tribunal de Justicia (1829), director general de Hacienda (1837) y diputado local y federal en varias ocasiones. En 1853 fue miembro del triunvirato que ejerció el Ejecutivo local y fue dos veces gobernador interino de Chihuahua (1845 y 1854).

Zuloaga, Tomás ◆ n. en Álamos, Son., y m. en Chihuahua, Chih. (¿1806?-1868). Militar y abogado. En Chihuahua, en 1820, se dio de alta en las compañías presidiales. Fue mayor de órdenes del gobernador José Joaquín Calvo y jefe político y comandante militar del partido de Paso del Norte. Participó en varias campañas contra los apaches y comanches y se dio de baja en 1839. Magistrado del Supremo Tribunal de Justicia y vocal de la Junta Departamental (1841), volvió al ejército en 1844 y apoyó el Plan de Tacubaya en enero de 1858. Fue después profesor del Instituto Científico y Literario de Chihuahua y diputado local. Sumiso al imperio de Maximiliano, fue designado prefecto municipal de la ciudad y prefecto imperial del departamento de Chihuahua (de septiembre a octubre de 1865). Tras el triunfo de la República fue condenado a dos años de destierro.

Zumárraga, Juan de ◆ n. en España y m. en la ciudad de México (1468-1548). Fraile franciscano. Era inquisidor de la provincia de Vizcaya cuando Carlos I de España lo nombró primer obispo de México. En 1528 llegó a la Nueva España, sin haber sido consagrado, junto con los primeros oidores, con los que tuvo numerosas desavenencias. Volvió a España en 1533 para ser sometido a juicio (en el que fue absuelto de las acusaciones hechas por el oidor Delgadillo) y fue consagrado en Valladolid. En 1534 regresó a la Nueva España y en 1547 el papa Paulo III lo hizo primer arzobispo de México. Durante su gestión introdujo la imprenta, intervino en la fundación de los colegios

Gabinete del presidente Félix Zuloaga
23 de enero al 23 de diciembre de 1858

Relaciones Exteriores:	
Luis G. Cuevas	24 de enero al 9 de julio de 1858
Joaquín M. del Castillo y Lanzas	10 de julio al 23 de diciembre de 1858
Gobernación:	
Hilario Elguero	24 de enero al 2 de julio de 1858
Juan M. Fernández de Jáuregui	3 de julio al 23 de diciembre de 1858
Justicia y Negocios Eclesiásticos:	
Manuel Larraínzar	24 de enero al 20 de abril de 1858
Mariano Alegría	21 al 23 de abril de 1858
Hilario Elguero	24 de abril al 9 de julio de 1858
Francisco Javier Miranda	10 de julio al 23 de diciembre de 1858
Fomento:	
Juan Hierro Maldonado	24 de enero al 9 de julio de 1858
José María Zaldívar	10 de julio al 23 de diciembre de 1858
Hacienda:	
Juan Hierro Maldonado	24 de enero al 24 de abril de 1858
Manuel Piña y Cuevas	24 de abril al 9 de julio de 1858
Pedro Jorrín	10 de julio al 23 de diciembre de 1858

Foto: Archivo General de la Nación/Fondo Teixidor

Retrato y firma de Juan de Zumárraga

Félix María Zuloaga

Glifo de Zumpahuacán, Estado de México

Autocaricatura de José Guadalupe Zuno

de Santa Cruz de Tlatelolco y de San Juan de Letrán, fundó el hospital del Amor de Dios y promovió la fundación de la Real y Pontificia Universidad. Editó la *Breve y más compendiosa doctrina* (1539), *Manual de adultos* (1540), *Doctrina cristiana breve* (1543), *Doctrina breve muy provechosa de las cosas que pertenecen a la fe católica y a nuestra cristiandad en estilo llano para común inteligencia* (1544), *Tripartito de doctrina cristiana*, de Juan Gerson (1544), *Compendio*, de Rickel (1544), *Doctrina*, de Pedro de Córdoba (1544) y *Doctrina cristiana breve*, de Alonso de Molina (1546). Autor de *Regla cristiana breve* (1547).

Zumaya, Francisco ◆ n. en España y m. en la Nueva España (1532-?). Pintor cuyo nombre era Francisco Ibía. Adoptó como apellido el nombre de su pueblo natal. Presumiblemente fue profesor y suegro del pintor Baltazar de Echave y Orio. Se cree que llegó a la ciudad de México hacia 1565. Doró los púlpitos de la capilla del Crucifijo y pintó cuatro ventanas para la capilla del sacramento de la vieja catedral de México. Algunos autores le atribuyen un *San Sebastián* y *Nuestra señora de las Nieves* o *Virgen del Perdón* del desaparecido Altar del Perdón de la Catedral Metropolitana (obras perdidas en el incendio de enero de 1967).

Zumaya, Manuel de ◆ n. en la ciudad de México y m. en Oaxaca, Oax. (¿1685?-1754). Músico. Ingresó en 1690 al coro infantil de la Catedral Metropolitana. En 1694 fue becado para estudiar ejecución con el profesor José de Ydiáquez, organista de la Catedral Metropolitana, y composición con Antonio de Salazar, maestro de capilla en la misma catedral. Fue protegido del deán Tomás Montaño y del virrey Fernando de Alencastre Noroña y Silva. Tradujo y musicalizó numerosas obras italianas. Organista adjunto de la Catedral (1700) y maestro de capilla de la misma (1715). En 1738 fue capellán personal de Montaño (designado en ese año obispo de Antequera) y cura provisional del sagrario oaxaqueño, cargo que perdió a

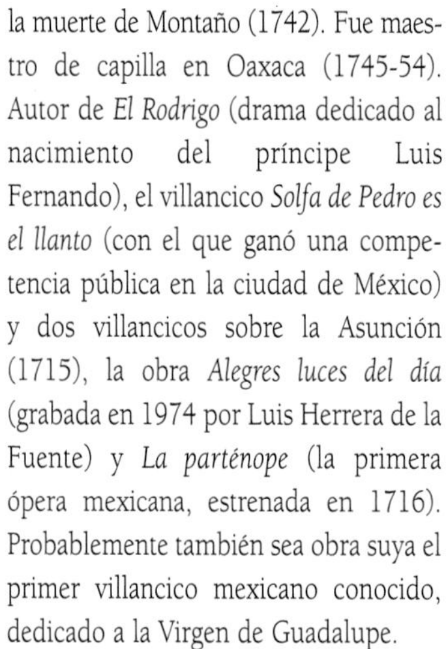

la muerte de Montaño (1742). Fue maestro de capilla en Oaxaca (1745-54). Autor de *El Rodrigo* (drama dedicado al nacimiento del príncipe Luis Fernando), el villancico *Solfa de Pedro es el llanto* (con el que ganó una competencia pública en la ciudad de México) y dos villancicos sobre la Asunción (1715), la obra *Alegres luces del día* (grabada en 1974 por Luis Herrera de la Fuente) y *La parténope* (la primera ópera mexicana, estrenada en 1716). Probablemente también sea obra suya el primer villancico mexicano conocido, dedicado a la Virgen de Guadalupe.

Zumpahuacán ◆ Municipio del Estado de México situado en el sur de la entidad, al sur-sureste de Toluca, en los límites con Guerrero. Superficie: 334.80 km². Habitantes: 13,178, de los cuales 2,928 forman la población económicamente activa. Hablan alguna lengua indígena 23 personas mayores de cinco años. En la jurisdicción se localiza la zona arqueológica de Zumpahuacán, aún sin explorar. En la cabecera, del mismo nombre, se halla la iglesia de San Pablo, edificada en el siglo XVI.

Zumpango, de ◆ Laguna del Estado de México situada en la porción noroccidental de la llamada región de Zumpango, al norte de Cuautitlán. En ella desemboca el río de las Avenidas de Pachuca. Con un programa de restauración iniciado en 1986, la Secretaría de Agricultura y Recursos Hidráulicos salvó la laguna, que estaba a punto de desecarse por completo.

Zumpango ◆ Municipio del Estado de México situado en el noreste de la entidad, y próximo a Tepotzotlán, en los límites con Hidalgo. Superficie: 208.63 km². Habitantes: 91,642, de los cuales 19,332 forman la población económicamente activa. Hablan alguna lengua indígena 274 personas mayores de cinco años (náhuatl 91 y mazahua 39). Parte de sus tierras fértiles son porciones desecadas de la laguna del mismo nombre. En su jurisdicción se localiza la zona arqueológica de Zumpango. Su cabecera, Zumpango de Ocampo, se localiza en la ribera oriental de la laguna y está limitada al este por el canal de desagüe del Distrito Federal. Al consumarse la conquista de México, la zona norte del valle de México fue convertida en corregimiento de Citlaltépec, cuya cabecera es el actual San Juan Zitlatépec, sufragáneo de la provincia de Guautitlán; hacia el siglo XVII era una provincia independiente que se llamó sucesivamente (por las sedes de su alcaldía mayor) Citlaltépec, Xilocingo y Zumpango de la Laguna (actual Zumpango de Ocampo). A partir de 1786 la provincia se convirtió en subdelegación de la intendencia de México.

Zumpango del Río ◆ Cabecera del municipio guerrerense Eduardo Neri (☛).

Zuno Hernández, Alberto ◆ n. y m. en Guadalajara, Jal. (1893-1960). Militar. Se unió en 1914 a la revolución constitucionalista y participó en las campañas antivillistas de Coahuila, Jalisco y Sonora. Comandante de la Línea del Río Yaqui, fundó en Sonora la primera escuela para soldados. En 1923 se encontraba en Jalisco cuando fue aprehendido por el delahuertista Enrique Estrada; escapó y se unió a las fuerzas de Eugenio Ortiz para combatir la rebelión. Fue jefe de armas en varias poblaciones de Veracruz y presidió el Comité Antialcohólico de Coahuila. General de brigada en 1939, en ese año se le nombró director del Colegio Militar, donde fundó la *Revista del Colegio Militar* y una cooperativa de consumo. En 1941 fue nombrado director del Departamento de Caballería. Autor de *El ejército como factor social y su acercamiento con el pueblo*, *El ejército y el pueblo soviéticos* y *Consideraciones sobre el servicio militar obligatorio*.

Zuno Hernández, José Guadalupe ◆ n. en la hacienda de San Agustín, municipio de La Barca, y m. en Guadalajara, Jal. (1891-1980). Escritor, pintor y caricaturista. Licenciado en derecho por la Universidad de Guadalajara (1931). En 1907 fue expulsado del Liceo de Varones de Guadalajara, por pertenecer a un grupo antirreeleccionis-

Francisco Zúñiga

ta. Pasó a la ciudad de México, donde estudió pintura en la Academia de San Carlos y con José Clemente Orozco. En 1909 se inició como caricaturista en *El Perico* y fundó en Guadalajara el Centro Bohemio y las publicaciones *Prensa Unida, Gil Blas, La Sátira, Rigoletto, 30-30, Etcétera* y *Basilio* (1912). En 1914 presentó su primera exposición pictórica. Diputado federal por Jalisco (1920-22), fue destituido por el Senado por "violaciones a la Constitución" e inhabilitado para ocupar puestos públicos durante siete años y seis meses. Presidente municipal de Guadalajara de mayo a diciembre de 1922. Fue gobernador de Jalisco (del 1 de marzo de 1923 al 23 de marzo de 1926). Durante su gobierno fundó la Universidad de Guadalajara (de la que después sería alumno y profesor) y, por su política anticlerical, tuvo numerosos enfrentamientos con el arzobispo Francisco Orozco Jiménez. Consejero del presidente Lázaro Cárdenas (1935), apoderado general de Ferronales, presidente del Tribunal de Arbitraje, profesor de la Escuela Nacional de Maestros, director de la Escuela de Bellas Artes y del Departamento de Extensión Universitaria de la Universidad de Guadalajara, dirigió en 1955 el Museo Regional de Guadalajara y en 1970 fue designado miembro de la Academia Internacional de Derecho. Suegro del presidente Luis Echeverría, el 28 de agosto de 1974 fue secuestrado por un comando del grupo guerrillero Fuerzas Revolucionarias Armadas del Pueblo. Autor de *Derecho y revolución* (1931, tesis de licenciatura), *Pasión y muerte de Hidalgo* (1954), *Las lacas michoacanas* (1954), *Orozco y la ironía plástica* (Premio Jalisco, 1954), *La muerte de un lago* (1955), *Notas sobre la plástica* (1955), *Don Pedro Moreno* (1956), *Nuestro liberalismo* (4 t., 1956-70), *Reminiscencias de una vida* (4 t., 1956-72), *Las artes populares en Jalisco* (1957), *El Museo Regional de Guadalajara* (1957), *Historia de las artes plásticas en Jalisco* (1957), *Don José María Estrada* (1957), *La ironía plástica en Jalisco* (1958), *José Guadalupe Posada y la ironía plástica* (1959), *La ironía plástica en Goya* (1959), *Introducción a la historia general de la caricatura* (1959), *Lecciones de derecho del trabajo* (1959), *Los insurgentes del lago de Chapala* (1960), *Historia general de la caricatura y la ironía plástica* (1960), *Historia de la caricatura de Jalisco* (1960), *Don Juan A. Mateos* (1960), *Historia de la caricatura en México* (1961), *El martirio de Cuauhtémoc* (1961), *El sacrificio de don Pedro Moreno* (1961), *El chacal Huerta* (1961), *La lámpara de la verdad* (1961), *Lecciones de historia del arte* (2 t., 1961-62), *El compositor infortunado* (1962), *La bárbara conquista de Tonalá* (1962), *Un cura, un obispo y un virrey* (1962), *La niña, la luna y el globo* (1962), *La muerte de Juárez* (1962), *La fábula del árbol que habla* (1963), *El coyotito hechicero* (1963), *Don Santos Degollado, el santo de la reforma* (1964), *Historia de la revolución en Jalisco* (1964), *La novela del mercado* (1964), *Lista de los artistas jaliscienses* (1965), *El zapote mágico* (1965), *Subasta de cuadros* (1966), *Biografía del general Eugenio Zúñiga* (1967), *Biografía del general Francisco Arce* (1967), *Historia de las artes plásticas en la Revolución Mexicana* (2 t., 1967-69), *La pléyade jalisciense del federalismo y la reforma* (1968), *Biografía del general don Ramón Corona* (1969), *Guía del Museo de Guadalajara* (1969), *Vida y muerte de Morelos* (1970), *Don Pedro Ogazón* (1970), *Don Prisciliano Sánchez* (1970), *Los valientes no asesinan* (1971) y *El pensamiento del hombre sobre el árbol* (1972).

ZÚÑIGA, DULCE MARÍA ◆ n. en Culiacán, Sin. (1961). Ensayista. Realizó sus estudios en la Universidad Paul Valéry de Montpellier, Francia, donde obtuvo el doctorado en Estudios Romances, con especialidad en italiano. Traductora de francés e italiano. Ha sido profesora en la licenciatura de letras y en la maestría de literatura del siglo XX en la Facultad de Filosofía y Letras de la Universidad de Guadalajara; investigadora titular y directora del Centro de Estudios Literarios de la misma universidad. Ha colaborado en *Los Universitarios, SEC, Jalisco en el Arte, La Gaceta* (de Cuba), *América Hispánica* (Río Janeiro), *Et Caetera, Zenzontli* y *Tiempo de Jalisco*. Ha publicado los ensayos: *Prácticas poéticas contemporáneas, Italia y Francia* (en colaboración con Franc Dueros y Dante Medina, 1988), *Intertextos: Calvino, Borges, Fuentes* (1989), *La novela infinita de Italo Calvino* (1991), *La tremenda corte: un caso de lingüisticidio* (1994). Becaria del Fonca (1991-1992) y del Sistema Nacional de Investigadores (1991-1994).

ZÚÑIGA, FRANCISCO ◆ n. en Costa Rica y m. en el DF (1912-1998). Escultor. Estudió dibujo en la Escuela de Bellas Artes de San José de Costa Rica

Evelia en un banquillo, obra de Francisco Zúñiga

Horacio Zúñiga

Retrato y firma de Gaspar de Zúñiga y Acevedo

Retrato y firma de Baltasar de Zúñiga y Guzmán

(1927) y en México, donde llegó en 1936, asistió a la Escuela de Talla Directa y fue alumno de Manuel Rodríguez Lozano (1936). Trabajó como ayudante de Oliverio Martínez en las esculturas del Monumento a la Revolución (1937) y de Guillermo Ruiz en trabajos monumentales de bronce (1938-42). Profesor fundador de la Escuela Nacional de Pintura, Escultura y Grabado, La Esmeralda, del INBA (1939-70), tuvo un taller en la Escuela de Artesanías. Adquirió la nacionalidad mexicana en 1986. Realizó su primera exposición individual en 1965. Autor de más de 900 esculturas: *Maternidad* (1935, en San José de Costa Rica), *El minero* (1949, en Angangueo), *La pesca y la cosecha* (1952, Veracruz), de los bajorelieves del edificio de la Secretaría de Comunicaciones y Transportes (1954), *Monumento a la libertad* (1956, San Salvador), *Morelos* (1963, Cartagena), *Juárez* (1963, Tegucigalpa), bustos de López Velarde, Manuel J. Othón, González Martínez, Antonio Caso y Gutiérrez Nájera (1963-64, en la Rotonda de los Hombres Ilustres), busto de Vasco de Quiroga (1971, España), *Monumento al agricultor* (1976, Costa Rica) y *La familia* (1978, Costa Rica). Miembro de la Academia Mexicana de las Artes (1987). Creador emérito del Sistema Nacional de Creadores (1993). Primer Premio Centroamericano de Escultura (1935), primer premio de la primera Bienal de Escultura al Aire Libre del Museo Middleheim, de Amberes (1971) y Premio Nacional de Cultura Magón 73 de Costa Rica (1974), Chancellor's Award de la Universidad de California en Los Ángeles (1982). Premio Elías Sourasky (1982) y Premio Nacional de Ciencias y Artes 1992.

ZÚÑIGA, HORACIO ♦ n. y m. en Toluca, Edo. de Méx. (1897-1956). Escritor. Realizó estudios de derecho en la Escuela Nacional de Jurisprudencia. Fue director de la Biblioteca y del Museo del Estado de México y profesor del Instituto Científico y Literario de Toluca, de la Escuela de Artes y Oficios y de las escuelas nacionales de Jurisprudencia, Preparatoria y de Maestros. Autor de los poemarios *Mirras, poemas orfébricos* (1913), *La selva sonora, poemas orquestales* (1933), *Tres poemas a la madre* (1936), *Realidad, El verbo peregrinante, Torre negra* (1938), *El ánfora, El hombre absurdo, Presente, El minuto azul, Selva sonora, Sinfonías* y *Espumas y oleajes* (1977); de la novelas: *El hombre absurdo* (1935), *Realidad* (1936) y *Miseria* (editada en 1991); y de los ensayos: *El verbo peregrinante, La miscelánea, Imágenes, ideas, palabras* y *El Estado de México.*

ZÚÑIGA, JULIÁN ♦ n. en Querétaro, Qro., y m. en el DF (1893-1971). Organista de la basílica de Guadalupe desde 1921 hasta su muerte. Estrenó el órgano monumental de ese templo en diciembre de 1931, durante las celebraciones del cuarto centenario de las apariciones de la Virgen de Guadalupe. Tocó en 80 de los cien conciertos transmitidos por radio desde la basílica y durante su vida profesional acompañó, entre otros, a los cantantes Fanny Anitúa, María Teresa Santillán, Ángel H. Ferreiro, María Romero, María Luis y Consuelo Escobar, Eugenia Rocabruna, Alfonso Ortiz Tirado, Armando Tokatian, Francisco Zárate Ríos, Ángel R. Esquivel, Joaquín Álvarez y a los coros del Seminario Conciliar de México, de los seminaristas del Espíritu Santo y del Orfeón de José Guadalupe Velázquez. Autor de las obras de música sacra *Misa en honor de la Virgen de Guadalupe, Sunnon Sanctisimae Trinitates, Salve, Alma de América* y el oratorio *Tepeyac.*

ZÚÑIGA Y ACEVEDO, GASPAR DE ♦ n. en España y m. en Perú (1560-1606). Desde 1578 estuvo al servicio de Felipe II de España en la campaña de Portugal y en la defensa de La Coruña, puerto atacado por el pirata Francis Drake. En 1595 fue designado virrey de la Nueva España y llegó a la ciudad de México en noviembre de ese año. Durante su gestión se multiplicaron las misiones jesuitas en el norte del virreinato, prohibió la venta de las tierras de los indios y dio a éstos facilidades para que las trabajaran, se efectuaron las expediciones de Sebastián Vizcaíno, en la costa del Pacífico, y de Diego de Montemayor, al Nuevo Reino de León. Las ciudades de Monterrey (en California y Nuevo León) llevan ese nombre en honor a Zúñiga, que era conde de la homónima ciudad española. En 1597 mudó el puerto de Veracruz al sitio que actualmente ocupa y fortificó la ciudad de Campeche, repetidamente atacada por piratas. En 1603 fue designado virrey de Perú, cargo que desempeñó hasta su muerte.

ZÚÑIGA Y GUZMÁN, BALTASAR DE ♦ n. y m. en España (1658-1727). Miembro del Consejo de Indias y virrey de Navarra y Cerdeña. Trigesimosexto virrey de la Nueva España (1716-22). Durante su gestión se efectuaron las reconquistas de Texas (ocupada por los

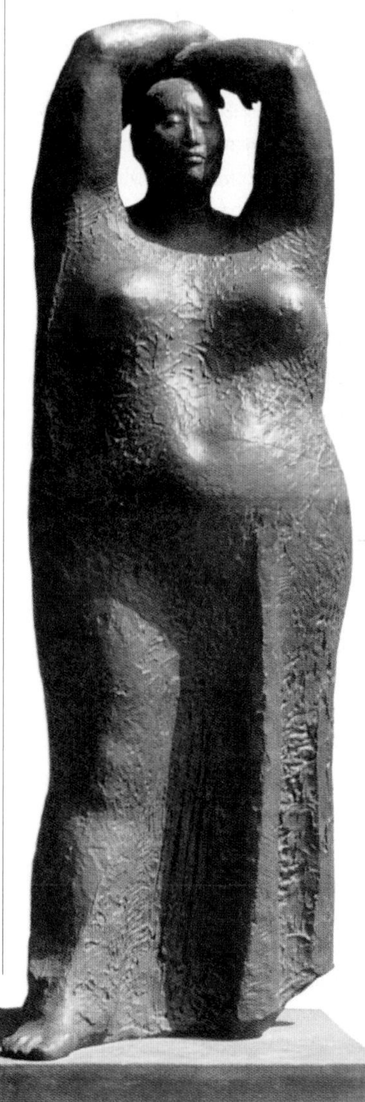
Juchiteca de pie, escultura en bronce de Francisco Zúñiga

franceses) y de Laguna de Términos (en poder de los ingleses), se sometió al cacique de Florida, Tixjanaque, y las ciudades de aquella península fueron fortificadas, se inició la pubicación del primer periódico de México, la *Gaceta* de Castorena, y se fundó el convento de Corpus Christi, para indias nobles. En 1722 volvió a España como presidente del Consejo de Indias.

Zúñiga y Miranda, Nicolás ◆ n. en Zacatecas y m. en el DF (1865-1925). Pasó en 1883 a la ciudad de México, donde se inscribió en la Escuela Nacional de Jurisprudencia. Se afirma que predijo el temblor del 24 de mayo de 1887, hecho que le dio notoriedad. Publicó periódicos de corta vida como *El Incensario* (1887) y *El Semanario de Zúñiga y Miranda* (1892). En 1893 fue a la cárcel, acusado de conspiración, un delito que no estaba tipificado. Después de 25 días incomunicado y casi sin comer, fue presentado ante un juez con síntomas de turbación mental. En 1896 formó el Club Político Nacional que lanzó su candidatura a la Presidencia de la República en contra de Porfirio Díaz. Se creía presidente legalmente electo, despojado mediante fraude; esta circunstancia y sus excentricidades, como su aparato para predecir sismos, lo convirtieron en personaje pintoresco de finales del siglo XIX y principios del XX. En 1909 ofreció sus servicios a los reyistas, quienes no lo tomaron en cuenta. Después de la caída de Díaz siguió su costumbre de participar en las elecciones presidenciales y aun llegó a obtener algunos votos en las de 1917.

Zúñiga y Ontiveros, Felipe de ◆ ¿n.? y m. en la ciudad de México (¿1717?-1793). Impresor. Hacia 1752 era copropietario, con su hermano Cristóbal, de la Imprenta Auterpiana, de la que quedó como único dueño en 1764. Decía ser "agrimensor titulado por Su Magestad, de tierras, aguas y minas de todo el reino". Editó, entre 1752 y 1780 las *Efemérides calculadas y pronosticadas según el meridiano de México* (con los pronósticos y explicaciones de los fenómenos meteorológicos) y en 1756 la *Respuesta satisfactoria a las anotaciones hechas a las efemérides mexicanas*. Publicaba cada año una lista de funcionarios residentes en la ciudad de México. Tal nómina se convirtió en 1767 en la *Guía de Forasteros*, de acuerdo con el privilegio concedido por el virrey Bucareli y extendido a su *Kalendario*, que se publicó hasta 1792. Fue el impresor de la *Gazeta de México* hasta 1792. Introdujo en la Nueva España los tipos fundidos de Dimas Rangel, al imprimir los *Estatutos de la Real Academia de San Carlos* (1785). Sus tipos, traídos de Madrid, hicieron que cambiara el nombre de su establecimiento por Imprenta Nueva Madrileña. Autor del opúsculo *Bomba hidráulica para levantar las aguas* (1770) y de un soneto que figuró en el *Fénix de los mineros ricos* (1779).

Zúñiga y Tejeda, Arcadio ◆ n. en Atoyac y m. ¿en Guadalajara?, Jal. (1858-1892). Músico y periodista. En 1879 abandonó la carrera de medicina para dedicarse a la composición musical. Colaboró en la publicación *La Lanza de San Baltasar*, fundó la sociedad Bohemia Literaria Jalisciense y un periódico llamado *Juan Soldado*. Su oposición al régimen porfirista le valió el destierro a Colima y a Michoacán. Volvió en 1884 a Guadalajara, donde fundó las publicaciones *Juan Panadero*, primero, y *El Hijo de Juan Panadero*, después. Autor de las composiciones musicales *La barca de oro, Quiero soñar, Los turbiones, La serenata, Sueño del alma, Lejos de ti, No sabes tú, mi niña, Ilusiones perdidas, Cantar llorando, La barca de plata* y *La golondrina*.

Zurita, Humberto ◆ n. en Torreón, Coah. (1952). Hizo estudios presbiteriales. Ingresó al grupo de teatro de su preparatoria donde se inició en *Los Fantoches* de Carlos Solórzano (tercer premio en el Concurso Nacional de Teatro Estudiantil del Injuve). En el DF estudió en el Centro Universitario de Teatro de la UNAM donde actuó, entre otras, en *El Avaro* de Moliere y *Señor Butterfly* de David Wang. Fue nombrado Revelación del Año en 1978 por la Asociación de Críticos de Teatro por *The Knack*. En cine ha participado en *Rastro de muerte* (1981), *Bajo la metralla* (1982), *El tres de copas* (1986), *Los placeres ocultos* (1988) y *Nada que ver* (1994), entre otras. Ha producido *Bésame en la boca* (1994), *Morena* (1994) y *El amor de tu vida S.A.* (1994), entre otras. Junto con su esposa, Christian Bach, ha producido teatro y ha actuado en televisión. También ha actuado en telenovelas como *Pura Sangre* y *El Candidato* (1999, de TV-Azteca), entre otras.

Zurita, Juan ◆ n. en Veracruz, Ver. (1917). Boxeador. El 8 de marzo de 1944 ganó el campeonato mundial pluma al derrotar en Los Ángeles a Sammy Angot, con lo que se convirtió en el primer mexicano en ganar el campeonato mundial de ese peso; perdió el título frente al estadounidense Ike Williams (18 de abril de 1945, en la ciudad de México). Retirado del boxeo, se dedicó al comercio.

Zurriago Literario, El ◆ Revista literaria fundada por José Justo Gómez de la Cortina, el conde de la Cortina. Publicó poesía, crítica y textos sobre política, economía y otros temas. Tuvo tres etapas: la primera entre agosto de 1839 y enero de 1840 como revista semanal; la segunda, de abril de 1843 a junio de 1844, como sección del diario *El Siglo XIX*; y la tercera, bajo el nombre abreviado de *El Zurriago*, de mayo a noviembre de 1851, otra vez como semanario autónomo.

Zych Delimat, Jan ◆ n. en Polonia y m. en el DF (1931-1995). Escritor. Estudió letras en la Universidad Jagelónica, especializándose como traductor del español. En su país difundió la literatura latinoamericana, que tradujo al polaco, como *El laberinto de la soledad* y *Piedra de sol*, de Octavio Paz, *Pedro Páramo*, de Juan Rulfo y la poesía completa de Pablo Neruda. Radicó en México desde 1977, donde colaboró en la revista *Vuelta* y tradujo al español la obra de Czeslaw Milosz, Zbigniew Herbert y Wyeslawa Szymborska. Autor de los poemarios *Violín verde* (1955), *La frontera caminante* (1961), *Sistema del corazón* (1965), *Elogio del colibrí* (1972) y *Cicatrices de la luz* (1978). Fue jurado del Premio de Poesía Aguascalientes.

ESTATUTOS DE LA REAL ACADEMIA DE SAN CARLOS DE NUEVA ESPAÑA.

EN LA IMPRENTA NUEVA MEXICANA DE DON FELIPE DE ZÚÑIGA Y ONTIVEROS, AÑO DE CIↃ. IↃCC. LXXXV.

Libro impreso por Felipe de Zúñiga y Ontiveros en 1785

Arcadio Zúñiga y Tejeda

Humberto Zurita

Dirección General: ◆ CONSUELO SÁIZAR ◆

Producción: Diagrama Casa Editorial, S.C.

Coordinación: ◆ PILAR TAPIA ◆

Diseño: ◆ ADRIANA DÍAZ ◆ Jesús Arana Trejo, Jorge Luis Flores Juárez, Elsa Garrido Calderón, Hermenegildo López, Guadalupe López Gómez, Marina Mejía Vázquez, Norma Salas Martínez y Gerardo Santillán Flores.
Color: ◆ VÍCTOR ORNELAS ◆ Manuel Díaz López, Roberto López Gómez, Juan Ortega Corona, Leonardo Wilson y Jorge Gálvez (Milán y Roma).
Iconografía: ◆ ENRIQUE MARTÍNEZ LIMÓN ◆ Geney Beltrán Félix, Verónica Sosa Romo, Sergio Dueñas García y Emiliano Galíndez ◆ Penélope Esparza, Anaïk Folange y Soledad Ribó.
Lectura: ◆ MANUEL ANDRADE ◆ Zamná Heredia y Roberto Núñez Narváez.

El autor contó con la colaboración de: ◆ REBECA FLORES ◆ Alberto Chimal, María Cristina Cruz, Verónica Ladrón de Guevara, Sergio Raúl López, Hugo Martínez, Esteban David Rodríguez, Yolanda Rosales, Rodolfo Zárate y Miguel Díaz Siles.

Fotografías: ◆ Archivo General de la Nación ◆ Cuartoscuro, Eikon, Época, Imagen Latina, Milenio y Reforma ◆ Guillermo Aguilera, Rogelio Baeza, Gabriela Bautista, Dante Bucio, Michael Calderwood, Pablo Cervantes, Gilberto Contreras, Jorge Contreras Chacel, Claudio Contreras Koob, Rogelio Cuéllar, Jesús Díaz, Arturo Fuentes, Pablo González de Alba, Mario Guzmán, Carlos Hahn, Ana Lourdes Herrera, Armando Herrera, Catalina Herrera, Héctor Herrera, Fabrizio León, Héctor López, Rafael Miranda, Jesús Miranda, Erick Solórzano y Boris de Swan.

Las imágenes que exhiben la leyenda "Fondo Editorial Grupo Azabache" son propiedad de Grupo Azabache, S.A. de C.V. y fueron creadas por alguno de los artistas siguientes: Jorge Pablo de Aguinaco, Guillermo Aldana, Lourdes Almeida, María de Lourdes Alonso, Ángela Arciniega, Pamela Atkinson, Pedro Berruecos, Michael Calderwood, Rafael Doniz, Fluvio Ellardi, Pablo Esteva, José P. Fernández Cueto, Javier Flores Cruz, Miguel Franco, Enrique Franco Torrijos, Bernardo García Díaz, Adolfo Gómez Amador, José I. González Manterola, Vicente Guijosa, Enrique Hambleton, Javier Hinojosa, Edward Koprowski, Jesús Eduardo López Reyes, Flavio de Luna Arce, Carlos Martínez, Francisco Mata Rosas, Marco A. Maza, Eduardo Meade, Armando Mendoza, Juan José Morín, Pablo Oseguera, Ernesto Ríos Lanz, Adalberto Ríos Szalay, Everardo Rivera, Gerardo Suter, Ignacio Urquiza, Eliu Vega y Michel Zabé.

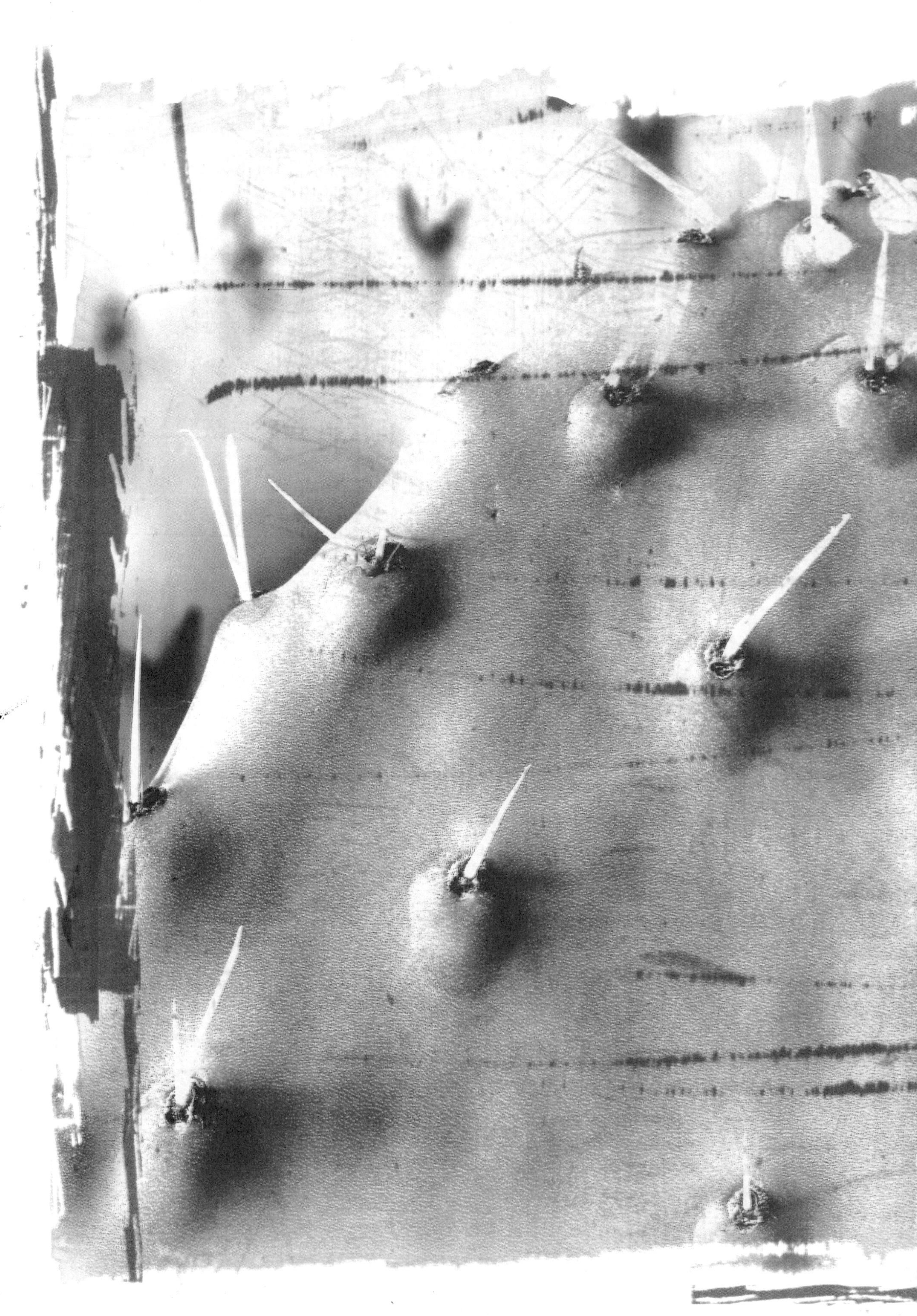